FEDERAL SECURITIES LAWS

SELECTED STATUTES, RULES AND FORMS

2018–2019 Edition

Compiled by

JOHN C. COFFEE, JR.
Adolf A. Berle Professor of Law
Columbia University School of Law

HILLARY A. SALE
Professor of Law, Georgetown University Law Center and
Affiliated Faculty, McDonough School of Business, Georgetown University

CHARLES K. WHITEHEAD
Myron C. Taylor Alumni Professor of Business Law
Cornell Law School

FOUNDATION PRESS

444 Cedar Street, Suite 700
St. Paul, MN 55101
1-877-888-1330

Printed in the United States of America

ISBN: 978-1-64242-673-1

PREFACE

The 2018–2019 Edition of Federal Statutes, Rules, and Forms follows the format of earlier editions. It contains many changes from the prior year's version:

- Changes to Regulation S–K;
- Changes to Regulation S–X;
- New Securities Act Rule 135d regarding communications involving security-based swaps;
- Amendment of Securities Act Rule 701;
- Temporary relief from certain crowdfunding reporting requirements in Securities Act Rule 203;
- Temporary Investment Company Act Rule 30b1–9(T) regarding monthly reports on Form N-PORT; and
- Amendments to Regulation ATS.

This edition has a cutoff date of November 15, 2018.

JOHN C. COFFEE, JR.
NEW YORK, NEW YORK

HILLARY A. SALE
WASHINGTON, D.C.

CHARLES K. WHITEHEAD
ITHACA, NEW YORK

TABLE OF CONTENTS

FEDERAL SECURITIES LAWS

SELECTED STATUTES, RULES AND FORMS

2018–2019 Edition

I. FEDERAL SECURITIES LAWS AND REGULATIONS

A. SECURITIES ACT OF 1933

15 U.S.C. § 77a et seq.

Section Act	15 U.S.C.	
1	77a	Short Title
2	77b	Definitions; Promotion of Efficiency, Competition, and Capital Formation
2A	77b–1	Swap Agreements
3	77c	Classes of Securities Under This Title
4	77d	Exempted Transactions
4A	77d–1	Requirements With Respect to Certain Small Transactions
5	77e	Prohibitions Relating to Interstate Commerce and the Mails
6	77f	Registration of Securities and Signing of Registration Statement
7	77g	Information Required in Registration Statement
8	77h	Taking Effect of Registration Statements and Amendments Thereto
8A	77h–1	Cease-and-Desist Proceedings
9	77i	Court Review of Orders
10	77j	Information Required in Prospectus
11	77k	Civil Liabilities on Account of False Registration Statement
12	77*l*	Civil Liabilities Arising in Connection with Prospectuses and Communications
13	77m	Limitation of Actions
14	77n	Contrary Stipulations Void
15	77*o*	Liability of Controlling Persons
16	77p	Additional Remedies; Limitations on Remedies
17	77q	Fraudulent Interstate Transactions
18	77r	Exemption from State Regulation of Securities Offerings
19	77s	Special Powers of Commission
20	77t	Injunctions and Prosecution of Offenses
21	77u	Hearings by Commission
22	77v	Jurisdiction of Offenses and Suits
23	77w	Unlawful Representations
24	77x	Penalties
25	77y	Jurisdiction of Other Government Agencies Over Securities
26	77z	Separability of Provisions
27	77z–1	Private Securities Litigation
27A	77z–2	Application of Safe Harbor for Forward–Looking Statements
27B	77z–2a	Conflicts of Interest Relating to Certain Securitizations
28	77z–3	General Exemptive Authority

SCHEDULES OF INFORMATION REQUIRED IN REGISTRATION STATEMENT (15 USC § 77aa)

Schedule A
Schedule B

SECURITIES ACT OF 1933

TITLE I

Short Title

Sec. 1. This subchapter may be cited as the "Securities Act of 1933."

Definitions; Promotion of Efficiency, Competition, and Capital Formation

Sec. 2. (a) *Definitions.* When used in this subchapter, unless the context otherwise requires—

(1) The term "security" means any note, stock, treasury stock, security future, security-based swap, bond, debenture, evidence of indebtedness, certificate of interest or participation in any profit-sharing agreement, collateral-trust certificate, preorganization certificate or subscription, transferable share, investment contract, voting-trust certificate, certificate of deposit for a security, fractional undivided interest in oil, gas, or other mineral rights, any put, call, straddle, option, or privilege on any security, certificate of deposit, or group or index of securities (including any interest therein or based on the value thereof), or any put, call, straddle, option, or privilege entered into on a national securities exchange relating to foreign currency, or, in general, any interest or instrument commonly known as a "security," or any certificate of interest or participation in, temporary or interim certificate for, receipt for, guarantee of, or warrant or right to subscribe to or purchase, any of the foregoing.

(2) The term "person" means an individual, a corporation, a partnership, an association, a joint-stock company, a trust, any unincorporated organization, or a government or political subdivision thereof. As used in this paragraph the term "trust" shall include only a trust where the interest or interests of the beneficiary or beneficiaries are evidenced by a security.

(3) The term "sale" or "sell" shall include every contract of sale or disposition of a security or interest in a security, for value. The term "offer to sell", "offer for sale", or "offer" shall include every attempt or offer to dispose of, or solicitation of an offer to buy, a security or interest in a security, for value. The terms defined in this paragraph and the term "offer to buy" as used in subsection (c) of section 5 shall not include preliminary negotiations or agreements between an issuer (or any person directly or indirectly controlling or controlled by an issuer, or under direct or indirect common control with an issuer) and any underwriter or among underwriters who are or are to be in privity of contract with an issuer (or any person directly or indirectly controlling or controlled by an issuer, or under direct or indirect common control with an issuer). Any security given or delivered with, or as a bonus on account of, any purchase of securities or any other thing, shall be conclusively presumed to constitute a part of the subject of such purchase and to have been offered and sold for value. The issue or transfer of a right or privilege, when originally issued or transferred with a security, giving the holder of such security the right to convert such security into another security of the same issuer or of another person, or giving a right to subscribe to another security of the same issuer or of another person, which right cannot be exercised until some future date, shall not be deemed to be an offer or sale of such other security; but the issue or transfer of such other security upon the exercise of such right of conversion or subscription shall be deemed a sale of such other security. Any offer or sale of a security futures product by or on behalf of the issuer of the securities underlying the security futures product, an affiliate of the issuer, or an underwriter, shall constitute a contract for sale of, sale of, offer for sales or offer to sell the underlying securities. Any offer or sale of a security-based swap by or on behalf of the issuer of the securities upon which security-based swap is based or is referenced, an affiliate of the issuer, or an underwriter, shall constitute a contract for sale of, sale of, offer for sale, or offer to sell such securities. The publication or distribution by a broker or dealer of a research report about an emerging growth company that is the subject of a proposed public offering of the common equity securities of such emerging growth company pursuant to a registration statement that the issuer proposes to file, or has filed, or that is effective shall be deemed for purposes of paragraph (10) of this subsection and section 5(c) not to constitute an offer for sale or of-

fer to sell a security, even if the broker or dealer is participating or will participate in the registered offering of the securities of the issuer. As used in this paragraph, the term "research report" means a written, electronic, or oral communication that includes information, opinions, or recommendations with respect to securities of an issuer or an analysis of a security or an issuer, whether or not it provides information reasonably sufficient upon which to base an investment decision.

(4) The term "issuer" means every person who issues or proposes to issue any security; except that with respect to certificates of deposit, voting-trust certificates, or collateral-trust certificates, or with respect to certificates of interest or shares in an unincorporated investment trust not having a board of directors (or persons performing similar functions) or of the fixed, restricted management, or unit type, the term "issuer" means the person or persons performing the acts and assuming the duties of depositor or manager pursuant to the provisions of the trust or other agreement or instrument under which such securities are issued; except that in the case of an unincorporated association which provides by its articles for limited liability of any or all of its members, or in the case of a trust, committee, or other legal entity, the trustees or members thereof shall not be individually liable as issuers of any security issued by the association, trust, committee, or other legal entity; except that with respect to equipment-trust certificates or like securities, the term "issuer" means the person by whom the equipment or property is or is to be used; and except that with respect to fractional undivided interests in oil, gas, or other mineral rights, the term "issuer" means the owner of any such right or of any interest in such right (whether whole or fractional) who creates fractional interests therein for the purpose of public offering.

(5) The term "Commission" means the Securities and Exchange Commission.

(6) The term "Territory" means Puerto Rico, the Virgin Islands, and the insular possessions of the United States.

(7) The term "interstate commerce" means trade or commerce in securities or any transportation or communication relating thereto among the several States or between the District of Columbia or any Territory of the United States and any State or other Territory, or between any foreign country and any State, Territory, or the District of Columbia, or within the District of Columbia.

(8) The term "registration statement" means the statement provided for in section 6, and includes any amendment thereto and any report, document, or memorandum filed as part of such statement or incorporated therein by reference.

(9) The term "write" or "written" shall include printed, lithographed, or any means of graphic communication.

(10) The term "prospectus" means any prospectus, notice, circular, advertisement, letter, or communication, written or by radio or television, which offers any security for sale or confirms the sale of any security; except that (a) a communication sent or given after the effective date of the registration statement (other than a prospectus permitted under subsection (b) of section 10) shall not be deemed a prospectus if it is proved that prior to or at the same time with such communication a written prospectus meeting the requirements of subsection (a) of section 10 at the time of such communication was sent or given to the person to whom the communication was made, and (b) a notice, circular, advertisement, letter, or communication in respect of a security shall not be deemed to be a prospectus if it states from whom a written prospectus meeting the requirements of section 10 may be obtained and, in addition, does no more than identify the security, state the price thereof, state by whom orders will be executed, and contain such other information as the Commission, by rules or regulations deemed necessary or appropriate in the public interest and for the protection of investors, and subject to such terms and conditions as may be prescribed therein, may permit.

(11) The term "underwriter" means any person who has purchased from an issuer with a view to, or offers or sells for an issuer in connection with, the distribution of any security, or participates or has a direct or indirect participation in any such undertaking, or participates or has a participation in the direct or indirect underwriting of any such undertaking; but such term shall not include a person whose interest is limited to a commission from an underwriter or dealer not in excess of the usual and customary distributors' or sellers' commission. As used in this paragraph the term "issuer" shall include, in addition to an issuer, any person directly or indirectly controlling or con-

trolled by the issuer, or any person under direct or indirect common control with the issuer.

(12) The term "dealer" means any person who engages either for all or part of his time, directly or indirectly, as agent, broker, or principal, in the business of offering, buying, selling, or otherwise dealing or trading in securities issued by another person.

(13) The term "insurance company" means a company which is organized as an insurance company, whose primary and predominant business activity is the writing of insurance or the reinsuring of risks underwritten by insurance companies, and which is subject to supervision by the insurance commissioner, or a similar official or agency of a State or territory or the District of Columbia; or any receiver or similar official or any liquidating agent for such company, in his capacity as such.

(14) The term "separate account" means an account established and maintained by an insurance company pursuant to the laws of any State or territory of the United States, the District of Columbia, or of Canada or any province thereof, under which income, gains and losses, whether or not realized, from assets allocated to such account, are, in accordance with the applicable contract, credited to or charged against such account without regard to other income, gains or losses of the insurance company.

(15) The term "accredited investor" shall mean—

(i) a bank as defined in section 3(a)(2) whether acting in its individual or fiduciary capacity; an insurance company as defined in paragraph (13) of this subsection; an investment company registered under the Investment Company Act of 1940 or a business development company as defined in section 2(a)(48) of that Act; a Small Business Investment Company licensed by the Small Business Administration; or an employee benefit plan, including an individual retirement account, which is subject to the provisions of the Employee Retirement Income Security Act of 1974, if the investment decision is made by a plan fiduciary, as defined in section 3(21) of such Act, which is either a bank, insurance company, or registered investment adviser; or

(ii) any person who, on the basis of such factors as financial sophistication, net worth, knowledge, and experience in financial matters, or amount of assets under management qualifies as an accredited investor under rules and regulations which the Commission shall prescribe.

(16) The terms "security future", "narrow-based security index", and "security futures product" have the same meanings as provided in section 3(a)(55) of the Securities Exchange Act of 1934.

(17) The terms "swap" and "security-based swap" have the same meanings as in section 1a of the Commodity Exchange Act.

(18) The terms "purchase" or "sale" of a security-based swap shall be deemed to mean the execution, termination (prior to its scheduled maturity date), assignment, exchange, or similar transfer or conveyance of, or extinguishing of rights or obligations under, a security-based swap, as the context may require.

(19) The term "emerging growth company" means an issuer that had total annual gross revenues of less than $1,000,000,000 (as such amount is indexed for inflation every 5 years by the Commission to reflect the change in the Consumer Price Index for All Urban Consumers published by the Bureau of Labor Statistics, setting the threshold to the nearest 1,000,000) during its most recently completed fiscal year. An issuer that is an emerging growth company as of the first day of that fiscal year shall continue to be deemed an emerging growth company until the earliest of—

(A) the last day of the fiscal year of the issuer during which it had total annual gross revenues of $1,000,000,000 (as such amount is indexed for inflation every 5 years by the Commission to reflect the change in the Consumer Price Index for All Urban Consumers published by the Bureau of Labor Statistics, setting the threshold to the nearest 1,000,000) or more;

(B) the last day of the fiscal year of the issuer following the fifth anniversary of the date of the first sale of common equity securities of the issuer pursuant to an effective registration statement under this title;

(C) the date on which such issuer has, during the previous 3-year period, issued more than $1,000,000,000 in non-convertible debt; or

(D) the date on which such issuer is deemed to be a "large accelerated filer", as defined in Rule 12b–2 under the Securities Act of 1934, or any successor thereto.

(b) *Consideration of Promotion of Efficiency, Competition, and Capital Formation.* Whenever pursuant to this title the Commission is engaged in rulemaking and is required to consider or determine whether an action is necessary or appropriate in the public interest, the Commission shall also consider, in addition to the protection of investors, whether the action will promote efficiency, competition, and capital formation.

Swap Agreements

Sec. 2A. (a) [Reserved.]

(b) *Security–Based Swap Agreements*

(1) The definition of "security" in section 2(a)(1) of this title does not include any security-based swap agreement (as defined in section 3(a)(78) of the Securities Exchange Act of 1934).

(2) The Commission is prohibited from registering, or requiring, recommending, or suggesting, the registration under this title of any security-based swap agreement (as defined in section 3(a)(78) of the Securities Exchange Act of 1934). If the Commission becomes aware that a registrant has filed a registration statement with respect to such a swap agreement, the Commission shall promptly so notify the registrant. Any such registration statement with respect to such a swap agreement shall be void and of no force or effect.

(3) The Commission is prohibited from—

(A) promulgating, interpreting, or enforcing rules; or

(B) issuing orders of general applicability;

under this title in a manner that imposes or specifies reporting or recordkeeping requirements, procedures, or standards as prophylactic measures against fraud, manipulation, or insider trading with respect to any security-based swap agreement (as defined in section 3(a)(78) of the Securities Exchange Act of 1934).

(4) References in this title to the "purchase" or "sale" of a security-based swap agreement shall be deemed to mean the execution, termination (prior to its scheduled maturity date), assignment, exchange, or similar transfer or conveyance of, or extinguishing of rights or obligations under, a security-based swap agreement (as defined in section 3(a)(78) of the Securities Exchange Act of 1934), as the context may require.

Classes of Securities Under This Title

Sec. 3. (a) *Exempted Securities.* Except as hereinafter expressly provided, the provisions of this title shall not apply to any of the following classes of securities:

(1) [Reserved]

(2) Any security issued or guaranteed by the United States or any territory thereof, or by the District of Columbia, or by any State of the United States, or by any political subdivision of a State or territory, or by any public instrumentality of one or more States or territories, or by any person controlled or supervised by and acting as an instrumentality of the Government of the United States pursuant to authority granted by the Congress of the United States; or any certificate of deposit for any of the foregoing; or any security issued or guaranteed by any bank; or any security issued by or representing an interest in or a direct obligation of a Federal Reserve bank; or any interest or participation in any common trust fund or similar fund that is excluded from the definition of the term "investment company" under section 3(c)(3) of the Investment Company Act of 1940; or any security which is an industrial development bond (as defined in section 103(c)(2) of the Internal Revenue Code of 1954) the interest on which is excludable from gross income under section 103(a)(1) of such Code if, by reason of the application of paragraph (4) or (6) of section 103(c) of such Code (determined as if paragraphs (4)(A), (5), and (7) were not included in such section 103(c)), paragraph (1) of such section 103(c) does not apply to such security; or any interest or participation in a single trust fund, or in a collective trust fund maintained by a bank, or any security arising out of a contract issued by an insurance company, which interest, participation, or security is issued in connection with (A) a stock bonus, pension, or profit-sharing plan which meets the requirements for qualification under section 401 of the Internal Revenue Code of 1954, (B) an annuity plan which meets the requirements for the deduction of the employer's contributions under section 404(a)(2) of such Code, (C) a governmental plan as defined in section 414(d) of such Code which has been established by an employer for the exclusive benefit of its employees or their beneficiaries for the purpose of distributing to such employees or their beneficiaries the corpus and income of the funds accumulated under such plan, if under such plan it is impossible, prior to the satisfaction of all liabilities with respect to such employees and their beneficiaries, for any part of the corpus or income to be used for, or diverted to, purposes other than the exclusive benefit of such employees or their

beneficiaries, or (D) a church plan, company, or account that is excluded from the definition of an investment company under section 3(c)(14) of the Investment Company Act of 1940, other than any plan described in subparagraph (A), (B), (C), or (D) of this paragraph (i) the contributions under which are held in a single trust fund or in a separate account maintained by an insurance company for a single employer and under which an amount in excess of the employer's contribution is allocated to the purchase of securities (other than interests or participations in the trust or separate account itself) issued by the employer or any company directly or indirectly controlling, controlled by, or under common control with the employer, (ii) which covers employees some or all of whom are employees within the meaning of section 401(c)(1) of such Code (other than a person participating in a church plan who is described in section 414(e)(3)(B) of the Internal Revenue Code of 1986), or (iii) which is a plan funded by an annuity contract described in section 403(b) of such Code (other than a retirement income account described in section 403(b)(9) of the Internal Revenue Code of 1986, to the extent that the interest or participation in such single trust fund or collective trust fund is issued to a church, a convention or association of churches, or an organization described in section 414(e)(3)(A) of such Code establishing or maintaining the retirement income account or to a trust established by any such entity in connection with the retirement income account). The Commission, by rules and regulations or order, shall exempt from the provisions of section 5 of this title any interest or participation issued in connection with a stock bonus, pension, profit-sharing, or annuity plan which covers employees some or all of whom are employees within the meaning of section 401(c)(1) of the Internal Revenue Code of 1954, if and to the extent that the Commission determines this to be necessary or appropriate in the public interest and consistent with the protection of investors and the purposes fairly intended by the policy and provisions of this title. For purposes of this paragraph, a security issued or guaranteed by a bank shall not include any interest or participation in any collective trust fund maintained by a bank; and the term "bank" means any national bank, or banking institution organized under the laws of any State, territory, or the District of Columbia, the business of which is substantially confined to banking and is supervised by the State or territorial banking commission or similar official; except that in the case of a common trust fund or similar fund, or a collective trust fund, the term "bank" has the same meaning as in the Investment Company Act of 1940;

(3) Any note, draft, bill of exchange, or banker's acceptance which arises out of a current transaction or the proceeds of which have been or are to be used for current transactions, and which has a maturity at the time of issuance of not exceeding nine months, exclusive of days of grace, or any renewal thereof the maturity of which is likewise limited;

(4) Any security issued by a person organized and operated exclusively for religious, educational, benevolent, fraternal, charitable, or reformatory purposes and not for pecuniary profit, and no part of the net earnings of which inures to the benefit of any person, private stockholder, or individual, or any security of a fund that is excluded from the definition of an investment company under section 3(c)(10)(B) of the Investment Company Act of 1940;

(5) Any security issued (A) by a savings and loan association, building and loan association, cooperative bank, homestead association, or similar institution, which is supervised and examined by State or Federal authority having supervision over any such institution; or (B) by (i) a farmer's cooperative organization exempt from tax under section 521 of the Internal Revenue Code of 1954, (ii) a corporation described in section 501(c)(16) of such Code and exempt from tax under section 501(a) of such Code, or (iii) a corporation described in section 501(c)(2) of such Code which is exempt from tax under section 501(a) of such Code and is organized for the exclusive purpose of holding title to property, collecting income therefrom, and turning over the entire amount thereof, less expenses, to an organization or corporation described in clause (i) or (ii);

(6) Any interest in a railroad equipment trust. For purposes of this paragraph "interest in a railroad equipment trust" means any interest in an equipment trust, lease, conditional sales contract or other similar arrangement entered into, issued, assumed, guaranteed by, or for the benefit of, a common carrier to finance the acquisition of rolling stock including motive power;

(7) Certificates issued by a receiver or by a trustee or debtor in possession in a case under title 11 of the United States Code, with the approval of the court;

(8) Any insurance or endowment policy or annuity contract or optional annuity contract, issued by a corporation subject to the supervision of the insurance commissioner, bank commissioner, or any agency or officer performing like functions, of any State or Territory of the United States or the District of Columbia;

(9) Except with respect to a security exchanged in a case under title 11 of the United States Code, any security exchanged by the issuer with its existing security holders exclusively where no commission or other remuneration is paid or given directly or indirectly for soliciting such exchange;

(10) Except with respect to a security exchanged in a case under title 11 of the United States Code, any security which is issued in exchange for one or more bona fide outstanding securities, claims or property interests, or partly in such exchange and partly for cash, where the terms and conditions of such issuance and exchange are approved, after a hearing upon the fairness of such terms and conditions at which all persons to whom it is proposed to issue securities in such exchange shall have the right to appear, by any court, or by any official or agency of the United States, or by any State or Territorial banking or insurance commission or other governmental authority expressly authorized by law to grant such approval;

(11) Any security which is a part of an issue offered and sold only to persons resident within a single State or Territory, where the issuer of such security is a person resident and doing business within, or, if a corporation, incorporated by and doing business within, such State or Territory.

(12) Any equity security issued in connection with the acquisition by a holding company of a bank under section 3(a) of the Bank Holding Company Act of 1956 or a savings association under section 10(e) of the Home Owners' Loan Act, if—

(A) the acquisition occurs solely as part of a reorganization in which security holders exchange their shares of a bank or savings association for shares of a newly formed holding company with no significant assets other than securities of the bank or savings association and the existing subsidiaries of the bank or savings association;

(B) the security holders receive, after that reorganization, substantially the same proportional share interests in the holding company as they held in the bank or savings association, except for nominal changes in shareholders' interests resulting from lawful elimination of fractional interests and the exercise of dissenting shareholders' rights under State or Federal law;

(C) the rights and interests of security holders in the holding company are substantially the same as those in the bank or savings association prior to the transaction, other than as may be required by law; and

(D) the holding company has substantially the same assets and liabilities, on a consolidated basis, as the bank or savings association had prior to the transaction.

For purposes of this paragraph, the term "savings association" means a savings association (as defined in section 3(b) of the Federal Deposit Insurance Act) the deposits of which are insured by the Federal Deposit Insurance Corporation.

(13) Any security issued by or any interest or participation in any church plan, company or account that is excluded from the definition of an investment company under section 3(c)(14) of the Investment Company Act of 1940.

(14) Any security futures product that is—

(A) cleared by a clearing agency registered under section 17A of the Securities Exchange Act of 1934 or exempt from registration under subsection (b)(7) of such section 17A; and

(B) traded on a national securities exchange or a national securities association registered pursuant to section 15A(a) of the Securities Exchange Act of 1934.

(b) *Additional Exemptions.*

(1) *Small Issues Exemptive Authority.* The Commission may from time to time by its rules and regulations, and subject to such terms and conditions as may be prescribed therein, add any class of securities to the securities exempted as provided in this section, if it finds that the enforcement of this title with respect to such securities is not necessary in the public interest and for the protection of investors by reason of the small amount involved or the limited character of the public offering; but no issue of securities shall be exempted under this subsection where the aggregate amount at which such issue is offered to the public exceeds $5,000,000.

(2) *Additional Issues.* The Commission shall by rule or regulation add a class of securities to the securities exempted pursuant to this section in accordance with the following terms and conditions:

(A) The aggregate offering amount of all securities offered and sold within the prior 12-month period in reliance on the exemption added in accordance with this paragraph shall not exceed $50,000,000.

(B) The securities may be offered and sold publicly.

(C) The securities shall not be restricted securities within the meaning of the Federal securities laws and the regulations promulgated thereunder.

(D) The civil liability provision in section 12(a)(2) shall apply to any person offering or selling such securities.

(E) The issuer may solicit interest in the offering prior to filing any offering statement, on such terms and conditions as the Commission may prescribe in the public interest or for the protection of investors.

(F) The Commission shall require the issuer to file audited financial statements with the Commission annually.

(G) Such other terms, conditions, or requirements as the Commission may determine necessary in the public interest and for the protection of investors, which may include—

(i) a requirement that the issuer prepare and electronically file with the Commission and distribute to prospective investors an offering statement, and any related documents, in such form and with such content as prescribed by the Commission, including audited financial statements, a description of the issuer's business operations, its financial condition, its corporate governance principles, its use of investor funds, and other appropriate matters; and

(ii) disqualification provisions under which the exemption shall not be available to the issuer or its predecessors, affiliates, officers, directors, underwriters, or other related persons, which shall be substantially similar to the disqualification provisions contained in the regulations adopted in accordance with section 926 of the Dodd–Frank Wall Street Reform and Consumer Protection Act.

(3) *Limitation.* Only the following types of securities may be exempted under a rule or regulation adopted pursuant to paragraph (2): equity securities, debt securities, and debt securities convertible or exchangeable to equity interests, including any guarantees of such securities.

(4) *Periodic Disclosures.* Upon such terms and conditions as the Commission determines necessary in the public interest and for the protection of investors, the Commission by rule or regulation may require an issuer of a class of securities exempted under paragraph (2) to make available to investors and file with the Commission periodic disclosures regarding the issuer, its business operations, its financial condition, its corporate governance principles, its use of investor funds, and other appropriate matters, and also may provide for the suspension and termination of such a requirement with respect to that issuer.

(5) *Adjustment.* Not later than 2 years after the date of enactment of the Small Company Capital Formation Act of 2011 and every 2 years thereafter, the Commission shall review the offering amount limitation described in paragraph (2)(A) and shall increase such amount as the Commission determines appropriate. If the Commission determines not to increase such amount, it shall report to the Committee on Financial Services of the House of Representatives and the Committee on Banking, Housing, and Urban Affairs of the Senate on its reasons for not increasing the amount.

(c) *Securities Issued by Small Investment Company.* The Commission may from time to time by its rules and regulations and subject to such terms and conditions as may be prescribed therein, add to the securities exempted as provided in this section any class of securities issued by a small business investment company under the Small Business Investment Act of 1958 if it finds, having regard to the purposes of that Act, that the enforcement of this Act with respect to such securities is not necessary in the public interest and for the protection of investors.

Exempted Transactions

Sec. 4.* (a) The provisions of section 5 shall not apply to—

(1) transactions by any person other than an issuer, underwriter, or dealer.

(2) transactions by an issuer not involving any public offering.

* In the JOBS Act, Congress divided Section 4 into Sections 4(a) and 4(b). Then, throughout the JOBS Act Congress referred to Section 4(6) rather than 4(a)(6).

(3) transactions by a dealer (including an underwriter no longer acting as an underwriter in respect of the security involved in such transaction), except—

(A) transactions taking place prior to the expiration of forty days after the first date upon which the security was bona fide offered to the public by the issuer or by or through an underwriter,

(B) transactions in a security as to which a registration statement has been filed taking place prior to the expiration of forty days after the effective date of such registration statement or prior to the expiration of forty days after the first date upon which the security was bona fide offered to the public by the issuer or by or through an underwriter after such effective date, whichever is later (excluding in the computation of such forty days any time during which a stop order issued under section 8 is in effect as to the security), or such shorter period as the Commission may specify by rules and regulations or order, and

(C) transactions as to securities constituting the whole or a part of an unsold allotment to or subscription by such dealer as a participant in the distribution of such securities by the issuer or by or through an underwriter.

With respect to transactions referred to in clause (B), if securities of the issuer have not previously been sold pursuant to an earlier effective registration statement the applicable period, instead of forty days, shall be ninety days, or such shorter period as the Commission may specify by rules and regulations or order.

(4) brokers' transactions executed upon customers' orders on any exchange or in the over-the-counter market but not the solicitation of such orders.

(5) transactions involving offers or sales by an issuer solely to one or more accredited investors, if the aggregate offering price of an issue of securities offered in reliance on this paragraph does not exceed the amount allowed under section 3(b)(1) of this title, if there is no advertising or public solicitation in connection with the transaction by the issuer or anyone acting on the issuer's behalf, and if the issuer files such notice with the Commission as the Commission shall prescribe.

(6) transactions involving the offer or sale of securities by an issuer (including all entities controlled by or under common control with the issuer), provided that—*

(A) the aggregate amount sold to all investors by the issuer, including any amount sold in reliance on the exemption provided under this paragraph during the 12-month period preceding the date of such transaction, is not more than $1,000,000;

(B) the aggregate amount sold to any investor by an issuer, including any amount sold in reliance on the exemption provided under this paragraph during the 12-month period preceding the date of such transaction, does not exceed—

(i) the greater of $2,000 or 5 percent of the annual income or net worth of such investor, as applicable, if either the annual income or the net worth of the investor is less than $100,000; and

(ii) 10 percent of the annual income or net worth of such investor, as applicable, not to exceed a maximum aggregate amount sold of $100,000, if either the annual income or net worth of the investor is equal to or more than $100,000;

(C) the transaction is conducted through a broker or funding portal that complies with the requirements of section 4A(a); and

(D) the issuer complies with the requirements of section 4A(b).

(7) transactions meeting the requirements of subsection (d).

(b) Offers and sales exempt under Rule 506 under the Securities Act of 1933 (as revised pursuant to section 201 of the Jumpstart Our Business Startups Act) shall not be deemed public offerings under the Federal securities laws as a result of general advertising or general solicitation.

(b)(1) With respect to securities offered and sold in compliance with Rule 506 of Regulation D under this Act, no person who meets the conditions set

* The JOBS Act directed that this section be amended by substituting "section 3(b)(1)" for "section 3(b)" in para. (5), and by adding a para. (6) to the end. Such amendments have been made in subsection (a) in order to effectuate the probable intent of Congress.

forth in paragraph (2) shall be subject to registration as a broker or dealer pursuant to section 15(a)(1) of this title,** solely because—***

(A) that person maintains a platform or mechanism that permits the offer, sale, purchase, or negotiation of or with respect to securities, or permits general solicitations, general advertisements, or similar or related activities by issuers of such securities, whether online, in person, or through any other means;

(B) that person or any person associated with that person co-invests in such securities; or

(C) that person or any person associated with that person provides ancillary services with respect to such securities.

(2) The exemption provided in paragraph (1) shall apply to any person described in such paragraph if—

(A) such person and each person associated with that person receives no compensation in connection with the purchase or sale of such security;

(B) such person and each person associated with that person does not have possession of customer funds or securities in connection with the purchase or sale of such security; and

(C) such person is not subject to a statutory disqualification as defined in section 3(a)(39) of this title and does not have any person associated with that person subject to such a statutory disqualification.

(3) For the purposes of this subsection, the term "ancillary services" means—

(A) the provision of due diligence services, in connection with the offer, sale, purchase, or negotiation of such security, so long as such services do not include, for separate compensation, investment advice or recommendations to issuers or investors; and

(B) the provision of standardized documents to the issuers and investors, so long as such person or entity does not negotiate the terms of the issuance for and on behalf of third parties and issuers are not required to use the standardized documents as a condition of using the service.

** Refers to Securities Act but should refer to section 15(a)(1) of the Securities Exchange Act of 1934.

*** Two subsec. (b) have been enacted.

(d) *Certain Accredited Investor Transactions.*—The transactions referred to in subsection (a)(7) are transactions meeting the following requirements:

(1) *Accredited Investor Requirement.*—Each purchaser is an accredited investor, as that term is defined in section 230.501(a) of title 17, Code of Federal Regulations (or any successor regulation).

(2) *Prohibition on General Solicitation or Advertising.*—Neither the seller, nor any person acting on the seller's behalf, offers or sells securities by any form of general solicitation or general advertising.

(3) *Information Requirement.*—In the case of a transaction involving the securities of an issuer that is neither subject to section 13 or 15(d) of the Securities Exchange Act of 1934 (15 U.S.C. 78m; 78o(d)), nor exempt from reporting pursuant to section 240.12g3–2(b) of title 17, Code of Federal Regulations, nor a foreign government (as defined in section 230.405 of title 17, Code of Federal Regulations) eligible to register securities under Schedule B, the seller and a prospective purchaser designated by the seller obtain from the issuer, upon request of the seller, and the seller in all cases makes available to a prospective purchaser, the following information (which shall be reasonably current in relation to the date of resale under this section):

(A) The exact name of the issuer and the issuer's predecessor (if any).

(B) The address of the issuer's principal executive offices.

(C) The exact title and class of the security.

(D) The par or stated value of the security.

(E) The number of shares or total amount of the securities outstanding as of the end of the issuer's most recent fiscal year.

(F) The name and address of the transfer agent, corporate secretary, or other person responsible for transferring shares and stock certificates.

(G) A statement of the nature of the business of the issuer and the products and services it offers, which shall be presumed reasonably current if the statement is as of 12 months before the transaction date.

(H) The names of the officers and directors of the issuer.

(I) The names of any persons registered as a broker, dealer, or agent that shall be paid or given, directly or indirectly, any commission or remuneration for such person's participation in the offer or sale of the securities.

(J) The issuer's most recent balance sheet and profit and loss statement and similar financial statements, which shall—

(i) be for such part of the 2 preceding fiscal years as the issuer has been in operation;

(ii) be prepared in accordance with generally accepted accounting principles or, in the case of a foreign private issuer, be prepared in accordance with generally accepted accounting principles or the International Financial Reporting Standards issued by the International Accounting Standards Board;

(iii) be presumed reasonably current if—

(I) with respect to the balance sheet, the balance sheet is as of a date less than 16 months before the transaction date; and

(II) with respect to the profit and loss statement, such statement is for the 12 months preceding the date of the issuer's balance sheet; and

(iv) if the balance sheet is not as of a date less than 6 months before the transaction date, be accompanied by additional statements of profit and loss for the period from the date of such balance sheet to a date less than 6 months before the transaction date.

(K) To the extent that the seller is a control person with respect to the issuer, a brief statement regarding the nature of the affiliation, and a statement certified by such seller that they have no reasonable grounds to believe that the issuer is in violation of the securities laws or regulations.

(4) *Issuers Disqualified.*—The transaction is not for the sale of a security where the seller is an issuer or a subsidiary, either directly or indirectly, of the issuer.

(5) *Bad Actor Prohibition.*—Neither the seller, nor any person that has been or will be paid (directly or indirectly) remuneration or a commission for their participation in the offer or sale of the securities, including solicitation of purchasers for the seller is subject to an event that would disqualify an issuer or other covered person under Rule 506(d)(1) of Regulation D (17 CFR 230.506(d)(1)) or is subject to a statutory disqualification described under section 3(a)(39) of the Securities Exchange Act of 1934.

(6) *Business Requirement.*—The issuer is engaged in business, is not in the organizational stage or in bankruptcy or receivership, and is not a blank check, blind pool, or shell company that has no specific business plan or purpose or has indicated that the issuer's primary business plan is to engage in a merger or combination of the business with, or an acquisition of, an unidentified person.

(7) *Underwriter Prohibition.*—The transaction is not with respect to a security that constitutes the whole or part of an unsold allotment to, or a subscription or participation by, a broker or dealer as an underwriter of the security or a redistribution.

(8) *Outstanding Class Requirement.*—The transaction is with respect to a security of a class that has been authorized and outstanding for at least 90 days prior to the date of the transaction.

(e) Additional Requirements.—

(1) *In General.*—With respect to an exempted transaction described under subsection (a)(7):

(A) Securities acquired in such transaction shall be deemed to have been acquired in a transaction not involving any public offering.

(B) Such transaction shall be deemed not to be a distribution for purposes of section 2(a)(11).

(C) Securities involved in such transaction shall be deemed to be restricted securities within the meaning of Rule 144 (17 CFR 230.144).

(2) *Rule of Construction.*—The exemption provided by subsection (a)(7) shall not be the exclusive means for establishing an exemption from the registration requirements of section 5.

Requirements With Respect to Certain Small Transactions

Sec. 4A. (a) *Requirements on Intermediaries.* A person acting as an intermediary in a transaction involving the offer or sale of securities for the account of others pursuant to section 4(a)(6) shall—

(1) register with the Commission as—

(A) a broker; or

(B) a funding portal (as defined in section 3(a)(80) of the Securities Exchange Act of 1934);

(2) register with any applicable self-regulatory organization (as defined in section 3(a)(26) of the Securities Exchange Act of 1934);

(3) provide such disclosures, including disclosures related to risks and other investor education materials, as the Commission shall, by rule, determine appropriate;

(4) ensure that each investor—

(A) reviews investor-education information, in accordance with standards established by the Commission, by rule;

(B) positively affirms that the investor understands that the investor is risking the loss of the entire investment, and that the investor could bear such a loss; and

(C) answers questions demonstrating—

(i) an understanding of the level of risk generally applicable to investments in startups, emerging businesses, and small issuers;

(ii) an understanding of the risk of illiquidity; and

(iii) an understanding of such other matters as the Commission determines appropriate, by rule;

(5) take such measures to reduce the risk of fraud with respect to such transactions, as established by the Commission, by rule, including obtaining a background and securities enforcement regulatory history check on each officer, director, and person holding more than 20 percent of the outstanding equity of every issuer whose securities are offered by such person;

(6) not later than 21 days prior to the first day on which securities are sold to any investor (or such other period as the Commission may establish), make available to the Commission and to potential investors any information provided by the issuer pursuant to subsection (b);

(7) ensure that all offering proceeds are only provided to the issuer when the aggregate capital raised from all investors is equal to or greater than a target offering amount, and allow all investors to cancel their commitments to invest, as the Commission shall, by rule, determine appropriate;

(8) make such efforts as the Commission determines appropriate, by rule, to ensure that no investor in a 12-month period has purchased securities offered pursuant to section 4(a)(6) that, in the aggregate, from all issuers, exceed the investment limits set forth in section 4(a)(6)(B);

(9) take such steps to protect the privacy of information collected from investors as the Commission shall, by rule, determine appropriate;

(10) not compensate promoters, finders, or lead generators for providing the broker or funding portal with the personal identifying information of any potential investor;

(11) prohibit its directors, officers, or partners (or any person occupying a similar status or performing a similar function) from having any financial interest in an issuer using its services; and

(12) meet such other requirements as the Commission may, by rule, prescribe, for the protection of investors and in the public interest.

(b) *Requirements for Issuers.* For purposes of section 4(6), an issuer who offers or sells securities shall—

(1) file with the Commission and provide to investors and the relevant broker or funding portal, and make available to potential investors—

(A) the name, legal status, physical address, and website address of the issuer;

(B) the names of the directors and officers (and any persons occupying a similar status or performing a similar function), and each person holding more than 20 percent of the shares of the issuer;

(C) a description of the business of the issuer and the anticipated business plan of the issuer;

(D) a description of the financial condition of the issuer, including, for offerings that, together with all other offerings of the issuer under section 4(6) within the preceding 12–month period, have, in the aggregate, target offering amounts of—

(i) $100,000 or less—

(I) the income tax returns filed by the issuer for the most recently completed year (if any); and

(II) financial statements of the issuer, which shall be certified by the principal executive officer of the issuer to be true and complete in all material respects;

(ii) more than $100,000, but not more than $500,000, financial statements reviewed by a public accountant who is independent of the issuer, using professional standards and procedures for such review or standards and procedures established by the Commission, by rule, for such purpose; and

(iii) more than $500,000 (or such other amount as the Commission may establish, by rule), audited financial statements;

(E) a description of the stated purpose and intended use of the proceeds of the offering sought by the issuer with respect to the target offering amount;

(F) the target offering amount, the deadline to reach the target offering amount, and regular updates regarding the progress of the issuer in meeting the target offering amount;

(G) the price to the public of the securities or the method for determining the price, provided that, prior to sale, each investor shall be provided in writing the final price and all required disclosures, with a reasonable opportunity to rescind the commitment to purchase the securities;

(H) a description of the ownership and capital structure of the issuer, including—

(i) terms of the securities of the issuer being offered and each other class of security of the issuer, including how such terms may be modified, and a summary of the differences between such securities, including how the rights of the securities being offered may be materially limited, diluted, or qualified by the rights of any other class of security of the issuer;

(ii) a description of how the exercise of the rights held by the principal shareholders of the issuer could negatively impact the purchasers of the securities being offered;

(iii) the name and ownership level of each existing shareholder who owns more than 20 percent of any class of the securities of the issuer;

(iv) how the securities being offered are being valued, and examples of methods for how such securities may be valued by the issuer in the future, including during subsequent corporate actions; and

(v) the risks to purchasers of the securities relating to minority ownership in the issuer, the risks associated with corporate actions, including additional issuances of shares, a sale of the issuer or of assets of the issuer, or transactions with related parties; and

(I) such other information as the Commission may, by rule, prescribe, for the protection of investors and in the public interest;

(2) not advertise the terms of the offering, except for notices which direct investors to the funding portal or broker;

(3) not compensate or commit to compensate, directly or indirectly, any person to promote its offerings through communication channels provided by a broker or funding portal, without taking such steps as the Commission shall, by rule, require to ensure that such person clearly discloses the receipt, past or prospective, of such compensation, upon each instance of such promotional communication;

(4) not less than annually, file with the Commission and provide to investors reports of the results of operations and financial statements of the issuer, as the Commission shall, by rule, determine appropriate, subject to such exceptions and termination dates as the Commission may establish, by rule; and

(5) comply with such other requirements as the Commission may, by rule, prescribe, for the protection of investors and in the public interest.

(c) *Liability for Material Misstatements and Omissions.*

(1) *Actions Authorized.*

(A) *In General.* Subject to paragraph (2), a person who purchases a security in a transaction exempted by the provisions of section 4(a)(6) may bring an action against an issuer described in paragraph (2), either at law or in equity in any court of competent jurisdiction, to recover the consideration paid for such security with interest thereon, less the amount of any income received thereon, upon the tender of such security, or for damages if such person no longer owns the security.

(B) *Liability.* An action brought under this paragraph shall be subject to the provisions of section 12(b) and section 13, as if the liability were created under section 12(a)(2).

(2) *Applicability.* An issuer shall be liable in an action under paragraph (1), if the issuer—

(A) by the use of any means or instruments of transportation or communication in interstate commerce or of the mails, by any means of any written or oral communication, in the offering or sale of a security in a transaction exempted by the provisions of section 4(a)(6), makes an untrue statement of a material fact or omits to state a material fact required to be stated or necessary in order to make the statements, in the light of the circumstances under which they were made, not misleading, provided that the purchaser did not know of such untruth or omission; and

(B) does not sustain the burden of proof that such issuer did not know, and in the exercise of reasonable care could not have known, of such untruth or omission.

(3) *Definition.* As used in this subsection, the term 'issuer' includes any person who is a director or partner of the issuer, and the principal executive officer or officers, principal financial officer, and controller or principal accounting officer of the issuer (and any person occupying a similar status or performing a similar function) that offers or sells a security in a transaction exempted by the provisions of section 4(a)(6), and any person who offers or sells the security in such offering.

(d) *Information Available to States.* The Commission shall make, or shall cause to be made by the relevant broker or funding portal, the information described in subsection (b) and such other information as the Commission, by rule, determines appropriate, available to the securities commission (or any agency or office performing like functions) of each State and territory of the United States and the District of Columbia.

(e) *Restrictions on Sales.* Securities issued pursuant to a transaction described in section 4(a)(6)—

(1) may not be transferred by the purchaser of such securities during the 1-year period beginning on the date of purchase, unless such securities are transferred—

(A) to the issuer of the securities;

(B) to an accredited investor;

(C) as part of an offering registered with the Commission; or

(D) to a member of the family of the purchaser or the equivalent, or in connection with the death or divorce of the purchaser or other similar circumstance, in the discretion of the Commission; and

(2) shall be subject to such other limitations as the Commission shall, by rule, establish.

(f) *Applicability.* Section 4(a)(6) shall not apply to transactions involving the offer or sale of securities by any issuer that—

(1) is not organized under and subject to the laws of a State or territory of the United States or the District of Columbia;

(2) is subject to the requirement to file reports pursuant to section 13 or section 15(d) of the Securities Exchange Act of 1934;

(3) is an investment company, as defined in section 3 of the Investment Company Act of 1940, or is excluded from the definition of investment company by section 3(b) or section 3(c) of that Act; or

(4) the Commission, by rule or regulation, determines appropriate.

(g) *Rule of Construction.* Nothing in this section or section 4(a)(6) shall be construed as preventing an issuer from raising capital through methods not described under section 4(a)(6).

(h) *Certain Calculations.*

(1) *Dollar Amounts.* Dollar amounts in section 4(a)(6) and subsection (b) of this section shall be adjusted by the Commission not less frequently than once every 5 years, by notice published in the Federal Register to reflect any change in the Consumer Price Index for All Urban Consumers published by the Bureau of Labor Statistics.

(2) *Income and Net Worth.* The income and net worth of a natural person under section 4(a)(6)(B) shall be calculated in accordance with any rules of the Commission under this title regarding the calculation of the income and net worth, respectively, of an accredited investor.

Prohibitions Relating to Interstate Commerce and the Mails

Sec. 5. (a) *Sale or Delivery After Sale of Unregistered Securities.* Unless a registration statement is in effect as to a security, it shall be unlawful for any person, directly or indirectly—

(1) to make use of any means or instruments of transportation or communication in interstate commerce or of the mails to sell such security through the use or medium of any prospectus or otherwise; or

(2) to carry or cause to be carried through the mails or in interstate commerce, by any means or

instruments of transportation, any such security for the purpose of sale or for delivery after sale.

(b) *Necessity of Prospectus Meeting Requirements of Section 10 of This Title.* It shall be unlawful for any person, directly or indirectly—

(1) to make use of any means or instruments of transportation or communication in interstate commerce or of the mails to carry or transmit any prospectus relating to any security with respect to which a registration statement has been filed under this title, unless such prospectus meets the requirements of section 10; or

(2) to carry or cause to be carried through the mails or in interstate commerce any such security for the purpose of sale or for delivery after sale, unless accompanied or preceded by a prospectus that meets the requirements of subsection (a) of section 10.

(c) *Necessity of Filing Registration Statement.* It shall be unlawful for any person, directly or indirectly, to make use of any means or instruments of transportation or communication in interstate commerce or of the mails to offer to sell or offer to buy through the use or medium of any prospectus or otherwise any security, unless a registration statement has been filed as to such security, or while the registration statement is the subject of a refusal order or stop order or (prior to the effective date of the registration statement) any public proceeding or examination under section 8.

(d) *Limitation.* Notwithstanding any other provision of this section, an emerging growth company or any person authorized to act on behalf of an emerging growth company may engage in oral or written communications with potential investors that are qualified institutional buyers or institutions that are accredited investors, as such terms are respectively defined in Rules 144A and 501(a) under the Securities Act of 1933, or any successor thereto, to determine whether such investors might have an interest in a contemplated securities offering, either prior to or following the date of filing of a registration statement with respect to such securities with the Commission, subject to the requirement of subsection (b)(2).

(e) Notwithstanding the provisions of section 3 or 4, unless a registration statement meeting the requirements of section 10(a) is in effect as to a security-based swap, it shall be unlawful for any person, directly or indirectly, to make use of any means or instruments of transportation or communication in interstate commerce or of the mails to offer to sell, offer to buy or purchase or sell a security-based swap to any person who is not an eligible contract participant as defined in section 1a(18) of the Commodity Exchange Act.

Registration of Securities and Signing of Registration Statement

Sec. 6. (a) *Method of Registration.* Any security may be registered with the Commission under the terms and conditions hereinafter provided, by filing a registration statement in triplicate, at least one of which shall be signed by each issuer, its principal executive officer or officers, its principal financial officer, its comptroller or principal accounting officer, and the majority of its board of directors or persons performing similar functions (or, if there is no board of directors or persons performing similar functions, by the majority of the persons or board having the power of management of the issuer), and in case the issuer is a foreign or Territorial person by its duly authorized representative in the United States; except that when such registration statement relates to a security issued by a foreign government, or political subdivision thereof, it need be signed only by the underwriter of such security. Signatures of all such persons when written on the said registration statements shall be presumed to have been so written by authority of the person whose signature is so affixed and the burden of proof, in the event such authority shall be denied, shall be upon the party denying the same. The affixing of any signature without the authority of the purported signer shall constitute a violation of this title. A registration statement shall be deemed effective only as to the securities specified therein as proposed to be offered.

(b) *Registration Fee.*

(1) *Fee Payment Required.* At the time of filing a registration statement, the applicant shall pay to the Commission a fee at a rate that shall be equal to $92 per $1,000,000 of the maximum aggregate price at which such securities are proposed to be offered, except that during fiscal year 2003 and any succeeding fiscal year such fee shall be adjusted pursuant to paragraph (2).

(2) *Annual Adjustment.* For each fiscal year, the Commission shall by order adjust the rate required by paragraph (1) for such fiscal year to a rate that, when applied to the baseline estimate of the aggregate maximum offering prices for such fiscal year, is reasonably likely to produce aggregate fee collections under this subsection that are equal to the target fee collection amount for such fiscal year.

(3) *Pro Rata Application.* The rates per $1,000,000 required by this subsection shall be applied pro rata to amounts and balances of less than $1,000,000.

(4) *Review and Effective Date.* In exercising its authority under this subsection, the Commission shall not be required to comply with the provisions of section 553 of title 5, United States Code. An adjusted rate prescribed under paragraph (2) and published under paragraph (5) shall not be subject to judicial review. An adjusted rate prescribed under paragraph (2) shall take effect on the first day of the fiscal year to which such rate applies.

(5) *Publication.* The Commission shall publish in the Federal Register notices of the rate applicable under this subsection and under sections 13(e) and 14(g) for each fiscal year not later than August 31 of the fiscal year preceding the fiscal year to which such rate applies, together with any estimates or projections on which such rate is based.

(6) *Definitions.* For purposes of this subsection:

(A) *Target Fee Collection Amount.* The target fee collection amount for each fiscal year is determined according to the following table:

Fiscal year:	Target fee collection amount
2002	$ 377,000,000
2003	$ 435,000,000
2004	$ 467,000,000
2005	$ 570,000,000
2006	$ 689,000,000
2007	$ 214,000,000
2008	$ 234,000,000
2009	$ 284,000,000
2010	$ 334,000,000
2011	$ 394,000,000
2012	$ 425,000,000
2013	$ 455,000,000
2014	$ 485,000,000
2015	$ 515,000,000
2016	$ 550,000,000
2017	$ 585,000,000
2018	$ 620,000,000
2019	$ 660,000,000
2020	$ 705,000,000
2021 and each fiscal year thereafter	An amount that is equal to the target fee collection amount for the prior fiscal year, adjusted by the rate of inflation.

(B) *Baseline Estimate of the Aggregate Maximum Offering Prices.* The baseline estimate of the aggregate maximum offering prices for any fiscal year is the baseline estimate of the aggregate maximum offering price at which securities are proposed to be offered pursuant to registration statements filed with the Commission during such fiscal year as determined by the Commission, after consultation with the Congressional Budget Office and the Office of Management and Budget, using the methodology required for projections pursuant to section 257 of the Balanced Budget and Emergency Deficit Control Act of 1985.

(c) *Time Registration Effective.* The filing with the Commission of a registration statement, or of an amendment to a registration statement, shall be deemed to have taken place upon the receipt thereof, but the filing of a registration statement shall not be deemed to have taken place unless it is accompanied by a United States postal money order or a certified bank check or cash for the amount of the fee required under subsection (b).

(d) *Information Available to Public.* The information contained in or filed with any registration statement shall be made available to the public under such regulations as the Commission may prescribe, and copies thereof, photostatic or otherwise, shall be furnished to every applicant at such reasonable charge as the Commission may prescribe.

(e) *Emerging Growth Companies.*

(1) *In General.* Any emerging growth company, prior to its initial public offering date, may

confidentially submit to the Commission a draft registration statement, for confidential nonpublic review by the staff of the Commission prior to public filing, provided that the initial confidential submission and all amendments thereto shall be publicly filed with the Commission not later than 15 days before the date on which the issuer conducts a road show, as such term is defined in Rule 433(h)(4) under the Securities Act of 1933, or any successor thereto. An issuer that was an emerging growth company at the time it submitted a confidential registration statement or, in lieu thereof, a publicly filed registration statement for review under this subsection but ceases to be an emerging growth company thereafter shall continue to be treated as an emerging market growth company for the purposes of this subsection through the earlier of the date on which the issuer consummates its initial public offering pursuant to such registrations statement or the end of the 1-year period beginning on the date the company ceases to be an emerging growth company.

(2) *Confidentiality.* Notwithstanding any other provision of this title, the Commission shall not be compelled to disclose any information provided to or obtained by the Commission pursuant to this subsection. For purposes of the Freedom of Information Act, section 552 of title 5, United States Code, this subsection shall be considered a statute described in subsection (b)(3)(B) of such section 552. Information described in or obtained pursuant to this subsection shall be deemed to constitute confidential information for purposes of section 24(b)(2) of the Securities Exchange Act of 1934.

Information Required in Registration Statement

Sec. 7. (a) *Information Required in Registration Statement.*

(1) *In General.* The registration statement, when relating to a security other than a security issued by a foreign government, or political subdivision thereof, shall contain the information, and be accompanied by the documents, specified in Schedule A, and when relating to a security issued by a foreign government, or political subdivision thereof, shall contain the information, and be accompanied by the documents, specified in Schedule B; except that the Commission may by rules or regulations provide that any such information or document need not be included in respect of any class of issuers or securities if it finds that the requirement of such information or document is inapplicable to such class and that disclosure fully adequate for the protection of investors is otherwise required to be included within the registration statement. If any accountant, engineer, or appraiser, or any person whose profession gives authority to a statement made by him, is named as having prepared or certified any part of the registration statement, or is named as having prepared or certified a report or valuation for use in connection with the registration statement, the written consent of such person shall be filed with the registration statement. If any such person is named as having prepared or certified a report or valuation (other than a public official document or statement) which is used in connection with the registration statement, but is not named as having prepared or certified such report or valuation for use in connection with the registration statement, the written consent of such person shall be filed with the registration statement unless the Commission dispenses with such filing as impracticable or as involving undue hardship on the person filing the registration statement. Any such registration statement shall contain such other information, and be accompanied by such other documents, as the Commission may by rules or regulations require as being necessary or appropriate in the public interest or for the protection of investors.

(2) *Treatment of Emerging Growth Companies.* An emerging growth company—

(A) need not present more than 2 years of audited financial statements in order for the registration statement of such emerging growth company with respect to an initial public offering of its common equity securities to be effective, and in any other registration statement to be filed with the Commission, an emerging growth company need not present selected financial data in accordance with Item 301 under Regulation S–K, for any period prior to the earliest audited period presented in connection with its initial public offering; and

(B) may not be required to comply with any new or revised financial accounting standard until such date that a company that is not an issuer (as defined under section 2(a) of the Sarbanes–Oxley Act of 2002) is required to comply with such new or revised accounting standard, if such standard applies to companies that are not issuers.

(b)(1) The Commission shall prescribe special rules with respect to registration statements filed by any issuer that is a blank check company. Such rules may, as the Commission determines necessary or appropriate in the public interest or for the protection of investors—

(A) require such issuers to provide timely disclosure, prior to or after such statement becomes effective under section 8, of (i) information regarding the company to be acquired and the specific application of the proceeds of the offering, or (ii) additional information necessary to prevent such statement from being misleading;

(B) place limitations on the use of such proceeds and the distribution of securities by such issuer until the disclosures required under subparagraph (A) have been made; and

(C) provide a right of rescission to shareholders of such securities.

(2) The Commission may, as it determines consistent with the public interest and the protection of investors, by rule or order exempt any issuer or class of issuers from the rules prescribed under paragraph (1).

(3) For purposes of paragraph (1) of this subsection, the term "blank check company" means any development stage company that is issuing a penny stock (within the meaning of section 3(a)(51) of the Securities Exchange Act of 1934) and that—

(A) has no specific business plan or purpose; or

(B) has indicated that its business plan is to merge with an unidentified company or companies.

(c) *Disclosure Requirements.*

(1) *In General.* The Commission shall adopt regulations under this subsection requiring each issuer of an asset-backed security to disclose, for each tranche or class of security, information regarding the assets backing that security.

(2) *Content of Regulations.* In adopting regulations under this subsection, the Commission shall—

(A) set standards for the format of the data provided by issuers of an asset-backed security, which shall, to the extent feasible, facilitate comparison of such data across securities in similar types of asset classes; and

(B) require issuers of asset-backed securities, at a minimum, to disclose asset-level or loan-level data, if such data are necessary for investors to independently perform due diligence, including—

(i) data having unique identifiers relating to loan brokers or originators;

(ii) the nature and extent of the compensation of the broker or originator of the assets backing the security; and

(iii) the amount of risk retention by the originator and the securitizer of such assets.

(d) *Registration Statement for Asset-Backed Securities.* Not later than 180 days after the date of enactment of this subsection, the Commission shall issue rules relating to the registration statement required to be filed by any issuer of an asset-backed security (as that term is defined in section 3(a)(77) of the Securities Exchange Act of 1934) that require any issuer of an asset-backed security—

(1) to perform a review of the assets underlying the asset-backed security; and

(2) to disclose the nature of the review under paragraph (1).

Taking Effect of Registration Statements and Amendments Thereto

Sec. 8. (a) *Effective Date of Registration Statement.* Except as hereinafter provided, the effective date of a registration statement shall be the twentieth day after the filing thereof or such earlier date as the Commission may determine, having due regard to the adequacy of the information respecting the issuer theretofore available to the public, to the facility with which the nature of the securities to be registered, their relationship to the capital structure of the issuer and the rights of holders thereof can be understood, and to the public interest and the protection of investors. If any amendment to any such statement is filed prior to the effective date of such statement, the registration statement shall be deemed to have been filed when such amendment was filed; except that an amendment filed with the consent of the Commission, prior to the effective date of the registration statement, or filed pursuant to an order of the Commission, shall be treated as a part of the registration statement.

(b) *Incomplete or Inaccurate Registration Statement.* If it appears to the Commission that a registration statement is on its face incomplete or inaccurate in any material respect, the Commission may, after notice by personal service or the sending of confirmed telegraphic notice not later than ten days after the filing of the registration statement, and opportunity for hearing (at a time fixed by the Commission) within ten days after such notice by personal service or the sending of such telegraphic notice, issue an order prior to the effective date of registration refusing to permit such statement to become effective until it has been amended in accordance with such order. When such statement has been amended in accordance with such order the Commission shall so declare and the registration shall become effective at the time provided in subsection (a) or upon the date of such declaration, whichever date is the later.

(c) *Effective Date of Amendment to Registration Statement.* An amendment filed after the effective date of the registration statement, if such amendment, upon its face, appears to the Commission not to be incomplete or inaccurate in any material respect, shall become effective on such date as the Commission may determine, having due regard to the public interest and the protection of investors.

(d) *Untrue Statements or Omissions in Registration Statement.* If it appears to the Commission at any time that the registration statement includes any untrue statement of a material fact or omits to state any material fact required to be stated therein or necessary to make the statements therein not misleading, the Commission may, after notice by personal service or the sending of confirmed telegraphic notice, and after opportunity for hearing (at a time fixed by the Commission) within fifteen days after such notice by personal service or the sending of such telegraphic notice, issue a stop order suspending the effectiveness of the registration statement. When such statement has been amended in accordance with such stop order the Commission shall so declare and thereupon the stop order shall cease to be effective.

(e) *Examination for Issuance of Stop Order.* The Commission is empowered to make an examination in any case in order to determine whether a stop order should issue under subsection (d). In making such examination the Commission or any officer or officers designated by it shall have access to and may demand the production of any books and papers of, and may administer oaths and affirmations to and examine, the issuer, underwriter, or any other person, in respect of any matter relevant to the examination, and may, in its discretion, require the production of a balance sheet exhibiting the assets and liabilities of the issuer, or its income statement, or both, to be certified to by a public or certified accountant approved by the Commission. If the issuer or underwriter shall fail to cooperate, or shall obstruct or refuse to permit the making of an examination, such conduct shall be proper ground for the issuance of a stop order.

(f) *Notice Requirements.* Any notice required under this section shall be sent to or served on the issuer, or, in case of a foreign government or political subdivision thereof, to or on the underwriter, or, in the case of a foreign or Territorial person, to or on its duly authorized representative in the United States named in the registration statement, properly directed in each case of telegraphic notice to the address given in such statement.

Cease-and-Desist Proceedings

Sec. 8A. (a) *Authority of Commission.* If the Commission finds, after notice and opportunity for hearing, that any person is violating, has violated, or is about to violate any provision of this title, or any rule or regulation thereunder, the Commission may publish its findings and enter an order requiring such person, and any other person that is, was, or would be a cause of the violation, due to an act or omission the person knew or should have known would contribute to such violation, to cease and desist from committing or causing such violation and any future violation of the same provision, rule or regulation. Such order may, in addition to requiring a person to cease and desist from committing or causing a violation, require such person to comply, or to take steps to effect compliance, with such provision, rule, or regulation, upon such terms and conditions and within such time as the Commission may specify in such order. Any such order may, as the Commission deems appropriate, require future compliance or steps to effect future compliance, either permanently or for such period of time as the Commission may specify, with such provision, rule, or regulation with respect to any security, any issuer, or any other person.

(b) *Hearing.* The notice instituting proceedings pursuant to subsection (a) shall fix a hearing date not earlier than 30 days nor later than 60 days after service of the notice unless an earlier or a later date is set by the Commission with the consent of any respondent so served.

(c) *Temporary Order.*

(1) *In General.* Whenever the Commission determines that the alleged violation or threatened violation specified in the notice instituting pro-

ceedings pursuant to subsection (a), or the continuation thereof, is likely to result in significant dissipation or conversion of assets, significant harm to investors, or substantial harm to the public interest, including, but not limited to, losses to the Securities Investor Protection Corporation, prior to the completion of the proceedings, the Commission may enter a temporary order requiring the respondent to cease and desist from the violation or threatened violation and to take such action to prevent the violation or threatened violation and to prevent dissipation or conversion of assets, significant harm to investors, or substantial harm to the public interest as the Commission deems appropriate pending completion of such proceedings. Such an order shall be entered only after notice and opportunity for a hearing, unless the Commission determines that notice and hearing prior to entry would be impracticable or contrary to the public interest. A temporary order shall become effective upon service upon the respondent and, unless set aside, limited, or suspended by the Commission or a court of competent jurisdiction, shall remain effective and enforceable pending the completion of the proceedings.

(2) *Applicability*. This subsection shall apply only to a respondent that acts, or, at the time of the alleged misconduct acted, as a broker, dealer, investment adviser, investment company, municipal securities dealer, government securities broker, government securities dealer, or transfer agent, or is, or was at the time of the alleged misconduct, an associated person of, or a person seeking to become associated with, any of the foregoing.

(d) *Review of Temporary Orders*.

(1) *Commission Review*. At any time after the respondent has been served with a temporary cease-and-desist order pursuant to subsection (c), the respondent may apply to the Commission to have the order set aside, limited, or suspended. If the respondent has been served with a temporary cease-and-desist order entered without a prior Commission hearing, the respondent may, within 10 days after the date on which the order was served, request a hearing on such application and the Commission shall hold a hearing and render a decision on such application at the earliest possible time.

(2) *Judicial Review*. Within—

(A) 10 days after the date the respondent was served with a temporary cease-and-desist order entered with a prior Commission hearing, or

(B) 10 days after the Commission renders a decision on an application and hearing under paragraph (1), with respect to any temporary cease-and-desist order entered without a prior Commission hearing,

the respondent may apply to the United States district court for the district in which the respondent resides or has its principal place of business, or for the District of Columbia, for an order setting aside, limiting, or suspending the effectiveness or enforcement of the order, and the court shall have jurisdiction to enter such an order. A respondent served with a temporary cease-and-desist order entered without a prior Commission hearing may not apply to the court except after hearing and decision by the Commission on the respondent's application under paragraph (1) of this subsection.

(3) *No Automatic Stay of Temporary Order*. The commencement of proceedings under paragraph (2) of this subsection shall not, unless specifically ordered by the court, operate as a stay of the Commission's order.

(4) *Exclusive Review*. Section 9(a) of this title shall not apply to a temporary order entered pursuant to this section.

(e) *Authority to Enter an Order Requiring an Accounting and Disgorgement*. In any cease-and-desist proceeding under subsection (a), the Commission may enter an order requiring accounting and disgorgement, including reasonable interest. The Commission is authorized to adopt rules, regulations, and orders concerning payments to investors, rates of interest, periods of accrual, and such other matters as it deems appropriate to implement this subsection.

(f) *Authority of the Commission to Prohibit Persons from Serving as Officers or Directors*. In any cease-and-desist proceeding under subsection (a), the Commission may issue an order to prohibit, conditionally or unconditionally, and permanently or for such period of time as it shall determine, any person who has violated section 17(a)(1) or the rules or regulations thereunder, from acting as an officer or director of any issuer that has a class of securities registered pursuant to section 12 of the Securities Exchange Act of 1934, or that is required to file reports pursuant to section 15(d) of that Act, if the conduct of that person demonstrates unfitness to serve as an officer or director of any such issuer.

(g) *Authority to Impose Money Penalties.*

(1) *Grounds.* In any cease-and-desist proceeding under subsection (a), the Commission may impose a civil penalty on a person if the Commission finds, on the record, after notice and opportunity for hearing, that—

(A) such person—

(i) is violating or has violated any provision of this title, or any rule or regulation issued under this title; or

(ii) is or was a cause of the violation of any provision of this title, or any rule or regulation thereunder; and

(B) such penalty is in the public interest.

(2) *Maximum Amount of Penalty.*

(A) *First Tier.* The maximum amount of a penalty for each act or omission described in paragraph (1) shall be $7,500 for a natural person or $75,000 for any other person.

(B) *Second Tier.* Notwithstanding subparagraph (A), the maximum amount of penalty for each such act or omission shall be $75,000 for a natural person or $375,000 for any other person, if the act or omission described in paragraph (1) involved fraud, deceit, manipulation, or deliberate or reckless disregard of a regulatory requirement.

(C) *Third Tier.* Notwithstanding subparagraphs (A) and (B), the maximum amount of penalty for each such act or omission shall be $150,000 for a natural person or $725,000 for any other person, if—

(i) the act or omission described in paragraph (1) involved fraud, deceit, manipulation, or deliberate or reckless disregard of a regulatory requirement; and

(ii) such act or omission directly or indirectly resulted in—

(I) substantial losses or created a significant risk of substantial losses to other persons; or

(II) substantial pecuniary gain to the person who committed the act or omission.

(3) *Evidence Concerning Ability to Pay.* In any proceeding in which the Commission may impose a penalty under this section, a respondent may present evidence of the ability of the respondent to pay such penalty. The Commission may, in its discretion, consider such evidence in determining whether such penalty is in the public interest. Such evidence may relate to the extent of the ability of the respondent to continue in business and the collectability of a penalty, taking into account any other claims of the United States or third parties upon the assets of the respondent and the amount of the assets of the respondent.

Court Review of Orders

Sec. 9. (a) Any person aggrieved by an order of the Commission may obtain a review of such order in the court of appeals of the United States, within any circuit wherein such person resides or has his principal place of business, or in the United States Court of Appeals for the District of Columbia, by filing in such Court, within sixty days after the entry of such order, a written petition praying that the order of the Commission be modified or be set aside in whole or in part. A copy of such petition shall be forthwith transmitted by the clerk of the court to the Commission, and thereupon the Commission shall file in the court the record upon which the order complained of was entered, as provided in section 2112 of title 28, United States Code. No objection to the order of the Commission shall be considered by the court unless such objection shall have been urged before the Commission. The finding of the Commission as to the facts, if supported by evidence, shall be conclusive. If either party shall apply to the court for leave to adduce additional evidence, and shall show to the satisfaction of the court that such additional evidence is material and that there were reasonable grounds for failure to adduce such evidence in the hearing before the Commission, the court may order such additional evidence to be taken before the Commission and to be adduced upon the hearing in such manner and upon such terms and conditions as to the court may seem proper. The Commission may modify its findings as to the facts by reason of the additional evidence so taken, and it shall file such modified or new findings, which, if supported by evidence, shall be conclusive, and its recommendation, if any, for the modification or setting aside of the original order. The jurisdiction of the court shall be exclusive and its judgment and decree, affirming, modifying, or setting aside, in whole or in part, any order of the Commission, shall be final, subject to review by the Supreme Court of the United States upon certiorari or certification as provided in section 1254 of title 28, United States Code.

(b) The commencement of proceedings under subsection (a) shall not, unless specifically ordered by the court, operate as a stay of the Commission's order.

Information Required in Prospectus

Sec. 10. (a) *Information in Registration Statement; Documents Not Required.* Except to the extent otherwise permitted or required pursuant to this subsection or subsections (c), (d), or (e)—

(1) a prospectus relating to a security other than a security issued by a foreign government or political subdivision thereof, shall contain the information contained in the registration statement, but it need not include the documents referred to in paragraphs (28) to (32), inclusive, of Schedule A;

(2) a prospectus relating to a security issued by a foreign government or political subdivision thereof shall contain the information contained in the registration statement, but it need not include the documents referred to in paragraphs (13) and (14) of Schedule B;

(3) notwithstanding the provisions of paragraphs (1) and (2) of this subsection (a) when a prospectus is used more than nine months after the effective date of the registration statement, the information contained therein shall be as of a date not more than sixteen months prior to such use, so far as such information is known to the user of such prospectus or can be furnished by such user without unreasonable effort or expense;

(4) there may be omitted from any prospectus any of the information required under this subsection (a) which the Commission may by rules or regulations designate as not being necessary or appropriate in the public interest or for the protection of investors.

(b) *Summarizations and Omissions Allowed by Rules and Regulations.* In addition to the prospectus permitted or required in subsection (a), the Commission shall by rules or regulations deemed necessary or appropriate in the public interest or for the protection of investors permit the use of a prospectus for the purposes of subsection (b)(1) of section 5 which omits in part or summarizes information in the prospectus specified in subsection (a). A prospectus permitted under this subsection shall, except to the extent the Commission by rules or regulations deemed necessary or appropriate in the public interest or for the protection of investors otherwise provides, be filed as part of the registration statement but shall not be deemed a part of such registration statement for the purposes of section 11. The Commission may at any time issue an order preventing or suspending the use of a prospectus permitted under this subsection (b), if it has reason to believe that such prospectus has not been filed (if required to be filed as part of the registration statement) or includes any untrue statement of a material fact or omits to state any material fact required to be stated therein or necessary to make the statements therein, in the light of the circumstances under which such prospectus is or is to be used, not misleading. Upon issuance of an order under this subsection, the Commission shall give notice of the issuance of such order and opportunity for hearing by personal service or the sending of confirmed telegraphic notice. The Commission shall vacate or modify the order at any time for good cause or if such prospectus has been filed or amended in accordance with such order.

(c) *Additional Information Required by Rules and Regulations.* Any prospectus shall contain such other information as the Commission may by rules or regulations require as being necessary or appropriate in the public interest or for the protection of investors.

(d) *Classification of Prospectuses.* In the exercise of its powers under subsections (a), (b), or (c), the Commission shall have authority to classify prospectuses according to the nature and circumstances of their use or the nature of the security, issue, issuer, or otherwise, and, by rules and regulations and subject to such terms and conditions as it shall specify therein, to prescribe as to each class the form and contents which it may find appropriate and consistent with the public interest and the protection of investors.

(e) *Information in Conspicuous Part of Prospectus.* The statements or information required to be included in a prospectus by or under authority of subsections (a), (b), (c), or (d), when written, shall be placed in a conspicuous part of the prospectus and, except as otherwise permitted by rules or regulations, in type as large as that used generally in the body of the prospectus.

(f) *Prospectus Consisting of Radio or Television Broadcast.* In any case where a prospectus consists of a radio or television broadcast, copies thereof shall be filed with the Commission under such rules and regulations as it shall prescribe. The Commission may by rules and regulations require the filing with it of forms and prospectuses used in connection with the offer or sale of securities registered under this title.

Civil Liabilities on Account of False Registration Statement

Sec. 11. (a) *Persons Possessing Cause of Action; Persons Liable.* In case any part of the registration statement, when such part became effective, contained an untrue statement of a material fact or omitted to state a material fact required to be stated therein or necessary to make the statements therein not misleading, any person acquiring such security (unless it is proved that at the time of such acquisition he knew of such untruth or omission) may, either at law or in equity, in any court of competent jurisdiction, sue—

(1) every person who signed the registration statement;

(2) every person who was a director of (or person performing similar functions) or partner in the issuer at the time of the filing of the part of the registration statement with respect to which his liability is asserted;

(3) every person who, with his consent, is named in the registration statement as being or about to become a director, person performing similar functions, or partner;

(4) every accountant, engineer, or appraiser, or any person whose profession gives authority to a statement made by him, who has with his consent been named as having prepared or certified any part of the registration statement, or as having prepared or certified any report or valuation which is used in connection with the registration statement, with respect to the statement in such registration statement, report, or valuation, which purports to have been prepared or certified by him;

(5) every underwriter with respect to such security.

If such person acquired the security after the issuer has made generally available to its security holders an earning statement covering a period of at least twelve months beginning after the effective date of the registration statement, then the right of recovery under this subsection shall be conditioned on proof that such person acquired the security relying upon such untrue statement in the registration statement or relying upon the registration statement and not knowing of such omission, but such reliance may be established without proof of the reading of the registration statement by such person.

(b) *Persons Exempt from Liability upon Proof of Issues.* Notwithstanding the provisions of subsection (a) no person, other than the issuer, shall be liable as provided therein who shall sustain the burden of proof—

(1) that before the effective date of the part of the registration statement with respect to which his liability is asserted (A) he had resigned from or had taken such steps as are permitted by law to resign from, or ceased or refused to act in, every office, capacity, or relationship in which he was described in the registration statement as acting or agreeing to act, and (B) he had advised the Commission and the issuer in writing that he had taken such action and that he would not be responsible for such part of the registration statement; or

(2) that if such part of the registration statement became effective without his knowledge, upon becoming aware of such fact he forthwith acted and advised the Commission, in accordance with paragraph (1), and, in addition, gave reasonable public notice that such part of the registration statement had become effective without his knowledge; or

(3) that (A) as regards any part of the registration statement not purporting to be made on the authority of an expert, and not purporting to be a copy of or extract from a report or valuation of an expert, and not purporting to be made on the authority of a public official document or statement, he had, after reasonable investigation, reasonable ground to believe and did believe, at the time such part of the registration statement became effective, that the statements therein were true and that there was no omission to state a material fact required to be stated therein or necessary to make the statements therein not misleading; and (B) as regards any part of the registration statement purporting to be made upon his authority as an expert or purporting to be a copy of or extract from a report or valuation of himself as an expert, (i) he had, after reasonable investigation, reasonable ground to believe and did believe, at the time such part of the registration statement became effective, that the statements therein were true and that there was no omission to state a material fact required to be stated therein or necessary to make the statements therein not misleading, or (ii) such part of the registration statement did not fairly represent his statement as an expert or was not a

fair copy of or extract from his report or valuation as an expert; and (C) as regards any part of the registration statement purporting to be made on the authority of an expert (other than himself) or purporting to be a copy of or extract from a report or valuation of an expert (other than himself), he had no reasonable ground to believe and did not believe, at the time such part of the registration statement became effective, that the statements therein were untrue or that there was an omission to state a material fact required to be stated therein or necessary to make the statements therein not misleading, or that such part of the registration statement did not fairly represent the statement of the expert or was not a fair copy of or extract from the report or valuation of the expert; and (D) as regards any part of the registration statement purporting to be a statement made by an official person or purporting to be a copy of or extract from a public official document, he had no reasonable ground to believe and did not believe, at the time such part of the registration statement became effective, that the statements therein were untrue, or that there was an omission to state a material fact required to be stated therein or necessary to make the statements therein not misleading, or that such part of the registration statement did not fairly represent the statement made by the official person or was not a fair copy of or extract from the public official document.

(c) *Standard of Reasonableness.* In determining, for the purpose of paragraph (3) of subsection (b) of this section, what constitutes reasonable investigation and reasonable ground for belief, the standard of reasonableness shall be that required of a prudent man in the management of his own property.

(d) *Effective Date of Registration Statement with Regard to Underwriters.* If any person becomes an underwriter with respect to the security after the part of the registration statement with respect to which his liability is asserted has become effective, then for the purposes of paragraph (3) of subsection (b) of this section such part of the registration statement shall be considered as having become effective with respect to such person as of the time when he became an underwriter.

(e) *Measure of Damages; Undertaking for Payment of Costs.* The suit authorized under subsection (a) of this section may be to recover such damages as shall represent the difference between the amount paid for the security (not exceeding the price at which the security was offered to the public) and (1) the value thereof as of the time such suit was brought, or (2) the price at which such security shall have been disposed of in the market before suit, or (3) the price at which such security shall have been disposed of after suit but before judgment if such damages shall be less than the damages representing the difference between the amount paid for the security (not exceeding the price at which the security was offered to the public) and the value thereof as of the time such suit was brought: *Provided,* That if the defendant proves that any portion or all of such damages represents other than the depreciation in value of such security resulting from such part of the registration statement, with respect to which his liability is asserted, not being true or omitting to state a material fact required to be stated therein or necessary to make the statements therein not misleading, such portion of or all such damages shall not be recoverable. In no event shall any underwriter (unless such underwriter shall have knowingly received from the issuer for acting as an underwriter some benefit, directly or indirectly, in which all other underwriters similarly situated did not share in proportion to their respective interests in the underwriting) be liable in any suit or as a consequence of suits authorized under subsection (a) for damages in excess of the total price at which the securities underwritten by him and distributed to the public were offered to the public. In any suit under this or any other section of this subchapter the court may, in its discretion, require an undertaking for the payment of the costs of such suit, including reasonable attorney's fees, and if judgment shall be rendered against a party litigant, upon the motion of the other party litigant, such costs may be assessed in favor of such party litigant (whether or not such undertaking has been required) if the court believes the suit or the defense to have been without merit, in an amount sufficient to reimburse him for the reasonable expenses incurred by him, in connection with such suit, such costs to be taxed in the manner usually provided for taxing of costs in the court in which the suit was heard.

(f) *Joint and Several Liability; Liability of Outside Director.* (1) Except as provided in paragraph (2), all or any one or more of the persons specified in subsection (a) shall be jointly and severally liable, and every person who becomes liable to make any payment under this section may recover contribution as in cases of contract from any person who, if sued separately, would have been liable to make the same payment, unless the person who has become liable was, and the other was not, guilty of fraudulent misrepresentation.

(2)(A) The liability of an outside director under subsection (e) shall be determined in accordance with section 21D of the Securities Exchange Act of 1934.

(B) For purposes of this paragraph, the term "outside director" shall have the meaning given such term by rule or regulation of the Commission.

(g) *Offering Price to Public as Maximum Amount Recoverable.* In no case shall the amount recoverable under this section exceed the price at which the security was offered to the public.

Civil Liabilities Arising in Connection with Prospectuses and Communications

Sec. 12. (a) *In General.* Any person who—

(1) offers or sells a security in violation of section 5, or

(2) offers or sells a security (whether or not exempted by the provisions of section 3, other than paragraphs (2) and (14) of subsection (a) thereof), by the use of any means or instruments of transportation or communication in interstate commerce or of the mails, by means of a prospectus or oral communication, which includes an untrue statement of a material fact or omits to state a material fact necessary in order to make the statements, in the light of the circumstances under which they were made, not misleading (the purchaser not knowing of such untruth or omission), and who shall not sustain the burden of proof that he did not know, and in the exercise of reasonable care could not have known, of such untruth or omission,

shall be liable, subject to subsection (b) to the person purchasing such security from him, who may sue either at law or in equity in any court of competent jurisdiction, to recover the consideration paid for such security with interest thereon, less the amount of any income received thereon, upon the tender of such security, or for damages if he no longer owns the security.

(b) *Loss Causation.* In an action described in subsection (a)(2), if the person who offered or sold such security proves that any portion or all of the amount recoverable under subsection (a)(2) represents other than the depreciation in value of the subject security resulting from such part of the prospectus or oral communication, with respect to which the liability of that person is asserted, not being true or omitting to state a material fact required to be stated therein or necessary to make the statement not misleading, then such portion or amount, as the case may be, shall not be recoverable.

Limitation of Actions

Sec. 13. No action shall be maintained to enforce any liability created under section 11 or section 12(a)(2) unless brought within one year after the discovery of the untrue statement or the omission, or after such discovery should have been made by the exercise of reasonable diligence, or, if the action is to enforce a liability created under section 12(a)(1), unless brought within one year after the violation upon which it is based. In no event shall any such action be brought to enforce a liability created under section 11 or section 12(a)(1) more than three years after the security was bona fide offered to the public, or under section 12(a)(2) more than three years after the sale.

Contrary Stipulations Void

Sec. 14. Any condition, stipulation, or provision binding any person acquiring any security to waive compliance with any provision of this title or of the rules and regulations of the Commission shall be void.

Liability of Controlling Persons

Sec. 15. (a) *Controlling Persons.* Every person who, by or through stock ownership, agency, or otherwise, or who, pursuant to or in connection with an agreement or understanding with one or more other persons by or through stock ownership, agency, or otherwise, controls any person liable under sections 11 or 12, shall also be liable jointly and severally with and to the same extent as such controlled person to any person to whom such controlled person is liable, unless the controlling person had no knowledge of or reasonable ground to believe in the existence of the facts by reason of which the liability of the controlled person is alleged to exist.

(b) *Prosecution of Persons who Aid and Abet Violations.* For purposes of any action brought by the Commission under subparagraph (b) or (d) of section 20, any person that knowingly or recklessly provides substantial assistance to another person in violation of a provision of this Act, or of any rule or regulation issued under this Act, shall be deemed to be in violation of such provision to the same extent as the person to whom such assistance is provided.

Additional Remedies; Limitations on Remedies

Sec. 16. (a) *Remedies Additional.* Except as provided in subsection (b), the rights and remedies provided by this title shall be in addition to any and all other rights and remedies that may exist at law or in equity.

(b) *Class Action Limitations.* No covered class action based upon the statutory or common law of any State or subdivision thereof may be maintained in any State or Federal court by any private party alleging—

(1) an untrue statement or omission of a material fact in connection with the purchase or sale of a covered security; or

(2) that the defendant used or employed any manipulative or deceptive device or contrivance in connection with the purchase or sale of a covered security.

(c) *Removal of Covered Class Actions.* Any covered class action brought in any State court involving a covered security, as set forth in subsection (b), shall be removable to the Federal district court for the district in which the action is pending, and shall be subject to subsection (b).

(d) *Preservation of Certain Actions.*

(1) *Actions Under State Law of State of Incorporation.*

(A) *Actions Preserved.* Notwithstanding subsection (b) or (c), a covered class action described in subparagraph (B) of this paragraph that is based upon the statutory or common law of the State in which the issuer is incorporated (in the case of a corporation) or organized (in the case of any other entity) may be maintained in a State or Federal court by a private party.

(B) *Permissible Actions.* A covered class action is described in this subparagraph if it involves—

(i) the purchase or sale of securities by the issuer or an affiliate of the issuer exclusively from or to holders of equity securities of the issuer; or

(ii) any recommendation, position, or other communication with respect to the sale of securities of the issuer that—

(I) is made by or on behalf of the issuer or an affiliate of the issuer to holders of equity securities of the issuer; and

(II) concerns decisions of those equity holders with respect to voting their securities, acting in response to a tender or exchange offer, or exercising dissenters' or appraisal rights.

(2) *State Actions.*

(A) *In General.* Notwithstanding any other provision of this section, nothing in this section may be construed to preclude a State or political subdivision thereof or a State pension plan from bringing an action involving a covered security on its own behalf, or as a member of a class comprised solely of other States, political subdivisions, or State pension plans that are named plaintiffs, and that have authorized participation, in such action.

(B) *State Pension Plan Defined.* For purposes of this paragraph, the term "State pension plan" means a pension plan established and maintained for its employees by the government of the State or political subdivision thereof, or by any agency or instrumentality thereof.

(3) *Actions Under Contractual Agreements Between Issuers and Indenture Trustees.* Notwithstanding subsection (b) or (c), a covered class action that seeks to enforce a contractual agreement between an issuer and an indenture trustee may be maintained in a State or Federal court by a party to the agreement or a successor to such party.

(4) *Remand of Removed Actions.* In an action that has been removed from a State court pursuant to subsection (c), if the Federal court determines that the action may be maintained in State court pursuant to this subsection, the Federal court shall remand such action to such State court.

(e) *Preservation of State Jurisdiction.* The securities commission (or any agency or office performing like functions) of any State shall retain jurisdiction under the laws of such State to investigate and bring enforcement actions.

(f) *Definitions.* For purposes of this section, the following definitions shall apply:

(1) *Affiliate of the Issuer.* The term "affiliate of the issuer" means a person that directly or indirectly, through one or more intermediaries, controls or is controlled by or is under common control with, the issuer.

(2) *Covered Class Action.*

(A) *In General.* The term "covered class action" means—

(i) any single lawsuit in which—

(I) damages are sought on behalf of more than 50 persons or prospective class members, and questions of law or fact common to those persons or members of the prospective class, without reference to issues of individualized reliance on an alleged misstatement or omission, predominate over any questions affecting only individual persons or members; or

(II) one or more named parties seek to recover damages on a representative basis on behalf of themselves and other unnamed parties similarly situated, and questions of law or fact common to those persons or members of the prospective class predominate over any questions affecting only individual persons or members; or

(ii) any group of lawsuits filed in or pending in the same court and involving common questions of law or fact, in which—

(I) damages are sought on behalf of more than 50 persons; and

(II) the lawsuits are joined, consolidated, or otherwise proceed as a single action for any purpose.

(B) *Exception for Derivative Actions.* Notwithstanding subparagraph (A), the term "covered class action" does not include an exclusively derivative action brought by one or more shareholders on behalf of a corporation.

(C) *Counting of Certain Class Members.* For purposes of this paragraph, a corporation, investment company, pension plan, partnership, or other entity, shall be treated as one person or prospective class member, but only if the entity is not established for the purpose of participating in the action.

(D) *Rule of Construction.* Nothing in this paragraph shall be construed to affect the discretion of a State court in determining whether actions filed in such court should be joined, consolidated, or otherwise allowed to proceed as a single action.

(3) *Covered Security.* The term "covered security" means a security that satisfies the standards for a covered security specified in paragraph (1) or (2) of section 18(b) at the time during which it is alleged that the misrepresentation, omission, or manipulative or deceptive conduct occurred, except that such term shall not include any debt security that is exempt from registration under this title pursuant to rules issued by the Commission under section 4(a)(2).

Fraudulent Interstate Transactions

Sec. 17. (a) *Use of Interstate Commerce for Purpose of Fraud or Deceit.* It shall be unlawful for any person in the offer or sale of any securities (including security-based swaps) or any security-based swap agreement (as defined in section 3(a)(78) of the Securities Exchange Act of 1934) by the use of any means or instruments of transportation or communication in interstate commerce or by use of the mails, directly or indirectly—

(1) to employ any device, scheme, or artifice to defraud, or

(2) to obtain money or property by means of any untrue statement of a material fact or any omission to state a material fact necessary in order to make the statements made, in light of the circumstances under which they were made, not misleading; or

(3) to engage in any transaction, practice, or course of business which operates or would operate as a fraud or deceit upon the purchaser.

(b) *Use of Interstate Commerce for Purpose of Offering for Sale.* It shall be unlawful for any person, by the use of any means or instruments of transportation or communication in interstate commerce or by the use of the mails, to publish, give publicity to, or circulate any notice, circular, advertisement, newspaper, article, letter, investment service, or communication which, though not purporting to offer a security for sale, describes such security for a consideration received or to be received, directly or indirectly, from an issuer, underwriter, or dealer, without fully disclosing the receipt, whether past or prospective, of such consideration and the amount thereof.

(c) *Exemptions of Section 3 Not Applicable to This Section.* The exemptions provided in section 3 shall not apply to the provisions of this section.

(d) Authority with Respect to Security-Based Swap Agreements. The authority of the Commission under this section with respect to security-based swap agreements (as defined in section 3(a)(78) of the Se-

curities Exchange Act of 1934) shall be subject to the restrictions and limitations of section 2A(b) of this title.

Exemption from State Regulation of Securities Offerings

Sec. 18. (a) *Scope of Exemption.* Except as otherwise provided in this section, no law, rule, regulation, or order, or other administrative action of any State or any political subdivision thereof—

(1) requiring, or with respect to, registration or qualification of securities, or registration or qualification of securities transactions, shall directly or indirectly apply to a security that—

(A) is a covered security; or

(B) will be a covered security upon completion of the transaction;

(2) shall directly or indirectly prohibit, limit, or impose any conditions upon the use of—

(A) with respect to a covered security described in subsection (b), any offering document that is prepared by or on behalf of the issuer; or

(B) any proxy statement, report to shareholders, or other disclosure document relating to a covered security or the issuer thereof that is required to be and is filed with the Commission or any national securities organization registered under section 15A of the Securities Exchange Act of 1934, except that this subparagraph does not apply to the laws, rules, regulations, or orders, or other administrative actions of the State of incorporation of the issuer; or

(3) shall directly or indirectly prohibit, limit, or impose conditions, based on the merits of such offering or issuer, upon the offer or sale of any security described in paragraph (1).

(b) *Covered Securities.* For purposes of this section, the following are covered securities:

(1) *Exclusive Federal Registration of Nationally Traded Securities.* A security is a covered security if such security is—

(A) listed, or authorized for listing, on the New York Stock Exchange or the American Stock Exchange, or listed or authorized for listing on the National Market System of the Nasdaq Stock Market (or any successor to such entities);

(B) listed, or authorized for listing, on a national securities exchange (or tier or segment thereof) that has listing standards that the Commission determines by rule (on its own initiative or on the basis of a petition) are substantially similar to the listing standards applicable to securities described in subparagraph (A); or

(C) a security of the same issuer that is equal in seniority or that is a senior security to a security described in subparagraph (A) or (B).

(2) *Exclusive Federal Registration of Investment Companies.* A security is a covered security if such security is a security issued by an investment company that is registered, or that has filed a registration statement, under the Investment Company Act of 1940.

(3) *Sales to Qualified Purchasers.* A security is a covered security with respect to the offer or sale of the security to qualified purchasers, as defined by the Commission by rule. In prescribing such rule, the Commission may define the term "qualified purchaser" differently with respect to different categories of securities, consistent with the public interest and the protection of investors.

(4) *Exemption in Connection with Certain Exempt Offerings.* A security is a covered security with respect to a transaction that is exempt from registration under this title pursuant to—

(A) paragraph (1) or (3) of section 4, and the issuer of such security files reports with the Commission pursuant to section 13 or 15(d) of the Securities Exchange Act of 1934;

(B) section 4(a)(4);

(C) section 4(a)(6);

(D) a rule or regulation adopted pursuant to section 3(b)(2) and such security is—

(i) offered or sold on a national securities exchange; or

(ii) offered or sold to a qualified purchaser, as defined by the Commission pursuant to paragraph (3) with respect to that purchase or sale;

(E) section 3(a), other than the offer or sale of a security that is exempt from such registration pursuant to paragraph (4), (10) or (11) of such section, except that a municipal security that is exempt from such registration pursuant to paragraph (2) of such section is not a covered security with respect to the offer or sale of such security in the State in which the issuer of such security is located;

(F) Commission rules or regulations issued under section 4(a)(2), except that this subparagraph does not prohibit a State from imposing notice filing requirements that are substantially similar to those required by rule or regulation under section 4(a)(2) that are in effect on September 1, 1996; or

(G) Section 4(a)(7).

(c) *Preservation of Authority.*

(1) *Fraud Authority.* Consistent with this section, the securities commission (or any agency or office performing like functions) of any State shall retain jurisdiction under the laws of such State to investigate and bring enforcement actions, in connection with securities or securities transactions

(A) with respect to—

(i) fraud or deceit; or

(ii) unlawful conduct by a broker, dealer, or funding portal; and

(B) in connection to a transaction described under section 4(a)(6), with respect to—

(i) fraud or deceit; or

(ii) unlawful conduct by a broker, dealer, funding portal, or issuer.

(2) *Preservation of Filing Requirements.*

(A) *Notice Filings Permitted.* Nothing in this section prohibits the securities commission (or any agency or office performing like functions) of any State from requiring the filing of any document filed with the Commission pursuant to this title, together with annual or periodic reports of the value of securities sold or offered to be sold to persons located in the State (if such sales data is not included in documents filed with the Commission), solely for notice purposes and the assessment of any fee, together with a consent to service of process and any required fee.

(B) *Preservation of Fees.*

(i) *In General.* Until otherwise provided by law, rule, regulation, or order, or other administrative action of any State or any political subdivision thereof, adopted after the date of enactment of the National Securities Markets Improvement Act of 1996, filing or registration fees with respect to securities or securities transactions shall continue to be collected in amounts determined pursuant to State law as in effect on the day before such date.

(ii) *Schedule.* The fees required by this subparagraph shall be paid, and all necessary supporting data on sales or offers for sales required under subparagraph (A), shall be reported on the same schedule as would have been applicable had the issuer not relied on the exemption provided in subsection (a).

(C) *Availability of Preemption Contingent on Payment of Fees.*

(i) *In General.* During the period beginning on the date of enactment of the National Securities Markets Improvement Act of 1996 and ending 3 years after that date of enactment, the securities commission (or any agency or office performing like functions) of any State may require the registration of securities issued by any issuer who refuses to pay the fees required by subparagraph (B).

(ii) *Delays.* For purposes of this subparagraph, delays in payment of fees or underpayments of fees that are promptly remedied shall not constitute a refusal to pay fees.

(D) *Fees Not Permitted on Listed Securities.* Notwithstanding subparagraphs (A), (B), and (C), no filing or fee may be required with respect to any security that is a covered security pursuant to subsection (b)(1) of this section, or will be such a covered security upon completion of the transaction, or is a security of the same issuer that is equal in seniority or that is a senior security to a security that is a covered security pursuant to subsection (b)(1).

(F)* *Fees Not Permitted on Crowdfunded Securities.* Notwithstanding subparagraphs (A), (B), and (C), no filing or fee may be required with respect to any security that is a covered security pursuant to subsection (b)(4)(B), or will be such a covered security upon completion of the transaction, except for the securities commission (or any agency or office performing like functions) of the State of the principal place of business of the issuer, or any State in which purchasers of 50 percent or greater of the aggregate amount of the issue are residents, provided that for purposes of this subparagraph, the term 'State'

* No subparagraph (E) has been enacted.

includes the District of Columbia and the territories of the United States.

(3) *Enforcement of Requirements.* Nothing in this section shall prohibit the securities commission (or any agency or office performing like functions) of any State from suspending the offer or sale of securities within such State as a result of the failure to submit any filing or fee required under law and permitted under this section.

(d) *Definitions.* For purposes of this section, the following definitions shall apply:

(1) *Offering Document.* The term "offering document"—

(A) has the meaning given the term "prospectus" in section 2(a)(10), but without regard to the provisions of subparagraphs (a) and (b) of that section; and

(B) includes a communication that is not deemed to offer a security pursuant to a rule of the Commission.

(2) *Prepared by or on Behalf of the Issuer.* Not later than 6 months after the date of enactment of the National Securities Markets Improvement Act of 1996, the Commission shall, by rule, define the term "prepared by or on behalf of the issuer" for purposes of this section.

(3) *State.* The term "State" has the same meaning as in section 3 of the Securities Exchange Act of 1934.

(4) *Senior Security.* The term "senior security" means any bond, debenture, note, or similar obligation or instrument constituting a security and evidencing indebtedness, and any stock of a class having priority over any other class as to distribution of assets or payment of dividends.

Special Powers of Commission

Sec. 19. (a) The Commission shall have authority from time to time to make, amend, and rescind such rules and regulations as may be necessary to carry out the provisions of this title, including rules and regulations governing registration statements and prospectuses for various classes of securities and issuers, and defining accounting, technical, and trade terms used in this title. Among other things, the Commission shall have authority, for the purposes of this title, to prescribe the form or forms in which required information shall be set forth, the items or details to be shown in the balance sheet and earning statement, and the methods to be followed in the preparation of accounts, in the appraisal or valuation of assets and liabilities, in the determination of depreciation and depletion, in the differentiation of recurring and nonrecurring income, in the differentiation of investment and operating income, and in the preparation, where the Commission deems it necessary or desirable, of consolidated balance sheets or income accounts of any person directly or indirectly controlling or controlled by the issuer, or any person under direct or indirect common control with the issuer. The rules and regulations of the Commission shall be effective upon publication in the manner which the Commission shall prescribe. No provision of this title imposing any liability shall apply to any act done or omitted in good faith in conformity with any rule or regulation of the Commission, notwithstanding that such rule or regulation may, after such act or omission, be amended or rescinded or be determined by judicial or other authority to be invalid for any reason.

(b) *Recognition of Accounting Standards.*

(1) *In General.* In carrying out its authority under subsection (a) and under section 13(b) of the Securities Exchange Act of 1934, the Commission may recognize, as "generally accepted" for purposes of the securities laws, any accounting principles established by a standard setting body—

(A) that—

(i) is organized as a private entity;

(ii) has, for administrative and operational purposes, a board of trustees (or equivalent body) serving in the public interest, the majority of whom are not, concurrent with their service on such board, and have not been during the 2–year period preceding such service, associated persons of any registered public accounting firm;

(iii) is funded as provided in section 109 of the Sarbanes–Oxley Act of 2002;

(iv) has adopted procedures to ensure prompt consideration, by majority vote of its members, of changes to accounting principles necessary to reflect emerging accounting issues and changing business practices; and

(v) considers, in adopting accounting principles, the need to keep standards current in order to reflect changes in the business environment, the extent to which international convergence on high quality accounting standards is necessary or appropriate in the public interest and for the protection of its investors; and

(B) that the Commission determines has the capacity to assist the Commission in fulfilling the requirements of subsection (a) and section 13(b) of the Securities Exchange Act of 1934, because, at a minimum, the standard setting body is capable of improving the accuracy and effectiveness of financial reporting and the protection of investors under the securities laws.

(2) *Annual Report.* A standard setting body described in paragraph (1) shall submit an annual report to the Commission and the public, containing audited financial statements of that standard setting body.

(c) For the purpose of all investigations which, in the opinion of the Commission, are necessary and proper for the enforcement of this title, any member of the Commission or any officer or officers designated by it are empowered to administer oaths and affirmations, subpena witnesses, take evidence, and require the production of any books, papers, or other documents which the Commission deems relevant or material to the inquiry. Such attendance of witnesses and the production of such documentary evidence may be required from any place in the United States or any Territory at any designated place of hearing.

(d)(1) The Commission is authorized to cooperate with any association composed of duly constituted representatives of State governments whose primary assignment is the regulation of the securities business within those States, and which, in the judgment of the Commission, could assist in effectuating greater uniformity in Federal-State securities matters. The Commission shall, at its discretion, cooperate, coordinate, and share information with such an association for the purposes of carrying out the policies and projects set forth in paragraphs (2) and (3).

(2) It is the declared policy of this subsection that there should be greater Federal and State cooperation in securities matters, including—

(A) maximum effectiveness of regulation,

(B) maximum uniformity in Federal and State regulatory standards,

(C) minimum interference with the business of capital formation, and

(D) a substantial reduction in costs and paperwork to diminish the burdens of raising investment capital (particularly by small business) and to diminish the costs of the administration of the Government programs involved.

(3) The purpose of this subsection is to engender cooperation between the Commission, any such association of State securities officials, and other duly constituted securities associations in the following areas:

(A) the sharing of information regarding the registration or exemption of securities issues applied for in the various States;

(B) the development and maintenance of uniform securities forms and procedures; and

(C) the development of a uniform exemption from registration for small issuers which can be agreed upon among several States or between the States and the Federal Government. The Commission shall have the authority to adopt such an exemption as agreed upon for Federal purposes. Nothing in this Act shall be construed as authorizing preemption of State law.

(4) In order to carry out these policies and purposes, the Commission shall conduct an annual conference as well as such other meetings as are deemed necessary, to which representatives from such securities associations, securities self-regulatory organizations, agencies, and private organizations involved in capital formation shall be invited to participate.

(5) For fiscal year 1982, and for each of the three succeeding fiscal years, there are authorized to be appropriated such amounts as may be necessary and appropriate to carry out the policies, provisions, and purposes of this subsection. Any sums so appropriated shall remain available until expended.

(6) Notwithstanding any other provision of law, neither the Commission nor any other person shall be required to establish any procedures not specifically required by the securities laws, as that term is defined in section 3(a)(47) of the Securities Exchange Act of 1934, or by chapter 5 of title 5, United States Code, in connection with cooperation, coordination, or consultation with—

(A) any association referred to in paragraph (1) or (3) or any conference or meeting referred to in paragraph (4), while such association, conference, or meeting is carrying out activities in furtherance of the provisions of this subsection; or

(B) any forum, agency, or organization, or group referred to in section 503 of the Small Business Investment Incentive Act of 1980, while such forum, agency, organization, or group is carrying out activities in furtherance of the provisions of such section 503.

As used in this paragraph, the terms "association", "conference", "meeting", "forum", "agency", "organization", and "group" include any committee, subgroup, or representative of such entities.

(e) *Evaluation of Rules or Programs.* For the purpose of evaluating any rule or program of the Commission issued or carried out under any provision of the securities laws, as defined in section 3 of the Securities Exchange Act of 1934, and the purposes of considering, proposing, adopting, or engaging in any such rule or program or developing new rules or programs, the Commission may—

(1) gather information from and communicate with investors or other members of the public;

(2) engage in such temporary investor testing programs as the Commission determines are in the public interest or would protect investors; and

(3) consult with academics and consultants, as necessary to carry out this subsection.

(f) *Rule of Construction.* For purposes of the Paperwork Reduction Act, any action taken under subsection (e) shall not be construed to be a collection of information.

(g) *Funding for the GASB.*

(1) *In General.* The Commission may, subject to the limitations imposed by section 15B of the Securities Exchange Act of 1934, require a national securities association registered under the Securities Exchange Act of 1934 to establish—

(A) a reasonable annual accounting support fee to adequately fund the annual budget of the Governmental Accounting Standards Board (referred to in this subsection as the "GASB"); and

(B) rules and procedures, in consultation with the principal organizations representing State governors, legislators, local elected officials, and State and local finance officers, to provide for the equitable allocation, assessment, and collection of the accounting support fee established under subparagraph (A) from the members of the association, and the remittance of all such accounting support fees to the Financial Accounting Foundation.

(2) *Annual Budget.* For purposes of this subsection, the annual budget of the GASB is the annual budget reviewed and approved according to the internal procedures of the Financial Accounting Foundation.

(3) *Use of Funds.* Any fees or funds collected under this subsection shall be used to support the efforts of the GASB to establish standards of financial accounting and reporting recognized as generally accepted accounting principles applicable to State and local governments of the United States.

(4) *Limitation on Fee.* The annual accounting support fees collected under this subsection for a fiscal year shall not exceed the recoverable annual budgeted expenses of the GASB (which may include operating expenses, capital, and accrued items).

(5) *Rules of Construction.*

(A) *Fees Not Public Monies.* Accounting support fees collected under this subsection and other receipts of the GASB shall not be considered public monies of the United States.

(B) *Limitation on Authority of the Commission.* Nothing in this subsection shall be construed to—

(i) provide the Commission or any national securities association direct or indirect oversight of the budget or technical agenda of the GASB; or

(ii) affect the setting of generally accepted accounting principles by the GASB.

(C) *Noninterference with States.* Nothing in this subsection shall be construed to impair or limit the authority of a State or local government to establish accounting and financial reporting standards.

Injunctions and Prosecution of Offenses

Sec. 20. (a) *Investigation of Violations.* Whenever it shall appear to the Commission, either upon complaint or otherwise, that the provisions of this title, or of any rule or regulation prescribed under authority thereof, have been or are about to be violated, it may, in its discretion, either require or permit such person to file with it a statement in writing, under oath, or otherwise, as to all the facts and circumstances concerning the subject matter which it believes to be in the public interest to investigate, and may investigate such facts.

(b) *Action for Injunction or Criminal Prosecution in District Court.* Whenever it shall appear to the Commission that any person is engaged or about to engage in any acts or practices which constitute or will constitute a violation of the provisions of this title, or of any rule or regulation prescribed under authority thereof, the Commission may in its discretion, bring an action in any district court of the United States, or United States court of any Territory, to enjoin such acts or practices, and upon a proper showing, a permanent or temporary injunction or restraining order shall be granted without bond. The Commission may transmit such evidence as may be available concerning such acts or practices to the Attorney General who may, in his discretion, institute the necessary criminal proceedings under this title. Any such criminal proceeding may be brought either in the district wherein the transmittal of the prospectus or security complained of begins, or in the district wherein such prospectus or security is received.

(c) *Writ of Mandamus.* Upon application of the Commission, the district courts of the United States and the United States courts of any Territory shall have jurisdiction to issue writs of mandamus commanding any person to comply with the provisions of this title or any order of the Commission made in pursuance thereof.

(d) *Money Penalties in Civil Actions.*

(1) *Authority of Commission.* Whenever it shall appear to the Commission that any person has violated any provision of this subchapter, the rules or regulations thereunder, or a cease-and-desist order entered by the Commission pursuant to section 8A of this subchapter, other than by committing a violation subject to a penalty pursuant to section 21A of the Securities Exchange Act of 1934, the Commission may bring an action in a United States district court to seek, and the court shall have jurisdiction to impose, upon a proper showing, a civil penalty to be paid by the person who committed such violation.

(2) *Amount of Penalty.*

(A) *First Tier.* The amount of the penalty shall be determined by the court in light of the facts and circumstances. For each violation, the amount of the penalty shall not exceed the greater of (i) $5,000 for a natural person or $50,000 for any other person, or (ii) the gross amount of pecuniary gain to such defendant as a result of the violation.

(B) *Second Tier.* Notwithstanding subparagraph (A), the amount of penalty for each such violation shall not exceed the greater of (i) $50,000 for a natural person or $250,000 for any other person, or (ii) the gross amount of pecuniary gain to such defendant as a result of the violation, if the violation described in paragraph (1) involved fraud, deceit, manipulation, or deliberate or reckless disregard of a regulatory requirement.

(C) *Third Tier.* Notwithstanding subparagraphs (A) and (B), the amount of penalty for each such violation shall not exceed the greater of (i) $100,000 for a natural person or $500,000 for any other person, or (ii) the gross amount of pecuniary gain to such defendant as a result of the violation, if—

(I) the violation described in paragraph (1) involved fraud, deceit, manipulation, or deliberate or reckless disregard of a regulatory requirement; and

(II) such violation directly or indirectly resulted in substantial losses or created a significant risk of substantial losses to other persons.

(3) *Procedures for Collection.*

(A) *Payment of Penalty to Treasury.* A penalty imposed under this section shall be payable into the Treasury of the United States, except as otherwise provided in section 308 of the Sarbanes–Oxley Act of 2002 and section 21F of the Securities Exchange Act of 1934.

(B) *Collection of Penalties.* If a person upon whom such a penalty is imposed shall fail to pay such penalty within the time prescribed in the court's order, the Commission may refer the matter to the Attorney General who shall recover such penalty by action in the appropriate United States district court.

(C) *Remedy Not Exclusive.* The actions authorized by this subsection may be brought in addition to any other action that the Commission or the Attorney General is entitled to bring.

(D) *Jurisdiction and Venue.* For purposes of section 22 of this subchapter, actions under this section shall be actions to enforce a liability or a duty created by this subchapter.

(4) *Special Provisions Relating to a Violation of a Cease-and-Desist Order.* In an action to enforce a cease-and-desist order entered by the Commission pursuant to section 8A, each separate violation of such order shall be a separate offense, except that in the case of a violation through a continuing failure to comply with such an order, each day of the failure to comply with the order shall be deemed a separate offense.

(e) *Authority of a Court to Prohibit Persons from Serving as Officers and Directors.* In any proceeding under subsection (b), the court may prohibit, conditionally or unconditionally, and permanently or for such period of time as it shall determine, any person who violated section 17(a)(1) of this title from acting as an officer or director of any issuer that has a class of securities registered pursuant to section 12 of the Securities Exchange Act of 1934 or that is required to file reports pursuant to section 15(d) of such Act if the person's conduct demonstrates unfitness to serve as an officer or director of any such issuer.

(f) *Prohibition of Attorneys' Fees Paid from Commission Disgorgement Funds.* Except as otherwise ordered by the court upon motion by the Commission, or, in the case of an administrative action, as otherwise ordered by the Commission, funds disgorged as the result of an action brought by the Commission in Federal court, or as a result of any Commission administrative action, shall not be distributed as payment for attorneys' fees or expenses incurred by private parties seeking distribution of the disgorged funds.

(g) *Authority of a Court to Prohibit Persons From Participating in an Offering of Penny Stock.*

(1) *In General.* In any proceeding under subsection (a) against any person participating in, or, at the time of the alleged misconduct, who was participating in, an offering of penny stock, the court may prohibit that person from participating in an offering of penny stock, conditionally or unconditionally, and permanently or for such period of time as the court shall determine.

(2) *Definition.* For purposes of this subsection, the term "person participating in an offering of penny stock" includes any person engaging in activities with a broker, dealer, or issuer for purposes of issuing, trading, or inducing or attempting to induce the purchase or sale of, any penny stock. The Commission may, by rule or regulation, define such term to include other activities, and may, by rule, regulation, or order, exempt any person or class of persons, in whole or in part, conditionally or unconditionally, from inclusion in such term.

Hearings by Commission

Sec. 21. All hearings shall be public and may be held before the Commission or an officer or officers of the Commission designated by it, and appropriate records thereof shall be kept.

Jurisdiction of Offenses and Suits

Sec. 22. (a) *Federal and State Courts; Venue; Service of Process; Review; Removal; Costs.* The district courts of the United States and United States courts of any Territory shall have jurisdiction of offenses and violations under this title and under the rules and regulations promulgated by the Commission in respect thereto, and, concurrent with State and Territorial courts, except as provided in section 16 with respect to covered class actions, of all suits in equity and actions at law brought to enforce any liability or duty created by this title. Any such suit or action may be brought in the district wherein the defendant is found or is an inhabitant or transacts business, or in the district where the offer or sale took place, if the defendant participated therein, and process in such cases may be served in any other district of which the defendant is an inhabitant or wherever the defendants may be found. In any action or proceeding instituted by the Commission under this title in a United States district court for any judicial district, a subpoena issued to compel the attendance of a witness or the production of documents or tangible things (or both) at a hearing or trial may be served at any place within the United States. Rule 45(c)(3)(A)(ii) of the Federal Rules of Civil Procedure shall not apply to a subpoena issued under the preceding sentence. Judgments and decrees so rendered shall be subject to review as provided in sections 1254, 1291, 1292, and 1294 of title 28, United States Code. Except as provided in section 16(c), no case arising under this title and brought in any State court of competent jurisdiction shall be removed to any court of the United States. No costs shall be assessed for or against the Commission in any proceeding under this title brought by or against it in the Supreme Court or such other courts.

(b) *Contumacy or Refusal to Obey Subpoena; Contempt.* In case of contumacy or refusal to obey a subpena issued to any person, any of the said United States courts, within the jurisdiction of which said person guilty of contumacy or refusal to obey is found or resides, upon application by the Commission may issue to such person an order requiring such person to appear before the Commission, or one of its examiners designated by it, there to produce documentary evidence if so ordered, or there to give evidence touching the matter in question; and any failure to obey such order of the court may be punished by said court as a contempt thereof.

(c) *Extraterritorial Jurisdiction.* The district courts of the United States and the United States courts of any Territory shall have jurisdiction of an action or proceeding brought or instituted by the Commission or the United States alleging a violation of section 17(a) involving—

(1) conduct within the United States that constitutes significant steps in furtherance of the violation, even if the securities transaction occurs outside the United States and involves only foreign investors; or

(2) conduct occurring outside the United States that has a foreseeable substantial effect within the United States.

Unlawful Representations

Sec. 23. Neither the fact that the registration statement for a security has been filed or is in effect nor the fact that a stop order is not in effect with respect thereto shall be deemed a finding by the Commission that the registration statement is true and accurate on its face or that it does not contain an untrue statement of fact or omit to state a material fact, or be held to mean that the Commission has in any way passed upon the merits of, or given approval to, such security. It shall be unlawful to make, or cause to be made, to any prospective purchaser any representation contrary to the foregoing provisions of this section.

Penalties

Sec. 24. Any person who willfully violates any of the provisions of this title, or the rules and regulations promulgated by the Commission under authority thereof, or any person who willfully, in a registration statement filed under this title, makes any untrue statement of a material fact or omits to state any material fact required to be stated therein or necessary to make the statements therein not misleading, shall upon conviction be fined not more than $10,000 or imprisoned not more than five years, or both.

Jurisdiction of Other Government Agencies Over Securities

Sec. 25. Nothing in this title shall relieve any person from submitting to the respective supervisory units of the Government of the United States information, reports, or other documents that may be required by any provision of law.

Separability of Provisions

Sec. 26. If any provision of this Act, or the application of such provision to any person or circumstance, shall be held invalid, the remainder of this Act, or the application of such provision to persons or circumstances other than those as to which it is held invalid, shall not be affected thereby.

Private Securities Litigation

Sec. 27. (a) *Private Class Actions.*

(1) *In General.* The provisions of this subsection shall apply to each private action arising under this title that is brought as a plaintiff class action pursuant to the Federal Rules of Civil Procedure.

(2) *Certification Filed With Complaint.*

(A) *In General.* Each plaintiff seeking to serve as a representative party on behalf of a class shall provide a sworn certification, which shall be personally signed by such plaintiff and filed with the complaint, that—

(i) states that the plaintiff has reviewed the complaint and authorized its filing;

(ii) states that the plaintiff did not purchase the security that is the subject of the complaint at the direction of plaintiff's counsel or in order to participate in any private action arising under this title;

(iii) states that the plaintiff is willing to serve as a representative party on behalf of a class, including providing testimony at deposition and trial, if necessary;

(iv) sets forth all of the transactions of the plaintiff in the security that is the subject of the complaint during the class period specified in the complaint;

(v) identifies any other action under this title, filed during the 3-year period preceding the date on which the certification is signed by the plaintiff, in which the plaintiff has sought to serve, or served, as a representative party on behalf of a class; and

(vi) states that the plaintiff will not accept any payment for serving as a representative party on behalf of a class beyond the plaintiff's pro rata share of any recovery, except as ordered or approved by the court in accordance with paragraph (4).

(B) *Nonwaiver of Attorney-Client Privilege.* The certification filed pursuant to subparagraph (A) shall not be construed to be a waiver of the attorney-client privilege.

(3) *Appointment of Lead Plaintiff.*

(A) *Early Notice to Class Members.*

(i) *In General.* Not later than 20 days after the date on which the complaint is filed, the plaintiff or plaintiffs shall cause to be published, in a widely circulated national business-oriented publication or wire service, a notice advising members of the purported plaintiff class—

(I) of the pendency of the action, the claims asserted therein, and the purported class period; and

(II) that, not later than 60 days after the date on which the notice is published, any member of the purported class may move the court to serve as lead plaintiff of the purported class.

(ii) *Multiple Actions.* If more than one action on behalf of a class asserting substantially the same claim or claims arising under this title is filed, only the plaintiff or plaintiffs in the first filed action shall be required to cause notice to be published in accordance with clause (i).

(iii) *Additional Notices May Be Required Under Federal Rules.* Notice required under clause (i) shall be in addition to any notice required pursuant to the Federal Rules of Civil Procedure.

(B) *Appointment of Lead Plaintiff.*

(i) *In General.* Not later than 90 days after the date on which a notice is published under subparagraph (A)(i), the court shall consider any motion made by a purported class member in response to the notice, including any motion by a class member who is not individually named as a plaintiff in the complaint or complaints, and shall appoint as lead plaintiff the member or members of the purported plaintiff class that the court determines to be most capable of adequately representing the interests of class members (hereafter in this paragraph referred to as the "most adequate plaintiff") in accordance with this subparagraph.

(ii) *Consolidated Actions.* If more than one action on behalf of a class asserting substantially the same claim or claims arising under this title has been filed, and any party has sought to consolidate those actions for pretrial purposes or for trial, the court shall not make the determination required by clause (i) until after the decision on the motion to consolidate is rendered. As soon as practicable after such decision is rendered, the court shall appoint the most adequate plaintiff as lead plaintiff for the consolidated actions in accordance with this subparagraph.

(iii) *Rebuttable Presumption.*

(I) *In General.* Subject to subclause (II), for purposes of clause (i), the court shall adopt a presumption that the most adequate plaintiff in any private action arising under this title is the person or group of persons that—

(aa) has either filed the complaint or made a motion in response to a notice under subparagraph (A)(i);

(bb) in the determination of the court, has the largest financial interest in the relief sought by the class; and

(cc) otherwise satisfies the requirements of Rule 23 of the Federal Rules of Civil Procedure.

(II) *Rebuttal Evidence.* The presumption described in subclause (I) may be rebutted only upon proof by a member of the purported plaintiff class that the presumptively most adequate plaintiff—

(aa) will not fairly and adequately protect the interests of the class; or (bb) is subject to unique defenses that render such plaintiff incapable of adequately representing the class.

(iv) *Discovery.* For purposes of this subparagraph, discovery relating to whether a member or members of the purported plaintiff class is the most adequate plaintiff may be conducted by a plaintiff only if the plaintiff first demonstrates a reasonable basis for a finding that the presumptively most adequate plaintiff is incapable of adequately representing the class.

(v) *Selection of Lead Counsel.* The most adequate plaintiff shall, subject to the approval of the court, select and retain counsel to represent the class.

(vi) *Restrictions on Professional Plaintiffs.* Except as the court may otherwise permit, consistent with the purposes of this section, a person may be a lead plaintiff, or an officer, director, or fiduciary of a lead plaintiff, in no more than 5 securities class actions brought as plaintiff class actions pursuant to the Federal Rules of Civil Procedure during any 3–year period.

(4) *Recovery by Plaintiffs.* The share of any final judgment or of any settlement that is awarded to a representative party serving on behalf of a class shall be equal, on a per share basis, to the portion of the final judgment or settlement awarded to all other members of the class. Nothing in this paragraph shall be construed to limit the award of reasonable costs and expenses (including lost wages) directly relating to the representation of the class to any representative party serving on behalf of the class.

(5) *Restrictions on Settlements Under Seal.* The terms and provisions of any settlement agreement of a class action shall not be filed under seal, except that on motion of any party to the settlement, the court may order filing under seal for those portions of a settlement agreement as to which good cause is shown for such filing under seal. For purposes of this paragraph, good cause shall exist only if publication of a term or provision of a settlement agreement would cause direct and substantial harm to any party.

(6) *Restrictions on Payment of Attorneys' Fees and Expenses.* Total attorneys' fees and expenses awarded by the court to counsel for the plaintiff class shall not exceed a reasonable percentage of the amount of any damages and prejudgment interest actually paid to the class.

(7) *Disclosure of Settlement Terms to Class Members.* Any proposed or final settlement agreement that is published or otherwise disseminated to the class shall include each of the following statements, along with a cover page summarizing the information contained in such statements:

(A) *Statement of Plaintiff Recovery.* The amount of the settlement proposed to be distributed to the parties to the action, determined in the aggregate and on an average per share basis.

(B) *Statement of Potential Outcome of Case.*

(i) *Agreement on Amount of Damages.* If the settling parties agree on the average amount of damages per share that would be recoverable if the plaintiff prevailed on each claim alleged under this title, a statement concerning the average amount of such potential damages per share.

(ii) *Disagreement on Amount of Damages.* If the parties do not agree on the average amount of damages per share that would be recoverable if the plaintiff prevailed on each claim alleged under this title, a statement from each settling party concerning the issue or issues on which the parties disagree.

(iii) *Inadmissibility for Certain Purposes.* A statement made in accordance with clause (i) or (ii) concerning the amount of damages shall not be admissible in any Federal or State judicial action or administrative proceeding, other than an action or proceeding arising out of such statement.

(C) *Statement of Attorneys' Fees or Costs Sought.* If any of the settling parties or their counsel intend to apply to the court for an award of attorneys' fees or costs from any fund established as part of the settlement, a statement indicating which parties or counsel intend to make such an application, the amount of fees and costs that will be sought (including the amount of such fees and costs determined on an average per share basis), and a brief explanation supporting the fees and costs sought.

(D) *Identification of Lawyers' Representatives.* The name, telephone number, and address of one or more representatives of counsel for the plaintiff class who will be reasonably available to answer questions from class members concerning any matter contained in any notice of settlement published or otherwise disseminated to the class.

(E) *Reasons for Settlement.* A brief statement explaining the reasons why the parties are proposing the settlement.

(F) *Other Information.* Such other information as may be required by the court.

(8) *Attorney Conflict of Interest.* If a plaintiff class is represented by an attorney who directly owns or otherwise has a beneficial interest in the securities that are the subject of the litigation, the court shall make a determination of whether such ownership or other interest constitutes a conflict of interest sufficient to disqualify the attorney from representing the plaintiff class.

(b) *Stay of Discovery; Preservation of Evidence.*

(1) *In General.* In any private action arising under this title, all discovery and other proceedings shall be stayed during the pendency of any motion to dismiss, unless the court finds, upon the motion of any party, that particularized discovery is necessary to preserve evidence or to prevent undue prejudice to that party.

(2) *Preservation of Evidence.* During the pendency of any stay of discovery pursuant to this subsection, unless otherwise ordered by the court, any party to the action with actual notice of the allegations contained in the complaint shall treat all documents, data compilations (including electronically recorded or stored data), and tangible objects that are in the custody or control of such person and that are relevant to the allegations, as if they were the subject of a continuing request for production of documents from an opposing party under the Federal Rules of Civil Procedure.

(3) *Sanction for Willful Violation.* A party aggrieved by the willful failure of an opposing party to comply with paragraph (2) may apply to the court for an order awarding appropriate sanctions.

(4) *Circumvention of Stay of Discovery.* Upon a proper showing, a court may stay discovery proceedings in any private action in a State court as necessary in aid of its jurisdiction, or to protect or effectuate its judgments, in an action subject to a stay of discovery pursuant to this subsection.

(c) *Sanctions for Abusive Litigation.*

(1) *Mandatory Review by Court.* In any private action arising under this title, upon final adjudication of the action, the court shall include in the record specific findings regarding compliance by each party and each attorney representing any party with each requirement of Rule 11(b) of the Federal Rules of Civil Procedure as to any complaint, responsive pleading, or dispositive motion.

(2) *Mandatory Sanctions.* If the court makes a finding under paragraph (1) that a party or attorney violated any requirement of Rule 11(b) of the Federal Rules of Civil Procedure as to any complaint, responsive pleading, or dispositive motion, the court shall impose sanctions on such party or attorney in accordance with Rule 11 of the Federal Rules of Civil Procedure. Prior to making a finding that any party or attorney has violated Rule 11 of the Federal Rules of Civil Procedure, the court shall give such party or attorney notice and an opportunity to respond.

(3) *Presumption in Favor of Attorneys' Fees and Costs.*

(A) *In General.* Subject to subparagraphs (B) and (C), for purposes of paragraph (2), the court shall adopt a presumption that the appropriate sanction—

(i) for failure of any responsive pleading or dispositive motion to comply with any requirement of Rule 11(b) of the Federal Rules of Civil Procedure is an award to the opposing party of the reasonable attorneys' fees and other expenses incurred as a direct result of the violation; and

(ii) for substantial failure of any complaint to comply with any requirement of Rule 11(b) of the Federal Rules of Civil Procedure is an award to the opposing party of the reasonable attorneys' fees and other expenses incurred in the action.

(B) *Rebuttal Evidence.* The presumption described in subparagraph (A) may be rebutted only upon proof by the party or attorney against whom sanctions are to be imposed that—

(i) the award of attorneys' fees and other expenses will impose an unreasonable burden on that party or attorney and would be unjust, and the failure to make such an award would not impose a greater burden on the party in whose favor sanctions are to be imposed; or

(ii) the violation of Rule 11(b) of the Federal Rules of Civil Procedure was de minimis.

(C) *Sanctions.* If the party or attorney against whom sanctions are to be imposed meets its burden under subparagraph (B), the court shall award the sanctions that the court deems appropriate pursuant to Rule 11 of the Federal Rules of Civil Procedure.

(d) *Defendant's Right to Written Interrogatories.* In any private action arising under this title in which the plaintiff may recover money damages only on proof that a defendant acted with a particular state of mind, the court shall, when requested by a defendant, submit to the jury a written interrogatory on the issue of each such defendant's state of mind at the time the alleged violation occurred.

Application of Safe Harbor for Forward–Looking Statements

Sec. 27A. (a) *Applicability.* This section shall apply only to a forward-looking statement made by—

(1) an issuer that, at the time that the statement is made, is subject to the reporting requirements of section 13(a) or section 15(d) of the Securities Exchange Act of 1934;

(2) a person acting on behalf of such issuer;

(3) an outside reviewer retained by such issuer making a statement on behalf of such issuer; or

(4) an underwriter, with respect to information provided by such issuer or information derived from information provided by the issuer.

(b) *Exclusions.* Except to the extent otherwise specifically provided by rule, regulation, or order of the Commission, this section shall not apply to a forward-looking statement—

(1) that is made with respect to the business or operations of the issuer, if the issuer—

(A) during the 3-year period preceding the date on which the statement was first made—

(i) was convicted of any felony or misdemeanor described in clauses (i) through (iv) of section 15(b)(4)(B) of the Securities Exchange Act of 1934; or

(ii) has been made the subject of a judicial or administrative decree or order arising out of a governmental action that—

(I) prohibits future violations of the antifraud provisions of the securities laws;

(II) requires that the issuer cease and desist from violating the antifraud provisions of the securities laws; or

(III) determines that the issuer violated the antifraud provisions of the securities laws;

(B) makes the forward-looking statement in connection with an offering of securities by a blank check company;

(C) issues penny stock;

(D) makes the forward-looking statement in connection with a rollup transaction; or

(E) makes the forward-looking statement in connection with a going private transaction; or

(2) that is—

(A) included in a financial statement prepared in accordance with generally accepted accounting principles;

(B) contained in a registration statement of, or otherwise issued by, an investment company;

(C) made in connection with a tender offer;

(D) made in connection with an initial public offering;

(E) made in connection with an offering by, or relating to the operations of, a partnership, limited liability company, or a direct participation investment program; or

(F) made in a disclosure of beneficial ownership in a report required to be filed with the Commission pursuant to section 13(d) of the Securities Exchange Act of 1934.

(c) *Safe Harbor.*

(1) *In General.* Except as provided in subsection (b), in any private action arising under this title that is based on an untrue statement of a material fact or omission of a material fact necessary to make the statement not misleading, a person referred to in subsection (a) shall not be liable with respect to any forward-looking statement, whether written or oral, if and to the extent that—

(A) the forward-looking statement is—

(i) identified as a forward-looking statement, and is accompanied by meaningful cautionary statements identifying important factors that could cause actual results to differ materially from those in the forward looking statement; or

(ii) immaterial; or

(B) the plaintiff fails to prove that the forward-looking statement—

(i) if made by a natural person, was made with actual knowledge by that person that the statement was false or misleading; or

(ii) if made by a business entity was—

(I) made by or with the approval of an executive officer of that entity, and

(II) made or approved by such officer with actual knowledge by that officer that the statement was false or misleading.

(2) *Oral Forward–Looking Statements.* In the case of an oral forward-looking statement made by an issuer that is subject to the reporting requirements of section 13(a) or section 15(d) of the Securities Exchange Act of 1934, or by a person acting on behalf of such issuer, the requirement set forth in paragraph (1)(A) shall be deemed to be satisfied—

(A) if the oral forward-looking statement is accompanied by a cautionary statement—

(i) that the particular oral statement is a forward-looking statement; and

(ii) that the actual results could differ materially from those projected in the forward-looking statement; and

(B) if—

(i) the oral forward-looking statement is accompanied by an oral statement that additional information concerning factors that could cause actual results to differ materially from those in the forward-looking statement is contained in a readily available written document, or portion thereof;

(ii) the accompanying oral statement referred to in clause (i) identifies the document, or portion thereof, that contains the additional information about those factors relating to the forward-looking statement; and

(iii) the information contained in that written document is a cautionary statement that satisfies the standard established in paragraph (1)(A).

(3) *Availability.* Any document filed with the Commission or generally disseminated shall be deemed to be readily available for purposes of paragraph (2).

(4) *Effect on Other Safe Harbors.* The exemption provided for in paragraph (1) shall be in addition to any exemption that the Commission may establish by rule or regulation under subsection (g).

(d) *Duty to Update.* Nothing in this section shall impose upon any person a duty to update a forward-looking statement.

(e) *Dispositive Motion.* On any motion to dismiss based upon subsection (c)(1), the court shall consider any statement cited in the complaint and cautionary statement accompanying the forward-looking statement, which are not subject to material dispute, cited by the defendant.

(f) *Stay Pending Decision on Motion.* In any private action arising under this title, the court shall stay discovery (other than discovery that is specifically directed to the applicability of the exemption provided for in this section) during the pendency of any motion by a defendant for summary judgment that is based on the grounds that—

(1) the statement or omission upon which the complaint is based is a forward-looking statement within the meaning of this section; and

(2) the exemption provided for in this section precludes a claim for relief.

(g) *Exemption Authority.* In addition to the exemptions provided for in this section, the Commission may, by rule or regulation, provide exemptions from or under any provision of this title, including with respect to liability that is based on a statement or that is based on projections or other forward-looking information, if and to the extent that any such exemption is consistent with the public interest and the protection of investors, as determined by the Commission.

(h) *Effect on Other Authority of Commission.* Nothing in this section limits, either expressly or by implication, the authority of the Commission to exercise similar authority or to adopt similar rules and regulations with respect to forward-looking statements under any other statute under which the Commission exercises rulemaking authority.

(i) *Definitions.* For purposes of this section, the following definitions shall apply:

(1) *Forward–Looking Statement.* The term "forward-looking statement" means—

(A) a statement containing a projection of revenues, income (including income loss), earnings (including earnings loss) per share, capital expenditures, dividends, capital structure, or other financial items;

(B) a statement of the plans and objectives of management for future operations, including plans or objectives relating to the products or services of the issuer;

(C) a statement of future economic performance, including any such statement contained in a discussion and analysis of financial condition by the management or in the results of operations included pursuant to the rules and regulations of the Commission;

(D) any statement of the assumptions underlying or relating to any statement described in subparagraph (A), (B), or (C);

(E) any report issued by an outside reviewer retained by an issuer, to the extent that the report assesses a forward-looking statement made by the issuer; or

(F) a statement containing a projection or estimate of such other items as may be specified by rule or regulation of the Commission.

(2) *Investment Company.* The term "investment company" has the same meaning as in section 3(a) of the Investment Company Act of 1940.

(3) *Penny Stock.* The term "penny stock" has the same meaning as in section 3(a)(51) of the Securities Exchange Act of 1934, and the rules and regulations, or orders issued pursuant to that section.

(4) *Going Private Transaction.* The term "going private transaction" has the meaning given that term under the rules or regulations of the Commission issued pursuant to section 13(e) of the Securities Exchange Act of 1934.

(5) *Securities Laws.* The term "securities laws" has the same meaning as in section 3 of the Securities Exchange Act of 1934.

(6) *Person Acting on Behalf of an Issuer.* The term "person acting on behalf of an issuer" means an officer, director, or employee of the issuer.

(7) *Other Terms.* The terms "blank check company", "roll-up transaction", "partnership", "limited liability company", "executive officer of an entity" and "direct participation investment program", have the meanings given those terms by rule or regulation of the Commission.

Conflicts of Interest Relating to Certain Securitizations

[*This section shall take effect on the effective date of final rules issued by the Commission under subsection (b) of such section 27B, except that subsections (b) and (d) of such section 27B shall take effect on the date of enactment of the Dodd–Frank Act.*]

Sec. 27B. (a) *In General.* An underwriter, placement agent, initial purchaser, or sponsor, or any affiliate or subsidiary of any such entity, of an asset-backed security (as such term is defined in section 3 of the Securities and Exchange Act of 1934, which for the purposes of this section shall include a synthetic asset-backed security), shall not, at any time for a period ending on the date that is one year after the date of the first closing of the sale of the asset-backed security, engage in any transaction that would involve or result in any material conflict of interest with respect to any investor in a transaction arising out of such activity.

(b) *Rulemaking.* Not later than 270 days after the date of enactment of this section, the Commission shall issue rules for the purpose of implementing subsection (a).

(c) *Exception.* The prohibitions of subsection (a) shall not apply to—

(1) risk-mitigating hedging activities in connection with positions or holdings arising out of the underwriting, placement, initial purchase, or sponsorship of an asset-backed security, provided that such activities are designed to reduce the specific risks to the underwriter, placement agent, initial purchaser, or sponsor associated with positions or holdings arising out of such underwriting, placement, initial purchase, or sponsorship; or

(2) purchases or sales of asset-backed securities made pursuant to and consistent with—

(A) commitments of the underwriter, placement agent, initial purchaser, or sponsor, or any affiliate or subsidiary of any such entity, to provide liquidity for the asset-backed security, or

(B) bona fide market-making in the asset backed security.

(d) *Rule of Construction.* This subsection shall not otherwise limit the application of section 15G of the Securities Exchange Act of 1934.

General Exemptive Authority

Sec. 28. The Commission, by rule or regulation, may conditionally or unconditionally exempt any person, security, or transaction, or any class or classes of persons, securities, or transactions, from any provision or provisions of this title or of any rule or regulation issued under this title, to the extent that such exemption is necessary or appropriate in the public interest, and is consistent with the protection of investors.

Schedules of Information Required in Registration Statement

Schedule A

(1) The name under which the issuer is doing or intends to do business;

(2) the name of the State or other sovereign power under which the issuer is organized;

(3) the location of the issuer's principal business office, and if the issuer is a foreign or territorial person, the name and address of its agent in the United States authorized to receive notice;

(4) the names and addresses of the directors or persons performing similar functions, and the chief executive, financial and accounting officers, chosen or to be chosen if the issuer be a corporation, association, trust, or other entity; of all partners, if the issuer be a partnership; and of the issuer, if the issuer be an individual; and of the promoters in the case of a business to be formed, or formed within two years prior to the filing of the registration statement;

(5) the names and addresses of the underwriters;

(6) the names and addresses of all persons, if any, owning of record or beneficially, if known, more than 10 per centum of any class of stock of the issuer, or more than 10 per centum in the aggregate of the outstanding stock of the issuer as of a date within twenty days prior to the filing of the registration statement;

(7) the amount of securities of the issuer held by any person specified in paragraphs (4), (5), and (6) of this schedule, as of a date within twenty days prior to the filing of the registration statement, and, if possible, as of one year prior thereto, and the amount of the securities, for which the registration statement is filed, to which such persons have indicated their intention to subscribe;

(8) the general character of the business actually transacted or to be transacted by the issuer;

(9) a statement of the capitalization of the issuer, including the authorized and outstanding amounts of its capital stock and the proportion thereof paid up, the number and classes of shares in which such capital stock is divided, par value thereof, or if it has no par value, the stated or assigned value thereof, a description of the respective voting rights, preferences, conversion and exchange rights, rights to dividends, profits, or capital of each class, with respect to each other class, including the retirement and liquidation rights or values thereof;

(10) a statement of the securities, if any, covered by options outstanding or to be created in connection with the security to be offered, together with the names and addresses of all persons, if any, to be allotted more than 10 per centum in the aggregate of such options;

(11) the amount of capital stock of each class issued or included in the shares of stock to be offered;

(12) the amount of the funded debt outstanding and to be created by the security to be offered, with a brief description of the date, maturity, and character of such debt, rate of interest, character of amortization provisions, and the security, if any, therefor. If substitution of any security is permissible, a summarized statement of the conditions under which such substitution is permitted. If substitution is permissible without notice, a specific statement to that effect;

(13) the specific purposes in detail and the approximate amounts to be devoted to such purposes, so far as determinable, for which the security to be offered is to supply funds, and if the funds are to be raised in part from other sources, the amounts thereof and the sources thereof, shall be stated;

(14) the remuneration, paid or estimated to be paid, by the issuer or its predecessor, directly or indirectly, during the past year and ensuing year, to (a) the directors or persons performing similar functions, and (b) its officers and other persons, naming them wherever such remuneration exceeded $25,000 during any such year;

(15) the estimated net proceeds to be derived from the security to be offered;

(16) the price at which it is proposed that the security shall be offered to the public or the method by which such price is computed and any variation therefrom at which any portion of such security is proposed to be offered to any persons or classes of persons, other than the underwriters, naming them or specifying the class. A variation in price may be proposed prior to the date of the public offering of the security, but the Commission shall immediately be notified of such variation;

(17) all commissions or discounts paid or to be paid, directly or indirectly, by the issuer to the underwriters in respect of the sale of the security to be offered. Commissions shall include all cash, securities, contracts, or anything else of value, paid, to be set aside, disposed of, or understandings with or for the benefit of any other persons in which any underwriter is interested, made, in connection with the sale of such security. A commission paid or to be paid in connection with the sale of such security by a person in which the issuer has an interest or which is controlled or directed by, or under common control with, the issuer shall be deemed to have been paid by the issuer. Where any such commission is paid the amount of such commission paid to each underwriter shall be stated;

(18) the amount or estimated amounts, itemized in reasonable detail, of expenses, other than commissions specified in paragraph (17) of this schedule, incurred or borne by or for the account of the issuer in connection with the sale of the security to be offered or properly chargeable thereto, including legal, engineering, certification, authentication, and other charges;

(19) the net proceeds derived from any security sold by the issuer during the two years preceding the filing of the registration statement, the price at which such security was offered to the public, and the names of the principal underwriters of such security;

(20) any amount paid within two years preceding the filing of the registration statement or intended to be paid to any promoter and the consideration for any such payment;

(21) the names and addresses of the vendors and the purchase price of any property, or good will, acquired or to be acquired, not in the ordinary course of business, which is to be defrayed in whole or in part from the proceeds of the security to be offered, the amount of any commission payable to any person in connection with such acquisition, and the name or names of such person or persons, together with any expense incurred or to be incurred in connection with such acquisition, including the cost of borrowing money to finance such acquisition;

(22) full particulars of the nature and extent of the interest, if any, of every director, principal executive officer, and of every stockholder holding more than 10 per centum of any class of stock or more than 10 per centum in the aggregate of the stock of the issuer, in any property acquired, not in the ordinary course of business of the issuer, within two years preceding the filing of the registration statement or proposed to be acquired at such date;

(23) the names and addresses of counsel who have passed on the legality of the issue;

(24) dates of and parties to, and the general effect concisely stated of every material contract made, not in the ordinary course of business, which contract is to be executed in whole or in part at or after the filing of the registration statement or which contract has been made not more than two years before such filing. Any management contract or contract providing for special bonuses or profit-sharing arrangements, and every material patent or contract for a material patent right, and every contract by or with a public utility company or an affiliate thereof, providing for the giving or receiving of technical or financial advice or service (if such contract may involve a charge to any party thereto at a rate in excess of $2,500 per year in cash or securities or anything else of value), shall be deemed a material contract;

(25) a balance sheet as of a date not more than ninety days prior to the date of the filing of the registration statement showing all of the assets of the issuer, the nature and cost thereof, whenever determinable, in such detail and in such form as the Commission shall prescribe (with intangible items segregated), including any loan in excess of $20,000 to any officer, director, stockholder or person directly or indirectly controlling or controlled by the issuer,

or person under direct or indirect common control with the issuer. All the liabilities of the issuer in such detail and such form as the Commission shall prescribe, including surplus of the issuer showing how and from what sources such surplus was created, all as of a date not more than ninety days prior to the filing of the registration statement. If such statement be not certified by an independent public or certified accountant, in addition to the balance sheet required to be submitted under this schedule, a similar detailed balance sheet of the assets and liabilities of the issuer, certified by an independent public or certified accountant, of a date not more than one year prior to the filing of the registration statement, shall be submitted;

(26) a profit and loss statement of the issuer showing earnings and income, the nature and source thereof, and the expenses and fixed charges in such detail and such form as the Commission shall prescribe for the latest fiscal year for which such statement is available and for the two preceding fiscal years, year by year, or, if such issuer has been in actual business for less than three years, then for such time as the issuer has been in actual business, year by year. If the date of the filing of the registration statement is more than six months after the close of the last fiscal year, a statement from such closing date to the latest practicable date. Such statement shall show what the practice of the issuer has been during the three years or lesser period as to the character of the charges, dividends or other distributions made against its various surplus accounts, and as to depreciation, depletion, and maintenance charges, in such detail and form as the Commission shall prescribe, and if stock dividends or avails from the sale of rights have been credited to income, they shall be shown separately with a statement of the basis upon which the credit is computed. Such statement shall also differentiate between any recurring and nonrecurring income and between any investment and operating income. Such statement shall be certified by an independent public or certified accountant;

(27) if the proceeds, or any part of the proceeds, of the security to be issued is to be applied directly or indirectly to the purchase of any business, a profit and loss statement of such business certified by an independent public or certified accountant, meeting the requirements of paragraph (26) of this schedule, for the three preceding fiscal years, together with a balance sheet, similarly certified, of such business, meeting the requirements of paragraph (25) of this schedule of a date not more than ninety days prior to the filing of the registration statement or at the date such business was acquired by the issuer if the business was acquired by the issuer more than ninety days prior to the filing of the registration statement;

(28) a copy of any agreement or agreements (or, if identical agreements are used, the forms thereof) made with any underwriter, including all contracts and agreements referred to in paragraph (17) of this schedule;

(29) a copy of the opinion or opinions of counsel in respect to the legality of the issue, with a translation of such opinion, when necessary, into the English language;

(30) a copy of all material contracts referred to in paragraph (24) of this schedule, but no disclosure shall be required of any portion of any such contract if the Commission determines that disclosure of such portion would impair the value of the contract and would not be necessary for the protection of the investors;

(31) unless previously filed and registered under the provisions of this title, and brought up to date, (a) a copy of its articles of incorporation, with all amendments thereof and of its existing bylaws or instruments corresponding thereto, whatever the name, if the issuer be a corporation; (b) copy of all instruments by which the trust is created or declared, if the issuer is a trust; (c) a copy of its articles of partnership or association and all other papers pertaining to its organization, if the issuer is a partnership, unincorporated association, joint-stock company, or any other form of organization; and

(32) a copy of the underlying agreements or indentures affecting any stock, bonds, or debentures offered or to be offered.

In case of certificates of deposit, voting trust certificates, collateral trust certificates, certificates of interest or shares in unincorporated investment trusts, equipment trust certificates, interim or other receipts for certificates, and like securities, the Commission shall establish rules and regulations requiring the submission of information of a like character applicable to such cases, together with such other information as it may deem appropriate and necessary regarding the character, financial or otherwise, of the actual issuer of the securities and/or the person performing the acts and assuming the duties of depositor or manager.

Schedule B

(1) Name of borrowing government or subdivision thereof;

(2) specific purposes in detail and the approximate amounts to be devoted to such purposes, so far as determinable, for which the security to be offered is to supply funds, and if the funds are to be raised in part from other sources, the amounts thereof and the sources thereof, shall be stated;

(3) the amount of the funded debt and the estimated amount of the floating debt outstanding and to be created by the security to be offered, excluding intergovernmental debt, and a brief description of the date, maturity, character of such debt, rate of interest, character of amortization provisions, and the security, if any, therefor. If substitution of any security is permissible, a statement of the conditions under which such substitution is permitted. If substitution is permissible without notice, a specific statement to that effect;

(4) whether or not the issuer or its predecessor has, within a period of twenty years prior to the filing of the registration statement, defaulted on the principal or interest of any external security, excluding intergovernmental debt, and, if so, the date, amount, and circumstances of such default, and the terms of the succeeding arrangement, if any;

(5) the receipts, classified by source, and the expenditures, classified by purpose, in such detail and form as the Commission shall prescribe for the latest fiscal year for which such information is available and the two preceding fiscal years, year by year;

(6) the names and addresses of the underwriters;

(7) the name and address of its authorized agent, if any, in the United States;

(8) the estimated net proceeds to be derived from the sale in the United States of the security to be offered;

(9) the price at which it is proposed that the security shall be offered in the United States to the public or the method by which such price is computed. A variation in price may be proposed prior to the date of the public offering of the security, but the Commission shall immediately be notified of such variation;

(10) all commissions paid or to be paid, directly or indirectly, by the issuer to the underwriters in respect of the sale of the security to be offered. Commissions shall include all cash, securities, contracts, or anything else of value, paid, to be set aside, disposed of, or understandings with or for the benefit of any other persons in which the underwriter is interested, made, in connection with the sale of such security. Where any such commission is paid, the amount of such commission paid to each underwriter shall be stated;

(11) the amount or estimated amounts, itemized in reasonable detail, of expenses, other than the commissions specified in paragraph (10) of this schedule, incurred or borne by or for the account of the issuer in connection with the sale of the security to be offered or properly chargeable thereto, including legal, engineering, certification, and other charges;

(12) the names and addresses of counsel who have passed upon the legality of the issue;

(13) a copy of any agreement or agreements made with any underwriter governing the sale of the security within the United States; and

(14) an agreement of the issuer to furnish a copy of the opinion or opinions of counsel in respect to the legality of the issue, with a translation, where necessary, into the English language. Such opinion shall set out in full all laws, decrees, ordinances, or other acts of Government under which the issue of such security has been authorized.

SECURITIES ACT OF 1933

GENERAL RULES AND REGULATIONS

(Cite as 17 CFR § 230.__)

GENERAL

REGULATION S–K—STANDARD INSTRUCTIONS FOR FILING FORMS UNDER SECURITIES ACT OF 1933, SECURITIES EXCHANGE ACT OF 1934 AND ENERGY POLICY AND CONSERVATION ACT OF 1975

(Cite as 17 CFR § 229.___)

REGULATION M–A—MERGERS AND ACQUISITIONS

(Cite as 17 CFR § 229.1000 et seq.)

Item
1009. Persons/assets, retained, employed, compensated or used
1010. Financial statements
1011. Additional information
1012. The solicitation or recommendation
1013. Purposes, alternatives, reasons and effects in a going-private transaction
1014. Fairness of the going-private transaction
1015. Reports, opinions, appraisals and negotiations
1016. Exhibits

REGULATION AB—ASSET–BACKED SECURITIES

(Cite as 17 CFR § 229.1100 et seq.)

Item
1100. General
1101. Definitions
1102. Forepart of registration statement and outside cover page of the prospectus
1103. Transaction summary and risk factors
1104. Sponsors
1105. Static pool information
1106. Depositors
1107. Issuing entities
1108. Servicers
1109. Trustees
1110. Originators
1111. Pool assets
1112. Significant obligors of pool assets
1113. Structure of the transaction
1114. Credit enhancement and other support, except for certain derivative instruments
1115. Certain derivatives instruments
1116. Tax matters
1117. Legal proceedings
1118. Reports and additional information
1119. Affiliations and certain relationships and related transactions
1120. Ratings
1121. Distribution and pool performance information
1122. Compliance with applicable servicing criteria
1123. Services compliance statement
1124. Sponsor interest in the securities
1125. Schedule AL—asset-level information

DISCLOSURE BY REGISTRANTS ENGAGED IN OIL AND GAS PRODUCING ACTIVITIES

Item
1201. General instructions to oil and gas industry—specific disclosures
1202. Disclosure of reserves
1203. Proved undeveloped reserves
1204. Oil and gas production, production prices and production costs
1205. Drilling and other exploratory and development activities
1206. Present activities
1207. Delivery commitments
1208. Oil and gas properties, wells, operations, and acreage

REGULATION G

Rule
100. General rules regarding disclosure of non–GAAP financial measures
101. Definitions
102. No effect on antifraud liability

REGULATION S–X—FORM AND CONTENT OF AND REQUIREMENTS FOR FINANCIAL STATEMENTS, SECURITIES ACT OF 1933, SECURITIES EXCHANGE ACT OF 1934, PUBLIC UTILITY HOLDING COMPANY ACT OF 1935, INVESTMENT COMPANY ACT OF 1940, INVESTMENT ADVISERS ACT OF 1940, AND ENERGY POLICY AND CONSERVATION ACT OF 1975

(Cite as 17 CFR § 210.___)

Article 10—Interim Financial Statements

Article 11—Pro forma Financial Information

REGULATION S–T—GENERAL RULES AND REGULATIONS FOR ELECTRONIC FILINGS

(Cite as 17 CFR § 232.___)

GENERAL

ELECTRONIC FILING REQUIREMENTS

HARDSHIP EXEMPTIONS

PREPARATION OF ELECTRONIC SUBMISSIONS

XBRL—RELATED DOCUMENTS

EDGAR FUNCTIONS

Rule

501. Modular submissions and segmented filings

FORMS UNDER THE SECURITIES ACT OF 1933

Form

1–A. Regulation A offering statement under the Securities Act of 1933
2–A. Report of sales and uses of proceeds pursuant to Rule 257 of Regulation A
S–1. Registration statement under the Securities Act of 1933
S–3. Registration statement under the Securities Act of 1933 for certain issuers subject to the reporting requirements of the Exchange Act and whose securities are widely followed in the marketplace
S–4. Registration statement under the Securities Act of 1933 for securities to be issued in connection with a reorganization or recapitalization
144. Notice of proposed sale of securities pursuant to Rule 144 under the Securities Act of 1933
D. Notice of exempt offering of securities

SECURITIES ACT OF 1933

GENERAL RULES AND REGULATIONS

GENERAL

ATTENTION ELECTRONIC FILERS

THIS REGULATION SHOULD BE READ IN CONJUNCTION WITH REGULATION S–T (17 CFR 232), WHICH GOVERNS THE PREPARATION AND SUBMISSION OF DOCUMENTS IN ELECTRONIC FORMAT. MANY PROVISIONS RELATING TO THE PREPARATION AND SUBMISSION OF DOCUMENTS IN PAPER FORMAT CONTAINED IN THIS REGULATION ARE SUPERSEDED BY THE PROVISIONS OF REGULATION S–T FOR DOCUMENTS REQUIRED TO BE FILED IN ELECTRONIC FORMAT

Rule 100. Definitions of terms used in the rules and regulations

(a) As used in the rules and regulations prescribed by the Securities and Exchange Commission pursuant to the Securities Act of 1933, unless the context otherwise requires—

(1) The term *Commission* means the Securities and Exchange Commission.

(2) The term *Act* means the Securities Act of 1933.

(3) The term *rules and regulations* refers to all rules and regulations adopted by the Commission pursuant to the Act, including the forms and accompanying instructions thereto.

(4) The term *registrant* means the issuer of securities for which a registration statement is filed.

(5) The term *agent for service* means the person authorized in the registration statement to receive notices and communications from the Commission.

(6) The term *electronic filer* means a person or an entity that submits filings electronically pursuant to Rules 101, 901, 902 or 903 of Regulation S–T.

(7) The term *electronic filing* means a document under the federal securities laws that is transmitted or delivered to the Commission in electronic format.

(b) Unless otherwise specifically provided, the terms used in the rules and regulations shall have the meanings defined in the Act.

(c) A rule in the general rules and regulations which defines a term without express reference to the Act or to the rules and regulations or to a portion thereof defines such terms for all purposes as used both in the Act and in the rules and regulations, unless the context otherwise requires.

Rule 110. Business hours of the Commission

(a) *General.* The principal office of the Commission, at 100 F Street, NE, Washington, DC 20549, is open each day, except Saturdays, Sundays and federal holidays, from 9 a.m. to 5:30 p.m., Eastern Standard Time or Eastern Daylight Saving Time, whichever is currently in effect *provided that* hours for the filing of documents pursuant to the Act or the rules and regulations thereunder are as set forth in paragraphs (b), (c) and (d) of this rule.

(b) *Submissions Made in Paper.* Paper documents filed with or otherwise furnished to the Commission may be submitted each day, except Saturdays, Sundays and federal holidays from 8 a.m. to 5:30 p.m., Eastern Standard Time or Eastern Daylight Saving Time, whichever is currently in effect.

(c) *Filings by Direct Transmission.* Filings made by direct transmission may be submitted to the Commission each day, except Saturdays, Sundays and federal holidays, from 8 a.m. to 10 p.m., Eastern Standard Time or Eastern Daylight Saving Time, whichever is currently in effect.

(d) *Filings by Facsimile.* Registration statements and post-effective amendments thereto filed by facsimile transmission pursuant to Rule 462(b) and Rule 455 may be filed with the Commission each day, except Saturdays, Sundays and federal holidays, from 5:30 p.m. to 10 p.m., Eastern Standard Time or Eastern Daylight Savings Time, whichever is currently in effect.

Rule 111. Payment of fees

All payments of fees for registration statements under the Act shall be made by wire transfer, or by certified check, bank cashier's check, United States postal money order, or bank money order payable to the Securities and Exchange Commission, omitting the name or title of any official of the Commission. There will be no refunds. Payment of fees required by this rule shall be made in accordance with the directions set forth in 17 CFR 202.3a.

Rule 120. Inspection of registration statements

Except for material contracts or portions thereof accorded confidential treatment pursuant to Rule 406, all registration statements are available for public inspection, during business hours, at the principal office of the Commission in Washington, D.C. Electronic registration statements made through the Electronic Data Gathering, Analysis, and Retrieval system are publicly available through the Commission's Web site (http://www.sec.gov).

Rule 122. Nondisclosure of information obtained in the course of examinations and investigations

Information or documents obtained by officers or employees of the Commission in the course of any examination or investigation pursuant to section 8(e) or 20(a) shall, unless made a matter of public record, be deemed confidential. Except as provided by 17 CFR 203.2, officers and employees are hereby prohibited from making such confidential information or documents or any other non-public records of the Commission available to anyone other than a member, officer, or employee of the Commission, unless the Commission or the General Counsel, pursuant to delegated authority, authorizes the disclosure of such information or the production of such documents as not being contrary to the public interest. Any officer or employee who is served with a subpoena requiring the disclosure of such information or the production of such documents shall appear in court and, unless the authorization described in the preceding sentence shall have been given, shall respectfully decline to disclose the information or produce the documents called for, basing his or her refusal upon this rule. Any officer or employee who is served with such a subpoena shall promptly advise the General Counsel of the service of such subpoena, the nature of the information or documents sought, and any circumstances which may bear upon the desirability of making available such information or documents.

Rule 130. Definition of "rules and regulations" as used in certain sections of the Act

The term *rules and regulations* as used in sections 7, 10(a), (c) and (d) and 19(a) of the Act, shall include the forms for registration of securities under the Act and the related instructions thereto.

Rule 131. Definition of security issued under governmental obligation

(a) Any part of an obligation evidenced by any bond, note, debenture, or other evidence of indebtedness issued by any governmental unit specified in section 3(a)(2) of the Act which is payable from payments to be made in respect of property or money which is or will be used, under a lease, sale, or loan arrangement, by or for industrial or commercial enterprise, shall be deemed to be a separate *security* within the meaning of section 2(1) of the Act, issued by the lessee or obligor under the lease, sale or loan arrangement.

(b) An obligation shall not be deemed a separate *security* as defined in paragraph (a) of this rule if, (1) the obligation is payable from the general revenues of a governmental unit, specified in section 3(a)(2) of the Act, having other resources which may be used for payment of the obligation, or (2) the obligation relates to a public project or facility owned and operated by or on behalf of and under the control of a governmental unit specified in such section, or (3) the obligation relates to a facility which is leased to and under the control of an industrial or commercial enterprise but is a part of a public project which, as a whole, is owned by and under the general control of a governmental unit specified in such section, or an instrumentality thereof.

(c) This rule shall apply to transactions of the character described in paragraph (a) of this rule only with respect to bonds, notes, debentures or other evidences of indebtedness sold after December 31, 1968.

Rule 132. Definition of "common trust fund" as used in Section 3(a)(2) of the Act

The term *common trust fund* as used in section 3(a)(2) of the Act shall include a common trust fund which is maintained by a bank which is a member of an affiliated group, as defined in section 1504(a) of the Internal Revenue Code of 1954, and which is maintained exclusively for the collective investment and reinvestment of monies contributed thereto by one or more bank members of such affiliated group in the capacity of trustee, executor, administrator, or guardian, *Provided That*:

(a) The common trust fund is operated in compliance with the same state and federal regulatory requirements as would apply if the bank maintaining such fund and any other contributing banks were the same entity; and

(b) The rights of persons for whose benefit a contributing bank acts as trustee, executor, administrator, or guardian would not be diminished by reason of the maintenance of such common trust fund by another bank member of the affiliated group.

Rule 134. Communications not deemed a prospectus

Except as provided in paragraphs (e) and (g) of this section, the terms "prospectus" as defined in section 2(a)(10) of the Act or "free writing prospectus" as defined in Rule 405 shall not include a communication limited to the statements required or permitted by this section, provided that the communication is published or transmitted to any person only after a registration statement relating to the offering that includes a prospectus satisfying the requirements of section 10 of the Act (except as otherwise permitted in paragraph (a) of this section) has been filed.

(a) Such communication may include any one or more of the following items of information, which need not follow the numerical sequence of this paragraph, provided that, except as to paragraphs (a)(4), (a)(5), and (a)(6) of this section, the prospectus included in the filed registration statement does not have to include a price range otherwise required by rule:

(1) Factual information about the legal identity and business location of the issuer limited to the following: the name of the issuer of the security, the address, phone number, and e-mail address of the issuer's principal offices and contact for investors, the issuer's country of organization, and the geographic areas in which it conducts business;

(2) The title of the security or securities and the amount or amounts being offered, which title may include a designation as to whether the securities are convertible, exercisable, or exchangeable, and as to the ranking of the securities;

(3) A brief indication of the general type of business of the issuer, limited to the following:

(i) In the case of a manufacturing company, the general type of manufacturing, the principal products or classes of products manufactured, and the segments in which the company conducts business;

(ii) In the case of a public utility company, the general type of services rendered, a brief indication of the area served, and the segments in which the company conducts business;

(iii) In the case of an asset-backed issuer, the identity of key parties, such as sponsor, depositor, issuing entity, servicer or servicers, and trustee, the asset class of the transaction, and the identity of any credit enhancement or other support; and

(iv) In the case of any other type of company, a corresponding statement;

(4) The price of the security, or if the price is not known, the method of its determination or the *bona fide* estimate of the price range as specified by the issuer or the managing underwriter or underwriters;

(5) In the case of a fixed income security, the final maturity and interest rate provisions or, if the final maturity or interest rate provisions are not known, the probable final maturity or interest rate provisions, as specified by the issuer or the managing underwriter or underwriters;

(6) In the case of a fixed income security with a fixed (non-contingent) interest rate provision, the yield or, if the yield is not known, the probable yield range, as specified by the issuer or the managing underwriter or underwriters and the yield of fixed income securities with comparable maturity and security rating;

(7) A brief description of the intended use of proceeds of the offering, if then disclosed in the prospectus that is part of the filed registration statement;

(8) The name, address, phone number, and e-mail address of the sender of the communication and the fact that it is participating, or expects to participate, in the distribution of the security;

(9) The type of underwriting, if then included in the disclosure in the prospectus that is part of the filed registration statement;

(10) The names of underwriters participating in the offering of the securities, and their additional roles, if any, within the underwriting syndicate;

(11) The anticipated schedule for the offering (including the approximate date upon which the proposed sale to the public will begin) and a description of marketing events (including the dates, times, locations, and procedures for attending or otherwise accessing them);

(12) A description of the procedures by which the underwriters will conduct the offering and the procedures for transactions in connection with the offering with the issuer or an underwriter or participating dealer (including procedures regarding account opening and submitting indications of interest and conditional offers to buy), and procedures regarding directed share plans and other participation in offerings by officers, directors, and employees of the issuer;

(13) Whether, in the opinion of counsel, the security is a legal investment for savings banks, fiduciaries, insurance companies, or similar investors under the laws of any State or Territory or the District of Columbia, and the permissibility or status of the investment under the Employee Retirement Income Security Act of 1974;

(14) Whether, in the opinion of counsel, the security is exempt from specified taxes, or the extent to which the issuer has agreed to pay any tax with respect to the security or measured by the income therefrom;

(15) Whether the security is being offered through rights issued to security holders, and, if so, the class of securities the holders of which will be entitled to subscribe, the subscription ratio, the actual or proposed record date, the date upon which the rights were issued or are expected to be issued, the actual or anticipated date upon which they will expire, and the approximate subscription price, or any of the foregoing;

(16) Any statement or legend required by any state law or administrative authority;

(17) [Reserved].

(18) The names of selling security holders, if then disclosed in the prospectus that is part of the filed registration statement;

(19) The names of securities exchanges or other securities markets where any class of the issuer's securities are, or will be, listed;

(20) The ticker symbols, or proposed ticker symbols, of the issuer's securities;

(21) The CUSIP number as defined in Rule 17Ad–19(a)(5) under the Securities Exchange Act of 1934 assigned to the securities being offered; and

(22) Information disclosed in order to correct inaccuracies previously contained in a communication permissibly made pursuant to this rule.

(b) Except as provided in paragraph (c) of this rule, every communication used pursuant to this section shall contain the following:

(1) If the registration statement has not yet become effective, the following statement:

A registration statement relating to these securities has been filed with the Securities and Exchange Commission but has not yet become effective. These securities may not be sold nor may offers to buy be accepted prior to the time the registration statement becomes effective; and

(2) The name and address of a person or persons from whom a written prospectus for the offering meeting the requirements of section 10 of the Act (other than a free writing prospectus as defined in Rule 405) including as to the identified paragraphs above a price range where required by rule, may be obtained.

(c) Any of the statements or information specified in paragraph (b) of this rule may, but need not, be contained in a communication which:

(1) Does no more than state from whom and include the uniform resource locator (URL) where a written prospectus meeting the requirements of section 10 of the Act (other than a free writing prospectus as defined in Rule 405) may be obtained, identify the security, state the price thereof and state by whom orders will be executed; or

(2) Is accompanied or preceded by a prospectus or a summary prospectus, other than a free writing prospectus as defined in Rule 405, which meets the requirements of section 10 of the Act, including a price range where required by rule, at the date of such preliminary communication.

(d) A communication sent or delivered to any person pursuant to this section which is accompanied or preceded by a prospectus which meets the requirements of section 10 of the Act (other than a free writing prospectus as defined in Rule 405), including a price range where required by rule, at the date of such communication, may solicit from the recipient of the communication an offer to buy the security or request the recipient to indicate whether he or she might be interested in the security, if the communication contains substantially the following statement:

No offer to buy the securities can be accepted and no part of the purchase price can be received until the registration statement has become effective, and any such offer may be withdrawn or revoked, without obligation or commitment of any kind, at any time prior to notice of its acceptance given after the effective date.

Provided, that such statement need not be included in such a communication to a dealer.

(e) A section 10 prospectus included in any communication pursuant to this section shall remain a prospectus for all purposes under the Act.

(f) The provision in paragraphs (c)(2) and (d) of this rule that a prospectus that meets the requirements of section 10 of the Act precede or accompany a communication will be satisfied if such communication is an electronic communication containing an active hyperlink to such prospectus.

(g) This rule does not apply to a communication relating to an investment company registered under the Investment Company Act of 1940 (15 U.S.C. 80a–1 *et seq.*) or a business development company as defined in section 2(a)(48) of the Investment Company Act of 1940 (15 U.S.C. 80a–2(a)(48)).

Rule 134a. Options material not deemed a prospectus

Written materials, including advertisements, relating to standardized options, as that term is defined in Rule 9b–1 under the Securities Exchange Act of 1934, shall not be deemed to be a prospectus for the purposes of Section 2(10) of the Securities Act of 1933: *Provided,* That such materials are limited to explanatory information describing the general nature of the standardized options markets or one or more strategies; *And, Provided further,* That:

(a) The potential risks related to options trading generally and to each strategy addressed are explained;

(b) No past or projected performance figures, including annualized rates of return are used;

(c) No recommendation to purchase or sell any option contract is made;

(d) No specific security is identified other than

(1) An option or other security exempt from registration under the Act, or

(2) An index option, including the component securities of the index; and

(e) If there is a definitive options disclosure document, as defined in Rule 9b–1 under the Securities Exchange Act of 1934, the materials shall contain the name and address of a person or persons from whom a copy of such document may be obtained.

Rule 134b. Statements of additional information

For the purpose only of Section 5(b) of the Act (15 U.S.C. 77e(b)), the term "prospectus" as defined in Section 2(a)(10) of the Act (15 U.S.C. 77b(a)(10)) does not include a Statement of Additional Information filed as part of a registration statement on Form N–1A (17 CFR 239.15A and 17 CFR 274.11A), Form N–2 (17 CFR 239.14 and 17 CFR 274.11a–1), Form N–3 (17 CFR 239.17a and 17 CFR 274.11b), Form N–4 (17 CFR 239.17b and 274.11c), or Form N–6 (17 CFR 239.17c and 17 CFR 274.11d) transmitted prior to the effective date of the registration statement if it is accompanied or preceded by a preliminary prospectus meeting the requirements of Rule 430.

Rule 135. Notice of proposed registered offerings

(a) *When Notice is Not an Offer.* For purposes of section 5 of the Act (15 U.S.C. 77e) only, an issuer or a selling security holder (and any person acting on behalf of either of them) that publishes through any medium a notice of a proposed offering to be registered under the Act will not be deemed to offer its securities for sale through that notice if:

(1) *Legend.* The notice includes a statement to the effect that it does not constitute an offer of any securities for sale; and

(2) *Limited Notice Content.* The notice otherwise includes no more than the following information:

(i) The name of the issuer;

(ii) The title, amount and basic terms of the securities offered;

(iii) The amount of the offering, if any, to be made by selling security holders;

(iv) The anticipated timing of the offering;

(v) A brief statement of the manner and the purpose of the offering, without naming the underwriters;

(vi) Whether the issuer is directing its offering to only a particular class of purchasers;

(vii) Any statements or legends required by the laws of any state or foreign country or administrative authority; and

(viii) In the following offerings, the notice may contain additional information, as follows:

(A) *Rights Offering.* In a rights offering to existing security holders:

(*1*) The class of security holders eligible to subscribe;

(*2*) The subscription ratio and expected subscription price;

(*3*) The proposed record date;

(*4*) The anticipated issuance date of the rights; and

(*5*) The subscription period or expiration date of the rights offering.

(B) *Offering to Employees.* In an offering to employees of the issuer or an affiliated company:

(*1*) The name of the employer;

(*2*) The class of employees being offered the securities;

(*3*) The offering price; and

(*4*) The duration of the offering period.

(C) *Exchange Offer.* In an exchange offer:

(*1*) The basic terms of the exchange offer;

(*2*) The name of the subject company;

(*3*) The subject class of securities sought in the exchange offer.

(D) *Rule 145(a) Offering.* In a Rule 145(a) offering:

(*1*) The name of the person whose assets are to be sold in exchange for the securities to be offered;

(*2*) The names of any other parties to the transaction;

(*3*) A brief description of the business of the parties to the transaction;

(*4*) The date, time and place of the meeting of security holders to vote on or consent to the transaction; and

(*5*) A brief description of the transaction and the basic terms of the transaction.

(b) *Corrections of Misstatements About the Offering.* A person that publishes a notice in reliance on this section may issue a notice that contains no more information than is necessary to correct inaccuracies published about the proposed offering.

NOTE TO RULE 135: Communications under this section relating to business combination transactions must be filed as required by Rule 425(b).

Rule 135a. Generic advertising

(a) For the purposes only of section 5 of the Act, a notice, circular, advertisement, letter, sign, or other communication, published or transmitted to any person which does not specifically refer by name to the securities of a particular investment company, to the investment company itself, or to any other securities not exempt under section 3(a) of the Act, will not be deemed to offer any security for sale, provided:

(1) Such communication is limited to any one or more of the following:

(i) Explanatory information relating to securities of investment companies generally or to the nature of investment companies, or to services offered in connection with the ownership of such securities,

(ii) The mention or explanation of investment companies of different generic types or having various investment objectives, such as *balanced funds, growth funds, income funds, leveraged funds, specialty funds, variable annuities, bond funds,* and *no-load funds,*

(iii) Offers, descriptions, and explanations of various products and services not constituting a security subject to registration under the Act: *Provided,* That such offers, descriptions, and explanations do not relate directly to the desirability of owning or purchasing a security issued by a registered investment company,

(iv) Invitation to inquire for further information, and

(2) Such communication contains the name and address of a registered broker or dealer or other person sponsoring the communication.

(b) If such communication contains a solicitation of inquiries and prospectuses for investment company securities are to be sent or delivered in response to such inquiries, the number of such investment companies and, if applicable, the fact that the sponsor of the communication is the principal underwriter or investment adviser in respect to such investment companies shall be stated.

(c) With respect to any communication describing any type of security, service, or product, the broker, dealer, or other person sponsoring such communication must offer for sale a security, service, or product of the type described in such communication.

Rule 135b. Materials not deemed an offer to sell or offer to buy nor a prospectus

Materials meeting the requirements of Rule 9b–1 under the Securities Exchange Act of 1934 shall not be deemed an offer to sell or offer to buy a security for purposes solely of Section 5 (15 U.S.C. 77e) of the Act, nor shall such materials be deemed a prospectus for purposes of Sections 2(a)(10) and 12(a)(2) (15 U.S.C. 77b(a)(10) and 77l(a)(2)) of the Act, even if such materials are referred to in, deemed to be incorporated by reference into, or otherwise in any manner deemed to be a part of a Form S–20 prospectus.

Rule 135c. Notice of certain proposed unregistered offerings

(a) For the purposes only of section 5 of the Act, a notice given by an issuer required to file reports pursuant to section 13 or 15(d) of the Securities Exchange Act of 1934 or a foreign issuer that is exempt from registration under the Securities Exchange Act of 1934 pursuant to Rule 12g3–2(b) under the Securities Exchange Act of 1934 that it proposes to make, is making or has made an offering of securities not registered or required to be registered under the Act shall not be deemed to offer any securities for sale if:

(1) Such notice is not used for the purpose of conditioning the market in the United States for any of the securities offered;

(2) Such notice states that the securities offered will not be or have not been registered under the Act and may not be offered or sold in the United States absent registration or an applicable exemption from registration requirements; and

(3) Such notice contains no more than the following additional information:

(i) The name of the issuer;

(ii) The title, amount and basic terms of the securities offered, the amount of the offering, if any, made by selling security holders, the time of the offering and a brief statement of the manner and purpose of the offering without naming the underwriters;

(iii) In the case of a rights offering to security holders of the issuer, the class of securities the holders of which will be or were entitled to subscribe to the securities offered, the subscription ratio, the record date, the date upon which the rights are proposed to be or were issued, the term or expiration date of the rights and the subscription price, or any of the foregoing;

(iv) In the case of an offering of securities in exchange for other securities of the issuer or of another issuer, the name of the issuer and the title of the securities to be surrendered in exchange for the securities offered, the basis upon which the exchange may be made, or any of the foregoing;

(v) In the case of an offering to employees of the issuer or to employees of any affiliate of the issuer, the name of the employer and class or classes of employees to whom the securities are offered, the offering price or basis of the offering and the period during which the offering is to be or was made or any of the foregoing; and

(vi) Any statement or legend required by State or foreign law or administrative authority.

(b) Any notice contemplated by this section may take the form of a news release or a written communication directed to security holders or employees, as the case may be, or other published statements.

(c) Notwithstanding the provisions of paragraphs (a) and (b) of this rule, in the case of a rights offering of a security listed or subject to unlisted trading privileges on a national securities exchange or quoted on the NASDAQ inter-dealer quotation system information with respect to the interest rate, conversion ratio and subscription price may be disseminated through the facilities of the exchange, the consolidated transaction reporting system, the NASDAQ system or the Dow Jones broad tape, provided such information is already disclosed in a Form 8–K (17 CFR 249.308) on file with the Commission, in a Form 6–K (17 CFR 249.306) furnished to the Commission or, in the case of an issuer relying on Rule 12g3–2(b) under the Securities Exchange Act of 1934, in a submission made pursuant to that Section to the Commission.

(d) The issuer shall file any notice contemplated by this rule with the Commission under cover of Form 8–K (17 CFR 249.308) or furnish such notice under Form 6–K (17 CFR 249.306), as applicable, and, if relying on Rule 12g3–2(b) under the Securities Exchange Act of 1934, shall furnish such notice to the Commission in accordance with the provisions of that exemptive Section.

Rule 135d. Communications involving security-based swaps

(a) For the purposes only of Section 5 of the Act (15 U.S.C. 77e), the publication or distribution of quotes relating to security-based swaps that may be purchased only by persons who are eligible contract participants (as defined in Section 1a(18) of the Commodity Exchange Act (7 U.S.C. 1a(18))) and are traded or processed on or through a trading system or platform that either is registered as a national securities exchange under Section 6(a) of the Securities Exchange Act of 1934 (15 U.S.C. 78f(a)) or as a security-based swap execution facility under Section 3D(a) of the Securities Exchange Act of 1934 (15 U.S.C. 78c–4(a)), or is exempt from registration as a security-based swap execution facility under Section 3D(a) of the Securities Exchange Act of 1934 pursuant to a rule, regulation, or order of the Commission shall not be deemed to constitute an offer, an offer to sell, or a solicitation of an offer to buy or purchase any security-based swap or any guarantee of such security-based swap that is a security; and

(b) For the purposes only of Section 5 of the Act (15 U.S.C. 77e), a broker, dealer, or security-based swap dealer's publication or distribution of a research report (as defined in Rule 139(d)) that discusses security-based swaps that may be purchased only by persons who are eligible contract participants (as defined in Section 1a(18) of the Commodity Exchange Act (7 U.S.C. 1a(18))) shall not be deemed to constitute an offer, an offer to sell, or a solicitation of an offer to buy or purchase any security-based swap or any guarantee of such security-based swap that is a security, provided that the broker, dealer, or security-based swap dealer publishes or distributes research reports on the issuer underlying the security-based swap or its securities in the regular course of its business and the publication or distribution of the research report does not represent the initiation of publication of research reports about such issuer or its securities or the reinitiation of such publication following discontinuation of publication of such research reports. For purposes of this section, the term issuer as used in the definition of "research report" means the issuer of any security or loan referenced in the security-based swap, each issuer of a security in a narrow-based security index referenced in the security-based swap, or each issuer referenced in the security-based swap.

Rule 135e. Offshore press conferences, meetings with issuer representatives conducted offshore, and press–related materials released offshore

(a) For the purposes only of Section 5 of the Act, an issuer that is a foreign private issuer (as defined in Rule 405) or a foreign government issuer, a selling security holder of the securities of such issuers, or their representatives will not be deemed to offer any security for sale by virtue of providing any journalist with access to its press conferences held outside of the United States, to meetings with issuer or selling security holder representatives conducted outside of the United States, or to written press-related materials released outside the United States, at or in which a present or proposed offering of securities is discussed, if:

(1) The present or proposed offering is not being, or to be, conducted solely in the United States;

NOTE TO PARAGRAPH (a)(1): An offering will be considered not to be made solely in the United States under this paragraph (a)(1) only if there is an intent to make a bona fide offering offshore.

(2) Access is provided to both U.S. and foreign journalists; and

(3) Any written press-related materials pertaining to transactions in which any of the securities will be or are being offered in the United States satisfy the requirements of paragraph (b) of this rule.

(b) Any written press-related materials specified in paragraph (a)(3) of this rule must:

(1) State that the written press-related materials are not an offer of securities for sale in the United States, that securities may not be offered or sold in the United States absent registration or an exemption from registration, that any public offering of securities to be made in the United States will be made by means of a prospectus that may be obtained from the issuer or the selling security holder and that will contain detailed information about the company and management, as well as financial statements;

(2) If the issuer or selling security holder intends to register any part of the present or proposed offering in the United States, include a statement regarding this intention; and

(3) Not include any purchase order, or coupon that could be returned indicating interest in the offering, as part of, or attached to, the written press-related materials.

(c) For the purposes of this rule, *United States* means the United States of America, its territories and possessions, any State of the United States, and the District of Columbia.

Rule 136. Definition of certain terms in relation to assessable stock

(a) An *offer*, *offer to sell* or *offer for sale* of securities shall be deemed to be made to the holders of assessable stock of a corporation when such corporation shall give notice of an assessment to the holders of such assessable stock. A *sale* shall be deemed to occur when a stockholder shall pay or agree to pay all or any part of such an assessment.

(b) The term *transactions by any person other than an issuer, underwriter or dealer* in section 4(a)(1) of the Act shall not be deemed to include the offering or sale of assessable stock, at public auction or otherwise, upon the failure of the holder of such stock to pay an assessment levied thereon by the issuer, where the offer or sale is made for the purpose of realizing the amount of the assessment and any of the proceeds of such sale are to be received by the issuer. However, any person whose functions are limited to acting as auctioneer at such an auction sale shall not be deemed to be an underwriter of the securities offered or sold at the auction sale. Any person who acquires assessable stock at any such public auction or other sale with a view to the distribution thereof shall be deemed to be an underwriter of such assessable stock.

(c) The term *assessable stock* means stock which is subject to resale by the issuer pursuant to statute or otherwise in the event of a failure of the holder of such stock to pay any assessment levied thereon.

Rule 137. Publications or distributions of research reports by brokers or dealers that are not participating in an issuer's registered distribution of securities

Under the following conditions, the terms "offers," "participates," or "participation" in section 2(a)(11) of the Act shall not be deemed to apply to the publication or distribution of research reports with respect to the securities of an issuer which is the subject of an offering pursuant to a registration statement that the issuer proposes to file, or has filed, or that is effective:

(a) The broker or dealer (and any affiliate) that has distributed the report and, if different, the person (and any affiliate) that has published the report have not participated, are not participating, and do not propose to participate in the distribution of the securities that are or will be the subject of the registered offering.

(b) In connection with the publication or distribution of the research report, the broker or dealer (and any affiliate) that has distributed the report and, if different, the person (and any affiliate) that has published the report are not receiving and have not received consideration directly or indirectly from, and are not acting under any direct or indirect arrangement or understanding with:

(1) The issuer of the securities;

(2) A selling security holder;

(3) Any participant in the distribution of the securities that are or will be the subject of the registration statement; or

(4) Any other person interested in the securities that are or will be the subject of the registration statement.

Instruction to Rule 137(b): This paragraph (b) does not preclude payment of:

1. The regular price being paid by the broker or dealer for independent research, so long as the conditions of this paragraph (b) are satisfied; or

2. The regular subscription or purchase price for the research report.

(c) The broker or dealer publishes or distributes the research report in the regular course of its business.

(d) The issuer is not and during the past three years neither the issuer nor any of its predecessors was:

(1) A blank check company as defined in Rule 419(a)(2);

(2) A shell company, other than a business combination related shell company, each as defined in Rule 405; or

(3) An issuer for an offering of penny stock as defined in Rule 3a51–1 under the Securities Exchange Act of 1934.

(e) *Definition of Research Report.* For purposes of this section, research report means a written communication, as defined in Rule 405, that includes information, opinions, or recommendations with respect to securities of an issuer or an analysis of a security or an issuer, whether or not it provides information reasonably sufficient upon which to base an investment decision.

Rule 138. Publications or distributions of research reports by brokers or dealers about securities other than those they are distributing

(a) *Registered Offerings.* Under the following conditions, a broker's or dealer's publication or distribution of research reports about securities of an issuer shall be deemed for purposes of sections 2(a)(10) and 5(c) of the Act not to constitute an offer for sale or offer to sell a security which is the subject of an offering pursuant to a registration statement that the issuer proposes to file, or has filed, or that is effective, even if the broker or dealer is participating or will participate in the registered offering of the issuer's securities:

(1)(i) The research report relates solely to the issuer's common stock, or debt securities, or preferred stock convertible into its common stock, and the offering involves solely the issuer's non-convertible debt securities or non-convertible, non-participating preferred stock; or

(ii) The research report relates solely to the issuer's non-convertible debt securities or non-convertible, non-participating preferred stock, and the offering involves solely the issuer's common stock, or debt securities, or preferred stock convertible into its common stock.

Instruction to Paragraph (a)(1): If the issuer has filed a shelf registration statement under Rule 415(a)(1)(x) or pursuant to General Instruction I.D. of Form S–3 or General Instruction I.C. of Form F–3 (17 CFR 239.13 or 17 CFR 239.33) with respect to multiple classes of securities, the conditions of paragraph (a)(1) of this rule must be satisfied for the offering in which the broker or dealer is participating or will participate.

(2) The issuer as of the date of reliance on this rule:

(i) Is required to file reports, and has filed all periodic reports required during the preceding 12 months (or such shorter time that the issuer was required to file such reports) on Forms 10–K (17 CFR 249.310), 10–Q (17 CFR 249.308a) and 20–F (17 CFR 249.220f) pursuant to section 13 or section 15(d) of the Securities Exchange Act of 1934 (15 U.S.C. 78m or 78o(d)); or

(ii) Is a foreign private issuer that:

(A) Meets all of the registrant requirements of Form F–3 other than the reporting history provisions of General Instructions I.A.1. and I.A.2(a) of Form F–3;

(B) Either:

(*1*) Satisfies the public float threshold in General Instruction I.B.1. of Form F–3; or

(*2*) Is issuing non-convertible securities, other than common equity, and the issuer meets the provisions of General Instruction I.B.2. of Form F–3 (referenced in 17 CFR 239.33); and

(C) Either:

(*1*) Has its equity securities trading on a designated offshore securities market as defined in Rule 902(b) and has had them so traded for at least 12 months; or

(*2*) Has a worldwide market value of its outstanding common equity held by non-affiliates of $700 million or more.

(3) The broker or dealer publishes or distributes research reports on the types of securities in question in the regular course of its business; and

(4) The issuer is not, and during the past three years neither the issuer nor any of its predecessors was:

(i) A blank check company as defined in Rule 419(a)(2);

(ii) A shell company, other than a business combination related shell company, each as defined in Rule 405; or

(iii) An issuer for an offering of penny stock as defined in Rule 3a51–1 under the Securities Exchange Act of 1934.

(b) *Rule 144A Offerings.* If the conditions in paragraph (a) of this rule are satisfied, a broker's or dealer's publication or distribution of a research report shall not be considered an offer for sale or an offer to sell a security or general solicitation or general advertising, in connection with an offering relying on Rule 144A.

(c) *Regulation S Offerings.* If the conditions in paragraph (a) of this rule are satisfied, a broker's or dealer's publication or distribution of a research report shall not:

(1) Constitute directed selling efforts as defined in Rule 902(c) for offerings under Regulation S (Rules 901 through 905); or

(2) Be inconsistent with the offshore transaction requirement in Rule 902(h) for offerings under Regulation S.

(d) *Definition of Research Report.* For purposes of this rule, research report means a written communication, as defined in Rule 405, that includes information, opinions, or recommendations with respect to securities of an issuer or an analysis of a security or an issuer, whether or not it provides information reasonably sufficient upon which to base an investment decision.

Rule 139. Publications or distributions of research reports by brokers or dealers distributing securities

(a) *Registered Offerings.* Under the conditions of paragraph (a)(1) or (a)(2) of this rule, a broker's or dealer's publication or distribution of a research report about an issuer or any of its securities shall be deemed for purposes of sections 2(a)(10) and 5(c) of the Act not to constitute an offer for sale or offer to sell a security that is the subject of an offering pursuant to a registration statement that the issuer proposes to file, or has filed, or that is effective, even if the broker or dealer is participating or will participate in the registered offering of the issuer's securities:

(1) *Issuer–Specific Research Reports.* (i) The issuer either:

(A)(*1*) At the later of the time of filing its most recent Form S–3 (17 CFR 239.13) or Form F–3 (17 CFR 239.33) or the time of its most recent amendment to such registration statement for purposes of complying with section 10(a)(3) of the Act or, if no Form S–3 or Form F–3 has been filed, at the date of reliance on this section, meets the registrant requirements of such Form S–3 or Form F–3 and:

(*i*) At such date, meets the minimum float provisions of General Instruction I.B.1 of such Forms; or

(*ii*) At the date of reliance on this section, is, or if a registration statement has not been filed, will be, offering non-convertible securities, other than common equity, and meets the requirements for the General Instruction I.B.2. of Form S–3 or Form F–3; or

(*iii*) At the date of reliance on this section is a well-known seasoned issuer as defined in Rule 405, other than a majority-owned subsidiary that is a well-known seasoned issuer by virtue of paragraph (1)(ii) of the definition of well-known seasoned issuer in Rule 405; and

(*2*) As of the date of reliance on this section, has filed all periodic reports required during the preceding 12 months on Forms 10–K (17 CFR 249.310), 10–Q (17 CFR 249.308a), and 20–F (17 CFR 249.220f) pursuant to section 13 or section 15(d) of the Securities Exchange Act of 1934 (15 U.S.C. 78m or 78o(d)); or

(B) Is a foreign private issuer that as of the date of reliance on this rule:

(*1*) Meets all of the registrant requirements of Form F–3 other than the reporting history provisions of General Instructions I.A.1. and I.A.2(a) of Form F–3;

(*2*) Either:

(*i*) Satisfies the public float threshold in General Instruction I.B.1. of Form F–3; or

(*ii*) Is issuing non-convertible securities, other than common equity, and meets the provisions of General Instruction I.B.2. of Form F–3; and

(*3*) Either:

(*i*) Has its equity securities trading on a designated offshore securities market as defined in Rule 902(b) and has had them so traded for at least 12 months; or

(*ii*) Has a worldwide market value of its outstanding common equity held by non-affiliates of $700 million or more;

(ii) The issuer is not and during the past three years neither the issuer nor any of its predecessors was:

(A) A blank check company as defined in Rule 419(a)(2);

(B) A shell company, other than a business combination related shell company, each as defined in Rule 405; or

(C) An issuer for an offering of penny stock as defined in Rule 3a51–1 under the Securities Exchange Act of 1934; and

(iii) The broker or dealer publishes or distributes research reports in the regular course of its business and such publication or distribution does not represent the initiation of publication of research reports about such issuer or its securities or reinitiation of such publication following discontinuation of publication of such research reports.

(2) *Industry Reports.*

(i) The issuer is required to file reports pursuant to section 13 or section 15(d) of the Securities Exchange Act of 1934 or satisfies the conditions in paragraph (a)(1)(i)(B) of this rule;

(ii) The condition in paragraph (a)(1)(ii) of this rule is satisfied;

(iii) The research report includes similar information with respect to a substantial number of issuers in the issuer's industry or sub-industry, or contains a comprehensive list of securities currently recommended by the broker or dealer;

(iv) The analysis regarding the issuer or its securities is given no materially greater space or prominence in the publication than that given to other securities or issuers; and

(v) The broker or dealer publishes or distributes research reports in the regular course of its business and, at the time of the publication or distribution of the research report, is including similar information about the issuer or its securities in similar reports.

(b) *Rule 144A Offerings.* If the conditions in paragraph (a)(1) or (a)(2) of this rule are satisfied, a broker's or dealer's publication or distribution of a research report shall not be considered an offer for sale or an offer to sell a security or general solicitation or general advertising, in connection with an offering relying on Rule 144A.

(c) *Regulation S Offerings.* If the conditions in paragraph (a)(1) or (a)(2) of this rule are satisfied, a broker's or dealer's publication or distribution of a research report shall not:

(1) Constitute directed selling efforts as defined in Rule 902(c) for offerings under Regulation S (Rules 901 through 905); or

(2) Be inconsistent with the offshore transaction requirement in Rule 902(h) for offerings under Regulation S.

(d) *Definition of Research Report.* For purposes of this rule, research report means a written communication, as defined in Rule 405, that includes information, opinions, or recommendations with respect to securities of an issuer or an analysis of a security or an issuer, whether or not it provides information reasonably sufficient upon which to base an investment decision.

Instruction to Rule 139: *Projections.* A projection constitutes an analysis or information falling within the definition of research report. When a broker or dealer publishes or distributes projections of an issuer's sales or earnings in reliance on paragraph (a)(2) of this rule, it must:

1. Have previously published or distributed projections on a regular basis in order to satisfy the "regular course of its business" condition;

2. At the time of publishing or disseminating a research report, be publishing or distributing projections with respect to that issuer; and

3. For purposes of paragraph (a)(2)(iii) of this rule, include projections covering the same or similar periods with respect to either a substantial number of issuers in the issuer's industry or sub-industry or substantially all issuers represented in the comprehensive list of securities contained in the research report.

Rule 139a. Publications by brokers or dealers distributing asset-backed securities

The publication or distribution by a broker or dealer of information, an opinion or a recommendation with respect to asset-backed securities meeting the criteria of Form SF–3 (17 CFR 239.45) ("SF–3 ABS") shall not be deemed to constitute an offer for sale or offer to sell SF–3 ABS registered or proposed to be registered for purposes of sections 2(a)(10) and 5(c) of the Act (15 U.S.C. 77b(a)(10) and 77e(c)) (the "registered securities"), even if such broker or dealer is or will be a participant in the distribution of the registered securities, if the following conditions are met:

(a) The broker or dealer shall have previously published or distributed with reasonable regularity information, opinions or recommendations relating to SF–3 ABS backed directly (or, with respect to securitizations of other securities, indirectly) by substantially similar collateral as that directly or indirectly backing SF–3 ABS that is the subject of the information, opinion or recommendation that is proposed to be published or distributed.

(b) If the registered securities are proposed to be offered, offered or part of an unsold allotment or subscription, the information, opinion or recommendation shall not:

(1) Identify the registered securities;

(2) Give greater prominence to specific structural or collateral-related attributes of the registered securities than it gives to the same attributes of other asset-backed securities that it mentions; or

(3) Contain any *ABS informational and computational material* (as defined in Item 1101 of Regulation AB) relating to the registered securities.

(c) Sufficient information is available from one or more public sources to provide a reasonable basis for the view expressed by the broker or dealer with respect to the asset-backed securities that are the subject of the information, opinion or recommendation.

(d) If the material published by the broker or dealer identifies asset-backed securities backed directly or indirectly by substantially similar collateral as that directly or indirectly backing the registered securities and specifically recommends that such asset-backed securities by preferred over other asset-backed securities backed by different types of collateral, then the material shall explain in reasonable detail the reasons for such preference.

Rule 140. Definition of "distribution" in Section 2(11) for certain transactions

A person, the chief part of whose business consists of the purchase of the securities of one issuer, or of two or more affiliated issuers, and the sale of its own securities, including the levying of assessments on its assessable stock and the resale of such stock upon the failure of the holder thereof to pay any assessment levied thereon, to furnish the proceeds with which to acquire the securities of such issuer or affiliated issuers, is to be regarded as engaged in the distribution of the securities of such issuer or affiliated issuers within the meaning of section 2(11) of the Act.

Rule 141. Definition of "commission from an underwriter or dealer not in excess of the usual and customary distributors' or sellers' commissions" in Section 2(11), for certain transactions

(a) The term *commission* in section 2(11) shall include such remuneration, commonly known as a spread, as may be received by a distributor or dealer as a consequence of reselling securities bought from an underwriter or dealer at a price below the offering price of such securities, where such resales afford the distributor or dealer a margin of profit not in excess of what is usual and customary in such transactions.

(b) The term *commission from an underwriter or dealer* in section 2(11) shall include commissions paid by an underwriter or dealer directly or indirectly controlling or controlled by, or under direct or indirect common control with the issuer.

(c) The term *usual and customary distributors' or sellers' commission* in section 2(11) of the Act shall mean a commission or remuneration, commonly known as a spread, paid to or received by any person selling securities either for his own account or for the account of others, which is not in excess of the amount usual and customary in the distribution and sale of issues of similar type and size, and not in excess of the amount allowed to other persons, if any, for comparable service in the distribution of the particular issue; but such term shall not include amounts paid to any person whose function is the management of the distribution of all or a substantial part of the particular issue, or who performs the functions normally performed by an underwriter or underwriting syndicate.

Rule 142. Definition of "participates" and "participation," as used in Section 2(11), in relation to certain transactions

(a) The terms *participates* and *participation* in section 2(11) shall not include the interest of a person (1) who is not in privity of contract with the issuer nor directly or indirectly controlling, controlled by, or under common control with, the issuer, and (2) who has no association with any principal underwriter of the securities being distributed, and (3) whose function in the distribution is confined to an undertaking to purchase all or some specified proportion of the securities remaining unsold after the lapse of some specified period of time, and (4) who purchases such securities for investment and not with a view to distribution.

(b) As used in this rule:

(1) The term *issuer* shall have the meaning defined in section 2(4) and in the last sentence of section 2(11).

(2) The term *association* shall include a relationship between two persons under which one:

(i) Is directly or indirectly controlling, controlled by, or under common control with, the other, or

(ii) Has, in common with the other, one or more partners, officers, directors, trustees, branch managers, or other persons occupying a similar status or performing similar functions, or

(iii) Has a participation, direct or indirect, in the profits of the other, or has a financial stake, by debtor-creditor relationship, stock ownership, contract or otherwise, in the income or business of the other.

(3) The term *principal underwriter* shall have the meaning defined in Rule 405.

Rule 143. Definition of "has purchased," "sells for," "participates," and "participation," as used in Section 2(11), in relation to certain transactions of foreign governments for war purposes

The terms *has purchased, sells for, participates,* and *participation,* in section 2(11), shall not be deemed to apply to any action of a foreign government in acquiring, for war purposes and by or in anticipation of the exercise of war powers, from any person subject to its jurisdiction securities of a person organized under the laws of the United States or any State or Territory, or in disposing of such securities with a view to their distribution by underwriters in the United States, notwithstanding the fact that the price to be paid to such foreign government upon the disposition of such securities by it may be measured by or may be in direct or indirect relation to such price as may be realized by the underwriters.

Rule 144. Persons deemed not to be engaged in a distribution and therefore not underwriters

PRELIMINARY NOTE

Certain basic principles are essential to an understanding of the registration requirements in the Securities Act of 1933 (the Act or the Securities Act) and the purposes underlying Rule 144:

1. If any person sells a non-exempt security to any other person, the sale must be registered unless an exemption can be found for the transaction.

2. Section 4(a)(1) of the Securities Act provides one such exemption for a transaction "by a person other than an issuer, underwriter, or dealer." Therefore, an understanding of the term "underwriter" is important in determining whether or not the Section 4(a)(1) exemption from registration is available for the sale of the securities.

The term "underwriter" is broadly defined in Section 2(a)(11) of the Securities Act to mean any person who has purchased from an issuer with a view to, or offers or sells for an issuer in connection with, the distribution of any security, or participates, or has a direct or indirect participation in any such undertaking, or participates or has a participation in the direct or indirect underwriting of any such undertaking. The interpretation of this definition traditionally has focused on the words "with a view to" in the phrase "purchased from an issuer with a view to ... distribution." An investment banking firm which arranges with an issuer for the public sale of its securities is clearly an "underwriter" under that section. However, individual investors who are not professionals in the securities business also may be "underwriters" if they act as links in a chain of transactions through which securities move from an issuer to the public.

Since it is difficult to ascertain the mental state of the purchaser at the time of an acquisition of securities, prior to and since the adoption of Rule 144, subsequent acts and circumstances have been considered to determine whether the purchaser took the securities "with a view to distribution" at the time of the acquisition. Emphasis has been placed on factors such as the length of time the person held the securities and whether there has been an unforeseeable change in circumstances of the holder. Experience has shown, however, that reliance upon such factors alone has led to uncertainty in the application of the registration provisions of the Act.

The Commission adopted Rule 144 to establish specific criteria for determining whether a person is not engaged in a distribution. Rule 144 creates a safe harbor from the Section 2(a)(11) definition of "underwriter." A person satisfying the applicable conditions of the Rule 144 safe harbor is deemed not to be engaged in a distribution of the securities and therefore not an underwriter of the securities for purposes of Section 2(a)(11). Therefore, such a person is deemed not to be an underwriter when determining whether a sale is eligible for the Section 4(a)(1) exemption for "transactions by any person other than an issuer, underwriter, or dealer." If a sale of securities complies with all of the applicable conditions of Rule 144:

1. Any affiliate or other person who sells restricted securities will be deemed not to be engaged in a distribution and therefore not an underwriter for that transaction;

2. Any person who sells restricted or other securities on behalf of an affiliate of the issuer will be deemed not to be engaged in a distribution and therefore not an underwriter for that transaction; and

3. The purchaser in such transaction will receive securities that are not restricted securities.

Rule 144 is not an exclusive safe harbor. A person who does not meet all of the applicable conditions of Rule 144 still may claim any other available exemption under the Act for the sale of the securities. The Rule 144 safe harbor is not available to any person with respect to any transaction or series of transactions that, although in technical compliance with Rule 144, is part of a plan or scheme to evade the registration requirements of the Act.

(a) *Definitions.* The following definitions shall apply for the purposes of this rule.

(1) An *affiliate* of an issuer is a person that directly, or indirectly through one or more intermediaries, controls, or is controlled by, or is under common control with, such issuer.

(2) The term *person* when used with reference to a person for whose account securities are to be sold in reliance upon this rule includes, in addition to such person, all of the following persons:

(i) Any relative or spouse of such person, or any relative of such spouse, any one of whom has the same home as such person;

(ii) Any trust or estate in which such person or any of the persons specified in paragraph (a)(2)(i) of this section collectively own 10 percent or more of the total beneficial interest or of which any of such persons serve as trustee, executor or in any similar capacity; and

(iii) Any corporation or other organization (other than the issuer) in which such person or any of the persons specified in paragraph (a)(2)(i) of this rule are the beneficial owners collectively of 10 percent or more of any class of equity securities or 10 percent or more of the equity interest.

(3) The term *restricted securities* means:

(i) Securities acquired directly or indirectly from the issuer, or from an affiliate of the issuer, in a transaction or chain of transactions not involving any public offering;

(ii) Securities acquired from the issuer that are subject to the resale limitations of Rule 502(d) under Regulation D or Rule 701(c);

(iii) Securities acquired in a transaction or chain of transactions meeting the requirements of Rule 144A;

(iv) Securities acquired from the issuer in a transaction subject to the conditions of Regulation CE;

(v) Equity securities of domestic issuers acquired in a transaction or chain of transactions subject to the conditions of Rules 901 or 903 under Regulation S (Rules 901 through 905, and Preliminary Notes);

(vi) Securities acquired in a transaction made under Rule 801 to the same extent and proportion that the securities held by the security holder of the class with respect to which the rights offering was made were, as of the record date for the rights offering, "restricted securities" within the meaning of this paragraph (a)(3);

(vii) Securities acquired in a transaction made under Rule 802 to the same extent and proportion that the securities that were tendered or exchanged in the exchange offer or business combination were "restricted securities" within the meaning of this paragraph (a)(3); and

(viii) Securities acquired from the issuer in a transaction subject to an exemption under section 4(5) (15 U.S.C. 77d(5)) of the Act.

(4) The term *debt securities* means:

(i) Any security other than an equity security as defined in Rule 405;

(ii) Non-participatory preferred stock, which is defined as non-convertible capital stock, the holders of which are entitled to a preference in payment of dividends and in distribution of assets on liquidation, dissolution, or winding up of the issuer, but are not entitled to participate in residual earnings or assets of the issuer; and

(iii) Asset-backed securities, as defined in Item 1101 of Regulation AB.

(b) *Conditions to Be Met.* Subject to paragraph (i) of this rule, the following conditions must be met:

(1) *Non-Affiliates.* (i) If the issuer of the securities is, and has been for a period of at least 90 days immediately before the sale, subject to the reporting requirements of section 13 or 15(d) of the Securities Exchange Act of 1934 (the Exchange Act), any person who is not an affiliate of the issuer at the time of the sale, and has not been an affiliate during the preceding three months, who sells restricted securities of the issuer for his or her own account shall be deemed not to be an underwriter of those securities within the meaning of section 2(a)(11) of the Act if all of the conditions of paragraphs (c)(1) and (d) of this rule are met. The requirements of paragraph (c)(1) of this rule shall not apply to restricted securities sold for the account of a person who is not an affiliate of the issuer at the time of the sale and has not been an affiliate during the preceding three months, provided a period of one year has elapsed since the later of the date the securities were acquired from the issuer or from an affiliate of the issuer.

(ii) If the issuer of the securities is not, or has not been for a period of at least 90 days immediately before the sale, subject to the reporting requirements of section 13 or 15(d) of the Exchange Act, any person who is not an affiliate of the issuer at the time of the sale, and has not been an affiliate during the preceding three months, who sells restricted securities of the issuer for his or her own account shall be deemed not to be an underwriter of those securities within the meaning of section (2)(a)(11) of the Act if the condition of paragraph (d) of this rule is met.

(2) *Affiliates or Persons Selling on Behalf of Affiliates.* Any affiliate of the issuer, or any person who was an affiliate at any time during the 90 days immediately before the sale, who sells restricted securities, or any person who sells restricted or any other securities for the account of an affiliate of the issuer of such securities, or any person who sells restricted or any other securities for the account of a person who was an affiliate at any time during the 90 days immediately before the sale, shall be deemed not to be an underwriter of those securities within the meaning of section (2)(a)(11) of the Act if all of the conditions of this rule are met.

(c) *Current Public Information.* Adequate current public information with respect to the issuer of the securities must be available. Such information will be deemed to be available only if the applicable condition set forth in this paragraph is met:

(1) *Reporting Issuers.* The issuer is, and has been for a period of at least 90 days immediately before the sale, subject to the reporting requirements of section 13 or 15(d) of the Exchange Act and has:

(i) Filed all required reports under section 13 or 15(d) of the Exchange Act, as applicable, during the 12 months preceding such sale (or for such shorter period that the issuer was required to file such reports), other than Form 8–K reports (17 CFR 249.308); and

(ii) Submitted electronically every Interactive Data File (Rule 11 of Regulation S –T) required to be submitted pursuant to Rule 405 of Regulation S –T, during the 12 months preceding such sale (or for such shorter period that the issuer was required to submit such files); or

(2) *Non–Reporting Issuers.* If the issuer is not subject to the reporting requirements of section 13 or 15(d) of the Exchange Act, there is publicly available the information concerning the issuer specified in paragraphs (a)(5)(i) to (xiv), inclusive, and paragraph (a)(5)(xvi) of Rule 15c2–11 under the Securities Exchange Act of 1934, or, if the issuer is an insurance company, the information specified in section 12(g)(2)(G)(i) of the Exchange Act (15 U.S.C. 78*l*(g)(2)(G)(i)).

NOTE TO PARAGRAPH (c). With respect to paragraph (c)(1), the person can rely upon:

1. A statement in whichever is the most recent report, quarterly or annual, required to be filed and filed by the issuer that such issuer has:

a. Filed all reports required under section 13 or 15(d) of the Exchange Act, as applicable, during the preceding 12 months (or for such shorter period that the issuer was required to file such reports), other than Form 8–K reports (17 CFR 249.308), and has been subject to such filing requirements for the past 90 days; and

b. Submitted electronically every Interactive Data File (Rule 11 of Regulation S –T) required to be submitted pursuant to Rule 405 of Regulation S–T, during the preceding 12 months (or for such shorter period that the issuer was required to submit such files); or

2. A written statement from the issuer that it has complied with such reporting or submission requirements.

3. Neither type of statement may be relied upon, however, if the person knows or has reason to believe that the issuer has not complied with such requirements.

(d) *Holding Period for Restricted Securities.* If the securities sold are restricted securities, the following provisions apply:

(1) *General Rule.*

(i) If the issuer of the securities is, and has been for a period of at least 90 days immediately before the sale, subject to the reporting requirements of section 13 or 15(d) of the Exchange Act, a minimum of six months must elapse between the later of the date of the acquisition of the securities from the issuer, or from an affiliate of the issuer, and any resale of such securities in reliance on this rule for the account of either the acquiror or any subsequent holder of those securities.

(ii) If the issuer of the securities is not, or has not been for a period of at least 90 days immediately before the sale, subject to the reporting requirements of section 13 or 15(d) of the Exchange Act, a minimum of one year must elapse between the later of the date of the acquisition of the securities from the issuer, or from an affiliate of the issuer, and any resale of such securities in reliance on this rule for the account of either the acquiror or any subsequent holder of those securities.

(iii) If the acquiror takes the securities by purchase, the holding period shall not begin until the full purchase price or other consideration is paid or given by the person acquiring the securities from the issuer or from an affiliate of the issuer.

(2) *Promissory Notes, Other Obligations or Installment Contracts.* Giving the issuer or affiliate of the issuer from whom the securities were purchased a promissory note or other obligation to pay the purchase price, or entering into an installment purchase contract with such seller, shall not be deemed full payment of the purchase price unless the promissory note, obligation or contract:

(i) Provides for full recourse against the purchaser of the securities;

(ii) Is secured by collateral, other than the securities purchased, having a fair market value at least equal to the purchase price of the securities purchased; and

(iii) Shall have been discharged by payment in full prior to the sale of the securities.

(3) *Determination of Holding Period.* The following provisions shall apply for the purpose of determining the period securities have been held:

(i) *Stock Dividends, Splits and Recapitalizations.* Securities acquired from the issuer as a dividend or pursuant to a stock split, reverse split or recapitalization shall be deemed to have been acquired at the same time as the securities on which the dividend or, if more than one, the initial dividend was paid, the securities involved in the split or reverse split, or the securities surrendered in connection with the recapitalization.

(ii) *Conversions and Exchanges.* If the securities sold were acquired from the issuer solely in exchange for other securities of the same issuer, the newly acquired securities shall be deemed to have been acquired at the same time as the securities surrendered for conversion or exchange, even if the securities surrendered were not convertible or exchangeable by their terms.

NOTE TO PARAGRAPH (d)(3)(ii): If the surrendered securities originally did not provide for cashless conversion or exchange by their terms and the holder provided consideration, other than solely securities of the same issuer, in connection with the amendment of the surrendered securities to permit cashless conversion or exchange, then the newly acquired securities shall be deemed to have been acquired at the same time as such amendment to the surrendered securities, so long as, in the conversion or exchange, the securities sold were acquired from the issuer solely in exchange for other securities of the same issuer.

(iii) *Contingent Issuance of Securities.* Securities acquired as a contingent payment of the purchase price of an equity interest in a business, or the assets of a business, sold to the issuer or an affiliate of the issuer shall be deemed to have been acquired at the time of such sale if the issuer or affiliate was then committed to issue the securities subject only to conditions other than the payment of further consideration for such securities. An agreement entered into in connection with any such purchase to remain in the employment of, or not to compete with, the issuer or affiliate or the rendering of services pursuant to such agreement shall not be deemed to be the payment of further consideration for such securities.

(iv) *Pledged Securities.* Securities which are bona fide pledged by an affiliate of the issuer when sold by the pledgee, or by a purchaser, after a default in the obligation secured by the pledge, shall be deemed to have been acquired when they were acquired by the pledgor, except that if the securities were pledged without recourse they shall be deemed to have been acquired by the pledgee at the time of the pledge or by the purchaser at the time of purchase.

(v) *Gifts of Securities.* Securities acquired from an affiliate of the issuer by gift shall be deemed to have been acquired by the donee when they were acquired by the donor.

(vi) *Trusts.* Where a trust settlor is an affiliate of the issuer, securities acquired from the settlor by the trust, or acquired from the trust by the beneficiaries thereof, shall be deemed to have been acquired when such securities were acquired by the settlor.

(vii) *Estates.* Where a deceased person was an affiliate of the issuer, securities held by the estate of such person or acquired from such estate by the estate beneficiaries shall be deemed to have been acquired when they were acquired by the deceased person, except that no holding period is required if the estate is not an affiliate of the issuer or if the securities are sold by a beneficiary of the estate who is not such an affiliate.

NOTE: While there is no holding period or amount limitation for estates and beneficiaries which are not affiliates of the issuer, paragraphs (c) and (h) of the rule apply to securities sold by such persons in reliance upon the rule.

(viii) *Rule 145(a) Transactions.* The holding period for securities acquired in a transaction specified in Rule 145(a) shall be deemed to commence on the date the securities were acquired by the purchaser in such transaction except as otherwise provided in paragraphs (d)(3)(ii) and (ix) of this rule.

(ix) *Holding Company Formations.* Securities acquired from the issuer in a transaction effected solely for the purpose of forming a holding company shall be deemed to have been acquired at the same time as the securities of the predecessor issuer exchanged in the holding company formation where:

(A) The newly formed holding company's securities were issued solely in exchange for the securities of the predecessor company as part of a reorganization of the predecessor company into a holding company structure;

(B) Holders received securities of the same class evidencing the same proportional interest in the holding company as they held in the predecessor, and the rights and interests of the holders of such securities are substantially the same as those they possessed as holders of the predecessor company's securities; and

(C) Immediately following the transaction, the holding company has no significant assets other than securities of the predecessor company and its existing subsidiaries and has substantially the same assets and liabilities on a consolidated basis as the predecessor company had before the transaction.

(x) *Cashless Exercise of Options and Warrants.* If the securities sold were acquired from the issuer solely upon cashless exercise of options or warrants issued by the issuer, the newly acquired securities shall be deemed to have been acquired at the same time as the exercised options or warrants, even if the options or warrants exercised originally did not provide for cashless exercise by their terms.

NOTE 1 TO PARAGRAPH (d)(3)(x): If the options or warrants originally did not provide for cashless exercise by their terms and the holder provided consideration, other than solely securities of the same issuer, in connection with the amendment of the options or warrants to permit cashless exercise, then the newly acquired securities shall be deemed to have been acquired at the same time as such amendment to the options or warrants so long as the exercise itself was cashless.

NOTE 2 TO PARAGRAPH (d)(3)(x): If the options or warrants are not purchased for cash or property and do not create any investment risk to the holder, as in the case of employee stock options, the newly acquired securities shall be deemed to have been acquired at the time the options or warrants are exercised, so long as the full purchase price or other consideration for the newly acquired securities has been paid or given by the person acquiring the securities from the issuer or from an affiliate of the issuer at the time of exercise.

(e) *Limitation on Amount of Securities Sold.* Except as hereinafter provided, the amount of securities sold for the account of an affiliate of the issuer in reliance upon this rule shall be determined as follows:

(1) If any securities are sold for the account of an affiliate of the issuer, regardless of whether those securities are restricted, the amount of securities sold, together with all sales of securities of the same class sold for the account of such person within the preceding three months, shall not exceed the greatest of:

(i) One percent of the shares or other units of the class outstanding as shown by the most recent report or statement published by the issuer, or

(ii) The average weekly reported volume of trading in such securities on all national securities exchanges and/or reported through the automated quotation system of a registered securities association during the four calendar weeks preceding the filing of notice required by paragraph (h), or if no such notice is required the date of receipt of the order to execute the transaction by the broker or the date of execution of the transaction directly with a market maker, or

(iii) The average weekly volume of trading in such securities reported pursuant to an *effective transaction reporting plan* or an *effective national market system plan* as those terms are defined in Item 600 during the four-week period specified in paragraph (e)(1)(ii) of this rule.

(2) If the securities sold are debt securities, then the amount of debt securities sold for the account of an affiliate of the issuer, regardless of whether those securities are restricted, shall not exceed the greater of the limitation set forth in paragraph (e)(1) of this rule or, together with all sales of securities of the same tranche (or class when the securities are nonparticipatory preferred stock) sold for the account of such person within the preceding three months, ten percent of the principal amount of the tranche (or class when the securities are nonparticipatory preferred stock) attributable to the securities sold.

(3) *Determination of Amount.* For the purpose of determining the amount of securities specified in paragraph (e)(1) of this rule and, as applicable, paragraph (e)(2) of this rule, the following provisions shall apply:

(i) Where both convertible securities and securities of the class into which they are convertible are sold, the amount of convertible securities sold shall be deemed to be the amount of securities of the class into which they are convertible for the purpose of determining the aggregate amount of securities of both classes sold;

(ii) The amount of securities sold for the account of a pledgee of those securities, or for the account of a purchaser of the pledged securities, during any period of three months within six months (or within one year if the issuer of the securities is not, or has not been for a period of at least 90 days immediately before the sale, subject to the reporting requirements of section 13 or 15(d) of the Exchange Act) after a default in the obligation secured by the pledge, and the amount of securities sold during the same three-month period for the account of the pledgor shall not exceed, in the aggregate, the amount specified in paragraph (e)(1) or (2) of this rule, whichever is applicable;

NOTE TO PARAGRAPH (e)(3)(ii): Sales by a pledgee of securities pledged by a borrower will not be aggregated under paragraph (e)(3)(ii) with sales of the securities of the same issuer by other pledgees of such borrower in the absence of concerted action by such pledgees.

(iii) The amount of securities sold for the account of a donee of those securities during any three-month period within six months (or within one year if the issuer of the securities is not, or has not been for a period of at least 90 days immediately before the sale, subject to the reporting requirements of section 13 or 15(d) of the Exchange Act) after the donation, and the amount of securities sold during the same three-month period for the account of the donor, shall not exceed, in the aggregate, the amount specified in paragraph (e)(1) or (2) of this rule, whichever is applicable;

(iv) Where securities were acquired by a trust from the settlor of the trust, the amount of such securities sold for the account of the trust during any three-month period within six months (or within one year if the issuer of the securities is not, or has not been for a period of at least

90 days immediately before the sale, subject to the reporting requirements of section 13 or 15(d) of the Exchange Act) after the acquisition of the securities by the trust, and the amount of securities sold during the same three-month period for the account of the settlor, shall not exceed, in the aggregate, the amount specified in paragraph (e)(1) or (2) of this rule, whichever is applicable;

(v) The amount of securities sold for the account of the estate of a deceased person, or for the account of a beneficiary of such estate, during any three-month period and the amount of securities sold during the same three-month period for the account of the deceased person prior to his death shall not exceed, in the aggregate, the amount specified in paragraph (e)(1) or (2) of this rule, whichever is applicable: *Provided,* that no limitation on amount shall apply if the estate or beneficiary of the estate is not an affiliate of the issuer;

(vi) When two or more affiliates or other persons agree to act in concert for the purpose of selling securities of an issuer, all securities of the same class sold for the account of all such persons during any three-month period shall be aggregated for the purpose of determining the limitation on the amount of securities sold;

(vii) The following sales of securities need not be included in determining the amount of securities to be sold in reliance upon this rule:

(A) Securities sold pursuant to an effective registration statement under the Act;

(B) Securities sold pursuant to an exemption provided by Regulation A (Rules 251 through 263) under the Act;

(C) Securities sold in a transaction exempt pursuant to section 4 of the Act (15 U.S.C. 77d) and not involving any public offering; and

(D) Securities sold offshore pursuant to Regulation S (Rules 901 through 905, and Preliminary Notes) under the Act.

(f) *Manner of Sale.*

(1) The securities shall be sold in one of the following manners:

(i) *brokers' transactions* within the meaning of section 4(a)(4) of the Act;

(ii) transactions directly with a *market maker*, as that term is defined in section 3(a)(38) of the Exchange Act; or

(iii) *riskless principal transactions* where:

(A) the offsetting trades must be executed at the same price (exclusive of an explicitly disclosed markup or markdown, commission equivalent, or other fee);

(B) the transaction is permitted to be reported as riskless under the rules of a self-regulatory organization; and

(C) the requirements of paragraphs (g)(2) (applicable to any markup or markdown, commission equivalent, or other fee), (g)(3), and (g)(4) of this rule are met.

Note to Paragraph (f)(1): For purposes of this paragraph, a *riskless principal transaction* means a principal transaction where, after having received from a customer an order to buy, a broker or dealer purchases the security as principal in the market to satisfy the order to buy or, after having received from a customer an order to sell, sells the security as principal to the market to satisfy the order to sell.

(2) The person selling the securities shall not:

(i) Solicit or arrange for the solicitation of orders to buy the securities in anticipation of or in connection with such transaction, or

(ii) Make any payment in connection with the offer or sale of the securities to any person other than the broker or dealer who executes the order to sell the securities.

(3) Paragraph (f) of this rule shall not apply to:

(i) Securities sold for the account of the estate of a deceased person or for the account of a beneficiary of such estate provided the estate or estate beneficiary is not an affiliate of the issuer; or

(ii) Debt securities.

(g) *Brokers' Transactions.* The term *brokers' transactions* in Section 4(a)(4) of the Act shall for the purposes of this rule be deemed to include transactions by a broker in which such broker:

(1) Does no more than execute the order or orders to sell the securities as agent for the person for whose account the securities are sold;

(2) Receives no more than the usual and customary broker's commission;

(3) Neither solicits nor arranges for the solicitation of customers' orders to buy the securities in anticipation of or in connection with the transaction; *Provided,* that the foregoing shall not preclude:

(i) inquiries by the broker of other brokers or dealers who have indicated an interest in the securities within the preceding 60 days;

(ii) inquiries by the broker of his customers who have indicated an unsolicited bona fide interest in the securities within the preceding 10 business days;

(iii) the publication by the broker of bid and ask quotations for the security in an inter-dealer quotation system provided that such quotations are incident to the maintenance of a bona fide inter-dealer market for the security for the broker's own account and that the broker has published bona fide bid and ask quotations for the security in an inter-dealer quotation system on each of at least twelve days within the preceding thirty calendar days with no more than four business days in succession without such two-way quotations; or

(iv) the publication by the broker of bid and ask quotations for the security in an alternative trading system, as defined in Rule 300 of Regulation ATS, provided that the broker has published bona fide bid and ask quotations for the security in the alternative trading system on each of the last twelve business days; and

NOTE TO PARAGRAPH (g)(3)(ii): The broker should obtain and retain in his files written evidence of indications of bona fide unsolicited interest by his customers in the securities at the time such indications are received.

(4) After reasonable inquiry is not aware of circumstances indicating that the person for whose account the securities are sold is an underwriter with respect to the securities or that the transaction is a part of a distribution of securities of the issuer. Without limiting the foregoing, the broker shall be deemed to be aware of any facts or statements contained in the notice required by paragraph (h) of this section.

NOTES: (i) The broker, for his own protection, should obtain and retain in his files a copy of the notice required by paragraph (h) of this section.

(ii) The reasonable inquiry required by paragraph (g)(3) of this rule should include, but not necessarily be limited to, inquiry as to the following matters:

(a) The length of time the securities have been held by the person for whose account they are to be sold. If practicable, the inquiry should include physical inspection of the securities;

(b) The nature of the transaction in which the securities were acquired by such person;

(c) The amount of securities of the same class sold during the past three months by all persons whose sales are required to be taken into consideration pursuant to paragraph (e) of this section;

(d) Whether such person intends to sell additional securities of the same class through any other means;

(e) Whether such person has solicited or made any arrangement for the solicitation of buy orders in connection with the proposed sale of securities;

(f) Whether such person has made any payment to any other person in connection with the proposed sale of the securities; and

(g) The number of shares or other units of the class outstanding, or the relevant trading volume.

(h) *Notice of Proposed Sale.* (1) If the amount of securities to be sold in reliance upon this rule during any period of three months exceeds 5,000 shares or other units or has an aggregate sale price in excess of $50,000, three copies of a notice on Form 144 (17 CFR 239.144) shall be filed with the Commission. If such securities are admitted to trading on any national securities exchange, one copy of such notice also shall be transmitted to the principal exchange on which such securities are admitted.

(2) The Form 144 shall be signed by the person for whose account the securities are to be sold and shall be transmitted for filing concurrently with either the placing with a broker of an order to execute a sale of securities in reliance upon this rule or the execution directly with a market maker of such a sale. Neither the filing of such notice nor the failure of the Commission to comment on such notice shall be deemed to preclude the Commission from taking any action that it deems necessary or appropriate with respect to the sale of the securities referred to in such notice. The person filing the notice required by this paragraph shall have a bona fide intention to sell the securities referred to in the notice within a reasonable time after the filing of such notice.

(i) *Unavailability to Securities of Issuers with No or Nominal Operations and No or Nominal Non–Cash Assets.*

(1) This rule is not available for the resale of securities initially issued by an issuer defined below:

(i) An issuer, other than a business combination related shell company, as defined in Rule 405, or an asset-backed issuer, as defined in Item 1101(b) of Regulation AB, that has:

(A) No or nominal operations; and

(B) Either:

(*1*) No or nominal assets;

(*2*) Assets consisting solely of cash and cash equivalents; or

(3) Assets consisting of any amount of cash and cash equivalents and nominal other assets; or

(ii) An issuer that has been at any time previously an issuer described in paragraph (i)(1)(i).

(2) Notwithstanding paragraph (i)(1), if the issuer of the securities previously had been an issuer described in paragraph (i)(1)(i) but has ceased to be an issuer described in paragraph(i)(1)(i); is subject to the reporting requirements of section 13 or 15(d) of the Exchange Act; has filed all reports and other materials required to be filed by section 13 or 15(d) of the Exchange Act, as applicable, during the preceding 12 months (or for such shorter period that the issuer was required to file such reports and materials), other than Form 8–K reports (17 CFR 249.308); and has filed current "Form 10 information" with the Commission reflecting its status as an entity that is no longer an issuer described in paragraph (i)(1)(i), then those securities may be sold subject to the requirements of this rule after one year has elapsed from the date that the issuer filed "Form 10 information" with the Commission.

(3) The term "Form 10 information" means the information that is required by Form 10 or Form 20–F (17 CFR 249.210 or 249.220f), as applicable to the issuer of the securities, to register under the Exchange Act each class of securities being sold under this rule. The issuer may provide the Form 10 information in any filing of the issuer with the Commission. The Form 10 information is deemed filed when the initial filing is made with the Commission.

Rule 144A. Private resales of securities to institutions

PRELIMINARY NOTES

1. This rule relates solely to the application of section 5 of the Act and not to antifraud or other provisions of the federal securities laws.

2. Attempted compliance with this rule does not act as an exclusive election; any seller hereunder may also claim the availability of any other applicable exemption from the registration requirements of the Act.

3. In view of the objective of this rule and the policies underlying the Act, this rule is not available with respect to any transaction or series of transactions that, although in technical compliance with this rule, is part of a plan or scheme to evade the registration provisions of the Act. In such cases, registration under the Act is required.

4. Nothing in this rule obviates the need for any issuer or any other person to comply with the securities registration or broker-dealer registration requirements of the Securities Exchange Act of 1934 (the "Exchange Act"), whenever such requirements are applicable.

5. Nothing in this rule obviates the need for any person to comply with any applicable state law relating to the offer or sale of securities.

6. Securities acquired in a transaction made pursuant to the provisions of this rule are deemed to be *restricted securities* within the meaning of Rule 144(a)(3).

7. The fact that purchasers of securities from the issuer thereof may purchase such securities with a view to reselling such securities pursuant to this rule will not affect the availability to such issuer of an exemption under section 4(a)(2) of the Act, or Regulation D under the Act, from the registration requirements of the Act.

(a) *Definitions.* (1) For purposes of this rule, *qualified institutional buyer* shall mean:

(i) Any of the following entities, acting for its own account or the accounts of other qualified institutional buyers, that in the aggregate owns and invests on a discretionary basis at least $100 million in securities of issuers that are not affiliated with the entity:

(A) Any *insurance company* as defined in section 2(a)(13) of the Act;

NOTE: A purchase by an insurance company for one or more of its separate accounts, as defined by section 2(a)(37) of the Investment Company Act of 1940 (the "Investment Company Act"), which are neither registered under section 8 of the Investment Company Act nor required to be so registered, shall be deemed to be a purchase for the account of such insurance company.

(B) Any *investment company* registered under the Investment Company Act or any *business development company* as defined in section 2(a)(48) of that Act;

(C) Any *Small Business Investment Company* licensed by the U.S. Small Business Administration under section 301(c) or (d) of the Small Business Investment Act of 1958;

(D) Any *plan* established and maintained by a state, its political subdivisions, or any agency or instrumentality of a state or its political subdivisions, for the benefit of its employees;

(E) Any *employee benefit plan* within the meaning of title I of the Employee Retirement Income Security Act of 1974;

(F) Any trust fund whose trustee is a bank or trust company and whose participants are exclusively plans of the types identified in paragraph (a)(1)(i)(D) or (E) of this rule, except trust funds that include as participants individual retirement accounts or H.R. 10 plans.

(G) Any *business development company* as defined in section 202(a)(22) of the Investment Advisers Act of 1940;

(H) Any organization described in section 501(c)(3) of the Internal Revenue Code, corporation (other than a bank as defined in section 3(a)(2) of the Act or a savings and loan association or other institution referenced in section 3(a)(5)(A) of the Act or a foreign bank or savings and loan association or equivalent institution), partnership, or Massachusetts or similar business trust; and

(I) Any *investment adviser* registered under the Investment Advisers Act.

(ii) Any *dealer* registered pursuant to section 15 of the Exchange Act, acting for its own account or the accounts of other qualified institutional buyers, that in the aggregate owns and invests on a discretionary basis at least $10 million of securities of issuers that are not affiliated with the dealer, *Provided,* That securities constituting the whole or a part of an unsold allotment to or subscription by a dealer as a participant in a public offering shall not be deemed to be owned by such dealer;

(iii) Any *dealer* registered pursuant to section 15 of the Exchange Act acting in a riskless principal transaction on behalf of a qualified institutional buyer;

NOTE: A registered dealer may act as agent, on a non-discretionary basis, in a transaction with a qualified institutional buyer without itself having to be a qualified institutional buyer.

(iv) Any investment company registered under the Investment Company Act, acting for its own account or for the accounts of other qualified institutional buyers, that is part of a family of investment companies which own in the aggregate at least $100 million in securities of issuers, other than issuers that are affiliated with the investment company or are part of such family of investment companies. *Family of investment companies* means any two or more investment companies registered under the Investment Company Act, except for a unit investment trust whose assets consist solely of shares of one or more registered investment companies, that have the same investment adviser (or, in the case of unit investment trusts, the same depositor), *Provided* That, for purposes of this rule:

(A) Each series of a series company (as defined in Rule 18f–2 under the Investment Company Act) shall be deemed to be a separate investment company; and

(B) Investment companies shall be deemed to have the same adviser (or depositor) if their advisers (or depositors) are majority-owned subsidiaries of the same parent, or if one investment company's adviser (or depositor) is a majority-owned subsidiary of the other investment company's adviser (or depositor);

(v) Any entity, all of the equity owners of which are qualified institutional buyers, acting for its own account or the accounts of other qualified institutional buyers; and

(vi) Any *bank* as defined in section 3(a)(2) of the Act, any savings and loan association or other institution as referenced in section 3(a)(5)(A) of the Act, or any foreign bank or savings and loan association or equivalent institution, acting for its own account or the accounts of other qualified institutional buyers, that in the aggregate owns and invests on a discretionary basis at least $100 million in securities of issuers that are not affiliated with it and that has an audited net worth of at least $25 million as demonstrated in its latest annual financial statements, as of a date not more than 16 months preceding the date of sale under the Rule in the case of a U.S. bank or savings and loan association, and not more than 18 months preceding such date of sale for a foreign bank or savings and loan association or equivalent institution.

(2) In determining the aggregate amount of securities owned and invested on a discretionary basis by an entity, the following instruments and interests shall be excluded: bank deposit notes and certificates of deposit; loan participations; repurchase agreements; securities owned but subject to a repurchase agreement and currency, interest rate and commodity swaps.

(3) The aggregate value of securities owned and invested on a discretionary basis by an entity shall be the cost of such securities, except where the entity reports its securities holdings in its financial statements on the basis of their market value, and no current information with respect to the cost of those securities has been published. In the latter event, the securities may be valued at market for purposes of this rule.

(4) In determining the aggregate amount of securities owned by an entity and invested on a dis-

cretionary basis, securities owned by subsidiaries of the entity that are consolidated with the entity in its financial statements prepared in accordance with generally accepted accounting principles may be included if the investments of such subsidiaries are managed under the direction of the entity, except that, unless the entity is a reporting company under section 13 or 15(d) of the Exchange Act, securities owned by such subsidiaries may not be included if the entity itself is a majority-owned subsidiary that would be included in the consolidated financial statements of another enterprise.

(5) For purposes of this rule, *riskless principal transaction* means a transaction in which a dealer buys a security from any person and makes a simultaneous offsetting sale of such security to a qualified institutional buyer, including another dealer acting as riskless principal for a qualified institutional buyer.

(6) For purposes of this rule, *effective conversion premium* means the amount, expressed as a percentage of the security's conversion value, by which the price at issuance of a convertible security exceeds its conversion value.

(7) For purposes of this rule, *effective exercise premium* means the amount, expressed as a percentage of the warrant's exercise value, by which the sum of the price at issuance and the exercise price of a warrant exceeds its exercise value.

(b) *Sales by Persons Other Than Issuers or Dealers.* Any person, other than the issuer or a dealer, who offers or sells securities in compliance with the conditions set forth in paragraph (d) of this rule shall be deemed not to be engaged in a distribution of such securities and therefore not to be an underwriter of such securities within the meaning of sections 2(a)(11) and 4(a)(1) of the Act.

(c) *Sales by Dealers.* Any dealer who offers or sells securities in compliance with the conditions set forth in paragraph (d) of this rule shall be deemed not to be a participant in a distribution of such securities within the meaning of section 4(a)(3)(C) of the Act and not to be an underwriter of such securities within the meaning of section 2(a)(11) of the Act, and such securities shall be deemed not to have been offered to the public within the meaning of section 4(a)(3)(A) of the Act.

(d) *Conditions to Be Met.* To qualify for exemption under this rule, an offer or sale must meet the following conditions:

(1) The securities offered are sold only to a qualified institutional buyer or to a purchaser that the seller and any person acting on behalf of the seller reasonably believe is a qualified institutional buyer. In determining whether a prospective purchaser is a qualified institutional buyer, the seller and any person acting on its behalf shall be entitled to rely upon the following non-exclusive methods of establishing the prospective purchaser's ownership and discretionary investments of securities:

(i) The prospective purchaser's most recent publicly available financial statements, *Provided* That such statements present the information as of a date within 16 months preceding the date of sale of securities under this rule in the case of a U.S. purchaser and within 18 months preceding such date of sale for a foreign purchaser;

(ii) The most recent publicly available information appearing in documents filed by the prospective purchaser with the Commission or another United States federal, state, or local governmental agency or self-regulatory organization, or with a foreign governmental agency or self-regulatory organization, *Provided* That any such information is as of a date within 16 months preceding the date of sale of securities under this rule in the case of a U.S. purchaser and within 18 months preceding such date of sale for a foreign purchaser;

(iii) The most recent publicly available information appearing in a recognized securities manual, *Provided* That such information is as of a date within 16 months preceding the date of sale of securities under this rule in the case of a U.S. purchaser and within 18 months preceding such date of sale for a foreign purchaser; or

(iv) A certification by the chief financial officer, a person fulfilling an equivalent function, or other executive officer of the purchaser, specifying the amount of securities owned and invested on a discretionary basis by the purchaser as of a specific date on or since the close of the purchaser's most recent fiscal year, or, in the case of a purchaser that is a member of a family of investment companies, a certification by an executive officer of the investment adviser specifying the amount of securities owned by the family of investment companies as of a specific date on or since the close of the purchaser's most recent fiscal year;

(2) The seller and any person acting on its behalf takes reasonable steps to ensure that the purchaser is aware that the seller may rely on the exemption from the provisions of section 5 of the Act provided by this rule;

(3) The securities offered or sold:

(i) Were not, when issued, of the same class as securities listed on a national securities exchange registered under section 6 of the Exchange Act or quoted in a U.S. automated inter-dealer quotation system; *Provided,* That securities that are convertible or exchangeable into securities so listed or quoted at the time of issuance and that had an effective conversion premium of less than 10 percent, shall be treated as securities of the class into which they are convertible or exchangeable; and that warrants that may be exercised for securities so listed or quoted at the time of issuance, for a period of less than 3 years from the date of issuance, or that had an effective exercise premium of less than 10 percent, shall be treated as securities of the class to be issued upon exercise; and *Provided further,* That the Commission may from time to time, taking into account then-existing market practices, designate additional securities and classes of securities that will not be deemed of the same class as securities listed on a national securities exchange or quoted in a U.S. automated inter-dealer quotation system; and

(ii) Are not securities of an open-end investment company, unit investment trust or face-amount certificate company that is or is required to be registered under section 8 of the Investment Company Act; and

(4)(i) In the case of securities of an issuer that is neither subject to section 13 or 15(d) of the Exchange Act, nor exempt from reporting pursuant to Rule 12g3–2(b) under the Securities Exchange Act of 1934, nor a foreign government as defined in Rule 405 eligible to register securities under Schedule B of the Act, the holder and a prospective purchaser designated by the holder have the right to obtain from the issuer, upon request of the holder, and the prospective purchaser has received from the issuer, the seller, or a person acting on either of their behalf, at or prior to the time of sale, upon such prospective purchaser's request to the holder or the issuer, the following information (which shall be reasonably current in relation to the date of resale under this section); a very brief statement of the nature of the business of the issuer and the products and services it offers; and the issuer's most recent balance sheet and profit and loss and retained earnings statements, and similar financial statements for such part of the two preceding fiscal years as the issuer has been in operation (the financial statements should be audited to the extent reasonably available).

(ii) The requirement that the information be *reasonably current* will be presumed to be satisfied if:

(A) The balance sheet is as of a date less than 16 months before the date of resale, the statements of profit and loss and retained earnings are for the 12 months preceding the date of such balance sheet, and if such balance sheet is not as of a date less than 6 months before the date of resale, it shall be accompanied by additional statements of profit and loss and retained earnings for the period from the date of such balance sheet to a date less than 6 months before the date of resale; and

(B) The statement of the nature of the issuer's business and its products and services offered is as of a date within 12 months prior to the date of resale; or

(C) With regard to foreign private issuers, the required information meets the timing requirements of the issuer's home country or principal trading markets.

(e) Offers and sales of securities pursuant to this rule shall be deemed not to affect the availability of any exemption or safe harbor relating to any previous or subsequent offer or sale of such securities by the issuer or any prior or subsequent holder thereof.

Rule 145. Reclassification of securities, mergers, consolidations and acquisitions of assets

PRELIMINARY NOTE

Rule 145 is designed to make available the protection provided by registration under the Securities Act of 1933, as amended (Act), to persons who are offered securities in a business combination of the type described in paragraphs (a)(1), (2) and (3) of the rule. The thrust of the rule is that an *offer, offer to sell, offer for sale,* or *sale* occurs when there is submitted to security holders a plan or agreement pursuant to which such holders are required to elect, on the basis of what is in substance a new investment decision, whether to accept a new or different security in exchange for their existing security. Rule 145 embodies the Commission's determination that such transactions are subject to the registration requirements of the Act, and that the previously existing *no-sale* theory of Rule 133 is no longer consistent with the statutory purposes of the Act. See Release No. 33–5316 (October 6, 1972) [37 FR 23631]. Securities issued in transactions described in paragraph (a) of Rule 145 may be registered on Form S–4 or F–4 (17 CFR 239.25 or 239.34) or Form N–14 (17 CFR 239.23) under the Act.

Transactions for which statutory exemptions under the Act, including those contained in sections 3(a)(9), (10), (11) and 4(a)(2), are otherwise available are not affected by Rule 145.

NOTE 1 TO RULE 145: Reference is made to Rule 153a describing the prospectus delivery required in a transaction of the type referred to in Rule 145.

NOTE 2 TO RULE 145: A reclassification of securities covered by Rule 145 would be exempt from registration pursuant to section 3(a)(9) or (11) of the Act if the conditions of either of these sections are satisfied.

(a) *Transactions Within This Section.* An *offer*, *offer to sell*, *offer for sale*, or *sale* shall be deemed to be involved, within the meaning of section 2(3) of the Act, so far as the security holders of a corporation or other person are concerned where, pursuant to statutory provisions of the jurisdiction under which such corporation or other person is organized, or pursuant to provisions contained in its certificate of incorporation or similar controlling instruments, or otherwise, there is submitted for the vote or consent of such security holders a plan or agreement for:

(1) *Reclassifications.* A reclassification of securities of such corporation or other person, other than a stock split, reverse stock split, or change in par value, which involves the substitution of a security for another security;

(2) *Mergers or Consolidations.* A statutory merger or consolidation or similar plan or acquisition in which securities of such corporation or other person held by such security holders will become or be exchanged for securities of any person, unless the sole purpose of the transaction is to change an issuer's domicile solely within the United States; or

(3) *Transfers of Assets.* A transfer of assets of such corporation or other person, to another person in consideration of the issuance of securities of such other person or any of its affiliates, if:

(i) Such plan or agreement provides for dissolution of the corporation or other person whose security holders are voting or consenting; or

(ii) Such plan or agreement provides for a pro rata or similar distribution of such securities to the security holders voting or consenting; or

(iii) The board of directors or similar representatives of such corporation or other person, adopts resolutions relative to paragraph (a)(3) (i) or (ii) of this section within 1 year after the taking of such vote or consent; or

(iv) The transfer of assets is a part of a preexisting plan for distribution of such securities, notwithstanding paragraph (a)(3)(i), (ii), or (iii) of this section.

(b) *Communications Before a Registration Statement Is Filed.* Communications made in connection with or relating to a transaction described in paragraph (a) of this rule that will be registered under the Act may be made under Rule 135, Rule 165 or Rule 166.

(c) *Persons and Parties Deemed to Be Underwriters.* For purposes of this rule, if any party to a transaction specified in paragraph (a) of this rule is a shell company, other than a business combination related shell company, as those terms are defined in Rule 405, any party to that transaction, other than the issuer, or any person who is an affiliate of such party at the time such transaction is submitted for vote or consent, who publicly offers or sells securities of the issuer acquired in connection with any such transaction, shall be deemed to be engaged in a distribution and therefore to be an underwriter thereof within the meaning of Section 2(a)(11) of the Act.

(d) *Resale Provisions for Persons and Parties Deemed Underwriters.* Notwithstanding the provisions of paragraph (c), a person or party specified in that paragraph shall not be deemed to be engaged in a distribution and therefore not to be an underwriter of securities acquired in a transaction specified in paragraph (a) that was registered under the Act if:

(1) The issuer has met the requirements applicable to an issuer of securities in paragraph (i)(2) of Rule 144; and

(2) One of the following three conditions is met:

(i) Such securities are sold by such person or party in accordance with the provisions of paragraphs (c), (e), (f), and (g) of Rule 144 and at least 90 days have elapsed since the date the securities were acquired from the issuer in such transaction; or

(ii) Such person or party is not, and has not been for at least three months, an affiliate of the issuer, and at least six months, as determined in accordance with paragraph (d) of Rule 144, have elapsed since the date the securities were acquired from the issuer in such transaction, and the issuer meets the requirements of paragraph (c) of Rule 144; or

(iii) Such person or party is not, and has not been for at least three months, an affiliate of the issuer, and at least one year, as determined in accordance with paragraph (d) of Rule 144, has elapsed since the date the securities were acquired from the issuer in such transaction.

NOTE TO PARAGRAPHS (c) AND (d): Paragraph (d) is not available with respect to any transaction or series of transactions that, although in technical compliance with the rule, is part of a plan or scheme to evade the registration requirements of the Act.

(e) *Definitions.*

(1) The term *affiliate* as used in paragraphs (c) and (d) of this rule shall have the same meaning as the definition of that term in Rule 144.

(2) The term *party* as used in paragraphs (c) and (d) of this rule shall mean the corporations, business entities, or other persons, other than the issuer, whose assets or capital structure are affected by the transactions specified in paragraph (a) of this rule.

(3) The term *person* as used in paragraphs (c) and (d) of this rule, when used in reference to a person for whose account securities are to be sold, shall have the same meaning as the definition of that term in paragraph (a)(2) of Rule 144.

Rule 146. Rules under Section 18 of the Act

(a) *Prepared by or on Behalf of the Issuer.* An offering document (as defined in Section 18(d)(1) of the Act) is "prepared by or on behalf of the issuer" for purposes of Section 18 of the Act, if the issuer or an agent or representative:

(1) Authorizes the document's production, and

(2) Approves the document before its use.

(b) *Covered Securities for the Purpose of Section 18.*

(1) For purposes of Section 18(b) of the Act (15 U.S.C. 77r), the Commission finds that the following national securities exchanges, or segments or tiers thereof, have listing standards that are substantially similar to those of the New York Stock Exchange ("NYSE"), the NYSE American LLC ("NYSE American"), or the National Market System of the Nasdaq Stock Market ("Nasdaq/NGM"), and that securities listed, or authorized for listing, on such exchanges shall be deemed covered securities:

(i) Tier I of the NYSE Arca, Inc.;

(ii) Tier I of the NASDAQ PHLX LLC;

(iii) The Chicago Board Options Exchange, Incorporated;

(iv) Options listed on Nasdaq ISE, LLC;

(v) The Nasdaq Capital Market;

(vi) Tier I and Tier II of Bats BZX Exchange, Inc.; and

(vii) Investors Exchange LLC.

(2) The designation of securities in paragraphs (b)(1)(i) through (vii) of this section as covered securities is conditioned on such exchanges' listing standards (or segments or tiers thereof) continuing to be substantially similar to those of the NYSE, NYSE American, or Nasdaq/NGM.

Rule 147. Intrastate offers and sales

(a) This section shall not raise any presumption that the exemption provided by section 3(a)(11) of the Act (15 U.S.C. 77c(a)(11)) is not available for transactions by an issuer which do not satisfy all of the provisions of this section.

(b) *Manner of offers and sales.* An issuer, or any person acting on behalf of the issuer, shall be deemed to conduct an offering in compliance with section 3(a)(11) of the Act (15 U.S.C. 77c(a)(11)), where offers and sales are made only to persons resident within the same state or territory in which the issuer is resident and doing business, within the meaning of section 3(a)(11) of the Act, so long as the issuer complies with the provisions of paragraphs (c), (d), and (f) through (h) of this section.

(c) *Nature of the issuer.* The issuer of the securities shall at the time of any offers and sales be a person resident and doing business within the state or territory in which all of the offers and sales are made.

(1) The issuer shall be deemed to be a resident of the state or territory in which:

(i) It is incorporated or organized, and it has its principal place of business, if acorporation, limited partnership, trust or other form of business organization that is organized under state or territorial law. The issuer shall be deemed to have its principal place of business in a state or territory in which the officers, partners or managers of the issuer primarily direct, control and coordinate the activities of the issuer;

(ii) It has its principal place of business, as defined in paragraph (c)(1)(i) of this section, if a general partnership or other form of business organization that is not organized under any state or territorial law;

(iii) Such person's principal residence is located, if an individual.

Instruction to paragraph (c)(1): An issuer that has previously conducted an intrastate offering pursuant to this section (§ 230.147) or Rule 147A (§ 230.147A) may not conduct another intrastate offering pursuant to this section (§ 230.147) in a different state or territory, until the expiration of the time period specified in paragraph (e) of this section (§ 230.147(e)) or paragraph (e) of Rule 147A (§ 230.147A(e)), calculated on the basis of the date of the last sale in such offering.

(2) The issuer shall be deemed to be doing business within a state or territory if the issuer satisfies at least one of the following requirements:

(i) The issuer derived at least 80% of its consolidated gross revenues from the operation of a business or of real property located in or from the rendering of services within such state or territory;

Instruction to paragraph (c)(2)(i): Revenues must be calculated based on the issuer's most recent fiscal year, if the first offer of securities pursuant to this section is made during the first six months of the issuer's current fiscal year, and based on the first six months of the issuer's current fiscal year or during the twelve-month fiscal period ending with such six-month period, if the first offer of securities pursuant to this section is made during the last six months of the issuer's current fiscal year.

(ii) The issuer had at the end of its most recent semi-annual fiscal period prior to an initial offer of securities in any offering or subsequent offering pursuant to this section, at least 80% of its assets and those of its subsidiaries on a consolidated basis located within such state or territory;

(iii) The issuer intends to use and uses at least 80% of the net proceeds to the issuer from sales made pursuant to this section (§ 230.147) in connection with the operation of a business or of real property, the purchase of real property located in, or the rendering of services within such state or territory; or

(iv) A majority of the issuer's employees are based in such state or territory.

(d) *Residence of offerees and purchasers.* Offers and sales of securities pursuant to this section (§ 230.147) shall be made only to residents of the state or territory in which the issuer is resident,as determined pursuant to paragraph (c) of this section, or who the issuer reasonably believes, at the time of the offer and sale,are residents of the state or territory in which the issuer is resident. For purposes of determining the residence of offerees and purchasers:

(1) A corporation, partnership, limited liability company, trust or other form of business organization shall be deemed to be a resident of a state or territory if, at the time of the offer and sale to it, it has its principal place of business, as defined in paragraph (c)(1)(i) of this section, within such state or territory.

Instruction to paragraph (d)(1): A trust that is not deemed by the law of the state or territory of its creation to be a separate legal entity is deemed to be a resident of each state or territory in which its trustee is, or trustees are, resident.

(2) Individuals shall be deemed to be residents of a state or territory if such individuals have, at the time of the offer and sale to them, their principal residence in the state or territory.

(3) A corporation, partnership, trust or other form of business organization, which is organized for the specific purpose of acquiring securities offered pursuant to this section (§ 230.147), shall not be a resident of a state or territory unless all of the beneficial owners of such organization are residents of such state or territory.

Instruction to paragraph (d): Obtaining a written representation from purchasers of in-state residency status will not, without more, be sufficient to establish a reasonable belief that such purchasers are in-state residents.

(e) *Limitation on resales.* For a period of six months from the date of the sale by the issuer of a security pursuant to this section (§ 230.147), any resale of such security shall be made only to persons resident within the state or territory in which the issuer was resident, as determined pursuant to paragraph (c) of this section, at the time of the sale of the security by the issuer.

Instruction to paragraph (e): In the case of convertible securities, resales of either the convertible security, or if it is converted, the underlying security, could be made during the period described in paragraph (e) only to persons resident within such state or territory. For purposes of this paragraph (e), a conversion in reliance on section 3(a)(9) of the Act (15 U.S.C. 77c(a)(9)) does not begin a new period.

(f) *Precautions against interstate sales.* (1) The issuer shall, in connection with any securities sold by it pursuant to this section:

(i) Place a prominent legend on the certificate or other document evidencing the security stating that: "Offers and sales of these securities were made under an exemption from registration and have not been registered under the Securities Act of 1933. For a period of six months from the date of the sale by the issuer of these securities, any resale of these securities (or the underlying securities in the case of convertible securities) shall be made only to persons resident within the state or territory of [identify the name of the state or territory in which the issuer was resident at the time of the sale of the securities by the issuer].";

(ii) Issue stop transfer instructions to the issuer's transfer agent, if any, with respect to the securities, or, if the issuer transfers its own securities, make a notation in the appropriate records of the issuer; and

(iii) Obtain a written representation from each purchaser as to his or her residence.

(2) The issuer shall, in connection with the issuance of new certificates for any of the securities that are sold pursuant to this section (§ 230.147) that are presented for transfer during the time period specified in paragraph (e), take the steps required by paragraphs (f)(1)(i) and (ii) of this section.

(3) The issuer shall, at the time of any offer or sale by it of a security pursuant to this section (§ 230.147), prominently disclose to each offeree in the manner in which any such offer is communicated and to each purchaser of such security in writing a reasonable period of time before the date of sale, the following: "Sales will be made only to residents of [identify the name of the state or territory in which the issuer was resident at the time of the sale of the securities by the issuer]. Offers and sales of these securities are made under an exemption from registration and have not been registered under the Securities Act of 1933. For a period of six months from the date of the sale by the issuer of the securities, any resale of the securities (or the underlying securities in the case of convertible securities) shall be made only to persons resident within the state or territory of [identify the name of the state or territory in which the issuer was resident at the time of the sale of the securities by the issuer]."

(g) *Integration with other offerings.* Offers or sales made in reliance on this section will not be integrated with:

(1) Offers or sales of securities made prior to the commencement of offers and sales of securities pursuant to this section (§ 230.147); or

(2) Offers or sales made after completion of offers and sales of securities pursuant to this section (§ 230.147) that are:

(i) Registered under the Act, except as provided in paragraph (h) of this section (§ 230.147);

(ii) Exempt from registration under Regulation A (§§ 230.251 through 230.263);

(iii) Exempt from registration under Rule 701 (§ 230.701);

(iv) Made pursuant to an employee benefit plan;

(v) Exempt from registration under Regulation S (§§ 230.901 through 230.905);

(vi) Exempt from registration under section 4(a)(6) of the Act (15 U.S.C. 77d(a)(6)); or

(vii) Made more than six months after the completion of an offering conducted pursuant to this section (§ 230.147).

Instruction to paragraph (g): If none of the safe harbors applies, whether subsequent offers and sales of securities will be integrated with any securities offered or sold pursuant to this section (§ 230.147) will depend on the particular facts and circumstances.

(h) *Offerings limited to qualified institutional buyers and institutional accredited investors.* Where an issuer decides to register an offering under the Act after making offers in reliance on this section (§ 230.147) limited only to qualified institutional buyers and institutional accredited investors referenced in section 5(d) of the Act, such offers will not be subject to integration with any subsequent registered offering. If the issuer makes offers in reliance on this section (§ 230.147) to persons other than qualified institutional buyers and institutional accredited investors referenced in section 5(d) of the Act, such offers will not be subject to integration if the issuer (and any underwriter, broker, dealer, or agent used by the issuer in connection with the proposed offering) waits at least 30 calendar days between the last such offer made in reliance on this section (§ 230.147) and the filing of the registration statement with the Commission.

Rule 147A. Intrastate sales exemption

(a) *Scope of the exemption.* Offers and sales by or on behalf of an issuer of its securities made in accordance with this section (§ 30.147A) are exempt from section 5 of the Act (15 U.S.C. 77e). This exemption is not available to an issuer that is an investment company registered or required to be registered under the Investment Company Act of 1940 (15 U.S.C. 80a-1 et seq.).

(b) *Manner of offers and sales.* An issuer, or any person acting on behalf of the issuer, may rely on this exemption to make offers and sales using any form of general solicitation and general advertising, so long as the issuer complies with the provisions of paragraphs (c), (d), and (f) through (h) of this section.

(c) *Nature of the issuer*. The issuer of the securities shall at the time of any offers and sales be a person resident and doing business within the state or territory in which all of the sales are made.

(1) The issuer shall be deemed to be a resident of the state or territory in which it has its principal place of business. The issuer shall be deemed to have its principal place of business in a state or territory in which the officers, partners or managers of the issuer primarily direct, control and coordinate the activities of the issuer.

(2) The issuer shall be deemed to be doing business within a state or territory if the issuer satisfies at least one of the following requirements:

(i) The issuer derived at least 80% of its consolidated gross revenues from the operation of a business or of real property located in or from the rendering of services within such state or territory;

Instruction to paragraph (c)(2)(i): Revenues must be calculated based on the issuer's most recent fiscal year, if the first offer of securities pursuant to this section is made during the first six months of the issuer's current fiscal year, and based on the first six months of the issuer's current fiscal year or during the twelve-month fiscal period ending with such six-month period, if the first offer of securities pursuant to this section is made during the last six months of the issuer's current fiscal year.

(ii) The issuer had at the end of its most recent semi-annual fiscal period prior to an initial offer of securities in any offering or subsequent offering pursuant to this section, at least 80% of its assets and those of its subsidiaries on a consolidated basis located within such state or territory;

(iii) The issuer intends to use and uses at least 80% of the net proceeds to the issuer from sales made pursuant to this section (§ 230.147A) in connection with the operation of a business or of real property, the purchase of real property located in, or the rendering of services within such state or territory; or

(iv) A majority of the issuer's employees are based in such state or territory.

Instruction to paragraph (c): An issuer that has previously conducted an intrastate offering pursuant to this section (§ 230.147A) or Rule 147 (§ 230.147) may not conduct another intrastate offering pursuant to this section (§ 230.147A) in a different state or territory, until the expiration of the time period specified in paragraph (e) of this section (§ 230.147A(e)) or paragraph (e) of Rule 147 (§ 230.147(e)), calculated on the basis of the date of the last sale in such offering.

(d) *Residence of purchasers*. Sales of securities pursuant to this section (§ 230.147A) shall be made only to residents of the state or territory in which the issuer is resident, as determined pursuant to paragraph (c) of this section, or who the issuer reasonably believes, at the time of sale, are residents of the state or territory in which the issuer is resident. For purposes of determining the residence of purchasers:

(1) A corporation, partnership, limited liability company, trust or other form of business organization shall be deemed to be a resident of a state or territory if, at the time of sale to it, it has its principal place of business, as defined in paragraph (c)(1) of this section, within such state or territory.

Instruction to paragraph (d)(1): A trust that is not deemed by the law of the state or territory of its creation to be a separate legal entity is deemed to be a resident of each state or territory in which its trustee is, or trustees are, resident.

(2) Individuals shall be deemed to be residents of a state or territory if such individuals have, at the time of sale to them, their principal residence in the state or territory.

(3) A corporation, partnership, trust or other form of business organization, which is organized for the specific purpose of acquiring securities offered pursuant to this section (§ 230.147A), shall not be a resident of a state or territory unless all of the beneficial owners of such organization are residents of such state or territory.

Instruction to paragraph (d): Obtaining a written representation from purchasers of in-state residency status will not, without more, be sufficient to establish a reasonable belief that such purchasers are in-state residents.

(e) *Limitation on resales*. For a period of six months from the date of the sale by the issuer of a security pursuant to this section (§ 230.147A), any resale of such security shall be made only to persons resident within the state or territory in which the issuer was resident, as determined pursuant to paragraph (c) of this section, at the time of the sale of the security by the issuer.

Instruction to paragraph (e): In the case of convertible securities, resales of either the convertible security, or if it is converted, the underlying security, could be made during the period described in paragraph (e) only to persons resident within such state or territory. For purposes of this paragraph (e), a conversion in reliance on section 3(a)(9) of the Act (15 U.S.C. 77c(a)(9)) does not begin a new period.

(f) *Precautions against interstate sales.* (1) The issuer shall, in connection with any securities sold by it pursuant to this section:

(i) Place a prominent legend on the certificate or other document evidencing the security stating that: "Offers and sales of these securities were made under an exemption from registration and have not been registered under the Securities Act of 1933. For a period of six months from the date of the sale by the issuer of these securities, any resale of these securities (or the underlying securities in the case of convertible securities) shall be made only to persons resident within the state or territory of [identify the name of the state or territory in which the issuer was resident at the time of the sale of the securities by the issuer].";

(ii) Issue stop transfer instructions to the issuer's transfer agent, if any, with respect to the securities, or, if the issuer transfers its own securities, make a notation in the appropriate records of the issuer; and

(iii) Obtain a written representation from each purchaser as to his or her residence.

(2) The issuer shall, in connection with the issuance of new certificates for any of the securities that are sold pursuant to this section (§ 230.147A) that are presented for transfer during the time period specified in paragraph (e), take the steps required by paragraphs (f)(1)(i) and (ii) of this section.

(3) The issuer shall, at the time of any offer or sale by it of a security pursuant to this section (§ 230.147A), prominently disclose to each offeree in the manner in which any such offer is communicated and to each purchaser of such security in writing a reasonable period of time before the date of sale, the following: "Sales will be made only to residents of the state or territory of [identify the name of the state or territory in which the issuer was resident at the time of the sale of the securities by the issuer]. Offers and sales of these securities are made under an exemption from registration and have not been registered under the Securities Act of 1933. For a period of six months from the date of the sale by the issuer of the securities, any resale of the securities (or the underlying securities in the case of convertible securities) shall be made only to persons resident within the state or territory of [identify the name of the state or territory in which the issuer was resident at the time of the sale of the securities by the issuer]."

(g) *Integration with other offerings.* Offers or sales made in reliance on this section will not be integrated with:

(1) Offers or sales of securities made prior to the commencement of offers and sales of securities pursuant to this section (§ 230.147A); or

(2) Offers or sales of securities made after completion of offers and sales of securities pursuant to this section (§ 230.147A) that are:

(i) Registered under the Act, except as provided in paragraph (h) of this section (§230.147A);

(ii) Exempt from registration under Regulation A (§§ 230.251 through 230.263);

(iii) Exempt from registration under Rule 701 (§ 230.701);

(iv) Made pursuant to an employee benefit plan;

(v) Exempt from registration under Regulation S (§§ 230.901 through 230.905);

(vi) Exempt from registration under section 4(a)(6) of the Act (15 U.S.C.77d(a)(6)); or

(vii) Made more than six months after the completion of an offering conducted pursuant to this section (§ 230.147A).

Instruction to paragraph (g): If none of the safe harbors applies, whether subsequent offers and sales of securities will be integrated with any securities offered or sold pursuant to this section (§ 230.147A) will depend on the particular facts and circumstances.

(h) *Offerings limited to qualified institutional buyers and institutional accredited investors.* Where an issuer decides to register an offering under the Act after making offers in reliance on this section (§ 230.147A) limited only to qualified institutional buyers and institutional accredited investors referenced in section 5(d) of the Act, such offers will not be subject to integration with any subsequent registered offering. If the issuer makes offers in reliance on this section (§ 230.147A) to persons other than qualified institutional buyers and institutional accredited investors referenced in section 5(d) of the Act, such offers will not be subject to integration if the issuer (and any underwriter, broker, dealer, or agent used by the issuer in connection with the proposed offering) waits at least 30 calendar days between the last such offer made in reliance on this section (§ 230.147A) and the filing of the registration statement with the Commission.

Rule 148. [Reserved]

Rule 149. Definition of "exchanged" in Section 3(a)(9) for certain transactions

The term *exchanged* in section 3(a)(9) (sec. 202(c), 48 Stat. 906; 15 U.S.C. 77c(9)) shall be deemed to include the issuance of a security in consideration of the surrender, by the existing security holders of the issuer, of outstanding securities of the issuer, notwithstanding the fact that the surrender of the outstanding securities may be required by the terms of the plan of exchange to be accompanied by such payment in cash by the security holder as may be necessary to effect an equitable adjustment, in respect of dividends or interest paid or payable on the securities involved in the exchange, as between such security holder and other security holders of the same class accepting the offer of exchange.

Rule 150. Definition of "commission or other remuneration" in Section 3(a)(9), for certain transactions

The term *commission or other remuneration* in section 3(a)(9) of the Act shall not include payments made by the issuer, directly or indirectly, to its security holders in connection with an exchange of securities for outstanding securities, when such payments are part of the terms of the offer of exchange.

Rule 151. Safe harbor definition of certain "annuity contracts or optional annuity contracts" within the meaning of Section 3(a)(8)

(a) Any annuity contract or optional annuity contract (a *contract*) shall be deemed to be within the provisions of section 3(a)(8) of the Securities Act of 1933 (15 U.S.C. 77c(a)(8)), *Provided,* That

(1) The annuity or optional annuity contract is issued by a corporation (the *insurer*) subject to the supervision of the insurance commissioner, bank commissioner, or any agency or officer performing like functions, of any State or Territory of the United States or the District of Columbia;

(2) The insurer assumes the investment risk under the contract as prescribed in paragraph (b) of this rule; and

(3) The contract is not marketed primarily as an investment.

(b) The insurer shall be deemed to assume the investment risk under the contract if:

(1) The value of the contract does not vary according to the investment experience of a separate account;

(2) The insurer for the life of the contract

(i) Guarantees the principal amount of purchase payments and interest credited thereto, less any deduction (without regard to its timing) for sales, administrative or other expenses or charges; and

(ii) Credits a specified rate of interest (as defined in paragraph (c) of this rule) to net purchase payments and interest credited thereto; and

(3) The insurer guarantees that the rate of any interest to be credited in excess of that described in paragraph (b)(2)(ii) of this rule will not be modified more frequently than once per year.

(c) The term *specified rate of interest,* as used in paragraph (b)(2)(ii) of this rule, means a rate of interest under the contract that is at least equal to the minimum rate required to be credited by the relevant nonforfeiture law in the jurisdiction in which the contract is issued. If that jurisdiction does not have any applicable nonforfeiture law at the time the contract is issued (or if the minimum rate applicable to an existing contract is no longer mandated in that jurisdiction), the specified rate under the contract must at least be equal to the minimum rate then required for individual annuity contracts by the NAIC Standard Nonforfeiture Law.

Rule 151A. Certain contracts not "annuity contracts" or "optional annuity contracts" under Section 3(a)(8)

(a) *General.* Except as provided in paragraph (c) of this rule, a contract that is issued by a corporation subject to the supervision of the insurance commissioner, bank commissioner, or any agency or officer performing like functions, of any State or Territory of the United States or the District of Columbia, and that is subject to regulation under the insurance laws of that jurisdiction as an annuity is not an "annuity contract" or "optional annuity contract" under Section 3(a)(8) of the Securities Act (15 U.S.C. 77c(a)(8)) if:

(1) The contract specifies that amounts payable by the issuer under the contract are calculated at or after the end of one or more specified crediting periods, in whole or in part, by reference to the performance during the crediting period or periods of a security, including a group or index of securities; and

(2) Amounts payable by the issuer under the contract are more likely than not to exceed the amounts guaranteed under the contract.

(b) *Determination of Amounts Payable and Guaranteed.* In making the determination under paragraph (a)(2) of this rule:

(1) Amounts payable by the issuer under the contract and amounts guaranteed under the contract shall be determined by taking into account all charges under the contract, including, without limitation, charges that are imposed at the time that payments are made by the issuer; and

(2) A determination by the issuer at or prior to issuance of the contract shall be conclusive, provided that:

(i) Both the methodology and the economic, actuarial, and other assumptions used in the determination are reasonable;

(ii) The computations made by the issuer in support of the determination are materially accurate; and

(iii) The determination is made not more than six months prior to the date on which the form of contract is first offered.

(c) *Separate Accounts.* This rule does not apply to any contract whose value varies according to the investment experience of a separate account.

Rule 152. Definition of "transactions by an issuer not involving any public offering" in Section 4(a)(2) for certain transactions

The phrase *transactions by an issuer not involving any public offering* in section 4(a)(2) (48 Stat. 77, Sec. 203(a), 48 Stat. 906; 15 U.S.C. 77d) shall be deemed to apply to transactions not involving any public offering at the time of said transactions although subsequently thereto the issuer decides to make a public offering and/or files a registration statement.

Rule 152a. Offer or sale of certain fractional interests

Any offer or sale of a security, evidenced by a scrip certificate, order form or similar document which represents a fractional interest in a share of stock or similar security shall be deemed a transaction by a person other than an issuer, underwriter or dealer, within the meaning of section 4(a)(1) of the Act, if the fractional interest (a) resulted from a stock dividend, stock split, reverse stock split, conversion, merger or similar transaction, and (b) is offered or sold pursuant to arrangements for the purchase and sale of fractional interests among the person entitled to such fractional interests for the purpose of combining such interests into whole shares, and for the sale of such number of whole shares as may be necessary to compensate security holders for any remaining fractional interests not so combined, notwithstanding that the issuer or an affiliate of the issuer may act on behalf of or as agent for the security holders in effecting such transactions.

Rule 153. Definition of "preceded by a prospectus" as used in Section 5(b)(2), in relation to certain transactions

(a) *Definition of Preceded by a Prospectus.* The term preceded by a prospectus as used in section 5(b)(2) of the Act, regarding any requirement of a broker or dealer to deliver a prospectus to a broker or dealer as a result of a transaction effected between such parties on or through a national securities exchange or facility thereof, trading facility of a national securities association, or an alternative trading system, shall mean the satisfaction of the conditions in paragraph (b) of this rule.

(b) *Conditions.* Any requirement of a broker or dealer to deliver a prospectus for transactions covered by paragraph (a) of this rule will be satisfied if:

(1) Securities of the same class as the securities that are the subject of the transaction are trading on that national securities exchange or facility thereof, trading facility of a national securities association, or alternative trading system;

(2) The registration statement relating to the offering is effective and is not the subject of any pending proceeding or examination under section 8(d) or 8(e) of the Act;

(3) Neither the issuer, nor any underwriter or participating dealer is the subject of a pending proceeding under section 8A of the Act in connection with the offering; and

(4) The issuer has filed or will file with the Commission a prospectus that satisfies the requirements of section 10(a) of the Act.

(c) *Definitions.* (1) The term *national securities exchange*, as used in this rule, shall mean a securities exchange registered as a national securities exchange under section 6 of the Securities Exchange Act of 1934 (15 U.S.C. 78f).

(2) The term *trading facility*, as used in this rule, shall mean a trading facility sponsored and governed by the rules of a registered securities association or a national securities exchange.

(3) The term *alternative trading system*, as used in this rule, shall mean an alternative trading system as defined in Rule 300(a) of Regulation ATS under the Securities Exchange Act of 1934 registered with the Commission pursuant to Rule 301 of Regulation ATS under the Securities Exchange Act of 1934.

Rule 153a. Definition of "preceded by a prospectus" as used in Section 5(b)(2), in relation to certain transactions requiring approval of security holders

The term *preceded by a prospectus,* as used in section 5(b)(2) of the Act with respect to any requirement for the delivery of a prospectus to security holders of a corporation or other person, in connection with transactions of the character specified in paragraph (a) of Rule 145, shall mean the delivery of a prospectus:

(a) Prior to the vote of security holders on such transactions; or,

(b) With respect to actions taken by consent, prior to the earliest date on which the corporate action may be taken;

to all security holders of record of such corporation or other person, entitled to vote on or consent to the proposed transaction, at their address of record on the transfer records of the corporation or other person.

Rule 153b. Definition of "preceded by a prospectus", as used in Section 5(b)(2), in connection with certain transactions in standardized options

The term *preceded by a prospectus*, as used in Section 5(b)(2) of the Act with respect to any requirement for the delivery of a prospectus relating to standardized options registered on Form S–20, shall mean the delivery, prior to any transactions, of copies of such prospectus to each options market upon which the options are traded, for the purpose of redelivery to options customers upon their request, *Provided* That:

(a) Such options market shall thereto have requested of the issuer, from time to time, such number of copies of such prospectus as may have appeared reasonably necessary to comply with the requests of options customers, and shall have delivered promptly from its supply on hand a copy to any options customer making a request thereof; and

(b) The issuer shall have furnished such options market with such reasonable number of copies of such prospectus as may have been requested by the options market for the purpose stated above.

Rule 154. Delivery of prospectuses to investors at the same address

(a) *Delivery of a Single Prospectus.* If you must deliver a prospectus under the federal securities laws, for purposes of sections 5(b) and 2(a)(10) of the Act (15 U.S.C. 77e(b) and 77b(a)(10)) or Rule 15c2–8(b) under the Securities Exchange Act of 1934, you will be considered to have delivered a prospectus to investors who share an address if:

(1) You deliver a prospectus to the shared address;

(2) You address the prospectus to the investors as a group (for example, "ABC Fund [or Corporation] Shareholders," "Jane Doe and Household," "The Smith Family") or to each of the investors individually (for example, "John Doe and Richard Jones"); and

(3) The investors consent in writing to delivery of one prospectus.

(b) *Implied Consent.* You do not need to obtain written consent from an investor under paragraph (a)(3) of this rule if all of the following conditions are met:

(1) The investor has the same last name as the other investors, or you reasonably believe that the investors are members of the same family;

(2) You have sent the investor a notice at least 60 days before you begin to rely on this rule concerning delivery of prospectuses to that investor. The notice must be a separate written statement and:

(i) State that only one prospectus will be delivered to the shared address unless you receive contrary instructions;

(ii) Include a toll-free telephone number or be accompanied by a reply form that is pre-addressed with postage provided, that the investor can use to notify you that he or she wishes to receive a separate prospectus;

(iii) State the duration of the consent;

(iv) Explain how an investor can revoke consent;

(v) State that you will begin sending individual copies to an investor within 30 days after you receive revocation of the investor's consent; and

(vi) Contain the following prominent statement, or similar clear and understandable statement, in bold-face type: "Important Notice Regarding Delivery of Shareholder Documents."

This statement also must appear on the envelope in which the notice is delivered. Alternatively, if the notice is delivered separately from other communications to investors, this statement may appear either on the notice or on the envelope in which the notice is delivered;

NOTE TO PARAGRAPH (b)(2): The notice should be written in plain English. See Rule 421(d)(2) for a discussion of plain English principles.

(3) You have not received the reply form or other notification indicating that the investor wishes to continue to receive an individual copy of the prospectus, within 60 days after you sent the notice; and

(4) You deliver the prospectus to a post office box or to a residential street address. You can assume a street address is a residence unless you have information that indicates it is a business.

(c) *Revocation of Consent.* If an investor, orally or in writing, revokes consent to delivery of one prospectus to a shared address (provided under paragraphs (a)(3) or (b) of this rule), you must begin sending individual copies to that investor within 30 days after you receive the revocation. If the individual's consent concerns delivery of the prospectus of a registered open-end management investment company, at least once a year you must explain to investors who have consented how they can revoke their consent. The explanation must be reasonably designed to reach these investors.

(d) *Definition of Address.* For purposes of this rule, address means a street address, a post office box number, an electronic mail address, a facsimile telephone number, or other similar destination to which paper or electronic documents are delivered, unless otherwise provided in this rule. If you have reason to believe that an address is the street address of a multi-unit building, the address must include the unit number.

Rule 155. Integration of abandoned offerings

Compliance with paragraph (b) or (c) of this rule provides a non-exclusive safe harbor from integration of private and registered offerings. Because of the objectives of Rule 155 and the policies underlying the Act, Rule 155 is not available to any issuer for any transaction or series of transactions that, although in technical compliance with the rule, is part of a plan or scheme to evade the registration requirements of the Act.

(a) *Definition of Terms.* For the purposes of this rule only, a *private offering* means an unregistered offering of securities that is exempt from registration under Section 4(a)(2) or 4(5) of the Act (15 U.S.C. 77d(2) and 77d(5)) or Rule 506 of Regulation D.

(b) *Abandoned Private Offering Followed by a Registered Offering.* A private offering of securities will not be considered part of an offering for which the issuer later files a registration statement if:

(1) No securities were sold in the private offering;

(2) The issuer and any person(s) acting on its behalf terminate all offering activity in the private offering before the issuer files the registration statement;

(3) The Section 10(a) final prospectus and any Section 10 preliminary prospectus used in the registered offering disclose information about the abandoned private offering, including:

(i) The size and nature of the private offering;

(ii) The date on which the issuer abandoned the private offering;

(iii) That any offers to buy or indications of interest given in the private offering were rejected or otherwise not accepted; and

(iv) That the prospectus delivered in the registered offering supersedes any offering materials used in the private offering; and

(4) The issuer does not file the registration statement until at least 30 calendar days after termination of all offering activity in the private offering, unless the issuer and any person acting on its behalf offered securities in the private offering only to persons who were (or who the issuer reasonably believes were):

(i) Accredited investors (as that term is defined in Rule 501(a)); or

(ii) Persons who satisfy the knowledge and experience standard of Rule 506(b)(2)(ii).

(c) *Abandoned Registered Offering Followed by a Private Offering.* An offering for which the issuer filed a registration statement will not be considered part of a later commenced private offering if:

(1) No securities were sold in the registered offering;

(2) The issuer withdraws the registration statement under Rule 477;

(3) Neither the issuer nor any person acting on the issuer's behalf commences the private offering earlier than 30 calendar days after the effective date of withdrawal of the registration statement under Rule 477;

(4) The issuer notifies each offeree in the private offering that:

(i) The offering is not registered under the Act;

(ii) The securities will be "restricted securities" (as that term is defined in Rule 144(a)(3)) and may not be resold unless they are registered under the Act or an exemption from registration is available;

(iii) Purchasers in the private offering do not have the protection of Section 11 of the Act (15 U.S.C. 77k); and

(iv) A registration statement for the abandoned offering was filed and withdrawn, specifying the effective date of the withdrawal; and

(5) Any disclosure document used in the private offering discloses any changes in the issuer's business or financial condition that occurred after the issuer filed the registration statement that are material to the investment decision in the private offering.

Rule 156. Investment company sales literature

(a) Under the federal securities laws, including section 17(a) of the Securities Act of 1933 (15 U.S.C. 77q(a)) and section 10(b) of the Securities Exchange Act of 1934 (15 U.S.C. 78j(b)) and Rule 10b–5 thereunder, it is unlawful for any person, directly or indirectly, by the use of any means or instrumentality of interstate commerce or of the mails, to use sales literature which is materially misleading in connection with the offer or sale of securities issued by an investment company. Under these provisions, sales literature is materially misleading if it (1) contains an untrue statement of a material fact or (2) omits to state a material fact necessary in order to make a statement made, in the light of the circumstances of its use, not misleading.

(b) Whether or not a particular description, representation, illustration, or other statement involving a material fact is misleading depends on evaluation of the context in which it is made. In considering whether a particular statement involving a material fact is or might be misleading, weight should be given to all pertinent factors, including, but not limited to, those listed below.

(1) A statement could be misleading because of:

(i) Other statements being made in connection with the offer of sale or sale of the securities in question;

(ii) The absence of explanations, qualifications, limitations or other statements necessary or appropriate to make such statement not misleading; or

(iii) General economic or financial conditions or circumstances.

(2) Representations about past or future investment performance could be misleading because of statements or omissions made involving a material fact, including situations where:

(i) Portrayals of past income, gain, or growth of assets convey an impression of the net investment results achieved by an actual or hypothetical investment which would not be justified under the circumstances, including portrayals that omit explanations, qualifications, limitations, or other statements necessary or appropriate to make the portrayals not misleading; and

(ii) Representations, whether express or implied, about future investment performance, including:

(A) Representations, as to security of capital, possible future gains or income, or expenses associated with an investment;

(B) Representations implying that future gain or income may be inferred from or predicted based on past investment performance; or

(C) Portrayals of past performance, made in a manner which would imply that gains or income realized in the past would be repeated in the future.

(3) A statement involving a material fact about the characteristics or attributes of an investment company could be misleading because of:

(i) Statements about possible benefits connected with or resulting from services to be provided or methods of operation which do not give equal prominence to discussion of any risks or limitations associated therewith;

(ii) Exaggerated or unsubstantiated claims about management skill or techniques, characteristics of the investment company or an investment in securities issued by such company, services, security of investment or funds, effects of government supervision, or other attributes; and

(iii) Unwarranted or incompletely explained comparisons to other investment vehicles or to indexes.

(c) For purposes of this rule, the term *sales literature* shall be deemed to include any communication (whether in writing, by radio, or by television) used by any person to offer to sell or induce the sale of securities of any investment company. Communications between issuers, underwriters and dealers are included in this definition of sales literature if such communications, or the information contained therein, can be reasonably expected to be communicated to prospective investors in the offer or sale of securities or are designed to be employed in either written or oral form in the offer or sale of securities.

Rule 157. Small entities under the Securities Act for purposes of the Regulatory Flexibility Act

For purposes of Commission rulemaking in accordance with the provisions of Chapter Six of the Administrative Procedure Act, and unless otherwise defined for purposes of a particular rulemaking proceeding, the term *small business* or *small organization* shall—

(a) When used with reference to an issuer, other than an investment company, for purposes of the Act, mean an issuer whose total assets on the last day of its most recent fiscal year were $5 million or less and that is engaged or proposing to engage in small business financing. An issuer is considered to be engaged or proposing to engage in small business financing under this section if it is conducting or proposes to conduct an offering of securities which does not exceed the dollar limitation prescribed by section 3(b)(1) of the Act.

(b) When used with reference to an investment company that is an issuer for purposes of the Act, have the meaning ascribed to those terms by Rule 0–10 under the Investment Company Act of 1940.

Rule 158. Definitions of certain terms in the last paragraph of Section 11(a)

(a) An "earning statement" made generally available to security holders of the registrant pursuant to the last paragraph of section 11(a) of the Act shall be sufficient for the purposes of such paragraph if:

(1) There is included the information required for statements of comprehensive income (as defined in Rule 1–02 of Regulation S–X) contained either:

(i) In Item 8 of Form 10–K (17 CFR 239.310), Part I, Item 1 of Form 10–Q (17 CFR 240.308a), or Rule 14a–3(b) under the Securities Exchange Act of 1934;

(ii) In Item 17 of Form 20–F, if appropriate; or

(iii) In Form 40–F; and

(2) The information specified in the last paragraph of section 11(a) is contained in one report or any combination of reports either:

(i) On Form 10–K (17 CFR 249.308), Form 8–K, or in the annual report to security holders pursuant to Rule 14a–3 under the Securities Exchange Act of 1934; or

(ii) On Form 20–F, Form 40–F or Form 6–K.

NOTE 1 TO PARAGRAPH (a). A subsidiary issuing debt securities guaranteed by its parent will be deemed to have met the requirements of this paragraph (a) if the parent's statements of comprehensive income (as defined in Rule 1–02 of Regulation S–X) satisfy the criteria of this paragraph and information respecting the subsidiary is included to the same extent as was presented in the registration statement. An "earning statement" not meeting the requirements of this paragraph (a) may otherwise be sufficient for purposes of the last paragraph of section 11(a) of the Act.

(b) For purposes of the last paragraph of section 11(a) only, the "earning statement" contemplated by paragraph (a) of this Rule shall be deemed to be "made generally available to its security holders" if the registrant:

(1) Is required to file reports pursuant to section 13 or 15(d) of the Securities Exchange Act of 1934 and

(2) Has filed its report or reports on Form 10–K and Form 10–KSB, Form 10–Q and Form 10–QSB, Form 8–K, Form 20–F, Form 40–F or Form 6–K, or has supplied to the Commission copies of the annual report sent to security holders pursuant to Rule 14a–3(c) under the Securities Exchange Act of 1934, containing such information.

A registrant may use other methods to make an earning statement "generally available to its security holders" for purposes of the last paragraph of section 11(a).

(c) For purposes of the last paragraph of section 11(a) of the Act only, the effective date of the registration statement is deemed to be the date of the latest to occur of:

(1) The effective date of the registration statement;

(2) The effective date of the last post-effective amendment to the registration statement next preceding a particular sale of the issuer's registered securities to the public filed for the purposes of:

(i) Including any prospectus required by section 10(a)(3) of the Act; or

(ii) Reflecting in the prospectus any facts or events arising after the effective date of the registration statement (or the most recent post-effective amendment thereof) which, individually or in the aggregate, represent a fundamental change in the information set forth in the registration statement;

(3) The date of filing of the last report of the issuer incorporated by reference into the prospectus that is part of the registration statement or the date that a form of prospectus filed pursuant to Rule 424(b) or Rule 497(b), (c), (d), or (e) is deemed part of and included in the registration statement, and relied upon in either case in lieu of filing a post-effective amendment for purposes of paragraphs (c)(2)(i) and (ii) of this rule next preceding a particular sale of the issuer's registered securities to the public; or

(4) As to the issuer and any underwriter at that time only, the most recent effective date of the registration statement for purposes of liability under section 11 of the Act of the issuer and any such underwriter only at the time of or next preceding a particular sale of the issuer's registered securities to the public determined pursuant to Rule 430B.

(d) If an earnings statement was made available by "other methods" than those specified in paragraphs (a) and (b) of this rule, the earnings statement must be filed as exhibit 99 to the next periodic report required by section 13 or 15(d) of the Exchange Act covering the period in which the earnings statement was released.

Rule 159. Information available to purchaser at time of contract of sale

(a) For purposes of section 12(a)(2) of the Act only, and without affecting any other rights a purchaser may have, for purposes of determining whether a prospectus or oral statement included an untrue statement of a material fact or omitted to state a material fact necessary in order to make the statements, in the light of the circumstances under which they were made, not misleading at the time of sale (including, without limitation, a contract of sale), any information conveyed to the purchaser only after such time of sale (including such contract of sale) will not be taken into account.

(b) For purposes of section 17(a)(2) of the Act only, and without affecting any other rights the Commission may have to enforce that section, for purposes of determining whether a statement includes or represents any untrue statement of a material fact or any omission to state a material fact necessary in order to make the statements made, in light of the circumstances under which they were made, not misleading at the time of sale (including, without limitation, a contract of sale), any information conveyed to the purchaser only after such time of sale (including such contract of sale) will not be taken into account.

(c) For purposes of section 12(a)(2) of the Act only, knowing of such untruth or omission in respect of a sale (including, without limitation, a contract of sale), means knowing at the time of such sale (including such contract of sale).

Rule 159A. Certain definitions for purposes of Section 12(a)(2) of the Act

(a) *Definition of Seller for Purposes of Section 12(a)(2) of the Act.* For purposes of section 12(a)(2) of the Act only, in a primary offering of securities of the issuer, regardless of the underwriting method used to sell the issuer's securities, *seller* shall include the issuer of the securities sold to a person as part of the initial distribution of such securities, and the issuer shall be considered to offer or sell the securities to such person, if the securities are offered or sold to such person by means of any of the following communications:

(1) Any preliminary prospectus or prospectus of the issuer relating to the offering required to be filed pursuant to Rule 424 or Rule 497;

(2) Any free writing prospectus as defined in Rule 405 relating to the offering prepared by or on behalf of the issuer or used or referred to by the issuer and, in the case of an issuer that is an open-end management company registered under the Investment Company Act of 1940 (15 U.S.C. 80a–1 *et seq.*), any summary prospectus relating to the offering provided pursuant to Rule 498;

(3) The portion of any other free writing prospectus (or, in the case of an issuer that is an investment company registered under the Investment Company Act of 1940 or a business development company as defined in section 2(a)(48) of the Investment Company Act of 1940 (15 U.S.C. 80a–2(a)(48))), any advertisement pursuant to Rule 482 relating to the offering containing material information about the issuer or its securities provided by or on behalf of the issuer; and

(4) Any other communication that is an offer in the offering made by the issuer to such person.

NOTES TO PARAGRAPH (a) OF RULE 159A: 1. For purposes of paragraph (a) of this rule, information is provided or a communication is made by or on behalf of an issuer if an issuer or an agent or representative of the issuer authorizes or approves the information or communication before its provision or use. An offering participant other than the issuer shall not be an agent or representative of the issuer solely by virtue of its acting as an offering participant.

2. Paragraph (a) of this rule shall not affect in any respect the determination of whether any person other than

an issuer is a "seller" for purposes of section 12(a)(2) of the Act.

(b) *Definition of by Means of for Purposes of Section 12(a)(2) of the Act.* (1) For purposes of section 12(a)(2) of the Act only, an offering participant other than the issuer shall not be considered to offer or sell securities that are the subject of a registration statement by means of a free writing prospectus as to a purchaser unless one or more of the following circumstances shall exist:

(i) The offering participant used or referred to the free writing prospectus in offering or selling the securities to the purchaser;

(ii) The offering participant offered or sold securities to the purchaser and participated in planning for the use of the free writing prospectus by one or more other offering participants and such free writing prospectus was used or referred to in offering or selling securities to the purchaser by one or more of such other offering participants; or

(iii) The offering participant was required to file the free writing prospectus pursuant to the conditions to use in Rule 433.

(2) For purposes of section 12(a)(2) of the Act only, a person will not be considered to offer or sell securities by means of a free writing prospectus solely because another person has used or referred to the free writing prospectus or filed the free writing prospectus with the Commission pursuant to Rule 433.

Rule 160. Registered investment company exemption from Section 101(c)(1) of the Electronic Signatures in Global and National Commerce Act

A prospectus for an investment company registered under the Investment Company Act of 1940 (15 U.S.C. 80a–1 *et seq.*) that is sent or given for the sole purpose of permitting a communication not to be deemed a prospectus under section 2(a)(10)(a) of the Act (15 U.S.C. 77b(a)(10)(a)) shall be exempt from the requirements of section 101(c)(1) of the Electronic Signatures in Global and National Commerce Act.

Rule 161. Amendments to rules and regulations governing exemptions

The rules and regulations governing the exemption of securities under section 3(b) of the Act, as in effect at the time the securities are first bona fide offered to the public in conformity therewith, shall continue to govern the exemption of such securities notwithstanding the subsequent amendment of such rules and regulations. This rule shall not apply, however, to any new offering of such securities by an issuer or underwriter after the effective date of any such amendment, nor shall it apply to any offering after January 1, 1959, of securities by an issuer or underwriter pursuant to Regulation D or pursuant to Regulation A as in effect at any time prior to July 23, 1956.

Rule 162. Submission of tenders in registered exchange offers

(a) Notwithstanding section 5(a) of the Act (15 U.S.C. 77e(a)), an offeror may solicit tenders of securities in an exchange offer before a registration statement is effective as to the security offered, so long as no securities are purchased until the registration statement is effective and the tender offer has expired in accordance with the tender offer rules, and either:

(1) The exchange offer is subject to Rule 13e–4 or Rules 14d–1 through 14d–11 under the Securities Exchange Act of 1934; or

(2) The offeror provides withdrawal rights to the same extent as would be required if the exchange offer were subject to the requirements of Rule 13e–4 or Rules 14d–1 through 14d–11 under the Securities Exchange Act of 1934; and if a material change occurs in the information published, sent or given to security holders, the offeror complies with the provisions of Rule 13e–4(e)(3) or Rule 14d–4(b) and (d) under the Securities Exchange Act of 1934 in disseminating information about the material change to security holders, and including the minimum periods during which the offer must remain open (with withdrawal rights) after notice of the change is provided to security holders.

(b) Notwithstanding Section 5(b)(2) of the Act (15 U.S.C. 77e(b)(2)), a prospectus that meets the requirements of Section 10(a) of the Act (15 U.S.C. 77j(a)) need not be delivered to security holders in an exchange offer that commences before the effectiveness of a registration statement in accordance with the provisions of Rule 162(a), so long as a preliminary prospectus, prospectus supplements and revised prospectuses are delivered to security holders in accordance with Rule 13e–4(e)(2) or Rule 14d–4(b) under the Securities Exchange Act of 1934. This applies not only to exchange offers subject to those provisions, but also to exchange offers not subject to those provisions that meet the conditions in Rule 162(a)(2).

Instruction to Rule 162: Notwithstanding the provisions of Rule 162 of this section above, for going-private transactions (as defined by Rule 13e–3 under the Securities Exchange Act of 1934) and roll-up transactions (as described by Item 901 of Regulation S–K), a registration statement registering the securities to be offered must have become effective and only a prospectus that meets the requirements of Section 10(a) of the Securities Act may be delivered to security holders on the date of commencement.

Rule 163. Exemption from Section 5(c) of the Act for certain communications by or on behalf of well-known seasoned issuers

Preliminary Note to Rule 163

Attempted compliance with this rule does not act as an exclusive election and the issuer also may claim the availability of any other applicable exemption or exclusion. Reliance on this rule does not affect the availability of any other exemption or exclusion from the requirements of section 5 of the Act.

(a) In an offering by or on behalf of a well-known seasoned issuer, as defined in Rule 405, that will be or is at the time intended to be registered under the Act, an offer by or on behalf of such issuer is exempt from the prohibitions in section 5(c) of the Act on offers to sell, offers for sale, or offers to buy its securities before a registration statement has been filed, provided that:

(1) Any written communication that is an offer made in reliance on this exemption will be a free writing prospectus as defined in Rule 405 and a prospectus under section 2(a)(10) of the Act relating to a public offering of securities to be covered by the registration statement to be filed; and

(2) The exemption from section 5(c) of the Act provided in this rule for such written communication that is an offer shall be conditioned on satisfying the conditions in paragraph (b) of this rule.

(b) *Conditions.* (1) *Legend.* (i) Every written communication that is an offer made in reliance on this exemption shall contain substantially the following legend:

The issuer may file a registration statement (including a prospectus) with the SEC for the offering to which this communication relates. Before you invest, you should read the prospectus in that registration statement and other documents the issuer has filed with the SEC for more complete information about the issuer and this offering. You may get these documents for free by visiting EDGAR on the SEC Web site at www.sec.gov. Alternatively, the company will arrange to send you the prospectus after filing if you request it by calling toll-free 1–8[xx–xxx–xxxx].

(ii) The legend also may provide an e-mail address at which the documents can be requested and may indicate that the documents also are available by accessing the issuer's Web site, and provide the Internet address and the particular location of the documents on the Web site.

(iii) An immaterial or unintentional failure to include the specified legend in a free writing prospectus required by this rule will not result in a violation of section 5(c) of the Act or the loss of the ability to rely on this rule so long as:

(A) A good faith and reasonable effort was made to comply with the specified legend condition;

(B) The free writing prospectus is amended to include the specified legend as soon as practicable after discovery of the omitted or incorrect legend; and

(C) If the free writing prospectus has been transmitted without the specified legend, the free writing prospectus is retransmitted with the legend by substantially the same means as, and directed to substantially the same prospective purchasers to whom, the free writing prospectus was originally transmitted.

(2) *Filing Condition.* (i) Subject to paragraph (b)(2)(ii) of this rule, every written communication that is an offer made in reliance on this exemption shall be filed by the issuer with the Commission promptly upon the filing of the registration statement, if one is filed, or an amendment, if one is filed, covering the securities that have been offered in reliance on this exemption.

(ii) The condition that an issuer shall file a free writing prospectus with the Commission under this rule shall not apply in respect of any communication that has previously been filed with, or furnished to, the Commission or that the issuer would not be required to file with the Commission pursuant to the conditions of Rule 433 if the communication was a free writing prospectus used after the filing of the registration statement. The condition that the issuer shall file a free writing prospectus with the Commission under this rule shall be satisfied if the issuer satisfies the filing conditions (other than timing of filing which is provided in this rule) that would apply under Rule 433 if the communication was a free writing prospectus used after the filing of the registration statement.

(iii) An immaterial or unintentional failure to file or delay in filing a free writing prospectus to the extent provided in this rule will not result in a violation of section 5(c) of the Act or the loss of the ability to rely on this rule so long as:

(A) A good faith and reasonable effort was made to comply with the filing condition; and

(B) The free writing prospectus is filed as soon as practicable after discovery of the failure to file.

(3) *Ineligible Offerings*. The exemption in paragraph (a) of this rule shall not be available to:

(i) Communications relating to business combination transactions that are subject to Rule 165 or Rule 166;

(ii) Communications by an issuer that is an investment company registered under the Investment Company Act of 1940 (15 U.S.C. 80a–1 *et seq.*); or

(iii) Communications by an issuer that is a business development company as defined in section 2(a)(48) of the Investment Company Act of 1940 (15 U.S.C. 80a–2(a)(48)).

(c) For purposes of this rule, a communication is made by or on behalf of an issuer if the issuer or an agent or representative of the issuer, other than an offering participant who is an underwriter or dealer, authorizes or approves the communication before it is made.

(d) For purposes of this rule, a communication for which disclosure would be required under section 17(b) of the Act as a result of consideration given or to be given, directly or indirectly, by or on behalf of an issuer is deemed to be an offer by the issuer and, if a written communication, is deemed to be a free writing prospectus of the issuer.

(e) A communication exempt from section 5(c) of the Act pursuant to this rule will not be considered to be in connection with a securities offering registered under the Securities Act for purposes of Rule 100(b)(2)(iv) of Regulation FD under the Securities Exchange Act of 1934.

Rule 163A. Exemption From Section 5(c) of the Act for certain communications made by or on behalf of issuers more than 30 days before a registration statement is filed

PRELIMINARY NOTE TO RULE 163A

Attempted compliance with this rule does not act as an exclusive election and the issuer also may claim the availability of any other applicable exemption or exclusion. Reliance on this rule does not affect the availability of any other exemption or exclusion from the requirements of section 5 of the Act.

(a) Except as excluded pursuant to paragraph (b) of this rule, in all registered offerings by issuers, any communication made by or on behalf of an issuer more than 30 days before the date of the filing of the registration statement that does not reference a securities offering that is or will be the subject of a registration statement shall not constitute an offer to sell, offer for sale, or offer to buy the securities being offered under the registration statement for purposes of section 5(c) of the Act, provided that the issuer takes reasonable steps within its control to prevent further distribution or publication of such communication during the 30 days immediately preceding the date of filing the registration statement.

(b) The exemption in paragraph (a) of this rule shall not be available with respect to the following communications:

(1) Communications relating to business combination transactions that are subject to Rule 165 or Rule 166;

(2) Communications made in connection with offerings registered on Form S–8 (17 CFR 239.16b), other than by well-known seasoned issuers;

(3) Communications in offerings of securities of an issuer that is, or during the past three years was (or any of whose predecessors during the last three years was):

(i) A blank check company as defined in Rule 419(a)(2);

(ii) A shell company, other than a business combination related shell company, each as defined in Rule 405; or

(iii) An issuer for an offering of penny stock as defined in Rule 3a51–1 under the Securities Exchange Act of 1934; or

(4) Communications made by an issuer that is:

(i) An investment company registered under the Investment Company Act of 1940 (15 U.S.C. 80a–1 *et seq.*); or

(ii) A business development company as defined in section 2(a)(48) of the Investment Company Act of 1940 (15 U.S.C. 80a–2(a)(48)).

(c) For purposes of this rule, a communication is made by or on behalf of an issuer if the issuer or an agent or representative of the issuer, other than an offering participant who is an underwriter or dealer, authorizes or approves the communication before it is made.

(d) A communication exempt from section 5(c) of the Act pursuant to this rule will not be considered to be in connection with a securities offering registered under the Securities Act for purposes of Rule 100(b)(2)(iv) of Regulation FD under the Securities Exchange Act of 1934.

Rule 164. Post-filing free writing prospectuses in connection with certain registered offerings

PRELIMINARY NOTES TO RULE 164

1. This rule is not available for any communication that, although in technical compliance with this rule, is part of a plan or scheme to evade the requirements of section 5 of the Act.

2. Attempted compliance with this rule does not act as an exclusive election and the person relying on this rule also may claim the availability of any other applicable exemption or exclusion. Reliance on this rule does not affect the availability of any other exemption or exclusion from the requirements of section 5 of the Act.

(a) In connection with a registered offering of an issuer meeting the requirements of this rule, a free writing prospectus, as defined in Rule 405, of the issuer or any other offering participant, including any underwriter or dealer, after the filing of the registration statement will be a section 10(b) prospectus for purposes of section 5(b)(1) of the Act provided that the conditions set forth in Rule 433 are satisfied.

(b) An immaterial or unintentional failure to file or delay in filing a free writing prospectus as necessary to satisfy the filing conditions contained in Rule 433 will not result in a violation of section 5(b)(1) of the Act or the loss of the ability to rely on this rule so long as:

(1) A good faith and reasonable effort was made to comply with the filing condition; and

(2) The free writing prospectus is filed as soon as practicable after discovery of the failure to file.

(c) An immaterial or unintentional failure to include the specified legend in a free writing prospectus as necessary to satisfy the legend condition contained in Rule 433 will not result in a violation of section 5(b)(1) of the Act or the loss of the ability to rely on this rule so long as:

(1) A good faith and reasonable effort was made to comply with the legend condition;

(2) The free writing prospectus is amended to include the specified legend as soon as practicable after discovery of the omitted or incorrect legend; and

(3) If the free writing prospectus has been transmitted without the specified legend, the free writing prospectus must be retransmitted with the legend by substantially the same means as, and directed to substantially the same prospective purchasers to whom, the free writing prospectus was originally transmitted.

(d) Solely for purposes of this rule, an immaterial or unintentional failure to retain a free writing prospectus as necessary to satisfy the record retention condition contained in Rule 433 will not result in a violation of section 5(b)(1) of the Act or the loss of the ability to rely on this rule so long as a good faith and reasonable effort was made to comply with the record retention condition. Nothing in this paragraph will affect, however, any other record retention provisions applicable to the issuer or any offering participant.

(e) *Ineligible Issuers.* (1) This rule and Rule 433 are available only if at the eligibility determination date for the offering in question, determined pursuant to paragraph (h) of this rule, the issuer is not an ineligible issuer as defined in Rule 405 (or in the case of any offering participant, other than the issuer, the participant has a reasonable belief that the issuer is not an ineligible issuer);

(2) Notwithstanding paragraph (e)(1) of this rule, this rule and Rule 433 are available to an ineligible issuer with respect to a free writing prospectus that contains only descriptions of the terms of the securities in the offering or the offering (or in the case of an offering of asset-backed securities), contains only information specified in paragraphs (a)(1), (2), (3), (4), (6), (7), and (8) of the definition of ABS informational and computational materials in Item 1101 of Regulation AB, unless the issuer is or during the last three years the issuer or any of its predecessors was:

(i) A blank check company as defined in Rule 419(a)(2);

(ii) A shell company, other than a business combination related shell company, as defined in Rule 405; or

(iii) An issuer for an offering of penny stock as defined in Rule 3a51–1 under the Securities Exchange Act of 1934.

(f) *Excluded Issuers.* This rule and Rule 433 are not available if the issuer is an investment company registered under the Investment Company Act of 1940 (15 U.S.C. 80a–1 *et seq.*) or a business development company as defined in section 2(a)(48) of the Investment Company Act of 1940 (15 U.S.C. 80a–2(a)(48)).

(g) *Excluded Offerings.* This rule and Rule 433 are not available if the issuer is registering a business combination transaction as defined in Rule 165(f)(1) or the issuer, other than a well-known seasoned issuer, is registering an offering on Form S–8 (17 CFR 239.16b).

(h) For purposes of this rule and Rule 433, the determination date as to whether an issuer is an ineligible issuer in respect of an offering shall be:

(1) Except as provided in paragraph (h)(2) of this rule, the time of filing of the registration statement covering the offering; or

(2) If the offering is being registered pursuant to Rule 415, the earliest time after the filing of the registration statement covering the offering at which the issuer, or in the case of an underwritten offering the issuer or another offering participant, makes a *bona fide* offer, including without limitation through the use of a free writing prospectus, in the offering.

Rule 165. Offers made in connection with a business combination transaction

PRELIMINARY NOTE

This rule is available only to communications relating to business combinations. The exemption does not apply to communications that may be in technical compliance with this rule, but have the primary purpose or effect of conditioning the market for another transaction, such as a capital-raising or resale transaction.

(a) *Communications Before a Registration Statement Is Filed.* Notwithstanding section 5(c) of the Act (15 U.S.C. 77e(c)), the offeror of securities in a business combination transaction to be registered under the Act may make an offer to sell or solicit an offer to buy those securities from and including the first public announcement until the filing of a registration statement related to the transaction, so long as any written communication (other than non-public communications among participants) made in connection with or relating to the transaction (*i.e.*, prospectus) is filed in accordance with Rule 425 and the conditions in paragraph (c) of this rule are satisfied.

(b) *Communications After a Registration Statement Is Filed.* Notwithstanding section 5(b)(1) of the Act (15 U.S.C. 77e(b)(1)), any written communication (other than non–public communications among participants) made in connection with or relating to a business combination transaction (*i.e.*, prospectus) after the filing of a registration statement related to the transaction need not satisfy the requirements of section 10 (15 U.S.C. 77j) of the Act, so long as the prospectus is filed in accordance with Rule 424 or Rule 425 and the conditions in paragraph (c) of this rule are satisfied.

(c) *Conditions.* To rely on paragraphs (a) and (b) of this rule:

(1) Each prospectus must contain a prominent legend that urges investors to read the relevant documents filed or to be filed with the Commission because they contain important information. The legend also must explain to investors that they can get the documents for free at the Commission's web site and describe which documents are available free from the offeror; and

(2) In an exchange offer, the offer must be made in accordance with the applicable tender offer rules (Rules 14d–1 through 14e–8 under the Securities Exchange Act of 1934); and, in a transaction involving the vote of security holders, the offer must be made in accordance with the applicable proxy or information statement rules (Rules 14a–1 through 14a–101 and Rules 14c–1 through 14c–101 under the Securities Exchange Act of 1934).

(d) *Applicability.* This rule is applicable not only to the offeror of securities in a business combination transaction, but also to any other participant that may need to rely on and complies with this section in communicating about the transaction.

(e) *Failure to File or Delay in Filing.* An immaterial or unintentional failure to file or delay in filing a prospectus described in this rule will not result in a violation of section 5(b)(1) or (c) of the Act (15 U.S.C. 77e(b)(1) and (c)), so long as:

(1) A good faith and reasonable effort was made to comply with the filing requirement; and

(2) The prospectus is filed as soon as practicable after discovery of the failure to file.

(f) *Definitions.* (1) A *business combination transaction* means any transaction specified in Rule 145(a) or exchange offer;

(2) A *participant* is any person or entity that is a party to the business combination transaction and any persons authorized to act on their behalf; and

(3) *Public announcement* is any oral or written communication by a participant that is reasonably designed to, or has the effect of, informing the public or security holders in general about the business combination transaction.

Rule 166. Exemption from Section 5(c) for certain communications in connection with business combination transactions

PRELIMINARY NOTE

This rule is available only to communications relating to business combinations. The exemption does not apply to communications that may be in technical compliance with this rule, but have the primary purpose or effect of conditioning the market for another transaction, such as a capital-raising or resale transaction.

(a) *Communications.* In a registered offering involving a business combination transaction, any communication made in connection with or relating to the transaction before the first public announcement of the offering will not constitute an offer to sell or a solicitation of an offer to buy the securities offered for purposes of section 5(c) of the Act (15 U.S.C. 77e(c)), so long as the participants take all reasonable steps within their control to prevent further distribution or publication of the communication until either the first public announcement is made or the registration statement related to the transaction is filed.

(b) *Definitions.* The terms business combination transaction, participant and public announcement have the same meaning as set forth in Rule 165(f).

Rule 167. Communications in connection with certain registered offerings of asset–backed securities

Preliminary Note

This rule is available only to communications in connection with certain offerings of asset-backed securities. The exemption does not apply to communications that may be in technical compliance with this rule, but have the primary purpose or effect of conditioning the market for another transaction or are part of a plan or scheme to evade the requirements of section 5 of the Act (15 U.S.C. 77e).

(a) In an offering of asset-backed securities registered on Form SF–3 (17 CFR 239.45), *ABS informational and computational material* regarding such securities used after the effective date of the registration statement and before the sending or giving to investors of a final prospectus that meets the requirements of section 10(a) of the Act (15 U.S.C. 77j(a)) regarding such offering is exempt from section 5(b)(1) of the Act (15 U.S.C. 77e(b)(1)), if the conditions in paragraph (b) of this rule are met.

(b) *Conditions.* To rely on paragraph (a) of this rule:

(1) The communications shall be filed to the extent required pursuant to Rule 426.

(2) Every communication used pursuant to this rule shall include prominently on the cover page or otherwise at the beginning of such communication:

(i) The issuing entity's name and the depositor's name, if applicable;

(ii) The Commission file number for the related registration statement;

(iii) A statement that such communication is *ABS informational and computational material* used in reliance on Securities Act Rule 167; and

(iv) A legend that urges investors to read the relevant documents filed or to be filed with the Commission because they contain important information. The legend also shall explain to investors that they can get the documents for free at the Commission's Web site and describe which documents are available free from the issuer or an underwriter.

(c) This rule is applicable not only to the offeror of the asset-backed securities, but also to any other participant that may need to rely on and complies with this rule in communicating about the transaction. A participant for purposes of this rule is any person or entity that is a party to the asset-backed securities transaction and any persons authorized to act on their behalf.

(d) Failure by a particular underwriter to cause the filing of a prospectus described in this rule will not affect the ability of any other underwriter who has complied with the procedures to rely on the exemption.

(e) An immaterial or unintentional failure to file or delay in filing a prospectus described in this rule will not result in a violation of section 5(b)(1) of the Act (15 U.S.C. 77e(b)(1)), so long as:

(1) A good faith and reasonable effort was made to comply with the filing requirement; and

(2) The prospectus is filed as soon as practicable after discovery of the failure to file.

(f) Terms used in this rule have the same meaning as in Item 1101 of Regulation AB.

Rule 168. Exemption from Sections 2(a)(10) and 5(c) of the Act for certain communications of regularly released factual business information and forward–looking information

Preliminary Notes to Rule 168

1. This rule is not available for any communication that, although in technical compliance with this rule, is part of a plan or scheme to evade the requirements of section 5 of the Act.

2. This rule provides a non-exclusive safe harbor for factual business information and forward-looking information released or disseminated as provided in this rule. Attempted compliance with this rule does not act as an exclusive election and the issuer also may claim the availability of any other applicable exemption or exclusion. Reliance on this rule does not affect the availability of any other exemption or exclusion from the definition of prospectus in section 2(a)(10) or the requirements of section 5 of the Act.

3. The availability of this rule for a release or dissemination of a communication that contains or incorporates factual business information or forward-looking information will not be affected by another release or dissemination of a communication that contains all or a portion of the same factual business information or forward-looking information that does not satisfy the conditions of this rule.

(a) For purposes of sections 2(a)(10) and 5(c) of the Act, the regular release or dissemination by or on behalf of an issuer (and, in the case of an asset-backed issuer, the other persons specified in paragraph (a)(3) of this rule) of communications containing factual business information or forward-looking information shall be deemed not to constitute an offer to sell or offer for sale of a security which is the subject of an offering pursuant to a registration statement that the issuer proposes to file, or has filed, or that is effective, if the conditions of this rule are satisfied by any of the following:

(1) An issuer that is required to file reports pursuant to section 13 or section 15(d) of the Securities Exchange Act of 1934 (15 U.S.C. 78m or 78o(d));

(2) A foreign private issuer that:

(i) Meets all of the registrant requirements of Form F–3 (17 CFR 239.33) other than the reporting history provisions of General Instructions I.A.1. and I.A.2.(a) of Form F–3;

(ii) Either:

(A) Satisfies the public float threshold in General Instruction I.B.1. of Form F–3; or

(B) Is issuing non-convertible securities, other than common equity, and meets the provisions of General Instruction I.B.2. of Form F–3 (referenced in 17 CFR 239.33); and

(iii) Either:

(A) Has its equity securities trading on a designated offshore securities market as defined in Rule 902(b) and has had them so traded for at least 12 months; or

(B) Has a worldwide market value of its outstanding common equity held by non-affiliates of $700 million or more; or

(3) An asset-backed issuer or a depositor, sponsor, or servicer (as such terms are defined in Item 1101 of Regulation AB or an affiliated depositor, whether or not such other person is the issuer).

(b) *Definitions.* (1) *Factual business information* means some or all of the following information that is released or disseminated under the conditions in paragraph (d) of this rule, including, without limitation, such factual business information contained in reports or other materials filed with, furnished to, or submitted to the Commission pursuant to the Securities Exchange Act of 1934 (15 U.S.C. 78a *et seq.*):

(i) Factual information about the issuer, its business or financial developments, or other aspects of its business;

(ii) Advertisements of, or other information about, the issuer's products or services; and

(iii) Dividend notices.

(2) *Forward-looking information* means some or all of the following information that is released or disseminated under the conditions in paragraph (d) of this rule, including, without limitation, such forward-looking information contained in reports or other materials filed with, furnished to, or submitted to the Commission pursuant to the Securities Exchange Act of 1934:

(i) Projections of the issuer's revenues, income (loss), earnings (loss) per share, capital expenditures, dividends, capital structure, or other financial items;

(ii) Statements about the issuer management's plans and objectives for future operations, including plans or objectives relating to the products or services of the issuer;

(iii) Statements about the issuer's future economic performance, including statements of the type contemplated by the management's discussion and analysis of financial condition and results of operation described in Item 303 of Regulations S–B and S–K or the operating and financial review and prospects described in Item 5 of Form 20–F (17 CFR 249.220f); and

(iv) Assumptions underlying or relating to any of the information described in paragraphs (b)(2)(i), (b)(2)(ii) and (b)(2)(iii) of this rule.

(3) For purposes of this rule, the release or dissemination of a communication is by or on behalf of the issuer if the issuer or an agent or representative of the issuer, other than an offering participant who is an underwriter or dealer, authorizes or approves such release or dissemination before it is made.

(4) For purposes of this rule, in the case of communications of a person specified in paragraph (a)(3) of this rule other than the asset-backed issuer, the release or dissemination of a communication is by or on behalf of such other person if such other person or its agent or representative, other than

an underwriter or dealer, authorizes or approves such release or dissemination before it is made.

(c) *Exclusion.* A communication containing information about the registered offering or released or disseminated as part of the offering activities in the registered offering is excluded from the exemption of this rule.

(d) *Conditions to Exemption.* The following conditions must be satisfied:

(1) The issuer (or in the case of an asset-backed issuer, the issuer and the other persons specified in paragraph (a)(3) of this rule, taken together) has previously released or disseminated information of the type described in this rule in the ordinary course of its business;

(2) The timing, manner, and form in which the information is released or disseminated is consistent in material respects with similar past releases or disseminations; and

(3) The issuer is not an investment company registered under the Investment Company Act of 1940 (15 U.S.C. 80a–1 *et seq.*) or a business development company as defined in section 2(a)(48) of the Investment Company Act of 1940 (15 U.S.C. 80a–2(a)(48)).

Rule 169. Exemption from Sections 2(a)(10) and 5(c) of the Act for certain communications of regularly released factual business information

Preliminary Notes to Rule 169

1. This rule is not available for any communication that, although in technical compliance with this rule, is part of a plan or scheme to evade the requirements of section 5 of the Act.

2. This rule provides a non-exclusive safe harbor for factual business information released or disseminated as provided in this rule. Attempted compliance with this rule does not act as an exclusive election and the issuer also may claim the availability of any other applicable exemption or exclusion. Reliance on this rule does not affect the availability of any other exemption or exclusion from the definition of prospectus in section 2(a)(10) or the requirements of section 5 of the Act.

3. The availability of this rule for a release or dissemination of a communication that contains or incorporates factual business information will not be affected by another release or dissemination of a communication that contains all or a portion of the same factual business information that does not satisfy the conditions of this rule.

(a) For purposes of sections 2(a)(10) and 5(c) of the Act, the regular release or dissemination by or on behalf of an issuer of communications containing factual business information shall be deemed not to constitute an offer to sell or offer for sale of a security by an issuer which is the subject of an offering pursuant to a registration statement that the issuer proposes to file, or has filed, or that is effective, if the conditions of this rule are satisfied.

(b) *Definitions.* (1) *Factual business information* means some or all of the following information that is released or disseminated under the conditions in paragraph (d) of this rule:

(i) Factual information about the issuer, its business or financial developments, or other aspects of its business; and

(ii) Advertisements of, or other information about, the issuer's products or services.

(2) For purposes of this rule, the release or dissemination of a communication is by or on behalf of the issuer if the issuer or an agent or representative of the issuer, other than an offering participant who is an underwriter or dealer, authorizes or approves such release or dissemination before it is made.

(c) *Exclusions.* A communication containing information about the registered offering or released or disseminated as part of the offering activities in the registered offering is excluded from the exemption of this rule.

(d) *Conditions to Exemption.* The following conditions must be satisfied:

(1) The issuer has previously released or disseminated information of the type described in this rule in the ordinary course of its business;

(2) The timing, manner, and form in which the information is released or disseminated is consistent in material respects with similar past releases or disseminations;

(3) The information is released or disseminated for intended use by persons, such as customers and suppliers, other than in their capacities as investors or potential investors in the issuer's securities, by the issuer's employees or agents who historically have provided such information; and

(4) The issuer is not an investment company registered under the Investment Company Act of 1940 (15 U.S.C. 80a–1 *et seq.*) or a business development company as defined in section 2(a)(48) of the Investment Company Act of 1940 (15 U.S.C. 80a–2(a)(48)).

Rule 170. Prohibition of use of certain financial statements

Financial statements which purport to give effect to the receipt and application of any part of the proceeds from the sale of securities for cash shall not be used unless such securities are to be offered through underwriters and the underwriting arrangements are such that the underwriters are or will be committed to take and pay for all of the securities, if any are taken, prior to or within a reasonable time after the commencement of the public offering, or if the securities are not so taken to refund to all subscribers the full amount of all subscription payments made for the securities. The caption of any such financial statement shall clearly set forth the assumptions upon which such statement is based. The caption shall be in type at least as large as that used generally in the body of the statement.

Rule 171. Disclosure detrimental to the national defense or foreign policy

(a) Any requirement to the contrary notwithstanding, no registration statement, prospectus, or other document filed with the Commission or used in connection with the offering or sale of any securities shall contain any document or information which, pursuant to Executive order, has been classified by an appropriate department or agency of the United States for protection in the interests of national defense or foreign policy.

(b) Where a document or information is omitted pursuant to paragraph (a) of this rule, there shall be filed, in lieu of such document or information, a statement from an appropriate department or agency of the United States to the effect that such document or information has been classified or that the status thereof is awaiting determination. Where a document is omitted pursuant to paragraph (a) of this rule, but information relating to the subject matter of such document is nevertheless included in material filed with the Commission pursuant to a determination of an appropriate department or agency of the United States that disclosure of such information would not be contrary to the interests of national defense or foreign policy, a statement from such department or agency to that effect shall be submitted for the information of the Commission. A registrant may rely upon any such statement in filing or omitting any document or information to which the statement relates.

(c) The Commission may protect any information in its possession which may require classification in the interests of national defense or foreign policy pending determination by an appropriate department or agency as to whether such information should be classified.

(d) It shall be the duty of the registrant to submit the documents or information referred to in paragraph (a) of this rule to the appropriate department or agency of the United States prior to filing them with the Commission and to obtain and submit to the Commission, at the time of filing such documents or information, or in lieu thereof, as the case may be, the statements from such department or agency required by paragraph (b) of this rule. All such statements shall be in writing.

Rule 172. Delivery of prospectuses

(a) *Sending Confirmations and Notices of Allocations.* After the effective date of a registration statement, the following are exempt from the provisions of section 5(b)(1) of the Act if the conditions set forth in paragraph (c) of this rule are satisfied:

(1) Written confirmations of sales of securities in an offering pursuant to a registration statement that contain information limited to that called for in Rule 10b–10 under the Securities Exchange Act of 1934 and other information customarily included in written confirmations of sales of securities, which may include notices provided pursuant to Rule 173; and

(2) Notices of allocation of securities sold or to be sold in an offering pursuant to the registration statement that may include information identifying the securities (including the CUSIP number) and otherwise may include only information regarding pricing, allocation and settlement, and information incidental thereto.

(b) *Transfer of the Security.* Any obligation under section 5(b)(2) of the Act to have a prospectus that satisfies the requirements of section 10(a) of the Act precede or accompany the carrying or delivery of a security in a registered offering is satisfied if the conditions in paragraph (c) of this rule are met.

(c) *Conditions.*

(1) The registration statement relating to the offering is effective and is not the subject of any pending proceeding or examination under section 8(d) or 8(e) of the Act;

(2) Neither the issuer, nor an underwriter or participating dealer is the subject of a pending proceeding under section 8A of the Act in connection with the offering; and

(3) The issuer has filed with the Commission a prospectus with respect to the offering that satisfies the requirements of section 10(a) of the Act or the issuer will make a good faith and reasonable effort to file such a prospectus within the time required under Rule 424 and, in the event that the issuer

fails to file timely such a prospectus, the issuer files the prospectus as soon as practicable thereafter.

(4) The condition in paragraph (c)(3) of this rule shall not apply to transactions by dealers requiring delivery of a final prospectus pursuant to section 4(3) of the Act.

(d) *Exclusions.* This rule shall not apply to any:

(1) Offering of any investment company registered under the Investment Company Act of 1940 (15 U.S.C. 80a–1 *et seq.*);

(2) Offering of any business development company as defined in section 2(a)(48) of the Investment Company Act of 1940 (15 U.S.C. 80a–2(a)(48));

(3) A business combination transaction as defined in Rule 165(f)(1); or

(4) Offering registered on Form S–8 (17 CFR 239.16b).

Rule 173. Notice of registration

(a) In a transaction that represents a sale by the issuer or an underwriter, or a sale where there is not an exclusion or exemption from the requirement to deliver a final prospectus meeting the requirements of section 10(a) of the Act pursuant to section 4(a)(3) of the Act or Rule 174, each underwriter or dealer selling in such transaction shall provide to each purchaser from it, not later than two business days following the completion of such sale, a copy of the final prospectus or, in lieu of such prospectus, a notice to the effect that the sale was made pursuant to a registration statement or in a transaction in which a final prospectus would have been required to have been delivered in the absence of Rule 172.

(b) If the sale was by the issuer and was not effected by or through an underwriter or dealer, the responsibility to send a prospectus, or in lieu of such prospectus, such notice as set forth in paragraph (a) of this rule, shall be the issuer's.

(c) Compliance with the requirements of this rule is not a condition to reliance on Rule 172.

(d) A purchaser may request from the person responsible for sending a notice a copy of the final prospectus if one has not been sent.

(e) After the effective date of the registration statement with respect to an offering, notices as set forth in paragraph (a) of this rule, are exempt from the provisions of section 5(b)(1) of the Act.

(f) *Exclusions.* This rule shall not apply to any:

(1) Transaction solely between brokers or dealers in reliance on Rule 153;

(2) Offering of any investment company registered under the Investment Company Act of 1940 (15 U.S.C. 80a–1 *et seq.*);

(3) Offering of any business development company as defined in section 2(a)(48) of the Investment Company Act of 1940 (15 U.S.C. 80a–2(a)(48));

(4) A business combination transaction as defined in Rule 165(f)(1); or

(5) Offering registered on Form S–8 (17 CFR 239.16b).

Rule 174. Delivery of prospectus by dealers; exemptions under Section 4(a)(3) of the Act

The obligations of a dealer (including an underwriter no longer acting as an underwriter in respect of the security involved in such transactions) to deliver a prospectus in transactions in a security as to which a registration statement has been filed taking place prior to the expiration of the 40– or 90–day period specified in section 4(a)(3) of the Act after the effective date of such registration statement or prior to the expiration of such period after the first date upon which the security was bona fide offered to the public by the issuer or by or through an underwriter after such effective date, whichever is later, shall be subject to the following provisions:

(a) No prospectus need be delivered if the registration statement is on Form F–6 (17 CFR 239.36).

(b) No prospectus need be delivered if the issuer is subject, immediately prior to the time of filing the registration statement, to the reporting requirements of Section 13 or 15(d) of the Securities Exchange Act of 1934.

(c) Where a registration statement relates to offerings to be made from time to time no prospectus need be delivered after the expiration of the initial prospectus delivery period specified in section 4(a)(3) of the Act following the first bona fide offering of securities under such registration statement.

(d) If (1) the registration statement relates to the security of an issuer that is not subject, immediately prior to the time of filing the registration statement, to the reporting requirements of Section 13 or 15(d) of the Securities Exchange Act of 1934, and (2) as of the offering date, the security is listed on a registered national securities exchange or authorized for inclusion in an electronic inter-dealer quotation system sponsored and governed by the rules of a registered securities association, no prospectus need be delivered after the expiration of twenty-five calendar days after the offering date. For purposes of this provision, the term *offering date* refers to the later of the effective date of the registration statement or the first date on which the security was bona fide offered to the public.

(e) Notwithstanding the foregoing, the period during which a prospectus must be delivered by a dealer shall be:

(1) As specified in section 4(a)(3) of the Act if the registration statement was the subject of a stop order issued under section 8 of the Act; or

(2) As the Commission may provide upon application or on its own motion in a particular case.

(f) Nothing in this rule shall affect the obligation to deliver a prospectus pursuant to the provisions of section 5 of the Act by a dealer who is acting as an underwriter with respect to the securities involved or who is engaged in a transaction as to securities constituting the whole or part of an unsold allotment to or subscription by such dealer as a participant in the distribution of such securities by the issuer or by or through an underwriter.

(g) If the registration statement relates to an offering of securities of a "blank check company," as defined in Rule 419 under the Act the statutory period for prospectus delivery specified in section 4(a)(3) of the Act shall not terminate until 90 days after the date funds and securities are released from the escrow or trust account pursuant to Rule 419 under the Act.

(h) Any obligation pursuant to Section 4(a)(3) of the Act and this rule to deliver a prospectus, other than pursuant to paragraph (g) of this rule, may be satisfied by compliance with the provisions of Rule 172.

Rule 175. Liability for certain statements by issuers

(a) A statement within the coverage of paragraph (b) of this rule which is made by or on behalf of an issuer or by an outside reviewer retained by the issuer shall be deemed not to be a fraudulent statement (as defined in paragraph (d) of this rule), unless it is shown that such statement was made or reaffirmed without a reasonable basis or was disclosed other than in good faith.

(b) This rule applies to the following statements:

(1) A forward-looking statement (as defined in paragraph (c) of this rule) made in a document filed with the Commission, in Part I of a quarterly report on Form 10–Q (17 CFR 249.308a), or in an annual report to securityholders meeting the requirements of Rules 14a–3(b) and (c) or 14c–3(a) and (b) under the Securities Exchange Act of 1934, a statement reaffirming such forward-looking statement after the date the document was filed or the annual report was made publicly available, or a forward-looking statement made before the date the document was filed or the date the annual report was publicly available if such statement is reaffirmed in a filed document, in Part I of a quarterly report on Form 10–Q, or in an annual report made publicly available within a reasonable time after the making of such forward-looking statement; *Provided,* That

(i) At the time such statements are made or reaffirmed, either the issuer is subject to the reporting requirements of section 13(a) or 15(d) of the Securities Exchange Act of 1934 and has complied with the requirements of Rule 13a–1 or 15d–1 under the Securities Exchange Act of 1934 thereunder, if applicable, to file its most recent annual report on Form 10–K, Form 20–F, or Form 40–F; or if the issuer is not subject to the reporting requirements of section 13(a) or 15(d) of the Securities Exchange Act of 1934, the statements are made in a registration statement filed under the Act, offering statement or solicitation of interest written document or broadcast script under Regulation A or pursuant to section 12(b) or (g) of the Securities Exchange Act of 1934; and

(ii) The statements are not made by or on behalf of an issuer that is an investment company registered under the Investment Company Act of 1940; and

(2) Information that is disclosed in a document filed with the Commission, in Part I of a quarterly report on Form 10–Q (17 CFR 249.308a) or in an annual report to shareholders meeting the requirements of Rules 14a–3 (b) and (c) or 14c–3 (a) and (b) under the Securities Exchange Act of 1934 and that relates to:

(i) The effects of changing prices on the business enterprise, presented voluntarily or pursuant to Item 303 of Regulation S–K, "Management's Discussion and Analysis of Financial Condition and Results of Operations," Item 5 of Form 20–F (17 CFR 249.220(f)), "Operating and Financial Review and Prospects," Item 302 of Regulation S–K, "Supplementary Financial Information," or Rule 3–20(c) of Regulation S–X; or

(ii) The value of proved oil and gas reserves (such as a standardized measure of discounted future net cash flows relating to proved oil and gas reserves as set forth in FASB ASC paragraphs 932–235–50–29 through 932–235–50–36 (Extractive Activities—Oil and Gas Topic)) presented voluntarily or pursuant to Item 302 of Regulation S–K.

(c) For the purpose of this rule the term "forward-looking statement" shall mean and shall be limited to:

(1) A statement containing a projection of revenues, income (loss), earnings (loss) per share, capital expenditures, dividends, capital structure or other financial items;

(2) A statement of management's plans and objectives for future operations;

(3) A statement of future economic performance contained in management's discussion and analysis of financial condition and results of operations included pursuant to Item 303 of Regulation S–K or Item 9 of Form 20–F; or

(4) Disclosed statements of the assumptions underlying or relating to any of the statements described in paragraphs (c)(1), (2) or (3) of this rule.

(d) For the purpose of this rule the term *fraudulent statement* shall mean a statement which is an untrue statement of a material fact, a statement false or misleading with respect to any material fact, an omission to state a material fact necessary to make a statement not misleading, or which constitutes the employment of a manipulative, deceptive, or fraudulent device, contrivance, scheme, transaction, act, practice, course of business, or an artifice to defraud, as those terms are used in the Securities Act of 1933 or the rules or regulations promulgated thereunder.

Rule 176. Circumstances affecting the determination of what constitutes reasonable investigation and reasonable grounds for belief under Section 11 of the Securities Act

In determining whether or not the conduct of a person constitutes a reasonable investigation or a reasonable ground for belief meeting the standard set forth in section 11(c), relevant circumstances include, with respect to a person other than the issuer:

(a) The type of issuer;

(b) The type of security;

(c) The type of person;

(d) The office held when the person is an officer;

(e) The presence or absence of another relationship to the issuer when the person is a director or proposed director;

(f) Reasonable reliance on officers, employees, and others whose duties should have given them knowledge of the particular facts (in the light of the functions and responsibilities of the particular person with respect to the issuer and the filing);

(g) When the person is an underwriter, the type of underwriting arrangement, the role of the particular person as an underwriter and the availability of information with respect to the registrant; and

(h) Whether, with respect to a fact or document incorporated by reference, the particular person had any responsibility for the fact or document at the time of the filing from which it was incorporated.

Rule 180. Exemption from registration of interests and participations issued in connection with certain H.R. 10 plans

(a) Any interest or participation in a single trust fund or in a collective trust fund maintained by a bank, or any security arising out of a contract issued by an insurance company, issued to an employee benefit plan shall be exempt from the provisions of section 5 of the Act if the following terms and conditions are met:

(1) The plan covers employees, some or all of whom are employees within the meaning of section 401(c)(1) of the Internal Revenue Code of 1954, and is either: (i) a pension or profit-sharing plan which meets the requirements for qualification under section 401 of such Code, or (ii) an annuity plan which meets the requirements for the deduction of the employer's contribution under section 404(a)(2) of such Code;

(2) The plan covers only employees of a single employer or employees of interrelated partnerships; and

(3) The issuer of such interest, participation or security shall have reasonable grounds to believe and, after making reasonable inquiry, shall believe immediately prior to any issuance that:

(i) The employer is a law firm, accounting firm, investment banking firm, pension consulting firm or investment advisory firm that is engaged in furnishing services of a type that involve such knowledge and experience in financial and business matters that the employer is able to represent adequately its interests and those of its employees; or

(ii) In connection with the plan, the employer prior to adopting the plan obtains the advice of a person or entity that (A) is not a financial institution providing any funding vehicle for the plan, and is neither an affiliated person as defined in section 2(a)(3) of the Investment Company Act of 1940 of, nor a person who has a material business relationship with, a financial institution providing a funding vehicle for the plan; and (B) is, by virtue of knowledge and experience in financial and business matters, able to represent adequately the interests of the employer and its employees.

(b) Any interest or participation issued to a participant in either a pension or profit-sharing plan which meets the requirements for qualification under section 401 of the Internal Revenue Code of 1954 or an annuity plan which meets the requirements for the deduction of the employer's contribution under section 404(a)(2) of such Code, and which covers employees, some or all of whom are employees within the meaning of section 401(c)(1) of such Code, shall be exempt from the provisions of section 5 of the Act.

Rule 190. Registration of underlying securities in asset–backed securities transactions

(a) In an offering of asset-backed securities where the asset pool includes securities of another issuer ("underlying securities"), unless the underlying securities are themselves exempt from registration under section 3 of the Act (15 U.S.C. 77c), the offering of the relevant underlying securities itself must be registered as a primary offering of such securities in accordance with paragraph (b) of this rule unless all of the following are true. Terms used in this rule have the same meaning as in Item 1101 of Regulation AB.

(1) Neither the issuer of the underlying securities nor any of its affiliates has a direct or indirect agreement, arrangement, relationship or understanding, written or otherwise, relating to the underlying securities and the asset-backed securities transaction;

(2) Neither the issuer of the underlying securities nor any of its affiliates is an affiliate of the sponsor, depositor, issuing entity or underwriter of the asset-backed securities transaction;

(3) If the underlying securities are restricted securities, as defined in Rule 144 (a)(3), Rule 144 must be available for the sale of the securities, provided however, that notwithstanding any other provision of Rule 144, Rule 144 shall only be so available if at least two years have elapsed since the later of the date the securities were acquired from the issuer of the underlying securities or from an affiliate of the issuer of the underlying securities; and

(4) The depositor would be free to publicly resell the underlying securities without registration under the Act. For example, the offering of the asset-backed security does not constitute part of a distribution of the underlying securities. An offering of asset-backed securities with an asset pool containing underlying securities that at the time of the purchase for the asset pool are part of a subscription or unsold allotment would be a distribution of the underlying securities. For purposes of this rule, in an offering of asset-backed securities involving a sponsor, depositor or underwriter that was an underwriter or an affiliate of an underwriter in a registered offering of the underlying securities, the distribution of the asset-backed securities will not constitute part of a distribution of the underlying securities if the underlying securities were purchased at arm's length in the secondary market at least three months after the last sale of any unsold allotment or subscription by the affiliated underwriter that participated in the registered offering of the underlying securities.

(b) If all of the conditions in paragraph (a) of this rule are not met, the offering of the relevant underlying securities itself must be registered as a primary offering of such securities in accordance with the following:

(1) If the offering of asset-backed securities is registered on Form SF–3 (17 CFR 239.45), the offering of the underlying securities itself must be eligible to be registered under Form SF–3, Form S–3 (17 CFR 239.13), or F–3 (17 CFR 239.33) as a primary offering of such securities;

(2) The plan of distribution in the registration statement for the offering of the underlying securities contemplates this type of distribution at the time of the commencement of the offering of the asset-backed securities;

(3) The prospectus for the asset-backed securities offering describes the plan of distribution for both the underlying securities and the asset-backed securities;

(4) The prospectus relating to the offering of the underlying securities is delivered simultaneously with the delivery of the prospectus relating to the offering of the asset-backed securities, and the prospectus for the asset-backed securities includes disclosure that the prospectus for the offer-

ing of the underlying securities will be delivered along with, or is combined with, the prospectus for the offering of the asset-backed securities;

(5) The prospectus for the asset-backed securities offering identifies the issuing entity, depositor, sponsor and each underwriter for the offering of the asset-backed securities as an underwriter for the offering of the underlying securities; and

(6) Neither prospectus disclaims or limits responsibility by the issuing entity, sponsor, depositor, trustee or any underwriter for information regarding the underlying securities.

(c) Notwithstanding paragraphs (a) and (b) of this rule, if the asset pool for the asset-backed securities includes a pool asset representing an interest in or the right to the payments or cash flows of another asset pool, then that pool asset is not considered an "underlying security" for purposes of this rule (although its distribution in connection with the asset-backed securities transaction may need to be separately registered) if the following conditions are met:

(1) Both the issuing entity for the asset-backed securities and the entity issuing the pool asset were established under the direction of the same sponsor and depositor;

(2) The pool asset is created solely to satisfy legal requirements or otherwise facilitate the structuring of the asset-backed securities transaction;

(3) The pool asset is not part of a scheme to avoid registration or the requirements of this rule; and

(4) The pool asset is held by the issuing entity and is a part of the asset pool for the asset-backed securities.

(d) Notwithstanding paragraph (c) of this section (that is, although the pool asset described in paragraph (c) of this section is an not an "underlying security" for purposes of this section), if the pool assets for the asset-backed securities are collateral certificates or special units of beneficial interest, those collateral certificates or special units of beneficial interest must be registered concurrently with the registration of the asset-backed securities. However, pursuant to Rule 457(t) no separate registration fee for the certificates or special units of beneficial interest is required to be paid.

Rule 191. Definition of "issuer" in Section 2(a)(4) of the Act in relation to asset-backed securities

The following applies with respect to asset-backed securities under the Act. Terms used in this rule have the same meaning as in Item 1101 of Regulation AB.

(a) The depositor for the asset-backed securities acting solely in its capacity as depositor to the issuing entity is the "issuer" for purposes of the asset-backed securities of that issuing entity.

(b) The person acting in the capacity as the depositor specified in paragraph (a) of this section is a different "issuer" from that same person acting as a depositor for another issuing entity or for purposes of that person's own securities.

Rule 193. Review of underlying assets in asset-backed securities transactions

An issuer of an "asset-backed security," as that term is defined in Section 3(a)(79) of the Securities Exchange Act of 1934 (15 U.S.C. 78c(a)(79)), offering and selling such a security pursuant to a registration statement shall perform a review of the pool assets underlying the asset-backed security. At a minimum, such review must be designed and effected to provide reasonable assurance that the disclosure regarding the pool assets in the form of prospectus filed pursuant to Rule 424 is accurate in all material respects. The issuer may conduct the review or an issuer may employ a third party engaged for purposes of performing the review. If the findings and conclusions of the review are attributed to the third party, the third party must be named in the registration statement and consent to being named as an expert in accordance with Rule 436.

Instruction to Rule 193: An issuer of an "asset-backed security" may rely on one or more third parties to fulfill its obligation to perform a review under this section, provided that the reviews performed by the third parties and the issuer, in the aggregate, comply with the minimum standard in this section. The issuer must comply with the requirements of this section for each third party engaged by the issuer to perform the review for purposes of this section. An issuer may not rely on a review performed by an unaffiliated originator for purposes of performing the review required under this section.

Rule 194. Definition of the terms "swap" and "security-based swap" as used in the Act

(a) The term *swap* as used in section 2(a)(17) of the Act has the same meaning as provided in section 3(a)(69) of the Securities Exchange Act of 1934 and the rules and regulations thereunder.

(b) The term *security-based swap* as used in section 2(a)(17) of the Act has the same meaning as provided in section 3(a)(68) of the Securities Exchange Act of 1934 and the rules and regulations thereunder.

Rule 215. Accredited investor

The term *accredited investor* as used in section 2(15)(ii) of the Securities Act of 1933 (15 U.S.C. 77b(15)(ii)) shall include the following persons:

(a) Any savings and loan association or other institution specified in section 3(a)(5)(A) of the Act whether acting in its individual or fiduciary capacity; any broker or dealer registered pursuant to section 15 of the Securities Exchange Act of 1934; any plan established and maintained by a state, its political subdivisions, or any agency or instrumentality of a state or its political subdivisions, for the benefit of its employees, if such plan has total assets in excess of $5,000,000; any employee benefit plan within the meaning of Title I of the Employee Retirement Income Security Act of 1974, if the investment decision is made by a plan fiduciary, as defined in section 3(21) of such Act, which is a savings and loan association, or if the employee benefit plan has total assets in excess of $5,000,000 or, if a self-directed plan, with investment decisions made solely by persons that are accredited investors;

(b) Any private business development company as defined in section 202(a)(22) of the Investment Advisers Act of 1940;

(c) Any organization described in section 501(c)(3) of the Internal Revenue Code, corporation, Massachusetts or similar business trust, or partnership, not formed for the specific purpose of acquiring the securities offered, with total assets in excess of $5,000,000;

(d) Any director, executive officer, or general partner of the issuer of the securities being offered or sold, or any director, executive officer, or general partner of a general partner of that issuer;

(e) Any natural person whose individual net worth, or joint net worth with that person's spouse, exceeds $1,000,000.

(1) Except as provided in paragraph (e)(2) of this section, for purposes of calculating net worth under this paragraph (e):

(i) The person's primary residence shall not be included as an asset;

(ii) Indebtedness that is secured by the person's primary residence, up to the estimated fair market value of the primary residence at the time of the sale of securities, shall not be included as a liability (except that if the amount of such indebtedness outstanding at the time of the sale of securities exceeds the amount outstanding 60 days before such time, other than as a result of the acquisition of the primary residence, the amount of such excess shall be included as a liability); and

(iii) Indebtedness that is secured by the person's primary residence in excess of the estimated fair market value of the primary residence shall be included as a liability.

(2) Paragraph (1) of this section will not apply to any calculation of a person's net worth made in connection with a purchase of securities in accordance with a right to purchase such securities, provided that:

(i) Such right was held by the person on July 20, 2010;

(ii) The person qualified as an accredited investor on the basis of net worth at the time the person acquired such right; and

(iii) The person held securities of the same issuer, other than such right, on July 20, 2010.

(f) Any natural person who had an individual income in excess of $200,000 in each of the two most recent years or joint income with that person's spouse in excess of $300,000 in each of those years and has a reasonable expectation of reaching the same income level in the current year;

(g) Any trust, with total assets in excess of $5,000,000, not formed for the specific purpose of acquiring the securities offered, whose purchase is directed by a sophisticated person as described in Rule 506(b)(2)(ii); and

(h) Any entity in which all of the equity owners are accredited investors.

SPECIAL EXEMPTIONS

Rule 236. Exemption of shares offered in connection with certain transactions

Shares of stock or similar security offered to provide funds to be distributed to shareholders of the issuer of such securities in lieu of issuing fractional shares, scrip certificates or order forms, in connection with a stock dividend, stock split, reverse stock split, conversion, merger or similar transaction, shall be exempt from registration under the Act if the following conditions are met:

(a) The issuer of such shares is required to file and has filed reports with the Commission pursuant to section 13 or 15(d) of the Securities Exchange Act of 1934.

(b) The aggregate gross proceeds from the sale of all shares offered in connection with the transaction for the purpose of providing such funds does not exceed $300,000.

(c) At least ten days prior to the offering of the shares, the issuer shall furnish to the Commission in writing the following information: (1) That it proposes to offer shares in reliance upon the exemption provided by this rule; (2) the estimated number of shares to be so offered; (3) the aggregate market value of such shares as of the latest practicable date; and (4) a brief description of the transaction in connection with which the shares are to be offered.

Rule 237. Exemption for offers and sales to certain Canadian tax-deferred retirement savings accounts

(a) *Definitions.* As used in this rule:

(1) *Canadian law* means the federal laws of Canada, the laws of any province or territory of Canada, and the rules or regulations of any federal, provincial, or territorial regulatory authority, or any self-regulatory authority, of Canada.

(2) *Canadian Retirement Account* means a trust or other arrangement, including, but not limited to, a "Registered Retirement Savings Plan" or "Registered Retirement Income Fund" administered under Canadian law, that is managed by the Participant and:

(i) Operated to provide retirement benefits to a Participant; and

(ii) Established in Canada, administered under Canadian law, and qualified for tax-deferred treatment under Canadian law.

(3) *Eligible Security* means a security issued by a Qualified Company that:

(i) Is offered to a Participant, or sold to his or her Canadian Retirement Account, in reliance on this rule; and

(ii) May also be purchased by Canadians other than Participants.

(4) *Foreign Government* means the government of any foreign country or of any political subdivision of a foreign country.

(5) *Foreign Issuer* means any issuer that is a Foreign Government, a national of any foreign country or a corporation or other organization incorporated or organized under the laws of any foreign country, except an issuer meeting the following conditions:

(i) More than 50 percent of the outstanding voting securities of the issuer are held of record either directly or through voting trust certificates or depositary receipts by residents of the United States; and

(ii) Any of the following:

(A) The majority of the executive officers or directors are United States citizens or residents;

(B) More than 50 percent of the assets of the issuer are located in the United States; or

(C) The business of the issuer is administered principally in the United States.

(iii) For purposes of this definition, the term *resident,* as applied to security holders, means any person whose address appears on the records of the issuer, the voting trustee, or the depositary as being located in the United States.

(6) *Participant* means a natural person who is a resident of the United States, or is temporarily present in the United States, and who contributes to, or is or will be entitled to receive the income and assets from, a Canadian Retirement Account.

(7) *Qualified Company* means a Foreign Issuer whose securities are qualified for investment on a tax-deferred basis by a Canadian Retirement Account under Canadian law.

(8) *United States* means the United States of America, its territories and possessions, any State of the United States, and the District of Columbia.

(b) *Exemption.* The offer to a Participant, or the sale to his or her Canadian Retirement Account, of Eligible Securities by any person is exempt from Section 5 of the Act (15 U.S.C. 77e) if the person:

(1) Includes in any written offering materials delivered to a Participant, or to his or her Canadian Retirement Account, a prominent statement that the Eligible Security is not registered with the U.S. Securities and Exchange Commission and the Eligible Security is being offered or sold in the United States under an exemption from registration.

(2) Has not asserted that Canadian law, or the jurisdiction of the courts of Canada, does not apply in a proceeding involving an Eligible Security.

Rule 238. Exemption for standardized options

(a) *Exemption.* Except as expressly provided in paragraphs (b) and (c) of this rule, the Act does not apply to any standardized option, as that term is defined by Rule 9b–1(a)(4) under the Securities Exchange Act of 1934, that is:

(1) Issued by a clearing agency registered under section 17A of the Securities Exchange Act of 1934 (15 U.S.C. 78q–1); and

(2) Traded on a national securities exchange registered pursuant to section 6(a) of the Securities Exchange Act of 1934 (15 U.S.C. 78f(a)) or on a national securities association registered pursuant to section 15A(a) of the Securities Exchange Act of 1934 (15 U.S.C. 78o–3(a)).

(b) *Limitation.* The exemption provided in paragraph (a) of this rule does not apply to the provisions of section 17 of the Act (15 U.S.C. 77q).

(c) *Offers and Sales.* Any offer or sale of a standardized option by or on behalf of the issuer of the securities underlying the standardized option, an affiliate of the issuer, or an underwriter, will constitute a contract for sale of, sale of, offer for sale, or offer to sell the underlying securities as defined in section 2(a)(3) of the Act (15 U.S.C. 77b(a)(3)).

Rule 239. Exemption for offers and sales of certain security–based swaps

(a) Provided that the conditions of paragraph (b) of this section are satisfied and except as expressly provided in paragraph (c) of this section, the Act does not apply to any offer or sale of a security-based swap that:

(1) Is issued or will be issued by a clearing agency that is either registered as a clearing agency under Section 17A of the Securities Exchange Act of 1934 (15 U.S.C. 78q–1) or exempt from registration under Section 17A of the Securities Exchange Act of 1934 pursuant to a rule, regulation, or order of the Commission ("eligible clearing agency"), and

(2) The Commission has determined is required to be cleared or that is permitted to be cleared pursuant to the eligible clearing agency's rules.

(b) The exemption provided in paragraph (a) of this section applies only to an offer or sale of a security-based swap described in paragraph (a) of this section if the following conditions are satisfied:

(1) The security-based swap is offered or sold in a transaction involving the eligible clearing agency in its function as a central counterparty with respect to such security-based swap;

(2) The security-based swap is sold only to an eligible contract participant (as defined in Section 1a(18) of the Commodity Exchange Act (7 U.S.C. 1a(18))); and

(3) The eligible clearing agency posts on its publicly available website at a specified Internet address or includes in its agreement covering the security-based swap that the eligible clearing agency provides or makes available to its counterparty the following:

(i) A statement identifying any security, issuer, loan, or narrow-based security index underlying the security-based swap;

(ii) A statement indicating the security or loan to be delivered (or class of securities or loans), or if cash settled, the security, loan, or narrow-based security index (or class of securities or loans) whose value is to be used to determine the amount of the settlement obligation under the security-based swap; and

(iii) A statement of whether the issuer of any security or loan, each issuer of a security in a narrow-based security index, or each referenced issuer underlying the security-based swap is subject to the reporting requirements of Sections 13 or 15(d) of the Securities Exchange Act of 1934 (15 U.S.C. 78m and 78o) and, if not subject to such reporting requirements, whether public information, including financial information, about any such issuer is available and where the information is available.

(c) The exemption provided in paragraph (a) of this section does not apply to the provisions of Section 17(a) of the Act (15 U.S.C. 77q(a)).

Rule 240. Exemption for certain security–based swaps

(a) Except as expressly provided in paragraph (b) of this section, the Act does not apply to the offer or sale of any security-based swap that is:

(1) A *security-based swap agreement*, as defined in Section 2A of the Act (15 U.S.C. 77b(b)–1) as in effect prior to July 16, 2011; and

(2) Entered into between eligible contract participants (as defined in Section 1a(12) of the Commodity Exchange Act (7 U.S.C. 1a(12)) as in effect prior to July 16, 2011, other than a person who is an eligible contract participant under Section 1a(12)(C) of the Commodity Exchange Act as in effect prior to July 16, 2011).

(b) The exemption provided in paragraph (a) of this section does not apply to the provisions of Section 17(a) of the Act (15 U.S.C. 77q(a)).

(c) This rule will expire on February 11, 2017.

REGULATION A—CONDITIONAL SMALL ISSUES EXEMPTION

Rule 251. Scope of exemption

(a) *Tier 1 and Tier 2.* A public offer or sale of eligible securities, as defined in Rule 261, pursuant to Regulation A shall be exempt under section 3(b) from the registration requirements of the Act.

(1) *Tier 1.* Offerings pursuant to Regulation A in which the sum of all cash and other consideration to be received for the securities being offered ("aggregate offering price") plus the gross proceeds for all securities sold pursuant to other offering statements within the 12 months before the start of and during the current offering of securities ("aggregate sales") does not exceed $20,000,000, including not more than $6,000,000 offered by all selling securityholders that are affiliates of the issuer ("Tier 1 offerings").

(2) *Tier 2.* Offerings pursuant to Regulation A in which the sum of the aggregate offering price and aggregate sales does not exceed $50,000,000, including not more than $15,000,000 offered by all selling securityholders that are affiliates of the issuer ("Tier 2 offerings").

(3) *Additional limitation on secondary sales in first year.* The portion of the aggregate offering price attributable to the securities of selling securityholders shall not exceed 30% of the aggregate offering price of a particular offering in:

(i) The issuer's first offering pursuant to Regulation A; or

(ii) Any subsequent Regulation A offering that is qualified within one year of the qualification date of the issuer's first offering.

NOTE TO PARAGRAPH (a). Where a mixture of cash and non-cash consideration is to be received, the aggregate offering price must be based on the price at which the securities are offered for cash. Any portion of the aggregate offering price or aggregate sales attributable to cash received in a foreign currency must be translated into United States currency at a currency exchange rate in effect on, or at a reasonable time before, the date of the sale of the securities. If securities are not offered for cash, the aggregate offering price or aggregate sales must be based on the value of the consideration as established by bona fide sales of that consideration made within a reasonable time, or, in the absence of sales, on the fair value as determined by an accepted standard. Valuations of non-cash consideration must be reasonable at the time made. If convertible securities or warrants are being offered and such securities are convertible, exercisable, or exchangeable within one year of the offering statement's qualification or at the discretion of the issuer, the underlying securities must also be qualified and the aggregate offering price must include the actual or maximum estimated conversion, exercise, or exchange price of such securities.

(b) *Issuer.* The issuer of the securities:

(1) Is an entity organized under the laws of the United States or Canada, or any State, Province, Territory or possession thereof, or the District of Columbia, with its principal place of business in the United States or Canada;

(2) Is not subject to section 13 or 15(d) of the Securities Exchange Act of 1934 immediately before the offering;

(3) Is not a development stage company that either has no specific business plan or purpose, or has indicated that its business plan is to merge with or acquire an unidentified company or companies;

(4) Is not an investment company registered or required to be registered under the Investment Company Act of 1940 or a business development company as defined in section 2(a)(48) of the Investment Company Act of 1940;

(5) Is not issuing fractional undivided interests in oil or gas rights, or a similar interest in other mineral rights;

(6) Is not, and has not been, subject to any order of the Commission entered pursuant to Section 12(j) of the Exchange Act within five years before the filing of the offering statement;

(7) Has filed with the Commission all reports required to be filed, if any, pursuant to Rule 257 during the two years before the filing of the offering statement (or for such shorter period that the issuer was required to file such reports); and

(8) Is not disqualified under Rule 262.

(c) *Integration with other offerings.* Offers or sales made in reliance on this Regulation A will not be integrated with:

(1) Prior offers or sales of securities; or

(2) Subsequent offers or sales of securities that are:

(i) Registered under the Securities Act, except as provided in Rule 255(e);

(ii) Exempt from registration under Rule 701;

(iii) Made pursuant to an employee benefit plan;

(iv) Exempt from registration under Regulation S (Rules 901 through 905);

(v) Made more than six months after the completion of the Regulation A offering; or

(vi) Exempt from registration under Section 4(a)(6) of the Securities Act.

NOTE TO PARAGRAPH (c). If these safe harbors do not apply, whether subsequent offers and sales of securities will be integrated with the Regulation A offering will depend on the particular facts and circumstances.

(d) *Offering conditions*—(1) *Offers*. (i) Except as allowed by Rule 255, no offer of securities may be made unless an offering statement has been filed with the Commission.

(ii) After the offering statement has been filed, but before it is qualified:

(A) Oral offers may be made;

(B) Written offers pursuant to Rule 254 may be made; and

(C) Solicitations of interest and other communications pursuant to Rule 255 may be made.

(iii) Offers may be made after the offering statement has been qualified, but any written offers must be accompanied with or preceded by the most recent offering circular filed with the Commission for such offering.

(2) *Sales*. (i) No sale of securities may be made:

(A) Until the offering statement has been qualified;

(B) By issuers that are not currently required to file reports pursuant to Rule 257(b), until a Preliminary Offering Circular is delivered at least 48 hours before the sale to any person that before qualification of the offering statement had indicated an interest in purchasing securities in the offering, including those persons that responded to an issuer's solicitation of interest materials; and

(C) In a Tier 2 offering of securities that are not listed on a registered national securities exchange upon qualification, unless the purchaser is either an accredited investor (as defined in Rule 501) or the aggregate purchase price to be paid by the purchaser for the securities (including the actual or maximum estimated conversion, exercise, or exchange price for any underlying securities that have been qualified) is no more than ten percent (10%) of the greater of such purchaser's:

(*1*) Annual income or net worth if a natural person (with annual income and net worth for such natural person purchasers determined as provided in Rule 501); or

(*2*) Revenue or net assets for such purchaser's most recently completed fiscal year end if a non-natural person.

NOTE TO PARAGRAPH (d)(2)(i)(C). When securities underlying warrants or convertible securities are being qualified pursuant to Tier 2 of Regulation A one year or more after the qualification of an offering for which investment limitations previously applied, purchasers of the underlying securities for which investment limitations would apply at that later date may determine compliance with the ten percent (10%) investment limitation using the conversion, exercise, or exchange price to acquire the underlying securities at that later time without aggregating such price with the price of the overlying warrants or convertible securities.

(D) The issuer may rely on a representation of the purchaser when determining compliance with the ten percent (10%) investment limitation in this paragraph (d)(2)(i)(C), provided that the issuer does not know at the time of sale that any such representation is untrue.

(ii) In a transaction that represents a sale by the issuer or an underwriter, or a sale by a dealer within 90 calendar days after qualification of the offering statement, each underwriter or dealer selling in such transaction must deliver to each purchaser from it, not later than two business days following the completion of such sale, a copy of the Final Offering Circular, subject to the following provisions:

(A) If the sale was by the issuer and was not effected by or through an underwriter or dealer, the issuer is responsible for delivering the Final Offering Circular as if the issuer were an underwriter;

(B) For continuous or delayed offerings pursuant to paragraph (d)(3) of this section, the 90 calendar day period for dealers shall commence on the day of the first bona fide offering of securities under such offering statement;

(C) If the security is listed on a registered national securities exchange, no offering circular need be delivered by a dealer more than 25 calendar days after the later of the qualification date of the offering statement or the first date on which the security was bona fide offered to the public;

(D) No offering circular need be delivered by a dealer if the issuer is subject, immediately prior to the time of the filing of the offering statement, to the reporting requirements of Rule 257(b); and

(E) The Final Offering Circular delivery requirements set forth in paragraph (d)(2)(ii) of this section may be satisfied by delivering a notice to the effect that the sale was made pursuant to a qualified offering statement that includes the uniform resource locator ("URL"), which, in the case of an electronic-only offering, must be an active hyperlink, where the Final Offering Circular, or the offering statement of which such Final Offering Circular is part, may be obtained on the Commission's Electronic Data Gathering, Analysis and Retrieval System ("EDGAR") and contact information sufficient to notify a purchaser where a request for a Final Offering Circular can be sent and received in response.

(3) *Continuous or delayed offerings.* (i) Continuous or delayed offerings may be made under this Regulation A, so long as the offering statement pertains only to:

(A) Securities that are to be offered or sold solely by or on behalf of a person or persons other than the issuer, a subsidiary of the issuer, or a person of which the issuer is a subsidiary;

(B) Securities that are to be offered and sold pursuant to a dividend or interest reinvestment plan or an employee benefit plan of the issuer;

(C) Securities that are to be issued upon the exercise of outstanding options, warrants, or rights;

(D) Securities that are to be issued upon conversion of other outstanding securities;

(E) Securities that are pledged as collateral; or

(F) Securities the offering of which will be commenced within two calendar days after the qualification date, will be made on a continuous basis, may continue for a period in excess of 30 calendar days from the date of initial qualification, and will be offered in an amount that, at the time the offering statement is qualified, is reasonably expected to be offered and sold within two years from the initial qualification date. These securities may be offered and sold only if not more than three years have elapsed since the initial qualification date of the offering statement under which they are being offered and sold; provided, however, that if a new offering statement has been filed pursuant to this paragraph (d)(3)(i)(F), securities covered by the prior offering statement may continue to be offered and sold until the earlier of the qualification date of the new offering statement or 180 calendar days after the third anniversary of the initial qualification date of the prior offering statement. Before the end of such three-year period, an issuer may file a new offering statement covering the securities. The new offering statement must include all the information that would be required at that time in an offering statement relating to all offerings that it covers. Before the qualification date of the new offering statement, the issuer may include as part of such new offering statement any unsold securities covered by the earlier offering statement by identifying on the cover page of the new offering circular, or the latest amendment, the amount of such unsold securities being included. The offering of securities on the earlier offering statement will be deemed terminated as of the date of qualification of the new offering statement. Securities may be sold pursuant to this paragraph (d)(3)(i)(F) only if the issuer is current in its annual and semiannual filings pursuant to Rule 257(b), at the time of such sale.

(ii) At the market offerings, by or on behalf of the issuer or otherwise, are not permitted under this Regulation A. As used in this paragraph (d)(3)(ii), the term at the market offering means an offering of equity securities into an existing trading market for outstanding shares of the same class at other than a fixed price.

(e) *Confidential treatment.* A request for confidential treatment may be made under Rule 406 for information required to be filed, and Rule 83 for information not required to be filed.

(f) *Electronic filing.* Documents filed or otherwise provided to the Commission pursuant to this Regulation A must be submitted in electronic format by means of EDGAR in accordance with the EDGAR rules set forth in Regulation S–T.

Rule 252. Offering statement

(a) *Documents to be included.* The offering statement consists of the contents required by Form 1–A and any other material information necessary to make the required statements, in light of the circumstances under which they are made, not misleading.

(b) *Paper, printing, language and pagination.* Except as otherwise specified in this rule, the requirements for offering statements are the same as those specified in Rule 403 for registration statements under the Act. No fee is payable to the Commission upon either the submission or filing of an offering statement on Form 1–A, or any amendment to an offering statement.

(c) *Signatures*. The issuer, its principal executive officer, principal financial officer, principal accounting officer, and a majority of the members of its board of directors or other governing body, must sign the offering statement in the manner prescribed by Form 1–A. If a signature is by a person on behalf of any other person, evidence of authority to sign must be filed, except where an executive officer signs for the issuer.

(d) *Non-public submission*. An issuer whose securities have not been previously sold pursuant to a qualified offering statement under this Regulation A or an effective registration statement under the Securities Act may submit a draft offering statement to the Commission for non-public review by the staff of the Commission before public filing, provided that the offering statement shall not be qualified less than 21 calendar days after the public filing with the Commission of:

(1) The initial non-public submission;

(2) All non-public amendments; and

(3) All non-public correspondence submitted by or on behalf of the issuer to the Commission staff regarding such submissions (subject to any separately approved confidential treatment request under Rule 251(e).

(e) *Qualification*. An offering statement and any amendment thereto can be qualified only at such date and time as the Commission may determine.

(f) *Amendments*. (1) (i) Amendments to an offering statement must be signed and filed with the Commission in the same manner as the initial filing. Amendments to an offering statement must be filed under cover of Form 1–A and must be numbered consecutively in the order in which filed.

(ii) Every amendment that includes amended audited financial statements must include the consent of the certifying accountant to the use of such accountant's certification in connection with the amended financial statements in the offering statement or offering circular and to being named as having audited such financial statements.

(iii) Amendments solely relating to Part III of Form 1–A must comply with the requirements of paragraph (f)(1)(i) of this section, except that such amendments may be limited to Part I of Form 1–A, an explanatory note, and all of the information required by Part III of Form 1–A.

(2) Post-qualification amendments must be filed in the following circumstances for ongoing offerings:

(i) At least every 12 months after the qualification date to include the financial statements that would be required by Form 1–A as of such date; or

(ii) To reflect any facts or events arising after the qualification date of the offering statement (or the most recent post-qualification amendment thereof) which, individually or in the aggregate, represent a fundamental change in the information set forth in the offering statement.

Rule 253. Offering circular

(a) *Contents*. An offering circular must include the information required by Form 1–A for offering circulars.

(b) *Information that may be omitted*. Notwithstanding paragraph (a) of this section, a qualified offering circular may omit information with respect to the public offering price, underwriting syndicate (including any material relationships between the issuer or selling securityholders and the unnamed underwriters, brokers or dealers), underwriting discounts or commissions, discounts or commissions to dealers, amount of proceeds, conversion rates, call prices and other items dependent upon the offering price, delivery dates, and terms of the securities dependent upon the offering date; provided, that the following conditions are met:

(1) The securities to be qualified are offered for cash.

(2) The outside front cover page of the offering circular includes a bona fide estimate of the range of the maximum offering price and the maximum number of shares or other units of securities to be offered or a bona fide estimate of the principal amount of debt securities offered, subject to the following conditions:

(i) The range must not exceed $2 for offerings where the upper end of the range is $10 or less or 20% if the upper end of the price range is over $10; and

(ii) The upper end of the range must be used in determining the aggregate offering price under Rule 251(a).

(3) The offering statement does not relate to securities to be offered by competitive bidding.

(4) The volume of securities (the number of equity securities or aggregate principal amount of debt securities) to be offered may not be omitted in reliance on this paragraph (b).

NOTE TO PARAGRAPH (b). A decrease in the volume of securities offered or a change in the bona fide estimate of the offering price range from that indicated in the offering circular filed as part of a qualified offering statement may be disclosed in the offering circular filed with the Commission pursuant to Rule 253(g), so long as the decrease in the volume of securities offered or change in the price range would not materially change the disclosure contained in the offering statement at qualification. Notwithstanding the foregoing, any decrease in the volume of securities offered and any deviation from the low or high end of the price range may be reflected in the offering circular supplement filed with the Commission pursuant to Rule 253(g) (1) or (3) if, in the aggregate, the decrease in volume and/or change in price represent no more than a 20% change from the maximum aggregate offering price calculable using the information in the qualified offering statement. In no circumstances may this paragraph be used to offer securities where the maximum aggregate offering price would result in the offering exceeding the limit set forth in Rule 251(a) or if the change would result in a Tier 1 offering becoming a Tier 2 offering. An offering circular supplement may not be used to increase the volume of securities being offered. Additional securities may only be offered pursuant to a new offering statement or post-qualification amendment qualified by the Commission.

(c) *Filing of omitted information.* The information omitted from the offering circular in reliance upon paragraph (b) of this section must be contained in an offering circular filed with the Commission pursuant to paragraph (g) of this section; except that if such offering circular is not so filed by the later of 15 business days after the qualification date of the offering statement or 15 business days after the qualification of a post-qualification amendment thereto that contains an offering circular, the information omitted in reliance upon paragraph (b) of this section must be contained in a qualified post-qualification amendment to the offering statement.

(d) *Presentation of information.* (1) Information in the offering circular must be presented in a clear, concise and understandable manner and in a type size that is easily readable. Repetition of information should be avoided; cross-referencing of information within the document is permitted.

(2) Where an offering circular is distributed through an electronic medium, issuers may satisfy legibility requirements applicable to printed documents by presenting all required information in a format readily communicated to investors.

(e) *Date.* An offering circular must be dated approximately as of the date it was filed with the Commission.

(f) *Cover page legend.* The cover page of every offering circular must display the following statement highlighted by prominent type or in another manner:

The United States Securities and Exchange Commission does not pass upon the merits of or give its approval to any securities offered or the terms of the offering, nor does it pass upon the accuracy or completeness of any offering circular or other solicitation materials. These securities are offered pursuant to an exemption from registration with the Commission; however, the Commission has not made an independent determination that the securities offered are exempt from registration.

(g) *Offering circular supplements.* (1) An offering circular that discloses information previously omitted from the offering circular in reliance upon Rule 253(b) must be filed with the Commission no later than two business days following the earlier of the date of determination of the offering price or the date such offering circular is first used after qualification in connection with a public offering or sale.

(2) An offering circular that reflects information other than that covered in paragraph (g) (1) of this section that constitutes a substantive change from or addition to the information set forth in the last offering circular filed with the Commission must be filed with the Commission no later than five business days after the date it is first used after qualification in connection with a public offering or sale. If an offering circular filed pursuant to this paragraph (g) (2) consists of an offering circular supplement attached to an offering circular that previously had been filed or was not required to be filed pursuant to paragraph (g) of this section because it did not contain substantive changes from an offering circular that previously was filed, only the offering circular supplement need be filed under paragraph (g) of this section, provided that the cover page of the offering circular supplement identifies the date(s) of the related offering circular and any offering circular supplements thereto that together constitute the offering circular with respect to the securities currently being offered or sold.

(3) An offering circular that discloses information, facts or events covered in both para-

graphs (g)(1) and (2) of this section must be filed with the Commission no later than two business days following the earlier of the date of the determination of the offering price or the date it is first used after qualification in connection with a public offering or sale.

(4) An offering circular required to be filed pursuant to paragraph (g) of this section that is not filed within the time frames specified in paragraphs (g)(1) through (3) of this section, as applicable, must be filed pursuant to this paragraph (g)(4) as soon as practicable after the discovery of such failure to file.

(5) Each offering circular filed under this section must contain in the upper right corner of the cover page the paragraphs of paragraphs (g)(1) through (4) of this section under which the filing is made, and the file number of the offering statement to which the offering circular relates.

Rule 254. Preliminary offering circular

After the filing of an offering statement, but before its qualification, written offers of securities may be made if they meet the following requirements:

(a) *Outside front cover page.* The outside front cover page of the material bears the caption Preliminary Offering Circular, the date of issuance, and the following legend, which must be highlighted by prominent type or in another manner:

An offering statement pursuant to Regulation A relating to these securities has been filed with the Securities and Exchange Commission. Information contained in this Preliminary Offering Circular is subject to completion or amendment. These securities may not be sold nor may offers to buy be accepted before the offering statement filed with the Commission is qualified. This Preliminary Offering Circular shall not constitute an offer to sell or the solicitation of an offer to buy nor may there be any sales of these securities in any state in which such offer, solicitation or sale would be unlawful before registration or qualification under the laws of any such state. We may elect to satisfy our obligation to deliver a Final Offering Circular by sending you a notice within two business days after the completion of our sale to you that contains the URL where the Final Offering Circular or the offering statement in which such Final Offering Circular was filed may be obtained.

(b) *Other contents.* The Preliminary Offering Circular contains substantially the information required to be in an offering circular by Form 1–A, except that certain information may be omitted under Rule 253(b) subject to the conditions set forth in such rule.

(c) *Filing.* The Preliminary Offering Circular is filed as a part of the offering statement.

Rule 255. Solicitations of interest and other communications

(a) *Solicitation of interest.* At any time before the qualification of an offering statement, including before the non-public submission or public filing of such offering statement, an issuer or any person authorized to act on behalf of an issuer may communicate orally or in writing to determine whether there is any interest in a contemplated securities offering. Such communications are deemed to be an offer of a security for sale for purposes of the antifraud provisions of the federal securities laws. No solicitation or acceptance of money or other consideration, nor of any commitment, binding or otherwise, from any person is permitted until qualification of the offering statement.

(b) *Conditions.* The communications must:

(1) State that no money or other consideration is being solicited, and if sent in response, will not be accepted;

(2) State that no offer to buy the securities can be accepted and no part of the purchase price can be received until the offering statement is qualified, and any such offer may be withdrawn or revoked, without obligation or commitment of any kind, at any time before notice of its acceptance given after the qualification date;

(3) State that a person's indication of interest involves no obligation or commitment of any kind; and

(4) After the public filing of the offering statement:

(i) State from whom a copy of the most recent version of the Preliminary Offering Circular may be obtained, including a phone number and address of such person;

(ii) Provide the URL where such Preliminary Offering Circular, or the offering statement in which such Preliminary Offering Circular was filed, may be obtained; or

(iii) Include a complete copy of the Preliminary Offering Circular.

(c) *Indications of interest.* Any written communication under this rule may include a means by which a person may indicate to the issuer that such person is interested in a potential offering. This issuer may require the name, address, telephone number, and/or e-mail address in any response form included pursuant to this paragraph (c).

(d) *Revised solicitations of interest.* If solicitation of interest materials are used after the public filing of the offering statement and such solicitation of interest materials contain information that is inaccurate or inadequate in any material respect, revised solicitation of interest materials must be redistributed in a substantially similar manner as such materials were originally distributed. Notwithstanding the foregoing in this paragraph (d), if the only information that is inaccurate or inadequate is contained in a Preliminary Offering Circular provided with the solicitation of interest materials pursuant to paragraphs (b)(4)(i) or (ii) of this section, no such redistribution is required in the following circumstances:

(1) in the case of paragraph (b)(4)(i) of this section, the revised Preliminary Offering Circular will be provided to any persons making new inquiries and will be recirculated to any persons making any previous inquiries; or

(2) in the case of paragraph (b)(4)(ii) of this section, the URL continues to link directly to the most recent Preliminary Offering Circular or to the offering statement in which such revised Preliminary Offering Circular was filed.

(e) *Abandoned offerings.* Where an issuer decides to register an offering under the Securities Act after soliciting interest in a contemplated, but subsequently abandoned, Regulation A offering, the abandoned Regulation A offering would not be subject to integration with the registered offering if the issuer engaged in solicitations of interest pursuant to this rule only to qualified institutional buyers and institutional accredited investors permitted by Section 5(d) of the Securities Act. If the issuer engaged in solicitations of interest to persons other than qualified institutional buyers and institutional accredited investors, an abandoned Regulation A offering would not be subject to integration if the issuer (and any underwriter, broker, dealer, or agent used by the issuer in connection with the proposed offering) waits at least 30 calendar days between the last such solicitation of interest in the Regulation A offering and the filing of the registration statement with the Commission.

Rule 256. Definition of "qualified purchaser"

For purposes of Section 18(b)(3) of the Securities Act, a "qualified purchaser" means any person to whom securities are offered or sold pursuant to a Tier 2 offering of this Regulation A.

Rule 257. Periodic and current reporting; exit report

(a) *Tier 1*: Exit report. Each issuer that has filed an offering statement for a Tier 1 offering that has been qualified pursuant to this Regulation A must file an exit report on Form 1–Z not later than 30 calendar days after the termination or completion of the offering.

(b) *Tier 2*: Periodic and current reporting. Each issuer that has filed an offering statement for a Tier 2 offering that has been qualified pursuant to this Regulation A must file with the Commission the following periodic and current reports:

(1) *Annual reports.* An annual report on Form 1–K for the fiscal year in which the offering statement became qualified and for any fiscal year thereafter, unless the issuer's obligation to file such annual report is suspended under paragraph (d) of this section. Annual reports must be filed within the period specified in Form 1–K.

(2) *Special financial report.* (i) A special financial report on Form 1–K or Form 1–SA if the offering statement did not contain the following:

(A) audited financial statements for the issuer's most recent fiscal year (or for the life of the issuer if less than a full fiscal year) preceding the fiscal year in which the issuer's offering statement became qualified; or

(B) unaudited financial statements covering the first six months of the issuer's current fiscal year if the offering statement was qualified during the last six months of that fiscal year.

(ii) The special financial report described in paragraph (b)(2)(i)(A) of this section must be filed under cover of Form 1–K within 120 calendar days after the qualification date of the offering statement and must include audited financial statements for such fiscal year or other period specified in that paragraph, as the case may be. The special financial report described in paragraph (b)(2)(i)(B) of this section must be filed under cover of Form 1–SA within 90 calendar days after the qualification date of the offering statement and must include the semiannual financial statements for the first six months of the issuer's fiscal year, which may be unaudited.

(iii) A special financial report must be signed in accordance with the requirements of the form on which it is filed.

(3) *Semiannual report.* A semiannual report on Form 1–SA within the period specified in Form 1–SA. Semiannual reports must cover the first six months of each fiscal year of the issuer, commencing with the first six months of the fiscal year immediately following the most recent fiscal year for which full financial statements were included in the offering statement, or, if the offering statement included financial statements for the first six months of the fiscal year following the most recent full fiscal year, for the first six months of the following fiscal year.

(4) *Current reports.* Current reports on Form 1–U with respect to the matters and within the period specified in that form, unless substantially the same information has been previously reported to the Commission by the issuer under cover of Form 1–K or Form 1–SA.

(5) *Reporting by successor issuers.* Where in connection with a succession by merger, consolidation, exchange of securities, acquisition of assets or otherwise, securities of any issuer that is not required to file reports pursuant to paragraph (b) of this section are issued to the holders of any class of securities of another issuer that is required to file such reports, the duty to file reports pursuant to paragraph (b) of this section shall be deemed to have been assumed by the issuer of the class of securities so issued. The successor issuer must, after the consummation of the succession, file reports in accordance with paragraph (b) of this section, unless that issuer is exempt from filing such reports or the duty to file such reports is terminated or suspended under paragraph (d) of this section.

(c) *Amendments.* All amendments to the reports described in paragraphs (a) and (b) of this section must be filed under cover of the form amended, marked with the letter A to designate the document as an amendment, *e.g.*, "1–K/A," and in compliance with pertinent requirements applicable to such reports. Amendments filed pursuant to this paragraph (c) must set forth the complete text of each item as amended, but need not include any items that were not amended. Amendments must be numbered sequentially and be filed separately for each report amended. Amendments must be signed on behalf of the issuer by a duly authorized representative of the issuer. An amendment to any report required to include certifications as specified in the applicable form must include new certifications by the appropriate persons.

(d) *Suspension of duty to file reports.* (1) The duty to file reports under this rule shall be automatically suspended if and so long as the issuer is subject to the duty to file reports required by section 13 or 15(d) of the Exchange Act.

(2) The duty to file reports under paragraph (b) of this section with respect to a class of securities held of record (as defined in Rule 12g5–1) by less than 300 persons, or less than 1,200 persons for a bank (as defined in Section 3(a)(6) of the Exchange Act), or a bank holding company (as defined in section 2 of the Bank Holding Company Act of 1956), shall be suspended for such class of securities immediately upon filing with the Commission an exit report on Form 1–Z if the issuer of such class has filed all reports due pursuant to this rule before the date of such Form 1–Z filing for the shorter of:

(i) The period since the issuer became subject to such reporting obligation; or

(ii) Its most recent three fiscal years and the portion of the current year preceding the date of filing Form 1–Z.

(3) For the purposes of paragraph (d)(2) of this section, the term class shall be construed to include all securities of an issuer that are of substantially similar character and the holders of which enjoy substantially similar rights and privileges. If the Form 1–Z is subsequently withdrawn or if it is denied because the issuer was ineligible to use the form, the issuer must, within 60 calendar days, file with the Commission all reports which would have been required if such exit report had not been filed. If the suspension resulted from the issuer's merger into, or consolidation with, another issuer or issuers, the notice must be filed by the successor issuer.

(4) The ability to suspend reporting, as described in paragraph (d)(2) of this section, is not available for any class of securities if:

(i) During that fiscal year a Tier 2 offering statement was qualified;

(ii) The issuer has not filed an annual report under this rule or the Exchange Act for the fiscal year in which a Tier 2 offering statement was qualified; or

(iii) Offers or sales of securities of that class are being made pursuant to a Tier 2 Regulation A offering.

(e) *Termination of duty to file reports.* If the duty to file reports is suspended pursuant to paragraph (d)(1) of this section and such suspension ends because the issuer terminates or suspends its duty to file reports under the Exchange Act, the issuer's obligation to file reports under paragraph (b) of this section shall:

(1) Automatically terminate if the issuer is eligible to suspend its duty to file reports under paragraphs (d)(2) and (3) of this section; or

(2) Recommence with the report covering the most recent financial period after that included in any effective registration statement or filed Exchange Act report.

Rule 258. Suspension of the exemption

(a) *Suspension.* The Commission may at any time enter an order temporarily suspending a Regulation A exemption if it has reason to believe that:

(1) No exemption is available or any of the terms, conditions or requirements of Regulation A have not been complied with;

(2) The offering statement, any sales or solicitation of interest material, or any report filed pursuant to Rule 257 contains any untrue statement of a material fact or omits to state a material fact necessary in order to make the statements made, in light of the circumstances under which they are made, not misleading;

(3) The offering is being made or would be made in violation of section 17 of the Securities Act;

(4) An event has occurred after the filing of the offering statement that would have rendered the exemption hereunder unavailable if it had occurred before such filing;

(5) Any person specified in Rule 262(a) has been indicted for any crime or offense of the character specified in Rule 262(a)(1), or any proceeding has been initiated for the purpose of enjoining any such person from engaging in or continuing any conduct or practice of the character specified in Rule 262(a)(2), or any proceeding has been initiated for the purposes of Rule 262(a)(3)-(8); or

(6) The issuer or any promoter, officer, director, or underwriter has failed to cooperate, or has obstructed or refused to permit the making of an investigation by the Commission in connection with any offering made or proposed to be made in reliance on Regulation A.

(b) *Notice and hearing.* Upon the entry of an order under paragraph (a) of this section, the Commission will promptly give notice to the issuer, any underwriter, and any selling securityholder:

(1) That such order has been entered, together with a brief statement of the reasons for the entry of the order; and

(2) That the Commission, upon receipt of a written request within 30 calendar days after the entry of the order, will, within 20 calendar days after receiving the request, order a hearing at a place to be designated by the Commission.

(c) *Suspension order.* If no hearing is requested and none is ordered by the Commission, an order entered under paragraph (a) of this section shall become permanent on the 30th calendar day after its entry and shall remain in effect unless or until it is modified or vacated by the Commission. Where a hearing is requested or is ordered by the Commission, the Commission will, after notice of and opportunity for such hearing, either vacate the order or enter an order permanently suspending the exemption.

(d) *Permanent suspension.* The Commission may, at any time after notice of and opportunity for hearing, enter an order permanently suspending the exemption for any reason upon which it could have entered a temporary suspension order under paragraph (a) of this section. Any such order shall remain in effect until vacated by the Commission.

(e) *Notice procedures.* All notices required by this rule must be given by personal service, registered or certified mail to the addresses given by the issuer, any underwriter and any selling securityholder in the offering statement.

Rule 259. Withdrawal or abandonment of offering statements

(a) *Withdrawal.* If none of the securities that are the subject of an offering statement has been sold and such offering statement is not the subject of a proceeding under Rule 258, the offering statement may be withdrawn with the Commission's consent. The application for withdrawal must state the reason the offering statement is to be withdrawn and must be signed by an authorized representative of the issuer. Any withdrawn document will remain in the Commission's files, as well as the related request for withdrawal.

(b) *Abandonment.* When an offering statement has been on file with the Commission for nine months without amendment and has not become qualified, the Commission may, in its discretion, declare the offering statement abandoned. If the offering statement has been amended, the nine-month period shall be computed from the date of the latest amendment.

Rule 260. Insignificant deviations from a term, condition or requirement of Regulation A

(a) *Failure to comply.* A failure to comply with a term, condition or requirement of Regulation A will not result in the loss of the exemption from the requirements of section 5 of the Securities Act for any offer or sale to a particular individual or entity, if the person relying on the exemption establishes that:

(1) The failure to comply did not pertain to a term, condition or requirement directly intended to protect that particular individual or entity;

(2) The failure to comply was insignificant with respect to the offering as a whole, provided that any failure to comply with Rule 251(a), (b), and (d)(1) and (3) shall be deemed to be significant to the offering as a whole; and

(3) A good faith and reasonable attempt was made to comply with all applicable terms, conditions and requirements of Regulation A.

(b) *Action by Commission.* A transaction made in reliance upon Regulation A must comply with all applicable terms, conditions and requirements of the regulation. Where an exemption is established only through reliance upon paragraph (a) of this section, the failure to comply shall nonetheless be actionable by the Commission under section 20 of the Securities Act.

(c) *Suspension.* This provision provides no relief or protection from a proceeding under Rule 258.

Rule 261. Definitions

As used in this Regulation A, all terms have the same meanings as in Rule 405, except that all references to registrant in those definitions shall refer to the issuer of the securities to be offered and sold under Regulation A. In addition, these terms have the following meanings:

(a) *Affiliated issuer.* An affiliate (as defined in Rule 501) of the issuer that is issuing securities in the same offering.

(b) *Business day.* Any day except Saturdays, Sundays or United States federal holidays.

(c) *Eligible securities.* Equity securities, debt securities, and securities convertible or exchangeable to equity interests, including any guarantees of such securities, but not including asset-backed securities as such term is defined in Item 1101(c) of Regulation AB.

(d) *Final order.* A written directive or declaratory statement issued by a federal or state agency described in Rule 262(a)(3) under applicable statutory authority that provides for notice and an opportunity for hearing, which constitutes a final disposition or action by that federal or state agency.

(e) *Final offering circular.* The more recent of: the current offering circular contained in a qualified offering statement; and any offering circular filed pursuant to Rule 253(g). If, however, the issuer is relying on Rule 253(b), the Final Offering Circular is the most recent of the offering circular filed pursuant to Rule 253(g)(1) or (3) and any subsequent offering circular filed pursuant to Rule 253(g).

(f) *Offering statement.* An offering statement prepared pursuant to Regulation A.

(g) *Preliminary offering circular.* The offering circular described in Rule 254.

Rule 262. Disqualification provisions

(a) *Disqualification events.* No exemption under this Regulation A shall be available for a sale of securities if the issuer; any predecessor of the issuer; any affiliated issuer; any director, executive officer, other officer participating in the offering, general partner or managing member of the issuer; any beneficial owner of 20% or more of the issuer's outstanding voting equity securities, calculated on the basis of voting power; any promoter connected with the issuer in any capacity at the time of filing, any offer after qualification, or such sale; any person that has been or will be paid (directly or indirectly) remuneration for solicitation of purchasers in connection with such sale of securities; any general partner or managing member of any such solicitor; or any director, executive officer or other officer participating in the offering of any such solicitor or general partner or managing member of such solicitor:

(1) Has been convicted, within ten years before the filing of the offering statement (or five years, in the case of issuers, their predecessors and affiliated issuers), of any felony or misdemeanor:

(i) In connection with the purchase or sale of any security;

(ii) Involving the making of any false filing with the Commission; or

(iii) Arising out of the conduct of the business of an underwriter, broker, dealer, municipal securities dealer, investment adviser or paid solicitor of purchasers of securities;

(2) Is subject to any order, judgment or decree of any court of competent jurisdiction, entered within five years before the filing of the offering statement, that, at the time of such filing, restrains or enjoins such person from engaging or continuing to engage in any conduct or practice:

(i) In connection with the purchase or sale of any security;

(ii) Involving the making of any false filing with the Commission; or

(iii) Arising out of the conduct of the business of an underwriter, broker, dealer, municipal securities dealer, investment adviser or paid solicitor of purchasers of securities;

(3) Is subject to a final order (as defined in Rule 261) of a state securities commission (or an agency or officer of a state performing like functions); a state authority that supervises or examines banks, savings associations, or credit unions; a state insurance commission (or an agency or officer of a state performing like functions); an appropriate federal banking agency; the U.S. Commodity Futures Trading Commission; or the National Credit Union Administration that:

(i) At the time of the filing of the offering statement, bars the person from:

(A) Association with an entity regulated by such commission, authority, agency, or officer;

(B) Engaging in the business of securities, insurance or banking; or

(C) Engaging in savings association or credit union activities; or

(ii) Constitutes a final order based on a violation of any law or regulation that prohibits fraudulent, manipulative, or deceptive conduct entered within ten years before such filing of the offering statement;

(4) Is subject to an order of the Commission entered pursuant to section 15(b) or 15B(c) of the Securities Exchange Act of 1934 or section 203(e) or (f) of the Investment Advisers Act of 1940 that, at the time of the filing of the offering statement:

(i) Suspends or revokes such person's registration as a broker, dealer, municipal securities dealer or investment adviser;

(ii) Places limitations on the activities, functions or operations of such person; or

(iii) Bars such person from being associated with any entity or from participating in the offering of any penny stock;

(5) Is subject to any order of the Commission entered within five years before the filing of the offering statement that, at the time of such filing, orders the person to cease and desist from committing or causing a violation or future violation of:

(i) Any scienter-based anti-fraud provision of the federal securities laws, including without limitation section 17(a)(1) of the Securities Act of 1933, section 10(b) of the Securities Exchange Act of 1934 and Rule 10b–5, section 15(c)(1) of the Securities Exchange Act of 1934 and section 206(1) of the Investment Advisers Act of 1940, or any other rule or regulation thereunder; or

(ii) Section 5 of the Securities Act of 1933.

(6) Is suspended or expelled from membership in, or suspended or barred from association with a member of, a registered national securities exchange or a registered national or affiliated securities association for any act or omission to act constituting conduct inconsistent with just and equitable principles of trade;

(7) Has filed (as a registrant or issuer), or was or was named as an underwriter in, any registration statement or offering statement filed with the Commission that, within five years before the filing of the offering statement, was the subject of a refusal order, stop order, or order suspending the Regulation A exemption, or is, at the time of such filing, the subject of an investigation or proceeding to determine whether a stop order or suspension order should be issued; or

(8) Is subject to a United States Postal Service false representation order entered within five years before the filing of the offering statement, or is, at the time of such filing, subject to a temporary restraining order or preliminary injunction with respect to conduct alleged by the United States Postal Service to constitute a scheme or device for obtaining money or property through the mail by means of false representations.

(b) *Transition, waivers, reasonable care exception.* Paragraph (a) of this section shall not apply:

(1) With respect to any order under Rule 262(a)(3) or (5) that occurred or was issued before June 19, 2015;

(2) Upon a showing of good cause and without prejudice to any other action by the Commission, if the Commission determines that it is not necessary under the circumstances that an exemption be denied;

(3) If, before the filing of the offering statement, the court or regulatory authority that entered the relevant order, judgment or decree advises in writing (whether contained in the relevant judgment, order or decree or separately to the Commission or its staff) that disqualification under paragraph (a) of this section should not arise as a consequence of such order, judgment or decree; or

(4) If the issuer establishes that it did not know and, in the exercise of reasonable care, could not have known that a disqualification existed under paragraph (a) of this section.

NOTE TO PARAGRAPH (b)(4). An issuer will not be able to establish that it has exercised reasonable care unless it has made, in light of the circumstances, factual inquiry into whether any disqualifications exist. The nature and scope of the factual inquiry will vary based on the facts and circumstances concerning, among other things, the issuer and the other offering participants.

(c) *Affiliated issuers*. For purposes of paragraph (a) of this section, events relating to any affiliated issuer that occurred before the affiliation arose will be not considered disqualifying if the affiliated entity is not:

(1) In control of the issuer; or

(2) Under common control with the issuer by a third party that was in control of the affiliated entity at the time of such events.

(d) *Disclosure of prior "bad actor" events*. The issuer must include in the offering circular a description of any matters that would have triggered disqualification under paragraphs (a)(3) and (5) of this section but occurred before June 19, 2015. The failure to provide such information shall not prevent an issuer from relying on Regulation A if the issuer establishes that it did not know and, in the exercise of reasonable care, could not have known of the existence of the undisclosed matter or matters.

Rule 263. Consent to service of process

(a) If the issuer is not organized under the laws of any of the states or territories of the United States of America, it shall furnish to the Commission a written irrevocable consent and power of attorney on Form F–X at the time of filing the offering statement required by Rule 252.

(b) Any change to the name or address of the agent for service of the issuer shall be communicated promptly to the Commission through amendment of the requisite form and referencing the file number of the relevant offering statement.

REGULATION C—REGISTRATION

ATTENTION ELECTRONIC FILERS

THIS REGULATION SHOULD BE READ IN CONJUNCTION WITH REGULATION S–T (17 CFR 232), WHICH GOVERNS THE PREPARATION AND SUBMISSION OF DOCUMENTS IN ELECTRONIC FORMAT. MANY PROVISIONS RELATING TO THE PREPARATION AND SUBMISSION OF DOCUMENTS IN PAPER FORMAT CONTAINED IN THIS REGULATION ARE SUPERSEDED BY THE PROVISIONS OF REGULATION S–T FOR DOCUMENTS REQUIRED TO BE FILED IN ELECTRONIC FORMAT.

Rule 400. Application of Rules 400 to 494, inclusive

Rules 400 to 494 shall govern every registration of securities under the Act, except that any provision in a form, or an item of Regulation S–K referred to in such form, covering the same subject matter as any such rule shall be controlling unless otherwise specifically provided in Rules 400 to 494.

GENERAL REQUIREMENTS

Rule 401. Requirements as to proper form

(a) The form and contents of a registration statement and prospectus shall conform to the applicable rules and forms as in effect on the initial filing date of such registration statement and prospectus.

(b) If an amendment to a registration statement and prospectus is filed for the purpose of meeting the requirements of section 10(a)(3) of the Act or pursuant to the provisions of section 24(e) or 24(f) of the Investment Company Act of 1940, the form and contents of such an amendment shall conform to the applicable rules and forms as in effect on the filing date of such amendment.

(c) An amendment to a registration statement and prospectus, other than an amendment described in paragraph (b) of this rule, may be filed on any shorter Securities Act registration form for which it is eligible on the filing date of the amendment. At the issuer's option, the amendment also may be filed on the same Securities Act registration form used for the most recent amendment described in paragraph (b) of this rule or, if no such amendment has been filed, the initial registration statement and prospectus.

(d) The form and contents of a prospectus forming part of a registration statement which is the subject of a stop order entered under section 8(d) of the Act, if used after the date such stop order ceases to be effective, shall conform to the applicable rules and forms as in effect on the date such stop order ceases to be effective.

(e) A prospectus filed as part of an amendment to an effective registration statement, or other amendment to such registration statement, on any form may be prepared in accordance with the requirements of any other form which would then be appropriate for the registration of securities to which the prospectus or other amendment relates, provided that all of the other requirements of such other form and applicable rules (including any required undertakings) are met.

(f) Notwithstanding the provisions of this rule, a registrant (1) shall comply with the rules and forms as in effect at a date different from those specified in paragraphs (a), (b), (c) and (d) of this rule if the rules or forms or amendments thereto specifically so provide; and (2) may comply voluntarily with the rules and forms as in effect at dates subsequent to those specified in paragraphs (a), (b), (c) and (d) of this rule, provided that all of the requirements of the particular rules and forms in effect at such dates (including any required undertakings) are met.

(g)(1) Subject to paragraphs (g)(2), (g)(3), and (g)(4) of this rule, except for registration statements and post-effective amendments that become effective immediately pursuant to Rule 462 and Rule 464, a registration statement or any amendment thereto is deemed filed on the proper registration form unless the Commission objects to the registration form before the effective date.

(2) An automatic shelf registration statement as defined in Rule 405 and any post-effective amendment thereto are deemed filed on the proper registration form unless and until the Commission notifies the issuer of its objection to the use of such form. Following any such notification, the issuer must amend its automatic shelf registration statement onto the registration form it is then eligible to use, *provided, however*, that any continuous offering of securities pursuant to Rule 415 that the issuer has commenced pursuant to the registration statement before the Commission has notified the issuer of its objection to the use of such form may continue until the effective date of a new registration statement or post-effective amendment to the registration statement that the issuer has filed on the proper registration form, if the issuer files promptly after notification the new registration statement or post-effective amendment and if the offering is permitted to be made under the new registration statement or post-effective amendment.

(3) Violations of General Instruction I.B.6. of Form S–3 or General Instruction I.B.5. of Form F–3 will also violate the requirements as to proper form under this rule notwithstanding that the registration statement may have been declared effective previously.

(4) Notwithstanding that the registration statement may have become effective previously, requirements as to proper form under this section will have been violated for any offering of securities where the requirements of General Instruction I.A. of Form SF–3 (17 CFR 239.45) have not been met as of ninety days after the end of the depositor's fiscal year end prior to such offering.

Rule 402. Number of copies; binding; signatures

(a) Three copies of the complete registration statement, including exhibits and all other papers and documents filed as a part of the statement, shall be filed with the Commission. Each copy shall be bound, in one or more parts, without stiff covers. The binding shall be made on the side or stitching margin in such manner as to leave the reading matter legible. At least one such copy of every registration shall be signed by the persons specified in section 6(a) of the Act. Unsigned copies shall be conformed.

(b) Ten additional copies of the registration statement, similarly bound, shall be furnished for use in the examination of the registration statement, public inspection, copying and other purposes. Where a registration statement incorporates into the prospectus documents which are required to be delivered with the prospectus in lieu of prospectus presentation, the ten additional copies of the registration statement shall be accompanied by ten copies of such documents. No other exhibits are required to accompany such additional copies.

(c) Notwithstanding any other provision of this rule, if a registration statement is filed on Form S–8 (17 CFR 239.16b), three copies of the complete registration statement, including exhibits and all other papers and documents filed as a part of the statement, shall be filed with the Commission. Each copy shall be bound, in one or more parts, without stiff covers. The binding shall be made on the side or stitching margin in such manner as to leave the reading matter legible. At least one such copy shall be signed by the persons specified in section 6(a) of the Act. Unsigned copies shall be conformed. Three additional copies of the registration statement, similarly bound, also shall be furnished to the Commission for use in the examination of the registration statement, public inspection, copying and other purposes. No exhibits are required to accompany the additional copies of registration statements filed on Form S–8.

(d) Notwithstanding any other provision of this rule, if a registration statement is filed pursuant to Rule 462(b) and Rule 110(d), one copy of the complete registration statement, including exhibits and all other papers and documents filed as a part thereof shall be filed with the Commission. Such copy should not be bound and may contain facsimile versions of manual signatures in accordance with paragraph (e) of this rule.

(e) *Signatures.* Where the Act or the rules thereunder, including paragraphs (a) and (c) of this rule, require a document filed with or furnished to the Commission to be signed, such document shall be manually signed, or signed using either typed signatures or duplicated or facsimile versions of manual signatures. Where typed, duplicated or facsimile signatures are used, each signatory to the filing shall manually sign a signature page or other document authenticating, acknowledging or otherwise adopting his or her signature that appears in the filing. Such document shall be executed before or at the time the filing is made and shall be retained by the registrant for a period of five years. Upon request, the registrant shall furnish to the Commission or its staff a copy of any or all documents retained pursuant to this rule.

Rule 403. Requirements as to paper, printing, language and pagination

(a) Registration statements, applications and reports shall be filed on good quality, unglazed, white paper no larger than 8½ × 11 inches in size, insofar as practicable. To the extent that the reduction of larger documents would render them illegible, such documents may be filed on paper larger than 8½ × 11 inches in size.

(b) The registration statement and, insofar as practicable, all papers and documents filed as a part thereof shall be printed, lithographed, mimeographed or typewritten. However, the statement or any portion thereof may be prepared by any similar process which, in the opinion of the Commission, produces copies suitable for a permanent record. Irrespective of the process used, all copies of any such material shall be clear, easily readable and suitable for repeated photocopying. Debits in credit categories and credits in debit categories shall be designated so as to be clearly distinguishable as such on photocopies.

(c)(1) All Securities Act filings and submissions must be in the English language, except as otherwise provided by this rule. If a registration statement or other filing requires the inclusion of a document that is in a foreign language, the filer must submit instead a fair and accurate English translation of the entire foreign language document, except as provided by paragraph (c)(3) of this rule.

(2) If a registration statement or other filing or submission subject to review by the Division of Corporation Finance requires the inclusion of a foreign language document as an exhibit or attachment, the filer must submit a fair and accurate English translation of the foreign language document if consisting of any of the following, or an amendment of any of the following:

(i) Articles of incorporation, memoranda of association, bylaws, and other comparable documents, whether original or restated;

(ii) Instruments defining the rights of security holders, including indentures qualified or to be qualified under the Trust Indenture Act of 1939;

(iii) Voting agreements, including voting trust agreements;

(iv) Contracts to which directors, officers, promoters, voting trustees or security holders named in a registration statement are parties;

(v) Contracts upon which a filer's business is substantially dependent;

(vi) Audited annual and interim consolidated financial information; and

(vii) Any document that is or will be the subject of a confidential treatment request under Rule 406 or Rule 24b–2 under the Securities Exchange Act of 1934.

(3)(i) A filer may submit an English summary instead of an English translation of a foreign language document as an exhibit or attachment to a filing subject to review by the Division of Corporation Finance as long as:

(A) The foreign language document does not consist of any of the subject matter enumerated in paragraph (c)(2) of this rule; or

(B) The applicable form permits the use of an English summary.

(ii) Any English summary submitted under paragraph (c)(3) of this rule must:

(A) Fairly and accurately summarize the terms of each material provision of the foreign language document; and

(B) Fairly and accurately describe the terms that have been omitted or abridged.

(4) When submitting an English summary or English translation of a foreign language document under this rule, a filer must identify the submission as either an English summary or English translation. A filer may submit a copy of the unabridged foreign language document when including an English summary or English translation of a foreign language document in a filing. A filer must provide a copy of any foreign language document upon the request of Commission staff.

(5) A Canadian issuer may file an exhibit or other part of a registration statement on Form F–7, F–8, F–9, F–10, or F–80 (17 CFR 239.37, 239.38, 239.39, 239.40, or 239.41), that contains text in both French and English if the issuer included the French text to comply with the requirements of the Canadian securities administrator or other Canadian authority and, for an electronic filing, if the filing is an HTML document, as defined in Regulation S–T Rule 11.

(d) The manually signed original (or in the case of duplicate originals, one duplicate original) of all registrations, applications, statements, reports or other documents filed under the Act shall be numbered sequentially (in addition to any internal numbering which otherwise may be present) by handwritten, typed, printed or other legible form of notation from the first page of the document through the last page of that document and any exhibits or attachments thereto. Further, the total number of pages contained in a numbered original shall be set forth on the first page of the document.

Rule 404. Preparation of registration statement

(a) A registration statement shall consist of the facing sheet of the applicable form; a prospectus containing the information called for by Part I of such form; the information, list of exhibits, undertakings and signatures required to be set forth in Part II of such form; financial statements and schedules; exhibits; any other information or documents filed as part of the registration statement; and all documents or information incorporated by reference in the foregoing (whether or not required to be filed).

(b) All general instructions, instructions to items of the form, and instructions as to financial statements, exhibits, or prospectuses are to be omitted from the registration statement in all cases.

(c) The prospectus shall contain the information called for by all of the items of Part I of the applicable form, except that unless otherwise specified, no reference need be made to inapplicable items, and negative answers to any item in Part I may be omitted. A copy of the prospectus may be filed as a part of the registration statement in lieu of furnishing the information in item-and-answer form. Wherever a copy of the prospectus is filed in lieu of information in item-and-answer form, the text of the items of the form is to be omitted from the registration statement, as well as from the prospectus, except to the extent provided in paragraph (d) of this rule.

(d) Where any items of a form call for information not required to be included in the prospectus, generally Part II of such form, the text of such items, including the numbers and captions thereof, together with the answers thereto shall be filed with the prospectus under cover of the facing sheet of the form as a part of the registration statement. However, the text of such items may be omitted provided the answers are so prepared as to indicate the coverage of the item without the necessity of reference to the text of the item. If any such item is inapplicable, or the answer thereto is in the negative, a statement to that effect shall be made. Any financial statements not required to be included in the prospectus shall also be filed as a part of the registration statement proper, unless incorporated by reference pursuant to Rule 411.

Rule 405. Definitions of terms

Unless the context otherwise requires, all terms used in Rules 400 to 494, inclusive, or in the forms for registration have the same meanings as in the Act and in the general rules and regulations. In addition, the following definitions apply, unless the context otherwise requires:

Affiliate. An *affiliate* of, or person *affiliated* with, a specified person, is a person that directly, or indirectly through one or more intermediaries, controls or is controlled by, or is under common control with, the person specified.

Amount. The term *amount*, when used in regard to securities, means the principal amount if relating to evidences of indebtedness, the number of shares if relating to shares, and the number of units if relating to any other kind of security.

Associate. The term *associate*, when used to indicate a relationship with any person, means (1) a corporation or organization (other than the registrant or a majority-owned subsidiary of the registrant) of which such person is an officer or partner or is, directly or indirectly, the beneficial owner of 10 percent or more of any class of equity securities, (2) any trust or other estate in which such person has a substantial beneficial interest or as to which such person serves as trustee or in a similar capacity, and (3) any relative or spouse of such person, or any relative of such spouse, who has the same home as such person or who is a director or officer of the registrant or any of its parents or subsidiaries.

Automatic Shelf Registration Statement. The term *automatic shelf registration* statement means a registration statement filed on Form S–3 or Form F–3 (17 CFR 239.13 or 17 CFR 239.33) by a well-known seasoned issuer pursuant to General Instruction I.D. or I.C. of such forms, respectively.

Business Combination Related Shell Company. The term *business combination related shell company* means a shell company (as defined in Rule 405) that is:

(1) Formed by an entity that is not a shell company solely for the purpose of changing the corporate domicile of that entity solely within the United States; or

(2) Formed by an entity that is not a shell company solely for the purpose of completing a business combination transaction (as defined in Rule 165(f)) among one or more entities other than the shell company, none of which is a shell company.

Business Development Company. The term *business development company* refers to a company which has elected to be regulated as a business development company under sections 55 through 65 of the Investment Company Act of 1940.

Certified. The term *certified*, when used in regard to financial statements, means examined and reported upon with an opinion expressed by an independent public or certified public accountant.

Charter. The term *charter* includes articles of incorporation, declarations of trust, articles of association or partnership, or any similar instrument, as amended, affecting (either with or without filing with any governmental agency) the organization or creation of an incorporated or unincorporated person.

Commission. The term *Commission* means the Securities and Exchange Commission.

Common Equity. The term *common equity* means any class of common stock or an equivalent interest, including but not limited to a unit of beneficial interest in a trust or a limited partnership interest.

Control. The term *control* (including the terms *controlling, controlled by* and *under common control with*) means the possession, direct or indirect, of the power to direct or cause the direction of the management and policies of a person, whether through the ownership of voting securities, by contract, or otherwise.

Depositary Share. The term *depositary share* means a security, evidenced by an American Depositary Receipt, that represents a foreign security or a multiple of or fraction thereof deposited with a depositary.

Director. The term *director* means any director of a corporation or any person performing similar functions with respect to any organization whether incorporated or unincorporated.

Dividend or Interest Reinvestment Plan. The term *dividend or interest reinvestment plan* means a plan which is offered solely to the existing security holders of the registrant, which allows such persons to reinvest dividends or interest paid to them on securities issued by the registrant, and also may allow additional cash amounts to be contributed by the participants in the plan, provided the securities to be registered are newly issued, or are purchased for the account of plan participants, at prices not in excess of current market prices at the time of purchase, or at prices not in excess of an amount determined in accordance with a pricing formula specified in the plan and based upon average or current market prices at the time of purchase.

Electronic Filer. The term *electronic filer* means a person or an entity that submits filings electronically pursuant to Rules 100 and 101 of Regulation S–T.

Electronic Filing. The term *electronic filing* means a document under the federal securities laws that is transmitted or delivered to the Commission in electronic format.

Emerging Growth Company. (1) The term emerging growth company means an issuer that had total annual gross revenues of less than $1,070,000,000 during its most recently completed fiscal year.

(2) An issuer that is an emerging growth company as of the first day of that fiscal year shall con-

tinue to be deemed an emerging growth company until the earliest of:

(i) the last day of the fiscal year of the issuer during which it had total annual gross revenues of $1,070,000,000 or more;

(ii) the last day of the fiscal year of the issuer following the fifth anniversary of the date of the first sale of common equity securities of the issuer pursuant to an effective registration statement under the Securities Act of 1933;

(iii) the date on which such issuer has, during the previous three year period, issued more than $1,000,000,000 in non-convertible debt; or

(iv) the date on which such issuer is deemed to be a large accelerated filer, as defined in Rule 12b-2 of the Exchange Act (§ 240.12b–2 of this chapter), or any successor thereto.

Employee. The term *employee* does not include a director, trustee, or officer.

Employee Benefit Plan. The term *employee benefit plan* means any written purchase, savings, option, bonus, appreciation, profit sharing, thrift, incentive, pension or similar plan or written compensation contract solely for employees, directors, general partners, trustees (where the registrant is a business trust), officers, or consultants or advisors. However, consultants or advisors may participate in an employee benefit plan only if:

(1) They are natural persons;

(2) They provide *bona fide* services to the registrant; and

(3) The services are not in connection with the offer or sale of securities in a capital-raising transaction, and do not directly or indirectly promote or maintain a market for the registrant's securities.

Equity Security. The term *equity security* means any stock or similar security, certificate of interest or participation in any profit sharing agreement, preorganization certificate or subscription, transferable share, voting trust certificate or certificate of deposit for an equity security, limited partnership interest, interest in a joint venture, or certificate of interest in a business trust; any security future on any such security; or any security convertible, with or without consideration into such a security, or carrying any warrant or right to subscribe to or purchase such a security; or any such warrant or right; or any put, call, straddle, or other option or privilege of buying such a security from or selling such a security to another without being bound to do so.

Executive Officer. The term *executive officer*, when used with reference to a registrant, means its president, any vice president of the registrant in charge of a principal business unit, division or function (such as sales, administration or finance), any other officer who performs a policy making function or any other person who performs similar policy making functions for the registrant. Executive officers of subsidiaries may be deemed executive officers of the registrant if they perform such policy making functions for the registrant.

Fiscal Year. The term *fiscal year* means the annual accounting period or, if no closing date has been adopted, the calendar year ending on December 31.

Foreign Government. The term *foreign government* means the government of any foreign country or of any political subdivision of a foreign country.

Foreign Issuer. The term *foreign issuer* means any issuer which is a foreign government, a national of any foreign country or a corporation or other organization incorporated or organized under the laws of any foreign country.

Foreign Private Issuer. (1) The term *foreign private issuer* means any foreign issuer other than a foreign government except an issuer meeting the following conditions as of the last business day of its most recently completed second fiscal quarter:

(i) More than 50 percent of the outstanding voting securities of such issuer are directly or indirectly owned of record by residents of the United States; and

(ii) Any of the following:

(A) The majority of the executive officers or directors are United States citizens or residents;

(B) More than 50 percent of the assets of the issuer are located in the United States; or

(C) The business of the issuer is administered principally in the United States.

(2) In the case of a new registrant with the Commission, the determination of whether an issuer is a foreign private issuer shall be made as of a date within 30 days prior to the issuer's filing of an initial registration statement under either the Act or the Securities Exchange Act of 1934.

(3) Once an issuer qualifies as a foreign private issuer, it will immediately be able to use the forms and rules designated for foreign private issuers until it fails to qualify for this status at the end of its most recently completed second fiscal quarter. An issuer's

determination that it fails to qualify as a foreign private issuer governs its eligibility to use the forms and rules designated for foreign private issuers beginning on the first day of the fiscal year following the determination date. Once an issuer fails to qualify for foreign private issuer status, it will remain unqualified unless it meets the requirements for foreign private issuer status as of the last business day of its second fiscal quarter.

NOTE TO PARAGRAPH (1) OF THE DEFINITION OF *Foreign private issuer*: To determine the percentage of outstanding voting securities held by U.S. residents:

A. Use the method of calculating record ownership in Rule 12g3-2(a) of this chapter, except that:

(1) The inquiry as to the amount of shares represented by accounts of customers resident in the United States may be limited to brokers, dealers, banks and other nominees located in:

(i) The United States,

(ii) The issuer's jurisdiction of incorporation, and

(iii) The jurisdiction that is the primary trading market for the issuer's voting securities, if different than the issuer's jurisdiction of incorporation; and

(2) Notwithstanding Rule 12g5-1(a)(8) of this chapter, the issuer shall not exclude securities held by persons who received the securities pursuant to an employee compensation plan.

B. If, after reasonable inquiry, the issuer is unable to obtain information about the amount of shares represented by accounts of customers resident in the United States, the issuer may assume, for purposes of this definition, that the customers are residents of the jurisdiction in which the nominee has its principal place of business.

C. Count shares of voting securities beneficially owned by residents of the United States as reported on reports of beneficial ownership provided to the issuer or filed publicly and based on information otherwise provided to the issuer.

Free Writing Prospectus. Except as otherwise specifically provided or the context otherwise requires, a *free writing prospectus* is any written communication as defined in this rule that constitutes an offer to sell or a solicitation of an offer to buy the securities relating to a registered offering that is used after the registration statement in respect of the offering is filed (or, in the case of a well-known seasoned issuer, whether or not such registration statement is filed) and is made by means other than:

(1) A prospectus satisfying the requirements of section 10(a) of the Act, Rule 430, Rule 430A, Rule 430B, Rule 430C, Rule 430D, or Rule 431;

(2) A written communication used in reliance on Rule 167 and Rule 426; or

(3) A written communication that constitutes an offer to sell or solicitation of an offer to buy such securities that falls within the exception from the definition of prospectus in clause (a) of section 2(a)(10) of the Act.

Graphic Communication. The term *graphic communication*, which appears in the definition of "write, written" in section 2(a)(9) of the Act and in the definition of written communication in this rule, shall include all forms of electronic media, including, but not limited to, audiotapes, videotapes, facsimiles, CD–ROM, electronic mail, Internet Web sites, substantially similar messages widely distributed (rather than individually distributed) on telephone answering or voice mail systems, computers, computer networks and other forms of computer data compilation. Graphic communication shall not include a communication that, at the time of the communication, originates live, in real-time to a live audience and does not originate in recorded form or otherwise as a graphic communication, although it is transmitted through graphic means.

Ineligible Issuer. (1) *An ineligible issuer* is an issuer with respect to which any of the following is true as of the relevant date of determination:

(i) Any issuer that is required to file reports pursuant to section 13 or 15(d) of the Securities Exchange Act of 1934 (15 U.S.C. 78m or 78o(d)) that has not filed all reports and other materials required to be filed during the preceding 12 months (or for such shorter period that the issuer was required to file such reports pursuant to sections 13 or 15(d) of the Securities Exchange Act of 1934), other than reports on Form 8–K (17 CFR 249.308) required solely pursuant to an item specified in General Instruction I.A.3(b) of Form S–3 (17 CFR 239.13) (or in the case of an asset–backed issuer), to the extent the depositor or any issuing entity previously established, directly or indirectly, by the depositor (as such terms are defined in Item 1101 of Regulation AB are or were at any time during the preceding 12 calendar months required to file reports pursuant to section 13 or 15(d) of the Securities Exchange Act of 1934 with respect to a class of asset-backed securities involving the same asset class, such depositor and each such issuing entity must have filed all reports and other material required to be filed for such period (or such shorter period that each such entity was required to file such reports), other than reports on Form 8–K required solely pursuant to an item specified in General Instruction I.A.2 of Form SF–3);

(ii) The issuer is, or during the past three years the issuer or any of its predecessors was:

(A) A blank check company as defined in Rule 419(a)(2);

(B) A shell company, other than a business combination related shell company, each as defined in this rule;

(C) An issuer in an offering of penny stock as defined in Rule 3a51–1 under the Securities Exchange Act of 1934;

(iii) The issuer is a limited partnership that is offering and selling its securities other than through a firm commitment underwriting;

(iv) Within the past three years, a petition under the federal bankruptcy laws or any state insolvency law was filed by or against the issuer, or a court appointed a receiver, fiscal agent or similar officer with respect to the business or property of the issuer subject to the following:

(A) In the case of an involuntary bankruptcy in which a petition was filed against the issuer, ineligibility will occur upon the earlier to occur of:

(*1*) 90 days following the date of the filing of the involuntary petition (if the case has not been earlier dismissed); or

(*2*) The conversion of the case to a voluntary proceeding under federal bankruptcy or state insolvency laws; and

(B) Ineligibility will terminate under this paragraph (1)(iv) if an issuer has filed an annual report with audited financial statements subsequent to its emergence from that bankruptcy, insolvency, or receivership process;

(v) Within the past three years, the issuer or any entity that at the time was a subsidiary of the issuer was convicted of any felony or misdemeanor described in paragraphs (i) through (iv) of section 15(b)(4)(B) of the Securities Exchange Act of 1934 (15 U.S.C. 78o(b)(4)(B)(i) through (iv));

(vi) Within the past three years (but in the case of a decree or order agreed to in a settlement, not before December 1, 2005), the issuer or any entity that at the time was a subsidiary of the issuer was made the subject of any judicial or administrative decree or order arising out of a governmental action that:

(A) Prohibits certain conduct or activities regarding, including future violations of, the anti-fraud provisions of the federal securities laws;

(B) Requires that the person cease and desist from violating the anti-fraud provisions of the federal securities laws; or

(C) Determines that the person violated the anti-fraud provisions of the federal securities laws;

(vii) The issuer has filed a registration statement that is the subject of any pending proceeding or examination under section 8 of the Act or has been the subject of any refusal order or stop order under section 8 of the Act within the past three years; or

(viii) The issuer is the subject of any pending proceeding under section 8A of the Act in connection with an offering.

(2) An issuer shall not be an ineligible issuer if the Commission determines, upon a showing of good cause, that it is not necessary under the circumstances that the issuer be considered an ineligible issuer. Any such determination shall be without prejudice to any other action by the Commission in any other proceeding or matter with respect to the issuer or any other person.

(3) The date of determination of whether an issuer is an ineligible issuer is as follows:

(i) For purposes of determining whether an issuer is a well-known seasoned issuer, at the date specified for purposes of such determination in paragraph (2) of the definition of well-known seasoned issuer in this rule; and

(ii) For purposes of determining whether an issuer or offering participant may use free writing prospectuses in respect of an offering in accordance with the provisions of Rules 164 and 433, at the date in respect of the offering specified in paragraph (h) of Rule 164.

Majority–Owned Subsidiary. The term *majority-owned subsidiary* means a subsidiary more than 50 percent of whose outstanding securities representing the right, other than as affected by events of default, to vote for the election of directors, is owned by the subsidiary's parent and/or one or more of the parent's other majority-owned subsidiaries.

Material. The term *material,* when used to qualify a requirement for the furnishing of information as to any subject, limits the information required to those matters to which there is a substantial likelihood that a reasonable investor would attach importance in determining whether to purchase the security registered.

Officer. The term *officer* means a president, vice president, secretary, treasurer or principal financial officer, comptroller or principal accounting officer, and any person routinely performing corresponding functions with respect to any organization whether incorporated or unincorporated.

Parent. A *parent* of a specified person is an affiliate controlling such person directly, or indirectly through one or more intermediaries.

Predecessor. The term *predecessor* means a person the major portion of the business and assets of which another person acquired in a single succession, or in a series of related successions in each of which the acquiring person acquired the major portion of the business and assets of the acquired person.

Principal Underwriter. The term *principal underwriter* means an underwriter in privity of contract with the issuer of the securities as to which he is underwriter, the term "issuer" having the meaning given in sections 2(4) and 2(11) of the Act.

Promoter. (1) The term *promoter* includes—

(i) Any person who, acting alone or in conjunction with one or more other persons, directly or indirectly takes initiative in founding and organizing the business or enterprise of an issuer; or

(ii) Any person who, in connection with the founding and organizing of the business or enterprise of an issuer, directly or indirectly receives in consideration of services or property, or both services and property, 10 percent or more of any class of securities of the issuer or 10 percent or more of the proceeds from the sale of any class of such securities. However, a person who receives such securities or proceeds either solely as underwriting commissions or solely in consideration of property shall not be deemed a promoter within the meaning of this paragraph if such person does not otherwise take part in founding and organizing the enterprise.

(2) All persons coming within the definition of *promoter* in paragraph (1) of this definition may be referred to as *founders* or *organizers* or by another term provided that such term is reasonably descriptive of those persons' activities with respect to the issuer.

Prospectus. Unless otherwise specified or the context otherwise requires, the term *prospectus* means a prospectus meeting the requirements of section 10(a) of the Act.

Registrant. The term *registrant* means the issuer of the securities for which the registration statement is filed.

Share. The term *share* means a share of stock in a corporation or unit of interest in an unincorporated person.

Shell Company: The term *shell company* means a registrant, other than an asset-backed issuer as defined in Item 1101(b) of Regulation AB, that has:

(1) No or nominal operations; and

(2) Either:

(i) No or nominal assets;

(ii) Assets consisting solely of cash and cash equivalents; or

(iii) Assets consisting of any amount of cash and cash equivalents and nominal other assets.

NOTE: For purposes of this definition, the determination of a registrant's assets (including cash and cash equivalents) is based solely on the amount of assets that would be reflected on the registrant's balance sheet prepared in accordance with generally accepted accounting principles on the date of that determination.

Significant Subsidiary. The term *significant subsidiary* means a subsidiary, including its subsidiaries, which meets any of the following conditions:

(1) The registrant's and its other subsidiaries' investments in and advances to the subsidiary exceed 10 percent of the total assets of the registrant and its subsidiaries consolidated as of the end of the most recently completed fiscal year (for a proposed combination between entities under common control, this condition is also met when the number of common shares exchanged or to be exchanged by the registrant exceeds 10 percent of its total common shares outstanding at the date the combination is initiated); or

(2) The registrant's and its other subsidiaries' proportionate share of the total assets (after intercompany eliminations) of the subsidiary exceeds 10 percent of the total assets of the registrants

and its subsidiaries consolidated as of the end of the most recently completed fiscal year; or

(3) The registrant's and its other subsidiaries' equity in the income from continuing operations before income taxes of the subsidiary exclusive of amounts attributable to any noncontrolling interests exceeds 10 percent of such income of the registrant and its subsidiaries consolidated for the most recently completed fiscal year.

NOTE 1: A registrant that files its financial statements in accordance with or provides a reconciliation to U.S. Generally Accepted Accounting Principles shall make the prescribed tests using amounts determined under U.S. Generally Accepted Accounting Principles. A foreign private issuer that files its financial statements in accordance with IFRS as issued by the IASB shall make the prescribed tests using amounts determined under IFRS as issued by the IASB.

COMPUTATIONAL NOTE 1 TO PARAGRAPH (3): For purposes of making the prescribed income test the following guidance should be applied:

1. When a loss exclusive of amounts attributable to any noncontrolling interests has been incurred by either the parent and its subsidiaries consolidated or the tested subsidiary, but not both, the equity in the income or loss of the tested subsidiary exclusive of amounts attributable to any noncontrolling interests should be excluded from such income of the registrant and its subsidiaries consolidated for purposes of the computation.

2. If income of the registrant and its subsidiaries consolidated exclusive of amounts attributable to any noncontrolling interests for the most recent fiscal year is at least 10 percent lower than the average of the income for the last five fiscal years, such average income should be substituted for purposes of the computation. Any loss years should be omitted for purposes of computing average income.

Smaller Reporting Company. As used in this part, the term *smaller reporting company* means an issuer that is not an investment company, an asset-backed issuer (as defined in Item 1101 of Regulation AB), or a majority-owned subsidiary of a parent that is not a smaller reporting company and that:

(1) Had a public float of less than $250 million; or

(2) Had annual revenues of less than $100 million and either:

(i) No public float; or

(ii) A public float of less than $700 million.

(3) Whether an issuer is a smaller reporting company is determined on an annual basis.

(i) For issuers that are required to file reports under section 13(a) or 15(d) of the Exchange Act:

(A) Public float is measured as of the last business day of the issuer's most recently completed second fiscal quarter and computed by multiplying the aggregate worldwide number of shares of its voting and non-voting common equity held by non-affiliates by the price at which the common equity was last sold, or the average of the bid and asked prices of common equity, in the principal market for the common equity;

(B) Annual revenues are as of the most recently completed fiscal year for which audited financial statements are available; and

(C) An issuer must reflect the determination of whether it came within the definition of smaller reporting company in its quarterly report on Form 10–Q for the first fiscal quarter of the next year, indicating on the cover page of that filing, and in subsequent filings for that fiscal year, whether it is a smaller reporting company, except that, if a determination based on public float indicates that the issuer is newly eligible to be a smaller reporting company, the issuer may choose to reflect this determination beginning with its first quarterly report on Form 10–Q following the determination, rather than waiting until the first fiscal quarter of the next year.

(ii) For determinations based on an initial registration statement under the Securities Act or Exchange Act for shares of its common equity:

(A) Public float is measured as of a date within 30 days of the date of the filing of the registration statement and computed by multiplying the aggregate worldwide number of shares of its voting and non-voting common equity held by non-affiliates before the registration plus, in the case of a Securities Act registration statement, the number of shares of its voting and non-voting common equity included in the registration statement by the estimated public offering price of the shares;

(B) Annual revenues are as of the most recently completed fiscal year for which audited financial statements are available; and

(C) The issuer must reflect the determination of whether it came within the definition of smaller reporting company in the registration statement and must appropriately indicate on the cover page of the filing, and subsequent filings for the fiscal year in which the filing is made, whether it is a smaller reporting company. The issuer must re-determine its status at the end of its second fiscal quarter and then reflect any change in status as provided in paragraph (3)(i)(C) of this definition. In the case of a determination based on an initial Securities Act registration statement, an issuer that was not determined to be a smaller reporting company has the option to re-determine its status at the conclusion of the offering covered by the registration statement based on the actual offering price and number of shares sold.

(iii) Once an issuer determines that it does not qualify for smaller reporting company status because it exceeded one or more of the current thresholds, it will remain unqualified unless when making its annual determination either:

(A) It determines that its public float was less than $200 million; or

(B) It determines that its public float and its annual revenues meet the requirements for subsequent qualification included in the following chart:

Prior Annual Revenues	**Prior Public Float**	
	None or less than $700 million	**$700 million or more**
Less than $100 million	Neither threshold exceeded.	**Public float** Less than $560 million; and **Revenues** Less than $100 million.
$100 million or more	**Public float** None or less than $700 million; and **Revenues** Less than $80 million.	**Public float** Less than $560 million; and **Revenues** Less than 80 million.

Instruction 1 to definition of "smaller reporting company": A registrant that qualifies as a smaller reporting company under the public float thresholds identified in paragraphs (1) and (3)(iii)(A) of this definition will qualify as a smaller reporting company regardless of its revenues.

Subsidiary. A *subsidiary* of a specified person is an affiliate controlled by such person directly, or indirectly through one or more intermediaries. (See also *majority owned subsidiary*, *significant subsidiary*, *totally held subsidiary*, and *wholly owned subsidiary*.)

Succession. The term *succession* means the direct acquisition of the assets comprising a going business, whether by merger, consolidation, purchase, or other direct transfer. The term does not include the acquisition of control of a business unless followed by the direct acquisition of its assets. The terms *succeed* and *successor* have meanings correlative to the foregoing.

Totally Held Subsidiary. The term *totally held subsidiary* means a subsidiary (1) substantially all of whose outstanding securities are owned by its parent and/or the parent's other totally held subsidiaries, and (2) which is not indebted to any person other than its parent and/or the parent's other totally held subsidiaries in an amount which is material in relation to the particular subsidiary, excepting indebtedness incurred in the ordinary course of business which is not overdue and which matures within one year from the date of its creation, whether evidenced by securities or not.

Voting Securities. The term *voting securities* means securities the holders of which are presently entitled to vote for the election of directors.

Well-Known Seasoned Issuer. A *well-known seasoned issuer* is an issuer that, as of the most recent determination date determined pursuant to paragraph (2) of this definition:

(1)(i) Meets all the registrant requirements of General Instruction I.A. of Form S–3 or Form F–3 (17 CFR 239.13 or 17 CFR 239.33) and either:

(A) As of a date within 60 days of the determination date, has a worldwide market value of its outstanding voting and non-voting common equity held by non-affiliates of $700 million or more; or

(B)(*1*) As of a date within 60 days of the determination date, has issued in the last three years at least $1 billion aggregate principal amount of non-convertible securities, other than common equity, in primary offerings for cash, not exchange, registered under the Act; and

(*2*) Will register only non-convertible securities, other than common equity, and full and unconditional guarantees permitted pursuant to paragraph (1)(ii) of this definition unless, at the determination date, the issuer also is eligible to register a primary offering of its securities relying on General Instruction I.B.1. of Form S–3 or Form F–3.

(*3*) Provided that as to a parent issuer only, for purposes of calculating the aggregate principal amount of outstanding non-convertible securities under paragraph (1)(i)(B)(1) of this definition, the parent issuer may include the aggregate principal amount of non-convertible securities, other than common equity, of its majority-owned subsidiaries issued in registered primary offerings for cash, not exchange, that it has fully and unconditionally guaranteed, within the meaning of Rule 3–10 of Regulation S–X in the last three years; or

(ii) Is a majority-owned subsidiary of a parent that is a well-known seasoned issuer pursuant to paragraph (1)(i) of this definition and, as to the subsidiaries' securities that are being or may be offered on that parent's registration statement:

(A) The parent has provided a full and unconditional guarantee, as defined in Rule 3–10 of Regulation S–X, of the payment obligations on the subsidiary's securities and the securities are non-convertible securities, other than common equity;

(B) The securities are guarantees of:

(*1*) Non-convertible securities, other than common equity, of its parent being registered; or

(*2*) Non-convertible securities, other than common equity, of another majority-owned subsidiary being registered where there is a full and unconditional guarantee, as defined in Rule 3–10 of Regulation S–X, of such non-convertible securities by the parent; or

(C) The securities of the majority-owned subsidiary meet the conditions of General Instruction I.B.2 of Form S–3 or Form F–3.

(iii) Is not an ineligible issuer as defined in this rule.

(iv) Is not an asset-backed issuer as defined in Item 1101 of Regulation AB.

(v) Is not an investment company registered under the Investment Company Act of 1940 (15 U.S.C. 80a–1 *et seq.*) or a business development company as defined in section 2(a)(48) of the Investment Company Act of 1940 (15 U.S.C. 80a–2(a)(48)).

(2) For purposes of this definition, the determination date as to whether an issuer is a well-known seasoned issuer shall be the latest of:

(i) The time of filing of its most recent shelf registration statement; or

(ii) The time of its most recent amendment (by post-effective amendment, incorporated report filed pursuant to section 13 or 15(d) of the Securities Exchange Act of 1934) (15 U.S.C. 78m or 78o(d), or form of prospectus) to a shelf registration statement for purposes of complying with section 10(a)(3) of the Act (or if such amendment has not been made within the time period required by section 10(a)(3) of the Act, the date on which such amendment is required); or

(iii) In the event that the issuer has not filed a shelf registration statement or amended a shelf registration statement for purposes of complying with section 10(a)(3) of the Act for sixteen months, the time of filing of the issuer's most recent annual report on Form 10–K (17 CFR 249.310) or Form 20–F (17 CFR 249.220f) (or if such report has not been filed by its due date, such due date).

Wholly Owned Subsidiary. The term *wholly owned subsidiary* means a subsidiary substantially all of whose outstanding voting securities are owned by its parent and/or the parent's other wholly owned subsidiaries.

Written Communication. Except as otherwise specifically provided or the context otherwise requires, a *written communication* is any communication that is written, printed, a radio or television broadcast, or a graphic communication as defined in this rule.

NOTE to definition of "written communication." A communication that is a radio or television broadcast is a written communication regardless of the means of transmission of the broadcast.

Rule 406. Confidential treatment of information filed with the Commission

PRELIMINARY NOTES

(1) Confidential treatment of supplemental information or other information not required to be filed under the Act should be requested under 17 CFR 200.83 and not under this rule.

(2) All confidential treatment requests shall be submitted in paper format only, whether or not the filer is an electronic filer. *See* Rule 101(c)(1)(i) of Regulation S–T.

(a) Any person submitting any information in a document required to be filed under the Act may make written objection to its public disclosure by following the procedure in paragraph (b) of this rule, which shall be the exclusive means of requesting confidential treatment of information included in any document (hereinafter referred to as the *material filed*) required to be filed under the Act, *except* that if the material filed is a registration statement on Form S–8 (17 CFR 239.16b) or on Form S–3, F–2,

F–3 (17 CFR 239.13, 239.32 or 239.33) relating to a dividend or interest reinvestment plan, or on Form S–4 (17 CFR 239.25) complying with General Instruction G of that Form, or if the material filed is a registration statement that does not contain a delaying amendment pursuant to Rule 473, the person shall comply with the procedure in paragraph (b) *prior* to the filing of a registration statement.

(b) The person shall omit from the material filed the portion thereof which it desires to keep undisclosed (hereinafter called the *confidential portion*). In lieu thereof, the person shall indicate at the appropriate place in the material filed that the confidential portion has been so omitted and filed separately with the Commission. The person shall file with the material filed:

(1) One copy of the confidential portion, marked "Confidential Treatment," of the material filed with the Commission. The copy shall contain an appropriate identification of the item or other requirement involved and, notwithstanding that the confidential portion does not constitute the whole of the answer or required disclosure, the entire answer or required disclosure, except that in the case where the confidential portion is part of a financial statement or schedule, only the particular financial statement or schedule need be included. The copy of the confidential portion shall be in the same form as the remainder of the material filed;

(2) An application making objection to the disclosure of the confidential portion. Such application shall be on a sheet or sheets separate from the confidential portion, and shall contain

(i) An identification of the portion;

(ii) A statement of the grounds of the objection referring to and analyzing the applicable exemption(s) from disclosure under 17 CFR 200.80, the Commission's rule adopted under the Freedom of Information Act (5 U.S.C. 552), and a justification of the period of time for which confidential treatment is sought;

(iii) A detailed explanation of why, based on the facts and circumstances of the particular case, disclosure of the information is unnecessary for the protection of investors;

(iv) A written consent to the furnishing of the confidential portion to other government agencies, offices or bodies and to the Congress; and

(v) The name, address and telephone number of the person to whom all notices and orders issued under this rule at any time should be directed;

(3) The copy of the confidential portion and the application filed in accordance with this paragraph (b) shall be enclosed in a separate envelope marked "Confidential Treatment" and addressed to The Secretary, Securities and Exchange Commission, Washington, DC 20549.

(c) Pending a determination as to the objection, the material for which confidential treatment has been applied will not be made available to the public.

(d) If it is determined by the Division, acting pursuant to delegated authority, that the application should be granted, an order to that effect will be entered, and a notation to that effect will be made at the appropriate place in the material filed. Such a determination will not preclude reconsideration whenever appropriate, such as upon receipt of any subsequent request under the Freedom of Information Act and, if appropriate, revocation of the confidential status of all or a portion of the information in question.

(e) If the Commission denies the application, or the Division, acting pursuant to delegated authority, denies the application and Commission review is not sought pursuant to 17 CFR 201.431, confirmed telegraphic notice of the order of denial will be sent to the person named in the application pursuant to paragraph (b)(2)(v) of this rule. In such case, if the material filed may be withdrawn pursuant to an applicable statute, rule, or regulation, the registrant shall have the right to withdraw the material filed in accordance with the terms of the applicable statute, rule, or regulation, but without the necessity of stating any grounds for the withdrawal or of obtaining the further assent of the Commission. In the event of such withdrawal, the confidential portion will be returned to the registrant. If the material filed may not be so withdrawn, the confidential portion will be made available for public inspection in the same manner as if confidential treatment had been revoked under paragraph (h) of this rule.

(f) If a right of withdrawal pursuant to paragraph (e) of this rule is not exercised, the confidential portion will be made available for public inspection as part of the material filed, and the registrant shall amend the material filed to include all information required to be set forth in regard to such confidential portion.

(g) In any case where a prior grant of confidential treatment has been revoked, the person named in the application pursuant to paragraph (b)(2)(v) of this rule will be so informed by registered or certified mail. Pursuant to 17 CFR 201.431, persons making objections to disclosure may petition the Commission for review of a determination by the Division revoking confidential treatment.

(h) Upon revocation of confidential treatment, the confidential portion shall be made available to the public at the time and according to the conditions specified in paragraphs (h)(1)–(2):

(1) Upon the lapse of five days after the dispatch of notice by registered or certified mail of a determination disallowing an objection, if prior to the lapse of such five days the person shall not have communicated to the Secretary of the Commission his intention to seek review by the Commission under 17 CFR 201.431 of the determination made by the Division; or

(2) If such a petition for review shall have been filed under 17 CFR 201.431, upon final disposition adverse to the petitioner.

(i) If the confidential portion is made available to the public, one copy thereof shall be attached to each copy of the material filed with the Commission.

Rule 408. Additional information

(a) In addition to the information expressly required to be included in a registration statement, there shall be added such further material information, if any, as may be necessary to make the required statements, in the light of the circumstances under which they are made, not misleading.

(b) Notwithstanding paragraph (a) of this rule, unless otherwise required to be included in the registration statement, the failure to include in a registration statement information included in a free writing prospectus will not, solely by virtue of inclusion of the information in a free writing prospectus (as defined in Rule 405), be considered an omission of material information required to be included in the registration statement.

Rule 409. Information unknown or not reasonably available

Information required need be given only insofar as it is known or reasonably available to the registrant. If any required information is unknown and not reasonably available to the registrant, either because the obtaining thereof could involve unreasonable effort or expense, or because it rests peculiarly within the knowledge of another person not affiliated with the registrant, the information may be omitted, subject to the following conditions:

(a) The registrant shall give such information on the subject as it possesses or can acquire without unreasonable effort or expense, together with the sources thereof.

(b) The registrant shall include a statement either showing that unreasonable effort or expense would be involved or indicating the absence of any affiliation with the person within whose knowledge the information rests and stating the result of a request made to such person for the information.

Rule 410. Disclaimer of control

If the existence of control is open to reasonable doubt in any instance, the registrant may disclaim the existence of control and any admission thereof; in such case, however, the registrant shall state the material facts pertinent to the possible existence of control.

Rule 411. Incorporation by reference

(a) *Prospectus.* Except as provided by this rule, Item 1100(c) of Regulation AB for registered offerings of asset-backed securities, or unless otherwise provided in the appropriate form, information shall not be incorporated by reference in a prospectus. Where a summary or outline of the provisions of any document is required in the prospectus, the summary or outline may incorporate by reference particular items, sections or paragraphs of any exhibit and may be qualified in its entirety by such reference.

(b) *Information Not Required in a Prospectus.* Except for exhibits covered by Paragraph (c) of this rule, information may be incorporated by reference in answer, or partial answer, to any item that calls for information not required to be included in a prospectus subject to the following provisions:

(1) Non-financial information may be incorporated by reference to any document;

(2) Financial information may be incorporated by reference to any document, provided any financial statement so incorporated meets the requirements of the forms on which the statement is filed. Financial statements or other financial data required to be given in comparative form for two or more fiscal years or periods shall not be incorporated by reference unless the information incorporated by reference includes the entire period for which the comparative data is given;

(3) Information contained in any part of the registration statement, including the prospectus, may be incorporated by reference in answer, or partial answer, to any item that calls for information not required to be included in the prospectus; and

(4) Unless the information is incorporated by reference to a document which complies with the time limitations of 17 CFR 228.10(f) and Item 10(d) of Regulation S–K, then the document, or part thereof, containing the incorporated information is required to be filed as an exhibit.

(c) *Exhibits.* Any document or part thereof filed with the Commission pursuant to any Act administered by the Commission may, subject to the limitations of 17 CFR 228.10(f) and Item 10(d) of Regulation S–K, be incorporated by reference as an exhibit to any registration statement. If any modification has occurred in the text of any document incorporated by reference since the filing thereof, the registrant shall file with the reference a statement containing the text of such modification and the date thereof.

(d) *General.* Any incorporation by reference of information pursuant to this rule shall be subject to the provisions of Rule 24 of the Commission's Rules of Practice restricting incorporation by reference of documents which incorporate by reference other information. Information incorporated by reference shall be clearly identified in the reference by page, paragraph, caption or otherwise. If the information is incorporated by reference to a previously filed document, the file number of such document shall be included. Where only certain pages of a document are incorporated by reference and filed with the statement, the document from which the information is taken shall be clearly identified in the reference. An express statement that the specified matter is incorporated by reference shall be made at the particular place in the registration statement where the information is required. Information shall not be incorporated by reference in any case where such incorporation would render the statement incomplete, unclear or confusing.

Rule 412. Modified or superseded documents

(a) Any statement contained in a document incorporated or deemed to be incorporated by reference or deemed to be part of a registration statement or the prospectus that is part of the registration statement shall be deemed to be modified or superseded for purposes of the registration statement or the prospectus that is part of the registration statement to the extent that a statement contained in the prospectus that is part of the registration statement or in any other subsequently filed document which also is or is deemed to be incorporated by reference or deemed to be part of the registration statement or prospectus that is part of the registration statement modifies or replaces such statement. Any statement contained in a document that is deemed to be incorporated by reference or deemed to be part of a registration statement or the prospectus that is part of the registration statement after the most recent effective date or after the date of the most recent prospectus that is part of the registration statement may modify or replace existing statements contained in the registration statement or the prospectus that is part of the registration statement.

(b) The modifying or superseding statement may, but need not, state that it has modified or superseded a prior statement or include any other information set forth in the document which is not so modified or superseded. The making of a modifying or superseding statement shall not be deemed an admission that the modified or superseded statement, when made, constituted an untrue statement of a material fact, an omission to state a material fact necessary to make a statement not misleading, or the employment of a manipulative, deceptive, or fraudulent device, contrivance, scheme, transaction, act, practice, course of business or artifice to defraud, as those terms are used in the Act, the Securities Exchange Act of 1934, the Investment Company Act of 1940, or the rules and regulations thereunder.

(c) Any statement so modified shall not be deemed in its unmodified form to constitute part of the registration statement or prospectus for purpose of the Act. Any statement so superseded shall not be deemed to constitute a part of the registration statement or the prospectus for purposes of the Act.

Rule 413. Registration of additional securities and additional classes of securities

(a) Except as provided in section 24(f) of the Investment Company Act of 1940 (15 U.S.C. 80a–24(f)) and in paragraph (b) of this rule, where a registration statement is already in effect, the registration of additional securities shall only be effected through a separate registration statement relating to the additional securities.

(b) Notwithstanding paragraph (a) of this rule, the following additional securities or additional classes of securities may be added to an automatic shelf registration statement already in effect by filing a post-effective amendment to that automatic shelf registration statement:

(1) Securities of a class different than those registered on the effective automatic shelf registration statement identified as provided in Rule 430B(a); or

(2) Securities of a majority-owned subsidiary that are permitted to be included in an automatic shelf registration statement, provided that the subsidiary and the securities are identified as provided in Rule 430B and the subsidiary satisfies the signature requirements of an issuer in the post-effective amendment.

Rule 414. Registration by certain successor issuers

If any issuer, except a foreign issuer exempted by Rule 3a12–3 under the Securities Exchange Act of 1934, incorporated under the laws of any State or foreign government and having securities registered under the Act has been succeeded by an issuer incorporated under the laws of another State or foreign government for the purpose of changing the State or country of incorporation of the enterprises, or if any issuer has been succeeded by an issuer for the purpose of changing its form of organization, the registration statement of the predecessor issuer shall be deemed the registration statement of the successor issuer for the purpose of continuing the offering provided:

(a) Immediately prior to the succession the successor issuer had no assets or liabilities other than nominal assets or liabilities;

(b) The succession was effected by a merger or similar succession pursuant to statutory provisions or the terms of the organic instruments under which the successor issuer acquired all of the assets and assumed all of the liabilities and obligations of the predecessor issuer;

(c) The succession was approved by security holders of the predecessor issuer at a meeting for which proxies were solicited pursuant to section 14(a) of the Securities Exchange Act of 1934 or section 20(a) of the Investment Company Act of 1940 or information was furnished to security holders pursuant to section 14(c) of the Securities Exchange Act of 1934; and

(d) The successor issuer has filed an amendment to the registration statement of the predecessor issuer expressly adopting such statements as its own registration statement for all purposes of the Act and the Securities Exchange Act of 1934 and setting forth any additional information necessary to reflect any material changes made in connection with or resulting from the succession, or necessary to keep the registration statement from being misleading in any material respect, and such amendment has become effective.

Rule 415. Delayed or continuous offering and sale of securities

(a) Securities may be registered for an offering to be made on a continuous or delayed basis in the future, *Provided,* That:

(1) The registration statement pertains only to:

(i) Securities which are to be offered or sold solely by or on behalf of a person or persons other than the registrant, a subsidiary of the registrant or a person of which the registrant is a subsidiary;

(ii) Securities which are to be offered and sold pursuant to a dividend or interest reinvestment plan or an employee benefit plan of the registrant;

(iii) Securities which are to be issued upon the exercise of outstanding options, warrants or rights;

(iv) Securities which are to be issued upon conversion of other outstanding securities;

(v) Securities which are pledged as collateral;

(vi) Securities which are registered on Form F–6 (17 CFR 239.36);

(vii) Asset-backed securities (as defined in Item 1101(c) of Regulation AB) registered (or qualified to be registered) on Form SF–3 (17 CFR 239.45) which are to be offered and sold on an immediate or delayed basis by or on behalf of the registrant;

Instruction to Paragraph (a)(1)(vii): The requirements of General Instruction I.B.1 of Form SF–3 (17 CFR 239.45) must be met for any offerings of an asset-backed security (as defined in Item 1101(c) of Regulation AB) registered in reliance on this paragraph (a)(1)(vii).

(viii) Securities which are to be issued in connection with business combination transactions;

(ix) Securities, other than asset-backed securities (as defined in 17 CFR 229.1101(c)), the offering of which will be commenced promptly, will be made on a continuous basis and may continue for a period in excess of 30 days from the date of initial effectiveness;

(x) Securities registered (or qualified to be registered) on Form S–3 or Form F–3 (17 CFR 239.13 or 17 CFR 239.33) which are to be offered and sold on an immediate, continuous or delayed basis by or on behalf of the registrant, a majority-owned subsidiary of the registrant or a person of which the registrant is a majority-owned subsidiary; or

(xi) Shares of common stock which are to be offered and sold on a delayed or continuous basis by or on behalf of a registered closed-end management investment company or business development company that makes periodic repurchase offers pursuant to Rule 23c–3 under the Investment Company Act of 1940.

(xii) Asset-backed securities (as defined in Item 1101(c) of Regulation AB) that are to be offered and sold on a continuous basis if the offering is commenced promptly and being conducted on the condition that the consideration paid for such securities will be promptly refunded to the purchaser unless:

(A) All of the securities being offered are sold at a specified price within a specified time; and

(B) The total amount due to the seller is received by him by a specified date.

(2) Securities in paragraph (a)(1)(viii) of this rule and securities in paragraph (a)(1)(ix) of this rule that are not registered on Form S–3 or Form F–3 (17 CFR 239.13 or 239.33) may only be registered in an amount which, at the time the registration statement becomes effective, is reasonably expected to be offered and sold within two years from the initial effective date of the registration.

(3) The registrant furnishes the undertakings required by Item 512(a) of Regulation S–K, except that a registrant that is an investment company filing on Form N–2 must furnish the undertakings required by Item 34.4 of Form N–2 (17 CFR 239.14 and 274.11a–1).

(4) In the case of a registration statement pertaining to an at the market offering of equity securities by or on behalf of the registrant, the offering must come within paragraph (a)(1)(x) of this rule. As used in this paragraph, the term "at the market offering" means an offering of equity securities into an existing trading market for outstanding shares of the same class at other than a fixed price.

(5) Securities registered on an automatic shelf registration statement and securities described in paragraphs (a)(1)(vii), (ix), and (x) of this rule may be offered and sold only if not more than three years have elapsed since the initial effective date of the registration statement under which they are being offered and sold, *provided, however*, that if a new registration statement has been filed pursuant to paragraph (a)(6) of this rule:

(i) If the new registration statement is an automatic shelf registration statement, it shall be immediately effective pursuant to Rule 462(e); or

(ii) If the new registration statement is not an automatic shelf registration statement:

(A) Securities covered by the prior registration statement may continue to be offered and sold until the earlier of the effective date of the new registration statement or 180 days after the third anniversary of the initial effective date of the prior registration statement; and

(B) A continuous offering of securities covered by the prior registration statement that commenced within three years of the initial effective date may continue until the effective date of the new registration statement if such offering is permitted under the new registration statement.

(6) Prior to the end of the three-year period described in paragraph (a)(5) of this rule, an issuer may file a new registration statement covering securities described in such paragraph (a)(5) of this rule, which may, if permitted, be an automatic shelf registration statement. The new registration statement and prospectus included therein must include all the information that would be required at that time in a prospectus relating to all offering(s) that it covers. Prior to the effective date of the new registration statement (including at the time of filing in the case of an automatic shelf registration statement), the issuer may include on such new registration statement any unsold securities covered by the earlier registration statement by identifying on the bottom of the facing page of the new registration statement or latest amendment thereto the amount of such unsold securities being included and any filing fee paid in connection with such unsold securities, which will continue to be applied to such unsold securities. The offering of securities on the earlier registration statement will be deemed terminated as of the date of effectiveness of the new registration statement.

(b) This rule shall not apply to any registration statement pertaining to securities issued by a face-amount certificate company or redeemable securities issued by an open-end management company or unit investment trust under the Investment Company Act of 1940 or any registration statement filed by any foreign government or political subdivision thereof.

Rule 416. Securities to be issued as a result of stock splits, stock dividends, and anti-dilution provisions and interests to be issued pursuant to certain employee benefit plans

(a) If a registration statement purports to register securities to be offered pursuant to terms which provide for a change in the amount of securities being offered or issued to prevent dilution resulting from stock splits, stock dividends or similar transactions, such registration statement shall, unless otherwise expressly provided, be deemed to cover the additional securities to be offered or issued in connection with any such provision.

(b) If prior to completion of the distribution of the securities covered by a registration statement, additional securities of the same class are issued or issuable as a result of a stock split or stock dividend, the registration statement shall, unless otherwise expressly provided therein, be deemed to cover such additional securities resulting from the split of, or the stock dividend on, the registered securities. If prior to completion of the distribution of the securities covered by a registration statement, all the securities of a class which includes the registered securities are combined by a reverse split into a lesser amount of securities of the same class, the amount of undistributed securities of such class deemed to be covered by the registration statement shall be proportionately reduced. If paragraph (a) of this rule is not applicable, the registration statement shall be amended prior to the offering of such additional or lesser amount of securities to reflect the change in the amount of securities registered.

(c) Where a registration statement on Form S–8 relates to securities to be offered pursuant to an employee benefit plan, including interests in such plan that constitute separate securities required to be registered under the Act, such registration statement shall be deemed to register an indeterminate amount of such plan interests.

Rule 417. Date of financial statements

Whenever financial statements of any person are required to be furnished as of a date within a specified period prior to the date of filing the registration statement and the last day of such period falls on a Saturday, Sunday, or holiday, such registration statement may be filed on the first business day following the last day of the specified period.

Rule 418. Supplemental information

(a) The Commission or its staff may, where it is deemed appropriate, request supplemental information concerning the registrant, the registration statement, the distribution of the securities, market activities and underwriters' activities. Such information includes, but is not limited to, the following items which the registrant should be prepared to furnish promptly upon request:

(1)(i) Any reports or memoranda which have been prepared for external use by the registrant or a principal underwriter, as defined in Rule 405, in connection with the proposed offering;

(ii) A statement as to the actual or proposed use and distribution of the reports or memoranda specified in paragraph (a)(1)(i) of this rule, identifying each class of persons who have received or will receive such reports or memoranda and the number of copies distributed to each such class;

(2) In the case of a registration statement relating to a business combination as defined in Rule 145(a), exchange offer, tender offer or similar transaction, any feasibility studies, management analyses, fairness opinions or similar reports prepared by or for any of the parties to the subject transaction in connection with such transaction;

(3) Except in the case of a registrant eligible to use Form S–3 (17 CFR 239.13), any engineering, management or similar reports or memoranda relating to broad aspects of the business, operations or products of the registrant, which have been prepared within the past twelve months for or by the registrant and any affiliate of the registrant or any principal underwriter, as defined in Rule 405, of the securities being registered except for:

(i) Reports solely comprised of recommendations to buy, sell or hold the securities of the registrant, unless such recommendations have changed within the past six months; and

(ii) Any information contained in documents already filed with the Commission.

(4) Where there is a registration of an at-the-market offering, as defined in Rule 100 of Regulation M under the Securities Exchange Act of 1934, of more than 10 percent of the securities outstanding, where the offering includes securities owned by officers, directors or affiliates of the registrant and where there is no underwriting agreement, information (i) concerning contractual arrangements between selling security holders of a limited group or of several groups of related shareholders to comply with the anti-manipulation rules until the offering by all members of the group is com-

pleted and to inform the exchange, brokers and selling security holders when the distribution by the members of the group is over; or (ii) concerning the registrant's efforts to notify members of a large group of unrelated sellers of the applicable Commission rules and regulations;

(5) Where the registrant recently has introduced a new product or has begun to do business in a new industry segment or has made public its intentions to introduce a new product or to do business in a new industry segment, and this action requires the investment of a material amount of the assets of the registrant or otherwise is material, copies of any studies prepared for the registrant by outside persons or any internal studies, documents, reports or memoranda the contents of which were material to the decision to develop the product or to do business in the new segment including, but not limited to, documents relating to financial requirements and engineering, competitive, environmental and other considerations, but excluding technical documents;

(6) Where reserve estimates are referred to in a document, a copy of the full report of the engineer or other expert who estimated the reserves;

(7) With respect to the extent of the distribution of a preliminary prospectus, information concerning:

(i) The date of the preliminary prospectus distributed;

(ii) The dates or approximate dates of distribution;

(iii) The number of prospective underwriters and dealers to whom the preliminary prospectus was furnished;

(iv) The number of prospectuses so distributed;

(v) The number of prospectuses distributed to others, identifying them in general terms; and

(vi) The steps taken by such underwriters and dealers to comply with the provisions of Rule 15c2–8 under the Securities Exchange Act of 1934; and

(8) Any free writing prospectuses used in connection with the offering.

(b) Supplemental information described in paragraph (a) of this rule shall not be required to be filed with or deemed part of and included in the registration statement, unless otherwise required. The information shall be returned to the registrant upon request, provided that:

(1) Such request is made at the time such information is furnished to the staff;

(2) The return of such information is consistent with the protection of investors;

(3) The return of such information is consistent with the provisions of the Freedom of Information Act [5 U.S.C. 552]; and

(4) The information was not filed in electronic format.

Rule 419. Offerings by blank check companies

(a) *Scope of the Rule and Definitions.* (1) The provisions of this rule shall apply to every registration statement filed under the Act relating to an offering by a blank check company.

(2) For purposes of this rule, the term "blank check company" shall mean a company that:

(i) Is a development stage company that has no specific business plan or purpose or has indicated that its business plan is to engage in a merger or acquisition with an unidentified company or companies, or other entity or person; and

(ii) Is issuing "penny stock," as defined in Rule 3a51–1 under the Securities Exchange Act of 1934.

(3) For purposes of this rule the term "purchaser" shall mean any person acquiring securities directly or indirectly in the offering, for cash or otherwise, including promoters or others receiving securities as compensation in connection with the offering.

(b) *Deposit of Securities and Proceeds in Escrow or Trust Account.* (1) *General.* (i) Except as otherwise provided in this rule or prohibited by other applicable law, all securities issued in connection with an offering by a blank check company and the gross proceeds from the offering shall be deposited promptly into:

(A) An escrow account maintained by an "insured depository institution," as that term is defined in section 3(c)(2) of the Federal Deposit Insurance Act (12 U.S.C. 1813(C)(2)); or

(B) A separate bank account established by a broker or dealer registered under the Exchange Act maintaining net capital equal to or exceeding $25,000 (as calculated pursuant to Rule 15c3–1 under the Securities Exchange Act of 1934), in which the broker or dealer acts as trustee for persons having the beneficial interests in the account.

(ii) If funds and securities are deposited into an escrow account maintained by an insured depository institution, the deposit account records of the insured depository institution must provide that funds in the escrow account are held for the benefit of the purchasers named and identified in accordance with 12 CFR 330.1 of the regulations of the Federal Deposit Insurance Corporation, and the records of the escrow agent, maintained in good faith and in the regular course of business, must show the name and interest of each party to the account. If funds and securities are deposited in a separate bank account established by a broker or dealer acting as a trustee, the books and records of the broker-dealer must indicate the name, address, and interest of each person for whom the account is held.

(2) *Deposit and Investment of Proceeds.* (i) All offering proceeds, after deduction of cash paid for underwriting commissions, underwriting expenses and dealer allowances, and amounts permitted to be released to the registrant pursuant to paragraph (b)(2)(vi) of this rule shall be deposited promptly into the escrow or trust account; *provided, however,* that no deduction may be made for underwriting commissions, underwriting expenses or dealer allowances payable to an affiliate of the registrant.

(ii) Deposited proceeds shall be in the form of checks, drafts, or money orders payable to the order of the escrow agent or trustee.

(iii) Deposited proceeds and interest or dividends thereon, if any, shall be held for the sole benefit of the purchasers of the securities.

(iv) Deposited proceeds shall be invested in one of the following:

(A) An obligation that constitutes a "deposit," as that term is defined in section 3(1) of the Federal Deposit Insurance Act (12 U.S.C. 1813(1));

(B) Securities of any open-end investment company registered under the Investment Company Act of 1940 (15 U.S.C. 80a–1 *et seq.*) that holds itself out as a money market fund meeting the conditions of paragraph (d) of Rule 2a–7 under the Investment Company Act; or

(C) Securities that are direct obligations of, or obligations guaranteed as to principal or interest by, the United States.

NOTE TO RULE 419(b)(2)(iv): Issuers are cautioned that investments in government securities are inappropriate unless such securities can be readily sold or otherwise disposed of for cash at the time required without any dissipation of offering proceeds invested.

(v) Interest or dividends earned on the funds, if any, shall be held in the escrow or trust account until the funds are released in accordance with the provisions of this rule. If funds held in the escrow or trust account are released to a purchaser of the securities, the purchasers shall receive interest or dividends earned, if any, on such funds up to the date of release. If funds held in the escrow or trust account are released to the registrant, interest or dividends earned on such funds up to the date of release may be released to the registrant.

(vi) The registrant may receive up to 10 percent of the proceeds remaining after payment of underwriting commissions, underwriting expenses and dealer allowances permitted by paragraph (b)(2)(i) of this rule, exclusive of interest or dividends, as those proceeds are deposited into the escrow or trust account.

(3) *Deposit of Securities.* (i) All securities issued in connection with the offering, whether or not for cash consideration, and any other securities issued with respect to such securities, including securities issued with respect to stock splits, stock dividends, or similar rights, shall be deposited directly into the escrow or trust account promptly upon issuance. The identity of the purchaser of the securities shall be included on the stock certificates or other documents evidencing such securities. See also Rule 15g–8 regarding restrictions on sales of, or offers to sell, securities deposited in the escrow or trust account.

(ii) Securities held in the escrow or trust account are to remain as issued and deposited and shall be held for the sole benefit of the purchasers, who shall have voting rights, if any, with respect to securities held in their names, as provided by applicable state law. No transfer or other disposition of securities held in the escrow or trust account or any interest related to such securities shall be permitted other than by will or the laws of descent and distribution, or pursuant to a qualified domestic relations order as defined by the Internal Revenue Code of 1986 as amended (26 U.S.C. 1 *et seq.*) or Title 1 of the

Employee Retirement Income Security Act (29 U.S.C. 1001 *et seq.*), or the rules thereunder.

(iii) Warrants, convertible securities or other derivative securities relating to securities held in the escrow or trust account may be exercised or converted in accordance with their terms; *provided, however,* that securities received upon exercise or conversion, together with any cash or other consideration paid in connection with the exercise or conversion, are promptly deposited into the escrow or trust account.

(4) *Escrow or Trust Agreement.* A copy of the executed escrow or trust agreement shall be filed as an exhibit to the registration statement and shall contain the provisions of paragraphs (b)(2), (b)(3), and (e)(3) of this rule.

(5) *Request for Supplemental Information.* Upon request by the Commission or the staff, the registrant shall furnish as supplemental information the names and addresses of persons for whom securities are held in the escrow or trust account.

NOTE TO RULE 419(b): With respect to a blank check offering subject to both Rule 419 and Rule 15c2–4 under the Securities Exchange Act of 1934, the requirements of Rule 15c2–4 are applicable only until the conditions of the offering governed by that Rule are met (*e.g.,* reaching the minimum in a "part-or-none" offering). When those conditions are satisfied, Rule 419 continues to govern the use of offering proceeds.

(c) *Disclosure of Offering Terms.* The initial registration statement shall disclose the specific terms of the offering, including, but not limited to:

(1) The terms and provisions of the escrow or trust agreement and the effect thereof upon the registrant's right to receive funds and the effect of the escrow or trust agreement upon the purchaser's funds and securities required to be deposited into the escrow or trust account, including, if applicable, any material risk of non-insurance of purchasers' funds resulting from deposits in excess of the insured amounts; and

(2) The obligation of the registrant to provide, and the right of the purchaser to receive, information regarding an acquisition, including the requirement that pursuant to this rule, purchasers confirm in writing their investment in the registrant's securities as specified in paragraph (e) of this rule.

(d) *Probable Acquisition Post-Effective Amendment Requirement.* If, during any period in which offers or sales are being made, a significant acquisition becomes probable, the registrant shall file promptly a post-effective amendment disclosing the information specified by the applicable registration statement form and Industry Guides, including financial statements of the registrant and the company to be acquired as well as pro forma financial information required by the form and applicable rules and regulations. Where warrants, rights or other derivative securities issued in the initial offering are exercisable, there is a continuous offering of the underlying security.

(e) *Release of Deposited and Funds Securities.* (1) *Post-effective Amendment for Acquisition Agreement.* Upon execution of an agreement(s) for the acquisition(s) of a business(es) or assets that will constitute the business (or a line of business) of the registrant and for which the fair value of the business(es) or net assets to be acquired represents at least 80 percent of the maximum offering proceeds, including proceeds received or to be received upon the exercise or conversion of any securities offered, but excluding amounts payable to non-affiliates for underwriting commissions, underwriting expenses, and dealer allowances, the registrant shall file a post-effective amendment that:

(i) Discloses the information specified by the applicable registration statement form and Industry Guides, including financial statements of the registrant and the company acquired or to be acquired and pro forma financial information required by the form and applicable rules and regulations;

(ii) Discloses the results of the initial offering, including but not limited to:

(A) The gross offering proceeds received to date, specifying the amounts paid for underwriter commissions, underwriting expenses and dealer allowances, amounts disbursed to the registrant, and amounts remaining in the escrow or trust account; and

(B) The specific amount, use and application of funds disbursed to the registrant to date, including, but not limited to, the amounts paid to officers, directors, promoters, controlling shareholders or affiliates, either directly or indirectly, specifying the amounts and purposes of such payments; and

(iii) Discloses the terms of the offering as described pursuant to paragraph (e)(2) of this rule.

(2) *Terms of the Offering.* The terms of the offering must provide, and the registrant must satisfy, the following conditions:

(i) Within five business days after the effective date of the post-effective amendment(s), the registrant shall send by first class mail or other equally prompt means, to each purchaser of securities held in escrow or trust, a copy of the prospectus contained in the post-effective amendment and any amendment or supplement thereto;

(ii) Each purchaser shall have no fewer than 20 business days and no more than 45 business days from the effective date of the post-effective amendment to notify the registrant in writing that the purchaser elects to remain an investor. If the registrant has not received such written notification by the 45th business day following the effective date of the post-effective amendment, funds and interest or dividends, if any, held in the escrow or trust account shall be sent by first class mail or other equally prompt means to the purchaser within five business days;

(iii) The acquisition(s) meeting the criteria set forth in paragraph (e)(1) of this rule will be consummated if a sufficient number of purchasers confirm their investments; and

(iv) If a consummated acquisition(s) meeting the requirements of this rule has not occurred by a date 18 months after the effective date of the initial registration statement, funds held in the escrow or trust account shall be returned by first class mail or equally prompt means to the purchaser within five business days following that date.

(3) *Conditions for Release of Deposited Securities and Funds.* Funds held in the escrow or trust account may be released to the registrant and securities may be delivered to the purchaser or other registered holder identified on the deposited securities only at the same time as or after:

(i) The escrow agent or trustee has received a signed representation from the registrant, together with other evidence acceptable to the escrow agent or trustee, that the requirements of paragraphs (e)(1) and (e)(2) of this rule have been met; and

(ii) Consummation of an acquisition(s) meeting the requirements of paragraph (e)(2)(iii) of this rule.

(4) *Prospectus Supplement.* If funds and securities are released from the escrow or trust account to the registrant pursuant to this paragraph, the prospectus shall be supplemented to indicate the amount of funds and securities released and the date of release.

Notes to Rule 419(e): 1. With respect to a blank check offering subject to both Rule 419 and Rule 10b–9 under the Securities Exchange Act of 1934 the requirements of Rule 10b–9 are applicable only until the conditions of the offering governed by that Rule are met (*e.g.*, reaching the minimum in a "part-or-none" offering). When those conditions are satisfied, Rule 419 continues to govern the use of offering proceeds.

2. If the business(es) or assets are acquired for cash, the fair value shall be presumed to be equal to the cash paid. If all or part of the consideration paid consists of securities or other non-cash consideration, the fair value shall be determined by an accepted standard, such as bona fide sales of the assets or similar assets made within a reasonable time, forecasts of expected cash flows, independent appraisals, etc. Such valuation must be reasonable at the time made.

(f) *Financial Statements.* The registrant shall:

(1) Furnish to security holders audited financial statements for the first full fiscal year of operations following consummation of an acquisition pursuant to paragraph (e) of this rule, together with the information required by Item 303(a) of Regulation S–K (17 CFR 229.303(a)), no later than 90 days after the end of such fiscal year; and

(2) File the financial statements and additional information with the Commission under cover of Form 8–K (17 CFR 249.308); *provided, however,* that such financial statements and related information need not be filed separately if the registrant is filing reports pursuant to Section 13(a) or 15(d) of the Exchange Act.

FORM AND CONTENT OF PROSPECTUSES

Rule 420. Legibility of prospectus

(a) The body of all printed prospectuses and all notes to financial statements and other tabular data included therein shall be in roman type at least as large and as legible as 10-point modern type. However, (a) to the extent necessary for convenient presentation, financial statements and other tabular data, including tabular data in notes, and (b) prospectuses deemed to be omitting prospectuses under Rule 482 may be in roman type at least as large and as legible as 8-point modern type. All such type shall be leaded at least 2 points.

(b) Where a prospectus is distributed through an electronic medium, issuers may satisfy legibility requirements applicable to printed documents, such as paper size, type size and font, bold-face type, italics and red ink, by presenting all required information in a format readily communicated to investors, and where indicated, in a manner reasonably calculated to draw investor attention to specific information.

Rule 421. Presentation of information in prospectuses

(a) The information required in a prospectus need not follow the order of the items or other requirements in the form. Such information shall not, however, be set forth in such fashion as to obscure any of the required information or any information necessary to keep the required information from being incomplete or misleading. Where an item requires information to be given in a prospectus in tabular form it shall be given in substantially the tabular form specified in the item.

(b) You must present the information in a prospectus in a clear, concise and understandable manner. You must prepare the prospectus using the following standards:

(1) Present information in clear, concise sections, paragraphs, and sentences. Whenever possible, use short, explanatory sentences and bullet lists;

(2) Use descriptive headings and subheadings;

(3) Avoid frequent reliance on glossaries or defined terms as the primary means of explaining information in the prospectus. Define terms in a glossary or other section of the document only if the meaning is unclear from the context. Use a glossary only if it facilitates understanding of the disclosure; and

(4) Avoid legal and highly technical business terminology.

NOTE TO RULE 421(b): In drafting the disclosure to comply with this rule, you should avoid the following:

1. Legalistic or overly complex presentations that make the substance of the disclosure difficult to understand;

2. Vague "boilerplate" explanations that are imprecise and readily subject to different interpretations;

3. Complex information copied directly from legal documents without any clear and concise explanation of the provision(s); and

4. Disclosure repeated in different sections of the document that increases the size of the document but does not enhance the quality of the information.

(c) All information required to be included in a prospectus shall be clearly understandable without the necessity of referring to the particular form or to the general rules and regulations. Except as to financial statements and information required in a tabular form, the information set forth in a prospectus may be expressed in condensed or summarized form. In lieu of repeating information in the form of notes to financial statements, references may be made to other parts of the prospectus where such information is set forth.

(d)(1) To enhance the readability of the prospectus, you must use plain English principles in the organization, language, and design of the front and back cover pages, the summary, and the risk factors section.

(2) You must draft the language in these sections so that at a minimum it substantially complies with each of the following plain English writing principles:

(i) Short sentences;

(ii) Definite, concrete, everyday words;

(iii) Active voice;

(iv) Tabular presentation or bullet lists for complex material, whenever possible;

(v) No legal jargon or highly technical business terms; and

(vi) No multiple negatives.

(3) In designing these sections or other sections of the prospectus, you may include pictures, logos, charts, graphs, or other design elements so long as the design is not misleading and the required information is clear. You are encouraged to use tables, schedules, charts and graphic illustrations of the results of operations, balance sheet, or other financial data that present the data in an understandable manner. Any presentation must be consistent with the financial statements and non-financial information in the prospectus. You must draw the graphs and charts to scale. Any information you provide must not be misleading.

Instruction to Rule 421: You should read Securities Act Release No. 33–7497 (January 28, 1998) for information on plain English principles.

Rule 423. Date of prospectuses

Except for a form of prospectus used after the effective date of the registration statement and before the determination of the offering price as permitted by Rule 430A(c) under the Securities Act or before the opening of bids as permitted by Rule 445(c) under the Securities Act, each prospectus used after the effective date of the registration statement shall be dated approximately as of such effective date; provided, however, that a revised or amended prospectus used thereafter need only bear the approximate date of its issuance. Each supplement to a prospectus shall be dated separately the approximate date of its issuance.

Rule 424. Filing of prospectuses, number of copies

(a) Except as provided in paragraph (f) of this rule, five copies of every form of prospectus sent or given to any person prior to the effective date of the registration statement which varies from the form or forms of prospectus included in the registration statement as filed pursuant to Rule 402(a) shall be filed as a part of the registration statement not later than the date such form of prospectus is first sent or given to any person: *Provided, however,* that only a form of prospectus that contains substantive changes from or additions to a prospectus previously filed with the Commission as part of a registration statement need be filed pursuant to this paragraph (a).

(b) Ten copies of each form of prospectus purporting to comply with section 10 of the Act, except for documents constituting a prospectus pursuant to Rule 428(a) or free writing prospectuses pursuant to Rule 164 and Rule 433, shall be filed with the Commission in the form in which it is used after the effectiveness of the registration statement and identified as required by paragraph (e) of this rule; *provided, however*, that only a form of prospectus that contains substantive changes from or additions to a previously filed prospectus is required to be filed; *Provided, further*, that this paragraph (b) shall not apply in respect of a form of prospectus contained in a registration statement and relating solely to securities offered at competitive bidding, which prospectus is intended for use prior to the opening of bids. Ten copies of the form of prospectus shall be filed or transmitted for filing as follows:

(1) A form of prospectus that discloses information previously omitted from the prospectus filed as part of an effective registration statement in reliance upon Rule 430A under the Securities Act shall be filed with the commission no later than the second business day following the earlier of the date of determination of the offering price or the date it is first used after effectiveness in connection with a public offering or sales, or transmitted by a means reasonably calculated to result in filing with the Commission by that date.

(2) A form of prospectus that is used in connection with a primary offering of securities pursuant to Rule 415(a)(1)(x) or a primary offering of securities registered for issuance on a delayed basis pursuant to Rule 415(a)(1)(vii) or (viii) and that, in the case of Rule 415(a)(1)(viii) discloses the public offering price, description of securities or similar matters, and in the case of Rule 415(a)(1)(vii) and (x) discloses information previously omitted from the prospectus filed as part of an effective registration statement in reliance on Rule 430B, or, in the case of asset-backed securities, Rule 430D shall be filed with the Commission no later than the second business day following the earlier of the date of the determination of the offering price or the date it is first used after effectiveness in connection with a public offering or sales, or transmitted by a means reasonably calculated to result in filing with the Commission by that date.

(3) A form of prospectus that reflects facts or events other than those covered in paragraphs (b)(1), (2) and (6) of this rule that constitute a substantive change from or addition to the information set forth in the last form of prospectus filed with the Commission under this rule or as part of a registration statement under the Securities Act shall be filed with the Commission no later than the fifth business day after the date it is first used after effectiveness in connection with a public offering or sales, or transmitted by a means reasonably calculated to result in filing with the Commission by that date.

(4) A form of prospectus that discloses information, facts or events covered in both paragraphs (b)(1) and (3) shall be filed with the Commission no later than the second business day following the earlier of the date of the determination of the offering price or the date it is first used after effectiveness in connection with a public offering or sales, or transmitted by a means reasonably calculated to result in filing with the Commission by that date.

(5) A form of prospectus that discloses information, facts or events covered in both paragraphs (b)(2) and (3) shall be filed with the Commission no later than the second business day following the earlier of the date of the determination of the offering price or the date it is first used after effectiveness in connection with a public offering or sales, or transmitted by a means reasonably calculated to result in filing with the Commission by that date.

(6) A form of prospectus used in connection with an offering of securities under Canada's National Policy Statement No. 45 pursuant to Rule 415 under the Securities Act that is not made in the United States shall be filed with the Commission no later than the date it is first used in Canada, or transmitted by a means reasonably calculated to result in filing with the Commission by that date.

(7) A form of prospectus that identifies selling security holders and the amounts to be sold by them that was previously omitted from the registration statement and the prospectus in reliance upon Rule 430B shall be filed with the Commission no later than the second business day following the earlier of the date of sale or the date of first use or transmitted by a means reasonably calculated to result in filing with the Commission by that date.

(8) A form of prospectus otherwise required to be filed pursuant to paragraph (b) of this rule that is not filed within the time frames specified in paragraph (b) of this rule must be filed pursuant to this paragraph as soon as practicable after the discovery of such failure to file.

NOTE TO PARAGRAPH (b)(8) OF RULE 424: A form of prospectus required to be filed pursuant to another paragraph of Rule 424(b) that is filed under Rule 424(b)(8) shall nonetheless be "required to be filed" under such other paragraph.

Instruction to Paragraph (b): Notwithstanding Rule 424(b)(2) and (b)(5) above, a form of prospectus or prospectus supplement relating to an offering of asset-backed securities under Rule 415(a)(1)(vii) or Rule 415(a)(1)(xii) that is required to be filed pursuant to paragraph (b) of this rule shall be filed with the Commission no later than the second business day following the date it is first used after effectiveness in connection with a public offering or sales, or transmitted by a means reasonably calculated to result in filing with the Commission by that date.

(c) If a form of prospectus, other than one filed pursuant to paragraph (b)(1) or (b)(4) of this rule, consists of a prospectus supplement attached to a form of prospectus that (1) previously had been filed or (2) was not required to be filed pursuant to paragraph (b) because it did not contain substantive changes from a prospectus that previously was filed, only the prospectus supplement need be filed under paragraph (b) of this rule, provided that the first page of each prospectus supplement includes a cross reference to the date(s) of the related prospectus and any prospectus supplements thereto that together constitute the prospectus required to be delivered by Section 5(b) of the Securities Act (15 U.S.C. 77e(b)) with respect to the securities currently being offered or sold. The cross reference may be set forth in longhand, provided it is legible.

Note: Any prospectus supplement being filed separately that is smaller than a prospectus page should be attached to an 8½" × 11" sheet of paper.

(d) Every prospectus consisting of a radio or television broadcast shall be reduced to writing. Five copies of every such prospectus shall be filed with the Commission in accordance with the requirements of this rule.

(e) Each copy of a form of prospectus filed under this rule shall contain in the upper right corner of the cover page the paragraph of this rule, including the subparagraph if applicable, under which the filing is made, and the file number of the registration statement to which the prospectus relates. The information required by this paragraph may be set forth in longhand, provided it is legible.

(f) This rule shall not apply with respect to prospectuses of an investment company registered under the Investment Company Act of 1940 or a business development company.

(g) A form of prospectus filed pursuant to this rule that operates to reflect the payment of filing fees for an offering or offerings pursuant to Rule 456(b) must include on its cover page the calculation of registration fee table reflecting the payment of such filing fees for the securities that are the subject of the payment.

(h)(1) Three copies of a form of prospectus relating to an offering of asset-backed securities pursuant to Rule 415(a)(1)(vii) or Rule 415(a)(1)(xii) disclosing information previously omitted from the prospectus filed as part of an effective registration statement in reliance on Rule 430D shall be filed with the Commission at least three business days before the date of the first sale in the offering, or if used earlier, the earlier of:

(i) The applicable number of business days before the date of the first sale; or

(ii) The second business day after first use.

(2) Three copies of a prospectus supplement relating to an offering of asset-backed securities pursuant to Rule 415(a)(vii) or Rule 415(a)(1)(xii) that reflects any material change from the information contained in a prospectus filed in accordance with Rule 424(h)(1) shall be filed with the Commission at least forty-eight hours before the date and time of the first sale in the offering. The prospectus supplement must clearly delineate what material information has changed and how the information has changed from the prospectus filed in accordance with Rule 424(h)(1).

Instruction to Paragraph (h): The filing requirements of this paragraph (h) do not apply if a filing is made solely to add fees pursuant to Rule 457 and for no other purpose.

Rule 425. Filing of certain prospectuses and communications under Rule 135 in connection with business combination transactions

(a) All written communications made in reliance on Rule 165 are prospectuses that must be filed with the Commission under this rule on the date of first use.

(b) All written communications that contain no more information than that specified in Rule 135 must be filed with the Commission on or before the date of first use except as provided in paragraph (d)(1) of this rule. A communication limited to the information specified in Rule 135 will not be deemed an offer in accordance with Rule 135 even though it is filed under this rule.

(c) Each prospectus or Rule 135 communication filed under this section must identify the filer, the company that is the subject of the offering and the Commission file number for the related registration statement or, if that file number is unknown, the subject company's Exchange Act or Investment Company Act file number, in the upper right corner of the cover page.

(d) Notwithstanding paragraph (a) of this rule, the following need not be filed under this rule:

(1) Any written communication that is limited to the information specified in Rule 135 and does not contain new or different information from that which was previously publicly disclosed and filed under this rule.

(2) Any research report used in reliance on Rule 137, Rule 138 and Rule 139;

(3) Any confirmation described in Rule 10b–10 under the Securities Exchange Act of 1934; and

(4) Any prospectus filed under Rule 424.

NOTES TO RULE 425:

1. File five copies of the prospectus or Rule 135 communication if paper filing is permitted.

2. No filing is required under Rule 13e–4(c), Rule 14a–12(b), Rule 14d–2(b), or Rule 14d–9(a) under the Securities Exchange Act of 1934, if the communication is filed under this rule. Communications filed under this rule also are deemed filed under the other applicable rules.

Rule 426. Filing of certain prospectuses under Rule 167 in connection with certain offerings of asset–backed securities

(a) All written communications made in reliance on Rule 167 are prospectuses that must be filed with the Commission in accordance with paragraphs (b) and (c) of this rule on Form 8–K (17 CFR 249.308) and incorporated by reference to the related registration statement for the offering of asset-backed securities. Each prospectus filed under this section must identify the Commission file number of the related registration statement on the cover page of the related Form 8–K in addition to any other information required by that form. The information contained in any such prospectus shall be deemed to be a part of the registration statement as of the earlier of the time of filing of such information or the time of the filing of the final prospectus that meets the requirements of section 10(a) of the Act (15 U.S.C. 77j(a)) relating to such offering pursuant to Rule 424(b).

(b) Except as specified in paragraph (c) of this rule, ABS *informational and computational material* made in reliance on Rule 167 that meet the conditions in paragraph (b)(1) of this rule must be filed within the time frame specified in paragraph (b)(2) of this rule.

(1) *Conditions for Which Materials Must Be Filed.* The materials are provided to prospective investors under the following conditions:

(i) If a prospective investor has indicated to the issuer or an underwriter that it will purchase all or a portion of the class of asset-backed securities to which such materials relate, all materials relating to such class that are or have been provided to such prospective investor; and

(ii) For any other prospective investor, all materials provided to such prospective investor after the final terms have been established for all classes of the offering.

(2) *Time Frame to File the Materials.* The materials must be filed by the later of:

(i) The due date for filing the final prospectus relating to such offering that meets the requirements of section 10(a) of the Act (15 U.S.C. 77j(a)) pursuant to Rule 424(b); or

(ii) Two business days after first use.

(c) Notwithstanding paragraphs (a) and (b) of this rule, the following need not be filed under this rule:

(1) *ABS informational and computational material* that relate to abandoned structures or that are furnished to a prospective investor prior to the time the final terms have been established for all classes of the offering where such prospective investor has not indicated to the issuer or an underwriter its intention to purchase the asset-backed securities.

(2) Any *ABS informational and computational material* if a prospectus that meets the requirements of section 10(a) of the Act (15 U.S.C. 77j(a)) relating to the offering of such asset-backed securities accompanies or precedes the use of such material.

(3) Any *ABS informational and computational material* that does not contain new or different information from that which was previously disclosed and filed under this rule.

(4) Any written communication that is limited to the information specified in Rules 134, 135 or 135c.

(5) Any research report used in reliance on Rules 137, 138, 139 or 139a.

(6) Any confirmation described in Rule 10b–10 under the Securities Exchange Act of 1934.

(7) Any prospectus filed under Rule 424.

(8) Any free writing prospectus used in reliance on Rule 164 and Rule 433.

(d) Terms used in this rule have the same meaning as in Item 1101 of Regulation AB.

Instruction to Rule 426: The issuer may aggregate data presented in *ABS informational and computational material* that are to be filed and file such data in consolidated form. Any such aggregation, however, must not result in either the omission of any information contained in such material otherwise to be filed, or a presentation that makes the information misleading.

Rule 427. Contents of prospectus used after nine months

There may be omitted from any prospectus used more than 9 months after the effective date of the registration statement any information previously required to be contained in the prospectus insofar as later information covering the same subjects, including the latest available certified financial statement, as of a date not more than 16 months prior to the use of the prospectus is contained therein.

Rule 428. Documents constituting a Section 10(a) prospectus for Form S–8 registration statement; requirements relating to offerings of securities registered on Form S–8

(a)(1) Where securities are to be offered pursuant to a registration statement on Form S–8 (17 CFR 239.16b), the following, taken together, shall constitute a prospectus that meets the requirements of section 10(a) of the Act:

(i) The document(s), or portions thereof as permitted by paragraph (b)(1)(ii) of this rule, containing the employee benefit plan information required by Item 1 of the Form;

(ii) The statement of availability of registrant information, employee benefit plan annual reports and other information required by Item 2; and

(iii) The documents containing registrant information and employee benefit plan annual reports that are incorporated by reference in the registration statement pursuant to Item 3.

(2) The registrant shall maintain a file of the documents that, pursuant to paragraph (a) of this rule, at any time are part of the section 10(a) prospectus, except for documents required to be incorporated by reference in the registration statement pursuant to Item 3 of Form S–8. Each such document shall be included in the file until five years after it is last used as part of the Section 10(a) prospectus to offer or sell securities pursuant to the plan. With respect to documents containing specifically designated portions that constitute part of the section 10(a) prospectus pursuant to paragraph (b)(1)(ii) of this rule, the entire document shall be maintained in the file. Upon request, the registrant shall furnish to the Commission or its staff a copy of any or all of the documents included in the file.

(b) Where securities are offered pursuant to a registration statement on Form S–8:

(1)(i) The registrant shall deliver or cause to be delivered, to each employee who is eligible to participate (or selected by the registrant to participate, in the case of a stock option or other plan with selective participation) in an employee benefit plan to which the registration statement relates, the information required by Part I of Form S–8. The information shall be in written form and shall be updated in writing in a timely manner to reflect any material changes during any period in which offers or sales are being made. When updating information is furnished, documents previously furnished need not be re-delivered, but the registrant shall furnish promptly without charge to each employee, upon written or oral request, a copy of all documents containing the plan information required by Part I that then constitute part of the section 10(a) prospectus.

(ii) The registrant may designate an entire document or only portions of a document as constituting part of the section 10(a) prospectus. If the registrant designates only portions of a document as constituting part of the prospectus, rather than the entire document, a statement clearly identifying such portions, for example, by reference to section headings, section numbers, paragraphs or page numbers within the document must be included in a conspicuous place in the forepart of the document, or such portions must be specifically designated throughout the text of the document. Registrants shall not designate only words or sentences within a paragraph as part of a prospectus. Unless the portions of a document constituting part of the section 10(a) prospectus are clearly identified, the entire document shall constitute part of the prospectus.

(iii) The registrant shall date any document constituting part of the section 10(a) prospectus or containing portions constituting part of the prospectus and shall include the following printed, stamped or typed legend in a conspicuous place in the forepart of the document, substituting the bracketed language as appropriate: "This document [Specifically designated portions of this document] constitutes [constitute] part of a prospectus covering securities that have been registered under the Securities Act of 1933."

(iv) The registrant shall revise the document(s) containing the plan information sent or given to newly eligible participants pursuant to paragraph (b)(1)(i) of this rule, if documents containing updating information would obscure the readability of the plan information.

(2) The registrant shall deliver or cause to be delivered with the document(s) containing the information required by Part I of Form S–8, to each employee to whom such information is sent or given, a copy of any one of the following:

(i) The registrant's annual report to security holders containing the information required by Rule 14a–3(b) under the Securities Exchange Act of 1934 (*Exchange Act*) for its latest fiscal year;

(ii) The registrant's annual report on Form 10–K (17 CFR 249.310), 20–F (17 CFR 249.220f) or, in the case of registrants described in General Instruction A.(2) of Form 40–F (17 CFR 249.240f), for its latest fiscal year;

(iii) The latest prospectus filed pursuant to Rule 424(b) under the Act that contains audited financial statements for the registrant's latest fiscal year, *Provided* that the financial statements are not incorporated by reference from another filing, and *Provided* further that such prospectus contains substantially the information required by Rule 14a–3(b) under the Securities Exchange Act of 1934 or the registration statement was on Form S–1 (17 CFR 239.11) or F–1 (17 CFR 239.31); or

(iv) The registrant's effective Exchange Act registration statement on Form 10 (17 CFR 249.210), 20–F or, in the case of registrants described in General Instruction A.(2) of Form 40–F, containing audited financial statements for the registrant's latest fiscal year.

Instructions: If a registrant has previously sent or given an employee a copy of any document specified in clauses (i)–(iv) of paragraph (b)(2) for the latest fiscal year, it need not be re-delivered, but the registrant shall furnish promptly, without charge, a copy of such document upon written or oral request of the employee.

2. If the latest fiscal year of the registrant has ended within 120 days (or 190 days with respect to foreign private issuers) prior to the delivery of the documents containing the information specified by Part I of Form S–8, the registrant may deliver a document containing financial statements for the fiscal year preceding the latest fiscal year, *Provided that* within the 120 or 190 day period a document containing financial statements for the latest fiscal year is furnished to each employee.

(3) The registrant shall deliver or cause to be delivered promptly, without charge, to each employee to whom information is required to be delivered, upon written or oral request, a copy of the information that has been incorporated by reference pursuant to Item 3 of Form S–8 (not including exhibits to the information that is incorporated by reference unless such exhibits are specifically incorporated by reference into the information that the registration statement incorporates).

(4) Where interests in a plan are registered, the registrant shall deliver or cause to be delivered promptly, without charge, to each employee to whom information is required to be delivered, upon written or oral request, a copy of the then latest annual report of the plan filed pursuant to Section 15(d) of the Securities Exchange Act of 1934, whether on Form 11–K (17 CFR 249.311) or included as part of the registrant's annual report on Form 10–K.

(5) The registrant shall deliver or cause to be delivered to all employees participating in a stock option plan or plan fund that invests in registrant securities (and other plan participants who request such information orally or in writing) who do not otherwise receive such material, copies of all reports, proxy statements and other communications distributed to its security holders general-

ly, provided that such material is sent or delivered no later than the time it is sent to security holders.

(c) As used in this Rule, the term *employee benefit plan* is defined in Rule 405 of Regulation C and the term *employee* is defined in General Instruction A.1 of Form S–8.

Rule 429. Prospectus relating to several registration statements

(a) Where a registrant has filed two or more registration statements, it may file a single prospectus in the latest registration statement in order to satisfy the requirements of the Act and the rules and regulations thereunder for that offering and any other offering(s) registered on the earlier registration statement(s). The combined prospectus in the latest registration statement must include all of the information that currently would be required in a prospectus relating to all offering(s) that it covers. The combined prospectus may be filed as part of the initial filing of the latest registration statement, in a pre-effective amendment to it or in a post-effective amendment to it.

(b) Where a registrant relies on paragraph (a) of this rule, the registration statement containing the combined prospectus shall act, upon effectiveness, as a post-effective amendment to any earlier registration statement whose prospectus has been combined in the latest registration statement. The registrant must identify any earlier registration statement to which the combined prospectus relates by setting forth the Commission file number at the bottom of the facing page of the latest registration statement.

Rule 430. Prospectus for use prior to effective date

(a) A form of prospectus filed as a part of the registration statement shall be deemed to meet the requirements of section 10 of the Act for the purpose of section 5(b)(1) thereof prior to the effective date of the registration statement, provided such form of prospectus contains substantially the information required by the Act and the rules and regulations thereunder to be included in a prospectus meeting the requirements of section 10(a) of the Act for the securities being registered, or contains substantially that information except for the omission of information with respect to the offering price, underwriting discounts or commissions, discounts or commissions to dealers, amount of proceeds, conversion rates, call prices, or other matters dependent upon the offering price. Every such form of prospectus shall be deemed to have been filed as a part of the registration statement for the purpose of section 7 of the Act.

(b) A form of prospectus filed as part of a registration statement on Form N–1A (17 CFR 239.15A and 17 CFR 274.11A), Form N–2 (17 CFR 239.14 and 17 CFR 274.11a–1), Form N–3 (17 CFR 239.17a and 17 CFR 274.11b), Form N–4 (17 CFR 239.17b and 17 CFR 274.11c), or Form N–6 (17 CFR 239.17c and 17 CFR 274.11d) shall be deemed to meet the requirements of Section 10 of the Act (15 U.S.C. 77j) for the purpose of Section 5(b)(1) thereof (15 U.S.C. 77e(b)(1)) prior to the effective date of the registration statement, provided that:

(1) Such form of prospectus meets the requirements of paragraph (a) of this rule; and

(2) Such registration statement contains a form of Statement of Additional Information that is made available to persons receiving such prospectus upon written or oral request, and without charge, unless the form of prospectus contains the information otherwise required to be disclosed in the form of Statement of Additional Information. Every such form of prospectus shall be deemed to have been filed as part of the registration statement for the purpose of section 7 of the Act.

Rule 430A. Prospectus in a registration statement at the time of effectiveness

(a) The form of prospectus filed as part of a registration statement that is declared effective may omit information with respect to the public offering price, underwriting syndicate (including any material relationships between the registrant and underwriters not named therein), underwriting discounts or commissions, discounts or commissions to dealers, amount of proceeds, conversion rates, call prices and other items dependent upon the offering price, delivery dates, and terms of the securities dependent upon the offering date; and such form of prospectus need not contain such information in order for the registration statement to meet the requirements of Section 7 of the Securities Act (15 U.S.C. 77g) for the purposes of Section 5 thereof (15 U.S.C. 77e), *Provided*, That:

(1) The securities to be registered are offered for cash;

(2) The registrant furnishes the undertakings required by Item 512(i) of Regulation S–K (17 CFR 229.512(i)); and

(3) The information omitted in reliance upon paragraph (a) from the form of prospectus filed as part of a registration statement that is declared effective is contained in a form of prospectus filed with the Commission pursuant to Rule 424(b) or

Rule 497(h) under the Securities Act; except that if such form of prospectus is not so filed by the later of fifteen business days after the effective date of the registration statement or fifteen business days after the effectiveness of a post-effective amendment thereto that contains a form of prospectus, or transmitted by a means reasonably calculated to result in filing with the Commission by that date, the information omitted in reliance upon paragraph (a) must be contained in an effective post-effective amendment to the registration statement.

Instruction to Paragraph (a): A decrease in the volume of securities offered or change in the bona fide estimate of the maximum offering price range from that indicated in the form of prospectus filed as part of a registration statement that is declared effective may be disclosed in the form of prospectus filed with the Commission pursuant to Rule 424(b) or Rule 497(h) under the Securities Act so long as the decrease in the volume or change in the price range would not materially change the disclosure contained in the registration statement at effectiveness. Notwithstanding the foregoing, any increase or decrease in volume (if the total dollar value of securities offered would not exceed that which was registered) and any deviation from the low or high end of the range may be reflected in the form of prospectus filed with the Commission pursuant to Rule 424(b)(1) or Rule 497(h) if, in the aggregate, the changes in volume and price represent no more than a 20% change in the maximum aggregate offering price set forth in the "Calculation of Registration Fee" table in the effective registration statement.

(b) The information omitted in reliance upon paragraph (a) from the form of prospectus filed as part of an effective registration statement, and contained in the form of prospectus filed with the Commission pursuant to Rule 424(b) or Rule 497(h) under the Securities Act, shall be deemed to be a part of the registration statement as of the time it was declared effective.

(c) When used prior to determination of the offering price of the securities, a form of prospectus relating to the securities offered pursuant to a registration statement that is declared effective with information omitted from the form of prospectus filed as part of such effective registration statement in reliance upon this Rule 430A need not contain information omitted pursuant to paragraph (a), in order to meet the requirements of Section 10 of the Securities Act (15 U.S.C. 77j) for the purpose of Section 5(b)(1) (15 U.S.C. 77e(b)(1)) thereof. This provision shall not limit the information required to be contained in a form of prospectus meeting the requirements of Section 10(a) of the Act for the purposes of Section 5(b)(2) thereof or exception (a) of Section 2(10) (15 U.S.C. 77b(a)(10)) thereof.

(d) This rule shall not apply to registration statements for securities to be offered by competitive bidding.

(e) In the case of a registration statement filed on Form N–1A (17 CFR 239.15A and 17 CFR 274.11A), Form N–2 (17 CFR 239.14 and 17 CFR 274.11a–1), Form N–3 (17 CFR 239.17a and 17 CFR 274.11b), Form N–4 (17 CFR 239.17b and 17 CFR 274.11c), or Form N–6 (17 CFR 239.17c and 17 CFR 274.11d), the references to "form of prospectus" in paragraphs (a) and (b) of this section and the accompanying Note shall be deemed also to refer to the form of Statement of Additional Information filed as part of such a registration statement.

(f) This rule may apply to registration statements that are immediately effective pursuant to Rule 462(e) and (f).

NOTE: If information is omitted in reliance upon paragraph (a) from the form of prospectus filed as part of an effective registration statement, or effective post-effective amendment thereto, the registrant must ascertain promptly whether a form of prospectus transmitted for filing under Rule 424(b) or Rule 497(h) under the Securities Act actually was received for filing by the Commission and, in the event that it was not, promptly file such prospectus.

Rule 430B. Prospectus in a registration statement after effective date

(a) A form of prospectus filed as part of a registration statement for offerings pursuant to Rule 415(a)(1)(x) may omit from the information required by the form to be in the prospectus information that is unknown or not reasonably available to the issuer pursuant to Rule 409. In addition, a form of prospectus filed as part of an automatic shelf registration statement for offerings pursuant to Rule 415(a), other than Rule 415(a)(1)(viii), also may omit information as to whether the offering is a primary offering or an offering on behalf of persons other than the issuer, or a combination thereof, the plan of distribution for the securities, a description of the securities registered other than an identification of the name or class of such securities, and the identification of other issuers. Each such form of prospectus shall be deemed to have been filed as part of the registration statement for the purpose of section 7 of the Act.

(b) A form of prospectus filed as part of a registration statement for offerings pursuant to Rule 415(a)(1)(i) by an issuer eligible to use Form S–3 or Form F–3 (17 CFR 239.13 or 17 CFR 239.33) for primary offerings pursuant to General Instruction I.B.1 of such forms, may omit the information specified in paragraph (a) of this rule, and may also omit the identities of selling security holders and amounts of securities to be registered on their behalf if:

(1) The registration statement is an automatic shelf registration statement as defined in Rule 405; or

(2) All of the following conditions are satisfied:

(i) The initial offering transaction of the securities (or securities convertible into such securities) the resale of which are being registered on behalf of each of the selling security holders, was completed;

(ii) The securities (or securities convertible into such securities) were issued and outstanding prior to the original date of filing the registration statement covering the resale of the securities;

(iii) The registration statement refers to any unnamed selling security holders in a generic manner by identifying the initial offering transaction in which the securities were sold; and

(iv) The issuer is not and during the past three years neither the issuer nor any of its predecessors was:

(A) A blank check company as defined in Rule 419(a)(2);

(B) A shell company, other than a business combination related shell company, each as defined in Rule 405; or

(C) An issuer in an offering of penny stock as defined in Rule 3a51–1 of the Securities Exchange Act of 1934.

(c) A form of prospectus that is part of a registration statement that omits information in reliance upon paragraph (a) or (b) of this rule meets the requirements of Section 10 of the Act for the purpose of Section 5(b)(1) thereof. This provision shall not limit the information required to be contained in a form of prospectus in order to meet the requirements of section 10(a) of the Act for the purposes of section 5(b)(2) thereof or exception (a) of section 2(a)(10) thereof.

(d) Information omitted from a form of prospectus that is part of an effective registration statement in reliance on paragraph (a) or (b) of this rule may be included subsequently in the prospectus that is part of a registration statement by:

(1) A post-effective amendment to the registration statement;

(2) A prospectus filed pursuant to Rule 424(b); or

(3) If the applicable form permits, including the information in the issuer's periodic or current reports filed pursuant to section 13 or 15(d) of the Securities Exchange Act of 1934 (15 U.S.C. 78m or 78o(d)) that are incorporated or deemed incorporated by reference into the prospectus that is part of the registration statement in accordance with applicable requirements, subject to the provisions of paragraph (h) of this rule.

(e) Information omitted from a form of prospectus that is part of an effective registration statement in reliance on paragraph (a) or (b) of this rule and contained in a form of prospectus required to be filed with the Commission pursuant to Rule 424(b), other than as provided in paragraph (f) of this rule, shall be deemed part of and included in the registration statement as of the date such form of filed prospectus is first used after effectiveness.

(f)(1) Information omitted from a form of prospectus that is part of an effective registration statement in reliance on paragraph (a) or (b) of this rule and is contained in a form of prospectus required to be filed with the Commission pursuant to Rule 424(b)(2), (b)(5), or (b)(7), shall be deemed to be part of and included in the registration statement on the earlier of the date such subsequent form of prospectus is first used or the date and time of the first contract of sale of securities in the offering to which such subsequent form of prospectus relates.

(2) The date on which a form of prospectus is deemed to be part of and included in the registration statement pursuant to paragraph (f)(1) of this rule shall be deemed, for purposes of liability under section 11 of the Act of the issuer and any underwriter at the time only, to be a new effective date of the part of such registration statement relating to the securities to which such form of prospectus relates, such part of the registration statement consisting of all information included in the registration statement and any prospectus relating to the offering of such securities (including information relating to the offering in a prospectus already included in the registration statement) as of such date and all information relating to the offering included in reports and materials incorporated by reference into such registration statement and prospectus as of such date, and in each case not modified or superseded pursuant to Rule 412. The offering of such securities at that time shall be deemed to be the initial *bona fide* offering thereof.

(3) If a registration statement is amended to include or is deemed to include, through incorporation by reference or otherwise, except as otherwise

provided in Rule 436, a report or opinion of any person made on such person's authority as an expert whose consent would be required under section 7 of the Act because of being named as having prepared or certified part of the registration statement, then for purposes of this rule and for liability purposes under section 11 of the Act, the part of the registration statement for which liability against such person is asserted shall be considered as having become effective with respect to such person as of the time the report or opinion is deemed to be part of the registration statement and a consent required pursuant to section 7 of the Act has been provided as contemplated by section 11 of the Act.

(4) Except for an effective date resulting from the filing of a form of prospectus filed for purposes of including information required by section 10(a)(3) of the Act or pursuant to Item 512(a)(1)(ii) of Regulation S–K, the date a form of prospectus is deemed part of and included in the registration statement pursuant to this paragraph shall not be an effective date established pursuant to paragraph (f)(2) of this rule as to:

(i) Any director (or person acting in such capacity) of the issuer;

(ii) Any person signing any report or document incorporated by reference into the registration statement, except for such a report or document incorporated by reference for purposes of including information required by section 10(a)(3) of the Act or pursuant to Item 512(a)(1)(ii) of Regulation S–K (such person except for such reports being deemed not to be a person who signed the registration statement within the meaning of section 11(a) of the Act).

(5) The date a form of prospectus is deemed part of and included in the registration statement pursuant to paragraph (f)(2) of this rule shall not be an effective date established pursuant to paragraph (f)(2) of this rule as to:

(i) Any accountant with respect to financial statements or other financial information contained in the registration statement as of a prior effective date and for which the accountant previously provided a consent to be named as required by section 7 of the Act, unless the form of prospectus contains new audited financial statements or other financial information as to which the accountant is an expert and for which a new consent is required pursuant to section 7 of the Act or Rule 436; and

(ii) Any other person whose report or opinion as an expert or counsel has, with their consent, previously been included in the registration statement as of a prior effective date, unless the form of prospectus contains a new report or opinion for which a new consent is required pursuant to section 7 of the Act or Rule 436.

(g) Notwithstanding paragraph (e) or (f) of this rule or paragraph (a) of Rule 412, no statement made in a registration statement or prospectus that is part of the registration statement or made in a document incorporated or deemed incorporated by reference into the registration statement or prospectus that is part of the registration statement after the effective date of such registration statement or portion thereof in respect of an offering determined pursuant to this rule will, as to a purchaser with a time of contract of sale prior to such effective date, supersede or modify any statement that was made in the registration statement or prospectus that was part of the registration statement or made in any such document immediately prior to such effective date.

(h) Where a form of prospectus filed pursuant to Rule 424(b) relating to an offering does not include disclosure of omitted information regarding the terms of the offering, the securities, or the plan of distribution, or selling security holders for the securities that are the subject of the form of prospectus, because such omitted information has been included in periodic or current reports filed pursuant to section 13 or 15(d) of the Securities Exchange Act of 1934 incorporated or deemed incorporated by reference into the prospectus, the issuer shall file a form of prospectus identifying the periodic or current reports that are incorporated or deemed incorporated by reference into the prospectus that is part of the registration statement that contain such omitted information. Such form of prospectus shall be required to be filed, depending on the nature of the incorporated information, pursuant to Rule 424(b)(2), (b)(5), or (b)(7).

(i) Issuers relying on this rule shall furnish the undertakings required by Item 512(a) of Regulation S–K.

NOTE TO RULE 430B: The provisions of paragraph (b) of Rule 401 shall apply to any prospectus filed for purposes of including information required by section 10(a)(3) of the Act.

Rule 430C. Prospectus in a registration statement pertaining to an offering other than pursuant to Rule 430A or Rule 430B after the effective date

(a) In offerings made other than in reliance on Rule 430B or Rule 430D and other than for prospectuses filed in reliance on Rule 430A, information contained in a form of prospectus required to be filed with the Commission pursuant to Rule 424(b) or Rule 497(b), (c), (d), or (e), shall be deemed to be part of and included in the registration statement on the date it is first used after effectiveness.

(b) Notwithstanding paragraph (a) of this rule or paragraph (a) of Rule 412, no statement made in a registration statement or prospectus that is part of the registration statement or made in a document incorporated or deemed incorporated by reference into the registration statement or prospectus that is part of the registration statement will, as to a purchaser with a time of contract of sale prior to such first use, supersede or modify any statement that was made in the registration statement or prospectus that was part of the registration statement or made in any such document immediately prior to such date of first use.

(c) Nothing in this rule shall affect the information required to be included in an issuer's registration statement and prospectus.

(d) Issuers subject to paragraph (a) of this rule shall furnish the undertakings required by Item 512(a) of Regulation S–K, or Item 34.4 of Form N–2 (17 CFR 239.14 and 274.11a–1), as applicable.

Rule 430D. Prospectus in a registration statement after effective date for asset-backed securities offerings

(a) A form of prospectus filed as part of a registration statement for primary offerings of asset-backed securities pursuant to Rule 415(a)(1)(vii) or Rule 415(a)(1)(xii) may omit from the information required by the form to be in the prospectus information that is unknown or not reasonably available to the issuer pursuant to Rule 409.

(b) Information omitted from a form of prospectus that is part of an effective registration statement in reliance on paragraph (a) of this section (other than information with respect to offering price, underwriting syndicate (including any material relationships between the registrant and underwriters not named therein), underwriting discounts or commissions, discounts or commissions to dealers, amount of proceeds or other maters dependent upon the offering price to the extent such information is unknown or not reasonably available to the issuer pursuant to Rule 409) shall be disclosed in a form of prospectus required to be filed with the Commission pursuant to Rule 424(h). Each such form of prospectus shall be deemed to have been filed as part of the registration statement for the purpose of section 7 of the Act (15 U.S.C. 77g).

(c) A form of prospectus filed as part of a registration statement that omits information in reliance upon paragraph (a) of this section meets the requirements of section 10 of the Act (15 U.S.C. 77j) for the purpose of section 5(b)(1) of the Act (15 U.S.C. 77e(b)(1)). This provision shall not limit the information required to be contained in a form of prospectus in order to meet the requirements of section 10(a) of the Act for the purposes of section 5(b)(2) (15 U.S.C. 77e(b)(2)) or exception (a) of section 2(a)(10) of the Act (15 U.S.C. 77b(a)(10)(a)).

(d)(1) Except as provided in paragraph (b) or (d)(2) of this section, information omitted from a form of prospectus that is part of an effective registration statement in reliance on paragraph (a) of this section may be included subsequently in the prospectus that is part of a registration statement by:

(i) A post-effective amendment to the registration statement;

(ii) A prospectus filed pursuant to § 230.424(b); or

(iii) If the applicable form permits, including the information in the issuer's periodic or current reports filed pursuant to section 13 or 15(d) of the Securities Exchange Act of 1934 (15 U.S.C. 78m or 78o(d)) that are incorporated or deemed incorporated by reference into the prospectus that is part of the registration statement in accordance with the applicable requirements, subject to the provisions of paragraph (h) of this section.

(2) Information omitted from a form of prospectus that is part of an effective registration statement in reliance on paragraph (a) of this section that adds a new structural feature or credit enhancement must be included subsequently in the prospectus that is part of a registration statement by a post-effective amendment to the registration statement.

(e)(1) Information omitted from a form of prospectus that is part of an effective registration statement in reliance on paragraph (a) of this section and contained in a form of prospectus required to be filed with the Commission pursuant to Rule 424(b), other than as provided in paragraph (f) of this section, shall be deemed part of and included in the registration statement as of the date such form of filed prospectus is first used after effectiveness.

(2) Information omitted from a form of prospectus that is part of an effective registration statement in reliance on paragraph (a) of this section and contained in a form of prospectus required to be filed with the Commission pursuant to § 230.424(h) shall be deemed part of and included in the registration statement the earlier of the date such form of filed prospectus is filed with the Commission pursuant to Rule 424(h) or, if used earlier than the date of filing, the date it is first used after effectiveness.

(f)(1) Information omitted from a form of prospectus that is part of an effective registration statement in reliance on paragraph (a) of this section, and is contained in a form of prospectus required to be filed with the Commission pursuant to Rule 424(b)(2) or (b)(5), shall be deemed to be part of and included in the registration statement on the earlier of the date such subsequent form of prospectus is first used or the date and time of the first contract of sale of securities in the offering to which such subsequent form of prospectus relates.

(2) The date on which a form of prospectus is deemed to be part of and included in the registration statement pursuant to paragraph (f)(1) of this section shall be deemed, for purposes of liability under section 11 of the Act (15 U.S.C. 77k) of the issuer and any underwriter at the time only, to be a new effective date of the part of such registration statement relating to the securities to which such form of prospectus relates, such part of the registration statement consisting of all information included in the registration statement and any prospectus relating to the offering of such securities (including information relating to the offering in a prospectus already included in the registration statement) as of such date and all information relating to the offering included in reports and materials incorporated by reference into such registration statement and prospectus as of such date, and in each case not modified or superseded pursuant to § 230.412. The offering of such securities at that time shall be deemed to be the initial bona fide offering thereof.

(3) If a registration statement is amended to include or is deemed to include, through incorporation by reference or otherwise, except as otherwise provided in § 230.436, a report or opinion of any person made on such person's authority as an expert whose consent would be required under section 7 of the Act (15 U.S.C. 77g) because of being named as having prepared or certified part of the registration statement, then for purposes of this section and for liability purposes under section 11 of the Act (15 U.S.C. 77k), the part of the registration statement for which liability against such person is asserted shall be considered as having become effective with respect to such person as of the time the report or opinion is deemed to be part of the registration statement and a consent required pursuant to section 7 of the Act has been provided as contemplated by section 11 of the Act.

(4) Except for an effective date resulting from the filing of a form of prospectus filed for purposes of including information required by section 10(a)(3) of the Act (15 U.S.C. 77j(a)(3)) or pursuant to Item 512(a)(1)(ii) of Regulation S–K (17 CFR 229.512(a)(1)(ii)), the date a form of prospectus is deemed part of and included in the registration statement pursuant to this paragraph shall not be an effective date established pursuant to paragraph (f)(2) of this section as to:

(i) Any director (or person acting in such capacity) of the issuer;

(ii) Any person signing any report or document incorporated by reference into the registration statement, except for such a report or document incorporated by reference for purposes of including information required by section 10(a)(3) of the Act (15 U.S.C. 77j(a)(3)) or pursuant to Item 512(a)(1)(ii) of Regulation S–K (17 CFR 229.512(a)(1)(ii)) (such person except for such reports being deemed not to be a person who signed the registration statement within the meaning of section 11(a) of the Act (15 U.S.C. 77k(a)).

(5) The date a form of prospectus is deemed part of and included in the registration statement pursuant to paragraph (f)(2) of this section shall not be an effective date established pursuant to paragraph (f)(2) of this section as to:

(i) Any accountant with respect to financial statements or other financial information contained in the registration statement as of a prior effective date and for which the accountant previously provided a consent to be named as required by section 7 of the Act (15 U.S.C. 77g), unless the form of prospectus contains new audited financial statements or other financial information as to which the accountant is an expert and for which a new consent is required pursuant to section 7 of the Act or Rule 436; and

(ii) Any other person whose report or opinion as an expert or counsel has, with their consent, previously been included in the registration statement as of a prior effective date, unless the form of prospectus contains a new report or opinion for which a new consent is required pursuant to section 7 of the Act (15 U.S.C. 77g) or Rule 436.

(g) Notwithstanding paragraph (e) or (f) of this section or Rule 412(a), no statement made in a registration statement or prospectus that is part of the registration statement or made in a document incorporated or deemed incorporated by reference into the registration statement or prospectus that is part of the registration statement after the effective date of such registration statement or portion thereof in respect of an offering determined pursuant to this section will, as to a purchaser with a time of contract of sale prior to such effective date, supersede or modify any statement that was made in the registration statement or prospectus that was part of the registration statement or made in any such document immediately prior to such effective date.

(h) Where a form of prospectus filed pursuant to Rule 424(b) relating to an offering does not include disclosure of omitted information regarding the terms of the offering, the securities or the plan of distribution for the securities that are the subject of the form of prospectus, because such omitted information has been included in periodic or current reports filed pursuant to section 13 or 15(d) of the Securities Exchange Act of 1934 (15 U.S.C. 78m or 78o(d)) incorporated or deemed incorporated by reference into the prospectus, the issuer shall file a form of prospectus identifying the periodic or current reports that are incorporated or deemed incorporated by reference into the prospectus that is part of the registration statement that contain such omitted information. Such form of prospectus shall be required to be filed, depending on the nature of the incorporated information, pursuant to Rule 424(b)(2) or (b)(5).

(i) Issuers relying on this section shall furnish the undertakings required by Item 512(a) of Regulation S–K (17 CFR 229.512(a)).

Rule 431. Summary prospectuses

(a) A summary prospectus prepared and filed (except a summary prospectus filed by an open-end management investment company registered under the Investment Company Act of 1940) as part of a registration statement in accordance with this rule shall be deemed to be a prospectus permitted under section 10(b) of the Act (15 U.S.C. 77j(b)) for the purposes of section 5(b)(1) of the Act (15 U.S.C. 77e(b)(1)) if the form used for registration of the securities to be offered provides for the use of a summary prospectus and the following conditions are met:

(1)(i) The registrant is organized under the laws of the United States or any State or Territory or the District of Columbia and has its principal business operations in the United States or its territories; or

(ii) The registrant is a foreign private issuer eligible to use Form F–2 (17 CFR 239.32);

(2) The registrant has a class of securities registered pursuant to section 12(b) of the Securities Exchange Act of 1934 or has a class of equity securities registered pursuant to section 12(g) of that Act or is required to file reports pursuant to section 15(d) of that Act;

(3) The registrant: (i) Has been subject to the requirements of section 12 or 15(d) of the Securities Exchange Act of 1934 and has filed all the material required to be filed pursuant to sections 13, 14 or 15(d) of that Act for a period of at least thirty-six calendar months immediately preceding the filing of the registration statement; and (ii) has filed in a timely manner all reports required to be filed during the twelve calendar months and any portion of a month immediately preceding the filing of the registration statement and, if the registrant has used (during the twelve calendar months and any portion of a month immediately preceding the filing of the registration statement) Rule 12b–25(b) under the Securities Exchange Act of 1934 with respect to a report or portion of a report, that report or portion thereof has actually been filed within the time period prescribed by that Rule; and

(4) Neither the registrant nor any of its consolidated or unconsolidated subsidiaries has, since the end of its last fiscal year for which certified financial statements of the registrant and its consolidated subsidiaries were included in a report filed pursuant to section 13(a) or 15(d) of the Securities Exchange Act of 1934: (i) failed to pay any dividend or sinking fund installment on preferred stock; or (ii) defaulted on any installment or installments on indebtedness for borrowed money, or on any rental on one or more long term leases, which defaults in the aggregate are material to

the financial position of the registrant and its consolidated and unconsolidated subsidiaries, taken as a whole.

(b) A summary prospectus shall contain the information specified in the instructions as to summary prospectuses in the form used for registration of the securities to be offered. Such prospectus may include any other information the substance of which is contained in the registration statement except as otherwise specifically provided in the instructions as to summary prospectuses in the form used for registration. It shall not include any information the substance of which is not contained in the registration statement except that a summary prospectus may contain any information specified in Rule 134(a). No reference need be made to inapplicable terms and negative answers to any item of the form may be omitted.

(c) All information included in a summary prospectus, other than the statement required by paragraph (e) of this rule, may be expressed in such condensed or summarized form as may be appropriate in the light of the circumstances under which the prospectus is to be used. The information need not follow the numerical sequence of the items of the form used for registration. Every summary prospectus shall be dated approximately as of the date of its first use.

(d) When used prior to the effective date of the registration statement, a summary prospectus shall be captioned a "Preliminary Summary Prospectus" and shall comply with the applicable requirements relating to a preliminary prospectus.

(e) A statement to the following effect shall be prominently set forth in conspicuous print at the beginning or at the end of every summary prospectus:

> "Copies of a more complete prospectus may be obtained from" (Insert name(s), address(es) and telephone number(s)).

Copies of a summary prospectus filed with the Commission pursuant to paragraph (g) of this rule may omit the names of persons from whom the complete prospectus may be obtained.

(f) Any summary prospectus published in a newspaper, magazine or other periodical need only be set in type at least as large as 7 point modern type. Nothing in this rule shall prevent the use of reprints of a summary prospectus published in a newspaper, magazine, or other periodical, if such reprints are clearly legible.

(g) Eight copies of every proposed summary prospectus shall be filed as a part of the registration statement, or as an amendment thereto, at least 5 days (exclusive of Saturdays, Sundays and holidays) prior to the use thereof, or prior to the release for publication by any newspaper, magazine or other person, whichever is earlier. The Commission may, however, in its discretion, authorize such use or publication prior to the expiration of the 5-day period upon a written request for such authorization. Within 7 days after the first use or publication thereof, 5 additional copies shall be filed in the exact form in which it was used or published.

Rule 432. Additional information required to be included in prospectuses relating to tender offers

Notwithstanding the provisions of any form for the registration of securities under the Act, any prospectus relating to securities to be offered in connection with a tender offer for, or a request or invitation for tenders of, securities subject to either Rule 13e–4 under the Securities Exchange Act of 1934 or section 14(d) of the Securities Exchange Act of 1934 (15 U.S.C. 78n(d)) must include the information required by Rules 13e–4(d)(1) or 14d–6(d)(1) under the Securities Exchange Act of 1934, as applicable, in all tender offers, requests or invitations that are published, sent or given to security holders.

Rule 433. Conditions to permissible post-filing free writing prospectuses

(a) *Scope of Rule.* This rule applies to any free writing prospectus with respect to securities of any issuer (except as set forth in Rule 164 that are the subject of a registration statement that has been filed under the Act). Such a free writing prospectus that satisfies the conditions of this rule may include information the substance of which is not included in the registration statement. Such a free writing prospectus that satisfies the conditions of this rule will be a prospectus permitted under section 10(b) of the Act for purposes of sections 2(a)(10), 5(b)(1), and 5(b)(2) of the Act and will, for purposes of considering it a prospectus, be deemed to be public, without regard to its method of use or distribution, because it is related to the public offering of securities that are the subject of a filed registration statement.

(b) *Permitted Use of Free Writing Prospectus.* Subject to the conditions of this paragraph (b) and satisfaction of the conditions set forth in paragraphs (c) through (g) of this rule, a free writing prospectus may be used under this rule and Rule 164 in connection with a registered offering of securities:

(1) *Eligibility and Prospectus Conditions for Seasoned Issuers and Well-Known Seasoned Is-*

suers. Subject to the provisions of Rule 164(e), (f), and (g), the issuer or any other offering participant may use a free writing prospectus in the following offerings after a registration statement relating to the offering has been filed that includes a prospectus that, other than by reason of this rule or Rule 431, satisfies the requirements of section 10 of the Act:

(i) Offerings of securities registered on Form S–3 (17 CFR 239.33) pursuant to General Instruction I.B.1, I.B.2, I.C., or I.D. thereof;

(ii) Offerings of securities registered on Form F–3 (17 CFR 239.13) pursuant to General Instruction I.A.5, I.B.1, I.B.2, or I.C. thereof;

(iii) Any other offering not excluded from reliance on this rule and Rule 164 of securities of a well-known seasoned issuer; and

(iv) Any other offering not excluded from reliance on this rule and Rule 164 of securities of an issuer eligible to use Form S–3 or Form F–3 for primary offerings pursuant to General Instruction I.B.1 of such Forms.

(2) *Eligibility and Prospectus Conditions for Non–Reporting and Unseasoned Issuers*. If the issuer does not fall within the provisions of paragraph (b)(1) of this rule, then, subject to the provisions of Rule 164(e), (f), and (g), any person participating in the offer or sale of the securities may use a free writing prospectus as follows:

(i) If the free writing prospectus is or was prepared by or on behalf of or used or referred to by an issuer or any other offering participant, if consideration has been or will be given by the issuer or other offering participant for the dissemination (in any format) of any free writing prospectus (including any published article, publication, or advertisement), or if section 17(b) of the Act requires disclosure that consideration has been or will be given by the issuer or other offering participant for any activity described therein in connection with the free writing prospectus, then a registration statement relating to the offering must have been filed that includes a prospectus that, other than by reason of this rule or Rule 431, satisfies the requirements of section 10 of the Act, including a price range where required by rule, and the free writing prospectus shall be accompanied or preceded by the most recent such prospectus; *provided, however*, that use of the free writing prospectus is not conditioned on providing the most recent such prospectus if a prior such prospectus has been provided and there is no material change from the prior prospectus reflected in the most recent prospectus; *provided further*, that after effectiveness and availability of a final prospectus meeting the requirements of section 10(a) of the Act, no such earlier prospectus may be provided in satisfaction of this condition, and such final prospectus must precede or accompany any free writing prospectus provided after such availability, whether or not an earlier prospectus had been previously provided.

NOTES TO PARAGRAPH (b)(2)(i) OF RULE 433:

1. The condition that a free writing prospectus shall be accompanied or preceded by the most recent prospectus satisfying the requirements of section 10 of the Act would be satisfied if a free writing prospectus that is an electronic communication contained an active hyperlink to such most recent prospectus; and

2. A communication for which disclosure would be required under section 17(b) of the Act as a result of consideration given or to be given, directly or indirectly, by or on behalf of an issuer or other offering participant is an offer by the issuer or such other offering participant as the case may be and is, if written, a free writing prospectus of the issuer or other offering participant.

(ii) Where paragraph (b)(2)(i) of this rule does not apply, a registration statement relating to the offering has been filed that includes a prospectus that, other than by reason of this rule or Rule 431 satisfies the requirements of section 10 of the Act, including a price range where required by rule. For purposes of paragraph (f) of this rule, the prospectus included in the registration statement relating to the offering that has been filed does not have to include a price range otherwise required by rule.

(3) *Successors*. A successor issuer will be considered to satisfy the applicable provisions of this paragraph (b) if:

(i) Its predecessor and it, taken together, satisfy the conditions, provided that the succession was primarily for the purpose of changing the state or other jurisdiction of incorporation of the predecessor or forming a holding company and the assets and liabilities of the successor at the time of succession were substantially the same as those of the predecessor; or

(ii) All predecessors met the conditions at the time of succession and the issuer has continued to do so since the succession.

(c) *Information in a Free Writing Prospectus*.

(1) A free writing prospectus used in reliance on this rule may include information the substance

of which is not included in the registration statement but such information shall not conflict with:

(i) Information contained in the filed registration statement, including any prospectus or prospectus supplement that is part of the registration statement (including pursuant to Rule 430B, Rule 430C, or Rule 430D) and not superseded or modified; or

(ii) Information contained in the issuer's periodic and current reports filed or furnished to the Commission pursuant to section 13 or 15(d) of the Securities Exchange Act of 1934 (15 U.S.C. 78m or 78o(d)) that are incorporated by reference into the registration statement and not superseded or modified.

(2)(i) A free writing prospectus used in reliance on this rule shall contain substantially the following legend:

The issuer has filed a registration statement (including a prospectus) with the SEC for the offering to which this communication relates. Before you invest, you should read the prospectus in that registration statement and other documents the issuer has filed with the SEC for more complete information about the issuer and this offering. You may get these documents for free by visiting EDGAR on the SEC Web site at www.sec.gov. Alternatively, the issuer, any underwriter or any dealer participating in the offering will arrange to send you the prospectus if you request it by calling toll-free 1–8[xx–xxx–xxxx].

(ii) The legend also may provide an e-mail address at which the documents can be requested and may indicate that the documents also are available by accessing the issuer's Web site and provide the Internet address and the particular location of the documents on the Web site.

(d) *Filing Conditions.*

(1) Except as provided in paragraphs (d)(3), (d)(4), (d)(5), (d)(6), (d)(7), (d)(8), and (f) of this rule, the following shall be filed with the Commission under this rule by a means reasonably calculated to result in filing no later than the date of first use. The free writing prospectus filed for purposes of this rule will not be filed as part of the registration statement:

(i) The issuer shall file:

(A) Any issuer free writing prospectus, as defined in paragraph (h) of this rule;

(B) Any issuer information that is contained in a free writing prospectus prepared by or on behalf of or used by any other offering participant (but not information prepared by or on behalf of a person other than the issuer on the basis of or derived from that issuer information); and

(C) A description of the final terms of the issuer's securities in the offering or of the offering contained in a free writing prospectus or portion thereof prepared by or on behalf of the issuer or any offering participant, after such terms have been established for all classes in the offering; and

(ii) Any offering participant, other than the issuer, shall file any free writing prospectus that is used or referred to by such offering participant and distributed by or on behalf of such person in a manner reasonably designed to lead to its broad unrestricted dissemination.

(2) Each free writing prospectus or issuer information contained in a free writing prospectus filed under this rule shall identify in the filing the Commission file number for the related registration statement or, if that file number is unknown, a description sufficient to identify the related registration statement.

(3) The condition to file a free writing prospectus under paragraph (d)(1) of this rule shall not apply if the free writing prospectus does not contain substantive changes from or additions to a free writing prospectus previously filed with the Commission.

(4) The condition to file issuer information contained in a free writing prospectus of an offering participant other than the issuer shall not apply if such information is included (including through incorporation by reference) in a prospectus or free writing prospectus previously filed that relates to the offering.

(5) Notwithstanding the provisions of paragraph (d)(1) of this rule:

(i) To the extent a free writing prospectus or portion thereof otherwise required to be filed contains a description of terms of the issuer's securities in the offering or of the offering that does not reflect the final terms, such free writing prospectus or portion thereof is not required to be filed; and

(ii) A free writing prospectus or portion thereof that contains only a description of the final terms of the issuer's securities in the offering or of the offerings shall be filed by the issuer within two days of the later of the date such final terms have been established for all classes of the offering and the date of first use.

(6)(i) Notwithstanding the provisions of paragraph (d) of this rule, in an offering of asset-backed securities, a free writing prospectus or portion thereof required to be filed that contains only ABS informational and computational materials as defined in Item 1101(a) of Regulation AB, may be filed under this rule within the timeframe permitted by Rule 426(b) and such filing will satisfy the filing conditions under this rule.

(ii) In the event that a free writing prospectus is used in reliance on this rule and Rule 164 and the conditions of this rule and Rule 164 (which may include the conditions of paragraph (d)(6)(i) of this rule) are satisfied with respect thereto, then the use of that free writing prospectus shall not be conditioned on satisfaction of the provisions, including without limitation the filing conditions, of Rule 167 and Rule 426. In the event that ABS informational and computational materials are used in reliance on Rule 167 and Rule 426 and the conditions of those rules are satisfied with respect thereto, then the use of those materials shall not be conditioned on the satisfaction of the conditions of Rule 164 and this rule.

(7) The condition to file a free writing prospectus or issuer information pursuant to this paragraph (d) for a free writing prospectus used at the same time as a communication in a business combination transaction subject to Rule 425 shall be satisfied if:

(i) The free writing prospectus or issuer information is filed in accordance with the provisions of Rule 425, including the filing timeframe of Rule 425;

(ii) The filed material pursuant to Rule 425 indicates on the cover page that it also is being filed pursuant to Rule 433; and

(iii) The filed material pursuant to Rule 425 contains the information specified in paragraph (c)(2) of this rule.

(8) Notwithstanding any other provision of this paragraph (d):

(i) A road show for an offering that is a written communication is a free writing prospectus, provided that, except as provided in paragraph (d)(8)(ii) of this rule, a written communication that is a road show shall not be required to be filed; and

(ii) In the case of a road show that is a written communication for an offering of common equity or convertible equity securities by an issuer that is, at the time of the filing of the registration statement for the offering, not required to file reports with the Commission pursuant to section 13 or section 15(d) of the Securities Exchange Act of 1934, such a road show is required to be filed pursuant to this rule unless the issuer of the securities makes at least one version of a *bona fide* electronic road show available without restriction by means of graphic communication to any person, including any potential investor in the securities (and if there is more than one version of a road show for the offering that is a written communication, the version available without restriction is made available no later than the other versions).

NOTE TO PARAGRAPH (d)(8): A communication that is provided or transmitted simultaneously with a road show and is provided or transmitted in a manner designed to make the communication available only as part of the road show and not separately is deemed to be part of the road show. Therefore, if the road show is not a written communication, such a simultaneous communication (even if it would otherwise be a graphic communication or other written communication) is also deemed not to be written. If the road show is written and not required to be filed, such a simultaneous communication is also not required to be filed. Otherwise, a written communication that is an offer contained in a separate file from a road show, whether or not the road show is a written communication, or otherwise transmitted separately from a road show, will be a free writing prospectus subject to any applicable filing conditions of paragraph (d) of this rule.

(e) *Treatment of Information on, or Hyperlinked from, an Issuer's Web Site.* (1) An offer of an issuer's securities that is contained on an issuer's Web site or hyperlinked by the issuer from the issuer's Web site to a third party's Web site is a written offer of such securities by the issuer and, unless otherwise exempt or excluded from the requirements of Section 5(b)(1) of the Act, the filing conditions of paragraph (d) of this rule apply to such offer.

(2) Notwithstanding paragraph (e)(1) of this rule, historical issuer information that is identified as such and located in a separate section of the issuer's Web site containing historical issuer information, that has not been incorporated by reference into or otherwise included in a prospectus of the issuer for the offering and that has not otherwise been used or referred to in connection with the offering, will not be considered a current

offer of the issuer's securities and therefore will not be a free writing prospectus.

(f) *Free Writing Prospectuses Published or Distributed by Media.* Any written offer for which an issuer or any other offering participant or any person acting on its behalf provided, authorized, or approved information that is prepared and published or disseminated by a person unaffiliated with the issuer or any other offering participant that is in the business of publishing, radio or television broadcasting or otherwise disseminating written communications would be considered at the time of publication or dissemination to be a free writing prospectus prepared by or on behalf of the issuer or such other offering participant for purposes of this rule subject to the following:

(1) The conditions of paragraph (b)(2)(i) of this rule will not apply and the conditions of paragraphs (c)(2) and (d) of this rule will be deemed to be satisfied if:

(i) No payment is made or consideration given by or on behalf of the issuer or other offering participant for the written communication or its dissemination; and

(ii) The issuer or other offering participant in question files the written communication with the Commission, and includes in the filing the legend required by paragraph (c)(2) of this rule, within four business days after the issuer or other offering participant becomes aware of the publication, radio or television broadcast, or other dissemination of the written communication.

(2) The filing obligation under paragraph (f)(1)(ii) of this rule shall be subject to the following:

(i) The issuer or other offering participant shall not be required to file a free writing prospectus if the substance of that free writing prospectus has previously been filed with the Commission;

(ii) Any filing made pursuant to paragraph (f)(1)(ii) of this rule may include information that the issuer or offering participant in question reasonably believes is necessary or appropriate to correct information included in the communication; and

(iii) In lieu of filing the actual written communication as published or disseminated as required by paragraph (f)(1)(ii) of this rule, the issuer or offering participant in question may file a copy of the materials provided to the media, including transcripts of interviews or similar materials, provided the copy or transcripts contain all the information provided to the media.

(3) For purposes of this paragraph (f) of this rule, an issuer that is in the business of publishing or radio or television broadcasting may rely on this paragraph (f) as to any publication or radio or television broadcast that is a free writing prospectus in respect of an offering of securities of the issuer if the issuer or an affiliate:

(i) Is the publisher of a *bona fide* newspaper, magazine, or business or financial publication of general and regular circulation or *bona fide* broadcaster of news including business and financial news;

(ii) Has established policies and procedures for the independence of the content of the publications or broadcasts from the offering activities of the issuer; and

(iii) Publishes or broadcasts the communication in the ordinary course.

(g) *Record Retention.* Issuers and offering participants shall retain all free writing prospectuses they have used, and that have not been filed pursuant to paragraph (d) or (f) of this rule, for three years following the initial bona fide offering of the securities in question.

NOTE TO PARAGRAPH (g) OF RULE 433: To the extent that the record retention requirements of Rule 17a–4 under the Securities Exchange Act of 1934 apply to free writing prospectuses required to be retained by a broker-dealer under this rule, such free writing prospectuses are required to be retained in accordance with such requirements.

(h) *Definitions.* For purposes of this rule:

(1) An *issuer free writing prospectus* means a free writing prospectus prepared by or on behalf of the issuer or used or referred to by the issuer and, in the case of an asset-backed issuer, prepared by or on behalf of a depositor, sponsor, or servicer (as defined in Item 1101 of Regulation AB) or affiliated depositor or used or referred to by any such person.

(2) *Issuer information* means material information about the issuer or its securities that has been provided by or on behalf of the issuer.

(3) A written communication or information is prepared or provided by or on behalf of a person if the person or an agent or representative of the person authorizes the communication or information or approves the communication or information before it is used. An offering participant other

than the issuer shall not be an agent or representative of the issuer solely by virtue of its acting as an offering participant.

(4) *A road show* means an offer (other than a statutory prospectus or a portion of a statutory prospectus filed as part of a registration statement) that contains a presentation regarding an offering by one or more members of the issuer's management (and in the case of an offering of asset-backed securities, management involved in the securitization or servicing function of one or more of the depositors, sponsors, or servicers (as such terms are defined in Item 1101 of Regulation AB) or an affiliated depositor) and includes discussion of one or more of the issuer, such management, and the securities being offered; and

(5) *A bona fide electronic road show* means a road show that is a written communication transmitted by graphic means that contains a presentation by one or more officers of an issuer or other persons in an issuer's management (and in the case of an offering of asset-backed securities, management involved in the securitization or servicing function of one or more of the depositors, sponsors, or servicers (as such terms are defined in Item 1101 of Regulation AB) or an affiliated depositor) and, if more than one road show that is a written communication is being used, includes discussion of the same general areas of information regarding the issuer, such management, and the securities being offered as such other issuer road show or shows for the same offering that are written communications.

NOTE TO RULE 433: This rule does not affect the operation of the provisions of clause (a) of section 2(a)(10) of the Act providing an exception from the definition of "prospectus."

WRITTEN CONSENTS

Rule 436. Consents required in special cases

(a) If any portion of the report or opinion of an expert or counsel is quoted or summarized as such in the registration statement or in a prospectus, the written consent of the expert or counsel shall be filed as an exhibit to the registration statement and shall expressly state that the expert or counsel consents to such quotation or summarization.

(b) If it is stated that any information contained in the registration statement has been reviewed or passed upon by any persons and that such information is set forth in the registration statement upon the authority of or in reliance upon such persons as experts, the written consents of such persons shall be filed as exhibits to the registration statement.

(c) Notwithstanding the provisions of paragraph (b) of this rule, a report on unaudited interim financial information (as defined in paragraph (d) of this rule) by an independent accountant who has conducted a review of such interim financial information shall not be considered a part of a registration statement prepared or certified by an accountant or a report prepared or certified by an accountant within the meaning of sections 7 and 11 of the Act.

(d) The term *report on unaudited interim financial information* shall mean a report which consists of the following:

(1) A statement that the review of interim financial information was made in accordance with established professional standards for such reviews;

(2) An identification of the interim financial information reviewed;

(3) A description of the procedures for a review of interim financial information;

(4) A statement that a review of interim financial information is substantially less in scope than an audit conducted in accordance with the standards of the Public Company Accounting Oversight Board (United States) ("PCAOB"), the objective of which is an expression of an opinion regarding the financial statements taken as a whole, and, accordingly, no such opinion is expressed; and

(5) A statement about whether the accountant is aware of any material modifications that should be made to the accompanying financial information so that it conforms with generally accepted accounting principles.

(e) Where a counsel is named as having acted for the underwriters or selling security holders, no consent will be required by reason of his being named as having acted in such capacity.

(f) Where the opinion of one counsel relies upon the opinion of another counsel, the consent of the counsel whose prepared opinion is relied upon need not be furnished.

(g)(1) Notwithstanding the provisions of paragraphs (a) and (b) of this rule, the security rating assigned to a class of debt securities, a class of convertible debt securities, or a class of preferred stock by a nationally recognized statistical rating organization, or with respect to registration statements on Form F–9 (17 CFR 239.39) by any other rating organization specified in the Instruction to paragraph (a)(2) of General Instruction I of Form F–9, shall not be considered a part of the registration statement prepared or certified by a person within the meaning of sections 7 and 11 of the Act.*

(2) For the purpose of paragraph (g)(1) of this rule, the term *nationally recognized statistical rating organization* shall have the same meaning as used in Rule 15c3–1(c)(2)(vi)(F) under the Securities Exchange Act of 1934.

Rule 437. Application to dispense with consent

An application to the Commission to dispense with any written consent of an expert pursuant to section 7 of the Act shall be made by the registrant and shall be supported by an affidavit or affidavits establishing that the obtaining of such consent is impracticable or involves undue hardship on the registrant. Such application shall be filed and the consent of the Commission shall be obtained prior to the effective date of the registration statement.

Rule 438. Consents of persons about to become directors

If any person who has not signed the registration statement is named therein as about to become a director, the written consent of such person shall be filed with the registration statement. Any such consent, however, may be omitted if there is filed with the registration statement a statement by the registrant, supported by an affidavit or affidavits, setting forth the reasons for such omission and establishing that the obtaining of such consent is impracticable or involves undue hardship on the registrant.

Rule 439. Consent to use of material incorporated by reference

(a) If the Act or the rules and regulations of the Commission require the filing of a written consent to the use of any material in connection with the registration statement, such consent shall be filed as an exhibit to the registration statement even though the material is incorporated therein by reference. Where the filing of a written consent is required with respect to material incorporated in the registration statement by reference, which is to be filed subsequent to the effective date of the registration statement, such consent shall be filed as an amendment to the registration statement no later than the date on which such material is filed with the Commission, unless express consent to incorporation by reference is contained in the material to be incorporated by reference.

* Sec. 439G declared this section to have no force or effect.

(b) Notwithstanding paragraph (a) of this rule, any required consent may be incorporated by reference into a registration statement filed pursuant to Rule 462(b) or a post-effective amendment filed pursuant to Rule 462(e) from a previously filed registration statement relating to that offering, provided that the consent contained in the previously filed registration statement expressly provides for such incorporation.

Rules 445 to 447. [Reserved]

FILINGS; FEES; EFFECTIVE DATE

Rule 455. Place of filing

All registration statements and other papers filed with the Commission shall be filed at its principal office. Such material may be filed by delivery to the Commission; provided, however, that only registration statements and post-effective amendments thereto filed pursuant to Rule 462(b) and Rule 110(d) may be filed by means of facsimile transmission.

Rule 456. Date of filing; timing of fee payment

(a) The date on which any papers are actually received by the Commission shall be the date of filing thereof, if all the requirements of the Act and the rules with respect to such filing have been complied with and the required fee paid. The failure to pay an insignificant amount of the required fee at the time of filing, as the result of a *bona fide* error, shall not be deemed to affect the date of filing.

(b)(1) Notwithstanding paragraph (a) of this rule, a well-known seasoned issuer that registers securities offerings on an automatic shelf registration statement, or registers additional securities or classes of securities thereon pursuant to Rule 413(b), may, but is not required to, defer payment of all or any part of the registration fee to the Commission required by section 6(b)(2) of the Act on the following conditions:

(i) If the issuer elects to defer payment of the registration fee, it shall pay the registration fees (pay-as-you-go registration fees) calculated in accordance with Rule 457(r) in advance of or in connection with an offering of securities from the registration statement within the time required to file the prospectus supplement pursuant to Rule 424(b) for the offering, provided, however, that if the issuer fails, after a good faith effort to pay the filing fee within the time required by this rule, the issuer may still be considered to have paid the fee in a timely manner if it is paid within four business days of its original due date; and

(ii) The issuer reflects the amount of the pay-as-you-go registration fee paid or to be paid in accordance with paragraph (b)(1)(i) of this rule by updating the "Calculation of Registration Fee" table to indicate the class and aggregate offering price of securities offered and the amount of registration fee paid or to be paid in connection with the offering or offerings either in a post-effective amendment filed at the time of the fee payment or on the cover page of a prospectus filed pursuant to Rule 424(b).

(2) A registration statement filed relying on the pay-as-you-go registration fee payment provisions of paragraph (b)(1) of this rule will be considered filed as to the securities or classes of securities identified in the registration statement for purposes of this rule and section 5 of the Act when it is received by the Commission, if it complies with all other requirements of the Act and the rules with respect to it.

(3) The securities sold pursuant to a registration statement will be considered registered, for purposes of section 6(a) of the Act, if the pay-as-you-go registration fee has been paid and the prospectus including the amended "Calculation of Registration Fee" table is filed pursuant to paragraph (b)(1) of this rule.

(c)(1) Notwithstanding paragraph (a) of this section, an asset-backed issuer that registers asset-backed securities offerings on Form SF–3 (17 CFR 239.45), may, but is not required to, defer payment of all or any part of the registration fee to the Commission required by section 6(b)(1) of the Act (15 U.S.C. 77f(b)(1)) on the following conditions:

(i) If the issuer elects to defer payment of the registration fee, it shall pay the registration fees (pay-as-you-go registration fees) calculated in accordance with Rule 457(s) in advance of or in connection with an offering of securities from the registration statement at the time of filing the prospectus pursuant to Rule 424(h) for the offering; and

(ii) The issuer reflects the amount of the pay-as-you-go registration fee paid or to be paid in accordance with paragraph (c)(1)(i) of this section by updating the "Calculation of Registration Fee" table to indicate the class and aggregate offering price of securities offered and the amount of registration fee paid or to be paid in connection with the offering or offerings on the cover page of a prospectus filed pursuant to Rule 424(h).

(2) A registration statement filed relying on the pay-as-you-go registration fee payment provisions of paragraph (c)(1) of this section will be considered filed as to the securities or classes of securities identified in the registration statement for purposes of this section and section 5 of the Act (15 U.S.C. 77e) when it is received by the Commission, if it complies with all other requirements of the Act and the rules with respect to it.

(3) The securities sold pursuant to a registration statement will be considered registered, for purpose of section 6(a) of the Act (15 U.S.C. 77f(a)), if the pay-as-you-go registration fee has been paid and prospectus including the amended "Calculation of Registration Fee" table is filed pursuant to paragraph (c)(1) of this section.

Rule 457. Computation of fee

(a) If a filing fee based on a bona fide estimate of the maximum offering price, computed in accordance with this rule where applicable, has been paid, no additional filing fee shall be required as a result of changes in the proposed offering price. If the number of shares or other units of securities, or the principal amount of debt securities to be offered is increased by an amendment filed prior to the effective date of the registration statement, an additional filing fee, computed on the basis of the offering price of the additional securities, shall be paid. There will be no refund once the statement is filed.

(b) A required fee shall be reduced in an amount equal to any fee paid with respect to such transaction pursuant to sections 13(e) and 14(g) of the Securities Exchange Act of 1934 or any applicable provision of this rule; the fee requirements under sections 13(e) and 14(g) shall be reduced in an amount equal to the fee paid the Commission with respect to a transaction under this rule. No part of a filing fee is refundable.

(c) Where securities are to be offered at prices computed upon the basis of fluctuating market prices, the registration fee is to be calculated upon the basis of the price of securities of the same class, as follows: either the average of the high and low prices reported in the consolidated reporting system (for exchange traded securities and last sale reported over-the-counter securities) or the average of the bid and asked price (for other over-the-counter securities) as of a specified date within 5 business days prior to the date of filing the registration statement.

(d) Where securities are to be offered at varying prices based upon fluctuating values of underlying assets, the registration fee is to be calculated upon the basis of the market value of such assets as of a specified date within fifteen days prior to the date of filing, in accordance with the method to be used in calculating the daily offering price.

(e) Where securities are to be offered to existing security holders and the portion, if any, not taken by such security holders is to be reoffered to the general public, the registration fee is to be calculated upon the basis of the proposed offering price to such security holders or the proposed reoffering price to the general public, whichever is higher.

(f) Where securities are to be offered in exchange for other securities (except where such exchange results from the exercise of a conversion privilege) or in a reclassification or recapitalization which involves the substitution of a security for another security, a merger, a consolidation, or a similar plan of acquisition, the registration fee is to be calculated as follows:

(1) Upon the basis of the market value of the securities to be received by the registrant or canceled in the exchange or transaction as established by the price of securities of the same class, as determined in accordance with paragraph (c) of this rule.

(2) If there is no market for the securities to be received by the registrant or cancelled in the exchange or transaction, the book value of such securities computed as of the latest practicable date prior to the date of filing the registration statement shall be used, unless the issuer of such securities is in bankruptcy or receivership, or has an accumulated capital deficit, in which case one-third of the principal amount, par value or stated value of such securities shall be used.

(3) If any cash is to be received by the registrant in connection with the exchange or transaction, the amount thereof shall be added to the value of the securities to be received by the registrant or cancelled as computed in accordance with (e)(1) or (2) of this rule. If any cash is to be paid by the registrant in connection with the exchange or transaction, the amount thereof shall be deducted from the value of the securities to be received by the registrant in exchange as computed in accordance with (e)(1) or (2) of this rule.

(4) Securities to be offered directly or indirectly for certificates of deposit shall be deemed to be offered for the securities represented by the certificates of deposit.

(5) If a filing fee is paid under this paragraph for the registration of an offering and the registration statement also covers the resale of such securities, no additional filing fee is required to be paid for the resale transaction.

(g) Where securities are to be offered pursuant to warrants or other rights to purchase such securities and the holders of such warrants or rights may be deemed to be underwriters, as defined in section 2(11) of the Act, with respect to the warrants or rights or the securities subject thereto, the registration fee is to be calculated upon the basis of the price at which the warrants or rights or securities subject thereto are to be offered to the public. If such offering price cannot be determined at the time of filing the registration statement, the registration fee is to be calculated upon the basis of the highest of the following: (1) the price at which the warrants or rights may be exercised, if known at the time of filing the registration statement; (2) the offering price of securities of the same class included in the registration statement; or (3) the price of securities of the same class, as determined in accordance with paragraph (c) of this rule. If the fee is to be calculated upon the basis of the price at which the warrants or rights may be exercised and they are exercisable over a period of time at progressively higher prices, the fee shall be calculated on the basis of the highest price at which they may be exercised. If the warrants or rights are to be registered for distribution in the same registration statement as the securities to be offered pursuant thereto, no separate registration fee shall be required.

(h)(1) Where securities are to be offered pursuant to an employee benefit plan, the aggregate offering price and the amount of the registration fee shall be computed with respect to the maximum number of the registrant's securities issuable under the plan that are covered by the registration statement. If the offering price is not known, the fee shall be computed upon the basis of the price of securities of the same class, as determined in accordance with paragraph (c) of this rule. In the case of an employee stock option plan, the aggregate offering price and the fee shall be computed upon the basis of the price at which the options may be exercised, or, if such price is not known, upon the basis of the price of securities of the same class, as determined in accordance with paragraph (c) of this rule. If there is no market for the securities to be offered, the book value of such securities computed as of the latest practicable date prior to the date of filing the registration statement shall be used.

(2) If the registration statement registers securities of the registrant and also registers interests in the plan constituting separate securities, no separate fee is required with respect to the plan interests.

(3) Where a registration statement includes securities to be offered pursuant to an employee benefit plan and covers the resale of the same securities, no additional filing fee shall be paid with respect to the securities to be offered for resale. A filing fee determined in accordance with paragraph (c) of this rule shall be paid with respect to any additional securities to be offered for resale.

(i) Where convertible securities and the securities into which conversion is offered are registered at the same time, the registration fee is to be calculated on the basis of the proposed offering price of the convertible securities alone, except that if any additional consideration is to be received in connection with the exercise of the conversion privilege the maximum amount which may be received shall be added to the proposed offering price of the convertible securities.

(j) Where securities are sold prior to the registration thereof and are subsequently registered for the purpose of making an offer of rescission of such sale or sales, the registration fee is to be calculated on the basis of the amount at which such securities were sold, except that where securities repurchased pursuant to such offer of rescission are to be reoffered to the general public at a price in excess of such amount the registration fee is to be calculated on the basis of the proposed reoffering price.

(k) Notwithstanding the other provisions of this rule, the proposed maximum aggregate offering price of Depositary Shares evidenced by American Depositary Receipts shall, only for the purpose of calculating the registration fee, be computed upon the basis of the maximum aggregate fees or charges to be imposed in connection with the issuance of such receipts.

(*l*) Notwithstanding the other provisions of this rule, the proposed maximum aggregate offering price of any put or call option which is traded on an exchange and registered by such exchange or a facility thereof or which is traded over the counter shall, for the purpose of calculating the registration fee, be computed upon the basis of the maximum aggregate fees or charges to be imposed by such registrant in connection with the issuance of such option.

(m) Notwithstanding the other provisions of this rule, where the securities to be registered include (1) any note, draft, bill of exchange, or bankers' acceptance which meets all the conditions of section 3(a)(3) hereof, and (2) any note, draft, bill of exchange or bankers' acceptance which has a maturity at the time of issuance of not exceeding nine months exclusive of days of grace, or any renewal thereof the maturity date of which is likewise limited, but which otherwise does not meet the conditions of section 3(a)(3), the registration fee shall be calculated by taking one-fiftieth of 1 per centum of the maximum principal amount of only those securities not meeting the conditions of section 3(a)(3).

(n) Where the securities to be offered are guarantees of other securities which are being registered concurrently, no separate fee for the guarantees shall be payable.

(*o*) Where an issuer registers an offering of securities, the registration fee may be calculated on the basis of the maximum aggregate offering price of all the securities listed in the "Calculation of Registration Fee" table. The number of shares or units of securities need not be included in the "Calculation of Registration Fee" Table. If the maximum aggregate offering price increases prior to the effective date of the registration statement, a pre-effective amendment must be filed to increase the maximum dollar value being registered and the additional filing fee shall be paid.

(p) Where all or a portion of the securities offered under a registration statement remain unsold after the offering's completion or termination, or withdrawal of the registration statement, the aggregate total dollar amount of the filing fee associated with those unsold securities (whether computed under Rule 457(a) or (*o*)) may be offset against the total filing fee due for a subsequent registration statement or registration statements. The subsequent registration statement(s) must be filed within five years of the initial filing date of the earlier registration statement, and must be filed by the same registrant (including a successor within the meaning of Rule 405), a majority-owned subsidiary of that registrant, or a parent that owns more than 50 percent of the registrant's outstanding voting securities. A note should be added to the "Calculation of Registration Fee" table in the subsequent registration statement(s) stating the dollar amount of the filing fee previously paid that is offset against the currently due filing fee, the file number of the earlier registration statement from which the filing fee is offset, and the name of the registrant and the initial filing date of that earlier registration statement.

(q) Notwithstanding any other provisions of this rule, no filing fee is required for the registration of an indeterminate amount of securities to be offered solely for market-making purposes by an affiliate of the registrant.

(r) Where securities are to be offered pursuant to an automatic shelf registration statement, the registration fee is to be calculated in accordance with this rule. When the issuer elects to defer payment of the fees pursuant to Rule 456(b), the "Calculation of Registration Fee" table in the registration statement must indicate that the issuer is relying on Rule 456(b) but does not need to include the number of shares or units of securities or the maximum aggregate offering price of any securities until the issuer updates the "Calculation of Registration Fee" table to reflect payment of the registration fee, including a pay-as-you-go registration fee in accordance with Rule 456(b). The registration fee shall be calculated based on the fee payment rate in effect on the date of the fee payment.

(s) Where securities are asset-backed securities being offered pursuant to a registration statement on Form SF–3 (17 CFR 239.45), the registration fee is to be calculated in accordance with this section. When the issuer elects to defer payment of the fees pursuant to Rule 456(c), the "Calculation of Registration Fee" table in the registration statement must indicate that the issuer is relying on Rule 456(c) but does not need to include the number of units of securities or the maximum aggregate offering price of any securities until the issuer updates the "Calculation of Registration Fee" table to reflect payment of the registration fee, including a pay-as-you-go registration fee in accordance with Rule 456(c). The registration fee shall be calculated based on the fee payment rate in effect on the date of the fee payment.

(t) Where the security to be offered is a collateral certificate or is a special unit of beneficial interest, underlying asset-backed securities (as defined in § 229.1101(c) of this chapter) which are being registered concurrently, no separate fee for the certificate or the special unit of beneficial interest shall be payable.

Rule 459. Calculation of effective date

Saturdays, Sundays, and holidays shall be counted in computing the effective date of registration statements under section 8(a) of the Act. In the case of statements which become effective on the 20th day after filing, the 20th day shall be deemed to begin at the expiration of 19 periods of 24 hours each from 5:30 p.m. Eastern Standard Time or Eastern Daylight-Saving Time, whichever is in effect at the principal office of the Commission on the date of filing.

Rule 460. Distribution of preliminary prospectus

(a) Pursuant to the statutory requirement that the Commission in ruling upon requests for acceleration of the effective date of a registration statement shall have due regard to the adequacy of the information respecting the issuer theretofore available to the public, the Commission may consider whether the persons making the offering have taken reasonable steps to make the information contained in the registration statement conveniently available to underwriters and dealers who it is reasonably anticipated will be invited to participate in the distribution of the security to be offered or sold.

(b)(1) As a minimum, reasonable steps to make the information conveniently available would involve the distribution, to each underwriter and dealer who it is reasonably anticipated will be invited to participate in the distribution of the security, a reasonable time in advance of the anticipated effective date of the registration statement, of as many copies of the proposed form of preliminary prospectus permitted by Rule 430 as appears to be reasonable to secure adequate distribution of the preliminary prospectus.

(2) In the case of a registration statement filed by a closed-end investment company on Form N–2 (17 CFR 239.14 and 274.11a–1), reasonable steps to make information conveniently available would involve distribution of a sufficient number of copies of the Statement of Additional Information required by Rule 430(b) as it appears to be reasonable to secure their adequate distribution either to each underwriter or dealer who it is reasonably anticipated will be invited to participate in the distribution of the security, or to the underwriter, dealer or other source named on the cover page of the preliminary prospectus as being the person investors should contact in order to obtain the Statement of Additional Information.

(c) The granting of acceleration will not be conditioned upon

(1) The distribution of a preliminary prospectus in any state where such distribution would be illegal; or

(2) The distribution of a preliminary prospectus

(i) in the case of a registration statement relating solely to securities to be offered at competitive bidding, provided the undertaking in Item 512(d)(1) of Regulation S–K is included in the registration statement and distribution of prospectuses pursuant to such undertaking is made prior to the publication or distribution of the invitation for bids, or

(ii) In the case of a registration statement relating to a security issued by a face-amount certificate company or a redeemable security issued by an open-end management company or unit investment trust if any other security of the same class is currently being offered or sold, pursuant to an effective registration statement by the issuer or by or through an underwriter, or

(iii) In the case of an offering of subscription rights unless it is contemplated that the distribution will be made through dealers and the underwriters intend to make the offering during the stockholders' subscription period, in which case copies of the preliminary prospectus must be distributed to dealers prior to the effective date of the registration statement in the same fashion as is required in the case of other offerings through underwriters, or

(iv) In the case of a registration statement pertaining to a security to be offered pursuant to an exchange offer or transaction described in Rule 145.

Rule 461. Acceleration of effective date

(a) Requests for acceleration of the effective date of a registration statement shall be made by the registrant and the managing underwriters of the proposed issue, or, if there are no managing underwriters, by the principal underwriters of the proposed issue, and shall state the date upon which it is desired that the registration statement shall become effective. Such requests may be made in writing or orally, provided that, if an oral request is to be made, a letter indicating that fact and stating that the registrant and the managing or principal underwriters are aware of their obligations under the Act must accompany the registration statement for a pre-effective amendment thereto at the time of filing with the Commission. Written requests may be sent to the Commission by facsimile transmission. If, by reason of the expected arrangement in connection with the offering, it is to be requested that the registration statement shall become effective at a particular hour of the day, the Commission must be advised to that effect not later than the second business day before the day which it is desired that the registration statement shall become effective. A person's request for acceleration will be considered confirmation of such person's awareness of the person's obligations under the Act. Not later than the time of filing the last amendment prior to the effective date of the registration statement, the registrant shall inform the Commission as to whether or not the amount of compensation to be allowed or paid to the underwriters and any other arrangements among the registrant, the underwriters and other broker dealers participating in the distribution, as described in the registration statement, have been reviewed to the extent required by the National Association of Securities Dealers, Inc. and such Association has issued a statement expressing no objections to the compensation and other arrangements.

(b) Having due regard to the adequacy of information respecting the registrant theretofore available to the public, to the facility with which the nature of the securities to be registered, their relationship to the capital structure of the registrant issuer and the rights of holders thereof can be understood, and to the public interest and the protection of investors, as provided in section 8(a) of the Act, it is the general policy of the Commission, upon request, as provided in paragraph (a) of this rule, to permit acceleration of the effective date of the registration statement as soon as possible after the filing of appropriate amendments, if any. In determining the date on which a registration statement shall become effective, the following are included in the situations in which the Commission considers that the statutory standards of section 8(a) may not be met and may refuse to accelerate the effective date:

(1) Where there has not been a bona fide effort to make the prospectus reasonably concise, readable, and in compliance with the plain English requirements of Rule 421(d) of Regulation C in order to facilitate an understanding of the information in the prospectus.

(2) Where the form of preliminary prospectus, which has been distributed by the issuer or underwriter, is found to be inaccurate or inadequate in any material respect, until the Commission has received satisfactory assurance that appropriate correcting material has been sent to all underwriters and dealers who received such preliminary prospectus or prospectuses in quantity sufficient for their information and the information of others to whom the inaccurate or inadequate material was sent.

(3) Where the Commission is currently making an investigation of the issuer, a person controlling the issuer, or one of the underwriters, if any, of the securities to be offered, pursuant to any of the Acts administered by the Commission.

(4) Where one or more of the underwriters, although firmly committed to purchase securities covered by the registration statement, is subject to and does not meet the financial responsibility requirements of Rule 15c3–1 under the Securities Exchange Act of 1934. For the purposes of this paragraph underwriters will be deemed to be firmly committed even though the obligation to purchase is subject to the usual conditions as to receipt of opinions of counsel, accountants, etc., the accuracy of warranties or representations, the happening of calamities or the occurrence of other events the determination of which is not expressed to be in the sole or absolute discretion of the underwriters.

(5) Where there have been transactions in securities of the registrant by persons connected with or proposed to be connected with the offering which may have artificially affected or may artificially affect the market price of the security being offered.

(6) Where the amount of compensation to be allowed or paid to the underwriters and any other arrangements among the registrant, the underwriters and other broker dealers participating in the distribution, as described in the registration statement, if required to be reviewed by the National Association of Securities Dealers, Inc. (NASD), have been reviewed by the NASD and the NASD has not issued a statement expressing no objections to the compensation and other arrangements.

(7) Where, in the case of a significant secondary offering at the market, the registrant, selling security holders and underwriters have not taken sufficient measures to insure compliance with Rules 100 through 105 of Regulation M.

(c) Insurance against liabilities arising under the Act, whether the cost of insurance is borne by the registrant, the insured or some other person, will not be considered a bar to acceleration, unless the registrant is a registered investment company or a business development company and the cost of such insurance is borne by other than an insured officer or director of the registrant. In the case of such a registrant, the Commission may refuse to accelerate the effective date of the registration statement when the registrant is organized or administered pursuant to any instrument (including a contract for insurance against liabilities arising under the Act) that protects or purports to protect any director or officer of the company against any liability to the company or its security holders to which he or she would otherwise be subject by reason of willful misfeasance, bad faith, gross negligence or reckless disregard of the duties involved in the conduct of his or her office.

Rule 462. Immediate effectiveness of certain registration statements and post–effective amendments

(a) A registration statement on Form S–8 (17 CFR 239.16b) and a registration statement on Form S–3 (17 CFR 239.13) or on Form F–3 (17 CFR 239.33) for a dividend or interest reinvestment plan shall become effective upon filing with the Commission.

(b) A registration statement and any post-effective amendment thereto shall become effective upon filing with the Commission if:

(1) The registration statement is for registering additional securities of the same class(es) as were included in an earlier registration statement for the same offering and declared effective by the Commission;

(2) The new registration statement is filed prior to the time confirmations are sent or given; and

(3) The new registration statement registers additional securities in an amount and at a price that together represent no more than 20% of the maximum aggregate offering price set forth for each class of securities in the "Calculation of Registration Fee" table contained in such earlier registration statement.

(c) If the prospectus contained in a post-effective amendment filed prior to the time confirmations are sent or given contains no substantive changes from or additions to the prospectus previously filed as part of the effective registration statement, other than price-related information omitted from the registration statement in reliance on Rule 430A of the Act, such post-effective amendment shall become effective upon filing with the Commission.

(d) A post-effective amendment filed solely to add exhibits to a registration statement shall become effective upon filing with the Commission.

(e) An automatic shelf registration statement, including an automatic shelf registration statement filed in accordance with Rule 415(a)(6), and any post-effective amendment thereto, including a post-effective amendment filed to register additional classes of securities pursuant to Rule 413(b), shall become effective upon filing with the Commission.

(f) A post-effective amendment filed pursuant to paragraph (e) of this rule for purposes of adding a new issuer and its securities as permitted by Rule 413(b) that satisfies the requirements of Form S–3 or Form F–3 (17 CFR 239.13 or 239.33), as applicable, including the signatures required by Rule 402(e), and contains a prospectus satisfying the requirements of Rule 430B, shall become effective upon filing with the Commission.

Rule 463. Report of offering of securities and use of proceeds therefrom

(a) Except as provided in this rule, following the effective date of the first registration statement filed under the Act by an issuer, the issuer or successor issuer shall report the use of proceeds pursuant to Item 701 of Regulation S–B or S–K or Item 14(e) of Form 20–F, as applicable, on its first periodic report filed pursuant to Sections 13(a) and 15(d) (15 U.S.C. 78m(a) and 78o(d)) of the Securities Exchange Act of 1934 after effectiveness, and thereafter on each of its subsequent periodic reports filed pursuant to Sections 13(a) and 15(d) of the Securities Exchange Act of 1934 through the later of disclosure of the application of all the offering proceeds or disclosure of the termination of the offering.

(b) A successor issuer shall comply with paragraph (a) of this rule only if a report of the use of proceeds is required with respect to the first effective registration statement of the predecessor issuer.

(c) For purposes of this rule:

(1) The term *offering proceeds* shall not include any amount(s) received for the account(s) of any selling security holder(s).

(2) The term *application* shall not include the temporary investment of proceeds by the issuer pending final application.

(d) This rule shall not apply to any effective registration statement for securities to be issued:

(1) In a business combination described in Rule 145(a);

(2) By an issuer which pursuant to a business combination described in Rule 145(a) has succeeded to another issuer that prior to such business combination had a registration statement become effective under the Act and on the date of such business combination was not subject to paragraph (a) of this rule;

(3) Pursuant to an employee benefit plan;

(4) Pursuant to a dividend or interest reinvestment plan;

(5) As American depository receipts for foreign securities;

(6) By any investment company registered under the Investment Company Act of 1940 and any issuer that has elected to be regulated as a business development company under sections 54 through 65 of the Investment Company Act of 1940 (15 U.S.C. 80a–53 through 80a–64);

(7) By any public utility company or public utility holding company required to file reports with any State or Federal authority;

(8) In a merger in which a vote or consent of the security holders of the company being acquired is not required pursuant to applicable state law; or

(9) In an exchange offer for the securities of the issuer or another entity.

Rule 464. Effective date of post-effective amendments to registration statements filed on Form S–8 and on certain forms S–3, S–4, F–2 and F–3

Provided. That, at the time of filing of each post-effective amendment with the Commission, the issuer continues to meet the requirements of filing on Form S–8 (17 CFR 239.16b); or on Form S–3, F–2 or F–3 (17 CFR 239.13, 239.32 or 239.33) for a registration statement relating to a dividend or interest reinvestment plan; or in the case of a registration statement on Form S–4 (17 CFR 239.25) that there is continued compliance with General Instruction G of that Form:

(a) The post-effective amendment shall become effective upon filing with the Commission; and

(b) With respect to securities sold on or after the filing date pursuant to a prospectus which forms a part of a Form S–8 registration statement; or a Form S–3, F–2, or F–3 registration statement relating to a dividend or interest reinvestment plan; or a Form S–4 registration statement complying with General Instruction G of that Form and which has been amended to include or incorporate new full year financial statements or to comply with the provisions of section 10(a)(3) of the Act, the effective date of the registration statement shall be deemed to be the filing date of the post-effective amendment.

Rule 466. Effective date of certain registration statements on Form F–6

(a) A depositary that previously has filed a registration statement on Form F–6 (17 CFR 239.36) may designate a date and time for a registration statement (including post-effective amendments) on Form F–6 to become effective and such registration statement shall become effective in accordance with such designation if the following conditions are met:

(1) The depositary previously has filed a registration statement on Form F–6 (17 CFR 239.36), which the Commission has declared effective, with identical terms of deposit, except for the number of foreign securities a Depositary Share represents, and the depositary so certifies; and

(2) The designation of the effective date and time is set forth on the facing-page of the registration statement, or in any pre-effective amendment thereto. A pre-effective amendment containing such a designation properly made shall be deemed to have been filed with the consent of the Commission.

(b)(1) The Commission may, in the manner and under the circumstances set forth in paragraph (b)(2) of this rule, suspend the ability of a depositary to designate the date and time of effectiveness of a registration statement, and such suspension shall remain in effect until the Commission furnishes written notice to the depositary that the suspension has been terminated. Any suspension, so long as it is in effect, shall apply to any registration statement that has been filed but has not, at the time of such suspension, become effective and to any registration statement the depositary files after such suspension. Any such suspension applies only to the ability to designate the date and time of effectiveness under paragraph (a) of this rule and does not otherwise affect the registration statement.

(2) Any suspension under paragraph (b)(1) of this rule becomes effective when the Commission furnishes written notice thereof to the depositary. The Commission may issue a suspension if it appears to the Commission: (i) that any registration statement containing a designation under this rule is incomplete or inaccurate in any material respect, whether or not such registration has become effective, or (ii) that the depositary has not complied with any of the conditions of this rule. The depositary may petition the Commission to review the suspension. The Commission will order a hearing on the matter if a request for such a hearing is included in the petition.

Rule 467. Effectiveness of registration statements and post-effective amendments thereto made on Forms F–7, F–8, F–10 and F–80

(a) A registration statement on Form F–7, Form F–8 or Form F–80 (17 CFR 239.37, 17 CFR 239.38 or 17 CFR 239.41) and any amendment thereto, shall become effective upon filing with the Commission. A registration statement on Form F–10 (17 CFR 239.40), and any amendment thereto, relating to an offering being made contemporaneously in the United States and Canada shall become effective upon filing with the Commission, unless designated as preliminary material on the Form.

(b) Where no contemporaneous offering is being made in Canada, a registrant filing on Form F–10 may designate on the facing page of the registration statement, or any amendment thereto, a date and time for such filing to become effective that is not earlier than seven calendar days after the date of filing with the Commission, and such registration statement or amendment shall become effective in accordance with such designation; provided, however, That such registration statement or amendment may become effective prior to seven calendar days after the date of filing with the Commission if the securities regulatory authority in the review jurisdiction issues a receipt or notification of clearance with respect thereto before such time elapses, in which case the registration statement or amendment shall become effective by order of the Commission as soon as practicable after receipt of written notification by the Commission from the registrant or the applicable Canadian securities regulatory authority of the issuance of such receipt or notification of clearance.

AMENDMENTS; WITHDRAWALS

Rule 470. Formal requirements for amendments

Except for telegraphic amendments filed pursuant to Rule 473, amendments to a registration statement shall be filed under cover of an appropriate facing sheet, shall be numbered consecutively in the order in which filed, and shall indicate on the facing sheet the applicable registration form on which the amendment is prepared and the file number of the registration statement.

Rule 471. Signatures to amendments

(a) Except as provided in Rule 447 and in Rule 478, every amendment to a registration statement shall be signed by the persons specified in section 6(a) of the Act. At least one copy of every amendment filed with the Commission shall be signed. Unsigned copies shall be conformed.

(b) Where the Act or the rules thereunder require a document filed with or furnished to the Commission to be signed, such document shall be manually signed, or signed using either typed signatures or duplicated or facsimile versions of manual signatures. Where typed, duplicated or facsimile signatures are used, each signatory to the filing shall manually sign a signature page or other document authenticating, acknowledging or otherwise adopting his or her signature that appears in the filing. Such document shall be executed before or at the time the filing is made and shall be retained by the registrant for a period of five years. Upon request, the registrant shall furnish to the Commission or its staff a copy of any or all documents retained pursuant to this rule.

Rule 472. Filing of amendments; number of copies

(a) Except for telegraphic amendments filed pursuant to Rule 473, there shall be filed with the Commission three complete, unmarked copies of every amendment, including exhibits and all other papers and documents filed as part of the amendment, and eight additional copies of such amendment at least five of which shall be marked to indicate clearly and precisely, by underlining or in some other appropriate manner, the changes effected in the registration statement by the amendment. Where the amendment to the registration statement incorporates into the prospectus documents which are required to be delivered with the prospectus in lieu of prospectus presentation, the eight additional copies shall be accompanied by eight copies of such documents. No other exhibits are required to accompany such additional copies.

(b) Every amendment which relates to a prospectus shall include copies of the prospectus as amended. Each such copy of the amended prospectus shall be accompanied by a copy of the cross reference sheet required by Rule 481(a), where applicable, if the amendment of the prospectus resulted in any change in the accuracy of the cross reference sheet previously filed. Notwithstanding the foregoing provisions of this paragraph, only copies of the changed pages of the prospectus, and the cross reference sheet if amended, need be included in an amendment filed pursuant to an undertaking referred to in Item 512(d) of Regulation S–K.

(c) Every amendment of a financial statement which is not included in the prospectus shall include copies of the financial statement as amended. Every amendment relating to a certified financial statement shall include the consent of the certifying accountant to the use of his certificate in connection with the amended financial statement in the registration statement or prospectus and to being named as having certified such financial statement.

(d) Notwithstanding any other provision of this rule, if a registration statement filed on Form S–8 (17 CFR 239.16b) is amended, there shall be filed with the Commission three complete, unmarked copies of every amendment, including exhibits and all other papers and documents filed as part of the amendment. Three additional, unmarked copies of such amendments shall be furnished to the Commission. No exhibits are required to accompany the additional copies of amendments to registration statements filed on Form S–8.

(e) Notwithstanding any other provision of this rule, if a post-effective amendment is filed pursuant to Rule 462(b) and Rule 110(d), one copy of the complete post-effective amendment, including exhibits and all other papers and documents filed as a part thereof shall be filed with the Commission. Such copy should not be bound and may contain facsimile versions of manual signatures in accordance with Rule 402(e).

Rule 473. Delaying amendments

(a) An amendment in the following form filed with a registration statement, or as an amendment to a registration statement which has not become effective, shall be deemed, for the purpose of section 8(a) of the Act, to be filed on such date or dates as may be necessary to delay the effective date of such registration statement (1) until the registrant shall file a further amendment which specifically states as provided in paragraph (b) of this rule that such registration statement shall thereafter become effective in accordance with section 8(a) of the Act, or (2) until the registration statement shall become effective on such date as the Commission, acting pursuant to section 8(a), may determine:

> The registrant hereby amends this registration statement on such date or dates as may be necessary to delay its effective date until the registrant shall file a further amendment which specifically states that this registration statement shall thereafter become effective in accordance with section 8(a) of the Securities Act of 1933 or until the registration statement shall become effective on such date as the Commission acting pursuant to said section 8(a), may determine.

(b) An amendment which for the purpose of paragraph (a)(1) of this rule specifically states that a registration statement shall thereafter become effective in accordance with section 8(a) of the Act, shall be in the following form:

This registration statement shall hereafter become effective in accordance with the provisions of section 8(a) of the Securities Act of 1933.

(c) An amendment pursuant to paragraph (a) of this rule which is filed with a registration statement shall be set forth on the facing page thereof following the calculation of the registration fee. Any such amendment filed after the filing of the registration statement, any amendment altering the proposed date of public sale of the securities being registered, or any amendment filed pursuant to paragraph (b) of this rule may be made by telegram, letter, or facsimile transmission. Each such telegraphic amendment shall be confirmed in writing within a reasonable time by the filing of a signed copy of the amendment. Such confirmation shall not be deemed an amendment.

(d) [Effective until Dec. 31, 2012.] No amendments pursuant to paragraph (a) of this section may be filed with a registration statement on Form F–7, F–8 or F–80 (17 CFR 239.37, 17 CFR 239.38 or 17 CFR 239.41); on Form F–9 or F–10 (17 CFR 239.39 or 17 CFR 239.40) relating to an offering being made contemporaneously in the United States and the issuer's home jurisdiction; on Form S–8 (17 CFR 239.16b); on Form S–3 or F–3 (17 CFR 239.13 or 17 CFR 239.33) relating to a dividend or interest reinvestment plan; on Form S–3 or Form F–3 relating to an automatic shelf registration statement; or on Form S–4 (17 CFR 239.25) complying with General Instruction G of that Form.

(d) [Effective Dec. 31, 2012.] No amendments pursuant to paragraph (a) of this section may be filed with a registration statement on Form F–7, F–8 or F–80 (17 CFR 239.37, 17 CFR 239.38 or 17 CFR 239.41); on F–10 (17 CFR 239.40) relating to an offering being made contemporaneously in the United States and the issuer's home jurisdiction; on Form S–8 (17 CFR 239.16b); on Form S–3 or F–3 (17 CFR 239.13 or 17 CFR 239.33) relating to a dividend or interest reinvestment plan; on Form S–3 or Form F–3 relating to an automatic shelf registration statement; or on Form S–4 (17 CFR 239.25) complying with General Instruction G of that Form.

Rule 474. Date of filing of amendments

The date on which amendments are actually received by the Commission shall be the date of filing thereof, if all the requirements of the Act and the rules with respect to such filing have been complied with.

Rule 475. Amendment filed with consent of Commission

An application for the Commission's consent to the filing of an amendment with the effect provided in section 8(a) of the Act may be filed before or after or concurrently with the filing of the amendment. The application shall be signed and shall state fully the grounds upon which it is made. The Commission's consent shall be deemed to have been given and the amendment shall be treated as a part of the registration statement only when the Commission shall after the filing of such amendment enter an order to that effect.

Rule 475a. Certain pre–effective amendments deemed filed with the consent of the Commission

Amendments to a registration statement on Form F–2 (17 CFR 239.32) relating to a dividend or interest reinvestment plan, or on Form S–4 (17 CFR 239.25) complying with General Instruction G of that Form, filed prior to the effectiveness of such registration statement shall be deemed to have been filed with a consent of the Commission and shall accordingly be treated as part of the registration statement.

Rule 476. Amendment filed pursuant to order of Commission

An amendment filed prior to the effective date of a registration statement shall be deemed to have been filed pursuant to an order of the Commission within the meaning of section 8(a) of the Act so as to be treated as a part of the registration statement only when the Commission shall after the filing of such amendment enter an order declaring that it has been filed pursuant to the Commission's previous order.

Rule 477. Withdrawal of registration statement or amendment

(a) Except as provided in paragraph (b) of this rule, any registration statement or any amendment or exhibit thereto may be withdrawn upon application if the Commission, finding such withdrawal consistent with the public interest and the protection of investors, consents thereto.

(b) Any application for withdrawal of a registration statement filed on Form F–2 (17 CFR 239.32) relating to a dividend or interest reinvestment plan, or on Form S–4 (17 CFR 239.25) complying with

General Instruction G of that Form, and/or any pre-effective amendment thereto, will be deemed granted upon filing if such filing is made prior to the effective date. Any other application for withdrawal of an entire registration statement made before the effective date of the registration statement will be deemed granted at the time the application is filed with the Commission unless, within 15 calendar days after the registrant files the application, the Commission notifies the registrant that the application for withdrawal will not be granted.

(c) The registrant must sign any application for withdrawal and must state fully in it the grounds on which the registrant makes the application. The fee paid upon the filing of the registration statement will not be refunded to the registrant. The registrant must state in the application that no securities were sold in connection with the offering. If the registrant applies for withdrawal in anticipation of reliance on Rule 155(c), the registrant must, without discussing any terms of the private offering, state in the application that the registrant may undertake a subsequent private offering in reliance on Rule 155(c).

(d) Any withdrawn document will remain in the Commission's public files, as well as the related request for withdrawal.

Rule 478. Powers to amend or withdraw registration statement

All persons signing a registration statement shall be deemed, in the absence of a statement to the contrary, to confer upon the registrant, and upon the agent for service named in the registration statement, the following powers:

(a) A power to amend the registration statement (1) by the filing of an amendment as provided in Rule 473; (2) by filing any written consent; (3) by correcting typographical errors; or (4) by reducing the amount of securities registered, pursuant to an undertaking contained in the registration statement.

(b) A power to make application pursuant to Rule 475 for the Commission's consent to the filing of an amendment.

(c) A power to withdraw the registration statement or any amendment or exhibit thereto.

(d) A power to consent to the entry of an order under section 8(b) of the Act, waiving notice and hearing, such order being entered without prejudice to the right of the registrant thereafter to have the order vacated upon a showing to the Commission that the registration statement as amended is no longer incomplete or inaccurate on its face in any material respect.

Rule 479. Procedure with respect to abandoned registration statements and post-effective amendments

When a registration statement, or a post-effective amendment to such a statement, has been on file with the Commission for a period of nine months and has not become effective the Commission may, in its discretion, proceed in the following manner to determine whether such registration statement or amendment has been abandoned by the registrant. If the registration statement has been amended, otherwise than for the purpose of delaying the effective date thereof, or if the post-effective amendment has been amended, the nine-month period shall be computed from the date of the latest such amendment.

(a) A notice will be sent to the registrant, and to the agent for service named in the registration statement, by registered or certified mail, return receipt requested, addressed to the most recent addresses for the registrant and the agent for service reflected in the registration statement. Such notice will inform the registrant and the agent for service that the registration statement or amendment is out of date and must be either amended to comply with the applicable requirements of the Act and the rules and regulations thereunder or be withdrawn within 30 days after the date of such notice.

(b) If the registrant or the agent for service fails to respond to such notice by filing a substantive amendment or withdrawing the registration statement and does not furnish a satisfactory explanation as to why it has not done so within such 30 days, the Commission may, where consistent with the public interest and the protection of investors, enter an order declaring the registration statement or amendment abandoned.

(c) When such an order is entered by the Commission the papers comprising the registration statement or amendment will not be removed from the files of the Commission but an order shall be included in the file for the registration statement in the following manner: "Declared abandoned by order dated ________."

INVESTMENT COMPANIES; BUSINESS DEVELOPMENT COMPANIES

NOTE: The rules which comprise this section of Regulation C (Rules 480 to 489) are applicable only to investment companies and business development companies, except Rule 489, which applies to certain entities excepted from the definition of investment company by rules under the Investment Company Act of 1940. The rules comprising the rest of Regulation C (Rules 400 to 479 and Rules 490 to 494) are, unless the context specifically indicates otherwise, also applicable to investment companies and business development companies. See Rule 400.

Rule 480. Title of securities

If a registration statement is prepared on a form available solely to investment companies registered under the Investment Company Act of 1940, or a business development company which is selling or proposing to sell its securities pursuant to a registration statement which has been filed under the Act, wherever the title of securities is required to be stated there shall be given such information as will indicate the type and general character of the securities, including the following:

(a) In the case of shares, the par or stated value, if any; the rate of dividends, if fixed, and whether cumulative or non-cumulative; a brief indication of the preference, if any; and, if convertible, a statement to that effect.

(b) In the case of funded debt, the rate of interest; the date of maturity, or, if the issue matures serially, a brief indication of the serial maturities such as "maturing serially from 1950 to 1960"; if the payment of principal or interest is contingent, an appropriate indication of such contingency; a brief indication of the priority of the issue; and, if convertible, a statement to that effect.

(c) In the case of any other kind of security, appropriate information of comparable character.

Rule 481. Information required in prospectuses

Disclose the following in registration statements prepared on a form available solely to investment companies registered under the Investment Company Act of 1940 or in registration statements filed under the Act for a company that has elected to be regulated as a business development company under Sections 55 through 65 of the Investment Company Act (15 U.S.C. 80a–54–80a–64):

(a) *Facing Page.* Indicate the approximate date of the proposed sale of the securities to the public.

(b) *Outside Front Cover Page.* If applicable, include the following in plain English as required by Rule 421(d):

(1) *Commission Legend.* Provide a legend that indicates that the Securities and Exchange Commission has not approved or disapproved of the securities or passed upon the accuracy or adequacy of the disclosure in the prospectus and that any contrary representation is a criminal offense. The legend may be in one of the following or other clear and concise language:

Example A: The Securities and Exchange Commission has not approved or disapproved these securities or passed upon the adequacy of this prospectus. Any representation to the contrary is a criminal offense.

Example B: The Securities and Exchange Commission has not approved or disapproved these securities or determined if this prospectus is truthful or complete. Any representation to the contrary is a criminal offense.

(2) *"Subject to Completion" Legend.*

(i) If a prospectus or Statement of Additional Information will be used before the effective date of the registration statement, include on the outside front cover page of the prospectus or Statement of Additional Information, a prominent statement that:

(A) The information in the prospectus or Statement of Additional Information will be amended or completed;

(B) A registration statement relating to these securities has been filed with the Securities and Exchange Commission;

(C) The securities may not be sold until the registration statement becomes effective; and

(D) In a prospectus, that the prospectus is not an offer to sell the securities and it is not soliciting an offer to buy the securities in any state where offers or sales are not permitted, or in a Statement of Additional Information, that the Statement of Additional Information is not a prospectus.

(ii) The legend may be in the following language or other clear and understandable language:

The information in this prospectus (or Statement of Additional Information) is not complete and may be changed. We may not sell these securities until the registration statement filed with the Securities and Exchange Commission is effective. This prospectus (or Statement of Additional Information) is not an offer to sell these securities and is not soliciting an offer to buy these securities in any state where the offer or sale is not permitted.

(iii) In the case of a prospectus that omits pricing information under Rule 430A, provide the information and legend in paragraph (b)(2) of this rule if the prospectus or Statement of

Additional Information is used before the initial public offering price is determined.

(c) *Table of Contents.* Include on either the outside front, inside front, or outside back cover page of the prospectus, a reasonably detailed table of contents. It must show the page number of the various sections or subdivisions of the prospectus. Include this table of contents immediately following the cover page in any prospectus delivered electronically.

(d) *Stabilization and Other Transactions.*

(1) Indicate on the front cover page of the prospectus if the underwriter has any arrangement with the issuer, such as an over-allotment option, under which the underwriter may purchase additional shares in connection with the offering, and state the amount of additional shares the underwriter may purchase under the arrangement. Provide disclosure in the prospectus that briefly describes any transaction that the underwriter intends to conduct during the offering that stabilizes, maintains, or otherwise affects the market price of the offered securities. Include information on stabilizing transactions, syndicate short covering transactions, penalty bids, or any other transactions that affect the offered security's price. Describe the nature of the transactions clearly and explain how the transactions affect the offered security's price. Identify the exchange or other market on which these transactions may occur. If true, disclose that the underwriter may discontinue these transactions at any time;

(2) If the stabilizing began before the effective date of the registration statement, disclose in the prospectus the amount of securities bought, the prices at which they were bought and the period within which they were bought. In the event that Rule 430A is used, the prospectus filed under Rule 497(h) or included in a post-effective amendment must contain information on the stabilizing transactions that took place before the determination of the public offering price shown in the prospectus; and

(3) If you are making a warrant or rights offering of securities to existing security holders and the securities not purchased by existing security holders are to be reoffered to the public, disclose in the prospectus used in connection with the reoffering:

(i) The amount of securities bought in stabilization activities during the offering period and the price or range of prices at which the securities were bought;

(ii) The amount of the offered securities subscribed for during the offering period;

(iii) The amount of the offered securities subscribed for by the underwriters during the offering period;

(iv) The amount of the offered securities sold during the offering period by the underwriters and the price or range of prices at which the securities were sold; and

(v) The amount of the offered securities to be reoffered to the public and the public offering price.

(e) *Dealer Prospectus Delivery Obligations.* On the outside back cover page of the prospectus, advise dealers of their prospectus delivery obligation, including the expiration date specified by Section 4(a)(3) of the Act (15 U.S.C. 77d(3)) and Rule 174. If the expiration date is not known on the effective date of the registration statement, include the expiration date in the copy of the prospectus filed under Rule 497. This information need not be included if dealers are not required to deliver a prospectus under Rule 174 or Section 24(d) of the Investment Company Act of 1940 (15 U.S.C. 80a–24). Use the following or other clear, plain language:

DEALER PROSPECTUS DELIVERY OBLIGATION

Until (insert date), all dealers that effect transactions in these securities, whether or not participating in this offering, may be required to deliver a prospectus. This is in addition to the dealers' obligation to deliver a prospectus when acting as underwriters and with respect to their unsold allotments or subscriptions.

(f) *Electronic Distribution.* Where a prospectus is distributed through an electronic medium, issuers may satisfy legibility requirements applicable to printed documents, such as paper size, type size and font, bold-face type, italics and red ink, by presenting all required information in a format readily communicated to investors, and where indicated, in a manner reasonably calculated to draw investor attention to specific information.

Rule 482. Advertising by an investment company as satisfying requirements of Section 10

(a) *Scope of Rule.* This rule applies to an advertisement or other sales material (*advertisement*) with respect to securities of an investment company registered under the Investment Company Act of 1940 (15 U.S.C. 80a–1 *et seq.*) (*1940 Act*), or a business development company, that is selling or proposing to sell its securities pursuant to a registration statement that has been filed under the Act. This rule does not apply to an advertisement that is excepted from the definition of prospectus by section 2(a)(10) of the Act (15 U.S.C. 77b(a)(10)) or Rule 498(d) or to a summary prospectus under Rule 498. An advertisement that complies with this rule, which may include information the substance of which is not included in the prospectus specified in section 10(a) of the Act (15 U.S.C. 77j(a)), will be deemed to be a prospectus under section 10(b) of the Act (15 U.S.C. 77j(b)) for the purpose of section 5(b)(1) of the Act (15 U.S.C. 77e(b)(1)).

Note to Paragraph (a): The fact that an advertisement complies with this rule does not relieve the investment company, underwriter, or dealer of any obligations with respect to the advertisement under the antifraud provisions of the federal securities laws. For guidance about factors to be weighed in determining whether statements, representations, illustrations, and descriptions contained in investment company advertisements are misleading, see Rule 156. In addition, an advertisement that complies with this rule is subject to the legibility requirements of Rule 420.

(b) *Required Disclosure.* This paragraph describes information that is required to be included in an advertisement in order to comply with this rule.

(1) *Availability of Additional Information.* An advertisement must include a statement that advises an investor to consider the investment objectives, risks, and charges and expenses of the investment company carefully before investing; explains that the prospectus and, if available, the summary prospectus contain this and other information about the investment company; identifies a source from which an investor may obtain a prospectus and, if available, a summary prospectus; and states that the prospectus and, if available, the summary prospectus should be read carefully before investing.

(2) *Advertisements Used Prior to Effectiveness of Registration Statement.* An advertisement that is used prior to effectiveness of the investment company's registration statement or the determination of the public offering price (in the case of a registration statement that becomes effective omitting information from the prospectus contained in the registration statement in reliance upon Rule 430A) must include the "Subject to Completion" legend required by Rule 481(b)(2).

(3) *Advertisements Including Performance Data.* An advertisement that includes performance data of an open-end management investment company or a separate account registered under the 1940 Act as a unit investment trust offering variable annuity contracts (*trust account*) must include the following:

(i) A legend disclosing that the performance data quoted represents past performance; that past performance does not guarantee future results; that the investment return and principal value of an investment will fluctuate so that an investor's shares, when redeemed, may be worth more or less than their original cost; and that current performance may be lower or higher than the performance data quoted. The legend should also identify either a toll-free (or collect) telephone number or a Web site where an investor may obtain performance data current to the most recent month-end unless the advertisement includes total return quotations current to the most recent month ended seven business days prior to the date of use. An advertisement for a money market fund that is a government money market fund, as defined in 17 CFR 270.2a–7(a)(16), or a retail money market fund, as defined in 17 CFR 270.2a–7(a)(25) may omit the disclosure about principal value fluctuation; and

Note to Paragraph (b)(3)(i): The date of use refers to the date or dates when an advertisement is used by investors, not the date on which an advertisement is published or submitted for publication. The date of use refers to the entire period of use by investors and not simply the first date on which an advertisement is used.

(ii) If a sales load or any other nonrecurring fee is charged, the maximum amount of the load or fee, and if the sales load or fee is not reflected, a statement that the performance data does not reflect the deduction of the sales load or fee, and that, if reflected, the load or fee would reduce the performance quoted.

(4) *Money market funds.* (i) An advertisement for an investment company that holds itself out to be a money market fund, that is not a government money market fund, as defined in 17 CFR 270.2a–7(a)(16), or a retail money market fund, as defined in 17 CFR 270.2a–7(a)(25), must include the following statement:

You could lose money by investing in the Fund. Because the share price of the Fund will fluctuate, when you sell your shares they may be worth more or less than what you originally paid for them. The Fund may impose a fee upon sale of your shares or may temporarily suspend your ability to sell shares if the Fund's liquidity falls below required minimums because of market conditions or other factors. An investment in the Fund is not insured or guaranteed by the Federal Deposit Insurance Corporation or any other government agency. The Fund's sponsor has no legal obligation to provide financial support to the Fund, and you should not expect that the sponsor will provide financial support to the Fund at any time.

(ii) An advertisement for an investment company that holds itself out to be a money market fund, that is a government money market fund, as defined in 17 CFR 270.2a–7(a)(16) or a retail money market fund, as defined in 17 CFR 270.2a–7(a)(25), and that is subject to the requirements of 17 CFR 270.2a–7(c)(2)(i) and/or (ii) (or is not subject to the requirements of 17 CFR 270.2a–7(c)(2)(i) and/or (ii) pursuant to 17 CFR 270.2a–7(c)(2)(iii), but has chosen to rely on the ability to impose liquidity fees and suspend redemptions consistent with the requirements of 17 CFR 270.2a–7(c)(2)(i) and/or (ii)), must include the following statement:

> You could lose money by investing in the Fund. Although the Fund seeks to preserve the value of your investment at $1.00 per share, it cannot guarantee it will do so. The Fund may impose a fee upon sale of your shares or may temporarily suspend your ability to sell shares if the Fund's liquidity falls below required minimums because of market conditions or other factors. An investment in the Fund is not insured or guaranteed by the Federal Deposit Insurance Corporation or any other government agency. The Fund's sponsor has no legal obligation to provide financial support to the Fund, and you should not expect that the sponsor will provide financial support to the Fund at any time.

(iii) An advertisement for an investment company that holds itself out to be a money market fund, that is a government money market fund, as defined in 17 CFR 270.2a–7(a)(16), that is not subject to the requirements of 17 CFR 270.2a–7(c)(2)(i) and/or (ii) pursuant to 17 CFR 270.2a–7(c)(2)(iii), and that has not chosen to rely on the ability to impose liquidity fees and suspend redemptions consistent with the requirements of 17 CFR 270.2a–7(c)(2)(i) and/or (ii)), must include the following statement:

> You could lose money by investing in the Fund. Although the Fund seeks to preserve the value of your investment at $1.00 per share, it cannot guarantee it will do so. An investment in the Fund is not insured or guaranteed by the Federal Deposit Insurance Corporation or any other government agency. The Fund's sponsor has no legal obligation to provide financial support to the Fund, and you should not expect that the sponsor will provide financial support to the Fund at any time.

NOTE TO PARAGRAPH (b)(4). If an affiliated person, promoter, or principal underwriter of the Fund, or an affiliated person of such a person, has contractually committed to provide financial support to the Fund, the statement may omit the last sentence ("The Fund's sponsor has no legal obligation to provide financial support to the Fund, and you should not expect that the sponsor will provide financial support to the Fund at any time.") for the term of the agreement. For purposes of this Note, the term "financial support" includes any capital contribution, purchase of a security from the Fund in reliance on 17 CFR 270.17a–9, purchase of any defaulted or devalued security at par, execution of letter of credit or letter of indemnity, capital support agreement (whether or not the Fund ultimately received support), performance guarantee, or any other similar action reasonably intended to increase or stabilize the value or liquidity of the fund's portfolio; however, the term "financial support" excludes any routine waiver of fees or reimbursement of fund expenses, routine inter–fund lending, routine inter–fund purchases of fund shares, or any action that would qualify as financial support as defined above, that the board of directors has otherwise determined not to be reasonably intended to increase or stabilize the value or liquidity of the fund's portfolio.

(5) *Presentation.* In a print advertisement, the statements required by paragraphs (b)(1) through (b)(4) of this rule must be presented in a type size at least as large as and of a style different from, but at least as prominent as, that used in the major portion of the advertisement, provided that when performance data is presented in a type size smaller than that of the major portion of the advertisement, the statements required by paragraph (b)(3) of this rule may appear in a type size no smaller than that of the performance data. If an advertisement is delivered through an electronic medium, the legibility requirements for the statements required by paragraphs (b)(1) through (b)(4) of this rule relating to type size and style may be satisfied by presenting the statements in any manner reasonably calculated to draw investor attention to them. In a radio or television advertisement, the statements required by paragraphs (b)(1) through (b)(4) of this rule must be given emphasis equal to that used in the major portion of the advertisement. The statements required by paragraph (b)(3) of this rule must be presented in close proximity to the performance data, and, in a print advertisement, must be presented in the body of the advertisement and not in a footnote.

(6) *Commission Legend.* An advertisement that complies with this rule need not contain the Commission legend required by Rule 481(b)(1).

(c) *Use of Applications.* An advertisement that complies with this rule may not contain or be accompanied by any application by which a prospective investor may invest in the investment company, except that a prospectus meeting the requirements of section 10(a) of the Act (15 U.S.C. 77j(a)) by which a unit investment trust offers variable annuity or variable life insurance contracts may contain a contract application although the prospectus includes, or is accompanied by, information about an investment company in which the unit investment trust invests that, pursuant to this rule, is deemed a prospectus under section 10(b) of the Act (15 U.S.C. 77j(b)).

(d) *Performance Data for Non-Money Market Funds.* In the case of an open-end management investment company or a trust account (other than a money market fund referred to in paragraph (e) of this rule), any quotation of the company's performance contained in an advertisement shall be limited to quotations of:

(1) *Current Yield.* A current yield that:

(i) Is based on the methods of computation prescribed in Form N–1A (17 CFR 239.15A and 274.11A), N–3 (17 CFR 239.17a and 274.11b), or N–4 (17 CFR 239.17b and 274.11c);

(ii) Is accompanied by quotations of total return as provided for in paragraph (d)(3) of this rule;

(iii) Is set out in no greater prominence than the required quotations of total return; and

(iv) Adjacent to the quotation and with no less prominence than the quotation, identifies the length of and the date of the last day in the base period used in computing the quotation.

(2) *Tax–Equivalent Yield.* A tax-equivalent yield that:

(i) Is based on the methods of computation prescribed in Form N–1A (17 CFR 239.15A and 274.11A), N–3 (17 CFR 239.17a and 274.11b), or N–4 (17 CFR 239.17b and 274.11c);

(ii) Is accompanied by quotations of yield as provided for in paragraph (d)(1) of this rule and total return as provided for in paragraph (d)(3) of this rule;

(iii) Is set out in no greater prominence than the required quotations of yield and total return;

(iv) Relates to the same base period as the required quotation of yield; and

(v) Adjacent to the quotation and with no less prominence than the quotation, identifies the length of and the date of the last day in the base period used in computing the quotation.

(3) *Average Annual Total Return.* Average annual total return for one, five, and ten year periods, except that if the company's registration statement under the Act (15 U.S.C. 77a *et seq.*) has been in effect for less than one, five, or ten years, the time period during which the registration statement was in effect is substituted for the period(s) otherwise prescribed. The quotations must:

(i) Be based on the methods of computation prescribed in Form N–1A (17 CFR 239.15A and 274.11A), N–3 (17 CFR 239.17a and 274.11b), or N–4 (17 CFR 239.17b and 274.11c);

(ii) Be current to the most recent calendar quarter ended prior to the submission of the advertisement for publication;

(iii) Be set out with equal prominence; and

(iv) Adjacent to the quotation and with no less prominence than the quotation, identify the length of and the last day of the one, five, and ten year periods.

(4) *After–Tax Return.* For an open-end management investment company, average annual total return (after taxes on distributions) and average annual total return (after taxes on distributions and redemption) for one, five, and ten year periods, except that if the company's registration statement under the Act (15 U.S.C. 77a *et seq.*) has been in effect for less than one, five, or ten years, the time period during which the registration statement was in effect is substituted for the period(s) otherwise prescribed. The quotations must:

(i) Be based on the methods of computation prescribed in Form N–1A (17 CFR 239.15A and 274.11A);

(ii) Be current to the most recent calendar quarter ended prior to the submission of the advertisement for publication;

(iii) Be accompanied by quotations of total return as provided for in paragraph (d)(3) of this rule;

(iv) Include both average annual total return (after taxes on distributions) and average annual total return (after taxes on distributions and redemption);

(v) Be set out with equal prominence and be set out in no greater prominence than the required quotations of total return; and

(vi) Adjacent to the quotations and with no less prominence than the quotations, identify the length of and the last day of the one, five, and ten year periods.

(5) *Other Performance Measures.* Any other historical measure of company performance (not subject to any prescribed method of computation) if such measurement:

(i) Reflects all elements of return;

(ii) Is accompanied by quotations of total return as provided for in paragraph (d)(3) of this rule;

(iii) In the case of any measure of performance adjusted to reflect the effect of taxes, is accompanied by quotations of total return as provided for in paragraph (d)(4) of this rule;

(iv) Is set out in no greater prominence than the required quotations of total return; and

(v) Adjacent to the measurement and with no less prominence than the measurement, identifies the length of and the last day of the period for which performance is measured.

(e) *Performance Data for Money Market Funds.* In the case of a money market fund:

(1) *Yield.* Any quotation of the money market fund's yield in an advertisement shall be based on the methods of computation prescribed in Form N–1A (17 CFR 239.15A and 274.11A), N–3 (17 CFR 239.17a and 274.11b), or N–4 (17 CFR 239.17b and 274.11c) and may include:

(i) A quotation of current yield that, adjacent to the quotation and with no less prominence than the quotation, identifies the length of and the date of the last day in the base period used in computing that quotation;

(ii) A quotation of effective yield if it appears in the same advertisement as a quotation of current yield and each quotation relates to an identical base period and is presented with equal prominence; or

(iii) A quotation or quotations of tax-equivalent yield or tax-equivalent effective yield if it appears in the same advertisement as a quotation of current yield and each quotation relates to the same base period as the quotation of current yield, is presented with equal prominence, and states the income tax rate used in the calculation.

(2) *Total Return.* Accompany any quotation of the money market fund's total return in an advertisement with a quotation of the money market fund's current yield under paragraph (e)(1)(i) of this rule. Place the quotations of total return and current yield next to each other, in the same size print, and if there is a material difference between the quoted total return and the quoted current yield, include a statement that the yield quotation more closely reflects the current earnings of the money market fund than the total return quotation.

(f) *Advertisements That Make Tax Representations.* An advertisement for an open-end management investment company (other than a company that is permitted under Rule 35d–1(a)(4) of the Investment Company Act of 1940 to use a name suggesting that the company's distributions are exempt from federal income tax or from both federal and state income tax) that represents or implies that the company is managed to limit or control the effect of taxes on company performance must accompany any quotation of the company's performance permitted by paragraph (d) of this rule with quotations of total return as provided for in paragraph (d)(4) of this rule.

(g) *Timeliness of Performance Data.* All performance data contained in any advertisement must be as of the most recent practicable date considering the type of investment company and the media through which the data will be conveyed, except that any advertisement containing total return quotations will be considered to have complied with this paragraph provided that:

(1)(i) The total return quotations are current to the most recent calendar quarter ended prior to the submission of the advertisement for publication; and

(ii) Total return quotations current to the most recent month ended seven business days prior to the date of use are provided at the toll-free (or collect) telephone number or Web site identified pursuant to paragraph (b)(3)(i) of this rule; or

(2) The total return quotations are current to the most recent month ended seven business days prior to the date of use of the advertisement.

NOTE TO PARAGRAPH (g): The date of use refers to the date or dates when an advertisement is used by investors, not the date on which an advertisement is published or submitted for publication. The date of use refers to the entire period of use by investors and not simply the first date on which an advertisement is used.

(h) *Filing.* An advertisement that complies with this rule need not be filed as part of the registration statement filed under the Act.

NOTE TO PARAGRAPH (h): These advertisements, unless filed with NASD Regulation, Inc., are required to be filed in accordance with the requirements of Rule 497.

Rule 483. Exhibits for certain registration statements

If a registration statement is prepared on a form available solely to investment companies registered under the Investment Company Act of 1940, or a business development company which is selling or proposing to sell its securities pursuant to a registration statement which has been filed under the Act, the following provisions apply:

(a) Such registration statement shall contain an exhibit index, which should immediately precede the exhibits filed with such registration statement. The exhibit index shall indicate by handwritten, typed, printed or other legible form of notation in the manually signed original registration statement the page number in the sequential numbering system where such exhibit can be found. Where exhibits are incorporated by reference, this fact shall be noted in the exhibit index referred to in the preceding sentence. Further, the first page of the manually signed registration statement shall list the page in the filing where the exhibit index is located.

(b) If any name is signed to the registration statement pursuant to a power of attorney, copies of such powers of attorney shall be filed as an exhibit to the registration statement. In addition, if the name of any officer signing on behalf of the registrant, or attesting the registrant's seal, is signed pursuant to a power of attorney, certified copies of a resolution of the registrant's board of directors authorizing such signature shall also be filed as an exhibit to the registration statement. A power of attorney that is filed with the Commission shall relate to a specific filing, an amendment thereto, or a related registration statement that is to be effective upon filing pursuant to Rule 462(b) under the Act.

(c)(1) All written consents are required to be filed as an exhibit to the registration statement, together with a list thereof. Such consents shall be dated and manually signed. Where the consent of an expert or counsel is contained in his report or opinion, a reference shall be made in the list to the report or opinion containing the consent.

(2) In a registration statement filed pursuant to Rule 462(b) by a closed-end company, any required consent may be incorporated by reference into the registration statement from a previously filed registration statement related to the offering, provided that the consent contained in the previously filed registration statement expressly provides for such incorporation. Any consent filed in a Rule 462(b) registration statement may contain duplicated or facsimile versions of required signatures, and such signatures shall be considered manually filed for the purposes of the Act and the rules thereunder.

(d) The registrant—

(1) May file such exhibits as it may desire in addition to those required by the appropriate form. Such exhibits shall be so marked as to indicate clearly the subject matters to which they refer;

(2) In any case where two or more indentures, contracts, franchises, or other documents required to be filed as exhibits are substantially identical in all material respects except as to the parties thereto, the dates of execution, or other details, need file a copy of only one of such documents, with a schedule identifying the other documents omitted and setting forth the material details in which such documents differ from the document of which a copy is filed. The Commission may at any time in its discretion require filing of copies of any documents so omitted; and

(3) If an exhibit to a registration statement (other than an opinion or consent), filed in preliminary form, has been changed only (i) to insert information as to interest, dividend or conversion rates, redemption or conversion prices, purchase or offering prices, underwriters' or dealers' commission, names, addresses or participation of underwriters or similar matters, which information appears elsewhere in an amendment to the registration statement, or (ii) to correct typographical errors, insert signatures or make other similar immaterial changes, then, notwithstanding any contrary requirement of any rule or form, need not refile such exhibit as so amended; provided the registrant states in the amendment to the registration statement the basis provided by this rule for not refiling such exhibit. Any such incomplete exhibit

may not, however, be incorporated by reference in any subsequent filing under any Act administered by the Commission.

Rule 484. Undertaking required in certain registration statements

If a registration statement is prepared on a form available solely to investment companies registered under the Investment Company Act of 1940, or a business development company which is selling or proposing to sell its securities pursuant to a registration statement which has been filed under the Act, if

(a) Any acceleration is requested of the effective date of the registration statement pursuant to Rule 461, and

(b)(1) Any provision or arrangement exists whereby the registrant may indemnify a director, officer or controlling person of the registrant against liabilities arising under the Act, or

(2) The underwriting agreement contains provisions by which indemnification against such liabilities is given by the registrant to the underwriter or controlling persons of the underwriter and the director, officer or controlling person of the registrant is such an underwriter or controlling person thereof or a member of any firm which is an underwriter, and

(3) The benefits of such indemnification are not waived by such persons; the registration statement shall include a brief description of the indemnification provisions and an undertaking in substantially the following form:

> Insofar as indemnification for liability arising under the Securities Act of 1933 may be permitted to directors, officers and controlling persons of the registrant pursuant to the foregoing provisions, or otherwise, the registrant has been advised that in the opinion of the Securities and Exchange Commission such indemnification is against public policy as expressed in the Act and is, therefore, unenforceable. In the event that a claim for indemnification against such liabilities (other than the payment by the registrant of expenses incurred or paid by a director, officer or controlling person of the registrant in the successful defense of any action, suit or proceeding) is asserted by such director, officer or controlling person in connection with the securities being registered, the registrant will, unless in the opinion of its counsel the matter has been settled by controlling precedent, submit to a court of appropriate jurisdiction the question whether such indemnification by it is against public policy as expressed in the Act and will be governed by the final adjudication of such issue.

Rule 485. Effective date of post-effective amendments filed by certain registered investment companies

(a) *Automatic Effectiveness.* (1) Except as otherwise provided in this rule, a post-effective amendment to a registration statement filed by a registered open-end management investment company, unit investment trust or separate account as defined in section 2(a)(37) of the Investment Company Act of 1940 shall become effective on the sixtieth day after the filing thereof, or a later date designated by the registrant on the facing sheet of the amendment, which date shall be no later than eighty days after the date on which the amendment is filed.

(2) A post-effective amendment filed by a registered open-end management investment company for the purpose of adding a series shall become effective on the seventy-fifth day after the filing thereof or a later date designated by the registrant on the facing sheet of the amendment, which date shall be no later than ninety-five days after the date on which the amendment is filed.

(3) The Commission, having due regard to the public interest and the protection of investors, may declare an amendment filed under this paragraph (a) effective on an earlier date.

(b) *Immediate Effectiveness.* Except as otherwise provided in this rule, a post-effective amendment to a registration statement filed by a registered open-end management investment company, unit investment trust or separate account as defined in section 2(a)(37) of the Investment Company Act of 1940 shall become effective on the date upon which it is filed with the Commission, or a later date designated by the registrant on the facing sheet of the amendment, which date shall be not later than thirty days after the date on which the amendment is filed, except that a post-effective amendment including a designation of a new effective date pursuant to paragraph (b)(1)(iii) of this rule shall become effective on the new effective date designated therein, *Provided,* that the following conditions are met:

(1) It is filed for no purpose other than one or more of the following:

(i) Bringing the financial statements up to date under section 10(a)(3) of the Securities Act of 1933 or Rules 3–12 or 3–18 of Regulation S–X;

(ii) Complying with an undertaking to file an amendment containing financial statements, which may be unaudited, within four to six months after the effective date of the registrant's registration statement under the Securities Act of 1933;

(iii) Designating a new effective date for a previously filed post-effective amendment pursuant to paragraph (a) of this rule, which has not yet become effective, *Provided,* that the new effective date shall be no earlier than the effective date designated in the previously filed amendment under paragraph (a) of this rule and no later than thirty days after that date;

(iv) Disclosing or updating the information required by Item 5(b) or 10(a)(2) of Form N–1A [17 CFR 239.15A and 274.11A];

(v) Making any non-material changes which the registrant deems appropriate;

(vi) In the case of a separate account registered as a unit investment trust, to make changes in the disclosure in the unit investment trust's registration statement to reflect changes to disclosure in the registration statement of the investment company in which the unit investment trust invests all of its assets; and

(vii) Any other purpose which the Commission shall approve.

(2) The registrant represents that the amendment is filed solely for one or more of the purposes specified in paragraph (b)(1) of this rule and that no material event requiring disclosure in the prospectus, other than one listed in paragraph (b)(1) of this rule or one for which the Commission has approved a filing under paragraph (b)(1)(vii) of this rule, has occurred since the latest of the following three dates:

(i) the effective date of the registrant's registration statement;

(ii) the effective date of its most recent post-effective amendment to its registration statement which included a prospectus; or

(iii) the filing date of a post-effective amendment filed under paragraph (a) of this rule which has not become effective.

(3) The amendment recites on its facing sheet that the registrant proposes that the amendment will become effective under paragraph (b) of this rule.

(4) The representations of the registrant referred to in paragraph (b)(2) of this rule shall be made by certification on the signature page of the post-effective amendment that the amendment meets all the requirements for effectiveness under paragraph (b) of this rule. If counsel prepared or reviewed the post-effective amendment filed under paragraph (b) of this rule, counsel shall furnish to the Commission at the time the amendment is filed a written representation that the amendment does not contain disclosures that would render it ineligible to become effective under paragraph (b) of this rule.

(c) *Incomplete or Inaccurate Amendments; Suspension of Use of Paragraph (b) of This Rule.* (1) No amendment shall become effective under paragraph (a) of this rule if, prior to the effective date of the amendment, it should appear to the Commission that the amendment may be incomplete or inaccurate in any material respect, and the Commission furnishes to the registrant written notice that the effective date of the amendment is to be suspended. Following such action by the Commission, the registrant may file with the Commission at any time a petition for review of the suspension. The Commission will order a hearing on the matter if a request for such a hearing is included in the petition. If the Commission has suspended the effective date of an amendment, the amendment shall become effective on such date as the Commission may determine, having due regard to the public interest and the protection of investors.

(2) The Commission may, in the manner and under the circumstances set forth in this paragraph (c)(2), suspend the ability of registrant to file a post-effective amendment under paragraph (b) of this rule. The notice of such suspension shall be in writing and shall specify the period for which such suspension shall remain in effect. The Commission may issue a suspension if it appears to the Commission that a registrant which files a post-effective amendment under paragraph (b) of this rule has not complied with the conditions of that paragraph. Any suspension under this paragraph (c)(2) shall become effective at such time as the Commission furnishes written notice thereof to the registrant. Any such suspension, so long as it is in effect, shall apply to any post-effective amendment that has been filed but has not, at the time of such suspension, become effective, and to any post-effective amendment that may be filed after the suspension. Any suspension shall apply only to the ability to file a post-effective

amendment pursuant to paragraph (b) of this rule and shall not otherwise affect any post-effective amendment. Following this action by the Commission the registrant may file with the Commission at any time a petition for review of the suspension. The Commission will order a hearing on the matter if a request for a hearing is included in the petition.

(3) A registrant's ability to file a post-effective amendment, other than an amendment filed solely for purposes of submitting an Interactive Data File, under paragraph (b) of this rule is automatically suspended if a registrant fails to submit any Interactive Data File as required by General Instruction C.3.(g) of Form N–1A (17 CFR 239.15A and 274.11A). A suspension under this paragraph (c)(3) shall become effective at such time as the registrant fails to submit an Interactive Data File as required by General Instruction C.3.(g) of Form N–1A. Any such suspension, so long as it is in effect, shall apply to any post-effective amendment that is filed after the suspension becomes effective, but shall not apply to any post-effective amendment that was filed before the suspension became effective. Any suspension shall apply only to the ability to file a post-effective amendment pursuant to paragraph (b) of this rule and shall not otherwise affect any post-effective amendment. Any suspension under this paragraph (c)(3) shall terminate as soon as a registrant has submitted the Interactive Data File as required by General Instruction C.3.(g) of Form N–1A.

(d) *Subsequent Amendments.* (1) Except as provided in paragraph (d)(2) of this rule, a post-effective amendment that includes a prospectus shall not become effective under paragraph (a) of this rule if a subsequent post-effective amendment relating to the prospectus is filed before such amendment becomes effective.

(2) A post-effective amendment that includes a prospectus shall become effective under paragraph (a) of this rule notwithstanding the filing of a subsequent post-effective amendment relating to the prospectus, *Provided,* that the following conditions are met:

(i) the subsequent amendment is filed under paragraph (b) of this rule; and

(ii) the subsequent amendment designates as its effective date either:

(A) the date on which the prior post-effective amendment was to become effective under paragraph (a) of this rule; or

(B) a new effective date designated under paragraph (b)(1)(iii) of this rule.

In this case the prior post-effective amendment filed under paragraph (a) of this rule and any prior post-effective amendment filed under paragraph (b) of this rule shall also become effective on the new effective date designated under paragraph (b)(1)(iii) of this rule.

(3) Notwithstanding paragraphs (d)(1) and (d)(2) of this rule, if another post-effective amendment relating to the same prospectus is filed under paragraph (a) of this rule before the prior amendments filed pursuant to paragraphs (a) and (b) of this rule have become effective, none of such prior amendments shall become effective under this rule.

(e) *Certain Separate Accounts.* For purposes of this rule, a post-effective amendment to a registration statement for an offering of securities by a registered open-end management investment company or unit investment trust as those terms are used in paragraphs (a), (b), and (e) of this rule and as such amendments are referred to in paragraphs (c) and (d) of this rule, shall include a post-effective amendment to an offering of securities by an insurance company funded through a separate account, as defined in section 2(a)(37) of the Investment Company Act of 1940, where the separate account need not register under the Investment Company Act of 1940 under section 3(c)(11) thereof.

(f) *Electronic Filers.* When ascertaining the date of filing, electronic filers should not presume a registration statement has been accepted until notice of acceptance has been received from the Commission.

NOTE: To determine the date of automatic effectiveness, the day following the filing date is the first day of the time period. For example, a post-effective amendment filed under paragraph (a) of this rule on November 1 would become effective on December 31.

Rule 486. Effective date of post–effective amendments and registration statements filed by certain closed–end management investment companies

(a) *Automatic Effectiveness.* Except as otherwise provided in this rule, a post-effective amendment to a registration statement, or a registration statement filed for the purpose of registering additional shares of common stock for which a registration statement filed on Form N–2 (17 CFR 239.14 and 274.11a–1) is effective, filed by a registered closed-end management investment company or business development company which makes periodic repurchase offers under Rule 23c–3 under the Investment Company

Act of 1940, shall become effective on the sixtieth day after the filing thereof, or a later date designated by the registrant on the facing sheet of the amendment or registration statement, which date shall not be later than eighty days after the date on which the amendment or registration statement is filed, *Provided,* that the Commission, having due regard to the public interest and the protection of investors, may declare an amendment or registration statement filed under this paragraph (a) effective on an earlier date.

(b) *Immediate Effectiveness.* Except as otherwise provided in this rule, a post-effective amendment to a registration statement, or a registration statement for additional shares of common stock, filed by a registered closed-end management investment company or business development company which makes periodic repurchase offers under Rule 23c–3 under the Investment Company Act of 1940, shall become effective on the date on which it is filed with the Commission, or a later date designated by the registrant on the facing sheet of the amendment or registration statement, which date shall be not later than thirty days after the date on which the amendment or registration statement is filed, except that a post-effective amendment including a designation of a new effective date under paragraph (b)(1)(iii) of this rule shall become effective on the new effective date designated therein, *Provided,* that the following conditions are met:

(1) It is filed for no purpose other than one or more of the following:

(i) Registering additional shares of common stock for which a registration statement filed on Form N–2 (17 CFR 239.14 and 274.11a–1) is effective;

(ii) Bringing the financial statements up to date under section 10(a)(3) of the Act or Rule 3–18 of Regulation S–X;

(iii) Designating a new effective date for a previously filed post-effective amendment or registration statement for additional shares under paragraph (a) of this rule, which has not yet become effective, *Provided,* that the new effective date shall be no earlier than the effective date designated in the previously filed amendment or registration statement under paragraph (a) of this rule and no later than thirty days after that date;

(iv) Disclosing or updating the information required by Item 9c of Form N–2 [17 CFR 239.14 and 274.11a–1];

(v) Making any non-material changes which the registrant deems appropriate; and

(vi) Any other purpose which the Commission shall approve.

(2) The registrant represents that the amendment is filed solely for one or more of the purposes specified in paragraph (b)(1) of this rule and that no material event requiring disclosure in the prospectus, other than one listed in paragraph (b)(1) or one for which the Commission has approved a filing under paragraph (b)(1)(vi) of this rule, has occurred since the latest of the following three dates:

(i) the effective date of the registrant's registration statement;

(ii) the effective date of its most recent post-effective amendment to its registration statement which included a prospectus; or

(iii) the filing date of a post-effective amendment or registration statement filed under paragraph (a) of this rule which has not become effective; and

(3) The amendment or registration statement recites on the facing sheet thereof that the registrant proposes that the amendment or registration statement will become effective under paragraph (b) of this rule.

(4) The representations of the registrant referred to in paragraph (b)(2) of this rule shall be made by certification on the signature page of the post-effective amendment or registration statement that the amendment or registration statement meets all of the requirements for effectiveness under paragraph (b) of this rule. If counsel prepared or reviewed the post-effective amendment or registration statement filed under paragraph (b) of this rule, counsel shall furnish to the Commission at the time the amendment or registration statement is filed a written representation that the amendment or registration statement does not contain disclosure which would render it ineligible to become effective under paragraph (b) of this rule.

(c) *Incomplete or Inaccurate Amendments; Suspension of Use of Paragraph (b) of This Rule.* (1) No amendment or registration statement shall become effective under paragraph (a) of this rule if, prior to the effective date of the amendment or registration statement, it should appear to the Commission that the amendment or registration statement may be incomplete or inaccurate in any material respect, and the Commission furnishes to the registrant written notice that the effective date of the amendment or registration statement is to be suspended. Following such action by the Commission, the registrant may file with the Commission at any time a petition for review of the suspension. The Commission will order a hearing on the matter if a request for such a hearing is included in the petition. If the Commission has suspended the effective date of an amendment or registration statement, the amendment or registration statement shall become effective on such date as the Commission may determine, having due regard to the public interest and the protection of investors.

(2) The Commission may, in the manner and under the circumstances set forth in this paragraph (c)(2), suspend the ability of a registrant to file a post-effective amendment or registration statement under paragraph (b) of this rule. The notice of such suspension shall be in writing and shall specify the period for which such suspension shall remain in effect. The Commission may issue a suspension if it appears to the Commission that a registrant which files a post-effective amendment under paragraph (b) of this rule has not complied with the conditions of that paragraph. Any suspension under this paragraph shall become effective at such time as the Commission furnishes written notice thereof to the company. Any such suspension, so long as it is in effect, shall apply to any post-effective amendment or registration statement that has been filed but has not, at the time of such suspension, become effective, and to any post-effective amendment or registration statement that may be filed after the suspension. Any suspension shall apply only to the ability to file a post-effective amendment or registration statement under paragraph (b) of this rule and shall not otherwise affect any post-effective amendment or registration statement. Following this action by the Commission, the registrant may file with the Commission at any time a petition for review of the suspension. The Commission will order a hearing on the matter if a request for a hearing is included in the petition.

(d) *Subsequent Amendments.* (1) Except as provided in paragraph (d)(2) of this rule, a post-effective amendment or registration statement which includes a prospectus shall not become effective under paragraph (a) of this rule if a subsequent post-effective amendment or registration statement relating to the prospectus is filed before such amendment or registration statement becomes effective.

(2) A post-effective amendment or registration statement which includes a prospectus shall become effective under paragraph (a) of this rule notwithstanding the filing of a subsequent post-effective amendment or registration statement relating to the prospectus, *Provided,* that the following conditions are met:

(i) the subsequent amendment or registration statement is filed under paragraph (b) of this rule; and

(ii) the subsequent amendment or registration statement designates as its effective date either:

(A) the date on which the prior post-effective amendment or registration statement was to become effective under paragraph (a) of this rule or

(B) a new effective date designated under paragraph (b)(1)(iii) of this rule.

In this case the prior post-effective amendment or registration statement filed under paragraph (a) of this rule and any prior post-effective amendment or registration statement filed under paragraph (b) of this rule shall also become effective on the new effective date designated under paragraph (b)(1)(iii) of this rule.

(3) Notwithstanding paragraphs (d)(1) and (d)(2) of this rule, if another post-effective amendment or registration statement relating to the same prospectus is filed under paragraph (a) of this rule before the prior amendments or registration statements filed under paragraphs (a) and (b) of this rule have become effective, none of such prior amendments or registration statements shall become effective under this rule.

(e) *Condition to Use of Paragraphs (a) or (b).* A post-effective amendment or new registration statement shall not become effective under paragraphs (a) or (b) of this rule unless within two years prior to the filing thereof a post-effective amendment or registration statement relating to the common stock of the registrant has become effective.

(f) *Electronic Filers.* When ascertaining the date of filing, electronic filers should not presume a registration statement has been accepted until notice of acceptance has been received from the Commission.

NOTE: To determine the date of automatic effectiveness, the day following the filing date is the first day of the time period. For example, a post-effective amendment filed under paragraph (a) of this rule on November 1 would become effective on December 31.

Rule 487. Effectiveness of registration statements filed by certain unit investment trusts

(a)(1) A unit investment trust registered under the Investment Company Act of 1940 that files a registration statement pursuant to the Act in connection with the offering of the securities of a series of the unit investment trust, except the first series of such trust, may designate a date and time for such registration statement to become effective. If the registrant complies with the conditions set forth in paragraph (b) of this rule, the registration statement shall become effective in accordance with such designation.

(2) The registrant may designate the date and time of effectiveness in the registration statement or in any pre-effective amendment thereto. A pre-effective amendment to a registration statement with respect to which such a designation is properly made shall be deemed to have been filed with the consent of the Commission and shall accordingly be treated as part of the registration statement.

(b) Availability of effectiveness of a registration statement in accordance with paragraph (a) of this rule is conditioned upon compliance with the following:

(1) The registrant is not engaged in the business of investing in securities issued by one or more open-end management investment companies;

(2) The designation provided for in paragraph (a) of this rule is set forth on the facing sheet of such registration statement or a pre-effective amendment thereto;

(3) The registrant identifies one or more previous series of the trust for which the effective date of the registration statement was determined by the Commission or its staff, and makes the following representations:

(i) That the portfolio securities deposited in the series with respect to which the registration statement or pre-effective amendment is being filed do not differ materially in type or quality from those deposited in such previous series identified by the registrant; and

(ii) That, except to the extent necessary to identify the specific portfolio securities deposited in, and to provide essential financial information for, the series with respect to which the registration statement or pre-effective amendment thereto is being filed, the registration statement or pre-effective amendment thereto does not contain disclosures that differ in any material respect from those contained in the registration statement of such previous series identified by the registrant;

(4) The registrant represents that it has complied with Rule 460 under the Act;

(5) The identification and representations provided for in paragraphs (b)(3) and (b)(4) of this rule are made on the signature page of the registration statement or a pre-effective amendment thereto; and

(6) If counsel prepared or reviewed such registration statement or a pre-effective amendment thereto, such counsel shall furnish to the Commission at the time the registration statement or pre-effective amendment thereto is filed a written representation that such registration statement or pre-effective amendment does not contain disclosures which would render such registration statement ineligible to become effective pursuant to paragraph (a) of this rule.

(c)(1) The Commission may, in the manner and under the circumstances set forth in paragraph (c)(2) of this rule, suspend the ability of a unit investment trust to designate the date and time of effectiveness of a series of such trust. Any such suspension, so long as it is in effect, shall apply to any registration statement that has been filed but has not, at the time of such suspension, become effective, and to any registration statement with respect to any series of such trust that may be filed after such suspension. Any suspension shall apply only to the ability to designate the date and time of effectiveness pursuant to paragraph (a) of this rule and shall not otherwise affect any registration statement.

(2) Any suspension pursuant to paragraph (c)(1) of this rule shall become effective at such time as the Commission furnishes written notice thereof to the company or the sponsor of the unit investment trust. The notice of such suspension shall be in writing and shall specify the period for which such suspension shall remain in effect. The Commission may issue such suspension if it appears to the Commission that any registration statement containing a designation pursuant to this rule is incomplete or inaccurate in any material respect, whether or not such registration statement has become effective, or that the registrant has not complied with the conditions of this rule. Following such action by the Commission, the registrant may file with the Commission at any time a peti-

tion for review of the suspension. The Commission will order a hearing on the matter if a request for a hearing is included in the petition.

(d) When ascertaining the date of filing, electronic filers should not presume a registration statement has been accepted until notice of acceptance has been received from the Commission.

Rule 488. Effective date of registration statements relating to securities to be issued in certain business combination transactions

(a) A registration statement filed on Form N–14 by a registered open-end management investment company for the purpose of registering securities to be issued in an exchange offer or other business combination transaction pursuant to Rule 145 under the Securities Act of 1933 (15 U.S.C. 77a et seq.) shall become effective on the thirtieth day after the date upon which it is filed with the Commission, or such later date designated by the registrant on the facing sheet of the registration statement, which date shall be not later than fifty days after the date on which the registration statement is filed, unless the Commission having due regard to the public interest and the protection of investors declares such amendment effective on an earlier date, provided the following conditions are met:

(1) Any prospectus filed as a part of the registration statement does not include disclosure relating to any other proposal to be acted on at a meeting of the shareholders of either company other than proposals related to an exchange offer, or a business combination transaction pursuant to Rule 145(a), and any other proposal relating to:

(i) Uncontested election of directors,

(ii) Ratification of the selection of accountants,

(iii) The continuation of a current advisory contract,

(iv) Increases in the number or amount of shares authorized to be issued by the registrant; and

(v) Continuation of any current contract relating to the distribution of shares issued by the registrant; and

(2) The registration statement recites on the facing sheet that the registrant proposes that the filing become effective pursuant to this rule.

(b) No registration statement shall become effective pursuant to paragraph (a) of this rule if, prior to the effective date of the registration statement, it should appear to the Commission that the registration statement may be incomplete or inaccurate in any material respect and the Commission furnishes to the registrant written notice that the effective date is to be suspended. Following such action by the Commission, the registrant may file with the Commission at any time a petition for review of the suspension. The Commission will order a hearing on the matter if a request for such a hearing is included in the petition. If the Commission has suspended the effective date of the registration statement, it shall become effective on such date as the Commission may determine, having due regard to the public interest and the protection of investors.

(c) When ascertaining the date of filing, electronic filers should not presume a registration statement has been accepted until notice of acceptance has been received from the Commission.

Rule 489. Filing of form by foreign banks and insurance companies and certain of their holding companies and finance subsidiaries

(a) The following foreign issuers shall file Form F–N [17 CFR 239.43] under the Act appointing an agent for service of process when filing a registration statement under the Act:

(1) A foreign issuer that is a foreign bank or foreign insurance company excepted from the definition of investment company by Rule 3a–6 under the Investment Company Act of 1940 (the "1940 Act");

(2) A foreign issuer that is a finance subsidiary of a foreign bank or foreign insurance company, as those terms are defined in Rule 3a–6 under the 1940 Act, if the finance subsidiary is excepted from the definition of investment company by Rule 3a–5 under the Investment Company Act of 1940; or

(3) A foreign issuer that is excepted from the definition of investment company by Rule 3a–1 under the Investment Company Act of 1940 because some or all of its majority-owned subsidiaries are foreign banks or insurance companies excepted from the definition of investment company by Rule 3a–6 under the Investment Company Act of 1940.

(b) The requirements of paragraph (a) of this rule shall not apply to:

(1) A foreign issuer that has filed Form F–X (17 CFR 239.42) under the Securities Act of 1933 with respect to the securities being offered; and

(2) A foreign issuer filing a registration statement relating to debt securities or non-voting preferred stock that has on file with the Commission a currently accurate Form N–6C9 (17 CFR 274.304, rescinded) under the Investment Company Act of 1940.

(c) Six copies of Form F–N, one of which shall be manually signed, shall be filed with the Commission at its principal office.

REGISTRATION BY FOREIGN GOVERNMENTS OR POLITICAL SUBDIVISIONS THEREOF

Rule 490. Information to be furnished under Paragraph (3) of Schedule B

Any issuer filing a registration statement pursuant to Schedule B of the Act need not furnish the detailed information specified in paragraph (3) as to issues of outstanding funded debt the aggregate amount of which outstanding is less than 5 percent of the total funded debt outstanding and to be created by the security to be offered, provided the amount thereof is included in the statement of the total amount of funded debt outstanding and a statement is made as to the title, amount outstanding, rate of interest, and date of maturity of each such issue.

Rule 491. Information to be furnished under Paragraph (6) of Schedule B

Any foreign government filing a registration statement pursuant to Schedule B of the Act need state, in furnishing the information required by paragraph (6), the names and addresses only of principal underwriters, namely, underwriters in privity of contract with the registrant, provided they are designated as principal underwriters and a brief statement is made as to the discounts and commissions to be received by subunderwriters or dealers.

Rule 492. Omissions from prospectuses

In the case of a security for which a registration statement conforming to Schedule B is in effect, the following information, contained in the registration statement, may be omitted from any prospectus: Information in answer to paragraph (3) of the Schedule with respect to the amortization and retirement provisions for debt not being registered, and with respect to the provisions for the substitution of security for such debt; the addresses of underwriters in answer to paragraph (6); information in answer to paragraph (11); the addresses of counsel in answer to paragraph (12); the copy of any agreement or agreements required by paragraph (13); the agreement required by paragraph (14); and all information, whether contained in the registration statement itself or in any exhibit thereto, not required by Schedule B.

Rule 493. Additional Schedule B disclosure and filing requirements

(a) The copy of the opinion or opinions of counsel required by paragraph (14) of Schedule B shall be filed either as a part of the registration statement as originally filed, or as an amendment to the registration statement.

(b) A foreign government or political subdivision of a foreign government must file a registration statement submitted under Schedule B of the Act on the Commission's Electronic Data Gathering and Retrieval System (EDGAR) unless it has obtained a hardship exemption under Items 201 or 202 of Regulation S–T.

(c) A foreign government or political subdivision must disclose in its Schedule B registration statement:

(1) That the Commission maintains an Internet site that contains reports and other information regarding issuers that file electronically with the Commission; and

(2) The address for the Commission Internet site (http://www.sec.gov). A foreign government or political subdivision filing on EDGAR is further encouraged to give its Internet address, if available.

Rule 494. Newspaper prospectuses

(a) This rule shall apply only to newspaper prospectuses relating to securities, as to which a registration statement has become effective, issued by a foreign national government with which the United States maintains diplomatic relations. The term "newspaper prospectus" means an advertisement of securities in newspapers, magazines or other periodicals which are admitted to the mails as second-class matter and which are not distributed by the advertiser. The term does not include reprints, reproductions or detached copies of such advertisements. A newspaper prospectus shall not be deemed a prospectus meeting the requirements of Section 10 for the purpose of Section 2(10)(a) or 5(b)(2) of the Act.

(b) All information included in a newspaper prospectus may be expressed in such condensed or summarized form as may be necessary in the light of the circumstances under which newspaper prospectuses are authorized to be used. The information need not follow the order in which the information is set forth in the registration statement or in the full prospectus. No information need be set forth in tabular form.

(c) The following statement shall be set forth at the head of every newspaper prospectus in conspicuous print:

These securities, though registered, have not been approved or disapproved by the Securities and Exchange Commission, which does not pass on the merits of any registered securities.

(d) There shall be set forth at the foot of every newspaper prospectus in conspicuous print a statement to the following effect:

Further information, particularly financial information, is contained in the registration statement filed with the Commission and in a more complete prospectus which must be furnished to each purchaser and is obtainable from the following persons:

(Insert names.)

(e) If the registrant or any of the underwriters knows or has reasonable grounds to believe that it is intended to stabilize the price of any security to facilitate the offering of the registered security, there shall be placed in the newspaper prospectus, in capital letters, the statement required by Item 502(d) of Regulation S–K to be included in the full prospectus.*

(f) A newspaper prospectus shall contain the information specified in paragraphs (f) (1) to (9) of this rule. All other information and documents contained in the registration statement may be omitted. The following information shall be included:

(1) The name of the borrowing government;

(2) A brief description of the securities to be offered;

(3) The price at which it is proposed to offer the security to the public in the United States;

(4) The purpose and approximate amounts to be devoted to such purposes, so far as determinable, for which the security to be offered is to supply funds; and if funds for such purposes are to be raised in part from other sources, the amounts and the sources thereof:

(5) A brief statement as to the amount of funded and floating debt outstanding and to be created, excluding inter-governmental debt;

(6) A condensed or summarized statement of receipt and expenditures for the last three fiscal years for which data are available;

(7) A condensed or summarized statement of the balance of international payments for the last three fiscal years for which data are available;

(8) If the issuer or its predecessor has defaulted on the principal or interest of any external debt, excluding intergovernmental debt, during the last twenty years, the date, amount and circumstances of such default and the general effect of any succeeding arrangement;

(9) Underwriting discounts and commissions per unit and in the aggregate.

(g) A newspaper prospectus may also include, in condensed, summarized or graphic form, additional information the substance of which is contained in the registration statement. A newspaper prospectus shall not contain any information the substance of which is not set forth in the registration statement.

(h) All information included in a newspaper prospectus shall be set forth in type at least as large as seven-point modern type: *Provided, however*, That such information shall not be so arranged as to be misleading or obscure the information required to be included in such a prospectus.

(i) Five copies of every proposed newspaper prospectus, in the size and form in which it is intended to be published shall be filed with the Commission at least three business days before definitive copies thereof are submitted to the newspaper, magazine or other periodical for publication. Within seven days after publication, five additional copies shall be filed in the exact form in which it was published and shall be accompanied by a statement of the date and manner of its publication.

Rule 495. Preparation of registration statement

(a) A registration statement on Form N–1A (17 CFR 239.15A and 17 CFR 274.11A), Form N–2 (17 CFR 239.14 and 274.11a–1), Form N–3 (17 CFR 239.17a and 274.11b), Form N–4 (17 CFR 239.17b and 274.11c), or Form N–6 (17 CFR 239.17c and 274.11d), shall consist of the facing sheet of the applicable form; a prospectus containing the information called for by such form; the information, list of exhibits, undertakings and signatures required to be set forth in such form; financial statements and schedules; exhibits; and other information or documents filed as part of the registration statement; and all documents or information incorporated by

* There is no paragraph (d) to Item 502 of Regulation S–K.

reference in the foregoing (whether or not required to be filed).

(b) All general instructions, instructions to items of the form, and instructions as to financial statements, exhibits, or prospectuses are to be omitted from the registration statement in all cases.

(c) In the case of a registration statement filed on Form N–1A (17 CFR 239.15A and 274.11A), Form N–2 (17 CFR 239.14 and 274.11a–1), Form N–3 (17 CFR 239.17a and 274.11b), Form N–4 (17 CFR 239.17b and 274.11c), or Form N–6 (17 CFR 239.17c and 274.11d), Parts A and B shall contain the information called for by each of the items of the applicable Part, except that unless otherwise specified, no reference need be made to inapplicable items, and negative answers to any item may be omitted. Copies of Parts A and B may be filed as part of the registration statement in lieu of furnishing the information in item-and-answer form. Wherever such copies are filed in lieu of information in item-and-answer form, the text of the items of the form is to be omitted from the registration statement, as well as from Parts A and B, except to the extent provided in paragraph (d) of the section.

(d) In the case of a registration statement filed on Form N–1A (17 CFR 239.15A and 274.11A), Form N–2 (17 CFR 239.14 and 274.11a–1), Form N–3 (17 CFR 239.17a and 274.11b), Form N–4 (17 CFR 239.17b and 274.11c), or Form N–6 (17 CFR 239.17c and 274.11d), where any item of those forms calls for information not required to be included in Parts A and B (generally Part C of such form), the text of such items, including the numbers and captions thereof, together with the answers thereto, shall be filed with Parts A or B under cover of the facing sheet of the form as part of the registration statement. However, the text of such items may be omitted, provided the answers are so prepared as to indicate the coverage of the item without the necessity of reference to the text of the item. If any such item is inapplicable, or the answer thereto is in the negative, a statement to that effect shall be made. Any financial statements not required to be included in Parts A and B shall also be filed as part of the registration statement proper, unless incorporated by reference pursuant to Rule 411.

(e) *Electronic Filings.* When ascertaining the date of filing, electronic filers should not presume a registration statement has been accepted until notice of acceptance has been received from the Commission.

Rule 496. Contents of prospectus and statement of additional information used after nine months

In the case of a registration statement filed on Form N–1A (17 CFR 239.15A and 274.11A), Form N–2 (17 CFR 239.14 and 274.11a–1), Form N–3 (17 CFR 239.17a and 274.11b), Form N–4 (17 CFR 239.17b and 274.11c), or Form N–6 (17 CFR 239.17c and 274.11d), there may be omitted from any prospectus or Statement of Additional Information used more than 9 months after the effective date of the registration statement any information previously required to be contained in the prospectus or the Statement of Additional Information insofar as later information covering the same subjects, including the latest available certified financial statements, as of a date not more than 16 months prior to the use of the prospectus or the Statement of Additional Information is contained therein.

Rule 497. Filing of investment company prospectuses—number of copies

(a) Five copies of every form of prospectus sent or given to any person prior to the effective date of the registration statement that varies from the form or forms of prospectus included in the registration statement filed pursuant to Rule 402(a) shall be filed as part of the registration statement not later than the date that form of prospectus is first sent or given to any person, except that an investment company advertisement under Rule 482 shall be filed under this paragraph (a) (but not as part of the registration statement) unless filed under paragraph (i) of this rule.

(b) Within 5 days after the effective date of a registration statement or the commencement of a public offering after the effective date of a registration statement, whichever occurs later, 10 copies of each form of prospectus used after the effective date in connection with such offering shall be filed with the Commission in the exact form in which it was used.

(c) For investment companies filing on Form N–1A (17 CFR 239.15A and 274.11A), Form N–2 (17 CFR 239.14 and 274.11a–1), Form N–3 (17 CFR 239.17a and 274.11b), Form N–4 (17 CFR 239.17b and 274.11c), or Form N–6 (17 CFR 239.17c and 274.11d), within five days after the effective date of a registration statement or the commencement of a public offering after the effective date of a registration statement, whichever occurs later, ten copies of each form of prospectus and form of Statement of Additional Information used after the effective date in connection with such offering shall be filed with the Commission in the exact form in which it was used. Investment companies filing on Form N–1A must, if applicable pursuant to General Instruction C.3.(g) of Form N–1A, submit an Interactive Data File (Rule 11 of Regulation S–T).

(d) After the effective date of a registration statement no prospectus which purports to comply with section 10 of the Act and which varies from any form of prospectus filed pursuant to paragraph (b) or (c) of this rule shall be used until 10 copies thereof have been filed with, or mailed for filing to, the Commission.

(e) For investment companies filing on Form N–1A (17 CFR 239.15A and 274.11A), Form N–2 (17 CFR 239.14 and 274.11a–1), Form N–3 (17 CFR 239.17a and 274.11b), Form N–4 (17 CFR 239.17b and 274.11c), or Form N–6 (17 CFR 239.17c and 274.11d), after the effective date of a registration statement, no prospectus that purports to comply with Section 10 of the Act (15 U.S.C. 77j) or Statement of Additional Information that varies from any form of prospectus or form of Statement of Additional Information filed pursuant to paragraph (c) of this rule shall be used until five copies thereof have been filed with, or mailed for filing to the Commission. Investment companies filing on Form N–1A must, if applicable pursuant to General Instruction C.3.(g) of Form N–1A, submit an Interactive Data File (Rule 11 of Regulation S–T).

(f) Every prospectus consisting of a radio or television broadcast shall be reduced in writing. Five copies of every such prospectus shall be filed with the Commission in accordance with the requirements of this rule.

(g) Each copy of a prospectus under this rule shall contain in the upper right hand corner of the cover page the paragraph of this rule under which the filing is made and the file number of the registration statement to which the prospectus relates. In addition, each investment company advertisement deemed to be a Section 10(b) prospectus pursuant to Rule 482 shall contain in the upper right hand corner of the cover page the legend "Rule 482 ad." The information required by this paragraph may be set forth in longhand, provided it is legible.

(h) No later than the second business day following the earlier of the date of the determination of the offering price or the date it is first used after effectiveness in connection with a public offering or sales, ten copies of every form of prospectus and Statement of Additional Information, where applicable, that discloses the information previously omitted from the prospectus filed as part of an effective registration statement in reliance upon Rule 430A under the Securities Act shall be filed with the Commission in the exact form in which it is used, or transmitted by a means reasonably calculated to result in filing with the Commission by that date.

(i) An investment company advertisement deemed to be a Section 10(b) prospectus pursuant to Rule 482 shall be considered to be filed with the Commission upon filing with a national securities association registered under Section 15A of the Securities Exchange Act of 1934 (15 U.S.C. 78(*o*)) that has adopted rules providing standards for the investment company advertising practices of its members and has established and implemented procedures to review that advertising.

(j) In lieu of filing under paragraph (b) or (c) of this rule, a registrant may file a certification that:

(1) The form of prospectus and Statement of Additional Information that would have been filed under paragraph (b) or (c) of this rule would not have differed from that contained in the most recent registration statement or amendment, and

(2) The text of the most recent registration statement or amendment has been filed electronically.

(k) *Summary Prospectus Filing Requirements.* This paragraph (k), and not the other provisions of Rule 497, shall govern the filing of summary prospectuses under Rule 498. Each definitive form of a summary prospectus under Rule 498 shall be filed with the Commission no later than the date that it is first used.

Rule 498. Summary prospectuses for open–end management investment companies

(a) *Definitions.* For purposes of this rule:

(1) *Class* means a class of shares issued by a Fund that has more than one class that represent interests in the same portfolio of securities under 17 CFR 270.18f–3 or under an order exempting the Fund from sections 18(f), 18(g), and 18(i) of the Investment Company Act (15 U.S.C. 80a–18(f), 80a–18(g), and 80a–18(i)).

(2) *Exchange–Traded Fund* means a Fund or a Class, the shares of which are traded on a national securities exchange, and that has formed and operates pursuant to an exemptive order granted by the Commission or in reliance on an exemptive rule adopted by the Commission.

(3) *Fund* means an open-end management investment company, or any Series of such a company, that has, or is included in, an effective registration statement on Form N–1A (17 CFR 239.15A and 274.11A) and that has a current prospectus that satisfies the requirements of section 10(a) of the Act (15 U.S.C. 77j(a)).

(4) *Series* means shares offered by a Fund that represent undivided interests in a portfolio of investments and that are preferred over all other series of shares for assets specifically allocated to that series in accordance with Rule 18f–2(a) under the Investment Company Act of 1940.

(5) *Statement of Additional Information* means the statement of additional information required by Part B of Form N–1A.

(6) *Statutory Prospectus* means a prospectus that satisfies the requirements of section 10(a) of the Act.

(7) *Summary Prospectus* means the summary prospectus described in paragraph (b) of this rule.

(b) *General Requirements for Summary Prospectus.* This paragraph describes the requirements for a Fund's Summary Prospectus. A Summary Prospectus that complies with this paragraph (b) will be deemed to be a prospectus that is authorized under section 10(b) of the Act (15 U.S.C. 77j(b)) and section 24(g) of the Investment Company Act (15 U.S.C. 80a–24(g)) for the purposes of section 5(b)(1) of the Act (15 U.S.C. 77e(b)(1)).

(1) *Cover Page or Beginning of Summary Prospectus.* Include on the cover page of the Summary Prospectus or at the beginning of the Summary Prospectus:

(i) The Fund's name and the Class or Classes, if any, to which the Summary Prospectus relates.

(ii) The exchange ticker symbol of the Fund's shares or, if the Summary Prospectus relates to one or more Classes of the Fund's shares, adjacent to each such Class, the exchange ticker symbol of such Class of the Fund's shares. If the Fund is an Exchange–Traded Fund, also identify the principal U.S. market or markets on which the Fund shares are traded.

(iii) A statement identifying the document as a "Summary Prospectus."

(iv) The approximate date of the Summary Prospectus's first use.

(v) The following legend:

Before you invest, you may want to review the Fund's prospectus, which contains more information about the Fund and its risks. You can find the Fund's prospectus and other information about the Fund online at [____]. You can also get this information at no cost by calling [____] or by sending an e-mail request to [____].

(A) The legend must provide an Internet address, other than the address of the Commission's electronic filing system; toll free (or collect) telephone number; and e-mail address that investors can use to obtain the Statutory Prospectus and other information. The Internet Web site address must be specific enough to lead investors directly to the Statutory Prospectus and other materials that are required to be accessible under paragraph (e)(1) of this rule, rather than to the home page or other section of the Web site on which the materials are posted. The Web site could be a central site with prominent links to each document. The legend may indicate, if applicable, that the Statutory Prospectus and other information are available from a financial intermediary (such as a broker-dealer or bank) through which shares of the Fund may be purchased or sold.

(B) If a Fund incorporates any information by reference into the Summary Prospectus, the legend must identify the type of document (*e.g.*, Statutory Prospectus) from which the information is incorporated and the date of the document. If a Fund incorporates by reference a part of a document, the legend must clearly identify the part by page, paragraph, caption, or otherwise. If information is incorporated from a source other than the Statutory Prospectus, the legend must explain that the incorporated information may be obtained, free of charge, in the same manner as the Statutory Prospectus. A Fund may modify the legend to include a statement to the effect that the Summary Prospectus is intended for use in connection with a defined contribution plan that meets the requirements for qualification under section 401(k) of the Internal Revenue Code (26 U.S.C. 401(k)), a tax-deferred arrangement under section 403(b) or 457 of the Internal Revenue Code (26 U.S.C. 403(b) or 457), or a variable contract as defined in section 817(d) of the Internal Revenue Code

(26 U.S.C. 817(d)), as applicable, and is not intended for use by other investors.

(2) *Contents of the Summary Prospectus.* Except as otherwise provided in this paragraph (b), provide the information required or permitted by Items 2 through 8 of Form N–1A, and only that information, in the order required by the form. A Summary Prospectus may omit the explanation and information required by Instruction 2(c) to Item 4(b)(2) of Form N–1A.

(3) *Incorporation by Reference.*

(i) Except as provided by paragraph (b)(3)(ii) of this rule, information may not be incorporated by reference into a Summary Prospectus. Information that is incorporated by reference into a Summary Prospectus in accordance with paragraph (b)(3)(ii) of this rule need not be sent or given with the Summary Prospectus.

(ii) A Fund may incorporate by reference into a Summary Prospectus any or all of the information contained in the Fund's Statutory Prospectus and Statement of Additional Information, and any information from the Fund's reports to shareholders under Rule 30e–1 under the Investment Company Act of 1940 that the Fund has incorporated by reference into the Fund's Statutory Prospectus, provided that:

(A) The conditions of paragraphs (b)(1)(v)(B) and (e) of this rule are met;

(B) A Fund may not incorporate by reference into a Summary Prospectus information that paragraphs (b)(1) and (2) of this rule require to be included in the Summary Prospectus; and

(C) Information that is permitted to be incorporated by reference into the Summary Prospectus may be incorporated by reference into the Summary Prospectus only by reference to the specific document that contains the information, not by reference to another document that incorporates such information by reference.

(iii) For purposes of Rule 159, information is conveyed to a person not later than the time that a Summary Prospectus is received by the person if the information is incorporated by reference into the Summary Prospectus in accordance with paragraph (b)(3)(ii) of this rule.

(4) *Multiple Funds and Classes.* A Summary Prospectus may describe only one Fund, but may describe more than one Class of a Fund.

(c) *Transfer of the Security.* Any obligation under section 5(b)(2) of the Act (15 U.S.C. 77e(b)(2)) to have a Statutory Prospectus precede or accompany the carrying or delivery of a Fund security in an offering registered on Form N–1A is satisfied if:

(1) A Summary Prospectus is sent or given no later than the time of the carrying or delivery of the Fund security;

(2) The Summary Prospectus is not bound together with any materials, except that a Summary Prospectus for a Fund that is available as an investment option in a variable annuity or variable life insurance contract may be bound together with the Statutory Prospectus for the contract and Summary Prospectuses and Statutory Prospectuses for other investment options available in the contract, provided that:

(i) All of the Funds to which the Summary Prospectuses and Statutory Prospectuses that are bound together relate are available to the person to whom such documents are sent or given; and

(ii) A table of contents identifying each Summary Prospectus and Statutory Prospectus that is bound together, and the page number on which it is found, is included at the beginning or immediately following a cover page of the bound materials;

(3) The Summary Prospectus that is sent or given satisfies the requirements of paragraph (b) of this rule at the time of the carrying or delivery of the Fund security; and

(4) The conditions set forth in paragraph (e) of this rule are satisfied.

(d) *Sending Communications.* A communication relating to an offering registered on Form N–1A sent or given after the effective date of a Fund's registration statement (other than a prospectus permitted or required under section 10 of the Act) shall not be deemed a prospectus under section 2(a)(10) of the Act (15 U.S.C. 77b(a)(10)) if:

(1) It is proved that prior to or at the same time with such communication a Summary Prospectus was sent or given to the person to whom the communication was made;

(2) The Summary Prospectus is not bound together with any materials, except as permitted by paragraph (c)(2) of this rule;

(3) The Summary Prospectus that was sent or given satisfies the requirements of paragraph (b) of this rule at the time of such communication; and

(4) The conditions set forth in paragraph (e) of this rule are satisfied.

(e) *Availability of Fund's Statutory Prospectus and Certain Other Fund Documents.*

(1) The Fund's current Summary Prospectus, Statutory Prospectus, Statement of Additional Information, and most recent annual and semi-annual reports to shareholders under 17 CFR 270.30e–1 are publicly accessible, free of charge, at the Web site address specified on the cover page or at the beginning of the Summary Prospectus on or before the time that the Summary Prospectus is sent or given and current versions of those documents remain on the Web site through the date that is at least 90 days after:

(i) In the case of reliance on paragraph (c) of this rule, the date that the Fund security is carried or delivered; or

(ii) In the case of reliance on paragraph (d) of this rule, the date that the communication is sent or given.

(2) The materials that are accessible in accordance with paragraph (e)(1) of this rule must be presented on the Web site in a format, or formats, that:

(i) Are human-readable and capable of being printed on paper in human-readable format;

(ii) Permit persons accessing the Statutory Prospectus or Statement of Additional Information to move directly back and forth between each section heading in a table of contents of such document and the section of the document referenced in that section heading; provided that, in the case of the Statutory Prospectus, the table of contents is either required by Rule 481(c) or contains the same section headings as the table of contents required by Rule 481(c); and

(iii) Permit persons accessing the Summary Prospectus to move directly back and forth between:

(A) Each section of the Summary Prospectus and any section of the Statutory Prospectus and Statement of Additional Information that provides additional detail concerning that section of the Summary Prospectus; or

(B) Links located at both the beginning and end of the Summary Prospectus, or that remain continuously visible to persons accessing the Summary Prospectus, and tables of contents of both the Statutory Prospectus and the Statement of Additional Information that meet the requirements of paragraph (e)(2)(ii) of this rule.

(3) Persons accessing the materials specified in paragraph (e)(1) of this rule must be able to permanently retain, free of charge, an electronic version of such materials in a format, or formats, that meet each of the requirements of paragraphs (e)(2)(i) and (ii) of this rule.

(4) The conditions set forth in paragraphs (e)(1), (e)(2), and (e)(3) of this rule shall be deemed to be met, notwithstanding the fact that the materials specified in paragraph (e)(1) of this rule are not available for a time in the manner required by paragraphs (e)(1), (e)(2), and (e)(3) of this rule, provided that:

(i) The Fund has reasonable procedures in place to ensure that the specified materials are available in the manner required by paragraphs (e)(1), (e)(2), and (e)(3) of this rule; and

(ii) The Fund takes prompt action to ensure that the specified documents become available in the manner required by paragraphs (e)(1), (e)(2), and (e)(3) of this rule, as soon as practicable following the earlier of the time at which it knows or reasonably should have known that the documents are not available in the manner required by paragraphs (e)(1), (e)(2), and (e)(3) of this rule.

(f) *Other Requirements.*

(1) *Delivery upon Request.* If paragraph (c) or (d) of this rule is relied on with respect to a Fund, the Fund (or a financial intermediary through which shares of the Fund may be purchased or sold) must send, at no cost to the requestor and by U.S. first class mail or other reasonably prompt means, a paper copy of the Fund's Statutory Prospectus, Statement of Additional Information, and most recent annual and semi-annual reports to shareholders to any person requesting such a copy within three business days after receiving a request for a paper copy. If paragraph (c) or (d) of this rule is relied on with respect to a Fund, the Fund (or a fi-

nancial intermediary through which shares of the Fund may be purchased or sold) must send, at no cost to the requestor and by e-mail, an electronic copy of the Fund's Statutory Prospectus, Statement of Additional Information, and most recent annual and semi-annual reports to shareholders to any person requesting such a copy within three business days after receiving a request for an electronic copy. The requirement to send an electronic copy of a document by e-mail may be satisfied by sending a direct link to the document on the Internet; provided that a current version of the document is directly accessible through the link from the time that the e-mail is sent through the date that is six months after the date that the e-mail is sent and the e-mail explains both how long the link will remain useable and that, if the recipient desires to retain a copy of the document, he or she should access and save the document.

(2) *Greater Prominence.* If paragraph (c) or (d) of this section is relied on with respect to a Fund, the Fund's Summary Prospectus shall be given greater prominence than any materials that accompany the Fund's Summary Prospectus, with the exception of other Summary Prospectuses, Statutory Prospectuses, or a Notice of Internet Availability of Proxy Materials under Rule 14a–16 of this chapter.

(3) *Convenient for Reading and Printing.* If paragraph (c) or (d) of this rule is relied on with respect to a Fund:

(i) The materials that are accessible in accordance with paragraph (e)(1) of this rule must be presented on the Web site in a format, or formats, that are convenient for both reading online and printing on paper; and

(ii) Persons accessing the materials that are accessible in accordance with paragraph (e)(1) of this rule must be able to permanently retain, free of charge, an electronic version of such materials in a format, or formats, that are convenient for both reading online and printing on paper.

(4) *Information in Summary Prospectus Must Be the Same as Information in Statutory Prospectus.* If paragraph (c) or (d) of this rule is relied on with respect to a Fund, the information provided in response to Items 2 through 8 of Form N–1A in the Fund's Summary Prospectus must be the same as the information provided in response to Items 2 through 8 of Form N–1A in the Fund's Statutory Prospectus except as expressly permitted by paragraph (b)(2) of this rule.

(5) *Compliance with Paragraph (f) Not a Condition to Reliance on Paragraphs (c) and (d).* Compliance with this paragraph (f) is not a condition to the ability to rely on paragraph (c) or (d) of this rule with respect to a Fund, and failure to comply with paragraph (f) does not negate the ability to rely on paragraph (c) or (d).

REGULATION D—RULES GOVERNING THE LIMITED OFFER AND SALE OF SECURITIES WITHOUT REGISTRATION UNDER THE SECURITIES ACT OF 1933

Rule 500. Use of Regulation D

Users of Regulation D should note the following:

(a) Regulation D relates to transactions exempted from the registration requirements of section 5 of the Securities Act of 1933 (the "Act"). Such transactions are not exempt from the antifraud, civil liability, or other provisions of the federal securities laws. Issuers are reminded of their obligation to provide such further material information, if any, as may be necessary to make the information required under Regulation D, in light of the circumstances under which it is furnished, not misleading.

(b) Nothing in Regulation D obviates the need to comply with any applicable state law relating to the offer and sale of securities. Regulation D is intended to be a basic element in a uniform system of federal-state limited offering exemptions consistent with the provisions of sections 18 and 19(c) of the Act. In those states that have adopted Regulation D, or any version of Regulation D, special attention should be directed to the applicable state laws and regulations, including those relating to registration of persons who receive remuneration in connection with the offer and sale of securities, to disqualification of issuers and other persons associated with offerings based on state administrative orders or judgments, and to requirements for filings of notices of sales.

(c) Attempted compliance with any rule in Regulation D does not act as an exclusive election; the issuer can also claim the availability of any other applicable exemption. For instance, an issuer's failure to satisfy all the terms and conditions of rule 506(b) shall not raise any presumption that the exemption provided by section 4(a)(2) of the Act is not available.

(d) Regulation D is available only to the issuer of the securities and not to any affiliate of that issuer or to any other person for resales of the issuer's securities. Regulation D provides an exemption only for the transactions in which the securities are offered or sold by the issuer, not for the securities themselves.

(e) Regulation D may be used for business combinations that involve sales by virtue of rule 145(a) or otherwise.

(f) In view of the objectives of Regulation D and the policies underlying the Act, Regulation D is not available to any issuer for any transaction or chain of transactions that, although in technical compliance with Regulation D, is part of a plan or scheme to evade the registration provisions of the Act. In such cases, registration under the Act is required.

(g) Securities offered and sold outside the United States in accordance with Regulation S need not be registered under the Act. See Release No. 33–6863. Regulation S may be relied upon for such offers and sales even if coincident offers and sales are made in accordance with Regulation D inside the United States. Thus, for example, persons who are offered and sold securities in accordance with Regulation S would not be counted in the calculation of the number of purchasers under Regulation D. Similarly, proceeds from such sales would not be included in the aggregate offering price. The provisions of this paragraph (g), however, do not apply if the issuer elects to rely solely on Regulation D for offers or sales to persons made outside the United States.

Rule 501. Definitions and terms used in Regulation D

As used in Regulation D (Rules 500–508), the following terms shall have the meaning indicated:

(a) *Accredited Investor. Accredited investor* shall mean any person who comes within any of the following categories, or who the issuer reasonably believes comes within any of the following categories, at the time of the sale of the securities to that person:

(1) Any bank as defined in section 3(a)(2) of the Act, or any savings and loan association or other institution as defined in section 3(a)(5)(A) of the Act whether acting in its individual or fiduciary capacity; any broker or dealer registered pursuant to section 15 of the Securities Exchange Act of 1934; any insurance company as defined in section 2(a)(13) of the Act; any investment company registered under the Investment Company Act of 1940 or a business development company as defined in section 2(a)(48) of that Act; any Small Business Investment Company licensed by the U.S. Small Business Administration under section 301(c) or (d) of the Small Business Investment Act of 1958; any plan established and maintained by a state, its political subdivisions, or any agency or instrumentality of a state or its political subdivisions, for the benefit of its employees, if such plan has total assets in excess of $5,000,000; any employee benefit plan within the meaning of the Employee Retirement Income Security Act of 1974, if the investment decision is made by a plan fiduciary, as defined in section 3(21) of such act, which is either a bank, savings and loan association, insurance company, or registered investment adviser, or if the employee benefit plan has total assets in excess of $5,000,000 or, if a self-directed plan, with investment decisions made solely by persons that are accredited investors;

(2) Any private business development company as defined in section 202(a)(22) of the Investment Advisers Act of 1940;

(3) Any organization described in section 501(c)(3) of the Internal Revenue Code, corporation, Massachusetts or similar business trust, or partnership, not formed for the specific purpose of acquiring the securities offered, with total assets in excess of $5,000,000;

(4) Any director, executive officer, or general partner of the issuer of the securities being offered or sold, or any director, executive officer, or general partner of a general partner of that issuer;

(5) Any natural person whose individual net worth, or joint net worth with that person's spouse, exceeds $1,000,000.

(i) Except as provided in paragraph (a)(5)(ii) of this section, for purposes of calculating net worth under this paragraph (a)(5):

(A) The person's primary residence shall not be included as an asset;

(B) Indebtedness that is secured by the person's primary residence, up to the estimated fair market value of the primary residence at the time of the sale of securities, shall not be included as a liability (except that if the amount of such indebtedness outstanding at the time of sale of securities exceeds the amount outstanding 60 days before such time, other than as a result of the acquisition of the primary residence, the amount of such excess shall be included as a liability); and

(C) Indebtedness that is secured by the person's primary residence in excess of the estimated fair market value of the primary residence at the time of the sale of securities shall be included as a liability;

(ii) Paragraph (a)(5)(i) of this section will not apply to any calculation of a person's net worth made in connection with a purchase of securities in accordance with a right to purchase such securities, provided that:

(A) Such right was held by the person on July 20, 2010;

(B) The person qualified as an accredited investor on the basis of net worth at the time the person acquired such right; and

(C) The person held securities of the same issuer, other than such right, on July 20, 2010.

(6) Any natural person who had an individual income in excess of $200,000 in each of the two most recent years or joint income with that person's spouse in excess of $300,000 in each of those years and has a reasonable expectation of reaching the same income level in the current year;

(7) Any trust, with total assets in excess of $5,000,000, not formed for the specific purpose of acquiring the securities offered, whose purchase is directed by a sophisticated person as described in Rule 506(b)(2)(ii); and

(8) Any entity in which all of the equity owners are accredited investors.

(b) *Affiliate.* An *affiliate* of, or person *affiliated* with, a specified person shall mean a person that directly, or indirectly through one or more intermediaries, controls or is controlled by, or is under common control with, the person specified.

(c) *Aggregate Offering Price. Aggregate offering price* shall mean the sum of all cash, services, property, notes, cancellation of debt, or other consideration to be received by an issuer for issuance of its securities. Where securities are being offered for both cash and non-cash consideration, the aggregate offering price shall be based on the price at which the securities are offered for cash. Any portion of the aggregate offering price attributable to cash received in a foreign currency shall be translated into United States currency at the currency exchange rate in effect at a reasonable time prior to or on the date of the sale of the securities. If securities are not offered for cash, the aggregate offering price shall be based on the value of the consideration as established by bona fide sales of that consideration made within a reasonable time, or, in the absence of sales, on the fair value as determined by an accepted standard. Such valuations of non-cash consideration must be reasonable at the time made.

(d) *Business Combination. Business combination* shall mean any transaction of the type specified in paragraph (a) of Rule 145 under the Act and any transaction involving the acquisition by one issuer, in exchange for all or a part of its own or its parent's stock, of stock of another issuer if, immediately after the acquisition, the acquiring issuer has control of the other issuer (whether or not it had control before the acquisition).

(e) *Calculation of Number of Purchasers.* For purposes of calculating the number of purchasers under Rule 506(b) only, the following shall apply:

(1) The following purchasers shall be excluded:

(i) Any relative, spouse or relative of the spouse of a purchaser who has the same primary residence as the purchaser;

(ii) Any trust or estate in which a purchaser and any of the persons related to him as specified in paragraph (e)(1)(i) or (e)(1)(iii) of this Rule 501 collectively have more than 50 percent of the beneficial interest (excluding contingent interests);

(iii) Any corporation or other organization of which a purchaser and any of the persons related to him as specified in paragraph (e)(1)(i) or (e)(1)(ii) of this Rule 501 collectively are beneficial owners of more than 50 percent of the equity securities (excluding directors' qualifying shares) or equity interests; and

(iv) Any accredited investor.

(2) A corporation, partnership or other entity shall be counted as one purchaser. If, however, that entity is organized for the specific purpose of acquiring the securities offered and is not an accredited investor under paragraph (a)(8) of this Rule 501, then each beneficial owner of equity securities or equity interests in the entity shall count as a separate purchaser for all provisions of Regulation D (Rules 501–508), except to the extent provided in paragraph (e)(1) of this Rule.

(3) A non-contributory employee benefit plan within the meaning of Title I of the Employee Retirement Income Security Act of 1974 shall be counted as one purchaser where the trustee makes all investment decisions for the plan.

NOTE: The issuer must satisfy all the other provisions of Regulation D for all purchasers whether or not they are included in calculating the number of purchasers. Clients of an investment adviser or customers of a broker or dealer shall be considered the "purchasers" under Regulation D regardless of the amount of discretion given to the investment adviser or broker or dealer to act on behalf of the client or customer.

(f) *Executive Officer. Executive officer* shall mean the president, any vice president in charge of a principal business unit, division or function (such as sales, administration or finance), any other officer who performs a policy making function, or any other person who performs similar policy making functions for the issuer. Executive officers of subsidiaries may be deemed executive officers of the issuer if they perform such policy making functions for the issuer.

(g) *Final order. Final order* shall mean a written directive or declaratory statement issued by a federal or state agency described in Rule 506(d)(1)(iii) under applicable statutory authority that provides for notice and an opportunity for hearing, which constitutes a final disposition or action by that federal or state agency.

(h) *Issuer.* The definition of the term *issuer* in section 2(a)(4) of the Act shall apply, except that in the case of a proceeding under the Federal Bankruptcy Code (11 U.S.C. 101 *et seq.*), the trustee or debtor in possession shall be considered the issuer in an offering under a plan or reorganization, if the securities are to be issued under the plan.

(i) *Purchaser Representative. Purchaser representative* shall mean any person who satisfies all of the following conditions or who the issuer reasonably believes satisfies all of the following conditions:

(1) Is not an affiliate, director, officer or other employee of the issuer, or beneficial owner of 10 percent or more of any class of the equity securities or 10 percent or more of the equity interest in the issuer, except where the purchaser is:

(i) A relative of the purchaser representative by blood, marriage or adoption and not more remote than a first cousin;

(ii) A trust or estate in which the purchaser representative and any persons related to him as specified in paragraph (h)(1)(i) or (h)(1)(iii) of this Rule 501 collectively have more than 50 percent of the beneficial interest (excluding contingent interest) or of which the purchaser representative serves as trustee, executor, or in any similar capacity; or

(iii) A corporation or other organization of which the purchaser representative and any persons related to him as specified in paragraph (h)(1)(i) or (h)(1)(ii) of this Rule 501 collectively are the beneficial owners of more than 50 percent of the equity securities (excluding directors' qualifying shares) or equity interests;

(2) Has such knowledge and experience in financial and business matters that he is capable of evaluating, alone, or together with other purchaser representatives of the purchaser, or together with the purchaser, the merits and risks of the prospective investment;

(3) Is acknowledged by the purchaser in writing, during the course of the transaction, to be his purchaser representative in connection with evaluating the merits and risks of the prospective investment; and

(4) Discloses to the purchaser in writing a reasonable time prior to the sale of securities to that purchaser any material relationship between himself or his affiliates and the issuer or its affiliates that then exists, that is mutually understood to be contemplated, or that has existed at any time during the previous two years, and any compensation received or to be received as a result of such relationship.

RULE 501 NOTE 1: A person acting as a purchaser representative should consider the applicability of the registration and antifraud provisions relating to brokers and dealers under the Securities Exchange Act of 1934 (*Exchange Act*) (15 U.S.C. 78a *et seq.*, as amended) and relating to investment advisers under the Investment Advisers Act of 1940.

RULE 501 NOTE 2: The acknowledgment required by paragraph (h)(3) and the disclosure required by paragraph (h)(4) of this Rule 501 must be made with specific reference to each prospective investment. Advance blanket acknowledgment, such as for *all securities transactions* or *all private placements,* is not sufficient.

RULE 501 NOTE 3: Disclosure of any material relationships between the purchaser representative or his affiliates and the issuer or its affiliates does not relieve the purchaser representative of his obligation to act in the interest of the purchaser.

Rule 502. General conditions to be met

The following conditions shall be applicable to offers and sales made under Regulation D (Rules 500–508):

(a) *Integration.* All sales that are part of the same Regulation D offering must meet all of the terms and conditions of Regulation D. Offers and sales that are made more than six months before the start of a Regulation D offering or are made more than six months after completion of a Regulation D offering will not be considered part of that Regulation D offering, so long as during those six month periods there are no offers or sales of securities by or for the issuer that are of the same or a similar class as those offered or sold under Regulation D, other than those offers or sales of securities under an employee benefit plan as defined in Rule 405 under the Act.

NOTE: The term *offering* is not defined in the Act or in Regulation D. If the issuer offers or sells securities for which the safe harbor rule in paragraph (a) of this Rule 502 is unavailable, the determination as to whether separate sales of securities are part of the same offering (*i.e.* are considered *integrated*) depends on the particular facts and circumstances. Generally, transactions otherwise meeting the requirements of an exemption will not be integrated with simultaneous offerings being made outside the United States in compliance with Regulation S. See Release No. 33–6863.

The following factors should be considered in determining whether offers and sales should be integrated for purposes of the exemptions under Regulation D:

(a) Whether the sales are part of a single plan of financing;

(b) Whether the sales involve issuance of the same class of securities;

(c) Whether the sales have been made at or about the same time;

(d) Whether the same type of consideration is being received; and

(e) Whether the sales are made for the same general purpose.

See Release No. 33–4552 (November 6, 1962).

(b) *Information Requirements.* (1) *When Information Must Be Furnished.* If the issuer sells securities under Rule 506(b) to any purchaser that is not an accredited investor, the issuer shall furnish the information specified in paragraph (b)(2) of this Rule 502 to such purchaser a reasonable time prior to sale. The issuer is not required to furnish the specified information to purchasers when it sells securities under Rule 504, or to any accredited investor.

NOTE: When an issuer provides information to investors pursuant to paragraph (b)(1), it should consider providing such information to accredited investors as well, in view of the anti-fraud provisions of the federal securities laws.

(2) *Type of Information to Be Furnished.* (i) If the issuer is not subject to the reporting requirements of section 13 or 15(d) of the Exchange Act, at a reasonable time prior to the sale of securities the issuer shall furnish to the purchaser, to the extent material to an understanding of the issuer, its business, and the securities being offered:

(A) *Non-financial Statement Information.* If the issuer is eligible to use Regulation A (Rules 251–263), the same kind of information as would be required in Part II of Form 1–A (17 CFR 239.90). If the issuer is not eligible to use Regulation A, the same kind of information as required in Part I of a registration statement filed under the Securities Act on the form that the issuer would be entitled to use.

(B) *Financial Statement Information.* (*1*) *Offerings Up to $2,000,000.* The information required in Article 8 of Regulation S–X, except that only the issuer's balance sheet, which shall be dated within 120 days of the start of the offering, must be audited.

(*2*) *Offerings Up to $7,500,000.* The financial statement information required in Form S–1 (17 CFR 239.10) for smaller reporting companies. If an issuer, other than a limited partnership, cannot obtain audited financial statements without unreasonable effort or expense, then only the issuer's balance sheet, which shall be dated within 120 days of the start of the offering, must be audited. If the issuer is a limited partnership and cannot obtain the required financial statements without unreasonable effort or expense, it may furnish financial statements that have been prepared on the basis of Federal income tax requirements and examined and reported on in accordance with generally accepted auditing standards by an independent public or certified accountant.

(*3*) *Offerings Over $7,500,000.* The financial statement as would be required in a registration statement filed under the Act on the form that the issuer would be entitled to use. If an issuer, other than a limited partnership, cannot obtain audited financial statements without unreasonable effort or expense, then only the issuer's balance sheet, which shall be dated within 120 days of the start of the offering, must be audited. If the issuer is a limited partnership and cannot obtain the required financial statements without unreasonable effort or expense, it may furnish financial statements that have been prepared on the basis of Federal income tax requirements and examined and reported on in accordance with generally accepted auditing standards by an independent public or certified accountant.

(C) If the issuer is a foreign private issuer eligible to use Form 20–F, the issuer shall disclose the same kind of information required to be included in a registration statement filed under the Act on the form that the issuer would be entitled to use. The financial statements need be certified only to the extent required by paragraph (b)(2)(i)(B)(1), (2) or (3) of this rule, as appropriate.

(ii) If the issuer is subject to the reporting requirements of section 13 or 15(d) of the Exchange Act, at a reasonable time prior to the sale of securities the issuer shall furnish to the purchaser the information specified in paragraph (b)(2)(ii)(A) or (B) of this rule, and in either event the information specified in paragraph (b)(2)(ii)(C) of this Rule 502:

(A) The issuer's annual report to shareholders for the most recent fiscal year, if such annual report meets the requirements of Rules 14a–3 or 14c–3 under the Exchange Act, the definitive proxy statement filed in connection with that annual report, and if requested by the purchaser in writing, a copy of the issuer's most recent Form 10–K (17 CFR 249.310) under the Exchange Act.

(B) The information contained in an annual report on Form 10–K (17 CFR 249.310) under the Exchange Act or in a registration statement on Form S–1 (17 CFR 239.11) or S–11 (17 CFR 239.18) under the Act or on Form 10 (17 CFR 249.210) under the Exchange Act, whichever filing is the most recent required to be filed.

(C) The information contained in any reports or documents required to be filed by the issuer under sections 13(a), 14(a), 14(c), and 15(d) of the Exchange Act since the distribution or filing of the report or registration statement specified in paragraph (b)(2)(ii)(A) or (B), and a brief description of the securities being offered, the use of the proceeds from the offering, and any material changes in the issuer's affairs that are not disclosed in the documents furnished.

(D) If the issuer is a foreign private issuer, the issuer may provide in lieu of the information specified in paragraphs (b)(2)(ii)(A) or (B) of this rule, the information contained in its most recent filing on Form 20–F or Form F–1 (17 CFR 239.31).

(iii) Exhibits required to be filed with the Commission as part of a registration statement or report, other than an annual report to shareholders or parts of that report incorporated by reference in a Form 10–K report, need not be furnished to each purchaser that is not an accredited investor if the contents of material exhibits are identified and such exhibits are made available to a purchaser, upon his or her written request, a reasonable time prior to his or her purchase.

(iv) At a reasonable time prior to the sale of securities to any purchaser that is not an accredited investor in a transaction under Rule 506(b), the issuer shall furnish to the purchaser a brief description in writing of any material written information concerning the offering that has been provided by the issuer to any accredited investor but not previously delivered to such unaccredited purchaser. The issuer shall furnish any portion or all of this information to the purchaser, upon his written request a reasonable time prior to his purchase.

(v) The issuer shall also make available to each purchaser at a reasonable time prior to his purchase of securities in a transaction under Rule 506(b) the opportunity to ask questions and receive answers concerning the terms and conditions of the offering and to obtain any additional information which the issuer possesses or can acquire without unreasonable effort or expense that is necessary to verify the accuracy of information furnished under paragraph (b)(2)(i) or (ii) of this Rule 502.

(vi) For business combinations or exchange offers, in addition to information required by Form S–4 (17 CFR 239.25) the issuer shall provide to each purchaser at the time the plan is submitted to security holders, or, with an exchange, during the course of the transaction and prior to sale, written information about any terms or arrangements of the proposed transactions that are materially different from those for all other security holders. For purposes of this subsection, an issuer which is not subject to the reporting requirements of section 13 or 15(d) of the Exchange Act may satisfy the requirements of Part I.B. or C. of Form S–4 by compliance with paragraph (b)(2)(i) of this Rule 502.

(vii) At a reasonable time prior to the sale of securities to any purchaser that is not an accredited investor in a transaction under Rule 506(b), the issuer shall advise the purchaser of the limitations on resale in the manner contained in paragraph (d)(2) of this Rule. Such disclosure may be contained in other materials required to be provided by this paragraph.

(c) *Limitation on Manner of Offering.* Except as provided in Rule 504(b)(1) or Rule 506(c), neither the issuer nor any person acting on its behalf shall offer or sell the securities by any form of general solicitation or general advertising, including, but not limited to, the following:

(1) Any advertisement, article, notice or other communication published in any newspaper, magazine, or similar media or broadcast over television or radio; and

(2) Any seminar or meeting whose attendees have been invited by any general solicitation or general advertising; *Provided, however*, that publication by an issuer of a notice in accordance with Rule 135c or filing with the Commission by an issuer of a notice of sales on Form D (17 CFR 239.500) in which the issuer has made a good faith and reasonable attempt to comply with the requirements of such form, shall not be deemed to constitute general solicitation or general advertising for purposes of this rule; *Provided further*, that, if the requirements of Rule 135e are satisfied, providing any journalist with access to press conferences held outside of the United States, to meetings with issuer or selling security holder representatives conducted outside of the United States, or to written press-related materials released outside the United States, at or in which a present or proposed offering of securities is discussed, will not be deemed to constitute general solicitation or general advertising for purposes of this rule.

(d) *Limitations on Resale.* Except as provided in Rule 504(b)(1), securities acquired in a transaction under Regulation D shall have the status of securities acquired in a transaction under Section 4(a)(2) of the Act and cannot be resold without registration under the Act or an exemption therefrom. The issuer shall exercise reasonable care to assure that the purchasers of the securities are not underwriters within the meaning of section 2(a)(11) of the Act, which reasonable care may be demonstrated by the following:

(1) Reasonable inquiry to determine if the purchaser is acquiring the securities for himself or for other persons;

(2) Written disclosure to each purchaser prior to sale that the securities have not been registered under the Act and, therefore, cannot be resold unless they are registered under the Act or unless an exemption from registration is available; and

(3) Placement of a legend on the certificate or other document that evidences the securities stating that the securities have not been registered under the Act and setting forth or referring to the restrictions on transferability and sale of the securities.

While taking these actions will establish the requisite reasonable care, it is not the exclusive method to demonstrate such care. Other actions by the issuer may satisfy this provision. In addition, Rule 502(b)(2)(vii) requires the delivery of written disclosure of the limitations on resale to investors in certain instances.

Rule 503. Filing of notice of sales

(a) *When Notice of Sales on Form D Is Required and Permitted to Be Filed.* (1) An issuer offering or selling securities in reliance on Rule 504 or 506 must file with the Commission a notice of sales containing the information required by Form D (17 CFR 239.500) for each new offering of securities no later than 15 calendar days after the first sale of securities in the offering, unless the end of that period falls on a Saturday, Sunday or holiday, in which case the due date would be the first business day following.

(2) An issuer may file an amendment to a previously filed notice of sales on Form D at any time.

(3) An issuer must file an amendment to a previously filed notice of sales on Form D for an offering:

(i) To correct a material mistake of fact or error in the previously filed notice of sales on Form D, as soon as practicable after discovery of the mistake or error;

(ii) To reflect a change in the information provided in the previously filed notice of sales on Form D, as soon as practicable after the change, except that no amendment is required to reflect a change that occurs after the offering terminates or a change that occurs solely in the following information:

(A) The address or relationship to the issuer of a related person identified in response to Item 3 of the notice of sales on Form D;

(B) An issuer's revenues or aggregate net asset value;

(C) The minimum investment amount, if the change is an increase, or if the change, together with all other changes in that amount since the previously filed notice of sales on Form D, does not result in a decrease of more than 10%;

(D) Any address or state(s) of solicitation shown in response to Item 12 of the notice of sales on Form D;

(E) The total offering amount, if the change is a decrease, or if the change, together with all other changes in that amount since the previously filed notice of sales on Form D, does not result in an increase of more than 10%;

(F) The amount of securities sold in the offering or the amount remaining to be sold;

(G) The number of non-accredited investors who have invested in the offering, as long as the change does not increase the number to more than 35;

(H) The total number of investors who have invested in the offering; or

(I) The amount of sales commissions, finders' fees or use of proceeds for payments to executive officers, directors or promoters, if the change is a decrease, or if the change, together with all other changes in that amount since the previously filed notice of sales on Form D, does not result in an increase of more than 10%; and

(iii) Annually, on or before the first anniversary of the filing of the notice of sales on Form D or the filing of the most recent amendment to the notice of sales on Form D, if the offering is continuing at that time.

(4) An issuer that files an amendment to a previously filed notice of sales on Form D must provide current information in response to all requirements of the notice of sales on Form D regardless of why the amendment is filed.

(b) *How Notice of Sales on Form D Must Be Filed and Signed.*

(1) A notice of sales on Form D must be filed with the Commission in electronic format by means of the Commission's Electronic Data Gathering, Analysis, and Retrieval System (EDGAR) in accordance with EDGAR rules set forth in Regulation S–T (17 CFR Part 232).

(2) Every notice of sales on Form D must be signed by a person duly authorized by the issuer.

Rule 504. Exemption for limited offerings and sales of securities not exceeding $5,000,000

(a) *Exemption.* Offers and sales of securities that satisfy the conditions in paragraph (b) of this Rule 504 by an issuer that is not:

(1) subject to the reporting requirements of section 13 or 15(d) of the Exchange Act;

(2) an investment company; or

(3) a development stage company that either has no specific business plan or purpose or has indicated that its business plan is to engage in a merger or acquisition with an unidentified company or companies, or other entity or person, shall be exempt from the provision of section 5 of the Act under section 3(b) of the Act.

(b) *Conditions to Be Met.* (1) *General conditions.* To qualify for exemption under this Rule 504, offers and sales must satisfy the terms and conditions of Rules 501 and 502(a), (c) and (d), except that the provisions of Rule 502 (c) and (d) will not apply to offers and sales of securities under this Rule 504 that are made:

(i) Exclusively in one or more states that provide for the registration of the securities, and require the public filing and delivery to investors of a substantive disclosure document before sale, and are made in accordance with those state provisions;

(ii) In one or more states that have no provision for the registration of the securities or the public filing or delivery of a disclosure document before sale, if the securities have been registered in at least one state that provides for such registration, public filing and delivery before sale, offers and sales are made in that state in accordance with such provisions, and the disclosure document is delivered before sale to all purchasers (including those in the states that have no such procedure); or

(iii) Exclusively according to state law exemptions from registration that permit general solicitation and general advertising so long as sales are made only to "accredited investors" as defined in Rule 501(a).

(2) The aggregate offering price for an offering of securities under this Rule 504, as defined in Rule 501(c), shall not exceed $5,000,000, less the aggregate offering price for all securities sold within the twelve months before the start of and during the

offering of securities under this Rule 504 or in violation of section 5(a) of the Securities Act.

Instruction to paragraph (b)(2): If a transaction under Rule 504 fails to meet the limitation on the aggregate offering price, it does not affect the availability of Rule 504 for the other transactions considered in applying such limitation. For example, if an issuer sold $5,000,000 of its securities on January 1, 2014 under Rule 504 and an additional $500,000 of its securities on July 1, 2014, Rule 504 would not be available for the later sale, but would still be applicable to the January 1, 2014 sale.

(3) Disqualifications. No exemption under this section shall be available for the securities of any issuer if such issuer would be subject to disqualification under Rule 506(d) on or after January 20, 2017; provided that disclosure of prior "bad actor" events shall be required in accordance with Rule 506(e).

Instruction to paragraph (b)(3): For purposes of disclosure of prior "bad actor" events pursuant to Rule 506(e), an issuer shall furnish to each purchaser, a reasonable time prior to sale, a description in writing of any matters that would have triggered disqualification under this paragraph (b)(3) but occurred before January 20, 2017.

Rule 505. [Removed and Reserved]

Rule 506. Exemption for limited offers and sales without regard to dollar amount of offering

(a) *Exemption*. Offers and sales of securities by an issuer that satisfy the conditions in paragraph (b) or (c) of this Rule 506 shall be deemed to be transactions not involving any public offering within the meaning of section 4(a)(2) of the Act.

(b) *Conditions to Be Met in Offerings Subject to Limitation on Manner of Offering*. (1) *General Conditions*. To qualify for an exemption under this Rule 506, offers and sales must satisfy all the terms and conditions of Rules 501 and 502.

(2) *Specific Conditions*. (i) *Limitation on Number of Purchasers*. There are no more than or the issuer reasonably believes that there are no more than 35 purchasers of securities from the issuer in any offering under this Rule 506.

NOTE TO PARAGRAPH (b)(2)(i): See Rule 501(e) for the calculation of the number of purchasers and Rule 502(a) for what may or may not constitute an offering under Rule 506(b).

(ii) *Nature of Purchasers*. Each purchaser who is not an accredited investor either alone or with his purchaser representative(s) has such knowledge and experience in financial and business matters that he is capable of evaluating the merits and risks of the prospective investment, or the issuer reasonably believes immediately prior to making any sale that such purchaser comes within this description.

(c) *Conditions to be met in offerings not subject to limitation on manner of offering*

(1) *General conditions*. To qualify for exemption under this section, sales must satisfy all the terms and conditions Rules 501 and 502(a) and (d).

(2) *Specific conditions*.

(i) *Nature of purchasers*. All purchasers of securities sold in any offering under paragraph (c) of this section are accredited investors.

(ii) *Verification of accredited investor status*. The issuer shall take reasonable steps to verify that purchasers of securities sold in any offering under paragraph (c) of this section are accredited investors. The issuer shall be deemed to take reasonable steps to verify if the issuer uses, at its option, one of the following non-exclusive and non-mandatory methods of verifying that a natural person who purchases securities in such offering is an accredited investor; provided, however, that the issuer does not have knowledge that such person is not an accredited investor:

(A) In regard to whether the purchaser is an accredited investor on the basis of income, reviewing any Internal Revenue Service form that reports the purchaser's income for the two most recent years (including, but not limited to, Form W–2, Form 1099, Schedule K–1 to Form 1065, and Form 1040) and obtaining a written representation from the purchaser that he or she has a reasonable expectation of reaching the income level necessary to qualify as an accredited investor during the current year;

(B) In regard to whether the purchaser is an accredited investor on the basis of net worth, reviewing one or more of the following types of documentation dated within the prior three months and obtaining a written representation from the purchaser that all liabilities necessary to make a determination of net worth have been disclosed:

(*1*) With respect to assets: bank statements, brokerage statements and other statements of securities holdings, certificates of deposit, tax assessments, and appraisal reports issued by independent third parties; and

(*2*) With respect to liabilities: a consumer report from at least one of the nationwide consumer reporting agencies; or

(C) Obtaining a written confirmation from one of the following persons or entities that such person or entity has taken reasonable steps to verify that the purchaser is an accredited investor within the prior three months and has determined that such purchaser is an accredited investor:

(*1*) A registered broker-dealer;

(*2*) An investment adviser registered with the Securities and Exchange Commission;

(*3*) A licensed attorney who is in good standing under the laws of the jurisdictions in which he or she is admitted to practice law; or

(*4*) A certified public accountant who is duly registered and in good standing under the laws of the place of his or her residence or principal office.

(D) In regard to any person who purchased securities in an issuer's Rule 506(b) offering as an accredited investor prior to the effective date of paragraph (c) of this section and continues to hold such securities, for the same issuer's Rule 506(c) offering, obtaining a certification by such person at the time of sale that he or she qualifies as an accredited investor.

Instructions to paragraph (c)(2)(ii)(A) through (C) of this section:

1. The issuer is not required to use any of these methods in verifying the accredited investor status of natural persons who are purchasers. These methods are examples of the types of non-exclusive and non-mandatory methods that satisfy the verification requirement in Rule 506(c)(2)(ii).

2. In the case of a person who qualifies as an accredited investor based on joint income with that person's spouse, the issuer would be deemed to satisfy the verification requirement in Rule 506(c)(2)(ii)(A) by reviewing copies of Internal Revenue Service forms that report income for the two most recent years in regard to, and obtaining written representations from, both the person and the spouse.

3. In the case of a person who qualifies as an accredited investor based on joint net worth with that person's spouse, the issuer would be deemed to satisfy the verification requirement in Rule 506(c)(2)(ii)(B) by reviewing such documentation in regard to, and obtaining written representations from, both the person and the spouse.

(d) *"Bad Actor" disqualification.* (1) No exemption under this section shall be available for a sale of securities if the issuer; any predecessor of the issuer; any affiliated issuer; any director, executive officer, other officer participating in the offering, general partner or managing member of the issuer; any beneficial owner of 20% or more of the issuer's outstanding voting equity securities, calculated on the basis of voting power; any promoter connected with the issuer in any capacity at the time of such sale; any investment manager of an issuer that is a pooled investment fund; any person that has been or will be paid (directly or indirectly) remuneration for solicitation of purchasers in connection with such sale of securities; any general partner or managing member of any such investment manager or solicitor; or any director, executive officer or other officer participating in the offering of any such investment manager or solicitor or general partner or managing member of such investment manager or solicitor:

(i) Has been convicted, within ten years before such sale (or five years, in the case of issuers, their predecessors and affiliated issuers), of any felony or misdemeanor:

(A) In connection with the purchase or sale of any security;

(B) Involving the making of any false filing with the Commission; or

(C) Arising out of the conduct of the business of an underwriter, broker, dealer, municipal securities dealer, investment adviser or paid solicitor of purchasers of securities;

(ii) Is subject to any order, judgment or decree of any court of competent jurisdiction, entered within five years before such sale, that, at the time of such sale, restrains or enjoins such person from engaging or continuing to engage in any conduct or practice:

(A) In connection with the purchase or sale of any security;

(B) Involving the making of any false filing with the Commission; or

(C) Arising out of the conduct of the business of an underwriter, broker, dealer, municipal securities dealer, investment adviser or paid solicitor of purchasers of securities;

(iii) Is subject to a final order of a state securities commission (or an agency or officer of a state performing like functions); a state authority that supervises or examines banks, savings associations, or credit unions; a state insurance commission (or an agency or officer of a state performing like functions); an appropriate federal banking agency; the U.S. Commodity Futures Trading Commission; or the National Credit Union Administration that:

(A) At the time of such sale, bars the person from:

(*1*) Association with an entity regulated by such commission, authority, agency, or officer;

(*2*) Engaging in the business of securities, insurance or banking; or

(*3*) Engaging in savings association or credit union activities; or

(B) Constitutes a final order based on a violation of any law or regulation that prohibits fraudulent, manipulative, or deceptive conduct entered within ten years before such sale;

(iv) Is subject to an order of the Commission entered pursuant to section 15(b) or 15B(c) of the Securities Exchange Act of 1934 or section 203(e) or (f) of the Investment Advisers Act of 1940 that, at the time of such sale:

(A) Suspends or revokes such person's registration as a broker, dealer, municipal securities dealer or investment adviser;

(B) Places limitations on the activities, functions or operations of such person; or

(C) Bars such person from being associated with any entity or from participating in the offering of any penny stock;

(v) Is subject to any order of the Commission entered within five years before such sale that, at the time of such sale, orders the person to cease and desist from committing or causing a violation or future violation of:

(A) Any scienter-based anti-fraud provision of the federal securities laws, including without limitation section 17(a)(1) of the Securities Act of 1933, section 10(b) of the Securities Exchange Act of 1934 and Rule 10b–5, section 15(c)(1) of the Securities Exchange Act of 1934, and section 206 (1) of the Investment Advisers Act of 1940, or any other rule or regulation thereunder; or

(B) Section 5 of the Securities Act of 1933.

(vi) Is suspended or expelled from membership in, or suspended or barred from association with a member of, a registered national securities exchange or a registered national or affiliated securities association for any act or omission to act constituting conduct inconsistent with just and equitable principles of trade;

(vii) Has filed (as a registrant or issuer), or was or was named as an underwriter in, any registration statement or Regulation A offering statement filed with the Commission that, within five years before such sale, was the subject of a refusal order, stop order, or order suspending the Regulation A exemption, or is, at the time of such sale, the subject of an investigation or proceeding to determine whether a stop order or suspension order should be issued; or

(viii) Is subject to a United States Postal Service false representation order entered within five years before such sale, or is, at the time of such sale, subject to a temporary restraining order or preliminary injunction with respect to conduct alleged by the United States Postal Service to constitute a scheme or device for obtaining money or property through the mail by means of false representations.

(2) Paragraph (d)(1) of this section shall not apply:

(i) With respect to any conviction, order, judgment, decree, suspension, expulsion or bar that occurred or was issued before September 23, 2013;

(ii) Upon a showing of good cause and without prejudice to any other action by the Commission, if the Commission determines that it is not necessary under the circumstances that an exemption be denied;

(iii) If, before the relevant sale, the court or regulatory authority that entered the relevant order, judgment or decree advises in writing (whether contained in the relevant judgment, order or decree or separately to the Commission or its staff) that disqualification under paragraph (d)(1) of this section should not arise as a consequence of such order, judgment or decree; or

(iv) If the issuer establishes that it did not know and, in the exercise of reasonable care, could not have known that a disqualification existed under paragraph (d)(1) of this section.

Instruction to paragraph (d)(2)(iv). An issuer will not be able to establish that it has exercised reasonable care unless it has made, in light of the circumstances, factual inquiry into whether any disqualifications exist. The nature and scope of the factual inquiry will vary based on the facts and circumstances concerning, among other things, the issuer and the other offering participants.

(3) For purposes of paragraph (d)(1) of this section, events relating to any affiliated issuer that occurred before the affiliation arose will be not considered disqualifying if the affiliated entity is not:

(i) In control of the issuer; or

(ii) Under common control with the issuer by a third party that was in control of the affiliated entity at the time of such events.

(e) *Disclosure of prior "bad actor" events.* The issuer shall furnish to each purchaser, a reasonable time prior to sale, a description in writing of any matters that would have triggered disqualification under paragraph (d)(1) of this section but occurred before September 23, 2013. The failure to furnish such information timely shall not prevent an issuer from relying on this section if the issuer establishes that it did not know and, in the exercise of reasonable care, could not have known of the existence of the undisclosed matter or matters.

Instruction to paragraph (e). An issuer will not be able to establish that it has exercised reasonable care unless it has made, in light of the circumstances, factual inquiry into whether any disqualifications exist. The nature and scope of the factual inquiry will vary based on the facts and circumstances concerning, among other things, the issuer and the other offering participants.

Rule 507. Disqualifying provision relating to exemptions under Rules 504 and 506

(a) No exemption under Rules 504 or 506 shall be available for an issuer if such issuer, any of its predecessors or affiliates have been subject to any order, judgment, or decree of any court of competent jurisdiction temporarily, preliminary or permanently enjoining such person for failure to comply with Rule 503.

(b) Paragraph (a) of this rule shall not apply if the Commission determines, upon a showing of good cause, that it is not necessary under the circumstances that the exemption be denied.

Rule 508. Insignificant deviations from a term, condition or requirement of Regulation D

(a) A failure to comply with a term, condition or requirement of Rules 504 or 506 will not result in the loss of the exemption from the requirements of section 5 of the Act for any offer or sale to a particular individual or entity, if the person relying on the exemption shows:

(1) The failure to comply did not pertain to a term, condition or requirement directly intended to protect that particular individual or entity; and

(2) The failure to comply was insignificant with respect to the offering as a whole, provided that any failure to comply with paragraph (c) of Rule 502, paragraph (b)(2) of Rule 504 and paragraph (b)(2)(i) of Rule 506 shall be deemed to be significant to the offering as a whole; and

(3) A good faith and reasonable attempt was made to comply with all applicable terms, conditions and requirements of Rules 504 or 506.

(b) A transaction made in reliance on Rules 504 or 506 shall comply with all applicable terms, conditions and requirements of Regulation D. Where an exemption is established only through reliance upon paragraph (a) of this rule, the failure to comply shall nonetheless be actionable by the Commission under section 20 of the Act.

EXEMPTION FOR CERTAIN COMPENSATORY BENEFIT PLANS

Rule 701. Exemption for offers and sales of securities pursuant to certain compensatory benefit plans and contracts relating to compensation

PRELIMINARY NOTES

1. This rule relates to transactions exempted from the registration requirements of section 5 of the Act (15 U.S.C. 77e). These transactions are not exempt from the antifraud, civil liability, or other provisions of the federal securities laws. Issuers and persons acting on their behalf have an obligation to provide investors with disclosure adequate to satisfy the antifraud provisions of the federal securities laws.

2. In addition to complying with this rule, the issuer also must comply with any applicable state law relating to the offer and sale of securities.

3. An issuer that attempts to comply with this rule, but fails to do so, may claim any other exemption that is available.

4. This rule is available only to the issuer of the securities. Affiliates of the issuer may not use this rule to offer or sell securities. This rule also does not cover resales of securities by any person. This rule provides an exemption only for the transactions in which the securities are offered or sold by the issuer, not for the securities themselves.

5. The purpose of this rule is to provide an exemption from the registration requirements of the Act for securities issued in compensatory circumstances. This rule is not available for plans or schemes to circumvent this purpose, such as to raise capital. This rule also is not available to exempt any transaction that is in technical compliance with this rule but is part of a plan or scheme to evade the reg-

istration provisions of the Act. In any of these cases, registration under the Act is required unless another exemption is available.

(a) *Exemption.* Offers and sales made in compliance with all of the conditions of this rule are exempt from section 5 of the Act (15 U.S.C. 77e).

(b) *Issuers Eligible to Use This Rule.* (1) *General.* This rule is available to any issuer that is not subject to the reporting requirements of section 13 or 15(d) of the Securities Exchange Act of 1934 (the "Exchange Act") (15 U.S.C. 78m or 78o(d)) and is not an investment company registered or required to be registered under the Investment Company Act of 1940 (15 U.S.C. 80a–1 *et seq.*).

(2) *Issuers that Become Subject to Reporting.* If an issuer becomes subject to the reporting requirements of section 13 or 15(d) of the Exchange Act (15 U.S.C. 78m or 78o(d)) after it has made offers complying with this rule, the issuer may nevertheless rely on this rule to sell the securities previously offered to the persons to whom those offers were made.

(3) *Guarantees by Reporting Companies.* An issuer subject to the reporting requirements of section 13 or 15(d) of the Exchange Act (15 U.S.C. 78m, 78o(d)) may rely on this rule if it is merely guaranteeing the payment of a subsidiary's securities that are sold under this rule.

(c) *Transactions Exempted by This Rule.* This rule exempts offers and sales of securities (including plan interests and guarantees pursuant to paragraph (d)(2)(ii) of this rule) under a written compensatory benefit plan (or written compensation contract) established by the issuer, its parents, its majority-owned subsidiaries or majority-owned subsidiaries of the issuer's parent, for the participation of their employees, directors, general partners, trustees (where the issuer is a business trust), officers, or consultants and advisors, and their family members who acquire such securities from such persons through gifts or domestic relations orders. This rule exempts offers and sales to former employees, directors, general partners, trustees, officers, consultants and advisors only if such persons were employed by or providing services to the issuer at the time the securities were offered. In addition, the term "employee" includes insurance agents who are exclusive agents of the issuer, its subsidiaries or parents, or derive more than 50% of their annual income from those entities.

(1) *Special Requirements for Consultants and Advisors.* This rule is available to consultants and advisors only if:

(i) They are natural persons;

(ii) They provide *bona fide* services to the issuer, its parents, its majority-owned subsidiaries or majority-owned subsidiaries of the issuer's parent; and

(iii) The services are not in connection with the offer or sale of securities in a capital-raising transaction, and do not directly or indirectly promote or maintain a market for the issuer's securities.

(2) *Definition of "Compensatory Benefit Plan."* For purposes of this rule, a *compensatory benefit plan* is any purchase, savings, option, bonus, stock appreciation, profit sharing, thrift, incentive, deferred compensation, pension or similar plan.

(3) *Definition of "Family Member."* For purposes of this rule, *family member* includes any child, stepchild, grandchild, parent, stepparent, grandparent, spouse, former spouse, sibling, niece, nephew, mother-in-law, father-in-law, son-in-law, daughter-in-law, brother-in-law, or sister-in-law, including adoptive relationships, any person sharing the employee's household (other than a tenant or employee), a trust in which these persons have more than fifty percent of the beneficial interest, a foundation in which these persons (or the employee) control the management of assets, and any other entity in which these persons (or the employee) own more than fifty percent of the voting interests.

(d) *Amounts that May Be Sold.* (1) *Offers.* Any amount of securities may be offered in reliance on this rule. However, for purposes of this rule, sales of securities underlying options must be counted as sales on the date of the option grant.

(2) *Sales.* The aggregate sales price or amount of securities sold in reliance on this rule during any consecutive 12–month period must not exceed the greatest of the following:

(i) $1,000,000;

(ii) 15% of the total assets of the issuer (or of the issuer's parent if the issuer is a wholly-owned subsidiary and the securities represent obligations that the parent fully and unconditionally guarantees), measured at the issuer's most recent balance sheet date (if no older than its last fiscal year end); or

(iii) 15% of the outstanding amount of the class of securities being offered and sold in reliance on this rule, measured at the issuer's most recent balance sheet date (if no older than its last fiscal year end).

(3) *Rules for Calculating Prices and Amounts.* (i) *Aggregate Sales Price.* The term *aggregate sales price* means the sum of all cash, property, notes, cancellation of debt or other consideration received or to be received by the issuer for the sale of the securities. Non-cash consideration must be valued by reference to *bona fide* sales of that consideration made within a reasonable time or, in the absence of such sales, on the fair value as determined by an accepted standard. The value of services exchanged for securities issued must be measured by reference to the value of the securities issued. Options must be valued based on the exercise price of the option.

(ii) *Time of the Calculation.* With respect to options to purchase securities, the aggregate sales price is determined when an option grant is made (without regard to when the option becomes exercisable). With respect to other securities, the calculation is made on the date of sale. With respect to deferred compensation or similar plans, the calculation is made when the irrevocable election to defer is made.

(iii) *Derivative Securities.* In calculating outstanding securities for purposes of paragraph (d)(2)(iii) of this rule, treat the securities underlying all currently exercisable or convertible options, warrants, rights or other securities, other than those issued under this exemption, as outstanding. In calculating the amount of securities sold for other purposes of paragraph (d)(2) of this rule, count the amount of securities that would be acquired upon exercise or conversion in connection with sales of options, warrants, rights or other exercisable or convertible securities, including those to be issued under this exemption.

(iv) *Other Exemptions.* Amounts of securities sold in reliance on this rule do not affect "aggregate offering prices" in other exemptions, and amounts of securities sold in reliance on other exemptions do not affect the amount that may be sold in reliance on this rule.

(e) *Disclosure that Must be Provided.* The issuer must deliver to investors a copy of the compensatory benefit plan or the contract, as applicable. In addition, if the aggregate sales price or amount of securities sold during any consecutive 12-month period exceeds $10 million, the issuer must deliver the following disclosure to investors a reasonable period of time before the date of sale:

(1) If the plan is subject to the Employee Retirement Income Security Act of 1974 ("ERISA") (29 U.S.C. 1104–1107), a copy of the summary plan description required by ERISA;

(2) If the plan is not subject to ERISA, a summary of the material terms of the plan;

(3) Information about the risks associated with investment in the securities sold pursuant to the compensatory benefit plan or compensation contract; and

(4) Financial statements required to be furnished by Part F/S of Form 1–A (Regulation A Offering Statement) (17 CFR 239.90) under Regulation A (Rules 251 through 263). Foreign private issuers as defined in Rule 405 must provide a reconciliation to generally accepted accounting principles in the United States (U.S. GAAP) if their financial statements are not prepared in accordance with U.S. GAAP or International Financial Reporting Standards as issued by the International Accounting Standards Board (Item 17 of Form 20–F (17 CFR 249.220f)). The financial statements required by this rule must be as of a date no more than 180 days before the sale of securities in reliance on this exemption.

(5) If the issuer is relying on paragraph (d)(2)(ii) of this rule to use its parent's total assets to determine the amount of securities that may be sold, the parent's financial statements must be delivered. If the parent is subject to the reporting requirements of section 13 or 15(d) of the Exchange Act (15 U.S.C. 78m or 78o(d)), the financial statements of the parent required by Rule 10–01 of Regulation S–X and Item 310 of Regulation S–B, as applicable, must be delivered.

(6) If the sale involves a stock option or other derivative security, the issuer must deliver disclosure a reasonable period of time before the date of exercise or conversion. For deferred compensation or similar plans, the issuer must deliver disclosure to investors a reasonable period of time before the date the irrevocable election to defer is made.

(f) *No Integration with Other Offerings.* Offers and sales exempt under this rule are deemed to be a part of a single, discrete offering and are not subject to integration with any other offers or sales, whether registered under the Act or otherwise exempt from the registration requirements of the Act.

(g) *Resale Limitations.* (1) Securities issued under this rule are deemed to be "restricted securities" as defined in Rule 144.

(2) Resales of securities issued pursuant to this rule must be in compliance with the registration requirements of the Act or an exemption from those requirements.

(3) Ninety days after the issuer becomes subject to the reporting requirements of section 13 or 15(d) of the Exchange Act (15 U.S.C. 78m or 78o(d)), securities issued under this rule may be resold by persons who are not affiliates (as defined in Rule 144) in reliance on Rule 144, without compliance with paragraphs (c) and (d) of Rule 144, and by affiliates without compliance with paragraph (d) of Rule 144.

EXEMPTIONS FOR CROSS–BORDER RIGHTS OFFERINGS, EXCHANGE OFFERS AND BUSINESS COMBINATIONS

GENERAL NOTES TO RULES 800, 801 AND 802

1. Rules 801 and 802 relate only to the applicability of the registration provisions of the Act (15 U.S.C. 77e) and not to the applicability of the anti-fraud, civil liability or other provisions of the federal securities laws.

2. The exemptions provided by Rules 801 and 802 are not available for any securities transaction or series of transactions that technically complies with Rules 801 and 802 but are part of a plan or scheme to evade the registration provisions of the Act.

3. An issuer who relies on Rule 801 or an offeror who relies on Rule 802 must still comply with the securities registration or broker-dealer registration requirements of the Securities Exchange Act of 1934 (15 U.S.C. 78a *et seq.*) and any other applicable provisions of the federal securities laws.

4. An issuer who relies on Rule 801 or an offeror who relies on Rule 802 must still comply with any applicable state laws relating to the offer and sale of securities.

5. Attempted compliance with Rules 801 or 802 does not act as an exclusive election; an issuer making an offer or sale of securities in reliance on Rules 801 or 802 may also rely on any other applicable exemption from the registration requirements of the Act.

6. Rules 801 and 802 provide exemptions only for the issuer of the securities and not for any affiliate of that issuer or for any other person for resales of the issuer's securities. These sections provide exemptions only for the transaction in which the issuer or other person offers or sells the securities, not for the securities themselves. Securities acquired in a Rules 801 or 802 transaction may be resold in the United States only if they are registered under the Act or an exemption from registration is available.

7. Unregistered offers and sales made outside the United States will not affect contemporaneous offers and sales made in compliance with Rules 801 or 802. A transaction that complies with Rules 801 or 802 will not be integrated with offerings exempt under other provisions of the Act, even if both transactions occur at the same time.

8. Securities acquired in a rights offering under Rule 801 are "restricted securities" within the meaning of Rule 144(a)(3) to the same extent and proportion that the securities held by the security holder as of the record date for the rights offering were restricted securities. Likewise, securities acquired in an exchange offer or business combination subject to Rule 802 are "restricted securities" within the meaning of Rule 144(a)(3) to the same extent and proportion that the securities tendered or exchanged by the security holder in that transaction were restricted securities.

9. Rule 801 does not apply to a rights offering by an investment company registered or required to be registered under the Investment Company Act of 1940 (15 U.S.C. 80a–1 *et seq.*), other than a registered closed-end investment company. Rule 802 does not apply to exchange offers or business combinations by an investment company registered or required to be registered under the Investment Company Act of 1940 (15 U.S.C. 80a–1 *et seq.*), other than a registered closed-end investment company.

Rule 800. Definitions for Rules 800, 801, and 802

The following definitions apply in Rules 800, 801 and 802.

(a) *Business Combination. Business combination* means a statutory amalgamation, merger, arrangement or other reorganization requiring the vote of security holders of one or more of the participating companies. It also includes a statutory short form merger that does not require a vote of security holders.

(b) *Equity Security. Equity security* means the same as in Rules 3a11–1 under the Securities Exchange Act of 1934, but for purposes of this rule only does not include:

(1) Any debt security that is convertible into an equity security, with or without consideration;

(2) Any debt security that includes a warrant or right to subscribe to or purchase an equity security;

(3) Any such warrant or right; or

(4) Any put, call, straddle, or other option or privilege that gives the holder the option of buying or selling a security but does not require the holder to do so.

(c) *Exchange Offer. Exchange offer* means a tender offer in which securities are issued as consideration.

(d) *Foreign Private Issuer. Foreign private issuer* means the same as in Rule 405 of Regulation C.

(e) *Foreign Subject Company. Foreign subject company* means any foreign private issuer whose securities are the subject of the exchange offer or business combination.

(f) *Home Jurisdiction. Home jurisdiction* means both the jurisdiction of the foreign subject company's (or in the case of a rights offering, the foreign private issuer's) incorporation, organization or chartering and the principal foreign market where the foreign subject company's (or in the case of a rights offering, the issuer's) securities are listed or quoted.

(g) *Rights Offering. Rights offering* means offers and sales for cash of equity securities where:

(1) The issuer grants the existing security holders of a particular class of equity securities (including holders of depositary receipts evidencing those securities) the right to purchase or subscribe for additional securities of that class; and

(2) The number of additional shares an existing security holder may purchase initially is in proportion to the number of securities he or she holds of record on the record date for the rights offering. If an existing security holder holds depositary receipts, the proportion must be calculated as if the underlying securities were held directly.

(h) *U.S. Holder*. U.S. holder means any security holder resident in the United States. To determine the percentage of outstanding securities held by U.S. holders:

(1) Calculate the percentage of outstanding securities held by U.S. holders as of a date no more than 60 days before or 30 days after the public announcement of a business combination conducted under Rule 802 or of the record date in a rights offering conducted under Rule 801. For a business combination conducted under Rule 802, if you are unable to calculate as of a date within these time frames, the calculation may be made as of the most recent practicable date before public announcement, but in no event earlier than 120 days before public announcement.

(2) Include securities underlying American Depositary Shares convertible or exchangeable into the securities that are the subject of the tender offer when calculating the number of subject securities outstanding, as well as the number held by U.S. holders. Exclude from the calculation other types of securities that are convertible or exchangeable into the securities that are the subject of the tender offer, such as warrants, options and convertible securities. Exclude from those calculations securities held by the acquiror in an exchange offer or business combination;

(3) Use the method of calculating record ownership in Rule 12g3–2(a) under the Securities Exchange Act of 1934, except that your inquiry as to the amount of securities represented by accounts of customers resident in the United States may be limited to brokers, dealers, banks and other nominees located in the United States, the subject company's jurisdiction of incorporation or that of each participant in a business combination, and the jurisdiction that is the primary trading market for the subject securities, if different from the subject company's jurisdiction of incorporation;

(4) If, after reasonable inquiry, you are unable to obtain information about the amount of securities represented by accounts of customers resident in the United States, you may assume, for purposes of this provision, that the customers are residents of the jurisdiction in which the nominee has its principal place of business.

(5) Count securities as owned by U.S. holders when publicly filed reports of beneficial ownership or information that is otherwise provided to you indicates that the securities are held by U.S. residents.

(6) For exchange offers conducted pursuant to Rule 802 by persons other than the issuer of the subject securities or its affiliates that are not made pursuant to an agreement with the issuer of the subject securities, the issuer of the subject securities will be presumed to be a foreign private issuer and U.S. holders will be presumed to hold 10 percent or less of the outstanding subject securities, unless paragraphs (h)(7)(i), (ii) or (iii) of this rule indicate otherwise.

(7) For rights offerings and business combinations, including exchange offers conducted pursuant to Rule 802, where the offeror is unable to conduct the analysis of U.S. ownership set forth in paragraph (h)(3) of this rule, the issuer of the subject securities will be presumed to be a foreign private issuer and U.S. holders will be presumed to hold 10 percent or less of the outstanding subject securities so long as there is a primary trading market for the subject securities outside the United States, as defined in Rule 12h–6(f)(5) under the Securities Exchange Act of 1934, unless:

(i) Average daily trading volume of the subject securities in the United States for a recent twelve-month period ending on a date no more than 60 days before the public announcement of the business combination or of the record date for a rights offering exceeds 10 percent of the average daily trading volume of that class of securities on a worldwide basis for the same period; or

(ii) The most recent annual report or annual information filed or submitted by the issuer with securities regulators of the home jurisdiction or with the Commission or any jurisdiction in which the subject securities trade before the public announcement of the offer indicates that U.S. holders hold more than 10 percent of the outstanding subject class of securities; or

(iii) The acquiror or issuer knows or has reason to know, before the public announcement of the offer, that the level of U.S. ownership exceeds 10 percent of such securities. As an example, an acquiror or issuer is deemed to know information about U.S. ownership of the subject class of securities that is publicly available and that appears in any filing with the Commission or any regulatory body in the issuer's jurisdiction of incorporation or (if different) the non-U.S. jurisdiction in which the primary trading market for the subject securities is located. The acquiror in a business combination is deemed to know information about U.S. ownership available from the issuer. The acquiror or issuer is deemed to know information obtained or readily available from any other source that is reasonably reliable, including from persons it has retained to advise it about the transaction, as well as from third-party information providers. These examples are not intended to be exclusive.

(i) *United States. United States* means the United States of America, its territories and possessions, any State of the United States, and the District of Columbia.

Rule 801. Exemption in connection with a rights offering

A rights offering is exempt from the provisions of Section 5 of the Act (15 U.S.C. 77e), so long as the following conditions are satisfied:

(a) *Conditions.* (1) *Eligibility of Issuer.* The issuer is a foreign private issuer on the date the securities are first offered to U.S. holders.

(2) *Limitation on U.S. Ownership.* U.S. holders hold no more than 10 percent of the outstanding class of securities that is the subject of the rights offering (as determined under the definition of "U.S. holder" in Rule 800(h)).

(3) *Equal Treatment.* The issuer permits U.S. holders to participate in the rights offering on terms at least as favorable as those offered the other holders of the securities that are the subject of the offer. The issuer need not, however, extend the rights offering to security holders in those states or jurisdictions that require registration or qualification.

(4) *Informational Documents.*

(i) If the issuer publishes or otherwise disseminates an informational document to the holders of the securities in connection with the rights offering, the issuer must furnish that informational document, including any amendments thereto, in English, to the Commission on Form CB (17 CFR 239.800) by the first business day after publication or dissemination. If the issuer is a foreign company, it must also file a Form F–X (17 CFR 239.42) with the Commission at the same time as the submission of Form CB to appoint an agent for service in the United States.

(ii) The issuer must disseminate any informational document to U.S. holders, including any amendments thereto, in English, on a comparable basis to that provided to security holders in the home jurisdiction.

(iii) If the issuer disseminates by publication in its home jurisdiction, the issuer must publish the information in the United States in a manner reasonably calculated to inform U.S. holders of the offer.

(5) *Eligibility of Securities.* The securities offered in the rights offering are equity securities of the same class as the securities held by the offerees in the United States directly or through American Depositary Receipts.

(6) *Limitation on Transferability of Rights.* The terms of the rights prohibit transfers of the rights by U.S. holders except in accordance with Regulation S (Rules 901 through 905).

(b) *Legends.* The following legend or an equivalent statement in clear, plain language, to the extent applicable, appears on the cover page or other prominent portion of any informational document the issuer disseminates to U.S. holders:

This rights offering is made for the securities of a foreign company. The offer is subject to the disclosure requirements of a foreign country that are different from those of the United States. Financial statements included in the document, if any, have been prepared in accordance with foreign accounting standards that may not be comparable to the financial statements of United States companies.

It may be difficult for you to enforce your rights and any claim you may have arising under the federal securities laws, since the issuer is located in a foreign country, and some or all of its officers and directors may be residents of a foreign country. You may not be able to sue the foreign company or its officers or directors in a foreign court for violations of the U.S. securities laws. It may be difficult to compel a foreign company and its affiliates to subject themselves to a U.S. court's judgment.

Rule 802. Exemption for offerings in connection with an exchange offer or business combination for the securities of foreign private issuers

Offers and sales in any exchange offer for a class of securities of a foreign private issuer, or in any exchange of securities for the securities of a foreign private issuer in any business combination, are exempt from the provisions of section 5 of the Act (15 U.S.C. 77e), if they satisfy the following conditions:

(a) *Conditions to Be Met.* (1) *Limitation on U.S. Ownership.* Except in the case of an exchange offer or business combination that is commenced during the pendency of a prior exchange offer or business combination made in reliance on this paragraph, U.S. holders of the foreign subject company must hold no more than 10 percent of the securities that are the subject of the exchange offer or business combination (as determined under the definition of "U.S. holder" in Rule 800(h)). In the case of a business combination in which the securities are to be issued by a successor registrant, U.S. holders may hold no more than 10 percent of the class of securities of the successor registrant, as if measured immediately after completion of the business combination.

(2) *Equal treatment.* The offeror must permit U.S. holders to participate in the exchange offer or business combination on terms at least as favorable as those offered any other holder of the subject securities. The offeror, however, need not extend the offer to security holders in those states or jurisdictions that require registration or qualification, except that the offeror must offer the same cash alternative to security holders in any such state that it has offered to security holders in any other state or jurisdiction.

(3) *Informational documents.* (i) If the offeror publishes or otherwise disseminates an informational document to the holders of the subject securities in connection with the exchange offer or business combination, the offeror must furnish that informational document, including any amendments thereto, in English, to the Commission on Form CB (17 CFR 239.800) by the first business day after publication or dissemination. If the offeror is a foreign company, it must also file a Form F–X (17 CFR 239.42) with the Commission at the same time as the submission of the Form CB to appoint an agent for service of process in the United States.

(ii) The offeror must disseminate any informational document to U.S. holders, including any amendments thereto, in English, on a comparable basis to that provided to security holders in the foreign subject company's home jurisdiction.

(iii) If the offeror disseminates by publication in its home jurisdiction, the offeror must publish the information in the United States in a manner reasonably calculated to inform U.S. holders of the offer.

(b) *Legends.* The following legend or an equivalent statement in clear, plain language, to the extent applicable, must be included on the cover page or other prominent portion of any informational document the offeror publishes or disseminates to U.S. holders:

This exchange offer or business combination is made for the securities of a foreign company. The offer is subject to disclosure requirements of a foreign country that are different from those of the United States. Financial statements included in the document, if any, have been prepared in accordance with foreign accounting standards that may not be comparable to the financial statements of United States companies.

It may be difficult for you to enforce your rights and any claim you may have arising under the federal securities laws, since the issuer is located in a foreign country, and some or all of its officers and directors may be residents of a foreign country. You may not be able to sue a foreign company or its officers or directors in a foreign court for violations of the U.S. securities laws. It may be difficult to compel a foreign company and its affiliates to subject themselves to a U.S. court's judgment.

You should be aware that the issuer may purchase securities otherwise than under the exchange offer, such as in open market or privately negotiated purchases.

REGULATION S—RULES GOVERNING OFFERS AND SALES MADE OUTSIDE THE UNITED STATES WITHOUT REGISTRATION UNDER THE SECURITIES ACT OF 1933

PRELIMINARY NOTES

1. The following rules relate solely to the application of Section 5 of the Securities Act of 1933 (the "Act") and not to antifraud or other provisions of the federal securities laws.

2. In view of the objective of these rules and the policies underlying the Act, Regulation S is not available with respect to any transaction or series of transactions that, although in technical compliance with these rules, is part of a plan or scheme to evade the registration provisions of the Act. In such cases, registration under the Act is required.

3. Nothing in these rules obviates the need for any issuer or any other person to comply with the securities registration or broker-dealer registration requirements of the Securities Exchange Act (the "Exchange Act"), whenever such requirements are applicable.

4. Nothing in these rules obviates the need to comply with any applicable state law relating to the offer and sale of securities.

5. Attempted compliance with any rule in Regulation S does not act as an exclusive election; a person making an offer or sale of securities may also claim the availability of any applicable exemption from the registration requirements of the Act. The availability of the Regulation S safe harbor to offers and sales that occur outside of the United States will not be affected by the subsequent offer and sale of these securities into the United States or to U.S. persons during the distribution compliance period, as long as the subsequent offer and sale are made pursuant to registration or an exemption therefrom under the Act.

6. Regulation S is available only for offers and sales of securities outside the United States. Securities acquired overseas, whether or not pursuant to Regulation S, may be resold in the United States only if they are registered under the Act or an exemption from registration is available.

7. Nothing in these rules precludes access by journalists for publications with a general circulation in the United States to offshore press conferences, press releases and meetings with company press spokespersons in which an offshore offering or tender offer is discussed, provided that the information is made available to the foreign and United States press generally and is not intended to induce purchases of securities by persons in the United States or tenders of securities by United States holders in the case of exchange offers. Where applicable, issuers and bidders may also look to Rule 135e and Rule 14d–1(c) under the Securities Exchange Act of 1934.

8. The provisions of this Regulation S shall not apply to offers and sales of securities issued by open-end investment companies or unit investment trusts registered or required to be registered or closed-end investment companies required to be registered, but not registered, under the Investment Company Act of 1940 (the "1940 Act").

Rule 901. General statement

For the purposes only of section 5 of the Act (15 U.S.C. § 77e), the terms *offer*, *offer to sell*, *sell*, *sale*, and *offer to buy* shall be deemed to include offers and sales that occur within the United States and shall be deemed not to include offers and sales that occur outside the United States.

Rule 902. Definitions

As used in Regulation S, the following terms shall have the meanings indicated.

(a) *Debt Securities.* "Debt securities" of an issuer is defined to mean any security other than an equity security as defined in Rule 405, as well as the following:

(1) Non-participatory preferred stock, which is defined as non-convertible capital stock, the holders of which are entitled to a preference in payment of dividends and in distribution of assets on liquidation, dissolution, or winding up of the issuer, but are not entitled to participate in residual earnings or assets of the issuer; and

(2) Asset-backed securities, which are securities of a type that either:

(i) Represent an ownership interest in a pool of discrete assets, or certificates of interest or participation in such assets (including any rights designed to assure servicing, or the receipt or timeliness of receipt by holders of such assets, or certificates of interest or participation in such assets, of amounts payable thereunder), provided that the assets are not generated or originated between the issuer of the security and its affiliates; or

(ii) Are secured by one or more assets or certificates of interest or participation in such assets, and the securities, by their terms, provide for payments of principal and interest (if any) in relation to payments or reasonable projections of payments on assets meeting the requirements of paragraph (a)(2)(i) of this rule, or certificates of interest or participations in assets meeting such requirements.

(iii) For purposes of paragraph (a)(2) of this rule, the term "assets" means securities, installment sales, accounts receivable, notes, leases or other contracts, or other assets that by their terms convert into cash over a finite period of time.

(b) *Designated Offshore Securities Market.* "Designated offshore securities market" means:

(1) The Eurobond market, as regulated by the International Securities Market Association; the Alberta Stock Exchange; the Amsterdam Stock Exchange; the Australian Stock Exchange Limited; the Bermuda Stock Exchange; the Bourse de Bruxelles; the Copenhagen Stock Exchange; the European Association of Securities Dealers Automated Quotation; the Frankfurt Stock Exchange; the Helsinki Stock Exchange; The Stock Exchange of Hong Kong Limited; the Irish Stock Exchange; the Istanbul Stock Exchange; the Johannesburg Stock Exchange; the London Stock Exchange; the Bourse de Luxembourg; the Mexico Stock Exchange; the Borsa Valori di Milan; the Montreal Stock Exchange; the Oslo Stock Exchange; the Bourse de Paris; the Stock Exchange of Singapore Ltd.; the Stockholm Stock Exchange; the Tokyo Stock Exchange; the Toronto Stock Exchange; the Vancouver Stock Exchange; the Warsaw Stock Exchange and the Zurich Stock Exchange; and

(2) Any foreign securities exchange or non-exchange market designated by the Commission. Attributes to be considered in determining whether to designate an offshore securities market, among others, include:

(i) Organization under foreign law;

(ii) Association with a generally recognized community of brokers, dealers, banks, or other professional intermediaries with an established operating history;

(iii) Oversight by a governmental or self-regulatory body;

(iv) Oversight standards set by an existing body of law;

(v) Reporting of securities transactions on a regular basis to a governmental or self-regulatory body;

(vi) A system for exchange of price quotations through common communications media; and

(vii) An organized clearance and settlement system.

(c) *Directed Selling Efforts.* (1) "Directed selling efforts" means any activity undertaken for the purpose of, or that could reasonably be expected to have the effect of, conditioning the market in the United States for any of the securities being offered in reliance on this Regulation S (Rules 901 through 905, and Preliminary Notes). Such activity includes placing an advertisement in a publication "with a general circulation in the United States" that refers to the offering of securities being made in reliance upon this Regulation S.

(2) Publication "with a general circulation in the United States":

(i) Is defined as any publication that is printed primarily for distribution in the United States, or has had, during the preceding twelve months, an average circulation in the United States of 15,000 or more copies per issue; and

(ii) Will encompass only the U.S. edition of any publication printing a separate U.S. edition if the publication, without considering its U.S. edition would not constitute a publication with a general circulation in the United States.

(3) The following are not "directed selling efforts":

(i) Placing an advertisement required to be published under U.S. or foreign law, or under rules or regulations of a U.S. or foreign regulatory or self-regulatory authority, provided the advertisement contains no more information than legally required and includes a statement to the effect that the securities have not been registered under the Act and may not be offered or sold in the United States (or to a U.S. person, if the advertisement relates to an offering under Category 2 or 3 (paragraph (b)(2) or (b)(3)) in Rule 903) absent registration or an applicable exemption from the registration requirements;

(ii) Contact with persons excluded from the definition of "U.S. person" pursuant to paragraph (k)(2)(vi) of this rule or persons holding accounts excluded from the definition of "U.S. person" pursuant to paragraph (k)(2)(i) of this rule, solely in their capacities as holders of such accounts;

(iii) A tombstone advertisement in any publication with a general circulation in the United States, provided:

(A) The publication has less than 20% of its circulation, calculated by aggregating the circulation of its U.S. and comparable non-U.S. editions, in the United States;

(B) Such advertisement contains a legend to the effect that the securities have not been registered under the Act and may not be offered or sold in the United States (or to a U.S.

person, if the advertisement relates to an offering under Category 2 or 3 (paragraph (b)(2) or (b)(3)) in Rule 903) absent registration or an applicable exemption from the registration requirements; and

(C) Such advertisement contains no more information than:

(*1*) The issuer's name;

(*2*) The amount and title of the securities being sold;

(*3*) A brief indication of the issuer's general type of business;

(*4*) The price of the securities;

(*5*) The yield of the securities, if debt securities with a fixed (non-contingent) interest provision;

(*6*) The name and address of the person placing the advertisement, and whether such person is participating in the distribution;

(*7*) The names of the managing underwriters;

(*8*) The dates, if any, upon which the sales commenced and concluded;

(*9*) Whether the securities are offered or were offered by rights issued to security holders and, if so, the class of securities that are entitled or were entitled to subscribe, the subscription ratio, the record date, the dates (if any) upon which the rights were issued and expired, and the subscription price; and

(*10*) Any legend required by law or any foreign or U.S. regulatory or self-regulatory authority.

(iv) Bona fide visits to real estate, plants or other facilities located in the United States and tours thereof conducted for a prospective investor by an issuer, a distributor, any of their respective affiliates or a person acting on behalf of any of the foregoing;

(v) Distribution in the United States of a foreign broker-dealer's quotations by a third-party system that distributes such quotations primarily in foreign countries if:

(A) Securities transactions cannot be executed between foreign broker-dealers and persons in the United States through the system; and

(B) The issuer, distributors, their respective affiliates, persons acting on behalf of any of the foregoing, foreign broker-dealers and other participants in the system do not initiate contacts with U.S. persons or persons within the United States, beyond those contacts exempted under Rule 15a–6 under the Securities Exchange Act of 1934;

(vi) Publication by an issuer of a notice in accordance with Rules 135 or 135c;

(vii) Providing any journalist with access to press conferences held outside of the United States, to meetings with the issuer or selling security holder representatives conducted outside the United States, or to written press-related materials released outside the United States, at or in which a present or proposed offering of securities is discussed, if the requirements of Rule 135e are satisfied; and

(viii) Publication or distribution of a research report by a broker or dealer in accordance with Rule 138(c) or Rule 139(b).

(d) *Distributor*. "Distributor" means any underwriter, dealer, or other person who participates, pursuant to a contractual arrangement, in the distribution of the securities offered or sold in reliance on this Regulation S (Rules 901 through 905, and Preliminary Notes).

(e) *Domestic Issuer/Foreign Issuer*. "Domestic issuer" means any issuer other than a "foreign government" or "foreign private issuer" (both as defined in Rule 405). "Foreign issuer" means any issuer other than a "domestic issuer."

(f) *Distribution Compliance Period*. "Distribution compliance period" means a period that begins when the securities were first offered to persons other than distributors in reliance upon this Regulation S (Rules 901 through 905, and Preliminary Notes) or the date of closing of the offering, whichever is later, and continues until the end of the period of time specified in the relevant provision of Rule 903, except that:

(1) All offers and sales by a distributor of an unsold allotment or subscription shall be deemed to be made during the distribution compliance period;

(2) In a continuous offering, the distribution compliance period shall commence upon completion of the distribution, as determined and certified by the managing underwriter or person performing similar functions;

(3) In a continuous offering of non-convertible debt securities offered and sold in identifiable tranches, the distribution compliance period for securities in a tranche shall commence upon completion of the distribution of such tranche, as determined and certified by the managing underwriter or person performing similar functions; and

(4) That in a continuous offering of securities to be acquired upon the exercise of warrants, the distribution compliance period shall commence upon completion of the distribution of the warrants, as determined and certified by the managing underwriter or person performing similar functions, if requirements of Rule 903(b)(5) are satisfied.

(g) *Offering Restrictions.* "Offering restrictions" means:

(1) Each distributor agrees in writing:

(i) That all offers and sales of the securities prior to the expiration of the distribution compliance period specified in Category 2 or 3 (paragraph (b)(2) or (b)(3)) in Rule 903, as applicable, shall be made only in accordance with the provisions of Rules 903 or 904; pursuant to registration of the securities under the Act; or pursuant to an available exemption from the registration requirements of the Act; and

(ii) For offers and sales of equity securities of domestic issuers, not to engage in hedging transactions with regard to such securities prior to the expiration of the distribution compliance period specified in Category 2 or 3 (paragraph (b)(2) or (b)(3)) in Rule 903, as applicable, unless in compliance with the Act; and

(2) All offering materials and documents (other than press releases) used in connection with offers and sales of the securities prior to the expiration of the distribution compliance period specified in Category 2 or 3 (paragraph (b)(2) or (b)(3)) in Rule 903, as applicable, shall include statements to the effect that the securities have not been registered under the Act and may not be offered or sold in the United States or to U.S. persons (other than distributors) unless the securities are registered under the Act, or an exemption from the registration requirements of the Act is available. For offers and sales of equity securities of domestic issuers, such offering materials and documents also must state that hedging transactions involving those securities may not be conducted unless in compliance with the Act. Such statements shall appear:

(i) On the cover or inside cover page of any prospectus or offering circular used in connection with the offer or sale of the securities;

(ii) In the underwriting section of any prospectus or offering circular used in connection with the offer or sale of the securities; and

(iii) In any advertisement made or issued by the issuer, any distributor, any of their respective affiliates, or any person acting on behalf of any of the foregoing. Such statements may appear in summary form on prospectus cover pages and in advertisements.

(h) *Offshore Transaction.* (1) An offer or sale of securities is made in an "offshore transaction" if:

(i) The offer is not made to a person in the United States; and

(ii) Either:

(A) At the time the buy order is originated, the buyer is outside the United States, or the seller and any person acting on its behalf reasonably believe that the buyer is outside the United States; or

(B) For purposes of:

(*1*) Rule 903, the transaction is executed in, on or through a physical trading floor of an established foreign securities exchange that is located outside the United States; or

(*2*) Rule 904, the transaction is executed in, on or through the facilities of a designated offshore securities market described in paragraph (b) of this rule, and neither the seller nor any person acting on its behalf knows that the transaction has been pre-arranged with a buyer in the United States.

(2) Notwithstanding paragraph (h)(1) of this rule, offers and sales of securities specifically targeted at identifiable groups of U.S. citizens abroad, such as members of the U.S. armed forces serving overseas, shall not be deemed to be made in "offshore transactions."

(3) Notwithstanding paragraph (h)(1) of this rule, offers and sales of securities to persons excluded from the definition of "U.S. person" pursuant to paragraph (k)(2)(vi) of this rule or persons holding accounts excluded from the definition of

"U.S. person" pursuant to paragraph (k)(2)(i) of this rule solely in their capacities as holders of such accounts, shall be deemed to be made in "offshore transactions."

(4) Notwithstanding paragraph (h)(1) of this rule, publication or distribution of a research report in accordance with Rule 138(c) or Rule 139(b) by a broker or dealer at or around the time of an offering in reliance on Regulation S (Rules 901 through 905) will not cause the transaction to fail to be an offshore transaction as defined in this rule.

(i) *Reporting Issuer.* "Reporting issuer" means an issuer other than an investment company registered or required to register under the 1940 Act that:

(1) Has a class of securities registered pursuant to Section 12(b) or 12(g) of the Exchange Act (15 U.S.C. 78l(b) or 78l(g)) or is required to file reports pursuant to Section 15(d) of the Exchange Act (15 U.S.C. 78o(d)); and

(2) Has filed all the material required to be filed pursuant to Section 13(a) or 15(d) of the Exchange Act (15 U.S.C. 78m(a) or 78o(d)) for a period of at least twelve months immediately preceding the offer or sale of securities made in reliance upon this Regulation S (Rules 901 through 905, and Preliminary Notes) (or for such shorter period that the issuer was required to file such material).

(j) *Substantial U.S. Market Interest.* (1) "Substantial U.S. market interest" with respect to a class of an issuer's equity securities means:

(i) The securities exchanges and inter-dealer quotation systems in the United States in the aggregate constituted the single largest market for such class of securities in the shorter of the issuer's prior fiscal year or the period since the issuer's incorporation; or

(ii) 20 percent or more of all trading in such class of securities took place in, on or through the facilities of securities exchanges and inter-dealer quotation systems in the United States and less than 55 percent of such trading took place in, on or through the facilities of securities markets of a single foreign country in the shorter of the issuer's prior fiscal year or the period since the issuer's incorporation.

(2) "Substantial U.S. market interest" with respect to an issuer's debt securities means:

(i) Its debt securities, in the aggregate, are held of record (as that term is defined in Rule 12g5–1 under the Securities Exchange Act of 1934 and used for purposes of paragraph (j)(2) of this rule) by 300 or more U.S. persons;

(ii) $1 billion or more of: The principal amount outstanding of its debt securities, the greater of liquidation preference or par value of its securities described in Rule 902(a)(1), and the principal amount or principal balance of its securities described in Rule 902(a)(2), in the aggregate is held of record by U.S. persons; and

(iii) 20 percent or more of: The principal amount outstanding of its debt securities, the greater of liquidation preference or par value of its securities described in Rule 902(a)(1), and the principal amount or principal balance of its securities described in Rule 902(a)(2), in the aggregate, is held of record by U.S. persons.

(3) Notwithstanding paragraph (j)(2) of this rule, substantial U.S. market interest with respect to an issuer's debt securities is calculated without reference to securities that qualify for the exemption provided by Section 3(a)(3) of the Act (15 U.S.C. 77c(a)(3)).

(k) *U.S. Person.* (1) "U.S. person" means:

(i) Any natural person resident in the United States;

(ii) Any partnership or corporation organized or incorporated under the laws of the United States;

(iii) Any estate of which any executor or administrator is a U.S. person;

(iv) Any trust of which any trustee is a U.S. person;

(v) Any agency or branch of a foreign entity located in the United States;

(vi) Any non-discretionary account or similar account (other than an estate or trust) held by a dealer or other fiduciary for the benefit or account of a U.S. person;

(vii) Any discretionary account or similar account (other than an estate or trust) held by a dealer or other fiduciary organized, incorporated, or (if an individual) resident in the United States; and

(viii) Any partnership or corporation if:

(A) Organized or incorporated under the laws of any foreign jurisdiction; and

(B) Formed by a U.S. person principally for the purpose of investing in securities not registered under the Act, unless it is organized or incorporated, and owned, by accredited investors (as defined in Rule 501(a)) who are not natural persons, estates or trusts.

(2) The following are not "U.S. persons":

(i) Any discretionary account or similar account (other than an estate or trust) held for the benefit or account of a non-U.S. person by a dealer or other professional fiduciary organized, incorporated, or (if an individual) resident in the United States;

(ii) Any estate of which any professional fiduciary acting as executor or administrator is a U.S. person if:

(A) An executor or administrator of the estate who is not a U.S. person has sole or shared investment discretion with respect to the assets of the estate; and

(B) The estate is governed by foreign law;

(iii) Any trust of which any professional fiduciary acting as trustee is a U.S. person, if a trustee who is not a U.S. person has sole or shared investment discretion with respect to the trust assets, and no beneficiary of the trust (and no settlor if the trust is revocable) is a U.S. person;

(iv) An employee benefit plan established and administered in accordance with the law of a country other than the United States and customary practices and documentation of such country;

(v) Any agency or branch of a U.S. person located outside the United States if:

(A) The agency or branch operates for valid business reasons; and

(B) The agency or branch is engaged in the business of insurance or banking and is subject to substantive insurance or banking regulation, respectively, in the jurisdiction where located; and

(vi) The International Monetary Fund, the International Bank for Reconstruction and Development, the Inter–American Development Bank, the Asian Development Bank, the African Development Bank, the United Nations, and their agencies, affiliates and pension plans, and any other similar international organizations, their agencies, affiliates and pension plans.

(*l*) United States. "United States" means the United States of America, its territories and possessions, any State of the United States, and the District of Columbia.

Rule 903. Offers or sales of securities by the issuer, a distributor, any of their respective affiliates, or any person acting on behalf of any of the foregoing; conditions relating to specific securities

(a) An offer or sale of securities by the issuer, a distributor, any of their respective affiliates, or any person acting on behalf of any of the foregoing, shall be deemed to occur outside the United States within the meaning of Rule 901 if:

(1) The offer or sale is made in an offshore transaction;

(2) No directed selling efforts are made in the United States by the issuer, a distributor, any of their respective affiliates, or any person acting on behalf of any of the foregoing; and

(3) The conditions of paragraph (b) of this rule, as applicable, are satisfied.

(b) *Additional Conditions.* (1) *Category 1.* No conditions other than those set forth in Rule 903(a) apply to securities in this category. Securities are eligible for this category if:

(i) The securities are issued by a foreign issuer that reasonably believes at the commencement of the offering that:

(A) There is no substantial U.S. market interest in the class of securities to be offered or sold (if equity securities are offered or sold);

(B) There is no substantial U.S. market interest in its debt securities (if debt securities are offered or sold);

(C) There is no substantial U.S. market interest in the securities to be purchased upon exercise (if warrants are offered or sold); and

(D) There is no substantial U.S. market interest in either the convertible securities or the underlying securities (if convertible securities are offered or sold);

(ii) The securities are offered and sold in an overseas directed offering, which means:

(A) An offering of securities of a foreign issuer that is directed into a single country other than the United States to the residents thereof and that is made in accordance with the local laws and customary practices and documentation of such country; or

(B) An offering of non-convertible debt securities of a domestic issuer that is directed into a single country other than the United States to the residents thereof and that is made in accordance with the local laws and customary practices and documentation of such country, provided that the principal and interest of the securities (or par value, as applicable) are denominated in a currency other than U.S. dollars and such securities are neither convertible into U.S. dollar-denominated securities nor linked to U.S. dollars (other than through related currency or interest rate swap transactions that are commercial in nature) in a manner that in effect converts the securities to U.S. dollar-denominated securities.

(iii) The securities are backed by the full faith and credit of a foreign government; or

(iv) The securities are offered and sold to employees of the issuer or its affiliates pursuant to an employee benefit plan established and administered in accordance with the law of a country other than the United States, and customary practices and documentation of such country, provided that:

(A) The securities are issued in compensatory circumstances for bona fide services rendered to the issuer or its affiliates in connection with their businesses and such services are not rendered in connection with the offer or sale of securities in a capital-raising transaction;

(B) Any interests in the plan are not transferable other than by will or the laws of descent or distribution;

(C) The issuer takes reasonable steps to preclude the offer and sale of interests in the plan or securities under the plan to U.S. residents other than employees on temporary assignment in the United States; and

(D) Documentation used in connection with any offer pursuant to the plan contains a statement that the securities have not been registered under the Act and may not be offered or sold in the United States unless registered or an exemption from registration is available.

(2) *Category 2.* The following conditions apply to securities that are not eligible for Category 1 (paragraph (b)(1)) of this rule and that are equity securities of a reporting foreign issuer, or debt securities of a reporting issuer or of a non-reporting foreign issuer.

(i) Offering restrictions are implemented;

(ii) The offer or sale, if made prior to the expiration of a 40–day distribution compliance period, is not made to a U.S. person or for the account or benefit of a U.S. person (other than a distributor); and

(iii) Each distributor selling securities to a distributor, a dealer, as defined in section 2(a)(12) of the Act (15 U.S.C. 77b(a)(12)), or a person receiving a selling concession, fee or other remuneration in respect of the securities sold, prior to the expiration of a 40–day distribution compliance period, sends a confirmation or other notice to the purchaser stating that the purchaser is subject to the same restrictions on offers and sales that apply to a distributor.

(3) *Category 3.* The following conditions apply to securities that are not eligible for Category 1 or 2 (paragraph (b)(1) or (b)(2)) of this rule:

(i) Offering restrictions are implemented;

(ii) In the case of debt securities:

(A) The offer or sale, if made prior to the expiration of a 40–day distribution compliance period, is not made to a U.S. person or for the account or benefit of a U.S. person (other than a distributor); and

(B) The securities are represented upon issuance by a temporary global security which is not exchangeable for definitive securities until the expiration of the 40–day distribution compliance period and, for persons other than distributors, until certification of beneficial ownership of the securities by a non-U.S. person or a U.S. person who purchased securities in a transaction that did not require registration under the Act;

(iii) In the case of equity securities:

(A) The offer or sale, if made prior to the expiration of a one-year distribution compliance period (or six–month distribution compliance period if the issuer is a reporting issuer), is not made to a U.S. person or for the account or benefit of a U.S. person (other than a distributor); and

(B) The offer or sale, if made prior to the expiration of a one-year distribution compliance period (or six-month distribution compliance period if the issuer is a reporting issuer), is made pursuant to the following conditions:

(*1*) The purchaser of the securities (other than a distributor) certifies that it is not a U.S. person and is not acquiring the securities for the account or benefit of any U.S. person or is a U.S. person who purchased securities in a transaction that did not require registration under the Act;

(*2*) The purchaser of the securities agrees to resell such securities only in accordance with the provisions of this Regulation S (Rules 901 through 905, and Preliminary Notes), pursuant to registration under the Act, or pursuant to an available exemption from registration; and agrees not to engage in hedging transactions with regard to such securities unless in compliance with the Act;

(*3*) The securities of a domestic issuer contain a legend to the effect that transfer is prohibited except in accordance with the provisions of this Regulation S (Rules 901 through 905, and Preliminary Notes), pursuant to registration under the Act, or pursuant to an available exemption from registration; and that hedging transactions involving those securities may not be conducted unless in compliance with the Act;

(*4*) The issuer is required, either by contract or a provision in its bylaws, articles, charter or comparable document, to refuse to register any transfer of the securities not made in accordance with the provisions of this Regulation S (Rules 901 through 905, and Preliminary Notes), pursuant to registration under the Act, or pursuant to an available exemption from registration; provided, however, that if the securities are in bearer form or foreign law prevents the issuer of the securities from refusing to register securities transfers, other reasonable procedures (such as a legend described in paragraph (b)(3)(iii)(B)(3) of this rule) are implemented to prevent any transfer of the securities not made in accordance with the provisions of this Regulation S; and

(iv) Each distributor selling securities to a distributor, a dealer (as defined in section 2(a)(12) of the Act (15 U.S.C. 77b(a)(12))), or a person receiving a selling concession, fee or other remuneration, prior to the expiration of a 40–day distribution compliance period in the case of debt securities, or a one-year distribution compliance period (or six-month distribution compliance period if the issuer is a reporting issuer) in the case of equity securities, sends a confirmation or other notice to the purchaser stating that the purchaser is subject to the same restrictions on offers and sales that apply to a distributor.

(4) *Guaranteed Securities.* Notwithstanding paragraphs (b)(1) through (b)(3) of this rule, in offerings of debt securities fully and unconditionally guaranteed as to principal and interest by the parent of the issuer of the debt securities, only the requirements of paragraph (b) of this rule that are applicable to the offer and sale of the guarantee must be satisfied with respect to the offer and sale of the guaranteed debt securities.

(5) *Warrants.* An offer or sale of warrants under Category 2 or 3 (paragraph (b)(2) or (b)(3)) of this rule also must comply with the following requirements:

(i) Each warrant must bear a legend stating that the warrant and the securities to be issued upon its exercise have not been registered under the Act and that the warrant may not be exercised by or on behalf of any U.S. person unless registered under the Act or an exemption from such registration is available;

(ii) Each person exercising a warrant is required to give:

(A) Written certification that it is not a U.S. person and the warrant is not being exercised on behalf of a U.S. person; or

(B) A written opinion of counsel to the effect that the warrant and the securities delivered upon exercise thereof have been registered under the Act or are exempt from registration thereunder; and

(iii) Procedures are implemented to ensure that the warrant may not be exercised within the United States, and that the securities may not be delivered within the United States upon exercise, other than in offerings deemed to meet the definition of "offshore transaction" pursuant to Rule 902(h), unless registered under the Act or an exemption from such registration is available.

Rule 904. Offshore resales

(a) An offer or sale of securities by any person other than the issuer, a distributor, any of their respective affiliates (except any officer or director who is an affiliate solely by virtue of holding such position), or any person acting on behalf of any of the foregoing, shall be deemed to occur outside the United States within the meaning of Rule 901 if:

(1) The offer or sale are made in an offshore transaction;

(2) No directed selling efforts are made in the United States by the seller, an affiliate, or any person acting on their behalf; and

(3) The conditions of paragraph (b) of this rule, if applicable, are satisfied.

(b) *Additional Conditions.* (1) *Resales by Dealers and Persons Receiving Selling Concessions.* In the case of an offer or sale of securities prior to the expiration of the distribution compliance period specified in Category 2 or 3 (paragraph (b)(2) or (b)(3)) of Rule 903, as applicable, by a dealer, as defined in Section 2(a)(12) of the Act (15 U.S.C. 77(b)(a)(12)), or a person receiving a selling concession, fee or other remuneration in respect of the securities offered or sold:

(i) Neither the seller nor any person acting on its behalf knows that the offeree or buyer of the securities is a U.S. person; and

(ii) If the seller or any person acting on the seller's behalf knows that the purchaser is a dealer, as defined in Section 2(a)(12) of the Act (15 U.S.C. 77b(a)(12)), or is a person receiving a selling concession, fee or other remuneration in respect of the securities sold, the seller or a person acting on the seller's behalf sends to the purchaser a confirmation or other notice stating that the securities may be offered and sold during the distribution compliance period only in accordance with the provisions of this Regulation S (Rules 901 through 905, and Preliminary Notes); pursuant to registration of the securities under the Act; or pursuant to an available exemption from the registration requirements of the Act.

(2) *Resales by Certain Affiliates.* In the case of an offer or sale of securities by an officer or director of the issuer or a distributor, who is an affiliate of the issuer or distributor solely by virtue of holding such position, no selling concession, fee or other remuneration is paid in connection with such offer or sale other than the usual and customary broker's commission that would be received by a person executing such transaction as agent.

Rule 905. Resale limitations

Equity securities of domestic issuers acquired from the issuer, a distributor, or any of their respective affiliates in a transaction subject to the conditions of Rule 901 or Rule 903 are deemed to be "restricted securities" as defined in Rule 144. Resales of any of such restricted securities by the offshore purchaser must be made in accordance with this Regulation S (Rules 901 through 905, and Preliminary Notes), the registration requirements of the Act or an exemption therefrom. Any "restricted securities," as defined in Rule 144, that are equity securities of a domestic issuer will continue to be deemed to be restricted securities, notwithstanding that they were acquired in a resale transaction made pursuant to Rule 901 or Rule 904.

REGULATION CE—COORDINATED EXEMPTIONS FOR CERTAIN ISSUES OF SECURITIES EXEMPT UNDER STATE LAW

Rule 1001. Exemption for transactions exempt from qualification under § 25102(n) of the California Corporations Code

PRELIMINARY NOTES

(1) Nothing in this rule is intended to be or should be construed as in any way relieving issuers or persons acting on behalf of issuers from providing disclosure to prospective investors necessary to satisfy the antifraud provisions of the federal securities laws. This rule only provides an exemption from the registration requirements of the Securities Act of 1933 ("the Act") [15 U.S.C. 77a *et seq.*].

(2) Nothing in this rule obviates the need to comply with any applicable state law relating to the offer and sales of securities.

(3) Attempted compliance with this rule does not act as an exclusive election; the issuer also can claim the availability of any other applicable exemption.

(4) This exemption is not available to any issuer for any transaction which, while in technical compliance with the provision of this rule, is part of a plan or scheme to evade the registration provisions of the Act. In such cases, registration under the Act is required.

(a) *Exemption.* Offers and sales of securities that satisfy the conditions of paragraph (n) of § 25102 of the California Corporations Code, and paragraph (b) of this section, shall be exempt from the provisions of Section 5 of the Securities Act of 1933 by virtue of Section 3(b) of that Act.

(b) *Limitation on and Computation of Offering Price.* The sum of all cash and other consideration to be received for the securities shall not exceed $5,000,000, less the aggregate offering price for all other securities sold in the same offering of securities, whether pursuant to this or another exemption.

(c) *Resale Limitations.* Securities issued pursuant to this Rule 1001 are deemed to be "restricted securities" as defined in Securities Act Rule 144. Resales of such securities must be made in compliance with the registration requirements of the Act or an exemption therefrom.

REGULATION CROWDFUNDING, GENERAL RULES AND REGULATIONS

(Cite as 17 CFR §227.__)

Subpart A – General Crowdfunding Exemption and Requirements

Rule 100. Crowdfunding exemption and requirements

(a) *Exemption*. An issuer may offer or sell securities in reliance on section 4(a)(6) of the Securities Act of 1933 (the "Securities Act") (15 U.S.C. 77d(a)(6)), provided that:

(1) The aggregate amount of securities sold to all investors by the issuer in reliance on section 4(a)(6) of the Securities Act (15 U.S.C. 77d(a)(6)) during the 12-month period preceding the date of such offer or sale, including the securities offered in such transaction, shall not exceed $1,070,000;

(2) The aggregate amount of securities sold to any investor across all issuers in reliance on section 4(a)(6) of the Securities Act (15 U.S.C. 77d(a)(6)) during the 12-month period preceding the date of such transaction, including the securities sold to such investor in such transaction, shall not exceed:

(i) The greater of $2,200 or 5 percent of the lesser of the investor's annual income or net worth if either the investor's annual income or net worth is less than $107,000; or

(ii) 10 percent of the lesser of the investor's annual income or net worth, not to exceed an amount sold of $107,000, if both the investor's annual income and net worth are equal to or more than $107,000;

Instruction 1 to paragraph (a)(2). To determine the investment limit for a natural person, the person's annual income and net worth shall be calculated as those values are calculated for purposes of determining accredited investor status in accordance with Rule 501 of this chapter.

Instruction 2 to paragraph (a)(2). A person's annual income and net worth may be calculated jointly with that person's spouse; however, when such a joint calculation is used, the aggregate investment of the investor spouses may not exceed the limit that would apply to an individual investor at that income or net worth level.

Instruction 3 to paragraph (a)(2). An issuer offering and selling securities in reliance on section 4(a)(6) of the Securities Act (15 U.S.C. 77d(a)(6)) may rely on the efforts of an intermediary required by Rule 303(b) to ensure that the aggregate amount of securities purchased by an investor in offerings pursuant to section 4(a)(6) of the Securities Act will not cause the investor to exceed the limit set forth in section 4(a)(6) of the Securities Act and Rule 100(a)(2), *provided that* the issuer does not know that the investor has exceeded the investor limits or would exceed the investor limits as a result of purchasing securities in the issuer's offering.

(3) The transaction is conducted through an intermediary that complies with the requirements in section 4A(a) of the Securities Act (15 U.S.C. 77d-1(a)) and the related requirements in this part, and the transaction is conducted exclusively through the intermediary's platform; and

Instruction to paragraph (a)(3). An issuer shall not conduct an offering or concurrent offerings in reliance on section 4(a)(6) of the Securities Act of 1933 (15 U.S.C. 77d(a)(6)) using more than one intermediary.

(4) The issuer complies with the requirements in section 4A(b) of the Securities Act (15 U.S.C. 77d-1(b)) and the related requirements in this part; *provided, however,* that the failure to comply with Rules 202, 227.203(a)(3) and 227.203(b) shall not prevent an issuer from relying on the exemption provided by section 4(a)(6) of the Securities Act (15 U.S.C. 77d(a)(6)).

(b) *Applicability.* The crowdfunding exemption shall not apply to transactions involving the offer or sale of securities by any issuer that:

(1) Is not organized under, and subject to, the laws of a State or territory of the United States or the District of Columbia;

(2) Is subject to the requirement to file reports pursuant to section 13 or section 15(d) of the Securities Exchange Act of 1934 (the "Exchange Act") (15 U.S.C. 78m or 78o(d));

(3) Is an investment company, as defined in section 3 of the Investment Company Act of 1940 (15 U.S.C. 80a-3), or is excluded from the definition of investment company by section 3(b) or section 3(c) of that Act (15 U.S.C. 80a-3(b) or 80a-3(c));

(4) Is not eligible to offer or sell securities in reliance on section 4(a)(6) of the Securities Act (15 U.S.C. 77d(a)(6)) as a result of a disqualification as specified in Rule 503(a);

(5) Has sold securities in reliance on section 4(a)(6) of the Securities Act (15 U.S.C. 77d(a)(6)) and has not filed with the Commission and provided to investors, to the extent required, the ongoing annual reports required by this part during the two years immediately preceding the filing of the required offering statement; or

Instruction to paragraph (b)(5). An issuer delinquent in its ongoing reports can again rely on section 4(a)(6) of the Securities Act (15 U.S.C. 77d(a)(6)) once it has filed with the Commission and provided to investors both of the annual reports required during the two years immediately preceding the filing of the required offering statement.

(6) Has no specific business plan or has indicated that its business plan is to engage in a merger or acquisition with an unidentified company or companies.

(c) *Issuer.* For purposes of Rule 201(r), calculating aggregate amounts offered and sold in Rule 100(a) and Rule 201(t), and determining whether an issuer has previously sold securities in Rule 201(t)(3), *issuer* includes all entities controlled by or under common control with the issuer and any predecessors of the issuer.

Instruction to paragraph (c). The term *control* means the possession, direct or indirect, of the power to direct or cause the direction of the management and policies of the entity, whether through the ownership of voting securities, by contract or otherwise.

(d) *Investor.* For purposes of this part, *investor* means any investor or any potential investor, as the context requires.

Subpart B – Requirements for Issuers

Rule 201. Disclosure requirements

An issuer offering or selling securities in reliance on section 4(a)(6) of the Securities Act (15 U.S.C. 77d(a)(6)) and in accordance with section 4A of the Securities Act (15 U.S.C. 77d-1) and this part must file with the Commission and provide to investors and the relevant intermediary the following information:

(a) The name, legal status (including its form of organization, jurisdiction in which it is organized and date of organization), physical address and website of the issuer;

(b) The names of the directors and officers (and any persons occupying a similar status or performing a similar function) of the issuer, all positions and offices with the issuer held by such persons, the period of time in which such persons served in the position or office and their business experience during the past three years, including:

(1) Each person's principal occupation and employment, including whether any officer is employed by another employer; and

(2) The name and principal business of any corporation or other organization in which such occupation and employment took place.

Instruction to paragraph (b). For purposes of this paragraph (b), the term *officer* means a president, vice president, secretary, treasurer or principal financial officer, comptroller or principal accounting officer, and any person routinely performing similar functions.

(c) The name of each person, as of the most recent practicable date but no earlier than 120 days prior to the date the offering statement or report is filed, who is a beneficial owner of 20 percent or more of the issuer's outstanding voting equity securities, calculated on the basis of voting power;

(d) A description of the business of the issuer and the anticipated business plan of the issuer;

(e) The current number of employees of the issuer;

(f) A discussion of the material factors that make an investment in the issuer speculative or risky;

(g) The target offering amount and the deadline to reach the target offering amount, including a statement that if the sum of the investment commitments does not equal or exceed the target offering amount at the offering deadline, no securities will be sold in the offering, investment commitments will be cancelled and committed funds will be returned;

(h) Whether the issuer will accept investments in excess of the target offering amount and, if so, the maximum amount that the issuer will accept and how oversubscriptions will be allocated, such as on a pro-rata, first come-first served, or other basis;

(i) A description of the purpose and intended use of the offering proceeds;

Instruction to paragraph (i). An issuer must provide a reasonably detailed description of any intended use of proceeds, such that investors are provided with enough information to understand how the offering proceeds will be used. If an issuer has identified a range of possible uses, the issuer should identify and describe each probable use and the factors the issuer may consider in allocating proceeds among the potential uses. If the issuer will accept proceeds in excess of the target offering amount, the issuer must describe the purpose, method for allocating oversubscriptions, and intended use of the excess proceeds with similar specificity.

(j) A description of the process to complete the transaction or cancel an investment commitment, including a statement that:

(1) Investors may cancel an investment commitment until 48 hours prior to the deadline identified in the issuer's offering materials;

(2) The intermediary will notify investors when the target offering amount has been met;

(3) If an issuer reaches the target offering amount prior to the deadline identified in its offering materials, it may close the offering early if it provides notice about the new offering deadline at least five business days prior to such new offering deadline (absent a material change that would require an extension of the offering and reconfirmation of the investment commitment); and

(4) If an investor does not cancel an investment commitment before the 48-hour period prior to the offering deadline, the funds will be released to the issuer upon closing of the offering and the investor will receive securities in exchange for his or her investment;

(k) A statement that if an investor does not reconfirm his or her investment commitment after a material change is made to the offering, the investor's investment commitment will be cancelled and the committed funds will be returned;

(*l*) The price to the public of the securities or the method for determining the price, provided that, prior to any sale of securities, each investor shall be provided in writing the final price and all required disclosures;

(m) A description of the ownership and capital structure of the issuer, including:

(1) The terms of the securities being offered and each other class of security of the issuer, including the number of securities being offered and/or outstanding, whether or not such securities have voting rights, any limitations on such voting rights, how the terms of the securities being offered may be modified and a summary of the differences between such securities and each other class of security of the issuer, and how the rights of the securities being offered may be materially limited, diluted or qualified by the rights of any other class of security of the issuer;

(2) A description of how the exercise of rights held by the principal shareholders of the issuer could affect the purchasers of the securities being offered;

(3) The name and ownership level of each person, as of the most recent practicable date but no earlier than 120 days prior to the date the offering statement or report is filed, who is the beneficial owner of 20 percent or more of the issuer's outstanding voting equity securities, calculated on the basis of voting power;

(4) How the securities being offered are being valued, and examples of methods for how such securities may be valued by the issuer in the future, including during subsequent corporate actions;

(5) The risks to purchasers of the securities relating to minority ownership in the issuer and the risks associated with corporate actions including additional issuances of securities, issuer repurchases of securities, a sale of the issuer or of assets of the issuer or transactions with related parties; and

(6) A description of the restrictions on transfer of the securities, as set forth in Rule 501;

(n) The name, SEC file number and Central Registration Depository (CRD) number (as applicable) of the intermediary through which the offering is being conducted;

(*o*) A description of the intermediary's financial interests in the issuer's transaction and in the issuer, including:

(1) The amount of compensation to be paid to the intermediary, whether as a dollar amount or a percentage of the offering amount, or a good faith estimate if the exact amount is not available at the time of the filing, for conducting the offering, including the amount of referral and any other fees associated with the offering, and

(2) Any other direct or indirect interest in the issuer held by the intermediary, or any arrangement for the intermediary to acquire such an interest;

(p) A description of the material terms of any indebtedness of the issuer, including the amount, interest rate, maturity date and any other material terms;

(q) A description of exempt offerings conducted within the past three years;

Instruction to paragraph (q). In providing a description of any prior exempt offerings, disclose: (1) The date of the offering; (2) The offering exemption relied upon; (3) The type of securities offered; and (4) The amount of securities sold and the use of proceeds.

(r) A description of any transaction since the beginning of the issuer's last fiscal year, or any currently proposed transaction, to which the issuer was or is to be a party and the amount involved exceeds five percent of the aggregate amount of capital raised by the issuer in reliance on section 4(a)(6) of the Securities Act (15 U.S.C. 77d(a)(6)) during the preceding 12-month period, inclusive of the amount the issuer seeks to raise in the current offering under section 4(a)(6) of the Securities Act, in which any of the following persons had or is to have a direct or indirect material interest:

(1) Any director or officer of the issuer;

(2) Any person who is, as of the most recent practicable date but no earlier than 120 days prior to the date the offering statement or report is filed, the beneficial owner of 20 percent or more of the issuer's outstanding voting equity securities, calculated on the basis of voting power;

(3) If the issuer was incorporated or organized within the past three years, any promoter of the issuer; or

(4) Any member of the family of any of the foregoing persons, which includes a child, stepchild, grandchild, parent, stepparent, grandparent, spouse or spousal equivalent, sibling, mother-in-law, father-in-law, son-in-law, daughter-in-law, brother-in-law, or sister-in-law, and shall include adoptive relationships. The term *spousal equivalent* means a cohabitant occupying a relationship generally equivalent to that of a spouse.

Instruction 1 to paragraph (r). For each transaction identified, disclose the name of the specified person and state his or her relationship to the issuer, and the nature and, where practicable, the approximate amount of his or her interest in the transaction. The amount of such interest shall be computed without regard to the amount of the profit or loss involved in the transaction. Where it is not practicable to state the approximate amount of the interest, the approximate amount involved in the transaction shall be disclosed.

Instruction 2 to paragraph (r). For purposes of paragraph (r), a transaction includes, but is not limited to, any financial transaction, arrangement or relationship (including any indebtedness or guarantee of indebtedness) or any series of similar transactions, arrangements or relationships.

(s) A discussion of the issuer's financial condition, including, to the extent material, liquidity, capital resources and historical results of operations;

Instruction 1 to paragraph (s). The discussion must cover each period for which financial statements of the issuer are provided. An issuer also must include a discussion of any material changes or trends known to management in the financial condition and results of operations of the issuer subsequent to the period for which financial statements are provided.

Instruction 2 to paragraph (s). For issuers with no prior operating history, the discussion should focus on financial milestones and operational, liquidity and other challenges. For issuers with an operating history, the discussion should focus on whether historical results and cash flows are representative of what investors should expect in the future. Issuers should take into account the proceeds of the offering and any other known or pending sources of capital. Issuers also should discuss how the proceeds from the offering will affect the issuer's liquidity, whether receiving these funds and any other additional funds is necessary to the viability of the business, and how quickly the issuer anticipates using its available cash. In addition, issuers should describe the other available sources of capital to the business, such as lines of credit or required contributions by shareholders.

Instruction 3 to paragraph (s). References to the issuer in this paragraph and its instructions refer to the issuer and its predecessors, if any.

(t) For offerings that, together with all other amounts sold under section 4(a)(6) of the Securities Act (15 U.S.C. 77d(a)(6)) within the preceding 12-month period, have, in the aggregate, the following target offering amounts:

(1) $107,000 or less, the amount of total income, taxable income and total tax, or the equivalent line items, as reported on the federal income tax returns filed by the issuer for the most recently completed year (if any), which shall be certified by the principal executive officer of the issuer to reflect accurately the information reported on the issuer's federal income tax returns, and financial statements of the issuer, which shall be certified by the principal executive officer of the issuer to be true and complete in all material respects. If financial statements of the issuer are available that have either been reviewed or audited by a public accountant that is independent of the issuer, the issuer must provide those financial statements instead and need not include the information reported on the federal income tax returns or the certifications of the principal executive officer;

(2) More than $107,000, but not more than $535,000, financial statements of the issuer reviewed by a public accountant that is independent of the issuer. If financial statements of the issuer are available that have been audited by a public accountant that is independent of the issuer, the issuer must provide those financial statements instead and need not include the reviewed financial statements; and

(3) More than $535,000, financial statements of the issuer audited by a public accountant that is independent of the issuer; *provided, however*, that for issuers that have not previously sold securities in reliance on section 4(a)(6) of the Securities Act (15 U.S.C. 77d(a)(6)), offerings that have a target offering amount of more than $535,000, but not more than $1,070,000, financial statements of the issuer reviewed by a public accountant that is independent of the issuer. If financial statements of the issuer are available that have been audited by a public accountant that is independent of the issuer, the issuer must provide those financial statements instead and need not include the reviewed financial statements.

Instruction 1 to paragraph (t). To determine the financial statements required under this paragraph (t), an issuer must aggregate amounts sold in reliance on section 4(a)(6) of the Securities Act (15 U.S.C. 77d(a)(6)) within the preceding 12-month period and the offering amount in the offering for which disclosure is being provided. If the issuer will accept proceeds in excess of the target offering amount, the issuer must include the maximum offering amount that the issuer will accept in the calculation to determine the financial statements required under this paragraph (t).

Instruction 2 to paragraph (t). An issuer may voluntarily meet the requirements of this paragraph (t) for a higher aggregate target offering amount.

Instruction 3 to paragraph (t). The financial statements must be prepared in accordance with U.S. generally accepted accounting principles and include balance sheets, statements of comprehensive income, statements of cash flows, statements of changes in stockholders' equity and notes to the financial statements. If the financial statements are not audited, they must be labeled as "unaudited." The financial statements must cover the two most recently completed fiscal years or the period(s) since inception, if shorter.

Instruction 4 to paragraph (t). For an offering conducted in the first 120 days of a fiscal year, the financial statements provided may be for the two fiscal years prior to the issuer's most recently completed fiscal year; however, financial statements for the two most recently completed fiscal years must be provided if they are otherwise available. If more than 120 days have passed since the end of the issuer's most recently completed fiscal year, the financial statements provided must be for the issuer's two most recently completed fiscal years. If the 120th day falls on a Saturday, Sunday, or holiday, the next business day shall be considered the 120th day for purposes of determining the age of the financial statements.

Instruction 5 to paragraph (t). An issuer may elect to delay complying with any new or revised financial accounting standard that applies to companies that are not issuers (as defined under section 2(a) of the Sarbanes-Oxley Act of 2002 (15 U.S.C. 7201(a)) until the date that such companies are required to comply with such new or revised accounting standard. Issuers electing this accommodation must disclose it at the time the issuer files its offering statement and apply the election to all standards. Issuers electing not to use this accommodation must forgo this accommodation for all financial accounting standards and may not elect to rely on this accommodation in any future filings.

Instruction 6 to paragraph (t). An issuer required to provide information from a tax return under paragraph (t)(1) of this section before filing a tax return with the U.S. Internal Revenue Service for the most recently completed fiscal year may provide information from its tax return for the prior year (if any), provided that the issuer provides information from the tax return for the most recently completed fiscal year when it is filed with the U.S. Internal Revenue Service (if the tax return is filed during the offering period). An issuer that requested an extension from the U.S. Internal Revenue Service would not be required to provide information from the tax return until the date the return is filed, if filed during the offering period. If an issuer has not yet filed a tax return and is not required to file a tax return before the end of the offering period, then the tax return information does not need to be provided.

Instruction 7 to paragraph (t). An issuer providing financial statements that are not audited or reviewed and tax information as specified under paragraph (t)(1) of this section must have its principal executive officer provide the following certification:

I, [identify the certifying individual], certify that: (1) the financial statements of [identify the issuer] included in this Form are true and complete in all material respects; and (2) the tax return information of [identify the issuer] included in this Form reflects accurately the information reported on the tax return for [identify the issuer] filed for the fiscal year ended [date of most recent tax return]. [Signature and title].

Instruction 8 to paragraph (t). Financial statement reviews shall be conducted in accordance with the Statements on Standards for Accounting and Review Services issued by the Accounting and Review Services Committee of the American Institute of Certified Public Accountants. A signed review report must accompany the reviewed financial statements, and an issuer must notify the public accountant of the issuer's intended use of the review report in the offering. An issuer will not be in compliance with the requirement to provide reviewed financial statements if the review report includes modifications.

Instruction 9 to paragraph (t). Financial statement audits shall be conducted in accordance with either auditing standards issued by the American Institute of Certified Public Accountants (referred to as U.S. Generally Accepted Auditing Standards) or the standards of the Public Company Accounting Oversight Board. A signed audit report must accompany audited financial statements, and an issuer must notify the public accountant of the issuer's intended use of the audit report in the offering. An issuer will not be in compliance with the requirement to provide audited financial statements if the audit report includes a qualified opinion, an adverse opinion, or a disclaimer of opinion.

Instruction 10 to paragraph (t). To qualify as a public accountant that is independent of the issuer for purposes of this part, the accountant must satisfy the independence standards of either:

(i) 17 CFR 210.2-01 of this chapter, or

(ii) The American Institute of Certified Public Accountants. The public accountant that audits or reviews the financial statements provided by an issuer must be:

(A) Duly registered and in good standing as a certified public accountant under the laws of the place of his or her residence or principal office; or

(B) In good standing and entitled to practice as a public accountant under the laws of his or her place of residence or principal office.

Instruction 11 to paragraph (t). Except as set forth in Rule 100(c), references to the issuer in this paragraph (t) and its instructions (2) through (10) refer to the issuer and its predecessors, if any.

(u) Any matters that would have triggered disqualification under Rule 503(a) but occurred before May 16, 2016. The failure to provide such disclosure shall not prevent an issuer from continuing to rely on the exemption provided by section 4(a)(6) of the Securities Act (15 U.S.C. 77d(a)(6)) if the issuer establishes that it did not know and, in the exercise of reasonable care, could not have known of the existence of the undisclosed matter or matters;

Instruction to paragraph (u). An issuer will not be able to establish that it could not have known of a disqualification unless it has made factual inquiry into whether any disqualifications exist. The nature and scope of the factual inquiry will vary based on the facts and circumstances concerning, among other things, the issuer and the other offering participants.

(v) Updates regarding the progress of the issuer in meeting the target offering amount, to be provided in accordance with Rule 203;

(w) Where on the issuer's website investors will be able to find the issuer's annual report, and the date by which such report will be available on the issuer's website;

(x) Whether the issuer or any of its predecessors previously failed to comply with the ongoing reporting requirements of Rule 202; and

(y) Any material information necessary in order to make the statements made, in light of the circumstances under which they were made, not misleading.

Instruction to Rule 201. If disclosure provided pursuant to any paragraph of this section also satisfies the requirements of one or more other paragraphs of this section, it is not necessary to repeat the disclosure. Instead of repeating information, an issuer may include a cross-reference to disclosure contained elsewhere in the offering statement or report, including to information in the financial statements.

Rule 202. Ongoing reporting requirements

(a) An issuer that has offered and sold securities in reliance on section 4(a)(6) of the Securities Act (15 U.S.C. 77d(a)(6)) and in accordance with section 4A of the Securities Act (15 U.S.C. 77d-1) and this part must file with the Commission and post on the issuer's website an annual report along with the financial statements of the issuer certified by the principal executive officer of the issuer to be true and complete in all material respects and a description of the financial condition of the issuer as described in Rule 201(s). If, however, an issuer has available financial statements that have either been reviewed or audited by a public accountant that is independent of the issuer, those financial statements must be provided and the certification by the principal executive officer will not be required. The annual report also must include the disclosure required by paragraphs (a), (b), (c), (d), (e), (f), (m), (p), (q), (r), and (x) of Rule 201. The report must be filed in accordance with the requirements of Rule 203 and Form C (Rule 900 of this chapter) and no later than 120 days after the end of the fiscal year covered by the report.

Instruction 1 to paragraph (a). Instructions (3), (8), (9), (10), and (11) to paragraph (t) of Rule 201 shall apply for purposes of this section.

Instruction 2 to paragraph (a). An issuer providing financial statements that are not audited or reviewed must have its principal executive officer provide the following certification:

I, [identify the certifying individual], certify that the financial statements of [identify the issuer] included in this Form are true and complete in all material respects. [Signature and title].

(b) An issuer must continue to comply with the ongoing reporting requirements until one of the following occurs:

(1) The issuer is required to file reports under section 13(a) or section 15(d) of the Exchange Act (15 U.S.C. 78m(a) or 78o(d));

(2) The issuer has filed, since its most recent sale of securities pursuant to this part, at least one annual report pursuant to this section and has fewer than 300 holders of record;

(3) The issuer has filed, since its most recent sale of securities pursuant to this part, the annual reports required pursuant to this section for at least the three most recent years and has total assets that do not exceed $10,000,000;

(4) The issuer or another party repurchases all of the securities issued in reliance on section 4(a)(6) of the Securities Act (15 U.S.C. 77d(a)(6)), including any payment in full of debt securities or any complete redemption of redeemable securities; or

(5) The issuer liquidates or dissolves its business in accordance with state law.

(c) *Temporary Relief from Certain Reporting Requirements.*

(1) An issuer that is not able to meet a filing deadline for any report or form required to be filed by this section (Rule 202), Rule 203(a)(3) (17 CFR 227.203(a)(3)), or Rule 203(b) (17 CFR 227.203(b)), as applicable:

(i) During the period from and including August 25, 2017 to and including October 26, 2017 due to Hurricane Harvey and its aftermath shall be deemed to have satisfied the filing deadline for such report or form if the issuer files such report or form with the Commission on or before October 27, 2017;

(ii) During the period from and including September 6, 2017 to and including November 7, 2017 due to Hurricane Irma and its aftermath shall be deemed to have satisfied the filing deadline for such report or form if the issuer files such report or form with the Commission on or before November 8, 2017; or

(iii) During the period from and including September 20, 2017 to and including November 21, 2017 due to Hurricane Maria and its aftermath shall be deemed to have satisfied the filing deadline for such report or form if the issuer files such report or form with the Commission on or before November 22, 2017.

(2) In any report or form filed pursuant to paragraph (c)(1) of this section, the issuer must disclose that it is relying on this paragraph (c) (Rule 202(c) of Regulation Crowdfunding) and state the reasons why, in good faith, it could not file such report or form on a timely basis.

Rule 203. Filing requirements and form

(a) *Form C: Offering statement and amendments* (Rule 900 of this chapter). (1) *Offering statement.* An issuer offering or selling securities in reliance on section 4(a)(6) of the Securities Act (15 U.S.C. 77d(a)(6)) and in accordance with section 4A of the Securities Act (15 U.S.C. 77d-1) and this part must file with the Commission and provide to investors and the relevant intermediary a Form C: Offering Statement (Form C) (Rule 900 of this chapter) prior to the commencement of the offering of securities. The Form C must include the information required by Rule 201.

(2) *Amendments to offering statement.* An issuer must file with the Commission and provide to investors and the relevant intermediary an amendment to the offering statement filed on Form C (Rule 900 of this chapter) to disclose any material changes, additions or updates to information that it provides to investors through the intermediary's platform, for any offering that has not yet been completed or terminated. The amendment must be filed on Form C: Amendment (Form C/A) (Rule 900 of this chapter), and if the amendment reflects material changes, additions or updates, the issuer shall check the box indicating that investors must reconfirm an investment commitment within five business days or the investor's commitment will be considered cancelled.

(3) *Progress updates.* (i) An issuer must file with the Commission and provide to investors and the relevant intermediary a Form C: Progress Update

(Form C-U) (Rule 900 of this chapter) to disclose its progress in meeting the target offering amount no later than five business days after each of the dates when the issuer reaches 50 percent and 100 percent of the target offering amount.

(ii) If the issuer will accept proceeds in excess of the target offering amount, the issuer must file with the Commission and provide to investors and the relevant intermediary, no later than five business days after the offering deadline, a final Form C-U (Rule 900 of this chapter) to disclose the total amount of securities sold in the offering.

(iii) The requirements of paragraphs (a)(3)(i) and (ii) of this section shall not apply to an issuer if the relevant intermediary makes publicly available on the intermediary's platform frequent updates regarding the progress of the issuer in meeting the target offering amount; however, the issuer must still file a Form C-U (Rule 900 of this chapter) to disclose the total amount of securities sold in the offering no later than five business days after the offering deadline.

Instruction to paragraph (a)(3). If multiple Forms C-U (Rule 900 of this chapter) are triggered within the same five business day period, the issuer may consolidate such progress updates into one Form C-U, so long as the Form C-U discloses the most recent threshold that was met and the Form C-U is filed with the Commission and provided to investors and the relevant intermediary by the day on which the first progress update is due.

Instruction 1 to paragraph (a). An issuer would satisfy the requirement to provide to the relevant intermediary the information required by this paragraph (a) if it provides to the relevant intermediary a copy of the disclosures filed with the Commission.

Instruction 2 to paragraph (a). An issuer would satisfy the requirement to provide to investors the information required by this paragraph (a) if the issuer refers investors to the information on the intermediary's platform by means of a posting on the issuer's website or by e- mail.

(b) *Form C: Annual report and termination of reporting (Rule 900 of this chapter).* (1) *Annual reports.* An issuer that has sold securities in reliance on section 4(a)(6) of the Securities Act (15 U.S.C. 77d(a)(6)) and in accordance with section 4A of the Securities Act (15 U.S.C. 77d- 1) and this part must file an annual report on Form C: Annual Report (Form C-AR) (Rule 900 of this chapter) with the Commission no later than 120 days after the end of the fiscal year covered by the report. The annual report shall include the information required by Rule 202(a).

(2) *Amendments to annual report.* An issuer must file with the Commission an amendment to the annual report filed on Form C: Annual Report (Form C-AR) (Rule 900 of this chapter) to make a material change to the previously filed annual report as soon as practicable after discovery of the need for the material change. The amendment must be filed on Form C: Amendment to Annual Report (Form C-AR/A) (Rule 900 of this chapter).

(3) *Termination of reporting.* An issuer eligible to terminate its obligation to file annual reports with the Commission pursuant to Rule 202(b) must file with the Commission, within five business days from the date on which the issuer becomes eligible to terminate its reporting obligation, Form C: Termination of Reporting (Form C-TR) (Rule 900 of this chapter) to advise investors that the issuer will cease reporting pursuant to this part.

Rule 204. Advertising

(a) An issuer may not, directly or indirectly, advertise the terms of an offering made in reliance on section 4(a)(6) of the Securities Act (15 U.S.C. 77d(a)(6)), except for notices that meet the requirements of paragraph (b) of this section.

Instruction to paragraph (a). For purposes of this paragraph (a), *issuer* includes persons acting on behalf of the issuer.

(b) A notice may advertise any of the terms of an issuer's offering made in reliance on section 4(a)(6) of the Securities Act (15 U.S.C. 77d(a)(6)) if it directs investors to the intermediary's platform and includes no more than the following information:

(1) A statement that the issuer is conducting an offering pursuant to section 4(a)(6) of the Securities Act (15 U.S.C. 77d(a)(6)), the name of the intermediary through which the offering is being conducted and a link directing the potential investor to the intermediary's platform;

(2) The terms of the offering; and

(3) Factual information about the legal identity and business location of the issuer, limited to the name of the issuer of the security, the address, phone number and website of the issuer, the e-mail address of a representative of the issuer and a brief description of the business of the issuer.

(c) Notwithstanding the prohibition on advertising any of the terms of the offering, an issuer, and persons acting on behalf of the issuer, may communicate with investors and potential investors about the terms of the offering through communication channels provided by the intermediary on the intermediary's platform, provided that an issuer identifies itself as the issuer in all communications.

Persons acting on behalf of the issuer must identify their affiliation with the issuer in all communications on the intermediary's platform. *Instruction to Rule 204.* For purposes of this section, *terms of the offering* means the amount of securities offered, the nature of the securities, the price of the securities and the closing date of the offering period.

Rule 205. Promoter compensation

(a) An issuer, or person acting on behalf of the issuer, shall be permitted to compensate or commit to compensate, directly or indirectly, any person to promote the issuer's offerings made in reliance on section 4(a)(6) of the Securities Act (15 U.S.C. 77d(a)(6)) through communication channels provided by an intermediary on the intermediary's platform, but only if the issuer or person acting on behalf of the issuer, takes reasonable steps to ensure that the person promoting the offering clearly discloses the receipt, past or prospective, of such compensation with any such communication.

Instruction to paragraph (a). The disclosure required by this paragraph is required, with each communication, for persons engaging in promotional activities on behalf of the issuer through the communication channels provided by the intermediary, regardless of whether or not the compensation they receive is specifically for the promotional activities. This includes persons hired specifically to promote the offering as well as to persons who are otherwise employed by the issuer or who undertake promotional activities on behalf of the issuer.

(b) Other than as set forth in paragraph (a) of this section, an issuer or person acting on behalf of the issuer shall not compensate or commit to compensate, directly or indirectly, any person to promote the issuer's offerings made in reliance on section 4(a)(6) of the Securities Act (15 U.S.C. 77d(a)(6)), unless such promotion is limited to notices permitted by, and in compliance with, Rule 204.

Subpart C – Requirements for Intermediaries

Rule 300. Intermediaries

(a) *Requirements.* A person acting as an intermediary in a transaction involving the offer or sale of securities in reliance on section 4(a)(6) of the Securities Act (15 U.S.C. 77d(a)(6)) must:

(1) Be registered with the Commission as a broker under section 15(b) of the Exchange Act (15 U.S.C. 78*o*(b)) or as a funding portal in accordance with the requirements of Rule 400; and

(2) Be a member a national securities association registered under section 15A of the Exchange Act (15 U.S.C. 78*o*-3).

(b) *Financial interests.* Any director, officer or partner of an intermediary, or any person occupying a similar status or performing a similar function, may not have a financial interest in an issuer that is offering or selling securities in reliance on section 4(a)(6) of the Securities Act (15 U.S.C. 77d(a)(6)) through the intermediary's platform, or receive a financial interest in an issuer as compensation for the services provided to or for the benefit of the issuer in connection with the offer or sale of such securities. An intermediary may not have a financial interest in an issuer that is offering or selling securities in reliance on section 4(a)(6) of the Securities Act (15 U.S.C. 77d(a)(6)) through the intermediary's platform unless:

(1) the intermediary receives the financial interest from the issuer as compensation for the services provided to, or for the benefit of, the issuer in connection with the offer or sale of the securities being offered or sold in reliance on section 4(a)(6) of the Securities Act (15 U.S.C. 77d(a)(6)) through the intermediary's platform; and

(2) the financial interest consists of securities of the same class and having the same terms, conditions and rights as the securities being offered or sold in reliance on section 4(a)(6) of the Securities Act (15 U.S.C. 77d(a)(6)) through the intermediary's platform. For purposes of this paragraph, a *financial interest in an issuer* means a direct or indirect ownership of, or economic interest in, any class of the issuer's securities.

(c) *Definitions.* For purposes of this part: (1) *Associated person of a funding portal* or *person associated with a funding portal* means any partner, officer, director or manager of a funding portal (or any person occupying a similar status or performing similar functions), any person directly or indirectly controlling or controlled by such funding portal, or any employee of a funding portal, except that any person associated with a funding portal whose functions are solely clerical or ministerial shall not be included in the meaning of such term for purposes of section 15(b) of the Exchange Act (15 U.S.C. 78*o*(b)) (other than paragraphs (4) and (6) of section 15(b) of the Exchange Act).

(2) *Funding portal* means a broker acting as an intermediary in a transaction involving the offer or sale of securities in reliance on section 4(a)(6) of

the Securities Act (15 U.S.C. 77d(a)(6)), that does not:

(i) Offer investment advice or recommendations;

(ii) Solicit purchases, sales or offers to buy the securities displayed on its platform;

(iii) Compensate employees, agents, or other persons for such solicitation or based on the sale of securities displayed or referenced on its platform; or (iv) Hold, manage, possess, or otherwise handle investor funds or securities.

(3) *Intermediary* means a broker registered under section 15(b) of the Exchange Act (15 U.S.C. 78o(b)) or a funding portal registered under Rule 400 and includes, where relevant, an associated person of the registered broker or registered funding portal.

(4) *Platform* means a program or application accessible via the Internet or other similar electronic communication medium through which a registered broker or a registered funding portal acts as an intermediary in a transaction involving the offer or sale of securities in reliance on section 4(a)(6) of the Securities Act (15 U.S.C. 77d(a)(6)).

Instruction to paragraph (c)(4). An intermediary through which a crowdfunding transaction is conducted may engage in back office or other administrative functions other than on the intermediary's platform.

Rule 301. Measures to reduce risk of fraud

An intermediary in a transaction involving the offer or sale of securities in reliance on section 4(a)(6) of the Securities Act (15 U.S.C. 77d(a)(6)) must:

(a) Have a reasonable basis for believing that an issuer seeking to offer and sell securities in reliance on section 4(a)(6) of the Securities Act (15 U.S.C. 77d(a)(6)) through the intermediary's platform complies with the requirements in section 4A(b) of the Act (15 U.S.C. 77d-1(b)) and the related requirements in this part. In satisfying this requirement, an intermediary may rely on the representations of the issuer concerning compliance with these requirements unless the intermediary has reason to question the reliability of those representations;

(b) Have a reasonable basis for believing that the issuer has established means to keep accurate records of the holders of the securities it would offer and sell through the intermediary's platform, provided that an intermediary may rely on the representations of the issuer concerning its means of recordkeeping unless the intermediary has reason to question the reliability of those representations. An intermediary will be deemed to have satisfied this requirement if the issuer has engaged the services of a transfer agent that is registered under Section 17A of the Exchange Act (15 U.S.C. 78q-1(c)).

(c) Deny access to its platform to an issuer if the intermediary: (1) Has a reasonable basis for believing that the issuer or any of its officers, directors (or any person occupying a similar status or performing a similar function) or beneficial owners of 20 percent or more of the issuer's outstanding voting equity securities, calculated on the basis of voting power, is subject to a disqualification under Rule 503. In satisfying this requirement, an intermediary must, at a minimum, conduct a background and securities enforcement regulatory history check on each issuer whose securities are to be offered by the intermediary and on each officer, director or beneficial owner of 20 percent or more of the issuer's outstanding voting equity securities, calculated on the basis of voting power.

(2) Has a reasonable basis for believing that the issuer or the offering presents the potential for fraud or otherwise raises concerns about investor protection. In satisfying this requirement, an intermediary must deny access if it reasonably believes that it is unable to adequately or effectively assess the risk of fraud of the issuer or its potential offering. In addition, if an intermediary becomes aware of information after it has granted access that causes it to reasonably believe that the issuer or the offering presents the potential for fraud or otherwise raises concerns about investor protection, the intermediary must promptly remove the offering from its platform, cancel the offering, and return (or, for funding portals, direct the return of) any funds that have been committed by investors in the offering.

Rule 302. Account opening

(a) *Accounts and electronic delivery.* (1) No intermediary or associated person of an intermediary may accept an investment commitment in a transaction involving the offer or sale of securities in reliance on section 4(a)(6) of the Securities Act (15 U.S.C. 77d(a)(6)) until the investor has opened an account with the intermediary and the intermediary has obtained from the investor consent to electronic delivery of materials.

(2) An intermediary must provide all information that is required to be provided by the intermediary under subpart C of this part (Rules 300 through 305), including, but not limited to, educational materials, notices and confirmations,

through electronic means. Unless otherwise indicated in the relevant rule of subpart C of this part, in satisfying this requirement, an intermediary must provide the information through an electronic message that contains the information, through an electronic message that includes a specific link to the information as posted on intermediary's platform, or through an electronic message that provides notice of what the information is and that it is located on the intermediary's platform or on the issuer's website. Electronic messages include, but are not limited to, e-mail, social media messages, instant messages or other electronic media messages.

(b) *Educational materials.* (1) In connection with establishing an account for an investor, an intermediary must deliver educational materials to such investor that explain in plain language and are otherwise designed to communicate effectively and accurately:

(i) The process for the offer, purchase and issuance of securities through the intermediary and the risks associated with purchasing securities offered and sold in reliance on section 4(a)(6) of the Securities Act (15 U.S.C. 77d(a)(6));

(ii) The types of securities offered and sold in reliance on section 4(a)(6) of the Securities Act (15 U.S.C. 77d(a)(6)) available for purchase on the intermediary's platform and the risks associated with each type of security, including the risk of having limited voting power as a result of dilution;

(iii) The restrictions on the resale of a security offered and sold in reliance on section 4(a)(6) of the Securities Act (15 U.S.C. 77d(a)(6));

(iv) The types of information that an issuer is required to provide under Rule 202, the frequency of the delivery of that information and the possibility that those obligations may terminate in the future;

(v) The limitations on the amounts an investor may invest pursuant to Rule 100(a)(2);

(vi) The limitations on an investor's right to cancel an investment commitment and the circumstances in which an investment commitment may be cancelled by the issuer;

(vii) The need for the investor to consider whether investing in a security offered and sold in reliance on section 4(a)(6) of the Securities Act (15 U.S.C. 77d(a)(6)) is appropriate for that investor;

(viii) That following completion of an offering conducted through the intermediary, there may or may not be any ongoing relationship between the issuer and intermediary; and

(ix) That under certain circumstances an issuer may cease to publish annual reports and, therefore, an investor may not continually have current financial information about the issuer.

(2) An intermediary must make the most current version of its educational material available on its platform at all times and, if at any time, the intermediary makes a material revision to its educational materials, it must make the revised educational materials available to all investors before accepting any additional investment commitments or effecting any further transactions in securities offered and sold in reliance on section 4(a)(6) of the Securities Act (15 U.S.C. 77d(a)(6)).

(c) *Promoters.* In connection with establishing an account for an investor, an intermediary must inform the investor that any person who promotes an issuer's offering for compensation, whether past or prospective, or who is a founder or an employee of an issuer that engages in promotional activities on behalf of the issuer on the intermediary's platform, must clearly disclose in all communications on the intermediary's platform, respectively, the receipt of the compensation and that he or she is engaging in promotional activities on behalf of the issuer.

(d) *Compensation disclosure.* When establishing an account for an investor, an intermediary must clearly disclose the manner in which the intermediary is compensated in connection with offerings and sales of securities in reliance on section 4(a)(6) of the Securities Act (15 U.S.C. 77d(a)(6)).

Rule 303. Requirements with respect to transactions

(a) *Issuer information.* An intermediary in a transaction involving the offer or sale of securities in reliance on section 4(a)(6) of the Securities Act (15 U.S.C. 77d(a)(6)) must make available to the Commission and to investors any information required to be provided by the issuer of the securities under Rules 201 and 203(a).

(1) This information must be made publicly available on the intermediary's platform, in a manner that reasonably permits a person accessing the platform to save, download, or otherwise store the information;

(2) This information must be made publicly available on the intermediary's platform for a

minimum of 21 days before any securities are sold in the offering, during which time the intermediary may accept investment commitments;

(3) This information, including any additional information provided by the issuer, must remain publicly available on the intermediary's platform until the offer and sale of securities in reliance on section 4(a)(6) of the Securities Act (15 U.S.C. 77d(a)(6)) is completed or cancelled; and

(4) An intermediary may not require any person to establish an account with the intermediary to access this information.

(b) *Investor qualification.* Each time before accepting any investment commitment (including any additional investment commitment from the same person), an intermediary must:

(1) Have a reasonable basis for believing that the investor satisfies the investment limitations established by section 4(a)(6)(B) of the Act (15 U.S.C. 77d(a)(6)(B)) and this part. An intermediary may rely on an investor's representations concerning compliance with the investment limitation requirements concerning the investor's annual income, net worth, and the amount of the investor's other investments made pursuant to section 4(a)(6) of the Securities Act (15 U.S.C. 77d(a)(6)) unless the intermediary has reason to question the reliability of the representation.

(2) Obtain from the investor: (i) A representation that the investor has reviewed the intermediary's educational materials delivered pursuant to Rule 302(b), understands that the entire amount of his or her investment may be lost, and is in a financial condition to bear the loss of the investment; and

(ii) A questionnaire completed by the investor demonstrating the investor's understanding that:

(A) There are restrictions on the investor's ability to cancel an investment commitment and obtain a return of his or her investment;

(B) It may be difficult for the investor to resell securities acquired in reliance on section 4(a)(6) of the Securities Act (15 U.S.C. 77d(a)(6)); and

(C) Investing in securities offered and sold in reliance on section 4(a)(6) of the Securities Act (15 U.S.C. 77d(a)(6)) involves risk, and the investor should not invest any funds in an offering made in reliance on section 4(a)(6) of the Securities Act unless he or she can afford to lose the entire amount of his or her investment.

(c) *Communication channels.* An intermediary must provide on its platform communication channels by which persons can communicate with one another and with representatives of the issuer about offerings made available on the intermediary's platform, provided:

(1) If the intermediary is a funding portal, it does not participate in these communications other than to establish guidelines for communication and remove abusive or potentially fraudulent communications;

(2) The intermediary permits public access to view the discussions made in the communication channels;

(3) The intermediary restricts posting of comments in the communication channels to those persons who have opened an account with the intermediary on its platform; and

(4) The intermediary requires that any person posting a comment in the communication channels clearly and prominently disclose with each posting whether he or she is a founder or an employee of an issuer engaging in promotional activities on behalf of the issuer, or is otherwise compensated, whether in the past or prospectively, to promote the issuer's offering.

(d) *Notice of investment commitment.* An intermediary must promptly, upon receipt of an investment commitment from an investor, give or send to the investor a notification disclosing:

(1) The dollar amount of the investment commitment;

(2) The price of the securities, if known;

(3) The name of the issuer; and

(4) The date and time by which the investor may cancel the investment commitment.

(e) *Maintenance and transmission of funds.* (1) An intermediary that is a registered broker must comply with the requirements of Rule 15c2-4.

(2) An intermediary that is a funding portal must direct investors to transmit the money or other consideration directly to a qualified third party that has agreed in writing to hold the funds for the benefit of, and to promptly transmit or return the funds to, the persons entitled thereto in accordance with paragraph (e)(3) of this section.

For purposes of this subpart C (Rules 300 through 305), a qualified third party means a:

(i) Registered broker or dealer that carries customer or broker or dealer accounts and holds funds or securities for those persons; or

(ii) Bank or credit union (where such credit union is insured by National Credit Union Administration) that has agreed in writing either to hold the funds in escrow for the persons who have the beneficial interests therein and to transmit or return such funds directly to the persons entitled thereto when so directed by the funding portal as described in paragraph (e)(3) of this section, or to maintain a bank or credit union account (or accounts) for the exclusive benefit of investors and the issuer.

(3) A funding portal that is an intermediary in a transaction involving the offer or sale of securities in reliance on section 4(a)(6) of the Securities Act (15 U.S.C. 77d(a)(6)) shall promptly direct the qualified third party to:

(i) Transmit funds from the qualified third party to the issuer when the aggregate amount of investment commitments from all investors is equal to or greater than the target amount of the offering and the cancellation period as set forth in Rule 304 has elapsed, *provided that* in no event may the funding portal direct this transmission of funds earlier than 21 days after the date on which the intermediary makes publicly available on its platform the information required to be provided by the issuer under §Rule 201 and 227.203(a);

(ii) Return funds to an investor when an investment commitment has been cancelled in accordance with Rule 304 (including for failure to obtain effective reconfirmation as required under Rule 304(c)); and

(iii) Return funds to investors when an issuer does not complete the offering. 578

(f) *Confirmation of transaction.* (1) An intermediary must, at or before the completion of a transaction in a security in reliance on section 4(a)(6) of the Securities Act (15 U.S.C. 77d(a)(6)), give or send to each investor a notification disclosing:

(i) The date of the transaction;

(ii) The type of security that the investor is purchasing;

(iii) The identity, price, and number of securities purchased by the investor, as well as the number of securities sold by the issuer in the transaction and the price(s) at which the securities were sold;

(iv) If a debt security, the interest rate and the yield to maturity calculated from the price paid and the maturity date;

(v) If a callable security, the first date that the security can be called by the issuer; and

(vi) The source, form and amount of any remuneration received or to be received by the intermediary in connection with the transaction, including any remuneration received or to be received by the intermediary from persons other than the issuer.

(2) An intermediary satisfying the requirements of paragraph (f)(1) of this section is exempt from the requirements of §240.10b-10 of this chapter with respect to a transaction in a security offered and sold in reliance on section 4(a)(6) of the Securities Act (15 U.S.C. 77d(a)(6)).

Rule 304. Completion of offerings, cancellations and reconfirmations

(a) *Generally*. An investor may cancel an investment commitment for any reason until 48 hours prior to the deadline identified in the issuer's offering materials. During the 48 hours prior to such deadline, an investment commitment may not be cancelled except as provided in paragraph (c) of this section.

(b) *Early completion of offering*. If an issuer reaches the target offering amount prior to the deadline identified in its offering materials pursuant to Rule 201(g), the issuer may close the offering on a date earlier than the deadline identified in its offering materials pursuant to Rule 201(g), *provided that:*

(1) The offering remains open for a minimum of 21 days pursuant to Rule 303(a);

(2) The intermediary provides notice to any potential investors, and gives or sends notice to investors that have made investment commitments in the offering, of:

(i) The new, anticipated deadline of the offering;

(ii) The right of investors to cancel investment commitments for any reason until 48 hours prior to the new offering deadline; and

(iii) Whether the issuer will continue to accept investment commitments during the 48- hour period prior to the new offering deadline.

(3) The new offering deadline is scheduled for and occurs at least five business days after the notice required in paragraph (b)(2) of this section is provided; and

(4) At the time of the new offering deadline, the issuer continues to meet or exceed the target offering amount.

(c) *Cancellations and reconfirmations based on material changes.* (1) If there is a material change to the terms of an offering or to the information provided by the issuer, the intermediary must give or send to any investor who has made an investment commitment notice of the material change and that the investor's investment commitment will be cancelled unless the investor reconfirms his or her investment commitment within five business days of receipt of the notice. If the investor fails to reconfirm his or her investment within those five business days, the intermediary within five business days thereafter must:

(i) Give or send the investor a notification disclosing that the commitment was cancelled, the reason for the cancellation and the refund amount that the investor is expected to receive; and

(ii) Direct the refund of investor funds.

(2) If material changes to the offering or to the information provided by the issuer regarding the offering occur within five business days of the maximum number of days that an offering is to remain open, the offering must be extended to allow for a period of five business days for the investor to reconfirm his or her investment.

(d) *Return of funds if offering is not completed.* If an issuer does not complete an offering, an intermediary must within five business days:

(1) Give or send each investor a notification of the cancellation, disclosing the reason for the cancellation, and the refund amount that the investor is expected to receive;

(2) Direct the refund of investor funds; and

(3) Prevent investors from making investment commitments with respect to that offering on its platform.

Rule 305. Payments to third parties

(a) *Prohibition on payments for personally identifiable information.* An intermediary may not compensate any person for providing the intermediary with the personally identifiable information of any investor or potential investor in securities offered and sold in reliance on section 4(a)(6) of the Securities Act (15 U.S.C. 77d(a)(6)).

(b) For purposes of this rule, personally identifiable information means information that can be used to distinguish or trace an individual's identity, either alone or when combined with other personal or identifying information that is linked or linkable to a specific individual.

Subpart D – Funding Portal Regulation

Rule 400. Registration of funding portals

(a) *Registration.* A funding portal must register with the Commission, by filing a complete Form Funding Portal (§ 249.2000 of this chapter) in accordance with the instructions on the form, and become a member of a national securities association registered under section 15A of the Exchange Act (15 U.S.C. 78*o*-3). The registration will be effective the later of:

(1) Thirty calendar days after the date that the registration is received by the Commission; or

(2) The date the funding portal is approved for membership by a national securities association registered under section 15A of the Exchange Act (15 U.S.C. 78o-3).

(b) *Amendments to registration.* A funding portal must file an amendment to Form Funding Portal (§ 249.2000 of this chapter) within 30 days of any of the information previously submitted on Form Funding Portal becoming inaccurate for any reason.

(c) *Successor registration.* (1) If a funding portal succeeds to and continues the business of a registered funding portal, the registration of the predecessor will remain effective as the registration of the successor if the successor, within 30 days after such succession, files a registration on Form Funding Portal (Rule 2000 of this chapter) and the predecessor files a withdrawal on Form Funding Portal; *provided, however*, that the registration of the predecessor funding portal will be deemed withdrawn 45 days after registration on Form Funding Portal is filed by the successor.

(2) Notwithstanding paragraph (c)(1) of this section, if a funding portal succeeds to and continues the business of a registered funding portal and the

succession is based solely on a change of the predecessor's date or state of incorporation, form of organization, or composition of a partnership, the successor may, within 30 days after the succession, amend the registration of the predecessor on Form Funding Portal (Rule 2000 of this chapter) to reflect these changes.

(d) *Withdrawal.* A funding portal must promptly file a withdrawal of registration on Form Funding Portal (Rule 2000 of this chapter) in accordance with the instructions on the form upon ceasing to operate as a funding portal. Withdrawal will be effective on the later of 30 days after receipt by the Commission (after the funding portal is no longer operational), or within such longer period of time as to which the funding portal consents or which the Commission by order may determine as necessary or appropriate in the public interest or for the protection of investors.

(e) *Applications and reports.* The applications and reports provided for in this section shall be considered filed when a complete Form Funding Portal (Rule 2000 of this chapter) is submitted with the Commission. Duplicate originals of the applications and reports provided for in this section must be filed with surveillance personnel designated by any registered national securities association of which the funding portal is a member.

(f) *Nonresident funding portals.* Registration pursuant to this section by a nonresident funding portal shall be conditioned upon there being an information sharing arrangement in place between the Commission and the competent regulator in the jurisdiction under the laws of which the nonresident funding portal is organized or where it has its principal place of business, that is applicable to the nonresident funding portal.

(1) *Definition.* For purposes of this section, the term *nonresident funding portal* shall mean a funding portal incorporated in or organized under the laws of a jurisdiction outside of the United States or its territories, or having its principal place of business in any place not in the United States or its territories.

(2) *Power of attorney.* (i) Each nonresident funding portal registered or applying for registration pursuant to this section shall obtain a written consent and power of attorney appointing an agent in the United States, other than the Commission or a Commission member, official or employee, upon whom may be served any process, pleadings or other papers in any action under the federal securities laws. This consent and power of attorney must be signed by the nonresident funding portal and the named agent(s) for service of process.

(ii) Each nonresident funding portal registered or applying for registration pursuant to this section shall, at the time of filing its application on Form Funding Portal (Rule 2000 of this chapter), furnish to the Commission the name and address of its United States agent for service of process on Schedule C to the Form.

(iii) Any change of a nonresident funding portal's agent for service of process and any change of name or address of a nonresident funding portal's existing agent for service of process shall be communicated promptly to the Commission through amendment of the Schedule C to Form Funding Portal (Rule 2000 of this chapter).

(iv) Each nonresident funding portal must promptly appoint a successor agent for service of process if the nonresident funding portal discharges its identified agent for service of process or if its agent for service of process is unwilling or unable to accept service on behalf of the nonresident funding portal.

(v) Each nonresident funding portal must maintain, as part of its books and records, the written consent and power of attorney identified in paragraph (f)(2)(i) of this section for at least three years after the agreement is terminated.

(3) *Access to books and records; inspections and examinations*—(i) *Certification and opinion of counsel.* Any nonresident funding portal applying for registration pursuant to this section shall:

(A) Certify on Schedule C to Form Funding Portal (§ 249.2000 of this chapter) that the nonresident funding portal can, as a matter of law, and will provide the Commission and any registered national securities association of which it becomes a member with prompt access to the books and records of such nonresident funding portal and can, as a matter of law, and will submit to onsite inspection and examination by the Commission and any registered national securities association of which it becomes a member; and

(B) Provide an opinion of counsel that the nonresident funding portal can, as a matter of law, provide the Commission and any registered national securities association of which it becomes a member with prompt access to the books and records of such nonresident funding portal and can, as a matter of law, submit to onsite inspection and examination by the Commission and any registered national securities association of which it becomes a member.

(ii) *Amendments*. The nonresident funding portal shall re-certify, on Schedule C to Form Funding Portal (Rule 2000 of this chapter), within 90 days after any changes in the legal or regulatory framework that would impact the nonresident funding portal's ability to provide, or the manner in which it provides, the Commission, or any registered national securities association of which it is a member, with prompt access to its books and records or that would impact the Commission's or such registered national securities association's ability to inspect and examine the nonresident funding portal. The re-certification shall be accompanied by a revised opinion of counsel describing how, as a matter of law, the nonresident funding portal can continue to meet its obligations under paragraphs (f)(3)(i)(A) and (B) of this section.

Rule 401. Exemption

A funding portal that is registered with the Commission pursuant to Rule 400 is exempt from the broker registration requirements of section 15(a)(1) of the Exchange Act (15 U.S.C. 78*o*(a)(1)) in connection with its activities as a funding portal.

Rule 402. Conditional safe harbor

(a) *General*. Under section 3(a)(80) of the Exchange Act (15 U.S.C. 78c(a)(80)), a funding portal acting as an intermediary in a transaction involving the offer or sale of securities in reliance on section 4(a)(6) of the Securities Act (15 U.S.C. 77d(a)(6)) may not: offer investment advice or recommendations; solicit purchases, sales, or offers to buy the securities offered or displayed on its platform or portal; compensate employees, agents, or other persons for such solicitation or based on the sale of securities displayed or referenced on its platform or portal; hold, manage, possess, or otherwise handle investor funds or securities; or engage in such other activities as the Commission, by rule, determines appropriate. This section is intended to provide clarity with respect to the ability of a funding portal to engage in certain activities, consistent with the prohibitions under section 3(a)(80) of the Exchange Act. No presumption shall arise that a funding portal has violated the prohibitions under section 3(a)(80) of the Exchange Act or this part by reason of the funding portal or its associated persons engaging in activities in connection with the offer or sale of securities in reliance on section 4(a)(6) of the Securities Act that do not meet the conditions specified in paragraph (b) of this section. The antifraud provisions and all other applicable provisions of the federal securities laws continue to apply to the activities described in paragraph (b) of this section.

(b) *Permitted activities*. A funding portal may, consistent with the prohibitions under section 3(a)(80) of the Exchange Act (15 U.S.C. 78c(a)(80)) and this part:

(1) Determine whether and under what terms to allow an issuer to offer and sell securities in reliance on section 4(a)(6) of the Securities Act (15 U.S.C. 77d(a)(6)) through its platform; provided that a funding portal otherwise complies with this part;

(2) Apply objective criteria to highlight offerings on the funding portal's platform where:

(i) The criteria are reasonably designed to highlight a broad selection of issuers offering securities through the funding portal's platform, are applied consistently to all issuers and offerings and are clearly displayed on the funding portal's platform;

(ii) The criteria may include, among other things, the type of securities being offered (for example, common stock, preferred stock or debt securities); the geographic location of the issuer; the industry or business segment of the issuer; the number or amount of investment commitments made, progress in meeting the issuer's target offering amount or, if applicable, the maximum offering amount; and the minimum or maximum investment amount; provided that the funding portal may not highlight an issuer or offering based on the advisability of investing in the issuer or its offering; and

(iii) The funding portal does not receive special or additional compensations for highlighting one or more issuers or offerings on its platform;

(3) Provide search functions or other tools that investors can use to search, sort, or categorize the offerings available through the funding portal's platform according to objective criteria where;

(i) The criteria may include, among other things, the type of securities being offered (for example, common stock, preferred stock or debt securities); the geographic location of the issuer; the industry or business segment of the issuer; the number or amount of investment commitments made, progress in meeting the issuer's target offering amount or, if applicable, the maximum offering amount; and the minimum or maximum investment amount; and

(ii) The criteria may not include, among other things, the advisability of investing in the issuer or its offering, or an assessment of any characteristic of the issuer, its business plan, its key management or risks associated with an investment.

(4) Provide communication channels by which investors can communicate with one another and with representatives of the issuer through the funding portal's platform about offerings through the platform, so long as the funding portal (and its associated persons):

(i) Does not participate in these communications, other than to establish guidelines for communication and remove abusive or potentially fraudulent communications;

(ii) Permits public access to view the discussions made in the communication channels;

(iii) Restricts posting of comments in the communication channels to those persons who have opened an account on its platform; and

(iv) Requires that any person posting a comment in the communication channels clearly disclose with each posting whether he or she is a founder or an employee of an issuer engaging in promotional activities on behalf of the issuer, or is otherwise compensated, whether in the past or prospectively, to promote an issuer's offering;

(5) Advise an issuer about the structure or content of the issuer's offering, including assisting the issuer in preparing offering documentation;

(6) Compensate a third party for referring a person to the funding portal, so long as the third party does not provide the funding portal with personally identifiable information of any potential investor, and the compensation, other than that paid to a registered broker or dealer, is not based, directly or indirectly, on the purchase or sale of a security in reliance on section 4(a)(6) of the Securities Act (15 U.S.C. 77d(a)(6)) offered on or through the funding portal's platform;

(7) Pay or offer to pay any compensation to a registered broker or dealer for services, including referrals pursuant to paragraph (b)(6) of this section, in connection with the offer or sale of securities by the funding portal in reliance on section 4(a)(6) of the Act(15 U.S.C. 77d(a)(6)), provided that:

(i) Such services are provided pursuant to a written agreement between the funding portal and the registered broker or dealer;

(ii) Such services and compensation are permitted under this part; and

(iii) Such services and compensation comply with the rules of any registered national securities association of which the funding portal is a member;

(8) Receive any compensation from a registered broker or dealer for services provided by the funding portal in connection with the offer or sale of securities by the funding portal in reliance on section 4(a)(6) of the Securities Act (15 U.S.C. 77d(a)(6)), provided that:

(i) Such services are provided pursuant to a written agreement between the funding portal and the registered broker or dealer;

(ii) Such compensation is permitted under this part; and

(iii) Such compensation complies with the rules of any registered national securities association of which the funding portal is a member;

(9) Advertise the existence of the funding portal and identify one or more issuers or offerings available on the portal on the basis of objective criteria, as long as:

(i) The criteria are reasonably designed to identify a broad selection of issuers offering securities through the funding portal's platform, and are applied consistently to all potential issuers and offerings;

(ii) The criteria may include, among other things, the type of securities being offered (for example, common stock, preferred stock or debt securities); the geographic location of the issuer; the industry or business segment of the issuer; the expressed interest by investors, as measured by number or amount of investment commitments made, progress in meeting the issuer's target offering amount or, if applicable, the maximum offering amount; and the minimum or maximum investment amount; and

(iii) The funding portal does not receive special or additional compensation for identifying the issuer or offering in this manner;

(10) Deny access to its platform to, or cancel an offering of an issuer, pursuant to Rule 301(c)(2), if the funding portal has a reasonable basis for believing that the issuer or the offering presents the potential for fraud or otherwise raises concerns about investor protection;

(11) Accept, on behalf of an issuer, an investment commitment for securities offered in reliance on section 4(a)(6) of the Securities Act (15 U.S.C. 77d(a)(6)) by that issuer on the funding portal's platform;

(12) Direct investors where to transmit funds or remit payment in connection with the purchase of securities offered and sold in reliance on section 4(a)(6) of the Securities Act (15 U.S.C. 77d(a)(6)); and

(13) Direct a qualified third party, as required by Rule 303(e), to release proceeds to an issuer upon completion of a crowdfunding offering or to return proceeds to investors in the event an investment commitment or an offering is cancelled.

Rule 403. Compliance

(a) *Policies and procedures*. A funding portal must implement written policies and procedures reasonably designed to achieve compliance with the federal securities laws and the rules and regulations thereunder relating to its business as a funding portal.

(b) *Privacy*. A funding portal must comply with the requirements of part 248 of this chapter as they apply to brokers.

(c) *Inspections and examinations*. A funding portal shall permit the examination and inspection of all of its business and business operations that relate to its activities as a funding portal, such as its premises, systems, platforms, and records by representatives of the Commission and of the registered national securities association of which it is a member.

Rule 404. Records to be made and kept by funding portals

(a) *Generally*. A funding portal shall make and preserve the following records for five years, the first two years in an easily accessible place:

(1) All records related to an investor who purchases or attempts to purchase securities through the funding portal;

(2) All records related to issuers who offer and sell or attempt to offer and sell securities through the funding portal and the control persons of such issuers;

(3) Records of all communications that occur on or through its platform;

(4) All records related to persons that use communication channels provided by a funding portal to promote an issuer's securities or communicate with potential investors;

(5) All records required to demonstrate compliance with the requirements of subparts C (Rules 300 through 305) and D (Rules 400 through 404) of this part;

(6) All notices provided by such funding portal to issuers and investors generally through the funding portal's platform or otherwise, including, but not limited to, notices addressing hours of funding portal operations (if any), funding portal malfunctions, changes to funding portal procedures, maintenance of hardware and software, instructions pertaining to access to the funding portal and denials of, or limitations on, access to the funding portal;

(7) All written agreements (or copies thereof) entered into by such funding portal relating to its business as such;

(8) All daily, monthly and quarterly summaries of transactions effected through the funding portal, including:

(i) Issuers for which the target offering amount has been reached and funds distributed; and

(ii) Transaction volume, expressed in:

(A) Number of transactions;

(B) Number of securities involved in a transaction;

(C) Total amounts raised by, and distributed to, issuers; and

(D) Total dollar amounts raised across all issuers, expressed in U.S. dollars; and

(9) A log reflecting the progress of each issuer who offers or sells securities through the funding portal toward meeting the target offering amount.

(b) *Organizational documents*. A funding portal shall make and preserve during the operation of the funding portal and of any successor funding portal, all organizational documents relating to the funding portal, including but not limited to, partnership agreements, articles of incorporation or charter, minute books and stock certificate books (or other similar type documents).

(c) *Format.* The records required to be maintained and preserved pursuant to paragraph (a) of this section must be produced, reproduced, and maintained in the original, non-alterable format in which they were created or as permitted under Rule 17a-4(f) of this chapter.

(d) *Third parties.* The records required to be made and preserved pursuant to this section may be prepared or maintained by a third party on behalf of a funding portal. An agreement with a third party shall not relieve a funding portal from the responsibility to prepare and maintain records as specified in this rule. A funding portal must file with the registered national securities association of which it is a member, a written undertaking in a form acceptable to the registered national securities association, signed by a duly authorized person of the third party, stating in effect that such records are the property of the funding portal and will be surrendered promptly on request of the funding portal. The undertaking shall include the following provision:

> With respect to any books and records maintained or preserved on behalf of [name of funding portal], the undersigned hereby acknowledges that the books and records are the property of [name of funding portal], and hereby undertakes to permit examination of such books and records at any time, or from time to time, during business hours by representatives of the Securities and Exchange Commission and the registered national securities association of which the funding portal is a member, and to promptly furnish to the Commission, its representatives, and the registered national securities association of which the funding portal is a member, a true, correct, complete and current hard copy of any, all, or any part of, such books and records.

(e) *Review of records.* All records of a funding portal are subject at any time, or from time to time, to reasonable periodic, special, or other examination by the representatives of the Commission and the registered national securities association of which a funding portal is a member. Every funding portal shall furnish promptly to the Commission, its representatives, and the registered national securities association of which the funding portal is a member true, correct, complete and current copies of such records of the funding portal that are requested by the representatives of the Commission and the registered national securities association.

(f) *Financial recordkeeping and reporting of currency and foreign transactions.* A funding portal that is subject to the requirements of the Currency and Foreign Transactions Reporting Act of 1970 (15 U.S.C. 5311 *et seq.*) shall comply with the reporting, recordkeeping and record retention requirements of 31 CFR chapter X. Where 31 CFR chapter X and Rule 404(a) and (b) require the same records or reports to be preserved for different periods of time, such records or reports shall be preserved for the longer period of time.

Subpart E – Miscellaneous Provisions

Rule 501. Restrictions on resales

(a) Securities issued in a transaction exempt from registration pursuant to section 4(a)(6) of the Securities Act (15 U.S.C. 77d(a)(6)) and in accordance with section 4A of the Securities Act (15 U.S.C. 77d-1) and this part may not be transferred by any purchaser of such securities during the one-year period beginning when the securities were issued in a transaction exempt from registration pursuant to section 4(a)(6) of the Securities Act (15 U.S.C. 77d(a)(6)), unless such securities are transferred:

(1) To the issuer of the securities;

(2) To an accredited investor;

(3) As part of an offering registered with the Commission; or

(4) To a member of the family of the purchaser or the equivalent, to a trust controlled by the purchaser, to a trust created for the benefit of a member of the family of the purchaser or the equivalent, or in connection with the death or divorce of the purchaser or other similar circumstance.

(b) For purposes of this Rule 501, the term *accredited investor* shall mean any person who comes within any of the categories set forth in Rule 501(a) of this chapter, or who the seller reasonably believes comes within any of such categories, at the time of the sale of the securities to that person.

(c) For purposes of this section, the term *member of the family of the purchaser or the equivalent* includes a child, stepchild, grandchild, parent, stepparent, grandparent, spouse or spousal equivalent, sibling, mother-in-law, father-in-law, son-in-law, daughter-in-law, brother-in- law, or sister-in-law of the purchaser, and shall include adoptive relationships. For purposes of this paragraph (c), the term *spousal equivalent* means a cohabitant occupying a relationship generally equivalent to that of a spouse.

Rule 502. Insignificant deviations from a term, condition or requirement of this part (Regulation Crowdfunding)

(a) A failure to comply with a term, condition, or requirement of this part will not result in the loss of the exemption from the requirements of Section 5 of the Securities Act (15 U.S.C. 77e) for any offer or sale to a particular individual or entity, if the issuer relying on the exemption shows:

(1) The failure to comply was insignificant with respect to the offering as a whole;

(2) The issuer made a good faith and reasonable attempt to comply with all applicable terms, conditions and requirements of this part; and

(3) The issuer did not know of such failure where the failure to comply with a term, condition or requirement of this part was the result of the failure of the intermediary to comply with the requirements of section 4A(a) of the Securities Act (15 U.S.C. 77d-1(a)) and the related rules, or such failure by the intermediary occurred solely in offerings other than the issuer's offering.

(b) Paragraph (a) of this section shall not preclude the Commission from bringing an enforcement action seeking any appropriate relief for an issuer's failure to comply with all applicable terms, conditions and requirements of this part.

Rule 503. Disqualification provisions

(a) *Disqualification events.* No exemption under this section 4(a)(6) of the Securities Act (15 U.S.C. 77d(a)(6)) shall be available for a sale of securities if the issuer; any predecessor of the issuer; any affiliated issuer; any director, officer, general partner or managing member of the issuer; any beneficial owner of 20 percent or more of the issuer's outstanding voting equity securities, calculated on the basis of voting power; any promoter connected with the issuer in any capacity at the time of such sale; any person that has been or will be paid (directly or indirectly) remuneration for solicitation of purchasers in connection with such sale of securities; or any general partner, director, officer or managing member of any such solicitor:

(1) Has been convicted, within 10 years before the filing of the offering statement (or five years, in the case of issuers, their predecessors and affiliated issuers), of any felony or misdemeanor:

(i) In connection with the purchase or sale of any security;

(ii) Involving the making of any false filing with the Commission; or

(iii) Arising out of the conduct of the business of an underwriter, broker, dealer, municipal securities dealer, investment adviser, funding portal or paid solicitor of purchasers of securities;

(2) Is subject to any order, judgment or decree of any court of competent jurisdiction, entered within five years before the filing of the information required by section 4A(b) of the Securities Act (15 U.S.C. 77d-1(b)) that, at the time of such filing, restrains or enjoins such person from engaging or continuing to engage in any conduct or practice:

(i) In connection with the purchase or sale of any security;

(ii) Involving the making of any false filing with the Commission; or

(iii) Arising out of the conduct of the business of an underwriter, broker, dealer, municipal securities dealer, investment adviser, funding portal or paid solicitor of purchasers of securities;

(3) Is subject to a final order of a state securities commission (or an agency or officer of a state performing like functions); a state authority that supervises or examines banks, savings associations or credit unions; a state insurance commission (or an agency or officer of a state performing like functions); an appropriate federal banking agency; the U.S. Commodity Futures Trading Commission; or the National Credit Union Administration that:

(i) At the time of the filing of the information required by section 4A(b) of the Securities Act (15 U.S.C. 77d-1(b)), bars the person from:

(A) Association with an entity regulated by such commission, authority, agency or officer;

(B) Engaging in the business of securities, insurance or banking; or

(C) Engaging in savings association or credit union activities; or

(ii) Constitutes a final order based on a violation of any law or regulation that prohibits fraudulent, manipulative or deceptive conduct entered within ten years before such filing of the offering statement;

Instruction to paragraph (a)(3). Final order shall mean a written directive or declaratory statement issued by a federal or state agency, described in Rule 503(a)(3), under applicable statutory authority that provides for notice and an opportunity for hearing, which constitutes a final disposition or action by that federal or state agency.

(4) Is subject to an order of the Commission entered pursuant to section 15(b) or 15B(c) of the Exchange Act (15 U.S.C. 78*o*(b) or 78*o*-4(c)) or Section 203(e) or (f) of the Investment Advisers Act of 1940 (15 U.S.C. 80b-3(e) or (f)) that, at the time of the filing of the information required by section 4A(b) of the Securities Act (15 U.S.C. 77d-1(b)):

(i) Suspends or revokes such person's registration as a broker, dealer, municipal securities dealer, investment adviser or funding portal;

(ii) Places limitations on the activities, functions or operations of such person; or

(iii) Bars such person from being associated with any entity or from participating in the offering of any penny stock;

(5) Is subject to any order of the Commission entered within five years before the filing of the information required by section 4A(b) of the Securities Act (15 U.S.C. 77d-1(b)) that, at the time of such filing, orders the person to cease and desist from committing or causing a violation or future violation of:

(i) Any scienter-based anti-fraud provision of the federal securities laws, including without limitation Section 17(a)(1) of the Securities Act (15 U.S.C. 77q(a)(1)), Section 10(b) of the Exchange Act (15 U.S.C. 78j(b)) and 17 CFR 240.10b-5, section 15(c)(1) of the Exchange Act (15 U.S.C. 78o(c)(1)) and Section 206(1) of the Investment Advisers Act of 1940 (15 U.S.C. 80b-6(1)) or any other rule or regulation thereunder; or

(ii) Section 5 of the Securities Act (15 U.S.C. 77e);

(6) Is suspended or expelled from membership in, or suspended or barred from association with a member of, a registered national securities exchange or a registered national or affiliated securities association for any act or omission to act constituting conduct inconsistent with just and equitable principles of trade;

(7) Has filed (as a registrant or issuer), or was or was named as an underwriter in, any registration statement or Regulation A (Rules 251 through 263) offering statement filed with the Commission that, within five years before the filing of the information required by section 4A(b) of the Securities Act (15 U.S.C. 77d-1(b)), was the subject of a refusal order, stop order, or order suspending the Regulation A exemption, or is, at the time of such filing, the subject of an investigation or proceeding to determine whether a stop order or suspension order should be issued; or

(8) Is subject to a United States Postal Service false representation order entered within five years before the filing of the information required by section 4A(b) of the Securities Act (15 U.S.C. 77d-1(b)), or is, at the time of such filing, subject to a temporary restraining order or preliminary injunction with respect to conduct alleged by the United States Postal Service to constitute a scheme or device for obtaining money or property through the mail by means of false representations.

(b) *Transition, waivers, reasonable care exception.* Paragraph (a) of this section shall not apply:

(1) With respect to any conviction, order, judgment, decree, suspension, expulsion or bar that occurred or was issued before May 16, 2016;

(2) Upon a showing of good cause and without prejudice to any other action by the Commission, if the Commission determines that it is not necessary under the circumstances that an exemption be denied;

(3) If, before the filing of the information required by section 4A(b) of the Securities Act (15 U.S.C. 77d-1(b)), the court or regulatory authority that entered the relevant order, judgment or decree advises in writing (whether contained in the relevant judgment, order or decree or separately to the Commission or its staff) that disqualification under paragraph (a) of this section should not arise as a consequence of such order, judgment or decree; or

(4) If the issuer establishes that it did not know and, in the exercise of reasonable care, could not have known that a disqualification existed under paragraph (a) of this section.

Instruction to paragraph (b)(4). An issuer will not be able to establish that it has exercised reasonable care unless it has made, in light of the circumstances, factual inquiry into whether any disqualifications exist. The nature and scope of the factual inquiry will vary based on the facts and circumstances concerning, among other things, the issuer and the other offering participants.

(c) *Affiliated issuers.* For purposes of paragraph (a) of this section, events relating to any affiliated issuer that occurred before the affiliation arose will be not considered disqualifying if the affiliated entity is not:

(1) In control of the issuer; or

(2) Under common control with the issuer by a third party that was in control of the affiliated entity at the time of such events.

(d) *Intermediaries.* A person that is subject to a statutory disqualification as defined in section 3(a)(39) of the Exchange Act (15 U.S.C. 78c(a)(39)) may not act as, or be an associated person of, an intermediary in a transaction involving the offer or sale of securities in reliance on section 4(a)(6) of the Securities Act (15 U.S.C. 77d(a)(6)) unless so permitted pursuant to Commission rule or order.

Instruction to paragraph (d). § 240.17f-2 of this chapter generally requires the fingerprinting of every person who is a partner, director, officer or employee of a broker, subject to certain exceptions.

REGULATION S–K—STANDARD INSTRUCTIONS FOR FILING FORMS UNDER SECURITIES ACT OF 1933, SECURITIES EXCHANGE ACT OF 1934 AND ENERGY POLICY AND CONSERVATION ACT OF 1975

(Cite as 17 CFR § 229.__)

Item

SUBPART 700—MISCELLANEOUS

701. Recent Sales of Unregistered Securities; Use of Proceeds from Registered Securities
702. Indemnification of Directors and Officers
703. Purchases of Equity Securities by the Issuer and Affiliated Purchasers

SUBPART 800—LIST OF INDUSTRY GUIDES

801. Securities Act Industry Guides
802. Exchange Act Industry Guides

SUBPART 900—ROLL–UP TRANSACTIONS

901. Definitions
902. Individual partnership supplements
903. Summary
904. Risk factors and other considerations
905. Comparative information
906. Allocation of roll–up consideration
907. Background of the roll–up transaction
908. Reasons for and alternatives to the roll–up transaction
909. Conflicts of interest
910. Fairness of the transaction
911. Reports, opinions and appraisals
912. Source and amount of funds and transactional expenses
913. Other provisions of the transaction
914. Pro forma financial statements: selected financial data
915. Federal income tax consequences

SUBPART 1000—MERGERS AND ACQUISITIONS (REGULATION M–A)

1000. Definitions
1001. Summary term sheet
1002. Subject company information
1003. Identity and background of filing person
1004. Terms of the transaction
1005. Past contacts, transactions, negotiations and agreements
1006. Purposes of the transaction and plans or proposals
1007. Source and amount of funds or other consideration
1008. Interest in securities of the subject company
1009. Persons/assets, retained, employed, compensated or used
1010. Financial statements
1011. Additional information
1012. The solicitation or recommendation
1013. Purposes, alternatives, reasons and effects in a going–private transaction
1014. Fairness of the going–private transaction
1015. Reports, opinions, appraisals and negotiations
1016. Exhibits

SUBPART 1100—ASSET–BACKED SECURITIES (REGULATION AB)

1100. General
1101. Definitions
1102. Forepart of registration statement and outside cover page of the prospectus
1103. Transaction summary and risk factors
1104. Sponsors
1105. Static pool information
1106. Depositors
1107. Issuing entities
1108. Servicers
1109. Trustees and transaction parties
1110. Originators

Subpart 1—General

ATTENTION ELECTRONIC FILERS

THIS REGULATION SHOULD BE READ IN CONJUNCTION WITH REGULATION S–T (17 CFR 232), WHICH GOVERNS THE PREPARATION AND SUBMISSION OF DOCUMENTS IN ELECTRONIC FORMAT. MANY PROVISIONS RELATING TO THE PREPARATION AND SUBMISSION OF DOCUMENTS IN PAPER FORMAT CONTAINED IN THIS REGULATION ARE SUPERSEDED BY THE PROVISIONS OF REGULATION S–T FOR DOCUMENTS REQUIRED TO BE FILED IN ELECTRONIC FORMAT.

Item 10. General

(a) *Application of Regulation S–K.* This part (together with the General Rules and Regulations under the Securities Act of 1933, 15 U.S.C. 77a et seq., as amended (*Securities Act*), and the Securities Exchange Act of 1934, 15 U.S.C. 78a et seq., as amended (*Exchange Act*) (17 CFR 230 and 17 CFR 240), the Interpretative Releases under these Acts (17 CFR 231 and 17 CFR 241) and the forms under these Acts (17 CFR 239 and 17 CFR 249) states the requirements applicable to the content of the non-financial statement portions of):

(1) Registration statements under the Securities Act (17 CFR 239) to the extent provided in the forms to be used for registration under such Act; and

(2) Registration statements under section 12 (subpart C of 17 CFR 249), annual or other reports under sections 13 and 15(d) (subparts D and E of 17 CFR 249), going-private transaction statements under section 13 (17 CFR 240), tender offer statements under sections 13 and 14 (17 CFR 240), annual reports to security holders and proxy and information statements under section 14 (17 CFR 240), and any other documents required to be filed under the Exchange Act, to the extent provided in the forms and rules under that Act.

(b) *Commission Policy on Projections.* The Commission encourages the use in documents specified in Rule 175 under the Securities Act and Rule 3b–6 under the Exchange Act of management's projections of future economic performance that have a reasonable basis and are presented in an appropriate format. The guidelines set forth herein represent the Commission's views on important factors to be considered in formulating and disclosing such projections.

(1) *Basis for Projections.* The Commission believes that management must have the option to present in Commission filings its good faith assessment of a registrant's future performance. Management, however, must have a reasonable basis for such an assessment. Although a history of operations or experience in projecting may be among the factors providing a basis for management's assessment, the Commission does not believe that a registrant always must have had such a history or experience in order to formulate projections with a reasonable basis. An outside review of management's projections may furnish additional support for having a reasonable basis for a projection. If management decides to include a report of such a review in a Commission filing, there also should be disclosure of the qualifications of the reviewer, the extent of the review, the relationship between the reviewer and the registrant, and other material factors concerning the process by which any outside review was sought or obtained. Moreover, in the case of a registration statement under the Securities Act, the reviewer would be deemed an expert and an appropriate consent must be filed with the registration statement.

(2) *Format for Projections.* In determining the appropriate format for projections included in Commission filings, consideration must be given to, among other things, the financial items to be projected, the period to be covered, and the manner of presentation to be used. Although traditionally projections have been given for three financial items generally considered to be of primary importance to investors (revenues, net income (loss) and earnings (loss) per share), projection information need not necessarily be limited to these three items. However, management should take care to assure that the choice of items projected is not susceptible of misleading inferences through selective projection of only favorable items. Revenues, net income (loss) and earnings (loss) per share usually are presented together in order to avoid any misleading inferences that may arise when the individual items reflect contradictory trends. There may be instances, however, when it is appropriate to present earnings (loss) from continuing operations in addition to or in lieu of net income (loss). It generally would be misleading to present sales or revenue projections without one of the foregoing measures of income. The period that appropriately may be covered by a projection depends to a large extent on the particular circumstances of the company involved. For certain companies in certain industries, a projection covering a two or three year period may be entirely reasonable. Other companies may not have a reasonable basis for projections beyond the current year. Accordingly, management should select the period most appropriate in the circumstances. In addition, management, in making a projection, should disclose what, in its opinion, is the most probable specific amount or the most reasonable range for each financial item projected based on the selected assumptions. Ranges, however, should not be so wide as to make the disclosures meaningless. Moreover, several projections based on varying assumptions may be judged by management to be more meaningful than a single number or range and would be permitted.

(3) *Investor Understanding.* (i) When management chooses to include its projections in a Commission filing, the disclosures accompanying the projections should facilitate investor understanding of the basis for and limitations of projections. In this regard investors should be cautioned against attributing undue certainty to management's assessment, and the Commission believes that investors would be aided by a statement indicating management's intention regarding the furnishing of updated projections. The Commission also believes that investor understanding would be enhanced by disclosure of the assumptions which in management's opinion are most significant to the projections or are the key factors upon which the financial results of the enterprise depend and encourages disclosure of assumptions in a manner that will provide a framework for analysis of the projection.

(ii) Management also should consider whether disclosure of the accuracy or inaccuracy of previous projections would provide investors with important insights into the limitations of projections. In this regard, consideration should be given to presenting the projections in a format that will facilitate subsequent analysis of the reasons for differences between actual and forecast results. An important benefit may arise from the systematic analysis of variances between projected and actual results on a continuing basis, since such disclosure may highlight for investors the most significant risk and profit-sensitive areas in a business operation.

(iii) With respect to previously issued projections, registrants are reminded of their responsibility to make full and prompt disclosure of material facts, both favorable and unfavorable, regarding their financial condition. This responsibility may extend to situations where management knows or has reason to know that its previously disclosed projections no longer have a reasonable basis.

(iv) Since a registrant's ability to make projections with relative confidence may vary with all the facts and circumstances, the responsibility for determining whether to discontinue or to resume making projections is best left to management. However, the Commission encourages registrants not to discontinue or to resume projections in Commission filings without a reasonable basis.

(c) *Commission Policy on Security Ratings.* In view of the importance of security ratings ("ratings") to investors and the marketplace, the Commission permits registrants to disclose, on a voluntary basis, ratings assigned by rating organizations to classes of debt securities, convertible debt securities and preferred stock in registration statements and periodic reports. Set forth herein are the Commission's views on important matters to be considered in disclosing security ratings.

(1) *Securities Act Filings.* (i) If a registrant includes in a registration statement filed under the Securities Act any rating(s) assigned to a class of securities, it should consider including:

(A) Any other rating intended for public dissemination assigned to such class by a nationally recognized statistical rating organizations ("NRSRO") ("additional NRSRO rating") that is available on the date of the initial filing of the document and that is materially different from any rating disclosed; and

(B) the name of each rating organization whose rating is disclosed; each such rating organization's definition or description of the category in which it rated the class of securities; the relative rank of each rating within the assigning rating organization's overall classification system; and a statement informing investors that a security rating is not a recommendation to buy, sell or hold securities, that it may be subject to revision or withdrawal at any time by the assigning rating organization, and that each rating should be evaluated independently of any other rating. The registrant also should include the written consent of any rating organization that is not a NRSRO whose rating is included. With respect to the written consent of any NRSRO whose rating is included, see Rule 436(g) under the Securities Act.

(ii) If a change in a rating already included is available subsequent to the filing of the registration statement, but prior to its effectiveness, the registrant should consider including such rating change in the final prospectus. If the rating change is material or if a materially different rating from any disclosed becomes available during this period, the registrant should consider amending the registration statement to include the rating change or additional rating and recirculating the preliminary prospectus.

(iii) If a materially different additional NRSRO rating or a material change in a rating already included becomes available during any period in which offers or sales are being made, the registrant should consider disclosing such additional rating or rating change by means of post-effective amendment or sticker to the prospectus pursuant to Rule 424(b) under the Securities Act, unless, in the case of a registration statement on Form S–3 (17 CFR 239.13), it has been disclosed in a document incorporated by reference into the registration statement subsequent to its effectiveness and prior to the termination of the offering.

(2) *Exchange Act Filings.* (i) If a registrant includes in a registration statement or periodic report filed under the Exchange Act any rating(s) assigned to a class of securities, it should consider including the information specified in paragraphs (c)(1)(i)(A) and (B) of this item.

(ii) If there is a material change in the rating(s) assigned by any NRSRO(s) to any outstanding class(es) of securities of a registrant subject to the reporting requirements of section 13(a) or 15(d) of the Exchange Act, the registrant should consider filing a report on Form 8–K (17 CFR 249.308) or other appropriate report under the Exchange Act disclosing such rating change.

(d) *Incorporation by Reference.* Where rules, regulations, or instructions to forms of the Commission permit incorporation by reference, a document may be so incorporated by reference to the specific document and to the prior filing or submission in which such document was physically filed or submitted. Except where a registrant or issuer is expressly required to incorporate a document or documents by reference (or for purposes of Item 1100(c) of Regulation AB with respect to an asset-backed issuer, as that term is defined in Item 1101 of Regulation AB), reference may not be made to any document which incorporates another document by reference if the pertinent portion of the document containing the information or financial statements to be incorporated by reference includes an incorporation by reference to another document. No document on file with the Commission for more than five years may be incorporated by reference except:

(1) Documents contained in registration statements, which may be incorporated by reference as long as the registrant has a reporting requirement with the Commission; or

(2) Documents that the registrant specifically identifies by physical location by SEC file number reference, provided such materials have not been disposed of by the Commission pursuant to its Records Control Schedule (17 CFR 200.80f).

(e) *Use of Non–GAAP Financial Measures in Commission Filings.* (1) Whenever one or more non–GAAP financial measures are included in a filing with the Commission:

(i) The registrant must include the following in the filing:

(A) A presentation, with equal or greater prominence, of the most directly comparable financial measure or measures calculated and presented in accordance with Generally Accepted Accounting Principles (GAAP);

(B) A reconciliation (by schedule or other clearly understandable method), which shall be quantitative for historical non–GAAP measures presented, and quantitative, to the extent available without unreasonable efforts, for forward-looking information, of the differences between the non–GAAP financial measure disclosed or released with the most directly comparable financial measure or measures calculated and presented in accordance with GAAP identified in paragraph (e)(1)(i)(A) of this section;

(C) A statement disclosing the reasons why the registrant's management believes that presentation of the non–GAAP financial measure provides useful information to investors regarding the registrant's financial condition and results of operations; and

(D) To the extent material, a statement disclosing the additional purposes, if any, for which the registrant's management uses the non–GAAP financial measure that are not disclosed pursuant to paragraph (e)(1)(i)(C) of this section; and

(ii) A registrant must not:

(A) Exclude charges or liabilities that required, or will require, cash settlement, or would have required cash settlement absent an ability to settle in another manner, from non–GAAP liquidity measures, other than the measures earnings before interest and taxes (EBIT) and earnings before interest, taxes, depreciation, and amortization (EBITDA);

(B) Adjust a non–GAAP performance measure to eliminate or smooth items identified as non-recurring, infrequent or unusual, when the nature of the charge or gain is such that it is reasonably likely to recur within two years or there was a similar charge or gain within the prior two years;

(C) Present non–GAAP financial measures on the face of the registrant's financial statements prepared in accordance with GAAP or in the accompanying notes;

(D) Present non–GAAP financial measures on the face of any *pro forma* financial information required to be disclosed by Article 11 of Regulation S–X (Rules 11–01 through 11–03); or

(E) Use titles or descriptions of non–GAAP financial measures that are the same as, or confusingly similar to, titles or descriptions used for GAAP financial measures; and

(iii) If the filing is not an annual report on Form 10–K or Form 20–F (17 CFR 249.220f), a registrant need not include the information required by paragraphs (e)(1)(i)(C) and (e)(1)(i)(D) of this item if that information was included in its most recent annual report on Form 10–K or Form 20–F or a more recent filing, provided that the required information is updated to the extent necessary to meet the requirements of paragraphs (e)(1)(i)(C) and (e)(1)(i)(D) of this section at the time of the registrant's current filing.

(2) For purposes of this paragraph (e), a non–GAAP financial measure is a numerical measure

of a registrant's historical or future financial performance, financial position or cash flows that:

(i) Excludes amounts, or is subject to adjustments that have the effect of excluding amounts, that are included in the most directly comparable measure calculated and presented in accordance with GAAP in the statement of comprehensive income, balance sheet or statement of cash flows (or equivalent statements) of the issuer; or

(ii) Includes amounts, or is subject to adjustments that have the effect of including amounts, that are excluded from the most directly comparable measure so calculated and presented.

(3) For purposes of this paragraph (e), GAAP refers to generally accepted accounting principles in the United States, except that:

(i) In the case of foreign private issuers whose primary financial statements are prepared in accordance with non-U.S. generally accepted accounting principles, GAAP refers to the principles under which those primary financial statements are prepared; and

(ii) In the case of foreign private issuers that include a non–GAAP financial measure derived from or based on a measure calculated in accordance with U.S. generally accepted accounting principles, GAAP refers to U.S. generally accepted accounting principles for purposes of the application of the requirements of this paragraph (e) to the disclosure of that measure.

(4) For purposes of this paragraph (e), non–GAAP financial measures exclude:

(i) Operating and other statistical measures; and

(ii) Ratios or statistical measures calculated using exclusively one or both of:

(A) Financial measures calculated in accordance with GAAP; and

(B) Operating measures or other measures that are not non–GAAP financial measures.

(5) For purposes of this paragraph (e), non–GAAP financial measures exclude financial measures required to be disclosed by GAAP, Commission rules, or a system of regulation of a government or governmental authority or self-regulatory organization that is applicable to the registrant. However, the financial measure should be presented outside of the financial statements unless the financial measure is required or expressly permitted by the standard-setter that is responsible for establishing the GAAP used in such financial statements.

(6) The requirements of paragraph (e) of this section shall not apply to a non–GAAP financial measure included in disclosure relating to a proposed business combination, the entity resulting therefrom or an entity that is a party thereto, if the disclosure is contained in a communication that is subject to Rule 425, Rule 14a–12 or Rule 14d–2(b)(2) under the Securities Exchange Act of 1934 or Item 1015 of Regulation M–A.

(7) The requirements of paragraph (e) of this section shall not apply to investment companies registered under section 8 of the Investment Company Act of 1940 (15 U.S.C. 80a–8).

Note to Paragraph (e): A non–GAAP financial measure that would otherwise be prohibited by paragraph (e)(1)(ii) of this section is permitted in a filing of a foreign private issuer if:

1. The non–GAAP financial measure relates to the GAAP used in the registrant's primary financial statements included in its filing with the Commission;

2. The non–GAAP financial measure is required or expressly permitted by the standard-setter that is responsible for establishing the GAAP used in such financial statements; and

3. The non–GAAP financial measure is included in the annual report prepared by the registrant for use in the jurisdiction in which it is domiciled, incorporated or organized or for distribution to its security holders.

(f) *Smaller Reporting Companies.* The requirements of this part apply to smaller reporting companies. A smaller reporting company may comply with either the requirements applicable to smaller reporting companies or the requirements applicable to other companies for each item, unless the requirements for smaller reporting companies specify that smaller reporting companies must comply with the smaller reporting company requirements. The following items of this part set forth requirements for smaller reporting companies that are different from requirements applicable to other companies:

Index of Scaled Disclosure Available to Smaller Reporting Companies

Item 101	Description of business
Item 201	Market price of and dividends on registrant's common equity and related stockholder matters

Item 301	Selected financial data
Item 302	Supplementary financial information
Item 303	Management's discussion and analysis of financial condition and results of operations
Item 305	Quantitative and qualitative disclosures about market risk
Item 402	Executive compensation
Item 404	Transactions with related persons, promoters and certain control persons
Item 407	Corporate governance
Item 503	Prospectus summary, risk factors, and ratio of earnings to fixed charges
Item 504	Use of proceeds
Item 601	Exhibits

(1) *Definition of Smaller Reporting Company.* As used in this part, the term *smaller reporting company* means an issuer that is not an investment company, an asset-backed issuer (as defined in Item 1101 of Regulation AB), or a majority-owned subsidiary of a parent that is not a smaller reporting company and that:

(i) Had a public float of less than $250 million; or

(ii) Had annual revenues of less than $100 million and either:

(A) No public float; or

(B) A public float of less than $700 million.

(2) *Determination.* Whether an issuer is a smaller reporting company is determined on an annual basis.

(i) For issuers that are required to file reports under section 13(a) or 15(d) of the Exchange Act:

(A) Public float is measured as of the last business day of the issuer's most recently completed second fiscal quarter and computed by multiplying the aggregate worldwide number of shares of its voting and non-voting common equity held by non-affiliates by the price at which the common equity was last sold, or the average of the bid and asked prices of common equity, in the principal market for the common equity;

(B) Annual revenues are as of the most recently completed fiscal year for which audited financial statements are available; and

(C) An issuer must reflect the determination of whether it came within the definition of smaller reporting company in its quarterly report on Form 10–Q for the first fiscal quarter of the next year, indicating on the cover page of that filing, and in subsequent filings for that fiscal year, whether it is a smaller reporting company, except that, if a determination based on public float indicates that the issuer is newly eligible to be a smaller reporting company, the issuer may choose to reflect this determination beginning with its first quarterly report on Form 10–Q following the determination, rather than waiting until the first fiscal quarter of the next year.

(ii) For determinations based on an initial registration statement under the Securities Act or Exchange Act for shares of its common equity:

(A) Public float is measured as of a date within 30 days of the date of the filing of the registration statement and computed by multiplying the aggregate worldwide number of shares of its voting and non-voting common equity held by non-affiliates before the registration plus, in the case of a Securities Act registration statement, the number of shares of its voting and non-voting common equity included in the registration statement by the estimated public offering price of the shares;

(B) Annual revenues are as of the most recently completed fiscal year for which audited financial statements are available; and

(C) The issuer must reflect the determination of whether it came within the definition of smaller reporting company in the registration statement and must appropriately indicate on the cover page of the filing, and subsequent filings for the fiscal year in which the filing is made, whether it is a smaller reporting company. The issuer must re-determine its status at the end of its second fiscal quarter and then reflect any change in status as provided in paragraph (f)(2)(i)(C) of this section. In the case of a determination based on an initial Securities Act registration statement, an issuer that was not determined to be a smaller reporting company has the option to re-determine its status at the conclusion of the offering covered by the registration statement based on the actual offering price and number of shares sold.

(iii) Once an issuer determines that it does not qualify for smaller reporting company status because it exceeded one or more of the current thresholds, it will remain unqualified unless when making its annual determination either:

(A) It determines that its public float was less than $200 million; or

(B) It determines that its public float and its annual revenues meet the requirements for subsequent qualification included in the following chart:

Prior Annual Revenues	Prior Public Float: None or less than $700 million	Prior Public Float: $700 million or more
Less than $100 million	Neither threshold exceeded.	**Public float** Less than $560 million; and **Revenues** Less than $100 million.
$100 million or more	**Public float** None or less than $700 million; and **Revenues** Less than $80 million.	**Public float** Less than $560 million; and **Revenues** Less than $80 million.

Instruction 1 to paragraph (f): A registrant that qualifies as a smaller reporting company under the public float thresholds identified in paragraphs (f)(1)(i) and (f)(2)(iii)(A) of this section will qualify as a smaller reporting company regardless of its revenues.

Subpart 100—Business

Item 101. Description of business

(a) *General Development of Business.* Describe the general development of the business of the registrant, its subsidiaries and any predecessor(s) during the past five years, or such shorter period as the registrant may have been engaged in business. Information shall be disclosed for earlier periods if material to an understanding of the general development of the business.

(1) In describing developments, information shall be given as to matters such as the following: the year in which the registrant was organized and its form of organization; the nature and results of any bankruptcy, receivership or similar proceedings with respect to the registrant or any of its significant subsidiaries; the nature and results of any other material reclassification, merger or consolidation of the registrant or any of its significant subsidiaries; the acquisition or disposition of any material amount of assets otherwise than in the ordinary course of business; and any material changes in the mode of conducting the business.

(2) Registrants; (i) Filing a registration statement on Form S–1 (17 CFR 239.11) under the Securities Act or on Form 10 (17 CFR 249.210) under the Exchange Act, (ii) Not subject to the reporting requirements of section 13(a) or 15(d) of the Exchange Act immediately before the filing of such registration statement, and (iii) That (including predecessors) have not received revenue from operations during each of the three fiscal years immediately before the filing of such registration statement, shall provide the following information:

(A) if the registration statement is filed prior to the end of the registrant's second fiscal quarter, a description of the registrant's plan of operation for the remainder of the fiscal year; or

(B) if the registration statement is filed subsequent to the end of the registrant's second fiscal quarter, a description of the registrant's plan of operation for the remainder of the fiscal year and for the first six months of the next fiscal year. If such information is not available, the reasons for its not being available shall be stated. Disclosure relating to any plan shall include such matters as:

(1) In the case of a registration statement on Form S–1, a statement in narrative form indicating the registrant's opinion as to the period of time that the proceeds from the

offering will satisfy cash requirements and whether in the next six months it will be necessary to raise additional funds to meet the expenditures required for operating the business of the registrant; the specific reasons for such opinion shall be set forth and categories of expenditures and sources of cash resources shall be identified; however, amounts of expenditures and cash resources need not be provided; in addition, if the narrative statement is based on a cash budget, such budget shall be furnished to the Commission as supplemental information, but not as part of the registration statement;

(2) An explanation of material product research and development to be performed during the period covered in the plan;

(3) Any anticipated material acquisition of plant and equipment and the capacity thereof;

(4) Any anticipated material changes in number of employees in the various departments such as research and development, production, sales or administration; and

(5) Other material areas which may be peculiar to the registrant's business.

(b) [Reserved]

(c) *Narrative Description of Business.* (1) Describe the business done and intended to be done by the registrant and its subsidiaries, focusing upon the registrant's dominant segment or each reportable segment about which financial information is presented in the financial statements. To the extent material to an understanding of the registrant's business taken as a whole, the description of each such segment shall include the information specified in paragraphs (c)(1)(i) through (x) of this Item. The matters specified in paragraphs (c)(1)(xi) through (xiii) of this Item shall be discussed with respect to the registrant's business in general; where material, the segments to which these matters are significant shall be identified.

(i) The principal products produced and services rendered by the registrant in the segment and the principal markets for, and methods of distribution of, the segment's principal products and services. In addition, state for each of the last three fiscal years the amount or percentage of total revenue contributed by any class of similar products or services which accounted for 10 percent or more of consolidated revenue in any of the last three fiscal years or 15 percent or more of consolidated revenue, if total revenue did not exceed $50,000,000 during any of such fiscal years.

(ii) A description of the status of a product or segment (e.g. whether in the planning stage, whether prototypes exist, the degree to which product design has progressed or whether further engineering is necessary), if there has been a public announcement of, or if the registrant otherwise has made public information about, a new product or segment that would require the investment of a material amount of the assets of the registrant or that otherwise is material. This paragraph is not intended to require disclosure of otherwise nonpublic corporate information the disclosure of which would affect adversely the registrant's competitive position.

(iii) The sources and availability of raw materials.

(iv) The importance to the segment and the duration and effect of all patents, trademarks, licenses, franchises and concessions held.

(v) The extent to which the business of the segment is or may be seasonal.

(vi) The practices of the registrant and the industry (respective industries) relating to working capital items (e.g., where the registrant is required to carry significant amounts of inventory to meet rapid delivery requirements of customers or to assure itself of a continuous allotment of goods from suppliers; where the registrant provides rights to return merchandise; or where the registrant has provided extended payment terms to customers).

(vii) The dependence of the segment upon a single customer, or a few customers, the loss of any one or more of which would have a material adverse effect on the segment. The name of any customer and its relationship, if any, with the registrant or its subsidiaries shall be disclosed if sales to the customer by one or more segments are made in an aggregate amount equal to 10 percent or more of the registrant's consolidated revenues and the loss of such customer would have a material adverse effect on the registrant and its subsidiaries taken as a whole. The names of other customers may be included, unless in the particular case the effect of including the names would be misleading. For purposes of this paragraph, a group of customers under common control or customers that are affiliates of each other shall be regarded as a single customer.

(viii) The dollar amount of backlog orders believed to be firm, as of a recent date and as of a comparable date in the preceding fiscal year, together with an indication of the portion thereof not reasonably expected to be filled within the current fiscal year, and seasonal or other material aspects of the backlog. (There may be included as firm orders government orders that are firm but not yet funded and contracts awarded but not yet signed, provided an appropriate statement is added to explain the nature of such orders and the amount thereof. The portion of orders already included in sales or operating revenues on the basis of percentage of completion or program accounting shall be excluded.)

(ix) A description of any material portion of the business that may be subject to renegotiation of profits or termination of contracts or subcontracts at the election of the Government.

(x) Competitive conditions in the business involved including, where material, the identity of the particular markets in which the registrant competes, an estimate of the number of competitors and the registrant's competitive position, if known or reasonably available to the registrant. Separate consideration shall be given to the principal products or services or classes of products or services of the segment, if any. Generally, the names of competitors need not be disclosed. The registrant may include such names, unless in the particular case the effect of including the names would be misleading. Where, however, the registrant knows or has reason to know that one or a small number of competitors is dominant in the industry it shall be identified. The principal methods of competition (e.g., price, service, warranty or product performance) shall be identified, and positive and negative factors pertaining to the competitive position of the registrant, to the extent that they exist, shall be explained if known or reasonably available to the registrant.

(xi) [Reserved]

(xii) Appropriate disclosure also shall be made as to the material effects that compliance with Federal, State and local provisions which have been enacted or adopted regulating the discharge of materials into the environment, or otherwise relating to the protection of the environment, may have upon the capital expenditures, earnings and competitive position of the registrant and its subsidiaries. The registrant shall disclose any material estimated capital expenditures for environmental control facilities for the remainder of its current fiscal year and its succeeding fiscal year and for such further periods as the registrant may deem material.

(xiii) The number of persons employed by the registrant.

(d) [Reserved]

(e) *Available Information.* Disclose the information in paragraphs (e)(1), (e)(2) and (e)(3) of this section in any registration statement you file under the Securities Act (15 U.S.C. 77a *et seq.*), and disclose the information in paragraph (e)(3) of this section in your annual report on Form 10-K (17 CFR 249.310). Further disclose the information in paragraph (e)(4) of this section if you are an accelerated filer or a large accelerated filer (as defined in Rule 12b–2 under the Securities Exchange Act of 1934) filing an annual report on Form 10–K (17 CFR 249.310):

(1) Whether you file reports with the Securities and Exchange Commission. If you are a reporting company, identify the reports and other information you file with the SEC.

(2) State that the SEC maintains an Internet site that contains reports, proxy and information statements, and other information regarding issuers that file electronically with the SEC and state the address of that site (http://www.sec.gov).

(3) Disclose your Internet address, if you have one.

(4)(i) Whether you make available free of charge or through your Internet website, if you have one, your annual report on Form 10–K, quarterly reports on Form 10–Q (17 CFR 249.308a), current reports on Form 8–K (17 CFR 249.308), and amendments to those reports filed or furnished pursuant to Section 13(a) or 15(d) of the Securities Exchange Act of 1934 (15 U.S.C. 78m(a) or 78o(d)) as soon as reasonably practicable after you electronically file such material with, or furnish it to, the SEC;

(ii) If you do not make your filings available in this manner, the reasons you do not do so (including, where applicable, that you do not have an Internet website); and

(iii) If you do not make your filings available in this manner, whether you voluntarily will provide electronic or paper copies of your filings free of charge upon request.

(f) *Reports to Security Holders.* Disclose the following information in any registration statement you file under the Securities Act:

(1) If the SEC's proxy rules or regulations, or stock exchange requirements, do not require you to send an annual report to security holders or to holders of American depository receipts, describe briefly the nature and frequency of reports that you will give to security holders. Specify whether the reports that you give will contain financial information that has been examined and reported on, with an opinion expressed "by" an independent public or certified public accountant.

(2) For a foreign private issuer, if the report will not contain financial information prepared in accordance with U.S. generally accepted accounting principles, you must state whether the report will include a reconciliation of this information with U.S. generally accepted accounting principles.

(g) *Enforceability of Civil Liabilities Against Foreign Persons.* Disclose the following if you are a foreign private issuer filing a registration statement under the Securities Act:

(1) Whether or not investors may bring actions under the civil liability provisions of the U.S. federal securities laws against the foreign private issuer, any of its officers and directors who are residents of a foreign country, any underwriters or experts named in the registration statement that are residents of a foreign country, and whether investors may enforce these civil liability provisions when the assets of the issuer or these other persons are located outside of the United States. The disclosure must address the following matters:

(i) The investor's ability to effect service of process within the United States on the foreign private issuer or any person;

(ii) The investor's ability to enforce judgments obtained in U.S. courts against foreign persons based upon the civil liability provisions of the U.S. federal securities laws;

(iii) The investor's ability to enforce, in an appropriate foreign court, judgments of U.S. courts based upon the civil liability provisions of the U.S. federal securities laws; and

(iv) The investor's ability to bring an original action in an appropriate foreign court to enforce liabilities against the foreign private issuer or any person based upon the U.S. federal securities laws.

(2) If you provide this disclosure based on an opinion of counsel, name counsel in the prospectus and file as an exhibit to the registration statement a signed consent of counsel to the use of its name and opinion.

(h) *Smaller Reporting Companies.* A smaller reporting company, as defined by Item 10(f)(1) of Regulation S–K, may satisfy its obligations under this Item by describing the development of its business during the last three years. If the smaller reporting company has not been in business for three years, give the same information for predecessor(s) of the smaller reporting company if there are any. This business development description should include:

(1) Form and year of organization;

(2) Any bankruptcy, receivership or similar proceeding; and

(3) Any material reclassification, merger, consolidation, or purchase or sale of a significant amount of assets not in the ordinary course of business.

(4) *Business of the Smaller Reporting Company.* Briefly describe the business and include, to the extent material to an understanding of the smaller reporting company:

(i) Principal products or services and their markets;

(ii) Distribution methods of the products or services;

(iii) Status of any publicly announced new product or service;

(iv) Competitive business conditions and the smaller reporting company's competitive position in the industry and methods of competition;

(v) Sources and availability of raw materials and the names of principal suppliers;

(vi) Dependence on one or a few major customers;

(vii) Patents, trademarks, licenses, franchises, concessions, royalty agreements or labor contracts, including duration;

(viii) Need for any government approval of principal products or services. If government approval is necessary and the smaller reporting company has not yet received that approval, discuss the status of the approval within the government approval process;

(ix) Effect of existing or probable governmental regulations on the business;

(x) [Reserved]

(xi) Costs and effects of compliance with environmental laws (federal, state and local); and

(xii) Number of total employees and number of full-time employees.

(5) *Reports to Security Holders.* Disclose the following in any registration statement you file under the Securities Act of 1933:

(i) If you are not required to deliver an annual report to security holders, whether you will voluntarily send an annual report and whether the report will include audited financial statements;

(ii) Whether you file reports with the Securities and Exchange Commission. If you are a reporting company, identify the reports and other information you file with the Commission; and

(iii) State that the Commission maintains an Internet site that contains reports, proxy and information statements, and other information regarding issuers that file electronically with the Commission and state the address of that site (http://www.sec.gov). Disclose your Internet address, if available.

(6) *Foreign Issuers.* Provide the information required by Item 101(g) of Regulation S–K.

Instructions to Item 101:

1. In determining what information about the segments is material to an understanding of the registrant's business taken as a whole and therefore required to be disclosed, pursuant to paragraph (c) of this Item, the registrant should take into account both quantitative and qualitative factors such as the significance of the matter to the registrant (e.g., whether a matter with a relatively minor impact on the registrant's business is represented by management to be important to its future profitability), the pervasiveness of the matter (e.g., whether it affects or may affect numerous items in the segment information), and the impact of the matter (e.g., whether it distorts the trends reflected in the segment information). Situations may arise when information should be disclosed about a segment, although the information in quantitative terms may not appear significant to the registrant's business taken as a whole.

2. Base the determination of whether the information about segments is required for a particular year upon an evaluation of interperiod comparability. For instance, interperiod comparability would require a registrant to report segment information in the current period even if not material under the criteria for reportability of FASB ASC Topic 280, *Segment Reporting*, if a segment has been significant in the immediately preceding period and the registrant expects it to be significant in the future.

3. The Commission, upon written request of the registrant and where consistent with the protection of investors, may permit the omission of any of the information required by this Item or the furnishing in substitution thereof of appropriate information of comparable character.

Item 102. Description of property

State briefly the location and general character of the principal plants, mines and other materially important physical properties of the registrant and its subsidiaries. In addition, identify the segment(s), as reported in the financial statements, that use the properties described. If any such property is not held in fee or is held subject to any major encumbrance, so state and describe briefly how held.

Instructions to Item 102:

1. What is required is such information as reasonably will inform investors as to the suitability, adequacy, productive capacity and extent of utilization of the facilities by the registrant. Detailed descriptions of the physical characteristics of individual properties or legal descriptions by metes and bounds are not required and shall not be given.

2. In determining whether properties should be described, the registrant should take into account both quantitative and qualitative factors. See Instruction 1 to Item 101 of Regulation S–K.

3. In the case of an extractive enterprise, not involved in oil and gas producing activities, material information shall be given as to production, reserves, locations, development, and the nature of the registrant's interest. If individual properties are of major significance to an industry segment:

A. More detailed information concerning these matters shall be furnished; and

B. Appropriate maps shall be used to disclose location data of significant properties except in cases for which numerous maps would be required.

4. A registrant engaged in oil and gas producing activities shall provide the information required by Subpart 1200 of Regulation S–K.

5. In the case of extractive reserves other than oil and gas reserves, estimates other than proven or probable reserves (and any estimated values of such reserves) shall not be disclosed in any document publicly filed with the Commission, unless such information is required to be disclosed in the document by foreign or state law; provided, however, that where such estimates previously have been provided to a person (or any of its affiliates) that is offer-

ing to acquire, merge, or consolidate with the registrant, or otherwise to acquire the registrant's securities, such estimates may be included in documents relating to such acquisition.

6. The definitions in Rule 4–10(a) of Regulation S–X shall apply to this Item with respect to oil and gas operations.

7. The attention of issuers engaged in significant mining operations is directed to the information called for in Guide 7 (Item 801(g) and Item 802(g) of Regulation S–K).

8. The attention of certain issuers engaged in oil and gas producing activities is directed to the information called for in Securities Act Industry Guide 4 (referred to in Item 801(d) of Regulation S–K).

9. The attention of issuers engaged in real estate activities is directed to the information called for in Guide 5 (17 CFR 229.801(e)).

Item 103. Legal proceedings

Describe briefly any material pending legal proceedings, other than ordinary routine litigation incidental to the business, to which the registrant or any of its subsidiaries is a party or of which any of their property is the subject. Include the name of the court or agency in which the proceedings are pending, the date instituted, the principal parties thereto, a description of the factual basis alleged to underlie the proceeding and the relief sought. Include similar information as to any such proceedings known to be contemplated by governmental authorities.

Instructions to Item 103:

1. If the business ordinarily results in actions for negligence or other claims, no such action or claim need be described unless it departs from the normal kind of such actions.

2. No information need be given with respect to any proceeding that involves primarily a claim for damages if the amount involved, exclusive of interest and costs, does not exceed 10 percent of the current assets of the registrant and its subsidiaries on a consolidated basis. However, if any proceeding presents in large degree the same legal and factual issues as other proceedings pending or known to be contemplated, the amount involved in such other proceedings shall be included in computing such percentage.

3. Notwithstanding Instructions 1 and 2, any material bankruptcy, receivership, or similar proceeding with respect to the registrant or any of its significant subsidiaries shall be described.

4. Any material proceedings to which any director, officer or affiliate of the registrant, any owner of record or beneficially of more than five percent of any class of voting securities of the registrant, or any associate of any such director, officer, affiliate of the registrant, or security holder is a party adverse to the registrant or any of its subsidiaries or has a material interest adverse to the registrant or any of its subsidiaries also shall be described.

5. Notwithstanding the foregoing, an administrative or judicial proceeding (including, for purposes of A and B of this Instruction, proceedings which present in large degree the same issues) arising under any Federal, State or local provisions that have been enacted or adopted regulating the discharge of materials into the environment or primary for the purpose of protecting the environment shall not be deemed "ordinary routine litigation incidental to the business" and shall be described if:

A. Such proceeding is material to the business or financial condition of the registrant;

B. Such proceeding involves primarily a claim for damages, or involves potential monetary sanctions, capital expenditures, deferred charges or charges to income and the amount involved, exclusive of interest and costs, exceeds 10 percent of the current assets of the registrant and its subsidiaries on a consolidated basis; or

C. A governmental authority is a party to such proceeding and such proceeding involves potential monetary sanctions, unless the registrant reasonably believes that such proceeding will result in no monetary sanctions, or in monetary sanctions, exclusive of interest and costs, of less than $100,000; provided, however, that such proceedings which are similar in nature may be grouped and described generically.

Item 104. Mine safety disclosure

(a) A registrant that is the operator, or that has a subsidiary that is an operator, of a coal or other mine shall provide the information specified below for the time period covered by the report:

(1) For each coal or other mine of which the registrant or a subsidiary of the registrant is an operator, identify the mine and disclose:

(i) The total number of violations of mandatory health or safety standards that could significantly and substantially contribute to the cause and effect of a coal or other mine safety or health hazard under section 104 of the Federal Mine Safety and Health Act of 1977 (30 U.S.C. 814) for which the operator received a citation from the Mine Safety and Health Administration.

(ii) The total number of orders issued under section 104(b) of such Act (30 U.S.C. 814(b)).

(iii) The total number of citations and orders for unwarrantable failure of the mine operator to comply with mandatory health or safety standards under section 104(d) of such Act (30 U.S.C. 814(d)).

(iv) The total number of flagrant violations under section 110(b)(2) of such Act (30 U.S.C. 820(b)(2)).

(v) The total number of imminent danger orders issued under section 107(a) of such Act (30 U.S.C. 817(a)).

(vi) The total dollar value of proposed assessments from the Mine Safety and Health Administration under such Act (30 U.S.C. 801 et seq.).

Instruction to Item 104(a)(1)(vi): Registrants must provide the total dollar value of assessments proposed by MSHA relating to any type of violation during the period covered by the report, regardless of whether the registrant has challenged or appealed the assessment.

(vii) The total number of mining-related fatalities.

Instruction to Item 104(a)(1)(vii): Registrants must report all fatalities occurring at a coal or other mine during the period covered by the report unless the fatality has been determined by MSHA to be unrelated to mining activity.

(2) A list of coal or other mines, of which the registrant or a subsidiary of the registrant is an operator, that receive written notice from the Mine Safety and Health Administration of:

(i) A pattern of violations of mandatory health or safety standards that are of such nature as could have significantly and substantially contributed to the cause and effect of coal or other mine health or safety hazards under section 104(e) of such Act (30 U.S.C. 814(e)); or

(ii) The potential to have such a pattern.

(3) Any pending legal action before the Federal Mine Safety and Health Review Commission involving such coal or other mine.

Instruction to Item 104(a)(3): The registrant must report the total number of legal actions that were pending before the Federal Mine Safety and Health Review Commission as of the last day of the time period covered by the report, as well as the aggregate number of legal actions instituted and the aggregate number of legal actions resolved during the reporting period. With respect to the total number of legal actions that were pending before the Federal Mine Safety and Health Review Commission as of the last day of the time period covered by the report, the registrant must also report the number of such legal actions that are (a) contests of citations and orders referenced in Subpart B of 29 CFR Part 2700; (b) contests of proposed penalties referenced in Subpart C of 29 CFR Part 2700; (c) complaints for compensation referenced in Subpart D of 29 CFR Part 2700; (d) complaints of discharge, discrimination or interference in Subpart F of 29 CFR Part 2700; and (f) appeals of judges' decisions or orders to the Federal Mine Safety and Health Review Commission referenced in Subpart H of 29 CFR Part 2700.

(b) *Definitions.* For purposes of this Item.

(1) The term *coal or other mine* means a coal or other mine, as defined in section 3 of the Federal Mine Safety and Health Act of 1977 (30 U.S.C. 802), that is subject to the provisions of such Act (30 U.S.C. 801 et seq.).

(2) The term *operator* has the meaning given the term in section 3 of the Federal Mine Safety and Health Act of 1977 (30 U.S.C. 802).

(3) The term *subsidiary* has the meaning given the term in Rule 12b–2 under the Securities Exchange Act of 1934.

Instruction to Item 104:

1. The registrant must provide the information by this Item as specified by Item 601(b)(95) of Regulation S–K. In addition, the registrant must provide a statement, in an appropriately captioned section of the periodic report, that the information concerning mine safety violations or other regulatory matters required by Section 1503(a) of the Dodd–Frank Wall Street Reform and Consumer Protection Act and this Item is included in exhibit 95 to the periodic report.

2. When the disclosure required by this item is included in an exhibit to an annual report on Form 10–K, the information is to be provided for the registrant's fiscal year.

Subpart 200—Securities of the Registrant

Item 201. Market price of and dividends on the registrant's common equity and related stockholder matters

(a) *Market Information.* (1)(i) Identify the principal United States market(s) and the corresponding trading symbol(s) for each class of the registrant's common equity. In the case of foreign registrants, also identify the principal foreign public trading market(s), if any, and the corresponding trading symbol(s) for each class of the registrant's common equity.

(ii) If the principal United States market for such common equity is not an exchange, indicate, as applicable, that any over-the-counter market quotations reflect inter-dealer prices, without retail mark-up, mark-down or commission and may not necessarily represent actual transactions.

(iii) Where there is no established public trading market for a class of common equity, furnish a statement to that effect and, if applicable, state the range of high and low bid information for each full quarterly period within the two most recent fiscal years and any subsequent interim period for which financial statements are included, or are required to be included by 17 CFR 210.3–01 through 210.3–20 (Article 3 of Regulation S–X), indicating the source of such quotations. Reference to quotations shall be qualified by appropriate explanation. For purposes of this Item the existence of limited or sporadic quotations should not of itself be deemed to constitute an "established public trading market."

(2) If the information called for by this paragraph (a) is being presented in a registration statement on Form S–1 (17 CFR 239.11) under the Securities Act or on Form 10 (17 CFR 249.210) under the Exchange Act relating to a class of common equity for which at the time of filing there is no established United States public trading market, indicate the amount(s) of common equity: (i) [Reserved]; (ii) that could be sold pursuant to Rule 144 or that the registrant has agreed to register under the Securities Act for sale by security holders; or (iii) that is being, or has been publicly proposed to be, publicly offered by the registrant (unless such common equity is being offered pursuant to an employee benefit plan or dividend reinvestment plan), the offering of which could have a material effect on the market price of the registrant's common equity.

(b) *Holders.* (1) Set forth the approximate number of holders of each class of common equity of the registrant as of the latest practicable date.

(2) If the information called for by this paragraph (b) is being presented in a registration statement filed pursuant to the Securities Act or a proxy statement or information statement filed pursuant to the Exchange Act that relates to an acquisition, business combination or other reorganization, indicate the effect of such transaction on the amount and percentage of present holdings of the registrant's common equity owned beneficially by (i) any person (including any group as that term is used in section 13(d)(3) of the Exchange Act) who is known to the registrant to be the beneficial owner of more than five percent of any class of the registrant's common equity and (ii) each director and nominee and (iii) all directors and officers as a group, and the registrant's present commitments to such persons with respect to the issuance of shares of any class of its common equity.

(c) *Dividends.* (1) [Reserved]

(2) Where registrants have a record of paying no cash dividends although earnings indicate an ability to do so, they are encouraged to consider the question of their intention to pay cash dividends in the foreseeable future and, if no such intention exists, to make a statement of that fact in the filing. Registrants which have a history of paying cash dividends also are encouraged to indicate whether they currently expect that comparable cash dividends will continue to be paid in the future and, if not, the nature of the change in the amount or rate of cash dividend payments.

(d) *Securities Authorized for Issuance Under Equity Compensation Plans.* (1) In the following tabular format, provide the information specified in paragraph (d)(2) of this Item as of the end of the most recently completed fiscal year with respect to compensation plans (including individual compensation arrangements) under which equity securities of the registrant are authorized for issuance, aggregated as follows:

(i) All compensation plans previously approved by security holders; and

(ii) All compensation plans not previously approved by security holders.

EQUITY COMPENSATION PLAN INFORMATION

Plan category	Number of securities to be issued upon exercise of outstanding options, warrants and rights	Weighted-average exercise price of outstanding options, warrants and rights	Number of securities remaining available for future issuance under equity compensation plans (excluding securities reflected in column (a))
	(a)	(b)	(c)
Equity compensation plans approved by security holders			
Equity compensation plans not approved by security holders			
Total			

(2) The table shall include the following information as of the end of the most recently completed fiscal year for each category of equity compensation plan described in paragraph (d)(1) of this Item:

(i) The number of securities to be issued upon the exercise of outstanding options, warrants and rights (column (a));

(ii) The weighted-average exercise price of the outstanding options, warrants and rights disclosed pursuant to paragraph (d)(2)(i) of this Item (column (b)); and

(iii) Other than securities to be issued upon the exercise of the outstanding options, warrants and rights disclosed in paragraph (d)(2)(i) of this Item, the number of securities remaining available for future issuance under the plan (column (c)).

(3) For each compensation plan under which equity securities of the registrant are authorized for issuance that was adopted without the approval of security holders, describe briefly, in narrative form, the material features of the plan.

Instructions to Paragraph (d):

1. Disclosure shall be provided with respect to any compensation plan and individual compensation arrangement of the registrant (or parent, subsidiary or affiliate of the registrant) under which equity securities of the registrant are authorized for issuance to employees or non-employees (such as directors, consultants, advisors, vendors, customers, suppliers or lenders) in exchange for consideration in the form of goods or services as described in FASB ASC Topic 718, *Compensation—Stock Compensation*, and FASB ASC Subtopic 505–50, *Equity—Equity–Based Payments to Non–Employees*. No disclosure is required with respect to:

a. Any plan, contract or arrangement for the issuance of warrants or rights to all security holders of the registrant as such on a pro rata basis (such as a stock rights offering) or

b. Any employee benefit plan that is intended to meet the qualification requirements of Section 401(a) of the Internal Revenue Code (26 U.S.C. 401(a)).

2. For purposes of this paragraph, an "individual compensation arrangement" includes, but is not limited to, the following: a written compensation contract within the meaning of "employee benefit plan" under Rule 405 and a plan (whether or not set forth in any formal document) applicable to one person as provided under Item 402(a)(6)(ii) of Regulation S–K.

3. If more than one class of equity security is issued under its equity compensation plans, a registrant should aggregate plan information for each class of security.

4. A registrant may aggregate information regarding individual compensation arrangements with the plan information required under paragraph (d)(1)(i) and (ii) of this Item, as applicable.

5. A registrant may aggregate information regarding a compensation plan assumed in connection with a merger, consolidation or other acquisition transaction pursuant to which the registrant may make subsequent grants or awards of its equity securities with the plan information required under paragraph (d)(1)(i) and (ii) of this Item, as applicable. A registrant shall disclose on an aggregated basis in a footnote to the table the information required under paragraph (d)(2)(i) and (ii) of this Item with respect to any individual options, warrants or rights assumed in connection with a merger, consolidation or other acquisition transaction.

6. To the extent that the number of securities remaining available for future issuance disclosed in column (c) includes securities available for future issuance under any compensation plan or individual compensation arrangement other than upon the exercise of an option, warrant or right, disclose the number of securities and type of plan separately for each such plan in a footnote to the table.

7. If the description of an equity compensation plan set forth in a registrant's financial statements contains the disclosure required by paragraph (d)(3) of this Item, a cross-reference to such description will satisfy the requirements of paragraph (d)(3) of this Item.

8. If an equity compensation plan contains a formula for calculating the number of securities available for issuance under the plan, including, without limitation, a formula that automatically increases the number of securities available for issuance by a percentage of the number of outstanding securities of the registrant, a description of this formula shall be disclosed in a footnote to the table.

9. Except where it is part of a document that is incorporated by reference into a prospectus, the information required by this paragraph need not be provided in any registration statement filed under the Securities Act.

(e) *Performance Graph.* (1) Provide a line graph comparing the yearly percentage change in the registrant's cumulative total shareholder return on a class of common stock registered under section 12 of the Exchange Act (as measured by dividing the sum of the cumulative amount of dividends for the measurement period, assuming dividend reinvestment, and the difference between the registrant's share price at the end and the beginning of the measurement period; by the share price at the beginning of the measurement period) with:

(i) The cumulative total return of a broad equity market index assuming reinvestment of dividends, that includes companies whose equity securities are traded on the same exchange or are of comparable market capitalization; *provided, however*, that if the registrant is a company within the Standard & Poor's 500 Stock Index, the registrant must use that index; and

(ii) The cumulative total return, assuming reinvestment of dividends, of:

(A) A published industry or line-of-business index;

(B) Peer issuer(s) selected in good faith. If the registrant does not select its peer issuer(s) on an industry or line-of-business basis, the registrant shall disclose the basis for its selection; or

(C) Issuer(s) with similar market capitalization(s), but only if the registrant does not use a published industry or line-of-business index and does not believe it can reasonably identify a peer group. If the registrant uses this alternative, the graph shall be accompanied by a statement of the reasons for this selection.

(2) For purposes of paragraph (e)(1) of this Item, the term "measurement period" shall be the period beginning at the "measurement point" established by the market close on the last trading day before the beginning of the registrant's fifth preceding fiscal year, through and including the end of the registrant's last completed fiscal year. If the class of securities has been registered under section 12 of the Exchange Act (15 U.S.C. 78*l*) for a shorter period of time, the period covered by the comparison may correspond to that time period.

(3) For purposes of paragraph (e)(1)(ii)(A) of this Item, the term "published industry or line-of-business index" means any index that is prepared by a party other than the registrant or an affiliate and is accessible to the registrant's security holders; *provided, however*, that registrants may use an index prepared by the registrant or affiliate if such index is widely recognized and used.

(4) If the registrant selects a different index from an index used for the immediately preceding fiscal year, explain the reason(s) for this change and also compare the registrant's total return with that of both the newly selected index and the index used in the immediately preceding fiscal year.

Instructions to Item 201(e):

1. In preparing the required graphic comparisons, the registrant should:

a. Use, to the extent feasible, comparable methods of presentation and assumptions for the total return calculations required by paragraph (e)(1) of this Item; *provided, however*, that if the registrant constructs its own peer group index under paragraph (e)(1)(ii)(B), the same methodology must be used in calculating both the registrant's total return and that on the peer group index; and

b. Assume the reinvestment of dividends into additional shares of the same class of equity securities at the frequency with which dividends are paid on such securities during the applicable fiscal year.

2. In constructing the graph:

a. The closing price at the measurement point must be converted into a fixed investment, stated in dollars, in the registrant's stock (or in the stocks represented by a given index) with cumulative returns for each subsequent fiscal year measured as a change from that investment; and

b. Each fiscal year should be plotted with points showing the cumulative total return as of that point. The value of the investment as of each point plotted on a given return line is the number of shares held at that point multiplied by the then-prevailing share price.

3. The registrant is required to present information for the registrant's last five fiscal years, and may choose to graph a longer period; but the measurement point, however, shall remain the same.

4. Registrants may include comparisons using performance measures in addition to total return, such as return on average common shareholders' equity.

5. If the registrant uses a peer issuer(s) comparison or comparison with issuer(s) with similar market capitalizations, the identity of those issuers must be disclosed and the returns of each component issuer of the group must be weighted according to the respective issuer's stock market capitalization at the beginning of each period for which a return is indicated.

6. *Smaller Reporting Company*. A registrant that qualifies as a "smaller reporting company," as defined by Item 10(f)(1) of Regulation S–K, is not required to provide the information required by paragraph (e) of this Item.

7. The information required by paragraph (e) of this Item need not be provided in any filings other than an annual report to security holders required by Rule 14a–3 or Rule 14c–3 under the Securities Exchange Act of 1934 that precedes or accompanies a registrant's proxy or information statement relating to an annual meeting of security holders at which directors are to be elected (or special meeting or written consents in lieu of such meeting). Such information will not be deemed to be incorporated by reference into any filing under the Securities Act or the Exchange Act, except to the extent that the registrant specifically incorporates it by reference.

8. The information required by paragraph (e) of this Item shall not be deemed to be "soliciting material" or to be "filed" with the Commission or subject to Regulation 14A or 14C (Rules 14a–1 through 14a–104 or 14c–1 through 14c–101 under the Securities Exchange Act of 1934), other than as provided in this item, or to the liabilities of section 18 of the Exchange Act (15 U.S.C. 78r), except to the extent that the registrant specifically requests that such information be treated as soliciting material or specifically incorporates it by reference into a filing under the Securities Act or the Exchange Act.

Instruction 1 to Item 201. [Reserved]

Instruction 2 to Item 201. Bid information reported pursuant to this Item shall be adjusted to give retroactive effect to material changes resulting from stock dividends, stock splits and reverse stock splits.

Instruction 3 to Item 201. The computation of the approximate number of holders of registrant's common equity may be based upon the number of record holders or also may include individual participants in security position listings. See Rule 17Ad–8 under the Exchange Act. The method of computation that is chosen shall be indicated.

Instruction 4 to Item 201. If the registrant is a foreign issuer, describe briefly:

A. Any governmental laws, decrees or regulations in the country in which the registrant is organized that restrict the export or import of capital, including, but not limited to, foreign exchange controls, or that affect the remittance of dividends or other payments to nonresident holders of the registrant's common equity; and

B. All taxes, including withholding provisions, to which United States common equity holders are subject under existing laws and regulations of the foreign country in which the registrant is organized. Include a brief description of pertinent provisions of any reciprocal tax treaty between such foreign country and the United States regarding withholding. If there is no such treaty, so state.

Instruction 5 to Item 201. If the registrant is a foreign private issuer whose common equity of the class being registered is wholly or partially in bearer form, the response to this Item shall so indicate together with as much information as the registrant is able to provide with respect to security holdings in the United States. If the securities being registered trade in the United States in the form of American Depositary Receipts or similar certificates, the response to this Item shall so indicate together with the name of the depositary issuing such receipts and the number of shares or other units of the underlying security representing the trading units in such receipts.

Item 202. Description of registrant's securities

NOTE: If the securities being described have been accepted for listing on an exchange, the exchange may be identified. The document should not however, convey the impression that the registrant may apply successfully for listing of the securities on an exchange or that, in the case of an underwritten offering, the underwriters may request the registrant to apply for such listing, unless there is reasonable assurance that the securities to be offered will be acceptable to a securities exchange for listing.

(a) *Capital Stock.* If capital stock is to be registered, state the title of the class and describe such of the matters listed in paragraphs (a)(1) through (5) as are relevant. A complete legal description of the securities need not be given.

(1) Outline briefly: (i) dividend rights; (ii) terms of conversion; (iii) sinking fund provisions; (iv) redemption provisions; (v) voting rights, including any provisions specifying the vote required by security holders to take action; (vi) any classification of the Board of Directors, and the impact of such classification where cumulative voting is permitted or required; (vii) liquidation rights; (viii) preemption rights; and (ix) liability to further calls or to assessment by the registrant and for liabilities of the registrant imposed on its stockholders under state statutes (e.g., to laborers, servants or employees of the registrant), unless such disclosure would be immaterial because the financial resources of the registrant or other factors make it improbable that liability under such state statutes would be imposed; (x) any restriction on alienability of the securities to be registered; and (xi) any provision discriminating against any existing or prospective holder of such securities as a result of such security holder owning a substantial amount of securities.

(2) If the rights of holders of such stock may be modified otherwise than by a vote of a majority or more of the shares outstanding, voting as a class, so state and explain briefly.

(3) If preferred stock is to be registered, describe briefly any restriction on the repurchase or redemption of shares by the registrant while there is any arrearage in the payment of dividends or sinking fund installments. If there is no such restriction, so state.

(4) If the rights evidenced by, or amounts payable with respect to, the shares to be registered are, or may be, materially limited or qualified by the rights of any other authorized class of securities, include the information regarding such other securities as will enable investors to understand such limitations or qualifications. No information need be given, however, as to any class of securities all of which will be retired, provided appropriate steps to ensure such retirement will be completed prior to or upon delivery by the registrant of the shares.

(5) Describe briefly or cross-reference to a description in another part of the document, any provision of the registrant's charter or by-laws that would have an effect of delaying, deferring or preventing a change in control of the registrant and that would operate only with respect to an extraordinary corporate transaction involving the registrant (or any of its subsidiaries), such as a merger, reorganization, tender offer, sale or transfer of substantially all of its assets, or liquidation. Provisions and arrangements required by law or imposed by governmental or judicial authority need not be described or discussed pursuant to this paragraph (a)(5). Provisions or arrangements adopted by the registrant to effect, or further, compliance with laws or governmental or judicial mandate are not subject to the immediately preceding sentence where such compliance did not require the specific provisions or arrangements adopted.

(b) *Debt Securities.* If debt securities are to be registered, state the title of such securities, the principal amount being offered, and, if a series, the total amount authorized and the total amount outstanding as of the most recent practicable date; and describe such of the matter listed in paragraphs (b)(1) through (10) as are relevant. A complete legal description of the securities need not be given. For purposes solely of this Item, debt securities that differ from one another only as to the interest rate or maturity shall be regarded as securities of the same class. Outline briefly:

(1) Provisions with respect to maturity, interest, conversion, redemption, amortization, sinking fund, or retirement;

(2) Provisions with respect to the kind and priority of any lien securing the securities, together with a brief identification of the principal properties subject to such lien;

(3) Provisions with respect to the subordination of the rights of holders of the securities to other security holders or creditors of the registrant; where debt securities are designated as subordinated in accordance with Instruction 1 to this Item, set forth the aggregate amount of outstanding indebtedness as of the most recent practicable date that by the terms of such debt securities would be senior to such subordinated debt and describe briefly any limitation on the issuance of such additional senior indebtedness or state that there is no such limitation;

(4) Provisions restricting the declaration of dividends or requiring the maintenance of any asset ratio or the creation or maintenance of reserves;

(5) Provisions restricting the incurrence of additional debt or the issuance of additional securities; in the case of secured debt, whether the securities being registered are to be issued on the basis of unbonded bondable property, the deposit of cash or otherwise; as of the most recent practicable date, the approximate amount of unbonded bondable property available as a basis for the issuance of bonds; provisions permitting the withdrawal of cash deposited as a basis for the issuance of bonds; and provisions permitting the release or substitution of assets securing the issue; *Provided, however,* That provisions permitting the release of assets upon the deposit of equivalent funds or the pledge of equivalent property, the release of property no longer required in the business, obsolete property, or property taken by eminent domain or the application of insurance moneys, and other similar provisions need not be described;

(6) The general type of event that constitutes a default and whether or not any periodic evidence is required to be furnished as to the absence of default or as to compliance with the terms of the indenture;

(7) Provisions relating to modification of the terms of the security or the rights of security holders;

(8) If the rights evidenced by the securities to be registered are, or may be, materially limited or qualified by the rights of any other authorized class of securities, the information regarding such other securities as will enable investors to understand the rights evidenced by the securities; to the extent not otherwise disclosed pursuant to this Item; no information need be given, however, as to any class of securities all of which will be retired, provided appropriate steps to ensure such retirement will be completed prior to or upon delivery by the registrant of the securities;

(9) If debt securities are to be offered at a price such that they will be deemed to be offered at an "original issue discount" as defined in paragraph (a) of section 1273 of the Internal Revenue Code (26 U.S.C. 1273), or if a debt security is sold in a package with another security and the allocation of the offering price between the two securities may have the effect of offering the debt security at such an original issue discount, the tax effects thereof pursuant to section 1271–1278;

(10) The name of the trustee(s) and the nature of any material relationship with the registrant or with any of its affiliates; the percentage of securities of the class necessary to require the trustee to take action; and what indemnification the trustee may require before proceeding to enforce the lien.

(c) *Warrants and Rights.* If the securities described are to be offered pursuant to warrants or rights state:

(1) The amount of securities called for by such warrants or rights;

(2) The period during which and the price at which the warrants or rights are exercisable;

(3) The amount of warrants or rights outstanding;

(4) Provisions for changes to or adjustments in the exercise price; and

(5) Any other material terms of such rights on warrants.

(d) *Other Securities.* If securities other than capital stock, debt, warrants or rights are to be registered, include a brief description (comparable to that required in paragraphs (a), (b) and (c) of Item 202) of the rights evidenced thereby.

(e) *Market Information for Securities Other Than Common Equity.* If securities other than common equity are to be registered and there is an established public trading market for such securities (as that term is used in Item 201 of Regulation S–K) provide market information with respect to such securities comparable to that required by paragraph (a) of Item 201 of Regulation S–K.

(f) *American Depositary Receipts.* If Depositary Shares represented by American Depositary Receipts are being registered, furnish the following information:

(1) The name of the depositary and the address of its principal executive office.

(2) State the title of the American Depositary Receipts and identify the deposited security. Describe briefly the terms of deposit, including the provisions, if any, with respect to:

(i) The amount of deposited securities represented by one unit of American Depositary Receipts;

(ii) The procedure for voting, if any, the deposited securities;

(iii) The collection and distribution of dividends;

(iv) The transmission of notices, reports and proxy soliciting material;

(v) The sale or exercise of rights;

(vi) The deposit or sale of securities resulting from dividends, splits or plans of reorganization;

(vii) Amendment, extension or termination of the deposit;

(viii) Rights of holders of receipts to inspect the transfer books of the depositary and the list of holders of receipts;

(ix) Restrictions upon the right to deposit or withdraw the underlying securities;

(x) Limitation upon the liability of the depositary.

(3) Describe all fees and charges which may be imposed directly or indirectly against the holder of the American Depositary Receipts, indicating the type of service, the amount of fee or charges and to whom paid.

Instructions to Item 202:

1. Wherever the title of securities is required to be stated, there shall be given such information as will indicate the type and general character of the securities, including the following:

A. In the case of shares, the par or stated value, if any; the rate of dividends, if fixed, and whether cumulative or non-cumulative; a brief indication of the preference, if any; and if convertible or redeemable, a statement to that effect;

B. In the case of debt, the rate of interest; the date of maturity or, if the issue matures serially, a brief indication of the serial maturities, such as "maturing serially from 1955 to 1960"; if the payment of principal or interest is contingent, an appropriate indication of such contingency; a brief indication of the priority of the issue; and, if convertible or callable, a statement to that effect; or

C. In the case of any other kind of security, appropriate information of comparable character.

2. If the registrant is a foreign registrant, include (to the extent not disclosed in the document pursuant to Item 201 of Regulation S–K or otherwise) in the description of the securities:

A. A brief description of any limitations on the right of nonresident or foreign owners to hold or vote such securities imposed by foreign law or by the charter or other constituent document of the registrant, or if no such limitations are applicable, so state;

B. A brief description of any governmental laws, decrees or regulations in the country in which the registrant is organized affecting the remittance of dividends, interest and other payments to nonresident holders of the securities being registered;

C. A brief outline of all taxes, including withholding provisions, to which United States security holders are subject under existing laws and regulations of the foreign country in which the registrant is organized; and

D. A brief description of pertinent provisions of any reciprocal tax treaty between such foreign country and the United States regarding withholding or, if there is no such treaty, so state.

3. Section 305(a)(2) of the Trust Indenture Act of 1939 (15 U.S.C. 77aaa *et seq.*), as amended ("Trust Indenture Act"), shall not be deemed to require the inclusion in a registration statement or in a prospectus of any information not required by this Item.

4. Where convertible securities or stock purchase warrants are being registered that are subject to redemption or call, the description of the conversion terms of the securities or material terms of the warrants shall disclose:

A. Whether the right to convert or purchase the securities will be forfeited unless it is exercised before the date specified in a notice of the redemption or call;

B. The expiration or termination date of the warrants;

C. The kinds, frequency and timing of notice of the redemption or call, including the cities or newspapers in which notice will be published (where the securities provide for a class of newspapers or group of cities in which the publication may be made at the discretion of the registrant, the registrant should describe such provision); and

D. In the case of bearer securities, that investors are responsible for making arrangements to prevent loss of the right to convert or purchase in the event of redemption of call, for example, by reading the newspapers in which the notice of redemption or call may be published.

5. The response to paragraph (f) shall include information with respect to fees and charges in connection with (A) the deposit or substitution of the underlying securities; (B) receipt and distribution of dividends; (C) the sale or exercise of rights; (D) the withdrawal of the underlying security; and (E) the transferring, splitting or grouping of receipts. Information with respect to the right to collect the fees and charges against dividends received and deposited securities shall be included in response to this item.

6. For asset-backed securities, see also Item 1113 of Regulation AB.

Subpart 300—Financial Information

Item 301. Selected financial data

Furnish in comparative columnar form the selected financial data for the registrant referred to below, for

(a) Each of the last five fiscal years of the registrant (or for the life of the registrant and its predecessors, if less), and

(b) Any additional fiscal years necessary to keep the information from being misleading.

(c) *Smaller Reporting Companies.* A registrant that qualifies as a smaller reporting company, as defined by Item 10(f)(1) of Regulation S–K, is not required to provide the information required by this Item.

Instructions to Item 301:

1. The purpose of the selected financial data shall be to supply in a convenient and readable format selected financial data which highlight certain significant trends in the registrant's financial condition and results of operations.

2. Subject to appropriate variation to conform to the nature of the registrant's business, the following items shall be included in the table of financial data: net sales or operating revenues; income (loss) from continuing operations; income (loss) from continuing operations per common share; total assets; long-term obligations and redeemable preferred stock (including long-term debt, capital leases, and redeemable preferred stock as defined in Rule 5–02.27(a)) of Regulation S–X; and cash dividends declared per common share. Registrants may include additional items which they believe would enhance an understanding of and would highlight other trends in their financial condition and results of operations.

Briefly describe, or cross-reference to a discussion thereof, factors such as accounting changes, business combinations or dispositions of business operations, that materially affect the comparability of the information reflected in selected financial data. Discussion of, or reference to, any material uncertainties should also be included where such matters might cause the data reflected herein not to be indicative of the registrant's future financial condition or results of operations.

3. All references to the registrant in the table of selected financial data and in this Item shall mean the registrant and its subsidiaries consolidated.

4. If interim period financial statements are included, or are required to be included, by Article 3 of Regulation S–X, registrants should consider whether any or all of the selected financial data need to be updated for such interim periods to reflect a material change in the trends indicated; where such updating information is necessary, registrants shall provide the information on a comparative basis unless not necessary to an understanding of such updating information.

5. A foreign private issuer shall disclose also the following information in all filings containing financial statements:

A. In the forepart of the document and as of the latest practicable date, the exchange rate into U.S. currency of the foreign currency in which the financial statements are denominated;

B. A history of exchange rates for the five most recent years and any subsequent interim period for which financial statements are presented setting forth the rates for period end, the average rates, and the range of high and low rates for each year; and

C. If equity securities are being registered, a five year summary of dividends per share stated in both the currency in which the financial statements are denominated and United States currency based on the exchange rates at each respective payment date.

6. A foreign private issuer shall present the selected financial data in the same currency as its financial statements. The issuer may present the selected financial data on the basis of the accounting principles used in its primary financial statements but in such case shall present this data also on the basis of any reconciliations of such data to United States generally accepted accounting principles and Regulation S–X made pursuant to Rule 4–01 of Regulation S–X.

7. For purposes of this rule, the rate of exchange means the noon buying rate in New York City for cable transfers in foreign currencies as certified for customs purposes by the Federal Reserve Bank of New York. The average rate means the average of the exchange rates on the last day of each month during a year.

(d) *Emerging Growth Company.* An emerging growth company, as defined in Rule 405 of the Securities Act of 1933 (§230.405 of this chapter) or Rule 12b-2 of the Securities Exchange Act of 1934 (§240.12b-2 of this chapter), that is providing the information called for by this Item in: (1) a Securities Act registration statement, need not present selected financial data for any period prior to the earliest audited financial statements presented in connection with the registrant's initial public offering of its common equity securities; or (2) a registration statement, periodic report, or other report filed under the Exchange Act, need not present selected financial data for any period prior to the earliest audited financial statements presented in connection with its first registration statement that became effective under the Exchange Act or the Securities Act.

Item 302. Supplementary financial information

(a) *Selected Quarterly Financial Data.* Registrants specified in paragraph (a)(5) of this Item shall provide the information specified below.

(1) Disclosure shall be made of net sales, gross profit (net sales less costs and expenses associated directly with or allocated to products sold or services rendered), income (loss) from continuing operations, per share data based upon income (loss) from continuing operations, net income (loss), per share data based upon net income (loss) and net income (loss) attributable to the registrant, for each full quarter within the two most recent fiscal years and any subsequent interim period for which financial statements are included or are required to be included by 17 CFR 210.3–01 through 210.3–20 (Article 3 of Regulation S–X).

(2) When the data supplied pursuant to paragraph (a) of this section vary from the amounts previously reported on the Form 10–Q (17 CFR 249.308a) filed for any quarter, such as would be the case when a combination between entities under common control occurs or where an error is corrected, reconcile the amounts given with those previously reported and describe the reason for the difference.

(3) Describe the effect of any discontinued operations and unusual or infrequently occurring items recognized in each full quarter within the two most recent fiscal years and any subsequent interim period for which financial statements are included or are required to be included by 17 CFR 210.3–01 through 17 CFR 210.3–20 (Article 3 of Regulation S–X), as well as the aggregate effect and the nature of year-end or other adjustments which are material to the results of that quarter.

(4) If the financial statements to which this information relates have been reported on by an accountant, appropriate professional standards and procedures, as enumerated in the Statements of Auditing Standards issued by the Auditing Standards Board of the American Institute of Certified Public Accountants, shall be followed by the reporting accountant with regard to the data required by this paragraph (a).

(5) This paragraph (a) applies to any registrant, except a foreign private issuer, that has securities registered pursuant to sections 12(b) (15 U.S.C. 78*l*(b)) (other than mutual life insurance companies) or 12(g) of the Exchange Act (15 U.S.C. 78*l*(g)).

(b) *Information About Oil and Gas Producing Activities.* Registrants engaged in oil and gas producing activities shall present the information about oil and gas producing activities (as those activities are defined in Regulation S–X, Rule 4–10(a)) specified in FASB ASC Topic 932, *Extractive Activities—Oil and Gas*, if such oil and gas producing activities are regarded as significant under one or more of the tests set forth in FASB ASC Subtopic 932–235, *Extractive Activities—Oil and Gas—Notes to Financial Statements*, for "Significant Activities."

Instruction 1 to paragraph (b). (a) FASB ASC Subtopic 932-235 disclosures that relate to annual periods shall be presented for each annual period for which a statement of comprehensive income (as defined in Rule 1–02 of Regulation S–X) is required, (b) FASB ASC Subtopic 932–235 disclosures required as of the end of an annual period shall be presented as of the date of each audited balance sheet required, and (c) FASB ASC Subtopic 932-235 disclosures required as of the beginning of an annual period shall be presented as of the beginning of each annual period for which a statement of comprehensive income (as defined in Rule 1–02 of Regulation S–X) is required.

Instruction 2 to paragraph (b). This paragraph, together with 17 CFR 210.4–10 (Article 4 of Regulation S–X), prescribes financial reporting standards for the preparation of accounts by persons engaged, in whole or in part, in the production of crude oil or natural gas in the United States, pursuant to Section 503 of the Energy Policy and Conservation Act of 1975 (42 U.S.C. 8383) ("EPCA") and Section 11(c) of the Energy Supply and Environmental Coordination Act of 1974 (15 U.S.C. 796) ("ESECA") as amended by Section 506 of EPCA. The application of the paragraph to those oil and gas producing operations of companies regulated for ratemaking purposes on an individual-company-cost-of-service basis may, however, give appropriate recognition to differences arising because of the effect of the ratemaking process.

Instruction 3 to paragraph (b). Any person exempted by the Department of Energy from any record-keeping or reporting requirements pursuant to Section 11(c) of ESECA, as amended, is similarly exempted from the related provisions of this paragraph in the preparation of accounts pursuant to EPCA. This exemption does not affect the applicability of this paragraph to filings pursuant to the federal securities laws.

(c) *Smaller Reporting Companies.* A registrant that qualifies as a smaller reporting company, as defined by Item 10(f)(1) of Regulation S–K, is not required to provide the information required by this Item.

Item 303. Management's discussion and analysis of financial condition and results of operations

(a) *Full Fiscal Years.* Discuss registrant's financial condition, changes in financial condition and results of operations. The discussion shall provide information as specified in paragraphs (a)(1) through (5) of this Item and also shall provide such other information that the registrant believes to be necessary to an understanding of its financial condition, changes in financial condition and results of operations. Discussions of liquidity and capital resources may be combined whenever the two topics are interrelated. Where in the registrant's judgment a discussion of segment information and/or of other subdivisions (e.g., geographic areas) of the registrant's business would be appropriate to an understanding of such business, the discussion shall focus on each relevant, reportable segment and/or other subdivision of the business and on the registrant as a whole.

(1) *Liquidity.* Identify any known trends or any known demands, commitments, events or uncertainties that will result in or that are reasonably likely to result in the registrant's liquidity increasing or decreasing in any material way. If a material deficiency is identified, indicate the course of action that the registrant has taken or proposes to take to remedy the deficiency. Also identify and separately describe internal and external sources of liquidity, and briefly discuss any material unused sources of liquid assets.

(2) *Capital Resources.* (i) Describe the registrant's material commitments for capital expenditures as of the end of the latest fiscal period, and indicate the general purpose of such commitments and the anticipated source of funds needed to fulfill such commitments.

(ii) Describe any known material trends, favorable or unfavorable, in the registrant's capital resources. Indicate any expected material changes in the mix and relative cost of such resources. The discussion shall consider changes between equity, debt and any off-balance sheet financing arrangements.

(3) *Results of Operations.* (i) Describe any unusual or infrequent events or transactions or any significant economic changes that materially affected the amount of reported income from continuing operations and, in each case, indicate the extent to which income was so affected. In addition, describe any other significant components of revenues or expenses that, in the registrant's judgment, should be described in order to understand the registrant's results of operations.

(ii) Describe any known trends or uncertainties that have had or that the registrant reasonably expects will have a material favorable or unfavorable impact on net sales or revenues or income from continuing operations. If the registrant knows of events that will cause a material change in the relationship between costs and revenues (such as known future increases in costs of labor or materials or price increases or inventory adjustments), the change in the relationship shall be disclosed.

(iii) To the extent that the financial statements disclose material increases in net sales or revenues, provide a narrative discussion of the extent to which such increases are attributable to increases in prices or to increases in the volume or amount of goods or services being sold or to the introduction of new products or services.

(iv) For the three most recent fiscal years of the registrant, or for those fiscal years in which the registrant has been engaged in business, whichever period is shortest, discuss the impact of inflation and changing prices on the registrant's net sales and revenues and on income from continuing operations.

(4) *Off–Balance Sheet Arrangements.* (i) In a separately-captioned section, discuss the registrant's off-balance sheet arrangements that have or are reasonably likely to have a current or future effect on the registrant's financial condition, changes in financial condition, revenues or expenses, results of operations, liquidity, capital expenditures or capital resources that is material to investors. The disclosure shall include the items specified in paragraphs (a)(4)(i)(A), (B), (C) and (D) of this Item to the extent necessary to an understanding of such arrangements and effect and shall also include such other information that the registrant believes is necessary for such an understanding.

(A) The nature and business purpose to the registrant of such off-balance sheet arrangements;

(B) The importance to the registrant of such off-balance sheet arrangements in respect of its liquidity, capital resources, market risk support, credit risk support or other benefits;

(C) The amounts of revenues, expenses and cash flows of the registrant arising from such arrangements; the nature and amounts of any interests retained, securities issued and other indebtedness incurred by the registrant in connection with such arrangements; and the nature and amounts of any other obligations or liabilities (including contingent obligations or liabilities) of the registrant arising from such arrangements that are or are reasonably likely to become material and the triggering events or circumstances that could cause them to arise; and

(D) Any known event, demand, commitment, trend or uncertainty that will result in or is reasonably likely to result in the termination, or material reduction in availability to the registrant, of its off-balance sheet arrangements that provide material benefits to it, and the course of action that the registrant has taken or proposes to take in response to any such circumstances.

(ii) As used in this paragraph (a)(4), the term *off-balance sheet arrangement* means any transaction, agreement or other contractual arrangement to which an entity unconsolidated with the registrant is a party, under which the registrant has:

(A) Any obligation under a guarantee contract that has any of the characteristics identified in FASB ASC paragraph 460–10–15–4 (Guarantees Topic), as may be modified or supplemented, and that is not excluded from the initial recognition and measurement provisions of FASB ASC paragraphs 460–10–15–7, 460–10–25–1, and 460–10–30–1;

(B) A retained or contingent interest in assets transferred to an unconsolidated entity or similar arrangement that serves as credit liquidity or market risk support to such entity for such assets;

(C) Any obligation, including a contingent obligation, under a contract that would be accounted for as a derivative instrument, except that it is both indexed to the registrant's own stock and classified in stockholders' equity in the registrant's statement of financial position, and therefore excluded from the scope of FASB ASC Topic 815, *Derivatives and Hedging*, pursuant to FASB ASC subparagraph 815–10–15–74(a), as may be modified or supplemented; or

(D) Any obligation, including a contingent obligation, arising out of a variable interest (as defined in the FASB ASC Master Glossary, as may be modified or supplemented) in an unconsolidated entity that is held by, and material to, the registrant, where such entity provides financing, liquidity, market risk or credit risk support to, or engages in leasing, hedging or research and development services with, the registrant.

Instructions to paragraph 303(a). 1. The registrant's discussion and analysis shall be of the financial statements and other statistical data that the registrant believes will enhance a reader's understanding of its financial condition, changes in financial condition and results of operations. Generally, the discussion shall cover the three-year period covered by the financial statements and shall use year-to-year comparisons or any other formats that in the registrant's judgment enhance a reader's understanding. However, where trend information is relevant, reference to the five-year selected financial data appearing pursuant to Item 301 of Regulation S-K (§229.301) may be necessary. A smaller reporting company's discussion shall cover the two-year period required in Article 8 of Regulation S-X and shall use year-to-year comparisons or any other formats that in the registrant's judgment enhance a reader's understanding. An emerging growth company, as defined in Rule 405 of the Securities Act (§230.405 of this chapter) or Rule 12b-2 of the Exchange Act (§240.12b-2 of this chapter), may provide the discussion required in paragraph (a) of this Item for its two most recent fiscal years if, pursuant to Section 7(a) of the Securities Act of 1933 (15 U.S.C 77g(a)), it provides audited financial statements for two years in a Securities Act registration statement for the initial public offering of the emerging growth company's common equity securities.

Instructions to Paragraph 303(a)(4):

1. No obligation to make disclosure under paragraph (a)(4) of this Item shall arise in respect of an off-balance sheet arrangement until a definitive agreement that is unconditionally binding or subject only to customary closing conditions exists or, if there is no such agreement, when settlement of the transaction occurs.

2. Registrants should aggregate off-balance sheet arrangements in groups or categories that provide material information in an efficient and understandable manner and should avoid repetition and disclosure of immaterial information. Effects that are common or similar with respect to a number of off-balance sheet arrangements must be analyzed in the aggregate to the extent the aggregation increases understanding. Distinctions in arrangements and their effects must be discussed to the extent the information is material, but the discussion should avoid repetition and disclosure of immaterial information.

3. For purposes of paragraph (a)(4) of this Item only, contingent liabilities arising out of litigation, arbitration or regulatory actions are not considered to be off-balance sheet arrangements.

4. Generally, the disclosure required by paragraph (a)(4) shall cover the most recent fiscal year. However, the discussion should address changes from the previous year where such discussion is necessary to an understanding of the disclosure.

5. In satisfying the requirements of paragraph (a)(4) of this Item, the discussion of off-balance sheet arrangements need not repeat information provided in the footnotes to the financial statements, provided that such discussion clearly cross-references to specific information in the relevant footnotes and integrates the substance of the footnotes into such discussion in a manner designed to inform readers of the significance of the information that is not included within the body of such discussion.

(5) *Tabular Disclosure of Contractual Obligations.* (i) In a tabular format, provide the information specified in this paragraph (a)(5) as of the latest fiscal year end balance sheet date with respect to the registrant's known contractual obligations specified in the table that follows this paragraph (a)(5)(i). The registrant shall provide amounts,

aggregated by type of contractual obligation. The registrant may disaggregate the specified categories of contractual obligations using other categories suitable to its business, but the presentation must include all of the obligations of the registrant that fall within the specified categories. A presentation covering at least the periods specified shall be included. The tabular presentation may be accompanied by footnotes to describe provisions that create, increase or accelerate obligations, or other pertinent data to the extent necessary for an understanding of the timing and amount of the registrant's specified contractual obligations.

		Payments due by period			
Contractual obligations	Total	Less than 1 year	1–3 years	3–5 years	More than 5 years
[Long–Term Debt Obligations]	....	....	....	....	....
[Capital Lease Obligations]	....	....	....	....	....
[Operating Lease Obligations]	....	....	....	....	....
[Purchase Obligations]	....	....	....	....	....
[Other Long–Term Liabilities Reflected on the Registrant's Balance Sheet under GAAP]	....	....	....	....	....
Total	....	....	....	....	....

(ii) *Definitions*: The following definitions apply to this paragraph (a)(5):

(A) *Long–Term Debt Obligation* means a payment obligation under long-term borrowings referenced in FASB ASC paragraph 470–10–50–1 (Debt Topic), as may be modified or supplemented.

(B) *Capital Lease Obligation* means a payment obligation under a lease classified as a capital lease pursuant to FASB ASC Topic 840, *Lease*, as may be modified or supplemented.

(C) *Operating Lease Obligation* means a payment obligation under a lease classified as an operating lease and disclosed pursuant to FASB ASC Topic 840, as may be modified or supplemented.

(D) *Purchase Obligation* means an agreement to purchase goods or services that is enforceable and legally binding on the registrant that specifies all significant terms, including: fixed or minimum quantities to be purchased; fixed, minimum or variable price provisions; and the approximate timing of the transaction.

Instructions to Paragraph 303(a):

1. The registrant's discussion and analysis shall be of the financial statements and other statistical data that the registrant believes will enhance a reader's understanding of its financial condition, changes in financial condition and results of operations. Generally, the discussion shall cover the three year period covered by the financial statements and shall use year-to-year comparisons or any other formats that in the registrant's judgment enhance a reader's understanding. However, where trend information is relevant, reference to the five year selected financial data appearing pursuant to Item 301 of Regulation S–K may be necessary. A smaller reporting company's discussion shall cover the two-year period required in Article 8 of Regulation S–X and shall use year-to-year comparisons or any other formats that in the registrant's judgment enhance a reader's understanding.

2. The purpose of the discussion and analysis shall be to provide to investors and other users information relevant to an assessment of the financial condition and results of operations of the registrant as determined by evaluating the amounts and certainty of cash flows from operations and from outside sources.

3. The discussion and analysis shall focus specifically on material events and uncertainties known to management that would cause reported financial information not to be necessarily indicative of future operating results or of future financial condition. This would include descriptions and amounts of (A) matters that would have an impact on future operations and have not had an impact in the past, and (B) matters that have had an impact on reported operations and are not expected to have an impact upon future operations.

4. Where the consolidated financial statements reveal material changes from year to year in one or more line items, the causes for the changes shall be described to the extent necessary to an understanding of the registrant's businesses as a whole; *Provided, however,* That if the causes for a change in one line item also relate to other line items, no repetition is required and a line-by-line analysis of the financial statements as a whole is not required

or generally appropriate. Registrants need not recite the amounts of changes from year to year which are readily computable from the financial statements. The discussion shall not merely repeat numerical data contained in the consolidated financial statements.

5. The term "liquidity" as used in this Item refers to the ability of an enterprise to generate adequate amounts of cash to meet the enterprise's needs for cash. Except where it is otherwise clear from the discussion, the registrant shall indicate those balance sheet conditions or income or cash flow items which the registrant believes may be indicators of its liquidity condition. Liquidity generally shall be discussed on both a long-term and short-term basis. The issue of liquidity shall be discussed in the context of the registrant's own business or businesses. For example a discussion of working capital may be appropriate for certain manufacturing, industrial or related operations but might be inappropriate for a bank or public utility.

6. Where financial statements presented or incorporated by reference in the registration statement are required by Rule 4–08(e)(3) of Regulation S–X to include disclosure of restrictions on the ability of both consolidated and unconsolidated subsidiaries to transfer funds to the registrant in the form of cash dividends, loans or advances, the discussion of liquidity shall include a discussion of the nature and extent of such restrictions and the impact such restrictions have had and are expected to have on the ability of the parent company to meet its cash obligations.

7. Any forward-looking information supplied is expressly covered by the safe harbor rule for projections. See Rule 175 under the Securities Act, Rule 3b–6 under the Exchange Act and Securities Act Release No. 6084 (June 25, 1979) (44 FR 38810).

8. Registrants are only required to discuss the effects of inflation and other changes in prices when considered material. This discussion may be made in whatever manner appears appropriate under the circumstances. All that is required is a brief textual presentation of management's views. No specific numerical financial data need be presented except as: Rule 3–20(c) of Regulation S–X otherwise requires. However, registrants may elect to voluntarily disclose supplemental information on the effects of changing prices as provided for in FASB ASC Topic 255, *Changing Prices*, or through other supplemental disclosures. The Commission encourages experimentation with these disclosures in order to provide the most meaningful presentation of the impact of price changes on the registrant's financial statements.

9. Registrants that elect to disclose supplementary information on the effects of changing prices as specified by FASB ASC Topic 255 may combine such explanations with the discussion and analysis required pursuant to this Item or may supply such information separately with appropriate cross-reference.

10. All references to the registrant in the discussion and in this Item shall mean the registrant and its subsidiaries consolidated.

11. Foreign private registrants also shall discuss briefly any pertinent governmental economic, fiscal, monetary, or political policies or factors that have materially affected or could materially affect, directly or indirectly, their operations or investments by United States nationals.

12. If the registrant is a foreign private issuer, the discussion shall focus on the primary financial statements presented in the registration statement or report. There shall be a reference to the reconciliation to United States generally accepted accounting principles, and a discussion of any aspects of the difference between foreign and United States generally accepted accounting principles, not discussed in the reconciliation, that the registrant believes is necessary for an understanding of the financial statements as a whole.

13. The attention of bank holding companies is directed to the information called for in Guide 3 (Items 801(c) and 802(c) of Regulation S–K).

14. The attention of property-casualty insurance companies is directed to the information called for in Guide 6 (Item 801(f) of Regulation S–K).

(b) *Interim Periods.* If interim period financial statements are included or are required to be included by Article 3 of Regulation S–X, a management's discussion and analysis of the financial condition and results of operations shall be provided so as to enable the reader to assess material changes in financial condition and results of operations between the periods specified in paragraphs (b)(1) and (2) of this Item. The discussion and analysis shall include a discussion of material changes in those items specifically listed in paragraph (a) of this Item, except that the impact of inflation and changing prices on operations for interim periods need not be addressed.

(1) *Material Changes in Financial Condition.* Discuss any material changes in financial condition from the end of the preceding fiscal year to the date of the most recent interim balance sheet provided. If the interim financial statements include an interim balance sheet as of the corresponding interim date of the preceding fiscal year, any material changes in financial condition from that date to the date of the most recent interim balance sheet provided also shall be discussed. If discussions of changes from both the end and the corresponding interim date of the preceding fiscal year are required, the discussions may be combined at the discretion of the registrant.

(2) *Material Changes in Results of Operations.* Discuss any material changes in the registrant's results of operations with respect to the most recent fiscal year-to-date period for which a statement of comprehensive income (or statement of operations if comprehensive income is presented in two separate but consecutive financial statements or if no other comprehensive income) is provided and the corresponding year-to-date period of the preceding fiscal year. If the registrant is required to or has elected to provide a statement of comprehensive income (or statement of operations if comprehensive income is presented in two separate but consecutive financial statements or if no other comprehensive income) for the most recent fiscal quarter, such discussion also shall cover material changes with respect to that fiscal quarter and the

corresponding fiscal quarter in the preceding fiscal year. In addition, if the registrant has elected to provide a statement of comprehensive income (or statement of operations if comprehensive income is presented in two separate but consecutive financial statements or if no other comprehensive income) for the twelve-month period ended as of the date of the most recent interim balance sheet provided, the discussion also shall cover material changes with respect to that twelve-month period and the twelve-month period ended as of the corresponding interim balance sheet date of the preceding fiscal year. Notwithstanding the above, if for purposes of a registration statement a registrant subject to Rule 3–03(b) of Regulation S–X of this chapter provides a statement of comprehensive income (or statement of operations if comprehensive income is presented in two separate but consecutive financial statements or if no other comprehensive income) for the twelve-month period ended as of the date of the most recent interim balance sheet provided in lieu of the interim statements of comprehensive income (or statement of operations if comprehensive income is presented in two separate but consecutive financial statements or if no other comprehensive income) otherwise required, the discussion of material changes in that twelve-month period will be in respect to the preceding fiscal year rather than the corresponding preceding period.

Instructions to Paragraph (b) of Item 303:

Instruction 1 to paragraph (b). If interim financial statements are presented together with financial statements for full fiscal years, the discussion of the interim financial information shall be prepared pursuant to this paragraph (b) and the discussion of the full fiscal year's information shall be prepared pursuant to paragraph (a) of this Item. Such discussions may be combined.

Instruction 2 to paragraph (b). In preparing the discussion and analysis required by this paragraph (b), the registrant may presume that users of the interim financial information have read or have access to the discussion and analysis required by paragraph (a) for the preceding fiscal year.

Instruction 3 to paragraph (b). The discussion and analysis required by this paragraph (b) is required to focus only on material changes. Where the interim financial statements reveal material changes from period to period in one or more significant line items, the causes for the changes shall be described if they have not already been disclosed: Provided, however, That if the causes for a change in one line item also relate to other line items, no repetition is required. Registrants need not recite the amounts of changes from period to period which are readily computable from the financial statements. The discussion shall not merely repeat numerical data contained in the financial statements. The information provided shall include that which is available to the registrant without undue effort or expense and which does not clearly appear in the registrant's condensed interim financial statements.

Instruction 4 to paragraph (b). The registrant's discussion of material changes in results of operations shall identify any significant elements of the registrant's income or loss from continuing operations which do not arise from or are not necessarily representative of the registrant's ongoing business.

Instruction 5 to paragraph (b). [Reserved]

Instruction 6 to paragraph (b). Any forward-looking information supplied is expressly covered by the safe harbor rule for projections. See Rule 175 under the Securities Act [17 CFR 230.175], Rule 3b–6 under the Exchange Act [17 CFR 249.3b–6] and Securities Act Release No. 6084 (June 25, 1979) (44 FR 38810).

Instruction 7 to paragraph (b). The registrant is not required to include the table required by paragraph (a)(5) of this Item for interim periods. Instead, the registrant should disclose material changes outside the ordinary course of the registrant's business in the specified contractual obligations during the interim period.

Instruction 8 to paragraph (b). The term statement of comprehensive income shall mean a statement of comprehensive income as defined in Rule 1–02 of Regulation S–X.

(c) *Safe Harbor.* (1) The safe harbor provided in section 27A of the Securities Act of 1933 (15 U.S.C. 77z–2) and section 21E of the Securities Exchange Act of 1934 (15 U.S.C. 78u–5) ("statutory safe harbors") shall apply to forward-looking information provided pursuant to paragraphs (a)(4) and (5) of this Item, provided that the disclosure is made by: an issuer; a person acting on behalf of the issuer; an outside reviewer retained by the issuer making a statement on behalf of the issuer, or an underwriter, with respect to information provided by the issuer or information derived from information provided by the issuer.

(2) For purposes of paragraph (c) of this Item only:

(i) All information required by paragraphs (a)(4) and (5) of this Item is deemed to be a *forward looking statement* as that term is defined in the statutory safe harbors, except for historical facts.

(ii) With respect to paragraph (a)(4) of this Item, the meaningful cautionary statements element of the statutory safe harbors will be satisfied if a registrant satisfies all requirements of that same paragraph (a)(4) of this Item.

(d) *Smaller Reporting Companies.* A smaller reporting company, as defined by Item 10(f)(1) of Regulation S–K, may provide the information required in paragraph (a)(3)(iv) of this Item for the last two most recent fiscal years of the registrant if it provides financial information on net sales and revenues and on income from continuing operations for only two years. A smaller reporting company is not required to provide the information required by paragraph (a)(5) of this Item.

Item 304. Changes in and disagreements with accountants on accounting and financial disclosure

(a)(1) If during the registrant's two most recent fiscal years or any subsequent interim period, an independent accountant who was previously engaged as the principal accountant to audit the registrant's financial statements, or an independent accountant who was previously engaged to audit a significant subsidiary and on whom the principal accountant expressed reliance in its report, has resigned (or indicated it has declined to stand for re-election after the completion of the current audit) or was dismissed, then the registrant shall

(i) State whether the former accountant resigned, declined to stand for re-election or was dismissed and the date thereof.

(ii) State whether the principal accountant's report on the financial statements for either of the past two years contained an adverse opinion or a disclaimer of opinion, or was qualified or modified as to uncertainty, audit scope, or accounting principles; and also describe the nature of each such adverse opinion, disclaimer of opinion, modification, or qualification.

(iii) State whether the decision to change accountants was recommended or approved by:

(A) Any audit or similar committee of the board of directors, if the issuer has such a committee; or

(B) The board of directors, if the issuer has no such committee.

(iv) State whether during the registrant's two most recent fiscal years and any subsequent interim period preceding such resignation, declination or dismissal there were any disagreements with the former accountant on any matter of accounting principles or practices, financial statement disclosure, or auditing scope or procedure, which disagreement(s), if not resolved to the satisfaction of the former accountant, would have caused it to make reference to the subject matter of the disagreement(s) in connection with its report. Also, (A) describe each such disagreement; (B) state whether any audit or similar committee of the board of directors, or the board of directors, discussed the subject matter of each of such disagreements with the former accountant; and (C) state whether the registrant has authorized the former accountant to respond fully to the inquiries of the successor accountant concerning the subject matter of each of such disagreements and, if not, describe the nature of any limitation thereon and the reason therefor. The disagreements required to be reported in response to this Item include both those resolved to the former accountant's satisfaction and those not resolved to the former accountant's satisfaction. Disagreements contemplated by this Item are those that occur at the decision-making level; i.e., between personnel of the registrant responsible for presentation of its financial statements and personnel of the accounting firm responsible for rendering its report.

(v) Provide the information required by paragraph (a)(1)(iv) of this Item for each of the kinds of events (even though the registrant and the former accountant did not express a difference of opinion regarding the event) listed in paragraphs (a)(1)(v)(A) through (D) of this section, that occurred within the registrant's two most recent fiscal years and any subsequent interim period preceding the former accountant's resignation, declination to stand for re-election, or dismissal ("reportable events"). If the event led to a disagreement or difference of opinion, then the event should be reported as a disagreement under paragraph (a)(1)(iv) and need not be repeated under this paragraph.

(A) The accountant's having advised the registrant that the internal controls necessary for the registrant to develop reliable financial statements do not exist;

(B) The accountant's having advised the registrant that information has come to the accountant's attention that has led it to no longer be able to rely on management's representations, or that has made it unwilling to be associated with the financial statements prepared by management;

(C)(*1*) The accountant's having advised the registrant of the need to expand significantly the scope of its audit, or that information has come to the accountant's attention during the time period covered by Item 304(a)(1)(iv), that if further investigated may:

(*i*) Materially impact the fairness or reliability of either: a previously issued audit report or the underlying financial statements, or the financial statements issued or to be issued covering the fiscal period(s) subsequent to the date of the most recent financial statements covered by an audit report (including information that may prevent it from rendering an unqualified audit report on those financial statements), or

(*ii*) Cause it to be unwilling to rely on management's representations or be associated with the registrant's financial statements, and

(*2*) Due to the accountant's resignation (due to audit scope limitations or otherwise) or dismissal, or for any other reason, the accountant did not so expand the scope of its audit or conduct such further investigation; or

(D)(*1*) the accountant's having advised the registrant that information has come to the accountant's attention that it has concluded materially impacts the fairness or reliability of either (*i*) a previously issued audit report or the underlying financial statements, or (*ii*) the financial statements issued or to be issued covering the fiscal period(s) subsequent to the date of the most recent financial statements covered by an audit report (including information that, unless resolved to the accountant's satisfaction, would prevent it from rendering an unqualified audit report on those financial statements), and

(*2*) Due to the accountant's resignation, dismissal or declination to stand for re-election, or for any other reason, the issue has not been resolved to the accountant's satisfaction prior to its resignation, dismissal or declination to stand for re-election.

(2) If during the registrant's two most recent fiscal years or any subsequent interim period, a new independent accountant has been engaged as either the principal accountant to audit the registrant's financial statements, or as an independent accountant to audit a significant subsidiary and on whom the principal accountant is expected to express reliance in its report, then the registrant shall identify the newly engaged accountant and indicate the date of such accountant's engagement. In addition, if during the registrant's two most recent fiscal years, and any subsequent interim period prior to engaging that accountant, the registrant (or someone on its behalf) consulted the newly engaged accountant regarding

(i) Either: the application of accounting principles to a specified transaction, either completed or proposed; or the type of audit opinion that might be rendered on the registrant's financial statements, and either a written report was provided to the registrant or oral advice was provided that the new accountant concluded was an important factor considered by the registrant in reaching a decision as to the accounting, auditing or financial reporting issue; or

(ii) Any matter that was either the subject of a disagreement (as defined in paragraph 304(a)(1)(iv) and the related instructions to this item) or a reportable event (as described in paragraph 304(a)(1)(v)), then the registrant shall:

(A) So state and identify the issues that were the subjects of those consultations;

(B) Briefly describe the views of the newly engaged accountant as expressed orally or in writing to the registrant on each such issue and, if written views were received by the registrant, file them as an exhibit to the report or registration statement requiring compliance with this Item 304(a);

(C) State whether the former accountant was consulted by the registrant regarding any such issues, and if so, provide a summary of the former accountant's views; and

(D) Request the newly engaged accountant to review the disclosure required by this Item 304(a) before it is filed with the Commission and provide the new accountant the opportunity to furnish the registrant with a letter addressed to the Commission containing any new information, clarification of the registrant's expression of its views, or the respects in which it does not agree with the statements made by the registrant in response to Item 304(a). The registrant shall file any such letter as an exhibit to the report or registration statement containing the disclosure required by this Item.

(3) The registrant shall provide the former accountant with a copy of the disclosures it is making in response to this Item 304(a) that the former accountant shall receive no later than the day that the disclosures are filed with the Commission. The registrant shall request the former accountant to furnish the registrant with a letter addressed to the Commission stating whether it agrees with the statements made by the registrant in response to this Item 304(a) and, if not, stating the respects

in which it does not agree. The registrant shall file the former accountant's letter as an exhibit to the report or registration statement containing this disclosure. If the former accountant's letter is unavailable at the time of filing such report or registration statement, then the registrant shall request the former accountant to provide the letter as promptly as possible so that the registrant can file the letter with the Commission within ten business days after the filing of the report or registration statement. Notwithstanding the ten business day period, the registrant shall file the letter by amendment within two business days of receipt; if the letter is received on a Saturday, Sunday or holiday on which the Commission is not open for business, then the two business day period shall begin to run on and shall include the first business day thereafter. The former accountant may provide the registrant with an interim letter highlighting specific areas of concern and indicating that a more detailed letter will be forthcoming within the ten business day period noted above. If not filed with the report or registration statement containing the registrant's disclosure under this Item 304(a), then the interim letter, if any, shall be filed by the registrant by amendment within two business days of receipt.

(b) If: (1) In connection with a change in accountants subject to paragraph (a) of this Item 304, there was any disagreement of the type described in paragraph (a)(1)(iv) or any reportable event as described in paragraph (a)(1)(v) of this Item:

(2) During the fiscal year in which the change in accountants took place or during the subsequent fiscal year, there have been any transactions or events similar to those which involved such disagreement or reportable event; and

(3) Such transactions or events were material and were accounted for or disclosed in a manner different from that which the former accountants apparently would have concluded was required, the registrant shall state the existence and nature of the disagreement or reportable event and also state the effect on the financial statements if the method had been followed which the former accountants apparently would have concluded was required.

These disclosures need not be made if the method asserted by the former accountants ceases to be generally accepted because of authoritative standards or interpretations subsequently issued.

Instructions to Item 304:

1. The disclosure called for by paragraph (a) of this Item need not be provided if it has been previously reported as that term is defined in Rule 12b–2 under the Exchange Act; the disclosure called for by paragraph (a) must be provided, however, notwithstanding prior disclosure, if required pursuant to Item 9 of Schedule 14A under the Securities Exchange Act of 1934. The disclosure called for by paragraph (b) of this section must be furnished, where required, notwithstanding any prior disclosure about accountant changes or disagreements.

2. When disclosure is required by paragraph (a) of this section in an annual report to security holders pursuant to Rule 14a–3 or Rule 14c–3 under the Securities Exchange Act of 1934, or in a proxy or information statement filed pursuant to the requirements of Schedule 14A or 14C (Rules 14a–101 or 14c–101 under the Securities Exchange Act of 1934), in lieu of a letter pursuant to paragraph (a)(2)(D) or (a)(3), prior to filing such materials with or furnishing such materials to the Commission, the registrant shall furnish the disclosure required by paragraph (a) of this section to any former accountant engaged by the registrant during the period set forth in paragraph (a) of this section and to the newly engaged accountant. If any such accountant believes that the statements made in response to paragraph (a) of this section are incorrect or incomplete, it may present its views in a brief statement, ordinarily expected not to exceed 200 words, to be included in the annual report or proxy or information statement. This statement shall be submitted to the registrant within ten business days of the date the accountant receives the registrant's disclosure. Further, unless the written views of the newly engaged accountant required to be filed as an exhibit by paragraph (a)(2)(B) of this Item 304 have been previously filed with the Commission the registrant shall file a Form 8–K concurrently with the annual report or proxy or information statement for the purpose of filing the written views as exhibits thereto.

3. The information required by Item 304(a) need not be provided for a company being acquired by the registrant that is not subject to the filing requirements of either section 13(a) or 15(d) of the Securities Exchange Act of 1934, or, because of section 12(i) of the Securities Exchange Act of 1934, has not furnished an annual report to security holders pursuant to Rule 14a–3 or Rule 14c–3 for its latest fiscal year.

4. The term "disagreements" as used in this Item shall be interpreted broadly, to include any difference of opinion concerning any matter of accounting principles or practices, financial statement disclosure, or auditing scope or procedure which (if not resolved to the satisfaction of the former accountant) would have caused it to make reference to the subject matter of the disagreement in connection with its report. It is not necessary for there to have been an argument to have had a disagreement, merely a difference of opinion. For purposes of this Item, however, the term disagreements does not include initial differences of opinion based on incomplete facts or preliminary information that were later resolved to the former accountant's satisfaction by, and providing the registrant and the accountant do not continue to have a difference of opinion upon, obtaining additional relevant facts or information.

5. In determining whether any disagreement or reportable event has occurred, an oral communication from the engagement partner or another person responsible for rendering the accounting firm's opinion (or their designee) will generally suffice as the accountant advising the registrant of a reportable event or as a statement of a disagreement at the "decision-making-level" within the accounting firm and require disclosure under this Item.

Item 305. Quantitative and qualitative disclosures about market risk

(a) *Quantitative Information About Market Risk.* (1) Registrants shall provide, in their reporting currency, quantitative information about market risk as of the end of the latest fiscal year, in accordance with one of the following three disclosure alternatives. In preparing this quantitative information, registrants shall categorize market risk sensitive instruments into instruments entered into for trading purposes and instruments entered into for purposes other than trading purposes. Within both the trading and other than trading portfolios, separate quantitative information shall be presented, to the extent material, for each market risk exposure category (*i.e.,* interest rate risk, foreign currency exchange rate risk, commodity price risk, and other relevant market risks, such as equity price risk). A registrant may use one of the three alternatives set forth in this section for all of the required quantitative disclosures about market risk. A registrant also may choose, from among the three alternatives, one disclosure alternative for market risk sensitive instruments entered into for trading purposes and another disclosure alternative for market risk sensitive instruments entered into for other than trading purposes. Alternatively, a registrant may choose any disclosure alternative, from among the three alternatives, for each risk exposure category within the trading and other than trading portfolios. The three disclosure alternatives are:

(i)(A)*(1)* Tabular presentation of information related to market risk sensitive instruments; such information shall include fair values of the market risk sensitive instruments and contract terms sufficient to determine future cash flows from those instruments, categorized by expected maturity dates.

(2) Tabular information relating to contract terms shall allow readers of the table to determine expected cash flows from the market risk sensitive instruments for each of the next five years. Comparable tabular information for any remaining years shall be displayed as an aggregate amount.

(3) Within each risk exposure category, the market risk sensitive instruments shall be grouped based on common characteristics. Within the foreign currency exchange rate risk category, the market risk sensitive instruments shall be grouped by functional currency and within the commodity price risk category, the market risk sensitive instruments shall be grouped by type of commodity.

(4) See the Appendix to this Item for a suggested format for presentation of this information; and

(B) Registrants shall provide a description of the contents of the table and any related assumptions necessary to understand the disclosures required under paragraph (a)(1)(i)(A) of this Item 305; or

(ii)(A) Sensitivity analysis disclosures that express the potential loss in future earnings, fair values, or cash flows of market risk sensitive instruments resulting from one or more selected hypothetical changes in interest rates, foreign currency exchange rates, commodity prices, and other relevant market rates or prices over a selected period of time. The magnitude of selected hypothetical changes in rates or prices may differ among and within market risk exposure categories; and

(B) Registrants shall provide a description of the model, assumptions, and parameters, which are necessary to understand the disclosures required under paragraph (a)(1)(ii)(A) of this Item 305; or

(iii)(A) Value at risk disclosures that express the potential loss in future earnings, fair values, or cash flows of market risk sensitive instruments over a selected period of time, with a selected likelihood of occurrence, from changes in interest rates, foreign currency exchange rates, commodity prices, and other relevant market rates or prices;

(B)*(1)* For each category for which value at risk disclosures are required under paragraph (a)(1)(iii)(A) of this Item 305, provide either:

(i) The average, high and low amounts, or the distribution of the value at risk amounts for the reporting period; or

(ii) The average, high and low amounts, or the distribution of actual changes in fair values, earnings, or cash flows from the market risk sensitive instruments occurring during the reporting period; or

(iii) The percentage or number of times the actual changes in fair values, earnings, or cash flows from the market risk sensitive instruments exceeded the value

at risk amounts during the reporting period;

(2) Information required under paragraph (a)(1)(iii)(B)*(1)* of this Item 305 is not required for the first fiscal year end in which a registrant must present Item 305 information; and

(C) Registrants shall provide a description of the model, assumptions, and parameters, which are necessary to understand the disclosures required under paragraphs (a)(1)(iii)(A) and (B) of this Item 305.

(2) Registrants shall discuss material limitations that cause the information required under paragraph (a)(1) of this Item 305 not to reflect fully the net market risk exposures of the entity. This discussion shall include summarized descriptions of instruments, positions, and transactions omitted from the quantitative market risk disclosure information or the features of instruments, positions, and transactions that are included, but not reflected fully in the quantitative market risk disclosure information.

(3) Registrants shall present summarized market risk information for the preceding fiscal year. In addition, registrants shall discuss the reasons for material quantitative changes in market risk exposures between the current and preceding fiscal years. Information required by this paragraph (a)(3), however, is not required if disclosure is not required under paragraph (a)(1) of this Item 305 for the current fiscal year. Information required by this paragraph (a)(3) is not required for the first fiscal year end in which a registrant must present Item 305 information.

(4) If registrants change disclosure alternatives or key model characteristics, assumptions, and parameters used in providing quantitative information about market risk (*e.g.,* changing from tabular presentation to value at risk, changing the scope of instruments included in the model, or changing the definition of loss from fair values to earnings), and if the effects of any such change is material, the registrant shall:

(i) Explain the reasons for the change; and

(ii) Either provide summarized comparable information, under the new disclosure method, for the year preceding the current year or, in addition to providing disclosure for the current year under the new method, provide disclosures for the current year and preceding fiscal year under the method used in the preceding year.

Instructions to Paragraph 305(a):

1. Under paragraph 305(a)(1):

A. For each market risk exposure category within the trading and other than trading portfolios, registrants may report the average, high, and low sensitivity analysis or value at risk amounts for the reporting period, as an alternative to reporting year-end amounts.

B. In determining the average, high, and low amounts for the fiscal year under instruction 1.A. of the Instructions to Paragraph 305(a), registrants should use sensitivity analysis or value at risk amounts relating to at least four equal time periods throughout the reporting period (*e.g.,* four quarter-end amounts, 12 month-end amounts, or 52 week-end amounts).

C. Functional currency means functional currency as defined by generally accepted accounting principles (see, *e.g.,* FASB ASC Master Glossary).

D. Registrants using the sensitivity analysis and value at risk disclosure alternatives are encouraged, but not required, to provide quantitative amounts that reflect the aggregate market risk inherent in the trading and other than trading portfolios.

2. Under paragraph 305(a)(1)(i):

A. Examples of contract terms sufficient to determine future cash flows from market risk sensitive instruments include, but are not limited to:

i. Debt instruments—principal amounts and weighted average effective interest rates;

ii. Forwards and futures—contract amounts and weighted average settlement prices;

iii. Options—contract amounts and weighted average strike prices;

iv. Swaps—notional amounts, weighted average pay rates or prices, and weighted average receive rates or prices; and

v. Complex instruments—likely to be a combination of the contract terms presented in 2.A.i. through iv. of this Instruction;

B. When grouping based on common characteristics, instruments should be categorized, at a minimum, by the following characteristics, when material:

i. Fixed rate or variable rate assets or liabilities;

ii. Long or short forwards and futures;

iii. Written or purchased put or call options with similar strike prices;

iv. Receive fixed and pay variable swaps, receive variable and pay fixed swaps, and receive variable and pay variable swaps;

v. The currency in which the instruments' cash flows are denominated;

vi. Financial instruments for which foreign currency transaction gains and losses are reported in the same manner as translation adjustments under generally accepted accounting principles (see, *e.g.,* FASB ASC paragraph 830–20–35–3 (Foreign Currency Matters Topic); and

vii. Derivatives used to manage risks inherent in anticipated transactions;

C. Registrants may aggregate information regarding functional currencies that are economically related, managed together for internal risk management purposes, and have statistical correlations of greater than 75% over each of the past three years;

D. Market risk sensitive instruments that are exposed to rate or price changes in more than one market risk exposure category should be presented within the tabular information for each of the risk exposure categories to which those instruments are exposed;

E. If a currency swap eliminates all foreign currency exposures in the cash flows of a foreign currency denominated debt instrument, neither the currency swap nor the foreign currency denominated debt instrument are required to be disclosed in the foreign currency risk exposure category. However, both the currency swap and the foreign currency denominated debt instrument should be disclosed in the interest rate risk exposure category; and

F. The contents of the table and related assumptions that should be described include, but are not limited to:

i. The different amounts reported in the table for various categories of the market risk sensitive instruments (*e.g.*, principal amounts for debt, notional amounts for swaps, and contract amounts for options and futures);

ii. The different types of reported market rates or prices (*e.g.*, contractual rates or prices, spot rates or prices, forward rates or prices); and

iii. Key prepayment or reinvestment assumptions relating to the timing of reported amounts.

3. Under paragraph 305(a)(1)(ii):

A. Registrants should select hypothetical changes in market rates or prices that are expected to reflect reasonably possible near-term changes in those rates and prices. In this regard, absent economic justification for the selection of a different amount, registrants should use changes that are not less than 10 percent of end of period market rates or prices;

B. For purposes of instruction 3.A. of the Instructions to Paragraph 305(a), the term *reasonably possible* has the same meaning as defined by generally accepted accounting principles (see, *e.g.*, FASB ASC Master Glossary);

C. For purposes of instruction 3.A. of the Instructions to Paragraph 305(a), the term near term means a period of time going forward up to one year from the date of the financial statements (see FASB ASC Master Glossary);

D. Market risk sensitive instruments that are exposed to rate or price changes in more than one market risk exposure category should be included in the sensitivity analysis disclosures for each market risk category to which those instruments are exposed;

E. Registrants with multiple foreign currency exchange rate exposures should prepare foreign currency sensitivity analysis disclosures that measure the aggregate sensitivity to changes in all foreign currency exchange rate exposures, including the effects of changes in both transactional currency/functional currency exchange rate exposures and functional currency/reporting currency exchange rate exposures. For example, assume a French division of a registrant presenting its financial statements in U.S. dollars ($US) invests in a deutschmark (DM)-denominated debt security. In these circumstances, the $US is the reporting currency and the DM is the transactional currency. In addition, assume this division determines that the French franc (FF) is its functional currency according to FASB ASC Topic 830, *Foreign Currency Matters*. In preparing the foreign currency sensitivity analysis disclosures, this registrant should report the aggregate potential loss from hypothetical changes in both the DM/FF exchange rate exposure and the FF/$US exchange rate exposure; and

F. Model, assumptions, and parameters that should be described include, but are not limited to, how *loss* is defined by the model (*e.g.*, loss in earnings, fair values, or cash flows), a general description of the modeling technique (*e.g.*, duration modeling, modeling that measures the change in net present values arising from selected hypothetical changes in market rates or prices, and a description as to how optionality is addressed by the model), the types of instruments covered by the model (*e.g.*, derivative financial instruments, other financial instruments, derivative commodity instruments, and whether other instruments are included voluntarily, such as certain commodity instruments and positions, cash flows from anticipated transactions, and certain financial instruments excluded under instruction 3.C.ii. of the General Instructions to Paragraphs 305(a) and 305(b)), and other relevant information about the model's assumptions and parameters, (*e.g.*, the magnitude and timing of selected hypothetical changes in market rates or prices used, the method by which discount rates are determined, and key prepayment or reinvestment assumptions).

4. Under paragraph 305(a)(1)(iii):

A. The confidence intervals selected should reflect reasonably possible near-term changes in market rates and prices. In this regard, absent economic justification for the selection of different confidence intervals, registrants should use intervals that are 95 percent or higher;

B. For purposes of instruction 4.A. of the Instructions to Paragraph 305(a), the term *reasonably possible* has the same meaning as defined by generally accepted accounting principles (see, *e.g.*, FASB ASC Master Glossary);

C. For purposes of instruction 4.A. of the Instructions to Paragraphs 305(a), the term *near term* means a period of time going forward up to one year from the date of the financial statements (see FASB ASC Master Glossary);

D. Registrants with multiple foreign currency exchange rate exposures should prepare foreign currency value at risk analysis disclosures that measure the aggregate sensitivity to changes in all foreign currency exchange rate exposures, including the aggregate effects of changes in both transactional currency/functional currency exchange rate exposures and functional currency/reporting currency exchange rate exposures. For example, assume a French division of a registrant presenting its financial statements in U.S. dollars ($US) invests in a deutschmark (DM)-denominated debt security. In these circumstances, the $US is the reporting currency and the DM is the transactional currency. In addition, assume this division determines that the French franc (FF) is its functional currency according to FASB ASC Topic 830, *Foreign Currency Matters*. In preparing the foreign currency value at risk disclosures, this registrant should report the aggregate potential loss from hypothetical changes in both the DM/FF exchange rate exposure and the FF/$US exchange rate exposure; and

E. Model, assumptions, and parameters that should be described include, but are not limited to, how *loss* is defined by the model (*e.g.*, loss in earnings, fair values, or cash flows), the type of model used (*e.g.*, variance/covariance, historical simulation, or Monte Carlo simulation and a description as to how optionality is addressed by the model), the types of instruments covered by the model (*e.g.*, derivative financial instruments, other financial instruments, derivative commodity instruments, and whether other instruments are included voluntarily, such as certain commodity instruments and positions, cash flows from anticipated transactions, and certain financial instruments excluded under instruction 3.C.ii. of the General Instructions to Paragraphs 305(a) and 305(b)), and other relevant information about the model's assumptions and parameters, (*e.g.*, holding periods, confidence intervals, and, when appropriate, the methods used for aggregating value at risk amounts across market risk exposure categories, such as by assuming perfect positive correlation, independence, or actual observed correlation).

5. Under paragraph 305(a)(2), limitations that should be considered include, but are not limited to:

A. The exclusion of certain market risk sensitive instruments, positions, and transactions from the disclosures required under paragraph 305(a)(1) (*e.g.*, derivative commodity instruments not permitted by contract or business custom to be settled in cash or with another financial instrument, commodity positions, cash flows from anticipated transactions, and certain financial instruments excluded under instruction 3.C.ii. of the General Instructions to Paragraphs 305(a) and 305(b)). Failure to include such instruments, positions, and transactions in preparing the disclosures under paragraph 305(a)(1) may be a limitation because the resulting disclosures may not fully reflect the net market risk of a registrant; and

B. The ability of disclosures required under paragraph 305(a)(1) to reflect fully the market risk that may be inherent in instruments with leverage, option, or prepayment features (*e.g.*, options, including written options, structured notes, collateralized mortgage obligations, leveraged swaps, and options embedded in swaps).

(b) *Qualitative Information About Market Risk.* (1) To the extent material, describe:

(i) The registrant's primary market risk exposures;

(ii) How those exposures are managed. Such descriptions shall include, but not be limited to, a discussion of the objectives, general strategies, and instruments, if any, used to manage those exposures; and

(iii) Changes in either the registrant's primary market risk exposures or how those exposures are managed, when compared to what was in effect during the most recently completed fiscal year and what is known or expected to be in effect in future reporting periods.

(2) Qualitative information about market risk shall be presented separately for market risk sensitive instruments entered into for trading purposes and those entered into for purposes other than trading.

Instructions to Paragraph 305(b):

1. For purposes of disclosure under paragraph 305(b), primary market risk exposures means:

A. The following categories of market risk: interest rate risk, foreign currency exchange rate risk, commodity price risk, and other relevant market rate or price risks (*e.g.*, equity price risk); and

B. Within each of these categories, the particular markets that present the primary risk of loss to the registrant. For example, if a registrant has a material exposure to foreign currency exchange rate risk and, within this category of market risk, is most vulnerable to changes in dollar/yen, dollar/pound, and dollar/peso exchange rates, the registrant should disclose those exposures. Similarly, if a registrant has a material exposure to interest rate risk and, within this category of market risk, is most vulnerable to changes in short-term U.S. prime interest rates, it should disclose the existence of that exposure.

2. For purposes of disclosure under paragraph 305(b), registrants should describe primary market risk exposures that exist as of the end of the latest fiscal year, and how those exposures are managed.

General Instructions to Paragraphs 305(a) and 305(b):

1. The disclosures called for by paragraphs 305(a) and 305(b) are intended to clarify the registrant's exposures to market risk associated with activities in derivative financial instruments, other financial instruments, and derivative commodity instruments.

2. In preparing the disclosures under paragraphs 305(a) and 305(b), registrants are required to include derivative financial instruments, other financial instruments, and derivative commodity instruments.

3. For purposes of paragraphs 305(a) and 305(b), derivative financial instruments, other financial instruments, and derivative commodity instruments (collectively referred to as "market risk sensitive instruments") are defined as follows:

A. *Derivative financial instruments* has the same meaning as defined by generally accepted accounting principles (see *e.g.*, FASB ASC Master Glossary), and includes futures, forwards, swaps, options, and other financial instruments with similar characteristics;

B. *Other financial instruments* means all financial instruments as defined by generally accepted accounting principles for which fair value disclosures are required (see *e.g.*, FASB ASC paragraph 825–10–50–8 (Financial Instruments Topic)), except for derivative financial instruments, as defined above;

C. i. Other financial instruments include, but are not limited to, trade accounts receivable, investments, loans, structured notes, mortgage-backed securities, trade accounts payable, indexed debt instruments, interest-only and principal-only obligations, deposits, and other debt obligations;

ii. Other financial instruments exclude employers' and plans' obligations for pension and other post-retirement benefits, substantively extinguished debt, insurance contracts, lease contracts, warranty obligations and rights, unconditional purchase obligations, investments accounted for under the equity method, noncontrolling interests in consolidated enterprises, and equity instruments issued by the registrant and classified in stockholders' equity in the statement of financial position (*see e.g.*, FASB ASC paragraph 825–10–50–8). For purposes of this item, trade accounts receivable and trade accounts payable need not be considered other financial instruments when their carrying amounts approximate fair market value; and

D. *Derivative commodity instruments* include, to the extent such instruments are not derivative financial instruments, commodity futures, commodity forwards, commodity swaps, commodity options, and other commodity instruments with similar characteristics that are permitted by contract or business custom to be settled in cash or with another financial instrument. For purposes of this paragraph, settlement in cash includes settlement in cash of the net change in value of the derivative commodity instrument (*e.g.,* net cash settlement based on changes in the price of the underlying commodity).

4. A. In addition to providing required disclosures for the market risk sensitive instruments defined in instruction 2. of the General Instructions to Paragraphs 305(a) and 305(b), registrants are encouraged to include other market risk sensitive instruments, positions, and transactions within the disclosures required under paragraphs 305(a) and 305(b). Such instruments, positions, and transactions might include commodity positions, derivative commodity instruments that are not permitted by contract or business custom to be settled in cash or with another financial instrument, cash flows from anticipated transactions, and certain financial instruments excluded under instruction 3.C.ii. of the General Instructions to Paragraphs 305(a) and 305(b).

B. Registrants that voluntarily include other market risk sensitive instruments, positions and transactions within their quantitative disclosures about market risk under the sensitivity analysis or value at risk disclosure alternatives are not required to provide separate market risk disclosures for any voluntarily selected instruments, positions, or transactions. Instead, registrants selecting the sensitivity analysis and value at risk disclosure alternatives are permitted to present comprehensive market risk disclosures, which reflect the combined market risk exposures inherent in both the required and any voluntarily selected instruments, position, or transactions. Registrants that choose the tabular presentation disclosure alternative should present voluntarily selected instruments, positions, or transactions in a manner consistent with the requirements in Item 305(a) for market risk sensitive instruments.

C. If a registrant elects to include voluntarily a particular type of instrument, position, or transaction in their quantitative disclosures about market risk, that registrant should include all, rather than some, of those instruments, positions, or transactions within those disclosures. For example, if a registrant holds in inventory a particular type of commodity position and elects to include that commodity position within their market risk disclosures, the registrant should include the entire commodity position, rather than only a portion thereof, in their quantitative disclosures about market risk.

5. A. Under paragraphs 305(a) and 305(b), a materiality assessment should be made for each market risk exposure category within the trading and other than trading portfolios.

B. For purposes of making the materiality assessment under instruction 5.A. of the General Instructions to Paragraphs 305(a) and 305(b), registrants should evaluate both:

i. The materiality of the fair values of derivative financial instruments, other financial instruments, and derivative commodity instruments outstanding as of the end of the latest fiscal year; and

ii. The materiality of potential, near-term losses in future earnings, fair values, and/or cash flows from reasonably possible near-term changes in market rates or prices.

iii. If either paragraphs B.i. or B.ii. in this instruction of the General Instructions to Paragraphs 305(a) and 305(b) are material, the registrant should disclose quantitative and qualitative information about market risk, if such market risk for the particular market risk exposure category is material.

C. For purposes of instruction 5.B.i. of the General Instructions to Paragraphs 305(a) and 305(b), registrants generally should not net fair values, except to the extent allowed under generally accepted accounting principles (see, *e.g.,* FASB ASC Subtopic 210–20, *Balance Sheet–Offsetting*). For example, under this instruction, the fair value of assets generally should not be netted with the fair value of liabilities.

D. For purposes of instructions 5.B.ii. of the General Instructions to Paragraphs 305(a) and 305(b), registrants should consider, among other things, the magnitude of:

i. Past market movements

ii. Reasonably possible, near-term market movements; and

iii. Potential losses that may arise from leverage, option, and multiplier features.

E. For purposes of instructions 5.B.ii. and 5.D.ii. of the General Instructions to Paragraphs 305(a) and 305(b), the term *near term* means a period of time going forward up to one year from the date of the financial statements (see FASB ASC Master Glossary).

F. For the purposes of instructions 5.B.ii and 5.D.ii. of the General Instructions to Paragraphs 305(a) and 305(b), the term *reasonably possible* has the same meaning as defined by generally accepted accounting principles (see, *e.g.,* FASB ASC Master Glossary).

6. For purposes of paragraphs 305(a) and 305(b), registrants should present the information outside of, and not incorporate the information into, the financial statements (including the footnotes to the financial statements). In addition, registrants are encouraged to provide the required information in one location. However, alternative presentation, such as inclusion of all or part of the information in Management's Discussion and Analysis, may be used at the discretion of the registrant. If information is disclosed in more than one location, registrants should provide cross-references to the locations of the related disclosures.

7. For purposes of the instructions to paragraphs 305(a) and 305(b), trading purposes means dealing and other trading activities measured at fair value with gains and losses recognized in earnings. In addition, anticipated transactions means transactions (other than transactions involving existing assets or liabilities or transactions necessitated by existing firm commitments) an enterprise expects, but is not obligated, to carry out in the normal course of business.

(c) *Interim Periods.* If interim period financial statements are included or are required to be included by Article 3 of Regulation S–X (17 CFR 210), discussion and analysis shall be provided so as to enable the reader to assess the sources and effects of material changes in information that would be provided under Item 305 of Regulation S–K from the end of the preceding fiscal year to the date of the most recent interim balance sheet.

Instructions to Paragraph 305(c):

1. Information required under paragraph (c) of this Item 305 is not required until after the first fiscal year end in which this Item 305 is applicable.

(d) *Safe Harbor.* (1) The safe harbor provided in Section 27A of the Securities Act of 1933 (15 U.S.C. 77z–2) and Section 21E of the Securities Exchange Act of 1934 (15 U.S.C. 78u–5) ("statutory safe harbors") shall apply, with respect to all types of issuers and transactions, to information provided pursuant to paragraphs (a), (b), and (c) of this Item 305, provided that the disclosure is made by: an issuer; a person acting on behalf of the issuer; an outside reviewer retained by the issuer making a statement on behalf of the issuer; or an underwriter, with respect to information provided by the issuer or information derived from information provided by the issuer.

(2) For purposes of paragraph (d) of this Item 305 only:

(i) All information required by paragraphs (a), (b)(1)(i), (b)(1)(iii), and (c) of this Item 305 is considered *forward looking statements* for purposes of the statutory safe harbors, except for historical facts such as the terms of particular contracts and the number of market risk sensitive instruments held during or at the end of the reporting period; and

(ii) With respect to paragraph (a) of this Item 305, the *meaningful cautionary statements* prong of the statutory safe harbors will be satisfied if a registrant satisfies all requirements of that same paragraph (a) of this Item 305.

(e) *Smaller Reporting Companies.* A smaller reporting company, as defined in Item 10(f)(1) of Regulation S–K, is not required to provide the information required by this Item.

General Instructions to Paragraphs 305(a), 305(b), 305(c), 305(d), and 305(e):

1. Bank registrants, thrift registrants, and non-bank and non-thrift registrants with market capitalizations on January 28, 1997 in excess of $2.5 billion should provide Item 305 disclosures in filings with the Commission that include annual financial statements for fiscal years ending after June 15, 1997. Non-bank and non-thrift registrants with market capitalizations on January 28, 1997 of $2.5 billion or less should provide Item 305 disclosures in filings with the Commission that include financial statements for fiscal years ending after June 15, 1998.

2. A. For purposes of instruction 1. of the General Instructions to Paragraphs 305(a), 305(b), 305(c), 305(d), and 305(e), *bank registrants and thrift registrants* include any registrant which has control over a depository institution.

B. For purposes of instruction 2.A. of the General Instructions to Paragraphs 305(a), 305(b), 305(c), 305(d), and 305(e), a registrant has control over a depository institution if:

i. The registrant directly or indirectly or acting through one or more other persons owns, controls, or has power to vote 25% or more of any class of voting securities of the depository institution;

ii. The registrant controls in any manner the election of a majority of the directors or trustees of the depository institution; or

iii. The Federal Reserve Board or Office of Thrift Supervision determines, after notice and opportunity for hearing, that the registrant directly or indirectly exercises a controlling influence over the management or policies of the depository institution.

C. For purposes of instruction 2.B. of the General Instructions to Paragraphs 305(a), 305(b), 305(c), 305(d), and 305(e), a depository institution means any of the following:

i. An insured depository institution as defined in section 3(c)(2) of the Federal Deposit Insurance Act (12 U.S.C.A. Sec. 1813(c));

ii. An institution organized under the laws of the United States, any State of the United States, the District of Columbia, any territory of the United States, Puerto Rico, Guam, American Somoa, or the Virgin Islands, which both accepts demand deposits or deposits that the depositor may withdraw by check or similar means for payment to third parties or others and is engaged in the business of making commercial loans.

D. For purposes of instruction 1. of the General Instructions to Paragraphs 305(a), 305(b), 305(c), 305(d) and 305(e), *market capitalization* is the aggregate market value of common equity as set forth in General Instruction I.B.1. of Form S–3; provided however, that common equity held by affiliates is included in the calculation of market capitalization; and provided further that instead of using the 60 day period prior to filing referenced in General Instruction I.B.1. of Form S–3, the measurement date is January 28, 1997.

Appendix to Item 305—Tabular Disclosures

The tables set forth below are illustrative of the format that might be used when a registrant elects to present the information required by paragraph (a)(1)(i)(A) of Item 305 regarding terms and information about derivative financial instruments, other financial instruments, and derivative commodity instruments. These examples are for illustrative purposes only. Registrants are not required to display the information in the specific format illustrated below. Alternative methods of display are permissible as long as the disclosure requirements of the section are satisfied. Furthermore, these examples were designed primarily to illustrate possible formats for presentation of the information required by the disclosure item and do not purport to illustrate the broad range of derivative financial instruments, other financial instruments, and derivative commodity instruments utilized by registrants.

INTEREST RATE SENSITIVITY

The table below provides information about the Company's derivative financial instruments and other financial instruments that are sensitive to changes in interest rates, including interest rate swaps and debt obligations. For debt obligations, the table presents principal cash flows and related weighted average interest rates by expected maturity dates. For interest rate swaps, the table presents notional amounts and weighted average interest rates by expected (contractual) maturity dates. Notional amounts are used to calculate the contractual payments to be exchanged under the contract. Weighted average variable rates are based on implied forward rates in the yield curve at the reporting date. The information is presented in U.S. dollar equivalents, which is the Company's reporting currency. The instrument's actual cash flows are denominated in both U.S. dollars ($US) and German deutschmarks (DM), as indicated in parentheses.

December 31, 19X1

	Expected maturity date							
	19X2	19X3	19X4	19X5	19X6	Thereafter	Total	Fair value
Liabilities	(US$ Equivalent in millions)							
Long-term Debt:								
Fixed Rate ($US)	$XXX	$XXX	$XXX	$XXX	$XXX	$XXX	$XXX	$XXX
Average interest rate	X.X%	X.X%	X.X%	X.X%	X.X%	X.X%	X.X%	
Fixed Rate (DM)	XXX	XXX	XXX	XXX	XXX	XXX	XXX	XXX
Average interest rate	X.X%	X.X%	X.X%	X.X%	X.X%	X.X%	X.X%	
Variable Rate ($US)	XXX	XXX	XXX	XXX	XXX	XXX	XXX	XXX
Average interest rate	X.X%	X.X%	X.X%	X.X%	X.X%	X.X%	X.X%	
Interest Rate Derivatives	(In millions)							
Interest Rate Swaps:								
Variable to Fixed ($US)	$XXX	$XXX	$XXX	$XXX	$XXX	$XXX	$XXX	$XXX
Average pay rate	X.X%	X.X%	X.X%	X.X%	X.X%	X.X%	X.X%	
Average receive rate..........	X.X%	X.X%	X.X%	X.X%	X.X%	X.X%	X.X%	
Fixed to Variable ($US)	XXX	XXX	XXX	XXX	XXX	XXX	XXX	XXX
Average pay rate	X.X%	X.X%	X.X%	X.X%	X.X%	X.X%	X.X%	
Average receive rate..........	X.X%	X.X%	X.X%	X.X%	X.X%	X.X%	X.X%	

EXCHANGE RATE SENSITIVITY

The table below provides information about the Company's derivative financial instruments, other financial instruments, and firmly committed sales transactions by functional currency and presents such information in U.S. dollar equivalents.[1] The table summarizes information on instruments and transactions that are sensitive to foreign currency exchange rates, including foreign currency forward exchange agreements, deutschmark (DM)-denominated debt obligations, and firmly committed DM sales transactions. For debt obligations, the table presents principal cash flows and related weighted average interest rates by expected maturity dates. For firmly committed DM-sales transactions, sales amounts are presented by the expected transaction date, which are not expected to exceed two years. For foreign currency forward exchange agreements, the table presents the notional amounts and weighted average exchange rates by expected (contractual) maturity dates. These notional amounts generally are used to calculate the contractual payments to be exchanged under the contract.

December 31, 19X1

	Expected maturity date							
	19X2	19X3	19X4	19X5	19X6	There-after	Total	Fair value
On–Balance Sheet Financial Instruments	(US$ Equivalent in millions)							
$US Functional Currency [2]:								
Liabilities								
Long–Term Debt:								
Fixed Rate (DM)	$XXX	$XXX	$XXX	$XXX	$XXX	$XXX	$XXX	$XXX
Average interest rate	X.X	X.X	X.X	X.X	X.X	X.X	X.X	....
Anticipated Transactions and Related Derivatives [3]	Expected maturity or transaction date (US$ Equivalent in millions)							
$US Functional Currency:								
	December 31, 19X1							

	Expected maturity date							
	19X2	19X3	19X4	19X5	19X6	There-after	Total	Fair value
Firmly committed Sales Contracts (DM)	$XXX	$XXX	....	....	....	....	$XXX	$XXX
Forward Exchange Agreements								
(Receive $US/Pay DM):								
Contract Amount	XXX	XXX	....	....	....	....	XXX	XXX
Average Contractual Exchange Rate	X.X	X.X	....	....	....	....	X.X	....

[1] The information is presented in U.S. dollars because that is the registrant's reporting currency.
[2] Similar tabular information would be provided for other functional currencies.
[3] Pursuant to General Instruction 4. to Items 305(a) and 305(b) of Regulation S–K, registrants may include cash flows from anticipated transactions and operating cash flows resulting from non-financial and non-commodity instruments.

COMMODITY PRICE SENSITIVITY

The table below provides information about the Company's corn inventory and futures contracts that are sensitive to changes in commodity prices, specifically corn prices. For inventory, the table presents the carrying amount and fair value at December 31, 19X1. For the futures contracts the table presents the notional amounts in bushels, the weighted average contract prices, and the total dollar contract amount by expected maturity dates, the latest of which occurs one year from the reporting date. Contract amounts are used to calculate the contractual payments and quantity of corn to be exchanged under the futures contracts.

December 31, 19X1		
	Carrying amount	Fair value
	(In millions)	
On Balance Sheet Commodity Position and Related Derivatives		
Corn Inventory [4]..	$XXX	$XXX
	Expected maturity 1992	Fair value
Related Derivatives		
Futures Contracts (Short):		
Contract Volumes (100,000 bushels)........................	XXX	....
Weighted Average Price (Per 100,000 bushels)........	$X.XX	....
Contract Amount ($US in millions)........................	$XXX	$XXX

[4] Pursuant to General Instruction 4. to Items 305(a) and 305(b) of Regulation S–K, registrants may include information on commodity positions, such as corn inventory.

Item 306. [Reserved]

Item 307. Disclosure controls and procedures

Disclose the conclusions of the registrant's principal executive and principal financial officers, or persons performing similar functions, regarding the effectiveness of the registrant's disclosure controls and procedures (as defined in Rule 13a–15(e) or Rule 15d–15(e) under the Securities Exchange Act of 1934) as of the end of the period covered by the report, based on the evaluation of these controls and procedures required by paragraph (b) of Rule 13a–15 or Rule 15d–15 under the Securities Exchange Act of 1934.

Item 308. Internal control over financial reporting

(a) *Management's Annual Report on Internal Control over Financial Reporting.* Provide a report of management on the registrant's internal control over financial reporting (as defined in Rule 13a–15(f) or Rule 15d–15(f) under the Securities Exchange Act of 1934) that contains:

(1) A statement of management's responsibility for establishing and maintaining adequate internal control over financial reporting for the registrant;

(2) A statement identifying the framework used by management to evaluate the effectiveness of the registrant's internal control over financial reporting as required by paragraph (c) of Rule 13a–15 or Rule 15d–15 under the Securities Exchange Act of 1934;

(3) Management's assessment of the effectiveness of the registrant's internal control over financial reporting as of the end of the registrant's most recent fiscal year, including a statement as to whether or not internal control over financial reporting is effective. This discussion must include disclosure of

any material weakness in the registrant's internal control over financial reporting identified by management. Management is not permitted to conclude that the registrant's internal control over financial reporting is effective if there are one or more material weaknesses in the registrant's internal control over financial reporting; and

(4) If the registrant is an accelerated filer or a large accelerated filer (as defined in Rule 12b–2 under the Securities and Exchange Act of 1934), or otherwise includes in its annual report a registered public accounting firm's attestation report on internal control over financial reporting, a statement that the registered public accounting firm that audited the financial statements included in the annual report containing the disclosure required by this Item has issued an attestation report on the registrant's internal control over financial reporting.

(b) *Attestation report of the registered public accounting firm.* If the registrant, other than a registrant that is an emerging growth company, as defined in Rule 405 of the Securities Act of 1933 (§230.405 of this chapter) or Rule 12b-2 of the Securities Exchange Act of 1934 (§240.12b-2 of this chapter), is an accelerated filer or a large accelerated filer (as defined in §240.12b-2 of this chapter), provide the registered public accounting firm's attestation report on the registrant's internal control over financial reporting in the registrant's annual report containing the disclosure required by this Item.

(c) *Changes in Internal Control over Financial Reporting.* Disclose any change in the registrant's internal control over financial reporting identified in connection with the evaluation required by paragraph (d) of Rule 13a–15 or Rule 15d–15 under the Securities Exchange Act of 1934 that occurred during the registrant's last fiscal quarter (the registrant's fourth fiscal quarter in the case of an annual report) that has materially affected, or is reasonably likely to materially affect, the registrant's internal control over financial reporting.

Instructions to Item 308:

1. A registrant need not comply with paragraphs (a) and (b) of this Item until it either had been required to file an annual report pursuant to section 13(a) or 15(d) of the Exchange Act (15 U.S.C. 78m or 78o(d)) for the prior fiscal year or had filed an annual report with the Commission for the prior fiscal year. A registrant that does not comply shall include a statement in the first annual report that it files in substantially the following form: "This annual report does not include a report of management's assessment regarding internal control over financial reporting or an attestation report of the company's registered public accounting firm due to a transition period established by rules of the Securities and Exchange Commission for newly public companies."

2. The registrant must maintain evidential matter, including documentation, to provide reasonable support for management's assessment of the effectiveness of the registrant's internal control over financial reporting.

Subpart 400—Management and Certain Security Holders

Item 401. Directors, executive officers, promoters and control persons

(a) *Identification of Directors.* List the names and ages of all directors of the registrant and all persons nominated or chosen to become directors; indicate all positions and offices with the registrant held by each such person; state his term of office as director and any period(s) during which he has served as such; describe briefly any arrangement or understanding between him and any other person(s) (naming such person(s)) pursuant to which he was or is to be selected as a director or nominee.

Instructions to Paragraph (a) of Item 401:

1. Do not include arrangements or understandings with directors or officers of the registrant acting solely in their capacities as such.

2. No nominee or person chosen to become a director who has not consented to act as such shall be named in response to this Item. In this regard, with respect to proxy statements, see Rule 14a–4(d) under the Exchange Act.

3. If the information called for by this paragraph (a) is being presented in a proxy or information statement, no information need be given respecting any director whose term of office as a director will not continue after the meeting to which the statement relates.

4. With regard to proxy statements in connection with action to be taken concerning the election of directors, if fewer nominees are named than the number fixed by or pursuant to the governing instruments, state the reasons for this procedure and that the proxies cannot be voted for a greater number of persons than the number of nominees named.

5. With regard to proxy statements in connection with action to be taken concerning the election of directors, if the solicitation is made by persons other than management, information shall be given as to nominees of the persons making the solicitation. In all other instances, information shall be given as to directors and persons nominated for election or chosen by management to become directors.

(b) *Identification of Executive Officers.* List the names and ages of all executive officers of the registrant and all persons chosen to become executive officers; indicate all positions and offices with the registrant held by each such person; state his term of office as officer and the period during which he has served as such and describe briefly any arrangement or understanding between him and any other person(s) (naming such person) pursuant to which he was or is to be selected as an officer.

Instructions to Paragraph (b) of Item 401:

1. Do not include arrangements or understandings with directors or officers of the registrant acting solely in their capacities as such.

2. No person chosen to become an executive officer who has not consented to act as such shall be named in response to this Item.

3. The information regarding executive officers called for by this Item need not be furnished in proxy or information statements prepared in accordance with Schedule 14A under the Securities Exchange Act of 1934 (Rule 14a–101) by registrants relying on General Instruction G of Form 10–K under the Securities Exchange Act of 1934 (17 CFR 249.310); provided, that such information is furnished in a separate item captioned "Executive officers of the registrant" and included in Part I of the registrant's annual report on Form 10–K.

(c) *Identification of Certain Significant Employees.* Where the registrant employs persons such as production managers, sales managers, or research scientists who are not executive officers but who make or are expected to make significant contributions to the business of the registrant, such persons shall be identified and their background disclosed to the same extent as in the case of executive officers. Such disclosure need not be made if the registrant was subject to section 13(a) or 15(d) of the Exchange Act or was exempt from section 13(a) by section 12(g)(2)(G) of such Act immediately prior to the filing of the registration statement, report, or statement to which this Item is applicable.

(d) *Family Relationships.* State the nature of any family relationship between any director, executive officer, or person nominated or chosen by the registrant to become a director or executive officer.

Instruction to Paragraph 401(d): The term "family relationship" means any relationship by blood, marriage, or adoption, not more remote than first cousin.

(e) *Business Experience.* (1) *Background.* Briefly describe the business experience during the past five years of each director, executive officer, person nominated or chosen to become a director or executive officer, and each person named in answer to paragraph (c) of Item 401, including: each person's principal occupations and employment during the past five years; the name and principal business of any corporation or other organization in which such occupations and employment were carried on; and whether such corporation or organization is a parent, subsidiary or other affiliate of the registrant. In addition, for each director or person nominated or chosen to become a director, briefly discuss the specific experience, qualifications, attributes or skills that led to the conclusion that the person should serve as a director for the registrant at the time that the disclosure is made, in light of the registrant's business and structure. If material, this disclosure should cover more than the past five years, including information about the person's particular areas of expertise or other relevant qualifications. When an executive officer or person named in response to paragraph (c) of Item 401 has been employed by the registrant or a subsidiary of the registrant for less than five years, a brief explanation shall be included as to the nature of the responsibility undertaken by the individual in prior positions to provide adequate disclosure of his or her prior business experience. What is required is information relating to the level of his or her professional competence, which may include, depending upon the circumstances, such specific information as the size of the operation supervised.

(2) *Directorships.* Indicate any other directorships held, including any other directorships held during the past five years, held by each director or person nominated or chosen to become a director in any company with a class of securities registered pursuant to section 12 of the Exchange Act or subject to the requirements of section 15(d) of such Act or any company registered as an investment company under the Investment Company Act of 1940, 15 U.S.C. 80a–1, *et seq.*, as amended, naming such company.

Instruction to Paragraph (e) of Item 401: For the purposes of paragraph (e)(2), where the other directorships of each director or person nominated or chosen to become a director include directorships of two or more registered investment companies that are part of a "fund complex" as that term is defined in Item 22(a) of Schedule 14A under the Exchange Act (Rule 14a–101), the registrant may, rather than listing each such investment company, identify the fund complex and provide the number of investment company directorships held by the director or nominee in such fund complex.

(f) *Involvement in Certain Legal Proceedings.* Describe any of the following events that occurred during the past ten years and that are material to an evaluation of the ability or integrity of any director, person nominated to become a director or executive officer of the registrant:

(1) A petition under the Federal bankruptcy laws or any state insolvency law was filed by or against, or a receiver, fiscal agent or similar officer was appointed by a court for the business or property of such person, or any partnership in which he was a general partner at or within two years before the time of such filing, or any corporation or business association of which he was an executive

officer at or within two years before the time of such filing;

(2) Such person was convicted in a criminal proceeding or is a named subject of a pending criminal proceeding (excluding traffic violations and other minor offenses);

(3) Such person was the subject of any order, judgment, or decree, not subsequently reversed, suspended or vacated, of any court of competent jurisdiction, permanently or temporarily enjoining him from, or otherwise limiting, the following activities:

(i) Acting as a futures commission merchant, introducing broker, commodity trading advisor, commodity pool operator, floor broker, leverage transaction merchant, any other person regulated by the Commodity Futures Trading Commission, or an associated person of any of the foregoing, or as an investment adviser, underwriter, broker or dealer in securities, or as an affiliated person, director or employee of any investment company, bank, savings and loan association or insurance company, or engaging in or continuing any conduct or practice in connection with such activity;

(ii) Engaging in any type of business practice; or

(iii) Engaging in any activity in connection with the purchase or sale of any security or commodity or in connection with any violation of Federal or State securities laws or Federal commodities laws;

(4) Such person was the subject of any order, judgment or decree, not subsequently reversed, suspended or vacated, of any Federal or State authority barring, suspending or otherwise limiting for more than 60 days the right of such person to engage in any activity described in paragraph (f)(3)(i) of this Item, or to be associated with persons engaged in any such activity;

(5) Such person was found by a court of competent jurisdiction in a civil action or by the Commission to have violated any Federal or State securities law, and the judgment in such civil action or finding by the Commission has not been subsequently reversed, suspended, or vacated;

(6) Such person was found by a court of competent jurisdiction in a civil action or by the Commodity Futures Trading Commission to have violated any Federal commodities law, and the judgment in such civil action or finding by the Commodity Futures Trading Commission has not been subsequently reversed, suspended or vacated;

(7) Such person was the subject of, or a party to, any Federal or State judicial or administrative order, judgment, decree, or finding, not subsequently reversed, suspended or vacated, relating to an alleged violation of:

(i) Any Federal or State securities or commodities law or regulation; or

(ii) Any law or regulation respecting financial institutions or insurance companies including, but not limited to, a temporary or permanent injunction, order of disgorgement or restitution, civil money penalty or temporary or permanent cease-and-desist order, or removal or prohibition order; or

(iii) Any law or regulation prohibiting mail or wire fraud or fraud in connection with any business entity; or

(8) Such person was the subject of, or a party to, any sanction or order, not subsequently reversed, suspended or vacated, of any self-regulatory organization (as defined in Section 3(a)(26) of the Exchange Act (15 U.S.C. 78c(a)(26))), any registered entity (as defined in Section 1(a)(29) of the Commodity Exchange Act (7 U.S.C. 1(a)(29))), or any equivalent exchange, association, entity or organization that has disciplinary authority over its members or persons associated with a member.

Instructions to Paragraph (f) of Item 401:

1. For purposes of computing the ten-year period referred to in this paragraph, the date of a reportable event shall be deemed the date on which the final order, judgment or decree was entered, or the date on which any rights of appeal from preliminary orders, judgments, or decrees have lapsed. With respect to bankruptcy petitions, the computation date shall be the date of filing for uncontested petitions or the date upon which approval of a contested petition became final.

2. If any event specified in this paragraph (f) has occurred and information in regard thereto is omitted on the grounds that it is not material, the registrant may furnish to the Commission, at time of filing (or at the time preliminary materials are filed, or ten days before definitive materials are filed if preliminary filing is not required, pursuant to Rule 14a–6 or 14c–5 under the Exchange Act), as supplemental information and not as part of the registration statement, report, or proxy or information statement, materials to which the omission relates, a description of the event and a statement of the reasons for the omission of information in regard thereto.

3. The registrant is permitted to explain any mitigating circumstances associated with events reported pursuant to this paragraph.

4. If the information called for by this paragraph (f) is being presented in a proxy or information statement, no information need be given respecting any director whose

term of office as a director will not continue after the meeting to which the statement relates.

5. This paragraph (f)(7) shall not apply to any settlement of a civil proceeding among private litigants.

(g) *Promoters and Control Persons.* (1) Registrants, which have not been subject to the reporting requirements of Section 13(a) or 15(d) of the Exchange Act (15 U.S.C. 78m(a) or 78*o*(d)) for the twelve months immediately prior to the filing of the registration statement, report, or statement to which this Item is applicable, and which had a promoter at any time during the past five fiscal years, shall describe with respect to any promoter, any of the events enumerated in paragraphs (f)(1) through (f)(6) of this Item that occurred during the past five years and that are material to a voting or investment decision.

(2) Registrants, which have not been subject to the reporting requirements of Section 13(a) or 15(d) of the Exchange Act for the twelve months immediately prior to the filing of the registration statement, report, or statement to which this Item is applicable, shall describe with respect to any control person, any of the events enumerated in paragraphs (f)(1) through (f)(6) of this Item that occurred during the past five years and that are material to a voting or investment decision.

Instructions to Paragraph (g) of Item 401:

1. Instructions 1. through 3. to paragraph (f) shall apply to this paragraph (g).

2. Paragraph (g) shall not apply to any subsidiary of a registrant which has been reporting pursuant to Section 13(a) or 15(d) of the Exchange Act for the twelve months immediately prior to the filing of the registration statement, report or statement.

Item 402. Executive compensation

(a) *General.* (1) *Treatment of Foreign Private Issuers.* A foreign private issuer will be deemed to comply with this Item if it provides the information required by Items 6.B and 6.E.2 of Form 20–F (17 CFR 249.220f), with more detailed information provided if otherwise made publicly available or required to be disclosed by the issuer's home jurisdiction or a market in which its securities are listed or traded.

(2) *All Compensation Covered.* This Item requires clear, concise and understandable disclosure of all plan and non-plan compensation awarded to, earned by, or paid to the named executive officers designated under paragraph (a)(3) of this Item, and directors covered by paragraph (k) of this Item, by any person for all services rendered in all capacities to the registrant and its subsidiaries, unless otherwise specifically excluded from disclosure in this Item. All such compensation shall be reported pursuant to this Item, even if also called for by another requirement, including transactions between the registrant and a third party where a purpose of the transaction is to furnish compensation to any such named executive officer or director. No amount reported as compensation for one fiscal year need be reported in the same manner as compensation for a subsequent fiscal year; amounts reported as compensation for one fiscal year may be required to be reported in a different manner pursuant to this Item.

(3) *Persons Covered.* Disclosure shall be provided pursuant to this Item for each of the following (the "named executive officers"):

(i) All individuals serving as the registrant's principal executive officer or acting in a similar capacity during the last completed fiscal year ("PEO"), regardless of compensation level;

(ii) All individuals serving as the registrant's principal financial officer or acting in a similar capacity during the last completed fiscal year ("PFO"), regardless of compensation level;

(iii) The registrant's three most highly compensated executive officers other than the PEO and PFO who were serving as executive officers at the end of the last completed fiscal year; and

(iv) Up to two additional individuals for whom disclosure would have been provided pursuant to paragraph (a)(3)(iii) of this Item but for the fact that the individual was not serving as an executive officer of the registrant at the end of the last completed fiscal year.

Instructions to Item 402(a)(3):

1. *Determination of Most Highly Compensated Executive Officers.* The determination as to which executive officers are most highly compensated shall be made by reference to total compensation for the last completed fiscal year (as required to be disclosed pursuant to paragraph (c)(2)(x) of this Item) reduced by the amount required to be disclosed pursuant to paragraph (c)(2)(viii) of this Item, provided, however, that no disclosure need be provided for any executive officer, other than the PEO and PFO, whose total compensation, as so reduced, does not exceed $100,000.

2. *Inclusion of Executive Officer of Subsidiary.* It may be appropriate for a registrant to include as named executive officers one or more executive officers or other employees of subsidiaries in the disclosure required by this Item. See Rule 3b–7 under the Exchange Act.

3. *Exclusion of Executive Officer Due to Overseas Compensation.* It may be appropriate in limited circumstances for a registrant not to include in the disclosure required by this Item an individual, other than its PEO or PFO, who is one of the registrant's most highly compensated executive officers due to the payment of amounts of cash compensation relating to overseas assignments attributed predominantly to such assignments.

(4) *Information for Full Fiscal Year*. If the PEO or PFO served in that capacity during any part of a fiscal year with respect to which information is required, information should be provided as to all of his or her compensation for the full fiscal year. If a named executive officer (other than the PEO or PFO) served as an executive officer of the registrant (whether or not in the same position) during any part of the fiscal year with respect to which information is required, information shall be provided as to all compensation of that individual for the full fiscal year.

(5) *Omission of Table or Column*. A table or column may be omitted if there has been no compensation awarded to, earned by, or paid to any of the named executive officers or directors required to be reported in that table or column in any fiscal year covered by that table.

(6) *Definitions*. For purposes of this Item:

(i) The term *stock* means instruments such as common stock, restricted stock, restricted stock units, phantom stock, phantom stock units, common stock equivalent units or any similar instruments that do not have option-like features, and the term *option* means instruments such as stock options, stock appreciation rights and similar instruments with option-like features. The term *stock appreciation rights* ("*SARs*") refers to SARs payable in cash or stock, including SARs payable in cash or stock at the election of the registrant or a named executive officer. The term *equity* is used to refer generally to stock and/or options.

(ii) The term *plan* includes, but is not limited to, the following: Any plan, contract, authorization or arrangement, whether or not set forth in any formal document, pursuant to which cash, securities, similar instruments, or any other property may be received. A plan may be applicable to one person. Except with respect to the disclosure required by paragraph (t) of this Item, registrants may omit information regarding group life, health, hospitalization, or medical reimbursement plans that do not discriminate in scope, terms or operation, in favor of executive officers or directors of the registrant and that are available generally to all salaried employees.

(iii) The term *incentive plan* means any plan providing compensation intended to serve as incentive for performance to occur over a specified period, whether such performance is measured by reference to financial performance of the registrant or an affiliate, the registrant's stock price, or any other performance measure. An *equity incentive plan* is an incentive plan or portion of an incentive plan under which awards are granted that fall within the scope of FASB ASC Topic 718, *Compensation—Stock Compensation*. A *non-equity incentive plan* is an incentive plan that is not an equity incentive plan. The term *incentive plan award* means an award provided under an incentive plan.

(iv) The terms *date of grant* or *grant date* refer to the grant date determined for financial statement reporting purposes pursuant to FASB ASC Topic 718.

(v) *Closing market price* is defined as the price at which the registrant's security was last sold in the principal United States market for such security as of the date for which the closing market price is determined.

(b) *Compensation Discussion and Analysis*.

(1) Discuss the compensation awarded to, earned by, or paid to the named executive officers. The discussion shall explain all material elements of the registrant's compensation of the named executive officers. The discussion shall describe the following:

(i) The objectives of the registrant's compensation programs;

(ii) What the compensation program is designed to reward;

(iii) Each element of compensation;

(iv) Why the registrant chooses to pay each element;

(v) How the registrant determines the amount (and, where applicable, the formula) for each element to pay;

(vi) How each compensation element and the registrant's decisions regarding that element fit into the registrant's overall compensation objectives and affect decisions regarding other elements; and

(vii) Whether and, if so, how the registrant has considered the results of the most recent shareholder advisory vote on executive compensation required by section 14A of the Exchange Act (15 U.S.C. 78n–1) or Rule 14a–20 of the Securities Exchange Act of 1934 in determining compensation policies and decisions and, if so, how that consideration has affected the registrant's executive compensation decisions and policies.

(2) While the material information to be disclosed under Compensation Discussion and Analysis will vary depending upon the facts and circumstances, examples of such information may include, in a given case, among other things, the following:

(i) The policies for allocating between long-term and currently paid out compensation;

(ii) The policies for allocating between cash and non-cash compensation, and among different forms of non-cash compensation;

(iii) For long-term compensation, the basis for allocating compensation to each different form of award (such as relationship of the award to the achievement of the registrant's long-term goals, management's exposure to downside equity performance risk, correlation between cost to registrant and expected benefits to the registrant);

(iv) How the determination is made as to when awards are granted, including awards of equity-based compensation such as options;

(v) What specific items of corporate performance are taken into account in setting compensation policies and making compensation decisions;

(vi) How specific forms of compensation are structured and implemented to reflect these items of the registrant's performance, including whether discretion can be or has been exercised (either to award compensation absent attainment of the relevant performance goal(s) or to reduce or increase the size of any award or payout), identifying any particular exercise of discretion, and stating whether it applied to one or more specified named executive officers or to all compensation subject to the relevant performance goal(s);

(vii) How specific forms of compensation are structured and implemented to reflect the named executive officer's individual performance and/or individual contribution to these items of the registrant's performance, describing the elements of individual performance and/or contribution that are taken into account;

(viii) Registrant policies and decisions regarding the adjustment or recovery of awards or payments if the relevant registrant performance measures upon which they are based are restated or otherwise adjusted in a manner that would reduce the size of an award or payment;

(ix) The factors considered in decisions to increase or decrease compensation materially;

(x) How compensation or amounts realizable from prior compensation are considered in setting other elements of compensation (*e.g.*, how gains from prior option or stock awards are considered in setting retirement benefits);

(xi) With respect to any contract, agreement, plan or arrangement, whether written or unwritten, that provides for payment(s) at, following, or in connection with any termination or change-in-control, the basis for selecting particular events as triggering payment (*e.g.*, the rationale for providing a single trigger for payment in the event of a change-in-control);

(xii) The impact of the accounting and tax treatments of the particular form of compensation;

(xiii) The registrant's equity or other security ownership requirements or guidelines (specifying applicable amounts and forms of ownership), and any registrant policies regarding hedging the economic risk of such ownership;

(xiv) Whether the registrant engaged in any benchmarking of total compensation, or any material element of compensation, identifying the benchmark and, if applicable, its components (including component companies); and

(xv) The role of executive officers in determining executive compensation.

Instructions to Item 402(b):

1. The purpose of the Compensation Discussion and Analysis is to provide to investors material information that is necessary to an understanding of the registrant's compensation policies and decisions regarding the named executive officers.

2. The Compensation Discussion and Analysis should be of the information contained in the tables and otherwise disclosed pursuant to this Item. The Compensation Discussion and Analysis should also cover actions regarding executive compensation that were taken after the registrant's last fiscal year's end. Actions that should be addressed might include, as examples only, the adoption or implementation of new or modified programs and policies or specific decisions that were made or steps that were taken that could affect a fair understanding of the named executive officer's compensation for the last fiscal year. Moreover, in some situations it may be necessary to discuss prior years in order to give context to the disclosure provided.

3. The Compensation Discussion and Analysis should focus on the material principles underlying the registrant's executive compensation policies and decisions and the most important factors relevant to analysis of those policies and decisions. The Compensation Discussion and Analysis shall reflect the individual circumstances of the registrant and shall avoid boilerplate language and repetition of the more detailed information set forth in the tables and narrative disclosures that follow.

4. Registrants are not required to disclose target levels with respect to specific quantitative or qualitative performance-related factors considered by the compensation committee or the board of directors, or any other factors or criteria involving confidential trade secrets or confidential commercial or financial information, the disclosure of which would result in competitive harm for the registrant. The standard to use when determining whether disclosure would cause competitive harm for the registrant is the same standard that would apply when a registrant requests confidential treatment of confidential trade secrets or confidential commercial or financial information pursuant to Rule 406 under the Securities Exchange Act of 1933 and Rule 24b–2 under the Securities Exchange Act of 1934, each of which incorporates the criteria for non-disclosure when relying upon Exemption 4 of the Freedom of Information Act (5 U.S.C. 552(b)(4)) and Rule 80(b)(4) (17 CFR 200.80(b)(4)) thereunder. A registrant is not required to seek confidential treatment under the procedures in Securities Act Rule 406 and Exchange Act Rule 24b–2 if it determines that the disclosure would cause competitive harm in reliance on this instruction; however, in that case, the registrant must discuss how difficult it will be for the executive or how likely it will be for the registrant to achieve the undisclosed target levels or other factors.

5. Disclosure of target levels that are non–GAAP financial measures will not be subject to Regulation G (Rule 100–102) and Item 10(e) of Regulation S–K; however, disclosure must be provided as to how the number is calculated from the registrant's audited financial statements.

(c) *Summary Compensation Table.*

(1) *General.* Provide the information specified in paragraph (c)(2) of this Item, concerning the compensation of the named executive officers for each of the registrant's last three completed fiscal years, in a Summary Compensation Table in the tabular format specified below.

SUMMARY COMPENSATION TABLE

Name and Principal Position	Year	Salary ($)	Bonus ($)	Stock Awards ($)	Option Awards ($)	Non–Equity Incentive Plan Compensation ($)	Change in Pension Value and Nonqualified Deferred Compensation Earnings ($)	All Other Compensation ($)	Total ($)
(a)	(b)	(c)	(d)	(e)	(f)	(g)	(h)	(i)	(j)
PEO									
PFO									
A									
B									
C									

(2) The Table shall include:

(i) The name and principal position of the named executive officer (column (a));

(ii) The fiscal year covered (column (b));

(iii) The dollar value of base salary (cash and non-cash) earned by the named executive officer during the fiscal year covered (column (c));

(iv) The dollar value of bonus (cash and non-cash) earned by the named executive officer during the fiscal year covered (column (d));

Instructions to Item 402(c)(2)(iii) and (iv):

1. If the amount of salary or bonus earned in a given fiscal year is not calculable through the latest practicable date, a footnote shall be included disclosing that the amount of salary or bonus is not calculable through the latest practicable date and providing the date that the amount of salary or bonus is expected to be determined, and such amount must then be disclosed in a filing under Item 5.02(f) of Form 8–K (17 CFR 249.308).

2. Registrants shall include in the salary column (column (c)) or bonus column (column (d)) any amount of salary or bonus forgone at the election of a named executive officer under which stock, equity-based or other forms of non-cash compensation instead have been received by the named executive officer. However, the receipt of any such form of non-cash compensation instead of salary or bonus must be disclosed in a footnote added to the salary or bonus column and, where applicable, referring to the Grants of Plan–Based Awards Table (required by paragraph (d) of this Item) where the stock, option or non-equity incentive plan award elected by the named executive officer is reported.

(v) For awards of stock, the aggregate grant date fair value computed in accordance with FASB ASC Topic 718 (column (e));

(vi) For awards of options, with or without tandem SARs (including awards that subsequently have been transferred), the aggregate grant date fair value computed in accordance with FASB ASC Topic 718 (column (f));

Instructions to Item 402(c)(2)(v) and (vi):

1. For awards reported in columns (e) and (f), include a footnote disclosing all assumptions made in the valuation by reference to a discussion of those assumptions in the registrant's financial statements, footnotes to the financial statements, or discussion in the Management's Discussion and Analysis. The sections so referenced are deemed part of the disclosure provided pursuant to this Item.

2. If at any time during the last completed fiscal year, the registrant has adjusted or amended the exercise price

of options or SARs previously awarded to a named executive officer, whether through amendment, cancellation or replacement grants, or any other means ("repriced"), or otherwise has materially modified such awards, the registrant shall include, as awards required to be reported in column (f), the incremental fair value, computed as of the repricing or modification date in accordance with FASB ASC Topic 718, with respect to that repriced or modified award.

3. For any awards that are subject to performance conditions, report the value at the grant date based upon the probable outcome of such conditions. This amount should be consistent with the estimate of aggregate compensation cost to be recognized over the service period determined as of the grant date under FASB ASC Topic 718, excluding the effect of estimated forfeitures. In a footnote to the table, disclose the value of the award at the grant date assuming that the highest level of performance conditions will be achieved if an amount less than the maximum was included in the table.

(vii) The dollar value of all earnings for services performed during the fiscal year pursuant to awards under non-equity incentive plans as defined in paragraph (a)(6)(iii) of this Item, and all earnings on any outstanding awards (column (g));

Instructions to Item 402(c)(2)(vii):

1. If the relevant performance measure is satisfied during the fiscal year (including for a single year in a plan with a multi-year performance measure), the earnings are reportable for that fiscal year, even if not payable until a later date, and are not reportable again in the fiscal year when amounts are paid to the named executive officer.

2. All earnings on non-equity incentive plan compensation must be identified and quantified in a footnote to column (g), whether the earnings were paid during the fiscal year, payable during the period but deferred at the election of the named executive officer, or payable by their terms at a later date.

(viii) The sum of the amounts specified in paragraphs (c)(2)(viii)(A) and (B) of this Item (column (h)) as follows:

(A) The aggregate change in the actuarial present value of the named executive officer's accumulated benefit under all defined benefit and actuarial pension plans (including supplemental plans) from the pension plan measurement date used for financial statement reporting purposes with respect to the registrant's audited financial statements for the prior completed fiscal year to the pension plan measurement date used for financial statement reporting purposes with respect to the registrant's audited financial statements for the covered fiscal year; and

(B) Above-market or preferential earnings on compensation that is deferred on a basis that is not tax-qualified, including such earnings on nonqualified defined contribution plans;

Instructions to Item 402(c)(2)(viii):

1. The disclosure required pursuant to paragraph (c)(2)(viii)(A) of this Item applies to each plan that provides for the payment of retirement benefits, or benefits that will be paid primarily following retirement, including but not limited to tax-qualified defined benefit plans and supplemental executive retirement plans, but excluding tax-qualified defined contribution plans and nonqualified defined contribution plans. For purposes of this disclosure, the registrant should use the same amounts required to be disclosed pursuant to paragraph (h)(2)(iv) of this Item for the covered fiscal year and the amounts that were or would have been required to be reported for the executive officer pursuant to paragraph (h)(2)(iv) of this Item for the prior completed fiscal year.

2. Regarding paragraph (c)(2)(viii)(B) of this Item, interest on deferred compensation is above-market only if the rate of interest exceeds 120% of the applicable federal long-term rate, with compounding (as prescribed under section 1274(d) of the Internal Revenue Code, (26 U.S.C. 1274(d))) at the rate that corresponds most closely to the rate under the registrant's plan at the time the interest rate or formula is set. In the event of a discretionary reset of the interest rate, the requisite calculation must be made on the basis of the interest rate at the time of such reset, rather than when originally established. Only the above-market portion of the interest must be included. If the applicable interest rates vary depending upon conditions such as a minimum period of continued service, the reported amount should be calculated assuming satisfaction of all conditions to receiving interest at the highest rate. Dividends (and dividend equivalents) on deferred compensation denominated in the registrant's stock ("deferred stock") are preferential only if earned at a rate higher than dividends on the registrant's common stock. Only the preferential portion of the dividends or equivalents must be included. Footnote or narrative disclosure may be provided explaining the registrant's criteria for determining any portion considered to be above-market.

3. The registrant shall identify and quantify by footnote the separate amounts attributable to each of paragraphs (c)(2)(viii)(A) and (B) of this Item. Where such amount pursuant to paragraph (c)(2)(viii)(A) is negative, it should be disclosed by footnote but should not be reflected in the sum reported in column (h).

(ix) All other compensation for the covered fiscal year that the registrant could not properly report in any other column of the Summary Compensation Table (column (i)). Each compensation item that is not properly reportable in columns (c)–(h), regardless of the amount of the compensation item, must be included in column (i). Such compensation must include, but is not limited to:

(A) Perquisites and other personal benefits, or property, unless the aggregate amount of such compensation is less than $10,000;

(B) All "gross-ups" or other amounts reimbursed during the fiscal year for the payment of taxes;

(C) For any security of the registrant or its subsidiaries purchased from the registrant or its subsidiaries (through deferral of salary or bonus, or otherwise) at a discount from the market price of such security at the date of purchase, unless that discount is available generally, either to all security holders or to all salaried employees of the registrant, the compensation cost, if any, computed in accordance with FASB ASC Topic 718.

(D) The amount paid or accrued to any named executive officer pursuant to a plan or arrangement in connection with:

(*1*) Any termination, including without limitation through retirement, resignation, severance or constructive termination (including a change in responsibilities) of such executive officer's employment with the registrant and its subsidiaries; or

(*2*) A change in control of the registrant;

(E) Registrant contributions or other allocations to vested and unvested defined contribution plans;

(F) The dollar value of any insurance premiums paid by, or on behalf of, the registrant during the covered fiscal year with respect to life insurance for the benefit of a named executive officer; and

(G) The dollar value of any dividends or other earnings paid on stock or option awards, when those amounts were not factored into the grant date fair value required to be reported for the stock or option award in column (e) or (f); and

Instructions to Item 402(c)(2)(ix):

1. Non-equity incentive plan awards and earnings and earnings on stock and options, except as specified in paragraph (c)(2)(ix)(G) of this Item, are required to be reported elsewhere as provided in this Item and are not reportable as All Other Compensation in column (i).

2. Benefits paid pursuant to defined benefit and actuarial plans are not reportable as All Other Compensation in column (i) unless accelerated pursuant to a change in control; information concerning these plans is reportable pursuant to paragraphs (c)(2)(viii)(A) and (h) of this Item.

3. Any item reported for a named executive officer pursuant to paragraph (c)(2)(ix) of this Item that is not a perquisite or personal benefit and whose value exceeds $10,000 must be identified and quantified in a footnote to column (i). This requirement applies only to compensation for the last fiscal year. All items of compensation are required to be included in the Summary Compensation Table without regard to whether such items are required to be identified other than as specifically noted in this Item.

4. Perquisites and personal benefits may be excluded as long as the total value of all perquisites and personal benefits for a named executive officer is less than $10,000. If the total value of all perquisites and personal benefits is $10,000 or more for any named executive officer, then each perquisite or personal benefit, regardless of its amount, must be identified by type. If perquisites and personal benefits are required to be reported for a named executive officer pursuant to this rule, then each perquisite or personal benefit that exceeds the greater of $25,000 or 10% of the total amount of perquisites and personal benefits for that officer must be quantified and disclosed in a footnote. The requirements for identification and quantification apply only to compensation for the last fiscal year. Perquisites and other personal benefits shall be valued on the basis of the aggregate incremental cost to the registrant. With respect to the perquisite or other personal benefit for which footnote quantification is required, the registrant shall describe in the footnote its methodology for computing the aggregate incremental cost. Reimbursements of taxes owed with respect to perquisites or other personal benefits must be included in column (i) and are subject to separate quantification and identification as tax reimbursements (paragraph (c)(2)(ix)(B) of this Item) even if the associated perquisites or other personal benefits are not required to be included because the total amount of all perquisites or personal benefits for an individual named executive officer is less than $10,000 or are required to be identified but are not required to be separately quantified.

5. For purposes of paragraph (c)(2)(ix)(D) of this Item, an accrued amount is an amount for which payment has become due.

(x) The dollar value of total compensation for the covered fiscal year (column (j)). With respect to each named executive officer, disclose the sum of all amounts reported in columns (c) through (i).

Instructions to Item 402(c):

1. Information with respect to fiscal years prior to the last completed fiscal year will not be required if the registrant was not a reporting company pursuant to section 13(a) or 15(d) of the Exchange Act (15 U.S.C. 78m(a) or 78o(d)) at any time during that year, except that the registrant will be required to provide information for any such year if that information previously was required to be provided in response to a Commission filing requirement.

2. All compensation values reported in the Summary Compensation Table must be reported in dollars and rounded to the nearest dollar. Reported compensation values must be reported numerically, providing a single numerical value for each grid in the table. Where compensation was paid to or received by a named executive officer in a different currency, a footnote must be provided to identify that currency and describe the rate and methodology used to convert the payment amounts to dollars.

3. If a named executive officer is also a director who receives compensation for his or her services as a director, reflect that compensation in the Summary Compensation Table and provide a footnote identifying and itemizing such compensation and amounts. Use the categories in the Director Compensation Table required pursuant to paragraph (k) of this Item.

4. Any amounts deferred, whether pursuant to a plan established under section 401(k) of the Internal Revenue Code (26 U.S.C. 401(k)), or otherwise, shall be included in the appropriate column for the fiscal year in which earned.

(d) *Grants of Plan-Based Awards Table.* (1) Provide the information specified in paragraph (d)(2) of this Item, concerning each grant of an award made to a named executive officer in the last completed fiscal year under any plan, including awards that subsequently have been transferred, in the following tabular format:

GRANTS OF PLAN–BASED AWARDS

Name	Grant Date	Estimated Future Payouts Under Non–Equity Incentive Plan Awards			Estimated Future Payouts Under Equity Incentive Plan Awards			All Other Stock Awards: Number of Shares of Stock or Units (#)	All Other Option Awards: Number of Securities Underlying Options (#)	Exercise of Base Price of Option Awards ($/Sh)	Grant Date Fair Value of Stock and Option Awards
		Threshold ($)	Target ($)	Maximum ($)	Threshold (#)	Target (#)	Maximum (#)				
(a)	(b)	(c)	(d)	(e)	(f)	(g)	(h)	(i)	(j)	(k)	(*l*)
PEO											
PFO											
A											
B											
C											

(2) The Table shall include:

(i) The name of the named executive officer (column (a));

(ii) The grant date for equity-based awards reported in the table (column (b)). If such grant date is different than the date on which the compensation committee (or a committee of the board of directors performing a similar function or the full board of directors) takes action or is deemed to take action to grant such awards, a separate, adjoining column shall be added between columns (b) and (c) showing such date;

(iii) The dollar value of the estimated future payout upon satisfaction of the conditions in question under non-equity incentive plan awards granted in the fiscal year, or the applicable range of estimated payouts denominated in dollars (threshold, target and maximum amount) (columns (c) through (e)).

(iv) The number of shares of stock, or the number of shares underlying options to be paid out or vested upon satisfaction of the conditions in question under equity incentive plan awards granted in the fiscal year, or the applicable range of estimated payouts denominated in the number of shares of stock, or the number of shares underlying options under the award (threshold, target and maximum amount) (columns (f) through (h)).

(v) The number of shares of stock granted in the fiscal year that are not required to be disclosed in columns (f) through (h) (column (i));

(vi) The number of securities underlying options granted in the fiscal year that are not required to be disclosed in columns (f) through (h) (column (j));

(vii) The per-share exercise or base price of the options granted in the fiscal year (column (k)). If such exercise or base price is less than the closing market price of the underlying security on the date of the grant, a separate, adjoining column showing the closing market price on the date of the grant shall be added after column (k); and

(viii) The grant date fair value of each equity award computed in accordance with FASB ASC Topic 718 (column (*l*)). If at any time during the last completed fiscal year, the registrant has adjusted or amended the exercise or base price of options, SARs or similar option-like instruments previously awarded to a named executive officer, whether through amendment, cancellation or replacement grants, or any other means ("repriced"), or otherwise has materially modified such awards, the incremental fair value, computed as of the repricing or modification date in accordance with FASB ASC Topic 718, with respect to that repriced or modified award, shall be reported.

Instructions to Item 402(d):

1. Disclosure on a separate line shall be provided in the Table for each grant of an award made to a named executive officer during the fiscal year. If grants of awards were made to a named executive officer during the fiscal year under more than one plan, identify the particular plan under which each such grant was made.

2. For grants of incentive plan awards, provide the information called for by columns (c), (d) and (e), or (f), (g) and (h), as applicable. For columns (c) and (f), *threshold* refers to the minimum amount payable for a certain level of performance under the plan. For columns (d) and (g), *target* refers to the amount payable if the specified performance target(s) are reached. For columns (e) and (h), *maximum* refers to the maximum payout possible under the plan. If the award provides only for a single estimated payout, that amount must be reported as the *target* in columns (d) and (g). In columns (d) and (g), registrants must provide a representative amount based on the previous fiscal year's performance if the target amount is not determinable.

3. In determining if the exercise or base price of an option is less than the closing market price of the underlying security on the date of the grant, the registrant may use either the closing market price as specified in paragraph (a)(6)(v) of this Item, or if no market exists, any other formula prescribed for the security. Whenever the exercise or base price reported in column (k) is not the closing market price, describe the methodology for determining the exercise or base price either by a footnote or accompanying textual narrative.

4. A tandem grant of two instruments, only one of which is granted under an incentive plan, such as an option granted in tandem with a performance share, need be reported only in column (i) or (j), as applicable. For example, an option granted in tandem with a performance share would be reported only as an option grant in column (j), with the tandem feature noted either by a footnote or accompanying textual narrative.

5. Disclose the dollar amount of consideration, if any, paid by the executive officer for the award in a footnote to the appropriate column.

6. If non-equity incentive plan awards are denominated in units or other rights, a separate, adjoining column between columns (b) and (c) shall be added quantifying the units or other rights awarded.

7. Options, SARs and similar option-like instruments granted in connection with a repricing transaction or other material modification shall be reported in this Table. However, the disclosure required by this Table does not apply to any repricing that occurs through a pre-existing formula or mechanism in the plan or award that results in the periodic adjustment of the option or SAR exercise or base price, an antidilution provision in a plan or award, or a recapitalization or similar transaction equally affecting all holders of the class of securities underlying the options or SARs.

8. For any equity awards that are subject to performance conditions, report in column (*l*) the value at the grant date based upon the probable outcome of such conditions. This amount should be consistent with the estimate of aggregate compensation cost to be recognized over the service period determined as of the grant date under FASB ASC Topic 718, excluding the effect of estimated forfeitures.

(e) *Narrative Disclosure to Summary Compensation Table and Grants of Plan–Based Awards Table.* (1) Provide a narrative description of any material factors necessary to an understanding of the information disclosed in the tables required by paragraphs (c) and (d) of this Item. Examples of such factors may include, in given cases, among other things:

(i) The material terms of each named executive officer's employment agreement or arrangement, whether written or unwritten;

(ii) If at any time during the last fiscal year, any outstanding option or other equity-based award was repriced or otherwise materially modified (such as by extension of exercise periods, the change of vesting or forfeiture conditions, the change or elimination of applicable performance criteria, or the change of the bases upon which returns are determined), a description of each such repricing or other material modification;

(iii) The material terms of any award reported in response to paragraph (d) of this Item, including a general description of the formula or criteria to be applied in determining the amounts payable, and the vesting schedule. For example, state where applicable that dividends will be paid on stock, and if so, the applicable dividend rate and whether that rate is preferential. Describe any performance-based conditions, and any other material conditions, that are applicable to the award. For purposes of the Table required by paragraph (d) of this Item and the narrative disclosure required by paragraph (e) of this Item, performance-based conditions include both performance conditions and market conditions, as those terms are defined in FASB ASC Topic 718; and

(iv) An explanation of the amount of salary and bonus in proportion to total compensation.

Instructions to Item 402(e)(1):

1. The disclosure required by paragraph (e)(1)(ii) of this Item would not apply to any repricing that occurs through a pre-existing formula or mechanism in the plan or award that results in the periodic adjustment of the option or SAR exercise or base price, an antidilution provision in a plan or award, or a recapitalization or similar transaction equally affecting all holders of the class of securities underlying the options or SARs.

2. Instructions 4 and 5 to Item 402(b) apply regarding disclosure pursuant to paragraph (e)(1) of this item of target levels with respect to specific quantitative or qualitative performance-related factors considered by the compensation committee or the board of directors, or any other factors or criteria involving confidential trade secrets or confidential commercial or financial information, the disclosure of which would result in competitive harm for the registrant.

(2) [Reserved.]

(f) *Outstanding Equity Awards at Fiscal Year–End Table.* (1) Provide the information specified in paragraph (f)(2) of this Item, concerning unexercised options; stock that has not vested; and equity incentive plan awards for each named executive officer outstanding as of the end of the registrant's last completed fiscal year in the following tabular format:

OUTSTANDING EQUITY AWARDS AT FISCAL YEAR–END

	Option Awards					Stock Awards			
Name	Number of Securities Underlying Unexercised Options (#) Exercisable	Number of Securities Underlying Unexercised Options (#) Unexercisable	Equity Incentive Plan Awards: Number of Securities Underlying Unexercised Unearned Options (#)	Option Exercise Price ($)	Option Expiration Date	Number of Shares or Units of Stock That Have Not Vested (#)	Market Value of Shares or Units of Stock That Have Not Vested ($)	Equity Incentive Plan Awards: Number of Unearned Shares, Units or Other Rights That Have Not Vested (#)	Equity Incentive Plan Awards: Market or Payout Value of Unearned Shares, Units or Other Rights That Have Not Vested ($)
(a)	(b)	(c)	(d)	(e)	(f)	(g)	(h)	(i)	(j)
PEO									
PFO									
A									
B									
C									

(2) The Table shall include:

(i) The name of the named executive officer (column (a));

(ii) On an award-by-award basis, the number of securities underlying unexercised options, including awards that have been transferred other than for value, that are exercisable and that are not reported in column (d) (column (b));

(iii) On an award-by-award basis, the number of securities underlying unexercised options, including awards that have been transferred other than for value, that are unexercisable and that are not reported in column (d) (column (c));

(iv) On an award-by-award basis, the total number of shares underlying unexercised options awarded under any equity incentive plan that have not been earned (column (d));

(v) For each instrument reported in columns (b), (c) and (d), as applicable, the exercise or base price (column (e));

(vi) For each instrument reported in columns (b), (c) and (d), as applicable, the expiration date (column (f));

(vii) The total number of shares of stock that have not vested and that are not reported in column (i) (column (g));

(viii) The aggregate market value of shares of stock that have not vested and that are not reported in column (j) (column (h));

(ix) The total number of shares of stock, units or other rights awarded under any equity incentive plan that have not vested and that have not been earned, and, if applicable the number of shares underlying any such unit or right (column (i)); and

(x) The aggregate market or payout value of shares of stock, units or other rights awarded under any equity incentive plan that have not vested and that have not been earned (column (j)).

Instructions to Item 402(f)(2):

1. Identify by footnote any award that has been transferred other than for value, disclosing the nature of the transfer.

2. The vesting dates of options, shares of stock and equity incentive plan awards held at fiscal-year end must be disclosed by footnote to the applicable column where the outstanding award is reported.

3. Compute the market value of stock reported in column (h) and equity incentive plan awards of stock reported in column (j) by multiplying the closing market price of the registrant's stock at the end of the last completed fiscal year by the number of shares or units of stock or the amount of equity incentive plan awards, respectively. The number of shares or units reported in columns (d) or (i), and the payout value reported in column (j), shall be based on achieving threshold performance goals, except that if the previous fiscal year's performance has exceeded the threshold, the disclosure shall be based on the next higher performance measure (target or maximum) that exceeds the previous fiscal year's performance. If the award provides only for a single estimated payout, that amount should be reported. If the target amount is not determinable, registrants must provide a representative amount based on the previous fiscal year's performance.

4. Multiple awards may be aggregated where the expiration date and the exercise and/or base price of the

instruments is identical. A single award consisting of a combination of options, SARs and/or similar option-like instruments shall be reported as separate awards with respect to each tranche with a different exercise and/or base price or expiration date.

5. Options or stock awarded under an equity incentive plan are reported in columns (d) or (i) and (j), respectively, until the relevant performance condition has been satisfied. Once the relevant performance condition has been satisfied, even if the option or stock award is subject to forfeiture conditions, options are reported in column (b) or (c), as appropriate, until they are exercised or expire, or stock is reported in columns (g) and (h) until it vests.

(g) *Option Exercises and Stock Vested Table.* (1) Provide the information specified in paragraph (g)(2) of this Item, concerning each exercise of stock options, SARs and similar instruments, and each vesting of stock, including restricted stock, restricted stock units and similar instruments, during the last completed fiscal year for each of the named executive officers on an aggregated basis in the following tabular format:

OPTION EXERCISES AND STOCK VESTED

		Option Awards		Stock Awards	
	Name	Number of Shares Acquired on Exercise (#)	Value Realized on Exercise ($)	Number of Shares Acquired on Vesting (#)	Value Realized on Vesting ($)
	(a)	(b)	(c)	(d)	(e)
PEO					
PFO					
A					
B					
C					

(2) The Table shall include:

(i) The name of the executive officer (column (a));

(ii) The number of securities for which the options were exercised (column (b));

(iii) The aggregate dollar value realized upon exercise of options, or upon the transfer of an award for value (column (c));

(iv) The number of shares of stock that have vested (column (d)); and

(v) The aggregate dollar value realized upon vesting of stock, or upon the transfer of an award for value (column (e)).

Instruction to Item 402(g)(2):

Report in column (c) the aggregate dollar amount realized by the named executive officer upon exercise of the options or upon the transfer of such instruments for value. Compute the dollar amount realized upon exercise by determining the difference between the market price of the underlying securities at exercise and the exercise or base price of the options. Do not include the value of any related payment or other consideration provided (or to be provided) by the registrant to or on behalf of a named executive officer, whether in payment of the exercise price or related taxes. (Any such payment or other consideration provided by the registrant is required to be disclosed in accordance with paragraph (c)(2)(ix) of this Item.) Report in column (e) the aggregate dollar amount realized by the named executive officer upon the vesting of stock or the transfer of such instruments for value. Compute the aggregate dollar amount realized upon vesting by multiplying the number of shares of stock or units by the market value of the underlying shares on the vesting date. For any amount realized upon exercise or vesting for which receipt has been deferred, provide a footnote quantifying the amount and disclosing the terms of the deferral.

(h) *Pension Benefits.* (1) Provide the information specified in paragraph (h)(2) of this Item with respect to each plan that provides for payments or other benefits at, following, or in connection with retirement, in the following tabular format:

PENSION BENEFITS

	Name	Plan Name	Number of Years Credited Service (#)	Present Value of Accumulated Benefit ($)	Payments During Last Fiscal Year ($)
	(a)	(b)	(c)	(d)	(e)
PEO					
PFO					

A					
B					
C					

(2) The Table shall include:

(i) The name of the executive officer (column (a));

(ii) The name of the plan (column (b));

(iii) The number of years of service credited to the named executive officer under the plan, computed as of the same pension plan measurement date used for financial statement reporting purposes with respect to the registrant's audited financial statements for the last completed fiscal year (column (c));

(iv) The actuarial present value of the named executive officer's accumulated benefit under the plan, computed as of the same pension plan measurement date used for financial statement reporting purposes with respect to the registrant's audited financial statements for the last completed fiscal year (column (d)); and

(v) The dollar amount of any payments and benefits paid to the named executive officer during the registrant's last completed fiscal year (column (e)).

Instructions to Item 402(h)(2):

1. The disclosure required pursuant to this Table applies to each plan that provides for specified retirement payments and benefits, or payments and benefits that will be provided primarily following retirement, including but not limited to tax-qualified defined benefit plans and supplemental executive retirement plans, but excluding tax-qualified defined contribution plans and nonqualified defined contribution plans. Provide a separate row for each such plan in which the named executive officer participates.

2. For purposes of the amount(s) reported in column (d), the registrant must use the same assumptions used for financial reporting purposes under generally accepted accounting principles, except that retirement age shall be assumed to be the normal retirement age as defined in the plan, or if not so defined, the earliest time at which a participant may retire under the plan without any benefit reduction due to age. The registrant must disclose in the accompanying textual narrative the valuation method and all material assumptions applied in quantifying the present value of the current accrued benefit. A benefit specified in the plan document or the executive's contract itself is not an assumption. Registrants may satisfy all or part of this disclosure by reference to a discussion of those assumptions in the registrant's financial statements, footnotes to the financial statements, or discussion in the Management's Discussion and Analysis. The sections so referenced are deemed part of the disclosure provided pursuant to this Item.

3. For purposes of allocating the current accrued benefit between tax qualified defined benefit plans and related supplemental plans, apply the limitations applicable to tax qualified defined benefit plans established by the Internal Revenue Code and the regulations thereunder that applied as of the pension plan measurement date.

4. If a named executive officer's number of years of credited service with respect to any plan is different from the named executive officer's number of actual years of service with the registrant, provide footnote disclosure quantifying the difference and any resulting benefit augmentation.

(3) Provide a succinct narrative description of any material factors necessary to an understanding of each plan covered by the tabular disclosure required by this paragraph. While material factors will vary depending upon the facts, examples of such factors may include, in given cases, among other things:

(i) The material terms and conditions of payments and benefits available under the plan, including the plan's normal retirement payment and benefit formula and eligibility standards, and the effect of the form of benefit elected on the amount of annual benefits. For this purpose, normal retirement means retirement at the normal retirement age as defined in the plan, or if not so defined, the earliest time at which a participant may retire under the plan without any benefit reduction due to age;

(ii) If any named executive officer is currently eligible for early retirement under any plan, identify that named executive officer and the plan, and describe the plan's early retirement payment and benefit formula and eligibility standards. For this purpose, early retirement means retirement at the early retirement age as defined in the plan, or otherwise available to the executive under the plan;

(iii) The specific elements of compensation (*e.g.*, salary, bonus, etc.) included in applying the payment and benefit formula, identifying each such element;

(iv) With respect to named executive officers' participation in multiple plans, the different purposes for each plan; and

(v) Registrant policies with regard to such matters as granting extra years of credited service.

(i) *Nonqualified Defined Contribution and other Nonqualified Deferred Compensation Plans*. (1) Provide the information specified in paragraph (i)(2) of this Item with respect to each defined contribution or other plan that provides for the deferral of compensation on a basis that is not tax-qualified in the following tabular format:

NONQUALIFIED DEFERRED COMPENSATION

	Name (a)	Executive Contributions in Last FY ($) (b)	Registrant Contributions in Last FY ($) (c)	Aggregate Earnings in Last FY ($) (d)	Aggregate Withdrawals/ Distributions ($) (e)	Aggregate Balance at Last FYE ($) (f)
PEO						
PFO						
A						
B						
C						

(2) The Table shall include:

(i) The name of the executive officer (column (a));

(ii) The dollar amount of aggregate executive contributions during the registrant's last fiscal year (column (b));

(iii) The dollar amount of aggregate registrant contributions during the registrant's last fiscal year (column (c));

(iv) The dollar amount of aggregate interest or other earnings accrued during the registrant's last fiscal year (column (d));

(v) The aggregate dollar amount of all withdrawals by and distributions to the executive during the registrant's last fiscal year (column (e)); and

(vi) The dollar amount of total balance of the executive's account as of the end of the registrant's last fiscal year (column (f)).

Instruction to Item 402(i)(2):

Provide a footnote quantifying the extent to which amounts reported in the contributions and earnings columns are reported as compensation in the last completed fiscal year in the registrant's Summary Compensation Table and amounts reported in the aggregate balance at last fiscal year end (column (f)) previously were reported as compensation to the named executive officer in the registrant's Summary Compensation Table for previous years.

(3) Provide a succinct narrative description of any material factors necessary to an understanding of each plan covered by tabular disclosure required by this paragraph. While material factors will vary depending upon the facts, examples of such factors may include, in given cases, among other things:

(i) The type(s) of compensation permitted to be deferred, and any limitations (by percentage of compensation or otherwise) on the extent to which deferral is permitted;

(ii) The measures for calculating interest or other plan earnings (including whether such measure(s) are selected by the executive or the registrant and the frequency and manner in which selections may be changed), quantifying interest rates and other earnings measures applicable during the registrant's last fiscal year; and

(iii) Material terms with respect to payouts, withdrawals and other distributions.

(j) *Potential Payments upon Termination or Change-in-Control*. Regarding each contract, agreement, plan or arrangement, whether written or unwritten, that provides for payment(s) to a named executive officer at, following, or in connection with any termination, including without limitation resignation, severance, retirement or a constructive termination of a named executive officer, or a change in control of the registrant or a change in the named executive officer's responsibilities, with respect to each named executive officer:

(1) Describe and explain the specific circumstances that would trigger payment(s) or the provision of other benefits, including perquisites and health care benefits;

(2) Describe and quantify the estimated payments and benefits that would be provided in each covered circumstance, whether they would or could be lump sum, or annual, disclosing the duration, and by whom they would be provided;

(3) Describe and explain how the appropriate payment and benefit levels are determined under the various circumstances that trigger payments or provision of benefits;

(4) Describe and explain any material conditions or obligations applicable to the receipt of payments or benefits, including but not limited to non-compete, non-solicitation, non-disparagement or confidentiality agreements, including the duration of such agreements and provisions regarding waiver of breach of such agreements; and

(5) Describe any other material factors regarding each such contract, agreement, plan or arrangement.

Instructions to Item 402(j):

1. The registrant must provide quantitative disclosure under these requirements, applying the assumptions that the triggering event took place on the last business day of the registrant's last completed fiscal year, and the price per share of the registrant's securities is the closing market price as of that date. In the event that uncertainties exist as to the provision of payments and benefits or the amounts involved, the registrant is required to make a reasonable estimate (or a reasonable estimated range of amounts) applicable to the payment or benefit and disclose material assumptions underlying such estimates or estimated ranges in its disclosure. In such event, the disclosure would require forward-looking information as appropriate.

2. Perquisites and other personal benefits or property may be excluded only if the aggregate amount of such compensation will be less than $10,000. Individual perquisites and personal benefits shall be identified and quantified as required by Instruction 4 to paragraph (c)(2)(ix) of this Item. For purposes of quantifying health care benefits, the registrant must use the assumptions used for financial reporting purposes under generally accepted accounting principles.

3. To the extent that the form and amount of any payment or benefit that would be provided in connection with any triggering event is fully disclosed pursuant to paragraph (h) or (i) of this Item, reference may be made to that disclosure. However, to the extent that the form or amount of any such payment or benefit would be enhanced or its vesting or other provisions accelerated in connection with any triggering event, such enhancement or acceleration must be disclosed pursuant to this paragraph.

4. Where a triggering event has actually occurred for a named executive officer and that individual was not serving as a named executive officer of the registrant at the end of the last completed fiscal year, the disclosure required by this paragraph for that named executive officer shall apply only to that triggering event.

5. The registrant need not provide information with respect to contracts, agreements, plans or arrangements to the extent they do not discriminate in scope, terms or operation, in favor of executive officers of the registrant and that are available generally to all salaried employees.

(k) *Compensation of Directors*. (1) Provide the information specified in paragraph (k)(2) of this Item, concerning the compensation of the directors for the registrant's last completed fiscal year, in the following tabular format:

DIRECTOR COMPENSATION

Name	Fees Earned or Paid in Cash ($)	Stock Awards ($)	Option Awards ($)	Non–Equity Incentive Plan Compensation ($)	Change in Pension Value and Nonqualified Deferred Compensation Earnings	All Other Compensation ($)	Total ($)
(a)	(b)	(c)	(d)	(e)	(f)	(g)	(h)
A							
B							
C							
D							
E							

(2) The Table shall include:

(i) The name of each director unless such director is also a named executive officer under paragraph (a) of this Item and his or her compensation for service as a director is fully reflected in the Summary Compensation Table pursuant to paragraph (c) of this Item and otherwise as required pursuant to paragraphs (d) through (j) of this Item (column (a));

(ii) The aggregate dollar amount of all fees earned or paid in cash for services as a director, including annual retainer fees, committee and/or chairmanship fees, and meeting fees (column (b));

(iii) For awards of stock, the aggregate grant date fair value computed in accordance with FASB ASC Topic 718 (column (c));

(iv) For awards of options, with or without tandem SARs (including awards that subsequently have been transferred), the aggregate grant date fair value computed in accordance with FASB ASC Topic 718 (column (d));

Instruction to Item 402(k)(2)(iii) and (iv):

For each director, disclose by footnote to the appropriate column; the grant date fair value of each equity award computed in accordance with FASB ASC Topic 718; for each option, SAR or similar option like instrument for which the registrant has adjusted or amended the exercise for base price during the last complete fiscal year, whether through amendment, cancellation or replacement grants, or any other means ("repriced"), or otherwise has materially modified such awards, the incremental fair value, computed as of the repricing or modification date in accordance with FASB ASC Topic 718; and the aggregate number of stock awards and the aggregate number of option awards outstanding at fiscal year end. However, the disclosure required by this Instruction does not apply to any repricing that occurs through a pre-existing formula or mechanism in the plan or award that results in the periodic adjustment of the option or SAR exercise or base price, an antidilution provision in a plan or award, or a recapitalization or similar transaction equally affecting all holders of the class of securities underlying the options or SARs.

(v) The dollar value of all earnings for services performed during the fiscal year pursuant to non-equity incentive plans as defined in paragraph (a)(6)(iii) of this Item, and all earnings on any outstanding awards (column (e));

(vi) The sum of the amounts specified in paragraphs (k)(2)(vi)(A) and (B) of this Item (column (f)) as follows:

(A) The aggregate change in the actuarial present value of the director's accumulated benefit under all defined benefit and actuarial pension plans (including supplemental plans) from the pension plan measurement date used for financial statement reporting purposes with respect to the registrant's audited financial statements for the prior completed fiscal year to the pension plan measurement date used for financial statement reporting purposes with respect to the registrant's audited financial statements for the covered fiscal year; and

(B) Above-market or preferential earnings on compensation that is deferred on a basis that is not tax-qualified, including such earnings on nonqualified defined contribution plans;

(vii) All other compensation for the covered fiscal year that the registrant could not properly report in any other column of the Director Compensation Table (column (g)). Each compensation item that is not properly reportable in columns (b)–(f), regardless of the amount of the compensation item, must be included in column (g). Such compensation must include, but is not limited to:

(A) Perquisites and other personal benefits, or property, unless the aggregate amount of such compensation is less than $10,000;

(B) All "gross-ups" or other amounts reimbursed during the fiscal year for the payment of taxes;

(C) For any security of the registrant or its subsidiaries purchased from the registrant or its subsidiaries (through deferral of salary or bonus, or otherwise) at a discount from the market price of such security at the date of purchase, unless that discount is available generally, either to all security holders or to all salaried employees of the registrant, the compensation cost, if any, computed in accordance with FASB ASC Topic 718;

(D) The amount paid or accrued to any director pursuant to a plan or arrangement in connection with:

(*1*) The resignation, retirement or any other termination of such director; or

(*2*) A change in control of the registrant;

(E) Registrant contributions or other allocations to vested and unvested defined contribution plans;

(F) Consulting fees earned from, or paid or payable by the registrant and/or its subsidiaries (including joint ventures);

(G) The annual costs of payments and promises of payments pursuant to director legacy programs and similar charitable award programs;

(H) The dollar value of any insurance premiums paid by, or on behalf of, the registrant during the covered fiscal year with respect to life insurance for the benefit of a director; and

(I) The dollar value of any dividends or other earnings paid on stock or option awards, when those amounts were not factored into the grant date fair value required to be reported for the stock or option award in column (c) or (d); and

Instructions to Item 402(k)(2)(vii):

1. Programs in which registrants agree to make donations to one or more charitable institutions in a director's name, payable by the registrant currently or upon a designated event, such as the retirement or death of the director, are charitable awards programs or director legacy programs for purposes of the disclosure required by paragraph (k)(2)(vii)(G) of this Item. Provide footnote disclosure of the total dollar amount payable under the program and other material terms of each such program for which tabular disclosure is provided.

2. Any item reported for a director pursuant to paragraph (k)(2)(vii) of this Item that is not a perquisite or personal benefit and whose value exceeds $10,000 must be identified and quantified in a footnote to column (g). All items of compensation are required to be included in the Director Compensation Table without regard to whether such items are required to be identified other than as specifically noted in this Item.

3. Perquisites and personal benefits may be excluded as long as the total value of all perquisites and personal benefits for a director is less than $10,000. If the total value of all perquisites and personal benefits is $10,000 or more for any director, then each perquisite or personal benefit, regardless of its amount, must be identified by type. If perquisites and personal benefits are required to be reported for a director pursuant to this rule, then each perquisite or personal benefit that exceeds the greater of $25,000 or 10% of the total amount of perquisites and personal benefits for that director must be quantified and disclosed in a footnote. Perquisites and other personal benefits shall be valued on the basis of the aggregate incremental cost to the registrant. With respect to the perquisite or other personal benefit for which footnote quantification is required, the registrant shall describe in the footnote its methodology for computing the aggregate incremental cost. Reimbursements of taxes owed with respect to perquisites or other personal benefits must be included in column (g) and are subject to separate quantification and identification as tax reimbursements (paragraph (k)(2)(vii)(B) of this Item) even if the associated perquisites or other personal benefits are not required to be included because the total amount of all perquisites or personal benefits for an individual director is less than $10,000 or are required to be identified but are not required to be separately quantified.

(viii) The dollar value of total compensation for the covered fiscal year (column (h)). With respect to each director, disclose the sum of all amounts reported in columns (b) through (g).

Instruction to Item 402(k)(2): Two or more directors may be grouped in a single row in the Table if all elements of their compensation are identical. The names of the directors for whom disclosure is presented on a group basis should be clear from the Table.

(3) *Narrative to Director Compensation Table*.

Provide a narrative description of any material factors necessary to an understanding of the director compensation disclosed in this Table. While material factors will vary depending upon the facts, examples of such factors may include, in given cases, among other things:

(i) A description of standard compensation arrangements (such as fees for retainer, committee service, service as chairman of the board or a committee, and meeting attendance); and

(ii) Whether any director has a different compensation arrangement, identifying that director and describing the terms of that arrangement.

Instruction to Item 402(k): In addition to the Instruction to paragraphs (k)(2)(iii) and (iv) and the Instructions to paragraph (k)(2)(vii) of this Item, the following apply equally to paragraph (k) of this Item: Instructions 2 and 4 to paragraph (c) of this Item; Instructions to paragraphs (c)(2)(iii) and (iv) of this Item; Instructions to paragraphs (c)(2)(v) and (vi) of this Item; Instructions to paragraph (c)(2)(vii) of this Item; Instructions to paragraph (c)(2)(viii) of this Item; and Instructions 1 and 5 to paragraph (c)(2)(ix) of this Item. These Instructions apply to the columns in the Director Compensation Table that are analogous to the columns in the Summary Compensation Table to which they refer and to disclosures under paragraph (k) of this Item that correspond to analogous disclosures provided for in paragraph (c) of this Item to which they refer.

(*l*) *Smaller reporting companies and emerging growth companies*. A registrant that qualifies as a "smaller reporting company," as defined by Item 10(f) (§229.10(f)(1)), or is an "emerging growth company," as defined in Rule 405 of the Securities Act (§230.405 of this chapter) or Rule 12b-2 of the Exchange Act (§240.12b-2 of this chapter), may provide the scaled disclosure in paragraphs (m) through (r) instead of paragraphs (a) through (k), (s), and (u) of this Item.

(m) *Smaller Reporting Companies—General*. (1) *All Compensation Covered*. This Item requires clear, concise and understandable disclosure of all plan and non-plan compensation awarded to, earned by, or paid to the named executive officers designated under paragraph (m)(2) of this Item, and directors covered by paragraph (r) of this Item, by any person for all services rendered in all capacities to the smaller reporting company and its subsidiaries, unless otherwise specifically excluded from disclosure in this Item. All such compensation shall be reported pursuant to this Item, even if also called for by another requirement, including transactions between the smaller reporting company and a third party where a purpose of the transaction is to furnish compensation to any such named executive officer or director. No amount reported as compensation for one fiscal year need be reported in the same manner as compensation for a subsequent fiscal year; amounts reported as compensation for one fiscal year may be required to be reported in a different manner pursuant to this Item.

(2) *Persons Covered.* Disclosure shall be provided pursuant to this Item for each of the following (the "named executive officers"):

(i) All individuals serving as the smaller reporting company's principal executive officer or acting in a similar capacity during the last completed fiscal year ("PEO"), regardless of compensation level;

(ii) The smaller reporting company's two most highly compensated executive officers other than the PEO who were serving as executive officers at the end of the last completed fiscal year; and

(iii) Up to two additional individuals for whom disclosure would have been provided pursuant to paragraph (m)(2)(ii) of this Item but for the fact that the individual was not serving as an executive officer of the smaller reporting company at the end of the last completed fiscal year.

Instructions to Item 402(m)(2):

1. *Determination of Most Highly Compensated Executive Officers.* The determination as to which executive officers are most highly compensated shall be made by reference to total compensation for the last completed fiscal year (as required to be disclosed pursuant to paragraph (n)(2)(x) of this Item) reduced by the amount required to be disclosed pursuant to paragraph (n)(2)(viii) of this Item, *provided, however,* that no disclosure need be provided for any executive officer, other than the PEO, whose total compensation, as so reduced, does not exceed $100,000.

2. *Inclusion of Executive Officer of a Subsidiary.* It may be appropriate for a smaller reporting company to include as named executive officers one or more executive officers or other employees of subsidiaries in the disclosure required by this Item. See Rule 3b–7 under the Exchange Act (17 CFR 240.3b–7).

3. *Exclusion of Executive Officer Due to Overseas Compensation.* It may be appropriate in limited circumstances for a smaller reporting company not to include in the disclosure required by this Item an individual, other than its PEO, who is one of the smaller reporting company's most highly compensated executive officers due to the payment of amounts of cash compensation relating to overseas assignments attributed predominantly to such assignments.

(3) *Information for Full Fiscal Year.* If the PEO served in that capacity during any part of a fiscal year with respect to which information is required, information should be provided as to all of his or her compensation for the full fiscal year. If a named executive officer (other than the PEO) served as an executive officer of the smaller reporting company (whether or not in the same position) during any part of the fiscal year with respect to which information is required, information shall be provided as to all compensation of that individual for the full fiscal year.

(4) *Omission of Table or Column.* A table or column may be omitted if there has been no compensation awarded to, earned by, or paid to any of the named executive officers or directors required to be reported in that table or column in any fiscal year covered by that table.

(5) *Definitions.* For purposes of this Item:

(i) The term *stock* means instruments such as common stock, restricted stock, restricted stock units, phantom stock, phantom stock units, common stock equivalent units or any similar instruments that do not have option-like features, and the term *option* means instruments such as stock options, stock appreciation rights and similar instruments with option-like features. The term *stock appreciation rights* ("*SARs*") refers to SARs payable in cash or stock, including SARs payable in cash or stock at the election of the smaller reporting company or a named executive officer. The term *equity* is used to refer generally to stock and/or options.

(ii) The term *plan* includes, but is not limited to, the following: Any plan, contract, authorization or arrangement, whether or not set forth in any formal document, pursuant to which cash, securities, similar instruments, or any other property may be received. A plan may be applicable to one person. Except with respect to disclosure required by paragraph (t) of this Item, smaller reporting companies may omit information regarding group life, health, hospitalization, or medical reimbursement plans that do not discriminate in scope, terms or operation, in favor of executive officers or directors of the smaller reporting company and that are available generally to all salaried employees.

(iii) The term *incentive plan* means any plan providing compensation intended to serve as incentive for performance to occur over a specified period, whether such performance is measured by references to financial performance of the smaller reporting company or an affiliate, the smaller reporting company's stock price, or any other performance measure. An equity incentive plan is an incentive plan or portion of an incentive plan under which awards are granted that fall within the scope of FASB ASC Topic 718. A *non-equity incentive plan* is an incentive plan or portion of an incentive plan that is not an equity incentive plan. The term *incentive plan award* means an award provided under an incentive plan.

(iv) The terms *date of grant* or *grant date* refer to the grant date determined for financial statement reporting purposes pursuant to FASB ASC Topic 718.

(v) *Closing market price* is defined as the price at which the smaller reporting company's security was last sold in the principal United States market for such security as of the date for which the closing market price is determined.

(n) *Smaller Reporting Companies—Summary Compensation Table.* (1) *General.* Provide the information specified in paragraph (n)(2) of this Item, concerning the compensation of the named executive officers for each of the smaller reporting company's last two completed fiscal years, in a Summary Compensation Table in the tabular format specified below.

SUMMARY COMPENSATION TABLE

Name and principal position (a)	Year (b)	Salary ($) (c)	Bonus ($) (d)	Stock awards ($) (e)	Option awards ($) (f)	Non-equity incentive plan compensation ($) (g)	Nonqualified deferred compensation earnings ($) (h)	All other compensation ($) (i)	Total ($) (j)
PEO									
A									
B									

(2) The Table shall include:

(i) The name and principal position of the named executive officer (column (a));

(ii) The fiscal year covered (column (b));

(iii) The dollar value of base salary (cash and non-cash) earned by the named executive officer during the fiscal year covered (column (c));

(iv) The dollar value of bonus (cash and non-cash) earned by the named executive officer during the fiscal year covered (column (d));

Instructions to Item 402(n)(2)(iii) and (iv):

1. If the amount of salary or bonus earned in a given fiscal year is not calculable through the latest practicable date, a footnote shall be included disclosing that the amount of salary or bonus is not calculable through the latest practicable date and providing the date that the amount of salary or bonus is expected to be determined, and such amount must then be disclosed in a filing under Item 5.02(f) of Form 8–K (17 CFR 249.308).

2. Smaller reporting companies shall include in the salary column (column (c)) or bonus column (column (d)) any amount of salary or bonus forgone at the election of a named executive officer under which stock, equity-based or other forms of non-cash compensation instead have been received by the named executive officer. However, the receipt of any such form of non-cash compensation instead of salary or bonus must be disclosed in a footnote added to the salary or bonus column and, where applicable, referring to the narrative disclosure to the Summary Compensation Table (required by paragraph (*o*) of this Item) where the material terms of the stock, option or non-equity incentive plan award elected by the named executive officer are reported.

(v) For awards of stock, the aggregate grant date fair value computed in accordance with FASB ASC Topic 718 (column (e));

(vi) For awards of options, with or without tandem SARs (including awards that subsequently have been transferred), the aggregate grant date fair value computed in accordance with FASB ASC Topic 718 (column (f));

Instructions to Item 402(n)(2)(v) and (n)(2)(vi):

1. For awards reported in columns (e) and (f), include a footnote disclosing all assumptions made in the valuation by reference to a discussion of those assumptions in the smaller reporting company's financial statements, footnotes to the financial statements, or discussion in the Management's Discussion and Analysis. The sections so referenced are deemed part of the disclosure provided pursuant to this Item.

2. If at any time during the last completed fiscal year, the smaller reporting company has adjusted or amended the exercise price of options or SARs previously awarded to a named executive officer, whether through amendment, cancellation or replacement grants, or any other means ("repriced"), or otherwise has materially modified such awards, the smaller reporting company shall include, as awards required to be reported in column (f), the incremental fair value, computed as of the repricing or modification date in accordance with FASB ASC Topic 718, with respect to that repriced or modified award.

3. For any awards that are subject to performance conditions, report the value at the grant date based upon the probable outcome of such conditions. This amount should be consistent with the estimate of aggregate compensation cost to be recognized over the service period determined as of the grant date under FASB ASC Topic 718, excluding the effect of estimated forfeitures. In a footnote to the

table, disclose the value of the award at the grant date assuming that the highest level of performance conditions will be achieved if an amount less than the maximum was included in the table.

(vii) The dollar value of all earnings for services performed during the fiscal year pursuant to awards under non-equity incentive plans as defined in paragraph (m)(5)(iii) of this Item, and all earnings on any outstanding awards (column (g));

Instructions to Item 402(n)(2)(vii):

1. If the relevant performance measure is satisfied during the fiscal year (including for a single year in a plan with a multi-year performance measure), the earnings are reportable for that fiscal year, even if not payable until a later date, and are not reportable again in the fiscal year when amounts are paid to the named executive officer.

2. All earnings on non-equity incentive plan compensation must be identified and quantified in a footnote to column (g), whether the earnings were paid during the fiscal year, payable during the period but deferred at the election of the named executive officer, or payable by their terms at a later date.

(viii) Above-market or preferential earnings on compensation that is deferred on a basis that is not tax-qualified, including such earnings on nonqualified defined contribution plans (column (h));

Instruction to Item 402(n)(2)(viii): Interest on deferred compensation is above-market only if the rate of interest exceeds 120% of the applicable federal long-term rate, with compounding (as prescribed under section 1274(d) of the Internal Revenue Code, (26 U.S.C. 1274(d))) at the rate that corresponds most closely to the rate under the smaller reporting company's plan at the time the interest rate or formula is set. In the event of a discretionary reset of the interest rate, the requisite calculation must be made on the basis of the interest rate at the time of such reset, rather than when originally established. Only the above-market portion of the interest must be included. If the applicable interest rates vary depending upon conditions such as a minimum period of continued service, the reported amount should be calculated assuming satisfaction of all conditions to receiving interest at the highest rate. Dividends (and dividend equivalents) on deferred compensation denominated in the smaller reporting company's stock ("deferred stock") are preferential only if earned at a rate higher than dividends on the smaller reporting company's common stock. Only the preferential portion of the dividends or equivalents must be included. Footnote or narrative disclosure may be provided explaining the smaller reporting company's criteria for determining any portion considered to be above-market.

(ix) All other compensation for the covered fiscal year that the smaller reporting company could not properly report in any other column of the Summary Compensation Table (column (i)). Each compensation item that is not properly reportable in columns (c) through (h), regardless of the amount of the compensation item, must be included in column (i). Such compensation must include, but is not limited to:

(A) Perquisites and other personal benefits, or property, unless the aggregate amount of such compensation is less than $10,000;

(B) All "gross-ups" or other amounts reimbursed during the fiscal year for the payment of taxes;

(C) For any security of the smaller reporting company or its subsidiaries purchased from the smaller reporting company or its subsidiaries (through deferral of salary or bonus, or otherwise) at a discount from the market price of such security at the date of purchase, unless that discount is available generally either to all security holders or to all salaried employees of the smaller reporting company, the compensation cost, if any, computed in accordance with FASB ASC Topic 718;

(D) The amount paid or accrued to any named executive officer pursuant to a plan or arrangement in connection with:

(*1*) Any termination, including without limitation through retirement, resignation, severance or constructive termination (including a change in responsibilities) of such executive officer's employment with the smaller reporting company and its subsidiaries; or

(*2*) A change in control of the smaller reporting company;

(E) Smaller reporting company contributions or other allocations to vested and unvested defined contribution plans;

(F) The dollar value of any insurance premiums paid by, or on behalf of, the smaller reporting company during the covered fiscal year with respect to life insurance for the benefit of a named executive officer; and

(G) The dollar value of any dividends or other earnings paid on stock or option awards, when those amounts were not factored into the grant date fair value required to be reported for the stock or option award in column (e) or (f); and

Instructions to Item 402(n)(2)(ix):

1. Non-equity incentive plan awards and earnings and earnings on stock or options, except as specified in paragraph (n)(2)(ix)(G) of this Item, are required to be reported elsewhere as provided in this Item and are not reportable as All Other Compensation in column (i).

2. Benefits paid pursuant to defined benefit and actuarial plans are not reportable as All Other Compensation in column (i) unless accelerated pursuant to a change in

control; information concerning these plans is reportable pursuant to paragraph (q)(1) of this Item.

3. Reimbursements of taxes owed with respect to perquisites or other personal benefits must be included in the columns as tax reimbursements (paragraph (n)(2)(ix)(B) of this Item) even if the associated perquisites or other personal benefits are not required to be included because the aggregate amount of such compensation is less than $10,000.

4. Perquisites and other personal benefits shall be valued on the basis of the aggregate incremental cost to the smaller reporting company.

5. For purposes of paragraph (n)(2)(ix)(D) of this Item, an accrued amount is an amount for which payment has become due.

(x) The dollar value of total compensation for the covered fiscal year (column (j)). With respect to each named executive officer, disclose the sum of all amounts reported in columns (c) through (i).

Instructions to Item 402(n):

1. Information with respect to the fiscal year prior to the last completed fiscal year will not be required if the smaller reporting company was not a reporting company pursuant to section 13(a) or 15(d) of the Exchange Act (15 U.S.C. 78m(a) or 78o(d)) at any time during that year, except that the smaller reporting company will be required to provide information for any such year if that information previously was required to be provided in response to a Commission filing requirement.

2. All compensation values reported in the Summary Compensation Table must be reported in dollars and rounded to the nearest dollar. Reported compensation values must be reported numerically, providing a single numerical value for each grid in the table. Where compensation was paid to or received by a named executive officer in a different currency, a footnote must be provided to identify that currency and describe the rate and methodology used to convert the payment amounts to dollars.

3. If a named executive officer is also a director who receives compensation for his or her services as a director, reflect that compensation in the Summary Compensation Table and provide a footnote identifying and itemizing such compensation and amounts. Use the categories in the Director Compensation Table required pursuant to paragraph (r) of this Item.

4. Any amounts deferred, whether pursuant to a plan established under section 401(k) of the Internal Revenue Code (26 U.S.C. 401(k)), or otherwise, shall be included in the appropriate column for the fiscal year in which earned.

(o) *Smaller Reporting Companies—Narrative Disclosure to Summary Compensation Table.* Provide a narrative description of any material factors necessary to an understanding of the information disclosed in the Table required by paragraph (n) of this Item. Examples of such factors may include, in given cases, among other things:

(1) The material terms of each named executive officer's employment agreement or arrangement, whether written or unwritten;

(2) If at any time during the last fiscal year, any outstanding option or other equity-based award was repriced or otherwise materially modified (such as by extension of exercise periods, the change of vesting or forfeiture conditions, the change or elimination of applicable performance criteria, or the change of the bases upon which returns are determined), a description of each such repricing or other material modification;

(3) The waiver or modification of any specified performance target, goal or condition to payout with respect to any amount included in non-stock incentive plan compensation or payouts reported in column (g) to the Summary Compensation Table required by paragraph (n) of this Item, stating whether the waiver or modification applied to one or more specified named executive officers or to all compensation subject to the target, goal or condition;

(4) The material terms of each grant, including but not limited to the date of exercisability, any conditions to exercisability, any tandem feature, any reload feature, any tax-reimbursement feature, and any provision that could cause the exercise price to be lowered;

(5) The material terms of any non-equity incentive plan award made to a named executive officer during the last completed fiscal year, including a general description of the formula or criteria to be applied in determining the amounts payable and vesting schedule;

(6) The method of calculating earnings on nonqualified deferred compensation plans including nonqualified defined contribution plans; and

(7) An identification to the extent material of any item included under All Other Compensation (column (i)) in the Summary Compensation Table. Identification of an item shall not be considered material if it does not exceed the greater of $25,000 or 10% of all items included in the specified category in question set forth in paragraph (n)(2)(ix) of this Item. All items of compensation are required to be included in the Summary Compensation Table without regard to whether such items are required to be identified.

Instruction to Item 402(o): The disclosure required by paragraph (o)(2) of this Item would not apply to any repricing that occurs through a pre-existing formula or mechanism in the plan or award that results in the periodic adjustment of the option or SAR exercise or base price, an antidilution provision in a plan or award, or a recapitalization or similar transaction equally affecting all holders of the class of securities underlying the options or SARs.

(p) *Smaller Reporting Companies—Outstanding Equity Awards at Fiscal Year–End Table.* (1) Provide the information specified in paragraph (p)(2) of this Item, concerning unexercised options; stock that has not vested; and equity incentive plan awards for each named executive officer outstanding as of the end of the smaller reporting company's last completed fiscal year in the following tabular format:

OUTSTANDING EQUITY AWARDS AT FISCAL YEAR–END

	Option awards					Stock awards			
Name	Number of Securities Underlying Unexercised Options (#) Exercisable	Number of Securities Underlying Unexercised Options (#) Unexercisable	Equity Incentive Plan Awards: Number of Securities Underlying Unexercised Unearned Options (#)	Option Exercise Price ($)	Option Expiration Date	Number of Shares or Units of Stock That Have Not Vested (#)	Market Value of Shares or Units of Stock That Have Not Vested ($)	Equity Incentive Plan Awards: Number of Unearned Shares, Units or Other Rights That Have Not Vested (#)	Equity Incentive Plan Awards: Market or Payout Value of Unearned Shares, Units or Other Rights That Have Not Vested ($)
(a)	(b)	(c)	(d)	(e)	(f)	(g)	(h)	(i)	(j)
PEO									
A									
B									

(2) The Table shall include:

(i) The name of the named executive officer (column (a));

(ii) On an award-by-award basis, the number of securities underlying unexercised options, including awards that have been transferred other than for value, that are exercisable and that are not reported in column (d) (column (b));

(iii) On an award-by-award basis, the number of securities underlying unexercised options, including awards that have been transferred other than for value, that are unexercisable and that are not reported in column (d) (column (c));

(iv) On an award-by-award basis, the total number of shares underlying unexercised options awarded under any equity incentive plan that have not been earned (column (d));

(v) For each instrument reported in columns (b), (c) and (d), as applicable, the exercise or base price (column (e));

(vi) For each instrument reported in columns (b), (c) and (d), as applicable, the expiration date (column (f));

(vii) The total number of shares of stock that have not vested and that are not reported in column (i) (column (g));

(viii) The aggregate market value of shares of stock that have not vested and that are not reported in column (j) (column (h));

(ix) The total number of shares of stock, units or other rights awarded under any equity incentive plan that have not vested and that have not been earned, and, if applicable the number of shares underlying any such unit or right (column (i)); and

(x) The aggregate market or payout value of shares of stock, units or other rights awarded under any equity incentive plan that have not vested and that have not been earned (column (j)).

Instructions to Item 402(p)(2):

1. Identify by footnote any award that has been transferred other than for value, disclosing the nature of the transfer.

2. The vesting dates of options, shares of stock and equity incentive plan awards held at fiscal-year end must be disclosed by footnote to the applicable column where the outstanding award is reported.

3. Compute the market value of stock reported in column (h) and equity incentive plan awards of stock reported in column (j) by multiplying the closing market price of the

smaller reporting company's stock at the end of the last completed fiscal year by the number of shares or units of stock or the amount of equity incentive plan awards, respectively. The number of shares or units reported in column (d) or (i), and the payout value reported in column (j), shall be based on achieving threshold performance goals, except that if the previous fiscal year's performance has exceeded the threshold, the disclosure shall be based on the next higher performance measure (target or maximum) that exceeds the previous fiscal year's performance. If the award provides only for a single estimated payout, that amount should be reported. If the target amount is not determinable, smaller reporting companies must provide a representative amount based on the previous fiscal year's performance.

4. Multiple awards may be aggregated where the expiration date and the exercise and/or base price of the instruments is identical. A single award consisting of a combination of options, SARs and/or similar option-like instruments shall be reported as separate awards with respect to each tranche with a different exercise and/or base price or expiration date.

5. Options or stock awarded under an equity incentive plan are reported in columns (d) or (i) and (j), respectively, until the relevant performance condition has been satisfied. Once the relevant performance condition has been satisfied, even if the option or stock award is subject to forfeiture conditions, options are reported in column (b) or (c), as appropriate, until they are exercised or expire, or stock is reported in columns (g) and (h) until it vests.

(q) *Smaller Reporting Companies—Additional Narrative Disclosure.* Provide a narrative description of the following to the extent material:

(1) The material terms of each plan that provides for the payment of retirement benefits, or benefits that will be paid primarily following retirement, including but not limited to tax-qualified defined benefit plans, supplemental executive retirement plans, tax-qualified defined contribution plans and nonqualified defined contribution plans.

(2) The material terms of each contract, agreement, plan or arrangement, whether written or unwritten, that provides for payment(s) to a named executive officer at, following, or in connection with the resignation, retirement or other termination of a named executive officer, or a change in control of the smaller reporting company or a change in the named executive officer's responsibilities following a change in control, with respect to each named executive officer.

(r) *Smaller Reporting Companies—Compensation of Directors.* (1) Provide the information specified in paragraph (r)(2) of this Item, concerning the compensation of the directors for the smaller reporting company's last completed fiscal year, in the following tabular format:

DIRECTOR COMPENSATION

Name	Fees earned or paid in cash ($)	Stock awards ($)	Option awards ($)	Non-equity incentive plan compensation ($)	Non-qualified deferred compensation earnings ($)	All other compensation ($)	Total ($)
(a)	(b)	(c)	(d)	(e)	(f)	(g)	(h)
A							
B							
C							
D							
E							

(2) The Table shall include:

(i) The name of each director unless such director is also a named executive officer under paragraph (m) of this Item and his or her compensation for service as a director is fully reflected in the Summary Compensation Table pursuant to paragraph (n) of this Item and otherwise as required pursuant to paragraphs (*o*) through (q) of this Item (column (a));

(ii) The aggregate dollar amount of all fees earned or paid in cash for services as a director, including annual retainer fees, committee and/or chairmanship fees, and meeting fees (column (b));

(iii) For awards of stock, the aggregate grant date fair value computed in accordance with FASB ASC Topic 718 (column (c));

(iv) For awards of options, with or without tandem SARs (including awards that subsequently have been transferred), the aggregate grant date fair value computed in accordance with FASB ASC Topic 718 (column (d));

Instruction to Item 402(r)(2)(iii) and (iv): For each director, disclose by footnote to the appropriate column, the aggregate number of stock awards and the aggregate number of option awards outstanding at fiscal year end.

(v) The dollar value of all earnings for services performed during the fiscal year pursuant to non-equity incentive plans as defined in paragraph (m)(5)(iii) of this Item, and all earnings on any outstanding awards (column (e));

(vi) Above-market or preferential earnings on compensation that is deferred on a basis that is not tax-qualified, including such earnings on non-qualified defined contribution plans (column (f));

(vii) All other compensation for the covered fiscal year that the smaller reporting company could not properly report in any other column of the Director Compensation Table (column (g)). Each compensation item that is not properly reportable in columns (b) through (f), regardless of the amount of the compensation item, must be included in column (g) and must be identified and quantified in a footnote if it is deemed material in accordance with paragraph (o)(7) of this Item. Such compensation must include, but is not limited to:

(A) Perquisites and other personal benefits, or property, unless the aggregate amount of such compensation is less than $10,000;

(B) All "gross-ups" or other amounts reimbursed during the fiscal year for the payment of taxes;

(C) For any security of the smaller reporting company or its subsidiaries purchased from the smaller reporting company or its subsidiaries (through deferral of salary or bonus, or otherwise) at a discount from the market price of such security at the date of purchase, unless that discount is available generally either to all security holders or to all salaried employees of the smaller reporting company, the compensation cost, if any, computed in accordance with FASB ASC Topic 718;

(D) The amount paid or accrued to any director pursuant to a plan or arrangement in connection with:

(*1*) The resignation, retirement or any other termination of such director; or

(*2*) A change in control of the smaller reporting company;

(E) Smaller reporting company contributions or other allocations to vested and unvested defined contribution plans;

(F) Consulting fees earned from, or paid or payable by the smaller reporting company and/or its subsidiaries (including joint ventures);

(G) The annual costs of payments and promises of payments pursuant to director legacy programs and similar charitable award programs;

(H) The dollar value of any insurance premiums paid by, or on behalf of, the smaller reporting company during the covered fiscal year with respect to life insurance for the benefit of a director; and

(I) The dollar value of any dividends or other earnings paid on stock or option awards, when those amounts were not factored into the grant date fair value required to be reported for the stock or option award in column (c) or (d); and

Instruction to Item 402(r)(2)(vii): Programs in which smaller reporting companies agree to make donations to one or more charitable institutions in a director's name, payable by the smaller reporting company currently or upon a designated event, such as the retirement or death of the director, are charitable awards programs or director legacy programs for purposes of the disclosure required by paragraph (r)(2)(vii)(G) of this Item. Provide footnote disclosure of the total dollar amount payable under the program and other material terms of each such program for which tabular disclosure is provided.

(viii) The dollar value of total compensation for the covered fiscal year (column (h)). With respect to each director, disclose the sum of all amounts reported in columns (b) through (g).

Instruction to Item 402(r)(2): Two or more directors may be grouped in a single row in the Table if all elements of their compensation are identical. The names of the directors for whom disclosure is presented on a group basis should be clear from the Table.

(3) *Narrative to Director Compensation Table.* Provide a narrative description of any material factors necessary to an understanding of the director compensation disclosed in this Table. While material factors will vary depending upon the facts, examples of such factors may include, in given cases, among other things:

(i) A description of standard compensation arrangements (such as fees for retainer, committee service, service as chairman of the board or a committee, and meeting attendance); and

(ii) Whether any director has a different compensation arrangement, identifying that director and describing the terms of that arrangement.

Instruction to Item 402(r): In addition to the Instruction to paragraph (r)(2)(vii) of this Item, the following apply equally to paragraph (r) of this Item: Instructions 2 and 4 to paragraph (n) of this Item; the Instructions to paragraphs (n)(2)(iii) and (iv) of this Item; the Instructions to paragraphs (n)(2)(v) and (vi) of this Item; the Instructions to paragraph (n)(2)(vii) of this Item; the Instruction to paragraph (n)(2)(viii) of this Item; the Instructions to paragraph (n)(2)(ix) of this Item; and paragraph (*o*)(7) of this Item. These Instructions apply to the columns in the Director Compensation Table that are analogous to the columns in the Summary Compensation Table to which they refer and to disclosures under paragraph (r) of this Item that correspond to analogous disclosures provided for in paragraph (n) of this Item to which they refer.

(s) *Narrative Disclosure of the Registrant's Compensation Policies and Practices as they Relate to the Registrant's Risk Management.* To the extent that risks arising from the registrant's compensation policies and practices for its employees are reasonably likely to have a material adverse effect on the registrant, discuss the registrant's policies and practices of compensating its employees, including non-executive officers, as they relate to risk management practices and risk-taking incentives. While the situations requiring disclosure will vary depending on the particular registrant and compensation policies and practices, situations that may trigger disclosure include, among others, compensation policies and practices: at a business unit of the company that carries a significant portion of the registrant's risk profile; at a business unit with compensation structured significantly differently than other units within the registrant; at a business unit that is significantly more profitable than others within the registrant; at a business unit where compensation expense is a significant percentage of the unit's revenues; and that vary significantly from the overall risk and reward structure of the registrant, such as when bonuses are awarded upon accomplishment of a task, while the income and risk to the registrant from the task extend over a significantly longer period of time. The purpose of this paragraph (s) is to provide investors material information concerning how the registrant compensates and incentivizes its employees that may create risks that are reasonably likely to have a material adverse effect on the registrant. While the information to be disclosed pursuant to this paragraph (s) will vary depending upon the nature of the registrant's business and the compensation approach, the following are examples of the issues that the registrant may need to address for the business units or employees discussed:

(1) The general design philosophy of the registrant's compensation policies and practices for employees whose behavior would be most affected by the incentives established by the policies and practices, as such policies and practices relate to or affect risk taking by employees on behalf of the registrant, and the manner of their implementation;

(2) The registrant's risk assessment or incentive considerations, if any, in structuring its compensation policies and practices or in awarding and paying compensation;

(3) How the registrant's compensation policies and practices relate to the realization of risks resulting from the actions of employees in both the short term and the long term, such as through policies requiring claw backs or imposing holding periods;

(4) The registrant's policies regarding adjustments to its compensation policies and practices to address changes in its risk profile;

(5) Material adjustments the registrant has made to its compensation policies and practices as a result of changes in its risk profile; and

(6) The extent to which the registrant monitors its compensation policies and practices to determine whether its risk management objectives are being met with respect to incentivizing its employees.

(t) *Golden parachute compensation.*

(1) In connection with any proxy or consent solicitation material providing the disclosure required by section 14A(b)(1) of the Exchange Act (15 U.S.C. 78n-1(b)(1)) or any proxy or consent solicitation that includes disclosure under Item 14 of Schedule 14A (§240.14a-101) pursuant to Note A of Schedule 14A (excluding any proxy or consent solicitation of an "emerging growth company," as defined in Rule 405 of the Securities Act (§230.405 of this chapter) or Rule 12b-2 of the Exchange Act (§240.12b-2 of this chapter)), with respect to each named executive officer of the acquiring company and the target company, provide the information specified in paragraphs (t)(2) and (3) of this section regarding any agreement or understanding, whether written or unwritten, between such named executive officer and the acquiring company or target company, concerning any type of compensation, whether present, deferred or contingent, that is based on or otherwise relates to an acquisition, merger, consolidation, sale or other disposition of all or substantially all assets of the issuer, as follows:

GOLDEN PARACHUTE COMPENSATION

Name	Cash ($)	Equity ($)	Pension/ NQDC ($)	Perquisites/ Benefits ($)	Tax Reimbursement ($)	Other ($)	Total($)
(a)	(b)	(c)	(d)	(e)	(f)	(g)	(h)
PEO							
PFO							
A							
B							
C							

(2) The table shall include, for each named executive officer:

(i) The name of the named executive officer (column (a));

(ii) The aggregate dollar value of any cash severance payments, including but not limited to payments of base salary, bonus, and pro-rated non-equity incentive compensation plan payments (column (b));

(iii) The aggregate dollar value of:

(A) Stock awards for which vesting would be accelerated;

(B) In-the-money option awards for which vesting would be accelerated; and

(C) Payments in cancellation of stock and option awards (column (c));

(iv) The aggregate dollar value of pension and nonqualified deferred compensation benefit enhancements (column (d));

(v) The aggregate dollar value of perquisites and other personal benefits or property, and health care and welfare benefits (column (e));

(vi) The aggregate dollar value of any tax reimbursements (column (f));

(vii) The aggregate dollar value of any other compensation that is based on or otherwise relates to the transaction not properly reported in columns (b) through (f) (column (g)); and

(viii) The aggregate dollar value of the sum of all amounts reported in columns (b) through (g) (column (h)).

Instructions to Item 402(t)(2):

1. If this disclosure is included in a proxy or consent solicitation seeking approval of an acquisition, merger, consolidation, or proposed sale or other disposition of all or substantially all the assets of the registrant, or in a proxy or consent solicitation that includes disclosure under Item 14 of Schedule 14A pursuant to Note A of Schedule 14A, the disclosure provided by this table shall be quantified assuming that the triggering event took place on the latest practicable date, and that the price per share of the registrant's securities shall be determined as follows: if the shareholders are to receive a fixed dollar amount, the price per share shall be that fixed dollar amount, and if such value is not a fixed dollar amount, the price per share shall be the average closing market price of the registrant's securities over the first five business days following the first public announcement of the transaction. Compute the dollar value of in-the-money option awards for which vesting would be accelerated by determining the difference between this price and the exercise or base price of the options. Include only compensation that is based on or otherwise relates to the subject transaction. Apply Instruction 1 to Item 402(t) with respect to those executive officers for whom disclosure was required in the issuer's most recent filing with the Commission under the Securities Act (15 U.S.C. 77a et seq.) or Exchange Act (15 U.S.C. 78a et seq.) that required disclosure pursuant to Item 402(c).

2. If this disclosure is included in a proxy solicitation for the annual meeting at which directors are elected for purposes of subjecting the disclosed agreements or understandings to a shareholder vote under section 14A(a)(1) of the Exchange Act (15 U.S.C. 78n–1(a)(1)), the disclosure provided by this table shall be quantified assuming that the triggering event took place on the last business day of the registrant's last completed fiscal year, and the price per share of the registrant's securities is the closing market price as of that date. Compute the dollar value of in-the-money option awards for which vesting would be accelerated by determining the difference between this price and the exercise or base price of the options.

3. In the event that uncertainties exist as to the provision of payments and benefits or the amounts involved, the registrant is required to make a reasonable estimate applicable to the payment or benefit and disclose material assumptions underlying such estimates in its disclosure. In such event, the disclosure would require forward-looking information as appropriate.

4. For each of columns (b) through (g), include a footnote quantifying each separate form of compensation included in the aggregate total reported. Include the value of all perquisites and other personal benefits or property. Individual perquisites and personal benefits shall be identified and quantified as required by Instruction 4 to Item 402(c)(2)(ix) of this section. For purposes of quantifying health care benefits, the registrant must use the assumptions used for financial reporting purposes under generally accepted accounting principles.

5. For each of columns (b) through (h), include a footnote quantifying the amount payable attributable to a double-trigger arrangement (i.e., amounts triggered by a change-in-control for which payment is conditioned upon the executive officer's termination without cause or resignation for good reason within a limited time period fol-

lowing the change-in-control), specifying the time-frame in which such termination or resignation must occur in order for the amount to become payable, and the amount payable attributable to a single-trigger arrangement (i.e., amounts triggered by a change-in-control for which payment is not conditioned upon such a termination or resignation of the executive officer).

6. A registrant conducting a shareholder advisory vote pursuant to Rule 14a–21(c) of the Securities Exchange Act of 1934 to cover new arrangements and understandings, and/or revised terms of agreements and understandings that were previously subject to a shareholder advisory vote pursuant to Rule 14a–21(a) of the Securities Exchange Act of 1934, shall provide two separate tables. One table shall disclose all golden parachute compensation, including both the arrangements and amounts previously disclosed and subject to a shareholder advisory vote under section 14A(a)(1) of the Exchange Act (15 U.S.C. 78n–1(a)(1)) and Rule 14a–21(a) of the Securities Exchange Act of 1934 and the new arrangements and understandings and/or revised terms of agreements and understandings that were previously subject to a shareholder advisory vote. The second table shall disclose only the new arrangements and/or revised terms subject to the separate shareholder vote under section 14A(b)(2) of the Exchange Act and Rule 14a–21(c) of the Securities Exchange Act of 1934.

7. In cases where this Item 402(t)(2) requires disclosure of arrangements between an acquiring company and the named executive officers of the soliciting target company, the registrant shall clarify whether these agreements are included in the separate shareholder advisory vote pursuant to Rule 14a–21(c) under the Exchange Act by providing a separate table of all agreements and understandings subject to the shareholder advisory vote required by section 14A(b)(2) of the Exchange Act (15 U.S.C. 78n–1(b)(2)) and Rule 14a–21(c) of the Securities Exchange Act of 1934, if different from the full scope of golden parachute compensation subject to Item 402(t) disclosure.

(3) Provide a succinct narrative description of any material factors necessary to an understanding of each such contract, agreement, plan or arrangement and the payments quantified in the tabular disclosure required by this paragraph. Such factors shall include, but not be limited to a description of:

(i) The specific circumstances that would trigger payment(s);

(ii) Whether the payments would or could be lump sum, or annual, disclosing the duration, and by whom they would be provided; and

(iii) Any material conditions or obligations applicable to the receipt of payment or benefits, including but not limited to non-compete, non-solicitation, non-disparagement or confidentiality agreements, including the duration of such agreements and provisions regarding waiver or breach of such agreements.

Instructions to Item 402(t):

1. A registrant that does not qualify as a "smaller reporting company," as defined by Item 10(f)(1), must provide the information required by this Item 402(t) with respect to the individuals covered by Items 402(a)(3)(i), (ii) and (iii) of this section. A registrant that qualifies as a "smaller reporting company," as defined by Item 10(f)(1) of this chapter, must provide the information required by this Item 402(t) with respect to the individuals covered by Items 402(m)(2)(i) and (ii) of this section.

2. The obligation to provide the information in this Item 402(t) shall not apply to agreements and understandings described in paragraph (t)(1) of this section with senior management of foreign private issuers, as defined in Rule 3b–4 of the Securities Exchange Act of 1934.

(u) *Pay ratio disclosure*.--

(1) Disclose:

(i) The median of the annual total compensation of all employees of the registrant, except the PEO of the registrant;

(ii) The annual total compensation of the PEO of the registrant; and

(iii) The ratio of the amount in paragraph (u)(1)(i) of this Item to the amount in paragraph (u)(1)(ii) of this Item. For purposes of the ratio required by this paragraph (u)(1)(iii), the amount in paragraph (u)(1)(i) of this Item shall equal one, or, alternatively, the ratio may be expressed narratively as the multiple that the amount in paragraph (u)(1)(ii) of this Item bears to the amount in paragraph (u)(1)(i) of this Item.

(2) For purposes of this paragraph (u):

(i) *Total compensation* for the median of annual total compensation of all employees of the registrant and the PEO of the registrant shall be determined in accordance with paragraph (c)(2)(x) of this Item 402. In determining the total compensation, all references to "named executive officer" in this Item 402 and the instructions thereto may be deemed to refer instead, as applicable, to "employee" and, for non-salaried employees, references to "base salary" and "salary" in this Item 402 and the instructions thereto may be deemed to refer instead, as applicable, to "wages plus overtime";

(ii) *Annual total compensation* means total compensation for the registrant's last completed fiscal year; and

(iii) *Registrant* means the registrant and its consolidated subsidiaries.

(3) For purposes of this paragraph (u), *employee* or *employee* of the registrant means an individu-

al employed by the registrant or any of its consolidated subsidiaries, whether as a full- time, part-time, seasonal, or temporary worker, as of a date chosen by the registrant within the last three months of the registrant's last completed fiscal year. The definition of employee or employee of the registrant does not include those workers who are employed, and whose compensation is determined, by an unaffiliated third party but who provide services to the registrant or its consolidated subsidiaries as independent contractors or "leased" workers;

(4) For purposes of this paragraph (u), an employee located in a jurisdiction outside the United States (a "non-U.S. employee") may be exempt from the definition of employee or employee of the registrant under either of the following conditions:

(i) The employee is employed in a foreign jurisdiction in which the laws or regulations governing data privacy are such that, despite its reasonable efforts to obtain or process the information necessary for compliance with this paragraph (u), the registrant is unable to do so without violating such data privacy laws or regulations. The registrant's reasonable efforts shall include, at a minimum, using or seeking an exemption or other relief under any governing data privacy laws or regulations. If the registrant chooses to exclude any employees using this exemption, it shall list the excluded jurisdictions, identify the specific data privacy law or regulation, explain how complying with this paragraph (u) violates such data privacy law or regulation (including the efforts made by the registrant to use or seek an exemption or other relief under such law or regulation), and provide the approximate number of employees exempted from each jurisdiction based on this exemption. In addition, if a registrant excludes any non-U.S. employees in a particular jurisdiction under this exemption, it must exclude all non-U.S. employees in that jurisdiction. Further, the registrant shall obtain a legal opinion from counsel that opines on the inability of the registrant to obtain or process the information necessary for compliance with this paragraph (u) without violating the jurisdiction's laws or regulations governing data privacy, including the registrant's inability to obtain an exemption or other relief under any governing laws or regulations. The registrant shall file the legal opinion as an exhibit to the filing in which the pay ratio disclosure is included.

(ii) The registrant's non-U.S. employees account for 5% or less of the registrant's total employees. In that circumstance, if the registrant chooses to exclude any non-U.S. employees under this exemption, it must exclude all non-U.S. employees. Additionally, if a registrant's non-U.S. employees exceed 5% of the registrant's total U.S. and non-U.S. employees, it may exclude up to 5% of its total employees who are non-U.S. employees; *provided, however*, if a registrant excludes any non-U.S. employees in a particular jurisdiction, it must exclude all non-U.S. employees in that jurisdiction. If more than 5% of a registrant's employees are located in any one non-U.S. jurisdiction, the registrant may not exclude any employees in that jurisdiction under this exemption.

(A) In calculating the number of non-U.S. employees that may be excluded under this Item 402(u)(4)(ii) ("*de minimis*" exemption), a registrant shall count against the total any non- U.S. employee exempted under the data privacy law exemption under Item 402(u)(4)(i) ("data privacy" exemption). A registrant may exclude any non-U.S. employee from a jurisdiction that meets the data privacy exemption, even if the number of excluded employees exceeds 5% of the registrant's total employees. If, however, the number of employees excluded under the data privacy exemption equals or exceeds 5% of the registrant's total employees, the registrant may not use the *de minimis* exemption. Additionally, if the number of employees excluded under the data privacy exemption is less than 5% of the registrant's total employees, the registrant may use the *de minimis* exemption to exclude no more than the number of non-U.S. employees that, combined with the data privacy exemption, does not exceed 5% of the registrant's total employees.

(B) If a registrant excludes non-U.S. employees under the *de minimis* exemption, it must disclose the jurisdiction or jurisdictions from which those employees are being excluded, the approximate number of employees excluded from each jurisdiction under the *de minimis* exemption, the total number of its U.S. and non-U.S. employees irrespective of any exemption (data privacy or *de minimis*), and the total number of its U.S. and non-U.S. employees used for its *de minimis* calculation.

Instruction 1 to Item 402(u). Disclosing the date chosen for identifying the median employee.

A registrant shall disclose the date within the last three months of its last completed fiscal year that it selected pursuant to paragraph (u)(3) of this Item to identify its median employee. If the registrant changes the date it uses to identify the median employee from the prior year, the registrant shall disclose this change and provide a brief explanation about the reason or reasons for the change.

Instruction 2 to Item 402(u). Identifying the median employee.

A registrant is required to identify its median employee only once every three years and calculate total compensation for that employee each year; *provided that*, during a registrant's last completed fiscal year there has been no change in its employee population or employee compensation arrangements that it reasonably believes would result in a significant change to its pay ratio disclosure. If there have been no changes that the registrant reasonably believes would significantly affect its pay ratio disclosure, the registrant shall disclose that it is using the same median employee in its pay ratio calculation and describe briefly the basis for its reasonable belief. For example, the registrant could disclose that there has been no change in its employee population or employee compensation arrangements that it believes would significantly impact the pay ratio disclosure. If there has been a change in the registrant's employee population or employee compensation arrangements that the registrant reasonably believes would result in a significant change in its pay ratio disclosure, the registrant shall re-identify the median employee for that fiscal year. If it is no longer appropriate for the registrant to use the median employee identified in year one as the median employee in years two or three because of a change in the original median employee's circumstances that the registrant reasonably believes would result in a significant change in its pay ratio disclosure, the registrant may use another employee whose compensation is substantially similar to the original median employee based on the compensation measure used to select the original median employee.

Instruction 3 to Item 402(u). Updating for the last completed fiscal year.

Pay ratio information (i.e., the disclosure called for by paragraph (u)(1) of this Item) with respect to the registrant's last completed fiscal year is not required to be disclosed until the filing of its annual report on Form 10-K for that last completed fiscal year or, if later, the filing of a definitive proxy or information statement relating to its next annual meeting of shareholders (or written consents in lieu of such a meeting) following the end of such fiscal year; *provided that*, the required pay ratio information must, in any event, be filed as provided in General Instruction G(3) of Form 10-K (17 CFR 249.310) not later than 120 days after the end of such fiscal year.

Instruction 4 to Item 402(u). Methodology and use of estimates.

1. Registrants may use reasonable estimates both in the methodology used to identify the median employee and in calculating the annual total compensation or any elements of total compensation for employees other than the PEO.

2. In determining the employees from which the median employee is identified, a registrant may use its employee population or statistical sampling and/or other reasonable methods.

3. A registrant may identify the median employee using annual total compensation or any other compensation measure that is consistently applied to all employees included in the calculation, such as information derived from the registrant's tax and/or payroll records. In using a compensation measure other than annual total compensation to identify the median employee, if that measure is recorded on a basis other than the registrant's fiscal year (such as information derived from tax and/or payroll records), the registrant may use the same annual period that is used to derive those amounts. Where a compensation measure other than annual total compensation is used to identify the median employee, the registrant must disclose the compensation measure used.

4. In identifying the median employee, whether using annual total compensation or any other compensation measure that is consistently applied to all employees included in the calculation, the registrant may make cost-of-living adjustments to the compensation of employees in jurisdictions other than the jurisdiction in which the PEO resides so that the compensation is adjusted to the cost of living in the jurisdiction in which the PEO resides. If the registrant uses a cost-of-living adjustment to identify the median employee, and the median employee identified is an employee in a jurisdiction other than the jurisdiction in which the PEO resides, the registrant must use the same cost-of-living adjustment in calculating the median employee's annual total compensation and disclose the median employee's jurisdiction. The registrant also shall briefly describe the cost-of-living adjustments it used to identify the median employee and briefly describe the cost-of-living adjustments it used to calculate the median employee's annual total compensation, including the measure used as the basis for the cost-of-living adjustment. A registrant electing to present the pay ratio in this manner also shall disclose the median employee's annual total compensation and pay ratio without the cost-of-living adjustment. To calculate this pay ratio, the registrant will need to identify the median employee without using any cost-of-living adjustments.

5. The registrant shall briefly describe the methodology it used to identify the median employee. It shall also briefly describe any material assumptions, adjustments (including any cost-of-living adjustments), or estimates it used to identify the median employee or to determine total compensation or any elements of total compensation, which shall be consistently applied. The registrant shall clearly identify any estimates used. The required descriptions should be a brief overview; it is not necessary for the registrant to provide technical analyses or formulas. If a registrant changes its methodology or its material assumptions, adjustments, or estimates from those used in its pay ratio disclosure for the prior fiscal year, and if the effects of any such change are significant, the registrant shall briefly describe the change and the reasons for the change. Registrants must also disclose if they changed from using the cost-of-living adjustment to not using that adjustment and if they changed from not using the cost-of-living adjustment to using it.

6. Registrants may, at their discretion, include personal benefits that aggregate less than $10,000 and compensation under non-discriminatory benefit plans in calculating the annual total compensation of the median employee as long as these items are also included in calculating the PEO's annual total compensation. The registrant shall also explain any difference between the PEO's annual total compensation used in the pay ratio disclosure and the total compensation amounts reflected in the Summary Compensation Table, if material.

Instruction 5 to Item 402(u). Permitted annualizing adjustments.

A registrant may annualize the total compensation for all permanent employees (full-time or part-time) that were employed by the registrant for less than the full fiscal year (such as newly hired employees or permanent employees on an unpaid leave of absence during the period). A registrant may not annualize the total compensation for employees in temporary or seasonal positions. A registrant may not make a full-time equivalent adjustment for any employee.

Instruction 6 to Item 402(u). PEO compensation not available.

A registrant that is relying on Instruction 1 to Item 402(c)(2)(iii) and (iv) in connection with the salary or bonus of the PEO for the last completed fiscal year, shall disclose that the pay ratio required by paragraph (u) of this Item is not calculable until the PEO salary or bonus, as applicable, is determined and shall disclose the date that the PEO's actual total compensation is expected to be determined. The disclosure required by paragraph (u) of this Item shall then be disclosed in the filing under Item 5.02(f) of Form 8-K (17 CFR 249.308) that discloses the PEO's salary or bonus in accordance with Instruction 1 to Item 402(c)(2)(iii) and (iv).

Instruction 7 to Item 402(u). Transition periods for registrants.

1. Upon becoming subject to the requirements of Section 13(a) or 15(d) of the Exchange Act (15 U.S.C. 78m or 78o(d)), a registrant shall comply with paragraph (u) of this Item with respect to compensation for the first fiscal year following the year in which it became subject to such requirements, but not for any fiscal year commencing before January 1, 2017. The registrant may omit the disclosure required by paragraph (u) of this Item from any filing until the filing of its annual report on Form 10-K (17 CFR 249.310) for such fiscal year or, if later, the filing of a proxy or information statement relating to its next annual meeting of shareholders (or written consents in lieu of such a meeting) following the end of such year; *provided that*, such disclosure shall, in any event, be filed as provided in General Instruction G(3) of Form 10-K not later than 120 days after the end of such fiscal year.

2. A registrant may omit any employees that became its employees as the result of the business combination or acquisition of a business for the fiscal year in which the transaction becomes effective, but the registrant must disclose the approximate number of employees it is omitting. Those employees shall be included in the total employee count for the triennial calculations of the median employee in the year following the transaction for purposes of evaluating whether a significant change had occurred. The registrant shall identify the acquired business excluded for the fiscal year in which the business combination or acquisition becomes effective. 3. A registrant shall comply with paragraph (u) of this Item with respect to compensation for the first fiscal year commencing on or after the date the registrant ceases to be a smaller reporting company, but not for any fiscal year commencing before January 1, 2017.

Instruction 8 to Item 402(u). Emerging growth companies.

A registrant is not required to comply with paragraph (u) of this Item if it is an emerging growth company as defined in Section 2(a)(19) of the Securities Act (15 U.S.C. 77(b)(a)(19)) or Section 3(a)(80) of the Exchange Act (15 U.S.C. 78c(a)(80)). A registrant shall comply with paragraph (u) of this Item with respect to compensation for the first fiscal year commencing on or after the date the registrant ceases to be an emerging growth company, but not for any fiscal year commencing before January 1, 2017.

Instruction 9 to Item 402(u). Additional information.

Registrants may present additional information, including additional ratios, to supplement the required ratio, but are not required to do so. Any additional information shall be clearly identified, not misleading, and not presented with greater prominence than the required ratio.

Instruction 10 to Item 402(u). Multiple PEOs during the year.

A registrant with more than one non-concurrent PEO serving during its fiscal year may calculate the annual total compensation for its PEO in either of the following manners:

1. The registrant may calculate the compensation provided to each person who served as PEO during the year for the time he or she served as PEO and combine those figures; or

2. The registrant may look to the PEO serving in that position on the date it selects to identify the median employee and annualize that PEO's compensation. Regardless of the alternative selected, the registrant shall disclose which option it chose and how it calculated its PEO's annual total compensation.

Instruction 11 to Item 402(u). Employees' personally identifiable information.

Registrants are not required to, and should not, disclose any personally identifiable information about that employee other than his or her compensation. Registrants may choose to generally identify an employee's position to put the employee's compensation in context, but registrants are not required to provide this information and should not do so if providing the information could identify any specific individual.

Instruction to Item 402: Specify the applicable fiscal year in the title to each table required under this Item which calls for disclosure as of or for a completed fiscal year.

Item 403. Security ownership of certain beneficial owners and management

(a) *Security Ownership of Certain Beneficial Owners*. Furnish the following information, as of the most recent practicable date, substantially in the tabular form indicated, with respect to any person (including any "group" as that term is used in section 13(d)(3) of the Exchange Act) who is known to the registrant to be the beneficial owner of more than five percent of any class of the registrant's voting securities. The address given in column (2) may be a business, mailing or residence address. Show in column (3) the total number of shares beneficially owned and in column (4) the percentage of class so owned. Of the number of shares shown in column (3), indicate by footnote or otherwise the amount known to be shares with respect to which such listed beneficial owner has the right to acquire beneficial ownership as specified in Rule 13d–3(d)(1) under the Exchange Act.

(1) Title of class	(2) Name and address of beneficial owner	(3) Amount and nature of beneficial ownership	(4) Percent of class

(b) *Security Ownership of Management*. Furnish the following information, as of the most recent practicable date, in substantially the tabular form indicated, as to each class of equity securities of the registrant or any of its parents or subsidiaries, including directors' qualifying shares, beneficially owned by all directors and nominees, naming them, each of the named executive officers as defined in Item 402(a)(3) of Regulation S–K, and directors and executive officers of the registrant as a group, without naming them. Show in column (3) the total number of shares beneficially owned and in column (4) the percent of the class so owned. Of the number of shares shown in column (3), indicate, by footnote or otherwise, the amount of shares that are pledged as security and the amount of shares with respect to which such persons have the right to acquire beneficial ownership as specified in Rule 13d–3(d)(1) under the Securities Exchange Act of 1934.

(1) Title of Class	(2) Name of Beneficial Owner	(3) Amount and Nature of Beneficial Ownership	(4) Percent of Class

(c) *Changes in Control.* Describe any arrangements, known to the registrant, including any pledge by any person of securities of the registrant or any of its parents, the operation of which may at a subsequent date result in a change in control of the registrant.

Instructions to Item 403:

1. The percentages are to be calculated on the basis of the amount of outstanding securities, excluding securities held by or for the account of the registrant or its subsidiaries, plus securities deemed outstanding pursuant to Rule 13d–3(d)(1) under the Exchange Act. For purposes of paragraph (b), if the percentage of shares beneficially owned by any director or nominee, or by all directors and officers of the registrant as a group, does not exceed one percent of the class so owned, the registrant may, in lieu of furnishing a precise percentage, indicate this fact by means of an asterisk and explanatory footnote or other similar means.

2. For the purposes of this Item, beneficial ownership shall be determined in accordance with Rule 13d–3 under the Exchange Act. Include such additional subcolumns or other appropriate explanation of column (3) necessary to reflect amounts as to which the beneficial owner has (A) sole voting power, (B) shared voting power, (C) sole investment power, or (D) shared investment power.

3. The registrant shall be deemed to know the contents of any statements filed with the Commission pursuant to section 13(d) or 13(g) of the Securities Exchange Act of 1934. When applicable, a registrant may rely upon information set forth in such statements unless the registrant knows or has reason to believe that such information is not complete or accurate or that a statement or amendment should have been filed and was not.

4. For purposes of furnishing information pursuant to paragraph (a) of this Item, the registrant may indicate the source and date of such information.

5. Where more than one beneficial owner is known to be listed for the same securities, appropriate disclosure should be made to avoid confusion. For purposes of paragraph (b), in computing the aggregate number of shares owned by directors and officers of the registrant as a group, the same shares shall not be counted more than once.

6. Paragraph (c) of this Item does not require a description of ordinary default provisions contained in the charter, trust indentures or other governing instruments relating to securities of the registrant.

7. Where the holder(s) of voting securities reported pursuant to paragraph (a) hold more than five percent of any class of voting securities of the registrant pursuant to any voting trust or similar agreement, state the title of such securities, the amount held or to be held pursuant to the trust or agreement (if not clear from the table) and the duration of the agreement. Give the names and addresses of the voting trustees and outline briefly their voting rights and other powers under the trust or agreement.

Item 404. Transactions with related persons, promoters and certain control persons

(a) *Transactions with Related Persons.* Describe any transaction, since the beginning of the registrant's last fiscal year, or any currently proposed transaction, in which the registrant was or is to be a participant and the amount involved exceeds $120,000, and in which any related person had or will have a direct or indirect material interest. Disclose the following information regarding the transaction:

(1) The name of the related person and the basis on which the person is a related person.

(2) The related person's interest in the transaction with the registrant, including the related person's position(s) or relationship(s) with, or ownership in, a firm, corporation, or other entity that is a party to, or has an interest in, the transaction.

(3) The approximate dollar value of the amount involved in the transaction.

(4) The approximate dollar value of the amount of the related person's interest in the transaction, which shall be computed without regard to the amount of profit or loss.

(5) In the case of indebtedness, disclosure of the amount involved in the transaction shall include the largest aggregate amount of principal outstanding during the period for which disclosure is provided, the amount thereof outstanding as of the latest practicable date, the amount of principal paid during the periods for which disclosure is provided, the amount of interest paid during the period for which disclosure is provided, and the rate or amount of interest payable on the indebtedness.

(6) Any other information regarding the transaction or the related person in the context of the transaction that is material to investors in light of the circumstances of the particular transaction.

Instructions to Item 404(a):

1. For the purposes of paragraph (a) of this Item, the term *related person* means:

a. Any person who was in any of the following categories at any time during the specified period for which disclosure under paragraph (a) of this Item is required:

i. Any director or executive officer of the registrant;

ii. Any nominee for director, when the information called for by paragraph (a) of this Item is being presented in a proxy or information statement relating to the election of that nominee for director; or

iii. Any immediate family member of a director or executive officer of the registrant, or of any nominee for director when the information called for by paragraph (a) of this Item is being presented in a proxy or information statement relating to the election of that nominee for director, which means any child, stepchild, parent, stepparent, spouse, sibling, mother-in-law, father-in-law, son-in-law, daughter-in-law, brother-in-law, or sister-in-law of such director, executive officer or nominee for director, and any person (other than a tenant or employee) sharing the household of such director, executive officer or nominee for director; and

b. Any person who was in any of the following categories when a transaction in which such person had a direct or indirect material interest occurred or existed:

i. A security holder covered by Item 403(a) of Regulation S–K; or

ii. Any immediate family member of any such security holder, which means any child, stepchild, parent, stepparent, spouse, sibling, mother-in-law, father-in-law, son-in-law, daughter-in-law, brother-in-law, or sister-in-law of such security holder, and any person (other than a tenant or employee) sharing the household of such security holder.

2. For purposes of paragraph (a) of this Item, *a transaction* includes, but is not limited to, any financial transaction, arrangement or relationship (including any indebtedness or guarantee of indebtedness) or any series of similar transactions, arrangements or relationships.

3. The amount involved in the transaction shall be computed by determining the dollar value of the amount involved in the transaction in question, which shall include:

a. In the case of any lease or other transaction providing for periodic payments or installments, the aggregate amount of all periodic payments or installments due on or after the beginning of the registrant's last fiscal year, including any required or optional payments due during or at the conclusion of the lease or other transaction providing for periodic payments or installments; and

b. In the case of indebtedness, the largest aggregate amount of all indebtedness outstanding at any time since the beginning of the registrant's last fiscal year and all amounts of interest payable on it during the last fiscal year.

4. In the case of a transaction involving indebtedness:

a. The following items of indebtedness may be excluded from the calculation of the amount of indebtedness and need not be disclosed: amounts due from the related person for purchases of goods and services subject to usual trade terms, for ordinary business travel and expense payments and for other transactions in the ordinary course of business;

b. Disclosure need not be provided of any indebtedness transaction for the related persons specified in Instruction 1.b. to paragraph (a) of this Item; and

c. If the lender is a bank, savings and loan association, or broker-dealer extending credit under Federal Reserve Regulation T (12 CFR part 220) and the loans are not disclosed as nonaccrual, past due, restructured or potential problems (see Item III.C.1. and 2. of Industry Guide 3, Statistical Disclosure by Bank Holding Companies (17 CFR 229.802(c))), disclosure under paragraph (a) of this Item may consist of a statement, if such is the case, that the loans to such persons:

i. Were made in the ordinary course of business;

ii. Were made on substantially the same terms, including interest rates and collateral, as those prevailing at the time for comparable loans with persons not related to the lender; and

iii. Did not involve more than the normal risk of collectibility or present other unfavorable features.

5. a. Disclosure of an employment relationship or transaction involving an executive officer and any related compensation solely resulting from that employment relationship or transaction need not be provided pursuant to paragraph (a) of this Item if:

i. The compensation arising from the relationship or transaction is reported pursuant to Item 402 of Regulation S–K; or

ii. The executive officer is not an immediate family member (as specified in Instruction 1 to paragraph (a) of this Item) and such compensation would have been reported under Item 402 of Regulation S–K as compensation earned for services to the registrant if the executive officer was a named executive officer as that term is defined in Item 402(a)(3) of Regulation S–K, and such compensation had been approved, or recommended to the board of directors of the registrant for approval, by the compensation committee of the board of directors (or group of independent directors performing a similar function) of the registrant.

b. Disclosure of compensation to a director need not be provided pursuant to paragraph (a) of this Item if the compensation is reported pursuant to Item 402(k) of Regulation S–K.

6. A person who has a position or relationship with a firm, corporation, or other entity that engages in a transaction with the registrant shall not be deemed to have an indirect material interest within the meaning of paragraph (a) of this Item where:

a. The interest arises only:

i. From such person's position as a director of another corporation or organization that is a party to the transaction; or

ii. From the direct or indirect ownership by such person and all other persons specified in Instruction 1 to paragraph (a) of this Item, in the aggregate, of less than a ten percent equity interest in another person (other than a partnership) which is a party to the transaction; or iii. From both such position and ownership; or

b. The interest arises only from such person's position as a limited partner in a partnership in which the person and all other persons specified in Instruction 1 to paragraph (a) of this Item, have an interest of less than ten percent, and the person is not a general partner of and does not hold another position in the partnership.

7. Disclosure need not be provided pursuant to paragraph (a) of this Item if:

a. The transaction is one where the rates or charges involved in the transaction are determined by competitive bids, or the transaction involves the rendering of services as a common or contract carrier, or public utility, at rates or charges fixed in conformity with law or governmental authority;

b. The transaction involves services as a bank depositary of funds, transfer agent, registrar, trustee under a trust indenture, or similar services; or

c. The interest of the related person arises solely from the ownership of a class of equity securities of the registrant and all holders of that class of equity securities of the registrant received the same benefit on a pro rata basis.

(b) *Review, Approval or Ratification of Transactions with Related Persons.* (1) Describe the registrant's policies and procedures for the review, approval, or ratification of any transaction required to be reported under paragraph (a) of this Item. While the material features of such policies and procedures will vary depending on the particular circumstances, examples of such features may include, in given cases, among other things:

(i) The types of transactions that are covered by such policies and procedures;

(ii) The standards to be applied pursuant to such policies and procedures;

(iii) The persons or groups of persons on the board of directors or otherwise who are responsible for applying such policies and procedures; and

(iv) A statement of whether such policies and procedures are in writing and, if not, how such policies and procedures are evidenced.

(2) Identify any transaction required to be reported under paragraph (a) of this Item since the beginning of the registrant's last fiscal year where such policies and procedures did not require review, approval or ratification or where such policies and procedures were not followed.

Instruction to Item 404(b): Disclosure need not be provided pursuant to this paragraph regarding any transaction that occurred at a time before the related person became one of the enumerated persons in Instruction 1.a.i., ii., or iii. to Item 404(a) if such transaction did not continue after the related person became one of the enumerated persons in Instruction 1.a.i., ii., or iii. to Item 404(a).

(c) *Promoters and Certain Control Persons.* (1) Registrants that are filing a registration statement on Form S–1 under the Securities Act (17 CFR 239.11) or on Form 10 under the Exchange Act (17 CFR 249.210) and that had a promoter at any time during the past five fiscal years shall:

(i) State the names of the promoter(s), the nature and amount of anything of value (including money, property, contracts, options or rights of any kind) received or to be received by each promoter, directly or indirectly, from the registrant and the nature and amount of any assets, services or other consideration therefore received or to be received by the registrant; and

(ii) As to any assets acquired or to be acquired by the registrant from a promoter, state the amount at which the assets were acquired or are to be acquired and the principle followed or to be followed in determining such amount, and identify the persons making the determination and their relationship, if any, with the registrant or any promoter. If the assets were acquired by the promoter within two years prior to their transfer to the registrant, also state the cost thereof to the promoter.

(2) Registrants shall provide the disclosure required by paragraphs (c)(1)(i) and (c)(1)(ii) of this Item as to any person who acquired control of a registrant that is a shell company, or any person that is part of a group, consisting of two or more persons that agree to act together for the purpose of acquiring, holding, voting or disposing of equity securities of a registrant, that acquired control of a registrant that is a shell company. For purposes of this Item, *shell company* has the same meaning as in Rule 405 under the Securities Act and Rule 12b–2 under the Exchange Act.

(d) *Smaller Reporting Companies.* A registrant that qualifies as a "smaller reporting company," as defined by Item 10(f)(1) of Regulation S–K, must provide the following information in order to comply with this Item:

(1) The information required by paragraph (a) of this Item for the period specified there for a transaction in which the amount involved exceeds the lesser of $120,000 or one percent of the average of the smaller reporting company's total assets at year end for the last two completed fiscal years;

(2) The information required by paragraph (c) of this Item; and

(3) A list of all parents of the smaller reporting company showing the basis of control and as to each parent, the percentage of voting securities owned or other basis of control by its immediate parent, if any.

Instruction to Item 404(d):

1. Include information for any material underwriting discounts and commissions upon the sale of securities by the smaller reporting company where any of the persons specified in paragraph (a) of this Item was or is to be a principal underwriter or is a controlling person or member of a firm that was or is to be a principal underwriter.

2. For smaller reporting companies information shall be given for the period specified in paragraph (a) of this Item and, in addition, for the fiscal year preceding the small reporting company's last fiscal year.

Instructions to Item 404:

1. If the information called for by this Item is being presented in a registration statement filed pursuant to the Securities Act or the Exchange Act, information shall be given for the periods specified in the Item and, in addition, for the two fiscal years preceding the registrant's last fiscal year, unless the information is being incorporated by reference into a registration statement on Form S–4 (17 CFR 239.25), in which case, information shall be given for the periods specified in the Item.

2. A foreign private issuer will be deemed to comply with this Item if it provides the information required by Item 7.B. of Form 20–F (17 CFR 249.220f) with more detailed information provided if otherwise made publicly available or required to be disclosed by the issuer's home jurisdiction or a market in which its securities are listed or traded.

Item 405. Compliance with Section 16(a) of the Exchange Act

Every registrant having a class of equity securities registered pursuant to section 12 of the Exchange Act (15 U.S.C. 78(*l*)), every closed-end investment company registered under the Investment Company Act of 1940 (15 U.S.C. 80a–1 *et seq.*) shall:

(a) Based solely upon a review of Forms 3 and 4 (17 CFR 249.103 and 249.104) and amendments thereto furnished to the registrant under Rule 16a–3(e) during its most recent fiscal year and Forms 5 and amendments thereto (17 CFR 249.105) furnished to the registrant with respect to its most recent fiscal year, and any written representation referred to in paragraph (b)(1) of this item.

(1) Under the caption "Section 16(a) Beneficial Ownership Reporting Compliance," identify each person who, at any time during the fiscal year, was a director, officer, beneficial owner of more than ten percent of any class of equity securities of the registrant registered pursuant to section 12 of the Exchange Act, or any other person subject to section 16 of the Exchange Act with respect to the registrant because of the requirements of section 30 of the Investment Company Act ("reporting person") that failed to file on a timely basis, as disclosed in the above Forms, reports required by section 16(a) of the Exchange Act during the most recent fiscal year or prior fiscal years.

(2) For each such person, set forth the number of late reports, the number of transactions that were not reported on a timely basis, and any known failure to file a required Form. A known failure to file would include, but not be limited to, a failure to file a Form 3, which is required of all reporting persons, and a failure to file a Form 5 in the absence of the written representation referred to in paragraph (b)(1) of this section, unless the registrant otherwise knows that no Form 5 is required.

NOTE: The disclosure requirement is based on a review of the forms submitted to the registrant during and with respect to its most recent fiscal year, as specified above. Accordingly, a failure to file timely need only be disclosed once. For example, if in the most recently concluded fiscal year a reporting person filed a Form 4 disclosing a transaction that took place in the prior fiscal year, and should have been reported in that year, the registrant should disclose that late filing and transaction pursuant to this Item 405 with respect to the most recently concluded fiscal year, but not in material filed with respect to subsequent years.

(b) With respect to the disclosure required by paragraph (a) of this item, if the registrant:

(1) Receives a written representation from the reporting person that no Form 5 is required; and

(2) Maintains the representation for two years, making a copy available to the Commission or its staff upon request, the registrant need not identify such reporting person pursuant to paragraph (a) of this section as having failed to file a Form 5 with respect to that fiscal year.

Item 406. Code of ethics

(a) Disclose whether the registrant has adopted a code of ethics that applies to the registrant's principal executive officer, principal financial officer, principal accounting officer or controller, or persons performing similar functions. If the registrant has not adopted such a code of ethics, explain why it has not done so.

(b) For purposes of this Item 406, the term *code of ethics* means written standards that are reasonably designed to deter wrongdoing and to promote:

(1) Honest and ethical conduct, including the ethical handling of actual or apparent conflicts of interest between personal and professional relationships;

(2) Full, fair, accurate, timely, and understandable disclosure in reports and documents that a

registrant files with, or submits to, the Commission and in other public communications made by the registrant;

(3) Compliance with applicable governmental laws, rules and regulations;

(4) The prompt internal reporting of violations of the code to an appropriate person or persons identified in the code; and

(5) Accountability for adherence to the code.

(c) The registrant must:

(1) File with the Commission a copy of its code of ethics that applies to the registrant's principal executive officer, principal financial officer, principal accounting officer or controller, or persons performing similar functions, as an exhibit to its annual report;

(2) Post the text of such code of ethics on its Internet website and disclose, in its annual report, its Internet address and the fact that it has posted such code of ethics on its Internet Web site; or

(3) Undertake in its annual report filed with the Commission to provide to any person without charge, upon request, a copy of such code of ethics and explain the manner in which such request may be made.

(d) If the registrant intends to satisfy the disclosure requirement under Item 5.05 of Form 8–K regarding an amendment to, or a waiver from, a provision of its code of ethics that applies to the registrant's principal executive officer, principal financial officer, principal accounting officer or controller, or persons performing similar functions and that relates to any element of the code of ethics definition enumerated in paragraph (b) of this Item by posting such information on its Internet website, disclose the registrant's Internet address and such intention.

Instructions to Item 406:

1. A registrant may have separate codes of ethics for different types of officers. Furthermore, a *code of ethics* within the meaning of paragraph (b) of this Item may be a portion of a broader document that addresses additional topics or that applies to more persons than those specified in paragraph (a). In satisfying the requirements of paragraph (c), a registrant need only file, post or provide the portions of a broader document that constitutes a *code of ethics* as defined in paragraph (b) and that apply to the persons specified in paragraph (a).

2. If a registrant elects to satisfy paragraph (c) of this Item by posting its code of ethics on its website pursuant to paragraph (c)(2), the code of ethics must remain accessible on its Web site for as long as the registrant remains subject to the requirements of this Item and chooses to comply with this Item by posting its code on its Web site pursuant to paragraph (c)(2).

Item 407. Corporate governance

(a) *Director Independence.* Identify each director and, when the disclosure called for by this paragraph is being presented in a proxy or information statement relating to the election of directors, each nominee for director, that is independent under the independence standards applicable to the registrant under paragraph (a)(1) of this Item. In addition, if such independence standards contain independence requirements for committees of the board of directors, identify each director that is a member of the compensation, nominating or audit committee that is not independent under such committee independence standards. If the registrant does not have a separately designated audit, nominating or compensation committee or committee performing similar functions, the registrant must provide the disclosure of directors that are not independent with respect to all members of the board of directors applying such committee independence standards.

(1) In determining whether or not the director or nominee for director is independent for the purposes of paragraph (a) of this Item, the registrant shall use the applicable definition of independence, as follows:

(i) If the registrant is a listed issuer whose securities are listed on a national securities exchange or in an inter-dealer quotation system which has requirements that a majority of the board of directors be independent, the registrant's definition of independence that it uses for determining if a majority of the board of directors is independent in compliance with the listing standards applicable to the registrant. When determining whether the members of a committee of the board of directors are independent, the registrant's definition of independence that it uses for determining if the members of that specific committee are independent in compliance with the independence standards applicable for the members of the specific committee in the listing standards of the national securities exchange or inter-dealer quotation system that the registrant uses for determining if a majority of the board of directors are independent. If the registrant does not have independence standards for a committee, the independence standards for that specific committee in the listing standards of the national securities exchange or inter-dealer quotation system that the registrant uses for determining if a majority of the board of directors are independent.

(ii) If the registrant is not a listed issuer, a definition of independence of a national securities exchange or of an inter-dealer quotation system which has requirements that a majority of the board of directors be independent, and state which definition is used. Whatever such definition the registrant chooses, it must use the same definition with respect to all directors and nominees for director. When determining whether the members of a specific committee of the board of directors are independent, if the national securities exchange or national securities association whose standards are used has independence standards for the members of a specific committee, use those committee specific standards.

(iii) If the information called for by paragraph (a) of this Item is being presented in a registration statement on Form S–1 (17 CFR 239.11) under the Securities Act or on a Form 10 (17 CFR 249.210) under the Exchange Act where the registrant has applied for listing with a national securities exchange or in an inter-dealer quotation system that has requirements that a majority of the board of directors be independent, the definition of independence that the registrant uses for determining if a majority of the board of directors is independent, and the definition of independence that the registrant uses for determining if members of the specific committee of the board of directors are independent, that is in compliance with the independence listing standards of the national securities exchange or inter-dealer quotation system on which it has applied for listing, or if the registrant has not adopted such definitions, the independence standards for determining if the majority of the board of directors is independent and if members of the committee of the board of directors are independent of that national securities exchange or inter-dealer quotation system.

(2) If the registrant uses its own definitions for determining whether its directors and nominees for director, and members of specific committees of the board of directors, are independent, disclose whether these definitions are available to security holders on the registrant's Web site. If so, provide the registrant's Web site address. If not, include a copy of these policies in an appendix to the registrant's proxy statement or information statement that is provided to security holders at least once every three fiscal years or if the policies have been materially amended since the beginning of the registrant's last fiscal year. If a current copy of the policies is not available to security holders on the registrant's Web site, and is not included as an appendix to the registrant's proxy statement or information statement, identify the most recent fiscal year in which the policies were so included in satisfaction of this requirement.

(3) For each director and nominee for director that is identified as independent, describe, by specific category or type, any transactions, relationships or arrangements not disclosed pursuant to Item 404(a) of Regulation S–K, or for investment companies, Item 22(b) of Schedule 14A (Rule 14a–101 under the Securities Exchange Act of 1934), that were considered by the board of directors under the applicable independence definitions in determining that the director is independent.

Instructions to Item 407(a):

1. If the registrant is a listed issuer whose securities are listed on a national securities exchange or in an inter-dealer quotation system which has requirements that a majority of the board of directors be independent, and also has exemptions to those requirements (for independence of a majority of the board of directors or committee member independence) upon which the registrant relied, disclose the exemption relied upon and explain the basis for the registrant's conclusion that such exemption is applicable. The same disclosure should be provided if the registrant is not a listed issuer and the national securities exchange or inter-dealer quotation system selected by the registrant has exemptions that are applicable to the registrant. Any national securities exchange or inter-dealer quotation system which has requirements that at least 50 percent of the members of a small business issuer's board of directors must be independent shall be considered a national securities exchange or inter-dealer quotation system which has requirements that a majority of the board of directors be independent for the purposes of the disclosure required by paragraph (a) of this Item.

2. Registrants shall provide the disclosure required by paragraph (a) of this Item for any person who served as a director during any part of the last completed fiscal year, except that no information called for by paragraph (a) of this Item need be given in a registration statement filed at a time when the registrant is not subject to the reporting requirements of section 13(a) or 15(d) of the Exchange Act (15 U.S.C. 78m(a) or 78*o*(d)) respecting any director who is no longer a director at the time of effectiveness of the registration statement.

3. The description of the specific categories or types of transactions, relationships or arrangements required by paragraph (a)(3) of this Item must be provided in such detail as is necessary to fully describe the nature of the transactions, relationships or arrangements.

(b) *Board Meetings and Committees; Annual Meeting Attendance*. (1) State the total number of meetings of the board of directors (including regularly scheduled and special meetings) which were held during the last full fiscal year. Name each incumbent director who during the last full fiscal year attended fewer than 75 percent of the aggregate of:

(i) The total number of meetings of the board of directors (held during the period for which he has been a director); and

(ii) The total number of meetings held by all committees of the board on which he served (during the periods that he served).

(2) Describe the registrant's policy, if any, with regard to board members' attendance at annual meetings of security holders and state the number of board members who attended the prior year's annual meeting.

Instruction to Item 407(b)(2): In lieu of providing the information required by paragraph (b)(2) of this Item in the proxy statement, the registrant may instead provide the registrant's Web site address where such information appears.

(3) State whether or not the registrant has standing audit, nominating and compensation committees of the board of directors, or committees performing similar functions. If the registrant has such committees, however designated, identify each committee member, state the number of committee meetings held by each such committee during the last fiscal year and describe briefly the functions performed by each such committee. Such disclosure need not be provided to the extent it is duplicative of disclosure provided in accordance with paragraph (c), (d) or (e) of this Item.

(c) *Nominating Committee*. (1) If the registrant does not have a standing nominating committee or committee performing similar functions, state the basis for the view of the board of directors that it is appropriate for the registrant not to have such a committee and identify each director who participates in the consideration of director nominees.

(2) Provide the following information regarding the registrant's director nomination process:

(i) State whether or not the nominating committee has a charter. If the nominating committee has a charter, provide the disclosure required by Instruction 2 to this Item regarding the nominating committee charter;

(ii) If the nominating committee has a policy with regard to the consideration of any director candidates recommended by security holders, provide a description of the material elements of that policy, which shall include, but need not be limited to, a statement as to whether the committee will consider director candidates recommended by security holders;

(iii) If the nominating committee does not have a policy with regard to the consideration of any director candidates recommended by security holders, state that fact and state the basis for the view of the board of directors that it is appropriate for the registrant not to have such a policy;

(iv) If the nominating committee will consider candidates recommended by security holders, describe the procedures to be followed by security holders in submitting such recommendations;

(v) Describe any specific minimum qualifications that the nominating committee believes must be met by a nominating committee-recommended nominee for a position on the registrant's board of directors, and describe any specific qualities or skills that the nominating committee believes are necessary for one or more of the registrant's directors to possess;

(vi) Describe the nominating committee's process for identifying and evaluating nominees for director, including nominees recommended by security holders, and any differences in the manner in which the nominating committee evaluates nominees for director based on whether the nominee is recommended by a security holder, and whether, and if so how, the nominating committee (or the board) considers diversity in identifying nominees for director. If the nominating committee (or the board) has a policy with regard to the consideration of diversity in identifying director nominees, describe how this policy is implemented, as well as how the nominating committee (or the board) assesses the effectiveness of its policy;

(vii) With regard to each nominee approved by the nominating committee for inclusion on the registrant's proxy card (other than nominees who are executive officers or who are directors standing for re-election), state which one or more of the following categories of persons or entities recommended that nominee: security holder, non-management director, chief executive officer, other executive officer, third-party search firm, or other specified source. With regard to each such nominee approved by a nominating committee of an investment company, state which one or more of the following additional categories of persons or entities recommended that nominee: security holder, director, chief executive officer, other executive officer, or employee of the investment company's investment adviser, principal underwriter, or any affiliated person of the investment adviser or principal underwriter;

(viii) If the registrant pays a fee to any third party or parties to identify or evaluate or assist in identifying or evaluating potential nominees, disclose the function performed by each such third party; and

(ix) If the registrant's nominating committee received, by a date not later than the 120th calendar day before the date of the registrant's proxy statement released to security holders in connection with the previous year's annual meeting, a recommended nominee from a security holder that beneficially owned more than 5% of the registrant's voting common stock for at least one year as of the date the recommendation was made, or from a group of security holders that beneficially owned, in the aggregate, more than 5% of the registrant's voting common stock, with each of the securities used to calculate that ownership held for at least one year as of the date the recommendation was made, identify the candidate and the security holder or security holder group that recommended the candidate and disclose whether the nominating committee chose to nominate the candidate, *provided, however*, that no such identification or disclosure is required without the written consent of both the security holder or security holder group and the candidate to be so identified.

Instructions to Item 407(c)(2)(ix):

1. For purposes of paragraph (c)(2)(ix) of this Item, the percentage of securities held by a nominating security holder may be determined using information set forth in the registrant's most recent quarterly or annual report, and any current report subsequent thereto, filed with the Commission pursuant to the Securities Exchange Act of 1934 (or, in the case of a registrant that is an investment company registered under the Investment Company Act of 1940, the registrant's most recent report on Form N–CSR (17 CFR 249.331 and 274.128)), unless the party relying on such report knows or has reason to believe that the information contained therein is inaccurate.

2. For purposes of the registrant's obligation to provide the disclosure specified in paragraph (c)(2)(ix) of this Item, where the date of the annual meeting has been changed by more than 30 days from the date of the previous year's meeting, the obligation under that Item will arise where the registrant receives the security holder recommendation a reasonable time before the registrant begins to print and mail its proxy materials.

3. For purposes of paragraph (c)(2)(ix) of this Item, the percentage of securities held by a recommending security holder, as well as the holding period of those securities, may be determined by the registrant if the security holder is the registered holder of the securities. If the security holder is not the registered owner of the securities, he or she can submit one of the following to the registrant to evidence the required ownership percentage and holding period:

a. A written statement from the "record" holder of the securities (usually a broker or bank) verifying that, at the time the security holder made the recommendation, he or she had held the required securities for at least one year; or

b. If the security holder has filed a Schedule 13D (Rule 13d–101 under the Securities Exchange Act of 1934), Schedule 13G (Rule 13d–102 under the Securities Exchange Act of 1934), Form 3 (17 CFR 249.103), Form 4 (17 CFR 249.104), and/or Form 5 (17 CFR 249.105), or amendments to those documents or updated forms, reflecting ownership of the securities as of or before the date of the recommendation, a copy of the schedule and/or form, and any subsequent amendments reporting a change in ownership level, as well as a written statement that the security holder continuously held the securities for the one-year period as of the date of the recommendation.

4. For purposes of the registrant's obligation to provide the disclosure specified in paragraph (c)(2)(ix) of this Item, the security holder or group must have provided to the registrant, at the time of the recommendation, the written consent of all parties to be identified and, where the security holder or group members are not registered holders, proof that the security holder or group satisfied the required ownership percentage and holding period as of the date of the recommendation.

Instruction to Item 407(c)(2): For purposes of paragraph (c)(2) of this Item, the term *nominating committee* refers not only to nominating committees and committees performing similar functions, but also to groups of directors fulfilling the role of a nominating committee, including the entire board of directors.

(3) Describe any material changes to the procedures by which security holders may recommend nominees to the registrant's board of directors, where those changes were implemented after the registrant last provided disclosure in response to the requirements of paragraph (c)(2)(iv) of this Item, or paragraph (c)(3) of this Item.

Instructions to Item 407(c)(3):

1. The disclosure required in paragraph (c)(3) of this Item need only be provided in a registrant's quarterly or annual reports.

2. For purposes of paragraph (c)(3) of this Item, adoption of procedures by which security holders may recommend nominees to the registrant's board of directors, where the registrant's most recent disclosure in response to the requirements of paragraph (c)(2)(iv) of this Item, or paragraph (c)(3) of this Item, indicated that the registrant did not have in place such procedures, will constitute a material change.

(d) *Audit Committee*. (1) State whether or not the audit committee has a charter. If the audit committee has a charter, provide the disclosure required by Instruction 2 to this Item regarding the audit committee charter.

(2) If a listed issuer's board of directors determines, in accordance with the listing standards applicable to the issuer, to appoint a director to the audit committee who is not independent (apart from the requirements in Rule 10A–3 un-

der the Securities Exchange Act of 1934), including as a result of exceptional or limited or similar circumstances, disclose the nature of the relationship that makes that individual not independent and the reasons for the board of directors' determination.

(3)(i) The audit committee must state whether:

(A) The audit committee has reviewed and discussed the audited financial statements with management;

(B) The audit committee has discussed with the independent auditors the matters required to be discussed by the statement on Auditing Standards No. 61, as amended (AICPA, *Professional Standards, Vol. 1. AU section 380),*[1] *as adopted by the Public Company Accounting Oversight Board in Rule 3200T;*

(C) The audit committee has received the written disclosures and the letter from the independent accountant required by applicable requirements of the Public Company Accounting Oversight Board regarding the independent accountant's communications with the audit committee concerning independence, and has discussed with the independent accountant the independent accountant's independence; and

(D) Based on the review and discussions referred to in paragraphs (d)(3)(i)(A) through (d)(3)(i)(C) of this Item, the audit committee recommended to the board of directors that the audited financial statements be included in the company's annual report on Form 10–K (17 CFR 249.310) (or, for closed-end investment companies registered under the Investment Company Act of 1940 (15 U.S.C. 80a–1 *et seq.*), the annual report to shareholders required by section 30(e) of the Investment Company Act of 1940 (15 U.S.C. 80a–29(e)) and Rule 30d–1 thereunder) for the last fiscal year for filing with the Commission.

(ii) The name of each member of the company's audit committee (or, in the absence of an audit committee, the board committee performing equivalent functions or the entire board of directors) must appear below the disclosure required by paragraph (d)(3)(i) of this Item.

1. Available at www.pcaobus.org/standards/interim_standards/auditing_standards/index_au.asp?series=300&section=300.

(4)(i) If the registrant meets the following requirements, provide the disclosure in paragraph (d)(4)(ii) of this Item:

(A) The registrant is a listed issuer, as defined in Rule 10A–3 under the Securities Exchange Act of 1934;

(B) The registrant is filing either an annual report on Form 10–K (17 CFR 249.310), or a proxy statement or information statement pursuant to the Exchange Act (15 U.S.C. 78a *et seq.*) if action is to be taken with respect to the election of directors; and

(C) The registrant is neither:

(*1*) A subsidiary of another listed issuer that is relying on the exemption in Rule 10A–3(c)(2) under the Securities Exchange Act of 1934; nor

(*2*) Relying on any of the exemptions in Rule 10A–3(c)(4) through (c)(7) under the Securities Exchange Act of 1934.

(ii)(A) State whether or not the registrant has a separately-designated standing audit committee established in accordance with section 3(a)(58)(A) of the Securities Exchange Act of 1934 (15 U.S.C. 78c(a)(58)(A)), or a committee performing similar functions. If the registrant has such a committee, however designated, identify each committee member. If the entire board of directors is acting as the registrant's audit committee as specified in section 3(a)(58)(B) of the Exchange Act (15 U.S.C. 78c(a)(58)(B)), so state.

(B) If applicable, provide the disclosure required by Rule 10A–3(d) under the Securities Exchange Act of 1934 regarding an exemption from the listing standards for audit committees.

(5) *Audit Committee Financial Expert*.

(i)(A) Disclose that the registrant's board of directors has determined that the registrant either:

(*1*) Has at least one audit committee financial expert serving on its audit committee; or

(*2*) Does not have an audit committee financial expert serving on its audit committee.

(B) If the registrant provides the disclosure required by paragraph (d)(5)(i)(A)(*1*) of this Item, it must disclose the name of the audit committee financial expert and whether that person is *independent*, as independence for audit committee members is defined in the listing standards applicable to the listed issuer.

(C) If the registrant provides the disclosure required by paragraph (d)(5)(i)(A)(*2*) of this Item, it must explain why it does not have an audit committee financial expert.

Instruction to Item 407(d)(5)(i): If the registrant's board of directors has determined that the registrant has more than one audit committee financial expert serving on its audit committee, the registrant may, but is not required to, disclose the names of those additional persons. A registrant choosing to identify such persons must indicate whether they are independent pursuant to paragraph (d)(5)(i)(B) of this Item.

(ii) For purposes of this Item, an *audit committee financial expert* means a person who has the following attributes:

(A) An understanding of generally accepted accounting principles and financial statements;

(B) The ability to assess the general application of such principles in connection with the accounting for estimates, accruals and reserves;

(C) Experience preparing, auditing, analyzing or evaluating financial statements that present a breadth and level of complexity of accounting issues that are generally comparable to the breadth and complexity of issues that can reasonably be expected to be raised by the registrant's financial statements, or experience actively supervising one or more persons engaged in such activities;

(D) An understanding of internal control over financial reporting; and

(E) An understanding of audit committee functions.

(iii) A person shall have acquired such attributes through:

(A) Education and experience as a principal financial officer, principal accounting officer, controller, public accountant or auditor or experience in one or more positions that involve the performance of similar functions;

(B) Experience actively supervising a principal financial officer, principal accounting officer, controller, public accountant, auditor or person performing similar functions;

(C) Experience overseeing or assessing the performance of companies or public accountants with respect to the preparation, auditing or evaluation of financial statements; or

(D) Other relevant experience.

(iv) *Safe Harbor*. (A) A person who is determined to be an audit committee financial expert will not be deemed an *expert* for any purpose, including without limitation for purposes of section 11 of the Securities Act of 1933 (15 U.S.C. 77k), as a result of being designated or identified as an audit committee financial expert pursuant to this Item 407.

(B) The designation or identification of a person as an audit committee financial expert pursuant to this Item 407 does not impose on such person any duties, obligations or liability that are greater than the duties, obligations and liability imposed on such person as a member of the audit committee and board of directors in the absence of such designation or identification.

(C) The designation or identification of a person as an audit committee financial expert pursuant to this Item does not affect the duties, obligations or liability of any other member of the audit committee or board of directors.

Instructions to Item 407(d)(5):

1. The disclosure under paragraph (d)(5) of this Item is required only in a registrant's annual report. The registrant need not provide the disclosure required by paragraph (d)(5) of this Item in a proxy or information statement unless that registrant is electing to incorporate this information by reference from the proxy or information statement into its annual report pursuant to General Instruction G(3) to Form 10–K (17 CFR 249.310).

2. If a person qualifies as an audit committee financial expert by means of having held a position described in paragraph (d)(5)(iii)(D) of this Item, the registrant shall provide a brief listing of that person's relevant experience. Such disclosure may be made by reference to disclosures required under Item 401(e) of Regulation S–K.

3. In the case of a foreign private issuer with a two-tier board of directors, for purposes of paragraph (d)(5) of this Item, the term *board of directors* means the supervisory or non-management board. In the case of a foreign private issuer meeting the requirements of Rule 10A–3(c)(3) under the Securities Exchange Act of 1934, for purposes of paragraph (d)(5) of this Item, the term *board of directors* means the issuer's board of auditors (or similar body) or statutory auditors, as applicable. Also, in the case of a foreign private issuer, the term *generally accepted accounting principles* in paragraph (d)(5)(ii)(A) of this Item means the body of generally accepted accounting principles used by that issuer in its primary financial statements filed with the Commission.

4. A registrant that is an Asset–Backed Issuer (as defined in Item 1101 of Regulation AB) is not required to dis-

close the information required by paragraph (d)(5) of this Item.

Instructions to Item 407(d):

1. The information required by paragraphs (d)(1)–(3) of this Item shall not be deemed to be "soliciting material," or to be "filed" with the Commission or subject to Regulation 14A or 14C (17 CFR 240.14a–1 through 240.14b–2 or 240.14c–1 through 240.14c–101), other than as provided in this Item, or to the liabilities of section 18 of the Exchange Act (15 U.S.C. 78r), except to the extent that the registrant specifically requests that the information be treated as soliciting material or specifically incorporates it by reference into a document filed under the Securities Act or the Exchange Act. Such information will not be deemed to be incorporated by reference into any filing under the Securities Act or the Exchange Act, except to the extent that the registrant specifically incorporates it by reference.

2. The disclosure required by paragraphs (d)(1)–(3) of this Item need only be provided one time during any fiscal year.

3. The disclosure required by paragraph (d)(3) of this Item need not be provided in any filings other than a registrant's proxy or information statement relating to an annual meeting of security holders at which directors are to be elected (or special meeting or written consents in lieu of such meeting).

(e) *Compensation Committee*. (1) If the registrant does not have a standing compensation committee or committee performing similar functions, state the basis for the view of the board of directors that it is appropriate for the registrant not to have such a committee and identify each director who participates in the consideration of executive officer and director compensation.

(2) State whether or not the compensation committee has a charter. If the compensation committee has a charter, provide the disclosure required by Instruction 2 to this Item regarding the compensation committee charter.

(3) Provide a narrative description of the registrant's processes and procedures for the consideration and determination of executive and director compensation, including:

(i)(A) The scope of authority of the compensation committee (or persons performing the equivalent functions); and

(B) The extent to which the compensation committee (or persons performing the equivalent functions) may delegate any authority described in paragraph (e)(3)(i)(A) of this Item to other persons, specifying what authority may be so delegated and to whom;

(ii) Any role of executive officers in determining or recommending the amount or form of executive and director compensation; and

(iii) Any role of compensation consultants in determining or recommending the amount or form of executive and director compensation (other than any role *limited* to consulting on any broad-based plan that does not discriminate in scope, terms, or operation, in favor of executive officers or directors of the registrant, and that is available generally to all salaried employees; or providing information that either is not customized for a particular registrant or that is customized based on parameters that are not developed by the compensation consultant, and about which the compensation consultant does not provide advice) during the registrant's last completed fiscal year, identifying such consultants, stating whether such consultants were engaged directly by the compensation committee (or persons performing the equivalent functions) or any other person, describing the nature and scope of their assignment, and the material elements of the instructions or directions given to the consultants with respect to the performance of their duties under the engagement:

(A) If such compensation consultant was engaged by the compensation committee (or persons performing the equivalent functions) to provide advice or recommendations on the amount or form of executive and director compensation (other than any role *limited* to consulting on any broad-based plan that does not discriminate in scope, terms, or operation, in favor of executive officers or directors of the registrant, and that is available generally to all salaried employees; or providing information that either is not customized for a particular registrant or that is customized based on parameters that are not developed by the compensation consultant, and about which the compensation consultant does not provide advice) and the compensation consultant or its affiliates also provided additional services to the registrant or its affiliates in an amount in excess of $120,000 during the registrant's last completed fiscal year, then disclose the aggregate fees for determining or recommending the amount or form of executive and director compensation and the aggregate fees for such additional services. Disclose whether the decision to engage the compensation consultant or its affiliates for these other services was made, or recommended, by management, and whether the compensation committee or the board approved such other services of the compensation consultant or its affiliates.

(B) If the compensation committee (or persons performing the equivalent functions) has not engaged a compensation consultant, but management has engaged a compensation consultant to provide advice or recommendations on the amount or form of executive and director compensation (other than any role *limited* to consulting on any broad-based plan that does not discriminate in scope, terms, or operation, in favor of executive officers or directors of the registrant, and that is available generally to all salaried employees; or providing information that either is not customized for a particular registrant or that is customized based on parameters that are not developed by the compensation consultant, and about which the compensation consultant does not provide advice) and such compensation consultant or its affiliates has provided additional services to the registrant in an amount in excess of $120,000 during the registrant's last completed fiscal year, then disclose the aggregate fees for determining or recommending the amount or form of executive and director compensation and the aggregate fees for any additional services provided by the compensation consultant or its affiliates.

(iv) With regard to any compensation consultant identified in response to Item 407(e)(3)(iii) whose work has raised any conflict of interest, disclose the nature of the conflict and how the conflict is being addressed.

Instruction to Item 407(e)(3)(iv): For purposes of this paragraph, the factors listed in Rule 10C–1(b)(4)(i) through (vi) of this chapter are among the factors that should be considered in determining whether a conflict of interest exists.

(4) Under the caption "Compensation Committee Interlocks and Insider Participation":

(i) Identify each person who served as a member of the compensation committee of the registrant's board of directors (or board committee performing equivalent functions) during the last completed fiscal year, indicating each committee member who:

(A) Was, during the fiscal year, an officer or employee of the registrant;

(B) Was formerly an officer of the registrant; or

(C) Had any relationship requiring disclosure by the registrant under any paragraph of Item 404 of Regulation S–K. In this event, the disclosure required by Item 404 of Regulation S–K shall accompany such identification.

(ii) If the registrant has no compensation committee (or other board committee performing equivalent functions), the registrant shall identify each officer and employee of the registrant, and any former officer of the registrant, who, during the last completed fiscal year, participated in deliberations of the registrant's board of directors concerning executive officer compensation.

(iii) Describe any of the following relationships that existed during the last completed fiscal year:

(A) An executive officer of the registrant served as a member of the compensation committee (or other board committee performing equivalent functions or, in the absence of any such committee, the entire board of directors) of another entity, one of whose executive officers served on the compensation committee (or other board committee performing equivalent functions or, in the absence of any such committee, the entire board of directors) of the registrant;

(B) An executive officer of the registrant served as a director of another entity, one of whose executive officers served on the compensation committee (or other board committee performing equivalent functions or, in the absence of any such committee, the entire board of directors) of the registrant; and

(C) An executive officer of the registrant served as a member of the compensation committee (or other board committee performing equivalent functions or, in the absence of any such committee, the entire board of directors) of another entity, one of whose executive officers served as a director of the registrant.

(iv) Disclosure required under paragraph (e)(4)(iii) of this Item regarding a compensation committee member or other director of the registrant who also served as an executive officer of another entity shall be accompanied by the disclosure called for by Item 404 with respect to that person.

Instruction to Item 407(e)(4): For purposes of paragraph (e)(4) of this Item, the term *entity* shall not include an entity exempt from tax under section 501(c)(3) of the Internal Revenue Code (26 U.S.C. 501(c)(3)).

(5) Under the caption "Compensation Committee Report:"

(i) The compensation committee (or other board committee performing equivalent functions or, in the absence of any such committee, the entire board of directors) must state whether:

(A) The compensation committee has reviewed and discussed the Compensation Discussion and Analysis required by Item 402(b) of Regulation S–K with management; and

(B) Based on the review and discussions referred to in paragraph (e)(5)(i)(A) of this Item, the compensation committee recommended to the board of directors that the Compensation Discussion and Analysis be included in the registrant's annual report on Form 10–K (17 CFR 249.310), proxy statement on Schedule 14A (Rule 14a–101 under the Securities Exchange Act of 1934) or information statement on Schedule 14C (Rule 14c–101 under the Securities Exchange Act of 1934).

(ii) The name of each member of the registrant's compensation committee (or other board committee performing equivalent functions or, in the absence of any such committee, the entire board of directors) must appear below the disclosure required by paragraph (e)(5)(i) of this Item.

Instructions to Item 407(e)(5):

1. The information required by paragraph (e)(5) of this Item shall not be deemed to be "soliciting material," or to be "filed" with the Commission or subject to Regulation 14A or 14C (17 CFR 240.14a–1 through 240.14b–2 or 240.14c–1 through 240.14c–101), other than as provided in this Item, or to the liabilities of section 18 of the Securities Exchange Act of 1934 (15 U.S.C. 78r), except to the extent that the registrant specifically requests that the information be treated as soliciting material or specifically incorporates it by reference into a document filed under the Securities Act of 1933 or the Securities Exchange Act of 1934.

2. The disclosure required by paragraph (e)(5) of this Item need not be provided in any filings other than an annual report on Form 10–K (17 CFR 249.310), a proxy statement on Schedule 14A (Rule 14a–101 under the Securities Exchange Act of 1934) or an information statement on Schedule 14C (Rule 14c–101 under the Securities Exchange Act of 1934). Such information will not be deemed to be incorporated by reference into any filing under the Securities Act or the Exchange Act, except to the extent that the registrant specifically incorporates it by reference. If the registrant elects to incorporate this information by reference from the proxy or information statement into its annual report on Form 10–K pursuant to General Instruction G(3) to Form 10–K, the disclosure required by paragraph (e)(5) of this Item will be deemed furnished in the annual report on Form 10–K and will not be deemed incorporated by reference into any filing under the Securities Act or the Exchange Act as a result as a result of furnishing the disclosure in this manner.

3. The disclosure required by paragraph (e)(5) of this Item need only be provided one time during any fiscal year.

(f) *Shareholder Communications.* (1) State whether or not the registrant's board of directors provides a process for security holders to send communications to the board of directors and, if the registrant does not have such a process for security holders to send communications to the board of directors, state the basis for the view of the board of directors that it is appropriate for the registrant not to have such a process.

(2) If the registrant has a process for security holders to send communications to the board of directors:

(i) Describe the manner in which security holders can send communications to the board and, if applicable, to specified individual directors; and

(ii) If all security holder communications are not sent directly to board members, describe the registrant's process for determining which communications will be relayed to board members.

Instructions to Item 407(f):

1. In lieu of providing the information required by paragraph (f)(2) of this Item in the proxy statement, the registrant may instead provide the registrant's Web site address where such information appears.

2. For purposes of the disclosure required by paragraph (f)(2)(ii) of this Item, a registrant's process for collecting and organizing security holder communications, as well as similar or related activities, need not be disclosed provided that the registrant's process is approved by a majority of the independent directors or, in the case of a registrant that is an investment company, a majority of the directors who are not "interested persons" of the investment company as defined in section 2(a)(19) of the Investment Company Act of 1940 (15 U.S.C. 80a–2(a)(19)).

3. For purposes of this paragraph, communications from an officer or director of the registrant will not be viewed as "security holder communications." Communications from an employee or agent of the registrant will be viewed as "security holder communications" for purposes of this paragraph only if those communications are made solely in such employee's or agent's capacity as a security holder.

4. For purposes of this paragraph, security holder proposals submitted pursuant to Rule 14a–8 under the Securities Exchange Act of 1934, and communications made in connection with such proposals, will not be viewed as "security holder communications."

(g) *Smaller Reporting Companies.* A registrant that qualifies as a "smaller reporting company," as defined by Item 10(f)(1) of Regulation S–K, is not required to provide:

(1) The disclosure required in paragraph (d)(5) of this Item in its first annual report filed pursuant to section 13(a) or 15(d) of the Exchange Act

(15 U.S.C. 78m (a) or 78o(d)) following the effective date of its first registration statement filed under the Securities Act (15 U.S.C. 77a *et seq.*) or Exchange Act (15 U.S.C. 78a *et seq.*); and

(2) Need not provide the disclosures required by paragraphs (e)(4) and (e)(5) of this Item.

(h) *Board Leadership Structure and Role in Risk Oversight.* Briefly describe the leadership structure of the registrant's board, such as whether the same person serves as both principal executive officer and chairman of the board, or whether two individuals serve in those positions, and, in the case of a registrant that is an investment company, whether the chairman of the board is an "interested person" of the registrant as defined in section 2(a)(19) of the Investment Company Act (15 U.S.C. 80a–2(a)(19)). If one person serves as both principal executive officer and chairman of the board, or if the chairman of the board of a registrant that is an investment company is an "interested person" of the registrant, disclose whether the registrant has a lead independent director and what specific role the lead independent director plays in the leadership of the board. This disclosure should indicate why the registrant has determined that its leadership structure is appropriate given the specific characteristics or circumstances of the registrant. In addition, disclose the extent of the board's role in the risk oversight of the registrant, such as how the board administers its oversight function, and the effect that this has on the board's leadership structure.

Instructions to Item 407:

1. For purposes of this Item:

a. *Listed issuer* means a listed issuer as defined in Rule 10A–3 under the Securities Exchange Act of 1934;

b. *National securities exchange* means a national securities exchange registered pursuant to section 6(a) of the Exchange Act (15 U.S.C. 78f(a));

c. *Inter-dealer quotation system* means an automated inter-dealer quotation system of a national securities association registered pursuant to section 15A(a) of the Exchange Act (15 U.S.C. 78o–3(a)); and

d. *National securities association* means a national securities association registered pursuant to section 15A(a) of the Exchange Act (15 U.S.C. 78o–3(a)) that has been approved by the Commission (as that definition may be modified or supplemented).

2. With respect to paragraphs (c)(2)(i), (d)(1) and (e)(2) of this Item, disclose whether a current copy of the applicable committee charter is available to security holders on the registrant's Web site, and if so, provide the registrant's Web site address. If a current copy of the charter is not available to security holders on the registrant's Web site, include a copy of the charter in an appendix to the registrant's proxy or information statement that is provided to security holders at least once every three fiscal years, or if the charter has been materially amended since the beginning of the registrant's last fiscal year. If a current copy of the charter is not available to security holders on the registrant's Web site, and is not included as an appendix to the registrant's proxy or information statement, identify in which of the prior fiscal years the charter was so included in satisfaction of this requirement.

Subpart 500—Registration Statement and Prospectus Provisions

Item 501. Forepart of registration statement and outside front cover page of prospectus

The registrant must furnish the following information in plain English. See Rule 421(d) of Regulation C.

(a) *Front Cover Page of the Registration Statement.* Where appropriate, include the delaying amendment legend from Rule 473 of Regulation C.

(b) *Outside Front Cover Page of the Prospectus.* Limit the outside cover page to one page. If the following information applies to your offering, disclose it on the outside cover page of the prospectus.

(1) *Name.* The registrant's name. A foreign registrant must give the English translation of its name.

Instruction to Paragraph 501(b)(1): If your name is the same as that of a company that is well known, include information to eliminate any possible confusion with the other company. If your name indicates a line of business in which you are not engaged or you are engaged only to a limited extent, include information to eliminate any misleading inference as to your business. In some circumstances, disclosure may not be sufficient and you may be required to change your name. You will not be required to change your name if you are an established company, the character of your business has changed, and the investing public is generally aware of the change and the character of your current business.

(2) *Title and Amount of Securities.* The title and amount of securities offered. Separately state the amount of securities offered by selling security holders, if any. If the underwriter has any arrangement with the issuer, such as an over-allotment option, under which the underwriter may purchase additional shares in connection with the offering, indicate that this arrangement exists and state the amount of additional shares that the underwriter may purchase under the arrangement. Give a brief description of the securities except where the information is clear from the title of the security. For example, you are not required to describe common stock that has full voting, div-

idend and liquidation rights usually associated with common stock.

(3) *Offering Price of the Securities.* Where you offer securities for cash, the price to the public of the securities, the underwriter's discounts and commissions, the net proceeds you receive, and any selling shareholder's net proceeds. Show this information on both a per share or unit basis and for the total amount of the offering. If you make the offering on a minimum/maximum basis, show this information based on the total minimum and total maximum amount of the offering. You may present the information in a table, term sheet format, or other clear presentation. You may present the information in any format that fits the design of the cover page so long as the information can be easily read and is not misleading:

Instructions to Paragraph 501(b)(3):

1. If a preliminary prospectus is circulated and you are not subject to the reporting requirements of Section 13(a) or 15(d) of the Securities Exchange Act of 1934, provide, as applicable:

(A) A bona fide estimate of the range of the maximum offering price and the maximum number of securities offered; or

(B) A bona fide estimate of the principal amount of the debt securities offered.

2. If it is impracticable to state the price to the public, explain the method by which the price is to be determined. If the securities are to be offered at the market price, or if the offering price is to be determined by a formula related to the market price, indicate the market and market price of the securities as of the latest practicable date.

3. If you file a registration statement on Form S–8, you are not required to comply with this paragraph (b)(3).

(4) *Market for the Securities.* Whether any national securities exchange or the Nasdaq Stock Market lists the securities offered, naming the particular market(s), and identifying the trading symbol(s) for those securities;

(5) *Risk Factors.* A cross-reference to the risk factors section, including the page number where it appears in the prospectus. Highlight this cross-reference by prominent type or in another manner;

(6) *State Legend.* Any legend or statement required by the law of any state in which the securities are to be offered. You may combine this with any legend required by the SEC, if appropriate;

(7) *Commission Legend.* A legend that indicates that neither the Securities and Exchange Commission nor any state securities commission has approved or disapproved of the securities or passed upon the accuracy or adequacy of the disclosures in the prospectus and that any contrary representation is a criminal offense. You may use one of the following or other clear, plain language:

Example A: Neither the Securities and Exchange Commission nor any state securities commission has approved or disapproved of these securities or passed upon the adequacy or accuracy of this prospectus. Any representation to the contrary is a criminal offense.

Example B: Neither the Securities and Exchange Commission nor any state securities commission has approved or disapproved of these securities or determined if this prospectus is truthful or complete. Any representation to the contrary is a criminal offense.

(8) *Underwriting.* (i) Name(s) of the lead or managing underwriter(s) and an identification of the nature of the underwriting arrangements;

(ii) If the offering is not made on a firm commitment basis, a brief description of the underwriting arrangements. You may use any clear, concise, and accurate description of the underwriting arrangements. You may use the following descriptions of underwriting arrangements where appropriate:

Example A: Best efforts offering. The underwriters are not required to sell any specific number or dollar amount of securities but will use their best efforts to sell the securities offered.

Example B: Best efforts, minimum-maximum offering. The underwriters must sell the minimum number of securities offered (*insert number*) if any are sold. The underwriters are required to use only their best efforts to sell the maximum number of securities offered (*insert number*).

(iii) If you offer the securities on a best efforts or best efforts minimum/maximum basis, the date the offering will end, any minimum purchase requirements, and any arrangements to place the funds in an escrow, trust, or similar account. If you have not made any of these arrangements, state this fact and describe the effect on investors;

(9) *Date of Prospectus.* The date of the prospectus;

(10) *Prospectus "Subject to Completion" Legend.* If you use the prospectus before the effective date of the registration statement, a prominent statement that:

(i) The information in the prospectus will be amended or completed;

(ii) A registration statement relating to these securities has been filed with the Securities and Exchange Commission;

(iii) The securities may not be sold until the registration statement becomes effective; and

(iv) The prospectus is not an offer to sell the securities and it is not soliciting an offer to buy the securities in any state where offers or sales are not permitted. The legend may be in the following or other clear, plain language:

> The information in this prospectus is not complete and may be changed. We may not sell these securities until the registration statement filed with the Securities and Exchange Commission is effective. This prospectus is not an offer to sell these securities and it is not soliciting an offer to buy these securities in any state where the offer or sale is not permitted.

(11) If you use Rule 430A to omit pricing information and the prospectus is used before you determine the public offering price, the information and legend in paragraph (b)(10) of this item.

Instruction to Item 501: For asset-backed securities, see also Item 1102 of Regulation AB.

Item 502. Inside front and outside back cover pages of prospectus

The registrant must furnish this information in plain English. See Rule 421(d) of Regulation C.

(a) *Table of Contents*. On either the inside front or outside back cover page of the prospectus, provide a reasonably detailed table of contents. It must show the page number of the various sections or subdivisions of the prospectus. Include a specific listing of the risk factors section required by Item 503 of this Regulation S–K. You must include the table of contents immediately following the cover page in any prospectus you deliver electronically.

(b) *Dealer Prospectus Delivery Obligation*. On the outside back cover page of the prospectus, advise dealers of their prospectus delivery obligation, including the expiration date specified by Section 4(a)(3) of the Securities Act (15 U.S.C. 77d(3)) and Rule 174. If you do not know the expiration date on the effective date of the registration statement, include the expiration date in the copy of the prospectus you file under Rule 424(b). You do not have to include this information if dealers are not required to deliver a prospectus under Rule 174 or Section 24(d) of the Investment Company Act (15 U.S.C. 80a–24). You may use the following or other clear, plain language:

> DEALER PROSPECTUS DELIVERY OBLIGATION
>
> Until (*insert date*), all dealers that effect transactions in these securities, whether or not participating in this offering, may be required to deliver a prospectus. This is in addition to the dealers' obligation to deliver a prospectus when acting as underwriters and with respect to their unsold allotments or subscriptions.

Item 503. Prospectus summary and risk factors

The registrant must furnish this information in plain English. See Rule 421(d) of Regulation C.

(a) *Prospectus Summary*. Provide a summary of the information in the prospectus where the length or complexity of the prospectus makes a summary useful. The summary should be brief. The summary should not contain, and is not required to contain, all of the detailed information in the prospectus. If you provide summary business or financial information, even if you do not caption it as a summary, you still must provide that information in plain English.

Instruction to Paragraph 503(a): The summary should not merely repeat the text of the prospectus but should provide a brief overview of the key aspects of the offering. Carefully consider and identify those aspects of the offering that are the most significant and determine how best to highlight those points in clear, plain language.

(b) *Address and Telephone Number*. Include, either on the cover page or in the summary section of the prospectus, the complete mailing address and telephone number of your principal executive offices.

(c) *Risk Factors*. Where appropriate, provide under the caption "Risk Factors" a discussion of the most significant factors that make the offering speculative or risky. This discussion must be concise and organized logically. Do not present risks that could apply to any issuer or any offering. Explain how the risk affects the issuer or the securities being offered. Set forth each risk factor under a subcaption that adequately describes the risk. The risk factor discussion must immediately follow the summary section. If you do not include a summary section, the risk factor section must immediately follow the cover page of the prospectus or the pricing information section that immediately follows the cover page. Pricing information means price and price-related information that you may omit from the prospectus in an effective registration statement based on Rule 430A(a). The risk factors may include, among other things, the following:

(1) Your lack of an operating history;

(2) Your lack of profitable operations in recent periods;

(3) Your financial position;

(4) Your business or proposed business; or

(5) The lack of a market for your common equity securities or securities convertible into or exercisable for common equity securities.

Instruction to Item 503: For asset-backed securities, see also Item 1103 of Regulation AB (17 CFR 229.1103).

Item 504. Use of proceeds

State the principal purposes for which the net proceeds to the registrant from the securities to be offered are intended to be used and the approximate amount intended to be used for each such purpose. Where registrant has no current specific plan for the proceeds, or a significant portion thereof, the registrant shall so state and discuss the principal reasons for the offering.

Instructions to Item 504:

1. Where less than all the securities to be offered may be sold and more than one use is listed for the proceeds, indicate the order of priority of such purposes and discuss the registrant's plans if substantially less than the maximum proceeds are obtained. Such discussion need not be included if underwriting arrangements with respect to such securities are such that, if any securities are sold to the public, it reasonably can be expected that the actual proceeds will not be substantially less than the aggregate proceeds to the registrant shown pursuant to Item 501 of Regulation S–K.

2. Details of proposed expenditures need not be given; for example, there need be furnished only a brief outline of any program of construction or addition of equipment. Consideration should be given as to the need to include a discussion of certain matters addressed in the discussion and analysis of registrant's financial condition and results of operations, such as liquidity and capital expenditures.

3. If any material amounts of other funds are necessary to accomplish the specified purposes for which the proceeds are to be obtained, state the amounts of such other funds needed for each such specified purpose and the sources thereof.

4. If any material part of the proceeds is to be used to discharge indebtedness, set forth the interest rate and maturity of such indebtedness. If the indebtedness to be discharged was incurred within one year, describe the use of the proceeds of such indebtedness other than short-term borrowings used for working capital.

5. If any material amount of the proceeds is to be used to acquire assets, otherwise than in the ordinary course of business, describe briefly and state the cost of the assets and, where such assets are to be acquired from affiliates of the registrant or their associates, give the names of the persons from whom they are to be acquired and set forth the principle followed in determining the cost to the registrant.

6. Where the registrant indicates that the proceeds may, or will, be used to finance acquisitions of other businesses, the identity of such businesses, if known, or, if not known, the nature of the businesses to be sought, the status of any negotiations with respect to the acquisition, and a brief description of such business shall be included. Where, however, pro forma financial statements reflecting such acquisition are not required by Regulation S–X, including Rule 8–05 for smaller reporting companies, to be included in the registration statement, the possible terms of any transaction, the identification of the parties thereto or the nature of the business sought need not be disclosed, to the extent that the registrant reasonably determines that public disclosure of such information would jeopardize the acquisition. Where Regulation S–X, including Rule 8–04 for smaller reporting companies, as applicable, would require financial statements of the business to be acquired to be included, the description of the business to be acquired shall be more detailed.

7. The registrant may reserve the right to change the use of proceeds, provided that such reservation is due to certain contingencies that are discussed specifically and the alternatives to such use in that event are indicated.

Item 505. Determination of offering price

(a) *Common Equity.* Where common equity is being registered for which there is no established public trading market for purposes of paragraph (a) of Item 201 of Regulation S–K or where there is a material disparity between the offering price of the common equity being registered and the market price of outstanding shares of the same class, describe the various factors considered in determining such offering price.

(b) *Warrants, Rights and Convertible Securities.* Where warrants, rights or convertible securities exercisable for common equity for which there is no established public trading market for purposes of paragraph (a) of Item 201 of Regulation S–K are being registered, describe the various factors considered in determining their exercise or conversion price.

Item 506. Dilution

Where common equity securities are being registered and there is substantial disparity between the public offering price and the effective cash cost to officers, directors, promoters and affiliated persons of common equity acquired by them in transactions during the past five years, or which they have the right to acquire, and the registrant is not subject to the reporting requirements of section 13(a) or 15(d) of the Exchange Act immediately prior to filing of the registration statement, there shall be included a comparison of the public contribution under the proposed public offering and the effective cash contribution of such persons. In such cases, and in other instances where common equity securities are being registered by a registrant that has had losses in each of its last three fiscal years and there is a material dilution of the purchasers' equity interest, the following shall be disclosed:

(a) The net tangible book value per share before and after the distribution;

(b) The amount of the increase in such net tangible book value per share attributable to the cash payments made by purchasers of the shares being offered; and

(c) the amount of the immediate dilution from the public offering price which will be absorbed by such purchasers.

Item 507. Selling security holders

If any of the securities to be registered are to be offered for the account of security holders, name each such security holder, indicate the nature of any position, office, or other material relationship which the selling security holder has had within the past three years with the registrant or any of its predecessors or affiliates, and state the amount of securities of the class owned by such security holder prior to the offering, the amount to be offered for the security holder's account, the amount and (if one percent or more) the percentage of the class to be owned by such security holder after completion of the offering.

Item 508. Plan of distribution

(a) *Underwriters and Underwriting Obligation.* If the securities are to be offered through underwriters, name the principal underwriters, and state the respective amounts underwritten. Identify each such underwriter having a material relationship with the registrant and state the nature of the relationship. State briefly the nature of the obligation of the underwriter(s) to take the securities.

Instruction to Paragraph 508(a): All that is required as to the nature of the underwriters' obligation is whether the underwriters are or will be committed to take and to pay for all of the securities if any are taken, or whether it is merely an agency or the type of "best efforts" arrangement under which the underwriters are required to take and to pay for only such securities as they may sell to the public. Conditions precedent to the underwriters' taking the securities, including "market-outs," need not be described except in the case of an agency or "best efforts" arrangement.

(b) *New Underwriters.* Where securities being registered are those of a registrant that has not previously been required to file reports pursuant to section 13(a) or 15(d) of the Securities Exchange Act of 1934, or where a prospectus is required to include reference on its cover page to material risks pursuant to Item 501 of Regulation S–K, and any one or more of the managing underwriter(s) (or where there are no managing underwriters, a majority of the principal underwriters) has been organized, reactivated, or first registered as a broker-dealer within the past three years, these facts concerning such underwriter(s) shall be disclosed in the prospectus together with, where applicable, the disclosures that the principal business function of such underwriter(s) will be to sell the securities to be registered, or that the promoters of the registrant have a material relationship with such underwriter(s). Sufficient details shall be given to allow full appreciation of such underwriter(s) experience and its relationship with the registrant, promoters and their controlling persons.

(c) *Other Distributions.* Outline briefly the plan of distribution of any securities to be registered that are to be offered otherwise than through underwriters.

(1) If any securities are to be offered pursuant to a dividend or interest reinvestment plan the terms of which provide for the purchase of some securities on the market, state whether the registrant or the participant pays fees, commissions, and expenses incurred in connection with the plan. If the participant will pay such fees, commissions and expenses, state the anticipated cost to participants by transaction or other convenient reference.

(2) If the securities are to be offered through the selling efforts of brokers or dealers, describe the plan of distribution and the terms of any agreement, arrangement, or understanding entered into with broker(s) or dealer(s) prior to the effective date of the registration statement, including volume limitations on sales, parties to the agreement and the conditions under which the agreement may be terminated. If known, identify the broker(s) or dealer(s) which will participate in the offering and state the amount to be offered through each.

(3) If any of the securities being registered are to be offered otherwise than for cash, state briefly the general purposes of the distribution, the basis, upon which the securities are to be offered, the amount of compensation and other expenses of distribution, and by whom they are to be borne. If the distribution is to be made pursuant to a plan of acquisition, reorganization, readjustment or succession, describe briefly the general effect of the plan and state when it became or is to become operative. As to any material amount of assets to be acquired under the plan, furnish information corresponding to that required by Instruction 5 of Item 504 of Regulation S–K.

(d) *Offerings on Exchange.* If the securities are to be offered on an exchange, indicate the exchange. If the registered securities are to be offered in connection with the writing of exchange-traded call options, describe briefly such transactions.

(e) *Underwriter's Compensation.* Provide a table that sets out the nature of the compensation and the amount of discounts and commissions to be paid to the underwriter for each security and in total. The table must show the separate amounts to be paid by the company and the selling shareholders. In addition, include in the table all other items considered by the Financial Industry Regulatory Authority ("FINRA") to be underwriting compensation for purposes of FINRA rules.

Instructions to Paragraph 508(e):

1. The term "commissions" is defined in paragraph (17) of Schedule A of the Securities Act. Show separately in the table the cash commissions paid by the registrant and selling security holders. Also show in the table commissions paid by other persons. Disclose any finder's fee or similar payments in the table.

2. Disclose the offering expenses specified in Item 511 of Regulation S–K.

3. If the underwriter has any arrangement with the issuer, such as an over-allotment option, under which the underwriter may purchase additional shares in connection with the offering, indicate that this arrangement exists and state the amount of additional shares that the underwriter may purchase under the arrangement. Where the underwriter has such an arrangement, present maximum-minimum information in a separate column to the table, based on the purchase of all or none of the shares subject to the arrangement. Describe the key terms of the arrangement in the narrative.

(f) *Underwriter's Representative on Board of Directors.* Describe any arrangement whereby the underwriter has the right to designate or nominate a member or members of the board of directors of the registrant. The registrant shall disclose the identify of any director so designated or nominated, and indicate whether or not a person so designated or nominated, or allowed to be designated or nominated by the underwriter is or may be a director, officer, partner, employee or affiliate of the underwriter.

(g) *Indemnification of Underwriters.* If the underwriting agreement provides for indemnification by the registrant of the underwriters or their controlling persons against any liability arising under the Securities Act, furnish a brief description of such indemnification provisions.

(h) *Dealers' Compensation.* State briefly the discounts and commissions to be allowed or paid to dealers, including all cash, securities, contracts or other considerations to be received by any dealer in connection with the sale of the securities. If any dealers are to act in the capacity of subunderwriters and are to be allowed or paid any additional discounts or commissions for acting in such capacity, a general statement to that effect will suffice without giving the additional amounts to be sold.

(i) *Finders.* Identify any finder and, if applicable, describe the nature of any material relationship between such finder and the registrant, its officers, directors, principal stockholders, finders or promoters or the principal underwriter(s), or if there is a managing underwriter(s), the managing underwriter(s), (including, in each case, affiliates or associates thereof).

(j) *Discretionary Accounts.* If the registrant was not, immediately prior to the filing of the registration statement, subject to the requirements of section 13(a) or 15(d) of the Exchange Act, identify any principal underwriter that intends to sell to any accounts over which it exercises discretionary authority and include an estimate of the amount of securities so intended to be sold. The response to this paragraph shall be contained in a pre-effective amendment which shall be circulated if the information is not available when the registration statement is filed.

(k) *Passive Market Making.* If the underwriters or any selling group members intend to engage in passive market making transactions as permitted by Rule 103 of Regulation M, indicate such intention and briefly describe passive market making.

(*l*) *Stabilization and Other Transactions.* (1) Briefly describe any transaction that the underwriter intends to conduct during the offering that stabilizes, maintains, or otherwise affects the market price of the offered securities. Include information on stabilizing transactions, syndicate short covering transactions, penalty bids, or any other transaction that affects the offered security's price. Describe the nature of the transactions clearly and explain how the transactions affect the offered security's price. Identify the exchange or other market on which these transactions may occur. If true, disclose that the underwriter may discontinue these transactions at any time;

(2) If the stabilizing began before the effective date of the registration statement, disclose the amount of securities bought, the prices at which they were bought and the period within which they were bought. If you use Rule 430A, the prospectus you file under Rule 424(b) or include in a post-effective amendment must contain information on the stabilizing transactions that took place before the determination of the public offering price; and

(3) If you are making a warrants or rights offering of securities to existing security holders and any securities not purchased by existing security holders are to be reoffered to the public, disclose in a supplement to the prospectus or in the prospectus used in connection with the reoffering:

(i) The amount of securities bought in stabilization activities during the offering period and the price or range of prices at which the securities were bought;

(ii) The amount of the offered securities subscribed for during the offering period;

(iii) The amount of the offered securities subscribed for by the underwriter during the offering period;

(iv) The amount of the offered securities sold during the offering period by the underwriter and the price or price ranges at which the securities were sold; and

(v) The amount of the offered securities that will be reoffered to the public and the public offering price.

Item 509. Interests of named experts and counsel

If (a) any expert named in the registration statement as having prepared or certified any part thereof (or is named as having prepared or certified a report or valuation for use in connection with the registration statement), or (b) counsel for the registrant, underwriters or selling security holders named in the prospectus as having given an opinion upon the validity of the securities being registered or upon other legal matters in connection with the registration or offering of such securities, was employed for such purpose on a contingent basis, or at the time of such preparation, certification or opinion or at any time thereafter, through the date of effectiveness of the registration statement or that part of the registration statement to which such preparation, certification or opinion relates, had, or is to receive in connection with the offering, a substantial interest, direct or indirect, in the registrant or any of its parents or subsidiaries or was connected with the registrant or any of its parents or subsidiaries as a promoter, managing underwriter (or any principal underwriter, if there are no managing underwriters) voting trustee, director, officer, or employee, furnish a brief statement of the nature of such contingent basis, interest, or connection.

Instructions to Item 509:

1. The interest of an expert (other than an accountant) or counsel will not be deemed substantial and need not be disclosed if the interest, including the fair market value of all securities of the registrant owned, received and to be received, or subject to options, warrants or rights received or to be received by the expert or counsel does not exceed $50,000. For the purpose of this Instruction, the term "expert" or counsel includes the firm, corporation, partnership or other entity, if any, by which such expert or counsel is employed or of which he is a member or of counsel to and all attorneys in the case of counsel, and all nonclerical personnel in the case of named experts, participating in such matter on behalf of such firm, corporation, partnership or entity.

2. Accountants, providing a report on the financial statements, presented or incorporated by reference in the registration statement, should note Rule 2–01 of Regulation S–X for the Commission's requirements regarding "Qualification of Accountants" which discusses disqualifying interests.

Item 510. Disclosure of Commission position on indemnification for Securities Act liabilities

In addition to the disclosure prescribed by Item 702 of Regulation S–K, if the undertaking required by paragraph (h) of Item 512 of Regulation S–K is not required to be included in the registration statement because acceleration of the effective date of the registration statement is not being requested, and if waivers have not been obtained comparable to those specified in paragraph (h), a brief description of the indemnification provisions relating to directors, officers and controlling persons of the registrant against liability arising under the Securities Act (including any provision of the underwriting agreement which relates to indemnification of the underwriter or its controlling persons by the registrant against such liabilities where a director, officer or controlling person of the registrant is such an underwriter or controlling person thereof or a member of any firm which is such an underwriter) shall be included in the prospectus, together with a statement in substantially the following form:

> Insofar as indemnification for liabilities arising under the Securities Act of 1933 may be permitted to directors, officers or persons controlling the registrant pursuant to the foregoing provisions, the registrant has been informed that in the opinion of the Securities and Exchange Commission such indemnification is against public policy as expressed in the Act and is therefore unenforceable.

Item 511. Other expenses of issuance and distribution

Furnish a reasonably itemized statement of all expenses in connection with the issuance and distribution of the securities to be registered, other than underwriting discounts and commissions. If any of the securities to be registered are to be offered for the account of security holders, indicate the portion of such expenses to be borne by such security holder.

Instruction to Item 511: Insofar as practicable, registration fees, Federal taxes, States taxes and fees, trustees' and transfer agent's fees, costs of printing and engraving, and legal, accounting, and engineering fees shall be itemized separately. Include as a separate item any premium paid by the registrant or any selling security holder on any policy obtained in connection with the offering and sale of the securities being registered which insures or indemnifies directors or officers against any liabilities they may incur in connection with the registration, offering, or sale of such securities. The information may be given as subject to future contingencies. If the amounts of any items are not known, estimates, identified as such, shall be given.

Item 512. Undertakings

Include each of the following undertakings that is applicable to the offering being registered.

(a) *Rule 415 Offering.*[1] Include the following if the securities are registered pursuant to Rule 415 under the Securities Act:

The undersigned registrant hereby undertakes:

(1) To file, during any period in which offers or sales are being made, a post-effective amendment to this registration statement:

(i) To include any prospectus required by section 10(a)(3) of the Securities Act of 1933;

(ii) To reflect in the prospectus any facts or events arising after the effective date of the registration statement (or the most recent post-effective amendment thereof) which, individually or in the aggregate, represent a fundamental change in the information set forth in the registration statement. Notwithstanding the foregoing, any increase or decrease in volume of securities offered (if the total dollar value of securities offered would not exceed that which was registered) and any deviation from the low or high end of the estimated maximum offering range may be reflected in the form of prospectus filed with the Commission pursuant to Rule 424(b) if, in the aggregate, the changes in volume and price represent no more than 20% change in the maximum aggregate offering price set forth in the "Calculation of Registration Fee" table in the effective registration statement.

(iii) To include any material information with respect to the plan of distribution not previously disclosed in the registration statement or any material change to such information in the registration statement.

Provided, however, That:

(A) Paragraphs (a)(1)(i) and (a)(1)(ii) of this section do not apply if the registration statement is on Form S–8 (17 CFR 239.16b), and the information required to be included in a post-effective amendment by those paragraphs is contained in reports filed with or furnished to the Commission by the registrant pursuant to section 13 or section 15(d) of the Securities Exchange Act of 1934 (15 U.S.C. 78m or 78o(d)) that are incorporated by reference in the registration statement; and

(B) Paragraphs (a)(1)(i), (a)(1)(ii) and (a)(1)(iii) of this section do not apply if the registration statement is on Form S–3 (17 CFR 239.13), Form SF–3 (17 CFR 239.45) or Form F–3 (17 CFR 239.33) and the information required to be included in a post-effective amendment by those paragraphs is contained in reports filed with or furnished to the Commission by the registrant pursuant to section 13 or section 15(d) of the Securities Exchange Act of 1934 that are incorporated by reference in the registration statement, or is contained in a form of prospectus filed pursuant to Rule 424(b) that is part of the registration statement.

(C) *Provided further, however*, that paragraphs (a)(1)(i) and (a)(1)(ii) do not apply if the registration statement is for an offering of asset-backed securities on Form SF–1 (17 CFR 239.44) or Form SF–3 (17 CFR 239.45), and the information required to be included in a post-effective amendment is provided pursuant to Item 1100(c) of Regulation AB.

(2) That, for the purpose of determining any liability under the Securities Act of 1933, each such post-effective amendment shall be deemed to be a new registration statement relating to the securities offered therein, and the offering of such securities at that time shall be deemed to be the initial bona fide offering thereof.

(3) To remove from registration by means of a post-effective amendment any of the securities being registered which remain unsold at the termination of the offering.

(4) If the registrant is a foreign private issuer, to file a post-effective amendment to the registration statement to include any financial statements required by Item 8.A of Form 20–F (17 CFR 249.220f of this chapter) at the start of any delayed offering or throughout a continuous offering. Financial statements and information otherwise required by Section 10(a)(3) of the Act (15 U.S.C. 77j(a)(3)) need not be furnished, provided that the registrant includes in the prospectus, by means of a post-effective amendment, financial statements required pursuant

1. Paragraph (a) reflects proposals made in Securities Act Release No. 6334 (Aug. 6, 1981).

to this paragraph (a)(4) and other information necessary to ensure that all other information in the prospectus is at least as current as the date of those financial statements. Notwithstanding the foregoing, with respect to registration statements on Form F–3 (17 CFR 239.33 of this chapter), a post-effective amendment need not be filed to include financial statements and information required by Section 10(a)(3) of the Act or Item 8.A of Form 20–F if such financial statements and information are contained in periodic reports filed with or furnished to the Commission by the registrant pursuant to section 13 or section 15(d) of the Securities Exchange Act of 1934 that are incorporated by reference in the Form F–3.

(5) That, for the purpose of determining liability under the Securities Act of 1933 to any purchaser:

(i) If the registrant is relying on Rule 430B:

(A) Each prospectus filed by the registrant pursuant to Rule 424(b)(3) shall be deemed to be part of the registration statement as of the date the filed prospectus was deemed part of and included in the registration statement; and

(B) Each prospectus required to be filed pursuant to Rule 424(b)(2), (b)(5), or (b)(7) as part of a registration statement in reliance on Rule 430B relating to an offering made pursuant to Rule 415(a)(1)(i), (vii), or (x) for the purpose of providing the information required by section 10(a) of the Securities Act of 1933 shall be deemed to be part of and included in the registration statement as of the earlier of the date such form of prospectus is first used after effectiveness or the date of the first contract of sale of securities in the offering described in the prospectus. As provided in Rule 430B, for liability purposes of the issuer and any person that is at that date an underwriter, such date shall be deemed to be a new effective date of the registration statement relating to the securities in the registration statement to which that prospectus relates, and the offering of such securities at that time shall be deemed to be the initial bona fide offering thereof. Provided, however, that no statement made in a registration statement or prospectus that is part of the registration statement or made in a document incorporated or deemed incorporated by reference into the registration statement or prospectus that is part of the registration statement will, as to a purchaser with a time of contract of sale prior to such effective date, supersede or modify any statement that was made in the registration statement or prospectus that was part of the registration statement or made in any such document immediately prior to such effective date; or

(ii) If the registrant is subject to Rule 430C, each prospectus filed pursuant to Rule 424(b) as part of a registration statement relating to an offering, other than registration statements relying on Rule 430B or other than prospectuses filed in reliance on Rule 430A, shall be deemed to be part of and included in the registration statement as of the date it is first used after effectiveness. *Provided, however*, that no statement made in a registration statement or prospectus that is part of the registration statement or made in a document incorporated or deemed incorporated by reference into the registration statement or prospectus that is part of the registration statement will, as to a purchaser with a time of contract of sale prior to such first use, supersede or modify any statement that was made in the registration statement or prospectus that was part of the registration statement or made in any such document immediately prior to such date of first use.

(iii) If the registrant is relying on Rule 430D of this chapter:

(A) Each prospectus filed by the registrant pursuant to Rules 230.424(b)(3) and (h) of this chapter shall be deemed to be part of the registration statement as of the date the filed prospectus was deemed part of and included in the registration statement; and

(B) Each prospectus required to be filed pursuant to Rule 230.424(b)(2), (b)(5), or (b)(7) of this chapter as part of a registration statement in reliance on Rule 430D of this chapter relating to an offering made pursuant to Rule 415(a)(1)(vii) or (a)(1)(xii) of this chapter for the purpose of providing the information required by section 10(a) of the Securities Act of 1933 (15 U.S.C. 77j(a)) shall be deemed to be part of and included in the registration statement as of the earlier of the date such form of prospectus is first used after effectiveness or the date of the first contract of sale of securities in the offering described in the prospectus. As provided in Rule 430D of this chapter, for liability purposes of the issuer and any person that is at that date an underwriter, such date shall be deemed to be a new effective date of the registration statement relating to the securities in the registration statement to which that prospectus relates, and the offering of such securities at that time shall be deemed to be the initial *bona fide* offering thereof. *Provided, however,* that no statement made in a registration statement or prospectus that is part of the registration statement or made in a document incorporated or deemed incorporated by reference into the registration statement or prospectus that is part of the registration statement will, as to a purchaser with a time of contract of sale prior to such effective date, supersede or modify any statement that was made in the registration statement or prospectus that was part of the registration statement or made in any such document immediately prior to such effective date; or

(6) That, for the purpose of determining liability of the registrant under the Securities Act of 1933 to any purchaser in the initial distribution of the securities:

The undersigned registrant undertakes that in a primary offering of securities of the undersigned registrant pursuant to this registration statement, regardless of the underwriting method used to sell the securities to the purchaser, if the securities are offered or sold to such purchaser by means of any of the following communications, the undersigned registrant will be a seller to the purchaser and will be considered to offer or sell such securities to such purchaser:

(i) Any preliminary prospectus or prospectus of the undersigned registrant relating to the offering required to be filed pursuant to Rule 424;

(ii) Any free writing prospectus relating to the offering prepared by or on behalf of the undersigned registrant or used or referred to by the undersigned registrant;

(iii) The portion of any other free writing prospectus relating to the offering containing material information about the undersigned registrant or its securities provided by or on behalf of the undersigned registrant; and

(iv) Any other communication that is an offer in the offering made by the undersigned registrant to the purchaser.

(7) If the registrant is relying on Rule 430D of this chapter, with respect to any offering of securities registered on Form SF–3 (17 CFR 239.45), to file the information previously omitted from the prospectus filed as part of an effective registration statement in accordance with Rule 424(h) and Rule 430D of this chapter.

(b) *Filings Incorporating Subsequent Exchange Act Documents by Reference.* Include the following if the registration statement incorporates by reference any Exchange Act document filed subsequent to the effective date of the registration statement:

The undersigned registrant hereby undertakes that, for purposes of determining any liability under the Securities Act of 1933, each filing of the registrant's annual report pursuant to section 13(a) or section 15(d) of the Securities Exchange Act of 1934 (and, where applicable, each filing of an employee benefit plan's annual report pursuant to section 15(d) of the Securities Exchange Act of 1934) that is incorporated by reference in the registration statement shall be deemed to be a new registration statement relating to the securities offered therein, and the offering of such securities at that time shall be deemed to be the initial bona fide offering thereof.

(c) *Warrants and Rights Offerings.* Include the following, with appropriate modifications to suit the particular case, if the securities to be registered are to be offered to existing security holders pursuant to warrants or rights and any securities not taken by security holders are to be reoffered to the public:

The undersigned registrant hereby undertakes to supplement the prospectus, after the expiration of the subscription period, to set forth the results of the subscription offer, the transactions by the underwriters during the subscription period, the amount of unsubscribed securities to be purchased by the underwriters, and the terms of any subsequent reoffering thereof. If any public offering by the underwriters is to be made on terms differing from those set forth on the cover page of the prospectus, a post-effective amendment will be filed to set forth the terms of such offering.

(d) *Competitive Bids.* Include the following, with appropriate modifications to suit the particular case, if the securities to be registered are to be offered at competitive bidding:

The undersigned registrant hereby undertakes (1) to use its best efforts to distribute prior to the opening of bids, to prospective bidders, underwriters, and dealers, a reasonable number of copies of a prospectus which at that time meets the requirements of section 10(a) of the Act, and relating to the securities offered at competitive bidding, as contained in the registration statement, together with any supplements thereto and (2) to file an amendment to the registration statement reflecting the results of bidding, the terms of the reoffering and related matters to the extent required by the applicable form, not later than the first use, authorized by the issuer after the opening of bids, of a prospectus relating to the securities offered at competitive bidding, unless no further public offering of such securities by the issuer and no reoffering of such securities by the purchasers is proposed to be made.

(e) *Incorporated Annual and Quarterly Reports.* Include the following if the registration statement specifically incorporates by reference (other than by indirect incorporation by reference through a Form 10–K (17 CFR 249.310) report) in the prospectus all or any part of the annual report to security holders meeting the requirements of Rule 14a–3 or Rule 14c–3 under the Exchange Act:

The undersigned registrant hereby undertakes to deliver or cause to be delivered with the prospectus, to each person to whom the prospectus is sent or given, the latest annual report to security holders that is incorporated by reference in the prospectus and furnished pursuant to and meeting the requirements of Rule 14a–3 or Rule 14c–3 under the Securities Exchange Act of 1934; and, where interim financial information required to be presented by Article 3 of Regulation S–X are not set forth in the prospectus, to deliver, or cause to be delivered to each person to whom the prospectus is sent or given, the latest quarterly report that is specifically incorporated by reference in the prospectus to provide such interim financial information.

(f) *Equity Offerings of Nonreporting Registrants.* Include the following if equity securities of a registrant that prior to the offering had no obligation to file reports with the Commission pursuant to section 13(a) or 15(d) of the Exchange Act are being registered for sale in an underwritten offering:

The undersigned registrant hereby undertakes to provide to the underwriter at the closing specified in the underwriting agreements certificates in such denominations and registered in such names as required by the underwriter to permit prompt delivery to each purchaser.

(g) *Registration on Form S–4 or F–4 of Securities Offered for Resale.* Include the following if the securities are being registered on Form S–4 or F–4 (17 CFR 239.25, or 34) in connection with a transaction specified in paragraph (a) of Rule 145.

(1) The undersigned registrant hereby undertakes as follows: that prior to any public reoffering of the securities registered hereunder through use of a prospectus which is a part of this registration statement, by any person or party who is deemed to be an underwriter within the meaning of Rule 145(c), the issuer undertakes that such reoffering prospectus will contain the information called for by the applicable registration form with respect to reofferings by persons who may be deemed underwriters, in addition to the information called for by the other Items of the applicable form.

(2) The registrant undertakes that every prospectus (i) that is filed pursuant to paragraph (h)(1) immediately preceding, or (ii) that purports to meet the requirements of section 10(a)(3) of the Act and is used in connection with an offering of securities subject to Rule 415, will be filed as a part of an amendment to the registration statement and will not be used until such amendment is effective, and that, for purposes of determining any liability under the Securities Act of 1933, each such post-effective amendment shall be deemed to be a new registration statement relating to the securities offered therein, and the offering of such securities at that time shall be deemed to be the initial bona fide offering thereof.

(h) *Request for Acceleration of Effective Date or Filing of Registration Statement Becoming Effective Upon Filing.* Include the following if acceleration is requested of the effective date of the registration statement pursuant to Rule 461 under the Securities Act, if a Form S–3 or Form F–3 will become effective upon filing with the Commission pursuant to Rule 462(e) or (f) under the Securities Act, or if the registration statement is filed on Form S–8, and:

(1) Any provision or arrangement exists whereby the registrant may indemnify a director, officer

or controlling person of the registrant against liabilities arising under the Securities Act, or

(2) The underwriting agreement contains a provision whereby the registrant indemnifies the underwriter or controlling persons of the underwriter against such liabilities and a director, officer or controlling person of the registrant is such an underwriter or controlling person thereof or a member of any firm which is such an underwriter, and

(3) The benefits of such indemnification are not waived by such persons:

Insofar as indemnification for liabilities arising under the Securities Act of 1933 may be permitted to directors, officers and controlling persons of the registrant pursuant to the foregoing provisions, or otherwise, the registrant has been advised that in the opinion of the Securities and Exchange Commission such indemnification is against public policy as expressed in the Act and is, therefore, unenforceable. In the event that a claim for indemnification against such liabilities (other than the payment by the registrant of expenses incurred or paid by a director, officer or controlling person of the registrant in the successful defense of any action, suit or proceeding) is asserted by such director, officer or controlling person in connection with the securities being registered, the registrant will, unless in the opinion of its counsel the matter has been settled by controlling precedent, submit to a court of appropriate jurisdiction the question whether such indemnification by it is against public policy as expressed in the Act and will be governed by the final adjudication of such issue.

(i) Include the following in a registration statement permitted by Rule 430A under the Securities Act of 1933:

The undersigned registrant hereby undertakes that:

(1) For purposes of determining any liability under the Securities Act of 1933, the information omitted from the form of prospectus filed as part of this registration statement in reliance upon Rule 430A and contained in a form of prospectus filed by the registrant pursuant to Rule 424(b)(1) or (4) or 497(h) under the Securities Act shall be deemed to be part of this registration statement as of the time it was declared effective.

(2) For the purpose of determining any liability under the Securities Act of 1933, each post-effective amendment that contains a form of prospectus shall be deemed to be a new registration statement relating to the securities offered therein, and the offering of such securities at that time shall be deemed to be the initial bona fide offering thereof.

(j) *Qualification of Trust Indentures Under the Trust Indenture Act of 1939 for Delayed Offerings.* Include the following if the registrant intends to rely on section 305(b)(2) of the Trust Indenture Act of 1939 for determining the eligibility of the trustee under indentures for securities to be issued, offered, or sold on a delayed basis by or on behalf of the registrant:

The undersigned registrant hereby undertakes to file an application for the purpose of determining the eligibility of the trustee to act under subsection (a) of section 310 of the Trust Indenture Act ("Act") in accordance with the rules and regulations prescribed by the Commission under section 305(b)(2) of the Act.

(k) Filings regarding asset-backed securities incorporating by reference subsequent Exchange Act documents by third parties. Include the following if the registration statement incorporates by reference any Exchange Act document filed subsequent to the effective date of the registration statement pursuant to Item 1100(c) of Regulation AB:

The undersigned registrant hereby undertakes that, for purposes of determining any liability under the Securities Act of 1933, each filing of the annual report pursuant to section 13(a) or section 15(d) of the Securities Exchange Act of 1934 of a third party that is incorporated by reference in the registration statement in accordance with Item 1100(c)(1) of Regulation AB shall be deemed to be a new registration statement relating to the securities offered therein, and the offering of such securities at that time shall be deemed to be the initial bona fide offering thereof.

Subpart 600—Exhibits

Item 601. Exhibits

(a) *Exhibits and Index Required.* (1) Subject to Rule 411(c) under the Securities Act and Rule 12b–32 under the Exchange Act regarding incorporation of exhibits by reference, the exhibits required by in the exhibit table shall be filed as indicated, as part of the registration statement or report.

(2) Each registration statement or report shall contain an exhibit index, which must appear before the required signatures in the registration statement or report. For convenient reference, each exhibit shall be listed in the exhibit index according to the number assigned to it in the exhibit table. If an exhibit is incorporated by reference, this must be noted in the exhibit index. Each exhibit identified in the exhibit index (other than an exhibit filed in eXtensible Business Reporting Language or an exhibit that is filed with Form ABS-EE) must include an active link to an exhibit that is filed with the registration statement or report or, if the exhibit is incorporated by reference, an active hyperlink to the exhibit separately filed on EDGAR. If a registration statement or report is amended, each amendment must include hyperlinks to the exhibits required with the amendment. For a description of each of the exhibits included in the exhibit table, see paragraph (b) of this section.

(3) This Item applies only to the forms specified in the exhibit table. With regard to forms not listed in that table, reference shall be made to the appropriate form for the specific exhibit filing requirements applicable thereto.

(4) If a material contract or plan of acquisition, reorganization, arrangement, liquidation or succession is executed or becomes effective during the reporting period reflected by a Form 10–Q or Form 10–K, it shall be filed as an exhibit to the Form 10–Q or Form 10–K filed for the corresponding period. Any amendment or modification to a previously filed exhibit to a Form 10, 10–K, or 10–Q document shall be filed as an exhibit to a Form 10–Q and Form 10–K. Such amendment or modification need not be filed where such previously filed exhibit would not be currently required.

Instructions to Item 601:

1. If an exhibit to a registration statement (other than an opinion or consent), filed in preliminary form, has been changed only (A) to insert information as to interest, dividend or conversion rates, redemption or conversion prices, purchase or offering prices, underwriters' or dealers' commissions, names, addresses or participation of underwriters or similar matters, which information appears elsewhere in an amendment to the registration statement or a prospectus filed pursuant to Rule 424(b) under the Securities Act, or (B) to correct typographical errors, insert signatures or make other similar immaterial changes, then, notwithstanding any contrary requirement of any rule or form, the registrant need not refile such exhibit as so amended. Any such incomplete exhibit may not, however, be incorporated by reference in any subsequent filing under any Act administered by the Commission.

2. In any case where two or more indentures, contracts, franchises, or other documents required to be filed as exhibits are substantially identical in all material respects except as to the parties thereto, the dates of execution, or other details, the registrant need file a copy of only one of such documents, with a schedule identifying the other documents omitted and setting forth the material details in which such documents differ from the document a copy of which is filed. The Commission may at any time in its discretion require filing of copies of any documents so omitted.

3. Only copies, rather than originals, need be filed of each exhibit required except as otherwise specifically noted.

4. *Electronic Filings.* Whenever an exhibit is filed in paper pursuant to a hardship exemption (Rules 201 and 202 of Regulation S–T), the letter "P" (paper) shall be placed next to the exhibit in the list of exhibits required by Item 601(a)(2) of this Rule. Whenever an electronic confirming copy of an exhibit is filed pursuant to a grant of a hardship exemption (Rules 201 or 202(d) of Regulation S–T), the exhibit index shall specify where the confirming electronic copy can be located; in addition, the designation "CE" (confirming electronic) should be placed next to the listed exhibit in the exhibit index.

EXHIBIT TABLE

	Securities Act Forms								Exchange Act Forms					
	S–1	S–3	S–4[1]	S–8	S–11	F–1	F–3	F–4[1]	10	8–K[2]	10–D	10–Q	10–K	ABS-EE
(1) Underwriting agreement	X	X	X	—	X	X	X	X	—	X	—	—	—	—
(2) Plan of acquisition, reorganization, arrangement, liquidation or succession	X	X	X	—	X	X	X	X	X	X	—	X	X	—
(3) (i) Articles of incorporation	X	—	X	—	X	X	—	X	X	X	X	X	X	—
(ii) Bylaws	X	—	X	—	X	X	—	X	X	X	X	X	X	—
(4) Instruments defining the rights of security holders, including indentures	X	X	X	X	X	X	X	X	X	X	X	X	X	—
(5) Opinion re legality	X	X	X	X	X	X	X	X	—	—	—	—	—	—

(6) [Reserved]	N/A	N/A	N/A	N/A	N/A	N/A	N/A	N/A	N/A	N/A	N/A	N/A	N/A	N/A
(7) Correspondence from an independent accountant regarding non-reliance on a previously issued audit report or completed interim review	—	—	—	—	—	—	—	—	—	X	—	—	—	—
(8) Opinion re tax matters	X	X	X	—	X	X	X	X	—	—	—	—	—	—
(9) Voting trust agreement	X	—	X	—	X	X	—	X	X	—	—	—	X	—
(10) Material contracts	X	—	X	—	X	X	—	X	X	—	X	X	X	—
(11) [Reserved]														
(12) [Reserved]														
(13) Annual report to security holders, Form 10–Q or quarterly report to security holders[3]	—	—	X	—	—	—	—	—	—	—	—	X	X	—
(14) Code of Ethics	X	—	X	—	—	—	—	—	—	—	—	—	—	—
(15) Letter re unaudited interim financial information	X	X	X	X	X	X	X	X	—	—	—	X	—	—
(16) Letter re change in certifying accountant[4]	X	—	X	—	X	—	—	—	X	X	—	—	X	—
(17) Correspondence on departure of director	—	—	—	—	—	—	—	—	—	X	—	—	—	—
(18) Letter re change in accounting principles	—	—	—	—	—	—	—	—	—	—	—	X	X	—
(19) [Reserved]														
(20) Other documents or statements to security holders	—	—	—	—	—	—	—	—	—	X	—	—	—	—
	Securities Act Forms								Exchange Act Forms					
	S–1	S–3	S–4[1]	S–8	S–11	F–1	F–3	F–4[1]	10	8–K[2]	10–D	10–Q	10–K	ABS-EE
(21) Subsidiaries of the registrant	X	—	X	—	X	X	—	X	X	—	—	—	X	—
(22) [Reserved]														
(23) Consents of experts and counsel	X	X	X	X	X	X	X	X	—	X[5]	X[5]	X[5]	X[5]	—
(24) Power of attorney	X	X	X	X	X	X	X	X	X	X	—	X	X	—
(25) Statement of eligibility of trustee	X	X	X	—	—	X	X	X	—	—	—	—	—	—
(26) [Reserved]														
(27) through (30) [Reserved]														
(31) (i) Rule 13a–14(a)/15d–14(a) Certifications	—	—	—	—	—	—	—	—	—	—	—	X	X	—
(ii) Rule 13a–14/15d–14 Certifications	—	X												
(32) Section 1350 Certifications[6]	—	—	—	—	—	—	—	—	—	—	—	X	X	—
(33) Report on assessment of compliance with servicing criteria for asset-backed issuers	—	—	—	—	—	—	—	—	—	—	—	—	X	—
(34) Attestation report on assessment of compliance with servicing criteria for asset-backed securities	—	—	—	—	—	—	—	—	—	—	—	—	X	—

(35) Servicer compliance statement	—	—	—	—	—	—	—	—	—	—	—	—	X	—
(36) Depositor Certification for shelf offerings asset-backed securities	—	—	—	—	—	—	—	—	—	—	—	—	—	—
(37) through (94) [Reserved]	N/A	N/A	N/A	N/A	N/A	N/A	N/A	N/A	N/A	N/A	N/A	N/A	N/A	N/A
(95) Mine Safety Disclosure Exhibit	—	—	—	—	—	—	—	—	—	—	—	X	X	—
(96) through (98) [Reserved]	N/A	N/A	N/A	N/A	N/A	N/A	N/A	N/A	N/A	N/A	N/A	N/A	N/A	N/A
(99) Additional exhibits	X	X	X	X	X	X	X	X	X	X	X	X	X	—
[Reserved]														
(101) Interactive Data File	X	X	X	—	X	X	X	X	—	X	—	X	X	—
(102) Asset Data File	—	—	—	—	—	—	—	—	—	—	X	—	—	X
(103) Asset Related Documents	—	—	—	—	—	—	—	—	—	—	X	—	—	X
(104) [Reserved]	N/A	N/A	N/A	N/A	N/A	N/A	N/A	N/A	N/A	N/A	N/A	N/A	N/A	N/A
(105) [Reserved]	N/A	N/A	N/A	N/A	N/A	N/A	N/A	N/A	N/A	N/A	N/A	N/A	N/A	N/A
(106) Static Pool	—	—	X	X	—	—	—	—	—	X	—	—	—	—

[1] An exhibit need not be provided about a company if: (1) With respect to such company an election has been made under Form S–4 or F–4 to provide information about such company at a level prescribed by Form S–3 or F–3; and (2) the form, the level of which has been elected under Form S–4 or F–4, would not require such company to provide such exhibit if it were registering a primary offering.

[2] A Form 8–K exhibit is required only if relevant to the subject matter reported on the Form 8–K report. For example, if the Form 8–K pertains to the departure of a director, only the exhibit described in paragraph (b)(17) of this section need be filed. A required exhibit may be incorporated by reference from a previous filing.

[3] Where incorporated by reference into the text of the prospectus and delivered to security holders along with the prospectus as permitted by the registration statement; or, in the case of the Form 10–K, where the annual report to security holders is incorporated by reference into the text of the Form 10–K.

[4] If required pursuant to Item 304 of Regulation S–K.

[5] Where the opinion of the expert or counsel has been incorporated by reference into a previously filed Securities Act registration statement.

[6] Pursuant to Rules 13a–13(b)(3) and 15d–13(b)(3) under the Securities Exchange Act of 1934, asset-backed issuers are not required to file reports on Form 10–Q.

Instructions to the Exhibit Table. 1. The exhibit table indicates those documents that must be filed as exhibits to the respective forms listed.

2. The "X" designation indicates the documents which are required to be filed with each form even if filed previously with another document, *Provided, However,* that such previously filed documents may be incorporated by reference to satisfy the filing requirements.

3. The number used in the far left column of the table refers to the appropriate subsection in paragraph (b) where a description of the exhibit can be found. Whenever necessary, alphabetical or numerical subparts may be used.

(b) *Description of Exhibits.* Set forth below is a description of each document listed in the exhibit tables.

(1) *Underwriting Agreement.* Each underwriting contract or agreement with a principal underwriter pursuant to which the securities being registered are to be distributed; if the terms of such documents have not been determined, the proposed forms thereof. Such agreement may be filed as an exhibit to a report on Form 8–K (17 CFR 249.308) which is incorporated by reference into a registration statement subsequent to its effectiveness.

(2) *Plan of Acquisition, Reorganization, Arrangement, Liquidation or Succession.* Any material plan of acquisition, disposition, reorganization, readjustment, succession, liquidation or arrangement and any amendments thereto described in the statement or report. Schedules (or similar attachments) to these exhibits shall not be filed unless such schedules contain information which is material to an investment decision and which is not otherwise disclosed in the agreement or the disclosure document. The plan filed shall contain a list briefly identifying the contents of all omitted schedules, together with an agreement to furnish supplementally a copy of any omitted schedule to the Commission upon request.

(3)(i) *Articles of Incorporation.* The articles of incorporation of the registrant or instruments corresponding thereto as currently in effect and any amendments thereto. Whenever the registrant files an amendment to its articles of incorporation, it must file a complete copy of the articles as amended. However, if such amendment is being reported on Form 8–K (17 CFR 249.308), the registrant is required to file only the text of the amendment as a Form 8–K exhibit. In such case, a complete copy of the articles of incorporation as amended must be filed as an exhibit to the next Securities Act registration statement or periodic report filed by the registrant to which this exhibit requirement applies. Where it is impracticable for the registrant to file a charter amendment authorizing new securities with the appropriate state authority prior to the effective date of the registration statement registering such securities, the registrant may file as an exhibit to the registration statement the form of amendment to be filed with the state authority. In such a case, if material changes are made after the copy is filed, the registrant must also file the changed copy.

(ii) *Bylaws.* The bylaws of the registrant or instruments corresponding thereto as currently in effect and any amendments thereto. Whenever the registrant files an amendment to the bylaws, it must file a complete copy of the amended bylaws. However, if such amendment is being reported on Form 8–K (17 CFR 249.308), the registrant is required to file only the text of the amendment as a Form 8–K exhibit. In such case, a complete copy of the bylaws as amended must be filed as an exhibit to the next Securities Act registration statement or periodic report filed by the registrant to which this exhibit requirement applies.

(4) *Instruments Defining the Rights of Security Holders, Including Indentures.* (i) All instruments defining the rights of holders of the equity or debt securities being registered including, where applicable, the relevant portion of the articles of incorporation or by-laws of the registrant.

(ii) Except as set forth in paragraph (b)(4)(iii) of this Item for filings on Forms S–1, S–4, S–11, N–14 and F–4 under the Securities Act (17 CFR 239.11, 239.25, 239.18, 239.23 and 239.34) and Forms 10 and 10–K under the Exchange Act (17 CFR 249.210 and 249.310) all instruments defining the rights of holders of long-term debt of the registrant and its consolidated subsidiaries and for any of its unconsolidated subsidiaries for which financial statements are required to be filed.

(iii) Where the instrument defines the rights of holders of long-term debt of the registrant and its consolidated subsidiaries and for any of its unconsolidated subsidiaries for which financial statements are required to be filed, there need not be filed:

(A) Any instrument with respect to long-term debt not being registered if the total amount of securities authorized thereunder does not exceed 10 percent of the total assets of the registrant and its subsidiaries on a consolidated basis and if there is filed an agreement to furnish a copy of such agreement to the Commission upon request;

(B) Any instrument with respect to any class of securities if appropriate steps to assure the redemption or retirement of such class will be taken prior to or upon delivery by the registrant of the securities being registered; or

(C) Copies of instruments evidencing scrip certificates for fractions of shares.

(iv) If any of the securities being registered are, or will be, issued under an indenture to be qualified under the Trust Indenture Act, the copy of such indenture which is filed as an exhibit shall include or be accompanied by:

(A) a reasonably itemized and informative table of contents; and

(B) a cross-reference sheet showing the location in the indenture of the provisions inserted pursuant to sections 310 through 318(a) inclusive of the Trust Indenture Act of 1939.

(v) With respect to Forms 8–K and 10–Q under the Exchange Act that are filed and that disclose, in the text of the Form 10–Q, the interim financial statements, or the footnotes thereto the creation of a new class of securities or indebtedness or the modification of existing rights of security holders, file all instruments defining the rights of holders of these securities or indebtedness. However, there need not be filed any instrument with respect to long-term debt not being registered which meets the exclusion set forth above in paragraph (b)(4)(iii)(A) of this Item.

Instruction 1 to Paragraph (b)(4): There need not be filed any instrument which defines the rights of participants (not as security holders) pursuant to an employee benefit plan.

Instruction 2 to Paragraph (b)(4) (for electronic filings): If the instrument defining the rights of security holders is in the form of a certificate, the text appearing on the certificate shall be reproduced in an electronic filing together with a description of any other graphic and image material appearing on the certificate, as provided in Rule 304 of Regulation S–T.

(5) *Opinion re Legality.* (i) An opinion of counsel as to the legality of the securities being registered, indicating whether they will, when sold, be legally issued, fully paid and non-assessable, and, if debt securities, whether they will be binding obligations of the registrant.

(ii) If the securities being registered are issued under a plan and the plan is subject to the requirements of ERISA furnish either:

(A) An opinion of counsel which confirms compliance of the provisions of the written documents constituting the plan with the requirements of ERISA pertaining to such provisions; or

(B) A copy of the Internal Revenue Service determination letter that the plan is qualified under section 401 of the Internal Revenue Code; or

(iii) If the securities being registered are issued under a plan which is subject to the requirements of ERISA and the plan has been amended subsequent to the filing of (ii)(A) or (B) above, furnish either:

(A) An opinion of counsel which confirms compliance of the amended provisions of the plan with the requirements of ERISA pertaining to such provisions; or

(B) A copy of the Internal Revenue Service determination letter that the amended plan is qualified under section 401 of the Internal Revenue Code.

NOTE: Attention is directed to Item 8 of Form S–8 for exemptions to this exhibit requirement applicable to that Form.

(6) [Reserved]

(7) *Correspondence from an Independent Accountant Regarding Non–Reliance on a Previously Issued Audit Report or Completed Interim Review.* Any written notice from the registrant's current or previously engaged independent accountant that the independent accountant is withdrawing a previously issued audit report or that a previously issued audit report or completed interim review, covering one or more years or interim periods for which the registrant is required to provide financial statements under Regulation S–X, should no longer be relied upon. In addition, any letter, pursuant to Item 4.02(c) of Form 8–K (17 CFR 249.308), from the independent accountant to the Commission stating whether the independent accountant agrees with the statements made by the registrant describing the events giving rise to the notice.

(8) *Opinion re Tax Matters.* For filings on Form S–11 under the Securities Act (17 CFR 239.18) or those to which Securities Act Industry Guide 5 applies, an opinion of counsel or of an independent public or certified public accountant or, in lieu thereof, a revenue ruling from the Internal Revenue Service, supporting the tax matters and consequences to the shareholder as described in the filing when such tax matters are material to the transaction for which the registration statement is being filed. This exhibit otherwise need only be filed with the other applicable registration forms where the tax consequences are material to an investor and a representation as to tax consequences is set forth in the filing. If a tax opinion is set forth in full in the filing, an indication that such is the case may be made in lieu of filing the otherwise required exhibit. Such tax opinions may be conditioned or may be qualified, so long as such conditions and qualifications are adequately described in the filing.

(9) *Voting Trust Agreement.* Any voting trust agreements and amendments thereto.

(10) *Material Contracts.* (i) Every contract not made in the ordinary course of business which is material to the registrant and is to be performed in whole or in part at or after the filing of the registration statement or report or was entered into not more than two years before such filing. Only contracts need be filed as to which the registrant or subsidiary of the registrant is a party or has succeeded to a party by assumption or assignment or in which the registrant or such subsidiary has a beneficial interest.

(ii) If the contract is such as ordinarily accompanies the kind of business conducted by the registrant and its subsidiaries, it will be deemed to have been made in the ordinary course of business and need not be filed unless it falls within one or more of the following categories, in which case it shall be filed except where immaterial in amount or significance:

(A) Any contract to which directors, officers, promoters, voting trustees, security holders named in the registration statement or report, or underwriters are parties other than contracts involving only the purchase or sale of current assets having a determinable market price, at such market price;

(B) Any contract upon which the registrant's business is substantially dependent, as in the case of continuing contracts to sell the major part of registrant's products or services or to purchase the major part of registrant's requirements of goods, services or raw materials or any franchise or license or other agreement to use a patent, formula, trade secret, process or trade name upon which registrant's business depends to a material extent;

(C) Any contract calling for the acquisition or sale of any property, plant or equipment for a consideration exceeding 15 percent of such fixed assets of the registrant on a consolidated basis; or

(D) Any material lease under which a part of the property described in the registration statement or report is held by the registrant.

(iii)(A) Any management contract or any compensatory plan, contract or arrangement, including but not limited to plans relating to options, warrants or rights, pension, retirement or deferred compensation or bonus, incentive or profit sharing (or if not set forth in any formal document, a written description thereof) in which any director or any of the named executive officers of the registrant, as defined by Item 402(a)(3) of Regulation S–K, participates shall be deemed material and shall be filed; and any other management contract or any other compensatory plan, contract, or arrangement in which any other executive officer of the registrant participates shall be filed unless immaterial in amount or significance.

(B) Any compensatory plan, contract or arrangement adopted without the approval of security holders pursuant to which equity may be awarded, including, but not limited to, options, warrants or rights (or if not set forth in any formal document, a written description thereof), in which any employee (whether or not an executive officer of the registrant) participates shall be filed unless immaterial in amount or significance. A compensation plan assumed by a registrant in connection with a merger, consolidation or other acquisition transaction pursuant to which the registrant may make further grants or awards of its equity securities shall be considered a compensation plan of the registrant for purposes of the preceding sentence.

(C) Notwithstanding paragraph (iii)(A) above, the following management contracts or compensatory plans, contracts or arrangements need not be filed:

(*1*) Ordinary purchase and sales agency agreements.

(*2*) Agreements with managers of stores in a chain organization or similar organization.

(*3*) Contracts providing for labor or salesmen's bonuses or payments to a class of security holders, as such.

(*4*) Any compensatory plan, contract or arrangement which pursuant to its terms is available to employees, officers or directors generally and which in operation provides for the same method of allocation of benefits between management and nonmanagement participants.

(*5*) Any compensatory plan, contract or arrangement if the registrant is a foreign private issuer that furnishes compensatory information under Item 402(a)(1) of Regulation S–K and the public filing of the plan, contract or arrangement, or portion thereof, is not required in the registrant's home country and is not otherwise publicly disclosed by the registrant.

(*6*) Any compensatory plan, contract, or arrangement if the registrant is a wholly owned subsidiary of a company that has a class of securities registered pursuant to section 12 or files reports pursuant to section 15(d) of the Exchange Act and is filing a report on Form 10–K or registering debt instruments or preferred stock that are not voting securities on Form S–1.

Instruction 1 to Paragraph (b)(10): With the exception of management contracts, in order to comply with paragraph (iii) above, registrants need only file copies of the various compensatory plans and need not file each individual director's or executive officer's personal agreement under the plans unless there are particular provisions in such personal agreements whose disclosure in an exhibit is necessary to an investor's understanding of that individual's compensation under the plan.

Instruction 2 to Paragraph (b)(10): If a material contract is executed or becomes effective during the reporting period reflected by a Form 10–Q or Form 10–K, it shall be filed as an exhibit to the Form 10–Q or Form 10–K filed for the corresponding period. *See* paragraph (a)(4) of this Item. With respect to quarterly reports on Form 10–Q, only those contracts executed or becoming effective during the most recent period reflected in the report shall be filed.

(11) [Reserved]

(12) [Reserved]

(13) *Annual Report to Security Holders, Form 10–Q, or Quarterly Report to Security Holders.* (i) The registrant's annual report to security holders for its last fiscal year, its Form 10–Q (if specifically incorporated by reference in the prospectus) or its quarterly report to security holders, if all or a portion thereof is incorporated by reference in the filing. Such report, except for those portions thereof that are expressly incorporated by reference in the filing, is to be furnished for the information of the Commission and is not to be deemed "filed" as part of the filing. If the financial statements in the report have been incorporated by reference in the filing, the accountant's certificate shall be manually signed in one copy. See Rule 411(b).

(ii) *Electronic Filings.* If all, or any portion, of the annual or quarterly report to security holders is incorporated by reference into any electronic filing, all, or such portion of the annual or quarterly report to security holders so incorporated, shall be filed in electronic format as an exhibit to the filing.

(14) *Code of Ethics.* Any code of ethics, or amendment thereto, that is the subject of the disclosure required by Item 406 of Regulation S–K or Item 5.05 of Form 8–K, to the extent that the registrant intends to satisfy the Item 406 or Item 10 requirements through filing of an exhibit.

(15) *Letter re Unaudited Interim Financial Information.* A letter, where applicable, from the independent accountant that acknowledges awareness of the use in a registration statement of a report on unaudited interim financial information that pursuant to Rule 436(c) under the Securities Act is not considered a part of a registration statement prepared or certified by an accountant or a report prepared or certified by an accountant within the meaning of sections 7 and 11 of that Act. Such letter may be filed with the registration statement, an amendment thereto, or a report on Form 10–Q which is incorporated by reference into the registration statement.

(16) *Letter re Change in Certifying Accountant.* A letter from the registrant's former independent accountant regarding its concurrence or disagreement with the statements made by the registrant in the current report concerning the resignation or dismissal as the registrant's principal accountant.

(17) *Correspondence on Departure of Director.* Any written correspondence from a former director concerning the circumstances surrounding the former director's retirement, resignation, refusal to stand for re-election or removal, including any letter from the former director to the registrant stating whether the former director agrees with statements made by the registrant describing the former director's departure.

(18) *Letter re Change in Accounting Principles.* Unless previously filed, a letter from the registrant's independent accountant indicating whether any change in accounting principles or practices followed by the registrant, or any change in the method of applying any such accounting principles or practices, which affected the financial statements being filed with the Commission in the report or which is reasonably certain to affect the financial statements of future fiscal years is to an alternative principle which in his judgment is preferable under the circumstances. No such letter need be filed when such change is made in response to a standard adopted by the Financial Accounting Standards Board that creates a new accounting principle, that expresses a preference for an accounting principle, or that rejects a specific accounting principle.

(19) [Reserved]

(20) *Other Documents or Statements to Security Holders.* If the registrant makes available to its stockholders or otherwise publishes, within the period prescribed for filing the report, a document or statement containing information meeting some or all of the requirements of this form the information called for may be incorporated by reference to such published document or statement provided copies thereof are filed as an exhibit to the report on this form.

(21) *Subsidiaries of the Registrant.* (i) List all subsidiaries of the registrant, the state or other jurisdiction of incorporation or organization of each, and the names under which such subsidiaries do business. This list may be incorporated by

reference from a document which includes a complete and accurate list.

(ii) The names of particular subsidiaries may be omitted if the unnamed subsidiaries, considered in the aggregate as a single subsidiary, would not constitute a significant subsidiary as of the end of the year covered by this report. (See the definition of "significant subsidiary" in Rule 1–02(w) (17 CFR 210.1–02(w))of Regulation S–X.) The names of consolidated wholly-owned multiple subsidiaries carrying on the same line of business, such as chain stores or small loan companies, may be omitted, provided the name of the immediate parent, the line of business, the number of omitted subsidiaries operating in the United States and the number operating in foreign countries are given. This instruction shall not apply, however, to banks, insurance companies, savings and loan associations or to any subsidiary subject to regulation by another Federal agency.

(22) [Reserved]

(23) *Consents of Experts and Counsel.* (i) *Securities Act Filings.* All written consents required to be filed shall be dated and manually signed. Where the consent of an expert or counsel is contained in his report or opinion or elsewhere in the registration statement or document filed therewith, a reference shall be made in the index to the report, the part of the registration statement or document or opinion, containing the consent.

(ii) *Exchange Act Reports.* Where the filing of a written consent is required with respect to material incorporated by reference in a previously filed registration statement under the Securities Act, such consent may be filed as exhibit to the material incorporated by reference. Such consents shall be dated and manually signed.

(24) *Power of Attorney.* If any name is signed to the registration statement or report pursuant to a power of attorney, manually signed copies of such power of attorney shall be filed. Where the power of attorney is contained elsewhere in the registration statement or documents filed therewith a reference shall be made in the index to the part of the registration statement or document containing such power of attorney. In addition, if the name of any officer signing on behalf of the registrant is signed pursuant to a power of attorney, certified copies of a resolution of the registrant's board of directors authorizing such signature shall also be filed. A power of attorney that is filed with the Commission shall relate to a specific filing or an amendment thereto, provided, however, that a power of attorney relating to a registration statement under the Securities Act or an amendment thereto also may relate to any registration statement for the same offering that is to be effective upon filing pursuant to Rule 462(b) under the Securities Act. A power of attorney that confers general authority shall not be filed with the Commission.

(25) *Statement of Eligibility of Trustee.* (i) A statement of eligibility and qualification of each person designated to act as trustee under an indenture to be qualified under the Trust Indenture Act of 1939. Such statement of eligibility shall be bound separately from the other exhibits.

(ii) *Electronic Filings.* The requirement to bind separately the statement of eligibility and qualification of each person designated to act as a trustee under the Trust Indenture Act of 1939 from other exhibits shall not apply to statements submitted in electronic format. Rather, such statements must be submitted as exhibits in the same electronic submission as the registration statement to which they relate, or in an amendment thereto, except that electronic filers that rely on Trust Indenture Act Section 305(b)(2) for determining the eligibility of the trustee under indentures for securities to be issued, offered or sold on a delayed basis by or on behalf of the registrant shall file such statements separately in the manner prescribed by 17 CFR 260.5b–1 through 17 CFR 260.5b–3 and by the EDGAR Filer Manual.

(26)–(30) [Reserved].

(31)(i) *Rule 13a–14(a)/15d–14(a) Certifications.* The certifications required by Rules 13a–14(a) or 15d–14(a) under the Securities Exchange Act of 1934 exactly as set forth below:

*Certifications** I, [identify the certifying individual], certify that:

1. I have reviewed this [specify report] of [identify registrant];

2. Based on my knowledge, this report does not contain any untrue statement of a material fact or omit to state a material fact necessary to make the statements made, in light of the circumstances under which such statements were made, not misleading with respect to the period covered by this report;

3. Based on my knowledge, the financial statements, and other financial information included in this report, fairly present in all material respects the financial condition, results of operations and cash flows of the registrant as of, and for, the periods presented in this report;

4. The registrant's other certifying officer(s) and I are responsible for establishing and maintaining disclosure controls and procedures (as defined in Exchange Act Rules 13a–15(e) and 15d–15(e)) and internal control over financial reporting (as defined in Exchange Act Rules 13a–15(f) and 15d–15(f)) for the registrant and have:

(a) Designed such disclosure controls and procedures, or caused such disclosure controls and procedures to be designed under our supervision, to ensure that material information relating to the registrant, including its consolidated subsidiaries, is made known to us by others within those entities, particularly during the period in which this report is being prepared;

(b) Designed such internal control over financial reporting, or caused such internal control over financial reporting to be designed under our supervision, to provide reasonable assurance regarding the reliability of financial reporting and the preparation of financial statements for external purposes in accordance with generally accepted accounting principles;

(c) Evaluated the effectiveness of the registrant's disclosure controls and procedures and presented in this report our conclusions about the effectiveness of the disclosure controls and procedures, as of the end of the period covered by this report based on such evaluation; and

(d) Disclosed in this report any change in the registrant's internal control over financial reporting that occurred during the registrant's most recent fiscal quarter (the registrant's fourth fiscal quarter in the case of an annual report) that has materially affected, or is reasonably likely to materially affect, the registrant's internal control over financial reporting; and

5. The registrant's other certifying officer(s) and I have disclosed, based on our most recent evaluation of internal control over financial reporting, to the registrant's auditors and the audit committee of the registrant's board of directors (or persons performing the equivalent functions):

(a) All significant deficiencies and material weaknesses in the design or operation of internal control over financial reporting which are reasonably likely to adversely affect the registrant's ability to record, process, summarize and report financial information; and

(b) Any fraud, whether or not material, that involves management or other employees who have a significant role in the registrant's internal control over financial reporting.

Date: ________

____
[Signature]

____
[Title]

*Provide a separate certification for each principal executive officer and principal financial officer of the registrant. See Rules 13a–14(a) and 15d–14(a).

(ii) *Rule 13a–14(d)/15d–14(d) Certifications.* If an asset-backed issuer (as defined in Item 1101 of Regulation AB), the certifications required by Rule 13a–14(d) or Rule 15d–14(d) under the Securities Exchange Act of 1934 exactly as set forth below:

Certifications[1]

I, [identify the certifying individual], certify that:

1. I have reviewed this report on Form 10–K and all reports on Form 10–D required to be filed in respect of the period covered by this report on Form 10–K of [identify the issuing entity] (the "Exchange Act periodic reports");

2. Based on my knowledge, the Exchange Act periodic reports, taking as a whole, do not contain any untrue statement of a material fact or omit to state a material fact necessary to make the statements made, in light of the circumstances under which such statements were made, not misleading with respect to the period covered by this report;

3. Based on my knowledge, all of the distribution, servicing and other information required to be provided under Form 10–D for the period covered by this report is included in the Exchange Act periodic reports;

4. [I am responsible for reviewing the activities performed by the servicer(s) and based on my knowledge and the compliance review(s) conducted in preparing the servicer compliance statement(s) required in this report under Item 1123 of Regulation AB, and except as disclosed in the Exchange Act periodic reports, the servicer(s) [has/have] fulfilled [its/their] obligations under the servicing agreements(s) in all material respects; and]

[Based on my knowledge and the servicer compliance statement(s) required in this report under Item 1123 of Regulation AB, and except as disclosed in the Exchange Act periodic reports, the servicer(s) [has/have] fulfilled [its/their] obligations under the servicing agreements(s) in all material respects; and][2]

5. All of the reports on assessment of compliance with servicing criteria for asset-backed securities and their related attestation reports on assessment of compliance with servicing criteria for asset-backed securities required to be included in this report in accordance with Item 1122 of Regulation AB and Rules 13a–18 and 15d–18 under the Securities Exchange Act of 1934 have been included as an exhibit to this report, except as otherwise disclosed in this report.

1. With respect to asset-backed issuers, the certification must be signed by either: (1) The senior officer in charge of securitization of the depositor if the depositor is signing the report on Form 10–K; or (2) The senior officer in charge of the servicing function of the servicer if the servicer is signing the report on Form 10–K on behalf of the issuing entity. See Rules 13a–14(e) and 15d–14(e) under the Securities Exchange Act of 1934. If multiple servicers are involved in servicing the pool assets, the senior officer in charge of the servicing function of the master servicer (or entity performing the equivalent function) must sign if a representative of the servicer is to sign the certification. If there is a master servicer and one or more underlying servicers, the references in the certification relate to the master servicer. A natural person must sign the certification in his or her individual capacity, although the title of that person in the organization of which he or she is an officer may be included under the signature.

2. The first version of paragraph 4 is to be used when the servicer is signing the report on behalf of the issuing entity. The second version of paragraph 4 is to be used when the depositor is signing the report.

Any material instances of noncompliance described in such reports have been disclosed in this report on Form 10–K.[3]

[In giving the certifications above, I have reasonably relied on information provided to me by the following unaffiliated parties [name of servicer, sub-servicer, co-servicer, depositor or trustee].][4]

Date: _______________

____

[Signature]
[Title]

(32) *Section 1350 Certifications.* (i) The certifications required by Rule 13a–14(b) (17 CFR 240.13a–14(b)) or Rule 15d–14(b) (17 CFR 240.15d–14(b)) and Section 1350 of Chapter 63 of Title 18 of the United States Code (18 U.S.C. 1350).

(ii) A certification furnished pursuant to this item will not be deemed "filed" for purposes of Section 18 of the Securities Exchange Act of 1934 (15 U.S.C. 78r), or otherwise subject to the liability of that section. Such certification will not be deemed to be incorporated by reference into any filing under the Securities Act or the Exchange Act, except to the extent that the registrant specifically incorporates it by reference.

(33) *Report on Assessment of Compliance with Servicing Criteria for Asset–Backed Securities.* Each report on assessment of compliance with servicing criteria required by Item 1122(a) of Regulation AB.

3. The certification refers to the reports prepared by parties participating in the servicing function that are required to be included as an exhibit to the Form 10–K. See Item 1122 of Regulation AB and Rules 13a–18 and 15d–18 under the Securities Exchange Act of 1934. If a report that is otherwise required to be included is not attached, disclosure that the report is not included and an associated explanation must be provided in the Form 10–K report. The certification refers to the reports prepared by parties participating in the servicing function that are required to be included as an exhibit to the Form 10–K. See Item 1122 of Regulation AB and Rules 13a–18 and 15d–18 under the Securities Exchange Act of 1934. If a report that is otherwise required to be included is not attached, disclosure that the report is not included and an associated explanation must be provided in the Form 10–K report. The certification refers to the reports prepared by parties participating in the servicing function that are required to be included as an exhibit to the Form 10–K. See Item 1122 of Regulation AB and Rules 13a–18 and 15d–18 under the Securities Exchange Act of 1934. If a report that is otherwise required to be included is not attached, disclosure that the report is not included and an associated explanation must be provided in the Form 10–K report.

4. Because the signer of the certification must rely in certain circumstances on information provided by unaffiliated parties outside of the signer's control, this paragraph must be included if the signer is reasonably relying on information that unaffiliated trustees, depositors, servicers, sub-servicers or co-servicers have provided.

(34) *Attestation Report on Assessment of Compliance with Servicing Criteria for Asset–Backed Securities.* Each attestation report on assessment of compliance with servicing criteria for asset-backed securities required by Item 1122(b) of Regulation AB.

(35) *Servicer Compliance Statement.* Each servicer compliance statement required by Item 1123 of Regulation AB.

(36) *Certification for shelf offerings of asset-backed securities.* Provide the certification required by General Instruction I.B.1.(a) of Form SF–3 (17 CFR 239.45) exactly as set forth below:

Certification

I [identify the certifying individual] certify as of [the date of the final prospectus under Rule 424 of this chapter] that:

1. I have reviewed the prospectus relating to [title of all securities, the offer and sale of which are registered] (the "securities") and am familiar with, in all material respects, the following: the characteristics of the securitized assets underlying the offering (the "securitized assets"), the structure of the securitization, and all material underlying transaction agreements as described in the prospectus;

2. Based on my knowledge, the prospectus does not contain any untrue statement of a material fact or omit to state a material fact necessary to make the statements made, in light of the circumstances under which such statements were made, not misleading;

3. Based on my knowledge, the prospectus and other information included in the registration statement of which it is a part fairly present, in all material respects, the characteristics of the securitized assets, the structure of the securitization and the risks of ownership of the securities, including the risks relating to the securitized assets that would affect the cash flows available to service payments or distributions on the securities in accordance with their terms; and

4. Based on my knowledge, taking into account all material aspects of the characteristics of the securitized assets, the structure of the securitization, and the related risks as described in the prospectus, there is a reasonable basis to conclude that the securitization is structured to produce, but is not guaranteed by this certification to produce, expected cash flows at times and in amounts to service scheduled payments of interest and the ultimate repayment of principal on the securities (or other scheduled or required distributions on the securities, however denominated) in accordance with their terms as described in the prospectus.

5. The foregoing certifications are given subject to any and all defenses available to me under the federal securities laws, including any and all defenses available to an executive officer that signed the registration statement of which the prospectus referred to in this certification is part.

Date: _______________

____

[Signature]
[Title]

The certification must be signed by the chief executive officer of the depositor, as required by General Instruction I.B.1.(a) of Form SF–3.

(37)–(94) [Reserved]

(95) *Mine Safety Disclosure Exhibit.* A registrant that is an operator, or that has a subsidiary that is an operator, of a coal or other mine must provide the information required by Item 104 of Regulation S–K in an exhibit to its Exchange Act annual or quarterly report. For purposes of this Item:

1. The term *coal or other mine* means a coal or other mine, as defined in section 3 of the Federal Mine Safety and Health Act of 1977 (30 U.S.C. 802), that is subject to the provisions of such Act (30 U.S.C. 801 et seq).

2. The term *operator* has the meaning given the term in section 3 of the Federal Mine Safety and Health Act of 1977 (30 U.S.C. 802).

3. The term *subsidiary* has the meaning given the term in Rule 12b–2 under the Securities Exchange Act of 1934.

(96)–(98) [Reserved]

(99) *Additional Exhibits.* (i) Any additional exhibits which the registrant may wish to file shall be so marked as to indicate clearly the subject matters to which they refer.

(ii) Any document (except for an exhibit) or part thereof which is incorporated by reference in the filing and is not otherwise required to be filed by this Item or is not a Commission filed document incorporated by reference in a Securities Act registration statement.

(iii) If pursuant to Section 11(a) of the Securities Act of 1933 (15 U.S.C. 77k(a)) an issuer makes generally available to its security holders an earnings statement covering a period of at least 12 months beginning after the effective date of the registration statement, and if such earnings statement is made available by "other methods" than those specified in paragraphs (a) or (b) of Rule 158, it must be filed as an exhibit to the Form 10–Q or the Form 10–K, as appropriate, covering the period in which the earnings statement was released.

(100) [Reserved]

(101) *Interactive Data File.* Where a registrant prepares its financial statements in accordance with either generally accepted accounting principles as used in the United States or International Financial Reporting Standards as issued by the International Accounting Standards Board, an Interactive Data File (Rule 11 of Regulation S–T) is:

(i) *Required to Be Submitted.* Required to be submitted to the Commission in the manner provided by Rule 405 of Regulation S–T if the registrant does not prepare its financial statements in accordance with 17 CFR 210.6–01 through 210.6–10 (Article 6 of Regulation S–X), except that an Interactive Data File:

(A) First is required for a periodic report on Form 10–Q (17 CFR §249.308a), Form 20–F (17 CFR 249.220f), or Form 40–F (17 CFR 249.), as applicable;

(B) Is required for a registration statement under the Securities Act only if the registration statement contains a price or price range; and

(C) Is required for a Form 8–K (17 CFR 249.308) only when the Form 8– K contains audited annual financial statements that are a revised version of financial statements that previously were filed with the Commission and that have been revised pursuant to applicable accounting standards to reflect the effects of certain subsequent events, including a discontinued operation, a change in reportable segments or a change in accounting principle. In such case, the Interactive Data File will be required only as to such revised financial statements regardless of whether the Form 8–K contains other financial statements.

(ii) *Permitted to be submitted.* Permitted to be submitted to the Commission in the manner provided by Rule 405 of Regulation S–T if the:

(A) Registrant does not prepare its financial statements in accordance with 17 CFR 210.6–01 through 210.6–10 (Article 6 of Regulation S–X); and

(B) Interactive Data File is not required to be submitted to the Commission under paragraph (b)(101)(i) of this section.

Instruction 1 to paragraphs (b)(101)(i) and (ii): When an Interactive Data File is submitted as provided by paragraph(a)(3)(i) of Rule 405 of Regulation S–T, the exhibit index must include the word "Inline" within the title description for any eXtensible Business Reporting Language (XBRL)-related exhibit.

(iii) *Not permitted to be submitted.* Not permitted to be submitted to the Commission if the registrant prepares its financial statements in accordance with 17 CFR 210.6–01 through 210.6–10 (Article 6 of Regulation S–X).

(102) *Asset Data File*. An Asset Data File (as defined in Rule 232.11 of this chapter) filed pursuant to Item 1111(h)(3) of Regulation AB (17 CFR 229.1111(h)(3)).

(103) *Asset Related Document*. Additional asset-level information or explanatory language pursuant to Item 1111(h)(4) and (5) of Regulation AB (17 CFR 229.1111(h)(4) and (h)(5)).

(104) [Reserved].

(105) [Reserved].

(106) *Static Pool*. If not included in the prospectus filed in accordance with Rule 424(b)(2) or (5) and (h) of this chapter, static pool disclosure as required by Rule 229.1105.

Subpart 700—Miscellaneous

Item 701. Recent sales of unregistered securities; use of proceeds from registered securities

Furnish the following information as to all securities of the registrant sold by the registrant within the past three years which were not registered under the Securities Act of 1933. Include sales of reacquired securities, as well as new issues, securities issued in exchange for property, services, or other securities, and new securities resulting from the modification of outstanding securities.

(a) *Securities Sold*. Give the date of sale and the title and amount of securities sold.

(b) *Underwriters and Other Purchasers*. Give the names of the principal underwriters, if any. As to any such securities not publicly offered, name the persons or identify the class of persons to whom the securities were sold.

(c) *Consideration*. As to securities sold for cash, state the aggregate offering price and the aggregate underwriting discounts or commissions. As to any securities sold otherwise than for cash, state the nature of the transaction and the nature and aggregate amount of consideration received by the registrant.

(d) *Exemption from Registration Claimed*. Indicate the section of the Securities Act or the rule of the Commission under which exemption from registration was claimed and state briefly the facts relied upon to make the exemption available.

(e) *Terms of Conversion or Exercise*. If the information called for by this paragraph (e) is being presented on Form 8–K, Form 10–Q, Form 10–K or Form 10–D under the Securities Exchange Act of 1934 (17 CFR 249.308, 249.308(a), 249.310 or 249.312), and where the securities sold by the registrant are convertible or exchangeable into equity securities, or are warrants or options representing equity securities, disclose the terms of conversion or exercise of the securities.

(f) *Use of Proceeds*. As required by Rule 463, following the effective date of the first registration statement filed under the Securities Act of 1933 by an issuer, the issuer or successor issuer shall report the use of proceeds on its first periodic report filed pursuant to sections 13(a) and 15(d) of the Exchange Act (15 U.S.C. 78m(a) and 78*o*(d)) after effectiveness of its Securities Act of 1933 registration statement, and thereafter on each of its subsequent periodic reports filed pursuant to sections 13(a) and 15(d) of the Securities Exchange Act of 1934 through the later of disclosure of the application of all the offering proceeds or disclosure of the termination of the offering. If a report of the use of proceeds is required with respect to the first effective registration statement of the predecessor issuer, the successor issuer shall provide such a report. The information provided pursuant to paragraphs (f)(2) through (f)(4) of this Item need only be provided with respect to the first periodic report filed pursuant to sections 13(a) and 15(d) of the Securities Exchange Act of 1934 after effectiveness of the registration statement filed under the Securities Act of 1933. Subsequent periodic reports filed pursuant to sections 13(a) and 15(d) of the Exchange Act need only provide the information required in paragraphs (f)(2) through (f)(4) of this Item if any of such required information has changed since the last periodic report filed. In disclosing the use of proceeds in the first periodic report filed pursuant to the Securities Exchange Act of 1934, the issuer or successor issuer should include the following information:

(1) The effective date of the Securities Act registration statement for which the use of proceeds information is being disclosed and the Commission file number assigned to the registration statement;

(2) If the offering has commenced, the offering date, and if the offering has not commenced, an explanation why it has not;

(3) If the offering terminated before any securities were sold, an explanation for such termination; and

(4) If the offering did not terminate before any securities were sold, disclose:

(i) Whether the offering has terminated and, if so, whether it terminated before the sale of all securities registered;

(ii) The name(s) of the managing underwriter(s), if any;

(iii) The title of each class of securities registered and, where a class of convertible securities is being registered, the title of any class of securities into which such securities may be converted;

(iv) For each class of securities (other than a class of securities into which a class of convertible securities registered may be converted without additional payment to the issuer) the following information, provided for both the account of the issuer and the account(s) of any selling security holder(s): the amount registered, the aggregate price of the offering amount registered, the amount sold and the aggregate offering price of the amount sold to date;

(v) From the effective date of the Securities Act registration statement to the ending date of the reporting period, the amount of expenses incurred for the issuer's account in connection with the issuance and distribution of the securities registered for underwriting discounts and commissions, finders' fees, expenses paid to or for underwriters, other expenses and total expenses. Indicate if a reasonable estimate for the amount of expenses incurred is provided instead of the actual amount of expense. Indicate whether such payments were:

(A) Direct or indirect payments to directors, officers, general partners of the issuer or their associates; to persons owning ten (10) percent or more of any class of equity securities of the issuer; and to affiliates of the issuer; or

(B) Direct or indirect payments to others;

(vi) The net offering proceeds to the issuer after deducting the total expenses described in paragraph (f)(4)(v) of this Item;

(vii) From the effective date of the Securities Act registration statement to the ending date of the reporting period, the amount of net offering proceeds to the issuer used for construction of plant, building and facilities; purchase and installation of machinery and equipment; purchases of real estate; acquisition of other business(es); repayment of indebtedness; working capital; temporary investments (which should be specified); and any other purposes for which at least five (5) percent of the issuer's total offering proceeds or $100,000 (whichever is less) has been used (which should be specified). Indicate if a reasonable estimate for the amount of net offering proceeds applied is provided instead of the actual amount of net offering proceeds used. Indicate whether such payments were:

(A) Direct or indirect payments to directors, officers, general partners of the issuer or their associates; to persons owning ten (10) percent or more of any class of equity securities of the issuer; and to affiliates of the issuer; or

(B) Direct or indirect payments to others; and

(viii) If the use of proceeds in paragraph (f)(4)(vii) of this Item represents a material change in the use of proceeds described in the prospectus, the issuer should describe briefly the material change.

Instructions:

1. Information required by this Item 701 need not be set forth as to notes, drafts, bills of exchange, or bankers' acceptances which mature not later than one year from the date of issuance.

2. If the sales were made in a series of transactions, the information may be given by such totals and periods as will reasonably convey the information required.

Item 702. Indemnification of directors and officers

State the general effect of any statute, charter provisions, by-laws, contract or other arrangements under which any controlling persons, director or officer of the registrant is insured or indemnified in any manner against liability which he may incur in his capacity as such.

Item 703. Purchases of equity securities by the issuer and affiliated purchasers

(a) In the following tabular format, provide the information specified in paragraph (b) of this Item with respect to any purchase made by or on behalf of the business issuer or any "affiliated purchaser," as defined in Rule 10b–18(a)(3) under the Securities Exchange Act of 1934, of shares or other units of any class of the issuer's equity securities that is registered by the issuer pursuant to section 12 of the Exchange Act (15 U.S.C. 78l).

ISSUER PURCHASES OF EQUITY SECURITIES

Period	(a) Total Number of Shares (or Units) Purchased	(b) Average Price Paid per Share (or Unit)	(c) Total Number of Shares (or Units) Purchased as Part of Publicly Announced Plans or Programs	(d) Maximum Number (or Approximate Dollar Value) of Shares (or Units) that May Yet Be Purchased Under the Plans or Programs
Month #1 (identify beginning and ending dates)				
Month #2 (identify beginning and ending dates)				
Month #3 (identify beginning and ending dates)				
Total				

(b) The table shall include the following information for each class or series of securities for each month included in the period covered by the report:

(1) The total number of shares (or units) purchased (column (a));

Instruction to Paragraph (b)(1) of Item 703: Include in this column all issuer repurchases, including those made pursuant to publicly announced plans or programs and those not made pursuant to publicly announced plans or programs. Briefly disclose, by footnote to the table, the number of shares purchased other than through a publicly announced plan or program and the nature of the transaction (e.g., whether the purchases were made in open-market transactions, tender offers, in satisfaction of the company's obligations upon exercise of outstanding put options issued by the company, or other transactions).

(2) The average price paid per share (or unit) (column (b));

(3) The total number of shares (or units) purchased as part of publicly announced repurchase plans or programs (column (c)); and

(4) The maximum number (or approximate dollar value) of shares (or units) that may yet be purchased under the plans or programs (column (d)).

Instructions to paragraphs (b)(3) and (b)(4) of Item 703:

1. In the table, disclose this information in the aggregate for all plans or programs publicly announced.

2. By footnote to the table, indicate:

a. The date each plan or program was announced;

b. The dollar amount (or share or unit amount) approved;

c. The expiration date (if any) of each plan or program;

d. Each plan or program that has expired during the period covered by the table; and

e. Each plan or program the issuer has determined to terminate prior to expiration, or under which the issuer does not intend to make further purchases.

Instruction to Item 703: Disclose all purchases covered by this Item, including purchases that do not satisfy the conditions of the safe harbor of Rule 10b–18 under the Securities Exchange Act of 1934.

Subpart 800—List of Industry Guides

Item 801. Securities Act industry guides

(a) [Reserved]

(b) [Reserved]

(c) *Guide 3.* Statistical disclosure by bank holding companies.

(d) *Guide 4.* Prospectuses relating to interests in oil and gas programs.

(e) *Guide 5.* Preparation of registration statements relating to interests in real estate limited partnerships.

(f) *Guide 6.* Disclosures concerning unpaid claims and claim adjustment expenses of property-casualty insurance underwriters.

(g) *Guide 7.* Description of Property by Issuers Engaged or To Be Engaged in Significant Mining Operations.

Item 802. Exchange Act industry guides

(a) [Reserved]

(b) [Reserved]

(c) *Guide 3.* Statistical disclosure by bank holding companies.

(d) *Guide 4.* Disclosures concerning unpaid claims and claim adjustment expenses of property-casualty underwriters.

(e)–(f) [Reserved]

(g) *Guide 7.* Description of Property by Issuers Engaged or To Be Engaged in Significant Mining Operations.

Subpart 900—Roll-Up Transactions

Item 901. Definitions

For the purposes of this Item 900:

(a) *General partner* means the person or persons responsible under state law for managing or directing the management of the business and affairs of a partnership that is the subject of a roll-up transaction including, but not limited to, the general partner(s), board of directors, board of trustees, or other person(s) having a fiduciary duty to such partnership.

(b)(1) *Partnership* means any:

(i) Finite-life limited partnership; or

(ii) Other finite-life entity.

(2)(i) Except as provided in paragraph (b)(2)(ii) of this Item, a limited partnership or other entity is "finite-life" if:

(A) It operates as a conduit vehicle for investors to participate in the ownership of assets for a limited period of time; and

(B) It has as a policy or purpose distributing to investors proceeds from the sale, financing or refinancing of assets or cash from operations, rather than reinvesting such proceeds or cash in the business (whether for the term of the entity or after an initial period of time following commencement of operations).

(ii) A real estate investment trust as defined in I.R.C. section 856 is not *finite-life* solely because of the distribution to investors of net income as provided by the I.R.C. if its policies or purposes do not include the distribution to investors of proceeds from the sale, financing or refinancing of assets, rather than the reinvestment of such proceeds in the business.

(3) *Partnership* does not include any entity registered under the Investment Company Act of 1940 (15 U.S.C. 80a–1 *et seq.*) or any Business Development Company as defined in section 2(a)(48) of that Act (15 U.S.C. 80a–2(a)(48)).

(c)(1) Except as provided in paragraph (c)(2) or (c)(3) of this Item, *roll-up transaction* means a transaction involving the combination or reorganization of one or more partnerships, directly or indirectly, in which some or all of the investors in any of such partnerships will receive new securities, or securities in another entity.

(2) Notwithstanding paragraph (c)(1) of this Item, *roll-up transaction* shall not include:

(i) A transaction wherein the interests of all of the investors in each of the partnerships are repurchased, recalled, or exchanged in accordance with the terms of the preexisting partnership agreement for securities in an operating company specifically identified at the time of the formation of the original partnership;

(ii) A transaction in which the securities to be issued or exchanged are not required to be and are not registered under the Securities Act of 1933 (15 U.S.C. 77a *et seq.*);

(iii) A transaction that involves only issuers that are not required to register or report under Section 12 of the Securities Exchange Act of 1934 (15 U.S.C. 78*l*), both before and after the transaction;

(iv) A transaction that involves the combination or reorganization of one or more partnerships in which a non-affiliated party succeeds to the interests of a general partner or sponsor, if:

(A) Such action is approved by not less than 66⅔% of the outstanding units of each of the participating partnerships; and

(B) As a result of the transaction, the existing general partners will receive only compensation to which they are entitled as expressly provided for in the preexisting partnership agreements;

(v) A transaction in which the securities offered to investors are securities of another entity that are reported under a transaction reporting plan declared effective before December 17, 1993 by the Commission under Section 11A of the Securities Exchange Act of 1934 (15 U.S.C. 78k–1), if:

(A) Such other entity was formed, and such class of securities was reported and regularly traded, not less than 12 months before the date on which soliciting material is mailed to investors; and

(B) The securities of that entity issued to investors in the transaction do not exceed 20% of the total outstanding securities of the entity, exclusive of any securities of such class held by or for the account of the entity or a subsidiary of the entity; and

(C) For purposes of paragraph (c)(2)(v) of this Item, a *regularly traded* security means any security with a minimum closing price of $2.00 or more for a majority of the business days during the preceding three-month period and a six-month minimum average daily trading volume of 1,000 shares;

(vi) A transaction in which all of the investors' partnership securities are reported under a transaction reporting plan declared effective before December 17, 1993 by the Commission under Section 11A of the Securities Exchange Act of 1934 (15 U.S.C. 78k–1) and such investors receive new securities or securities in another entity that are reported under a transaction reporting plan declared effective before December 17, 1993 by the Commission under Section 11A of the Securities Exchange Act of 1934 (15 U.S.C. 78k–1), except that, for purposes of this paragraph, securities that are reported under a transaction reporting plan declared effective before December 17, 1993 by the Commission under Section 11A of the Securities Exchange Act of 1934 shall not include securities listed on the American Stock Exchange's Emerging Company Marketplace;

(vii) A transaction in which the investors in any of the partnerships involved in the transaction are not subject to a significant adverse change with respect to voting rights, the terms of existence of the entity, management compensation or investment objectives; or

(viii) A transaction in which all investors are provided an option to receive or retain a security under substantially the same terms and conditions as the original issue.

(3) The Commission, upon written request or upon its own motion, may exempt by rule or order any security or class of securities, any transaction or class of transactions, or any person or class of persons, in whole or in part, conditionally or unconditionally, from the definition of roll-up transaction or the requirements imposed on roll-up transactions by Items 902–915 of Regulation S–K, if it finds such action to be consistent with the public interest and the protection of investors.

(d) *Sponsor* means the person proposing the roll-up transaction.

(e) *Successor* means the surviving entity after completion of the roll-up transaction or the entity whose securities are being offered or sold to, or acquired by, limited partners of the partnerships or the limited partnerships to be combined or reorganized.

Instruction to Item 901: If a transaction is a roll-up transaction as defined in Item 901(c) of this subpart, the requirements of this subpart apply to each entity proposed to be included in the roll-up transaction, whether or not the entity is a "partnership" as defined in Item 901(b) of this subpart.

Item 902. Individual partnership supplements

(a) If two or more entities are proposed to be included in the roll-up transaction, provide the information specified in this Item in a separate supplement to the disclosure document for each entity.

(b) The separate supplement required by paragraph (a) of this Item shall be filed as part of the registration statement, shall be delivered with the prospectus to investors in the partnership covered thereby, and shall include:

(1) A statement in the forepart of the supplement to the effect that:

(i) Supplements have been prepared for each partnership;

(ii) The effects of the roll-up transaction may be different for investors in the various partnerships; and

(iii) Upon receipt of a written request by an investor or his representative who has been so designated in writing, a copy of any supplement will be transmitted promptly, without charge, by the general partner or sponsor.

This statement must include the name and address of the person to whom investors should make their request.

(2) A brief description of each material risk and effect of the roll-up transaction, including, but not limited to, federal income tax consequences, for investors in the partnership, with appropriate cross references to the discussions of the risks, effects and tax consequences of the roll-up transaction required in the principal disclosure document pursuant to Items 904 and 915 of this subpart (Items 904 and 915 of Regulation S–K). Such discussion shall address the effect of the roll-up transaction on the partnership's financial condition and results of operations.

(3) A statement concerning whether the general partner reasonably believes that the roll-up transaction is fair or unfair to investors in the partnership, together with a brief discussion of the bases for such belief, with appropriate cross references to the discussion of the fairness of the roll-up transaction required in the principal disclosure document pursuant to Item 910 of this subpart (Item 910 of Regulation S–K). If there are material differences between the fairness analysis for the partnership and for the other partnerships, such differences shall be described briefly in the supplement.

(4) A brief, narrative description of the method of calculating the value of the partnership and allocating interests in the successor to the partnership, and a table showing such calculation and allocation. Such table shall include the following information (or other information of a comparable character necessary to a thorough understanding of the calculation and allocation):

(i) The appraised value of each separately appraised significant asset (as defined in Item 911(c)(5) of this subpart) (Item 911(c)(5) of Regulation S–K) held by the partnership, or, if appraisals have not been obtained for each significant asset, the value assigned for purposes of the valuation of the partnership to each significant asset for which an appraisal has not been obtained;

(ii) The dollar amount of any mortgages or other similar liabilities to which each of such assets is subject;

(iii) Cash and cash equivalent assets held by the partnership;

(iv) Other assets held by the partnership;

(v) Other liabilities of the partnership;

(vi) The value assigned to the partnership;

(vii) The value assigned to the partnership per interest held by investors in the partnership (on an equivalent interest basis, such as per $1,000 original investment);

(viii) The aggregate number of interests in the successor to be allocated to the partnership and the percentage of the total interests of the successor;

(ix) The number of interests in the successor to be allocated to investors in the partnership for each interest held by such investors (on an equivalent interest basis, such as per $1,000 original investment); and

(x) The value assigned to the general partner's interest in the partnership, and the number of interests in the successor or other consideration to be allocated in the roll-up transaction to the general partner for such general partnership interest or otherwise as compensation or reimbursement for claims against or interests in the partnership, such as foregone fees, unearned fees and for fees to be earned on the sale or refinancing of an asset.

(5) The amounts of compensation paid, and cash distributions made, to the general partner and its affiliates by the partnership for the last three fiscal years and the most recently completed interim period and the amounts that would have been paid if the compensation and distributions structure to be in effect after the roll-up transaction had been in effect during such period. If any proposed change(s) in the business or operations of the successor after the roll-up transaction would change materially the compensation and distributions that would have been paid by the successor (e.g., if properties will be sold or purchased after the roll-up transaction and no properties were sold or purchased during the period covered by the table), describe such changes and the effects thereof on the compensation and distributions to be paid by the successor.

(6) Cash distributions made to investors during each of the last five fiscal years and most recently completed interim period, identifying any such distributions which represent a return of capital.

(7) An appropriate cross reference to selected financial information concerning the partnership and the pro forma financial statements included in the principal disclosure document in response to Item 914(b)(2) of this subpart (Item 914(b)(2) of Regulation S–K).

Item 903. Summary

(a) Provide in the forepart of the disclosure document a clear, concise and comprehensible summary of the roll-up transaction.

(b) The summary required by paragraph (a) of this Item shall include a summary description of each of the following items, as well as any other material terms or consequences of the roll-up transaction necessary to an understanding of such transaction:

(1) Each material risk and effect on investors, including, but not limited to:

(i) Changes in the business plan, voting rights, cash distribution policies, form of ownership interest or management compensation;

(ii) The general partner's conflicts of interest in connection with the roll-up transaction and in connection with the successor's future operations; and

(iii) The likelihood that securities received by investors in the roll-up transaction will trade at prices substantially below the value assigned to such securities in the roll-up transaction and/or the value of the successor's assets;

(2) The material terms of the roll-up transaction, including the valuation method used to allocate securities in the successor to investors in the partnerships;

(3) Whether the general partner reasonably believes that the roll-up transaction is fair or unfair to investors in each partnership, including a brief discussion of the bases for such belief;

(4) Any opinion from an outside party concerning the fairness of the roll-up transaction, including whether the opinion addresses the fairness of all possible combinations of partnerships or portions of partnerships, and contacts with any outside party concerning fairness opinions, valuations or reports in connection with the roll-up transaction required to be disclosed pursuant to Item 911(a)(5) of this subpart (Item 911(a)(5) of Regulation S–K);

(5) The background of and reasons for the roll-up transaction, as well as alternatives to the roll-up transaction described in response to Item 908(b) of this subpart (Item 908(b) of Regulation S–K);

(6) Rights of investors to exercise dissenters' or appraisal rights or similar rights and to obtain a list of investors in the partnership in which the investor holds an interest; and

(7) If any affiliates of the general partner or the sponsor may participate in the business of the successor or receive compensation from the successor, an organizational chart showing the relationships between the general partner, the sponsor and their affiliates.

Instruction to Item 903: The description of the material risks and effects of the roll-up transaction required by paragraph (b)(1) of this Item 903 of Reg. S–K must be presented prominently in the forepart of the summary.

Item 904. Risk factors and other considerations

(a) Immediately following the summary required by Item 903 of this subpart (Item 903 of Regulation S–K), describe in reasonable detail each material risk and effect of the roll-up transaction on investors in each partnership, including, but not limited to:

(1) The potential risks, adverse effects and benefits of the roll-up transaction for investors and for the general partner, including those which result from each matter described in response to Item 905 of this subpart (Item 905 of Regulation S–K), with appropriate cross references to the comparative information required by Item 905;

(2) The material risks arising from an investment in the successor; and

(3) The likelihood that securities of the successor received by investors in the roll-up transaction will trade in the securities markets at a price substantially below the value assigned to such securities in the roll-up transaction and/or the value of the assets of the successor, and the effects on investors of such a trading market discount.

(b) Quantify each risk or effect to the extent practicable.

(c) State whether any of such risks or effects may be different for investors in any partnership and, if so, identify such partnership(s) and describe such difference(s).

Instruction to Item 904: The requirement to quantify the effects of the roll-up transaction shall include, but not be limited to:

(i) If cost savings resulting from combined administration of the partnerships is identified as a potential benefit of the roll-up transaction, the amount of cost savings and a comparison of such amount to the costs of the roll-up transaction; and

(ii) If there may be a material conflict of interest of the sponsor or general partner arising from its receipt of payments or other consideration as a result of the roll-up transaction, the amount of such payments and other consideration to be obtained in the roll-up transaction and a comparison of such amounts to the amounts to which the sponsor or general partner would be entitled without the roll-up transaction.

Item 905. Comparative information

(a)(1) Describe the voting and other rights of investors in the successor under the successor's governing instruments and under applicable law. Compare such rights to the voting and other rights of investors in each partnership subject to the transaction under the partnerships' governing instruments and under applicable law. Describe the effects of the change(s) in such rights.

(2) Describe the duties owed by the general partner of the successor to investors in the successor under the successor's governing instruments and under applicable law. Compare such duties to the duties owed by the general partner of each partnership to investors in the partnership under the partnership's governing instruments and under applicable law. Describe the effects of the change(s) in such duties.

(b)(1) Describe each item of compensation (including reimbursement of expenses) payable by the successor after the roll-up transaction to the general partner and its affiliates or to any affiliate of the successor. Compare such compensation to the compensation currently payable to the general partner and its affiliates by each partnership. Describe the effects of the change(s) in compensation arrangements.

(2) Describe each instance in which cash or other distributions may be made by the successor to the general partner and its affiliates or to any affiliate of the successor. Compare such distributions to the distributions currently paid or payable to the general partner and its affiliates by each partnership. Describe the effects of the change(s) in distribution arrangements. If distributions similar to those currently paid or payable by any partnership to the general partner or its affiliates will not be made by the successor, state whether or not other compensation arrangements with the successor described in response to paragraph (b)(1) of this Item (e.g., incentive fees payable upon sale of a property) will, in effect, replace such distributions.

(3) Provide a table demonstrating the changes in such compensation and distributions setting forth among other things:

(i) The actual amounts of compensation and distributions, separately identified, paid by the partnerships on a combined basis to the general partner and its affiliates for the partnerships' last three fiscal years and most recently ended interim periods; and

(ii) The amounts of compensation and distributions that would have been paid if the compensation and distributions structure to be in effect after the roll-up transaction had been in effect during such period.

(4) If any proposed change(s) in the business or operations of the successor after the roll-up transaction would change materially the compensation and distributions that would have been paid by the successor from that shown in the table provided in response to paragraph (b)(3)(ii) of this Item (e.g., if properties will be sold or purchased after the roll-up transaction and no properties were sold or purchased during the period covered by the table), describe such changes and the effects thereof on the compensation and distributions to be paid by the successor.

(5) Describe the material conflicts that may arise between the interests of the sponsor or general partner and the interests of investors in the successor as a result of the compensation and distribution arrangements described in response to paragraphs (b)(1) and (2) of this Item and describe any steps that will be taken to resolve any such conflicts.

(c) Describe any provisions in the governing instruments of the successor and any policies of the general partner of the successor relating to distributions to investors of cash from operations, proceeds from the sale, financing or refinancing of assets, and any other distributions. Compare such provisions and policies to those of each of the partnerships. Describe the effects of any change(s) in such provisions or policies.

(d)(1) Describe each material investment policy of the successor, including, without limitation, policies with respect to borrowings by the successor. Compare such investment policies to the investment policies of each of the partnerships. Describe the effects of any change(s) in such policies.

(2) Describe any plans of the general partner, sponsor or of any person who will be an affiliate of the successor with respect to:

(i) A sale of any material assets of the partnerships;

(ii) A purchase of any material assets; and

(iii) Borrowings.

(3)(i) State whether or not specific assets have been identified for sale, financing, refinancing or purchase following the roll-up transaction.

(ii) If specific assets have been so identified, describe the assets and the proposed transaction.

(e) Describe any other similar terms or policies of the successor that are material to an investment in the successor. Compare any such terms or policies to those of each of the partnerships. Describe the effects of any change(s) in any such terms or policies.

Instructions to Item 905:

(1) The information provided in response to this Item should be illustrated in tables or other readily understandable formats, which should be included together with the disclosures required by this Item.

(2) The information required by this Item shall be set forth in appropriate separate sections of the principal disclosure document.

Item 906. Allocation of roll-up consideration

(a) Describe in reasonable detail the method used to allocate interests in the successor to investors in the partnerships and the reasons why such method was used.

(b) Provide a table showing the calculation of the valuation of each partnership and the allocation of interests in the successor to investors. Such table shall include for each partnership the following information (or other information of a comparable character necessary to an understanding of the calculation and allocation):

(1) The value assigned to each significant category of assets of the partnership and the total value assigned to the partnership;

(2) The total value assigned to all partnerships;

(3) The aggregate amount of interests in the successor to be allocated to each partnership and the percentage of the total amount of all such interests represented thereby; and

(4) The amount of interests of the successor to be issued to investors per interest held in each partnership (on an equivalent interest basis, such as per $1,000 invested).

(c) If interests in the successor will be allocated to the general partner in exchange for its general partner interest or otherwise or if the general partner will receive other consideration in connection with the roll-up transaction:

(1) Describe in reasonable detail the method used to allocate interests in the successor to the general partner or to determine the amount of consideration payable to the general partner and the reasons such method(s) was used; and

(2) Identify the consideration paid by the general partner for interests in the partnerships that will be exchanged in the roll-up transaction.

Item 907. Background of the roll-up transaction

(a)(1) Furnish a summary of the background of the transaction. Such summary shall include, but not be limited to, a description of any contacts, negotiations or transactions concerning any of the following matters:

(i) A merger, consolidation, or combination of any of the partnerships;

(ii) An acquisition of any of the partnerships or a material amount of any of their assets;

(iii) A tender offer for or other acquisition of securities of any class issued by any of the partnerships; or

(iv) A change in control of any of the partnerships.

(2) The summary required by paragraph (a)(1) of this Item shall:

(i) Cover the period beginning with each partnership's second full fiscal year preceding the date of the filing of the roll-up transaction;

(ii) Include contacts, negotiations or transactions between the general partner or its affiliates and any person who would have a direct interest in the matters listed in paragraph (a)(1)(i)–(iv) of this Item; and

(iii) Identify the person who initiated such contacts, negotiations or transactions.

(b) Briefly describe the background of each partnership, including, but not limited to:

(1) The amount of capital raised from investors, the extent to which net proceeds from the original offering of interests have been invested, the extent to which funds have been invested as planned and the amount not yet invested; and

(2) The partnership's investment objectives and the extent to which the partnership has achieved its investment objectives.

(c) Discuss whether the general partner (including any affiliated person materially dependent on the general partner's compensation arrangement with the partnership) or any partnership has experienced since the commencement of the most recently completed fiscal year or is likely to experience any material adverse financial developments. If so, describe such developments and the effect of the transaction on such matters.

Item 908. Reasons for and alternatives to the roll–up transaction

(a) Describe the reason(s) for the roll-up transaction.

(b)(1) If the general partner or sponsor considered alternatives to the roll-up transaction being proposed, describe such alternative(s) and state the reason(s) for their rejection.

(2) Whether or not described in response to paragraph (b)(1) of this Item, describe in reasonable detail the potential alternative of continuation of the partnerships in accordance with their existing business plans, including the effects of such continuation and the material risks and benefits that likely would arise in connection therewith, and, if applicable, the general partner's reasons for not considering such alternative.

(3) Whether or not described in response to paragraph (b)(1) of this Item, describe in reasonable detail the potential alternative of liquidation of the partnerships, the procedures required to accomplish liquidation, the effects of liquidation, the material risks and benefits that likely would arise in connection with liquidation, and, if applicable, the general partner's reasons for not considering such alternative.

(c) State the reasons for the structure of the roll-up transaction and for undertaking such transaction at this time.

(d) State whether the general partner initiated the roll-up transaction and, if not, whether the general partner participated in the structuring of the transaction.

(e) State whether the general partner recommends the roll-up transaction and briefly describe the reasons for such recommendation.

Item 909. Conflicts of interest

(a) Briefly describe the general partner's fiduciary duties to each partnership subject to the roll-up transaction and each actual or potential material conflict of interest between the general partner and the investors relating to the roll-up transaction.

(b)(1) State whether or not the general partner has retained an unaffiliated representative to act on behalf of investors for purposes of negotiating the terms of the roll-up transaction. If no such representative has been retained, describe the reasons therefor and the risks arising from the absence of separate representation.

(2) If an unaffiliated representative has been retained to represent investors:

(i) Identify such unaffiliated representative;

(ii) Briefly describe the representative's qualifications, including a brief description of any other transaction similar to the roll-up transaction in which the representative has served in a similar capacity within the past five years;

(iii) Describe the method of selection of such representative, including a statement as to whether or not any investors were consulted in the selection of the representative and, if so, the names of such investors;

(iv) Describe the scope and terms of the engagement of the representative, including, but not limited to, what party will be responsible for paying the representative's fees and whether such fees are contingent upon the outcome of the roll-up transaction;

(v) Describe any material relationship between the representative or its affiliates and:

(A) The general partner, sponsor, any affiliate of the general partner or sponsor; or

(B) Any other person having a material interest in the roll-up transaction,

which existed during the past two years or is mutually understood to be contemplated and any compensation received or to be received as a result of such relationship;

(vi) Describe in reasonable detail the actions taken by the representative on behalf of investors; and

(vii) Describe the fiduciary duties or other legal obligations of the representative to investors in each of the partnerships.

Item 910. Fairness of the transaction

(a) State whether the general partner reasonably believes that the roll-up transaction is fair or unfair to investors and the reasons for such belief. Such discussion must address the fairness of the roll-up transaction to investors in each of the partnerships and as a whole. If the roll-up transaction may be completed with a combination of partnerships consisting of less than all partnerships, or with portions of partnerships, the belief stated must address each possible combination.

(b) Discuss in reasonable detail the material factors upon which the belief stated in paragraph (a) of this Item is based and, to the extent practicable, the weight assigned to each such factor. Such discussion should include an analysis of the extent, if any, to which such belief is based on the factors set forth in Instructions (2) and (3) to this Item, paragraph (b)(1) of Item 909 of this subpart (Item 909(b)(1) of Regulation S–K) and Item 911 of this subpart (Item 911 of Regulation S–K). This discussion also must:

(1) Compare the value of the consideration to be received in the roll-up transaction to the value of the consideration that would be received pursuant to each of the alternatives discussed in response to Item 908(b) of this subpart (Item 908(b) of Regulation S–K); and

(2) Describe any material differences among the partnerships (e.g., different types of assets or different investment objectives) relating to the fairness of the transaction.

(c) If any offer of the type described in Instruction (2)(viii) to this Item has been received, describe such offer and state the reason(s) for its rejection.

(d) Describe any factors known to the general partner that may affect materially the value of the consideration to be received by investors in the roll-up transaction, the values assigned to the partnerships for purposes of the comparisons to alternatives required by paragraph (b) of this Item and the fairness of the transaction to investors.

(e) State whether the general partner's statements in response to paragraphs (a) and (b) of this Item are based, in whole or in part, on any report, opinion or appraisal described in response to Item 911 of this subpart (Item 911 of Regulation S–K). If so, describe any material uncertainties known to the general partner that relate to the conclusions in any such report, opinion or appraisal including, but not limited to, developments or trends that have affected or are reasonably likely to affect materially such conclusions.

Instructions to Item 910:

(1) A statement that the general partner has no reasonable belief as to the fairness of the roll-up transaction to investors will not be considered sufficient disclosure in response to paragraph (a) of this Item.

(2) The factors which are important in determining the fairness of a roll-up transaction to investors and the weight, if any, which should be given to them in a particular context will vary. Normally such factors will include, among others, those referred to in paragraph (b)(1) of Item 909 and whether the consideration offered to investors constitutes fair value in relation to:

(i) Current market prices, if any;

(ii) Historic market prices, if any;

(iii) Net book value;

(iv) Going concern value;

(v) Liquidation value;

(vi) Purchases of limited partnership interests by the general partner or sponsor or their affiliates since the commencement of the partnership's second full fiscal year preceding the date of filing of the disclosure document for the roll-up transaction;

(vii) Any report, opinion, or appraisal described in Item 911 of this subpart (Item 911 of Regulation S–K); and

(viii) Offers of which the general partner or sponsor is aware made during the preceding eighteen months for a merger, consolidation, or combination of any of the partnerships; an acquisition of any of the partnerships or a material amount of their assets; a tender offer for or other acquisition of securities of any class issued by any of the partnerships; or a change in control of any of the partnerships.

(3) The discussion concerning fairness should specifically address material terms of the transaction including whether the consideration offered to investors constitutes fair value in relation to:

(i) The form and amount of consideration to be received by investors and the sponsor in the roll-up transaction;

(ii) The methods used to determine such consideration; and

(iii) The compensation to be paid to the sponsor in the future.

(4) Conclusory statements, such as "The roll-up transaction is fair to investors in relation to net book value, going concern value, liquidation value and future prospects of the partnership," will not be considered sufficient disclosure in response to paragraph (b) of this Item.

(5) Consideration should be given to presenting the comparative numerical data as to the value of the consideration being received by investors, liquidation value and other values in a tabular format. Financial and other information concerning the partnerships should be prepared based upon the most recent available information, such as, in the case of financial information, the periods covered by interim selected financial information included in the prospectus in accordance with Item 914 of this subpart (Item 914 of Regulation S–K).

Item 911. Reports, opinions and appraisals

(a)(1) *All Material Reports, Opinions or Appraisals.* State whether or not the general partner or sponsor has received any report, opinion (other than an opinion of counsel) or appraisal from an outside party which is materially related to the roll-up transaction including, but not limited to, any such report, opinion or appraisal relating to the consideration or the fairness of the consideration to be offered to investors in connection with the roll-up transaction or the fairness of such transaction to the general partner or investors.

(2) With respect to any report, opinion or appraisal described in paragraph (a)(1) of this Item;

(i) Identify such outside party;

(ii) Briefly describe the qualifications of such outside party;

(iii) Describe the method of selection of such outside party;

(iv) Describe any material relationship between:

(A) The outside party or its affiliates; and

(B) The general partner, sponsor, the successor or any of their affiliates, which existed during the past two years or is mutually understood to be contemplated and any compensation received or to be received as a result of such relationship;

(v) If such report, opinion or appraisal relates to the fairness of the consideration, state whether the general partner, sponsor or affiliate determined the amount of consideration to be paid or whether the outside party recommended the amount of consideration to be paid.

(vi) Furnish a summary concerning such report, opinion or appraisal which shall include, but not be limited to, the procedures followed; the findings and recommendations; the bases for and methods of arriving at such findings and recommendations; instructions received from the general partner, sponsor or its affiliates; and any limitation imposed by the general partner, sponsor or affiliate on the scope of the investigation. If any limitation was imposed by the general partner, sponsor or affiliate on the scope of the investigation, including, but not limited to, access to its personnel, premises, and relevant books and records, state the reasons therefor.

(vii) State whether any compensation paid to such outside party is contingent on the approval or completion of the roll-up transaction and, if so, the reasons for compensating such parties on a contingent basis.

(3) Furnish a statement to the effect that upon written request by an investor or his representative who has been so designated in writing, a copy of any such report, opinion or appraisal shall be transmitted promptly, without charge, by the general partner or sponsor. The statement also must include the name and address of the person to whom investors or their representatives should make their request.

(4) All reports, opinions or appraisals referred to in paragraph (a)(1) of this Item shall be filed as exhibits to the registration statement.

(5)(i) Describe any contacts in connection with the roll-up transaction between the sponsor or the general partner and any outside party with respect to the preparation by such party of an opinion concerning the fairness of the roll-up transaction, a valuation of a partnership or its assets, or any other report with respect to the roll-up transaction. No description is required, however, of contacts with respect to reports, opinions or appraisals filed as exhibits pursuant to paragraph (a)(4) of this Item.

(ii) The description of contacts with any outside party required by paragraph (a)(5)(i) of this Item shall include the following:

(A) The identity of each such party;

(B) The nature of the contact;

(C) The actions taken by such party;

(D) Any views, preliminary or final, expressed on the proposed subject matter of the report, opinion or appraisal; and

(E) Any reasons such party did not provide a report, opinion or appraisal.

(b) *Fairness Opinions*: (1) If any report, opinion or appraisal relates to the fairness of the roll-up transaction to investors in the partnerships, state whether or not the report, opinion or appraisal addresses the fairness of:

(i) The roll-up transaction as a whole and to investors in each partnership; and

(ii) All possible combinations of partnerships in the roll-up transaction (including portions of partnerships if the transaction is structured to permit portions of partnerships to participate). If all possible combinations are not addressed:

(A) Identify the combinations that are addressed;

(B) Identify the person(s) that determined which combinations would be addressed and state the reasons for the selection of the combinations; and

(C) State that if the roll-up transaction is completed with a combination of partnerships not addressed, no report, opinion or appraisal concerning the fairness of the roll-up transaction will have been obtained.

(2) If the sponsor or the general partner has not obtained any opinion on the fairness of the proposed roll-up transaction to investors in each of the affected partnerships, state the sponsor's or general partner's reasons for concluding that such an opinion is not necessary in order to permit the limited partners or shareholders to make an informed decision on the proposed transaction.

(c) *Appraisals.* If the report, opinion or appraisal consists of an appraisal of the assets of the partnerships:

(1) Describe the purpose(s) for which the appraisals were obtained and their use in connection with the roll-up transaction;

(2) Describe which assets are covered by the appraisals and state the aggregate appraised value of the assets covered by the appraisals (including such value net of associated indebtedness). Provide a description of, and valuation of, any assets subject to any material qualifications by the appraiser and a summary of such qualifications;

(3) Identify the date as of which the appraisals were prepared. State whether and in what circumstances the appraisals will be updated. State whether any events have occurred or conditions have changed since the date of the appraisals that may have caused a material change in the value of the assets;

(4) Include as an appendix to the prospectus one or more tables setting forth the following information:

(i) The appraised value of any separately appraised asset that is significant to the partnership holding such asset;

(ii) If the appraiser considered different valuation approaches in preparing the appraisals of the assets identified in response to paragraph (c)(4)(i) of this Item, the value of each such asset under each valuation approach considered by the appraiser, identifying the valuation approach used by the appraiser in determining the appraised value and the reason such approach was chosen; and

(iii) All material assumptions used by the appraiser in appraising the assets identified in response to paragraph (c)(4)(i) of this Item, and, if the appraiser used different assumptions for any of such assets, the reasons the different assumptions were chosen.

(5) For purposes of this Item and Item 902 of this subpart (Item 902 of Regulation S–K), an asset is "significant" to a partnership if it represents more than 10% of the value of the partnership's assets as of the end of the most recently-completed fiscal year or recently-completed interim period or if 10% or more of the partnership's cash flow or net income for the most recently-completed fiscal year or most recently-completed subsequent interim period was derived from such asset.

Instructions to Item 911:

(1) The reports, opinions and appraisals required to be identified in response to paragraph (a) of this Item include any reports, opinions and appraisals which materially relate to the roll-up transaction whether or not relied upon, such as reports or opinions regarding alternatives to the roll-up transaction whether or not the alternatives were rejected.

(2) The information called for by paragraph (a)(2) of this Item should be given with respect to the firm which provides the report, opinion or appraisal rather than the employees of such firm who prepared it.

(3) With respect to appraisals, a summary prepared by the appraisers should not be included in lieu of the description of the appraisals required by paragraph (c) of this Item. A clear and concise summary description of the appraisals is required.

Item 912. Source and amount of funds and transactional expenses

(a) State the source and total amount of funds or other consideration to be used in the roll-up transaction.

(b)(1) Furnish a reasonably itemized statement of all expenses incurred or estimated to be incurred in connection with the roll-up transaction including, but not limited to, filing fees, legal, financial advisory, accounting and appraisal fees, solicitation expenses and printing costs. Identify the persons responsible for paying any or all of such expenses.

(2) State whether or not any partnership subject to the roll-up transaction will be, directly or indirectly, responsible for any or all of the expenses of the transaction. If any partnership will be so responsible, state the amount to be provided by each partnership and the sources of capital to finance such amount.

(c) If all or any part of the consideration to be used by the sponsor or successor in the roll-up transaction is expected to be, directly or indirectly, provided by any partnership, state the amount to be provided by each partnership and the sources of capital to finance such amount.

(d) If all or any part of the funds or other consideration is, or is expected to be, directly or indirectly borrowed by the sponsor or successor for the purpose of the roll-up transaction:

(1) Provide a summary of each such loan agreement containing the identity of the parties, the term, the collateral, the stated and effective interest rates, and other material terms or conditions; and

(2) Briefly describe any plans or arrangements to finance or repay such borrowing, or, if no plans or arrangements have been made, make a statement to that effect.

(e) If the source of all or any part of the funds to be used in the roll-up transaction is a loan made in the ordinary course of business by a bank as defined by section 3(a)(6) of the Securities Exchange Act of 1934 and section 13(d) or 14(d) is applicable to such transaction, the name of such bank shall not be made available to the public if the person filing the statement so requests in writing and files such request, naming such bank, with the Secretary of the Commission.

Item 913. Other provisions of the transaction

(a) State whether or not appraisal rights are provided under applicable state law, under the partnership's governing instruments or will be voluntarily accorded by the successor, the general partner or the sponsor (or any of their affiliates) in connection with the roll-up transaction. If so, summarize such appraisal rights. If appraisal rights will not be available to investors who object to the transaction, briefly outline the rights which may be available to such investors under such law.

(b) If any provision has been made to allow investors to obtain access to the books and records of the partnership or to obtain counsel or appraisal services at the expense of the successor, the general partner, the partnership, the sponsor (or any of their affiliates), describe such provision.

(c) Discuss the investors' rights under federal and state law to obtain a partnership's list of investors.

Item 914. Pro forma financial statements: selected financial data

(a) In addition to the information required by Item 301 of Regulation S–K, Selected Financial Data, and Item 302 of Regulation S–K, Supplementary Financial Information, for each partnership proposed to be included in a roll-up transaction provide: Ratio of earnings to fixed charges, cash and cash equivalents, total assets at book value, total assets at the value assigned for purposes of the roll-up transaction (if applicable), total liabilities, general and limited partners' equity, net increase (decrease) in cash and cash equivalents, net cash provided by operating activities, distributions; and per unit data for net income (loss), book value, value assigned for purposes of the roll-up transaction (if applicable), and distributions (separately identifying distributions that represent a return of capital). This information should be provided for the same period(s) for which Selected Financial Data and Supplementary Financial Information are required to be provided. Additional or other information should be provided if material to an understanding of each partnership proposed to be included in a roll-up transaction.

(b) Provide pro forma financial information (including oil and gas reserves and cash flow disclosure, if appropriate), assuming:

(1) All partnerships participate in the roll-up transaction; and

(2) Participation in a roll-up transaction of those partnerships that on a combined basis have the lowest combined net cash provided by operating activities for the last fiscal year of such partnerships, *provided* participation by such partnerships satisfies all conditions to consummation of the roll-up transaction. If the combination of all partnerships proposed to be included in a roll-up transaction results in such lowest combined net cash provided by operating activities, this shall be noted and no separate pro forma financial statements are required.

(c) The pro forma financial statements required by paragraph (b) of this Item shall disclose the effect of the roll-up transaction on the successor's:

(1) Balance sheet as of the later of the end of the most recent fiscal year or the latest interim period;

(2) Statement of income (with separate line items to reflect income (loss) excluding and including the roll-up expenses and payments), earnings per share amounts, and ratio of earnings to fixed

charges for the most recent fiscal year and the latest interim period;

(3) Statement of cash flows for the most recent fiscal year and the latest interim period; and

(4) Book value per share as of the later of the end of the most recent fiscal year or the latest interim period.

Instructions to Item 914:

(1) Notwithstanding the provisions of this Item, any or all of the information required by paragraphs (b) and (c) of this Item that is not material for the exercise of prudent judgment in regard to the matter to be acted upon, may be omitted.

(2) If the roll-up transaction is structured to permit participation by portions of partnerships, consideration should be given to the effect of such participation in preparing the pro forma financial statements reflecting a partial roll-up.

Item 915. Federal income tax consequences

(a) Provide a brief, clear and understandable summary of the material Federal income tax consequences of the roll-up transaction and an investment in the successor. Where a tax opinion has been provided, briefly summarize the substance of such opinion, including identification of the material consequences upon which counsel has not been asked, or is unable, to opine. If any of the material Federal income tax consequences are not expected to be the same for investors in all partnerships, the differences shall be described.

(b) State whether or not the opinion of counsel is included as an appendix to the prospectus. If filed as an exhibit to the registration statement and not included as an appendix to the prospectus, include a statement to the effect that, upon receipt of a written request by an investor or his representative who has been so designated in writing, a copy of the opinion of counsel will be transmitted promptly, without charge, by the general partner or sponsor. The statement should include the name and address of the person to whom investors should make their request.

Subpart 1000—Mergers and Acquisitions (Regulation M–A)

Item 1000. Definitions

The following definitions apply to the terms used in Regulation M–A (Items 1000 through 1016), unless specified otherwise:

(a) *Associate* has the same meaning as in Rule 12b–2 under the Securities Exchange Act of 1934;

(b) *Instruction C* means General Instruction C to Schedule 13E–3 (17 CFR 240.13e–100) and General Instruction C to Schedule TO (17 CFR 240.14d–100);

(c) *Issuer tender offer* has the same meaning as in Rule 13e–4(a)(2) under the Securities Exchange Act of 1934;

(d) *Offeror* means any person who makes a tender offer or on whose behalf a tender offer is made;

(e) *Rule 13e–3* transaction has the same meaning as in Rule 13e–3(a)(3) under the Securities Exchange Act of 1934;

(f) *Subject company* means the company or entity whose securities are sought to be acquired in the transaction (e.g., the target), or that is otherwise the subject of the transaction;

(g) *Subject securities* means the securities or class of securities that are sought to be acquired in the transaction or that are otherwise the subject of the transaction; and

(h) *Third-party tender offer* means a tender offer that is not an issuer tender offer.

Item 1001. Summary term sheet

Summary Term Sheet. Provide security holders with a summary term sheet that is written in plain English. The summary term sheet must briefly describe in bullet point format the most material terms of the proposed transaction. The summary term sheet must provide security holders with sufficient information to understand the essential features and significance of the proposed transaction. The bullet points must cross-reference a more detailed discussion contained in the disclosure document that is disseminated to security holders.

Instructions to Item 1001:

1. The summary term sheet must not recite all information contained in the disclosure document that will be provided to security holders. The summary term sheet is intended to serve as an overview of all material matters that are presented in the accompanying documents provided to security holders.

2. The summary term sheet must begin on the first or second page of the disclosure document provided to security holders.

3. Refer to Rule 421(b) and (d) of Regulation C of the Securities Act (Rule 421) for a description of plain English disclosure.

Item 1002. Subject company information

(a) *Name and Address.* State the name of the subject company (or the issuer in the case of an issuer tender offer), and the address and telephone number of its principal executive offices.

(b) *Securities.* State the exact title and number of shares outstanding of the subject class of equity securities as of the most recent practicable date. This may be based upon information in the most recently available filing with the Commission by the subject company unless the filing person has more current information.

(c) *Trading Market and Price.* Identify the principal market in which the subject securities are traded and state the high and low sales prices for the subject securities in the principal market (or, if there is no principal market, the range of high and low bid quotations and the source of the quotations) for each quarter during the past two years. If there is no established trading market for the securities (except for limited or sporadic quotations), so state.

(d) *Dividends.* State the frequency and amount of any dividends paid during the past two years with respect to the subject securities. Briefly describe any restriction on the subject company's current or future ability to pay dividends. If the filing person is not the subject company, furnish this information to the extent known after making reasonable inquiry.

(e) *Prior Public Offerings.* If the filing person has made an underwritten public offering of the subject securities for cash during the past three years that was registered under the Securities Act of 1933 or exempt from registration under Regulation A (Rule 251 through Rule 263), state the date of the offering, the amount of securities offered, the offering price per share (adjusted for stock splits, stock dividends, etc. as appropriate) and the aggregate proceeds received by the filing person.

(f) *Prior Stock Purchases.* If the filing person purchased any subject securities during the past two years, state the amount of the securities purchased, the range of prices paid and the average purchase price for each quarter during that period. Affiliates need not give information for purchases made before becoming an affiliate.

Item 1003. Identity and background of filing person

(a) *Name and Address.* State the name, business address and business telephone number of each filing person. Also state the name and address of each person specified in Instruction C to the schedule (except for Schedule 14D–9 (17 CFR 240.14d–101)). If the filing person is an affiliate of the subject company, state the nature of the affiliation. If the filing person is the subject company, so state.

(b) *Business and Background of Entities.* If any filing person (other than the subject company) or any person specified in Instruction C to the schedule is not a natural person, state the person's principal business, state or other place of organization, and the information required by paragraphs (c)(3) and (c)(4) of this item for each person.

(c) *Business and Background of Natural Persons.* If any filing person or any person specified in Instruction C to the schedule is a natural person, provide the following information for each person:

(1) Current principal occupation or employment and the name, principal business and address of any corporation or other organization in which the employment or occupation is conducted;

(2) Material occupations, positions, offices or employment during the past five years, giving the starting and ending dates of each and the name, principal business and address of any corporation or other organization in which the occupation, position, office or employment was carried on;

(3) A statement whether or not the person was convicted in a criminal proceeding during the past five years (excluding traffic violations or similar misdemeanors). If the person was convicted, describe the criminal proceeding, including the dates, nature of conviction, name and location of court, and penalty imposed or other disposition of the case;

(4) A statement whether or not the person was a party to any judicial or administrative proceeding during the past five years (except for matters that were dismissed without sanction or settlement) that resulted in a judgment, decree or final order enjoining the person from future violations of, or prohibiting activities subject to, federal or state securities laws, or a finding of any violation of federal or state securities laws. Describe the proceeding, including a summary of the terms of the judgment, decree or final order; and

(5) Country of citizenship.

(d) *Tender Offer.* Identify the tender offer and the class of securities to which the offer relates, the name of the offeror and its address (which may be based on the offeror's Schedule TO (17 CFR 240.14d–100) filed with the Commission).

Instruction to Item 1003: If the filing person is making information relating to the transaction available on the Internet, state the address where the information can be found.

Item 1004. Terms of the transaction

(a) *Material Terms.* State the material terms of the transaction.

(1) *Tender Offers.* In the case of a tender offer, the information must include:

(i) The total number and class of securities sought in the offer;

(ii) The type and amount of consideration offered to security holders;

(iii) The scheduled expiration date;

(iv) Whether a subsequent offering period will be available, if the transaction is a third-party tender offer;

(v) Whether the offer may be extended, and if so, how it could be extended;

(vi) The dates before and after which security holders may withdraw securities tendered in the offer;

(vii) The procedures for tendering and withdrawing securities;

(viii) The manner in which securities will be accepted for payment;

(ix) If the offer is for less than all securities of a class, the periods for accepting securities on a pro rata basis and the offeror's present intentions in the event that the offer is oversubscribed;

(x) An explanation of any material differences in the rights of security holders as a result of the transaction, if material;

(xi) A brief statement as to the accounting treatment of the transaction, if material; and

(xii) The federal income tax consequences of the transaction, if material.

(2) *Mergers or Similar Transactions.* In the case of a merger or similar transaction, the information must include:

(i) A brief description of the transaction;

(ii) The consideration offered to security holders;

(iii) The reasons for engaging in the transaction;

(iv) The vote required for approval of the transaction;

(v) An explanation of any material differences in the rights of security holders as a result of the transaction, if material;

(vi) A brief statement as to the accounting treatment of the transaction, if material; and

(vii) The federal income tax consequences of the transaction, if material.

Instruction to Item 1004(a): If the consideration offered includes securities exempt from registration under the Securities Act of 1933, provide a description of the securities that complies with Item 202 of Regulation S–K. This description is not required if the issuer of the securities meets the requirements of General Instructions I.A, I.B.1 or I.B.2, as applicable, or I.C. of Form S–3 (17 CFR 239.13) and elects to furnish information by incorporation by reference; only capital stock is to be issued; and securities of the same class are registered under section 12 of the Exchange Act and either are listed for trading or admitted to unlisted trading privileges on a national securities exchange; or are securities for which bid and offer quotations are reported in an automated quotations system operated by a national securities association.

(b) *Purchases.* State whether any securities are to be purchased from any officer, director or affiliate of the subject company and provide the details of each transaction.

(c) *Different Terms.* Describe any term or arrangement in the Rule 13e–3 transaction that treats any subject security holders differently from other subject security holders.

(d) *Appraisal Rights.* State whether or not dissenting security holders are entitled to any appraisal rights. If so, summarize the appraisal rights. If there are no appraisal rights available under state law for security holders who object to the transaction, briefly outline any other rights that may be available to security holders under the law.

(e) *Provisions for Unaffiliated Security Holders.* Describe any provision made by the filing person in connection with the transaction to grant unaffiliated security holders access to the corporate files of the filing person or to obtain counsel or appraisal services at the expense of the filing person. If none, so state.

(f) *Eligibility for Listing or Trading.* If the transaction involves the offer of securities of the filing person in exchange for equity securities held by unaffiliated security holders of the subject company, describe whether or not the filing person will take steps to assure that the securities offered are or will be eligible for trading on an automated quotations system operated by a national securities association.

Item 1005. Past contacts, transactions, negotiations and agreements

(a) *Transactions*. Briefly state the nature and approximate dollar amount of any transaction, other than those described in paragraphs (b) or (c) of this item, that occurred during the past two years, between the filing person (including any person specified in Instruction C of the schedule) and;

(1) The subject company or any of its affiliates that are not natural persons if the aggregate value of the transactions is more than one percent of the subject company's consolidated revenues for:

(i) The fiscal year when the transaction occurred; or

(ii) The past portion of the current fiscal year, if the transaction occurred in the current year; and

Instruction to Item 1005(a)(1): The information required by this Item may be based on information in the subject company's most recent filing with the Commission, unless the filing person has reason to believe the information is not accurate.

(2) Any executive officer, director or affiliate of the subject company that is a natural person if the aggregate value of the transaction or series of similar transactions with that person exceeds $60,000.

(b) *Significant Corporate Events*. Describe any negotiations, transactions or material contacts during the past two years between the filing person (including subsidiaries of the filing person and any person specified in Instruction C of the schedule) and the subject company or its affiliates concerning any:

(1) Merger;

(2) Consolidation;

(3) Acquisition;

(4) Tender offer for or other acquisition of any class of the subject company's securities;

(5) Election of the subject company's directors; or

(6) Sale or other transfer of a material amount of assets of the subject company.

(c) *Negotiations or Contacts*. Describe any negotiations or material contacts concerning the matters referred to in paragraph (b) of this item during the past two years between:

(1) Any affiliates of the subject company; or

(2) The subject company or any of its affiliates and any person not affiliated with the subject company who would have a direct interest in such matters.

Instruction to Paragraphs (b) and (c) of Item 1005: Identify the person who initiated the contacts or negotiations.

(d) *Conflicts of Interest*. If material, describe any agreement, arrangement or understanding and any actual or potential conflict of interest between the filing person or its affiliates and:

(1) The subject company, its executive officers, directors or affiliates; or

(2) The offeror, its executive officers, directors or affiliates.

Instruction to Item 1005(d): If the filing person is the subject company, no disclosure called for by this paragraph is required in the document disseminated to security holders, so long as substantially the same information was filed with the Commission previously and disclosed in a proxy statement, report or other communication sent to security holders by the subject company in the past year. The document disseminated to security holders, however, must refer specifically to the discussion in the proxy statement, report or other communication that was sent to security holders previously. The information also must be filed as an exhibit to the schedule.

(e) *Agreements Involving the Subject Company's Securities*. Describe any agreement, arrangement, or understanding, whether or not legally enforceable, between the filing person (including any person specified in Instruction C of the schedule) and any other person with respect to any securities of the subject company. Name all persons that are a party to the agreements, arrangements, or understandings and describe all material provisions.

Instructions to Item 1005(e):

1. The information required by this Item includes: the transfer or voting of securities, joint ventures, loan or option arrangements, puts or calls, guarantees of loans, guarantees against loss, or the giving or withholding of proxies, consents or authorizations.

2. Include information for any securities that are pledged or otherwise subject to a contingency, the occurrence of which would give another person the power to direct the voting or disposition of the subject securities. No disclosure, however, is required about standard default and similar provisions contained in loan agreements.

Item 1006. Purposes of the transaction and plans or proposals

(a) *Purposes*. State the purposes of the transaction.

(b) *Use of Securities Acquired*. Indicate whether the securities acquired in the transaction will be retained, retired, held in treasury, or otherwise disposed of.

(c) *Plans*. Describe any plans, proposals or negotiations that relate to or would result in:

(1) Any extraordinary transaction, such as a merger, reorganization or liquidation, involving the subject company or any of its subsidiaries;

(2) Any purchase, sale or transfer of a material amount of assets of the subject company or any of its subsidiaries;

(3) Any material change in the present dividend rate or policy, or indebtedness or capitalization of the subject company;

(4) Any change in the present board of directors or management of the subject company, including, but not limited to, any plans or proposals to change the number or the term of directors or to fill any existing vacancies on the board or to change any material term of the employment contract of any executive officer;

(5) Any other material change in the subject company's corporate structure or business, including, if the subject company is a registered closed-end investment company, any plans or proposals to make any changes in its investment policy for which a vote would be required by Section 13 of the Investment Company Act of 1940 (15 U.S.C. 80a–13);

(6) Any class of equity securities of the subject company to be delisted from a national securities exchange or cease to be authorized to be quoted in an automated quotations system operated by a national securities association;

(7) Any class of equity securities of the subject company becoming eligible for termination of registration under section 12(g)(4) of the Act (15 U.S.C. 78*l*);

(8) The suspension of the subject company's obligation to file reports under Section 15(d) of the Act (15 U.S.C. 78*o*);

(9) The acquisition by any person of additional securities of the subject company, or the disposition of securities of the subject company; or

(10) Any changes in the subject company's charter, bylaws or other governing instruments or other actions that could impede the acquisition of control of the subject company.

(d) *Subject Company Negotiations*. If the filing person is the subject company:

(1) State whether or not that person is undertaking or engaged in any negotiations in response to the tender offer that relate to:

(i) A tender offer or other acquisition of the subject company's securities by the filing person, any of its subsidiaries, or any other person; or

(ii) Any of the matters referred to in paragraphs (c)(1) through (c)(3) of this item; and

(2) Describe any transaction, board resolution, agreement in principle, or signed contract that is entered into in response to the tender offer that relates to one or more of the matters referred to in paragraph (d)(1) of this item.

Instruction to Item 1006(d)(1): If an agreement in principle has not been reached at the time of filing, no disclosure under paragraph (d)(1) of this item is required of the possible terms of or the parties to the transaction if in the opinion of the board of directors of the subject company disclosure would jeopardize continuation of the negotiations. In that case, disclosure indicating that negotiations are being undertaken or are underway and are in the preliminary stages is sufficient.

Item 1007. Source and amount of funds or other consideration

(a) *Source of Funds*. State the specific sources and total amount of funds or other consideration to be used in the transaction. If the transaction involves a tender offer, disclose the amount of funds or other consideration required to purchase the maximum amount of securities sought in the offer.

(b) *Conditions*. State any material conditions to the financing discussed in response to paragraph (a) of this item. Disclose any alternative financing arrangements or alternative financing plans in the event the primary financing plans fall through. If none, so state.

(c) *Expenses*. Furnish a reasonably itemized statement of all expenses incurred or estimated to be incurred in connection with the transaction including, but not limited to, filing, legal, accounting and appraisal fees, solicitation expenses and printing costs and state whether or not the subject company has paid or will be responsible for paying any or all expenses.

(d) *Borrowed Funds*. If all or any part of the funds or other consideration required is, or is expected, to be borrowed, directly or indirectly, for the purpose of the transaction:

(1) Provide a summary of each loan agreement or arrangement containing the identity of the parties, the term, the collateral, the stated and effective interest rates, and any other material terms or conditions of the loan; and

(2) Briefly describe any plans or arrangements to finance or repay the loan, or, if no plans or arrangements have been made, so state.

Instruction to Item 1007(d): If the transaction is a third-party tender offer and the source of all or any part of the funds used in the transaction is to come from a loan made in the ordinary course of business by a bank as defined by section 3(a)(6) of the Act (15 U.S.C. 78c), the name of the bank will not be made available to the public if the filing person so requests in writing and files the request, naming the bank, with the Secretary of the Commission.

Item 1008. Interest in securities of the subject company

(a) *Securities Ownership*. State the aggregate number and percentage of subject securities that are beneficially owned by each person named in response to Item 1003 of Regulation M–A and by each associate and majority-owned subsidiary of those persons. Give the name and address of any associate or subsidiary.

Instructions to Item 1008(a):

1. For purposes of this section, beneficial ownership is determined in accordance with Rule 13d–3 under the Securities Exchange Act of 1934. Identify the shares that the person has a right to acquire.

2. The information required by this section may be based on the number of outstanding securities disclosed in the subject company's most recently available filing with the Commission, unless the filing person has more current information.

3. The information required by this section with respect to officers, directors and associates of the subject company must be given to the extent known after making reasonable inquiry.

(b) *Securities Transactions*. Describe any transaction in the subject securities during the past 60 days. The description of transactions required must include, but not necessarily be limited to:

(1) The identity of the persons specified in the Instruction to this section who effected the transaction;

(2) The date of the transaction;

(3) The amount of securities involved;

(4) The price per share; and

(5) Where and how the transaction was effected.

Instructions to Item 1008(b):

1. Provide the required transaction information for the following persons:

(a) The filing person (for all schedules);

(b) Any person named in Instruction C of the schedule and any associate or majority-owned subsidiary of the issuer or filing person (for all schedules except Schedule 14D–9 (17 CFR 240.14d–101));

(c) Any executive officer, director, affiliate or subsidiary of the filing person (for Schedule 14D–9 (17 CFR 240.14d–101));

(d) The issuer and any executive officer or director of any subsidiary of the issuer or filing person (for an issuer tender offer on Schedule TO (17 CFR 240.14d–100)); and

(e) The issuer and any pension, profit-sharing or similar plan of the issuer or affiliate filing the schedule (for a going-private transaction on Schedule 13E–3 (17 CFR 240.13e–100)).

2. Provide the information required by this Item if it is available to the filing person at the time the statement is initially filed with the Commission. If the information is not initially available, it must be obtained and filed with the Commission promptly, but in no event later than three business days after the date of the initial filing, and if material, disclosed in a manner reasonably designed to inform security holders. The procedure specified by this instruction is provided to maintain the confidentiality of information in order to avoid possible misuse of inside information.

Item 1009. Persons/assets, retained, employed, compensated or used

(a) *Solicitations or Recommendations*. Identify all persons and classes of persons that are directly or indirectly employed, retained, or to be compensated to make solicitations or recommendations in connection with the transaction. Provide a summary of all material terms of employment, retainer or other arrangement for compensation.

(b) *Employees and Corporate Assets*. Identify any officer, class of employees or corporate assets of the subject company that has been or will be employed or used by the filing person in connection with the transaction. Describe the purpose for their employment or use.

Instruction to Item 1009(b): Provide all information required by this item except for the information required by paragraph (a) of this item and Item 1007 of Regulation M–A.

Item 1010. Financial statements

(a) *Financial Information*. Furnish the following financial information:

(1) Audited financial statements for the two fiscal years required to be filed with the company's most recent annual report under sections 13 and 15(d) of the Securities Exchange Act of 1934 (15 U.S.C. 78m; 15 U.S.C. 78*o*);

(2) Unaudited balance sheets, comparative year-to-date statements of comprehensive income (as defined in Rule 1–02 of Regulation S–X of this chapter) and related earnings per share data and statements of cash flows required to be included in the company's most recent quarterly report filed under the Exchange Act; and

(3) [Reserved]

(4) Book value per share as of the date of the most recent balance sheet presented.

(b) *Pro Forma Information*. If material, furnish pro forma information disclosing the effect of the transaction on:

(1) The company's balance sheet as of the date of the most recent balance sheet presented under paragraph (a) of this item;

(2) The company's statement of comprehensive income and earnings per share for the most recent fiscal year and the latest interim period provided under paragraph (a)(2) of this section; and

(3) The company's book value per share as of the date of the most recent balance sheet presented under paragraph (a) of this item.

(c) *Summary Information*. Furnish a fair and adequate summary of the information specified in paragraphs (a) and (b) of this item for the same periods specified. A fair and adequate summary includes:

(1) The summarized financial information specified in Rule 1–02(bb)(1) of Regulation S–X;

(2) Income per common share from continuing operations (basic and diluted, if applicable);

(3) Net income per common share (basic and diluted, if applicable);

(4) [Reserved];

(5) Book value per share as of the date of the most recent balance sheet; and

(6) If material, pro forma data for the summarized financial information specified in paragraphs (c)(1) through (c)(5) of this item disclosing the effect of the transaction.

Item 1011. Additional information

(a) *Agreements, Regulatory Requirements and Legal Proceedings*. If material to a security holder's decision whether to sell, tender or hold the securities sought in the tender offer, furnish the following information:

(1) Any present or proposed material agreement, arrangement, understanding or relationship between the offeror or any of its executive officers, directors, controlling persons or subsidiaries and the subject company or any of its executive officers, directors, controlling persons or subsidiaries (other than any agreement, arrangement or understanding disclosed under any other sections of Regulation M–A (Items 1000 through 1016));

Instruction to Paragraph (a)(1): In an issuer tender offer disclose any material agreement, arrangement, understanding or relationship between the offeror and any of its executive officers, directors, controlling persons or subsidiaries.

(2) To the extent known by the offeror after reasonable investigation, the applicable regulatory requirements which must be complied with or approvals which must be obtained in connection with the tender offer;

(3) The applicability of any anti-trust laws;

(4) The applicability of margin requirements under section 7 of the Act (15 U.S.C. 78g) and the applicable regulations; and

(5) Any material pending legal proceedings relating to the tender offer, including the name and location of the court or agency in which the proceedings are pending, the date instituted, the principal parties, and a brief summary of the proceedings and the relief sought.

Instruction to Item 1011(a)(5): A copy of any document relating to a major development (such as pleadings, an answer, complaint, temporary restraining order, injunction, opinion, judgment or order) in a material pending legal proceeding must be furnished promptly to the Commission staff on a supplemental basis.

(b) Furnish the information required by Item 402(t)(2) and (3) of this part and in the tabular format set forth in Item 402(t)(1) of this part with respect to each named executive officer

(1) Of the subject company in a Rule 13e–3 transaction; or

(2) Of the issuer whose securities are the subject of a third-party tender offer, regarding any agreement or understanding, whether written or unwritten, between such named executive officer and the subject company, issuer, bidder, or the acquiring company, as applicable, concerning any type of compensation, whether present, deferred or contingent, that is based upon or otherwise relates to the Rule 13e–3 transaction or third-party tender offer.

Instructions to Item 1011(b):

1. The obligation to provide the information in paragraph (b) of this section shall not apply where the issuer whose securities are the subject of the Rule 13e-3 transaction or tender offer is a foreign private issuer, as defined in §240.3b-4 of this chapter, or an emerging growth company, as defined in Rule 405 of the Securities Act (§230.405 of this chapter) or Rule 12b-2 of the Exchange Act (§240.12b-2 of this chapter).

2. For purposes of Instruction 1 to Item 402(t)(2) of this part: If the disclosure is included in a Schedule 13E–3 (17 CFR 240.13e–100) or Schedule 14D–9 (17 CFR 14d–101), the disclosure provided by this table shall be quantified assuming that the triggering event took place on the latest practicable date and that the price per share of the securities of the subject company in a Rule 13e–3 transaction,

or of the issuer whose securities are the subject of the third-party tender offer, shall be determined as follows: if the shareholders are to receive a fixed dollar amount, the price per share shall be that fixed dollar amount, and if such value is not a fixed dollar amount, the price per share shall be the average closing market price of such securities over the first five business days following the first public announcement of the transaction. Compute the dollar value of in-the-money option awards for which vesting would be accelerated by determining the difference between this price and the exercise or base price of the options. Include only compensation that is based on or otherwise relates to the subject transaction. Apply Instruction 1 to Item 402(t) with respect to those executive officers for whom disclosure was required in the most recent filing by the subject company in a Rule 13e–3 transaction or by the issuer whose securities are the subject of a third-party tender offer, with the Commission under the Securities Act (15 U.S.C. 77a et seq.) or Exchange Act (15 U.S.C. 78a et seq.) that required disclosure pursuant to Item 402(c).

(c) *Other Material Information.* Furnish such additional material information, if any, as may be necessary to make the required statements, in light of the circumstances under which they are made, not materially misleading.

Item 1012. The solicitation or recommendation

(a) *Solicitation or Recommendation.* State the nature of the solicitation or the recommendation. If this statement relates to a recommendation, state whether the filing person is advising holders of the subject securities to accept or reject the tender offer or to take other action with respect to the tender offer and, if so, describe the other action recommended. If the filing person is the subject company and is not making a recommendation, state whether the subject company is expressing no opinion and is remaining neutral toward the tender offer or is unable to take a position with respect to the tender offer.

(b) *Reasons.* State the reasons for the position (including the inability to take a position) stated in paragraph (a) of this item. Conclusory statements such as "The tender offer is in the best interests of shareholders" are not considered sufficient disclosure.

(c) *Intent to Tender.* To the extent known by the filing person after making reasonable inquiry, state whether the filing person or any executive officer, director, affiliate or subsidiary of the filing person currently intends to tender, sell or hold the subject securities that are held of record or beneficially owned by that person.

(d) *Intent to Tender or Vote in a Going-Private Transaction.* To the extent known by the filing person after making reasonable inquiry, state whether or not any executive officer, director or affiliate of the issuer (or any person specified in Instruction C to the schedule) currently intends to tender or sell subject securities owned or held by that person and/or how each person currently intends to vote subject securities, including any securities the person has proxy authority for. State the reasons for the intended action.

Instruction to Item 1012(d): Provide the information required by this section if it is available to the filing person at the time the statement is initially filed with the Commission. If the information is not available, it must be filed with the Commission promptly, but in no event later than three business days after the date of the initial filing, and if material, disclosed in a manner reasonably designed to inform security holders.

(e) *Recommendations of Others.* To the extent known by the filing person after making reasonable inquiry, state whether or not any person specified in paragraph (d) of this item has made a recommendation either in support of or opposed to the transaction and the reasons for the recommendation.

Item 1013. Purposes, alternatives, reasons and effects in a going-private transaction

(a) *Purposes.* State the purposes for the Rule 13e–3 transaction.

(b) *Alternatives.* If the subject company or affiliate considered alternative means to accomplish the stated purposes, briefly describe the alternatives and state the reasons for their rejection.

(c) *Reasons.* State the reasons for the structure of the Rule 13e–3 transaction and for undertaking the transaction at this time.

(d) *Effects.* Describe the effects of the Rule 13e–3 transaction on the subject company, its affiliates and unaffiliated security holders, including the federal tax consequences of the transaction.

Instructions to Item 1013:

1. Conclusory statements will not be considered sufficient disclosure in response to this item.
2. The description required by paragraph (d) of this item must include a reasonably detailed discussion of both the benefits and detriments of the Rule 13e–3 transaction to the subject company, its affiliates and unaffiliated security holders. The benefits and detriments of the Rule 13e–3 transaction must be quantified to the extent practicable.
3. If this statement is filed by an affiliate of the subject company, the description required by paragraph (d) of this item must include, but not be limited to, the effect of the Rule 13e–3 transaction on the affiliate's interest in the net book value and net earnings of the subject company in terms of both dollar amounts and percentages.

Item 1014. Fairness of the going-private transaction

(a) *Fairness.* State whether the subject company or affiliate filing the statement reasonably believes that the Rule 13e–3 transaction is fair or unfair to unaffiliated security holders. If any director dissented to or abstained from voting on the Rule 13e–3 transaction, identify the director, and indicate, if known, after making reasonable inquiry, the reasons for the dissent or abstention.

(b) *Factors Considered in Determining Fairness.* Discuss in reasonable detail the material factors upon which the belief stated in paragraph (a) of this item is based and, to the extent practicable, the weight assigned to each factor. The discussion must include an analysis of the extent, if any, to which the filing person's beliefs are based on the factors described in Instruction 2 of this item, paragraphs (c), (d) and (e) of this item and Item 1015 of Regulation M–A.

(c) *Approval of Security Holders.* State whether or not the transaction is structured so that approval of at least a majority of unaffiliated security holders is required.

(d) *Unaffiliated Representative.* State whether or not a majority of directors who are not employees of the subject company has retained an unaffiliated representative to act solely on behalf of unaffiliated security holders for purposes of negotiating the terms of the Rule 13e–3 transaction and/or preparing a report concerning the fairness of the transaction.

(e) *Approval of Directors.* State whether or not the Rule 13e–3 transaction was approved by a majority of the directors of the subject company who are not employees of the subject company.

(f) *Other Offers.* If any offer of the type described in paragraph (viii) of Instruction 2 to this item has been received, describe the offer and state the reasons for its rejection.

Instructions to Item 1014:

1. A statement that the issuer or affiliate has no reasonable belief as to the fairness of the Rule 13e–3 transaction to unaffiliated security holders will not be considered sufficient disclosure in response to paragraph (a) of this item.

2. The factors that are important in determining the fairness of a transaction to unaffiliated security holders and the weight, if any, that should be given to them in a particular context will vary. Normally such factors will include, among others, those referred to in paragraphs (c), (d) and (e) of this item and whether the consideration offered to unaffiliated security holders constitutes fair value in relation to:

(i) Current market prices;

(ii) Historical market prices;

(iii) Net book value;

(iv) Going concern value;

(v) Liquidation value;

(vi) Purchase prices paid in previous purchases disclosed in response to Item 1002(f) of Regulation M–A;

(vii) Any report, opinion, or appraisal described in Item 1015 of Regulation M–A; and

(viii) Firm offers of which the subject company or affiliate is aware made by any unaffiliated person, other than the filing persons, during the past two years for:

(A) The merger or consolidation of the subject company with or into another company, or vice versa;

(B) The sale or other transfer of all or any substantial part of the assets of the subject company; or

(C) A purchase of the subject company's securities that would enable the holder to exercise control of the subject company.

3. Conclusory statements, such as "The Rule 13e–3 transaction is fair to unaffiliated security holders in relation to net book value, going concern value and future prospects of the issuer" will not be considered sufficient disclosure in response to paragraph (b) of this item.

Item 1015. Reports, opinions, appraisals and negotiations

(a) *Report, Opinion or Appraisal.* State whether or not the subject company or affiliate has received any report, opinion (other than an opinion of counsel) or appraisal from an outside party that is materially related to the Rule 13e–3 transaction, including, but not limited to: Any report, opinion or appraisal relating to the consideration or the fairness of the consideration to be offered to security holders or the fairness of the transaction to the issuer or affiliate or to security holders who are not affiliates.

(b) *Preparer and Summary of the Report, Opinion or Appraisal.* For each report, opinion or appraisal described in response to paragraph (a) of this section or any negotiation or report described in response to Item 1014(d) of Regulation M–A or Item 14(b)(6) of Schedule 14A concerning the terms of the transaction:

(1) Identify the outside party and/or unaffiliated representative;

(2) Briefly describe the qualifications of the outside party and/or unaffiliated representative;

(3) Describe the method of selection of the outside party and/or unaffiliated representative;

(4) Describe any material relationship that existed during the past two years or is mutually understood to be contemplated and any compensation received or to be received as a result of the relationship between:

(i) The outside party, its affiliates, and/or unaffiliated representative; and

(ii) The subject company or its affiliates;

(5) If the report, opinion or appraisal relates to the fairness of the consideration, state whether the subject company or affiliate determined the amount of consideration to be paid or whether the outside party recommended the amount of consideration to be paid; and

(6) Furnish a summary concerning the negotiation, report, opinion or appraisal. The summary must include, but need not be limited to, the procedures followed; the findings and recommendations; the bases for and methods of arriving at such findings and recommendations; instructions received from the subject company or affiliate; and any limitation imposed by the subject company or affiliate on the scope of the investigation.

Instruction to Item 1015(b): The information called for by paragraphs (b)(1), (2) and (3) of this item must be given with respect to the firm that provides the report, opinion or appraisal rather than the employees of the firm that prepared the report.

(c) *Availability of Documents*. Furnish a statement to the effect that the report, opinion or appraisal will be made available for inspection and copying at the principal executive offices of the subject company or affiliate during its regular business hours by any interested equity security holder of the subject company or representative who has been so designated in writing. This statement also may provide that a copy of the report, opinion or appraisal will be transmitted by the subject company or affiliate to any interested equity security holder of the subject company or representative who has been so designated in writing upon written request and at the expense of the requesting security holder.

Item 1016. Exhibits

File as an exhibit to the schedule:

(a) Any disclosure materials furnished to security holders by or on behalf of the filing person, including:

(1) Tender offer materials (including transmittal letter);

(2) Solicitation or recommendation (including those referred to in Item 1012 of Regulation M–A);

(3) Going-private disclosure document;

(4) Prospectus used in connection with an exchange offer where securities are registered under the Securities Act of 1933; and

(5) Any other disclosure materials;

(b) Any loan agreement referred to in response to Item 1007(d) of Regulation M–A;

Instruction to Item 1016(b): If the filing relates to a third-party tender offer and a request is made under Item 1007(d) of Regulation M–A, the identity of the bank providing financing may be omitted from the loan agreement filed as an exhibit.

(c) Any report, opinion or appraisal referred to in response to Item 1014(d) or Item 1015 of Regulation M–A;

(d) Any document setting forth the terms of any agreement, arrangement, understanding or relationship referred to in response to Item 1005(e) or Item 1011(a)(1) of Regulation M–A;

(e) Any agreement, arrangement or understanding referred to in response to Item 1005(d) of Regulation M–A, or the pertinent portions of any proxy statement, report or other communication containing the disclosure required by Item 1005(d) of Regulation M–A;

(f) A detailed statement describing security holders' appraisal rights and the procedures for exercising those appraisal rights referred to in response to Item 1004(d) of Regulation M–A;

(g) Any written instruction, form or other material that is furnished to persons making an oral solicitation or recommendation by or on behalf of the filing person for their use directly or indirectly in connection with the transaction; and

(h) Any written opinion prepared by legal counsel at the filing person's request and communicated to the filing person pertaining to the tax consequences of the transaction.

EXHIBIT TABLE TO ITEM 1016 OF REGULATION M–A

	13E–3	TO	14D–9
Disclosure Material . .	X	X	X
Loan Agreement	X	X	. . . .
Report, Opinion or Appraisal	X	. . . .	. . . .
Contracts, Arrangements or Understandings	X	X	X
Statement re: Appraisal Rights	X	. . . .	. . . .
Oral Solicitation Materials	X	X	X
Tax Opinion	. . . .	X	. . . .

Subpart 1100—Asset–Backed Securities (Regulation AB)

Item 1100. General

(a) *Application of Regulation AB.* Regulation AB (Items 1100 through 1125) is the source of various disclosure items and requirements for "asset-backed securities" filings under the Securities Act of 1933 (15 U.S.C. 77a *et seq.*) (the "Securities Act") and the Securities Exchange Act of 1934 (the "Exchange Act") (15 U.S.C. 78a *et seq.*). Unless otherwise specified, definitions to be used in this Regulation AB, including the definition of "asset-backed security," are set forth in Item 1101.

(b) *Presentation of Historical Delinquency and Loss Information.* Several Items in Regulation AB call for the presentation of historical information and data on delinquencies and loss information. In providing such information:

(1) Present delinquency experience in 30 or 31 day increments, as applicable, beginning at least with assets that are 30 or 31 days delinquent, as applicable, through the point that assets are written off or charged off as uncollectable. At a minimum, present such information by number of accounts and dollar amount. Present statistical information in a tabular or graphical format, if such presentation will aid understanding.

(2) Disclose the total amount of delinquent assets as a percentage of the aggregate asset pool.

(3) Present loss and cumulative loss information, as applicable, regarding charge-offs, charge-off rate, gross losses, recoveries and net losses (with a description of how these terms are defined), the number and amount of assets experiencing a loss and the number and amount of assets with a recovery, the ratio of aggregate net losses to average portfolio balance and the average of net loss on all assets that have experienced a net loss.

(4) Categorize all delinquency and loss information by pool asset type.

(5) In a registration statement under the Securities Act or the Exchange Act or in a prospectus to be filed pursuant to Rule 424, describe how delinquencies, charge-offs and uncollectable accounts are defined or determined, addressing the effect of any grace period, re-aging, restructure, partial payments considered current or other practices on delinquency and loss experience.

(6) Describe any other material information regarding delinquencies and losses particular to the pool asset type(s), such as repossession information, foreclosure information and real estate owned (REO) or similar information.

(c) *Presentation of Certain Third Party Information.* If information of a third party is required in a filing by Item 1112(b) of this Regulation AB (Information regarding significant obligors) (17 CFR 229.1112(b)), Items 1114(b)(2) or 1115(b) of this Regulation AB (Information regarding significant provider of enhancement or other support) (Rule 229.1114(b)(2) or 1115(b)), or Item 1125 of this Regulation AB (Asset-level information) (Rule 229.1125) such information, in lieu of including such information, may be provided as follows:

(1) *Incorporation by Reference.* If the following conditions are met, you may incorporate by reference (by means of a statement to that effect) the reports filed by the third party (or the entity that consolidates the third party) pursuant to section 13(a) or 15(d) of the Exchange Act (15 U.S.C. 78m(a) or 78o(d)):

(i) Such third party or the entity that consolidates the third party is required to file reports with the Commission pursuant to section 13(a) or 15(d) of the Exchange Act.

(ii) Such third party or the entity that consolidates the third party has filed all reports and other materials required to be filed by such requirements during the preceding 12 months (or such shorter period that such party was required to file such reports and materials).

(iii) The reports filed by such third party, or entity that consolidates the third party, include (or properly incorporate by reference) the financial statements of such third party.

(iv) If incorporated by reference into a prospectus or registration statement, the prospectus also states that all documents subsequently filed by such third party, or the entity that consolidates the third party, pursuant to section 13(a) or 15(d) of the Exchange Act prior to the termination of the offering also shall be deemed to be incorporated by reference into the prospectus.

Instructions to Item 1100(c)(1):

1. In addition to the conditions in paragraph (c)(1) of this item, any information incorporated by reference must comply with all applicable Commission rules pertaining to incorporation by reference, such as Item 10(d) of Regulation S–K, Rule 303 of Regulation S–T, Rule 411 of Regulation C, and Rules 12b–23 and 12b–32 under the Exchange Act.

2. In addition, any applicable requirements under the Securities Act or the rules and regulations of the Commission regarding the filing of a written consent for the use of incorporated material apply to the material incorporated by reference. See, for example, Rule 439.

3. Any undertakings set forth in Item 512 of Regulation S–K apply to any material incorporated by reference in a registration statement or prospectus.

4. If neither the third party nor any of its affiliates has had a direct or indirect agreement, arrangement, relationship or understanding, written or otherwise, relating to the ABS transaction, and neither the third party nor any of its affiliates is an affiliate of the sponsor, depositor, issuing entity or underwriter of the ABS transaction, then paragraph (c)(1)(ii) of this item is qualified by the knowledge of the registrant.

5. If you are relying on paragraph (c)(1) of this item to provide information required by Item 1112 of this Regulation AB regarding a significant obligor that is an asset-backed issuer and the pool assets relating to such significant obligor are asset-backed securities, then for purposes of paragraph (c)(1)(iii) of this item, the term "financial statements" means the information required by Instruction 3 of Item 1112 of this Regulation AB. Such information required by Instruction 3.a. of Item 1112 of this Regulation AB may be incorporated by reference from a prospectus that contains such information and is included in an effective Securities Act registration statement or filed pursuant to Rule 424.

(2) *Reference Information for Significant Obligors.* If the third party information relates to a significant obligor and the following conditions are met, you may include a reference to the third party's periodic reports (or the third party's parent with respect to paragraph (c)(2)(ii)(C) of this item) under section 13(a) or 15(d) of the Exchange Act (15 U.S.C. 78m(a) or 78o(d)) that are on file with the Commission (or otherwise publicly available with respect to paragraph (c)(2)(ii)(F) of this item), along with a statement of how those reports may be accessed, including the third party's name and Commission file number, if applicable (See, e.g., Item 1118 of this Regulation AB):

(i) Neither the third party nor any of its affiliates has had a direct or indirect agreement, arrangement, relationship or understanding, written or otherwise, relating to the asset-backed securities transaction, and neither the third party nor any of its affiliates is an affiliate of the sponsor, depositor, issuing entity or underwriter of the asset-backed securities transaction.

(ii) To the knowledge of the registrant, any of the following is true:

(A) The third party is eligible to use Form S–3 or F–3 (17 CFR 239.13 or 239.33) for a primary offering of non-investment grade securities pursuant to General Instruction I.B.1 of such forms.

(B) The third party meets the requirements of General Instruction I.A. of Form S–3 or General Instructions 1.A.1, 2, 3, 4 and 6 of Form F–3 and the pool assets relating to such third party are non-convertible investment grade securities, as described in General Instruction 1.B.2 of Form S–3 or Form F–3.

(C) If the third party does not meet the conditions of paragraph (c)(2)(ii)(A) or (c)(2)(ii)(B) of this item and the pool assets relating to the third party are fully and unconditionally guaranteed by a direct or indirect parent of the third party, General Instruction I.C.3 of Form S–3 or General Instruction I.A.5(iii) of Form F–3 is met with respect to the pool assets relating to such third party and the requirements of Rule 3–10 of Regulation S–X are satisfied regarding the information in the reports to be referenced.

(D) If the pool assets relating to the third party are guaranteed by a wholly owned subsidiary of the third party and the subsidiary does not meet the conditions of paragraph (c)(2)(ii)(A) or (c)(2)(ii)(B) of this item, the criteria in either paragraph (c)(2)(ii)(A) or paragraph (c)(2)(ii)(B) of this item are met with respect to the third party and the requirements of Rule 3–10 of Regulation S–X are satisfied regarding the information in the reports to be referenced.

(E) The pool assets relating to such third party are asset-backed securities and the third party is filing reports pursuant to section 12 or 15(d) of the Exchange Act (15 U.S.C. 78l or 78o(d)) and has filed all the material that would be required to be filed pursuant to section 13, 14 or 15(d) of the Exchange Act (15 U.S.C. 78m, 78n or 78o(d)) for a period of at least twelve calendar months and any portion of a month immediately preceding the filing referencing the third party's reports (or such shorter period that such third party was required to file such materials).

(F) The third party is a U.S. government-sponsored enterprise, has outstanding securities held by non-affiliates with an aggregate market value of $75 million or more, and makes information publicly available on an annual and quarterly basis, including audited financial statements prepared in accordance with generally accepted accounting principles covering the same periods that would be required for audited financial statements under Regulation S–X (Rules 1–01 through 12–29 and non-financial information consistent with that required by Regulation S–K (Items 10 through 1123)).

Instruction to Item 1100(c)(2): If you are relying on paragraph (c)(2)(ii)(E) of this rule because the pool assets relating to such third party are asset-backed securities, then for purposes of a registration statement under the Securities Act or the Exchange Act or a prospectus to be filed pursuant to Rule 424 for your securities, you also must include a reference (including Commission reporting number and filing date) to the prospectus for the third party asset-backed securities that:

(a) Is either included in an effective Securities Act registration statement or filed pursuant to Rule 424 under the Securities Act of 1933; and

(b) Contains the information required by Instruction 3.a. of Item 1112 of this Regulation AB.

(d) *Other Participants to the Transaction and Pool Assets Representing Interests in Certain Other Asset Pools.*

(1) If the asset-backed securities transaction involves additional or intermediate parties not specifically identified in this Regulation AB, the disclosure required by this Regulation AB includes information to the extent material regarding any such party and its role, function and experience in relation to the asset-backed securities and the asset pool. Describe the material terms of any agreement with such party regarding the transaction, and file such agreement as an exhibit.

(2) If the asset pool backing the asset-backed securities includes one or more pool assets representing an interest in or the right to the payments or cash flows of another asset pool, then for purposes of this Regulation AB and Rules 13a–18 and 15d–18 under the Securities Exchange Act of 1934, references to the asset pool and the pool assets of the issuing entity also include the other asset pool and its pool assets if the following conditions are met:

(i) Both the issuing entity for the asset-backed securities and the entity issuing the pool asset to be included in the issuing entity's asset pool were established under the direction of the same sponsor or depositor.

(ii) The pool asset was created solely to satisfy legal requirements or otherwise facilitate the structuring of the asset-backed securities transaction.

Instruction to Item 1100(d)(2): Reference to the underlying asset pool includes, without limitation, compliance with applicable servicing criteria referenced in Rules 13a–18 and 15d–18 under the Securities Exchange Act of 1934 and the servicer compliance statement required by Item 1123 of this Regulation AB. In addition, provide clear and concise disclosure, including by flow chart or other illustration, of the transaction and the various parties involved.

(e) *Foreign Asset–Backed Securities.* If the asset-backed securities are issued by a foreign issuer (as defined in Rule 405), backed by pool assets that are foreign assets, or affected by enhancement or support contemplated by Items 1114 or 1115 of this Regulation AB provided by a foreign entity, then in providing the disclosure required by this Regulation AB (including, but not limited to, Items 1104 and 1110 of this Regulation AB regarding origination and securitization practices, Item 1107 of this Regulation AB regarding the sale or transfer of the pool assets, bankruptcy remoteness and collateral protection, Item 1108 of this Regulation AB regarding servicing, Item 1109 of this Regulation AB regarding the rights, duties and responsibilities of the trustee, Item 1111 of this Regulation AB regarding the terms, nature and treatment of the pool assets and Items 1114 or 1115 of this Regulation AB, as applicable, regarding the enhancement provider), the filing must describe any pertinent governmental, legal or regulatory or administrative matters and any pertinent tax matters, exchange controls, currency restrictions or other economic, fiscal, monetary or potential factors in the applicable home jurisdiction that could materially affect payments on, the performance of, or other matters relating to, the assets contained in the pool or the asset-backed securities. See also Instruction 2 to Item 202 of Regulation S–K. In addition, in a registration statement under the Securities Act, provide the information required by Item 101(g) of Regulation S–K. Disclosure also is required in Forms 10–D (17 CFR 249.312) and 10–K (17 CFR 249.310) with respect to the asset-backed securities regarding any material impact caused by foreign legal and regulatory developments during the period covered by the report which have not been previously described in a Form 10–D, 10–K or 8–K (17 CFR 249.308) filed under the Exchange Act.

(f) *Filing of Required Exhibits.* Where agreements or other documents in this Regulation AB (Rules 229.1100 through 229.1125) are specified to be filed as exhibits to a Securities Act registration statement, such agreements or other documents, if applicable, may be incorporated by reference as an exhibit to the registration statement, such as by filing a Form 8–K (Rule 249.308 of this chapter) in the case of offerings registered on Form SF–3 (Rule

239.45 of this chapter). Final agreements must be filed and made part of the registration statement no later than the date the final prospectus is required to be filed under Rule 230.424 of this chapter.

Item 1101. Definitions

The following definitions apply to the terms used in Regulation AB (Items 1100 through 1123), unless specified otherwise:

(a) *ABS informational and computational material* means a written communication consisting solely of one or some combination of the following:

(1) Factual information regarding the asset-backed securities being offered and the structure and basic parameters of the securities, such as the number of classes, seniority, payment priorities, terms of payment, the tax, Employment Retirement Income Security Act of 1974, as amended, (29 U.S.C. 1001 *et seq.*) ("ERISA") or other legal conclusions of counsel, and descriptive information relating to each class (e.g., principal amount, coupon, minimum denomination, anticipated price, yield, weighted average life, credit enhancements, anticipated ratings, and other similar information relating to the proposed structure of the offering);

(2) Factual information regarding the pool assets underlying the asset-backed securities, including origination, acquisition and pool selection criteria, information regarding any prefunding or revolving period applicable to the offering, information regarding significant obligors, data regarding the contractual and related characteristics of the underlying pool assets (e.g., weighted average coupon, weighted average maturity, delinquency and loss information and geographic distribution) and other factual information concerning the parameters of the asset pool appropriate to the nature of the underlying assets, such as the type of assets comprising the pool and the programs under which the loans were originated;

(3) Identification of key parties to the transaction, such as servicers, trustees, depositors, sponsors, originators and providers of credit enhancement or other support, including a brief description of each such party's roles, responsibilities, background and experience;

(4) Static pool data, as referenced in Item 1105 of this Regulation AB, such as for the sponsor's and/or servicer's portfolio, prior transactions or the asset pool itself;

(5) Statistical information displaying for a particular class of asset-backed securities the yield, average life, expected maturity, interest rate sensitivity, cash flow characteristics, total rate of return, option adjusted spread or other financial or statistical information relating to the class or classes under specified prepayment, interest rate, loss or other hypothetical scenarios. Examples of such information under the definition include:

(i) Statistical results of interest rate sensitivity analyses regarding the impact on yield or other financial characteristics of a class of securities from changes in interest rates at one or more assumed prepayment speeds;

(ii) Statistical information showing the cash flows that would be associated with a particular class of asset-backed securities at a specified prepayment speed; and

(iii) Statistical information reflecting the financial impact of losses based on a variety of loss or default experience, prepayment, interest rate and related assumptions.

(6) The names of underwriters participating in the offering of the securities, and their additional roles, if any, within the underwriting syndicate;

(7) The anticipated schedule for the offering (including the approximate date upon which the proposed sale to the public will begin) and a description of marketing events (including the dates, times, locations, and procedures for attending or otherwise accessing them); and

(8) A description of the procedures by which the underwriters will conduct the offering and the procedures for transactions in connection with the offering with an underwriter or participating dealer (including procedures regarding account-opening and submitting indications of interest and conditional offers to buy).

(b) *Asset-backed issuer* means an issuer whose reporting obligation results from either the registration of an offering of asset-backed securities under the Securities Act, or the registration of a class of asset-backed securities under section 12 of the Exchange Act (15 U.S.C. 78*l*).

(c)(1) *Asset-backed security* means a security that is primarily serviced by the cash flows of a discrete pool of receivables or other financial assets, either fixed or revolving, that by their terms convert into cash within a finite time period, plus any rights or other assets designed to assure the servicing or timely distributions of proceeds to the security holders; provided that in the case of financial assets that are leases, those assets may convert to cash partially by the cash proceeds from the disposition of the physical property underlying such leases.

(2) The following additional conditions apply in order to be considered an *asset-backed security*:

(i) Neither the depositor nor the issuing entity is an investment company under the Investment Company Act of 1940 (15 U.S.C. 80a–1 *et seq.*) nor will become an investment company as a result of the asset-backed securities transaction.

(ii) The activities of the issuing entity for the asset-backed securities are limited to passively owning or holding the pool of assets, issuing the asset-backed securities supported or serviced by those assets, and other activities reasonably incidental thereto.

(iii) No non-performing assets are part of the asset pool as of the measurement date.

(iv) Delinquent assets do not constitute 50% or more, as measured by dollar volume, of the asset pool as of the measurement date.

(v) With respect to securities that are backed by leases, the portion of the securitized pool balance attributable to the residual value of the physical property underlying the leases, as determined in accordance with the transaction agreements for the securities, does not constitute:

(A) For master trusts, 25% of the aggregate principal balance of the total asset pool whose cash flows support the securities; and

(B) For other offerings, 25% of the proceeds of the offering.

(3) Notwithstanding the requirement in paragraph (c)(1) of this item that the asset pool be a discrete pool of assets, the following are considered to be a discrete pool of assets for purposes of being considered an asset-backed security:

(i) *Master Trusts.* The offering related to the securities contemplates adding additional assets to the pool that backs such securities in connection with future issuances of asset-backed securities backed by such pool. The offering related to the securities also may contemplate additions to the asset pool, to the extent consistent with paragraphs (c)(3)(ii) and (c)(3)(iii) of this item, in connection with maintaining minimum pool balances in accordance with the transaction agreements for master trusts with revolving periods or receivables or other financial assets that arise under revolving accounts.

(ii) *Prefunding Periods.* The offering related to the securities contemplates a prefunding account where a portion of the proceeds of that offering is to be used for the future acquisition of additional pool assets, if the duration of the prefunding period does not extend for more than one year from the date of issuance of the securities and the portion of the proceeds for such prefunding account does not involve in excess of:

(A) For master trusts, 25% of the aggregate principal balance of the total asset pool whose cash flows support the securities; and

(B) For other offerings, 25% of the proceeds of the offering.

(iii) *Revolving Periods.* The offering related to the securities contemplates a revolving period where cash flows from the pool assets may be used to acquire additional pool assets, provided, that, for securities backed by receivables or other financial assets that do not arise under revolving accounts, the revolving period does not extend for more than three years from the date of issuance of the securities and the additional pool assets are of the same general character as the original pool assets.

Instructions to Item 1101(c):

1. For purposes of determining non-performing, delinquency and residual value thresholds, the "measurement date" means either:

a. The designated cut-off date for the transaction (i.e., the date on and after which collections on the pool assets accrue for the benefit of asset-backed security holders), if applicable; or

b. In the case of master trusts, the date as of which delinquency and loss information or securitized pool balance information, as applicable, is presented in the prospectus for the asset-backed securities to be filed pursuant to Rule 424(b).

2. Non-performing and delinquent assets that are not funded or purchased by proceeds from the securities and that are not considered in cash flow calculations for the securities need not be considered as part of the asset pool for purposes of determining non-performing and delinquency thresholds.

3. For purposes of determining non-performing, delinquency and residual value thresholds for master trusts, calculations are to be measured against the total asset pool whose cash flows support the securities.

4. For purposes of determining residual value thresholds, residual values need not be included in measuring against the thresholds to the extent a separate party is obligated for such amounts (e.g., through a residual value guarantee, residual value insurance or where the lessee is obligated to cover any residual losses).

(d) *Delinquent*, for purposes of determining if a pool asset is delinquent, means if a pool asset is more than 30 or 31 days or a single payment cycle, as applicable, past due from the contractual due date, as determined in accordance with any of the following:

(1) The transaction agreements for the asset-backed securities;

(2) The delinquency recognition policies of the sponsor, any affiliate of the sponsor that originated the pool asset or the servicer of the pool asset; or

(3) The delinquency recognition policies applicable to such pool asset established by the primary safety and soundness regulator of any entity listed in paragraph (d)(2) of this item or the program or regulatory entity that oversees the program under which the pool asset was originated.

(e) *Depositor* means the depositor who receives or purchases and transfers or sells the pool assets to the issuing entity. For asset-backed securities transactions where there is not an intermediate transfer of the assets from the sponsor to the issuing entity, the term depositor refers to the sponsor. For asset-backed securities transactions where the person transferring or selling the pool assets is itself a trust, the depositor of the issuing entity is the depositor of that trust.

(f) *Issuing entity* means the trust or other entity created at the direction of the sponsor or depositor that owns or holds the pool assets and in whose name the asset-backed securities supported or serviced by the pool assets are issued.

(g) *Non-performing*, for purposes of determining if a pool asset is non-performing, means a pool asset if any of the following is true:

(1) The pool asset would be treated as wholly or partially charged-off under the requirements in the transaction agreements for the asset-backed securities;

(2) The pool asset would be treated as wholly or partially charged-off under the charge-off policies of the sponsor, an affiliate of the sponsor that originates the pool asset or a servicer that services the pool asset; or

(3) The pool asset would be treated as wholly or partially charged-off under the charge-off policies applicable to such pool asset established by the primary safety and soundness regulator of any entity listed in paragraph (g)(2) of this item or the program or regulatory entity that oversees the program under which the pool asset was originated.

(h) *NRSRO* has the same meaning as the term "nationally recognized statistical rating organization" as used in Rule 15c3–1(c)(2)(vi)(F) under the Securities Exchange Act of 1934.

(i) *Obligor* means any person who is directly or indirectly committed by contract or other arrangement to make payments on all or part of the obligations on a pool asset.

(j) *Servicer* means any person responsible for the management or collection of the pool assets or making allocations or distributions to holders of the asset-backed securities. The term servicer does not include a trustee for the issuing entity or the asset-backed securities that makes allocations or distributions to holders of the asset-backed securities if the trustee receives such allocations or distributions from a servicer and the trustee does not otherwise perform the functions of a servicer.

(k) *Significant obligor* means any of the following:

(1) An obligor or a group of affiliated obligors on any pool asset or group of pool assets if such pool asset or group of pool assets represents 10% or more of the asset pool.

(2) A single property or group of related properties securing a pool asset or a group of pool assets if such pool asset or group of pool assets represents 10% or more of the asset pool.

(3) A lessee or group of affiliated lessees if the related lease or group of leases represents 10% or more of the asset pool.

Instructions to Item 1101(k):

1. Regarding paragraph (k)(3) of this item, the calculation must focus on the leases whose cash flow supports the asset-backed securities directly or indirectly (including the residual value of the physical property underlying the leases if a portion of the securitized pool balance is attributable to the residual value of such property), regardless of whether the asset pool contains the leases themselves, mortgages on properties that are the subject of the leases or other assets related to the leases.

2. If separate pool assets, or properties underlying pool assets, are cross-defaulted and/or cross-collateralized, such pool assets are to be aggregated and considered together in determining concentration levels.

3. If the pool asset is a mortgage or lease relating to real estate, the pool asset is non-recourse to the obligor, and the obligor does not manage the property or does not own other assets and has no other operations, then the obligor need not be considered a separate significant obligor from the real estate. Otherwise, the obligor is a separate significant obligor.

4. The determination of significant obligors is to be made as of the designated cut-off date for the transaction

(i.e., the date on and after which collections on the pool assets accrue for the benefit of asset-backed security holders), provided, that, in the case of master trusts, the determination is to be made as of the cut-off date (or issuance date if there is not a cut-off date) for each issuance of asset-backed securities backed by the same asset pool. In addition, if disclosure is required pursuant to either Item 6.05 of Form 8–K (17 CFR 249.308) or in a Form 10–D (17 CFR 249.312) pursuant to Item 1121(b) of this Regulation AB, the determination of significant obligors is to be made against the asset pool described in such report. However, if the percentage concentration regarding an obligor falls below 10% subsequent to the determination dates discussed in this Instruction, the obligor no longer need be considered a significant obligor.

(*l*) *Sponsor* means the person who organizes and initiates an asset-backed securities transaction by selling or transferring assets, either directly or indirectly, including through an affiliate, to the issuing entity.

(m) *Asset representations reviewer* means any person appointed to review the underlying assets for compliance with the representations and warranties on the underlying pool assets and is not affiliated with any sponsor, depositor, servicer, or trustee of the transaction, or any of their affiliates. The asset representations reviewer shall not be the party to determine whether noncompliance with representations or warranties constitutes a breach of any contractual provision. The asset representations reviewer also shall not be the same party or an affiliate of any party hired by the sponsor or underwriter to perform pre-closing due diligence work on the pool assets.

Item 1102. Forepart of registration statement and outside cover page of the prospectus

In addition to the information required by Item 501 of Regulation S–K, provide the following information on the outside front cover page of the prospectus. Present information regarding multiple classes in tables if doing so will aid understanding. If information regarding multiple classes cannot appear on the cover page due to space limitations, include the information in the summary or in an immediately preceding separate table.

(a) Identify the sponsor, the depositor and the issuing entity (if known). Such identifying information should include a Central Index Key number for the depositor and the issuing entity, and if applicable, the sponsor.

(b) In identifying the title of the securities, include the series number, if applicable. If there is more than one class of securities offered, state the class designations of the securities offered.

(c) Identify the asset type(s) being securitized.

(d) Include a statement, if applicable and appropriately modified to the transaction, that the securities represent the obligations of the issuing entity only and do not represent the obligations of or interest in the sponsor, depositor or any of their affiliates.

(e) Identify the aggregate principal amount of all securities offered and the principal amount, if any, of each class of securities offered. If a class has no principal amount, disclose that fact, and, if applicable, state the notional amount, clearly identifying that the amount is a notional one. If the amounts are approximate, disclose that fact.

(f) Indicate the interest rate or specified rate of return of each class of security offered. If a class of securities does not bear interest or a specified return, disclose that fact. If the rate is based on a formula or is calculated in reference to a generally recognized interest rate index, such as a U.S. Treasury securities index, either provide the formula on the cover, or indicate that the rate is variable, indicate the index upon which the rate is based and indicate that further disclosure of how the rate is determined is included in the transaction summary.

(g) Identify the distribution frequency, by class or series where applicable, and the first expected distribution date for the asset-backed securities.

(h) Briefly describe any credit enhancement or other support for the transaction and identify any enhancement or support provider referenced in Items 1114(b) or 1115 of this Regulation AB.

Instruction to Item 1102: Also see Item 1113(f)(2) of this Regulation AB regarding the title of any class of securities with an optional redemption or termination feature that may be exercised when 25% or more of the original principal balance of the pool assets are still outstanding.

Item 1103. Transaction summary and risk factors

(a) *Prospectus Summary.* In providing the information required by Item 503(a) of Regulation S–K, provide the following information in the prospectus summary, as applicable. Present information regarding multiple classes in tables if doing so will aid understanding. Consider using diagrams to illustrate the relationships among the parties, the structure of the securities offered (including, for example, the flow of funds or any subordination features) and any other material features of the transaction.

(1) Identify the participants in the transaction, including the sponsor, depositor, issuing entity, trustee and servicers contemplated by Item 1108(a)(2) of this Regulation AB, and their respec-

tive roles. Describe the roles briefly if they are not apparent from the title of the role. Identify any originator contemplated by Item 1110 of this Regulation AB and any significant obligor.

(2) Briefly identify the pool assets and summarize briefly the size and material characteristics of the asset pool. Identify the cut-off date or similar date for establishing the composition of the asset pool, if applicable.

Instruction to Item 1103(a)(2): What is required is summary disclosure tailored to the particular asset pool backing the asset-backed securities. While the material characteristics will vary depending on the nature of the pool assets, summary disclosure may include, among other things, statistical information of: The types of underwriting or origination programs, exceptions to underwriting or origination criteria and, if applicable, modifications made to the pool assets after origination. Include a cross-reference in the prospectus summary to the more detailed statistical information found in the prospectus.

(3) State briefly the basic terms of each class of securities offered. In particular:

(i) Identify the classes offered by the prospectus and any classes issued in the same transaction or residual or equity interests in the transaction that are not being offered by the prospectus.

(ii) State the interest rate or rate of return on each class of securities offered, to the extent that the rates on any class of securities were not disclosed in full on the prospectus cover page.

(iii) State the expected final and final scheduled maturity or principal distribution dates, if applicable, of each class of securities offered.

(iv) Identify the denominations in which the securities may be issued.

(v) Identify the distribution frequency on the securities.

(vi) Summarize the flow of funds, payment priorities and allocations among the classes of securities offered, the classes of securities that are not offered, and fees and expenses, to the extent necessary to understand the payment characteristics of the classes that are offered by the prospectus.

(vii) Identify any events in the transaction agreements that can trigger liquidation or amortization of the asset pool or other performance triggers that would alter the transaction structure or the flow of funds.

(viii) Identify any optional or mandatory redemption or termination features.

(ix) Identify any credit enhancement or other support for the transaction, as referenced in Items 1114(a) and 1115 of this Regulation AB, and briefly describe what protection or support is provided by the enhancement. Identify any enhancement provider referenced in Items 1114(b) and 1115 of this Regulation AB. Summarize how losses not covered by credit enhancement or support will be allocated to the securities.

(4) Identify any outstanding series or classes of securities that are backed by the same asset pool or otherwise have claims on the pool assets. In addition, state if additional series or classes of securities may be issued that are backed by the same asset pool and briefly identify the circumstances under which those additional securities may be issued. Specify if security holder approval is necessary for such issuances and if security holders will receive notice of such issuances.

(5) If the transaction will include prefunding or revolving periods, indicate:

(i) The term or duration of the prefunding or revolving period.

(ii) For prefunding periods, the amount of proceeds to be deposited in the prefunding account.

(iii) For revolving periods, the maximum amount of additional assets that may be acquired during the revolving period, if applicable.

(iv) The percentage of the asset pool and any class or series of the asset-backed securities represented by the prefunding account or the revolving period, if applicable.

(v) Any limitation on the ability to add pool assets.

(vi) The requirements for assets that may be added to the pool.

(6) If pool assets can otherwise be added, removed or substituted (for example, in the event of a breach in representations or warranties regarding pool assets), summarize briefly the circumstances under which such actions can occur.

(7) Summarize the amount or formula for calculating the fee that the servicer will receive for performing its duties, and identify from what source those fees will be paid and the distribution priority of those fees.

(8) Summarize the federal income tax issues material to investors of each class of securities offered.

(9) Indicate whether the issuance or sale of any class of offered securities is conditioned on the assignment of a rating by one or more rating agencies. If so, identify each rating agency and the minimum rating that must be assigned.

(b) *Risk Factors*. In providing the information required by Item 503(c) of Regulation S–K, identify any risks that may be different for investors in any offered class of asset-backed securities, and if so, identify such classes and describe such difference(s).

Item 1104. Sponsors

Provide the following information about the sponsor:

(a) State the sponsor's name and describe the sponsor's form of organization.

(b) Describe the general character of the sponsor's business.

(c) Describe the sponsor's securitization program and state how long the sponsor has been engaged in the securitization of assets. The description must include, to the extent material, a general discussion of the sponsor's experience in securitizing assets of any type as well as a more detailed discussion of the sponsor's experience in and overall procedures for originating or acquiring and securitizing assets of the type included in the current transaction. Include to the extent material information regarding the size, composition and growth of the sponsor's portfolio of assets of the type to be securitized and information or factors related to the sponsor that may be material to an analysis of the origination or performance of the pool assets, such as whether any prior securitizations organized by the sponsor have defaulted or experienced an early amortization triggering event.

(d) Describe the sponsor's material roles and responsibilities in its securitization program, including whether the sponsor or an affiliate is responsible for originating, acquiring, pooling or servicing the pool assets, and the sponsor's participation in structuring the transaction.

(e) *Repurchases and Replacements*.

(1) If the underlying transaction agreements provide a covenant to repurchase or replace an underlying asset for breach of a representation or warranty, provide in the body of the prospectus for the prior three years, the information required by Rule 15Ga–1(a) under the Securities Exchange Act of 1934 concerning all assets securitized by the sponsor that were the subject of a demand to repurchase or replace for breach of the representations and warranties concerning the pool assets for all asset-backed securities (as that term is defined in Section 3(a)(79) of the Securities Exchange Act of 1934) where the underlying transaction agreements included a covenant to repurchase or replace an underlying asset of the same asset class held by non-affiliates of the sponsor, except that:

(i) For prospectuses to be filed pursuant to Rule 424 prior to February 14, 2014, information may be limited to the prior year; and

(ii) For prospectuses to be filed pursuant to Rule 424 on or after February 14, 2013 but prior to February 14, 2014, information may be limited to the prior two years

(2) Include a reference to the most recent Form ABS–15G filed by the securitizer (as that term is defined in Section 15G(a) of the Securities Exchange Act of 1934) in response to Rule 15Ga–1 and disclose the CIK number of the securitizer

(3) For prospectuses to be filed pursuant to Rule 424, the information presented shall not be more than 135 days old.

(f) If the sponsor is required to repurchase or replace any asset for breach of a representation and warranty pursuant to the transaction agreements, provide information regarding the sponsor's financial condition to the extent that there is a material risk that the effect on its ability to comply with the provisions in the transaction agreements relating to the repurchase obligations for those assets resulting from such financial condition could have a material impact on pool performance or performance of the asset-backed securities.

(g) Describe any interest that the sponsor, or any affiliate of the sponsor, has retained in the transaction, including the amount and nature of that interest. Disclose any hedge (security specific or portfolio) materially related to the credit risk of the securities that was entered into by the sponsor or, if known, by an affiliate of the sponsor to offset the risk position held.

Instruction to Item 1104(g): The disclosure required under this item shall separately state the amount and nature of any interest or asset retained in compliance with law, including any amounts that are retained by parties other than the sponsor in order to satisfy such requirements.

Item 1105. Static pool information

Describe the static pool information presented. Provide appropriate introductory and explanatory information to introduce the characteristics, the methodology used in determining or calculating the characteristics and any terms or abbreviations used. Include a description of how the static pool differs from the pool underlying the securities being offered, such as the extent to which the pool underlying the securities being offered was originated with the same or differing underwriting criteria, loan terms, and risk tolerances than the static pools presented. In addition to a narrative description, the static pool information should be presented graphically if doing so would aid in understanding.

(a) For amortizing asset pools, unless the registrant determines that such information is not material:

(1) Provide static pool information, to the extent material, regarding delinquencies, cumulative losses and prepayments for prior securitized pools of the sponsor for that asset type.

(2) If the sponsor has less than three years of experience securitizing assets of the type to be included in the offered asset pool, consider providing instead static pool information, to the extent material, regarding delinquencies, cumulative losses and prepayments by vintage origination years regarding originations or purchases by the sponsor, as applicable, for that asset type. A vintage origination year represents assets originated during the same year.

(3) In providing the information required by paragraphs (a)(1) and (a)(2) of this item:

(i) Provide the requested information for prior pools or vintage origination years, as applicable, relating to the following time period, to the extent material:

(A) Five years, or

(B) For so long as the sponsor has been either securitizing assets of the same asset type (in the case of paragraph (a)(1) of this item) or making originations or purchases of assets of the same asset type (in the case of paragraph (a)(2) of this item) if less than five years.

(ii) Present delinquency, cumulative loss and prepayment data for each prior securitized pool or vintage origination year, as applicable, over the life of the prior securitized pool or vintage origination year. The most recent periodic increment for the data must be as of a date no later than 135 days of the date of first use of the prospectus.

Instruction to Item 1105(a)(3)(ii): Present historical delinquency and loss information in accordance with Item 1100(b) of this Regulation AB (§ 229.1100(b)) through no less than 120 days.

(iii) Provide summary information for the original characteristics of the prior securitized pools or vintage origination years, as applicable and material. While the material summary characteristics may vary, these characteristics may include, among other things, the following: number of pool assets; original pool balance; weighted average initial loan balance; weighted average interest or note rate; weighted average original term; weighted average remaining term; weighted average and minimum and maximum standardized credit score or other applicable measure of obligor credit quality; product type; loan purpose; loan-to-value information; distribution of assets by loan or note rate; and geographic distribution information.

(iv) Provide graphical illustration of delinquencies, prepayments and losses for each prior securitized pool or by vintage origination year regarding originations or purchases by the sponsor, as applicable for that asset type.

(b) For revolving asset master trusts, unless the registrant determines that such information is not material, provide, to the extent material, data regarding delinquencies, cumulative losses, prepayments, payment rate, yield and standardized credit scores or other applicable measure of obligor credit quality in separate increments based on the date of origination of the pool assets. While the material increments may vary, consider presenting such data at a minimum in 12–month increments through the first five years of the account's life (e.g., 0–12 months, 13–24 months, 25–36 months, 37–48 months, 49–60 months and 61 months or more).

(c) If the information that would otherwise be required by paragraph (a)(1), (a)(2) or (b) of this section is not material, but alternative static pool information would provide material disclosure, provide such alternative information instead. Similarly, information contemplated by paragraph (a)(1), (a)(2) or (b) of this section regarding a party or parties other than the sponsor may be provided in addition to or in lieu of such information regarding the sponsor if appropriate to provide material disclosure. In addition, provide other explanatory disclosure, including why alternative disclosure is being provided and explain the absence of any static pool information contemplated by paragraph (a)(1), (a)(2) or (b) of this section, as applicable.

(d) The following information provided in response to this item shall not be deemed to be a prospectus or part of a prospectus for the asset-backed securities nor shall such information be deemed to be part of the registration statement for the asset-backed securities:

(1) With respect to information regarding prior securitized pools of the sponsor that do not include the currently offered pool, information regarding prior securitized pools that were established before January 1, 2006; and

(2) With respect to information regarding the currently offered pool, information about the pool for periods before January 1, 2006.(e) For prospectuses to be filed pursuant to Rule 424 that include information specified in paragraph (d)(1) or (d)(2) of this item, the prospectus shall disclose that such information is not deemed to be part of that prospectus or the registration statement for the asset-backed securities.

(f) If any of the information identified in paragraph (d)(1) or (d)(2) of this item that is to be provided in response to this item is unknown and not available to the registrant without unreasonable effort or expense, such information may be omitted, provided the registrant provides the information on the subject it possesses or can acquire without unreasonable effort or expense, and the registrant includes a statement in the prospectus showing that unreasonable effort or expense would be involved in obtaining the omitted information.

Item 1106. Depositors

If the depositor is not the same entity as the sponsor, provide separately the information regarding the depositor called for by paragraphs (a) and (b) of Item 1104 of this Regulation AB, and, to the extent the information would be material and materially different from the sponsor, paragraphs (c) and (d) of Item 1104 of this Regulation AB. In addition, provide the following information:

(a) The ownership structure of the depositor.

(b) The general character of any activities the depositor is engaged in other than securitizing assets and the time period during which it has been so engaged.

(c) Any continuing duties of the depositor after issuance of the asset-backed securities being registered regarding the asset-backed securities or the pool assets.

Item 1107. Issuing entities

Provide the following information about the issuing entity:

(a) State the issuing entity's name and describe the issuing entity's form of organization, including the State or other jurisdiction under whose laws the issuing entity is organized. File the issuing entity's governing documents as an exhibit.

(b) Describe the permissible activities and restrictions on the activities of the issuing entity under its governing documents, including any restrictions on the ability to issue or invest in additional securities, to borrow money or to make loans to other persons. Describe any provisions in the issuing entity's governing documents allowing for modification of the issuing entity's governing documents, including its permissible activities.

(c) Describe any specific discretionary activities with regard to the administration of the asset pool or the asset-backed securities, and identify the person or persons authorized to exercise such discretion.

(d) Describe any assets owned or to be owned by the issuing entity, apart from the pool assets, as well as any liabilities of the issuing entity, apart from the asset-backed securities. Disclose the fiscal year end of the issuing entity.

(e) If the issuing entity has executive officers, a board of directors or persons performing similar functions, provide the information required by Items 401, 402, 403 404 and 407(a), (c)(3), (d)(4), (d)(5) and (e)(4) of Regulation S–K for the issuing entity.

(f) Describe the terms of any management or administration agreement regarding the issuing entity. File any such agreement as an exhibit.

(g) Describe the capitalization of the issuing entity and the amount or nature of any equity contribution to the issuing entity by the sponsor, depositor or other party.

(h) Describe the sale or transfer of the pool assets to the issuing entity as well as the creation (and perfection and priority status) of any security interest in favor of the issuing entity, the trustee, the asset-backed security holders or others, including the material terms of any agreement providing for such sale, transfer or creation of a security interest. File any such agreements as an exhibit. In addition to an appropriate narrative description, also provide this information graphically or in a flow chart if it will aid understanding.

(i) If the pool assets are securities, as defined under the Securities Act of 1933, state the market price of the securities and the basis on which the market price was determined.

(j) If expenses incurred in connection with the selection and acquisition of the pool assets are to be payable from offering proceeds, disclose the amount of such expenses. If such expenses are to be paid to the sponsor, servicer contemplated by Item 1108(a)(2) of this Regulation AB, depositor, issuing entity, originator contemplated by Item 1110 of this Regulation AB, underwriter, or any affiliate of the foregoing, separately identify the type and amount of expenses paid to each such party.

(k) Describe to the extent material any provisions or arrangements included to address any one or more of the following issues:

(1) Whether any security interests granted in connection with the transaction are perfected, maintained and enforced.

(2) Whether declaration of bankruptcy, receivership or similar proceeding with respect to the issuing entity can occur.

(3) Whether in the event of a bankruptcy, receivership or similar proceeding with respect to the sponsor, originator, depositor or other seller of the pool assets, the issuing entity's assets will become part of the bankruptcy estate or subject to the bankruptcy control of a third party.

(4) Whether in the event of a bankruptcy, receivership or similar proceeding with respect to the issuing entity, the issuing entity's assets will become subject to the bankruptcy control of a third party.

(*l*) If applicable law prohibits the issuing entity from holding the pool assets directly (for example, an "eligible lender" trustee must hold student loans originated under the Federal Family Education Loan Program of the Higher Education Act of 1965 (20 U.S.C. 1001 *et seq.*)), describe the arrangements instituted to hold the pool assets on behalf of the issuing entity. Include disclosure regarding the arrangements taken, as applicable, regarding the items in paragraph (k) of this item with respect to any such additional entity that holds such assets on behalf of the issuing entity.

Item 1108. Servicers

Provide the following information for the servicer.

(a) *Multiple Servicers.* Where servicing of the pool assets utilizes multiple servicers (e.g., master servicers that oversee the actions of other servicers, primary servicers that have primary contact with the obligor, or special servicers for specific servicing functions):

(1) Provide a clear introductory description of the roles, responsibilities and oversight requirements of the entire servicing structure and the parties involved. In addition to an appropriate narrative discussion of the allocation of servicing responsibilities, also consider presenting the information graphically if doing so will aid understanding.

(2) Identify:

(i) Each master servicer;

(ii) Each affiliated servicer;

(iii) Each unaffiliated servicer that services 10% or more of the pool assets; and

(iv) Any other material servicer responsible for calculating or making distributions to holders of the asset-backed securities, performing work-outs or foreclosures, or other aspect of the servicing of the pool assets or the asset-backed securities upon which the performance of the pool assets or the asset-backed securities is materially dependent.

(3) Provide the information in paragraphs (b), (c), (d), and (e) of this item, as applicable depending on the servicer's role, for each servicer identified in paragraphs (a)(2)(i), (ii) and (iv) of this item and each unaffiliated servicer identified in paragraph (a)(2)(iii) of this item that services 20% or more of the pool assets.

(b) *Identifying Information and Experience.* (1) State the servicer's name and describe the servicer's form of organization.

(2) State how long the servicer has been servicing assets. Provide, to the extent material, a general discussion of the servicer's experience in servicing assets of any type as well as a more detailed discussion of the servicer's experience in, and procedures for the servicing function it will perform in the current transaction for assets of the type included in the current transaction. Include to the extent material information regarding the size, composition and growth of the servicer's portfolio of serviced assets of the type included in the

current transaction and information on factors related to the servicer that may be material to an analysis of the servicing of the assets or the asset-backed securities, as applicable.

(3) Describe any material changes to the servicer's policies or procedures in the servicing function it will perform in the current transaction for assets of the same type included in the current transaction during the past three years.

(4) Provide information regarding the servicer's financial condition to the extent that there is a material risk that the effect on one or more aspects of servicing resulting from such financial condition could have a material impact on pool performance or performance of the asset-backed securities.

(c) *Servicing Agreements and Servicing Practices.* (1) Describe the material terms of the servicing agreement and the servicer's duties regarding the asset-backed securities transaction. File the servicing agreement as an exhibit.

(2) Describe to the extent material the manner in which collections on the assets will be maintained, such as through a segregated collection account, and the extent of commingling of funds that occurs or may occur from the assets with other funds, serviced assets or other assets of the servicer.

(3) Describe to the extent material any special or unique factors involved in servicing the particular type of assets included in the current transaction, such as subprime assets, and the servicer's processes and procedures designed to address such factors.

(4) Describe to the extent material the terms of any arrangements whereby the servicer is required or permitted to provide advances of funds regarding collections, cash flows or distributions, including interest or other fees charged for such advances and terms of recovery by the servicer of such advances. To the extent material, provide statistical information regarding servicer advances on the pool assets and the servicer's overall servicing portfolio for the past three years.

(5) Describe to the extent material the servicer's process for handling delinquencies, losses, bankruptcies and recoveries, such as through liquidation of the underlying collateral, note sale by a special servicer or borrower negotiation or workouts.

(6) If the servicer has custodial responsibility for the assets, describe material arrangements regarding the safekeeping and preservation of the assets, such as the physical promissory notes, and procedures to reflect the segregation of the assets from other serviced assets. If no servicer has custodial responsibility for the assets, disclose that fact, identify the party that has such responsibility and provide the information called for by this paragraph for such party.

(7) Describe any limitations on the servicer's liability under the transaction agreements regarding the asset-backed securities transaction.

(d) *Back-up Servicing.* Describe the material terms regarding the servicer's removal, replacement, resignation or transfer, including:

(1) Provisions for selection of a successor servicer and financial or other requirements that must be met by a successor servicer.

(2) The process for transferring servicing to a successor servicer.

(3) Provisions for payment of expenses associated with a servicing transfer and any additional fees charged by a successor servicer. Specify the amount of any funds set aside for a servicing transfer.

(4) Arrangements, if any, regarding a back-up servicer for the assets and the identity of any such back-up servicer.

(e) Describe any interest that the servicer, or any affiliate of the servicer, has retained in the transaction, including the amount and nature of that interest. Disclose any hedge (security specific or portfolio) materially related to the credit risk of the securities that was entered into by the servicer or, if known, by an affiliate of the servicer to offset the risk position held.

Instruction to Item 1108(e): The disclosure required under this item shall separately state the amount and nature of any interest or asset retained in compliance with law, including any amounts that are retained by parties other than the servicer in order to satisfy such requirements.

Item 1109. Trustees and other transaction parties

(a) *Trustees.* Provide the following information for each trustee:

(1) State the trustee's name and describe the trustee's form of organization.

(2) Describe to what extent the trustee has had prior experience serving as a trustee for asset-backed securities transactions involving similar pool assets, if applicable.

(3) Describe the trustee's duties and responsibilities regarding the asset-backed securities under the governing documents and under applicable law. In addition, describe any actions required by the trustee, including whether notices are required to investors, rating agencies or other third parties, upon an event of default, potential event of default (and how defined) or other breach of a transaction covenant and any required percentage of a class or classes of asset-backed securities that is needed to require the trustee to take action.

(4) Describe any limitations on the trustee's liability under the transaction agreements regarding the asset-backed securities transaction.

(5) Describe any indemnification provisions that entitle the trustee to be indemnified from the cash flow that otherwise would be used to pay the asset-backed securities.

(6) Describe any contractual provisions or under- standings regarding the trustee's removal, replacement or resignation, as well as how the expenses associated with changing from one trustee to another trustee will be paid.

(b) *Asset representations reviewer*. Provide the following for each asset representations reviewer:

(1) State the asset representations reviewer's name and describe its form of organization.

(2) Describe to what extent the asset representations reviewer has had prior experience serving as an asset representations reviewer for asset-backed securities transactions involving similar pool assets.

(3) Describe the asset representations reviewer's duties and responsibilities regarding the asset-backed securities under the governing documents and under applicable law. In addition, describe any actions required of the asset representations reviewer, including whether notices are required to investors, rating agencies or other third parties, and any required percentage of a class or classes of asset-backed securities that is needed to require the asset representations reviewer to take action.

(4) Disclose the manner and amount in which the asset representations reviewer is compensated.

(5) Describe any limitations on the asset representations reviewer's liability under the transaction agreements regarding the asset-backed securities transaction.

(6) Describe any indemnification provisions that entitle the asset representations reviewer to be indemnified from the cash flow that otherwise would be used to pay holders of the asset- backed securities.

(7) Describe any contractual provisions or understandings regarding the asset representations reviewer's removal, replacement or resignation, as well as how the expenses associated with changing from one asset representations reviewer to another asset representations reviewer will be paid.

Instruction to Item 1109: If multiple trustees are involved in the transaction, provide a description of the roles and responsibilities of each trustee.

Item 1110. Originators

(a) Identify any originator or group of affiliated originators, apart from the sponsor or its affiliates, that originated, or is expected to originate, 10% or more of the pool assets. Also identify any originator(s) originating less than 10% of the pool assets if the cumulative amount originated by parties other than the sponsor or its affiliates is more than 10% of the pool assets.

(b) Provide the following information for any originator or group of affiliated originators, apart from the sponsor or its affiliates, that originated, or is expected to originate, 20% or more of the pool assets:

(1) The originator's form of organization.

(2) To the extent material, a description of the originator's origination program and how long the originator has been engaged in originating assets. The description must include a discussion of the originator's experience in originating assets of the type included in the current transaction. In providing the description, include, if material, information regarding the size and composition of the originator's origination portfolio as well as information material to an analysis of the performance of the pool assets, such as the originator's credit-granting or underwriting criteria for the asset types being securitized.

(3) Describe any interest that the originator, or any affiliate of the originator, has retained in the transaction, including the amount and nature of that interest. Disclose any hedge (security specific or portfolio) materially related to the credit risk of the securities that was entered into by the originator or, if known, by an affiliate of the originator to offset the risk position held.

Instruction to Item 1110(b)(3): The disclosure required under this item shall separately state the amount and nature of any interest or asset retained in compliance with law, including any amounts that are retained by parties other than the originator in order to satisfy such requirements.

(c) For any originator identified under paragraph (b) of this section, if such originator is required to repurchase or replace a pool asset for breach of a representation and warranty pursuant to the transaction agreements, provide information regarding the originator's financial condition to the extent that there is a material risk that the effect on its ability to comply with the provisions in the transaction agreements relating to the repurchase obligations for those assets resulting from such financial condition could have a material impact on pool performance or performance of the asset-backed securities.

Item 1111. Pool assets

Describe the pool assets, including the information required by this Item 1111. Present statistical information in tabular or graphical format, if such presentation will aid understanding. Present statistical information in appropriate distributional groups or incremental ranges in addition to presenting appropriate overall pool totals, averages and weighted averages, if such presentation will aid in the understanding of the data. In addition to presenting the number, amount and percentage of pool assets by distributional group or range, also provide statistical information for each group or range by variables, to the extent material, such as, average balance, weighted average coupon, average age and remaining term, average loan-to-value or similar ratio and weighted average standardized credit score or other applicable measure of obligor credit quality. These variables are just examples and should be tailored to the particular asset class backing the asset-backed securities. Consider providing minimums and maximums when presenting averages on an aggregate basis and within each group or range. In addition, provide historical data on the pool assets as appropriate (e.g., the lesser of three years or the time such assets have existed) to allow material evaluation of the pool data. In making any calculations regarding overall pool balances, disregard any funds set aside for a prefunding account.

(a) *Information Regarding Pool Asset Types and Selection Criteria.* Provide the following information:

(1) A brief description of the type or types of pool assets to be securitized.

(2) A general description of the material terms of the pool assets.

(3) A description of the solicitation, credit-granting or underwriting criteria used to originate or purchase the pool assets, including, to the extent known, any changes in such criteria and the extent to which such policies and criteria are or could be overridden.

(4) The method and criteria by which the pool assets were selected for the transaction.

(5) The cut-off date or similar date for establishing the composition of the asset pool, if applicable.

(6) If legal or regulatory provisions (such as bankruptcy, consumer protection, predatory lending, privacy, property rights or foreclosure laws or regulations) may materially affect pool asset performance or payments or expected payments on the asset-backed securities, briefly identify these provisions and their effects on such items.

Instruction to Item 1111(a)(6): Unless a material concentration of assets exists, it is not necessary to provide details of the laws in each jurisdiction. Even in that case, a legalistic description or recitation of the laws or regulations in a particular jurisdiction is not required.

(7)(i) The nature of a review of the assets performed by an issuer or sponsor (required by Rule 193 under the Securities Act of 1933), including whether the issuer of any asset-backed security engaged a third party for purposes of performing the review of the pool assets underlying an asset-backed security; and

(ii) The findings and conclusions of the review of the assets by the issuer, sponsor, or third party described in paragraph (a)(7)(i) of this section.

Instruction to Item 1111(a)(7): The disclosure required under this item shall provide an understanding of how the review related to the disclosure regarding the assets. For example, if benchmarks or criteria different from that specified in the prospectus were used to evaluate the assets, these should be described, as well as the findings and conclusions. If the review is of a sample of assets in the pool, disclose the size of the sample and the criteria used to select the assets sampled. If the issuer has engaged a third party for purposes of performing the review of assets, and attributes the findings and conclusions of the review to the third party in the disclosure required by this item, the issuer must provide the name of the third-party reviewer and comply with the requirements of Rule 436 under the Securities Act of 1933.

(8) If any assets in the pool deviate from the disclosed underwriting criteria or other criteria or benchmark used to evaluate the assets, or any assets in the sample or assets otherwise known to deviate if only a sample was reviewed, disclose how those assets deviate from the disclosed underwriting criteria or other criteria or benchmark used to evaluate the assets and include data on the

amount and characteristics of those assets that did not meet the disclosed standards. Disclose which entity (e.g., sponsor, originator, or underwriter) or entities determined that those assets should be included in the pool, despite not having met the disclosed underwriting standards or other criteria or benchmark used to evaluate the assets, and what factors were used to make the determination, such as compensating factors or a determination that the exception was not material. If compensating or other factors were used, provide data on the amount of assets in the pool or in the sample that are represented as meeting each such factor and the amount of assets that do not meet those factors. If multiple entities are involved in the decision to include assets despite not having met the disclosed underwriting standards, this should be described and each participating entity should be disclosed.

(b) *Pool Characteristics*. Describe the material characteristics of the asset pool. Provide appropriate introductory and explanatory information to introduce the characteristics, the methodology used in determining or calculating the characteristics and any terms or abbreviations used. While the material characteristics will vary depending on the nature of the pool assets, such characteristics may include, among other things:

(1) Number of each type of pool assets.

(2) Asset size, such as original balance and outstanding balance as of a designated cut-off date.

(3) Interest rate or rate of return, including type of interest rate if the pool includes different types, such as fixed and floating rates.

(4) Capitalized or uncapitalized accrued interest.

(5) Age, maturity, remaining term, average life (based on different prepayment assumptions), current payment/prepayment speeds and pool factors, as applicable.

(6) Servicer distribution, if different servicers service different pool assets.

(7) If a loan or similar receivable:

(i) Amortization period.

(ii) Loan purpose (e.g., whether a purchase or refinance) and status, if applicable (e.g., repayment or deferment).

(iii) Loan-to-value (LTV) ratios and debt service coverage ratios (DSCR), as applicable.

(iv) Type and/or use of underlying property, product or collateral (e.g., occupancy type for residential mortgages or industry sector for commercial mortgages).

(8) If a receivable or other financial asset that arises under a revolving account, such as a credit card receivable:

(i) Monthly payment rate.

(ii) Maximum credit lines.

(iii) Average account balance.

(iv) Yield percentages.

(v) Type of asset.

(vi) Finance charges, fees and other income earned.

(vii) Balance reductions granted for refunds, returns, fraudulent charges or other reasons.

(viii) Percentage of full-balance and minimum payments made.

(9) If the asset pool includes commercial mortgages, the following information, to the extent material:

(i) For all commercial mortgages:

(A) The location and present use of each mortgaged property.

(B) Net operating income and net cash flow information, as well as the components of net operating income and net cash flow, for each mortgaged property.

(C) Current occupancy rates for each mortgaged property.

(D) The identity, square feet occupied by and lease expiration dates for the three largest tenants at each mortgaged property.

(E) The nature and amount of all other material mortgages, liens or encumbrances against such properties and their priority.

(ii) For each commercial mortgage that represents, by dollar value, 10% or more of the asset pool, as measured as of the cut-off date:

(A) Any proposed program for the renovation, improvement or development of such properties, including the estimated cost thereof and the method of financing to be used.

(B) The general competitive conditions to which such properties are or may be subject.

(C) Management of such properties.

(D) Occupancy rate expressed as a percentage for each of the last five years.

(E) Principal business, occupations and professions carried on in, or from the properties.

(F) Number of tenants occupying 10% or more of the total rentable square footage of such properties and principal nature of business of such tenant, and the principal provisions of the leases with those tenants including, but not limited to: rental per annum, expiration date, and renewal options.

(G) The average effective annual rental per square foot or unit for each of the last three years prior to the date of filing.

(H) Schedule of the lease expirations for each of the ten years starting with the year in which the registration statement is filed (or the year in which the prospectus supplement is dated, as applicable), stating:

(*1*) The number of tenants whose leases will expire.

(*2*) The total area in square feet covered by such leases.

(*3*) The annual rental represented by such leases.

(*4*) The percentage of gross annual rental represented by such leases.

Instruction to Item 1111(b)(9): What is required is information material to an investor's understanding of the asset-backed securities. Detailed descriptions of the physical characteristics of individual properties or legal descriptions by metes and bounds are not required.

(10) Whether the pool asset is secured or unsecured, and if secured, the type(s) of collateral.

(11) Standardized credit scores of obligors and other information regarding obligor credit quality.

(12) Billing and payment procedures, including frequency of payment, payment options, fees, charges and origination or payment incentives.

(13) Information about the origination channel and origination process for the pool assets, such as originator information (and how acquired) and the level of origination documentation required, as applicable.

(14) Geographic distribution, such as by state or other material geographic region. If 10% or more of the pool assets are or will be located in any one state or other geographic region, describe any economic or other factors specific to such state or region that may materially impact the pool assets or pool asset cash flows.

Instruction to Item 1111(b)(14): For most assets, such as credit card accounts, motor vehicle leases, trade receivables and student loans, the location of the asset is the underlying obligor's billing address. For assets involving real estate, such as mortgages, the location of the asset is where the physical property underlying the asset is located.

(15) Other concentrations material to the asset type (e.g., school type for student loans). If material, provide information required by paragraph (b)(14) of this item regarding such concentrations, as applicable.

(c) *Delinquency and Loss Information.* Provide delinquency and loss information for the asset pool, including statistical information regarding delinquencies and losses.

(d) *Sources of Pool Cash Flow.* If the cash flows from the pool assets that are to be used to support the asset-backed securities are to come from more than one source (such as separate cash flows from lease payments and from the sale of the residual asset at the termination of the lease), provide the following information:

(1) Disclose the specific sources of funds that will be used to make the payments and distributions on the asset-backed securities, and, if applicable, provide information on the relative amount and percentage of funds that are to be derived from each source, including a description of any assumptions, data, models and methodology used to derive such amounts. If payments on different classes or different categories of payments on or related to the asset-backed securities (e.g., principal, interest or expenses) are to come from different or segregated cash flows from the pool assets or other sources, disclose the source of funds that will be used for such payments.

(2) *Residual Value Information.* If the asset pool includes leases or other assets where a portion of the securitized pool balance is attributable to the residual value of the underlying physical property underlying the leases, disclose the following:

(i) How the residual values used to structure the transaction were estimated, including an explanation of any material discount rates, models or assumptions used and who selected such rates, models or assumptions.

(ii) Any material procedures or requirements incorporated to preserve residual values during the term of the lease, such as lessee responsibilities, prohibitions on subletting, indemnification or required insurance or guarantees.

(iii) The procedures by which the residual values will be realized and by whom those procedures will be carried out, including information on the experience of such party, any affiliations with a party described in Item 1119(a) of this Regulation AB and the compensation arrangements with such party.

(iv) Whether the pool assets are open-end leases (e.g., where the lessee is required to cover the shortfall between the residual value of the leased property and the sale proceeds) or closed-end leases (e.g., where the lessor is responsible for such shortfalls), and where both types of leases are included in the asset pool, the percentage of each.

(v) To the extent material, any lessor obligations that are required under the leases, and the effect or potential effect on the asset-backed securities from failure by the lessor to perform its obligations.

(vi) Statistical information regarding estimated residual values for the pool assets.

(vii) Summary historical statistics on turn-in rates, if applicable, and residual value realization rates by the party responsible for such process over the past three years, or such longer period as is material to an evaluation of the pool assets.

(viii) The effect on security holders if not enough cash flow is received from the realization of the residual values, whether there are any provisions to address this contingency, and how any cash flow greater than that necessary to pay security holders will be allocated.

(e) *Representations and Warranties and Modification Provisions Relating to the Pool Assets.*

Provide the following information:

(1) *Representations and Warranties.* Summarize any representations and warranties made concerning the pool assets by the sponsor, transferor, originator or other party to the transaction, and describe briefly the remedies available if those representations and warranties are breached, such as repurchase obligations.

(2) *Modification Provisions.* Describe any provisions in the transaction agreements governing the modification of the terms of any asset, including how such modification may affect the cash flows from the assets or to the securities.

(f) *Claims on Pool Assets.* Describe any material direct or contingent claim that parties other than the holders of the asset-backed securities have on any pool assets. Also, describe any material cross-collateralization or cross-default provisions relating to the pool assets.

(g) *Revolving Periods, Prefunding Accounts and Other Changes to the Asset Pool.* If the transaction contemplates a prefunding or revolving period, provide the following information, as applicable. Provide similar information regarding any other circumstances where pool assets may be added, substituted or removed from the asset pool, such as in the event of additional issuances of asset-backed securities in a master trust or a breach of a pool asset representation or warranty:

(1) The term or duration of any prefunding or revolving period.

(2) For prefunding periods, the amount of proceeds to be deposited in the prefunding account.

(3) For revolving periods, the maximum amount of additional assets that may be acquired during the revolving period, if applicable.

(4) The percentage of the asset pool and any class or series of the asset-backed securities represented by the prefunding account or the revolving account, if applicable.

(5) Triggers or events that would trigger limits on or terminate the prefunding or revolving period and the effects of such triggers. In particular for a revolving period, describe the operation of the revolving period and the amortization period.

(6) When and how new pool assets may be acquired during the prefunding or revolving period, and if, when and how pool assets can be removed or substituted. Describe any limits on the amount, type or speed with which pool assets may be acquired, substituted or removed.

(7) The acquisition or underwriting criteria for additional pool assets to be acquired during the prefunding or revolving period, including a description of any differences from the criteria used to select the current asset pool.

(8) Which party has the authority to add, remove or substitute assets from the asset pool or determine if such pool assets meet the acquisition or underwriting criteria for additional pool assets. In addition, disclose whether or not there will be any independent verification of such person's exercise of authority or determinations.

(9) Any requirements to add or remove minimum amounts of pool assets and any effects of not meeting those requirements.

(10) If applicable, the procedures and standards for the temporary investment of funds in a prefunding or revolving account pending use (including the disposition of gains and losses on pending funds) and a description of the financial products or instruments eligible for such accounts.

(11) The circumstances under which funds in a prefunding or revolving account will be returned to investors or otherwise disposed of.

(12) A statement of whether, and if so, how, investors will be notified of changes to the asset pool.

(h) *Asset-Level Information.*

(1) If the asset pool includes residential mortgages, commercial mortgages, automobile loans, automobile leases, debt securities or resecuritizations of asset-backed securities, provide asset-level information for each asset or security in the pool in the manner specified in Schedule AL (Item 1125 of Regulation AB).

(2) File the disclosures as an Asset Data File (as defined in Rule 11 of Regulation S–T) in the format required by the EDGAR Filer Manual. See Rule 301 of Regulation S–T.

(3) File the Asset Data File as an exhibit to Form ABS–EE (17 CFR 249.1401) in accordance with Item 601(b)(102) of Regulation S–K (Item 601(b)(102)).

(4) A registrant may provide additional explanatory disclosure related to an Asset Data File by filing an asset related document as an exhibit to Form ABS–EE (17 CFR 249.1401) in accordance with Item 601(b)(103) of Regulation S–K (Item 601(b)(103)).

(5) A registrant may provide other asset-level information in addition to the information required by Schedule AL (Item 1125 of Regulation S–K) by filing an asset related document as an exhibit to Form ABS–EE (17 CFR 249.1401) in accordance with Item 601(b)(103) of Regulation S–K (Item 601(b)(103)). The asset related document(s) must contain the definitions and formulas for each additional data point and the related tagged data and may contain explanatory disclosure about each additional data point.

Instruction to Item 1111(h): All of the information required by this Item must be provided at the time of every filing for each asset that was in the asset pool during the reporting period, including assets removed prior to the end of the reporting period.

Item 1112. Significant obligors of pool assets

(a) *Descriptive Information.* Provide the Following Information for each significant obligor:

(1) The name of the obligor.

(2) The organizational form and general character of the business of the obligor.

(3) The nature of the concentration of the pool assets with the obligor.

(4) The material terms of the pool assets and the agreements with the obligor involving the pool assets.

(b) *Financial Information.* (1) If the pool assets relating to a significant obligor represent 10% or more, but less than 20%, of the asset pool, provide selected financial data required by Item 301 of Regulation S–K for the significant obligor, provided, however, that for a significant obligor under Item 1101(k)(2) of this Regulation AB, only net operating income for the most recent fiscal year and interim period is required.

(2) If pool assets relating to a significant obligor represent 20% or more of the asset pool, provide financial statements meeting the requirements of Regulation S–X (Rules 1–01 through 12–29), except Rules 3–05 and Article 11 of Regulation S–X (11–01 through 11–03), of the significant obligor. Financial statements of such obligor and its subsidiaries consolidated (as required by Rule 14a–3(b) under the Securities Exchange Act of 1934) shall be filed under this item.

Instructions to Item 1112(b):

1. No information need be provided pursuant to paragraph (b) of this item if the obligations of the significant obligor as they relate to the pool assets are backed by the full faith and credit of the United States.

2. If the significant obligor is an asset-backed issuer and the pool assets relating to the significant obligor are asset-backed securities, provide the following information in lieu of the information required by paragraph (b) of this item:

a. For a registration statement under the Securities Act of 1933 or the Securities Exchange Act of 1934 or a prospectus to be filed pursuant to Rule 424, the information required by Items 1104 through 1115, 1117 and 1119 of this Regulation AB regarding such asset-backed securities; and

b. For an Exchange Act report on Form 10–K or Form 10–D (17 CFR 249.310 or 249.312), the information required by General Instruction J. of Form 10–K regarding such asset-backed securities for the period for which the last Form 10–K of the asset-backed securities was due (or would have been due if such asset-backed securities are not required to file reports with the Commission pursuant to section 13(a) or 15(d) of the Securities Exchange Act of 1934) (15 U.S.C. 78m(a) or 78o(d)).

3. If the significant obligor is a foreign business (as defined Rule 1–02 of Regulation S–X):

a. Paragraph (b)(1) of this item may be complied with by providing the information required by Item 3.A. of Form 20–F (17 CFR 249.220f). If a reconciliation to U.S. generally accepted accounting principles called for by Instruction 2. to Item 3.A. of Form 20–F is unavailable or not obtainable without unreasonable cost or expense, at a minimum provide a narrative description of all material variations in accounting principles, practices and methods used in preparing the non-U.S. GAAP financial statements used as a basis for the selected financial data from those accepted in the U.S.

b. Paragraph (b)(2) of this item may be complied with by providing financial statements meeting the requirements of Item 17 of Form 20–F for the periods specified by Item 8.A. of Form 20–F.

Item 1113. Structure of the transaction

(a) *Description of the Securities and Transaction Structure.* In providing the information required by Item 202 of Regulation S–K, address the following specific factors relating to the asset-backed securities, as applicable:

(1) The types or categories of securities that may be offered, such as interest-weighted or principal-weighted classes (including IO (interest only) or PO (principal only) securities), planned amortization or companion classes or residual or subordinated interests.

(2) The flow of funds for the transaction, including the payment allocations, rights and distribution priorities among all classes of the issuing entity's securities, and within each class, with respect to cash flows, credit enhancement or other support and any other structural features designed to enhance credit, facilitate the timely payment of monies due on the pool assets or owing to security holders, adjust the rate of return on the asset-backed securities, or preserve monies that will or might be distributed to security holders. In addition to an appropriate narrative discussion of the allocation and priority structure of pool cash flows, present the flow of funds graphically if doing so will aid understanding. In the flow of funds discussion, provide information regarding any requirements directing cash flows from the pool assets (such as to reserve accounts, cash collateral accounts or expenses) and the purpose and operation of such requirements.

(3) In describing the interest rate or rate of return on the asset-backed securities and how such amounts are payable, explain how the rate is determined and how frequently it will be determined. If the rate to be paid can be a combination of two or more rates (such as the lesser of a variable rate or the actual weighted average net coupon on the pool assets), provide clear information regarding each rate and when each rate applies.

(4) How principal, if any, will be paid on the asset-backed securities, including maturity dates, amortization or principal distribution schedules, principal distribution dates, formulas for calculating principal distributions from the cash flows and other factors that will affect the timing or amount of principal payments for each class of securities.

(5) The denominations in which the asset-backed securities may be issued.

(6) Any specified changes to the transaction structure that would be triggered upon a default or event of default (such as a change in distribution priority among classes).

(7) Any liquidation, amortization, performance or similar triggers or events, and the rights of investors or changes to the transaction structure or flow of funds if such events were to occur.

(i) Describe how the delinquency threshold that triggers a review by the asset representations reviewer was determined to be appropriate. In describing the appropriateness of such delinquency threshold, compare such delinquency threshold against the delinquencies disclosed for prior securitized pools of the sponsor for that asset type in accordance with Item 1105 of Regulation AB (17 CFR 229.1105).

(ii) [Reserved]

(8) Whether the servicer or other party is required to provide periodic evidence of the absence of a default or of compliance with the terms of the transaction agreements.

(9) If applicable, the extent, expressed as a percentage, the transaction is overcollateralized or undercollateralized as measured by comparing the principal balance of the asset-backed securities to the asset pool.

(10) Any provisions contained in other securities that could result in a cross-default or cross-collateralization.

(11) Any minimum standards, restrictions or suitability requirements regarding potential investors in purchasing the securities or any restrictions on ownership or transfer of the securities.

(12) Security holder vote required to amend the transaction documents and allocation of voting rights among security holders.

(b) *Distribution Frequency and Cash Maintenance.* (1) Disclose the frequency of distribution dates for the asset-backed securities and the collection periods for the pool assets.

(2) Describe how cash held pending distribution or other uses is held and invested. Also describe the length of time cash will be held pending distributions to security holders. Identify the party or parties with access to cash balances and the authority to invest cash balances. Specify who determines any decisions regarding the deposit, transfer or disbursement of pool asset cash flows and whether there will be any independent verification of the transaction accounts or account activity.

(c) *Fees and Expenses.* Provide in a separate table an itemized list of all fees and expenses to be paid or payable out of the cash flows from the pool assets. In itemizing the fees and expenses, also indicate their general purpose, the party receiving such fees or expenses, the source of funds for such fees or expenses (if different from other fees or expenses or if such fees or expenses are to be paid from a specified portion of the cash flows) and the distribution priority of such expenses. If the amount of such fees or expenses is not fixed, provide the formula used to determine such fees or expenses. The tabular presentation should be accompanied by footnotes or other accompanying narrative disclosure to the extent necessary for an understanding of the timing or amount of such fees or expenses, such as any restrictions or limits on fees or whether the estimate may change in certain instances, such as in an event of default (and how the fees would change in such an instance or the factors that would affect the change). In addition, through footnote or other accompanying narrative disclosure, describe if any, and if so how, such fees or expenses can be changed without notice to, or approval by, security holders and any restrictions on the ability to change a fee or expense amount, such as due to a change in transaction party.

(d) *Excess Cash Flow.* (1) Describe the disposition of residual or excess cash flows. Identify who owns any residual or retained interests to the cash flows if such person is affiliated with the sponsor, depositor, issuing entity or any entity identified in Item 1119(a) of this Regulation AB or if such person has rights that may alter the transaction structure beyond receipt of residual or excess cash flows. Describe such rights, as material.

(2) Disclose any requirements in the transaction agreements to maintain a minimum amount of excess cash flow or spread from, or retained interest in, the transaction and any actions that would be required or changes to the transaction structure that would occur if such requirements were not met.

(3) To the extent material to an understanding of the asset-backed securities, disclose any features or arrangements to facilitate a securitization of the excess cash flow or retained interest from the transaction, including whether any material changes to the transaction structure may be made without the consent of asset-backed security holders in connection with these securitizations.

(e) *Master Trusts.* If one or more additional series or classes have been or may be issued that are backed by the same asset pool, provide information regarding the additional securities to the extent material to an understanding of their effect on the securities being offered, including the following:

(1) Relative priority of such additional securities to the securities being offered and rights to the underlying pool assets and their cash flows.

(2) Allocation of cash flow from the asset pool and any expenses or losses among the various series or classes.

(3) Terms under which such additional series or classes may be issued and pool assets increased or changed.

(4) The terms of any security holder approval or notification of such additional securities.

(5) Which party has the authority to determine whether such additional securities may be issued. In addition, if there are conditions to such additional issuance, disclose whether or not there will be an independent verification of such person's exercise of authority or determinations.

(f) *Optional or Mandatory Redemption or Termination.* (1) If any class of the asset-backed securities includes an optional or mandatory redemption or termination feature, provide the following information:

(i) Terms for triggering the redemption or termination.

(ii) The identity of the party that holds the redemption or termination option or obligation, as well as whether such party is an affiliate of the sponsor, depositor, issuing entity or any entity identified in Item 1119(a) of this Regulation AB.

(iii) The amount of the redemption or repurchase price or formula for determining such amount.

(iv) The procedures for redemption or termination, including any notices to security holders.

(v) If the amount allocated to security holders is reduced by losses, the policy regarding any amounts recovered after redemption or termination.

(2) The title of any class of securities with an optional redemption or termination feature that may be exercised when 25% or more of the original principal balance of the pool assets is still outstanding must include the word "callable," *provided, however*, that in the case of a master trust, a title of a class of securities must include the word "callable" when an optional redemption or termination feature may be exercised when 25% or more of the original principal balance of the particular series in which the class was issued is still outstanding.

(g) *Prepayment, Maturity and Yield Considerations.*

(1) Describe any models, including the related material assumptions and limitations, used as a means to identify cash flow patterns with respect to the pool assets.

(2) Describe to the extent material the degree to which each class of securities is sensitive to changes in the rate of payment on the pool assets (*e.g.*, prepayment or interest rate sensitivity), and describe the consequences of such changing rate of payment. Provide statistical information of such effects, such as the effect of prepayments on yield and weighted average life.

(3) Describe any special allocations of prepayment risks among the classes of securities, and whether any class protects other classes from the effects of the uncertain timing of cash flow.

Item 1114. Credit enhancement and other support, except for certain derivatives instruments

(a) *Descriptive Information.* To the extent material, describe the following, including a clear discussion of the manner in which each potential item is designed to affect or ensure timely payment of the asset-backed securities:

(1) Any external credit enhancement designed to ensure that the asset-backed securities or pool assets will pay in accordance with their terms, such as bond insurance, letters of credit or guarantees.

(2) Any mechanisms to ensure that payments on the asset-backed securities are timely, such as liquidity facilities, lending facilities, guaranteed investment contracts and minimum principal payment agreements.

(3) Any derivatives whose primary purpose is to provide credit enhancement related to pool assets or the asset-backed securities.

(4) Any internal credit enhancement as a result of the structure of the transaction that increases the likelihood that payments will be made on one or more classes of the asset-backed securities in accordance with their terms, such as subordination provisions, overcollateralization, reserve accounts, cash collateral accounts or spread accounts.

Instructions to Item 1114(a):

1. Include a description of the material terms of any enhancement or support described, including any limits on the timing or amount of the enhancement or support or any conditions that must be met before the enhancement or support can be accessed. The enhancement or support agreement is to be filed as an exhibit. Also describe any provisions regarding the substitution of enhancement or support.

2. This Item should not be construed as allowing anything other than an asset-backed security whose payment is based primarily by reference to the performance of the receivables or other financial assets in the asset pool.

(b) *Information Regarding Significant Enhancement Providers.*

(1) *Descriptive Information.* If an entity or group of affiliated entities providing enhancement or other support described in paragraph (a) of this item is liable or contingently liable to provide payments representing 10% or more of the cash flow supporting any offered class of asset-backed securities, provide the following information:

(i) The name of such enhancement provider.

(ii) The organizational form of enhancement provider.

(iii) The general character of the business of such enhancement provider.

(2) *Financial Information.* (i) If any entity or group of affiliated entities providing enhancement or other support described in paragraph (a) of this item is liable or contingently liable to provide payments representing 10% or more, but less than 20%, of the cash flow supporting any offered class of the asset-backed securities, provide financial data required by item 301 of Regulation S–K for each such entity or group of affiliated entities.

(ii) If any entity or group of affiliated entities providing enhancement or other support described in paragraph (a) of this section is liable or contingently liable to provide payments representing 20% or more of the cash flow supporting any offered class of the asset-backed securities, provide financial statements meeting the requirements of Regulation S–X (Rules 1–01 through 12–29), except Rule 3–05 and Article 11 of Regulation S–X (Rules 11–01 through 11–03), of such entity or group of affiliated entities. Financial statements of such enhancement provider and its subsidiaries consolidated (as required by Rule 14a–3(b) under the Securities Exchange Act of 1934) shall be filed under this item.

Instructions to Item 1114(b):

1. The requirements in paragraph (b) of this item apply to all providers of external credit enhancement or other support, other than those described in Item 1115 of this Regulation AB. Enhancement may support payment on the pool assets or payments on the asset-backed securities themselves.

2. No information need be provided pursuant to paragraph (b)(2) of this item if the obligations of the enhancement provider are backed by the full faith and credit of the United States.

3. If the pool assets are student loans originated under the Federal Family Education Loan Program of the Higher Education Act of 1965 (20 U.S.C. 1001 et seq.) and the enhancement provider for the pool assets is a guarantee agency as defined under the Higher Education Act, then the following information may be provided in lieu of providing financial information required pursuant to paragraph (b)(2) of this item:

a. The number of pool assets and aggregate outstanding principal balance of pool assets guaranteed by the guarantee agency (both by number and percentage of the asset pool as of the cut-off date or other applicable date).

b. Disclosure of the following with respect to the guarantee agency, as applicable, including a brief description regarding the method of calculation, covering at least five federal fiscal years:

i. Aggregate principal amount of all student loans guaranteed.

ii. Reserve ratio.

iii. Recovery rate.

iv. Loss rate.

v. Claims rate.

4. If the enhancement provider is a foreign business (as defined Rule 1–02 of Regulation S–X):

a. Paragraph (b)(2)(i) of this item may be complied with by providing the information required by Item 3.A. of Form 20–F (17 CFR 249.220(f)). If a reconciliation to U.S. generally accepted accounting principles called for by Instruction 2. to Item 3.A. of Form 20–F is unavailable or not obtainable without unreasonable cost or expense, at a minimum provide a narrative description of all material variations in accounting principles, practices and methods used in preparing the non-U.S. GAAP financial statements used as a basis for the selected financial data from those accepted in the U.S.

b. Paragraph (b)(2)(ii) of this item may be complied with by providing financial statements meeting the requirements of Item 17 of Form 20–F for the periods specified by Item 8.A. of Form 20–F.

Item 1115. Certain derivatives instruments

This item relates to derivative instruments, such as interest rate and currency swap agreements, that are used to alter the payment characteristics of the cashflows from the issuing entity and whose primary purpose is not to provide credit enhancement related to the pool assets or the asset-backed securities. For purposes of this section, the "significance estimate" of the derivative instrument is to be determined based on a reasonable good-faith estimate of maximum probable exposure, made in substantially the same manner as that used in the sponsor's internal risk management process in respect of similar instruments. The "significance percentage" is the percentage that the amount of the significance estimate represents of the aggregate principal balance of the pool assets, provided, that if the derivative instrument relates only to one or more classes of the asset-backed securities, the "significance percentage" is the percentage that the amount of the significance estimate represents of the aggregate principal balance of such classes.

(a) *Descriptive Information.*

(1) Describe the following regarding the external counterparty:

(i) The name of the derivative counterparty.

(ii) The organizational form of the derivative counterparty.

(iii) The general character of the business of the derivative counterparty.

(2) Describe the operation and material terms of the derivative instrument, including any limits on the timing or amount of payments or any conditions to payments.

(3) Describe any material provisions regarding substitution of the derivative instrument.

(4) At a minimum, disclose whether the significance percentage, as calculated in accordance with this section, is less than 10%, at least 10% but less than 20%, or 20% or more.

(5) File the agreement relating to the derivative instrument as an exhibit.

(b) *Financial Information.*

(1) If the aggregate significance percentage related to any entity or group of affiliated entities providing derivative instruments contemplated by this section is 10% or more, but less than 20%, provide financial data required by Item 301 of Regulation S–K for such entity or group of affiliated entities.

(2) If the aggregate significance percentage related to any entity or group of affiliated entities providing derivative instruments contemplated by this section is 20% or more, provide financial statements meeting the requirements of Regulation S–X (Rules 1–01 through 12–29), except Rule 3–05 and Article 11 of Regulation S–X (Rules 11–01 through 11–03), of such entity or group of affiliated entities. Financial statements of such entity and its subsidiaries consolidated (as required by Rule 14a–3(b) under the Securities Exchange Act of 1934) shall be filed under this item.

Instructions to Item 1115:

1. Instructions 2 and 4 to Item 1114(b) of this Regulation AB apply to the information contemplated by paragraph (b) of this item.

2. This Item should not be construed as allowing anything other than an asset-backed security whose payment is based primarily by reference to the performance of the receivables or other financial assets in the asset pool.

Item 1116. Tax matters

Provide a brief, clear and understandable summary of:

(a) The tax treatment of the asset-backed securities transaction under federal income tax laws.

(b) The material federal income tax consequences of purchasing, owning and selling the asset-backed securities. If any of the material federal income tax consequences are not expected to be the same for investors in all classes offered by the registration statement, describe the material differences.

(c) The substance of counsel's tax opinion, including identification of the material consequences upon which counsel has not been asked, or is unable, to opine.

Item 1117. Legal proceedings

Describe briefly any legal proceedings pending against the sponsor, depositor, trustee, issuing entity, servicer contemplated by Item 1108(a)(3) of this Regulation AB, originator contemplated by Item 1110(b) of this Regulation AB, or other party contemplated by Item 1100(d)(1) of this Regulation AB, or of which any property of the foregoing is the subject, that is material to security holders. Include similar information as to any such proceedings known to be contemplated by governmental authorities.

Item 1118. Reports and additional information

(a) *Reports Required Under the Transaction Documents.* Describe the reports or other documents provided to security holders required under the transaction agreements, including information included, schedule and manner of distribution or other availability, and the entity or entities that will prepare and provide the reports.

(b) *Reports to Be Filed with the Commission.*

(1) Specify the names, and if available, the Commission file numbers of the entity or entities under which reports about the asset-backed securities will be filed with the Securities and Exchange Commission. Identify the reports and other information filed with the Commission.

(2) State that the Commission maintains an Internet site that contains reports, proxy and information statements, and other information regarding issuers that file electronically with the Commission and state the address of that site (http://www.sec.gov).

(c) *Web Site Access to Reports.*

(1) State whether the issuing entity's annual reports on Form 10–K (17 CFR 249.310), distribution reports on Form 10–D (17 CFR 249.312), current reports on Form 8–K (17 CFR 249.308), and amendments to those reports filed or furnished pursuant to section 13(a) or 15(d) of the Exchange Act (15 U.S.C. 78m(a) or 78o(d)) will be made available on the Web site of a specified transaction party (e.g., the sponsor, depositor, servicer, issuing entity or trustee) as soon as reasonably practicable after such material is electronically filed with, or furnished to, the Commission.

(2) Disclose whether other reports to security holders or information about the asset-backed securities will be made available in this manner.

(3) If filings and other reports will be made available in this manner, disclose the Web site address where such filings may be found.

(4) If filings and other reports will not be made available in this manner, describe the reasons why they will not and whether an identified transaction party voluntarily will provide electronic or paper copies of those filings and other reports free of charge upon request.

Item 1119. Affiliations and certain relationships and related transactions

(a) Describe if so, and how, the sponsor, depositor or issuing entity is an affiliate (as defined in Rule 405) of any of the following parties as well as, to the extent known and material, if so, and how, any of the following parties are affiliates of any of the other following parties:

(1) Servicer contemplated by Item 1108(a)(3) of this Regulation AB.

(2) Trustee.

(3) Originator contemplated by Item 1110 of this Regulation AB.

(4) Significant obligor contemplated by Item 1112 of this Regulation AB.

(5) Enhancement or support provider contemplated by Items 1114 or 1115 of this Regulation AB.

(6) Any other material parties related to the asset-backed securities contemplated by Item 1100(d)(1) of this Regulation AB.

(7) Asset representations reviewer.

(b) Describe whether there is, and if so the general character of, any business relationship, agreement, arrangement, transaction or understanding that is entered into outside the ordinary course of business or is on terms other than would be obtained in an arm's length transaction with an unrelated third party, apart from the asset-backed securities transaction, between the sponsor, depositor or issuing entity and any of the parties in paragraphs (a)(1) through (a)(6) of this Item, or any affiliates of such parties, that currently exists or that existed during the past two years and that is material to an investor's understanding of the asset-backed securities.

Instruction to Item 1119(b): What is required is information material to an investor's understanding of the asset-backed securities. A detailed description or itemized listing of all commercial relationships among the parties is not required. Instead, the disclosure should indicate whether any relationships outside of the asset-backed securities transaction do exist that are outside the normal course and the general character of those relationships.

(c) Notwithstanding paragraph (b) of this item, describe, to the extent material, any specific relationships involving or relating to the asset-backed securities transaction or the pool assets, including the material terms and approximate dollar amount involved, between the sponsor, depositor or issuing entity and any of the parties in paragraphs (a)(1) through (a)(6) of this item, or any affiliates of such parties, that currently exists or that existed during the past two years.

Instruction to Item 1119: With respect to disclosure in an annual report on Form 10–K, information required by this Item 1119 may be omitted to the extent that substantially the same information had been provided previously in an annual report on Form 10–K (17 CFR 249.310) for the asset-backed securities or in an effective registration statement under the Securities Act or a prospectus timely filed pursuant to Rule 424 under the same Central Index Key (CIK) code as the current annual report on Form 10–K.

Item 1120. Ratings

Disclose whether the issuance or sale of any class of offered securities is conditioned on the assignment of a rating by one or more rating agencies, whether or not NRSROs. If so, identify each rating agency and the minimum rating that must be assigned. Describe any arrangements to have such rating monitored while the asset-backed securities are outstanding.

Item 1121. Distribution and pool performance information

(a) Describe the distribution for the related distribution period and the performance of the asset pool during the distribution period. Provide appropriate introductory and explanatory information to introduce any material terms, parties or abbreviations used (or a cross-reference to a Commission filing where such information may be found). Present statistical information in tabular or graphical format, if such presentation will aid understanding. While the material information regarding the related distribution and pool performance will vary depending on the nature of the transaction, such information may include, among other things:

(1) Any applicable record dates, accrual dates, determination dates for calculating distributions and actual distribution dates for the distribution period.

(2) Cash flows received and the sources thereof for distributions, fees and expenses (including portfolio yield, if applicable).

(3) Calculated amounts and distribution of the flow of funds for the period itemized by type and priority of payment, including:

(i) Fees or expenses accrued and paid, with an identification of the general purpose of such fees and the party receiving such fees or expenses.

(ii) Payments accrued or paid with respect to enhancement or other support identified in Item 1114 of this Regulation AB (such as insurance premiums or other enhancement maintenance fees), with an identification of the general purpose of such payments and the party receiving such payments.

(iii) Principal, interest and other distributions accrued and paid on the asset-backed securities by type and by class or series and any principal or interest shortfalls or carryovers.

(iv) The amount of excess cash flow or excess spread and the disposition of excess cash flow.

(4) Beginning and ending principal balances of the asset-backed securities.

(5) Interest rates applicable to the pool assets and the asset-backed securities, as applicable. Consider providing interest rate information for pool assets in appropriate distributional groups or incremental ranges.

(6) Beginning and ending balances of transaction accounts, such as reserve accounts, and material account activity during the period.

(7) Any amounts drawn on any credit enhancement or other support identified in Item 1114 of this Regulation AB, as applicable, and the amount of coverage remaining under any such enhancement, if known and applicable.

(8) Number and amount of pool assets at the beginning and ending of each period, and updated pool composition information, such as weighted average coupon, weighted average life, weighted average remaining term, pool factors and prepayment amounts. For asset-backed securities backed by leases where a portion of the securitized pool balance is attributable to residual values of the physical property underlying the leases, this information also would include turn-in rates and residual value realization rates.

(9) Delinquency and loss information for the period. Present historical delinquency and loss information in accordance with Item 1100(b) of this Regulation AB through no less than 120 days.

(10) Information on the amount, terms and general purpose of any advances made or reimbursed during the period, including the general use of funds advanced and the general source of funds for reimbursements.

(11) Any material modifications, extensions or waivers to pool asset terms, fees, penalties or payments during the distribution period or that have cumulatively become material over time.

(12) Material breaches of pool asset representations or warranties or transaction covenants.

(13) Information on ratio, coverage or other tests used for determining any early amortization, liquidation or other performance trigger and whether the trigger was met.

(14) Information regarding any new issuance of asset-backed securities backed by the same asset pool, any pool asset changes (other than in connection with a pool asset converting into cash in accordance with its terms), such as additions or removals in connection with a prefunding or revolving period and pool asset substitutions and repurchases (and purchase rates, if applicable), and cash flows available for future purchases, such as the balances of any prefunding or revolving accounts, if applicable. Disclose any material changes in the solicitation, credit-granting, underwriting, origination, acquisition or pool selection criteria or procedures, as applicable, used to originate, acquire or select the new pool assets.

(b) During a prefunding or revolving period, or if there has been a new issuance of asset-backed securities backed by the same pool under a master trust during the fiscal year of the issuing entity, provide the information required by Items 1110, 1111 and 1112 of this Regulation AB applied taking the revised pool composition into account in the Form 10–D report (17 CFR 249.312) for the last required distribution of the fiscal year of the issuing entity. In addition, provide such updated information in the first Form 10–D report for the period in which the prefunding or revolving period ends (if applicable). However, no disclosure need be provided by this paragraph if the information has not materially changed from that previously provided in an Exchange Act report relating to the asset-backed securities or in an effective registration statement under the Securities Act or a prospectus timely filed pursuant to Rule 424 under the same Central Index Key (CIK) code regarding a subsequent issuance of asset-backed securities backed by a pool of assets that includes the pool assets that are the subject of this paragraph.

(c) *Repurchases and Replacements.* (1) Provide the information required by Rule 15Ga–1(a) under the Securities Exchange Act of 1934 concerning all assets of the pool that were subject to a demand to repurchase or replace for breach of the representation and warranties.

(2) Include a reference to the most recent Form ABS–15G (17 CFR 249.1400) filed by the securitizer (as that term is defined in Section 15G(a) of the Securities Exchange Act of 1934) and disclose the CIK number of the securitizer.

(d) *Asset Review.* (1) If during the distribution period a review of the underlying assets for compliance with the representations and warranties on the underlying assets is required, provide the following information, as applicable:

(i) A description of the event(s) that triggered the review during the distribution period; and

(ii) If the asset representations reviewer provided to the trustee during the distribution period a report of the findings and conclusions of the review, a summary of the report.

(2) *Change in Asset Representations Reviewer.* If during the distribution period an asset representations reviewer has resigned or has been removed, replaced or substituted, or if a new asset representations reviewer has been appointed, state the date the event occurred and the circumstances surrounding the change. If a new asset representations reviewer has been appointed, provide the disclosure required by Item 1109(b) (17 CFR 229.1109(b)), as applicable, regarding such asset representations reviewer.

(e) *Investor Communication.* Disclose any request received from an investor to communicate with other investors during the reporting period received by the party responsible for making the Form 10–D filings on or before the end date of a distribution period. The disclosure regarding the request to communicate is required to include the name of the investor making the request, the date the request was received, a statement to the effect that the party responsible for filing the Form 10–D (17 CFR 249.312) has received a request from such investor, stating that such investor is interested in communicating with other investors with regard to the possible exercise of rights under the transaction agreements, and a description of the method by which other investors may contact the requesting investor.

Instruction to Item 1121(e). The party responsible for filing the Form 10–D (17 CFR 249.312) is required to disclose an investor's interest to communicate only where the communication relates to an investor exercising its rights under the terms of the transaction agreement.

Item 1122. Compliance with applicable servicing criteria

(a) *Reports on Assessment of Compliance with Servicing Criteria for Asset–Backed Securities.* As required by paragraph (b) of Rule 13a–18 or 15d–18 under the Securities Exchange Act of 1934, provide as an exhibit from each party participating in the servicing function a report on an assessment of compliance with the servicing criteria set forth in paragraph (d) of this item that contains the following:

(1) A statement of the party's responsibility for assessing compliance with the servicing criteria applicable to it;

(2) A statement that the party used the criteria in paragraph (d) of this item to assess compliance with the applicable servicing criteria;

(3) The party's assessment of compliance with the applicable servicing criteria as of and for the period ending the end of the fiscal year covered by the Form 10–K report (17 CFR 249.310). This discussion must include disclosure of any material instance of noncompliance identified by the party; and

(4) A statement that a registered public accounting firm has issued an attestation report on the party's assessment of compliance with the applicable servicing criteria as of and for the period ending the end of the fiscal year covered by the Form 10–K report.

(b) *Registered Public Accounting Firm Attestation Reports.* Provide the registered public accounting firm's attestation report required by paragraph (c) of Rule 13a–18 or Rule 15d–18 under the Securities Exchange Act of 1934 on the party's assessment of compliance with the applicable servicing criteria as an exhibit.

(c) *Additional Disclosure for the Form 10–K Report.* (1) If any party's report on assessment of compliance with servicing criteria required by paragraph (a) of this section, or related registered public accounting firm attestation report required by paragraph (b) of this section, identifies any material instance of noncompliance with the servicing criteria, identify the material instance of noncompliance in the report on Form 10–K (17 CFR 249.310). Also disclose whether the identified instance was determined to have involved the servicing of the assets backing the asset-backed securities covered in this Form 10–K report.

(2) Discuss any steps taken to remedy a material instance of noncompliance previously identified by an asserting party for its activities with respect to asset-backed securities transactions taken as a whole involving such party and that are backed by the same asset type backing the asset-backed securities.

(3) If any party's report on assessment of compliance with servicing criteria required by paragraph (a) of this item, or related registered public accounting firm attestation report required by paragraph (b) of this item, is not included as an exhibit to the Form 10–K report, disclosure that the report is not included and an associated explanation must be provided in the report on Form 10–K.

(d) *Servicing Criteria*. (1) *General Servicing Considerations.*

(i) Policies and procedures are instituted to monitor any performance or other triggers and events of default in accordance with the transaction agreements.

(ii) If any material servicing activities are outsourced to third parties, policies and procedures are instituted to monitor the third party's performance and compliance with such servicing activities.

(iii) Any requirements in the transaction agreements to maintain a back-up servicer for the pool assets are maintained.

(iv) A fidelity bond and errors and omissions policy is in effect on the party participating in the servicing function throughout the reporting period in the amount of coverage required by and otherwise in accordance with the terms of the transaction agreements.

(v) Aggregation of information, as applicable, is mathematically accurate and the information conveyed accurately reflects the information.

(2) *Cash Collection and Administration*. (i) Payments on pool assets are deposited into the appropriate custodial bank accounts and related bank clearing accounts no more than two business days of receipt, or such other number of days specified in the transaction agreements.

(ii) Disbursements made via wire transfer on behalf of an obligor or to an investor are made only by authorized personnel.

(iii) Advances of funds or guarantees regarding collections, cash flows or distributions, and any interest or other fees charged for such advances, are made, reviewed and approved as specified in the transaction agreements.

(iv) The related accounts for the transaction, such as cash reserve accounts or accounts established as a form of overcollateralization, are separately maintained (e.g., with respect to commingling of cash) as set forth in the transaction agreements.

(v) Each custodial account is maintained at a federally insured depository institution as set forth in the transaction agreements. For purposes of this criterion, "federally insured depository institution" with respect to a foreign financial institution means a foreign financial institution that meets the requirements of Rule 13k–1(b)(1) under the Securities Exchange Act of 1934.

(vi) Unissued checks are safeguarded so as to prevent unauthorized access.

(vii) Reconciliations are prepared on a monthly basis for all asset-backed securities related bank accounts, including custodial accounts and related bank clearing accounts. These reconciliations:

(A) Are mathematically accurate;

(B) Are prepared within 30 calendar days after the bank statement cutoff date, or such other number of days specified in the transaction agreements;

(C) Are reviewed and approved by someone other than the person who prepared the reconciliation; and

(D) Contain explanations for reconciling items. These reconciling items are resolved within 90 calendar days of their original identification, or such other number of days specified in the transaction agreements.

(3) *Investor Remittances and Reporting*. (i) Reports to investors, including those to be filed with the Commission, are maintained in accordance with the transaction agreements and applicable Commission requirements. Specifically, such reports:

(A) Are prepared in accordance with timeframes and other terms set forth in the transaction agreements;

(B) Provide information calculated in accordance with the terms specified in the transaction agreements;

(C) Are filed with the Commission as required by its rules and regulations; and

(D) Agree with investors' or the trustee's records as to the total unpaid principal balance and number of pool assets serviced by the servicer.

(ii) Amounts due to investors are allocated and remitted in accordance with timeframes, distribution priority and other terms set forth in the transaction agreements.

(iii) Disbursements made to an investor are posted within two business days to the servicer's investor records, or such other number of days specified in the transaction agreements.

(iv) Amounts remitted to investors per the investor reports agree with cancelled checks, or other form of payment, or custodial bank statements.

(4) *Pool Asset Administration.* (i) Collateral or security on pool assets is maintained as required by the transaction agreements or related pool asset documents.

(ii) Pool assets and related documents are safeguarded as required by the transaction agreements.

(iii) Any additions, removals or substitutions to the asset pool are made, reviewed and approved in accordance with any conditions or requirements in the transaction agreements.

(iv) Payments on pool assets, including any payoffs, made in accordance with the related pool asset documents are posted to the applicable servicer's obligor records maintained no more than two business days after receipt, or such other number of days specified in the transaction agreements, and allocated to principal, interest or other items (e.g., escrow) in accordance with the related pool asset documents.

(v) The servicer's records regarding the pool assets agree with the servicer's records with respect to an obligor's unpaid principal balance.

(vi) Changes with respect to the terms or status of an obligor's pool asset (e.g., loan modifications or re-agings) are made, reviewed and approved by authorized personnel in accordance with the transaction agreements and related pool asset documents.

(vii) Loss mitigation or recovery actions (e.g., forbearance plans, modifications and deeds in lieu of foreclosure, foreclosures and repossessions, as applicable) are initiated, conducted and concluded in accordance with the timeframes or other requirements established by the transaction agreements.

(viii) Records documenting collection efforts are maintained during the period a pool asset is delinquent in accordance with the transaction agreements. Such records are maintained on at least a monthly basis, or such other period specified in the transaction agreements, and describe the entity's activities in monitoring delinquent pool assets including, for example, phone calls, letters and payment rescheduling plans in cases where delinquency is deemed temporary (e.g., illness or unemployment).

(ix) Adjustments to interest rates or rates of return for pool assets with variable rates are computed based on the related pool asset documents.

(x) Regarding any funds held in trust for an obligor (such as escrow accounts):

(A) Such funds are analyzed, in accordance with the obligor's pool asset documents, on at least an annual basis, or such other period specified in the transaction agreements;

(B) Interest on such funds is paid, or credited, to obligors in accordance with applicable pool asset documents and state laws; and

(C) Such funds are returned to the obligor within 30 calendar days of full repayment of the related pool asset, or such other number of days specified in the transaction agreements.

(xi) Payments made on behalf of an obligor (such as tax or insurance payments) are made on or before the related penalty or expiration dates, as indicated on the appropriate bills or notices for such payments, provided that such support has been received by the servicer at least 30 calendar days prior to these dates, or such other number of days specified in the transaction agreements.

(xii) Any late payment penalties in connection with any payment to be made on behalf of an obligor are paid from the servicer's funds and not charged to the obligor, unless the late payment was due to the obligor's error or omission.

(xiii) Disbursements made on behalf of an obligor are posted within two business days to the obligor's records maintained by the servicer, or such other number of days specified in the transaction agreements.

(xiv) Delinquencies, charge-offs and uncollectable accounts are recognized and recorded in accordance with the transaction agreements.

(xv) Any external enhancement or other support, identified in Item 1114(a)(1) through (3) or Item 1115 of this Regulation AB, is maintained as set forth in the transaction agreements.

Instructions to Item 1122: The assessment should cover all asset-backed securities transactions involving such party and that are backed by the same asset type backing the class of asset-backed securities which are the subject of the Commission filing. The asserting party may take into account divisions among transactions that are consistent with actual practices. However, if the asserting party includes in its platform less than all of the transactions backed by the same asset type that it services, a description of the scope of the platform should be included in the assessment.

2. If certain servicing criteria are not applicable to the asserting party based on the activities it performs with respect to asset-backed securities transactions taken as a whole involving such party and that are backed by the same asset type backing the class of asset-backed securities, the inapplicability of the criteria must be disclosed in that asserting party's and the related registered public accounting firm's reports.

3. If multiple parties are participating in the servicing function, a separate assessment report and attestation report must be included for each party participating in the servicing function. A party participating in the servicing function means any entity (e.g., master servicer, primary servicers, trustees) that is performing activities that address the criteria in paragraph (d) of this item, unless such entity's activities relate only to 5% or less of the pool assets.

4. If the asset pool backing the asset-backed securities includes a pool asset representing an interest in or the right to the payments or cash flows of another asset pool and both the issuing entity for the asset-backed securities and the entity issuing the asset to be included in the issuing entity's asset pool were established under the direction of the same sponsor and depositor, see also Item 1100(d)(2) of this Regulation AB.

Item 1123. Servicer compliance statement

Provide as an exhibit a statement of compliance from the servicer, signed by an authorized officer of such servicer, to the effect that:

(a) A review of the servicer's activities during the reporting period and of its performance under the applicable servicing agreement has been made under such officer's supervision.

(b) To the best of such officer's knowledge, based on such review, the servicer has fulfilled all of its obligations under the agreement in all material respects throughout the reporting period or, if there has been a failure to fulfill any such obligation in any material respect, specifying each such failure known to such officer and the nature and status thereof.

Instruction to Item 1123: If multiple servicers are involved in servicing the pool assets, a separate servicer compliance statement is required from each servicer that meets the criteria in Item 1108(a)(2)(i) through (iii) of this Regulation AB.

Item 1124. Sponsor interest in the securities

Provide information about any material change in the sponsor's, or an affiliate's, interest in the securities resulting from the purchase, sale or other acquisition or disposition of the securities by the sponsor, or an affiliate, during the period covered by the report. Describe the change, including the amount of change and the sponsor's, or the affiliate's, resulting interest in the transaction after the change.

Instruction to Item 1124: The disclosure required under this item shall separately state the resulting amount and nature of any interest or asset retained in compliance with law, including any amounts that are retained by parties other than the sponsor in order to satisfy such requirement.

Item 1125. Schedule AL—asset-level information

The following definitions apply to the terms used in this schedule unless otherwise specified:

Debt service Reduction. A modification of the terms of a loan resulting from a bankruptcy proceeding, such as a reduction of the amount of the monthly payment on the related mortgage loan.

Deficient Valuation. A bankruptcy proceeding whereby the bankruptcy court may establish the value of the mortgaged property at an amount less than the then-outstanding principal balance of the mortgage loan secured by the mortgaged property or may reduce the outstanding principal balance of a mortgage loan.

Underwritten. The amount of revenues or expenses adjusted based on a number of assumptions made by the mortgage originator or seller.

Item 1. Residential Mortgages. If the asset pool includes residential mortgages, provide the following data and the data under Item 1 for each loan in the asset pool:

(a) *Asset Numbers.* (1) Asset number type. Identify the source of the asset number used to specifically identify each asset in the pool.

(2) Asset number. Provide the unique ID number of the asset.

Instruction to Paragraph (a)(2): The asset number must reference a single asset within the pool and should be the same number that will be used to identify the asset for all reports that would be required of an issuer under Sections 13 or 15(d) of the Exchange Act (15 U.S.C. 78m or 78o(d)). If an asset is removed and replaced with another asset, the asset added to the pool should be assigned a unique asset number applicable to only that asset.

(3) Asset group number. For structures with multiple collateral groups, indicate the collateral group number in which the asset falls.

(b) *Reporting Period.* (1) Reporting period begin date. Specify the beginning date of the reporting period.

(2) Reporting period end date. Specify the ending date of the reporting period.

(c) *General Information About the Residential Mortgage.* (1) Original loan purpose. Specify the code which describes the purpose of the loan at the time the loan was originated.

(2) Originator. Identify the name of the entity that originated the loan.

(3) Original loan amount. Indicate the amount of the loan at the time the loan was originated.

(4) Original loan maturity date. Indicate the month and year in which the final payment on the loan is scheduled to be made at the time the loan was originated.

(5) Original amortization term. Indicate the number of months that would have been required to retire the mortgage loan through regular payments, as determined at the origination date of the loan. In the case of an interest-only loan, the original amortization term is the original term to maturity (other than in the case of a balloon loan). In the case of a balloon loan, the original amortization term is the number of months used to calculate the principal and interest payment due each month (other than the balloon payment).

(6) Original interest rate. Provide the rate of interest at the time the loan was originated.

(7) Accrual type. Provide the code that describes e method used to calculate interest on the loan.

3) Original interest rate type. Indicate whether nterest rate on the loan is fixed, adjustable, r other.

(9) Original interest only term. Indicate the number of months in which the obligor is permitted to pay only interest on the loan beginning from when the loan was originated.

(10) Underwriting indicator. Indicate whether the loan or asset met the criteria for the first level of solicitation, credit-granting or underwriting criteria used to originate the pool asset.

(11) Original lien position. Indicate the code that describes the priority of the lien against the subject property at the time the loan was originated.

(12) Information related to junior liens. If the loan is a first mortgage with subordinate liens, provide the following additional information for each non-first mortgage if obtained or available:

(i) Most recent junior loan balance. Provide the most recent combined balance of any subordinate liens.

(ii) Date of most recent junior loan balance. Provide the date of the most recent junior loan balance.

(13) Information related to non-first mortgages. For non-first mortgages, provide the following information if obtained or available:

(i) Most recent senior loan amount. Provide the total amount of the balances of all associated senior loans.

(ii) Date of most recent senior loan amount. Provide the date(s) of the most recent senior loan amount.

(iii) Loan type of most senior lien. Indicate the code that describes the loan type of the first mortgage.

(iv) Hybrid period of most senior lien. For non-first mortgages where the associated first mortgage is a hybrid ARM, provide the number of months remaining in the initial fixed interest rate period for the first mortgage.

(v) Negative amortization limit of most senior lien. For non-first mortgages where the associated first mortgage features negative amortization, indicate the negative amortization limit of the mortgage as a percentage of the original unpaid principal balance.

(vi) Origination date of most senior lien. Provide the origination date of the associated first mortgage.

(14) Prepayment penalty indicator. Indicate yes or no as to whether the loan includes a penalty charged to the obligor in the event of a prepayment.

(15) Negative amortization indicator. Indicate yes or no as to whether the loan allows negative amortization.

(16) Modification indicator. Indicate yes or no as to whether the loan has been modified from its original terms.

(17) Number of modifications. Provide the number of times that the loan has been modified.

(18) Mortgage insurance requirement indicator. Indicate yes or no as to whether mortgage insurance is or was required as a condition for originating the loan.

(19) Balloon indicator. Indicate yes or no as to whether the loan documents require a lump-sum to fully pay off the loan.

(20) Covered/High cost loan indicator. Indicate yes, no or unknown as to whether as of the end of the reporting period the loan is categorized as "high cost," "higher priced" or "covered" according to applicable federal, state or local statutes, ordinances or regulations.

(21) Servicer-placed hazard insurance. Indicate yes, no or unknown as to whether as of the end of the reporting period the hazard insurance on the property is servicer-placed.

(22) Refinance cash-out amount. For any refinance loan that is a cash-out refinance provide the amount the obligor received after all other loans to be paid by the mortgage proceeds have been satisfied. For any refinance loan that is a no-cash-out refinance provide the result of the following calculation: [NEW LOAN AMOUNT] – [PAID OFF FIRST MORTGAGE LOAN AMOUNT] – [PAID OFF SECOND MORTGAGE LOAN AMOUNT] – [CLOSING COSTS].

(23) Total origination and discount points. Provide the amount paid to the lender to increase the lender's effective yield and, in the case of discount points, to reduce the interest rate paid by the obligor.

(24) Broker. Indicate yes or no as to whether a broker originated or was involved in the origination of the loan.

(25) *Channel.* Specify the code that describes the source from which the issuer *obtained* the loan.

(26) NMLS company number. Specify the National Mortgage License System (NMLS) registration number of the company that originated the loan.

(27) Buy down period. Indicate the total number of months during which any buy down is in effect, representing the accumulation of all buy down periods.

(28) Loan delinquency advance days count. Indicate the number of days after which a servicer can stop advancing funds on a delinquent loan.

(29) Information related to ARMs. If the loan is an ARM, provide the following additional information:

(i) Original ARM Index. Specify the code that describes the type and source of index to be used to determine the interest rate at each adjustment.

(ii) ARM Margin. Indicate the number of percentage points that is added to the index value to establish the new interest rate at each interest rate adjustment date.

(iii) Fully indexed interest rate. Indicate the fully indexed interest rate to which the obligor was underwritten.

(iv) Initial fixed rate period for hybrid ARM. If the interest rate is initially fixed for a period of time, indicate the number of months between the first payment date of the loan and the first interest rate adjustment date.

(v) Initial interest rate decrease. Indicate the maximum percentage by which the interest rate may decrease at the first interest rate adjustment date.

(vi) Initial interest rate increase. Indicate the maximum percentage by which the interest rate may increase at the first interest rate adjustment date.

(vii) Index look-back. Provide the number of days prior to an interest rate effective date used to determine the appropriate index rate.

(viii) Subsequent interest rate reset period. Indicate the number of months between subsequent rate adjustments.

(ix) Lifetime rate ceiling. Indicate the percentage of the maximum interest rate that can be in effect during the life of the loan.

(x) Lifetime rate floor. Indicate the percentage of the minimum interest rate that can be in effect during the life of the loan.

(xi) Subsequent interest rate decrease. Provide the maximum number of percentage points by which the interest rate may decrease at each rate adjustment date after the initial adjustment.

(xii) Subsequent interest rate increase. Provide the maximum number of percentage points by which the interest rate may increase at each rate adjustment date after the initial adjustment.

(xiii) Subsequent payment reset period. Indicate the number of months between payment adjustments after the first interest rate adjustment date.

(xiv) ARM round indicator. Indicate the code that describes whether an adjusted interest rate is rounded to the next higher adjustable rate mortgage round factor, to the next lower round factor, or to the nearest round factor.

(xv) ARM round percentage. Indicate the percentage to which an adjusted interest rate is to be rounded.

(xvi) Option ARM indicator. Indicate yes or no as to whether the loan is an option ARM.

(xvii) Payment method after recast. Specify the code that describes the means of computing the lowest monthly payment available to the obligor after recast.

(xviii) Initial minimum payment. Provide the amount of the initial minimum payment the obligor is permitted to make.

(xix) Convertible indicator. Indicate yes or no as to whether the obligor of the loan has an option to convert an adjustable interest rate to a fixed interest rate during a specified conversion window.

(xx) HELOC indicator. Indicate yes or no as to whether the loan is a home equity line of credit (HELOC).

(xxi) HELOC draw period. Indicate the original maximum number of months from the month the loan was originated during which the obligor may draw funds against the HELOC account.

(30) Information related to prepayment penalties. If the obligor is subject to prepayment penalties, provide the following additional information:

(i) Prepayment penalty calculation. Specify the code that describes the method for calculating the prepayment penalty for the loan.

(ii) Prepayment penalty type. Specify the code that describes the type of prepayment penalty.

(iii) Prepayment penalty total term. Provide the total number of months after the origination of the loan that the prepayment penalty may be in effect.

(iv) Prepayment penalty hard term. For hybrid prepayment penalties, provide the number of months after the origination of the loan during which a "hard" prepayment penalty applies.

(31) Information related to negative amortization. If the loan allows for negative amortization, provide the following additional information:

(i) Negative amortization limit. Specify the maximum amount of negative amortization that is allowed before recalculating a fully amortizing payment based on the new loan balance.

(ii) Initial negative amortization recast period. Indicate the number of months after the origination of the loan that negative amortization is allowed.

(iii) Subsequent negative amortization recast period. Indicate the number of months after which the payment is required to recast after the first amortization recast period.

(iv) Negative amortization balance amount. Provide the amount of the negative amortization balance accumulated as of the end of the reporting period.

(v) Initial fixed payment period. Indicate the number of months after the origination of the loan during which the payment is fixed.

(vi) Initial periodic payment cap. Indicate the maximum percentage by which a payment can increase in the first amortization recast period.

(vii) Subsequent periodic payment cap. Indicate the maximum percentage by which a payment can increase in one amortization recast period after the initial cap.

(viii) Initial minimum payment reset period. Provide the maximum number of months after the origination of the loan that an obligor can initially pay the minimum payment before a new minimum payment is determined.

(ix) Subsequent minimum payment reset period. Provide the maximum number of months after the initial period an obligor can pay the minimum payment before a new minimum payment is determined.

(x) Minimum payment. Provide the amount of the minimum payment due during the reporting period.

(d) *Information Related to the Property.* (1) Geographic location. Specify the location of the property by providing the two-digit zip code.

(2) Occupancy status. Specify the code that describes the property occupancy status at the time the loan was originated.

(3) Most recent occupancy status. If a property inspection has been performed after the loan is originated, provide the code that describes the manner in which the property is occupied.

(4) Property type. Specify the code that describes the type of property that secures the loan.

(5) Most recent property value. If an additional property valuation was obtained by any transaction party or its affiliates after the original appraised property value, provide the most recent property value obtained.

(6) Most recent property valuation type. Specify the code that describes the method by which the most recent property value was reported.

(7) Most recent property valuation date. Specify the date on which the most recent property value was reported.

(8) Most recent AVM model name. Provide the code indicating the name of the AVM model if an AVM was used to determine the most recent property value.

(9) Most recent AVM confidence score. If an additional AVM was obtained by any transaction party or its affiliates after the original valuation, provide the confidence score presented on the most recent AVM report.

(10) Original combined loan-to-value. Provide the ratio obtained by dividing the amount of all known outstanding mortgage liens on a property at origination by the lesser of the original appraised property value or the sales price.

(11) Original loan-to-value. Provide the ratio obtained by dividing the amount of the original mortgage loan at origination by the lesser of the original appraised property value or the sales price.

(e) *Information Related to the Obligor.* (1) Original number of obligors. Indicate the number of obligors who are obligated to repay the mortgage note at the time the loan was originated.

(2) Original obligor credit score. Provide the standardized credit score of the obligor used to evaluate the obligor during the loan origination process.

(3) Original obligor credit score type. Specify the type of the standardized credit score used to evaluate the obligor during the loan origination process.

(4) Most recent obligor credit score. If an additional credit score was obtained by any transaction party or its affiliates after the original credit score, provide the most recently obtained standardized credit score of the obligor.

(5) Most recent obligor credit score type. Specify the type of the most recently obtained standardized credit score of the obligor.

(6) Date of most recent obligor credit score. Provide the date of the most recently obtained standardized credit score of the obligor.

(7) Obligor income verification level. Indicate the code describing the extent to which the obligor's income was verified during the loan origination process.

(8) 4506 – T Indicator. Indicate yes or no whether a Transcript of Tax Return (received pursuant to the filing of IRS Form 4506–T) was obtained and considered.

(9) Originator front-end debt-to-income (DTI). Provide the front-end DTI ratio used by the originator to qualify the loan.

(10) Originator back-end DTI. Provide the back-end DTI ratio used by the originator to qualify the loan.

(11) Obligor employment verification. Indicate the code describing the extent to which the obligor's employment was verified during the loan origination process.

(12) Length of employment – obligor. Indicate whether the obligor was employed by its current employer for greater than 24 months at the time the loan was originated.

(13) Obligor asset verification. Indicate the code describing the extent to which the obligor's assets used to qualify the loan was verified during the loan origination process.

(14) Original pledged assets. If the obligor(s) pledged financial assets to the lender instead of making a down payment, provide the total value of assets pledged as collateral for the loan at the time of origination.

(15) Qualification method. Specify the code that describes the type of mortgage payment used to qualify the obligor for the loan.

(f) *Information Related to Mortgage Insurance.* If mortgage insurance is required on the mortgage, provide the following additional information:

(1) Mortgage insurance company name. Provide the name of the entity providing mortgage insurance for the loan.

(2) Mortgage insurance coverage. Indicate the total percentage of the original loan balance that is covered by mortgage insurance.

(3) Pool insurance company. Provide the name of the pool insurance provider.

(4) Pool insurance stop loss percent. Provide the aggregate amount that the pool insurance company will pay, calculated as a percentage of the pool balance.

(5) Mortgage insurance coverage plan type. Specify the code that describes the coverage category of the mortgage insurance applicable to the loan.

(g) *Information Related to Activity on the Loan.* (1) Asset added indicator. Indicate yes or no whether the asset was added to the pool during the reporting period.

Instruction to Paragraph (g)(1): A response to this data point is required only when assets are added to the asset pool after the final prospectus under Rule 424 of the Securities Act of 1933 is filed.

(2) Remaining term to maturity. Indicate the number of months from the end of the reporting period to the loan maturity date.

(3) Modification indicator – reporting period. Indicate yes or no whether the asset was modified during the reporting period.

(4) Next payment due date. For loans that have not been paid off, indicate the next payment due date.

(5) Advancing method. Specify the code that indicates a servicer's responsibility for advancing principal or interest on delinquent loans.

(6) Servicing advance methodology. Indicate the code that describes the manner in which principal and/or interest are advanced by the servicer.

(7) Stop principal and interest advance date. Provide the first payment due date for which the servicer ceased advancing principal or interest.

(8) Reporting period beginning loan balance. Indicate the outstanding principal balance of the loan as of the beginning of the reporting period.

(9) Reporting period beginning scheduled loan balance. Indicate the scheduled principal balance of the loan as of the beginning of the reporting period.

(10) Next reporting period payment amount due. Indicate the total payment due to be collected in the next reporting period.

(11) Reporting period interest rate. Indicate the interest rate in effect during the reporting period.

(12) Next interest rate. For loans that have not been paid off, indicate the interest rate that is in effect for the next reporting period.

(13) Servicing fee – percentage. If the servicing fee is based on a percentage, provide the percentage used to calculate the aggregate servicing fee.

(14) Servicing fee – flat-fee. If the servicing fee is based on a flat-fee amount, indicate the monthly servicing fee paid to all servicers.

(15) Other assessed but uncollected servicer fees. Provide the cumulative amount of late charges and other fees that have been assessed by the servicer, but not paid by the obligor.

(16) Other loan-level servicing fee(s) retained by the servicer. Provide the amount of all other fees earned by loan administrators during the reporting period that reduced the amount of funds remitted to the issuing entity (including subservicing, master servicing, trustee fees, etc.).

(17) Scheduled interest amount. Indicate the interest payment amount that was scheduled to be collected during the reporting period.

(18) Other interest adjustments. Indicate any unscheduled interest adjustments during the reporting period.

(19) Scheduled principal amount. Indicate the principal payment amount that was scheduled to be collected during the reporting period.

(20) Other principal adjustments. Indicate any other amounts that caused the principal balance of the loan to be decreased or increased during the reporting period.

(21) Reporting period ending actual balance. Indicate the actual balance of the loan as of the end of the reporting period.

(22) Reporting period ending scheduled balance. Indicate the scheduled principal balance of the loan as of the end of the reporting period.

(23) Reporting period scheduled payment amount. Indicate the total payment amount that was scheduled to be collected during the reporting period (including all fees and escrows).

(24) Total actual amount paid. Indicate the total payment (including all escrows) paid to the servicer during the reporting period.

(25) Actual interest collected. Indicate the gross amount of interest collected during the reporting period, whether or not from the obligor.

(26) Actual principal collected. Indicate the amount of principal collected during the reporting period, whether or not from the obligor.

(27) Actual other amounts collected. Indicate the total of any amounts, other than principal and interest, collected during the reporting period, whether or not from the obligor.

(28) Paid through date. Provide the date the loan's scheduled principal and interest is paid through as of the end of the reporting period.

(29) Interest paid through date. Provide the date through which interest is paid with the payment received during the reporting period, which is the effective date from which interest will be calculated for the application of the next payment.

(30) Paid-in-full amount. Provide the scheduled loan "paid-in-full" amount (principal) (do not include the current month's scheduled principal). Applies to all liquidations and loan payoffs.

(31) Information related to servicer advances.

(i) Servicer advanced amount – principal. Provide the total amount the servicer advanced for the reporting period for due but unpaid principal on the loan.

(ii) Servicer advanced amounts repaid – principal. Provide the total amount of any payments made by the obligor during the reporting period that was applied to outstanding advances of due but unpaid principal on the loan.

(iii) Servicer advances cumulative – principal. Provide the outstanding cumulative amount of principal advances made by the servicer as of the end of the reporting period, including amounts advanced for the reporting period.

(iv) Servicer advanced amount – interest. Provide the total amount the servicer advanced for the reporting period for due but unpaid interest on the loan.

(v) Servicer advanced amounts repaid – interest. Provide the total amount of any payments made by the obligor during the reporting period that was applied to outstanding advances of due but unpaid interest on the loan.

(vi) Servicer advances cumulative – interest. Provide the outstanding cumulative amount of interest advances made by the servicer as of the end of the reporting period, including amounts advanced for the reporting period.

(vii) Servicer advanced amount – taxes and insurance. Provide the total amount the servicer advanced for the reporting period for due but unpaid property tax and insurance payments (escrow amounts).

(viii) Servicer advanced amount repaid – taxes and insurance. Provide the total amount of any payment made by the obligor during the reporting period that was applied to outstanding advances of due but unpaid escrow amounts.

(ix) Servicer advances cumulative – taxes and insurance. Provide the outstanding cumulative amount of escrow advances made by the servicer as of the end of the reporting period, including amounts advanced for the reporting period.

(x) Servicer advanced amount – corporate. Provide the total amount the servicer advanced for property inspection and preservation expenses for the reporting period.

(xi) Servicer advanced amount repaid – corporate. Provide the total amount of any payments made by the obligor during the reporting period that was applied to outstanding corporate advances.

(xii) Servicer advances cumulative – corporate. Provide the outstanding cumulative amount of corporate advances made by the servicer as of the end of the reporting period, including amounts advanced for the reporting period.

Instruction to Paragraph (g)(31): For loans modified or liquidated during a reporting period the data provided in response to this paragraph (g)(31) is to be information as of the liquidation date or modification date, as applicable.

(32) Zero balance loans. If the loan balance was reduced to zero during the reporting period, provide the following additional information about the loan.

(i) Zero balance effective date. Provide the date on which the loan balance was reduced to zero.

(ii) Zero balance code. Provide the code that indicates the reason the loan's balance was reduced to zero.

(33) Most recent 12-month pay history. Provide the string that indicates the payment status per month listed from oldest to most recent.

(34) Number of payments past due. Indicate the number of payments the obligor is past due as of the end of the reporting period.

(35) Information related to activity on ARM loans. If the loan is an ARM, provide the following additional information.

(i) Rate at next reset. Provide the interest rate that will be used to determine the next scheduled interest payment, if known.

(ii) Next payment change date. Provide the next date that the amount of scheduled principal and/or interest is scheduled to change.

(iii) Next interest rate change date. Provide the next scheduled date on which the interest rate is scheduled to change.

(iv) Payment at next reset. Provide the principal and interest payment due after the next scheduled interest rate change, if known.

(v) Exercised ARM conversion option indicator. Indicate yes or no whether the obligor exercised an option to convert an ARM loan to a fixed interest rate loan during the reporting period.

(h) *Information Related to Servicers.* (1) Primary servicer. Indicate the name of the entity that serviced the loan during the reporting period.

(2) Most recent servicing transfer received date. If a loan's servicing has been transferred, provide the effective date of the most recent servicing transfer.

(3) Master servicer. Provide the name of the entity that served as master servicer during the reporting period, if applicable.

(4) Special servicer. Provide the name of the entity that served as special servicer during the reporting period, if applicable.

(5) Subservicer. Provide the name of the entity that served as a subservicer during the reporting period, if applicable.

(i) *Asset Subject to Demand.* Indicate yes or no whether during the reporting period the loan was the subject of a demand to repurchase or replace for breach of representations and warranties, including investor demands upon a trustee. If the loan is the subject of a demand to repurchase or replace for breach of representations and warranties, including investor demands upon a trustee, provide the following additional information:

(1) Status of asset subject to demand. Indicate the code that describes the status of the repurchase or replacement demand as of the end of the reporting period.

(2) Repurchase amount. Provide the amount paid to repurchase the loan from the pool.

(3) Demand resolution date. Indicate the date the loan repurchase or replacement demand was resolved.

(4) Repurchaser. Specify the name of the repurchaser.

(5) Repurchase or replacement reason. Indicate the code that describes the reason for the repurchase or replacement.

(j) *Information Related to Leases That Have Been Charged off.* If the lease has been charged off, provide the following additional information:

(1) Charged-off principal amount. Specify the total amount of uncollected principal charged off.

(2) Charged-off interest amount. Specify the total amount of uncollected interest charged off.

(k) *Reserved.*

(*l*) *Loss Mitigation Type Indicator.* Indicate the code that describes the type of loss mitigation the servicer is pursuing with the obligor, loan, or property as of the end of the reporting period.

(m) *Information Related to Lease Modifications.* If the lease has been modified from its original terms, provide the following additional information about the most recent loan modification:

(1) Most recent loan modification event type. Specify the code that describes the most recent action that has resulted in a change or changes to the loan note terms.

(2) Effective date of the most recent loan modification. Provide the date on which the most recent modification of the loan has gone into effect.

(3) Post-modification maturity date. Provide the loan's maturity date as of the modification effective payment date.

(4) Post-modification interest rate type. Indicate whether the interest rate type on the loan after the modification is fixed, adjustable, step, or other.

(5) Post-modification amortization type. Indicate the amortization type after modification.

(6) Post-modification interest rate. Provide the interest rate in effect as of the modification effective payment date.

(7) Post-modification first payment date. Indicate the date of the first payment due after the loan modification.

(8) Post-modification loan balance. Provide the loan balance as of the modification effective payment date as reported on the modification documents.

(9) Post-modification principal and interest payment. Provide total principal and interest payment amount as of the modification effective payment date.

(10) Total capitalized amount. Provide the amount added to the principal balance of the loan due to the modification.

(11) Income verification indicator (at modification). Indicate yes or no whether a Transcript of Tax Return (received pursuant to the filing of IRS Form 4506-T) was obtained and considered during the loan modification process.

(12) Modification front-end DTI. Provide the front-end DTI ratio used to qualify the modification.

(13) Modification back-end DTI. Provide the back-end DTI ratio used to qualify the modification.

(14) Total deferred amount. Provide the deferred amount that is non-interest bearing.

(15) Forgiven principal amount (cumulative). Provide the total amount of all principal balance reductions as a result of loan modifications over the life of the loan.

(16) Forgiven principal amount (reporting period). Provide the total principal balance reduction as a result of a loan modification during the reporting period.

(17) Forgiven interest amount (cumulative). Provide the total amount of all interest forgiven as a result of loan modifications over the life of the loan.

(18) Forgiven interest amount (reporting period). Provide the total gross interest forgiven as a result of a loan modification during the reporting period.

(19) Actual ending balance – total debt owed. For a loan with principal forbearance, provide the sum of the actual ending balance field plus the principal deferred amount. For all other loans, provide the actual ending balance.

(20) Scheduled ending balance – total debt owed. For a loan with principal forbearance, provide the sum of the scheduled ending balance field plus the deferred amount. For all other loans, provide the scheduled ending balance.

(21) Information related to ARM loan modifications. If the loan was an ARM before and after the most recent modification, provide the following additional information:

(i) Post-modification ARM indicator. Indicate whether the loan's existing ARM parameters have changed per the modification agreement.

(ii) Post-modification ARM index. Specify the code that describes the index on which an adjustable interest rate is based as of the modification effective payment date.

(iii) Post-modification margin. Provide the margin as of the modification effective payment date. The margin is the number of percentage points added to the index to establish the new rate.

(iv) Post-modification interest reset period (if changed). Provide the number of months of the interest reset period of the loan as of the modification effective payment date.

(v) Post-modification next reset date. Provide the next interest reset date as of the modification effective payment date.

(vi) Post-modification index lookback. Provide the number of days prior to an interest rate effective date used to determine the appropriate index rate as of the modification effective payment date.

(vii) Post-modification ARM round indicator. Indicate the code that describes whether an adjusted interest rate is rounded to the next higher adjustable rate mortgage round factor, to the next lower round factor, or to the nearest round factor as of the modification effective payment date.

(viii) Post-modification ARM round percentage. Indicate the percentage to which an adjusted interest rate is to be rounded as of the modification effective payment date.

(ix) Post-modification initial minimum payment. Provide the amount of the initial minimum payment the obligor is permitted to make as of the modification effective payment date.

(x) Post-modification next payment adjustment date. Provide the due date on which the next payment adjustment is scheduled to occur for an ARM loan per the modification agreement.

(xi) Post-modification ARM payment recast frequency. Provide the payment recast frequency of the loan (in months) per the modification agreement.

(xii) Post-modification lifetime rate floor. Provide the minimum rate of interest that may be applied to an adjustable rate loan over the course of the loan's life as of the modification effective payment date.

(xiii) Post-modification lifetime rate ceiling. Provide the maximum rate of interest that may be applied to an adjustable rate loan over the course of the loan's life as of the modification effective payment date.

(xiv) Post-modification initial interest rate increase. Indicate the maximum percentage by which the interest rate may increase at the first interest rate adjustment date after the loan modification.

(xv) Post-modification initial interest rate decrease. Provide the maximum percentage by which the interest rate may adjust downward on the first interest rate adjustment date after the loan modification.

(xvi) Post-modification subsequent interest rate increase. Provide the maximum number of percentage points by which the rate may increase at each rate adjustment date after the initial rate adjustment as of the modification effective payment date.

(xvii) Post-modification subsequent interest rate decrease. Provide the maximum number of percentage points by which the interest rate may decrease at each rate adjustment date after the initial adjustment as of the modification effective payment date.

(xviii) Post-modification payment cap. Provide the percentage value by which a payment may increase or decrease in one period as of the modification effective payment date.

(xix) Post-modification payment method after recast. Specify the code that describes the means of computing the lowest monthly payment available to the obligor after recast as of the modification effective payment date.

(xx) Post-modification ARM interest rate teaser period. Provide the duration in months that the teaser interest rate is in effect as of the modification effective payment date.

(xxi) Post-modification payment teaser period. Provide the duration in months that the teaser payment is in effect as of the modification effective payment date.

(xxii) Post-modification ARM negative amortization indicator. Indicate yes or no whether a negative amortization feature is part of the loan as of the modification effective payment date.

(xxiii) Post-modification ARM negative amortization cap. Provide the maximum percentage of negative amortization allowed on the loan as of the modification effective payment date.

(22) Information related to loan modifications involving interest-only periods. If the loan terms for the most recent loan modification include an interest only period, provide the following additional information:

(i) Post-modification interest-only term. Provide the number of months of the interest- only period from the modification effective payment date.

(ii) Post-modification interest-only last payment date. Provide the date of the last interest-only payment as of the modification effective payment date.

(23) Post-modification balloon payment amount. Provide the new balloon payment amount due at

maturity as a result of the loan modification, not including deferred amounts.

(24) Information related to step loans. If the loans terms for the most recent loan modification agreement call for the interest rate to step up over time, provide the following additional information:

(i) Post-modification interest rate step indicator. Indicate whether the terms of the modification agreement call for the interest rate to step up over time.

(ii) Post-modification step interest rate. Provide the rate(s) that will apply at each change date as stated in the loan modification agreement. All rates must be provided, not just the first change rate, unless there is only a single change date.

(iii) Post-modification step date. Provide the date(s) at which the next rate and/or payment change will occur per the loan modification agreement. All dates must be provided, not just the first change, unless there is only a single change date.

(iv) Post-modification – step principal and interest. Provide the principal and interest payment(s) that will apply at each change date as stated in the loan modification agreement. All payments must be provided, not just the first change payment, unless there is only a single change date.

(v) Post-modification – number of steps. Provide the total number of step rate adjustments under the step agreement.

(vi) Post-modification maximum future rate under step agreement. Provide the maximum interest rate to which the loan will step up.

(vii) Post-modification date of maximum rate under step agreement. Provide the date on which the maximum interest rate will be reached.

(25) Non-interest bearing principal deferred amount (cumulative). Provide the total amount of principal deferred (or forborne) by the modification that is not subject to interest accrual.

(26) Non-interest bearing principal deferred amount (reporting period). Provide the total amount of principal deferred by the modification that is not subject to interest accrual.

(27) Recovery of deferred principal (reporting period). Provide the amount of deferred principal collected from the obligor during the reporting period.

(28) Non-interest bearing deferred paid-in-full amount. If the loan had a principal forbearance and was paid in full or liquidated, provide the amount paid towards the amount of the principal forbearance.

(29) Non-interest bearing deferred interest and fees amount (reporting period). Provide the total amount of interest and expenses deferred by the modification that is not subject to interest accrual during the reporting period.

(30) Non-interest bearing deferred interest and fees amount (cumulative). Provide the total amount of interest and expenses deferred by the modification that is not subject to interest accrual.

(31) Recovery of deferred interest and fees (reporting period). Provide the amount of deferred interest and fees collected during the reporting period.

(n) *Information Related to Forbearance or Trial Modification.* If the type of loss mitigation is forbearance or a trial modification, provide the following additional information. A forbearance plan refers to a period during which either no payment or a payment amount less than the contractual obligation is required from the obligor. A trial modification refers to a temporary loan modification during which an obligor's application for a permanent loan modification is under evaluation.

(1) Most recent forbearance plan or trial modification start date. Provide the date on which a payment change pursuant to the most recent forbearance plan or trial modification started.

(2) Most recent forbearance plan or trial modification scheduled end date. Provide the date on which a payment change pursuant to the most recent forbearance plan or trial modification is scheduled to end.

(3) Most recent trial modification violated date. Provide the date on which the obligor ceased complying with the terms of the most recent trial modification.

(o) *Information Related to Repayment Plan.* If the type of loss mitigation is a repayment plan, provide the following additional information. A repayment plan refers to a period during which an obligor has agreed to make monthly mortgage payments greater than the contractual installment in an effort to bring a delinquent loan current.

(1) Most recent repayment plan start date. Provide the date on which the most recent repayment plan started.

(2) Most recent repayment plan scheduled end date. Provide the date on which the most recent repayment plan is scheduled to end.

(3) Most recent repayment plan violated date. Provide the date on which the obligor ceased complying with the terms of the most recent repayment plan.

(p) *Information Related to Short Sales.* Short sale refers to the process in which a servicer workers with a delinquent obligor to sell the property prior to the foreclosure sale. If the type of loss mitigation is short sale, provide the following information:

(1) Short sale accepted offer amount. Provide the amount accepted for a pending short sale.

(2) [Reserved]

(q) *Information Related to Loss Mitigation Exit.* If the loan has exited loss mitigation efforts during the reporting period, provide the following additional information:

(1) Most recent loss mitigation exit date. Provide the date on which the servicer deemed the most recent loss mitigation effort to have ended.

(2) Most recent loss mitigation exit code. Indicate the code that describes the reason the most recent loss mitigation effort ended.

(r) *Information Related to Loans in the Foreclosure Process.* If the loan is in foreclosure, provide the following additional information:

(1) Attorney referral date. Provide the date on which the loan was referred to a foreclosure attorney.

(2) Foreclosure delay reason. Indicate the code that describes the reason for delay within the foreclosure process.

(3) Foreclosure exit date. If the loan exited foreclosure during the reporting period, provide the date on which the loan exited foreclosure.

(4) Foreclosure exit reason. If the loan exited foreclosure during the reporting period, indicate the code that describes the reason the foreclosure proceeding ended.

(5) NOI Date. If a notice of intent (NOI) has been sent, provide the date on which the servicer sent the NOI correspondence to the obligor informing the obligor of the acceleration of the loan and pending initiation of foreclosure action.

(s) *Information Related to REO.* REO (Real Estate Owned) refers to property owned by a lender after an unsuccessful sale at a foreclosure auction. If the loan is REO, provide the following additional information:

(1) Most recent accepted REO offer amount. If an REO offer has been accepted, provide the amount accepted for the REO sale.

(2) Most recent accepted REO offer date. If an REO offer has been accepted, provide the date on which the REO sale amount was accepted.

(3) Gross liquidation proceeds. If the REO sale has closed, provide the gross amount due to the issuing entity as reported on Line 420 of the HUD-1 settlement statement.

(4) Net sales proceeds. If the REO sale has closed, provide the net proceeds received from the escrow closing (before servicer reimbursement).

(5) Reporting period loss amount passed to issuing entity. Provide the cumulative loss amount passed through to the issuing entity during the reporting period, including subsequent loss adjustments and any forgiven principal as a result of a modification that was passed through to the issuing entity.

(6) Cumulative total loss amount passed to issuing entity. Provide the loss amount passed through to the issuing entity to date, including any forgiven principal as a result of a modification that was passed through to the issuing entity.

(7) Subsequent recovery amount. Provide the reporting period amount recovered subsequent to the initial gain/loss recognized at the time of liquidation.

(8) Eviction indicator. Indicate whether an eviction process has begun.

(9) REO exit date. If the loan exited REO during the reporting period, provide the date on which the loan exited REO status.

(10) REO exit reason. If the loan exited REO during the reporting period, indicate the code that describes the reason the loan exited REO status.

(t) *Information Related to Losses.*

(1) Information related to loss claims.

(i) UPB at liquidation. Provide the actual unpaid principal balance (UPB) at the time of liquidation.

(ii) Servicing fees claimed. Provide the amount of accrued servicing fees claimed at time of servicer reimbursement after liquidation.

(iii) Servicer advanced amounts reimbursed—principal. Provide the total amount of unpaid principal advances made by the servicer that were reimbursed to the servicer.

(iv) Servicer advanced amounts reimbursed—interest. Provide the total amount of unpaid interest advances made by the servicer that were reimbursed to the servicer.

(v) Servicer advanced amount reimbursed—taxes and insurance. Provide the total amount of any unpaid escrow amounts advanced by the servicer that were reimbursed to the servicer.

(vi) Servicer advanced amount reimbursed—corporate. Provide the total amount of any outstanding advances of property inspection and preservation expenses made by the servicer that were reimbursed to the servicer.

(vii) REO management fees. If the loan is in REO, provide the total amount of REO management fees (including auction fees) paid over the life of the loan.

(viii) Cash for keys/cash for deed. Provide the total amount paid to the obligor or tenants in exchange for vacating the property, or the payment to the obligor to accelerate a deed-in-lieu process or complete a redemption period.

(ix) Performance incentive fees. Provide the total amount paid to the servicer in exchange for carrying out a deed-in-lieu or short sale or similar activities.

(2) [Reserved]

(u) *Information Related to Mortgage Insurance Claims.* If a mortgage insurance claim (MI claim) has been submitted to the primary mortgage insurance company for reimbursement, provide the following additional information:

(1) MI claim filed date. Provide the date on which the servicer filed an MI claim.

(2) MI claim amount. Provide the amount of the MI claim filed by the servicer.

(3) MI claim paid date. If the MI claim has been paid, provide the date on which the MI company paid the MI claim.

(4) MI claim paid amount. If the MI claim has been decided, provide the amount of the claim paid by the MI company.

(5) MI claim denied/rescinded date. If the MI claim has been denied or rescinded, provide the final MI denial date after all servicer appeals.

(6) Marketable title transferred date. If the deed for the property has been conveyed to the MI company, provide the date of actual title conveyance to the MI company.

(v) *Information Related to Delinquent Loans.* (1) Non-pay status. Indicate the code that describes the delinquency status of the loan.

(2) Reporting action code. Further indicate the code that defines the default/delinquent status of the loan.

Item 2. Commercial Mortgages. If the asset pool includes commercial mortgages, provide the following data for each loan in the asset pool:

(a) *Asset Numbers.* (1) Asset number type. Identify the source of the asset number used to specifically identify each asset in the pool.

(2) Asset number. Provide the unique ID number of the asset.

Instruction to Paragraph (a)(2): The asset number must reference a single asset within the pool and should be the same number that will be used to identify the asset for all reports that would be required of an issuer under Sections 13 or 15(d) of the Exchange Act (15 U.S.C. 78m or 78o(d)). If an asset is removed and replaced with another asset, the asset added to the pool should be assigned a unique asset number applicable to only that asset.

(3) Group ID. Indicate the alpha-numeric code assigned to each loan group within a securitization.

(b) *Reporting period.* (1) Reporting period begin date. Specify the beginning date of the reporting period.

(2) Reporting period end date. Specify the ending date of the reporting period.

(c) *General Information About the Commercial Mortgage.* (1) Originator. Identify the name or MERS organization number of the originator entity.

(2) Origination date. Provide the date the loan was originated.

(3) Original loan amount. Indicate the amount of the loan at the time the loan was originated.

(4) Original loan term. Indicate the term of the loan in months at the time the loan was originated.

(5) Maturity date. Indicate the date the final scheduled payment is due per the loan documents.

(6) Original amortization term. Indicate the number of months that would have been required to retire the loan through regular payments, as determined at the origination date of the loan.

(7) Original interest rate. Provide the rate of interest at the time the loan was originated.

(8) Interest rate at securitization. Indicate the annual gross interest rate used to calculate interest for the loan as of securitization.

(9) Interest accrual method. Provide the code that indicates the "number of days" convention used to calculate interest.

(10) Original interest rate type. Indicate whether the interest rate on the loan is fixed, adjustable, step or other.

(11) Original interest-only term. Indicate the number of months in which the obligor is permitted to pay only interest on the loan.

(12) First loan payment due date. Provide the date on which the borrower must pay the first full interest and/or principal payment due on the mortgage in accordance with the loan documents.

(13) Underwriting indicator. Indicate whether the loan or asset met the criteria for the first level of solicitation, credit-granting or underwriting criteria used to originate the pool asset.

(14) Lien position at securitization. Indicate the code that describes the lien position for the loan as of securitization.

(15) Loan structure. Indicate the code that describes the type of loan structure including the seniority of participated mortgage loan components. The code relates to the loan within the securitization.

(16) Payment type. Indicate the code that describes the type or method of payment for a loan.

(17) Periodic principal and interest payment at securitization. Provide the total amount of principal and interest due on the loan in effect as of securitization.

(18) Scheduled principal balance at securitization. Indicate the outstanding scheduled principal balance of the loan as of securitization.

(19) Payment frequency. Indicate the code that describes the frequency mortgage loan payments are required to be made.

(20) Number of properties at securitization. Provide the number of properties which serve as mortgage collateral for the loan as of securitization.

(21) Number of properties. Provide the number of properties which serve as mortgage collateral for the loan as of the end of the reporting period.

(22) Grace days allowed. Provide the number of days after a mortgage payment is due in which the lender will not require a late payment charge in accordance with the loan documents. Does not include penalties associated with default interest.

(23) Interest only indicator. Indicate yes or no whether this is a loan for which scheduled interest only is payable, whether for a temporary basis or until the full loan balance is due.

(24) Balloon indicator. Indicate yes or no whether the loan documents require a lump- sum payment of principal at maturity.

(25) Prepayment premium indicator. Indicate yes or no whether the obligor is subject to prepayment penalties.

(26) Negative amortization indicator. Indicate yes or no whether negative amortization (interest shortage) amounts are permitted to be added back to the unpaid principal balance of the loan if monthly payments should fall below the true amortized amount.

(27) Modification indicator. Indicate yes or no whether the loan has been modified from its original terms.

(28) Information related to ARMs. If the loan is an ARM, provide the following additional information for each loan:

(i) ARM index. Specify the code that describes the index on which an adjustable interest rate is based.

(ii) First rate adjustment date. Provide the date on which the first interest rate adjustment becomes effective (subsequent to loan securitization).

(iii) First payment adjustment date. Provide the date on which the first adjustment to the regular payment amount becomes effective (after securitization).

(iv) ARM margin. Indicate the spread added to the index of an ARM loan to determine the interest rate at securitization.

(v) Lifetime rate cap. Indicate the maximum interest rate that can be in effect during the life of the loan.

(vi) Lifetime rate floor. Indicate the minimum interest rate that can be in effect during the life of the loan.

(vii) Periodic rate increase limit. Provide the maximum amount the interest rate can increase from any period to the next.

(viii) Periodic rate decrease limit. Provide the maximum amount the interest rate can decrease from any period to the next.

(ix) Periodic pay adjustment maximum amount. Provide the maximum amount the principal and interest constant can increase or decrease on any adjustment date.

(x) Periodic pay adjustment maximum percentage. Provide the maximum percentage amount the payment can increase or decrease from any period to the next.

(xi) Rate reset frequency. Indicate the code describing the frequency which the periodic mortgage rate is reset due to an adjustment in the ARM index.

(xii) Pay reset frequency. Indicate the code describing the frequency which the periodic mortgage payment will be adjusted.

(xiii) Index look back in days. Provide the number of days prior to an interest rate adjustment effective date used to determine the appropriate index rate.

(29) Information related to prepayment penalties. If the obligor is subject to prepayment penalties, provide the following additional information for each loan:

(i) Prepayment lock-out end date. Provide the effective date after which the lender allows prepayment of a loan.

(ii) Yield maintenance end date. Provide the date after which yield maintenance prepayment penalties are no longer effective.

(iii) Prepayment premium end date. Provide the effective date after which prepayment premiums are no longer effective.

(30) Information related to negative amortization. If the loan allows for negative amortization, provide the following additional information for each loan:

(i) Maximum negative amortization allowed (% of original balance). Provide the maximum percentage of the original loan balance that can be added to the original loan balance as the result of negative amortization.

(ii) Maximum negative amortization allowed. Provide the maximum amount of the original loan balance that can be added to the original loan balance as the result of negative amortization.

(iii) Negative amortization/deferred interest capitalized amount. Indicate the amount for the reporting period that was capitalized (added to) the principal balance.

(iv) Deferred interest – cumulative. Indicate the cumulative deferred interest for the reporting period and prior reporting cycles net of any deferred interest collected.

(v) Deferred interest collected. Indicate the amount of deferred interest collected during the reporting period.

(d) *Information Related to the Property.* Provide the following information for each of the properties that collateralizes a loan identified above:

(1) Property name. Provide the name of the property which serves as mortgage collateral. If the property has been defeased, then populate with “defeased.”

(2) Property address. Specify the address of the property which serves as mortgage collateral. If multiple properties, then print “various.” If the property has been defeased then leave field empty. For substituted properties, populate with the new property information.

(3) Property city. Specify the city name where the property which serves as mortgage collateral is located. If the property has been defeased, then leave field empty.

(4) Property state. Indicate the two character abbreviated code representing the state in which the property which serves as mortgage collateral is located.

(5) Property zip code. Indicate the zip (or postal) code for the property which serves as mortgage collateral.

(6) Property county. Indicate the county in which the property which serves as mortgage collateral is located.

(7) Property type. Indicate the code that describes how the property is being used.

(8) Net rentable square feet. Provide the net rentable square feet area of the property.

(9) Net rentable square feet at securitization. Provide the net rentable square feet area of the property as determined at the time the property is contributed to the pool as collateral.

(10) Number of units/beds/rooms. If the property type is multifamily, self-storage, healthcare, lodging or mobile home park, provide the number of units/beds/rooms of the property.

(11) Number of units/beds/rooms at securitization. If the property type is multifamily, self-storage, healthcare, lodging or mobile home park, provide the number of units/beds/rooms of the property at securitization.

(12) Year built. Provide the year that the property was built.

(13) Year last renovated. Provide the year that the last major renovation/new construction was completed on the property.

(14) Valuation amount at securitization. Provide the valuation amount of the property as of the valuation date at securitization.

(15) Valuation source at securitization. Specify the code that identifies the source of the property valuation.

(16) Valuation date at securitization. Provide the date the valuation amount at securitization was determined.

(17) Most recent value. If an additional property valuation was obtained by any transaction party or its affiliates after the valuation obtained at securitization, provide the most recent valuation amount.

(18) Most recent valuation date. Provide the date of the most recent valuation.

(19) Most recent valuation source. Specify the code that identifies the source of the most recent property valuation.

(20) Physical occupancy at securitization. Provide the percentage of rentable space occupied by tenants.

(21) Most recent physical occupancy. Provide the most recent available percentage of rentable space occupied by tenants.

(22) Property status. Provide the code that describes the status of the property.

(23) Defeasance option start date. Provide the date when the defeasance option becomes available.

(24) Defeasance status. Provide the code that indicates if a loan has or is able to be defeased.

(25) Largest tenant.

(i) Largest tenant. Identify the tenant that leases the largest square feet of the property based on the most recent annual lease rollover review.

Instruction to Paragraph (d)(25)(i): If the tenant is not occupying the space but is still paying rent, print "Dark" after tenant name. If tenant has sub-leased the space, print "Sub- leased/name" after tenant name.

(ii) Square feet of largest tenant. Provide total number of square feet leased by the largest tenant based on the most recent annual lease rollover review.

(iii) Date of lease expiration of largest tenant. Provide the date of lease expiration for the largest tenant.

(26) Second largest tenant.

(i) Second largest tenant. Identify the tenant that leases the second largest square feet of the property based on the most recent annual lease rollover review.

Instruction to Paragraph (d)(26)(i): If the tenant is not occupying the space but is still paying rent, print "Dark" after tenant name. If tenant has sub-leased the space, print "Sub- leased/name" after tenant name.

(ii) Square feet of second largest tenant. Provide the total number of square feet leased by the second largest tenant based on the most recent annual lease rollover review.

(iii) Date of lease expiration of second largest tenant. Provide the date of lease expiration for the second largest tenant.

(27) Third largest tenant.

(i) Third largest tenant. Identify the tenant that leases the third largest square feet of the property based on the most recent annual lease rollover review.

Instruction to Paragraph (d)(27)(i): If the tenant is not occupying the space but is still paying rent, print "Dark" after tenant name. If tenant has sub-leased the space, print "Sub- leased/name" after tenant name.

(ii) Square feet of third largest tenant. Provide the total number square feet leased by the third largest tenant based on the most recent annual lease rollover review.

(iii) Date of lease expiration of third largest tenant. Provide the date of lease expiration for the third largest tenant.

(28) Financial information related to the property. Provide the following information as of the most recent date available:

(i) Date of financials as of securitization. Provide the date of the operating statement for the property used to underwrite the loan.

(ii) Most recent financial as of start date. Specify the first date of the period for the most recent, hard copy operating statement (e.g., year-to-date or trailing 12 months).

(iii) Most recent financial as of end date. Specify the last day of the period for the most recent, hard copy operating statement (e.g., year-to-date or trailing 12 months).

(iv) Revenue at securitization. Provide the total underwritten revenue amount from all sources for a property as of securitization.

(v) Most recent revenue. Provide the total revenues for the most recent operating statement reported.

(vi) Operating expenses at securitization. Provide the total underwritten operating expenses as of securitization. Include real estate taxes, insurance, management fees, utilities, and repairs and maintenance. Exclude capital expenditures, tenant improvements, and leasing commissions.

(vii) Operating expenses. Provide the total operating expenses for the most recent operating statement. Include real estate taxes, insurance, management fees, utilities, and repairs and maintenance. Exclude capital expenditures, tenant improvements, and leasing commissions.

(viii) Net operating income at securitization. Provide the total underwritten revenues less total underwritten operating expenses prior to application of mortgage payments and capital items for all properties as of securitization.

(ix) Most recent net operating income. Provide the total revenues less total operating expenses before capital items and debt service per the most recent operating statement.

(x) Net cash flow at securitization. Provide the total underwritten revenue less total underwritten operating expenses and capital costs as of securitization.

(xi) Most recent net cash flow. Provide the total revenue less the total operating expenses and capital costs but before debt service per the most recent operating statement.

(xii) Net operating income or net cash flow indicator at securitization. Indicate the code that describes the method used to calculate at securitization net operating income or net cash flow.

(xiii) Net operating income or net cash flow indicator. Indicate the code that describes the method used to calculate net operating income or net cash flow.

(xiv) Most recent debt service amount. Provide the amount of total scheduled or actual payments that cover the same number of months as the most recent financial operating statement.

(xv) Debt service coverage ratio (net operating income) at securitization. Provide the ratio of underwritten net operating income to debt service as of securitization.

(xvi) Most recent debt service coverage ratio (net operating income). Provide the ratio of net operating income to debt service during the most recent operating statement reported.

(xvii) Debt service coverage ratio (net cash flow) at securitization. Provide the ratio of underwritten net cash flow to debt service as of securitization.

(xviii) Most recent debt service coverage ratio (net cash flow). Provide the ratio of net cash flow to debt service for the most recent financial operating statement.

(xix) Debt service coverage ratio indicator at securitization. If there are multiple properties underlying the loan, indicate the code that describes how the debt service coverage ratio was calculated.

(xx) Most recent debt service coverage ratio indicator. Indicate the code that describes how the debt service coverage ratio was calculated for the most recent financial operating statement.

(xxi) Date of the most recent annual lease rollover review. Provide the date of the most recent annual lease rollover review.

(e) *Information Related to Activity on the Loan.* (1) Asset added indicator. Indicate yes or no whether the asset was added during the reporting period.

Instruction to Paragraph (e)(1): A response to this data point is required only when assets are added to the asset pool after the final prospectus under Rule 424 of the Securities Act of 1933 is filed.

(2) Modification indicator – reporting period. Indicate yes or no whether the loan was modified during the reporting period.

(3) Reporting period beginning scheduled loan balance. Indicate the scheduled balance as of the beginning of the reporting period.

(4) Total scheduled principal and interest due. Provide the total amount of principal and interest due on the loan in the month corresponding to the current distribution date.

(5) Reporting period interest rate. Indicate the annualized gross interest rate used to calculate the scheduled interest amount due for the reporting period.

(6) Servicer and trustee fee rate. Indicate the sum of annual fee rates payable to the servicers and trustee.

(7) Scheduled interest amount. Provide the amount of gross interest payment that was scheduled to be collected during the reporting period.

(8) Other interest adjustment. Indicate any unscheduled interest adjustments during the reporting period.

(9) Scheduled principal amount. Indicate the principal payment amount that was scheduled to be collected during the reporting period.

(10) Unscheduled principal collections. Provide the principal prepayments and other unscheduled payments of principal received on the loan during the reporting period.

(11) Other principal adjustments. Indicate any other amounts that caused the principal balance of the loan to be decreased or increased during the reporting period, which are not considered unscheduled principal collections and are not scheduled principal amounts.

(12) Reporting period ending actual balance. Indicate the outstanding actual balance of the loan as of the end of the reporting period.

(13) Reporting period ending scheduled balance. Indicate the scheduled or stated principal balance for the loan (as defined in the servicing agreement) as of the end of the reporting period.

(14) Paid through date. Provide the date the loan's scheduled principal and interest is paid through as of the end of the reporting period.

(15) Hyper-amortizing date. Provide the date after which principal and interest may amortize at an accelerated rate, and/or interest expense to the mortgagor increases substantially.

(16) Information related to servicer advances.

(i) Servicing advance methodology. Indicate the code that describes the manner in which principal and/or interest are advanced by the servicer.

(ii) Non-recoverability determined. Indicate yes or no whether the master servicer/special servicer has ceased advancing principal and interest and/or servicing the loan.

(iii) Total principal and interest advance outstanding. Provide the total outstanding principal and interest advances made (or scheduled to be made by the distribution date) by the servicer(s).

(iv) Total taxes and insurance advances outstanding. Provide the total outstanding tax and insurance advances made by the servicer(s) as of the end of the reporting period.

(v) Other expenses advance outstanding. Provide the total outstanding other or miscellaneous advances made by the servicer(s) as of the end of the reporting period.

(17) Payment status of loan. Provide the code that indicates the payment status of the loan.

(18) Information related to activity on ARM loans. If the loan is an ARM, provide the following additional information:

(i) ARM index rate. Provide the index rate used to determine the gross interest for the reporting period.

(ii) Next interest rate. Provide the annualized gross interest rate that will be used to determine the next scheduled interest payment.

(iii) Next interest rate change adjustment date. Provide the next date that the interest rate is scheduled to change.

(iv) Next payment adjustment date. Provide the date that the amount of scheduled principal and/or interest is next scheduled to change.

(f) *Information Related to Servicers*. (1) Primary servicer. Identify the name of the entity that services or will have the right to service the asset.

(2) Most recent special servicer transfer date. Provide the date the transfer letter, e-mail, etc.

provided by the master servicer is accepted by the special servicer.

(3) Most recent master servicer return date. Provide the date of the return letter, email, etc. provided by the special servicer which is accepted by the master servicer.

(g) *Asset Subject to Demand.* Indicate yes or no whether during the reporting period the loan was the subject of a demand to repurchase or replace for breach of representations and warranties, including investor demands upon a trustee. If the loan is the subject of a demand to repurchase or replace for breach of representations and warranties, including investor demands upon a trustee, provide the following additional information:

(1) Status of asset subject to demand. If the loan is the subject of a demand to repurchase or replace for breach of representations and warranties, including investor demands upon a trustee, indicate the code that describes the status of the repurchase demand as of the end of the reporting period.

(2) Repurchase amount. Provide the amount paid to repurchase the loan from the pool.

(3) Demand resolution date. Indicate the date the loan repurchase or replacement demand was resolved.

(4) Repurchaser. Specify the name of the repurchaser.

(5) Repurchase or replacement reason. Indicate the code that describes the reason for the repurchase.

(h) *Realized Loss to Trust.* Indicate the difference between net proceeds (after liquidation expenses) and the scheduled or stated principal of the loan as of the beginning of the reporting period.

(i) *Information Related to Prepayments.* If a prepayment was received, provide the following additional information for each loan:

(1) Liquidation/Prepayment code. Indicate the code assigned to any unscheduled principal payments or liquidation proceeds received during the reporting period.

(2) Liquidation/Prepayment date. Provide the effective date on which an unscheduled principal payment or liquidation proceeds were received.

(3) Prepayment premium/yield maintenance received. Indicate the amount received from a borrower during the reporting period in exchange for allowing a borrower to pay off a loan prior to the maturity or anticipated repayment date.

(j) *Workout Strategy.* Indicate the code that best describes the steps being taken to resolve the loan.

(k) *Information Related to Modifications.* If the loan has been modified from its original terms, provide the following additional information about the most recent loan modification:

(1) Date of last modification. Indicate the date of the most recent modification. A modification includes any material change to the loan document, excluding assumptions.

(2) Modification code. Indicate the code that describes the type of loan modification.

(3) Post-modification interest rate. Indicate the new initial interest rate to which the loan was modified.

(4) Post-modification payment amount. Indicate the new initial principal and interest payment amount to which the loan was modified.

(5) Post-modification maturity date. Indicate the new maturity date of the loan after the modification.

(6) Post-modification amortization period. Indicate the new amortization period in months after the modification.

Item 3. Automobile Loans. If the asset pool includes automobile loans, provide the following data for each loan in the asset pool:

(a) *Asset Numbers.* (1) Asset number type. Identify the source of the asset number used to specifically identify each asset in the pool.

(2) Asset number. Provide the unique ID number of the asset.

Instruction to Paragraph (a)(2): The asset number must reference a single asset within the pool and should be the same number that will be used to identify the asset for all reports that would be required of an issuer under Sections 13 or 15(d) of the Exchange Act (15 U.S.C. 78m or 78o(d)). If an asset is removed and replaced with another asset, the asset added to the pool should be assigned a unique asset number applicable to only that asset.

(b) *Reporting Period.* (1) Reporting period begin date. Specify the beginning date of the reporting period.

(2) Reporting period end date. Specify the ending date of the reporting period.

(c) *General Information About the Automobile loan.* (1) Originator. Identify the name of the entity that originated the loan.

(2) Origination date. Provide the date the loan was originated.

(3) Original loan amount. Indicate the amount of the loan at the time the loan was originated.

(4) Original loan term. Indicate the term of the loan in months at the time the loan was originated.

(5) Loan maturity date. Indicate the month and year in which the final payment on the loan is scheduled to be made.

(6) Original interest rate. Provide the rate of interest at the time the loan was originated.

(7) Interest calculation type. Indicate whether the interest rate calculation method is simple or other.

(8) Original interest rate type. Indicate whether the interest rate on the loan is fixed, adjustable or other.

(9) Original interest-only term. Indicate the number of months from origination in which the obligor is permitted to pay only interest on the loan beginning from when the loan was originated.

(10) Original first payment date. Provide the date of the first scheduled payment that was due after the loan was originated.

(11) Underwriting indicator. Indicate whether the loan or asset met the criteria for the first level of solicitation, credit-granting or underwriting criteria used to originate the pool asset.

(12) Grace period. Indicate the number of months during which interest accrues but no payments are due from the obligor.

(13) Payment type. Specify the code indicating how often payments are required or if a balloon payment is due.

(14) Subvented. Indicate yes or no to whether a form of subsidy is received on the loan, such as cash incentives or favorable financing for the buyer.

(d) *Information Related to the Vehicle.* (1) Vehicle manufacturer. Provide the name of the manufacturer of the vehicle.

(2) Vehicle model. Provide the name of the model of the vehicle.

(3) New or used. Indicate whether the vehicle financed is new or used at the time of origination.

(4) Model year. Indicate the model year of the vehicle.

(5) Vehicle type. Indicate the code describing the vehicle type.

(6) Vehicle value. Indicate the value of the vehicle at the time of origination.

(7) Source of vehicle value. Specify the code that describes the source of the vehicle value.

(e) *Information Related to the Obligor.* (1) Obligor credit score type. Specify the type of the standardized credit score used to evaluate the obligor during the loan origination process.

(2) Obligor credit score. Provide the standardized credit score of the obligor used to evaluate the obligor during the loan origination process.

(3) Obligor income verification level. Indicate the code describing the extent to which the obligor's income was verified during the loan origination process.

(4) Obligor employment verification. Indicate the code describing the extent to which the obligor's employment was verified during the loan origination process.

(5) Co-obligor present indicator. Indicate whether the loan has a co-obligor.

(6) Payment-to-income ratio. Provide the scheduled monthly payment amount as a percentage of the total monthly income of the obligor and any other obligor at the origination date. Provide the methodology for determining monthly income in the prospectus.

(7) Geographic location of obligor. Specify the location of the obligor by providing the current U.S. state or territory.

(f) *Information Related to Activity on the Loan.* (1) Asset added indicator. Indicate yes or no whether the asset was added during the reporting period.

Instruction to Paragraph (f)(1): A response to this data point is required only when assets are added to the asset pool after the final prospectus under Rule 424 under the Securities Act of 1933 is filed.

(2) Remaining term to maturity. Indicate the number of months from the end of the reporting period to the loan maturity date.

(3) Modification indicator – reporting period. Indicates yes or no whether the asset was modified from its original terms during the reporting period.

(4) Servicing advance method. Specify the code that indicates a servicer's responsibility for advancing principal or interest on delinquent loans.

(5) Reporting period beginning loan balance. Indicate the outstanding principal balance of the loan as of the beginning of the reporting period.

(6) Next reporting period payment amount due. Indicate the total payment due to be collected in the next reporting period.

(7) Reporting period interest rate. Indicate the current interest rate for the loan in effect during the reporting period.

(8) Next interest rate. For loans that have not been paid off, indicate the interest rate that is in effect for the next reporting period.

(9) Servicing fee—percentage. If the servicing fee is based on a percentage, provide the percentage used to calculate the aggregate servicing fee.

(10) Servicing fee—flat-fee. If the servicing fee is based on a flat-fee amount, indicate the monthly servicing fee paid to all servicers.

(11) Other loan-level servicing fee(s) retained by servicer. Provide the amount of all other fees earned by loan administrators that reduce the amount of funds remitted to the issuing entity (including subservicing, master servicing, trustee fees, etc.).

(12) Other assessed but uncollected servicer fees. Provide the cumulative amount of late charges and other fees that have been assessed by the servicer, but not paid by the obligor.

(13) Scheduled interest amount. Indicate the interest payment amount that was scheduled to be collected during the reporting period.

(14) Scheduled principal amount. Indicate the principal payment amount that was scheduled to be collected during the reporting period.

(15) Other principal adjustments. Indicate any other amounts that caused the principal balance of the loan to be decreased or increased during the reporting period.

(16) Reporting period ending actual balance. Indicate the actual balance of the loan as of the end of the reporting period.

(17) Reporting period scheduled payment amount. Indicate the total payment amount that was scheduled to be collected during the reporting period (including all fees).

(18) Total actual amount paid. Indicate the total payment paid to the servicer during the reporting period.

(19) Actual interest collected. Indicate the gross amount of interest collected during the reporting period, whether or not from the obligor.

(20) Actual principal collected. Indicate the amount of principal collected during the reporting period, whether or not from the obligor.

(21) Actual other amounts collected. Indicate the total of any amounts, other than principal and interest, collected during the reporting period, whether or not from the obligor.

(22) Servicer advanced amount. If amounts were advanced by the servicer during the reporting period, specify the amount.

(23) Interest paid through date. Provide the date through which interest is paid with the payment received during the reporting period, which is the effective date from which interest will be calculated for the application of the next payment.

(24) Zero balance loans. If the loan balance was reduced to zero during the reporting period, provide the following additional information about the loan:

(i) Zero balance effective date. Provide the date on which the loan balance was reduced to zero.

(ii) Zero balance code. Provide the code that indicates the reason the loan's balance was reduced to zero.

(25) Current delinquency status. Indicate the number of days the obligor is delinquent past the obligor's payment due date, as determined by the governing transaction agreement.

(g) *Information Related to Servicers.* (1) Primary loan servicer. Provide the name of the entity that services or will have the right to service the loan.

(2) Most recent servicing transfer received date. If a loan's servicing has been transferred, provide the effective date of the most recent servicing transfer.

(h) *Asset Subject to Demand.* Indicate yes or no whether during the reporting period the loan was the subject of a demand to repurchase or replace for breach of representations and warranties, including investor demands upon a trustee. If the loan is the subject of a demand to repurchase or replace for breach of representations and warranties, including investor demands upon a trustee, provide the following additional information:

(1) Status of asset subject to demand. Indicate the code that describes the status of the repur-

chase or replacement demand as of the end of the reporting period.

(2) Repurchase amount. Provide the amount paid to repurchase the loan.

(3) Demand resolution date. Indicate the date the loan repurchase or replacement demand was resolved.

(4) Repurchaser. Specify the name of the repurchaser.

(5) Repurchase or replacement reason. Indicate the code that describes the reason for the repurchase or replacement.

(i) *Information Related to Leases That Have Been Charged off.* If the lease has been charged off, provide the following additional information:

(1) Charged-off principal amount. Specify the amount of uncollected principal charged off.

(2) Amounts recovered. If the loan was previously charged off, specify any amounts received after charge-off.

(j) *Information Related to Leases Modifications.* If the lease has been modified from its original terms, provide the following additional information about the most recent lease modification:

(1) Modification type. Indicate the code that describes the reason the asset was modified during the reporting period.

(2) Payment extension. Provide the number of months the loan was extended during the reporting period.

(k) *Repossessed.* Indicate yes or no whether the vehicle has been repossessed. If the vehicle has been repossessed, provide the following additional information:

(1) Repossession proceeds. Provide the total amount of proceeds received on disposition (net of repossession fees and expenses).

(2) [Reserved]

Item 4. Automobile Leases. If the asset pool includes automobile leases, provide the following data for each lease in the asset pool:

(a) *Asset Numbers.* (1) Asset number type. Identify the source of the asset number used to specifically identify each asset in the pool.

(2) Asset number. Provide the unique ID number of the asset.

Instruction to Paragraph (a)(2): The asset number must reference a single asset within the pool and should be the same number that would be used to identify the asset for all reports that would be required of an issuer under Sections 13 or 15(d) of the Exchange Act (15 U.S.C. 78m or 78o(d)). If an asset is removed and replaced with another asset, the asset added to the pool should be assigned a unique asset number applicable to only that asset.

(b) *Reporting Period.* (1) Reporting period begin date. Specify the beginning date of the reporting period.

(2) Reporting period end date. Specify the ending date of the reporting period.

(c) *General Information About the Automobile Lease.* (1) Originator. Identify the name of the entity that originated the lease.

(2) Origination date. Provide the date the lease was originated.

(3) Acquisition cost. Provide the original acquisition cost of the lease.

(4) Original lease term. Indicate the term of the lease in months at the time the lease was originated.

(5) Scheduled termination date. Indicate the month and year in which the final lease payment is scheduled to be made.

(6) Original first payment date. Provide the date of the first scheduled payment after origination.

(7) Underwriting indicator. Indicate whether the lease met the criteria for the first level of solicitation, credit-granting or underwriting criteria used to originate the pool asset.

(8) Grace period. Indicate the number of months during the term of the lease when no payments are due from the lessee.

(9) Payment type. Specify the code indicating the payment frequency of the lease.

(10) Subvented. Indicate yes or no whether a form of subsidy is received on the lease, such as cash incentives or favorable financing for the lessee.

(d) *Information Related to the Vehicle.* (1) Vehicle manufacturer. Provide the name of the manufacturer of the leased vehicle.

(2) Vehicle model. Provide the name of the model of the leased vehicle.

(3) New or used. Indicate whether the leased vehicle is new or used.

(4) Model year. Indicate the model year of the leased vehicle.

(5) Vehicle type. Indicate the code describing the vehicle type.

(6) Vehicle value. Indicate the value of the vehicle at the time of origination.

(7) Source of vehicle value. Specify the code that describes the source of the vehicle value.

(8) Base residual value. Provide the securitized residual value of the leased vehicle.

(9) Source of base residual value. Specify the code that describes the source of the base residual value.

(10) Contractual residual value. Provide the residual value, as stated on the contract, that the lessee would need to pay to purchase the vehicle at the end of the lease term.

(e) *Information Related to the Lessee.* (1) Lessee credit score type. Specify the type of the standardized credit score used to evaluate the lessee during the lease origination process.

(2) Lessee credit score. Provide the standardized credit score of the lessee used to evaluate the lessee during the lease origination process.

(3) Lessee income verification level. Indicate the code describing the extent to which the lessee's income was verified during the lease origination process.

(4) Lessee employment verification. Indicate the code describing the extent to which the lessee's employment was verified during the lease origination process.

(5) Co-lessee present indicator. Indicate whether the lease has a co-lessee.

(6) Payment-to-income ratio. Provide the scheduled monthly payment amount as a percentage of the total monthly income of the lessee and any other co-lessee at the origination date. Provide the methodology for determining monthly income in the prospectus.

(7) Geographic location of lessee. Specify the location of the lessee by providing the current U.S. state or territory.

(f) *Information Related to Activity on the Lease.* (1) Asset added indicator. Indicate yes or no whether the asset was added during the reporting period.

Instruction to Paragraph (f)(1): A response to this data point is required only when assets are added to the asset pool after the final prospectus under Rule 424 of the Securities Act of 1933 is filed.

(2) Remaining term to maturity. Indicate the number of months from the end of the reporting period to the lease maturity date.

(3) Modification indicator – reporting period. Indicates yes or no whether the asset was modified from its original terms during the reporting period.

(4) Servicing advance method. Specify the code that indicates a servicer's responsibility for advancing principal or interest on delinquent leases.

(5) Reporting period securitization value. Provide the sum of the present values, as of the beginning of the reporting period, of the remaining scheduled monthly payment amounts and the base residual value of the leased vehicle, computed using the securitization value discount rate.

(6) Securitization value discount rate. Provide the discount rate of the lease for the securitization transaction.

(7) Next reporting period payment amount due. Indicate the total payment due to be collected in the next reporting period.

(8) Servicing fee – percentage. If the servicing fee is based on a percentage, provide the percentage used to calculate the aggregate servicing fee.

(9) Servicing fee – flat-fee. If the servicing fee is based on a flat-fee amount, indicate the monthly servicing fee paid to all servicers.

(10) Other lease-level servicing fee(s) retained by servicer. Provide the amount of all other fees earned by lease administrators that reduce the amount of funds remitted to the issuing entity (including subservicing, master servicing, trustee fees, etc.).

(11) Other assessed but uncollected servicer fees. Provide the cumulative amount of late charges and other fees that have been assessed by the servicer, but not paid by the lessee.

(12) Reporting period ending actual balance. Indicate the actual balance of the lease as of the end of the reporting period.

(13) Reporting period scheduled payment amount. Indicate the total payment amount that was scheduled to be collected during the reporting period (including all fees).

(14) Total actual amount paid. Indicate the total lease payment received during the reporting period.

(15) Actual other amounts collected. Indicate the total of any amounts, other than the scheduled lease payment, collected during the reporting period, whether or not from the lessee.

(16) Reporting period ending actual securitization value. Provide the sum of the present values, as of the end of the reporting period, of the remaining scheduled monthly payment amounts and the base residual value of the leased vehicle, computed using the securitization value discount rate.

(17) Servicer advanced amount. If amounts were advanced by the servicer during the reporting period, specify the amount.

(18) Paid through date. Provide the date through which scheduled payments have been made with the payment received during the reporting period, which is the effective date from which amounts due will be calculated for the application of the next payment.

(19) Zero balance leases. If the lease balance was reduced to zero during the reporting period, provide the following additional information about the lease:

(i) Zero balance effective date. Provide the date on which the lease balance was reduced to zero.

(ii) Zero balance code. Provide the code that indicates the reason the lease's balance was reduced to zero.

(20) Current delinquency status. Indicate the number of days the lessee is delinquent past the lessee's payment due date, as determined by the governing transaction agreement.

(g) *Information Related to Servicers.* (1) Primary lease servicer. Provide the name of the entity that services or will have the right to service the lease.

(2) Most recent servicing transfer received date. If a lease's servicing has been transferred, provide the effective date of the most recent servicing transfer.

(h) *Asset Subject to Demand.* Indicate yes or no whether during the reporting period the lease was the subject of a demand to repurchase or replace for breach of representations and warranties, including investor demands upon a trustee. If the lease is the subject of a demand to repurchase or replace for breach of representations and warranties, including investor demands upon a trustee, provide the following additional information:

(1) Status of asset subject to demand. Indicate the code that describes the status of the repurchase or replacement demand as of the end of the reporting period.

(2) Repurchase amount. Provide the amount paid to repurchase the lease from the pool.

(3) Demand resolution date. Indicate the date the lease repurchase or replacement demand was resolved.

(4) Repurchaser. Specify the name of the repurchaser.

(5) Repurchase or replacement reason. Indicate the code that describes the reason for the repurchase or replacement.

(i) *Information Related to Leases That Have Been Charged off.* If the lease has been charged off, provide the following additional information:

(1) Charge-off amounts. Provide the amount charged off on the lease.

(2) [Reserved]

(j) *Information Related to Lease Modifications.* If the lease has been modified from its original terms, provide the following additional information about the most recent lease modification:

(1) Modification type. Indicate the code that describes the reason the lease was modified during the reporting period.

(2) Lease extension. Provide the number of months the lease was extended during the reporting period.

(k) *Information Related to Lease Terminations.* If the lease was terminated, provide the following additional information:

(1) Termination indicator. Specify the code that describes the reason why the lease was terminated.

(2) Excess fees. Specify the amount of excess fees received upon return of the vehicle, such as excess wear and tear or excess mileage.

(3) Liquidation proceeds. Provide the liquidation proceeds net of repossession fees, auction fees and other expenses in accordance with standard industry practice.

Item 5. Debt Securities. If the asset pool includes debt securities, provide the following data for each security in the asset pool:

(a) *Asset Numbers.* (1) Asset number type. Identify the source of the asset number used to specifically identify each asset in the pool.

(2) Asset number. Provide the standard industry identifier assigned to the asset. If a standard industry identifier is not assigned to the asset, provide a unique ID number for the asset.

Instruction to Paragraph (a)(2): The asset number must reference a single asset within the pool and should be the same number that will be used to identify the asset for all reports that would be required of an issuer under Sections 13 or 15(d) of the Exchange Act (15 U.S.C. 78m or 78o(d)). If an asset is removed and replaced with another asset, the asset added to the pool should be assigned a unique asset number applicable to only that asset.

(3) Asset group number. For structures with multiple collateral groups, indicate the collateral group number in which the asset falls.

(b) *Reporting Period.* (1) Reporting period begin date. Specify the beginning date of the reporting period.

(2) Reporting period end date. Specify the ending date of the reporting period.

(c) *General Information About the Underlying Security.* (1) Issuer. Provide the name of the issuer.

(2) Original issuance date. Provide the date the underlying security was issued. For revolving asset master trusts, provide the issuance date of the receivable that will be added to the asset pool.

(3) Original security amount. Indicate the amount of the underlying security at the time the underlying security was issued.

(4) Original security term. Indicate the initial number of months between the month the underlying security was issued and the security's maturity date.

(5) Security maturity date. Indicate the month and year in which the final payment on the underlying security is scheduled to be made.

(6) Original amortization term. Indicate the number of months in which the underlying security would be retired if the amortizing principal and interest payment were to be paid each month.

(7) Original interest rate. Provide the rate of interest at the time the underlying security was issued.

(8) Accrual type. Provide the code that describes the method used to calculate interest on the underlying security.

(9) Interest rate type. Indicate the code that indicates whether the interest rate on the underlying security is fixed, adjustable, step or other.

(10) Original interest-only term. Indicate the number of months from the date the underlying security was issued in which the obligor is permitted to pay only interest on the underlying security.

(11) First payment date from issuance. Provide the date of the first scheduled payment.

(12) Underwriting indicator. Indicate whether the loan or asset met the criteria for the first level of solicitation, credit-granting or underwriting criteria used to originate the pool asset.

(13) Title of underlying security. Specify the title of the underlying security.

(14) Denomination. Give the minimum denomination of the underlying security.

(15) Currency. Specify the currency of the underlying security.

(16) Trustee. Specify the name of the trustee.

(17) Underlying SEC file number. Specify the registration statement file number of the registration of the offer and sale of the underlying security.

(18) Underlying CIK number. Specify the CIK number of the issuer of the underlying security.

(19) Callable. Indicate whether the security is callable.

(20) Payment frequency. Indicate the code describing the frequency of payments that will be made on the underlying security.

(21) Zero coupon indicator. Indicate yes or no whether an underlying security or agreement is interest bearing.

(d) *Information Related to Activity on the Underlying Security.* (1) Asset added indicator. Indicate yes or no whether the underlying security was added to the asset pool during the reporting period.

Instruction to Paragraph (d)(1): A response to this data point is required only when assets are added to the asset pool after the final prospectus under Rule 424 of the Securities Act of 1933 is filed.

(2) Modification indicator. Indicates yes or no whether the underlying security was modified from its original terms.

(3) Reporting period beginning asset balance. Indicate the outstanding principal balance of the underlying security as of the beginning of the reporting period.

(4) Reporting period beginning scheduled asset balance. Indicate the scheduled principal balance of the underlying security as of the beginning of the reporting period.

(5) Reporting period scheduled payment amount. Indicate the total payment amount that was scheduled to be collected during the reporting period.

(6) Reporting period interest rate. Indicate the interest rate in effect on the underlying security.

(7) Total actual amount paid. Indicate the total payment paid to the servicer during the reporting period.

(8) Actual interest collected. Indicate the gross amount of interest collected during the reporting period.

(9) Actual principal collected. Indicate the amount of principal collected during the reporting period.

(10) Actual other amounts collected. Indicate the total of any amounts, other than principal and interest, collected during the reporting period.

(11) Other principal adjustments. Indicate any other amounts that caused the principal balance of the underlying security to be decreased or increased during the reporting period.

(12) Other interest adjustments. Indicate any unscheduled interest adjustments during the reporting period.

(13) Scheduled interest amount. Indicate the interest payment amount that was scheduled to be collected during the reporting period.

(14) Scheduled principal amount. Indicate the principal payment amount that was scheduled to be collected during the reporting period.

(15) Reporting period ending actual balance. Indicate the actual balance of the underlying security as of the end of the reporting period.

(16) Reporting period ending scheduled balance. Indicate the scheduled principal balance of the underlying security as of the end of the reporting period.

(17) Servicing fee – percentage. If the servicing fee is based on a percentage, provide the percentage used to calculate the aggregate servicing fee.

(18) Servicing fee – flat-fee. If the servicing fee is based on a flat-fee amount, indicate the monthly servicing fee paid to all servicers as an amount.

(19) Zero balance loans. If the loan balance was reduced to zero during the reporting period, provide the following additional information about the loan:

(i) Zero balance code. Provide the code that indicates the reason the underlying security's balance was reduced to zero.

(ii) Zero balance effective date. Provide the date on which the underlying security's balance was reduced to zero.

(20) Remaining term to maturity. Indicate the number of months from the end of the reporting period to the maturity date of the underlying security.

(21) Current delinquency status. Indicate the number of days the obligor is delinquent as determined by the governing transaction agreement.

(22) Number of days payment is past due. If the obligor has not made the full scheduled payment, indicate the number of days since the scheduled payment date.

(23) Number of payments past due. Indicate the number of payments the obligor is past due as of the end of the reporting period.

(24) Next reporting period payment amount due. Indicate the total payment due to be collected in the next reporting period.

(25) Next due date. For assets that have not been paid off, indicate the next payment due date on the underlying security.

(e) *Information Related to Servicers.* (1) Primary servicer. Indicate the name or MERS organization number of the entity that serviced the underlying security during the reporting period.

(2) Most recent servicing transfer received date. If the servicing of the underlying security has been transferred, provide the effective date of the most recent servicing transfer.

(f) *Asset Subject to Demand.* Indicate yes or no whether during the reporting period the asset was the subject of a demand to repurchase or replace for breach of representations and warranties, including investor demands upon a trustee. If the asset is the subject of a demand to repurchase or replace for breach of representations and warranties, including investor demands upon a trustee, provide the following additional information:

(1) Status of asset subject to demand. Indicate the code that describes the status of the repur-

chase or replacement demand as of the end of the reporting period.

(2) Repurchase amount. Provide the amount paid to repurchase the underlying security from the pool.

(3) Demand resolution date. Indicate the date the underlying security repurchase or replacement demand was resolved.

(4) Repurchaser. Specify the name of the repurchaser.

(5) Repurchase or replacement reason. Indicate the code that describes the reason for the repurchase or replacement.

Item 6. Resecuritizations.

(a) If the asset pool includes asset-backed securities, provide the asset-level information specified in Item 5. Debt Securities in this Schedule AL for each security in the asset pool.

(b) If the asset pool includes asset-backed securities issued after [insert date 60 days plus two years after publication in the Federal Register], provide the asset-level information specified in Item 1111(h) of Regulation AB for the assets backing each security in the asset pool.

Subpart 1200—Disclosure by Registrants Engaged in Oil and Gas Producing Activities

Item 1201. General instructions to oil and gas industry—specific disclosures

(a) If oil and gas producing activities are material to the registrant's or its subsidiaries' business operations or financial position, the disclosure specified in this Subpart 229.1200 should be included under appropriate captions (with cross references, where applicable, to related information disclosed in financial statements). However, limited partnerships and joint ventures that conduct, operate, manage, or report upon oil and gas drilling or income programs, that acquire properties either for drilling and production, or for production of oil, gas, or geothermal steam or water, need not include such disclosure.

(b) To the extent that Items 1202 through 1208 call for disclosures in tabular format, as specified in the particular Item, a registrant may modify such format for ease of presentation, to add information or to combine two or more required tables.

(c) The definitions in Rule 4–10(a) of Regulation S–X shall apply for purposes of this Item 1200.

(d) For purposes of this Item 1200, the term *by geographic area* means, as appropriate for meaningful disclosure in the circumstances:

(1) By individual country;

(2) By groups of countries within a continent; or

(3) By continent.

Item 1202. Disclosure of reserves

(a) *Summary of Oil and Gas Reserves at Fiscal Year End*. (1) Provide the information specified in paragraph (a)(2) of this Item in tabular format as provided below:

Summary of Oil and Gas Reserves as of Fiscal–Year End Based on Average Fiscal–Year Prices

Reserves Category	Reserves				
	Oil	Natural Gas	Synthetic Oil	Synthetic Gas	Product A
	(mbbls)	(mmcf)	(mbbls)	(mmcf)	(measure)
PROVED					
Developed					
Continent A					
Continent B					
Country A					
Country B					
Other Countries in Continent B					
Undeveloped					
Continent A					
Continent B					

Country A	
Country B	
Other Countries in Continent B	
TOTAL PROVED	
PROBABLE	
Developed	
Undeveloped	
POSSIBLE	
Developed	
Undeveloped	

(2) Disclose, in the aggregate and by geographic area and for each country containing 15% or more of the registrant's proved reserves, expressed on an oil-equivalent-barrels basis, reserves estimated using prices and costs under existing economic conditions, for the product types listed in paragraph (a)(4) of this Item, in the following categories:

(i) Proved developed reserves;

(ii) Proved undeveloped reserves;

(iii) Total proved reserves;

(iv) Probable developed reserves (optional);

(v) Probable undeveloped reserves (optional);

(vi) Possible developed reserves (optional); and

(vii) Possible undeveloped reserves (optional).

Instruction 1 to paragraph (a)(2). Disclose updated reserves tables as of the close of each fiscal year.

Instruction 2 to paragraph (a)(2). The registrant is permitted, but not required, to disclose probable or possible reserves pursuant to paragraphs (a)(2)(iv) through (a)(2)(vii) of this Item.

Instruction 3 to paragraph (a)(2). If the registrant discloses amounts of a product in barrels of oil equivalent, disclose the basis for such equivalency.

Instruction 4 to paragraph (a)(2). A registrant need not provide disclosure of the reserves in a country containing 15% or more of the registrant's proved reserves if that country's government prohibits disclosure of reserves in that country. In addition, a registrant need not provide disclosure of the reserves in a country containing 15% or more of the registrant's proved reserves if that country's government prohibits disclosure in a particular field and disclosure of reserves in that country would have the effect of disclosing reserves in particular fields.

(3) Reported total reserves shall be simple arithmetic sums of all estimates for individual properties or fields within each reserves category. When probabilistic methods are used, reserves should not be aggregated probabilistically beyond the field or property level; instead, they should be aggregated by simple arithmetic summation.

(4) Disclose separately material reserves of the following product types:

(i) Oil;

(ii) Natural gas;

(iii) Synthetic oil;

(iv) Synthetic gas; and

(v) Sales products of other non-renewable natural resources that are intended to be upgraded into synthetic oil and gas.

(5) If the registrant discloses probable or possible reserves, discuss the uncertainty related to such reserves estimates.

(6) If the registrant has not previously disclosed reserves estimates in a filing with the Commission or is disclosing material additions to its reserves estimates, the registrant shall provide a general discussion of the technologies used to establish the appropriate level of certainty for reserves estimates from material properties included in the total reserves disclosed. The particular properties do not need to be identified.

(7) *Preparation of Reserves Estimates or Reserves Audit.* Disclose and describe the internal controls the registrant uses in its reserves estimation effort. In addition, disclose the qualifications of the technical person primarily responsible for overseeing the preparation of the reserves estimates and, if the registrant represents that a third party conducted a reserves audit, disclose the qualifications of the technical person primarily responsible for overseeing such reserves audit.

(8) *Third Party Reports.* If the registrant represents that a third party prepared, or conducted a reserves audit of, the registrant's reserves estimates, or any estimated valuation thereof, or conducted a process review, the registrant shall file report of the third party as an exhibit to the r vant registration statement or other Comm

filing. If the report relates to the preparation of, or a reserves audit of, the registrant's reserves estimates, it must include the following disclosure, if applicable to the type of filing:

(i) The purpose for which the report was prepared and for whom it was prepared;

(ii) The effective date of the report and the date on which the report was completed;

(iii) The proportion of the registrant's total reserves covered by the report and the geographic area in which the covered reserves are located;

(iv) The assumptions, data, methods, and procedures used, including the percentage of the registrant's total reserves reviewed in connection with the preparation of the report, and a statement that such assumptions, data, methods, and procedures are appropriate for the purpose served by the report;

(v) A discussion of primary economic assumptions;

(vi) A discussion of the possible effects of regulation on the ability of the registrant to recover the estimated reserves;

(vii) A discussion regarding the inherent uncertainties of reserves estimates;

(viii) A statement that the third party has used all methods and procedures as it considered necessary under the circumstances to prepare the report;

(ix) A brief summary of the third party's conclusions with respect to the reserves estimates; and

(x) The signature of the third party.

(9) For purposes of this Item 1202, the term *reserves audit* means the process of reviewing certain of the pertinent facts interpreted and assumptions underlying a reserves estimate prepared by another party and the rendering of an opinion about the appropriateness of the methodologies employed, the adequacy and quality of the data relied upon, the depth and thoroughness of the reserves estimation process, the classification of reserves appropriate to the relevant definitions used, and the reasonableness of the estimated reserves quantities.

(b) *Reserves sensitivity analysis (optional).* (1) The registrant may, but is not required to, provide the information specified in paragraph (b)(2) of this Item in tabular format as provided below:

Price Case	Proved Reserves					Probable Reserves					Possible Reserves				
	Oil	Gas	Syn. Oil	Syn. Gas	Product A	Oil	Gas	Syn. Oil	Syn. Gas	Product A	Oil	Gas	Syn. Oil	Syn. Gas	Product A
	mbbls	mmcf	mbbls	mmcf	measure	mbbls	mmcf	mbbls	mmcf	measure	mmcf	mbbls	mbbls	mmcf	measure
Scenario 1.															
Scenario 2.															

(2) The registrant may, but is not required to, disclose, in the aggregate, an estimate of reserves estimated for each product type based on different price and cost criteria, such as a range of prices and costs that may reasonably be achieved, including standardized futures prices or management's own forecasts.

(3) If the registrant provides disclosure under this paragraph (b), disclose the price and cost schedules and assumptions on which the disclosed values are based.

Instruction to Item 1202: Estimates of oil or gas resourc- ther than reserves, and any estimated values of such hall not be disclosed in any document publicly mission, unless such information is re- e document by foreign or state at where such estimates previ- to a person (or any of its affili- quire, merge, or consolidate with e to acquire the registrant's secu- be included in documents related

Item 1203. Proved undeveloped reserves

(a) Disclose the total quantity of proved undeveloped reserves at year end.

(b) Disclose material changes in proved undeveloped reserves that occurred during the year, including proved undeveloped reserves converted into proved developed reserves.

(c) Discuss investments and progress made during the year to convert proved undeveloped reserves to proved developed reserves, including, but not limited to, capital expenditures.

(d) Explain the reasons why material amounts of proved undeveloped reserves in individual fields or countries remain undeveloped for five years or more after disclosure as proved undeveloped reserves.

Item 1204. Oil and gas production, production prices and production costs

(a) For each of the last three fiscal years disclose production, by final product sold, of oil, gas, and other products. Disclosure shall be made by geographical area and for each country and field that contains 15% or more of the registrant's total proved reserves expressed on an oil-equivalent-barrels basis unless prohibited by the country in which the reserves are located.

(b) For each of the last three fiscal years disclose, by geographical area:

(1) The average sales price (including transfers) per unit of oil, gas and other products produced; and

(2) The average production cost, not including ad valorem and severance taxes, per unit of production.

Instruction 1 to Item 1204. Generally, net production should include only production that is owned by the registrant and produced to its interest, less royalties and production due others. However, in special situations (e.g., foreign production) net production before any royalties may be provided, if more appropriate. If "net before royalty" production figures are furnished, the change from the usage of "net production" should be noted.

Instruction 2 to Item 1204. Production of natural gas should include only marketable production of natural gas on an "as sold" basis. Production will include dry, residue, and wet gas, depending on whether liquids have been extracted before the registrant transfers title. Flared gas, injected gas, and gas consumed in operations should be omitted. Recovered gas-lift gas and reproduced gas should not be included until sold. Synthetic gas, when marketed as such, should be included in natural gas sales.

Instruction 3 to Item 1204. If any product, such as bitumen, is sold or custody is transferred prior to conversion to synthetic oil or gas, the product's production, transfer prices, and production costs should be disclosed separately from all other products.

Instruction 4 to Item 1204. The transfer price of oil and gas (natural and synthetic) produced should be determined in accordance with FASB ASC paragraph 932–235–50–24 (Extractive Activities—Oil and Gas Topic).

Instruction 5 to Item 1204. The average production cost, not including ad valorem and severance taxes, per unit of production should be computed using production costs disclosed pursuant to FASB ASC Topic 932, *Extractive Activities—Oil and Gas.* Units of production should be expressed in common units of production with oil, gas, and other products converted to a common unit of measure on the basis used in computing amortization.

Item 1205. Drilling and other exploratory and development activities

(a) For each of the last three fiscal years, by geographical area, disclose:

(1) The number of net productive and dry exploratory wells drilled; and

(2) The number of net productive and dry development wells drilled.

(b) *Definitions.* For purposes of this Item 1205, the following terms shall be defined as follows:

(1) A *dry well* is an exploratory, development, or extension well that proves to be incapable of producing either oil or gas in sufficient quantities to justify completion as an oil or gas well.

(2) A *productive well* is an exploratory, development, or extension well that is not a dry well.

(3) *Completion* refers to installation of permanent equipment for production of oil or gas, or, in the case of a dry well, to reporting to the appropriate authority that the well has been abandoned.

(4) The *number of wells drilled* refers to the number of wells completed at any time during the fiscal year, regardless of when drilling was initiated.

(c) Disclose, by geographic area, for each of the last three years, any other exploratory or development activities conducted, including implementation of mining methods for purposes of oil and gas producing activities.

Item 1206. Present activities

(a) Disclose, by geographical area, the registrant's present activities, such as the number of wells in the process of being drilled (including wells temporarily suspended), waterfloods in process of being installed, pressure maintenance operations, and any other related activities of material importance.

(b) Provide the description of present activities as of a date at the end of the most recent fiscal year or as close to the date that the registrant files the document as reasonably possible.

(c) Include only those wells in the process of being drilled at the "as of" date and express them in terms of both gross and net wells.

(d) Do not include wells that the registrant plans to drill, but has not commenced drilling unless there are factors that make such information material.

Item 1207. Delivery commitments

(a) If the registrant is committed to provide a fixed and determinable quantity of oil or gas in the near future under existing contracts or agreements, disclose material information concerning the estimated availability of oil and gas from any principal sources, including the following:

(1) The principal sources of oil and gas that the registrant will rely upon and the total amounts that the registrant expects to receive from each principal source and from all sources combined;

(2) The total quantities of oil and gas that are subject to delivery commitments; and

(3) The steps that the registrant has taken to ensure that available reserves and supplies are sufficient to meet such commitments for the next one to three years.

(b) Disclose the information required by this Item:

(1) In a form understandable to investors; and

(2) Based upon the facts and circumstances of the particular situation, including, but not limited to:

(i) Disclosure by geographic area;

(ii) Significant supplies dedicated or contracted to the registrant;

(iii) Any significant reserves or supplies subject to priorities or curtailments which may affect quantities delivered to certain classes of customers, such as customers receiving services under low priority and interruptible contracts;

(iv) Any priority allocations or price limitations imposed by Federal or State regulatory agencies, as well as other factors beyond the registrant's control that may affect the registrant's ability to meet its contractual obligations (the registrant need not provide detailed discussions of price regulation);

(v) Any other factors beyond the registrant's control, such as other parties having control over drilling new wells, competition for the acquisition of reserves and supplies, and the availability of foreign reserves and supplies, which may affect the registrant's ability to acquire additional reserves and supplies or to maintain or increase the availability of reserves and supplies; and

(vi) Any impact on the registrant's earnings and financing needs resulting from its inability to meet short-term or long-term contractual obligations. (See Items 303 and 1209 of Regulation S–K.)

(c) If the registrant has been unable to meet any significant delivery commitments in the last three years, describe the circumstances concerning such events and their impact on the registrant.

(d) For purposes of this Item, *available reserves* are estimates of the amounts of oil and gas which the registrant can produce from current proved developed reserves using presently installed equipment under existing economic and operating conditions and an estimate of amounts that others can deliver to the registrant under long-term contracts or agreements on a per-day, per-month, or per-year basis.

Item 1208. Oil and gas properties, wells, operations, and acreage

(a) Disclose, as of a reasonably current date or as of the end of the fiscal year, the total gross and net productive wells, expressed separately for oil and gas (including synthetic oil and gas produced through wells) and the total gross and net developed acreage (*i.e.*, acreage assignable to productive wells) by geographic area.

(b) Disclose, as of a reasonably current date or as of the end of the fiscal year, the amount of undeveloped acreage, both leases and concessions, if any, expressed in both gross and net acres by geographic area, together with an indication of acreage concentrations, and, if material, the minimum remaining terms of leases and concessions.

(c) *Definitions*. For purposes of this Item 1208, the following terms shall be defined as indicated:

(1) A *gross well or acre* is a well or acre in which the registrant owns a working interest. The number of gross wells is the total number of wells in which the registrant owns a working interest. Count one or more completions in the same bore hole as one well. In a footnote, disclose the number of wells with multiple completions. If one of the multiple completions in a well is an oil completion, classify the well as an oil well.

(2) A *net well or acre* is deemed to exist when the sum of fractional ownership working interests in gross wells or acres equals one. The number of net wells or acres is the sum of the fractional working interests owned in gross wells or acres expressed as whole numbers and fractions of whole numbers.

(3) *Productive wells* include producing wells and wells mechanically capable of production.

(4) Undeveloped acreage encompasses those leased acres on which wells have not been drilled or completed to a point that would permit the production of economic quantities of oil or gas regardless of whether such acreage contains proved reserves. Do not confuse undeveloped acreage with undrilled acreage held by production under the terms of the lease.

REGULATION G

(Cite as 17 CFR § 244.__)

Rule 100. General rules regarding disclosure of non–GAAP financial measures

(a) Whenever a registrant, or person acting on its behalf, publicly discloses material information that includes a non–GAAP financial measure, the registrant must accompany that non–GAAP financial measure with:

(1) A presentation of the most directly comparable financial measure calculated and presented in accordance with Generally Accepted Accounting Principles (GAAP); and

(2) A reconciliation (by schedule or other clearly understandable method), which shall be quantitative for historical non–GAAP measures presented, and quantitative, to the extent available without unreasonable efforts, for forward-looking information, of the differences between the non–GAAP financial measure disclosed or released with the most comparable financial measure or measures calculated and presented in accordance with GAAP identified in paragraph (a)(1) of this section.

(b) A registrant, or a person acting on its behalf, shall not make public a non–GAAP financial measure that, taken together with the information accompanying that measure and any other accompanying discussion of that measure, contains an untrue statement of a material fact or omits to state a material fact necessary in order to make the presentation of the non–GAAP financial measure, in light of the circumstances under which it is presented, not misleading.

(c) This section shall not apply to a disclosure of a non–GAAP financial measure that is made by or on behalf of a registrant that is a foreign private issuer if the following conditions are satisfied:

(1) The securities of the registrant are listed or quoted on a securities exchange or inter-dealer quotation system outside the United States;

(2) The non–GAAP financial measure is not derived from or based on a measure calculated and presented in accordance with generally accepted accounting principles in the United States; and

(3) The disclosure is made by or on behalf of the registrant outside the United States, or is included in a written communication that is released by or on behalf of the registrant outside the United States.

(d) This section shall not apply to a non–GAAP financial measure included in disclosure relating to a proposed business combination, the entity resulting therefrom or an entity that is a party thereto, if the disclosure is contained in a communication that is subject to Rule 425, Rules 14a–12 or 14d–2(b)(2) under the Securities Exchange Act of 1934 or Item 1015 of Regulation M–A.

NOTES TO RULE 100:

1. If a non–GAAP financial measure is made public orally, telephonically, by Web cast, by broadcast, or by similar means, the requirements of paragraphs (a)(1)(i) and (a)(1)(ii) of this section will be satisfied if:

(i) The required information in those paragraphs is provided on the registrant's Web site at the time the non–GAAP financial measure is made public; and

(ii) The location of the web site is made public in the same presentation in which the non–GAAP financial measure is made public.

2. The provisions of paragraph (c) of this section shall apply notwithstanding the existence of one or more of the following circumstances:

(i) A written communication is released in the United States as well as outside the United States, so long as the communication is released in the United States contemporaneously with or after the release outside the United States and is not otherwise targeted at persons located in the United States;

(ii) Foreign journalists, U.S. journalists or other third parties have access to the information;

(iii) The information appears on one or more web sites maintained by the registrant, so long as the web sites, taken together, are not available exclusively to, or targeted at, persons located in the United States; or

(iv) Following the disclosure or release of the information outside the United States, the information is included in a submission by the registrant to the Commission made under cover of a Form 6–K.

Rule 101. Definitions

This section defines certain terms as used in Regulation G (Rules 100 through 102).

(a)(1) *Non–GAAP financial measure.* A non–GAAP financial measure is a numerical measure of a registrant's historical or future financial performance, financial position or cash flows that:

(i) Excludes amounts, or is subject to adjustments that have the effect of excluding amounts, that are included in the most directly comparable measure calculated and presented in accordance with GAAP in the statement of income, balance sheet or statement of cash flows (or equivalent statements) of the issuer; or

(ii) Includes amounts, or is subject to adjustments that have the effect of including amounts, that are excluded from the most directly comparable measure so calculated and presented.

(2) A non–GAAP financial measure does not include operating and other financial measures and ratios or statistical measures calculated using exclusively one or both of:

(i) Financial measures calculated in accordance with GAAP; and

(ii) Operating measures or other measures that are not non–GAAP financial measures.

(3) A non–GAAP financial measure does not include financial measures required to be disclosed by GAAP, Commission rules, or a system of regulation of a government or governmental authority or self-regulatory organization that is applicable to the registrant.

(b) *GAAP*. GAAP refers to generally accepted accounting principles in the United States, except that:

(1) In the case of foreign private issuers whose primary financial statements are prepared in accordance with non-U.S. generally accepted accounting principles, GAAP refers to the principles under which those primary financial statements are prepared; and

(2) In the case of foreign private issuers that include a non–GAAP financial measure derived from a measure calculated in accordance with U.S. generally accepted accounting principles, GAAP refers to U.S. generally accepted accounting principles for purposes of the application of the requirements of Regulation G to the disclosure of that measure.

(c) *Registrant*. A registrant subject to this regulation is one that has a class of securities registered under Section 12 of the Securities Exchange Act of 1934 (15 U.S.C. 78*l*), or is required to file reports under Section 15(d) of the Securities Exchange Act of 1934 (15 U.S.C. 78o(d)), excluding any investment company registered under Section 8 of the Investment Company Act of 1940 (15 U.S.C. 80a–8).

(d) *United States*. United States means the United States of America, its territories and possessions, any State of the United States, and the District of Columbia.

Rule 102. No effect on antifraud liability

Neither the requirements of this Regulation G (17 CFR 244.100 through 244.102) nor a person's compliance or non-compliance with the requirements of this Regulation shall in itself affect any person's liability under Section 10(b) (15 U.S.C. 78j(b)) of the Securities Exchange Act of 1934 or Rule 10b–5 under the Securities Exchange Act of 1934.

REGULATION S–X—FORM AND CONTENT OF AND REQUIREMENTS FOR FINANCIAL STATEMENTS, SECURITIES ACT OF 1933, SECURITIES EXCHANGE ACT OF 1934, PUBLIC UTILITY HOLDING COMPANY ACT OF 1935, INVESTMENT COMPANY ACT OF 1940, INVESTMENT ADVISERS ACT OF 1940, AND ENERGY POLICY AND CONSERVATION ACT OF 1975

(Cite as 17 CFR § 210.____)

Article 1—Application of Regulation S–X

Rule	
1–01	Application of Regulation S–X
1–02	Definitions of terms used in Regulation S–X

Article 2—Qualifications and Reports of Accountants

2–01	Qualifications of accountants
2–02	Accountants' reports and attestation reports
2–03	Examination of financial statements by foreign government auditors
2–04	Examination of financial statements of persons other than the registrant
2–05	Examination of financial statements by more than one accountant
2–06	Retention of audit and review records
2–07	Communication with Audit Committees

Article 3—General Instructions as to Financial Statements

3–01	Consolidated balance sheets
3–02	Consolidated statements of comprehensive income and cash flows
3–03	Instructions to statement of comprehensive income requirements
3–04	Changes in stockholders' equity and noncontrolling interests
3–05	Financial statements of businesses acquired or to be acquired
3–06	Financial statements covering a period of nine to twelve months
3–07	[Reserved]
3–08	[Reserved]
3–09	Separate financial statements of subsidiaries not consolidated and 50 percent or less owned persons
3–10	Financial statements of guarantors and issuers of guaranteed securities registered or being registered
3–11	Financial statements of an inactive registrant
3–12	Age of financial statements at effective date of registration statement or at mailing date of proxy statement
3–13	Filing of other financial statements in certain cases
3–14	Special instructions for real estate operations to be acquired
3–15	Special provisions as to real estate investment trusts
3–16	Financial statements of affiliates whose securities collateralize an issue registered or being registered
3–17	Financial statements of natural persons
3–18	Special provisions as to registered management investment companies and companies required to be registered as management investment companies
3–19	[Reserved]
3–20	Currency for financial statements
3–21	[Reserved]

Article 3A—Consolidated and Combined Financial Statements

3A–01	[Reserved]
3A–02	Consolidated financial statements of the registrant and its subsidiaries
3A–03	Statement as to principles of consolidation or combination followed
3A–04	[Reserved]

Article 4—Rules of General Application

Article 5—Commercial and Industrial Companies

Article 6—Registered Investment Companies

Article 6A—Employee Stock Purchase, Savings and Similar Plans

Article 7—Insurance Companies

Article 8—Financial Statements of Smaller Reporting Companies

Article 9—Bank Holding Companies

Article 10—Interim Financial Statements

Article 11—Pro forma Financial Information

APPLICATION OF REGULATION S–X

ATTENTION ELECTRONIC FILERS

THIS REGULATION SHOULD BE READ IN CONJUNCTION WITH REGULATION S–T, WHICH GOVERNS THE PREPARATION AND SUBMISSION OF DOCUMENTS IN ELECTRONIC FORMAT. MANY PROVISIONS RELATING TO THE PREPARATION AND SUBMISSION OF DOCUMENTS IN PAPER FORMAT CONTAINED IN THIS REGULATION ARE SUPERSEDED BY THE PROVISIONS OF REGULATION S–T FOR DOCUMENTS REQUIRED TO BE FILED IN ELECTRONIC FORMAT.

Rule 1–01. Application of Regulation S–X

(a) This part (together with the Financial Reporting Releases (17 CFR 211)) sets forth the form and content of and requirements for financial statements required to be filed as a part of:

(1) Registration statements under the Securities Act of 1933 (17 CFR 239), except as otherwise specifically provided in the forms which are to be used for registration under this Act;

(2) Registration statements under section 12 (Subpart C of 17 CFR 249), annual or other reports under sections 13 and 15(d) (Subparts D and E of 17 CFR 249), and proxy and information statements under Section 14 of the Securities Exchange Act of 1934 except as otherwise specifically provided in the forms which are to be used for registration and reporting under these sections of this Act; and

(3) Registration statements and shareholder reports under the Investment Company Act of 1940 (17 CFR 274), except as otherwise specifically provided in the forms which are to be used for registration under this Act.

(b) The term *financial statements* as used in this Part shall be deemed to include all notes to the statements and all related schedules.

(c) In addition to filings pursuant to the Federal securities laws, Rule 4–10 of Regulation S–X applies to the preparation of accounts by persons engaged, in whole or in part, in the production of crude oil or natural gas in the United States pursuant to section 503 of the Energy Policy and Conservation Act of 1975 (42 U.S.C. 6383)(EPCA) and section 1(c) of the Energy Supply and Environmental Coordination Act of 1974 (15 U.S.C. 796), as amended by section 505 of EPCA.

Rule 1–02. Definitions of terms used in Regulation S–X

Unless the context otherwise requires, terms defined in the general rules and regulations or in the instructions to the applicable form, when used in Regulation S–X (this part 210), shall have the respective meanings given in such instructions or rules. In addition, the following terms shall have the meanings indicated in this section unless the context otherwise requires.

(a)(1) *Accountant's Report.* The term accountant's report, when used in regard to financial statements, means a document in which an independent public or certified public accountant indicates the scope of the audit (or examination) which he has made and sets forth his opinion regarding the financial statements taken as a whole, or an assertion to the effect that an overall opinion cannot be expressed. When an overall opinion cannot be expressed, the reasons therefor shall be stated.

(2) *Attestation Report on Internal Control over Financial Reporting.* The term *attestation report on internal control over financial reporting* means a report in which a registered public accounting firm expresses an opinion, either unqualified or adverse, as to whether the registrant maintained, in all material respects, effective internal control over financial reporting (as defined in Rule 13a–15(f) or Rule 15d–15(f) under the Securities Exchange Act of 1934), except in the rare circumstance of a scope limitation that cannot be overcome by the registrant or the registered public accounting firm which would result in the accounting firm disclaiming an opinion.

(3) *Attestation Report on Assessment of Compliance with Servicing Criteria for Asset-Backed Securities.* The term attestation report on assessment of compliance with servicing criteria for asset-backed securities means a report in which a registered public accounting firm, as required by Rule 13a–18(c) or Rule 15d–18(c) under the Securities Exchange Act of 1934, expresses an opinion, or states that an opinion cannot be expressed, concerning an asserting party's assessment of compliance with servicing criteria, as required by Rule 13a–18(b) or Rule 15d–18(b) under the Securities Exchange Act of 1934, in accordance with standards on attestation engagements. When an overall opinion cannot be expressed, the registered public accounting firm must state why it is unable to express such an opinion.

(4) *Definitions of Terms Related to Internal Control over Financial Reporting.* The term *material weakness* means a deficiency, or a combination of deficiencies, in internal control over financial reporting (as defined in Rule 13a–15(f) or Rule 15d–15(f) under the Securities Exchange Act of 1934) such that there is a reasonable possibility that a material misstatement of the registrant's annual or interim financial statements will not be prevented or detected on a timely basis. The term *significant deficiency* means a deficiency, or a combination of deficiencies, in internal control over financial reporting that is less severe than a material weakness, yet important enough to merit attention by those responsible for oversight of the registrant's financial reporting.

(b) *Affiliate.* An affiliate of, or a person affiliated with, a specific person is a person that directly, or indirectly through one or more intermediaries, controls, or is controlled by, or is under common control with, the person specified.

(c) *Amount.* The term amount, when used in regard to securities, means the principal amount if relating to evidences of indebtedness, the number of shares if relating to shares, and the number of units if relating to any other kind of security.

(d) *Audit (or Examination).* The term audit (or examination), when used in regard tofinancial statements of issuers as defined by Section 2(a)(7) of the Sarbanes-Oxley Act of 2002, means an examination of the financial statements by an independent accountant in accordance with the standards of the Public Company Accounting Oversight Board (United States) ("PCAOB") for the purpose of expressing an opinion thereon. When used in regard to financial statements of entities that are not issuers as defined by Section 2(a)(7) of the Sarbanes-Oxley Act of 2002, the term means an examination of the financial statements by an independent accountant in accordance with either the standards of the PCAOB or U.S. generally accepted auditing standards ("U.S. GAAS") as specified or permitted in the regulations and forms applicable to those entities for the purpose of expressing an opinion thereon. The standards of the PCAOB and U.S. GAAS may be modified or supplemented by the Commission.

(e) *Bank Holding Company.* The term bank holding company means a person which is engaged, either directly or indirectly, primarily in the business of owning securities of one or more banks for the purpose, and with the effect, of exercising control.

(f) *Certified.* The term certified, when used in regard to financial statements, means examined and reported upon with an opinion expressed by an independent public or certified public accountant.

(g) *Control.* The term control (including the terms *controlling, controlled by* and *under common control with*) means the possession, direct or indirect, of the power to direct or cause the direction of the management and policies of a person, whether through the ownership of voting shares, by contract, or otherwise.

(h) *Development Stage Company.* A company shall be considered to be in the development stage if it is devoting substantially all of its efforts to establishing a new business and either of the following conditions exists: (1) Planned principal operations have not commenced. (2) Planned principal operations have commenced, but there has been no significant revenue therefrom.

(i) *Equity Security.* The term *equity security* means any stock or similar security; or any security convertible, with or without consideration, into such a security, or carrying any warrant or right to subscribe to or purchase such a security; or any such warrant or right.

(j) *Fifty-Percent-Owned Person.* The term *50–percent-owned person*, in relation to a specified person, means a person approximately 50 percent of whose outstanding voting shares is owned by the specified person either directly, or indirectly through one or more intermediaries.

(k) *Fiscal Year.* The term *fiscal year* means the annual accounting period or, if no closing date has been adopted, the calendar year ending on December 31.

(*l*) *Foreign Business.* A business that is majority owned by persons who are not citizens or residents of the United States and is not organized under the laws of the United States or any state thereof, and either:

(1) More than 50 percent of its assets are located outside the United States; or

(2) The majority of its executive officers and directors are not United States citizens or residents.

(m) *Insurance Holding Company.* The term insurance holding company means a person which is engaged, either directly or indirectly, primarily in the business of owning securities of one or more insurance companies for the purpose, and with the effect, of exercising control.

(n) *Majority-Owned Subsidiary.* The term majority-owned subsidiary means a subsidiary more than 50 percent of whose outstanding voting shares is owned by its parent and/or the parent's other majority-owned subsidiaries.

(o) *Material.* The term *material*, when used to qualify a requirement for the furnishing of information as to any subject, limits the information required to those matters about which an average prudent investor ought reasonably to be informed.

(p) *Parent.* A parent of a specified person is an affiliate controlling such person directly, or indirectly through one or more intermediaries.

(q) *Person.* The term *person* means an individual, a corporation, a partnership, an association, a joint-stock company, a business trust, or an unincorporated organization.

(r) *Principal Holder of Equity Securities.* The term principal holder of equity securities, used in respect of a registrant or other person named in a particular statement or report, means a holder of record or a known beneficial owner of more than 10 percent of any class of equity securities of the registrant or other person, respectively, as of the date of the related balance sheet filed.

(s) *Promoter.* The term *promoter* includes:

(1) Any person who, acting alone or in conjunction with one or more other persons, directly or indirectly takes initiative in founding and organizing the business or enterprise of an issuer;

(2) Any person who, in connection with the founding and organizing of the business or enterprise of an issuer, directly or indirectly receives in consideration of services or property, or both services and property, 10 percent or more of any class of securities of the issuer or 10 percent or more of the proceeds from the sale of any class of securities. However, a person who receives such securities or proceeds either solely as underwriting commissions or solely in consideration of property shall not be deemed a promoter within the meaning of this paragraph if such person does not otherwise take part in founding and organizing the enterprise.

(t) *Registrant.* The term *registrant* means the issuer of the securities for which an application, a registration statement, or a report is filed.

(u) *Related Parties.* The term *related parties* is used as that term is defined in the FASB ASC Master Glossary.

(v) *Share.* The term *share* means a share of stock in a corporation or unit of interest in an unincorporated person.

(w) *Significant Subsidiary.* The term *significant subsidiary* means a subsidiary, including its subsidiaries, which meets any of the following conditions:

(1) The registrant's and its other subsidiaries' investments in and advances to the subsidiary exceed 10 percent of the total assets of the registrant and its subsidiaries consolidated as of the

end of the most recently completed fiscal year (for a proposed combination between entities under common control, this condition is also met when the number of common shares exchanged or to be exchanged by the registrant exceeds 10 percent of its total common shares outstanding at the date the combination is initiated); or

(2) The registrant's and its other subsidiaries' proportionate share of the total assets (after intercompany eliminations) of the subsidiary exceeds 10 percent of the total assets of the registrants and its subsidiaries consolidated as of the end of the most recently completed fiscal year; or

(3) The registrant's and its other subsidiaries' equity in the income from continuing operations before income taxes of the subsidiary exclusive of amounts attributable to any noncontrolling interests exceeds 10 percent of such income of the registrant and its subsidiaries consolidated for the most recently completed fiscal year.

NOTE TO PARAGRAPH (w): A registrant that files its financial statements in accordance with or provides a reconciliation to U.S. Generally Accepted Accounting Principles shall make the prescribed tests using amounts determined under U.S. Generally Accepted Accounting Principles. A foreign private issuer that files its financial statements in accordance with IFRS as issued by the IASB shall make the prescribed tests using amounts determined under IFRS as issued by the IASB.

COMPUTATIONAL NOTE 1 TO PARAGRAPH (3): For purposes of making the prescribed income test the following guidance should be applied:

1. When a loss exclusive of amounts attributable to any noncontrolling interests has been incurred by either the parent and its subsidiaries consolidated or the tested subsidiary, but not both, the equity in the income or loss of the tested subsidiary exclusive of amounts attributable to any noncontrolling interests should be excluded from such income of the registrant and its subsidiaries consolidated for purposes of the computation.

2. If income of the registrant and its subsidiaries consolidated exclusive of amounts attributable to any noncontrolling interests for the most recent fiscal year is at least 10 percent lower than the average of the income for the last five fiscal years, such average income should be substituted for purposes of the computation. Any loss years should be omitted for purposes of computing average income.

3. Where the test involves combined entities, as in the case of determining whether summarized financial data should be presented, entities reporting losses shall not be aggregated with entities reporting income.

(x) *Subsidiary*. A *subsidiary* of a specified person is an affiliate controlled by such person directly, or indirectly through one or more intermediaries.

(y) *Totally Held Subsidiary*. The term *totally held subsidiary* means a subsidiary (1) substantially all of whose outstanding equity securities are owned by its parent and/or the parent's other totally held subsidiaries, and (2) which is not indebted to any person other than its parent and/or the parent's other totally held subsidiaries, in an amount which is material in relation to the particular subsidiary, excepting indebtedness incurred in the ordinary course of business which is not overdue and which matures within 1 year from the date of its creation, whether evidenced by securities or not. Indebtedness of a subsidiary which is secured by its parent by guarantee, pledge, assignment, or otherwise is to be excluded for purposes of paragraph (x)(2) of this section.

(z) *Voting Shares*. The term *voting shares* means the sum of all rights, other than as affected by events of default, to vote for election of directors and/or the sum of all interests in an unincorporated person.

(aa) *Wholly Owned Subsidiary*. The term *wholly owned subsidiary* means a subsidiary substantially all of whose outstanding voting shares are owned by its parent and/or the parent's other wholly owned subsidiaries.

(bb) *Summarized Financial Information*. (1) Except as provided in paragraph (aa)(2), *summarized financial information* referred to in this regulation shall mean the presentation of summarized information as to the assets, liabilities and results of operations of the entity for which the information is required. Summarized financial information shall include the following disclosures:

(i) Current assets, noncurrent assets, current liabilities, noncurrent liabilities, and, when applicable, redeemable preferred stocks (see Rule 5-02.27 of Regulation S-X) and noncontrolling interests (for specialized industries in which classified balance sheets are normally not presented, information shall be provided as to the nature and amount of the majority components of assets and liabilities);

(ii) Net sales or gross revenues, gross profit (or, alternatively, costs and expenses applicable to net sales or gross revenues), income or loss from continuing operations, net income or loss, and net income or loss attributable to the entity (for specialized industries, other information may be substituted for sales and related costs and expenses if necessary for a more meaningful presentation); and

(2) Summarized financial information for unconsolidated subsidiaries and 50 percent or less owned persons referred to in and required by Rule 10-01(b) of Regulation S-X for interim periods shall include the information required by paragraph (aa)(1)(ii) of this rule.

(cc) *Statement(s) of Comprehensive Income.* The term statement(s) of comprehensive income means a financial statement that includes all changes in equity during a period except those resulting from investments by owners and distributions to owners. Comprehensive income comprises all components of net income and all components of other comprehensive income. The statement of comprehensive income may be presented either in a single continuous financial statement or in two separate but consecutive financial statements. A statement(s) of operations or variations thereof may be used in place of a statement(s) of comprehensive income if there was no other comprehensive income during the period(s).

(dd) *Restricted Net Assets.* The term restricted net assets shall mean that amount of the registrant's proportionate share of net assets of consolidated subsidiaries (after intercompany eliminations) which as of the end of the most recent fiscal year may not be transferred to the parent company by subsidiaries in the form of loans, advances or cash dividends without the consent of a third party (i.e., lender, regulatory agency, foreign government, etc.). Not all limitations on transferability of assets are considered to be restrictions for purposes of this rule, which considers only specific third party restrictions on the ability of subsidiaries to transfer funds outside of the entity. For example, the presence of subsidiary debt which is secured by certain of the subsidiary's assets does not constitute a restriction under this rule. However, if there are any loan provisions prohibiting dividend payments, loans or advances to the parent by a subsidiary, these are considered restrictions for purposes of computing restricted net assets. When a loan agreement requires that a subsidiary maintain certain working capital, net tangible asset, or net asset levels, or where formal compensating arrangements exist, there is considered to be a restriction under the rule because the lender's intent is normally to preclude the transfer by dividend or otherwise of funds to the parent company. Similarly, a provision which requires that a subsidiary reinvest all of its earnings is a restriction, since this precludes loans, advances or dividends in the amount of such undistributed earnings by the entity. Where restrictions on the amount of funds which may be loaned or advanced differ from the amount restricted as to transfer in the form of cash dividends, the amount least restrictive to the subsidiary shall be used. Redeemable preferred stocks (Rule 5–02.27) and noncontrolling interests shall be deducted in computing net assets for purposes of this test.

QUALIFICATIONS AND REPORTS OF ACCOUNTANTS

Rule 2–01. Qualifications of accountants

Preliminary Note to Rule 2–01

1. Rule 2–01 is designed to ensure that auditors are qualified and independent of their audit clients both in fact and in appearance. Accordingly, the rule sets forth restrictions on financial, employment, and business relationships between an accountant and an audit client and restrictions on an accountant providing certain non-audit services to an audit client.

2. Rule 210.2–01(b) sets forth the general standard of auditor independence. Paragraphs (c)(1) to (c)(5) reflect the application of the general standard to particular circumstances. The rule does not purport to, and the Commission could not, consider all circumstances that raise independence concerns, and these are subject to the general standard in Rule 2–01(b). In considering this standard, the Commission looks in the first instance to whether a relationship or the provision of a service: creates a mutual or conflicting interest between the accountant and the audit client; places the accountant in the position of auditing his or her own work; results in the accountant acting as management or an employee of the audit client; or places the accountant in a position of being an advocate for the audit client.

3. These factors are general guidance only and their application may depend on particular facts and circumstances. For that reason, Rule 2–01 provides that, in determining whether an accountant is independent, the Commission will consider all relevant facts and circumstances. For the same reason, registrants and accountants are encouraged to consult with the Commission's Office of the Chief Accountant before entering into relationships, including relationships involving the provision of services, that are not explicitly described in the rule.

(a) The Commission will not recognize any person as a certified public accountant who is not duly registered and in good standing as such under the laws of the place of his residence or principal office. The Commission will not recognize any person as a public accountant who is not in good standing and entitled to practice as such under the laws of the place of his residence or principal office.

(b) The Commission will not recognize an accountant as independent, with respect to an audit client, if the accountant is not, or a reasonable investor with knowledge of all relevant facts and circumstances would conclude that the accountant is not, capable of exercising objective and impartial judgment on all issues encompassed within the accountant's engagement. In determining whether an accountant is independent, the Commission will consider all relevant circumstances, including all relationships between the accountant and the audit client, and not just those relating to reports filed with the Commission.

(c) This paragraph sets forth a non-exclusive specification of circumstances inconsistent with paragraph (b) of this rule.

(1) *Financial Relationships.* An accountant is not independent if, at any point during the audit and professional engagement period, the accountant has a direct financial interest or a material indirect financial interest in the accountant's audit client, such as:

(i) Investments in audit clients. An accountant is not independent when:

(A) The accounting firm, any covered person in the firm, or any of his or her immediate family members, has any direct investment in an audit client, such as stocks, bonds, notes, options, or other securities. The term direct investment includes an investment in an audit client through an intermediary if:

(*1*) The accounting firm, covered person, or immediate family member, alone or together with other persons, supervises or participates in the intermediary's investment decisions or has control over the intermediary; or

(*2*) The intermediary is not a diversified management investment company, as defined by section 5(b)(1) of the Investment Company Act of 1940 (15 U.S.C. 80a–5(b)(1)), and has an investment in the audit client that amounts to 20% or more of the value of the intermediary's total investments.

(B) Any partner, principal, shareholder, or professional employee of the accounting firm, any of his or her immediate family members, any close family member of a covered person in the firm, or any group of the above persons has filed a Schedule 13D or 13G (17 CFR 240.13d–101 or 240.13d–102) with the Commission indicating beneficial ownership of more than five percent of an audit client's equity securities or controls an audit client, or a close family member of a partner, principal, or shareholder of the accounting firm controls an audit client.

(C) The accounting firm, any covered person in the firm, or any of his or her immediate family members, serves as voting trustee of a trust, or executor of an estate, containing the securities of an audit client, unless the accounting firm, covered person in the firm, or immediate family member has no authority to make investment decisions for the trust or estate.

(D) The accounting firm, any covered person in the firm, any of his or her immediate family members, or any group of the above persons has any material indirect investment in an audit client. For purposes of this paragraph, the term *material indirect investment* does not include ownership by any covered person in the firm, any of his or her immediate family members, or any group of the above persons of 5% or less of the outstanding shares of a diversified management investment company, as defined by section 5(b)(1) of the Investment Company Act of 1940 (15 U.S.C. 80a–5(b)(1)), that invests in an audit client.

(E) The accounting firm, any covered person in the firm, or any of his or her immediate family members:

(*1*) Has any direct or material indirect investment in an entity where:

(*i*) An audit client has an investment in that entity that is material to the audit client and has the ability to exercise significant influence over that entity; or

(*ii*) The entity has an investment in an audit client that is material to that entity and has the ability to exercise significant influence over that audit client;

(*2*) Has any material investment in an entity over which an audit client has the ability to exercise significant influence; or

(*3*) Has the ability to exercise significant influence over an entity that has the ability to exercise significant influence over an audit client.

(ii) *Other Financial Interests in Audit Client.* An accountant is not independent when the accounting firm, any covered person in the firm, or any of his or her immediate family members has:

(A) *Loans/Debtor-Creditor Relationship.* Any loan (including any margin loan) to or from an audit client, or an audit client's officers, directors, or record or beneficial owners of more than ten percent of the audit client's equity securities, except for the following loans obtained from a financial institution under its normal lending procedures, terms, and requirements:

(*1*) Automobile loans and leases collateralized by the automobile;

(*2*) Loans fully collateralized by the cash surrender value of an insurance policy;

(*3*) Loans fully collateralized by cash deposits at the same financial institution; and

(*4*) A mortgage loan collateralized by the borrower's primary residence provided the loan was not obtained while the covered person in the firm was a covered person.

(B) *Savings and Checking Accounts.* Any savings, checking, or similar account at a bank, savings and loan, or similar institution that is an audit client, if the account has a balance that exceeds the amount insured by the Federal Deposit Insurance Corporation or any similar insurer, except that an accounting firm account may have an uninsured balance provided that the likelihood of the bank, savings and loan, or similar institution experiencing financial difficulties is remote.

(C) *Broker-Dealer Accounts.* Brokerage or similar accounts maintained with a broker-dealer that is an audit client, if:

(*1*) Any such account includes any asset other than cash or securities (within the meaning of "security" provided in the Securities Investor Protection Act of 1970 ("SIPA") (15 U.S.C. 78aaa *et seq.*));

(*2*) The value of assets in the accounts exceeds the amount that is subject to a Securities Investor Protection Corporation advance, for those accounts, under Section 9 of SIPA (15 U.S.C. 78fff–3); or

(*3*) With respect to non-U.S. accounts not subject to SIPA protection, the value of assets in the accounts exceeds the amount insured or protected by a program similar to SIPA.

(D) *Futures Commission Merchant Accounts.* Any futures, commodity, or similar account maintained with a futures commission merchant that is an audit client.

(E) *Credit Cards.* Any aggregate outstanding credit card balance owed to a lender that is an audit client that is not reduced to $10,000 or less on a current basis taking into consideration the payment due date and any available grace period.

(F) *Insurance Products.* Any individual policy issued by an insurer that is an audit client unless:

(*1*) The policy was obtained at a time when the covered person in the firm was not a covered person in the firm; and

(*2*) The likelihood of the insurer becoming insolvent is remote.

(G) *Investment Companies.* Any financial interest in an entity that is part of an investment company complex that includes an audit client.

(iii) *Exceptions.* Notwithstanding paragraphs (c)(1)(i) and (c)(1)(ii) of this rule, an accountant will not be deemed not independent if:

(A) *Inheritance and Gift.* Any person acquires an unsolicited financial interest, such as through an unsolicited gift or inheritance, that would cause an accountant to be not independent under paragraph (c)(1)(i) or (c)(1)(ii) of this section, and the financial interest is disposed of as soon as practicable, but no later than 30 days after the person has knowledge of and the right to dispose of the financial interest.

(B) *New Audit Engagement.* Any person has a financial interest that would cause an accountant to be not independent under paragraph (c)(1)(i) or (c)(1)(ii) of this rule, and:

(*1*) The accountant did not audit the client's financial statements for the immediately preceding fiscal year; and

(*2*) The accountant is independent under paragraph (c)(1)(i) and (c)(1)(ii) of this section before the earlier of:

(*i*) Signing an initial engagement letter or other agreement to provide audit, review, or attest services to the audit client; or

(*ii*) Commencing any audit, review, or attest procedures (including planning the audit of the client's financial statements).

(C) *Employee Compensation and Benefit Plans.* An immediate family member of a person who is a covered person in the firm only by virtue of paragraphs (f)(11)(iii) or (f)(11)(iv) of this rule has a financial interest that would cause an accountant to be not independent under paragraph (c)(1)(i) or (c)(1)(ii) of this rule, and the acquisition of the financial interest was an unavoidable consequence of participation in his or her employer's employee compensation or benefits program, provided that the financial interest, other than unexercised employee stock options, is disposed of as soon as practicable, but no later than 30 days after the person has the right to dispose of the financial interest.

(iv) *Audit clients' financial relationships.* An accountant is not independent when:

(A) *Investments by the Audit Client in the Accounting Firm.* An audit client has, or has agreed to acquire, any direct investment in the accounting firm, such as stocks, bonds, notes, options, or other securities, or the audit client's officers or directors are record or beneficial owners of more than 5% of the equity securities of the accounting firm.

(B) *Underwriting.* An accounting firm engages an audit client to act as an underwriter, broker-dealer, market-maker, promoter, or analyst with respect to securities issued by the accounting firm.

(2) *Employment Relationships.* An accountant is not independent if, at any point during the audit and professional engagement period, the accountant has an employment relationship with an audit client, such as:

(i) *Employment at Audit Client of Accountant.* A current partner, principal, shareholder, or professional employee of the accounting firm is employed by the audit client or serves as a member of the board of directors or similar management or governing body of the audit client.

(ii) *Employment at Audit Client of Certain Relatives of Accountant.* A close family member of a covered person in the firm is in an accounting role or financial reporting oversight role at an audit client, or was in such a role during any period covered by an audit for which the covered person in the firm is a covered person.

(iii) *Employment at Audit Client of Former Employee of Accounting Firm.* (A) A former partner, principal, shareholder, or professional employee of an accounting firm is in an accounting role or financial reporting oversight role at an audit client, unless the individual:

(*1*) Does not influence the accounting firm's operations or financial policies;

(*2*) Has no capital balances in the accounting firm; and

(*3*) Has no financial arrangement with the accounting firm other than one providing for regular payment of a fixed dollar amount (which is not dependent on the revenues, profits, or earnings of the accounting firm):

(*i*) Pursuant to a fully funded retirement plan, rabbi trust, or, in jurisdictions in which a rabbi trust does not exist, a similar vehicle; or

(*ii*) In the case of a former professional employee who was not a partner, principal, or shareholder of the accounting firm and who has been disassociated from the accounting firm for more than five years, that is immaterial to the former professional employee; and

(B) A former partner, principal, shareholder, or professional employee of an accounting firm is in a financial reporting oversight role at an issuer (as defined in section 10A(f) of the Securities Exchange Act of 1934 (15 U.S.C. 78j–1(f))), except an issuer that is an investment company registered under section 8 of the Investment Company Act of 1940 (15 U.S.C. 80a–8), unless the individual:

(*1*) Employed by the issuer was not a member of the audit engagement team of the issuer during the one year period preceding the date that audit procedures commenced for the fiscal period that included the date of initial employment of the audit engagement team member by the issuer;

(*2*) For purposes of paragraph (c)(2)(iii)(B)(1) of this rule, the following individuals are not considered to be members of the audit engagement team:

(*i*) Persons, other than the lead partner and the concurring partner, who provided ten or fewer hours of audit, review, or attest services during the period covered by paragraph (c)(2)(iii)(B)(1) of this rule;

(*ii*) Individuals employed by the issuer as a result of a business combination between an issuer that is an audit client and the employing entity, provided employment was not in contemplation of the business combination and the audit committee of the successor issuer is aware of the prior employment relationship; and (*iii*) Individuals that are employed by the issuer due to an emergency or other unusual situation provided that the audit committee determines that the relationship is in the interest of investors;

(*3*) For purposes of paragraph (c)(2)(iii)(B)(*1*) of this section, audit procedures are deemed to have commenced for a fiscal period the day following the filing of the issuer's periodic annual report with the Commission covering the previous fiscal period; or

(C) A former partner, principal, shareholder, or professional employee of an accounting firm is in a financial reporting oversight role with respect to an investment company registered under section 8 of the Investment Company Act of 1940 (15 U.S.C. 80a–8), if:

(*1*) The former partner, principal, shareholder, or professional employee of an accounting firm is employed in a financial reporting oversight role related to the operations and financial reporting of the registered investment company at an entity in the investment company complex, as defined in (f)(14) of this rule, that includes the registered investment company; and

(*2*) The former partner, principal, shareholder, or professional employee of an accounting firm employed by the registered investment company or any entity in the investment company complex was a member of the audit engagement team of the registered investment company or any other registered investment company in the investment company complex during the one year period preceding the date that audit procedures commenced that included the date of initial employment of the audit engagement team member by the registered investment company or any entity in the investment company complex.

(*3*) For purposes of paragraph (c)(2)(iii)(C)(2) of this rule, the following individuals are not considered to be members of the audit engagement team:

(*i*) Persons, other than the lead partner and concurring partner, who provided ten or fewer hours of audit, review or attest services during the period covered by paragraph (c)(2)(iii)(C)(2) of this rule;

(*ii*) Individuals employed by the registered investment company or any entity in the investment company complex as a result of a business combination between a registered investment company or any entity in the investment company complex that is an audit client and the employing entity, provided employment was not in contemplation of the business combination and the audit committee of the registered investment company is aware of the prior employment relationship; and

(*iii*) Individuals that are employed by the registered investment company or any entity in the investment company complex due to an emergency or other unusual situation provided that the audit committee determines that the relationship is in the interest of investors.

(*4*) For purposes of paragraph (c)(2)(iii)(C)(2) of this rule, audit procedures are deemed to have commenced the day following the filing of the registered investment company's periodic annual report with the Commission.

(iv) *Employment at Accounting Firm of Former Employee of Audit Client*. A former officer, director, or employee of an audit client becomes a partner, principal, shareholder, or professional employee of the accounting firm, unless the individual does not participate in, and is not in a position to influence, the audit of the financial statements of the audit client covering any period during which he or she was employed by or associated with that audit client.

(3) *Business Relationships*. An accountant is not independent if, at any point during the audit and professional engagement period, the accounting firm or any covered person in the firm has any direct or material indirect business relationship with an audit client, or with persons associated with the audit client in a decision-making capacity, such as an audit client's officers, directors, or substantial stockholders. The relationships described in this paragraph do not include a relationship in which the accounting firm or covered person in the firm provides professional services to an audit client or is a consumer in the ordinary course of business.

(4) *Non-Audit Services*. An accountant is not independent if, at any point during the audit and

professional engagement period, the accountant provides the following non-audit services to an audit client:

(i) *Bookkeeping or Other Services Related to the Accounting Records or Financial Statements of the Audit Client.* Any service, unless it is reasonable to conclude that the results of these services will not be subject to audit procedures during an audit of the audit client's financial statements, including:

(A) Maintaining or preparing the audit client's accounting records;

(B) Preparing the audit client's financial statements that are filed with the Commission or that form the basis of financial statements filed with the Commission; or

(C) Preparing or originating source data underlying the audit client's financial statements.

(ii) *Financial Information Systems Design and Implementation.* Any service, unless it is reasonable to conclude that the results of these services will not be subject to audit procedures during an audit of the audit client's financial statements, including:

(A) Directly or indirectly operating, or supervising the operation of, the audit client's information system or managing the audit client's local area network; or

(B) Designing or implementing a hardware or software system that aggregates source data underlying the financial statements or generates information that is significant to the audit client's financial statements or other financial information systems taken as a whole.

(iii) *Appraisal or Valuation Services, Fairness Opinions, or Contribution-in-Kind Reports.* Any appraisal service, valuation service, or any service involving a fairness opinion or contribution-in-kind report for an audit client, unless it is reasonable to conclude that the results of these services will not be subject to audit procedures during an audit of the audit client's financial statements.

(iv) *Actuarial Services.* Any actuarially-oriented advisory service involving the determination of amounts recorded in the financial statements and related accounts for the audit client other than assisting a client in understanding the methods, models, assumptions, and inputs used in computing an amount, unless it is reasonable to conclude that the results of these services will not be subject to audit procedures during an audit of the audit client's financial statements.

(v) *Internal Audit Outsourcing Services.* Any internal audit service that has been outsourced by the audit client that relates to the audit client's internal accounting controls, financial systems, or financial statements, for an audit client unless it is reasonable to conclude that the results of these services will not be subject to audit procedures during an audit of the audit client's financial statements.

(vi) *Management Functions.* Acting, temporarily or permanently, as a director, officer, or employee of an audit client, or performing any decision-making, supervisory, or ongoing monitoring function for the audit client.

(vii) *Human Resources.* (A) Searching for or seeking out prospective candidates for managerial, executive, or director positions;

(B) Engaging in psychological testing, or other formal testing or evaluation programs;

(C) Undertaking reference checks of prospective candidates for an executive or director position;

(D) Acting as a negotiator on the audit client's behalf, such as determining position, status or title, compensation, fringe benefits, or other conditions of employment; or

(E) Recommending, or advising the audit client to hire, a specific candidate for a specific job (except that an accounting firm may, upon request by the audit client, interview candidates and advise the audit client on the candidate's competence for financial accounting, administrative, or control positions).

(viii) *Broker-Dealer, Investment Adviser, or Investment Banking Services.* Acting as a broker-dealer (registered or unregistered), promoter, or underwriter, on behalf of an audit client, making investment decisions on behalf of the audit client or otherwise having discretionary authority over an audit client's investments, executing a transaction to buy or sell an audit client's investment, or having custody of assets of the audit client, such as taking temporary possession of securities purchased by the audit client.

(ix) *Legal Services.* Providing any service to an audit client that, under circumstances in which the service is provided, could be provided only by someone licensed, admitted, or otherwise qualified to practice law in the jurisdiction in which the service is provided.

(x) *Expert Services Unrelated to the Audit.* Providing an expert opinion or other expert service for an audit client, or an audit client's legal representative, for the purpose of advocating an audit client's interests in litigation or in a regulatory or administrative proceeding or investigation. In any litigation or regulatory or administrative proceeding or investigation, an accountant's independence shall not be deemed to be impaired if the accountant provides factual accounts, including in testimony, of work performed or explains the positions taken or conclusions reached during the performance of any service provided by the accountant for the audit client.

(5) *Contingent Fees.* An accountant is not independent if, at any point during the audit and professional engagement period, the accountant provides any service or product to an audit client for a contingent fee or a commission, or receives a contingent fee or commission from an audit client.

(6) *Partner Rotation.* (i) Except as provided in paragraph (c)(6)(ii) of this rule, an accountant is not independent of an audit client when:

(A) Any audit partner as defined in paragraph (f)(7)(ii) of this rule performs:

(*1*) The services of a lead partner, as defined in paragraph (f)(7)(ii)(A) of this section, or concurring partner, as defined in paragraph (f)(7)(ii)(B) of this rule, for more than five consecutive years; or

(*2*) One or more of the services defined in paragraphs (f)(7)(ii)(C) and (D) of this rule for more than seven consecutive years;

(B) Any audit partner: (*1*) Within the five consecutive year period following the performance of services for the maximum period permitted under paragraph (c)(6)(i)(A)(1) of this rule, performs for that audit client the services of a lead partner, as defined in paragraph (f)(7)(ii)(A) of this section, or concurring partner, as defined in paragraph (f)(7)(ii)(B) of this rule, or a combination of those services, or

(*2*) Within the two consecutive year period following the performance of services for the maximum period permitted under paragraph (c)(6)(i)(A)(2) of this rule, performs one or more of the services defined in paragraph (f)(7)(ii) of this rule.

(ii) Any accounting firm with less than five audit clients that are issuers (as defined in section 10A(f) of the Securities Exchange Act of 1934 (15 U.S.C. 78j–1(f))) and less than ten partners shall be exempt from paragraph (c)(6)(i) of this section provided the Public Company Accounting Oversight Board conducts a review at least once every three years of each of the audit client engagements that would result in a lack of auditor independence under this paragraph.

(iii) For purposes of paragraph (c)(6)(i) of this rule, an audit client that is an investment company registered under section 8 of the Investment Company Act of 1940 (15 U.S.C. 80a–8), does not include an affiliate of the audit client that is an entity in the same investment company complex, as defined in paragraph (f)(14) of this section, except for another registered investment company in the same investment company complex. For purposes of calculating consecutive years of service under paragraph (c)(6)(i) of this rule with respect to investment companies in an investment company complex, audits of registered investment companies with different fiscal year-ends that are performed in a continuous 12–month period count as a single consecutive year.

(7) *Audit Committee Administration of the Engagement.* An accountant is not independent of an issuer (as defined in section 10A(f) of the Securities Exchange Act of 1934 (15 U.S.C. 78j–1(f))), other than an issuer that is an Asset–Backed Issuer as defined in Item 1101 of Regulation AB, or an investment company registered under section 8 of the Investment Company Act of 1940 (15 U.S.C. 80a–8), other than a unit investment trust as defined by section 4(2) of the Investment Company Act of 1940 (15 U.S.C. 80a–4(2)), unless:

(i) In accordance with Section 10A(i) of the Securities Exchange Act of 1934 (15 U.S.C. 78j–1(i)) either:

(A) Before the accountant is engaged by the issuer or its subsidiaries, or the registered investment company or its subsidiaries, to render audit or non-audit services, the engagement is approved by the issuer's or registered investment company's audit committee; or

(B) The engagement to render the service is entered into pursuant to pre-approval policies and procedures established by the audit committee of the issuer or registered investment company, provided the policies and procedures are detailed as to the particular service and the audit committee is informed of each service and such policies and procedures do not include delegation of the audit committees responsibilities under the Securities Exchange Act of 1934 to management; or

(C) With respect to the provision of services other than audit, review or attest services the pre-approval requirement is waived if:

(*1*) The aggregate amount of all such services provided constitutes no more than five percent of the total amount of revenues paid by the audit client to its accountant during the fiscal year in which the services are provided;

(*2*) Such services were not recognized by the issuer or registered investment company at the time of the engagement to be non-audit services; and

(*3*) Such services are promptly brought to the attention of the audit committee of the issuer or registered investment company and approved prior to the completion of the audit by the audit committee or by one or more members of the audit committee who are members of the board of directors to whom authority to grant such approvals has been delegated by the audit committee.

(ii) A registered investment company's audit committee also must pre-approve its accountant's engagements for non-audit services with the registered investment company's investment adviser (not including a sub-adviser whose role is primarily portfolio management and is sub-contracted or overseen by another investment adviser) and any entity controlling, controlled by, or under common control with the investment adviser that provides ongoing services to the registered investment company in accordance with paragraph (c)(7)(i) of this rule, if the engagement relates directly to the operations and financial reporting of the registered investment company, except that with respect to the waiver of the pre-approval requirement under paragraph (c)(7)(i)(C) of this rule, the aggregate amount of all services provided constitutes no more than five percent of the total amount of revenues paid to the registered investment company's accountant by the registered investment company, its investment adviser and any entity controlling, controlled by, or under common control with the investment adviser that provides ongoing services to the registered investment company during the fiscal year in which the services are provided that would have to be pre-approved by the registered investment company's audit committee pursuant to this rule.

(8) *Compensation.* An accountant is not independent of an audit client if, at any point during the audit and professional engagement period, any audit partner earns or receives compensation based on the audit partner procuring engagements with that audit client to provide any products or services other than audit, review or attest services. Any accounting firm with fewer than ten partners and fewer than five audit clients that are issuers (as defined in section 10A(f) of the Securities Exchange Act of 1934 (15 U.S.C. 78j–1(f))) shall be exempt from the requirement stated in the previous sentence.

(d) *Quality Controls.* An accounting firm's independence will not be impaired solely because a covered person in the firm is not independent of an audit client provided:

(1) The covered person did not know of the circumstances giving rise to the lack of independence;

(2) The covered person's lack of independence was corrected as promptly as possible under the relevant circumstances after the covered person or accounting firm became aware of it; and

(3) The accounting firm has a quality control system in place that provides reasonable assurance, taking into account the size and nature of the accounting firm's practice, that the accounting firm and its employees do not lack independence, and that covers at least all employees and associated entities of the accounting firm participating in the engagement, including employees and associated entities located outside of the United States.

(4) For an accounting firm that annually provides audit, review, or attest services to more than 500 companies with a class of securities registered with the Commission under section 12 of the Securities Exchange Act of 1934 (15 U.S.C. 78*l*), a quality control system will not provide such rea-

sonable assurance unless it has at least the following features:

(i) Written independence policies and procedures;

(ii) With respect to partners and managerial employees, an automated system to identify their investments in securities that might impair the accountant's independence;

(iii) With respect to all professionals, a system that provides timely information about entities from which the accountant is required to maintain independence;

(iv) An annual or on-going firm-wide training program about auditor independence;

(v) An annual internal inspection and testing program to monitor adherence to independence requirements;

(vi) Notification to all accounting firm members, officers, directors, and employees of the name and title of the member of senior management responsible for compliance with auditor independence requirements;

(vii) Written policies and procedures requiring all partners and covered persons to report promptly to the accounting firm when they are engaged in employment negotiations with an audit client, and requiring the firm to remove immediately any such professional from that audit client's engagement and to review promptly all work the professional performed related to that audit client's engagement; and

(viii) A disciplinary mechanism to ensure compliance with this section.

(e)(1) *Transition and Grandfathering.* Provided the following relationships did not impair the accountant's independence under pre-existing requirements of the Commission, the Independence Standards, Board, or the accounting profession in the United States, the existence of the relationship on May 6, 2003 will not be deemed to impair an accountant's independence:

(i) Employment relationships that commenced at the issuer prior to May 6, 2003 as described in paragraph (c)(2)(iii)(B) of this rule.

(ii) Compensation earned or received, as described in paragraph (c)(8) of this rule during the fiscal year of the accounting firm that includes the effective date of this rule.

(iii) Until May 6, 2004, the provision of services described in paragraph (c)(4) of this rule provided those services are pursuant to contracts in existence on May 6, 2003.

(iv) The provision of services by the accountant under contracts in existence on May 6, 2003 that have not been pre-approved by the audit committee as described in paragraph (c)(7) of this rule.

(v) Until the first day of the issuer's fiscal year beginning after May 6, 2003 by a "lead" partner and other audit partner (other than the "concurring" partner) providing services in excess of those permitted under paragraph (c)(6) of this rule. An accountant's independence will not be deemed to be impaired until the first day of the issuer's fiscal year beginning after May 6, 2004 by a "concurring" partner providing services in excess of those permitted under paragraph (c)(6) of this section. For the purposes of calculating periods of service under paragraph (c)(6) of this rule:

(A) For the "lead" and "concurring" partner, the period of service includes time served as the "lead" or "concurring" partner prior to May 6, 2003; and

(B) For audit partners other than the "lead" partner or "concurring" partner, and for audit partners in foreign firms, the period of service does not include time served on the audit engagement team prior to the first day of issuer's fiscal year beginning on or after May 6, 2003.

(2) *Settling Financial Arrangements with Former Professionals.* To the extent not required by pre-existing requirements of the Commission, the Independence Standards Board, or the accounting profession in the United States, the requirement in paragraph (c)(2)(iii) of this rule to settle financial arrangements with former professionals applies to situations that arise after the effective date of this rule.

(f) *Definitions of Terms.* For purposes of this rule:

(1) *Accountant,* as used in paragraphs (b) through (e) of this rule, means a registered public accounting firm, certified public accountant or public accountant performing services in connection with an engagement for which independence is required. References to the accountant include any accounting firm with which the certified public accountant or public accountant is affiliated.

(2) *Accounting firm* means an organization (whether it is a sole proprietorship, incorporated association, partnership, corporation, limited liability company, limited liability partnership, or other legal entity) that is engaged in the practice of public accounting and furnishes reports or other documents filed with the Commission or otherwise prepared under the securities laws, and all of the organization's departments, divisions, parents, subsidiaries, and associated entities, including those located outside of the United States. Accounting firm also includes the organization's pension, retirement, investment, or similar plans.

(3)(i) *Accounting role* means a role in which a person is in a position to or does exercise more than minimal influence over the contents of the accounting records or anyone who prepares them.

(ii) Financial reporting oversight role means a role in which a person is in a position to or does exercise influence over the contents of the financial statements or anyone who prepares them, such as when the person is a member of the board of directors or similar management or governing body, chief executive officer, president, chief financial officer, chief operating officer, general counsel, chief accounting officer, controller, director of internal audit, director of financial reporting, treasurer, or any equivalent position.

(4) *Affiliate of the audit* client means:

(i) An entity that has control over the audit client, or over which the audit client has control, or which is under common control with the audit client, including the audit client's parents and subsidiaries;

(ii) An entity over which the audit client has significant influence, unless the entity is not material to the audit client;

(iii) An entity that has significant influence over the audit client, unless the audit client is not material to the entity; and

(iv) Each entity in the investment company complex when the audit client is an entity that is part of an investment company complex.

(5) *Audit and professional engagement* period includes both:

(i) The period covered by any financial statements being audited or reviewed (the "audit period"); and

(ii) The period of the engagement to audit or review the audit client's financial statements or to prepare a report filed with the Commission (the "professional engagement period"):

(A) The professional engagement period begins when the accountant either signs an initial engagement letter (or other agreement to review or audit a client's financial statements) or begins audit, review, or attest procedures, whichever is earlier; and

(B) The professional engagement period ends when the audit client or the accountant notifies the Commission that the client is no longer that accountant's audit client.

(iii) For audits of the financial statements of foreign private issuers, the "audit and professional engagement period" does not include periods ended prior to the first day of the last fiscal year before the foreign private issuer first filed, or was required to file, a registration statement or report with the Commission, provided there has been full compliance with home country independence standards in all prior periods covered by any registration statement or report filed with the Commission.

(6) *Audit client* means the entity whose financial statements or other information is being audited, reviewed, or attested and any affiliates of the audit client, other than, for purposes of paragraph (c)(1)(i) of this rule, entities that are affiliates of the audit client only by virtue of paragraph (f)(4)(ii) or (f)(4)(iii) of this rule.

(7)(i) *Audit engagement team* means all partners, principals, shareholders and professional employees participating in an audit, review, or attestation engagement of an audit client, including audit partners and all persons who consult with others on the audit engagement team during the audit, review, or attestation engagement regarding technical or industry-specific issues, transactions, or events.

(ii) *Audit partner* means a partner or persons in an equivalent position, other than a partner who consults with others on the audit engagement team during the audit, review, or attestation engagement regarding technical or industry-specific issues, transactions, or events, who is a member of the audit engagement team who has responsibility for decision-making on significant auditing, accounting, and reporting matters that affect the financial statements, or who maintains regular contact with management and the audit committee and includes the following:

(A) The lead or coordinating audit partner having primary responsibility for the audit or review (the "lead partner");

(B) The partner conducting a quality review under applicable professional standards and any applicable rules of the Commission to evaluate the significant judgments and the related conclusions reached in forming the overall conclusion on the audit or review engagement ("Engagement Quality Reviewer" or "Engagement Quality Control Reviewer");

(C) Other audit engagement team partners who provide more than ten hours of audit, review, or attest services in connection with the annual or interim consolidated financial statements of the issuer or an investment company registered under section 8 of the Investment Company Act of 1940 (15 U.S.C. 80a–8); and

(D) Other audit engagement team partners who serve as the "lead partner" in connection with any audit or review related to the annual or interim financial statements of a subsidiary of the issuer whose assets or revenues constitute 20% or more of the assets or revenues of the issuer's respective consolidated assets or revenues.

(8) *Chain of command* means all persons who:

(i) Supervise or have direct management responsibility for the audit, including at all successively senior levels through the accounting firm's chief executive;

(ii) Evaluate the performance or recommend the compensation of the audit engagement partner; or

(iii) Provide quality control or other oversight of the audit.

(9) *Close family members* means a person's spouse, spousal equivalent, parent, dependent, nondependent child, and sibling.

(10) *Contingent fee* means, except as stated in the next sentence, any fee established for the sale of a product or the performance of any service pursuant to an arrangement in which no fee will be charged unless a specified finding or result is attained, or in which the amount of the fee is otherwise dependent upon the finding or result of such product or service. Solely for the purposes of this section, a fee is not a "contingent fee" if it is fixed by courts or other public authorities, or, in tax matters, if determined based on the results of judicial proceedings or the findings of governmental agencies. Fees may vary depending, for example, on the complexity of services rendered.

(11) *Covered persons* in the firm means the following partners, principals, shareholders, and employees of an accounting firm:

(i) The "audit engagement team";

(ii) The "chain of command";

(iii) Any other partner, principal, shareholder, or managerial employee of the accounting firm who has provided ten or more hours of non-audit services to the audit client for the period beginning on the date such services are provided and ending on the date the accounting firm signs the report on the financial statements for the fiscal year during which those services are provided, or who expects to provide ten or more hours of non-audit services to the audit client on a recurring basis; and

(iv) Any other partner, principal, or shareholder from an "office" of the accounting firm in which the lead audit engagement partner primarily practices in connection with the audit.

(12) *Group* means two or more persons who act together for the purposes of acquiring, holding, voting, or disposing of securities of a registrant.

(13) *Immediate family members* means a person's spouse, spousal equivalent, and dependents.

(14) *Investment company complex.* (i) *Investment company complex* includes:

(A) An investment company and its investment adviser or sponsor;

(B) Any entity controlled by or controlling an investment adviser or sponsor in paragraph (f)(14)(i)(A) of this section, or any entity under common control with an investment adviser or sponsor in paragraph (f)(14)(i)(A) of this rule if the entity:

(*1*) Is an investment adviser or sponsor; or

(*2*) Is engaged in the business of providing administrative, custodian, underwriting, or transfer agent services to any investment company, investment adviser, or sponsor; and

(C) Any investment company or entity that would be an investment company but for the exclusions provided by section 3(c) of the Investment Company Act of 1940 (15 U.S.C. 80a–3(c)) that has an investment adviser or sponsor included in this definition by either paragraph (f)(14)(i)(A) or (f)(14)(i)(B) of this rule.

(ii) An investment adviser, for purposes of this definition, does not include a sub-adviser whose role is primarily portfolio management and is subcontracted with or overseen by another investment adviser.

(iii) Sponsor, for purposes of this definition, is an entity that establishes a unit investment trust.

(15) *Office* means a distinct sub-group within an accounting firm, whether distinguished along geographic or practice lines.

(16) *Rabbi trust* means an irrevocable trust whose assets are not accessible to the accounting firm until all benefit obligations have been met, but are subject to the claims of creditors in bankruptcy or insolvency.

(17) *Audit committee* means a committee (or equivalent body) as defined in section 3(a)(58) of the Securities Exchange Act of 1934 (15 U.S.C. 78c(a)(58)).

Rule 2–02. Accountants' reports and attestation reports

(a) *Technical Requirements for Accountants' Reports.* The accountant's report:

(1) Shall be dated;

(2) Shall be signed manually;

(3) Shall indicate the city and State where issued; and

(4) Shall identify without detailed enumeration the financial statements covered by the report.

(b) *Representations as to the Audit Included in Accountants' Reports.* The accountant's report: (1) Shall state the applicable professional standards under which the audit was conducted; and (2) Shall designate any auditing procedures deemed necessary by the accountant under the circumstances of the particular case, which have been omitted, and the reasons for their omission. Nothing in this rule shall be construed to imply authority for the omission of any procedure which independent accountants would ordinarily employ in the course of an audit made for the purpose of expressing the opinions required by paragraph (c) of this rule.

(c) *Opinions to Be Expressed in Accountants' Reports.* The accountant's report shall state clearly: (1) The opinion of the accountant in respect of the financial statements covered by the report and the accounting principles and practices reflected therein; and (2) the opinion of the accountant as to the consistency of the application of the accounting principles, or as to any changes in such principles which have a material effect on the financial statements.

(d) *Exceptions Identified in Accountants' Reports.* Any matters to which the accountant takes exception shall be clearly identified, the exception thereto specifically and clearly stated, and, to the extent practicable, the effect of each such exception on the related financial statements given. (See section 101 of the Codification of Financial Reporting Policies.)

(e) Paragraph (e) of this rule applies only to registrants that are providing financial statements in a filing for a period with respect to which Arthur Andersen LLP or a foreign affiliate of Arthur Andersen LLP ("Andersen") issued an accountants' report. Notwithstanding any other Commission rule or regulation, a registrant that cannot obtain an accountants' report that meets the technical requirements of paragraph (a) of this section after reasonable efforts may include in the document a copy of the latest signed and dated accountants' report issued by Andersen for such period in satisfaction of that requirement, if prominent disclosure that the report is a copy of the previously issued Andersen accountants' report and that the report has not been reissued by Andersen is set forth on such copy.

(f) *Attestation Report on Internal Control over Financial Reporting.*

(1) Every registered public accounting firm that issues or prepares an accountant's report for a registrant, other than a registrant that is neither an accelerated filer nor a large accelerated filer (as defined in §240.12b-2 of this chapter), or is an emerging growth company, as defined in Rule 405 of the Securities Act (§230.405 of this chapter) or Rule 12b-2 of the Exchange Act (§240.12b-2 of this chapter), or an investment company registered under Section 8 of the Investment Company Act of 1940 (15 U.S.C. 80a-8), that is included in an annual report required by section 13(a) or 15(d) of the Securities Exchange Act of 1934 (15 U.S.C. 78a et seq.) containing an assessment by management of the effectiveness of the registrant's internal control over financial reporting must include

an attestation report on internal control over financial reporting.

(2) If an attestation report on internal control over financial reporting is included in an annual report required by section 13(a) or 15(d) of the Securities Exchange Act of 1934, it shall clearly state the opinion of the accountant, either unqualified or adverse, as to whether the registrant maintained, in all material respects, effective internal control over financial reporting, except in the rare circumstance of a scope limitation that cannot be overcome by the registrant or the registered public accounting firm which would result in the accounting firm disclaiming an opinion. The attestation report on internal control over financial reporting shall be dated, signed manually, identify the period covered by the report and indicate that the accountant has audited the effectiveness of internal control over financial reporting. The attestation report on internal control over financial reporting may be separate from the accountant's report.

(g) *Attestation Report on Assessment of Compliance with Servicing Criteria for Asset-Backed Securities.* The attestation report on assessment of compliance with servicing criteria for asset-backed securities, as required by Rule 13a–18(c) or Rule 15d–18(c) under the Securities Exchange Act of 1934, shall be dated, signed manually, identify the period covered by the report and clearly state the opinion of the registered public accounting firm as to whether the asserting party's assessment of compliance with the servicing criteria is fairly stated in all material respects, or must include an opinion to the effect that an overall opinion cannot be expressed. If an overall opinion cannot be expressed, explain why.

Rule 2–03. Examination of financial statements by foreign government auditors

Notwithstanding any requirements as to examination by independent accountants, the financial statements of any foreign governmental agency may be examined by the regular and customary auditing staff of the respective government if public financial statements of such governmental agency are customarily examined by such auditing staff.

Rule 2–04. Examination of financial statements of persons other than the registrant

If a registrant is required to file financial statements of any other person, such statements need not be examined if examination of such statements would not be required if such person were itself a registrant.

Rule 2–05. Examination of financial statements by more than one accountant

If, with respect to the examination of the financial statements, part of the examination is made by an independent accountant other than the principal accountant and the principal accountant elects to place reliance on the work of the other accountant and makes reference to that effect in his report, the separate report of the other accountant shall be filed. However, notwithstanding the provisions of this section, reports of other accountants which may otherwise be required in filings need not be presented in annual reports to security holders furnished pursuant to the proxy and information statement rules under the Securities Exchange Act of 1934 [17 CFR 240.14a–3 and 240.14c–3].

Rule 2–06. Retention of audit and review records

(a) For a period of seven years after an accountant concludes an audit or review of an issuer's financial statements to which section 10A(a) of the Securities Exchange Act of 1934 (15 U.S.C. 78j–1(a)) applies, or of the financial statements of any investment company registered under section 8 of the Investment Company Act of 1940 (15 U.S.C. 80a–8), the accountant shall retain records relevant to the audit or review, including workpapers and other documents that form the basis of the audit or review, and memoranda, correspondence, communications, other documents, and records (including electronic records), which:

(1) Are created, sent or received in connection with the audit or review, and

(2) Contain conclusions, opinions, analyses, or financial data related to the audit or review.

(b) For the purposes of paragraph (a) of this rule, *workpapers* means documentation of auditing or review procedures applied, evidence obtained, and conclusions reached by the accountant in the audit or review engagement, as required by standards established or adopted by the Commission or by the Public Company Accounting Oversight Board.

(c) Memoranda, correspondence, communications, other documents, and records (including electronic records) described in paragraph (a) of this rule shall be retained whether they support the auditor's final conclusions regarding the audit or review, or contain information or data, relating to a significant matter, that is inconsistent with the auditor's final conclusions regarding that matter or the audit or review. Significance of a matter shall be determined based on an objective analysis of the facts and circumstances. Such documents and records include, but are not limited to, those documenting a consultation on or resolution of differences in professional judgment.

(d) For the purposes of paragraph (a) of this rule, the term issuer means an issuer as defined in section 10A(f) of the Securities Exchange Act of 1934 (15 U.S.C. 78j–1(f)).

Rule 2–07. Communication with audit committees

(a) Each registered public accounting firm that performs for an audit client that is an issuer (as defined in section 10A(f) of the Securities Exchange Act of 1934 (15 U.S.C. 78j–1(f))), other than an issuer that is an Asset–Backed Issuer as defined in Item 1101 of Regulation AB, or an investment company registered under section 8 of the Investment Company Act of 1940 (15 U.S.C. 80a–8), other than a unit investment trust as defined by section 4(2) of the Investment Company Act of 1940 (15 U.S.C. 80a–4(2)), any audit required under the securities laws shall report, prior to the filing of such audit report with the Commission (or in the case of a registered investment company, annually, and if the annual communication is not within 90 days prior to the filing, provide an update, in the 90 day period prior to the filing, of any changes to the previously reported information), to the audit committee of the issuer or registered investment company:

(1) All critical accounting policies and practices to be used;

(2) All alternative treatments within Generally Accepted Accounting Principles for policies and practices related to material items that have been discussed with management of the issuer or registered investment company, including:

(i) Ramifications of the use of such alternative disclosures and treatments; and

(ii) The treatment preferred by the registered public accounting firm;

(3) Other material written communications between the registered public accounting firm and the management of the issuer or registered investment company, such as any management letter or schedule of unadjusted differences;

(4) If the audit client is an investment company, all non-audit services provided to any entity in an investment company complex, as defined in Rule 2–01 (f)(14), that were not pre-approved by the registered investment company's audit committee pursuant to Rule 2–01 (c)(7).

(b) [Reserved]

General Instructions as to Financial Statements

Note: These instructions specify the balance sheets and statements of income and cash flows to be included in disclosure documents prepared in accordance with Regulation S–X. Other portions of Regulation S–X govern the examination, form and content of such financial statements, including the basis of consolidation and the schedules to be filed. The financial statements described below shall be audited unless otherwise indicated.

For filings under the Securities Act of 1933, attention is directed to Rule 411(b) regarding incorporation by reference to financial statements and to section 10(a)(3) of the Act regarding information required in the prospectus.

For filings under the Securities Exchange Act of 1934, attention is directed to Rule 12b–23 regarding incorporation by reference and Rule 12b–36 regarding use of financial statements filed under other Acts.

GENERAL INSTRUCTIONS AS TO FINANCIAL STATEMENTS

Rule 3–01. Consolidated balance sheets

(a) There shall be filed, for the registrant and its subsidiaries consolidated, audited balance sheets as of the end of each of the two most recent fiscal years. If the registrant has been in existence for less than one fiscal year, there shall be filed an audited balance sheet as of a date within 135 days of the date of filing the registration statement.

(b) If the filing, other than a filing on Form 10–K or Form 10, is made within 45 days after the end of the registrant's fiscal year and audited financial statements for the most recent fiscal year are not available, the balance sheets may be as of the end of the two preceding fiscal years and the filing shall include an additional balance sheet as of an interim date at least as current as the end of the registrant's third fiscal quarter of the most recently completed fiscal year.

(c) The instruction in paragraph (b) of this rule is also applicable to filings, other than on Form 10–K or Form 10, made after 45 days but within the number of days of the end of the registrant's fiscal year specified in paragraph (i) of this rule: *Provided*, That the following conditions are met:

(1) The registrant files annual, quarterly and other reports pursuant to Section 13 or 15(d) of

the Securities Exchange Act of 1934 and all reports due have been filed;

(2) For the most recent fiscal year for which audited financial statements are not yet available the registrant reasonably and in good faith expects to report income attributable to the registrant, after taxes; and

(3) For at least one of the two fiscal years immediately preceding the most recent fiscal year the registrant reported income attributable to the registrant, after taxes.

(d) For filings made after 45 days but within the number of days of the end of the registrant's fiscal year specified in paragraph (i) of this rule where the conditions set forth in paragraph (c) of this rule are not met, the filing must include the audited balance sheets required by paragraph (a) of this rule.

(e) For filings made after the number of days specified in paragraph (i)(2) of this rule, the filing shall also include a balance sheet as of an interim date within the following number of days of the date of filing:

(1) 130 days for large accelerated filers and accelerated filers (as defined in Rule 12b–2 under the Securities Exchange Act of 1934); and

(2) 135 days for all other registrants.

(f) Any interim balance sheet provided in accordance with the requirements of this section may be unaudited and need not be presented in greater detail than is required by Rule 10–01 of Regulation S–X. Notwithstanding the requirements of this section, the most recent interim balance sheet included in a filing shall be at least as current as the most recent balance sheet filed with the Commission on Form 10–Q.

(g) For filings by registered management investment companies, the requirements

(h) Any foreign private issuer, other than a registered management investment company or an employee plan, may file the financial statements required by Item 8.A of Form 20–F (17 CFR 249.220) in lieu of the financial statements specified in this rule.

(i)(1) For purposes of paragraphs (c) and (d) of this rule, the number of days shall be:

(i) 60 days (75 days for fiscal years ending before December 15, 2006) for large accelerated filers (as defined in Rule 12b–2 under the Securities Exchange Act of 1934);

(ii) 75 days for accelerated filers (as defined in Rule 12b–2 under the Securities Exchange Act of 1934); and

(iii) 90 days for all other registrants.

(2) For purposes of paragraph (e) of this rule, the number of days shall be:

(i) 129 days subsequent to the end of the registrant's most recent fiscal year for large accelerated filers and accelerated filers (as defined in Rule 12b–2 under the Securities Exchange Act of 1934); and

(ii) 134 days subsequent to the end of the registrant's most recent fiscal year for all other registrants.

Rule 3–02. Consolidated statements of comprehensive income and cash flows

(a) There shall be filed, for the registrant and its subsidiaries consolidated and for its predecessors, audited statements of comprehensive income and cash flows for each of the three fiscal years preceding the date of the most recent audited balance sheet being filed or such shorter period as the registrant (including predecessors) has been in existence. A registrant that is an emerging growth company, as defined in Rule 405 or Rule 240.12b–2 under the Securities Exchange Act of 1934, may, in a Securities Act registration statement for the initial public offering of the emerging growth company's equity securities, provide audited statements of comprehensive income and cash flows for each of the two fiscal years preceding the date of the most recent audited balance sheet (or such shorter period as the registrant has been in existence).

(b) In addition, for any interim period between the latest audited balance sheet and the date of the most recent interim balance sheet being filed, and for the corresponding period of the preceding fiscal year, statements of comprehensive income and cash flows shall be provided. Such interim financial statements may be unaudited and need not be presented in greater detail than is required by Rule 10–01.

(c) For filings by registered management investment companies, the requirements of Rule 3–18 of Regulation S–X shall apply in lieu of the requirements of this rule.

(d) Any foreign private issuer, other than a registered management investment company or an employee plan, may file the financial statements required by Item 8.A of Form 20–F (17 CFR 249.220) in lieu of the financial statements specified in this rule.

Rule 3–03. Instructions to statement of comprehensive income requirements

(a) The statements required shall be prepared in compliance with the applicable requirements of this regulation.

(b) If the registrant is engaged primarily (1) in the generation, transmission or distribution of electricity, the manufacture, mixing, transmission or distribution of gas, the supplying or distribution of water, or the furnishing of telephone or telegraph service; or (2) in holding securities of companies engaged in such businesses, it may at its option include statements of comprehensive income and cash flows (which may be unaudited) for the twelve-month period ending on the date of the most recent balance sheet being filed, in lieu of the statements of comprehensive income and cash flows for the interim periods specified.

(c) If a period or periods reported on include operations of a business prior to the date of acquisition, or for other reasons differ from reports previously issued for any period, the statements shall be reconciled as to sales or revenues and net income in the statement or in a note thereto with the amounts previously reported: *Provided, however*, That such reconciliations need not be made (1) if they have been made in filings with the Commission in prior years or (2) the financial statements which are being retroactively adjusted have not previously been filed with the Commission or otherwise made public.

(d) Any unaudited interim financial statements furnished shall reflect all adjustments which are, in the opinion of management, necessary to a fair statement of the results for the interim periods presented. A statement to that effect shall be included. If all such adjustments are of a normal recurring nature, a statement to that effect shall be made; otherwise, there shall be furnished information describing in appropriate detail the nature and amount of any adjustments other than normal recurring adjustments entering into the determination of the results shown.

Rule 3–04. Changes in stockholders' equity and noncontrolling interests

An analysis of the changes in each caption of stockholders' equity and noncontrolling interests presented in the balance sheets shall be given in a note or separate statement. This analysis shall be presented in the form of a reconciliation of the beginning balance to the ending balance for each period for which a statement of comprehensive income is required to be filed with all significant reconciling items described by appropriate captions with contributions from and distributions to owners shown separately. Also, state separately the adjustments to the balance at the beginning of the earliest period presented for items which were retroactively applied to periods prior to that period. With respect to any dividends, state the amount per share and in the aggregate for each class of shares. Provide a separate schedule in the notes to the financial statements that shows the effects of any changes in the registrant's ownership interest in a subsidiary on the equity attributable to the registrant.

Rule 3–05. Financial statements of businesses acquired or to be acquired

(a) *Financial Statements Required.* (1) Financial statements prepared and audited in accordance with this regulation should be furnished for the periods specified in paragraph (b) below if any of the following conditions exist:

(i) A business combination has occurred or is probable (for purposes of this rule, this encompasses the acquisition an interest in a business accounted for by the equity method); or

(ii) Consummation of a combination between entities under common control is probable.

(2) For purposes of determining whether the provisions of this rule apply, the determination of whether a business has been acquired should be made in accordance with the guidance set forth in Rule 11–01(d) of Regulation S–X.

(3) Acquisitions of a group of related businesses that are probable or that have occurred subsequent to the latest fiscal year-end for which audited financial statements of the registrant have been filed shall be treated under this section as if they are a single business combination. The required financial statements of related businesses may be presented on a combined basis for any periods they are under common control or management. For purposes of this section, businesses shall be deemed to be related if:

(i) They are under common control or management;

(ii) The acquisition of one business is conditional on the acquisition of each other business; or

(iii) Each acquisition is conditioned on a single common event.

(4) This rule shall not apply to a business which is totally held by the registrant prior to consummation of the transaction.

(b) *Periods to Be Presented.* (1) If securities are being registered to be offered to the security holders of the business to be acquired, the financial statements specified in Rules 3–01 and 3–02 of Regulation S–X shall be furnished for the business to be acquired, except as provided otherwise for filings on Form N–14, S–4 or F–4 (17 CFR 239.23, 239.25 or 239.34). The financial statements covering fiscal years shall be audited except as provided in Item 14 of Schedule 14A (17 CFR 240.14a–101) with respect to certain proxy statements or in registration statements filed on Forms N–14, S–4 or F–4 (17 CFR 239.23, 239.25 or 239.34).

(2) In all cases not specified in paragraph (b)(1) of this section, financial statements of the business acquired or to be acquired shall be filed for the periods specified in this paragraph (b)(2) or such shorter period as the business has been in existence. The periods for which such financial statements are to be filed shall be determined using the conditions specified in the definition of significant subsidiary in Rule 1–02(w) of Regulation S–X as follows:

(i) If none of the conditions exceeds 20 percent, financial statements are not required. However, if the aggregate impact of the individually insignificant businesses acquired since the date of the most recent audited balance sheet filed for the registrant exceeds 50%, financial statements covering at least the substantial majority of the businesses acquired shall be furnished. Such financial statements shall be for at least the most recent fiscal year and any interim periods specified in Rules 3–01 and 3–02.

(ii) If any of the conditions exceeds 20 percent, but none exceed 40 percent, financial statements shall be furnished for at least the most recent fiscal year and any interim periods specified in Rules 3–01 and 3–02.

(iii) If any of the conditions exceeds 40 percent, but none exceed 50 percent, financial statements shall be furnished for at least the two most recent fiscal years and any interim periods specified in Rules 3–01 and 3–02.

(iv) If any of the conditions exceed 50 percent, the full financial statements specified in Rule 3–01 and Rule 3–02 shall be furnished. However, financial statements for the earliest of the three fiscal years required may be omitted if net revenues reported by the acquired business in its most recent fiscal year are less than $100 million.

(3) The determination shall be made by comparing the most recent annual financial statements of each such business, or group of related businesses on a combined basis, to the registrant's most recent annual consolidated financial statements filed at or prior to the date of acquisition. However, if the registrant made a significant acquisition subsequent to the latest fiscal year-end and filed a report on Form 8–K (17 CFR 249.308) which included audited financial statements of such acquired business for the periods required by this section and the pro forma financial information required by Rule 11, such determination may be made by using pro forma amounts for the latest fiscal year in the report on Form 8–K (17 CFR 249.308) rather than by using the historical amounts of the registrant. The tests may not be made by "annualizing" data.

(4) Financial statements required for the periods specified in paragraph (b)(2) of this rule may be omitted to the extent specified as follows:

(i) Registration statements not subject to the provisions of Rule 419 under the Securities Act of 1933 (Regulation C) and proxy statements need not include separate financial statements of the acquired or to be acquired business if it does not exceed any of the conditions of significance in the definition of significant subsidiary in Rule 1–02 at the 50 percent level, and either:

(A) The consummation of the acquisition has not yet occurred; or

(B) The date of the final prospectus or prospectus supplement relating to an offering as filed with the Commission pursuant to Rule 424(b) under the Securities Exchange Act of 1934, or mailing date in the case of a proxy statement, is no more than 74 days after consummation of the business combination, and the financial statements have not previously been filed by the registrant.

(ii) An issuer, other than a foreign private issuer required to file reports on Form 6–K, that omits from its initial registration statement financial statements of a recently consummated business combination pursuant to paragraph (b)(4)(i) of this section shall furnish those financial statements and any pro forma information specified by Article 11 under cover of Form 8–K

(17 CFR 249.308) no later than 75 days after consummation of the acquisition.

(iii) Separate financial statements of the acquired business need not be presented once the operating results of the acquired business have been reflected in the audited consolidated financial statements of the registrant for a complete fiscal year unless such financial statements have not been previously filed or unless the acquired business is of such significance to the registrant that omission of such financial statements would materially impair an investor's ability to understand the historical financial results of the registrant. For example, if, at the date of acquisition, the acquired business met at least one of the conditions in the definition of significant subsidiary in Rule 1–02 at the 80 percent level, the statements of comprehensive income of the acquired business should normally continue to be furnished for such periods prior to the purchase as may be necessary when added to the time for which audited statements of comprehensive income after the purchase are filed to cover the equivalent of the period specified in Rule 3–02.

(iv) A separate audited balance sheet of the acquired business is not required when the registrant's most recent audited balance sheet required by Rule 3–01 is for a date after the date the acquisition was consummated.

(c) *Financial Statements of Foreign Business.* If the business acquired or to be acquired is a foreign business, financial statements of the business meeting the requirements of Item 17 of Form 20–F (17 CFR 249.220f) will satisfy this rule.

Rule 3–06. Financial statements covering a period of nine to twelve months

Except with respect to registered investment companies, the filing of financial statements covering a period of 9 to 12 months shall be deemed to satisfy a requirement for filing financial statements for a period of 1 year where:

(a) The issuer has changed its fiscal year;

(b) The issuer has made a significant business acquisition for which financial statements are required under Rule 3–05 and the financial statements covering the interim period pertain to the business being acquired; or

(c) The Commission so permits pursuant to Rule 3–13.

Where there is a requirement for filing financial statements for a time period exceeding one year but not exceeding three consecutive years (with not more than 12 months included in any period reported upon), the filing of financial statements covering a period of nine to 12 months shall satisfy a filing requirement of financial statements for one year of that time period only if the conditions described in either paragraph (a), (b), or (c) of this rule exist and financial statements are filed that cover the full fiscal year or years for all other years in the time period.

Rules 3–07 to 3–08. [Reserved]

Rule 3–09. Separate financial statements of subsidiaries not consolidated and 50 percent or less owned persons

(a) If any of the conditions set forth in Rule 1–02(w), substituting 20 percent for 10 percent in the tests used therein to determine a significant subsidiary, are met for a majority-owned subsidiary not consolidated by the registrant or by a subsidiary of the registrant, separate financial statements of such subsidiary shall be filed. Similarly, if either the first or third condition set forth in Rule 1–02(w), substituting 20 percent for 10 percent, is met by a 50 percent or less owned person accounted for by the equity method either by the registrant or a subsidiary of the registrant, separate financial statements of such 50 percent or less owned person shall be filed.

(b) Insofar as practicable, the separate financial statements required by this section shall be as of the same dates and for the same periods as the audited consolidated financial statements required by Rules 210.3–01 and 3–02. However, these separate financial statements are required to be audited only for those fiscal years in which either the first or third condition set forth in Rule 1–02(w), substituting 20 percent for 10 percent, is met. For purposes of a filing on Form 10–K (17 CFR 249.310):

(1) If the registrant is an accelerated filer (as defined in Rule 12b–2 under the Securities Exchange Act of 1934) but the 50 percent or less owned person is not an accelerated filer, the required financial statements may be filed as an amendment to the report within 90 days, or within six months if the 50 percent or less owned person is a foreign business, after the end of the registrant's fiscal year.

(2) If the fiscal year of any 50 percent or less owned person ends within the *registrant's number of filing days* before the date of the filing, or if the fiscal year ends after the date of the filing, the required financial statements may be filed as an

amendment to the report within the *subsidiary's number of filing days*, or within six months if the 50 percent or less owned person is a foreign business, after the end of such subsidiary's or person's fiscal year.

(3) The term *registrant's number of filing days* means:

(i) 60 days (75 days for fiscal years ending before December 15, 2006) if the registrant is a large accelerated filer;

(ii) 75 days if the registrant is an accelerated filer; and

(iii) 90 days for all other registrants.

(4) The term *subsidiary's number of filing days* means:

(i) 60 days (75 days for fiscal years ending before December 15, 2006) if the 50 percent or less owned person is a large accelerated filer;

(ii) 75 days if the 50 percent or less owned person is an accelerated filer; and

(iii) 90 days for all other 50 percent or less owned persons.

(c) Notwithstanding the requirements for separate financial statements in paragraph (a) of this section, where financial statements of two or more majority-owned subsidiaries not consolidated are required, combined or consolidated statements of such subsidiaries may be filed subject to principles of inclusion and exclusion which clearly exhibit the financial position, cash flows and results of operations of the combined or consolidated group. Similarly, where financial statements of two or more 50 percent or less owned persons are required, combined or consolidated statements of such persons may be filed subject to the same principles of inclusion or exclusion referred to above.

(d) If the 50 percent or less owned person is a foreign business, financial statements of the business meeting the requirements of Item 17 of Form 20–F (17 CFR 249.220f) will satisfy this section.

Rule 3–10. Financial statements of guarantors and issuers of guaranteed securities registered or being registered

(a)(1) *General Rule.* Every issuer of a registered security that is guaranteed and every guarantor of a registered security must file the financial statements required for a registrant by Regulation S–X.

(2) *Operation of this Rule.* Paragraphs (b), (c), (d), (e) and (f) of this rule are exceptions to the general rule of paragraph (a)(1) of this section. Only one of these paragraphs can apply to a single issuer or guarantor. Paragraph (g) of this rule is a special rule for recently acquired issuers or guarantors that overrides each of these exceptions for a specific issuer or guarantor. Paragraph (h) of this rule defines the following terms used in this rule: 100% owned, full and unconditional, annual report, quarterly report, no independent assets or operations, minor, finance subsidiary and operating subsidiary. Paragraph (i) of this rule states the requirements for preparing the condensed consolidating financial information required by paragraphs (c), (d), (e) and (f) of this rule.

NOTE TO PARAGRAPH (a)(2): Where paragraphs (b), (c), (d), (e) and (f) of this rule specify the filing of financial statements of the parent company, the financial statements of an entity that is not an issuer or guarantor of the registered security cannot be substituted for those of the parent company.

(3) *Foreign Private Issuers.* Where any provision of this rule requires compliance with Rules 3–01 and 3–02, a foreign private issuer may comply by providing financial statements for the periods specified by Item 8.A of Form 20–F (17 CFR 249.220f).

(b) *Finance Subsidiary Issuer of Securities Guaranteed by its Parent Company.* When a finance subsidiary issues securities and its parent company guarantees those securities, the registration statement, parent company annual report, or parent company quarterly report need not include financial statements of the issuer if:

(1) The issuer is 100% owned by the parent company guarantor;

(2) The guarantee is full and unconditional;

(3) No other subsidiary of the parent company guarantees the securities; and

(4) The parent company's financial statements are filed for the periods specified by Rules 3–01 and 3–02 and include a footnote stating that the issuer is a 100%-owned finance subsidiary of the parent company and the parent company has fully and unconditionally guaranteed the securities. The footnote also must include the narrative disclosures specified in paragraphs (i)(9) and (i)(10) of this rule.

NOTE TO PARAGRAPH (b): Paragraph (b) is available if a subsidiary issuer satisfies the requirements of this paragraph but for the fact that, instead of the parent company guaranteeing the security, the subsidiary issuer co-issued the security, jointly and severally, with the parent company. In this situation, the narrative information required by paragraph (b)(4) must be modified accordingly.

(c) *Operating Subsidiary Issuer of Securities Guaranteed by its Parent Company*. When an operating subsidiary issues securities and its parent company guarantees those securities, the registration statement, parent company annual report, or parent company quarterly report need not include financial statements of the issuer if:

(1) The issuer is 100% owned by the parent company guarantor;

(2) The guarantee is full and unconditional;

(3) No other subsidiary of the parent company guarantees the securities; and

(4) The parent company's financial statements are filed for the periods specified by Rules 3–01 and 3–02 and include, in a footnote, condensed consolidating financial information for the same periods with a separate column for:

(i) The parent company;

(ii) The subsidiary issuer;

(iii) Any other subsidiaries of the parent company on a combined basis;

(iv) Consolidating adjustments; and

(v) The total consolidated amounts.

NOTES TO PARAGRAPH (c):

1. Instead of the condensed consolidating financial information required by paragraph (c)(4), the parent company's financial statements may include a footnote stating, if true, that the parent company has no independent assets or operations, the guarantee is full and unconditional, and any subsidiaries of the parent company other than the subsidiary issuer are minor. The footnote also must include the narrative disclosures specified in paragraphs (i)(9) and (i)(10) of this rule.

2. If the alternative disclosure permitted by Note 1 to this paragraph is not applicable because the parent company has independent assets or operations, the condensed consolidating financial information described in paragraph (c)(4) may omit the column for "any other subsidiaries of the parent company on a combined basis" if those other subsidiaries are minor.

3. Paragraph (c) is available if a subsidiary issuer satisfies the requirements of this paragraph but for the fact that, instead of the parent company guaranteeing the security, the subsidiary issuer co-issued the security, jointly and severally, with the parent company. In this situation, the narrative information required by paragraph (i)(8) of this rule must be modified accordingly.

(d) *Subsidiary Issuer of Securities Guaranteed by its Parent Company and One or More Other Subsidiaries of that Parent Company*. When a subsidiary issues securities and both its parent company and one or more other subsidiaries of that parent company guarantee those securities, the registration statement, parent company annual report, or parent company quarterly report need not include financial statements of the issuer or any subsidiary guarantor if:

(1) The issuer and all subsidiary guarantors are 100% owned by the parent company guarantor;

(2) The guarantees are full and unconditional;

(3) The guarantees are joint and several; and

(4) The parent company's financial statements are filed for the periods specified by Rules 3–01 and 3–02 and include, in a footnote, condensed consolidating financial information for the same periods with a separate column for:

(i) The parent company;

(ii) The subsidiary issuer;

(iii) The guarantor subsidiaries of the parent company on a combined basis;

(iv) Any other subsidiaries of the parent company on a combined basis;

(v) Consolidating adjustments; and

(vi) The total consolidated amounts.

NOTES TO PARAGRAPH (d):

1. Paragraph (d) applies in the same manner whether the issuer is a finance subsidiary or an operating subsidiary.

2. The condensed consolidating financial information described in paragraph (d)(4) may omit the column for "any other subsidiaries of the parent company on a combined basis" if those other subsidiaries are minor.

3. Paragraph (d) is available if a subsidiary issuer satisfies the requirements of this paragraph but for the fact that, instead of the parent company guaranteeing the security, the subsidiary issuer co-issued the security, jointly and severally, with the parent company. In this situation, the narrative information required by paragraph (i)(8) of this rule must be modified accordingly.

4. If all of the requirements in paragraph (d) are satisfied except that the guarantee of a subsidiary is not joint and several with, as applicable, the parent company's guarantee or the guarantees of the parent company and the other subsidiaries, then each subsidiary guarantor whose guarantee is not joint and several need not include separate financial statements, but the condensed consolidating financial information should include a separate column for each guarantor whose guarantee is not joint and several.

5. Instead of the condensed consolidating financial information required by paragraph (d)(4), the parent company's financial statements may include a footnote stating, if true, that the parent company has no independent assets or operations, the subsidiary issuer is a 100% owned finance subsidiary of the parent company, the parent company has guaranteed the securities, all of the parent company's subsidiaries other than the subsidiary issuer have guaranteed the securities, all of the guarantees are full and unconditional, and all of the guarantees are joint and several. The footnote also must include the narrative disclosures specified in paragraphs (i)(9) and (i)(10) of this rule.

(e) *Single Subsidiary Guarantor of Securities Issued by the Parent Company of that Subsidiary.* When a parent company issues securities and one of its subsidiaries guarantees those securities, the registration statement, parent company annual report, or parent company quarterly report need not include financial statements of the subsidiary guarantor if:

(1) The subsidiary guarantor is 100% owned by the parent company issuer;

(2) The guarantee is full and unconditional;

(3) No other subsidiary of that parent guarantees the securities; and

(4) The parent company's financial statements are filed for the periods specified by Rules 3–01 and 3–02 and include, in a footnote, condensed consolidating financial information for the same periods with a separate column for:

(i) The parent company;

(ii) The subsidiary guarantor;

(iii) Any other subsidiaries of the parent company on a combined basis;

(iv) Consolidating adjustments; and

(v) The total consolidated amounts.

NOTES TO PARAGRAPH (e):

1. Paragraph (e) applies in the same manner whether the guarantor is a finance subsidiary or an operating subsidiary.

2. Instead of the condensed consolidating financial information required by paragraph (e)(4), the parent company's financial statements may include a footnote stating, if true, that the parent company has no independent assets or operations, the guarantee is full and unconditional, and any subsidiaries of the parent company other than the subsidiary guarantor are minor. The footnote also must include the narrative disclosures specified in paragraphs (i)(9) and (i)(10) of this rule.

3. If the alternative disclosure permitted by Note 2 to this paragraph is not applicable because the parent company has independent assets or operations, the condensed consolidating financial information described in paragraph (e)(4) may omit the column for "any other subsidiaries of the parent company on a combined basis" if those other subsidiaries are minor.

4. If, instead of guaranteeing the subject security, a subsidiary co-issues the security jointly and severally with its parent company, this paragraph (e) does not apply. Instead, the appropriate financial information requirement would depend on whether the subsidiary is a finance subsidiary or an operating subsidiary. If the subsidiary is a finance subsidiary, paragraph (b) applies. If the subsidiary is an operating company, paragraph (c) applies.

(f) *Multiple Subsidiary Guarantors of Securities Issued by the Parent Company of Those Subsidiaries.* When a parent company issues securities and more than one of its subsidiaries guarantee those securities, the registration statement, parent company annual report, or parent company quarterly report need not include financial statements of the subsidiary guarantors if:

(1) Each of the subsidiary guarantors is 100% owned by the parent company issuer;

(2) The guarantees are full and unconditional;

(3) The guarantees are joint and several; and

(4) The parent company's financial statements are filed for the periods specified by Rules 3–01 and 3–02 and include, in a footnote, condensed consolidating financial information for the same periods with a separate column for:

(i) The parent company;

(ii) The subsidiary guarantors on a combined basis;

(iii) Any other subsidiaries of the parent company on a combined basis;

(iv) Consolidating adjustments; and

(v) The total consolidated amounts.

NOTES TO PARAGRAPH (f):

1. Instead of the condensed consolidating financial information required by paragraph (f)(4), the parent company's financial statements may include a footnote stating, if true, that the parent company has no independent assets or operations, the guarantees are full and unconditional and joint and several, and any subsidiaries of the parent company other than the subsidiary guarantors are minor. The footnote also must include the narrative disclosures specified in paragraphs (i)(9) and (i)(10) of this section.

2. If the alternative disclosure permitted by Note 1 to this paragraph is not applicable because the parent company has independent assets or operations, the condensed consolidating financial information described in paragraph (f)(4) may omit the column for "any other subsidiaries of the parent company on a combined basis" if those other subsidiaries are minor.

3. If any of the subsidiary guarantees is not joint and several with the guarantees of the other subsidiaries, then each subsidiary guarantor whose guarantee is not joint and several need not include separate financial statements, but the condensed consolidating financial information must include a separate column for each subsidiary guarantor whose guarantee is not joint and several.

(g) *Recently Acquired Subsidiary Issuers or Subsidiary Guarantors.* (1) The Securities Act registration statement of the parent company must include the financial statements specified in paragraph (g)(2) of this rule for any subsidiary that otherwise meets the conditions in paragraph (c), (d), (e) or (f) of this rule for omission of separate financial statements if:

(i) The subsidiary has not been included in the audited consolidated results of the parent company for at least nine months of the most recent fiscal year; and

(ii) The net book value or purchase price, whichever is greater, of the subsidiary is 20% or more of the principal amount of the securities being registered.

(2) Financial statements required.

(i) Audited financial statements for a subsidiary described in paragraph (g)(1) of this section must be filed for the subsidiary's most recent fiscal year preceding the acquisition. In addition, unaudited financial statements must be filed for any interim periods specified in Rules 3–01 and 3–02.

(ii) The financial statements must conform to the requirements of Regulation S-X (Rules 10.1–01 through 12–29), except that supporting schedules need not be filed. If the subsidiary is a foreign business, financial statements of the subsidiary meeting the requirements of Item 17 of Form 20–F (17 CFR 249.220f) will satisfy this item.

(3) Instructions to paragraph (g).

(i) The significance test of paragraph (g)(1)(ii) of this rule should be computed using net book value of the subsidiary as of the most recent fiscal year end preceding the acquisition.

(ii) Information required by this paragraph (g) is not required to be included in an annual report or quarterly report.

(iii) Acquisitions of a group of subsidiary issuers or subsidiary guarantors that are related prior to their acquisition shall be aggregated for purposes of applying the 20% test in paragraph (g)(1)(ii) of this rule. Subsidiaries shall be deemed to be related prior to their acquisition if:

(A) They are under common control or management;

(B) The acquisition of one subsidiary is conditioned on the acquisition of each subsidiary; or

(C) The acquisition of each subsidiary is conditioned on a single common event.

(h) *Definitions*. For the purposes of this section:

(1) A subsidiary is "100% owned" if all of its outstanding voting shares are owned, either directly or indirectly, by its parent company. A subsidiary not in corporate form is 100% owned if the sum of all interests are owned, either directly or indirectly, by its parent company other than:

(i) Securities that are guaranteed by its parent and, if applicable, other 100%-owned subsidiaries of its parent; and

(ii) Securities that guarantee securities issued by its parent and, if applicable, other 100%-owned subsidiaries of its parent.

(2) A guarantee is "full and unconditional," if, when an issuer of a guaranteed security has failed to make a scheduled payment, the guarantor is obligated to make the scheduled payment immediately and, if it doesn't, any holder of the guaranteed security may immediately bring suit directly against the guarantor for payment of all amounts due and payable.

(3) *Annual report* refers to an annual report on Form 10–K or Form 20–F (17 CFR 249.310 or 249.220f).

(4) *Quarterly report* refers to a quarterly report on Form 10–Q (17 CFR 249.308a).

(5) A parent company has no independent assets or operations if each of its total assets, revenues, income from continuing operations before income taxes, and cash flows from operating activities (excluding amounts related to its investment in its consolidated subsidiaries) is less than 3% of the corresponding consolidated amount.

(6) A subsidiary is minor if each of its total assets, stockholders' equity, revenues, income from continuing operations before income taxes, and cash flows from operating activities is less than 3% of the parent company's corresponding consolidated amount.

Note to Paragraph (h)(6): When considering a group of subsidiaries, the definition applies to each subsidiary in that group individually and to all subsidiaries in that group in the aggregate.

(7) A subsidiary is a finance subsidiary if it has no assets, operations, revenues or cash flows other than those related to the issuance, administration and repayment of the security being registered and any other securities guaranteed by its parent company.

(8) A subsidiary is an operating subsidiary if it is not a finance subsidiary.

(i) Instructions for preparation of the condensed consolidating financial information required by paragraphs (c), (d), (e) and (f) of this rule.

(1) Follow the general guidance in Rule 10–01 for the form and content for condensed financial statements and present the financial information in sufficient detail to allow investors to determine the assets, results of operations and cash flows of each of the consolidating groups;

(2) The financial information should be audited for the same periods that the parent company financial statements are required to be audited;

(3) The parent company column should present investments in all subsidiaries based upon their proportionate share of their subsidiary's net assets;

(4) The parent company's basis shall be "pushed down" to the applicable subsidiary columns to the extent that push down would be required or permitted in separate financial statements of the subsidiary;

(5) All subsidiary issuer or subsidiary guarantor columns should present the following investments in subsidiaries under the equity method:

(i) Non-guarantor subsidiaries;

(ii) Subsidiary issuers or subsidiary guarantors that are not 100% owned or whose guarantee is not full and unconditional;

(iii) Subsidiary guarantors whose guarantee is not joint and several with the guarantees of the other subsidiaries; and

(iv) Subsidiary guarantors with differences in domestic or foreign laws that affect the enforceability of the guarantees;

(6) Provide a separate column for each subsidiary issuer or subsidiary guarantor that is not 100% owned, whose guarantee is not full and unconditional, or whose guarantee is not joint and several with the guarantees of other subsidiaries. Inclusion of a separate column does not relieve that issuer or guarantor from the requirement to file separate financial statements under paragraph (a) of this rule. However, paragraphs (b) through (f) of this rule will provide this relief if the particular paragraph is satisfied except that the guarantee is not joint and several;

(7) Provide separate columns for each guarantor by legal jurisdiction if differences in domestic or foreign laws affect the enforceability of the guarantees;

(8) Include the following disclosure, if true:

(i) Each subsidiary issuer or subsidiary guarantor is 100% owned by the parent company;

(ii) All guarantees are full and unconditional; and

(iii) Where there is more than one guarantor, all guarantees are joint and several;

(9) Disclose any significant restrictions on the ability of the parent company or any guarantor to obtain funds from its subsidiaries by dividend or loan;

(10) Provide the disclosures prescribed by Rule 4–08(e)(3) with respect to the subsidiary issuers and subsidiary guarantors;

(11) The disclosure:

(i) May not omit any financial and narrative information about each guarantor if the information would be material for investors to evaluate the sufficiency of the guarantee;

(ii) Shall include sufficient information so as to make the financial information presented not misleading; and

(iii) Need not repeat information that would substantially duplicate disclosure elsewhere in the parent company's consolidated financial statements; and

(12) Where the parent company's consolidated financial statements are prepared on a comprehensive basis other than U.S. Generally Accepted Accounting Principles or International Financial Reporting Standards as issued by the International Accounting Standards Board, reconcile the information in each column to U.S. Generally Accepted Accounting Principles to the extent necessary to allow investors to evaluate the sufficiency of the guarantees. The reconciliation may be limited to the information specified by Item 17 of Form 20–F (17 CFR 249.220f). The reconciling information need not duplicate information included elsewhere in the reconciliation of the consolidated financial statements.

Rule 3–11. Financial statements of an inactive registrant

If a registrant is an inactive entity as defined below, the financial statements required by this regulation for purposes of reports pursuant to the Securities Exchange Act of 1934 may be unaudited. An inactive entity is one meeting all of the following conditions:

(a) Gross receipts from all sources for the fiscal year are not in excess of $100,000;

(b) The registrant has not purchased or sold any of its own stock, granted options therefor, or levied assessments upon outstanding stock;

(c) Expenditures for all purposes for the fiscal year are not in excess of $100,000;

(d) No material change in the business has occurred during the fiscal year, including any bankruptcy, reorganization, readjustment or succession or any material acquisition or disposition of plants, mines, mining equipment, mine rights or leases; and

(e) No exchange upon which the shares are listed, or governmental authority having jurisdiction, requires the furnishing to it or the publication of audited financial statements.

Rule 3-12. Age of financial statements at effective date of registration statement or at mailing date of proxy statement

(a) If the financial statements in a filing are as of a date the number of days specified in paragraph (g) of this section or more before the date the filing is expected to become effective, or proposed mailing date in the case of a proxy statement, the financial statements shall be updated, except as specified in the following paragraphs, with a balance sheet as of an interim date within the number of days specified in paragraph (g) of this section and with statements of comprehensive income and cash flows for the interim period between the end of the most recent fiscal year and the date of the interim balance sheet provided and for the corresponding period of the preceding fiscal year. Such interim financial statements may be unaudited and need not be presented in greater detail than is required by Rule 10-01. Notwithstanding the above requirements, the most recent interim financial statements shall be at least as current as the most recent financial statements filed with the Commission on Form 10-Q.

(b) Where the anticipated effective date of a filing, or in the case of a proxy statement the proposed mailing date, falls within the number of days subsequent to the end of the fiscal year specified in paragraph (g) of this rule, the filing need not include financial statements more current than as of the end of the third fiscal quarter of the most recently completed fiscal year unless the audited financial statements for such fiscal year are available or unless the anticipated effective date or proposed mailing date falls after 45 days subsequent to the end of the fiscal year and the registrant does not meet the conditions prescribed under paragraph (c) of Rule 3-01. If the anticipated effective date or proposed mailing date falls after 45 days subsequent to the end of the fiscal year and the registrant does not meet the conditions prescribed under paragraph (c) of Rule 3-01, the filing must include audited financial statements for the most recently completed fiscal year.

(c) Where a filing is made near the end of a fiscal year and audited financial statements for that fiscal year are not included in the filing, the filing shall be updated with such audited financial statements if they become available prior to the anticipated effective date, or proposed mailing date in the case of a proxy statement.

(d) The age of the registrant's most recent audited financial statements included in a registration statement filed under the Securities Act of 1933 or filed on Form 10 (17 CFR 249.210) under the Securities Exchange Act of 1934 shall not be more than one year and 45 days old at the date the registration statement becomes effective if the registration statement relates to the security of an issuer that was not subject, immediately before the time of filing the registration statement, to the reporting requirements of section 13 or 15(d) of the Securities Exchange Act of 1934.

(e) For filings by registered management investment companies, the requirements of Rule 3-18 shall apply in lieu of the requirements of this rule.

(f) Any foreign private issuer may file financial statements whose age is specified in Item 8.A of Form 20-F (17 CFR 249.220f). Financial statements of a foreign business which are furnished pursuant to Rules 3-05 or 3-09 because it is an acquired business or a 50 percent or less owned person may be of the age specified in Item 8.A of Form 20-F.

(g)(1) For purposes of paragraph (a) of this rule, the number of days shall be:

(i) 130 days for large accelerated filers and accelerated filers (as defined in Rule 12b-2 under the Securities Exchange Act of 1934); and

(ii) 135 days for all other registrants.

(2) For purposes of paragraph (b) of this rule, the number of days shall be:

(i) 60 days (75 days for fiscal years ending before December 15, 2006) for large accelerated filers (as defined in Rule 12b-2 under the Securities Exchange Act of 1934);

(ii) 75 days for accelerated filers (as defined in Rule 12b–2 under the Securities Exchange Act of 1934); and

(iii) 90 days for all other registrants.

Rule 3–13. Filing of other financial statements in certain cases

The Commission may, upon the informal written request of the registrant, and where consistent with the protection of investors, permit the omission of one or more of the financial statements herein required or the filing in substitution therefor of appropriate statements of comparable character. The Commission may also by informal written notice require the filing of other financial statements in addition to, or in substitution for, the statements herein required in any case where such statements are necessary or appropriate for an adequate presentation of the financial condition of any person whose financial statements are required, or whose statements are otherwise necessary for the protection of investors.

Rule 3–14. Special instructions for real estate operations to be acquired

(a) If, during the period for which statements of comprehensive income are required, the registrant has acquired one or more properties which in the aggregate are significant, or since the date of the latest balance sheet required has acquired or proposes to acquire one or more properties which in the aggregate are significant, the following shall be furnished with respect to such properties:

(1) Audited income statements (not including earnings per unit) for the three most recent fiscal years, which shall exclude items not comparable to the proposed future operations of the property such as mortgage interest, leasehold rental, depreciation, corporate expenses and Federal and state income taxes: *Provided, however*, That such audited statements need be presented for only the most recent fiscal year if (i) The property is not acquired from a related party; (ii) Material factors considered by the registrant in assessing the property are described with specificity in the filing with regard to the property, including sources of revenue (including, but not limited to, competition in the rental market, comparative rents, occupancy rates) and expense (including, but not limited to, utility rates, ad valorem tax rates, maintenance expenses, capital improvements anticipated); and (iii) The registrant indicates in the appropriate filing that, after reasonable inquiry, the registrant is not aware of any material factors relating to that specific property other than those discussed in response to paragraph (a)(1)(ii) of this rule that would cause the reported financial information not to be necessarily indicative of future operating results.

NOTE 1 TO PARAGRAPH (a)(1). The discussion of material factors considered should be combined with that required by Item 15 of Form S–11.

(2) If the property is to be operated by the registrant, there shall be furnished a statement showing the estimated taxable operating results of the registrant based on the most recent twelve month period including such adjustments as can be factually supported. If the property is to be acquired subject to a net lease the estimated taxable operating results shall be based on the rent to be paid for the first year of the lease. In either case, the estimated amount of cash to be made available by operations shall be shown. There shall be stated in an introductory paragraph the principal assumptions which have been made in preparing the statements of estimated taxable operating results and cash to be made available by operations.

(3) If appropriate under the circumstances, there shall be given in tabular form for a limited number of years the estimated cash distribution per unit showing the portion thereof reportable as taxable income and the portion representing a return of capital together with an explanation of annual variations, if any. If taxable net income per unit will become greater than the cash available for distribution per unit, that fact and approximate year of occurrence shall be stated, if significant.

(b) Information required by this rule is not required to be included in a filing on Form 10–K.

Rule 3–15. Special provisions as to real estate investment trusts

(a) [Reserved]

(a) [Reserved]

(c) The tax status of distributions per unit shall be stated (e.g., ordinary income, capital gain, return of capital).

Rule 3–16. Financial statements of affiliates whose securities collateralize an issue registered or being registered

(a) For each of the registrant's affiliates whose securities constitute a substantial portion of the collateral for any class of securities registered or being registered, there shall be filed the financial statements that would be required if the affiliate were a registrant and required to file financial statements. However, financial statements need not be filed pursuant to this rule for any person whose statements are otherwise separately included in the filing on an individual basis or on a basis consolidated with its subsidiaries.

(b) For the purposes of this rule, securities of a person shall be deemed to constitute a substantial portion of collateral if the aggregate principal amount, par value, or book value of the securities as carried by the registrant, or the market value of such securities, whichever is the greatest, equals 20 percent or more of the principal amount of the secured class of securities.

Rule 3–17. Financial statements of natural persons

(a) In lieu of the financial statements otherwise required, a natural person may file an unaudited balance sheet as of a date within 90 days of date of filing and unaudited statements of comprehensive income for each of the three most recent fiscal years.

(b) Financial statements conforming with the instructions as to financial statements of subsidiaries not consolidated and 50 percent or less owned persons under Rule 3–09(a) shall be separately presented for: (1) Each business owned as a sole proprietor, (2) each partnership, business trust, unincorporated association, or similar business organization of which the person holds a controlling interest and (3) each corporation of which the person, directly or indirectly, owns securities representing more than 50 percent of the voting power.

(c) Separate financial statements may be omitted, however, for each corporation, business trust, unincorporated association, or similar business organization if the person's total investment in such entity does not exceed 5 percent of his total assets and the person's total income from such entity does not exceed 5 percent of his gross income; *Provided*, that the person's aggregate investment in and income from all such omitted entities shall not exceed 15 percent of his total assets and gross income, respectively.

Rule 3–18. Special provisions as to registered management investment companies and companies required to be registered as management investment companies

(a) For filings by registered management investment companies, the following financial statements shall be filed:

(1) An audited balance sheet or statement of assets and liabilities as of the end of the most recent fiscal year;

(2) An audited statement of operations for the most recent fiscal year conforming to the requirements of Rule 6–07.

(3) An audited statement of cash flows for the most recent fiscal year if necessary to comply with generally accepted accounting principles. (Further references in this rule to the requirement for such statement are likewise applicable only to the extent that they are consistent with the requirements of generally accepted accounting principles.)

(4) Audited statements of changes in net assets conforming to the requirements of Rule 6–09 for the two most recent fiscal years.

(b) If the filing is made within 60 days after the end of the registrant's fiscal year and audited financial statements for the most recent fiscal year are not available, the balance sheet or statement of assets and liabilities may be as of the end of the preceding fiscal year and the filing shall include an additional balance sheet or statement of assets and liabilities as of an interim date within 245 days of the date of filing. In addition, the statements of operations and cash flows (if required by generally accepted accounting principles) shall be provided for the preceding fiscal year and the statement of changes in net assets shall be provided for the two preceding fiscal years and each of the statements shall be provided for the interim period between the end of the preceding fiscal year and the date of the most recent balance sheet or statement of assets and liabilities being filed. Financial statements for the corresponding period of the preceding fiscal year need not be provided.

(c) If the most current balance sheet or statement of assets and liabilities in a filing is as of a date 245 days or more prior to the date the filing is expected to become effective, the financial statements shall be updated with a balance sheet or statement of assets and liabilities as of an interim date within 245 days. In addition, the statements of operations, cash flows, and changes in net assets shall be provided for the interim period between the end of the most recent fiscal year for which a balance sheet or statement of assets and liabilities is presented and the date of the most recent interim balance sheet or statement of assets and liabilities filed.

(d) Interim financial statements provided in accordance with these requirements may be unaudited but shall be presented in the same detail as required by Rules 6–01 to 6–10. When unaudited financial statements are presented in a registration statement, they shall include the statement required by Rule 3–03(d).

Rule 3–19. [Reserved]

Rule 3–20. Currency for financial statements

(a)(1) A foreign private issuer, as defined in Rule 405 under the Securities Act of 1933, shall state amounts in its primary financial statements in the currency which it deems appropriate.

(2) An issuer that is not a foreign private issuer shall present its financial statements in U.S. dollars.

(b)(1) The currency in which amounts in the financial statements are stated shall be disclosed prominently on the face of the financial statements. If dividends on publicly-held equity securities will be declared in a currency other than the reporting currency, a note to the financial statements shall identify that currency. If there are material exchange restrictions or controls relating to the issuer's reporting currency, the currency of the issuer's domicile, or the currency in which the issuer will pay dividends, prominent disclosure of this fact shall be made in the financial statements. If the reporting currency is not the U.S. dollar, dollar-equivalent financial statements or convenience translations shall not be presented, except a translation may be presented of the most recent fiscal year and any subsequent interim period presented using the exchange rate as of the most recent balance sheet included in the filing, except that a rate as of the most recent practicable date shall be used if materially different.

(2) If there are material exchange restrictions or controls relating to the currency of a subsidiary's domicile, the currency held by a subsidiary, or the currency in which a subsidiary will pay dividends or transfer funds to the issuer or other subsidiaries, prominent disclosure of this fact shall be made in the financial statements.

(c) If the financial statements of a foreign private issuer are stated in a currency of a country that has experienced cumulative inflationary effects exceeding a total of 100 percent over the most recent three year period, and have not been recast or otherwise supplemented to include information on a historical cost/constant currency or current cost basis prescribed or permitted by appropriate authoritative standards, the issuer shall present supplementary information to quantify the effects of changing prices upon its financial position and results of operations.

(d) Notwithstanding the currency used for reporting purposes, the issuer shall measure separately its own transactions, and those of each of its material operations (e.g., branches, divisions, subsidiaries, joint ventures, and similar entities) that is included in the issuer's consolidated financial statements and not located in a hyperinflationary environment, using the particular currency of the primary economic environment in which the issuer or the operation conducts its business. Assets and liabilities so determined shall be translated into the reporting currency at the exchange rate at the balance sheet date; all revenues, expenses, gains, and losses shall be translated at the exchange rate existing at the time of the transaction or, if appropriate, a weighted average of the exchange rates during the period; and all translation effects of exchange rate changes shall be included as a separate component ("cumulative translation adjustment") of shareholder's equity. For purposes of this paragraph, the currency of an operation's primary economic environment is normally the currency in which cash is primarily generated and expended; a hyperinflationary environment is one that has cumulative inflation of approximately 100% or more over the most recent three year period. Departures from the methodology presented in this paragraph shall be quantified pursuant to Item 17(c)(2) of Form 20–F (17 CFR 249.220f).

(e) The issuer shall state its primary financial statements in the same currency for all periods for which financial information is presented. If the financial statements are stated in a currency that is different from that used in financial statements previously filed with the Commission, the issuer shall recast its financial statements as if the newly adopted currency had been used since at least the earliest period presented in the filing. The decision to change and the reason for the change in the reporting currency shall be disclosed in a note to the financial statements in the period in which the change occurs.

Rule 3–21. [Reserved]

CONSOLIDATED AND COMBINED FINANCIAL STATEMENTS

Rule 3A–01. [Reserved]

Rule 3A–02. Consolidated financial statements of the registrant and its subsidiaries

In deciding upon consolidation policy, the registrant must consider what financial presentation is most meaningful in the circumstances and should follow in the consolidated financial statements principles of inclusion or exclusion which will clearly exhibit the financial position and results of operations of the registrant. There is a presumption that consolidated financial statements are more meaningful than separate financial statements and that they are usually necessary for a fair presentation when one entity directly or indirectly has a controlling financial interest in another entity. Other particular facts and circumstances may require combined financial statements, an equity method of accounting, or valuation allowances in order to achieve a fair presentation.

(a) *Majority Ownership*: Among the factors that the registrant should consider in determining the most meaningful presentation is majority ownership. Generally, registrants shall consolidate entities that are majority owned and shall not consolidate entities that are not majority owned. The determination of majority ownership requires a careful analysis of the facts and circumstances of a particular relationship among entities. In rare situations, consolidation of a majority owned subsidiary may not result in a fair presentation, because the registrant, in substance, does not have a controlling financial interest (for example, when the subsidiary is in legal reorganization or in bankruptcy). In other situations, consolidation of an entity, notwithstanding the lack of technical majority ownership, is necessary to present fairly the financial position and results of operations of the registrant, because of the existence of a parent-subsidiary relationship by means other than record ownership of voting stock.

(b) [Reserved]

Rule 3A–03. Statement as to principles of consolidation or combination followed

(a) [Reserved]

(b) As to each consolidated financial statement and as to each combined financial statement, if there has been a change in the persons included or excluded in the corresponding statement for the preceding fiscal period filed with the Commission that has a material effect on the financial statements, the persons included and the persons excluded shall be disclosed.

Rule 3A–04. [Reserved]

RULES OF GENERAL APPLICATION

Rule 4–01. Form, order, and terminology

(a) Financial statements should be filed in such form and order, and should use such generally accepted terminology, as will best indicate their significance and character in the light of the provisions applicable thereto. The information required with respect to any statement shall be furnished as a minimum requirement to which shall be added such further material information as is necessary to make the required statements, in the light of the circumstances under which they are made, not misleading.

(1) Financial statements filed with the Commission which are not prepared in accordance with generally accepted accounting principles will be presumed to be misleading or inaccurate, despite footnote or other disclosures, unless the Commission has otherwise provided. This article and other articles of Regulation S–X provide clarification of certain disclosures which must be included in any event, in financial statements filed with the Commission.

(2) In all filings of foreign private issuers (see Rule 405 under the Securities Act of 1933), except as stated otherwise in the applicable form, the financial statements may be prepared according to a comprehensive set of accounting principles, other than those generally accepted in the United States or International Financial Reporting Standards as issued by the International Accounting Standards Board, if a reconciliation to U. S. Generally Accepted Accounting Principles and the provisions of Regulation S–X of the type specified in Item 18 of Form 20–F (17 CFR 249.220f) is also filed as part of the financial statements. Alternatively, the financial statements may be prepared according to U.S. Generally Accepted Accounting Principles or International Financial Reporting Standards as issued by the International Accounting Standards Board.

(b) All money amounts required to be shown in financial statements may be expressed in whole dollars or multiples thereof, as appropriate: *Provided*, That, when stated in other than whole dollars, an indication to that effect is inserted immediately beneath the caption of the statement or schedule, at the top of the money columns, or at an appropriate point in narrative material.

(c) Negative amounts (red figures) shall be shown in a manner which clearly distinguishes the negative attribute. When determining methods of display, consideration should be given to the limitations of reproduction and microfilming processes.

Rule 4–02. Items not material

If the amount which would otherwise be required to be shown with respect to any item is not material, it need not be separately set forth. The combination of insignificant amounts is permitted.

Rule 4–03. Inapplicable captions and omission of unrequired or inapplicable financial statements

(a) No caption should be shown in any financial statement as to which the items and conditions are not present.

(b) Financial statements not required or inapplicable because the required matter is not present need not be filed.

(c) The reasons for the omission of any required financial statements shall be indicated.

Rule 4–04. Omission of substantially identical notes

If a note covering substantially the same subject matter is required with respect to two or more financial statements relating to the same or affiliated persons, for which separate sets of notes are presented, the required information may be shown in a note to only one of such statements: *Provided*, That a clear and specific reference thereto is made in each of the other statements with respect to which the note is required.

Rule 4–05. [Reserved]

Rule 4–06. [Reserved]

Rule 4–07. Discount on shares

Discount on shares, or any unamortized balance thereof, shall be shown separately as a deduction from the applicable account(s) as circumstances require.

Rule 4–08. General notes to financial statements

If applicable to the person for which the financial statements are filed, the following shall be set forth on the face of the appropriate statement or in appropriately captioned notes. The information shall be provided for each statement required to be filed, except that the information required by paragraphs (b), (c), (d), (e) and (f) of this section shall be provided as of the most recent audited balance sheet being filed and for paragraph (j) of this section as specified therein. When specific statements are presented separately, the pertinent notes shall accompany such statements unless cross-referencing is appropriate.

(a) [Reserved]

(b) *Assets Subject to Lien*. Assets mortgaged, pledged, or otherwise subject to lien, and the approximate amounts thereof, shall be designated and the obligations collateralized briefly identified.

(c) *Defaults*. The facts and amounts concerning any default in principal, interest, sinking fund, or redemption provisions with respect to any issue of securities or credit agreements, or any breach of covenant of a related indenture or agreement, which default or breach existed at the date of the most recent balance sheet being filed and which has not been subsequently cured, shall be stated in the notes to the financial statements. If a default or breach exists but acceleration of the obligation has been waived for a stated period of time beyond the date of the most recent balance sheet being filed, state the amount of the obligation and the period of the waiver.

(d) *Preferred Shares*. Aggregate preferences on involuntary liquidation, if other than par or stated value, shall be shown parenthetically in the equity section of the balance sheet.

(e) *Restrictions Which Limit the Payment of Dividends by the Registrant*. (1) Describe the most significant restrictions on the payment of dividends by the registrant, indicating their sources, their pertinent provisions, and the amount of retained earnings or net income restricted or free of restrictions.

(2) Disclose the amount of consolidated retained earnings which represents undistributed earnings of 50 percent or less owned persons accounted for by the equity method.

(3) The disclosures in paragraphs (e)(3)(i) and (ii) of this section shall be provided when material.

(f) *Significant Changes in Bonds, Mortgages and Similar Debt.* Any significant changes in the authorized amounts of bonds, mortgages and similar debt since the date of the latest balance sheet being filed for a particular person or group shall be stated.

(g) *Summarized Financial Information of Subsidiaries Not Consolidated and 50 Percent or Less Owned Persons.* (1) The summarized information as to assets, liabilities and results of operations as detailed in Rule 1–02(bb) shall be presented in notes to the financial statements on an individual or group basis for:

(i) Subsidiaries not consolidated; or

(ii) For 50 percent or less owned persons accounted for by the equity method by the registrant or by a subsidiary of the registrant, if the criteria in Rule 1–02(w) for a significant subsidiary are met:

(A) Individually by any subsidiary not consolidated or any 50% or less owned person; or

(B) On an aggregated basis by any combination of such subsidiaries and persons.

(2) Summarized financial information shall be presented insofar as is practicable as of the same dates and for the same periods as the audited consolidated financial statements provided and shall include the disclosures prescribed by Rule 1–02(bb). Summarized information of subsidiaries not consolidated shall not be combined for disclosure purposes with the summarized information of 50 percent or less owned persons.

(h) *Income Tax Expense.* (1) Disclosure shall be made in the statement of comprehensive income or a note thereto, of the components of income (loss) before income tax expense (benefit) as either domestic or foreign.

NOTE 1 TO PARAGRAPH (h)(1): Amounts applicable to United States Federal income taxes, to foreign income taxes and the other income taxes shall be stated separately for each major component. Amounts applicable to foreign income (loss) and amounts applicable to foreign or other income taxes which are less than five percent of the total of income before taxes or the component of tax expense, respectively, need not be separately disclosed. For purposes of this rule, foreign income (loss) is defined as income (loss) generated from a registrant's foreign operations, i.e., operations that are located outside of the registrant's home country.

(2) In the reconciliation between the amount of reported total income tax expense (benefit) and the amount computed by multiplying the income (loss) before tax by the applicable statutory Federal income tax rate, if no individual reconciling item amounts to more than five percent of the amount computed by multiplying the income before tax by the applicable statutory Federal income tax rate, and the total difference to be reconciled is less than five percent of such computed amount, no reconciliation need be provided unless it would be significant in appraising the trend of earnings. Reconciling items that are individually less than five percent of the computed amount may be aggregated in the reconciliation. Where the reporting person is a foreign entity, the income tax rate in that person's country of domicile should normally be used in making the above computation, but different rates should not be used for subsidiaries or other segments of a reporting entity. When the rate used by a reporting person is other than the United States Federal corporate income tax rate, the rate used and the basis for using such rate shall be disclosed.

(i) [Reserved]

(j) [Reserved]

(k) *Related Party Transactions That Affect the Financial Statements.* (1) Amounts of related party transactions should be stated on the face of the balance sheet, statement of comprehensive income, or statement of cash flows.

(2) In cases where separate financial statements are presented for the registrant, certain investees, or subsidiaries, any intercompany profits or losses resulting from transactions with related parties and the effects thereof shall be disclosed.

(*l*) [Reserved]

(m) *Repurchase and Reverse Repurchase Agreements.* (1) Repurchase agreements (assets sold under agreements to repurchase).

(i) If, as of the most recent balance sheet date, the carrying amount (or market value, if higher than the carrying amount or if there is no carrying amount) of the securities or other assets sold under agreements to repurchase (repurchase agreements) exceeds 10% of total assets, disclose separately in the balance sheet the aggregate amount of liabilities incurred pursuant to repurchase agreements including accrued interest payable thereon.

(ii)(A) If, as of the most recent balance sheet date, the carrying amount (or market value, if higher than the carrying amount) of securities or other assets sold under repurchase agreements, other than securities or assets specified in paragraph (m)(1)(ii)(B) of this rule, exceeds 10% of total assets, disclose in an appropriately captioned footnote containing a tabular presentation, segregated as to type of such securities or assets sold under agreements to repurchase (e.g., U.S. Treasury obligations, U.S. Government agency obligations and loans), the following information as of the balance sheet date for each such agreement or group of agreements (other than agreements involving securities or assets specified in paragraph (m)(1)(ii)(B) of this rule) maturing (*1*) overnight; (*2*) term up to 30 days; (*3*) term of 30 to 90 days; (*4*) term over 90 days and (*5*) demand:

(*i*) The carrying amount and market value of the assets sold under agreement to repurchase, including accrued interest plus any cash or other assets on deposit under the repurchase agreements; and

(*ii*) The repurchase liability associated with such transaction or group of transactions and the interest rate(s) thereon.

(B) For purposes of paragraph (m)(1)(ii)(A) of this rule only, do not include securities or other assets for which unrealized changes in market value are reported in current income or which have been obtained under reverse repurchase agreements.

(iii) If, as of the most recent balance sheet date, the amount at risk under repurchase agreements with any individual counterparty or group of related counterparties exceeds 10% of stockholders' equity (or in the case of investment companies, net asset value), disclose the name of each such counterparty or group of related counterparties, the amount at risk with each, and the weighted average maturity of the repurchase agreements with each. The amount at risk under repurchase agreements is defined as the excess of carrying amount (or market value, if higher than the carrying amount or if there is no carrying amount) of the securities or other assets sold under agreement to repurchase, including accrued interest plus any cash or other assets on deposit to secure the repurchase obligation, over the amount of the repurchase liability (adjusted for accrued interest). (Cash deposits in connection with repurchase agreements shall not be reported as unrestricted cash pursuant to Rule 5–02.1.)

(2) *Reverse Repurchase Agreements (Assets Purchased Under Agreements to Resell).* (i) If, as of the most recent balance sheet date, the aggregate carrying amount of "reverse repurchase agreements" (securities or other assets purchased under agreements to resell) exceeds 10% of total assets: (A) Disclose separately such amount in the balance sheet; and (B) Disclose in an appropriately captioned footnote: (*1*) The registrant's policy with regard to taking possession of securities or other assets purchased under agreements to resell; and (*2*) whether or not there are any provisions to ensure that the market value of the underlying assets remains sufficient to protect the registrant in the event of default by the counterparty and if so, the nature of those provisions.

(ii) If, as of the most recent balance sheet date, the amount at risk under reverse repurchase agreements with any individual counterparty or group of related counterparties exceeds 10% of stockholders' equity (or in the case of investment companies, net asset value), disclose the name of each such counterparty or group of related counterparties, the amount at risk with each, and the weighted average maturity of the reverse repurchase agreements with each. The amount at risk under reverse repurchase agreements is defined as the excess of the carrying amount of the reverse repurchase agreements over the market value of assets delivered pursuant to the agreements by the counterparty to the registrant (or to a third party agent that has affirmatively agreed to act on behalf of the registrant) and not returned to the counterparty, except in exchange for their approximate market value in a separate transaction.

(n) *Accounting Policies for Certain Derivative Instruments.* Disclosures regarding accounting policies shall include, to the extent material, where in the statement of cash flows derivative financial instruments, and their related gains and losses, as defined by U.S. generally accepted accounting principles, are reported.

Rule 4–09. [Reserved]

Rule 4–10. Financial accounting and reporting for oil and gas producing activities pursuant to the federal securities laws and the Energy Policy and Conservation Act of 1975

This rule prescribes financial accounting and reporting standards for registrants with the Commission engaged in oil and gas producing activities in filings under the Federal securities laws and for the preparation of accounts by persons engaged, in whole or in part, in the production of crude oil or natural gas in the United States, pursuant to section 503 of the Energy Policy and Conservation Act of 1975 (42 U.S.C. 6383)(EPCA) and section 11(c) of the Energy Supply and Environmental Coordination Act of 1974 (15 U.S.C. 796) (ESECA), as amended by section 505 of EPCA. The application of this rule to those oil and gas producing operations of companies regulated for ratemaking purposes on an individual-company-cost-of-service basis may, however, give appropriate recognition to differences arising because of the effect of the ratemaking process.

Exemption. Any person exempted by the Department of Energy from any record-keeping or reporting requirements pursuant to section 11(c) of ESECA, as amended, is similarly exempted from the related provisions of this rule in the preparation of accounts pursuant to EPCA. This exemption does not affect the applicability of this rule to filings pursuant to the Federal securities laws.

DEFINITIONS

(a) *Definitions.* The following definitions apply to the terms listed below as they are used in this rule:

(1) *Acquisition of Properties.* Costs incurred to purchase, lease or otherwise acquire a property, including costs of lease bonuses and options to purchase or lease properties, the portion of costs applicable to minerals when land including mineral rights is purchased in fee, brokers' fees, recording fees, legal costs, and other costs incurred in acquiring properties.

(2) *Analogous Reservoir.* Analogous reservoirs, as used in resources assessments, have similar rock and fluid properties, reservoir conditions (depth, temperature, and pressure) and drive mechanisms, but are typically at a more advanced stage of development than the reservoir of interest and thus may provide concepts to assist in the interpretation of more limited data and estimation of recovery. When used to support proved reserves, an "analogous reservoir" refers to a reservoir that shares the following characteristics with the reservoir of interest:

(i) Same geological formation (but not necessarily in pressure communication with the reservoir of interest);

(ii) Same environment of deposition;

(iii) Similar geological structure; and

(iv) Same drive mechanism.

Instruction to Paragraph (a)(2): Reservoir properties must, in the aggregate, be no more favorable in the analog than in the reservoir of interest.

(3) *Bitumen.* Bitumen, sometimes referred to as natural bitumen, is petroleum in a solid or semi-solid state in natural deposits with a viscosity greater than 10,000 centipoise measured at original temperature in the deposit and atmospheric pressure, on a gas free basis. In its natural state it usually contains sulfur, metals, and other non-hydrocarbons.

(4) *Condensate.* Condensate is a mixture of hydrocarbons that exists in the gaseous phase at original reservoir temperature and pressure, but that, when produced, is in the liquid phase at surface pressure and temperature.

(5) *Deterministic Estimate.* The method of estimating reserves or resources is called deterministic when a single value for each parameter (from the geoscience, engineering, or economic data) in the reserves calculation is used in the reserves estimation procedure.

(6) *Developed Oil and Gas Reserves.* Developed oil and gas reserves are reserves of any category that can be expected to be recovered:

(i) Through existing wells with existing equipment and operating methods or in which the cost of the required equipment is relatively minor compared to the cost of a new well; and

(ii) Through installed extraction equipment and infrastructure operational at the time of the reserves estimate if the extraction is by means not involving a well.

(7) *Development Costs.* Costs incurred to obtain access to proved reserves and to provide facilities for extracting, treating, gathering and storing the oil and gas. More specifically, development costs, including depreciation and applicable operating costs of support equipment and facilities and other costs of development activities, are costs incurred to:

(i) Gain access to and prepare well locations for drilling, including surveying well locations for the purpose of determining specific development drilling sites, clearing ground, draining, road building, and relocating public roads, gas lines, and power lines, to the extent necessary in developing the proved reserves.

(ii) Drill and equip development wells, development-type stratigraphic test wells, and service wells, including the costs of platforms and of well equipment such as casing, tubing, pumping equipment, and the wellhead assembly.

(iii) Acquire, construct, and install production facilities such as lease flow lines, separators, treaters, heaters, manifolds, measuring devices, and production storage tanks, natural gas cycling and processing plants, and central utility and waste disposal systems.

(iv) Provide improved recovery systems.

(8) *Development Project.* A development project is the means by which petroleum resources are brought to the status of economically producible. As examples, the development of a single reservoir or field, an incremental development in a producing field, or the integrated development of a group of several fields and associated facilities with a common ownership may constitute a development project.

(9) *Development Well.* A well drilled within the proved area of an oil or gas reservoir to the depth of a stratigraphic horizon known to be productive.

(10) *Economically Producible.* The term economically producible, as it relates to a resource, means a resource which generates revenue that exceeds, or is reasonably expected to exceed, the costs of the operation. The value of the products that generate revenue shall be determined at the terminal point of oil and gas producing activities as defined in paragraph (a)(16) of this rule.

(11) *Estimated Ultimate Recovery (EUR).* Estimated ultimate recovery is the sum of reserves remaining as of a given date and cumulative production as of that date.

(12) *Exploration Costs.* Costs incurred in identifying areas that may warrant examination and in examining specific areas that are considered to have prospects of containing oil and gas reserves, including costs of drilling exploratory wells and exploratory-type stratigraphic test wells. Exploration costs may be incurred both before acquiring the related property (sometimes referred to in part as prospecting costs) and after acquiring the property. Principal types of exploration costs, which include depreciation and applicable operating costs of support equipment and facilities and other costs of exploration activities, are:

(i) Costs of topographical, geographical and geophysical studies, rights of access to properties to conduct those studies, and salaries and other expenses of geologists, geophysical crews, and others conducting those studies. Collectively, these are sometimes referred to as geological and geophysical or G & G costs.

(ii) Costs of carrying and retaining undeveloped properties, such as delay rentals, ad valorem taxes on properties, legal costs for title defense, and the maintenance of land and lease records.

(iii) Dry hole contributions and bottom hole contributions.

(iv) Costs of drilling and equipping exploratory wells.

(v) Costs of drilling exploratory-type stratigraphic test wells.

(13) *Exploratory Well.* An exploratory well is a well drilled to find a new field or to find a new reservoir in a field previously found to be productive of oil or gas in another reservoir. Generally, an exploratory well is any well that is not a development well, an extension well, a service well, or a stratigraphic test well as those items are defined in this rule.

(14) *Extension Well.* An extension well is a well drilled to extend the limits of a known reservoir.

(15) *Field.* An area consisting of a single reservoir or multiple reservoirs all grouped on or related to the same individual geological structural feature and/or stratigraphic condition. There may be two or more reservoirs in a field that are separated vertically by intervening impervious, strata, or laterally by local geologic barriers, or by both. Reservoirs that are associated by being in overlapping or adjacent fields may be treated as a single or common operational field. The geological terms *structural feature* and *stratigraphic condition* are intended to identify localized geological features as opposed to the broader terms of basins, trends, provinces, plays, areas-of-interest, etc.

(16) *Oil and Gas Producing Activities.* (i) Oil and gas producing activities include:

(A) The search for crude oil, including condensate and natural gas liquids, or natural gas ("oil and gas") in their natural states and original locations;

(B) The acquisition of property rights or properties for the purpose of further exploration or for the purpose of removing the oil or gas from such properties;

(C) The construction, drilling, and production activities necessary to retrieve oil and gas from their natural reservoirs, including the acquisition, construction, installation, and maintenance of field gathering and storage systems, such as:

(*1*) Lifting the oil and gas to the surface; and

(*2*) Gathering, treating, and field processing (as in the case of processing gas to extract liquid hydrocarbons); and

(D) Extraction of saleable hydrocarbons, in the solid, liquid, or gaseous state, from oil sands, shale, coalbeds, or other nonrenewable natural resources which are intended to be upgraded into synthetic oil or gas, and activities undertaken with a view to such extraction.

Instruction 1 to Paragraph (a)(16)(i). The oil and gas production function shall be regarded as ending at a "terminal point", which is the outlet valve on the lease or field storage tank. If unusual physical or operational circumstances exist, it may be appropriate to regard the terminal point for the production function as:

a. The first point at which oil, gas, or gas liquids, natural or synthetic, are delivered to a main pipeline, a common carrier, a refinery, or a marine terminal; and

b. In the case of natural resources that are intended to be upgraded into synthetic oil or gas, if those natural resources are delivered to a purchaser prior to upgrading, the first point at which the natural resources are delivered to a main pipeline, a common carrier, a refinery, a marine terminal, or a facility which upgrades such natural resources into synthetic oil or gas.

Instruction 2 to Paragraph (a)(16)(i). For purposes of this paragraph (a)(16), the term *saleable hydrocarbons* means hydrocarbons that are saleable in the state in which the hydrocarbons are delivered.

(ii) Oil and gas producing activities do not include:

(A) Transporting, refining, or marketing oil and gas;

(B) Processing of produced oil, gas or natural resources that can be upgraded into synthetic oil or gas by a registrant that does not have the legal right to produce or a revenue interest in such production;

(C) Activities relating to the production of natural resources other than oil, gas, or natural resources from which synthetic oil and gas can be extracted; or

(D) Production of geothermal steam.

(17) *Possible Reserves.* Possible reserves are those additional reserves that are less certain to be recovered than probable reserves.

(i) When deterministic methods are used, the total quantities ultimately recovered from a project have a low probability of exceeding proved plus probable plus possible reserves. When probabilistic methods are used, there should be at least a 10% probability that the total quantities ultimately recovered will equal or exceed the proved plus probable plus possible reserves estimates.

(ii) Possible reserves may be assigned to areas of a reservoir adjacent to probable reserves where data control and interpretations of available data are progressively less certain. Frequently, this will be in areas where geoscience and engineering data are unable to define clearly the area and vertical limits of commercial production from the reservoir by a defined project.

(iii) Possible reserves also include incremental quantities associated with a greater percentage recovery of the hydrocarbons in place than the recovery quantities assumed for probable reserves.

(iv) The proved plus probable and proved plus probable plus possible reserves estimates must be based on reasonable alternative technical and commercial interpretations within the reservoir or subject project that are clearly documented, including comparisons to results in successful similar projects.

(v) Possible reserves may be assigned where geoscience and engineering data identify directly adjacent portions of a reservoir within the same accumulation that may be separated from proved areas by faults with displacement less than formation thickness or other geological discontinuities and that have not been penetrated by a wellbore, and the registrant believes that such adjacent portions are in communication with the known (proved) reservoir. Possible reserves may be assigned to areas that are structurally higher or lower than the proved area if these areas are in communication with the proved reservoir.

(vi) Pursuant to paragraph (a)(22)(iii) of this rule, where direct observation has defined a highest known oil (HKO) elevation and the potential exists for an associated gas cap, proved oil reserves should be assigned in the structurally higher portions of the reservoir above the HKO only if the higher contact can be established with reasonable certainty through reliable technology. Portions of the reservoir that do not meet this reasonable certainty criterion may be assigned as probable and possible oil or gas based on reservoir fluid properties and pressure gradient interpretations.

(18) *Probable Reserves.* Probable reserves are those additional reserves that are less certain to be recovered than proved reserves but which, together with proved reserves, are as likely as not to be recovered.

(i) When deterministic methods are used, it is as likely as not that actual remaining quantities recovered will exceed the sum of estimated proved plus probable reserves. When probabilistic methods are used, there should be at least a 50% probability that the actual quantities recovered will equal or exceed the proved plus probable reserves estimates.

(ii) Probable reserves may be assigned to areas of a reservoir adjacent to proved reserves where data control or interpretations of available data are less certain, even if the interpreted reservoir continuity of structure or productivity does not meet the reasonable certainty criterion. Probable reserves may be assigned to areas that are structurally higher than the proved area if these areas are in communication with the proved reservoir.

(iii) Probable reserves estimates also include potential incremental quantities associated with a greater percentage recovery of the hydrocarbons in place than assumed for proved reserves.

(iv) See also guidelines in paragraphs (a)(17)(iv) and (a)(17)(vi) of this rule.

(19) *Probabilistic Estimate.* The method of estimation of reserves or resources is called probabilistic when the full range of values that could reasonably occur for each unknown parameter (from the geoscience and engineering data) is used to generate a full range of possible outcomes and their associated probabilities of occurrence.

(20) *Production Costs.* (i) Costs incurred to operate and maintain wells and related equipment and facilities, including depreciation and applicable operating costs of support equipment and facilities and other costs of operating and maintaining those wells and related equipment and facilities. They become part of the cost of oil and gas produced. Examples of production costs (sometimes called lifting costs) are:

(A) Costs of labor to operate the wells and related equipment and facilities.

(B) Repairs and maintenance.

(C) Materials, supplies, and fuel consumed and supplies utilized in operating the wells and related equipment and facilities.

(D) Property taxes and insurance applicable to proved properties and wells and related equipment and facilities.

(E) Severance taxes.

(ii) Some support equipment or facilities may serve two or more oil and gas producing activities and may also serve transportation, refining, and marketing activities. To the extent that the support equipment and facilities are used in oil and gas producing activities, their depreciation and applicable operating costs become exploration, development or production costs, as appropriate. Depreciation, depletion, and amortization of capitalized acquisition, exploration, and development costs are not production costs but also become part of the cost of oil and gas produced along with production (lifting) costs identified above.

(21) *Proved Area.* The part of a property to which proved reserves have been specifically attributed.

(22) *Proved Oil and Gas Reserves.* Proved oil and gas reserves are those quantities of oil and gas, which, by analysis of geoscience and engineering data, can be estimated with reasonable certainty to be economically producible—from a given date forward, from known reservoirs, and under existing economic conditions, operating methods, and government regulations—prior to the time at which contracts providing the right to operate expire, unless evidence indicates that renewal is reasonably certain, regardless of whether deterministic or probabilistic methods are used for the estimation. The project to extract the hydrocarbons must have commenced or the operator must be reasonably certain that it will commence the project within a reasonable time.

(i) The area of the reservoir considered as proved includes:

(A) The area identified by drilling and limited by fluid contacts, if any, and

(B) Adjacent undrilled portions of the reservoir that can, with reasonable certainty, be judged to be continuous with it and to contain economically producible oil or gas on the basis of available geoscience and engineering data.

(ii) In the absence of data on fluid contacts, proved quantities in a reservoir are limited by the lowest known hydrocarbons (LKH) as seen in a well penetration unless geoscience, engineering, or performance data and reliable technology establishes a lower contact with reasonable certainty.

(iii) Where direct observation from well penetrations has defined a highest known oil (HKO) elevation and the potential exists for an associated gas cap, proved oil reserves may be assigned in the structurally higher portions of the reservoir only if geoscience, engineering, or performance data and reliable technology establish the higher contact with reasonable certainty.

(iv) Reserves which can be produced economically through application of improved recovery techniques (including, but not limited to, fluid injection) are included in the proved classification when:

(A) Successful testing by a pilot project in an area of the reservoir with properties no more favorable than in the reservoir as a whole, the operation of an installed program in the reservoir or an analogous reservoir, or other evidence using reliable technology establishes the reasonable certainty of the engineering analysis on which the project or program was based; and

(B) The project has been approved for development by all necessary parties and entities, including governmental entities.

(v) Existing economic conditions include prices and costs at which economic producibility from a reservoir is to be determined. The price shall be the average price during the 12–month period prior to the ending date of the period covered by the report, determined as an unweighted arithmetic average of the first-day-of-the-month price for each month within such period, unless prices are defined by contractual arrangements, excluding escalations based upon future conditions.

(23) *Proved Properties*. Properties with proved reserves.

(24) *Reasonable Certainty*. If deterministic methods are used, reasonable certainty means a high degree of confidence that the quantities will be recovered. If probabilistic methods are used, there should be at least a 90% probability that the quantities actually recovered will equal or exceed the estimate. A high degree of confidence exists if the quantity is much more likely to be achieved than not, and, as changes due to increased availability of geoscience (geological, geophysical, and geochemical), engineering, and economic data are made to estimated ultimate recovery (EUR) with time, reasonably certain EUR is much more likely to increase or remain constant than to decrease.

(25) *Reliable Technology*. Reliable technology is a grouping of one or more technologies (including computational methods) that has been field tested and has been demonstrated to provide reasonably certain results with consistency and repeatability in the formation being evaluated or in an analogous formation.

(26) *Reserves*. Reserves are estimated remaining quantities of oil and gas and related substances anticipated to be economically producible, as of a given date, by application of development projects to known accumulations. In addition, there must exist, or there must be a reasonable expectation that there will exist, the legal right to produce or a revenue interest in the production, installed means of delivering oil and gas or related substances to market, and all permits and financing required to implement the project.

NOTE TO PARAGRAPH (a)(26): Reserves should not be assigned to adjacent reservoirs isolated by major, potentially sealing, faults until those reservoirs are penetrated and evaluated as economically producible. Reserves should not be assigned to areas that are clearly separated from a known accumulation by a non-productive reservoir (*i.e.*, absence of reservoir, structurally low reservoir, or negative test results). Such areas may contain prospective resources (*i.e.*, potentially recoverable resources from undiscovered accumulations).

(27) *Reservoir*. A porous and permeable underground formation containing a natural accumulation of producible oil and/or gas that is confined by impermeable rock or water barriers and is individual and separate from other reservoirs.

(28) *Resources*. Resources are quantities of oil and gas estimated to exist in naturally occurring accumulations. A portion of the resources may be estimated to be recoverable, and another portion may be considered to be unrecoverable. Resources include both discovered and undiscovered accumulations.

(29) *Service Well*. A well drilled or completed for the purpose of supporting production in an existing field. Specific purposes of service wells include gas injection, water injection, steam injection, air

injection, saltwater disposal, water supply for injection, observation, or injection for in-situ combustion.

(30) *Stratigraphic Test Well.* A stratigraphic test well is a drilling effort, geologically directed, to obtain information pertaining to a specific geologic condition. Such wells customarily are drilled without the intent of being completed for hydrocarbon production. The classification also includes tests identified as core tests and all types of expendable holes related to hydrocarbon exploration. Stratigraphic tests are classified as "exploratory type" if not drilled in a known area or "development type" if drilled in a known area.

(31) *Undeveloped Oil and Gas Reserves.* Undeveloped oil and gas reserves are reserves of any category that are expected to be recovered from new wells on undrilled acreage, or from existing wells where a relatively major expenditure is required for recompletion.

(i) Reserves on undrilled acreage shall be limited to those directly offsetting development spacing areas that are reasonably certain of production when drilled, unless evidence using reliable technology exists that establishes reasonable certainty of economic producibility at greater distances.

(ii) Undrilled locations can be classified as having undeveloped reserves only if a development plan has been adopted indicating that they are scheduled to be drilled within five years, unless the specific circumstances, justify a longer time.

(iii) Under no circumstances shall estimates for undeveloped reserves be attributable to any acreage for which an application of fluid injection or other improved recovery technique is contemplated, unless such techniques have been proved effective by actual projects in the same reservoir or an analogous reservoir, as defined in paragraph (a)(2) of this rule, or by other evidence using reliable technology establishing reasonable certainty.

(32) *Unproved Properties.* Properties with no proved reserves.

Successful Efforts Method

(b) A reporting entity that follows the successful efforts method shall comply with the accounting and financial reporting disclosure requirements of FASB ASC Topic 932, *Extractive Activities—Oil and Gas.*

Full Cost Method

(c) *Application of the Full Cost Method of Accounting.* A reporting entity that follows the full cost method shall apply that method to all of its operations and to the operations of its subsidiaries, as follows:

(1) *Determination of Cost Centers.* Cost centers shall be established on a country-by-country basis.

(2) *Costs to Be Capitalized.* All costs associated with property acquisition, exploration, and development activities (as defined in paragraph (a) of this section) shall be capitalized within the appropriate cost center. Any internal costs that are capitalized shall be limited to those costs that can be directly identified with acquisition, exploration, and development activities undertaken by the reporting entity for its own account, and shall not include any costs related to production, general corporate overhead, or similar activities.

(3) *Amortization of Capitalized Costs.* Capitalized costs within a cost center shall be amortized on the unit-of-production basis using proved oil and gas reserves, as follows:

(i) Costs to be amortized shall include (A) all capitalized costs, less accumulated amortization, other than the cost of properties described in paragraph (ii) below; (B) the estimated future expenditures (based on current costs) to be incurred in developing proved reserves; and (C) estimated dismantlement and abandonment costs, net of estimated salvage values.

(ii) The cost of investments in unproved properties and major development projects may be excluded from capitalized costs to be amortized, subject to the following:

(A) All costs directly associated with the acquisition and evaluation of unproved properties may be excluded from the amortization computation until it is determined whether or not proved reserves can be assigned to the properties, subject to the following conditions:

(*1*) Until such a determination is made, the properties shall be assessed at least annually to ascertain whether impairment has occurred. Unevaluated properties whose costs are individually significant shall be assessed individually. Where it is not practicable to individually assess the amount of impairment of properties for which costs are not individually significant, such properties may be grouped for purposes of assessing impairment. Impairment may be estimated by applying factors based on historical experience and other data such as primary lease terms of the properties, average holding periods of unproved properties, and geographic and geologic data to groupings of individually insignificant properties and projects. The amount of impairment assessed under either of these methods shall be added to the costs to be amortized.

(*2*) The costs of drilling exploratory dry holes shall be included in the amortization base immediately upon determination that the well is dry.

(*3*) If geological and geophysical costs cannot be directly associated with specific unevaluated properties, they shall be included in the amortization base as incurred. Upon complete evaluation of a property, the total remaining excluded cost (net of any impairment) shall be included in the full cost amortization base.

(B) Certain costs may be excluded from amortization when incurred in connection with major development projects expected to entail significant costs to ascertain the quantities of proved reserves attributable to the properties under development (e.g., the installation of an offshore drilling platform from which development wells are to be drilled, the installation of improved recovery programs, and similar major projects undertaken in the expectation of significant additions to proved reserves). The amounts which may be excluded are applicable portions of (1) the costs that relate to the major development project and have not previously been included in the amortization base, and (2) the estimated future expenditures associated with the development project. The excluded portion of any common costs associated with the development project should be based, as is most appropriate in the circumstances, on a comparison of either (i) existing proved reserves to total proved reserves expected to be established upon completion of the project, or (ii) the number of wells to which proved reserves have been assigned and total number of wells expected to be drilled. Such costs may be excluded from costs to be amortized until the earlier determination of whether additional reserves are proved or impairment occurs.

(C) Excluded costs and the proved reserves related to such costs shall be transferred into the amortization base on an ongoing (well-by-well or property-by-property) basis as the project is evaluated and proved reserves established or impairment determined. Once proved reserves are established, there is no further justification for continued exclusion from the full cost amortization base even if other factors prevent immediate production or marketing.

(iii) Amortization shall be computed on the basis of physical units, with oil and gas converted to a common unit of measure on the basis of their approximate relative energy content, unless economic circumstances (related to the effects of regulated prices) indicate that use of units of revenue is a more appropriate basis of computing amortization. In the latter case, amortization shall be computed on the basis of current gross revenues (excluding royalty payments and net profits disbursements) from production in relation to future gross revenues, based on current prices (including consideration of changes in existing prices provided only by contractual arrangements), from estimated production of proved oil and gas reserves. The effect of a significant price increase during the year on estimated future gross revenues shall be reflected in the amortization provision only for the period after the price increase occurs.

(iv) In some cases it may be more appropriate to depreciate natural gas cycling and processing plants by a method other than the unit-of-production method.

(v) Amortization computations shall be made on a consolidated basis, including investees accounted for on a proportionate consolidation basis. Investees accounted for on the equity method shall be treated separately.

(4) *Limitation on Capitalized Costs.* (i) For each cost center, capitalized costs, less accumulated amortization and related deferred income taxes, shall not exceed an amount (the cost center ceiling) equal to the sum of:

(A) The present value of estimated future net revenues computed by applying current prices of oil and gas reserves (with consideration of price changes only to the extent provided by contractual arrangements) to estimated future production of proved oil and gas reserves as of the date of the latest balance sheet presented, less estimated future expenditures (based on current costs) to be incurred in developing and producing the proved reserves computed using a discount factor of ten percent and assuming continuation of existing economic conditions; plus

(B) the cost of properties not being amortized pursuant to paragraph (i)(3)(ii) of this rule; plus

(C) the lower of cost or estimated fair value of unproven properties included in the costs being amortized; less

(D) income tax effects related to differences between the book and tax basis of the properties referred to in paragraphs (i)(4)(i)(B) and (C) of this rule.

(ii) If unamortized costs capitalized within a cost center, less related deferred income taxes, exceed the cost center ceiling, the excess shall be charged to expense and separately disclosed during the period in which the excess occurs. Amounts thus required to be written off shall not be reinstated for any subsequent increase in the cost center ceiling.

(5) *Production Costs.* All costs relating to production activities, including workover costs incurred solely to maintain or increase levels of production from an existing completion interval, shall be charged to expense as incurred.

(6) *Other Transactions.* The provisions of paragraph (h) of this rule, "Mineral property conveyances and related transactions if the successful efforts method of accounting is followed," shall apply also to those reporting entities following the full cost method except as follows:

(i) *Sales and Abandonments of Oil and Gas Properties.* Sales of oil and gas properties, whether or not being amortized currently, shall be accounted for as adjustments of capitalized costs, with no gain or loss recognized, unless such adjustments would significantly alter the relationship between capitalized costs and proved reserves of oil and gas attributable to a cost center. For instance, a significant alteration would not ordinarily be expected to occur for sales involving less than 25 percent of the reserve quantities of a given cost center. If gain or loss is recognized on such a sale, total capitalization costs within the cost center shall be allocated between the reserves sold and reserves retained on the same basis used to compute amortization, unless there are substantial economic differences between the properties sold and those retained, in which case capitalized costs shall be allocated on the basis of the relative fair values of the properties. Abandonments of oil and gas properties shall be accounted for as adjustments of capitalized costs; that is, the cost of abandoned properties shall be charged to the full cost center and amortized (subject to the limitation on capitalized costs in paragraph (b) of this rule).

(ii) *Purchases of Reserves.* Purchases of oil and gas reserves in place ordinarily shall be accounted for as additional capitalized costs within the applicable cost center; however, significant purchases of production payments or properties with lives substantially shorter than the composite productive life of the cost center shall be accounted for separately.

(iii) *Partnerships, Joint Ventures and Drilling Arrangements.* (A) Except as provided in paragraph (i)(6)(i) of this rule, all consideration received from sales or transfers of properties in connection with partnerships, joint venture operations, or various other forms of drilling arrangements involving oil and gas exploration and development activities (e.g., carried interest, turnkey wells, management fees, etc.) shall be credited to the full cost account, except to the extent of amounts that represent reimbursement of organization, offering, general and administrative expenses, etc., that are identifiable with the transaction, if such amounts are currently incurred and charged to expense.

(B) Where a registrant organizes and manages a limited partnership involved only in the purchase of proved developed properties and subsequent distribution of income from such properties, management fee income may be recognized provided the properties involved do not require aggregate development expenditures in connection with production of existing proved reserves in excess of 10% of the partnership's recorded cost of such properties. Any income not recognized as a result of this limitation would be credited to the full cost account and recognized through a lower amortization provision as reserves are produced.

(iv) *Other Services.* No income shall be recognized in connection with contractual services performed (e.g. drilling, well service, or equipment supply services, etc.) in connection with properties in which the registrant or an affiliate (as defined in Rule 1–02(b)) holds an ownership or other economic interest, except as follows:

(A) Where the registrant acquires an interest in the properties in connection with the service contract, income may be recognized to the extent the cash consideration received exceeds the related contract costs plus the registrant's share of costs incurred and estimated to be incurred in connection with the properties. Ownership interests acquired within one year of the date of such a contract are considered to be acquired in connection with the service for purposes of applying this rule. The amount of any guarantees or similar arrangements undertaken as part of this contract should be considered as part of the costs related to the properties for purposes of applying this rule.

(B) Where the registrant acquired an interest in the properties at least one year before the date of the service contract through transactions unrelated to the service contract, and that interest is unaffected by the service contract, income from such contract may be recognized subject to the general provisions for elimination of inter-company profit under generally accepted accounting principles.

(C) Notwithstanding the provisions of paragraphs (i)(6)(iv)(A) and (B) of this rule, no income may be recognized for contractual services performed on behalf of investors in oil and gas producing activities managed by the registrant or an affiliate. Furthermore, no income may be recognized for contractual services to the extent that the consideration received for such services represents an interest in the underlying property.

(D) Any income not recognized as a result of these rules would be credited to the full cost account and recognized through a lower amortization provision as reserves are produced.

(7) *Disclosures*. Reporting entities that follow the full cost method of accounting shall disclose all of the information required by paragraph (k) of this rule, with each cost center considered as a separate geographic area, except that reasonable groupings may be made of cost centers that are not significant in the aggregate. In addition:

(i) For each cost center for each year that a statement of comprehensive income is required, disclose the total amount of amortization expense (per equivalent physical unit of production if amortization is computed on the basis of physical units or per dollar of gross revenue from production if amortization is computed on the basis of gross revenue).

(ii) State separately on the face of the balance sheet the aggregate of the capitalized costs of unproved properties and major development projects that are excluded, in accordance with paragraph (i)(3) of this rule, from the capitalized costs being amortized. Provide a description in the notes to the financial statements of the current status of the significant properties or projects involved, including the anticipated timing of the inclusion of the costs in the amortization computation. Present a table that shows, by category of cost, (A) the total costs excluded as of the most recent fiscal year; and (B) the amounts of such excluded costs, incurred (*1*) in each of the three most recent fiscal years and (*2*) in the aggregate for any earlier fiscal years in which the costs were incurred. Categories of cost to be disclosed include acquisition costs, exploration costs, development costs in the case of significant development projects and capitalized interest.

(8) For purposes of this paragraph (c), the term "current price" shall mean the average price during the 12–month period prior to the ending date of the period covered by the report, determined as an unweighted arithmetic average of the first-day-of-the-month price for each month within such period, unless prices are defined by contractual arrangements, excluding escalations based upon future conditions.

INCOME TAXES

(d) *Income Taxes*. Comprehensive interperiod income tax allocation by a method which complies with generally accepted accounting principles shall be followed for intangible drilling and development costs and other costs incurred that enter into the determination of taxable income and pretax accounting income in different periods.

COMMERCIAL AND INDUSTRIAL COMPANIES

Rule 5–01. Application of Rules 5–01 to 5–04

Rules 5–01 to 5–04 shall be applicable to financial statements filed for all persons except—

(a) Registered investment companies (see Rules 6–01 to 6–10).

(b) Employee stock purchase, savings and similar plans (see Rules 6A–01 to 6A–05).

(c) Insurance companies (see Rules 7–01 to 7–05).

(d) Bank holding companies and banks (see Rules 9–01 to 9–07).

(e) Brokers and dealers when filing Form X–17A–5 [249.617] (see Rules 17a–5 and 17a–10 under the Securities Exchange Act of 1934).

Rule 5–02. Balance sheets

The purpose of this rule is to indicate the various line items and certain additional disclosures which, if applicable, and except as otherwise permitted by the Commission, should appear on the face of the balance sheets or related notes filed for the persons to whom this article pertains (see Rule 4–01(a)).

ASSETS AND OTHER DEBTS

Current Assets, When Appropriate

1. *Cash and Cash Items.* Separate disclosure shall be made of the cash and cash items which are restricted as to withdrawal or usage. The provisions of any restrictions shall be described in a note to the financial statements. Restrictions may include legally restricted deposits held as compensating balances against short-term borrowing arrangements, contracts entered into with others, or company statements of intention with regard to particular deposits; however, time deposits and short-term certificates of deposit are not generally included in legally restricted deposits. In cases where compensating balance arrangements exist but are not agreements which legally restrict the use of cash amounts shown on the balance sheet, describe in the notes to the financial statements these arrangements and the amount involved, if determinable, for the most recent audited balance sheet required and for any subsequent unaudited balance sheet required in the notes to the financial statements. Compensating balances that are maintained under an agreement to assure future credit availability shall be disclosed in the notes to the financial statements along with the amount and terms of such agreement.

2. *Marketable Securities.* The accounting and disclosure requirements for current marketable equity securities are specified by generally accepted accounting principles. With respect to all other current marketable securities, state, parenthetically or otherwise, the basis of determining the aggregate amount shown in the balance sheet, along with the alternatives of the aggregate cost or the aggregate market value at the balance sheet date.

3. *Accounts and Notes Receivable.* (a) State separately amounts receivable from (1) customers (trade); (2) related parties (see Rule 4–08(k)); (3) underwriters, promoters, and employees (other than related parties) which arose in other than the ordinary course of business; and (4) others.

(b) If the aggregate amount of notes receivable exceeds 10 percent of the aggregate amount of receivables, the above information shall be set forth separately, in the balance sheet or in a note thereto, for accounts receivable and notes receivable.

(c) If receivables include amounts due under long-term contracts (see Rule 5–02.6(d)), state separately in the balance sheet or in a note to the financial statements the following amounts:

(1) Balances billed but not paid by customers under retainage provisions in contracts.

(2) Amounts representing the recognized sales value of performance and such amounts that had not been billed and were not billable to customers at the date of the balance sheet. Include a general description of the prerequisites for billing.

(3) Billed or unbilled amounts representing claims or other similar items subject to uncertainty concerning their determination or ultimate realization. Include a description of the nature and status of the principal items comprising such amount.

(4) With respect to (1) through (3) above, also state the amounts included in each item which are expected to be collected after one year. Also state, by year, if practicable, when the amounts of retainage (see (1) above) are expected to be collected.

4. *Allowances for Doubtful Accounts and Notes Receivable.* The amount is to be set forth separately in the balance sheet or in a note thereto.

5. *Unearned Income.*

6. *Inventories.* (a) State separately in the balance sheet or in a note thereto, if practicable, the amounts of major classes of inventory such as: (1) Finished goods; (2) inventoried costs relating to long-term contracts or programs (see paragraph (d) of this section); (3) work in process; (4) raw materials; and (5) supplies. If the method of calculating a LIFO inventory does not allow for the practical determination of amounts assigned to major classes of inventory, the amounts of those classes may be stated under cost flow assumptions other than LIFO with the excess of such total amount over the aggregate LIFO amount shown as a deduction to arrive at the amount of the LIFO inventory.

(b) The basis of determining the amounts shall be stated.

If cost is used to determine any portion of the inventory amounts, the description of this method shall include the nature of the cost elements included in inventory. Elements of cost include, among other items, retained costs representing the excess of manufacturing or production costs over the amounts charged to cost of sales or delivered or in-process units, initial tooling or other deferred startup costs, or general and administrative costs.

The method by which amounts are removed from inventory (e.g., average cost, first-in, first-out, last-in, first-out, estimated average cost per unit) shall be described. If the estimated average cost per unit is used as a basis to determine amounts removed from inventory under a total program or similar basis of accounting, the principal assumptions (including, where meaningful, the aggregate number of units expected to be delivered under the program, the number of units delivered to date and the number of units on order) shall be disclosed.

If any general and administrative costs are charged to inventory, state in a note to the financial statements the aggregate amount of the general and administrative costs incurred in each period and the actual or estimated amount remaining in inventory at the date of each balance sheet.

(c) If the LIFO inventory method is used, the excess of replacement or current cost over stated LIFO value shall, if material, be stated parenthetically or in a note to the financial statements.

(d) For purposes of Rules 5–02.3 and 5–02.6, long-term contracts or programs include (1) all contracts or programs for which gross profits are recognized on a percentage-of-completion method of accounting or any variant thereof (e.g., delivered unit, cost to cost, physical completion), and (2) any contracts or programs accounted for on a completed contract basis of accounting where, in either case, the contracts or programs have associated with them material amounts of inventories or unbilled receivables and where such contracts or programs have been or are expected to be performed over a period of more than twelve months. Contracts or programs of shorter duration may also be included, if deemed appropriate.

For all long-term contracts or programs, the following information, if applicable, shall be stated in a note to the financial statements:

(i) The aggregate amount of manufacturing or production costs and any related deferred costs (e.g., initial tooling costs) which exceeds the aggregate estimated cost of all in-process and delivered units on the basis of the estimated average cost of all units expected to be produced under long-term contracts and programs not yet complete, as well as that portion of such amount which would not be absorbed in cost of sales based on existing firm orders at the latest balance sheet date. In addition, if practicable, disclose the amount of deferred costs by type of cost (e.g., initial tooling, deferred production, etc.).

(ii) The aggregate amount representing claims or other similar items subject to uncertainty concerning their determination or ultimate realization, and include a description of the nature and status of the principal items comprising such aggregate amount.

(iii)The amount of progress payments netted against inventory at the date of the balance sheet.

7. *Prepaid Expenses.*

8. *Other Current Assets*. State separately, in the balance sheet or in a note thereto, any amounts in excess of five percent of total current assets.

9. *Total Current Assets, When Appropriate.*

10. *Securities of Related Parties.* (See Rule 4–08(k).)

11. *Indebtedness of Related Parties—Not Current.* (See Rule 4–08(k).)

12. *Other Investments.* The accounting and disclosure requirements for non-current marketable equity securities are specified by generally accepted accounting principles. With respect to other security investments and any other investment, state, parenthetically or otherwise, the basis of determining the aggregate amounts shown in the balance sheet, along with the alternate of the aggregate cost or aggregate market value at the balance sheet date.

13. *Property, Plant and Equipment.*

(a) State the basis of determining the amounts.

(b) Tangible and intangible utility plant of a public utility company shall be segregated so as to show separately the original cost, plant acquisition adjustments, and plant adjustments, as required by the system of accounts prescribed by the applicable regulatory authorities. This rule shall not be applicable in respect to companies which are not required to make such a classification.

14. *Accumulated Depreciation, Depletion, and Amortization of Property, Plant and Equipment.* The amount is to be set forth separately in the balance sheet or in a note thereto.

15. *Intangible Assets.* State separately each class of such assets which is in excess of five percent of the total assets, along with the basis of determining the respective amounts. Any significant addition or deletion shall be explained in a note.

16. *Accumulated Depreciation and Amortization of Intangible Assets.* The amount is to be set forth separately in the balance sheet or in a note thereto.

17. *Other Assets.* State separately, in the balance sheet or in a note thereto, any other item not properly classified in one of the preceding asset captions which is in excess of five percent to total assets. Any significant addition or deletion should be explained in a note. With respect to any significant deferred charge, state the policy for deferral and amortization.

18. *Total Assets.*

LIABILITIES AND STOCKHOLDERS' EQUITY

Current Liabilities, When Appropriate

19. *Accounts and Notes Payable.* (a) State separately amounts payable to (1) banks for borrowings; (2) factors or other financial institutions for borrowings; (3) holders of commercial paper; (4) trade creditors; (5) related parties (see Rule 4–08(k)); (6) underwriters, promoters, and employees (other than related parties); and (7) others. Amounts applicable to (1), (2) and (3) may be stated separately in the balance sheet or in a note thereto.

(b) The amount and terms (including commitment fees and the conditions under which lines may be withdrawn) of unused lines of credit for short-term financing shall be disclosed, if significant, in the notes to the financial statements. The weighted average interest rate on short term borrowings outstanding as of the date of each balance sheet presented shall be furnished in a note. The amount of these lines of credit which support a commercial paper borrowing arrangement or similar arrangements shall be separately identified.

20. *Other Current Liabilities.* State separately, in the balance sheet or in a note thereto, any item in excess of 5 percent of total current liabilities. Such items may include, but are not limited to, accrued payrolls, accrued interest, taxes, indicating the current portion of deferred income taxes, and the current portion of long-term debt. Remaining items may be shown in one amount.

21. *Total Current Liabilities, When Appropriate.*

Long–Term Debt

22. *Bonds, Mortgages and Other Long-Term Debt, Including Capitalized Leases.* (a) State separately, in the balance sheet or in a note thereto, each issue or type of obligation and such information as will indicate:

(1) The general character of each type of debt including the rate of interest; (2) the date of maturity,

or, if maturing serially, a brief indication of the serial maturities, such as "maturing serially from 1980 to 1990"; (3) if the payment of principal or interest is contingent, an appropriate indication of such contingency; (4) a brief indication of priority; and (5) if convertible, the basis. For amounts owed to related parties, see Rule 4–08(k).

(b) The amount and terms (including commitment fees and the conditions under which commitments may be withdrawn) of unused commitments for long-term financing arrangements that would be disclosed under this rule if used shall be disclosed in the notes to the financial statements if significant.

23. *Indebtedness to Related Parties—Noncurrent.* Include under this caption indebtedness to related parties as required under Rule 4–08(k).

24. *Other Liabilities.* State separately, in the balance sheet or in a note thereto, any item not properly classified in one of the preceding liability captions which is in excess of 5 percent of total liabilities.

25. *Commitments and Contingent Liabilities.*

26. *Deferred Credits.* State separately in the balance sheet amounts for (a) deferred income taxes, (b) deferred tax credits, and (c) material items of deferred income.

Redeemable Preferred Stocks

27. *Preferred Stocks Subject to Mandatory Redemption Requirements or Whose Redemption is Outside the Control of the Issuer.* (a) Include under this caption amounts applicable to any class of stock which has any of the following characteristics: (1) it is redeemable at a fixed or determinable price on a fixed or determinable date or dates, whether by operation of a sinking fund or otherwise; (2) it is redeemable at the option of the holder; or (3) it has conditions for redemption which are not solely within the control of the issuer, such as stocks which must be redeemed out of future earnings. Amounts attributable to preferred stock which is not redeemable or is redeemable solely at the option of the issuer shall be included under Rule 5–02.28 unless it meets one or more of the above criteria.

(b) State on the face of the balance sheet the title of each issue, the carrying amount, and redemption amount. (If there is more than one issue, these amounts may be aggregated on the face of the balance sheet and details concerning each issue may be presented in the note required by paragraph (c) below.) Show also the dollar amount of any shares subscribed but unissued, and show the deduction of subscriptions receivable therefrom. If the carrying value is different from the redemption amount, describe the accounting treatment for such difference in the note required by paragraph (c) below. Also state in this note or on the face of the balance sheet, for each issue, the number of shares authorized and the number of shares issued or outstanding, as appropriate (See Rule 4–07).

(c) State in a separate note captioned "Redeemable Preferred Stocks" (1) a general description of each issue, including its redemption features (e.g. sinking fund, at option of holders, out of future earnings) and the rights, if any, of holders in the event of default, including the effect, if any, on junior securities in the event a required dividend, sinking fund, or other redemption payment(s) is not made; (2) the combined aggregate amount of redemption requirements for all issues each year for the five years following the date of the latest balance sheet; and (3) the changes in each issue for each period for which a statement of comprehensive income is required to be filed. (See also Rule 4–08(d).)

(d) Securities reported under this caption are not to be included under a general heading "stockholders' equity" or combined in a total with items described in captions 29, 30 or 31 which follow.

Non-Redeemable Preferred Stocks

28. *Preferred Stocks Which Are Not Redeemable or Are Redeemable Solely at the Option of the Issuer.* State on the face of the balance sheet, or if more than one issue is outstanding state in a note, the title of each issue and the dollar amount thereof. Show also the dollar amount of any shares subscribed but unissued, and show the deduction of subscriptions receivable therefrom. State on the face of the balance sheet or in a note, for each issue, the number of shares authorized and the number of shares issued or outstanding, as appropriate (see Rule 4–07). Show in a note or separate statement the changes in each class of preferred shares reported under this caption for each period for which a statement of comprehensive income is required to be filed. (See also Rule 4–08(d).)

Common Stocks

29. *Common Stocks.* For each class of common shares state, on the face of the balance sheet, the number of shares issued or outstanding, as appropriate (see Rule 4–07), and the dollar amount thereof. If convertible, this fact should be indicated on the face of the balance sheet. For each class of common shares state, on the face of the balance sheet or in a note, the title of the issue, the number of shares authorized, and, if convertible, the basis of conversion (see also Rule 4–08(d)). Show also the dollar amount of any common shares subscribed but unissued, and show the deduction of subscriptions receivable therefrom. Show in a note or statement the changes in each class of common shares for each period for which a statement of comprehensive income is required to be filed.

Other Stockholders' Equity

30. *Other Stockholders' Equity.* (a) Separate captions shall be shown for (1) additional paid-in capital, (2) other additional capital, (3) retained earnings (i) appropriated and (ii) unappropriated (See Rule 4–08(e)), and (4) accumulated other comprehensive income.

NOTE TO PARAGRAPH 30. (a). Additional paid-in capital and other additional capital may be combined with the stock caption to which it applies, if appropriate.

(b) For a period of at least 10 years subsequent to the effective date of a quasi-reorganization, any description of retained earnings shall indicate the point in time from which the new retained earnings dates and for a period of at least three years shall indicate, on the face of the balance sheet, the total amount of the deficit eliminated.

Noncontrolling Interests

31. *Noncontrolling Interests in Consolidated Subsidiaries.* State separately in a note the amounts represented by preferred stock and the applicable dividend requirements if the preferred stock is material in relation to the consolidated equity.

32. *Total Liabilities and Equity.*

Rule 5–03. Statements of Comprehensive Income

(a) The purpose of this rule is to indicate the various line items which, if applicable, and except as otherwise permitted by the Commission, should appear on the face of the statements of comprehensive income filed for the persons to whom this article pertains (see Rule 4–01(a)).

(b) If income is derived from more than one of the subcaptions described under Rule 5–03.1, each class which is not more than 10 percent of the sum of the items may be combined with another class. If these items are combined, related costs and expenses as described under Rule 5–03.2 shall be combined in the same manner.

1. *Net Sales and Gross Revenues.* State separately:

(a) Net sales of tangible products (gross sales less discounts, returns and allowances), (b) operating revenues of public utilities or others; (c) income from rentals; (d) revenues from services; and (e) other revenues. Amounts earned from transactions with related parties shall be disclosed as required under Rule 4–08(k). A public utility company using a uniform system of accounts or a form for annual report prescribed by federal or state authorities, or a similar system or report, shall follow the general segregation of operating revenues and operating expenses reported under Rule 5–03.2 prescribed by such system or report. If the total of sales and revenues reported under this caption includes excise taxes in an amount equal to 1 percent or more of such total, the amount of such excise taxes shall be shown on the face of the statement parenthetically or otherwise.

2. *Costs and Expenses Applicable to Sales and Revenues.* State separately the amount of (a) cost of tangible goods sold, (b) operating expenses of public utilities or others, (c) expenses applicable to rental income, (d) cost of services, and (e) expenses applicable to other revenues. Merchandising organizations, both wholesale and retail, may include occupancy and buying costs under caption 2(a). Amounts of costs and expenses incurred from transactions with related parties shall be disclosed as required under Rule 4–08(k).

3. *Other Operating Costs and Expenses.* State separately any material amounts not included under caption 2 above.

4. *Selling, General and Administrative Expenses.*

5. *Provision for Doubtful Accounts and Notes.*

6. *Other General Expenses.* Include items not normally included in caption 4 above. State separately any material item.

7. *Non-Operating Income.* State separately in the statement of comprehensive income or in a note thereto amounts earned from (a) dividends, (b) interest on securities, (c) profits on securities (net of losses), and (d) miscellaneous other income. Amounts earned from transactions in securities of related parties shall be disclosed as required under Rule 210.4–08(k). Material amounts included under miscellaneous other income shall be separately stated in the statement of comprehensive income or in a note thereto, indicating clearly the nature of the transactions out of which the items arose.

8. *Interest and Amortization of Debt Discount and Expense.*

9. *Non-Operating Expenses.* State separately in the statement of comprehensive income or in a note thereto amounts of (a) losses on securities (net of profits) and (b) miscellaneous income deductions. Material amounts included under miscellaneous income deductions shall be separately stated in the statement of comprehensive income or in a note thereto, indicating clearly the nature of the transactions out of which the items arose.

10. *Income or Loss Before Income Tax Expense and Appropriate Items Below.*

11. *Income Tax Expense.* Include under this caption only taxes based on income (see Rule 4–08(h)).

12. *Equity in Earnings of Unconsolidated Subsidiaries and 50 Percent or Less Owned Persons.* State, parenthetically or in a note, the amount of dividends received from such persons. If justified by the circumstances, this item may be presented in a different position and a different manner (see Rule 4–01(a)).

13. *Income or Loss from Continuing Operations.*

14. *Discontinued Operations.*

15. [Reserved]

16. [Reserved]

17. [Reserved]

18. *Net Income or Loss.*

19. *Net Income Attributable to the Noncontrolling Interest.*

20. *Net Income Attributable to the Controlling Interest.*

21. *Other Comprehensive Income.* State separately the components of and the total for other comprehensive income. Present the components either net of related tax effects or before related tax effects with one amount shown for the aggregate income tax expense or benefit. State the amount of income tax expense or benefit allocated to each component, including reclassification adjustments, in the statement of comprehensive income or in a note.

22. *Comprehensive Income.*

23. *Comprehensive Income Attributable to the Noncontrolling Interest.*

24. *Comprehensive Income Attributable to the Controlling Interest.*

25. *Earnings Per Share Data.*

Rule 5–04. What schedules are to be filed

(a) Except as expressly provided otherwise in the applicable form:

(1) The schedules specified below in this rule as Schedules II and III shall be filed as of the date of the most recent audited balanced sheet for each person or group.

(2) Schedule II of this section shall be filed for each period for which an audited statement of comprehensive income is required to be filed for each person or group.

(3) Schedules I and IV shall be filed as of the date and for periods specified in the schedule.

(b) When information is required in schedules for both the registrant and the registrant and its subsidiaries consolidated it may be presented in the form of a single schedule: Provided, That items pertaining to the registrant are separately shown and that such single schedule affords a properly summarized presentation of the facts. If the information required by any schedule (including the notes thereto) may be shown in the related financial statement or in a note thereto without making such statement unclear or confusing, that procedure may be followed and the schedule omitted.

(c) The schedules shall be examined by the independent accountant if the related financial statements are so examined.

Schedule I—Condensed Financial Information of Registrant. The schedule prescribed by Rule 210.12–04 shall be filed when the restricted net assets (Rule 210.1.02(dd)) of consolidated subsidiaries exceed 25 percent of consolidated net assets as of the end of the most recently completed fiscal year.

Schedule II—Valuation and Qualifying Accounts. The schedule prescribed by Rule 12–09 shall be filed in support of valuation and qualifying accounts included in each balance sheet but not included in Schedule VI. (See Rule 4–02.)

Schedule III—Real Estate and Accumulated Depreciation. The schedule prescribed by Rule 12–28 shall be filed for real estate (and the related accumulated depreciation) held by persons a substantial portion of whose business is that of acquiring and holding for investment real estate or interests in real estate, or interests in other persons a substantial portion of whose business is that of acquiring and holding real estate or interests in real estate for investment. Real estate used in the business shall be excluded from the schedule.

Schedule IV—Mortgage Loans on Real Estate. The schedule prescribed by Rule 12–29 shall be filed by persons specified under Schedule XI for investments in mortgage loans on real estate.

Schedule V—Supplemental Information Concerning Property-Casualty Insurance Operations. The schedule prescribed by Rule 12–18 shall be filed when a registrant, its subsidiaries or 50%-or-less-owned equity basis investees, have liabilities for property-casualty ("P/C") insurance claims. The required information shall be presented as of the same dates and for the same periods for which the information is reflected in the audited consolidated financial statements required by Rules 3–01 and 3–02. The schedule may be omitted if reserves for unpaid P/C claims and claims adjustment expenses of the registrant and its consolidated subsidiaries, its unconsolidated subsidiaries and its 50%-or-less-owned equity basis investees did not, in the aggregate, exceed one-half of common stockholders' equity of the registrant and its consolidated subsidiaries as of the beginning of the fiscal year. For purposes of this test only the proportionate share of the registrant and its other subsidiaries in the reserves for unpaid claims and claim adjustment expenses of 50%-or-less-owned equity basis investees taken in the aggregate after intercompany eliminations shall be taken into account.

REGISTERED INVESTMENT COMPANIES

Rule 6–01. Application of Rules 6–01 to 6–10

Rules 6–01 to 6–10 shall be applicable to financial statements filed for registered investment companies and business development companies.

Rule 6–02. Definition of certain terms

The following terms shall have the meaning indicated in this rule unless the context otherwise requires. (Also see Rule 1–02 of this part.)

(a) *Affiliate.* The term affiliate means an affiliated person as defined in section 2(a)(3) of the Investment Company Act of 1940 unless otherwise indicated. The term control has the meaning in section 2(a)(9) of that Act.

(b) *Value.* As used in Rules 6–01 to 6–10, the term value shall have the meaning given in section 2(a)(41)(B) of the Investment Company Act of 1940.

(c) *Balance Sheets; Statements of Net Assets.* As used in Rules 6–01 to 6–10, the term balance sheets shall include statements of assets and liabilities as well as statements of net assets unless the context clearly indicates the contrary.

(d) *Qualified Assets.* (1) For companies issuing face-amount certificates subsequent to December 31, 1940 under the provisions of section 28 of the Investment Company Act of 1940, the term qualified assets means qualified investments as that term is defined in section 28(b) of the Act. A statement to that effect shall be made in the balance sheet.

(2) For other companies, the term qualified assets means cash and investments which such companies do maintain or are required, by applicable governing legal instruments, to maintain in respect of outstanding face-amount certificates.

(3) Loans to certificate holders may be included as qualified assets in an amount not in excess of certificate reserves carried on the books of account in respect of each individual certificate upon which the loans were made.

Rule 6–03. Special rules of general application to registered investment companies and business development companies

The financial statements filed for persons to which Rules 6–01 to 6–10 are applicable shall be prepared in accordance with the following special rules in addition to the general rules in Rules 1–01 to 4–10 (Articles 1, 2, 3, and 4). Where the requirements of a special rule differ from those prescribed in a general rule, the requirements of the special rule shall be met.

(a) *Content of Financial Statements.* The financial statements shall be prepared in accordance with the requirements of this part (Regulation S–X) notwithstanding any provision of the articles of incorporation, trust indenture or other governing legal instruments specifying certain accounting procedures inconsistent with those required in Rules 6–01 to 6–10.

(b) *Audited Financial Statements.* Where, under Article 3 of this part, financial statements are required to be audited, the independent accountant shall have been selected and ratified in accordance with section 32 of the Investment Company Act of 1940.

(c) *Consolidated and Combined Statements.* (1) Consolidated and combined statements filed for registered investment companies and business development companies shall be prepared in accordance with Rule 3A–02 and Rule 3A–03 (Article 3A), except that:

(i) [Reserved]

(ii) A consolidated statement of the registrant and any of its investment company subsidiaries shall not be filed unless accompanied by a consolidating statement which sets forth the individual statements of each significant subsidiary included in the consolidated statement: Provided, however, That a consolidating statement need not be filed if all included subsidiaries are totally held; and

(iii) Consolidated or combined statements filed for subsidiaries not consolidated with the registrant shall not include any investment companies unless accompanied by consolidating or combining statements which set forth the individual statements of each included investment company which is a significant subsidiary.

(2) If consolidating or combining statements are filed, the amounts included under each caption in which financial data pertaining to affiliates is required to be furnished shall be subdivided to show separately the amounts:

(i) Eliminated in consolidation; and

(ii) Not eliminated in consolidation.

(d) *Valuation of Investments.* The balance sheets of registered investment companies, other than issuers of face-amount certificates, and business development companies, shall reflect all investments at value, with the aggregate cost of each category of investment reported under Rules 6–04.1, 6–04.2, 6–04.3 and 6–04.9 or the aggregate cost of each category of investment reported under Rule 6–05.1 shown parenthetically. State in a note the methods used in determining value of investments. As required by section 28(b) of the Investment Company Act of 1940 (15 U.S.C. 80a–28(b)), *qualified* assets of face-amount certificate companies shall be valued in accordance with certain provisions of the Code of the District of Columbia. For guidance as to valuation of securities, see §§ 404.03 to 404.05 of the Codification of Financial Reporting Policies.

(e) *Qualified Assets.* State in a note the nature of any investments and other assets maintained or required to be maintained, by applicable legal instruments, in respect of outstanding face-amount certificates. If the nature of the qualifying assets and amount thereof are not subject to the provisions of section 28 of the Investment Company Act of 1940, a statement to that effect shall be made.

(f) *Restricted Securities.* State in a note unless disclosed elsewhere the following information as to investment securities which cannot be offered for public sale without first being registered under the Securities Act of 1933 (restricted securities):

(1) The policy of the person with regard to acquisition of restricted securities.

(2) The policy of the person with regard to valuation of restricted securities. Specific comments shall be given as to the valuation of an investment in one or more issues of securities of a company or group of affiliated companies if any part of such investment is restricted and the aggregate value of the investment in all issues of such company or affiliated group exceeds five percent of the value of total assets. (As used in this paragraph, the term affiliated shall have the meaning given in Rule 6–02(a).)

(3) A description of the person's rights with regard to demanding registration of any restricted securities held at the date of the latest balance sheet.

(g) *Income Recognition.* Dividends shall be included in income on the ex-dividend date; interest shall be accrued on a daily basis. Dividends declared on short positions existing on the record date shall be recorded on the ex-dividend date and included as an expense of the period.

(h) *Federal Income Taxes.* (1) The company's status as a *regulated investment company* as defined in subtitle A, chapter 1, subchapter M of the Internal Revenue Code, as amended, shall be stated in a note referred to in the appropriate statements. Such note shall also indicate briefly the principal assumptions on which the company relied in making or not making provisions for income taxes. However, a company which retains realized capital gains and designates such gains as a distribution to shareholders in accordance with section 852(b)(3)(D) of the Internal Revenue Code shall, on the last day of its taxable year (and not earlier), make provision for taxes on such undistributed capital gains realized during such year.

(2) State the following amounts based on cost for Federal income tax purposes:

(i) Aggregate gross unrealized appreciation for all investments in which there is an excess of value over tax cost;

(ii) The aggregate gross unrealized depreciation for all investments in which there is an excess of tax cost over value;

(iii) The net unrealized appreciation or depreciation; and

(iv) The aggregate cost of investments for Federal income tax purposes.

NOTE TO PARAGRAPHS (h)(2)(i) AND (ii): The information required by paragraphs (h)(2)(i) and (ii) of this rule may be based on reasonable estimates if it is impracticable to determine the exact amounts involved.

(i) *Issuance and Repurchase by a Registered Investment Company of Its Own Securities.* Disclose for each class of the company's securities:

(1) The number of shares, units, or principal amount of bonds sold during the period of report, the amount received therefor, and, in the case of shares sold by closed-end management investment companies, the difference, if any, between the amount received and the net asset value or preference in involuntary liquidation (whichever is appropriate) of securities of the same class prior to such sale; and

(2) The number of shares, units, or principal amount of bonds repurchased during the period of report and the cost thereof. Closed-end management investment companies shall furnish the following additional information as to securities repurchased during the period of report:

(i) As to bonds and preferred shares, the aggregate difference between cost and the face amount or preference in involuntary liquidation and, if applicable net assets taken at value as of the date of repurchase were less than such face amount or preference, the aggregate difference between cost and such net asset value;

(ii) As to common shares, the weighted average discount per share, expressed as a percentage, between cost of repurchase and the net asset value applicable to such shares at the date of repurchases.

The information required by paragraphs (h)(i)(2) (i) and (ii) of this rule may be based on reasonable estimates if it is impracticable to determine the exact amounts involved.

(j) *Series Companies.* (1) The information required by this part shall, in the case of a person which in essence is comprised of more than one separate investment company, be given as if each class or series of such investment company were a separate investment company; this shall not prevent the inclusion, at the option of such person, of information applicable to other classes or series of such person on a comparative basis, except as to footnotes which need not be comparative.

(2) If the particular class or series for which information is provided may be affected by other classes or series of such investment company, such as by the offset of realized gains in one series with realized losses in another, or through contingent liabilities, such situation shall be disclosed.

(k) *Certificate Reserves.* (1) For companies issuing face-amount certificates subsequent to December 31, 1940 under the provisions of section 28 of the Investment Company Act of 1940, balance sheets shall reflect reserves for outstanding certificates computed in accordance with the provisions of section 28(a) of the Act.

(2) For other companies, balance sheets shall reflect reserves for outstanding certificates determined as follows:

(i) For certificates of the installment type, such amount which, together with the lesser of future payments by certificate holders as and when accumulated at a rate not to exceed 3 1/2 per centum per annum (or such other rate as may be appropriate under the circumstances of a particular case) compounded annually, shall provide the minimum maturity or face amount of the certificate when due.

(ii) For certificates of the fully-paid type, such amount which, as and when accumulated at a rate not to exceed 3 1/2 per centum per annum (or such other rate as may be appropriate under the circumstances of a particular case) compounded annually, shall provide the amount or amounts payable when due.

(iii) Such amount or accrual therefor, as shall have been credited to the account of any certificate holder in the form of any credit, or any dividend, or any interest in addition to the minimum maturity or face amount specified in the certificate, plus any accumulations on any amount so credited or accrued at rates required under the terms of the certificate.

(iv) An amount equal to all advance payments made by certificate holders, plus any accumulations thereon at rates required under the terms of the certificate.

(v) Amounts for other appropriate contingency reserves, for death and disability benefits or for reinstatement rights on any certificate providing for such benefits or rights.

(*l*) *Inapplicable Captions.* Attention is directed to the provisions of Rules 4–02 and 4–03 which permit the omission of separate captions in financial statements as to which the items and conditions are not present, or the amounts involved not significant. However, amounts involving directors, officers, and affiliates shall nevertheless be separately set forth except as otherwise specifically permitted under a particular caption.

Rule 6–04. Balance sheets

This rule is applicable to balance sheets filed by registered investment companies and business development companies except for persons who substitute a statement of net assets in accordance with the requirements specified in Rule 6–05, and issuers of face-amount certificates which are subject to the special provisions of Rule 6–06. Balance sheets filed under this rule shall comply with the following provisions:

ASSETS

1. *Investments in Securities of Unaffiliated Issuers.*

2. *Investments in and Advances to Affiliates.* State separately investments in and advances to: (a) Controlled companies and (b) other affiliates.

3. *Other Investments.* State separately amounts of assets related to (a) variation margin receivable on futures contracts, (b) forward foreign currency contracts; (c) swap contracts; and (d) investments—other than those presented in Rules 12–12, 12–12A, 12–12B, 12–13, 12–13A, 12–13B, and 12–13C.

4. *Cash.* Include under this caption cash on hand and demand deposits. Provide in a note to the financial statements the information required under Rule 5–02.1 regarding restrictions and compensating balances.

5. *Receivables.* (a) State separately amounts receivable from (1) sales of investments; (2) subscriptions to capital shares; (3) dividends and interest; (4) directors and officers; and (5) others.

(b) If the aggregate amount of notes receivable exceeds 10 percent of the aggregate amount of receivables, the above information shall be set forth separately, in the balance sheet or in a note thereto, for accounts receivable and notes receivable.

6. *Deposits for Securities Sold Short and Other Investments.* State separately amounts held by others in connection with: (a) Short sales; (b) open option contracts (c) futures contracts, (d) forward foreign currency contracts; (e) swap contracts; and (f) investments—other than those presented in Rules 12–12, 12–12A, 12–12B, 12–13, 12–13A, 12–13B, and 12–13C.

7. *Other Assets.* State separately (a) prepaid and deferred expenses; (b) pension and other special funds; (c) organization expenses; and (d) any other significant item not properly classified in another asset caption.

8. *Total Assets.*

LIABILITIES

9. *Other Investments.* State separately amounts of liabilities related to: (a) Securities sold short; (b) open option contracts written; (c) variation margin payable on futures contracts, (d) forward foreign currency contracts; (e) swap contracts; and (f) investments—other than those presented in Rules 12–12, 12–12A, 12–12B, 12–13, 12–13A, 12–13B, and 12–13C.

10. *Accounts Payable and Accrued Liabilities.* State separately amounts payable for: (a) Other purchases of securities; (b) capital shares redeemed; (c) dividends or other distributions on capital shares; and (d) others. State separately the amount of any other liabilities which are material.

11. *Deposits for Securities Loaned.* State the value of securities loaned and indicate the nature of the collateral received as security for the loan, including the amount of any cash received.

12. *Other Liabilities.* State separately (a) amounts payable for investment advisory, management and service fees; and (b) the total amount payable to: (1) Officers and directors; (2) controlled companies; and (3) other affiliates, excluding any amounts owing to noncontrolled affiliates which arose in the ordinary course of business and which are subject to usual trade terms.

13. *Notes Payable, Bonds and Similar Debt.* (a) State separately amounts payable to: (1) Banks or other financial institutions for borrowings; (2) controlled companies; (3) other affiliates; and (4) others, showing for each category amounts payable within one year and amounts payable after one year.

(b) Provide in a note the information required under Rule 5–02.19(b) regarding unused lines of credit for short-term financing and Rule 5–02.22(b) regarding unused commitments for long-term financing arrangements.

14. *Total Liabilities.*

15. *Commitments and Contingent Liabilities.*

NET ASSETS

16. *Units of Capital.*

(a) Disclose the title of each class of capital shares or other capital units, the number authorized, the number outstanding, and the dollar amount thereof.

(b) Unit investment trusts, including those which are issuers of periodic payment plan certificates, also shall state in a note to the financial statements: (1) The total cost to the investors of each class of units or shares; (2) the adjustment for market depreciation or appreciation; (3) other deductions from the total cost to the investors for fees, loads and other charges, including an explanation of such deductions; and (4) the net amount applicable to the investors.

17. *Total Distributable Earnings (Loss).* Disclose total distributable earnings (loss), which generally comprise:

(a) accumulated undistributed investment income-net,

(b) accumulated undistributed net realized gains (losses) on investment transactions, and

(c) net unrealized appreciation (depreciation) in value of investments at the balance sheet date.

18. *Other Elements of Capital.* Disclose any other elements of capital or residual interests appropriate to the capital structure of the reporting entity.

19. *Net Assets Applicable to Outstanding Units of Capital.* State the net asset value per share.

Rule 6–05. Statements of net assets

In lieu of the balance sheet otherwise required by Rule 6–04 of this part, persons may substitute a statement of net assets if at least 95 percent of the amount of the person's total assets are represented by investments in securities of unaffiliated issuers. If presented in such instances, a statement of net assets shall consist of the following:

STATEMENTS OF NET ASSETS

1. A schedule of investments in securities of unaffiliated issuers as prescribed in Rule 12–12.

2. The excess (or deficiency) of other assets over (under) total liabilities stated in one amount, except that any amounts due from or to officers, directors, controlled persons, or other affiliates, excluding any amounts owing to noncontrolled affiliates which arose in the ordinary course of business and which are subject to usual trade terms, shall be stated separately.

3. Disclosure shall be provided in the notes to the financial statements for any item required under Rules 6–04.10 to 6–04.13.

4. The balance of the amounts captioned as net assets. The number of outstanding shares and net asset value per share shall be shown parenthetically.

5. The information required by (i) Rule 6–04.16, (ii) Rule 6–04.17 and (iii) Rule 6–04.18 shall be furnished in a note to the financial statements.

Rule 6–06. Special provisions applicable to the balance sheets of issuers of face-amount certificates

Balance sheets filed by issuers of face-amount certificates shall comply with the following provisions:

ASSETS

1. *Investments.* State separately each major category: such as, real estate owned, first mortgage loans on real estate, other mortgage loans on real estate, investments in securities of unaffiliated issuers, and investments in and advances to affiliates.

2. *Cash.* Include under this caption cash on hand and demand deposits. Provide in a note to the financial statements the information required under Rule 5–02.1 regarding restrictions and compensating balances.

3. *Receivables.* (a) State separately amounts receivable from (1) sales of investments; (2) dividends and interest; (3) directors and officers; and (4) others.

(b) If the aggregate amount of notes receivable exceeds 10 percent of the aggregate amount of receivables, the above information shall be set forth separately, in the balance sheet or in a note thereto, for accounts receivable and notes receivable.

4. *Total Qualified Assets.* State in a note to the financial statements the amount of qualified assets on deposit classified as to general categories of assets and as to general types of depositories, such as banks and states, together with a statement as to the purpose of the deposits.

5. *Other Assets.* State separately: (a) Investments in securities of unaffiliated issuers not included in qualifying assets in Rule 1 above; (b) investments in and advances to affiliates not included in qualifying assets in Rule 1 above; and (c) any other significant item not properly classified in another asset caption.

6. *Total Assets.*

LIABILITIES

7. *Certificate Reserves.* Issuers of face-amount certificates shall state separately reserves for: (a) Certificates of the installment type; (b) certificates of the fully-paid type; (c) advance payments; (d) additional amounts accrued for or credited to the account of certificate holders in the form of any credit, dividend, or interest in addition to the minimum amount specified in the certificate; and (e) other certificate reserves. State in an appropriate manner the basis used in determining the reserves, including the rates of interest of accumulation.

8. *Notes Payable, Bonds and Similar Debt.* (a) State separately amounts payable to: (1) Banks or other financial institutions for borrowings; (2) controlled companies; (3) other affiliates; and (4) others, showing for each category amounts payable within one year and amounts payable after one year.

(b) Provide in a note the information required under Rule 5–02.19(b) regarding unused lines of credit for short-term financing and Rule 5–02.22(b) regarding unused commitments for long-term financing arrangements.

9. *Accounts Payable and Accrued Liabilities.* State separately (a) amounts payable for investment advisory, management and service fees; and (b) the total amount payable to: (1) Officers and directors; (2) controlled companies; and (3) other affiliates, excluding any amounts owing to noncontrolled affiliates which arose in the ordinary course of

business and which are subject to usual trade terms. State separately the amount of any other liabilities which are material.

10. *Total Liabilities.*

11. *Commitments and Contingent Liabilities.*

STOCKHOLDERS' EQUITY

12. *Capital Shares.* Disclose the title of each class of capital shares or other capital units, the number authorized, the number outstanding and the dollar amount thereof. Show also the dollar amount of any capital shares subscribed but unissued, and show the deduction for subscriptions receivable therefrom.

13. *Other Elements of Capital.* (a) Disclose any other elements of capital or residual interests appropriate to the capital structure of the reporting entity.

(b) A summary of each account under this caption setting forth the information prescribed in Rule 3–04 shall be given in a note or separate statement for each period in which a statement of operations is presented.

14. *Total Liabilities and Stockholders' Equity.*

Rule 6–07. Statements of operations.

Statements of operations, or statements of comprehensive income, where applicable, filed by registered investment companies, other than issuers of face-amount certificates, subject to the special provisions of Rule 6–08, and business development companies, shall comply with the following provisions:

STATEMENTS OF OPERATIONS

1. *Investment Income.* State separately income from: (a) Dividends; (b) interest on securities; and (c) other income. Any other category of income which exceeds five percent of the total shown under this caption (e.g. income from non-cash dividends, income from payment-in-kind interest) shall be stated separately. If income from investments in or indebtedness of affiliates is included hereunder, such income shall be segregated under an appropriate caption subdivided to show separately income from: (1) Controlled companies; and (2) other affiliates. If income from non-cash dividends or payment in kind interest are included in income, the bases of recognition and measurement used in respect to such amounts shall be disclosed.

2. *Expenses.* (a) State separately the total amount of investment advisory, management and service fees, and expenses in connection with research, selection, supervision, and custody of investments. Amounts of expenses incurred from transactions with affiliated persons shall be disclosed together with the identity of and related amount applicable to each such person accounting for five percent or more of the total expenses shown under this caption together with a description of the nature of the affiliation. Expenses incurred within the person's own organization in connection with research, selection and supervision of investments shall be stated separately. Reductions or reimbursements of management or service fees shall be shown as a negative amount or as a reduction of total expenses shown under this caption.

(b) State separately any other expense item the amount of which exceeds five percent of the total expenses shown under this caption.

(c) A note to the financial statements shall include information concerning management and service fees, the rate of fee, and the base and method of computation. State separately the amount and a description of any fee reductions or reimbursements representing: (1) Expense limitation agreements or commitments; and (2) offsets received from broker-dealers showing separately for each amount received or due from (i) unaffiliated persons; and (ii) affiliated persons. If no management or service fees were incurred for a period, state the reason therefor.

(d) If any expenses were paid otherwise than in cash, state the details in a note.

(e) State in a note to the financial statements the amount of brokerage commissions (including dealer markups) paid to affiliated broker-dealers in connection with purchase and sale of investment securities. Open-end management companies shall state in a note the net amounts of sales charges deducted from the proceeds of sale of capital shares which were retained by any affiliated principal underwriter or other affiliated broker-dealer.

(f) State separately all amounts paid in accordance with a plan adopted under Rule 12b–1 of the Investment Company Act of 1940 [17 CFR 270.12b–1]. Reimbursement to the fund of expenses incurred under such plan (12b–1 expense reimbursement) shall be shown as a negative amount and deducted from current 12b–1 expenses. If 12b–1 expense reimbursements exceed current 12b–1 costs, such excess shall be shown as a negative amount used in the calculation of total expenses under this caption.

(g) (1) *Brokerage/Service Arrangements.* If a broker-dealer or an affiliate of the broker-dealer has, in connection with directing the person's brokerage transactions to the broker-dealer, provided, agreed to provide, paid for, or agreed to pay for, in whole or in part, services provided to the person (other than brokerage and research services as those terms are used in section 28(e) of the Securities Exchange Act of 1934 [15 U.S.C. 78bb(e)]), include in the expense items set forth under this caption the amount that would have been incurred by the person for the services had it paid for the services directly in an arms-length transaction.

(2) *Expense Offset Arrangements.* If the person has entered into an agreement with any other person pursuant to which such other person reduces, or pays a third party which reduces, by a specified or reasonably ascertainable amount, its fees for services provided to the person in exchange for use of the person's assets, include in the expense items set forth under this caption the amount of fees that would have been incurred by the person if the person had not entered into the agreement.

(3) *Financial Statement Presentation.* Show the total amount by which expenses are increased pursuant to paragraphs (1) and (2) of this paragraph 2.(g) as a corresponding reduction in total expenses under this caption. In a note to the financial statements, state separately the total amounts by which expenses are increased pursuant to paragraphs (1) and (2) of this paragraph 2.(g), and list each category of expense that is increased by an amount equal to at least 5 percent of total expenses. If applicable, the note should state that the person could have employed the assets used by another person to produce income if it had not entered into an arrangement described in paragraph 2.(g)(2) of this rule.

3. *Interest and Amortization of Debt Discount and Expense.* Provide in the body of the statements or in the footnotes, the average dollar amount of borrowings and the average interest rate.

4. *Investment Income Before Income Tax Expense.*

5. *Income Tax Expense.* Include under this caption only taxes based on income.

6. *Investment Income-Net.*

7. *Realized and Unrealized Gain (Loss) on Investments-Net.* (a) State separately the net realized gain or loss from: (1) Transactions in investment securities of unaffiliated issuers, (2) transactions in investment securities of affiliated issuers, (3) expiration or closing of option contracts written, (4) closed short positions in securities, (5) expiration or closing of futures contracts, (6) settlement of forward foreign currency contracts, (7) expiration or closing of swap contracts, and (8) transactions in other investments held during the period.

(b) Distributions of realized gains by other investment companies shall be shown separately under this caption.

(c) State separately the amount of the net increase or decrease during the period in the unrealized appreciation or depreciation in the value of: (1) Investment securities of unaffiliated issuers, (2) investment securities of affiliated issuers, (3) option contracts written, (4) short positions in securities, (5) futures contracts, (6) forward foreign currency contracts, (7) swap contracts, and (8) other investments held at the end of the period.

(d) State separately any: (1) Federal income taxes and (2) other income taxes applicable to realized and unrealized gain (loss) on investments, distinguishing taxes payable currently from deferred income taxes.

8. *Net Gain (Loss) on Investments.*

9. *Net Increase (Decrease) in Net Assets Resulting from Operations.*

Rule 6–08. Special provisions applicable to the statements of operations of issuers of face-amount certificates

Statements of operations filed by issuers of face-amount certificates shall comply with the following provisions:

STATEMENTS OF OPERATIONS

1. *Investment Income.* State separately income from: (a) Interest on mortgages; (b) interest on securities; (c) dividends; (d) rental income; and (e) other investment income. If income from investments in or indebtedness of affiliates is included hereunder, such income shall be segregated under an appropriate caption subdivided to show separately income from: (1) Controlled companies; and (2) other affiliates. If non-cash dividends are included in income, the bases of recognition and measurement used in respect to such amounts shall be disclosed. Any other category of income which exceeds five percent of the total shown under this caption shall be stated separately.

2. *Investment Expenses.* (a) State separately the total amount of investment advisory, management and service fees, and expenses in connection with research, selection, supervision, and custody of investments. Amounts of expenses incurred from transactions with affiliated persons shall be disclosed together with the identity of and related amount applicable to each such person accounting for five percent or more of the total expenses shown under this caption together with a description of the nature of the affiliation. Expenses incurred within the person's own organization in connection with research, selection and supervision of investments shall be stated separately. Reductions or reimbursements of management or service fees shall be shown as a negative amount or as a reduction of total expenses shown under this caption.

(b) State separately any other expense item the amount of which exceeds five percent of the total expenses shown under this caption.

(c) A note to the financial statements shall include information concerning management and service fees, the rate of fee, and the base and method of computation. State separately the amount and a description of any fee reductions or reimbursements representing: (1) Expense limitation agreements or commitments; and (2) offsets received from broker-dealers showing separately for each amount received or due from: (i) Unaffiliated persons; and (ii) affiliated persons. If no management or service fees were incurred for a period, state the reason therefor.

(d) If any expenses were paid otherwise than in cash, state the details in a note.

(e) State in a note to the financial statements the amount of brokerage commissions (including dealer markups) paid to affiliated broker-dealers in connection with purchase and sale of investment securities.

3. *Interest and Amortization of Debt Discount and Expense.*

4. *Provision for Certificate Reserves.* State separately any provision for additional credits, or dividends, or interests, in addition to the minimum maturity or face amount specified in the certificates. State also in an appropriate manner reserve recoveries from surrenders or other causes.

5. *Investment Income Before Income Tax Expense.*

6. *Income Tax Expense.* Include under this caption only taxes based on income.

7. *Investment Income-Net.*

8. *Realized Gain (Loss) on Investments-Net.* (a) State separately the net realized gain or loss on transactions in: (1) Investment securities of unaffiliated issuers, (2) investment securities of affiliated issuers, and (3) other investments.

(b) Distributions of capital gains by other investment companies shall be shown separately under this caption.

(c) State separately any: (1) Federal income taxes and (2) other income taxes applicable to realized gain (loss) on investments, distinguishing taxes payable currently from deferred income taxes.

9. *Net Income or Loss.*

Rule 6–09. Statements of changes in net assets

Statements of changes in net assets filed for persons to whom this article is applicable shall comply with the following provisions:

STATEMENTS OF CHANGES IN NET ASSETS

1. *Operations.* State separately: (a) Investment income-net as shown by Rule 6–07.6; (b) realized gain (loss) on investments-net of any Federal or other income taxes applicable to such amounts; (c) increase (decrease) in unrealized appreciation or depreciation-net of any Federal or other income taxes applicable to such amounts; and (d) net increase (decrease) in net assets resulting from operations as shown by Rule 6–07.9.

2. *Net Equalization Charges and Credits.* State the net amount of accrued undivided earnings separately identified in the price of capital shares issued and repurchased.

3. *Distributions to Shareholders.* State total distributions to shareholders which generally come from: (a) investment income-net; (b) realized gain from investment transactions-net; and (c) other sources, except tax return of capital distributions, which shall be disclosed separately.

4. *Capital Share Transactions.* (a) State the increase or decrease in net assets derived from the net change in the number of outstanding shares or units.

(b) Disclose in the body of the statements or in the notes, for each class of the person's shares, the number and value of shares issued in reinvestment of dividends as well as the number and dollar amounts received for shares sold and paid for shares redeemed.

5. *Total Increase (Decrease).*

6. *Net Assets at the Beginning of the Period.*

7. *Net Assets at the End of the Period.*

Rule 6-10. What schedules are to be filed

(a) When information is required in schedules for both the person and its subsidiaries consolidated, it may be presented in the form of a single schedule, provided that items pertaining to the registrant are separately shown and that such single schedule affords a properly summarized presentation of the facts.

(b) The schedules shall be examined by an independent accountant if the related financial statements are so examined.

(c) *Management Investment Companies.* (1) Except as otherwise provided in the applicable form, the schedules specified in this paragraph shall be filed for management investment companies as of the dates of the most recent audited balance sheet and any subsequent unaudited statement being filed for each person or group.

Schedule I—Investments in Securities of Unaffiliated Issuers. The schedule prescribed by Rule 12-12 shall be filed in support of caption 1 of each balance sheet.

Schedule II—Investments in and Advances to Affiliates. The schedule prescribed by Rules 12-14 shall be filed in support of caption 2 of each balance sheet.

Schedule III—Investments—Securities Sold Short. The schedule prescribed by Rule 12-12A shall be filed in support of caption 9(a) of each balance sheet.

Schedule IV—Open Option Contracts Written. The schedule prescribed by Rule 12-13 shall be filed in support of caption 9(b) of each balance sheet.

Schedule V—Open Futures Contracts. The schedule prescribed by Rule 12-13A shall be filed in support of captions 3(a) and 9(c) of each balance sheet.

Schedule VI—Open Forward Foreign Currency Contracts. The schedule prescribed by Rule 12-13B shall be filed in support of captions 3(b) and 9(d) of each balance sheet.

Schedule VII—Open Swap Contracts. The schedule prescribed by Rule 12-13C shall be filed in support of captions 3(c) and 9(e) of each balance sheet.

Schedule VIII—Investments—Other Than Those Presented in Rules 12-12, 12-12A, 12-12B, 12-13, 12-13A, 12-13B and 12-13C. The schedule prescribed by Rule 12-13D shall be filed in support of captions 3(d) and 9(f) of each balance sheet.

(2) When permitted by the applicable form, the schedule specified in this paragraph may be filed for management investment companies as of the dates of the most recent audited balance sheet and any subsequent unaudited statement being filed for each person or group.

Schedule IX—Summary Schedule of Investments in Securities of Unaffiliated Issuers. The schedule prescribed by Rule 12-12B may be filed in support of caption 1 of each balance sheet.

(d) *Unit Investment Trusts.* Except as otherwise provided in the applicable form:

(1) Schedules I and II, specified below in this rule, shall be filed for unit investment trusts as of the dates of the most recent audited balance sheet and any subsequent unaudited statement being filed for each person or group.

(2) Schedule III, specified below in this rule, shall be filed for unit investment trusts for each period for which a statement of operations is required to be filed for each person or group.

Schedule I—Investment in Securities. The schedule prescribed by Rule 12-12 shall be filed in support of caption 1 of each balance sheet (Rule 6-04).

Schedule II—Allocation of Trust Assets to Series of Trust Shares. If the trust assets are specifically allocated to different series of trust shares, and if such allocation is not shown in the balance sheet in columnar form or by the filing of separate statements for each series of trust shares, a schedule shall be filed showing the amount of trust assets, indicated by each balance sheet filed, which is applicable to each series of trust shares.

Schedule III—Allocation of Trust Income and Distributable Funds to Series of Trust Shares. If the trust income and distributable funds are specifically allocated to different series of trust shares and if such allocation is not shown in the statement of operations in columnar form or by the filing of separate statements for each series of trust shares, a schedule shall be submitted showing the amount of income and distributable funds, indicated by each statement of operations filed, which is applicable to each series of trust shares.

(e) *Face-Amount Certificate Investment Companies.* Except as otherwise provided in the applicable form:

(1) Schedules I, V and X, specified below, shall be filed for face-amount certificate investment companies as of the dates of the most recent audited balance sheet and any subsequent unaudited statement being filed for each person or group.

(2) All other schedules specified below in this rule shall be filed for face-amount certificate investment companies for each period for which a statement of operations is filed, except as indicated for Schedules III and IV.

Schedule I—Investment in Securities of Unaffiliated Issuers. The schedule prescribed by Rule 12–21 shall be filed in support of caption 1 and, if applicable, caption 5(a) of each balance sheet. Separate schedules shall be furnished in support of each caption, if applicable.

Schedule II—Investments in and Advances to Affiliates and Income Thereon. The schedule prescribed by Rule 12–22 shall be filed in support of captions 1 and 5(b) of each balance sheet and caption 1 of each statement of operations. Separate schedules shall be furnished in support of each caption, if applicable.

Schedule III—Mortgage Loans on Real Estate and Interest Earned on Mortgages. The schedule prescribed by Rule 12–23 shall be filed in support of captions 1 and 5(c) of each balance sheet and caption 1 of each statement of operations, except that only the information required by column G and note 8 of the schedule need be furnished in support of statements of operations for years for which related balance sheets are not required.

Schedule IV—Real Estate Owned and Rental Income. The schedule prescribed by Rule 12–24 shall be filed in support of captions 1 and 5(a) of each balance sheet and caption 1 of each statement of operations for rental income included therein, except that only the information required by columns H, I and J, and item "Rent from properties sold during the period" and note 4 of the schedule need be furnished in support of statements of operations for years for which related balance sheets are not required.

Schedule V—Qualified Assets on Deposit. The schedule prescribed by Rule 12–27 shall be filed in support of the information required by caption 4 of Rule 6–06 as to total amount of qualified assets on deposit.

Schedule VI—Certificate Reserves. The schedule prescribed by Rule 12–26 shall be filed in support of caption 7 of each balance sheet.

Schedule VII—Valuation and Qualifying Accounts. The schedule prescribed by Rule 12–09 shall be filed in support of all other reserves included in the balance sheet.

EMPLOYEE STOCK PURCHASE, SAVINGS AND SIMILAR PLANS

Rules 6A–01. Application of Rules 6A–01 to 6A–05

(a) Rules 6A–01 to 6A–05 shall be applicable to financial statements filed for employee stock purchase, savings and similar plans.

(b) [Reserved]

Rule 6A–02. Special rules applicable to employee stock purchase, savings and similar plans

The financial statements filed for persons to which this article is applicable shall be prepared in accordance with the following special rules in addition to the general rules in Rules 1–01 to 4–10 of Regulation S–X. Where the requirements of a special rule differ from those prescribed in a general rule, the requirements of the special rule shall be met.

(a) *Investment Programs.* If the participating employees have an option as to the manner in which their deposits and contributions may be invested, a description of each investment program shall be given in a footnote or otherwise. The number of employees under each investment program shall be stated.

(b) *Net Asset Value Per Unit.* Where appropriate, the number of units and the net asset value per unit shall be given by footnote or otherwise.

(c) *Federal Income Taxes.* (1) If the plan is not subject to Federal income taxes, a note shall so state indicating briefly the principal assumptions on which the plan relied in not making provision for such taxes.

(2) State the Federal income tax status of the employee with respect to the plan.

(d) *Valuation of Assets.* The statement of financial condition shall reflect all investments at value, showing cost parenthetically. For purposes of this rule, the term value shall mean (1) market value for those securities having readily available market quotations and (2) fair value as determined in good faith by the trustee(s) for the plan (or by the person or persons who exercise similar responsibilities) with respect to other securities and assets.

Rule 6A–03. Statements of financial condition

Statements of financial condition filed under this rule shall comply with the following provisions:

PLAN ASSETS

1. *Investments in Securities of Participating Employers.* State separately each class of securities of the participating employer or employers.

2. *Investments in Securities of Unaffiliated Issuers.*

(a) United States Government bonds and other obligations. Include only direct obligations of the United States Government.

(b) Other securities. State separately (1) marketable securities and (2) other securities.

3. *Investments. Other than securities.* State separately each major class.

4. *Dividends and Interest Receivable.*

5. *Cash.*

6. *Other Assets.* State separately (a) total of amounts due from participating employers or any of their directors,

officers and principal holders of equity securities; (b) total of amounts due from trustees or managers of the plan; and (c) any other significant amounts.

LIABILITIES AND PLAN EQUITY

7. *Liabilities.* State separately (a) total of amounts payable to participating employers; (b) total of amounts payable to participating employees; and (c) any other significant amounts.

8. *Reserves and Other Credits.* State separately each significant item and describe each such item by using an appropriate caption or by a footnote referred to in the caption.

9. *Plan Equity at Close of Period.*

Rule 6A–04 Statements of comprehensive income and changes in plan equity

Statements of comprehensive income and changes in plan equity filed under this rule shall comply with the following provisions:

1. *Net Investment Income.* (a) Income. State separately income from (1) cash dividends; (2) interest, and (3) other sources. Income from investments in or indebtedness of participating employers shall be segregated under the appropriate subcaption.

(b) Expenses. State separately any significant amounts.

(c) Net investment income.

2. *Realized Gain or Loss on Investments.* (a) State separately the net of gains or losses arising from transactions in (1) investments in securities of the participating employer or employers; (2) other investments in securities; and (3) other investments.

(b) State in a footnote or otherwise for each category of investment in paragraph (a) above the aggregate cost, the aggregate proceeds and the net gain or loss. State the principle followed in determining the cost of securities sold, e.g., average cost or first-in, first-out.

3. *Unrealized Appreciation or Depreciation of Investments.* (a) State the amount of increase or decrease in unrealized appreciation or depreciation of investments during the period.

(b) State in a footnote or otherwise the amount of unrealized appreciation or depreciation of investments at the beginning of the period of report, at the end of the period of report, and the increase or decrease during the period.

4. *Contributions and Deposits.* (a) State separately (1) total of amounts deposited by participating employees, and (2) total of amounts contributed by the participating employer or employers.

(b) If employees of more than one employer participate in the plan, state in tabular form in a footnote or otherwise the amount contributed by each employer and the deposits of the employees of each such employer.

5. *Withdrawals, Lapses and Forfeitures.* State separately (a) balances of employees' accounts withdrawn, lapsed or forfeited during the period; (b) amounts disbursed in settlement of such accounts; and (c) disposition of balances remaining after settlement specified in (b).

6. *Plan Equity at Beginning of Period.*

7. *Plan Equity at End of Period.*

Rule 6A–05. What schedules are to be filed

(a) Schedule I of this section shall be filed as of the most recent audited statement of financial condition and any subsequent unaudited statement of financial condition being filed. Schedule II of this section shall be filed as of the date of each statement of financial condition being filed. Schedule III of this section shall be filed for each period for which a statement of comprehensive income and changes in plan equity is filed. All schedules shall be audited if the related statements are audited.

Schedule I—Investments. A schedule substantially in form prescribed by Rule 12–12 of Regulation S–X shall be filed in support of captions 1, 2 and 3 of each statement of financial condition unless substantially all of the information is given in the statement of financial condition by footnote or otherwise.

Schedule II—Allocation of Plan Assets and Liabilities to Investment Program. If the plan provides for separate investment programs with separate funds, and if the allocation of assets and liabilities to the several funds is not shown in the statement of financial condition in columnar form or by the submission of separate statements for each fund, a schedule shall be submitted showing the allocation of each caption of each statement of financial condition filed to the applicable fund.

Schedule III—Allocation of Plan Income and Changes in Plan Equity to Investment Programs. If the plan provides for separate investment programs with separate funds, and if the allocation of income and changes in plan equity to the several funds is not shown in the statement of comprehensive income and changes in plan equity in columnar form or by the submission of separate statements for each fund, a schedule shall be submitted showing the allocation of each caption of each statement of comprehensive income and changes in plan equity filed to the applicable fund.

(b) [Reserved]

INSURANCE COMPANIES

Rule 7–01. Application of Rules 7–01 to 7–05

This article shall be applicable to financial statements filed for insurance companies.

Rule 7–02. General requirement

(a) The requirements of the general rules in Rules 1–01 to 4–10 of Regulation S–X (Articles 1, 2, 3, 3A and 4) shall be applicable except where they differ from requirements of Rules 7–01 to 7–05 of Regulation S–X.

(b) Financial statements filed for mutual life insurance companies and wholly owned stock insurance company subsidiaries of mutual life insurance companies may be prepared in accordance with statutory accounting requirements. Financial statements prepared in accordance with statutory accounting requirements may be condensed as appropriate, but the amounts to be reported for net gain from operations (or net income or loss) and total capital and surplus (or surplus as regards policyholders) shall be the same as those reported on the corresponding Annual Statement.

Rule 7–03. Balance sheets

(a) The purpose of this rule is to indicate the various items which, if applicable, and except as otherwise permitted by the Commission, should appear on the face of the balance sheets and in the notes thereto filed for persons to whom this article pertains. (See Rule 4–01(a) of Regulation S–X.)

Assets

1. *Investments—Other than Investments in Related Parties.*

(a) *Fixed maturities.*

(b) *Equity securities.*

(c) *Mortgage loans on real estate.*

(d) *Investment real estate.*

(e) *Policy loans.*

(f) *Other long-term investments.*

(g) *Short-term investments.*

(h) *Total investments.*

Notes: (1) State parenthetically or otherwise in the balance sheet (a) the basis of determining the amounts shown in the balance sheet and (b) as to fixed maturities and equity securities either aggregate cost or aggregate value at the balance sheet date, whichever is the alternate amount of the carrying value in the balance sheet. Consideration shall be given to the discussion of "Valuation of Securities" in § 404.03 of the Codification of Financial Reporting Policies.

(2) Include under fixed maturities: bonds, notes, marketable certificates of deposit with maturities beyond one year, and redeemable preferred stocks. Include under equity securities: common stocks and nonredeemable preferred stocks.

(3) State separately in the balance sheet or in a note thereto the amount of accumulated depreciation and amortization deducted from investment real estate. Subcaption (d) shall not include real estate acquired in settling title claims, mortgage guaranty claims, and similar insurance claims. Real estate acquired in settling claims shall be included in caption 10, "Other Assets," or shown separately, if material.

(4) Include under subcaption (g) investments maturing within one year, such as commercial paper maturing within one year, marketable certificates of deposit maturing within one year, savings accounts, time deposits and other cash accounts and cash equivalents earning interest. State in a note any amounts subject to withdrawal or usage restrictions. (See Rule 5–02.1 of Regulation S–X.)

(5) State separately in a note the amount of any class of investments included in subcaption (f) if such amount exceeds ten percent of stockholders' equity.

(6) State in a note the name of any person in which the total amount invested in the person and its affiliates, included in the above subcaptions, exceeds ten percent of total stockholders' equity. For this disclosure, include in the amount invested in a person and its affiliates the aggregate of indebtedness and stocks issued by such person and its affiliates that is included in the several subcaptions above, and the amount of any real estate included in subcaption (d) that was purchased or acquired from such person and its affiliates. Indicate the amount included in each subcaption. An investment in bonds and notes of the United States Government or of a United States Government agency or authority which exceeds ten percent of total stockholders' equity need not be reported.

(7) State in a note the amount of investments included under each subcaption (a), (c), (d) and (f) which have been non-income producing for the twelve months preceding the balance sheet date.

2. *Cash.* Cash on hand or on deposit that is restricted as to withdrawal or usage shall be disclosed separately on the balance sheet. The provisions of any restrictions shall be described in a note to the financial statements. Restrictions may include legally restricted deposits held as compensating balances against short-term borrowing arrangements, contracts entered into with others, or company statements of intention with regard to particular deposits. In cases where compensating balance arrangements exist but are not agreements which legally restrict the use of cash amounts shown on the balance sheet, describe in the notes to the financial statements these arrangements and the amount involved, if determinable, for the most recent audited balance sheet required. Compensating balances that are maintained under an agreement to assure future credit availability shall be disclosed in the notes to the financial statements along with the amount and terms of the agreement.

3. *Securities and Indebtedness of Related Parties.* State separately (a) investments in related parties and (b) indebtedness from such related parties. (See Rule 4–08(k) of Regulation S–X.)

4. *Accrued Investment Income.*

5. *Accounts and Notes Receivable.* Include under this caption (a) amounts receivable from agents and insureds, (b) uncollected premiums and (c) other receivables. State separately in the balance sheet or in a note thereto any category of other receivable which is in excess of five percent of total assets. State separately in the balance sheet or in a note thereto the amount of allowance for doubtful accounts that was deducted.

6. *Reinsurance Recoverable.*

7. *Deferred Policy Acquisition Costs.*

8. *Property and Equipment.*

(a) State the basis of determining the amounts.

(b) State separately in the balance sheet or in a note thereto the amount of accumulated depreciation and amortization of property and equipment.

9. *Title Plant.*

10. *Other Assets.* State separately in the balance sheet or in a note thereto any other asset the amount of which exceeds five percent of total assets.

11. *Separate Account Assets.* Include under this caption the portion of separate account assets representing contract holder funds required to be reported in an insurance entity's financial statements as a summary total. An

equivalent summary total for the related liability shall be included under caption 18.

12. *Total Assets.*

LIABILITIES AND STOCKHOLDERS' EQUITY

13. *Policy Liabilities and Accruals.* (a) State separately in the balance sheet the amounts of (1) future policy benefits and losses, claims and loss expenses, (2) unearned premiums and (3) other policy claims and benefits payable.

(b) [Reserved]

14. *Other Policyholders' Funds.* (a) Include amounts of supplementary contracts without life contingencies, policyholders' dividend accumulations, undistributed earnings on participating business, dividends to policyholders and retrospective return premiums (not included elsewhere) and any similar items. State separately in the balance sheet or in a note thereto any item the amount of which is in excess of five percent of total liabilities.

(b) State in a note to the financial statements the relative significance of participating insurance expressed as percentages of (1) insurance in force and (2) premium income; and the method by which earnings and dividends allocable to such insurance is determined.

15. *Other Liabilities.* (a) Include under this caption such items as accrued payrolls, accrued interest and taxes. State separately in the balance sheet or in a note thereto any item included in other liabilities the amount of which exceeds five percent of total liabilities.

(b) State separately in the balance sheet or in a note thereto the amount of (1) income taxes payable and (2) deferred income taxes. Disclose separately the amount of deferred income taxes applicable to unrealized appreciation of equity securities.

16. *Notes Payable, Bonds, Mortgages and Similar Obligations, Including Capitalized Leases.* (a) State separately in the balance sheet the amounts of (1) short-term debt and (2) long-term debt including capitalized leases.

(b) The disclosure required by Rule 5–02.19(b) of Regulation S–X shall be given if the aggregate of short-term borrowings from banks, factors and other financial institutions and commercial paper issued exceeds five percent of total liabilities.

(c) The disclosure requirements of Rule 5–02.22 of Regulation S–X shall be followed for long-term debt.

17. *Indebtedness to Related Parties.* (See Rule 4–0.8(k) of Regulation S–X.)

18. *Liabilities Related to Separate Accounts.* [See caption 11.]

19. *Commitments and Contingent Liabilities.*

REDEEMABLE PREFERRED STOCKS

20. *Preferred Stocks Subject to Mandatory Redemption Requirements or Whose Redemption is Outside the Control of the Issuer.* The classification and disclosure requirements of Rule 5–02.27 of Regulation S–X shall be followed.

NONREDEEMABLE PREFERRED STOCKS

21. *Preferred Stocks Which Are Not Redeemable or Are Redeemable Solely at the Option of the Issuer.* The classification and disclosure requirements of Rule 5–02.28 of Regulation S–X shall be followed.

COMMON STOCKS

22. *Common Stocks.* The classification and disclosure requirements of Rule 5–02.29 of Regulation S–X shall be followed.

OTHER STOCKHOLDERS' EQUITY

23. *Other Stockholders' Equity.* (a) Separate captions shall be shown for (1) additional paid-in capital, (2) other additional capital, (3) accumulated other comprehensive income, (4) retained earnings (i) appropriated and (ii) unappropriated. (See Rule 4–08(e) of Regulation S–X.) Additional paid-in capital and other additional capital may be combined with the stock caption to which they apply, if appropriate.

(b) The classification and disclosure requirements of Rule 5–02.30(b) of Regulation S–X shall be followed for dating and effect of a quasi-reorganization.

(c) State in a note the following information separately for (1) life insurance legal entities, and (2) property and liability insurance legal entities: the amount of statutory stockholders' equity as of the date of each balance sheet presented and the amount of statutory net income or loss for each period for which a statement of comprehensive income is presented.

NONCONTROLLING INTERESTS

24. *Noncontrolling interests in consolidated subsidiaries.* The disclosure requirements of Rule 5–02.31 of Regulation S–X shall be followed.

25. *Total Liabilities and Equity.*

Rule 7–04. Statements of Comprehensive Income

The purpose of this section is to indicate the various items which, if applicable, should appear on the face of the statements of comprehensive income and in the notes thereto filed for persons to whom this article pertains. (See Rule 4–01(a).)

REVENUES

1. *Premiums.* Include premiums from reinsurance assumed and deduct premiums on reinsurance ceded. Where applicable, the amounts included in this caption should represent premiums earned.

2. *Net Investment Income.* State in a note to the financial statements, in tabular form, the amounts of (a) investment income from each category of investments listed in the subcaptions of Rule 7–03.1 of Regulation S–X that exceeds five percent of total investment income, (b) total investment income, (c) applicable expenses, and (d) net investment income.

3. *Realized Investment Gains and Losses.* Disclose the following amounts:

(a) Net realized investment gains and losses, which shall be shown separately regardless of size.

(b) Indicate in a footnote the registrant's policy with respect to whether investment income and realized gains and losses allocable to policyholders and separate accounts are included in the investment income and realized gain and loss amounts reported in the statement of comprehensive income. If the statement of comprehensive income includes investment income and realized gains and losses allocable to policyholders and separate accounts, indicate the amounts of such allocable investment income and realized gains and losses and the manner in which the insurance enterprise's obligation with respect to allocation of such investment income and realized gains and losses is otherwise accounted for in the financial statements.

(c) [Reserved]

(d) For each period for which a statement of comprehensive income is filed, include in a note an analysis of realized and unrealized investment gains and losses on fixed maturities and equity securities. For each period, state separately for fixed maturities [see Rule 7–03.1(a)] and for equity securities [see Rule 7–03.1(b)] the following amounts:

(1) Realized investment gains and losses, and

(2) The change during the period in the difference between value and cost.

The change in the difference between value and cost shall be given for both categories of investments even though they may be shown on the related balance sheet on a basis other than value.

4. *Other Income.* Include all revenues not included in captions 1 and 2 above. State separately in the statement any amounts in excess of five percent of total revenue, and disclose the nature of the transactions from which the items arose.

BENEFITS, LOSSES AND EXPENSES

5. *Benefits, Claims, Losses and Settlement Expenses.*

6. *Policyholders' Share of Earnings on Participating Policies, Dividends and Similar Items.* (See Rule 7–03.14(b) of Regulation S–X.)

7. *Underwriting, Acquisition and Insurance Expenses.* State separately in the statement of comprehensive income or in a note thereto (a) the amount included in this caption representing deferred policy acquisition costs amortized to income during the period, and (b) the amount of other operating expenses. State separately in the statement of comprehensive income any material amount included in all other operating expenses.

8. *Income or Loss Before Income Tax Expense and Appropriate Items Below.*

9. *Income Tax Expense.* Include under this caption only taxes based on income (See Rule 4–08(h).)

10. *Equity in Earnings of Unconsolidated Subsidiaries and 50% or Less Owned Persons.* State, parenthetically or in a note, the amount of dividends received from such persons. If justified by the circumstances, this item may be presented in a different position and a different manner. (See Rule 4–01(a) of Regulation S–X.)

11. *Income or Loss from Continuing Operations.*

12. *Discontinued Operations.*

13. [Reserved]

14. [Reserved]

15. [Reserved]

16. *Net Income or Loss.*

17. *Net Income Attributable to the Noncontrolling Interest.*

18. *Net Income Attributable to the Controlling Interest.*

19. *Other Comprehensive Income.* State separately the components of and the total for other comprehensive income. Present the components either net of related tax effects or before related tax effects with one amount shown for the aggregate income tax expense or benefit. State the amount of income tax expense or benefit allocated to each component, including reclassification adjustments, in the statement of comprehensive income or in a note.

20. *Comprehensive Income.*

21. *Comprehensive Income Attributable to the Noncontrolling Interest.*

22. *Comprehensive Income Attributable to the Controlling Interest.*

23. *Earnings Per Share Data.*

Rule 7–05. What schedules are to be filed

(a) Except as expressly provided otherwise in the applicable form:

(1) The schedule specified below in this section as Schedules I shall be as of the date of the most recent audited balance sheet for each person or group.

(2) The schedules specified in this section as Schedule IV and V shall be filed for each period for which an audited statement of comprehensive income is required to be filed for each person or group.

(3) Schedules II, III and V shall be filed as of the date and for periods specified in the schedule.

(b) When information is required in schedules for both the registrant and the registrant and its subsidiaries consolidated it may be presented in the form of a single schedule: Provided, That items pertaining to the registrant are shown separately and that such single schedule affords a properly summarized presentation of the facts. If the information required by any schedule (including the notes thereto) may be shown in the related financial statement or in a note thereto without making such statement unclear or confusing, that procedure may be followed and the schedule omitted.

(c) The schedules shall be examined by the independent accountant.

Schedule I—Summary of Investments—Other Than Investments in Related Parties. The schedule prescribed by Rule 12–15 of Regulation S–X shall be filed in support of caption 1 of the most recent audited balance sheet.

Schedule II—Condensed Financial Information of Registrant. The schedule prescribed by Rule 12–04 shall be filed when the restricted net assets (Rule 1.02(dd)) of consolidated subsidiaries exceed 25 percent of consolidated net assets as of the end of the most recently completed fiscal year.

Schedule III—Supplementary Insurance Information. The schedule prescribed by Rule 12–16 shall be filed giving segment detail in support of various balance sheet and statement of comprehensive income captions. The required balance sheet information shall be presented as of the date of each audited balance sheet filed, and the statement of comprehensive income information shall be presented for each period for which an audited statement of comprehensive income is required to be filed, for each person or group.

Schedule IV—Reinsurance. The schedule prescribed by Rule 12–17 of Regulation S–X shall be filed for reinsurance ceded and assumed.

Schedule V—Valuation and Qualifying Accounts. The schedule prescribed by Rule 12–09 of Regulation S–X shall be filed in support of valuation and qualifying accounts included in the balance sheet (see Rule 4–02 of Regulation S–X).

Schedule VI—Supplemental Information Concerning Property–Casualty Insurance Operations. The information required by Rule 12–18 of Regulation S–X shall be presented as of the same dates and for the same periods for which the information is reflected in the audited consolidated financial statements required by Rules 3–01 and 3–02 of Regulation S–X. The schedule may be omitted if reserves for unpaid property-casualty claims and claim adjustment expenses of the registrant and its consolidated subsidiaries, its unconsolidated subsidiaries and its 50%-or-less-owned equity basis investees did not in the aggregate, exceed one-half of common stockholders' equity of the registrant and its consolidated subsidiaries as of the beginning of the fiscal year. For purposes of this test, only the proportionate share of the registrant and its other subsidiaries in the reserves for unpaid claims and claim adjustment expenses of 50%-or-less-owned equity investees taken in the aggregate after intercompany eliminations shall be taken into account. Article 12—Form and Content of Schedules (17 CFR 210).

FINANCIAL STATEMENTS OF SMALLER REPORTING COMPANIES

Rule 8–01. Preliminary notes to Article 8

Rules 8–01 to 8–08 of Regulation S–X shall be applicable to financial statements filed for smaller reporting companies. These section are not applicable to financial statements prepared for the purposes of Item 17 or Item 18 of Form 20–F.

NOTE 1 TO Rule 8: Financial statements of a smaller reporting company, as defined by Item 10(f)(1) of Regulation S–K, its predecessors or any businesses to which the smaller reporting company is a successor shall be prepared in accordance with generally accepted accounting principles in the United States.

NOTE 2 TO Rule 8: Smaller reporting companies electing to prepare their financial statements with the form and content required in this article need not apply the other form and content requirements in Regulation S–X with the exception of the following:

a. The report and qualifications of the independent accountant shall comply with the requirements of Rule 2–01 through Rule 2–07 (Article 2 of this part); and

b. The description of accounting policies shall comply with Article 4–08(n); and

c. Smaller reporting companies engaged in oil and gas producing activities shall follow the financial accounting and reporting standards specified in Article 4–10 with respect to such activities.

To the extent that Article 11–01 (Pro Forma Presentation Requirements) offers enhanced guidelines for the preparation, presentation and disclosure of pro forma financial information, smaller reporting companies may wish to consider these items.

NOTE 3 TO Rule 8: Financial statements for a subsidiary of a smaller reporting company that issues securities guaranteed by the smaller reporting company or guarantees securities issued by the smaller reporting company must be presented as required by Rule 3–10 of Regulation S–X, except that the periods presented are those required by Rule 8–02 of Regulation S–X.

NOTE 4 TO Rule 8: Financial statements for a smaller reporting company's affiliates whose securities constitute a substantial portion of the collateral for any class of securities registered or being registered must be presented as required by Rule 3–16 of Regulation S–X, except that the periods presented are those required by Rule 8–02 of Regulation S–X.

NOTE 5 TO Rule 8: The Commission, where consistent with the protection of investors, may permit the omission of one or more of the financial statements or the substitution of appropriate statements of comparable character. The Commission by informal written notice may require the filing of other financial statements where necessary or appropriate.

Rule 8–02 Annual financial statements

Smaller reporting companies shall file an audited balance sheet as of the end of each of the most recent two fiscal years, or as of a date within 135 days if the issuer has existed for a period of less than one fiscal year, and audited statements of comprehensive income, cash flows and changes in stockholders' equity for each of the two fiscal years preceding the date of the most recent audited balance sheet (or such shorter period as the registrant has been in business).

Rule 8–03. Interim financial statements

Interim financial statements may be unaudited; however, before filing, interim financial statements included in quarterly reports on Form 10–Q (17 CFR 249.308(a)) must be reviewed by an independent public accountant using applicable professional standards and procedures for conducting such reviews, as may be modified or supplemented by the Commission. If, in any filing, the issuer states that interim financial statements have been reviewed by an independent public accountant, a report of the accountant on the review must be filed with the interim financial statements. Interim financial statements shall include a balance sheet as of the end of the issuer's most recent fiscal quarter, a balance sheet as of the end of the preceding fiscal year, and statements of comprehensive income and statements of cash flows for the interim period up to the date of such balance sheet and the comparable period of the preceding fiscal year.

(a) *Condensed Format.* Interim financial statements may be condensed as follows:

(1) Balance sheets should include separate captions for each balance sheet component presented in the annual financial statements that represents 10% or more of total assets. Cash and retained earnings should be presented regardless of relative significance to total assets. Registrants that present a classified balance sheet in their annual financial statements should present totals for current assets and current liabilities.

(2) Statements of comprehensive income (or the statement of net income if comprehensive income is presented in two separate but consecutive financial statements) should include net sales or gross revenue, each cost and expense category presented in the annual financial statements that exceeds 20% of sales or gross revenues, provision for income taxes, and discontinued operations. (Financial institutions should substitute net interest income for sales for purposes of determining items to be disclosed.)

(3) Cash flow statements should include cash flows from operating, investing and financing activities as well as cash at the beginning and end of each period and the increase or decrease in such balance.

(4) Additional line items may be presented to facilitate the usefulness of the interim financial statements, including their comparability with annual financial statements.

(5) Provide the information required by Rule 3–04 for the current and comparative year-to-date periods, with subtotals for each interim period.

(b) *Disclosure Required and Additional Instructions as to Content.*

(1) *Footnotes.* Footnote and other disclosures should be provided as needed for fair presentation and to ensure that the financial statements are not misleading.

(2) [Reserved]

(3) *Significant Equity Investees.* Sales, gross profit, net income (loss) from continuing operations, net income, and net income attributable to the investee must be disclosed for equity investees that constitute 20 percent or more of a registrant's consolidated assets, equity or income from continuing operations attributable to the registrant.

(4) *Significant Dispositions.* If a significant disposition has occurred during the most recent interim period and the transaction required the filing of a Form 8–K (17 CFR 249.308), pro forma data must be presented that reflects revenue, income from continuing operations, net income, net income attributable to the registrant and income per share for the current interim period and the corresponding interim period of the preceding fiscal year.

(5) *Material Accounting Changes.* The registrant's independent accountant must provide a letter in the first Form 10–Q (17 CFR 249.308a) filed after the change indicating whether or not the change is to a preferable method. Disclosure must be provided of any retroactive change to prior period financial statements, including the effect of any such change on income and income per share.

INSTRUCTION 1 TO Rule 8–03: Where Rule 8–01 through Rule 8–08 (Article 8 of this part) are applicable to a Form 10–Q (17 CFR 249.308a of this chapter) and the interim period is more than one quarter, statements of comprehensive income must also be provided for the most recent interim quarter and the comparable quarter of the preceding fiscal year.

INSTRUCTION 2 TO RULE 8–03: Interim financial statements must include all adjustments that, in the opinion of management, are necessary in order to make the financial statements not misleading. An affirmative statement that the financial statements have been so adjusted must be included with the interim financial statements.

Rule 8–04. Financial statements of businesses acquired or to be acquired

(a) If a business combination has occurred or is probable, financial statements of the business acquired or to be acquired shall be furnished for the periods specified in paragraph (c) of this rule:

(1) This encompasses the purchase of an interest in a business accounted for by the equity method.

(2) Acquisitions of a group of related businesses that are probable or that have occurred subsequent to the latest fiscal year end for which audited financial statements of the issuer have been filed shall be treated as if they are a single business combination for purposes of this rule. The required financial statements of related businesses may be presented on a combined basis for any periods they are under common control or management. A group of businesses is deemed to be related if:

(i) They are under common control or management;

(ii) The acquisition of one business is conditioned on the acquisition of each other business; or

(iii) Each acquisition is conditioned on a single common event.

(3) Annual financial statements required by this rule shall be audited. The form and content of the financial statements shall be in accordance with Rules 8–02 and 8–03 of Regulation S–X.

(b) The periods for which financial statements are to be presented are determined by comparison of the most recent annual financial statements of the business acquired or to be acquired and the smaller reporting company's most recent annual financial statements filed at or before the date of acquisition to evaluate each of the following conditions:

(1) Compare the smaller reporting company's investments in and advances to the acquiree to the total consolidated assets of the smaller reporting company as of the end of the most recently completed fiscal year.

(2) Compare the smaller reporting company's proportionate share of the total assets (after intercompany eliminations) of the acquiree to the total consolidated assets of the smaller reporting company as of the end of the most recently completed fiscal year.

(3) Compare the smaller reporting company's equity in the income from continuing operations before income taxes of the acquiree exclusive of amounts attributable to any noncontrolling interests to such consolidated income of the smaller reporting company for the most recently completed fiscal year.

COMPUTATIONAL NOTE TO RULE 8–04(b): For purposes of making the prescribed income test the following guidance should be applied: If income of the smaller reporting company and its subsidiaries consolidated exclusive of amounts attributable to any noncontrolling interests for the most recent fiscal year is at least 10 percent lower than the average of the income for the last five fiscal years, such average income should be substituted for purposes of the computation. Any loss years should be omitted for purposes of computing average income.

(c)(1) If none of the conditions specified in paragraph (b) of this rule exceeds 20%, financial statements are not required. If any of the conditions exceed 20%, but none exceeds 40%, financial statements shall be furnished for the most recent fiscal year and any interim periods specified in Rule 8–03 of Regulation S–X. If any of the conditions exceed 40%, financial statements shall be furnished for the two most recent fiscal years and any interim periods specified in Rule 8–03 of Regulation S–X.

(2) The separate audited balance sheet of the acquired business is not required when the smaller reporting company's most recent audited balance sheet filed is for a date after the acquisition was consummated.

(3) If the aggregate impact of individually insignificant businesses acquired since the date of the most recent audited balance sheet filed for the registrant exceeds 50%, financial statements covering at least the substantial majority of the businesses acquired shall be furnished. Such financial statements shall be for the most recent fiscal year and any interim periods specified in Rule 8–03 of Regulation S–X.

(4) Registration statements not subject to the provisions of Rule 419 (Regulation C) and proxy statements need not include separate financial statements of the acquired or to be acquired business if it does not meet or exceed any of the conditions specified in paragraph (b) of this rule at the 50 percent level, and either:

(i) The consummation of the acquisition has not yet occurred; or

(ii) The effective date of the registration statement, or mailing date in the case of a proxy statement, is no more than 74 days after consummation of the business combination, and the financial statements have not been filed previously by the registrant.

(5) An issuer that omits from its initial registration statement financial statements of a recently consummated business combination pursuant to paragraph (c)(4) of this rule shall furnish those financial statements and any pro forma information specified by Rule 8–05 of Regulation S–X under cover of Form 8–K (17 CFR 249.308) no later than 75 days after consummation of the acquisition.

(d) If the smaller reporting company made a significant business acquisition after the latest fiscal year end and filed a report on Form 8–K, which included audited financial statements of such acquired business for the periods required by paragraph (c) of this rule and the pro forma financial information required by Rule 8–05 of Regulation S–X, the determination of significance may be made by using pro forma amounts for the latest fiscal year in the report on Form 8–K rather than by using the historical amounts of the registrant. The tests may not be made by "annualizing" data.

(e) If the business acquired or to be acquired is a foreign business, financial statements of the business meeting the requirements of Item 17 of Form 20–F (17 CFR 249.220f) will satisfy this rule.

Rule 8–05. Pro forma financial information

(a) Pro forma information showing the effects of the acquisition shall be furnished if financial statements of a business acquired or to be acquired are presented.

(b) Pro forma statements should be condensed, in columnar form showing pro forma adjustments and results, and should include the following:

(1) If the transaction was consummated during the most recent fiscal year or subsequent interim period, pro forma statements of comprehensive income reflecting the combined operations of the entities for the latest fiscal year and interim period, if any; or

(2) If consummation of the transaction has occurred or is probable after the date of the most recent balance sheet required by Rule 8–02 or Rule 8–03, a pro forma balance sheet giving effect to the combination as of the date of the most recent balance sheet. For a purchase, pro forma statements of comprehensive income reflecting the combined operations of the entities for the latest fiscal year and interim period, if any, are required.

Rule 8–06. Real estate operations acquired or to be acquired

If, during the period for which statements of comprehensive income are required, the smaller reporting company has acquired one or more properties that in the aggregate are significant, or since the date of the latest balance sheet required by Rule 8–02 or Rule 8–03, has acquired or proposes to acquire one or more properties that in the aggregate are significant, the following shall be furnished with respect to such properties:

(a) Audited income statements (not including earnings per unit) for the two most recent years, which shall exclude items not comparable to the proposed future operations of the property such as mortgage interest, leasehold rental, depreciation, corporate expenses and federal and state income taxes; *Provided, however*, that such audited statements need be presented for only the most recent fiscal year if:

(1) The property is not acquired from a related party;

(2) Material factors considered by the smaller reporting company in assessing the property are described with specificity in the registration statement with regard to the property, including source of revenue (including, but not limited to, competition in the rental market, comparative rents, occupancy rates) and expenses (including but not limited to, utilities, *ad valorem* tax rates, maintenance expenses, and capital improvements anticipated); and

(3) The smaller reporting company indicates that, after reasonable inquiry, it is not aware of any material factors relating to the specific property other than those discussed in response to paragraph (a)(2) of this rule that would cause the reported financial information not to be necessarily indicative of future operating results.

(b) If the property will be operated by the smaller reporting company, a statement shall be furnished showing the estimated taxable operating results of the smaller reporting company based on the most recent twelve-month period, including such adjustments as can be factually supported. If the property will be acquired subject to a net lease, the estimated taxable operating results shall be based on the rent to be paid for the first year of the lease. In either case, the estimated amount of cash to be made available by operations shall be shown. Disclosure must be provided of the principal assumptions that have been made in preparing the statements of estimated taxable operating results and cash to be made available by operations.

(c) If appropriate under the circumstances, a table should be provided that shows, for a limited number of years, the estimated cash distribution per unit, indicating the portion reportable as taxable income and the portion representing a return of capital with an explanation of annual variations, if any. If taxable net income per unit will be greater than the cash available for distribution per unit, that fact and the approximate year of occurrence shall be stated, if significant.

Rule 8–07. Limited partnerships

(a) Smaller reporting companies that are limited partnerships must provide the balance sheets of the general partners as described in paragraphs (b) through (d) of this rule.

(b) Where a general partner is a corporation, the audited balance sheet of the corporation as of the end of its most recently completed fiscal year must be filed. Receivables, other than trade receivables, from affiliates of the general partner should be deducted from shareholders' equity of the general partner. Where an affiliate has committed itself to increase or maintain the general partner's capital, the audited balance sheet of such affiliate must also be presented.

(c) Where a general partner is a partnership, there shall be filed an audited balance sheet of such partnership as of the end of its most recently completed fiscal year.

(d) Where the general partner is a natural person, there shall be filed, as supplemental information, a balance sheet of such natural person as of a recent date. Such balance sheet need not be audited. The assets and liabilities should be carried at estimated fair market value, with provisions for estimated income taxes on unrealized gains. The net worth of such general partner(s), based on such balance sheet(s), singly or in the aggregate, shall be disclosed in the registration statement.

Rule 8–08. Age of financial statements

At the date of filing, financial statements included in filings other than filings on Form 10–K must be not less current than the financial statements that would be required in Forms 10–K and 10–Q if such reports were required to be filed. If required financial statements are as of a date 135 days or more before the date a registration statement becomes effective or proxy material is expected to be mailed, the financial statements shall be updated to include financial statements for an interim period ending within 135 days of the effective or expected mailing date. Interim financial statements must be prepared and presented in accordance with paragraph (b) of this rule.

(a) When the anticipated effective or mailing date falls within 45 days after the end of the fiscal year, the filing may include financial statements only as current as of the end of the third fiscal quarter; *Provided, however*, that if the audited financial statements for the recently completed fiscal year are available or become available before effectiveness or mailing, they must be included in the filing; and

(b) If the effective date or anticipated mailing date falls after 45 days but within 90 days of the end of the smaller reporting company's fiscal year, the smaller reporting company is not required to provide the audited financial statements for such year end provided that the following conditions are met:

(1) If the smaller reporting company is a reporting company, all reports due must have been filed;

(2) For the most recent fiscal year for which audited financial statements are not yet available, the smaller reporting company reasonably and in good faith expects to report income from continuing operations attributable to the registrant before taxes; and

(3) For at least one of the two fiscal years immediately preceding the most recent fiscal year the smaller reporting company reported income from continuing operations attributable to the registrant before taxes.

BANK HOLDING COMPANIES

Rule 9–01. Application of Rules 9–01 to 9–07

This article is applicable to consolidated financial statements filed for bank holding companies and to any financial statements of banks that are included in filings with the Commission.

Rule 9–02. General requirement

The requirements of the general rules in Rules 1 to 4 of Regulation S–X (Articles 1, 2, 3, 3A and 4) should be complied with where applicable.

Rule 9–03. Balance sheets

The purpose of this rule is to indicate the various items which, if applicable, should appear on the face of the balance sheets or in the notes thereto.

Assets

1. *Cash and Due from Banks*. The amounts in this caption should include all noninterest bearing deposits with other banks.

(a) Any withdrawal and usage restrictions (including requirements of the Federal Reserve to maintain certain average reserve balances) or compensating balance requirements should be disclosed (see Rule 5–02–1 of Regulation S–X).

2. *Interest-Bearing Deposits in Other Banks*.

3. *Federal Funds Sold and Securities Purchased Under Resale Agreements or Similar Arrangements*.

4. *Trading Account Assets*. Include securities or any other investments held for trading purposes only.

5. *Other Short-Term Investments*.

6. *Investment Securities Include Securities Held for Investment Only*. Disclose the aggregate book value of investment securities; show on the balance sheet the aggregate market value at the balance sheet date. The aggregate amounts should include securities pledged, loaned or sold

under repurchase agreements and similar arrangements; borrowed securities and securities purchased under resale agreements or similar arrangements should be excluded.

7. *Loans.* Disclose separately (1) total loans, (2) the related allowance for losses and (3) unearned income.

(a) Disclose on the balance sheet or in a note the amount of total loans in each of the following categories:

(1) Commercial, financial and agricultural

(2) Real estate—construction

(3) Real estate—mortgage

(4) Installment loans to individuals

(5) Lease financing

(6) Foreign

(7) Other (State separately any other loan category regardless of relative size if necessary to reflect any unusual risk concentration).

(b) A series of categories other than those specified in (a) above may be used to present details of loans if considered a more appropriate presentation.

(c) The amount of foreign loans must be presented if the disclosures provided by Rule 9–05 of Regulation S–X are required.

(d) [Reserved]

(e)(1)(i) As of each balance sheet date, disclose in a note the aggregate dollar amount of loans (exclusive of loans to any such persons which in the aggregate do not exceed $60,000 during the latest year) made by the registrant or any of its subsidiaries to directors, executive officers, or principal holders of equity securities (Rule 1–02 of Regulation S–X) of the registrant or any of its significant subsidiaries (Rule 1–02 of Regulation S–X), or to any associate of such persons. For the latest fiscal year, an analysis of activity with respect to such aggregate loans to related parties should be provided. The analysis should include the aggregate amount at the beginning of the period, new loans, repayments, and other changes. (Other changes, if significant, should be explained.)

(ii) This disclosure need not be furnished when the aggregate amount of such loans at the balance sheet date (or with respect to the latest fiscal year, the maximum amount outstanding during the period) does not exceed 5 percent of stockholders equity at the balance sheet date.

(2) If a significant portion of the aggregate amount of loans outstanding at the end of the fiscal year disclosed pursuant to (e)(1)(i) above relates to loans which are disclosed as nonaccrual, past due, restructured or potential problems (see Item III.C. 1. or 2. of Industry Guide 3, Statistical Disclosure by Bank Holding Companies), so state and disclose the aggregate amounts of such loans along with such other information necessary to an understanding of the effects of the transactions on the financial statements.

(3) Notwithstanding the aggregate disclosure called for by paragraph (e)(1) of this section, if any loans were not made in the ordinary course of business during any period for which a statement of comprehensive income is required to be filed, provide an appropriate description of each such loan.

(4) Definition of terms. For purposes of this rule, the following definitions shall apply:

Associate means (i) a corporation, venture or organization of which such person is a general partner or is, directly or indirectly, the beneficial owner of 10 percent or more of any class of equity securities; (ii) any trust or other estate in which such person has a substantial beneficial interest or for which such person serves as trustee or in a similar capacity and (iii) any member of the immediate family of any of the foregoing persons.

Executive officers means the president, any vice president in charge of a principal business unit, division or function (such as loans, investments, operations, administration or finance), and any other officer or person who performs similar policymaking functions.

Immediate Family means such person's spouse; parents; children; siblings; mothers and fathers-in-law; sons and daughters-in-law; and brothers and sisters-in-law.

Ordinary course of business means those loans which were made on substantially the same terms, including interest rate and collateral, as those prevailing at the same time for comparable transactions with unrelated persons and did not involve more than the normal risk of collectibility or present other unfavorable features.

8. *Premises and Equipment.*

9. *Due from Customers on Acceptances.* Include amounts receivable from customers on unmatured drafts and bills of exchange that have been accepted by a bank subsidiary or by other banks for the account of a subsidiary and that are outstanding—that is, not held by a subsidiary bank, on the reporting date. (If held by a bank subsidiary, they should be reported as "loans" under Rule 9–03.7 of Regulation S–X.)

10. *Other Assets.* Disclose separately on the balance sheet or in a note thereto any of the following assets or any other asset the amount of which exceeds thirty percent of stockholders equity. The remaining assets may be shown as one amount.

(1) Goodwill.

(2) Other intangible assets (net of amortization).

(3) Investments in and indebtedness of affiliates and other persons.

(4) Other real estate.

(a) Disclose in a note the basis at which other real estate is carried. A reduction to fair market value from the carrying value of the related loan at the time of acquisition shall be accounted for as a loan loss. Any allowance for losses on other real estate which has been established subsequent to acquisition should be deducted from other real estate. For each period for which a statement of comprehensive income is required, disclosures should be made in a note as to the changes in the allowances, including balance at beginning and end of period, provision charged to income, and losses charged to the allowance.

11. Total Assets.

Liabilities and Stockholders' Equity

Liabilities.

12. *Deposits.* Disclose separately the amounts of noninterest bearing deposits and interest bearing deposits.

(a) The amount of noninterest bearing deposits and interest bearing deposits in foreign banking offices must be presented if the disclosure provided by Rule 9–05 is required.

13. *Short-Term Borrowing.* Disclosure separately on the balance sheet or in a note, amounts payable for (1) Federal

funds purchased and securities sold under agreements to repurchase; (2) commercial paper, and (3) other short-term borrowings.

(a) Disclose any unused lines of credit for short-term financing: (Rule 5–02.19(b) of Regulation S–X).

14. *Bank Acceptances Outstanding.* Disclose the aggregate of unmatured drafts and bills of exchange accepted by a bank subsidiary, or by some other bank as its agent, less the amount of such acceptances acquired by the bank subsidiary through discount or purchase.

15. *Other Liabilities.* Disclose separately on the balance sheet or in a note any of the following liabilities or any other items which are individually in excess of thirty percent of stockholders' equity (except that amounts in excess of 5 percent of stockholders' equity should be disclosed with respect to item (4)). The remaining items may be shown as one amount.

(1) Income taxes payable.

(2) Deferred income taxes.

(3) Indebtedness to affiliates and other persons the investments in which are accounted for by the equity method.

(4) Indebtedness to directors, executive officers, and principal holders of equity securities of the registrant or any of its significant subsidiaries (the guidance in Rule 9–03.7(e) of Regulation S–X shall be used to identify related parties for purposes of this disclosure).

(5) Accounts payable and accrued expenses.

16. *Long-Term Debt.* Disclose in a note the information required by Rule 5–02.22 of Regulation S–X.

17. *Commitments and Contingent Liabilities.*

Redeemable Preferred Stocks

18. Preferred stocks subject to mandatory redemption requirements or whose redemption is outside the control of the issuer. See Rule 5–02.27 of Regulation S–X.

Non-Redeemable Preferred Stocks

19. Preferred stocks which are not redeemable or are redeemable solely at the option of the issuer. See Rule 5–02.28 of Regulation S–X.

Common Stocks

20. Common stocks. See Rule 5–02.29 of Regulation S–X.

Other Stockholders' Equity

21. Other stockholders' equity. See Rule 5–02.30 of Regulation S–X.

Noncontrolling Interests

22. Noncontrolling interests in consolidated subsidiaries. The disclosure requirements of Rule 5–02.31 of Regulation S–X shall be followed.

23. Total liabilities and equity.

Rule 9–04. Statements of comprehensive income

The purpose of this section is to indicate the various items which, if applicable, should appear on the face of the statement of comprehensive income or in the notes thereto.

1. *Interest and Fees on Loans.* Include commitment and origination fees, late charges and current amortization of premium and accretion of discount on loans which are related to or are an adjustment of the loan interest rate.

2. *Interest and Dividends on Investment Securities.* Disclosure separately (1) taxable interest income, (2) nontaxable interest income, and (3) dividends.

3. *Trading Account Interest.*

4. *Other Interest Income.*

5. *Total Interest Income (total of lines 1 through 4).*

6. *Interest on Deposits.*

7. *Interest on Short-Term Borrowings.*

8. *Interest on Long-Term Debt.*

9. *Total Interest Expense (total of lines 6 through 8).*

10. *Net Interest Income (line 5 minus line 9).*

11. *Provision for Loan Losses.*

12. *Net Interest Income After Provision for Loan Losses.*

13. *Other Income.* Disclose separately any of the following amounts, or any other item of other income, which exceed one percent of the aggregate of total interest income and other income. The remaining amounts may be shown as one amount, except for investment securities gains or losses which shall be shown separately regardless of size.

(a) Commissions and fees and fiduciary activities.

(b) Commissions, broker's fees and markups on securities underwriting and other securities activities.

(c) Insurance commissions, fees and premiums.

(d) Fees for other customer services.

(e) Profit or loss on transactions in securities in dealer trading account.

(f) Equity in earnings of unconsolidated subsidiaries and 50 percent or less owned persons.

(g) Gains or losses on disposition of equity in securities of subsidiaries or 50 percent or less owned persons.

(h) Investment securities gains or losses. Related income taxes shall be disclosed.

14. *Other Expenses.* Disclose separately any of the following amounts, or any other item of other expense, which exceed one percent of the aggregate of total interest income and other income. The remaining amounts may be shown as one amount.

(a) Salaries and employee benefits.

(b) Net occupancy expense of premises.

(c) [Reserved]

(d) Net cost of operation of other real estate (including provisions for real estate losses, rental income and gains and losses on sales of real estate).

15. *Income or Loss Before Income Tax Expense.*

16. *Income Tax Expense.* The information required by Rule 4–08(h) of Regulation S–X should be disclosed.

17. [Reserved]

18. [Reserved]

19. [Reserved]

20. *Net Income or Loss.*

21. *Net Income Attributable to the Noncontrolling Interest.*

22. *Net Income Attributable to the Controlling Interest.*

23. *Other Comprehensive Income.* State separately the components of and the total for other comprehensive income. Present the components either net of related tax effects or before related tax effects with one amount shown for the aggregate income tax expense or benefit. State the amount of income tax expense or benefit allocated to each component, including reclassification adjustments, in the statement of comprehensive income or in a note.

24. *Comprehensive Income.*

25. *Comprehensive Income Attributable to the Noncontrolling Interest.*

26. *Comprehensive Income Attributable to the Controlling Interest.*

27. *Earnings per Share Data.*

Rule 9–05. Foreign activities

(a) *General Requirement.* Separate disclosure concerning foreign activities shall be made for each period in which either (1) assets, or (2) revenue, or (3) income (loss) before income tax expense, or (4) net income (loss), each as associated with foreign activities, exceeded ten percent of the corresponding amount in the related financial statements.

(b) *Disclosures.* (1) Disclose total identifiable assets (net of valuation allowances) associated with foreign activities.

(2) For each period for which a statement of comprehensive income is filed, state the amount of revenue, income (loss) before taxes, and net income (loss) associated with foreign activities. Disclose significant estimates and assumptions (including those related to the cost of capital) used in allocating revenue and expenses to foreign activities; describe the nature and effects of any changes in such estimates and assumptions which have a significant impact on interperiod comparability.

(3) The information in paragraph (b)(1) and (2) of this rule shall be presented separately for each significant geographic area and in the aggregate for all other geographic areas not deemed significant.

(c) *Definitions.* (1) *Foreign activities* include loans and other revenues producing assets and transactions in which the debtor or customer, whether an affiliated or unaffiliated person, is domiciled outside the United States.

(2) The term *revenue* includes the total of the amount reported at Rules 9–04.5 and 9–04.13 of Regulation S–X.

(3) A *significant geographic area* is one in which assets or revenue or income before income tax or net income exceed 10 percent of the comparable amount as reported in the financial statements.

Rule 9–06. Condensed financial information of registrant

The information prescribed by Rule 12–04 shall be presented in a note to the financial statements when the restricted net assets (Rule 1–02(dd)) of consolidated subsidiaries exceed 25 percent of consolidated net assets as of the end of the most recently completed fiscal year. The investment in and indebtedness of and to bank subsidiaries shall be stated separately in the condensed balance sheet from amounts for other subsidiaries; the amount of cash dividends paid to the registrant for each of the last three years by bank subsidiaries shall be stated separately in the condensed statement of comprehensive income from amounts for other subsidiaries.

Rule 9–07. [Reserved]

INTERIM FINANCIAL STATEMENTS

Rule 10–01. Interim financial statements

(a) *Condensed Statements.* Interim financial statements shall follow the general form and content of presentation prescribed by the other sections of this Regulation with the following exceptions:

(1) Interim financial statements required by this rule need only be provided as to the registrant and its subsidiaries consolidated and may be unaudited. Separate statements of other entities which may otherwise be required by this Regulation may be omitted.

(2) Interim balance sheets shall include only major captions (i.e., numbered captions) prescribed by the applicable sections of this Regulation with the exception of inventories. Data as to raw materials, work in process and finished goods inventories shall be included either on the face of the balance sheet or in the notes to the financial statements, if applicable. Where any major balance sheet caption is less than 10% of total assets, and the amount in the caption has not increased or decreased by more than 25% since the end of the preceding fiscal year, the caption may be combined with others.

(3) Interim statements of comprehensive income shall also include major captions prescribed by the applicable sections of 17 CFR 210 (Regulation S–X). When any major statement of comprehensive

income (or statement of net income if comprehensive income is presented in two separate but consecutive financial statements) caption is less than 15% of average net income for the most recent three fiscal years and the amount in the caption has not increased or decreased by more than 20% as compared to the corresponding interim period of the preceding fiscal year, the caption may be combined with others. In calculating average net income, loss years should be excluded. If losses were incurred in each of the most recent three years, the average loss shall be used for purposes of this test. Notwithstanding these tests, Rule 4–02 applies and de minimis amounts therefore need not be shown separately, except that registrants reporting under Rule 9 shall show investment securities gains or losses separately regardless of size.

(4) The statement of cash flows may be abbreviated starting with a single figure of net cash flows from operating activities and showing cash changes from investing and financing activities individually only when they exceed 10% of the average of net cash flows from operating activities for the most recent three years. Notwithstanding this test, Rule 4–02 of Regulation S–X applies and de minimis amounts therefore need not be shown separately.

(5) The interim financial information shall include disclosures either on the face of the financial statements or in accompanying footnotes sufficient so as to make the interim information presented not misleading. Registrants may presume that users of the interim financial information have read or have access to the audited financial statements for the preceding fiscal year and that the adequacy of additional disclosure needed for a fair presentation may be determined in that context. Accordingly, footnote disclosure which would substantially duplicate the disclosure contained in the most recent annual report to security holders or latest audited financial statements, such as a statement of significant accounting policies and practices, details of accounts which have not changed significantly in amount or composition since the end of the most recently completed fiscal year, and detailed disclosures prescribed by Rule 4–08 may be omitted.

(6) Detailed schedules otherwise required by this Regulation may be omitted for purposes of preparing interim financial statements.

(7) Provide the information required by Rule 3–04 for the current and comparative year-to-date periods, with subtotals for each interim period.

(b) *Other Instructions as to Content.* The following additional instructions shall be applicable for purposes of preparing interim financial statements:

(1) Summarized statement of comprehensive income information shall be given separately as to each subsidiary not consolidated or 50 percent or less owned persons or as to each group of such subsidiaries or fifty percent or less owned persons for which separate individual or group statements would otherwise be required for annual periods. Such summarized information, however, need not be furnished for any such unconsolidated subsidiary or person which would not be required pursuant to Rule 13a–13 or Rule 15d–13 under the Securities Exchange Act of 1934 to file quarterly financial information with the Commission if it were a registrant.

(2) The basis of the earnings per share computation shall be stated together with the number of shares used in the computation.

(3) If, during the most recent interim period presented, the registrant or any of its consolidated subsidiaries entered into a combination between entities under common control, supplemental disclosure of the separate results of the combined entities for periods prior to the combination shall be given, with appropriate explanations.

(4) [Reserved]

(5) [Reserved]

(6) For filings on Form 10–Q (17 CFR 249.308(a)), a letter from the registrant's independent accountant shall be filed as an exhibit (in accordance with the provisions of Item 601 of Regulation S–K) in the first Form 10–Q after the date of an accounting change indicating whether or not the change is to an alternative principle which, in the accountant's judgment, is preferable under the circumstances; except that no letter from the accountant need be filed when the change is made in response to a standard adopted by the Financial Accounting Standards Board that requires such change.

(7) Any material retroactive prior period adjustment made during any period covered by the interim financial statements shall be disclosed, together with the effect thereof upon net income—total and per share—of any prior period included and upon the balance of retained earnings. If results of operations for any period presented have been adjusted retroactively by such an item subsequent

to the initial reporting of such period, similar disclosure of the effect of the change shall be made.

(8) Any unaudited interim financial statements furnished shall reflect all adjustments which are, in the opinion of management, necessary to a fair statement of the results for the interim periods presented. A statement to that effect shall be included. If all such adjustments are of a normal recurring nature, a statement to that effect shall be made; otherwise, there shall be furnished information describing in appropriate detail the nature and amount of any adjustments other than normal recurring adjustments entering into the determination of the results shown.

(c) *Periods to Be Covered.* The periods for which interim financial statements are to be provided in registration statements are prescribed elsewhere in this Regulation (see Rules 3–01 and 3–02 of Regulation S–X). For filings on Form 10–Q, financial statements shall be provided as set forth in this paragraph (c):

(1) An interim balance sheet as of the end of the most recent fiscal quarter and a balance sheet as of the end of the preceding fiscal year shall be provided. The balance sheet as of the end of the preceding fiscal year may be condensed to the same degree as the interim balance sheet provided. An interim balance sheet as of the end of the corresponding fiscal quarter of the preceding fiscal year need not be provided unless necessary for an understanding of the impact of seasonal fluctuations on the registrant's financial condition.

(2) Interim statements of comprehensive income shall be provided for the most recent fiscal quarter, for the period between the end of the preceding fiscal year and the end of the most recent fiscal quarter, and for the corresponding periods of the preceding fiscal year. Such statements may also be presented for the cumulative twelve month period ended during the most recent fiscal quarter and for the corresponding preceding period.

(3) Interim statements of cash flows shall be provided for the period between the end of the preceding fiscal year and the end of the most recent fiscal quarter, and for the corresponding period of the preceding fiscal year. Such statements may also be presented for the cumulative twelve month period ended during the most recent fiscal quarter and for the corresponding preceding period.

(4) Registrants engaged in seasonal production and sale of a single-crop agricultural commodity may provide interim statements of comprehensive income and cash flows for the twelve month period ended during the most recent fiscal quarter and for the corresponding preceding period in lieu of the year-to-date statements specified in paragraphs (c)(2) and (c)(3) of this section.

(d) *Interim Review by Independent Public Accountant.* Prior to filing, interim financial statements included in quarterly reports on Form 10–Q (17 CFR 249.308(a)) must be reviewed by an independent public accountant using applicable professional standards and procedures for conducting such reviews, as may be modified or supplemented by the Commission. If, in any filing, the company states that interim financial statements have been reviewed by an independent public accountant, a report of the accountant on the review must be filed with the interim financial statements.

(e) *Filing of Other Interim Financial Information in Certain Cases.* The Commission may, upon the informal written request of the registrant, and where consistent with the protection of investors, permit the omission of any of the interim financial information herein required or the filing in substitution thereof of appropriate information of comparable character. The Commission may also by informal written notice require the filing of other information in addition to, or in substitution for, the interim information herein required in any case where such information is necessary or appropriate for an adequate presentation of the financial condition of any person for which interim financial information is required, or whose financial information is otherwise necessary for the protection of investors.

PRO FORMA FINANCIAL INFORMATION

Rule 11–01. Presentation requirements

(a) Pro forma financial information shall be furnished when any of the following conditions exist:

(1) During the most recent fiscal year or subsequent interim period for which a balance sheet is required by Rule 3–01 of Regulation S–X, a significant business combination has occurred (for purposes of these rules, this encompasses the acquisition of an interest in a business accounted for by the equity method);

(2) After the date of the most recent balance sheet filed pursuant to Rule 3–01 of Regulation S–X, consummation of a significant business combination or a combination of entities under common control has occurred or is probable;

(3) Securities being registered by the registrant are to be offered to the security holders of a significant business to be acquired or the proceeds from the offered securities will be applied directly or indirectly to the purchase of a specific significant business;

(4) The disposition of a significant portion of a business either by sale, abandonment or distribution to shareholders by means of a spin-off, split-up or split-off has occurred or is probable and such disposition is not fully reflected in the financial statements of the registrant included in the filing;

(5) During the most recent fiscal year or subsequent interim period for which a balance sheet is required by Rule 3–01 of Regulation S–X, the registrant has acquired one or more real estate operations or properties which in the aggregate are significant, or since the date of the most recent balance sheet filed pursuant to that section the registrant has acquired or proposes to acquire one or more operations or properties which in the aggregate are significant.

(6) Pro forma financial information required by Item 914 of Regulation S–K is required to be provided in connection with a roll-up transaction as defined in Item 901(c) of Regulation S–K.

(7) The registrant previously was a part of another entity and such presentation is necessary to reflect operations and financial position of the registrant as an autonomous entity; or

(8) Consummation of other events or transactions has occurred or is probable for which disclosure of pro forma financial information would be material to investors.

(b) A business combination or disposition of a business shall be considered significant if:

(1) A comparison of the most recent annual financial statements of the business acquired or to be acquired and the registrant's most recent annual consolidated financial statements filed at or prior to the date of acquisition indicates that the business would be a significant subsidiary pursuant to the conditions specified in Rule 1–02(w) of Regulation S–X, substituting 20 percent for 10 percent each place it appears therein; or

(2) The business to be disposed of meets the conditions of a significant subsidiary in Rule 1–02(w) of Regulation S–X.

(c) The pro forma effects of a business combination need not be presented pursuant to this section if separate financial statements of the acquired business are not included in the filing.

(d) For purposes of this rule, the term business should be evaluated in light of the facts and circumstances involved and whether there is sufficient continuity of the acquired entity's operations prior to and after the transactions so that disclosure of prior financial information is material to an understanding of future operations. A presumption exists that a separate entity, a subsidiary, or a division is a business. However, a lesser component of an entity may also constitute a business. Among the facts and circumstances which should be considered in evaluating whether an acquisition of a lesser component of an entity constitutes a business are the following:

(1) Whether the nature of the revenue-producing activity of the component will remain generally the same as before the transaction; or

(2) Whether any of the following attributes remain with the component after the transaction:

(i) Physical facilities,

(ii) Employee base,

(iii) Market distribution system,

(iv) Sales force,

(v) Customer base,

(vi) Operating rights,

(vii) Production techniques, or

(viii) Trade names.

(e) This rule does not apply to transactions between a parent company and its totally held subsidiary.

Rule 11–02. Preparation requirements

(a) *Objective.* Pro forma financial information should provide investors with information about the continuing impact of a particular transaction by showing how it might have affected historical financial statements if the transaction had been consummated at an earlier time. Such statements should assist investors in analyzing the future prospects of the registrant because they illustrate the possible scope of the change in the registrant's historical financial position and results of operations caused by the transaction.

(b) *Form and Content.* (1) Pro forma financial information shall consist of a pro forma condensed balance sheet, pro forma condensed statements of comprehensive income, and accompanying explanatory notes. In certain circumstances (i.e., where a limited number of pro forma adjustments are required and those adjustments are easily understood), a narrative description of the pro forma effects of the transaction may be furnished in lieu of the statements described herein.

(2) The pro forma financial information shall be accompanied by an introductory paragraph which briefly sets forth a description of (i) the transaction, (ii) the entities involved, and (iii) the periods for which the pro forma information is presented. In addition, an explanation of what the pro forma presentation shows shall be set forth.

(3) The pro forma condensed financial information need only include major captions (i.e., the numbered captions) prescribed by the applicable sections of part 210 of this chapter (Regulation S–X). Where any major balance sheet caption is less than 10 percent of total assets, the caption may be combined with others. When any major statement of comprehensive income caption is less than 15 percent of average net income attributable to the registrant for the most recent three fiscal years, the caption may be combined with others. In calculating average net income attributable to the registrant, loss years should be excluded unless losses were incurred in each of the most recent three years, in which case the average loss shall be used for purposes of this test. Notwithstanding these tests, de minimis amounts need not be shown separately.

(4) Pro forma statements shall ordinarily be in columnar form showing condensed historical statements, pro forma adjustments, and the pro forma results.

(5) The pro forma condensed statement of comprehensive income shall disclose income (loss) from continuing operations before nonrecurring charges or credits directly attributable to the transaction. Material nonrecurring charges or credits and related tax effects which result directly from the transaction and which will be included in the income of the registrant within the 12 months succeeding the transaction shall be disclosed separately. It should be clearly indicated that such charges or credits were not considered in the pro forma condensed statement of comprehensive income. If the transaction for which pro forma financial information is presented relates to the disposition of a business, the pro forma results should give effect to the disposition and be presented under an appropriate caption.

(6) Pro forma adjustments related to the pro forma condensed statement of comprehensive income shall be computed assuming the transaction was consummated at the beginning of the fiscal year presented and shall include adjustments which give effect to events that are (i) directly attributable to the transaction, (ii) expected to have a continuing impact on the registrant, and (iii) factually supportable. Pro forma adjustments related to the pro forma condensed balance sheet shall be computed assuming the transaction was consummated at the end of the most recent period for which a balance sheet is required by Rule 3–01 and shall include adjustments which give effect to events that are directly attributable to the transaction and factually supportable regardless of whether they have a continuing impact or are nonrecurring. All adjustments should be referenced to notes which clearly explain the assumptions involved.

(7) Historical primary and fully diluted per share data based on continuing operations (or net income if the registrant does not report discontinued operations) for the registrant, and primary and fully diluted pro forma per share data based on continuing operations before nonrecurring charges or credits directly attributable to the transaction shall be presented on the face of the pro forma condensed statement of comprehensive income together with the number of shares used to compute such per share data. For transactions involving the issuance of securities, the number of shares used in the calculation of the pro forma per share data should be based on the weighted average number of shares outstanding during the period adjusted to give effect to shares subsequently issued or assumed to be issued had the particular transaction or event taken place at the beginning of the period presented. If a convertible security is being issued in the transaction, consideration should be given to the possible dilution of the pro forma per share data.

(8) If the transaction is structured in such a manner that significantly different results may occur, additional pro forma presentations shall be made which give effect to the range of possible results.

Instruction 1 to paragraph (b). The historical statement of comprehensive income used in the pro forma financial information shall not report discontinued operations. If the historical statement of comprehensive income includes such items, only the portion of the statement of comprehensive income through "income from continuing operations" (or the appropriate modification thereof) should be used in preparing pro forma results.

Instruction 2 to paragraph (b). For a business combination, pro forma adjustments for the statement of comprehensive income shall include amortization, depreciation and other adjustments based on the allocated purchase price of net assets acquired. In some transactions, such as in financial institution acquisitions, the purchase adjustments may include significant discounts of the historical cost of the acquired assets to their fair value at the acquisition date. When such adjustments will result in a significant effect on earnings (losses) in periods immediately subsequent to the acquisition which will be progressively eliminated over a relatively short period, the effect of the purchase adjustments on reported results of operations for each of the next five years should be disclosed in a note.

Instruction 3 to paragraph (b). For a disposition transaction, the pro forma financial information shall begin with the historical financial statements of the existing entity and show the deletion of the business to be divested along with the pro forma adjustments necessary to arrive at the remainder of the existing entity. For example, pro forma adjustments would include adjustments of interest expense arising from revised debt structures and expenses which will be or have been incurred on behalf of the business to be divested such as advertising costs, executive salaries and other costs.

Instruction 4 to paragraph (b). For entities which were previously a component of another entity, pro forma adjustments should include adjustments similar in nature to those referred to in Instruction 3 above. Adjustments may also be necessary when charges for corporate overhead, interest, or income taxes have been allocated to the entity on a basis other than one deemed reasonable by management.

Instruction 5 to paragraph (b). Adjustments to reflect the acquisition of real estate operations or properties for the pro forma statement of comprehensive income shall include a depreciation charge based on the new accounting basis for the assets, interest financing on any additional or refinanced debt, and other appropriate adjustments that can be factually supported. See also Instruction 4 to paragraph (b) of this section.

Instruction 6 to paragraph (b). When consummation of more than one transaction has occurred or is probable during a fiscal year, the pro forma financial information may be presented on a combined basis; however, in some circumstances (e.g., depending upon the combination of probable and consummated transactions, and the nature of the filing) it may be more useful to present the pro forma financial information on a disaggregated basis even though some or all of the transactions would not meet the tests of significance individually. For combined presentations, a note should explain the various transactions and disclose the maximum variances in the pro forma financial information which would occur for any of the possible combinations. If the pro forma financial information is presented in a proxy or information statement for purposes of obtaining shareholder approval of one of the transactions, the effects of that transaction must be clearly set forth.

Instruction 7 to paragraph (b). Tax effects, if any, of pro forma adjustments normally should be calculated at the statutory rate in effect during the periods for which pro forma condensed statements of comprehensive income are presented and should be reflected as a separate pro forma adjustment.

(c) *Periods to Be Presented.* (1) A pro forma condensed balance sheet as of the end of the most recent period for which a consolidated balance sheet of the registrant is required by Rule 3–01 of Regulation S–X shall be filed unless the transaction is already reflected in such balance sheet.

(2)(i) Pro forma condensed statements of comprehensive income shall be filed for only the most recent fiscal year and for the period from the most recent fiscal year end to the most recent interim date for which a balance sheet is required. A pro forma condensed statement of comprehensive income may be filed for the corresponding interim period of the preceding fiscal year. A pro forma condensed statement of comprehensive income shall not be filed when the historical statement of comprehensive income reflects the transaction for the entire period.

(ii) For combinations between entities under common control, the pro forma statements of comprehensive income (which are in effect a restatement of the historical statements of comprehensive income as if the combination had been consummated) shall be filed for all periods for which historical statements of comprehensive income of the registrant are required.

(3) Pro forma condensed statements of comprehensive income shall be presented using the registrant's fiscal year end. If the most recent fiscal year end of any other entity involved in the transaction differs from the registrant's most recent fiscal year end by more than 93 days, the other entity's statement of comprehensive income shall be brought up to within 93 days of the registrant's most recent fiscal year end, if practicable. This updating could be accomplished by adding subsequent interim period results to the most recent fiscal year-end information and deducting the comparable preceding year interim period results. Disclosure shall be made of the periods combined and of the sales or revenues and income for any periods which were excluded from or included more than once in the condensed pro forma statements of comprehensive income (e.g., an interim period that is included both as part of the fiscal year and the subsequent interim period). For investment companies subject to Rule 6–01 through Rule 6–10, the periods covered by the pro forma statements must be the same.

(4) Whenever unusual events enter into the determination of the results shown for the most recently completed fiscal year, the effect of such unusual events should be disclosed and consideration should be given to presenting a pro forma condensed statement of comprehensive income for the most recent twelve-month period in addition to those required in paragraph (c)(2)(i) of this section if the most recent twelve-month period is more representative of normal operations.

Rule 11–03. Presentation of financial forecast

(a) A financial forecast may be filed in lieu of the pro forma condensed statements of comprehensive income required by Rule 11–02(b)(1).

(1) The financial forecast shall cover a period of at least 12 months from the latest of (i) the most recent balance sheet included in the filing or (ii) the consummation date or estimated consummation date of the transaction.

(2) The forecasted statement of comprehensive income shall be presented in the same degree of detail as the pro forma condensed statement of comprehensive income required by Rule 11–02(b)(3).

(3) Assumptions particularly relevant to the transaction and effects thereof should be clearly set forth.

(4) Historical condensed financial information of the registrant and the business acquired or to be acquired, if any, shall be presented for at least a recent 12 month period in parallel columns with the financial forecast.

(b) Such financial forecast shall be presented in accordance with the guidelines established by the American Institute of Certified Public Accountants.

(c) Forecasted earnings per share data shall be substituted for pro forma per share data.

(d) This rule does not permit the filing of a financial forecast in lieu of pro forma information required by generally accepted accounting principles.

REGULATION S–T—GENERAL RULES AND REGULATIONS FOR ELECTRONIC FILINGS

(Cite as 17 CFR § 232.___)

GENERAL

Rule

ELECTRONIC FILING REQUIREMENTS

HARDSHIP EXEMPTIONS

PREPARATION OF ELECTRONIC SUBMISSIONS

INTERACTIVE DATA

EDGAR FUNCTIONS

GENERAL

Rule 10. Application of Part 232

(a) This part, in conjunction with the EDGAR Filer Manual and the electronic filing provisions of applicable rules, regulations and forms, shall govern the electronic submission of documents filed or otherwise submitted to the Commission and shall be controlling for an electronic format document in the manner and respects provided in this part.

(b) Each registrant, third party filer, or agent to whom the Commission previously has not assigned a Central Index Key (CIK) code, must, before filing on EDGAR:

(1) File electronically the information required by Form ID (17 CFR 239.63, 249.446, 269.7 and 274.402), the uniform application form for access codes to file on EDGAR, and

(2) File, by uploading as a Portable Document Format (PDF) attachment to the Form ID filing, a notarized document, manually signed by the applicant over the applicant's typed signature, that includes the information required to be included in the Form ID filing and confirms the authenticity of the Form ID filing.

NOTE: The Commission strongly urges any person or entity about to become subject to the disclosure and filing requirements of the federal securities laws to submit a Form ID well in advance of the first required filing, including a registration statement relating to an initial public offering, in order to facilitate electronic filing on a timely basis.

Rule 11. Definition of terms used in Part 232

Unless otherwise specifically provided, the terms used in Regulation S–T (17 CFR 232) have the same meanings as in the federal securities laws and the rules, regulations and forms promulgated thereunder. In addition, the following definitions of terms apply specifically to electronic format documents and shall apply wherever they appear in laws, rules, regulations and forms governing such documents, unless the context otherwise specifies:

Animated Graphics. The term *animated graphics* means text or images that do not remain static but that may move when viewed in a browser.

ASCII Document. The term *ASCII document* means an electronic text document with contents limited to American Standard Code for Information Interchange (ASCII) characters and that is tagged with Standard Generalized Mark Up Language (SGML) tags in the format required for ASCII/SGML documents by the EDGAR Filer Manual.

Asset Data File. The term Asset Data File means the machine-readable computer code that presents information in eXtensible Markup Language (XML) electronic format pursuant to § 229.1111(h) of this chapter.

Business Development Company. The term *business development company* has the meaning set forth in section 2(a)(48) of the Investment Company Act.

Direct Transmission. The term *direct transmission* means the transmission of one or more electronic submissions via a telephonic communication session.

Disruptive Code. The term *disruptive code* means any active content or other executable code, or any program or set of electronic computer instructions inserted into a computer, operating system, or program that replicates itself or that actually or potentially modifies or in any way alters, damages, destroys or disrupts the file content or the operation of any computer, computer file, computer database, computer system, computer network or software, and as otherwise set forth in the EDGAR Filer Manual.

EDGAR. The term EDGAR (Electronic Data Gathering, Analysis, and Retrieval) means the computer system for the receipt, acceptance, review and dissemination of documents submitted in electronic format.

EDGAR Filer Manual. The term *EDGAR Filer Manual* means the current version of the manual prepared by the Commission setting out the technical format requirements for an electronic submission.

NOTE: See Rule 301 of Regulation S–T (17 CFR 232.301).

Electronic Document. The term *electronic document* means the portion of an electronic submission separately tagged as an individual document in the format required by the EDGAR Filer Manual.

Electronic Filer. The term *electronic filer* means a person or an entity that submits filings electronically pursuant to Rules 100 and 101 of Regulation S–T.

Electronic Filing. The term *electronic filing* means one or more electronic documents filed under the federal securities laws that are transmitted or delivered to the Commission in electronic format.

Electronic Format. The term *electronic format* means the computerized format of a document prepared in accordance with the EDGAR Filer Manual.

Electronic Submission. The term *electronic submission* means any document, such as a filing, correspondence, or modular submission, or any discrete set of documents, transmitted or delivered to the Commission in electronic format.

Exchange Act. The term *Exchange Act* means the Securities Exchange Act of 1934.

Executable Code. The term *executable code* means instructions to a computer to carry out operations that use features beyond the viewer's, reader's, or Internet browser's native ability to interpret and display HTML, PDF, and static graphic files. Such code may be in binary (machine language) or in script form. Executable code includes disruptive code.

Header Information. The term *header information* means information designated by the EDGAR Filer Manual to precede the text of each electronic submission and document submitted therewith via EDGAR that identifies characteristics of the submission and documents in order to facilitate electronic processing by the EDGAR system.

HTML Document. The term *HTML document* means an electronic text document tagged with HyperText Markup Language tags in the format required by the EDGAR Filer Manual.

Hyperlinks. The term *hyperlinks* means the representation of an Internet address in a form that an Internet browser application can recognize as an Internet address.

Interactive Data File. The term *Interactive Data File* means the machine-readable computer code that presents information in eXtensible Business Reporting Language (XBRL) electronic format pursuant to Rule 405 of Regulation S–T and as specified by the EDGAR Filer Manual. When a filing is submitted using Inline XBRL as provided by Rule 405(a)(3) of Regulation S–T, a portion of the Interactive Data File is embedded into a filing with the remainder submitted as an exhibit to the filing.

Interactive Data Financial Report. The term Interactive Data Financial Report means the machine-readable computer code that presents information in eXtensible Business Reporting Language (XBRL) electronic format pursuant to Rule 407.

Investment Company Act. The term *Investment Company Act* means the Investment Company Act of 1940.

Modular Submission. The term *modular submission* means an electronic submission that contains one or more documents, or portions of a document, submitted for storage in the non-public EDGAR data storage area for purposes of subsequent inclusion in one or more electronic filings pursuant to Rule 501(a) of Regulation S–T.

Official Filing. The term *official filing* means any filing that is received and accepted by the Commission, regardless of filing medium and exclusive of header information, tags and any other technical information required in an electronic filing; except that electronic identification of investment company type and inclusion of identifiers for series and class (or contract, in the case of separate accounts of insurance companies) as required by Rule 313 of Regulation S–T are deemed part of the official filing.

Original. The term *original,* when used or implied in the securities laws, rules, regulations or forms, includes the writing itself or any counterpart intended to have the same effect by a person executing or issuing it. If data are stored in a computer or similar device, any printout or other output readable by sight, shown to reflect the data accurately, is an original.

Paper Format. The term *paper format* means a paper document.

Registrant. The term *registrant* means an issuer of securities for which a Securities Act registration statement is required to be filed and/or an issuer of securities with respect to which an Exchange Act registration statement or report is required to be filed and/or an investment company required to file an Investment Company Act registration statement or report.

Related Official Filing. The term *Related Official Filing* means the ASCII or HTML format part of the official filing with which all or part of an Interactive Data File appears as an exhibit or, in the case of a filing on Form N–1A (17 CFR 239.15A and 274.11A), the ASCII or HTML format part of an official filing that contains the information to which an Interactive Data File corresponds.

Related Official Financial Report Filing. The term *Related Official Financial Report Filing* means the ASCII or HTML format part of the official filing with which an Interactive Data Financial Report appears as an exhibit.

Securities Act. The term *Securities Act* means the Securities Act of 1933.

Segmented Filing. The term *segmented filing* means an electronic format document assembled from segments previously submitted to the non-public EDGAR data storage for one-time inclusion in an electronic filing pursuant to Rule 501(b) of Regulation S–T.

Tag. The term *tag* means an identifier that highlights specific information to EDGAR that is in the format required by the EDGAR Filer Manual.

Third Party Filer. The term *third party filer* means any person or entity that files documents with the Commission with respect to another entity.

Trust Indenture Act. The term *Trust Indenture Act* means the Trust Indenture Act of 1939.

Unofficial PDF Copy. The term *unofficial PDF copy* means an optional copy of an electronic document that may be included in an EDGAR submission tagged as a Portable Document Format document in the format required by the EDGAR Filer Manual and submitted in accordance with Rule 104 of Regulation S–T.

Rule 12. Business hours of the Commission

(a) *General.* The principal office of the Commission, at 100 F Street, N.E., Washington, DC 20549, is open each day, except Saturdays, Sundays, and federal holidays, from 9 a.m. to 5:30 p.m., Eastern Standard Time or Eastern Daylight Saving Time, whichever is currently in effect, *provided that* hours for the filing of documents pursuant to the Acts or the rules and regulations thereunder are as set forth in paragraphs (b) and (c) of this rule.

(b) *Submissions Made in Paper.* Filers may submit paper documents filed with or otherwise furnished to the Commission each day, except Saturdays, Sundays and federal holidays, from 8 a.m. to 5:30 p.m., Eastern Standard Time or Eastern Daylight Saving Time, whichever is currently in effect.

(c) *Submissions by Direct Transmission.* Electronic filings and other documents may be submitted by direct transmission, via dial-up modem or Internet, to the Commission each day, except Saturdays, Sundays and federal holidays, from 8 a.m. to 10 p.m., Eastern Standard Time or Eastern Daylight Saving Time, whichever is currently in effect.

Rule 13. Date of filing; adjustment of filing date

(a) *General.* (1) Except as provided in paragraph (b) of this rule, the business day on which a filing is received by the Commission shall be the date of filing thereof, if:

(i) All requirements of the Acts and rules applicable to such filing have been complied with;

(ii) The filing conforms to the applicable technical standards regarding electronic format in the EDGAR Filer Manual; and

(iii) With respect to Securities Act filings, including filings under section 24(f) of the Investment Company Act (15 U.S.C. 80a–24(f)), the required fee payment has been confirmed, *provided that* the failure to pay an insignificant amount of the fee at the time of the filing, as a result of a *bona fide* error, shall not affect the date of filing.

(2) If the conditions of paragraph (a)(1) of this rule are otherwise satisfied, all filings submitted by direct transmission commencing on or before 5:30 p.m. Eastern Standard Time or Eastern Daylight Saving Time, whichever is currently in effect, shall be deemed filed on the same business day, and all filings submitted by direct transmission commencing after 5:30 p.m. Eastern Standard Time or Eastern Daylight Saving Time, whichever is currently in effect, shall be deemed filed as of the next business day.

(3) Notwithstanding paragraph (a)(2) of this rule, any registration statement or any post-effective amendment thereto filed pursuant to Rule 462(b) by direct transmission commencing on or before 10 p.m. Eastern Standard Time or Eastern Daylight Savings Time, whichever is currently in effect, shall be deemed filed on the same business day.

(4) Notwithstanding paragraph (a)(2) of this rule, a Form 3, 4 or 5 (17 CFR 249.103, 249.104 and 249.105) or a Schedule 14N (17 CFR 240.14n–101) submitted by direct transmission on or before 10 p.m. Eastern Standard Time or Eastern Daylight Saving Time, whichever is currently in effect, shall be deemed filed on the same business day.

NOTE: Electronic filings that have an automatic or immediate effective date must be deemed filed, as provided in paragraph (a) of this rule, before any waiting period for automatic effectiveness commences or before the filing becomes immediately effective, whichever applies.

(b) Adjustment of the Filing Date. If an electronic filer in good faith attempts to file a document with the Commission in a timely manner but the filing is delayed due to technical difficulties beyond the electronic filer's control, the electronic filer may request an adjustment of the filing date of such document. The Commission, or the staff acting pursuant to delegated authority, may grant the request if it appears that such adjustment is appropriate and consistent with the public interest and the protection of investors.

(c) *Payment of Fees.* Fees required with respect to a filing that is submitted electronically shall be paid in accordance with the procedures set forth in Instructions for Filing Fees—Rule 3a of the Commission's Informal and Other Procedures (17 CFR 202.3a).

NOTE: All filing fees paid by electronic filers must be submitted to the lockbox depository, as provided in Rule 3a, including those pertaining to documents filed in paper pursuant to a hardship exemption.

(d) Where the Commission's rules, schedules and forms provide that a document must be filed on the same day it is published, furnished, sent or given to security holders or others, an electronic filer may file the document with the Commission electronically before or on the date the document is published, furnished, sent or given, or if such publication or distribution does not occur during the official business hours of the Commission, as soon as practicable on the next business day. Any associated time periods shall be calculated on the basis of the publication or distribution date (as applicable), and not on the basis of the date of filing.

Rule 14. Paper filings not accepted without exemption

The Commission will not accept in paper format any filing required to be submitted electronically under Rules 100 and 101 of Regulation S–T, unless the filing satisfies the requirements for a temporary or continuing hardship exemption under Rule 201 or 202 of Regulation S–T.

ELECTRONIC FILING REQUIREMENTS

Rule 100. Persons and entities subject to mandated electronic filing

The following persons or entities shall be subject to the electronic filing requirements of this part 232:

(a) Registrants and other entities whose filings are subject to review by the Division of Corporation Finance;

(b) Registrants whose filings are subject to review by the Division of Investment Management;

(c) Persons or entities whose filings are subject to review by the Division of Market Regulation; and

(d) Any party (including natural persons) that files a document jointly with, or as a third party filer with respect to, a person or entity that is subject to mandated electronic filing requirements.

Rule 101. Mandated electronic submissions and exceptions

(a) *Mandated Electronic Submissions.* (1) The following filings, including any related correspondence and supplemental information, except as otherwise provided, shall be submitted in electronic format:

(i) Registration statements and prospectuses filed pursuant to the Securities Act (15 U.S.C. 77a, *et seq.*) or registration statements filed pursuant to Sections 12(b) or 12(g) of the Exchange Act (15 U.S.C. 78*l* (b) or (g));

(ii) Statements and applications filed with the Commission pursuant to the Trust Indenture Act (15 U.S.C. 77aaa, *et seq.*), other than applications for exemptive relief filed pursuant to section 304 (15 U.S.C. 77ddd) and section 310 (15 U.S.C. 77jjj) of that Act;

(iii) Statements, reports and schedules filed with the Commission pursuant to sections 13, 14, 15(d) or 16(a) of the Exchange Act (15 U.S.C. 78m, 78n, 78o(d) and 78p(a)), and proxy materials required to be furnished for the information of the Commission in connection with annual reports on Form 10–K (17 CFR 249.310) or Form 10–KSB (17 CFR 249.310b) filed pursuant to section 15(d) of the Exchange Act.

NOTE 1. Electronic filers filing Schedules 13D and 13G with respect to foreign private issuers should include in the submission header all zeroes (i.e., 00–0000000) for the IRS tax identification number because the EDGAR system requires an IRS number tag to be inserted for the subject company as a prerequisite to acceptance of the filing.

NOTE 2. Foreign private issuers must file or submit their Form 6–K reports (17 CFR 249.306) in electronic format, except as otherwise permitted by paragraphs (b)(1) and (b)(7) of this rule.

(iv) Documents filed with the Commission pursuant to sections 8, 17, 20, 23(c), 24(b), 24(e),

24(f), and 30 of the Investment Company Act (15 U.S.C. 80a–8, 80a–17, 80a–20, 80a–23(c), 80a–24(b), 80a–24(e), 80a–24(f), and 80a–29) and any application for an order under any section of the Investment Company Act (15 U.S. C. 80a–1 *et seq.*);

(v) Documents relating to offerings exempt from registration under the Securities Act filed with the Commission pursuant to Regulation E (Rules 601–610a under the Securities Act of 1933);

(vi) Form CB (17 CFR 239.800 and 249.480) filed or submitted under Rules 801 or 802 or Rules 13e–4(h)(8), 14d–1(c), or 14e–2(d) under the Securities Exchange Act of 1934;

(vii) Form F–X (17 CFR 239.42) when filed in connection with a Form CB (17 CFR 239.800 and 249.480) or a Form 1–A (17 CFR 239.90);

(viii) Form F–N (17 CFR 239.43) filed by foreign banks and insurance companies and certain of their holding companies and finance subsidiaries under Rule 489;

(ix) Form ID (17 CFR 239.63, 249.446, 269.7 and 274.402); the Form ID authenticating document required by Rule 10(b) of Regulation S–T also shall be filed in electronic format as an uploaded Portable Document Format (PDF) attachment to the Form ID filing. Other related correspondence and supplemental information submitted after the Form ID filing shall not be submitted in electronic format;

(x) Form 25 (17 CFR 249.25); and

(xi) Form TA–1 (17 CFR 249.100), Form TA–2 (17 CFR 249.102), and Form TA–W (17 CFR 249.101);

(xii) Forms 15 and 15F (17 CFR 249.323 and 17 CFR 249.324);

(xiii) Form D (17 CFR 239.500).

(xiv) Form NRSRO (§ 249b.300 of this chapter), and the information and documents in Exhibits 1 through 9 to Form NRSRO, filed with or furnished to, as applicable, the Commission under § 240.17g–1(e), (f), and (g) of this chapter and the annual reports filed with or furnished to, as applicable, the Commission under § 240.17g–3 of this chapter. The filings or furnishings must be made on EDGAR as PDF documents in the format required by the EDGAR Filer Manual, as defined in Rule 11 of Regulation S–T. Notwithstanding Rule 104 of Regulation S–T, the PDF documents filed or furnished under this paragraph will be considered as officially filed with or furnished to, as applicable, the Commission.

(xv) Form ABS–EE (17 CFR 249.1401);

(xvi) Form ABS–15G (as defined in 17 CFR 249.1400); and

(xvii) Filings made pursuant to Regulation A (Rules 251 to 263).

(xvii) Documents filed with the Commission pursuant to section 13(n) of the Exchange Act and the rules and regulations thereunder, including Form SDR (17 CFR 249.1500) and reports filed pursuant to Rules 13n–11(d) and (f) under the Exchange Act.*

(2) The following amendments to filings and applications, including any related correspondence and supplemental information except as otherwise provided, shall be submitted as follows:

(i) Any amendment to a filing or application submitted by or relating to a registrant or an applicant that is required to file electronically, including any amendment to a paper filing or application, shall be submitted in electronic format;

(ii) The first electronic amendment to a paper format Schedule 13D (Rule 13d–101 under the Securities Exchange Act of 1934) or Schedule 13G (Rule 13d–102 under the Securities Exchange Act of 1934), shall restate the entire text of the Schedule 13D or 13G, but previously filed paper exhibits to such Schedules are not required to be restated electronically. See Rule 102 of Regulation S–T regarding amendments to exhibits previously filed in paper format. Notwithstanding the foregoing, if the sole purpose of filing the first electronic Schedule 13D or 13G amendment is to report a change in beneficial ownership that would terminate the filer's obligation to report, the amendment need not include a restatement of the entire text of the Schedule being amended.

(3) Supplemental information, including documents related to applications under any section of the Investment Company Act, shall be submitted in electronic format except as provided in paragraph (c)(2) of this rule. The information shall be stored in the non-public EDGAR data storage area as correspondence. Supplemental informa-

* The SEC promulgated two (xvii) provisions in two different releases: 33-9741 (3.25.15) and 34-74246 (2.11.15)

tion that is submitted in electronic format shall not be returned.

NOTE TO PARAGRAPH (a)(3): Failure to submit a required electronic filing pursuant to this paragraph (a), as well as any required confirming electronic copy of a paper filing made in reliance on a hardship exemption, as provided in Rules 201 and 202 of Regulation S–T, will result in ineligibility to use Forms S–2, S–3, S–8, SF–3, F–2 and F–3 (17 CFR 239.12, 239.13, 239.16b, 239.32, 239.33, and 239.45), restrict incorporation by reference of the document submitted in paper (see Rule 303 of Regulation S–T), or toll certain time periods associated with tender offers (see Rule 13e–4(f)(12) and Rule 14e–1(e) under the Securities Exchange Act of 1934).

(b) *Permitted Electronic Submissions.* The following documents may be submitted to the Commission in electronic format, at the option of the electronic filer:

(1) Annual reports to security holders furnished for the information of the Commission under Rule 14a–3(c) or Rule 14c–3(b) under the Securities Exchange Act of 1934, under the requirements of Form 10–K or Form 10–KSB (17 CFR 249.310 or 249.310b) filed by registrants under Exchange Act Section 15(d) (15 U.S.C. 78o(d)), or by foreign private issuers filed on Form 6–K (17 CFR 249.306 of this chapter) under Rule 13a–16 or Rule 15d–16 under the Securities Exchange Act of 1934;

(2) Notices of exempt solicitation furnished for the information of the Commission pursuant to Rule 14a–6(g) under the Securities Exchange Act of 1934 and notices of exempt preliminary roll-up communications furnished for the information of the Commission pursuant to Rule 14a–6(n);

(3) Form 11–K (17 CFR 249.311). Registrants who satisfy their Form 11–K filing obligations by filing amendments to Forms 10–K or 10–KSB, as provided by Rule 15d–21 under the Securities Exchange Act of 1934, also may choose to file such amendments in paper or electronic format;

(4) Form 144 (17 CFR 239.144), where the issuer of the securities is subject to the reporting requirements of Section 13 or 15(d) of the Exchange Act (15 U.S.C. 78m or 78o(d), respectively);

(5) Periodic reports and reports with respect to distributions of primary obligations filed by:

(i) The International Bank for Reconstruction and Development under Section 15(a) of the Bretton Woods Agreements Act (22 U.S.C. 286k–1(a)) and Part 285 of this chapter;

(ii) The Inter–American Development Bank under Section 11(a) of the Inter–American Development Bank Act (22 U.S.C. 283h(a)) and Part 286 of this chapter;

(iii) The Asian Development Bank under Section 11(a) of the Asian Development Bank Act (22 U.S.C. 285h(a)) and Part 287 of this chapter;

(iv) The African Development Bank under Section 9(a) of the African Development Bank Act (22 U.S.C. 290i–9(a)) and Part 288 of this chapter;

(v) The International Finance Corporation under Section 13(a) of the International Finance Corporation Act (22 U.S.C. 282k(a)) and Part 289 of this chapter; and

(vi) The European Bank for Reconstruction and Development under Section 9(a) of the European Bank for Reconstruction and Development Act (22 U.S.C. 290*l*–7(a)) and Part 290 of this chapter;

(6) A report or other document submitted by a foreign private issuer under cover of Form 6–K (17 CFR 249.306) that the issuer must furnish and make public under the laws of the jurisdiction in which the issuer is incorporated, domiciled or legally organized (the foreign private issuer's "home country"), or under the rules of the home country exchange on which the issuer's securities are traded, as long as the report or other document is not a press release, is not required to be and has not been distributed to the issuer's security holders, and, if discussing a material event, has already been the subject of a Form 6–K or other Commission filing or submission on EDGAR;

(7) [Reserved]

(8) Form F–X (Rule 42 of Regulation S–T) if filed by a Canadian issuer when qualifying an offering statement pursuant to the provisions of Regulation A (Rules 251–263 under the Securities Act of 1933); and

(9) Documents filed with the Commission pursuant to section 33 of the Investment Company Act (15 U.S.C. 80a–32); and

(10) Form D (17 CFR 239.500) but this temporary Rule 101(b)(10) of Regulation S–T will expire on March 16, 2009.

(c) *Documents to Be Submitted in Paper Only.* Except as otherwise provided in paragraph (d) of this section, the following shall not be submitted in electronic format:

(1)(i) Confidential treatment requests and the information with respect to which confidential treatment is requested;

(ii) Preliminary proxy materials and information statements with respect to a matter specified in Item 14 of Schedule 14A for which confidential treatment has been requested in the manner prescribed by Rule 14a–6(e)(2) or Rule 14c–5(d)(2) under the Securities Exchange Act of 1934;

(2) Supplemental information, if the submitter requests that the information be protected from public disclosure under the Freedom of Information Act (5 U.S.C. 552) pursuant to a request for confidential treatment under 17 CFR 200.83 or if the submitter requests that the information be returned after staff review and the information is of the type typically returned by the staff pursuant to Rule 418(b) or Rule 12b–4 under the Securities Exchange Act of 1934;

(3) Shareholder proposals and all related correspondence submitted pursuant to Rule 14a–8 under the Securities Exchange Act of 1934;

(4) No-action and interpretive letter requests (17 CFR 200.81 and 15 U.S.C. 78*l* (h));

(5) Applications for exemptive relief filed pursuant to Sections 304 and 310 of the Trust Indenture Act;

(6) Filings on Form 144 where the issuer of the securities is not subject to the reporting requirements of section 13 or 15(d) of the Exchange Act;

(7) Promotional and sales material submitted pursuant to Securities Act Industry Guide 5 (17 CFR 229.801(e)) or otherwise supplementally furnished for review by the staff of the Division of Corporation Finance;

(8) Documents and symbols in a foreign language (see Rule 306 of Regulation S–T);

(9) Exchange Act filings submitted to the Division of Market Regulation other than those that are submitted in electronic format as mandated or permitted electronic submissions under paragraph (a) and (b) of this rule or that are submitted electronically in a filing system other than EDGAR; and

(10) Documents relating to investigations and litigation submitted pursuant to Subpart D of Part 201 of this chapter.

(11) [Reserved];

(12) [Reserved];

(13) [Reserved];

(14) [Reserved];

(d) All documents, including any information with respect to which confidential treatment is requested, filed pursuant to section 13(n) of the Exchange Act and the rules and regulations thereunder shall be filed in electronic format.

Rule 102. Exhibits

(a) Exhibits to an electronic filing that have not previously been filed with the Commission shall be filed in electronic format, absent a hardship exemption. Previously filed exhibits, whether in paper or electronic format, may be incorporated by reference into an electronic filing to the extent permitted by § 229.10(d) of this chapter, Rule 411 under the Securities Act (§230.411 of this chapter), Rule 12b-23 or 12b-32 under the Exchange Act (§240.12b-23 or §240.12b-32 of this chapter), Rules 0-4, 8b-23, and 8b-32 under the Investment Company Act (§§270.0-4, 270.8b-23 and 270.8b-32 of this chapter) and Rule 303 of Regulation S-T (§232.303). An electronic filer may, at its option, restate in electronic format any exhibit incorporated by reference that originally was filed in paper format.

NOTE TO PARAGRAPH (a): Exhibits to a Commission schedule filed pursuant to Section 13 or 14(d) of the Exchange Act may be filed in paper under cover of Form SE where such exhibits previously were filed in paper (prior to a registrant's becoming subject to mandated electronic filing or pursuant to a hardship exemption) and are required to be refiled pursuant to the schedule's general instructions. *See* Rule 311(b) of Regulation S–T.

(b) Amendments to all exhibits shall be filed in electronic format, absent a hardship exemption.

(c) Notwithstanding any other provision of this rule, an electronic filer shall, upon amendment, restate in electronic format its articles of incorporation, by-laws or investment advisory agreement (in the case of a registered investment company or a business development company).

(d) Each electronic filing requiring exhibits must include an exhibit index which must appear before the required signatures in the document. The index must list each exhibit filed, whether filed electronically or in paper. For electronic filings on Form F-10 (§239.40 of this chapter), Form 20-F (§249.220f of this chapter), or filings subject to Item 601 of Regulation S-K (§229.601 of this chapter), each exhibit identified in the exhibit index (other than an exhibit filed in eXtensible Business Reporting Language or an exhibit that is filed with Form ABS-EE (§249.1401 of this chapter)) must include an active link to an exhibit that is filed with the document or, if the exhibit is incorporated by reference, an active hyperlink to the exhibit separately filed on EDGAR. Whenever a filer files an exhibit in paper pursuant to a temporary or continuing hardship exemption (§232.201 or §232.202) or pursuant to §232.311, the filer must place the letter "P" next to the listed exhibit in the exhibit index of the electronic filing to reflect the fact that the filer filed the exhibit in paper. In addition, if the exhibit is filed in paper pursuant to §232.311, the filer must place the designation "Rule 311" next to the letter "P" in the exhibit index. If the exhibit is filed in paper pursuant to a temporary or continuing hardship exemption, the filer must place the letters "TH" or "CH," respectively, next to the letter "P" in the exhibit index. Whenever an electronic confirming copy of an exhibit is filed pursuant to a hardship exemption (§232.201 or §232.202(d)), the exhibit index should specify where the confirming electronic copy can be located; in addition, the designation "CE" (confirming electronic) should be placed next to the listed exhibit in the exhibit index.

(e) Notwithstanding the provisions of paragraphs (a) through (d) of this rule, any incorporation by reference by a registered investment company or a business development company must relate only to documents that have been filed in electronic format on the EDGAR system, unless the document has been filed in paper under a hardship exemption (Rule 201 or Rule 202 of Regulation S–T) and any required confirming electronic copy has been submitted.

Rule 103. Liability for transmission errors or omissions in documents filed via EDGAR

An electronic filer shall not be subject to the liability and anti-fraud provisions of the federal securities laws with respect to an error or omission in an electronic filing resulting solely from electronic transmission errors beyond the control of the filer, where the filer corrects the error or omission by the filing of an amendment in electronic format as soon as reasonably practicable after the electronic filer becomes aware of the error or omission.

Rule 104. Unofficial PDF copies included in an electronic submission

(a) An electronic submission, other than a Form 3 (17 CFR 249.103), a Form 4 (17 CFR 249.104), a Form 5 (17 CFR 249.105), a Form ID (17 CFR 239.63, 249.446, 269.7 and 274.402), a Form TA–1 (17 CFR 249.100), a Form TA–2 (17 CFR 249.102), a Form TA–W (17 CFR 249.101) or a Form D (17 CFR 239.500), may include one unofficial PDF copy of each electronic document contained within that submission, tagged in the format required by the EDGAR Filer Manual.

(b) Except as provided in paragraphs (c) and (f) of this rule, each unofficial PDF copy must be substantively equivalent to its associated electronic document contained in the electronic submission. An unofficial PDF copy may contain graphic and image material (but not animated graphics, or audio or video material), notwithstanding the fact that its HTML or ASCII document counterpart may not contain such material but instead may contain a fair and accurate narrative description or tabular representation of any omitted graphic or image material.

(c) If a filer omits an unofficial PDF copy from, or submits one or more flawed unofficial PDF copies in, the electronic submission of an official filing, the filer may add or resubmit an unofficial PDF copy by electronically submitting an amendment to the filing to which it relates. The amendment must include an explanatory note that the purpose of the amendment is to add or to correct an unofficial PDF copy.

(1) If such an amendment is filed, the official amendment may consist solely of the cover page (or first page of the document), the explanatory note, and the signature page and exhibit index (where appropriate). The corresponding unofficial copy must include the complete text of the official filing document for which the amendment is being submitted.

(2) If the amendment is being filed to add or resubmit an unofficial PDF copy of one or more exhibits, the submission may consist of the following: the official filing—consisting of the cover page (or first page of the document), the explanatory note, the signature page (where appropriate), the exhibit index, and a separate electronic exhibit document for each exhibit for which an unofficial PDF copy is being submitted—and the corresponding unofficial PDF copy of each exhibit document. However, the text of the official exhibit document need not repeat the text of the exhibit; that document may contain only the following legend: RESUBMITTED TO ADD/REPLACE UNOFFICIAL PDF COPY OF EXHIBIT.

(d) An unofficial PDF copy is not filed for purposes of section 11 of the Securities Act (15 U.S.C. 77k), section 18 of the Exchange Act (15 U.S.C. 78r), section 323 of the Trust Indenture Act (15 U.S.C. 77www), or section 34(b) of the Investment Company Act (15 U.S.C. 80a–33(b)), or otherwise subject to the liabilities of such sections, and is not part of any registration statement to which it relates. An unofficial PDF copy is, however, subject to all other civil liability and anti-fraud provisions of the above Acts or other laws.

(e) Unofficial PDF copies that are prospectuses are subject to liability under Section 12 of the Securities Act (15 U.S.C. 77*l*).

(f) An unofficial PDF copy of a correspondence document contained in an electronic submission need not be substantively equivalent to that correspondence document.

Rule 105. Use of HTML and hyperlinks

(a) Electronic filers must submit the following documents in ASCII: Form N–SAR (17 CFR 274.101) and Form 13F (17 CFR 249.325). Notwithstanding the provisions of this rule, electronic filers may submit exhibits to Form N–SAR in HTML.

(b) Electronic filers may not include in any HTML document hyperlinks to sites, locations, or documents outside the HTML document, except links to officially filed documents within the current submission and to documents previously filed electronically and located in the EDGAR database on the Commission's public website (www.sec.gov). Electronic filers also may include within an HTML document links to different sections within that single HTML document.

(c) If a filer includes an external hyperlink within a filed document, the information contained in the linked material will not be considered part of the document for determining compliance with reporting obligations, but the inclusion of the link will cause the filer to be subject to the civil liability and antifraud provisions of the federal securities laws with reference to the information contained in the linked material.

(d) Electronic filers submitting Form F-10 (§239.40 of this chapter), Form 20-F (§249.220f of this chapter), or a registration statement or report subject to Item 601 of Regulation S-K (§229.601 of this chapter), must submit such registration statement or report in HTML and each exhibit identified in the exhibit index (other than an exhibit filed in eXtensible Business Reporting Language or an exhibit filed with Form ABS-EE (§249.1401 of this chapter)) must include an active link to an exhibit that is filed with the registration statement or report or, if the exhibit is incorporated by reference, an active hyperlink to the exhibit separately filed on EDGAR, unless such exhibit is filed in paper pursuant to a temporary or continuing hardship exemption under Rules 201 or 202 of Regulation S-T (§232.201 or §232.202) or pursuant to Rule 311 of Regulation S-T (§232.311).

Instructions to paragraph (d).

(1) No hyperlink is required for any exhibit incorporated by reference that has not been filed with the Commission in electronic format.

(2) An electronic filer must correct an inaccurate or nonfunctioning link or hyperlink to an exhibit, in the case of a registration statement that is not yet effective, by filing an amendment to the registration statement containing the inaccurate or nonfunctioning link or hyperlink; or, in the case of a registration statement that has become effective or an Exchange Act report, an electronic filer must correct the inaccurate or nonfunctioning link or hyperlink in the next Exchange Act periodic report that requires, or includes, an exhibit pursuant to Item 601 of Regulation S-K (§229.601 of this chapter) or, in the case of a foreign private issuer (as defined in §229.405 of this chapter), Form 20-F (§249.220f of this chapter) or Form F-10 (§239.40 of this chapter). Alternatively, an electronic filer may correct an inaccurate or nonfunctioning link or hyperlink in a registration statement that has become effective by filing a post-effective amendment to the registration statement.

Rule 106. Prohibition against electronic submissions containing executable code

(a) Electronic submissions must not contain executable code. Attempted submissions identified as containing executable code will be suspended, unless the executable code is contained only in one or more PDF documents, in which case the submission will be accepted but the PDF document(s) containing executable code will be deleted and not disseminated.

(b) If an electronic submission has been accepted, and the Commission staff later determines that the accepted submission contains executable code, the staff may delete from the EDGAR system the entire accepted electronic submission or any document contained in the accepted electronic submission. The Commission staff may direct the electronic filer to resubmit electronically replacement document(s) or a replacement submission in its entirety, in compliance with this provision and the EDGAR Filer Manual.

NOTE TO Rule 106: A violation of this rule or the relevant EDGAR Filer Manual section also may be a violation of the Computer Fraud and Abuse Act of 1986, as amended, and other statutes and laws.

HARDSHIP EXEMPTIONS

Rule 201. Temporary hardship exemption

(a) If an electronic filer experiences unanticipated technical difficulties preventing the timely preparation and submission of an electronic filing, other than a Form 3 (17 CFR 249.103), a Form 4 (17 CFR 249.104), a Form 5 (§ 17 CFR 249.105), a Form ID (17 CFR 239.63, 249.446, 269.7 and 274.402), a Form TA–1 (17 CFR 249.100), a Form TA–2 (17 CFR 249.102), a Form TA–W (17 CFR 249.101), a Form D (17 CFR 239.500), an application for an order under any section of the Investment Company Act (15 U.S.C. 80a–1 *et seq.*), an Interactive Data File (Rule 11 of Regulation S–T), or an Asset Data File (Rule 11 of Regulation S–T), the electronic filer may file the subject filing, under cover of Form TH (17 CFR 239.65, 249.447, 269.10 and 274.404 of this chapter), in paper format no later than one business day after the date on which the filing was to be made.

(1) An electronic imaged copy of the paper format document shall be the official filing for purposes of the federal securities laws.

(2) The following legend shall be set forth in capital letters on the cover page of the paper format document:

IN ACCORDANCE WITH RULE 201 OF REGULATION S–T, THIS (*specify document*) IS BEING FILED IN PAPER PURSUANT TO A TEMPORARY HARDSHIP EXEMPTION

(3) Signatures to the paper format document may be in typed form rather than manual format. See Rule 302 of Regulation S–T. All other requirements relating to paper format filings shall be satisfied.

(4) If the exemption pertains to a document filed pursuant to section 13(a) or 15(d) of the Exchange Act (15 U.S.C. 78m and 78*o*(d)) or section 30 of the Investment Company Act and the paper format document is filed in the manner specified in paragraph (a) of this rule, the filing shall be deemed to have been filed by its required due date.

NOTES TO PARAGRAPH (a):

1. Where a temporary hardship exemption relates to an exhibit only, the filer must file the paper format exhibit and a Form TH (17 CFR 239.65, 249.447, 269.10, and 274.404) under cover of Form SE (17 CFR 239.64, 249.444, 269.8, and 274.403).

2. Filers unable to submit a report within a prescribed time period because of electronic difficulties shall comply with the provisions of this rule and shall not use Form 12b–25 (17 CFR 249.322) as a notification of late filing.

(b) An electronic format copy of the filed paper format document shall be submitted to the Commission within six business days of filing the paper format document. Failure to submit the confirming electronic copy of a paper filing made in reliance on the temporary hardship exemption, as required in this paragraph (b), will result in ineligibility to use Form SF–3 (*see* 17 CFR 239.45). The electronic format version shall contain the following statement in capital letters at the top of the first page of the document:

THIS DOCUMENT IS A COPY OF THE (*specify document*) FILED ON (DATE) PURSUANT TO A RULE 201 TEMPORARY HARDSHIP EXEMPTION

NOTE 1 TO PARAGRAPH (b): As provided elsewhere in this chapter, failure to submit the confirming electronic copy of a paper filing made in reliance on the temporary hardship exemption, as required in paragraph (b) of this rule, will result in ineligibility to use Forms S–3, S–8, and F–3 (see 17 CFR 239.13, 239.16b, and 239.33, respectively), restrict incorporation by reference into an electronic filing of the document submitted in paper (*see* Rule 303 of Regulation S–T), and toll certain time periods associated with tender offers (*see* Rule 13e–4(f)(13) and Rule 14e–1(e) under the Securities Exchange Act of 1934).

NOTE 2 TO PARAGRAPH (b): If the exemption relates to an exhibit only, the requirement to submit a confirming electronic copy shall be satisfied by refiling the exhibit in electronic format in an amendment to the filing to which it relates. The confirming copy tag should not be used. The amendment should note that the purpose of the amendment is to add an electronic copy of an exhibit previously filed in paper pursuant to a temporary hardship exemption.

(c) If an electronic filer experiences unanticipated technical difficulties preventing the timely preparation and submission of an Interactive Data File (Rule 11 of Regulation S–T) as required pursuant to Rule 405 of Regulation S–T, the electronic filer still can timely satisfy the requirement to submit the Interactive Data File in the following manner:

(1) Substitute for the Interactive Data File exhibit a document that sets forth the following legend:

IN ACCORDANCE WITH THE TEMPORARY HARDSHIP EXEMPTION PROVIDED BY RULE 201 OF REGULATION S-T,

THE DATE BY WHICH THE INTERACTIVE DATA FILE IS REQUIRED TO BE SUBMITTED HAS BEEN EXTENDED BY SIX BUSINESS DAYS; and

(2) Submit the required Interactive Data File no later than six business days after the Interactive Data File originally was required to be submitted.

NOTE 1 TO PARAGRAPH (c): As provided elsewhere in this chapter, electronic filers unable to submit the Interactive Data File under the circumstances specified by paragraph (c) of this rule, must comply with the provisions of this rule and cannot use Form 12b–25 (17 CFR 249.322) as a notification of late filing. As also provided elsewhere in this chapter, failure to submit the Interactive Data File as required by the end of the six-business-day period specified by paragraph (c) of this rule will result in ineligibility to use Forms S–3, S–8, and F–3 (17 CFR 239.13, 239.16b, and 239.33 of this chapter, respectively), constitute a failure to have filed all required reports for purposes of the current public information requirements of Rule 144(c)(1), and, pursuant to Rule 485(c)(3), suspend the ability to file post-effective amendments under Rule 485(b).

(d) If an electronic filer experiences unanticipated technical difficulties preventing the timely preparation and submission of an Asset Data File (Item 11 of Regulation S–T) and any asset related document pursuant to Items 601(b)(102) and 601(b)(103) (17 CFR 229.601(b)(102) and 229.601(b)(103)) the electronic filer still can timely satisfy the requirement to submit the Asset Data File or any asset related document in the following manner by:

(1) Posting on a Web site the Asset Data File and any asset related documents unrestricted as to access and free of charge;

(2) Substituting for the Asset Data File and any asset related documents in the required Form ABS–EE (17 CFR 249.1401), a statement specifying the Web site address and that sets forth the following legend; and

IN ACCORDANCE WITH THE TEMPORARY HARDSHIP EXEMPTION PROVIDED BY RULE 201 OF REGULATION S–T, THE DATE BY WHICH THE ASSET DATA FILE IS REQUIRED TO BE SUBMITTED HAS BEEN EXTENDED BY SIX BUSINESS DAYS.

(3) Submitting the required Asset Data File and asset related documents no later than six business days after the Asset Data File originally was required to be submitted.

Rule 202. Continuing hardship exemption

(a) An electronic filer may apply in writing for a continuing hardship exemption if all or part of a filing, group of filings or submission, other than a Form ID (17 CFR 239.63, 249.446, 269.7, and 274.402), a Form D (17 CFR 239.500), or an Asset Data File (Rule 11), otherwise to be filed or submitted in electronic format cannot be so filed or submitted, as applicable, without undue burden or expense. Such written application shall be made at least ten business days before the required due date of the filing(s) or submission(s) or the proposed filing or submission date, as appropriate, or within such shorter period as may be permitted. The written application shall contain the information set forth in paragraph (b) of this rule.

(1) The application shall not be deemed granted until the applicant is notified by the Commission or the staff.

(2) If the Commission, or the staff acting pursuant to delegated authority, denies the application for a continuing hardship exemption, the electronic filer shall file or submit the required document or Interactive Data File in electronic format, as applicable, on the required due date or the proposed filing or submission date, or such other date as may be permitted.

(3) If the Commission, or the staff acting pursuant to delegated authority, determines that the grant of the exemption is appropriate and consistent with the public interest and the protection of investors and so notifies the applicant, the electronic filer shall follow the procedures set forth in paragraph (c) of this rule.

(b) The request for the continuing hardship exemption shall include, but not be limited to, the following:

(1) The reason(s) that the necessary hardware and software is not available without unreasonable burden and expense;

(2) The burden and expense involved to employ alternative means to make the electronic submission; and/or

(3) The reasons for not submitting electronically the document, group of documents or Interactive Data File, as well as the justification for the requested time period.

(c) If the request is granted with respect to:

(1) Electronic filing of a document or group of documents, not electronic submission of an Interactive Data File, then the electronic filer shall submit the document or group of documents for which the continuing hardship exemption is granted in

paper format on the required due date specified in the applicable form, rule or regulation, or the proposed filing date, as appropriate and the following legend shall be placed in capital letters at the top of the cover page of the paper format document(s):

IN ACCORDANCE WITH RULE 202 OF REGULATION S–T, THIS (*specify document*) IS BEING FILED IN PAPER PURSUANT TO A CONTINUING HARDSHIP EXEMPTION.

(2) Electronic submission of an Interactive Data File, then the electronic filer shall substitute for the Interactive Data File exhibit a document that sets forth one of the following legends, as appropriate:

IN ACCORDANCE WITH A CONTINUING HARDSHIP EXEMPTION OBTAINED UNDER RULE 202 OF REGULATION S–T, THE DATE BY WHICH THE INTERACTIVE DATA FILE IS REQUIRED TO BE SUBMITTED HAS BEEN EXTENDED TO (*specify date*); or

IN ACCORDANCE WITH A CONTINUING HARDSHIP EXEMPTION OBTAINED UNDER RULE 202 OF REGULATION S–T, THE INTERACTIVE DATA FILE IS NOT REQUIRED TO BE SUBMITTED.

(d) If a continuing hardship exemption is granted for a limited period of time for:

(1) Electronic filing of a document or group of documents, not electronic submission of an Interactive Data File, then the grant may be conditioned upon the filing of the document or group of documents that is the subject of the exemption in electronic format upon the expiration of the period for which the exemption is granted. The electronic format version shall contain the following statement in capital letters at the top of the first page of the document:

THIS DOCUMENT IS A COPY OF THE (*specify document*) FILED ON (DATE) PURSUANT TO A RULE 202(d) CONTINUING HARDSHIP EXEMPTION.

(2) Electronic submission of an Interactive Data File, then the grant may be conditioned upon the electronic submission of the Interactive Data File that is the subject of the exemption upon the expiration of the period for which the exemption is granted.

NOTE 1 TO RULE 202: Where a continuing hardship exemption is granted with respect to an exhibit only, the paper format exhibit shall be filed under cover of Form SE (17 CFR 239.64, 249.444, 269.8 and 274.403).

NOTE 2 TO RULE 202: If the exemption relates to an exhibit only and a confirming electronic copy of the exhibit is required to be submitted, the exhibit should be refiled in electronic format in an amendment to the filing to which it relates. The confirming copy tag should not be used. The amendment should note that the purpose of the amendment is to add an electronic copy of an exhibit previously filed in paper pursuant to a continuing hardship exemption.

NOTE 3 TO RULE 202: As provided elsewhere in this chapter, failure to submit a required confirming electronic copy of a paper filing made in reliance on a continuing hardship exemption granted pursuant to paragraph (d) of this rule will result in ineligibility to use Forms S–3, S–8, and F–3 (*see*, 17 CFR 239.13, 239.16b, and 239.33 of this chapter, respectively), restrict incorporation by reference into an electronic filing of the document submitted in paper (*see* Rule 303 of Regulation S-T), and toll certain time periods associated with tender offers (*see* Rule 13e–4(f)(13) and Rule 14e–1(e) under the Securities Exchange Act of 1934).

NOTE 4 TO RULE 202: As provided elsewhere in this chapter, failure to submit the Interactive Data File as required by Rule 405 of Regulation S-T by the end of the continuing hardship exemption if granted for a limited period of time, will result in ineligibility to use Forms S-3, S-8, and F-3 (17 CFR 239.13, 239.16b, and 239.33, respectively), constitute a failure to have filed all required reports for purposes of the current public information requirements of Rule 144(c)(1) under the Securities Act of 1933, and, pursuant to Rule 485(c)(3) of the Securities Act of 1933, suspend the ability to file post-effective amendments under Rule 485(b).

PREPARATION OF ELECTRONIC SUBMISSIONS

Rule 301. EDGAR filer manual

Filers must prepare electronic filings in the manner prescribed by the EDGAR Filer Manual, promulgated by the Commission, which sets forth the technical formatting requirements for electronic submissions. The requirements for becoming an EDGAR Filer and updating company data are set forth in the updated EDGAR Filer Manual, Volume I: "General Information," Version 30 (March 2018). The requirements for filing on EDGAR are set forth in the updated EDGAR Filer Manual, Volume II: "EDGAR Filing," Version 47 (July 2018). Additional provisions applicable to Form N-SAR filers are set forth in the EDGAR Filer Manual, Volume III: "N-SAR Supplement," Version 6 (January 2017). All of these provisions have been incorporated by reference into the Code of Federal Regulations, which action was approved by the Director of the Federal Register in accordance with 5 U.S.C. 552(a) and 1 CFR part 51. You must comply with these requirements in order for documents to be timely received and accepted. The EDGAR Filer Manual is available for website viewing and printing; the address for the Filer Manual is https://www.sec.gov/info/edgar/edmanuals.htm. You can obtain paper copies of the EDGAR Filer Manual at the following address: Public Reference Room, U.S. Securities and Exchange Commission, 100 F Street NE., Washington, DC 20549, on official business days between the hours of 10:00 a.m. and 3:00 p.m. You can also inspect the document at the National Archives and Records Administration (NARA). For information on the availability of this material at NARA, call 202-741-6030, or go to: https://www.archives.gov/federal- register/cfr/ibr-locations.html.

Rule 302. Signatures

(a) Required signatures to, or within, any electronic submission (including, without limitation, signatories within the certifications required by Rules 13a–14, 15d–14 and 30a–2 under the Securities Exchange Act of 1934) must be in typed form rather than manual format. Signatures in an HTML document that are not required may, but are not required to, be presented in an HTML graphic or image file within the electronic filing, in compliance with the formatting requirements of the EDGAR Filer Manual. When used in connection with an electronic filing the term "signature" means an electronic entry in the form of a magnetic impulse or other form of computer data compilation of any letters or series of letters or characters comprising a name, executed, adopted or authorized as a signature. Signatures are not required in unofficial PDF copies submitted in accordance with Rule 104 of Regulation S–T.

(b) Each signatory to an electronic filing (including, without limitation, each signatory to the certifications required by Rules 13a–14 and 15d–14 under the Securities Exchange Act of 1934 and 17 CFR 270.30a–2) shall manually sign a signature page or other document authenticating, acknowledging or otherwise adopting his or her signature that appears in typed form within the electronic filing. Such document shall be executed before or at the time the electronic filing is made and shall be retained by the filer for a period of five years. Upon request, an electronic filer shall furnish to the Commission or its staff a copy of any or all documents retained pursuant to this rule.

(c) Where the Commission's rules require a registrant to furnish to a national securities exchange or national securities association paper copies of a document filed with the Commission in electronic format, signatures to such paper copies may be in typed form.

Rule 303. Incorporation by reference

(a) The following documents shall not be incorporated by reference into an electronic filing:

(1) Any document filed in paper in violation of mandated electronic filing requirements;

(2) Any document filed in paper pursuant to a hardship exemption for which a required confirming electronic copy has not been submitted.

(3) For a registered investment company or a business development company, documents that have not been filed in electronic format, unless the document has been filed in paper under a hardship exemption (Rule 201 or Rule 202) and any required confirming copy has been submitted.

(b) If a filer incorporates by reference into an electronic filing any portion of an annual or quarterly report to security holders, it must also file the portion of the annual or quarterly report to security holders in electronic format as an exhibit to the filing, as required by Regulation S–K Item 601(b)(13) and Regulation S–B Item 601(b)(13) (17 CFR 228.601(b)(13)). If a foreign private issuer incorporates by reference into an electronic filing any portion of an annual or other report to security holders, or of a Form 6–K report (17 CFR 249.306) filed or submitted in paper, it must also file the incorporated portion in electronic format as an exhibit to the filing. The requirements of this paragraph do not apply to incorporation by reference by an investment company from an annual or quarterly report to security holders.

Rule 304. Graphic, image, audio and video material

(a) If a filer includes graphic, image, audio or video material in a document delivered to investors and others that is not reproduced in an electronic filing, the electronically filed version of that document must include a fair and accurate narrative description, tabular representation or transcript of the omitted material. Such descriptions, representations or transcripts may be included in the text of the electronic filing at the point where the graphic, image, audio or video material is presented in the delivered version, or they may be listed in an appendix to the electronic filing. Immaterial differences between the delivered and electronically filed versions, such as pagination, color, type size or style, or corporate logo need not be described.

NOTE TO PARAGRAPH (A): If the omitted graphic, image, audio or video material includes data, filers must include a tabular representation or other appropriate representation of that data in the electronically filed version of the document.

(b)(1) The graphic, image, audio and video material in the version of a document delivered to investors and others is deemed part of the electronic filing and subject to the civil liability and anti-fraud provisions of the federal securities laws.

(2) Narrative descriptions, tabular representations or transcripts of graphic, image, audio and video material included in an electronic filing or appendix thereto also are deemed part of the filing. However, to the extent such descriptions, representations or transcripts represent a good faith effort to fairly and accurately describe omitted graphic, image, audio or video material, they are not subject to the civil liability and anti-fraud provisions of the federal securities laws.

(c) An electronic filer must retain for a period of five years a copy of each publicly distributed document, in the format used, that contains graphic, image, audio or video material where such material is not included in the version filed with the Commission. The five-year period shall commence as of the filing date, or the date that appears on the document, whichever is later. Upon request, an electronic filer shall furnish to the Commission or its staff a copy of any or all of the documents contained in the file.

(d) For electronically filed ASCII documents, the performance graph that is to appear in registrant annual reports to security holders required by Exchange Act Rule 14a–3 or Exchange Act Rule 14c–3 to precede or accompany proxy statements or information statements relating to annual meetings of security holders at which directors are to be elected (or special meetings or written consents in lieu of such meetings), as required by Item 201(e) of Regulation S–K, and the line graph that is to appear in registrant annual reports to security holders, as required by paragraph (b)(7)(ii) of Item 27 of Form N–1A (17 CFR 274.11A), must be furnished to the Commission by presenting the data in tabular or chart form within the electronic ASCII document, in compliance with paragraph (a) of this rule and the formatting requirements of the EDGAR Filer Manual.

(e) Notwithstanding the provisions of paragraphs (a) through (d) of this rule, electronically filed HTML documents must present the following information in an HTML graphic or image file within the electronic submission in compliance with the formatting requirements of the EDGAR Filer Manual: the performance graph that is to appear in registrant annual reports to security holders required by Exchange Act Rule 14a–3 or Exchange Act Rule 14c–3 to precede or accompany registrant proxy statements or information statements relating to annual meetings of security holders at which directors are to be elected (or special meetings or written consents in lieu of such meetings), as required by Item 201(e) of Regulation S–K; the line graph that is to appear in registrant annual reports to security holders, as required by paragraph (b)(7)(ii) of Item 27 of Form N–1A (17 CFR 274.11A); and any other graphic material required by rule or form to be filed with the Commission. Filers may, but are not required to, submit any other graphic material in a HTML document by presenting the data in an HTML graphic or image file within the electronic filing, in compliance with the formatting requirements of the EDGAR Filer Manual. However, filers may not present in a graphic or image file information such as text or tables that users must be able to search and/or download into spreadsheet form (*e.g.*, financial statements); filers must present such material as text in an ASCII document or as text or an HTML table in an HTML document.

(f) Electronic filers may not include animated graphics in any EDGAR document.

Rule 305. Number of characters per line; tabular and columnar information

(a) The narrative portion of a document shall not exceed 80 characters per line, including blank spaces, and shall not be presented in multi-column newspaper format. Non-narrative information (*e.g.*, financial statements) may be presented in tabular or columnar format and may exceed 80 positions only if it is tagged as specified in the EDGAR Filer Manual. In no event shall information presented in tabular or columnar format exceed 132 positions wide.

(b) Paragraph (a) of this rule does not apply to HTML documents, Interactive Data Files (Rule 11) or Interactive Data Financial Reports (Rule 11).

Rule 306. Foreign language documents and symbols

(a) All electronic filings and submissions must be in the English language, except as otherwise provided by paragraph (d) of this rule. If a filing or submission requires the inclusion of a document that is in a foreign language, a party must submit instead a fair and accurate English translation of the foreign language document in accordance with Rule 403(c) or Rule 12b–12(d) under the Securities Exchange Act of 1934, except as otherwise provided by paragraph (c) of this rule. Alternatively, if the foreign language document is an exhibit or attachment to a filing or submission subject to review by the Division of Corporation Finance, a party may provide a fair and accurate English summary of the foreign language document if permitted by Rule 403(c)(3) or Rule 12b–12(d)(3) under the Securities Exchange Act of 1934.

(b) When including an English summary or English translation of a foreign language document in an electronic filing or submission, a party may also submit a copy of the unabridged foreign language document in paper under cover of Form SE (17 CFR 239.64, 249.444, 269.8, and 274.403) in accordance with Rule 311 of Regulation S–T. A filer must provide a copy of any foreign language document upon the request of Commission staff.

(c) A foreign government or its political subdivision must electronically file a fair and accurate English translation, if available, of its latest annual budget as presented to its legislative body, as Exhibit B to Form 18 (17 CFR 249.218) or Exhibit (c) to Form 18–K (17 CFR 249.318). If no English translation is available, a foreign government or political subdivision must submit a copy of the foreign language version of its latest annual budget in paper under cover of Form SE (17 CFR 239.64, 249.444, 269.8, and 274.403).

(d) A Canadian issuer may file an HTML document, as defined in Rule 11 of Regulation S–T, that contains text in both French and English if the issuer included the French text to comply with the requirements of the Canadian securities administrator or other Canadian authority, and the French text is in an exhibit to or part of:

(1) A registration statement on Form F–7, F–8, F–9, F–10, or F–80 (17 CFR 239.37, 239.38, 239.39, 239.40, and 239.41);

(2) A registration statement or annual report on Form 40–F (17 CFR 249.240f); or

(3) A Schedule 13E–4F, Schedule 14D–1F, or Schedule 14D–9F.

(e) Foreign currency denominations must be expressed in words or letters in the English language rather than representative symbols, except that HTML documents may include any representative foreign currency symbols that the EDGAR Filer Manual specifies. The limitations of this paragraph do not apply to unofficial PDF copies submitted in accordance with Rule 104 of Regulation S–T.

Rule 307. Bold face type

(a) Provisions requiring presentation of information in bold face type shall be satisfied in an electronic format document by presenting such information in capital letters.

(b) Paragraph (a) of this rule does not apply to HTML documents.

Rule 308. Type size and font; legibility

Provisions relating to type size, font and other legibility requirements shall not apply to electronic format documents.

Rule 309. Paper size; binding; sequential numbering; number of copies

(a) Requirements as to paper size, binding, and sequential page numbering shall not apply to electronic format documents.

(b) An electronic format document, submitted in the manner prescribed by the EDGAR Filer Manual, shall satisfy any requirement that more than one copy of such document be filed with or provided to the Commission.

Rule 310. Marking changed material

Provisions requiring the marking of changed materials are satisfied in ASCII and HTML documents by inserting the tag <R> before and the tag </R> following a paragraph containing changed material. HTML documents may be marked to show changed materials within paragraphs. Financial statements and notes thereto need not be marked for changed material.

Rule 311. Documents submitted in paper under cover of Form SE

Form SE (17 CFR 239.64, 249.444, 259.603, 269.8, and 274.403) shall be filed as a paper cover sheet to the following documents submitted to the Commission in paper:

(a) Exhibits filed in paper pursuant to a hardship exemption shall be filed under cover of Form SE. See Rules 201 and 202 of Regulation S–T.

(b) Exhibits to a Commission schedule filed pursuant to Section 13 or 14(d) of the Exchange Act may be filed in paper under cover of Form SE where such exhibits previously were filed in paper (prior to a registrant's becoming subject to mandated electronic filing or pursuant to a hardship exemption) and are required to be refiled pursuant to the schedule's general instructions.

(c) A party may submit a copy of an unabridged foreign language document in paper under cover of Form SE if the electronic filing or submission includes an English summary or English translation of the foreign language document in accordance with Rule 306(b) or if permitted by the applicable form.

(d) A foreign government or political subdivision that is not filing in electronic format an English translation of its latest annual budget submitted as Exhibit B to Form 18 (17 CFR 249.218) or Exhibit (c) to Form 18–K (17 CFR 249.318) must file a copy of the foreign language version of its latest annual budget in paper under cover of Form SE in accordance with Rule 306(c) of Regulation S–T.

(e) The Form SE shall be submitted in the following manner:

(1) If the subject of a temporary hardship exemption is an exhibit only, the filer must file the exhibit and a Form TH (17 CFR 239.65, 249.447, 269.10, and 274.404) under cover of Form SE (17 CFR 239.64, 249.444, 269.8, and 274.403) no later than one business day after the date the exhibit was to be filed electronically.

(2) An exhibit filed pursuant to a continuing hardship exemption, or any other document filed in paper under cover of Form SE (other than an exhibit filed pursuant to a temporary hardship exemption), as allowed by paragraphs (a) through (d) of this rule, may be filed up to six business days prior to, or on the date of filing of, the electronic format document to which it relates but shall not be filed after such filing date. If a paper document is submitted in this manner, requirements that the document be filed with, provided with or accompany the electronic filing shall be satisfied.

(f) Any requirements as to delivery or furnishing the information to persons other than the Commission shall not be affected by this rule.

Rule 312. Accommodation for certain information in filings with respect to asset–backed securities

(a) For filings with respect to asset-backed securities filed on or before June 30, 2012, the information provided in response to Item 1105 of Regulation AB may be provided under the following conditions on an Internet Web site for inclusion in the prospectus for the asset-backed securities, and will be deemed to be included in the prospectus included in the registration statement, in lieu of reproducing the information in the electronically filed version of that document. Terms used in this rule have the same meaning as in Item 1101 of Regulation AB.

(1) The prospectus in the registration statement at the time of effectiveness shall disclose the intention to provide such information through a Web site and the prospectus to be filed pursuant to Rule 424 shall provide the specific Internet address where the information is posted.

(2) Such information shall be provided through the Web site unrestricted as to access and free of charge.

(3) Such information shall remain available on the Web site for a period of not less than five years. If a subsequent update or change is made to the information, the date of such update or change shall be clearly indicated on the Web site.

(4) The registrant shall retain all versions of such information provided through the Web site for a period of not less than five years in a form that permits delivery to an investor or the Commission. Upon request, the registrant shall furnish to the Commission or its staff a copy of any or all information retained pursuant to this requirement.

(5) The registration statement shall contain the undertakings required by Item 512(*l*) of Regulation S–K that:

(i) Except as otherwise provided by this rule, such information provided through the specified

Internet address is deemed to be a part of the prospectus included in the registration statement for the asset-backed securities.

(ii) The registrant shall provide to any person without charge, upon request, a copy of such information provided through the specified Internet address as of the date of the prospectus included in the registration statement if a subsequent update or change is made to that information.

NOTE TO PARAGRAPH (a): With respect to paragraphs (a)(3) and (a)(4) of this rule, the five-year period shall commence from the filing date of the prospectus filed pursuant to Rule 424, or the date of first use of the prospectus, whichever is earlier.

(b) This rule does not affect any obligation to provide any other information in the filing electronically on EDGAR.

Rule 313. Identification of investment company type and series and/or class (or contract)

(a) Registered investment companies and business development companies must indicate their investment company type, based on whether the registrant's last effective registration statement or amendment (other than a merger/proxy filing on Form N–14) (17 CFR 239.23) was filed on Form N–1 (17 CFR 239.15 and 274.11), Form N–1A (17 CFR 239.15A 49 and 274.11A), Form N–2 (17 CFR 239.14 and 274.11a–1), Form N–3 (17 CFR 239.17A and 274.11b), Form N–4 (17 CFR 239.17b and 274.11c), Form N–5 (17 CFR 239.24 and 274.5), Form N–6 (17 CFR 239.17c and 274.11d), Form S–1 (17 CFR 239.11), Form S–3 (17 CFR 239.13), or Form S–6 (17 CFR 239.16) in those EDGAR submissions identified in the EDGAR Filer Manual.

(b) Registered investment companies whose last effective registration statement or amendment (other than a merger/proxy filing on Form N–14) (17 CFR 239.23) was filed on Form N–1A (17 CFR 239.15A and 274.11A), Form N–3 (17 CFR 239.17A and 274.11b), Form N–4 (17 CFR 239.17b and 274.11c), or Form N–6 (17 CFR 239.17c and 274.11d) must, under the procedures set forth in the EDGAR Filer Manual:

(1) Provide electronically, and keep current, information concerning their existing and new series and/or classes (or contracts, in the case of separate accounts), including series and/or class (contract) name and ticker symbol, if any, and be issued series and/or class (or contract) identification numbers;

(2) Deactivate for EDGAR purposes any series and/or class (or contract, in the case of separate accounts) that are no longer offered, go out of existence, or deregister following the last filing for that series and/or class (or contract, in the case of separate accounts), but the registrant must not deactivate the last remaining series unless the registrant deregisters; and

(3) For those EDGAR submissions identified in the EDGAR Filer Manual, include all series and/or class (or contract) identifiers of each series and/or class (or contract) on behalf of which the filing is made.

(c) Registered investment companies whose last effective registration statement or amendment (other than a merger/proxy filing on Form N–14 (17 CFR 239.23)) was filed on Form N–1A (17 CFR 239.15A and 274.11A), Form N–3 (17 CFR 239.17A and 274.11b), Form N–4 (17 CFR 239.17b and 274.11c), or Form N–6 (17 CFR 239.17c and 274.11d) must provide electronically, as specified in the EDGAR Filer Manual, in the EDGAR submission identifying information concerning the acquiring fund and the target fund (and the series and/or classes (contracts), if any, of each if in existence at the time of the filing) in connection with merger filings on Form N–14 (17 CFR 239.23), under Rule 425, and in compliance with Regulation 14A (Rule 14a–1 under the Securities Exchange Act of 1934), Schedule 14A (Rule 14a–101 under the Securities Exchange Act of 1934), and all other applicable rules and regulations adopted pursuant to Section 14(a) of the Exchange Act, as referenced in Investment Company Act Rule 20a–1 (17 CFR 270.20a–1).

(d) Non-registrant third party filers making proxy filings with respect to investment companies must designate in the EDGAR submission the type of investment company (as referenced in paragraph (a) of this rule) and include series and/or class (or contract) identifiers in designated EDGAR proxy submission types, in accordance with the EDGAR Filer Manual.

Rule 314. Accommodation for certain securitizers of asset-backed securities

The information required in response to Rule 15Ga–1 under the Securities Exchange Act of 1934 by a municipal securitizer will be deemed to satisfy the electronic submission requirements of Rule 101 under the following conditions:

(a) For purposes of this section, a municipal securitizer is a securitizer (as that term is defined in Section 15G(a) of the Securities Exchange Act of 1934) that is any State or Territory of the United States, the District of Columbia, any political subdivision of any State, Territory or the District of Columbia, or any public instrumentality of one or more States, Territories or the District of Columbia; and

(b) The information required by Rule 15Ga–1 is provided to the Municipal Securities Rulemaking Board in an electronic format available to the public on the Municipal Securities Rulemaking Board's Internet Web site.

INTERACTIVE DATA

Rule 401. [Reserved]

Rule 402. [Reserved]

Rule 403. [Reserved]

Rule 404. [Reserved]

Rule 405. Interactive data file submissions

This section applies to electronic filers that submit Interactive Data Files. Item 601(b)(101) of Regulation S–K, paragraph (101) of Part II—Information Not Required to be Delivered to Offerees or Purchasers of Form F–10 (17 CFR 239.40), paragraph 101 of the Instructions as to Exhibits of Form 20–F (17 CFR 249.220f), paragraph B.(15) of the General Instructions to Form 40–F (17 CFR 249.240f), paragraph C.(6) of the General Instructions to Form 6–K (17 CFR 249.306), and General Instruction C.3.(g) of Form N–1A (17 CFR 239.15A and 274.11A) specify when electronic filers are required or permitted to submit an Interactive Data File (Rule 11 of Regulation S–T), as further described in the note to this section. This section imposes content, format and submission requirements for an Interactive Data File, but does not change the substantive content requirements for the financial and other disclosures in the Related Official Filing (Rule 11 of Regulation S–T).

(a) *Content, Format, and Submission Requirements—General.* An Interactive Data File must:

(1) Comply with the content, format, and submission requirements of this rule;

(2) Be submitted only by an electronic filer either required or permitted to submit an Interactive Data File as specified by Item 601(b)(101) of Regulation S–K, paragraph (101) of Part II—Information Not Required to be Delivered to Offerees or Purchasers of Form F–10 (17 CFR 239.40), paragraph 101 of the Instructions as to Exhibits of Form 20–F (17 CFR 249.220f), paragraph B.(15) of the General Instructions to Form 40–F (17 CFR 249.240f), paragraph C.(6) of the General Instructions to Form 6-K (17 CFR 249.306), or General Instruction C.3.(g) of Form N-1A (17 CFR 239.15A and 274.11A), as applicable;

(3) Be submitted using Inline XBRL:

(i) If the electronic filer is not an open-end management investment company registered under the Investment Company Act of 1940 (15 U.S.C. 80a et seq.) and is not within one of the categories specified in paragraph (f)(1)(i) of this rule, as partly embedded into a filing with the remainder simultaneously submitted as an exhibit to:

(A) A filing that contains the disclosure this section requires to be tagged; or

(B) An amendment to a filing that contains the disclosure this section requires to be tagged if the amendment is filed no more than 30 days after the earlier of the due date or filing date of the filing and the Interactive Data File is the first Interactive Data File the electronic filer submits; or

(ii) If the electronic filer is an open-end management investment company registered under the Investment Company Act of 1940 and is not within one of the categories specified in paragraph (f)(1)(ii) of this rule, as partly embedded into a filing with the remainder simultaneously submitted as an exhibit to a filing that contains the disclosure this section requires to be tagged; and

(4) Be submitted in accordance with the EDGAR Filer Manual and, as applicable, either Item 601(b)(101) of Regulation S–K, paragraph (101) of Part II—Information Not Required to be Delivered to Offerees or Purchasers of Form F–10 (17 CFR 239.40), paragraph 101 of the Instructions as to Exhibits of Form 20–F (17 CFR 249.220f), paragraph B.(15) of the General Instructions to Form 40–F (17 CFR 249.240f), paragraph C.(6) of the General Instructions to Form 6–K (17 CFR 249.306), or General Instruction C.3.(g) of Form N–1A (17 CFR 239.15A and 274.11A).

(b)(1) *Content—Categories of Information Presented.* If the electronic filer is not an open-end management investment company registered under the Investment Company Act of 1940, an Interactive Data File must consist of only a complete set of information for all periods required to be presented in the corresponding data in the Related Official Filing, no more and no less, from all of the following categories:

(i) The complete set of the electronic filer's financial statements (which includes the face of the financial statements and all footnotes); and

(ii) All schedules set forth in Article 12 of Regulation S–X related to the electronic filer's financial statements.

NOTE TO PARAGRAPH (b)(1): It is not permissible for the Interactive Data File to present only partial face financial statements, such as by excluding comparative financial information for prior periods.

(2) If the electronic filer is an open-end management investment company registered under the Investment Company Act of 1940, an Interactive Data File must consist of only a complete set of information for all periods required to be presented in the corresponding data in the Related Official Filing, no more and no less, from the risk/return summary information set forth in Items 2, 3, and 4 of Form N–1A.

(c) *Format—Generally*. An Interactive Data File must comply with the following requirements, except as modified by paragraph (d) or (e) of this rule, as applicable, with respect to the corresponding data in the Related Official Filing consisting of footnotes to financial statements or financial statement schedules as set forth in Article 12 of Regulation S–X:

(1) *Data Elements and Labels*. (i) *Element Accuracy*. Each data element (*i.e.*, all text, line item names, monetary values, percentages, numbers, dates and other labels) contained in the Interactive Data File reflects the same information in the corresponding data in the Related Official Filing;

(ii) *Element Specificity*. No data element contained in the corresponding data in the Related Official Filing is changed, deleted or summarized in the Interactive Data File;

(iii) *Standard and Special Labels and Elements*. Each data element contained in the Interactive Data File is matched with an appropriate tag from the most recent version of the standard list of tags specified by the EDGAR Filer Manual. A tag is appropriate only when its standard definition, standard label and other attributes as and to the extent identified in the list of tags match the information to be tagged, except that:

(A) *Labels*. An electronic filer must create and use a new special label to modify a tag's existing standard label when that tag is an appropriate tag in all other respects (*i.e.*, in order to use a tag from the standard list of tags only its label needs to be changed); and

(B) *Elements*. An electronic filer must create and use a new special element if and only if an appropriate tag does not exist in the standard list of tags for reasons other than or in addition to an inappropriate standard label; and

(2) *Additional Mark–Up Related Content*. The Interactive Data File contains any additional mark-up related content (*e.g.*, the eXtensible Business Reporting Language tags themselves, identification of the core XML documents used and other technology related content) not found in the corresponding data in the Related Official Filing that is necessary to comply with the EDGAR Filer Manual requirements.

(d) *Format—Footnotes—Generally*. The part of the Interactive Data File for which the corresponding data in the Related Official Filing consists of footnotes to financial statements must comply with the requirements of paragraphs (c)(1) and (2) of this rule, as modified by this paragraph (d). Footnotes to financial statements must be tagged as follows:

(1) Each complete footnote must be block-text tagged;

(2) Each significant accounting policy within the significant accounting policies footnote must be block-text tagged;

(3) Each table within each footnote must be block-text tagged; and

(4) Within each footnote,

(i) Each amount (*i.e.*, monetary value, percentage, and number) must be tagged separately; and

(ii) Each narrative disclosure may be tagged separately to the extent the electronic filer chooses.

(e) *Format—Schedules—Generally*. The part of the Interactive Data File for which the corresponding data in the Related Official Filing consists of financial statement schedules as set forth in Article 12 of Regulation S–X must comply with the requirements of paragraphs (c)(1) and (2) of this rule, as modified by this paragraph (e). Financial statement schedules as set forth in Article 12 of Regulation S–X must be tagged as follows:

(1) Each complete financial statement schedule must be block-text tagged; and

(2) Within each financial statement schedule,

(i) Each amount (*i.e.*, monetary value, percentage and number) must be tagged separately; and

(ii) Each narrative disclosure may be tagged separately to the extent the electronic filer chooses.

(f) *Format—Phase-in for Inline XBRL Submissions.* (1) The following electronic filers may choose to submit an Interactive Data File:

(i) In the manner specified in paragraph (f)(2) of this rule rather than as specified by paragraph (a)(3)(i) of this rule: any electronic filer that is not an open-end management investment company registered under the Investment Company Act of 1940 if it is within one of the following categories, provided, however, that an Interactive Data File first is required to be submitted in the manner specified by paragraph (a)(3)(i) of this rule for a periodic report on Form 10–Q (17 CFR 249.308a) if the filer reports on Form 10–Q:

(A) A large accelerated filer (Rule 12b–2 of the Securities Exchange Act of 1934) that prepares its financial statements in accordance with generally accepted accounting principles as used in the United States and none of the financial statements for which an Interactive Data File is required is for a fiscal period that ends on or after June 15, 2019;

(B) An accelerated filer (Rule 12b–2 of the Securities Exchange Act of 1934) that prepares its financial statements in accordance with generally accepted accounting principles as used in the United States and none of the financial statements for which an Interactive Data File is required is for a fiscal period that ends on or after June 15, 2020; and

(C) A filer not specified in paragraph (f)(1)(i)(A) or (B) of this rule that prepares its financial statements in accordance with either generally accepted accounting principles as used in the United States or International Financial Reporting Standards as issued by the International Accounting Standards Board and none of the financial statements for which an Interactive Data File is required is for a fiscal period that ends on or after June 15, 2021.

(ii) In the manner specified in paragraph (f)(3) of this rule rather than as specified by paragraph (a)(3)(ii) of this rule: any electronic filer that is an open-end management investment company registered under the Investment Company Act of 1940 that, together with other investment companies in the same "group of related investment companies," as such term is defined in 17 CFR 270.0–10, has assets of:

(A) $1 billion or more as of the end of the most recent fiscal year until it files an initial registration statement (or post-effective amendment that is an annual update to an effective registration statement) that becomes effective on or after September 17, 2020; and

(B) Less than $1 billion as of the end of the most recent fiscal year until it files an initial registration statement (or post-effective amendment that is an annual update to an effective registration statement) that becomes effective on or after September 17, 2021.

(2) The electronic filers specified in paragraph (f)(1)(i) of this rule may submit the Interactive Data File solely as an exhibit to:

(i) A filing that contains the disclosure this section requires to be tagged; or

(ii) An amendment to a filing that contains the disclosure this section requires to be tagged if the amendment is filed no more than 30 days after the earlier of the due date or filing date of the filing and the Interactive Data File is the first Interactive Data File the electronic filer submits.

(3) The electronic filers specified in paragraph (f)(1)(ii) of this rule may submit the Interactive Data File solely as an exhibit to a filing that contains the disclosure this section requires to be tagged, up to 15 business days after the effective date of the registration statement or post-effective amendment that contains the related information, or the filing of a form of prospectus made pursuant to paragraph (c) or (e) of Rule 497.

Note to Rule 405: Item 601(b)(101) of Regulation S–K specifies the circumstances under which an Interactive Data File must be submitted and the circumstances under which it is permitted to be submitted, with respect to Forms S–1 (17 CFR 239.11), S–3 (17 CFR 239.13), S–4 (17 CFR 239.25), S–11 (17 CFR 239.18), F–1 (17 CFR 239.31), F–3 (17 CFR 239.33), F–4 (17 CFR 239.34), 10–K (17 CFR 249.310), 10–Q (17 CFR 249.308a), and 8–K (17 CFR 249.308). Paragraph (101) of Part II—Information not Required to be Delivered to Offerees or Purchasers of Form F–10 (17 CFR 239.40) specifies the circumstances under which an Interactive Data File must be submitted and the circumstances under which it is permitted to be submitted, with respect to Form F–10. Paragraph 101 of the Instructions as to Exhibits of Form 20–F (17 CFR 249.220f) specifies the circumstances under which an Interactive Data File must be submitted and the circumstances under which it is permitted to be submitted, with respect to Form 20-F. Paragraph B.(15) of the General Instructions to Form 40–F (17 CFR 249.240f) and Paragraph C.(6) of the General Instructions to Form 6–K (17 CFR 249.306) specify the circumstances under which an Interactive Data File must be submitted and the circumstances under which it is permitted to be submitted, with respect to Form 40–F and Form 6–K (17 CFR 249.240f and §249.306), respectively. Item 601(b)(101) of Regulation S–K, paragraph (101) of Part II—Information not Required to be Delivered to Offerees or Purchasers of Form F–10, paragraph 101 of the Instructions as to Exhibits of Form 20–F, paragraph B.(15) of the General Instructions to Form 40–F, and paragraph C.(6) of the General Instructions to Form 6–K all prohibit submission of an Interactive Data File by an issuer that prepares its financial statements in accordance with Article 6 of Regulation S–X. For an issuer that is an open-end management investment company registered under the Investment Company Act of 1940, General Instruction C.3.(g) of Form N–1A (17 CFR 239.15A and 274.11A) specifies the circumstances under which an Interactive Data File must be submitted.

Rule 407. Interactive data financial report filings

Section 407 of Regulation S–T applies to electronic filers that file Interactive Data Financial Reports (Rule 11) as required by Rule 13n–11(f)(5). Section 407 imposes content, format, and filing requirements for Interactive Data Financial Reports, but does not change the substantive content requirements for the financial and other disclosures in the Related Official Financial Report Filing (Rule 11). Rule 13n–11(f)(5) specifies the circumstances under which an Interactive Data Financial Report must be filed as an exhibit.

(a) *Content, format, and filing requirements – General.* Interactive Data Financial Reports must:

(1) Comply with the content, format, and filing requirements of this section;

(2) Be filed only by an electronic filer that is required to file an Interactive Data Financial Report pursuant to Rule 13n–11(f)(5) as an exhibit to a filing; and

(3) Be filed in accordance with the EDGAR Filer Manual and Rules 13n–11(f)(5) and (g).

(b) *Content – categories of information presented.* An Interactive Data Financial Report must consist of only a complete set of information for all periods required to be presented in the corresponding data in the Related Official Financial Report Filing, no more and no less, for the following categories, as applicable:

(1) The complete set of the electronic filer's financial statements (which includes the face of the financial statements and all footnotes); and

(2) All schedules set forth in Article 12 of Regulation S–X related to the electronic filer's financial statements.

NOTE TO PARAGRAPH (b): It is not permissible for the Interactive Data Financial Report to present only partial face financial statements, such as by excluding comparative financial information for prior periods.

(c) *Format – Generally.* An Interactive Data Financial Report must comply with the following requirements, except as modified by paragraph (d) or (e) of this section, as applicable, with respect to the corresponding data in the Related Official Financial Report Filing consisting of footnotes to financial statements or financial statement schedules as set forth in Article 12 of Regulation S–X:

(1) *Data elements and labels*—(i) *Element accuracy.* Each data element (*i.e.*, all text, line item names, monetary values, percentages, numbers, dates and other labels) contained in the Interactive Data Financial Report reflects the same information in the corresponding data in the Related Official Financial Report Filing;

(ii) *Element specificity.* No data element contained in the corresponding data in the Related Official Financial Report Filing is changed, deleted or summarized in the Interactive Data Financial Report;

(iii) *Standard and special labels and elements.* Each data element contained in the Interactive Data Financial Report is matched with an appropriate tag from the most recent version of the standard list of tags specified by the EDGAR Filer Manual. A tag is appropriate only when its standard definition, standard label, and other attributes as and to the extent identified in the list of tags match the information to be tagged, except that:

(A) *Labels.* An electronic filer must create and use a new special label to modify a tag's existing standard label when that tag is an appropriate tag in all other respects (i.e., in order to use a tag from the standard list of tags only its label needs to be changed); and

(B) *Elements.* An electronic filer must create and use a new special element if and only if an appropriate tag does not exist in the standard list of tags for reasons other than or in addition to an inappropriate standard label; and

(2) *Additional mark-up related content.* The Interactive Data Financial Report contains any additional mark-up related content (*e.g.*, the eXtensible Business Reporting Language tags themselves, identification of the core XML documents used and other technology-related content) not found in the corresponding data in the Related Official Financial Report Filing that is necessary to comply with the EDGAR Filer Manual requirements.

(d) *Format – Footnotes - Generally.* The part of the Interactive Data Financial Report for which the corresponding data in the Related Official Financial Report Filing consists of footnotes to financial statements must comply with the requirements of paragraphs (c)(1) and (2) of this section, as modified by this paragraph (d). Each complete footnote must be block-text tagged.

(e) *Format – Schedules - Generally.* The part of the Interactive Data Financial Report for which the corresponding data in the Related Official Financial Report Filing consists of financial statement schedules as set forth in Article 12 of Regulation S–X must comply with the requirements of paragraphs (c)(1) and (2) of this section, as modified by this paragraph (e). Each complete schedule must be block-text tagged.

EDGAR FUNCTIONS

Rule 501. Modular submissions and segmented filings

An electronic filer may use the following procedures to submit information to the EDGAR system for subsequent inclusion in an electronic filing:

(a) *Modular Submissions.* (1) One or more electronic format documents may be submitted for storage in the non-public EDGAR data storage area as a modular submission for subsequent inclusion in one or more electronic submissions.

(2) An electronic filer shall be permitted a maximum of ten modular submissions in the non-public EDGAR data storage area at any time, not to exceed a total of one megabyte of digital information. If an electronic filer attempts to submit a modular filing which would cause either of these limits to be exceeded, EDGAR will suspend the modular submission and notify the electronic filer by electronic mail. After six business days, the modular submission held in suspense will be deleted from the system.

(3) A modular submission may be corrected or amended only by resubmitting the entire modular submission.

(b) *Segmented Filings.* (1) Segments of a document intended to become an electronic filing may be submitted to the non-public EDGAR data storage area for assembly as a segmented filing.

(2) Segments shall be submitted no more than six business days in advance of the anticipated filing date and are not limited in number or size. They may be submitted from several geographic locations by more than one filing entity. Segments may be included in only one electronic filing. Once used, segments will be removed from the non-public EDGAR data storage area. The assembly of segments into a segmented filing shall be effected pursuant to the applicable provisions of the EDGAR Filer Manual. If segments are not prepared in accordance with the EDGAR Filer Manual, the filing will not be constructed. The filing date of a segmented filing shall be the date upon which the filing is assembled and satisfies the requirements of Rule 13(a) of Regulation S–T.

(3) Segments may be corrected or amended only by resubmitting the entire segment.

(c) A modular submission or segment shall not:

(1) be publicly available;

(2) be deemed filed with the Commission for purposes of Securities Act of 1933 section 11 (15 U.S.C. 77k), Securities Exchange Act of 1934 section 18 (15 U.S.C. 78r), Trust Indenture Act section 323 (15 U.S.C. 77www), or Investment Company Act section 34(b) (15 U.S.C. 80a–33(b)) prior to its inclusion in a filing; or

(3) be deemed to constitute an official filing prior to its inclusion in a filing under the federal securities laws. Once a modular submission or segment has been included in an electronic filing, the liability and anti-fraud provisions of the Securities Act of 1933, the Securities Exchange Act of 1934, the Trust Indenture Act, and the Investment Company Act shall apply to the electronic filing.

UNITED STATES
SECURITIES AND EXCHANGE COMMISSION

FORM 1–A

REGULATION A OFFERING STATEMENT

UNDER THE SECURITIES ACT OF 1933

GENERAL INSTRUCTIONS

I. Eligibility Requirements for Use of Form 1-A.

This Form is to be used for securities offerings made pursuant to Regulation A (17 CFR 230.251 et seq.). Careful attention should be directed to the terms, conditions and requirements of Regulation A, especially Rule 251, because the exemption is not available to all issuers or for every type of securities transaction. Further, the aggregate offering price and aggregate sales of securities in any 12-month period is strictly limited to $20 million for Tier 1 offerings and $50 million for Tier 2 offerings, including no more than $6 million offered by all selling securityholders that are affiliates of the issuer for Tier 1 offerings and $15 million by all selling securityholders that are affiliates of the issuer for Tier 2 offerings. Please refer to Rule 251 of Regulation A for more details.

II. Preparation, Submission and Filing of the Offering Statement.

An offering statement must be prepared by all persons seeking exemption under the provisions of Regulation A. Parts I, II and III must be addressed by all issuers. Part II, which relates to the content of the required offering circular, provides alternative formats, of which the issuer must choose one. General information regarding the preparation, format, content, and submission or filing of the offering statement is contained in Rule 252. Information regarding non-public submission of the offering statement is contained in Rule 252(d). Requirements relating to the offering circular are contained in Rules 253 and 254. The offering statement must be submitted or filed with the Securities and Exchange Commission in electronic format by means of the Commission's Electronic Data Gathering, Analysis and Retrieval System (EDGAR) in accordance with the EDGAR rules set forth in Regulation S-T (17 CFR Part 232) for such submission or filing.

III. Incorporation by Reference and Cross-Referencing.

An issuer may incorporate by reference to other documents previously submitted or filed on EDGAR. Cross-referencing within the offering statement is also encouraged to avoid repetition of information. For example, you may respond to an item of this Form by providing a cross-reference to the location of the information in the financial statements, instead of repeating such information. Incorporation by reference and cross-referencing are subject to the following additional conditions:

(a) The use of incorporation by reference and cross-referencing in Part II of this Form is limited to the following items:

(1) Items 2-14 of Part II if following the Offering Circular format;

(2) Items 3-11 (other than Item 11(e)) of Form S-1 if following the Part I of Form S-1 format; or

(3) Items 3-26, 28, and 30 of Form S-11 if following the Part I of Form S-11 format.

(b) Descriptions of where the information incorporated by reference or cross-referenced can be found must be specific and must clearly identify the relevant document and portion thereof where such information can be found. For exhibits incorporated by reference, this description must be noted in the exhibits index for each relevant exhibit. All descriptions of where information incorporated by reference can be found must be accompanied by a hyperlink to the incorporated document on EDGAR, which hyperlink need not remain active after the filing of the offering statement. Inactive hyperlinks must be updated in any amendment to the offering statement otherwise required.

(c) Reference may not be made to any document if the portion of such document containing the pertinent information includes an incorporation by reference to another document. Incorporation by reference to documents not available on EDGAR is not permitted. Incorporating information into the financial statements from elsewhere is not permitted. Information shall not be incorporated by reference or cross-referenced in any case where such incorporation would render the statement or report incomplete, unclear, or confusing.

(d) If any substantive modification has occurred in the text of any document incorporated by reference since such document was filed, the issuer must file with the reference a statement containing the text and date of such modification.

IV. Supplemental Information.

The information specified below must be furnished to the Commission as supplemental information, if applicable. Supplemental information shall not be required to be filed with or deemed part of the offering statement, unless otherwise required. The information shall be returned to the issuer upon request made in writing at the time of submission, provided that the return of such information is consistent with the protection of investors and the provisions of the Freedom of Information Act [5 U.S.C. 552] and the information was not filed in electronic format.

(a) A statement as to whether or not the amount of compensation to be allowed or paid to the underwriter has been cleared with the Financial Industry Regulatory Authority (FINRA).

(b) Any engineering, management, market, or similar report referenced in the offering circular or provided for external use by the issuer or by a principal underwriter in connection with the proposed offering. There must also be furnished at the same time a statement as to the actual or proposed use and distribution of such report or memorandum. Such statement must identify each class of persons who have received or will receive the report or memorandum, and state the number of copies distributed to each such class along with a statement as to the actual or proposed use and distribution of such report or memorandum.

(c) Such other information as requested by the staff in support of statements, representations and other assertions contained in the offering statement or any correspondence to the staff.

Correspondence appropriately responding to any staff comments made on the offering statement must also be furnished electronically. When applicable, such correspondence must clearly indicate where changes responsive to the staff's comments may be found in the offering statement.

PART I—NOTIFICATION

The following information must be provided in the XML-based portion of Form 1-A available through the EDGAR portal and must be completed or updated before uploading each offering statement or amendment thereto. The format of Part I shown below may differ from the electronic version available on EDGAR. The

electronic version of Part I will allow issuers to attach Part II and Part III for filing by means of EDGAR. All items must be addressed, unless otherwise indicated.

*** * * * * ***

☐ No changes to the information required by Part I have occurred since the last filing of this offering statement.

ITEM 1. Issuer Information

Exact name of issuer as specified in the issuer's charter: ______________________

Jurisdiction of incorporation/organization: ______________________

Year of incorporation: ____________

CIK: ____________

Primary Standard Industrial Classification Code: ______________

I.R.S. Employer Identification Number: ______________

Total number of full-time employees: ______________

Total number of part-time employees: ______________

Contact Information

Address of Principal Executive Offices: ______________________

____

Telephone: ( ) ____________

Provide the following information for the person the Securities and Exchange Commission's staff should call in connection with any pre-qualification review of the offering statement:

Name: ______________________

Address: ______________________

Telephone: ( ) ______________

Provide up to two e-mail addresses to which the Securities and Exchange Commission's staff may send any comment letters relating to the offering statement. After qualification of the offering statement, such e-mail addresses are not required to remain active: ______________________

____

Financial Statements

Industry Group (select one): ☐ Banking ☐ Insurance ☐ Other

Use the financial statements for the most recent fiscal period contained in this offering statement to provide the following information about the issuer. The following table does not include all of the line items from the financial statements. Long Term Debt would include notes payable, bonds, mortgages, and similar obligations. To determine "Total Revenues" for all companies selecting "Other" for their industry group, refer to Article 5-03(b)(1) of Regulation S-X. For companies selecting "Insurance," refer to Article 7-04 of Regulation S-X for calculation of "Total Revenues" and paragraphs 5 and 7(a) for "Costs and Expenses Applicable to Revenues".

[If "Other" is selected, display the following options in the Financial Statements table:]

Balance Sheet Information

Cash and Cash Equivalents: ________________
Investment Securities: ________________
Accounts and Notes Receivable: ________________
Property, Plant and Equipment (PP&E): ________________
Total Assets: ________________
Accounts Payable and Accrued Liabilities: ________________
Long Term Debt: ________________
Total Liabilities: ________________
Total Stockholders' Equity: ________________
Total Liabilities and Equity: ________________

Statement of Comprehensive Income Information

Total Revenues: ________________
Costs and Expenses Applicable to Revenues: ________________
Depreciation and Amortization: ________________
Net Income: ________________
Earnings Per Share – Basic: ________________
Earnings Per Share – Diluted: ________________

[If "Banking" is selected, display the following options in the Financial Statements table:]

Balance Sheet Information

Cash and Cash Equivalents: ________________
Investment Securities: ________________
Loans: ________________
Property and Equipment: ________________
Total Assets: ________________
Accounts Payable and Accrued Liabilities: ________________
Deposits: ________________
Long Term Debt: ________________
Total Liabilities: ________________
Total Stockholders' Equity: ________________
Total Liabilities and Equity: ________________

Statement of Comprehensive Income Information
Total Interest Income: ____________
Total Interest Expense: Depreciation ____________
and Amortization: Net Income: ____________
Earnings Per Share – Basic: ____________
Earnings Per Share – Diluted: ____________

[If "Insurance" is selected, display the following options in the Financial Statements table:]

Balance Sheet Information
Cash and Cash Equivalents: ____________
Total Investments: ____________
Accounts and Notes Receivable: ____________
Property and Equipment: ____________
Total Assets: ____________
Accounts Payable and Accrued Liabilities: ____________
Policy Liabilities and Accruals: ____________
Long Term Debt: ____________
Total Liabilities: ____________
Total Stockholders' Equity: ____________
Total Liabilities and Equity: ____________

Statement of Comprehensive Income Information
Total Revenues: ____________
Costs and Expenses Applicable to Revenues: ____________
Depreciation and Amortization: ____________
Net Income: ____________
Earnings Per Share – Basic: ____________
Earnings Per Share – Diluted:

[End of section that varies based on the selection of Industry Group]

Name of Auditor (if any): ____________

Outstanding Securities

	Name of Class (if any)	Units Outstanding	CUSIP (if any)	Name of Trading Center or Quotation Medium (if any)
Common Equity				
Preferred Equity				
Debt Securities				

ITEM 2. Issuer Eligibility

☐ Check this box to certify that all of the following statements are true for the issuer(s):

- Organized under the laws of the United States or Canada, or any State, Province, Territory or possession thereof, or the District of Columbia.
- Principal place of business is in the United States or Canada.
- Not subject to section 13 or 15(d) of the Securities Exchange Act of 1934.
- Not a development stage company that either (a) has no specific business plan or purpose, or (b) has indicated that its business plan is to merge with an unidentified company or companies.
- Not an investment company registered or required to be registered under the Investment Company Act of 1940.
- Not issuing fractional undivided interests in oil or gas rights, or a similar interest in other mineral rights.
- Not issuing asset-backed securities as defined in Item 1101(c) of Regulation AB.
- Not, and has not been, subject to any order of the Commission entered pursuant to Section 12(j) of the Exchange Act (15 U.S.C. 78l(j)) within five years before the filing of this offering statement.
- Has filed with the Commission all the reports it was required to file, if any, pursuant to Rule 257 during the two years immediately before the filing of the offering statement (or for such shorter period that the issuer was required to file such reports).

ITEM 3. Application of Rule 262

☐ Check this box to certify that, as of the time of this filing, each person described in Rule 262 of Regulation A is either not disqualified under that rule or is disqualified but has received a waiver of such disqualification.

☐ Check this box if "bad actor" disclosure under Rule 262(d) is provided in Part II of the offering statement.

ITEM 4. Summary Information Regarding the Offering and Other Current or Proposed Offerings

Check the appropriate box to indicate whether you are conducting a Tier 1 or Tier 2 offering:

☐ Tier 1 ☐ Tier 2

Check the appropriate box to indicate whether the annual financial statements have been audited:

☐ Unaudited ☐ Audited

Types of Securities Offered in this Offering Statement (select all that apply):

☐ Equity (common or preferred stock)
☐ Debt
☐ Option, warrant or other right to acquire another security
☐ Security to be acquired upon exercise of option, warrant or other right to acquire security
☐ Tenant-in-common securities
☐ Other (describe) ______________________________

Does the issuer intend to offer the securities on a delayed or continuous basis pursuant to Rule 251(d)(3)?
Yes ☐ No ☐

Does the issuer intend this offering to last more than one year?
Yes ☐ No ☐

Does the issuer intend to price this offering after qualification pursuant to Rule 253(b)?
Yes ☐ No ☐

Will the issuer be conducting a best efforts offering?
Yes ☐ No ☐

Has the issuer used solicitation of interest communications in connection with the proposed offering?
Yes ☐ No ☐

Does the proposed offering involve the resale of securities by affiliates of the issuer?
Yes ☐ No ☐

Number of securities offered: ______________________________

Number of securities of that class already outstanding: ______________________________

The information called for by this item below may be omitted if undetermined at the time of filing or submission, except that if a price range has been included in the offering statement, the midpoint of that range must be used to respond. Please refer to Rule 251(a) for the definition of "aggregate offering price" or "aggregate sales" as used in this item. Please leave the field blank if undetermined at this time and include a zero if a particular item is not applicable to the offering.

Price per security: $ ____________________

The portion of the aggregate offering price attributable to securities being offered on behalf of the issuer:
$ ____________________

The portion of the aggregate offering price attributable to securities being offered on behalf of selling security-holders:
$ ____________________

The portion of aggregate offering attributable to all the securities of the issuer sold pursuant to a qualified offering statement within the 12 months before the qualification of this offering statement:
$ ____________________

The estimated portion of aggregate sales attributable to securities that may be sold pursuant to any other qualified offering statement concurrently with securities being sold under this offering statement:
$ ____________________

Total: $ ____________________ (the sum of the aggregate offering price and aggregate sales in the four preceding paragraphs).

Anticipated fees in connection with this offering and names of service providers:

	Name of Service Provider	Fees
Underwriters:	____________	$ ____________
Sales Commissions:	____________	$ ____________
Finders' Fees:	____________	$ ____________
Audit:	____________	$ ____________
Legal:	____________	$ ____________
Promoters:	____________	$ ____________
Blue Sky Compliance:	____________	$ ____________

CRD Number of any broker or dealer listed: ____________________
Estimated net proceeds to the issuer: $ ____________________

Clarification of responses (if necessary):

ITEM 5. Jurisdictions in Which Securities are to be Offered

Using the list below, select the jurisdictions in which the issuer intends to offer the securities:

[List will include all U.S. and Canadian jurisdictions, with an option to add and remove them individually, add all and remove all.]

Using the list below, select the jurisdictions in which the securities are to be offered by underwriters, dealers or sales persons or check the appropriate box:

☐ None

☐ Same as the jurisdictions in which the issuer intends to offer the securities.

[List will include all U.S. and Canadian jurisdictions, with an option to add and remove them individually, add all and remove all.]

ITEM 6. Unregistered Securities Issued or Sold Within One Year

☐ None

As to any unregistered securities issued by the issuer or any of its predecessors or affiliated issuers within one year before the filing of this Form 1-A, state:

(a) Name of such issuer.

(b) (1) Title of securities issued

(2) Total amount of such securities issued

(3) Amount of such securities sold by or for the account of any person who at the time was a director, officer, promoter or principal securityholder of the issuer of such securities, or was an underwriter of any securities of such issuer

(c) (1) Aggregate consideration for which the securities were issued and basis for computing the amount thereof. ______________________________

____

____

(2) Aggregate consideration for which the securities listed in (b)(3) of this item (if any) were issued and the basis for computing the amount thereof (if different from the basis described in (c)(1)).

(d) Indicate the section of the Securities Act or Commission rule or regulation relied upon for exemption from the registration requirements of such Act and state briefly the facts relied upon for such exemption: ______________________________

____

____

PART II — INFORMATION REQUIRED IN OFFERING CIRCULAR

(a) Financial statement requirements regardless of the applicable disclosure format are specified in Part F/S of this Form 1-A. The narrative disclosure contents of offering circulars are specified as follows:

(1) The information required by:

(i) the Offering Circular format described below; or

(ii) The information required by Part I of Form S-1 (17 CFR 239.11) or Part I of Form S-11 (17

CFR 239.18), except for the financial statements, selected financial data, and supplementary financial information called for by those forms. An issuer choosing to follow the Form S-1 or Form S-11 format may follow the requirements for smaller reporting companies if it meets the definition of that term in Rule 405 (17 CFR 230.405). An issuer may only use the Form S-11 format if the offering is eligible to be registered on that form;

The cover page of the offering circular must identify which disclosure format is being followed.

(2) The offering circular must describe any matters that would have triggered disqualification under Rule 262(a)(3) or (a)(5) but for the provisions set forth in Rule 262(b)(1);

(3) The legend required by Rule 253(f) of Regulation A must be included on the offering circular cover page (for issuers following the S-1 or S-11 disclosure models this legend must be included instead of the legend required by Item 501(b)(7) of Regulation S-K);

(4) For preliminary offering circulars, the legend required by Rule 254(a) must be included on the offering circular cover page (for issuers following the S-1 or S-11 disclosure models, this legend must be included instead of the legend required by Item 501(b)(10) of Regulation S-K); and

(5) For Tier 2 offerings where the securities will not be listed on a registered national securities exchange upon qualification, the offering circular cover page must include the following legend highlighted by prominent type or in another manner:

> Generally, no sale may be made to you in this offering if the aggregate purchase price you pay is more than 10% of the greater of your annual income or net worth. Different rules apply to accredited investors and non-natural persons. Before making any representation that your investment does not exceed applicable thresholds, we encourage you to review Rule 251(d)(2)(i)(C) of Regulation A. For general information on investing, we encourage you to refer to www.investor.gov.

(b) The Commission encourages the use of management's projections of future economic performance that have a reasonable basis and are presented in an appropriate format. See Rule 175, 17 CFR 230.175.

(c) Offering circulars need not follow the order of the items or the order of other requirements of the disclosure form except to the extent otherwise specifically provided. Such information may not, however, be set forth in such a fashion as to obscure any of the required information or any information necessary to keep the required information from being incomplete or misleading. Information requested to be presented in a specified tabular format must be given in substantially the tabular format specified. For incorporation by reference, please refer to General Instruction III of this Form.

OFFERING CIRCULAR

Item 1. Cover Page of Offering Circular

The cover page of the offering circular must be limited to one page and must include the information specified in this item.

(a) Name of the issuer.

Instruction to Item 1(a):

If your name is the same as, or confusingly similar to, that of a company that is well known, include information to eliminate any possible confusion with the other company. If your name indicates a line of business in which you are not engaged or you are engaged only to a limited extent, include information to eliminate any misleading inference as to your business. In some circumstances, disclosure may not be sufficient and you may be required to change your name. You will not be required to change your name if you are an established company, the character of your business has changed, and the investing public is generally aware of the change and the character of your current business.

(b) Full mailing address of the issuer's principal executive offices and the issuer's telephone number (including the area code) and, if applicable, website address.

(c) Date of the offering circular.

(d) Title and amount of securities offered. Separately state the amount of securities offered by selling securityholders, if any. Include a cross-reference to the section where the disclosure required by Item 14 of Part II of this Form 1-A has been provided;

(e) The information called for by the applicable table below as to all the securities being offered, in substantially the tabular format indicated. If necessary, you may estimate any underwriting discounts and commissions and the proceeds to the issuer or other persons.

	Price to public	Underwriting discount and commissions	Proceeds to issuer	Proceeds to other persons
Per share/unit:				
Total:				

If the securities are to be offered on a best efforts basis, the cover page must set forth the termination date, if any, of the offering, any minimum required sale and any arrangements to place the funds received in an escrow, trust, or similar arrangement. The following table must be used instead of the preceding table.

	Price to public	Underwriting discount and commissions	Proceeds to issuer	Proceeds to other persons
Per share/unit:				
Total Minimum:				
Total Maximum:				

Instructions to Item 1(e):

1. The term "commissions" includes all cash, securities, contracts, or anything else of value, paid, to be set aside, disposed of, or understandings with or for the benefit of any other persons in which any underwriter is interested, made in connection with the sale of such security.

2. Only commissions paid by the issuer in cash are to be indicated in the table. Commissions paid by other persons or any form of non-cash compensation must be briefly identified in a footnote to the table with a cross-reference to a more complete description elsewhere in the offering circular.

3. Before the commencement of sales pursuant to Regulation A, the issuer must inform the Commission whether or not the amount of compensation to be allowed or paid to the underwriters, as described in the offering statement, has been cleared with FINRA.

4. If the securities are not to be offered for cash, state the basis upon which the offering is to be made.

5. Any finder's fees or similar payments must be disclosed on the cover page with a reference to a more complete discussion in the offering circular. Such disclosure must identify the finder, the nature of the services rendered and the nature of any relationship between the finder and the issuer, its officers, directors, promoters, principal stockholders and underwriters (including any affiliates of such persons).

6. The amount of the expenses of the offering borne by the issuer, including underwriting expenses to be borne by the issuer, must be disclosed in a footnote to the table.

(f) The name of the underwriter or underwriters.

(g) Any legend or information required by the law of any state in which the securities are to be offered.

(h) A cross-reference to the risk factors section, including the page number where it appears in the offering circular. Highlight this cross-reference by prominent type or in another manner.

(i) Approximate date of commencement of proposed sale to the public.

(j) If the issuer intends to rely on Rule 253(b) and a preliminary offering circular is circulated, provide (1) a bona fide estimate of the range of the maximum offering price and the maximum number of securities offered or (2) a bona fide estimate of the principal amount of the debt securities offered. The range must not exceed $2 for offerings where the upper end of the range is $10 or less and 20% if the upper end of the price range is over $10.

Instruction to Item 1(j):

The upper limit of the price range must be used in determining the aggregate offering price for purposes of Rule 251(a).

Item 2. Table of Contents

On the page immediately following the cover page of the offering circular, provide a reasonably detailed table of contents. It must show the page numbers of the various sections or subdivisions of the offering circular. Include a specific listing of the risk factors section required by Item 3 of Part II of this Form 1-A.

Item 3. Summary and Risk Factors

(a) An issuer may provide a summary of the information in the offering circular where the length or complexity of the offering circular makes a summary useful. The summary should be brief and must not contain all of the detailed information in the offering circular.

(b) Immediately following the Table of Contents required by Item 2 or the Summary, there must be set forth under an appropriate caption, a carefully organized series of short, concise paragraphs, summarizing the most significant factors that make the offering speculative or substantially risky. Issuers should avoid generalized statements and include only factors that are specific to the issuer.

Item 4. Dilution

Where there is a material disparity between the public offering price and the effective cash cost to officers, directors, promoters and affiliated persons for shares acquired by them in a transaction during the past year, or that they have a right to acquire, there must be included a comparison of the public contribution under the proposed public offering and the average effective cash contribution of such persons.

Item 5. Plan of Distribution and Selling Securityholders

(a) If the securities are to be offered through underwriters, give the names of the principal underwriters, and state the respective amounts underwritten. Identify each such underwriter having a material relationship to the issuer and state the nature of the relationship. State briefly the nature of the underwriters' obligation to take the securities.

Instructions to Item 5(a):

1. All that is required as to the nature of the underwriters' obligation is whether the underwriters are or will be committed to take and to pay for all of the securities if any are taken, or whether it is merely an agency or the type of best efforts arrangement under which the underwriters are required to take and to pay for only such securities as they may sell to the public. Conditions precedent to the underwriters' taking the securities, including market outs, need not be described except in the case of an agency or best efforts arrangement.

2. It is not necessary to disclose each member of a selling group. Disclosure may be limited to those underwriters who are in privity of contract with the issuer with respect to the offering.

(b) State briefly the discounts and commissions to be allowed or paid to dealers, including all cash, securities, contracts or other consideration to be received by any dealer in connection with the sale of the securities.

(c) Outline briefly the plan of distribution of any securities being issued that are to be offered through the selling efforts of brokers or dealers or otherwise than through underwriters.

(d) If any of the securities are to be offered for the account of securityholders, identify each selling securityholder, state the amount owned by the securityholder prior to the offering, the amount offered for his or her account and the amount to be owned after the offering. Provide such disclosure in a tabular format. At the bottom of the table, provide the total number of securities being offered for the account of all securityholders and describe what percent of the pre-offering outstanding securities of such class the offering represents.

Instruction to Item 5(d):

The term "securityholder" in this paragraph refers to beneficial holders, not nominee holders or other such holders of record. If the selling securityholder is an entity, disclosure of the persons who have sole or shared voting or investment power must be included.

(e) Describe any arrangements for the return of funds to subscribers if all of the securities to be offered are not sold. If there are no such arrangements, so state.

(f) If there will be a material delay in the payment of the proceeds of the offering by the underwriter to the issuer, the salient provisions in this regard and the effects on the issuer must be stated.

(g) Describe any arrangement to (1) limit or restrict the sale of other securities of the same class as those to be offered for the period of distribution, (2) stabilize the market for any of the securities to be offered, or (3) withhold commissions, or otherwise to hold each underwriter or dealer responsible for the distribution of its participation.

(h) Identify any underwriter that intends to confirm sales to any accounts over which it exercises discretionary authority and include an estimate of the amount of securities so intended to be confirmed.

Instruction to Item 5:

Attention is directed to the provisions of Rules 10b-9 [17 CFR 240.10b-9] and 15c2-4 [17 CFR 240.15c2-4] under the Securities Exchange Act of 1934. These rules outline, among other things, antifraud provisions concerning the return of funds to subscribers and the transmission of proceeds of an offering to a seller.

Item 6. Use of Proceeds to Issuer

State the principal purposes for which the net proceeds to the issuer from the securities to be offered are intended to be used and the approximate amount intended to be used for each such purpose. If the issuer will not receive any of proceeds from the offering, so state.

Instructions to Item 6:

1. If any substantial portion of the proceeds has not been allocated for particular purposes, a statement to that effect must be made together with a statement of the amount of proceeds not so allocated.

2. State whether or not the proceeds will be used to compensate or otherwise make payments to officers or directors of the issuer or any of its subsidiaries.

3. For best efforts offerings, describe any anticipated material changes in the use of proceeds if all of the securities being qualified on the offering statement are not sold.

4. If an issuer must provide the disclosure described in Item 9(c) the use of proceeds and plan of operations should be consistent.

5. If any material amounts of other funds are to be used in conjunction with the proceeds, state the amounts and sources of such other funds and whether such funds are firm or contingent.

6. If any material part of the proceeds is to be used to discharge indebtedness, describe the material terms of such indebtedness. If the indebtedness to be discharged was incurred within one year, describe the use of the proceeds arising from such indebtedness.

7. If any material amount of the proceeds is to be used to acquire assets, otherwise than in the ordinary course of business, briefly describe and state the cost of the assets. If the assets are to be acquired from affiliates of the issuer or their associates, give the names of the persons from whom they are to be acquired and set forth the basis used in determining the purchase price to the issuer.

8. The issuer may reserve the right to change the use of proceeds, so long as the reservation is prominently disclosed in the section where the use of proceeds is discussed. It is not necessary to describe the possible alternative uses of proceeds unless the issuer believes that a change in circumstances leading to an alternative use of proceeds is likely to occur.

Item 7. Description of Business

(a) Narrative description of business.

(1) Describe the business done and intended to be done by the issuer and its subsidiaries and the general development of the business during the past three years or such shorter period as the issuer may have been in business. Such description must include, but not be limited to, a discussion of the following factors if such factors are material to an understanding of the issuer's business:

(i) The principal products and services of the issuer and the principal market for and method of distribution of such products and services.

(ii) The status of a product or service if the issuer has made public information about a new product or service that would require the investment of a material amount of the assets of the issuer or is otherwise material.

(iii) [Reserved]

(iv) The total number of persons employed by the issuer, indicating the number employed full time.

(v) Any bankruptcy, receivership or similar proceeding.

(vi) Any legal proceedings material to the business or financial condition of the issuer.

(vii) Any material reclassification, merger, consolidation, or purchase or sale of a significant amount of assets not in the ordinary course of business.

(2) The issuer must also describe those distinctive or special characteristics of the issuer's operation or industry that are reasonably likely to have a material impact upon the issuer's future financial performance. Examples of factors that might be discussed include dependence on one or a few major customers or suppliers (including suppliers of raw materials or financing), effect of existing or probable governmental regulation (including environmental regulation), material terms of and/or expiration of material labor contracts or patents, trademarks, licenses, franchises, concessions or royalty agreements, unusual competitive conditions in the industry, cyclicality of the industry and anticipated raw material or energy shortages to the extent management may not be able to secure a continuing source of supply.

(b) [Reserved]

(c) Industry Guides. The disclosure guidelines in all Securities Act Industry Guides must be followed. To the extent that the industry guides are codified into Regulation S-K, the Regulation S-K industry disclosure items must be followed.

(d) For offerings of limited partnership or limited liability company interests, an issuer must comply with the Commission's interpretive views on substantive disclosure requirements set forth in Securities Act Release No. 6900 (June 17, 1991).

Item 8. Description of Property

State briefly the location and general character of any principal plants or other material physical properties of the issuer and its subsidiaries. If any such property is not held in fee or is held subject to any major encumbrance, so state and briefly describe how held. Include information regarding the suitability, adequacy, productive capacity and extent of utilization of the properties and facilities used in the issuer's business.

Instruction to Item 8:

Detailed descriptions of the physical characteristics of individual properties or legal descriptions by metes and bounds are not required and should not be given.

Item 9. Management's Discussion and Analysis of Financial Condition and Results of Operations

Discuss the issuer's financial condition, changes in financial condition and results of operations for each year and interim period for which financial statements are required, including the causes of material changes from year to year or period to period in financial statement line items, to the extent necessary for an understanding of the issuer's business as a whole. Information provided also must relate to the segment information of the issuer. Provide the information specified below as well as such other information that is necessary for an investor's understanding of the issuer's financial condition, changes in financial condition and results of operations.

(a) Operating results. Provide information regarding significant factors, including unusual or infrequent events or transactions or new developments, materially affecting the issuer's income from operations, and, in each case, indicating the extent to which income was so affected. Describe any other significant component of revenue or expenses necessary to understand the issuer's results of operations. To the extent that the financial statements disclose material changes in net sales or revenues, provide a narrative discussion of the extent to which such changes are attributable to changes in prices or to changes in the volume or amount of products or services being sold or to the introduction of new products or services.

Instruction to Item 9(a):

1. The discussion and analysis shall focus specifically on material events and uncertainties known to management that would cause reported financial information not to be necessarily indicative of future operating results or of future financial condition. This would include descriptions and amounts of (A) matters that would have an impact on future operations that have not had an impact in the past, and (B) matters that have had an impact on reported operations that are not expected to have an impact upon future operations.

2. Where the consolidated financial statements reveal material changes from year to year in one or more line items, the causes for the changes shall be described to the extent necessary to an understanding of the issuer's businesses as a whole. If the causes for a change in one line item also relate to other line items, no repetition is required and a line-by-line analysis of the financial statements as a whole is not required or generally appropriate. Issuers need not recite the amounts of changes from year to year which are readily computable from the financial statements. The discussion must not merely repeat numerical data contained in the consoli-dated financial statements.

3. When interim period financial statements are included, discuss any material changes in financial condition from the end of the preceding fiscal year to the date of the most recent interim balance sheet provided. Discuss any material changes in the issuer's results of operations with respect to the most recent fiscal year-to-date period for which a statement of comprehensive income (or statement of net income if comprehensive income is presented in two separate but consecutive financial statements or if no other comprehensive income) is provided and the corresponding year-to-date period of the preceding fiscal year.

(b) Liquidity and capital resources. Provide information regarding the following:

(1) the issuer's liquidity (both short and long term), including a description and evaluation of the internal and external sources of liquidity and a brief discussion of any material unused sources of liquidity. If a material deficiency in liquidity is identified, indicate the course of action that the issuer has taken or proposes to take to remedy the deficiency.

(2) the issuer's material commitments for capital expenditures as of the end of the latest fiscal year and any subsequent interim period and an indication of the general purpose of such commitments and the anticipated sources of funds needed to fulfill such commitments.

(c) Plan of Operations. Issuers (including predecessors) that have not received revenue from operations during each of the three fiscal years immediately before the filing of the offering statement (or since inception, whichever is shorter) must describe, if formulated, their plan of operation for the 12 months following the commencement of the proposed offering. If such information is not available, the reasons for its unavailability must be stated. Disclosure relating to any plan must include, among other things, a statement indicating whether, in the issuer's opinion, the proceeds from the offering will satisfy its cash requirements or whether it anticipates it will be necessary to raise additional funds in the next six months to implement the plan of operations.

(d) Trend information. The issuer must identify the most significant recent trends in production, sales and inventory, the state of the order book and costs and selling prices since the latest financial year. The issuer also must discuss, for at least the current financial year, any known trends, uncertainties, demands, commitments or events that are reasonably likely to have a material effect on the issuer's net sales or revenues, income from continuing operations, profitability, liquidity or capital resources, or that would cause reported financial information not necessarily to be indicative of future operating results or financial condition.

Item 10. Directors, Executive Officers and Significant Employees

(a) For each of the directors, persons nominated or chosen to become directors, executive officers, persons chosen to become executive officers, and significant employees, provide the information specified below in substantially the following tabular format:

Name	Position	Age	Term of Office(1)	Approximate hours per week for part-time employees(2)
Executive Officers:				
Directors:				
Significant Employees:				

(1) Provide the month and year of the start date and, if applicable, the end date. To the extent you are unable to provide specific dates, provide such other description in the table or in an appropriate footnote clarifying the term of office. If the person is a nominee or chosen to become a director or executive officer, it must be indicated in this column or by footnote.

(2) For executive officers and significant employees that are working part-time, indicate approximately the average number of hours per week or month such person works or is anticipated to work. This column may be left blank for directors. The entire column may be omitted if all those listed in the table work full time for the issuer.

In a footnote to the table, briefly describe any arrangement or understanding between the persons described above and any other persons (naming such persons) pursuant to which the person was or is to be selected to his or her office or position.

Instructions to Item 10(a):

1. No nominee or person chosen to become a director or person chosen to be an executive officer who has not consented to act as such may be named in response to this item.

2. The term "executive officer" means the president, secretary, treasurer, any vice president in charge of a principal business function (such as sales, administration, or finance) and any other person who performs similar policy making functions for the issuer.

3. The term "significant employee" means persons such as production managers, sales managers, or research scientists, who are not executive officers, but who make or are expected to make significant contributions to the business of the issuer.

(b) Family relationships. State the nature of any family relationship between any director, executive officer, person nominated or chosen by the issuer to become a director or executive officer or any significant employee.

Instruction to Item 10(b):

The term "family relationship" means any relationship by blood, marriage, or adoption, not more remote than first cousin.

(c) Business experience. Give a brief account of the business experience during the past five years of each director, executive officer, person nominated or chosen to become a director or executive officer, and each significant employee, including his or her principal occupations and employment during that period and the name and principal business of any corporation or other organization in which such occupations and employment were carried on. When an executive officer or significant employee has been employed by the issuer for less than five years, a brief explanation must be included as to the nature of the responsibilities undertaken by the individual in prior positions to provide adequate disclosure of this prior business experience. What is required is information relating to the level of the employee's professional competence, which may include, depending upon the circumstances, such specific information as the size of the operation supervised.

(d) Involvement in certain legal proceedings. Describe any of the following events which occurred during the past five years and which are material to an evaluation of the ability or integrity of any director, person nominated to become a director or executive officer of the issuer:

(1) A petition under the federal bankruptcy laws or any state insolvency law was filed by or against, or a receiver, fiscal agent or similar officer was appointed by a court for the business or property of such person, or any partnership in which he was general partner at or within two years before the time of such filing, or any corporation or business association of which he was an executive officer at or within two years before the time of such filing; or

(2) Such person was convicted in a criminal proceeding (excluding traffic violations and other minor offenses).

Item 11. Compensation of Directors and Executive Officers

(a) Provide, in substantially the tabular format indicated, the annual compensation of each of the three highest paid persons who were executive officers or directors during the issuer's last completed fiscal year.

Name	Capacities in which compensation was received (e.g., Chief Executive Officer, director, etc.)	Cash compensation ($)	Other compensation ($)	Total compensation ($)

(b) Provide the aggregate annual compensation of the issuer's directors as a group for the issuer's last completed fiscal year. Specify the total number of directors in the group.

(c) For Tier 1 offerings, the annual compensation of the three highest paid persons who were executive officers or directors and the aggregate annual compensation of the issuer's directors may be provided as a group, rather than as specified in paragraphs (a) and (b) of this item. In such case, issuers must specify the total number of persons in the group.

(d) Briefly describe all proposed compensation to be made in the future pursuant to any ongoing plan or arrangement to the individuals specified in paragraphs (a) and (b) of this item. The description must include a summary of how each plan operates, any performance formula or measure in effect (or the criteria used to determine payment amounts), the time periods over which the measurements of benefits will be determined, payment schedules, and any recent material amendments to the plan. Information need not be included with respect to any group life, health, hospitalization, or medical reimbursement plans that do not discriminate in scope, terms or operation in favor of executive officers or directors of the issuer and that are available generally to all salaried employees.

Instructions to Item 11:

1. In case of compensation paid or to be paid otherwise than in cash, if it is impracticable to determine the cash value thereof, state in a note to the table the nature and amount thereof.

2. This item is to be answered on an accrual basis if practicable; if not so answered, state the basis used.

Item 12. Security Ownership of Management and Certain Securityholders

(a) Include the information specified in paragraph (b) of this item as of the most recent practicable date (stating the date used), in substantially the tabular format indicated, with respect to voting securities beneficially owned by:

(1) all executive officers and directors as a group, individually naming each director or executive officer who beneficially owns more than 10% of any class of the issuer's voting securities;

(2) any other securityholder who beneficially owns more than 10% of any class of the issuer's voting securities as such beneficial ownership would be calculated if the issuer were subject to Rule 13d-3(d)(1) of the Securities Exchange Act of 1934.

(b) Beneficial Ownership Table:

Title of class	Name and address of beneficial owner(1)	Amount and nature of beneficial ownership	Amount and nature of beneficial ownership acquirable(2)	Percent of class(3)

(1) The address given in this column may be a business, mailing, or residential address. The address may be included in an appropriate footnote to the table rather than in this column.

(2) This column must include the amount of equity securities each beneficial owner has the right to acquire using the manner specified in Rule 13d-3(d)(1) of the Securities Exchange Act of 1934. An appropriate footnote must be included if the column heading does not sufficiently describe the circumstances upon which such securities could be acquired.

(3) This column must use the amounts contained in the two preceding columns to calculate the percent of class owned by such beneficial owner.

Item 13. Interest of Management and Others in Certain Transactions

(a) Describe briefly any transactions or any currently proposed transactions during the issuer's last two completed fiscal years and the current fiscal year, to which the issuer or any of its subsidiaries was or is to be a participant and the amount involved exceeds $50,000 for Tier 1 or the lesser of $120,000 and one percent of the average of the issuer's total assets at year end for the last two completed fiscal years for Tier 2, and in which any of the following persons had or is to have a direct or indirect material interest, naming the person and stating his or her relationship to the issuer, the nature of the person's interest in the transaction and, where practicable, the amount of such interest:

(1) Any director or executive officer of the issuer;

(2) Any nominee for election as a director;

(3) Any securityholder named in answer to Item 12(a)(2);

(4) If the issuer was incorporated or organized within the past three years, any promoter of the issuer; or

(5) Any immediate family member of the above persons. An "immediate family member" of a person means such person's child, stepchild, parent, stepparent, spouse, sibling, mother-in-law, father-in-law, son-in-law, daughter-in-law, brother-in-law, sister-in-law, or any person (other than a tenant or employee) sharing such person's household.

Instructions to Item 13(a):

1. For purposes of calculating the amount of the transaction described above, all periodic installments in the case of any lease or other agreement providing for periodic payments must be aggregated to the extent they occurred within the time period described in this item.

2. No information need be given in answer to this item as to any transaction where:

(a) The rates of charges involved in the transaction are determined by competitive bids, or the transaction involves the rendering of services as a common or contract carrier at rates or charges fixed in conformity with law or governmental authority;

(b) The transaction involves services as a bank depositary of funds, transfer agent, registrar, trustee under a trust indenture, or similar services;

(c) The interest of the specified person arises solely from the ownership of securities of the issuer and the specified person receives no extra or special benefit not shared on a pro-rata basis by all of the holders of securities of the class.

3. This item calls for disclosure of indirect as well as direct material interests in transactions. A person who has a position or relationship with a firm, corporation, or other entity which engages in a transaction with the issuer or its subsidiaries may have an indirect interest in such transaction by reason of the position or relationship. However, a person is deemed not to have a material indirect interest in a transaction within the meaning of this item where:

(a) the interest arises only (i) from the person's position as a director of another corporation or organization (other than a partnership) that is a party to the transaction, or (ii) from the direct or indirect ownership by the person and all other persons specified in paragraphs (1) through (5) of this item, in the aggregate, of less than a 10 percent equity interest in another person (other than a partnership) that is a party to the transaction, or (iii) from both such position and ownership;

(b) the interest arises only from the person's position as a limited partner in a partnership in which the person and all other persons specified in paragraphs (1) through (5) of this item had an interest of less than 10 percent; or

(c) the interest of the person arises solely from the holding of an equity interest (unless the equity interest confers management rights similar to a general partner interest) or a creditor interest in another person that is a party to the transaction with the issuer or any of its subsidiaries and the transaction is not material to the other person.

4. Include the name of each person whose interest in any transaction is described and the nature of the relationships by reason of which such interest is required to be described. The amount of the interest of any specified person must be computed without regard to the amount of the profit or loss involved in the transaction. Where it is not practicable to state the approximate amount of the interest, the approximate amount involved in the transaction must be disclosed.

5. Information must be included as to any material underwriting discounts and commissions upon the sale of securities by the issuer where any of the specified persons was or is to be a principal underwriter or is a controlling person, or member, of a firm which was or is to be a principal underwriter. Information need not be given concerning ordinary management fees paid by underwriters to a managing underwriter pursuant to an agreement among underwriters, the parties to which do not include the issuer or its subsidiaries.

6. As to any transaction involving the purchase or sale of assets by or to any issuer or any subsidiary, otherwise than in the ordinary course of business, state the cost of the assets to the purchaser and, if acquired by the seller within two years before the transaction, the cost to the seller.

7. Information must be included in answer to this item with respect to transactions not excluded above which involve compensation from the issuer or its subsidiaries, directly or indirectly, to any of the specified persons for services in any capacity unless the interest of such persons arises solely from the ownership individually and in the aggregate of less than 10 percent of any class of equity securities of another corporation furnishing the services to the issuer or its subsidiaries.

(b) If any expert named in the offering statement as having prepared or certified any part of the offering statement was employed for such purpose on a contingent basis or, at the time of such preparation or certification or at any time thereafter, had a material interest in the issuer or any of its parents or subsidiaries or was connected with the issuer or any of its subsidiaries as a promoter, underwriter, voting trustee, director, officer or employee, describe the nature of such contingent basis, interest or connection.

Item 14. Securities Being Offered

(a) If capital stock is being offered, state the title of the class and furnish the following information regarding all classes of capital stock outstanding:

(1) Outline briefly: (i) dividend rights; (ii) voting rights; (iii) liquidation rights; (iv) preemptive rights; (v) conversion rights; (vi) redemption provisions; (vii) sinking fund provisions; (viii) liability to further calls or to assessment by the issuer; (ix) any classification of the Board of Directors, and the impact of classification where cumulative voting is permitted or required; (x) restrictions on alienability of the securities being offered; (xi) any provision discriminating against any existing or prospective holder of such securities as a result of such securityholder owning a substantial amount of securities; and (xii) any rights of holders that may be modified otherwise than by a vote of a majority or more of the shares outstanding, voting as a class.

(2) Briefly describe potential liabilities imposed on securityholders under state statutes or foreign law, for example, to employees of the issuer, unless such disclosure would be immaterial because the financial resources of the issuer or other factors are such as to make it unlikely that the liability will ever be imposed.

(3) If preferred stock is to be offered or is outstanding, describe briefly any restriction on the repurchase or redemption of shares by the issuer while there is any arrearage in the payment of dividends or sinking fund installments. If there is no such restriction, so state.

(b) If debt securities are being offered, outline briefly the following:

(1) Provisions with respect to interest, conversion, maturity, redemption, amortization, sinking fund or retirement.

(2) Provisions with respect to the kind and priority of any lien securing the issue, together with a brief identification of the principal properties subject to such lien.

(3) Material affirmative and negative covenants.

Instruction to Item 14(b):

In the case of secured debt there must be stated: (i) the approximate amount of unbonded property available for use against the issuance of bonds, as of the most recent practicable date, and (ii) whether the securities being issued are to be issued against such property, against the deposit of cash, or otherwise.

(c) If securities described are to be offered pursuant to warrants, rights, or convertible securities, state briefly:

(1) the amount of securities issuable upon the exercise or conversion of such warrants, convertible securities or rights;

(2) the period during which and the price at which the warrants, convertible securities or rights are exercisable;

(3) the amounts of warrants, convertible securities or rights outstanding; and

(4) any other material terms of such securities.

(d) In the case of any other kind of securities, include a brief description with comparable information to that required in (a), (b) and (c) of Item 14.

Part F/S

(a) General Rules

(1) The appropriate financial statements set forth below of the issuer, or the issuer and its predecessors or any businesses to which the issuer is a successor must be filed as part of the offering statement and included in the offering circular that is distributed to investors.

(2) Unless the issuer is a Canadian company, financial statements must be prepared in accordance with generally accepted accounting principles in the United States (US GAAP). If the issuer is a Canadian company, such financial statements must be prepared in accordance with either US GAAP or International Financial Reporting Standards (IFRS) as issued by the International Accounting Standards Board (IASB). If the financial statements comply with IFRS, such compliance must be explicitly and unreservedly stated in the notes to the financial statements and if the financial statements are audited, the auditor's report must include an opinion on whether the financial statements comply with IFRS as issued by the IASB.

(3) The issuer may elect to delay complying with any new or revised financial accounting standard until the date that a company that is not an issuer (as defined under section 2(a) of the Sarbanes-Oxley Act of 2002 (15 U.S.C. 7201(a)) is required to comply with such new or revised accounting standard, if such standard also applies to companies that are not issuers. Issuers electing such extension of time accommodation must disclose it at the time the issuer files its offering statement and apply the election to all standards. Issuers electing not to use this accommodation must forgo this accommodation for all financial accounting standards and may not elect to rely on this accommodation in any future filings.

(b) Financial Statements for Tier 1 Offerings

(1) The financial statements prepared pursuant to this paragraph (b), including (b)(7), need not be prepared in accordance with Regulation S-X.

(2) The financial statements prepared pursuant to paragraph (b), including (b)(7), need not be audited. If the financial statements are not audited, they shall be labeled as "unaudited". However, if an audit of these financial statements is obtained for other purposes and that audit was performed in accordance with either U.S. generally accepted auditing standards or the Standards of the Public Company Accounting Oversight Board by an auditor that is independent pursuant to either the independence standards of the American Institute of Certified Public Accountants (AICPA) or Rule 2 01 of Regulation S-X, those audited financial statements must be filed, and an audit opinion complying with Rule 2-02 of Regulation S-X must be filed along with such financial statements. The auditor may, but need not, be registered with the Public Company Accounting Oversight Board.

(3) *Consolidated Balance Sheets*. Age of balance sheets at filing and at qualification:

(A) If the filing is made, or the offering statement is qualified, more than three months but no more than nine months after the most recently completed fiscal year end, include a balance sheet as of the two most recently completed fiscal year ends.

(B) If the filing is made, or the offering statement is qualified, more than nine months after the most recently completed fiscal year end, include a balance sheet as of the two most recently completed fiscal year ends and an interim balance sheet as of a date no earlier than six months after the most recently completed fiscal year end.

(C) If the filing is made, or the offering statement is qualified, within three months after the most recently completed fiscal year end, include a balance sheet as of the two fiscal year ends preceding the most recently completed fiscal year end and an interim balance sheet as of a date no earlier than six months after the date of the most recent fiscal year end balance sheet that is required.

(D) If the filing is made, or the offering statement is qualified, during the period from inception until three months after reaching the annual balance sheet date for the first time, include a balance sheet as of a date within nine months of filing or qualification.

(4) *Statements of Comprehensive Income, Cash Flows, and Changes in Stockholders' Equity.* File consolidated statements of comprehensive income (either in a single continuous financial statement or in two separate but consecutive financial statements; or a statement of net income if there was no other comprehensive income), cash flows, and changes in stockholders' equity for each of the two fiscal years preceding the date of the most recent balance sheet being filed or such shorter period as the issuer has been in existence.

(5) *Interim Financial Statements.*

(i) If a consolidated interim balance sheet is required by (b)(3) of Part F/S, consolidated interim statements of comprehensive income (either in a single continuous financial statement or in two separate but consecutive financial statements; or a statement of net income if there was no other comprehensive income) and cash flows shall be provided and must cover at least the first six months of the issuer's fiscal year and the corresponding period of the preceding fiscal year. An analysis of the changes in each caption of stockholders' equity presented in the balance sheets must be provided in a note or separate statement. This analysis shall be presented in the form of a reconciliation of the beginning balance to the ending balance for each period for which a statement of comprehensive income is required to be filed with all significant reconciling items described by appropriate captions with contributions from and distributions to owners shown separately. Dividends per share for each class of shares shall also be provided.

(ii) Interim financial statements of issuers that report under U.S. GAAP may be condensed as described in Rule 8-03(a) of Regulation S-X.

(iii) The interim statements of comprehensive income for all issuers must be accompanied by a statement that in the opinion of management all adjustments necessary in order to make the interim financial statements not misleading have been included.

(6) *Oil and Gas Producing Activities.* Issuers engaged in oil and gas producing activities must follow the financial accounting and reporting standards specified in Rule 4-10 of Regulation S-X.

(7) *Financial Statements of Other Entities.* The circumstances described below may require you to file financial statements of other entities in the offering statement. The financial statements of other entities must be presented for the same periods as if the other entity was the issuer as described above in paragraphs (b)(3) and (b)(4) unless a shorter period is specified by the rules below. The financial statement of other entities shall follow the same audit requirement as paragraph (b)(2) of this Part F/S.

(i) *Financial Statements of Guarantors and Issuers of Guaranteed Securities.* Financial statements of a subsidiary that issues securities guaranteed by the parent or guarantees securities issued by the parent must be presented as required by Rule 3-10 of Regulation S-X.

(ii) *Financial Statements of Affiliates Whose Securities Collateralize an Issuance.* Financial statements for an issuer's affiliates whose securities constitute a substantial portion of the collateral for any class of securities being offered must be presented as required by Rule 3-16 of Regulation S-X.

(iii) *Financial Statements of Businesses Acquired or to be Acquired.* File the financial statements required by Rule 8-04 of Regulation S-X.

(iv) *Pro Forma Financial Information.* If financial statements are presented under paragraph (b)(7)(iii) above, file pro forma information showing the effects of the acquisition as described in Rule 8-05 of Regulation S-X.

(v) *Real Estate Operations Acquired or to be Acquired.* File the financial information required by Rule 8-06 of Regulation S-X.

Instructions to paragraph (b) in Part F/S:

1. Issuers should refer to Rule 257(b)(2) to determine whether a special financial report will be required after qualification of the offering statement.

2. If the last day that the financial statements included in the offering statement can be accepted, according to the age requirements of this item falls on a Saturday, Sunday, or holiday, such offering statement may be filed on the first business day following the last day of the specified period.

3. As an alternative, an issuer may—but need not—elect to comply with the provisions of paragraph (c).

(c) Financial Statement Requirements for Tier 2 Offerings

(1) In addition to the general rules in paragraph (a), provide the financial statements required by paragraph (b) of this Part F/S, except the following rules should be followed in the preparation of the financial statements:

(i) Issuers that report under U.S. GAAP and, when applicable, other entities for which financial statements are required, must comply with Article 8 of Regulation S-X, as if they were conducting a registered offering on Form S-1, except the age of financial statements may follow paragraphs (b)(3)-(4) of this Part F/S.

(ii) Audited financial statements are required for Tier 2 offerings for the issuer and, when applicable, for financial statements of other entities. However, interim financial statements may be unaudited.

(iii) The audit must be conducted in accordance with either U.S. Generally Accepted Auditing Standards or the standards of the Public Company Accounting Oversight Board (United States) and the report and qualifications of the independent accountant shall comply with the requirements of Article 2 of Regulation S-X. Accounting firms conducting audits for the financial statements included in the offering circular may, but need not, be registered with the Public Company Accounting Oversight Board.

PART III—EXHIBITS

Item 16. Index to Exhibits

(a) An exhibits index must be presented at the beginning of Part III.

(b) Each exhibit must be listed in the exhibit index according to the number assigned to it under Item 17 below.

(c) For incorporation by reference, please refer to General Instruction III of this Form.

Item 17. Description of Exhibits

As appropriate, the following documents must be filed as exhibits to the offering statement.

1. *Underwriting agreement*—Each underwriting contract or agreement with a principal underwriter or letter pursuant to which the securities are to be distributed; where the terms have yet to be finalized, proposed formats may be provided.

2. *Charter and bylaws*—The charter and bylaws of the issuer or instruments corresponding thereto as currently in effect and any amendments thereto.

3. *Instruments defining the rights of securityholders*—

(a) All instruments defining the rights of any holder of the issuer's securities, including but not limited to (i) holders of equity or debt securities being issued; (ii) holders of long-term debt of the issuer, and of all subsidiaries for which consolidated or unconsolidated financial statements are required to be filed.

(b) The following instruments need not be filed if the issuer agrees to file them with the Commission upon request: (i) instruments defining the rights of holders of long-term debt of the issuer and all of its subsidiaries for which consolidated financial statements are required to be filed if such debt is not being issued pursuant to this Regulation A offering and the total amount of such authorized issuance does not exceed 5% of the total assets of the issuer and its subsidiaries on a consolidated basis; (ii) any instrument with respect to a class of securities that is to be retired or redeemed before the issuance or upon delivery of the securities being issued pursuant to this Regulation A offering and appropriate steps have been taken to assure such retirement or redemption; and (iii) copies of instruments evidencing scrip certificates or fractions of shares.

4. *Subscription agreement*—The form of any subscription agreement to be used in connection with the purchase of securities in this offering.

5. *Voting trust agreement*—Any voting trust agreements and amendments.

6. *Material contracts*

(a) Every contract not made in the ordinary course of business that is material to the issuer and is to be performed in whole or in part at or after the filing of the offering statement or was entered into not more than two years before such filing. Only contracts need be filed as to which the issuer or subsidiary of the issuer is a party or has succeeded to a party by assumption or assignment or in which the issuer or such subsidiary has a beneficial interest. Schedules (or similar attachments) to material contracts may be excluded if not material to an investment decision or if the material information contained in such schedules is otherwise disclosed in the agreement or the offering statement. The material contract filed must contain a list briefly identifying the contents of all omitted schedules, together with an agreement to furnish supplementally a copy of any omitted schedule to the Commission upon request.

(b) If the contract is such as ordinarily accompanies the kind of business conducted by the issuer and its subsidiaries, it is made in the ordinary course of business and need not be filed unless it falls within one or more of the following categories, in which case it must be filed except where immaterial in amount or significance: (i) any contract to which directors, officers, promoters, voting trustees, securityholders named in the offering statement, or underwriters are parties, except where the contract merely involves the purchase or sale of current assets having a determinable market price, at such market price; (ii) any contract upon which the issuer's business is substantially dependent, as in the case of continuing contracts to sell the major part of the issuer's products or services or to purchase the major part of the issuer's requirements of goods, services or raw materials or any franchise or license or other agreement to use a patent, formula, trade secret, process or trade name upon which the issuer's business depends to a material extent; (iii) any contract calling for the acquisition or sale of any property, plant or equipment for a consideration exceeding 15% of such fixed assets of the issuer on a consolidated basis; or (iv) any material lease under which a part of the property described in the offering statement is held by the issuer.

(c) Any management contract or any compensatory plan, contract or arrangement including, but not limited to, plans relating to options, warrants or rights, pension, retirement or deferred compensation or bonus, incentive or profit sharing (or if not set forth in any formal document, a written description) is deemed material and must be filed except for the following: (i) ordinary purchase and sales agency agreements; (ii) agreements with managers of stores in a chain organization or similar organization; (iii) contracts providing for labor or salesperson's bonuses or payments to a class of securityholders, as such; (iv) any compensatory plan, contract or arrangement that pursuant to its terms is available to employees generally and that in operation provides for the same method of allocation of benefits between management and non-management participants.

7. *Plan of acquisition, reorganization, arrangement, liquidation, or succession*—Any material plan of acquisition, disposition, reorganization, readjustment, succession, liquidation or arrangement and any amendments thereto described in the offering statement. Schedules (or similar attachments) to these exhibits must not be

filed unless such schedules contain information that is material to an investment decision and that is not otherwise disclosed in the agreement or the offering statement. The plan filed must contain a list briefly identifying the contents of all omitted schedules, together with an agreement to furnish supplementally a copy of any omitted schedule to the Commission upon request.

8. *Escrow agreements*—Any escrow agreement or similar arrangement which has been executed in connection with the Regulation A offering.

9. *Letter re change in certifying accountant*—A letter from the issuer's former independent accountant regarding its concurrence or disagreement with the statements made by the issuer in the current report concerning the resignation or dismissal as the issuer's principal accountant.

10. *Power of attorney*—If any name is signed to the offering statement pursuant to a power of attorney, signed copies of the power of attorney must be filed. Where the power of attorney is contained elsewhere in the offering statement or documents filed therewith, a reference must be made in the index to the part of the offering statement or document containing such power of attorney. In addition, if the name of any officer signing on behalf of the issuer is signed pursuant to a power of attorney, certified copies of a resolution of the issuer's board of directors authorizing such signature must also be filed. A power of attorney that is filed with the Commission must relate to a specific filing or an amendment thereto. A power of attorney that confers general authority may not be filed with the Commission.

11. *Consents*—

(a) Experts: The written consent of

(i) any accountant, counsel, engineer, geologist, appraiser or any persons whose profession gives authority to a statement made by them and who is named in the offering statement as having prepared or certified any part of the document or is named as having prepared or certified a report or evaluation whether or not for use in connection with the offering statement;

(ii) the expert that authored any portion of a report quoted or summarized as such in the offering statement, expressly stating their consent to the use of such quotation or summary;

(iii) any persons who are referenced as having reviewed or passed upon any information in the offering statement, and that such information is being included on the basis of their authority or in reliance upon their status as experts.

(b) All written consents must be dated and signed.

12. *Opinion re legality*—An opinion of counsel as to the legality of the securities covered by the Offering Statement, indicating whether they will when sold, be legally issued, fully paid and non-assessable, and if debt securities, whether they will be binding obligations of the issuer.

13. *"Testing the waters" materials*—Any written communication or broadcast script used under the authorization of Rule 255. Such materials need not be filed if they are substantively the same as materials previously filed with the offering statement.

14. *Appointment of agent for service of process*—A Canadian issuer must file Form F-X.

15. *Additional exhibits*—

(a) Any non-public, draft offering statement previously submitted pursuant to Rule 252(d) and any related, non-public correspondence submitted by or on behalf of the issuer.

(b) Any additional exhibits which the issuer may wish to file, which must be so marked as to indicate clearly the subject matters to which they refer.

SIGNATURES

Pursuant to the requirements of Regulation A, the issuer certifies that it has reasonable grounds to believe that it meets all of the requirements for filing on Form 1-A and has duly caused this offering statement to be signed on its behalf by the undersigned, thereunto duly authorized, in the City of _____, State of _____, on _____ (*date*).

(Exact name of issuer as specified in its charter) ____________________

By (Signature and Title) ____________________

This offering statement has been signed by the following persons in the capacities and on the dates indicated.

(Signature) ____________________

(Title) ____________________

(Date) __________

Instructions to Signatures:

1. The offering statement must be signed by the issuer, its principal executive officer, principal financial officer, principal accounting officer, and a majority of the members of its board of directors or other governing body. If a signature is by a person on behalf of any other person, evidence of authority to sign must be filed with the offering statement, except where an executive officer signs on behalf of the issuer.

2. The offering statement must be signed using a typed signature. Each signatory to the filing must also manually sign a signature page or other document authenticating, acknowledging or otherwise adopting his or her signature that appears in the filing. Such document must be executed before or at the time the filing is made and must be retained by the issuer for a period of five years. Upon request, the issuer must furnish to the Commission or its staff a copy of any or all documents retained pursuant to this section.

3. The name and title of each person signing the offering statement must be typed or printed beneath the signature.

FORM 2–A

REPORT OF SALES AND USES OF PROCEEDS PURSUANT TO RULE 257 OF REGULATION A

File No. 24 __–__–__

For period ending __/__/__

Indicate whether the report is an initial report [ ]
amendment [ ]
or final report [ ]

If the report is an amendment, indicate the number of such amendment. ❑❑
If the offering has terminated, indicate the date of termination __/__/__

GENERAL INSTRUCTIONS

The report shall be filed in accordance with the provisions of Rule 257 of Regulation A.

Answer each item in the box(es) or spaces provided. If additional space is required for any response, continue the response on an attached sheet.

If the issuer is required to file any report(s) on this form subsequent to its initial filing, each subsequent filing shall be deemed an amendment to the initial filing. Do not report in any amendment responses to Items 3–11 unless the information has changed.

No fee is required to accompany this filing.

Seven copies of the form shall be filed with the main office of the Commission in Washington, D.C. At least one copy of the form shall be manually signed; other copies may bear typed or printed signatures.

1. ____
   Exact name of issuer as specified in its charter.
2. Date of qualification of the offering statement:
   ❑❑ ❑❑ ❑❑
3. Has the offering commenced? [ ] Yes [ ] No.
   If yes, date of commencement: ❑❑ ❑❑ ❑❑
   If no, explain briefly:
   ____
4. Did the offering terminate before any securities were sold? [ ] Yes [ ] No.
   If yes, explain briefly:
   ____
   If "yes", do not answer Items 5–11.
5. Did the offering terminate prior to the sale of all the securities qualified under Regulation A?
   [ ] Yes [ ] No.
   If yes, explain briefly:
   ____
6. Indicate the total number of shares or other units offered and sold to date:
   _______ (issuer's account) _______ (selling securityholders)
   Indicate the number of shares or other units still being offered:
   _______ (issuer's account) _______ (selling securityholders)
7. Total amount of dollars received from the public to date. $ ________
   Total amount allocable to selling securityholders: $ ________
   Underwriting discount or commission allowed $ ________
   Underwriting expenses paid $ ________
   Finders' Fees $ ________
   Other expenses paid to date by or for issuer:
   Legal (including organization) $ ________
   Accounting $ ________
   Engineering $ ________
   Printing and Advertising $ ________

Other (specify) $ ______
______ $ ______
______ $ ______
______ $ ______
Total costs and expenses $ ______
Total net proceeds remaining. $ ______

8. Uses of net proceeds to date.

Instructions:

1. Do not include any amount in "working capital" to which a more specific category is applicable.
2. Round all amounts to the nearest dollar.
3. Specify under "other purposes" any purpose for which at least 5% of the issuer's proceeds or $50,000, whichever is less, has been used.

Salaries and fees $ ______
Construction of plant, building and facilities $ ______
Purchases and installation of machinery and equipment $ ______
Purchase of real estate $ ______
Acquisition of other business(es) $ ______
Repayment of indebtedness $ ______
Working capital $ ______
Development expense (product development, research, patent costs, etc.) $ ______
Temporary investment (specify) $ ______
______ $ ______
______ $ ______
______ $ ______
Other purposes (specify) $ ______
______ $ ______

9. Do the use(s) of proceeds in Item 8 represent a material change in the use(s) of proceeds described in the offering circular? [ ] Yes [ ] No.
If yes, explain briefly:
______

10. State the number of shares held by each promoter, director, officer or controlling person of the issuer, if different from the amount stated in the offering circular.
______

11. List the names and addresses of all brokers and dealers who have, to the knowledge of the issuer or underwriters, participated in the distribution of the securities during the period covered by this report.
______

SIGNATURE

Pursuant to the requirements of Rule 257 and Regulation A, ______ has caused this report to be signed on its behalf by the undersigned thereunto duly authorized.

______
Issuer

By ______
Signature

______
Date

Instruction: The report shall be signed by an executive officer, general partner or counsel of the issuer or by any other duly authorized person. The name and any title of the person who signs the report shall be typed or printed beneath the signature.

2. REGISTRATION AND OTHER FORMS UNDER THE 1933 ACT

FORM S–1

REGISTRATION STATEMENT UNDER THE SECURITIES ACT OF 1933

____
(Exact name of registrant as specified in its charter)

____
(State or other jurisdiction of incorporation or organization)

____
(Primary Standard Industrial Classification Code Number)

____
(I.R.S. Employer Identification Number)

____
(Address, including zip code, and telephone number, including area code, of registrant's principal executive offices)

____
(Name, address, including zip code, and telephone number, including area code, of agent for service)

____
(Approximate date of commencement of proposed sale to the public)

If any of the securities being registered on this Form are to be offered on a delayed or continuous basis pursuant to Rule 415 under the Securities Act of 1933, check the following box: ❑

If this Form is filed to register additional securities for an offering pursuant to Rule 462(b) under the Securities Act of 1933, please check the following box and list the Securities Act registration statement number of the earlier effective registration statement for the same offering. ❑

If this Form is a post-effective amendment filed pursuant to Rule 462(c) under the Securities Act, check the following box and list the Securities Act registration statement number of the earlier effective registration statement for the same offering. ❑

If this Form is a post-effective amendment filed pursuant to Rule 462(d) under the Securities Act, check the following box and list the Securities Act registration statement number of the earlier effective registration statement for the same offering. ❑

Indicate by check mark whether the registrant is a large accelerated filer, an accelerated filer, a non-accelerated filer, a smaller reporting company, or an emerging growth company. See the definitions of "large accelerated filer," "accelerated filer," "smaller reporting company," and "emerging growth company" in Rule 12b–2 of the Exchange Act.

Large accelerated filer ❑

Accelerated filer ❑

Non-accelerated filer ❑

Smaller reporting company ❑

Emerging growth company ❑

If an emerging growth company, indicate by check mark if the registrant has elected not to use the extended transition period for complying with any new or revised financial accounting standards provided pursuant to Section 7(a)(2)(B) of the Securities Act. ❑

Calculation of Registration Fee

Title of Each Class of Securities to be Registered	Amount to be Registered	Proposed Maximum Offering Price Per Unit	Proposed Maximum Aggregate Offering Price	Amount of Registration Fee

NOTE: Specific details relating to the fee calculation shall be furnished in notes to the table, including references to provisions of Rule 457 (17 CFR 230.457) relied upon, if the basis of the calculation is not otherwise evident from the information presented in the table. If the filing fee is calculated pursuant to Rule 457(*o*) under the Securities Act, only the title of the class of securities to be registered, the proposed maximum aggregate offering price for that class of securities and the amount of registration fee need to appear in the Calculation of Registration Fee table. Any difference between the dollar amount of securities registered for such offerings and the dollar amount of securities sold may be carried forward on a future registration statement pursuant to Rule 429 under the Securities Act.

GENERAL INSTRUCTIONS

I. Eligibility Requirements for Use of Form S–1

This Form shall be used for the registration under the Securities Act of 1933 ("Securities Act") of securities of all registrants for which no other form is authorized or prescribed, except that this Form shall not be used for securities of foreign governments or political subdivisions thereof or asset-backed securities, as defined in 17 CFR 229.1101(c).

II. Application of General Rules and Regulations

A. Attention is directed to the General Rules and Regulations under the Securities Act, particularly those comprising Regulation C (17 CFR 230.400 to 230.494) thereunder. That Regulation contains general requirements regarding the preparation and filing of the registration statement.

B. Attention is directed to Regulation S–K (17 CFR Part 229) for the requirements applicable to the content of the nonfinancial statement portions of registration statements under the Securities Act. Where this Form directs the registrant to furnish information required by Regulation S–K and the item of Regulation S–K so provides, information need only be furnished to the extent appropriate.

III. Exchange Offers

If any of the securities being registered are to be offered in exchange for securities of any other issuer the prospectus shall also include the information which would be required by Item 11 if the securities of such other issuer were registered on this Form. There shall also be included the information concerning such securities of such other issue which would be called for by Item 9 if such securities were being registered. In connection with this instruction, reference is made to Rule 409.

IV. Roll–Up Transactions

If the securities to be registered on this Form will be issued in a roll-up transaction as defined in Item 901(c) of Regulation S–K (17 CFR 229.901(c)), attention is directed to the requirements of Form S–4 applicable to roll-up transactions, including, but not limited to, General Instruction I.

V. Registration of Additional Securities

With respect to the registration of additional securities for an offering pursuant to Rule 462(b) under the Securities Act, the registrant may file a registration statement consisting only of the following: the facing page; a statement that the contents of the earlier registration statement, identified by file number, are incorporated by reference; required opinions and consents; the signature page; and any price-related information omitted from the earlier registration statement in reliance on Rule 430A that the registrant chooses to include in the new registration statement. The information contained in such a Rule 462(b) registration statement shall be deemed to be a part of the earlier registration statement as of the date of effectiveness of the Rule 462(b) registration statement. Any opinion or consent required in the Rule 462(b) registration statement may be incorporated by reference from the earlier registration statement with respect to the offering, if: (i) such opinion or consent expressly provides for such incorporation; and (ii) such opinion relates to the securities registered pursuant to Rule 462(b). *See* Rule 411(c) and Rule 439(b) under the Securities Act.

VI. Offerings of Asset–Backed Securities

The following applies if a registration statements on this Form S–1 is being used to register an offering of asset-backed securities. Terms used in this General Instruction VI, have the same meaning as in Item 1101 of Regulation AB (17 CFR 229.1101).

A. *Items that May Be Omitted.*

Such registrants may omit the information called for by Item 11, Information with Respect to the Registrant.

B. *Substitute Information to Be Included.*

In addition to the Items that are otherwise required by this Form, the registrant must furnish in the prospectus the information required by Items 1102 through 1120 of Regulation AB (17 CFR 229.1102 through 229.1120).

C. *Signatures.*

The registration statement must be signed by the depositor, the depositor's principal executive officer or officers, principal financial officer and controller or principal accounting officer, and by at least a majority of the depositor's board of directors or persons performing similar functions.

VII. Eligibility to Use Incorporation by Reference

If a registrant meets the following requirements immediately prior to the time of filing a registration statement on this Form, it may elect to provide information required by Items 3 through 11 of this Form in accordance with Item 11A and Item 12 of this Form:

A. The registrant is subject to the requirement to file reports pursuant to Section 13 or Section 15(d) of the Securities Exchange Act of 1934 ("Exchange Act").

B. The registrant has filed all reports and other materials required to be filed by Sections 13(a), 14, or 15(d) of the Exchange Act during the preceding 12 months (or for such shorter period that the registrant was required to file such reports and materials).

C. The registrant has filed an annual report required under Section 13(a) or Section 15(d) of the Exchange Act for its most recently completed fiscal year.

D. The registrant is not:

1. And during the past three years neither the registrant nor any of its predecessors was:

(a) A blank check company as defined in Rule 419(a)(2);

(b) A shell company, other than a business combination related shell company, each as defined in Rule 405; or

(c) A registrant for an offering of penny stock as defined in Rule 3a51-1 under the Securities Exchange Act of 1934.

2. Registering an offering that effectuates a business combination transaction as defined in Rule 165(f)(1).

E. If a registrant is a successor registrant it shall be deemed to have satisfied conditions A., B., C., and D.2 above if:

1. Its predecessor and it, taken together, do so, provided that the succession was primarily for the purpose of changing the state of incorporation of the predecessor or forming a holding company and that the assets and liabilities of the successor at the time of succession were substantially the same as those of the predecessor; or

2. All predecessors met the conditions at the time of succession and the registrant has continued to do so since the succession.

F. The registrant makes its periodic and current reports filed pursuant to Section 13 or Section 15(d) of the Exchange Act that are incorporated by reference pursuant to Item 11A or Item 12 of this Form readily available and accessible on a Web site maintained by or for the registrant and containing information about the registrant.

PART I—INFORMATION REQUIRED IN PROSPECTUS

Item 1. Forepart of the Registration Statement and Outside Front Cover Page of Prospectus.

Set forth in the forepart of the registration statement and on the outside front cover page of the prospectus the information required by Item 501 of Regulation S-K (17 CFR 229.501).

Item 2. Inside Front and Outside Back Cover Pages of Prospectus.

Set forth on the inside front cover page of the prospectus or, where permitted, on the outside back cover page, the information required by Item 502 of Regulation S-K (17 CFR 229.502).

Item 3. Summary Information and Risk Factors.

Furnish the information required by Item 503 of Regulation S-K (17 CFR 229.503).

Item 4. Use of Proceeds.

Furnish the information required by Item 504 of Regulation S-K (17 CFR 229.504).

Item 5. Determination of Offering Price.

Furnish the information required by Item 505 of Regulation S-K (17 CFR 229.505).

Item 6. Dilution.

Furnish the information required by Item 506 of Regulation S-K (17 CFR 229.506).

Item 7. Selling Security Holders.

Furnish the information required by Item 507 of Regulation S-K (17 CFR 229.507).

Item 8. Plan of Distribution.

Furnish the information required by Item 508 of Regulation S-K (17 CFR 229.508).

Item 9. Description of Securities to Be Registered.

Furnish the information required by Item 202 of Regulation S-K (17 CFR 229.202).

Item 10. Interests of Named Experts and Counsel.

Furnish the information required by Item 509 of Regulation S-K (17 CFR 229.509).

Item 11. Information with Respect to the Registrant.

Furnish the following information with respect to the registrant:

(a) Information required by Item 101 of Regulation S–K (17 CFR 229.101), description of business;

(b) Information required by Item 102 of Regulation S–K (17 CFR 229.102), description of property;

(c) Information required by Item 103 of Regulation S–K (17 CFR 229.103), legal proceedings;

(d) Where common equity securities are being offered, information required by Item 201 of Regulation S–K (17 CFR 229.201), market price of and dividends on the registrant's common equity and related stockholder matters;

(e) Financial statements meeting the requirements of Regulation S–X (17 CFR Part 210) (Schedules required under Regulation S–X shall be filed as "Financial Statements Schedules" pursuant to Item 15, Exhibits and Financial Statement Schedules, of this form), as well as any financial information required by Rule 3–05 and Article 11 of Regulation S–X. A smaller reporting company may provide the information in Rule 8–04 and 8–05 of Regulation S–X in lieu of the financial information required by Rule 3–05 and Article 11 of Regulation S–X;

(f) Information required by Item 301 of Regulation S–K (17 CFR 229.301), selected financial data;

(g) Information required by Item 302 of Regulation S–K (17 CFR 229.302), supplementary financial information;

(h) Information required by Item 303 of Regulation S–K (17 CFR 229.303), management's discussion and analysis of financial condition and results of operations;

(i) Information required by Item 304 of Regulation S–K (17 CFR 229.304), changes in and disagreements with accountants on accounting and financial disclosure;

(j) Information required by Item 305 of Regulation S–K (17 CFR 229.305), quantitative and qualitative disclosures about market risk.

(k) Information required by Item 401 of Regulation S–K (17 CFR 229.401), directors and executive officers;

(*l*) Information required by Item 402 of Regulation S–K (17 CFR 229.402), executive compensation, and information required by paragraph (e)(4) of Item 407 of Regulation S–K (17 CFR 229.407), corporate governance;

(m) Information required by Item 403 of Regulation S–K (17 CFR 229.403), security ownership of certain beneficial owners and management; and

(n) Information required by Item 404 of Regulation S–K (17 CFR 229.404), transactions with related persons, promoters and certain control persons, and Item 407(a) of Regulation S–K (17 CFR 229.407(a)), corporate governance.

Item 11A. Material Changes

If the registrant elects to incorporate information by reference pursuant to General Instruction VII, describe any and all material changes in the registrant's affairs which have occurred since the end of the latest fiscal year for which audited financial statements were included in the latest Form 10–K and that have not been described in a Form 10–Q or Form 8–K filed under the Exchange Act.

Item 12. Incorporation of Certain Information by Reference

If the registrant elects to incorporate information by reference pursuant to General Instruction VII.:

(a) It must specifically incorporate by reference into the prospectus contained in the registration statement the following documents by means of a statement to that effect in the prospectus listing all such documents:

(1) The registrant's latest annual report on Form 10–K filed pursuant to Section 13(a) or Section 15(d) of the Exchange Act that contains financial statements for the registrant's latest fiscal year for which a Form 10–K was required to have been filed; and

(2) All other reports filed pursuant to Section 13(a) or 15(d) of the Exchange Act or proxy or information statements filed pursuant to Section 14 of the Exchange Act since the end of the fiscal year covered by the annual report referred to in paragraph (a)(1) above.

NOTE TO ITEM 12(a). Attention is directed to Rule 439 (17 CFR 230.439) regarding consent to use of material incorporated by reference.

(b)(1) The registrant must state:

(i) That it will provide to each person, including any beneficial owner, to whom a prospectus is delivered, a copy of any or all of the reports or documents that have been incorporated by reference in the prospectus contained in the registration statement but not delivered with the prospectus;

(ii) That it will provide these reports or documents upon written or oral request;

(iii) That it will provide these reports or documents at no cost to the requester;

(iv) The name, address, telephone number, and e-mail address, if any, to which the request for these reports or documents must be made; and

(v) The registrant's Web site address, including the uniform resource locator (URL) where the incorporated reports and other documents may be accessed.

NOTE TO ITEM 12(b)(1). If the registrant sends any of the information that is incorporated by reference in the prospectus contained in the registration statement to security holders, it also must send any exhibits that are specifically incorporated by reference in that information.

(2) The registrant must:

(i) Identify the reports and other information that it files with the SEC; and

(ii) state that the SEC maintains an Internet site that contains reports, proxy and information statements, and other information regarding issuers that file electronically with the SEC and state the address of that site (http://www.sec.gov). Disclose your Internet address, if available.

Item 12A. Disclosure of Commission Position on Indemnification for Securities Act Liabilities

Furnish the information required by Item 510 of Regulation S–K (17 CFR 229.510).

PART II—INFORMATION NOT REQUIRED IN PROSPECTUS

Item 13. Other Expenses of Issuance and Distribution

Furnish the information required by Item 511 of Regulation S–K (17 CFR 229.511).

Item 14. Indemnification of Directors and Officers

Furnish the information required by Item 702 of Regulation S–X (17 CFR 229.702).

Item 15. Recent Sales of Unregistered Securities

Furnish the information required by Item 701 of Regulation S–K (17 CFR 229.701).

Item 16. Exhibits and Financial Statement Schedules

(a) Subject to the rules regarding incorporation by reference, furnish the exhibits as required by Item 601 of Regulation S–K (17 CFR 229.601).

(b) Furnish the financial statement schedules required by Regulation S–X (17 CFR Part 210) and Item 11(e) of this Form. These schedules shall be lettered or numbered in the manner described for exhibits in paragraph (a).

Item 17. Undertakings

Furnish the undertakings required by Item 512 of Regulation S–K (17 CFR 229.512).

SIGNATURES

Pursuant to the requirements of the Securities Act of 1933, the registrant has duly caused this registration statement to be signed on its behalf by the undersigned, thereunto duly authorized in the City of ______, State of ______, on ______, 20__.

(Registrant) ____________________

By (Signature and Title) ____________________

Pursuant to the requirements of the Securities Act of 1933, this registration statement has been signed by the following persons in the capacities and on the dates indicated.

(Signature) ____________________

(Title) ____________________

(Date) ____________________

Instructions: 1. The registration statement shall be signed by the registrant, its principal executive officer or officers, its principal financial officer, its controller or principal accounting officer and by at least a majority of the board of directors or persons performing similar functions. If the registrant is a foreign person, the registration statement shall also be signed by its authorized representative in the United States. Where the registrant is a limited partnership, the registration statement shall be signed by a majority of the board of directors of any corporate general partner signing the registration statement.

2. The name of each person who signs the registration statement shall be typed or printed beneath his signature. Any person who occupies more than one of the specified positions shall indicate each capacity in which he signs the registration statement. Attention is directed to Rule 402 concerning manual signatures and to Item 601 of Regulation S–K concerning signatures pursuant to powers of attorney.

INSTRUCTIONS AS TO SUMMARY PROSPECTUSES

1. A summary prospectus used pursuant to Rule 431 (17 CFR 230.431) shall at the time of its use contain such of the information specified below as is then included in the registration statement. All other information and documents contained in the registration statement may be omitted.

(a) As to Item 1, the aggregate offering price to the public, the aggregate underwriting discounts and commissions and the offering price per unit to the public;

(b) As to Item 4, a brief statement of the principal purposes for which the proceeds are to be used;

(c) As to Item 7, a statement as to the amount of the offering, if any, to be made for the account of security holders;

(d) As to Item 8, the name of the managing underwriter or underwriters and a brief statement as to the nature of the underwriter's obligation to take the securities; if any securities to be registered are to be offered otherwise than through underwriters, a brief statement as to the manner of distribution; and, if securities are to be offered otherwise than for cash, a brief statement as to the general purposes of the distribution, the basis upon which the securities are to be offered, the amount of compensation and other expenses of distribution, and by whom they are to be borne;

(e) As to Item 9, a brief statement as to dividend rights, voting rights, conversion rights, interest, maturity;

(f) As to Item 11, a brief statement of the general character of the business done and intended to be done, the selected financial data (Item 301 of Regulation S–K (17 CFR 229.301)) and a brief statement of the nature and present status of any material pending legal proceedings; and

(g) A tabular presentation of notes payable, long term debt, deferred credits, minority interests, if material, and the equity section of the latest balance sheet filed, as may be appropriate.

2. The summary prospectus shall not contain a summary or condensation of any other required financial information except as provided above.

3. Where securities being registered are to be offered in exchange for securities of any other issuer, the summary prospectus also shall contain that information as to Items 9 and 11 specified in paragraphs (e) and (f) above which would be required if the securities of such other issuer were registered on this Form.

4. The Commission may, upon the request of the registrant, and where consistent with the protection of investors, permit the omission of any of the information herein required or the furnishing in substitution therefor of appropriate information of comparable character. The Commission may also require the inclusion of other information in addition to, or in substitution for, the information herein required in any case where such information is necessary or appropriate for the protection of investors.

SECURITIES AND EXCHANGE COMMISSION

FORM S–3

REGISTRATION STATEMENT UNDER THE SECURITIES ACT OF 1933

(Exact name of registrant as specified in its charter)

(State or other jurisdiction of incorporation or organization)

(I.R.S. Employer Identification Number)

(Address, including zip code, and telephone number, including area code, of registrant's principal executive offices)

(Name, address, including zip code, and telephone number, including area code, of agent for service)

(Approximate date of commencement of proposed sale to the public)

If the only securities being registered on this Form are being offered pursuant to dividend or interest reinvestment plans, please check the following box. ❑

If any of the securities being registered on this Form are to be offered on a delayed or continuous basis pursuant to Rule 415 under the Securities Act of 1933, other than securities offered only in connection with dividend or interest reinvestment plans, check the following box. ❑

If this Form is filed to register additional securities for an offering pursuant to Rule 462(b) under the Securities Act, please check the following box and list the Securities Act registration statement number of the earlier effective registration statement for the same offering: ❑

If this Form is a post-effective amendment filed pursuant to Rule 462(c) under the Securities Act, check the following box and list the Securities Act registration statement number of the earlier effective registration statement for the same offering. ❑

If this Form is a registration statement pursuant to General Instruction I.D. or a post-effective amendment thereto that shall become effective upon filing with the Commission pursuant to Rule 462(e) under the Securities Act, check the following box. ❑

If this Form is a post-effective amendment to a registration statement filed pursuant to General Instruction I.D. filed to register additional securities or additional classes of securities pursuant to Rule 413(b) under the Securities Act, check the following box. ❑

Indicate by check mark whether the registrant is a large accelerated filer, an accelerated filer, a non-accelerated filer, a smaller reporting company, or an emerging growth company. See the definitions of "large accelerated filer," "accelerated filer," "smaller reporting company," and "emerging growth company" in Rule 12b–2 of the Exchange Act.

Large accelerated filer ❑

Accelerated filer ❑

Non-accelerated filer ❑

Smaller reporting company ❑

Emerging growth company ❑

If an emerging growth company, indicate by check mark if the registrant has elected not to use the extended transition period for complying with any new or revised financial accounting standards provided pursuant to Section 7(a)(2)(B) of the Securities Act. ❑

Calculation of Registration Fee

Title of each class of securities to be registered	Amount to be registered	Proposed maximum offering price per unit	Proposed maximum aggregate offering price	Amount of registration fee

Notes to the "Calculation of Registration Fee" Table ("Fee Table"):

1. Specific details relating to the fee calculation shall be furnished in notes to the Fee Table, including references to provisions of Rule 457 (17 CFR 230.457) relied upon, if the basis of the calculation is not otherwise evident from the information presented in the Fee Table.

2. If the filing fee is calculated pursuant to Rule 457(*o*) under the Securities Act, only the title of the

class of securities to be registered, the proposed maximum aggregate offering price for that class of securities, and the amount of registration fee need to appear in the Fee Table. Where two or more classes of securities are being registered pursuant to General Instruction II.D., however, the Fee Table need only specify the maximum aggregate offering price for all classes; the Fee Table need not specify by each class the proposed maximum aggregate offering price (see General Instruction II.D.).

3. If the filing fee is calculated pursuant to Rule 457(r) under the Securities Act, the Fee Table must state that it registers an unspecified amount of securities of each identified class of securities and must provide that the issuer is relying on Rule 456(b) and Rule 457(r). If the Fee Table is amended in a post-effective amendment to the registration statement or in a prospectus filed in accordance with Rule 456(b)(1)(ii) (17 CFR 230.456(b)(1)(ii)), the Fee Table must specify the aggregate offering price for all classes of securities in the referenced offering or offerings and the applicable registration fee.

4. Any difference between the dollar amount of securities registered for such offerings and the dollar amount of securities sold may be carried forward on a future registration statement pursuant to Rule 457 under the Securities Act.

GENERAL INSTRUCTIONS

I. Eligibility Requirements for Use of Form S-3

This instruction sets forth registrant requirements and transaction requirements for the use of Form S-3. Any registrant which meets the requirements of I.A. below ("Registrant Requirements") may use this Form for the registration of securities under the Securities Act of 1933 ("Securities Act") which are offered in any transaction specified in I.B. below ("Transaction Requirement") provided that the requirement applicable to the specified transaction are met. With respect to majority-owned subsidiaries, see Instruction I.C. below. With respect to well-known seasoned issuers and majority-owned subsidiaries of well-known seasoned issuers, see Instruction I.D. below.

A. Registrant Requirements. Registrants must meet the following conditions in order to use this Form S-3 for registration under the Securities Act of securities offered in the transactions specified in I.B. below:

1. The registrant is organized under the laws of the United States or any State or Territory or the District of Columbia and has its principal business operations in the United States or its territories.

2. The registrant has a class of securities registered pursuant to Section 12(b) of the Securities Exchange Act of 1934 ("Exchange Act") or a class of equity securities registered pursuant to Section 12(g) of the Exchange Act or is required to file reports pursuant to Section 15(d) of the Exchange Act.

3. The registrant:

(a) has been subject to the requirements of Section 12 or 15(d) of the Exchange Act and has filed all the material required to be filed pursuant to Section 13, 14 or 15(d) for a period of at least twelve calendar months immediately preceding the filing of the registration statement on this Form; and

(b) has filed in a timely manner all reports required to be filed during the twelve calendar months and any portion of a month immediately preceding the filing of the registration statement, other than a report that is required solely pursuant to Item 1.01, 1.02, 1.04, 2.03, 2.04, 2.05, 2.06, 4.02(a) or 5.02(e) of Form 8-K (17 CFR 249.308). If the registrant has used (during the twelve calendar months and any portion of a month immediately preceding the filing of the registration statement) Rule 12b-25(b) (17 CFR 240.12b-25(b)) under the Exchange Act with respect to a report or a portion of a report, that report or portion thereof has actually been filed within the time period prescribed by that rule.

4. Neither the registrant nor any of its consolidated or unconsolidated subsidiaries have, since the end of the last fiscal year for which certified financial statements of the registrant and its consolidated subsidiaries were included in a report filed pursuant to Section 13(a) or 15(d) of the Exchange Act: (a) failed to pay any dividend or sinking fund installment on preferred stock; or (b) defaulted (i) on any installment or installments on indebtedness for borrowed money, or (ii) on any rental on one or more long term leases, which defaults in the aggregate are material to the financial position of the registrant and its consolidated and unconsolidated subsidiaries, taken as a whole.

5. A foreign issuer, other than a foreign government, which satisfies all of the above provisions of these registrant eligibility requirements except the provisions in I. A. 1. relating to organization and principal business shall be deemed to have met these registrant eligibility requirements provided that such a foreign issuer files the same reports with the Commission under Section 13(a) or

15(d) of the Exchange Act as a domestic registrant pursuant to I. A. 3. above.

6. If the registrant is a successor registrant, it shall be deemed to have met conditions 1., 2., 3., and 5., above if: (a) its predecessor and it, taken together, do so, provided that the succession was primarily for the purpose of changing the state of incorporation of the predecessor or forming a holding company and that the assets and liabilities of the successor at the time of succession were substantially the same as those of the predecessor, or (b) if all predecessors met the conditions at the time of succession and the registrant has continued to do so since the succession.

7. *Electronic Filings.* In addition to satisfying the foregoing conditions, a registrant subject to the electronic filing requirements of Rule 101 of Regulation S–T shall have:

(a) Filed with the Commission all required electronic filings, including electronic copies of documents submitted in paper pursuant to a hardship exemption as provided by Rule 201 or Rule 202(d) of Regulation S–T; and

(b) Submitted electronically to the Commission all Interactive Data Files required to be submitted pursuant to Rule 405 of Regulation S–T during the twelve calendar months and any portion of a month immediately preceding the filing of the registration statement on this Form (or for such shorter period of time that the registrant was required to submit such files).

B. Transaction Requirements. Security offerings meeting any of the following conditions and made by a registrant meeting the Registrant Requirements specified in I.A. above may be registered on this Form:

1. *Primary Offerings by Certain Registrants.* Securities to be offered for cash by or on behalf of a registrant, or outstanding securities to be offered for cash for the account of any person other than the registrant, including securities acquired by standby underwriters in connection with the call or redemption by the registrant of warrants or a class of convertible securities; *Provided* That the aggregate market value of the voting and non-voting common equity held by non-affiliates of the registrant is $75 million or more.

Instruction. For the purposes of this Form, "common equity" is as defined in Securities Act Rule 405 (17 CFR 230.405). The aggregate market value of the registrant's outstanding voting and non-voting common equity shall be computed by use of the price at which the common equity was last sold, or the average of the bid and asked prices of such common equity, in the principal market for such common equity as of a date within 60 days prior to the date of filing. See the definition of "affiliate" in Securities Act Rule 405 (17 CFR 230.405).

2. *Primary Offerings of Non-Convertible Securities Other than Common Equity.* Non- convertible securities, other than common equity, to be offered for cash by or on behalf of a registrant, provided the registrant:

(i) has issued (as of a date within 60 days prior to the filing of the registration statement) at least $1 billion in non-convertible securities, other than common equity, in primary offerings for cash, not exchange, registered under the Securities Act, over the prior three years; or

(ii) has outstanding (as of a date within 60 days prior to the filing of the registration statement) at least $750 million of non-convertible securities, other than common equity, issued in primary offerings for cash, not exchange, registered under the Securities Act; or

(iii) is a wholly-owned subsidiary of a well-known seasoned issuer (as defined in 17 CFR 230.405); or

(iv) is a majority-owned operating partnership of a real estate investment trust that qualifies as a well-known seasoned issuer (as defined in 17 CFR 230.405).

Instruction. For purposes of Instruction I.B.2(i) above, an insurance company, as defined in Section 2(a)(13) of the Securities Act, when using this Form to register offerings of securities subject to regulation under the insurance laws of any State or Territory of the United States or the District of Columbia ("insurance contracts"), may include purchase payments or premium payments for insurance contracts, including purchase payments or premium payments for variable insurance contracts (not including purchase payments or premium payments initially allocated to investment options that are not registered under the Securities Act), issued in offerings registered under the Securities Act over the prior three years. For purposes of Instruction I.B.2(ii) above, an insurance company, as defined in Section 2(a)(13) of the Securities Act, when using this Form to register offerings of insurance contracts, may include the contract value, as of the measurement date, of any outstanding insurance contracts, including variable insurance contracts (not including the value allocated as of the measurement date to investment options that are not registered under the Securities Act), issued in offerings registered under the Securities Act.

3. *Transactions Involving Secondary Offerings.* Outstanding securities to be offered for the account of any person other than the issuer, including securities acquired by standby underwriters in connection with the call or redemption by the issuer of warrants or a class of convertible securities, if securities of the same class are listed and registered on a national securities exchange

or are quoted on the automated quotation system of a national securities association. (In addition, attention is directed to General Instruction C to Form S–8 (17 CFR 239.16b) for the registration of employee benefit plan securities for resale.)

4. *Rights Offerings, Dividend or Interest Reinvestment Plans, and Conversions or Warrants and Options.*

(a) Securities to be offered (1) upon the exercise of outstanding rights granted by the issuer of the securities to be offered, if such rights are granted on a *pro rata* basis to all existing security holders of the class of securities to which the rights attach, (2) under a dividend or interest reinvestment plan, or (3) upon the conversion of outstanding convertible securities or the exercise of outstanding warrants or options issued by the issuer of the securities to be offered, or by an affiliate of such issuer.

(b) However, Form S–3 is available for registering these securities only if the issuer has sent, within the twelve calendar months immediately before the registration statement is filed, material containing the information required by Rule 14a–3(b) (17 CFR 240.14a–3(b)) under the Exchange Act to:

(1) All record holders of the rights,

(2) All participants in the plans, or

(3) All record holders of the convertible securities, warrants or options, respectively.

(c) The issuer also must have provided, within the twelve calendar months immediately before the Form S–3 registration statement is filed, the information required by Items 401, 402, 403 and 407(c)(3), (d)(4), (d)(5) and (e)(4) of Regulation S–K (17 CFR 229.401–229.403 and 229.407(c)(3), (d)(4), (d)(5) and (e)(4)) to:

(1) Holders of rights exercisable for common stock,

(2) Holders of securities convertible into common stock, and

(3) Participants in plans that may invest in common stock, securities convertible into common stock, or warrants or options exercisable for common stock, respectively.

5. This Form shall not be used to register offerings of asset-backed securities, as defined in Item 1101(c) of Regulation AB.

6. *Limited Primary Offerings by Certain Other Registrants.* Securities to be offered for cash by or on behalf of a registrant; *provided that*:

(a) the aggregate market value of securities sold by or on behalf of the registrant pursuant to this Instruction I.B.6. during the period of 12 calendar months immediately prior to, and including, the sale is no more than one-third of the aggregate market value of the voting and non-voting common equity held by non-affiliates of the registrant;

(b) the registrant is not a shell company (as defined in Rule 405) and has not been a shell company for at least 12 calendar months previously and if it has been a shell company at any time previously, has filed current Form 10 information with the Commission at least 12 calendar months previously reflecting its status as an entity that is not a shell company; and

(c) the registrant has at least one class of common equity securities listed and registered on a national securities exchange.

Instructions.

1. "Common equity" is as defined in Securities Act Rule 405 (17 CFR 230.405). For purposes of computing the aggregate market value of the registrant's outstanding voting and non-voting common equity pursuant to General Instruction I.B.6., registrants shall use the price at which the common equity was last sold, or the average of the bid and asked prices of such common equity, in the principal market for such common equity as of a date within 60 days prior to the date of sale. See the definition of "affiliate" in Securities Act Rule 405 (17 CFR 230.405).

2. For purposes of computing the aggregate market value of all securities sold by or on behalf of the registrant in offerings pursuant to General Instruction I.B.6. during any period of 12 calendar months, registrants shall aggregate the gross proceeds of such sales; *provided*, that, in the case of derivative securities convertible into or exercisable for shares of the registrant's common equity, registrants shall calculate the aggregate market value of any underlying equity shares in lieu of the market value of the derivative securities. The aggregate market value of the underlying equity shall be calculated by multiplying the maximum number of common equity shares into which the derivative securities are convertible or for which they are exercisable as of a date within 60 days prior to the date of sale, by the same per share market price of the registrant's equity used for purposes of calculating the aggregate market value of the registrant's outstanding voting and non-voting common equity pursuant to Instruction 1 to General Instruction I.B.6. If the derivative securities have been converted or exercised, the aggregate market value of the underlying equity shall be calculated by multiplying the actual number of shares into which the securities were converted or received upon exercise, by the market price of such shares on the date of conversion or exercise.

3. If the aggregate market value of the registrant's outstanding voting and nonvoting common equity computed pursuant to General Instruction I.B.6. equals or exceeds $75 million subsequent to the effective date of this regis-

tration statement, then the one-third limitation on sales specified in General Instruction I.B.6(a) shall not apply to additional sales made pursuant to this registration statement on or subsequent to such date and instead the registration statement shall be considered filed pursuant to General Instruction I.B.1.

4. The term "Form 10 information" means the information that is required by Form 10 or Form 20–F (17 CFR 249.210 or 249.220f), as applicable to the registrant, to register under the Securities Exchange Act of 1934 each class of securities being registered using this form. A registrant may provide the Form 10 information in another Commission filing with respect to the registrant.

5. The date used in Instruction 2 to General Instruction I.B.6. shall be the same date used in Instruction 1 to General Instruction I.B.6.

6. A registrant's eligibility to register a primary offering on Form S–3 pursuant to General Instruction I.B.6. does not mean that the registrant meets the requirements of Form S–3 for purposes of any other rule or regulation of the Commission apart from Rule 415(a)(1)(x) (17 CFR 230.415 (a)(1)(x)).

7. Registrants must set forth on the outside front cover of the prospectus the calculation of the aggregate market value of the registrant's outstanding voting and nonvoting common equity pursuant to General Instruction I.B.6. and the amount of all securities offered pursuant to General Instruction I.B.6. during the prior 12 calendar month period that ends on, and includes, the date of the prospectus.

8. For purposes of General Instruction I.B.6(c), a "national securities exchange" shall mean an exchange registered as such under Section 6(a) of the Securities Exchange Act of 1934.

C. Majority-Owned Subsidiaries. If a registrant is a majority-owned subsidiary, security offerings may be registered on this Form if:

1. the registrant-subsidiary itself meets the Registrant Requirements and the applicable Transaction Requirement;

2. the parent of the registrant-subsidiary meets the Registrant Requirements and the conditions of Transaction Requirements B.2. (Primary Offerings of Non-Convertible Securities Other than Common Equity) are met;

3. the parent of the registrant-subsidiary meets the Registrant Requirements and the applicable Transaction Requirement, and provides a full and unconditional guarantee, as defined in Rule 3–10 of Regulation S–X (17 CFR 210.3–10), of the payment obligations on the securities being registered, and the securities being registered are non-convertible securities, other than common equity;

4. the parent of the registrant-subsidiary meets the Registrant Requirements and the applicable Transaction Requirement, and the securities of the registrant-subsidiary being registered are full and unconditional guarantees, as defined in Rule 3–10 of Regulation S–X, of the payment obligations on the parent's non-convertible securities, other than common equity, being registered; or

5. the parent of the registrant-subsidiary meets the Registrant Requirements and the applicable Transaction Requirement, and the securities of the registrant-subsidiary being registered are guarantees of the payment obligations on the non-convertible securities, other than common equity, being registered by another majority-owned subsidiary of the parent where the parent provides a full and unconditional guarantee, as defined in Rule 3–10 of Regulation S–X, of such non-convertible securities.

Note to General Instruction I.C.: With regard to paragraphs I.C.3, I.C.4, and I.C.5 above, the guarantor is the issuer of a separate security consisting of the guarantee, which must be concurrently registered, but may be registered on the same registration statement as are the non-convertible guaranteed securities.

D. Automatic Shelf Offerings by Well–Known Seasoned Issuers.

Any registrant that is a well-known seasoned issuer, as defined in Rule 405 (17 CFR 230.405), at the most recent eligibility determination date specified in paragraph (2) of that definition may use this Form for registration under the Securities Act of securities offerings, other than pursuant to Rule 415(a)(1)(vii) or (viii) (17 CFR 230.415(a)(1)(vii) or (viii)), as follows:

(1) The securities to be offered are:

(a) Any securities to be offered pursuant to Rule 415, Rule 430A, or Rule 430B (17 CFR 230.415, 230.430A, or 230.430B) by:

(i) A registrant that is a well-known seasoned issuer by reason of paragraph (1)(i)(A) of the definition in Rule 405; or

(ii) A registrant that is a well-known seasoned issuer only by reason of paragraph (1)(i)(B) of the definition in Rule 405 if the registrant also is eligible to register a primary offering of its securities pursuant to Transaction Requirement I.B.1 of this Form;

(b) Non-convertible securities, other than common equity, to be offered pursuant to Rule 415, Rule 430A, or Rule 430B by a registrant that is a well-known seasoned issuer only by reason of paragraph (1)(i)(B) of the definition in Rule 405 and does not fall within Transaction Requirement I.B.1 of this Form;

(c) Securities of majority-owned subsidiaries of the parent registrant to be offered pursuant to Rule 415, Rule 430A, or Rule 430B if the parent registrant is a well-known seasoned issuer and the securities of the majority-owned subsidiary being registered meet the following requirements:

(i) Securities of a majority-owned subsidiary that is a well-known seasoned issuer at the time it becomes a registrant, other than by virtue of paragraph (1)(ii) of the definition of well-known seasoned issuer in Rule 405;

(ii) Securities of a majority-owned subsidiary that are non-convertible securities, other than common equity, and the parent registrant provides a full and unconditional guarantee, as defined in Rule 3–10 of Regulation S–X, of the payment obligations on the non-convertible securities;

(iii) Securities of a majority-owned subsidiary that are a guarantee of:

(A) Non-convertible securities, other than common equity, of the parent registrant being registered;

(B) Non-convertible securities, other than common equity, of another majority-owned subsidiary being registered and the parent has provided a full and unconditional guarantee, as defined in Rule 3–10 of Regulation S–X, of the payment obligations on such non-convertible securities; or

(iv) Securities of a majority-owned subsidiary that meet the conditions of Transaction Requirement I.B.2. of this Form (Primary Offerings of Non-Convertible Securities Other than Common Equity).

(d) Securities to be offered for the account of any person other than the issuer ("selling security holders"), provided that the registration statement and the prospectus are not required to separately identify the selling security holders or the securities to be sold by such persons until the filing of a prospectus, prospectus supplement, post-effective amendment to the registration statement, or periodic or current report under the Exchange Act that is incorporated by reference into the registration statement and prospectus, identifying the selling security holders and the amount of securities to be sold by each of them and, if included in a periodic or current report, a prospectus or prospectus supplement is filed, as required by Rule 430B, pursuant to Rule 424(b)(7) (17 CFR 230.424(b)(7));

2. The registrant pays the registration fee pursuant to Rule 456(b) and Rule 457(r) (17 CFR 230.456(b) and 230.456(r)) or in accordance with Rule 456(a) (17 CFR 230.456(a));

3. If the registrant is a majority-owned subsidiary, it is required to file and has filed reports pursuant to Section 13 or Section 15(d) of the Exchange Act and satisfies the requirements of the Form with regard to incorporation by reference or information about the majority-owned subsidiary is included in the registration statement (or a post-effective amendment to the registration statement);

4. The registrant may register additional securities or classes of its or its majority-owned subsidiaries' securities on a post-effective amendment pursuant to Rule 413(b) (17 CFR 230.413(b)); and

5. An automatic shelf registration statement and post-effective amendment will become effective immediately pursuant to Rule 462(e) and (f) (17 CFR 230.462(e) and (f)) upon filing. All filings made on or in connection with automatic shelf registration statements on this Form become public upon filing with the Commission.

II. Application of General Rules and Regulations

A. Attention is directed to the General Rules and Regulations under the Securities Act, particularly Regulation C thereunder (17 CFR 230.400 to 230.400 to 230.494). That Regulation contains general requirements regarding the preparation and filing of registration statements.

B. Attention is directed to Regulation S–K (17 CFR Part 229) for the requirements applicable to the content of the non-financial statement portions of registration statements under the Securities Act. Where this Form directs the registrant to furnish information required by Regulation S–K and the item of Regulation S–K so provides, information need only be furnished to the extent appropriate. Notwithstanding Items 501 and 502 of Regulation S–K, no table of contents is required to be included in the prospectus or registration statement prepared on this form. In addition to the information expressly required to be included in a registration statement on this Form S–3, registrants also may provide such other information as they may deem appropriate.

C. A smaller reporting company, defined in Rule 405 (17 CFR 230.405), that is eligible to use Form S–3 shall use the disclosure items in Regulation S–K (17 CFR 229.10 *et seq.*) with specific attention to the scaled disclosure provided for smaller reporting companies, if any. Smaller reporting companies may provide the financial information called for by

Article 8 of Regulation S–X in lieu of the financial information called for by Item 11 in this form.

D. Non–Automatic Shelf Registration Statements. Where two or more classes of securities being registered on this Form pursuant to General Instruction I.B.1. or I.B.2. are to be offered pursuant to Rule 415(a)(1)(x) (17 CFR 230.415(a)(1)(x)), and where this Form is not an automatic shelf registration statement, Rule 457(*o*) permits the registration fee to be calculated on the basis of the maximum offering price of all the securities listed in the Fee Table. In this event, while the Fee Table would list each of the classes of securities being registered and the aggregate proceeds to be raised, the Fee Table need not specify by each class information as to the amount to be registered, proposed maximum offering price per unit, and proposed maximum aggregate offering price.

E. Automatic Shelf Registration Statements. Where securities are being registered on this Form pursuant to General Instruction I.D., Rule 456(b) permits, but does not require, the registrant to pay the registration fee on a pay-as-you-go basis and Rule 457(r) permits, but does not require, the registration fee to be calculated on the basis of the aggregate offering price of the securities to be offered in an offering or offerings off the registration statement. If a registrant elects to pay all or a portion of the registration fee on a deferred basis, the Fee Table in the initial filing must identify the classes of securities being registered and provide that the registrant elects to rely on Rule 456(b) and Rule 457(r), but the Fee Table does not need to specify any other information. When the registrant amends the Fee Table in accordance with Rule 456(b)(1)(ii), the amended Fee Table must include either the dollar amount of securities being registered if paid in advance of or in connection with an offering or offerings or the aggregate offering price for all classes of securities referenced in the offerings and the applicable registration fee.

F. Information in Automatic and Non–Automatic Shelf Registration Statements. Where securities are being registered on this Form pursuant to General Instruction I.B.1, I.B.2, I.C., or I.D., information is only required to be furnished as of the date of initial effectiveness of the registration statement to the extent required by Rule 430A or Rule 430B. Required information about a specific transaction must be included in the prospectus in the registration statement by means of a prospectus that is deemed to be part of and included in the registration statement pursuant to Rule 430A or Rule 430B, a post-effective amendment to the registration statement, or a periodic or current report under the Exchange Act incorporated by reference into the registration statement and the prospectus and identified in a prospectus filed, as required by Rule 430B, pursuant to Rule 424(b) (17 CFR 230.424(b)).

G. Selling Security Holder Offerings. Where a registrant eligible to register primary offerings on this Form pursuant to General Instruction I.B.1 registers securities offerings on this Form pursuant to General Instruction I.B.1 or I.B.3 for the account of persons other than the registrant, if the offering of the securities, or securities convertible into such securities, that are being registered on behalf of the selling security holders was completed and the securities, or securities convertible into such securities, were issued and outstanding prior to the original date of filing the registration statement covering the resale of the securities, the registrant may, as permitted by Rule 430B(b), in lieu of identifying selling security holders prior to effectiveness of the resale registration statement, refer to unnamed selling security holders in a generic manner by identifying the initial transaction in which the securities were sold. Following effectiveness, the registrant must include in a prospectus filed pursuant to Rule 424(b)(7), a post-effective amendment to the registration statement, or an Exchange Act report incorporated by reference into the prospectus that is part of the registration statement (which Exchange Act report is identified in a prospectus filed, as required by Rule 430B, pursuant to Rule 424(b)(7)) the names of previously unidentified selling security holders and amounts of securities that they intend to sell. If this Form is being filed pursuant to General Instruction I.D. by a well-known seasoned issuer to register securities being offered for the account of persons other than the issuer, the registration statement and the prospectus included in the registration statement do not need to designate the securities that will be offered for the account of such persons, identify them, or identify the initial transaction in which the securities, or securities convertible into such securities, were sold until the registrant files a post-effective amendment to the registration statement, a prospectus pursuant to Rule 424(b), or an Exchange Act report (and prospectus filed, as required by Rule 430B, pursuant to Rule 424(b)(7)) containing information for the offering on behalf of such persons.

III. Dividend or Interest Reinvestment Plans: Filing and Effectiveness of Registration Statement; Requests for Confidential Treatment

A registration statement on this Form S–3 relating solely to securities offered pursuant to dividend or interest reinvestment plans will become effective automatically (Rule 462, § 230.462 of this chapter) upon filing (Rule 456, § 230.456 of this chapter). Post-effective amendments to such a registration statement on this Form shall become effective upon filing (Rule 464, § 230.464 of this chapter). All filings made on or in connection with this Form become public upon filing with the Commission. As a result, requests for confidential treatment made under Rule 406 (17 CFR 230.406) must be processed with the Commission staff prior to the filing of such a registration statement. The number of copies of the registration statement and of each amendment required by Rules 402 and 472 (17 CFR 230.402 and 230.472) shall be filed with the Commission: *provided, however,* That the number of additional copies referred to in Rule 402(b) may be reduced from ten to three and the number of additional copies referred to in Rule 472(a) may be reduced from eight to three, one of which shall be marked clearly and precisely to indicate changes.

IV. Registration of Additional Securities and Additional Classes of Securities

A. Registration of Additional Securities Pursuant to Rule 462(b). With respect to the registration of additional securities for an offering pursuant to Rule 462(b) under the Securities Act, the registrant may file a registration statement consisting only of the following: the facing page; a statement that the contents of the earlier registration statement, identified by file number, are incorporated by reference; required opinions and consents; the signature page; and any price-related information omitted from the earlier registration statement in reliance on Rule 430A that the registrant chooses to include in the new registration statement. The information contained in such a Rule 462(b) registration statement shall be deemed to be a part of the earlier registration statement as of the date of effectiveness of the Rule 462(b) registration statement. Any opinion or consent required in the Rule 462(b) registration statement may be incorporated by reference from the earlier registration statement with respect to the offering, if: (i) such opinion or consent expressly provides for such incorporation; and (ii) such opinion relates to the securities registered pursuant to Rule 462(b). *See* Rule 411(c) and Rule 439(b) under the Securities Act.

B. Registration of Additional Securities or Classes of Securities or Additional Registrants After Effectiveness. A well-known seasoned issuer relying on General Instruction I.D. of this Form may register additional securities or classes of securities, pursuant to Rule 413(b) by filing a post-effective amendment to the effective registration statement. The well-known seasoned issuer may add majority-owned subsidiaries as additional registrants whose securities are eligible to be sold as part of the automatic shelf registration statement by filing a post-effective amendment identifying the additional registrants, and the registrant and the additional registrants and other persons required to sign the registration statement must sign the post-effective amendment. The post-effective amendment must consist of the facing page; any disclosure required by this Form that is necessary to update the registration statement to reflect the additional securities, additional classes of securities, or additional registrants; any required opinions and consents; and the signature page. Required information, consents, or opinions may be included in the prospectus and the registration statement through a post-effective amendment or may be provided through a document incorporated or deemed incorporated by reference into the registration statement and the prospectus that is part of the registration statement, or, as to the required information only, contained in a prospectus filed pursuant to Rule 424(b) that is deemed part of and included in the registration statement and prospectus that is part of the registration statement.

PART I—INFORMATION REQUIRED IN PROSPECTUS

Item 1. Forepart of the Registration Statement and Outside Front Cover Pages of Prospectus

Set forth in the forepart of the registration statement and on the outside front cover page of the prospectus the information required by Item 501 of Regulation S–K (17 CFR 229.501).

Item 2. Inside Front and Outside Back Cover Pages of Prospectus

Set forth on the inside front cover page of the prospectus or, where permitted, on the outside back cover page, the information required by Item 502 of Regulation S–K (17 CFR 229.502).

Item 3. Summary Information and Risk Factors

Furnish the information required by Item 503 of Regulation S–K (17 CFR 229.503).

Item 4. Use of Proceeds

Furnish the information required by Item 504 of Regulation S–K (17 CFR 229.504).

Item 5. Determination of Offering Price

Furnish the information required by Item 505 of Regulation S–K (17 CFR 229.505).

Item 6. Dilution

Furnish the information required by Item 506 of Regulation S–K (17 CFR 229.506).

Item 7. Selling Security Holders

Furnish the information required by Item 507 of Regulation S–K (17 CFR 229.507).

Item 8. Plan of Distribution

Furnish the information required by Item 508 of Regulation S–K (17 CFR 229.508).

Item 9. Description of Securities to Be Registered

Furnish the information required by Item 202 of Regulation S–K (17 CFR 229.202), unless capital stock is to be registered and securities of the same class are registered pursuant to Section 12 of the Exchange Act.

Item 10. Interests of Named Experts and Counsel

Furnish the information required by Item 509 of Regulation S–K (17 CFR 229.509).

Item 11. Material Changes

(a) Describe any and all material changes in the registrant's affairs that have occurred since the end of the latest fiscal year for which certified financial statements were included in the latest annual report to security holders and that have not been described in a report on Form 10–Q (17 CFR 249.308a) or Form 8–K (17 CFR 249.208a) filed under the Exchange Act.

(b) Include in the prospectus, if not incorporated by reference therein from the reports filed under the Exchange Act specified in Item 12(a), a proxy or information statement filed pursuant to Section 14 of the Exchange Act, a prospectus previously filed pursuant to Rule 424(b) or (c) under the Securities Act (17 CFR 230.424 (b) or (c)) or, where no prospectus is required to be filed pursuant to Rule 424(b), the prospectus included in the registration statement at effectiveness, or a Form 8–K filed during either of the two preceding years: (i) information required by Rule 3–05 and Article 11 of Regulation S–X (17 CFR Part 210); (ii) restated financial statements prepared in accordance with Regulation S–X if there has been a change in accounting principles or a correction in an error where such change or correction requires a material retroactive restatement of financial statements; (iii) restated financial statements prepared in accordance with Regulation S–X where a combination of entities under common control has been consummated subsequent to the most recent fiscal year and the transferred businesses, considered in the aggregate, are significant pursuant to Rule 11–01(b), or (iv) any financial information required because of a material disposition of assets outside the normal course of business.

Item 12. Incorporation of Certain Information by Reference

(a) The documents listed in (1) and (2) below shall be specifically incorporated by reference into the prospectus by means of a statement to that effect in the prospectus listing all such documents:

(1) the registrant's latest annual report on Form 10–K (17 CFR 249.310) filed pursuant to Section 13(a) or 15(d) of the Exchange Act that contains financial statements for the registrant's latest fiscal year for which a Form 10–K was required to be filed; and

(2) all other reports filed pursuant to Section 13(a) or 15(d) of the Exchange Act since the end of the fiscal year covered by the annual report referred to in (1) above; and

(3) if capital stock is to be registered and securities of the same class are registered under Section 12 of the Exchange Act, the description of such class of securities which is contained in a registration statement filed under the Exchange Act, including any amendment or reports filed for the purpose of updating such description.

(b) The prospectus shall also state that all documents subsequently filed by the registrant pursuant to Sections 13(a), 13(c), 14 or 15(d) of the Exchange Act, prior to the termination of the offering shall be deemed to be incorporated by reference into the prospectus.

Instruction. Attention is directed to Rule 439 (17 CFR 230.439) regarding consent to use of material incorporated by reference.

(c)(1) You must state (i) that you will provide to each person, including any beneficial owner, to whom a prospectus is delivered, a copy of any or all of the information that has been incorporated by reference in the prospectus but not delivered with the prospectus;

(ii) that you will provide this information upon written or oral request;

(iii) that you will provide this information at no cost to the requester; and

(iv) the name, address, and telephone number to which the request for this information must be made.

Note to Item 12(c)(1). If you send any of the information that is incorporated by reference in the prospectus to security holders, you also must send any exhibits that are specifically incorporated by reference in that information.

(2) You must (i) identify the reports and other information that you file with the SEC; and

(ii) state that the SEC maintains an Internet site that contains reports, proxy and information statements, and other information regarding issuers that file electronically with the SEC and state the address of that site (http://www.sec.gov). Disclose your Internet address, if available.

(d) Any information required in the prospectus in response to Item 3 through Item 11 of this Form may be included in the prospectus through documents filed pursuant to Section 13(a), 14, or 15(d) of the Exchange Act that are incorporated or deemed incorporated by reference into the prospectus that is part of the registration statement.

Item 13. Disclosure of Commission Position on Indemnification for Securities Act Liabilities

Furnish the information required by Item 510 of Regulation S–K (17 CFR 229.510).

PART II—INFORMATION NOT REQUIRED IN PROSPECTUS

Item 14. Other Expenses of Issuance and Distribution

Furnish the information required by Item 511 of Regulation S–K (17 CFR 229.511).

Item 15. Indemnification of Directors and Officers

Furnish the information required by Item 702 of Regulation S–K (17 CFR 229.702).

Item 16. Exhibits

Subject to the rules regarding incorporation by reference, furnish the exhibits required by Item 601 of Regulation S–K (17 CFR 229.601).

Item 17. Undertakings

Furnish the undertakings required by Item 512 of Regulation S–K (17 CFR 229.512).

SIGNATURES

Pursuant to the requirements of the Securities Act of 1933, the registrant certifies that it has reasonable grounds to believe that it meets all of the requirements for filing on Form S–3 and has duly caused this registration statement to be signed on its behalf by the undersigned, thereunto duly authorized, in the City of _______, State of _______, on _______, 20__.

(Registrant) ____________________

By (Signature and Title) ____________________

Pursuant to the requirements of the Securities Act of 1933, this registration statement has been signed by the following persons in the capacities and on the dates indicated.

(Signature) ____________________

(Title) ____________________

(Date)

Instructions. 1. The registration statement shall be signed by the registrant, its principal executive officer or officers, its principal financial officer, its controller or principal accounting officer, and by at least a majority of the board of directors or persons performing similar functions. If the registrant is a foreign person, the registration statement shall also be signed by its authorized representative in the United States. Where the registrant is a limited partnership, the registration statement shall be signed by a majority of the board of directors of any corporate general partner signing the registration statement.

2. The name of each person who signs the registration statement shall be typed or printed beneath his signature. Any person who occupies more than one of the specified positions shall indicate each capacity in which he signs the registration statement. Attention is directed to Rule 402 concerning manual signatures and Item 601 of Regulation S–K concerning signatures pursuant to powers of attorney.

FORM S–4

REGISTRATION STATEMENT UNDER THE SECURITIES ACT OF 1933

(Exact name of registrant as specified in its charter)

(State or other jurisdiction of incorporation or organization)

(Primary Standard Industrial Classification Code Number)

(I.R.S. Employer Identification Number)

(Address, including zip code, and telephone number, including area code, of registrant's principal executive offices)

(Name, address, including zip code, and telephone number, including area code, of agent for service)

Approximate date of commencement of proposed sale of the securities to the public: ____________

If the securities being registered on this Form are being offered in connection with the formation of a holding company and there is compliance with General Instruction G, check the following box. ❑

If this Form is filed to register additional securities for an offering pursuant to Rule 462(b) under the Securities Act, check the following box and list the Securities Act registration statement number of the earlier effective registration statement for the same offering. ❑

If this Form is a post-effective amendment filed pursuant to Rule 462(d) under the Securities Act, check the following box and list the Securities Act registration statement number of the earlier effective registration statement for the same offering. ❑

Indicate by check mark whether the registrant is a large accelerated filer, an accelerated filer, a non-accelerated filer, a smaller reporting company, or an emerging growth company. See the definitions of "large accelerated filer," "accelerated filer," "smaller reporting company," and "emerging growth company" in Rule 12b–2 of the Exchange Act.

Large accelerated filer ❑

Accelerated filer ❑

Non-accelerated filer ❑

Smaller reporting company ❑

Emerging growth company ❑

If an emerging growth company, indicate by check mark if the registrant has elected not to use the extended transition period for complying with any new or revised financial accounting standards provided pursuant to Section 7(a)(2)(B) of the Securities Act. ❑

If applicable, place an X in the box to designate the appropriate rule provision relied upon in conducting this transaction:

Exchange Act Rule 13e–4(i) (Cross-Border Issuer Tender Offer) ❑

Exchange Act Rule 14d–1(d) (Cross-Border Third-Party Tender Offer) ❑

Calculation of Registration Fee

Title of each class of securities to be registered	Amount to be registered	Proposed maximum offering price per unit	Proposed maximum aggregate offering price	Amount of registration fee

Note: Specific details relating to the fee calculation shall be furnished in notes to the table, including references to provisions of Rule 457 (17 CFR 230.457) relied upon, if the basis of the calculation is not otherwise evident from the information presented in the table.

GENERAL INSTRUCTIONS

A. Rule as to Use of Form S–4.

1. This Form may be used for registration under the Securities Act of 1933 ("Securities Act") of securities to be issued (1) in a transaction of the type specified in paragraph (a) of Rule 145 (17 CFR 230.145); (2) in a merger in which the applicable state law would not require the solicitation of the votes or consents of all of the security holders of the company being acquired; (3) in an exchange offer for securities of the issuer or another entity; (4) in a public reoffering or resale of any such securities acquired pursuant to this regis-

tration statement; or (5) in more than one of the kinds of transaction listed in (1) through (4) registered on one registration statement.

2. If the registrant meets the requirements of and elects to comply with the provisions in any item of this Form or Form F–4 (17 CFR 239.34) that provides for incorporation by reference of information about the registrant or the company being acquired, the prospectus must be sent to the security holders no later than 20 business days prior to the date on which the meeting of such security holders is held or, if no meeting is held, at least 20 business days prior to either (1) the date of such votes, consents or authorizations, or (2) the date the transaction is consummated or the votes, consents or authorizations may be used to effect the transaction. Attention is directed to Sections 13(e), 14(d) and 14(e) of the Securities Exchange Act of 1934 ("Exchange Act") the rules and regulations thereunder regarding other time periods in connection with exchange offers and going private transactions.

3. This Form shall not be used if the registrant is a registered investment company or a business development company as defined in Section 2(a)(48) of the Investment Company Act of 1940.

B. Information With Respect to the Registrant.

1. Information with respect to the registrant shall be provided in accordance with the items referenced in one of the following subparagraphs:

a. Items 10 and 11 of this Form, if the registrant elects this alternative and meets the following requirements of Form S–3 (17 CFR 239.13) (hereinafter, with respect to the registrant, "meets the requirements for use of Form S–3") for this offering of securities:

(i) the registrant meets the requirements of General Instruction I. A. of Form S–3; and

(ii) one of the following is met:

A. The registrant meets the aggregate market value requirement of General Instruction I.B.1. of Form S–3; or

B. Non-convertible debt or preferred securities are to be offered pursuant to this registration statement and the requirements of General Instruction I.B.2. of Form S–3 have been met for the securities to be registered on this registration statement; or

C. The registrant is a majority-owned subsidiary and one of the conditions of General Instruction I.C. of Form S–3 is met.

b. Items 12 and 13 of this Form, if the registrant meets the requirements for use of Form S–3 and elects this alternative; or

c. Item 14 of this Form, if the registrant does not meet the requirements for use of Form S–3, or if it otherwise elects this alternative.

2. If the registrant is a real estate entity of the type described in General Instruction A to Form S–11 (17 CFR 239.18), the information prescribed by Items 12, 13, 14, 15 and 16 of Form S–11 shall be furnished about the registrant in addition to the information provided pursuant to Items 10 through 14 of this Form. The information prescribed by such Items of Form S–11 may be incorporated by reference into the prospectus if (a) a registrant qualifies for and elects to provide information pursuant to alternative 1.a. or 1.b. of this instruction and (b) the documents incorporated by reference pursuant to such elected alternative contain such information.

C. Information With Respect to the Company Being Acquired.

1. Information with respect to the company whose securities are being acquired (hereinafter including, where securities of the registrant are being offered in exchange for securities of another company, such other company) shall be provided in accordance with the items referenced in one of the following subparagraphs:

a. Item 15 of this Form, if the company being acquired meets the requirements of General Instructions I.A. and I.B.1. of Form S–3 (hereinafter, with respect to the company being acquired, "meets the requirements for use of Form S–3") of Form S–3 and this alternative is elected;

b. Item 16 of this Form, if the company being acquired meets the requirements for use of Form S–3 and this alternative is elected; or

c. Item 17 of this Form, if the company being acquired does not meet the requirements for use of Form S–3 or if this alternative is otherwise elected.

2. If the company being acquired is a real estate entity of the type described in General Instruction A to Form S–11, the information that would be required by Items 13, 14, 15 and 16(a) of Form S–11 if securities of such company were being registered shall be furnished about such company being acquired in addition to the information provided pursuant to this Form. The information prescribed by such Items of Form S–11 may be incorporated by reference into the prospectus if (a) the company being acquired would qualify for use of the level of dis-

closure prescribed by alternative 1.a. or 1.b. of this instruction and such alternative is elected and (b) the documents incorporated by reference pursuant to such elected alternative contain such information.

D. Application of General Rules and Regulations.

1. Attention is directed to the General Rules and Regulations under the Securities Act, particularly those comprising Regulation C thereunder (17 CFR 230.400 et seq.). That Regulation contains general requirements regarding the preparation and filing of registration statements.

2. Attention is directed to Regulation S–K (17 CFR Part 229) for the requirements applicable to the content of nonfinancial statement portions of registration statements under the Securities Act. Where this Form directs the registrant to furnish information required by Regulation S–K and the item of Regulation S–K so provides, information need only be furnished to the extent appropriate.

3. A "small business issuer," defined in Rule 405 under the Securities Act of 1933, shall refer to the disclosure items in Regulation S–B (17 CFR 228.10 *et seq.*) and not Regulation S–K except with respect to disclosure called for by subpart 900 of Regulation S–K. Small business issuers shall provide or incorporate by reference the information called for by Item 310 of Regulation S–B.

E. Compliance With Exchange Act Rules.

1. If a corporation or other person submits a proposal to its security holders entitled to vote on, or consent to, the transaction in which the securities being registered are to be issued, and such person's submission to its security holders is subject to Regulation 14A (17 CFR 240.14a–1 through 14b–b) or 14C (17 CFR 240.14c–1 through 14c–101) under the Exchange Act, then the provisions of such Regulations shall apply in all respects to such person's submission, except that (a) the prospectus may be in the form of a proxy or information statement and may contain the information required by this Form in lieu of that required by Schedule 14A (17 CFR 240.14a–101) or 14C (17 CFR 240.14c–101) of Regulation 14A or 14C under the Exchange Act; and (b) copies of the preliminary and definitive proxy or information statement, form of proxy or other material filed as a part of the registration statement shall be deemed filed pursuant to such person's obligations under such Regulations.

2. If the proxy or information material sent to security holders is not subject to Regulation 14A or 14C, all such material shall be filed as a part of the registration statement at the time the statement is filed or as an amendment thereto prior to the use of such material.

3. If the transaction in which the securities being registered are to be issued is subject to Section 13(e), 14(d) or 14(e) of the Exchange Act, the provisions of those sections and the rules and regulations thereunder shall apply to the transaction in addition to the provisions of this Form.

F. Transactions Involving Foreign Private Issuers.

If a U.S. registrant is acquiring a foreign private issuer, as defined by Rule 405 (17 CFR 230.405), such registrant may use this Form and may present information about the foreign private issuer pursuant to Form F–4. If the registrant is a foreign private issuer, such registrant may use Form F–4 and

1. if the company being acquired is a foreign private issuer, may present information about such foreign company pursuant to Form F–4 or

2. if the company being acquired is a U.S. company, may present information about such company pursuant to this Form.

G. Filing and Effectiveness of Registration Statement Involving Formation of Hold–Companies; Requests for Confidential Treatment; Number of Copies.

Original registration statements on this Form S–4 will become effective automatically on the twentieth day after the date of filing (Rule 456, § 230.456 of this chapter), pursuant to the provisions of Section 8(a) of the Act (Rule 459, § 230.459 of this chapter) provided:

1. The transaction in connection with which securities are being registered involves the organization of a bank or savings and loan holding company for the sole purpose of issuing common stock to acquire all of the common stock of the company that is organizing the holding company; and

2. The following conditions are met:

a. the financial institution furnishes its security holders with an annual report that includes financial statements prepared on the basis of generally accepted accounting principles;

b. there are no anticipated changes in the security holders' relative equity ownership interest in the underlying company's assets except for redemption of no more than a nominal number of shares of unaffiliated persons who dissent;

c. in the aggregate, only nominal borrowings are to be incurred for such purposes as organizing the holding company to pay non-affiliated persons who dissent, or to meet minimum capital requirements;

d. there are no new classes of stock authorized other than those corresponding to the stock of the company being acquired immediately prior to the reorganization;

e. there are no plans or arrangements to issue any additional shares to acquire any business other than the company being acquired; and

f. there has been no material adverse change in the financial condition of the company being acquired since the latest fiscal year end included in the annual report to security holders.

Pre-effective amendments with respect to such a registration statement may be filed prior to effectiveness, and such amendments will be deemed to have been filed with the consent of the Commission (Rule 475a, 17 CFR 230.475). Accordingly, the filing of a pre-effective amendment to such a registration statement will not commence a new twenty-day period. Post-effective amendments to such a registration statement on this Form shall become effective upon the date of filing (Rule 464, 17 CFR 230.464). Delaying amendments are not permitted in connection with either original filings or amendments on such a registration statement (Rule 473(d) 17 CFR 230.473(d)), and any attempt to interpose a delaying amendment of any kind will be ineffective. All filings made on or in connection with this Form pursuant to this instruction become public upon filing with the Commission. As a result, requests for confidential treatment made under Rule 406 (17 CFR 230.406) must be processed by the Commission's staff prior to the filing of such a registration statement. The number of copies of such a registration statement and of each amendment required by Rules 402 and 472 (17 CFR 230.402 and 230.472) shall be filed with the Commission; *provided, however,* that the number of additional copies referred to in Rule 402(b) may be reduced from ten to three and the number of additional copies referred to in Rule 472(a) may be reduced from eight to three, one of which shall be marked to clearly and precisely indicate changes.

H. Registration Statements Subject to Rule 415(a)(1)(viii) (17 CFR 230.415(a)(1)(viii)).

If the registration statement relates to offerings of securities pursuant to Rule 415(a)(1)(viii), required information about the type of contemplated transaction or the company to be acquired only need be furnished as of the date of initial effectiveness of the registration statement to the extent practicable. The required information about the specific transaction and the particular company being acquired, however, must be included in the prospectus by means of a post-effective amendment; *Provided, however,* that where the transaction in which the securities are being offered pursuant to a registration statement under the Securities Act of 1933 would itself qualify for an exemption from Section 5 of the Act, absent the existence of other similar (prior or subsequent) transactions, a prospectus supplement could be used to furnish the information necessary in connection with such transaction.

I. Roll–Up Transactions.

1. If securities to be registered on this Form will be issued in a roll-up transaction as defined in Item 901(c) of Regulation S–K (17 CFR 229.901(c)), then the disclosure provisions of subpart 229.900 of Regulation S–K (17 CFR 229.900) shall apply to the transaction in addition to the provisions of this Form. A smaller reporting company, defined in § 230.405, that is engaged in a roll-up transaction shall refer to the disclosure items in subpart 900 of Regulation S–K. To the extent that the disclosure requirements of subpart 229.900 are inconsistent with the disclosure requirements of any other applicable forms or schedules, the requirements of subpart 229.900 are controlling.

2. If securities to be registered on this Form will be issued in a roll-up transaction as defined in Item 901(c) of Regulation S–K (17 CFR 229.901(c)), the prospectus must be distributed to security holders no later than the lesser of 60 calendar days prior to the date on which action is to be taken or the maximum number of days permitted for giving notice under applicable state law.

3. Attention is directed to the proxy rules (17 CFR 240.14a–1–240.14a–104) and Rule 14e–7 of the tender offer rules (17 CFR 240.14e–7) if securities to be registered on this Form will be issued in a roll-up transaction. Such rules contain provisions specifically applicable to roll-up transactions, whether or not the entities involved have securities registered pursuant to Section 12 of the Exchange Act.

J. Where two or more classes of securities being registered on the form are to be offered on a delayed or continuous basis pursuant to Rule 415(a)(1)(viii), Rule 457(*o*) under the Securities Act permits the registration fee to be calculated on the basis of the maximum offering price of all the securities listed in the "Calculation of Registration Fee" Table ("Fee Table"). In this event, while the Fee Table would list each of the classes of securities being registered and the aggregate proceeds to be raised, the Fee Table need not specify by each class information as to the amount to be registered, proposed maximum offering price per unit, and proposed maximum aggregate offering price.

K. Registration of Additional Securities.

With respect to the registration of additional securities for an offering pursuant to Rule 462(b) under the Securities Act, the registrant may file a registration statement consisting only of the following: the facing page; a statement that the contents of the earlier registration statement, identified by file number, are incorporated by reference; required opinions and consents; the signature page; and any price-related information omitted from the earlier registration statement in reliance on Rule 430A that the registrant chooses to include in the new registration statement. The information contained in such a Rule 462(b) registration statement shall be deemed to be a part of the earlier registration statement as of the date of effectiveness of the Rule 462(b) registration statement. Any opinion or consent required in the Rule 462(b) registration statement may be incorporated by reference from the earlier registration statement with respect to the offering, if: (i) such opinion or consent expressly provides for such incorporation; and (ii) such opinion relates to the securities registered pursuant to Rule 462(b). See Rule 411(c) and Rule 439(b) under the Securities Act.

PART I—INFORMATION REQUIRED IN THE PROSPECTUS

A. INFORMATION ABOUT THE TRANSACTION

Item 1. Forepart of Registration Statement and Outside Front Cover Page of Prospectus.

Set forth in the forepart of the registration statement and on the outside front cover page of the prospectus the information required by Item 501 of Regulation S–K (17 CFR 229.501).

Item 2. Inside Front and Outside Back Cover Pages of Prospectus.

Provide the information required by Item 502 of Regulation S–K. In addition, on the inside front cover page, you must state

(1) that the prospectus incorporates important business and financial information about the company that is not included in or delivered with the document; and

(2) that this information is available without charge to security holders upon written or oral request. Give the name, address, and telephone number to which security holders must make this request. In addition, you must state that to obtain timely delivery, security holders must request the information no later than five business days before the date they must make their investment decision. Specify the date by which security holders must request this information. You must highlight this statement by print type or otherwise.

NOTE TO ITEM 2. If you send any of the information that is incorporated by reference in the prospectus to security holders, you also must send any exhibits that are specifically incorporated by reference in that information.

Item 3. Risk Factors and Other Information.

Provide in the forepart of the prospectus a summary containing the information required by Item 503 of Regulation S–K (17 CFR 229.503) and the following:

(a) The name, complete mailing address (including the Zip Code), and telephone number (including the area code) of the principal executive offices of the registrant and the company being acquired;

(b) A brief description of the general nature of the business conducted by the registrant and by the company being acquired;

(c) A brief description of the transaction in which the securities being registered are to be offered;

(d) The information required by Item 301 of Regulation S–K (17 CFR 229.301) (selected financial data) for (i) the registrant; (ii) the company being acquired; and (iii) if material, the registrant, on a pro forma basis, giving effect to the transaction. To the extent the information is required to be presented in the prospectus pursuant to Items 12, 14, 16 or 17, it need not be repeated pursuant to this Item;

(e) If material, the information required by Item 301 of Regulation S–K for the registrant on a pro forma basis, giving effect to the transaction. To the extent the information is required to be presented in the prospectus pursuant to Items 12 or 14, it need not be repeated pursuant to this Item.

(f) In comparative columnar form, historical and pro forma per share data of the registrant and historical and equivalent pro forma per share data of the company being acquired for the following items:

(1) book value per share as of the date financial data is presented pursuant to Item 301 of Regulation S–K (17 CFR 229.301) (selected financial data);

(2) cash dividends declared per share for the periods for which financial data is presented pursuant to Item 301 of Regulation S–K (17 CFR 229.301) (selected financial data);

(3) income (loss) per share from continuing operations for the periods for which financial data is presented pursuant to Item 301 of Regulation S–K (17 CFR 229.301) (selected financial data).

Instruction to Paragraphs (e) and (f): For a business combination, the financial information required by paragraphs (e) and (f) shall be presented only for the most recent fiscal year and interim period. For a combination between entities under common control, the financial information required by paragraphs (e) and (f) (except for information with regard to book value) shall be presented for the most recent three fiscal years and interim period. For a combination between entities under common control, information with regard to book value shall be presented as of the end of the most recent fiscal year and interim period. Equivalent pro forma per share amounts shall be calculated by multiplying the pro forma income (loss) per share before non-recurring charges or credits directly attributable to the transaction, pro forma book value per share, and the pro forma dividends per share of the registrant by the exchange ratio so that the per share amounts are equated to the respective values for one share of the company being acquired.

(g) In comparative columnar form, the market value of securities of the company being acquired (on an historical and equivalent per share basis) and the market value of the securities of the registrant (on an historical basis) as of the date preceding public announcement of the proposed transaction, or, if no such public announcement was made, as of the day preceding the day the agreement with respect to the transaction was entered into;

(h) With respect to the registrant and the company being acquired, a brief statement comparing the percentage of outstanding shares entitled to vote held by directors, executive officers and their affiliates and the vote required for approval of the proposed transaction;

(i) A statement as to whether any federal or state regulatory requirements must be complied with or approval must be obtained in connection with the transaction, and if so, the status of such compliance or approval;

(j) A statement about whether or not dissenters' rights of appraisal exist, including a cross-reference to the information provided pursuant to Item 18 or 19 of this Form; and

(k) A brief statement about the tax consequences of the transaction, or if appropriate, consisting of a cross-reference to the information provided pursuant to Item 4 of this Form.

Item 4. Terms of the Transaction.

(a) Furnish a summary of the material features of the proposed transaction. The summary shall include, where applicable:

(1) A brief summary of the terms of the acquisition agreement;

(2) The reasons of the registrant and of the company being acquired for engaging in the transaction;

(3) The information required by Item 202 of Regulation S–K (17 CFR 229.202), description of registrant's securities, unless: (i) the registrant would meet the requirements for use of Form S–3, (ii) capital stock is to be registered and (iii) securities of the same class are registered under Section 12 of the Exchange Act and (i) listed for trading or admitted to unlisted trading privileges on a national securities exchange; or (ii) are securities for which bid and offer quotations are reported in an automated quotations system operated by a national securities association;

(4) An explanation of any material differences between the rights of security holders of the company being acquired and the rights of holders of the securities being offered;

(5) A brief statement as to the accounting treatment of the transaction; and

(6) The federal income tax consequences of the transaction.

(b) If a report, opinion or appraisal materially relating to the transaction has been received from an outside party, and such report, opinion or appraisal is referred to in the prospectus, furnish the same information as would be required by Item 1015(b) of Regulation M–A (17 CFR 229.1015(b)).

(c) Incorporate the acquisition agreement by reference into the prospectus by means of a statement to that effect.

Item 5. Pro Forma Financial Information.

Furnish financial information required by Article 11 of Regulation S–X (17 CFR 210.11–01 *et seq.*) with respect to this transaction. A smaller reporting company may provide the information in Rule 8–05 of Regulation S–X (17 CFR 210.8–05) in lieu of the financial information required by Article 11 of Regulation S–X.

Instruction: 1. Any other Article 11 information that is presented (rather than incorporated by reference) pursuant to other Items of this Form shall be presented together with the information provided pursuant to Item 5, but the presentation shall clearly distinguish between this transaction and any other.

2. If pro forma financial information with respect to all other transactions is incorporated by reference pursuant to Item 11 or 15 of this Form only the pro forma results need be presented as part of the pro forma financial information required by this Item.

Item 6. Material Contracts with the Company Being Acquired.

Describe any past, present or proposed material contracts, arrangements, understandings, relationships, negotiations or transactions during the periods for which financial statements are presented or incorporated by reference pursuant to Part I.B. or C.

of this Form between the company being acquired or its affiliates and the registrant or its affiliates, such as those concerning: a merger, consolidation or acquisition; a tender offer or other acquisition of securities; an election of directors; or a sale or other transfer of a material amount of assets.

Item 7. Additional Information Required for Reoffering by Persons and Parties Deemed to Be Underwriters.

If any of the securities are to be reoffered to the public by any person or party who is deemed to be an underwriter thereof, furnish the following information in the prospectus, at the time it is being used for the reoffer of the securities to the extent it is not already furnished therein:

(a) The information required by Item 507 of Regulation S–K (17 CFR 229.507), selling security holders; and

(b) Information with respect to the consummation of the transaction pursuant to which the securities were acquired and any material change in the registrant's affairs subsequent to the transaction.

Item 8. Interests of Named Experts and Counsel.

Furnish the information required by Item 509 of Regulation S–K (17 CFR 229.509).

Item 9. Disclosure of Commission Position on Indemnification for Securities Act Liabilities.

Furnish the information required by Item 510 of Regulation S–K (17 CFR 229.510).

B. INFORMATION ABOUT THE REGISTRANT

Item 10. Information with Respect to S–3 Registrants.

If the registrant meets the requirements for use of Form S–3 and elects to furnish information in accordance with the provisions of this Item, furnish information as required below:

(a) Describe any and all material changes in the registrant's affairs that have occurred since the end of the latest fiscal year for which audited financial statements were included in the latest annual report to security holders and that have not been described in a report on Form 10–Q (17 CFR 249.308a) or Form 8–K (17 CFR 249.308) filed under the Exchange Act.

(b) Include in the prospectus, if not incorporated by reference from the reports filed under the Exchange Act specified in Item 11 of this Form, a proxy or information statement filed pursuant to Section 14 of the Exchange Act, a prospectus previously filed pursuant to Rule 424 under the Securities Act (17 CFR 230.424), or a Form 8–K filed during either of the two preceding fiscal years:

(1) Financial information required by Rule 3–05 (17 CFR 210.3–05) and Article 11 of Regulation S–X with respect to transactions other than that pursuant to which the securities being registered are to be issued;

(2) Restated financial statements prepared in accordance with Regulation S–X (17 CFR Part 210), if there has been a change in accounting principles or a correction of an error where such change or correction requires a material retroactive restatement of financial statements;

(3) Restated financial statements prepared in accordance with Regulation S–X where a combination under common control has been consummated subsequent to the most recent fiscal year and the acquired businesses, considered in the aggregate, are significant pursuant to Rule 11–01(b) of Regulation S–X (17 CFR 210.11–01(b)); or

(4) Any financial information required because of a material disposition of assets outside the normal course of business.

Item 11. Incorporation of Certain Information by Reference.

If the registrant meets the requirements of Form S–3 and elects to furnish information in accordance with the provisions of Item 10 of this Form:

(a) Incorporate by reference into the prospectus, by means of a statement to that effect listing all documents so incorporated, the documents listed in paragraphs (1), (2) and, if applicable, (3) below.

(1) The registrant's latest annual report on Form 10–K (17 CFR 249.310) filed pursuant to Section 13(a) or 15(d) of the Exchange Act which contains financial statements for the registrant's latest fiscal year for which a Form 10–K was required to be filed;

(2) All other reports filed pursuant to Section 13(a) or 15(d) of the Exchange Act since the end of the fiscal year covered by the annual report referred to in Item 11(a)(1) of this Form; and

(3) If capital stock is to be registered and securities of the same class are registered under Section 12 of the Exchange Act and: (i) listed for trading or admitted to unlisted trading privileges on a national securities exchange; or (ii) are securities for which bid and offer quotations are reported

in an automated quotations system operated by a national securities association, the description of such class of securities which is contained in a registration statement filed under the Exchange Act, including any amendment or reports filed for the purpose of updating such description.

(b) The prospectus also shall state that all documents subsequently filed by the registrant pursuant to Sections 13(a), 13(c), 14 or 15(d) of the Exchange Act, prior to one of the following dates, whichever is applicable, shall be deemed to be incorporated by reference into the prospectus:

(1) If a meeting of security holders is to be held, the date on which such meeting is held;

(2) If a meeting of security holders is not to be held, the date on which the transaction is consummated;

(3) If securities of the registrant are being offered in exchange for securities of any other issuer, the date the offering is terminated; or

(4) If securities are being offered in a reoffering or resale of securities acquired pursuant to this registration statement, the date the reoffering is terminated.

(c) You must

(1) identify the reports and other information that you file with the SEC; and

(2) state that the SEC maintains an Internet site that contains reports, proxy and information statements, and other information regarding issuers that file electronically with the SEC and state the address of that site (http://www.sec.gov). Disclose your Internet address, if available.

Instruction. Attention is directed to Rule 439 (§ 230.439 of this chapter) regarding consent to the use of material incorporated by reference.

Item 12. Information With Respect to S–3 Registrants.

If the registrant meets the requirements for use of Form S–3 and elects to comply with this Item, furnish the information required by either paragraph (a) or paragraph (b) of this Item. The information required by paragraph (b) shall be furnished if the registrant satisfies the conditions of paragraph (c) of this Item.

(a) If the registrant elects to deliver this prospectus together with a copy of either its latest Form 10–K filed pursuant to Section 13(a) or 15(d) of the Exchange Act or its latest annual report to security holders, which at the time of original preparation met the requirements of either Rule 14a–3 or Rule 14c–3:

(1) Indicate that the prospectus is accompanied by either a copy of the registrant's latest Form 10–K or a copy of its latest annual report to security holders, whichever the registrant elects to deliver pursuant to paragraph (a) of this Item.

(2) Provide financial and other information with respect to the registrant in the form required by Part I of Form 10–Q as of the end of the most recent fiscal quarter which ended after the end of the latest fiscal year for which certified financial statements were included in the latest Form 10–K or the latest report to security holders (whichever the registrant elects to deliver pursuant to paragraph (a) of this Item), and more than forty-five days before the effective date of this registration statement (or as of a more recent date) by one of the following means:

(i) including such information in the prospectus;

(ii) providing without charge to each person to whom a prospectus is delivered a copy of the registrant's latest Form 10–Q; or

(iii) providing without charge to each person to whom a prospectus is delivered a copy of the registrant's latest quarterly report that was delivered to security holders and included the required financial information.

(3) If not reflected in the registrant's latest Form 10–K or its latest annual report to security holders (whichever the registrant elects to deliver pursuant to paragraph (a) of this Item) provide information required by Rule 3–05 (17 CFR 210.3–05) and Article 11 (17 CFR 210.11–01–210.11–03) of Regulation S–X. Smaller reporting companies may provide the information required by Rules 8–04 and 8–05 of Regulation S–X.

(4) Describe any and all material changes in the registrant's affairs that have occurred since the end of the latest fiscal year for which audited financial statements were included in the latest Form 10–K or latest annual report to security holders (whichever the registrant elects to deliver pursuant to paragraph (a) of this Item) and that were not described in a Form 10–Q or quarterly report delivered with the prospectus in accordance with paragraph (a)(2)(ii) or (iii) of this Item.

Instruction. Where the registrant elects to deliver the documents identified in paragraph (a) with a preliminary prospectus, such documents need not be redelivered with the final prospectus.

(b) If the registrant does not elect to deliver its latest Form 10–K or its latest annual report to security holders:

(1) Furnish a brief description of the business done by the registrant and its subsidiaries during the most recent fiscal year as required by Rule 14a–3 to be included in an annual report to security holders. The description also should take into account changes in the registrant's business that have occurred between the end of the latest fiscal year and the effective date of the registration statement.

(2) Include financial statements and information as required by Rule 14a–3(b)(1) (17 CFR 240.14a–3(b)(1)) to be included in an annual report to security holders. In addition, provide:

(i) the interim financial information required by Rule 10–01 of Regulation S–X (17 CFR 210.10) for a filing on Form 10–Q;

(ii) financial information required by Rule 3–05 and Article 11 of Regulation S–X with respect to transactions other than that pursuant to which the securities being registered are to be issued;

(iii) restated financial statements prepared in accordance with Regulation S–X if there has been a change in accounting principles or a correction of an error where such change or correction requires a material retroactive restatement of financial statements;

(iv) restated financial statements prepared in accordance with Regulation S–X where a combination under common control has been consummated subsequent to the most recent fiscal year and the businesses transferred, considered in the aggregate, are significant pursuant to Rule 11–01(b) of Regulation S–X; and

(v) any financial information required because of a material disposition of assets outside of the normal course of business;

(3) Furnish the information required by the following:

(i) Item 101(b), (c)(1)(i) and (d) of Regulation S–K (17 CFR 229.101), industry segments, classes of similar products or services, foreign and domestic operations and export sales;

(ii) where common equity securities are being offered, Item 201 of Regulation S–K (17 CFR 229.201), market price of and dividends on the registrant's common equity and related stockholder matters;

(iii) Item 301 of Regulation S–K (17 CFR 229.301), selected financial data;

(iv) Item 302 of Regulation S–K (17 CFR 229.302), supplementary financial information;

(v) Item 303 of Regulation S–K (17 CFR 229.303), management's discussion and analysis of financial condition and results of operations;

(vi) Item 304 of Regulation S–K (17 CFR 229.304), changes in and disagreements with accountants on accounting and financial disclosure; and

(vii) Item 305 of Regulation S–K (17 CFR 229.305), quantitative and qualitative disclosures about market risk.

(c) The registrant shall furnish the information required by paragraph (b) of this Item if:

(1) The registrant was required to make a material retroactive restatement of financial statements because of

(i) a change in accounting principles; or

(ii) a correction of an error; or

(iii) A combination under common control was effected subsequent to the most recent fiscal year and the acquired businesses considered in the aggregate meet the test of a significant subsidiary; OR

(2) the registrant engaged in a material disposition of assets outside the normal course of business; AND

(3) such restatement of financial statements or disposition of assets was not reflected in the registrant's latest annual report to security holders and/or its latest Form 10–K filed pursuant to Sections 13(a) or 15(d) of the Exchange Act.

Item 13. Incorporation of Certain Information by Reference.

If the registrant meets the requirements of Form S–3 and elects to furnish information in accordance with the provisions of Item 12 of this Form:

(a) Incorporate by reference into the prospectus, by means of a statement to that effect in the prospectus listing all documents so incorporated, the documents listed in paragraphs (1) and (2) of this Item and, if applicable, the portions of the documents listed in paragraphs (3) and (4) thereof.

(1) The registrant's latest annual report on Form 10–K filed pursuant to Section 13(a) or 15(d) of the Exchange Act which contains audited financial statements for the registrant's latest fiscal year for which a Form 10–K was required to be filed.

(2) All other reports filed pursuant to Section 13(a) or 15(d) of the Exchange Act since the end of the fiscal year covered by the annual report referred to in paragraph (a)(1) of this Item.

(3) If the registrant elects to deliver its latest annual report to security holders pursuant to Item 12 of this Form, the information furnished in accordance with the following:

(i) Item 101(b), (c)(1)(i) and (d) of Regulation S–K, segments, classes of similar products or services, foreign and domestic operations and export sales;

(ii) Where common equity securities are being issued, Item 201 of Regulation S–K, market price of and dividends on the registrant's common equity and related stockholder matters;

(iii) Item 301 of Regulation S–K, selected financial data;

(iv) Item 302 of Regulation S–K, supplementary financial information;

(v) Item 303 of Regulation S–K, management's discussion and analysis of financial condition and results of operations;

(vi) Item 304 of Regulation S–K, changes in and disagreements with accountants on accounting and financial disclosure; and

(vii) Item 305 of Regulation S–K (17 CFR 229.305) quantitative and qualitative disclosures about market risk.

(4) If the registrant elects, pursuant to Item 12(a)(2)(iii) of this Form, to provide a copy of its latest quarterly report which was delivered to security holders, financial information equivalent to that required to be presented in Part I of Form 10–Q.

Instruction. Attention is directed to Rule 439 regarding consent to the use of material incorporated by reference.

(b) The registrant also may state, if it so chooses, that specifically described portions of its annual or quarterly report to security holders, other than those portions required to be incorporated by reference pursuant to paragraphs (a)(3) and (4) of this Item, are not part of the registration statement. In such case, the description of portions that are not incorporated by reference or that are excluded shall be made with clarity and in reasonable detail.

(c) *Electronic Filings.* Electronic filers electing to deliver and incorporate by reference all, or any portion, of the quarterly or annual report to security holders pursuant to this Item shall file as an exhibit such quarterly or annual report to security holders, or such portion thereof that is incorporated by reference, in electronic format.

(d) You must

(1) identify the reports and other information that you file with the SEC; and

(2) state that the SEC maintains an Internet site that contains reports, proxy and information statements, and other information regarding issuers that file electronically with the SEC and state the address of that site (http://www.sec.gov). Disclose your Internet address, if available.

Item 14. Information with Respect to Registrants Other Than S–3 Registrants.

If the registrant does not meet the requirements for use of Form S–3, or otherwise elects to comply with this Item in lieu of Item 10 or 12, furnish the information required by:

(a) Item 101 of Regulation S–K, description of business;

(b) Item 102 of Regulation S–K, description of property;

(c) Item 103 of Regulation S–K, legal proceedings;

(d) Where common equity securities are being issued, Item 201 of Regulation S–K, market price of and dividends on the registrant's common equity and related stockholder matters;

(e) Financial statements meeting the requirements of Regulation S–X, (schedules required by Regulation S–X shall be filed as "Financial Statement Schedules" pursuant to Item 21 of this Form), as well as financial information required by Rule 3–05 and Article 11 of Regulation S–X with respect to transactions other than that pursuant to which the securities being registered are to be issued;

(f) Item 301 of Regulation S–K, selected financial data;

(g) Item 302 of Regulation S–K, supplementary financial information;

(h) Item 303 of Regulation S–K, management's discussion and analysis of financial condition and results of operations;

(i) Item 304 of Regulation S–K, changes in and disagreements with accountants on accounting and financial disclosure; and

(j) Item 305 of Regulation S–K (17 CFR 229.305), quantitative and qualitative disclosures about market risk.

C. INFORMATION ABOUT THE COMPANY BEING ACQUIRED

Item 15. Information with Respect to S–3 Companies.

If the company being acquired meets the requirements for use of Form S–3 and compliance with this Item is elected, furnish the information that would be required by Items 10 and 11 of this Form if securities of such company were being registered.

Item 16. Information with Respect to S–3 Companies.

(a) If the company being acquired meets the requirements for use of Form S–3 and elects to comply with this Item, furnish the information that would be required by Items 12 and 13 of this Form if securities of such company were being registered.

(b) *Electronic Filings.* In addition to satisfying the requirements of paragraph (a) of this Item, electronic filers that elect to deliver and incorporate by reference all, or any portion, of the quarterly or annual report to security holders of a company being acquired pursuant to this Item shall file as an exhibit such quarterly or annual report to security holders, or such portion thereof that is incorporated by reference, in electronic format.

Item 17. Information with Respect to Companies Other Than S–3 Companies.

If the company being acquired does not meet the requirements for use of Form S–3, or compliance with this Item is otherwise elected in lieu of Item 15 or 16, furnish the information required by paragraph (a) or (b) of this Item, whichever is applicable.

(a) If the company being acquired is subject to the reporting requirements of Section 13(a) or 15(d) of the Exchange Act, or compliance with this subparagraph in lieu of subparagraph (b) of this Item is selected, furnish the information that would be required by Item 14 of this Form if the securities of such company were being registered; *however,* only those schedules required by Rules 12–15, 28 and 29 of Regulation S–X (17 CFR 210.12–15, 28, 29) need be provided with respect to the company being acquired.

(b) If the company being acquired is not subject to the reporting requirements of either Section 13(a) or 15(d) of the Exchange Act; or, because of Section 12(i) of the Exchange Act, has not furnished an annual report to security holders pursuant to Rule 14a–3 (17 CFR 240.14a–3) or Rule 14c–3 (17 CFR 240.14c–3) for its latest fiscal year; furnish the information that would be required by the following if securities of such company were being registered:

(1) a brief description of the business done by the company which indicates the general nature and scope of the business;

(2) Item 201 of Regulation S–K, market price of and dividends on the registrant's common equity and related stockholder matters;

(3) Item 301 of Regulation S–K, selected financial data;

(4) Item 302 of Regulation S–K, supplementary financial information;

(5) Item 303 of Regulation S–K, management's discussion and analysis of financial condition and results of operations;

(6) Item 304(b) of Regulation S–K (17 CFR 229.304), changes in and disagreements with accountants on accounting and financial disclosure;

(7) Financial statements that would be required in an annual report sent to security holders under Rules 14a–3(b)(1) and (b)(2) (17 CFR 240.14b–3), if an annual report was required. If the registrant's security holders are not voting, the transaction is not a roll-up transaction (as described by Item 901 of Regulation S–K (17 CFR 229.901)), and:

(i) the company being acquired is significant to the registrant in excess of the 20% level as determined under 17 CFR 210.3–05(b)(2), provide financial statements of the company being acquired for the latest fiscal year in conformity with GAAP. In addition, if the company being acquired has provided its security holders with financial statements prepared in conformity with GAAP for either or both of the two fiscal years before the latest fiscal year, provide the financial statements for those years; or

(ii) the company being acquired is significant to the registrant at or below the 20% level, no financial information (including pro forma and comparative per share information) for the company being acquired need be provided.

Instructions:

1. The financial statements required by this paragraph for the latest fiscal year need be audited only to the extent practicable. The financial statements for the fiscal years before the latest fiscal year need not be audited if they were not previously audited.

2. If the financial statements required by this paragraph are prepared on the basis of a comprehensive body of accounting principles other than U.S. GAAP or International Financial Reporting Standards as issued by the International Accounting Standards Board, provide a reconciliation to U.S. GAAP in accordance with Item 17 of Form 20–F (17 CFR 249.220f) unless a reconciliation is unavailable or not obtainable without unreasonable cost or expense. At a minimum, provide a narrative description of all material

variations in accounting principles, practices and methods used in preparing the non-U.S. GAAP financial statements from those accepted in the U.S. when the financial statements are prepared on a basis other than U.S. GAAP.

3. If this Form is used to register resales to the public by any person who is deemed an underwriter within the meaning of Rule 145(c) (17 CFR 230.145(c)) with respect to the securities being reoffered, the financial statements must be audited for the fiscal years required to be presented under paragraph (b)(2) of Rule 3–05 of Regulation S–X (17 CFR 210.3–05(b)(2)).

4. In determining the significance of an acquisition for purposes of this paragraph, apply the tests prescribed in Rule 1–02(w) (17 CFR 210.1–02(w)).

(8) the quarterly financial and other information as would have been required had the company being acquired been required to file Part I of Form 10–Q (17 CFR 249.308a) for the most recent quarter for which such a report would have been on file at the time the registration statement becomes effective or for a period ending as of a more recent date.

(9) schedules required by Rules 12–15, 28 and 29 of Regulation S–X.

(10) Item 305 of Regulation S–K (17 CFR 229.305), quantitative and qualitative disclosures about market risk.

D. VOTING AND MANAGEMENT INFORMATION

Item 18. Information if Proxies, Consents or Authorizations are to be Solicited.

(a) If proxies, consents or authorizations are to be solicited, furnish the following information, except as provided by paragraph (b) of this Item:

(1) The information required by Item 1 of Schedule 14A, date, time and place information;

(2) The information required by Item 2 of Schedule 14A, revocability of proxy;

(3) The information required by Item 3 of Schedule 14A, dissenters' rights of appraisal;

(4) The information required by Item 4 of Schedule 14A, persons making the solicitation;

(5) With respect to both the registrant and the company being acquired, the information required by:

(i) Item 5 of Schedule 14A, interest of certain persons in matters to be acted upon; and

(ii) Item 6 of Schedule 14A, voting securities and principal holders thereof;

(6) The information required by Item 21 of Schedule 14A, vote required for approval; and

(7) With respect to each person who will serve as a director or an executive officer of the surviving or acquiring company, the information required by:

(i) Item 401 of Regulation S–K (17 CFR 229.401), directors and executive officers;

(ii) Item 402 of Regulation S–K (17 CFR 229.402), executive compensation, and paragraph (e)(4) of Item 407 of Regulation S–K (17 CFR 229.407(e)(4)), corporate governance;

(iii) Item 404 of Regulation S–K (17 CFR 229.404), transactions with related persons, promoters and certain control persons, and Item 407(a) of Regulation S–K (17 CFR 229.407(a)), corporate governance.

(b) If the registrant or the company being acquired meets the requirements for use of Form S–3, any information required by paragraphs (a)(5)(ii) and (7) of this Item with respect to such company may be incorporated by reference from its latest annual report on Form 10–K.

Item 19. Information if Proxies, Consents or Authorizations are not to be Solicited or in an Exchange Offer.

(a) If the transaction is an exchange offer or if proxies, consents or authorizations are not to be solicited, furnish, where applicable, the following information, except as provided by paragraph (c) of this item:

(1) The information required by Item 2 of Schedule 14C, statement that proxies are not to be solicited;

(2) The date, time and place of the meeting of security holders, unless such information is otherwise disclosed in material furnished to security holders with the prospectus;

(3) The information required by Item 3 of Schedule 14A, dissenters' rights of appraisal;

(4) With respect to both the registrant and the company being acquired, a brief description of any material interest, direct or indirect, by security holdings or otherwise, of affiliates of the registrant and of the company being acquired, in the proposed transaction;

Instruction. This subparagraph shall not apply to any interest arising from the ownership of securities of the registrant where the security holder receives no extra or special benefit not shared on a pro rata basis by all other holders of the same class.

(5) With respect to both the registrant and the company being acquired, the information required by Item 6 of Schedule 14A, voting securities and principal holders thereof;

(6) The information required by Item 21 of Schedule 14A, vote required for approval;

(7) With respect to each person who will serve as a director or an executive officer of the surviving or acquiring company the information required by:

(i) Item 401 of Regulation S–K, directors and executive officers;

(ii) Item 402 of Regulation S–K (17 CFR 229.402), executive compensation, and paragraph (e)(4) of Item 407 of Regulation S–K (17 CFR 229.407(e)(4)), corporate governance;

(iii) Item 404 of Regulation S–K (17 CFR 229.404), transactions with related persons, promoters and certain controls persons, and Item 407(a) of Regulation S–K (17 CFR 229.407(a)), corporate governance.

(b) If the transaction is an exchange offer, furnish the information required by paragraphs (a)(4), (a)(5), and (a)(7) of this Item, except as provided by paragraph (c) of this Item.

(c) If the registrant or the company being acquired meets the requirements for use of Form S–3, any information required by paragraphs (a)(5) and (7) of this Item with respect to such company may be incorporated by reference from its latest annual report on Form 10–K.

PART II—INFORMATION NOT REQUIRED IN PROSPECTUS

Item 20. Indemnification of Directors and Officers.

Furnish the information required by Item 702 of Regulation S–K (17 CFR 229.702).

Item 21. Exhibits and Financial Statement Schedules.

(a) Subject to the rules regarding incorporation by reference, furnish the exhibits as required by Item 601 of Regulation S–K (17 CFR 229.601).

(b) Furnish the financial statement schedules required by Regulation S–X and Item 14(e), Item 17(a) or Item 17(b)(9) of this Form. These schedules should be lettered or numbered in the manner described for exhibits in paragraph (a) of this Item.

(c) If information is provided pursuant to Item 4(b) of this Form, furnish the report, opinion or appraisal as an exhibit hereto, unless it is furnished as part of the prospectus.

Item 22. Undertakings.

(a) Furnish the undertakings required by Item 512 of Regulation S–K (17 CFR 229.512).

(b) Furnish the following undertaking:

The undersigned registrant hereby undertakes to respond to requests for information that is incorporated by reference into the prospectus pursuant to Items 4, 10(b), 11, or 13 of this Form, within one business day of receipt of such request, and to send the incorporated documents by first class mail or other equally prompt means. This includes information contained in documents filed subsequent to the effective date of the registration statement through the date of responding to the request.

(c) Furnish the following undertaking:

The undersigned registrant hereby undertakes to supply by means of a post-effective amendment all information concerning a transaction, and the company being acquired involved therein, that was not the subject of and included in the registration statement when it became effective.

SIGNATURES

Pursuant to the requirements of the Securities Act, the registrant has duly caused this registration statement to be signed on its behalf by the undersigned, thereunto duly authorized, in the City of ____________, State of ____________, on ____________, 20__

(Registrant)

By (Signature and Title) ____________

Pursuant to the requirements of the Securities Act of 1933, this registration statement has been signed by the following persons in the capacities and on the dates indicated.

(Signature) ____________

(Title) ____________

(Date) ____________

Instructions: 1. The registration statement shall be signed by the registrant, its principal executive officer or officers, its principal financial officer, its controller or principal accounting officer, and by at least a majority of the board of directors or persons performing similar functions. If the registrant is a foreign person, the registration statement shall also be signed by its authorized representative in the United States. Where the registrant is a limited partnership, the registration statement shall be signed by a majority of the board of directors of any corporate general partner signing the registration statement.

2. The name of each person who signs the registration statement shall be typed or printed beneath his signature. Any person who occupies more than one of the specified positions shall indicate each capacity in which he signs the registration statement. Attention is directed to Rule 402 (17 CFR 230.402) concerning manual signatures and Item 601 concerning signatures pursuant to powers of attorney.

OMB APPROVAL
OMB Number: 3235-0101
Expires: December 31, 2009
Estimated average burden hours per response 2.00

SEC USE ONLY
DOCUMENT SEQUENCE NO.
CUSIP NUMBER
WORK LOCATION

UNITED STATES
SECURITIES AND EXCHANGE COMMISSION
Washington, D.C. 20549

FORM 144

NOTICE OF PROPOSED SALE OF SECURITIES PURSUANT TO RULE 144 UNDER THE SECURITIES ACT OF 1933

ATTENTION: *Transmit for filing 3 copies of this form concurrently with either placing an order with a broker to execute sale or executing a sale directly with a market maker.*

1 (a) NAME OF ISSUER *(Please type or print)*			(b) IRS IDENT. NO.	(c) S.E.C. FILE NO.
1 (d) ADDRESS OF ISSUER STREET	CITY	STATE	ZIP CODE	(e) TELEPHONE NO. AREA CODE NUMBER
2 (a) NAME OF PERSON FOR WHOSE ACCOUNT THE SECURITIES ARE TO BE SOLD	(b) RELATIONSHIP TO ISSUER	(c) ADDRESS STREET CITY	STATE	ZIP CODE

INSTRUCTION: The person filing this notice should contact the issuer to obtain the I.R.S. Identification Number and the S.E.C. File Number.

3 (a) Title of the Class of Securities To Be Sold	(b) Name and Address of Each Broker Through Whom the Securities are to be Offered or Each Market Maker who is Acquiring the Securities	SEC USE ONLY Broker-Dealer File Number	(c) Number of Shares or Other Units To Be Sold *(See instr. 3(c))*	(d) Aggregate Market Value *(See instr. 3(d))*	(e) Number of Shares or Other Units Outstanding *(See instr. 3(e))*	(f) Approximate Date of Sale *(See instr. 3(f))* (MO. DAY YR.)	(g) Name of Each Securities Exchange *(See instr. 3(g))*

INSTRUCTIONS:

1. (a) Name of issuer
   (b) Issuer's I.R.S. Identification Number
   (c) Issuer's S.E.C. file number, if any
   (d) Issuer's address, including zip code
   (e) Issuer's telephone number, including area code

2. (a) Name of person for whose account the securities are to be sold
   (b) Such person's relationship to the issuer (e.g., officer, director, 10% stockholder, or member of immediate family of any of the foregoing)
   (c) Such person's address, including zip code

3. (a) Title of the class of securities to be sold
   (b) Name and address of each broker through whom the securities are intended to be sold
   (c) Number of shares or other units to be sold (if debt securities, give the aggregate face amount)
   (d) Aggregate market value of the securities to be sold as of a specified date within 10 days prior to the filing of this notice
   (e) Number of shares or other units of the class outstanding, or if debt securities the face amount thereof outstanding, as shown by the most recent report or statement published by the issuer
   (f) Approximate date on which the securities are to be sold
   (g) Name of each securities exchange, if any, on which the securities are intended to be sold

Potential persons who are to respond to the collection of information contained in this form are not required to respond unless the form displays a currently valid OMB control number.

SEC 1147 (08-07)

TABLE I — SECURITIES TO BE SOLD

Furnish the following information with respect to the acquisition of the securities to be sold and with respect to the payment of all or any part of the purchase price or other consideration therefor:

Title of the Class	Date you Acquired	Nature of Acquisition Transaction	Name of Person from Whom Acquired (If gift, also give date donor acquired)	Amount of Securities Acquired	Date of Payment	Nature of Payment

INSTRUCTIONS: If the securities were purchased and full payment therefor was not made in cash at the time of purchase, explain in the table or in a note thereto the nature of the consideration given. If the consideration consisted of any note or other obligation, or if payment was made in installments describe the arrangement and state when the note or other obligation was discharged in full or the last installment paid.

TABLE II — SECURITIES SOLD DURING THE PAST 3 MONTHS

Furnish the following information as to all securities of the issuer sold during the past 3 months by the person for whose account the securities are to be sold.

Name and Address of Seller	Title of Securities Sold	Date of Sale	Amount of Securities Sold	Gross Proceeds

REMARKS:

INSTRUCTIONS:
See the definition of "person" in paragraph (a) of Rule 144. Information is to be given not only as to the person for whose account the securities are to be sold but also as to all other persons included in that definition. In addition, information shall be given as to sales by all persons whose sales are required by paragraph (c) of Rule 144 to be aggregated with sales for the account of the person filing this notice.

ATTENTION:
The person for whose account the securities to which this notice relates are to be sold hereby represents by signing this notice that he does not know any material adverse information in regard to the current and prospective operations of the Issuer of the securities to be sold which has not been publicly disclosed. If such person has adopted a written trading plan or given trading instructions to satisfy Rule 10b5-1 under the Exchange Act, by signing the form and indicating the date that the plan was adopted or the instruction given, that person makes such representation as of the plan adoption or instruction date.

DATE OF NOTICE

DATE OF PLAN ADOPTION OR GIVING OF INSTRUCTION, IF RELYING ON RULE 10B5-1

(SIGNATURE)

The notice shall be signed by the person for whose account the securities are to be sold. At least one copy of the notice shall be manually signed. Any copies not manually signed shall bear typed or printed signatures.

ATTENTION: Intentional misstatements or omission of facts constitute Federal Criminal Violations (See 18 U.S.C. 1001)

SEC 1147 (04-07)

This form is a sample of the online form. Form D is available only for online filing. For more information, visit http://www.sec.gov/info/smallbus/secg/formdguide.htm.

[Effective Sept. 15, 2008]
UNITED STATES
SECURITIES AND EXCHANGE COMMISSION
Washington, DC 20549

OMB APPROVAL
OMB Number: 3235–0076
Expires: April 30, 2008
Estimated average burden
hours per response: .. 4.00

FORM D
NOTICE OF EXEMPT OFFERING OF SECURITIES
Intentional misstatements or omissions of fact constitute federal criminal violations. See 18 U.S.C. 1001.
You must follow the accompanying instructions in submitting this notice.

1. Issuer's Identity
Name of Issuer ____________
Previous Name(s) ____________ ❑ None
Jurisdiction of Incorporation/Organization (dropdown or other list selection feature)
Entity Type
❑ Corporation
❑ Limited Partnership
❑ Limited Liability Company
❑ General Partnership
❑ Business Trust
❑ Other (Specify)
Year of Incorporation/Organization
❑ Yet to Be Formed
❑ Within Last Five Years (Specify Year)
❑ Over Five Years Ago

2. Principal Place of Business and Contact Information
Street Address ____________
City ______ **State/Province** (dropdown or other list selection feature)
Zip/Postal Code ______
Country
❑ U.S.
❑ Canada
❑ Other (dropdown or other list selection feature for countries if answer is "Other" than U.S. or Canada)
Telephone Number __________

3. Related Persons

Full Name	Relationship	Address
	❑ Executive Officer	
	❑ Director	
	❑ Promoter	

Clarification of Response (if Necessary): ____________

4. **Industry Group** (dropdown or other list selection feature)
- ❑ Agriculture
- ❑ Banking & Financial Services—Commercial Banking
- ❑ Banking & Financial Services—Insurance
- ❑ Banking & Financial Services—Investing
- ❑ Banking & Financial Services—Investment Banking
- ❑ Banking & Financial Services—Pooled Investment Fund (If the Pooled Investment Fund checkbox is selected, pop-ups or other features also will require the filer to select one of the lower level checkboxes designating a specific type of investment fund and select a "yes" or "no" checkbox as to whether the filer is registered as an investment company under the Investment Company Act of 1940. If the "Hedge Fund" or "Other Investment Fund" option is selected, the filer will be asked to specify its aggregate net asset value range or to "Decline to Disclose" that value or specify that the information request is "Not Applicable.")
  - ❑ Pooled Investment Fund—Hedge Fund
  - ❑ Pooled Investment Fund—Private Equity Fund
  - ❑ Pooled Investment Fund—Venture Capital Fund
  - ❑ Pooled Investment Fund—Other Investment Fund
- ❑ Other Banking & Financial Services
- ❑ Business Services
- ❑ Energy—Coal Mining
- ❑ Energy—Electric Utilities
- ❑ Energy—Energy Conservation
- ❑ Energy—Environmental Services
- ❑ Energy—Oil & Gas
- ❑ Energy—Other Energy
- ❑ Health Care—Biotechnology
- ❑ Health Care—Health Insurance
- ❑ Health Care—Hospitals & Physicians
- ❑ Health Care—Pharmaceuticals
- ❑ Health Care—Other Health Care
- ❑ Manufacturing
- ❑ Real Estate—Commercial
- ❑ Real Estate—Construction
- ❑ Real Estate—REITS & Finance
- ❑ Real Estate—Residential
- ❑ Real Estate—Other Real Estate
- ❑ Retailing
- ❑ Restaurants
- ❑ Technology—Computers
- ❑ Technology—Telecommunications
- ❑ Technology—Other Technology
- ❑ Travel—Airlines & Airports
- ❑ Travel—Lodging & Conventions
- ❑ Travel—Tourism & Travel Services
- ❑ Travel—Other Travel
- ❑ Other

5. **Issuer Size**

Revenue Range (for issuers that do not specify "Hedge Fund" or "Other Investment Fund" in response to Item 4)
- ❑ No Revenues
- ❑ $1—$1,000,000
- ❑ $1,000,001—$5,000,000
- ❑ $5,000,001—$25,000,000
- ❑ $25,000,001—$100,000,000

❑ Over $100,000,000
❑ Decline to Disclose
❑ Not Applicable

Aggregate Net Asset Value Range (for issuers that specify "Hedge Fund" or "Other Investment Fund" in response to Item 4)

❑ No Aggregate Net Asset Value
❑ $1—$5,000,000
❑ $5,000,001—$25,000,000
❑ $25,000,001—$100,000,000
❑ Over $100,000,000
❑ Decline to Disclose
❑ Not Applicable

6. Federal Exemption(s) and Exclusion(s) Claimed (select all that apply)

❑ Rule 504(b)(1) (not (i), (ii) or (iii))
❑ Rule 506(b)
❑ Rule 506(c)
❑ Rule 504(b)(1)(i)
❑ Securities Act Section 4(a)(5)
❑ Rule 504(b)(1)(ii)
❑ Investment Company Act Section 3(c) **(If the filer selects the Investment Company Act Section 3(c) check-box, a pop-up or other feature will require the filer to select all claimed exclusions from the definition of "investment company" from among Sections 3(c)(1) through Section 3(c)(14) (except for Section 3(c)(8)).)**
❑ Rule 504(b)(1)(iii)

7. Type of Filing

❑ New Notice (dropdown or other feature to select "Date of First Sale" or "First Sale Yet to Occur")
❑ Amendment

8. Duration of Offering

Does the issuer intend this offering to last more than one year?

❑ Yes ❑ No

9. Type(s) of Securities Offered (select all that apply)

❑ Equity
❑ Debt
❑ Option, Warrant or Other Right to Acquire Another Security
❑ Security to be Acquired Upon Exercise of Option, Warrant or Other Right to Acquire Security
❑ Pooled Investment Fund Interests
❑ Tenant-in-Common Securities
❑ Mineral Property Securities
❑ Other (Describe: ______________)

10. Business Combination Transaction

Is this offering being made in connection with a business combination transaction, such as a merger, acquisition or exchange offer?

❑ Yes ❑ No

Clarification of Response (if Necessary): ______________

11. Minimum Investment

Minimum investment accepted from any outside investor $______

12. Sales Compensation

Recipient	Recipient CRD Number	Associated Broker or Dealer	Broker or Dealer CRD Number	Street Address	State(s) of Solicitation
					(dropdown or other list selection feature)

13. Offering and Sales Amounts

Total Offering Amount $________ or ❑ Indefinite
Total Amount Sold $________
Total Remaining to be Sold $________ *[auto subtract]* or ❑ Indefinite
Clarification of Response (if Necessary): ________

14. Investors

❑ Select if securities in the offering have been or may be sold to persons who do not qualify as *accredited investors,* and enter the number of such non-accredited investors who already have invested in the offering: ________

Regardless whether securities in the offering have been or may be sold to persons who do not qualify as accredited investors, enter the total number of investors who already have invested in the offering: ________

15. Sales Commissions and Finders' Fees Expenses

Provide separately the amounts of sales commissions and finders' fees expenses, if any. If the amount of an expenditure is not known, provide an estimate and check the box next to the amount(s).

Sales Commissions $________ ❑ Estimate
Finders' Fees $________ ❑ Estimate
Clarification of Response (if Necessary):

16. Use of Proceeds

Provide the amount of the gross proceeds of the offering that has been or is proposed to be used for payments to any of the persons required to be named as executive officers, directors or promoters in response to Item 3 above. If the amount is unknown, provide an estimate and check the box next to the amount.

$________ ❑ Estimate
Clarification of Response (if Necessary): ________

Signature and Submission

Terms of Submission: Please verify the information you have entered and review the Terms of Submission below before signing and clicking SUBMIT below to file this notice. In submitting this notice, each issuer named above is:

- Notifying the SEC and/or each State in which this notice is filed of the offering of securities described and undertaking to furnish them, upon written request in accordance with applicable law, the information furnished to offerees.

(This undertaking does not affect any limits Section 102(a) of the National Securities Markets Improvement Act of 1996 ("NSMIA") [Pub. L. No. 104–290, 110 Stat. 3416 (Oct. 11, 1996)] imposes on the ability of States to require information. As a result, if the securities that are the subject of this Form D are "covered securities" for purposes of NSMIA, whether in all instances or due to the nature of the offering that is the subject of this Form D, States cannot routinely require offering materials under this undertaking or otherwise and can require offering materials only to the extent NSMIA permits them to do so under NSMIA's preservation of their anti-fraud authority.)

- Irrevocably appointing each of the Secretary of the SEC and the Securities Administrator or other legally designated officer of the State in which the issuer maintains its principal place of business and any State in which this notice is filed, as its agents for service of process, and agreeing that these persons may accept service on its behalf, of any notice, process or pleading, and further agreeing that such service may be made by registered or certified mail, in any Federal or state action, administrative proceeding, or arbitration brought against the issuer in any place subject to the jurisdiction of the United States, if the action, proceeding or arbitration (a) arises out of any activity in connection with the offering of securities that is the subject of this notice, and (b) is founded, directly or indirectly, upon the provisions of: (i) the Securities Act of 1933, the Securities Exchange Act of 1934, the Trust Indenture Act of 1939, the Investment Company Act of 1940, or the Investment Advisers Act of 1940, or any rule or regulation under any of these statutes; or (ii) the laws of the State in which the issuer maintains its principal place of business or any State in which this notice is filed.

• Certifying that, if the issuer is claiming a Regulation D exemption for the offering, the issuer is not disqualified from relying on Rule 504 or 506 for one of the reasons stated in Rule 504(b)(3) or Rule 506(d).

Each issuer identified above has read this notice, knows the contents to be true, and has duly caused this notice to be signed on its behalf by the undersigned duly authorized person.

Signature ________ Title: ____________________ Date: ________

By clicking on SUBMIT below, you are agreeing to the Terms of Submission above.

<u>Persons who respond to the collection of information contained in this form are not required to respond unless the form displays a currently valid OMB control number.</u>

<u>Instructions for Submitting Notice</u>

General Instructions

Who Must File:

• Each issuer of securities that sells its securities in reliance on an exemption provided in Regulation D or Section 4(a)(5) of the Securities Act of 1933 must file this notice containing the information requested with the U.S. Securities and Exchange Commission (SEC) and with the state(s) requiring it. If more than one issuer has sold its securities in the same transaction, all issuers should be identified in one filing with the SEC, but some states may require a separate filing for each issuer or security sold.

When to File:

• An issuer must file a new notice with the SEC for each new offering of securities no later than 15 calendar days after the "date of first sale" of securities in the offering as explained in Instruction 7. For this purpose, the date of first sale is the date on which the first investor is irrevocably contractually committed to invest, which, depending on the terms and conditions of the contract, could be the date on which the issuer receives the investor's subscription agreement or check. An issuer may file the notice at any time before that if it has determined to make the offering. An issuer must file a new notice with each state that requires it at the time set by the state. For state filing information, go to <u>www.NASAA.org</u>. A mandatory capital commitment call does not constitute a new offering, but is made under the original offering, so no new Form D filing is required.

• An issuer may file an amendment to a previously filed notice at any time.

• An issuer must file an amendment to a previously filed notice for an offering:

  - to correct a material mistake of fact or error in the previously filed notice, as soon as practicable after discovery of the mistake or error;
  - to reflect a change in the information provided in the previously filed notice, except as provided below, as soon as practicable after the change; and
  - annually, on or before the first anniversary of the most recent previously filed notice, if the offering is continuing at that time.

• **When Amendment is Not Required:** An issuer is not required to file an amendment to a previously filed notice to reflect a change that occurs after the offering terminates or a change that occurs solely in the following information:

  - the address or relationship to the issuer of a related person identified in response to Item 3;
  - an issuer's revenues or aggregate net asset value;
  - the minimum investment amount, if the change is an increase, or if the change, together with all other changes in that amount since the previously filed notice, does not result in a decrease of more than 10%;
  - any address or state(s) of solicitation shown in response to Item 12;

- the total offering amount, if the change is a decrease, or if the change, together with all other changes in that amount since the previously filed notice, does not result in an increase of more than 10%;
- the amount of securities sold in the offering or the amount remaining to be sold;
- the number of non-accredited investors who have invested in the offering, as long as the change does not increase the number to more than 35;
- the total number of investors who have invested in the offering;
- the amount of sales commissions, finders' fees or use of proceeds for payments to executive officers, directors or promoters, if the change is a decrease, or if the change, together with all other changes in that amount since the previously filed notice, does not result in an increase of more than 10%.

- **Saturdays, Sundays and Holidays:** If the date on which a notice or an amendment to a previously filed notice is required to be filed falls on a Saturday, Sunday or holiday, the due date is the first business day following.
- **Amendment Content:** An issuer that files an amendment to a previously filed notice must provide current information in response to all items of this Form D, regardless of why the amendment is filed.
- **How to File:** Issuers must file this notice with the SEC in electronic format. For state filing information, go to www.NASAA.org.
- **Filing Fee:** There is no federal filing fee. For information on state filing fees, go to www.NASAA.org.
- **Definitions of Terms:** Terms used but not defined in this form that are defined in Rule 405 and Rule 501 under the Securities Act of 1933, 17 CFR 230.405 and 230.501, have the meanings given to them in those rules.

Item-by-Item Instructions

1. Issuer's Identity. Identify each legal entity issuing any securities being reported as being offered by entering its full name; any previous name used within the past five years; and its jurisdiction of incorporation or organization, type of legal entity, and year of incorporation or organization within the past five years or status as formed over five years ago or not yet formed. If more than one entity is issuing the securities, identify a primary issuer in the first fields shown and identify additional issuers in the fields that appear.

2. Principal Place of Business and Contact Information. Enter a full street address of the issuer's principal place of business. Post office box numbers and "In care of" addresses are not acceptable. Enter a contact telephone number for the issuer. If you identified more than one issuer in response to Item 1, enter the requested information for the primary issuer you identified in response to that item and, at your option, for any or all of the other issuers you identified in the fields that appear.

3. Related Persons. Enter the full name and address of each person having the specified relationships with any issuer and identify each relationship:

- Each executive officer and director of the issuer and person performing similar functions (title alone is not determinative) for the issuer, such as the general and managing partners of partnerships and managing members of limited liability companies; and
- Each person who has functioned directly or indirectly as a promoter of the issuer within the past five years of the later of the first sale of securities or the date upon which the Form D filing was required to be made.

If necessary to prevent the information supplied from being misleading, also provide a clarification in the space provided.

4. Industry Group. Select the issuer's industry group. If the issuer or issuers can be categorized in more than one industry group, select the industry group that most accurately reflects the use of the bulk of the proceeds of the offering. For purposes of this filing, use the ordinary dictionary and commonly understood meanings of the terms identifying the industry group.

5. Issuer Size.

- Revenue Range (for issuers that do not specify "Hedge Fund" or "Other Investment Fund" in response to Item 4): Enter the revenue range of the issuer or of all the issuers together for the most recently completed fiscal year available, or, if not in existence for a fiscal year, revenue range to date. Domestic SEC reporting companies should state revenues in accordance with Regulation

S–X under the Securities Exchange Act of 1934. Domestic non-reporting companies should state revenues in accordance with U.S. Generally Accepted Accounting Principles (GAAP). Foreign issuers should calculate revenues in U.S. dollars and state them in accordance with U.S. GAAP, home country GAAP or International Financial Reporting Standards. If the issuer(s) declines to disclose its revenue range, enter "Decline to Disclose." If the issuer's(s') business is intended to produce revenue but did not, enter "No Revenues." If the business is not intended to produce revenue (for example, the business seeks asset appreciation only), enter "Not Applicable."

- Aggregate Net Asset Value (for issuers that specify "Hedge Fund" or "Other Investment Fund" in response to Item 4): Enter the aggregate net asset value range of the issuer or of all the issuers together as of the most recent practicable date. If the issuer(s) declines to disclose its aggregate net asset value range, enter "Decline to Disclose."

6. Federal Exemption(s) and Exclusion(s) Claimed. Select the provision(s) being claimed to exempt the offering and resulting sales from the federal registration requirements under the Securities Act of 1933 and, if applicable, to exclude the issuer from the definition of "investment company" under the Investment Company Act of 1940. Select "Rule 504(b)(1) (not (i), (ii) or (iii))" only if the issuer is relying on the exemption in the introductory sentence of Rule 504 for offers and sales that satisfy all the terms and conditions of Rules 501 and 502(a), (c) and (d).

7. Type of Filing. Indicate whether the issuer is filing a new notice or an amendment to a notice that was filed previously. If this is a new notice, enter the date of the first sale of securities in the offering or indicate that the first sale has "Yet to Occur." For this purpose, the date of first sale is the date on which the first investor is irrevocably contractually committed to invest, which, depending on the terms and conditions of the contract, could be the date on which the issuer receives the investor's subscription agreement or check.

8. Duration of Offering. Indicate whether the issuer intends the offering to last for more than one year.

9. Type(s) of Securities Offered. Select the appropriate type or types of securities offered as to which this notice is filed. If the securities are debt convertible into other securities, however, select "Debt" and any other appropriate types of securities except for "Equity." For purposes of this filing, use the ordinary dictionary and commonly understood meanings of these categories. For instance, equity securities would be securities that represent proportional ownership in an issuer, such as ordinary common and preferred stock of corporations and partnership and limited liability company interests; debt securities would be securities representing money loaned to an issuer that must be repaid to the investor at a later date; pooled investment fund interests would be securities that represent ownership interests in a pooled or collective investment vehicle; tenant-in-common securities would be securities that include an undivided fractional interest in real property other than a mineral property; and mineral property securities would be securities that include an undivided interest in an oil, gas or other mineral property.

10. Business Combination Transaction. Indicate whether or not the offering is being made in connection with a business combination, such as an exchange (tender) offer or a merger, acquisition, or other transaction of the type described in paragraph (a)(1), (2) or (3) of Rule 145 under the Securities Act of 1933. Do not include an exchange (tender) offer for a class of the issuer's own securities. If necessary to prevent the information supplied from being misleading, also provide a clarification in the space provided.

11. Minimum Investment. Enter the minimum dollar amount of investment that will be accepted from any outside investor. If the offering provides a minimum investment amount for outside investors that can be waived, provide the lowest amount below which a waiver will not be granted. If there is no minimum investment amount, enter "0." Investors will be considered outside investors if they are not employees, officers, directors, general partners, trustees (where the issuer is a business trust), consultants, advisors or vendors of the issuer, its parents, its majority owned subsidiaries, or majority owned subsidiaries of the issuer's parent.

12. Sales Compensation. Enter the requested information for each person that has been or will be paid directly or indirectly any commission or other similar compensation in cash or other consideration in connection with sales of securities in the offering, including finders. Enter the CRD number for every person identified and any broker and dealer listed that has a CRD number. CRD numbers can be found at http://brokercheck.finra.org. A person that does not have a CRD number need not obtain one in order to be listed, and must be listed when required regardless of whether the person has a CRD number. In addition, enter the State(s) in which the named person has solicited or intends to solicit investors. If more than five persons to be listed are associated persons of the same broker or dealer, enter only the name of the broker or dealer, its CRD number and street address, and the State(s) in which the named person has solicited or intends to solicit investors.

13. Offering and Sales Amounts. Enter the dollar amount of securities being offered under a claim of federal exemption identified in Item 6 above. Also enter the dollar amount of securities sold in the offering as of the filing date. Select the "Indefinite" box if the amount being offered is undetermined or cannot be calculated at the present time, such as if the offering includes securities to be acquired upon the exercise or exchange of other securities or property and the exercise price or exchange value is not currently known or knowable. If an amount is definite but difficult to calculate without unreasonable effort or expense, provide a good faith estimate. The total offering and sold amounts should include all cash and other consideration to be received for the securities, including cash to be paid in the future under mandatory capital commitments. In offerings for consideration other than cash, the amounts entered should be based on the issuer's good faith valuation of the consideration. If necessary to prevent the information supplied from being misleading, also provide a clarification in the space provided.

14. Investors. Indicate whether securities in the offering have been or may be sold to persons who do not qualify as accredited investors as defined in Rule 501(a) and provide the number of such investors who already have already invested in the offering. In addition, regardless whether securities in the offering have been or may be sold to persons who do not qualify as accredited investors, specify the total number of investors who already have invested.

15. Sales Commission and Finders' Fees Expenses. The information on sales commissions and finders' fees expenses may be given as subject to future contingencies.

16. Use of Proceeds. No additional instructions.

Signature and Submission. An individual who is a duly authorized representative of each issuer identified must sign, date and submit this notice for the issuer. The capacity in which the individual signed should be set forth in the "Title" space.

Each individual must:

- sign with a typed signature; and
- manually sign a signature page or other document authenticating, acknowledging or otherwise adopting the signature that appears in typed fiorm in the Form D filing on or before the time of filting the Form D.

Each issuer must:

- provide a copy of the manually signed document.

B. SECURITIES EXCHANGE ACT OF 1934

15 U.S.C. § 78a et seq.

Act	15 U.S.C.	
1	78a	Short Title
2	78b	Necessity for Regulation
3	78c	Definitions and Application
3A	78c–1	Swap Agreements
3B	78c–2	Securities-Related Derivatives
3C	78c–3	Clearing for Security-Based Swaps
3D	78c–4	Security-Based Swap Execution Facilities
3E	78c–5	Segregation of Assets Held as Collateral in Security-Based Swap Transactions
4	78d	Securities and Exchange Commission
4A	78d–1	Delegation of Functions by Commission
4B	78d–2	Transfer of Functions with Respect to Assignment of Personnel to Chairman
4C	78d–3	Appearance and Practice Before the Commission
4D	78d–4	Additional Duties of Inspector General
4E	78d–5	Deadline for Completing Enforcement Investigations and Compliance Examinations and Inspections
5	78e	Transactions on Unregistered Exchanges
6	78f	National Securities Exchanges
7	78g	Margin Requirements
8	78h	Restrictions on Borrowing and Lending by Members, Brokers, and Dealers
9	78i	Prohibition Against Manipulation of Security Prices
10	78j	Regulation of the Use of Manipulative and Deceptive Devices
10A	78j–1	Audit Requirements
10B	78j–2	Position Limits and Position Accountability for Security-Based Swaps and Large Trader Reporting
10C	78j–3	Compensation Committees
10D	78j–4	Recovery of Erroneously Awarded Compensation Policy
11	78k	Trading by Members of Exchanges, Brokers, and Dealers
11A	78k–1	National Market System for Securities; Securities Information Processors
12	78*l*	Registration Requirements for Securities
13	78m	Periodical and Other Reports
13A	78m–1	Reporting and Recordkeeping for Certain Security-Based Swaps
14	78n	Proxies
14A	78n–1	Shareholder Approval of Executive Compensation
14B	78–2	Corporate Governance
15	78*o*	Registration and Regulation of Brokers and Dealers
15A	78*o*–3	Registered Securities Associations
15B	78*o*–4	Municipal Securities
15C	78*o*–5	Government Securities Brokers and Dealers
15D	78*o*–6	Securities Analysts and Research Reports
15E	78*o*–7	Registration of Nationally Recognized Statistical Rating Organizations
15F	78*o*–8	Registration and Regulation of Security-Based Swap Dealers and Major Security-Based Swap Participants
15G	78*o*–11	Credit Risk Retention
16	78p	Directors, Officers, and Principal Stockholders
17	78q	Accounts and Records, Examinations of Exchanges, Members, and Others
17A	78q–1	National System for Clearance and Settlement of Securities Transactions
17B	78q–2	Automated Quotation Systems for Penny Stocks
18	78r	Liability for Misleading Statements
19	78s	Registration, Responsibilities, and Oversight of Self–Regulatory Organizations
20	78t	Liability of Controlling Persons and Persons Who Aid and Abet Violations
20A	78t–1	Liability to Contemporaneous Traders for Insider Trading
21	78u	Investigations; Injunctions and Prosecution of Offenses

Act	15 U.S.C.	
21A	78u–1	Civil Penalties for Insider Trading
21B	78u–2	Civil Remedies in Administrative Proceedings
21C	78u–3	Cease–and–Desist Proceedings
21D	78u–4	Private Securities Litigation
21E	78u–5	Application of Safe Harbor for Forward-Looking Statements
21F	78u–6	Securities Whistleblower Incentives and Protection
22	78v	Hearings by Commission
23	78w	Rules, Regulations, and Orders; Annual Reports
24	78x	Public Availability of Information
25	78y	Court Review of Orders and Rules
26	78z	Unlawful Representations
27	78aa	Jurisdiction of Offenses and Suits
27A	78aa–1	Special Provision Relating to Statute of Limitations on Private Causes of Action
28	78bb	Effect on Existing Law
29	78cc	Validity of Contracts
30	78dd	Foreign Securities Exchanges
30A	78dd–1	Prohibited Foreign Trade Practices by Issuers
31	78ee	Transaction Fees
32	78ff	Penalties
33	78gg	Separability of Provisions
34	78hh	Effective Date
35	78kk	Authorization of Appropriations
35A	78*ll*	Requirements for the EDGAR System
36	78mm	General Exemptive Authority
37	78nn	Tennessee Valley Authority
38	78oo	Federal National Mortgage Association, Federal Home Loan Mortgage Corporation, Federal Home Loan Banks
39	78pp	Investor Advisory Committee

SECURITIES EXCHANGE ACT OF 1934

Short Title

Sec. 1. This Act may be cited as the "Securities Exchange Act of 1934."

Necessity for Regulation

Sec. 2. For the reasons hereinafter enumerated, transactions in securities as commonly conducted upon securities exchanges and over-the-counter markets are effected with a national public interest which makes it necessary to provide for regulation and control of such transactions and of practices and matters related thereto, including transactions by officers, directors, and principal security holders, to require appropriate reports, to remove impediments to and perfect the mechanisms of a national market system for securities and a national system for the clearance and settlement of securities transactions and the safeguarding of securities and funds related thereto, and to impose requirements necessary to make such regulation and control reasonably complete and effective, in order to protect interstate commerce, the national credit, the Federal taxing power, to protect and make more effective the national banking system and Federal Reserve System, and to insure the maintenance of fair and honest markets in such transactions:

(1) Such transactions (a) are carried on in large volume by the public generally and in large part originate outside the States in which the exchanges and over-the-counter markets are located and/or are effected by means of the mails and instrumentalities of interstate commerce; (b) constitute an important part of the current of interstate commerce; (c) involve in large part the securities of issuers engaged in interstate commerce; (d) involve the use of credit, directly affect the financing of trade, industry, and transportation in interstate commerce, and directly affect and influence the volume of interstate commerce; and affect the national credit.

(2) The prices established and offered in such transactions are generally disseminated and quoted throughout the United States and foreign countries and constitute a basis for determining and establishing the prices at which securities are bought and sold, the amount of certain taxes owing to the United States and to the several States by owners, buyers, and sellers of securities, and the value of collateral for bank loans.

(3) Frequently the prices of securities on such exchanges and markets are susceptible to manipulation and control, and the dissemination of such prices gives rise to excessive speculation, resulting in sudden and unreasonable fluctuations in the prices of securities which (a) cause alternately unreasonable expansion and unreasonable contraction of the volume of credit available for trade, transportation, and industry in interstate commerce, (b) hinder the proper appraisal of the value of securities and thus prevent a fair calculation of taxes owing to the United States and to the several States by owners, buyers, and sellers of securities, and (c) prevent the fair valuation of collateral for bank loans and/or obstruct the effective operation of the national banking system and Federal Reserve System.

(4) National emergencies, which produce widespread unemployment and the dislocation of trade, transportation, and industry, and which burden interstate commerce and adversely affect the general welfare, are precipitated, intensified, and prolonged by manipulation and sudden and unreasonable fluctuations of security prices and by excessive speculation on such exchanges and markets, and to meet such emergencies the Federal Government is put to such great expense as to burden the national credit.

Definitions and Application

Sec. 3. (a) *Definitions.* When used in this title, unless the context otherwise requires—

(1) The term "exchange" means any organization, association, or group of persons, whether incorporated or unincorporated, which constitutes, maintains, or provides a market place or facilities for bringing together purchasers and sellers of securities or for otherwise performing with respect to securities the functions commonly performed by a stock exchange as that term is generally understood, and includes the market place and the market facilities maintained by such exchange.

(2) The term "facility" when used with respect to an exchange includes its premises, tangible or intangible property whether on the premises or not, any right to the use of such premises or property or any service thereof for the purpose of effecting or reporting a transaction on an exchange (including, among other things, any system of communication to or from the exchange, by ticker or oth-

erwise, maintained by or with the consent of the exchange), and any right of the exchange to the use of any property or service.

(3)(A) The term "member" when used with respect to a national securities exchange means (i) any natural person permitted to effect transactions on the floor of the exchange without the services of another person acting as broker, (ii) any registered broker or dealer with which such a natural person is associated, (iii) any registered broker or dealer permitted to designate as a representative such a natural person, and (iv) any other registered broker or dealer which agrees to be regulated by such exchange and with respect to which the exchange undertakes to enforce compliance with the provisions of this chapter, the rules and regulations thereunder, and its own rules. For purposes of sections 6(b)(1), 6(b)(4), 6(b)(6), 6(b)(7), 6(d), 17(d), 19(d), 19(e), 19(g), 19(h), and 21 of this title, the term "member" when used with respect to a national securities exchange also means, to the extent of the rules of the exchange specified by the Commission, any person required by the Commission to comply with such rules pursuant to section 6(f) of this title.

(B) The term "member" when used with respect to a registered securities association means any broker or dealer who agrees to be regulated by such association and with respect to whom the association undertakes to enforce compliance with the provisions of this title, the rules and regulations thereunder, and its own rules.

(4) *Broker*.

(A) *In General*. The term "broker" means any person engaged in the business of effecting transactions in securities for the account of others.

(B) *Exception for Certain Bank Activities*. A bank shall not be considered to be a broker because the bank engages in any one or more of the following activities under the conditions described:

(i) *Third Party Brokerage Arrangements*. The bank enters into a contractual or other written arrangement with a broker or dealer registered under this title under which the broker or dealer offers brokerage services on or off the premises of the bank if—

(I) such broker or dealer is clearly identified as the person performing the brokerage services;

(II) the broker or dealer performs brokerage services in an area that is clearly marked and, to the extent practicable, physically separate from the routine deposit-taking activities of the bank;

(III) any materials used by the bank to advertise or promote generally the availability of brokerage services under the arrangement clearly indicate that the brokerage services are being provided by the broker or dealer and not by the bank;

(IV) any materials used by the bank to advertise or promote generally the availability of brokerage services under the arrangement are in compliance with the Federal securities laws before distribution;

(V) bank employees (other than associated persons of a broker or dealer who are qualified pursuant to the rules of a self-regulatory organization) perform only clerical or ministerial functions in connection with brokerage transactions including scheduling appointments with the associated persons of a broker or dealer, except that bank employees may forward customer funds or securities and may describe in general terms the types of investment vehicles available from the bank and the broker or dealer under the arrangement;

(VI) bank employees do not receive incentive compensation for any brokerage transaction unless such employees are associated persons of a broker or dealer and are qualified pursuant to the rules of a self-regulatory organization, except that the bank employees may receive compensation for the referral of any customer if the compensation is a nominal one-time cash fee of a fixed dollar amount and the payment of the fee is not contingent on whether the referral results in a transaction;

(VII) such services are provided by the broker or dealer on a basis in which all customers that receive any services are fully disclosed to the broker or dealer;

(VIII) the bank does not carry a securities account of the customer except as permitted under clause (ii) or (viii) of this subparagraph; and

(IX) the bank, broker, or dealer informs each customer that the brokerage services are provided by the broker or dealer and not by the bank and that the securities are not deposits or other obligations of the bank, are not guaranteed by the bank, and are not insured by the Federal Deposit Insurance Corporation.

(ii) *Trust Activities.* The bank effects transactions in a trustee capacity, or effects transactions in a fiduciary capacity in its trust department or other department that is regularly examined by bank examiners for compliance with fiduciary principles and standards, and—

(I) is chiefly compensated for such transactions, consistent with fiduciary principles and standards, on the basis of an administration or annual fee (payable on a monthly, quarterly, or other basis), a percentage of assets under management, or a flat or capped per order processing fee equal to not more than the cost incurred by the bank in connection with executing securities transactions for trustee and fiduciary customers, or any combination of such fees; and

(II) does not publicly solicit brokerage business, other than by advertising that it effects transactions in securities in conjunction with advertising its other trust activities.

(iii) *Permissible Securities Transactions.* The bank effects transactions in—

(I) commercial paper, bankers acceptances, or commercial bills;

(II) exempted securities;

(III) qualified Canadian government obligations as defined in section 24 of title 12, in conformity with section 15C of this title and the rules and regulations thereunder, or obligations of the North American Development Bank; or

(IV) any standardized, credit enhanced debt security issued by a foreign government pursuant to the March 1989 plan of then Secretary of the Treasury Brady, used by such foreign government to retire outstanding commercial bank loans.

(iv) *Certain Stock Purchase Plans.*

(I) *Employee Benefit Plans.* The bank effects transactions, as part of its transfer agency activities, in the securities of an issuer as part of any pension, retirement, profit-sharing, bonus, thrift, savings, incentive, or other similar benefit plan for the employees of that issuer or its affiliates (as defined in section 2 of the Bank Holding Company Act of 1956), if the bank does not solicit transactions or provide investment advice with respect to the purchase or sale of securities in connection with the plan.

(II) *Dividend Reinvestment Plans.* The bank effects transactions, as part of its transfer agency activities, in the securities of an issuer as part of that issuer's dividend reinvestment plan, if—

(aa) the bank does not solicit transactions or provide investment advice with respect to the purchase or sale of securities in connection with the plan; and

(bb) the bank does not net shareholders' buy and sell orders, other than for programs for odd-lot holders or plans registered with the Commission.

(III) *Issuer Plans.* The bank effects transactions, as part of its transfer agency activities, in the securities of an issuer as part of a plan or program for the purchase or sale of that issuer's shares, if—

(aa) the bank does not solicit transactions or provide investment advice with respect to the purchase or sale of securities in connection with the plan or program; and

(bb) the bank does not net shareholders' buy and sell orders, other than for programs for odd-lot holders or plans registered with the Commission.

(IV) *Permissible Delivery of Materials.* The exception to being considered a broker for a bank engaged in activities described in subclauses (I), (II), and (III) will not be affected by delivery of written or electronic plan materials by a bank to employees of the issuer, shareholders of the issuer, or members of affinity groups of the issuer, so long as such materials are—

(aa) comparable in scope or nature to that permitted by the Commission as of the date of the enactment of the Gramm–Leach–Bliley Act; or

(bb) otherwise permitted by the Commission.

(v) *Sweep Accounts*. The bank effects transactions as part of a program for the investment or reinvestment of deposit funds into any no-load, open-end management investment company registered under the Investment Company Act of 1940 that holds itself out as a money market fund.

(vi) *Affiliate Transactions*. The bank effects transactions for the account of any affiliate of the bank (as defined in section 2 of the Bank Holding Company Act of 1956) other than—

(I) a registered broker or dealer; or

(II) an affiliate that is engaged in merchant banking, as described in section 4(k)(4)(H) of the Bank Holding Company Act of 1956.

(vii) *Private Securities Offerings*. The bank—

(I) effects sales as part of a primary offering of securities not involving a public offering, pursuant to section 3(b), 4(2), or 4(5) of the Securities Act of 1933 or the rules and regulations issued thereunder;

(II) at any time after the date that is 1 year after the date of the enactment of the Gramm–Leach–Bliley Act, is not affiliated with a broker or dealer that has been registered for more than 1 year in accordance with this Act, and engages in dealing, market making, or underwriting activities, other than with respect to exempted securities; and

(III) if the bank is not affiliated with a broker or dealer, does not effect any primary offering described in subclause (I) the aggregate amount of which exceeds 25 percent of the capital of the bank, except that the limitation of this subclause shall not apply with respect to any sale of government securities or municipal securities.

(viii) *Safekeeping and Custody Activities*.

(I) *In General*. The bank, as part of customary banking activities—

(aa) provides safekeeping or custody services with respect to securities, including the exercise of warrants and other rights on behalf of customers;

(bb) facilitates the transfer of funds or securities, as a custodian or a clearing agency, in connection with the clearance and settlement of its customers' transactions in securities;

(cc) effects securities lending or borrowing transactions with or on behalf of customers as part of services provided to customers pursuant to division (aa) or (bb) or invests cash collateral pledged in connection with such transactions;

(dd) holds securities pledged by a customer to another person or securities subject to purchase or resale agreements involving a customer, or facilitates the pledging or transfer of such securities by book entry or as otherwise provided under applicable law, if the bank maintains records separately identifying the securities and the customer; or

(ee) serves as a custodian or provider of other related administrative services to any individual retirement account, pension, retirement, profit sharing, bonus, thrift savings, incentive, or other similar benefit plan.

(II) *Exception for Carrying Broker Activities*. The exception to being considered a broker for a bank engaged in activities described in subclause (I) shall not apply if the bank, in connection with such activities, acts in the United States as a carrying broker (as such term, and different formulations thereof, are used in section 15(c)(3) of this title and the rules and regulations thereunder) for any broker or dealer, unless such carrying broker activities are engaged in with respect to government securities (as defined in paragraph (42) of this subsection).

(ix) *Identified Banking Products*. The bank effects transactions in identified banking products as defined in section 206 of the Gramm–Leach–Bliley Act.

(x) *Municipal Securities*. The bank effects transactions in municipal securities.

(xi) *De Minimis Exception.* The bank effects, other than in transactions referred to in clauses (i) through (x), not more than 500 transactions in securities in any calendar year, and such transactions are not effected by an employee of the bank who is also an employee of a broker or dealer.

(C) *Execution by Broker or Dealer.* The exception to being considered a broker for a bank engaged in activities described in clauses (ii), (iv), and (viii) of subparagraph (B) shall not apply if the activities described in such provisions result in the trade in the United States of any security that is a publicly traded security in the United States, unless—

(i) the bank directs such trade to a registered broker or dealer for execution;

(ii) the trade is a cross trade or other substantially similar trade of a security that—

(I) is made by the bank or between the bank and an affiliated fiduciary; and

(II) is not in contravention of fiduciary principles established under applicable Federal or State law; or

(iii) the trade is conducted in some other manner permitted under rules, regulations, or orders as the Commission may prescribe or issue.

(D) *Fiduciary Capacity.* For purposes of subparagraph (B)(ii), the term "fiduciary capacity" means—

(i) in the capacity as trustee, executor, administrator, registrar of stocks and bonds, transfer agent, guardian, assignee, receiver, or custodian under a uniform gift to minor act, or as an investment adviser if the bank receives a fee for its investment advice;

(ii) in any capacity in which the bank possesses investment discretion on behalf of another; or

(iii) in any other similar capacity.

(E) *Exception for Entities Subject to Section 15(e).* The term "broker" does not include a bank that—

(i) was, on the day before the date of enactment of the Gramm–Leach–Bliley Act, subject to section 15(e); and

(ii) is subject to such restrictions and requirements as the Commission considers appropriate.

(F) *Joint Rulemaking Required.* The Commission and the Board of Governors of the Federal Reserve System shall jointly adopt a single set of rules or regulations to implement the exceptions in subparagraph (B).

(5) *Dealer.*

(A) *In General.* The term "dealer" means any person engaged in the business of buying and selling securities (not including security-based swaps, other than security-based swaps with or for persons that are not eligible contract participants) for such person's own account through a broker or otherwise.

(B) *Exception for Person Not Engaged in the Business of Dealing.* The term "dealer" does not include a person that buys or sells securities (not including security-based swaps, other than security-based swaps with or for persons that are not eligible contract participants) for such person's own account, either individually or in a fiduciary capacity, but not as a part of a regular business.

(C) *Exception for Certain Bank Activities.* A bank shall not be considered to be a dealer because the bank engages in any of the following activities under the conditions described:

(i) *Permissible Securities Transactions.* The bank buys or sells—

(I) commercial paper, bankers acceptances, or commercial bills;

(II) exempted securities;

(III) qualified Canadian government obligations as defined in section 5136 of the Revised Statutes of the United States, in conformity with section 15(c) of this title and the rules and regulations thereunder, or obligations of the North American Development Bank; or

(IV) any standardized, credit enhanced debt security issued by a foreign government pursuant to the March 1989 plan of then Secretary of the Treasury Brady, used by such foreign government to retire outstanding commercial bank loans.

(ii) *Investment, Trustee, and Fiduciary Transactions*. The bank buys or sells securities for investment purposes—

(I) for the bank; or

(II) for accounts for which the bank acts as a trustee or fiduciary.

(iii) *Asset–Backed Transactions*. The bank engages in the issuance or sale to qualified investors, through a grantor trust or other separate entity, of securities backed by or representing an interest in notes, drafts, acceptances, loans, leases, receivables, other obligations (other than securities of which the bank is not the issuer), or pools of any such obligations predominantly originated by—

(I) the bank;

(II) an affiliate of any such bank other than a broker or dealer; or

(III) a syndicate of banks of which the bank is a member, if the obligations or pool of obligations consists of mortgage obligations or consumer-related receivables.

(iv) *Identified Banking Products*. The bank buys or sells identified banking products, as defined in section 206 of the Gramm–Leach–Bliley Act.

(6) The term "bank" means (A) a banking institution organized under the laws of the United States or a Federal savings association, as defined in section 2(5) of the Home Owners' Loan Act, (B) a member bank of the Federal Reserve System, (C) any other banking institution or savings association, as defined in section 2(4) of the Home Owners' Loan Act, whether incorporated or not, doing business under the laws of any State or of the United States, a substantial portion of the business of which consists of receiving deposits or exercising fiduciary powers similar to those permitted to national banks under the authority of the Comptroller of the Currency pursuant to the first section of Public Law 87–722, and which is supervised and examined by State or Federal authority having supervision over banks or savings associations, and which is not operated for the purpose of evading the provisions of this title, and (D) a receiver, conservator, or other liquidating agent of any institution or firm included in clauses (A), (B), or (C) of this paragraph.

(7) The term "director" means any director of a corporation or any person performing similar functions with respect to any organization, whether incorporated or unincorporated.

(8) The term "issuer" means any person who issues or proposes to issue any security; except that with respect to certificates of deposit for securities, voting-trust certificates, or collateral-trust certificates, or with respect to certificates of interest or shares in an unincorporated investment trust not having a board of directors or of the fixed, restricted management, or unit type, the term "issuer" means the person or persons performing the acts and assuming the duties of depositor or manager pursuant to the provisions of the trust or other agreement or instrument under which such securities are issued; and except that with respect to equipment-trust certificates or like securities, the term "issuer" means the person by whom the equipment or property is, or is to be, used.

(9) The term "person" means a natural person, company, government, or political subdivision, agency, or instrumentality of a government.

(10) The term "security" means any note, stock, treasury stock, security future, security-based swap,* bond, debenture, certificate of interest or participation in any profit-sharing agreement or in any oil, gas, or other mineral royalty or lease, any collateral-trust certificate, preorganization certificate or subscription, transferable share, investment contract, voting-trust certificate, certificate of deposit for a security, any put, call, straddle, option, or privilege on any security, certificate of deposit, or group or index of securities (including any interest therein or based on the value thereof), or any put, call, straddle, option, or privilege entered into on a national securities exchange relating to foreign currency, or in general, any instrument commonly known as a "security"; or any certificate of interest or participation in, temporary or interim certificate for, receipt for, or warrant or right to subscribe to or purchase, any of the foregoing; but shall not include currency or

* On February 5, 2014, The SEC issued an Order Extending Temporary Exemptions under the Securities Exchange Act of 1934 in Connection with the Revision of the Definition of "Security" to Encompass Security-Based Swaps. This order grants temporary exemptions, subject to exceptions (including anti-fraud and manipulation provisions), to the inclusion of security-based swaps in the definition of a security. The purpose of this Order is to maintain the status quo. The Order's impact is broad and includes, for example, issues related to brokers, dealers, and exchanges. The SEC release number is 34–71485. The order from that release is reproduced in the back of the statutory supplement.

any note, draft, bill of exchange, or banker's acceptance which has a maturity at the time of issuance of not exceeding nine months, exclusive of days of grace, or any renewal thereof the maturity of which is likewise limited.

(11) The term "equity security" means any stock or similar security; or any security future on any such security; or any security convertible, with or without consideration, into such a security, or carrying any warrant or right to subscribe to or purchase such a security; or any such warrant or right; or any other security which the Commission shall deem to be of similar nature and consider necessary or appropriate, by such rules and regulations as it may prescribe in the public interest or for the protection of investors, to treat as an equity security.

(12)(A) The term "exempted security" or "exempted securities" includes—

(i) government securities, as defined in paragraph (42) of this subsection;

(ii) municipal securities, as defined in paragraph (29) of this subsection;

(iii) any interest or participation in any common trust fund or similar fund that is excluded from the definition of the term "investment company" under section 3(c)(3) of the Investment Company Act of 1940;

(iv) any interest or participation in a single trust fund, or a collective trust fund maintained by a bank, or any security arising out of a contract issued by an insurance company, which interest, participation, or security is issued in connection with a qualified plan as defined in subparagraph (C) of this paragraph;

(v) any security issued by or any interest or participation in any pooled income fund, collective trust fund, collective investment fund, or similar fund that is excluded from the definition of an investment company under section 3(c)(10)(B) of the Investment Company Act of 1940;

(vi) solely for purposes of sections 12, 13, 14, and 16 of this title, any security issued by or any interest or participation in any church plan, company, or account that is excluded from the definition of an investment company under section 3(c)(14) of the Investment Company Act of 1940; and

(vii) such other securities (which may include, among others, unregistered securities, the market in which is predominantly intrastate) as the Commission may, by such rules and regulations as it deems consistent with the public interest and the protection of investors, either unconditionally or upon specified terms and conditions or for stated periods, exempt from the operation of any one or more provisions of this title which by their terms do not apply to an "exempted security" or to "exempted securities".

(B)(i) Notwithstanding subparagraph (A)(i) of this paragraph, government securities shall not be deemed to be "exempted securities" for the purposes of section 17A of this title.

(ii) Notwithstanding subparagraph (A)(ii) of this paragraph, municipal securities shall not be deemed to be "exempted securities" for the purposes of sections 15, and 17A of this title.

(C) For purposes of subparagraph (A)(iv) of this paragraph, the term "qualified plan" means (i) a stock bonus, pension, or profit-sharing plan which meets the requirements for qualification under section 401 of the Internal Revenue Code of 1954, (ii) an annuity plan which meets the requirements for the deduction of the employer's contribution under section 404(a)(2) of such Code, (iii) a governmental plan as defined in section 414(d) of such Code which has been established by an employer for the exclusive benefit of its employees or their beneficiaries for the purpose of distributing to such employees or their beneficiaries the corpus and income of the funds accumulated under such plan, if under such plan it is impossible, prior to the satisfaction of all liabilities with respect to such employees and their beneficiaries, for any part of the corpus or income to be used for, or diverted to, purposes other than the exclusive benefit of such employees or their beneficiaries, or (iv) a church plan, company, or account that is excluded from the definition of an investment company under section 3(c)(14) of the Investment Company Act of 1940, other than any plan described in clause (i), (ii), or (iii) of this subparagraph which (I) covers employees some or all of whom are employees within the meaning of section 401(c) of such Code, or (II) is a plan funded by an annuity contract described in section 403(b) of such Code.

(13) The terms "buy" and "purchase" each include any contract to buy, purchase, or otherwise acquire. For security futures products, such term includes any contract, agreement, or transaction for future delivery. For security-based swaps, such terms include the execution, termination (prior to its scheduled maturity date), assignment, exchange, or similar transfer or conveyance of, or extinguishing of rights or obligations under, a security-based swap, as the context may require.

(14) The terms "sale" and "sell" each include any contract to sell or otherwise dispose of. For security futures products, such term includes any contract, agreement, or transaction for future delivery. For security-based swaps, such terms include the execution, termination (prior to its scheduled maturity date), assignment, exchange, or similar transfer or conveyance of, or extinguishing of rights or obligations under, a security-based swap, as the context may require.

(15) The term "Commission" means the Securities and Exchange Commission established by section 4 of this title.

(16) The term "State" means any State of the United States, the District of Columbia, Puerto Rico, the Virgin Islands, or any other possession of the United States.

(17) The term "interstate commerce" means trade, commerce, transportation, or communication among the several States, or between any foreign country and any State, or between any State and any place or ship outside thereof. The term also includes intrastate use of (A) any facility of a national securities exchange or of a telephone or other interstate means of communication, or (B) any other interstate instrumentality.

(18) The term "person associated with a broker or dealer" or "associated person of a broker or dealer" means any partner, officer, director, or branch manager of such broker or dealer (or any person occupying a similar status or performing similar functions), any person directly or indirectly controlling, controlled by, or under common control with such broker or dealer, or any employee of such broker or dealer, except that any person associated with a broker or dealer whose functions are solely clerical or ministerial shall not be included in the meaning of such term for purposes of section 15(b) of this title (other than paragraph (6) thereof).

(19) The terms "investment company", "affiliated person", "insurance company", "separate account", and "company" have the same meanings as in the Investment Company Act of 1940.

(20) The terms "investment adviser" and "underwriter" have the same meanings as in the Investment Advisers Act of 1940.

(21) The term "person associated with a member" or "associated person of a member" when used with respect to a member of a national securities exchange or registered securities association means any partner, officer, director, or branch manager of such member (or any person occupying a similar status or performing similar functions), any person directly or indirectly controlling, controlled by, or under common control with such member, or any employee of such member.

(22)(A) The term "securities information processor" means any person engaged in the business of (i) collecting, processing, or preparing for distribution or publication, or assisting, participating in, or coordinating the distribution or publication of, information with respect to transactions in or quotations for any security (other than an exempted security) or (ii) distributing or publishing (whether by means of a ticker tape, a communications network, a terminal display device, or otherwise) on a current and continuing basis, information with respect to such transactions or quotations. The term "securities information processor" does not include any bona fide newspaper, news magazine, or business or financial publication of general and regular circulation, any self-regulatory organizations, any bank, broker, dealer, building and loan, savings and loan, or homestead association, or cooperative bank, if such bank, broker, dealer, association, or cooperative bank would be deemed to be a securities information processor solely by reason of functions performed by such institutions as part of customary banking, brokerage, dealing, association, or cooperative bank activities, or any common carrier, as defined in section 3 of the Communications Act of 1934, subject to the jurisdiction of the Federal Communications Commission or a State commission, as defined in section 3 of that Act, unless the Commission determines that such carrier is engaged in the business of collecting, processing, or preparing for distribution or publication, information with respect to transactions in or quotations for any security.

(B) The term "exclusive processor" means any securities information processor or self-regulatory organization which, directly or indirectly, engages on an exclusive basis on behalf of any national securities exchange or registered securities association, or any national securities exchange or registered securities association which engages on an exclusive basis on its own behalf, in collecting, processing, or preparing for distribution or publication any information with respect to (i) transactions or quotations on or effected or made by means of any facility of such exchange or (ii) quotations distributed or published by means of any electronic system operated or controlled by such association.

(23)(A) The term "clearing agency" means any person who acts as an intermediary in making payments or deliveries or both in connection with transactions in securities or who provides facilities for comparison of data respecting the terms of settlement of securities transactions, to reduce the number of settlements of securities transactions, or for the allocation of securities settlement responsibilities. Such term also means any person, such as a securities depository, who (i) acts as a custodian of securities in connection with a system for the central handling of securities whereby all securities of a particular class or series of any issuer deposited within the system are treated as fungible and may be transferred, loaned, or pledged by bookkeeping entry without physical delivery of securities certificates, or (ii) otherwise permits or facilitates the settlement of securities transactions or the hypothecation or lending of securities without physical delivery of securities certificates.

(B) The term "clearing agency" does not include (i) any Federal Reserve bank, Federal home loan bank, or Federal land bank; (ii) any national securities exchange or registered securities association solely by reason of its providing facilities for comparison of data respecting the terms of settlement of securities transactions effected on such exchange or by means of any electronic system operated or controlled by such association; (iii) any bank, broker, dealer, building and loan, savings and loan, or homestead association, or cooperative bank if such bank, broker, dealer, association, or cooperative bank would be deemed to be a clearing agency solely by reason of functions performed by such institution as part of customary banking, brokerage, dealing, association, or cooperative banking activities, or solely by reason of acting on behalf of a clearing agency or a participant therein in connection with the furnishing by the clearing agency of services to its participants or the use of services of the clearing agency by its participants, unless the Commission, by rule, otherwise provides as necessary or appropriate to assure the prompt and accurate clearance and settlement of securities transactions or to prevent evasion of this title; (iv) any life insurance company, its registered separate accounts, or a subsidiary of such insurance company solely by reason of functions commonly performed by such entities in connection with variable annuity contracts or variable life policies issued by such insurance company or its separate accounts; (v) any registered open-end investment company or unit investment trust solely by reason of functions commonly performed by it in connection with shares in such registered open-end investment company or unit investment trust, or (vi) any person solely by reason of its performing functions described in paragraph (25)(E) of this subsection.

(24) The term "participant" when used with respect to a clearing agency means any person who uses a clearing agency to clear or settle securities transactions or to transfer, pledge, lend, or hypothecate securities. Such term does not include a person whose only use of a clearing agency is (A) through another person who is a participant or (B) as a pledgee of securities.

(25) The term "transfer agent" means any person who engages on behalf of an issuer of securities or on behalf of itself as an issuer of securities in (A) countersigning such securities upon issuance; (B) monitoring the issuance of such securities with a view to preventing unauthorized issuance, a function commonly performed by a person called a registrar; (C) registering the transfer of such securities; (D) exchanging or converting such securities; or (E) transferring record ownership of securities by bookkeeping entry without physical issuance of securities certificates. The term "transfer agent" does not include any insurance company or separate account which performs such functions solely with respect to variable annuity contracts or variable life policies which it issues or any registered clearing agency which performs such functions solely with respect to options contracts which it issues.

(26) The term "self-regulatory organization" means any national securities exchange, registered securities association, or registered clearing agency, or (solely for purposes of sections 19(b), 19(c) and 23(b) of this title) the Municipal Securi-

ties Rulemaking Board established by section 15B of this title.

(27) The term "rules of an exchange", "rules of an association", or "rules of a clearing agency" means the constitution, articles of incorporation, bylaws, and rules, or instruments corresponding to the foregoing, of an exchange, association of brokers and dealers, or clearing agency, respectively, and such of the stated policies, practices, and interpretations of such exchange, association, or clearing agency as the Commission, by rule, may determine to be necessary or appropriate in the public interest or for the protection of investors to be deemed to be rules of such exchange, association, or clearing agency.

(28) The term "rules of a self-regulatory organization" means the rules of an exchange which is a national securities exchange, the rules of an association of brokers and dealers which is a registered securities association, the rules of a clearing agency which is a registered clearing agency, or the rules of the Municipal Securities Rulemaking Board.

(29) The term "municipal securities" means securities which are direct obligations of, or obligations guaranteed as to principal or interest by, a State or any political subdivision thereof, or any agency or instrumentality of a State or any political subdivision thereof, or any municipal corporate instrumentality of one or more States, or any security which is an industrial development bond (as defined in section 103(c)(2) of the Internal Revenue Code the interest on which is excludable from gross income under section 103(a)(1) of such Code if, by reason of the application of paragraph (4) or (6) of section 103(c) of such Code (determined as if paragraphs (4)(A), (5), and (7) were not included in such section 103(c)), paragraph (1) of such section 103(c)) does not apply to such security.

(30) The term "municipal securities dealer" means any person (including a separately identifiable department or division of a bank) engaged in the business of buying and selling municipal securities for his own account, through a broker or otherwise, but does not include—

(A) any person insofar as he buys or sells such securities for his own account, either individually or in some fiduciary capacity, but not as a part of a regular business; or

(B) a bank, unless the bank is engaged in the business of buying and selling municipal securities for its own account other than in a fiduciary capacity, through a broker or otherwise: *Provided, however*, That if the bank is engaged in such business through a separately identifiable department or division (as defined by the Municipal Securities Rulemaking Board in accordance with section 15B(b)(2)(H) of this title), the department or division and not the bank itself shall be deemed to be the municipal securities dealer.

(31) The term "municipal securities broker" means a broker engaged in the business of effecting transactions in municipal securities for the account of others.

(32) The term "person associated with a municipal securities dealer" when used with respect to a municipal securities dealer which is a bank or a division or department of a bank means any person directly engaged in the management, direction, supervision, or performance of any of the municipal securities dealer's activities with respect to municipal securities, and any person directly or indirectly controlling such activities or controlled by the municipal securities dealer in connection with such activities.

(33) The term "municipal securities investment portfolio" means all municipal securities held for investment and not for sale as part of a regular business by a municipal securities dealer or by a person, directly or indirectly, controlling, controlled by, or under common control with a municipal securities dealer.

(34) The term "appropriate regulatory agency" means—

(A) When used with respect to a municipal securities dealer:

(i) the Comptroller of the Currency, in the case of a national bank a subsidiary or a department or division of any such bank, a Federal savings association (as defined in section 3(b)(2) of the Federal Deposit Insurance Act), the deposits of which are insured by the Federal Deposit Insurance Corporation, or a subsidiary or department or division of any such Federal savings association;

(ii) the Board of Governors of the Federal Reserve System, in the case of a State member bank of the Federal Reserve System, a subsidiary or a department or division thereof, a bank holding company, a subsidiary of a bank holding company which is a bank other than a bank specified in clause (i), (iii), or (iv) of this subparagraph, a subsidiary or a department or division of such subsidiary, or a savings and loan holding company;

(iii) the Federal Deposit Insurance Corporation, in the case of a bank insured by the Federal Deposit Insurance Corporation (other than a member of the Federal Reserve System), a subsidiary or department or division of any such bank, a State savings association (as defined in section 3(b)(3) of the Federal Deposit Insurance Act), the deposits of which are insured by the Federal Deposit Insurance Corporation, or a subsidiary or a department or division of any such State savings association; and

(iv) the Commission in the case of all other municipal securities dealers.

(B) When used with respect to a clearing agency or transfer agent:

(i) the Comptroller of the Currency, in the case of a national bank, a subsidiary of any such bank, a Federal savings association (as defined in section 3(b)(2) of the Federal Deposit Insurance Act), the deposits of which are insured by the Federal Deposit Insurance Corporation, or a subsidiary of any such Federal savings association;

(ii) the Board of Governors of the Federal Reserve System, in the case of a State member bank of the Federal Reserve System, a subsidiary thereof, a bank holding company, a subsidiary of a bank holding company that is a bank other than a bank specified in clause (i) or (iii) of this subparagraph, or a savings and loan holding company;

(iii) the Federal Deposit Insurance Corporation, in the case of a bank insured by the Federal Deposit Insurance Corporation (other than a member of the Federal Reserve System), a subsidiary of any such bank, a State savings association (as defined in section 3(b)(3) of the Federal Deposit Insurance Act), the deposits of which are insured by the Federal Deposit Insurance Corporation, or a subsidiary of any such State savings association; and

(iv) the Commission in the case of all other clearing agencies and transfer agents.

(C) When used with respect to a participant or applicant to become a participant in a clearing agency or a person requesting or having access to services offered by a clearing agency:

(i) the Comptroller of the Currency, in the case of a national bank or a Federal savings association (as defined in section 3(b)(2) of the Federal Deposit Insurance Act), the deposits of which are insured by the Federal Deposit Insurance Corporation when the appropriate regulatory agency for such clearing agency is not the Commission;

(ii) the Board of Governors of the Federal Reserve System in the case of a State member bank of the Federal Reserve System, a bank holding company, or a subsidiary of a bank holding company, a subsidiary of a bank holding company that is a bank other than a bank specified in clause (i) or (iii) of this subparagraph, or a savings and loan holding company when the appropriate regulatory agency for such clearing agency is not the Commission;

(iii) the Federal Deposit Insurance Corporation, in the case of a bank insured by the Federal Deposit Insurance Corporation (other than a member of the Federal Reserve System) or a State savings association (as defined in section 3(b)(3) of the Federal Deposit Insurance Act), the deposits of which are insured by the Federal Deposit Insurance Corporation; and when the appropriate regulatory agency for such clearing agency is not the Commission;

(iv) the Commission in all other cases.

(D) When used with respect to an institutional investment manager which is a bank the deposits of which are insured in accordance with the Federal Deposit Insurance Act:

(i) the Comptroller of the Currency, in the case of a national bank or a Federal savings association (as defined in section 3(b)(2) of the Federal Deposit Insurance Act), the deposits of which are insured by the Federal Deposit Insurance Corporation;

(ii) the Board of Governors of the Federal Reserve System, in the case of any other member bank of the Federal Reserve System; and

(iii) the Federal Deposit Insurance Corporation, in the case of any other insured bank or a State savings association (as defined in section 3(b)(3) of the Federal Deposit Insurance Act), the deposits of which are insured by the Federal Deposit Insurance Corporation.

(E) When used with respect to a national securities exchange or registered securities association, member thereof, person associated with a member thereof, applicant to become a member thereof or to become associated with a member thereof, or person requesting or having access to services offered by such exchange or association or member thereof, or the Municipal Securities Rulemaking Board, the Commission.

(F) When used with respect to a person exercising investment discretion with respect to an account;

(i) the Comptroller of the Currency, in the case of a national bank or a Federal savings association (as defined in section 3(b)(2) of the Federal Deposit Insurance Act), the deposits of which are insured by the Federal Deposit Insurance Corporation;

(ii) the Board of Governors of the Federal Reserve System, in the case of any other member bank of the Federal Reserve System;

(iii) the Federal Deposit Insurance Corporation, in the case of any other bank the deposits of which are insured in accordance with the Federal Deposit Insurance Act or a State savings association (as defined in section 3(b)(3) of the Federal Deposit Insurance Act), the deposits of which are insured by the Federal Deposit Insurance Corporation; and

(iv) the Commission, in the case of all other such persons.

(G) When used with respect to a government securities broker or government securities dealer, or person associated with a government securities broker or government securities dealer:

(i) the Comptroller of the Currency, in the case of a national bank, a Federal savings association (as defined in section 3(b)(2) of the Federal Deposit Insurance Act), the deposits of which are insured by the Federal Deposit Insurance Corporation or a Federal branch or Federal agency of a foreign bank (as such terms are used in the International Banking Act of 1978);

(ii) the Board of Governors of the Federal Reserve System, in the case of a State member bank of the Federal Reserve System, a foreign bank, an uninsured State branch or State agency of a foreign bank, a commercial lending company owned or controlled by a foreign bank (as such terms are used in the International Banking Act of 1978), or a corporation organized or having an agreement with the Board of Governors of the Federal Reserve System pursuant to section 25 or section 25A of the Federal Reserve Act;

(iii) the Federal Deposit Insurance Corporation, in the case of a bank insured by the Federal Deposit Insurance Corporation (other than a member of the Federal Reserve System or a Federal savings bank) a State savings association (as defined in section 3(b)(3) of the Federal Deposit Insurance Act), the deposits of which are insured by the Federal Deposit Insurance Corporation, or an insured State branch of a foreign bank (as such terms are used in the International Banking Act of 1978); and

(iv) the Commission, in the case of all other government securities brokers and government securities dealers.

(H) When used with respect to an institution described in subparagraph (D), (F), or (G) of section 2(c)(2), or held under section 4(f), of the Bank Holding Company Act of 1956—

(i) the Comptroller of the Currency, in the case of a national bank;

(ii) the Board of Governors of the Federal Reserve System, in the case of a State member bank of the Federal Reserve System or any corporation chartered under section 25A of the Federal Reserve Act;

(iii) the Federal Deposit Insurance Corporation, in the case of any other bank the deposits of which are insured in accordance with the Federal Deposit Insurance Act; or

(iv) the Commission in the case of all other such institutions.

As used in this paragraph, the terms "bank holding company" and "subsidiary of a bank holding company" have the meanings given them in section 2 of the Bank Holding Company Act of 1956. As used in this paragraph, the term "savings and loan holding company" has the same meaning as in section 10(a) of the Home Owners' Loan Act.

(35) A person exercises "investment discretion" with respect to an account if, directly or indirectly, such person (A) is authorized to determine what securities or other property shall be purchased or sold by or for the account, (B) makes decisions as

to what securities or other property shall be purchased or sold by or for the account even though some other person may have responsibility for such investment decisions, or (C) otherwise exercises such influence with respect to the purchase and sale of securities or other property by or for the account as the Commission, by rule, determines, in the public interest or for the protection of investors, should be subject to the operation of the provisions of this chapter and the rules and regulations thereunder.

(36) A class of persons or markets is subject to "equal regulation" if no member of the class has a competitive advantage over any other member thereof resulting from a disparity in their regulation under this title which the Commission determines is unfair and not necessary or appropriate in furtherance of the purposes of this title.

(37) The term "records" means accounts, correspondence, memorandums, tapes, discs, papers, books, and other documents or transcribed information of any type, whether expressed in ordinary or machine language.

(38) The term "market maker" means any specialist permitted to act as a dealer, any dealer acting in the capacity of block positioner, and any dealer who, with respect to a security, holds himself out (by entering quotations in an inter-dealer communications system or otherwise) as being willing to buy and sell such security for his own account on a regular or continuous basis.

(39) A person is subject to a "statutory disqualification" with respect to membership or participation in, or association with a member of, a self-regulatory organization, if such person—

(A) has been and is expelled or suspended from membership or participation in, or barred or suspended from being associated with a member of, any self-regulatory organization, foreign equivalent of a self-regulatory organization, foreign or international securities exchange, contract market designated pursuant to section 5 of the Commodity Exchange Act, or any substantially equivalent foreign statute or regulation, or futures association registered under section 17 of such Act, or any substantially equivalent foreign statute or regulation, or has been and is denied trading privileges on any such contract market or foreign equivalent;

(B) is subject to—

(i) an order of the Commission, other appropriate regulatory agency, or foreign financial regulatory authority—

(I) denying, suspending for a period not exceeding 12 months, or revoking his registration as a broker, dealer, municipal securities dealer, government securities broker, government securities dealer, security-based swap dealer, or major security-based swap participant or limiting his activities as a foreign person performing a function substantially equivalent to any of the above; or

(II) barring or suspending for a period not exceeding 12 months his being associated with a broker, dealer, municipal securities dealer, government securities broker, government securities dealer, security-based swap dealer, major security-based swap participant, or foreign person performing a function substantially equivalent to any of the above;

(ii) an order of the Commodity Futures Trading Commission denying, suspending, or revoking his registration under the Commodity Exchange Act; or

(iii) an order by a foreign financial regulatory authority denying, suspending, or revoking the person's authority to engage in transactions in contracts of sale of a commodity for future delivery or other instruments traded on or subject to the rules of a contract market, board of trade, or foreign equivalent thereof;

(C) by his conduct while associated with a broker, dealer, municipal securities dealer, government securities broker, government securities dealer, security-based swap dealer, or major security-based swap participant, or while associated with an entity or person required to be registered under the Commodity Exchange Act, has been found to be a cause of any effective suspension, expulsion, or order of the character described in subparagraph (A) or (B) of this paragraph, and in entering such a suspension, expulsion, or order, the Commission, an appropriate regulatory agency, or any such self-regulatory organization shall have jurisdiction to find whether or not any person was a cause thereof;

(D) by his conduct while associated with any broker, dealer, municipal securities dealer, government securities broker, government securities dealer, security-based swap dealer, major security-based swap participant, or any other entity engaged in transactions in securities, or while associated with an entity engaged in transactions in contracts of sale of a commodity for future delivery or other instruments traded on or subject to the rules of a contract market, board of trade, or foreign equivalent thereof, has been found to be a cause of any effective suspension, expulsion, or order by a foreign or international securities exchange or foreign financial regulatory authority empowered by a foreign government to administer or enforce its laws relating to financial transactions as described in subparagraph (A) or (B) of this paragraph;

(E) has associated with him any person who is known, or in the exercise of reasonable care should be known, to him to be a person described by subparagraph (A), (B), (C), or (D) of this paragraph; or

(F) has committed or omitted any act, or is subject to an order or finding, enumerated in subparagraph (D), (E), (H), or (G) of paragraph (4) of section 15(b) of this title, has been convicted of any offense specified in subparagraph (B) of such paragraph (4) or any other felony within ten years of the date of the filing of an application for membership or participation in, or to become associated with a member of, such self-regulatory organization, is enjoined from any action, conduct, or practice specified in subparagraph (C) of such paragraph (4), has willfully made or caused to be made in any application for membership or participation in, or to become associated with a member of, a self-regulatory organization, report required to be filed with a self-regulatory organization, or proceeding before a self-regulatory organization, any statement which was at the time, and in the light of the circumstances under which it was made, false or misleading with respect to any material fact, or has omitted to state in any such application, report, or proceeding any material fact which is required to be stated therein.

(40) The term "financial responsibility rules" means the rules and regulations of the Commission or the rules and regulations prescribed by any self-regulatory organization relating to financial responsibility and related practices which are designated by the Commission, by rule or regulation, to be financial responsibility rules.

(41) The term "mortgage related security" means a security that meets standards of credit-worthiness as established by the Commission, and either:

(A) represents ownership of one or more promissory notes or certificates of interest or participation in such notes (including any rights designed to assure servicing of, or the receipt or timeliness of receipt by the holders of such notes, certificates, or participations of amounts payable under, such notes, certificates, or participations), which notes:

(i) are directly secured by a first lien on a single parcel of real estate, including stock allocated to a dwelling unit in a residential cooperative housing corporation, upon which is located a dwelling or mixed residential and commercial structure, on a residential manufactured home as defined in section 603(6) of the National Manufactured Housing Construction and Safety Standards Act of 1974, whether such manufactured home is considered real or personal property under the laws of the State in which it is to be located or on one or more parcels of real estate upon which is located one or more commercial structures; and

(ii) were originated by a savings and loan association, savings bank, commercial bank, credit union, insurance company, or similar institution which is supervised and examined by a Federal or State authority, or by a mortgagee approved by the Secretary of Housing and Urban Development pursuant to sections 203 and 211 of the National Housing Act, or, where such notes involve a lien on the manufactured home, by any such institution or by any financial institution approved for insurance by the Secretary of Housing and Urban Development pursuant to section of the National Housing Act; or

(B) is secured by one or more promissory notes or certificates of interest or participations in such notes (with or without recourse to the issuer thereof) and, by its terms, provides for payments of principal in relation to payments, or reasonable projections of payments, on notes meeting the requirements of subparagraphs (A) (i) and (ii) or certificates of interest or participations in promissory notes meeting such requirements.

For the purpose of this paragraph, the term "promissory note", when used in connection with a manufactured home, shall also include a loan, advance, or credit sale as evidence by a retail installment sales contract or other instrument.

(42) The term "government securities" means—

(A) securities which are direct obligations of, or obligations guaranteed as to principal or interest by, the United States;

(B) securities which are issued or guaranteed by the Tennessee Valley Authority or by corporations in which the United States has a direct or indirect interest and which are designated by the Secretary of the Treasury for exemption as necessary or appropriate in the public interest or for the protection of investors;

(C) securities issued or guaranteed as to principal or interest by any corporation the securities of which are designated, by statute specifically naming such corporation, to constitute exempt securities within the meaning of the laws administered by the Commission;

(D) for purposes of sections 15C and 17A, any put, call, straddle, option, or privilege on a security described in subparagraph (A), (B), or (C) other than a put, call, straddle, option, or privilege—

(i) that is traded on one or more national securities exchanges; or

(ii) for which quotations are disseminated through an automated quotation system operated by a registered securities association; or

(E) for purposes of sections 15, 15C, and 17A as applied to a bank, a qualified Canadian government obligation as defined in section 5136 of the Revised Statutes of the United States.

(43) The term "government securities broker" means any person regularly engaged in the business of effecting transactions in government securities for the account of others, but does not include—

(A) any corporation the securities of which are government securities under subparagraph (B) or (C) of paragraph (42) of this subsection; or

(B) any person registered with the Commodity Futures Trading Commission, any contract market designated by the Commodity Futures Trading Commission, such contract market's affiliated clearing organization, or any floor trader on such contract market, solely because such person effects transactions in government securities that the Commission, after consultation with the Commodity Futures Trading Commission, has determined by rule or order to be incidental to such person's futures-related business.

(44) The term "government securities dealer" means any person engaged in the business of buying and selling government securities for his own account, through a broker or otherwise, but does not include—

(A) any person insofar as he buys or sells such securities for his own account, either individually or in some fiduciary capacity, but not as a part of a regular business;

(B) any corporation the securities of which are government securities under subparagraph (B) or (C) of paragraph (42) of this subsection;

(C) any bank, unless the bank is engaged in the business of buying and selling government securities for its own account other than in a fiduciary capacity, through a broker or otherwise; or

(D) any person registered with the Commodity Futures Trading Commission, any contract market designated by the Commodity Futures Trading Commission, such contract market's affiliated clearing organization, or any floor trader on such contract market, solely because such person effects transactions in government securities that the Commission, after consultation with the Commodity Futures Trading Commission, has determined by rule or order to be incidental to such person's futures-related business.

(45) The term "person associated with a government securities broker or government securities dealer" means any partner, officer, director, or branch manager of such government securities broker or government securities dealer (or any person occupying a similar status or performing similar functions), and any other employee of such government securities broker or government securities dealer who is engaged in the management, direction, supervision, or performance of any activities relating to government securities, and any person directly or indirectly controlling, controlled by, or under common control with such government securities broker or government securities dealer.

(46) The term "financial institution" means—

(A) a bank (as defined in paragraph (6) of this subsection);

(B) a foreign bank (as such term is used in the International Banking Act of 1978); and

(C) a savings association (as defined in section 3(b) of the Federal Deposit Insurance Act the deposits of which are insured by the Federal Deposit Insurance Corporation.

(47) The term "securities laws" means the Securities Act of 1933, the Securities Exchange Act of 1934, the Sarbanes–Oxley Act of 2002, the Trust Indenture Act of 1939, the Investment Company Act of 1940, the Investment Advisers Act of 1940, and the Securities Investor Protection Act of 1970.

(48) The term "registered broker or dealer" means a broker or dealer registered or required to register pursuant to section 15 or 15B of this title, except that in paragraph (3) of this subsection and sections 6 and 15A of this title the term means such a broker or dealer and a government securities broker or government securities dealer registered or required to register pursuant to section 15C(a)(1)(A) of this title.

(49) The term "person associated with a transfer agent" and "associated person of a transfer agent" mean any person (except an employee whose functions are solely clerical or ministerial) directly engaged in the management, direction, supervision, or performance of any of the transfer agent's activities with respect to transfer agent functions, and any person directly or indirectly controlling such activities or controlled by the transfer agent in connection with such activities.

(50) The term "foreign securities authority" means any foreign government, or any governmental body or regulatory organization empowered by a foreign government to administer or enforce its laws as they relate to securities matters.

(51)(A) The term "penny stock" means any equity security other than a security that is—

(i) registered or approved for registration and traded on a national securities exchange that meets such criteria as the Commission shall prescribe by rule or regulation for purposes of this paragraph;

(ii) authorized for quotation on an automated quotation system sponsored by a registered securities association, if such system (I) was established and in operation before January 1, 1990, and (II) meets such criteria as the Commission shall prescribe by rule or regulation for purposes of this paragraph;

(iii) issued by an investment company registered under the Investment Company Act of 1940;

(iv) excluded, on the basis of exceeding a minimum price, net tangible assets of the issuer, or other relevant criteria, from the definition of such term by rule or regulation which the Commission shall prescribe for purposes of this paragraph; or

(v) exempted, in whole or in part, conditionally or unconditionally, from the definition of such term by rule, regulation, or order prescribed by the Commission.

(B) The Commission may, by rule, regulation, or order, designate any equity security or class of equity securities described in clause (i) or (ii) of subparagraph (A) as within the meaning of the term "penny stock" if such security or class of securities is traded other than on a national securities exchange or through an automated quotation system described in clause (ii) of subparagraph (A).

(C) In exercising its authority under this paragraph to prescribe rules, regulations, and orders, the Commission shall determine that such rule, regulation, or order is consistent with the public interest and the protection of investors.

(52) The term "foreign financial regulatory authority" means any (A) foreign securities authority, (B) other governmental body or foreign equivalent of a self-regulatory organization empowered by a foreign government to administer or enforce its laws relating to the regulation of fiduciaries, trusts, commercial lending, insurance, trading in contracts of sale of a commodity for future delivery, or other instruments traded on or subject to the rules of a contract market, board of trade, or foreign equivalent, or other financial activities, or (C) membership organization a function of which is to regulate participation of its members in activities listed above.

(53)(A) The term "small business related security" means a security that meets standards of credit-worthiness as established by the Commission, and either—

(i) represents an interest in 1 or more promissory notes or leases of personal property evidencing the obligation of a small business concern and originated by an insured depository institution, insured credit union, insurance company, or similar institution which is supervised and examined by a Federal or State authority, or a finance company or leasing company; or

(ii) is secured by an interest in 1 or more promissory notes or leases of personal property (with or without recourse to the issuer or lessee) and provides for payments of principal in relation to payments, or reasonable projections of payments, on notes or leases described in clause (i).

(B) For purposes of this paragraph—

(i) an "interest in a promissory note or a lease of personal property" includes ownership rights, certificates of interest or participation in such notes or leases, and rights designed to assure servicing of such notes or leases, or the receipt or timely receipt of amounts payable under such notes or leases;

(ii) the term "small business concern" means a business that meets the criteria for a small business concern established by the Small Business Administration under section 3(a) of the Small Business Act;

(iii) the term "insured depository institution" has the same meaning as in section 3 of the Federal Deposit Insurance Act; and

(iv) the term "insured credit union" has the same meaning as in section 101 of the Federal Credit Union Act.

(54) *Qualified Investor.*

(A) *Definition.* Except as provided in subparagraph (B), for purposes of this title, the term "qualified investor" means—

(i) any investment company registered with the Commission under section 8 of the Investment Company Act of 1940;

(ii) any issuer eligible for an exclusion from the definition of investment company pursuant to section 3(c)(7) of the Investment Company Act of 1940;

(iii) any bank (as defined in paragraph (6) of this subsection), savings association (as defined in section 3(b) of the Federal Deposit Insurance Act, broker, dealer, insurance company (as defined in section 2(a)(13) of the Securities Act of 1933), or business development company (as defined in section 2(a)(48) of the Investment Company Act of 1940);

(iv) any small business investment company licensed by the United States Small Business Administration under section 301(c) or (d) of the Small Business Investment Act of 1940;

(v) any State sponsored employee benefit plan, or any other employee benefit plan, within the meaning of the Employee Retirement Income Security Act of 1974, other than an individual retirement account, if the investment decisions are made by a plan fiduciary, as defined in section 3(21) of the Act, which is either a bank, savings and loan association, insurance company, or registered investment adviser;

(vi) any trust whose purchases of securities are directed by a person described in clauses (i) through (v) of this subparagraph;

(vii) any market intermediary exempt under section 3(c)(2) of the Investment Company Act of 1940;

(viii) any associated person of a broker or dealer other than a natural person;

(ix) any foreign bank (as defined in section 1(b)(7) of the International Banking Act of 1978);

(x) the government of any foreign country;

(xi) any corporation, company, or partnership that owns and invests on a discretionary basis, not less than $25,000,000 in investments;

(xii) any natural person who owns and invests on a discretionary basis, not less than $25,000,000 in investments;

(xiii) any government or political subdivision, agency, or instrumentality of a government who owns and invests on a discretionary basis not less than $50,000,000 in investments; or

(xiv) any multinational or supranational entity or any agency or instrumentality thereof.

(B) *Altered Thresholds for Asset-Backed Securities and Loan Participations.* For purposes of section 3(a)(5)(C)(iii) of this title and section 206(a)(5) of the Gramm–Leach–Bliley Act, the term "qualified investor" has the meaning given such term by subparagraph (A) of this paragraph except that clauses (xi) and (xii) shall be applied by substituting "$10,000,000" for "$25,000,000".

(C) *Additional Authority*. The Commission may, by rule or order, define a "qualified investor" as any other person, taking into consideration such factors as the financial sophistication of the person, net worth, and knowledge and experience in financial matters.

(55)(A) The term "security future" means a contract of sale for future delivery of a single security or of a narrow-based security index, including any interest therein or based on the value thereof, except an exempted security under section 3(a)(12) of this title as in effect on the date of enactment of the Futures Trading Act of 1982 (other than any municipal security as defined in section 3(a)(29) as in effect on the date of enactment of the Futures Trading Act of 1982). The term "security future" does not include any agreement, contract, or transaction excluded from the Commodity Exchange Act under section 2(c), 2(d), 2(f) or 2(g) of the Commodity Exchange Act (as in effect on the date of enactment of the Commodity Futures Modernization Act of 2000) or title IV of the Commodity Futures Modernization Act of 2000.

(B) The term "narrow-based security index" means an index—

(i) that has 9 or fewer component securities;

(ii) in which a component security comprises more than 30 percent of the index's weighting;

(iii) in which the five highest weighted component securities in the aggregate comprise more than 60 percent of the index's weighting; or

(iv) in which the lowest weighted component securities comprising, in the aggregate, 25 percent of the index's weighting have an aggregate dollar value of average daily trading volume of less than $50,000,000 (or in the case of an index with 15 or more component securities, $30,000,000), except that if there are two or more securities with equal weighting that could be included in the calculation of the lowest weighted component securities comprising, in the aggregate, 25 percent of the index's weighting, such securities shall be ranked from lowest to highest dollar value of average daily trading volume and shall be included in the calculation based on their ranking starting with the lowest ranked security.

(C) Notwithstanding subparagraph (B), an index is not a narrow-based security index if—

(i)(I) it has at least nine component securities;

(II) no component security comprises more than 30 percent of the index's weighting; and

(III) each component security is—

(aa) registered pursuant to section 12 of the Securities Exchange Act of 1934;

(bb) one of 750 securities with the largest market capitalization; and

(cc) one of 675 securities with the largest dollar value of average daily trading volume;

(ii) a board of trade was designated as a contract market by the Commodity Futures Trading Commission with respect to a contract of sale for future delivery on the index, before the date of enactment of the Commodity Futures Modernization Act of 2000;

(iii)(I) a contract of sale for future delivery on the index traded on a designated contract market or registered derivatives transaction execution facility for at least 30 days as a contract of sale for future delivery on an index that was not a narrow-based security index; and

(II) it has been a narrow-based security index for no more than 45 business days over 3 consecutive calendar months;

(iv) a contract of sale for future delivery on the index is traded on or subject to the rules of a foreign board of trade and meets such requirements as are jointly established by rule or regulation by the Commission and the Commodity Futures Trading Commission;

(v) no more than 18 months have passed since the date of enactment of the Commodity Futures Modernization Act of 2000 and—

(I) it is traded on or subject to the rules of a foreign board of trade;

(II) the offer and sale in the United States of a contract of sale for future delivery on the index was authorized before the date of enactment of the Commodity Futures Modernization Act of 2000; and

(III) the conditions of such authorization continue to be met; or

(vi) a contract of sale for future delivery on the index is traded on or subject to the rules of a board of trade and meets such requirements as are jointly established by rule, regulation, or order by the Commission and the Commodity Futures Trading Commission.

(D) Within 1 year after the enactment of the Commodity Futures Modernization Act of 2000, the Commission and the Commodity Futures Trading Commission jointly shall adopt rules or regulations that set forth the requirements under clause (iv) of subparagraph (C).

(E) An index that is a narrow-based security index solely because it was a narrow-based security index for more than 45 business days over 3 consecutive calendar months pursuant to clause (iii) of subparagraph (C) shall not be a narrow-based security index for the 3 following calendar months.

(F) For purposes of subparagraphs (B) and (C) of this paragraph—

(i) the dollar value of average daily trading volume and the market capitalization shall be calculated as of the preceding 6 full calendar months; and

(ii) the Commission and the Commodity Futures Trading Commission shall, by rule or regulation, jointly specify the method to be used to determine market capitalization and dollar value of average daily trading volume.

(56) The term "security futures product" means a security future or any put, call, straddle, option, or privilege on any security future.

(57)(A) The term "margin", when used with respect to a security futures product, means the amount, type, and form of collateral required to secure any extension or maintenance of credit, or the amount, type, and form of collateral required as a performance bond related to the purchase, sale, or carrying of a security futures product.

(B) The terms "margin level" and "level of margin", when used with respect to a security futures product, mean the amount of margin required to secure any extension or maintenance of credit, or the amount of margin required as a performance bond related to the purchase, sale, or carrying of a security futures product.

(C) The terms "higher margin level" and "higher level of margin", when used with respect to a security futures product, mean a margin level established by a national securities exchange registered pursuant to section 6(g) that is higher than the minimum amount established and in effect pursuant to section 7(c)(2)(B) of this title.

(58) *Audit Committee.* The term "audit committee" means—

(A) a committee (or equivalent body) established by and amongst the board of directors of an issuer for the purpose of overseeing the accounting and financial reporting processes of the issuer and audits of the financial statements of the issuer; and

(B) if no such committee exists with respect to an issuer, the entire board of directors of the issuer.

(59) *Registered Public Accounting Firm.* The term "registered public accounting firm" has the same meaning as in section 2 of the Sarbanes–Oxley Act of 2002.

(60) *Credit Rating.* The term "credit rating" means an assessment of the creditworthiness of an obligor as an entity or with respect to specific securities or money market instruments.

(61) *Credit Rating Agency.* The term "credit rating agency" means any person—

(A) engaged in the business of issuing credit ratings on the Internet or through another readily accessible means, for free or for a reasonable fee, but does not include a commercial credit reporting company;

(B) employing either a quantitative or qualitative model, or both, to determine credit ratings; and

(C) receiving fees from either issuers, investors, or other market participants, or a combination thereof.

(62) *Nationally Recognized Statistical Rating Organization.* The term "nationally recognized statistical rating organization" means a credit rating agency that—

(A) issues credit ratings certified by qualified institutional buyers, in accordance with section 15E(a)(1)(B)(ix), with respect to—

(i) financial institutions, brokers, or dealers;

(ii) insurance companies;

(iii) corporate issuers;

(iv) issuers of asset-backed securities (as that term is defined in section 1101(c) of part 229 of title 17, Code of Federal Regulations, as in effect on the date of enactment of this paragraph;

(v) issuers of government securities, municipal securities, or securities issued by a foreign government; or

(vi) a combination of one or more categories of obligors described in any of clauses (i) through (v); and

(B) is registered under section 15E.

(63) *Person Associated with a Nationally Recognized Statistical Rating Organization.* The term "person associated with" a nationally recognized statistical rating organization means any partner, officer, director, or branch manager of a nationally recognized statistical rating organization (or any person occupying a similar status or performing similar functions), any person directly or indirectly controlling, controlled by, or under common control with a nationally recognized statistical rating organization, or any employee of a nationally recognized statistical rating organization.

(64) *Qualified Institutional Buyer.* The term "qualified institutional buyer" has the meaning given such term in Rule 144A(a) under the Securities Act of 1933, or any successor thereto.

(65) *Eligible Contract Participant.* The term "eligible contract participant" has the same meaning as in section 1a of the Commodity Exchange Act.

(66) *Major Swap Participant.* The term "major swap participant" has the same meaning as in section 1a of the Commodity Exchange Act.

(67) *Major Security–Based Swap Participant.*

(A) *In General.* The term "major security-based swap participant" means any person—

(i) who is not a security-based swap dealer; and

(ii)(I) who maintains a substantial position in security-based swaps for any of the major security-based swap categories, as such categories are determined by the Commission, excluding both positions held for hedging or mitigating commercial risk and positions maintained by any employee benefit plan (or any contract held by such a plan) as defined in paragraphs (3) and (32) of section 3 of the Employee Retirement Income Security Act of 1974 for the primary purpose of hedging or mitigating any risk directly associated with the operation of the plan;

(II) whose outstanding security-based swaps create substantial counterparty exposure that could have serious adverse effects on the financial stability of the United States banking system or financial markets; or

(III) that is a financial entity that—

(aa) is highly leveraged relative to the amount of capital such entity holds and that is not subject to capital requirements established by an appropriate Federal banking agency; and

(bb) maintains a substantial position in outstanding security-based swaps in any major security-based swap category, as such categories are determined by the Commission.

(B) *Definition of Substantial Position.* For purposes of subparagraph (A), the Commission shall define, by rule or regulation, the term "substantial position" at the threshold that the Commission determines to be prudent for the effective monitoring, management, and oversight of entities that are systemically important or can significantly impact the financial system of the United States. In setting the definition under this subparagraph, the Commission shall consider the person's relative position in uncleared as opposed to cleared security-based swaps and may take into consideration the value and quality of collateral held against counterparty exposures.

(C) *Scope of Designation.* For purposes of subparagraph (A), a person may be designated as a major security-based swap participant for 1 or more categories of security-based swaps without being classified as a major security-based swap participant for all classes of security-based swaps.

(68) *Security–Based Swap.*

(A) *In General.* Except as provided in subparagraph (B), the term "security-based swap" means any agreement, contract, or transaction that—

(i) is a swap, as that term is defined under section 1a of the Commodity Exchange Act (without regard to paragraph (47)(B)(x) of such section); and

(ii) is based on—

(I) an index that is a narrow-based security index, including any interest therein or on the value thereof;

(II) a single security or loan, including any interest therein or on the value thereof; or

(III) the occurrence, nonoccurrence, or extent of the occurrence of an event relating to a single issuer of a security or the issuers of securities in a narrow-based security index, provided that such event directly affects the financial statements, financial condition, or financial obligations of the issuer.

(B) *Rule of Construction Regarding Master Agreements*. The term "security-based swap" shall be construed to include a master agreement that provides for an agreement, contract, or transaction that is a security-based swap pursuant to subparagraph (A), together with all supplements to any such master agreement, without regard to whether the master agreement contains an agreement, contract, or transaction that is not a security-based swap pursuant to subparagraph (A), except that the master agreement shall be considered to be a security-based swap only with respect to each agreement, contract, or transaction under the master agreement that is a security-based swap pursuant to subparagraph (A).

(C) *Exclusions*. The term "security-based swap" does not include any agreement, contract, or transaction that meets the definition of a security-based swap only because such agreement, contract, or transaction references, is based upon, or settles through the transfer, delivery, or receipt of an exempted security under paragraph (12), as in effect on the date of enactment of the Futures Trading Act of 1982 (other than any municipal security as defined in paragraph (29) as in effect on the date of enactment of the Futures Trading Act of 1982), unless such agreement, contract, or transaction is of the character of, or is commonly known in the trade as, a put, call, or other option.

(D) *Mixed Swap*. The term "security-based swap" includes any agreement, contract, or transaction that is as described in subparagraph (A) and also is based on the value of 1 or more interest or other rates, currencies, commodities, instruments of indebtedness, indices, quantitative measures, other financial or economic interest or property of any kind (other than a single security or a narrow-based security index), or the occurrence, non-occurrence, or the extent of the occurrence of an event or contingency associated with a potential financial, economic, or commercial consequence (other than an event described in subparagraph (A)(ii)(III)).

(E) *Rule of Construction Regarding Use of the Term Index*. The term "index" means an index or group of securities, including any interest therein or based on the value thereof.

(69) *Swap*. The term "swap" has the same meaning as in section 1a of the Commodity Exchange Act.

(70) *Person Associated with a Security–Based Swap Dealer or Major Security–Based Swap Participant*.

(A) *In General*. The term "person associated with a security-based swap dealer or major security-based swap participant" or "associated person of a security-based swap dealer or major security-based swap participant" means—

(i) any partner, officer, director, or branch manager of such security-based swap dealer or major security-based swap participant (or any person occupying a similar status or performing similar functions);

(ii) any person directly or indirectly controlling, controlled by, or under common control with such security-based swap dealer or major security-based swap participant; or

(iii) any employee of such security-based swap dealer or major security-based swap participant.

(B) *Exclusion*. Other than for purposes of section 15F(*l*)(2), the term "person associated with a security-based swap dealer or major security-based swap participant" or "associated person of a security-based swap dealer or major security-based swap participant" does not include any person associated with a security-based swap dealer or major security-based swap participant whose functions are solely clerical or ministerial.

(71) *Security-Based Swap Dealer*.

(A) *In General*. The term "security-based swap dealer" means any person who—

(i) holds themself out as a dealer in security-based swaps;

(ii) makes a market in security-based swaps;

(iii) regularly enters into security-based swaps with counterparties as an ordinary course of business for its own account; or

(iv) engages in any activity causing it to be commonly known in the trade as a dealer or market maker in security-based swaps.

(B) *Designation by Type or Class*. A person may be designated as a security-based swap dealer for a single type or single class or category of security-based swap or activities and considered not to be a security-based swap dealer for other types, classes, or categories of security-based swaps or activities.

(C) *Exception*. The term "security-based swap dealer" does not include a person that enters into security-based swaps for such person's own account, either individually or in a fiduciary capacity, but not as a part of regular business.

(D) *De Minimis Exception*. The Commission shall exempt from designation as a security-based swap dealer an entity that engages in a de minimis quantity of security-based swap dealing in connection with transactions with or on behalf of its customers. The Commission shall promulgate regulations to establish factors with respect to the making of any determination to exempt.

(72) *Appropriate Federal Banking Agency*. The term "appropriate Federal banking agency" has the same meaning as in section 3(q) of the Federal Deposit Insurance Act.

(73) *Board*. The term "Board" means the Board of Governors of the Federal Reserve System.

(74) *Prudential Regulator*. The term "prudential regulator" has the same meaning as in section 1a of the Commodity Exchange Act.

(75) *Security-Based Swap Data Repository*. The term "security-based swap data repository" means any person that collects and maintains information or records with respect to transactions or positions in, or the terms and conditions of, security-based swaps entered into by third parties for the purpose of providing a centralized recordkeeping facility for security-based swaps.

(76) *Swap Dealer*. The term "swap dealer" has the same meaning as in section 1a of the Commodity Exchange Act.

(77) *Security-Based Swap Execution Facility*. The term "security-based swap execution facility" means a trading system or platform in which multiple participants have the ability to execute or trade security-based swaps by accepting bids and offers made by multiple participants in the facility or system, through any means of interstate commerce, including any trading facility, that—

(A) facilitates the execution of security-based swaps between persons; and

(B) is not a national securities exchange.

(78) *Security–Based Swap Agreement*.

(A) *In General*. For purposes of sections 9, 10, 16, 20, and 21A of this Act, and section 17 of the Securities Act of 1933, the term "security-based swap agreement" means a swap agreement as defined in section 206A of the Gramm–Leach–Bliley Act of which a material term is based on the price, yield, value, or volatility of any security or any group or index of securities, or any interest therein.

(B) *Exclusions*. The term "security-based swap agreement" does not include any security-based swap.

(79) *Asset–Backed Security*. The term "asset-backed security"—

(A) means a fixed-income or other security collateralized by any type of self-liquidating financial asset (including a loan, a lease, a mortgage, or a secured or unsecured receivable) that allows the holder of the security to receive payments that depend primarily on cash flow from the asset, including—

(i) a collateralized mortgage obligation;

(ii) a collateralized debt obligation;

(iii) a collateralized bond obligation;

(iv) a collateralized debt obligation of asset-backed securities;

(v) a collateralized debt obligation of collateralized debt obligations; and

(vi) a security that the Commission, by rule, determines to be an asset-backed security for purposes of this section; and

(B) does not include a security issued by a finance subsidiary held by the parent company or a company controlled by the parent company, if none of the securities issued by the finance subsidiary are held by an entity that is not controlled by the parent company.

(80) *Emerging Growth Company.* The term "emerging growth company" means an issuer that had total annual gross revenues of less than $1,000,000,000 (as such amount is indexed for inflation every 5 years by the Commission to reflect the change in the Consumer Price Index for All Urban Consumers published by the Bureau of Labor Statistics, setting the threshold to the nearest 1,000,000) during its most recently completed fiscal year. An issuer that is an emerging growth company as of the first day of that fiscal year shall continue to be deemed an emerging growth company until the earliest of—

(A) the last day of the fiscal year of the issuer during which it had total annual gross revenues of $1,000,000,000 (as such amount is indexed for inflation every 5 years by the Commission to reflect the change in the Consumer Price Index for All Urban Consumers published by the Bureau of Labor Statistics, setting the threshold to the nearest 1,000,000) or more;

(B) the last day of the fiscal year of the issuer following the fifth anniversary of the date of the first sale of common equity securities of the issuer pursuant to an effective registration statement under the Securities Act of 1933;

(C) the date on which such issuer has, during the previous 3-year period, issued more than $1,000,000,000 in non-convertible debt; or

(D) the date on which such issuer is deemed to be a "large accelerated filer", as defined in Rule 12b–2 under the Securities Exchange Act of 1934, or any successor thereto.

(80) *Funding Portal.* The term "funding portal" means any person acting as an intermediary in a transaction involving the offer or sale of securities for the account of others, solely pursuant to section 4(6) of the Securities Act of 1933, that does not—

(A) offer investment advice or recommendations;

(B) solicit purchases, sales, or offers to buy the securities offered or displayed on its website or portal;

(C) compensate employees, agents, or other persons for such solicitation or based on the sale of securities displayed or referenced on its website or portal;

(D) hold, manage, possess, or otherwise handle investor funds or securities; or

(E) engage in such other activities as the Commission, by rule, determines appropriate.*

(b) *Power to Define Technical, Trade, Accounting, and Other Terms.* The Commission and the Board of Governors of the Federal Reserve System, as to matters within their respective jurisdictions, shall have power by rules and regulations to define technical, trade, accounting, and other terms used in this title, consistently with the provisions and purposes of this title.

(c) *Application to Governmental Departments or Agencies.* No provision of this title shall apply to, or be deemed to include, any executive department or independent establishment of the United States, or any lending agency which is wholly owned, directly or indirectly, by the United States, or any officer, agent, or employee of any such department, establishment, or agency, acting in the course of his official duty as such, unless such provision makes specific reference to such department, establishment, or agency.

(d) *Issuers of Municipal Securities.* No issuer of municipal securities or officer or employee thereof acting in the course of his official duties as such shall be deemed to be a "broker", "dealer", or "municipal securities dealer" solely by reason of buying, selling, or effecting transactions in the issuer's securities.

(e) *Charitable Organizations.*

(1) *Exemption.* Notwithstanding any other provision of this title, but subject to paragraph (2) of this subsection, a charitable organization, as defined in section 3(c)(10)(D) of the Investment Company Act of 1940, or any trustee, director, officer, employee, or volunteer of such a charitable organization acting within the scope of such person's employment or duties with such organization, shall not be deemed to be a "broker", "dealer", "municipal securities broker", "municipal securities dealer", "government securities broker", or "government securities dealer" for purposes of this title solely because such organization or person buys, holds, sells, or trades in securities for its own account in its capacity as trustee or administrator of, or otherwise on behalf of or for the account of—

* The JOBS Act created two paragraph (80)'s.

(A) such a charitable organization;

(B) a fund that is excluded from the definition of an investment company under section 3(c)(10)(B) of the Investment Company Act of 1940; or

(C) a trust or other donative instrument described in section 3(c)(10)(B) of the Investment Company Act of 1940, or the settlors (or potential settlors) or beneficiaries of any such trust or other instrument.

(2) *Limitation on Compensation.* The exemption provided under paragraph (1) shall not be available to any charitable organization, or any trustee, director, officer, employee, or volunteer of such a charitable organization, unless each person who, on or after 90 days after the date of enactment of this subsection, solicits donations on behalf of such charitable organization from any donor to a fund that is excluded from the definition of an investment company under section 3(c)(10)(B) of the Investment Company Act of 1940, is either a volunteer or is engaged in the overall fund raising activities of a charitable organization and receives no commission or other special compensation based on the number or the value of donations collected for the fund.

(f) *Consideration of Promotion of Efficiency, Competition, and Capital Formation.* Whenever pursuant to this title the Commission is engaged in rulemaking, or in the review of a rule of a self-regulatory organization, and is required to consider or determine whether an action is necessary or appropriate in the public interest, the Commission shall also consider, in addition to the protection of investors, whether the action will promote efficiency, competition, and capital formation.

(g) *Church Plans.* No church plan described in section 414(e) of the Internal Revenue Code of 1986, no person or entity eligible to establish and maintain such a plan under the Internal Revenue Code of 1986, no company or account that is excluded from the definition of an investment company under section 3(c)(14) of the Investment Company Act of 1940, and no trustee, director, officer or employee of or volunteer for such plan, company, account, person, or entity, acting within the scope of that person's employment or activities with respect to such plan, shall be deemed to be a "broker", "dealer", "municipal securities broker", "municipal securities dealer", "government securities broker", "government securities dealer", "clearing agency", or "transfer agent" for purposes of this title—

(1) solely because such plan, company, person, or entity buys, holds, sells, trades in, or transfers securities or acts as an intermediary in making payments in connection with transactions in securities for its own account in its capacity as trustee or administrator of, or otherwise on behalf of, or for the account of, any church plan, company, or account that is excluded from the definition of an investment company under section 3(c)(14) of the Investment Company Act of 1940; and

(2) if no such person or entity receives a commission or other transaction-related sales compensation in connection with any activities conducted in reliance on the exemption provided by this subsection.

(h) *Limited Exemption for Funding Portals.*

(1) *In General.* The Commission shall, by rule, exempt, conditionally or unconditionally, a registered funding portal from the requirement to register as a broker or dealer under section 15(a)(1), provided that such funding portal—

(A) remains subject to the examination, enforcement, and other rulemaking authority of the Commission;

(B) is a member of a national securities association registered under section 15A; and

(C) is subject to such other requirements under this title as the Commission determines appropriate under such rule.

(2) *National Securities Association Membership.* For purposes of sections 15(b)(8) and 15A, the term 'broker or dealer' includes a funding portal and the term 'registered broker or dealer' includes a registered funding portal, except to the extent that the Commission, by rule, determines otherwise, provided that a national securities association shall only examine for and enforce against a registered funding portal rules of such national securities association written specifically for registered funding portals.

Swap Agreements

Sec. 3A. (a) [Reserved.]

(b) *Security-Based Swap Agreements.*

(1) The definition of "security" in section 3(a)(10) of this title does not include any security-based swap agreement.

(2) The Commission is prohibited from registering, or requiring, recommending, or suggesting, the registration under this title of any secu-

rity-based swap agreement. If the Commission becomes aware that a registrant has filed a registration application with respect to such a swap agreement, the Commission shall promptly so notify the registrant. Any such registration with respect to such a swap agreement shall be void and of no force or effect.

(3) Except as provided in section 16(a) with respect to reporting requirements, the Commission is prohibited from—

(A) promulgating, interpreting, or enforcing rules; or

(B) issuing orders of general applicability; under this title in a manner that imposes or specifies reporting or recordkeeping requirements, procedures, or standards as prophylactic measures against fraud, manipulation, or insider trading with respect to any security-based swap agreement.

(4) References in this title to the "purchase" or "sale" of a security-based swap agreement shall be deemed to mean the execution, termination (prior to its scheduled maturity date), assignment, exchange, or similar transfer or conveyance of, or extinguishing of rights or obligations under, a security-based swap agreement, as the context may require.

Securities-Related Derivatives

Sec. 3B. (a) Any agreement, contract, or transaction (or class thereof) that is exempted by the Commodity Futures Trading Commission pursuant to section 4(c)(1) of the Commodity Exchange Act with the condition that the Commission exercise concurrent jurisdiction over such agreement, contract, or transaction (or class thereof) shall be deemed a security for purposes of the securities laws.

(b) With respect to any agreement, contract, or transaction (or class thereof) that is exempted by the Commodity Futures Trading Commission pursuant to section 4(c)(1) of the Commodity Exchange Act with the condition that the Commission exercise concurrent jurisdiction over such agreement, contract, or transaction (or class thereof), references in the securities laws to the "purchase" or "sale" of a security shall be deemed to include the execution, termination (prior to its scheduled maturity date), assignment, exchange, or similar transfer or conveyance of, or extinguishing of rights or obligations under such agreement, contract, or transaction, as the context may require.

Clearing for Security-Based Swaps

[*This section shall take effect on the later of 360 days after July 21, 2010, or, to the extent a provision requires a rulemaking, not less than 60 days after publication of the final rule or regulation.*]

Sec. 3C. (a) *In General.*

(1) *Standard for Clearing.* It shall be unlawful for any person to engage in a security-based swap unless that person submits such security-based swap for clearing to a clearing agency that is registered under this Act or a clearing agency that is exempt from registration under this Act if the security-based swap is required to be cleared.

(2) *Open Access.* The rules of a clearing agency described in paragraph (1) shall—

(A) prescribe that all security-based swaps submitted to the clearing agency with the same terms and conditions are economically equivalent within the clearing agency and may be offset with each other within the clearing agency; and

(B) provide for non-discriminatory clearing of a security-based swap executed bilaterally or on or through the rules of an unaffiliated national securities exchange or security-based swap execution facility.

(b) *Commission Review.*

(1) *Commission-Initiated Review.*

(A) The Commission on an ongoing basis shall review each security-based swap, or any group, category, type, or class of security-based swaps to make a determination that such security-based swap, or group, category, type, or class of security-based swaps should be required to be cleared.

(B) The Commission shall provide at least a 30 day public comment period regarding any determination under subparagraph (A).

(2) *Swap Submissions.*

(A) A clearing agency shall submit to the Commission each security-based swap, or any group, category, type, or class of security-based swaps that it plans to accept for clearing and provide notice to its members (in a manner to be determined by the Commission) of such submission.

(B) Any security-based swap or group, category, type, or class of security-based swaps listed for clearing by a clearing agency as of the date of enactment of this subsection shall be considered submitted to the Commission.

(C) The Commission shall—

(i) make available to the public any submission received under subparagraphs (A) and (B);

(ii) review each submission made under subparagraphs (A) and (B), and determine whether the security-based swap, or group, category, type, or class of security-based swaps, described in the submission is required to be cleared; and

(iii) provide at least a 30–day public comment period regarding its determination whether the clearing requirement under subsection (a)(1) shall apply to the submission.

(3) *Deadline.* The Commission shall make its determination under paragraph (2)(C) not later than 90 days after receiving a submission made under paragraphs (2)(A) and (2)(B), unless the submitting clearing agency agrees to an extension for the time limitation established under this paragraph.

(4) *Determination.*

(A) In reviewing a submission made under paragraph (2), the Commission shall review whether the submission is consistent with section 17A.

(B) In reviewing a security-based swap, group of security-based swaps or class of security-based swaps pursuant to paragraph (1) or a submission made under paragraph (2), the Commission shall take into account the following factors:

(i) The existence of significant outstanding notional exposures, trading liquidity and adequate pricing data.

(ii) The availability of rule framework, capacity, operational expertise and resources, and credit support infrastructure to clear the contract on terms that are consistent with the material terms and trading conventions on which the contract is then traded.

(iii) The effect on the mitigation of systemic risk, taking into account the size of the market for such contract and the resources of the clearing agency available to clear the contract.

(iv) The effect on competition, including appropriate fees and charges applied to clearing.

(v) The existence of reasonable legal certainty in the event of the insolvency of the relevant clearing agency or 1 or more of its clearing members with regard to the treatment of customer and security-based swap counterparty positions, funds, and property.

(C) In making a determination under subsection (b)(1) or paragraph (2)(C) that the clearing requirement shall apply, the Commission may require such terms and conditions to the requirement as the Commission determines to be appropriate.

(5) *Rules.* Not later than 1 year after the date of the enactment of this section, the Commission shall adopt rules for a clearing agency's submission for review, pursuant to this subsection, of a security-based swap, or a group, category, type, or class of security-based swaps, that it seeks to accept for clearing. Nothing in this paragraph limits the Commission from making a determination under paragraph (2)(C) for security-based swaps described in paragraph (2)(B).

(c) *Stay of Clearing Requirement.*

(1) *In General.* After making a determination pursuant to subsection (b)(2), the Commission, on application of a counterparty to a security-based swap or on its own initiative, may stay the clearing requirement of subsection (a)(1) until the Commission completes a review of the terms of the security-based swap (or the group, category, type, or class of security-based swaps) and the clearing arrangement.

(2) *Deadline.* The Commission shall complete a review undertaken pursuant to paragraph (1) not later than 90 days after issuance of the stay, unless the clearing agency that clears the security-based swap, or group, category, type, or class of security-based swaps, agrees to an extension of the time limitation established under this paragraph.

(3) *Determination.* Upon completion of the review undertaken pursuant to paragraph (1), the Commission may—

(A) determine, unconditionally or subject to such terms and conditions as the Commission determines to be appropriate, that the security-based swap, or group, category, type, or class of security-based swaps, must be cleared pursuant to this subsection if it finds that such clearing is consistent with subsection (b)(4); or

(B) determine that the clearing requirement of subsection (a)(1) shall not apply to the security-based swap, or group, category, type, or class of security-based swaps.

(4) *Rules.* Not later than 1 year after the date of the enactment of this section, the Commission shall adopt rules for reviewing, pursuant to this subsection, a clearing agency's clearing of a security-based swap, or a group, category, type, or class of security-based swaps, that it has accepted for clearing.

(d) *Prevention of Evasion.*

(1) *In General.* The Commission shall prescribe rules under this section (and issue interpretations of rules prescribed under this section), as determined by the Commission to be necessary to prevent evasions of the mandatory clearing requirements under this Act.

(2) *Duty of Commission to Investigate and Take Certain Actions.* To the extent the Commission finds that a particular security-based swap or any group, category, type, or class of security-based swaps that would otherwise be subject to mandatory clearing but no clearing agency has listed the security-based swap or the group, category, type, or class of security-based swaps for clearing, the Commission shall—

(A) investigate the relevant facts and circumstances;

(B) within 30 days issue a public report containing the results of the investigation; and

(C) take such actions as the Commission determines to be necessary and in the public interest, which may include requiring the retaining of adequate margin or capital by parties to the security-based swap or the group, category, type, or class of security-based swaps.

(3) *Effect on Authority.* Nothing in this subsection—

(A) authorizes the Commission to adopt rules requiring a clearing agency to list for clearing a security-based swap or any group, category, type, or class of security-based swaps if the clearing of the security-based swap or the group, category, type, or class of security-based swaps would threaten the financial integrity of the clearing agency; and

(B) affects the authority of the Commission to enforce the open access provisions of subsection (a)(2) with respect to a security-based swap or the group, category, type, or class of security-based swaps that is listed for clearing by a clearing agency.

(e) *Reporting Transition Rules.* Rules adopted by the Commission under this section shall provide for the reporting of data, as follows:

(1) Security-based swaps entered into before the date of the enactment of this section shall be reported to a registered security-based swap data repository or the Commission no later than 180 days after the effective date of this section.

(2) Security-based swaps entered into on or after such date of enactment shall be reported to a registered security-based swap data repository or the Commission no later than the later of—

(A) 90 days after such effective date; or

(B) such other time after entering into the security-based swap as the Commission may prescribe by rule or regulation.

(f) *Clearing Transition Rules.*

(1) Security-based swaps entered into before the date of the enactment of this section are exempt from the clearing requirements of this subsection if reported pursuant to subsection (e)(1).

(2) Security-based swaps entered into before application of the clearing requirement pursuant to this section are exempt from the clearing requirements of this section if reported pursuant to subsection (e)(2).

(g) *Exceptions.*

(1) *In General.* The requirements of subsection (a)(1) shall not apply to a security-based swap if 1 of the counterparties to the security-based swap—

(A) is not a financial entity;

(B) is using security-based swaps to hedge or mitigate commercial risk; and

(C) notifies the Commission, in a manner set forth by the Commission, how it generally meets its financial obligations associated with entering into non–cleared security-based swaps.

(2) *Option to Clear.* The application of the clearing exception in paragraph (1) is solely at the discretion of the counterparty to the security–based swap that meets the conditions of subparagraphs (A) through (C) of paragraph (1).

(3) *Financial Entity Definition.*

(A) *In General.* For the purposes of this subsection, the term financial entity means—

(i) a swap dealer;

(ii) a security-based swap dealer;

(iii) a major swap participant;

(iv) a major security-based swap participant;

(v) a commodity pool as defined in section 1a(10) of the Commodity Exchange Act;

(vi) a private fund as defined in section 202(a) of the Investment Advisers Act of 1940;

(vii) an employee benefit plan as defined in paragraphs (3) and (32) of section 3 of the Employee Retirement Income Security Act of 1974;

(viii) a person predominantly engaged in activities that are in the business of banking or financial in nature, as defined in section 4(k) of the Bank Holding Company Act of 1956.

(B) *Exclusion.* The Commission shall consider whether to exempt small banks, savings associations, farm credit system institutions, and credit unions, including—

(i) depository institutions with total assets of $10,000,000,000 or less;

(ii) farm credit system institutions with total assets of $10,000,000,000 or less; or

(iii) credit unions with total assets of $10,000,000,000 or less.

(4) *Treatment of Affiliates.*

(A) *In General.* An affiliate of a person that qualifies for an exception under this subsection (including affiliate entities predominantly engaged in providing financing for the purchase of the merchandise or manufactured goods of the person) may qualify for the exception only if the affiliate—

(i) enters into the security-based swap to hedge or mitigate the commercial risk of the person or other affiliate of the person that is not a financial entity, and the commercial risk that the affiliate is hedging or mitigating has been transferred to the affiliate;

(ii) is directly and wholly-owned by another affiliate qualified for the exception under this paragraph or an entity that is not a financial entity;

(iii) is not indirectly majority-owned by a financial entity;

(iv) is not ultimately owned by a parent company that is a financial entity; and

(v) does not provide any services, financial or otherwise, to any affiliate that is a nonbank financial company supervised by the Board of Governors (as defined under section 102 of the Financial Stability Act of 2010).

(B) *Limitation on Qualifying Affiliates.* The exception in subparagraph (A) shall not apply if the affiliate is—

(i) a swap dealer;

(ii) a security-based swap dealer;

(iii) a major swap participant;

(iv) a major security-based swap participant;

(v) a commodity pool;

(vi) a bank holding company;

(vii) a private fund, as defined in section 202(a) of the Investment Advisers Act of 1940;

(viii) an employee benefit plan or government plan, as defined in paragraphs (3) and (32) of section 3 of the Employee Retirement Income Security Act of 1974;

(ix) an insured depository institution;

(x) a farm credit system institution;

(xi) a credit union;

(xii) a nonbank financial company supervised by the Board of Governors (as defined under section 102 of the Financial Stability Act of 2010); or

(xiii) an entity engaged in the business of insurance and subject to capital requirements established by an insurance governmental authority of a State, a territory of the United States, the District of Columbia, a country other than the United States, or a political subdivision of a country other than the United States that is engaged in the supervision of insurance companies under insurance law.

(C) *Limitation on Affiliates' Affiliates.* Unless the Commission determines, by order, rule, or regulation, that it is in the public interest, the exception in subparagraph (A) shall not apply with respect to an affiliate if such affiliate is itself affiliated with—

(i) a major security-based swap participant;

(ii) a security-based swap dealer;

(iii) a major swap participant; or

(iv) a swap dealer.

(D) *Conditions on transactions.* With respect to an affiliate that qualifies for the exception in subparagraph (A)—

(i) such affiliate may not enter into any security-based swap other than for the purpose of hedging or mitigating commercial risk; and

(ii) neither such affiliate nor any person affiliated with such affiliate that is not a financial entity may enter into a security-based swap with or on behalf of any affiliate that is a financial entity or otherwise assume, net, combine, or consolidate the risk of security-based swaps entered into by any such financial entity, except one that is an affiliate that qualifies for the exception under subparagraph (A).

(E) *Transition Rule for Affiliates.* An affiliate, subsidiary, or a wholly owned entity of a person that qualifies for an exception under subparagraph (A) and is predominantly engaged in providing financing for the purchase or lease of merchandise or manufactured goods of the person shall be exempt from the margin requirement described in section 15F(e) and the clearing requirement described in subsection (a) with regard to security-based swaps entered into to mitigate the risk of the financing activities for not less than a 2-year period beginning on the date of enactment of this subparagraph [July 21, 2010].

(F) *Risk Management Program.* Any security-based swap entered into by an affiliate that qualifies for the exception in subparagraph (A) shall be subject to a centralized risk management program of the affiliate, which is reasonably designed both to monitor and manage the risks associated with the security-based swap and to identify each of the affiliates on whose behalf a security-based swap was entered into.

(5) *Election of Counterparty.*

(A) *Security-Based Swaps Required to be Cleared.* With respect to any security-based swap that is subject to the mandatory clearing requirement under subsection (a) and entered into by a security-based swap dealer or a major security-based swap participant with a counterparty that is not a swap dealer, major swap participant, security-based swap dealer, or major security-based swap participant, the counterparty shall have the sole right to select the clearing agency at which the security-based swap will be cleared.

(B) *Security-Based Swaps Not Required to be Cleared.* With respect to any security-based swap that is not subject to the mandatory clearing requirement under subsection (a) and entered into by a security-based swap dealer or a major security-based swap participant with a counterparty that is not a swap dealer, major swap participant, security-based swap dealer, or major security-based swap participant, the counterparty—

(i) may elect to require clearing of the security-based swap; and

(ii) shall have the sole right to select the clearing agency at which the security-based swap will be cleared.

(6) *Abuse of Exception.* The Commission may prescribe such rules or issue interpretations of the rules as the Commission determines to be necessary to prevent abuse of the exceptions described in this subsection. The Commission may also request information from those persons claiming the clearing exception as necessary to prevent abuse of the exceptions described in this subsection.

(h) *Trade Execution.*

(1) *In General.* With respect to transactions involving security-based swaps subject to the clearing requirement of subsection (a)(1), counterparties shall—

(A) execute the transaction on an exchange; or

(B) execute the transaction on a security-based swap execution facility registered under section 3D or a security-based swap execution facility that is exempt from registration under section 3D(e).

(2) *Exception.* The requirements of subparagraphs (A) and (B) of paragraph (1) shall not apply if no exchange or security-based swap execution facility makes the security-based swap available to trade or for security-based swap transactions subject to the clearing exception under subsection (g).

(i) *Board Approval.* Exemptions from the requirements of this section to clear a security-based swap or execute a security-based swap through a national securities exchange or security-based swap execution facility shall be available to a counterparty that is an issuer of securities that are registered under section 12 or that is required to file reports pursuant to section 15(d), only if an appropriate committee of the issuer's board or governing body has reviewed and approved the issuer's decision to enter into security-based swaps that are subject to such exemptions.

(j) *Designation of Chief Compliance Officer.*

(1) *In General.* Each registered clearing agency shall designate an individual to serve as a chief compliance officer.

(2) *Duties.* The chief compliance officer shall—

(A) report directly to the board or to the senior officer of the clearing agency;

(B) in consultation with its board, a body performing a function similar thereto, or the senior officer of the registered clearing agency, resolve any conflicts of interest that may arise;

(C) be responsible for administering each policy and procedure that is required to be established pursuant to this section;

(D) ensure compliance with this title (including regulations issued under this title) relating to agreements, contracts, or transactions, including each rule prescribed by the Commission under this section;

(E) establish procedures for the remediation of noncompliance issues identified by the compliance officer through any—

(i) compliance office review;

(ii) look–back;

(iii) internal or external audit finding;

(iv) self–reported error; or

(v) validated complaint; and

(F) establish and follow appropriate procedures for the handling, management response, remediation, retesting, and closing of noncompliance issues.

(3) *Annual Reports.*

(A) *In General.* In accordance with rules prescribed by the Commission, the chief compliance officer shall annually prepare and sign a report that contains a description of—

(i) the compliance of the registered clearing agency or security-based swap execution facility of the compliance officer with respect to this title (including regulations under this title); and

(ii) each policy and procedure of the registered clearing agency of the compliance officer (including the code of ethics and conflict of interest policies of the registered clearing agency).

(B) *Requirements.* A compliance report under subparagraph (A) shall—

(i) accompany each appropriate financial report of the registered clearing agency that is required to be furnished to the Commission pursuant to this section; and

(ii) include a certification that, under penalty of law, the compliance report is accurate and complete.

Security-Based Swap Execution Facilities

[*This section shall take effect on the later of 360 days after July 21, 2010, or to the extent a provision requires a rulemaking, not less than 60 days after publication of the final rule or regulation.*]

Sec. 3D. (a) *Registration.*

(1) *In General.* No person may operate a facility for the trading or processing of security-based swaps, unless the facility is registered as a security-based swap execution facility or as a national securities exchange under this section.

(2) *Dual Registration.* Any person that is registered as a security-based swap execution facility under this section shall register with the Commission regardless of whether the person also is registered with the Commodity Futures Trading Commission as a swap execution facility.

(b) *Trading and Trade Processing.* A security-based swap execution facility that is registered under subsection (a) may—

(1) make available for trading any security-based swap; and

(2) facilitate trade processing of any security–based swap.

(c) *Identification of Facility Used To Trade Security–Based Swaps by National Securities Exchanges.* A national securities exchange shall, to the extent that the exchange also operates a security-based swap execution facility and uses the same electronic trade execution system for listing and executing trades of security-based swaps on or through the exchange and the facility, identify whether electronic trading of such security-based swaps is taking place on or through the national securities exchange or the security-based swap execution facility.

(d) *Core Principles for Security–Based Swap Execution Facilities.*

(1) *Compliance with Core Principles.*

(A) *In General.* To be registered, and maintain registration, as a security-based swap execution facility, the security-based swap execution facility shall comply with—

(i) the core principles described in this subsection; and

(ii) any requirement that the Commission may impose by rule or regulation.

(B) *Reasonable Discretion of Security–Based Swap Execution Facility.* Unless otherwise determined by the Commission, by rule or regulation, a security-based swap execution facility described in subparagraph (A) shall have reasonable discretion in establishing the manner in which it complies with the core principles described in this subsection.

(2) *Compliance with Rules.* A security-based swap execution facility shall—

(A) establish and enforce compliance with any rule established by such security-based swap execution facility, including—

(i) the terms and conditions of the security-based swaps traded or processed on or through the facility; and

(ii) any limitation on access to the facility;

(B) establish and enforce trading, trade processing, and participation rules that will deter abuses and have the capacity to detect, investigate, and enforce those rules, including means—

(i) to provide market participants with impartial access to the market; and

(ii) to capture information that may be used in establishing whether rule violations have occurred; and

(C) establish rules governing the operation of the facility, including rules specifying trading procedures to be used in entering and executing orders traded or posted on the facility, including block trades.

(3) *Security-Based Swaps Not Readily Susceptible to Manipulation.* The security-based swap execution facility shall permit trading only in security-based swaps that are not readily susceptible to manipulation.

(4) *Monitoring of Trading and Trade Processing.* The security-based swap execution facility shall—

(A) establish and enforce rules or terms and conditions defining, or specifications detailing—

(i) trading procedures to be used in entering and executing orders traded on or through the facilities of the security-based swap execution facility; and

(ii) procedures for trade processing of security-based swaps on or through the facilities of the security-based swap execution facility; and

(B) monitor trading in security-based swaps to prevent manipulation, price distortion, and disruptions of the delivery or cash settlement process through surveillance, compliance, and disciplinary practices and procedures, including methods for conducting realtime monitoring of trading and comprehensive and accurate trade reconstructions.

(5) *Ability to Obtain Information.* The security-based swap execution facility shall—

(A) establish and enforce rules that will allow the facility to obtain any necessary information to perform any of the functions described in this subsection;

(B) provide the information to the Commission on request; and

(C) have the capacity to carry out such international information–sharing agreements as the Commission may require.

(6) *Financial Integrity of Transactions.* The security-based swap execution facility shall establish and enforce rules and procedures for ensuring the financial integrity of security-based swaps entered on or through the facilities of the security-based swap execution facility, including the clearance and settlement of security-based swaps pursuant to section 3C(a)(1).

(7) *Emergency Authority.* The security-based swap execution facility shall adopt rules to provide for the exercise of emergency authority, in

consultation or cooperation with the Commission, as is necessary and appropriate, including the authority to liquidate or transfer open positions in any security-based swap or to suspend or curtail trading in a security-based swap.

(8) *Timely Publication of Trading Information.*

(A) *In General.* The security-based swap execution facility shall make public timely information on price, trading volume, and other trading data on security-based swaps to the extent prescribed by the Commission.

(B) *Capacity of Security–Based Swap Execution Facility.* The security-based swap execution facility shall be required to have the capacity to electronically capture and transmit and disseminate trade information with respect to transactions executed on or through the facility.

(9) *Recordkeeping and Reporting.*

(A) *In General.* A security-based swap execution facility shall—

(i) maintain records of all activities relating to the business of the facility, including a complete audit trail, in a form and manner acceptable to the Commission for a period of 5 years; and

(ii) report to the Commission, in a form and manner acceptable to the Commission, such information as the Commission determines to be necessary or appropriate for the Commission to perform the duties of the Commission under this title.

(B) *Requirements.* The Commission shall adopt data collection and reporting requirements for security-based swap execution facilities that are comparable to corresponding requirements for clearing agencies and security-based swap data repositories.

(10) *Antitrust Considerations.* Unless necessary or appropriate to achieve the purposes of this title, the security-based swap execution facility shall not—

(A) adopt any rules or taking any actions that result in any unreasonable restraint of trade; or

(B) impose any material anticompetitive burden on trading or clearing.

(11) *Conflicts of Interest.* The security-based swap execution facility shall—

(A) establish and enforce rules to minimize conflicts of interest in its decision–making process; and

(B) establish a process for resolving the conflicts of interest.

(12) *Financial Resources.*

(A) *In General.* The security-based swap execution facility shall have adequate financial, operational, and managerial resources to discharge each responsibility of the security-based swap execution facility, as determined by the Commission.

(B) *Determination of Resource Adequacy.* The financial resources of a security-based swap execution facility shall be considered to be adequate if the value of the financial resources—

(i) enables the organization to meet its financial obligations to its members and participants notwithstanding a default by the member or participant creating the largest financial exposure for that organization in extreme but plausible market conditions; and

(ii) exceeds the total amount that would enable the security-based swap execution facility to cover the operating costs of the security-based swap execution facility for a 1–year period, as calculated on a rolling basis.

(13) *System Safeguards.* The security-based swap execution facility shall—

(A) establish and maintain a program of risk analysis and oversight to identify and minimize sources of operational risk, through the development of appropriate controls and procedures, and automated systems, that—

(i) are reliable and secure; and

(ii) have adequate scalable capacity;

(B) establish and maintain emergency procedures, backup facilities, and a plan for disaster recovery that allow for—

(i) the timely recovery and resumption of operations; and

(ii) the fulfillment of the responsibilities and obligations of the security-based swap execution facility; and

(C) periodically conduct tests to verify that the backup resources of the security-based swap execution facility are sufficient to ensure continued—

(i) order processing and trade matching;

(ii) price reporting;

(iii) market surveillance; and

(iv) maintenance of a comprehensive and accurate audit trail.

(14) *Designation of Chief Compliance Officer.*

(A) *In General.* Each security-based swap execution facility shall designate an individual to serve as a chief compliance officer.

(B) *Duties.* The chief compliance officer shall—

(i) report directly to the board or to the senior officer of the facility;

(ii) review compliance with the core principles in this subsection;

(iii) in consultation with the board of the facility, a body performing a function similar to that of a board, or the senior officer of the facility, resolve any conflicts of interest that may arise;

(iv) be responsible for establishing and administering the policies and procedures required to be established pursuant to this section;

(v) ensure compliance with this title and the rules and regulations issued under this title, including rules prescribed by the Commission pursuant to this section;

(vi) establish procedures for the remediation of noncompliance issues found during—

(I) compliance office reviews;

(II) look backs;

(III) internal or external audit findings;

(IV) self–reported errors; or

(V) through validated complaints; and

(vii) establish and follow appropriate procedures for the handling, management response, remediation, retesting, and closing of noncompliance issues.

(C) *Annual Reports.*

(i) *In General.* In accordance with rules prescribed by the Commission, the chief compliance officer shall annually prepare and sign a report that contains a description of—

(I) the compliance of the security-based swap execution facility with this title; and

(II) the policies and procedures, including the code of ethics and conflict of interest policies, of the security-based security-based swap execution facility.

(ii) *Requirements.* The chief compliance officer shall—

(I) submit each report described in clause (i) with the appropriate financial report of the security-based swap execution facility that is required to be submitted to the Commission pursuant to this section; and

(II) include in the report a certification that, under penalty of law, the report is accurate and complete.

(e) *Exemptions.* The Commission may exempt, conditionally or unconditionally, a security-based swap execution facility from registration under this section if the Commission finds that the facility is subject to comparable, comprehensive supervision and regulation on a consolidated basis by the Commodity Futures Trading Commission.

(f) *Rules.* The Commission shall prescribe rules governing the regulation of security-based swap execution facilities under this section.

Segregation of Assets Held as Collateral in Security–Based Swap Transactions

[*This section shall take effect on the later of 360 after July 21, 2010, or to the extent a provision requires a rulemaking not less than 60 days after the publication of the final rule or regulation.*]

Sec. 3E. (a) *Registration Requirement.* It shall be unlawful for any person to accept any money, securities, or property (or to extend any credit in lieu of money, securities, or property) from, for, or on behalf of a security-based swaps customer to margin, guarantee, or secure a security-based swap cleared by or through a clearing agency (including money, securities, or property accruing to the customer as the result of such a security-based swap), unless the person shall have registered under this title with the Commission as a broker, dealer, or security-based swap dealer, and the registration shall not have expired nor been suspended nor revoked.

(b) *Cleared Security–Based Swaps.*

(1) *Segregation Required.* A broker, dealer, or security-based swap dealer shall treat and deal with all money, securities, and property of any security-based swaps customer received to margin, guarantee, or secure a security-based swap cleared by or though a clearing agency (including

money, securities, or property accruing to the security-based swaps customer as the result of such a security-based swap) as belonging to the security-based swaps customer.

(2) *Commingling Prohibited.* Money, securities, and property of a security-based swaps customer described in paragraph (1) shall be separately accounted for and shall not be commingled with the funds of the broker, dealer, or security-based swap dealer or be used to margin, secure, or guarantee any trades or contracts of any security-based swaps customer or person other than the person for whom the same are held.

(c) *Exceptions.*

(1) *Use of Funds.*

(A) *In General.* Notwithstanding subsection (b), money, securities, and property of a security-based swaps customer of a broker, dealer, or security-based swap dealer described in subsection (b) may, for convenience, be commingled and deposited in the same 1 or more accounts with any bank or trust company or with a clearing agency.

(B) *Withdrawal.* Notwithstanding subsection (b), such share of the money, securities, and property described in subparagraph (A) as in the normal course of business shall be necessary to margin, guarantee, secure, transfer, adjust, or settle a cleared security-based swap with a clearing agency, or with any member of the clearing agency, may be withdrawn and applied to such purposes, including the payment of commissions, brokerage, interest, taxes, storage, and other charges, lawfully accruing in connection with the cleared security-based swap.

(2) *Commission Action.* Notwithstanding subsection (b), in accordance with such terms and conditions as the Commission may prescribe by rule, regulation, or order, any money, securities, or property of the security-based swaps customer of a broker, dealer, or security-based swap dealer described in subsection (b) may be commingled and deposited as provided in this section with any other money, securities, or property received by the broker, dealer, or security-based swap dealer and required by the Commission to be separately accounted for and treated and dealt with as belonging to the security-based swaps customer of the broker, dealer, or security-based swap dealer.

(d) *Permitted Investments.* Money described in subsection (b) may be invested in obligations of the United States, in general obligations of any State or of any political subdivision of a State, and in obligations fully guaranteed as to principal and interest by the United States, or in any other investment that the Commission may by rule or regulation prescribe, and such investments shall be made in accordance with such rules and regulations and subject to such conditions as the Commission may prescribe.

(e) *Prohibition.* It shall be unlawful for any person, including any clearing agency and any depository institution, that has received any money, securities, or property for deposit in a separate account or accounts as provided in subsection (b) to hold, dispose of, or use any such money, securities, or property as belonging to the depositing broker, dealer, or security-based swap dealer or any person other than the swaps customer of the broker, dealer, or security-based swap dealer.

(f) *Segregation Requirements for Uncleared Security–Based Swaps.*

(1) *Segregation of Assets Held as Collateral in Uncleared Security–Based Swap Transactions.*

(A) *Notification.* A security-based swap dealer or major security-based swap participant shall be required to notify the counterparty of the security-based swap dealer or major security-based swap participant at the beginning of a security-based swap transaction that the counterparty has the right to require segregation of the funds of other property supplied to margin, guarantee, or secure the obligations of the counterparty.

(B) *Segregation and Maintenance of Funds.* At the request of a counterparty to a security-based swap that provides funds or other property to a security-based swap dealer or major security-based swap participant to margin, guarantee, or secure the obligations of the counterparty, the security-based swap dealer or major security-based swap participant shall—

(i) segregate the funds or other property for the benefit of the counterparty; and

(ii) in accordance with such rules and regulations as the Commission may promulgate, maintain the funds or other property in a segregated account separate from the assets and other interests of the security-based swap dealer or major security-based swap participant.

(2) *Applicability.* The requirements described in paragraph (1) shall—

(A) apply only to a security-based swap between a counterparty and a security-based swap dealer or major security-based swap participant that is not submitted for clearing to a clearing agency; and

(B)(i) not apply to variation margin payments; or

(ii) not preclude any commercial arrangement regarding—

(I) the investment of segregated funds or other property that may only be invested in such investments as the Commission may permit by rule or regulation; and

(II) the related allocation of gains and losses resulting from any investment of the segregated funds or other property.

(3) *Use of Independent Third–Party Custodians.* The segregated account described in paragraph (1) shall be—

(A) carried by an independent third–party custodian; and

(B) designated as a segregated account for and on behalf of the counterparty.

(4) *Reporting Requirement.* If the counterparty does not choose to require segregation of the funds or other property supplied to margin, guarantee, or secure the obligations of the counterparty, the security-based swap dealer or major security-based swap participant shall report to the counterparty of the security-based swap dealer or major security-based swap participant on a quarterly basis that the back office procedures of the security-based swap dealer or major security-based swap participant relating to margin and collateral requirements are in compliance with the agreement of the counterparties.

(g) *Bankruptcy.* A security-based swap, as defined in section 3(a)(68) shall be considered to be a security as such term is used in section 101(53A)(B) and subchapter III of title 11, United States Code. An account that holds a security-based swap, other than a portfolio margining account referred to in section 15(c)(3)(C) shall be considered to be a securities account, as that term is defined in section 741 of title 11, United States Code. The definitions of the terms "purchase" and "sale" in section 3(a)(13) and (14) shall be applied to the terms "purchase" and "sale", as used in section 741 of title 11, United States Code. The term "customer", as defined in section 741 of title 11, United States Code, excludes any person, to the extent that such person has a claim based on any open repurchase agreement, open reverse repurchase agreement, stock borrowed agreement, non–cleared option, or non–cleared security-based swap except to the extent of any margin delivered to or by the customer with respect to which there is a customer protection requirement under section 15(c)(3) or a segregation requirement.

Securities and Exchange Commission

Sec. 4. (a) *Establishment; Composition; Limitations on Commissioners; Terms of Office.* There is hereby established a Securities and Exchange Commission (hereinafter referred to as the "Commission") to be composed of five commissioners to be appointed by the President by and with the advice and consent of the Senate. Not more than three of such commissioners shall be members of the same political party, and in making appointments members of different political parties shall be appointed alternately as nearly as may be practicable. No commissioner shall engage in any other business, vocation, or employment than that of serving as commissioner, nor shall any commissioner participate, directly or indirectly, in any stock-market operations or transactions of a character subject to regulation by the Commission pursuant to this title. Each commissioner shall hold office for a term of five years and until his successor is appointed and has qualified, except that he shall not so continue to serve beyond the expiration of the next session of Congress subsequent to the expiration of said fixed term of office, and except (1) any commissioner appointed to fill a vacancy occurring prior to the expiration of the term for which his predecessor was appointed shall be appointed for the remainder of such term, and (2) the terms of office of the commissioners first taking office after the enactment of this title shall expire as designated by the President at the time of nomination, one at the end of one year, one at the end of two years, one at the end of three years, one at the end of four years, and one at the end of five years, after the enactment of this title.

(b) *Appointment and Compensation of Staff and Leasing Authority.*

(1) *Appointment and Compensation.* The Commission shall appoint and compensate officers, attorneys, economists, examiners, and other employees in accordance with section 4802 of title 5, United States Code.

(2) *Reporting of Information.* In establishing and adjusting schedules of compensation and ben-

efits for officers, attorneys, economists, examiners, and other employees of the Commission under applicable provisions of law, the Commission shall inform the heads of the agencies referred to under section 1206 of the Financial Institutions Reform, Recovery, and Enforcement Act of 1989 and Congress of such compensation and benefits and shall seek to maintain comparability with such agencies regarding compensation and benefits.

(3) *Leasing Authority.* Notwithstanding any other provision of law, the Commission is authorized to enter directly into leases for real property for office, meeting, storage, and such other space as is necessary to carry out its functions, and shall be exempt from any General Services Administration space management regulations or directives.

(c) *Acceptance of Travel Support for Commission Activities From Non–Federal Sources; Regulations.* Notwithstanding any other provision of law, in accordance with regulations which the Commission shall prescribe to prevent conflicts of interest, the Commission may accept payment and reimbursement, in cash or in kind, from non-Federal agencies, organizations, and individuals for travel, subsistence, and other necessary expenses incurred by Commission members and employees in attending meetings and conferences concerning the functions or activities of the Commission. Any payment or reimbursement accepted shall be credited to the appropriated funds of the Commission. The amount of travel, subsistence, and other necessary expenses for members and employees paid or reimbursed under this subsection may exceed per diem amounts established in official travel regulations, but the Commission may include in its regulations under this subsection a limitation on such amounts.

(d) *Acceptance of Relocation Expenses from Former Employers by Professional Fellows Program Participants.* Notwithstanding any other provision of law, former employers of participants in the Commission's professional fellows programs may pay such participants their actual expenses for relocation to Washington, District of Columbia, to facilitate their participation in such programs, and program participants may accept such payments.

(e) *Fee Payments.* Notwithstanding any other provision of law, whenever any fee is required to be paid to the Commission pursuant to any provision of the securities laws or any other law, the Commission may provide by rule that such fee shall be paid in a manner other than in cash and the Commission may also specify the time that such fee shall be determined and paid relative to the filing of any statement or document with the Commission.

(f) *Reimbursement of Expenses for Assisting Foreign Securities Authorities.* Notwithstanding any other provision of law, the Commission may accept payment and reimbursement, in cash or in kind, from a foreign securities authority, or made on behalf of such authority, for necessary expenses incurred by the Commission, its members, and employees in carrying out any investigation pursuant to section 21(a)(2) of this title or in providing any other assistance to a foreign securities authority. Any payment or reimbursement accepted shall be considered a reimbursement to the appropriated funds of the Commission.

(g) *Office of the Investor Advocate.*

(1) *Office Established.* There is established within the Commission the Office of the Investor Advocate (in this subsection referred to as the "Office").

(2) *Investor Advocate.*

(A) *In General.* The head of the Office shall be the Investor Advocate, who shall—

(i) report directly to the Chairman; and

(ii) be appointed by the Chairman, in consultation with the Commission, from among individuals having experience in advocating for the interests of investors in securities and investor protection issues, from the perspective of investors.

(B) *Compensation.* The annual rate of pay for the Investor Advocate shall be equal to the highest rate of annual pay for other senior executives who report to the Chairman of the Commission.

(C) *Limitation on Service.* An individual who serves as the Investor Advocate may not be employed by the Commission—

(i) during the 2–year period ending on the date of appointment as Investor Advocate; or

(ii) during the 5–year period beginning on the date on which the person ceases to serve as the Investor Advocate.

(3) *Staff of Office.* The Investor Advocate, after consultation with the Chairman of the Commission, may retain or employ independent counsel, research staff, and service staff, as the Investor Advocate deems necessary to carry out the functions, powers, and duties of the Office.

(4) *Functions of the Investor Advocate.* The Investor Advocate shall—

(A) assist retail investors in resolving significant problems such investors may have with the Commission or with self–regulatory organizations;

(B) identify areas in which investors would benefit from changes in the regulations of the Commission or the rules of self–regulatory organizations;

(C) identify problems that investors have with financial service providers and investment products;

(D) analyze the potential impact on investors of—

(i) proposed regulations of the Commission; and

(ii) proposed rules of self–regulatory organizations registered under this title; and

(E) to the extent practicable, propose to the Commission changes in the regulations or orders of the Commission and to Congress any legislative, administrative, or personnel changes that may be appropriate to mitigate problems identified under this paragraph and to promote the interests of investors.

(5) *Access to Documents.* The Commission shall ensure that the Investor Advocate has full access to the documents of the Commission and any self–regulatory organization, as necessary to carry out the functions of the Office.

(6) *Annual Reports.*

(A) *Report on Objectives.*

(i) *In General.* Not later than June 30 of each year after 2010, the Investor Advocate shall submit to the Committee on Banking, Housing, and Urban Affairs of the Senate and the Committee on Financial Services of the House of Representatives a report on the objectives of the Investor Advocate for the following fiscal year.

(ii) *Contents.* Each report required under clause (i) shall contain full and substantive analysis and explanation.

(B) *Report on Activities.*

(i) *In General.* Not later than December 31 of each year after 2010, the Investor Advocate shall submit to the Committee on Banking, Housing, and Urban Affairs of the Senate and the Committee on Financial Services of the House of Representatives a report on the activities of the Investor Advocate during the immediately preceding fiscal year.

(ii) *Contents.* Each report required under clause (i) shall include—

(I) appropriate statistical information and full and substantive analysis;

(II) information on steps that the Investor Advocate has taken during the reporting period to improve investor services and the responsiveness of the Commission and self–regulatory organizations to investor concerns;

(III) a summary of the most serious problems encountered by investors during the reporting period;

(IV) an inventory of the items described in subclause (III) that includes—

(aa) identification of any action taken by the Commission or the self–regulatory organization and the result of such action;

(bb) the length of time that each item has remained on such inventory; and

(cc) for items on which no action has been taken, the reasons for inaction, and an identification of any official who is responsible for such action;

(V) recommendations for such administrative and legislative actions as may be appropriate to resolve problems encountered by investors; and

(VI) any other information, as determined appropriate by the Investor Advocate.

(iii) *Independence.* Each report required under this paragraph shall be provided directly to the Committees listed in clause (i) without any prior review or comment from the Commission, any commissioner, any other officer or employee of the Commission, or the Office of Management and Budget.

(iv) *Confidentiality.* No report required under clause (i) may contain confidential information.

(7) *Regulations.* The Commission shall, by regulation, establish procedures requiring a formal response to all recommendations submitted to the

Commission by the Investor Advocate, not later than 3 months after the date of such submission.

(8) *Ombudsman.*

(A) *Appointment.* Not later than 180 days after the date on which the first Investor Advocate is appointed under paragraph (2)(A)(i), the Investor Advocate shall appoint an Ombudsman, who shall report directly to the Investor Advocate.

(B) *Duties.* The Ombudsman appointed under subparagraph (A) shall—

(i) act as a liaison between the Commission and any retail investor in resolving problems that retail investors may have with the Commission or with self-regulatory organizations;

(ii) review and make recommendations regarding policies and procedures to encourage persons to present questions to the Investor Advocate regarding compliance with the securities laws; and

(iii) establish safeguards to maintain the confidentiality of communications between the persons described in clause (ii) and the Ombudsman.

(C) *Limitation.* In carrying out the duties of the Ombudsman under subparagraph (B), the Ombudsman shall utilize personnel of the Commission to the extent practicable. Nothing in this paragraph shall be construed as replacing, altering, or diminishing the activities of any ombudsman or similar office of any other agency.

(D) *Report.* The Ombudsman shall submit a semi-annual report to the Investor Advocate that describes the activities and evaluates the effectiveness of the Ombudsman during the preceding year. The Investor Advocate shall include the reports required under this section in the reports required to be submitted by the Inspector Advocate under paragraph (6).

(h) *Examiners.*

(1) *Division of Trading and Markets.* The Division of Trading and Markets of the Commission, or any successor organizational unit, shall have a staff of examiners who shall—

(A) perform compliance inspections and examinations of entities under the jurisdiction of that Division; and

(B) report to the Director of that Division.

(2) *Division of Investment Management.* The Division of Investment Management of the Commission, or any successor organizational unit, shall have a staff of examiners who shall—

(A) perform compliance inspections and examinations of entities under the jurisdiction of that Division; and

(B) report to the Director of that Division.

(i) *Securities and Exchange Commission Reserve Fund.*

(1) *Reserve Fund Established.* There is established in the Treasury of the United States a separate fund, to be known as the "Securities and Exchange Commission Reserve Fund" (referred to in this subsection as the "Reserve Fund").

(2) *Reserve Fund Amounts.*

(A) *In General.* Except as provided in subparagraph (B), any registration fees collected by the Commission under section 6(b) of the Securities Act of 1933 or section 24(f) of the Investment Company Act of 1940 shall be deposited into the Reserve Fund.

(B) *Limitations.* For any 1 fiscal year—

(i) the amount deposited in the Fund may not exceed $50,000,000; and

(ii) the balance in the Fund may not exceed $100,000,000.

(C) *Excess Fees.* Any amounts in excess of the limitations described in subparagraph (B) that the Commission collects from registration fees under section 6(b) of the Securities Act of 1933 or section 24(f) of the Investment Company Act of 1940 shall be deposited in the General Fund of the Treasury of the United States and shall not be available for obligation by the Commission.

(3) *Use of Amounts in Reserve Fund.* The Commission may obligate amounts in the Reserve Fund, not to exceed a total of $100,000,000 in any 1 fiscal year, as the Commission determines is necessary to carry out the functions of the Commission. Any amounts in the reserve fund shall remain available until expended. Not later than 10 days after the date on which the Commission obligates amounts under this paragraph, the Commission shall notify Congress of the date, amount, and purpose of the obligation.

(4) *Rule of Construction.* Amounts collected and deposited in the Reserve Fund shall not be con-

strued to be Government funds or appropriated monies and shall not be subject to apportionment for the purpose of chapter 15 of title 31, United States Code, or under any other authority.

(j) *Office of the Advocate for Small Business Capital Formation.*

(1) *Office Established.* There is established within the Commission the Office of the Advocate for Small Business Capital Formation (hereafter in this subsection referred to as the "Office")—

(2) *Advocate for Small Business Capital Formation.*

(A) *In General.* The head of the Office shall be the Advocate for Small Business Capital Formation, who shall—

(i) report directly to the Commission; and

(ii) be appointed by the Commission, from among individuals having experience in advocating for the interests of small businesses and encouraging small business capital formation.

(B) *Compensation.* The annual rate of pay for the Advocate for Small Business Capital Formation shall be equal to the highest rate of annual pay for other senior executives who report directly to the Commission.

(C) *No Current Employee of the Commission.* An individual may not be appointed as the Advocate for Small Business Capital Formation if the individual is currently employed by the Commission.

(3) *Staff of Office.* The Advocate for Small Business Capital Formation, after consultation with the Commission, may retain or employ independent counsel, research staff, and service staff, as the Advocate for Small Business Capital Formation determines to be necessary to carry out the functions of the Office.

(4) *Functions of the Advocate for Small Business Capital Formation.* The Advocate for Small Business Capital Formation shall—

(A) assist small businesses and small business investors in resolving significant problems such businesses and investors may have with the Commission or with self-regulatory organizations;

(B) identify areas in which small businesses and small business investors would benefit from changes in the regulations of the Commission or the rules of self-regulatory organizations;

(C) identify problems that small businesses have with securing access to capital, including any unique challenges to minority-owned and women-owned small businesses;

(D) analyze the potential impact on small businesses and small business investors of—

(i) proposed regulations of the Commission that are likely to have a significant economic impact on small businesses and small business capital formation; and

(ii) proposed rules that are likely to have a significant economic impact on small businesses and small business capital formation of self-regulatory organizations registered under this title;

(E) conduct outreach to small businesses and small business investors, including through regional roundtables, in order to solicit views on relevant capital formation issues;

(F) to the extent practicable, propose to the Commission changes in the regulations or orders of the Commission and to Congress any legislative, administrative, or personnel changes that may be appropriate to mitigate problems identified under this paragraph and to promote the interests of small businesses and small business investors;

(G) consult with the Investor Advocate on proposed recommendations made under subparagraph (F); and

(H) advise the Investor Advocate on issues related to small businesses and small business investors.

(5) *Access to Documents.* The Commission shall ensure that the Advocate for Small Business Capital Formation has full access to the documents and information of the Commission and any self-regulatory organization, as necessary to carry out the functions of the Office.

(6) *Annual Report on Activities.*

(A) *In General.* Not later than December 31 of each year after 2015, the Advocate for Small Business Capital Formation shall submit to the Committee on Banking, Housing, and Urban Affairs of the Senate and the Committee on Financial Services of the House of Representatives a report on the activities of the Advocate for Small Business Capital Formation during the immediately preceding fiscal year.

(B) *Contents.* Each report required under subparagraph (A) shall include—

(i) appropriate statistical information and full and substantive analysis;

(ii) information on steps that the Advocate for Small Business Capital Formation has taken during the reporting period to improve small business services and the responsiveness of the Commission and self-regulatory organizations to small business and small business investor concerns;

(iii) a summary of the most serious issues encountered by small businesses and small business investors, including any unique issues encountered by minority-owned and women-owned small businesses and their investors, during the reporting period;

(iv) an inventory of the items summarized under clause (iii) (including items summarized under such clause for any prior reporting period on which no action has been taken or that have not been resolved to the satisfaction of the Advocate for Small Business Capital Formation as of the beginning of the reporting period covered by the report) that includes—

(I) identification of any action taken by the Commission or the self-regulatory organization and the result of such action;

(II) the length of time that each item has remained on such inventory; and

(III) for items on which no action has been taken, the reasons for inaction, and an identification of any official who is responsible for such action;

(v) recommendations for such changes to the regulations, guidance and orders of the Commission and such legislative actions as may be appropriate to resolve problems with the Commission and self-regulatory organizations encountered by small businesses and small business investors and to encourage small business capital formation; and

(vi) any other information, as determined appropriate by the Advocate for Small Business Capital Formation.

(C) *Confidentiality.* No report required by subparagraph (A) may contain confidential information.

(D) *Independence.* Each report required under subparagraph (A) shall be provided directly to the committees of Congress listed in such subparagraph without any prior review or comment from the Commission, any commissioner, any other officer or employee of the Commission, or the Office of Management and Budget.

(7) *Regulations.* The Commission shall establish procedures requiring a formal response to all recommendations submitted to the Commission by the Advocate for Small Business Capital Formation, not later than 3 months after the date of such submission.

(8) *Government-Business Forum on Small Business Capital Formation.* The Advocate for Small Business Capital Formation shall be responsible for planning, organizing, and executing the annual Government-Business Forum on Small Business Capital Formation described in section 503 of the Small Business Investment Incentive Act of 1980.

(9) *Rule of Construction.* Nothing in this subsection may be construed as replacing or reducing the responsibilities of the Investor Advocate with respect to small business investors.

Delegation of Functions by Commission

Sec. 4A. (a) *Authorization; Functions Delegable; Eligible Persons; Application of Other Laws.* In addition to its existing authority, the Securities and Exchange Commission shall have the authority to delegate, by published order or rule, any of its functions to a division of the Commission, an individual Commissioner, an administrative law judge, or an employee or employee board, including functions with respect to hearing, determining, ordering, certifying, reporting, or otherwise acting as to any work, business, or matter. Nothing in this section shall be deemed to supersede the provisions of section 556(b) of Title 5, United States Code, or to authorize the delegation of the function of rulemaking as defined in subchapter II of chapter 5 of Title 5, United States Code, with reference to general rules as distinguished from rules of particular applicability, or of the making of any rule pursuant to section 19(c) of this title.

(b) *Right of Review; Procedure.* With respect to the delegation of any of its functions, as provided in subsection (a) of this section, the Commission shall retain a discretionary right to review the action of any such division of the Commission, individual Commissioner, administrative law judge, employee, or employee board, upon its own initiative or upon petition of a party to or intervenor in such action, within such time and in such manner as the Commission by rule shall prescribe. The vote of one member of the Commission shall be sufficient to bring any such action before the Commission for review. A person or party shall be entitled to review by the Commission if he or it is adversely affected by action at a delegated level which (1) denies any request for action pursuant to section 8(a) or section 8(c) of the Securities Act of 1933 or the first sentence of section 12(d) of this title; (2) suspends trading in a security pursuant to section 12(k) of this title; or (3) is pursuant to any provision of this title in a case of adjudication, as defined in section 551 of Title 5, United States Code, not required by this title to be determined on the record after notice and opportunity for hearing (except to the extent there is involved a matter described in section 554(a)(1) through (6) of such Title 5).

(c) *Finality of Delegated Action.* If the right to exercise such review is declined, or if no such review is sought within the time stated in the rules promulgated by the Commission, then the action of any such division of the Commission, individual Commissioner, administrative law judge, employee, or employee board, shall, for all purposes, including appeal or review thereof, be deemed the action of the Commission.

Transfer of Functions with Respect to Assignment of Personnel to Chairman

Sec. 4B. In addition to the functions transferred by the provisions of Reorganization Plan Numbered 10 of 1950 (64 Stat. 1265), there are hereby transferred from the Commission to the Chairman of the Commission the functions of the Commission with respect to the assignment of Commission personnel, including Commissioners, to perform such functions as may have been delegated by the Commission to the Commission personnel, including Commissioners, pursuant to section 4A of this title.

Appearance and Practice Before the Commission

Sec. 4C. (a) *Authority to Censure.* The Commission may censure any person, or deny, temporarily or permanently, to any person the privilege of appearing or practicing before the Commission in any way, if that person is found by the Commission, after notice and opportunity for hearing in the matter—

(1) not to possess the requisite qualifications to represent others;

(2) to be lacking in character or integrity, or to have engaged in unethical or improper professional conduct; or

(3) to have willfully violated, or willfully aided and abetted the violation of, any provision of the securities laws or the rules and regulations issued thereunder.

(b) *Definition.* With respect to any registered public accounting firm or associated person, for purposes of this section, the term "improper professional conduct" means—

(1) intentional or knowing conduct, including reckless conduct, that results in a violation of applicable professional standards; and

(2) negligent conduct in the form of—

(A) a single instance of highly unreasonable conduct that results in a violation of applicable professional standards in circumstances in which the registered public accounting firm or associated person knows, or should know, that heightened scrutiny is warranted; or

(B) repeated instances of unreasonable conduct, each resulting in a violation of applicable professional standards, that indicate a lack of competence to practice before the Commission.

Additional Duties of Inspector General

Sec. 4D. (a) *Suggestion Submissions by Commission Employees.*

(1) *Hotline Established.* The Inspector General of the Commission shall establish and maintain a telephone hotline or other electronic means for the receipt of—

(A) suggestions by employees of the Commission for improvements in the work efficiency, effectiveness, and productivity, and the use of the resources, of the Commission; and

(B) allegations by employees of the Commission of waste, abuse, misconduct, or mismanagement within the Commission.

(2) *Confidentiality.* The Inspector General shall maintain as confidential—

(A) the identity of any individual who provides information by the means established under paragraph (1), unless the individual requests otherwise, in writing; and

(B) at the request of any such individual, any specific information provided by the individual.

(b) *Consideration of Reports*. The Inspector General shall consider any suggestions or allegations received by the means established under subsection (a)(1), and shall recommend appropriate action in relation to such suggestions or allegations.

(c) *Recognition*. The Inspector General may recognize any employee who makes a suggestion under subsection (a)(1) (or by other means) that would or does—

(1) increase the work efficiency, effectiveness, or productivity of the Commission; or

(2) reduce waste, abuse, misconduct, or mismanagement within the Commission.

(d) *Report*. The Inspector General of the Commission shall submit to Congress an annual report containing a description of—

(1) the nature, number, and potential benefits of any suggestions received under subsection (a);

(2) the nature, number, and seriousness of any allegations received under subsection (a);

(3) any recommendations made or actions taken by the Inspector General in response to substantiated allegations received under subsection (a); and

(4) any action the Commission has taken in response to suggestions or allegations received under subsection (a).

(e) *Funding*. The activities of the Inspector General under this subsection shall be funded by the Securities and Exchange Commission Investor Protection Fund established under section 21F.

Deadline for Completing Enforcement Investigations and Compliance Examinations and Inspections

Sec. 4E. (a) *Enforcement Investigations*.

(1) *In General*. Not later than 180 days after the date on which Commission staff provide a written Wells notification to any person, the Commission staff shall either file an action against such person or provide notice to the Director of the Division of Enforcement of its intent to not file an action.

(2) *Exceptions for Certain Complex Actions*. Notwithstanding paragraph (1), if the Director of the Division of Enforcement of the Commission or the Director's designee determines that a particular enforcement investigation is sufficiently complex such that a determination regarding the filing of an action against a person cannot be completed within the deadline specified in paragraph (1), the Director of the Division of Enforcement of the Commission or the Director's designee may, after providing notice to the Chairman of the Commission, extend such deadline as needed for one additional 180-day period. If after the additional 180-day period the Director of the Division of Enforcement of the Commission or the Director's designee determines that a particular enforcement investigation is sufficiently complex such that a determination regarding the filing of an action against a person cannot be completed within the additional 180-day period, the Director of the Division of Enforcement of the Commission or the Director's designee may, after providing notice to and receiving approval of the Commission, extend such deadline as needed for one or more additional successive 180-day periods.

(b) *Compliance Examinations and Inspections*.

(1) *In General*. Not later than 180 days after the date on which Commission staff completes the on-site portion of its compliance examination or inspection or receives all records requested from the entity being examined or inspected, whichever is later, Commission staff shall provide the entity being examined or inspected with written notification indicating either that the examination or inspection has concluded, has concluded without findings, or that the staff requests the entity undertake corrective action.

(2) *Exception for Certain Complex Actions*. Notwithstanding paragraph (1), if the head of any division or office within the Commission responsible for compliance examinations and inspections or his designee determines that a particular compliance examination or inspection is sufficiently complex such that a determination regarding concluding the examination or inspection, or regarding the staff requests the entity undertake corrective action, cannot be completed within the deadline specified in paragraph (1), the head of any division or office within the Commission responsible for compliance examinations and inspections or his designee may, after providing notice to the Chairman of the Commission, extend such deadline as needed for one additional 180-day period.

Transactions on Unregistered Exchanges

Sec. 5. It shall be unlawful for any broker, dealer, or exchange, directly or indirectly, to make use of the mails or any means or instrumentality of interstate commerce for the purpose of using any facility of an exchange within or subject to the jurisdiction of the United States to effect any transaction in a security, or to report any such transaction, unless such exchange (1) is registered as a national securities exchange under section 6 of this title, or (2) is exempted from such registration upon application by the exchange because, in the opinion of the Commission, by reason of the limited volume of transactions effected on such exchange, it is not practicable and not necessary or appropriate in the public interest or for the protection of investors to require such registration.

National Securities Exchanges

Sec. 6. (a) *Registration; Application.* An exchange may be registered as a national securities exchange under the terms and conditions hereinafter provided in this section and in accordance with the provisions of section 19(a) of this title, by filing with the Commission an application for registration in such form as the Commission, by rule, may prescribe containing the rules of the exchange and such other information and documents as the Commission, by rule, may prescribe as necessary or appropriate in the public interest or for the protection of investors.

(b) *Determination by Commission Requisite to Registration of Applicant as a National Securities Exchange.* An exchange shall not be registered as a national securities exchange unless the Commission determines that—

(1) Such exchange is so organized and has the capacity to be able to carry out the purposes of this title and to comply, and (subject to any rule or order of the Commission pursuant to section 17(d) or 19(g)(2) of this title) to enforce compliance by its members and persons associated with its members, with the provisions of this title, the rules and regulations thereunder, and the rules of the exchange.

(2) Subject to the provisions of subsection (c) of this section, the rules of the exchange provide that any registered broker or dealer or natural person associated with a registered broker or dealer may become a member of such exchange and any person may become associated with a member thereof.

(3) The rules of the exchange assure a fair representation of its members in the selection of its directors and administration of its affairs and provide that one or more directors shall be representative of issuers and investors and not be associated with a member of the exchange, broker, or dealer.

(4) The rules of the exchange provide for the equitable allocation of reasonable dues, fees, and other charges among its members and issuers and other persons using its facilities.

(5) The rules of the exchange are designed to prevent fraudulent and manipulative acts and practices, to promote just and equitable principles of trade, to foster cooperation and coordination with persons engaged in regulating, clearing, settling, processing information with respect to, and facilitating transactions in securities, to remove impediments to and perfect the mechanism of a free and open market and a national market system, and, in general, to protect investors and the public interest; and are not designed to permit unfair discrimination between customers, issuers, brokers, or dealers, or to regulate by virtue of any authority conferred by this title matters not related to the purposes of this title or the administration of the exchange.

(6) The rules of the exchange provide that (subject to any rule or order of the Commission pursuant to section 17(d) or 19(g)(2) of this title) its members and persons associated with its members shall be appropriately disciplined for violation of the provisions of this title, the rules or regulations thereunder, or the rules of the exchange, by expulsion, suspension, limitation of activities, functions, and operations, fine, censure, being suspended or barred from being associated with a member, or any other fitting sanction.

(7) The rules of the exchange are in accordance with the provisions of subsection (d) of this section, and in general, provide a fair procedure for the disciplining of members and persons associated with members, the denial of membership to any person seeking membership therein, the barring of any person from becoming associated with a member thereof, and the prohibition or limitation by the exchange of any person with respect to access to services offered by the exchange or a member thereof.

(8) The rules of the exchange do not impose any burden on competition not necessary or appropriate in furtherance of the purposes of this title.

(9)(A) The rules of the exchange prohibit the listing of any security issued in a limited partnership rollup transaction (as such term is defined in paragraphs (4) and (5) of section 14(h)), unless such transaction was conducted in accordance with procedures designed to protect the rights of limited partners, including—

(i) the right of dissenting limited partners to one of the following:

(I) an appraisal and compensation;

(II) retention of a security under substantially the same terms and conditions as the original issue;

(III) approval of the limited partnership rollup transaction by not less than 75 percent of the outstanding securities of each of the participating limited partnerships;

(IV) the use of a committee of limited partners that is independent, as determined in accordance with rules prescribed by the exchange, of the general partner or sponsor, that has been approved by a majority of the outstanding units of each of the participating limited partnerships, and that has such authority as is necessary to protect the interest of limited partners, including the authority to hire independent advisors, to negotiate with the general partner or sponsor on behalf of the limited partners, and to make a recommendation to the limited partners with respect to the proposed transaction; or

(V) other comparable rights that are prescribed by rule by the exchange and that are designed to protect dissenting limited partners;

(ii) the right not to have their voting power unfairly reduced or abridged;

(iii) the right not to bear an unfair portion of the costs of a proposed limited partnership rollup transaction that is rejected; and

(iv) restrictions on the conversion of contingent interests or fees into non-contingent interests or fees and restrictions on the receipt of a non-contingent equity interest in exchange for fees for services which have not yet been provided.

(B) As used in this paragraph, the term "dissenting limited partner" means a person who, on the date on which soliciting material is mailed to investors, is a holder of a beneficial interest in a limited partnership that is the subject of a limited partnership rollup transaction, and who casts a vote against the transaction and complies with procedures established by the exchange, except that for purposes of an exchange or tender offer, such person shall file an objection in writing under the rules of the exchange during the period during which the offer is outstanding.

(10)(A) The rules of the exchange prohibit any member that is not the beneficial owner of a security registered under section 12 from granting a proxy to vote the security in connection with a shareholder vote described in subparagraph (B), unless the beneficial owner of the security has instructed the member to vote the proxy in accordance with the voting instructions of the beneficial owner.

(B) A shareholder vote described in this subparagraph is a shareholder vote with respect to the election of a member of the board of directors of an issuer, executive compensation, or any other significant matter, as determined by the Commission, by rule, and does not include a vote with respect to the uncontested election of a member of the board of directors of any investment company registered under the Investment Company Act of 1940.

(C) Nothing in this paragraph shall be construed to prohibit a national securities exchange from prohibiting a member that is not the beneficial owner of a security registered under section 12 from granting a proxy to vote the security in connection with a shareholder vote not described in subparagraph (A).

(c) *Denial of Membership in National Exchanges; Denial of Association with Member; Conditions; Limitation of Membership.*

(1) A national securities exchange shall deny membership to (A) any person, other than a natural person, which is not a registered broker or dealer or (B) any natural person who is not, or is not associated with, a registered broker or dealer.

(2) A national securities exchange may, and in cases in which the Commission, by order, directs as necessary or appropriate in the public interest or for the protection of investors shall, deny membership to any registered broker or dealer or natural person associated with a registered broker or dealer, and bar from becoming associated with a member any person, who is subject to a

statutory disqualification. A national securities exchange shall file notice with the Commission not less than thirty days prior to admitting any person to membership or permitting any person to become associated with a member, if the exchange knew, or in the exercise of reasonable care should have known, that such person was subject to a statutory disqualification. The notice shall be in such form and contain such information as the Commission, by rule, may prescribe as necessary or appropriate in the public interest or for the protection of investors.

(3)(A) A national securities exchange may deny membership to, or condition the membership of, a registered broker or dealer if (i) such broker or dealer does not meet such standards of financial responsibility or operational capability or such broker or dealer or any natural persons associated with such broker or dealer does not meet such standards of training, experience, and competence as are prescribed by the rules of the exchange or (ii) such broker or dealer or person associated with such broker or dealer has engaged and there is a reasonable likelihood he may again engage in acts or practices inconsistent with just and equitable principles of trade. A national securities exchange may examine and verify the qualifications of an applicant to become a member and the natural persons associated with such an applicant in accordance with procedures established by the rules of the exchange.

(B) A national securities exchange may bar a natural person from becoming a member or associated with a member, or condition the membership of a natural person or association of a natural person with a member, if such natural person (i) does not meet such standards of training, experience, and competence as are prescribed by the rules of the exchange or (ii) has engaged and there is a reasonable likelihood he may again engage in acts or practices inconsistent with just and equitable principles of trade. A national securities exchange may examine and verify the qualifications of an applicant to become a person associated with a member in accordance with procedures established by the rules of the exchange and require any person associated with a member, or any class of such persons, to be registered with the exchange in accordance with procedures so established.

(C) A national securities exchange may bar any person from becoming associated with a member if such person does not agree (i) to supply the exchange with such information with respect to its relationship and dealings with the member as may be specified in the rules of the exchange and (ii) to permit the examination of its books and records to verify the accuracy of any information so supplied.

(4) A national securities exchange may limit (A) the number of members of the exchange and (B) the number of members and designated representatives of members permitted to effect transactions on the floor of the exchange without the services of another person acting as broker: *Provided, however,* That no national securities exchange shall have the authority to decrease the number of memberships in such exchange, or the number of members and designated representatives of members permitted to effect transactions on the floor of such exchange without the services of another person acting as broker, below such number in effect on May 1, 1975, or the date such exchange was registered with the Commission, whichever is later: *And provided further,* That the Commission, in accordance with the provisions of section 19(c) of this title, may amend the rules of any national securities exchange to increase (but not to decrease) or to remove any limitation on the number of memberships in such exchange or the number of members or designated representatives of members permitted to effect transactions on the floor of the exchange without the services of another person acting as broker, if the Commission finds that such limitation imposes a burden on competition not necessary or appropriate in furtherance of the purposes of this title.

(d) *Discipline of National Securities Exchange Members and Persons Associated with Members; Summary Proceedings.*

(1) In any proceeding by a national securities exchange to determine whether a member or person associated with a member should be disciplined (other than a summary proceeding pursuant to paragraph (3) of this subsection), the exchange shall bring specific charges, notify such member or person of, and give him an opportunity to defend against, such charges, and keep a record. A determination by the exchange to impose a disciplinary sanction shall be supported by a statement setting forth—

(A) any act or practice in which such member or person associated with a member has been found to have engaged, or which such member or person has been found to have omitted;

(B) the specific provision of this title, the rules or regulations thereunder, or the rules of the exchange which any such act or practice, or omission to act, is deemed to violate; and

(C) the sanction imposed and the reasons therefor.

(2) In any proceeding by a national securities exchange to determine whether a person shall be denied membership, barred from becoming associated with a member, or prohibited or limited with respect to access to services offered by the exchange or a member thereof (other than a summary proceeding pursuant to paragraph (3) of this subsection), the exchange shall notify such person of, and give him an opportunity to be heard upon, the specific grounds for denial, bar, or prohibition or limitation under consideration and keep a record. A determination by the exchange to deny membership, bar a person from becoming associated with a member, or prohibit or limit a person with respect to access to services offered by the exchange or a member thereof shall be supported by a statement setting forth the specific grounds on which the denial, bar, or prohibition or limitation is based.

(3) A national securities exchange may summarily (A) suspend a member or person associated with a member who has been and is expelled or suspended from any self-regulatory organization or barred or suspended from being associated with a member of any self-regulatory organization, (B) suspend a member who is in such financial or operating difficulty that the exchange determines and so notifies the Commission that the member cannot be permitted to continue to do business as a member with safety to investors, creditors, other members, or the exchange, or (C) limit or prohibit any person with respect to access to services offered by the exchange if subparagraph (A) or (B) of this paragraph is applicable to such person or, in the case of a person who is not a member, if the exchange determines that such person does not meet the qualification requirements or other prerequisites for such access and such person cannot be permitted to continue to have such access with safety to investors, creditors, members, or the exchange. Any person aggrieved by any such summary action shall be promptly afforded an opportunity for a hearing by the exchange in accordance with the provisions of paragraph (1) or (2) of this subsection. The Commission, by order, may stay any such summary action on its own motion or upon application by any person aggrieved thereby, if the Commission determines summarily or after notice and opportunity for hearing (which hearing may consist solely of the submission of affidavits or presentation of oral arguments) that such stay is consistent with the public interest and the protection of investors.

(e) *Commissions, Allowances, Discounts, and Other Fees.*

(1) On and after the date of the Securities Act Amendments of 1975, no national securities exchange may impose any schedule or fix rates of commissions, allowances, discounts, or other fees to be charged by its members: *Provided, however,* That until May 1, 1976, the preceding provisions of this paragraph shall not prohibit any such exchange from imposing or fixing any schedule of commissions, allowances, discounts, or other fees to be charged by its members for acting as broker on the floor of the exchange or as odd-lot dealer: *And provided further,* That the Commission, in accordance with the provisions of section 19(b) of this title as modified by the provisions of paragraph (3) of this subsection, may—

(A) permit a national securities exchange, by rule, to impose a reasonable schedule or fix reasonable rates of commissions, allowances, discounts, or other fees to be charged by its members for effecting transactions on such exchange prior to November 1, 1976, if the Commission finds that such schedule or fixed rates of commissions, allowances, discounts, or other fees are in the public interest; and

(B) permit a national securities exchange, by rule, to impose a schedule or fix rates of commissions, allowances, discounts, or other fees to be charged by its members for effecting transactions on such exchange after November 1, 1976, if the Commission finds that such schedule or fixed rates of commissions, allowances, discounts, or other fees (i) are reasonable in relation to the costs of providing the service for which such fees are charged (and the Commission publishes the standards employed in adjudging reasonableness) and (ii) do not impose any burden on competition not necessary or appropriate in furtherance of the purposes of this title, taking into consideration the competitive effects of permitting such schedule or fixed rates weighed against the competitive effects of other lawful actions which the Commission is authorized to take under this title.

(2) Notwithstanding the provisions of section 19(c) of this title, the Commission, by rule, may abrogate any exchange rule which imposes a schedule or fixes rates of commissions, allowances, discounts, or other fees, if the Commission determines that such schedule or fixed rates are no longer reasonable, in the public interest, or necessary to accomplish the purposes of this title.

(3)(A) Before approving or disapproving any proposed rule change submitted by a national securities exchange which would impose a schedule or fix rates of commissions, allowances, discounts, or other fees to be charged by its members for effecting transactions on such exchange, the Commission shall afford interested persons (i) an opportunity for oral presentation of data, views, and arguments and (ii) with respect to any such rule concerning transactions effected after November 1, 1976, if the Commission determines there are disputed issues of material fact, to present such rebuttal submissions and to conduct (or have conducted under subparagraph (B) of this paragraph) such cross-examination as the Commission determines to be appropriate and required for full disclosure and proper resolution of such disputed issues of material fact.

(B) The Commission shall prescribe rules and make rulings concerning any proceeding in accordance with subparagraph (A) of this paragraph designed to avoid unnecessary costs or delay. Such rules or rulings may (i) impose reasonable time limits on each interested person's oral presentations, and (ii) require any cross-examination to which a person may be entitled under subparagraph (A) of this paragraph to be conducted by the Commission on behalf of that person in such manner as the Commission determines to be appropriate and required for full disclosure and proper resolution of disputed issues of material fact.

(C)(i) If any class of persons, the members of which are entitled to conduct (or have conducted) cross-examination under subparagraphs (A) and (B) of this paragraph and which have, in the view of the Commission, the same or similar interests in the proceeding, cannot agree upon a single representative of such interests for purposes of cross-examination, the Commission may make rules and rulings specifying the manner in which such interests shall be represented and such cross-examination conducted.

(ii) No member of any class of persons with respect to which the Commission has specified the manner in which its interests shall be represented pursuant to clause (i) of this subparagraph shall be denied, pursuant to such clause (i), the opportunity to conduct (or have conducted) cross-examination as to issues affecting his particular interests if he satisfies the Commission that he has made a reasonable and good faith effort to reach agreement upon group representation and there are substantial and relevant issues which would not be presented adequately by group representation.

(D) A transcript shall be kept of any oral presentation and cross-examination.

(E) In addition to the bases specified in subsection 25(a), a reviewing Court may set aside an order of the Commission under section 19(b) approving an exchange rule imposing a schedule or fixing rates of commissions, allowances, discounts, or other fees, if the Court finds—

(1) a Commission determination under subparagraph (A) of this paragraph that an interested person is not entitled to conduct cross-examination or make rebuttal submissions, or

(2) a Commission rule or ruling under subparagraph (B) of this paragraph limiting the petitioner's cross-examination or rebuttal submissions,

has precluded full disclosure and proper resolution of disputed issues of material fact which were necessary for fair determination by the Commission.

(f) *Compliance of Non-Members with Exchange Rules*. The Commission, by rule or order, as it deems necessary or appropriate in the public interest and for the protection of investors, to maintain fair and orderly markets, or to assure equal regulation, may require—

(1) any person not a member or a designated representative of a member of a national securities exchange effecting transactions on such exchange without the services of another person acting as a broker, or

(2) any broker or dealer not a member of a national securities exchange effecting transactions on such exchange on a regular basis,

to comply with such rules of such exchange as the Commission may specify.

(g) *Notice Registration of Security Futures Product Exchanges.*

(1) *Registration Required.* An exchange that lists or trades security futures products may register as a national securities exchange solely for the purposes of trading security futures products if—

(A) the exchange is a board of trade, as that term is defined by the Commodity Exchange Act, that has been designated a contract market by the Commodity Futures Trading Commission and such designation is not suspended by order of the Commodity Futures Trading Commission; and

(B) such exchange does not serve as a market place for transactions in securities other than—

(i) security futures products; or

(ii) futures on exempted securities or groups or indexes of securities or options thereon that have been authorized under section 2(a)(1)(C) of the Commodity Exchange Act.

(2) *Registration by Notice Filing.*

(A) *Form and Content.* An exchange required to register only because such exchange lists or trades security futures products may register for purposes of this section by filing with the Commission a written notice in such form as the Commission, by rule, may prescribe containing the rules of the exchange and such other information and documents concerning such exchange, comparable to the information and documents required for national securities exchanges under section 6(a), as the Commission, by rule, may prescribe as necessary or appropriate in the public interest or for the protection of investors. If such exchange has filed documents with the Commodity Futures Trading Commission, to the extent that such documents contain information satisfying the Commission's informational requirements, copies of such documents may be filed with the Commission in lieu of the required written notice.

(B) *Immediate Effectiveness.* Such registration shall be effective contemporaneously with the submission of notice, in written or electronic form, to the Commission, except that such registration shall not be effective if such registration would be subject to suspension or revocation.

(C) *Termination.* Such registration shall be terminated immediately if any of the conditions for registration set forth in this subsection are no longer satisfied.

(3) *Public Availability.* The Commission shall promptly publish in the Federal Register an acknowledgment of receipt of all notices the Commission receives under this subsection and shall make all such notices available to the public.

(4) *Exemption of Exchanges from Specified Provisions.*

(A) *Transaction Exemptions.* An exchange that is registered under paragraph (1) of this subsection shall be exempt from, and shall not be required to enforce compliance by its members with, and its members shall not, solely with respect to those transactions effected on such exchange in security futures products, be required to comply with, the following provisions of this title and the rules thereunder:

(i) Subsections (b)(2), (b)(3), (b)(4), (b)(7), (b)(9), (c), (d), and (e) of this section.

(ii) Section 8.

(iii) Section 11.

(iv) Subsections (d), (f), and (k) of section 17.

(v) Subsections (a), (f), and (h) of section 19.

(B) *Rule Change Exemptions.* An exchange that registered under paragraph (1) of this subsection shall also be exempt from submitting proposed rule changes pursuant to section 19(b) of this title, except that—

(i) such exchange shall file proposed rule changes related to higher margin levels, fraud or manipulation, recordkeeping, reporting, listing standards, or decimal pricing for security futures products, sales practices for security futures products for persons who effect transactions in security futures products, or rules effectuating such exchange's obligation to enforce the securities laws pursuant to section 19(b)(7);

(ii) such exchange shall file pursuant to sections 19(b)(1) and 19(b)(2) of this title proposed rule changes related to margin, except for changes resulting in higher margin levels; and

(iii) such exchange shall file pursuant to section 19(b)(1) of this title proposed rule changes that have been abrogated by the Commission pursuant to section 19(b)(7)(C).

(5) *Trading in Security Futures Products.*

(A) *In General.* Subject to subparagraph (B), it shall be unlawful for any person to execute or trade a security futures product until the later of—

(i) 1 year after the date of enactment of the Commodity Futures Modernization Act of 2000; or

(ii) such date that a futures association registered under section 17 of the Commodity Exchange Act has met the requirements set forth in section 15A(k)(2) of this title.

(B) *Principal-to-Principal Transactions.* Notwithstanding subparagraph (A), a person may execute or trade a security futures product transaction if—

(i) the transaction is entered into—

(I) on a principal-to-principal basis between parties trading for their own accounts or as described in section 1a(18)(B)(ii) of the Commodity Exchange Act; and

(II) only between eligible contract participants (as defined in subparagraphs (A), (B)(ii), and (C) of such section 1a(18)) at the time at which the persons enter into the agreement, contract, or transaction; and

(ii) the transaction is entered into on or after the later of—

(I) 8 months after the date of enactment of the Commodity Futures Modernization Act of 2000; or

(II) such date that a futures association registered under section 17 of the Commodity Exchange Act has met the requirements set forth in section 15A(k)(2) of this title.

(h) *Trading in Security Futures Products.*

(1) *Trading on Exchange or Association Required.* It shall be unlawful for any person to effect transactions in security futures products that are not listed on a national securities exchange or a national securities association registered pursuant to section 15A(a).

(2) *Listing Standards Required.* Except as otherwise provided in paragraph (7), a national securities exchange or a national securities association registered pursuant to section 15A(a) of this title may trade only security futures products that (A) conform with listing standards that such exchange or association files with the Commission under section 19(b) and (B) meet the criteria specified in section 2(a)(1)(D)(i) of the Commodity Exchange Act.

(3) *Requirements for Listing Standards and Conditions for Trading.* Such listing standards shall—

(A) except as otherwise provided in a rule, regulation, or order issued pursuant to paragraph (4), require that any security underlying the security future, including each component security of a narrow-based security index, be registered pursuant to section 12 of this title;

(B) require that if the security futures product is not cash settled, the market on which the security futures product is traded have arrangements in place with a registered clearing agency for the payment and delivery of the securities underlying the security futures product;

(C) be no less restrictive than comparable listing standards for options traded on a national securities exchange or national securities association registered pursuant to section 15A(a) of this title;

(D) except as otherwise provided in a rule, regulation, or order issued pursuant to paragraph (4), require that the security future be based upon common stock and such other equity securities as the Commission and the Commodity Futures Trading Commission jointly determine appropriate;

(E) require that the security futures product is cleared by a clearing agency that has in place provisions for linked and coordinated clearing with other clearing agencies that clear security futures products, which permits the security futures product to be purchased on one market and offset on another market that trades such product;

(F) require that only a broker or dealer subject to suitability rules comparable to those of a national securities association registered pursuant to section 15A(a) of this title effect transactions in the security futures product;

(G) require that the security futures product be subject to the prohibition against dual trading in section 4j of the Commodity Exchange Act and the rules and regulations thereunder or the provisions of section 11(a) of this title and the rules and regulations thereunder, except to the extent otherwise permitted under this title and the rules and regulations thereunder;

(H) require that trading in the security futures product not be readily susceptible to manipulation of the price of such security futures product, nor to causing or being used in the manipulation of the price of any underlying security, option on such security, or option on a group or index including such securities;

(I) require that procedures be in place for coordinated surveillance among the market on which the security futures product is traded, any market on which any security underlying the security futures product is traded, and other markets on which any related security is traded to detect manipulation and insider trading;

(J) require that the market on which the security futures product is traded has in place audit trails necessary or appropriate to facilitate the coordinated surveillance required in subparagraph (I);

(K) require that the market on which the security futures product is traded has in place procedures to coordinate trading halts between such market and any market on which any security underlying the security futures product is traded and other markets on which any related security is traded; and

(L) require that the margin requirements for a security futures product comply with the regulations prescribed pursuant to section 7(c)(2)(B), except that nothing in this subparagraph shall be construed to prevent a national securities exchange or national securities association from requiring higher margin levels for a security futures product when it deems such action to be necessary or appropriate.

(4) *Authority to Modify Certain Listing Standard Requirements.*

(A) *Authority to Modify.* The Commission and the Commodity Futures Trading Commission, by rule, regulation, or order, may jointly modify the listing standard requirements specified in subparagraph (A) or (D) of paragraph (3) to the extent such modification fosters the development of fair and orderly markets in security futures products, is necessary or appropriate in the public interest, and is consistent with the protection of investors.

(B) *Authority to Grant Exemptions.* The Commission and the Commodity Futures Trading Commission, by order, may jointly exempt any person from compliance with the listing standard requirement specified in subparagraph (E) of paragraph (3) to the extent such exemption fosters the development of fair and orderly markets in security futures products, is necessary or appropriate in the public interest, and is consistent with the protection of investors.

(5) *Requirements for Other Persons Trading Security Future Products.* It shall be unlawful for any person (other than a national securities exchange or a national securities association registered pursuant to section 15A(a)) to constitute, maintain, or provide a marketplace or facilities for bringing together purchasers and sellers of security future products or to otherwise perform with respect to security future products the functions commonly performed by a stock exchange as that term is generally understood, unless a national securities association registered pursuant to section 15A(a) or a national securities exchange of which such person is a member—

(A) has in place procedures for coordinated surveillance among such person, the market trading the securities underlying the security future products, and other markets trading related securities to detect manipulation and insider trading;

(B) has rules to require audit trails necessary or appropriate to facilitate the coordinated surveillance required in subparagraph (A); and

(C) has rules to require such person to coordinate trading halts with markets trading the securities underlying the security future products and other markets trading related securities.

(6) *Deferral of Options on Security Futures Trading.* No person shall offer to enter into, enter into, or confirm the execution of any put, call, straddle, option, or privilege on a security future, except that, after 3 years after the date of enactment of this subsection, the Commission and the Commodity Futures Trading Commission may by order jointly determine to permit trading of puts, calls, straddles, options, or privileges on any security future authorized to be traded under the provisions of this Act and the Commodity Exchange Act.

(7) *Deferral of Linked and Coordinated Clearing.*

(A) Notwithstanding paragraph (2), until the compliance date, a national securities exchange or national securities association registered pursuant to section 15A(a) may trade a security futures product that does not—

(i) conform with any listing standard promulgated to meet the requirement specified in subparagraph (E) of paragraph (3); or

(ii) meet the criterion specified in section 2(a)(1)(D)(i)(IV) of the Commodity Exchange Act.

(B) The Commission and the Commodity Futures Trading Commission shall jointly publish in the Federal Register a notice of the compliance date no later than 165 days before the compliance date.

(C) For purposes of this paragraph, the term "compliance date" means the later of—

(i) 180 days after the end of the first full calendar month period in which the average aggregate comparable share volume for all security futures products based on single equity securities traded on all national securities exchanges, any national securities associations registered pursuant to section 15A(a), and all other persons equals or exceeds 10 percent of the average aggregate comparable share volume of options on single equity securities traded on all national securities exchanges and any national securities associations registered pursuant to section 15A(a); or

(ii) 2 years after the date on which trading in any security futures product commences under this title.

(i) *Rules to Avoid Duplicative Regulation of Dual Registrants.* Consistent with this title, each national securities exchange registered pursuant to subsection (a) of this section shall issue such rules as are necessary to avoid duplicative or conflicting rules applicable to any broker or dealer registered with the Commission pursuant to section 15(b) (except paragraph (11) thereof), that is also registered with the Commodity Futures Trading Commission pursuant to section 4f(a) of the Commodity Exchange Act (except paragraph (2) thereof), with respect to the application of—

(1) rules of such national securities exchange of the type specified in section 15(c)(3)(B) of this title involving security futures products; and

(2) similar rules of national securities exchanges registered pursuant to section 6(g) of this section and national securities associations registered pursuant to section 15A(k) involving security futures products.

(j) *Procedures and Rules for Security Future Products.* A national securities exchange registered pursuant to subsection (a) shall implement the procedures specified in section 6(h)(5)(A) of this title and adopt the rules specified in subparagraphs (B) and (C) of section 6(h)(5) of this title not later than 8 months after the date of receipt of a request from an alternative trading system for such implementation and rules.

(k) *Rules Relating to Security Futures Products Traded on Foreign Boards of Trade.*

(1) To the extent necessary or appropriate in the public interest, to promote fair competition, and consistent with the promotion of market efficiency, innovation, and expansion of investment opportunities, the protection of investors, and the maintenance of fair and orderly markets, the Commission and the Commodity Futures Trading Commission shall jointly issue such rules, regulations, or orders as are necessary and appropriate to permit the offer and sale of a security futures product traded on or subject to the rules of a foreign board of trade to United States persons.

(2) The rules, regulations, or orders adopted under paragraph (1) shall take into account, as appropriate, the nature and size of the markets that the securities underlying the security futures product reflect.

(*l*) *Security-Based Swaps.* It shall be unlawful for any person to effect a transaction in a security-based swap with or for a person that is not an eligible contract participant, unless such transaction is effected on a national securities exchange registered pursuant to subsection (b).

Margin Requirements

Sec. 7. (a) *Rules and Regulations for Extension of Credit; Standard for Initial Extension; Undermargined Accounts.* For the purpose of preventing the excessive use of credit for the purchase or carrying of securities, the Board of Governors of the Federal Reserve System shall, prior to the effective date of this section and from time to time thereafter, prescribe rules and regulations with respect to the amount of credit that may be initially extended and subsequently maintained on any security (other than an exempted security or a security futures product).

For the initial extension of credit, such rules and regulations shall be based upon the following standard: An amount not greater than whichever is the higher of—

(1) 55 per centum of the current market price of the security, or

(2) 100 per centum of the lowest market price of the security during the preceding thirty-six calendar months, but not more than 75 per centum of the current market price.

Such rules and regulations may make appropriate provision with respect to the carrying of undermargined accounts for limited periods and under specified conditions; the withdrawal of funds or securities; the substitution or additional purchases of securities; the transfer of accounts from one lender to another; special or different margin requirements for delayed deliveries, short sales, arbitrage transactions, and securities to which paragraph (2) of this subsection does not apply; the bases and the methods to be used in calculating loans, and margins and market prices; and similar administrative adjustments and details. For the purposes of paragraph (2) of this subsection, until July 1, 1936, the lowest price at which a security has sold on or after July 1, 1933, shall be considered as the lowest price at which such security has sold during the preceding thirty-six calendar months.

(b) *Lower and Higher Margin Requirements.* Notwithstanding the provisions of subsection (a) of this section, the Board of Governors of the Federal Reserve System may, from time to time, with respect to all or specified securities or transactions, or classes of securities, or classes of transactions, by such rules and regulations (1) prescribe such lower margin requirements for the initial extension or maintenance of credit as it deems necessary or appropriate for the accommodation of commerce and industry, having due regard to the general credit situation of the country, and (2) prescribe such higher margin requirements for the initial extension or maintenance of credit as it may deem necessary or appropriate to prevent the excessive use of credit to finance transactions in securities.

(c) *Unlawful Credit Extension to Customers.*

(1) *Prohibition.* It shall be unlawful for any member of a national securities exchange or any broker or dealer, directly or indirectly, to extend or maintain credit or arrange for the extension or maintenance of credit to or for any customer—

(A) on any security (other than an exempted security), except as provided in paragraph (2), in contravention of the rules and regulations which the Board of Governors of the Federal Reserve System (hereafter in this section referred to as the "Board") shall prescribe under subsections (a) and (b); or

(B) without collateral or on any collateral other than securities, except in accordance with such rules and regulations as the Board may prescribe—

(i) to permit under specified conditions and for a limited period any such member, broker, or dealer to maintain a credit initially extended in conformity with the rules and regulations of the Board; and

(ii) to permit the extension or maintenance of credit in cases where the extension or maintenance of credit is not for the purpose of purchasing or carrying securities or of evading or circumventing the provisions of subparagraph (A).

(2) *Margin Regulations.*

(A) *Compliance with Margin Rules Required.* It shall be unlawful for any broker, dealer, or member of a national securities exchange to, directly or indirectly, extend or maintain credit to or for, or collect margin from any customer on, any security futures product unless such activities comply with the regulations—

(i) which the Board shall prescribe pursuant to subparagraph (B); or

(ii) if the Board determines to delegate the authority to prescribe such regulations, which the Commission and the Commodity Futures Trading Commission shall jointly prescribe pursuant to subparagraph (B).

If the Board delegates the authority to prescribe such regulations under clause (ii) and the Commission and the Commodity Futures Trading Commission have not jointly prescribed such regulations within a reasonable period of time after the date of such delegation, the Board shall prescribe such regulations pursuant to subparagraph (B).

(B) *Criteria for Issuance of Rules.* The Board shall prescribe, or, if the authority is delegated pursuant to subparagraph (A)(ii), the Commission and the Commodity Futures Trading Commission shall jointly prescribe, such regulations to establish margin requirements, including the establishment of levels of margin (initial and maintenance) for security futures products under such terms, and at such levels, as the Board deems appropriate, or as the Commission and the Commodity Futures Trading Commission jointly deem appropriate—

(i) to preserve the financial integrity of markets trading security futures products;

(ii) to prevent systemic risk;

(iii) to require that—

(I) the margin requirements for a security future product be consistent with the margin requirements for comparable option contracts traded on any exchange registered pursuant to section 6(a) of this title; and

(II) initial and maintenance margin levels for a security future product not be lower than the lowest level of margin, exclusive of premium, required for any comparable option contract traded on any exchange registered pursuant to section 6(a) of this title, other than an option on a security future;

except that nothing in this subparagraph shall be construed to prevent a national securities exchange or national securities association from requiring higher margin levels for a security future product when it deems such action to be necessary or appropriate; and

(iv) to ensure that the margin requirements (other than levels of margin), including the type, form, and use of collateral for security futures products, are and remain consistent with the requirements established by the Board, pursuant to subparagraphs (A) and (B) of paragraph (1).

(3) *Exception.* This subsection and the rules and regulations issued under this subsection shall not apply to any credit extended, maintained, or arranged by a member of a national securities exchange or a broker or dealer to or for a member of a national securities exchange or a registered broker or dealer—

(A) a substantial portion of whose business consists of transactions with persons other than brokers or dealers; or

(B) to finance its activities as a market maker or an underwriter;

except that the Board may impose such rules and regulations, in whole or in part, on any credit otherwise exempted by this paragraph if the Board determines that such action is necessary or appropriate in the public interest or for the protection of investors.

(d) *Unlawful Credit Extension in Violation of Rules and Regulations; Exceptions to Application of Rules, Etc.*

(1) *Prohibition.* It shall be unlawful for any person not subject to subsection (c) to extend or maintain credit or to arrange for the extension or maintenance of credit for the purpose of purchasing or carrying any security, in contravention of such rules and regulations as the Board shall prescribe to prevent the excessive use of credit for the purchasing or carrying of or trading in securities in circumvention of the other provisions of this section. Such rules and regulations may impose upon all loans made for the purpose of purchasing or carrying securities limitations similar to those imposed upon members, brokers, or dealers by subsection (c) of this section and the rules and regulations thereunder.

(2) *Exceptions.* This subsection and the rules and regulations issued under this subsection shall not apply to any credit extended, maintained, or arranged—

(A) by a person not in the ordinary course of business;

(B) on an exempted security;

(C) to or for a member of a national securities exchange or a registered broker or dealer—

(i) a substantial portion of whose business consists of transactions with persons other than brokers or dealers; or

(ii) to finance its activities as a market maker or an underwriter;

(D) by a bank on a security other than an equity security; or

(E) as the Board shall, by such rules, regulations, or orders as it may deem necessary or appropriate in the public interest or for the protection of investors, exempt, either unconditionally or upon specified terms and conditions or for stated periods, from the operation of this subsection and the rules and regulations thereunder.

(3) *Board Authority.* The Board may impose such rules and regulations, in whole or in part, on any credit otherwise exempted by subparagraph (C) if it determines that such action is necessary or appropriate in the public interest or for the protection of investors.

(e) *Effective Date of This Section and Rules and Regulations.* The provisions of this section or the rules and regulations thereunder shall not apply on or before July 1, 1937, to any loan or extension of credit made prior to the enactment of this title, or to the maintenance, renewal, or extension of any such loan or credit, except to the extent that the Board of Governors of the Federal Reserve System may by rules and regulations prescribe as necessary to prevent the circumvention of the provisions of this section or the rules and regulations thereunder by means of withdrawals of funds or securities, substitutions of securities, or additional purchases or by any other device.

(f) *Unlawful Receipt of Credit; Exemptions.*

(1) It is unlawful for any United States person, or any foreign person controlled by a United States person or acting on behalf of or in conjunction with such person, to obtain, receive, or enjoy the beneficial use of a loan or other extension of credit from any lender (without regard to whether the lender's office or place of business is in a State or the transaction occurred in whole or in part within a State) for the purpose of (A) purchasing or carrying United States securities, or (B) purchasing or carrying within the United States of any other securities, if, under this section or rules and regulations prescribed thereunder, the loan or other credit transaction is prohibited or would be prohibited if it had been made or the transaction had otherwise occurred in a lender's office or other place of business in a State.

(2) For the purposes of this subsection—

(A) The term "United States person" includes a person which is organized or exists under the laws of any State or, in the case of a natural person, a citizen or resident of the United States; a domestic estate; or a trust in which one or more of the foregoing persons has a cumulative direct or indirect beneficial interest in excess of 50 per centum of the value of the trust.

(B) The term "United States security" means a security (other than an exempted security) issued by a person incorporated under the laws of any State, or whose principal place of business is within a State.

(C) The term "foreign person controlled by a United States person" includes any noncorporate entity in which United States persons directly or indirectly have more than a 50 per centum beneficial interest, and any corporation in which one or more United States persons, directly or indirectly, own stock possessing more than 50 per centum of the total combined voting power of all classes of stock entitled to vote, or more than 50 per centum of the total value of shares of all classes of stock.

(3) The Board of Governors of the Federal Reserve System may, in its discretion and with due regard for the purposes of this section, by rule or regulation exempt any class of United States persons or foreign persons controlled by a United States person from the application of this subsection.

(g) *Effect of Bona Fide Agreement for Delayed Delivery of Mortgage Related Security.* Subject to such rules and regulations as the Board of Governors of the Federal Reserve System may adopt in the public interest and for the protection of investors, no member of a national securities exchange or broker or dealer shall be deemed to have extended or maintained credit or arranged for the extension or maintenance of credit for the purpose of purchasing a security, within the meaning of this section, by reason of a bona fide agreement for delayed delivery of a mortgage related security or a small business related security against full payment of the purchase price thereof upon such delivery within one hundred and eighty days after the purchase, or within such shorter period as the Board of Governors of the Federal Reserve System may prescribe by rule or regulation.

Restrictions on Borrowing and Lending by Members, Brokers, and Dealers

Sec. 8. It shall be unlawful for any registered broker or dealer, member of a national securities exchange, or broker or dealer who transacts a business in securities through the medium of any member of a national securities exchange, directly or indirectly—

(a) In contravention of such rules and regulations as the Commission shall prescribe for the protection of investors to hypothecate or arrange for the hypothecation of any securities carried for the account of any customer under circumstances (1) that will permit the commingling of his securities without his written consent with the securities of any other customer, (2) that will permit such securities to be commingled with the securities of any person other than a bona fide customer, or (3) that will permit such securities to be hypothecated, or subjected to any lien or claim of the pledgee, for a sum in excess of the aggregate indebtedness of such customers in respect of such securities.

(b) To lend or arrange for the lending of any securities carried for the account of any customer without the written consent of such customer or in contravention of such rules and regulations as the Commission shall prescribe for the protection of investors.

Prohibition Against Manipulation of Security Prices

Sec. 9. (a) *Transactions Relating to Purchase or Sale of Security.* It shall be unlawful for any person, directly or indirectly, by the use of the mails or any means or instrumentality of interstate commerce, or of any facility of any national securities exchange, or for any member of a national securities exchange—

(1) For the purpose of creating a false or misleading appearance of active trading in any security other than a government security, or a false or misleading appearance with respect to the market for any such security, (A) to effect any transaction in such security which involves no change in the beneficial ownership thereof, or (B) to enter an order or orders for the purchase of such security with the knowledge that an order or orders of substantially the same size, at substantially the same time, and at substantially the same price, for the sale of any such security, has been or will be entered by or for the same or different parties, or (C) to enter any order or orders for the sale of any such security with the knowledge that an order or orders of substantially the same size, at substantially the same time, and at substantially the same price, for the purchase of such security, has been or will be entered by or for the same or different parties.

(2) To effect, alone or with 1 or more other persons, a series of transactions in any security registered on a national securities exchange, any security not so registered, or in connection with any security-based swap or security-based swap agreement with respect to such security creating actual or apparent active trading in such security, or raising or depressing the price of such security, for the purpose of inducing the purchase or sale of such security by others.

(3) If a dealer, broker, security-based swap dealer, major security-based swap participant, or other person selling or offering for sale or purchasing or offering to purchase the security, a security-based swap, or a security-based swap agreement with respect to such security, to induce the purchase or sale of any security registered on a national securities exchange, any security not so registered, any security-based swap, or any security-based swap agreement with respect to such security by the circulation or dissemination in the ordinary course of business of information to the effect that the price of any such security will or is likely to rise or fall because of market operations of any 1 or more persons conducted for the purpose of raising or depressing the price of such security.

(4) If a dealer, broker, security-based swap dealer, major security-based swap participant, or other person selling or offering for sale or purchasing or offering to purchase the security, a security-based swap, or security-based swap agreement with respect to such security, to make, regarding any security registered on a national securities exchange, any security not so registered, any security-based swap, or any security-based swap agreement with respect to such security, for the purpose of inducing the purchase or sale of such security, such security-based swap, or such security-based swap agreement any statement which was at the time and in the light of the circumstances under which it was made, false or misleading with respect to any material fact, and which that person knew or had reasonable ground to believe was so false or misleading.

(5) For a consideration, received directly or indirectly from a broker, dealer, security-based swap dealer, major security-based swap participant, or other person selling or offering for sale or purchasing or offering to purchase the security, a security-based swap, or security-based swap agreement with respect to such security, to induce the purchase of any security registered on a national securities exchange, any security not so registered, any security-based swap, or any security-based swap agreement with respect to such security by the circulation or dissemination of information to the effect that the price of any such security will or is likely to rise or fall because of the market operations of any 1 or more persons conducted for the purpose of raising or depressing the price of such security.

(6) To effect either alone or with one or more other persons any series of transactions for the

purchase and/or sale of any security other than a government security for the purpose of pegging, fixing, or stabilizing the price of such security in contravention of such rules and regulations as the Commission may prescribe as necessary or appropriate in the public interest or for the protection of investors.

(b) *Transactions Relating to Puts, Calls, Straddles, Options, Futures, or Security-Based Swaps.* It shall be unlawful for any person to effect, in contravention of such rules and regulations as the Commission may prescribe as necessary or appropriate in the public interest or for the protection of investors—

(1) any transaction in connection with any security whereby any party to such transaction acquires—

(A) any put, call, straddle, or other option or privilege of buying the security from or selling the security to another without being bound to do so;

(B) any security futures product on the security; or

(C) any security-based swap involving the security or the issuer of the security;

(2) any transaction in connection with any security with relation to which such person has, directly or indirectly, any interest in any—

(A) such put, call, straddle, option, or privilege;

(B) such security futures product; or

(C) such security-based swap; or

(3) any transaction in any security for the account of any person who such person has reason to believe has, and who actually has, directly or indirectly, any interest in any—

(A) such put, call, straddle, option, or privilege;

(B) such security futures product with relation to such security; or

(C) any security-based swap involving such security or the issuer of such security.

(c) *Endorsement or Guarantee of Puts, Calls, Straddles, or Options.* It shall be unlawful for any broker, dealer, or member of a national securities exchange directly or indirectly to endorse or guarantee the performance of any put, call, straddle, option, or privilege in relation to any security other than a government security, in contravention of such rules and regulations as the Commission may prescribe as necessary or appropriate in the public interest or for the protection of investors.

(d) *Transactions Relating to Short Sales of Securities.* It shall be unlawful for any person, directly or indirectly, by the use of the mails or any means or instrumentality of interstate commerce, or of any facility of any national securities exchange, or for any member of a national securities exchange to effect, alone or with one or more other persons, a manipulative short sale of any security. The Commission shall issue such other rules as are necessary or appropriate to ensure that the appropriate enforcement options and remedies are available for violations of this subsection in the public interest or for the protection of investors.

(e) *Registered Warrant, Right, or Convertible Security Not Included in "Put", "Call", "Straddle", or "Option".* The terms "put", "call", "straddle", "option", or "privilege" as used in this section shall not include any registered warrant, right, or convertible security.

(f) *Persons Liable; Suits at Law or in Equity.* Any person who willfully participates in any act or transaction in violation of subsection (a), (b), or (c) of this section, shall be liable to any person who shall purchase or sell any security at a price which was affected by such act or transaction, and the person so injured may sue in law or in equity in any court of competent jurisdiction to recover the damages sustained as a result of any such act or transaction. In any such suit the court may, in its discretion, require an undertaking for the payment of the costs of such suit, and assess reasonable costs, including reasonable attorneys' fees, against either party litigant. Every person who becomes liable to make any payment under this subsection may recover contribution as in cases of contract from any person who, if joined in the original suit, would have been liable to make the same payment. No action shall be maintained to enforce any liability created under this section, unless brought within one year after the discovery of the facts constituting the violation and within three years after such violation.

(g) *Section Not Applicable to Exempted Securities.* The provisions of subsection (a) shall not apply to an exempted security.

(h) *Foreign Currencies and Security Futures Products.*

(1) Notwithstanding any other provision of law, the Commission shall have the authority to regu-

late the trading of any put, call, straddle, option, or privilege on any security, certificate of deposit, or group or index of securities (including any interest therein or based on the value thereof), or any put, call, straddle, option, or privilege entered into on a national securities exchange relating to foreign currency (but not, with respect to any of the foregoing, an option on a contract for future delivery other than a security futures product).

(2) Notwithstanding the Commodity Exchange Act, the Commission shall have the authority to regulate the trading of any security futures product to the extent provided in the securities laws.

(i) *Limitations on Practices That Affect Market Volatility.* It shall be unlawful for any person, by the use of the mails or any means or instrumentality of interstate commerce or of any facility of any national securities exchange, to use or employ any act or practice in connection with the purchase or sale of any equity security in contravention of such rules or regulations as the Commission may adopt, consistent with the public interest, the protection of investors, and the maintenance of fair and orderly markets—

(1) to prescribe means reasonably designed to prevent manipulation of price levels of the equity securities market or a substantial segment thereof; and

(2) to prohibit or constrain, during periods of extraordinary market volatility, any trading practice in connection with the purchase or sale of equity securities that the Commission determines (A) has previously contributed significantly to extraordinary levels of volatility that have threatened the maintenance of fair and orderly markets; and (B) is reasonably certain to engender such levels of volatility if not prohibited or constrained.

In adopting rules under paragraph (2), the Commission shall, consistent with the purposes of this subsection, minimize the impact on the normal operations of the market and a natural person's freedom to buy or sell any equity security.

(j) *Limitation on Commission Authority.* The authority of the Commission under this section with respect to security-based swap agreements shall be subject to the restrictions and limitations of section 3A(b) of this title.

[*This subsection shall take effect on the later of 360 days after July 21, 2010, or, to the extent a provision requires a rulemaking, not less than 60 days after publication of the final rule or regulation.*]

(j) *Regulations Relating to Security-Based Swaps.* It shall be unlawful for any person, directly or indirectly, by the use of any means or instrumentality of interstate commerce or of the mails, or of any facility of any national securities exchange, to effect any transaction in, or to induce or attempt to induce the purchase or sale of, any security-based swap, in connection with which such person engages in any fraudulent, deceptive, or manipulative act or practice, makes any fictitious quotation, or engages in any transaction, practice, or course of business which operates as a fraud or deceit upon any person. The Commission shall, for the purposes of this subsection, by rules and regulations define, and prescribe means reasonably designed to prevent, such transactions, acts, practices, and courses of business as are fraudulent, deceptive, or manipulative, and such quotations as are fictitious.*

Regulation of the Use of Manipulative and Deceptive Devices

Sec. 10. It shall be unlawful for any person, directly or indirectly, by the use of any means or instrumentality of interstate commerce or of the mails, or of any facility of any national securities exchange—

(a)(1) To effect a short sale, or to use or employ any stop-loss order in connection with the purchase or sale, of any security other than a government security, in contravention of such rules and regulations as the Commission may prescribe as necessary or appropriate in the public interest or for the protection of investors.

(2) Paragraph (1) of this subsection shall not apply to security futures products.

(b) To use or employ, in connection with the purchase or sale of any security registered on a national securities exchange or any security not so registered, or any securities-based swap agreement any manipulative or deceptive device or contrivance in contravention of such rules and regulations as the Commission may prescribe as necessary or appropriate in the public interest or for the protection of investors.

(c)(1) To effect, accept, or facilitate a transaction involving the loan or borrowing of securities in contravention of such rules and regulations as the Commission may prescribe as necessary or appropriate in the public interest or for the protection of investors.

* Dodd-Frank created two subsection (j)'s in section 9.

(2) Nothing in paragraph (1) may be construed to limit the authority of the appropriate Federal banking agency (as defined in section 3(q) of the Federal Deposit Insurance Act), the National Credit Union Administration, or any other Federal department or agency having a responsibility under Federal law to prescribe rules or regulations restricting transactions involving the loan or borrowing of securities in order to protect the safety and soundness of a financial institution or to protect the financial system from systemic risk.

Rules promulgated under subsection (b) that prohibit fraud, manipulation, or insider trading (but not rules imposing or specifying reporting or recordkeeping requirements, procedures, or standards as prophylactic measures against fraud, manipulation, or insider trading), and judicial precedents decided under subsection (b) and rules promulgated thereunder that prohibit fraud, manipulation, or insider trading, shall apply to security-based swap agreements to the same extent as they apply to securities. Judicial precedents decided under section 17(a) of the Securities Act of 1933 and sections 9, 15, 16, 20, and 21A of this title, and judicial precedents decided under applicable rules promulgated under such sections, shall apply to security-based swap agreements to the same extent as they apply to securities.

Audit Requirements

Sec. 10A. (a) *In General.* Each audit required pursuant to this title of the financial statements of an issuer by a registered public accounting firm shall include, in accordance with generally accepted auditing standards, as may be modified or supplemented from time to time by the Commission—

(1) procedures designed to provide reasonable assurance of detecting illegal acts that would have a direct and material effect on the determination of financial statement amounts;

(2) procedures designed to identify related party transactions that are material to the financial statements or otherwise require disclosure therein; and

(3) an evaluation of whether there is substantial doubt about the ability of the issuer to continue as a going concern during the ensuing fiscal year.

(b) *Required Response to Audit Discoveries.*

(1) *Investigation and Report to Management.* If, in the course of conducting an audit pursuant to this title to which subsection (a) applies, the registered public accounting firm detects or otherwise becomes aware of information indicating that an illegal act (whether or not perceived to have a material effect on the financial statements of the issuer) has or may have occurred, the firm shall, in accordance with generally accepted auditing standards, as may be modified or supplemented from time to time by the Commission—

(A)(i) determine whether it is likely that an illegal act has occurred; and

(ii) if so, determine and consider the possible effect of the illegal act on the financial statements of the issuer, including any contingent monetary effects, such as fines, penalties, and damages; and

(B) as soon as practicable, inform the appropriate level of the management of the issuer and assure that the audit committee of the issuer, or the board of directors of the issuer in the absence of such a committee, is adequately informed with respect to illegal acts that have been detected or have otherwise come to the attention of such firm in the course of the audit, unless the illegal act is clearly inconsequential.

(2) *Response to Failure to Take Remedial Action.* If, after determining that the audit committee of the board of directors of the issuer, or the board of directors of the issuer in the absence of an audit committee, is adequately informed with respect to illegal acts that have been detected or have otherwise come to the attention of the firm in the course of the audit of such firm, the registered public accounting firm concludes that—

(A) the illegal act has a material effect on the financial statements of the issuer;

(B) the senior management has not taken, and the board of directors has not caused senior management to take, timely and appropriate remedial actions with respect to the illegal act; and

(C) the failure to take remedial action is reasonably expected to warrant departure from a standard report of the auditor, when made, or warrant resignation from the audit engagement;

the registered public accounting firm shall, as soon as practicable, directly report its conclusions to the board of directors.

(3) *Notice to Commission; Response to Failure to Notify.* An issuer whose board of directors receives

a report under paragraph (2) shall inform the Commission by notice not later than 1 business day after the receipt of such report and shall furnish the registered public accounting firm making such report with a copy of the notice furnished to the Commission. If the registered public accounting firm fails to receive a copy of the notice before the expiration of the required 1–business–day period, the registered public accounting firm shall—

(A) resign from the engagement; or

(B) furnish to the Commission a copy of its report (or the documentation of any oral report given) not later than 1 business day following such failure to receive notice.

(4) *Report After Resignation.* If a registered public accounting firm resigns from an engagement under paragraph (3)(A), the firm shall, not later than 1 business day following the failure by the issuer to notify the Commission under paragraph (3), furnish to the Commission a copy of the report of the firm (or the documentation of any oral report given).

(c) *Auditor Liability Limitation.* No registered public accounting firm shall be liable in a private action for any finding, conclusion, or statement expressed in a report made pursuant to paragraph (3) or (4) of subsection (b), including any rule promulgated pursuant thereto.

(d) *Civil Penalties in Cease–and–Desist Proceedings.* If the Commission finds, after notice and opportunity for hearing in a proceeding instituted pursuant to section 21C, that a registered public accounting firm has willfully violated paragraph (3) or (4) of subsection (b) of this section, the Commission may, in addition to entering an order under section 21C, impose a civil penalty against the registered public accounting firm and any other person that the Commission finds was a cause of such violation. The determination to impose a civil penalty and the amount of the penalty shall be governed by the standards set forth in section 21B.

(e) *Preservation of Existing Authority.* Except as provided in subsection (d), nothing in this section shall be held to limit or otherwise affect the authority of the Commission under this title.

(f) *Definitions.* As used in this section, the term “illegal act” means an act or omission that violates any law, or any rule or regulation having the force of law. As used in this section, the term “issuer” means an issuer (as defined in section 3), the securities of which are registered under section 12, or that is required to file reports pursuant to section 15(d), or that files or has filed a registration statement that has not yet become effective under the Securities Act of 1933, and that it has not withdrawn.

(g) *Prohibited Activities.* Except as provided in subsection (h), it shall be unlawful for a registered public accounting firm (and any associated person of that firm, to the extent determined appropriate by the Commission) that performs for any issuer any audit required by this title or the rules of the Commission under this title or beginning 180 days after the date of commencement of the operations of the Public Company Accounting Oversight Board established under section 101 of the Sarbanes–Oxley Act of 2002 (in this section referred to as the “Board”), the rules of the Board, to provide to that issuer, contemporaneously with the audit, any non-audit service, including—

(1) bookkeeping or other services related to the accounting records or financial statements of the audit client;

(2) financial information systems design and implementation;

(3) appraisal or valuation services, fairness opinions, or contribution-in-kind reports;

(4) actuarial services;

(5) internal audit outsourcing services;

(6) management functions or human resources;

(7) broker or dealer, investment adviser, or investment banking services;

(8) legal services and expert services unrelated to the audit; and

(9) any other service that the Board determines, by regulation, is impermissible.

(h) *Preapproval Required for Non-Audit Services.* A registered public accounting firm may engage in any non-audit service, including tax services, that is not described in any of paragraphs (1) through (9) of subsection (g) for an audit client, only if the activity is approved in advance by the audit committee of the issuer, in accordance with subsection (i).

(i) *Preapproval Requirements.*

(1) *In General.*

(A) *Audit Committee Action.* All auditing services (which may entail providing comfort letters in connection with securities underwritings or statutory audits required for insurance companies for purposes of State law) and non-audit services, other than as provided in subparagraph (B), provided to an issuer by the auditor of the issuer shall be preapproved by the audit committee of the issuer.

(B) *De Minimis Exception.* The preapproval requirement under subparagraph (A) is waived with respect to the provision of non-audit services for an issuer, if—

(i) the aggregate amount of all such non-audit services provided to the issuer constitutes not more than 5 percent of the total amount of revenues paid by the issuer to its auditor during the fiscal year in which the non-audit services are provided;

(ii) such services were not recognized by the issuer at the time of the engagement to be non-audit services; and

(iii) such services are promptly brought to the attention of the audit committee of the issuer and approved prior to the completion of the audit by the audit committee or by 1 or more members of the audit committee who are members of the board of directors to whom authority to grant such approvals has been delegated by the audit committee.

(2) *Disclosure to Investors.* Approval by an audit committee of an issuer under this subsection of a non-audit service to be performed by the auditor of the issuer shall be disclosed to investors in periodic reports required by section 13(a).

(3) *Delegation Authority.* The audit committee of an issuer may delegate to 1 or more designated members of the audit committee who are independent directors of the board of directors, the authority to grant preapprovals required by this subsection. The decisions of any member to whom authority is delegated under this paragraph to preapprove an activity under this subsection shall be presented to the full audit committee at each of its scheduled meetings.

(4) *Approval of Audit Services for Other Purposes.* In carrying out its duties under subsection (m)(2), if the audit committee of an issuer approves an audit service within the scope of the engagement of the auditor, such audit service shall be deemed to have been preapproved for purposes of this subsection.

(j) *Audit Partner Rotation.* It shall be unlawful for a registered public accounting firm to provide audit services to an issuer if the lead (or coordinating) audit partner (having primary responsibility for the audit), or the audit partner responsible for reviewing the audit, has performed audit services for that issuer in each of the 5 previous fiscal years of that issuer.

(k) *Reports to Audit Committees.* Each registered public accounting firm that performs for any issuer any audit required by this title shall timely report to the audit committee of the issuer—

(1) all critical accounting policies and practices to be used;

(2) all alternative treatments of financial information within generally accepted accounting principles that have been discussed with management officials of the issuer, ramifications of the use of such alternative disclosures and treatments, and the treatment preferred by the registered public accounting firm; and

(3) other material written communications between the registered public accounting firm and the management of the issuer, such as any management letter or schedule of unadjusted differences.

(*l*) *Conflicts of Interest.* It shall be unlawful for a registered public accounting firm to perform for an issuer any audit service required by this title, if a chief executive officer, controller, chief financial officer, chief accounting officer, or any person serving in an equivalent position for the issuer, was employed by that registered independent public accounting firm and participated in any capacity in the audit of that issuer during the 1-year period preceding the date of the initiation of the audit.

(m) *Standards Relating to Audit Committees.*

(1) *Commission Rules.*

(A) *In General.* Effective not later than 270 days after the date of enactment of this subsection, the Commission shall, by rule, direct the national securities exchanges and national securities associations to prohibit the listing of any security of an issuer that is not in compliance with the requirements of any portion of paragraphs (2) through (6).

(B) *Opportunity to Cure Defects.* The rules of the Commission under subparagraph (A) shall provide for appropriate procedures for an issuer to have an opportunity to cure any defects that would be the basis for a prohibition under subparagraph (A), before the imposition of such prohibition.

(2) *Responsibilities Relating to Registered Public Accounting Firms.* The audit committee of each issuer, in its capacity as a committee of the board of directors, shall be directly responsible for the appointment, compensation, and oversight of the work of any registered public accounting firm employed by that issuer (including resolution of disagreements between management and the auditor regarding financial reporting) for the purpose of preparing or issuing an audit report or related work, and each such registered public accounting firm shall report directly to the audit committee.

(3) *Independence.*

(A) *In General.* Each member of the audit committee of the issuer shall be a member of the board of directors of the issuer, and shall otherwise be independent.

(B) *Criteria.* In order to be considered to be independent for purposes of this paragraph, a member of an audit committee of an issuer may not, other than in his or her capacity as a member of the audit committee, the board of directors, or any other board committee—

(i) accept any consulting, advisory, or other compensatory fee from the issuer; or

(ii) be an affiliated person of the issuer or any subsidiary thereof.

(C) *Exemption Authority.* The Commission may exempt from the requirements of subparagraph (B) a particular relationship with respect to audit committee members, as the Commission determines appropriate in light of the circumstances.

(4) *Complaints.* Each audit committee shall establish procedures for—

(A) the receipt, retention, and treatment of complaints received by the issuer regarding accounting, internal accounting controls, or auditing matters; and

(B) the confidential, anonymous submission by employees of the issuer of concerns regarding questionable accounting or auditing matters.

(5) *Authority to Engage Advisers.* Each audit committee shall have the authority to engage independent counsel and other advisers, as it determines necessary to carry out its duties.

(6) *Funding.* Each issuer shall provide for appropriate funding, as determined by the audit committee, in its capacity as a committee of the board of directors, for payment of compensation—

(A) to the registered public accounting firm employed by the issuer for the purpose of rendering or issuing an audit report; and

(B) to any advisers employed by the audit committee under paragraph (5).

Position Limits and Position Accountability for Security-Based Swaps and Large Trade Reporting

Sec. 10B. (a) *Position Limits.* As a means reasonably designed to prevent fraud and manipulation, the Commission shall, by rule or regulation, as necessary or appropriate in the public interest or for the protection of investors, establish limits (including related hedge exemption provisions) on the size of positions in any security-based swap that may be held by any person. In establishing such limits, the Commission may require any person to aggregate positions in—

(1) any security-based swap and any security or loan or group of securities or loans on which such security-based swap is based, which such security-based swap references, or to which such security-based swap is related as described in paragraph (68) of section 3(a), and any other instrument relating to such security or loan or group or index of securities or loans; or

(2) any security-based swap and—

(A) any security or group or index of securities, the price, yield, value, or volatility of which, or of which any interest therein, is the basis for a material term of such security based swap as described in paragraph (68) of section 3(a); and

(B) any other instrument relating to the same security or group or index of securities described under subparagraph (A).

(b) *Exemptions.* The Commission, by rule, regulation, or order, may conditionally or unconditionally exempt any person or class of persons, any security-based swap or class of security-based swaps, or any transaction or class of transactions from any requirement the Commission may establish under this section with respect to position limits.

(c) *SRO Rules.*

(1) *In General.* As a means reasonably designed to prevent fraud or manipulation, the Commission, by rule, regulation, or order, as necessary or appropriate in the public interest, for the protec-

tion of investors, or otherwise in furtherance of the purposes of this title, may direct a self–regulatory organization—

(A) to adopt rules regarding the size of positions in any security-based swap that may be held by—

(i) any member of such self–regulatory organization; or

(ii) any person for whom a member of such self–regulatory organization effects transactions in such security-based swap; and

(B) to adopt rules reasonably designed to ensure compliance with requirements prescribed by the Commission under this subsection.

(2) *Requirement to Aggregate Positions.* In establishing the limits under paragraph (1), the self–regulatory organization may require such member or person to aggregate positions in—

(A) any security-based swap and any security or loan or group or narrow–based security index of securities or loans on which such security-based swap is based, which such security-based swap references, or to which such security-based swap is related as described in section 3(a)(68), and any other instrument relating to such security or loan or group or narrow–based security index of securities or loans; or

(B)(i) any security-based swap; and

(ii) any security-based swap and any other instrument relating to the same security or group or narrow–based security index of securities.

(d) *Large Trader Reporting.* The Commission, by rule or regulation, may require any person that effects transactions for such person's own account or the account of others in any securities–based swap or uncleared security-based swap and any security or loan or group or narrow–based security index of securities or loans as set forth in paragraphs (1) and (2) of subsection (a) under this section to report such information as the Commission may prescribe regarding any position or positions in any security-based swap or uncleared security-based swap and any security or loan or group or narrow–based security index of securities or loans and any other instrument relating to such security or loan or group or narrow–based security index of securities or loans as set forth in paragraphs (1) and (2) of subsection(a) under this section.

Compensation Committees

Sec. 10C. (a) *Independence of Compensation Committees.*

(1) *Listing Standards.* The Commission shall, by rule, direct the national securities exchanges and national securities associations to prohibit the listing of any equity security of an issuer, other than an issuer that is a controlled company, limited partnership, company in bankruptcy proceedings, open–ended management investment company that is registered under the Investment Company Act of 1940, or a foreign private issuer that provides annual disclosures to shareholders of the reasons that the foreign private issuer does not have an independent compensation committee, that does not comply with the requirements of this subsection.

(2) *Independence of Compensation Committees.* The rules of the Commission under paragraph (1) shall require that each member of the compensation committee of the board of directors of an issuer be—

(A) a member of the board of directors of the issuer; and

(B) independent.

(3) *Independence.* The rules of the Commission under paragraph (1) shall require that, in determining the definition of the term 'independence' for purposes of paragraph (2), the national securities exchanges and the national securities associations shall consider relevant factors, including—

(A) the source of compensation of a member of the board of directors of an issuer, including any consulting, advisory, or other compensatory fee paid by the issuer to such member of the board of directors; and

(B) whether a member of the board of directors of an issuer is affiliated with the issuer, a subsidiary of the issuer, or an affiliate of a subsidiary of the issuer.

(4) *Exemption Authority.* The rules of the Commission under paragraph (1) shall permit a national securities exchange or a national securities association to exempt a particular relationship from the requirements of paragraph (2), with respect to the members of a compensation committee, as the national securities exchange or national securities association determines is appropriate, taking into consideration the size of an issuer and any other relevant factors.

(b) *Independence of Compensation Consultants and Other Compensation Committee Advisers.*

(1) *In General.* The compensation committee of an issuer may only select a compensation consultant, legal counsel, or other adviser to the compensation committee after taking into consideration the factors identified by the Commission under paragraph (2).

(2) *Rules.* The Commission shall identify factors that affect the independence of a compensation consultant, legal counsel, or other adviser to a compensation committee of an issuer. Such factors shall be competitively neutral among categories of consultants, legal counsel, or other advisers and preserve the ability of compensation committees to retain the services of members of any such category, and shall include—

(A) the provision of other services to the issuer by the person that employs the compensation consultant, legal counsel, or other adviser;

(B) the amount of fees received from the issuer by the person that employs the compensation consultant, legal counsel, or other adviser, as a percentage of the total revenue of the person that employs the compensation consultant, legal counsel, or other adviser;

(C) the policies and procedures of the person that employs the compensation consultant, legal counsel, or other adviser that are designed to prevent conflicts of interest;

(D) any business or personal relationship of the compensation consultant, legal counsel, or other adviser with a member of the compensation committee; and

(E) any stock of the issuer owned by the compensation consultant, legal counsel, or other adviser.

(c) *Compensation Committee Authority Relating to Compensation Consultants.*

(1) *Authority to Retain Compensation Consultant.*

(A) *In General.* The compensation committee of an issuer, in its capacity as a committee of the board of directors, may, in its sole discretion, retain or obtain the advice of a compensation consultant.

(B) *Direct Responsibility of Compensation Committee.* The compensation committee of an issuer shall be directly responsible for the appointment, compensation, and oversight of the work of a compensation consultant.

(C) *Rule of Construction.* This paragraph may not be construed—

(i) to require the compensation committee to implement or act consistently with the advice or recommendations of the compensation consultant; or

(ii) to affect the ability or obligation of a compensation committee to exercise its own judgment in fulfillment of the duties of the compensation committee.

(2) *Disclosure.* In any proxy or consent solicitation material for an annual meeting of the shareholders (or a special meeting in lieu of the annual meeting) occurring on or after the date that is 1 year after the date of enactment of this section, each issuer shall disclose in the proxy or consent material, in accordance with regulations of the Commission, whether—

(A) the compensation committee of the issuer retained or obtained the advice of a compensation consultant; and

(B) the work of the compensation consultant has raised any conflict of interest and, if so, the nature of the conflict and how the conflict is being addressed.

(d) *Authority to Engage Independent Legal Counsel and Other Advisers.*

(1) *In General.* The compensation committee of an issuer, in its capacity as a committee of the board of directors, may, in its sole discretion, retain and obtain the advice of independent legal counsel and other advisers.

(2) *Direct Responsibility of Compensation Committee.* The compensation committee of an issuer shall be directly responsible for the appointment, compensation, and oversight of the work of independent legal counsel and other advisers.

(3) *Rule of Construction.* This subsection may not be construed—

(A) to require a compensation committee to implement or act consistently with the advice or recommendations of independent legal counsel or other advisers under this subsection; or

(B) to affect the ability or obligation of a compensation committee to exercise its own judgment in fulfillment of the duties of the compensation committee.

(e) *Compensation of Compensation Consultants, Independent Legal Counsel, and Other Advisers.* Each issuer shall provide for appropriate funding, as determined by the compensation committee in its capacity as a committee of the board of directors, for payment of reasonable compensation—

(1) to a compensation consultant; and

(2) to independent legal counsel or any other adviser to the compensation committee.

(f) *Commission Rules.*

(1) *In General.* Not later than 360 days after the date of enactment of this section, the Commission shall, by rule, direct the national securities exchanges and national securities associations to prohibit the listing of any security of an issuer that is not in compliance with the requirements of this section.

(2) *Opportunity to Cure Defects.* The rules of the Commission under paragraph (1) shall provide for appropriate procedures for an issuer to have a reasonable opportunity to cure any defects that would be the basis for the prohibition under paragraph (1), before the imposition of such prohibition.

(3) *Exemption Authority.*

(A) *In General.* The rules of the Commission under paragraph (1) shall permit a national securities exchange or a national securities association to exempt a category of issuers from the requirements under this section, as the national securities exchange or the national securities association determines is appropriate.

(B) *Considerations.* In determining appropriate exemptions under subparagraph (A), the national securities exchange or the national securities association shall take into account the potential impact of the requirements of this section on smaller reporting issuers.

(g) *Controlled Company Exemption.*

(1) *In General.* This section shall not apply to any controlled company.

(2) *Definition.* For purposes of this section, the term "controlled company" means an issuer—

(A) that is listed on a national securities exchange or by a national securities association; and

(B) that holds an election for the board of directors of the issuer in which more than 50 percent of the voting power is held by an individual, a group, or another issuer.

Recovery of Erroneously Awarded Compensation Policy

Sec. 10D. (a) *Listing Standards.* The Commission shall, by rule, direct the national securities exchanges and national securities associations to prohibit the listing of any security of an issuer that does not comply with the requirements of this section.

(b) *Recovery of Funds.* The rules of the Commission under subsection (a) shall require each issuer to develop and implement a policy providing—

(1) for disclosure of the policy of the issuer on incentive based compensation that is based on financial information required to be reported under the securities laws; and

(2) that, in the event that the issuer is required to prepare an accounting restatement due to the material noncompliance of the issuer with any financial reporting requirement under the securities laws, the issuer will recover from any current or former executive officer of the issuer who received incentive based compensation (including stock options awarded as compensation) during the 3-year period preceding the date on which the issuer is required to prepare an accounting restatement, based on the erroneous data, in excess of what would have been paid to the executive officer under the accounting restatement.

Trading by Members of Exchanges, Brokers, and Dealers

Sec. 11. (a) *Trading for Own Account or Account of Associated Person; Exception.*

(1) It shall be unlawful for any member of a national securities exchange to effect any transaction on such exchange for its own account, the account of an associated person, or an account with respect to which it or an associated person thereof exercises investment discretion: *Provided, however,* That this paragraph shall not make unlawful—

(A) any transaction by a dealer acting in the capacity of market maker;

(B) any transaction for the account of an odd-lot dealer in a security in which he is so registered;

(C) any stabilizing transaction effected in compliance with rules under section 10(b) of this title to facilitate a distribution of a security in which the member effecting such transaction is participating;

(D) any bona fide arbitrage transaction, any bona fide hedge transaction involving a long or short position in an equity security and a long or short position in a security entitling the holder to acquire or sell such equity security, or any risk arbitrage transaction in connection with a merger, acquisition, tender offer, or similar transaction involving a recapitalization;

(E) any transaction for the account of a natural person, the estate of a natural person, or a trust created by a natural person for himself or another natural person;

(F) any transaction to offset a transaction made in error;

(G) any other transaction for a member's own account provided that (i) such member is primarily engaged in the business of underwriting and distributing securities issued by other persons, selling securities to customers, and acting as broker, or any one or more of such activities, and whose gross income normally is derived principally from such business and related activities and (ii) such transaction is effected in compliance with rules of the Commission which, as a minimum, assure that the transaction is not inconsistent with the maintenance of fair and orderly markets and yields priority, parity, and precedence in execution to orders for the account of persons who are not members or associated with members of the exchange;

(H) any transaction for an account with respect to which such member or an associated person thereof exercises investment discretion if such member—

(i) has obtained, from the person or persons authorized to transact business for the account, express authorization for such member or associated person to effect such transactions prior to engaging in the practice of effecting such transactions;

(ii) furnishes the person or persons authorized to transact business for the account with a statement at least annually disclosing the aggregate compensation received by the exchange member in effecting such transactions; and

(iii) complies with any rules the Commission has prescribed with respect to the requirements of clauses (i) and (ii); and

(I) any other transaction of a kind which the Commission, by rule, determines is consistent with the purposes of this paragraph, the protection of investors, and the maintenance of fair and orderly markets.

(2) The Commission, by rule, as it deems necessary or appropriate in the public interest and for the protection of investors, to maintain fair and orderly markets, or to assure equal regulation of exchange markets and markets occurring otherwise than on an exchange, may regulate or prohibit:

(A) transactions on a national securities exchange not unlawful under paragraph (1) of this subsection effected by any member thereof for its own account (unless such member is acting in the capacity of market maker or odd-lot dealer), the account of an associated person, or an account with respect to which such member or an associated person thereof exercises investment discretion;

(B) transactions otherwise than on a national securities exchange effected by use of the mails or any means or instrumentality of interstate commerce by any member of a national securities exchange, broker, or dealer for the account of such member, broker, or dealer (unless such member, broker, or dealer is acting in the capacity of a market maker) the account of an associated person, or an account with respect to which such member, broker, or dealer or associated person thereof exercises investment discretion; and

(C) transactions on a national securities exchange effected by any broker or dealer not a member thereof for the account of such broker or dealer (unless such broker or dealer is acting in the capacity of market maker), the account of an associated person, or an account with respect to which such broker or dealer or associated person thereof exercises investment discretion.

(3) The provisions of paragraph (1) of this subsection insofar as they apply to transactions on a national securities exchange effected by a member thereof who was a member on February 1, 1978 shall not become effective until February 1, 1979. Nothing in this paragraph shall be construed to impair or limit the authority of the Commission to regulate or prohibit such transactions prior to February 1, 1979, pursuant to paragraph (2) of this subsection.

(b) *Registration of Members as Odd–Lot Dealers and Specialists.* When not in contravention of such rules and regulations as the Commission may prescribe as necessary or appropriate in the public interest and for the protection of investors, to maintain fair and orderly markets, or to remove impediments to and perfect the mechanism of a national market system, the rules of a national securities exchange may permit (1) a member to be registered as an odd-lot dealer and as such to buy and sell for his own account so far as may be reasonably necessary to carry on such odd-lot transactions, and (2) a member to be registered as a specialist. Under the rules and regulations of the Commission a specialist may be permitted to act as a broker and dealer or limited to acting as a broker or dealer. It shall be unlawful for a specialist or an official of the exchange to disclose information in regard to orders placed with such specialist which is not available to all members of the exchange, to any person other than an official of the exchange, a representative of the Commission, or a specialist who may be acting for such specialist: *Provided, however,* That the Commission, by rule, may require disclosure to all members of the exchange of all orders placed with specialists, under such rules and regulations as the Commission may prescribe as necessary or appropriate in the public interest or for the protection of investors. It shall also be unlawful for a specialist permitted to act as a broker and dealer to effect on the exchange as broker any transaction except upon a market or limited price order.

(c) *Exemptions from Provisions of Section and Rules and Regulations.* If because of the limited volume of transactions effected on an exchange, it is in the opinion of the Commission impracticable and not necessary or appropriate in the public interest or for the protection of investors to apply any of the foregoing provisions of this section or the rules and regulations thereunder, the Commission shall have power, upon application of the exchange and on a showing that the rules of such exchange are otherwise adequate for the protection of investors, to exempt such exchange and its members from any such provision or rules and regulations.

(d) *Prohibition on Extension of Credit by Broker–Dealer.* It shall be unlawful for a member of a national securities exchange who is both a dealer and a broker, or for any person who both as a broker and a dealer transacts a business in securities through the medium of a member or otherwise, to effect through the use of any facility of a national securities exchange or of the mails or of any means or instrumentality of interstate commerce, or otherwise in the case of a member, (1) any transaction in connection with which, directly or indirectly, he extends or maintains or arranges for the extension or maintenance of credit to or for a customer on any security (other than an exempted security) which was a part of a new issue in the distribution of which he participated as a member of a selling syndicate or group within thirty days prior to such transaction: *Provided,* That credit shall not be deemed extended by reason of a bona fide delayed delivery of (i) any such security against full payment of the entire purchase price thereof upon such delivery within thirty-five days after such purchase or (ii) any mortgage related security or any small business related security against full payment of the entire purchase price thereof upon such delivery within one hundred and eighty days after such purchase, or within such shorter period as the Commission may prescribe by rule or regulation, or (2) any transaction with respect to any security (other than an exempted security) unless, if the transaction is with a customer, he discloses to such customer in writing at or before the completion of the transaction whether he is acting as a dealer for his own account, as a broker for such customer, or as a broker for some other person.

National Market System for Securities; Securities Information Processors

Sec. 11A. (a) *Congressional Findings; Facilitating Establishment of National Market System for Securities; Designation of Qualified Securities.*

(1) The Congress finds that—

(A) The securities markets are an important national asset which must be preserved and strengthened.

(B) New data processing and communications techniques create the opportunity for more efficient and effective market operations.

(C) It is in the public interest and appropriate for the protection of investors and the maintenance of fair and orderly markets to assure—

(i) economically efficient execution of securities transactions;

(ii) fair competition among brokers and dealers, among exchange markets, and between exchange markets and markets other than exchange markets;

(iii) the availability to brokers, dealers, and investors of information with respect to quotations for and transactions in securities;

(iv) the practicability of brokers executing investors' orders in the best market; and

(v) an opportunity, consistent with the provisions of clauses (i) and (iv) of this subparagraph, for investors' orders to be executed without the participation of a dealer.

(D) The linking of all markets for qualified securities through communication and data processing facilities will foster efficiency, enhance competition, increase the information available to brokers, dealers, and investors, facilitate the offsetting of investors' orders, and contribute to best execution of such orders.

(2) The Commission is directed, therefore, having due regard for the public interest, the protection of investors, and the maintenance of fair and orderly markets, to use its authority under this title to facilitate the establishment of a national market system for securities (which may include subsystems for particular types of securities with unique trading characteristics) in accordance with the findings and to carry out the objectives set forth in paragraph (1) of this subsection. The Commission, by rule, shall designate the securities or classes of securities qualified for trading in the national market system from among securities other than exempted securities. (Securities or classes of securities so designated hereinafter in this section referred to as "qualified securities".)

(3) The Commission is authorized in furtherance of the directive in paragraph (2) of this subsection—

(A) to create one or more advisory committees pursuant to the Federal Advisory Committee Act (which shall be in addition to the National Market Advisory Board established pursuant to subsection (d) of this section) and to employ one or more outside experts;

(B) by rule or order, to authorize or require self-regulatory organizations to act jointly with respect to matters as to which they share authority under this title in planning, developing, operating, or regulating a national market system (or a subsystem thereof) or one or more facilities thereof; and

(C) to conduct studies and make recommendations to the Congress from time to time as to the possible need for modifications of the scheme of self-regulation provided for in this title so as to adapt it to a national market system.

(b) *Securities Information Processors; Registration; Withdrawal of Registration; Access to Services; Censure; Suspension or Revocation of Registration.*

(1) Except as otherwise provided in this section, it shall be unlawful for any securities information processor unless registered in accordance with this subsection, directly or indirectly, to make use of the mails or any means or instrumentality of interstate commerce to perform the functions of a securities information processor. The Commission, by rule or order, upon its own motion or upon application, may conditionally or unconditionally exempt any securities information processor or class of securities information processors or security or class of securities from any provision of this section or the rules or regulations thereunder, if the Commission finds that such exemption is consistent with the public interest, the protection of investors, and the purposes of this section, including the maintenance of fair and orderly markets in securities and the removal of impediments to and perfection of the mechanism of a national market system: *Provided, however,* That a securities information processor not acting as the exclusive processor of any information with respect to quotations for or transactions in securities is exempt from the requirement to register in accordance with this subsection unless the Commission, by rule or order, finds that the registration of such securities information processor is necessary or appropriate in the public interest, for the protection of investors, or for the achievement of the purposes of this section.

(2) A securities information processor may be registered by filing with the Commission an application for registration in such form as the Commission, by rule, may prescribe containing the address of its principal office, or offices, the names of the securities and markets for which it is then acting and for which it proposes to act as a securities information processor, and such other information and documents as the Commission, by rule, may prescribe with regard to performance capability, standards and procedures for the collection, processing, distribution, and publication of information with respect to quotations for and transactions in securities, personnel qualifications, financial condition, and such other matters as the Commission determines to be germane to the provisions of this title and the rules and regulations thereunder, or necessary or appropriate in furtherance of the purposes of this section.

(3) The Commission shall, upon the filing of an application for registration pursuant to paragraph (2) of this subsection, publish notice of the filing and afford interested persons an opportuni-

ty to submit written data, views, and arguments concerning such application. Within ninety days of the date of the publication of such notice (or within such longer period as to which the applicant consents) the Commission shall—

(A) by order grant such registration, or

(B) institute proceedings to determine whether registration should be denied. Such proceedings shall include notice of the grounds for denial under consideration and opportunity for hearing and shall be concluded within one hundred eighty days of the date of publication of notice of the filing of the application for registration. At the conclusion of such proceedings the Commission, by order, shall grant or deny such registration. The Commission may extend the time for the conclusion of such proceedings for up to sixty days if it finds good cause for such extension and publishes its reasons for so finding or for such longer periods as to which the applicant consents.

The Commission shall grant the registration of a securities information processor if the Commission finds that such securities information processor is so organized, and has the capacity, to be able to assure the prompt, accurate, and reliable performance of its functions as a securities information processor, comply with the provisions of this title and the rules and regulations thereunder, carry out its functions in a manner consistent with the purposes of this section, and, insofar as it is acting as an exclusive processor, operate fairly and efficiently. The Commission shall deny the registration of a securities information processor if the Commission does not make any such finding.

(4) A registered securities information processor may, upon such terms and conditions as the Commission deems necessary or appropriate in the public interest or for the protection of investors, withdraw from registration by filing a written notice of withdrawal with the Commission. If the Commission finds that any registered securities information processor is no longer in existence or has ceased to do business in the capacity specified in its application for registration, the Commission, by order, shall cancel the registration.

(5)(A) If any registered securities information processor prohibits or limits any person in respect of access to services offered, directly or indirectly, by such securities information processor, the registered securities information processor shall promptly file notice thereof with the Commission. The notice shall be in such form and contain such information as the Commission, by rule, may prescribe as necessary or appropriate in the public interest or for the protection of investors. Any prohibition or limitation on access to services with respect to which a registered securities information processor is required by this paragraph to file notice shall be subject to review by the Commission on its own motion, or upon application by any person aggrieved thereby filed within thirty days after such notice has been filed with the Commission and received by such aggrieved person, or within such longer period as the Commission may determine. Application to the Commission for review, or the institution of review by the Commission on its own motion, shall not operate as a stay of such prohibition or limitation, unless the Commission otherwise orders, summarily or after notice and opportunity for hearing on the question of a stay (which hearing may consist solely of the submission of affidavits or presentation of oral arguments). The Commission shall establish for appropriate cases an expedited procedure for consideration and determination of the question of a stay.

(B) In any proceeding to review the prohibition or limitation of any person in respect of access to services offered by a registered securities information processor, if the Commission finds, after notice and opportunity for hearing, that such prohibition or limitation is consistent with the provisions of this title and the rules and regulations thereunder and that such person has not been discriminated against unfairly, the Commission, by order, shall dismiss the proceeding. If the Commission does not make any such finding or if it finds, that such prohibition or limitation imposes any burden on competition not necessary or appropriate in furtherance of the purposes of this title, the Commission, by order, shall set aside the prohibition or limitation and require the registered securities information processor to permit such person access to services offered by the registered securities information processor.

(6) The Commission, by order, may censure or place limitations upon the activities, functions, or operations of any registered securities information processor or suspend for a period not exceeding twelve months or revoke the registration of any such processor, if the Commission finds, on the record after notice and opportunity for hearing, that such censure, placing of limitations, suspension,

or revocation is in the public interest, necessary or appropriate for the protection of investors or to assure the prompt, accurate, or reliable performance of the functions of such securities information processor, and that such securities information processor has violated or is unable to comply with any provision of this title or the rules or regulations thereunder.

(c) *Rules and Regulations Covering Use of Mails or Other Means or Instrumentalities of Interstate Commerce; Reports of Purchase or Sale of Qualified Securities; Limiting Registered Securities Transactions to National Securities Exchanges.*

(1) No self-regulatory organization, member thereof, securities information processor, broker, or dealer shall make use of the mails or any means or instrumentality of interstate commerce to collect, process, distribute, publish, or prepare for distribution or publication any information with respect to quotations for or transactions in any security other than an exempted security, to assist, participate in, or coordinate the distribution or publication of such information, or to effect any transaction in, or to induce or attempt to induce the purchase or sale of, any such security in contravention of such rules and regulations as the Commission shall prescribe as necessary or appropriate in the public interest, for the protection of investors, or otherwise in furtherance of the purposes of this title to—

(A) prevent the use, distribution, or publication of fraudulent, deceptive, or manipulative information with respect to quotations for and transactions in such securities;

(B) assure the prompt, accurate, reliable, and fair collection, processing, distribution, and publication of information with respect to quotations for and transactions in such securities and the fairness and usefulness of the form and content of such information;

(C) assure that all securities information processors may, for purposes of distribution and publication, obtain on fair and reasonable terms such information with respect to quotations for and transactions in such securities as is collected, processed, or prepared for distribution or publication by any exclusive processor of such information acting in such capacity;

(D) assure that all exchange members, brokers, dealers, securities information processors, and, subject to such limitations as the Commission, by rule, may impose as necessary or appropriate for the protection of investors or maintenance of fair and orderly markets, all other persons may obtain on terms which are not unreasonably discriminatory such information with respect to quotations for and transactions in such securities as is published or distributed by any self-regulatory organization or securities information processor;

(E) assure that all exchange members, brokers, and dealers transmit and direct orders for the purchase or sale of qualified securities in a manner consistent with the establishment and operation of a national market system; and

(F) assure equal regulation of all markets for qualified securities and all exchange members, brokers, and dealers effecting transactions in such securities.

(2) The Commission, by rule, as it deems necessary or appropriate in the public interest or for the protection of investors, may require any person who has effected the purchase or sale of any qualified security by use of the mails or any means or instrumentality of interstate commerce to report such purchase or sale to a registered securities information processor, national securities exchange, or registered securities association and require such processor, exchange, or association to make appropriate distribution and publication of information with respect to such purchase or sale.

(3)(A) The Commission, by rule, is authorized to prohibit brokers and dealers from effecting transactions in securities registered pursuant to section 12(b) otherwise than on a national securities exchange, if the Commission finds, on the record after notice and opportunity for hearing, that—

(i) as a result of transactions in such securities effected otherwise than on a national securities exchange the fairness or orderliness of the markets for such securities has been affected in a manner contrary to the public interest or the protection of investors;

(ii) no rule of any national securities exchange unreasonably impairs the ability of any dealer to solicit or effect transactions in such securities for his own account or unreasonably restricts competition among dealers in such securities or between dealers acting in the capacity of market makers who are specialists in such securities and such dealers who are not specialists in such securities, and

(iii) the maintenance or restoration of fair and orderly markets in such securities may not be assured through other lawful means under this title.

The Commission may conditionally or unconditionally exempt any security or transaction or any class of securities or transactions from any such prohibition if the Commission deems such exemption consistent with the public interest, the protection of investors, and the maintenance of fair and orderly markets.

(B) For the purposes of subparagraph (A) of this paragraph, the ability of a dealer to solicit or effect transactions in securities for his own account shall not be deemed to be unreasonably impaired by any rule of an exchange fairly and reasonably prescribing the sequence in which orders brought to the exchange must be executed or which has been adopted to effect compliance with a rule of the Commission promulgated under this title.

(4) The Commission is directed to review any and all rules of national securities exchanges which limit or condition the ability of members to effect transactions in securities otherwise than on such exchanges.

(5) No national securities exchange or registered securities association may limit or condition the participation of any member in any registered clearing agency.

(6) *Tick Size.*

(A) *Study and Report.* The Commission shall conduct a study examining the transition to trading and quoting securities in one penny increments, also known as decimalization. The study shall examine the impact that decimalization has had on the number of initial public offerings since its implementation relative to the period before its implementation. The study shall also examine the impact that this change has had on liquidity for small and middle capitalization company securities and whether there is sufficient economic incentive to support trading operations in these securities in penny increments. Not later than 90 days after the date of enactment of this paragraph, the Commission shall submit to Congress a report on the findings of the study.

(B) *Designation.* If the Commission determines that the securities of emerging growth companies should be quoted and traded using a minimum increment of greater than $0.01, the Commission may, by rule not later than 180 days after the date of enactment of this paragraph, designate a minimum increment for the securities of emerging growth companies that is greater than $0.01 but less than $0.10 for use in all quoting and trading of securities in any exchange or other execution venue.

(d) *National Market Advisory Board.*

(1) Not later than one hundred eighty days after the date of enactment of the Securities Acts Amendments of 1975, the Commission shall establish a National Market Advisory Board (hereinafter in this section referred to as the "Advisory Board") to be composed of fifteen members, not all of whom shall be from the same geographical area of the United States, appointed by the Commission for a term specified by the Commission of not less than two years or more than five years. The Advisory Board shall consist of persons associated with brokers and dealers (who shall be a majority) and persons not so associated who are representative of the public and, to the extent feasible, have knowledge of the securities markets of the United States.

(2) It shall be the responsibility of the Advisory Board to formulate and furnish to the Commission its views on significant regulatory proposals made by the Commission or any self-regulatory organization concerning the establishment, operation, and regulation of the markets for securities in the United States.

(3)(A) The Advisory Board shall study and make recommendations to the Commission as to the steps it finds appropriate to facilitate the establishment of a national market system. In so doing, the Advisory Board shall assume the responsibilities of any advisory committee appointed to advise the Commission with respect to the national market system which is in existence at the time of the establishment of the Advisory Board.

(B) The Advisory Board shall study the possible need for modifications of the scheme of self-regulation provided for in this title so as to adapt it to a national market system, including the need for the establishment of a new self-regulatory organization (hereinafter in this section referred to as a "National Market Regulatory Board" or "Regulatory Board") to administer the national market system. In the event the Advisory Board determines a National Market

Regulatory Board should be established, it shall make recommendations as to:

(i) the point in time at which a Regulatory Board should be established;

(ii) the composition of a Regulatory Board;

(iii) the scope of the authority of a Regulatory Board;

(iv) the relationship of a Regulatory Board to the Commission and to existing self-regulatory organizations; and

(v) the manner in which a Regulatory Board should be funded.

The Advisory Board shall report to the Congress, on or before December 31, 1976, the results of such study and its recommendations, including such recommendations for legislation as it deems appropriate.

(C) In carrying out its responsibilities under this paragraph, the Advisory Board shall consult with self-regulatory organizations, brokers, dealers, securities information processors, issuers, investors, representatives of Government agencies, and other persons interested or likely to participate in the establishment, operation, or regulation of the national market system.

(e) *National Markets System for Security Futures Products.*

(1) *Consultation and Cooperation Required.* With respect to security futures products, the Commission and the Commodity Futures Trading Commission shall consult and cooperate so that, to the maximum extent practicable, their respective regulatory responsibilities may be fulfilled and the rules and regulations applicable to security futures products may foster a national market system for security futures products if the Commission and the Commodity Futures Trading Commission jointly determine that such a system would be consistent with the congressional findings in subsection (a)(1). In accordance with this objective, the Commission shall, at least 15 days prior to the issuance for public comment of any proposed rule or regulation under this section concerning security futures products, consult and request the views of the Commodity Futures Trading Commission.

(2) *Application of Rules by Order of CFTC.* No rule adopted pursuant to this section shall be applied to any person with respect to the trading of security futures products on an exchange that is registered under section 6(g) unless the Commodity Futures Trading Commission has issued an order directing that such rule is applicable to such persons.

Registration Requirements for Securities

Sec. 12. (a) *General Requirement of Registration.* It shall be unlawful for any member, broker, or dealer to effect any transaction in any security (other than an exempted security) on a national securities exchange unless a registration is effective as to such security for such exchange in accordance with the provisions of this title and the rules and regulations thereunder. The provisions of this subsection shall not apply in respect of a security futures product traded on a national securities exchange.

(b) *Procedure for Registration; Information.* A security may be registered on a national securities exchange by the issuer filing an application with the exchange (and filing with the Commission such duplicate originals thereof as the Commission may require), which application shall contain—

(1) Such information, in such detail, as to the issuer and any person directly or indirectly controlling or controlled by, or under direct or indirect common control with, the issuer, and any guarantor of the security as to principal or interest or both, as the Commission may by rules and regulations require, as necessary or appropriate in the public interest or for the protection of investors, in respect of the following:

(A) the organization, financial structure and nature of the business;

(B) the terms, position, rights, and privileges of the different classes of securities outstanding;

(C) the terms on which their securities are to be, and during the preceding three years have been, offered to the public or otherwise;

(D) the directors, officers, and underwriters, and each security holder of record holding more than 10 per centum of any class of any equity security of the issuer (other than an exempted security), their remuneration and their interests in the securities of, and their material contracts with, the issuer and any person directly or indirectly controlling or controlled by, or under direct or indirect common control with, the issuer;

(E) remuneration to others than directors and officers exceeding $20,000 per annum;

(F) bonus and profit-sharing arrangements;

(G) management and service contracts;

(H) options existing or to be created in respect of their securities;

(I) material contracts, not made in the ordinary course of business, which are to be executed in whole or in part at or after the filing of the application or which were made not more than two years before such filing, and every material patent or contract for a material patent right shall be deemed a material contract;

(J) balance sheets for not more than the three preceding fiscal years, certified if required by the rules and regulations of the Commission by a registered public accounting firm;

(K) profit and loss statements for not more than the three preceding fiscal years, certified if required by the rules and regulations of the Commission by a registered public accounting firm; and

(L) any further financial statements which the Commission may deem necessary or appropriate for the protection of investors.

(2) Such copies of articles of incorporation, bylaws, trust indentures, or corresponding documents by whatever name known, underwriting arrangements, and other similar documents of, and voting trust agreements with respect to, the issuer and any person directly or indirectly controlling or controlled by, or under direct or indirect common control with, the issuer as the Commission may require as necessary or appropriate for the proper protection of investors and to insure fair dealing in the security.

(3) Such copies of material contracts, referred to in paragraph (1)(I) above, as the Commission may require as necessary or appropriate for the proper protection of investors and to insure fair dealing in the security.

(c) *Additional or Alternative Information.* If in the judgment of the Commission any information required under subsection (b) is inapplicable to any specified class or classes of issuers, the Commission shall require in lieu thereof the submission of such other information of comparable character as it may deem applicable to such class of issuers.

(d) *Effective Date of Registration; Withdrawal of Registration.* If the exchange authorities certify to the Commission that the security has been approved by the exchange for listing and registration, the registration shall become effective thirty days after the receipt of such certification by the Commission or within such shorter period of time as the Commission may determine. A security registered with a national securities exchange may be withdrawn or stricken from listing and registration in accordance with the rules of the exchange and, upon such terms as the Commission may deem necessary to impose for the protection of investors, upon application by the issuer or the exchange to the Commission; whereupon the issuer shall be relieved from further compliance with the provisions of this section and section 13 of this title and any rules or regulations under such sections as to the securities so withdrawn or stricken. An unissued security may be registered only in accordance with such rules and regulations as the Commission may prescribe as necessary or appropriate in the public interest or for the protection of investors.

(e) *Exemption from Provisions of Section for Period Ending Not Later than July 1, 1935.* Notwithstanding the foregoing provisions of this section, the Commission may by such rules and regulations as it deems necessary or appropriate in the public interest or for the protection of investors, permit securities listed on any exchange at the time the registration of such exchange as a national securities exchange becomes effective, to be registered for a period ending not later than July 1, 1935, without complying with the provisions of this section.

(f) *Unlisted Trading Privileges for Security Originally Listed on Another National Exchange.*

(1)(A) Notwithstanding the preceding subsections of this section, any national securities exchange, in accordance with the requirements of this subsection and the rules hereunder, may extend unlisted trading privileges to—

(i) any security that is listed and registered on a national securities exchange, subject to subparagraph (B); and

(ii) any security that is otherwise registered pursuant to this section, or that would be required to be so registered except for the exemption from registration provided in subparagraph (B) or (G) of subsection (g)(2), subject to subparagraph (E) of this paragraph.

(B) A national securities exchange may not extend unlisted trading privileges to a security described in subparagraph (A)(i) during such interval, if any, after the commencement of an initial public offering of such security, as is or may be required pursuant to subparagraph (C).

(C) Not later than 180 days after the date of enactment of the Unlisted Trading Privileges

Act of 1994, the Commission shall prescribe, by rule or regulation, the duration of the interval referred to in subparagraph (B), if any, as the Commission determines to be necessary or appropriate for the maintenance of fair and orderly markets, the protection of investors and the public interest, or otherwise in furtherance of the purposes of this title. Until the earlier of the effective date of such rule or regulation or 240 days after such date of enactment, such interval shall begin at the opening of trading on the day on which such security commences trading on the national securities exchange with which such security is registered and end at the conclusion of the next day of trading.

(D) The Commission may prescribe, by rule or regulation such additional procedures or requirements for extending unlisted trading privileges to any security as the Commission deems necessary or appropriate for the maintenance of fair and orderly markets, the protection of investors and the public interest, or otherwise in furtherance of the purposes of this title.

(E) No extension of unlisted trading privileges to securities described in subparagraph (A) (ii) may occur except pursuant to a rule, regulation, or order of the Commission approving such extension or extensions. In promulgating such rule or regulation or in issuing such order, the Commission—

(i) shall find that such extension or extensions of unlisted trading privileges is consistent with the maintenance of fair and orderly markets, the protection of investors and the public interest, and otherwise in furtherance of the purposes of this title;

(ii) shall take account of the public trading activity in such securities, the character of such trading, the impact of such extension on the existing markets for such securities, and the desirability of removing impediments to and the progress that has been made toward the development of a national market system; and

(iii) shall not permit a national securities exchange to extend unlisted trading privileges to such securities if any rule of such national securities exchange would unreasonably impair the ability of a dealer to solicit or effect transactions in such securities for its own account, or would unreasonably restrict competition among dealers in such securities or between such dealers acting in the capacity of market makers who are specialists and such dealers who are not specialists.

(F) An exchange may continue to extend unlisted trading privileges in accordance with this paragraph only if the exchange and the subject security continue to satisfy the requirements for eligibility under this paragraph, including any rules and regulations issued by the Commission pursuant to this paragraph, except that unlisted trading privileges may continue with regard to securities which had been admitted on such exchange prior to July 1, 1964, notwithstanding the failure to satisfy such requirements. If unlisted trading privileges in a security are discontinued pursuant to this subparagraph, the exchange shall cease trading in that security, unless the exchange and the subject security thereafter satisfy the requirements of this paragraph and the rules issued hereunder.

(G) For purposes of this paragraph—

(i) a security is the subject of an initial public offering if—

(I) the offering of the subject security is registered under the Securities Act of 1933; and

(II) the issuer of the security, immediately prior to filing the registration statement with respect to the offering, was not subject to the reporting requirements of section 13 or 15(d) of this title; and

(ii) an initial public offering of such security commences at the opening of trading on the day on which such security commences trading on the national securities exchange with which such security is registered.

(2)(A) At any time within 60 days of commencement of trading on an exchange of a security pursuant to unlisted trading privileges, the Commission may summarily suspend such unlisted trading privileges on the exchange. Such suspension shall not be reviewable under section 25 of this title and shall not be deemed to be a final agency action for purposes of section 704 of title 5, United States Code. Upon such suspension—

(i) the exchange shall cease trading in the security by the close of business on the date of such suspension, or at such time as the Commission may prescribe by rule or order for the maintenance of fair and orderly markets, the protection of investors and the public interest, or otherwise in furtherance of the purposes of this title; and

(ii) if the exchange seeks to extend unlisted trading privileges to the security, the exchange shall file an application to reinstate its ability to do so with the Commission pursuant to such procedures as the Commission may prescribe by rule or order for the maintenance of fair and orderly markets, the protection of investors and the public interest, or otherwise in furtherance of the purposes of this title.

(B) A suspension under subparagraph (A) shall remain in effect until the Commission, by order, grants approval of an application to reinstate, as described in subparagraph (A)(ii).

(C) A suspension under subparagraph (A) shall not affect the validity or force of an extension of unlisted trading privileges in effect prior to such suspension.

(D) The Commission shall not approve an application by a national securities exchange to reinstate its ability to extend unlisted trading privileges to a security unless the Commission finds, after notice and opportunity for hearing, that the extension of unlisted trading privileges pursuant to such application is consistent with the maintenance of fair and orderly markets, the protection of investors and the public interest, and otherwise in furtherance of the purposes of this title. If the application is made to reinstate unlisted trading privileges to a security described in paragraph (1)(A)(ii), the Commission—

(i) shall take account of the public trading activity in such security, the character of such trading, the impact of such extension on the existing markets for such a security, and the desirability of removing impediments to and the progress that has been made toward the development of a national market system; and

(ii) shall not grant any such application if any rule of the national securities exchange making application under this subsection would unreasonably impair the ability of a dealer to solicit or effect transactions in such security for its own account, or would unreasonably restrict competition among dealers in such security or between such dealers acting in the capacity of marketmakers who are specialists and such dealers who are not specialists.

(3) Notwithstanding paragraph (2), the Commission shall by rules and regulations suspend unlisted trading privileges in whole or in part for any or all classes of securities for a period not exceeding twelve months, if it deems such suspension necessary or appropriate in the public interest or for the protection of investors or to prevent evasion of the purposes of this title.

(4) On the application of the issuer of any security for which unlisted trading privileges on any exchange have been continued or extended pursuant to this subsection, or of any broker or dealer who makes or creates a market for such security, or of any other person having a bona fide interest in the question of termination or suspension of such unlisted trading privileges, or on its own motion, the Commission shall by order terminate, or suspend for a period not exceeding twelve months, such unlisted trading privileges for such security if the Commission finds, after appropriate notice and opportunity for hearing, that such termination or suspension is necessary or appropriate in the public interest or for the protection of investors.

(5) In any proceeding under this subsection in which appropriate notice and opportunity for hearing are required, notice of not less than ten days to the applicant in such proceeding, to the issuer of the security involved, to the exchange which is seeking to continue or extend or has continued or extended unlisted trading privileges for such security, and to the exchange, if any, on which such security is listed and registered, shall be deemed adequate notice, and any broker or dealer who makes or creates a market for such security, and any other person having a bona fide interest in such proceeding, shall upon application be entitled to be heard.

(6) Any security for which unlisted trading privileges are continued or extended pursuant to this subsection shall be deemed to be registered on a national securities exchange within the meaning of this title. The powers and duties of the Commission under this title shall be applicable to the rules of an exchange in respect of any such security. The Commission may, by such rules and regulations as it deems necessary or appropriate in the public interest or for the protection of investors, either unconditionally or upon specified terms and conditions, or for stated periods, exempt such securities

from the operation of any provision of section 13, 14, or 16 of this title.

(g) *Registration of Securities by Issuer; Exemptions.*

(1) Every issuer which is engaged in interstate commerce, or in a business affecting interstate commerce, or whose securities are traded by use of the mails or any means or instrumentality of interstate commerce shall—

(A) within 120 days after the last day of its first fiscal year ended on which the issuer has total assets exceeding $10,000,000 and a class of equity security (other than an exempted security) held of record by either—

(i) 2,000 persons, or

(ii) 500 persons who are not accredited investors (as such term is defined by the Commission), and

(B) in the case of an issuer that is a bank, a savings and loan holding company (as defined in Section 10 of the Home Owners' Loan Act), or a bank holding company, as such term is defined in section 2 of the Bank Holding Company Act of 1956, not later than 120 days after the last day of its first fiscal year ended after the effective date of this subsection, on which the issuer has total assets exceeding $10,000,000 and a class of equity security (other than an exempted security) held of record by 2,000 or more persons,

register such security by filing with the Commission a registration statement (and such copies thereof as the Commission may require) with respect to such security containing such information and documents as the Commission may specify comparable to that which is required in an application to register a security pursuant to subsection (b) of this section. Each such registration statement shall become effective sixty days after filing with the Commission or within such shorter period as the Commission may direct. Until such registration statement becomes effective it shall not be deemed filed for the purposes of section 18 of this title. Any issuer may register any class of equity security not required to be registered by filing a registration statement pursuant to the provisions of this paragraph. The Commission is authorized to extend the date upon which any issuer or class of issuers is required to register a security pursuant to the provisions of this paragraph.

(2) The provisions of this subsection shall not apply in respect of—

(A) any security listed and registered on a national securities exchange.

(B) any security issued by an investment company registered pursuant to section 8 of the Investment Company Act of 1940.

(C) any security, other than permanent stock, guaranty stock, permanent reserve stock, or any similar certificate evidencing nonwithdrawable capital, issued by a savings and loan association, building and loan association, cooperative bank, homestead association, or similar institution, which is supervised and examined by State or Federal authority having supervision over any such institution.

(D) any security of an issuer organized and operated exclusively for religious, educational, benevolent, fraternal, charitable, or reformatory purposes and not for pecuniary profit, and no part of the net earnings of which inures to the benefit of any private shareholder or individual; or any security of a fund that is excluded from the definition of an investment company under section 3(c)(10)(B) of the Investment Company Act of 1940.

(E) any security of an issuer which is a "cooperative association" as defined in the Agricultural Marketing Act, approved June 15, 1929, as amended, or a federation of such cooperative associations, if such federation possesses no greater powers or purposes than cooperative associations so defined.

(F) any security issued by a mutual or cooperative organization which supplies a commodity or service primarily for the benefit of its members and operates not for pecuniary profit, but only if the security is part of a class issuable only to persons who purchase commodities or services from the issuer, the security is transferable only to a successor in interest or occupancy of premises serviced or to be served by the issuer, and no dividends are payable to the holder of the security.

(G) any security issued by an insurance company if all of the following conditions are met:

(i) Such insurance company is required to and does file an annual statement with the Commissioner of Insurance (or other officer or agency performing a similar function) of its domiciliary State, and such annual statement conforms to that prescribed by the National Association of Insurance Commissioners or in the determination of such State commissioner, officer or agency substantially conforms to that so prescribed.

(ii) Such insurance company is subject to regulation by its domiciliary State of proxies, consents, or authorizations in respect of securities issued by such company and such regulation conforms to that prescribed by the National Association of Insurance Commissioners.

(iii) After July 1, 1966, the purchase and sales of securities issued by such insurance company by beneficial owners, directors, or officers of such company are subject to regulation (including reporting) by its domiciliary State substantially in the manner provided in section 16 of this title.

(H) any interest or participation in any collective trust funds maintained by a bank or in a separate account maintained by an insurance company which interest or participation is issued in connection with (i) a stock-bonus, pension, or profit-sharing plan which meets the requirements for qualification under section 401 of the Internal Revenue Code of 1954, (ii) an annuity plan which meets the requirements for deduction of the employer's contribution under section 404(a)(2) of such Code, or (iii) a church plan, company, or account that is excluded from the definition of an investment company under section 3(c)(14) of the Investment Company Act of 1940.

(3) The Commission may by rules or regulations or, on its own motion, after notice and opportunity for hearing, by order, exempt from this subsection any security of a foreign issuer, including any certificate of deposit for such a security, if the Commission finds that such exemption is in the public interest and is consistent with the protection of investors.

(4) Registration of any class of security pursuant to this subsection shall be terminated ninety days, or such shorter period as the Commission may determine, after the issuer files a certification with the Commission that the number of holders of record of such class of security is reduced to less than 300 persons, or, in the case of a bank, a savings and loan holding company (as defined in Section 10 of the Home Owners' Loan Act), or a bank holding company, as such term is defined in section 2 of the Bank Holding Company Act of 1956, 1,200 persons. The Commission shall after notice and opportunity for hearing deny termination of registration if it finds that the certification is untrue. Termination of registration shall be deferred pending final determination on the question of denial.

(5) For the purposes of this subsection the term "class" shall include all securities of an issuer which are of substantially similar character and the holders of which enjoy substantially similar rights and privileges. The Commission may for the purpose of this subsection define by rules and regulations the terms "total assets" and "held of record" as it deems necessary or appropriate in the public interest or for the protection of investors in order to prevent circumvention of the provisions of this subsection. For purposes of this subsection, a security futures product shall not be considered a class of equity security of the issuer of the securities underlying the security futures product. For purposes of determining whether an issuer is required to register a security with the Commission pursuant to paragraph (1), the definition of 'held of record' shall not include securities held by persons who received the securities pursuant to an employee compensation plan in transactions exempted from the registration requirements of section 5 of the Securities Act of 1933.

(6) *Exclusion for Persons Holding Certain Securities.* The Commission shall, by rule, exempt, conditionally or unconditionally, securities acquired pursuant to an offering made under section 4(6) of the Securities Act of 1933 from the provisions of this subsection.

(h) *Exemption by Rules and Regulations from Certain Provisions of Section.* The Commission may by rules and regulations, or upon application of an interested person, by order, after notice and opportunity for hearing, exempt in whole or in part any issuer or class of issuers from the provisions of subsection (g) of this section or from section 13, 14, or 15(d) or may exempt from section 16 any officer, director, or beneficial owner of securities of any issuer, any security of which is required to be registered pursuant to subsection (g) hereof, upon such terms and conditions and for such period as it deems necessary or appropriate, if the Commission finds, by reason of the number of public investors, amount of trading interest in the securities, the nature and extent of the activities of the issuer, income or assets of the issuer, or otherwise, that such action is not inconsistent with the public interest or the protection of investors. The Commission may, for the purposes of any of the above-mentioned sections or subsections of this title, classify issuers and prescribe requirements appropriate for each such class.

(i) *Securities Issued by Banks.* In respect of any securities issued by banks and savings associations the deposits of which are insured in accordance with the Federal Deposit Insurance Act, the powers, functions, and duties vested in the Commission to administer and enforce sections 10A(m), 12, 13, 14(a), 14(c), 14(d), 14(f), and 16 of this Act, and sections 302, 303, 304, 306, 401(b), 404, 406, and 407 of the Sarbanes-Oxley Act of 2002, (1) with respect to national banks and Federal savings associations, the accounts of which are insured by the Federal Deposit Insurance Corporation are vested in the Comptroller of the Currency, (2) with respect to all other member banks of the Federal Reserve System are vested in the Board of Governors of the Federal Reserve System, and (3) with respect to all other insured banks and State savings associations, the accounts of which are insured by the Federal Deposit Insurance Corporation, are vested in the Federal Deposit Insurance Corporation. The Comptroller of the Currency, the Board of Governors of the Federal Reserve System, and the Federal Deposit Insurance Corporation shall have the power to make such rules and regulations as may be necessary for the execution of the functions vested in them as provided in this subsection. In carrying out their responsibilities under this subsection, the agencies named in the first sentence of this subsection shall issue substantially similar regulations to regulations and rules issued by the Commission under sections 10A(m), 12, 13, 14(a), 14(c), 14(d), 14(f) and 16 of this Act, and sections 302, 303, 304, 306, 401(b), 404, 406, and 407 of the Sarbanes-Oxley Act of 2002, unless they find that implementation of substantially similar regulations with respect to insured banks and insured institutions are not necessary or appropriate in the public interest or for protection of investors, and publish such findings, and the detailed reasons therefor, in the Federal Register. Such regulations of the above-named agencies, or the reasons for failure to publish such substantially similar regulations to those of the Commission, shall be published in the Federal Register within 120 days of the date of enactment of this subsection, and, thereafter, within 60 days of any changes made by the Commission in its relevant regulations and rules.

(j) *Denial, Suspension, or Revocation of Registration; Notice and Hearing.* The Commission is authorized, by order, as it deems necessary or appropriate for the protection of investors to deny, to suspend the effective date of, to suspend for a period not exceeding twelve months, or to revoke the registration of a security, if the Commission finds, on the record after notice and opportunity for hearing, that the issuer of such security has failed to comply with any provision of this title or the rules and regulations thereunder. No member of a national securities exchange, broker, or dealer shall make use of the mails or any means or instrumentality of interstate commerce to effect any transaction in, or to induce the purchase or sale of, any security the registration of which has been and is suspended or revoked pursuant to the preceding sentence.

(k) *Trading Suspensions; Emergency Authority.*

(1) *Trading Suspensions.* If in its opinion the public interest and the protection of investors so require, the Commission is authorized by order—

(A) summarily to suspend trading in any security (other than an exempted security) for a period not exceeding 10 business days, and

(B) summarily to suspend all trading on any national securities exchange or otherwise, in securities other than exempted securities, for a period not exceeding 90 calendar days.

The action described in subparagraph (B) shall not take effect unless the Commission notifies the President of its decision and the President notifies the Commission that the President does not disapprove of such decision. If the actions described in subparagraph (A) or (B) involve a security futures product, the Commission shall consult with and consider the views of the Commodity Futures Trading Commission.

(2) *Emergency Orders.*

(A) *In General.* The Commission, in an emergency, may by order summarily take such action to alter, supplement, suspend, or impose requirements or restrictions with respect to any matter or action subject to regulation by the Commission or a self-regulatory organization under the securities laws, as the Commission determines is necessary in the public interest and for the protection of investors—

(i) to maintain or restore fair and orderly securities markets (other than markets in exempted securities);

(ii) to ensure prompt, accurate, and safe clearance and settlement of transactions in securities (other than exempted securities); or

(iii) to reduce, eliminate, or prevent the substantial disruption by the emergency of—

(I) securities markets (other than markets in exempted securities), investment companies, or any other significant portion or segment of such markets; or

(II) the transmission or processing of securities transactions (other than transactions in exempted securities).

(B) *Effective Period.* An order of the Commission under this paragraph shall continue in effect for the period specified by the Commission, and may be extended. Except as provided in subparagraph (C), an order of the Commission under this paragraph may not continue in effect for more than 10 business days, including extensions.

(C) *Extension.* An order of the Commission under this paragraph may be extended to continue in effect for more than 10 business days if, at the time of the extension, the Commission finds that the emergency still exists and determines that the continuation of the order beyond 10 business days is necessary in the public interest and for the protection of investors to attain an objective described in clause (i), (ii), or (iii) of subparagraph (A). In no event shall an order of the Commission under this paragraph continue in effect for more than 30 calendar days.

(D) *Security Futures.* If the actions described in subparagraph (A) involve a security futures product, the Commission shall consult with and consider the views of the Commodity Futures Trading Commission.

(E) *Exemption.* In exercising its authority under this paragraph, the Commission shall not be required to comply with the provisions of—

(i) section 19(c); or

(ii) section 553 of title 5, United States Code.

(3) *Termination of Emergency Actions by President.* The President may direct that action taken by the Commission under paragraph (1)(B) or paragraph (2) of this subsection shall not continue in effect.

(4) *Compliance With Orders.* No member of a national securities exchange, broker, or dealer shall make use of the mails or any means or instrumentality of interstate commerce to effect any transaction in, or to induce the purchase or sale of, any security in contravention of an order of the Commission under this subsection unless such order has been stayed, modified, or set aside as provided in paragraph (5) of this subsection or has ceased to be effective upon direction of the President as provided in paragraph (3).

(5) *Limitations on Review of Orders.* An order of the Commission pursuant to this subsection shall be subject to review only as provided in section 25(a) of this title. Review shall be based on an examination of all the information before the Commission at the time such order was issued. The reviewing court shall not enter a stay, writ of mandamus, or similar relief unless the court finds, after notice and hearing before a panel of the court, that the Commission's action is arbitrary, capricious, an abuse of discretion, or otherwise not in accordance with law.

(6) *Consultation.* Prior to taking any action described in paragraph (1)(B), the Commission shall consult with and consider the views of the Secretary of the Treasury, the Board of Governors of the Federal Reserve System, and the Commodity Futures Trading Commission, unless such consultation is impracticable in light of the emergency.

(7) *Definition.* For purposes of this subsection, the term "emergency" means—

(A) a major market disturbance characterized by or constituting—

(i) sudden and excessive fluctuations of securities prices generally, or a substantial threat thereof, that threaten fair and orderly markets; or

(ii) a substantial disruption of the safe or efficient operation of the national system for clearance and settlement of transactions in securities, or a substantial threat thereof; or

(B) a major disturbance that substantially disrupts, or threatens to substantially disrupt—

(i) the functioning of securities markets, investment companies, or any other significant portion or segment of the securities markets; or

(ii) the transmission or processing of securities transactions.

(*l*) *Issuance of Any Security in Contravention of Rules and Regulations; Application to Annuity Contracts and Variable Life Policies.* It shall be unlawful for an issuer, any class of whose securities is registered pursuant to this section or would be required to be so registered except for the exemption from registration provided by subsection (g)(2)(B) or (g)(2)

(G) of this section, by the use of any means or instrumentality of interstate commerce, or of the mails, to issue, either originally or upon transfer, any of such securities in a form or with a format which contravenes such rules and regulations as the Commission may prescribe as necessary or appropriate for the prompt and accurate clearance and settlement of transactions in securities. The provisions of this subsection shall not apply to variable annuity contracts or variable life policies issued by an insurance company or its separate accounts.

Periodical and Other Reports

Sec. 13. (a) *Reports by Issuer of Security; Contents.* Every issuer of a security registered pursuant to section 12 of this title shall file with the Commission, in accordance with such rules and regulations as the Commission may prescribe as necessary or appropriate for the proper protection of investors and to insure fair dealing in the security—

(1) such information and documents (and such copies thereof) as the Commission shall require to keep reasonably current the information and documents required to be included in or filed with an application or registration statement filed pursuant to section 12, except that the Commission may not require the filing of any material contract wholly executed before July 1, 1962.

(2) such annual reports (and such copies thereof), certified if required by the rules and regulations of the Commission by independent public accountants, and such quarterly reports (and such copies thereof), as the Commission may prescribe.

Every issuer of a security registered on a national securities exchange shall also file a duplicate original of such information, documents, and reports with the exchange. In any registration statement, periodic report, or other reports to be filed with the Commission, an emerging growth company need not present selected financial data in accordance with Item 301 under Regulation S–K, for any period prior to the earliest audited period presented in connection with its first registration statement that became effective under this Act or the Securities Act of 1933 and, with respect to any such statement or reports, an emerging growth company may not be required to comply with any new or revised financial accounting standard until such date that a company that is not an issuer (as defined under section 2(a) of the Sarbanes–Oxley Act of 2002) is required to comply with such new or revised accounting standard, if such standard applies to companies that are not issuers.

(b) *Form of Report; Books, Records, and Internal Accounting; Directives.* (1) The Commission may prescribe, in regard to reports made pursuant to this title, the form or forms in which the required information shall be set forth, the items or details to be shown in the balance sheet and the earnings statement, and the methods to be followed in the preparation of reports, in the appraisal or valuation of assets and liabilities, in the determination of depreciation and depletion, in the differentiation of recurring and nonrecurring income, in the differentiation of investment and operating income, and in the preparation, where the Commission deems it necessary or desirable, of separate and/or consolidated balance sheets or income accounts of any person directly or indirectly controlling or controlled by the issuer, or any person under direct or indirect common control with the issuer; but in the case of the reports of any person whose methods of accounting are prescribed under the provisions of any law of the United States, or any rule or regulation thereunder, the rules and regulations of the Commission with respect to reports shall not be inconsistent with the requirements imposed by such law or rule or regulation in respect of the same subject matter, (except that such rules and regulations of the Commission may be inconsistent with such requirements to the extent that the Commission determines that the public interest or the protection of investors so requires).

(2) Every issuer which has a class of securities registered pursuant to section 12 of this title and every issuer which is required to file reports pursuant to section 15(d) of this title shall—

(A) make and keep books, records, and accounts, which, in reasonable detail, accurately and fairly reflect the transactions and dispositions of the assets of the issuer;

(B) devise and maintain a system of internal accounting controls sufficient to provide reasonable assurances that—

(i) transactions are executed in accordance with management's general or specific authorization;

(ii) transactions are recorded as necessary (I) to permit preparation of financial statements in conformity with generally accepted accounting principles or any other criteria applicable to such statements, and (II) to maintain accountability for assets;

(iii) access to assets is permitted only in accordance with management's general or specific authorization; and

(iv) the recorded accountability for assets is compared with the existing assets at reasonable intervals and appropriate action is taken with respect to any differences; and

(C) notwithstanding any other provision of law, pay the allocable share of such issuer of a reasonable annual accounting support fee or fees, determined in accordance with section 109 of the Sarbanes–Oxley Act of 2002.

(3)(A) With respect to matters concerning the national security of the United States, no duty or liability under paragraph (2) of this subsection shall be imposed upon any person acting in cooperation with the head of any Federal department or agency responsible for such matters if such act in cooperation with such head of a department or agency was done upon the specific, written directive of the head of such department or agency pursuant to Presidential authority to issue such directives. Each directive issued under this paragraph shall set forth the specific facts and circumstances with respect to which the provisions of this paragraph are to be invoked. Each such directive shall, unless renewed in writing, expire one year after the date of issuance.

(B) Each head of a Federal department or agency of the United States who issues a directive pursuant to this paragraph shall maintain a complete file of all such directives and shall, on October 1 of each year, transmit a summary of matters covered by such directives in force at any time during the previous year to the Permanent Select Committee on Intelligence of the House of Representatives and the Select Committee on Intelligence of the Senate.

(4) No criminal liability shall be imposed for failing to comply with the requirements of paragraph (2) of this subsection except as provided in paragraph (5) of this subsection

(5) No person shall knowingly circumvent or knowingly fail to implement a system of internal accounting controls or knowingly falsify any book, record, or account described in paragraph (2).

(6) Where an issuer which has a class of securities registered pursuant to section 12 of this title or an issuer which is required to file reports pursuant to section 15(d) of this title holds 50 per centum or less of the voting power with respect to a domestic or foreign firm, the provisions of paragraph (2) require only that the issuer proceed in good faith to use its influence, to the extent reasonable under the issuer's circumstances, to cause such domestic or foreign firm to devise and maintain a system of internal accounting controls consistent with paragraph (2). Such circumstances include the relative degree of the issuer's ownership of the domestic or foreign firm and the laws and practices governing the business operations of the country in which such firm is located. An issuer which demonstrates good faith efforts to use such influence shall be conclusively presumed to have complied with the requirements of paragraph (2).

(7) For the purpose of paragraph (2) of this section, the terms "reasonable assurances" and "reasonable detail" mean such level of detail and degree of assurance as would satisfy prudent officials in the conduct of their own affairs.

(c) *Alternative Reports.* If in the judgment of the Commission any report required under subsection (a) is inapplicable to any specified class or classes of issuers, the Commission shall require in lieu thereof the submission of such reports of comparable character as it may deem applicable to such class or classes of issuers.

(d) *Reports by Persons Acquiring More than Five Per Centum of Certain Classes of Securities.*

(1) Any person who, after acquiring directly or indirectly the beneficial ownership of any equity security of a class which is registered pursuant to section 12 of this title, or any equity security of an insurance company which would have been required to be so registered except for the exemption contained in section 12(g)(2)(G) of this title, or any equity security issued by a closed-end investment company registered under the Investment Company Act of 1940 or any equity security issued by a Native Corporation pursuant to Section 37(d)(6) of the Alaska Native Claims Settlement Act, or otherwise becomes or is deemed to become a beneficial owner of any of the foregoing upon the purchase or sale of a security-based swap that the Commission may define by rule, and is directly or indirectly the beneficial owner of more than 5 per centum of such class shall, within ten days after such acquisition or within such shorter time as the Commission may establish by rule, file with the Commission, a statement containing such of the following information, and such additional information, as the Commission may by rules and regulations prescribe as necessary or appropriate

in the public interest or for the protection of investors—

(A) the background, and identity, residence, and citizenship of, and the nature of such beneficial ownership by, such person and all other persons by whom or on whose behalf the purchases have been or are to be effected;

(B) the source and amount of the funds or other consideration used or to be used in making the purchases, and if any part of the purchase price is represented or is to be represented by funds or other consideration borrowed or otherwise obtained for the purpose of acquiring, holding, or trading such security, a description of the transaction and the names of the parties thereto, except that where a source of funds is a loan made in the ordinary course of business by a bank, as defined in section 3(a)(6) of this title, if the person filing such statement so requests, the name of the bank shall not be made available to the public;

(C) if the purpose of the purchases or prospective purchases is to acquire control of the business of the issuer of the securities, any plans or proposals which such persons may have to liquidate such issuer, to sell its assets to or merge it with any other persons, or to make any other major change in its business or corporate structure;

(D) the number of shares of such security which are beneficially owned, and the number of shares concerning which there is a right to acquire, directly or indirectly, by (i) such person, and (ii) by each associate of such person, giving the background, identity, residence, and citizenship of each such associate; and

(E) information as to any contracts, arrangements, or understandings with any person with respect to any securities of the issuer, including but not limited to transfer of any of the securities, joint ventures, loan or option arrangements, puts or calls, guaranties of loans, guaranties against loss or guaranties of profits, division of losses or profits, or the giving or withholding of proxies, naming the persons with whom such contracts, arrangements, or understandings have been entered into, and giving the details thereof.

(2) If any material change occurs in the facts set forth in the statement filed with the Commission, an amendment shall be filed with the Commission, in accordance with such rules and regulations as the Commission may prescribe as necessary or appropriate in the public interest or for the protection of investors.

(3) When two or more persons act as a partnership, limited partnership, syndicate, or other group for the purpose of acquiring, holding, or disposing of securities of an issuer, such syndicate or group shall be deemed a "person" for the purposes of this subsection.

(4) In determining, for purposes of this subsection, any percentage of a class of any security, such class shall be deemed to consist of the amount of the outstanding securities of such class, exclusive of any securities of such class held by or for the account of the issuer or a subsidiary of the issuer.

(5) The Commission, by rule or regulation or by order, may permit any person to file in lieu of the statement required by paragraph (1) of this subsection or the rules and regulations thereunder, a notice stating the name of such person, the number of shares of any equity securities subject to paragraph (1) which are owned by him, the date of their acquisition and such other information as the Commission may specify, if it appears to the Commission that such securities were acquired by such person in the ordinary course of his business and were not acquired for the purpose of and do not have the effect of changing or influencing the control of the issuer nor in connection with or as a participant in any transaction having such purpose or effect.

(6) The provisions of this subsection shall not apply to—

(A) any acquisition or offer to acquire securities made or proposed to be made by means of a registration statement under the Securities Act of 1933;

(B) any acquisition of the beneficial ownership of a security which, together with all other acquisitions by the same person of securities of the same class during the preceding twelve months, does not exceed 2 per centum of that class;

(C) any acquisition of an equity security by the issuer of such security;

(D) any acquisition or proposed acquisition of a security which the Commission, by rules or regulations or by order, shall exempt from the provisions of this subsection as not entered into for the purpose of, and not having the effect of, changing or influencing the control of the issuer or otherwise as not comprehended within the purposes of this subsection.

(e) *Purchase of Securities by Issuer.*

(1) It shall be unlawful for an issuer which has a class of equity securities registered pursuant to section 12 of this title, or which is a closed-end investment company registered under the Investment Company Act of 1940, to purchase any equity security issued by it if such purchase is in contravention of such rules and regulations as the Commission, in the public interest or for the protection of investors, may adopt (A) to define acts and practices which are fraudulent, deceptive, or manipulative, and (B) to prescribe means reasonably designed to prevent such acts and practices. Such rules and regulations may require such issuer to provide holders of equity securities of such class with such information relating to the reasons for such purchase, the source of funds, the number of shares to be purchased, the price to be paid for such securities, the method of purchase, and such additional information, as the Commission deems necessary or appropriate in the public interest or for the protection of investors, or which the Commission deems to be material to a determination whether such security should be sold.

(2) For the purpose of this subsection, a purchase by or for the issuer or any person controlling, controlled by, or under common control with the issuer, or a purchase subject to control of the issuer or any such person, shall be deemed to be a purchase by the issuer. The Commission shall have power to make rules and regulations implementing this paragraph in the public interest and for the protection of investors, including exemptive rules and regulations covering situations in which the Commission deems it unnecessary or inappropriate that a purchase of the type described in this paragraph shall be deemed to be a purchase by the issuer for purposes of some or all of the provisions of paragraph (1) of this subsection.

(3) At the time of filing such statement as the Commission may require by rule pursuant to paragraph (1) of this subsection, the person making the filing shall pay to the Commission a fee at a rate that, subject to paragraph (4), is equal to $92 per $1,000,000 of the value of securities proposed to be purchased. The fee shall be reduced with respect to securities in an amount equal to any fee paid with respect to any securities issued in connection with the proposed transaction under section 6(b) of the Securities Act of 1933, or the fee paid under that section shall be reduced in an amount equal to the fee paid to the Commission in connection with such transaction under this paragraph.

(4) *Annual Adjustment*. For each fiscal year, the Commission shall by order adjust the rate required by paragraph (3) for such fiscal year to a rate that is equal to the rate (expressed in dollars per million) that is applicable under section 6(b) of the Securities Act of 1933 for such fiscal year.

(5) *Fee Collections.* Fees collected pursuant to this subsection for fiscal year 2012 and each fiscal year thereafter shall be deposited and credited as general revenue of the Treasury and shall not be available for obligation.

(6) *Effective Date; Publication.* In exercising its authority under this subsection, the Commission shall not be required to comply with the provisions of section 553 of title 5, United States Code. An adjusted rate prescribed under paragraph (4) shall be published and take effect in accordance with section 6(b) of the Securities Act of 1933.

(7) *Pro Rata Application.* The rates per $1,000,000 required by this subsection shall be applied pro rata to amounts and balances of less than $1,000,000.

(f) *Reports by Institutional Investment Managers.*

(1) Every institutional investment manager which uses the mails, or any means or instrumentality of interstate commerce in the course of its business as an institutional investment manager and which exercises investment discretion with respect to accounts holding equity securities of a class described in subsection (d)(1) of this section or otherwise becomes or is deemed to become a beneficial owner of any security of a class described in subsection (d)(1) upon the purchase or sale of a security-based swap that the Commission may define by rule, having an aggregate fair market value on the last trading day in any of the preceding twelve months of at least $100,000,000 or such lesser amount (but in no case less than $10,000,000) as the Commission, by rule, may determine, shall file reports with the Commission in such form, for such periods, and at such times after the end of such periods as the Commission, by rule, may prescribe, but in no event shall such reports be filed for periods longer than one year or shorter than one quarter. Such reports shall include for each such equity security held on the last day of the reporting period by accounts (in aggregate or by type as the Commission, by rule, may

prescribe) with respect to which the institutional investment manager exercises investment discretion (other than securities held in amounts which the Commission, by rule, determines to be insignificant for purposes of this subsection), the name of the issuer and the title, class, CUSIP number, number of shares or principal amount, and aggregate fair market value of each such security. Such reports may also include for accounts (in aggregate or by type) with respect to which the institutional investment manager exercises investment discretion such of the following information as the Commission, by rule, prescribes—

(A) the name of the issuer and the title, class, CUSIP number, number of shares or principal amount, and aggregate fair market value or cost or amortized cost of each other security (other than an exempted security) held on the last day of the reporting period by such accounts;

(B) the aggregate fair market value or cost or amortized cost of exempted securities (in aggregate or by class) held on the last day of the reporting period by such accounts;

(C) the number of shares of each equity security of a class described in section 13(d)(1) of this title held on the last day of the reporting period by such accounts with respect to which the institutional investment manager possesses sole or shared authority to exercise the voting rights evidenced by such securities;

(D) the aggregate purchases and aggregate sales during the reporting period of each security (other than an exempted security) effected by or for such accounts; and

(E) with respect to any transaction or series of transactions having a market value of at least $500,000 or such other amount as the Commission, by rule, may determine, effected during the reporting period by or for such accounts in any equity security of a class described in section 13(d)(1) of this title—

(i) the name of the issuer and the title, class, and CUSIP number of the security;

(ii) the number of shares or principal amount of the security involved in the transaction;

(iii) whether the transaction was a purchase or sale;

(iv) the per share price or prices at which the transaction was effected;

(v) the date or dates of the transaction;

(vi) the date or dates of the settlement of the transaction;

(vii) the broker or dealer through whom the transaction was effected;

(viii) the market or markets in which the transaction was effected; and

(ix) such other related information as the Commission, by rule, may prescribe.

(2) The Commission shall prescribe rules providing for the public disclosure of the name of the issuer and the title, class, CUSIP number, aggregate amount of the number of short sales of each security, and any additional information determined by the Commission following the end of the reporting period. At a minimum, such public disclosure shall occur every month.

(3) The Commission, by rule or order, may exempt, conditionally or unconditionally, any institutional investment manager or security or any class of institutional investment managers or securities from any or all of the provisions of this subsection or the rules thereunder.

(4) The Commission shall make available to the public for a reasonable fee a list of all equity securities of a class described in section 13(d)(1) of this title, updated no less frequently than reports are required to be filed pursuant to paragraph (1) of this subsection. The Commission shall tabulate the information contained in any report filed pursuant to this subsection in a manner which will, in the view of the Commission, maximize the usefulness of the information to other Federal and State authorities and the public. Promptly after the filing of any such report, the Commission shall make the information contained therein conveniently available to the public for a reasonable fee in such form as the Commission, by rule, may prescribe, except that the Commission, as it determines to be necessary or appropriate in the public interest or for the protection of investors, may delay or prevent public disclosure of any such information in accordance with section 552 of title 5, United States Code. Notwithstanding the preceding sentence, any such information identifying the securities held by the account of a natural person or an estate or trust (other than a business trust or investment company) shall not be disclosed to the public.

(5) In exercising its authority under this subsection, the Commission shall determine (and so

state) that its action is necessary or appropriate in the public interest and for the protection of investors or to maintain fair and orderly markets or, in granting an exemption, that its action is consistent with the protection of investors and the purposes of this subsection. In exercising such authority the Commission shall take such steps as are within its power, including consulting with the Comptroller General of the United States, the Director of the Office of Management and Budget, the appropriate regulatory agencies, Federal and State authorities which, directly or indirectly, require reports from institutional investment managers of information substantially similar to that called for by this subsection, national securities exchanges, and registered securities associations, (A) to achieve uniform, centralized reporting of information concerning the securities holdings of and transactions by or for accounts with respect to which institutional investment managers exercise investment discretion, and (B) consistently with the objective set forth in the preceding subparagraph, to avoid unnecessarily duplicative reporting by, and minimize the compliance burden on, institutional investment managers. Federal authorities which, directly or indirectly, require reports from institutional investment managers of information substantially similar to that called for by this subsection shall cooperate with the Commission in the performance of its responsibilities under the preceding sentence. An institutional investment manager which is a bank, the deposits of which are insured in accordance with the Federal Deposit Insurance Act, shall file with the appropriate regulatory agency a copy of every report filed with the Commission pursuant to this subsection.

(6)(A) For purposes of this subsection the term "institutional investment manager" includes any person, other than a natural person, investing in or buying and selling securities for its own account, and any person exercising investment discretion with respect to the account of any other person.

(B) The Commission shall adopt such rules as it deems necessary or appropriate to prevent duplicative reporting pursuant to this subsection by two or more institutional investment managers exercising investment discretion with respect to the same amount.

(g) *Statement of Equity Security Ownership.*

(1) Any person who is directly or indirectly the beneficial owner of more than 5 per centum of any security of a class described in subsection (d)(1) of this section or otherwise becomes or is deemed to become a beneficial owner of any security of a class described in subsection (d)(1) upon the purchase or sale of a security-based swap that the Commission may define by rule shall file with the Commission a statement setting forth, in such form and at such time as the Commission may, by rule, prescribe—

(A) such person's identity, residence, and citizenship; and

(B) the number and description of the shares in which such person has an interest and the nature of such interest.

(2) If any material change occurs in the facts set forth in the statement filed with the Commission, an amendment shall be filed with the Commission, in accordance with such rules and regulations as the Commission may prescribe as necessary or appropriate in the public interest or for the protection of investors.

(3) When two or more persons act as a partnership, limited partnership, syndicate, or other group for the purpose of acquiring, holding, or disposing of securities of an issuer, such syndicate or group shall be deemed a "person" for the purposes of this subsection.

(4) In determining, for purposes of this subsection, any percentage of a class of any security, such class shall be deemed to consist of the amount of the outstanding securities of such class, exclusive of any securities of such class held by or for the account of the issuer or a subsidiary of the issuer.

(5) In exercising its authority under this subsection, the Commission shall take such steps as it deems necessary or appropriate in the public interest or for the protection of investors (A) to achieve centralized reporting of information regarding ownership, (B) to avoid unnecessarily duplicative reporting by and minimize the compliance burden on persons required to report, and (C) to tabulate and promptly make available the information contained in any report filed pursuant to this subsection in a manner which will, in the view of the Commission, maximize the usefulness of the information to other Federal and State agencies and the public.

(6) The Commission may, by rule or order, exempt, in whole or in part, any person or class of persons from any or all of the reporting requirements of this subsection as it deems necessary or

appropriate in the public interest or for the protection of investors.

(h) *Large Trader Reporting.*

(1) *Identification Requirements for Large Traders.* For the purpose of monitoring the impact on the securities markets of securities transactions involving a substantial volume or a large fair market value or exercise value and for the purpose of otherwise assisting the Commission in the enforcement of this title, each large trader shall—

(A) provide such information to the Commission as the Commission may by rule or regulation prescribe as necessary or appropriate, identifying such large trader and all accounts in or through which such large trader effects such transactions; and

(B) identify, in accordance with such rules or regulations as the Commission may prescribe as necessary or appropriate, to any registered broker or dealer by or through whom such large trader directly or indirectly effects securities transactions, such large trader and all accounts directly or indirectly maintained with such broker or dealer by such large trader in or through which such transactions are effected.

(2) *Recordkeeping and Reporting Requirements for Brokers and Dealers.* Every registered broker or dealer shall make and keep for prescribed periods such records as the Commission by rule or regulation prescribes as necessary or appropriate in the public interest, for the protection of investors, or otherwise in furtherance of the purposes of this title, with respect to securities transactions that equal or exceed the reporting activity level effected directly or indirectly by or through such registered broker or dealer of or for any person that such broker or dealer knows is a large trader, or any person that such broker or dealer has reason to know is a large trader on the basis of transactions in securities effected by or through such broker or dealer. Such records shall be available for reporting to the Commission, or any self-regulatory organization that the Commission shall designate to receive such reports, on the morning of the day following the day the transactions were effected, and shall be reported to the Commission or a self-regulatory organization designated by the Commission immediately upon request by the Commission or such a self-regulatory organization. Such records and reports shall be in a format and transmitted in a manner prescribed by the Commission (including, but not limited to, machine readable form).

(3) *Aggregation Rules.* The Commission may prescribe rules or regulations governing the manner in which transactions and accounts shall be aggregated for the purpose of this subsection, including aggregation on the basis of common ownership or control.

(4) *Examination of Broker and Dealer Records.* All records required to be made and kept by registered brokers and dealers pursuant to this subsection with respect to transactions effected by large traders are subject at any time, or from time to time, to such reasonable periodic, special, or other examinations by representatives of the Commission as the Commission deems necessary or appropriate in the public interest, for the protection of investors, or otherwise in furtherance of the purposes of this title.

(5) *Factors to be Considered in Commission Actions.* In exercising its authority under this subsection, the Commission shall take into account—

(A) existing reporting systems;

(B) the costs associated with maintaining information with respect to transactions effected by large traders and reporting such information to the Commission or self-regulatory organizations; and

(C) the relationship between the United States and international securities markets.

(6) *Exemptions.* The Commission, by rule, regulation, or order, consistent with the purposes of this title, may exempt any person or class of persons or any transaction or class of transactions, either conditionally or upon specified terms and conditions or for stated periods, from the operation of this subsection, and the rules and regulations thereunder.

(7) *Authority of Commission to Limit Disclosure of Information.* Notwithstanding any other provision of law, the Commission shall not be compelled to disclose any information required to be kept or reported under this subsection. Nothing in this subsection shall authorize the Commission to withhold information from Congress, or prevent the Commission from complying with a request for information from any other Federal department or agency requesting information for purposes within the scope of its jurisdiction, or complying with an order of a court of the United States in an action brought by the United States

or the Commission. For purposes of section 552 of title 5, United States Code, this subsection shall be considered a statute described in subsection (b)(3)(B) of such section 552.

(8) *Definitions.* For purposes of this subsection—

(A) the term "large trader" means every person who, for his own account or an account for which he exercises investment discretion, effects transactions for the purchase or sale of any publicly traded security or securities by use of any means or instrumentality of interstate commerce or of the mails, or of any facility of a national securities exchange, directly or indirectly by or through a registered broker or dealer in an aggregate amount equal to or in excess of the identifying activity level;

(B) the term "publicly traded security" means any equity security (including an option on individual equity securities, and an option on a group or index of such securities) listed, or admitted to unlisted trading privileges, on a national securities exchange, or quoted in an automated interdealer quotation system;

(C) the term "identifying activity level" means transactions in publicly traded securities at or above a level of volume, fair market value, or exercise value as shall be fixed from time to time by the Commission by rule or regulation, specifying the time interval during which such transactions shall be aggregated;

(D) the term "reporting activity level" means transactions in publicly traded securities at or above a level of volume, fair market value, or exercise value as shall be fixed from time to time by the Commission by rule, regulation, or order, specifying the time interval during which such transactions shall be aggregated; and

(E) the term "person" has the meaning given in section 3(a)(9) of this title and also includes two or more persons acting as a partnership, limited partnership, syndicate, or other group, but does not include a foreign central bank.

(i) *Accuracy of Financial Reports.* Each financial report that contains financial statements, and that is required to be prepared in accordance with (or reconciled to) generally accepted accounting principles under this title and filed with the Commission shall reflect all material correcting adjustments that have been identified by a registered public accounting firm in accordance with generally accepted accounting principles and the rules and regulations of the Commission.

(j) *Off–Balance Sheet Transactions.* Not later than 180 days after the date of enactment of the Sarbanes–Oxley Act of 2002, the Commission shall issue final rules providing that each annual and quarterly financial report required to be filed with the Commission shall disclose all material off-balance sheet transactions, arrangements, obligations (including contingent obligations), and other relationships of the issuer with unconsolidated entities or other persons, that may have a material current or future effect on financial condition, changes in financial condition, results of operations, liquidity, capital expenditures, capital resources, or significant components of revenues or expenses.

(k) *Prohibition on Personal Loans to Executives.*

(1) *In General.* It shall be unlawful for any issuer (as defined in section 2 of the Sarbanes–Oxley Act of 2002), directly or indirectly, including through any subsidiary, to extend or maintain credit, to arrange for the extension of credit, or to renew an extension of credit, in the form of a personal loan to or for any director or executive officer (or equivalent thereof) of that issuer. An extension of credit maintained by the issuer on the date of enactment of this subsection, shall not be subject to the provisions of this subsection, provided that there is no material modification to any term of any such extension of credit or any renewal of any such extension of credit on or after that date of enactment.

(2) *Limitation.* Paragraph (1) does not preclude any home improvement and manufactured home loans (as that term is defined in section 5 of the Home Owners' Loan Act), consumer credit (as defined in section 103 of the Truth in Lending Act), or any extension of credit under an open end credit plan (as defined in section 103 of the Truth in Lending Act), or a charge card (as defined in section 127(c)(4)(e) of the Truth in Lending Act), or any extension of credit by a broker or dealer registered under section 15 of this title to an employee of that broker or dealer to buy, trade, or carry securities, that is permitted under rules or regulations of the Board of Governors of the Federal Reserve System pursuant to section 7 of this title (other than an extension of credit that would be used to purchase the stock of that issuer), that is—

(A) made or provided in the ordinary course of the consumer credit business of such issuer;

(B) of a type that is generally made available by such issuer to the public; and

(C) made by such issuer on market terms, or terms that are no more favorable than those offered by the issuer to the general public for such extensions of credit.

(3) *Rule of Construction for Certain Loans.* Paragraph (1) does not apply to any loan made or maintained by an insured depository institution (as defined in section 3 of the Federal Deposit Insurance Act, if the loan is subject to the insider lending restrictions of section 22(h) of the Federal Reserve Act.

(*l*) *Real Time Issuer Disclosures.* Each issuer reporting under section 13(a) or 15(d) of this title shall disclose to the public on a rapid and current basis such additional information concerning material changes in the financial condition or operations of the issuer, in plain English, which may include trend and qualitative information and graphic presentations, as the Commission determines, by rule, is necessary or useful for the protection of investors and in the public interest.

(m) *Public Availability of Security–Based Swap Transaction Data.*

(1) *In General.*

(A) *Definition of Real–Time Public Reporting.* In this paragraph, the term "real-time public reporting" means to report data relating to a security-based swap transaction, including price and volume, as soon as technologically practicable after the time at which the security-based swap transaction has been executed.

(B) *Purpose.* The purpose of this subsection is to authorize the Commission to make security-based swap transaction and pricing data available to the public in such form and at such times as the Commission determines appropriate to enhance price discovery.

(C) *General Rule.* The Commission is authorized to provide by rule for the public availability of security-based swap transaction, volume, and pricing data as follows:

(i) With respect to those security-based swaps that are subject to the mandatory clearing requirement described in section 3C(a)(1) (including those security-based swaps that are excepted from the requirement pursuant to section 3C(g)), the Commission shall require real–time public reporting for such transactions.

(ii) With respect to those security-based swaps that are not subject to the mandatory clearing requirement described in section 3C(a)(1), but are cleared at a registered clearing agency, the Commission shall require real–time public reporting for such transactions.

(iii) With respect to security-based swaps that are not cleared at a registered clearing agency and which are reported to a security-based swap data repository or the Commission under section 3C(a)(6), the Commission shall require real–time public reporting for such transactions, in a manner that does not disclose the business transactions and market positions of any person.

(iv) With respect to security-based swaps that are determined to be required to be cleared under section 3C(b) but are not cleared, the Commission shall require real–time public reporting for such transactions.

(D) *Registered Entities and Public Reporting.* The Commission may require registered entities to publicly disseminate the security-based swap transaction and pricing data required to be reported under this paragraph.

(E) *Rulemaking Required.* With respect to the rule providing for the public availability of transaction and pricing data for security-based swaps described in clauses (i) and (ii) of subparagraph (C), the rule promulgated by the Commission shall contain provisions—

(i) to ensure such information does not identify the participants;

(ii) to specify the criteria for determining what constitutes a large notional security-based swap transaction (block trade) for particular markets and contracts;

(iii) to specify the appropriate time delay for reporting large notional security-based swap transactions (block trades) to the public; and

(iv) that take into account whether the public disclosure will materially reduce market liquidity.

(F) *Timeliness of Reporting.* Parties to a security-based swap (including agents of the parties to a security-based swap) shall be responsible for reporting security-based swap transaction information to the appropriate registered entity in a timely manner as may be prescribed by the Commission.

(G) *Reporting of Swaps to Registered Security–Based Swap Data Repositories.* Each security-based swap (whether cleared or uncleared) shall be reported to a registered security-based swap data repository.

(H) *Registration of Clearing Agencies.* A clearing agency may register as a security-based swap data repository.

(2) *Semiannual and Annual Public Reporting of Aggregate Security–Based Swap Data.*

(A) *In General.* In accordance with subparagraph (B), the Commission shall issue a written report on a semiannual and annual basis to make available to the public information relating to—

(i) the trading and clearing in the major security-based swap categories; and

(ii) the market participants and developments in new products.

(B) *Use; Consultation.* In preparing a report under subparagraph (A), the Commission shall—

(i) use information from security-based swap data repositories and clearing agencies; and

(ii) consult with the Office of the Comptroller of the Currency, the Bank for International Settlements, and such other regulatory bodies as may be necessary.

(C) *Authority of Commission.* The Commission may, by rule, regulation, or order, delegate the public reporting responsibilities of the Commission under this paragraph in accordance with such terms and conditions as the Commission determines to be appropriate and in the public interest.

(n) *Security-Based Swap Data Repositories.*

(1) *Registration Requirement.* It shall be unlawful for any person, unless registered with the Commission, directly or indirectly, to make use of the mails or any means or instrumentality of interstate commerce to perform the functions of a security-based swap data repository.

(2) *Inspection and Examination.* Each registered security-based swap data repository shall be subject to inspection and examination by any representative of the Commission.

(3) *Compliance with Core Principles.*

(A) *In General.* To be registered, and maintain registration, as a security-based swap data repository, the security-based swap data repository shall comply with—

(i) the requirements and core principles described in this subsection; and

(ii) any requirement that the Commission may impose by rule or regulation.

(B) *Reasonable Discretion of Security–Based Swap Data Repository.* Unless otherwise determined by the Commission, by rule or regulation, a security-based swap data repository described in subparagraph (A) shall have reasonable discretion in establishing the manner in which the security-based swap data repository complies with the core principles described in this subsection.

(4) *Standard Setting.*

(A) *Data Identification.*

(i) *In General.* In accordance with clause (ii), the Commission shall prescribe standards that specify the data elements for each security-based swap that shall be collected and maintained by each registered security-based swap data repository.

(ii) *Requirement.* In carrying out clause (i), the Commission shall prescribe consistent data element standards applicable to registered entities and reporting counterparties.

(B) *Data Collection and Maintenance.* The Commission shall prescribe data collection and data maintenance standards for security-based swap data repositories.

(C) *Comparability.* The standards prescribed by the Commission under this subsection shall be comparable to the data standards imposed by the Commission on clearing agencies in connection with their clearing of security-based swaps.

(5) *Duties.* A security-based swap data repository shall—

(A) accept data prescribed by the Commission for each security-based swap under subsection (b);

(B) confirm with both counterparties to the security-based swap the accuracy of the data that was submitted;

(C) maintain the data described in subparagraph (A) in such form, in such manner, and for such period as may be required by the Commission;

(D)(i) provide direct electronic access to the Commission (or any designee of the Commission, including another registered entity); and

(ii) provide the information described in subparagraph (A) in such form and at such frequency as the Commission may require to comply with the public reporting requirements set forth in subsection (m);

(E) at the direction of the Commission, establish automated systems for monitoring, screening, and analyzing security-based swap data;

(F) maintain the privacy of any and all security-based swap transaction information that the security-based swap data repository receives from a security-based swap dealer, counterparty, or any other registered entity; and

(G) on a confidential basis pursuant to section 24, upon request, and after notifying the Commission of the request, make available security-based swap data obtained by the security-based swap data repository, including individual counterparty trade and position data, to—

(i) each appropriate prudential regulator;

(ii) the Financial Stability Oversight Council;

(iii) the Commodity Futures Trading Commission;

(iv) the Department of Justice; and

(v) any other person that the Commission determines to be appropriate, including—

(I) foreign financial supervisors (including foreign futures authorities);

(II) foreign central banks;

(III) foreign ministries; and

(IV) other foreign authorities.

(H) *Confidentiality Agreement*. Before the security-based swap data repository may share information with any entity described in subparagraph (G), the security-based swap data repository shall receive a written agreement from each entity stating that the entity shall abide by the confidentiality requirements described in section 24 relating to the information on security-based swap transactions that is provided.

(6) *Designation of Chief Compliance Officer*.

(A) *In General*. Each security-based swap data repository shall designate an individual to serve as a chief compliance officer.

(B) *Duties*. The chief compliance officer shall—

(i) report directly to the board or to the senior officer of the security-based swap data repository;

(ii) review the compliance of the security-based swap data repository with respect to the requirements and core principles described in this subsection;

(iii) in consultation with the board of the security-based swap data repository, a body performing a function similar to the board of the security-based swap data repository, or the senior officer of the security-based swap data repository, resolve any conflicts of interest that may arise;

(iv) be responsible for administering each policy and procedure that is required to be established pursuant to this section;

(v) ensure compliance with this title (including regulations) relating to agreements, contracts, or transactions, including each rule prescribed by the Commission under this section;

(vi) establish procedures for the remediation of noncompliance issues identified by the chief compliance officer through any—

(I) compliance office review;

(II) look–back;

(III) internal or external audit finding;

(IV) self–reported error; or

(V) validated complaint; and

(vii) establish and follow appropriate procedures for the handling, management response, remediation, retesting, and closing of noncompliance issues.

(C) *Annual Reports*.

(i) *In General*. In accordance with rules prescribed by the Commission, the chief compliance officer shall annually prepare and sign a report that contains a description of—

(I) the compliance of the security-based swap data repository of the chief compliance officer with respect to this title (including regulations); and

(II) each policy and procedure of the security-based swap data repository of the chief compliance officer (including the code of ethics and conflict of interest policies of the security-based swap data repository).

(ii) *Requirements.* A compliance report under clause (i) shall—

(I) accompany each appropriate financial report of the security-based swap data repository that is required to be furnished to the Commission pursuant to this section; and

(II) include a certification that, under penalty of law, the compliance report is accurate and complete.

(7) *Core Principles Applicable to Security–Based Swap Data Repositories.*

(A) *Antitrust Considerations.* Unless necessary or appropriate to achieve the purposes of this title, the swap data repository shall not—

(i) adopt any rule or take any action that results in any unreasonable restraint of trade; or

(ii) impose any material anticompetitive burden on the trading, clearing, or reporting of transactions.

(B) *Governance Arrangements.* Each security-based swap data repository shall establish governance arrangements that are transparent—

(i) to fulfill public interest requirements; and

(ii) to support the objectives of the Federal Government, owners, and participants.

(C) *Conflicts of Interest.* Each security-based swap data repository shall—

(i) establish and enforce rules to minimize conflicts of interest in the decision–making process of the security-based swap data repository; and

(ii) establish a process for resolving any conflicts of interest described in clause (i).

(D) *Additional Duties Developed by Commission.*

(i) *In General.* The Commission may develop 1 or more additional duties applicable to security-based swap data repositories.

(ii) *Consideration of Evolving Standards.* In developing additional duties under subparagraph (A), the Commission may take into consideration any evolving standard of the United States or the international community.

(iii) *Additional Duties for Commission Designees.* The Commission shall establish additional duties for any registrant described in section 13(m)(2)(C) in order to minimize conflicts of interest, protect data, ensure compliance, and guarantee the safety and security of the security-based swap data repository.

(8) *Required Registration for Security–Based Swap Data Repositories.* Any person that is required to be registered as a security-based swap data repository under this subsection shall register with the Commission, regardless of whether that person is also licensed under the Commodity Exchange Act as a swap data repository.

(9) *Rules.* The Commission shall adopt rules governing persons that are registered under this subsection.

(o) *Beneficial ownership.* For purposes of this section and section 16, a person shall be deemed to acquire beneficial ownership of an equity security based on the purchase or sale of a security-based swap, only to the extent that the Commission, by rule, determines after consultation with the prudential regulators and the Secretary of the Treasury, that the purchase or sale of the security-based swap, or class of security-based swap, provides incidents of ownership comparable to direct ownership of the equity security, and that it is necessary to achieve the purposes of this section that the purchase or sale of the security-based swaps, or class of security-based swap, be deemed the acquisition of beneficial ownership of the equity security.

(p) *Disclosures Relating to Conflict Minerals Originating in the Democratic Republic of the Congo.*

(1) *Regulations.*

(A) *In General.* Not later than 270 days after the date of the enactment of this subsection, the Commission shall promulgate regulations requiring any person described in paragraph (2) to disclose annually, beginning with the person's first full fiscal year that begins after the date of promulgation of such regulations, whether conflict minerals that are necessary as described in paragraph (2)(B), in the year for which such reporting is required, did originate in the Democratic Republic of the Congo or an adjoining country and, in cases in which such conflict minerals did originate in any such country, submit to the Commission a report that includes, with respect to the period covered by the report—

(i) a description of the measures taken by the person to exercise due diligence on the source and chain of custody of such minerals, which measures shall include an independent private sector audit of such report submitted through the Commission that is conducted in accordance with standards established by the Comptroller General of the United States, in accordance with rules promulgated by the Commission, in consultation with the Secretary of State; and

(ii) a description of the products manufactured or contracted to be manufactured that are not DRC conflict free ("DRC conflict free" is defined to mean the products that do not contain minerals that directly or indirectly finance or benefit armed groups in the Democratic Republic of the Congo or an adjoining country), the entity that conducted the independent private sector audit in accordance with clause (i), the facilities used to process the conflict minerals, the country of origin of the conflict minerals, and the efforts to determine the mine or location of origin with the greatest possible specificity.

(B) *Certification.* The person submitting a report under subparagraph (A) shall certify the audit described in clause (i) of such subparagraph that is included in such report. Such a certified audit shall constitute a critical component of due diligence in establishing the source and chain of custody of such minerals.

(C) *Unreliable Determination.* If a report required to be submitted by a person under subparagraph (A) relies on a determination of an independent private sector audit, as described under subparagraph (A)(i), or other due diligence processes previously determined by the Commission to be unreliable, the report shall not satisfy the requirements of the regulations promulgated under subparagraph (A)(i).

(D) *DRC Conflict Free.* For purposes of this paragraph, a product may be labeled as 'DRC conflict free' if the product does not contain conflict minerals that directly or indirectly finance or benefit armed groups in the Democratic Republic of the Congo or an adjoining country.

(E) *Information Available to the Public.* Each person described under paragraph (2) shall make available to the public on the Internet website of such person the information disclosed by such person under subparagraph (A).

(2) *Person Described.* A person is described in this paragraph if—

(A) the person is required to file reports with the Commission pursuant to paragraph (1)(A); and

(B) conflict minerals are necessary to the functionality or production of a product manufactured by such person.

(3) *Revisions and Waivers.* The Commission shall revise or temporarily waive the requirements described in paragraph (1) if the President transmits to the Commission a determination that—

(A) such revision or waiver is in the national security interest of the United States and the President includes the reasons therefor; and

(B) establishes a date, not later than 2 years after the initial publication of such exemption, on which such exemption shall expire.

(4) *Termination of Disclosure Requirements.* The requirements of paragraph (1) shall terminate on the date on which the President determines and certifies to the appropriate congressional committees, but in no case earlier than the date that is one day after the end of the 5–year period beginning on the date of the enactment of this subsection, that no armed groups continue to be directly involved and benefitting from commercial activity involving conflict minerals.

(5) *Definitions.* For purposes of this subsection, the terms "adjoining country", "appropriate congressional committees", "armed group", and "conflict mineral" have the meaning given those terms under section 1502 of the Dodd–Frank Wall Street Reform and Consumer Protection Act.

(q) *Disclosure of Payments by Resource Extraction Issuers.*

(1) *Definitions.* In this subsection—

(A) the term "commercial development of oil, natural gas, or minerals" includes exploration, extraction, processing, export, and other significant actions relating to oil, natural gas, or minerals, or the acquisition of a license for any such activity, as determined by the Commission;

(B) the term "foreign government" means a foreign government, a department, agency, or instrumentality of a foreign government, or a company owned by a foreign government, as determined by the Commission;

(C) the term "payment"—

(i) means a payment that is—

(I) made to further the commercial development of oil, natural gas, or minerals; and

(II) not de minimis; and

(ii) includes taxes, royalties, fees (including license fees), production entitlements, bonuses, and other material benefits, that the Commission, consistent with the guidelines of the Extractive Industries Transparency Initiative (to the extent practicable), determines are part of the commonly recognized revenue stream for the commercial development of oil, natural gas, or minerals;

(D) the term "resource extraction issuer" means an issuer that—

(i) is required to file an annual report with the Commission; and

(ii) engages in the commercial development of oil, natural gas, or minerals;

(E) the term "interactive data format" means an electronic data format in which pieces of information are identified using an interactive data standard; and

(F) the term "interactive data standard" means standardized list of electronic tags that mark information included in the annual report of a resource extraction issuer.

(2) *Disclosure.*

(A) *Information Required.* Not later than 270 days after the date of enactment of the Dodd–Frank Wall Street Reform and Consumer Protection Act, the Commission shall issue final rules that require each resource extraction issuer to include in an annual report of the resource extraction issuer information relating to any payment made by the resource extraction issuer, a subsidiary of the resource extraction issuer, or an entity under the control of the resource extraction issuer to a foreign government or the Federal Government for the purpose of the commercial development of oil, natural gas, or minerals, including—

(i) the type and total amount of such payments made for each project of the resource extraction issuer relating to the commercial development of oil, natural gas, or minerals; and

(ii) the type and total amount of such payments made to each government.

(B) *Consultation in Rulemaking.* In issuing rules under subparagraph (A), the Commission may consult with any agency or entity that the Commission determines is relevant.

(C) *Interactive Data Format.* The rules issued under subparagraph (A) shall require that the information included in the annual report of a resource extraction issuer be submitted in an interactive data format.

(D) *Interactive Data Standard.*

(i) *In General.* The rules issued under subparagraph (A) shall establish an interactive data standard for the information included in the annual report of a resource extraction issuer.

(ii) *Electronic Tags.* The interactive data standard shall include electronic tags that identify, for any payments made by a resource extraction issuer to a foreign government or the Federal Government—

(I) the total amounts of the payments, by category;

(II) the currency used to make the payments;

(III) the financial period in which the payments were made;

(IV) the business segment of the resource extraction issuer that made the payments;

(V) the government that received the payments, and the country in which the government is located;

(VI) the project of the resource extraction issuer to which the payments relate; and

(VII) such other information as the Commission may determine is necessary or appropriate in the public interest or for the protection of investors.

(E) *International Transparency Efforts.* To the extent practicable, the rules issued under subparagraph (A) shall support the commitment of the Federal Government to international transparency promotion efforts relating to the commercial development of oil, natural gas, or minerals.

(F) *Effective Date.* With respect to each resource extraction issuer, the final rules issued under subparagraph (A) shall take effect on the date on which the resource extraction issuer is required to submit an annual report relating to the fiscal year of the resource extraction issuer that ends not earlier than 1 year after the date on which the Commission issues final rules under subparagraph (A).

(3) *Public Availability of Information.*

(A) *In General.* To the extent practicable, the Commission shall make available online, to the public, a compilation of the information required to be submitted under the rules issued under paragraph (2)(A).

(B) *Other Information.* Nothing in this paragraph shall require the Commission to make available online information other than the information required to be submitted under the rules issued under paragraph (2)(A).

(4) *Authorization of Appropriations.* There are authorized to be appropriated to the Commission such sums as may be necessary to carry out this subsection.

(r) *Disclosure of Certain Activities Relating to Iran.*

(1) *In General.* Each issuer required to file an annual or quarterly report under subsection (a) shall disclose in that report the information required by paragraph (2) if, during the period covered by the report, the issuer or any affiliate of the issuer—

(A) knowingly engaged in an activity described in subsection (a) or (b) of section 5 of the Iran Sanctions Act of 1996 (Public Law 104–172; 50 U.S.C. 1701 note);

(B) knowingly engaged in an activity described in subsection (c)(2) of section 104 of the Comprehensive Iran Sanctions, Accountability, and Divestment Act of 2010 (22 U.S.C. 8513) or a transaction described in subsection (d)(1) of that section;

(C) knowingly engaged in an activity described in section 105A(b)(2) of that Act; or

(D) knowingly conducted any transaction or dealing with—

(i) any person the property and interests in property of which are blocked pursuant to Executive Order No. 13224 (66 Fed. Reg. 49079; relating to blocking property and prohibiting transactions with persons who commit, threaten to commit, or support terrorism);

(ii) any person the property and interests in property of which are blocked pursuant to Executive Order No. 13382 (70 Fed. Reg. 38567; relating to blocking of property of weapons of mass destruction proliferators and their supporters); or

(iii) any person or entity identified under section 560.304 of title 31, Code of Federal Regulations (relating to the definition of the Government of Iran) without the specific authorization of a Federal department or agency.

(2) *Information Required.* If an issuer or an affiliate of the issuer has engaged in any activity described in paragraph (1), the issuer shall disclose a detailed description of each such activity, including—

(A) the nature and extent of the activity;

(B) the gross revenues and net profits, if any, attributable to the activity; and

(C) whether the issuer or the affiliate of the issuer (as the case may be) intends to continue the activity.

(3) *Notice of Disclosures.* If an issuer reports under paragraph (1) that the issuer or an affiliate of the issuer has knowingly engaged in any activity described in that paragraph, the issuer shall separately file with the Commission, concurrently with the annual or quarterly report under subsection (a), a notice that the disclosure of that activity has been included in that annual or quarterly report that identifies the issuer and contains the information required by paragraph (2).

(4) *Public Disclosure of Information.* Upon receiving a notice under paragraph (3) that an annual or quarterly report includes a disclosure of

an activity described in paragraph (1), the Commission shall promptly—

(A) transmit the report to—

(i) the President;

(ii) the Committee on Foreign Affairs and the Committee on Financial Services of the House of Representatives; and

(iii) the Committee on Foreign Relations and the Committee on Banking, Housing, and Urban Affairs of the Senate; and

(B) make the information provided in the disclosure and the notice available to the public by posting the information on the Internet website of the Commission.

(5) *Investigations.* Upon receiving a report under paragraph (4) that includes a disclosure of an activity described in paragraph (1) (other than an activity described in subparagraph (D)(iii) of that paragraph), the President shall—

(A) initiate an investigation into the possible imposition of sanctions under the Iran Sanctions Act of 1996 (Public Law 104–172; 50 U.S.C. 1701 note), section 104 or 105A of the Comprehensive Iran Sanctions, Accountability, and Divestment Act of 2010, an Executive order specified in clause (i) or (ii) of paragraph (1)(D), or any other provision of law relating to the imposition of sanctions with respect to Iran, as applicable; and

(B) not later than 180 days after initiating such an investigation, make a determination with respect to whether sanctions should be imposed with respect to the issuer or the affiliate of the issuer (as the case may be).

(6) *Sunset.* The provisions of this subsection shall terminate on the date that is 30 days after the date on which the President makes the certification described in section 401(a) of the Comprehensive Iran Sanctions, Accountability, and Divestment Act of 2010 (22 U.S.C. 8551(a)).

Reporting and Recordkeeping for Certain Security–Based Swaps

[*Except for subparagraph 13A(a)(2)(C), which becomes effective on July 16, 2011, section 13A shall take effect, not less than 60 days after publication of the final rule or regulation implementing the provisions of the Dodd–Frank Act.*]

Sec. 13A. (a) *Required Reporting of Security–Based Swaps not Accepted by any Clearing Agency or Derivatives Clearing Organization.*

(1) *In General.* Each security-based swap that is not accepted for clearing by any clearing agency or derivatives clearing organization shall be reported to—

(A) a security-based swap data repository described in section 13(n); or

(B) in the case in which there is no security-based swap data repository that would accept the security-based swap, to the Commission pursuant to this section within such time period as the Commission may by rule or regulation prescribe.

(2) *Transition Rule for Preenactment Security–Based Swaps.*

(A) *Security-Based Swaps Entered into Before the Date of Enactment of the Wall Street Transparency and Accountability Act of 2010.* Each security-based swap entered into before the date of enactment of the Wall Street Transparency and Accountability Act of 2010, the terms of which have not expired as of the date of enactment of that Act, shall be reported to a registered security-based swap data repository or the Commission by a date that is not later than—

(i) 30 days after issuance of the interim final rule; or

(ii) such other period as the Commission determines to be appropriate.

(B) *Commission Rulemaking.* The Commission shall promulgate an interim final rule within 90 days of the date of enactment of this section providing for the reporting of each security-based swap entered into before the date of enactment as referenced in subparagraph (A).

(C) *Effective Date.* The reporting provisions described in this section shall be effective upon the date of the enactment of this section.*

* As noted above, this subparagraph became effective on July 16, 2011.

(3) *Reporting Obligations.*

(A) *Security-Based Swaps in which only 1 Counterparty is a Security-Based Swap Dealer or Major Security-Based Swap Participant.* With respect to a security-based swap in which only 1 counterparty is a security-based swap dealer or major security-based swap participant, the security-based swap dealer or major security-based swap participant shall report the security-based swap as required under paragraphs (1) and (2).

(B) *Security-Based Swaps in Which 1 Counterparty is a Security-Based Swap Dealer and the Other a Major Security-Based Swap Participant.* With respect to a security-based swap in which 1 counterparty is a security-based swap dealer and the other a major security-based swap participant, the security-based swap dealer shall report the security-based swap as required under paragraphs (1) and (2).

(C) *Other Security-Based Swaps.* With respect to any other security-based swap not described in subparagraph (A) or (B), the counterparties to the security-based swap shall select a counterparty to report the security-based swap as required under paragraphs (1) and (2).

(b) *Duties of Certain Individuals.* Any individual or entity that enters into a security-based swap shall meet each requirement described in subsection (c) if the individual or entity did not—

(1) clear the security-based swap in accordance with section 3C(a)(1); or

(2) have the data regarding the security-based swap accepted by a security-based swap data repository in accordance with rules (including timeframes) adopted by the Commission under this title.

(c) *Requirements.* An individual or entity described in subsection (b) shall—

(1) upon written request from the Commission, provide reports regarding the security-based swaps held by the individual or entity to the Commission in such form and in such manner as the Commission may request; and

(2) maintain books and records pertaining to the security-based swaps held by the individual or entity in such form, in such manner, and for such period as the Commission may require, which shall be open to inspection by—

(A) any representative of the Commission;

(B) an appropriate prudential regulator;

(C) the Commodity Futures Trading Commission;

(D) the Financial Stability Oversight Council; and

(E) the Department of Justice.

(d) *Identical Data.* In prescribing rules under this section, the Commission shall require individuals and entities described in subsection (b) to submit to the Commission a report that contains data that is not less comprehensive than the data required to be collected by security-based swap data repositories under this title.

Proxies

Sec. 14. (a)(1) *Solicitation of Proxies in Violation of Rules and Regulations.* It shall be unlawful for any person, by the use of the mails or by any means or instrumentality of interstate commerce or of any facility of a national securities exchange or otherwise, in contravention of such rules and regulations as the Commission may prescribe as necessary or appropriate in the public interest or for the protection of investors, to solicit or to permit the use of his name to solicit any proxy or consent or authorization in respect of any security (other than an exempted security) registered pursuant to section 12 of this title.

(2) The rules and regulations prescribed by the Commission under paragraph (1) may include—

(A) a requirement that a solicitation of proxy, consent, or authorization by (or on behalf of) an issuer include a nominee submitted by a shareholder to serve on the board of directors of the issuer; and

(B) a requirement that an issuer follow a certain procedure in relation to a solicitation described in subparagraph (A).

(b) *Giving or Refraining from Giving Proxy in Respect of Any Security Carried for Account of Customer.*

(1) It shall be unlawful for any member of a national securities exchange, or any broker or dealer registered under this title, or any bank, association, or other entity that exercises fiduciary powers, in contravention of such rules and regulations as the Commission may prescribe as necessary or appropriate in the public interest or for the protection of investors, to give, or to refrain from giving a proxy, consent, authorization, or information

statement in respect of any security registered pursuant to section 12 of this title, or any security issued by an investment company registered under the Investment Company Act of 1940, and carried for the account of a customer.

(2) With respect to banks, the rules and regulations prescribed by the Commission under paragraph (1) shall not require the disclosure of the names of beneficial owners of securities in an account held by the bank on the date of enactment of this paragraph, unless the beneficial owner consents to the disclosure. The provisions of this paragraph shall not apply in the case of a bank which the Commission finds has not made a good faith effort to obtain such consent from such beneficial owners.

(c) *Information to Holders of Record Prior to Annual or Other Meeting.* Unless proxies, consents, or authorizations in respect of a security registered pursuant to section 12 of this title, or a security issued by an investment company registered under the Investment Company Act of 1940, are solicited by or on behalf of the management of the issuer from the holders of record of such security in accordance with the rules and regulations prescribed under subsection (a) of this section, prior to any annual or other meeting of the holders of such security, such issuer shall, in accordance with rules and regulations prescribed by the Commission, file with the Commission and transmit to all holders of record of such security information substantially equivalent to the information which would be required to be transmitted if a solicitation were made, but no information shall be required to be filed or transmitted pursuant to this subsection before July 1, 1964.

(d) *Tender Offer by Owner of More than Five Per Centum of Class of Securities; Exceptions.* (1) It shall be unlawful for any person, directly or indirectly, by use of the mails or by any means or instrumentality of interstate commerce or of any facility of a national securities exchange or otherwise, to make a tender offer for, or a request or invitation for tenders of, any class of any equity security which is registered pursuant to section 12 of this title, or any equity security of an insurance company which would have been required to be so registered except for the exemption contained in section 12(g)(2)(G) of this title, or any equity security issued by a closed-end investment company registered under the Investment Company Act of 1940, if, after consummation thereof, such person would, directly or indirectly, be the beneficial owner of more than 5 per centum of such class, unless at the time copies of the offer or request or invitation are first published or sent or given to security holders such person has filed with the Commission a statement containing such of the information specified in section 13(d) of this title, and such additional information as the Commission may by rules and regulations prescribe as necessary or appropriate in the public interest or for the protection of investors. All requests or invitations for tenders or advertisements making a tender offer or requesting or inviting tenders of such a security shall be filed as a part of such statement and shall contain such of the information contained in such statement as the Commission may by rules and regulations prescribe. Copies of any additional material soliciting or requesting such tender offers subsequent to the initial solicitation or request shall contain such information as the Commission may by rules and regulations prescribe as necessary or appropriate in the public interest or for the protection of investors, and shall be filed with the Commission not later than the time copies of such material are first published or sent or given to security holders. Copies of all statements, in the form in which such material is furnished to security holders and the Commission, shall be sent to the issuer not later than the date such material is first published or sent or given to any security holders.

(2) When two or more persons act as a partnership, limited partnership, syndicate, or other group for the purpose of acquiring, holding, or disposing of securities of an issuer, such syndicate or group shall be deemed a "person" for purposes of this subsection.

(3) In determining, for purposes of this subsection, any percentage of a class of any security, such class shall be deemed to consist of the amount of the outstanding securities of such class, exclusive of any securities of such class held by or for the account of the issuer or a subsidiary of the issuer.

(4) Any solicitation or recommendation to the holders of such a security to accept or reject a tender offer or request or invitation for tenders shall be made in accordance with such rules and regulations as the Commission may prescribe as necessary or appropriate in the public interest or for the protection of investors.

(5) Securities deposited pursuant to a tender offer or request or invitation for tenders may be withdrawn by or on behalf of the depositor at any time until the expiration of seven days after the time definitive copies of the offer or request or invitation are first published or sent or given to security holders, and at any time after sixty days

from the date of the original tender offer or request or invitation, except as the Commission may otherwise prescribe by rules, regulations, or order as necessary or appropriate in the public interest or for the protection of investors.

(6) Where any person makes a tender offer, or request or invitation for tenders, for less than all the outstanding equity securities of a class, and where a greater number of securities is deposited pursuant thereto within ten days after copies of the offer or request or invitation are first published or sent or given to security holders than such person is bound or willing to take up and pay for, the securities taken up shall be taken up as nearly as may be pro rata, disregarding fractions, according to the number of securities deposited by each depositor. The provisions of this subsection shall also apply to securities deposited within ten days after notice of an increase in the consideration offered to security holders, as described in paragraph (7), is first published or sent or given to security holders.

(7) Where any person varies the terms of a tender offer or request or invitation for tenders before the expiration thereof by increasing the consideration offered to holders of such securities, such person shall pay the increased consideration to each security holder whose securities are taken up and paid for pursuant to the tender offer or request or invitation for tenders whether or not such securities have been taken up by such person before the variation of the tender offer or request or invitation.

(8) The provisions of this subsection shall not apply to any offer for, or request or invitation for tenders of, any security—

(A) if the acquisition of such security, together with all other acquisitions by the same person of securities of the same class during the preceding twelve months, would not exceed 2 per centum of that class;

(B) by the issuer of such security; or

(C) which the Commission, by rules or regulations or by order, shall exempt from the provisions of this subsection as not entered into for the purpose of, and not having the effect of, changing or influencing the control of the issuer or otherwise as not comprehended within the purposes of this subsection.

(e) *Untrue Statement of Material Fact or Omission of Fact with Respect to Tender Offer.* It shall be unlawful for any person to make any untrue statement of a material fact or omit to state any material fact necessary in order to make the statements made, in the light of the circumstances under which they are made, not misleading, or to engage in any fraudulent, deceptive, or manipulative acts or practices, in connection with any tender offer or request or invitation for tenders, or any solicitation of security holders in opposition to or in favor of any such offer, request, or invitation. The Commission shall, for the purposes of this subsection, by rules and regulations define, and prescribe means reasonably designed to prevent, such acts and practices as are fraudulent, deceptive, or manipulative.

(f) *Election or Designation of Majority of Directors of Issuer by Owner of More than Five Per Centum of Class of Securities at other than Meeting of Security Holders.* If, pursuant to any arrangement or understanding with the person or persons acquiring securities in a transaction subject to subsection (d) of this section or subsection (d) of section 13 of this title, any persons are to be elected or designated as directors of the issuer, otherwise than at a meeting of security holders, and the persons so elected or designated will constitute a majority of the directors of the issuer, then, prior to the time any such person takes office as a director, and in accordance with rules and regulations prescribed by the Commission, the issuer shall file with the Commission, and transmit to all holders of record of securities of the issuer who would be entitled to vote at a meeting for election of directors, information substantially equivalent to the information which would be required by subsection (a) or (c) of this section to be transmitted if such person or persons were nominees for election as directors at a meeting of such security holders.

(g) *Filing Fees.*

(1)(A) At the time of filing such preliminary proxy solicitation material as the Commission may require by rule pursuant to subsection (a) of this section that concerns an acquisition, merger, consolidation, or proposed sale or other disposition of substantially all the assets of a company, the person making such filing, other than a company registered under the Investment Company Act of 1940, shall pay to the Commission the following fees:

(i) for preliminary proxy solicitation material involving an acquisition, merger, or consolidation, if there is a proposed payment of cash or transfer of securities or property to shareholders, a fee at a rate that, subject to paragraph (4), is equal to $92 per $1,000,000 of such proposed payment, or of the value of such securities or other property proposed to be transferred; and

(ii) for preliminary proxy solicitation material involving a proposed sale or other disposition of substantially all of the assets of a company, a fee at a rate that, subject to paragraph (4), is equal to $92 per $1,000,000 of the cash or of the value of any securities or other property proposed to be received upon such sale or disposition.

(B) The fee imposed under subparagraph (A) shall be reduced with respect to securities in an amount equal to any fee paid to the Commission with respect to such securities in connection with the proposed transaction under section 6(b) of the Securities Act of 1933, or the fee paid under that section shall be reduced in an amount equal to the fee paid to the Commission in connection with such transaction under this subsection. Where two or more companies involved in an acquisition, merger, consolidation, sale, or other disposition of substantially all the assets of a company must file such proxy material with the Commission, each shall pay a proportionate share of such fee.

(2) At the time of filing such preliminary information statement as the Commission may require by rule pursuant to subsection (c) of this section, the issuer shall pay to the Commission the same fee as required for preliminary proxy solicitation material under paragraph (1) of this subsection.

(3) At the time of filing such statement as the Commission may require by rule pursuant to subsection (d)(1) of this section, the person making the filing shall pay to the Commission a fee at a rate that, subject to paragraph (4), is equal to $92 per $1,000,000 of the aggregate amount of cash or of the value of securities or other property proposed to be offered. The fee shall be reduced with respect to securities in an amount equal to any fee paid with respect to such securities in connection with the proposed transaction under section 6(b) of the Securities Act of 1933, or the fee paid under that section shall be reduced in an amount equal to the fee paid to the Commission in connection with such transaction under this subsection.

(4) *Annual Adjustment.* For each fiscal year, the Commission shall by order adjust the rate required by paragraphs (1) and (3) for such fiscal year to a rate that is equal to the rate (expressed in dollars per million) that is applicable under section 6(b) of the Securities Act of 1933 for such fiscal year.

(5) *Fee Collection.* Fees collected pursuant to this subsection for fiscal year 2012 and each fiscal year thereafter shall be deposited and credited as general revenue of the Treasury and shall not be available for obligation.

(6) *Review; Effective Date; Publication.* In exercising its authority under this subsection, the Commission shall not be required to comply with the provisions of section 553 of title 5, United States Code. An adjusted rate prescribed under paragraph (4) shall be published and take effect in accordance with section 6(b) of the Securities Act of 1933.

(7) *Pro Rata Application.* The rates per $1,000,000 required by this subsection shall be applied pro rata to amounts and balances of less than $1,000,000.

(8) Notwithstanding any other provision of law, the Commission may impose fees, charges, or prices for matters not involving any acquisition, merger, consolidation, sale, or other disposition of assets described in this subsection, as authorized by section 9701 of title 31, United States Code, or otherwise.

(h) *Proxy Solicitations and Tender Offers in Connection with Limited Partnership Rollup Transactions.*

(1) *Proxy Rules to Contain Special Provisions.* It shall be unlawful for any person to solicit any proxy, consent, or authorization concerning a limited partnership rollup transaction, or to make any tender offer in furtherance of a limited partnership rollup transaction, unless such transaction is conducted in accordance with rules prescribed by the Commission under subsections (a) and (d) as required by this subsection. Such rules shall—

(A) permit any holder of a security that is the subject of the proposed limited partnership rollup transaction to engage in preliminary communications for the purpose of determining whether to solicit proxies, consents, or authorizations in opposition to the proposed limited partnership rollup transaction, without regard to whether any such communication would otherwise be considered a solicitation of proxies, and without being required to file soliciting material with the Commission prior to making that determination, except that—

(i) nothing in this subparagraph shall be construed to limit the application of any provision of this title prohibiting, or reasonably designed to prevent, fraudulent, deceptive, or manipulative acts or practices under this title; and

(ii) any holder of not less than 5 percent of the outstanding securities that are the subject of the proposed limited partnership rollup transaction who engages in the business of buying and selling limited partnership interests in the secondary market shall be required to disclose such ownership interests and any potential conflicts of interests in such preliminary communications;

(B) require the issuer to provide to holders of the securities that are the subject of the limited partnership rollup transaction such list of the holders of the issuer's securities as the Commission may determine in such form and subject to such terms and conditions as the Commission may specify;

(C) prohibit compensating any person soliciting proxies, consents, or authorizations directly from security holders concerning such a limited partnership rollup transaction—

(i) on the basis of whether the solicited proxy, consent, or authorization either approves or disapproves the proposed limited partnership rollup transaction; or

(ii) contingent on the approval, disapproval, or completion of the limited partnership rollup transaction;

(D) set forth disclosure requirements for soliciting material distributed in connection with a limited partnership rollup transaction, including requirements for clear, concise, and comprehensible disclosure with respect to—

(i) any changes in the business plan, voting rights, form of ownership interest, or the compensation of the general partner in the proposed limited partnership rollup transaction from each of the original limited partnerships;

(ii) the conflicts of interest, if any, of the general partner;

(iii) whether it is expected that there will be a significant difference between the exchange values of the limited partnerships and the trading price of the securities to be issued in the limited partnership rollup transaction;

(iv) the valuation of the limited partnerships and the method used to determine the value of the interests of the limited partners to be exchanged for the securities in the limited partnership rollup transaction;

(v) the differing risks and effects of the limited partnership rollup transaction for investors in different limited partnerships proposed to be included, and the risks and effects of completing the limited partnership rollup transaction with less than all limited partnerships;

(vi) the statement by the general partner required under subparagraph (E);

(vii) such other matters deemed necessary or appropriate by the Commission;

(E) require a statement by the general partner as to whether the proposed limited partnership rollup transaction is fair or unfair to investors in each limited partnership, a discussion of the basis for that conclusion, and an evaluation and a description by the general partner of alternatives to the limited partnership rollup transaction, such as liquidation;

(F) provide that, if the general partner or sponsor has obtained any opinion (other than an opinion of counsel), appraisal, or report that is prepared by an outside party and that is materially related to the limited partnership rollup transaction, such soliciting materials shall contain or be accompanied by clear, concise, and comprehensible disclosure with respect to—

(i) the analysis of the transaction, scope of review, preparation of the opinion, and basis for and methods of arriving at conclusions, and any representations and undertakings with respect thereto;

(ii) the identity and qualifications of the person who prepared the opinion, the method of selection of such person, and any material past, existing, or contemplated relationships between the person or any of its affiliates and the general partner, sponsor, successor, or any other affiliate;

(iii) any compensation of the preparer of such opinion, appraisal, or report that is contingent on the transaction's approval or completion; and

(iv) any limitations imposed by the issuer on the access afforded to such preparer to the issuer's personnel, premises, and relevant books and records;

(G) provide that, if the general partner or sponsor has obtained any opinion, appraisal, or report as described in subparagraph (F) from any person whose compensation is contingent on the transaction's approval or completion or who has not been given access by the issuer to its personnel and premises and relevant books and records, the general partner or sponsor shall state the reasons therefor;

(H) provide that, if the general partner or sponsor has not obtained any opinion on the fairness of the proposed limited partnership rollup transaction to investors in each of the affected partnerships, such soliciting materials shall contain or be accompanied by a statement of such partner's or sponsor's reasons for concluding that such an opinion is not necessary in order to permit the limited partners to make an informed decision on the proposed transaction;

(I) require that the soliciting material include a clear, concise, and comprehensible summary of the limited partnership rollup transaction (including a summary of the matters referred to in clauses (i) through (vii) of subparagraph (D) and a summary of the matter referred to in subparagraphs (F), (G), and (H)), with the risks of the limited partnership rollup transaction set forth prominently in the fore part thereof;

(J) provide that any solicitation or offering period with respect to any proxy solicitation, tender offer, or information statement in a limited partnership rollup transaction shall be for not less than the lesser of 60 calendar days or the maximum number of days permitted under applicable State law; and

(K) contain such other provisions as the Commission determines to be necessary or appropriate for the protection of investors in limited partnership rollup transactions.

(2) *Exemptions.* The Commission may, consistent with the public interest, the protection of investors, and the purposes of this title, exempt by rule or order any security or class of securities, any transaction or class of transactions, or any person or class of persons, in whole or in part, conditionally or unconditionally, from the requirements imposed pursuant to paragraph (1) or from the definition contained in paragraph (4).

(3) *Effect on Commission Authority.* Nothing in this subsection limits the authority of the Commission under subsection (a) or (d) or any other provision of this title or precludes the Commission from imposing, under subsection (a) or (d) of this section or any other provision of this title, a remedy or procedure required to be imposed under this subsection.

(4) *Definition of Limited Partnership Rollup Transaction.* Except as provided in paragraph (5), as used in this subsection, the term "limited partnership rollup transaction" means a transaction involving the combination or reorganization of one or more limited partnerships, directly or indirectly, in which—

(A) some or all of the investors in any of such limited partnerships will receive new securities, or securities in another entity, that will be reported under a transaction reporting plan declared effective before the date of enactment of this subsection by the Commission under section 11A;

(B) any of the investors' limited partnership securities are not, as of the date of filing, reported under a transaction reporting plan declared effective before the date of enactment of this subsection, by the Commission under section 11A;

(C) investors in any of the limited partnerships involved in the transaction are subject to a significant adverse change with respect to voting rights, the term of existence of the entity, management compensation, or investment objectives; and

(D) any of such investors are not provided an option to receive or retain a security under substantially the same terms and conditions as the original issue.

(5) *Exclusions from Definition.* Notwithstanding paragraph (4), the term "limited partnership rollup transaction" does not include—

(A) a transaction that involves only a limited partnership or partnerships having an operating policy or practice of retaining cash available for distribution and reinvesting proceeds from the sale, financing, or refinancing of assets in accordance with such criteria as the Commission determines appropriate;

(B) a transaction involving only limited partnerships wherein the interests of the limited partners are repurchased, recalled, or exchanged in accordance with the terms of the preexisting limited partnership agreements for securities in an operating company specifically identified at the time of the formation of the original limited partnership;

(C) a transaction in which the securities to be issued or exchanged are not required to be and are not registered under the Securities Act of 1933;

(D) a transaction that involves only issuers that are not required to register or report under section 12, both before and after the transaction;

(E) a transaction, except as the Commission may otherwise provide by rule for the protection of investors, involving the combination or reorganization of one or more limited partnerships in which a non-affiliated party succeeds to the interests of a general partner or sponsor, if—

(i) such action is approved by not less than 66⅔ percent of the outstanding units of each of the participating limited partnerships; and

(ii) as a result of the transaction, the existing general partners will receive only compensation to which they are entitled as expressly provided for in the preexisting limited partnership agreements; or

(F) a transaction, except as the Commission may otherwise provide by rule for the protection of investors, in which the securities offered to investors are securities of another entity that are reported under a transaction reporting plan declared effective before the date of enactment of this subsection, by the Commission under section 11A, if—

(i) such other entity was formed, and such class of securities was reported and regularly traded, not less than 12 months before the date on which soliciting material is mailed to investors; and

(ii) the securities of that entity issued to investors in the transaction do not exceed 20 percent of the total outstanding securities of the entity, exclusive of any securities of such class held by or for the account of the entity or a subsidiary of the entity.

(i) *Disclosure of Pay Versus Performance.* The Commission shall, by rule, require each issuer to disclose in any proxy or consent solicitation material for an annual meeting of the shareholders of the issuer a clear description of any compensation required to be disclosed by the issuer under Item 402 of Regulation S–K (or any successor thereto), including, for any issuer other than an emerging growth company, information that shows the relationship between executive compensation actually paid and the financial performance of the issuer, taking into account any change in the value of the shares of stock and dividends of the issuer and any distributions. The disclosure under this subsection may include a graphic representation of the information required to be disclosed.

(j) *Disclosure of Hedging By Employees and Directors.* The Commission shall, by rule, require each issuer to disclose in any proxy or consent solicitation material for an annual meeting of the shareholders of the issuer whether any employee or member of the board of directors of the issuer, or any designee of such employee or member, is permitted to purchase financial instruments (including prepaid variable forward contracts, equity swaps, collars, and exchange funds) that are designed to hedge or offset any decrease in the market value of equity securities—

(1) granted to the employee or member of the board of directors by the issuer as part of the compensation of the employee or member of the board of directors; or

(2) held, directly or indirectly, by the employee or member of the board of directors.

Shareholder Approval of Executive Compensation

Sec. 14A. (a) *Separate Resolution Required.*

(1) *In General.* Not less frequently than once every 3 years, a proxy or consent or authorization for an annual or other meeting of the shareholders for which the proxy solicitation rules of the Commission require compensation disclosure shall include a separate resolution subject to shareholder vote to approve the compensation of executives, as disclosed pursuant to Item 402 of Regulation S–K, or any successor thereto.

(2) *Frequency of Vote.* Not less frequently than once every 6 years, a proxy or consent or authorization for an annual or other meeting of the shareholders for which the proxy solicitation rules of the Commission require compensation disclosure shall include a separate resolution subject to shareholder vote to determine whether votes on

the resolutions required under paragraph (1) will occur every 1, 2, or 3 years.

(3) *Effective Date.* The proxy or consent or authorization for the first annual or other meeting of the shareholders occurring after the end of the 6–month period beginning on the date of enactment of this section shall include—

(A) the resolution described in paragraph (1); and

(B) a separate resolution subject to shareholder vote to determine whether votes on the resolutions required under paragraph (1) will occur every 1, 2, or 3 years.

(b) *Shareholder Approval of Golden Parachute Compensation.*

(1) *Disclosure.* In any proxy or consent solicitation material (the solicitation of which is subject to the rules of the Commission pursuant to subsection (a)) for a meeting of the shareholders occurring after the end of the 6–month period beginning on the date of enactment of this section, at which shareholders are asked to approve an acquisition, merger, consolidation, or proposed sale or other disposition of all or substantially all the assets of an issuer, the person making such solicitation shall disclose in the proxy or consent solicitation material, in a clear and simple form in accordance with regulations to be promulgated by the Commission, any agreements or understandings that such person has with any named executive officers of such issuer (or of the acquiring issuer, if such issuer is not the acquiring issuer) concerning any type of compensation (whether present, deferred, or contingent) that is based on or otherwise relates to the acquisition, merger, consolidation, sale, or other disposition of all or substantially all of the assets of the issuer and the aggregate total of all such compensation that may (and the conditions upon which it may) be paid or become payable to or on behalf of such executive officer.

(2) *Shareholder Approval.* Any proxy or consent or authorization relating to the proxy or consent solicitation material containing the disclosure required by paragraph (1) shall include a separate resolution subject to shareholder vote to approve such agreements or understandings and compensation as disclosed, unless such agreements or understandings have been subject to a shareholder vote under subsection (a).

(c) *Rule of Construction.* The shareholder vote referred to in subsections (a) and (b) shall not be binding on the issuer or the board of directors of an issuer, and may not be construed—

(1) as overruling a decision by such issuer or board of directors;

(2) to create or imply any change to the fiduciary duties of such issuer or board of directors;

(3) to create or imply any additional fiduciary duties for such issuer or board of directors; or

(4) to restrict or limit the ability of shareholders to make proposals for inclusion in proxy materials related to executive compensation.

(d) *Disclosure of Votes.* Every institutional investment manager subject to section 13(f) shall report at least annually how it voted on any shareholder vote pursuant to subsections (a) and (b), unless such vote is otherwise required to be reported publicly by rule or regulation of the Commission.

(e) *Exemption.*

(1) *In General.* The Commission may, by rule or order, exempt any other issuer or class of issuers from the requirement under subsection (a) or (b). In determining whether to make an exemption under this subsection, the Commission shall take into account, among other considerations, whether the requirements under subsections (a) and (b) disproportionately burdens small issuers.

(2) *Treatment of Emerging Growth Companies.*

(A) *In General.* An emerging growth company shall be exempt from the requirements of subsections (a) and (b).

(B) *Compliance After Termination of Emerging Growth Company Treatment.* An issuer that was an emerging growth company but is no longer an emerging growth company shall include the first separate resolution described under subsection (a)(1) not later than the end of—

(i) in the case of an issuer that was an emerging growth company for less than 2 years after the date of first sale of common equity securities of the issuer pursuant to an effective registration statement under the Securities Act of 1933, the 3-year period beginning on such date; and

(ii) in the case of any other issuer, the 1-year period beginning on the date the issuer is no longer an emerging growth company.

Corporate Governance

Sec. 14B. Not later than 180 days after the date of enactment of this subsection, the Commission shall issue rules that require an issuer to disclose in the annual proxy sent to investors the reasons why the issuer has chosen—

(1) the same person to serve as chairman of the board of directors and chief executive officer (or in equivalent positions); or

(2) different individuals to serve as chairman of the board of directors and chief executive officer (or in equivalent positions of the issuer).

Registration and Regulation of Brokers and Dealers

Sec. 15. (a) *Registration of All Persons Utilizing Exchange Facilities to Effect Transactions; Exemptions.*

(1) It shall be unlawful for any broker or dealer which is either a person other than a natural person or a natural person not associated with a broker or dealer which is a person other than a natural person (other than such a broker or dealer whose business is exclusively intrastate and who does not make use of any facility of a national securities exchange) to make use of the mails or any means or instrumentality of interstate commerce to effect any transactions in, or to induce or attempt to induce the purchase or sale of, any security (other than an exempted security or commercial paper, bankers' acceptances, or commercial bills) unless such broker or dealer is registered in accordance with subsection (b) of this section.

(2) The Commission, by rule or order, as it deems consistent with the public interest and the protection of investors, may conditionally or unconditionally exempt from paragraph (1) of this subsection any broker or dealer or class of brokers or dealers specified in such rule or order.

(b) *Manner of Registration of Brokers and Dealers.*

(1) A broker or dealer may be registered by filing with the Commission an application for registration in such form and containing such information and documents concerning such broker or dealer and any persons associated with such broker or dealer as the Commission, by rule, may prescribe as necessary or appropriate in the public interest or for the protection of investors. Within forty-five days of the date of the filing of such application (or within such longer period as to which the applicant consents), the Commission shall—

(A) by order grant registration, or

(B) institute proceedings to determine whether registration should be denied. Such proceedings shall include notice of the grounds for denial under consideration and opportunity for hearing and shall be concluded within one hundred twenty days of the date of the filing of the application for registration. At the conclusion of such proceedings, the Commission, by order, shall grant or deny such registration. The Commission may extend the time for conclusion of such proceedings for up to ninety days if it finds good cause for such extension and publishes its reasons for so finding or for such longer period as to which the applicant consents.

The Commission shall grant such registration if the Commission finds that the requirements of this section are satisfied. The order granting registration shall not be effective until such broker or dealer has become a member of a registered securities association, or until such broker or dealer has become a member of a national securities exchange if such broker or dealer effects transactions solely on that exchange, unless the Commission has exempted such broker or dealer, by rule or order, from such membership. The Commission shall deny such registration if it does not make such a finding or if it finds that if the applicant were so registered, its registration would be subject to suspension or revocation under paragraph (4) of this subsection.

(2)(A) An application for registration of a broker or dealer to be formed or organized may be made by a broker or dealer to which the broker or dealer to be formed or organized is to be the successor. Such application, in such form as the Commission, by rule, may prescribe, shall contain such information and documents concerning the applicant, the successor, and any persons associated with the applicant or the successor, as the Commission, by rule, may prescribe as necessary or appropriate in the public interest or for the protection of investors. The grant or denial of registration to such an applicant shall be in accordance with the procedures set forth in paragraph (1) of this subsection. If the Commission grants such registration, the registration shall terminate on the forty-fifth day after the effective date thereof, unless prior thereto the successor shall, in accordance with such rules and regulations as the Commission may prescribe, adopt the application for registration as its own.

(B) Any person who is a broker or dealer solely by reason of acting as a municipal securities dealer or municipal securities broker, who so acts through a separately identifiable department or division, and who so acted in such a manner on the date of enactment of the Securities Acts Amendments of 1975, may, in accordance with such terms and conditions as the Commission, by rule, prescribes as necessary and appropriate in the public interest and for the protection of investors, register such separately identifiable department or division in accordance with this subsection. If any such department or division is so registered, the department or division and not such person himself shall be the broker or dealer for purposes of this title.

(C) Within six months of the date of the granting of registration to a broker or dealer, the Commission, or upon the authorization and direction of the Commission, a registered securities association or national securities exchange of which such broker or dealer is a member, shall conduct an inspection of the broker or dealer to determine whether it is operating in conformity with the provisions of this chapter and the rules and regulations thereunder: *Provided, however*, That the Commission may delay such inspection of any class of brokers or dealers for a period not to exceed six months.

(3) Any provision of this title (other than section 5 and subsection (a) of this section) which prohibits any act, practice, or course of business if the mails or any means or instrumentality of interstate commerce is used in connection therewith shall also prohibit any such act, practice, or course of business by any registered broker or dealer or any person acting on behalf of such a broker or dealer, irrespective of any use of the mails or any means or instrumentality of interstate commerce in connection therewith.

(4) The Commission, by order, shall censure, place limitations on the activities, functions, or operations of, suspend for a period not exceeding twelve months, or revoke the registration of any broker or dealer if it finds, on the record after notice and opportunity for hearing, that such censure, placing of limitations, suspension, or revocation is in the public interest and that such broker or dealer, whether prior or subsequent to becoming such, or any person associated with such broker or dealer, whether prior or subsequent to becoming so associated—

(A) has willfully made or caused to be made in any application for registration or report required to be filed with the Commission or with any other appropriate regulatory agency under this title, or in any proceeding before the Commission with respect to registration, any statement which was at the time and in the light of the circumstances under which it was made false or misleading with respect to any material fact, or has omitted to state in any such application or report any material fact which is required to be stated therein.

(B) has been convicted within ten years preceding the filing of any application for registration or at any time thereafter of any felony or misdemeanor or of a substantially equivalent crime by a foreign court of competent jurisdiction which the Commission finds—

(i) involves the purchase or sale of any security, the taking of a false oath, the making of a false report, bribery, perjury, burglary, any substantially equivalent activity however denominated by the laws of the relevant foreign government, or conspiracy to commit any such offense;

(ii) arises out of the conduct of the business of a broker, dealer, municipal securities dealer, municipal advisor, government securities broker, government securities dealer, investment adviser, bank, insurance company, fiduciary, transfer agent, nationally recognized statistical rating organization, foreign person performing a function substantially equivalent to any of the above, or entity or person required to be registered under the Commodity Exchange Act or any substantially equivalent foreign statute or regulation;

(iii) involves the larceny, theft, robbery, extortion, forgery, counterfeiting, fraudulent concealment, embezzlement, fraudulent conversion, or misappropriation of funds, or securities, or substantially equivalent activity however denominated by the laws of the relevant foreign government; or

(iv) involves the violation of section 152, 1341, 1342, or 1343 or chapter 25 or 47 of title 18, United States Code, or a violation of a substantially equivalent foreign statute.

(C) is permanently or temporarily enjoined by order, judgment, or decree of any court of competent jurisdiction from acting as an investment adviser, underwriter, broker, dealer, municipal securities dealer, municipal advisor, government securities broker, government securities dealer, security-based swap dealer, major security-based swap participant, transfer agent, nationally recognized statistical rating organization, foreign person performing a function substantially equivalent to any of the above, or entity or person required to be registered under the Commodity Exchange Act or any substantially equivalent foreign statute or regulation, or as an affiliated person or employee of any investment company, bank, insurance company, foreign entity substantially equivalent to any of the above, or entity or person required to be registered under the Commodity Exchange Act or any substantially equivalent foreign statute or regulation or from engaging in or continuing any conduct or practice in connection with any such activity, or in connection with the purchase or sale of any security.

(D) has willfully violated any provision of the Securities Act of 1933, the Investment Advisers Act of 1940, the Investment Company Act of 1940, the Commodity Exchange Act, this title, the rules or regulations under any of such statutes, or the rules of the Municipal Securities Rulemaking Board, or is unable to comply with any such provision.

(E) has willfully aided, abetted, counseled, commanded, induced, or procured the violation by any other person of any provision of the Securities Act of 1933, the Investment Advisers Act of 1940, the Investment Company Act of 1940, the Commodity Exchange Act, this title, the rules or regulations under any of such statutes, or the rules of the Municipal Securities Rulemaking Board, or has failed reasonably to supervise, with a view to preventing violations of the provisions of such statutes, rules, and regulations, another person who commits such a violation, if such other person is subject to his supervision. For the purposes of this subparagraph (E) no person shall be deemed to have failed reasonably to supervise any other person, if—

(i) there have been established procedures, and a system for applying such procedures, which would reasonably be expected to prevent and detect, insofar as practicable, any such violation by such other person, and

(ii) such person has reasonably discharged the duties and obligations incumbent upon him by reason of such procedures and system without reasonable cause to believe that such procedures and system were not being complied with.

(F) is subject to any order of the Commission barring or suspending the right of the person to be associated with a broker, dealer, security-based swap dealer, or a major security-based swap participant;

(G) has been found by a foreign financial regulatory authority to have—

(i) made or caused to be made in any application for registration or report required to be filed with a foreign financial regulatory authority, or in any proceeding before a foreign financial regulatory authority with respect to registration, any statement that was at the time and in the light of the circumstances under which it was made false or misleading with respect to any material fact, or has omitted to state in any application or report to the foreign financial regulatory authority any material fact that is required to be stated therein;

(ii) violated any foreign statute or regulation regarding transactions in securities, or contracts of sale of a commodity for future delivery, traded on or subject to the rules of a contract market or any board of trade;

(iii) aided, abetted, counseled, commanded, induced, or procured the violation by any person of any provision of any statutory provisions enacted by a foreign government, or rules or regulations thereunder, empowering a foreign financial regulatory authority regarding transactions in securities, or contracts of sale of a commodity for future delivery, traded on or subject to the rules of a contract market or any board of trade, or has been found, by a foreign financial regulatory authority, to have failed reasonably to supervise, with a view to preventing violations of such statutory provisions, rules, and regulations, another person who commits such a violation, if such other person is subject to his supervision; or

(H) is subject to any final order of a State securities commission (or any agency or officer performing like functions), State authority that supervises or examines banks, savings associations, or credit unions, State insurance commission (or any agency or office performing like functions), an appropriate Federal banking agency (as defined in section 3 of the Federal Deposit Insurance Act), or the National Credit Union Administration, that—

(i) bars such person from association with an entity regulated by such commission, authority, agency, or officer, or from engaging in the business of securities, insurance, banking, savings association activities, or credit union activities; or

(ii) constitutes a final order based on violations of any laws or regulations that prohibit fraudulent, manipulative, or deceptive conduct.

(5) Pending final determination whether any registration under this subsection shall be revoked, the Commission, by order, may suspend such registration, if such suspension appears to the Commission, after notice and opportunity for hearing, to be necessary or appropriate in the public interest or for the protection of investors. Any registered broker or dealer may, upon such terms and conditions as the Commission deems necessary or appropriate in the public interest or for the protection of investors, withdraw from registration by filing a written notice of withdrawal with the Commission. If the Commission finds that any registered broker or dealer is no longer in existence or has ceased to do business as a broker or dealer, the Commission, by order, shall cancel the registration of such broker or dealer.

(6)(A) With respect to any person who is associated, who is seeking to become associated, or, at the time of the alleged misconduct, who was associated or was seeking to become associated with a broker or dealer, or any person participating, or, at the time of the alleged misconduct, who was participating, in an offering of any penny stock, the Commission, by order, shall censure, place limitations on the activities or functions of such person, or suspend for a period not exceeding 12 months, or bar any such person from being associated with a broker, dealer, investment adviser, municipal securities dealer, municipal advisor, transfer agent, or nationally recognized statistical rating organization, or from participating in an offering of penny stock, if the Commission finds, on the record after notice and opportunity for a hearing, that such censure, placing of limitations, suspension, or bar is in the public interest and that such person—

(i) has committed or omitted any act, or is subject to an order or finding, enumerated in subparagraph (A), (D), (E), (H), or (G) of paragraph (4) of this subsection;

(ii) has been convicted of any offense specified in subparagraph (B) of such paragraph (4) within 10 years of the commencement of the proceedings under this paragraph; or

(iii) is enjoined from any action, conduct, or practice specified in subparagraph (C) of such paragraph (4).

(B) It shall be unlawful—

(i) for any person as to whom an order under subparagraph (A) is in effect, without the consent of the Commission, willfully to become, or to be, associated with a broker or dealer in contravention of such order, or to participate in an offering of penny stock in contravention of such order;

(ii) for any broker or dealer to permit such a person, without the consent of the Commission, to become or remain, a person associated with the broker or dealer in contravention of such order, if such broker or dealer knew, or in the exercise of reasonable care should have known, of such order; or

(iii) for any broker or dealer to permit such a person, without the consent of the Commission, to participate in an offering of penny stock in contravention of such order, if such broker or dealer knew, or in the exercise of reasonable care should have known, of such order and of such participation.

(C) For purposes of this paragraph, the term "person participating in an offering of penny stock" includes any person acting as any promoter, finder, consultant, agent, or other person who engages in activities with a broker, dealer, or issuer for purposes of the issuance or trading in any penny stock, or inducing or attempting to induce the purchase or sale of any penny stock. The Commission may, by rule or regulation, define such term to include other activities, and may, by rule, regulation, or order, exempt any person or class of persons, in whole or in part, conditionally or unconditionally, from such term.

(7) No registered broker or dealer or government securities broker or government securities dealer registered (or required to register) under section 15(a)(1)(A) shall effect any transaction in,

or induce the purchase or sale of, any security unless such broker or dealer meets such standards of operational capability and such broker or dealer and all natural persons associated with such broker or dealer meet such standards of training, experience, competence, and such other qualifications as the Commission finds necessary or appropriate in the public interest or for the protection of investors. The Commission shall establish such standards by rules and regulations, which may—

(A) specify that all or any portion of such standards shall be applicable to any class of brokers and dealers and persons associated with brokers and dealers;

(B) require persons in any such class to pass tests prescribed in accordance with such rules and regulations, which tests shall, with respect to any class of partners, officers, or supervisory employees (which latter term may be defined by the Commission's rules and regulations and as so defined shall include branch managers of brokers or dealers) engaged in the management of the broker or dealer, include questions relating to bookkeeping, accounting, internal control over cash and securities, supervision of employees, maintenance of records, and other appropriate matters; and

(C) provide that persons in any such class other than brokers and dealers and partners, officers, and supervisory employees of brokers or dealers, may be qualified solely on the basis of compliance with such standards of training and such other qualifications as the Commission finds appropriate.

The Commission, by rule, may prescribe reasonable fees and charges to defray its costs in carrying out this paragraph, including, but not limited to, fees for any test administered by it or under its direction. The Commission may cooperate with registered securities associations and national securities exchanges in devising and administering tests and may require registered brokers and dealers and persons associated with such brokers and dealers to pass tests administered by or on behalf of any such association or exchange and to pay such association or exchange reasonable fees or charges to defray the costs incurred by such association or exchange in administering such tests.

(8) It shall be unlawful for any registered broker or dealer to effect any transaction in, or induce or attempt to induce the purchase or sale of, any security (other than or commercial paper, bankers' acceptances, or commercial bills), unless such broker or dealer is a member of a securities association registered pursuant to section 15A of this title or effects transactions in securities solely on a national securities exchange of which it is a member.

(9) The Commission by rule or order, as it deems consistent with the public interest and the protection of investors, may conditionally or unconditionally exempt from paragraph (8) of this subsection any broker or dealer or class of brokers or dealers specified in such rule or order.

(10) For the purposes of determining whether a person is subject to a statutory disqualification under section 6(c)(2), 15A(g)(2), or 17A(b)(4)(A) of this title, the term "Commission" in paragraph (4)(B) of this subsection shall mean "exchange", "association", or "clearing agency", respectively.

(11) *Broker/Dealer Registration with Respect to Transactions in Security Futures Products.*

(A) *Notice Registration.*

(i) *Contents of Notice.* Notwithstanding paragraphs (1) and (2), a broker or dealer required to register only because it effects transactions in security futures products on an exchange registered pursuant to section 6(g) may register for purposes of this section by filing with the Commission a written notice in such form and containing such information concerning such broker or dealer and any persons associated with such broker or dealer as the Commission, by rule, may prescribe as necessary or appropriate in the public interest or for the protection of investors. A broker or dealer may not register under this paragraph unless that broker or dealer is a member of a national securities association registered under section 15A(k).

(ii) *Immediate Effectiveness.* Such registration shall be effective contemporaneously with the submission of notice, in written or electronic form, to the Commission, except that such registration shall not be effective if the registration would be subject to suspension or revocation under paragraph (4).

(iii) *Suspension.* Such registration shall be suspended immediately if a national securities association registered pursuant to section 15A(k) of this title suspends the membership of that broker or dealer.

(iv) *Termination.* Such registration shall be terminated immediately if any of the above stated conditions for registration set forth in this paragraph are no longer satisfied.

(B) *Exemptions for Registered Brokers and Dealers.* A broker or dealer registered pursuant to the requirements of subparagraph (A) shall be exempt from the following provisions of this title and the rules thereunder with respect to transactions in security futures products:

(i) Section 8.

(ii) Section 11.

(iii) Subsections (c)(3) and (c)(5) of this section.

(iv) Section 15B.

(v) Section 15C.

(vi) Subsections (d), (e), (f), (g), (h), and (i) of section 17.

(12) *Exemption for Security Futures Product Exchange Members.*

(A) *Registration Exemption.* A natural person shall be exempt from the registration requirements of this section if such person—

(i) is a member of a designated contract market registered with the Commission as an exchange pursuant to section 6(g);

(ii) effects transactions only in securities on the exchange of which such person is a member; and

(iii) does not directly accept or solicit orders from public customers or provide advice to public customers in connection with the trading of security futures products.

(B) *Other Exemptions.* A natural person exempt from registration pursuant to subparagraph (A) shall also be exempt from the following provisions of this title and the rules thereunder:

(i) Section 8.

(ii) Section 11.

(iii) Subsections (c)(3), (c)(5), and (e) of this section.

(iv) Section 15B.

(v) Section 15C.

(vi) Subsections (d), (e), (f), (g), (h), and (i) of section 17.

(c) *Use of Manipulative or Deceptive Devices; Contravention of Rules and Regulations.*

(1)(A) No broker or dealer shall make use of the mails or any means or instrumentality of interstate commerce to effect any transaction in, or to induce or attempt to induce the purchase or sale of, any security (other than commercial paper, bankers' acceptances, or commercial bills), or any security-based swap agreement by means of any manipulative, deceptive, or other fraudulent device or contrivance.

(B) No broker, dealer, or municipal securities dealer shall make use of the mails or any means or instrumentality of interstate commerce to effect any transaction in, or to induce or attempt to induce the purchase or sale of, any municipal security or any security-based swap agreement involving a municipal security by means of any manipulative, deceptive, or other fraudulent device or contrivance.

(C) No government securities broker or government securities dealer shall make use of the mails or any means or instrumentality of interstate commerce to effect any transaction in, or to induce or to attempt to induce the purchase or sale of, any government security or any security-based swap agreement involving a government security by means of any manipulative, deceptive, or other fraudulent device or contrivance.

(2)(A) No broker or dealer shall make use of the mails or any means or instrumentality of interstate commerce to effect any transaction in, or to induce or attempt to induce the purchase or sale of, any security (other than an exempted security or commercial paper, bankers' acceptances, or commercial bills) otherwise than on a national securities exchange of which it is a member, in connection with which such broker or dealer engages in any fraudulent, deceptive, or manipulative act or practice, or makes any fictitious quotation.

(B) No broker, dealer, or municipal securities dealer shall make use of the mails or any means or instrumentality of interstate commerce to effect any transaction in, or to induce or attempt to induce the purchase or sale of, any municipal security in connection with which such broker, dealer, or municipal securities dealer engages in any fraudulent, deceptive, or manipulative act or practice, or makes any fictitious quotation.

(C) No government securities broker or government securities dealer shall make use of the mails or any means or instrumentality of interstate commerce to effect any transaction in, or induce or attempt to induce the purchase or sale of, any government security in connection with which such government securities broker or government securities dealer engages in any fraudulent, deceptive, or manipulative act or practice, or makes any fictitious quotation.

(D) The Commission shall, for the purposes of this paragraph, by rules and regulations define, and prescribe means reasonably designed to prevent, such acts and practices as are fraudulent, deceptive, or manipulative and such quotations as are fictitious.

(E) The Commission shall, prior to adopting any rule or regulation under subparagraph (C), consult with and consider the views of the Secretary of the Treasury and each appropriate regulatory agency. If the Secretary of the Treasury or any appropriate regulatory agency comments in writing on a proposed rule or regulation of the Commission under such subparagraph (C) that has been published for comment, the Commission shall respond in writing to such written comment before adopting the proposed rule. If the Secretary of the Treasury determines, and notifies the Commission, that such rule or regulation, if implemented, would, or as applied does (i) adversely affect the liquidity or efficiency of the market for government securities; or (ii) impose any burden on competition not necessary or appropriate in furtherance of the purposes of this section, the Commission shall, prior to adopting the proposed rule or regulation, find that such rule or regulation is necessary and appropriate in furtherance of the purposes of this section notwithstanding the Secretary's determination.

(3)(A) No broker or dealer (other than a government securities broker or government securities dealer, except a registered broker or dealer) shall make use of the mails or any means or instrumentality of interstate commerce to effect any transaction in, or to induce or attempt to induce the purchase or sale of, any security (other than an exempted security (except a government security) or commercial paper, bankers' acceptances, or commercial bills) in contravention of such rules and regulations as the Commission shall prescribe as necessary or appropriate in the public interest or for the protection of investors to provide safeguards with respect to the financial responsibility and related practices of brokers and dealers including, but not limited to, the acceptance of custody and use of customers' securities and the carrying and use of customers' deposits or credit balances. Such rules and regulations shall (A) require the maintenance of reserves with respect to customers' deposits or credit balances, and (B) no later than September 1, 1975, establish minimum financial responsibility requirements for all brokers and dealers.

(B) Consistent with this title, the Commission, in consultation with the Commodity Futures Trading Commission, shall issue such rules, regulations, or orders as are necessary to avoid duplicative or conflicting regulations applicable to any broker or dealer registered with the Commission pursuant to section 15(b) (except paragraph (11) thereof), that is also registered with the Commodity Futures Trading Commission pursuant to section 4f(a) of the Commodity Exchange Act (except paragraph (2) thereof), with respect to the application of: (i) the provisions of section 8, section 15(c)(3), and section 17 of this title and the rules and regulations thereunder related to the treatment of customer funds, securities, or property, maintenance of books and records, financial reporting, or other financial responsibility rules, involving security futures products; and (ii) similar provisions of the Commodity Exchange Act and rules and regulations thereunder involving security futures products.

(C) Notwithstanding any provision of sections 2(a)(1)(C)(i) or 4d(a)(2) of the Commodity Exchange Act and the rules and regulations thereunder, and pursuant to an exemption granted by the Commission under section 36 of this title or pursuant to a rule or regulation, cash and securities may be held by a broker or dealer registered pursuant to subsection (b)(1) and also registered as a futures commission merchant pursuant to section 4f(a)(1) of the Commodity Exchange Act, in a portfolio margining account carried as a futures account subject to section 4d of the Commodity Exchange Act and the rules and regulations thereunder, pursuant to a portfolio margining program approved by the Commodity Futures Trading Commission, and subject to subchapter IV of chapter 7 of title 11 of the United States Code and the rules and regulations thereunder. The Commission shall consult with the Commodity Futures Trading Commission to adopt rules to ensure that such transactions and accounts are subject to comparable requirements to the extent practicable for similar products.

(4) If the Commission finds, after notice and opportunity for a hearing, that any person subject to the provisions of section 12, 13, 14, or subsection (d) of section 15 of this title or any rule or regulation thereunder has failed to comply with any such provision, rule, or regulation in any material respect, the Commission may publish its findings and issue an order requiring such person, and any person who was a cause of the failure to comply due to an act or omission the person knew or should have known would contribute to the failure to comply, to comply, or to take steps to effect compliance, with such provision or such rule or regulation thereunder upon such terms and conditions and within such time as the Commission may specify in such order.

(5) No dealer (other than a specialist registered on a national securities exchange) acting in the capacity of market maker or otherwise shall make use of the mails or any means or instrumentality of interstate commerce to effect any transaction in, or to induce or attempt to induce the purchase or sale of, any security (other than an exempted security or a municipal security) in contravention of such specified and appropriate standards with respect to dealing as the Commission, by rule, shall prescribe as necessary or appropriate in the public interest and for the protection of investors, to maintain fair and orderly markets, or to remove impediments to and perfect the mechanism of a national market system. Under the rules of the Commission a dealer in a security may be prohibited from acting as a broker in that security.

(6) No broker or dealer shall make use of the mails or any means or instrumentality of interstate commerce to effect any transaction in, or to induce or attempt to induce the purchase or sale of, any security (other than an exempted security, municipal security, commercial paper, bankers' acceptances, or commercial bills) in contravention of such rules and regulations as the Commission shall prescribe as necessary or appropriate in the public interest and for the protection of investors or to perfect or remove impediments to a national system for the prompt and accurate clearance and settlement of securities transactions, with respect to the time and method of, and the form and format of documents used in connection with, making settlements of and payments for transactions in securities, making transfers and deliveries of securities, and closing accounts. Nothing in this paragraph shall be construed (A) to affect the authority of the Board of Governors of the Federal Reserve System, pursuant to section 7 of this title, to prescribe rules and regulations for the purpose of preventing the excessive use of credit for the purchase or carrying of securities, or (B) to authorize the Commission to prescribe rules or regulations for such purpose.

(7) In connection with any bid for or purchase of a government security related to an offering of government securities by or on behalf of an issuer, no government securities broker, government securities dealer, or bidder for or purchaser of securities in such offering shall knowingly or willfully make any false or misleading written statement or omit any fact necessary to make any written statement made not misleading.

(8) *Prohibition of Referral Fees.* No broker or dealer, or person associated with a broker or dealer, may solicit or accept, directly or indirectly, remuneration for assisting an attorney in obtaining the representation of any person in any private action arising under this title or under the Securities Act of 1933.

(d) *Filing of Supplementary and Periodic Information.*

(1) *In General.* Each issuer which has filed a registration statement containing an undertaking which is or becomes operative under this subsection as in effect prior to the date of enactment of the Securities Acts Amendments of 1964, and each issuer which shall after such date file a registration statement which has become effective pursuant to the Securities Act of 1933, as amended, shall file with the Commission, in accordance with such rules and regulations as the Commission may prescribe as necessary or appropriate in the public interest or for the protection of investors, such supplementary and periodic information, documents, and reports as may be required pursuant to section 13 of this title in respect of a security registered pursuant to section 12 of this title. The duty to file under this subsection shall be automatically suspended if and so long as any issue of securities of such issuer is registered pursuant to section 12 of this title. The duty to file under this subsection shall also be automatically suspended as to any fiscal year, other than the fiscal year within which such registration statement became effective, if, at the beginning of such fiscal year, the securities of each class, other than any class of asset-backed securities, to which the registration statement relates are held of record by less than 300 persons, or, in the case of a bank, a savings and loan hold-

ing company (as defined in Section 10 of the Home Owners' Loan Act), or a bank holding company, as such term is defined in section 2 of the Bank Holding Company Act of 1956, 1,200 persons. For the purposes of this subsection, the term "class" shall be construed to include all securities of an issuer which are of substantially similar character and the holders of which enjoy substantially similar rights and privileges. The Commission may, for the purpose of this subsection, define by rules and regulations the term "held of record" as it deems necessary or appropriate in the public interest or for the protection of investors in order to prevent circumvention of the provisions of this subsection. Nothing in this subsection shall apply to securities issued by a foreign government or political subdivision thereof.

(2) *Asset-Backed Securities.*

(A) *Suspension of Duty to File.* The Commission may, by rule or regulation, provide for the suspension or termination of the duty to file under this subsection for any class of asset-backed security, on such terms and conditions and for such period or periods as the Commission deems necessary or appropriate in the public interest or for the protection of investors.

(B) *Classification of Issuers.* The Commission may, for purposes of this subsection, classify issuers and prescribe requirements appropriate for each class of issuers of asset-backed securities.

(e) *Notices to Customers Regarding Securities Lending.* Every registered broker or dealer shall provide notice to its customers that they may elect not to allow their fully paid securities to be used in connection with short sales. If a broker or dealer uses a customer's securities in connection with short sales, the broker or dealer shall provide notice to its customer that the broker or dealer may receive compensation in connection with lending the customer's securities. The Commission, by rule, as it deems necessary or appropriate in the public interest and for the protection of investors, may prescribe the form, content, time, and manner of delivery of any notice required under this paragraph.

(f) *Compliance with This Title by Members Not Required to Be Registered.* The Commission, by rule, as it deems necessary or appropriate in the public interest and for the protection of investors or to assure equal regulation, may require any member of a national securities exchange not required to register under section 15 of this title and any person associated with any such member to comply with any provision of this chapter (other than section 15(a)) or the rules or regulations thereunder which by its terms regulates or prohibits any act, practice, or course of business by a "broker or dealer" or "registered broker or dealer" or a "person associated with a broker or dealer," respectively.

(g) *Prevention of Misuse of Material, Nonpublic Information.* Every registered broker or dealer shall establish, maintain, and enforce written policies and procedures reasonably designed, taking into consideration the nature of such broker's or dealer's business, to prevent the misuse in violation of this title, or the rules or regulations thereunder, of material, nonpublic information by such broker or dealer or any person associated with such broker or dealer. The Commission, as it deems necessary or appropriate in the public interest or for the protection of investors, shall adopt rules or regulations to require specific policies or procedures reasonably designed to prevent misuse in violation of this title (or the rules or regulations thereunder) of material, nonpublic information.

(h) *Requirements for Transactions in Penny Stocks.*

(1) *In General.* No broker or dealer shall make use of the mails or any means or instrumentality of interstate commerce to effect any transaction in, or to induce or attempt to induce the purchase or sale of, any penny stock by any customer except in accordance with the requirements of this subsection and the rules and regulations prescribed under this subsection.

(2) *Risk Disclosure with Respect to Penny Stocks.* Prior to effecting any transaction in any penny stock, a broker or dealer shall give the customer a risk disclosure document that—

(A) contains a description of the nature and level of risk in the market for penny stocks in both public offerings and secondary trading;

(B) contains a description of the broker's or dealer's duties to the customer and of the rights and remedies available to the customer with respect to violations of such duties or other requirements of Federal securities laws;

(C) contains a brief, clear, narrative description of a dealer market, including "bid" and "ask" prices for penny stocks and the significance of the spread between the bid and ask prices;

(D) contains the toll free telephone number for inquiries on disciplinary actions established pursuant to section 15A(i) of this title;

(E) defines significant terms used in the disclosure document or in the conduct of trading in penny stocks; and

(F) contains such other information, and is in such form (including language, type size, and format), as the Commission shall require by rule or regulation.

(3) *Commission Rules Relating to Disclosure.* The Commission shall adopt rules setting forth additional standards for the disclosure by brokers and dealers to customers of information concerning transactions in penny stocks. Such rules—

(A) shall require brokers and dealers to disclose to each customer, prior to effecting any transaction in, and at the time of confirming any transaction with respect to any penny stock, in accordance with such procedures and methods as the Commission may require consistent with the public interest and the protection of investors—

(i) the bid and ask prices for penny stock, or such other information as the Commission may, by rule, require to provide customers with more useful and reliable information relating to the price of such stock;

(ii) the number of shares to which such bid and ask prices apply, or other comparable information relating to the depth and liquidity of the market for such stock; and

(iii) the amount and a description of any compensation that the broker or dealer and the associated person thereof will receive or has received in connection with such transaction;

(B) shall require brokers and dealers to provide, to each customer whose account with the broker or dealer contains penny stocks, a monthly statement indicating the market value of the penny stocks in that account or indicating that the market value of such stock cannot be determined because of the unavailability of firm quotes; and

(C) may, as the Commission finds necessary or appropriate in the public interest or for the protection of investors, require brokers and dealers to disclose to customers additional information concerning transactions in penny stocks.

(4) *Exemptions.* The Commission, as it determines consistent with the public interest and the protection of investors, may by rule, regulation, or order exempt in whole or in part, conditionally or unconditionally, any person or class of persons, or any transaction or class of transactions, from the requirements of this subsection. Such exemptions shall include an exemption for brokers and dealers based on the minimal percentage of the broker's or dealer's commissions, commission-equivalents, and markups received from transactions in penny stocks.

(5) *Regulations.* It shall be unlawful for any person to violate such rules and regulations as the Commission shall prescribe in the public interest or for the protection of investors or to maintain fair and orderly markets—

(A) as necessary or appropriate to carry out this subsection; or

(B) as reasonably designed to prevent fraudulent, deceptive, or manipulative acts and practices with respect to penny stocks.

(i) *Limitations on State Law.*

(1) *Capital, Margin, Books and Records, Bonding, and Reports.* No law, rule, regulation, or order, or other administrative action of any State or political subdivision thereof shall establish capital, custody, margin, financial responsibility, making and keeping records, bonding, or financial or operational reporting requirements for brokers, dealers, municipal securities dealers, government securities brokers, or government securities dealers that differ from, or are in addition to, the requirements in those areas established under this title. The Commission shall consult periodically the securities commissions (or any agency or office performing like functions) of the States concerning the adequacy of such requirements as established under this title.

(2) *Funding Portals.*

(A) *Limitation on State Laws.* Except as provided in subparagraph (B), no State or political subdivision thereof may enforce any law, rule, regulation, or other administrative action against a registered funding portal with respect to its business as such.

(B) *Examination and Enforcement Authority.* Subparagraph (A) does not apply with respect to the examination and enforcement of any law, rule, regulation, or administrative action of a State or political subdivision thereof in which the principal place of business of a registered funding portal is located, provided that such law, rule, regulation, or administrative action is not in addition to or different from the requirements for registered funding portals established by the Commission.

(C) *Definition.* For purposes of this paragraph, the term "State" includes the District of Columbia and the territories of the United States.

(3) *De Minimis Transactions by Associated Persons.* No law, rule, regulation, or order, or other administrative action of any State or political subdivision thereof may prohibit an associated person of a broker or dealer from effecting a transaction described in paragraph (3) for a customer in such State if—

(A) such associated person is not ineligible to register with such State for any reason other than such a transaction;

(B) such associated person is registered with a registered securities association and at least one State; and

(C) the broker or dealer with which such person is associated is registered with such State.

(4) *Described Transactions.*

(A) *In General.* A transaction is described in this paragraph if—

(i) such transaction is effected—

(I) on behalf of a customer that, for 30 days prior to the day of the transaction, maintained an account with the broker or dealer; and

(II) by an associated person of the broker or dealer—

(aa) to which the customer was assigned for 14 days prior to the day of the transaction; and

(bb) who is registered with a State in which the customer was a resident or was present for at least 30 consecutive days during the 1–year period prior to the day of the transaction; or

(ii) the transaction is effected—

(I) on behalf of a customer that, for 30 days prior to the day of the transaction, maintained an account with the broker or dealer; and

(II) during the period beginning on the date on which such associated person files an application for registration with the State in which the transaction is effected and ending on the earlier of—

(aa) 60 days after the date on which the application is filed; or

(bb) the date on which such State notifies the associated person that it has denied the application for registration or has stayed the pendency of the application for cause.

(B) *Rules of Construction.* For purposes of subparagraph (A)(i)(II)—

(i) each of up to 3 associated persons of a broker or dealer who are designated to effect transactions during the absence or unavailability of the principal associated person for a customer may be treated as an associated person to which such customer is assigned; and

(ii) if the customer is present in another State for 30 or more consecutive days or has permanently changed his or her residence to another State, a transaction is not described in this paragraph, unless the associated person of the broker or dealer files an application for registration with such State not later than 10 business days after the later of the date of the transaction, or the date of the discovery of the presence of the customer in the other State for 30 or more consecutive days or the change in the customer's residence.

(j) *Limitation.* The authority of the Commission under this section with respect to security-based swap agreements shall be subject to the restrictions and limitations of section 3A(b) of this title.*

(j) *Rulemaking to Extend Requirements to New Hybrid Products.*

(1) *Consultation.* Prior to commencing a rulemaking under this subsection, the Commission shall consult with and seek the concurrence of the Board concerning the imposition of broker or dealer registration requirements with respect to any new hybrid product. In developing and promulgating rules under this subsection, the Commission shall consider the views of the Board, including views with respect to the nature of the new hybrid product; the history, purpose, extent, and appropriateness of the regulation of the new product under the Federal banking laws; and the

* Dodd-Frank created two subsection (j)'s in section 15.

impact of the proposed rule on the banking industry.

(2) *Limitation.* The Commission shall not—

(A) require a bank to register as a broker or dealer under this section because the bank engages in any transaction in, or buys or sells, a new hybrid product; or

(B) bring an action against a bank for a failure to comply with a requirement described in subparagraph (A), unless the Commission has imposed such requirement by rule or regulation issued in accordance with this section.

(3) *Criteria for Rulemaking.* The Commission shall not impose a requirement under paragraph (2) of this subsection with respect to any new hybrid product unless the Commission determines that—

(A) the new hybrid product is a security; and

(B) imposing such requirement is necessary and appropriate in the public interest and for the protection of investors.

(4) *Considerations.* In making a determination under paragraph (3), the Commission shall consider—

(A) the nature of the new hybrid product; and

(B) the history, purpose, extent, and appropriateness of the regulation of the new hybrid product under the Federal securities laws and under the Federal banking laws.

(5) *Objection to Commission Regulation.*

(A) *Filing of Petition for Review.* The Board may obtain review of any final regulation described in paragraph (2) in the United States Court of Appeals for the District of Columbia Circuit by filing in such court, not later than 60 days after the date of publication of the final regulation, a written petition requesting that the regulation be set aside. Any proceeding to challenge any such rule shall be expedited by the Court of Appeals.

(B) *Transmittal of Petition and Record.* A copy of a petition described in subparagraph (A) shall be transmitted as soon as possible by the Clerk of the Court to an officer or employee of the Commission designated for that purpose. Upon receipt of the petition, the Commission shall file with the court the regulation under review and any documents referred to therein, and any other relevant materials prescribed by the court.

(C) *Exclusive Jurisdiction.* On the date of the filing of the petition under subparagraph (A), the court has jurisdiction, which becomes exclusive on the filing of the materials set forth in subparagraph (B), to affirm and enforce or to set aside the regulation at issue.

(D) *Standard of Review.* The court shall determine to affirm and enforce or set aside a regulation of the Commission under this subsection, based on the determination of the court as to whether—

(i) the subject product is a new hybrid product, as defined in this subsection;

(ii) the subject product is a security; and

(iii) imposing a requirement to register as a broker or dealer for banks engaging in transactions in such product is appropriate in light of the history, purpose, and extent of regulation under the Federal securities laws and under the Federal banking laws, giving deference neither to the views of the Commission nor the Board.

(E) *Judicial Stay.* The filing of a petition by the Board pursuant to subparagraph (A) shall operate as a judicial stay, until the date on which the determination of the court is final (including any appeal of such determination).

(F) *Other Authority to Challenge.* Any aggrieved party may seek judicial review of the Commission's rulemaking under this subsection pursuant to section 25 of this title.

(6) *Definitions.* For purposes of this subsection:

(A) *New Hybrid Product.* The term "new hybrid product" means a product that—

(i) was not subjected to regulation by the Commission as a security prior to November 12, 1999;

(ii) is not an identified banking product as such term is defined in section 206 of such Act; and

(iii) is not an equity swap within the meaning of section 206(a)(6) of such Act.

(B) *Board.* The term "Board" means the Board of Governors of the Federal Reserve System.

(k) *Registration or Succession to a United States Broker or Dealer.* In determining whether to permit a foreign person or an affiliate of a foreign person to register as a United States broker or dealer, or succeed to the registration of a United States broker or dealer, the Commission may consider whether, for a foreign person, or an affiliate of a foreign person that presents a risk to the stability of the United States financial system, the home country of the foreign person has adopted, or made demonstrable progress toward adopting, an appropriate system of financial regulation to mitigate such risk.*

(*l*) *Termination of a United States Broker or Dealer*. For a foreign person or an affiliate of a foreign person that presents such a risk to the stability of the United States financial system, the Commission may determine to terminate the registration of such foreign person or an affiliate of such foreign person as a broker or dealer in the United States, if the Commission determines that the home country of the foreign person has not adopted, or made demonstrable progress toward adopting, an appropriate system of financial regulation to mitigate such risk.

(k) *Standard of Conduct*.

(1) *In General*. Notwithstanding any other provision of this Act or the Investment Advisers Act of 1940, the Commission may promulgate rules to provide that, with respect to a broker or dealer, when providing personalized investment advice about securities to a retail customer (and such other customers as the Commission may by rule provide), the standard of conduct for such broker or dealer with respect to such customer shall be the same as the standard of conduct applicable to an investment adviser under section 211 of the Investment Advisers Act of 1940. The receipt of compensation based on commission or other standard compensation for the sale of securities shall not, in and of itself, be considered a violation of such standard applied to a broker or dealer. Nothing in this section shall require a broker or dealer or registered representative to have a continuing duty of care or loyalty to the customer after providing personalized investment advice about securities.

(2) *Disclosure of Range of Products Offered*. Where a broker or dealer sells only proprietary or other limited range of products, as determined by the Commission, the Commission may by rule require that such broker or dealer provide notice to each retail customer and obtain the consent or acknowledgment of the customer. The sale of only proprietary or other limited range of products by a broker or dealer shall not, in and of itself, be considered a violation of the standard set forth in paragraph (1).

(*l*) *Other Matters*. The Commission shall—

(1) facilitate the provision of simple and clear disclosures to investors regarding the terms of their relationships with brokers, dealers, and investment advisers, including any material conflicts of interest; and

(2) examine and, where appropriate, promulgate rules prohibiting or restricting certain sales practices, conflicts of interest, and compensation schemes for brokers, dealers, and investment advisers that the Commission deems contrary to the public interest and the protection of investors.**

(m) *Harmonization of Enforcement*. The enforcement authority of the Commission with respect to violations of the standard of conduct applicable to a broker or dealer providing personalized investment advice about securities to a retail customer shall include—

(1) the enforcement authority of the Commission with respect to such violations provided under this Act; and

(2) the enforcement authority of the Commission with respect to violations of the standard of conduct applicable to an investment adviser under the Investment Advisers Act of 1940, including the authority to impose sanctions for such violations, and the Commission shall seek to prosecute and sanction violators of the standard of conduct applicable to a broker or dealer providing personalized investment advice about securities to a retail customer under this Act to same extent as the Commission prosecutes and sanctions violators of the standard of conduct applicable to an investment advisor under the Investment Advisers Act of 1940.

(n) *Disclosures to Retail Investors*.

(1) *In General*. Notwithstanding any other provision of the securities laws, the Commission may issue rules designating documents or information that shall be provided by a broker or dealer to a retail investor before the purchase of an investment product or service by the retail investor.

(2) *Considerations*. In developing any rules under paragraph (1), the Commission shall consider whether the rules will promote investor protection, efficiency, competition, and capital formation.

(3) *Form and Contents of Documents and Information*. Any documents or information designat-

* Dodd–Frank created two (k)'s and two (*l*)'s in section 15.

ed under a rule promulgated under paragraph (1) shall—

(A) be in a summary format; and

(B) contain clear and concise information about—

(i) investment objectives, strategies, costs, and risks; and

(ii) any compensation or other financial incentive received by a broker, dealer, or other intermediary in connection with the purchase of retail investment products.

(o) *Authority To Restrict Mandatory Pre–Dispute Arbitration.* The Commission, by rule, may prohibit, or impose conditions or limitations on the use of, agreements that require customers or clients of any broker, dealer, or municipal securities dealer to arbitrate any future dispute between them arising under the Federal securities laws, the rules and regulations thereunder, or the rules of a self-regulatory organization if it finds that such prohibition, imposition of conditions, or limitations are in the public interest and for the protection of investors.

Registered Securities Associations

Sec. 15A. (a) *Registration; Application.* An association of brokers and dealers may be registered as a national securities association pursuant to subsection (b), or as an affiliated securities association pursuant to subsection (d) under the terms and conditions hereinafter provided in this section and in accordance with the provisions of section 19(a) of this title, by filing with the Commission an application for registration in such form as the Commission, by rule, may prescribe containing the rules of the association and such other information and documents as the Commission, by rule, may prescribe as necessary or appropriate in the public interest or for the protection of investors.

(b) *Determinations by Commission Requisite to Registration of Applicant as National Securities Association.* An association of brokers and dealers shall not be registered as a national securities association unless the Commission determines that—

(1) By reason of the number and geographical distribution of its members and the scope of their transactions, such association will be able to carry out the purposes of this section.

(2) Such association is so organized and has the capacity to be able to carry out the purposes of this title and to comply, and (subject to any rule or order of the Commission pursuant to section 17(d) or 19(g)(2) of this title) to enforce compliance by its members and persons associated with its members, with the provisions of this title, the rules and regulations thereunder, the rules of the Municipal Securities Rulemaking Board, and the rules of the association.

(3) Subject to the provisions of subsection (g) of this section, the rules of the association provide that any registered broker or dealer may become a member of such association and any person may become associated with a member thereof.

(4) The rules of the association assure a fair representation of its members in the selection of its directors and administration of its affairs and provide that one or more directors shall be representative of issuers and investors and not be associated with a member of the association, broker, or dealer.

(5) The rules of the association provide for the equitable allocation of reasonable dues, fees, and other charges among members and issuers and other persons using any facility or system which the association operates or controls.

(6) The rules of the association are designed to prevent fraudulent and manipulative acts and practices, to promote just and equitable principles of trade, to foster cooperation and coordination with persons engaged in regulating, clearing, settling, processing information with respect to, and facilitating transactions in securities, to remove impediments to and perfect the mechanism of a free and open market and a national market system, and, in general, to protect investors and the public interest; and are not designed to permit unfair discrimination between customers, issuers, brokers, or dealers, to fix minimum profits, to impose any schedule or fix rates of commissions, allowances, discounts, or other fees to be charged by its members, or to regulate by virtue of any authority conferred by this title matters not related to the purposes of this title or the administration of the association.

(7) The rules of the association provide that (subject to any rule or order of the Commission pursuant to section 17(d) or 19(g)(2) of this title) its members and persons associated with its members shall be appropriately disciplined for violation of any provision of this title, the rules or regulations thereunder, the rules of the Municipal Securities Rulemaking Board, or the rules of the association, by expulsion, suspension, limitation of activities, functions, and operations, fine, censure,

being suspended or barred from being associated with a member, or any other fitting sanction.

(8) The rules of the association are in accordance with the provisions of subsection (h) of this section, and, in general, provide a fair procedure for the disciplining of members and persons associated with members, the denial of membership to any person seeking membership therein, the barring of any person from becoming associated with a member thereof, and the prohibition or limitation by the association of any person with respect to access to services offered by the association or a member thereof.

(9) The rules of the association do not impose any burden on competition not necessary or appropriate in furtherance of the purposes of this title.

(10) The requirements of subsection (c) of this section, insofar as these may be applicable, are satisfied.

(11) The rules of the association include provisions governing the form and content of quotations relating to securities sold otherwise than on a national securities exchange which may be distributed or published by any member or person associated with a member, and the persons to whom such quotations may be supplied. Such rules relating to quotations shall be designed to produce fair and informative quotations, to prevent fictitious or misleading quotations, and to promote orderly procedures for collecting, distributing, and publishing quotations.

(12) The rules of the association to promote just and equitable principles of trade, as required by paragraph (6), include rules to prevent members of the association from participating in any limited partnership rollup transaction (as such term is defined in paragraphs (4) and (5) of section 14(h)) unless such transaction was conducted in accordance with procedures designed to protect the rights of limited partners, including—

(A) the right of dissenting limited partners to one of the following:

(i) an appraisal and compensation;

(ii) retention of a security under substantially the same terms and conditions as the original issue;

(iii) approval of the limited partnership rollup transaction by not less than 75 percent of the outstanding securities of each of the participating limited partnerships;

(iv) the use of a committee that is independent, as determined in accordance with rules prescribed by the association, of the general partner or sponsor, that has been approved by a majority of the outstanding securities of each of the participating partnerships, and that has such authority as is necessary to protect the interest of limited partners, including the authority to hire independent advisors, to negotiate with the general partner or sponsor on behalf of the limited partners, and to make a recommendation to the limited partners with respect to the proposed transaction; or

(v) other comparable rights that are prescribed by rule by the association and that are designed to protect dissenting limited partners;

(B) the right not to have their voting power unfairly reduced or abridged;

(C) the right not to bear an unfair portion of the costs of a proposed limited partnership rollup transaction that is rejected; and

(D) restrictions on the conversion of contingent interests or fees into non-contingent interests or fees and restrictions on the receipt of a non-contingent equity interest in exchange for fees for services which have not yet been provided.

As used in this paragraph, the term "dissenting limited partner" means a person who, on the date on which soliciting material is mailed to investors, is a holder of a beneficial interest in a limited partnership that is the subject of a limited partnership rollup transaction, and who casts a vote against the transaction and complies with procedures established by the association, except that for purposes of an exchange or tender offer, such person shall file an objection in writing under the rules of the association during the period in which the offer is outstanding.

(13) The rules of the association prohibit the authorization for quotation on an automated interdealer quotation system sponsored by the association of any security designated by the Commission as a national market system security resulting from a limited partnership rollup transaction (as such term is defined in paragraphs (4) and (5) of section 14(h)), unless such transaction was con-

ducted in accordance with procedures designed to protect the rights of limited partners, including—

(A) the right of dissenting limited partners to one of the following:

(i) an appraisal and compensation;

(ii) retention of a security under substantially the same terms and conditions as the original issue;

(iii) approval of the limited partnership rollup transaction by not less than 75 percent of the outstanding securities of each of the participating limited partnerships;

(iv) the use of a committee that is independent, as determined in accordance with rules prescribed by the association, of the general partner or sponsor, that has been approved by a majority of the outstanding securities of each of the participating partnerships, and that has such authority as is necessary to protect the interest of limited partners, including the authority to hire independent advisors, to negotiate with the general partner or sponsor on behalf of the limited partners, and to make a recommendation to the limited partners with respect to the proposed transaction; or

(v) other comparable rights that are prescribed by rule by the association and that are designed to protect dissenting limited partners;

(B) the right not to have their voting power unfairly reduced or abridged;

(C) the right not to bear an unfair portion of the costs of a proposed limited partnership rollup transaction that is rejected; and

(D) restrictions on the conversion of contingent interests or fees into non-contingent interests or fees and restrictions on the receipt of a non-contingent equity interest in exchange for fees for services which have not yet been provided.

As used in this paragraph, the term "dissenting limited partner" means a person who, on the date on which soliciting material is mailed to investors, is a holder of a beneficial interest in a limited partnership that is the subject of a limited partnership rollup transaction, and who casts a vote against the transaction and complies with procedures established by the association, except that for purposes of an exchange or tender offer, such person shall file an objection in writing under the rules of the association during the period during which the offer is outstanding.

(14) The rules of the association include provisions governing the sales, or offers of sales, of securities on the premises of any military installation to any member of the Armed Forces or a dependent thereof, which rules require—

(A) the broker or dealer performing brokerage services to clearly and conspicuously disclose to potential investors—

(i) that the securities offered are not being offered or provided by the broker or dealer on behalf of the Federal Government, and that its offer is not sanctioned, recommended, or encouraged by the Federal Government; and

(ii) the identity of the registered broker-dealer offering the securities;

(B) such broker or dealer to perform an appropriate suitability determination, including consideration of costs and knowledge about securities, prior to making a recommendation of a security to a member of the Armed Forces or a dependent thereof; and

(C) that no person receive any referral fee or incentive compensation in connection with a sale or offer of sale of securities, unless such person is an associated person of a registered broker or dealer and is qualified pursuant to the rules of a self-regulatory organization.

(15) The rules of the association provide that the association shall—

(A) request guidance from the Municipal Securities Rulemaking Board in interpretation of the rules of the Municipal Securities Rulemaking Board; and

(B) provide information to the Municipal Securities Rulemaking Board about the enforcement actions and examinations of the association under section 15B(b)(2)(E), so that the Municipal Securities Rulemaking Board may—

(i) assist in such enforcement actions and examinations; and

(ii) evaluate the ongoing effectiveness of the rules of the Board.

(c) *National Association Rules; Provision for Registration of Affiliated Securities. Association.* The Commission may permit or require the rules of an association applying for registration pursuant to subsection (b), to provide for the admission of an association registered as an affiliated securities association pursuant to subsection (d), to participation in said applicant association as an affiliate thereof, under terms permitting such powers and responsibilities to such affiliate, and under such other appropriate terms and conditions, as may be provided by the rules of said applicant association, if such rules appear to the Commission to be necessary or appropriate in the public interest or for the protection of investors and to carry out the purposes of this section. The duties and powers of the Commission with respect to any national securities association or any affiliated securities association shall in no way be limited by reason of any such affiliation.

(d) *Registration as Affiliated Association; Prerequisites; Association Rules.* An applicant association shall not be registered as an affiliated securities association unless it appears to the Commission that—

(1) such association, notwithstanding that it does not satisfy the requirements set forth in paragraph (1) of subsection (b), will, forthwith upon the registration thereof, be admitted to affiliation with an association registered as a national securities association pursuant to subsection (b), in the manner and under the terms and conditions provided by the rules of said national securities association in accordance with subsection (c); and

(2) such association and its rules satisfy the requirements set forth in paragraphs (2) to (10), inclusive, and paragraph (12), of subsection (b); except that in the case of any such association any restrictions upon membership therein of the type authorized by paragraph (3) of subsection (b) shall not be less stringent than in the case of the national securities association with which such association is to be affiliated.

(e) *Dealings with Nonmember Professionals.*

(1) The rules of a registered securities association may provide that no member thereof shall deal with any nonmember professional (as defined in paragraph (2) of this subsection) except at the same prices, for the same commissions or fees, and on the same terms and conditions as are by such member accorded to the general public.

(2) For the purposes of this subsection, the term "nonmember professional" shall include (A) with respect to transactions in securities other than municipal securities, any registered broker or dealer who is not a member of any registered securities association, except such a broker or dealer who deals exclusively in commercial paper, bankers' acceptances, and commercial bills, and (B) with respect to transactions in municipal securities, any municipal securities dealer (other than a bank or division or department of a bank) who is not a member of any registered securities association and any municipal securities broker who is not a member of any such association.

(3) Nothing in this subsection shall be so construed or applied as to prevent (A) any member of a registered securities association from granting to any other member of any registered securities association any dealer's discount, allowance, commission, or special terms, in connection with the purchase or sale of securities, or (B) any member of a registered securities association or any municipal securities dealer which is a bank or a division or department of a bank from granting to any member of any registered securities association or any such municipal securities dealer any dealer's discount, allowance, commission, or special terms in connection with the purchase or sale of municipal securities: *Provided, however*, That the granting of any such discount, allowance, commission, or special terms in connection with the purchase or sale of municipal securities shall be subject to rules of the Municipal Securities Rulemaking Board adopted pursuant to section 15B(b)(2)(K) of this title.

(f) *Transactions in Municipal Securities.* Nothing in subsection (b)(6) or (b)(11) of this section shall be construed to permit a registered securities association to make rules concerning any transaction by a registered broker or dealer in a municipal security.

(g) *Denial of Membership.*

(1) A registered securities association shall deny membership to any person who is not a registered broker or dealer.

(2) A registered securities association may, and in cases in which the Commission, by order, directs as necessary or appropriate in the public interest or for the protection of investors shall, deny membership to any registered broker or dealer, and bar from becoming associated with a member any person, who is subject to a statutory disqualification. A registered securities association shall file notice with the Commission not less than thirty days prior to admitting any registered broker or dealer to membership or permitting any person to become associated with a member, if the association knew, or in the exercise of reasonable care should have known, that such broker or dealer or person was subject to a statutory disqualification. The notice shall be in such form and contain such

information as the Commission, by rule, may prescribe as necessary or appropriate in the public interest or for the protection of investors.

(3)(A) A registered securities association may deny membership to, or condition the membership of, a registered broker or dealer if (i) such broker or dealer does not meet such standards of financial responsibility or operational capability or such broker or dealer or any natural person associated with such broker or dealer does not meet such standards of training, experience, and competence as are prescribed by the rules of the association or (ii) such broker or dealer or person associated with such broker or dealer has engaged and there is a reasonable likelihood he will again engage in acts or practices inconsistent with just and equitable principles of trade. A registered securities association may examine and verify the qualifications of an applicant to become a member and the natural persons associated with such an applicant in accordance with procedures established by the rules of the association.

(B) A registered securities association may bar a natural person from becoming associated with a member or condition the association of a natural person with a member if such natural person (i) does not meet such standards of training, experience, and competence as are prescribed by the rules of the association or (ii) has engaged and there is a reasonable likelihood he will again engage in acts or practices inconsistent with just and equitable principles of trade. A registered securities association may examine and verify the qualifications of an applicant to become a person associated with a member in accordance with procedures established by the rules of the association and require a natural person associated with a member, or any class of such natural persons, to be registered with the association in accordance with procedures so established.

(C) A registered securities association may bar any person from becoming associated with a member if such person does not agree (i) to supply the association with such information with respect to its relationship and dealings with the member as may be specified in the rules of the association and (ii) to permit examination of its books and records to verify the accuracy of any information so supplied.

(D) Nothing in subparagraph (A), (B), or (C) of this paragraph shall be construed to permit a registered securities association to deny membership to or condition the membership of, or bar any person from becoming associated with or condition the association of any person with, a broker or dealer that engages exclusively in transactions in municipal securities.

(4) A registered securities association may deny membership to a registered broker or dealer not engaged in a type of business in which the rules of the association require members to be engaged: *Provided, however,* That no registered securities association may deny membership to a registered broker or dealer by reason of the amount of such type of business done by such broker or dealer or the other types of business in which he is engaged.

(h) *Discipline of Registered Securities Association Members and Persons Associated with Members; Summary Proceedings.*

(1) In any proceeding by a registered securities association to determine whether a member or person associated with a member should be disciplined (other than a summary proceeding pursuant to paragraph (3) of this subsection) the association shall bring specific charges, notify such member or person of, and give him an opportunity to defend against, such charges, and keep a record. A determination by the association to impose a disciplinary sanction shall be supported by a statement setting forth—

(A) any act or practice in which such member or person associated with a member has been found to have engaged, or which such member or person has been found to have omitted;

(B) the specific provision of this chapter, the rules or regulations thereunder, the rules of the Municipal Securities Rulemaking Board, or the rules of the association which any such act or practice, or omission to act, is deemed to violate; and

(C) the sanction imposed and the reason therefor.

(2) In any proceeding by a registered securities association to determine whether a person shall be denied membership, barred from becoming associated with a member, or prohibited or limited with respect to access to services offered by the association or a member thereof (other than a summary proceeding pursuant to paragraph (3) of this subsection), the association shall notify such person of and give him an opportunity to be heard upon, the specific grounds for denial, bar, or

prohibition or limitation under consideration and keep a record. A determination by the association to deny membership, bar a person from becoming associated with a member, or prohibit or limit a person with respect to access to services offered by the association or a member thereof shall be supported by a statement setting forth the specific grounds on which the denial, bar, or prohibition or limitation is based.

(3) A registered securities association may summarily (A) suspend a member or person associated with a member who has been and is expelled or suspended from any self-regulatory organization or barred or suspended from being associated with a member of any self-regulatory organization, (B) suspend a member who is in such financial or operating difficulty that the association determines and so notifies the Commission that the member cannot be permitted to continue to do business as a member with safety to investors, creditors, other members, or the association, or (C) limit or prohibit any person with respect to access to services offered by the association if subparagraph (A) or (B) of this paragraph is applicable to such person or, in the case of a person who is not a member, if the association determines that such person does not meet the qualification requirements or other prerequisites for such access and such person cannot be permitted to continue to have such access with safety to investors, creditors, members, or the association. Any person aggrieved by any such summary action shall be promptly afforded an opportunity for a hearing by the association in accordance with the provisions of paragraph (1) or (2) of this subsection. The Commission, by order, may stay any such summary action on its own motion or upon application by any person aggrieved thereby, if the Commission determines summarily or after notice and opportunity for hearing (which hearing may consist solely of the submission of affidavits or presentation of oral arguments) that such stay is consistent with the public interest and the protection of investors.

(i) *Obligation to Maintain Registration, Disciplinary, and Other Data.*

(1) *Maintenance of System to Respond to Inquiries.* A registered securities association shall—

(A) establish and maintain a system for collecting and retaining registration information;

(B) establish and maintain a toll-free telephone listing, and a readily accessible electronic or other process, to receive and promptly respond to inquiries regarding—

(i) registration information on its members and their associated persons; and

(ii) registration information on the members and their associated persons of any registered national securities exchange that uses the system described in subparagraph (A) for the registration of its members and their associated persons; and

(C) adopt rules governing the process for making inquiries and the type, scope, and presentation of information to be provided in response to such inquiries in consultation with any registered national securities exchange providing information pursuant to subparagraph (B)(ii).

(2) *Recovery of Costs.* A registered securities association may charge persons making inquiries described in paragraph (1)(B), other than individual investors, reasonable fees for responses to such inquiries.

(3) *Process for Disputed Information.* Each registered securities association shall adopt rules establishing an administrative process for disputing the accuracy of information provided in response to inquiries under this subsection in consultation with any registered national securities exchange providing information pursuant to paragraph (1)(B)(ii).

(4) *Limitation on Liability.* A registered securities association, or an exchange reporting information to such an association, shall not have any liability to any person for any actions taken or omitted in good faith under this subsection.

(5) *Definition.* For purposes of this subsection, the term "registration information" means the information reported in connection with the registration or licensing of brokers and dealers and their associated persons, including disciplinary actions, regulatory, judicial, and arbitration proceedings, and other information required by law, or exchange or association rule, and the source and status of such information.

(j) *Registration for Sales of Private Securities Offerings.* A registered securities association shall create a limited qualification category for any associated person of a member who effects sales as part of a primary offering of securities not involving a public offering, pursuant to section 3(b), 4(2), or 4(6) of the Securities Act of 1933 and the rules and regulations thereunder, and shall deem qualified in such limited qualification category, without testing, any bank employee who, in the six month period preceding the date of enactment of the Gramm–Leach–Bliley Act, engaged in effecting such sales.

(k) *Limited Purpose National Securities Association.*

(1) *Regulation of Members with Respect to Security Futures Products.* A futures association registered under section 17 of the Commodity Exchange Act shall be a registered national securities association for the limited purpose of regulating the activities of members who are registered as brokers or dealers in security futures products pursuant to section 15(b)(11).

(2) *Requirements for Registration.* Such a securities association shall—

(A) be so organized and have the capacity to carry out the purposes of the securities laws applicable to security futures products and to comply, and (subject to any rule or order of the Commission pursuant to section 19(g)(2)) to enforce compliance by its members and persons associated with its members, with the provisions of the securities laws applicable to security futures products, the rules and regulations thereunder, and its rules;

(B) have rules that—

(i) are designed to prevent fraudulent and manipulative acts and practices, to promote just and equitable principles of trade, and, in general, to protect investors and the public interest, including rules governing sales practices and the advertising of security futures products reasonably comparable to those of other national securities associations registered pursuant to subsection (a) that are applicable to security futures products; and

(ii) are not designed to regulate by virtue of any authority conferred by this title matters not related to the purposes of this title or the administration of the association;

(C) have rules that provide that (subject to any rule or order of the Commission pursuant to section 19(g)(2)) its members and persons associated with its members shall be appropriately disciplined for violation of any provision of the securities laws applicable to security futures products, the rules or regulations thereunder, or the rules of the association, by expulsion, suspension, limitation of activities, functions, and operations, fine, censure, being suspended or barred from being associated with a member, or any other fitting sanction; and

(D) have rules that ensure that members and natural persons associated with members meet such standards of training, experience, and competence necessary to effect transactions in security futures products and are tested for their knowledge of securities and security futures products.

(3) *Exemption from Rule Change Submission.* Such a securities association shall be exempt from submitting proposed rule changes pursuant to section 19(b) of this title, except that—

(A) the association shall file proposed rule changes related to higher margin levels, fraud or manipulation, recordkeeping, reporting, listing standards, or decimal pricing for security futures products, sales practices for, advertising of, or standards of training, experience, competence, or other qualifications for security futures products for persons who effect transactions in security futures products, or rules effectuating the association's obligation to enforce the securities laws pursuant to section 19(b)(7);

(B) the association shall file pursuant to sections 19(b)(1) and 19(b)(2) proposed rule changes related to margin, except for changes resulting in higher margin levels; and

(C) the association shall file pursuant to section 19(b)(1) proposed rule changes that have been abrogated by the Commission pursuant to section 19(b)(7)(C).

(4) *Other Exemptions.* Such a securities association shall be exempt from and shall not be required to enforce compliance by its members, and its members shall not, solely with respect to their transactions effected in security futures products, be required to comply, with the following provisions of this title and the rules thereunder:

(A) Section 8.

(B) Subsections (b)(1), (b)(3), (b)(4), (b)(5), (b)(8), (b)(10), (b)(11), (b)(12), (b)(13), (c), (d), (e), (f), (g), (h), and (i) of this section.

(C) Subsections (d), (f), and (k) of section 17.

(D) Subsections (a), (f), and (h) of section 19.

(l) Rules to Avoid Duplicative Regulation of Dual Registrants. Consistent with this title, each national securities association registered pursuant to subsection (a) of this section shall issue such rules as are

necessary to avoid duplicative or conflicting rules applicable to any broker or dealer registered with the Commission pursuant to section 15B (except paragraph (11) thereof), that is also registered with the Commodity Futures Trading Commission pursuant to section 4f(a) of the Commodity Exchange Act (except paragraph (2) thereof), with respect to the application of—

(1) rules of such national securities association of the type specified in section 15(c)(3)(B) of this title involving security futures products; and

(2) similar rules of national securities associations registered pursuant to subsection (k) of this section and national securities exchanges registered pursuant to section 6(g) involving security futures products.

(m) *Procedures and Rules for Security Future Products.* A national securities association registered pursuant to subsection (a) shall, not later than 8 months after the date of enactment of the Commodity Futures Modernization Act of 2000, implement the procedures specified in section 6(h)(5)(A) of this title and adopt the rules specified in subparagraphs (B) and (C) of section 6(h)(5) of this title.

Municipal Securities

Sec. 15B. (a) *Registration of Municipal Securities Dealers.*

(1)(A) It shall be unlawful for any municipal securities dealer (other than one registered as a broker or dealer under section 15 of this title) to make use of the mails or any means or instrumentality of interstate commerce to effect any transaction in, or to induce or attempt to induce the purchase or sale of, any municipal security unless such municipal securities dealer is registered in accordance with this subsection.

(B) It shall be unlawful for a municipal advisor to provide advice to or on behalf of a municipal entity or obligated person with respect to municipal financial products or the issuance of municipal securities, or to undertake a solicitation of a municipal entity or obligated person, unless the municipal advisor is registered in accordance with this subsection.

(2) A municipal securities dealer or municipal advisor may be registered by filing with the Commission an application for registration in such form and containing such information and documents concerning such municipal securities dealer or municipal advisor and any persons associated with such municipal securities dealer or municipal advisor as the Commission, by rule, may prescribe as necessary or appropriate in the public interest or for the protection of investors. Within forty–five days of the date of the filing of such application (or within such longer period as to which the applicant consents), the Commission shall—

(A) by order grant registration, or

(B) institute proceedings to determine whether registration should be denied. Such proceedings shall include notice of the grounds for denial under consideration and opportunity for hearing and shall be concluded within one hundred twenty days of the date of the filing of the application for registration. At the conclusion of such proceedings the Commission, by order, shall grant or deny such registration. The Commission may extend the time for the conclusion of such proceedings for up to ninety days if it finds good cause for such extension and publishes its reasons for so finding or for such longer period as to which the applicant consents.

The Commission shall grant the registration of a municipal securities dealer or municipal advisor if the Commission finds that the requirements of this section are satisfied. The Commission shall deny such registration if it does not make such a finding or if it finds that if the applicant were so registered, its registration would be subject to suspension or revocation under subsection (c) of this section.

(3) Any provision of this title (other than section 5 or paragraph (1) of this subsection) which prohibits any act, practice, or course of business if the mails or any means or instrumentality of interstate commerce is used in connection therewith shall also prohibit any such act, practice, or course of business by any registered municipal securities dealer or municipal advisor or any person acting on behalf of such municipal securities dealer or municipal advisor, irrespective of any use of the mails or any means or instrumentality of interstate commerce in connection therewith.

(4) The Commission, by rule or order, upon its own motion or upon application, may conditionally or unconditionally exempt any broker, dealer, municipal securities dealer, or municipal advisor, or class of brokers, dealers, municipal securities dealers, or municipal advisors from any provision of this section or the rules or regulations thereunder, if the Commission finds that such exemption

is consistent with the public interest, the protection of investors, and the purposes of this section.

(5) No municipal advisor shall make use of the mails or any means or instrumentality of interstate commerce to provide advice to or on behalf of a municipal entity or obligated person with respect to municipal financial products, the issuance of municipal securities, or to undertake a solicitation of a municipal entity or obligated person, in connection with which such municipal advisor engages in any fraudulent, deceptive, or manipulative act or practice

(b) *Municipal Securities Rulemaking Board; Rules and Regulations.*

(1) The Municipal Securities Rulemaking Board shall be composed of 15 members, or such other number of members as specified by rules of the Board pursuant to paragraph (2)(B), which shall perform the duties set forth in this section. The members of the Board shall serve as members for a term of 3 years or for such other terms as specified by rules of the Board pursuant to paragraph (2)(B), and shall consist of (A) 8 individuals who are independent of any municipal securities broker, municipal securities dealer, or municipal advisor, at least 1 of whom shall be representative of institutional or retail investors in municipal securities, at least 1 of whom shall be representative of municipal entities, and at least 1 of whom shall be a member of the public with knowledge of or experience in the municipal industry (which members are hereinafter referred to as "public representatives"); and (B) 7 individuals who are associated with a broker, dealer, municipal securities dealer, or municipal advisor, including at least 1 individual who is associated with and representative of brokers, dealers, or municipal securities dealers that are not banks or subsidiaries or departments or divisions of banks (which members are hereinafter referred to as "broker–dealer representatives"), at least 1 individual who is associated with and representative of municipal securities dealers which are banks or subsidiaries or departments or divisions of banks (which members are hereinafter referred to as "bank representatives"), and at least 1 individual who is associated with a municipal advisor (which members are hereinafter referred to as "advisor representatives" and, together with the broker–dealer representatives and the bank representatives, are referred to as "regulated representatives"). Each member of the board shall be knowledgeable of matters related to the municipal securities markets. Prior to the expiration of the terms of office of the members of the Board, an election shall be held under rules adopted by the Board (pursuant to subsection (b)(2)(B) of this section) of the members to succeed such members.

(2) The Board shall propose and adopt rules to effect the purposes of this title with respect to transactions in municipal securities effected by brokers, dealers, and municipal securities dealers and advice provided to or on behalf of municipal entities or obligated persons by brokers, dealers, municipal securities dealers, and municipal advisors with respect to municipal financial products, the issuance of municipal securities, and solicitations of municipal entities or obligated persons undertaken by brokers, dealers, municipal securities dealers, and municipal advisors. The rules of the Board, as a minimum, shall:

(A) provide that no municipal securities broker or municipal securities dealer shall effect any transaction in, or induce or attempt to induce the purchase or sale of, any municipal security, and no broker, dealer, municipal securities dealer, or municipal advisor shall provide advice to or on behalf of a municipal entity or obligated person with respect to municipal financial products or the issuance of municipal securities, unless such municipal securities broker or municipal securities dealer meets such standards of operational capability and such municipal securities broker or municipal securities dealer and every natural person associated with such municipal securities broker or municipal securities dealer meets such standards of training, experience, competence, and such other qualifications as the Board finds necessary or appropriate in the public interest or for the protection of investors and municipal entities or obligated persons. In connection with the definition and application of such standards the Board may—

(i) appropriately classify municipal securities brokers, municipal securities dealers, and municipal advisors (taking into account relevant matters, including types of business done, nature of securities other than municipal securities sold, and character of business organization), and persons associated with municipal securities brokers, municipal securities dealers, and municipal advisors;

(ii) specify that all or any portion of such standards shall be applicable to any such class; and

(iii) require persons in any such class to pass tests administered in accordance with subsection (c)(7) of this section.

(B) establish fair procedures for the nomination and election of members of the Board and assure fair representation in such nominations and elections of public representatives, broker dealer representatives, bank representatives, and advisor representatives. Such rules—

(i) shall provide that the number of public representatives of the Board shall at all times exceed the total number of regulated representatives and that the membership shall at all times be as evenly divided in number as possible between public representatives and regulated representatives;

(ii) shall specify the length or lengths of terms members shall serve;

(iii) may increase the number of members which shall constitute the whole Board, provided that such number is an odd number; and

(iv) shall establish requirements regarding the independence of public representatives.

(C) be designed to prevent fraudulent and manipulative acts and practices, to promote just and equitable principles of trade, to foster cooperation and coordination with persons engaged in regulating, clearing, settling, processing information with respect to, and facilitating transactions in municipal securities and municipal financial products, to remove impediments to and perfect the mechanism of a free and open market in municipal securities and municipal financial products, and, in general, to protect investors, municipal entities, obligated persons, and the public interest; and not be designed to permit unfair discrimination among customers, municipal entities, obligated persons, municipal securities brokers, municipal securities dealers, or municipal advisors, to fix minimum profits, to impose any schedule or fix rates of commissions, allowances, discounts, or other fees to be charged by municipal securities brokers, municipal securities dealers, or municipal advisors, to regulate by virtue of any authority conferred by this title matters not related to the purposes of this title or the administration of the Board, or to impose any burden on competition not necessary or appropriate in furtherance of the purposes of this title.

(D) if the Board deems appropriate, provide for the arbitration of claims, disputes, and controversies relating to transactions in municipal securities and advice concerning municipal financial products: Provided, however, that no person other than a municipal securities broker, municipal securities dealer, municipal advisor, or person associated with such a municipal securities broker, municipal securities dealer, or municipal advisor may be compelled to submit to such arbitration except at his instance and in accordance with section 29 of this title.

(E) provide for the periodic examination in accordance with subsection (c)(7) of this section of municipal securities brokers, municipal securities dealers, and municipal advisors to determine compliance with applicable provisions of this title, the rules and regulations thereunder, and the rules of the Board. Such rules shall specify the minimum scope and frequency of such examinations and shall be designed to avoid unnecessary regulatory duplication or undue regulatory burdens for any such municipal securities broker, municipal securities dealer, or municipal advisor.

(F) include provisions governing the form and content of quotations relating to municipal securities which may be distributed or published by any municipal securities broker, municipal securities dealer, or person associated with such a municipal securities broker or municipal securities dealer, and the persons to whom such quotations may be supplied. Such rules relating to quotations shall be designed to produce fair and informative quotations, to prevent fictitious or misleading quotations, and to promote orderly procedures for collecting, distributing, and publishing quotations.

(G) prescribe records to be made and kept by municipal securities brokers, municipal securities dealers, and municipal advisors and the periods for which such records shall be preserved.

(H) define the term "separately identifiable department or division", as that term is used in section 3(a)(30) of this title, in accordance with specified and appropriate standards to assure that a bank is not deemed to be engaged in the business of buying and selling municipal securities through a separately identifiable department or division unless such department or division is organized and administered so as to permit independent examination and enforcement of applicable provisions of this title, the rules and regulations thereunder and the rules of the Board. A separately identifiable department or division of a bank may be engaged in activities other than those relating to municipal securities.

(I) provide for the operation and administration of the Board, including the selection of a Chairman from among the members of the Board, the compensation of the members of the Board, and the appointment and compensation of such employees, attorneys, and consultants as may be necessary or appropriate to carry out the Board's functions under this section.

(J) provide that each municipal securities broker, municipal securities dealer, and municipal advisor shall pay to the Board such reasonable fees and charges as may be necessary or appropriate to defray the costs and expenses of operating and administering the Board. Such rules shall specify the amount of such fees and charges, which may include charges for failure to submit to the Board, or to any information system operated by the Board, within the prescribed timeframes, any items of information or documents required to be submitted under any rule issued by the Board.

(K) establish the terms and conditions under which any broker, dealer, or municipal securities dealer may sell, or prohibit any broker, dealer, or municipal securities dealer from selling, any part of a new issue of municipal securities to a related account of a broker, dealer, or municipal securities dealer during the underwriting period.

(L) with respect to municipal advisors—

(i) prescribe means reasonably designed to prevent acts, practices, and courses of business as are not consistent with a municipal advisor's fiduciary duty to its clients;

(ii) provide continuing education requirements for municipal advisors;

(iii) provide professional standards; and

(iv) not impose a regulatory burden on small municipal advisors that is not necessary or appropriate in the public interest and for the protection of investors, municipal entities, and obligated persons, provided that there is robust protection of investors against fraud.

(3) The Board, in conjunction with or on behalf of any Federal financial regulator or self–regulatory organization, may—

(A) establish information systems; and

(B) assess such reasonable fees and charges for the submission of information to, or the receipt of information from, such systems from any persons which systems may be developed for the purposes of serving as a repository of information from municipal market participants or otherwise in furtherance of the purposes of the Board, a Federal financial regulator, or a self–regulatory organization, except that the Board—

(i) may not charge a fee to municipal entities or obligated persons to submit documents or other information to the Board or charge a fee to any person to obtain, directly from the Internet site of the Board, documents or information submitted by municipal entities, obligated persons, brokers, dealers, municipal securities dealers, or municipal advisors, including documents submitted under the rules of the Board or the Commission; and

(ii) shall not be prohibited from charging commercially reasonable fees for automated subscription–based feeds or similar services, or for charging for other data or document–based services customized upon request of any person, made available to commercial enterprises, municipal securities market professionals, or the general public, whether delivered through the Internet or any other means, that contain all or part of the documents or information, subject to approval of the fees by the Commission under section 19(b).

(4) The Board may provide guidance and assistance in the enforcement of, and examination for, compliance with the rules of the Board to the Commission, a registered securities association under section 15A, or any other appropriate regulatory agency, as applicable.

(5) The Board, the Commission, and a registered securities association under section 15A, or the designees of the Board, the Commission, or such association, shall meet not less frequently than 2 times a year—

(A) to describe the work of the Board, the Commission, and the registered securities association involving the regulation of municipal securities; and

(B) to share information about—

(i) the interpretation of the Board, the Commission, and the registered securities association of Board rules; and

(ii) examination and enforcement of compliance with Board rules.

(6) [Not enacted]

(7) Nothing in this section shall be construed to impair or limit the power of the Commission under this title.

(c) *Discipline of Municipal Securities Dealers; Censure; Suspension or Revocation of Registration; Other Sanctions; Investigations.*

(1) No broker, dealer, or municipal securities dealer shall make use of the mails or any means or instrumentality of interstate commerce to effect any transaction in, or to induce or attempt to induce the purchase or sale of, any municipal security, and no broker, dealer, municipal securities dealer, or municipal advisor shall make use of the mails or any means or instrumentality of interstate commerce to provide advice to or on behalf of a municipal entity or obligated person with respect to municipal financial products, the issuance of municipal securities, or to undertake a solicitation of a municipal entity or obligated person, in contravention of any rule of the Board. A municipal advisor and any person associated with such municipal advisor shall be deemed to have a fiduciary duty to any municipal entity for whom such municipal advisor acts as a municipal advisor, and no municipal advisor may engage in any act, practice, or course of business which is not consistent with a municipal advisor's fiduciary duty or that is in contravention of any rule of the Board.

(2) The Commission, by order, shall censure, place limitations on the activities, functions, or operations, suspend for a period not exceeding twelve months, or revoke the registration of any municipal securities dealer or municipal advisor, if it finds, on the record after notice and opportunity for hearing, that such censure, placing of limitations, denial, suspension, or revocation, is in the public interest and that such municipal securities dealer or municipal advisor has committed or omitted any act, or is subject to an order or finding, enumerated in subparagraph (A), (D), (E), (H), or (G) of paragraph (4) of section 15(b) of this title, has been convicted of any offense specified in subparagraph (B) of such paragraph (4) within ten years of the commencement of the proceedings under this paragraph, or is enjoined from any action, conduct, or practice specified in subparagraph (C) of such paragraph (4).

(3) Pending final determination whether any registration under this section shall be revoked, the Commission, by order, may suspend such registration, if such suspension appears to the Commission, after notice and opportunity for hearing, to be necessary or appropriate in the public interest or for the protection of investors or municipal entities or obligated person. Any registered municipal securities dealer or municipal advisor may, upon such terms and conditions as the Commission may deem necessary in the public interest or for the protection of investors or municipal entities or obligated person, withdraw from registration by filing a written notice of withdrawal with the Commission. If the Commission finds that any registered municipal securities dealer or municipal advisor is no longer in existence or has ceased to do business as a municipal securities dealer or municipal advisor, the Commission, by order, shall cancel the registration of such municipal securities dealer or municipal advisor.

(4) The Commission, by order, shall censure or place limitations on the activities or functions of any person associated, seeking to become associated, or, at the time of the alleged misconduct, associated or seeking to become associated with a municipal securities dealer, or suspend for a period not exceeding 12 months or bar any such person from being associated with a broker, dealer, investment adviser, municipal securities dealer, municipal advisor, transfer agent, or nationally recognized statistical rating organization, if the Commission finds, on the record after notice and opportunity for hearing, that such censure, placing of limitations, suspension, or bar is in the public interest and that such person has committed any act, or is subject to an order or finding, enumerated in subparagraph (A), (D), (E), (H), or (G) of paragraph (4) of Section 15(b) of this title, has been convicted of any offense specified in subparagraph (B) of such paragraph (4) within 10 years of the commencement of the proceedings under this paragraph, or is enjoined from any action, conduct, or practice specified in subparagraph (C) of such paragraph (4). It shall be unlawful for any person as to whom an order entered pursuant to this paragraph or paragraph (5) of this subsection

suspending or barring him from being associated with a municipal securities dealer is in effect willfully to become, or to be, associated with a municipal securities dealer without the consent of the Commission, and it shall be unlawful for any municipal securities dealer to permit such a person to become, or remain, a person associated with him without the consent of the Commission, if such municipal securities dealer knew, or, in the exercise of reasonable care should have known, of such order.

(5) With respect to any municipal securities dealer for which the Commission is not the appropriate regulatory agency, the appropriate regulatory agency for such municipal securities dealer may sanction any such municipal securities dealer in the manner and for the reasons specified in paragraph (2) of this subsection and any person associated with such municipal securities dealer in the manner and for the reasons specified in paragraph (4) of this subsection. In addition, such appropriate regulatory agency may, in accordance with section 8 of the Federal Deposit Insurance Act enforce compliance by such municipal securities dealer or any person associated with such municipal securities dealer with the provisions of this section, section 17 of this title, the rules of the Board, and the rules of the Commission pertaining to municipal securities dealers, persons associated with municipal securities dealers, and transactions in municipal securities. For purposes of the preceding sentence, any violation of any such provision shall constitute adequate basis for the issuance of any order under section 8(b) or 8(c) of the Federal Deposit Insurance Act, and the customers of any such municipal securities dealer shall be deemed to be "depositors" as that term is used in section 8(c) of that Act. Nothing in this paragraph shall be construed to affect in any way the powers of such appropriate regulatory agency to proceed against such municipal securities dealer under any other provision of law.

(6)(A) The Commission, prior to the entry of an order of investigation, or commencement of any proceedings, against any municipal securities dealer, or person associated with any municipal securities dealer, for which the Commission is not the appropriate regulatory agency, for violation of any provision of this section, section 15(c)(1) or 15(c)(2) of this title, any rule or regulation under any such section, or any rule of the Board, shall (i) give notice to the appropriate regulatory agency for such municipal securities dealer of the identity of such municipal securities dealer or person associated with such municipal securities dealer, the nature of and basis for such proposed action, and whether the Commission is seeking a monetary penalty against such municipal securities dealer or such associated person pursuant to section 21B of this title; and (ii) consult with such appropriate regulatory agency concerning the effect of such proposed action on sound banking practices and the feasibility and desirability of coordinating such action with any proceeding or proposed proceeding by such appropriate regulatory agency against such municipal securities dealer or associated person.

(B) The appropriate regulatory agency for a municipal securities dealer (if other than the Commission), prior to the entry of an order of investigation, or commencement of any proceedings, against such municipal securities dealer or person associated with such municipal securities dealer, for violation of any provision of this section, the rules of the Board, or the rules or regulations of the Commission pertaining to municipal securities dealers, persons associated with municipal securities dealers, or transactions in municipal securities shall (i) give notice to the Commission of the identity of such municipal securities dealer or person associated with such municipal securities dealer and the nature of and basis for such proposed action and (ii) consult with the Commission concerning the effect of such proposed action on the protection of investors or municipal entities or obligated person and the feasibility and desirability of coordinating such action with any proceeding or proposed proceeding by the Commission against such municipal securities dealer or associated person.

(C) Nothing in this paragraph shall be construed to impair or limit (other than by the requirement of prior consultation) the power of the Commission or the appropriate regulatory agency for a municipal securities dealer to initiate any action of a class described in this paragraph or to affect in any way the power of the Commission or such appropriate regulatory agency to initiate any other action pursuant to this title or any other provision of law.

(7)(A) Tests required pursuant to subsection (b)(2)(A)(iii) of this section shall be administered by or on behalf of and periodic examinations pursuant to subsection (b)(2)(E) of this section shall be conducted by—

(i) a registered securities association, in the case of municipal securities brokers and municipal securities dealers who are members of such association;

(ii) the appropriate regulatory agency for any municipal securities broker or municipal securities dealer, in the case of all other municipal securities brokers and municipal securities dealers; and

(iii) the Commission, or its designee, in the case of municipal advisors.

(B) A registered securities association shall make a report of any examination conducted pursuant to subsection (b)(2)(E) of this section and promptly furnish the Commission a copy thereof and any data supplied to it in connection with such examination. Subject to such limitations as the Commission, by rule, determines to be necessary or appropriate in the public interest or for the protection of investors or municipal entities or obligated person, the Commission shall, on request, make available to the Board a copy of any report of an examination of a municipal securities broker or municipal securities dealer made by or furnished to the Commission pursuant to this paragraph or section 17(c)(3) of this title.

(8) The Commission is authorized, by order, if in its opinion such action is necessary or appropriate in the public interest, for the protection of investors, or otherwise, in furtherance of the purposes of this chapter, to remove from office or censure any person who is, or at the time of the alleged violation or abuse was, a member or employee of the Board, who, the Commission finds, on the record after notice and opportunity for hearing, has willfully (A) violated any provision of this chapter, the rules and regulations thereunder, or the rules of the Board or (B) abused his authority.

(9)(A) Fines collected by the Commission for violations of the rules of the Board shall be equally divided between the Commission and the Board.

(B) Fines collected by a registered securities association under section 15A(7) with respect to violations of the rules of the Board shall be accounted for by such registered securities association separately from other fines collected under section 15A(7) and shall be allocated between such registered securities association and the Board, and such allocation shall require the registered securities association to pay to the Board 1/3 of all fines collected by the registered securities association reasonably allocable to violations of the rules of the Board, or such other portion of such fines as may be directed by the Commission upon agreement between the registered securities association and the Board.

(d) *Issuance of Municipal Securities.*

(1) Neither the Commission nor the Board is authorized under this title, by rule or regulation, to require any issuer of municipal securities, directly or indirectly through a purchaser or prospective purchaser of securities from the issuer, to file with the Commission or the Board prior to the sale of such securities by the issuer any application, report, or document in connection with the issuance, sale, or distribution of such securities.

(2) The Board is not authorized under this title to require any issuer of municipal securities, directly or indirectly through a municipal securities broker, municipal securities dealer, municipal advisor, or otherwise, to furnish to the Board or to a purchaser or a prospective purchaser of such securities any application, report, document, or information with respect to such issuer: Provided, however, That the Board may require municipal securities brokers and municipal securities dealers or municipal advisors to furnish to the Board or purchasers or prospective purchasers of municipal securities applications, reports, documents, and information with respect to the issuer thereof which is generally available from a source other than such issuer. Nothing in this paragraph shall be construed to impair or limit the power of the Commission under any provision of this title.

(e) *Definitions.* For purposes of this section—

(1) the term "Board" means the Municipal Securities Rulemaking Board established under subsection (b)(1);

(2) the term "guaranteed investment contract" includes any investment that has specified withdrawal or reinvestment provisions and a specifically negotiated or bid interest rate, and also includes any agreement to supply investments on 2 or more future dates, such as a forward supply contract;

(3) the term "investment strategies" includes plans or programs for the investment of the proceeds of municipal securities that are not municipal derivatives, guaranteed investment contracts, and the recommendation of and brokerage of municipal escrow investments;

(4) the term "municipal advisor"—

(A) means a person (who is not a municipal entity or an employee of a municipal entity) that—

(i) provides advice to or on behalf of a municipal entity or obligated person with respect to municipal financial products or the issuance of municipal securities, including advice with respect to the structure, timing, terms, and other similar matters concerning such financial products or issues; or

(ii) undertakes a solicitation of a municipal entity;

(B) includes financial advisors, guaranteed investment contract brokers, third–party marketers, placement agents, solicitors, finders, and swap advisors, if such persons are described in any of clauses (i) through (iii) of subparagraph (A); and

(C) does not include a broker, dealer, or municipal securities dealer serving as an underwriter (as defined in section 2(a)(11) of the Securities Act of 1933), any investment adviser registered under the Investment Advisers Act of 1940, or persons associated with such investment advisers who are providing investment advice, any commodity trading advisor registered under the Commodity Exchange Act or persons associated with a commodity trading advisor who are providing advice related to swaps, attorneys offering legal advice or providing services that are of a traditional legal nature, or engineers providing engineering advice;

(5) the term "municipal financial product" means municipal derivatives, guaranteed investment contracts, and investment strategies;

(6) the term "rules of the Board" means the rules proposed and adopted by the Board under subsection (b)(2);

(7) the term "person associated with a municipal advisor" or "associated person of an advisor" means—

(A) any partner, officer, director, or branch manager of such municipal advisor (or any person occupying a similar status or performing similar functions);

(B) any other employee of such municipal advisor who is engaged in the management, direction, supervision, or performance of any activities relating to the provision of advice to or on behalf of a municipal entity or obligated person with respect to municipal financial products or the issuance of municipal securities; and

(C) any person directly or indirectly controlling, controlled by, or under common control with such municipal advisor;

(8) the term 'municipal entity' means any State, political subdivision of a State, or municipal corporate instrumentality of a State, including—

(A) any agency, authority, or instrumentality of the State, political subdivision, or municipal corporate instrumentality;

(B) any plan, program, or pool of assets sponsored or established by the State, political subdivision, or municipal corporate instrumentality or any agency, authority, or instrumentality thereof; and

(C) any other issuer of municipal securities;

(9) the term "solicitation of a municipal entity or obligated person" means a direct or indirect communication with a municipal entity or obligated person made by a person, for direct or indirect compensation, on behalf of a broker, dealer, municipal securities dealer, municipal advisor, or investment adviser (as defined in section 202 of the Investment Advisers Act of 1940) that does not control, is not controlled by, or is not under common control with the person undertaking such solicitation for the purpose of obtaining or retaining an engagement by a municipal entity or obligated person of a broker, dealer, municipal securities dealer, or municipal advisor for or in connection with municipal financial products, the issuance of municipal securities, or of an investment adviser to provide investment advisory services to or on behalf of a municipal entity; and

(10) the term "obligated person" means any person, including an issuer of municipal securities, who is either generally or through an enterprise, fund, or account of such person, committed by contract or other arrangement to support the payment of all or part of the obligations on the municipal securities to be sold in an offering of municipal securities.

Government Securities Brokers and Dealers

Sec. 15C. (a) *Registration Requirements; Notice to Regulatory Agencies; Manner of Registration; Exemption of Registration Requirements.*

(1)(A) It shall be unlawful for any government securities broker or government securities dealer (other than a registered broker or dealer or a financial institution) to make use of the mails or any means or instrumentality of interstate commerce to effect any transaction in, or to induce or attempt to induce the purchase or sale of, any government security unless such government securities broker or government securities dealer is registered in accordance with paragraph (2) of this subsection.

(B)(i) It shall be unlawful for any government securities broker or government securities dealer that is a registered broker or dealer or a financial institution to make use of the mails or any means or instrumentality of interstate commerce to effect any transaction in, or to induce or attempt to induce the purchase or sale of, any government security unless such government securities broker or government securities dealer has filed with the appropriate regulatory agency written notice that it is a government securities broker or government securities dealer. When such a government securities broker or government securities dealer ceases to act as such it shall file with the appropriate regulatory agency a written notice that it is no longer acting as a government securities broker or government securities dealer.

(ii) Such notices shall be in such form and contain such information concerning a government securities broker or government securities dealer that is a financial institution and any persons associated with such government securities broker or government securities dealer as the Board of Governors of the Federal Reserve System shall, by rule, after consultation with each appropriate regulatory agency (including the Commission), prescribe as necessary or appropriate in the public interest or for the protection of investors. Such notices shall be in such form and contain such information concerning a government securities broker or government securities dealer that is a registered broker or dealer and any persons associated with such government securities broker or government securities dealer as the Commission shall, by rule, prescribe as necessary or appropriate in the public interest or for the protection of investors.

(iii) Each appropriate regulatory agency (other than the Commission) shall make available to the Commission the notices which have been filed with it under this subparagraph, and the Commission shall maintain and make available to the public such notices and the notices it receives under this subparagraph.

(2) A government securities broker or a government securities dealer subject to the registration requirement of paragraph (1)(A) of this subsection may be registered by filing with the Commission an application for registration in such form and containing such information and documents concerning such government securities broker or government securities dealer and any persons associated with such government securities broker or government securities dealer as the Commission, by rule, may prescribe as necessary or appropriate in the public interest or for the protection of investors. Within 45 days of the date of filing of such application (or within such longer period as to which the applicant consents), the Commission shall—

(A) by order grant registration, or

(B) institute proceedings to determine whether registration should be denied. Such proceedings shall include notice of the grounds for denial under consideration and opportunity for hearing and shall be concluded within 120 days of the date of the filing of the application for registration. At the conclusion of such proceedings, the Commission, by order, shall grant or deny such registration. The Commission may extend the time for the conclusion of such proceedings for up to 90 days if it finds good cause for such extension and publishes its reasons for so finding or for such longer period as to which the applicant consents.

The Commission shall grant the registration of a government securities broker or a government securities dealer if the Commission finds that the requirements of this section are satisfied. The order granting registration shall not be effective until such government securities broker or government securities dealer has become a member of a national securities exchange registered under section 6 of this title, or a securities association registered under section 15A of this title, unless the Commission has exempted such government securities broker or government securities dealer, by rule or order, from such membership. The Commission shall deny such registration if it does not make such a finding or if it finds that if the applicant were so registered, its registration would be subject to suspension or revocation under subsection (c) of this section.

(3) Any provision of this title (other than section 5 or paragraph (1) of this subsection) which prohibits any act, practice, or course of business if the mails or any means or instrumentality of interstate commerce is used in connection therewith shall also prohibit any such act, practice, or course of business by any government securities broker or government securities dealer registered or having filed notice under paragraph (1) of this subsection or any person acting on behalf of such government securities broker or government securities dealer, irrespective of any use of the mails or any means or instrumentality of interstate commerce in connection therewith.

(4) No government securities broker or government securities dealer that is required to register under paragraph (1)(A) and that is not a member of the Securities Investor Protection Corporation shall effect any transaction in any security in contravention of such rules as the Commission shall prescribe pursuant to this subsection to assure that its customers receive complete, accurate, and timely disclosure of the inapplicability of Securities Investor Protection Corporation coverage to their accounts.

(5) The Secretary of the Treasury (hereinafter in this section referred to as the "Secretary"), by rule or order, upon the Secretary's own motion or upon application, may conditionally or unconditionally exempt any government securities broker or government securities dealer, or class of government securities brokers or government securities dealers, from any provision of subsection (a), (b), or (d) of this section, other than subsection (d)(3) of this section, or the rules thereunder, if the Secretary finds that such exemption is consistent with the public interest, the protection of investors, and the purposes of this title.

(b) *Rules With Respect to Transactions in Government Securities.*

(1) The Secretary shall propose and adopt rules to effect the purposes of this title with respect to transactions in government securities effected by government securities brokers and government securities dealers as follows:

(A) Such rules shall provide safeguards with respect to the financial responsibility and related practices of government securities brokers and government securities dealers including, but not limited to, capital adequacy standards, the acceptance of custody and use of customers' securities, the carrying and use of customers' deposits or credit balances, and the transfer and control of government securities subject to repurchase agreements and in similar transactions.

(B) Such rules shall require every government securities broker and government securities dealer to make reports to and furnish copies of records to the appropriate regulatory agency, and to file with the appropriate regulatory agency, annually or more frequently, a balance sheet and income statement certified by an independent public accountant, prepared on a calendar or fiscal year basis, and such other financial statements (which shall, as the Secretary specifies, be certified) and information concerning its financial condition as required by such rules.

(C) Such rules shall require records to be made and kept by government securities brokers and government securities dealers and shall specify the periods for which such records shall be preserved.

(2) *Risk Assessment for Holding Company Systems.*

(A) *Obligations to Obtain, Maintain, and Report Information.* Every person who is registered as a government securities broker or government securities dealer under this section shall obtain such information and make and keep such records as the Secretary by rule prescribes concerning the registered person's policies, procedures, or systems for monitoring and controlling financial and operational risks to it resulting from the activities of any of its associated persons, other than a natural person. Such records shall describe, in the aggregate, each of the financial and securities activities conducted by, and customary sources of capital and funding of, those of its associated persons whose business activities are reasonably likely to have a material impact on the financial or operational condition of such registered person, including its capital, its liquidity, or its ability to conduct or finance its operations. The Secretary, by rule, may require summary reports of such information to be filed with the registered person's appropriate regulatory agency no more frequently than quarterly.

(B) *Authority to Require Additional Information.* If, as a result of adverse market conditions or based on reports provided pursuant to subparagraph (A) of this paragraph or other available information, the appropriate regulatory agency reasonably concludes that it has concerns regarding the financial or operational condition of any government securities broker or government securities dealer registered under this section, such agency may require the registered person to make reports concerning the financial and securities activities of any of such person's associated persons, other than a natural person, whose business activities are reasonably likely to have a material impact on the financial or operational condition of such registered person. The appropriate regulatory agency, in requiring reports pursuant to this subparagraph, shall specify the information required, the period for which it is required, the time and date on which the information must be furnished, and whether the information is to be furnished directly to the appropriate regulatory agency or to a self-regulatory organization with primary responsibility for examining the registered person's financial and operational condition.

(C) *Special Provisions with Respect to Associated Persons Subject to Federal Banking Regulation.*

(i) *Cooperation in Implementation.* In developing and implementing reporting requirements pursuant to subparagraph (A) of this paragraph with respect to associated persons subject to examination by or reporting requirements of a Federal banking agency, the Secretary shall consult with and consider the views of each such Federal banking agency. If a Federal banking agency comments in writing on a proposed rule of the Secretary under this paragraph that has been published for comment, the Secretary shall respond in writing to such written comment before adopting the proposed rule. The Secretary shall, at the request of a Federal banking agency, publish such comment and response in the Federal Register at the time of publishing the adopted rule.

(ii) *Use of Banking Agency Reports.* A registered government securities broker or government securities dealer shall be in compliance with any recordkeeping or reporting requirement adopted pursuant to subparagraph (A) of this paragraph concerning an associated person that is subject to examination by or reporting requirements of a Federal banking agency if such government securities broker or government securities dealer utilizes for such recordkeeping or reporting requirement copies of reports filed by the associated person with the Federal banking agency pursuant to section 5211 of the Revised Statutes, section 9 of the Federal Reserve Act, section 7(a) of the Federal Deposit Insurance Act, section 10(b) of the Home Owners' Loan Act, or section 8 of the Bank Holding Company Act of 1956. The Secretary may, however, by rule adopted pursuant to subparagraph (A), require any registered government securities broker or government securities dealer filing such reports with the appropriate regulatory agency to obtain, maintain, or report supplemental information if the Secretary makes an explicit finding, based on information provided by the appropriate regulatory agency, that such supplemental information is necessary to inform the appropriate regulatory agency regarding potential risks to such government securities broker or government securities dealer. Prior to requiring any such supplemental information, the Secretary shall first request the Federal banking agency to expand its reporting requirements to include such information.

(iii) *Procedure for Requiring Additional Information.* Prior to making a request pursuant to subparagraph (B) of this paragraph for information with respect to an associated person that is subject to examination by or reporting requirements of a Federal banking agency, the appropriate regulatory agency shall—

(I) notify such banking agency of the information required with respect to such associated person; and

(II) consult with such agency to determine whether the information required is available from such agency and for other purposes, unless the appropriate regulatory agency determines that any delay resulting from such consultation would be inconsistent with ensuring the financial and operational condition of the government securities broker or government securities dealer or the stability or integrity of the securities markets.

(iv) *Exclusion for Examination Reports.* Nothing in this subparagraph shall be construed to permit the Secretary or an appropriate regulatory agency to require any registered government securities broker or government securities dealer to obtain, maintain, or furnish any examination report of any Federal banking agency or any supervisory recommendations or analysis contained therein.

(v) *Confidentiality of Information Provided.* No information provided to or obtained by an appropriate regulatory agency from any Federal banking agency pursuant to a request under clause (iii) of this subparagraph regarding any associated person which is subject to examination by or reporting requirements of a Federal banking agency may be disclosed to any other person (other than a self-regulatory organization), without the prior written approval of the Federal banking agency. Nothing in this clause shall authorize the Secretary or any appropriate regulatory agency to withhold information from Congress, or prevent the Secretary or any appropriate regulatory agency from complying with a request for information from any other Federal department or agency requesting the information for purposes within the scope of its jurisdiction, or complying with an order of a court of the United States in an action brought by the United States or the Commission.

(vi) *Notice to Banking Agencies Concerning Financial and Operational Condition Concerns.* The Secretary or appropriate regulatory agency shall notify the Federal banking agency of any concerns of the Secretary or the appropriate regulatory agency regarding significant financial or operational risks resulting from the activities of any government securities broker or government securities dealer to any associated person thereof which is subject to examination by or reporting requirements of the Federal banking agency.

(vii) *Definition.* For purposes of this subparagraph, the term "Federal banking agency" shall have the same meaning as the term "appropriate Federal banking agency" in section 3(q) of the Federal Deposit Insurance Act.

(D) *Exemptions.* The Secretary by rule or order may exempt any person or class of persons, under such terms and conditions and for such periods as the Secretary shall provide in such rule or order, from the provisions of this paragraph, and the rules thereunder. In granting such exemptions, the Secretary shall consider, among other factors—

(i) whether information of the type required under this paragraph is available from a supervisory agency (as defined in section 1101(6) of the Right to Financial Privacy Act of 1978), a State insurance commission or similar State agency, the Commodity Futures Trading Commission, or a similar foreign regulator;

(ii) the primary business of any associated person;

(iii) the nature and extent of domestic or foreign regulation of the associated person's activities;

(iv) the nature and extent of the registered person's securities transactions; and

(v) with respect to the registered person and its associated persons, on a consolidated basis, the amount and proportion of assets devoted to, and revenues derived from, activities in the United States securities markets.

(E) *Conformity With Requirements Under Section 17(h).* In exercising authority pursuant to subparagraph (A) of this paragraph concerning information with respect to associated persons of government securities brokers and government securities dealers who are also associated persons of registered brokers or dealers reporting to the Commission pursuant to section 17(h) of this title, the requirements relating to such associated persons shall conform, to the greatest extent practicable, to the requirements under section 17(h).

(F) *Authority to Limit Disclosure of Information.* Notwithstanding any other provision of law, the Secretary and any appropriate regulatory agency shall not be compelled to disclose any information required to be reported under this paragraph, or any information supplied to the Secretary or any appropriate regulatory agency by any domestic or foreign regulatory agency that relates to the financial or operational condition of any associated person of a registered government securities broker or a government securities dealer. Nothing in this paragraph shall authorize the Secretary or any appropriate regulatory agency to withhold information from Congress, or prevent the Secretary or any appropriate regulatory agency from complying with a request for information from any other Federal department or agency requesting the information for purposes within the scope of its jurisdiction, or complying with an order of a court of the United States in an action brought by the United States or the Commission. For purposes of section 552 of title 5, United States Code, this paragraph shall be considered a statute described in subsection (b)(3)(B) of such section 552.

(3)(A) With respect to any financial institution that has filed notice as a government securities broker or government securities dealer or that is required to file notice under subsection (a)(1)(B), the appropriate regulatory agency for such government securities broker or government securities dealer may issue such rules and regulations with respect to transactions in government securities as may be necessary to prevent fraudulent and manipulative acts and practices and to promote just and equitable principles of trade. If the Secretary of the Treasury determines, and notifies the appropriate regulatory agency, that such rule or regulation, if implemented, would, or as applied does (i) adversely affect the liquidity or efficiency of the market for government securities; or (ii) impose any burden on competition not necessary or appropriate in furtherance of the purposes of this section, the appropriate regulatory agency shall, prior to adopting the proposed rule or regulation, find that such rule or regulation is necessary and appropriate in furtherance of the purposes of this section notwithstanding the Secretary's determination.

(B) The appropriate regulatory agency shall consult with and consider the views of the Secretary prior to approving or amending a rule or regulation under this paragraph, except where the appropriate regulatory agency determines that an emergency exists requiring expeditious and summary action and publishes its reasons therefor. If the Secretary comments in writing to the appropriate regulatory agency on a proposed rule or regulation that has been published for comment, the appropriate regulatory agency shall respond in writing to such written comment before approving the proposed rule or regulation.

(C) In promulgating rules under this section, the appropriate regulatory agency shall consider the sufficiency and appropriateness of then existing laws and rules applicable to government securities brokers, government securities dealers, and persons associated with government securities brokers and government securities dealers.

(4) Rules promulgated and orders issued under this section shall—

(A) be designed to prevent fraudulent and manipulative acts and practices and to protect the integrity, liquidity, and efficiency of the market for government securities, investors, and the public interest; and

(B) not be designed to permit unfair discrimination between customers, issuers, government securities brokers, or government securities dealers, or to impose any burden on competition not necessary or appropriate in furtherance of the purposes of this title.

(5) In promulgating rules and issuing orders under this section, the Secretary—

(A) may appropriately classify government securities brokers and government securities dealers (taking into account relevant matters, including types of business done, nature of securities other than government securities purchased or sold, and character of business organization) and persons associated with government securities brokers and government securities dealers;

(B) may determine, to the extent consistent with paragraph (2) of this subsection and with the public interest, the protection of investors, and the purposes of this title, not to apply, in whole or in part, certain rules under this section, or to apply greater, lesser, or different standards, to certain classes of government securities brokers, government securities dealers, or persons associated with government securities brokers or government securities dealers;

(C) shall consider the sufficiency and appropriateness of then existing laws and rules applicable to government securities brokers, government securities dealers, and persons associated with government securities brokers and government securities dealers; and

(D) shall consult with and consider the views of the Commission and the Board of Governors of the Federal Reserve System, except where the Secretary determines that an emergency exists requiring expeditious or summary action and publishes its reasons for such determination.

(6) If the Commission or the Board of Governors of the Federal Reserve System comments in writing on a proposed rule of the Secretary that has been published for comment, the Secretary shall

respond in writing to such written comment before approving the proposed rule.

(7) No government securities broker or government securities dealer shall make use of the mails or any means or instrumentality of interstate commerce to effect any transaction in, or to induce or attempt to induce the purchase or sale of, any government security in contravention of any rule under this section.

(c) *Sanctions for Violations.*

(1) With respect to any government securities broker or government securities dealer registered or required to register under subsection (a)(1)(A) of this section—

(A) The Commission, by order, shall censure, place limitations on the activities, functions, or operations of, suspend for a period not exceeding 12 months, or revoke the registration of such government securities broker or government securities dealer, if it finds, on the record after notice and opportunity for hearing, that such censure, placing of limitations, suspension, or revocation is in the public interest and that such government securities broker or government securities dealer, or any person associated with such government securities broker or government securities dealer (whether prior or subsequent to becoming so associated), has committed or omitted any act, or is subject to an order or finding, enumerated in subparagraph (A), (D), (E), (H), or (G) of paragraph (4) of section 15(b) of this title, has been convicted of any offense specified in subparagraph (B) of such paragraph (4) within 10 years of the commencement of the proceedings under this paragraph, or is enjoined from any action, conduct, or practice specified in subparagraph (C) of such paragraph (4).

(B) Pending final determination whether registration of any government securities broker or government securities dealer shall be revoked, the Commission, by order, may suspend such registration, if such suspension appears to the Commission, after notice and opportunity for hearing, to be necessary or appropriate in the public interest or for the protection of investors. Any registered government securities broker or registered government securities dealer may, upon such terms and conditions as the Commission may deem necessary in the public interest or for the protection of investors, withdraw from registration by filing a written notice of withdrawal with the Commission. If the Commission finds that any registered government securities broker or registered government securities dealer is no longer in existence or has ceased to do business as a government securities broker or government securities dealer, the Commission, by order, shall cancel the registration of such government securities broker or government securities dealer.

(C) The Commission, by order, shall censure or place limitations on the activities or functions of any person who is, or at the time of the alleged misconduct was, associated or seeking to become associated with a government securities broker or government securities dealer registered or required to register under subsection (a)(1)(A) of this section or suspend for a period not exceeding 12 months or bar any such person from being associated with such a government securities broker or government securities dealer, if the Commission finds, on the record after notice and opportunity for hearing, that such censure, placing of limitations, suspension, or bar is in the public interest and that such person has committed or omitted any act, or is subject to an order or finding, enumerated in subparagraph (A), (D), (E), (H), or (G) of paragraph (4) of section 15(b), has been convicted of any offense specified in subparagraph (B) of such paragraph (4) within 10 years of the commencement of the proceedings under this paragraph, or is enjoined from any action, conduct, or practice specified in subparagraph (C) of such paragraph (4).

(2)(A) With respect to any government securities broker or government securities dealer which is not registered or required to register under subsection (a)(1)(A) of this section, the appropriate regulatory agency for such government securities broker or government securities dealer may, in the manner and for the reasons specified in paragraph (1)(A) of this subsection, censure, place limitations on the activities, functions, or operations of, suspend for a period not exceeding 12 months, or bar from acting as a government securities broker or government securities dealer any such government securities broker or government securities dealer, and may sanction any person associated, seeking to become associated, or, at the time of the alleged misconduct, associated or seeking to become associated with such government securities broker or government securities dealer in the manner and for the reasons specified in paragraph (1)(C) of this subsection.

(B) In addition, where applicable, such appropriate regulatory agency may, in accordance with Section 8 of the Federal Deposit Insurance Act, Section 5 of the Home Owner's Loan Act of 1933, or Section 407 of the National Housing Act, enforce compliance by such government securities broker or government securities dealer or any person associated, seeking to become associated, or, at the time of the alleged misconduct, associated or seeking to become associated with such government securities broker or government securities dealer with the provisions of this section and the rules thereunder.

(C) For purposes of subparagraph (B) of this paragraph, any violation of any such provision shall constitute adequate basis for the issuance of any order under section 8(b) or 8(c) of the Federal Deposit Insurance Act, section 5(d)(2) or 5(d)(3) of the Home Owners' Loan Act of 1933, or section 407(e) or 407(f) of the National Housing Act, and the customers of any such government securities broker or government securities dealer shall be deemed, respectively, "depositors" as that term is used in section 8(c) of the Federal Deposit Insurance Act, "savings account holders" as that term is used in section 5(d)(3) of the Home Owners' Loan Act of 1933, or "insured members" as that term is used in section 407(f) of the National Housing Act.

(D) Nothing in this paragraph shall be construed to affect in any way the powers of such appropriate regulatory agency to proceed against such government securities broker or government securities dealer under any other provision of law.

(E) Each appropriate regulatory agency (other than the Commission) shall promptly notify the Commission after it has imposed any sanction under this paragraph on a government securities broker or government securities dealer, or a person associated with a government securities broker or government securities dealer, and the Commission shall maintain, and make available to the public, a record of such sanctions and any sanctions imposed by it under this subsection.

(3) It shall be unlawful for any person as to whom an order entered pursuant to paragraph (1) or (2) of this subsection suspending or barring him from being associated with a government securities broker or government securities dealer is in effect willfully to become, or to be, associated with a government securities broker or government securities dealer without the consent of the appropriate regulatory agency, and it shall be unlawful for any government securities broker or government securities dealer to permit such a person to become, or remain, a person associated with it without the consent of the appropriate regulatory agency, if such government securities broker or government securities dealer knew, or, in the exercise of reasonable care should have known, of such order.

(d) *Records of Brokers and Dealers Subject to Examination.*

(1) All records of a government securities broker or government securities dealer are subject at any time, or from time to time, to such reasonable periodic, special, or other examinations by representatives of the appropriate regulatory agency for such government securities broker or government securities dealer as such appropriate regulatory agency deems necessary or appropriate in the public interest, for the protection of investors, or otherwise in furtherance of the purposes of this title.

(2) Information received by an appropriate regulatory agency, the Secretary, or the Commission from or with respect to any government securities broker, government securities dealer, any person associated with a government securities broker or government securities dealer, or any other person subject to this section or rules promulgated thereunder, may be made available by the Secretary or the recipient agency to the Commission, the Secretary, the Department of Justice, the Commodity Futures Trading Commission, any appropriate regulatory agency, any self-regulatory organization, or any Federal Reserve Bank.

(3) *Government Securities Trade Reconstruction.*

(A) *Furnishing Records.* Every government securities broker and government securities dealer shall furnish to the Commission on request such records of government securities transactions, including records of the date and time of execution of trades, as the Commission may require to reconstruct trading in the course of a particular inquiry or investigation being conducted by the Commission for enforcement or surveillance purposes. In requiring information pursuant to this paragraph, the Commission shall specify the information required, the period for which it is required, the time and date on which the information must be furnished, and whether the information is to be furnished directly to the Commission, to the Federal Reserve Bank of New York, or to an appropriate regulatory agency or self-regulatory organization with responsibility for examining the government securities broker or government securities dealer. The Commission may require that such information be furnished in machine readable form notwithstanding any limitation in subparagraph (B). In utilizing its authority to require information in machine readable form, the Commission shall minimize the burden such requirement may place on small government securities brokers and dealers.

(B) *Limitation; Construction.* The Commission shall not utilize its authority under this paragraph to develop regular reporting requirements, except that the Commission may require information to be furnished under this paragraph as frequently as necessary for particular inquiries or investigations for enforcement or surveillance purposes. This paragraph shall not be construed as requiring, or as authorizing the Commission to require, any government securities broker or government securities dealer to obtain or maintain any information for purposes of this paragraph which is not otherwise maintained by such broker or dealer in accordance with any other provision of law or usual and customary business practice. The Commission shall, where feasible, avoid requiring any information to be furnished under this paragraph that the Commission may obtain from the Federal Reserve Bank of New York.

(C) *Procedures for Requiring Information.* At the time the Commission requests any information pursuant to subparagraph (A) with respect to any government securities broker or government securities dealer for which the Commission is not the appropriate regulatory agency, the Commission shall notify the appropriate regulatory agency for such government securities broker or government securities dealer and, upon request, furnish to the appropriate regulatory agency any information supplied to the Commission.

(D) *Consultation.* Within 90 days after the date of enactment of this paragraph, and annually thereafter, or upon the request of any other appropriate regulatory agency, the Commission shall consult with the other appropriate regulatory agencies to determine the availability of records that may be required to be furnished under this paragraph and, for those records available directly from the other appropriate regulatory agencies, to develop a procedure for furnishing such records expeditiously upon the Commission's request.

(E) *Exclusion for Examination Reports.* Nothing in this paragraph shall be construed so as to permit the Commission to require any government securities broker or government securities dealer to obtain, maintain, or furnish any examination report of any appropriate regulatory agency other than the Commission or any supervisory recommendations or analysis contained in any such examination report.

(F) *Authority to Limit Disclosure of Information.* Notwithstanding any other provision of law, the Commission and the appropriate regulatory agencies shall not be compelled to disclose any information required or obtained under this paragraph. Nothing in this paragraph shall authorize the Commission or any appropriate regulatory agency to withhold information from Congress, or prevent the Commission or any appropriate regulatory agency from complying with a request for information from any other Federal department or agency requesting information for purposes within the scope of its jurisdiction, or from complying with an order of a court of the United States in an action brought by the United States, the Commission, or the appropriate regulatory agency. For purposes of section 552 of title 5, United States Code, this subparagraph shall be considered a statute described in subsection (b)(3)(B) of such section 552.

(e) *Membership in National Securities Exchange; Exemptions.*

(1) It shall be unlawful for any government securities broker or government securities dealer registered or required to register with the Commission under subsection (a)(1)(A) to effect any transaction in, or induce or attempt to induce the purchase or sale of, any government security, unless such government securities broker or government securities dealer is a member of a national securities exchange registered under section 6 of this title or a securities association registered under section 15A of this title.

(2) The Commission, after consultation with the Secretary, by rule or order, as it deems consistent with the public interest and the protection

of investors, may conditionally or unconditionally exempt from paragraph (1) of this subsection any government securities broker or government securities dealer or class of government securities brokers or government securities dealers specified in such rule or order.

(f) *Large Position Reporting*.

(1) *Reporting Requirements*. The Secretary may adopt rules to require specified persons holding, maintaining, or controlling large positions in to-be-issued or recently issued Treasury securities to file such reports regarding such positions as the Secretary determines to be necessary and appropriate for the purpose of monitoring the impact in the Treasury securities market of concentrations of positions in Treasury securities and for the purpose of otherwise assisting the Commission in the enforcement of this title, taking into account any impact of such rules on the efficiency and liquidity of the Treasury securities market and the cost to taxpayers of funding the Federal debt. Unless otherwise specified by the Secretary, reports required under this subsection shall be filed with the Federal Reserve Bank of New York, acting as agent for the Secretary. Such reports shall, on a timely basis, be provided directly to the Commission by the person with whom they are filed.

(2) *Recordkeeping Requirements*. Rules under this subsection may require persons holding, maintaining, or controlling large positions in Treasury securities to make and keep for prescribed periods such records as the Secretary determines are necessary or appropriate to ensure that such persons can comply with reporting requirements under this subsection.

(3) *Aggregation Rules*. Rules under this subsection—

(A) may prescribe the manner in which positions and accounts shall be aggregated for the purpose of this subsection, including aggregation on the basis of common ownership or control; and

(B) may define which persons (individually or as a group) hold, maintain, or control large positions.

(4) *Definitional Authority; Determination of Reporting Threshold*.

(A) In prescribing rules under this subsection, the Secretary may, consistent with the purpose of this subsection, define terms used in this subsection that are not otherwise defined in section 3 of this title.

(B) Rules under this subsection shall specify—

(i) the minimum size of positions subject to reporting under this subsection, which shall be no less than the size that provides the potential for manipulation or control of the supply or price, or the cost of financing arrangements, of an issue or the portion thereof that is available for trading;

(ii) the types of positions (which may include financing arrangements) to be reported;

(iii) the securities to be covered; and

(iv) the form and manner in which reports shall be transmitted, which may include transmission in machine readable form.

(5) *Exemptions*. Consistent with the public interest and the protection of investors, the Secretary by rule or order may exempt in whole or in part, conditionally or unconditionally, any person or class of persons, or any transaction or class of transactions, from the requirements of this subsection.

(6) *Limitation on Disclosure of Information*. Notwithstanding any other provision of law, the Secretary and the Commission shall not be compelled to disclose any information required to be kept or reported under this subsection. Nothing in this subsection shall authorize the Secretary or the Commission to withhold information from Congress, or prevent the Secretary or the Commission from complying with a request for information from any other Federal department or agency requesting information for purposes within the scope of its jurisdiction, or from complying with an order of a court of the United States in an action brought by the United States, the Secretary, or the Commission. For purposes of section 552 of title 5, United States Code, this paragraph shall be considered a statute described in subsection (b)(3)(B) of such section 552.

(g) *Effect on Other Laws; Authority of Commission*.

(1) Nothing in this section except paragraph (2) of this subsection shall be construed to impair or limit the authority under any other provision of law of the Commission, the Secretary of the Treasury, the Board of Governors of the Federal Reserve System, the Comptroller of the Currency, the Federal Deposit Insurance Corporation, the

Secretary of Housing and Urban Development, and the Government National Mortgage Association.

(2) Notwithstanding any other provision of this title, the Commission shall not have any authority to make investigations of, require the filing of a statement by, or take any other action under this title against a government securities broker or government securities dealer, or any person associated with a government securities broker or government securities dealer, for any violation or threatened violation of the provisions of this section, other than subsection (d)(3), or the rules or regulations thereunder, unless the Commission is the appropriate regulatory agency for such government securities broker or government securities dealer. Nothing in the preceding sentence shall be construed to limit the authority of the Commission with respect to violations or threatened violations of any provision of this title other than this section, (except subsection (d)(3) of this section), the rules or regulations under any such other provision or investigations pursuant to section 78u(a)(2) of this title to assist a foreign securities authority.

(h) *Emergency Authority.* The Secretary may, by order, take any action with respect to a matter or action subject to regulation by the Secretary under this section, or the rules of the Secretary under this section, involving a government security or a market therein (or significant portion or segment of that market), that the Commission may take under section 12(k)(2) of this title with respect to transactions in securities (other than exempted securities) or a market therein (or significant portion or segment of that market).

Securities Analysts and Research Reports

Sec. 15D. (a) *Analyst Protections.* The Commission, or upon the authorization and direction of the Commission, a registered securities association or national securities exchange, shall have adopted, not later than 1 year after the date of enactment of this section, rules reasonably designed to address conflicts of interest that can arise when securities analysts recommend equity securities in research reports and public appearances, in order to improve the objectivity of research and provide investors with more useful and reliable information, including rules designed—

(1) to foster greater public confidence in securities research, and to protect the objectivity and independence of securities analysts, by—

(A) restricting the prepublication clearance or approval of research reports by persons employed by the broker or dealer who are engaged in investment banking activities, or persons not directly responsible for investment research, other than legal or compliance staff;

(B) limiting the supervision and compensatory evaluation of securities analysts to officials employed by the broker or dealer who are not engaged in investment banking activities; and

(C) requiring that a broker or dealer and persons employed by a broker or dealer who are involved with investment banking activities may not, directly or indirectly, retaliate against or threaten to retaliate against any securities analyst employed by that broker or dealer or its affiliates as a result of an adverse, negative, or otherwise unfavorable research report that may adversely affect the present or prospective investment banking relationship of the broker or dealer with the issuer that is the subject of the research report, except that such rules may not limit the authority of a broker or dealer to discipline a securities analyst for causes other than such research report in accordance with the policies and procedures of the firm;

(2) to define periods during which brokers or dealers who have participated, or are to participate, in a public offering of securities as underwriters or dealers should not publish or otherwise distribute research reports relating to such securities or to the issuer of such securities;

(3) to establish structural and institutional safeguards within registered brokers or dealers to assure that securities analysts are separated by appropriate informational partitions within the firm from the review, pressure, or oversight of those whose involvement in investment banking activities might potentially bias their judgment or supervision; and

(4) to address such other issues as the Commission, or such association or exchange, determines appropriate.

(b) *Disclosure.* The Commission, or upon the authorization and direction of the Commission, a registered securities association or national securities exchange, shall have adopted, not later than 1 year after the date of enactment of this section, rules reasonably designed to require each securities analyst to disclose in public appearances, and each registered broker or dealer to disclose in each research report, as applicable, conflicts of interest that are known or should have been known by the securities analyst or the broker or dealer, to exist at the time of the appearance or the date of distribution of the report, including—

(1) the extent to which the securities analyst has debt or equity investments in the issuer that is the subject of the appearance or research report;

(2) whether any compensation has been received by the registered broker or dealer, or any affiliate thereof, including the securities analyst, from the issuer that is the subject of the appearance or research report, subject to such exemptions as the Commission may determine appropriate and necessary to prevent disclosure by virtue of this paragraph of material non-public information regarding specific potential future investment banking transactions of such issuer, as is appropriate in the public interest and consistent with the protection of investors;

(3) whether an issuer, the securities of which are recommended in the appearance or research report, currently is, or during the 1-year period preceding the date of the appearance or date of distribution of the report has been, a client of the registered broker or dealer, and if so, stating the types of services provided to the issuer;

(4) whether the securities analyst received compensation with respect to a research report, based upon (among any other factors) the investment banking revenues (either generally or specifically earned from the issuer being analyzed) of the registered broker or dealer; and

(5) such other disclosures of conflicts of interest that are material to investors, research analysts, or the broker or dealer as the Commission, or such association or exchange, determines appropriate.

(c) *Limitation.* Notwithstanding subsection (a) or any other provision of law, neither the Commission nor any national securities association registered under section 15A may adopt or maintain any rule or regulation in connection with an initial public offering of the common equity of an emerging growth company—

(1) restricting, based on functional role, which associated persons of a broker, dealer, or member of a national securities association, may arrange for communications between a securities analyst and a potential investor; or

(2) restricting a securities analyst from participating in any communications with the management of an emerging growth company that is also attended by any other associated person of a broker, dealer, or member of a national securities association whose functional role is other than as a securities analyst.

(d) *Definitions.* In this section—

(1) the term "securities analyst" means any associated person of a registered broker or dealer that is principally responsible for, and any associated person who reports directly or indirectly to a securities analyst in connection with, the preparation of the substance of a research report, whether or not any such person has the job title of "securities analyst"; and

(2) the term "research report" means a written or electronic communication that includes an analysis of equity securities of individual companies or industries, and that provides information reasonably sufficient upon which to base an investment decision.

Registration of Nationally Recognized Statistical Rating Organizations

Sec. 15E. (a) *Registration Procedures.*

(1) *Application for Registration.*

(A) *In General.* A credit rating agency that elects to be treated as a nationally recognized statistical rating organization for purposes of this title (in this section referred to as the "applicant"), shall furnish to the Commission an application for registration, in such form as the Commission shall require, by rule or regulation issued in accordance with subsection (n), and containing the information described in subparagraph (B).

(B) *Required Information.* An application for registration under this section shall contain information regarding—

(i) credit ratings performance measurement statistics over short-term, mid-term, and long-term periods (as applicable) of the applicant;

(ii) the procedures and methodologies that the applicant uses in determining credit ratings;

(iii) policies or procedures adopted and implemented by the applicant to prevent the misuse, in violation of this title (or the rules and regulations hereunder), of material, nonpublic information;

(iv) the organizational structure of the applicant;

(v) whether or not the applicant has in effect a code of ethics, and if not, the reasons therefor;

(vi) any conflict of interest relating to the issuance of credit ratings by the applicant;

(vii) the categories described in any of clauses (i) through (v) of section 3(a)(62)(B) of this title with respect to which the applicant intends to apply for registration under this section;

(viii) on a confidential basis, a list of the 20 largest issuers and subscribers that use the credit rating services of the applicant, by amount of net revenues received therefrom in the fiscal year immediately preceding the date of submission of the application;

(ix) on a confidential basis, as to each applicable category of obligor described in any of clauses (i) through (v) of section 3(a)(62)(B) of this title, written certifications described in subparagraph (C), except as provided in subparagraph (D); and

(x) any other information and documents concerning the applicant and any person associated with such applicant as the Commission, by rule, may prescribe as necessary or appropriate in the public interest or for the protection of investors.

(C) *Written Certifications.* Written certifications required by subparagraph (B)(ix)—

(i) shall be provided from not fewer than 10 qualified institutional buyers, none of which is affiliated with the applicant;

(ii) may address more than one category of obligors described in any of clauses (i) through (v) of section 3(a)(62)(B) of this title;

(iii) shall include not fewer than 2 certifications for each such category of obligor; and

(iv) shall state that the qualified institutional buyer—

(I) meets the definition of a qualified institutional buyer under section 3(a)(64) of this title; and

(II) has used the credit ratings of the applicant for at least the 3 years immediately preceding the date of the certification in the subject category or categories of obligors.

(D) *Exemption from Certification Requirement.* A written certification under subparagraph (B)(ix) is not required with respect to any credit rating agency which has received, or been the subject of, a no-action letter from the staff of the Commission prior to August 2, 2006, stating that such staff would not recommend enforcement action against any broker or dealer that considers credit ratings issued by such credit rating agency to be ratings from a nationally recognized statistical rating organization.

(E) *Limitation on Liability of Qualified Institutional Buyers.* No qualified institutional buyer shall be liable in any private right of action for any opinion or statement expressed in a certification made pursuant to subparagraph (B)(ix).

(2) *Review of Application.*

(A) *Initial Determination.* Not later than 90 days after the date on which the application for registration is furnished to the Commission under paragraph (1) (or within such longer period as to which the applicant consents) the Commission shall—

(i) by order, grant such registration for ratings in the subject category or categories of obligors, as described in clauses (i) through (v) of section 3(a)(62)(B); or

(ii) institute proceedings to determine whether registration should be denied.

(B) *Conduct of Proceedings.*

(i) *Content.* Proceedings referred to in subparagraph (A)(ii) shall—

(I) include notice of the grounds for denial under consideration and an opportunity for hearing; and

(II) be concluded not later than 120 days after the date on which the application for registration is furnished to the Commission under paragraph (1).

(ii) *Determination.* At the conclusion of such proceedings, the Commission, by order, shall grant or deny such application for registration.

(iii) *Extension Authorized.* The Commission may extend the time for conclusion of such proceedings for not longer than 90 days, if it finds good cause for such extension and publishes its reasons for so finding, or for such longer period as to which the applicant consents.

(C) *Grounds for Decision.* The Commission shall grant registration under this subsection—

(i) if the Commission finds that the requirements of this section are satisfied; and

(ii) unless the Commission finds (in which case the Commission shall deny such registration) that—

(I) the applicant does not have adequate financial and managerial resources to consistently produce credit ratings with integrity and to materially comply with the procedures and methodologies disclosed under paragraph (1)(B) and with subsections (g), (h), (i), and (j); or

(II) if the applicant were so registered, its registration would be subject to suspension or revocation under subsection (d).

(3) *Public Availability of Information.* Subject to section 24, the Commission shall, by rule, require a nationally recognized statistical rating organization, upon the granting of registration under this section, to make the information and documents submitted to the Commission in its completed application for registration, or in any amendment submitted under paragraph (1) or (2) of subsection (b), publicly available on its website, or through another comparable, readily accessible means, except as provided in clauses (viii) and (ix) of paragraph (1)(B).

(b) *Update of Registration.*

(1) *Update.* Each nationally recognized statistical rating organization shall promptly amend its application for registration under this section if any information or document provided therein becomes materially inaccurate, except that a nationally recognized statistical rating organization is not required to amend—

(A) the information required to be filed under subsection (a)(1)(B)(i) by filing information under this paragraph, but shall amend such information in the annual submission of the organization under paragraph (2) of this subsection; or

(B) the certifications required to be provided under subsection (a)(1)(B)(ix) by filing information under this paragraph.

(2) *Certification.* Not later than 90 days after the end of each calendar year, each nationally recognized statistical rating organization shall file with the Commission an amendment to its registration, in such form as the Commission, by rule, may prescribe as necessary or appropriate in the public interest or for the protection of investors—

(A) certifying that the information and documents in the application for registration of such nationally recognized statistical rating organization (other than the certifications required under subsection (a)(1)(B)(ix)) continue to be accurate; and

(B) listing any material change that occurred to such information or documents during the previous calendar year.

(c) *Accountability for Ratings Procedures.*

(1) *Authority.* The Commission shall have exclusive authority to enforce the provisions of this section in accordance with this chapter with respect to any nationally recognized statistical rating organization, if such nationally recognized statistical rating organization issues credit ratings in material contravention of those procedures relating to such nationally recognized statistical rating organization, including procedures relating to the prevention of misuse of nonpublic information and conflicts of interest, that such nationally recognized statistical rating organization—

(A) includes in its application for registration under subsection (a)(1)(B)(ii); or

(B) makes and disseminates in reports pursuant to section 17(a) or the rules and regulations thereunder.

(2) *Limitation.* The rules and regulations that the Commission may prescribe pursuant to this chapter, as they apply to nationally recognized statistical rating organizations, shall be narrowly tailored to meet the requirements of this chapter applicable to nationally recognized statistical rating organizations. Notwithstanding any other provision of this section, or any other provision of law, neither the Commission nor any State (or political subdivision thereof) may regulate the substance of credit ratings or the procedures and methodologies by which any nationally recognized statistical rating organization determines credit ratings. Nothing in this paragraph may be construed to afford a defense against any action or proceeding brought by the Commission to enforce the antifraud provisions of the securities laws.

(3) *Internal Controls Over Processes for Determining Credit Ratings.*

(A) *In General.* Each nationally recognized statistical rating organization shall establish, maintain, enforce, and document an effective internal control structure governing the implementation of and adherence to policies, procedures, and methodologies for determining credit ratings, taking into consideration such factors as the Commission may prescribe, by rule.

(B) *Attestation Requirement.* The Commission shall prescribe rules requiring each nationally recognized statistical rating organization to submit to the Commission an annual internal controls report, which shall contain—

(i) a description of the responsibility of the management of the nationally recognized statistical rating organization in establishing and maintaining an effective internal control structure under subparagraph (A);

(ii) an assessment of the effectiveness of the internal control structure of the nationally recognized statistical rating organization; and

(iii) the attestation of the chief executive officer, or equivalent individual, of the nationally recognized statistical rating organization.

(d) *Censure, Denial, or Suspension of Registration; Notice and Hearing.*

(1) *In General.* The Commission, by order, shall censure, place limitations on the activities, functions, or operations of, suspend for a period not exceeding 12 months, or revoke the registration of any nationally recognized statistical rating organization, or with respect to any person who is associated with, who is seeking to become associated with, or, at the time of the alleged misconduct, who was associated or was seeking to become associated with a nationally recognized statistical rating organization, the Commission, by order, shall censure, place limitations on the activities or functions of such person, suspend for a period not exceeding 1 year, or bar such person from being associated with a nationally recognized statistical rating organization, if the Commission finds, on the record after notice and opportunity for hearing, that such censure, placing of limitations, suspension, bar or revocation is necessary for the protection of investors and in the public interest and that such nationally recognized statistical rating organization, or any person associated with such an organization, whether prior to or subsequent to becoming so associated—

(A) has committed or omitted any act, or is subject to an order or finding, enumerated in subparagraph (A), (D), (E), (H), or (G) of section 15(b)(4), has been convicted of any offense specified in section 15(b)(4)(B), or is enjoined from any action, conduct, or practice specified in subparagraph (C) of section 15(b)(4), during the 10-year period preceding the date of commencement of the proceedings under this subsection, or at any time thereafter;

(B) has been convicted during the 10-year period preceding the date on which an application for registration is filed with the Commission under this section, or at any time thereafter, of—

(i) any crime that is punishable by imprisonment for 1 or more years, and that is not described in section 15(b)(4)(B); or

(ii) a substantially equivalent crime by a foreign court of competent jurisdiction;

(C) is subject to any order of the Commission barring or suspending the right of the person to be associated with a nationally recognized statistical rating organization;

(D) fails to file the certifications required under subsection (b)(2);

(E) fails to maintain adequate financial and managerial resources to consistently produce credit ratings with integrity; [or]*

(F) has failed reasonably to supervise, with a view to preventing a violation of the securities laws, an individual who commits such a violation, if the individual is subject to the supervision of that person.

(2) *Suspension or Revocation for Particular Class of Securities.*

(A) *In General.* The Commission may temporarily suspend or permanently revoke the registration of a nationally recognized statistical rating organization with respect to a particular class or subclass of securities, if the Commission finds, on the record after notice and opportunity for hearing, that the nationally recognized statistical rating organization does not have adequate financial and managerial resources to consistently produce credit ratings with integrity.

* So in original. The word "or" probably should appear.

(B) *Considerations.* In making any determination under subparagraph (A), the Commission shall consider—

(i) whether the nationally recognized statistical rating organization has failed over a sustained period of time, as determined by the Commission, to produce ratings that are accurate for that class or subclass of securities; and

(ii) such other factors as the Commission may determine.

(e) *Termination of Registration.*

(1) *Voluntary Withdrawal.* A nationally recognized statistical rating organization may, upon such terms and conditions as the Commission may establish as necessary in the public interest or for the protection of investors, withdraw from registration by furnishing a written notice of withdrawal to the Commission.

(2) *Commission Authority.* In addition to any other authority of the Commission under this title, if the Commission finds that a nationally recognized statistical rating organization is no longer in existence or has ceased to do business as a credit rating agency, the Commission, by order, shall cancel the registration under this section of such nationally recognized statistical rating organization.

(f) *Representations.*

(1) *Ban on Representations of Sponsorship by United States or Agency Thereof.* It shall be unlawful for any nationally recognized statistical rating organization to represent or imply in any manner whatsoever that such nationally recognized statistical rating organization has been designated, sponsored, recommended, or approved, or that the abilities or qualifications thereof have in any respect been passed upon, by the United States or any agency, officer, or employee thereof.

(2) *Ban on Representation as NRSRO of Unregistered Credit Rating Agencies.* It shall be unlawful for any credit rating agency that is not registered under this section as a nationally recognized statistical rating organization to state that such credit rating agency is a nationally recognized statistical rating organization registered under this title.

(3) *Statement of Registration Under Securities Exchange Act of 1934 Provisions.* No provision of paragraph (1) shall be construed to prohibit a statement that a nationally recognized statistical rating organization is a nationally recognized statistical rating organization under this title, if such statement is true in fact and if the effect of such registration is not misrepresented.

(g) *Prevention of Misuse of Nonpublic Information.*

(1) *Organization Policies and Procedures.* Each nationally recognized statistical rating organization shall establish, maintain, and enforce written policies and procedures reasonably designed, taking into consideration the nature of the business of such nationally recognized statistical rating organization, to prevent the misuse in violation of this title, or the rules or regulations hereunder, of material, nonpublic information by such nationally recognized statistical rating organization or any person associated with such nationally recognized statistical rating organization.

(2) *Commission Authority.* The Commission shall issue final rules in accordance with subsection (n) of this section to require specific policies or procedures that are reasonably designed to prevent misuse in violation of this title (or the rules or regulations hereunder) of material, nonpublic information.

(h) *Management of Conflicts of Interest.*

(1) *Organization Policies and Procedures.* Each nationally recognized statistical rating organization shall establish, maintain, and enforce written policies and procedures reasonably designed, taking into consideration the nature of the business of such nationally recognized statistical rating organization and affiliated persons and affiliated companies thereof, to address and manage any conflicts of interest that can arise from such business.

(2) *Commission Authority.* The Commission shall issue final rules in accordance with subsection (n) of this section to prohibit, or require the management and disclosure of, any conflicts of interest relating to the issuance of credit ratings by a nationally recognized statistical rating organization, including, without limitation, conflicts of interest relating to—

(A) the manner in which a nationally recognized statistical rating organization is compensated by the obligor, or any affiliate of the obligor, for issuing credit ratings or providing related services;

(B) the provision of consulting, advisory, or other services by a nationally recognized statistical rating organization, or any person associated with such nationally recognized statistical rating organization, to the obligor, or any affiliate of the obligor;

(C) business relationships, ownership interests, or any other financial or personal interests between a nationally recognized statistical rating organization, or any person associated with such nationally recognized statistical rating organization, and the obligor, or any affiliate of the obligor;

(D) any affiliation of a nationally recognized statistical rating organization, or any person associated with such nationally recognized statistical rating organization, with any person that underwrites the securities or money market instruments that are the subject of a credit rating; and

(E) any other potential conflict of interest, as the Commission deems necessary or appropriate in the public interest or for the protection of investors.

(3) *Separation of Ratings from Sales and Marketing.*

(A) *Rules Required.* The Commission shall issue rules to prevent the sales and marketing considerations of a nationally recognized statistical rating organization from influencing the production of ratings by the nationally recognized statistical rating organization.

(B) *Contents of Rules.* The rules issued under subparagraph (A) shall provide for—

(i) exceptions for small nationally recognized statistical rating organizations with respect to which the Commission determines that the separation of the production of ratings and sales and marketing activities is not appropriate; and

(ii) suspension or revocation of the registration of a nationally recognized statistical rating organization, if the Commission finds, on the record, after notice and opportunity for a hearing, that—

(I) the nationally recognized statistical rating organization has committed a violation of a rule issued under this subsection; and

(II) the violation of a rule issued under this subsection affected a rating.

(4) *Look-Back Requirement.*

(A) *Review by the Nationally Recognized Statistical Rating Organization.* Each nationally recognized statistical rating organization shall establish, maintain, and enforce policies and procedures reasonably designed to ensure that, in any case in which an employee of a person subject to a credit rating of the nationally recognized statistical rating organization or the issuer, underwriter, or sponsor of a security or money market instrument subject to a credit rating of the nationally recognized statistical rating organization was employed by the nationally recognized statistical rating organization and participated in any capacity in determining credit ratings for the person or the securities or money market instruments during the 1-year period preceding the date an action was taken with respect to the credit rating, the nationally recognized statistical rating organization shall—

(i) conduct a review to determine whether any conflicts of interest of the employee influenced the credit rating; and

(ii) take action to revise the rating if appropriate, in accordance with such rules as the Commission shall prescribe.

(B) *Review by Commission.*

(i) *In General.* The Commission shall conduct periodic reviews of the policies described in subparagraph (A) and the implementation of the policies at each nationally recognized statistical rating organization to ensure they are reasonably designed and implemented to most effectively eliminate conflicts of interest.

(ii) *Timing of Reviews.* The Commission shall review the code of ethics and conflict of interest policy of each nationally recognized statistical rating organization—

(I) not less frequently than annually; and

(II) whenever such policies are materially modified or amended.

(5) *Report to Commission on Certain Employment Transitions.*

(A) *Report Required.* Each nationally recognized statistical rating organization shall report to the Commission any case such organization knows or can reasonably be expected to know where a person associated with such organization within the previous 5 years obtains employment with any obligor, issuer, underwriter, or sponsor of a security or money market instrument for which the organization issued a credit rating during the 12-month period prior to such employment, if such employee—

(i) was a senior officer of such organization;

(ii) participated in any capacity in determining credit ratings for such obligor, issuer, underwriter, or sponsor; or

(iii) supervised an employee described in clause (ii).

(B) *Public Disclosure.* Upon receiving such a report, the Commission shall make such information publicly available.

(i) *Prohibited Conduct.*

(1) *Prohibited Acts and Practices.* The Commission shall issue final rules in accordance with subsection (n) of this section to prohibit any act or practice relating to the issuance of credit ratings by a nationally recognized statistical rating organization that the Commission determines to be unfair, coercive, or abusive, including any act or practice relating to—

(A) conditioning or threatening to condition the issuance of a credit rating on the purchase by the obligor or an affiliate thereof of other services or products, including pre-credit rating assessment products, of the nationally recognized statistical rating organization or any person associated with such nationally recognized statistical rating organization;

(B) lowering or threatening to lower a credit rating on, or refusing to rate, securities or money market instruments issued by an asset pool or as part of any asset-backed or mortgage-backed securities transaction, unless a portion of the assets within such pool or part of such transaction, as applicable, also is rated by the nationally recognized statistical rating organization; or

(C) modifying or threatening to modify a credit rating or otherwise departing from its adopted systematic procedures and methodologies in determining credit ratings, based on whether the obligor, or an affiliate of the obligor, purchases or will purchase the credit rating or any other service or product of the nationally recognized statistical rating organization or any person associated with such organization.

(2) *Rule of Construction.* Nothing in paragraph (1), or in any rules or regulations adopted thereunder, may be construed to modify, impair, or supersede the operation of any of the antitrust laws (as defined in the first section of the Clayton Act, except that such term includes section 5 of the Federal Trade Commission Act, to the extent that such section 5 applies to unfair methods of competition).

(j) *Designation of Compliance Officer.*

(1) *In General.* Each nationally recognized statistical rating organization shall designate an individual responsible for administering the policies and procedures that are required to be established pursuant to subsections (g) and (h), and for ensuring compliance with the securities laws and the rules and regulations thereunder, including those promulgated by the Commission pursuant to this section.

(2) *Limitations.*

(A) *In General.* Except as provided in subparagraph (B), an individual designated under paragraph (1) may not, while serving in the designated capacity—

(i) perform credit ratings;

(ii) participate in the development of ratings methodologies or models;

(iii) perform marketing or sales functions; or

(iv) participate in establishing compensation levels, other than for employees working for that individual.

(B) *Exception.* The Commission may exempt a small nationally recognized statistical rating organization from the limitations under this paragraph, if the Commission finds that compliance with such limitations would impose an unreasonable burden on the nationally recognized statistical rating organization.

(3) *Other Duties.* Each individual designated under paragraph (1) shall establish procedures for the receipt, retention, and treatment of—

(A) complaints regarding credit ratings, models, methodologies, and compliance with the securities laws and the policies and procedures developed under this section; and

(B) confidential, anonymous complaints by employees or users of credit ratings.

(4) *Compensation.* The compensation of each compliance officer appointed under paragraph (1) shall not be linked to the financial performance of the nationally recognized statistical rating organization and shall be arranged so as to ensure the independence of the officer's judgment.

(5) *Annual Reports Required.*

(A) *Annual Reports Required.* Each individual designated under paragraph (1) shall submit to the nationally recognized statistical rating organization an annual report on the compliance of the nationally recognized statistical rating organization with the securities laws and the policies and procedures of the nationally recognized statistical rating organization that includes—

(i) a description of any material changes to the code of ethics and conflict of interest policies of the nationally recognized statistical rating organization; and

(ii) a certification that the report is accurate and complete.

(B) *Submission of Reports to the Commission.* Each nationally recognized statistical rating organization shall file the reports required under subparagraph (A) together with the financial report that is required to be submitted to the Commission under this section.

(k) *Statements of Financial Condition.* Each nationally recognized statistical rating organization shall, on a confidential basis, file with the Commission, at intervals determined by the Commission, such financial statements, certified (if required by the rules or regulations of the Commission) by an independent public accountant, and information concerning its financial condition, as the Commission, by rule, may prescribe as necessary or appropriate in the public interest or for the protection of investors.

(*l*) *Sole Method of Registration.*

(1) *In General.* On and after the effective date of this section, a credit rating agency may only be registered as a nationally recognized statistical rating organization for any purpose in accordance with this section.

(2) *Prohibition on Reliance on No–Action Relief.* On and after the effective date of this section—

(A) an entity that, before that date, received advice, approval, or a no-action letter from the Commission or staff thereof to be treated as a nationally recognized statistical rating organization pursuant to the Commission Rule 15c3–1, may represent itself or act as a nationally recognized statistical rating organization only—

(i) during Commission consideration of the application, if such entity has filed an application for registration under this section; and

(ii) on and after the date of approval of its application for registration under this section; and

(B) the advice, approval, or no-action letter described in subparagraph (A) shall be void.

(3) *Notice to Other Agencies.* Not later than 30 days after the date of enactment of this section, the Commission shall give notice of the actions undertaken pursuant to this section to each Federal agency which employs in its rules and regulations the term "nationally recognized statistical rating organization" (as that term is used under Commission Rule 15c3–1, as in effect on the date of enactment of this section).

(m) *Accountability.*

(1) *In General.* The enforcement and penalty provisions of this title shall apply to statements made by a credit rating agency in the same manner and to the same extent as such provisions apply to statements made by a registered public accounting firm or a securities analyst under the securities laws, and such statements shall not be deemed forward-looking statements for the purposes of section 21E.

(2) *Rulemaking.* The Commission shall issue such rules as may be necessary to carry out this subsection.

(n) *Regulations.*

(1) *New Provisions.* Such rules and regulations as are required by this section or are otherwise necessary to carry out this section, including the application form required under subsection (a)—

(A) shall be issued by the Commission in final form, not later than 270 days after the date of enactment of this section; and

(B) shall become effective not later than 270 days after the date of enactment of this section.

(2) *Review of Existing Regulations.* Not later than 270 days after the date of enactment of this section, the Commission shall—

(A) review its existing rules and regulations which employ the term "nationally recognized statistical rating organization" or "NRSRO"; and

(B) amend or revise such rules and regulations in accordance with the purposes of this section, as the Commission may prescribe as necessary or appropriate in the public interest or for the protection of investors.

(o) *NRSROs Subject to Commission Authority.*

(1) *In General.* No provision of the laws of any State or political subdivision thereof requiring the registration, licensing, or qualification as a credit rating agency or a nationally recognized statistical rating organization shall apply to any nationally recognized statistical rating organization or person employed by or working under the control of a nationally recognized statistical rating organization.

(2) *Limitation.* Nothing in this subsection prohibits the securities commission (or any agency or office performing like functions) of any State from investigating and bringing an enforcement action with respect to fraud or deceit against any nationally recognized statistical rating organization or person associated with a nationally recognized statistical rating organization.

(p) *Regulation of Nationally Recognized Statistical Rating Organizations.*

(1) *Establishment of Office of Credit Ratings.*

(A) *Office Established.* The Commission shall establish within the Commission an Office of Credit Ratings (referred to in this subsection as the "Office") to administer the rules of the Commission—

(i) with respect to the practices of nationally recognized statistical rating organizations in determining ratings, for the protection of users of credit ratings and in the public interest;

(ii) to promote accuracy in credit ratings issued by nationally recognized statistical rating organizations; and

(iii) to ensure that such ratings are not unduly influenced by conflicts of interest.

(B) *Director of the Office.* The head of the Office shall be the Director, who shall report to the Chairman.

(2) *Staffing.* The Office established under this subsection shall be staffed sufficiently to carry out fully the requirements of this section. The staff shall include persons with knowledge of and expertise in corporate, municipal, and structured debt finance.

(3) *Commission Examinations.*

(A) *Annual Examinations Required.* The Office shall conduct an examination of each nationally recognized statistical rating organization at least annually.

(B) *Conduct of Examinations.* Each examination under subparagraph (A) shall include a review of—

(i) whether the nationally recognized statistical rating organization conducts business in accordance with the policies, procedures, and rating methodologies of the nationally recognized statistical rating organization;

(ii) the management of conflicts of interest by the nationally recognized statistical rating organization;

(iii) implementation of ethics policies by the nationally recognized statistical rating organization;

(iv) the internal supervisory controls of the nationally recognized statistical rating organization;

(v) the governance of the nationally recognized statistical rating organization;

(vi) the activities of the individual designated by the nationally recognized statistical rating organization under subsection (j)(1);

(vii) the processing of complaints by the nationally recognized statistical rating organization; and

(viii) the policies of the nationally recognized statistical rating organization governing the post-employment activities of former staff of the nationally recognized statistical rating organization.

(C) *Inspection Reports.* The Commission shall make available to the public, in an easily understandable format, an annual report summarizing—

(i) the essential findings of all examinations conducted under subparagraph (A), as deemed appropriate by the Commission;

(ii) the responses by the nationally recognized statistical rating organizations to any material regulatory deficiencies identified by the Commission under clause (i); and

(iii) whether the nationally recognized statistical rating organizations have appropriately addressed the recommendations of the Commission contained in previous reports under this subparagraph.

(4) *Rulemaking Authority.* The Commission shall—

(A) establish, by rule, fines, and other penalties applicable to any nationally recognized statistical rating organization that violates the requirements of this section and the rules thereunder; and

(B) issue such rules as may be necessary to carry out this section.

(q) *Transparency of Ratings Performance.*

(1) *Rulemaking Required.* The Commission shall, by rule, require that each nationally recognized statistical rating organization publicly disclose information on the initial credit ratings determined by the nationally recognized statistical rating organization for each type of obligor, security, and money market instrument, and any subsequent changes to such credit ratings, for the purpose of allowing users of credit ratings to evaluate the accuracy of ratings and compare the performance of ratings by different nationally recognized statistical rating organizations.

(2) *Content.* The rules of the Commission under this subsection shall require, at a minimum, disclosures that—

(A) are comparable among nationally recognized statistical rating organizations, to allow users of credit ratings to compare the performance of credit ratings across nationally recognized statistical rating organizations;

(B) are clear and informative for investors having a wide range of sophistication who use or might use credit ratings;

(C) include performance information over a range of years and for a variety of types of credit ratings, including for credit ratings withdrawn by the nationally recognized statistical rating organization;

(D) are published and made freely available by the nationally recognized statistical rating organization, on an easily accessible portion of its website, and in writing, when requested;

(E) are appropriate to the business model of a nationally recognized statistical rating organization; and

(F) each nationally recognized statistical rating organization include an attestation with any credit rating it issues affirming that no part of the rating was influenced by any other business activities, that the rating was based solely on the merits of the instruments being rated, and that such rating was an independent evaluation of the risks and merits of the instrument.

(r) *Credit Ratings Methodologies.* The Commission shall prescribe rules, for the protection of investors and in the public interest, with respect to the procedures and methodologies, including qualitative and quantitative data and models, used by nationally recognized statistical rating organizations that require each nationally recognized statistical rating organization—

(1) to ensure that credit ratings are determined using procedures and methodologies, including qualitative and quantitative data and models, that are—

(A) approved by the board of the nationally recognized statistical rating organization, a body performing a function similar to that of a board; and

(B) in accordance with the policies and procedures of the nationally recognized statistical rating organization for the development and modification of credit rating procedures and methodologies;

(2) to ensure that when material changes to credit rating procedures and methodologies (including changes to qualitative and quantitative data and models) are made, that—

(A) the changes are applied consistently to all credit ratings to which the changed procedures and methodologies apply;

(B) to the extent that changes are made to credit rating surveillance procedures and methodologies, the changes are applied to then-current credit ratings by the nationally recognized statistical rating organization within a reasonable time period determined by the Commission, by rule; and

(C) the nationally recognized statistical rating organization publicly discloses the reason for the change; and

(3) to notify users of credit ratings—

(A) of the version of a procedure or methodology, including the qualitative methodology or quantitative inputs, used with respect to a particular credit rating;

(B) when a material change is made to a procedure or methodology, including to a qualitative model or quantitative inputs;

(C) when a significant error is identified in a procedure or methodology, including a qualitative or quantitative model, that may result in credit rating actions; and

(D) of the likelihood of a material change described in subparagraph (B) resulting in a change in current credit ratings.

(s) *Transparency of Credit Rating Methodologies And Information Reviewed.*

(1) *Form for Disclosures.* The Commission shall require, by rule, each nationally recognized statistical rating organization to prescribe a form to accompany the publication of each credit rating that discloses—

(A) information relating to—

(i) the assumptions underlying the credit rating procedures and methodologies;

(ii) the data that was relied on to determine the credit rating; and

(iii) if applicable, how the nationally recognized statistical rating organization used servicer or remittance reports, and with what frequency, to conduct surveillance of the credit rating; and

(B) information that can be used by investors and other users of credit ratings to better understand credit ratings in each class of credit rating issued by the nationally recognized statistical rating organization.

(2) *Format.* The form developed under paragraph (1) shall—

(A) be easy to use and helpful for users of credit ratings to understand the information contained in the report;

(B) require the nationally recognized statistical rating organization to provide the content described in paragraph (3)(B) in a manner that is directly comparable across types of securities; and

(C) be made readily available to users of credit ratings, in electronic or paper form, as the Commission may, by rule, determine.

(3) *Content of Form.*

(A) *Qualitative Content.* Each nationally recognized statistical rating organization shall disclose on the form developed under paragraph (1)—

(i) the credit ratings produced by the nationally recognized statistical rating organization;

(ii) the main assumptions and principles used in constructing procedures and methodologies, including qualitative methodologies and quantitative inputs and assumptions about the correlation of defaults across underlying assets used in rating structured products;

(iii) the potential limitations of the credit ratings, and the types of risks excluded from the credit ratings that the nationally recognized statistical rating organization does not comment on, including liquidity, market, and other risks;

(iv) information on the uncertainty of the credit rating, including—

(I) information on the reliability, accuracy, and quality of the data relied on in determining the credit rating; and

(II) a statement relating to the extent to which data essential to the determination of the credit rating were reliable or limited, including—

(aa) any limits on the scope of historical data; and

(bb) any limits in accessibility to certain documents or other types of information that would have better informed the credit rating;

(v) whether and to what extent third party due diligence services have been used by the nationally recognized statistical rating organization, a description of the information that such third party reviewed in conducting due diligence services, and a description of the findings or conclusions of such third party;

(vi) a description of the data about any obligor, issuer, security, or money market instrument that were relied upon for the purpose of determining the credit rating;

(vii) a statement containing an overall assessment of the quality of information available and considered in producing a rating for an obligor, security, or money market instrument, in relation to the quality of information available to the nationally recognized statistical rating organization in rating similar issuances;

(viii) information relating to conflicts of interest of the nationally recognized statistical rating organization; and

(ix) such additional information as the Commission may require.

(B) *Quantitative Content.* Each nationally recognized statistical rating organization shall disclose on the form developed under this subsection—

(i) an explanation or measure of the potential volatility of the credit rating, including—

(I) any factors that might lead to a change in the credit ratings; and

(II) the magnitude of the change that a user can expect under different market conditions;

(ii) information on the content of the rating, including—

(I) the historical performance of the rating; and

(II) the expected probability of default and the expected loss in the event of default;

(iii) information on the sensitivity of the rating to assumptions made by the nationally recognized statistical rating organization, including—

(I) 5 assumptions made in the ratings process that, without accounting for any other factor, would have the greatest impact on a rating if the assumptions were proven false or inaccurate; and

(II) an analysis, using specific examples, of how each of the 5 assumptions identified under subclause (I) impacts a rating;

(iv) such additional information as may be required by the Commission.

(4) *Due Diligence Services for Asset–Backed Securities.*

(A) *Findings.* The issuer or underwriter of any asset-backed security shall make publicly available the findings and conclusions of any third-party due diligence report obtained by the issuer or underwriter.

(B) *Certification Required.* In any case in which third-party due diligence services are employed by a nationally recognized statistical rating organization, an issuer, or an underwriter, the person providing the due diligence services shall provide to any nationally recognized statistical rating organization that produces a rating to which such services relate, written certification, as provided in subparagraph (C).

(C) *Format and Content.* The Commission shall establish the appropriate format and content for the written certifications required under subparagraph (B), to ensure that providers of due diligence services have conducted a thorough review of data, documentation, and other relevant information necessary for a nationally recognized statistical rating organization to provide an accurate rating.

(D) *Disclosure of Certification.* The Commission shall adopt rules requiring a nationally recognized statistical rating organization, at the time at which the nationally recognized statistical rating organization produces a rating, to disclose the certification described in subparagraph (B) to the public in a manner that allows the public to determine the adequacy and level of due diligence services provided by a third party.

(t) *Corporate Governance, Organization, and Management of Conflicts of Interest.*

(1) *Board of Directors.* Each nationally recognized statistical rating organization shall have a board of directors.

(2) *Independent Directors.*

(A) *In General.* At least 1/2 of the board of directors, but not fewer than 2 of the members thereof, shall be independent of the nationally recognized statistical rating agency. A portion of the independent directors shall include users of ratings from a nationally recognized statistical rating organization.

(B) *Independence Determination.* In order to be considered independent for purposes of this subsection, a member of the board of directors of a nationally recognized statistical rating organization—

(i) may not, other than in his or her capacity as a member of the board of directors or any committee thereof—

(I) accept any consulting, advisory, or other compensatory fee from the nationally recognized statistical rating organization; or

(II) be a person associated with the nationally recognized statistical rating organization or with any affiliated company thereof; and

(ii) shall be disqualified from any deliberation involving a specific rating in which the independent board member has a financial interest in the outcome of the rating.

(C) *Compensation and Term*. The compensation of the independent members of the board of directors of a nationally recognized statistical rating organization shall not be linked to the business performance of the nationally recognized statistical rating organization, and shall be arranged so as to ensure the independence of their judgment. The term of office of the independent directors shall be for a pre-agreed fixed period, not to exceed 5 years, and shall not be renewable.

(3) *Duties of Board of Directors*. In addition to the overall responsibilities of the board of directors, the board shall oversee—

(A) the establishment, maintenance, and enforcement of policies and procedures for determining credit ratings;

(B) the establishment, maintenance, and enforcement of policies and procedures to address, manage, and disclose any conflicts of interest;

(C) the effectiveness of the internal control system with respect to policies and procedures for determining credit ratings; and

(D) the compensation and promotion policies and practices of the nationally recognized statistical rating organization.

(4) *Treatment of NRSRO Subsidiaries*. If a nationally recognized statistical rating organization is a subsidiary of a parent entity, the board of the directors of the parent entity may satisfy the requirements of this subsection by assigning to a committee of such board of directors the duties under paragraph (3), if—

(A) at least ½ of the members of the committee (including the chairperson of the committee) are independent, as defined in this section; and

(B) at least 1 member of the committee is a user of ratings from a nationally recognized statistical rating organization.

(5) *Exception Authority*. If the Commission finds that compliance with the provisions of this subsection present an unreasonable burden on a small nationally recognized statistical rating organization, the Commission may permit the nationally recognized statistical rating organization to delegate such responsibilities to a committee that includes at least one individual who is a user of ratings of a nationally recognized statistical rating organization.

(u) *Duty to Report Tips Alleging Material Violations of Law*.

(1) *Duty to Report*. Each nationally recognized statistical rating organization shall refer to the appropriate law enforcement or regulatory authorities any information that the nationally recognized statistical rating organization receives from a third party and finds credible that alleges that an issuer of securities rated by the nationally recognized statistical rating organization has committed or is committing a material violation of law that has not been adjudicated by a Federal or State court.

(2) *Rule of Construction*. Nothing in paragraph (1) may be construed to require a nationally recognized statistical rating organization to verify the accuracy of the information described in paragraph (1).

(v) *Information From Sources Other Than the Issuer*. In producing a credit rating, a nationally recognized statistical rating organization shall consider information about an issuer that the nationally recognized statistical rating organization has, or receives from a source other than the issuer or underwriter, that the nationally recognized statistical rating organization finds credible and potentially significant to a rating decision.

Registration and Regulation of Security-Based Swap Dealers and Major Security-Based Swap Participants

[*Except for clause 15F(e)(3)(B)(ii) and paragraph 15F(h)(7), which became effective on July 16, 2011, section 15F shall take effect, not less than 60 days after publication of the final rule or regulation implementing the provisions of the Dodd–Frank Act.*]

Sec. 15F. (a) *Registration.*

(1) *Security-Based Swap Dealers.* It shall be unlawful for any person to act as a security-based swap dealer unless the person is registered as a security-based swap dealer with the Commission.

(2) *Major Security-Based Swap Participants.* It shall be unlawful for any person to act as a major security-based swap participant unless the person is registered as a major security-based swap participant with the Commission.

(b) *Requirements.*

(1) *In General.* A person shall register as a security-based swap dealer or major security-based swap participant by filing a registration application with the Commission.

(2) *Contents.*

(A) *In General.* The application shall be made in such form and manner as prescribed by the Commission, and shall contain such information, as the Commission considers necessary concerning the business in which the applicant is or will be engaged.

(B) *Continual Reporting.* A person that is registered as a security-based swap dealer or major security-based swap participant shall continue to submit to the Commission reports that contain such information pertaining to the business of the person as the Commission may require.

(3) *Expiration.* Each registration under this section shall expire at such time as the Commission may prescribe by rule or regulation.

(4) *Rules.* Except as provided in subsections (d) and (e), the Commission may prescribe rules applicable to security-based swap dealers and major security-based swap participants, including rules that limit the activities of non–bank security-based swap dealers and major security-based swap participants.

(5) *Transition.* Not later than 1 year after the date of enactment of the Wall Street Transparency and Accountability Act of 2010, the Commission shall issue rules under this section to provide for the registration of security-based swap dealers and major security-based swap participants.

(6) *Statutory Disqualification.* Except to the extent otherwise specifically provided by rule, regulation, or order of the Commission, it shall be unlawful for a security-based swap dealer or a major security-based swap participant to permit any person associated with a security-based swap dealer or a major security-based swap participant who is subject to a statutory disqualification to effect or be involved in effecting security-based swaps on behalf of the security-based swap dealer or major security-based swap participant, if the security-based swap dealer or major security-based swap participant knew, or in the exercise of reasonable care should have known, of the statutory disqualification.

(c) *Dual Registration.*

(1) *Security-Based Swap Dealer.* Any person that is required to be registered as a security-based swap dealer under this section shall register with the Commission, regardless of whether the person also is registered with the Commodity Futures Trading Commission as a swap dealer.

(2) *Major Security-Based Swap Participant.* Any person that is required to be registered as a major security-based swap participant under this section shall register with the Commission, regardless of whether the person also is registered with the Commodity Futures Trading Commission as a major swap participant.

(d) *Rulemaking.*

(1) *In General.* The Commission shall adopt rules for persons that are registered as security-based swap dealers or major security-based swap participants under this section.

(2) *Exception for Prudential Requirements.*

(A) *In General.* The Commission may not prescribe rules imposing prudential requirements on security-based swap dealers or major security-based swap participants for which there is a prudential regulator.

(B) *Applicability.* Subparagraph (A) does not limit the authority of the Commission to prescribe rules as directed under this section.

(e) *Capital and Margin Requirements.*

(1) *In General.*

(A) *Security-Based Swap Dealers and Major Security-Based Swap Participants that are Banks.* Each registered security-based swap dealer and major security-based swap participant for which there is not a prudential regulator shall meet such minimum capital requirements and minimum initial and variation margin requirements as the prudential regulator shall by rule or regulation prescribe under paragraph (2)(A).

(B) *Security-Based Swap Dealers and Major Security-Based Swap Participants that are not Banks.* Each registered security-based swap dealer and major security-based swap participant for which there is not a prudential regulator shall meet such minimum capital requirements and minimum initial and variation margin requirements as the Commission shall by rule or regulation prescribe under paragraph (2)(B).

(2) *Rules.*

(A) *Security-Based Swap Dealers and Major Security-Based Swap Participants that are Banks.* The prudential regulators, in consultation with the Commission and the Commodity Futures Trading Commission, shall adopt rules for security-based swap dealers and major security-based swap participants, with respect to their activities as a swap dealer or major swap participant, for which there is a prudential regulator imposing—

(i) capital requirements; and

(ii) both initial and variation margin requirements on all security-based swaps that are not cleared by a registered clearing agency.

(B) *Security-Based Swap Dealers and Major Security-Based Swap Participants that are not Banks.* The Commission shall adopt rules for security-based swap dealers and major security-based swap participants, with respect to their activities as a swap dealer or major swap participant, for which there is not a prudential regulator imposing—

(i) capital requirements; and

(ii) both initial and variation margin requirements on all swaps that are not cleared by a registered clearing agency.*

(C) *Capital.* In setting capital requirements for a person that is designated as a security-based swap dealer or a major security-based swap participant for a single type or single class or category of security-based swap or activities, the prudential regulator and the Commission shall take into account the risks associated with other types of security-based swaps or classes of security-based swaps or categories of security-based swaps engaged in and the other activities conducted by that person that are not otherwise subject to regulation applicable to that person by virtue of the status of the person.

(3) *Standards for Capital and Margin.*

(A) *In General.* To offset the greater risk to the security-based swap dealer or major security-based swap participant and the financial system arising from the use of security-based swaps that are not cleared, the requirements imposed under paragraph (2) shall—

(i) help ensure the safety and soundness of the security-based swap dealer or major security-based swap participant; and

(ii) be appropriate for the risk associated with the non–cleared security-based swaps held as a security-based swap dealer or major security-based swap participant.

(B) *Rule of Construction.*

(i) *In General.* Nothing in this section shall limit, or be construed to limit, the authority—

(I) of the Commission to set financial responsibility rules for a broker or dealer registered pursuant to section 15(b) (except for section 15(b)(11) thereof) in accordance with section 15(c)(3); or

(II) of the Commodity Futures Trading Commission to set financial responsibility rules for a futures commission merchant or introducing broker registered pursuant to section 4f(a) of the Commodity Exchange Act (except for section 4f(a)(3) thereof) in accordance with section 4f(b) of the Commodity Exchange Act.

(ii) *Futures Commission Merchants and Other Dealers.* A futures commission merchant, introducing broker, broker, or dealer shall maintain sufficient capital to comply with the stricter of any applicable capital requirements to which such futures commission merchant, introducing broker, broker, or dealer is subject to under this title or the Commodity Exchange Act.

(C) *Margin Requirements.* In prescribing margin requirements under this subsection, the prudential regulator with respect to securi-

* As noted above, this clause became effective on July 16, 2011.

ty-based swap dealers and major security-based swap participants that are depository institutions, and the Commission with respect to security-based swap dealers and major security-based swap participants that are not depository institutions shall permit the use of noncash collateral, as the regulator or the Commission determines to be consistent with—

(i) preserving the financial integrity of markets trading security-based swaps; and

(ii) preserving the stability of the United States financial system.

(D) *Comparability of Capital and Margin Requirements.*

(i) *In General.* The prudential regulators, the Commission, and the Securities and Exchange Commission shall periodically (but not less frequently than annually) consult on minimum capital requirements and minimum initial and variation margin requirements.

(ii) *Comparability.* The entities described in clause (i) shall, to the maximum extent practicable, establish and maintain comparable minimum capital requirements and minimum initial and variation margin requirements, including the use of noncash collateral, for—

(I) security-based swap dealers; and

(II) major security-based swap participants.

(4) *Applicability with Respect to Counterparties.* The requirements of paragraphs (2)(A)(ii) and (2)(B)(ii) shall not apply to a security-based swap in which a counterparty qualifies for an exception under section 3C(g)(1) or satisfies the criteria in section 3C(g)(4).

(f) *Reporting and Recordkeeping.*

(1) *In General.* Each registered security-based swap dealer and major security-based swap participant—

(A) shall make such reports as are required by the Commission, by rule or regulation, regarding the transactions and positions and financial condition of the registered security-based swap dealer or major security-based swap participant;

(B)(i) for which there is a prudential regulator, shall keep books and records of all activities related to the business as a security-based swap dealer or major security-based swap participant in such form and manner and for such period as may be prescribed by the Commission by rule or regulation; and

(ii) for which there is no prudential regulator, shall keep books and records in such form and manner and for such period as may be prescribed by the Commission by rule or regulation; and

(C) shall keep books and records described in subparagraph (B) open to inspection and examination by any representative of the Commission.

(2) *Rules.* The Commission shall adopt rules governing reporting and recordkeeping for security-based swap dealers and major security-based swap participants.

(g) *Daily Trading Records.*

(1) *In General.* Each registered security-based swap dealer and major security-based swap participant shall maintain daily trading records of the security-based swaps of the registered security-based swap dealer and major security-based swap participant and all related records (including related cash or forward transactions) and recorded communications, including electronic mail, instant messages, and recordings of telephone calls, for such period as may be required by the Commission by rule or regulation.

(2) *Information Requirements.* The daily trading records shall include such information as the Commission shall require by rule or regulation.

(3) *Counterparty Records.* Each registered security-based swap dealer and major security-based swap participant shall maintain daily trading records for each counterparty in a manner and form that is identifiable with each security-based swap transaction.

(4) *Audit Trail.* Each registered security-based swap dealer and major security-based swap participant shall maintain a complete audit trail for conducting comprehensive and accurate trade reconstructions.

(5) *Rules.* The Commission shall adopt rules governing daily trading records for security-based swap dealers and major security-based swap participants.

(h) *Business Conduct Standards.*

(1) *In General.* Each registered security-based swap dealer and major security-based swap par-

ticipant shall conform with such business conduct standards as prescribed in paragraph (3) and as may be prescribed by the Commission by rule or regulation that relate to—

(A) fraud, manipulation, and other abusive practices involving security-based swaps (including security-based swaps that are offered but not entered into);

(B) diligent supervision of the business of the registered security-based swap dealer and major security-based swap participant;

(C) adherence to all applicable position limits; and

(D) such other matters as the Commission determines to be appropriate.

(2) *Responsibilities with Respect to Special Entities.*

(A) *Advising Special Entities.* A security-based swap dealer or major security-based swap participant that acts as an advisor to special entity regarding a security-based swap shall comply with the requirements of paragraph (4) with respect to such special entity.

(B) *Entering of Security-Based Swaps with Respect to Special Entities.* A security-based swap dealer that enters into or offers to enter into security-based swap with a special entity shall comply with the requirements of paragraph (5) with respect to such special entity.

(C) *Special Entity Defined.* For purposes of this subsection, the term special entity means—

(i) a Federal agency;

(ii) a State, State agency, city, county, municipality, or other political subdivision of a State or;

(iii) any employee benefit plan, as defined in section 3 of the Employee Retirement Income Security Act of 1974;

(iv) any governmental plan, as defined in section 3 of the Employee Retirement Income Security Act of 1974; or

(v) any endowment, including an endowment that is an organization described in section 501(c)(3) of the Internal Revenue Code of 1986.

(3) *Business Conduct Requirements.* Business conduct requirements adopted by the Commission shall—

(A) establish a duty for a security-based swap dealer or major security-based swap participant to verify that any counterparty meets the eligibility standards for an eligible contract participant;

(B) require disclosure by the security-based swap dealer or major security-based swap participant to any counterparty to the transaction (other than a security-based swap dealer, major security-based swap participant, security-based swap dealer, or major security-based swap participant) of—

(i) information about the material risks and characteristics of the security-based swap;

(ii) any material incentives or conflicts of interest that the security-based swap dealer or major security-based swap participant may have in connection with the security-based swap; and

(iii)(I) for cleared security-based swaps, upon the request of the counterparty, receipt of the daily mark of the transaction from the appropriate derivatives clearing organization; and

(II) for uncleared security-based swaps, receipt of the daily mark of the transaction from the security-based swap dealer or the major security-based swap participant;

(C) establish a duty for a security-based swap dealer or major security-based swap participant to communicate in a fair and balanced manner based on principles of fair dealing and good faith; and

(D) establish such other standards and requirements as the Commission may determine are appropriate in the public interest, for the protection of investors, or otherwise in furtherance of the purposes of this Act.

(4) *Special Requirements for Security-Based Swap Dealers Acting as Advisors.*

(A) *In General.* It shall be unlawful for a security-based swap dealer or major security-based swap participant—

(i) to employ any device, scheme, or artifice to defraud any special entity or prospective customer who is a special entity;

(ii) to engage in any transaction, practice, or course of business that operates as a fraud or deceit on any special entity or prospective customer who is a special entity; or

(iii) to engage in any act, practice, or course of business that is fraudulent, deceptive, or manipulative.

(B) *Duty*. Any security-based swap dealer that acts as an advisor to a special entity shall have a duty to act in the best interests of the special entity.

(C) *Reasonable Efforts*. Any security-based swap dealer that acts as an advisor to a special entity shall make reasonable efforts to obtain such information as is necessary to make a reasonable determination that any security-based swap recommended by the security-based swap dealer is in the best interests of the special entity, including information relating to—

(i) the financial status of the special entity;

(ii) the tax status of the special entity;

(iii) the investment or financing objectives of the special entity; and

(iv) any other information that the Commission may prescribe by rule or regulation.

(5) *Special Requirements for Security-Based Swap Dealers as Counterparties to Special Entities*.

(A) *In General*. Any security-based swap dealer or major security-based swap participant that offers to or enters into a security-based swap with a special entity shall—

(i) comply with any duty established by the Commission for a security-based swap dealer or major security-based swap participant, with respect to a counterparty that is an eligible contract participant within the meaning of subclause (I) or (II) of clause (vii) of section 1a(18) of the Commodity Exchange Act, that requires the security-based swap dealer or major security-based swap participant to have a reasonable basis to believe that the counterparty that is a special entity has an independent representative that—

(I) has sufficient knowledge to evaluate the transaction and risks;

(II) is not subject to a statutory disqualification;

(III) is independent of the security-based swap dealer or major security-based swap participant;

(IV) undertakes a duty to act in the best interests of the counterparty it represents;

(V) makes appropriate disclosures;

(VI) will provide written representations to the special entity regarding fair pricing and the appropriateness of the transaction; and

(VII) in the case of employee benefit plans subject to the Employee Retirement Income Security Act of 1974, is a fiduciary as defined in section 3 of that Act; and

(ii) before the initiation of the transaction, disclose to the special entity in writing the capacity in which the security-based swap dealer is acting.

(B) *Commission Authority*. The Commission may establish such other standards and requirements under this paragraph as the Commission may determine are appropriate in the public interest, for the protection of investors, or otherwise in furtherance of the purposes of this Act.

(6) *Rules*. The Commission shall prescribe rules under this subsection governing business conduct standards for security-based swap dealers and major security-based swap participants.

(7) *Applicability*. This subsection shall not apply with respect to a transaction that is—

(A) initiated by a special entity on an exchange or security-based swaps execution facility; and

(B) the security-based swap dealer or major security-based swap participant does not know the identity of the counterparty to the transaction.

(i) *Documentation Standards*.

(1) *In General*. Each registered security-based swap dealer and major security-based swap participant shall conform with such standards as may be prescribed by the commission, by rule or regulation, that relate to timely and accurate confirmation, processing, netting, documentation, and valuation of all security-based swaps.

(2) *Rules*. The Commission shall adopt rules governing documentation standards for security-based swap dealers and major security-based swap participants.

(j) *Duties*. Each registered security-based swap dealer and major security-based swap participant shall, at all times, comply with the following requirements:

(1) *Monitoring of Trading.* The security-based swap dealer or major security-based swap participant shall monitor its trading in security-based swaps to prevent violations of applicable position limits.

(2) *Risk Management Procedures.* The security-based swap dealer or major security-based swap participant shall establish robust and professional risk management systems adequate for managing the day–to–day business of the security-based swap dealer or major security-based swap participant.

(3) *Disclosure of General Information.* The security-based swap dealer or major security-based swap participant shall disclose to the Commission and to the prudential regulator for the security-based swap dealer or major security-based swap participant, as applicable, information concerning—

(A) terms and conditions of its security-based swaps;

(B) security-based swap trading operations, mechanisms, and practices;

(C) financial integrity protections relating to security-based swaps; and

(D) other information relevant to its trading in security-based swaps.

(4) *Ability to Obtain Information.* The security-based swap dealer or major security-based swap participant shall—

(A) establish and enforce internal systems and procedures to obtain any necessary information to perform any of the functions described in this section; and

(B) provide the information to the Commission and to the prudential regulator for the security-based swap dealer or major security-based swap participant, as applicable, on request.

(5) *Conflicts of Interest.* The security-based swap dealer and major security-based swap participant shall implement conflict–of–interest systems and procedures that—

(A) establish structural and institutional safeguards to ensure that the activities of any person within the firm relating to research or analysis of the price or market for any security-based swap or acting in a role of providing clearing activities or making determinations as to accepting clearing customers are separated by appropriate informational partitions within the firm from the review, pressure, or oversight of persons whose involvement in pricing, trading, or clearing activities might potentially bias their judgment or supervision and contravene the core principles of open access and the business conduct standards described in this title; and

(B) address such other issues as the Commission determines to be appropriate.

(6) *Antitrust Considerations.* Unless necessary or appropriate to achieve the purposes of this title, the security-based swap dealer or major security-based swap participant shall not—

(A) adopt any process or take any action that results in any unreasonable restraint of trade; or

(B) impose any material anticompetitive burden on trading or clearing.

(7) *Rules.* The Commission shall prescribe rules under this subsection governing duties of security-based swap dealers and major security-based swap participants.

(k) *Designation of Chief Compliance Officer.*

(1) *In General.* Each security-based swap dealer and major security-based swap participant shall designate an individual to serve as a chief compliance officer.

(2) *Duties.* The chief compliance officer shall—

(A) report directly to the board or to the senior officer of the security-based swap dealer or major security-based swap participant;

(B) review the compliance of the security-based swap dealer or major security-based swap participant with respect to the security-based swap dealer and major security-based swap participant requirements described in this section;

(C) in consultation with the board of directors, a body performing a function similar to the board, or the senior officer of the organization, resolve any conflicts of interest that may arise;

(D) be responsible for administering each policy and procedure that is required to be established pursuant to this section;

(E) ensure compliance with this title (including regulations) relating to security-based swaps, including each rule prescribed by the Commission under this section;

(F) establish procedures for the remediation of noncompliance issues identified by the chief compliance officer through any—

(i) compliance office review;

(ii) look-back;

(iii) internal or external audit finding;

(iv) self-reported error; or

(v) validated complaint; and

(G) establish and follow appropriate procedures for the handling, management response, remediation, retesting, and closing of noncompliance issues.

(3) *Annual Reports.*

(A) *In General.* In accordance with rules prescribed by the Commission, the chief compliance officer shall annually prepare and sign a report that contains a description of—

(i) the compliance of the security-based swap dealer or major swap participant with respect to this title (including regulations); and

(ii) each policy and procedure of the security-based swap dealer or major security-based swap participant of the chief compliance officer (including the code of ethics and conflict of interest policies).

(B) *Requirements.* A compliance report under subparagraph (A) shall—

(i) accompany each appropriate financial report of the security-based swap dealer or major security-based swap participant that is required to be furnished to the Commission pursuant to this section; and

(ii) include a certification that, under penalty of law, the compliance report is accurate and complete.

(*l*) *Enforcement and Administrative Proceeding Authority.*

(1) *Primary Enforcement Authority.*

(A) *Securities and Exchange Commission.* Except as provided in subparagraph (B), (C), or (D), the Commission shall have primary authority to enforce subtitle B, and the amendments made by subtitle B of the Wall Street Transparency and Accountability Act of 2010, with respect to any person.

(B) *Prudential Regulators.* The prudential regulators shall have exclusive authority to enforce the provisions of subsection (e) and other prudential requirements of this title (including risk management standards), with respect to security-based swap dealers or major security-based swap participants for which they are the prudential regulator.

(C) *Referral.*

(i) *Violations of Nonprudential Requirements.* If the appropriate Federal banking agency for security-based swap dealers or major security-based swap participants that are depository institutions has cause to believe that such security-based swap dealer or major security-based swap participant may have engaged in conduct that constitutes a violation of the nonprudential requirements of this section or rules adopted by the Commission thereunder, the agency may recommend in writing to the Commission that the Commission initiate an enforcement proceeding as authorized under this title. The recommendation shall be accompanied by a written explanation of the concerns giving rise to the recommendation.

(ii) *Violations of Prudential Requirements.* If the Commission has cause to believe that a securities-based swap dealer or major securities–based swap participant that has a prudential regulator may have engaged in conduct that constitute a violation of the prudential requirements of subsection (e) or rules adopted thereunder, the Commission may recommend in writing to the prudential regulator that the prudential regulator initiate an enforcement proceeding as authorized under this title. The recommendation shall be accompanied by a written explanation of the concerns giving rise to the recommendation.

(D) *Backstop Enforcement Authority.*

(i) *Initiation of Enforcement Proceeding by Prudential Regulator.* If the Commission does not initiate an enforcement proceeding before the end of the 90–day period beginning on the date on which the Commission receives a written report under subsection (C)(i), the prudential regulator may initiate an enforcement proceeding.

(ii) *Initiation of Enforcement Proceeding by Commission.* If the prudential regulator does not initiate an enforcement proceeding before the end of the 90–day period beginning on the date on which the prudential regulator receives a written report under subsection (C)(ii), the Commission may initiate an enforcement proceeding.

(2) *Censure, Denial, Suspension; Notice and Hearing.* The Commission, by order, shall censure, place limitations on the activities, functions, or operations of, or revoke the registration of any security-based swap dealer or major security-based swap participant that has registered with the Commission pursuant to subsection (b) if the Commission finds, on the record after notice and opportunity for hearing, that such censure, placing of limitations, or revocation is in the public interest and that such security-based swap dealer or major security-based swap participant, or any person associated with such security-based swap dealer or major security-based swap participant effecting or involved in effecting transactions in security-based swaps on behalf of such security-based swap dealer or major security-based swap participant, whether prior or subsequent to becoming so associated—

(A) has committed or omitted any act, or is subject to an order or finding, enumerated in subparagraph (A), (D), or (E) of paragraph (4) of section 15(b);

(B) has been convicted of any offense specified in subparagraph (B) of such paragraph (4) within 10 years of the commencement of the proceedings under this subsection;

(C) is enjoined from any action, conduct, or practice specified in subparagraph (C) of such paragraph (4);

(D) is subject to an order or a final order specified in subparagraph (F) or (H), respectively, of such paragraph (4); or

(E) has been found by a foreign financial regulatory authority to have committed or omitted any act, or violated any foreign statute or regulation, enumerated in subparagraph (G) of such paragraph (4).

(3) *Associated Persons.* With respect to any person who is associated, who is seeking to become associated, or, at the time of the alleged misconduct, who was associated or was seeking to become associated with a security-based swap dealer or major security-based swap participant for the purpose of effecting or being involved in effecting security-based swaps on behalf of such security-based swap dealer or major security-based swap participant, the Commission, by order, shall censure, place limitations on the activities or functions of such person, or suspend for a period not exceeding 12 months, or bar such person from being associated with a security-based swap dealer or major security-based swap participant, if the Commission finds, on the record after notice and opportunity for a hearing, that such censure, placing of limitations, suspension, or bar is in the public interest and that such person—

(A) has committed or omitted any act, or is subject to an order or finding, enumerated in subparagraph (A), (D), or (E) of paragraph (4) of section 15(b);

(B) has been convicted of any offense specified in subparagraph (B) of such paragraph (4) within 10 years of the commencement of the proceedings under this subsection;

(C) is enjoined from any action, conduct, or practice specified in subparagraph (C) of such paragraph (4);

(D) is subject to an order or a final order specified in subparagraph (F) or (H), respectively, of such paragraph (4); or

(E) has been found by a foreign financial regulatory authority to have committed or omitted any act, or violated any foreign statute or regulation, enumerated in subparagraph (G) of such paragraph (4).

(4) *Unlawful Conduct.* It shall be unlawful—

(A) for any person as to whom an order under paragraph (3) is in effect, without the consent of the Commission, willfully to become, or to be, associated with a security-based swap dealer or major security-based swap participant in contravention of such order; or

(B) for any security-based swap dealer or major security-based swap participant to permit such a person, without the consent of the Commission, to become or remain a person associated with the security-based swap dealer or major security-based swap participant in contravention of such order, if such security-based swap dealer or major security-based swap participant knew, or in the exercise of reasonable care should have known, of such order.

Credit Risk Retention

Sec. 15G. (a) *Definitions.* In this section—

(1) the term "Federal banking agencies" means the Office of the Comptroller of the Currency, the Board of Governors of the Federal Reserve System, and the Federal Deposit Insurance Corporation;

(2) the term "insured depository institution" has the same meaning as in section 3(c) of the Federal Deposit Insurance Act;

(3) the term "securitizer" means—

(A) an issuer of an asset-backed security; or

(B) a person who organizes and initiates an asset-backed securities transaction by selling or transferring assets, either directly or indirectly, including through an affiliate, to the issuer; and

(4) the term "originator" means a person who—

(A) through the extension of credit or otherwise, creates a financial asset that collateralizes an asset-backed security; and

(B) sells an asset directly or indirectly to a securitizer.

(b) *Regulations Required.*

(1) *In General.* Not later than 270 days after the date of enactment of this section, the Federal banking agencies and the Commission shall jointly prescribe regulations to require any securitizer to retain an economic interest in a portion of the credit risk for any asset that the securitizer, through the issuance of an asset-backed security, transfers, sells, or conveys to a third party.

(2) *Residential Mortgages.* Not later than 270 days after the date of the enactment of this section, the Federal banking agencies, the Commission, the Secretary of Housing and Urban Development, and the Federal Housing Finance Agency, shall jointly prescribe regulations to require any securitizer to retain an economic interest in a portion of the credit risk for any residential mortgage asset that the securitizer, through the issuance of an asset-backed security, transfers, sells, or conveys to a third party.

(c) *Standards for Regulations.*

(1) *Standards.* The regulations prescribed under subsection (b) shall—

(A) prohibit a securitizer from directly or indirectly hedging or otherwise transferring the credit risk that the securitizer is required to retain with respect to an asset;

(B) require a securitizer to retain—

(i) not less than 5 percent of the credit risk for any asset—

(I) that is not a qualified residential mortgage that is transferred, sold, or conveyed through the issuance of an asset-backed security by the securitizer; or

(II) that is a qualified residential mortgage that is transferred, sold, or conveyed through the issuance of an asset-backed security by the securitizer, if 1 or more of the assets that collateralize the asset-backed security are not qualified residential mortgages; or

(ii) less than 5 percent of the credit risk for an asset that is not a qualified residential mortgage that is transferred, sold, or conveyed through the issuance of an asset-backed security by the securitizer, if the originator of the asset meets the underwriting standards prescribed under paragraph (2)(B);

(C) specify—

(i) the permissible forms of risk retention for purposes of this section;

(ii) the minimum duration of the risk retention required under this section; and

(iii) that a securitizer is not required to retain any part of the credit risk for an asset that is transferred, sold or conveyed through the issuance of an asset-backed security by the securitizer, if all of the assets that collateralize the asset-backed security are qualified residential mortgages;

(D) apply, regardless of whether the securitizer is an insured depository institution;

(E) with respect to a commercial mortgage, specify the permissible types, forms, and amounts of risk retention that would meet the requirements of subparagraph (B), which in the determination of the Federal banking agencies and the Commission may include—

(i) retention of a specified amount or percentage of the total credit risk of the asset;

(ii) retention of the first-loss position by a third-party purchaser that specifically negotiates for the purchase of such first loss position, holds adequate financial resources to back losses, provides due diligence on all individual assets in the pool before the issuance of the asset-backed securities, and meets the same standards for risk retention as the Federal banking agencies and the Commission require of the securitizer;

(iii) a determination by the Federal banking agencies and the Commission that the underwriting standards and controls for the asset are adequate; and

(iv) provision of adequate representations and warranties and related enforcement mechanisms; and

(F) establish appropriate standards for retention of an economic interest with respect to collateralized debt obligations, securities collateralized by collateralized debt obligations, and similar instruments collateralized by other asset-backed securities; and

(G) provide for—

(i) a total or partial exemption of any securitization, as may be appropriate in the public interest and for the protection of investors;

(ii) a total or partial exemption for the securitization of an asset issued or guaranteed by the United States, or an agency of the United States, as the Federal banking agencies and the Commission jointly determine appropriate in the public interest and for the protection of investors, except that, for purposes of this clause, the Federal National Mortgage Association and the Federal Home Loan Mortgage Corporation are not agencies of the United States;

(iii) a total or partial exemption for any asset-backed security that is a security issued or guaranteed by any State of the United States, or by any political subdivision of a State or territory, or by any public instrumentality of a State or territory that is exempt from the registration requirements of the Securities Act of 1933 by reason of section 3(a)(2) of that Act, or a security defined as a qualified scholarship funding bond in section 150(d)(2) of the Internal Revenue Code of 1986, as may be appropriate in the public interest and for the protection of investors; and

(iv) the allocation of risk retention obligations between a securitizer and an originator in the case of a securitizer that purchases assets from an originator, as the Federal banking agencies and the Commission jointly determine appropriate.

(2) *Asset Classes.*

(A) *Asset Classes.* The regulations prescribed under subsection (b) shall establish asset classes with separate rules for securitizers of different classes of assets, including residential mortgages, commercial mortgages, commercial loans, auto loans, and any other class of assets that the Federal banking agencies and the Commission deem appropriate.

(B) *Contents.* For each asset class established under subparagraph (A), the regulations prescribed under subsection (b) shall include underwriting standards established by the Federal banking agencies that specify the terms, conditions, and characteristics of a loan within the asset class that indicate a low credit risk with respect to the loan.

(d) *Originators.* In determining how to allocate risk retention obligations between a securitizer and an originator under subsection (c)(1)(E)(iv), the Federal banking agencies and the Commission shall—

(1) reduce the percentage of risk retention obligations required of the securitizer by the percentage of risk retention obligations required of the originator; and

(2) consider—

(A) whether the assets sold to the securitizer have terms, conditions, and characteristics that reflect low credit risk;

(B) whether the form or volume of transactions in securitization markets creates incentives for imprudent origination of the type of loan or asset to be sold to the securitizer; and

(C) the potential impact of the risk retention obligations on the access of consumers and businesses to credit on reasonable terms, which may not include the transfer of credit risk to a third party.

(e) *Exemptions, Exceptions, and Adjustments.*

(1) *In General.* The Federal banking agencies and the Commission may jointly adopt or issue exemptions, exceptions, or adjustments to the rules issued under this section, including exemptions, exceptions, or adjustments for classes of institutions or assets relating to the risk retention requirement and the prohibition on hedging under subsection (c)(1).

(2) *Applicable Standards.* Any exemption, exception, or adjustment adopted or issued by the Federal banking agencies and the Commission under this paragraph shall—

(A) help ensure high quality underwriting standards for the securitizers and originators of assets that are securitized or available for securitization; and

(B) encourage appropriate risk management practices by the securitizers and originators of assets, improve the access of consumers and businesses to credit on reasonable terms, or otherwise be in the public interest and for the protection of investors.

(3) *Certain Institutions and Programs Exempt.*

(A) *Farm Credit System Institutions.* Notwithstanding any other provision of this section, the requirements of this section shall not apply to any loan or other financial asset made, insured, guaranteed, or purchased by any institution that is subject to the supervision of the Farm Credit Administration, including the Federal Agricultural Mortgage Corporation.

(B) *Other Federal Programs.* This section shall not apply to any residential, multifamily, or health care facility mortgage loan asset, or securitization based directly or indirectly on such an asset, which is insured or guaranteed by the United States or an agency of the United States. For purposes of this subsection, the Federal National Mortgage Association, the Federal Home Loan Mortgage Corporation, and the Federal home loan banks shall not be considered an agency of the United States.

(4) *Exemption for Qualified Residential Mortgages.*

(A) *In General.* The Federal banking agencies, the Commission, the Secretary of Housing and Urban Development, and the Director of the Federal Housing Finance Agency shall jointly issue regulations to exempt qualified residential mortgages from the risk retention requirements of this subsection.

(B) *Qualified Residential Mortgage.* The Federal banking agencies, the Commission, the Secretary of Housing and Urban Development, and the Director of the Federal Housing Finance Agency shall jointly define the term 'qualified residential mortgage' for purposes of this subsection, taking into consideration underwriting and product features that historical loan performance data indicate result in a lower risk of default, such as—

(i) documentation and verification of the financial resources relied upon to qualify the mortgagor;

(ii) standards with respect to—

(I) the residual income of the mortgagor after all monthly obligations;

(II) the ratio of the housing payments of the mortgagor to the monthly income of the mortgagor;

(III) the ratio of total monthly installment payments of the mortgagor to the income of the mortgagor;

(iii) mitigating the potential for payment shock on adjustable rate mortgages through product features and underwriting standards;

(iv) mortgage guarantee insurance or other types of insurance or credit enhancement obtained at the time of origination, to the extent such insurance or credit enhancement reduces the risk of default; and

(v) prohibiting or restricting the use of balloon payments, negative amortization, prepayment penalties, interest-only payments, and other features that have been demonstrated to exhibit a higher risk of borrower default.

(C) *Limitation on Definition.* The Federal banking agencies, the Commission, the Secretary of Housing and Urban Development, and the Director of the Federal Housing Finance Agency in defining the term "qualified residential mortgage", as required by subparagraph (B), shall define that term to be no broader than the definition "qualified mortgage" as the term is defined under section 129C(c)(2) of the Truth in Lending Act, as amended by the Consumer Financial Protection Act of 2010, and regulations adopted thereunder.

(5) *Condition for Qualified Residential Mortgage Exemption.* The regulations issued under paragraph (4) shall provide that an asset-backed security that is collateralized by tranches of other asset-backed securities shall not be exempt from the risk retention requirements of this subsection.

(6) *Certification.* The Commission shall require an issuer to certify, for each issuance of an as-

set-backed security collateralized exclusively by qualified residential mortgages, that the issuer has evaluated the effectiveness of the internal supervisory controls of the issuer with respect to the process for ensuring that all assets that collateralize the asset-backed security are qualified residential mortgages.

(f) *Enforcement*. The regulations issued under this section shall be enforced by—

(1) the appropriate Federal banking agency, with respect to any securitizer that is an insured depository institution; and

(2) the Commission, with respect to any securitizer that is not an insured depository institution.

(g) *Authority of Commission*. The authority of the Commission under this section shall be in addition to the authority of the Commission to otherwise enforce the securities laws.

(h) *Authority to Coordinate on Rulemaking*. The Chairperson of the Financial Stability Oversight Council shall coordinate all joint rulemaking required under this section.

(i) *Effective Date of Regulations*. The regulations issued under this section shall become effective—

(1) with respect to securitizers and originators of asset-backed securities backed by residential mortgages, 1 year after the date on which final rules under this section are published in the Federal Register; and

(2) with respect to securitizers and originators of all other classes of asset-backed securities, 2 years after the date on which final rules under this section are published in the Federal Register.

Directors, Officers, and Principal Stockholders

Sec. 16. (a) *Disclosure Required*.

(1) *Directors, Officers, and Principal Stockholders Required to File*. Every person who is directly or indirectly the beneficial owner of more than 10 percent of any class of any equity security (other than an exempted security) which is registered pursuant to section 12, or who is a director or an officer of the issuer of such security, shall file the statements required by this subsection with the Commission.

(2) *Time of Filing*. The statements required by this subsection shall be filed—

(A) at the time of the registration of such security on a national securities exchange or by the effective date of a registration statement filed pursuant to section 12(g);

(B) within 10 days after he or she becomes such beneficial owner, director, or officer, or within such shorter time as the Commission may establish by rule;

(C) if there has been a change in such ownership, or if such person shall have purchased or sold a security-based swap agreement involving such equity security, before the end of the second business day following the day on which the subject transaction has been executed, or at such other time as the Commission shall establish, by rule, in any case in which the Commission determines that such 2-day period is not feasible.

(3) *Contents of Statements*. A statement filed—

(A) under subparagraph (A) or (B) of paragraph (2) shall contain a statement of the amount of all equity securities of such issuer of which the filing person is the beneficial owner; and

(B) under subparagraph (C) of such paragraph shall indicate ownership by the filing person at the date of filing, any such changes in such ownership, and such purchases and sales of the security-based swap agreements or security-based swaps as have occurred since the most recent such filing under such subparagraph.

(4) *Electronic Filing and Availability*. Beginning not later than 1 year after the date of enactment of the Sarbanes–Oxley Act of 2002—

(A) a statement filed under subparagraph (C) of paragraph (2) shall be filed electronically;

(B) the Commission shall provide each such statement on a publicly accessible Internet site not later than the end of the business day following that filing; and

(C) the issuer (if the issuer maintains a corporate website) shall provide that statement on that corporate website, not later than the end of the business day following that filing.

(b) *Profits from Purchase and Sale of Security within Six Months*. For the purpose of preventing the unfair use of information which may have been obtained by such beneficial owner, director, or officer by reason of his relationship to the issuer, any profit realized by him from any purchase and sale, or any sale and purchase, of any equity security of such issuer (other than an exempted security) or a security-based swap agreement involving any such equity security within any period of less than six months, unless such security or security-based swap agreement was acquired in good faith in connection with a debt previously contracted, shall inure to and be recoverable by the issuer, irrespective of any intention on the part of such beneficial owner, director, or officer in entering into such transaction of holding the security or security-based swap agreement purchased or of not repurchasing the security or security-based swap agreement sold for a period exceeding six months. Suit to recover such profit may be instituted at law or in equity in any court of competent jurisdiction by the issuer, or by the owner of any security of the issuer in the name and in behalf of the issuer if the issuer shall fail or refuse to bring such suit within sixty days after request or shall fail diligently to prosecute the same thereafter; but no such suit shall be brought more than two years after the date such profit was realized. This subsection shall not be construed to cover any transaction where such beneficial owner was not such both at the time of the purchase and sale, or the sale and purchase, of the security or security-based swap agreement or a security-based swap involved, or any transaction or transactions which the Commission by rules and regulations may exempt as not comprehended within the purpose of this subsection.

(c) *Conditions for Sale of Security by Beneficial Owner, Director, or Officers.* It shall be unlawful for any such beneficial owner, director, or officer, directly or indirectly, to sell any equity security of such issuer (other than an exempted security), if the person selling the security or his principal (1) does not own the security sold, or (2) if owning the security, does not deliver it against such sale within twenty days thereafter, or does not within five days after such sale deposit it in the mails or other usual channels of transportation; but no person shall be deemed to have violated this subsection if he proves that notwithstanding the exercise of good faith he was unable to make such delivery or deposit within such time, or that to do so would cause undue inconvenience or expense.

(d) *Securities Held in Investment Account, Transactions in Ordinary Course of Business, and Establishment of Primary or Secondary Market.* The provisions of subsection (b) of this section shall not apply to any purchase and sale, or sale and purchase, and the provisions of subsection (c) of this section shall not apply to any sale, of an equity security not then or theretofore held by him in an investment account, by a dealer in the ordinary course of his business and incident to the establishment or maintenance by him of a primary or secondary market (otherwise than on a national securities exchange or an exchange exempted from registration under section 5 of this title) for such security. The Commission may, by such rules and regulations as it deems necessary or appropriate in the public interest, define and prescribe terms and conditions with respect to securities held in an investment account and transactions made in the ordinary course of business and incident to the establishment or maintenance of a primary or secondary market.

(e) *Application of Section to Foreign or Domestic Arbitrage Transactions.* The provisions of this section shall not apply to foreign or domestic arbitrage transactions unless made in contravention of such rules and regulations as the Commission may adopt in order to carry out the purposes of this section.

(f) *Treatment of Transactions in Security Futures Products.* The provisions of this section shall apply to ownership of and transactions in security futures products.

(g) *Limitation on Commission Authority.* The authority of the Commission under this section with respect to security-based swap agreements shall be subject to the restrictions and limitations of section 3A(b) of this title.

Accounts and Records, Examinations of Exchanges, Members, and Others

Sec. 17. (a) *Rules and Regulations.*

(1) Every national securities exchange, member thereof, broker or dealer who transacts a business in securities through the medium of any such member, registered securities association, registered broker or dealer, registered municipal securities dealer, municipal advisor, registered securities information processor, registered transfer agent, nationally recognized statistical rating organization, and registered clearing agency and the Municipal Securities Rulemaking Board shall make and keep for prescribed periods such records, furnish such copies thereof, and make and disseminate such reports as the Commission, by rule, prescribes as necessary or appropriate in the public interest, for the protection of investors, or otherwise in furtherance of the purposes of this chapter. Any report that a nationally recognized statistical rating organization is required by Commission rules under this paragraph to make and

disseminate to the Commission shall be deemed furnished to the Commission.

(2) Every registered clearing agency shall also make and keep for prescribed periods such records, furnish such copies thereof, and make and disseminate such reports, as the appropriate regulatory agency for such clearing agency, by rule, prescribes as necessary or appropriate for the safeguarding of securities and funds in the custody or control of such clearing agency or for which it is responsible.

(3) Every registered transfer agent shall also make and keep for prescribed periods such records, furnish such copies thereof, and make such reports as the appropriate regulatory agency for such transfer agent, by rule, prescribes as necessary or appropriate in furtherance of the purposes of section 17A of this title.

(b) *Records Subject to Examination.*

(1) *Procedures for Cooperation with Other Agencies.* All records of persons described in subsection (a) of this section are subject at any time, or from time to time, to such reasonable periodic, special, or other examinations by representatives of the Commission and the appropriate regulatory agency for such persons as the Commission or the appropriate regulatory agency for such persons deems necessary or appropriate in the public interest, for the protection of investors, or otherwise in furtherance of the purposes of this title: *Provided, however,* That the Commission shall, prior to conducting any such examination of a—

(A) registered clearing agency, registered transfer agent, or registered municipal securities dealer for which it is not the appropriate regulatory agency, give notice to the appropriate regulatory agency for such clearing agency, transfer agent, or municipal securities dealer of such proposed examination and consult with such appropriate regulatory agency concerning the feasibility and desirability of coordinating such examination with examinations conducted by such appropriate regulatory agency with a view to avoiding unnecessary regulatory duplication or undue regulatory burdens for such clearing agency, transfer agent, or municipal securities dealer; or

(B) broker or dealer registered pursuant to section 15(b)(11), exchange registered pursuant to section 6(g) of this title, or national securities association registered pursuant to section 15A(k), give notice to the Commodity Futures Trading Commission of such proposed examination and consults with the Commodity Futures Trading Commission concerning the feasibility and desirability of coordinating such examination with examinations conducted by the Commodity Futures Trading Commission in order to avoid unnecessary regulatory duplication or undue regulatory burdens for such broker or dealer or exchange.

(2) *Furnishing Data and Reports to CFTC.* The Commission shall notify the Commodity Futures Trading Commission of any examination conducted of any broker or dealer registered pursuant to section 15(b)(11), exchange registered pursuant to section 6(g), or national securities association registered pursuant to section 15A(k) and, upon request, furnish to the Commodity Futures Trading Commission any examination report and data supplied to, or prepared by, the Commission in connection with such examination.

(3) *Use of CFTC Reports.* Prior to conducting an examination under paragraph (1), the Commission shall use the reports of examinations, if the information available therein is sufficient for the purposes of the examination, of—

(A) any broker or dealer registered pursuant to section 15(b)(11);

(B) exchange registered pursuant to section 6(g); or

(C) national securities association registered pursuant to section 15A(k);

that is made by the Commodity Futures Trading Commission, a national securities association registered pursuant to section 15A(k), or an exchange registered pursuant to section 6(g).

(4) *Rules of Construction.*

(A) Notwithstanding any other provision of this subsection, the records of a broker or dealer registered pursuant to section 15(b)(11), an exchange registered pursuant to section 6(g), or a national securities association registered pursuant to section 15A(k) described in this subparagraph shall not be subject to routine periodic examinations by the Commission.

(B) Any recordkeeping rules adopted under this subsection for a broker or dealer registered pursuant to section 15(b)(11), an exchange registered pursuant to section 6(g), or a national securities association registered pursuant to section 15A(k) shall be limited to records with respect to persons, accounts, agreements, contracts, and transactions involving security futures products.

(C) Nothing in the proviso in paragraph (1) shall be construed to impair or limit (other than by the requirement of prior consultation) the power of the Commission under this subsection to examine any clearing agency, transfer agent, or municipal securities dealer or to affect in any way the power of the Commission under any other provision of this title or otherwise to inspect, examine, or investigate any such clearing agency, transfer agent, or municipal securities dealer.

(c) *Copies of Reports Filed with Other Regulatory Agencies.*

(1) Every clearing agency, transfer agent, and municipal securities dealer for which the Commission is not the appropriate regulatory agency shall (A) file with the appropriate regulatory agency for such clearing agency, transfer agent, or municipal securities dealer a copy of any application, notice, proposal, report, or document filed with the Commission by reason of its being a clearing agency, transfer agent, or municipal securities dealer and (B) file with the Commission a copy of any application, notice, proposal, report, or document filed with such appropriate regulatory agency by reason of its being a clearing agency, transfer agent, or municipal securities dealer. The Municipal Securities Rulemaking Board shall file with each agency enumerated in section 3(a)(34)(A) copies of every proposed rule change filed with the Commission pursuant to section 19(b).

(2) The appropriate regulatory agency for a clearing agency, transfer agent, or municipal securities dealer for which the Commission is not the appropriate regulatory agency shall file with the Commission notice of the commencement of any proceeding and a copy of any order entered by such appropriate regulatory agency against any clearing agency, transfer agent, municipal securities dealer, or person associated with a transfer agent or municipal securities dealer, and the Commission shall file with such appropriate regulatory agency, if any, notice of the commencement of any proceeding and a copy of any order entered by the Commission against the clearing agency, transfer agent, or municipal securities dealer, or against any person associated with a transfer agent or municipal securities dealer for which the agency is the appropriate regulatory agency.

(3) The Commission and the appropriate regulatory agency for a clearing agency, transfer agent, or municipal securities dealer for which the Commission is not the appropriate regulatory agency shall each notify the other and make a report of any examination conducted by it of such clearing agency, transfer agent, or municipal securities dealer, and, upon request, furnish to the other a copy of such report and any data supplied to it in connection with such examination.

(4) The Commission or the appropriate regulatory agency may specify that documents required to be filed pursuant to this subsection with the Commission or such agency, respectively, may be retained by the originating clearing agency, transfer agent, or municipal securities dealer, or filed with another appropriate regulatory agency. The Commission or the appropriate regulatory agency (as the case may be) making such a specification shall continue to have access to the document on request.

(d) *Self-Regulatory Organizations.*

(1) The Commission, by rule or order, as it deems necessary or appropriate in the public interest and for the protection of investors, to foster cooperation and coordination among self-regulatory organizations, or to remove impediments to and foster the development of a national market system and national system for the clearance and settlement of securities transactions, may—

(A) with respect to any person who is a member of or participant in more than one self-regulatory organization, relieve any such self-regulatory organization of any responsibility under this title (i) to receive regulatory reports from such person, (ii) to examine such person for compliance, or to enforce compliance by such person, with specified provisions of this title, the rules and regulations thereunder, and its own rules, or (iii) to carry out other specified regulatory functions with respect to such person, and

(B) allocate among self-regulatory organizations the authority to adopt rules with respect to matters as to which, in the absence of such allocation, such self-regulatory organizations share authority under this title.

In making any such rule or entering any such order, the Commission shall take into consideration the regulatory capabilities and procedures of the self-regulatory organizations, availability of staff, convenience of location,

* Editor's note: second comma in the original.

unnecessary regulatory duplication, and such other factors as the Commission may consider germane to the protection of investors, cooperation and coordination among self-regulatory organizations, and the development of a national market system and a national system for the clearance and settlement of securities transactions. The Commission, by rule or order, as it deems necessary or appropriate in the public interest and for the protection of investors, may require any self-regulatory organization relieved of any responsibility pursuant to this paragraph, and any person with respect to whom such responsibility relates, to take such steps as are specified in any such rule or order to notify customers of, and persons doing business with, such person of the limited nature of such self-regulatory organization's responsibility for such person's acts, practices, and course of business.

(2) A self-regulatory organization shall furnish copies of any report of examination of any person who is a member of or a participant in such self-regulatory organization to any other self-regulatory organization of which such person is a member or in which such person is a participant upon the request of such person, such other self-regulatory organization, or the Commission.

(e) *Balance Sheet and Income Statement; Other Financial Statements and Information.*

(1)(A) Every registered broker or dealer shall annually file with the Commission a balance sheet and income statement certified by a independent public accounting firm, or by a registered public accounting firm if the firm is required to be registered under the Sarbanes-Oxley Act of 2002,,* prepared on a calendar or fiscal year basis, and such other financial statements (which shall, as the Commission specifies, be certified) and information concerning its financial condition as the Commission, by rule may prescribe as necessary or appropriate in the public interest or for the protection of investors.

(B) Every registered broker and dealer shall annually send to its customers its certified balance sheet and such other financial statements and information concerning its financial condition as the Commission, by rule, may prescribe pursuant to subsection (a) of this section.

(C) The Commission, by rule or order, may conditionally or unconditionally exempt any registered broker or dealer, or class of such brokers or dealers, from any provision of this paragraph if the Commission determines that such exemption is consistent with the public interest and the protection of investors.

(2) The Commission, by rule, as it deems necessary or appropriate in the public interest or for the protection of investors, may prescribe the form and content of financial statements filed pursuant to this title and the accounting principles and accounting standards used in their preparation.

(f) *Missing, Lost, Counterfeit, and Stolen Securities.*

(1) Every national securities exchange, member thereof, registered securities association, broker, dealer, municipal securities dealer, government securities broker, government securities dealer, registered transfer agent, registered clearing agency, participant therein, member of the Federal Reserve System, and bank whose deposits are insured by the Federal Deposit Insurance Corporation shall—

(A) report to the Commission or other person designated by the Commission and, in the case of securities issued pursuant to chapter 31 of Title 31, to the Secretary of the Treasury such information about securities that are missing, lost, counterfeit, stolen, or cancelled, in such form and within such time as the Commission, by rule, determines is necessary or appropriate in the public interest or for the protection of investors; such information shall be available on request for a reasonable fee, to any such exchange, member, association, broker, dealer, municipal securities dealer, government securities broker, government securities dealer, transfer agent, clearing agency, participant, member of the Federal Reserve System, or insured bank, and such other persons as the Commission, by rule, designates; and

(B) make such inquiry with respect to information reported pursuant to this subsection as the Commission, by rule, prescribes as necessary or appropriate in the public interest or for the protection of investors, to determine whether securities in their custody or control, for which they are responsible, or in which they are effecting, clearing, or settling a transaction have been reported as missing, lost, counterfeit, stolen, cancelled, or reported in such other manner as the Commission, by rule, may prescribe.

(2) Every member of a national securities exchange, broker, dealer, registered transfer agent, registered clearing agency, registered securities

information processor, national securities exchange, and national securities association shall require that each of its partners, directors, officers, and employees be fingerprinted and shall submit such fingerprints, or cause the same to be submitted, to the Attorney General of the United States for identification and appropriate processing. The Commission, by rule, may exempt from the provisions of this paragraph upon specified terms, conditions, and periods, any class of partners, directors, officers, or employees of any such member, broker, dealer, transfer agent, clearing agency, securities information processor, national securities exchange, or national securities association, if the Commission finds that such action is not inconsistent with the public interest or the protection of investors. Notwithstanding any other provision of law, in providing identification and processing functions, the Attorney General shall provide the Commission and self-regulatory organizations designated by the Commission with access to all criminal history record information.

(3)(A) In order to carry out the authority under paragraph (1) above, the Commission or its designee may enter into agreement with the Attorney General to use the facilities of the National Crime Information Center ("NCIC") to receive, store, and disseminate information in regard to missing, lost, counterfeit, or stolen securities and to permit direct inquiry access to NCIC's file on such securities for the financial community.

(B) In order to carry out the authority under paragraph (1) of this subsection, the Commission or its designee and the Secretary of the Treasury shall enter into an agreement whereby the Commission or its designee will receive, store, and disseminate information in the possession, and which comes into the possession, of the Department of the Treasury in regard to missing, lost, counterfeit, or stolen securities.

(4) In regard to paragraphs (1), (2), and (3), above insofar as such paragraphs apply to any bank or member of the Federal Reserve System, the Commission may delegate its authority to:

(A) the Comptroller of the Currency as to national banks;

(B) the Federal Reserve Board in regard to any member of the Federal Reserve System which is not a national bank; and

(C) the Federal Deposit Insurance Corporation for any State bank which is insured by the Federal Deposit Insurance Corporation but which is not a member of the Federal Reserve System.

(5) The Commission shall encourage the insurance industry to require their insured to report expeditiously instances of missing, lost, counterfeit, or stolen securities to the Commission or to such other person as the Commission may, by rule, designate to receive such information.

(g) *Persons Extending Credit.* Any broker, dealer, or other person extending credit who is subject to the rules and regulations prescribed by the Board of Governors of the Federal Reserve System pursuant to this title shall make such reports to the Board as it may require as necessary or appropriate to enable it to perform the functions conferred upon it by this title. If any such broker, dealer, or other person shall fail to make any such report or fail to furnish full information therein, or, if in the judgment of the Board it is otherwise necessary, such broker, dealer, or other person shall permit such inspections to be made by the Board with respect to the business operations of such broker, dealer, or other person as the Board may deem necessary to enable it to obtain the required information.

(h) *Risk Assessment for Holding Company Systems.*

(1) *Obligations to Obtain, Maintain, and Report Information.* Every person who is (A) a registered broker or dealer, or (B) a registered municipal securities dealer for which the Commission is the appropriate regulatory agency, shall obtain such information and make and keep such records as the Commission by rule prescribes concerning the registered person's policies, procedures, or systems for monitoring and controlling financial and operational risks to it resulting from the activities of any of its associated persons, other than a natural person. Such records shall describe, in the aggregate, each of the financial and securities activities conducted by, and the customary sources of capital and funding of, those of its associated persons whose business activities are reasonably likely to have a material impact on the financial or operational condition of such registered person, including its net capital, its liquidity, or its ability to conduct or finance its operations. The Commission, by rule, may require summary reports of such information to be filed with the Commission no more frequently than quarterly.

(2) *Authority to Require Additional Information.* If, as a result of adverse market conditions or based on reports provided to the Commission

pursuant to paragraph (1) of this subsection or other available information, the Commission reasonably concludes that it has concerns regarding the financial or operational condition of (A) any registered broker or dealer, or (B) any registered municipal securities dealer, government securities broker, or government securities dealer for which the Commission is the appropriate regulatory agency, the Commission may require the registered person to make reports concerning the financial and securities activities of any of such person's associated persons, other than a natural person, whose business activities are reasonably likely to have a material impact on the financial or operational condition of such registered person. The Commission, in requiring reports pursuant to this paragraph, shall specify the information required, the period for which it is required, the time and date on which the information must be furnished, and whether the information is to be furnished directly to the Commission or to a self-regulatory organization with primary responsibility for examining the registered person's financial and operational condition.

(3) *Special Provisions with Respect to Associated Persons Subject to Federal Banking Agency Regulation.*

(A) *Cooperation in Implementation.* In developing and implementing reporting requirements pursuant to paragraph (1) of this subsection with respect to associated persons subject to examination by or reporting requirements of a Federal banking agency, the Commission shall consult with and consider the views of each such Federal banking agency. If a Federal banking agency comments in writing on a proposed rule of the Commission under this subsection that has been published for comment, the Commission shall respond in writing to such written comment before adopting the proposed rule. The Commission shall, at the request of the Federal banking agency, publish such comment and response in the Federal Register at the time of publishing the adopted rule.

(B) *Use of Banking Agency Reports.* A registered broker, dealer, or municipal securities dealer shall be in compliance with any recordkeeping or reporting requirement adopted pursuant to paragraph (1) of this subsection concerning an associated person that is subject to examination by or reporting requirements of a Federal banking agency if such broker, dealer, or municipal securities dealer utilizes for such recordkeeping or reporting requirement copies of reports filed by the associated person with the Federal banking agency pursuant to section 5211 of the Revised Statutes, section 9 of the Federal Reserve Act, section 7(a) of the Federal Deposit Insurance Act, section 10(b) of the Home Owners' Loan Act, or section 8 of the Bank Holding Company Act of 1956. The Commission may, however, by rule adopted pursuant to paragraph (1), require any broker, dealer, or municipal securities dealer filing such reports with the Commission to obtain, maintain, or report supplemental information if the Commission makes an explicit finding that such supplemental information is necessary to inform the Commission regarding potential risks to such broker, dealer, or municipal securities dealer. Prior to requiring any such supplemental information, the Commission shall first request the Federal banking agency to expand its reporting requirements to include such information.

(C) *Procedure for Requiring Additional Information.* Prior to making a request pursuant to paragraph (2) of this subsection for information with respect to an associated person that is subject to examination by or reporting requirements of a Federal banking agency, the Commission shall—

(i) notify such agency of the information required with respect to such associated person; and

(ii) consult with such agency to determine whether the information required is available from such agency and for other purposes, unless the Commission determines that any delay resulting from such consultation would be inconsistent with ensuring the financial and operational condition of the broker, dealer, municipal securities dealer, government securities broker, or government securities dealer or the stability or integrity of the securities markets.

(D) *Exclusion for Examination Reports.* Nothing in this subsection shall be construed to permit the Commission to require any registered broker or dealer, or any registered municipal securities dealer, government securities broker, or government securities dealer for which the Commission is the appropriate regulatory agency, to obtain, maintain, or furnish any examination report of any Federal banking agency or any supervisory recommendations or analysis contained therein.

(E) *Confidentiality of Information Provided.* No information provided to or obtained by the Commission from any Federal banking agency pursuant to a request by the Commission under subparagraph (C) of this paragraph regarding any associated person which is subject to examination by or reporting requirements of a Federal banking agency may be disclosed to any other person (other than a self-regulatory organization), without the prior written approval of the Federal banking agency. Nothing in this subsection shall authorize the Commission to withhold information from Congress, or prevent the Commission from complying with a request for information from any other Federal department or agency requesting the information for purposes within the scope of its jurisdiction, or complying with an order of a court of the United States in an action brought by the United States or the Commission.

(F) *Notice to Banking Agencies Concerning Financial and Operational Condition Concerns.* The Commission shall notify the Federal banking agency of any concerns of the Commission regarding significant financial or operational risks resulting from the activities of any registered broker or dealer, or any registered municipal securities dealer, government securities broker, or government securities dealer for which the Commission is the appropriate regulatory agency, to any associated person thereof which is subject to examination by or reporting requirements of the Federal banking agency.

(G) *Definition.* For purposes of this paragraph, the term "Federal banking agency" shall have the same meaning as the term "appropriate Federal bank agency" in section 3(q) of the Federal Deposit Insurance Act.

(4) *Exemptions.* The Commission by rule or order may exempt any person or class of persons, under such terms and conditions and for such periods as the Commission shall provide in such rule or order, from the provisions of this subsection, and the rules thereunder. In granting such exemptions, the Commission shall consider, among other factors—

(A) whether information of the type required under this subsection is available from a supervisory agency (as defined in section 1101(6) of the Right to Financial Privacy Act of 1978, a State insurance commission or similar State agency, the Commodity Futures Trading Commission, or a similar foreign regulator;

(B) the primary business of any associated person;

(C) the nature and extent of domestic or foreign regulation of the associated person's activities;

(D) the nature and extent of the registered person's securities activities; and

(E) with respect to the registered person and its associated persons, on a consolidated basis, the amount and proportion of assets devoted to, and revenues derived from, activities in the United States securities markets.

(5) *Authority to Limit Disclosure of Information.* Notwithstanding any other provision of law, the Commission shall not be compelled to disclose any information required to be reported under this subsection, or any information supplied to the Commission by any domestic or foreign regulatory agency that relates to the financial or operational condition of any associated person of a registered broker, dealer, government securities broker, government securities dealer, or municipal securities dealer. Nothing in this subsection shall authorize the Commission to withhold information from Congress, or prevent the Commission from complying with a request for information from any other Federal department or agency requesting the information for purposes within the scope of its jurisdiction, or complying with an order of a court of the United States in an action brought by the United States or the Commission. For purposes of section 552 of title 5, United States Code, this subsection shall be considered a statute described in subsection (b)(3)(B) of such section 552. In prescribing regulations to carry out the requirements of this subsection, the Commission shall designate information described in or obtained pursuant to subparagraph (B) or (C) of paragraph (3) of this subsection as confidential information for purposes of section 24(b)(2) of this title.

(i) *Authority to Limit Disclosure of Information.* Notwithstanding any other provision of law, the Commission shall not be compelled to disclose any information required to be reported under subsection (h) or (i) of this section or any information supplied to the Commission by any domestic or foreign regulatory agency that relates to the financial or operational condition of any associated person of a broker or dealer, investment bank holding company, or any affiliate of an investment bank holding company. Nothing in this subsection shall authorize the Commission to withhold information from Congress, or prevent the Commission from complying with a request for information from any other Federal department or agency or any self-regulatory organization requesting the information for purposes within the scope of its jurisdiction, or complying with an order of a court of the United States in an action brought by the United States or the Commission. For purposes of section 552 of title 5, United States code, this subsection shall be considered a statute described in subsection (b)(3)(B) of such section 552. In prescribing regulations to carry out the requirements of this subsection, the Commission shall designate information described in or obtained pursuant to subparagraphs (A), (B), and (C) of subsection (i)(5) as confidential information for purposes of section 24(b)(2) of this title.

(j) *Coordination of Examining Authorities.*

(1) *Elimination of Duplication.* The Commission and the examining authorities, through cooperation and coordination of examination and oversight activities, shall eliminate any unnecessary and burdensome duplication in the examination process.

(2) *Coordination of Examinations.* The Commission and the examining authorities shall share such information, including reports of examinations, customer complaint information, and other nonpublic regulatory information, as appropriate to foster a coordinated approach to regulatory oversight of brokers and dealers that are subject to examination by more than one examining authority.

(3) *Examinations for Cause.* At any time, any examining authority may conduct an examination for cause of any broker or dealer subject to its jurisdiction.

(4) *Confidentiality.*

(A) *In General.* Section 24 shall apply to the sharing of information in accordance with this subsection. The Commission shall take appropriate action under section 24(c) to ensure that such information is not inappropriately disclosed.

(B) *Appropriate Disclosure Not Prohibited.* Nothing in this paragraph authorizes the Commission or any examining authority to withhold information from the Congress, or prevent the Commission or any examining authority from complying with a request for information from any other Federal department or agency requesting the information for purposes within the scope of its jurisdiction, or complying with an order of a court of the United States in an action brought by the United States or the Commission.

(5) *Definition.* For purposes of this subsection, the term "examining authority" means a self-regulatory organization registered with the Commission under this title (other than a registered clearing agency) with the authority to examine, inspect, and otherwise oversee the activities of a registered broker or dealer.

National System for Clearance and Settlement of Securities Transactions

Sec. 17A. (a) *Congressional Findings; Facilitating Establishment of System.*

(1) The Congress finds that—

(A) The prompt and accurate clearance and settlement of securities transactions, including the transfer of record ownership and the safeguarding of securities and funds related thereto, are necessary for the protection of investors and persons facilitating transactions by and acting on behalf of investors.

(B) Inefficient procedures for clearance and settlement impose unnecessary costs on investors and persons facilitating transactions by and acting on behalf of investors.

(C) New data processing and communications techniques create the opportunity for more efficient, effective, and safe procedures for clearance and settlement.

(D) The linking of all clearance and settlement facilities and the development of uniform standards and procedures for clearance and settlement will reduce unnecessary costs and increase the protection of investors and persons facilitating transactions by and acting on behalf of investors.

(2)(A) The Commission is directed, therefore, having due regard for the public interest, the protection of investors, the safeguarding of securities and funds, and maintenance of fair competition among brokers and dealers, clearing agencies, and transfer agents, to use its authority under this title—

(i) to facilitate the establishment of a national system for the prompt and accurate clearance and settlement of transactions in securities (other than exempt securities); and

(ii) to facilitate the establishment of linked or coordinated facilities for clearance and settlement of transactions in securities, securities options, contracts of sale for future delivery and options thereon, and commodity options;

in accordance with the findings and to carry out the objectives set forth in paragraph (1) of this subsection.

(B) The Commission shall use its authority under this title to assure equal regulation under this title of registered clearing agencies and registered transfer agents. In carrying out its responsibilities set forth in subparagraph (A)(ii) of this paragraph, the Commission shall coordinate with the Commodity Futures Trading Commission and consult with the Board of Governors of the Federal Reserve System.

(b) *Registration of Clearing Agencies; Application; Determinations by Commission Requisite to Registration of Applicant as Clearing Agency; Denial of Participation; Discipline; Summary Proceedings.*

(1) Except as otherwise provided in this section, it shall be unlawful for any clearing agency, unless registered in accordance with this subsection, directly or indirectly, to make use of the mails or any means or instrumentality of interstate commerce to perform the functions of a clearing agency with respect to any security (other than an exempted security). The Commission, by rule or order, upon its own motion or upon application, may conditionally or unconditionally exempt any clearing agency or security or any class of clearing agencies or securities from any provision of this section or the rules or regulations thereunder, if the Commission finds that such exemption is consistent with the public interest, the protection of investors, and the purposes of this section, including the prompt and accurate clearance and settlement of securities transactions and the safeguarding of securities and funds. A clearing agency or transfer agent shall not perform the functions of both a clearing agency and a transfer agent unless such clearing agency or transfer agent is registered in accordance with this subsection and subsection (c) of this section.*

(2) A clearing agency may be registered under the terms and conditions hereinafter provided in this subsection and in accordance with the provisions of section 19(a) of this title, by filing with the Commission an application for registration in such form as the Commission, by rule, may prescribe containing the rules of the clearing agency and such other information and documents as the Commission, by rule, may prescribe as necessary or appropriate in the public interest or for the prompt and accurate clearance and settlement of securities transactions.

(3) A clearing agency shall not be registered unless the Commission determines that—

(A) Such clearing agency is so organized and has the capacity to be able to facilitate the prompt and accurate clearance and settlement of securities transactions and derivative agreements, contracts, and transactions for which it is responsible, to safeguard securities and funds in its custody or control or for which it is responsible, to comply with the provisions of this title and the rules and regulations thereunder, to enforce (subject to any rule or order of the Commission pursuant to section 17(d) or 19(g)(2) of this title) compliance by its participants with the rules of the clearing agency, and to carry out the purposes of this section.

(B) Subject to the provisions of paragraph (4) of this subsection, the rules of the clearing agency provide that any (i) registered broker or dealer, (ii) other registered clearing agency, (iii) registered investment company, (iv) bank, (v) insurance company, or (vi) other person or class of persons as the Commission, by rule, may from time to time designate as appropriate to the development of a national system for the prompt and accurate clearance and settlement of securities transactions may become a participant in such clearing agency.

(C) The rules of the clearing agency assure a fair representation of its shareholders (or members) and participants in the selection of its directors and administration of its affairs. (The Commission may determine that the representation of participants is fair if they are afforded a reasonable opportunity to acquire voting stock of the clearing agency, directly or indirectly, in reasonable proportion to their use of such clearing agency.)

* On July 1, 2011, the SEC issued an Order Pursuant to Section 36 of the Securities Exchange Act of 1934 Granting Temporary Exemptions from Clearing Agency Registration Requirements under Section 17A(b) of the Exchange Act for Entities Providing Certain Clearing Services for Security-Based Swaps. This order provides a temporary exemption for persons that would be required to register as a clearing agency, provided that they comply with notice provisions. The SEC release number is 34–64796.

(D) The rules of the clearing agency provide for the equitable allocation of reasonable dues, fees, and other charges among its participants.

(E) The rules of the clearing agency do not impose any schedule of prices, or fix rates or other fees, for services rendered by its participants.

(F) The rules of the clearing agency are designed to promote the prompt and accurate clearance and settlement of securities transactions and, to the extent applicable, derivative agreements, contracts, and transactions, to assure the safeguarding of securities and funds which are in the custody or control of the clearing agency or for which it is responsible, to foster cooperation and coordination with persons engaged in the clearance and settlement of securities transactions, to remove impediments to and perfect the mechanism of a national system for the prompt and accurate clearance and settlement of securities transactions, and, in general, to protect investors and the public interest; and are not designed to permit unfair discrimination in the admission of participants or among participants in the use of the clearing agency, or to regulate by virtue of any authority conferred by this title matters not related to the purposes of this section or the administration of the clearing agency.

(G) The rules of the clearing agency provide that (subject to any rule or order of the Commission pursuant to section 17(d) or 19(g)(2) of this title) its participants shall be appropriately disciplined for violation of any provision of the rules of the clearing agency by expulsion, suspension, limitation of activities, functions, and operations, fine, censure, or any other fitting sanction.

(H) The rules of the clearing agency are in accordance with the provisions of paragraph (5) of this subsection, and, in general, provide a fair procedure with respect to the disciplining of participants, the denial of participation to any person seeking participation therein, and the prohibition or limitation by the clearing agency of any person with respect to access to services offered by the clearing agency.

(I) The rules of the clearing agency do not impose any burden on competition not necessary or appropriate in furtherance of the purposes of this title.

(4)(A) A registered clearing agency may, and in cases in which the Commission, by order, directs as appropriate in the public interest shall, deny participation to any person subject to a statutory disqualification. A registered clearing agency shall file notice with the Commission not less than thirty days prior to admitting any person to participation, if the clearing agency knew, or in the exercise of reasonable care should have known, that such person was subject to a statutory disqualification. The notice shall be in such form and contain such information as the Commission, by rule, may prescribe as necessary or appropriate in the public interest or for the protection of investors.

(B) A registered clearing agency may deny participation to, or condition the participation of, any person if such person does not meet such standards of financial responsibility, operational capability, experience, and competence as are prescribed by the rules of the clearing agency. A registered clearing agency may examine and verify the qualifications of an applicant to be a participant in accordance with procedures established by the rules of the clearing agency.

(5)(A) In any proceeding by a registered clearing agency to determine whether a participant should be disciplined (other than a summary proceeding pursuant to subparagraph (C) of this paragraph), the clearing agency shall bring specific charges, notify such participant of, and give him an opportunity to defend against such charges, and keep a record. A determination by the clearing agency to impose a disciplinary sanction shall be supported by a statement setting forth—

(i) any act or practice in which such participant has been found to have engaged, or which such participant has been found to have omitted;

(ii) the specific provisions of the rules of the clearing agency which any such act or practice, or omission to act, is deemed to violate; and

(iii) the sanction imposed and the reasons therefor.

(B) In any proceeding by a registered clearing agency to determine whether a person shall be denied participation or prohibited or limited with respect to access to services offered by the clearing agency, the clearing agency shall notify such person of, and give him an opportunity to be heard upon, the specific grounds for denial or prohibition or limitation under consideration and keep a record. A determination by the clearing agency to deny participation or prohibit or limit a person with respect to access to services offered by the clearing agency shall be supported by a statement setting forth the specific grounds on which the denial or prohibition or limitation is based.

(C) A registered clearing agency may summarily suspend and close the accounts of a participant who (i) has been and is expelled or suspended from any self-regulatory organization, (ii) is in default of any delivery of funds or securities to the clearing agency, or (iii) is in such financial or operating difficulty that the clearing agency determines and so notifies the appropriate regulatory agency for such participant that such suspension and closing of accounts are necessary for the protection of the clearing agency, its participants, creditors, or investors. A participant so summarily suspended shall be promptly afforded an opportunity for a hearing by the clearing agency in accordance with the provisions of subparagraph (A) of this paragraph. The appropriate regulatory agency for such participant, by order, may stay any such summary suspension on its own motion or upon application by any person aggrieved thereby, if such appropriate regulatory agency determines summarily or after notice and opportunity for hearing (which hearing may consist solely of the submission of affidavits or presentation of oral arguments) that such stay is consistent with the public interest and protection of investors.

(6) No registered clearing agency shall prohibit or limit access by any person to services offered by any participant therein.

(7)(A) A clearing agency that is regulated directly or indirectly by the Commodity Futures Trading Commission through its association with a designated contract market for security futures products that is a national securities exchange registered pursuant to section 6(g), and that would be required to register pursuant to paragraph (1) of this subsection only because it performs the functions of a clearing agency with respect to security futures products effected pursuant to the rules of the designated contract market with which such agency is associated, is exempted from the provisions of this section and the rules and regulations thereunder, except that if such a clearing agency performs the functions of a clearing agency with respect to a security futures product that is not cash settled, it must have arrangements in place with a registered clearing agency to effect the payment and delivery of the securities underlying the security futures product.

(B) Any clearing agency that performs the functions of a clearing agency with respect to security futures products must coordinate with and develop fair and reasonable links with any and all other clearing agencies that perform the functions of a clearing agency with respect to security futures products, in order to permit, as of the compliance date (as defined in section 6(h)(6)(C)), security futures products to be purchased on one market and offset on another market that trades such products.

(8) A registered clearing agency shall be permitted to provide facilities for the clearance and settlement of any derivative agreements, contracts, or transactions that are excluded from the Commodity Exchange Act, subject to the requirements of this section and to such rules and regulations as the Commission may prescribe as necessary or appropriate in the public interest, for the protection of investors, or otherwise in furtherance of the purposes of this title.

(c) *Registration of Transfer Agents.*

(1) Except as otherwise provided in this section, it shall be unlawful for any transfer agent, unless registered in accordance with this section, directly or indirectly, to make use of the mails or any means or instrumentality of interstate commerce to perform the function of a transfer agent with respect to any security registered under section 12 of this title or which would be required to be registered except for the exemption from registration provided by subsection (g)(2)(B) or (g)(2)(G) of that section. The appropriate regulatory agency, by rule or order, upon its own motion or upon application, may conditionally or unconditionally exempt any person or security or class of persons or securities from any provision of this section or any rule or regulation prescribed under this section, if the appropriate regulatory agency finds (A) that such exemption is in the public interest and consistent with the protection of investors and the purposes of this section, including the prompt and accurate clearance and settlement of securities transactions and the safeguarding of securities and funds, and (B) the Commission does not object to such exemption.

(2) A transfer agent may be registered by filing with the appropriate regulatory agency for such transfer agent an application for registration in such form and containing such information and

documents concerning such transfer agent and any persons associated with the transfer agent as such appropriate regulatory agency may prescribe as necessary or appropriate in furtherance of the purposes of this section. Except as hereinafter provided, such registration shall become effective 45 days after receipt of such application by such appropriate regulatory agency or within such shorter period of time as such appropriate regulatory agency may determine.

(3) The appropriate regulatory agency for a transfer agent, by order, shall deny registration to, censure, place limitations on the activities, functions, or operations of, suspend for a period not exceeding 12 months, or revoke the registration of such transfer agent, if such appropriate regulatory agency finds, on the record after notice and opportunity for hearing, that such denial, censure, placing of limitations, suspension, or revocation is in the public interest and that such transfer agent, whether prior or subsequent to becoming such, or any person associated with such transfer agent, whether prior or subsequent to becoming so associated—

(A) has committed or omitted any act, or is subject to an order or finding, enumerated in subparagraph (A), (D), (E), (G), or (H) of paragraph (4) of section 15(b) of this title, has been convicted of any offense specified in subparagraph (B) of such paragraph (4) within ten years of the commencement of the proceedings under this paragraph, or is enjoined from any action, conduct, or practice specified in subparagraph (C) of such paragraph (4); or

(B) is subject to an order entered pursuant to subparagraph (C) of paragraph (4) of this subsection barring or suspending the right of such person to be associated with a transfer agent.

(4)(A) Pending final determination whether any registration by a transfer agent under this subsection shall be denied, the appropriate regulatory agency for such transfer agent, by order, may postpone the effective date of such registration for a period not to exceed fifteen days, but if, after notice and opportunity for hearing (which may consist solely of affidavits and oral arguments), it shall appear to such appropriate regulatory agency to be necessary or appropriate in the public interest or for the protection of investors to postpone the effective date of such registration until final determination, such appropriate regulatory agency shall so order. Pending final determination whether any registration under this subsection shall be revoked, such appropriate regulatory agency, by order, may suspend such registration, if such suspension appears to such appropriate regulatory agency, after notice and opportunity for hearing, to be necessary or appropriate in the public interest or for the protection of investors.

(B) A registered transfer agent may, upon such terms and conditions as the appropriate regulatory agency for such transfer agent deems necessary or appropriate in the public interest, for the protection of investors, or in furtherance of the purposes of this section, withdraw from registration by filing a written notice of withdrawal with such appropriate regulatory agency. If such appropriate regulatory agency finds that any transfer agent for which it is the appropriate regulatory agency, is no longer in existence or has ceased to do business as a transfer agent, such appropriate regulatory agency, by order, shall cancel or deny the registration.

(C) The appropriate regulatory agency for a transfer agent, by order, shall censure or place limitations on the activities or functions of any person associated, seeking to become associated, or, at the time of the alleged misconduct, associated or seeking to become associated with the transfer agent, or suspend for a period not exceeding 12 months or bar any such person from being associated with any transfer agent, broker, dealer, investment adviser, municipal securities dealer, municipal advisor, or nationally recognized statistical rating organization, if the appropriate regulatory agency finds, on the record after notice and opportunity for hearing, that such censure, placing of limitations, suspension, or bar is in the public interest and that such person has committed or omitted any act, or is subject to an order or finding, enumerated in subparagraph (A), (D), (E), (H), or (G) or* paragraph (4) of Section 15(b) of this title, has been convicted of any offense specified in subparagraph (B) of such paragraph (4) within ten years of the commencement of the proceedings under this paragraph, or is enjoined from any action, conduct, or practice specified in subparagraph (C) of such paragraph (4). It shall be unlawful for any person as to whom such an order suspending or barring him from being associated with a transfer agent is in effect willfully to become, or to be, associated with a transfer agent without the consent of the appropriate

* Editor's note: Or in original. Probably should be of.

propriate regulatory agency that entered the order and the appropriate regulatory agency for that transfer agent. It shall be unlawful for any transfer agent to permit such a person to become, or remain, a person associated with it without the consent of such appropriate regulatory agencies, if the transfer agent knew, or in the exercise of reasonable care should have known, of such order. The Commission may establish, by rule, procedures by which a transfer agent reasonably can determine whether a person associated or seeking to become associated with it is subject to any such order, and may require, by rule, that any transfer agent comply with such procedures.

(d) *Activities of Clearing Agencies and Transfer Agents; Enforcement by Appropriate Regulatory Agencies.*

(1) No registered clearing agency or registered transfer agent shall, directly or indirectly, engage in any activity as clearing agency or transfer agent in contravention of such rules and regulations (A) as the Commission may prescribe as necessary or appropriate in the public interest, for the protection of investors, or otherwise in furtherance of the purposes of this title, or (B) as the appropriate regulatory agency for such clearing agency or transfer agent may prescribe as necessary or appropriate for the safeguarding of securities and funds.

(2) With respect to any clearing agency or transfer agent for which the Commission is not the appropriate regulatory agency, the appropriate regulatory agency for such clearing agency or transfer agent may, in accordance with section 8 of the Federal Deposit Insurance Act, enforce compliance by such clearing agency or transfer agent with the provisions of this section, sections 17 and 19 of this title, and the rules and regulations thereunder. For purpose of the preceding sentence, any violation of any such provision shall constitute adequate basis for the issuance of an order under section 8(b) or 8(c) of the Federal Deposit Insurance Act, and the participants in any such clearing agency and the persons doing business with any such transfer agent shall be deemed to be "depositors" as that term is used in section 8(c) of that Act.

(3)(A) With respect to any clearing agency or transfer agent for which the Commission is not the appropriate regulatory agency, the Commission and the appropriate regulatory agency for such clearing agency or transfer agent shall consult and cooperate with each other, and, as may be appropriate, with State banking authorities having supervision over such clearing agency or transfer agent toward the end that, to the maximum extent practicable, their respective regulatory responsibilities may be fulfilled and the rules and regulations applicable to such clearing agency or transfer agent may be in accord with both sound banking practices and a national system for the prompt and accurate clearance and settlement of securities transactions. In accordance with this objective—

(i) the Commission and such appropriate regulatory agency shall, at least fifteen days prior to the issuance for public comment of any proposed rule or regulation or adoption of any rule or regulation concerning such clearing agency or transfer agent, consult and request the views of the other; and

(ii) such appropriate regulatory agency shall assume primary responsibility to examine and enforce compliance by such clearing agency or transfer agent with the provisions of this section and sections 17 and 19 of this title.

(B) Nothing in the preceding subparagraph or elsewhere in this title shall be construed to impair or limit (other than by the requirement of notification) the Commission's authority to make rules under any provision of this title or to enforce compliance pursuant to any provision of this title by any clearing agency, transfer agent, or person associated with a transfer agent with the provisions of this title and the rules and regulations thereunder.

(4) Nothing in this section shall be construed to impair the authority of any State banking authority or other State or Federal regulatory authority having jurisdiction over a person registered as a clearing agency, transfer agent, or person associated with a transfer agent, to make and enforce rules governing such person which are not inconsistent with this title and the rules and regulations thereunder.

(5) A registered transfer agent may not, directly or indirectly, engage in any activity in connection with the guarantee of a signature of an endorser of a security, including the acceptance or rejection of such guarantee, in contravention of such rules and regulations as the Commission may prescribe as necessary or appropriate in the public interest,

for the protection of investors, to facilitate the equitable treatment of financial institutions which issue such guarantees, or otherwise in furtherance of the purposes of this title.

(e) *Physical Movement of Securities Certificates.* The Commission shall use its authority under this title to end the physical movement of securities certificates in connection with the settlement among brokers and dealers of transactions in securities consummated by means of the mails or any means or instrumentalities of interstate commerce.

(f) *Rules Concerning Transfer of Securities and Rights and Obligations of Involved or Affected Parties.*

(1) Notwithstanding any provision of State law, except as provided in paragraph (3), if the Commission makes each of the findings described in paragraph (2)(A), the Commission may adopt rules concerning—

(A) the transfer of certificated or uncertificated securities (other than government securities issued pursuant to chapter 31 of title 31, United States Code, or securities otherwise processed within a book-entry system operated by the Federal Reserve banks pursuant to a Federal book-entry regulation) or limited interests (including security interests) therein; and

(B) rights and obligations of purchasers, sellers, owners, lenders, borrowers, and financial intermediaries (including brokers, dealers, banks, and clearing agencies) involved in or affected by such transfers, and the rights of third parties whose interests in such securities devolve from such transfers.

(2)(A) The findings described in this paragraph are findings by the Commission that—

(i) such rule is necessary or appropriate for the protection of investors or in the public interest and is reasonably designed to promote the prompt, accurate, and safe clearance and settlement of securities transactions;

(ii) in the absence of a uniform rule, the safe and efficient operation of the national system for clearance and settlement of securities transactions will be, or is, substantially impeded; and

(iii) to the extent such rule will impair or diminish, directly or indirectly, rights of persons specified in paragraph (1)(B) under State law concerning transfers of securities (or limited interests therein), the benefits of such rule outweigh such impairment or diminution of rights.

(B) In making the findings described in subparagraph (A), the Commission shall give consideration to the recommendations of the Advisory Committee established under paragraph (4), and it shall consult with and consider the views of the Secretary of the Treasury and the Board of Governors of the Federal Reserve System. If the Secretary of the Treasury objects, in writing, to any proposed rule of the Commission on the basis of the Secretary's view on the issues described in clauses (i), (ii), and (iii) of subparagraph (A), the Commission shall consider all feasible alternatives to the proposed rule, and it shall not adopt any such rule unless the Commission makes an explicit finding that the rule is the most practicable method for achieving safe and efficient operation of the national clearance and settlement system.

(3) Any State may, prior to the expiration of 2 years after the Commission adopts a rule under this subsection, enact a statute that specifically refers to this subsection and the specific rule thereunder and establishes, prospectively from the date of enactment of the State statute, a provision that differs from that applicable under the Commission's rule.

(4)(A) Within 90 days after the date of enactment of this subsection, the Commission shall (and at such times thereafter as the Commission may determine, the Commission may), after consultation with the Secretary of the Treasury and the Board of Governors of the Federal Reserve System, establish an advisory committee under the Federal Advisory Committee Act. The Advisory Committee shall be directed to consider and report to the Commission on such matters as the Commission, after consultation with the Secretary of the Treasury and the Board of Governors of the Federal Reserve System, determines, including the areas, if any, in which State commercial laws and related Federal laws concerning the transfer of certificated or uncertificated securities, limited interests (including security interests) in such securities, or the creation or perfection of security interests in such securities do not provide the necessary certainty, uniformity, and clarity for purchasers, sellers, owners, lenders, borrowers, and financial intermediaries concerning their respective rights and obligations.

(B) The Advisory Committee shall consist of 15 members, of which—

(i) 11 shall be designated by the Commission in accordance with the Federal Advisory Committee Act; and

(ii) 2 each shall be designated by the Board of Governors of the Federal Reserve System and the Secretary of the Treasury.

(C) The Advisory Committee shall conduct its activities in accordance with the Federal Advisory Committee Act. Within 6 months of its designation, or such longer time as the Commission may designate, the Advisory Committee shall issue a report to the Commission, and shall cause copies of that report to be delivered to the Secretary of the Treasury and the Chairman of the Board of Governors of the Federal Reserve System.

(g) *Due Diligence for the Delivery of Dividends, Interest, and Other Valuable Property Rights.*

(1) *Revision of Rules Required.* The Commission shall revise its regulations in 17 CFR 240.17Ad–17, as in effect on December 8, 1997, to extend the application of such section to brokers and dealers and to provide for the following:

(A) A requirement that the paying agent provide a single written notification to each missing security holder that the missing security holder has been sent a check that has not yet been negotiated. The written notification may be sent along with a check or other mailing subsequently sent to the missing security holder but must be provided no later than 7 months after the sending of the not yet negotiated check.

(B) An exclusion for paying agents from the notification requirements when the value of the not yet negotiated check is less than $25.

(C) A provision clarifying that the requirements described in subparagraph (A) shall have no effect on State escheatment laws.

(D) For purposes of such revised regulations—

(i) a security holder shall be considered a "missing security holder" if a check is sent to the security holder and the check is not negotiated before the earlier of the paying agent sending the next regularly scheduled check or the elapsing of 6 months after the sending of the not yet negotiated check; and

(ii) the term "paying agent" includes any issuer, transfer agent, broker, dealer, investment adviser, indenture trustee, custodian, or any other person that accepts payments from the issuer of a security and distributes the payments to the holders of the security.

(2) *Rulemaking.* The Commission shall adopt such rules, regulations, and orders necessary to implement this subsection no later than 1 year after July 21, 2010. In proposing such rules, the Commission shall seek to minimize disruptions to current systems used by or on behalf of paying agents to process payment to account holders and avoid requiring multiple paying agents to send written notification to a missing security holder regarding the same not yet negotiated check.

[*Except for subsection 17A(h) and paragraphs 17(A)(l)(1) and (2), which became effective on July 16, 2011, the following subsections shall take effect, not less than 60 days after publication of final rules implementing the provisions of the Dodd–Frank Act.*]

(g) *Registration Requirement.* It shall be unlawful for a clearing agency, unless registered with the Commission, directly or indirectly to make use of the mails or any means or instrumentality of interstate commerce to perform the functions of a clearing agency with respect to a security-based swap.*

(h) *Voluntary Registration.* A person that clears agreements, contracts, or transactions that are not required to be cleared under this title may register with the Commission as a clearing agency.

(i) *Standards for Clearing Agencies Clearing Security–Based Swap Transactions.* To be registered and to maintain registration as a clearing agency that clears security-based swap transactions, a clearing agency shall comply with such standards as the Commission may establish by rule. In establishing any such standards, and in the exercise of its oversight of such a clearing agency pursuant to this title, the Commission may conform such standards or oversight to reflect evolving United States and international standards. Except where the Commission determines otherwise by rule or regulation, a clearing agency shall have reasonable discretion in establishing the manner in which it complies with any such standards.

(j) *Rules.* The Commission shall adopt rules governing persons that are registered as clearing agencies for security-based swaps under this title.

* Dodd-Frank created two (g)'s.

(k) *Exemptions.* The Commission may exempt, conditionally or unconditionally, a clearing agency from registration under this section for the clearing of security-based swaps if the Commission determines that the clearing agency is subject to comparable, comprehensive supervision and regulation by the Commodity Futures Trading Commission or the appropriate government authorities in the home country of the agency. Such conditions may include, but are not limited to, requiring that the clearing agency be available for inspection by the Commission and make available all information requested by the Commission.

(*l*) *Existing Depository Institutions and Derivative Clearing Organizations.*

(1) *In General.* A depository institution or derivative clearing organization registered with the Commodity Futures Trading Commission under the Commodity Exchange Act that is required to be registered as a clearing agency under this section is deemed to be registered under this section solely for the purpose of clearing security-based swaps to the extent that, before the date of enactment of this subsection—

(A) the depository institution cleared swaps as a multilateral clearing organization; or

(B) the derivative clearing organization cleared swaps pursuant to an exemption from registration as a clearing agency.

(2) *Conversion of Depository Institutions.* A depository institution to which this subsection applies may, by the vote of the shareholders owning not less than 51 percent of the voting interests of the depository institution, be converted into a State corporation, partnership, limited liability company, or similar legal form pursuant to a plan of conversion, if the conversion is not in contravention of applicable State law.

(3) *Sharing of Information.* The Commodity Futures Trading Commission shall make available to the Commission, upon request, all information determined to be relevant by the Commodity Futures Trading Commission regarding a derivatives clearing organization deemed to be registered with the Commission under paragraph (1).

(m) *Modification of Core Principles.* The Commission may conform the core principles established in this section to reflect evolving United States and international standards.

Automated Quotation Systems for Penny Stocks

Sec. 17B. (a) *Findings.* The Congress finds that—

(1) the market for penny stocks suffers from a lack of reliable and accurate quotation and last sale information available to investors and regulators;

(2) it is in the public interest and appropriate for the protection of investors and the maintenance of fair and orderly markets to improve significantly the information available to brokers, dealers, investors, and regulators with respect to quotations for and transactions in penny stocks; and

(3) a fully implemented automated quotation system for penny stocks would meet the information needs of investors and market participants and would add visibility and regulatory and surveillance data to that market.

(b) *Mandate to Facilitate the Establishment of Automated Quotation Systems.*

(1) *In General.* The Commission shall facilitate the widespread dissemination of reliable and accurate last sale and quotation information with respect to penny stocks in accordance with the findings set forth in subsection (a) of this section, with a view toward establishing, at the earliest feasible time, one or more automated quotation systems that will collect and disseminate information regarding all penny stocks.

(2) *Characteristics of Systems.* Each such automated quotation system shall—

(A) be operated by a registered securities association or a national securities exchange in accordance with such rules as the Commission and these entities shall prescribe;

(B) collect and disseminate quotation and transaction information;

(C) except as provided in subsection (c), provide bid and ask quotations of participating brokers or dealers, or comparably accurate and reliable pricing information, which shall constitute firm bids or offers for at least such minimum numbers of shares or minimum dollar amounts as the Commission and the registered securities association or national securities exchange shall require; and

(D) provide for the reporting of the volume of penny stock transactions, including last sale reporting, when the volume reaches appropriate levels that the Commission shall specify by rule or order.

(c) *Exemptive Authority.* The Commission may, by rule or order, grant such exemptions, in whole or in part, conditionally or unconditionally, to any penny stock or class of penny stocks from the requirements of subsection (b) as the Commission determines to be consistent with the public interest, the protection of investors, and the maintenance of fair and orderly markets.

(d) *Commission Reporting Requirements.* The Commission shall, in each of the first 5 annual reports (under section 23(b)(1) of this title) submitted more than 12 months after the date of enactment of this section, include a description of the status of the penny stock automated quotation system or systems required by subsection (b) of this section. Such description shall include—

(1) a review of the development, implementation, and progress of the project, including achievement of significant milestones and current project schedule; and

(2) a review of the activities of registered securities associations and national securities exchanges in the development of the system.

Liability for Misleading Statements

Sec. 18. (a) *Persons Liable; Persons Entitled to Recover; Defense of Good Faith; Suit at Law or in Equity; Costs, Etc.* Any person who shall make or cause to be made any statement in any application, report, or document filed pursuant to this title or any rule or regulation thereunder or any undertaking contained in a registration statement as provided in subsection (d) of section 15 of this title, which statement was at the time and in the light of the circumstances under which it was made false or misleading with respect to any material fact, shall be liable to any person (not knowing that such statement was false or misleading) who, in reliance upon such statement, shall have purchased or sold a security at a price which was affected by such statement, for damages caused by such reliance, unless the person sued shall prove that he acted in good faith and had no knowledge that such statement was false or misleading. A person seeking to enforce such liability may sue at law or in equity in any court of competent jurisdiction. In any such suit the court may, in its discretion, require an undertaking for the payment of the costs of such suit, and assess reasonable costs, including reasonable attorneys' fees, against either party litigant.

(b) *Contribution.* Every person who becomes liable to make payment under this section may recover contribution as in cases of contact from any person who, if joined in the original suit, would have been liable to make the same payment.

(c) *Period of Limitations.* No action shall be maintained to enforce any liability created under this section unless brought within one year after the discovery of the facts constituting the cause of action and within three years after such cause of action accrued.

Registration, Responsibilities, and Oversight of Self-Regulatory Organizations

Sec. 19. (a) *Registration Procedures; Notice of Filing; Other Regulatory Agencies.*

(1) The Commission shall, upon the filing of an application for registration as a national securities exchange, registered securities association, or registered clearing agency, pursuant to section 6, 15A, or 17A of this title, respectively, publish notice of such filing and afford interested persons an opportunity to submit written data, views, and arguments concerning such application. Within ninety days of the date of publication of such notice (or within such longer period as to which the applicant consents), the Commission shall—

(A) by order grant such registration, or

(B) institute proceedings to determine whether registration should be denied. Such proceedings shall include notice of the grounds for denial under consideration and opportunity for hearing and shall be concluded within one hundred eighty days of the date of a publication of notice of the filing of the application for registration. At the conclusion of such proceedings the Commission, by order, shall grant or deny such registration. The Commission may extend the time for conclusion of such proceedings for up to ninety days if it finds good cause for such extension and publishes its reasons for so finding or for such longer period as to which the applicant consents.

The Commission shall grant such registration if it finds that the requirements of this title and the rules and regulations thereunder with respect to the applicant are satisfied. The Commission shall deny such registration if it does not make such finding.

(2) With respect to an application for registration filed by a clearing agency for which the Commission is not the appropriate regulatory agency—

(A) The Commission shall not grant registration prior to the sixtieth day after the date of publication of notice of the filing of such application unless the appropriate regulatory agency for such clearing agency has notified the Commission of such appropriate regulatory agency's determination that such clearing agency is so organized and has the capacity to be able to safeguard securities and funds in its custody or control or for which it is responsible and that the rules of such clearing agency are designed to assure the safeguarding of such securities and funds.

(B) The Commission shall institute proceedings in accordance with paragraph (1)(B) of this subsection to determine whether registration should be denied if the appropriate regulatory agency for such clearing agency notifies the Commission within sixty days of the date of publication of notice of the filing of such application of such appropriate regulatory agency's (i) determination that such clearing agency may not be so organized or have the capacity to be able to safeguard securities or funds in its custody or control or for which it is responsible or that the rules of such clearing agency may not be designed to assure the safeguarding of such securities and funds and (ii) reasons for such determination.

(C) The Commission shall deny registration if the appropriate regulatory agency for such clearing agency notifies the Commission prior to the conclusion of proceedings instituted in accordance with paragraph (1)(B) of this subsection of such appropriate regulatory agency's (i) determination that such clearing agency is not so organized or does not have the capacity to be able to safeguard securities or funds in its custody or control or for which it is responsible or that the rules of such clearing agency are not designed to assure the safeguarding of such securities or funds and (ii) reasons for such determination.

(3) A self-regulatory organization may, upon such terms and conditions as the Commission, by rule, deems necessary or appropriate in the public interest or for the protection of investors, withdraw from registration by filing a written notice of withdrawal with the Commission. If the Commission finds that any self-regulatory organization is no longer in existence or has ceased to do business in the capacity specified in its application for registration, the Commission, by order, shall cancel its registration. Upon the withdrawal of a national securities association from registration or the cancellation, suspension, or revocation of the registration of a national securities association, the registration of any association affiliated therewith shall automatically terminate.

(b) *Proposed Rule Changes; Notice; Proceedings.*

(1) Each self-regulatory organization shall file with the Commission, in accordance with such rules as the Commission may prescribe, copies of any proposed rule or any proposed change in, addition to, or deletion from the rules of such self-regulatory organization (hereinafter in this subsection collectively referred to as a "proposed rule change") accompanied by a concise general statement of the basis and purpose of such proposed rule change. The Commission shall, as soon as practicable after the date of the filing of any proposed rule change, publish notice thereof together with the terms of substance of the proposed rule change or a description of the subjects and issues involved. The Commission shall give interested persons an opportunity to submit written data, views, and arguments concerning such proposed rule change. No proposed rule change shall take effect unless approved by the Commission or otherwise permitted in accordance with the provisions of this subsection.

(2) *Approval Process.*

(A) *Approval Process Established*

(i) *In General.* Except as provided in clause (ii), not later than 45 days after the date of publication of a proposed rule change under paragraph (1), the Commission shall—

(I) by order, approve or disapprove the proposed rule change; or

(II) institute proceedings under subparagraph (B) to determine whether the proposed rule change should be disapproved.

(ii) *Extension of Time Period.* The Commission may extend the period established under clause (i) by not more than an additional 45 days, if

(I) the Commission determines that a longer period is appropriate and publishes the reasons for such determination; or

(II) the self-regulatory organization that filed the proposed rule change consents to the longer period.

(B) *Proceedings*

(i) *Notice and Hearing.* If the Commission does not approve or disapprove a proposed rule change under subparagraph (A), the Commission shall provide to the self-regulatory organization that filed the proposed rule change—

(I) notice of the grounds for disapproval under consideration; and

(II) opportunity for hearing, to be concluded not later than 180 days after the date of publication of notice of the filing of the proposed rule change.

(ii) *Order of Approval or Disapproval.*

(I) *In General.* Except as provided in subclause (II), not later than 180 days after the date of publication under paragraph (1), the Commission shall issue an order approving or disapproving the proposed rule change.

(II) *Extension of Time Period.* The Commission may extend the period for issuance under clause (I) by not more than 60 days, if—

(aa) the Commission determines that a longer period is appropriate and publishes the reasons for such determination; or

(bb) the self-regulatory organization that filed the proposed rule change consents to the longer period.

(C) *Standards for Approval and Disapproval*

(i) *Approval.* The Commission shall approve a proposed rule change of a self-regulatory organization if it finds that such proposed rule change is consistent with the requirements of this chapter and the rules and regulations issued under this chapter that are applicable to such organization.

(ii) *Disapproval.* The Commission shall disapprove a proposed rule change of a self-regulatory organization if it does not make a finding described in clause (i).

(iii) *Time for Approval.* The Commission may not approve a proposed rule change earlier than 30 days after the date of publication under paragraph (1), unless the Commission finds good cause for so doing and publishes the reason for the finding.

(D) *Result of Failure to Institute or Conclude Proceedings.* A proposed rule change shall be deemed to have been approved by the Commission, if—

(i) the Commission does not approve or disapprove the proposed rule change or begin proceedings under subparagraph (B) within the period described in subparagraph (A); or

(ii) the Commission does not issue an order approving or disapproving the proposed rule change under subparagraph (B) within the period described in subparagraph (B)(ii).

(E) *Publication Date Based on Federal Register Publishing.* For purposes of this paragraph, if, after filing a proposed rule change with the Commission pursuant to paragraph (1), a self-regulatory organization publishes a notice of the filing of such proposed rule change, together with the substantive terms of such proposed rule change, on a publicly accessible website, the Commission shall thereafter send the notice to the Federal Register for publication thereof under paragraph (1) within 15 days of the date on which such website publication is made. If the Commission fails to send the notice for publication thereof within such 15 day period, then the date of publication shall be deemed to be the date on which such website publication was made.

(F) *Rulemaking*

(i) *In General.* Not later than 180 days after July 21, 2010, after consultation with other regulatory agencies, the Commission shall promulgate rules setting forth the procedural requirements of the proceedings required under this paragraph.

(ii) *Notice and Comment Not Required.* The rules promulgated by the Commission under clause (i) are not required to include republication of proposed rule changes or solicitation of public comment.

(3)(A) Notwithstanding the provisions of paragraph (2) of this subsection, a proposed rule change shall take effect upon filing with the Commission if designated by the self-regulatory organization as (i) constituting a stated policy, practice, or interpretation with respect to the meaning, administration, or enforcement of an existing rule of the self-regulatory organization,

(ii) establishing or changing a due, fee, or other charge imposed by the self-regulatory organization on any person, whether or not the person is a member of the self-regulatory organization, or (iii) concerned solely with the administration of the self-regulatory organization or other matters which the Commission, by rule, consistent with the public interest and the purposes of this subsection, may specify as without the provisions of such paragraph (2).

(B) Notwithstanding any other provision of this subsection, a proposed rule change may be put into effect summarily if it appears to the Commission that such action is necessary for the protection of investors, the maintenance of fair and orderly markets, or the safeguarding of securities or funds. Any proposed rule change so put into effect shall be filed promptly thereafter in accordance with the provisions of paragraph (1) of this subsection.

(C) Any proposed rule change of a self-regulatory organization which has taken effect pursuant to subparagraph (A) or (B) of this paragraph may be enforced by such organization to the extent it is not inconsistent with the provisions of this title, the rules and regulations thereunder, and applicable Federal and State law. At any time within the 60-day period beginning on the date of filing of such a proposed rule change in accordance with the provisions of paragraph (1), the Commission summarily may temporarily suspend the change in the rules of the self-regulatory organization made thereby, if it appears to the Commission that such action is necessary or appropriate in the public interest, for the protection of investors, or otherwise in furtherance of the purposes of this title. If the Commission takes such action, the Commission shall institute proceedings under paragraph (2)(B) to determine whether the proposed rule should be approved or disapproved. Commission action pursuant to this subparagraph shall not affect the validity or force of the rule change during the period it was in effect and shall not be reviewable under section 25 of this title nor deemed to be "final agency action" for purposes of section 704 of title 5, United States Code.

(4) With respect to a proposed rule change filed by a registered clearing agency for which the Commission is not the appropriate regulatory agency—

(A) The Commission shall not approve any such proposed rule change prior to the thirtieth day after the date of publication of notice of the filing thereof unless the appropriate regulatory agency for such clearing agency has notified the Commission of such appropriate regulatory agency's determination that the proposed rule change is consistent with the safeguarding of securities and funds in the custody or control of such clearing agency or for which it is responsible.

(B) The Commission shall institute proceedings in accordance with paragraph (2)(B) of this subsection to determine whether any such proposed rule change should be disapproved, if the appropriate regulatory agency for such clearing agency notifies the Commission within thirty days of the date of publication of notice of the filing of the proposed rule change of such appropriate regulatory agency's (i) determination that the proposed rule change may be inconsistent with the safeguarding of securities or funds in the custody or control of such clearing agency or for which it is responsible and (ii) reasons for such determination.

(C) The Commission shall disapprove any such proposed rule change if the appropriate regulatory agency for such clearing agency notifies the Commission prior to the conclusion of proceedings instituted in accordance with paragraph (2)(B) of this subsection of such appropriate regulatory agency's (i) determination that the proposed rule change is inconsistent with the safeguarding of securities or funds in the custody or control of such clearing agency or for which it is responsible and (ii) reasons for such determination.

(D)(i) The Commission shall order the temporary suspension of any change in the rules of a clearing agency made by a proposed rule change that has taken effect under paragraph (3), if the appropriate regulatory agency for the clearing agency notifies the Commission not later than 30 days after the date on which the proposed rule change was filed of—

(I) the determination by the appropriate regulatory agency that the rules of such clearing agency, as so changed, may be inconsistent with the safe-guarding of securities or funds in the custody or control of such clearing agency or for which it is responsible; and

(II) the reasons for the determination described in subclause (I).

(ii) If the Commission takes action under clause (i), the Commission shall institute proceedings under paragraph (2)(B) to determine if the proposed rule change should be approved or disapproved.

(5) The Commission shall consult with and consider the views of the Secretary of the Treasury prior to approving a proposed rule filed by a registered securities association that primarily concerns conduct related to transactions in government securities, except where the Commission determines that an emergency exists requiring expeditious or summary action and publishes its reasons therefor. If the Secretary of the Treasury comments in writing to the Commission on a proposed rule that has been published for comment, the Commission shall respond in writing to such written comment before approving the proposed rule. If the Secretary of the Treasury determines, and notifies the Commission, that such rule, if implemented, would, or as applied does (i) adversely affect the liquidity or efficiency of the market for government securities; or (ii) impose any burden on competition not necessary or appropriate in furtherance of the purposes of this section, the Commission shall, prior to adopting the proposed rule, find that such rule is necessary and appropriate in furtherance of the purposes of this section notwithstanding the Secretary's determination.

(6) In approving rules described in paragraph (5), the Commission shall consider the sufficiency and appropriateness of then existing laws and rules applicable to government securities brokers, government securities dealers, and persons associated with government securities brokers and government securities dealers.

(7) *Security Futures Product Rule Changes.*

(A) *Filing Required.* A self-regulatory organization that is an exchange registered with the Commission pursuant to section 6(g) of this title or that is a national securities association registered pursuant to section 15A(k) of this title shall file with the Commission, in accordance with such rules as the Commission may prescribe, copies of any proposed rule change or any proposed change in, addition to, or deletion from the rules of such self-regulatory organization (hereinafter in this paragraph collectively referred to as a "proposed rule change") that relates to higher margin levels, fraud or manipulation, recordkeeping, reporting, listing standards, or decimal pricing for security futures products, sales practices for security futures products for persons who effect transactions in security futures products, or rules effectuating such self-regulatory organization's obligation to enforce the securities laws. Such proposed rule change shall be accompanied by a concise general statement of the basis and purpose of such proposed rule change. The Commission shall, upon the filing of any proposed rule change, promptly publish notice thereof together with the terms of substance of the proposed rule change or a description of the subjects and issues involved. The Commission shall give interested persons an opportunity to submit data, views, and arguments concerning such proposed rule change.

(B) *Filing with CFTC.* A proposed rule change filed with the Commission pursuant to subparagraph (A) shall be filed concurrently with the Commodity Futures Trading Commission. Such proposed rule change may take effect upon filing of a written certification with the Commodity Futures Trading Commission under section 5c(c) of the Commodity Exchange Act, upon a determination by the Commodity Futures Trading Commission that review of the proposed rule change is not necessary, or upon approval of the proposed rule change by the Commodity Futures Trading Commission.

(C) *Abrogation of Rule Changes.* Any proposed rule change of a self-regulatory organization that has taken effect pursuant to subparagraph (B) may be enforced by such self-regulatory organization to the extent such rule is not inconsistent with the provisions of this title, the rules and regulations thereunder, and applicable Federal law. At any time within 60 days of the date of the filing of a written certification with the Commodity Futures Trading Commission under section 5c(c) of the Commodity Exchange Act, the date the Commodity Futures Trading Commission determines that review of such proposed rule change is not necessary, or the date the Commodity Futures Trading Commission approves such proposed rule change, the Commission, after consultation with the Commodity Futures Trading Commission, may summarily abrogate the proposed rule change and require that the proposed rule change be refiled in accordance with the provisions of paragraph (1), if it appears to the Commission that such proposed rule change unduly burdens competition or efficiency, conflicts with the securities laws, or is inconsistent with the public interest and the protection of investors. Commission action pursuant to the preceding sentence shall not affect the validity or force of the rule change during the period it was in effect and shall not be reviewable under section 25 of this title nor deemed to be a final agency action for purposes of section 704 of title 5, United States Code.

(D) *Review of Resubmitted Abrogated Rules.*

(i) *Proceedings.* Within 35 days of the date of publication of notice of the filing of a proposed rule change that is abrogated in accordance with subparagraph (C) and refiled in accordance with paragraph (1), or within such longer period as the Commission may designate up to 90 days after such date if the Commission finds such longer period to be appropriate and publishes its reasons for so finding or as to which the self-regulatory organization consents, the Commission shall—

(I) by order approve such proposed rule change; or

(II) after consultation with the Commodity Futures Trading Commission, institute proceedings to determine whether the proposed rule change should be disapproved. Proceedings under subclause (II) shall include notice of the grounds for disapproval under consideration and opportunity for hearing and be concluded within 180 days after the date of publication of notice of the filing of the proposed rule change. At the conclusion of such proceedings, the Commission, by order, shall approve or disapprove such proposed rule change. The Commission may extend the time for conclusion of such proceedings for up to 60 days if the Commission finds good cause for such extension and publishes its reasons for so finding or for such longer period as to which the self-regulatory organization consents.

(ii) *Grounds for Approval.* The Commission shall approve a proposed rule change of a self-regulatory organization under this subparagraph if the Commission finds that such proposed rule change does not unduly burden competition or efficiency, does not conflict with the securities laws, and is not inconsistent with the public interest or the protection of investors. The Commission shall disapprove such a proposed rule change of a self-regulatory organization if it does not make such finding. The Commission shall not approve any proposed rule change prior to the 30th day after the date of publication of notice of the filing thereof, unless the Commission finds good cause for so doing and publishes its reasons for so finding.

(8) *Decimal Pricing.* Not later than 9 months after the date on which trading in any security futures product commences under this title, all self-regulatory organizations listing or trading security futures products shall file proposed rule changes necessary to implement decimal pricing of security futures products. The Commission may not require such rules to contain equal minimum increments in such decimal pricing.

(9) *Consultation with CFTC.*

(A) *Consultation Required.* The Commission shall consult with and consider the views of the Commodity Futures Trading Commission prior to approving or disapproving a proposed rule change filed by a national securities association registered pursuant to section 15A(a) or a national securities exchange subject to the provisions of subsection (a) that primarily concerns conduct related to transactions in security futures products, except where the Commission determines that an emergency exists requiring expeditious or summary action and publishes its reasons therefor.

(B) *Responses to CFTC Comments and Findings.* If the Commodity Futures Trading Commission comments in writing to the Commission on a proposed rule that has been published for comment, the Commission shall respond in writing to such written comment before approving or disapproving the proposed rule. If the Commodity Futures Trading Commission determines, and notifies the Commission, that such rule, if implemented or as applied, would—

(i) adversely affect the liquidity or efficiency of the market for security futures products; or

(ii) impose any burden on competition not necessary or appropriate in furtherance of the purposes of this section,

the Commission shall, prior to approving or disapproving the proposed rule, find that such rule is necessary and appropriate in furtherance of the purposes of this section notwithstanding the Commodity Futures Trading Commission's determination.

[*This paragraph shall take effect on the later of 360 days after July 21, 2010, or, to the extent a provision requires a rulemaking, not less than 60 days after publication of the final rule or regulation.*]

(10) Notwithstanding paragraph (2), the time period within which the Commission is required by order to approve a proposed rule change or institute proceedings to determine whether the proposed rule change should be disapproved is stayed pending a determination by the Commission upon the request of the Commodity Futures Trading Commission or its Chairman that the Commission issue a determination as to whether a product that is the subject of such proposed rule change is a security pursuant to section 718 of the Wall Street Transparency and Accountability Act of 2010.

(10) *Rule of Construction Relating to Filing Date of Proposed Rule Changes.*

(A) *In General.* For purposes of this subsection, the date of filing of a proposed rule change shall be deemed to be the date on which the Commission receives the proposed rule change.

(B) *Exception.* A proposed rule change has not been received by the Commission for purposes of subparagraph (A) if, not later than 7 business days after the date of receipt by the Commission, the Commission notifies the self-regulatory organization that such proposed rule change does not comply with the rules of the Commission relating to the required form of a proposed rule change, except that if the Commission determines that the proposed rule change is unusually lengthy and is complex or raises novel regulatory issues, the Commission shall inform the self-regulatory organization of such determination not later than 7 business days after the date of receipt by the Commission and, for the purposes of subparagraph (A), a proposed rule change has not been received by the Commission, if, not later than 21 days after the date of receipt by the Commission, the Commission notifies the self-regulatory organization that such proposed rule change does not comply with the rules of the Commission relating to the required form of a proposed rule change.*

(c) *Amendment by Commission of Rules of Self-Regulatory Organizations.* The Commission, by rule, may abrogate, add to, and delete from (hereinafter in this subsection collectively referred to as "amend") the rules of a self-regulatory organization (other than a registered clearing agency) as the Commission deems necessary or appropriate to insure the fair administration of the self-regulatory organization, to conform its rules to requirements of this title and the rules and regulations thereunder applicable to such organization, or otherwise in furtherance of the purposes of this title, in the following manner:

(1) The Commission shall notify the self-regulatory organization and publish notice of the proposed rulemaking in the Federal Register. The notice shall include the text of the proposed amendment to the rules of the self-regulatory organization and a statement of the Commission's reasons, including any pertinent facts, for commencing such proposed rulemaking.

(2) The Commission shall give interested persons an opportunity for the oral presentation of data, views, and arguments, in addition to an opportunity to make written submissions. A transcript shall be kept of any oral presentation.

(3) A rule adopted pursuant to this subsection shall incorporate the text of the amendment to the rules of the self-regulatory organization and a statement of the Commission's basis for and purpose in so amending such rules. This statement shall include an identification of any facts on which the Commission considers its determination so to amend the rules of the self-regulatory agency to be based, including the reasons for the Commission's conclusions as to any of such facts which were disputed in the rulemaking.

(4)(A) Except as provided in paragraphs (1) through (3) of this subsection, rulemaking under this subsection shall be in accordance with the procedures specified in section 553 of title 5, United States Code for rulemaking not on the record.

(B) Nothing in this subsection shall be construed to impair or limit the Commission's power to make, or to modify or alter the procedures the Commission may follow in making rules and regulations pursuant to any other authority under this title.

(C) Any amendment to the rules of a self-regulatory organization made by the Commission pursuant to this subsection shall be considered for all purposes of this title to be part of the rules of such self-regulatory organization and shall not be considered to be a rule of the Commission.

(5) With respect to rules described in subsection (b)(5), the Commission shall consult with and con-

* Dodd-Frank added two (10)'s.

sider the views of the Secretary of the Treasury before abrogating, adding to, and deleting from such rules, except where the Commission determines that an emergency exists requiring expeditious or summary action and publishes its reasons therefor.

(d) *Notice of Disciplinary Action Taken by Self–Regulatory Organization Against a Member or Participant; Review of Action by Appropriate Regulatory Agency; Procedure.*

(1) If any self-regulatory organization imposes any final disciplinary sanction on any member thereof or participant therein, denies membership or participation to any applicant, or prohibits or limits any person in respect to access to services offered by such organization or member thereof or if any self-regulatory organization (other than a registered clearing agency) imposes any final disciplinary sanction on any person associated with a member or bars any person from becoming associated with a member, the self-regulatory organization shall promptly file notice thereof with the appropriate regulatory agency for the self-regulatory organization and (if other than the appropriate regulatory agency for the self-regulatory organization) the appropriate regulatory agency for such member, participant, applicant, or other person. The notice shall be in such form and contain such information as the appropriate regulatory agency for the self-regulatory organization, by rule, may prescribe as necessary or appropriate in furtherance of the purposes of this title.

(2) Any action with respect to which a self-regulatory organization is required by paragraph (1) of this subsection to file notice shall be subject to review by the appropriate regulatory agency for such member, participant, applicant, or other person, on its own motion, or upon application by any person aggrieved thereby filed within thirty days after the date such notice was filed with such appropriate regulatory agency and received by such aggrieved person, or within such longer period as such appropriate regulatory agency may determine. Application to such appropriate regulatory agency for review, or the institution of review by such appropriate regulatory agency on its own motion, shall not operate as a stay of such action unless such appropriate regulatory agency otherwise orders, summarily or after notice and opportunity for hearing on the question of a stay (which hearing may consist solely of the submission of affidavits or presentation of oral arguments). Each appropriate regulatory agency shall establish for appropriate cases an expedited procedure for consideration and determination of the question of a stay.

(3) The provisions of this subsection shall apply to an exchange registered pursuant to section 6(g) of this title or a national securities association registered pursuant to section 15A(k) of this title only to the extent that such exchange or association imposes any final disciplinary sanction for—

(A) a violation of the Federal securities laws or the rules and regulations thereunder; or

(B) a violation of a rule of such exchange or association, as to which a proposed change would be required to be filed under section 19 of this title, except that, to the extent that the exchange or association rule violation relates to any account, agreement, contract, or transaction, this subsection shall apply only to the extent such violation involves a security futures product.

(e) *Disposition of Review; Cancellation, Reduction, or Remission of Sanction.*

(1) In any proceeding to review a final disciplinary sanction imposed by a self-regulatory organization on a member thereof or participant therein or a person associated with such a member, after notice and opportunity for hearing (which hearing may consist solely of consideration of the record before the self-regulatory organization and opportunity for the presentation of supporting reasons to affirm, modify, or set aside the sanction)—

(A) if the appropriate regulatory agency for such member, participant, or person associated with a member finds that such member, participant, or person associated with a member has engaged in such acts or practices, or has omitted such acts, as the self-regulatory organization has found him to have engaged in or omitted, that such acts or practices, or omissions to act, are in violation of such provisions of this title, the rules or regulations thereunder, the rules of the self-regulatory organization, or, in the case of a registered securities association, the rules of the Municipal Securities Rulemaking Board as have been specified in the determination of the self-regulatory organization, and that such provisions are, and were applied in a manner, consistent with the purposes of this title, such appropriate regulatory agency, by order, shall so declare and, as appropriate, affirm the sanction imposed by the self-regulatory organization, modify the sanction in accordance with paragraph (2) of this subsection, or remand to the self-regulatory organization for further proceedings; or

(B) if such appropriate regulatory agency does not make any such finding it shall, by order, set aside the sanction imposed by the self-regulatory organization and, if appropriate, remand to the self-regulatory organization for further proceedings.

(2) If the appropriate regulatory agency for a member, participant, or person associated with a member, having due regard for the public interest and the protection of investors, finds after a proceeding in accordance with paragraph (1) of this subsection that a sanction imposed by a self-regulatory organization upon such member, participant, or person associated with a member imposes any burden on competition not necessary or appropriate in furtherance of the purposes of this title or is excessive or oppressive, the appropriate regulatory agency may cancel, reduce, or require the remission of such sanction.

(f) *Dismissal of Review Proceeding.* In any proceeding to review the denial of membership or participation in a self-regulatory organization to any applicant, the barring of any person from becoming associated with a member of a self-regulatory organization, or the prohibition or limitation by a self-regulatory organization of any person with respect to access to services offered by the self-regulatory organization or any member thereof, if the appropriate regulatory agency for such applicant or person, after notice and opportunity for hearing (which hearing may consist solely of consideration of the record before the self-regulatory organization and opportunity for the presentation of supporting reasons to dismiss the proceeding or set aside the action of the self-regulatory organization) finds that the specific grounds on which such denial, bar, or prohibition or limitation is based exist in fact, that such denial, bar, or prohibition or limitation is in accordance with the rules of the self-regulatory organization, and that such rules are, and were applied in a manner, consistent with the purposes of this title, such appropriate regulatory agency, by order, shall dismiss the proceeding. If such appropriate regulatory agency does not make any such finding or if it finds that such denial, bar, or prohibition or limitation imposes any burden on competition not necessary or appropriate in furtherance of the purposes of this title, such appropriate regulatory agency, by order, shall set aside the action of the self-regulatory organization and require it to admit such applicant to membership or participation, permit such person to become associated with a member, or grant such person access to services offered by the self-regulatory organization or member thereof.

(g) *Compliance with Rules and Regulations.*

(1) Every self-regulatory organization shall comply with the provisions of this title, the rules and regulations thereunder, and its own rules, and (subject to the provisions of section 17(d) of this title, paragraph (2) of this subsection, and the rules thereunder) absent reasonable justification or excuse enforce compliance—

(A) in the case of a national securities exchange, with such provisions by its members and persons associated with its members;

(B) in the case of a registered securities association, with such provisions and the provisions of the rules of the Municipal Securities Rulemaking Board by its members and persons associated with its members; and

(C) in the case of a registered clearing agency, with its own rules by its participants.

(2) The Commission, by rule, consistent with the public interest, the protection of investors, and the other purposes of this title, may relieve any self-regulatory organization of any responsibility under this title to enforce compliance with any specified provision of this title or the rules or regulations thereunder by any member of such organization or person associated with such a member, or any class of such members or persons associated with a member.

(h) *Suspension or Revocation of Self–Regulatory Organization's Registration; Censure; Other Sanctions.*

(1) The appropriate regulatory agency for a self-regulatory organization is authorized, by order, if in its opinion such action is necessary or appropriate in the public interest, for the protection of investors, or otherwise in furtherance of the purposes of this title, to suspend for a period not exceeding twelve months or revoke the registration of such self-regulatory organization, or to censure or impose limitations upon the activities, functions, and operations of such self-regulatory organization, if such appropriate regulatory agency finds, on the record after notice and opportunity for hearing, that such self-regulatory organization has violated or is unable to comply with any provision of this title, the rules or regulations thereunder, or its own rules or without reasonable

justification or excuse has failed to enforce compliance—

(A) in the case of a national securities exchange, with any such provision by a member thereof or a person associated with a member thereof;

(B) in the case of a registered securities association, with any such provision or any provision of the rules of the Municipal Securities Rulemaking Board by a member thereof or a person associated with a member thereof; or

(C) in the case of a registered clearing agency, with any provision of its own rules by a participant therein.

(2) The appropriate regulatory agency for a self-regulatory organization is authorized, by order, if in its opinion such action is necessary or appropriate in the public interest, for the protection of investors, or otherwise in furtherance of the purposes of this title, to suspend for a period not exceeding twelve months or expel from such self-regulatory organization any member thereof or participant therein, if such member or participant is subject to an order of the Commission pursuant to section 15(b)(4) of this title or if such appropriate regulatory agency finds, on the record after notice and opportunity for hearing, that such member or participant has willfully violated or has effected any transaction for any other person who, such member or participant had reason to believe, was violating with respect to such transaction—

(A) in the case of a national securities exchange, any provision of the Securities Act of 1933, the Investment Advisers Act of 1940, the Investment Company Act of 1940, this title, or the rules or regulations under any of such statutes;

(B) in the case of a registered securities association, any provision of the Securities Act of 1933, the Investment Advisers Act of 1940, the Investment Company Act of 1940, this title, the rules or regulations under any of such statutes, or the rules of the Municipal Securities Rulemaking Board; or

(C) in the case of a registered clearing agency, any provision of the rules of the clearing agency.

(3) The appropriate regulatory agency for a national securities exchange or registered securities association is authorized, by order, if in its opinion such action is necessary or appropriate in the public interest, for the protection of investors, or otherwise in furtherance of the purposes of this title, to suspend for a period not exceeding twelve months or to bar any person from being associated with a member of such national securities exchange or registered securities association, if such person is subject to an order of the Commission pursuant to section 15(b)(6) or if such appropriate regulatory agency finds, on the record after notice and opportunity for hearing, that such person has willfully violated or has effected any transaction for any other person who, such person associated with a member had reason to believe, was violating with respect to such transaction—

(A) in the case of a national securities exchange, any provision of the Securities Act of 1933, the Investment Advisers Act of 1940, the Investment Company Act of 1940, this title, or the rules or regulations under any of such statutes; or

(B) in the case of a registered securities association, any provision of the Securities Act of 1933, the Investment Advisers Act of 1940, the Investment Company Act of 1940, this title, the rules or regulations under any of the statutes, or the rules of the Municipal Securities Rulemaking Board.

(4) The appropriate regulatory agency for a self-regulatory organization is authorized, by order, if in its opinion such action is necessary or appropriate in the public interest, for the protection of investors, or otherwise in furtherance of the purposes of this chapter, to remove from office or censure any person who is, or at the time of the alleged misconduct was, an officer or director of such self-regulatory organization, if such appropriate regulatory agency finds, on the record after notice and opportunity for hearing, that such person has willfully violated any provision of this chapter, the rules or regulations thereunder, or the rules of such self-regulatory organization, willfully abused his authority, or without reasonable justification or excuse has failed to enforce compliance—

(A) in the case of a national securities exchange, with any such provision by any member or person associated with a member;

(B) in the case of a registered securities association, with any such provision or any provision of the rules of the Municipal Securities Rulemaking Board by any member or person associated with a member; or

(C) in the case of a registered clearing agency, with any provision of the rules of the clearing agency by any participant.

(i) *Appointment of Trustee.* If a proceeding under subsection (h)(1) of this section results in the suspension or revocation of the registration of a clearing agency, the appropriate regulatory agency for such clearing agency may, upon notice to such clearing agency, apply to any court of competent jurisdiction specified in section 21(d) or 27 of this title for the appointment of a trustee. In the event of such an application, the court may, to the extent it deems necessary or appropriate, take exclusive jurisdiction of such clearing agency and the records and assets thereof, wherever located; and the court shall appoint the appropriate regulatory agency for such clearing agency or a person designated by such appropriate regulatory agency as trustee with power to take possession and continue to operate or terminate the operations of such clearing agency in an orderly manner for the protection of participants and investors, subject to such terms and conditions as the court may prescribe.

Liability of Controlling Persons and Persons Who Aid and Abet Violations

Sec. 20. (a) *Joint and Several Liability; Good Faith Defense.* Every person who, directly or indirectly, controls any person liable under any provision of this title or of any rule or regulation thereunder shall also be liable jointly and severally with and to the same extent as such controlled person to any person to whom such controlled person is liable (including to the Commission in any action brought under paragraph (1) or (3) of section 21(d)), unless the controlling person acted in good faith and did not directly or indirectly induce the act or acts constituting the violation or cause of action.

(b) *Unlawful Activity Through or By Means of Any Other Person.* It shall be unlawful for any person, directly or indirectly, to do any act or thing which it would be unlawful for such person to do under the provisions of this title or any rule or regulation thereunder through or by means of any other person.

(c) *Hindering, Delaying, or Obstructing the Making or Filing of Any Document, Report, or Information.* It shall be unlawful for any director or officer of, or any owner of any securities issued by, any issuer required to file any document, report, or information under this title or any rule or regulation thereunder without just cause to hinder, delay, or obstruct the making or filing of any such document, report, or information.

(d) *Liability for Trading in Securities While in Possession of Material Nonpublic Information.* Wherever communicating, or purchasing or selling a security while in possession of, material nonpublic information would violate, or result in liability to any purchaser or seller of the security under any provisions of this title, or any rule or regulation thereunder, such conduct in connection with a purchase or sale of a put, call, straddle, option, privilege or security-based swap agreement with respect to such security or with respect to a group or index of securities including such security, shall also violate and result in comparable liability to any purchaser or seller of that security under such provision, rule, or regulation.

(e) *Prosecution of Persons Who Aid and Abet Violations.* For purposes of any action brought by the Commission under paragraph (1) or (3) of section 21(d), any person that knowingly or recklessly provides substantial assistance to another person in violation of a provision of this title, or of any rule or regulation issued under this title, shall be deemed to be in violation of such provision to the same extent as the person to whom such assistance is provided.

(f) *Limitation on Commission Authority.* The authority of the Commission under this section with respect to security-based swap agreements shall be subject to the restrictions and limitations of section 3A(b) of this title.

Liability to Contemporaneous Traders for Insider Trading

Sec. 20A. (a) *Private Rights of Action Based on Contemporaneous Trading.* Any person who violates any provision of this title or the rules or regulations thereunder by purchasing or selling a security while in possession of material, nonpublic information shall be liable in an action in any court of competent jurisdiction to any person who, contemporaneously with the purchase or sale of securities that is the subject of such violation, has purchased (where such violation is based on a sale of securities) or sold (where such violation is based on a purchase of securities) securities of the same class.

(b) *Limitations on Liability.*

(1) *Contemporaneous Trading Actions Limited to Profit Gained or Loss Avoided.* The total amount of damages imposed under subsection (a) shall not exceed the profit gained or loss avoided in the

transaction or transactions that are the subject of the violation.

(2) *Offsetting Disgorgements Against Liability.* The total amount of damages imposed against any person under subsection (a) shall be diminished by the amounts, if any, that such person may be required to disgorge, pursuant to a court order obtained at the instance of the Commission, in a proceeding brought under section 21(d) of this title relating to the same transaction or transactions.

(3) *Controlling Person Liability.* No person shall be liable under this section solely by reason of employing another person who is liable under this section, but the liability of a controlling person under this section shall be subject to section 20(a) of this title.

(4) *Statute of Limitations.* No action may be brought under this section more than 5 years after the date of the last transaction that is the subject of the violation.

(c) *Joint and Several Liability for Communicating.* Any person who violates any provision of this title or the rules or regulations thereunder by communicating material, nonpublic information shall be jointly and severally liable under subsection (a) with, and to the same extent as, any person or persons liable under subsection (a) to whom the communication was directed.

(d) *Authority Not to Restrict Other Express or Implied Rights of Action.* Nothing in this section shall be construed to limit or condition the right of any person to bring an action to enforce a requirement of this title or the availability of any cause of action implied from a provision of this title.

(e) *Provisions Not to Affect Public Prosecutions.* This section shall not be construed to bar or limit in any manner any action by the Commission or the Attorney General under any other provision of this title, nor shall it bar or limit in any manner any action to recover penalties, or to seek any other order regarding penalties.

Investigations; Injunctions and Prosecution of Offenses

Sec. 21. (a) *Authority and Discretion of Commission to Investigate Violations.*

(1) The Commission may, in its discretion, make such investigations as it deems necessary to determine whether any person has violated, is violating, or is about to violate any provision of this chapter, the rules or regulations thereunder, the rules of a national securities exchange or registered securities association of which such person is a member or a person associated, or, as to any act or practice, or omission to act, while associated with a member, formerly associated with a member, the rules of a registered clearing agency in which such person is a participant, or, as to any act or practice, or omission to act, while a participant, was a participant, the rules of the Public Company Accounting Oversight Board, of which such person is a registered public accounting firm, a person associated with such a firm, or, as to any act, practice, or omission to act, while associated with such firm, a person formerly associated with such a firm, or the rules of the Municipal Securities Rulemaking Board, and may require or permit any person to file with it a statement in writing, under oath or otherwise as the Commission shall determine, as to all the facts and circumstances concerning the matter to be investigated. The Commission is authorized in its discretion, to publish information concerning any such violations, and to investigate any facts, conditions, practices, or matters which it may deem necessary or proper to aid in the enforcement of such provisions, in the prescribing of rules and regulations under this chapter, or in securing information to serve as a basis for recommending further legislation concerning the matters to which this chapter relates.

(2) On request from a foreign securities authority, the Commission may provide assistance in accordance with this paragraph if the requesting authority states that the requesting authority is conducting an investigation which it deems necessary to determine whether any person has violated, is violating, or is about to violate any laws or rules relating to securities matters that the requesting authority administers or enforces. The Commission may, in its discretion, conduct such investigation as the Commission deems necessary to collect information and evidence pertinent to the request for assistance. Such assistance may be provided without regard to whether the facts stated in the request would also constitute a violation of the laws of the United States. In deciding whether to provide such assistance, the Commission shall consider whether (A) the requesting authority has agreed to provide reciprocal assistance in securities matters to the Commission; and (B) compliance with the request would prejudice the public interest of the United States.

(b) *Attendance of Witnesses; Production of Records.* For the purpose of any such investigation, or any other proceeding under this title, any member of the Commission or any officer designated by it is empowered to administer oaths and affirmations, subpena witnesses, compel their attendance, take evidence, and require the production of any books, papers, correspondence, memoranda, or other records which the Commission deems relevant or material to the inquiry. Such attendance of witnesses and the production of any such records may be required from any place in the United States or any State at any designated place of hearing.

(c) *Judicial Enforcement of Investigative Power of Commission; Refusal to Obey Subpoena; Criminal Sanctions.* In case of contumacy by, or refusal to obey a subpena issued to, any person, the Commission may invoke the aid of any court of the United States within the jurisdiction of which such investigation or proceeding is carried on, or where such person resides or carries on business, in requiring the attendance and testimony of witnesses and the production of books, papers, correspondence, memoranda, and other records. And such court may issue an order requiring such person to appear before the Commission or member or officer designated by the Commission, there to produce records, if so ordered, or to give testimony touching the matter under investigation or in question; and any failure to obey such order of the court may be punished by such court as a contempt thereof. All process in any such case may be served in the judicial district whereof such person is an inhabitant or wherever he may be found. Any person who shall, without just cause, fail or refuse to attend and testify or to answer any lawful inquiry or to produce books, papers, correspondence, memoranda, and other records, if in his power so to do, in obedience to the subpena of the Commission, shall be guilty of a misdemeanor and, upon conviction, shall be subject to a fine of not more than $1,000 or to imprisonment for a term of not more than one year, or both.

(d) *Injunction Proceedings; Authority of Court to Prohibit Persons from Serving as Officers and Directors; Money Penalties in Civil Actions.*

(1) Whenever it shall appear to the Commission that any person is engaged or is about to engage in acts or practices constituting a violation of any provision of this title, the rules or regulations thereunder, the rules of a national securities exchange or registered securities association of which such person is a member or a person associated with a member, the rules of a registered clearing agency in which such person is a participant, the rules of the Public Company Accounting Oversight Board, of which such person is a registered public accounting firm or a person associated with such a firm, or the rules of the Municipal Securities Rulemaking Board, it may in its discretion bring an action in the proper district court of the United States, the United States District Court for the District of Columbia, or the United States courts of any territory or other place subject to the jurisdiction of the United States, to enjoin such acts or practices, and upon a proper showing a permanent or temporary injunction or restraining order shall be granted without bond. The Commission may transmit such evidence as may be available concerning such acts or practices as may constitute a violation of any provision of this title or the rules or regulations thereunder to the Attorney General, who may, in his discretion, institute the necessary criminal proceedings under this title.

(2) *Authority of a Court to Prohibit Persons from Serving as Officers and Directors.* In any proceeding under paragraph (1) of this subsection, the court may prohibit, conditionally or unconditionally, and permanently or for such period of time as it shall determine, any person who violated section 10(b) of this title or the rules or regulations thereunder from acting as an officer or director of any issuer that has a class of securities registered pursuant to section 12 of this title or that is required to file reports pursuant to section 15(d) of this title if the person's conduct demonstrates unfitness to serve as an officer or director of any such issuer.

(3) *Money Penalties in Civil Actions.*

(A) *Authority of Commission.* Whenever it shall appear to the Commission that any person has violated any provision of this title, the rules or regulations thereunder, or a cease-and-desist order entered by the Commission pursuant to section 21C of this title, other than by committing a violation subject to a penalty pursuant to section 21A, the Commission may bring an action in a United States district court to seek, and the court shall have jurisdiction to impose, upon a proper showing, a civil penalty to be paid by the person who committed such violation.

(B) *Amount of Penalty.*

(i) *First Tier.* The amount of the penalty shall be determined by the court in light of the facts and circumstances. For each violation, the amount of the penalty shall not exceed the greater of (I) $5,000 for a natural person or $50,000 for any other person, or (II) the gross amount of pecuniary gain to such defendant as a result of the violation.

(ii) *Second Tier.* Notwithstanding clause (i), the amount of penalty for each such violation shall not exceed the greater of (I) $50,000 for a natural person or $250,000 for any other person, or (II) the gross amount of pecuniary gain to such defendant as a result of the violation, if the violation described in subparagraph (A) involved fraud, deceit, manipulation, or deliberate or reckless disregard of a regulatory requirement.

(iii) *Third Tier.* Notwithstanding clauses (i) and (ii), the amount of penalty for each such violation shall not exceed the greater of (I) $100,000 for a natural person or $500,000 for any other person, or (II) the gross amount of pecuniary gain to such defendant as a result of the violation, if—

(aa) the violation described in subparagraph (A) involved fraud, deceit, manipulation, or deliberate or reckless disregard of a regulatory requirement; and

(bb) such violation directly or indirectly resulted in substantial losses or created a significant risk of substantial losses to other persons.

(C) *Procedures for Collection.*

(i) *Payment of Penalty to Treasury.* A penalty imposed under this section shall be payable into the Treasury of the United States, except as otherwise provided in section 308 of the Sarbanes-Oxley Act of 2002 and section 21F of this title.

(ii) *Collection of Penalties.* If a person upon whom such a penalty is imposed shall fail to pay such penalty within the time prescribed in the court's order, the Commission may refer the matter to the Attorney General who shall recover such penalty by action in the appropriate United States district court.

(iii) *Remedy Not Exclusive.* The actions authorized by this paragraph may be brought in addition to any other action that the Commission or the Attorney General is entitled to bring.

(iv) *Jurisdiction and Venue.* For purposes of section 27 of this title, actions under this paragraph shall be actions to enforce a liability or a duty created by this title.

(D) *Special Provisions Relating to a Violation of a Cease-and-Desist Order.* In an action to enforce a cease-and-desist order entered by the Commission pursuant to section 21C of this title, each separate violation of such order shall be a separate offense, except that in the case of a violation through a continuing failure to comply with the order, each day of the failure to comply shall be deemed a separate offense.

(4) *Prohibition of Attorneys' Fees Paid From Commission Disgorgement Funds.* Except as otherwise ordered by the court upon motion by the Commission, or, in the case of an administrative action, as otherwise ordered by the Commission, funds disgorged as the result of an action brought by the Commission in Federal court, or as a result of any Commission administrative action, shall not be distributed as payment for attorneys' fees or expenses incurred by private parties seeking distribution of the disgorged funds.

(5) *Equitable Relief.* In any action or proceeding brought or instituted by the Commission under any provision of the securities laws, the Commission may seek, and any Federal court may grant, any equitable relief that may be appropriate or necessary for the benefit of investors.

(6) *Authority of a Court to Prohibit Persons from Participating in an Offering of Penny Stock.*

(A) *In General.* In any proceeding under paragraph (1) against any person participating in, or, at the time of the alleged misconduct who was participating in, an offering of penny stock, the court may prohibit that person from participating in an offering of penny stock, conditionally or unconditionally, and permanently or for such period of time as the court shall determine.

(B) *Definition.* For purposes of this paragraph, the term "person participating in an offering of penny stock" includes any person engaging in activities with a broker, dealer, or issuer for purposes of issuing, trading, or inducing or attempting to induce the purchase or sale of, any penny stock. The Commission may, by rule or regulation, define such term to include other activities, and may, by rule, regulation, or order, exempt any person or class of persons, in whole or in part, conditionally or unconditionally, from inclusion in such term.

(e) *Mandamus.* Upon application of the Commission the district courts of the United States and the United States courts of any territory or other place subject to the jurisdiction of the United States shall have jurisdiction to issue writs of mandamus, injunctions, and orders commanding (1) any person to comply with the provisions of this title, the rules, regulations, and orders thereunder, the rules of a national securities exchange or registered securities association of which such person is a member or person associated with a member, the rules of a registered clearing agency in which such person is a participant, the rules of the Public Company Accounting Oversight Board, of which such person is a registered public accounting firm or a person associated with such a firm, the rules of the Municipal Securities Rulemaking Board, or any undertaking contained in a registration statement as provided in subsection (d) of section 15 of this title, (2) any national securities exchange or registered securities association to enforce compliance by its members and persons associated with its members with the provisions of this title, the rules, regulations, and orders thereunder, and the rules of such exchange or association, or (3) any registered clearing agency to enforce compliance by its participants with the provisions of the rules of such clearing agency.

(f) *Rules of Self–Regulatory Organizations.* Notwithstanding any other provision of this title, the Commission shall not bring any action pursuant to subsection (d) or (e) of this section against any person for violation of, or to command compliance with, the rules of a self-regulatory organization or the Public Company Accounting Oversight Board unless it appears to the Commission that (1) such self-regulatory organization or the Public Company Accounting Oversight Board is unable or unwilling to take appropriate action against such person in the public interest and for the protection of investors, or (2) such action is otherwise necessary or appropriate in the public interest or for the protection of investors.

(g) *Consolidation of Actions; Consent of Commission.* Notwithstanding the provisions of section 1407(a) of title 28, United States Code, or any other provision of law, no action for equitable relief instituted by the Commission pursuant to the securities laws shall be consolidated or coordinated with other actions not brought by the Commission, even though such other actions may involve common questions of fact, unless such consolidation is consented to by the Commission.

(h) *Access to Records.*

(1) The Right to Financial Privacy Act of 1978 shall apply with respect to the Commission, except as otherwise provided in this subsection.

(2) Notwithstanding section 1105 or 1107 of the Right to Financial Privacy Act of 1978, the Commission may have access to and obtain copies of, or the information contained in financial records of a customer from a financial institution without prior notice to the customer upon an ex parte showing to an appropriate United States district court that the Commission seeks such financial records pursuant to a subpena issued in conformity with the requirements of section 19(b) of the Securities Act of 1933, section 21(b) of the Securities Exchange Act of 1934, section 42(b) of the Investment Company Act of 1940, or section 209(b) of the Investment Advisers Act of 1940, and that the Commission has reason to believe that—

(A) delay in obtaining access to such financial records, or the required notice, will result in—

(i) flight from prosecution;

(ii) destruction of or tampering with evidence;

(iii) transfer of assets or records outside the territorial limits of the United States;

(iv) improper conversion of investor assets; or

(v) impeding the ability of the Commission to identify or trace the source or disposition of funds involved in any securities transaction;

(B) such financial records are necessary to identify or trace the record or beneficial ownership interest in any security;

(C) the acts, practices or course of conduct under investigation involve—

(i) the dissemination of materially false or misleading information concerning any security, issuer, or market, or the failure to make disclosures required under the securities laws, which remain uncorrected; or

(ii) a financial loss to investors or other persons protected under the securities laws which remains substantially uncompensated; or

(D) the acts, practices or course of conduct under investigation—

(i) involve significant financial speculation in securities; or

(ii) endanger the stability of any financial or investment intermediary.

(3) Any application under paragraph (2) for a delay in notice shall be made with reasonable specificity.

(4)(A) Upon a showing described in paragraph (2), the presiding judge or magistrate shall enter an ex parte order granting the requested delay for a period not to exceed ninety days and an order prohibiting the financial institution involved from disclosing that records have been obtained or that a request for records has been made.

(B) Extensions of the period of delay of notice provided in subparagraph (A) of up to ninety days each may be granted by the court upon application, but only in accordance with this subsection or section 1109(a), (b)(1), or (b)(2) of the Right to Financial Privacy Act of 1978.

(C) Upon expiration of the period of delay of notification ordered under subparagraph (A) or (B), the customer shall be served with or mailed a copy of the subpena insofar as it applies to the customer together with the following notice which shall describe with reasonable specificity the nature of the investigation for which the Commission sought the financial records:

"Records or information concerning your transactions which are held by the financial institution named in the attached subpena were supplied to the Securities and Exchange Commission on (date). Notification was withheld pursuant to a determination by the (title of court so ordering) under section 21(h) of the Securities Exchange Act of 1934 that (state reason). The purpose of the investigation or official proceeding was (state purpose)."

(5) Upon application by the Commission, all proceedings pursuant to paragraphs (2) and (4) shall be held in camera and the records thereof sealed until expiration of the period of delay or such other date as the presiding judge or magistrate may permit.

(6) [Repealed]

(7)(A) Following the expiration of the period of delay of notification ordered by the court pursuant to paragraph (4) of this subsection, the customer may, upon motion, reopen the proceeding in the district court which issued the order. If the presiding judge or magistrate judge finds that the movant is the customer to whom the records obtained by the Commission pertain, and that the Commission has obtained financial records or information contained therein in violation of this subsection, other than paragraph (1), it may order that the customer be granted civil penalties against the Commission in an amount equal to the sum of—

(i) $100 without regard to the volume of records involved;

(ii) any out-of-pocket damages sustained by the customer as a direct result of the disclosure; and

(iii) if the violation is found to have been willful, intentional, and without good faith, such punitive damages as the court may allow, together with the costs of the action and reasonable attorney's fees as determined by the court.

(B) Upon a finding that the Commission has obtained financial records or information contained therein in violation of this subsection, other than paragraph (1), the court, in its discretion, may also or in the alternative issue injunctive relief to require the Commission to comply with this subsection with respect to any subpena which the Commission issues in the future for financial records of such customer for purposes of the same investigation.

(C) Whenever the court determines that the Commission has failed to comply with this subsection, other than paragraph (1), and the court finds that the circumstances raise questions of whether an officer or employee of the Commission acted in a willful and intentional manner and without good faith with respect to the violation, the Office of Personnel Management shall promptly initiate a proceeding to determine whether disciplinary action is warranted against the agent or employee who was primarily responsible for the violation. After investigating and considering the evidence submitted, the Office of Personnel Management shall submit its findings and recommendations to the Commission and shall send copies of the findings and recommendations to the officer or employee or his representative. The Commission shall take the corrective action that the Office of Personnel Management recommends.

(8) The relief described in paragraphs (7) and (10) shall be the only remedies or sanctions available to a customer for a violation of this subsection, other than paragraph (1), and nothing herein or in the Right to Financial Privacy Act of 1978 shall be deemed to prohibit the use in any inves-

tigation or proceeding of financial records, or the information contained therein, obtained by a subpena issued by the Commission. In the case of an unsuccessful action under paragraph (7), the court shall award the costs of the action and attorney's fees to the Commission if the presiding judge or magistrate finds that the customer's claims were made in bad faith.

(9)(A) The Commission may transfer financial records or the information contained therein to any government authority if the Commission proceeds as a transferring agency in accordance with section 1112 of the Right to Financial Privacy Act of 1978, except that the customer notice required under section 1112(b) or (c) of such Act may be delayed upon a showing by the Commission, in accordance with the procedure set forth in paragraphs (4) and (5), that one or more of subparagraphs (A) through (D) of paragraph (2) apply.

(B) The Commission may, without notice to the customer pursuant to section 1112 of the Right to Financial Privacy Act of 1978, transfer financial records or the information contained therein to a State securities agency or to the Department of Justice. Financial records or information transferred by the Commission to the Department of Justice or to a State securities agency pursuant to the provisions of this subparagraph may be disclosed or used only in an administrative, civil, or criminal action or investigation by the Department of Justice or the State securities agency which arises out of or relates to the acts, practices, or courses of conduct investigated by the Commission, except that if the Department of Justice or the State securities agency determines that the information should be disclosed or used for any other purpose, it may do so if it notifies the customer, except as otherwise provided in the Right to Financial Privacy Act of 1978, within 30 days of its determination, or complies with the requirements of section 1109 of such Act regarding delay of notice.

(10) Any government authority violating paragraph (9) shall be subject to the procedures and penalties applicable to the Commission under paragraph (7)(A) with respect to a violation by the Commission in obtaining financial records.

(11) Notwithstanding the provisions of this subsection, the Commission may obtain financial records from a financial institution or transfer such records in accordance with provisions of the Right to Financial Privacy Act of 1978.

(12) Nothing in this subsection shall enlarge or restrict any rights of a financial institution to challenge requests for records made by the Commission under existing law. Nothing in this subsection shall entitle a customer to assert any rights of a financial institution.

(13) Unless the context otherwise requires, all terms defined in the Right to Financial Privacy Act of 1978 which are common to this subsection shall have the same meaning as in such Act.

(i) *Information to CFTC.* The Commission shall provide the Commodity Futures Trading Commission with notice of the commencement of any proceeding and a copy of any order entered by the Commission against any broker or dealer registered pursuant to section 15(b)(11), any exchange registered pursuant to section 6(g), or any national securities association registered pursuant to section 15A(k).

Civil Penalties for Insider Trading

Sec. 21A. (a) *Authority To Impose Civil Penalties.*

(1) *Judicial Actions by Commission Authorized.* Whenever it shall appear to the Commission that any person has violated any provision of this title or the rules or regulations thereunder by purchasing or selling a security or security-based swap agreement while in possession of material, nonpublic information in, or has violated any such provision by communicating such information in connection with, a transaction on or through the facilities of a national securities exchange or from or through a broker or dealer, and which is not part of a public offering by an issuer of securities other than standardized options or security futures products, the Commission—

(A) may bring an action in a United States district court to seek and the court shall have jurisdiction to impose, a civil penalty to be paid by the person who committed such violation; and

(B) may, subject to subsection (b)(1) of this section bring an action in a United States district court to seek, and the court shall have jurisdiction to impose, a civil penalty to be paid by a person who, at the time of the violation, directly or indirectly controlled the person who committed such violation.

(2) *Amount of Penalty for Person Who Committed Violation.* The amount of the penalty which

may be imposed on the person who committed such violation shall be determined by the court in light of the facts and circumstances, but shall not exceed three times the profit gained or loss avoided as a result of such unlawful purchase, sale, or communication.

(3) *Amount of Penalty for Controlling Person.* The amount of the penalty which may be imposed on any person who, at the time of the violation, directly or indirectly controlled the person who committed such violation, shall be determined by the court in light of the facts and circumstances, but shall not exceed the greater of $1,000,000, or three times the amount of the profit gained or loss avoided as a result of such controlled person's violation. If such controlled person's violation was a violation by communication, the profit gained or loss avoided as a result of the violation shall, for purposes of this paragraph only, be deemed to be limited to the profit gained or loss avoided by the person or persons to whom the controlled person directed such communication.

(b) *Limitations on Liability.*

(1) *Liability of Controlling Persons.* No controlling person shall be subject to a penalty under subsection (a)(1)(B) unless the Commission establishes that—

(A) such controlling person knew or recklessly disregarded the fact that such controlled person was likely to engage in the act or acts constituting the violation and failed to take appropriate steps to prevent such act or acts before they occurred; or

(B) such controlling person knowingly or recklessly failed to establish, maintain, or enforce any policy or procedure required under section 15(f) of this title or section 204A of the Investment Advisers Act of 1940 and such failure substantially contributed to or permitted the occurrence of the act or acts constituting the violation.

(2) *Additional Restrictions on Liability.* No person shall be subject to a penalty under subsection (a) of this section solely by reason of employing another person who is subject to a penalty under such subsection, unless such employing person is liable as a controlling person under paragraph (1) of this subsection. Section 20(a) of this title shall not apply to actions under subsection (a) of this section.

(c) *Authority of Commission.* The Commission, by such rules, regulations, and orders as it considers necessary or appropriate in the public interest or for the protection of investors, may exempt, in whole or in part, either unconditionally or upon specific terms and conditions, any person or transaction or class of persons or transactions from this section.

(d) *Procedures for Collection.*

(1) *Payment of Penalty to Treasury.* A penalty imposed under this section shall be payable into the Treasury of the United States, except as otherwise provided in section 308 of the Sarbanes-Oxley Act of 2002 and section 21F of this title.

(2) *Collection of Penalties.* If a person upon whom such a penalty is imposed shall fail to pay such penalty within the time prescribed in the court's order, the Commission may refer the matter to the Attorney General who shall recover such penalty by action in the appropriate United States district court.

(3) *Remedy Not Exclusive.* The actions authorized by this section may be brought in addition to any other actions that the Commission or the Attorney General are entitled to bring.

(4) *Jurisdiction and Venue.* For purposes of section 27 of this title, actions under this section shall be actions to enforce a liability or a duty created by this title.

(5) *Statute of Limitations.* No action may be brought under this section more than 5 years after the date of the purchase or sale. This section shall not be construed to bar or limit in any manner any action by the Commission or the Attorney General under any other provision of this title, nor shall it bar or limit in any manner any action to recover penalties, or to seek any other order regarding penalties, imposed in an action commenced within 5 years of such transaction.

(e) *Definition.* For purposes of this section, "profit gained" or "loss avoided" is the difference between the purchase or sale price of the security and the value of that security as measured by the trading price of the security a reasonable period after public dissemination of the nonpublic information.

(f) *Limitation on Commission Authority.* The authority of the Commission under this section with respect to security-based swap agreements shall be subject to the restrictions and limitations of section 3A(b) of this title.

(g) *Duty of Members and Employees of Congress.*

(1) *In General.* Subject to the rule of construction under section 10 of the STOCK Act and solely

for purposes of the insider trading prohibitions arising under this Act, including section 10(b) and Rule 10b–5 thereunder, each Member of Congress or employee of Congress owes a duty arising from a relationship of trust and confidence to the Congress, the United States Government, and the citizens of the United States with respect to material, nonpublic information derived from such person's position as a Member of Congress or employee of Congress or gained from the performance of such person's official responsibilities.

(2) *Definitions.* In this subsection—

(A) the term "Member of Congress" means a member of the Senate or House of Representatives, a Delegate to the House of Representatives, and the Resident Commissioner from Puerto Rico; and

(B) the term "employee of Congress" means—

(i) any individual (other than a Member of Congress), whose compensation is disbursed by the Secretary of the Senate or the Chief Administrative Officer of the House of Representatives; and

(ii) any other officer or employee of the legislative branch (as defined in section 109(11) of the Ethics in Government Act of 1978).

(3) *Rule of Construction.* Nothing in this subsection shall be construed to impair or limit the construction of the existing antifraud provisions of the securities laws or the authority of the Commission under those provisions.

(h) *Duty of Other Federal Officials.*

(1) *In General.* Subject to the rule of construction under section 10 of the STOCK Act and solely for purposes of the insider trading prohibitions arising under this Act, including section 10(b), and Rule 10b–5 thereunder, each executive branch employee, each judicial officer, and each judicial employee owes a duty arising from a relationship of trust and confidence to the United States Government and the citizens of the United States with respect to material, nonpublic information derived from such person's position as an executive branch employee, judicial officer, or judicial employee or gained from the performance of such person's official responsibilities.

(2) *Definitions.* In this subsection—

(A) the term "executive branch employee"—

(i) has the meaning given the term "employee" under section 2105 of title 5, United States Code;

(ii) includes—

(I) the President;

(II) the Vice President; and

(III) an employee of the United States Postal Service or the Postal Regulatory Commission;

(B) the term "judicial employee" has the meaning given that term in section 109(8) of the Ethics in Government Act of 1978 (5 U.S.C. App. 109(8)); and

(C) the term "judicial officer" has the meaning given that term under section 109(10) of the Ethics in Government Act of 1978.

(3) *Rule of Construction.* Nothing in this subsection shall be construed to impair or limit the construction of the existing antifraud provisions of the securities laws or the authority of the Commission under those provisions.

(i) *Participation in Initial Public Offerings.* An individual described in section 101(f) of the Ethics in Government Act of 1978 may not purchase securities that are the subject of an initial public offering (within the meaning given such term in section 12(f)(1)(G)(i)) in any manner other than is available to members of the public generally.

Civil Remedies in Administrative Proceedings

Sec. 21B. (a) *Commission Authority to Assess Money Penalties.*

(1) *In General.* In any proceeding instituted pursuant to sections 15(b)(4), 15(b)(6), 15B, 15C, 15D, 15E, or 17A of this title against any person, the Commission or the appropriate regulatory agency may impose a civil penalty if it finds, on the record after notice and opportunity for hearing, that such penalty is in the public interest and that such person—

(A) has willfully violated any provision of the Securities Act of 1933, the Investment Company Act of 1940, the Investment Advisers Act of 1940, or this title, or the rules or regulations thereunder, or the rules of the Municipal Securities Rulemaking Board;

(B) has willfully aided, abetted, counseled, commanded, induced, or procured such a violation by any other person;

(C) has willfully made or caused to be made in any application for registration or report required to be filed with the Commission or with any other appropriate regulatory agency under this title, or in any proceeding before the Commission with respect to registration, any statement which was, at the time and in the light of the circumstances under which it was made, false or misleading with respect to any material fact, or has omitted to state in any such application or report any material fact which is required to be stated therein; or

(D) has failed reasonably to supervise, within the meaning of section 15(b)(4)(E), with a view to preventing violations of the provisions of such statutes, rules and regulations, another person who commits such a violation, if such other person is subject to his supervision.

(2) *Cease-and-Desist Proceedings.* In any proceeding instituted under section 21C against any person, the Commission may impose a civil penalty, if the Commission finds, on the record after notice and opportunity for hearing, that such person—

(A) is violating or has violated any provision of this title, or any rule or regulation issued under this title; or

(B) is or was a cause of the violation of any provision of this title, or any rule or regulation issued under this title.

(b) *Maximum Amount of Penalty.*

(1) *First Tier.* The maximum amount of penalty for each act or omission described in subsection (a) of this section shall be $5,000 for a natural person or $50,000 for any other person.

(2) *Second Tier.* Notwithstanding paragraph (1), the maximum amount of penalty for each such act or omission shall be $50,000 for a natural person or $250,000 for any other person if the act or omission described in subsection (a) of this section involved fraud, deceit, manipulation, or deliberate or reckless disregard of a regulatory requirement.

(3) *Third Tier.* Notwithstanding paragraphs (1) and (2), the maximum amount of penalty for each such act or omission shall be $100,000 for a natural person or $500,000 for any other person if—

(A) the act or omission described in subsection (a) of this section involved fraud, deceit, manipulation, or deliberate or reckless disregard of a regulatory requirement; and

(B) such act or omission directly or indirectly resulted in substantial losses or created a significant risk of substantial losses to other persons or resulted in substantial pecuniary gain to the person who committed the act or omission.

(c) *Determination of Public Interest.* In considering under this section whether a penalty is in the public interest, the Commission or the appropriate regulatory agency may consider—

(1) whether the act or omission for which such penalty is assessed involved fraud, deceit, manipulation, or deliberate or reckless disregard of a regulatory requirement;

(2) the harm to other persons resulting either directly or indirectly from such act or omission;

(3) the extent to which any person was unjustly enriched, taking into account any restitution made to persons injured by such behavior;

(4) whether such person previously has been found by the Commission, another appropriate regulatory agency, or a self-regulatory organization to have violated the Federal securities laws, State securities laws, or the rules of a self-regulatory organization, has been enjoined by a court of competent jurisdiction from violations of such laws or rules, or has been convicted by a court of competent jurisdiction of violations of such laws or of any felony or misdemeanor described in section 15(b)(4)(B) of this title;

(5) the need to deter such person and other persons from committing such acts or omissions; and

(6) such other matters as justice may require.

(d) *Evidence Concerning Ability to Pay.* In any proceeding in which the Commission or the appropriate regulatory agency may impose a penalty under this section, a respondent may present evidence of the respondent's ability to pay such penalty. The Commission or the appropriate regulatory agency may, in its discretion, consider such evidence in determining whether such penalty is in the public interest. Such evidence may relate to the extent of such person's ability to continue in business and the collectability of a penalty, taking into account any other claims of the United States or third parties upon such person's assets and the amount of such person's assets.

(e) *Authority to Enter Order Requiring Accounting and Disgorgement.* In any proceeding in which the Commission or the appropriate regulatory agency may impose a penalty under this section, the Commission or the appropriate regulatory agency may enter an order requiring accounting and disgorgement, including reasonable interest. The Commission is authorized to adopt rules, regulations, and orders concerning payments to investors, rates of interest, periods of accrual, and such other matters as it deems appropriate to implement this subsection.

(f) *Security-Based Swaps.*

(1) *Clearing Agency.* Any clearing agency that knowingly or recklessly evades or participates in or facilitates an evasion of the requirements of section 3C shall be liable for a civil money penalty in twice the amount otherwise available for a violation of section 3C.

(2) *Security-Based Swap Dealer or Major Security-Based Swap Participant.* Any security-based swap dealer or major security-based swap participant that knowingly or recklessly evades or participates in or facilitates an evasion of the requirements of section 3C shall be liable for a civil money penalty in twice the amount otherwise available for a violation of section 3C.

Cease-and-Desist Proceedings

Sec. 21C. (a) *Authority of the Commission.* If the Commission finds, after notice and opportunity for hearing, that any person is violating, has violated, or is about to violate any provision of this title, or any rule or regulation thereunder, the Commission may publish its findings and enter an order requiring such person, and any other person that is, was, or would be a cause of the violation, due to an act or omission the person knew or should have known would contribute to such violation, to cease and desist from committing or causing such violation and any future violation of the same provision, rule, or regulation. Such order may, in addition to requiring a person to cease and desist from committing or causing a violation, require such person to comply, or to take steps to effect compliance, with such provision, rule, or regulation, upon such terms and conditions and within such time as the Commission may specify in such order. Any such order may, as the Commission deems appropriate, require future compliance or steps to effect future compliance, either permanently or for such period of time as the Commission may specify, with such provision, rule, or regulation with respect to any security, any issuer, or any other person.

(b) *Hearing.* The notice instituting proceedings pursuant to subsection (a) shall fix a hearing date not earlier than 30 days nor later than 60 days after service of the notice unless an earlier or a later date is set by the Commission with the consent of any respondent so served.

(c) *Temporary Order.*

(1) *In General.* Whenever the Commission determines that the alleged violation or threatened violation specified in the notice instituting proceedings pursuant to subsection (a), or the continuation thereof, is likely to result in significant dissipation or conversion of assets, significant harm to investors, or substantial harm to the public interest, including, but not limited to, losses to the Securities Investor Protection Corporation, prior to the completion of the proceedings, the Commission may enter a temporary order requiring the respondent to cease and desist from the violation or threatened violation and to take such action to prevent the violation or threatened violation and to prevent dissipation or conversion of assets, significant harm to investors, or substantial harm to the public interest as the Commission deems appropriate pending completion of such proceedings. Such an order shall be entered only after notice and opportunity for a hearing, unless the Commission determines that notice and hearing prior to entry would be impracticable or contrary to the public interest. A temporary order shall become effective upon service upon the respondent and, unless set aside, limited, or suspended by the Commission or a court of competent jurisdiction, shall remain effective and enforceable pending the completion of the proceedings.

(2) *Applicability.* Paragraph (1) shall apply only to a respondent that acts, or, at the time of the alleged misconduct acted, as a broker, dealer, investment adviser, investment company, municipal securities dealer, government securities broker, government securities dealer, registered public accounting firm (as defined in section 2 of the Sarbanes–Oxley Act of 2002), or transfer agent, or is, or was at the time of the alleged misconduct, an associated person of, or a person seeking to become associated with, any of the foregoing.

(3) *Temporary Freeze.*

(A) *In General.*

(i) *Issuance of Temporary Order.* Whenever, during the course of a lawful investigation involving possible violations of the Federal securities laws by an issuer of publicly traded securities or any of its directors, officers, partners, controlling persons, agents, or employees, it shall appear to the Commission that it is likely that the issuer will make extraordinary payments (whether compensation or otherwise) to any of the foregoing persons, the Commission may petition a Federal district court for a temporary order requiring the issuer to escrow, subject to court supervision, those payments in an interest-bearing account for 45 days.

(ii) *Standard.* A temporary order shall be entered under clause (i), only after notice and opportunity for a hearing, unless the court determines that notice and hearing prior to entry of the order would be impracticable or contrary to the public interest.

(iii) *Effective Period.* A temporary order issued under clause (i) shall—

(I) become effective immediately;

(II) be served upon the parties subject to it; and

(III) unless set aside, limited or suspended by a court of competent jurisdiction, shall remain effective and enforceable for 45 days.

(iv) *Extensions Authorized.* The effective period of an order under this subparagraph may be extended by the court upon good cause shown for not longer than 45 additional days, provided that the combined period of the order shall not exceed 90 days.

(B) *Process on Determination of Violations.*

(i) *Violations Charged.* If the issuer or other person described in subparagraph (A) is charged with any violation of the Federal securities laws before the expiration of the effective period of a temporary order under subparagraph (A) (including any applicable extension period), the order shall remain in effect, subject to court approval, until the conclusion of any legal proceedings related thereto, and the affected issuer or other person, shall have the right to petition the court for review of the order.

(ii) *Violations Not Charged.* If the issuer or other person described in subparagraph (A) is not charged with any violation of the Federal securities laws before the expiration of the effective period of a temporary order under subparagraph (A) (including any applicable extension period), the escrow shall terminate at the expiration of the 45–day effective period (or the expiration of any extension period, as applicable), and the disputed payments (with accrued interest) shall be returned to the issuer or other affected person.

(d) *Review of Temporary Orders.*

(1) *Commission Review.* At any time after the respondent has been served with a temporary cease-and-desist order pursuant to subsection (c), the respondent may apply to the Commission to have the order set aside, limited, or suspended. If the respondent has been served with a temporary cease-and-desist order entered without a prior Commission hearing, the respondent may, within 10 days after the date on which the order was served, request a hearing on such application and the Commission shall hold a hearing and render a decision on such application at the earliest possible time.

(2) *Judicial Review.* Within—

(A) 10 days after the date the respondent was served with a temporary cease-and-desist order entered with a prior Commission hearing, or

(B) 10 days after the Commission renders a decision on an application and hearing under paragraph (1), with respect to any temporary cease-and-desist order entered without a prior Commission hearing,

the respondent may apply to the United States district court for the district in which the respondent resides or has its principal place of business, or for the District of Columbia, for an order setting aside, limiting, or suspending the effectiveness or enforcement of the order, and the court shall have jurisdiction to enter such an order. A respondent served with a temporary cease-and-desist order entered without a prior Commission hearing may not apply to the court except after hearing and decision by the Commission on the respondent's application under paragraph (1) of this subsection.

(3) *No Automatic Stay of Temporary Order.* The commencement of proceedings under paragraph (2) of this subsection shall not, unless specifically ordered by the court, operate as a stay of the Commission's order.

(4) *Exclusive Review.* Section 25 of this title shall not apply to a temporary order entered pursuant to this section.

(e) *Authority to Enter an Order Requiring an Accounting and Disgorgement.* In any cease-and-desist proceeding under subsection (a), the Commission may enter an order requiring accounting and disgorgement, including reasonable interest. The Commission is authorized to adopt rules, regulations, and orders concerning payments to investors, rates of interest, periods of accrual, and such other matters as it deems appropriate to implement this subsection.

(f) *Authority of the Commission to Prohibit Persons from Serving as Officers or Directors.* In any cease-and-desist proceeding under subsection (a), the Commission may issue an order to prohibit, conditionally or unconditionally, and permanently or for such period of time as it shall determine, any person who has violated section 10(b) or the rules or regulations thereunder, from acting as an officer or director of any issuer that has a class of securities registered pursuant to section 12, or that is required to file reports pursuant to section 15(d), if the conduct of that person demonstrates unfitness to serve as an officer or director of any such issuer.

Private Securities Litigation

Sec. 21D. (a) *Private Class Actions.*

(1) *In General.* The provisions of this subsection shall apply in each private action arising under this title that is brought as a plaintiff class action pursuant to the Federal Rules of Civil Procedure.

(2) *Certification Filed with Complaint.*

(A) *In General.* Each plaintiff seeking to serve as a representative party on behalf of a class shall provide a sworn certification, which shall be personally signed by such plaintiff and filed with the complaint, that—

(i) states that the plaintiff has reviewed the complaint and authorized its filing;

(ii) states that the plaintiff did not purchase the security that is the subject of the complaint at the direction of plaintiff's counsel or in order to participate in any private action arising under this title;

(iii) states that the plaintiff is willing to serve as a representative party on behalf of a class, including providing testimony at deposition and trial, if necessary;

(iv) sets forth all of the transactions of the plaintiff in the security that is the subject of the complaint during the class period specified in the complaint;

(v) identifies any other action under this title, filed during the 3-year period preceding the date on which the certification is signed by the plaintiff, in which the plaintiff has sought to serve as a representative party on behalf of a class; and

(vi) states that the plaintiff will not accept any payment for serving as a representative party on behalf of a class beyond the plaintiff's pro rata share of any recovery, except as ordered or approved by the court in accordance with paragraph (4).

(B) *Nonwaiver of Attorney–Client Privilege.* The certification filed pursuant to subparagraph (A) shall not be construed to be a waiver of the attorney-client privilege.

(3) *Appointment of Lead Plaintiff.*

(A) *Early Notice to Class Members.*

(i) *In General.* Not later than 20 days after the date on which the complaint is filed, the plaintiff or plaintiffs shall cause to be published, in a widely circulated national business-oriented publication or wire service, a notice advising members of the purported plaintiff class—

(I) of the pendency of the action, the claims asserted therein, and the purported class period; and

(II) that, not later than 60 days after the date on which the notice is published, any member of the purported class may move the court to serve as lead plaintiff of the purported class.

(ii) *Multiple Actions.* If more than one action on behalf of a class asserting substantially the same claim or claims arising under this title is filed, only the plaintiff or plaintiffs in the first filed action shall be required to cause notice to be published in accordance with clause (i).

(iii) *Additional Notices May Be Required Under Federal Rules.* Notice required under clause (i) shall be in addition to any notice required pursuant to the Federal Rules of Civil Procedure.

(B) *Appointment of Lead Plaintiff.*

(i) *In General.* Not later than 90 days after the date on which a notice is published under subparagraph (A)(i), the court shall consider any motion made by a purported class member in response to the notice, including any motion by a class member who is not individually named as a plaintiff in the complaint or complaints, and shall appoint as lead plaintiff the member or members of the purported plaintiff class that the court determines to be most capable of adequately representing the interests of class members (hereafter in this paragraph referred to as the "most adequate plaintiff") in accordance with this subparagraph.

(ii) *Consolidated Actions.* If more than one action on behalf of a class asserting substantially the same claim or claims arising under this title has been filed, and any party has sought to consolidate those actions for pretrial purposes or for trial, the court shall not make the determination required by clause (i) until after the decision on the motion to consolidate is rendered. As soon as practicable after such decision is rendered, the court shall appoint the most adequate plaintiff as lead plaintiff for the consolidated actions in accordance with this paragraph.

(iii) *Rebuttable Presumption.*

(I) *In General.* Subject to subclause (II), for purposes of clause (i), the court shall adopt a presumption that the most adequate plaintiff in any private action arising under this title is the person or group of persons that—

(aa) has either filed the complaint or made a motion in response to a notice under subparagraph (A)(i);

(bb) in the determination of the court, has the largest financial interest in the relief sought by the class; and

(cc) otherwise satisfies the requirements of Rule 23 of the Federal Rules of Civil Procedure.

(II) *Rebuttal Evidence.* The presumption described in subclause (I) may be rebutted only upon proof by a member of the purported plaintiff class that the presumptively most adequate plaintiff—

(aa) will not fairly and adequately protect the interests of the class; or

(bb) is subject to unique defenses that render such plaintiff incapable of adequately representing the class.

(iv) *Discovery.* For purposes of this subparagraph, discovery relating to whether a member or members of the purported plaintiff class is the most adequate plaintiff may be conducted by a plaintiff only if the plaintiff first demonstrates a reasonable basis for a finding that the presumptively most adequate plaintiff is incapable of adequately representing the class.

(v) *Selection of Lead Counsel.* The most adequate plaintiff shall, subject to the approval of the court, select and retain counsel to represent the class.

(vi) *Restrictions on Professional Plaintiffs.* Except as the court may otherwise permit, consistent with the purposes of this section, a person may be a lead plaintiff, or an officer, director, or fiduciary of a lead plaintiff, in no more than 5 securities class actions brought as plaintiff class actions pursuant to the Federal Rules of Civil Procedure during any 3–year period.

(4) *Recovery by Plaintiffs.* The share of any final judgment or of any settlement that is awarded to a representative party serving on behalf of a class shall be equal, on a per share basis, to the portion of the final judgment or settlement awarded to all other members of the class. Nothing in this paragraph shall be construed to limit the award of reasonable costs and expenses (including lost wages) directly relating to the representation of the class to any representative party serving on behalf of a class.

(5) *Restrictions on Settlements Under Seal.* The terms and provisions of any settlement agreement of a class action shall not be filed under seal, except that on motion of any party to the settlement, the court may order filing under seal for those portions of a settlement agreement as to which good cause is shown for such filing under seal. For purposes of this paragraph, good cause shall exist only if publication of a term or provision of a settlement agreement would cause direct and substantial harm to any party.

(6) *Restrictions on Payment of Attorneys' Fees and Expenses.* Total attorneys' fees and expenses

awarded by the court to counsel for the plaintiff class shall not exceed a reasonable percentage of the amount of any damages and prejudgment interest actually paid to the class.

(7) *Disclosure of Settlement Terms to Class Members.* Any proposed or final settlement agreement that is published or otherwise disseminated to the class shall include each of the following statements, along with a cover page summarizing the information contained in such statements:

(A) *Statement of Plaintiff Recovery.* The amount of the settlement proposed to be distributed to the parties to the action, determined in the aggregate and on an average per share basis.

(B) *Statement of Potential Outcome of Case.*

(i) *Agreement on Amount of Damages.* If the settling parties agree on the average amount of damages per share that would be recoverable if the plaintiff prevailed on each claim alleged under this title, a statement concerning the average amount of such potential damages per share.

(ii) *Disagreement on Amount of Damages.* If the parties do not agree on the average amount of damages per share that would be recoverable if the plaintiff prevailed on each claim alleged under this title, a statement from each settling party concerning the issue or issues on which the parties disagree.

(iii) *Inadmissibility for Certain Purposes.* A statement made in accordance with clause (i) or (ii) concerning the amount of damages shall not be admissible in any Federal or State judicial action or administrative proceeding, other than an action or proceeding arising out of such statement.

(C) *Statement of Attorneys' Fees or Costs Sought.* If any of the settling parties or their counsel intend to apply to the court for an award of attorneys' fees or costs from any fund established as part of the settlement, a statement indicating which parties or counsel intend to make such an application, the amount of fees and costs that will be sought (including the amount of such fees and costs determined on an average per share basis), and a brief explanation supporting the fees and costs sought. Such information shall be clearly summarized on the cover page of any notice to a party of any proposed or final settlement agreement.

(D) *Identification of Lawyers' Representatives.* The name, telephone number, and address of one or more representatives of counsel for the plaintiff class who will be reasonably available to answer questions from class members concerning any matter contained in any notice of settlement published or otherwise disseminated to the class.

(E) *Reasons for Settlement.* A brief statement explaining the reasons why the parties are proposing the settlement.

(F) *Other Information.* Such other information as may be required by the court.

(8) *Security for Payment of Costs in Class Actions.* In any private action arising under this title that is certified as a class action pursuant to the Federal Rules of Civil Procedure, the court may require an undertaking from the attorneys for the plaintiff class, the plaintiff class, or both, or from the attorneys for the defendant, the defendant, or both, in such proportions and at such times as the court determines are just and equitable, for the payment of fees and expenses that may be awarded under this subsection.

(9) *Attorney Conflict of Interest.* If a plaintiff class is represented by an attorney who directly owns or otherwise has a beneficial interest in the securities that are the subject of the litigation, the court shall make a determination of whether such ownership or other interest constitutes a conflict of interest sufficient to disqualify the attorney from representing the plaintiff class.

(b) *Requirements for Securities Fraud Actions.*

(1) *Misleading Statements and Omissions.* In any private action arising under this title in which the plaintiff alleges that the defendant—

(A) made an untrue statement of a material fact; or

(B) omitted to state a material fact necessary in order to make the statements made, in the light of the circumstances in which they were made, not misleading;

the complaint shall specify each statement alleged to have been misleading, the reason or reasons why the statement is misleading, and, if an allegation regarding the statement or omission is made on information and belief, the complaint shall state with particularity all facts on which that belief is formed.

(2) *Required State of Mind.*

(A) *In General.* Except as provided in subparagraph (B), in any private action arising under this title in which the plaintiff may recover money damages only on proof that the defendant acted with a particular state of mind, the complaint shall, with respect to each act or omission alleged to violate this title, state with particularity facts giving rise to a strong inference that the defendant acted with the required state of mind.

(B) *Exception.* In the case of an action for money damages brought against a credit rating agency or a controlling person under this title, it shall be sufficient, for purposes of pleading any required state of mind in relation to such action, that the complaint state with particularity facts giving rise to a strong inference that the credit rating agency knowingly or recklessly failed—

(i) to conduct a reasonable investigation of the rated security with respect to the factual elements relied upon by its own methodology for evaluating credit risk; or

(ii) to obtain reasonable verification of such factual elements (which verification may be based on a sampling technique that does not amount to an audit) from other sources that the credit rating agency considered to be competent and that were independent of the issuer and underwriter.

(3) *Motion to Dismiss; Stay of Discovery.*

(A) *Dismissal for Failure to Meet Pleading Requirements.* In any private action arising under this title, the court shall, on the motion of any defendant, dismiss the complaint if the requirements of paragraphs (1) and (2) are not met.

(B) *Stay of Discovery.* In any private action arising under this title, all discovery and other proceedings shall be stayed during the pendency of any motion to dismiss, unless the court finds upon the motion of any party that particularized discovery is necessary to preserve evidence or to prevent undue prejudice to that party.

(C) *Preservation of Evidence.*

(i) *In General.* During the pendency of any stay of discovery pursuant to this paragraph, unless otherwise ordered by the court, any party to the action with actual notice of the allegations contained in the complaint shall treat all documents, data compilations (including electronically recorded or stored data), and tangible objects that are in the custody or control of such person and that are relevant to the allegations, as if they were the subject of a continuing request for production of documents from an opposing party under the Federal Rules of Civil Procedure.

(ii) *Sanction for Willful Violation.* A party aggrieved by the willful failure of an opposing party to comply with clause (i) may apply to the court for an order awarding appropriate sanctions.

(D) *Circumvention of Stay of Discovery.* Upon a proper showing, a court may stay discovery proceedings in any private action in a State court, as necessary in aid of its jurisdiction, or to protect or effectuate its judgments, in an action subject to a stay of discovery pursuant to this paragraph.

(4) *Loss Causation.* In any private action arising under this title, the plaintiff shall have the burden of proving that the act or omission of the defendant alleged to violate this title caused the loss for which the plaintiff seeks to recover damages.

(c) *Sanctions for Abusive Litigation.*

(1) *Mandatory Review by Court.* In any private action arising under this title, upon final adjudication of the action, the court shall include in the record specific findings regarding compliance by each party and each attorney representing any party with each requirement of Rule 11(b) of the Federal Rules of Civil Procedure as to any complaint, responsive pleading, or dispositive motion.

(2) *Mandatory Sanctions.* If the court makes a finding under paragraph (1) that a party or attorney violated any requirement of Rule 11(b) of the Federal Rules of Civil Procedure as to any complaint, responsive pleading, or dispositive motion, the court shall impose sanctions on such party or attorney in accordance with Rule 11 of the Federal Rules of Civil Procedure. Prior to making a finding that any party or attorney has violated Rule 11 of the Federal Rules of Civil Procedure, the court shall give such party or attorney notice and an opportunity to respond.

(3) *Presumption in Favor of Attorneys' Fees and Costs.*

(A) *In General.* Subject to subparagraphs (B) and (C), for purposes of paragraph (2), the court shall adopt a presumption that the appropriate sanction—

(i) for failure of any responsive pleading or dispositive motion to comply with any requirement of Rule 11(b) of the Federal Rules of Civil Procedure is an award to the opposing party of the reasonable attorneys' fees and other expenses incurred as a direct result of the violation; and

(ii) for substantial failure of any complaint to comply with any requirement of Rule 11(b) of the Federal Rules of Civil Procedure is an award to the opposing party of the reasonable attorneys' fees and other expenses incurred in the action.

(B) *Rebuttal Evidence.* The presumption described in subparagraph (A) may be rebutted only upon proof by the party or attorney against whom sanctions are to be imposed that—

(i) the award of attorneys' fees and other expenses will impose an unreasonable burden on that party or attorney and would be unjust, and the failure to make such an award would not impose a greater burden on the party in whose favor sanctions are to be imposed; or

(ii) the violation of Rule 11(b) of the Federal Rules of Civil Procedure was de minimis.

(C) *Sanctions.* If the party or attorney against whom sanctions are to be imposed meets its burden under subparagraph (B), the court shall award the sanctions that the court deems appropriate pursuant to Rule 11 of the Federal Rules of Civil Procedure.

(d) *Defendant's Right to Written Interrogatories.* In any private action arising under this title in which the plaintiff may recover money damages, the court shall, when requested by a defendant, submit to the jury a written interrogatory on the issue of each such defendant's state of mind at the time the alleged violation occurred.

(e) *Limitation on Damages.*

(1) *In General.* Except as provided in paragraph (2), in any private action arising under this title in which the plaintiff seeks to establish damages by reference to the market price of a security, the award of damages to the plaintiff shall not exceed the difference between the purchase or sale price paid or received, as appropriate, by the plaintiff for the subject security and the mean trading price of that security during the 90–day period beginning on the date on which the information correcting the misstatement or omission that is the basis for the action is disseminated to the market.

(2) *Exception.* In any private action arising under this title in which the plaintiff seeks to establish damages by reference to the market price of a security, if the plaintiff sells or repurchases the subject security prior to the expiration of the 90–day period described in paragraph (1), the plaintiff's damages shall not exceed the difference between the purchase or sale price paid or received, as appropriate, by the plaintiff for the security and the mean trading price of the security during the period beginning immediately after dissemination of information correcting the misstatement or omission and ending on the date on which the plaintiff sells or repurchases the security.

(3) *Definition.* For purposes of this subsection, the "mean trading price" of a security shall be an average of the daily trading price of that security, determined as of the close of the market each day during the 90–day period referred to in paragraph (1).

(f) *Proportionate Liability.*

(1) *Applicability.* Nothing in this subsection shall be construed to create, affect, or in any manner modify, the standard for liability associated with any action arising under the securities laws.

(2) *Liability for Damages.*

(A) *Joint and Several Liability.* Any covered person against whom a final judgment is entered in a private action shall be liable for damages jointly and severally only if the trier of fact specifically determines that such covered person knowingly committed a violation of the securities laws.

(B) *Proportionate Liability.*

(i) *In General.* Except as provided in subparagraph (A), a covered person against whom a final judgment is entered in a private action shall be liable solely for the portion of the judgment that corresponds to the percentage of responsibility of that covered person, as determined under paragraph (3).

(ii) *Recovery by and Costs of Covered Person.* In any case in which a contractual relationship permits, a covered person that prevails in any private action may recover the attorney's fees and costs of that covered person in connection with the action.

(3) *Determination of Responsibility.*

* Editors note. The statute appears to be incorrect. The "[if]" has be inserted for clarifications.

(A) *In General.* In any private action, the court shall instruct the jury to answer special interrogatories, or if there is no jury, shall make findings, with respect to each covered person and each of the other persons claimed by any of the parties to have caused or contributed to the loss incurred by the plaintiff, including persons who have entered into settlements with the plaintiff or plaintiffs, concerning—

(i) whether such person violated the securities laws;

(ii) the percentage of responsibility of such person, measured as a percentage of the total fault of all persons who caused or contributed to the loss incurred by the plaintiff; and

(iii) whether such person knowingly committed a violation of the securities laws.

(B) *Contents of Special Interrogatories or Findings.* The responses to interrogatories, or findings, as appropriate, under subparagraph (A) shall specify the total amount of damages that the plaintiff is entitled to recover and the percentage of responsibility of each covered person found to have caused or contributed to the loss incurred by the plaintiff or plaintiffs.

(C) *Factors for Consideration.* In determining the percentage of responsibility under this paragraph, the trier of fact shall consider—

(i) the nature of the conduct of each covered person found to have caused or contributed to the loss incurred by the plaintiff or plaintiffs; and

(ii) the nature and extent of the causal relationship between the conduct of each such person and the damages incurred by the plaintiff or plaintiffs.

(4) *Uncollectible Share.*

(A) *In General.* Notwithstanding paragraph (2)(B), [if]* upon motion made not later than 6 months after a final judgment is entered in any private action, the court determines that all or part of the share of the judgment of the covered person is not collectible against that covered person, and is also not collectible against a covered person described in paragraph (2)(A), each covered person described in paragraph (2)(B) shall be liable for the uncollectible share as follows:

(i) *Percentage of Net Worth.* Each covered person shall be jointly and severally liable for the uncollectible share if the plaintiff establishes that—

(I) the plaintiff is an individual whose recoverable damages under the final judgment are equal to more than 10 percent of the net worth of the plaintiff; and

(II) the net worth of the plaintiff is equal to less than $200,000.

(ii) *Other Plaintiffs.* With respect to any plaintiff not described in subclauses (I) and (II) of clause (i), each covered person shall be liable for the uncollectible share in proportion to the percentage of responsibility of that covered person, except that the total liability of a covered person under this clause may not exceed 50 percent of the proportionate share of that covered person, as determined under paragraph (3)(B).

(iii) *Net Worth.* For purposes of this subparagraph, net worth shall be determined as of the date immediately preceding the date of the purchase or sale (as applicable) by the plaintiff of the security that is the subject of the action, and shall be equal to the fair market value of assets, minus liabilities, including the net value of the investments of the plaintiff in real and personal property (including personal residences).

(B) *Overall Limit.* In no case shall the total payments required pursuant to subparagraph (A) exceed the amount of the uncollectible share.

(C) *Covered Persons Subject to Contribution.* A covered person against whom judgment is not collectible shall be subject to contribution and to any continuing liability to the plaintiff on the judgment.

(5) *Right of Contribution.* To the extent that a covered person is required to make an additional payment pursuant to paragraph (4), that covered person may recover contribution—

(A) from the covered person originally liable to make the payment;

(B) from any covered person liable jointly and severally pursuant to paragraph (2)(A);

(C) from any covered person held proportionately liable pursuant to this paragraph who is liable to make the same payment and has paid less than his or her proportionate share of that payment; or

(D) from any other person responsible for the conduct giving rise to the payment that would have been liable to make the same payment.

(6) *Nondisclosure to Jury.* The standard for allocation of damages under paragraphs (2) and (3) and the procedure for reallocation of uncollectible shares under paragraph (4) shall not be disclosed to members of the jury.

(7) *Settlement Discharge.*

(A) *In General.* A covered person who settles any private action at any time before final verdict or judgment shall be discharged from all claims for contribution brought by other persons. Upon entry of the settlement by the court, the court shall enter a bar order constituting the final discharge of all obligations to the plaintiff of the settling covered person arising out of the action. The order shall bar all future claims for contribution arising out of the action—

(i) by any person against the settling covered person; and

(ii) by the settling covered person against any person, other than a person whose liability has been extinguished by the settlement of the settling covered person.

(B) *Reduction.* If a covered person enters into a settlement with the plaintiff prior to final verdict or judgment, the verdict or judgment shall be reduced by the greater of—

(i) an amount that corresponds to the percentage of responsibility of that covered person; or

(ii) the amount paid to the plaintiff by that covered person.

(8) *Contribution.* A covered person who becomes jointly and severally liable for damages in any private action may recover contribution from any other person who, if joined in the original action, would have been liable for the same damages. A claim for contribution shall be determined based on the percentage of responsibility of the claimant and of each person against whom a claim for contribution is made.

(9) *Statute of Limitations for Contribution.* In any private action determining liability, an action for contribution shall be brought not later than 6 months after the entry of a final, nonappealable judgment in the action, except that an action for contribution brought by a covered person who was required to make an additional payment pursuant to paragraph (4) may be brought not later than 6 months after the date on which such payment was made.

(10) *Definitions.* For purposes of this subsection—

(A) a covered person "knowingly commits a violation of the securities laws"—

(i) with respect to an action that is based on an untrue statement of material fact or omission of a material fact necessary to make the statement not misleading, if—

(I) that covered person makes an untrue statement of a material fact, with actual knowledge that the representation is false, or omits to state a fact necessary in order to make the statement made not misleading, with actual knowledge that, as a result of the omission, one of the material representations of the covered person is false; and

(II) persons are likely to reasonably rely on that misrepresentation or omission; and

(ii) with respect to an action that is based on any conduct that is not described in clause (i), if that covered person engages in that conduct with actual knowledge of the facts and circumstances that make the conduct of that covered person a violation of the securities laws;

(B) reckless conduct by a covered person shall not be construed to constitute a knowing commission of a violation of the securities laws by that covered person;

(C) the term "covered person" means—

(i) a defendant in any private action arising under this title; or

(ii) a defendant in any private action arising under section 11 of the Securities Act of 1933, who is an outside director of the issuer of the securities that are the subject of the action; and

(D) the term "outside director" shall have the meaning given such term by rule or regulation of the Commission.

Application of Safe Harbor for Forward-Looking Statements

Sec. 21E. (a) *Applicability.* This section shall apply only to a forward-looking statement made by—

(1) an issuer that, at the time that the statement is made, is subject to the reporting requirements of section 13(a) or section 15(d);

(2) a person acting on behalf of such issuer;

(3) an outside reviewer retained by such issuer making a statement on behalf of such issuer; or

(4) an underwriter, with respect to information provided by such issuer or information derived from information provided by such issuer.

(b) *Exclusions.* Except to the extent otherwise specifically provided by rule, regulation, or order of the Commission, this section shall not apply to a forward-looking statement—

(1) that is made with respect to the business or operations of the issuer, if the issuer—

(A) during the 3–year period preceding the date on which the statement was first made—

(i) was convicted of any felony or misdemeanor described in clauses (i) through (iv) of section 15(b)(4)(B); or

(ii) has been made the subject of a judicial or administrative decree or order arising out of a governmental action that—

(I) prohibits future violations of the antifraud provisions of the securities laws;

(II) requires that the issuer cease and desist from violating the antifraud provisions of the securities laws; or

(III) determines that the issuer violated the antifraud provisions of the securities laws;

(B) makes the forward-looking statement in connection with an offering of securities by a blank check company;

(C) issues penny stock;

(D) makes the forward-looking statement in connection with a rollup transaction; or

(E) makes the forward-looking statement in connection with a going private transaction; or

(2) that is—

(A) included in a financial statement prepared in accordance with generally accepted accounting principles;

(B) contained in a registration statement of, or otherwise issued by, an investment company;

(C) made in connection with a tender offer;

(D) made in connection with an initial public offering;

(E) made in connection with an offering by, or relating to the operations of, a partnership, limited liability company, or a direct participation investment program; or

(F) made in a disclosure of beneficial ownership in a report required to be filed with the Commission pursuant to section 13(d).

(c) *Safe Harbor.*

(1) *In General.* Except as provided in subsection (b), in any private action arising under this title that is based on an untrue statement of a material fact or omission of a material fact necessary to make the statement not misleading, a person referred to in subsection (a) shall not be liable with respect to any forward-looking statement, whether written or oral, if and to the extent that—

(A) the forward-looking statement is—

(i) identified as a forward-looking statement, and is accompanied by meaningful cautionary statements identifying important factors that could cause actual results to differ materially from those in the forward-looking statement; or

(ii) immaterial; or

(B) the plaintiff fails to prove that the forward-looking statement—

(i) if made by a natural person, was made with actual knowledge by that person that the statement was false or misleading; or

(ii) if made by a business entity, was—

(I) made by or with the approval of an executive officer of that entity; and

(II) made or approved by such officer with actual knowledge by that officer that the statement was false or misleading.

(2) *Oral Forward–Looking Statements.* In the case of an oral forward-looking statement made by an issuer that is subject to the reporting requirements of section 13(a) or section 15(d), or by a person acting on behalf of such issuer, the requirement set forth in paragraph (1)(A) shall be deemed to be satisfied—

(A) if the oral forward-looking statement is accompanied by a cautionary statement—

(i) that the particular oral statement is a forward-looking statement; and

(ii) that the actual results might differ materially from those projected in the forward-looking statement; and

(B) if—

(i) the oral forward-looking statement is accompanied by an oral statement that additional information concerning factors that could cause actual results to materially differ from those in the forward-looking statement is contained in a readily available written document, or portion thereof;

(ii) the accompanying oral statement referred to in clause (i) identifies the document, or portion thereof, that contains the additional information about those factors relating to the forward-looking statement; and

(iii) the information contained in that written document is a cautionary statement that satisfies the standard established in paragraph (1)(A).

(3) *Availability.* Any document filed with the Commission or generally disseminated shall be deemed to be readily available for purposes of paragraph (2).

(4) *Effect on Other Safe Harbors.* The exemption provided for in paragraph (1) shall be in addition to any exemption that the Commission may establish by rule or regulation under subsection (g).

(d) *Duty to Update.* Nothing in this section shall impose upon any person a duty to update a forward-looking statement.

(e) *Dispositive Motion.* On any motion to dismiss based upon subsection (c)(1), the court shall consider any statement cited in the complaint and any cautionary statement accompanying the forward-looking statement, which are not subject to material dispute, cited by the defendant.

(f) *Stay Pending Decision on Motion.* In any private action arising under this title, the court shall stay discovery (other than discovery that is specifically directed to the applicability of the exemption provided for in this section) during the pendency of any motion by a defendant for summary judgment that is based on the grounds that—

(1) the statement or omission upon which the complaint is based is a forward-looking statement within the meaning of this section; and

(2) the exemption provided for in this section precludes a claim for relief.

(g) *Exemption Authority.* In addition to the exemptions provided for in this section, the Commission may, by rule or regulation, provide exemptions from or under any provision of this title, including with respect to liability that is based on a statement or that is based on projections or other forward-looking information, if and to the extent that any such exemption is consistent with the public interest and the protection of investors, as determined by the Commission.

(h) *Effect on Other Authority of Commission.* Nothing in this section limits, either expressly or by implication, the authority of the Commission to exercise similar authority or to adopt similar rules and regulations with respect to forward-looking statements under any other statute under which the Commission exercises rulemaking authority.

(i) *Definitions.* For purposes of this section, the following definitions shall apply:

(1) *Forward–Looking Statement.* The term "forward-looking statement" means—

(A) a statement containing a projection of revenues, income (including income loss), earnings (including earnings loss) per share, capital expenditures, dividends, capital structure, or other financial items;

(B) a statement of the plans and objectives of management for future operations, including plans or objectives relating to the products or services of the issuer;

(C) a statement of future economic performance, including any such statement contained in a discussion and analysis of financial condition by the management or in the results of operations included pursuant to the rules and regulations of the Commission;

(D) any statement of the assumptions underlying or relating to any statement described in subparagraph (A), (B), or (C);

(E) any report issued by an outside reviewer retained by an issuer, to the extent that the report assesses a forward-looking statement made by the issuer; or

(F) a statement containing a projection or estimate of such other items as may be specified by rule or regulation of the Commission.

(2) *Investment Company.* The term "investment company" has the same meaning as in section 3(a) of the Investment Company Act of 1940.

(3) *Going Private Transaction.* The term "going private transaction" has the meaning given that term under the rules or regulations of the Commission issued pursuant to section 13(e).

(4) *Person Acting on Behalf of an Issuer.* The term "person acting on behalf of an issuer" means any officer, director, or employee of such issuer.

(5) *Other Terms.* The terms "blank check company", "roll-up transaction", "partnership", "limited liability company", "executive officer of an entity" and "direct participation investment program", have the meanings given those terms by rule or regulation of the Commission.

Securities Whistleblower Incentives and Protection

Sec. 21F. (a) *Definitions.* In this section the following definitions shall apply:

(1) *Covered Judicial or Administrative Action.* The term "covered judicial or administrative action" means any judicial or administrative action brought by the Commission under the securities laws that results in monetary sanctions exceeding $1,000,000.

(2) *Fund.* The term "Fund" means the Securities and Exchange Commission Investor Protection Fund.

(3) *Original Information.* The term 'original information' means information that—

(A) is derived from the independent knowledge or analysis of a whistleblower;

(B) is not known to the Commission from any other source, unless the whistleblower is the original source of the information; and

(C) is not exclusively derived from an allegation made in a judicial or administrative hearing, in a governmental report, hearing, audit, or investigation, or from the news media, unless the whistleblower is a source of the information.

(4) *Monetary Sanctions.* The term "monetary sanctions", when used with respect to any judicial or administrative action, means—

(A) any monies, including penalties, disgorgement, and interest, ordered to be paid; and

(B) any monies deposited into a disgorgement fund or other fund pursuant to section 308(b) of the Sarbanes–Oxley Act of 2002, as a result of such action or any settlement of such action.

(5) *Related Action.* The term "related action", when used with respect to any judicial or administrative action brought by the Commission under the securities laws, means any judicial or administrative action brought by an entity described in subclauses (I) through (IV) of subsection (h)(2)(D)(i) that is based upon the original information provided by a whistleblower pursuant to subsection (a) that led to the successful enforcement of the Commission action.

(6) *Whistleblower.* The term "whistleblower" means any individual who provides, or 2 or more individuals acting jointly who provide, information relating to a violation of the securities laws to the Commission, in a manner established, by rule or regulation, by the Commission.

(b) *Awards.*

(1) *In General.* In any covered judicial or administrative action, or related action, the Commission, under regulations prescribed by the Commission and subject to subsection (c), shall pay an award or awards to 1 or more whistleblowers who voluntarily provided original information to the Commission that led to the successful enforcement of the covered judicial or administrative action, or related action, in an aggregate amount equal to—

(A) not less than 10 percent, in total, of what has been collected of the monetary sanctions imposed in the action or related actions; and

(B) not more than 30 percent, in total, of what has been collected of the monetary sanctions imposed in the action or related actions.

(2) *Payment of Awards.* Any amount paid under paragraph (1) shall be paid from the Fund.

(c) *Determination of Amount of Award; Denial of Award.*

(1) *Determination of Amount of Award.*

(A) *Discretion.* The determination of the amount of an award made under subsection (b) shall be in the discretion of the Commission.

(B) *Criteria.* In determining the amount of an award made under subsection (b), the Commission—

(i) shall take into consideration—

(I) the significance of the information provided by the whistleblower to the success of the covered judicial or administrative action;

(II) the degree of assistance provided by the whistle blower and any legal representative of the whistleblower in a covered judicial or administrative action;

(III) the programmatic interest of the Commission in deterring violations of the securities laws by making awards to whistleblowers who provide information that lead to the successful enforcement of such laws; and

(IV) such additional relevant factors as the Commission may establish by rule or regulation; and

(ii) shall not take into consideration the balance of the Fund.

(2) *Denial of Award.* No award under subsection (b) shall be made—

(A) to any whistleblower who is, or was at the time the whistleblower acquired the original information submitted to the commission, a member, officer, or employee of—

(i) an appropriate regulatory agency;

(ii) the Department of Justice;

(iii) a self-regulatory organization;

(iv) the Public Company Accounting Oversight Board; or

(v) a law enforcement organization;

(B) to any whistleblower who is convicted of a criminal violation related to the judicial or administrative action for which the whistleblower otherwise could receive an award under this section;

(C) to any whistleblower who gains the information through the performance of an audit of financial statements required under the securities laws and for whom such submission would be contrary to the requirements of section 10A of the Securities Exchange Act of 1934; or

(D) to any whistleblower who fails to submit information to the Commission in such form as the Commission may, by rule, require.

(d) *Representation.*

(1) *Permitted Representation.* Any whistleblower who makes a claim for an award under subsection (b) may be represented by counsel.

(2) *Required Representation.*

(A) *In General.* Any whistleblower who anonymously makes a claim for an award under subsection (b) shall be represented by counsel if the whistleblower anonymously submits the information upon which the claim is based.

(B) *Disclosure of Identity.* Prior to the payment of an award, a whistleblower shall disclose the identity of the whistleblower and provide such other information as the Commission may require, directly or through counsel for the whistleblower.

(e) *No Contract Necessary.* No contract with the Commission is necessary for any whistleblower to receive an award under subsection (b), unless otherwise required by the Commission by rule or regulation.

(f) *Appeals.* Any determination made under this section, including whether, to whom, or in what amount to make awards, shall be in the discretion of the Commission. Any such determination, except the determination of the amount of an award if the award was made in accordance with subsection (b), may be appealed to the appropriate court of appeals of the United States not more than 30 days after the determination is issued by the Commission. The court shall review the determination made by the Commission in accordance with section 706 of title 5, United States Code.

(g) *Investor Protection Fund.*

(1) *Fund Established.* There is established in the Treasury of the United States a fund to be known as the 'Securities and Exchange Commission Investor Protection Fund'.

(2) *Use of Fund.* The Fund shall be available to the Commission, without further appropriation or fiscal year limitation, for—

(A) paying awards to whistleblowers as provided in subsection (b); and

(B) funding the activities of the Inspector General of the Commission under section 4(i).

(3) *Deposits and Credits.*

(A) *In General.* There shall be deposited into or credited to the Fund an amount equal to—

(i) any monetary sanction collected by the Commission in any judicial or administrative action brought by the Commission under the securities laws that is not added to a disgorgement fund or other fund under section 308 of the Sarbanes–Oxley Act of 2002 or otherwise distributed to victims of a violation of the securities laws, or the rules and regulations thereunder, underlying such action, unless the balance of the Fund at the time the monetary sanction is collected exceeds $300,000,000;

(ii) any monetary sanction added to a disgorgement fund or other fund under section 308 of the Sarbanes–Oxley Act of 2002 that is not distributed to the victims for whom the Fund was established, unless the balance of the disgorgement fund at the time the determination is made not to distribute the monetary sanction to such victims exceeds $200,000,000; and

(iii) all income from investments made under paragraph (4).

(B) *Additional Amounts.* If the amounts deposited into or credited to the Fund under subparagraph (A) are not sufficient to satisfy an award made under subsection (b), there shall be deposited into or credited to the Fund an amount equal to the unsatisfied portion of the award from any monetary sanction collected by the Commission in the covered judicial or administrative action on which the award is based.

(4) *Investments.*

(A) *Amounts In Fund May Be Invested.* The Commission may request the Secretary of the Treasury to invest the portion of the Fund that is not, in the discretion of the Commission, required to meet the current needs of the Fund.

(B) *Eligible Investments.* Investments shall be made by the Secretary of the Treasury in obligations of the United States or obligations that are guaranteed as to principal and interest by the United States, with maturities suitable to the needs of the Fund as determined by the Commission on the record.

(C) *Interest and Proceeds Credited.* The interest on, and the proceeds from the sale or redemption of, any obligations held in the Fund shall be credited to the Fund.

(5) *Reports to Congress.* Not later than October 30 of each fiscal year beginning after the date of enactment of this subsection, the Commission shall submit to the Committee on Banking, Housing, and Urban Affairs of the Senate, and the Committee on Financial Services of the House of Representatives a report on—

(A) the whistleblower award program, established under this section, including—

(i) a description of the number of awards granted; and

(ii) the types of cases in which awards were granted during the preceding fiscal year;

(B) the balance of the Fund at the beginning of the preceding fiscal year;

(C) the amounts deposited into or credited to the Fund during the preceding fiscal year;

(D) the amount of earnings on investments made under paragraph (4) during the preceding fiscal year;

(E) the amount paid from the Fund during the preceding fiscal year to whistleblowers pursuant to subsection (b);

(F) the balance of the Fund at the end of the preceding fiscal year; and

(G) a complete set of audited financial statements, including—

(i) a balance sheet;

(ii) income statement; and

(iii) cash flow analysis.

(h) *Protection of Whistleblowers.*

(1) *Prohibition Against Retaliation.*

(A) *In General.* No employer may discharge, demote, suspend, threaten, harass, directly or indirectly, or in any other manner discriminate against, a whistleblower in the terms and conditions of employment because of any lawful act done by the whistleblower—

(i) in providing information to the Commission in accordance with this section;

(ii) in initiating, testifying in, or assisting in any investigation or judicial or administrative action of the Commission based upon or related to such information; or

(iii) in making disclosures that are required or protected under the Sarbanes–Oxley Act of 2002, the Securities Exchange Act of 1934, including section 10A(m) of such Act, section 1513(e) of title 18, United States Code, and any other law, rule, or regulation subject to the jurisdiction of the Commission.

(B) *Enforcement.*

(i) *Cause of Action.* An individual who alleges discharge or other discrimination in violation of subparagraph (A) may bring an action under this subsection in the appropriate district court of the United States for the relief provided in subparagraph (C).

(ii) *Subpoenas.* A subpoena requiring the attendance of a witness at a trial or hearing conducted under this section may be served at any place in the United States.

(iii) *Statute of Limitations.*

(I) *In General.* An action under this subsection may not be brought—

(aa) more than 6 years after the date on which the violation of subparagraph (A) occurred; or

(bb) more than 3 years after the date when facts material to the right of action are known or reasonably should have been known by the employee alleging a violation of subparagraph (A).

(II) *Required Action Within 10 Years.* Notwithstanding subclause (I), an action under this subsection may not in any circumstance be brought more than 10 years after the date on which the violation occurs.

(C) *Relief.* Relief for an individual prevailing in an action brought under subparagraph (B) shall include—

(i) reinstatement with the same seniority status that the individual would have had, but for the discrimination;

(ii) 2 times the amount of back pay otherwise owed to the individual, with interest; and

(iii) compensation for litigation costs, expert witness fees, and reasonable attorneys' fees.

(2) *Confidentiality.*

(A) *In General.* Except as provided in subparagraphs (B) and (C), the Commission and any officer or employee of the Commission shall not disclose any information, including information provided by a whistleblower to the Commission, which could reasonably be expected to reveal the identity of a whistleblower, except in accordance with the provisions of section 552a of title 5, United States Code, unless and until required to be disclosed to a defendant or respondent in connection with a public proceeding instituted by the Commission or any entity described in subparagraph (C). For purposes of section 552 of title 5, United States Code, this paragraph shall be considered a statute described in subsection (b)(3)(B) of such section.

(B) *Exempted Statute.* For purposes of section 552 of title 5, United States Code, this paragraph shall be considered a statute described in subsection (b)(3)(B) of such section 552.

(C) *Rule of Construction.* Nothing in this section is intended to limit, or shall be construed to limit, the ability of the Attorney General to present such evidence to a grand jury or to share such evidence with potential witnesses or defendants in the course of an ongoing criminal investigation.

(D) *Availability to Government Agencies.*

(i) *In General.* Without the loss of its status as confidential in the hands of the Commission, all information referred to in subparagraph (A) may, in the discretion of the Commission, when determined by the Commission to be necessary to accomplish the purposes of this Act and to protect investors, be made available to—

(I) the Attorney General of the United States;

(II) an appropriate regulatory authority;

(III) a self-regulatory organization;

(IV) a State attorney general in connection with any criminal investigation;

(V) any appropriate State regulatory authority;

(VI) the Public Company Accounting Oversight Board;

(VII) a foreign securities authority; and

(VIII) a foreign law enforcement authority.

(ii) *Confidentiality.*

(I) *In General.* Each of the entities described in subclauses (I) through (VI) of clause (i) shall maintain such information as confidential in accordance with the requirements established under subparagraph (A).

(II) *Foreign Authorities.* Each of the entities described in subclauses (VII) and (VIII) of clause (i) shall maintain such information in accordance with such assurances of confidentiality as the Commission determines appropriate.

(3) *Rights Retained.* Nothing in this section shall be deemed to diminish the rights, privileges, or remedies of any whistleblower under any Federal or State law, or under any collective bargaining agreement.

(i) *Provision of False Information.* A whistleblower shall not be entitled to an award under this section if the whistleblower—

(1) knowingly and willfully makes any false, fictitious, or fraudulent statement or representation; or

(2) uses any false writing or document knowing the writing or document contains any false, fictitious, or fraudulent statement or entry.

(j) *Rulemaking Authority.* The Commission shall have the authority to issue such rules and regulations as may be necessary or appropriate to implement the provisions of this section consistent with the purposes of this section.

Hearings by Commission

Sec. 22. Hearings may be public and may be held before the Commission, any member or members thereof, or any officer or officers of the Commission designated by it, and appropriate records thereof shall be kept.

Rules, Regulations, and Orders; Annual Reports

Sec. 23. (a) *Power to Make Rules and Regulations; Considerations; Public Disclosure.*

(1) The Commission, the Board of Governors of the Federal Reserve System, and the other agencies enumerated in section 3(a)(34) of this title shall each have power to make such rules and regulations as may be necessary or appropriate to implement the provisions of this title for which they are responsible or for the execution of the functions vested in them by this title, and may for such purposes classify persons, securities, transactions, statements, applications, reports, and other matters within their respective jurisdictions, and prescribe greater, lesser, or different requirements for different classes thereof. No provision of this title imposing any liability shall apply to any act done or omitted in good faith in conformity with a rule, regulation, or order of the Commission, the Board of Governors of the Federal Reserve System, other agency enumerated in section 3(a)(34) of this title, or any self-regulatory organization, notwithstanding that such rule, regulation, or order may thereafter be amended or rescinded or determined by judicial or other authority to be invalid for any reason.

(2) The Commission and the Secretary of the Treasury, in making rules and regulations pursuant to any provisions of this chapter, shall consider among other matters the impact any such rule or regulation would have on competition. The Commission and the Secretary of the Treasury shall not adopt any such rule or regulation which would impose a burden on competition not necessary or appropriate in furtherance of the purposes of this title. The Commission and the Secretary of the Treasury shall include in the statement of basis and purpose incorporated in any rule or regulation adopted under this title, the reasons for the Commission's or the Secretary's determination that any burden on competition imposed by such rule or regulation is necessary or appropriate in furtherance of the purposes of this title.

(3) The Commission and the Secretary, in making rules and regulations pursuant to any provision of this title, considering any application for registration in accordance with section 19(a) of this title, or reviewing any proposed rule change of a self-regulatory organization in accordance with section 19(b) of this title, shall keep in a public file and make available for copying all written statements filed with the Commission and the Secretary and all written communications between the Commission or the Secretary and any person relating to the proposed rule, regulation, application, or proposed rule change: *Provided, however,* That the Commission and the Secretary shall not be required to keep in a public file or make available for copying any such statement or communication which it may withhold from the public in accordance with the provisions of section 552 of title 5, United States Code.

(b) *Reports to Congress*

(1) The Commission, the Board of Governors of the Federal Reserve System, and the other agencies enumerated in section 78c(a)(34) of this title, shall each make an annual report to the Congress on its work for the preceding year, and shall include in each such report whatever information, data, and recommendations for further legislation it considers advisable with regard to matters within its respective jurisdiction under this chapter.

(2) The appropriate regulatory agency for a self-regulatory organization shall include in its annual report to the Congress for each fiscal year, a summary of its oversight activities under this chapter with respect to such self-regulatory organization, including a description of any examination conducted as part of such activities of any such organization, any material recommendation presented as part of such activities to such organization for changes in its organization or rules, and any action by such organization in response to any such recommendation.

(3) The appropriate regulatory agency for any class of municipal securities dealers shall include in its annual report to the Congress for each fiscal year a summary of its regulatory activities pursuant to this chapter with respect to such municipal securities dealers, including the nature of and reason for any sanction imposed pursuant to this chapter against any such municipal securities dealer.

(4) The Commission shall also include in its annual report to the Congress for each fiscal year—

(A) a summary of the Commission's oversight activities with respect to self-regulatory organizations for which it is not the appropriate regulatory agency, including a description of any examination of any such organization, any material recommendation presented to any such organization for changes in its organization or rules, and any action by any such organization in response to any such recommendations;

(B) a statement and analysis of the expenses and operations of each self-regulatory organization in connection with the performance of its responsibilities under this chapter, for which purpose data pertaining to such expenses and operations shall be made available by such organization to the Commission at its request;

(C) the steps the Commission has taken and the progress it has made toward ending the physical movement of the securities certificate in connection with the settlement of securities transactions, and its recommendations, if any, for legislation to eliminate the securities certificate;

(D) the number of requests for exemptions from provisions of this chapter received, the number granted, and the basis upon which any such exemption was granted;

(E) a summary of the Commission's regulatory activities with respect to municipal securities dealers for which it is not the appropriate regulatory agency, including the nature of, and reason for, any sanction imposed in proceedings against such municipal securities dealers;

(F) a statement of the time elapsed between the filing of reports pursuant to section 78m(f) of this title and the public availability of the information contained therein, the costs involved in the Commission's processing of such reports and tabulating such information, the manner in which the Commission uses such information, and the steps the Commission has taken and the progress it has made toward requiring such reports to be filed and such information to be made available to the public in machine language;

(G) information concerning (i) the effects its rules and regulations are having on the viability of small brokers and dealers; (ii) its attempts to reduce any unnecessary reporting burden on such brokers and dealers; and (iii) its efforts to help to assure the continued participation of small brokers and dealers in the United States securities markets;

(H) a statement detailing its administration of the Freedom of Information Act, section 552 of Title 5, including a copy of the report filed pursuant to subsection (d) of such section; and

(I) the steps that have been taken and the progress that has been made in promoting the timely public dissemination and availability for analytical purposes (on a fair, reasonable, and nondiscriminatory basis) of information concerning government securities transactions and quotations, and its recommendations, if any, for legislation to assure timely dissemination of (i) information on transactions in regularly traded government securities sufficient to permit the determination of the prevailing market price for such securities, and (ii) reports of the highest published bids and lowest published offers for government securities (including the size at which persons are willing to trade with respect to such bids and offers).

(c) *Procedure for Adjudication*. The Commission, by rule, shall prescribe the procedure applicable to every case pursuant to this chapter of adjudication (as defined in section 551 of title 5, United States Code) not required to be determined on the record after notice and opportunity for hearing. Such rules shall, as a minimum, provide that prompt notice shall be given of any adverse action or final disposition and that such notice and the entry of any order shall be accompanied by a statement of written reasons.

(d) *Cease-and-Desist Procedures.* Within 1 year after the date of enactment of this subsection, the Commission shall establish regulations providing for the expeditious conduct of hearings and rendering of decisions under section 21C of this title, section 8A of the Securities Act of 1933, section 9(f) of the Investment Company Act of 1940, and section 203(k) of the Investment Advisers Act of 1940.

Public Availability of Information

Sec. 24. (a) *"Records" Defined.* For purposes of section 552 of title 5, United States Code, the term "records" includes all applications, statements, reports, contracts, correspondence, notices, and other documents filed with or otherwise obtained by the Commission pursuant to this title or otherwise.

(b) *Disclosure or Personal Use.* It shall be unlawful for any member, officer, or employee of the Commission to disclose to any person other than a member, officer, or employee of the Commission, or to use for personal benefit, any information contained in any application, statement, report, contract, correspondence, notice, or other document filed with or otherwise obtained by the Commission (1) in contravention of the rules and regulations of the Commission under section 552 of title 5, United States Code, or (2) in circumstances where the Commission has determined pursuant to such rules to accord confidential treatment to such information.

(c) *Confidential Disclosures.* The Commission may, in its discretion and upon a showing that such information is needed, provide all "records" (as defined in subsection (a)) and other information in its possession to such persons, both domestic and foreign, as the Commission by rule deems appropriate if the person receiving such records or information provides such assurances of confidentiality as the Commission deems appropriate.

(d) *Records Obtained from Foreign Securities Authorities.* Except as provided in subsection (g), the Commission shall not be compelled to disclose records obtained from a foreign securities authority if (1) the foreign securities authority has in good faith determined and represented to the Commission that public disclosure of such records would violate the laws applicable to that foreign securities authority, and (2) the Commission obtains such records pursuant to (A) such procedure as the Commission may authorize for use in connection with the administration or enforcement of the securities laws, or (B) a memorandum of understanding. For purposes of section 552 of Title 5, this subsection shall be considered a statute described in subsection (b)(3)(B) of such section 552.

(e) *Freedom of Information Act.* For purposes of section 552(b)(8) of Title 5, (commonly referred to as the Freedom of Information Act)—

(1) the Commission is an agency responsible for the regulation or supervision of financial institutions; and

(2) any entity for which the Commission is responsible for regulating, supervising, or examining under this title is a financial institution.

(f) *Sharing Privileged Information with Other Authorities.*

(1) *Privileged Information Provided by the Commission.* The Commission shall not be deemed to have waived any privilege applicable to any information by transferring that information to or permitting that information to be used by—

(A) any agency (as defined in section 6 of Title 18);

(B) the Public Company Accounting Oversight Board;

(C) any self-regulatory organization;

(D) any foreign securities authority;

(E) any foreign law enforcement authority; or

(F) any State securities or law enforcement authority.

(2) *Nondisclosure of Privileged Information Provided to the Commission.* The Commission shall not be compelled to disclose privileged information obtained from any foreign securities authority, or foreign law enforcement authority, if the authority has in good faith determined and represented to the Commission that the information is privileged.

(3) *Nonwaiver of Privileged Information Provided to the Commission.*

(A) *In General.* Federal agencies, State securities and law enforcement authorities, self-regulatory organizations, and the Public Company Accounting Oversight Board shall not be deemed to have waived any privilege applicable to any information by transferring that information to or permitting that information to be used by the Commission.

(B) *Exception.* The provisions of subparagraph (A) shall not apply to a self-regulatory organization or the Public Company Accounting Oversight Board with respect to information used by the Commission in an action against such organization.

(4) *Definitions.* For purposes of this subsection—

(A) the term "privilege" includes any work-product privilege, attorney-client privilege, governmental privilege, or other privilege recognized under Federal, State, or foreign law;

(B) the term "foreign law enforcement authority" means any foreign authority that is empowered under foreign law to detect, investigate or prosecute potential violations of law; and

(C) the term "State securities or law enforcement authority" means the authority of any State or territory that is empowered under State or territory law to detect, investigate, or prosecute potential violations of law.

(g) *Savings Provision.* Nothing in this section shall—

(1) alter the Commission's responsibilities under the Right to Financial Privacy Act, as limited by section 21(h) of this Act, with respect to transfers of records covered by such statutes, or

(2) authorize the Commission to withhold information from the Congress or prevent the Commission from complying with an order of a court of the United States in an action commenced by the United States or the Commission.

Court Review of Orders and Rules

Sec. 25. (a) *Final Commission Orders; Persons Aggrieved; Petition; Record; Findings; Affirmance, Modification, Enforcement or Setting Aside of Orders; Remand to Adduce Additional Evidence.*

(1) A person aggrieved by a final order of the Commission entered pursuant to this title may obtain review of the order in the United States Court of Appeals for the circuit in which he resides or has his principal place of business, or for the District of Columbia Circuit, by filing in such court, within sixty days after the entry of the order, a written petition requesting that the order be modified or set aside in whole or in part.

(2) A copy of the petition shall be transmitted forthwith by the clerk of the court to a member of the Commission or an officer designated by the Commission for that purpose. Thereupon the Commission shall file in the court the record on which the order complained of is entered, as provided in section 2112 of title 28, United States Code, and the Federal Rules of Appellate Procedure.

(3) On the filing of the petition, the court has jurisdiction, which becomes exclusive on the filing of the record, to affirm or modify and enforce or to set aside the order in whole or in part.

(4) The findings of the Commission as to the facts, if supported by substantial evidence, are conclusive.

(5) If either party applies to the court for leave to adduce additional evidence and shows to the satisfaction of the court that the additional evidence is material and that there was reasonable ground for failure to adduce it before the Commission, the court may remand the case to the Commission for further proceedings, in whatever manner and on whatever conditions the court considers appropriate. If the case is remanded to the Commission, it shall file in the court a supplemental record containing any new evidence, any further or modified findings, and any new order.

(b) *Commission Rules; Persons Adversely Affected; Petition; Record; Affirmance, Enforcement, or Setting Aside of Rules; Findings; Transfer of Proceedings.*

(1) A person adversely affected by a rule of the Commission promulgated pursuant to section 6, 9(h)(2), 11, 11A, 15(c)(5) or (6), 15A, 17, 17A, or 19 of this title may obtain review of this rule in the United States Court of Appeals for the circuit in which he resides or has his principal place of business or for the District of Columbia Circuit, by filing in such court, within sixty days after the promulgation of the rule, a written petition requesting that the rule be set aside.

(2) A copy of the petition shall be transmitted forthwith by the clerk of the court to a member of the Commission or an officer designated for that purpose. Thereupon, the Commission shall file in the court the rule under review and any documents referred to therein, the Commission's notice of proposed rulemaking and any documents referred to therein, all written submissions and the transcript of any oral presentations in the rulemaking, factual information not included in the foregoing that was considered by the Commission in the promulgation of the rule or proffered by the Commission as pertinent to the rule, the report of any advisory committee received or considered by the Commission in the rulemaking, and any other materials prescribed by the court.

(3) On the filing of the petition, the court has jurisdiction, which becomes exclusive on the filing of the materials set forth in paragraph (2) of this subsection, to affirm and enforce or to set aside the rule.

(4) The findings of the Commission as to the facts identified by the Commission as the basis, in whole or in part, of the rule, if supported by substantial evidence, are conclusive. The court shall affirm and enforce the rule unless the Commission's action in promulgating the rule is found to be arbitrary, capricious, an abuse of discretion, or otherwise not in accordance with law; contrary to constitutional right, power, privilege, or immunity; in excess of statutory jurisdiction, authority, or limitations, or short of statutory right; or without observance of procedure required by law.

(5) If proceedings have been instituted under this subsection in two or more courts of appeals with respect to the same rule, the Commission shall file the materials set forth in paragraph (2) of this subsection in that court in which a proceeding was first instituted. The other courts shall thereupon transfer all such proceedings to the court in which the materials have been filed. For the convenience of the parties in the interest of justice that court may thereafter transfer all the proceedings to any other court of appeals.

(c) *Objections Not Urged Before Commission; Stay of Orders and Rules; Transfer of Enforcement or Review Proceedings.*

(1) No objection to an order or rule of the Commission, for which review is sought under this section, may be considered by the court unless it was urged before the Commission or there was reasonable ground for failure to do so.

(2) The filing of a petition under this section does not operate as a stay of the Commission's order or rule. Until the court's jurisdiction becomes exclusive, the Commission may stay its order or rule pending judicial review if it finds that justice so requires. After the filing of a petition under this section, the court, on whatever conditions may be required and to the extent necessary to prevent irreparable injury, may issue all necessary and appropriate process to stay the order or rule or to preserve status or rights pending its review; but (notwithstanding section 705 of title 5, United States Code) no such process may be issued by the court before the filing of the record or the materials set forth in subsection (b)(2) of this section unless: (A) the Commission has denied a stay or failed to grant requested relief, (B) a reasonable period has expired since the filing of an application for a stay without a decision by the Commission, or (C) there was reasonable ground for failure to apply to the Commission.

(3) When the same order or rule is the subject of one or more petitions for review filed under this section and an action for enforcement filed in a district court of the United States under section 21(d) or (e) of this title, that court in which the petition or the action is first filed has jurisdiction with respect to the order or rule to the exclusion of any other court, and thereupon all such proceedings shall be transferred to that court; but, for the convenience of the parties in the interest of justice, that court may thereafter transfer all the proceedings to any other court of appeals or district court of the United States, whether or not a petition for review or an action for enforcement was originally filed in the transferee court. The scope of review by a district court under section 21(d) or (e) of this title is in all cases the same as by a court of appeals under this section.

(d) *Other Appropriate Regulatory Agencies.*

(1) For purposes of the preceding subsections of this section, the term "Commission" includes the agencies enumerated in section 3(a)(34) of this title insofar as such agencies are acting pursuant to this title and the Secretary of the Treasury insofar as he is acting pursuant to section 15C of this title.

(2) For purposes of subsection (a)(4) of this section and section 706 of title 5, United States Code, an order of the Commission pursuant to section 19(a) of this title denying registration to a clearing agency for which the Commission is not the appropriate regulatory agency or pursuant to section 19(b) of this title disapproving a proposed rule change by such a clearing agency shall be deemed to be an order of the appropriate regulatory agency for such clearing agency insofar as such order was entered by reason of a determination by such appropriate regulatory agency pursuant to section 19(a)(2)(C) or 19(b)(4)(C) of this title that such registration or proposed rule change would be inconsistent with the safeguarding of securities or funds.

Unlawful Representations

Sec. 26. No action or failure to act by the Commission or the Board of Governors of the Federal Reserve System, in the administration of this title shall be construed to mean that the particular authority has in any way passed upon the merits of, or given approval to, any security or any transaction or transactions therein, nor shall such action or failure to act with regard to any statement or report filed with or examined by such authority pursuant to this title or rules and regulations thereunder, be deemed a finding by such authority that such statement or report is true and accurate on its face or that it is not false or misleading. It shall be unlawful to make, or cause to be made, to any prospective purchaser or seller of a security any representation that any such action or failure to act by any such authority is to be so construed or has such effect.

Jurisdiction of Offenses and Suits

Sec. 27. (a) *In General.* The district courts of the United States and the United States courts of any Territory or other place subject to the jurisdiction of the United States shall have exclusive jurisdiction of violations of this title or the rules and regulations thereunder, and of all suits in equity and actions at law brought to enforce any liability or duty created by this title or the rules and regulations thereunder. Any criminal proceeding may be brought in the district wherein any act or transaction constituting the violation occurred. Any suit or action to enforce any liability or duty created by this title or rules and regulations thereunder, or to enjoin any violation of such title or rules and regulations, may be brought in any such district or in the district wherein the defendant is found or is an inhabitant or transacts business, and process in such cases may be served in any other district of which the defendant is an inhabitant or wherever the defendant may be found. In any action or proceeding instituted by the Commission under this title in a United States district court for any judicial district, a subpoena issued to compel the attendance of a witness or the production of documents or tangible things (or both) at a hearing or trial may be served at any place within the United States. Rule 45(c)(3)(A)(ii) of the Federal Rules of Civil Procedure shall not apply to a subpoena issued under the preceding sentence. Judgments and decrees so rendered shall be subject to review as provided in sections 1254, 1291, 1292, and 1294 of title 28, United States Code. No costs shall be assessed for or against the Commission in any proceeding under this title brought by or against it in the Supreme Court or such other courts.

(b) *Extraterritorial Jurisdiction.* The district courts of the United States and the United States courts of any Territory shall have jurisdiction of an action or proceeding brought or instituted by the Commission or the United States alleging a violation of the antifraud provisions of this title involving—

(1) conduct within the United States that constitutes significant steps in furtherance of the violation, even if the securities transaction occurs outside the United States and involves only foreign investors; or

(2) conduct occurring outside the United States that has a foreseeable substantial effect within the United States.

Special Provision Relating to Statute of Limitations on Private Causes of Action

Sec. 27A. (a) *Effect on Pending Causes of Action.* The limitation period for any private civil action implied under section 10(b) of this Act that was commenced on or before June 19, 1991, shall be the limitation period provided by the laws applicable in the jurisdiction, including principles of retroactivity, as such laws existed on June 19, 1991.

(b) *Effect on Dismissed Causes of Action.* Any private civil action implied under section 10(b) of this Act that was commenced on or before June 19, 1991—

(1) which was dismissed as time barred subsequent to June 19, 1991, and

(2) which would have been timely filed under the limitation period provided by the laws applicable in the jurisdiction, including principles of retroactivity, as such laws existed on June 19, 1991,

shall be reinstated on motion by the plaintiff not later than 60 days after the date of enactment of this section.

Effect on Existing Law

Sec. 28. (a) *Limitation on Judgments.*

(1) *In General.* No person permitted to maintain a suit for damages under the provisions of this title shall recover, through satisfaction of judgment in 1 or more actions, a total amount in excess of the actual damages to that person on account of the act complained of. Except as otherwise specifically provided in this title, nothing in this title shall affect the jurisdiction of the securities commission (or any agency or officer performing like functions) of any State over any security or any person insofar as it does not conflict with the provisions of this title or the rules and regulations under this title.

(2) *Rule of Construction.* Except as provided in subsection (f), the rights and remedies provided by this title shall be in addition to any and all other rights and remedies that may exist at law or in equity.

(3) *State Bucket Shop Laws.* No State law which prohibits or regulates the making or promoting of wagering or gaming contracts, or the operation of "bucket shops" or other similar or related activities, shall invalidate—

(A) any put, call, straddle, option, privilege, or other security subject to this title (except any security that has a pari-mutuel payout or otherwise is determined by the Commission, acting by rule, regulation, or order, to be appropriately subject to such laws), or apply to any activity which is incidental or related to the offer, purchase, sale, exercise, settlement, or closeout of any such security;

(B) any security-based swap between eligible contract participants; or

(C) any security-based swap effected on a national securities exchange registered pursuant to section 6(b).

(4) *Other State Provisions.* No provision of State law regarding the offer, sale, or distribution of securities shall apply to any transaction in a security-based swap or a security futures product, except that this paragraph may not be construed as limiting any State antifraud law of general applicability. A security-based swap may not be regulated as an insurance contract under any provision of State law.

(b) *Modification of Disciplinary Procedures.* Nothing in this title shall be construed to modify existing law with regard to the binding effect (1) on any member of or participant in any self-regulatory organization of any action taken by the authorities of such organization to settle disputes between its members or participants, (2) on any municipal securities dealer or municipal securities broker of any action taken pursuant to a procedure established by the Municipal Securities Rulemaking Board to settle disputes between municipal securities dealers and municipal securities brokers, or (3) of any action described in paragraph (1) or (2) on any person who has agreed to be bound thereby.

(c) *Continuing Validity of Disciplinary Sanctions.* The stay, setting aside, or modification pursuant to section 19(e) of this title of any disciplinary sanction imposed by a self-regulatory organization on a member thereof, person associated with a member, or participant therein, shall not affect the validity or force of any action taken as a result of such sanction by the self-regulatory organization prior to such stay, setting aside, or modification: *Provided,* That such action is not inconsistent with the provisions of this title or the rules or regulations thereunder. The rights of any person acting in good faith which arise out of any such action shall not be affected in any way by such stay, setting aside, or modification.

(d) *Physical Location of Facilities of Registered Clearing Agencies or Registered Transfer Agents Not to Subject Changes in Beneficial or Record Ownership of Securities to State or Local Taxes.* No State or political subdivision thereof shall impose any tax on any change in beneficial or record ownership of securities effected through the facilities of a registered clearing agency or registered transfer agent or any nominee thereof or custodian therefor or upon the delivery or transfer of securities to or through or receipt from such agency or agent or any nominee thereof or custodian therefor, unless such change in beneficial or record ownership or such transfer or delivery or receipt would otherwise be taxable by such State or political subdivision if the facilities of such registered clearing agency, registered transfer agent, or any nominee thereof or custodian therefor were not physically located in the taxing State or political subdivision. No State or political subdivision thereof shall impose any tax on securities which are deposited in or retained by a registered clearing agency, registered transfer agent, or any nominee thereof or custodian therefor, unless such securities would otherwise be taxable by such State or political subdivision if the facilities of such registered clearing agency, registered transfer agent, or any nominee thereof or custodian therefor were not physically located in the taxing State or political subdivision.

(e) *Exchange, Broker, and Dealer Commissions; Brokerage and Research Services.*

(1) No person using the mails, or any means or instrumentality of interstate commerce, in the exercise of investment discretion with respect to an account shall be deemed to have acted unlawfully or to have breached a fiduciary duty under State or Federal law unless expressly provided to the contrary by a law enacted by the Congress or any State subsequent to the date of enactment of the Securities Acts Amendments of 1975 [June 4, 1975], solely by reason of his having caused the account to pay a member of an exchange, broker, or dealer an amount of commission for effecting a securities transaction in excess of the amount

of commission another member of an exchange, broker, or dealer would have charged for effecting that transaction, if such person determined in good faith that such amount of commission was reasonable in relation to the value of the brokerage and research services provided by such member, broker, or dealer, viewed in terms of either that particular transaction or his overall responsibilities with respect to the accounts as to which he exercises investment discretion. This subsection is exclusive and plenary insofar as conduct is covered by the foregoing, unless otherwise expressly provided by contract: *Provided, however*, That nothing in this subsection shall be construed to impair or limit the power of the Commission under any other provision of this title or otherwise.

(2) A person exercising investment discretion with respect to an account shall make such disclosure of his policies and practices with respect to commissions that will be paid for effecting securities transactions, at such times and in such manner, as the appropriate regulatory agency, by rule, may prescribe as necessary or appropriate in the public interest or for the protection of investors.

(3) For purposes of this subsection a person provides brokerage and research services insofar as he—

(A) furnishes advice, either directly or through publications or writings, as to the value of securities, the advisability of investing in purchasing or selling securities, and the availability of securities or purchasers or sellers of securities;

(B) furnishes analyses and reports concerning issuers, industries, securities, economic factors and trends, portfolio strategy, and the performance of accounts; or

(C) effects securities transactions and performs functions incidental thereto (such as clearance, settlement, and custody) or required in connection therewith by rules of the Commission or a self-regulatory organization of which such person is a member or person associated with a member or in which such person is a participant.

(4) The provisions of this subsection shall not apply with regard to securities that are security futures products.

(f) *Limitations on Remedies.*

(1) *Class Action Limitations.* No covered class action based upon the statutory or common law of any State or subdivision thereof may be maintained in any State or Federal court by any private party alleging—

(A) a misrepresentation or omission of a material fact in connection with the purchase or sale of a covered security; or

(B) that the defendant used or employed any manipulative or deceptive device or contrivance in connection with the purchase or sale of a covered security.

(2) *Removal of Covered Class Actions.* Any covered class action brought in any State court involving a covered security, as set forth in paragraph (1), shall be removable to the Federal district court for the district in which the action is pending, and shall be subject to paragraph (1).

(3) *Preservation of Certain Actions.*

(A) *Actions Under State Law of State of Incorporation.*

(i) *Actions Preserved.* Notwithstanding paragraph (1) or (2), a covered class action described in clause (ii) of this subparagraph that is based upon the statutory or common law of the State in which the issuer is incorporated (in the case of a corporation) or organized (in the case of any other entity) may be maintained in a State or Federal court by a private party.

(ii) *Permissible Actions.* A covered class action is described in this clause if it involves—

(I) the purchase or sale of securities by the issuer or an affiliate of the issuer exclusively from or to holders of equity securities of the issuer; or

(II) any recommendation, position, or other communication with respect to the sale of securities of an issuer that—

(aa) is made by or on behalf of the issuer or an affiliate of the issuer to holders of equity securities of the issuer; and

(bb) concerns decisions of such equity holders with respect to voting their securities, acting in response to a tender or exchange offer, or exercising dissenters' or appraisal rights.

(B) *State Actions.*

(i) *In General.* Notwithstanding any other provision of this subsection, nothing in this subsection may be construed to preclude a State or political subdivision thereof or a

State pension plan from bringing an action involving a covered security on its own behalf, or as a member of a class comprised solely of other States, political subdivisions, or State pension plans that are named plaintiffs, and that have authorized participation, in such action.

(ii) *State Pension Plan Defined.* For purposes of this subparagraph, the term "State pension plan" means a pension plan established and maintained for its employees by the government of a State or political subdivision thereof, or by any agency or instrumentality thereof.

(C) *Actions Under Contractual Agreements Between Issuers and Indenture Trustees.* Notwithstanding paragraph (1) or (2), a covered class action that seeks to enforce a contractual agreement between an issuer and an indenture trustee may be maintained in a State or Federal court by a party to the agreement or a successor to such party.

(D) *Remand of Removed Actions.* In an action that has been removed from a State court pursuant to paragraph (2), if the Federal court determines that the action may be maintained in State court pursuant to this subsection, the Federal court shall remand such action to such State court.

(4) *Preservation of State Jurisdiction.* The securities commission (or any agency or office performing like functions) of any State shall retain jurisdiction under the laws of such State to investigate and bring enforcement actions.

(5) *Definitions.* For purposes of this subsection, the following definitions shall apply:

(A) *Affiliate of the Issuer.* The term "affiliate of the issuer" means a person that directly or indirectly, through one or more intermediaries, controls or is controlled by or is under common control with, the issuer.

(B) *Covered Class Action.* The term "covered class action" means—

(i) any single lawsuit in which—

(I) damages are sought on behalf of more than 50 persons or prospective class members, and questions of law or fact common to those persons or members of the prospective class, without reference to issues of individualized reliance on an alleged misstatement or omission, predominate over any questions affecting only individual persons or members; or

(II) one or more named parties seek to recover damages on a representative basis on behalf of themselves and other unnamed parties similarly situated, and questions of law or fact common to those persons or members of the prospective class predominate over any questions affecting only individual persons or members; or

(ii) any group of lawsuits filed in or pending in the same court and involving common questions of law or fact, in which—

(I) damages are sought on behalf of more than 50 persons; and

(II) the lawsuits are joined, consolidated, or otherwise proceed as a single action for any purpose.

(C) *Exception for Derivative Actions.* Notwithstanding subparagraph (B), the term "covered class action" does not include an exclusively derivative action brought by one or more shareholders on behalf of a corporation.

(D) *Counting of Certain Class Members.* For purposes of this paragraph, a corporation, investment company, pension plan, partnership, or other entity, shall be treated as one person or prospective class member, but only if the entity is not established for the purpose of participating in the action.

(E) *Covered Security.* The term "covered security" means a security that satisfies the standards for a covered security specified in paragraph (1) or (2) of section 18(b) of the Securities Act of 1933, at the time during which it is alleged that the misrepresentation, omission, or manipulative or deceptive conduct occurred, except that such term shall not include any debt security that is exempt from registration under the Securities Act of 1933 pursuant to rules issued by the Commission under section 4(a)(2) of that Act.

(F) *Rule of Construction.* Nothing in this paragraph shall be construed to affect the discretion of a State court in determining whether actions filed in such court should be joined, consolidated, or otherwise allowed to proceed as a single action.

Validity of Contracts

Sec. 29. (a) *Waiver Provisions.* Any condition, stipulation, or provision binding any person to waive compliance with any provision of this title or of any rule or regulation thereunder, or of any rule of a self-regulatory organization, shall be void.

(b) *Contract Provisions in Violation of Title.* Every contract made in violation of any provision of this title or of any rule or regulation thereunder, and every contract (including any contract for listing a security on an exchange) heretofore or hereafter made, the performance of which involves the violation of, or the continuance of any relationship or practice in violation of, any provision of this title or any rule or regulation thereunder, shall be void (1) as regards the rights of any person who, in violation of any such provision, rule, or regulation, shall have made or engaged in the performance of any such contract, and (2) as regards the rights of any person who, not being a party to such contract, shall have acquired any right thereunder with actual knowledge of the facts by reason of which the making or performance of such contract was in violation of any such provision, rule, or regulation: *Provided,* (A) That no contract shall be void by reason of this subsection because of any violation of any rule or regulation prescribed pursuant to paragraph (3) of subsection (c) of section 15 of this title, and (B) that no contract shall be deemed to be void by reason of this subsection in any action maintained in reliance upon this subsection, by any person to or for whom any broker or dealer sells, or from or for whom any broker or dealer purchases, a security in violation of any rule or regulation prescribed pursuant to paragraph (1) or (2) of subsection (c) of section 15 of this title, unless such action is brought within one year after the discovery that such sale or purchase involves such violation and within three years after such violation. The Commission may, in a rule or regulation prescribed pursuant to such paragraph (2), of such section 15(c) of this title, designate such rule or regulation, or portion thereof, as a rule or regulation, or portion thereof, a contract in violation of which shall not be void by reason of this subsection.

(c) *Validity of Loans, Extensions of Credit, and Creation of Liens; Actual Knowledge of Violation.* Nothing in this title shall be construed (1) to affect the validity of any loan or extension of credit (or any extension or renewal thereof) made or of any lien created prior or subsequent to the enactment of this title, unless at the time of the making of such loan or extension of credit (or extension or renewal thereof) or the creating of such lien, the person making such loan or extension of credit (or extension or renewal thereof) or acquiring such lien shall have actual knowledge of facts by reason of which the making of such loan or extension of credit (or extension or renewal thereof) or the acquisition of such lien is a violation of the provisions of this title or any rule or regulation thereunder, or (2) to afford a defense to the collection of any debt or obligation or the enforcement of any lien by any person who shall have acquired such debt, obligation, or lien in good faith for value and without actual knowledge of the violation of any provision of this title or any rule or regulation thereunder affecting the legality of such debt, obligation, or lien.

Foreign Securities Exchanges

Sec. 30. (a) It shall be unlawful for any broker or dealer, directly or indirectly, to make use of the mails or of any means or instrumentality of interstate commerce for the purpose of effecting on an exchange not within or subject to the jurisdiction of the United States, any transaction in any security the issuer of which is a resident of, or is organized under the laws of, or has its principal place of business in, a place within or subject to the jurisdiction of the United States, in contravention of such rules and regulations as the Commission may prescribe as necessary or appropriate in the public interest or for the protection of investors or to prevent the evasion of this title.

(b) The provisions of this title or of any rule or regulation thereunder shall not apply to any person insofar as he transacts a business in securities without the jurisdiction of the United States, unless he transacts such business in contravention of such rules and regulations as the Commission may prescribe as necessary or appropriate to prevent the evasion of this title.

(c) *Rule of Construction.* No provision of this title that was added by the Wall Street Transparency and Accountability Act of 2010, or any rule or regulation thereunder, shall apply to any person insofar as such person transacts a business in security-based swaps without the jurisdiction of the United States, unless such person transacts such business in contravention of such rules and regulations as the Commission may prescribe as necessary or appropriate to prevent the evasion of any provision of this title that was added by the Wall Street Transparency and Accountability Act of 2010. This subsection shall not be construed to limit the jurisdiction of the Commission under any provision of this title, as in effect prior to the date of enactment of the Wall Street Transparency and Accountability Act of 2010.

Prohibited Foreign Trade Practices by Issuers

Sec. 30A. (a) *Prohibition.* It shall be unlawful for any issuer which has a class of securities registered pursuant to section 78l of this title or which is required to file reports under section 15(d) of this title, or for any officer, director, employee, or agent of such issuer or any stockholder thereof acting on behalf of such issuer, to make use of the mails or any means or instrumentality of interstate commerce corruptly in furtherance of an offer, payment, promise to pay, or authorization of the payment of any money, or offer, gift, promise to give, or authorization of the giving of anything of value to—

(1) any foreign official for purposes of—

(A)(i) influencing any act or decision of such foreign official in his official capacity, (ii) inducing such foreign official to do or omit to do any act in violation of the lawful duty of such official, or (iii) securing any improper advantage; or

(B) inducing such foreign official to use his influence with a foreign government or instrumentality thereof to affect or influence any act or decision of such government or instrumentality,

in order to assist such issuer in obtaining or retaining business for or with, or directing business to, any person;

(2) any foreign political party or official thereof or any candidate for foreign political office for purposes of—

(A)(i) influencing any act or decision of such party, official, or candidate in its or his official capacity, (ii) inducing such party, official, or candidate to do or omit to do an act in violation of the lawful duty of such party, official, or candidate, or (iii) securing any improper advantage; or

(B) inducing such party, official, or candidate to use its or his influence with a foreign government or instrumentality thereof to affect or influence any act or decision of such government or instrumentality,

in order to assist such issuer in obtaining or retaining business for or with, or directing business to, any person; or

(3) any person, while knowing that all or a portion of such money or thing of value will be offered, given, or promised, directly or indirectly, to any foreign official, to any foreign political party or official thereof, or to any candidate for foreign political office, for purposes of—

(A)(i) influencing any act or decision of such foreign official, political party, party official, or candidate in his or its official capacity, (ii) inducing such foreign official, political party, party official, or candidate to do or omit to do any act in violation of the lawful duty of such foreign official, political party, party official, or candidate, or (iii) securing any improper advantage; or

(B) inducing such foreign official, political party, party official, or candidate to use his or its influence with a foreign government or instrumentality thereof to affect or influence any act or decision of such government or instrumentality,

in order to assist such issuer in obtaining or retaining business for or with, or directing business to, any person.

(b) *Exception for Routine Governmental Action.* Subsections (a) and (g) shall not apply to any facilitating or expediting payment to a foreign official, political party, or party official the purpose of which is to expedite or to secure the performance of a routine governmental action by a foreign official, political party, or party official.

(c) *Affirmative Defenses.* It shall be an affirmative defense to actions under subsection (a) or (g) that—

(1) the payment, gift, offer, or promise of anything of value that was made, was lawful under the written laws and regulations of the foreign official's, political party's, party official's, or candidate's country; or

(2) the payment, gift, offer, or promise of anything of value that was made, was a reasonable and bona fide expenditure, such as travel and lodging expenses, incurred by or on behalf of a foreign official, party, party official, or candidate and was directly related to—

(A) the promotion, demonstration, or explanation of products or services; or

(B) the execution or performance of a contract with a foreign government or agency thereof.

(d) *Guidelines by Attorney General.* Not later than one year after the date of the enactment of the Foreign Corrupt Practices Act Amendments of 1988, the Attorney General, after consultation with the Commission, the Secretary of Commerce, the United States Trade Representative, the Secretary of State, and the Secretary of the Treasury, and after obtaining the views of all interested persons through public notice and comment procedures, shall determine to what extent compliance with this section would be enhanced and the business community would be assisted by further clarification of the preceding provisions of this section and may, based on such determination and to the extent necessary and appropriate, issue—

(1) guidelines describing specific types of conduct, associated with common types of export sales arrangements and business contracts, which for purposes of the Department of Justice's present enforcement policy, the Attorney General determines would be in conformance with the preceding provisions of this section; and

(2) general precautionary procedures which issuers may use on a voluntary basis to conform their conduct to the Department of Justice's present enforcement policy regarding the preceding provisions of this section.

The Attorney General shall issue the guidelines and procedures referred to in the preceding sentence in accordance with the provisions of subchapter II of chapter 5 of title 5, United States Code, and those guidelines and procedures shall be subject to the provisions of chapter 7 of that title.

(e) *Opinions of Attorney General.*

(1) The Attorney General, after consultation with appropriate departments and agencies of the United States and after obtaining the views of all interested persons through public notice and comment procedures, shall establish a procedure to provide responses to specific inquiries by issuers concerning conformance of their conduct with the Department of Justice's present enforcement policy regarding the preceding provisions of this section. The Attorney General shall, within 30 days after receiving such a request, issue an opinion in response to that request. The opinion shall state whether or not certain specified prospective conduct would, for purposes of the Department of Justice's present enforcement policy, violate the preceding provisions of this section. Additional requests for opinions may be filed with the Attorney General regarding other specified prospective conduct that is beyond the scope of conduct specified in previous requests. In any action brought under the applicable provisions of this section, there shall be a rebuttable presumption that conduct, which is specified in a request by an issuer and for which the Attorney General has issued an opinion that such conduct is in conformity with the Department of Justice's present enforcement policy, is in compliance with the preceding provisions of this section. Such a presumption may be rebutted by a preponderance of the evidence. In considering the presumption for purposes of this paragraph, a court shall weigh all relevant factors, including but not limited to whether the information submitted to the Attorney General was accurate and complete and whether it was within the scope of the conduct specified in any request received by the Attorney General. The Attorney General shall establish the procedure required by this paragraph in accordance with the provisions of subchapter II of chapter 5 of title 5, United States Code, and that procedure shall be subject to the provisions of chapter 7 of that title.

(2) Any document or other material which is provided to, received by, or prepared in the Department of Justice or any other department or agency of the United States in connection with a request by an issuer under the procedure established under paragraph (1), shall be exempt from disclosure under section 552 of title 5, United States Code, and shall not, except with the consent of the issuer, be made publicly available, regardless of whether the Attorney General responds to such a request or the issuer withdraws such request before receiving a response.

(3) Any issuer who has made a request to the Attorney General under paragraph (1) may withdraw such request prior to the time the Attorney General issues an opinion in response to such request. Any request so withdrawn shall have no force or effect.

(4) The Attorney General shall, to the maximum extent practicable, provide timely guidance concerning the Department of Justice's present enforcement policy with respect to the preceding provisions of this section to potential exporters and small businesses that are unable to obtain specialized counsel on issues pertaining to such provisions. Such guidance shall be limited to responses to requests under paragraph (1) concerning conformity of specified prospective conduct with the Department of Justice's present enforcement policy regarding the preceding provisions of this section and general explanations of compli-

ance responsibilities and of potential liabilities under the preceding provisions of this section.

(f) *Definitions.* For purposes of this section:

(1)(A) The term "foreign official" means any officer or employee of a foreign government or any department, agency, or instrumentality thereof, or of a public international organization, or any person acting in an official capacity for or on behalf of any such government or department, agency, or instrumentality, or for or on behalf of any such public international organization.

(B) For purposes of subparagraph (A), the term "public international organization" means—

(i) an organization that is designated by Executive order pursuant to section 1 of the International Organizations Immunities Act; or

(ii) any other international organization that is designated by the President by Executive order for the purposes of this section, effective as of the date of publication of such order in the Federal Register.

(2)(A) A person's state of mind is "knowing" with respect to conduct, a circumstance, or a result if—

(i) such person is aware that such person is engaging in such conduct, that such circumstance exists, or that such result is substantially certain to occur; or

(ii) such person has a firm belief that such circumstance exists or that such result is substantially certain to occur.

(B) When knowledge of the existence of a particular circumstance is required for an offense, such knowledge is established if a person is aware of a high probability of the existence of such circumstance, unless the person actually believes that such circumstance does not exist.

(3)(A) The term "routine governmental action" means only an action which is ordinarily and commonly performed by a foreign official in—

(i) obtaining permits, licenses, or other official documents to qualify a person to do business in a foreign country;

(ii) processing governmental papers, such as visas and work orders;

(iii) providing police protection, mail pick-up and delivery, or scheduling inspections associated with contract performance or inspections related to transit of goods across country;

(iv) providing phone service, power and water supply, loading and unloading cargo, or protecting perishable products or commodities from deterioration; or

(v) actions of a similar nature.

(B) The term "routine governmental action" does not include any decision by a foreign official whether, or on what terms, to award new business to or to continue business with a particular party, or any action taken by a foreign official involved in the decision-making process to encourage a decision to award new business to or continue business with a particular party.

(g) *Alternative Jurisdiction.*

(1) It shall also be unlawful for any issuer organized under the laws of the United States, or a State, territory, possession, or commonwealth of the United States or a political subdivision thereof and which has a class of securities registered pursuant to section 12 of this title or which is required to file reports under section 15(d) of this title, or for any United States person that is an officer, director, employee, or agent of such issuer or a stockholder thereof acting on behalf of such issuer, to corruptly do any act outside the United States in furtherance of an offer, payment, promise to pay, or authorization of the payment of any money, or offer, gift, promise to give, or authorization of the giving of anything of value to any of the persons or entities set forth in paragraphs (1), (2), and (3) of subsection (a) of this section for the purposes set forth therein, irrespective of whether such issuer or such officer, director, employee, agent, or stockholder makes use of the mails or any means or instrumentality of interstate commerce in furtherance of such offer, gift, payment, promise, or authorization.

(2) As used in this subsection, the term "United States person" means a national of the United States (as defined in section 101 of the Immigration and Nationality Act or any corporation, partnership, association, joint-stock company, business trust, unincorporated organization, or sole proprietorship organized under the laws of the United States or any State, territory, possession, or commonwealth of the United States, or any political subdivision thereof.

Transaction Fees

Sec. 31. (a) *Recovery of Costs of Annual Appropriation.* The Commission shall, in accordance with this section, collect transaction fees and assessments that are designed to recover the costs to the Government of the annual appropriation to the Commission by Congress.

(b) *Exchange–Traded Securities.* Subject to subsection (j), each national securities exchange shall pay to the Commission a fee at a rate equal to $15 per $1,000,000 of the aggregate dollar amount of sales of securities (other than bonds, debentures, other evidences of indebtedness, security futures products, and options on securities indexes (excluding a narrow-based security index)) transacted on such national securities exchange.

(c) *Off-Exchange Trades of Exchange Registered and Last–Sale–Reported Securities.* Subject to subsection (j), each national securities association shall pay to the Commission a fee at a rate equal to $15 per $1,000,000 of the aggregate dollar amount of sales transacted by or through any member of such association otherwise than on a national securities exchange of securities (other than bonds, debentures, other evidences of indebtedness, security futures products, and options on securities indexes (excluding a narrow-based security index)) registered on a national securities exchange or subject to prompt last sale reporting pursuant to the rules of the Commission or a registered national securities association.

(d) *Assessments on Security Futures Transactions.* Each national securities exchange and national securities association shall pay to the Commission an assessment equal to $0.009 for each round turn transaction (treated as including one purchase and one sale of a contract of sale for future delivery) on a security future traded on such national securities exchange or by or through any member of such association otherwise than on a national securities exchange, except that for fiscal year 2007 and each succeeding fiscal year such assessment shall be equal to $0.0042 for each such transaction.

(e) *Dates for Payment.* The fees and assessments required by subsections (b), (c), and (d) of this section shall be paid—

(1) on or before March 15, with respect to transactions and sales occurring during the period beginning on the preceding September 1 and ending at the close of the preceding December 31; and

(2) on or before September 25, with respect to transactions and sales occurring during the period beginning on the preceding January 1 and ending at the close of the preceding August 31.

(f) *Exemptions.* The Commission, by rule, may exempt any sale of securities or any class of sales of securities from any fee or assessment imposed by this section, if the Commission finds that such exemption is consistent with the public interest, the equal regulation of markets and brokers and dealers, and the development of a national market system.

(g) *Publication.* The Commission shall publish in the Federal Register notices of the fee or assessment rates applicable under this section for each fiscal year not later than 30 days after the date on which an Act making a regular appropriation to the Commission for such fiscal year is enacted, together with any estimates or projections on which such fees are based.

(h) *Pro Rata Application.* The rates per $1,000,000 required by this section shall be applied pro rata to amounts and balances of less than $1,000,000.

(i) *Deposit of Fees.*

(1) *Offsetting Collections.* Fees collected pursuant to subsections (b), (c), and (d) of this section for any fiscal year—

(A) shall be deposited and credited as offsetting collections to the account providing appropriations to the Commission; and

(B) except as provided in subsection (k), shall not be collected for any fiscal year except to the extent provided in advance in appropriation Acts.

(2) *General Revenues Prohibited.* No fees collected pursuant to subsections (b), (c), and (d) of this section for fiscal year 2002 or any succeeding fiscal year shall be deposited and credited as general revenue of the Treasury.

(j) *Adjustments to Fee Rates.*

(1) *Annual Adjustment.* Subject to subsections (i)(1)(B) and (k), for each fiscal year, the Commission shall by order adjust each of the rates applicable under subsections (b) and (c) for such fiscal year to a uniform adjusted rate that, when applied to the baseline estimate of the aggregate dollar amount of sales for such fiscal year, is reasonably likely to produce aggregate fee collections under this section (including assessments collected un-

der subsection (d) of this section) that are equal to the regular appropriation to the Commission by Congress for such fiscal year.

(2) *Mid-Year Adjustment.* Subject to subsections (i)(1)(B) and (k), for each fiscal year, the Commission shall determine, by March 1 of such fiscal year, whether, based on the actual aggregate dollar volume of sales during the first 5 months of such fiscal year, the baseline estimate of the aggregate dollar volume of sales used under paragraph (1) for such fiscal year is reasonably likely to be 10 percent (or more) greater or less than the actual aggregate dollar volume of sales for such fiscal year. If the Commission so determines, the Commission shall by order, no later than March 1, adjust each of the rates applicable under subsections (b) and (c) for such fiscal year to a uniform adjusted rate that, when applied to the revised estimate of the aggregate dollar amount of sales for the remainder of such fiscal year, is reasonably likely to produce aggregate fee collections under this section (including fees collected during such five-month period and assessments collected under subsection (d) of this section) that are equal to the regular appropriation to the Commission by Congress for such fiscal year. In making such revised estimate, the Commission shall, after consultation with the Congressional Budget Office and the Office of Management and Budget, use the same methodology required by subsection (*l*).

(3) *Review.* In exercising its authority under this subsection, the Commission shall not be required to comply with the provisions of section 553 of title 5, United States Code. An adjusted rate prescribed under paragraph (1) or (2) and published under subsection (g) shall not be subject to judicial review.

(4) *Effective Date.*

(A) *Annual Adjustment.* Subject to subsections (i)(1)(B) and (k), an adjusted rate prescribed under paragraph (1) shall take effect on the later of—

(i) the first day of the fiscal year to which such rate applies; or

(ii) 60 days after the date on which an Act making a regular appropriation to the Commission for such fiscal year is enacted.

(B) *Mid-Year Adjustment.* An adjusted rate prescribed under paragraph (2) shall take effect on April 1 of the fiscal year to which such rate applies.

(k) *Lapse of Appropriation.* If on the first day of a fiscal year a regular appropriation to the Commission has not been enacted, the Commission shall continue to collect (as offsetting collections) the fees and assessments under subsections (b), (c), and (d) of this section at the rate in effect during the preceding fiscal year, until 60 days after the date such a regular appropriation is enacted.

(*l*) *Baseline Estimate of the Aggregate Dollar Amount of Sales.* The baseline estimate of the aggregate dollar amount of sales for any fiscal year is the baseline estimate of the aggregate dollar amount of sales of securities (other than bonds, debentures, other evidences of indebtedness, security futures products, and options on securities indexes (excluding a narrow-based security index)) to be transacted on each national securities exchange and by or through any member of each national securities association (otherwise than on a national securities exchange) during such fiscal year as determined by the Commission, after consultation with the Congressional Budget Office and the Office of Management and Budget, using the methodology required for making projections pursuant to section 257 of the Balanced Budget and Emergency Deficit Control Act of 1985.

(m) *Transmittal of Commission Budget Requests.*

(1) *Budget Required.* For fiscal year 2012, and each fiscal year thereafter, the Commission shall prepare and submit a budget to the President. Whenever the Commission submits a budget estimate or request to the President or the Office of Management and Budget, the Commission shall concurrently transmit copies of the estimate or request to the Committee on Appropriations of the Senate, the Committee on Appropriations of the House of Representatives, the Committee on Banking, Housing, and Urban Affairs of the Senate, and the Committee on Financial Services of the House of Representatives.

(2) *Submission to Congress.* The President shall submit each budget submitted under paragraph (1) to Congress, in unaltered form, together with the annual budget for the Administration submitted by the President.

(3) *Contents.* The Commission shall include in each budget submitted under paragraph (1)—

(A) an itemization of the amount of funds necessary to carry out the functions of the Commission.

(B) an amount to be designated as contingency funding to be used by the Commission to address unanticipated needs; and

(C) a designation of any activities of the Commission for which multi-year budget authority would be suitable.

Penalties

Sec. 32. (a) *Willful Violations; False and Misleading Statements.* Any person who willfully violates any provision of this title (other than Section 30A) or any rule or regulation thereunder the violation of which is made unlawful or the observance of which is required under the terms of this title, or any person who willfully and knowingly makes, or causes to be made, any statement in any application, report, or document required to be filed under this title or any rule or regulation thereunder or any undertaking contained in a registration statement as provided in subsection (d) of section 15 of this title, or by any self-regulatory organization in connection with an application for membership or participation therein or to become associated with a member thereof, which statement was false or misleading with respect to any material fact, shall upon conviction be fined not more than $5,000,000, or imprisoned not more than 20 years, or both, except that when such person is a person other than a natural person, a fine not exceeding $25,000,000 may be imposed; but no person shall be subject to imprisonment under this section for the violation of any rule or regulation if he proves that he had no knowledge of such rule or regulation.

(b) *Failure to File Information, Documents, or Reports.* Any issuer which fails to file information, documents, or reports required to be filed under subsection (d) of section 15 of this title or any rule or regulation thereunder shall forfeit to the United States the sum of $100 for each and every day such failure to file shall continue. Such forfeiture, which shall be in lieu of any criminal penalty for such failure to file which might be deemed to arise under subsection (a) of this section, shall be payable into the Treasury of the United States and shall be recoverable in a civil suit in the name of the United States.

(c) *Violations by Issuers, Officers, Directors, Stockholders, Employees, or Agents of Issuers.*

(1)(A) Any issuer that violates subsection (a) or (g) of section 30A shall be fined not more than $2,000,000.

(B) Any issuer that violates subsection (a) or (g) of section 30A shall be subject to a civil penalty of not more than $10,000 imposed in an action brought by the Commission.

(2)(A) Any officer, director, employee, or agent of an issuer, or stockholder acting on behalf of such issuer, who willfully violates subsection (a) or (g) of section 30A of this title shall be fined not more than $100,000, or imprisoned not more than 5 years, or both.

(B) Any officer, director, employee, or agent of an issuer, or stockholder acting on behalf of such issuer, who violates subsection (a) or (g) of section 30A of this title shall be subject to a civil penalty of not more than $10,000 imposed in an action brought by the Commission.

(3) Whenever a fine is imposed under paragraph (2) upon any officer, director, employee, agent, or stockholder of an issuer, such fine may not be paid, directly or indirectly, by such issuer.

Separability of Provisions

Sec. 33. If any provision of this Act, or the application of such provision to any person or circumstances, shall be held invalid, the remainder of the Act, and the application of such provision to persons or circumstances other than those as to which it is held invalid, shall not be affected thereby.

Effective Date

Sec. 34. This Act shall become effective on July 1, 1934, except that sections 6 and 12(b), (c), (d), and (e) shall become effective on September 1, 1934; and sections 5, 7, 8, 9(a)(6), 10, 11, 12(a), 13, 14, 15, 16, 17, 18, 19, and 30 shall become effective on October 1, 1934.

Authorization of Appropriations

Sec. 35. In addition to any other funds authorized to be appropriated to the Commission, there are authorized to be appropriated to carry out the functions, powers, and duties of the Commission—

(1) for fiscal year 2011, $1,300,000,000;

(2) for fiscal year 2012, $1,500,000,000;

(3) for fiscal year 2013, $1,750,000,000;

(4) for fiscal year 2014, $2,000,000,000; and

(5) for fiscal year 2015, $2,250,000,000.

Requirements for the EDGAR System

Sec. 35A. The Commission, by rule or regulation—

(1) shall provide that any information in the EDGAR system that is required to be disseminated by the contractor—

(A) may be sold or disseminated by the contractor only pursuant to a uniform schedule of fees prescribed by the Commission;

(B) may be obtained by a purchaser by direct interconnection with the EDGAR system;

(C) shall be equally available on equal terms to all persons; and

(D) may be used, resold, or redisseminated by any person who has lawfully obtained such information without restriction and without payment of additional fees or royalties; and

(2) shall require that persons, or classes of persons, required to make filings with the Commission submit such filings in a form and manner suitable for entry into the EDGAR system and shall specify the date that such requirement is effective with respect to that person or class; except that the Commission may exempt persons or classes of persons, or filings or classes of filings, from such rules or regulations in order to prevent hardships or to avoid imposing unreasonable burdens or as otherwise may be necessary or appropriate.

General Exemptive Authority

Sec. 36. (a) *Authority.*

(1) *In General.* Except as provided in subsection (b), but notwithstanding any other provision of this title, the Commission, by rule, regulation, or order, may conditionally or unconditionally exempt any person, security, or transaction, or any class or classes of persons, securities, or transactions, from any provision or provisions of this title or of any rule or regulation thereunder, to the extent that such exemption is necessary or appropriate in the public interest, and is consistent with the protection of investors.

(2) *Procedures.* The Commission shall, by rule or regulation, determine the procedures under which an exemptive order under this section shall be granted and may, in its sole discretion, decline to entertain any application for an order of exemption under this section.

(b) *Limitation.* The Commission may not, under this section, exempt any person, security, or transaction, or any class or classes of persons, securities, or transactions from section 15C or the rules or regulations issued thereunder or (for purposes of section 15C and the rules and regulations issued thereunder) from any definition in paragraph (42), (43), (44), or (45) of section 3(a).

(c) *Derivatives.* Unless the Commission is expressly authorized by any provision described in this subsection to grant exemptions, the Commission shall not grant exemptions, with respect to amendments made by subtitle B of the Wall Street Transparency and Accountability Act of 2010, with respect to paragraphs (65), (66), (68), (69), (70), (71), (72), (73), (74), (75), (76), and (79) of section 3(a), and sections 10B(a), 10B(b), 10B(c), 13A, 15F, 17A(g), 17A(h), 17A(i), 17A(j), 17A(k), and 17A(*l*); provided that the Commission shall have exemptive authority under this title with respect to security-based swaps as to the same matters that the Commodity Futures Trading Commission has under the Wall Street Transparency and Accountability Act of 2010 with respect to swaps, including under section (c) of the Commodity Exchange Act.

Tennessee Valley Authority

Sec. 37. (a) *In General.* Commencing with the issuance by the Tennessee Valley Authority of an annual report on Commission Form 10–K (or any successor thereto) for fiscal year 2006 and thereafter, the Tennessee Valley Authority shall file with the Commission, in accordance with such rules and regulations as the Commission has prescribed or may prescribe, such periodic, current, and supplementary information, documents, and reports as would be required pursuant to section 13 if the Tennessee Valley Authority were an issuer of a security registered pursuant to section 12. Notwithstanding the preceding sentence, the Tennessee Valley Authority shall not be required to register any securities under this chapter, and shall not be deemed to have registered any securities under this chapter.

(b) *Limited Treatment as Issuer.* Commencing with the issuance by the Tennessee Valley Authority of an annual report on Commission Form 10–K (or any successor thereto) for fiscal year 2006 and thereafter, the Tennessee Valley Authority shall be deemed to be an issuer for purposes of section 10A, other than for subsection (m)(1) or (m)(3) of section 10A of this title. The Tennessee Valley Authority shall not be required by this subsection to comply with the rules issued by any national securities exchange or national securities association in response to rules issued by the Commission pursuant to section 10A(m)(1).

(c) *No Effect on TVA Authority*. Nothing in this section shall be construed to diminish, impair, or otherwise affect the authority of the Board of Directors of the Tennessee Valley Authority to carry out its statutory functions under the Tennessee Valley Authority Act of 1933.

Federal National Mortgage Association, Federal Home Loan Mortgage Corporation, Federal Home Loan Banks

Sec. 38. (a) *Federal National Mortgage Association and Federal Home Loan Mortgage Corporation*. No class of equity securities of the Federal National Mortgage Association or the Federal Home Loan Mortgage Corporation shall be treated as an exempted security for purposes of section 12, 13, 14, or 16.

(b) *Federal Home Loan Banks*.

(1) *Registration*. Each Federal Home Loan Bank shall register a class of its common stock under section 12(g), not later than 120 days after the date of enactment of the Federal Housing Finance Regulatory Reform Act of 2008, and shall thereafter maintain such registration and be treated for purposes of this title as an "issuer", the securities of which are required to be registered under section 12, regardless of the number of members holding such stock at any given time.

(2) *Standards Relating to Audit Committees*. Each Federal Home Loan Bank shall comply with the rules issued by the Commission under section 10A(m).

(c) *Definitions*. For purposes of this section, the following definitions shall apply:

(1) *Federal Home Loan Bank; Member*. The terms "Federal Home Loan Bank" and "member", have the same meanings as in section 2 of the Federal Home Loan Bank Act.

(2) *Federal National Mortgage Association*. The term "Federal National Mortgage Association" means the corporation created by the Federal National Mortgage Association Charter Act.

(3) *Federal Home Loan Mortgage Corporation*. The term "Federal Home Loan Mortgage Corporation" means the corporation created by the Federal Home Loan Mortgage Corporation Act.

Investor Advisory Committee

Sec. 39. (a) *Establishment and Purpose*.

(1) *Establishment*. There is established within the Commission the Investor Advisory Committee (referred to in this section as the "Committee").

(2) *Purpose*. The Committee shall—

(A) advise and consult with the Commission on—

(i) regulatory priorities of the Commission;

(ii) issues relating to the regulation of securities products, trading strategies, and fee structures, and the effectiveness of disclosure;

(iii) initiatives to protect investor interest; and

(iv) initiatives to promote investor confidence and the integrity of the securities marketplace; and

(B) submit to the Commission such findings and recommendations as the Committee determines are appropriate, including recommendations for proposed legislative changes.

(b) *Membership*.

(1) *In General*. The members of the Committee shall be—

(A) the Investor Advocate;

(B) a representative of State securities commissions;

(C) a representative of the interests of senior citizens; and

(D) not fewer than 10, and not more than 20, members appointed by the Commission, from among individuals who—

(i) represent the interests of individual equity and debt investors, including investors in mutual funds;

(ii) represent the interests of institutional investors, including the interests of pension funds and registered investment companies;

(iii) are knowledgeable about investment issues and decisions; and

(iv) have reputations of integrity.

(2) *Term.* Each member of the Committee appointed under paragraph (1)(B) shall serve for a term of 4 years.

(3) *Members Not Commission Employees.* Members appointed under paragraph (1)(B) shall not be deemed to be employees or agents of the Commission solely because of membership on the Committee.

(c) *Chairman; Vice Chairman; Secretary; Assistant Secretary.*

(1) *In General.* The members of the Committee shall elect, from among the members of the Committee—

(A) a chairman, who may not be employed by an issuer;

(B) a vice chairman, who may not be employed by an issuer;

(C) a secretary; and

(D) an assistant secretary.

(2) *Term.* Each member elected under paragraph (1) shall serve for a term of 3 years in the capacity for which the member was elected under paragraph (1).

(d) *Meetings.*

(1) *Frequency of Meetings.* The Committee shall meet—

(A) not less frequently than twice annually, at the call of the chairman of the Committee; and

(B) from time to time, at the call of the Commission.

(2) *Notice.* The chairman of the Committee shall give the members of the Committee written notice of each meeting, not later than 2 weeks before the date of the meeting.

(e) *Compensation and Travel Expenses.* Each member of the Committee who is not a full-time employee of the United States shall—

(1) be entitled to receive compensation at a rate not to exceed the daily equivalent of the annual rate of basic pay in effect for a position at level V of the Executive Schedule under section 5316 of title 5, United States Code, for each day during which the member is engaged in the actual performance of the duties of the Committee; and

(2) while away from the home or regular place of business of the member in the performance of services for the Committee, be allowed travel expenses, including per diem in lieu of subsistence, in the same manner as persons employed intermittently in the Government service are allowed expenses under section 5703(b) of title 5, United States Code.

(f) *Staff.* The Commission shall make available to the Committee such staff as the chairman of the Committee determines are necessary to carry out this section.

(g) *Review by Commission.* The Commission shall—

(1) review the findings and recommendations of the Committee; and

(2) each time the Committee submits a finding or recommendation to the Commission, promptly issue a public statement—

(A) assessing the finding or recommendation of the Committee; and

(B) disclosing the action, if any, the Commission intends to take with respect to the finding or recommendation.

(h) *Committee Findings.* Nothing in this section shall require the Commission to agree to or act upon any finding or recommendation of the Committee.

(i) *Federal Advisory Committee Act.* The Federal Advisory Committee Act shall not apply with respect to the Committee and its activities.

(j) *Authorization of Appropriations.* There is authorized to be appropriated to the Commission such sums as are necessary to carry out this section.

RULES AND REGULATIONS UNDER THE SECURITIES EXCHANGE ACT OF 1934

(Cite as 17 CFR § 240.__)

RULES OF GENERAL APPLICATION

DEFINITION OF "EQUITY SECURITY" AS USED IN SECTIONS 12(g) AND 16

MISCELLANEOUS EXEMPTIONS

SECURITY-BASED SWAP DEALER AND PARTICIPANT DEFINITIONS

FURTHER DEFINITION OF SWAP, SECURITY–BASED SWAP, AND SECURITY–BASED SWAP AGREEMENT; MIXED SWAPS; SECURITY–BASED SWAP AGREEMENT RECORDKEEPING

MANIPULATIVE AND DECEPTIVE DEVICES AND CONTRIVANCES

REPORTS UNDER SECTION 10A

REQUIREMENTS UNDER SECTION 10C

ADOPTION OF FLOOR TRADING REGULATION (RULE 11a–1)

ADOPTION OF REGULATION ON CONDUCT OF SPECIALISTS

EXEMPTION OF CERTAIN SECURITIES FROM SECTION 11(d)(1)

SECURITIES EXEMPTED FROM REGISTRATION

REGULATION 12B. REGISTRATION AND REPORTING

GENERAL

FORMAL REQUIREMENTS

GENERAL REQUIREMENTS AS TO CONTENTS

EXHIBITS

SPECIAL PROVISIONS

CERTIFICATION BY EXCHANGES AND EFFECTIVENESS OF REGISTRATION

SUSPENSION OF TRADING, WITHDRAWAL, AND STRIKING FROM LISTING AND REGISTRATION

UNLISTED TRADING

EXTENSIONS AND TEMPORARY EXEMPTIONS; DEFINITIONS

REGULATION 13A. REPORTS OF ISSUERS OF SECURITIES REGISTERED PURSUANT TO SECTION 12

ANNUAL REPORTS

Rule

13a–14. Certification of disclosure in annual and quarterly reports
13a–15. Controls and procedures
13a–16. Reports of foreign private issuers on Form 6–K (17 CFR 249.306)
13a–17. Reports of asset-backed issuers on Form 10–D (17 CFR 249.312)
13a–18. Compliance with servicing criteria for asset-backed securities
13a–19. Reports by shell companies on Form 20–F
13a–20. Plain English presentation of specified information

REGULATION 13B–2. MAINTENANCE OF RECORD AND PREPARATION OF REQUIRED REPORTS

13b2–1. Falsification of accounting records
13b2–2. Representations and conduct in connection with the preparation of required reports and documents

REGULATION 13D–G

13d–1. Filing of Schedule 13D and 13G
13d–2. Filing of amendments to Schedules 13D or 13G
13d–3. Determination of beneficial owner
13d–4. Disclaimer of beneficial ownership
13d–5. Acquisition of securities
13d–6. Exemption of certain acquisitions
13d–7. Dissemination
13d–101. Schedule 13D—information to be included in statements filed pursuant to Rule 13d–1(a) and amendments thereto filed pursuant to Rule 13d–2(a)
13d–102. Schedule 13G—information to be included in statements filed pursuant to Rule 13d–1(b), (c), and (d) and amendments thereto filed pursuant to Rule 13d–2
13e–1. Purchase of securities by the issuer during a third-party tender offer
13e–2 [Reserved]
13e–3. Going private transactions by certain issuers or their affiliates
13e–4. Tender offers by issuers
13e–100. Schedule 13E–3 transaction statement under Section 13(e) of the Securities Exchange Act of 1934 and Rule 13e–3 thereunder
13e–101. [Reserved]
13e–102. Schedule 13E–4F. Tender offer statement pursuant to Section 13(e)(1) of the Securities Exchange Act of 1934 and Rule 13e–4 thereunder
13f–1. Reporting by institutional investment managers of information with respect to accounts over which they exercise investment discretion
13h–1. Large trader reporting
13k–1. Foreign bank exemption from the insider lending prohibition under Section 13(k)
13n–1. Registration of security-based swap data repository
13n–2. Withdrawal from registration; revocation and cancellation
13n–3. Registration of successor to registered security-based swap data repository
13n–4. Duties and core principles of security-based swap data repository
13n–5. Data collection and maintenance
13n–6. Automated systems
13n–7. Recordkeeping of security-based swap data repository
13n–8. Reports to be provided to the Commission
13n–9. Privacy requirements of security-based swap data repository
13n–10. Disclosure requirements of security-based swap data repository
13n–11. Chief compliance officer of security-based swap data repository; compliance reports and financial reports

REGULATION 14A. SOLICITATION OF PROXIES

REGULATION 14C. DISTRIBUTION OF INFORMATION PURSUANT TO SECTION 14(c)

REGULATION 14D

REGULATION 14E

REGULATION 14N: FILINGS REQUIRED BY CERTAIN NOMINATING SHAREHOLDERS

EXEMPTION OF CERTAIN OTC DERIVATIVES DEALERS

EXEMPTION OF CERTAIN SECURITIES FROM SECTION 15(a)

REGISTRATION OF BROKERS AND DEALERS

NATIONAL AND AFFILIATED SECURITIES ASSOCIATIONS

REGISTRATION OF GOVERNMENT SECURITIES BROKERS AND GOVERNMENT SECURITIES DEALERS

REGISTRATION OF SECURITY-BASED SWAP DEALERS AND MAJOR SECURITY-BASED SWAP PARTICIPANTS

BUSINESS CONDUCT STANDARDS FOR SECURITY-BASED SWAP DEALERS AND MAJOR SECURITY-BASED SWAP PARTICIPANTS

Rule

15Fh–5 Special requirements for security-based swap dealers and major security-based swap participants acting as counterparties to special entities
15Fh–6 Political contributions by certain security-based swap dealers
15Fi–1 Definitions
15Fi–2 Acknowledgment and verification of security-based swap transactions
15Fk–1 Designation of chief compliance officer for security-based swap dealers and major security-based swap participants

DISCLOSURE FOR ASSET-BACKED SECURITIES

15Ga–1. Repurchases and replacements relating to asset-backed securities
15Ga–2. Findings and conclusions of third-party due diligence reports

REPORTS OF DIRECTORS, OFFICERS, AND PRINCIPAL SHAREHOLDERS

16a–1. Definition of terms
16a–2. Persons and transactions subject to Section 16
16a–3. Reporting transactions and holdings
16a–4. Derivative securities
16a–5. Odd–lot dealers
16a–6. Small acquisitions
16a–7. Transactions effected in connection with a distribution
16a–8. Trusts
16a–9. Stock splits, stock dividends, and pro rata rights
16a–10. Exemptions under Section 16(a)
16a–11. Dividend or interest reinvestment plans
16a–12. Domestic relations orders
16a–13. Change in form of beneficial ownership

EXEMPTION OF CERTAIN TRANSACTIONS FROM SECTION 16(b)

16b–1. Transactions approved by a regulatory authority
16b–2. [Reserved]
16b–3. Transactions between an issuer and its officers or directors
16b–4. [Reserved]
16b–5. Bona fide gifts and inheritance
16b–6. Derivative securities
16b–7. Mergers, reclassifications, and consolidations
16b–8. Voting trusts

EXEMPTION OF CERTAIN TRANSACTIONS FROM SECTION 16(c)

16c–1. Brokers
16c–2. Transactions effected in connection with a distribution
16c–3. Exemption of sales of securities to be acquired
16c–4. Derivative securities

ARBITRAGE TRANSACTIONS

16e–1. Arbitrage transactions under Section 16

PRESERVATION OF RECORDS AND REPORTS OF CERTAIN STABILIZING ACTIVITIES

17a–1. Recordkeeping rule for national securities exchanges, national securities associations, registered clearing agencies and the Municipal Securities Rulemaking Board
17a–2. Recordkeeping requirements relating to stabilizing activities
17a–3. Records to be made by certain exchange members, brokers, and dealers

NATIONALLY RECOGNIZED STATISTICAL RATING ORGANIZATIONS

SUSPENSION AND EXPULSION OF EXCHANGE MEMBERS

IMPLEMENTATION OF THE WHISTLEBLOWER PROVISIONS OF SECTION 21F OF THE SECURITIES EXCHANGE ACT OF 1934

Rule	
21F–5.	Amount of award
21F–6.	Criteria for determining amount of award
21F–7.	Confidentiality of submissions
21F–8.	Eligibility
21F–9.	Procedures for submitting original information
21F–10.	Procedures for making a claim for a whistleblower award in SEC actions that result in monetary sanctions in excess of $1,000,000
21F–11.	Procedures for determining awards based upon a related action
21F–12.	Materials that may form as the basis for an award determination and that may comprise the record on appeal
21F–13.	Appeals
21F–14.	Procedures applicable to the payment of awards
21F–15.	No amnesty
21F–16.	Awards to whistleblowers who engage in culpable conduct
21F–17.	Staff communications with individuals reporting possible securities law violations

INSPECTION AND PUBLICATION OF INFORMATION FILED UNDER THE ACT

24b–1.	Documents to be kept public by exchanges
24b–2.	Nondisclosure of information filed with the Commission and with any exchange
24b–3.	Information filed by issuers and others under Sections 12, 13, 14, and 16
24c–1.	Access to nonpublic information
31.	Section 31 transaction fees
36a1–1.	Exemption from Section 7 for OTC derivatives dealers
36a1–2.	Exemption from SIPA for OTC derivatives dealers

REGULATION M

(Cite as 17 CFR § 242.___)

100.	Preliminary note; definitions
101.	Activities by distribution participants
102.	Activities by issuers and selling security holders during a distribution
103.	NASDAQ passive market making
104.	Stabilizing and other activities in connection with an offering
105.	Short selling in connection with a public offering

REGULATION SHO—REGULATION OF SHORT SALES

(Cite as 17 CFR § 242.___)

200.	Definition of "short sale" and marketing requirements
201.	Circuit breaker
203.	Borrowing and delivery requirements
204.	Close-out requirement

REGULATION ATS—ALTERNATIVE TRADING SYSTEMS

(Cite as 17 CFR § 242.___)

300.	Definitions
301.	Requirements for alternative trading systems
302.	Recordkeeping requirements for alternative trading systems
303.	Record preservation requirements for alternative trading systems
304.	NMS Stock ATSs

CUSTOMER MARGIN REQUIREMENTS FOR SECURITY FUTURES

(Cite as 17 CFR § 242.___)

REGULATION AC—ANALYST CERTIFICATION

(Cite as 17 CFR § 242.___)

REGULATION NMS—REGULATION OF THE NATIONAL MARKET SYSTEM

(Cite as 17 CFR § 242.___)

REGULATION SBSR—REGULATORY REPORTING AND PUBLIC DISSEMINATION OF SECURITY-BASED SWAP INFORMATION

(Cite as 17 CFR § 242.___)

REGULATION SCI—SYSTEMS COMPLIANCE AND INTEGRITY

(Cite as 17 CFR 242.__)

REGULATION FD

(Cite as 17 CFR § 243.___)

REGULATION BTR—BLACKOUT TRADING RESTRICTION

(Cite as 17 CFR § 245.___)

FORMS UNDER THE SECURITIES EXCHANGE ACT OF 1934

RULES AND REGULATIONS UNDER THE SECURITIES EXCHANGE ACT OF 1934

(Cite as 17 CFR § 240.__)

RULES OF GENERAL APPLICATION

ATTENTION ELECTRONIC FILERS

THIS REGULATION SHOULD BE READ IN CONJUNCTION WITH REGULATION S–T (17 CFR 232), WHICH GOVERNS THE PREPARATION AND SUBMISSION OF DOCUMENTS IN ELECTRONIC FORMAT. MANY PROVISIONS RELATING TO THE PREPARATION AND SUBMISSION OF DOCUMENTS IN PAPER FORMAT CONTAINED IN THIS REGULATION ARE SUPERSEDED BY THE PROVISIONS OF REGULATION S–T FOR DOCUMENTS REQUIRED TO BE FILED IN ELECTRONIC FORMAT.

Rule 0–1. Definitions

(a) As used in the rules and regulations prescribed by the Commission pursuant to Title I of the Securities Exchange Act of 1934, unless the context otherwise specifically requires—

(1) The term *Commission* means the Securities and Exchange Commission.

(2) The term *Act* means Title I of the Securities Exchange Act of 1934.

(3) The term *section* refers to a section of the Securities Exchange Act of 1934.[1]

(4) The term *rules and regulations* refers to all rules and regulations adopted by the Commission pursuant to the Act, including the forms for registration and reports and the accompanying instructions thereto.

(5) The term *electronic filer* means a person or an entity that submits filings electronically pursuant to Rules 100 and 101 of Regulation S–T (17 CFR 232.100 and 232.101).

(6) The term *electronic filing* means a document under the federal securities laws that is transmitted or delivered to the Commission in electronic format.

(b) Unless otherwise specifically stated, the terms used in the rules and regulations shall have the meaning defined in the Act.

(c) A rule or regulation which defines a term without express reference to the Act or to the rules and regulations, or to a portion thereof, defines such term for all purposes as used both in the Act and in the rules and regulations, unless the context otherwise specifically requires.

(d) Unless otherwise specified or the context otherwise requires, the term *prospectus* means a prospectus meeting the requirements of section 10(a) of the Securities Act of 1933 as amended.

Rule 0–2. Business hours of the Commission

(a) The principal office of the Commission, at 100 F Street, NE, Washington, DC 20549, is open each day, except Saturdays, Sundays, and Federal holidays, from 9 a.m. to 5:30 p.m., Eastern Standard Time or Eastern Daylight Saving Time, whichever currently is in effect in Washington, DC, *provided that* hours for the filing of documents pursuant to the Act or the rules and regulations thereunder are as set forth in paragraphs (b) and (c) of this rule.

(b) *Submissions Made in Paper*. Paper documents filed with or otherwise furnished to the Commission may be submitted to the Commission each day, except Saturdays, Sundays and federal holidays, from 8 a.m. to 5:30 p.m., Eastern Standard Time or Eastern Daylight Saving Time, whichever is currently in effect.

(c) *Electronic Filings*. Filings made by direct transmission may be submitted to the Commission each day, except Saturdays, Sundays and federal holidays, from 8 a.m. to 10 p.m., Eastern Standard Time or Eastern Daylight Saving Time, whichever is currently in effect.

Rule 0–3. Filing of material with the Commission

(a) All papers required to be filed with the Commission pursuant to the Act or the rules and regulations thereunder shall be filed at the principal office in Washington, DC Material may be filed by delivery

1. The provisions of paragraph (a)(3) of Rule 0–1 relate to the terminology of rules and regulations as published by the Securities and Exchange Commission and are inapplicable to the terminology appearing in the Code of Federal Regulations.

to the Commission, through the mails or otherwise. The date on which papers are actually received by the Commission shall be the date of filing thereof if all of the requirements with respect to the filing have been complied with, except that if the last day on which papers can be accepted as timely filed falls on a Saturday, Sunday or holiday, such papers may be filed on the first business day following.

(b) The manually signed original (or in the case of duplicate originals, one duplicate original) of all registrations, applications, statements, reports, or other documents filed under the Securities Exchange Act of 1934, as amended, shall be numbered sequentially (in addition to any internal numbering which otherwise may be present) by handwritten, typed, printed or other legible form of notation from the facing page of the document through the last page of that document and any exhibits or attachments thereto. Further, the total number of pages contained in a numbered original shall be set forth on the first page of the document.

(c) Each document filed shall contain an exhibit index, which should immediately precede the exhibits filed with such document. The index shall list each exhibit filed and identify by handwritten, typed, printed, or other legible form of notation in the manually signed original, the page number in the sequential numbering system described in paragraph (b) of this rule where such exhibit can be found or where it is stated that the exhibit is incorporated by reference. Further, the first page of the manually signed document shall list the page in the filing where the exhibit index is located.

Rule 0–4. Nondisclosure of information obtained in examinations and investigations

Information or documents obtained by officers or employees of the Commission in the course of any examination or investigation pursuant to section 17(a) (15 U.S.C. 78q(a)) or 21(a) (15 U.S.C. 78u(a)) shall, unless made a matter of public record, be deemed confidential. Except as provided by 17 CFR 203.2, officers and employees are hereby prohibited from making such confidential information or documents or any other non-public records of the Commission available to anyone other than a member, officer, or employee of the Commission, unless the Commission or the General Counsel, pursuant to delegated authority, authorizes the disclosure of such information or the production of such documents as not being contrary to the public interest. Any officer or employee who is served with a subpoena requiring the disclosure of such information or the production of such documents shall appear in court and, unless the authorization described in the preceding sentence shall have been given, shall respectfully decline to disclose the information or produce the documents called for, basing his or her refusal upon this rule. Any officer or employee who is served with such a subpoena shall promptly advise the General Counsel of the service of such subpoena, the nature of the information or documents sought, and any circumstances which may bear upon the desirability of making available such information or documents.

Rule 0–5. Reference to rule by obsolete designation

Wherever in any rule, form, or instruction book specific reference is made to a rule by number or other designation, which is now obsolete, such reference shall be deemed to be made to the corresponding rule or rules in these General Rules and Regulations.

Rule 0–6. Disclosure detrimental to the national defense or foreign policy

(a) Any requirement to the contrary notwithstanding, no registration statement, report, proxy statement or other document filed with the Commission or any securities exchange shall contain any document or information which, pursuant to Executive order, has been classified by an appropriate department or agency of the United States for protection in the interests of national defense or foreign policy.

(b) Where a document or information is omitted pursuant to paragraph (a) of this rule, there shall be filed, in lieu of such document or information, a statement from an appropriate department or agency of the United States to the effect that such document or information has been classified or that the status thereof is awaiting determination. Where a document is omitted pursuant to paragraph (a) of this rule, but information relating to the subject matter of such document is nevertheless included in material filed with the Commission pursuant to a determination of an appropriate department or agency of the United States that disclosure of such information would not be contrary to the interests of national defense or foreign policy, a statement from such department or agency to that effect shall be submitted for the information of the Commission. A registrant may rely upon any such statement in filing or omitting any document or information to which the statement relates.

(c) The Commission may protect any information in its possession which may require classification in the interests of national defense or foreign policy pending determination by an appropriate department or agency as to whether such information should be classified.

(d) It shall be the duty of the registrant to submit the documents or information referred to in paragraph (a) of this rule to the appropriate department or agency of the United States prior to filing them with the Commission and to obtain and submit to the Commission, at the time of filing such documents or information, or in lieu thereof, as the case may be, the statements from such department or agency required by paragraph (b) of this rule. All such statements shall be in writing.

Rule 0–8. Application of rules to registered broker-dealers

Any provision of any rule or regulation under the Act which prohibits any act, practice, or course of business by any person if the mails or any means or instrumentality of interstate commerce are used in connection therewith, shall also prohibit any such act, practice, or course of business by any broker or dealer registered pursuant to section 15(b) of the Act, or any person acting on behalf of such a broker or dealer, irrespective of any use of the mails or any means or instrumentality of interstate commerce.

Rule 0–9. Payment of fees

All payment of fees shall be made by wire transfer, or by certified check, bank cashier's check, United States postal money order, or bank money order payable to the Securities and Exchange Commission, omitting the name or title of any official of the Commission. Payment of filing fees required by this rule shall be made in accordance with the directions set forth in 17 CFR 202.3a.

Rule 0–10. Small entities under the Securities Exchange Act for purposes of the Regulatory Flexibility Act

For purposes of Commission rulemaking in accordance with the provisions of Chapter Six of the Administrative Procedure Act (5 U.S.C. 601 *et seq.*), and unless otherwise defined for purposes of a particular rulemaking proceeding, the term *small business* or *small organization* shall—

(a) When used with reference to an "issuer" or a "person," other than an investment company, mean an "issuer" or "person" that, on the last day of its most recent fiscal year, had total assets of $5 million or less;

(b) When used with reference to an "issuer" or "person" that is an investment company, have the meaning ascribed to those terms by Rule 0-10 under the Investment Company Act 1940;

(c) When used with reference to a broker or dealer, mean a broker or dealer that:

(1) Had total capital (net worth plus subordinated liabilities) of less than $500,000 on the date in the prior fiscal year as of which its audited financial statements were prepared pursuant to Rule 17a–5(d) or, if not required to file such statements, a broker or dealer that had total capital (net worth plus subordinated liabilities) of less than $500,000 on the last business day of the preceding fiscal year (or in the time that it has been in business, if shorter); and

(2) Is not affiliated with any person (other than a natural person) that is not a small business or small organization as defined in this rule;

(d) When used with reference to a clearing agency, mean a clearing agency that:

(1) Compared, cleared and settled less than $500 million in securities transactions during the preceding fiscal year (or in the time that it has been in business, if shorter);

(2) Had less than $200 million of funds and securities in its custody or control at all times during the preceding fiscal year (or in the time that it has been in business, if shorter); and

(3) Is not affiliated with any person (other than a natural person) that is not a small business or small organization as defined in this rule;

(e) When used with reference to an exchange, mean any exchange that:

(1) Has been exempted from the reporting requirements of Rule 601 of Regulation NMS; and

(2) Is not affiliated with any person (other than a natural person) that is not a small business or small organization as defined in this rule;

(f) When used with reference to a municipal securities dealer that is a bank (including any separately identifiable department or division of a bank), mean any such municipal securities dealer that:

(1) Had, or is a department of a bank that had, total assets of less than $10 million at all times during the preceding fiscal year (or in the time that it has been in business, if shorter);

(2) Had an average monthly volume of municipal securities transactions in the preceding fiscal year (or in the time it has been registered, if shorter) of less than $100,000; and

(3) Is not affiliated with any person (other than a natural person) that is not a small business or small organization as defined in this rule;

(g) When used with reference to a securities information processor, mean a securities information processor that:

(1) Had gross revenues of less than $10 million during the preceding fiscal year (or in the time it has been in business, if shorter);

(2) Provided service to fewer than 100 interrogation devices or moving tickers at all times during the preceding fiscal year (or in the time that it has been in business, if shorter); and

(3) Is not affiliated with any person (other than a natural person) that is not a small business or small organization under this rule; and

(h) When used with reference to a transfer agent, mean a transfer agent that:

(1) Received less than 500 items for transfer and less than 500 items for processing during the preceding six months (or in the time that it has been in business, if shorter);

(2) Transferred items only of issuers that would be deemed "small businesses" or "small organizations" as defined in this rule; and

(3) Maintained master shareholder files that in the aggregate contained less than 1,000 shareholder accounts or was the named transfer agent for less than 1,000 shareholder accounts at all times during the preceding fiscal year (or in the time that it has been in business, if shorter); and

(4) Is not affiliated with any person (other than a natural person) that is not a small business or small organization under this rule.

(i) For purposes of paragraph (c) of this rule, a broker or dealer is affiliated with another person if:

(1) Such broker or dealer controls, is controlled by, or is under common control with such other person; a person shall be deemed to control another person if that person has the right to vote 25 percent or more of the voting securities of such other person or is entitled to receive 25 percent or more of the net profits of such other person or is otherwise able to direct or cause the direction of the management or policies of such other person; or

(2) Such broker or dealer introduces transactions in securities, other than registered investment company securities or interests or participations in insurance company separate accounts, to such other person, or introduces accounts of customers or other brokers or dealers, other than accounts that hold only registered investment company securities or interests or participations in insurance company separate accounts, to such other person that carries such accounts on a fully disclosed basis.

(j) For purposes of paragraphs (d) through (h) of this rule, a person is affiliated with another person if that person controls, is controlled by, or is under common control with such other person; a person shall be deemed to control another person if that person has the right to vote 25 percent or more of the voting securities of such other person or is entitled to receive 25 percent or more of the net profits of such other person or is otherwise able to direct or cause the direction of the management or policies of such other person.

(k) For purposes of paragraph (g) of this rule, "interrogation device" shall refer to any device that may be used to read or receive securities information, including quotations, indications of interest, last sale data and transaction reports, and shall include proprietary terminals or personal computers that receive securities information via computer-to-computer interfaces or gateway access.

Rule 0–11. Filing fees for certain acquisitions, dispositions and similar transactions

(a) *General.* (1) At the time of filing a disclosure document described in paragraphs (b) through (d) of this rule relating to certain acquisitions, dispositions, business combinations, consolidations or similar transactions, the person filing the specified document shall pay a fee payable to the Commission to be calculated as set forth in paragraph (b) through (d) of this rule.

(2) Only one fee per transaction is required to be paid. A required fee shall be reduced in an amount equal to any fee paid with respect to such transaction pursuant to either section 6(b) of the Securities Act of 1933 or any applicable provision of this rule; the fee requirements under section 6(b) shall be reduced in an amount equal to the fee paid the Commission with respect to a transaction under this regulation. No part of a filing fee is refundable.

(3) If at any time after the initial payment the aggregate consideration offered is increased, an additional filing fee based upon such increase shall be paid with the required amended filing.

(4) When the fee is based upon the market value of securities, such market value shall be established by either the average of the high and low prices reported in the consolidated reporting system (for exchange traded securities and last sale reported over-the-counter securities) or the average of the bid and asked price (for other over-the-counter securities) as of a specified date within 5 business days prior to the date of the filing. If there is no market for the securities, the value shall be based upon the book value of the securities computed as of the latest practicable date prior to the date of the filing, unless the issuer of the securities is in bankruptcy or receivership or has an accumulated capital deficit, in which case one-third of the principal amount, par value or stated value of the securities shall be used.

(5) The cover page of the filing shall set forth the calculation of the fee in tabular format, as well as the amount offset by a previous filing and the identification of such filing, if applicable.

(b) *Section 13(e)(1) Filings.* At the time of filing such statement as the Commission may require pursuant to section 13(e)(1) of the Exchange Act, a fee of one-fiftieth of one percent of the value of the securities proposed to be acquired by the acquiring person. The value of the securities proposed to be acquired shall be determined as follows:

(1) The value of the securities to be acquired solely for cash shall be the amount of cash to be paid for them;

(2) The value of the securities to be acquired with securities or other non-cash consideration, whether or not in combination with a cash payment for the same securities, shall be based upon the market value of the securities to be received by the acquiring person as established in accordance with paragraph (a)(4) of this rule.

(c) *Proxy and Information Statement Filings.* At the time of filing a preliminary proxy statement pursuant to Rule 14a–6(a) or preliminary information statement pursuant to Rule 14c–5(a) that concerns a merger, consolidation, acquisition of a company, or proposed sale or other disposition of substantially all the assets of the registrant (including a liquidation), the following fee:

(1) For preliminary material involving a vote upon a merger, consolidation or acquisition of a company, a fee of one-fiftieth of one percent of the proposed cash payment or of the value of the securities and other property to be transferred to security holders in the transaction. The fee is payable whether the registrant is acquiring another company or being acquired.

(i) The value of securities or other property to be transferred to security holders, whether or not in combination with a cash payment for the same securities, shall be based upon the market value of the securities to be received by the acquiring person as established in accordance with paragraph (a)(4) of this rule.

(ii) Notwithstanding the above, where the acquisition, merger or consolidation is for the sole purpose of changing the registrant's domicile, no filing fee is required to be paid.

(2) For preliminary material involving a vote upon a proposed sale or other disposition of substantially all the assets of the registrant, a fee of one-fiftieth of one percent of the aggregate of the cash and the value of the securities (other than its own) and other property to be received by the registrant. In the case of a disposition in which the registrant will not receive any property, such as a liquidation or spin-off, the fee shall be one-fiftieth of one percent of the aggregate of the cash and the value of the securities and other property to be distributed to security holders.

(i) The value of the securities to be received (or distributed in the case of a spin-off or liquidation) shall be based upon the market value of such securities as established in accordance with paragraph (a)(4) of this rule.

(ii) The value of other property shall be a bona fide estimate of the fair market value of such property.

(3) Where two or more companies are involved in the transaction, each shall pay a proportionate share of such fee, determined by the persons involved.

(4) Notwithstanding the above, the fee required by this paragraph (c) shall not be payable for a proxy statement filed by a company registered under the Investment Company Act of 1940.

(d) *Section 14(d)(1) Filings.* At the time of filing such statement as the Commission may require pursuant to section 14(d)(1) of the Act, a fee of one-fiftieth of one percent of the aggregate of the cash or of the value of the securities or other property offered by the bidder. Where the bidder is offering securities or other non-cash consideration for some or all of the securities to be acquired, whether or not in combination with a cash payment for the same securities, the value of the consideration to be offered for such securities shall be based upon the market value of the securities to be received by the bidder as established in accordance with paragraph (a)(4) of this rule.

Rule 0–12. Commission procedures for filing applications for orders for exemptive relief under Section 36 of the Exchange Act

(a) The application shall be in writing in the form of a letter, must include any supporting documents necessary to make the application complete, and otherwise must comply with Rule 0–3. All applications must be submitted to the Office of the Secretary of the Commission. Requestors may seek confidential treatment of their applications to the extent provided under 17 CFR 200.81. If an application is incomplete, the Commission, through the Division handling the application, may request that the application be withdrawn unless the applicant can justify, based on all the facts and circumstances, why supporting materials have not been submitted and undertakes to submit the omitted materials promptly.

(b) An applicant may submit a request electronically. The electronic mailbox to use for these applications is described on the Commission's website at www.sec.gov in the "Exchange Act Exemptive Applications" section. In the event the electronic mailbox is revised in the future, applicants can find the appropriate mailbox by accessing the "Electronic Mailboxes at the Commission" section.

(c) An applicant also may submit a request in paper format. Five copies of every paper application and every amendment to such an application must be submitted to the Office of the Secretary at 100 F Street, NE, Washington, DC 20549–1090. Applications must be on white paper no larger than 8$^{1/2}$ by 11 inches in size. The left margin of applications must be at least 1$^{1/2}$ inches wide, and if the application is bound, it must be bound on the left side. All typewritten or printed material must be on one side of the paper only and must be set forth in black ink so as to permit photocopying.

(d) Every application (electronic or paper) must contain the name, address and telephone number of each applicant and the name, address, and telephone number of a person to whom any questions regarding the application should be directed. The Commission will not consider hypothetical or anonymous requests for exemptive relief. Each applicant shall state the basis for the relief sought, and identify the anticipated benefits for investors and any conditions or limitations the applicant believes would be appropriate for the protection of investors. Applicants should also cite to and discuss applicable precedent.

(e) Amendments to the application should be prepared and submitted as set forth in these procedures and should be marked to show what changes have been made.

(f) After the filing is complete, the applicable Division will review the application. Once all questions and issues have been answered to the satisfaction of the Division, the staff will make an appropriate recommendation to the Commission. After consideration of the recommendation by the Commission, the Commission's Office of the Secretary will issue an appropriate response and will notify the applicant. If the application pertains to a rule of the Exchange Act pursuant to which the Commission has delegated its authority to the appropriate Division, the Division Director or his or her designee will issue an appropriate response and notify the applicant.

(g) The Commission, in its sole discretion, may choose to publish in the Federal Register a notice that the application has been submitted. The notice would provide that any person may, within the period specified therein, submit to the Commission any information that relates to the Commission action requested in the application. The notice also would indicate the earliest date on which the Commission would take final action on the application, but in no event would such action be taken earlier than 25 days following publication of the notice in the Federal Register.

(h) The Commission may, in its sole discretion, schedule a hearing on the matter addressed by the application.

Rule 0–13. Commission procedures for filing applications to request a substituted compliance order under the Exchange Act

(a) The application shall be in writing in the form of a letter, must include any supporting documents necessary to make the application complete, and otherwise must comply with Rule 0–3. All applications must be submitted to the Office of the Secretary of the Commission, by a party that potentially would comply with requirements under the Exchange Act pursuant to a substituted compliance order, or by the relevant foreign financial regulatory authority or authorities. If an application is incomplete, the Commission may request that the application be withdrawn unless the applicant can justify, based on all the facts and circumstances, why supporting materials have not been submitted and undertakes to submit the omitted materials promptly.

(b) An applicant may submit a request electronically. The electronic mailbox to use for these applications is described on the Commission's website at www.sec.gov in the "Exchange Act Substituted Compliance Applications" section. In the event electronic mailboxes are revised in the future, applicants can find the appropriate mailbox by accessing the "Electronic Mailboxes at the Commission" section.

(c) All filings and submissions filed pursuant to this rule must be in the English language. If a filing or submission filed pursuant to this rule requires the inclusion of a document that is in a foreign language, a party must submit instead a fair and accurate English translation of the entire foreign language document. A party may submit a copy of the unabridged foreign language document when including an English translation of a foreign language document in a filing or submission filed pursuant to this rule. A party must provide a copy of any foreign language document upon the request of the Commission staff.

(d) An applicant also may submit a request in paper format. Five copies of every paper application and every amendment to such an application must be submitted to the Office of the Secretary at 100 F Street, NE, Washington, DC 20549-1090. Applications must be on white paper no longer than 8½ by 11 inches in size. The left margin of applications must be at least 1½ inches wide, and if the application is bound, it must be bound on the left side. All typewritten or printed material must be set forth in black ink so as to permit photocopying.

(e) Every application (electronic or paper) must contain the name, address, telephone number, and email address of each applicant and the name, address, telephone number, and email address of a person to whom any questions regarding the application should be directed. The Commission will not consider hypothetical or anonymous requests for a substituted compliance order. Each applicant shall provide the Commission with any supporting documentation it believes necessary for the Commission to make such determination, including information regarding applicable requirements established by the foreign financial regulatory authority or authorities, as well as the methods used by the foreign financial regulatory authority or authorities to monitor and enforce compliance with such rules. Applicants should also cite to and discuss applicable precedent.

(f) Amendments to the application should be prepared and submitted as set forth in these procedures and should be marked to show what changes have been made.

(g) After the filing is complete, the staff will review the application. Once all questions and issues have been answered to the satisfaction of the staff, the staff will make an appropriate recommendation to the Commission. After consideration of the recommendation and a vote by the Commission, the Commission's Office of the Secretary will issue an appropriate response and will notify the applicant.

(h) The Commission shall publish in the *Federal Register* a notice that a complete application has been submitted. The notice will provide that any person may, within the period specified therein, submit to the Commission any information that relates to the Commission action requested in the application. The notice also will indicate the earliest date on which the Commission would take final action on the application, but in no event would such action be taken earlier than 25 days following publication of the notice in the *Federal Register*.

(i) The Commission may, in its sole discretion, schedule a hearing on the matter addressed by the application.

Rule 3a1–1. Exemption from the definition of "exchange" under Section 3(a)(1) of the Act

(a) An organization, association, or group of persons shall be exempt from the definition of the term "exchange" under section 3(a)(1) of the Act, (15 U.S.C. 78c(a)(1)), if such organization, association, or group of persons:

(1) Is operated by a national securities association;

(2) Is in compliance with Regulation ATS, 17 CFR 242.300 through 242.304; or

(3) Pursuant to paragraph (a) of Rule 301 of Regulation ATS is not required to comply with Regulation ATS, 17 CFR 242.300 through 242.304.

(b) Notwithstanding paragraph (a) of this rule, an organization, association, or group of persons shall not be exempt under this rule from the definition of "exchange," if:

(1) During three of the preceding four calendar quarters such organization, association, or group of persons had:

(i) Fifty percent or more of the average daily dollar trading volume in any security and five percent or more of the average daily dollar trading volume in any class of securities; or

(ii) Forty percent or more of the average daily dollar trading volume in any class of securities; and

(2) The Commission determines, after notice to the organization, association, or group of persons, and an opportunity for such organization, association, or group of persons to respond, that such an exemption would not be necessary or appropriate in the public interest or consistent with the protection of investors taking into account the requirements for exchange registration under section 6 of the Act, (15 U.S.C. 78f), and the objectives of the national market system under section 11A of the Act, (15 U.S.C 78k–1).

(3) For purposes of paragraph (b) of this rule, each of the following shall be considered a "class of securities":

(i) Equity securities, which shall have the same meaning as in Rule 3a11–1;

(ii) Listed options, which shall mean any options traded on a national securities exchange or automated facility of a national securities exchange;

(iii) Unlisted options, which shall mean any options other than those traded on a national securities exchange or automated facility of a national securities association;

(iv) Municipal securities, which shall have the same meaning as in section 3(a)(29) of the Act, (15 U.S.C. 78c(a)(29));

(v) Corporate debt securities, which shall mean any securities that:

(A) Evidence a liability of the issuer of such securities;

(B) Have a fixed maturity date that is at least one year following the date of issuance; and

(C) Are not exempted securities, as defined in section 3(a)(12) of the Act, (15 U.S.C. 78c(a)(12));

(vi) Foreign corporate debt securities, which shall mean any securities that:

(A) Evidence a liability of the issuer of such debt securities;

(B) Are issued by a corporation or other organization incorporated or organized under the laws of any foreign country; and

(C) Have a fixed maturity date that is at least one year following the date of issuance; and

(vii) Foreign sovereign debt securities, which shall mean any securities that:

(A) Evidence a liability of the issuer of such debt securities;

(B) Are issued or guaranteed by the government of a foreign country, any political subdivision of a foreign country or any supranational entity; and

(C) Do not have a maturity date of a year or less following the date of issuance.

Rule 3a4–1. Associated persons of an issuer deemed not to be brokers

(a) An associated person of an issuer of securities shall not be deemed to be a broker solely by reason of his participation in the sale of the securities of such issuer if the associated person:

(1) Is not subject to a statutory disqualification, as that term is defined in Section 3(a)(39) of the Act, at the time of his participation; and

(2) Is not compensated in connection with his participation by the payment of commissions or other remuneration based either directly or indirectly on transactions in securities; and

(3) Is not at the time of his participation an associated person of a broker or dealer; and

(4) Meets the conditions of any one of paragraphs (a)(4)(i), (ii), or (iii) of this rule.

(i) The association person restricts his participation to transactions involving offers and sales of securities:

(A) To a registered broker or dealer; a registered investment company (or registered separate account); an insurance company; a bank; a savings and loan association; a trust company or similar institution supervised by a state or federal banking authority; or a trust for which a bank, a savings and loan association, a trust company, or a registered investment adviser either is the trustee or is authorized in writing to make investment decisions; or

(B) That are exempted by reason of section 3(a)(7), 3(a)(9) or 3(a)(10) of the Securities Act of 1933 from the registration provisions of that Act; or

(C) That are made pursuant to a plan or agreement submitted for the vote or consent of the security holders who will receive securities of the issuer in connection with a reclassification of securities of the issuer, a merger or consolidation or a similar plan of acquisition involving an exchange of securities, or a transfer of assets of any other person to the issuer in exchange for securities of the issuer; or

(D) That are made pursuant to a bonus, profit-sharing, pension, retirement, thrift, savings, incentive, stock purchase, stock ownership, stock appreciation, stock option, dividend reinvestment or similar plan for employees of an issuer or a subsidiary of the issuer;

(ii) The associated person meets all of the following conditions:

(A) The associated person primarily performs, or is intended primarily to perform at the end of the offering, substantial duties for or on behalf of the issuer otherwise than in connection with transactions in securities; and

(B) The associated person was not a broker or dealer, or an associated person of a broker or dealer, within the preceding 12 months; and

(C) The associated person does not participate in selling an offering of securities for any issuer more than once every 12 months other than in reliance on paragraphs (a)(4)(i) or (a)(4)(iii) of this rule, except that for securities issued pursuant to Rule 415 under the Securities Act of 1933, the 12 months shall begin with the last sale of any security included within one Rule 415 registration.

(iii) The associated person restricts his participation to any one or more of the following activities;

(A) Preparing any written communication or delivering such communication through the mails or other means that does not involve oral solicitation by the associated person of a potential purchaser; *Provided, however,* that the content of such communication is approved by a partner, officer or director of the issuer;

(B) Responding to inquiries of a potential purchaser in a communication initiated by the potential purchaser; *Provided, however,* that the content of such responses are limited to information contained in a registration statement filed under the Securities Act of 1933 or other offering document; or

(C) Performing ministerial and clerical work involved in effecting any transaction.

(b) No presumption shall arise that an associated person of an issuer has violated section 15(a) of the Act solely by reason of his participation in the sale of securities of the issuer if he does not meet the conditions specified in paragraph (a) of this rule.

(c) *Definitions.* When used in this rule:

(1) The term *associated person of an issuer* means any natural person who is a partner, officer, director, or employee of:

(i) The issuer;

(ii) A corporate general partner of a limited partnership that is the issuer;

(iii) A company or partnership that controls, is controlled by, or is under common control with, the issuer; or

(iv) An investment adviser registered under the Investment Advisers Act of 1940 to an investment company registered under the Investment Company Act of 1940 which is the issuer.

(2) The term *associated person of a broker or dealer* means any partner, officer, director, or branch manager of such broker or dealer (or any person occupying a similar status or performing similar functions), any person directly or indirectly controlling, controlled by, or under common control with such broker or dealer, or any employee of such broker or dealer, except that any person associated with a broker or dealer whose functions are solely clerical or ministerial and any person who is required under the laws of any state to register as a broker or dealer in that state solely because such person is an issuer of securities or associated person of an issuer of securities shall not be included in the meaning of such term for purposes of this rule.

Rule 3a4–2. [Reserved]

Rule 3a4–3. [Reserved]

Rule 3a4–4. [Reserved]

Rule 3a4–5. [Reserved]

Rule 3a4–6. [Reserved]

Rule 3a5–1. Exemption from the definition of "dealer" for a bank engaged in riskless principal transactions

(a) A bank is exempt from the definition of the term "dealer" to the extent that it engages in or effects riskless principal transactions if the number of such riskless principal transactions during a calendar year combined with transactions in which the bank is acting as an agent for a customer pursuant to section 3(a)(4)(B)(xi) of the Act (15 U.S.C. 78c(a)(4)(B)(xi)) during that same year does not exceed 500.

(b) For purposes of this rule, the term riskless principal transaction means a transaction in which, after having received an order to buy from a customer, the bank purchased the security from another person to offset a contemporaneous sale to such customer or, after having received an order to sell from a customer, the bank sold the security to another person to offset a contemporaneous purchase from such customer.

Rule 3a5–2. Exemption from the definition of "dealer" for banks effecting transactions in securities issued pursuant to Regulation S

(a) A bank is exempt from the definition of the term "dealer" under section 3(a)(5) of the Act (15 U.S.C. 78c(a)(5)), to the extent that, in a riskless principal transaction, the bank:

(1) Purchases an eligible security from an issuer or a broker-dealer and sells that security in compliance with the requirements of 17 CFR 230.903 to a purchaser who is not in the United States;

(2) Purchases from a person who is not a U.S. person under Rule 902(k) under the Securities Act of 1933 an eligible security after its initial sale with a reasonable belief that the eligible security was initially sold outside of the United States within the meaning of and in compliance with the requirements of Rule 903 under the Securities Act of 1933, and resells that security to a purchaser who is not in the United States or to a registered broker or dealer, provided that if the resale is made prior to the expiration of any applicable distribution compliance period specified in Rule 903(b)(2) or (b)(3) under the Securities Act of 1933, the resale is made in compliance with the requirements of Rule 904 under the Securities Act of 1933; or

(3) Purchases from a registered broker or dealer an eligible security after its initial sale with a reasonable belief that the eligible security was initially sold outside of the United States within the meaning of and in compliance with the requirements of Rule 903 under the Securities Act of 1933, and resells that security to a purchaser who is not in the United States, provided that if the resale is made prior to the expiration of any applicable distribution compliance period specified in Rule 903(b)(2) or (b)(3) under the Securities Act of 1933, the resale is made in compliance with the requirements of Rule 904 under the Securities Act of 1933.

(b) Definitions. For purposes of this rule:

(1) *Distributor* has the same meaning as in Rule 902(d) under the Securities Act of 1933.

(2) *Eligible security* means a security that:

(i) Is not being sold from the inventory of the bank or an affiliate of the bank; and

(ii) Is not being underwritten by the bank or an affiliate of the bank on a firm–commitment basis, unless the bank acquired the security from an unaffiliated distributor that did not purchase the security from the bank or an affiliate of the bank.

(3) *Purchaser* means a person who purchases an eligible security and who is not a U.S. person under Rule 902(k) under the Securities Act of 1933.

(4) *Riskless principal transaction* means a transaction in which, after having received an order to buy from a customer, the bank purchased the security from another person to offset a contemporaneous sale to such customer or, after having received an order to sell from a customer, the bank sold the security to another person to offset a contemporaneous purchase from such customer.

Rule 3a5–3. Exemption from the definition of "dealer" for banks engaging in securities lending transactions

(a) A bank is exempt from the definition of the term "dealer" under section 3(a)(5) of the Act (15 U.S.C. 78c(a)(5)), to the extent that, as a conduit lender, it engages in or effects securities lending transactions, and any securities lending services in connection with such transactions, with or on behalf of a person the bank reasonably believes to be:

(1) A qualified investor as defined in section 3(a)(54)(A) of the Act (15 U.S.C. 78c(a)(54)(A)); or

(2) Any employee benefit plan that owns and invests, on a discretionary basis, not less than $25,000,000 in investments.

(b) *Securities lending transaction* means a transaction in which the owner of a security lends the security temporarily to another party pursuant to a written securities lending agreement under which the lender retains the economic interests of an owner of such securities, and has the right to terminate the transaction and to recall the loaned securities on terms agreed by the parties.

(c) *Securities lending services* means:

(1) Selecting and negotiating with a borrower and executing, or directing the execution of the loan with the borrower;

(2) Receiving, delivering, or directing the receipt or delivery of loaned securities;

(3) Receiving, delivering, or directing the receipt or delivery of collateral;

(4) Providing mark-to-market, corporate action, recordkeeping or other services incidental to the administration of the securities lending transaction;

(5) Investing, or directing the investment of, cash collateral; or

(6) Indemnifying the lender of securities with respect to various matters.

(d) For the purposes of this rule, the term *conduit lender* means a bank that borrows or loans securities, as principal, for its own account, and contemporaneously loans or borrows the same securities, as principal, for its own account. A bank that qualifies under this definition as a conduit lender at the commencement of a transaction will continue to qualify, notwithstanding whether:

(1) The lending or borrowing transaction terminates and so long as the transaction is replaced within one business day by another lending or borrowing transaction involving the same securities; and

(2) Any substitutions of collateral occur.

DEFINITION OF "EQUITY SECURITY" AS USED IN SECTIONS 12(g) AND 16

Rule 3a11–1. Definition of the term "equity security"

The term *equity security* is hereby defined to include any stock or similar security, certificate of interest or participation in any profit sharing agreement, preorganization certificate or subscription, transferable share, voting trust certificate or certificate of deposit for an equity security, limited partnership interest, interest in a joint venture, or certificate of interest in a business trust; any security future on such security; or any security convertible, with or without consideration into such a security, or carrying any warrant or right to subscribe to or purchase such a security; or any such warrant or right; or any put, call, straddle, or other option or privilege of buying such a security from or selling such a security to another without being bound to do so.

MISCELLANEOUS EXEMPTIONS

Rule 3a12–1. Exemption of certain mortgages and interests in mortgages

Mortgages, as defined in section 302(d) of the Emergency Home Finance Act of 1970, which are or have been sold by the Federal Home Loan Mortgage Corporation are hereby exempted from the operation of such provisions of the Act as by their terms do not apply to an "exempted security" or to "exempted securities".

Rule 3a12–2. [Reserved]

Rule 3a12–3. Exemption from Sections 14(a), 14(b), 14(c), 14(f) and 16 for securities of certain foreign issuers

(a) Securities for which the filing of registration statements on Form 18 (17 CFR 249.218) are authorized shall be exempt from the operation of sections 14 and 16 of the Act.

(b) Securities registered by a foreign private issuer, as defined in Rule 3b–4, shall be exempt from sections 14(a), 14(b), 14(c), 14(f) and 16 of the Act.

Rule 3a12–4. Exemptions from Sections 15(a) and 15(c)(3) for certain mortgage securities

(a) When used in this rule the following terms shall have the meanings indicated:

(1) The term *whole loan mortgage* means an evidence of indebtedness secured by mortgage, deed of trust, or other lien upon real estate or upon leasehold interests therein where the entire mortgage, deed or other lien is transferred with the entire evidence of indebtedness.

(2) The term *aggregated whole loan mortgage* means two or more whole loan mortgages that are grouped together and sold to one person in one transaction.

(3) The term *participation interest* means an undivided interest representing one of only two such interests in a whole loan mortgage or in an aggregated whole loan mortgage, provided that the other interest is retained by the originator of such participation interest.

(4) The term *commitment* means a contract to purchase a whole loan mortgage, an aggregated whole loan mortgage or a participation interest which by its terms requires that the contract be fully executed within 2 years.

(5) The term *mortgage security* means a whole loan mortgage, an aggregated whole loan mortgage, a participation interest, or a commitment.

(b) A mortgage security shall be deemed an "exempted security" for purposes of subsections (a) and (c)(3) of section 15 of the Act provided that, in the case of and at the time of any sale of the mortgage security by a broker or dealer, such mortgage security is not in default and has an unpaid principal amount of at least $50,000.

Rule 3a12–5. Exemption of certain investment contract securities from Sections 7 and 11(d)(1)

(a) An investment contract security involving the direct ownership of specified residential real property shall be exempted from the provisions of section 7(c) and 11(d)(1) of the Act with respect to any transaction by a broker or dealer who, directly or indirectly, arranges for the extension or maintenance of credit on the security to or from a customer, if the credit:

(1) Is secured by a lien, mortgage, deed of trust, or any other similar security interest related only to real property; *Provided, however*, That this provision shall not prevent a lender from requiring (i) a security interest in the common areas and recreational facilities or furniture and fixtures incidental to the investment contract if the purchase of such furniture and fixtures is required by, or subject to the approval of, the issuer, as a condition of purchase; or (ii) an assignment of future rentals in the event of default by the purchaser or a co-signer or guarantor on the debt obligation other than the issuer, its affiliates, or any broker or dealer offering such securities;

(2) Is to be repaid by periodic payments of principal and interest pursuant to an amortization schedule established by the governing instruments; *Provided, however*, That this provision shall not prevent the extension of credit on terms which require the payment of interest only, if extended in compliance with the other provisions of this rule; and

(3) Is extended by a lender which is not, directly or indirectly controlling, controlled by, or under common control with the broker or dealer or the issuer of the securities or affiliates thereof.

(b) For purposes of this rule:

(1) *residential real property* shall mean real property containing living accommodations, whether used on a permanent or transient basis, and may include furniture or fixtures if required as a condition of purchase of the investment contract or if subject to the approval of the issuer.

(2) *direct ownership* shall mean ownership of a fee or leasehold estate or a beneficial interest in a trust the purchase of which, under applicable local law, is financed and secured by a security interest therein similar to a mortgage or deed of trust, but it shall not include an interest in a real estate investment trust, an interest in a general or limited partnership, or similar indirect interest in the ownership of real property.

Rule 3a12–6. Definition of "common trust fund" as used in Section 3(a)(12) of the Act

The term *common trust fund* as used in section 3(a)(12) of the Act (15 U.S.C. 78c(a)(12)) shall include a common trust fund which is maintained by a bank which is a member of an affiliated group, as defined in section 1504(a) of the Internal Revenue Code of 1954 (26 U.S.C. 1504(a)), and which is maintained exclusively for the collective investment and reinvestment of monies contributed thereto by one or more bank members of such affiliated group in the capacity of trustee, executor, administrator, or guardian, *Provided That*:

(a) The common trust fund is operated in compliance with the same state and federal regulatory requirements as would apply if the bank maintaining such fund and any other contributing banks were the same entity; and

(b) The rights of persons for whose benefit a contributing bank acts as trustee, executor, administrator, or guardian would not be diminished by reason of the maintenance of such common trust fund by another bank member of the affiliated group.

Rule 3a12–7. Exemption for certain derivative securities traded otherwise than on a national securities exchange

Any put, call, straddle, option, or privilege traded exclusively otherwise than on a national securities exchange and for which quotations are not disseminated through an automated quotation system of a registered securities association, which relates to any securities which are direct obligations of, or obligations guaranteed as to principal or interest by, the United States, or securities issued or guaranteed by a corporation in which the United States has a direct or indirect interest as shall be designated for exemption by the Secretary of the Treasury pursuant to section 3(a)(12) of the Act, shall be exempt from all provisions of the Act which by their terms do not apply to any "exempted security" or "exempted securities," provided that the securities underlying such put, call, straddle, option or privilege represent an obligation equal to or exceeding $250,000 principal amount.

Rule 3a12–8. Exemption for designated foreign government securities for purposes of futures trading

(a) When used in this rule, the following terms shall have the meaning indicated:

(1) The term *designated foreign government security* shall mean a security not registered under the Securities Act of 1933 nor the subject of any American depositary receipt so registered, and representing a debt obligation of the government of

(i) The United Kingdom of Great Britain and Northern Ireland;

(ii) Canada;

(iii) Japan;

(iv) The Commonwealth of Australia;

(v) The Republic of France;

(vi) New Zealand;

(vii) The Republic of Austria;

(viii) The Kingdom of Denmark;

(ix) The Republic of Finland;

(x) The Kingdom of the Netherlands;

(xi) Switzerland;

(xii) The Federal Republic of Germany;

(xiii) The Republic of Ireland;

(xiv) The Republic of Italy;

(xv) The Kingdom of Spain;

(xvi) The United Mexican States;

(xvii) The Federative Republic of Brazil;

(xviii) The Republic of Argentina;

(xix) The Republic of Venezuela;

(xx) The Kingdom of Belgium; or

(xxi) The Kingdom of Sweden.

(2) The term *qualifying foreign futures contracts* shall mean any contracts for the purchase or sale of a designated foreign government security for future delivery, as *future delivery* is defined in 7 U.S.C. 2, provided such contracts require delivery outside the United States, any of its possessions or territories, and are traded on or through a board of trade, as defined at 7 U.S.C. 2.

(b) Any designated foreign government security shall, for purposes only of the offer, sale or confirmation of sale of qualifying foreign futures contracts, be exempted from all provisions of the Act which by their terms do not apply to an "exempted security" or "exempted securities."

Rule 3a12–9. Exemption of certain direct participation program securities from the arranging provisions of Sections 7(c) and 11(d)(1)

(a) Direct participation program securities sold on a basis whereby the purchase price is paid to the issuer in one or more mandatory deferred payments shall be deemed to be exempted securities for purposes of the arranging provisions of Sections 7(c) and 11(d)(1) of the Act, provided that:

(1) The securities are registered under the Securities Act of 1933 or are sold or offered exclusively on an intrastate basis in reliance upon Section 3(a)(11) of that Act;

(2) The mandatory deferred payments bear a reasonable relationship to the capital needs and program objectives described in a business development plan disclosed to investors in a registration statement filed with the Commission under the Securities Act of 1933 or, where no registration statement is required to be filed with the Commission, as part of a statement filed with the relevant state securities administrator;

(3) Not less than 50 percent of the purchase price of the direct participation program security is paid by the investor at the time of sale;

(4) The total purchase price of the direct participation program security is due within three years in specified property programs or two years in non-specified property programs. Such pay-in periods are to be measured from the earlier of the completion of the offering or one year following the effective date of the offering.

(b) For purposes of this rule:

(1) *Direct participation program* shall mean a program financed through the sale of securities, other than securities that are listed on an exchange, quoted on NASDAQ, or will otherwise be actively traded during the pay-in period as a result of efforts by the issuer, underwriter, or other participants in the initial distribution of such securities, that provides for flow-through tax consequences to its investors; *Provided, however,* that the term "direct participation program" does not include real estate investment trusts, Subchapter S corporate offerings, tax qualified pension and profit sharing plans under Sections 401 and 403(a) of the Internal Revenue Code ("Code"), tax shelter annuities under Section 403(b) of the Code, individual retirement plans under Section 408 of the Code, and any issuer, including a separate account, that is registered under the Investment Company Act of 1940.

(2) *Business development plan* shall mean a specific plan describing the program's anticipated economic development and the amounts of future capital contributions, in the form of mandatory deferred payments, to be required at specified times or upon the occurrence of certain events.

(3) *Specified property program* shall mean a direct participation program in which, at the date of effectiveness, more than 75 percent of the net proceeds from the sale of program securities are committed to specific purchases or expenditures. *Non-specified property program* shall mean any other direct participation program.

Rule 3a12–10. Exemption of certain securities issued by the Resolution Funding Corporation

Securities that are issued by the Resolution Funding Corporation pursuant to section 21B(f) of the Federal Home Loan Bank Act (12 U.S.C. 1421 *et seq.*) are exempt from the operation of all provisions of the Act that by their terms do not apply to any "exempted security" or to "exempted securities."

Rule 3a12–11. Exemption from Sections 8(a), 14(a), 14(b), and 14(c) for debt securities listed on a national securities exchange

(a) Debt securities that are listed for trading on a national securities exchange shall be exempt from the restrictions on borrowing of Section 8(a) of the Act (15 U.S.C. 78h(a)).

(b) Debt securities registered pursuant to the provisions of Section 12(b) of the Act (15 U.S.C. 78*l* (b)) shall be exempt from Sections 14(a), 14(b), and 14(c) of the Act (15 U.S.C. 78n(a), (b), and (c)), *except that* Rules 14a–1, 14a–2(a), 14a–9, 14a–13, 14b–1, 14b–2, 14c–1, 14c–6 and 14c–7 shall continue to apply.

(c) For purposes of this rule, debt securities is defined to mean any securities that are not "equity securities" as defined in Section 3(a)(11) of the Act (15 U.S.C. 78c(a)(11)) and Rule 3a11–1 thereunder.

Rule 3a12–12. Exemption from certain provisions of Section 16 of the Act for asset-backed securities

Asset-backed securities, as defined in Item 1101 of Regulation AB, are exempt from section 16 of the Act (15 U.S.C. 78p).

Rule 3a40–1. Designation of financial responsibility rules

The term *financial responsibility rules* for purposes of the Securities Investor Protection Act of 1970 shall include:

(a) Any rule adopted by the Commission pursuant to sections 8, 15(c)(3), 17(a) or 17(e)(1)(A) of the Securities Exchange Act of 1934;

(b) Any rule adopted by the Commission relating to hypothecation or lending of customer securities;

(c) Any rule adopted by any self-regulatory organization relating to capital, margin, recordkeeping, hypothecation or lending requirements; and

(d) Any other rule adopted by the Commission or any self-regulatory organization relating to the protection of funds or securities.

Rule 3a43-1. Customer-related government securities activities incidental to futures-related business of a futures commission merchant registered with the Commodity Futures Trading Commission

(a) A futures commission merchant registered with the Commodity Futures Trading Commission ("CFTC") is not a government securities broker or government securities dealer solely because such futures commission merchant effects transactions in government securities that are defined in paragraph (b) of this rule as incidental to such person's futures-related business.

(b) Provided that the futures commission merchant maintains in a regulated account all funds and securities associated with such government securities transactions (except funds and securities associated with transactions under paragraph (b)(1)(i) of this rule) and does not advertise that it is in the business of effecting transactions in government securities otherwise than in connection with futures or options on futures trading or the investment of margin or excess funds related to such trading or the trading of any other instrument subject to CFTC jurisdiction, the following transactions in government securities are incidental to the futures-related business of such a futures commission merchant:

(1) Transactions as agent for a customer—

(i) To effect delivery pursuant to a futures contract; or

(ii) For risk reduction or arbitrage of existing or contemporaneously created positions in futures or options on futures;

(2) Transactions as agent for a customer for investment of margin and excess funds related to futures or options on futures trading or the trading of other instruments subject to CFTC jurisdiction, provided further that,

(i) Such transactions involve Treasury securities with a maturity of less than 93 days at the time of the transaction.

(ii) Such transactions generate no monetary profit for the futures commission merchant in excess of the costs of executing such transactions, or

(iii) Such transactions are unsolicited, and commissions and other income generated on transactions pursuant to this paragraph (b)(2)(iii) (including transactional fees paid by the futures commission merchant and charged to its customer) do not exceed 2% of such futures commission merchant's total commission revenues;

(3) Exchange of futures for physical transactions as agent for or as principal with a customer; and

(4) Any transaction or transactions that the Commission exempts, either unconditionally or on specified terms and conditions, as incidental to the futures-related business of a specified futures commission merchant, a specified category of futures commission merchants, or futures commission merchants generally.

(c) *Definitions.* (1) *Customer* means any person for whom the futures commission merchant effects or intends to effect transactions in futures, options on futures, or any other instruments subject to CFTC jurisdiction.

(2) *Regulated account* means a customer segregation account subject to the regulations of the CFTC; provided, however, that, where such regulations do not permit to be maintained in such an account or require to be maintained in a separate regulated account funds or securities in proprietary accounts or funds or securities used as margin for or excess funds related to futures contracts, options on futures or any other instruments subject to CFTC jurisdiction that trade outside the United States, its territories, or possessions, the term *regulated account* means such separate regulated account or any other account subject to record-keeping regulations of the CFTC.

(3) *Unsolicited transaction* means a transaction that is not effected in a discretionary account or recommended to a customer by the futures commission merchant, an associated person of a futures commission merchant, a business affiliate that is controlled by, controlling, or under common control with the futures commission merchant, or an introducing broker that is guaranteed by the futures commission merchant.

(4) *Futures* and *futures contracts* mean contracts of sale of a commodity for future delivery traded on or subject to the rules of a contract market designated by the CFTC or traded on or subject to the rules of any board of trade located outside the United States, its territories, or possessions.

(5) *Options on futures* means puts or calls on a futures contract traded on or subject to the rules of a contract market designated by the CFTC or traded or subject to the rules of any board of trade

located outside the United States, its territories, or possessions.

Rule 3a44-1. Proprietary government securities transactions incidental to the futures-related business of a CFTC-regulated person

(a) A person registered with the Commodity Futures Trading Commission ("CFTC"), a contract market designated by the CFTC, such a contract market's affiliated clearing organization, or any floor trader or such a contract market (hereinafter referred to collectively as a "CFTC-regulated person") is not a government securities dealer solely because such person effects transactions for its own account in government securities that are defined in paragraph (b) of this rule as incidental to such person's futures-related business.

(b) Provided that a CFTC-regulated person does not advertise or otherwise hold itself out as a government securities dealer except as permitted under Rule 3a43-1 the following transactions in government securities for its own account are incidental to the futures-related business of such a CFTC-regulated person:

(1) Transactions to effect delivery of a government security pursuant to a futures contract;

(2) Exchange of futures for physical transactions with (i) a government securities broker or government securities dealer that has registered with the Commission or filed notice pursuant to section 15C(a) of the Act or (ii) a CFTC-regulated person;

(3) Transactions (including repurchase agreements and reverse repurchase agreements) involving segregated customer funds and securities or funds and securities held by a clearing organization with (i) a government securities broker or government securities dealer that has registered with the Commission or filed notice pursuant to section 15C(a) of the Act or (ii) a bank;

(4) Transactions for risk reduction or arbitrage of existing or contemporaneously created positions in futures or options on futures with (i) a government securities broker or government securities dealer that has registered with the Commission or filed notice pursuant to section 15C(a) of the Act or (ii) a CFTC-regulated person;

(5) Repurchase and reverse repurchase agreement transactions between a futures commission merchant acting in a proprietary capacity and another CFTC-regulated person acting in a proprietary capacity and contemporaneous offsetting transactions between such a futures commission merchant and (i) a government securities broker or government securities dealer that has registered with the Commission or filed notice pursuant to section 15C(a) of the Act, (ii) a bank, or (iii) a CFTC-regulated person acting in a proprietary capacity; and

(6) Any transaction or transactions that the Commission exempts, either unconditionally or on specified terms and conditions, as incidental to the futures related business of a specified CFTC-regulated person, a specified category of CFTC-regulated persons, or CFTC-regulated persons generally.

(c) *Definitions.* (1) *Segregated customer funds* means funds subject to CFTC segregation requirements.

(2) *Futures* and *futures contracts* mean contracts of sale of a commodity for future delivery traded on or subject to the rules of a contract market designated by the CFTC or traded on or subject to the rules of any board of trade located outside the United States, its territories, or possessions.

(3) *Options on futures* means puts or calls on a futures contract traded on or subject to the rules of a contract market designated by the CFTC or traded on or subject to the rules of any board of trade located outside the United States, its territories, or possessions.

Rule 3a51-1. Definition of penny stock

For purposes of section 3(a)(51) of the Act, the term "penny stock" shall mean any equity security other than a security:

(a) That is an NMS stock, as defined in Rule 600(b)(47) of Regulation NMS, provided that:

(1) The security is registered, or approved for registration upon notice of issuance, on a national securities exchange that has been continuously registered as a national securities exchange since April 20, 1992 (the date of the adoption of Rule 3a51-1 by the Commission); and the national securities exchange has maintained quantitative listing standards that are substantially similar to or stricter than those listing standards that were in place on that exchange on January 8, 2004; or

(2) The security is registered, or approved for registration upon notice of issuance, on a national securities exchange, or is listed, or approved for listing upon notice of issuance on, an automated

quotation system sponsored by a registered national securities association, that:

(i) Has established initial listing standards that meet or exceed the following criteria:

(A) The issuer shall have:

(*1*) Stockholders' equity of $5,000,000;

(*2*) Market value of listed securities of $50 million for 90 consecutive days prior to applying for the listing (market value means the closing bid price multiplied by the number of securities listed); or

(*3*) Net income of $750,000 (excluding non-recurring items) in the most recently completed fiscal year or in two of the last three most recently completed fiscal years;

(B) The issuer shall have an operating history of at least one year or a market value of listed securities of $50 million (market value means the closing bid price multiplied by the number of securities listed);

(C) The issuer's stock, common or preferred, shall have a minimum bid price of $4 per share;

(D) In the case of common stock, there shall be at least 300 round lot holders of the security (a round lot holder means a holder of a normal unit of trading);

(E) In the case of common stock, there shall be at least 1,000,000 publicly held shares and such shares shall have a market value of at least $5 million (market value means the closing bid price multiplied by number of publicly held shares, and shares held directly or indirectly by an officer or director of the issuer and by any person who is the beneficial owner of more than 10 percent of the total shares outstanding are not considered to be publicly held);

(F) In the case of a convertible debt security, there shall be a principal amount outstanding of at least $10 million;

(G) In the case of rights and warrants, there shall be at least 100,000 issued and the underlying security shall be registered on a national securities exchange or listed on an automated quotation system sponsored by a registered national securities association and shall satisfy the requirements of paragraph (a) or (e) of this rule;

(H) In the case of put warrants (that is, instruments that grant the holder the right to sell to the issuing company a specified number of shares of the company's common stock, at a specified price until a specified period of time), there shall be at least 100,000 issued and the underlying security shall be registered on a national securities exchange or listed on an automated quotation system sponsored by a registered national securities association and shall satisfy the requirements of paragraph (a) or (e) of this rule;

(I) In the case of units (that is, two or more securities traded together), all component parts shall be registered on a national securities exchange or listed on an automated quotation system sponsored by a registered national securities association and shall satisfy the requirements of paragraph (a) or (e) of this rule; and

(J) In the case of equity securities (other than common and preferred stock, convertible debt securities, rights and warrants, put warrants, or units), including hybrid products and derivative securities products, the national securities exchange or registered national securities association shall establish quantitative listing standards that are substantially similar to those found in paragraphs (a)(2)(i)(A) through (a)(2)(i)(I) of this rule; and

(ii) Has established quantitative continued listing standards that are reasonably related to the initial listing standards set forth in paragraph (a)(2)(i) of this rule, and that are consistent with the maintenance of fair and orderly markets;

(b) That is issued by an investment company registered under the Investment Company Act of 1940;

(c) That is a put or call option issued by the Options Clearing Corporation;

(d) Except for purposes of section 7(b) of the Securities Act and Rule 419 under the Securities Act of 1933, that has a price of five dollars or more;

(1) For purposes of paragraph (d) of this rule:

(i) A security has a price of five dollars or more for a particular transaction if the security is purchased or sold in that transaction at a price of five dollars or more, excluding any broker or dealer commission, commission equivalent, mark-up, or mark-down; and

(ii) Other than in connection with a particular transaction, a security has a price of five dollars or more at a given time if the inside bid quotation is five dollars or more; *Provided, however*, that if there is no such inside bid quotation, a security has a price of five dollars or more at a given time if the average of three or more interdealer bid quotations at specified prices displayed at that time in an interdealer quotation system, as defined in Rule 15c2–7(c)(1), by three or more market makers in the security, is five dollars or more.

(iii) The term "inside bid quotation" shall mean the highest bid quotation for the security displayed by a market maker in the security on an automated interdealer quotation system that has the characteristics set forth in section 17B(b)(2) of the Act, or such other automated interdealer quotation system designated by the Commission for purposes of this rule, at any time in which at least two market makers are contemporaneously displaying on such system bid and offer quotations for the security at specified prices.

(2) If a security is a unit composed of one or more securities, the unit price divided by the number of shares of the unit that are not warrants, options, rights, or similar securities must be five dollars or more, as determined in accordance with paragraph (d)(1) of this rule, and any share of the unit that is a warrant, option, right, or similar security, or a convertible security, must have an exercise price or conversion price of five dollars or more;

(e)(1) That is registered, or approved for registration upon notice of issuance, on a national securities exchange that makes transaction reports available pursuant to Rule 601 of Regulation NMS, provided that:

(i) Price and volume information with respect to transactions in that security is required to be reported on a current and continuing basis and is made available to vendors of market information pursuant to the rules of the national securities exchange;

(ii) The security is purchased or sold in a transaction that is effected on or through the facilities of the national securities exchange, or that is part of the distribution of the security; and

(iii) The security satisfies the requirements of paragraph (a)(1) or (a)(2) of this rule;

(2) A security that satisfies the requirements of this paragraph (e), but does not otherwise satisfy the requirements of paragraph (a), (b), (c), (d), (f), or (g) of this rule, shall be a penny stock for purposes of section 15(b)(6) of the Act (15 U.S.C. 78o(b)(6));

(f) That is a security futures product listed on a national securities exchange or an automated quotation system sponsored by a registered national securities association; or

(g) Whose issuer has:

(1) Net tangible assets (*i.e.*, total assets less intangible assets and liabilities) in excess of \$2,000,000, if the issuer has been in continuous operation for at least three years, or \$5,000,000, if the issuer has been in continuous operation for less than three years; or

(2) Average revenue of at least \$6,000,000 for the last three years.

(3) For purposes of paragraph (g) of this rule, net tangible assets or average revenues must be demonstrated by financial statements dated less than fifteen months prior to the date of the transaction that the broker or dealer has reviewed and has a reasonable basis for believing are accurate in relation to the date of the transaction, and:

(i) If the issuer is other than a foreign private issuer, are the most recent financial statements for the issuer that have been audited and reported on by an independent public accountant in accordance with the provisions of Rule 2–02 of Regulation S–X; or

(ii) If the issuer is a foreign private issuer, are the most recent financial statements for the issuer that have been filed with the Commission or furnished to the Commission pursuant to Rule 12g3–2(b); *Provided, However*, that if financial statements for the issuer dated less than fifteen months prior to the date of the transaction have not been filed with or furnished to the Commission, financial statements dated within fifteen months prior to the transaction shall be prepared in accordance with generally accepted accounting principles in the country of incorporation, audited in compliance with the requirements of that jurisdiction, and reported on by an accountant duly registered and in good standing in accordance with the regulations of that jurisdiction.

(4) The broker or dealer shall preserve, as part of its records, copies of the financial statements

required by paragraph (g)(3) of this rule for the period specified in Rule 17a-4(b).

Rule 3a55-1. Method for determining market capitalization and dollar value of average daily trading volume; application of the definition of narrow-based security index

(a) *Market Capitalization.* For purposes of section 3(a)(55)(C)(i)(III)(bb) of the Act (15 U.S.C. 78c(a)(55)(C)(i)(III)(bb)):

(1) On a particular day, a security shall be 1 of 750 securities with the largest market capitalization as of the preceding 6 full calendar months when it is included on a list of such securities designated by the Commission and the CFTC as applicable for that day.

(2) In the event that the Commission and the CFTC have not designated a list under paragraph (a)(1) of this rule:

(i) The method to be used to determine market capitalization of a security as of the preceding 6 full calendar months is to sum the values of the market capitalization of such security for each U.S. trading day of the preceding 6 full calendar months, and to divide this sum by the total number of such trading days.

(ii) The 750 securities with the largest market capitalization shall be identified from the universe of all NMS securities as defined in Rule 600 of Regulation NMS that are common stock or depositary shares.

(b) *Dollar Value of ADTV.* (1) For purposes of section 3(a)(55)(B) of the Act (15 U.S.C. 78c(a)(55)(B)):

(i)(A) The method to be used to determine the dollar value of ADTV of a security is to sum the dollar value of ADTV of all reported transactions in such security in each jurisdiction as calculated pursuant to paragraphs (b)(1)(ii) and (iii).

(B) The dollar value of ADTV of a security shall include the value of all reported transactions for such security and for any depositary share that represents such security.

(C) The dollar value of ADTV of a depositary share shall include the value of all reported transactions for such depositary share and for the security that is represented by such depositary share.

(ii) For trading in a security in the United States, the method to be used to determine the dollar value of ADTV as of the preceding 6 full calendar months is to sum the value of all reported transactions in such security for each U.S. trading day during the preceding 6 full calendar months, and to divide this sum by the total number of such trading days.

(iii)(A) For trading in a security in a jurisdiction other than the United States, the method to be used to determine the dollar value of ADTV as of the preceding 6 full calendar months is to sum the value in U.S. dollars of all reported transactions in such security in such jurisdiction for each trading day during the preceding 6 full calendar months, and to divide this sum by the total number of trading days in such jurisdiction during the preceding 6 full calendar months.

(B) If the value of reported transactions used in calculating the ADTV of securities under paragraph (b)(1)(iii)(A) is reported in a currency other than U.S. dollars, the total value of each day's transactions in such currency shall be converted into U.S. dollars on the basis of a spot rate of exchange for that day obtained from at least one independent entity that provides or disseminates foreign exchange quotations in the ordinary course of its business.

(iv) The dollar value of ADTV of the lowest weighted 25% of an index is the sum of the dollar value of ADTV of each of the component securities comprising the lowest weighted 25% of such index.

(2) For purposes of section 3(a)(55)(C)(i)(III)(cc) of the Act (15 U.S.C. 78c(a)(55)(C)(i)(III)(cc)):

(i) On a particular day, a security shall be 1 of 675 securities with the largest dollar value of ADTV as of the preceding 6 full calendar months when it is included on a list of such securities designated by the Commission and the CFTC as applicable for that day.

(ii) In the event that the Commission and the CFTC have not designated a list under paragraph (b)(2) of this rule:

(A) The method to be used to determine the dollar value of ADTV of a security as of the preceding 6 full calendar months is to sum the value of all reported transactions in such security in the United States for each U.S. trading day during the preceding 6 full calendar months, and to divide this sum by the total number of such trading days.

(B) The 675 securities with the largest dollar value of ADTV shall be identified from the universe of all NMS securities as defined in Rule 600 of Regulation NMS that are common stock or depositary shares.

(c) *Depositary Shares and Section 12 Registration.* For purposes of section 3(a)(55)(C) of the Act (15 U.S.C. 78c(a)(55)(C)), the requirement that each component security of an index be registered pursuant to section 12 of the Act (15 U.S.C. 78*l*) shall be satisfied with respect to any security that is a depositary share if the deposited securities underlying the depositary share are registered pursuant to Section 12 of the Act and the depositary share is registered under the Securities Act of 1933 (15 U.S.C. 77a *et seq.*) on Form F–6 (17 CFR 239.36).

(d) *Definitions.* For purposes of this rule:

(1) *CFTC* means Commodity Futures Trading Commission.

(2) *Closing price* of a security means:

(i) If reported transactions in the security have taken place in the United States, the price at which the last transaction in such security took place in the regular trading session of the principal market for the security in the United States.

(ii) If no reported transactions in a security have taken place in the United States, the closing price of such security shall be the closing price of any depositary share representing such security divided by the number of shares represented by such depositary share.

(iii) If no reported transactions in a security or in a depositary share representing such security have taken place in the United States, the closing price of such security shall be the price at which the last transaction in such security took place in the regular trading session of the principal market for the security. If such price is reported in a currency other than U.S. dollars, such price shall be converted into U.S. dollars on the basis of a spot rate of exchange relevant for the time of the transaction obtained from at least one independent entity that provides or disseminates foreign exchange quotations in the ordinary course of its business.

(3) *Depositary share* has the same meaning as in Rule 12b–2.

(4) *Foreign financial regulatory authority* has the same meaning as in section 3(a)(52) of the Act (15 U.S.C. 78c(a)(52)).

(5) *Lowest Weighted 25% of an Index.* With respect to any particular day, the lowest weighted component securities comprising, in the aggregate, 25% of an index's weighting for purposes of section 3(a)(55)(B)(iv) of the Act (15 U.S.C. 78c(a)(55)(B)(iv)) ("lowest weighted 25% of an index") means those securities:

(i) That are the lowest weighted securities when all the securities in such index are ranked from lowest to highest based on the index's weighting methodology; and

(ii) For which the sum of the weight of such securities is equal to, or less than, 25% of the index's total weighting.

(6) *Market capitalization* of a security on a particular day:

(i) If the security is not a depositary share, is the product of:

(A) The closing price of such security on that same day; and

(B) The number of outstanding shares of such security on that same day.

(ii) If the security is a depositary share, is the product of:

(A) The closing price of the depositary share on that same day divided by the number of deposited securities represented by such depositary share; and

(B) The number of outstanding shares of the security represented by the depositary share on that same day.

(7) *Outstanding shares* of a security means the number of outstanding shares of such security as reported on the most recent Form 10–K, Form 10–Q, Form 10–KSB, Form 10–QSB, or Form 20–F (17 CFR 249.310, 249.308a, 249.310b, 249.308b, or 249.220f) filed with the Commission by the issuer of such security, including any change to such number of outstanding shares subsequently reported by the issuer on a Form 8–K (17 CFR 249.308).

(8) *Preceding 6 full calendar months* means, with respect to a particular day, the period of time beginning on the same day of the month 6 months before and ending on the day prior to such day.

(9) *Principal market* for a security means the single securities market with the largest reported trading volume for the security during the preceding 6 full calendar months.

(10) *Reported transaction* means:

(i) With respect to securities transactions in the United States, any transaction for which a transaction report is collected, processed, and made available pursuant to an effective transaction reporting plan, or for which a transaction report, last sale data, or quotation information is disseminated through an automated quotation system as described in section 3(a)(51)(A)(ii) of the Act (15 U.S.C. 78c(a)(51)(A)(ii)); and

(ii) With respect to securities transactions outside the United States, any transaction that has been reported to a foreign financial regulatory authority in the jurisdiction where such transaction has taken place.

(11) *U.S. trading day* means any day on which a national securities exchange is open for trading.

(12) *Weighting* of a component security of an index means the percentage of such index's value represented, or accounted for, by such component security.

Rule 3a55–2. Indexes underlying futures contracts trading for fewer than 30 days

(a) An index on which a contract of sale for future delivery is trading on a designated contract market, registered derivatives transaction execution facility, or foreign board of trade is not a narrow-based security index under section 3(a)(55) of the Act (15 U.S.C. 78c(a)(55)) for the first 30 days of trading, if:

(1) Such index would not have been a narrow-based security index on each trading day of the preceding 6 full calendar months with respect to a date no earlier than 30 days prior to the commencement of trading of such contract;

(2) On each trading day of the preceding 6 full calendar months with respect to a date no earlier than 30 days prior to the commencement of trading such contract:

(i) Such index had more than 9 component securities;

(ii) No component security in such index comprised more than 30 percent of the index's weighting;

(iii) The 5 highest weighted component securities in such index did not comprise, in the aggregate, more than 60 percent of the index's weighting; and

(iv) The dollar value of the trading volume of the lowest weighted 25% of such index was not less than $50 million (or in the case of an index with 15 or more component securities, $30 million); or

(3) On each trading day of the preceding 6 full calendar months, with respect to a date no earlier than 30 days prior to the commencement of trading such contract:

(i) Such index had at least 9 component securities;

(ii) No component security in such index comprised more than 30 percent of the index's weighting; and

(iii) Each component security in such index was:

(A) Registered pursuant to section 12 of the Act (15 U.S.C. 78) or was a depositary share representing a security registered pursuant to section 12 of the Act;

(B) 1 of 750 securities with the largest market capitalization that day; and

(C) 1 of 675 securities with the largest dollar value of trading volume that day.

(b) An index that is not a narrow-based security index for the first 30 days of trading pursuant to paragraph (a) of this rule, shall become a narrow-based security index if such index has been a narrow-based security index for more than 45 business days over 3 consecutive calendar months.

(c) An index that becomes a narrow-based security index solely because it was a narrow-based security index for more than 45 business days over 3 consecutive calendar months pursuant to paragraph (b) of this rule shall not be a narrow-based security index for the following 3 calendar months.

(d) *Definitions.* For purposes of this rule:

(1) *Market capitalization* has the same meaning as in Rule 3a55–1(d)(6).

(2) *Dollar value of trading volume* of a security on a particular day is the value in U.S. dollars of all reported transactions in such security on that day. If the value of reported transactions used in calculating dollar value of trading volume is reported in a currency other than U.S. dollars, the total value of each day's transactions shall be converted into U.S. dollars on the basis of a spot rate

of exchange for that day obtained from at least one independent entity that provides or disseminates foreign exchange quotations in the ordinary course of its business.

(3) *Lowest weighted 25% of an index* has the same meaning as in Rule 3a55–1(d)(5).

(4) *Preceding 6 full calendar months* has the same meaning as in Rule 3a55–1(d)(8).

(5) *Reported transaction* has the same meaning as in Rule 3a55–1(d)(10).

Rule 3a55–3. Futures contracts on security indexes trading on or subject to the rules of a foreign board of trade

When a contract of sale for future delivery on a security index is traded on or subject to the rules of a foreign board of trade, such index shall not be a narrow-based security index if it would not be a narrow-based security index if a futures contract on such index were traded on a designated contract market or registered derivatives transaction execution facility.

Rule 3a55–4. Exclusion from definition of narrow–based security index for indexes composed of debt securities

(a) An index is not a narrow-based security index if:

(1)(i) Each of the securities of an issuer included in the index is a security, as defined in section 2(a)(1) of the Securities Act of 1933 (15 U.S.C. 77b(a)(1)) and section 3(a)(10) of the Act (15 U.S.C. 78c(a)(10)) and the respective rules promulgated thereunder, that is a note, bond, debenture, or evidence of indebtedness;

(ii) None of the securities of an issuer included in the index is an equity security, as defined in section 3(a)(11) of the Act (15 U.S.C. 78c(a)(11)) and the rules promulgated thereunder;

(iii) The index is comprised of more than nine securities that are issued by more than nine non-affiliated issuers;

(iv) The securities of any issuer included in the index do not comprise more than 30 percent of the index's weighting;

(v) The securities of any five non-affiliated issuers included in the index do not comprise more than 60 percent of the index's weighting;

(vi) Except as provided in paragraph (a)(1)(viii) of this rule, for each security of an issuer included in the index one of the following criteria is satisfied:

(A) The issuer of the security is required to file reports pursuant to section 13 or section 15(d) of the Act (15 U.S.C. 78m and 78o(d));

(B) The issuer of the security has a worldwide market value of its outstanding common equity held by non-affiliates of $71 million or more;

(C) The issuer of the security has outstanding securities that are notes, bonds, debentures, or evidences of indebtedness having a total remaining principal amount of at least $1 billion;

(D) The security is an exempted security as defined in section 3(a)(12) of the Act (15 U.S.C. 78c(a)(12)) and the rules promulgated thereunder; or

(E) The issuer of the security is a government of a foreign country or a political subdivision of a foreign country;

(vii) Except as provided in paragraph (a)(1)(viii) of this rule, for each security of an issuer included in the index one of the following criteria is satisfied:

(A) The security has a total remaining principal amount of at least $250,000,000; or

(B) The security is a municipal security, as defined in section 3(a)(29) of the Act (15 U.S.C. 78c(a)(29)) and the rules promulgated thereunder that has a total remaining principal amount of at least $200,000,000 and the issuer of such municipal security has outstanding securities that are notes, bonds, debentures, or evidences of indebtedness having a total remaining principal amount of at least $1 billion; and

(viii) Paragraphs (a)(1)(vi) and (a)(1)(vii) of this rule will not apply to securities of an issuer included in the index if:

(A) All securities of such issuer included in the index represent less than 5 percent of the index's weighting; and

(B) Securities comprising at least 80 percent of the index's weighting satisfy the provisions of paragraphs (a)(1)(vi) and (a)(1)(vii) of this rule; or

(2)(i) The index includes exempted securities, other than municipal securities, as defined in section 3(a)(29) of the Act and the rules promulgated thereunder, that are:

(A) Notes, bonds, debentures, or evidences of indebtedness; and

(B) Not equity securities, as defined in section 3(a)(11) of the Act (15 U.S.C. 78c(a)(11)) and the rules promulgated thereunder; and

(ii) Without taking into account any portion of the index composed of such exempted securities, other than municipal securities, the remaining portion of the index would not be a narrow-based security index meeting all the conditions under paragraph (a)(1) of this rule.

(b) For purposes of this rule:

(1) An issuer is affiliated with another issuer if it controls, is controlled by, or is under common control with, that issuer.

(2) For purposes of this rule, *control* means ownership of 20 percent or more of an issuer's equity, or the ability to direct the voting of 20 percent or more of the issuer's voting equity.

(3) The term *issuer* includes a single issuer or group of affiliated issuers.

SECURITY-BASED SWAP DEALER AND PARTICIPANT DEFINITIONS

Rule 3a67–1. Definition of "major security–based swap participant"

(a) *General. Major security-based swap participant* means any person:

(1) That is not a security-based swap dealer; and

(2)(i) That maintains a substantial position in security-based swaps for any of the major security-based swap categories, excluding both positions held for hedging or mitigating commercial risk, and positions maintained by any employee benefit plan (or any contract held by such a plan) as defined in paragraphs (3) and (32) of section 3 of the Employee Retirement Income Security Act of 1974 (29 U.S.C. 1002) for the primary purpose of hedging or mitigating any risk directly associated with the operation of the plan;

(ii) Whose outstanding security-based swaps create substantial counterparty exposure that could have serious adverse effects on the financial stability of the United States banking system or financial markets; or

(iii) That is a financial entity that:

(A) Is highly leveraged relative to the amount of capital such entity holds and that is not subject to capital requirements established by an appropriate Federal banking agency (as defined in 15 U.S.C. 78c(a)(72)); and

(B) Maintains a substantial position in outstanding security-based swaps in any major security-based swap category.

(b) *Scope of Designation.* A person that is a major security-based swap participant in general shall be deemed to be a major security-based swap participant with respect to each security-based swap it enters into, regardless of the category of the security-based swap or the person's activities in connection with the security-based swap, unless the Commission limits the person's designation as a major security-based swap participant to specified categories of security-based swaps.

Rule 3a67–2. Categories of security–based swaps

For purposes of section 3(a)(67) of the Act, 15 U.S.C. 78c(a)(67), and the rules thereunder, the terms *major security-based swap category, category of security-based swaps* and any similar terms mean either of the following categories of security-based swaps:

(a) *Debt Security-Based Swaps.* Any security-based swap that is based, in whole or in part, on one or more instruments of indebtedness (including loans), or on a credit event relating to one or more issuers or securities, including but not limited to any security-based swap that is a credit default swap, total return swap on one or more debt instruments, debt swap, debt index swap, or credit spread.

(b) *Other Security-Based Swaps.* Any security-based swap not described in paragraph (a) of this section.

Rule 3a67–3. Definition of "substantial position"

(a) *General.* For purposes of section 3(a)(67) of the Act, and Rule 3a67–1, the term *substantial position* means security-based swap positions that equal or exceed either of the following thresholds in any major category of security-based swaps:

(1) $1 billion in daily average aggregate uncollateralized outward exposure; or

(2) $2 billion in:

(i) Daily average aggregate uncollateralized outward exposure; plus

(ii) Daily average aggregate potential outward exposure.

(b) *Aggregate Uncollateralized Outward Exposure.*

(1) *General. Aggregate uncollateralized outward exposure* in general means the sum of the current exposure, obtained by marking-to-market using industry standard practices, of each of the person's security-based swap positions with negative value in a major security-based swap category, less the value of the collateral the person has posted in connection with those positions.

(2) *Calculation of Aggregate Uncollateralized Outward Exposure.* In calculating this amount the person shall, with respect to each of its security-based swap counterparties in a given major security-based swap category:

(i) Determine the dollar value of the aggregate current exposure arising from each of its security-based swap positions with negative value (subject to the netting provisions described below) in that major category by marking-to-market using industry standard practices; and

(ii) Deduct from that dollar amount the aggregate value of the collateral the person has posted with respect to the security-based swap positions.

(iii) The aggregate uncollateralized outward exposure shall be the sum of those uncollateralized amounts across all of the person's security-based swap counterparties in the applicable major category.

(3) *Relevance of Netting Agreements.*

(i) If a person has one or more master netting agreements with a counterparty, the person may measure the current exposure arising from its security-based swaps in any major category on a net basis, applying the terms of those agreements. Calculation of current exposure may take into account offsetting positions entered into with that particular counterparty involving security-based swaps (in any security-based swap category) as well as swaps and securities financing transactions (consisting of securities lending and borrowing, securities margin lending and repurchase and reverse repurchase agreements), and other financial instruments that are subject to netting offsets for purposes of applicable bankruptcy law, to the extent these are consistent with the offsets permitted by the master netting agreements.

(ii) Such adjustments may not take into account any offset associated with positions that the person has with separate counterparties.

(4) *Allocation of Uncollateralized Outward Exposure.* If a person calculates current exposure with a particular counterparty on a net basis, as provided by paragraph (b)(3) of this section, the amount of current uncollateralized exposure attributable to each "major" category of security-based swaps should be calculated according to the following formula:

NOTE TO PARAGRAPH (b)(4). Where: $E_{SBS(MC)}$ equals the amount of aggregate current exposure attributable to the entity's security-based swap positions in the "major" category at issue (either security-based credit derivatives or other security-based swaps); $E_{net\ total}$ equals the entity's aggregate current exposure to the counterparty at issue, after accounting for the netting of positions and the posting of collateral; $OTM_{SBS(MC)}$ equals the current exposure associated with the entity's out-of-the-money positions in security-based swaps in the "major" category at issue, subject to those netting arrangements; and $OTM_{SBS(O)}$ equals the current exposure associated with the entity's out-of-the-money positions in the other "major" category of security-based swaps, subject to those netting arrangements; and $OTM_{non\text{-}SBS}$ equals the current exposure associated with the entity's out-of-the-money positions associated with instruments, other than security-based swaps, that are subject to those netting arrangements.

(c) *Aggregate Potential Outward Exposure.*

(1) *General. Aggregate potential outward exposure* means the sum of:

(i) The aggregate potential outward exposure for each of the person's security-based swap positions in a major security-based swap category that are neither cleared by a registered or exempt clearing agency nor subject to daily mark-to-market margining, as calculated in accordance with paragraph (c)(2) of this section; and

(ii) The aggregate potential outward exposure for each of the person's security-based swap positions in a major security-based swap category that are either cleared by a registered or exempt clearing agency or subject to daily mark-to-market margining, as calculated in accordance with paragraph (c)(3) of this section.

(2) *Calculation of Potential Outward Exposure for Security-Based Swaps That Are Not Cleared by a Registered or Exempt Clearing Agency or Subject to Daily Mark-To-Market Margining.*

(i) *General.*

(A) For positions in security-based swaps that are not cleared by a registered or exempt clearing agency or subject to daily mark-to-market margining, potential outward exposure equals the total notional principal amount of those positions, multiplied by the following factors on a position-by-position basis reflecting the type of security-based swap. For any security-based swap that is not of the "debt" type, the "equity and other" conversion factors are to be used:

Residual maturity	Debt	Equity and other
One year or less	0.10	0.06
Over one to five years	0.10	0.08
Over five years	0.10	0.10

If a security-based swap is structured such that on specified dates any outstanding exposure is settled and the terms are reset so that the market value of the security-based swap is zero, the remaining maturity equals the time until the next reset date.

(B) *Use of Effective Notional Amounts*. If the stated notional amount on a position is leveraged or enhanced by the structure of the position, the calculation in paragraph (c)(2)(i)(A) of this section shall be based on the effective notional amount of the position rather than on the stated notional amount.

(C) *Exclusion of Certain Positions*. The calculation in paragraph (c)(2)(i)(A) of this section shall exclude:

(*1*) Positions that constitute the purchase of an option, such that the person has no additional payment obligations under the position;

(*2*) Other positions for which the person has prepaid or otherwise satisfied all of its payment obligations; and

(*3*) Positions for which, pursuant to regulatory requirement, the person has assigned an amount of cash or U.S. Treasury securities that is sufficient to pay the person's maximum possible liability under the position, and the person may not use that cash or those Treasury securities for other purposes.

(D) *Adjustment for Certain Positions*. Notwithstanding paragraph (c)(2)(i)(A) of this section, the potential outward exposure associated with a position by which a person buys credit protection using a credit default swap, or associated with a position by which a person purchases an option for which the person retains additional payment obligations under the position, is capped at the net present value of the unpaid premiums.

(ii) Adjustment for netting agreements. Notwithstanding paragraph (c)(2)(i) of this section, for positions subject to master netting agreements the potential outward exposure associated with the person's security-based swaps with each counterparty equals a weighted average of the potential outward exposure for the person's security-based swaps with that counterparty as calculated under paragraph (c)(2)(i) of this section, and that amount reduced by the ratio of net current exposure to gross current exposure, consistent with the following equation as calculated on a counterparty-by-counterparty basis:

$$P_{Net} = 0.4 \text{ x } P_{Gross} + 0.6 \text{ x } NGR \text{ x } P_{Gross}$$

NOTE TO PARAGRAPH (c)(2)(ii). Where: P_{Net} is the potential outward exposure, adjusted for bilateral netting, of the person's security-based swaps with a particular counterparty; P_{Gross} is the potential outward exposure without adjustment for bilateral netting, as calculated pursuant to paragraph (c)(2)(i) of this section; and *NGR* is the ratio of:

(a) the current exposure arising from its security-based swaps in the major category as calculated on a net basis according to paragraphs (b)(3) and (b)(4) of this section, divided by

(b) the current exposure arising from its security-based swaps in the major category as calculated in the absence of those netting procedures.

(3) *Calculation of Potential Outward Exposure for Security-Based Swaps That Are Either Cleared by a Registered or Exempt Clearing Agency or Subject to Daily Mark-to-Market Margining*. For positions in security-based swaps that are cleared by a registered or exempt clearing agency or subject to daily mark-to-market margining:

(i) Potential outward exposure equals the potential outward exposure that would be attributed to such positions using the procedures in paragraph (c)(2) of this section, multiplied by:

(A) 0.1, in the case of positions cleared by a registered or exempt clearing agency; or

(B) 0.2, in the case of positions that are subject to daily mark-to-market margining but that are not cleared by a registered or exempt clearing agency.

(ii) Solely for purposes of calculating potential outward exposure:

(A) A security-based swap shall be considered to be subject to daily mark-to-market margining if, and for as long as, the counterparties follow the daily practice of exchanging collateral to reflect changes in the current exposure arising from the security-based swap (after taking into account any other financial positions addressed by a netting agreement between the counterparties).

(B) If the person is permitted by agreement to maintain a threshold for which it is not required to post collateral, the position still will be considered to be subject to daily mark-to-market margining for purposes of calculating potential outward exposure, but the total amount of that threshold (regardless of the actual exposure at any time) less any initial margin posted up to the amount of that threshold, shall be added to the person's aggregate uncollateralized outward exposure for purposes of paragraph (a)(2) of this section.

(C) If the minimum transfer amount under the agreement is in excess of $1 million, the position still will be considered to be subject to daily mark-to-market margining for purposes of calculating potential outward exposure, but the entirety of the minimum transfer amount shall be added to the person's aggregate uncollateralized outward exposure for purposes of paragraph (a)(2) of this section.

(D) A person may, at its discretion, calculate the potential outward exposure of positions in security-based swaps that are subject to daily mark-to-market margining in accordance with paragraph (c)(2) of this section in lieu of calculating the potential outward exposure of such positions in accordance with this paragraph (c)(3).

(d) *Calculation of Daily Average.* Measures of daily average aggregate uncollateralized outward exposure and daily average aggregate potential outward exposure shall equal the arithmetic mean of the applicable measure of exposure at the close of each business day, beginning the first business day of each calendar quarter and continuing through the last business day of that quarter.

(e) *Inter-Affiliate Activities.* In calculating its aggregate uncollateralized outward exposure and its aggregate potential outward exposure, a person shall not consider its security-based swap positions with counterparties that are majority-owned affiliates. For these purposes the parties are majority-owned affiliates if one party directly or indirectly owns a majority interest in the other, or if a third party directly or indirectly owns a majority interest in both counterparties to the security-based swap, where "majority interest" is the right to vote or direct the vote of a majority of a class of voting securities of an entity, the power to sell or direct the sale of a majority of a class of voting securities of an entity, or the right to receive upon dissolution or the contribution of a majority of the capital of a partnership.

Rule 3a67-4. Definition of "hedging or mitigating commercial risk"

For purposes of section 3(a)(67) of the Act, and Rule 3a67-1, a security-based swap position shall be deemed to be held for the purpose of hedging or mitigating commercial risk when:

(a)(1) Such position is economically appropriate to the reduction of risks that are associated with the present conduct and management of a commercial enterprise (or of a majority owned affiliate of the enterprise), or are reasonably expected to arise in the future conduct and management of the commercial enterprise, where such risks arise from:

(i) The potential change in the value of assets that a person owns, produces, manufactures, processes, or merchandises or reasonably anticipates owning, producing, manufacturing, processing, or merchandising in the ordinary course of business of the enterprise (or of an affiliate under common control with the enterprise);

(ii) The potential change in the value of liabilities that a person has incurred or reasonably anticipates incurring in the ordinary course of business of the enterprise (or of an affiliate under common control with the enterprise); or

(iii) The potential change in the value of services that a person provides, purchases, or reasonably anticipates providing or purchasing in the ordinary course of business of the enterprise (or of an affiliate under common control with the enterprise);

(2) Depending on the applicable facts and circumstances, the security-based swap positions described in paragraph (a)(1) of this section may be expected to encompass, among other positions:

(i) Positions established to manage the risk posed by a customer's, supplier's or counterparty's potential default in connection with: financing provided to a customer in connection with the sale of real property or a good, product or service; a customer's lease of real property or a good, product or service; a customer's agreement to purchase real property or a good, product or service in the future; or a supplier's commitment to provide or sell a good, product or service in the future;

(ii) Positions established to manage the default risk posed by a financial counterparty (different from the counterparty to the hedging position at issue) in connection with a separate transaction (including a position involving a credit derivative, equity swap, other security-based swap, interest rate swap, commodity swap, foreign exchange swap or other swap, option, or future that itself is for the purpose of hedging or mitigating commercial risk pursuant to this section or 17 CFR 1.3(kkk));

(iii) Positions established to manage equity or market risk associated with certain employee compensation plans, including the risk associated with market price variations in connection with stock-based compensation plans, such as deferred compensation plans and stock appreciation rights;

(iv) Positions established to manage equity market price risks connected with certain business combinations, such as a corporate merger or consolidation or similar plan or acquisition in which securities of a person are exchanged for securities of any other person (unless the sole purpose of the transaction is to change an issuer's domicile solely within the United States), or a transfer of assets of a person to another person in consideration of the issuance of securities of such other person or any of its affiliates;

(v) Positions established by a bank to manage counterparty risks in connection with loans the bank has made; and

(vi) Positions to close out or reduce any of the positions described in paragraphs (a)(2)(i) through (a)(2)(v) of this section; and

(b) Such position is:

(1) Not held for a purpose that is in the nature of speculation or trading; and

(2) Not held to hedge or mitigate the risk of another security-based swap position or swap position, unless that other position itself is held for the purpose of hedging or mitigating commercial risk as defined by this section or 17 CFR 1.3(kkk).

Rule 3a67-5. Definition of "substantial counterparty exposure"

(a) *General.* For purposes of section 3(a)(67) of the Act, and Rule 3a67-1, the term *substantial counterparty exposure that could have serious adverse effects on the financial stability of the United States banking system or financial markets* means a security-based swap position that satisfies either of the following thresholds:

(1) $2 billion in daily average aggregate uncollateralized outward exposure; or

(2) $4 billion in:

(i) Daily average aggregate uncollateralized outward exposure; plus

(ii) Daily average aggregate potential outward exposure.

(b) *Calculation.* For these purposes, *daily average aggregate uncollateralized outward exposure* and *daily average aggregate potential outward exposure* shall be calculated the same way as is prescribed in Rule 3a67-3, except that these amounts shall be calculated by reference to all of the person's security-based swap positions, rather than by reference to a specific major security-based swap category.

Rule 3a67-6. Definition of "financial entity"

(a) *General.* For purposes of section 3(a)(67) of the Act, and Rule 3a67-1, the term financial entity means:

(1) A swap dealer;

(2) A major swap participant;

(3) A commodity pool as defined in section 1a(10) of the Commodity Exchange Act (7 U.S.C. 1a(10));

(4) A private fund as defined in section 202(a) of the Investment Advisers Act of 1940 (15 U.S.C. 80b-2(a));

(5) An employee benefit plan as defined in paragraphs (3) and (32) of section 3 of the Employee Retirement Income Security Act of 1974 (29 U.S.C. 1002); and

(6) A person predominantly engaged in activities that are in the business of banking or financial in nature, as defined in section 4(k) of the Bank Holding Company Act of 1956 (12 U.S.C. 1843k).

(b) *Exclusion for Centralized Hedging Facilities.*

(1) *General.* Notwithstanding paragraph (a) of this section, for purposes of this section the term financial entity shall not encompass a person that

would be a financial entity solely as a result of the person's activities that facilitate hedging and/or treasury functions on behalf of one or more majority-owned affiliates that themselves do not constitute a financial entity.

(2) *Meaning of Majority-Owned.* For these purposes the counterparties to a security-based swap are majority-owned affiliates if one counterparty directly or indirectly owns a majority interest in the other, or if a third party directly or indirectly owns a majority interest in both counterparties to the security-based swap, where "majority interest" includes, but is not limited to, the right to vote or direct the vote of a majority of a class of voting securities of an entity, the power to sell or direct the sale of a majority of a class of voting securities of an entity, or the right to receive upon dissolution or the contribution of a majority of the capital of a partnership.

Rule 3a67–7. Definition of "highly leveraged"

(a) *General.* For purposes of section 3(a)(67) of the Act, and Rule 3a67–1, the term *highly leveraged* means the existence of a ratio of an entity's total liabilities to equity in excess of 12 to 1 as measured at the close of business on the last business day of the applicable fiscal quarter.

(b) *Measurement of Liabilities and Equity.* For purposes of this section, liabilities and equity generally should each be determined in accordance with U.S. generally accepted accounting principles; provided, however, that a person that is an employee benefit plan, as defined in paragraphs (3) and (32) of section 3 of the Employee Retirement Income Security Act of 1974 (29 U.S.C. 1002), may, for purposes of this paragraph (b):

(1) Exclude obligations to pay benefits to plan participants from the calculation of liabilities; and

(2) Substitute the total value of plan assets for equity.

Rule 3a67–8. Timing requirements, reevaluation period, and termination of status

(a) *Timing Requirements.* A person that is not registered as a major security-based swap participant, but that meets the criteria in Rule 3a67–1 to be a major security-based swap participant as a result of its security-based swap activities in a fiscal quarter, will not be deemed to be a major security-based swap participant until the earlier of the date on which it submits a complete application for registration pursuant to section 15F of the Act (15 U.S.C. 78*o*–10) or two months after the end of that quarter.

(b) *Reevaluation Period.* Notwithstanding paragraph (a) of this section, if a person that is not registered as a major security-based swap participant meets the criteria in Rule 3a67–1 to be a major security-based swap participant in a fiscal quarter, but does not exceed any applicable threshold by more than twenty percent in that quarter:

(1) That person will not immediately be deemed a major security-based swap participant pursuant to the timing requirements specified in paragraph (a) of this section; but

(2) That person will be deemed a major security-based swap participant pursuant to the timing requirements specified in paragraph (a) of this section at the end of the next fiscal quarter if the person exceeds any of the applicable daily average thresholds in that next fiscal quarter.

(c) *Termination of Status.* A person that is deemed to be a major security-based swap participant shall continue to be deemed a major security-based swap participant until such time that its security-based swap activities do not exceed any of the daily average thresholds set forth within Rule 3a67–1 for four consecutive fiscal quarters after the date on which the person becomes registered as a major security-based swap participant.

Rule 3a67–9. Calculation of major participant status by certain persons

A person shall not be deemed to be a major security-based swap participant, regardless of whether the criteria in Rule 3a67–1 otherwise would cause the person to be a major security-based swap participant, provided the person meets the conditions set forth in paragraph (a) of this section.

(a) *Conditions.*

(1) *Caps on Uncollateralized Exposure and Notional Positions.*

(i) *Maximum Potential Uncollateralized Exposure.* The express terms of the person's agreements or arrangements relating to security-based swaps with its counterparties at no time would permit the person to maintain a total uncollateralized exposure of more than $100 million to all such counterparties, including any exposure that may result from thresholds or minimum transfer amounts established by credit support annexes or similar arrangements; and

(ii) *Maximum Notional Amount of Security-Based Swap Positions.* The person does not maintain security-based swap positions in an effective notional amount of more than $2 billion in any major category of security-based swaps, or more than $4 billion in aggregate; or

(2) *Caps on Uncollateralized Exposure plus Monthly Calculation.*

(i) *Maximum Potential Uncollateralized Exposure.* The express terms of the person's agreements or arrangements relating to security-based swaps with its counterparties at no time would permit the person to maintain a total uncollateralized exposure of more than $200 million to all such counterparties (with regard to security-based swaps and any other instruments by which the person may have exposure to those counterparties), including any exposure that may result from thresholds or minimum transfer amounts established by credit support annexes or similar arrangements; and

(ii) *Calculation of Positions.*

(A) At the end of each month, the person performs the calculations prescribed by Rules 3a67–3 and 3a67–5 with regard to whether the aggregate uncollateralized outward exposure plus aggregate potential outward exposure as of that day constitute a substantial position in a major category of security-based swaps, or pose substantial counterparty exposure that could have serious adverse effects on the financial stability of the United States banking system or financial markets; these calculations shall disregard provisions of those rules that provide for the analyses to be determined based on a daily average over a calendar quarter; and

(B) Each such analysis produces thresholds of no more than:

(*1*) $1 billion in aggregate uncollateralized outward exposure plus aggregate potential outward exposure in any major category of security-based swaps; if the person is subject to Rule 3a67–3(a)(2)(iii), by virtue of being a highly leveraged financial entity that is not subject to capital requirements established by an appropriate Federal banking agency, this analysis shall account for all of the person's security-based swap positions in that major category (without excluding hedging positions), otherwise this analysis shall exclude the same hedging and related positions that are excluded from consideration pursuant to Rule 3a67–3(a)(2)(i); or

(*2*) $2 billion in aggregate uncollateralized outward exposure plus aggregate potential outward exposure (without any positions excluded from the analysis) with regard to all of the person's security-based swap positions.

(3) *Calculations Based on Certain Information.*

(i) At the end of each month:

(A)(*1*) The person's aggregate uncollateralized outward exposure with respect to its security-based swap positions is less than $500 million with respect to each of the major security-based swap categories; and

(*2*) The sum of the amount calculated under paragraph (a)(3)(i)(A)(1) of this section with respect to each major security-based swap category and the total notional principal amount of the person's security-based swap positions in each such major security-based swap category, adjusted by the multipliers set forth in Rule 3a67–3(c)(2)(i)(A) on a position-by-position basis reflecting the type of security-based swap, is less than $1 billion with respect to each of the major security-based swap categories.

(B)(*1*) The person's aggregate uncollateralized outward exposure with respect to its security-based swap positions across all major security-based swap categories is less than $500 million; and

(*2*) The sum of the amount calculated under paragraph (a)(3)(i)(B)(1) of this section and the product of the total effective notional principal amount of the person's security-based swap positions in all major security-based swap categories multiplied by 0.10 is less than $1 billion; or

(ii) For purposes of the calculations set forth in paragraph (a)(3)(i) of this section:

(A) The person's aggregate uncollateralized outward exposure for positions held with security-based swap dealers shall be equal to such exposure reported on the most recent reports of such exposure received from such security-based swap dealers; and

(B) The person's aggregate uncollateralized outward exposure for positions that are not reflected in any report of exposure from a security-based swap dealer (including all security-based swap positions it holds with persons other than security-based swap dealers) shall be calculated in accordance with Rule 3a67–3(b)(2).

(b) For purposes of the calculations set forth by this section, the person shall use the effective notional amount of a position rather than the stated notional amount of the position if the stated notional amount is leveraged or enhanced by the structure of the position.

(c) No presumption shall arise that a person is required to perform the calculations needed to determine if it is a major security-based swap participant, solely by reason that the person does not meet the conditions specified in paragraph (a) of this section.

Rule 3a67–10. Foreign major security-based swap participants

(a) *Definitions.* As used in this section, the following terms shall have the meanings indicated:

(1) *Conduit affiliate* has the meaning set forth in Rule 3a71–3(a)(1).

(2) *Foreign branch* has the meaning set forth in Rule 3a71–3(a)(2).

(3) *Transaction conducted through a foreign branch* has the meaning set for in Rule 3a71–3(a)(3).

(4) *U.S. person* has the meaning set forth in Rule 3a71–3(a)(4).

(5) *U.S. major security-based swap participant* means a major security-based swap participant, as defined in section 3(a)(67) of the Act (15 U.S.C. 78c(a)(67)), and the rules and regulations thereunder, that is a U.S. person.

(6) *Foreign major security-based swap participant* means a major security-based swap participant, as defined in section 3(a)(67) of the Act (15 U.S.C. 78c(a)(67)), and the rules and regulations thereunder, that is not a U.S. person.

(b) *Application of Major Security-Based Swap Participant Tests in the Cross-Border Context.* For purposes of calculating a person's status as a major security-based swap participant as defined in section 3(a)(67) under the, and the rules and regulations thereunder, a person shall include the following security-based swap positions:

(1) If such person is a U.S. person, all security-based swap positions that are entered into by the person, including positions entered into through a foreign branch;

(2) If such person is a conduit affiliate, all security-based swap positions that are entered into by the person; and

(3) If such person is a non-U.S. person other than a conduit affiliate, all of the following types of security-based swap positions that are entered into by the person:

(i) Security-based swap positions that are entered into with a U.S. person; provided, however, that this paragraph (i) shall not apply to:

(A) Positions with a U.S. person counterparty that arise from transactions conducted through foreign branch of the counterparty, when the counterparty is a registered security-based swap dealer; and

(B) Positions with a U.S. person counterparty that arise from transactions conducted through a foreign branch of the counterparty, when the transaction is entered into prior to 60 days following the earliest date on which the registration of security-based swap dealers is first required pursuant to the applicable final rules and regulations; and

(ii) Security-based swap positions for which the non-U.S. person's counterparty to the security-based swap has rights of recourse against a U.S. person; for these purposes a counterparty has rights of recourse against the U.S. person if the counterparty has a conditional or unconditional legally enforceable right, in whole or in part, to receive payments from, or otherwise collect from, the U.S. person in connection with the security-based swap.

(c) *Attributed Positions.*

(1) *In General.* For purposes of calculating a person's status as a major security-based swap participant as defined in section 3(a)(67) under the Act, and the rules and regulations thereunder, a person also shall include the following security-based swap positions:

(i) If such person is a U.S. person, any security-based swap position of a non-U.S. person for which the non-U.S. person's counterparty to the security-based swap has rights of recourse against that U.S. person.

NOTE TO PARAGRAPH (c)(1)(i): This paragraph describes attribution requirements for a U.S. person solely with respect to the guarantee of the obligations of a non-U.S. person under a security-based swap. The Commission and the Commodity Futures Trading Commission previously provided an interpretation about attribution to a U.S. parent, other affiliate, or guarantor to the extent that the counterparties to those positions have recourse against that parent, other affiliate, or guarantor in connection with the position. *See* Intermediary Definitions Adopting Release, *http://www.gpo.gov/fdsys/pkg/FR-2012-08-13/pdf/2012-18003.pdf*. The Commission explained that it intended to issue separate releases addressing the application of the major participant definition, and Title VII generally, to non-U.S. persons. *See id.* at note 1041.

(ii) If such person is a non-U.S. person:

(A) Any security-based swap position of a U.S. person for which that person's counterparty has rights of recourse against the non-U.S. person; and

(B) Any security-based swap position of another non-U.S. person entered into with a U.S. person counterparty who has rights of recourse against the first non-U.S. person, provided, however, that this paragraph (B) shall not apply to positions described in Rule 3a67–10(b)(3)(i)(A) and (B).

(2) *Exceptions.* Notwithstanding paragraph (c)(1) of this section, a person shall not include such security-based swap positions if the person whose performance is guaranteed in connection with the security-based swap is:

(i) Subject to capital regulation by the Commission or the Commodity Futures Trading Commission (including, but not limited to regulation as a swap dealer, major swap participant, security-based swap dealer, major security-based swap participant, futures commission merchant, broker, or dealer);

(ii) Regulated as a bank in the United States;

(iii) Subject to capital standards, adopted by the person's home country supervisor, that are consistent in all respects with the Capital Accord of the Basel Committee on Banking Supervision; or

(iv) Deemed not to be a major security-based swap participant pursuant to Rule 3a67–8(a).

(d) *Application of Customer Protection Requirements.*

(1) A registered foreign major security-based swap participant shall not be subject to the requirements relating to business conduct standards described in section 15F(h) of the Act (15 U.S.C. 78o–10(h)), and the rules and regulations thereunder, other than rules and regulations prescribed by the Commission pursuant to section 15F(h)(1)(B) of the Act (15 U.S.C. 78o– 10(h)(1)(B)), with respect to a security-based swap transaction with a counterparty that is not a U.S. person or with a counterparty that is a U.S. person in a transaction conducted through a foreign branch of the U.S. person.

(2) A registered U.S. major security-based swap participant shall not be subject to the requirements relating to business conduct standards described in section 15F(h) of the Act (15 U.S.C. 78o–10(h)), and the rules and regulations thereunder, other than rules and regulations prescribed by the Commission pursuant to section 15F(h)(1)(B) of the Act (15 U.S.C. 78o– 10(h)(1)(B)), with respect to a security-based swap transaction that constitutes a transaction conducted through a foreign branch of the registered U.S. major security-based swap participant with a non-U.S. person or with a U.S.-person counterparty that constitutes a transaction conducted through a foreign branch of that U.S.-person counterparty.

FURTHER DEFINITION OF SWAP, SECURITY–BASED SWAP, AND SECURITY–BASED SWAP AGREEMENT; MIXED SWAPS; SECURITY–BASED SWAP AGREEMENT RECORDKEEPING

Rule 3a68–1a. Meaning of "issuers of securities in a narrow–based security index" as used in Section 3(a)(68)(A)(ii)(III) of the Act

(a) Notwithstanding Rule 3a68–3(a), and solely for purposes of determining whether a credit default swap is a security-based swap under section 3(a)(68)(A)(ii)(III) of the Act, the term *issuers of securities in a narrow-based security index* as used in section 3(a)(68)(A)(ii)(III) of the Act means issuers of securities included in an index (including an index referencing loan borrowers or loans of such borrowers) in which:

(1)(i) There are nine or fewer non-affiliated issuers of securities that are reference entities included in the index, provided that an issuer of securities shall not be deemed a reference entity included in the index for purposes of this section unless:

(A) A credit event with respect to such reference entity would result in a payment by the credit protection seller to the credit protection buyer under the credit default swap based on the related notional amount allocated to such reference entity; or

(B) The fact of such credit event or the calculation in accordance with paragraph (a)(1)(i)(A) of this section of the amount owed with respect to such credit event is taken into account in determining whether to make any future payments under the credit default swap with respect to any future credit events;

(ii) The effective notional amount allocated to any reference entity included in the index comprises more than 30 percent of the index's weighting;

(iii) The effective notional amount allocated to any five non-affiliated reference entities included in the index comprises more than 60 percent of the index's weighting; or

(iv) Except as provided in paragraph (b) of this section, for each reference entity included in the index, none of the criteria in paragraphs (a)(1)(iv)(A) through (a)(1)(iv)(H) of this section is satisfied:

(A) The reference entity included in the index is required to file reports pursuant to section 13 or section 15(d) of the Act;

(B) The reference entity included in the index is eligible to rely on the exemption provided in Rule 12g3–2(b);

(C) The reference entity included in the index has a worldwide market value of its outstanding common equity held by non-affiliates of $700 million or more;

(D) The reference entity included in the index (other than a reference entity included in the index that is an issuing entity of an asset-backed security as defined in section 3(a)(79) of the Act has outstanding notes, bonds, debentures, loans, or evidences of indebtedness (other than revolving credit facilities) having a total remaining principal amount of at least $1 billion;

(E) The reference entity included in the index is the issuer of an exempted security as defined in section 3(a)(12) of the Act (other than any municipal security as defined in section 3(a)(29) of the Act;

(F) The reference entity included in the index is a government of a foreign country or a political subdivision of a foreign country;

(G) If the reference entity included in the index is an issuing entity of an asset-backed security as defined in section 3(a)(79) of the Act, such asset-backed security was issued in a transaction registered under the Securities Act of 1933 and has publicly available distribution reports; and

(H) For a credit default swap entered into solely between eligible contract participants as defined in section 3(a)(65) of the Act:

(*1*) The reference entity included in the index (other than a reference entity included in the index that is an issuing entity of an asset-backed security as defined in section 3(a)(79) of the Act makes available to the public or otherwise makes available to such eligible contract participant information about the reference entity included in the index pursuant to Rule 144A(d)(4)) of the Securities Act of 1933;

(*2*) Financial information about the reference entity included in the index (other than a reference entity included in the index that is an issuing entity of an asset-backed security as defined in section 3(a)(79) of the Act is otherwise publicly available; or

(*3*) In the case of a reference entity included in the index that is an issuing entity of an asset-backed security as defined in section 3(a)(79) of the Act, information of the type and level included in publicly available distribution reports for similar asset-backed securities is publicly available about both the reference entity included in the index and such asset-backed security; and

(2)(i) The index is not composed solely of reference entities that are issuers of exempted securities as defined in section 3(a)(12) of the Act, as in effect on the date of enactment of the Futures Trading Act of 1982 (other than any municipal security as defined in section 3(a)(29) of the Act, as in effect on the date of enactment of the Futures Trading Act of 1982); and

(ii) Without taking into account any portion of the index composed of reference entities that are issuers of exempted securities as defined in section 3(a)(12) of the Act, as in effect on the date of enactment of the Futures Trading Act of 1982 (other than any municipal security as defined in section 3(a)(29) of the Act, the remaining portion of the index would be within the term "issuer of securities in a narrow-based security index" under paragraph (a)(1) of this section.

(b) Paragraph (a)(1)(iv) of this section will not apply with respect to a reference entity included in the index if:

(1) The effective notional amounts allocated to such reference entity comprise less than five percent of the index's weighting; and

(2) The effective notional amounts allocated to reference entities included in the index that satisfy paragraph (a)(1)(iv) of this section comprise at least 80 percent of the index's weighting.

(c) For purposes of this section:

(1) A reference entity included in the index is affiliated with another reference entity included in the index (for purposes of paragraph (c)(4) of this section) or another entity (for purposes of paragraph (c)(5) of this section) if it controls, is controlled by, or is under common control with, that other reference entity included in the index or other entity, as applicable; provided that each reference entity included in the index that is an issuing entity of an asset-backed security as defined in section 3(a)(79) of the Act will not be considered affiliated with any other reference entity included in the index or any other entity that is an issuing entity of an asset-backed security.

(2) Control for purposes of this section means ownership of more than 50 percent of the equity of a reference entity included in the index (for purposes of paragraph (c)(4) of this section) or another entity (for purposes of paragraph (c)(5) of this section), or the ability to direct the voting of more than 50 percent of the voting equity of a reference entity included in the index (for purposes of paragraph (c)(4) of this section) or another entity (for purposes of paragraph (c)(5) of this section).

(3) In identifying a reference entity included in the index for purposes of this section, the term *reference entity* includes:

(i) An issuer of securities;

(ii) An issuer of securities that is an issuing entity of an asset-backed security as defined in section 3(a)(79) of the Act; and

(iii) An issuer of securities that is a borrower with respect to any loan identified in an index of borrowers or loans.

(4) For purposes of calculating the thresholds in paragraphs (a)(1)(i) through (a)(1)(iii) of this section, the term *reference entity included in the index* includes a single reference entity included in the index or a group of affiliated reference entities included in the index as determined in accordance with paragraph (c)(1) of this section (with each reference entity included in the index that is an issuing entity of an asset-backed security as defined in section 3(a)(79) of the Act being considered a separate reference entity included in the index).

(5) For purposes of determining whether one of the criterion in either paragraphs (a)(1)(iv)(A) through (a)(1)(iv)(D) of this section or paragraphs (a)(1)(iv)(H)(*1*) and (a)(1)(iv)(H)(*2*) of this section is met, the term *reference entity included in the index* includes a single reference entity included in the index or a group of affiliated entities as determined in accordance with paragraph (c)(1) of this section (with each issuing entity of an asset-backed security as defined in section 3(a)(79) of the Act being considered a separate entity).

Rule 3a68–1b. Meaning of "narrow-based security index" as used in Section 3(a)(68)(A)(ii)(I) of the Act

(a) Notwithstanding Rule 3a68–3(a), and solely for purposes of determining whether a credit default swap is a security-based swap under section 3(a)(68)(A)(ii)(I) of the Act, the term *narrow-based security index* as used in section 3(a)(68)(A)(ii)(I) of the Act means an index in which:

(1)(i) The index is composed of nine or fewer securities or securities that are issued by nine or fewer non-affiliated issuers, provided that a security shall not be deemed a component of the index for purposes of this section unless:

(A) A credit event with respect to the issuer of such security or a credit event with respect to such security would result in a payment by the credit protection seller to the credit protection buyer under the credit default swap based on the related notional amount allocated to such security; or

(B) The fact of such credit event or the calculation in accordance with paragraph (a)(1)(i)(A) of this section of the amount owed with respect to such credit event is taken into account in determining whether to make any future payments under the credit default swap with respect to any future credit events;

(ii) The effective notional amount allocated to the securities of any issuer included in the index comprises more than 30 percent of the index's weighting;

(iii) The effective notional amount allocated to the securities of any five non-affiliated issuers included in the index comprises more than 60 percent of the index's weighting; or

(iv) Except as provided in paragraph (b) of this section, for each security included in the index none of the criteria in paragraphs (a)(1)(iv)(A) through (a)(1)(iv)(H) of this section is satisfied:

(A) The issuer of the security included in the index is required to file reports pursuant to section 13 or section 15(d) of the Act;

(B) The issuer of the security included in the index is eligible to rely on the exemption provided in Rule 12g3–2(b);

(C) The issuer of the security included in the index has a worldwide market value of its outstanding common equity held by non-affiliates of $700 million or more;

(D) The issuer of the security included in the index (other than an issuer of the security that is an issuing entity of an asset-backed security as defined in section 3(a)(79) of the Act has outstanding notes, bonds, debentures, loans, or evidences of indebtedness (other than revolving credit facilities) having a total remaining principal amount of at least $1 billion;

(E) The security included in the index is an exempted security as defined in section 3(a)(12) of the Act (other than any municipal security as defined in section 3(a)(29) of the Act);

(F) The issuer of the security included in the index is a government of a foreign country or a political subdivision of a foreign country;

(G) If the security included in the index is an asset-backed security as defined in section 3(a)(79) of the Act, the security was issued in a transaction registered under the Securities Act of 1933 and has publicly available distribution reports; and

(H) For a credit default swap entered into solely between eligible contract participants as defined in section 3(a)(65) of the Act:

(*1*) The issuer of the security included in the index (other than an issuer of the security that is an issuing entity of an asset-backed security as defined in section 3(a)(79) of the Act) makes available to the public or otherwise makes available to such eligible contract participant information about such issuer pursuant to Rule 144A(d)(4) of the Securities Act of 1933;

(*2*) Financial information about the issuer of the security included in the index (other than an issuer of the security that is an issuing entity of an asset-backed security as defined in section 3(a)(79) of the Act is otherwise publicly available; or

(*3*) In the case of an asset-backed security as defined in section 3(a)(79) of the Act, information of the type and level included in public distribution reports for similar asset-backed securities is publicly available about both the issuing entity and such asset-backed security; and

(2)(i) The index is not composed solely of exempted securities as defined in section 3(a)(12) of the Act, as in effect on the date of enactment of the Futures Trading Act of 1982 (other than any municipal security as defined in section 3(a)(29) of the Act, as in effect on the date of enactment of the Futures Trading Act of 1982); and

(ii) Without taking into account any portion of the index composed of exempted securities as defined in section 3(a)(12) of the Act, as in effect on the date of enactment of the Futures Trading Act of 1982 (other than any municipal security as defined in section 3(a)(29) of the Act, the remaining portion of the index would be within the term "narrow-based security index" under paragraph (a)(1) of this section.

(b) Paragraph (a)(1)(iv) of this section will not apply with respect to securities of an issuer included in the index if:

(1) The effective notional amounts allocated to all securities of such issuer included in the index comprise less than five percent of the index's weighting; and

(2) The securities that satisfy paragraph (a)(1)(iv) of this section comprise at least 80 percent of the index's weighting.

(c) For purposes of this section:

(1) An issuer of securities included in the index is affiliated with another issuer of securities included in the index (for purposes of paragraph (c)(4) of this section) or another entity (for purposes of paragraph (c)(5) of this section) if it controls, is controlled by, or is under common control with, that other issuer or other entity, as applicable; provided that each issuer of securities included

in the index that is an issuing entity of an asset-backed security as defined in section 3(a)(79) of the Act will not be considered affiliated with any other issuer of securities included in the index or any other entity that is an issuing entity of an asset-backed security.

(2) Control for purposes of this section means ownership of more than 50 percent of the equity of an issuer of securities included in the index (for purposes of paragraph (c)(4) of this section) or another entity (for purposes of paragraph (c)(5) of this section), or the ability to direct the voting of more than 50 percent of the voting equity an issuer of securities included in the index (for purposes of paragraph (c)(4) of this section) or another entity (for purposes of paragraph (c)(5) of this section).

(3) In identifying an issuer of securities included in the index for purposes of this section, the term *issuer* includes:

(i) An issuer of securities; and

(ii) An issuer of securities that is an issuing entity of an asset-backed security as defined in section 3(a)(79) of the Act.

(4) For purposes of calculating the thresholds in paragraphs (a)(1)(i) through (a)(1)(iii) of this section, the term *issuer of the security included in the index* includes a single issuer of securities included in the index or a group of affiliated issuers of securities included in the index as determined in accordance with paragraph (c)(1) of this section (with each issuer of securities included in the index that is an issuing entity of an asset-backed security as defined in section 3(a)(79) of the Act being considered a separate issuer of securities included in the index).

(5) For purposes of determining whether one of the criterion in either paragraphs (a)(1)(iv)(A) through (a)(1)(iv)(D) of this section or paragraphs (a)(1)(iv)(H)(*1*) and (a)(1)(iv)(H)(*2*) of this section is met, the term *issuer of the security included in the index* includes a single issuer of securities included in the index or a group affiliated entities as determined in accordance with paragraph (c)(1) of this section (with each issuing entity of an asset-backed security as defined in section 3(a)(79) of the Act being considered a separate entity).

Rule 3a68–2. Requests for interpretation of swaps, security-based swaps, and mixed swaps

(a) *In General.* Any person may submit a request to the Commission and the Commodity Futures Trading Commission to provide a joint interpretation of whether a particular agreement, contract, or transaction (or class thereof) is:

(1) A swap, as that term is defined in section 3(a)(69) of the Act and the rules and regulations promulgated thereunder;

(2) A security-based swap, as that term is defined in section 3(a)(68) of the Act and the rules and regulations promulgated thereunder; or

(3) A mixed swap, as that term is defined in section 3(a)(68)(D) of the Act and the rules and regulations promulgated thereunder.

(b) *Request Process.* In making a request pursuant to paragraph (a) of this section, the requesting person must provide the Commission and the Commodity Futures Trading Commission with the following:

(1) All material information regarding the terms of the agreement, contract, or transaction (or class thereof);

(2) A statement of the economic characteristics and purpose of the agreement, contract, or transaction (or class thereof);

(3) The requesting person's determination as to whether the agreement, contract, or transaction (or class thereof) should be characterized as a swap, a security-based swap, or both (i.e., a mixed swap), including the basis for such determination; and

(4) Such other information as may be requested by the Commission or the Commodity Futures Trading Commission.

(c) *Request Withdrawal.* A person may withdraw a request made pursuant to paragraph (a) of this section at any time prior to the issuance of a joint interpretation or joint proposed rule by the Commission and the Commodity Futures Trading Commission in response to the request; provided, however, that notwithstanding such withdrawal, the Commission and the Commodity Futures Trading Commission may provide a joint interpretation of whether the agreement, contract, or transaction (or class thereof) is a swap, a security-based swap, or both (i.e., a mixed swap).

(d) *Request by the Commission or the Commodity Futures Trading Commission.* In the absence of a request for a joint interpretation under paragraph (a) of this section:

(1) If the Commission or the Commodity Futures Trading Commission receives a proposal to list, trade, or clear an agreement, contract, or trans-

action (or class thereof) that raises questions as to the appropriate characterization of such agreement, contract, or transaction (or class thereof) as a swap, a security-based swap, or both (i.e., a mixed swap), the Commission or the Commodity Futures Trading Commission, as applicable, promptly shall notify the other of the agreement, contract, or transaction (or class thereof); and

(2) The Commission or the Commodity Futures Trading Commission, or their Chairmen jointly, may submit a request for a joint interpretation as described in paragraph (a) of this section; such submission shall be made pursuant to paragraph (b) of this section, and may be withdrawn pursuant to paragraph (c) of this section.

(e) *Timeframe for Joint Interpretation.*

(1) If the Commission and the Commodity Futures Trading Commission determine to issue a joint interpretation as described in paragraph (a) of this section, such joint interpretation shall be issued within 120 days after receipt of a complete submission requesting a joint interpretation under paragraph (a) or (d) of this section.

(2) The Commission and the Commodity Futures Trading Commission shall consult with the Board of Governors of the Federal Reserve System prior to issuing any joint interpretation as described in paragraph (a) of this section.

(3) If the Commission and the Commodity Futures Trading Commission seek public comment with respect to a joint interpretation regarding an agreement, contract, or transaction (or class thereof), the 120–day period described in paragraph (e)(1) of this section shall be stayed during the pendency of the comment period, but shall recommence with the business day after the public comment period ends.

(4) Nothing in this section shall require the Commission and the Commodity Futures Trading Commission to issue any joint interpretation.

(5) If the Commission and the Commodity Futures Trading Commission do not issue a joint interpretation within the time period described in paragraph (e)(1) or (e)(3) of this section, each of the Commission and the Commodity Futures Trading Commission shall publicly provide the reasons for not issuing such a joint interpretation within the applicable timeframes.

(f) *Joint Proposed Rule.*

(1) Rather than issue a joint interpretation pursuant to paragraph (a) of this section, the Commission and the Commodity Futures Trading Commission may issue a joint proposed rule, in consultation with the Board of Governors of the Federal Reserve System, to further define one or more of the terms swap, security-based swap, or mixed swap.

(2) A joint proposed rule described in paragraph (f)(1) of this section shall be issued within the timeframe for issuing a joint interpretation set forth in paragraph (e) of this section.

Rule 3a68–3. Meaning of "narrow–based security index" as used in the definition of "security–based swap"

(a) *In General.* Except as otherwise provided in Rule 3a68–1a and Rule 3a68–1b, for purposes of section 3(a)(68) of the Act, the term *narrow-based security index* has the meaning set forth in section 3(a)(55) of the Act, and the rules, regulations, and orders of the Commission thereunder.

(b) *Tolerance Period for Swaps Traded on Designated Contract Markets, Swap Execution Facilities and Foreign Boards of Trade.* Notwithstanding paragraph (a) of this section, solely for purposes of swaps traded on or subject to the rules of a designated contract market, swap execution facility, or foreign board of trade pursuant to the Commodity Exchange Act, a security index underlying such swaps shall not be considered a narrow-based security index if:

(1)(i) A swap on the index is traded on or subject to the rules of a designated contract market, swap execution facility, or foreign board of trade pursuant to the Commodity Exchange Act for at least 30 days as a swap on an index that was not a narrow-based security index; or

(ii) Such index was not a narrow-based security index during every trading day of the six full calendar months preceding a date no earlier than 30 days prior to the commencement of trading of a swap on such index on a market described in paragraph (b)(1)(i) of this section; and

(2) The index has been a narrow-based security index for no more than 45 business days over three consecutive calendar months.

(c) *Tolerance Period for Security–Based Swaps Traded on National Securities Exchanges or Security–Based Swap Execution Facilities.* Notwithstanding paragraph (a) of this section, solely for purposes of security-based swaps traded on a national securities exchange or security-based swap execution facility, a security index underlying such security-based swaps shall be considered a narrow-based security index if:

(1)(i) A security-based swap on the index is traded on a national securities exchange or security-based swap execution facility for at least 30 days as a security-based swap on narrow-based security index; or

(ii) Such index was a narrow-based security index during every trading day of the six full calendar months preceding a date no earlier than 30 days prior to the commencement of trading of a security-based swap on such index on a market described in paragraph (c)(1)(i) of this section; and

(2) The index has been a security index that is not a narrow-based security index for no more than 45 business days over three consecutive calendar months.

(d) *Grace Period.*

(1) Solely with respect to a swap that is traded on or subject to the rules of a designated contract market, swap execution facility or foreign board of trade pursuant to the Commodity Exchange Act, an index that becomes a narrow-based security index under paragraph (b) of this section solely because it was a narrow-based security index for more than 45 business days over three consecutive calendar months shall not be a narrow-based security index for the following three calendar months.

(2) Solely with respect to a security-based swap that is traded on a national securities exchange or security-based swap execution facility, an index that becomes a security index that is not a narrow-based security index under paragraph (yyy)(3) of this section solely because it was not a narrow-based security index for more than 45 business days over three consecutive calendar months shall be a narrow-based security index for the following three calendar months.

Rule 3a68–4. Regulation of mixed swaps

(a) *In General.* The term mixed swap has the meaning set forth in section 3(a)(68)(D) of the Act.

(b) *Regulation of Bilateral Uncleared Mixed Swaps Entered Into by Dually–Registered Dealers or Major Participants.* A mixed swap:

(1) That is neither executed on nor subject to the rules of a designated contract market, national securities exchange, swap execution facility, security-based swap execution facility, or foreign board of trade;

(2) That will not be submitted to a derivatives clearing organization or registered or exempt clearing agency to be cleared; and

(3) Where at least one party is registered with the Commission as a security-based swap dealer or major security-based swap participant and also with the Commodity Futures Trading Commission as a swap dealer or major swap participant, shall be subject to:

(i) The following provisions of the Commodity Exchange Act, and the rules and regulations promulgated thereunder, set forth in the rules and regulations of the Commodity Futures Trading Commission:

(A) Examinations and information sharing: 7 U.S.C. 6s(f) and 12;

(B) Enforcement: 7 U.S.C. 2(a)(1)(B), 6(b), 6b, 6c, 6s(h)(1)(A), 6s(h)(4)(A), 9, 13b, 13a–1, 13a–2, 13, 13c(a), 13c(b), 15 and 26;

(C) Reporting to a swap data repository: 7 U.S.C. 6r;

(D) Real-time reporting: 7 U.S.C. 2(a)(13);

(E) Capital: 7 U.S.C. 6s(e); and

(F) Position Limits: 7 U.S.C. 6a; and

(ii) The provisions of the federal securities laws, as defined in section 3(a)(47) of the Act, and the rules and regulations promulgated thereunder.

(c) *Process for Determining Regulatory Treatment for Other Mixed Swaps.*

(1) *In General.* Any person who desires or intends to list, trade, or clear a mixed swap (or class thereof) that is not subject to paragraph (b) of this section may request the Commission and the Commodity Futures Trading Commission to issue a joint order permitting the requesting person (and any other person or persons that subsequently lists, trades, or clears that mixed swap) to comply, as to parallel provisions only, with specified parallel provisions of either the Act or the Commodity Exchange Act, and the rules and regulations thereunder (collectively, *specified parallel provisions*), instead of being required to comply with parallel provisions of both the Act and the Commodity Exchange Act. For purposes of this paragraph (c), *parallel provisions* means comparable provisions of the Act and the Commodity Exchange Act that were added or amended by the Wall Street Transparency and Accountability Act

of 2010 with respect to security-based swaps and swaps, and the rules and regulations thereunder.

(2) *Request Process.* A person submitting a request pursuant to paragraph (c)(1) of this section must provide the Commission and the Commodity Futures Trading Commission with the following:

(i) All material information regarding the terms of the specified, or specified class of, mixed swap;

(ii) The economic characteristics and purpose of the specified, or specified class of, mixed swap;

(iii) The specified parallel provisions, and the reasons the person believes such specified parallel provisions would be appropriate for the mixed swap (or class thereof); and

(iv) An analysis of:

(A) The nature and purposes of the parallel provisions that are the subject of the request;

(B) The comparability of such parallel provisions;

(C) The extent of any conflicts or differences between such parallel provisions; and

(D) Such other information as may be requested by the Commission or the Commodity Futures Trading Commission.

(3) *Request Withdrawal.* A person may withdraw a request made pursuant to paragraph (c)(1) of this section at any time prior to the issuance of a joint order under paragraph (c)(4) of this section by the Commission and the Commodity Futures Trading Commission in response to the request.

(4) *Issuance of Orders.* In response to a request under paragraph (c)(1) of this section, the Commission and the Commodity Futures Trading Commission, as necessary to carry out the purposes of the Wall Street Transparency and Accountability Act of 2010, may issue a joint order, after notice and opportunity for comment, permitting the requesting person (and any other person or persons that subsequently lists, trades, or clears that mixed swap) to comply, as to parallel provisions only, with the specified parallel provisions (or another subset of the parallel provisions that are the subject of the request, as the Commissions determine is appropriate), instead of being required to comply with parallel provisions of both the Act and the Commodity Exchange Act. In determining the contents of such joint order, the Commission and the Commodity Futures Trading Commission may consider, among other things:

(i) The nature and purposes of the parallel provisions that are the subject of the request;

(ii) The comparability of such parallel provisions; and

(iii) The extent of any conflicts or differences between such parallel provisions.

(5) *Timeframe.*

(i) If the Commission and the Commodity Futures Trading Commission determine to issue a joint order as described in paragraph (c)(4) of this section, such joint order shall be issued within 120 days after receipt of a complete request for a joint order under paragraph (c)(1) of this section, which time period shall be stayed during the pendency of the public comment period provided for in paragraph (c)(4) of this section and shall recommence with the business day after the public comment period ends.

(ii) Nothing in this section shall require the Commission and the Commodity Futures Trading Commission to issue any joint order.

(iii) If the Commission and the Commodity Futures Trading Commission do not issue a joint order within the time period described in paragraph (c)(5)(i) of this section, each of the Commission and the Commodity Futures Trading Commission shall publicly provide the reasons for not issuing such a joint order within that timeframe.

Rule 3a68–5. Regulation of certain futures contracts on foreign sovereign debt

Futures contracts on certain foreign sovereign debt. The term *security-based swap* as used in section 3(a)(68) of the Act does not include an agreement, contract, or transaction that is based on or references a qualifying foreign futures contract (as defined in Rule 3a12–8 on the debt securities of any one or more of the foreign governments enumerated in Rule 3a12–8, provided that such agreement, contract, or transaction satisfies the following conditions:

(a) The futures contract that the agreement, contract, or transaction references or upon which the agreement, contract, or transaction is based is a qualifying foreign futures contract that satisfies the conditions of Rule 3a12–8 applicable to qualifying foreign futures contracts;

(b) The agreement, contract, or transaction is traded on or through a board of trade (as defined in 7 U.S.C. 2);

(c) The debt securities upon which the qualifying foreign futures contract is based or referenced and any security used to determine the cash settlement amount pursuant to paragraph (4) of this section were not registered under the Securities Act of 1933 or the subject of any American depositary receipt registered under the Securities Act of 1933;

(d) The agreement, contract, or transaction may only be cash settled; and

(e) The agreement, contract or transaction is not entered into by the issuer of the debt securities upon which the qualifying foreign futures contract is based or referenced (including any security used to determine the cash payment due on settlement of such agreement, contract or transaction), an affiliate (as defined in the Securities Act of 1933 and the rules and regulations thereunder) of the issuer, or an underwriter of such issuer's debt securities.

Rule 3a69-1. Safe harbor definition of "security-based swap" and "swap" as used in Sections 3(a)(68) and 3(a)(69) of the Act—insurance

(a) This paragraph is a non-exclusive safe harbor. The terms *security-based swap* as used in section 3(a)(68) of the Act and *swap* as used in section 3(a)(69) of the Act do not include an agreement, contract, or transaction that:

(1) By its terms or by law, as a condition of performance on the agreement, contract, or transaction:

(i) Requires the beneficiary of the agreement, contract, or transaction to have an insurable interest that is the subject of the agreement, contract, or transaction and thereby carry the risk of loss with respect to that interest continuously throughout the duration of the agreement, contract, or transaction;

(ii) Requires that loss to occur and to be proved, and that any payment or indemnification therefor be limited to the value of the insurable interest;

(iii) Is not traded, separately from the insured interest, on an organized market or over the counter; and

(iv) With respect to financial guaranty insurance only, in the event of payment default or insolvency of the obligor, any acceleration of payments under the policy is at the sole discretion of the insurer; and

(2) Is provided:

(i)(A) By a person that is subject to supervision by the insurance commissioner (or similar official or agency) of any State, as defined in section 3(a)(16) of the Act, or by the United States or an agency or instrumentality thereof; and

(B) Such agreement, contract, or transaction is regulated as insurance under applicable State law or the laws of the United States;

(ii)(A) Directly or indirectly by the United States, any State or any of their respective agencies or instrumentalities; or

(B) Pursuant to a statutorily authorized program thereof; or

(iii) In the case of reinsurance only by a person to another person that satisfies the conditions set forth in paragraph (a)(2) of this section, provided that:

(A) Such person is not prohibited by applicable State law or the laws of the United States from offering such agreement, contract, or transaction to such person that satisfies the conditions set forth in paragraph (a)(2) of this section;

(B) The agreement, contract, or transaction to be reinsured satisfies the conditions set forth in paragraph (a)(1) or (3) of this section; and

(C) Except as otherwise permitted under applicable State law, the total amount reimbursable by all reinsurers for such agreement, contract, or transaction may not exceed the claims or losses paid by the person writing the risk being ceded or transferred by such person; or

(iv) In the case of non-admitted insurance by a person who:

(A) Is located outside of the United States and listed on the Quarterly Listing of Alien Insurers as maintained by the International Insurers Department of the National Association of Insurance Commissioners; or

(B) Meets the eligibility criteria for non-admitted insurers under applicable State law; or

(3) Is provided in accordance with the conditions set forth in paragraph (a)(2) of this section and is one of the following types of products:

(i) surety bond;

(ii) fidelity bond;

(iii) life insurance;

(iv) health insurance;

(v) long term care insurance;

(vi) title insurance;

(vii) property and casualty insurance;

(viii) annuity;

(ix) disability insurance;

(x) insurance against default on individual residential mortgages; and

(xi) reinsurance of any of the foregoing products identified in paragraphs (i) through (x) of this section.

(b) The terms security-based swap as used in section 3(a)(68) of the Act and swap as used in section 3(a)(69) of the Act do not include an agreement, contract, or transaction that was entered into on or before the effective date of this section and that, at such time that it was entered into, was provided in accordance with the conditions set forth in paragraph (a)(2) of this section.

Rule 3a69–2. Definition of "swap" as used in Section 3(a)(69) of the Act—additional products

(a) *In General.* The term *swap* has the meaning set forth in section 3(a)(69) of the Act.

(b) *Inclusion of Particular Products.*

(1) The term *swap* includes, without limiting the meaning set forth in section 3(a)(69) of the Act, the following agreements, contracts, and transactions:

(i) A cross-currency swap;

(ii) A currency option, foreign currency option, foreign exchange option and foreign exchange rate option;

(iii) A foreign exchange forward;

(iv) A foreign exchange swap;

(v) A forward rate agreement; and

(vi) A non-deliverable forward involving foreign exchange.

(2) The term *swap* does not include an agreement, contract, or transaction described in paragraph (b)(1) of this section that is otherwise excluded by section 1a(47)(B) of the Commodity Exchange Act.

(c) *Foreign Exchange Forwards and Foreign Exchange Swaps.* Notwithstanding paragraph (b)(2) of this section:

(1) A foreign exchange forward or a foreign exchange swap shall not be considered a swap if the Secretary of the Treasury makes a determination described in section 1a(47)(E)(i) of the Commodity Exchange Act.

(2) Notwithstanding paragraph (c)(1) of this section:

(i) The reporting requirements set forth in section 4r of the Commodity Exchange Act and regulations promulgated thereunder shall apply to a foreign exchange forward or foreign exchange swap; and

(ii) The business conduct standards set forth in section 4s(h) of the Commodity Exchange Act and regulations promulgated thereunder shall apply to a swap dealer or major swap participant that is a party to a foreign exchange forward or foreign exchange swap.

(3) For purposes of section 1a(47)(E) of the Commodity Exchange Act and this section, the term *foreign exchange forward* has the meaning set forth in section 1a(24) of the Commodity Exchange Act.

(4) For purposes of section 1a(47)(E) of the Commodity Exchange Act and this section, the term *foreign exchange swap* has the meaning set forth in section 1a(25) of the Commodity Exchange Act.

(5) For purposes of sections 1a(24) and 1a(25) of the Commodity Exchange Act and this section, the following transactions are not foreign exchange forwards or foreign exchange swaps:

(i) A currency swap or a cross-currency swap;

(ii) A currency option, foreign currency option, foreign exchange option, or foreign exchange rate option; and

(iii) A non-deliverable forward involving foreign exchange.

Rule 3a69–3. Books and records requirements for security–based swap agreements

(a) A person registered as a swap data repository under section 21 of the Commodity Exchange Act and the rules and regulations thereunder:

(1) Shall not be required to keep and maintain additional books and records regarding security-based swap agreements other than the books

and records regarding swaps required to be kept and maintained pursuant to section 21 of the Commodity Exchange Act and the rules and regulations thereunder; and

(2) Shall not be required to collect and maintain additional data regarding security-based swap agreements other than the data regarding swaps required to be collected and maintained by such persons pursuant to section 21 of the Commodity Exchange Act and the rules and regulations thereunder.

(b) A person shall not be required to keep and maintain additional books and records, including daily trading records, regarding security-based swap agreements other than the books and records regarding swaps required to be kept and maintained by such persons pursuant to section 4s of the Commodity Exchange Act and the rules and regulations thereunder if such person is registered as:

(1) A swap dealer under section 4s(a)(1) of the Commodity Exchange Act and the rules and regulations thereunder;

(2) A major swap participant under section 4s(a)(2) of the Commodity Exchange Act and the rules and regulations thereunder;

(3) A security-based swap dealer under section 15F(a)(1) of the Act and the rules and regulations thereunder; or

(4) A major security-based swap participant under section 15F(a)(2) of the Act and the rules and regulations thereunder.

(c) The term *security-based swap* agreement has the meaning set forth in section 3(a)(78) of the Act.

Rule 3a71–1. Definition of "security-based swap dealer"

(a) *General.* The term *security-based swap dealer* in general means any person who:

(1) Holds itself out as a dealer in security-based swaps;

(2) Makes a market in security-based swaps;

(3) Regularly enters into security-based swaps with counterparties as an ordinary course of business for its own account; or

(4) Engages in any activity causing it to be commonly known in the trade as a dealer or market maker in security-based swaps.

(b) *Exception.* The term security-based swap dealer does not include a person that enters into security-based swaps for such person's own account, either individually or in a fiduciary capacity, but not as a part of regular business.

(c) *Scope of Designation.* A person that is a security-based swap dealer in general shall be deemed to be a security-based swap dealer with respect to each security-based swap it enters into, regardless of the type, class, or category of the security-based swap or the person's activities in connection with the security-based swap, unless the Commission limits the person's designation as a security-based swap dealer to specified types, classes, or categories of security-based swaps or specified activities of the person in connection with security-based swaps.

(d) *Inter-Affiliate Activities.*

(1) *General.* In determining whether a person is a security-based swap dealer, that person's security-based swaps with majority-owned affiliates shall not be considered.

(2) *Meaning of Majority-Owned.* For these purposes the counterparties to a security-based swap are majority-owned affiliates if one counterparty directly or indirectly owns a majority interest in the other, or if a third party directly or indirectly owns a majority interest in both counterparties to the security-based swap, where "majority interest" is the right to vote or direct the vote of a majority of a class of voting securities of an entity, the power to sell or direct the sale of a majority of a class of voting securities of an entity, or the right to receive upon dissolution or the contribution of a majority of the capital of a partnership.

Rule 3a71–2. De minimis exception

(a) *Requirements.* For purposes of section 3(a)(71) of the Act (15 U.S.C. 78c(a)(71)) and Rule 3a71–1, a person that is not currently registered as a security-based swap dealer shall be deemed not to be a security-based swap dealer, and, therefore, shall not be subject to section 15F of the Act and the rules, regulations and interpretations issued thereunder, as a result of security-based swap dealing activity that meets the following conditions:

(1) *Notional Thresholds.* The security-based swap positions connected with the dealing activity in which the person—or any other entity controlling, controlled by or under common control with the person—engages over the course of the immediately preceding 12 months (or following the effective date of final rules implementing section 3(a)(68) of the Act) if that period is less than 12 months) have:

(i) An aggregate gross notional amount of no more than $3 billion, subject to a phase-in level of an aggregate gross notional amount of no more than $8 billion applied in accordance with paragraph (a)(2)(i) of this section, with regard to credit default swaps that constitute security-based swaps;

(ii) An aggregate gross notional amount of no more than $150 million, subject to a phase-in level of an aggregate gross notional amount of no more than $400 million applied in accordance with paragraph (a)(2)(i) of this section, with regard to security-based swaps not described in paragraph (a)(1)(i) of this section; and

(iii) An aggregate gross notional amount of no more than $25 million with regard to all security-based swaps in which the counterparty is a special entity (as that term is defined in section 15F(h)(2)(C) of the Act).

(2) *Phase-In Procedure.*

(i) *Phase-In Period.* For purposes of paragraphs (a)(1)(i) and (a)(1)(ii) of this section, a person that engages in security-based swap dealing activity that does not exceed either of the phase-in levels set forth in paragraphs (a)(1)(i) and (a)(1)(ii) of this section, as applicable, shall be deemed not to be a security-based swap dealer, and, therefore, shall not be subject to Section 15F of the Act and the rules, regulations and interpretations issued thereunder, as a result of its security-based swap dealing activity, until the "phase-in termination date" established as provided in paragraph (a)(2)(ii) of this section; provided, however, that this phase-in period shall not be available to the extent that a person engages in security-based swap dealing activity with counterparties that are natural persons, other than natural persons who qualify as eligible contract participants by virtue of section 1a(18)(A)(xi)(II) of the Commodity Exchange Act, (7 U.S.C. 1a(18)(A)(xi)(II)). The Commission shall announce the phase-in termination date on the Commission website and publish such date in the *Federal Register*.

(ii) *Establishment of Phase-In Termination Date.*

(A) Nine months after the publication of the staff report described in Appendix A of this section, and after giving due consideration to that report and any associated public comment, the Commission may either:

(*1*) Terminate the phase-in period set forth in paragraph (a)(2)(i) of this section, in which case the phase-in termination date shall be established by the Commission by order published in the Federal Register; or

(*2*) Determine that it is necessary or appropriate in the public interest to propose through rulemaking an alternative to the $3 billion and $150 million amounts set forth in paragraphs (a)(1)(i) and (a)(1)(ii) of this section, as applicable, that would constitute a de minimis quantity of security-based swap dealing in connection with transactions with or on behalf of customers within the meaning of section 3(a)(71)(D) of the Act, (15 U.S.C. 78c(a)(71)(D)), in which case the Commission shall by order published in the Federal Register provide notice of such determination to propose through rulemaking an alternative, which order shall also establish the phase-in termination date.

(B) If the phase-in termination date has not been previously established pursuant to paragraph (a)(2)(ii)(A) of this section, then in any event the phase-in termination date shall occur five years after the data collection initiation date defined in paragraph (a)(2)(iii) of this section.

(iii) *Data Collection Initiation Date.* The term "*data collection initiation date*" shall mean the date that is the later of: the last compliance date for the registration and regulatory requirements for security-based swap dealers and major security-based swap participants under Section 15F of the Act; or the first date on which compliance with the trade-by-trade reporting rules for credit-related and equity-related security-based swaps to a registered security-based swap data repository is required. The Commission shall announce the data collection initiation date on the Commission website and publish such date in the *Federal Register*.

(3) *Use of Effective Notional Amounts.* For purposes of paragraph (a)(1) of this section, if the stated notional amount of a security-based swap is leveraged or enhanced by the structure of the security-based swap, the calculation shall be based on the effective notional amount of the security-based swap rather than on the stated notional amount.

(b) *Registration Period for Persons that no Longer can Take Advantage of the Exception.* A person that has not registered as a security-based swap dealer by virtue of satisfying the requirements of paragraph (a) of this section, but that no longer can take advantage of the de minimis exception provided for in paragraph (a) of this section, will be deemed not to be a security-based swap dealer under section 3(a)(71) of the Act and subject to the requirements of section 15F of the Act and the rules, regulations and interpretations issued thereunder until the earlier of the date on which it submits a complete application for registration pursuant to section 15F(b) or two months after the end of the month in which that person becomes no longer able to take advantage of the exception.

(c) *Applicability to Registered Security-Based Swap Dealers.* A person who currently is registered as a security-based swap dealer may apply to withdraw that registration, while continuing to engage in security-based swap dealing activity in reliance on this section, so long as that person has been registered as a security-based swap dealer for at least 12 months and satisfies the conditions of paragraph (a) of this section.

(d) *Future Adjustments to Scope of the De Minimis Exception.* The Commission may by rule or regulation change the requirements of the de minimis exception described in paragraphs (a) through (c) of this section.

(e) *Voluntary Registration.* Notwithstanding paragraph (a) of this section, a person that chooses to register with the Commission as a security-based swap dealer shall be deemed to be a security-based swap dealer, and, therefore, shall be subject to Section 15F of the Act and the rules, regulations and interpretations issued thereunder.

Rule 3a71–2A. Report regarding the "security-based swap dealer" and "major security-based swap participant" definitions (Appendix A to Rule 3a71–2)

Appendix A to Rule 3a71–2 sets forth guidelines applicable to a report that the Commission has directed its staff to make in connection with the rules and interpretations further defining the Act's definitions of the terms "security-based swap dealer" (including the de minimis exception to that definition) and "major security-based swap participant." The Commission intends to consider this report in reviewing the effect and application of these rules based on the evolution of the security-based swap market following the implementation of the registration and regulatory requirements of Section 15F of the Act. The report may also be informative as to potential changes to the rules further defining those terms. In producing this report, the staff shall consider security-based swap data collected by the Commission pursuant to other Title VII rules, as well as any other applicable information as the staff may determine to be appropriate for its analysis.

(a) *Report Topics.* As appropriate, based on the availability of data and information, the report should address the following topics:

(1) *De Minimis Exception.* In connection with the de minimis exception to the definition of "security-based swap dealer," the report generally should assess whether any of the de minimis thresholds set forth in paragraph (a)(1) of Rule 3a71–2 should be increased or decreased;

(2) *General Security-Based Swap Dealer Analysis.* In connection with the definition of "security-based swap dealer," the report generally should consider the factors that are useful for identifying security-based swap dealing activity, including the application of the dealer-trader distinction for that purpose, and the potential use of more objective tests or safe harbors as part of the analysis;

(3) *General Major Security-Based Swap Participant Analysis.* In connection with the definition of "major security-based swap participant," the report generally should consider the tests used to identify the presence of a "substantial position" in a major category of security-based swaps, and the tests used to identify persons whose security-based swap positions create "substantial counterparty exposure," including the potential use of alternative tests or thresholds;

(4) *Commercial Risk Hedging Exclusion.* In connection with the definition of "major security-based swap participant," the report generally should consider the definition of "hedging or mitigating commercial risk," including whether that latter definition inappropriately permits certain positions to be excluded from the "substantial position" analysis, and whether the continued availability of the exclusion for such hedging positions should be conditioned on a person assessing and documenting the hedging effectiveness of those positions;

(5) *Highly Leveraged Financial Entities.* In connection with the definition of "major security-based swap participant," the report generally should consider the definition of "highly leveraged," including whether alternative approaches should be used to identify highly leveraged financial entities;

(6) *Inter-Affiliate Exclusions.* In connection with the definitions of "security-based swap dealer" and "major security-based swap participant,"

the report generally should consider the impact of rule provisions excluding inter-affiliate transactions from the relevant analyses, and should assess potential alternative approaches for such exclusions; and

(7) *Other Topics.* Any other analysis of security-based swap data and information the Commission or the staff deem relevant to this rule.

(b) *Timing of Report.* The report shall be completed no later than three years following the data collection initiation date, established pursuant to Rule 3a71-2(a)(2)(iii).

(c) *Public Comment on the Report.* Following completion of the report, the report shall be published in the Federal Register for public comment.

Rule 3a71-3. Cross-border security-based swap dealing activity

(a) *Definitions.* As used in this section, the following terms shall have the meanings indicated:

(1) *Conduit Affiliate*—

(i) *Definition. Conduit affiliate* means a person, other than a U.S. person, that:

(A) Is directly or indirectly majority-owned by one or more U.S. persons; and

(B) In the regular course of business enters into security-based swaps with one or more other non-U.S. persons, or with foreign branches of U.S. banks that are registered as security-based swap dealers, for the purpose of hedging or mitigating risks faced by, or otherwise taking positions on behalf of, one or more U.S. persons (other than U.S. persons that are registered as security-based swap dealers or major security-based swap participants) who are controlling, controlled by, or under common control with the person, and enters into offsetting security-based swaps or other arrangements with such U.S. persons to transfer risks and benefits of those security-based swaps.

(ii) *Majority-Ownership Standard.* The majority-ownership standard in paragraph (a)(1)(i)(A) of this section is satisfied if one or more persons described in Rule 3a71-3(a)(4)(i)(B) directly or indirectly own a majority interest in the non-U.S. person, where "majority interest" is the right to vote or direct the vote of a majority of a class of voting securities of an entity, the power to sell or direct the sale of a majority of a class of voting securities of an entity, or the right to receive upon dissolution, or the contribution of, a majority of the capital of a partnership.

(2) *Foreign branch* means any branch of a U.S. bank if:

(i) The branch is located outside the United States;

(ii) The branch operates for valid business reasons; and

(iii) The branch is engaged in the business of banking and is subject to substantive banking regulation in the jurisdiction where located.

(3) *Transaction Conducted Through a Foreign Branch*—

(i) *Definition. Transaction conducted through a foreign branch* means a security-based swap transaction that is arranged, negotiated, and executed by a U.S. person through a foreign branch of such U.S. person if:

(A) The foreign branch is the counterparty to such security-based swap transaction; and

(B) The security-based swap transaction is arranged, negotiated, and executed on behalf of the foreign branch solely by persons located outside the United States.

(ii) *Representations.* A person shall not be required to consider its counterparty's activity in connection with paragraph (a)(3)(i)(B) of this section in determining whether a security-based swap transaction is a transaction conducted through a foreign branch if such person receives a representation from its counterparty that the security-based swap transaction is arranged, negotiated, and executed on behalf of the foreign branch solely by persons located outside the United States, unless such person knows or has reason to know that the representation is not accurate; for the purposes of this final rule a person would have reason to know the representation is not accurate if a reasonable person should know, under all of the facts of which the person is aware, that it is not accurate.

(4) *U.S. Person*—

(i) Except as provided in paragraph (a)(4)(iii) of this section, *U.S. person* means any person that is:

(A) A natural person resident in the United States;

(B) A partnership, corporation, trust, investment vehicle, or other legal person organized, incorporated, or established under the laws of the United States or having its principal place of business in the United States;

(C) An account (whether discretionary or non-discretionary) of a U.S. person; or

(D) An estate of a decedent who was a resident of the United States at the time of death.

(ii) For purposes of this section, *principal place of business* means the location from which the officers, partners, or managers of the legal person primarily direct, control, and coordinate the activities of the legal person. With respect to an externally managed investment vehicle, this location is the office from which the manager of the vehicle primarily directs, controls, and coordinates the investment activities of the vehicle.

(iii) The term *U.S. person* does not include the International Monetary Fund, the International Bank for Reconstruction and Development, the Inter-American Development Bank, the Asian Development Bank, the African Development Bank, the United Nations, and their agencies and pension plans, and any other similar international organizations, their agencies and pension plans.

(iv) A person shall not be required to consider its counterparty to a security-based swap to be a U.S. person if such person receives a representation from the counterparty that the counterparty does not satisfy the criteria set forth in paragraph (a)(4)(i) of this section, unless such person knows or has reason to know that the representation is not accurate; for the purposes of this final rule a person would have reason to know the representation is not accurate if a reasonable person should know, under all of the facts of which the person is aware, that it is not accurate.

(5) *United States* means the United States of America, its territories and possessions, any State of the United States, and the District of Columbia.

(6) *U.S. security-based swap dealer* means a security-based swap dealer, as defined in section 3(a)(71) of the Act (15 U.S.C. 78c(a)(71)), and the rules and regulations thereunder, that is a U.S. person.

(7) *Foreign security-based swap dealer* means a security-based swap dealer, as defined in section 3(a)(71) of the Act (15 U.S.C. 78c(a)(71)), and the rules and regulations thereunder, that is not a U.S. person.

(8) *U.S. business* means:

(i) With respect to a foreign security-based swap dealer:

(A) Any security-based swap transaction entered into, or offered to be entered into, by or on behalf of such foreign security-based swap dealer, with a U.S. person (other than a transaction conducted through a foreign branch of that person); or

(B) Any security-based swap transaction arranged, negotiated, or executed by personnel of the foreign security-based swap dealer located in a U.S. branch or office, or by personnel of an agent of the foreign security-based swap dealer located in a U.S. branch or office; and

(ii) With respect to a U.S. security-based swap dealer, any transaction entered into or offered to be entered into by or on behalf of such U.S. security-based swap dealer, other than a transaction conducted through a foreign branch with a non-U.S. person or with a U.S.-person counterparty that constitutes a transaction conducted through a foreign branch of the counterparty.

(9) *Foreign business* means security-based swap transactions entered into, or offered to be entered into, by or on behalf of a security-based swap dealer, other than the U.S. business of such person.

(b) *Application of De Minimis Exception to Cross-Border Dealing Activity*. For purposes of calculating the amount of security-based swap positions connected with dealing activity under Rule 3a71–2(a)(1), except as provided in Rule 3a71–5, a person shall include the following security-based swap transactions:

(1)(i) If such a person is a U.S. person, all security-based swap transactions connected with the dealing activity in which such person engages, including transactions conducted through a foreign branch;

(ii) If such person is a conduit affiliate, all security-based swap transactions connected with the dealing activity in which such person engages; and

(iii) If such person is a non-U.S. person other than a conduit affiliate, all of the following types of transactions:

(A) Security-based swap transactions connected with the dealing activity in which such person engages that are entered into with a U.S. person; provided, however, that this paragraph (A) shall not apply to:

(*1*) Transactions with a U.S. person counterparty that constitute transactions conducted through a foreign branch of the counterparty, when the counterparty is a registered security-based swap dealer; and

(*2*) Transactions with a U.S. person counterparty that constitute transactions conducted through a foreign branch of the counterparty, when the transaction is entered into prior to 60 days following the earliest date on which the registration of security-based swap dealers is first required pursuant to the applicable final rules and regulations; and

(B) Security-based swap transactions connected with the dealing activity in which such person engages for which the counterparty to the security-based swap has rights of recourse against a U.S. person that is controlling, controlled by, or under common control with the non-U.S. person; for these purposes a counterparty has rights of recourse against the U.S. person if the counterparty has a conditional or unconditional legally enforceable right, in whole or in part, to receive payments from, or otherwise collect from, the U.S. person in connection with the security-based swap;

(C) Unless such person is a person described in paragraph (a)(4)(iii) of this section, security-based swap transactions connected with such person's security-based swap dealing activity that are arranged, negotiated, or executed by personnel of such non-U.S. person located in a U.S. branch or office, or by personnel of an agent of such non-U.S. person located in a U.S. branch or office; and

(2) If such person engages in transactions described in paragraph (b)(1) of this section, except as provided in Rule 3a71–4, all of the following types of security-based swap transactions:

(i) Security-based swap transactions connected with the dealing activity in which any U.S. person controlling, controlled by, or under common control with such person engages, including transactions conducted through a foreign branch;

(ii) Security-based swap transactions connected with the dealing activity in which any conduit affiliate controlling, controlled by, or under common control with such person engages; and

(iii) Security-based swap transactions connected with the dealing activity of any non-U.S. person, other than a conduit affiliate, that is controlling, controlled by, or under common control with such person, that are described in paragraph (b)(1)(iii) of this section.

(c) *Application of customer protection requirements.* A registered security-based swap dealer, with respect to its foreign business, shall not be subject to the requirements relating to business conduct standards described in section 15F(h) of the Act (15 U.S.C. 78o-10(h)), and the rules and regulations thereunder, other than the rules and regulations prescribed by the Commission pursuant to section 15F(h)(1)(B) of the Act (15 U.S.C. 78o-10(h)(1)(B)).

Rule 3a71–4. Exception from aggregation for affiliated groups with registered security-based swap dealers

Notwithstanding Rules 3a71–2(a)(1) and 3a71–3(b)(2), a person shall not include the security-based swap transactions of another person (an "affiliate") controlling, controlled by, or under common control with such person where such affiliate either is:

(a) Registered with the Commission as a security-based swap dealer; or

(b) Deemed not to be a security-based swap dealer pursuant to Rule 3a71–2(b).

Rule 3a71–5. Exception for cleared transactions executed on a swap execution facility

(a) For purposes of Rule 3a71–3(b)(1), a non-U.S. person, other than a conduit affiliate, shall not include its security-based swap transactions that are entered into anonymously on an execution facility or national securities exchange and are cleared through a clearing agency; and

(b) For purposes of Rule 3a71–3(b)(2), a person shall not include security-based swap transactions of an affiliated non-U.S. person, other than a conduit affiliate, when such transactions are entered into anonymously on an execution facility or national securities exchange and are cleared through a clearing agency.

(c) The exceptions in paragraphs (a) and (b) of this section shall not apply to any security-based swap transactions of a non–U.S. person or of an affiliated non–U.S. person connected with the person's security-based swap dealing activity that are arranged, negotiated, or executed by personnel of such non–U.S. person located in a U.S. branch or office, or by personnel of an agent of such non–U.S. person located in a U.S. branch or office.

Rule 3a71-6. Substituted compliance for security-based swap dealers and major security-based swap participants

(a) *Determinations*—(1) *In general.* Subject to paragraph (a)(2) of this section, the Commission may, conditionally or unconditionally, by order, make a determination with respect to a foreign financial regulatory system that compliance with specified requirements under such foreign financial regulatory system by a registered security-based swap dealer and/or by a registered major security-based swap participant (each a "security-based swap entity"), or class thereof, may satisfy the corresponding requirements identified in paragraph (d) of this section that would otherwise apply to such security-based swap entity (or class thereof).

(2) *Standard.* The Commission shall not make a substituted compliance determination under paragraph (a)(1) of this section unless the Commission:

(i) Determines that the requirements of such foreign financial regulatory system applicable to such security-based swap entity (or class thereof) or to the activities of such security-based swap entity (or class thereof) are comparable to otherwise applicable requirements, after taking into account such factors as the Commission determines are appropriate, such as the scope and objectives of the relevant foreign regulatory requirements (taking into account the applicable criteria set forth in paragraph (d) of this section), as well as the effectiveness of the supervisory compliance program administered, and the enforcement authority exercised, by a foreign financial regulatory authority or authorities in such system to support its oversight of such security-based swap entity (or class thereof) or of the activities of such security-based swap entity (or class thereof); and

(ii) Has entered into a supervisory and enforcement memorandum of understanding and/or other arrangement with the relevant foreign financial regulatory authority or authorities under such foreign financial regulatory system addressing supervisory and enforcement cooperation and other matters arising under the substituted compliance determination.

(3) *Withdrawal or modification.* The Commission may, on its own initiative, by order, modify or withdraw a substituted compliance determination under paragraph (a)(1) of this section, after appropriate notice and opportunity for comment.

(b) *Reliance by security-based swap entities.* A registered security-based swap entity may satisfy the requirements described in paragraph (d) of this section by complying with corresponding law, rules and regulations under a foreign financial regulatory system, provided:

(1) The Commission has made a substituted compliance determination pursuant to paragraph (a)(1) of this section regarding such foreign financial regulatory system providing that compliance with specified requirements under such foreign financial regulatory system by such registered security-based swap entity (or class thereof) may satisfy the corresponding requirements described in paragraph (d) of this section; and

(2) Such registered security-based swap entity satisfies any conditions set forth in a substituted compliance determination made by the Commission pursuant to paragraph (a)(1) of this section.

(c) *Requests for determinations.* (1) A party or group of parties that potentially would comply with specified requirements pursuant to paragraph (a)(1), or any foreign financial regulatory authority or authorities supervising such a party or its security-based swap activities, may file an application, pursuant to the procedures set forth in Rule 0-13, requesting that the Commission make a substituted compliance determination pursuant to paragraph (a)(1) of this section, with respect to one or more requirements described in paragraph (d) of this section.

(2) Such a party or group of parties may make a request under paragraph (c)(1) of this section only if:

(i) Each such party, or the party's activities, is directly supervised by the foreign financial regulatory authority or authorities with respect to the foreign regulatory requirements relating to the applicable requirements described in paragraph (d) of this section; and

(ii) Each such party provides the certification and opinion of counsel as described in Rule 15Fb2-4(c), as if the party were subject to that requirement at the time of the request.

(3) Such foreign financial authority or authorities may make a request under paragraph (c)(1) of this section only if each such authority provides adequate assurances that no law or policy of any relevant foreign jurisdiction would impede the ability of any entity that is directly supervised by the foreign financial regulatory authority and that may register with the Commission as a security-based swap dealer or major security-based swap participant to provide prompt access to the Commission to such entity's books and records or to submit to onsite inspection or examination by the Commission.

(d) *Eligible requirements.* The Commission may make a substituted compliance determination under paragraph (a)(1) of this section to permit security-based swap entities that are not U.S. persons (as defined in Rule 3a71-3(a)(4)), but not security-based swap entities that are U.S. persons, to satisfy the following requirements by complying with comparable foreign requirements:

(1) *Business conduct and supervision.* The business conduct and supervision requirements of sections 15F(h) and (j) of the Act (15 U.S.C. 78*o*–10(h) and (j)) and Rules 15Fh-3 through 15Fh-6, other than the antifraud provisions of section 15F(h)(4)(A) of the Act and Rule 15Fh-4(a), and other than the provisions of sections 15F(j)(3) and 15F(j)(4)(B) of the Act; provided, however, that prior to making such a substituted compliance determination the Commission intends to consider whether the information that is required to be provided to counterparties pursuant to the requirements of the foreign financial regulatory system, the counterparty protections under the requirements of the foreign financial regulatory system, the mandates for supervisory systems under the requirements of the foreign financial regulatory system, and the duties imposed by the foreign financial regulatory system, are comparable to those associated with the applicable provisions arising under the Act and its rules and regulations.

(2) *Chief compliance officer.* The chief compliance officer requirements of section 15F(k) of the Act (15 U.S.C. 78o–10(k)) and Rule 15Fk-1; provided, however, that prior to making such a substituted compliance determination the Commission intends to consider whether the requirements of the foreign financial regulatory system regarding chief compliance officer obligations are comparable to those required pursuant to the applicable provisions arising under the Act and its rules and regulations.

(3) *Trade acknowledgment and verification.* The trade acknowledgment and verification requirements of section 15F(i) of the Act (15 U.S.C. 78o-10(i)) and § 240.15Fi-2; provided, however, that prior to making such a substituted compliance determination the Commission intends to consider whether the information that is required to be provided pursuant to the requirements of the foreign financial regulatory system, and the manner and timeframe by which that information must be provided, are comparable to those required pursuant to the applicable provisions arising under the Act and its rules and regulations.

DEFINITIONS

Rule 3b–1. Definition of "listed"

The term *listed* means admitted to full trading privileges upon application by the issuer or its fiscal agent or, in the case of the securities of a foreign corporation, upon application by a banker engaged in distributing them; and includes securities for which authority to add to the list on official notice of issuance has been granted.

Rule 3b–2. Definition of "officer"

The term *officer* means a president, vice president, secretary, treasurer or principal financial officer, comptroller or principal accounting officer, and any person routinely performing corresponding functions with respect to any organization whether incorporated or unincorporated.

Rule 3b–3. [Reserved]

Rule 3b–4. Definition of "foreign government," "foreign issuer" and "foreign private issuer"

(a) The term *foreign government* means the government of any foreign country or of any political subdivision of a foreign country.

(b) The term *foreign issuer* means any issuer which is a foreign government, a national of any foreign country or a corporation or other organization incorporated or organized under the laws of any foreign country.

(c) The term *foreign private issuer* means any foreign issuer other than a foreign government except for an issuer meeting the following conditions as of the last business day of its most recently completed second fiscal quarter:

(1) More than 50 percent of the issuer's outstanding voting securities are directly or indirectly held of record by residents of the United States; and

(2) Any of the following:

(i) The majority of the executive officers or directors are United States citizens or residents;

(ii) More than 50 percent of the assets of the issuer are located in the United States; or

(iii) The business of the issuer is administered principally in the United States.

Note to Paragraph (c)(1): To determine the percentage of outstanding voting securities held by U.S. residents:

A. Use the method of calculating record ownership in § 240.12g3-2(a), except that:

(1) Your inquiry as to the amount of shares represented by accounts of customers resident in the United States may be limited to brokers, dealers, banks and other nominees located in:

(i) The United States,

(ii) Your jurisdiction of incorporation, and

(iii) The jurisdiction that is the primary trading market for your voting securities,if different than your jurisdiction of incorporation; and

(2) Notwithstanding Rule 12g5-1(a)(8) of this chapter, you shall not exclude securities held by persons who received the securities pursuant to an employee compensation plan.

B. If, after reasonable inquiry, you are unable to obtain information about the amount of shares represented by accounts of customers resident in the United States, you may assume, for purposes of this definition, that the customers are residents of the jurisdiction in which the nominee has its principal place of business.

C. Count shares of voting securities beneficially owned by residents of the United States as reported on reports of beneficial ownership provided to you or filed publicly and based on information otherwise provided to you.

(d) Notwithstanding paragraph (c) of this rule, in the case of a new registrant with the Commission, the determination of whether an issuer is a foreign private issuer will be made as of a date within 30 days prior to the issuer's filing of an initial registration statement under either the Act or the Securities Act of 1933.

(e) Once an issuer qualifies as a foreign private issuer, it will immediately be able to use the forms and rules designated for foreign private issuers until it fails to qualify for this status at the end of its most recently completed second fiscal quarter. An issuer's determination that it fails to qualify as a foreign private issuer governs its eligibility to use the forms and rules designated for foreign private issuers beginning on the first day of the fiscal year following the determination date. Once an issuer fails to qualify for foreign private issuer status, it will remain unqualified unless it meets the requirements for foreign private issuer status as of the last business day of its second fiscal quarter.

Rule 3b-5. Nonexempt securities issued under governmental obligations

(a) Any part of an obligation evidenced by any bond, note, debenture, or other evidence of indebtedness issued by any governmental unit specified in section 3(a)(12) of the Act which is payable from payments to be made in respect of property or money which is or will be used, under a lease, sale, or loan arrangement, by or for industrial or commercial enterprise, shall be deemed to be a separate "security" within the meaning of section 3(a)(10) of the Act, issued by the lessee or obligor under the lease, sale or loan arrangement.

(b) An obligation shall not be deemed a separate "security" as defined in paragraph (a) hereof if (1) the obligation is payable from the general revenues of a governmental unit, specified in section 3(a)(12) of the Act, having other resources which may be used for payment of the obligation, or (2) the obligation relates to a public project or facility owned and operated by or on behalf of and under the control of a governmental unit specified in such section, or (3) the obligation relates to a facility which is leased to and under the control of an industrial or commercial enterprise but is a part of a public project which, as a whole, is owned by and under the general control of a governmental unit specified in such section, or an instrumentality thereof.

(c) This rule shall apply to transactions of the character described in paragraph (a) only with respect to bonds, notes, debentures or other evidences of indebtedness sold after December 31, 1968.

Rule 3b-6. Liability for certain statements by issuers

(a) A statement within the coverage of paragraph (b) of this rule which is made by or on behalf of an issuer or by an outside reviewer retained by the issuer shall be deemed not to be a fraudulent statement (as defined in paragraph (d) of this rule), unless it is shown that such statement was made or reaffirmed without a reasonable basis or was disclosed other than in good faith.

(b) This rule applies to the following statements:

(1) A forward-looking statement (as defined in paragraph (c) of this rule) made in a document

filed with the Commission, in Part I of a quarterly report on Form 10–Q (17 CFR 249.308a), or in an annual report to security holders meeting the requirements of Rules 14a–3(b) and (c) or 14c–3(a) and (b), a statement reaffirming such forward-looking statement after to the date the document was filed or the annual report was made publicly available, or a forward-looking statement made before to the date the document was filed or the date the annual report was made publicly available if such statement is reaffirmed in a filed document, in Part I of a quarterly report on Form 10–Q, or in an annual report made publicly available within a reasonable time after the making of such forward-looking statement; *Provided*, That

(i) At the time such statements are made or reaffirmed, either the issuer is subject to the reporting requirements of section 13(a) or 15(d) of the Act and has complied with the requirements of Rule 13a–1 or 15d–1 thereunder, if applicable, to file its most recent annual report on Form 10–K or Form 20–F or Form 40–F; or if the issuer is not subject to the reporting requirements of section 13(a) or 15(d) of the Act, the statements are made in a registration statement filed under the Securities Act of 1933 offering statement or solicitation of interest, written document or broadcast script under Regulation A or pursuant to section 12 (b) or (g) of the Securities Exchange Act of 1934, and

(ii) The statements are not made by or on behalf of an issuer that is an investment company registered under the Investment Company Act of 1940; and

(2) Information that is disclosed in a document filed with the Commission in Part I of a quarterly report on Form 10–Q or in an annual report to security holders meeting the requirements of Rules 14a–3(b) and (c) or 14c–3(a) and (b) under the Act and that relates to:

(i) The effects of changing prices on the business enterprise, presented voluntarily or pursuant to Item 303 of Regulation S–K, "Management's Discussion and Analysis of Financial Condition and Results of Operations," Item 5 of Form 20–F, "Operating and Financial Review and Prospects," Item 302 of Regulation S–K "Supplementary Financial Information," or Rule 3–20(c) of Regulation S–X; or

(ii) The value of proved oil and gas reserves (such as standardized measure of discounted future net cash flows relating to proved oil and gas reserves as set forth in FASB ASC paragraphs 932–235–50–29 through 932–235–50–36 (Extractive Activities—Oil and Gas Topic)), presented voluntarily or pursuant to Item 302 of Regulation S–K.

(c) For the purpose of this rule the term *forward looking statement* shall mean and shall be limited to:

(1) A statement containing a projection of revenues, income (loss), earnings (loss) per share, capital expenditures, dividends, capital structure or other financial items;

(2) A statement of management's plans and objectives for future operations;

(3) A statement of future economic performance contained in management's discussion and analysis of financial condition and results of operations included pursuant to Item 303 of Regulation S–K; or Item 5 of Form 20–F or

(4) Disclosed statements of the assumptions underlying or relating to any of the statements described in paragraphs (d)(1), (2), or (3) of this rule.

(d) For the purpose of this rule the term *fraudulent statement* shall mean a statement which is an untrue statement of a material fact, a statement false or misleading with respect to any material fact, an omission to state a material fact necessary to make a statement not misleading, or which constitutes the employment of a manipulative, deceptive, or fraudulent device, contrivance, scheme, transaction, act, practice, course of business, or an artifice to defraud, as those terms are used in the Securities Exchange Act of 1934 or the rules or regulations promulgated thereunder.

Rule 3b–7. Definition of "executive officer"

The term *executive officer,* when used with reference to a registrant, means its president, any vice president of the registrant in charge of a principal business unit, division or function (such as sales, administration, or finance), any other officer who performs a policy making function or any other person who performs similar policy making functions for the registrant. Executive officers of subsidiaries may be deemed executive officers of the registrant if they perform such policy making functions for the registrant.

Rule 3b–8. Definitions of "Qualified OTC market maker," "qualified third market maker" and "qualified block positioner"

For the purposes of Regulation U under the Act (12 CFR 221):

(a) The term *Qualified OTC Market Maker* in an over-the-counter ("OTC") margin security means a dealer in any "OTC Margin Security" [as that term is defined in Rule 2(j) of Regulation U (12 CFR 221.2(j))] who (1) is a broker or dealer registered pursuant to Section 15 of the Act, (2) is subject to and is in compliance with Rule 15c3–1, (3) has and maintains minimum net capital, as defined in Rule 15c3–1, of the lesser of (i) $250,000 or (ii) $25,000 plus $5,000 for each security in excess of five with regard to which the broker or dealer is, or is seeking to become a Qualified OTC Market Maker, and (4) except when such activity is unlawful, meets all of the following conditions with respect to such security: (i) He regularly publishes bona fide, competitive bid and offer quotations in a recognized inter-dealer quotation system, (ii) he furnishes bona fide, competitive bid and offer quotations to other brokers and dealers on request, (iii) he is ready, willing and able to effect transactions in reasonable amounts, and at his quoted prices, with other brokers and dealers, and (iv) he has a reasonable average rate of inventory turnover in such security.

(b) The term *Qualified Third Market Maker* means a dealer in any stock registered on a national securities exchange ("exchange") who (1) is a broker or dealer registered pursuant to Section 15 of the Act, (2) is subject to and is in compliance with Rule 15c3–1, (3) has and maintains minimum net capital, as defined in Rule 15c3–1, of the lesser of (i) $500,000 or (ii) $100,000 plus $20,000 for each security in excess of five with regard to which the broker or dealer is, or is seeking to become, a Qualified Third Market Maker, and (4) except when such activity is unlawful, meets all of the following conditions with respect to such security: (i) He furnishes bona fide, competitive bid and offer quotations at all times to other brokers and dealers on request, (ii) he is ready, willing and able to effect transactions for his own account in reasonable amounts, and at his quoted prices with other brokers and dealers, and (iii) he has a reasonable average rate of inventory turnover in such security.

(c) The term *Qualified Block Positioner* means a dealer who (1) is a broker or dealer registered pursuant to section 15 of the Act, (2) is subject to and in compliance with Rule 15c3–1, (3) has and maintains minimum net capital, as defined in Rule 15c3–1 of $1,000,000 and (4) except when such activity is unlawful, meets all of the following conditions: (i) He engages in the activity of purchasing long or selling short from time to time, from or to a customer (other than a partner or a joint venture or other entity in which a partner, the dealer, or a person associated with such dealer, as defined in section 3(a)(18) of the Act, participates) a block of stock with a current market value of $200,000 or more in a single transaction, or in several transactions at approximately the same time, from a single source to facilitate a sale or purchase by such customer, (ii) he has determined in the exercise of reasonable diligence that the block could not be sold to or purchased from others on equivalent or better terms, and (iii) he sells the shares comprising the block as rapidly as possible commensurate with the circumstances.

Rule 3b–9. [Reserved]

Rule 3b–10. [Reserved]

Rule 3b–11. Definitions relating to limited partnership roll–up transactions for purposes of Sections 6(b)(9), 14(h) and 15A(b)(12)–(13)

For purposes of sections 6(b)(9), 14(h) and 15A(b)(12)–(13) of the Act (15 U.S.C. 78f(b)(9), 78n(h) and 78o–3(b)(12)–(13)):

(a) The term *limited partnership roll-up transaction* does not include a transaction involving only entities that are not "finite-life" as defined in Item 901(b)(2) of Regulation S–K.

(b) The term *limited partnership roll-up transaction* does not include a transaction involving only entities registered under the Investment Company Act of 1940 or any Business Development Company as defined in section 2(a)(48) of that Act (15 U.S.C. 80a–2(a)(48)).

(c) The term *regularly traded* shall be defined as in Item 901(c)(2)(v)(C) of Regulation S–K.

Rule 3b–12. Definition of OTC derivatives dealer

The term *OTC derivatives dealer* means any dealer that is affiliated with a registered broker or dealer (other than an OTC derivatives dealer), and whose securities activities:

(a) Are limited to:

(1) Engaging in dealer activities in eligible OTC derivative instruments that are securities;

(2) Issuing and reacquiring securities that are issued by the dealer, including warrants on securities, hybrid securities, and structured notes;

(3) Engaging in cash management securities activities;

(4) Engaging in ancillary portfolio management securities activities; and

(5) Engaging in such other securities activities that the Commission designates by order pursuant to Rule 15a–1(b)(1); and

(b) Consist primarily of the activities described in paragraphs (a)(1), (a)(2), and (a)(3) of this rule; and

(c) Do not consist of any other securities activities, including engaging in any transaction in any security that is not an eligible OTC derivative instrument, except as permitted under paragraphs (a)(3), (a)(4), and (a)(5) of this rule.

(d) For purposes of this rule, the term *hybrid security* means a security that incorporates payment features economically similar to options, forwards, futures, swap agreements, or collars involving currencies, interest or other rates, commodities, securities, indices, quantitative measures, or other financial or economic interests or property of any kind, or any payment or delivery that is dependent on the occurrence or nonoccurrence of any event associated with a potential financial, economic, or commercial consequence (or any combination, permutation, or derivative of such contract or underlying interest).

Rule 3b–13. Definition of eligible OTC derivative instrument

(a) Except as otherwise provided in paragraph (b) of this rule, the term *eligible OTC derivative instrument* means any contract, agreement, or transaction that:

(1) Provides, in whole or in part, on a firm or contingent basis, for the purchase or sale of, or is based on the value of, or any interest in, one or more commodities, securities, currencies, interest or other rates, indices, quantitative measures, or other financial or economic interests or property of any kind; or

(2) Involves any payment or delivery that is dependent on the occurrence or nonoccurrence of any event associated with a potential financial, economic, or commercial consequence; or

(3) Involves any combination or permutation of any contract, agreement, or transaction or underlying interest, property, or event described in paragraphs (a)(1) or (a)(2) of this rule.

(b) The term *eligible OTC derivative instrument* does not include any contract, agreement, or transaction that:

(1) Provides for the purchase or sale of a security, on a firm basis, unless:

(i) The settlement date for such purchase or sale occurs at least one year following the trade date or, in the case of an eligible forward contract, at least four months following the trade date; or

(ii) The material economic features of the contract, agreement, or transaction consist primarily of features of a type described in paragraph (a) of this rule other than the provision for the purchase or sale of a security on a firm basis; or

(2) Provides, in whole or in part, on a firm or contingent basis, for the purchase or sale of, or is based on the value of, or any interest in, any security (or group or index of securities), and is:

(i) Listed on, or traded on or through, a national securities exchange or registered national securities association, or facility or market thereof; or

(ii) Except as otherwise determined by the Commission by order pursuant to Rule 15a–1(b)(2), one of a class of fungible instruments that are standardized as to their material economic terms.

(c) The Commission may issue an order pursuant to Rule 15a–1(b)(3) clarifying whether certain contracts, agreements, or transactions are within the scope of eligible OTC derivative instrument.

(d) For purposes of this rule, the term *eligible forward contract* means a forward contract that provides for the purchase or sale of a security other than a government security, provided that, if such contract provides for the purchase or sale of margin stock (as defined in Regulation U of the Regulations of the Board of Governors of the Federal Reserve System, 12 CFR Part 221), such contract either:

(1) Provides for the purchase or sale of such stock by the issuer thereof (or an affiliate that is not a bank or a broker or dealer); or

(2) Provides for the transfer of transaction collateral in an amount that would satisfy the requirements, if any, that would be applicable assuming the OTC derivatives dealer party to such transaction were not eligible for the exemption from Regulation T of the Regulations of the Board of Governors of the Federal Reserve System, 12 CFR part 220, set forth in Rule 36a1–1.

Rule 3b–14. Definition of cash management securities activities

The term *cash management securities activities* means securities activities that are limited to transactions involving:

(a) Any taking possession of, and any subsequent sale or disposition of, collateral provided by a counterparty, or any acquisition of, and any subsequent sale or disposition of, collateral to be provided to a counterparty, in connection with any securities activities of the dealer permitted under Rule 15a–1 or any non-securities activities of the dealer that involve eligible OTC derivative instruments or other financial instruments;

(b) Cash management, in connection with any securities activities of the dealer permitted under Rule 15a–1 or any non-securities activities of the dealer that involve eligible OTC derivative instruments or other financial instruments; or

(c) Financing of positions of the dealer acquired in connection with any securities activities of the dealer permitted under Rule 15a–1 or any non-securities activities that involve eligible OTC derivative instruments or other financial instrument.

Rule 3b–15. Definition of ancillary portfolio management securities activities

(a) The term *ancillary portfolio management securities activities* means securities activities that:

(1) Are limited to transactions in connection with:

(i) Dealer activities in eligible OTC derivative instruments;

(ii) The issuance of securities by the dealer; or

(iii) Such other securities activities that the Commission designates by order pursuant to Rule 15a–1(b)(1); and

(2) Are conducted for the purpose of reducing the market or credit risk of the dealer or consist of incidental trading activities for portfolio management purposes; and

(3) Are limited to risk exposures within the market, credit, leverage, and liquidity risk parameters set forth in:

(i) The trading authorizations granted to the associated person (or to the supervisor of such associated person) who executes a particular transaction for, or on behalf of, the dealer; and

(ii) The written guidelines approved by the governing body of the dealer and included in the internal risk management control system for the dealer pursuant to Rule 15c3–4; and

(4) Are conducted solely by one or more associated persons of the dealer who perform substantial duties for, or on behalf of, the dealer in connection with its dealer activities in eligible OTC derivative instruments.

(b) The Commission may issue an order pursuant to Rule 15a–1(b)(4) clarifying whether certain securities activities are within the scope of ancillary portfolio management securities activities.

Rule 3b–16. Definitions of terms used in Section 3(a)(1) of the Act

(a) An organization, association, or group of persons shall be considered to constitute, maintain, or provide "a market place or facilities for bringing together purchasers and sellers of securities or for otherwise performing with respect to securities the functions commonly performed by a stock exchange," as those terms are used in section 3(a)(1) of the Act, (15 U.S.C. 78c(a)(1)), if such organization, association, or group of persons:

(1) Brings together the orders for securities of multiple buyers and sellers; and

(2) Uses established, non-discretionary methods (whether by providing a trading facility or by setting rules) under which such orders interact with each other, and the buyers and sellers entering such orders agree to the terms of a trade.

(b) An organization, association, or group of persons shall not be considered to constitute, maintain, or provide "a market place or facilities for bringing together purchasers and sellers of securities or for otherwise performing with respect to securities the functions commonly performed by a stock exchange," solely because such organization, association, or group of persons engages in one or more of the following activities:

(1) Routes orders to a national securities exchange, a market operated by a national securities association, or a broker-dealer for execution; or

(2) Allows persons to enter orders for execution against the bids and offers of a single dealer; and

(i) As an incidental part of these activities, matches orders that are not displayed to any person other than the dealer and its employees; or

(ii) In the course of acting as a market maker registered with a self-regulatory organization, displays the limit orders of such market maker's, or other broker-dealer's, customers; and

(A) Matches customer orders with such displayed limit orders; and

(B) As an incidental part of its market making activities, crosses or matches orders that are not displayed to any person other than the market maker and its employees.

(c) For purposes of this rule the term *order* means any firm indication of a willingness to buy or sell a security, as either principal or agent, including any bid or offer quotation, market order, limit order, or other priced order.

(d) For the purposes of this rule, the terms *bid* and *offer* shall have the same meaning as under Rule 600 of Regulation NMS.

(e) The Commission may conditionally or unconditionally exempt any organization, association, or group of persons from the definition in paragraph (a) of this rule.

Rule 3b–17. [Reserved]

Rule 3b–18. Definitions of terms used in Section 3(a)(5) of the Act

For the purposes of section 3(a)(5)(C) of the Act (15 U.S.C. 78c(a)(5)(C)):

(a) The term *affiliate* means any company that controls, is controlled by, or is under common control with another company.

(b) The term *consumer-related receivable* means any obligation incurred by any natural person to pay money arising out of a transaction in which the money, property, insurance, or services (being purchased) are primarily for personal, family, or household purposes.

(c) The term *member* as it relates to the term "syndicate of banks" means a bank that is a participant in a syndicate of banks and together with its affiliates, other than its broker or dealer affiliates, originates no less than 10% of the value of the obligations in a pool of obligations used to back the securities issued through a grantor trust or other separate entity.

(d) The term *obligation* means any note, draft, acceptance, loan, lease, receivable, or other evidence of indebtedness that is not a security issued by a person other than the bank.

(e) The term *originated* means:

(1) Funding an obligation at the time that the obligation is created; or

(2) Initially approving and underwriting the obligation, or initially agreeing to purchase the obligation, provided that:

(i) The obligation conforms to the underwriting standards or is evidenced by the loan documents of the bank or its affiliates, other than its broker or dealer affiliates; and

(ii) The bank or its affiliates, other than its broker or dealer affiliates, fund the obligation in a timely manner, not to exceed six months after the obligation is created.

(f) The term *pool* means more than one obligation or type of obligation grouped together to provide collateral for a securities offering.

(g) The term *predominantly originated* means that no less than 85% of the value of the obligations in any pool were originated by:

(1) The bank or its affiliates, other than its broker or dealer affiliates; or

(2) Banks that are members of a syndicate of banks and affiliates of such banks, other than their broker or dealer affiliates, if the obligations or pool of obligations consist of mortgage obligations or consumer-related receivables.

(3) For this purpose, the bank and its affiliates include any financial institution with which the bank or its affiliates have merged but does not include the purchase of a pool of obligations or the purchase of a line of business.

(h) The term *syndicate of banks* means a group of banks that acts jointly, on a temporary basis, to issue through a grantor trust or other separate entity, securities backed by obligations originated by each of the individual banks or their affiliates, other than their broker or dealer affiliates.

Rule 3b–19. Definition of "issuer" in Section 3(a)(8) of the Act in relation to asset-backed securities

The following applies with respect to asset-backed securities under the Act. Terms used in this rule have the same meaning as in Item 1101 of Regulation AB.

(a) The depositor for the asset-backed securities acting solely in its capacity as depositor to the issuing entity is the "issuer" for purposes of the asset-backed securities of that issuing entity.

(b) The person acting in the capacity as the depositor specified in paragraph (a) of this rule is a different "issuer" from that same person acting as a depositor for another issuing entity or for purposes of that person's own securities.

CLEARING OF SECURITY-BASED SWAPS

Rule 3Ca–1. Stay of clearing requirement and review by the Commission

(a) After making a determination pursuant to a clearing agency's security-based swap submission that a security-based swap, or any group, category, type or class of security-based swaps, is required to be cleared, the Commission, on application of a counterparty to a security-based swap or on the Commission's own initiative, may stay the clearing requirement until the Commission completes a review of the terms of the security-based swap (or group, category, type, or class of security-based swaps) and the clearing of the security-based swap (or group, category, type, or class of security-based swaps) by the clearing agency that has accepted it for clearing.

(b) A counterparty to a security-based swap applying for a stay of the clearing requirement for a security-based swap (or group, category, type, or class of security-based swaps) shall submit a written statement to the Commission that includes:

(1) A request for a stay of the clearing requirement;

(2) The identity of the counterparties to the security-based swap and a contact at the counterparty requesting the stay;

(3) The identity of the clearing agency clearing the security-based swap;

(4) The terms of the security-based swap subject to the clearing requirement and a description of the clearing arrangement; and

(5) Reasons why such stay should be granted and why the security-based swap should not be subject to a clearing requirement, specifically addressing the same factors a clearing agency must address in its security-based-swap submission pursuant to Rule 19b–4(*o*)(3).

(c) A stay of the clearing requirement may be granted with respect to a security-based swap, or the group, category, type, or class of security-based swaps, as determined by the Commission.

(d) The Commission's review shall include a quantitative and qualitative assessment of the factors specified in 19b–4(*o*)(3). Any clearing agency that has accepted for clearing a security-based swap, or any group, category, type or class of security-based swaps, that is subject to the stay of the clearing requirement shall provide information requested by the Commission as necessary to assess any of the factors it determines to be appropriate in the course of its review.

(e) Upon completion of its review, the Commission may:

(1) Determine, subject to any terms and conditions that the Commission determines to be appropriate in the public interest, that the security-based swap, or group, category, type, or class of security-based swaps must be cleared; or

(2) Determine that the clearing requirement will not apply to the security-based swap, or group, category, type, or class of security-based swaps, but clearing may continue on a non-mandatory basis.

Rule 3Ca–2. Submission of security–based swaps for clearing

Pursuant to section 3C(a)(1) of the Act (15 U.S.C. 78c–3(a)(1)), it shall be unlawful for any person to engage in a security-based swap unless that person submits such security-based swap for clearing to a clearing agency that is registered under this Act or a clearing agency that is exempt from registration under the Act if the security-based swap is required to be cleared. The phrase *submits such security-based swap for clearing to a clearing agency* in the clearing requirement of Section 3C(a)(1) of the Act shall mean that the security-based swap will be submitted for central clearing to a clearing agency that functions as a central counterparty.

REGISTRATION AND EXEMPTION OF EXCHANGES

Rule 6a–1. Application for registration as a national securities exchange or exemption from registration based on limited volume

(a) An application for registration as a national securities exchange, or for exemption from such registration based on limited volume, shall be filed on Form 1 (17 CFR 249.1), in accordance with the instructions contained therein.

(b) Promptly after the discovery that any information filed on Form 1 was inaccurate when filed, the exchange shall file with the Commission an amendment correcting such inaccuracy.

(c) Promptly after the discovery that any information in the statement, any exhibit, or any amendment was inaccurate when filed, the exchange shall file with the Commission an amendment correcting such inaccuracy.

(d) Whenever the number of changes to be reported in an amendment, or the number of amendments filed, are so great that the purpose of clarity will be promoted by the filing of a new complete statement and exhibits, an exchange may, at its election, or shall, upon request of the Commission, file as an amendment a complete new statement together with all exhibits which are prescribed to be filed in connection with Form 1.

Rule 6a–2. Amendments to application

(a) A national securities exchange, or an exchange exempted from such registration based on limited volume, shall file an amendment to Form 1, (17 CFR 249.1), which shall set forth the nature and effective date of the action taken and shall provide any new information and correct any information rendered inaccurate, on Form 1, (17 CFR 249.1), within 10 days after any action is taken that renders inaccurate, or that causes to be incomplete, any of the following:

(1) Information filed on the Execution Page of Form 1, or amendment thereto; or

(2) Information filed as part of Exhibits C, F, G, H, J, K or M, or any amendments thereto.

(b) On or before June 30 of each year, a national securities exchange, or an exchange exempted from such registration based on limited volume, shall file, as an amendment to Form 1, the following:

(1) Exhibits D and I as of the end of the latest fiscal year of the exchange; and

(2) Exhibits K, M, and N, which shall be up to date as of the latest date practicable within 3 months of the date the amendment is filed.

(c) On or before June 30, 2001 and every 3 years thereafter, a national securities exchange, or an exchange exempted from such registration based on limited volume, shall file, as an amendment to Form 1, complete Exhibits A, B, C and J. The information filed under this paragraph (c) shall be current as of the latest practicable date, but shall, at a minimum, be up to date within 3 months as of the date the amendment is filed.

(d)(1) If an exchange, on an annual or more frequent basis, publishes, or cooperates in the publication of, any of the information required to be filed by paragraphs (b)(2) and (c) of this rule, in lieu of filing such information, an exchange may:

(i) Identify the publication in which such information is available, the name, address, and telephone number of the person from whom such publication may be obtained, and the price of such publication; and

(ii) Certify to the accuracy of such information as of its publication date.

(2) If an exchange keeps the information required under paragraphs (b)(2) and (c) of this rule up to date and makes it available to the Commission and the public upon request, in lieu of filing such information, an exchange may certify that the information is kept up to date and is available to the Commission and the public upon request.

(3) If the information required to be filed under paragraphs (b)(2) and (c) of this rule is available continuously on an Internet web site controlled by an exchange, in lieu of filing such information with the Commission, such exchange may:

(i) Indicate the location of the Internet web site where such information may be found; and

(ii) Certify that the information available at such location is accurate as of its date.

(e) The Commission may exempt a national securities exchange, or an exchange exempted from such registration based on limited volume, from filing the amendment required by this rule for any affiliate or subsidiary listed in Exhibit C of the exchange's application for registration, as amended, that either:

(1) Is listed in Exhibit C of the application for registration or notice of registration, as amended, of one or more other national securities exchanges; or

(2) Was an inactive subsidiary throughout the subsidiary's latest fiscal year. Any such exemption may be granted upon terms and conditions the Commission deems necessary or appropriate in the public interest or for the protection of investors, provided however, that at least one national securities exchange shall be required to file the amendments required by this rule for an affiliate or subsidiary described in paragraph (e)(1) of this rule.

(f) A national securities exchange registered pursuant to section 6(g)(1) of the Act (15 U.S.C. 78f(g)(1)) shall be exempt from the requirements of this rule.

Rule 6a–3. Supplemental material to be filed by exchanges

(a)(1) A national securities exchange, or an exchange exempted from such registration based on limited volume, shall file with the Commission any material (including notices, circulars, bulletins, lists, and periodicals) issued or made generally available to members of, or participants or subscribers to, the exchange. Such material shall be filed with the Commission within 10 days after issuing or making such material available to members, participants or subscribers.

(2) If the information required to be filed under paragraph (a)(1) of this rule is available continuously on an Internet web site controlled by an exchange, in lieu of filing such information with the Commission, such exchange may:

(i) Indicate the location of the Internet web site where such information may be found; and

(ii) Certify that the information available at such location is accurate as of its date.

(b) Within 15 days after the end of each calendar month, a national securities exchange or an exchange exempted from such registration based on limited volume, shall file a report concerning the securities sold on such exchange during the calendar month. Such report shall set forth:

(1) The number of shares of stock sold and the aggregate dollar amount of such stock sold;

(2) The principal amount of bonds sold and the aggregate dollar amount of such bonds sold; and

(3) The number of rights and warrants sold and the aggregate dollar amount of such rights and warrants sold.

(c) A national securities exchange registered pursuant to Section 6(g)(1) of the Act (15 U.S.C. 78f(g)(1)) shall be exempt from the requirements of this rule.

Rule 6a–4. Notice of registration under Section 6(g) of the Act, amendment to such notice, and supplemental materials to be filed by exchanges registered under Section 6(g) of the Act

(a) *Notice of Registration.* (1) An exchange may register as a national securities exchange solely for the purposes of trading security futures products by filing Form 1–N (17 CFR 249.10) ("notice of registration"), in accordance with the instructions contained therein, if:

(i) The exchange is a board of trade, as that term in defined in the Commodity Exchange Act (7 U.S.C. 1a(2)), that:

(A) Has been designated a contract market by the Commodity Futures Trading Commission and such designation is not suspended by order of the Commodity Futures Trading Commission; or

(B) Is registered as a derivative transaction execution facility under Section 5a of the Commodity Exchange Act (7 U.S.C. 7a) and such registration is not suspended by the Commodity Futures Trading Commission; and

(ii) Such exchange does not serve as a market place for transactions in securities other than:

(A) Security futures products; or

(B) Futures on exempted securities or on groups or indexes of securities or options thereon that have been authorized under Section 2(a)(1)(C) of the Commodity Exchange Act (7 U.S.C. 2a).

(2) Promptly after the discovery that any information filed on Form 1–N (17 CFR 249.10) was inaccurate when filed, the exchange shall file with the Commission an amendment correcting such inaccuracy.

(b) *Amendment to Notice of Registration.* (1) A national securities exchange registered pursuant to section 6(g)(1) of the Act (15 U.S.C. 78f(g)(1)) ("Security Futures Product Exchange") shall file an amendment to Form 1–N (17 CFR 249.10), which shall set forth the nature and effective date of the action taken and shall provide any new information and correct any information rendered inaccurate, on Form 1–N (17 CFR 249.10), within:

(i) Ten days after any action is taken that renders inaccurate, or that causes to be incomplete, any information filed on the Execution Page of Form 1–N (17 CFR 249.10), or amendment thereto; or

(ii) 30 days after any action is taken that renders inaccurate, or that causes to be incomplete, any information filed as part of Exhibit F to Form 1–N (17 CFR 249.10), or any amendments thereto.

(2) A Security Futures Product Exchange shall maintain records relating to changes in information required in Exhibits C and E to Form 1–N (17 CFR 249.10) which shall be current of as of the latest practicable date, but shall, at a minimum, be up-

to-date within 30 days. A Security Futures Product Exchange shall make such records available to the Commission and the public upon request.

(3) On or before June 30, 2002, and by June 30 every year thereafter, a Security Futures Product Exchange shall file, as an amendment to Form 1–N (17 CFR 249.10), Exhibits F, H, and I, which shall be current of as of the latest practicable date, but shall, at a minimum, be up-to-date within three months as of the date the amendment is filed.

(4) On or before June 30, 2004, and by June 30 every three years thereafter, a Security Futures Product Exchange shall file, as an amendment to Form 1–N (17 CFR 249.10), complete Exhibits A, B, C, and E, which shall be current of as of the latest practicable date, but shall, at a minimum, be up-to-date within three months as of the date the amendment is filed.

(5)(i) If a Security Futures Product Exchange, on an annual or more frequent basis, publishes, or cooperates in the publication of, any of the information required to be filed by paragraphs (b)(3) and (b)(4) of this rule, in lieu of filing such information, a Security Futures Product Exchange may satisfy this filing requirement by:

(A) Identifying the publication in which such information is available, the name, address, and telephone number of the person from whom such publication may be obtained, and the price of such publication; and

(B) Certifying to the accuracy of such information as of its publication date.

(ii) If a Security Futures Product Exchange keeps the information required under paragraphs (b)(3) and (b)(4) of this rule up-to-date and makes it available to the Commission and the public upon request, in lieu of filing such information, a Security Futures Product Exchange may satisfy this filing requirement by certifying that the information is kept up-to-date and is available to the Commission and the public upon request.

(iii) If the information required to be filed under paragraphs (b)(3) and (b)(4) of this rule is available continuously on an Internet web site controlled by a Security Futures Product Exchange, in lieu of filing such information with the Commission, such Security Futures Product Exchange may satisfy this filing requirement by:

(A) Indicating the location of the Internet web site where such information may be found; and

(B) Certifying that the information available at such location is accurate as of its date.

(6)(i) The Commission may exempt a Security Futures Product Exchange from filing the amendment required by this rule for any affiliate or subsidiary listed in Exhibit C to Form 1–N (17 CFR 249.10), as amended, that either:

(A) Is listed in Exhibit C to Form 1 (17 CFR 249.1) or to Form 1–N (17 CFR 249.10), as amended, of one or more other national securities exchanges; or

(B) Was an inactive affiliate or subsidiary throughout the affiliate's or subsidiary's latest fiscal year.

(ii) Any such exemption may be granted upon terms and conditions the Commission deems necessary or appropriate in the public interest or for the protection of investors, provided however, that at least one national securities exchange shall be required to file the amendments required by this rule for an affiliate or subsidiary described in paragraph (b)(6)(i) of this rule.

(7) If a Security Futures Product Exchange has filed documents with the Commodity Futures Trading Commission, to the extent that such documents contain information satisfying the Commission's informational requirements, copies of such documents may be filed with the Commission in lieu of the required written notice.

(c) *Supplemental Material to Be Filed by Security Futures Product Exchanges.* (1)(i) A Security Futures Product Exchange shall file with the Commission any material related to the trading of security futures products (including notices, circulars, bulletins, lists, and periodicals) issued or made generally available to members of, participants in, or subscribers to, the exchange. Such material shall be filed with the Commission within ten days after issuing or making such material available to members, participants, or subscribers.

(ii) If the information required to be filed under paragraph (c)(1)(i) of this rule is available continuously on an Internet web site controlled by an exchange, in lieu of filing such information with the Commission, such exchange may:

(A) Indicate the location of the Internet web site where such information may be found; and

(B) Certify that the information available at such location is accurate as of its date.

(2) Within 15 days after the end of each calendar month, a Security Futures Product Exchange shall file a report concerning the security futures products traded on such exchange during the previous calendar month. Such a report shall:

(i) For each contract of sale for future delivery of a single security, the number of contracts traded on such exchange during the relevant calendar month and the total number of shares underlying such contracts traded; and

(ii) For each contract of sale for future delivery of a narrow-based security index, the number of contracts traded on such exchange during the relevant calendar month and the total number of shares represented by the index underlying such contracts traded.

Rule 6h–1. Settlement and regulatory halt requirements for security futures products

(a) For the purposes of this rule:

(1) *Opening price* means the price at which a security opened for trading, or a price that fairly reflects the price at which a security opened for trading, during the regular trading session of the national securities exchange or national securities association that lists the security. If the security is not listed on a national securities exchange or a national securities association, then *opening price* shall mean the price at which a security opened for trading, or a price that fairly reflects the price at which a security opened for trading, on the primary market for the security.

(2) *Regular trading session* of a security means the normal hours for business of a national securities exchange or national securities association that lists the security.

(3) *Regulatory halt* means a delay, halt, or suspension in the trading of a security, that is instituted by the national securities exchange or national securities association that lists the security, as a result of:

(i) A determination that there are matters relating to the security or issuer that have not been adequately disclosed to the public, or that there are regulatory problems relating to the security which should be clarified before trading is permitted to continue; or

(ii) The operation of circuit breaker procedures to halt or suspend trading in all equity securities trading on that national securities exchange or national securities association.

(b) *Final Settlement Prices for Security Futures Products.* (1) The final settlement price of a cash-settled security futures product must fairly reflect the opening price of the underlying security or securities.

(2) Notwithstanding paragraph (b)(1) of this rule, if an opening price for one or more securities underlying a security futures product is not readily available, the final settlement price of the security futures product shall fairly reflect:

(i) The price of the underlying security or securities during the most recent regular trading session for such security or securities; or

(ii) The next available opening price of the underlying security or securities.

(3) Notwithstanding paragraph (b)(1) or (b)(2) of this rule, if a clearing agency registered under section 17A of the Act (15 U.S.C. 78q–1), or exempt from registration pursuant to section 17A(b)(7) of the Act (15 U.S.C. 78q–1(b)(7)), to which the final settlement price of a security futures product is or would be reported determines, pursuant to its rules, that such final settlement price is not consistent with the protection of investors and the public interest, taking into account such factors as fairness to buyers and sellers of the affected security futures product, the maintenance of a fair and orderly market in such security futures product, and consistency of interpretation and practice, the clearing agency shall have the authority to determine, under its rules, a final settlement price for such security futures product.

(c) *Regulatory Trading Halts.* The rules of a national securities exchange or national securities association registered pursuant to section 15A(a) of the Act (15 U.S.C. 78o–3(a)) that lists or trades one or more security futures products must include the following provisions:

(1) Trading of a security futures product based on a single security shall be halted at all times that a regulatory halt has been instituted for the underlying security; and

(2) Trading of a security futures product based on a narrow-based security index shall be halted at all times that a regulatory halt has been instituted for one or more underlying securities that constitute 50 percent or more of the market capitalization of the narrow-based security index.

(d) The Commission may exempt from the requirements of this rule, either unconditionally or on specified terms and conditions, any national securities exchange or national securities association, if the Commission determines that such exemption is necessary or appropriate in the public interest and consistent with the protection of investors. An exemption granted pursuant to this paragraph shall not operate as an exemption from any Commodity Futures Trading Commission rules. Any exemption that may be required from such rules must be obtained separately from the Commodity Futures Trading Commission.

Rule 6h–2. Security future based on note, bond, debenture, or evidence of indebtedness

A security future may be based upon a security that is a note, bond, debenture, or evidence of indebtedness or a narrow-based security index composed of such securities.

Rule 7c2–1. [Reserved]

HYPOTHECATION OF CUSTOMERS' SECURITIES

Rule 8c–1. Hypothecation of customers' securities

(a) *General Provisions.* No member of a national securities exchange, and no broker or dealer who transacts a business in securities through the medium of any such member shall, directly or indirectly, hypothecate or arrange for or permit the continued hypothecation of any securities carried for the account of any customer under circumstances:

(1) That will permit the commingling of securities carried for the account of any such customer with securities carried for the account of any other customer, without first obtaining the written consent of each such customer to such hypothecation;

(2) That will permit such securities to be commingled with securities carried for the account of any person other than a bona fide customer of such member, broker or dealer under a lien for a loan made to such member, broker or dealer; or

(3) That will permit securities carried for the account of customers to be hypothecated, or subjected to any lien or liens or claim or claims of the pledges or pledgees, for a sum which exceeds the aggregate indebtedness of all customers in respect of securities carried for their accounts; except that this clause shall not be deemed to be violated by reason of an excess arising on any day through the reduction of the aggregate indebtedness of customers on such a day: *Provided,* That funds or securities in an amount sufficient to eliminate such excess are paid or placed in transfer to pledgees for the purpose of reducing the sum of the liens or claims to which securities carried for the account of customers are subjected as promptly as practicable after such reduction occurs, but before the lapse of one-half hour after the commencement of banking hours on the next banking day at the place where the largest principal amount of loans of such member, broker or dealer are payable and, in any event, before such member, broker or dealer on such day has obtained or increased any bank loan collateralized by securities carried for the account of customers.

(b) *Definitions.* For the purposes of this rule:

(1) The term *customer* shall not include any general or special partner or any director or officer of such member, broker or dealer, or any participant, as such, in any joint, group or syndicate account with such member, broker or dealer or with any partner, officer or director thereof. The term also shall not include any counterparty who has delivered collateral to an OTC derivatives dealer pursuant to a transaction in an eligible OTC derivative instrument, or pursuant to the OTC derivatives dealer's cash management securities activities or ancillary portfolio management securities activities, and who has received a prominent written notice from the OTC derivatives dealer that:

(i) Except as otherwise agreed in writing by the OTC derivatives dealer and the counterparty, the dealer may repledge or otherwise use the collateral in its business;

(ii) In the event of the OTC derivatives dealer's failure, the counterparty will likely be considered an unsecured creditor of the dealer as to that collateral;

(iii) The Securities Investor Protection Act of 1970 (15 U.S.C. 78aaa through 78lll) does not protect the counterparty; and

(iv) The collateral will not be subject to the requirements of Rule 8c–1, Rule 15c2–1, Rule 15c3–2, or Rule 15c3–3;

(2) The term *securities carried for the account of any customer* shall be deemed to mean:

(i) Securities received by or on behalf of such member, broker or dealer for the account of any customer;

(ii) Securities sold and appropriated by such member, broker or dealer to a customer, except that if such securities were subject to a lien when appropriated to a customer they shall not be deemed to be "securities carried for the account of any customer" pending their release from such lien as promptly as practicable;

(iii) Securities sold, but not appropriated, by such member, broker or dealer to a customer who has made any payment therefor, to the extent that such member, broker or dealer owns and has received delivery of securities of like kind, except that if such securities were subject to a lien when such payment was made they shall not be deemed to be "securities carried for the account of any customer" pending their release from such lien as promptly as practicable;

(3) "Aggregate indebtedness" shall not be deemed to be reduced by reason of uncollected items. In computing aggregate indebtedness, related guaranteed and guarantor accounts shall be treated as a single account and considered on a consolidated basis, and balances in accounts carrying both long and short positions shall be adjusted by treating the market value of the securities required to cover such short positions as though such market value were a debit; and

(4) In computing the sum of the liens or claims to which securities carried for the account of customers of a member, broker or dealer are subject, any rehypothecation of such securities by another member, broker or dealer who is subject to this rule or to Rule 15c2–1 shall be disregarded.

(c) *Exemption for Cash Accounts.* The provisions of paragraph (a)(1) of this rule shall not apply to any hypothecation of securities carried for the account of a customer in a special cash account within the meaning of 12 CFR 220.4(c): *Provided,* That at or before the completion of the transaction of purchase of such securities for, or of sale of such securities to, such customer, written notice is given or sent to such customer disclosing that such securities are or may be hypothecated under circumstances which will permit the commingling thereof with securities carried for the account of other customers. The term *the completion of the transaction* shall have the meaning given to such term by Rule 15c1–1(b).

(d) *Exemption for Clearinghouse Liens.* The provisions of paragraphs (a)(2), (a)(3), and (f) of this rule shall not apply to any lien or claim of the clearing corporation, or similar department or association, of a national securities exchange or a registered national securities association for a loan made and to be repaid on the same calendar day, which is incidental to the clearing of transactions in securities or loans through such corporation, department, or association: *Provided, however,* That for the purpose of paragraph (a)(3) of this rule, "aggregate indebtedness of all customers in respect of securities carried for their accounts" shall not include indebtedness in respect of any securities subject to any lien or claim exempted by this paragraph.

(e) *Exemption for Certain Liens on Securities of Noncustomers.* The provisions of paragraph (a)(2) of this rule shall not be deemed to prevent such member, broker, or dealer from permitting securities not carried for the account of a customer to be subjected (1) to a lien for a loan made against securities carried for the account of customers, or (2) to a lien for a loan made and to be repaid on the same calendar day. For the purpose of this exemption, a loan shall be deemed to be "made against securities carried for the account of customers" if only securities carried for the account of customers are used to obtain or to increase such loan or as substitutes for other securities carried for the account of customers.

(f) *Notice and Certification Requirements.* No person subject to this rule shall hypothecate any security carried for the account of a customer unless, at or prior to the time of each such hypothecation, he gives written notice to the pledgee that the security pledged is carried for the account of a customer and that such hypothecation does not contravene any provision of this rule, except that in the case of an omnibus account the member, broker or dealer for whom such account is carried may furnish a signed statement to the person carrying such account that all securities carried therein by such member, broker or dealer will be securities carried for the account of his customers and that the hypothecation thereof by such member, broker or dealer will not contravene any provision of this rule. The provisions of this paragraph shall not apply to any hypothecation of securities under any lien or claim of a pledgee securing a loan made and to be repaid on the same calendar day.

(g) The fact that securities carried for the accounts of customers and securities carried for the accounts of others are represented by one or more certificates in the custody of a clearing corporation or other subsidiary organization of either a national securities exchange or of a registered national securities association, or of a custodian bank, in accordance with a system for the central handling of securities established by a national securities exchange or a registered national securities association, pursuant to which system the hypothecation of such securities is effected by bookkeeping entries without physical delivery of such securities, shall not, in and of itself, result in a commingling of securities prohibited by paragraph (a)(1) or (a)(2) of this rule, whenever a participating member, broker or dealer hypothecates securities in accordance with such system: *Provided, however,* That (1) any such custodian of any securities held by or for such system shall agree that it will not for any reason, including the assertion of any claim, right or lien of any kind, refuse or refrain from promptly delivering any such securities (other than securities then hypothecated in accordance with such system) to such clearing corporation or other subsidiary organization or as directed by it, except that nothing in such agreement shall be deemed to require the custodian to deliver any securities in contravention of any notice of levy, seizure or similar notice, or order, or judgment, issued or directed by a governmental agency or court, or officer thereof, having jurisdiction over such custodian, which on its face affects such securities; (2) such systems shall have safeguards in the handling, transfer and delivery of securities and provisions for fidelity bond coverage of the employees and agents of the clearing corporation or other subsidiary organization and for periodic examinations by independent public accountants; and (3) the provisions of this paragraph shall not be effective with respect to any particular system unless the agreement required by paragraph (g)(1) of this rule and the safeguards and provisions required by paragraph (g)(2) of this rule shall have been deemed adequate by the Commission for the protection of investors, and unless any subsequent amendments to such agreement, safeguards or provisions shall have been deemed adequate by the Commission for the protection of investors.

Rule 9b–1. Options disclosure document

(a) *Definitions.* The following definitions shall apply for the purpose of this rule:

(1) *Options market* means a national securities exchange, an automated quotation system of a registered securities association or a foreign securities exchange on which standardized options are traded.

(2) *Options class* means all options contracts covering the same underlying instrument.

(3) *Options disclosure document* means a document, including all amendments and supplements thereto, prepared by one or more options markets which has been filed with the Commission or distributed in accordance with paragraph (b) of this rule. *Definitive options disclosure document* or *document* means an options disclosure document furnished to customers in accordance with paragraph (b) of this rule.

(4) *Standardized options* are options contracts trading on a national securities exchange, an automated quotation system of a registered securities association, or a foreign securities exchange which relate to options classes the terms of which are limited to specific expiration dates and exercise prices, or such other securities as the Commission may, by order, designate.

(b)(1) Five preliminary copies of an options disclosure document containing the information specified in paragraph (c) of this rule shall be filed with the Commission by an options market at least 60 days prior to the date definitive copies are furnished to customers, unless the Commission determines otherwise having due regard to the adequacy of the information disclosed and the public interest and protection of investors. Five copies of the definitive options disclosure document shall be filed with the Commission not later than the date the options disclosure document is furnished to customers. Notwithstanding the above, the use of an options disclosure document shall not be permitted unless the options class to which such document relates is the subject of an effective registration statement on Form S–20 under the Securities Act of 1933, or is exempt from registration under the Securities Act of 1933.

(2)(i) If the information contained in the options disclosure document becomes or will become materially inaccurate or incomplete or there is or will be an omission of material information necessary to make the options disclosure document not misleading, the options market shall amend or supplement its options disclosure document by filing five copies of an amendment or supplement to such options disclosure document with the Commission at least 30 days prior to the date definitive copies are furnished to customers, unless the Commission determines otherwise having due regard to the adequacy of the information disclosed and the public interest and protection of investors. Five copies of the definitive options disclosure document, as amended or supplemented, shall be filed with the Commission not later than the date the amendment or supplement, or the amended options disclosure document, is furnished to customers.

(ii) Notwithstanding paragraph (b)(2)(i) of this rule, an options market may distribute an amendment or supplement to an options disclosure document prior to such 30 day period if it determines, in good faith, that such delivery is necessary to ensure timely and accurate disclosure with respect to one or more of the options classes covered by the document. Five copies of any amendment or supplement distributed pursuant to this paragraph shall be filed with the Commission at the time of distribution. In that instance, if the Commission determines, having given due regard to the adequacy of the information disclosed and the public interest and the protection of investors, it may require refiling of the amendment pursuant to paragraph (b)(2)(i) of this rule.

(c) *Information Required in an Options Disclosure Document.* An options disclosure document shall contain the following information, unless otherwise provided by the Commission, with respect to the options classes covered by the document:

(1) A glossary of terms;

(2) A discussion of the mechanics of exercising the options;

(3) A discussion of the risks of being a holder or writer of the options;

(4) The identification of the market or markets in which the options are traded;

(5) A brief reference to the transaction costs, margin requirements and tax consequences of options trading;

(6) The identification of the issuer of the options;

(7) A general identification of the type of instrument or instruments underlying the options class or classes covered by the document;

(8) If the options are not exempt from registration under the Securities Act of 1933, the registration of the options on Form S–20 (17 CFR 239.20) and the availability of the prospectus and the information in part II of the registration statement; and

(9) Such other information as the Commission may specify.

(d) *Broker–Dealer Obligations.* (1) No broker or dealer shall accept an order from a customer to purchase or sell an option contract relating to an options class that is the subject of a definitive options disclosure document, or approve the customer's account for the trading of such option, unless the broker or dealer furnishes or has furnished to the customer a copy of the definitive options disclosure document.

(2) If a definitive options disclosure document relating to an options class is amended or supplemented, each broker and dealer shall promptly send a copy of the definitive amendment or supplement or a copy of the definitive options disclosure document as amended to each customer whose account is approved for trading the options class or classes to which the amendment or supplement relates.

Rule 10a–1. [Reserved]

Rule 10a–2. [Reserved]

MANIPULATIVE AND DECEPTIVE DEVICES AND CONTRIVANCES

Rule 10b–1. Prohibition of use of manipulative or deceptive devices or contrivances with respect to certain securities exempted from registration

The term *manipulative or deceptive device or contrivance*, as used in section 10(b) (15 U.S.C. 78j(b)), is hereby defined to include any act or omission to act with respect to any security exempted from the operation of section 12(a) (15 U.S.C. 78*l*(a)) pursuant to a rule which specifically provides that this rule shall be applicable to such security, if such act or omission to act would have been unlawful under section 9(a) (15 U.S.C. 78i(a)), or any rule or regulation heretofore or hereafter prescribed thereunder, if done or omitted to be done with respect to a security registered on a national securities exchange, and the use of any means or instrumentality of interstate commerce or of the mails or of any facility of any national securities exchange to use or employ any such device or contrivance in connection with the purchase or sale of any such security is hereby prohibited.

Rule 10b–2. [Reserved]

Rule 10b–3. Employment of manipulative and deceptive devices by brokers or dealers

(a) It shall be unlawful for any broker or dealer, directly or indirectly, by the use of any means or instrumentality of interstate commerce, or of the mails, or of any facility of any national securities exchange, to use or employ, in connection with the purchase or sale of any security otherwise than on a national securities exchange, any act, practice, or course of business defined by the Commission to be included within the term "manipulative, deceptive, or other fraudulent device or contrivance," as such term is used in section 15(c)(1) of the Act.

(b) It shall be unlawful for any municipal securities dealer directly or indirectly, by the use of any means or instrumentality of interstate commerce, or of the mails, or of any facility of any national securities exchange, to use or employ, in connection with the purchase or sale of any municipal security, any act, practice, or course of business defined by the Commission to be included within the term "manipulative, deceptive, or other fraudulent device or contrivance," as such term is used in section 15(c)(1) of the Act.

Rule 10b–4. [Reserved]

Rule 10b–5. Employment of manipulative and deceptive devices

It shall be unlawful for any person, directly or indirectly, by the use of any means or instrumentality of interstate commerce, or of the mails, or of any facility of any national securities exchange,

(a) To employ any device, scheme, or artifice to defraud,

(b) To make any untrue statement of a material fact or to omit to state a material fact necessary in order to make the statements made, in the light of the circumstances under which they were made, not misleading, or

(c) To engage in any act, practice, or course of business which operates or would operate as a fraud or deceit upon any person,

in connection with the purchase or sale of any security.

Rule 10b5–1. Trading "on the basis of" material nonpublic information in insider trading cases

PRELIMINARY NOTE TO RULE 10B5–1:

This provision defines when a purchase or sale constitutes trading "on the basis of" material nonpublic information in insider trading cases brought under Section 10(b) of the Act and Rule 10b–5 thereunder. The law of insider trading is otherwise defined by judicial opinions construing Rule 10b–5, and Rule 10b5–1 does not modify the scope of insider trading law in any other respect.

(a) *General.* The "manipulative and deceptive devices" prohibited by Section 10(b) of the Act (15 U.S.C. 78j) and Rule 10b–5 thereunder include, among other things, the purchase or sale of a security of any issuer, on the basis of material nonpublic information about that security or issuer, in breach of a duty of trust or confidence that is owed directly, indirectly, or derivatively, to the issuer of that security or the shareholders of that issuer, or to any other person who is the source of the material nonpublic information.

(b) *Definition of "on the basis of."* Subject to the affirmative defenses in paragraph (c) of this rule, a purchase or sale of a security of an issuer is "on the basis of" material nonpublic information about that security or issuer if the person making the purchase or sale was aware of the material nonpublic information when the person made the purchase or sale.

(c) *Affirmative Defenses.* (1)(i) Subject to paragraph (c)(1)(ii) of this rule, a person's purchase or sale is not "on the basis of" material nonpublic information if the person making the purchase or sale demonstrates that:

(A) Before becoming aware of the information, the person had:

(1) Entered into a binding contract to purchase or sell the security,

(2) Instructed another person to purchase or sell the security for the instructing person's account, or

(3) Adopted a written plan for trading securities;

(B) The contract, instruction, or plan described in paragraph (c)(1)(i)(A) of this rule:

(1) Specified the amount of securities to be purchased or sold and the price at which and the date on which the securities were to be purchased or sold;

(2) Included a written formula or algorithm, or computer program, for determining the amount of securities to be purchased or sold and the price at which and the date on which the securities were to be purchased or sold; or

(3) Did not permit the person to exercise any subsequent influence over how, when, or whether to effect purchases or sales; provided, in addition, that any other person who, pursuant to the contract, instruction, or plan, did exercise such influence must not have been aware of the material nonpublic information when doing so; and

(C) The purchase or sale that occurred was pursuant to the contract, instruction, or plan. A purchase or sale is not "pursuant to a contract, instruction, or plan" if, among other things, the person who entered into the contract, instruction, or plan altered or deviated from the contract, instruction, or plan to purchase or sell securities (whether by changing the amount, price, or timing of the purchase or sale), or entered into or altered a corresponding or hedging transaction or position with respect to those securities.

(ii) Paragraph (c)(1)(i) of this rule is applicable only when the contract, instruction, or plan to purchase or sell securities was given or entered into in good faith and not as part of a plan or scheme to evade the prohibitions of this rule.

(iii) This paragraph (c)(1)(iii) defines certain terms as used in paragraph (c) of this rule.

(A) *Amount*. "Amount" means either a specified number of shares or other securities or a specified dollar value of securities.

(B) *Price*. "Price" means the market price on a particular date or a limit price, or a particular dollar price.

(C) *Date*. "Date" means, in the case of a market order, the specific day of the year on which the order is to be executed (or as soon thereafter as is practicable under ordinary principles of best execution). "Date" means, in the case of a limit order, a day of the year on which the limit order is in force.

(2) A person other than a natural person also may demonstrate that a purchase or sale of securities is not "on the basis of" material nonpublic information if the person demonstrates that:

(i) The individual making the investment decision on behalf of the person to purchase or sell the securities was not aware of the information; and

(ii) The person had implemented reasonable policies and procedures, taking into consideration the nature of the person's business, to ensure that individuals making investment decisions would not violate the laws prohibiting trading on the basis of material nonpublic information. These policies and procedures may include those that restrict any purchase, sale, and causing any purchase or sale of any security as to which the person has material nonpublic information, or those that prevent such individuals from becoming aware of such information.

Rule 10b5–2. Duties of trust or confidence in misappropriation insider trading cases

PRELIMINARY NOTE TO RULE 10B5–2:

This section provides a non-exclusive definition of circumstances in which a person has a duty of trust or confidence for purposes of the "misappropriation" theory of insider trading under Section 10(b) of the Act and Rule 10b–5. The law of insider trading is otherwise defined by judicial opinions construing Rule 10b–5, and Rule 10b5–2 does not modify the scope of insider trading law in any other respect.

(a) *Scope of Rule.* This rule shall apply to any violation of Section 10(b) of the Act (15 U.S.C. 78j(b)) and Rule 10b–5 thereunder that is based on the purchase or sale of securities on the basis of, or the communication of, material nonpublic information misappropriated in breach of a duty of trust or confidence.

(b) *Enumerated "duties of trust or confidence."* For purposes of this rule, a "duty of trust or confidence" exists in the following circumstances, among others:

(1) Whenever a person agrees to maintain information in confidence;

(2) Whenever the person communicating the material nonpublic information and the person to whom it is communicated have a history, pattern, or practice of sharing confidences, such that the recipient of the information knows or reasonably should know that the person communicating the material nonpublic information expects that the recipient will maintain its confidentiality; or

(3) Whenever a person receives or obtains material nonpublic information from his or her spouse, parent, child, or sibling; *provided*, however, that the person receiving or obtaining the information may demonstrate that no duty of trust or confidence existed with respect to the information, by establishing that he or she neither knew nor reasonably should have known that the person who was the source of the information expected that the person would keep the information confidential, because of the parties' history, pattern, or practice of sharing and maintaining confidences, and because there was no agreement or understanding to maintain the confidentiality of the information.

Rule 10b–6. [Reserved]

Rule 10b–7. [Reserved]

Rule 10b–8. [Reserved]

Rule 10b–9. Prohibited representations in connection with certain offerings

(a) It shall constitute a *manipulative or deceptive device or contrivance,* as used in section 10(b) of the Act, for any person, directly or indirectly, in connection with the offer or sale of any security, to make any representation:

(1) To the effect that the security is being offered or sold on an "all-or-none" basis, unless the security is part of an offering or distribution being made on the condition that all or a specified amount of the consideration paid for such security will be promptly refunded to the purchaser unless (i) all of the securities being offered are sold at a specified price within a specified time, and (ii) the total amount due to the seller is received by him by a specified date; or

(2) To the effect that the security is being offered or sold on any other basis whereby all or part of the consideration paid for any such security will be refunded to the purchaser if all or some of the securities are not sold, unless the security is part of an offering or distribution being made on the condition that all or a specified part of the consideration paid for such security will be promptly refunded to the purchaser unless (i) a specified number of units of the security are sold at a specified price within a specified time, and (ii) the total amount due to the seller is received by him by a specified date.

(b) This rule shall not apply to any offer or sale of securities as to which the seller has a firm commitment from underwriters or others (subject only to customary conditions precedent, including "market outs") for the purchase of all the securities being offered.

Rule 10b–10. Confirmation of transactions

Preliminary Note

This rule requires broker-dealers to disclose specified information in writing to customers at or before completion of a transaction. The requirements under this rule that particular information be disclosed is not determinative of a broker-dealer's obligation under the general antifraud provisions of the federal securities laws to disclose additional information to a customer at the time of the customer's investment decision.

(a) *Disclosure Requirement.* It shall be unlawful for any broker or dealer to effect for or with an account of a customer any transaction in, or to induce the purchase or sale by such customer of, any security (other than U.S. Savings Bonds or municipal securities) unless such broker or dealer, at or before completion of such transaction, gives or sends to such customer written notification disclosing:

(1) The date and time of the transaction (or the fact that the time of the transaction will be furnished upon written request to such customer) and the identity, price, and number of shares or units (or principal amount) of such security purchased or sold by such customer; and

(2) Whether the broker or dealer is acting as agent for such customer, as agent for some other person, as agent for both such customer and some other person, or as principal for its own account; and if the broker or dealer is acting as principal, whether it is a market maker in the security (other than by reason of acting as a block positioner); and

(i) If the broker or dealer is acting as agent for such customer, for some other person, or for both such customer and some other person:

(A) The name of the person from whom the security was purchased, or to whom it was sold, for such customer or the fact that the information will be furnished upon written request of such customer; and

(B) The amount of any remuneration received or to be received by the broker from such customer in connection with the transaction unless remuneration paid by such customer is determined pursuant to written agreement with such customer, otherwise than on a transaction basis; and

(C) For a transaction in any NMS stock as defined in Rule 600 of Regulation NMS or a security authorized for quotation on an automated interdealer quotation system that has the characteristics set forth in section 17B of the Act (15 U.S.C. 78q–2), a statement whether payment for order flow is received by the broker or dealer for transactions in such securities and the fact that the source and nature of the compensation received in connection with the particular transaction will be furnished upon written request of the customer; *provided, however,* that brokers or dealers that do not receive payment for order flow in connection with any transaction have no disclosure obligations under this paragraph; and

(D) The source and amount of any other remuneration received or to be received by the broker in connection with the transaction: *Provided, however,* that if, in the case of a purchase, the broker was not participating in a distribution, or in the case of a sale, was not participating in a tender offer, the written notification may state whether any other remuneration has been or will be received and the fact that the source and amount of such other remuneration will be furnished upon written request of such customer; or

(ii) If the broker or dealer is acting as principal for its own account:

(A) In the case where such broker or dealer is not a market maker in an equity security and, if, after having received an order to buy from a customer, the broker or dealer purchased the equity security from another person to offset a contemporaneous sale to such customer or, after having received an order to sell from a customer, the broker or dealer sold the security to another person to offset a contemporaneous purchase from such customer, the difference between the price to the customer and the dealer's contemporaneous purchase (for customer purchases) or sale price (for customer sales); or

(B) In the case of any other transaction in an NMS stock as defined by Rule 600 of Regulation NMS, or an equity security that is traded on a national securities exchange and that is subject to last sale reporting, the reported trade price, the price to the customer in the transaction, and the difference, if any, between the reported trade price and the price to the customer.

(3) Whether any odd-lot differential or equivalent fee has been paid by such customer in connection with the execution of an order for an odd-lot number of shares or units (or principal amount) of a security and the fact that the amount of any such differential or fee will be furnished upon oral or written request: *Provided, however,* that such disclosure need not be made if the differential or fee is included in the remuneration disclosure, or exempted from disclosure, pursuant to paragraph (a)(2)(i)(B) of this rule; and

(4) In the case of any transaction in a debt security subject to redemption before maturity, a statement to the effect that such debt security may be redeemed in whole or in part before maturity, that such a redemption could affect the yield represented and the fact that additional information is available upon request; and

(5) In the case of a transaction in a debt security effected exclusively on the basis of a dollar price:

(i) The dollar price at which the transaction was effected, and

(ii) The yield to maturity calculated from the dollar price: *Provided, however,* that this paragraph (a)(5)(ii) shall not apply to a transaction in a debt security that either:

(A) Has a maturity date that may be extended by the issuer thereof, with a variable interest payable thereon; or

(B) Is an asset-backed security, that represents an interest in or is secured by a pool of receivables or other financial assets that are subject continuously to prepayment; and

(6) In the case of a transaction in a debt security effected on the basis of yield:

(i) The yield at which the transaction was effected, including the percentage amount and its characterization (*e.g.,* current yield, yield to maturity, or yield to call) and if effected at yield to call, the type of call, the call date and call price; and

(ii) The dollar price calculated from the yield at which the transaction was effected; and

(iii) If effected on a basis other than yield to maturity and the yield to maturity is lower than the represented yield, the yield to maturity as well as the represented yield: *Provided, however,* that this paragraph (a)(6)(iii) shall not apply to a transaction in a debt security that either:

(A) Has a maturity date that may be extended by the issuer thereof, with a variable interest rate payable thereon; or

(B) Is an asset-backed security, that represents an interest in or is secured by a pool of receivables or other financial assets that are subject continuously to prepayment; and

(7) In the case of a transaction in a debt security that is an asset-backed security, which represents an interest in or is secured by a pool of receivables or other financial assets that are subject continuously to prepayment, a statement indicating that the actual yield of such asset-backed security may vary according to the rate at which the underlying receivables or other financial assets are pre-

paid and a statement of the fact that information concerning the factors that affect yield (including at a minimum estimated yield, weighted average life, and the prepayment assumptions underlying yield) will be furnished upon written request of such customer; and

(8) That the broker or dealer is not a member of the Securities Investor Protection Corporation (SIPC), or that the broker or dealer clearing or carrying the customer account is not a member of SIPC, if such is the case: *Provided, however,* that this paragraph (a)(9) shall not apply in the case of a transaction in shares of a registered open-end investment company or unit investment trust if:

(i) The customer sends funds or securities directly to, or receives funds or securities directly from, the registered open-end investment company or unit investment trust, its transfer agent, its custodian, or other designated agent, and such person is not an associated person of the broker or dealer required by paragraph (a) of this rule to send written notification to the customer; and

(ii) The written notification required by paragraph (a) of this rule is sent on behalf of the broker or dealer to the customer by a person described in paragraph (a)(9)(i) of this rule.

(b) *Alternative Periodic Reporting.* A broker or dealer may effect transactions for or with the account of a customer without giving or sending to such customer the written notification described in paragraph (a) of this rule if:

(1) Such transactions are effected pursuant to a periodic plan or an investment company plan, or effected in shares of any open-end management investment company registered under the Investment Company Act of 1940 that holds itself out as a money market fund and attempts to maintain a stable net asset value per share: *Provided, however,* that no sales load is deducted upon the purchase or redemption of shares in the money market fund; and

(2) Such broker or dealer gives or sends to such customer within five business days after the end of each *quarterly* period, for transactions involving investment company and periodic plans, and after the end of each *monthly* period, for other transactions described in paragraph (b)(1) of this rule, a written statement disclosing each purchase or redemption, effected for or with, and each dividend or distribution credited to or reinvested for, the account of such customer during the month; the date of such transaction; the identity, number, and price of any securities purchased or redeemed by such customer in each such transaction; the total number of shares of such securities in such customer's account; any remuneration received or to be received by the broker or dealer in connection therewith; and that any other information required by paragraph (a) of this rule will be furnished upon written request: *Provided, however,* that the written statement may be delivered to some other person designated by the customer for distribution to the customer; and

(3) Such customer is provided with prior notification in writing disclosing the intention to send the written information referred to in paragraph (b)(1) of this rule in lieu of an immediate confirmation.

(c) A broker or dealer shall give or send to a customer information requested pursuant to this rule within five business days of receipt of the request; *Provided, however,* That in the case of information pertaining to a transaction effected more than 30 days prior to receipt of the request, the information shall be given or sent to the customer within 15 business days.

(d) *Definitions.* For the purposes of this rule:

(1) *Customer* shall not include a broker or dealer;

(2) *Completion of the transaction* shall have the meaning provided in Rule 15c1–1 under the Act;

(3) *Time of the transaction* means the time of execution, to the extent feasible, of the customer's order;

(4) *Debt security* as used in paragraphs (a)(3), (a)(4), and (a)(5) only, means any security, such as a bond, debenture, note, or any other similar instrument which evidences a liability of the issuer (including any such security that is convertible into stock or a similar security) and fractional or participation interests in one or more of any of the foregoing; *Provided, however,* That securities issued by an investment company registered under the Investment Company Act of 1940 shall not be included in this definition;

(5) *Periodic plan* means any written authorization for a broker acting as agent to purchase or sell for a customer a specific security or securities (other than securities issued by an open end investment company or unit investment trust registered under the Investment Company Act of 1940), in specific amounts (calculated in security

units or dollars), at specific time intervals and setting forth the commissions or charges to be paid by the customer in connection therewith (or the manner of calculating them); and

(6) *Investment company plan* means any plan under which securities issued by an open-end investment company or unit investment trust registered under the Investment Company Act of 1940 are purchased by a customer (the payments being made directly to, or made payable to, the registered investment company, or the principal underwriter, custodian, trustee, or other designated agent of the registered investment company), or sold by a customer pursuant to:

(i) An individual retirement or individual pension plan qualified under the Internal Revenue Code; or

(ii) A contractual or systematic agreement under which the customer purchases at the applicable public offering price, or redeems at the applicable redemption price, such securities in specified amounts (calculated in security units or dollars) at specified time intervals and setting forth the commissions or charges to be paid by such customer in connection therewith (or the manner of calculating them); or

(iii) Any other arrangement involving a group of two or more customers and contemplating periodic purchases of such securities by each customer through a person designated by the group; *Provided,* That such arrangement requires the registered investment company or its agent

(A) To give or send to the designated person, at or before the completion of the transaction for the purchase of such securities, a written notification of the receipt of the total amount paid by the group;

(B) To send to anyone in the group who was a customer in the prior quarter and on whose behalf payment has not been received in the current quarter a quarterly written statement reflecting that a payment was not received on his behalf; and

(C) To advise each customer in the group if a payment is not received from the designated person on behalf of the group within 10 days of a date certain specified in the arrangement for delivery of that payment by the designated person and thereafter to send to each such customer the written notification described in paragraph (a) of this rule for the next three succeeding payments.

(7) *NMS stock* shall have the meaning provided in Rule 600 of Regulation NMS.

(8) *Payment for order flow* shall mean any monetary payment, service, property, or other benefit that results in remuneration, compensation, or consideration to a broker or dealer from any broker or dealer, national securities exchange, registered securities association, or exchange member in return for the routing of customer orders by such broker or dealer to any broker or dealer, national securities exchange, registered securities association, or exchange member for execution, including but not limited to: research, clearance, custody, products or services; reciprocal agreements for the provision of order flow; adjustment of a broker or dealer's unfavorable trading errors; offers to participate as underwriter in public offerings; stock loans or shared interest accrued thereon; discounts, rebates, or any other reductions of or credits against any fee to, or expense or other financial obligation of, the broker or dealer routing a customer order that exceeds that fee, expense or financial obligation.

(9) *Asset-backed security* means a security that is primarily serviced by the cashflows of a discrete pool of receivables or other financial assets, either fixed or revolving, that by their terms convert into cash within a finite time period plus any rights or other assets designed to assure the servicing or timely distribution of proceeds to the security holders.

(e) *Security Futures Products.* The provisions of paragraphs (a) and (b) of this rule shall not apply to a broker or dealer registered pursuant to section 15(b)(11)(A) of the Act (15 U.S.C. 78*o*(b)(11)(A)) to the extent that it effects transactions for customers in security futures products in a futures account (as that term is defined in Rule 15c3–3(a)(15)) and a broker or dealer registered pursuant to section 15(b)(1) of the Act (15 U.S.C. 78*o*(b)(1)) that is also a futures commission merchant registered pursuant to section 4f(a)(1) of the Commodity Exchange Act (7 U.S.C. 6f(a)(1)), to the extent that it effects transactions for customers in security futures products in a futures account (as that term is defined in Rule 15c3–3(a)(15)), *Provided* that:

(1) The broker or dealer that effects any transaction for a customer in security futures products in a futures account gives or sends to the customer no later than the next business day after execu-

tion of any futures securities product transaction, written notification disclosing:

(i) The date the transaction was executed, the identity of the single security or narrow-based security index underlying the contract for the security futures product, the number of contracts of such security futures product purchased or sold, the price, and the delivery month;

(ii) The source and amount of any remuneration received or to be received by the broker or dealer in connection with the transaction, including, but not limited to, markups, commissions, costs, fees, and other charges incurred in connection with the transaction, provided, however, that if no remuneration is to be paid for an initiating transaction until the occurrence of the corresponding liquidating transaction, that the broker or dealer may disclose the amount of remuneration only on the confirmation for the liquidating transaction;

(iii) The fact that information about the time of the execution of the transaction, the identity of the other party to the contract, and whether the broker or dealer is acting as agent for such customer, as agent for some other person, as agent for both such customer and some other person, or as principal for its own account, and if the broker or dealer is acting as principal, whether it is engaging in a block transaction or an exchange of security futures products for physical securities, will be available upon written request of the customer; and

(iv) Whether payment for order flow is received by the broker or dealer for such transactions, the amount of this payment and the fact that the source and nature of the compensation received in connection with the particular transaction will be furnished upon written request of the customer; provided, however, that brokers or dealers that do not receive payment for order flow have no disclosure obligation under this paragraph.

(2) *Transitional Provision.* (i) Broker-dealers are not required to comply with paragraph (e)(1)(iii) of this rule until June 1, 2003, *Provided* that, if, not withstanding the absence of the disclosure required in that paragraph, the broker-dealer receives a written request from a customer for the information described in paragraph (e)(1)(iii) of this rule, the broker-dealer must make the information available to the customer; and

(ii) Broker-dealers are not required to comply with paragraph (e)(1)(iv) of this rule until June 1, 2003.

(f) The Commission may exempt any broker or dealer from the requirements of paragraphs (a) and (b) of this rule with regard to specific transactions or specific classes of transactions for which the broker or dealer will provide alternative procedures to effect the purposes of this rule; any such exemption may be granted subject to compliance with such alternative procedures and upon such other stated terms and conditions as the Commission may impose.

Rule 10b–13. [Reserved]

Rule 10b–16. Disclosure of credit terms in margin transactions

(a) It shall be unlawful for any broker or dealer to extend credit, directly or indirectly, to any customer in connection with any securities transaction unless such broker or dealer has established procedures to assure that each customer:

(1) Is given or sent at the time of opening the account, a written statement or statements disclosing (i) the conditions under which an interest charge will be imposed; (ii) the annual rate or rates of interest that can be imposed; (iii) the method of computing interest; (iv) if rates of interest are subject to change without prior notice, the specific conditions under which they can be changed; (v) the method of determining the debit balance or balances on which interest is to be charged and whether credit is to be given for credit balances in cash accounts; (vi) what other charges resulting from the extension of credit, if any, will be made and under what conditions; and (vii) the nature of any interest or lien retained by the broker or dealer in the security or other property held as collateral and the conditions under which additional collateral can be required: *Provided, however,* That the requirements of this subparagraph will be met in any case where the account is opened by telephone if the information required to be disclosed is orally communicated to the customer at that time and the required written statement or statements are sent to the customer immediately thereafter: *And provided, further,* That in the case of customers to whom credit is already being extended on the effective date of this rule, the written statement or statements required hereunder must be given or sent to said customers within 90 days after the effective date of this rule; and

(2) Is given or sent a written statement or statements, at least quarterly, for each account

in which credit was extended, disclosing (i) the balance at the beginning of the period; the date, amount and a brief description of each debit and credit entered during such period; the closing balance; and, if interest is charged for a period different from the period covered by the statement, the balance as of the last day of the interest period; (ii) the total interest charge for the period during which interest is charged (or, if interest is charged separately for separate accounts, the total interest charge for each such account), itemized to show the dates on which the interest period began and ended; the annual rate or rates of interest charged and the interest charge for each such different annual rate of interest; and either each different debit balance on which an interest calculation was based or the average debit balance for the interest period, except that if an average debit balance is used, a separate average debit balance must be disclosed for each interest rate applied; and (iii) all other charges resulting from the extension of credit in that account: *Provided, however,* That if the interest charge disclosed on a statement is for a period different from the period covered by the statement, there must be printed on the statement appropriate language to the effect that it should be retained for use in conjunction with the next statement containing the remainder of the required information: *And provided further,* That in the case of "equity funding programs" registered under the Securities Act of 1933, the requirements of this paragraph will be met if the broker or dealer furnishes to the customer, within 1 month after each extension of credit, a written statement or statements containing the information required to be disclosed under this paragraph.

(b) It shall be unlawful for any broker or dealer to make any changes in the terms and conditions under which credit charges will be made (as described in the initial statement made under paragraph (a) of this rule), unless the customer shall have been given not less than thirty (30) days written notice of such changes, except that no such prior notice shall be necessary where such changes are required by law: *Provided, however,* That if any change for which prior notice would otherwise be required under this paragraph results in a lower interest charge to the customer than would have been imposed before the change, notice of such change may be given within a reasonable time after the effective date of the change.

Rule 10b-17. Untimely announcements of record dates

(a) It shall constitute a "manipulative or deceptive device or contrivance" as used in section 10(b) of the Act for any issuer of a class of securities publicly traded by the use of any means or instrumentality of interstate commerce or of the mails or of any facility of any national securities exchange to fail to give notice in accordance with paragraph (b) of this rule of the following actions relating to such class of securities:

(1) A dividend or other distribution in cash or in kind, except an ordinary interest payment on a debt security, but including a dividend or distribution of any security of the same or another issuer;

(2) A stock split or reverse split; or

(3) A rights or other subscription offering.

(b) Notice shall be deemed to have been given in accordance with this rule only if:

(1) Given to the National Association of Securities Dealers, Inc., no later than 10 days prior to the record date involved or, in case of a rights subscription or other offering if such 10 days advance notice is not practical, on or before the record date and in no event later than the effective date of the registration statement to which the offering relates, and such notice includes:

(i) Title of the security to which the declaration relates;

(ii) Date of declaration;

(iii) Date of record for determining holders entitled to receive the dividend or other distribution or to participate in the stock or reverse split;

(iv) Date of payment or distribution or, in the case of a stock or reverse split or rights or other subscription offering, the date of delivery;

(v) For a dividend or other distribution including a stock or reverse split or rights or other subscription offering:

(A) In cash, the amount of cash to be paid or distributed per share, except if exact per share cash distributions cannot be given because of existing conversion rights which may be exercised during the notice period and which may affect the per share cash distribution, then a reasonable approximation of the per share distribution may be provided so long as the

actual per share distribution is subsequently provided on the record date.

(B) In the same security, the amount of the security outstanding immediately prior to and immediately following the dividend or distribution and the rate of the dividend or distribution.

(C) In any other security of the same issuer, the amount to be paid or distributed and the rate of the dividend or distribution.

(D) In any security of another issuer, the name of the issuer and title of that security, the amount to be paid or distributed, and the rate of the dividend or distribution and if that security is a right or a warrant, the subscription price.

(E) In any other property (including securities not covered under *(b)(1)(v)* through *(d)* of this rule) the identity of the property and its value and basis for assigning that value;

(vi) Method of settlement of fractional interests;

(vii) Details of any condition which must be satisfied or Government approval which must be secured to enable payment of distribution; and in

(viii) The case of stock or reverse split in addition to the aforementioned information;

(A) The name and address of the transfer or exchange agent; or

(2) The Commission, upon written request or upon its own motion, exempts the issuer from compliance with paragraph (b)(1) of this rule either unconditionally or on specified terms or conditions, as not constituting a manipulative or deceptive device or contrivance comprehended within the purpose of this rule or;

(3) Given in accordance with procedures of the national securities exchange or exchanges upon which a security of such issuer is registered pursuant to section 12 of the Act which contain requirements substantially comparable to those set forth in subparagraph (b)(1) of this rule.

(c) The provisions of this rule shall not apply, however, to redeemable securities issued by open-end investment companies registered with the Commission under the Investment Company Act of 1940.

Rule 10b–18. Purchases of certain equity securities by the issuer and others

Preliminary Notes to Rule 10b–18

1. Rule 10b–18 provides an issuer (and its affiliated purchasers) with a "safe harbor" from liability for manipulation under sections 9(a)(2) of the Act and Rule 10b–5 under the Act *solely* by reason of the manner, timing, price, and volume of their repurchases when they repurchase the issuer's common stock in the market in accordance with the section's manner, timing, price, and volume conditions. As a safe harbor, compliance with Rule 10b–18 is voluntary. To come within the safe harbor, however, an issuer's repurchases must satisfy (on a daily basis) each of the rule's four conditions. Failure to meet any one of the four conditions will remove all of the issuer's repurchases from the safe harbor for that day. The safe harbor, moreover, is not available for repurchases that, although made in technical compliance with the rule, are part of a plan or scheme to evade the federal securities laws.

2. Regardless of whether the repurchases are effected in accordance with Rule 10b–18, reporting issuers must report their repurchasing activity as required by Item 703 of Regulations S–K and S–B (17 CFR 229.703 and 228.703) and Item 15(e) of Form 20–F (17 CFR 249.220f) (regarding foreign private issuers), and closed-end management investment companies that are registered under the Investment Company Act of 1940 must report their repurchasing activity as required by Item 8 of Form N–CSR (17 CFR 249.331; 17 CFR 274.128).

(a) *Definitions*. Unless otherwise provided, all terms used in this rule shall have the same meaning as in the Act. In addition, the following definitions shall apply:

(1) *ADTV* means the average daily trading volume reported for the security during the four calendar weeks preceding the week in which the Rule 10b–18 purchase is to be effected.

(2) *Affiliate* means any person that directly or indirectly controls, is controlled by, or is under common control with, the issuer.

(3) *Affiliated purchaser* means:

(i) A person acting, directly or indirectly, in concert with the issuer for the purpose of acquiring the issuer's securities; or

(ii) An affiliate who, directly or indirectly, controls the issuer's purchases of such securities, whose purchases are controlled by the issuer, or whose purchases are under common control with those of the issuer; *Provided, however*, that "affiliated purchaser" shall not include a broker, dealer, or other person solely by reason of such broker, dealer, or other person effecting Rule 10b–18 purchases on behalf of the issuer or for its account, and shall not include an officer or director of the issuer solely by reason of that officer or director's participation in the decision to authorize Rule 10b–18 purchases by or on behalf of the issuer.

(4) *Agent independent of the issuer* has the meaning contained in Rule 100 of Regulation M.

(5) *Block* means a quantity of stock that either:

(i) Has a purchase price of $200,000 or more; or

(ii) Is at least 5,000 shares and has a purchase price of at least $50,000; or

(iii) Is at least 20 round lots of the security and totals 150 percent or more of the trading volume for that security or, in the event that trading volume data are unavailable, is at least 20 round lots of the security and totals at least one-tenth of one percent (.001) of the outstanding shares of the security, exclusive of any shares owned by any affiliate; *Provided, however*, That a block under paragraph (a)(5)(i), (ii), and (iii) shall not include any amount a broker or dealer, acting as principal, has accumulated for the purpose of sale or resale to the issuer or to any affiliated purchaser of the issuer if the issuer or such affiliated purchaser knows or has reason to know that such amount was accumulated for such purpose, nor shall it include any amount that a broker or dealer has sold short to the issuer or to any affiliated purchaser of the issuer if the issuer or such affiliated purchaser knows or has reason to know that the sale was a short sale.

(6) *Consolidated system* means a consolidated transaction or quotation reporting system that collects and publicly disseminates on a current and continuous basis transaction or quotation information in common equity securities pursuant to an effective transaction reporting plan or an effective national market system plan (as those terms are defined in Rule 600 of Regulation NMS).

(7) *Market-wide trading suspension* means a market-wide trading halt of 30 minutes or more that is:

(i) Imposed pursuant to the rules of a national securities exchange or a national securities association in response to a market-wide decline during a single trading session; or

(ii) Declared by the Commission pursuant to its authority under section 12(k) of the Act (15 U.S.C. 78*l*(k)).

(8) *Plan* has the meaning contained in Rule 100 of Regulation M.

(9) *Principal market* for a security means the single securities market with the largest reported trading volume for the security during the six full calendar months preceding the week in which the Rule 10b–18 purchase is to be effected.

(10) *Public float value* has the meaning contained in Rule 100 of Regulation M.

(11) *Purchase price* means the price paid per share as reported, exclusive of any commission paid to a broker acting as agent, or commission equivalent, mark-up, or differential paid to a dealer.

(12) *Riskless principal transaction* means a transaction in which a broker or dealer after having received an order from an issuer to buy its security, buys the security as principal in the market at the same price to satisfy the issuer's buy order. The issuer's buy order must be effected at the same price per-share at which the broker or dealer bought the shares to satisfy the issuer's buy order, exclusive of any explicitly disclosed markup or markdown, commission equivalent, or other fee. In addition, only the first leg of the transaction, when the broker or dealer buys the security in the market as principal, is reported under the rules of a self-regulatory organization or under the Act. For purposes of this rule, the broker or dealer must have written policies and procedures in place to assure that, at a minimum, the issuer's buy order was received prior to the offsetting transaction; the offsetting transaction is allocated to a riskless principal account or the issuer's account within 60 seconds of the execution; and the broker or dealer has supervisory systems in place to produce records that enable the broker or dealer to accurately and readily reconstruct, in a time-sequenced manner, all orders effected on a riskless principal basis.

(13) *Rule 10b–18 purchase* means a purchase (or any bid or limit order that would effect such purchase) of an issuer's common stock (or an equivalent interest, including a unit of beneficial interest in a trust or limited partnership or a depository share) by or for the issuer or any affiliated purchaser (including riskless principal transactions). However, it does *not* include any purchase of such security:

(i) Effected during the applicable restricted period of a distribution that is subject to Rule 102 of Regulation M;

(ii) Effected by or for an issuer plan by an agent independent of the issuer;

(iii) Effected as a fractional share purchase (a fractional interest in a security) evidenced by a script certificate, order form, or similar document;

(iv) Effected during the period from the time of public announcement (as defined in Rule 165(f) under the Securities Act of 1933) of a merger, acquisition, or similar transaction involving a recapitalization, until the earlier of the completion of such transaction or the completion of the vote by target shareholders. This exclusion does not apply to Rule 10b–18 purchases:

(A) Effected during such transaction in which the consideration is solely cash and there is no valuation period; or

(B) Where:

(*1*) The total volume of Rule 10b–18 purchases effected on any single day does not exceed the lesser of 25% of the security's four-week ADTV or the issuer's average daily Rule 10b–18 purchases during the three full calendar months preceding the date of the announcement of such transaction;

(*2*) The issuer's block purchases effected pursuant to paragraph (b)(4) of this rule do not exceed the average size and frequency of the issuer's block purchases effected pursuant to paragraph (b)(4) of this rule during the three full calendar months preceding the date of the announcement of such transaction; and

(*3*) Such purchases are not otherwise restricted or prohibited;

(v) Effected pursuant to Rule 13e–1;

(vi) Effected pursuant to a tender offer that is subject to Rule 13e–4 or specifically excepted from Rule 13e–4; or

(vii) Effected pursuant to a tender offer that is subject to section 14(d) of the Act (15 U.S.C. 78n(d)) and the rules and regulations thereunder.

(b) *Conditions to Be Met.* Rule 10b–18 purchases shall not be deemed to have violated the anti-manipulation provisions of sections 9(a)(2) or 10(b) of the Act (15 U.S.C. 78i(a)(2) 78j(b)) or Rule 10b–5 under the Act, solely by reason of the time, price, or amount of the Rule 10b–18 purchases, or the number of brokers or dealers used in connection with such purchases, if the issuer or affiliated purchaser of the issuer effects the Rule 10b–18 purchases according to each of the following conditions:

(1) *One Broker or Dealer.* Rule 10b–18 purchases must be effected from or through only one broker or dealer on any single day; *Provided, however*, that:

(i) The "one broker or dealer" condition shall not apply to Rule 10b–18 purchases that are not solicited by or on behalf of the issuer or its affiliated purchaser(s);

(ii) Where Rule 10b–18 purchases are effected by or on behalf of more than one affiliated purchaser of the issuer (or the issuer and one or more of its affiliated purchasers) on a single day, the issuer and all affiliated purchasers must use the same broker or dealer; and

(iii) Where Rule 10b–18 purchases are effected on behalf of the issuer by a broker-dealer that is not an electronic communication network (ECN) or other alternative trading system (ATS), that broker-dealer can access ECN or other ATS liquidity in order to execute repurchases on behalf of the issuer (or any affiliated purchaser of the issuer) on that day.

(2) *Time of Purchases.* Rule 10b–18 purchases must not be:

(i) The opening (regular way) purchase reported in the consolidated system;

(ii) Effected during the 10 minutes before the scheduled close of the primary trading session in the principal market for the security, and the 10 minutes before the scheduled close of the primary trading session in the market where the purchase is effected, for a security that has an ADTV value of $1 million or more and a public float value of $150 million or more; and

(iii) Effected during the 30 minutes before the scheduled close of the primary trading session in the principal market for the security, and the 30 minutes before the scheduled close of the primary trading session in the market where the purchase is effected, for all other securities;

(iv) However, for purposes of this rule, Rule 10b–18 purchases may be effected following the close of the primary trading session until the termination of the period in which last sale prices are reported in the consolidated system so long as such purchases are effected at prices that do not exceed the lower of the closing price of the primary trading session in the principal market for the security and any lower bids or sale prices subsequently reported in the consolidated system, and all of this rule's conditions are met. However, for purposes of this rule, the issuer may use one broker or dealer to effect Rule 10b–18 purchases during this period that may be different from the broker or dealer that it used during the primary trading session. However, the issuer's Rule 10b–18 purchase may not be the opening transaction of the session following the close of the primary trading session.

(3) *Price of Purchases.* Rule 10b–18 purchases must be effected at a purchase price that:

(i) Does not exceed the highest independent bid or the last independent transaction price, whichever is higher, quoted or reported in the consolidated system at the time the Rule 10b–18 purchase is effected;

(ii) For securities for which bids and transaction prices are not quoted or reported in the consolidated system, Rule 10b–18 purchases must be effected at a purchase price that does not exceed the highest independent bid or the last independent transaction price, whichever is higher, displayed and disseminated on any national securities exchange or on any inter-dealer quotation system (as defined in Rule 15c2–11) that displays at least two priced quotations for the security, at the time the Rule 10b–18 purchase is effected; and

(iii) For all other securities, Rule 10b–18 purchases must be effected at a price no higher than the highest independent bid obtained from three independent dealers.

(4) *Volume of Purchases.* The total volume of Rule 10b–18 purchases effected by or for the issuer and any affiliated purchasers effected on any single day must not exceed 25 percent of the ADTV for that security; *However*, once each week, in lieu of purchasing under the 25 percent of ADTV limit for that day, the issuer or an affiliated purchaser of the issuer may effect one block purchase if:

(i) No other Rule 10b–18 purchases are effected that day, and

(ii) The block purchase is *not* included when calculating a security's four week ADTV under this rule.

(c) *Alternative Conditions.* The conditions of paragraph (b) of this rule shall apply in connection with Rule 10b–18 purchases effected during a trading session following the imposition of a market-wide trading suspension, except:

(1) That the time of purchases condition in paragraph (b)(2) of this rule shall not apply, either:

(i) From the reopening of trading until the scheduled close of trading on the day that the market-wide trading suspension is imposed; or

(ii) At the opening of trading on the next trading day until the scheduled close of trading that day, if a market-wide trading suspension was in effect at the close of trading on the preceding day; and

(2) The volume of purchases condition in paragraph (b)(4) of this rule is modified so that the amount of Rule 10b–18 purchases must not exceed 100 percent of the ADTV for that security.

(d) *Other Purchases.* No presumption shall arise that an issuer or an affiliated purchaser has violated the anti-manipulation provisions of sections 9(a)(2) or 10(b) of the Act (15 U.S.C. 78i(a)(2) or 78j(b)), or Rule 10b–5 under the Act, if the Rule 10b–18 purchases of such issuer or affiliated purchaser do not meet the conditions specified in paragraph (b) or (c) of this rule.

Rule 10b–21. Deception in connection with a seller's ability or intent to deliver securities on the date delivery is due

PRELIMINARY NOTE TO RULE 10B–21

This rule is not intended to limit, or restrict, the applicability of the general antifraud provisions of the federal securities laws, such as section 10(b) of the Act and Rule 10b–5 thereunder.

(a) It shall also constitute a "manipulative or deceptive device or contrivance" as used in section 10(b) of this Act for any person to submit an order to sell an equity security if such person deceives a broker or dealer, a participant of a registered clearing agency, or a purchaser about its intention or ability to deliver the security on or before the settlement date, and such person fails to deliver the security on or before the settlement date.

(b) For purposes of this rule, the term *settlement date* shall mean the business day on which delivery of a security and payment of money is to be made through the facilities of a registered clearing agency in connection with the sale of a security.

REPORTS UNDER SECTION 10A

Rule 10A–1. Notice to the Commission pursuant to Section 10A of the Act

(a)(1) If any issuer with a reporting obligation under the Act receives a report requiring a notice to the Commission in accordance with section 10A(b)(3) of the Act, 15 U.S.C. 78j–1(b)(3), the issuer shall submit such notice to the Commission's Office of the Chief Accountant within the time period prescribed in that section. The notice may be provided by facsimile, telegraph, personal delivery, or any other means, *provided* it is received by the Office of the Chief Accountant within the required time period.

(2) The notice specified in paragraph (a)(1) of this rule shall be in writing and:

(i) Shall identify the issuer (including the issuer's name, address, phone number, and file number assigned to the issuer's filings by the Commission) and the independent accountant (including the independent accountant's name and phone number, and the address of the independent accountant's principal office);

(ii) Shall state the date that the issuer received from the independent accountant the report specified in section 10A(b)(2) of the Act, 15 U.S.C. 78j–1(b)(2);

(iii) Shall provide, at the election of the issuer, either:

(A) A summary of the independent accountant's report, including a description of the act that the independent accountant has identified as a likely illegal act and the possible effect of that act on all affected financial statements of the issuer of those related to the most current three-year period, whichever is shorter; or

(B) A copy of the independent accountant's report; and

(iv) May provide additional information regarding the issuer's views of and response to the independent accountant's report.

(3) Reports of the independent accountant submitted by the issuer to the Commission's Office of the Chief Accountant in accordance with paragraph (a)(2)(iii)(B) of this rule shall be deemed to have been made pursuant to section 10A(b)(3) or section 10A(b)(4) of the Act, 15 U.S.C. 78j–1(b)(3) or 78j–1(b)(4), for purposes of the safe harbor provided by section 10A(c) of the Act, 15 U.S.C. 78j–1(c).

(4) Submission of the notice in paragraphs (a)(1) and (a)(2) of this rule shall not relieve the issuer from its obligations to comply fully with all other reporting requirements, including, without limitation:

(i) The filing requirements of Form 8–K, 17 CFR 249.308, and Form N–SAR, 17 CFR 274.101, regarding a change in the issuer's certifying accountant and

(ii) The disclosure requirements of Item 304 of Regulation S–K.

(b)(1) Any independent accountant furnishing to the Commission a copy of a report (or the documentation of any oral report) in accordance with section 10A(b)(3) or section 10A(b)(4) of the Act, 15 U.S.C. 78j–1(b)(3) or 78j–1(b)(4), shall submit that report (or documentation) to the Commission's Office of the Chief Accountant within the time period prescribed by the appropriate section of the Act. The report (or documentation) may be submitted to the Commission's Office of the Chief Accountant by facsimile, telegraph, personal delivery, or any other means, *provided* it is received by the Office of the Chief Accountant within the time period set forth in section 10A(b)(3) or 10A(b)(4) of the Act, 15 U.S.C. 78j–1(b)(3) or 78j–(b)(4), whichever is applicable in the circumstances.

(2) If the report (or documentation) submitted to the Office of the Chief Accountant in accordance with paragraph (b)(1) of this rule does not clearly identify both the issuer (including the issuer's name, address, phone number, and file number assigned to the issuer's filings with the Commission) and the independent accountant (including the independent accountant's name and phone number, and the address of the independent accountant's principal office), then the independent accountant shall place that information in a prominent attachment to the report (or documentation) and shall submit that attachment to the Office of the Chief Accountant at the same time and in the same manner as the report (or documentation) is submitted to that Office.

(3) Submission of the report (or documentation) by the independent accountant as described in paragraphs (b)(1) and (b)(2) of this section shall not replace, or otherwise satisfy the need for, the

newly engaged and former accountants' letters under Items 304(a)(2)(D) and 304(a)(3) of Regulation S–K, respectively, and shall not limit, reduce, or affect in any way the independent accountant's obligations to comply fully with all other legal and professional responsibilities, including, without limitation, those under the standards of the Public Company Accounting Oversight Board (United States) ("PCAOB") and the rules or interpretations of the Commission that modify or supplement those auditing standards.

(c) A notice or report submitted to the Office of the Chief Accountant in accordance with paragraphs (a) and (b) of this rule shall be deemed to be an investigative record and shall be non-public and exempt from disclosure pursuant to the Freedom of Information Act to the same extent and for the same periods of time that the Commission's investigative records are non-public and exempt from disclosure under, among other applicable provisions, 5 U.S.C. 552(b)(7) and 17 CFR 200.80(b)(7). Nothing in this paragraph, however, shall relieve, limit, delay, or affect in any way, the obligation of any issuer or any independent accountant to make all public disclosures required by law, by any Commission disclosure item, rule, report, or form, or by any applicable accounting, auditing, or professional standard.

Instruction to Paragraph (c): Issuers and independent accountants may apply for additional bases for confidential treatment for a notice, report, or part thereof, in accordance with 17 CFR 200.83. That section indicates, in part, that any person who, pursuant to any requirement of law, submits any information or causes or permits any information to be submitted to the Commission, may request that the Commission afford it confidential treatment by reason of personal privacy or business confidentiality, or for any other reason permitted by Federal law.

Rule 10A–2. Auditor independence

It shall be unlawful for an auditor not to be independent under Rule 2–01(c)(2)(iii)(B), (c)(4), (c)(6), (c)(7), and Rule 210.2–07 of Regulation S–X.

Rule 10A–3. Listing standards relating to audit committees

(a) Pursuant to section 10A(m) of the Act (15 U.S.C. 78j–1(m)) and section 3 of the Sarbanes–Oxley Act of 2002 (15 U.S.C. 7202):

(1) *National Securities Exchanges*. The rules of each national securities exchange registered pursuant to section 6 of the Act (15 U.S.C. 78f) must, in accordance with the provisions of this rule, prohibit the initial or continued listing of any security of an issuer that is not in compliance with the requirements of any portion of paragraph (b) or (c) of this rule.

(2) *National Securities Associations*. The rules of each national securities association registered pursuant to section 15A of the Act (15 U.S.C. 78o–3) must, in accordance with the provisions of this rule, prohibit the initial or continued listing in an automated inter-dealer quotation system of any security of an issuer that is not in compliance with the requirements of any portion of paragraph (b) or (c) of this rule.

(3) *Opportunity to Cure Defects*. The rules required by paragraphs (a)(1) and (a)(2) of this rule must provide for appropriate procedures for a listed issuer to have an opportunity to cure any defects that would be the basis for a prohibition under paragraph (a) of this rule, before the imposition of such prohibition. Such rules also may provide that if a member of an audit committee ceases to be independent in accordance with the requirements of this rule for reasons outside the member's reasonable control, that person, with notice by the issuer to the applicable national securities exchange or national securities association, may remain an audit committee member of the listed issuer until the earlier of the next annual shareholders meeting of the listed issuer or one year from the occurrence of the event that caused the member to be no longer independent.

(4) *Notification of Noncompliance*. The rules required by paragraphs (a)(1) and (a)(2) of this rule must include a requirement that a listed issuer must notify the applicable national securities exchange or national securities association promptly after an executive officer of the listed issuer becomes aware of any material noncompliance by the listed issuer with the requirements of this rule.

(5) *Implementation*. (i) The rules of each national securities exchange or national securities association meeting the requirements of this rule must be operative, and listed issuers must be in compliance with those rules, by the following dates:

(A) July 31, 2005 for foreign private issuers and smaller reporting companies (as defined in Rule 12b–2); and

(B) For all other listed issuers, the earlier of the listed issuer's first annual shareholders meeting after January 15, 2004, or October 31, 2004.

(ii) Each national securities exchange and national securities association must provide to the Commission, no later than July 15, 2003, proposed rules or rule amendments that comply with this section.

(iii) Each national securities exchange and national securities association must have final rules or rule amendments that comply with this section approved by the Commission no later than December 1, 2003.

(b) *Required Standards*. (1) *Independence*. (i) Each member of the audit committee must be a member of the board of directors of the listed issuer, and must otherwise be independent; provided that, where a listed issuer is one of two dual holding companies, those companies may designate one audit committee for both companies so long as each member of the audit committee is a member of the board of directors of at least one of such dual holding companies.

(ii) *Independence Requirements for Non-Investment Company Issuers*. In order to be considered to be independent for purposes of this paragraph (b)(1), a member of an audit committee of a listed issuer that is not an investment company may not, other than in his or her capacity as a member of the audit committee, the board of directors, or any other board committee:

(A) Accept directly or indirectly any consulting, advisory, or other compensatory fee from the issuer or any subsidiary thereof, provided that, unless the rules of the national securities exchange or national securities association provide otherwise, compensatory fees do not include the receipt of fixed amounts of compensation under a retirement plan (including deferred compensation) for prior service with the listed issuer (provided that such compensation is not contingent in any way on continued service); or

(B) Be an affiliated person of the issuer or any subsidiary thereof.

(iii) *Independence Requirements for Investment Company Issuers*. In order to be considered to be independent for purposes of this paragraph (b)(1), a member of an audit committee of a listed issuer that is an investment company may not, other than in his or her capacity as a member of the audit committee, the board of directors, or any other board committee:

(A) Accept directly or indirectly any consulting, advisory, or other compensatory fee from the issuer or any subsidiary thereof, provided that, unless the rules of the national securities exchange or national securities association provide otherwise, compensatory fees do not include the receipt of fixed amounts of compensation under a retirement plan (including deferred compensation) for prior service with the listed issuer (provided that such compensation is not contingent in any way on continued service); or

(B) Be an "interested person" of the issuer as defined in section 2(a)(19) of the Investment Company Act of 1940 (15 U.S.C. 80a–2(a)(19)).

(iv) *Exemptions from the Independence Requirements*. (A) For an issuer listing securities pursuant to a registration statement under section 12 of the Act (15 U.S.C. 78l), or for an issuer that has a registration statement under the Securities Act of 1933 covering an initial public offering of securities to be listed by the issuer, where in each case the listed issuer was not, immediately prior to the effective date of such registration statement, required to file reports with the Commission pursuant to section 13(a) or 15(d) of the Act (15 U.S.C. 78m(a) or 78o(d)):

(*1*) All but one of the members of the listed issuer's audit committee may be exempt from the independence requirements of paragraph (b)(1)(ii) of this rule for 90 days from the date of effectiveness of such registration statement; and

(*2*) A minority of the members of the listed issuer's audit committee may be exempt from the independence requirements of paragraph (b)(1)(ii) of this rule for one year from the date of effectiveness of such registration statement.

(B) An audit committee member that sits on the board of directors of a listed issuer and an affiliate of the listed issuer is exempt from the requirements of paragraph (b)(1)(ii)(B) of this rule if the member, except for being a director on each such board of directors, otherwise meets the independence requirements of paragraph (b)(1)(ii) of this rule for each such entity, including the receipt of only ordinary-course compensation for serving as a member of the board of directors, audit committee or any other board committee of each such entity.

(C) An employee of a foreign private issuer who is not an executive officer of the foreign private issuer is exempt from the requirements of paragraph (b)(1)(ii) of this rule if the employee is elected or named to the board of directors or audit committee of the foreign private issuer pursuant to the issuer's governing law or documents, an employee collective bargaining or similar agreement or other home country legal or listing requirements.

(D) An audit committee member of a foreign private issuer may be exempt from the requirements of paragraph (b)(1)(ii)(B) of this rule if that member meets the following requirements:

(*1*) The member is an affiliate of the foreign private issuer or a representative of such an affiliate;

(*2*) The member has only observer status on, and is not a voting member or the chair of, the audit committee; and

(*3*) Neither the member nor the affiliate is an executive officer of the foreign private issuer.

(E) An audit committee member of a foreign private issuer may be exempt from the requirements of paragraph (b)(1)(ii)(B) of this rule if that member meets the following requirements:

(*1*) The member is a representative or designee of a foreign government or foreign governmental entity that is an affiliate of the foreign private issuer; and

(*2*) The member is not an executive officer of the foreign private issuer.

(F) In addition to paragraphs (b)(1)(iv)(A) through (E) of this rule, the Commission may exempt from the requirements of paragraphs (b)(1)(ii) or (b)(1)(iii) of this rule a particular relationship with respect to audit committee members, as the Commission determines appropriate in light of the circumstances.

(2) *Responsibilities Relating to Registered Public Accounting Firms.* The audit committee of each listed issuer, in its capacity as a committee of the board of directors, must be directly responsible for the appointment, compensation, retention and oversight of the work of any registered public accounting firm engaged (including resolution of disagreements between management and the auditor regarding financial reporting) for the purpose of preparing or issuing an audit report or performing other audit, review or attest services for the listed issuer, and each such registered public accounting firm must report directly to the audit committee.

(3) *Complaints.* Each audit committee must establish procedures for:

(i) The receipt, retention, and treatment of complaints received by the listed issuer regarding accounting, internal accounting controls, or auditing matters; and

(ii) The confidential, anonymous submission by employees of the listed issuer of concerns regarding questionable accounting or auditing matters.

(4) *Authority to Engage Advisers.* Each audit committee must have the authority to engage independent counsel and other advisers, as it determines necessary to carry out its duties.

(5) *Funding.* Each listed issuer must provide for appropriate funding, as determined by the audit committee, in its capacity as a committee of the board of directors, for payment of:

(i) Compensation to any registered public accounting firm engaged for the purpose of preparing or issuing an audit report or performing other audit, review or attest services for the listed issuer;

(ii) Compensation to any advisers employed by the audit committee under paragraph (b)(4) of this rule; and

(iii) Ordinary administrative expenses of the audit committee that are necessary or appropriate in carrying out its duties.

(c) *General Exemptions.* (1) At any time when an issuer has a class of securities that is listed on a national securities exchange or national securities association subject to the requirements of this rule, the listing of other classes of securities of the listed issuer on a national securities exchange or national securities association is not subject to the requirements of this rule.

(2) At any time when an issuer has a class of common equity securities (or similar securities) that is listed on a national securities exchange or national securities association subject to the requirements of this rule, the listing of classes of securities of a direct or indirect consolidated subsidiary or an at least 50% beneficially owned subsidiary of the issuer (except classes of equity securities, other than non-convertible, non-partic-

ipating preferred securities, of such subsidiary) is not subject to the requirements of this rule.

(3) The listing of securities of a foreign private issuer is not subject to the requirements of paragraphs (b)(1) through (b)(5) of this rule if the foreign private issuer meets the following requirements:

(i) The foreign private issuer has a board of auditors (or similar body), or has statutory auditors, established and selected pursuant to home country legal or listing provisions expressly requiring or permitting such a board or similar body;

(ii) The board or body, or statutory auditors is required under home country legal or listing requirements to be either:

(A) Separate from the board of directors; or

(B) Composed of one or more members of the board of directors and one or more members that are not also members of the board of directors;

(iii) The board or body, or statutory auditors, are not elected by management of such issuer and no executive officer of the foreign private issuer is a member of such board or body, or statutory auditors;

(iv) Home country legal or listing provisions set forth or provide for standards for the independence of such board or body, or statutory auditors, from the foreign private issuer or the management of such issuer;

(v) Such board or body, or statutory auditors, in accordance with any applicable home country legal or listing requirements or the issuer's governing documents, are responsible, to the extent permitted by law, for the appointment, retention and oversight of the work of any registered public accounting firm engaged (including, to the extent permitted by law, the resolution of disagreements between management and the auditor regarding financial reporting) for the purpose of preparing or issuing an audit report or performing other audit, review or attest services for the issuer; and

(vi) The audit committee requirements of paragraphs (b)(3), (b)(4) and (b)(5) of this rule apply to such board or body, or statutory auditors, to the extent permitted by law.

(4) The listing of a security futures product cleared by a clearing agency that is registered pursuant to section 17A of the Act (15 U.S.C. 78q–1) or that is exempt from the registration requirements of section 17A pursuant to paragraph (b)(7)(A) of such section is not subject to the requirements of this section.

(5) The listing of a standardized option, as defined in Rule 9b–1(a)(4), issued by a clearing agency that is registered pursuant to section 17A of the Act (15 U.S.C. 78q–1) is not subject to the requirements of this rule.

(6) The listing of securities of the following listed issuers are not subject to the requirements of this rule:

(i) Asset-Backed Issuers (as defined in Item 1101 of Regulation AB);

(ii) Unit investment trusts (as defined in 15 U.S.C. 80a–4(2)); and

(iii) Foreign governments (as defined in Rule 3b–4(a)).

(7) The listing of securities of a listed issuer is not subject to the requirements of this rule if:

(i) The listed issuer, as reflected in the applicable listing application, is organized as a trust or other unincorporated association that does not have a board of directors or persons acting in a similar capacity; and

(ii) The activities of the listed issuer that is described in paragraph (c)(7)(i) of this rule are limited to passively owning or holding (as well as administering and distributing amounts in respect of) securities, rights, collateral or other assets on behalf of or for the benefit of the holders of the listed securities.

(d) *Disclosure*. Any listed issuer availing itself of an exemption from the independence standards contained in paragraph (b)(1)(iv) of this rule (except paragraph (b)(1)(iv)(B) of this rule), the general exemption contained in paragraph (c)(3) of this rule or the last sentence of paragraph (a)(3) of this rule, must:

(1) Disclose its reliance on the exemption and its assessment of whether, and if so, how, such reliance would materially adversely affect the ability of the audit committee to act independently and to satisfy the other requirements of this rule in any proxy or information statement for a meet-

ing of shareholders at which directors are elected that is filed with the Commission pursuant to the requirements of section 14 of the Act (15 U.S.C. 78n); and

(2) Disclose the information specified in paragraph (d)(1) of this rule in, or incorporate such information by reference from such proxy or information statement filed with the Commission into, its annual report filed with the Commission pursuant to the requirements of section 13(a) or 15(d) of the Act (15 U.S.C. 78m(a) or 78o(d)).

(e) *Definitions.* Unless the context otherwise requires, all terms used in this rule have the same meaning as in the Act. In addition, unless the context otherwise requires, the following definitions apply for purposes of this rule:

(1)(i) The term *affiliate* of, or a person *affiliated* with, a specified person, means a person that directly, or indirectly through one or more intermediaries, controls, or is controlled by, or is under common control with, the person specified.

(ii)(A) A person will be deemed not to be in control of a specified person for purposes of this rule if the person:

(*1*) Is not the beneficial owner, directly or indirectly, of more than 10% of any class of voting equity securities of the specified person; and

(*2*) Is not an executive officer of the specified person.

(B) Paragraph (e)(1)(ii)(A) of this rule only creates a safe harbor position that a person does not control a specified person. The existence of the safe harbor does not create a presumption in any way that a person exceeding the ownership requirement in paragraph (e)(1)(ii)(A)(*1*) of this rule controls or is otherwise an affiliate of a specified person.

(iii) The following will be deemed to be affiliates:

(A) An executive officer of an affiliate;

(B) A director who also is an employee of an affiliate;

(C) A general partner of an affiliate; and

(D) A managing member of an affiliate.

(iv) For purposes of paragraph (e)(1)(i) of this rule, dual holding companies will not be deemed to be affiliates of or persons affiliated with each other by virtue of their dual holding company arrangements with each other, including where directors of one dual holding company are also directors of the other dual holding company, or where directors of one or both dual holding companies are also directors of the businesses jointly controlled, directly or indirectly, by the dual holding companies (and, in each case, receive only ordinary-course compensation for serving as a member of the board of directors, audit committee or any other board committee of the dual holding companies or any entity that is jointly controlled, directly or indirectly, by the dual holding companies).

(2) In the case of foreign private issuers with a two-tier board system, the term *board of directors* means the supervisory or non-management board.

(3) In the case of a listed issuer that is a limited partnership or limited liability company where such entity does not have a board of directors or equivalent body, the term *board of directors* means the board of directors of the managing general partner, managing member or equivalent body.

(4) The term *control* (including the terms *controlling, controlled by* and under *common control with*) means the possession, direct or indirect, of the power to direct or cause the direction of the management and policies of a person, whether through the ownership of voting securities, by contract, or otherwise.

(5) The term *dual holding companies* means two foreign private issuers that:

(i) Are organized in different national jurisdictions;

(ii) Collectively own and supervise the management of one or more businesses which are conducted as a single economic enterprise; and

(iii) Do not conduct any business other than collectively owning and supervising such businesses and activities reasonably incidental thereto.

(6) The term *executive officer* has the meaning set forth in Rule 3b–7.

(7) The term *foreign private issuer* has the meaning set forth in Rule 3b–4(c).

(8) The term *indirect acceptance by a member of an audit committee of any consulting, advisory or other compensatory fee* includes acceptance of such a fee by a spouse, a minor child or stepchild or a child or stepchild sharing a home with the member or by an entity in which such member is a partner, member, an officer such as a managing director occupying a comparable position or executive officer, or occupies a similar position (except limited partners, non-managing members and those occupying similar positions who, in each case, have no active role in providing services to the entity) and which provides accounting, consulting, legal, investment banking or financial advisory services to the issuer or any subsidiary of the issuer.

(9) The terms *listed* and *listing* refer to securities listed on a national securities exchange or listed in an automated inter-dealer quotation system of a national securities association or to issuers of such securities.

Instructions to Rule 10A–3

1. The requirements in paragraphs (b)(2) through (b)(5), (c)(3)(v) and (c)(3)(vi) of this rule do not conflict with, and do not affect the application of, any requirement or ability under a listed issuer's governing law or documents or other home country legal or listing provisions that requires or permits shareholders to ultimately vote on, approve or ratify such requirements. The requirements instead relate to the assignment of responsibility as between the audit committee and management. In such an instance, however, if the listed issuer provides a recommendation or nomination regarding such responsibilities to shareholders, the audit committee of the listed issuer, or body performing similar functions, must be responsible for making the recommendation or nomination.

2. The requirements in paragraphs (b)(2) through (b)(5), (c)(3)(v), (c)(3)(vi) and Instruction 1 of this rule do not conflict with any legal or listing requirement in a listed issuer's home jurisdiction that prohibits the full board of directors from delegating such responsibilities to the listed issuer's audit committee or limits the degree of such delegation. In that case, the audit committee, or body performing similar functions, must be granted such responsibilities, which can include advisory powers, with respect to such matters to the extent permitted by law, including submitting nominations or recommendations to the full board.

3. The requirements in paragraphs (b)(2) through (b)(5), (c)(3)(v) and (c)(3)(vi) of this rule do not conflict with any legal or listing requirement in a listed issuer's home jurisdiction that vests such responsibilities with a government entity or tribunal. In that case, the audit committee, or body performing similar functions, must be granted such responsibilities, which can include advisory powers, with respect to such matters to the extent permitted by law.

4. For purposes of this rule, the determination of a person's beneficial ownership must be made in accordance with Rule 13d–3.

REQUIREMENTS UNDER SECTION 10C

Rule 10C–1. Listing standards relating to compensation committees

(a) Pursuant to section 10C(a) of the Act (15 U.S.C. 78j–3(a)) and section 952 of the Dodd–Frank Wall Street Reform and Consumer Protection Act of 2010 (Pub. L. 111–203, 124 Stat. 1900):

(1) *National Securities Exchanges*. The rules of each national securities exchange registered pursuant to section 6 of the Act (15 U.S.C. 78f), to the extent such national securities exchange lists equity securities, must, in accordance with the provisions of this section, prohibit the initial or continued listing of any equity security of an issuer that is not in compliance with the requirements of any portion of paragraph (b) or (c) of this section.

(2) *National Securities Associations*. The rules of each national securities association registered pursuant to section 15A of the Act (15 U.S.C. 78o–3), to the extent such national securities association lists equity securities in an automated inter-dealer quotation system, must, in accordance with the provisions of this section, prohibit the initial or continued listing in an automated inter-dealer quotation system of any equity security of an issuer that is not in compliance with the requirements of any portion of paragraph (b) or (c) of this section.

(3) *Opportunity to Cure Defects*. The rules required by paragraphs (a)(1) and (a)(2) of this section must provide for appropriate procedures for a listed issuer to have a reasonable opportunity to cure any defects that would be the basis for a prohibition under paragraph (a) of this section, before the imposition of such prohibition. Such rules may provide that if a member of a compensation committee ceases to be independent in accordance with the requirements of this section for reasons outside the member's reasonable control, that person, with notice by the issuer to the applicable national securities exchange or national securities association, may remain a compensation committee member of the listed issuer until the earlier of the next annual shareholders meeting of the listed issuer or one year from the occurrence of the event that caused the member to be no longer independent.

(4) *Implementation*. (i) Each national securities exchange and national securities association that lists equity securities must provide to the Commis-

sion, no later than 90 days after publication of this section in the Federal Register, proposed rules or rule amendments that comply with this section. Each submission must include, in addition to any other information required under section 19(b) of the Act (15 U.S.C. 78s(b)) and the rules thereunder, a review of whether and how existing or proposed listing standards satisfy the requirements of this rule, a discussion of the consideration of factors relevant to compensation committee independence conducted by the national securities exchange or national securities association, and the definition of independence applicable to compensation committee members that the national securities exchange or national securities association proposes to adopt or retain in light of such review.

(ii) Each national securities exchange and national securities association that lists equity securities must have rules or rule amendments that comply with this section approved by the Commission no later than one year after publication of this section in the Federal Register.

(b) *Required Standards.* The requirements of this section apply to the compensation committees of listed issuers.

(1) *Independence.* (i) Each member of the compensation committee must be a member of the board of directors of the listed issuer, and must otherwise be independent.

(ii) *Independence Requirements.* In determining independence requirements for members of compensation committees, the national securities exchanges and national securities associations shall consider relevant factors, including, but not limited to:

(A) The source of compensation of a member of the board of directors of an issuer, including any consulting, advisory or other compensatory fee paid by the issuer to such member of the board of directors; and

(B) Whether a member of the board of directors of an issuer is affiliated with the issuer, a subsidiary of the issuer or an affiliate of a subsidiary of the issuer.

(iii) *Exemptions from the Independence Requirements.* (A) The listing of equity securities of the following categories of listed issuers is not subject to the requirements of paragraph (b)(1) of this section:

(1) Limited partnerships;

(2) Companies in bankruptcy proceedings;

(3) Open-end management investment companies registered under the Investment Company Act of 1940; and

(4) Any foreign private issuer that discloses in its annual report the reasons that the foreign private issuer does not have an independent compensation committee.

(B) In addition to the issuer exemptions set forth in paragraph (b)(1)(iii)(A) of this section, a national securities exchange or a national securities association, pursuant to section 19(b) of the Act (15 U.S.C. 78s(b)) and the rules thereunder, may exempt from the requirements of paragraph (b)(1) of this section a particular relationship with respect to members of the compensation committee, as each national securities exchange or national securities association determines is appropriate, taking into consideration the size of an issuer and any other relevant factors.

(2) *Authority to Retain Compensation Consultants, Independent Legal Counsel and Other Compensation Advisers.*

(i) The compensation committee of a listed issuer, in its capacity as a committee of the board of directors, may, in its sole discretion, retain or obtain the advice of a compensation consultant, independent legal counsel or other adviser.

(ii) The compensation committee shall be directly responsible for the appointment, compensation and oversight of the work of any compensation consultant, independent legal counsel and other adviser retained by the compensation committee.

(iii) Nothing in this paragraph shall be construed:

(A) To require the compensation committee to implement or act consistently with the advice or recommendations of the compensation consultant, independent legal counsel or other adviser to the compensation committee; or

(B) To affect the ability or obligation of a compensation committee to exercise its own judgment in fulfillment of the duties of the compensation committee.

(3) *Funding.* Each listed issuer must provide for appropriate funding, as determined by the compensation committee, in its capacity as a com-

mittee of the board of directors, for payment of reasonable compensation to a compensation consultant, independent legal counsel or any other adviser retained by the compensation committee.

(4) *Independence of Compensation Consultants and Other Advisers*. The compensation committee of a listed issuer may select a compensation consultant, legal counsel or other adviser to the compensation committee only after taking into consideration the following factors, as well as any other factors identified by the relevant national securities exchange or national securities association in its listing standards:

(i) The provision of other services to the issuer by the person that employs the compensation consultant, legal counsel or other adviser;

(ii) The amount of fees received from the issuer by the person that employs the compensation consultant, legal counsel or other adviser, as a percentage of the total revenue of the person that employs the compensation consultant, legal counsel or other adviser;

(iii) The policies and procedures of the person that employs the compensation consultant, legal counsel or other adviser that are designed to prevent conflicts of interest;

(iv) Any business or personal relationship of the compensation consultant, legal counsel or other adviser with a member of the compensation committee;

(v) Any stock of the issuer owned by the compensation consultant, legal counsel or other adviser; and

(vi) Any business or personal relationship of the compensation consultant, legal counsel, other adviser or the person employing the adviser with an executive officer of the issuer.

Instruction to Paragraph (b)(4) of this Section: A listed issuer's compensation committee is required to conduct the independence assessment outlined in paragraph (b)(4) with respect to any compensation consultant, legal counsel or other adviser that provides advice to the compensation committee, other than in-house legal counsel.

(5) *General Exemptions*. (i) The national securities exchanges and national securities associations, pursuant to section 19(b) of the Act (15 U.S.C. 78s(b)) and the rules thereunder, may exempt from the requirements of this section certain categories of issuers, as the national securities exchange or national securities association determines is appropriate, taking into consideration, among other relevant factors, the potential impact of such requirements on smaller reporting issuers.

(ii) The requirements of this section shall not apply to any controlled company or to any smaller reporting company.

(iii) The listing of a security futures product cleared by a clearing agency that is registered pursuant to section 17A of the Act (15 U.S.C. 78q–1) or that is exempt from the registration requirements of section 17A(b)(7)(A) (15 U.S.C. 78q–1(b)(7)(A)) is not subject to the requirements of this section.

(iv) The listing of a standardized option, as defined in Rule 9b–1(a)(4), issued by a clearing agency that is registered pursuant to section 17A of the Act (15 U.S.C. 78q–1) is not subject to the requirements of this section.

(c) *Definitions*. Unless the context otherwise requires, all terms used in this section have the same meaning as in the Act and the rules and regulations thereunder. In addition, unless the context otherwise requires, the following definitions apply for purposes of this section:

(1) In the case of foreign private issuers with a two-tier board system, the term *board of directors* means the supervisory or non-management board.

(2) The term *compensation committee* means:

(i) a committee of the board of directors that is designated as the compensation committee; or

(ii) in the absence of a committee of the board of directors that is designated as the compensation committee, a committee of the board of directors performing functions typically performed by a compensation committee, including oversight of executive compensation, even if it is not designated as the compensation committee or also performs other functions; or

(iii) for purposes of this section other than paragraphs (b)(2)(i) and (b)(3), in the absence of a committee as described in (i) or (ii) above, the members of the board of directors who oversee executive compensation matters on behalf of the board of directors.

(3) The term *controlled company* means an issuer:

(i) That is listed on a national securities exchange or by a national securities association; and

(ii) Of which more than 50 percent of the voting power for the election of directors is held by an individual, a group or another company.

(4) The terms *listed* and *listing* refer to equity securities listed on a national securities exchange or listed in an automated inter-dealer quotation system of a national securities association or to issuers of such securities.

(5) The term *open-end management investment company* means an open-end company, as defined by Section 5(a)(1) of the Investment Company Act of 1940 (15 U.S.C. 80a–5(a)(1)), that is registered under that Act.

ADOPTION OF FLOOR TRADING REGULATION (RULE 11a–1)

Rule 11a–1. Regulation of floor trading

(a) No member of a national securities exchange, while on the floor of such exchange, shall initiate, directly or indirectly, any transaction in any security admitted to trading on such exchange, for any account in which such member has an interest, or for any such account with respect to which such member has discretion as to the time of execution, the choice of security to be bought or sold, the total amount of any security to be bought or sold, or whether any such transaction shall be one of purchase or sale.

(b) The provisions of paragraph (a) of this rule shall not apply to:

(1) Any transaction by a registered specialist in a security in which he is so registered on such exchange;

(2) Any transaction for the account of an odd-lot dealer in a security in which he is so registered on such exchange;

(3) Any stabilizing transaction effected in compliance with Rule 104 of Regulation M to facilitate a distribution of such security in which such member is participating;

(4) Any bona fide arbitrage transaction;

(5) Any transaction made with the prior approval of a floor official of such exchange to permit such member to contribute to the maintenance of a fair and orderly market in such security, or any purchase or sale to reverse any such transaction;

(6) Any transaction to offset a transaction made in error; or

(7) Any transaction effected in conformity with a plan designed to eliminate floor trading activities which are not beneficial to the market and which plan has been adopted by an exchange and declared effective by the Commission. For the purpose of this rule, a plan filed with the Commission by a national securities exchange shall not become effective unless the Commission, having due regard for the maintenance of fair and orderly markets, for the public interest, and for the protection of investors, declares the plan to be effective.

(c) For the purpose of this rule the term "on the floor of such exchange" shall include the trading floor; the rooms, lobbies, and other premises immediately adjacent thereto for use of members generally; other rooms, lobbies and premises made available primarily for use by members generally; and the telephone and other facilities in any such place.

(d) Any national securities exchange may apply for an exemption from the provisions of this rule in compliance with the provisions of section 11(c) of the Act.

Rule 11a1–1(T). Transactions yielding priority, parity, and precedence

(a) A transaction effected on a national securities exchange for the account of a member which meets the requirements of Section 11(a)(1)(G)(i) of the Act shall be deemed, in accordance with the requirements of Section 11(a)(1)(G)(ii), to be not inconsistent with the maintenance of fair and orderly markets and to yield priority, parity, and precedence in execution to orders for the account of persons who are not members or associated with members of the exchange if such transaction is effected in compliance with each of the following requirements:

(1) A member shall disclose that a bid or offer for its account is for its account to any member with whom such bid or offer is placed or to whom it is communicated, and any such member through whom that bid or offer is communicated shall disclose to others participating in effecting the order that it is for the account of a member.

(2) Immediately before executing the order, a member (other than the specialist in such security) presenting any order for the account of a member on the exchange shall clearly announce or otherwise indicate to the specialist and to other members then present for the trading in such

security on the exchange that he is presenting an order for the account of a member.

(3) Notwithstanding rules of priority, parity, and precedence otherwise applicable, any member presenting for execution a bid or offer for its own account or for the account of another member shall grant priority to any bid or offer at the same price for the account of a person who is not, or is not associated with, a member, irrespective of the size of any such bid or offer or the time when entered.

(b) A member shall be deemed to meet the requirements of section 11(a)(1)(G)(i) of the Act if during its preceding fiscal year more than 50 percent of its gross revenues was derived from one or more of the sources specified in that section. In addition to any revenue which independently meets the requirements of section 11(a)(1)(G)(i), revenue derived from any transaction specified in paragraph (A), (B), or (D) of section 11(a)(1) of the Act or specified in Rule 11a1–4(T) shall be deemed to be revenue derived from one or more of the sources specified in section 11(a)(1)(G)(i). A member may rely on a list of members which are stated to meet the requirements of section 11(a)(1)(G)(i) if such list is prepared, and updated at least annually, by the exchange. In preparing any such list, an exchange may rely on a report which sets forth a statement of gross revenues of a member if covered by a report of independent accountants for such member to the effect that such report has been prepared in accordance with generally accepted accounting principles.

Rule 11a1–2. Transactions for certain accounts of associated persons of members

A transaction effected by a member of a national securities exchange for the account of an associated person thereof shall be deemed to be of a kind which is consistent with the purposes of section 11(a)(1) of the Act, the protection of investors, and the maintenance of fair and orderly markets if the transaction is effected:

(a) For the account of and for the benefit of an associated person, if, assuming such transaction were for the account of a member, or

(b) For the account of an associated person but for the benefit of an account carried by such associated person, if, assuming such account were carried on the same basis by a member.

The member would have been permitted, under section 11(a) of the Act and the other rules thereunder, to effect the transaction; *Provided, however,* That a transaction may not be effected by a member for the account of and for the benefit of an associated person under section 11(a)(1)(G) of the Act and Rule 11a1–1(T) thereunder unless the associated person derived, during its preceding fiscal year, more than 50 percent of its gross revenues from one or more of the sources specified in section 11(a)(1)(G)(i) of the Act.

Rule 11a1–3(T). Bona fide hedge transactions in certain securities

A bona fide hedge transaction effected on a national securities exchange by a member for its own account or an account of an associated person thereof and involving a long or short position in a security entitling the holder to acquire or sell an equity security, and a long or short position in one or more other securities entitling the holder to acquire or sell such equity security, shall be deemed to be of a kind which is consistent with the purposes of section 11(a)(1) of the Act, the protection of investors, and the maintenance of fair and orderly markets.

Rule 11a1–4(T). Bond transactions on national securities exchanges

A transaction in a bond, note, debenture, or other form of indebtedness effected on a national securities exchange by a member for its own account or the account of an associated person thereof shall be deemed to be of a kind which is consistent with the purposes of section 11(a)(1) of the Act, the protection of investors, and the maintenance of fair and orderly markets.

Rule 11a1–5. Transactions by registered competitive market makers and registered equity market makers

Any transaction by a New York Stock Exchange registered competitive market maker or an American Stock Exchange registered equity market maker effected in compliance with their respective governing rules shall be deemed to be of a kind which is consistent with the purposes of section 11(a)(1) of the Act, the protection of investors, and the maintenance of fair and orderly markets.

Rule 11a1–6. Transactions for certain accounts of OTC derivatives dealers

A transaction effected by a member of a national securities exchange for the account of an OTC derivatives dealer that is an associated person of that member shall be deemed to be of a kind that is consistent with the purposes of section 11(a)(1) of the Act (15 U.S.C. 78k(a)(1)), the protection of investors, and the maintenance of fair and orderly markets if, assuming such transaction were for the account of a member, the member would have been permitted, under section 11(a) of the Act and the other rules thereunder (with the exception of Rule 11a1–2), to effect the transaction.

Rule 11a2–2(T). Transactions effected by exchange members through other members

(a) A member of a national securities exchange (the "initiating member") may not effect a transaction on that exchange for its own account, the account of an associated person, or an account with respect to which it or an associated person thereof exercises investment discretion unless:

(1) The transaction is of a kind described in paragraphs A through H of Section 11(a)(1) of the Act and is effected in accordance with applicable rules and regulations thereunder; or

(2) The transaction is effected in compliance with each of the following conditions:

(i) The transaction is executed on the floor, or through use of the facilities, of the exchange by a member (the "executing member") which is not an associated person of the initiating member;

(ii) The order for the transaction is transmitted from off the exchange floor;

(iii) Neither the initiating member nor an associated person of the initiating member participates in the execution of the transaction at any time after the order for the transaction has been so transmitted; and

(iv) In the case of a transaction effected for an account with respect to which the initiating member or an associated person thereof exercises investment discretion, neither the initiating member nor any associated person thereof retains any compensation in connection with effecting the transaction; *Provided, however*, That this condition shall not apply to the extent that the person or persons authorized to transact business for the account have expressly provided otherwise by written contract referring to Section 11(a) of the Act and this rule executed on or after March 15, 1978, by each of them and by such exchange member or associated person exercising investment discretion.

(b) For purposes of this rule, a member "effects" a securities transaction when it performs any function in connection with the processing of that transaction, including, but not limited to, (1) transmission or an order for execution, (2) execution of the order, (3) clearance and settlement of the transaction, and (4) arranging for the performance of any such function.

(c) For purposes of this rule, the term "compensation in connection with effecting the transaction" refers to compensation directly or indirectly received or calculated on a transaction-related basis for the performance of any function involved in effecting a securities transaction.

(d) A member, or an associated person of a member, authorized by written contract to retain compensation in connection with effecting transactions pursuant to paragraph (a)(2)(iv) of this rule shall furnish at least annually to the person or persons authorized to transact business for the account a statement setting forth the total amount of all compensation retained by the member or any associated person thereof in connection with effecting transactions for that account during the period covered by the statement, which amount shall be exclusive of all amounts paid to others during that period for services rendered in effecting such transactions.

(e) A transaction effected in compliance with the requirements of this rule shall be deemed to be of a kind which is consistent with the purposes of Section 11(a)(1) of the Act, the protection of investors, and the maintenance of fair and orderly markets.

(f) The provisions of this rule shall not apply to transactions by exchange members to which, by operation of section 11(a)(3) of the Act, section 11(a)(1) of the Act is not effective.

ADOPTION OF REGULATION ON CONDUCT OF SPECIALISTS

Rule 11b–1. Regulation of specialists

(a)(1) The rules of a national securities exchange may permit a member of such exchange to register as a specialist and to act as a dealer.

(2) The rules of a national securities exchange permitting a member of such exchange to register as a specialist and to act as a dealer shall include:

(i) Adequate minimum capital requirements in view of the markets for securities on such exchange;

(ii) Requirements, as a condition of a specialist's registration, that a specialist engage in a course of dealings for his own account to assist in the maintenance, so far as practicable, of a fair and orderly market, and that a finding by the exchange of any substantial or continued failure by a specialist to engage in such a course of dealings will result in the suspension or cancellation of such specialist's registration in one or more of the securities in which such specialist is registered;

(iii) Provisions restricting his dealings so far as practicable to those reasonably necessary to permit him to maintain a fair and orderly market or necessary to permit him to act as an odd-lot dealer;

(iv) Provisions stating the responsibilities of a specialist acting as a broker in securities in which he is registered; and

(v) Procedures to provide for the effective and systematic surveillance of the activities of specialists.

(b) If after appropriate notice and opportunity for hearing the Commission finds that a member of a national securities exchange registered with such exchange as a specialist in specified securities has, for any account in which he, his member organization, or any participant therein has any beneficial interest, direct or indirect, effected transactions in such securities which were not part of a course of dealings reasonably necessary to permit such specialist to maintain a fair and orderly market, or to act as an odd-lot dealer, in the securities in which he is registered and were not effected in a manner consistent with the rules adopted by such exchange pursuant to paragraph (a)(2)(iii) of this rule, the Commission may by order direct such exchange to cancel, or to suspend for such period as the Commission may determine, such specialist's registration in one or more of the securities in which such specialist is registered: *Provided, however*, If such exchange has itself suspended or canceled such specialist's registration in one or more of the securities in which such specialist is registered, no further sanction shall be imposed pursuant to this paragraph (b) except in a case where the Commission finds substantial or continued misconduct by a specialist: *And provided, further*, That the provisions of this paragraph (b) shall not apply to a member of a national securities exchange exempted pursuant to the provisions of paragraph (d) of this rule.

(c) For the purposes of this rule, the term *rules* of an exchange shall mean its constitution, articles of incorporation, by-laws, or rules or instruments corresponding thereto, whatever the name, and its stated policies.

(d) Any national securities exchange may apply for an exemption from the provisions of this rule in compliance with the provisions of section 11(c) of the Act.

EXEMPTION OF CERTAIN SECURITIES FROM SECTION 11(d)(1)

Rule 11d1–1. Exemption of certain Securities from Section 11(d)(1)

A security shall be exempt from the provisions of section 11(d)(1) with respect to any transaction by a broker and dealer who, directly or indirectly, extends or maintains or arranges for the extension or maintenance of credit on the security to or for a customer if:

(a) The broker and dealer has not sold the security to the customer or bought the security for the customer's account; or

(b) The security is acquired by the customer in exchange with the issuer thereof for an outstanding security of the same issuer on which credit was lawfully maintained for the customer at the time of the exchange; or

(c) The customer is a broker or dealer or bank; or

(d) The security is acquired by the customer through the exercise of a right evidenced by a warrant or certificate expiring within 90 days after issuance, provided such right was originally issued to the customer as a stockholder of the corporation issuing the security upon which credit is to be extended. The right shall be deemed to be issued to the customer as a stockholder if he actually owned the stock giving rise to the right when such right accrued, even though such stock was not registered in his name; and in determining such fact the broker and dealer may rely upon a signed statement of the customer which the broker and dealer accepts in good faith; or

(e) Such broker and dealer would otherwise be subject to the prohibition of section 11(d)(1) with respect to 50 percent or less of all the securities of the same class which are outstanding or currently being distributed, and such broker and dealer sold the security to the customer or bought the security for the customer's account on a day when he was not participating in the distribution of any new issue of such security. A broker-dealer shall be deemed to be participating in a distribution of a new issue if (1) he owns, directly or indirectly, any undistributed security of such issue, or (2) he is engaged in any stabilizing activities to facilitate a distribution of such issue, or (3) he is a party to any syndicate agreement under which such stabilizing activities are being or may be undertaken, or (4) he is a party to an executory agreement to purchase or distribute such issue.

Rule 11d1–2. Exemption from Section 11(d)(1) for certain investment company securities held by broker–dealers as collateral in margin accounts

Any securities issued by a registered open-end investment company or unit investment trust as defined in the Investment Company Act of 1940 shall be exempted from the provisions of section 11(d)(1) with respect to any transaction by a person who is a broker and a dealer who, directly or indirectly, extends or maintains or arranges for the extension or maintenance of credit on such security, provided such security has been owned by the person to whom credit would be provided for more than 30 days, or purchased by such person pursuant to a plan for the automatic reinvestment of the dividends of such company or trust.

Rule 11d2–1. Exemption from Section 11(d)(2) for certain broker–dealers effecting transactions for customers security futures products in futures accounts

A broker or dealer registered pursuant to section 15(b)(1) of the Act (15 U.S.C. 78*o*(b)(1)) that is also a futures commission merchant registered pursuant to section 4f(a)(1) of the Commodity Exchange Act (7 U.S.C. 6f(a)(1)), to the extent that it effects transactions for customers in security futures products in a futures account (as that term is defined in Rule 15c3–3(a)(15)), is exempt from section 11(d)(2) of the Act (15 U.S.C. 78k(d)(2)).

SECURITIES EXEMPTED FROM REGISTRATION

Rule 12a–4. Exemption of certain warrants from Section 12(a)

(a) When used in this rule, the following terms shall have the meaning indicated unless the context otherwise requires:

(1) The term *warrant* means any warrant or certificate evidencing a right to subscribe to or otherwise acquire another security, issued or unissued.

(2) The term *beneficiary security* means a security to the holders of which a warrant or right to subscribe to or otherwise acquire another security is granted.

(3) The term *subject security* means a security which is the subject of a warrant or right to subscribe to or otherwise acquire such security.

(4) The term *in the process of admission to dealing,* in respect of a specified security means that (i) an application has been filed pursuant to section 12(b) and (c) of the Act for the registration of such security on a national securities exchange; or (ii) the Commission has granted an application made pursuant to section 12(f) of the Act to continue or extend unlisted trading privileges to such security on a national securities exchange; or (iii) written notice has been filed with the Commission by a national securities exchange to the effect that such security has been approved for admission to dealing as a security exempted from the operation of section 12(a) of the Act.

(b) Any issued or unissued warrant granted to the holders of a security admitted to dealing on a national securities exchange shall be exempt from the operation of section 12(a) of the Act to the extent necessary to render lawful the effecting of transactions therein on any national securities exchange (i) on which the beneficiary security is admitted to dealing or (ii) on which the subject security is admitted to dealing or is in the process of admission to dealing, subject to the following terms and conditions:

(1) Such warrant by its terms expires within 90 days after the issuance thereof;

(2) A registration statement under the Securities Act of 1933 is in effect as to such warrant and as to each subject security, or the applicable terms of any exemption from such registration have been met in respect to such warrant and each subject security; and,

(3) Within five days after the exchange has taken official action to admit such warrant to dealing, it shall notify the Commission of such action.

(c) Notwithstanding paragraph (b) above, no exemption pursuant to this rule shall be available for transactions in any such warrant on any exchange on which the beneficiary security is admitted to dealing unless:

(1) Each subject security is admitted to dealing or is in process of admission to dealing on a national securities exchange, or,

(2) There is available from a registration statement and periodic reports or other data filed by the issuer of the subject security, pursuant to any act administered by the Commission, information substantially equivalent to that available with respect to a security listed and registered on a national securities exchange.

(d) Notwithstanding the foregoing, an unissued warrant shall not be exempt pursuant to this rule unless:

(1) Formal or official announcement has been made by the issuer specifying (i) the terms upon which such warrant and each subject security is to be issued, (ii) the date, if any, as of which the security holders entitled to receive such warrant will be determined, (iii) the approximate date of the issuance of such warrant, and (iv) the approximate date of the issuance of each subject security; and

(2) The members of the exchange are subject to rules which provide that the performance of the contract to purchase and sell an unissued warrant shall be conditioned upon the issuance of such warrant.

(e) The Commission may by order deny or revoke the exemption of a warrant under this rule, if, after appropriate notice and opportunity for hearing to the issuer of such warrant and to the exchange or exchanges on which such warrant is admitted to dealing as an exempted security, it finds that:

(1) Any of the terms or conditions of this rule have not been met with respect to such exemption; or

(2) At any time during the period of such exemption transactions have been effected on any such exchanges in such warrant which (i) create or induce a false, misleading or artificial appearance of activity, (ii) unduly or improperly influence the market price, or (iii) make a price which does not reflect the true state of the market; or

(3) Any other facts exist which make such denial or revocation necessary or appropriate in the public interest or for the protection of investors.

(f) If it appears necessary or appropriate in the public interest or for the protection of investors, the Commission may summarily suspend the exemption of such warrant pending the determination by the Commission whether such exemption shall be denied or revoked.

(g) Rule 10b–1 shall be applicable to any warrant exempted by this rule.

Rule 12a–5. Temporary exemption of substituted or additional securities

(a)(1) Subject to the conditions of paragraph (a)(2) of this rule, whenever the holders of a security admitted to trading on a national securities exchange (hereinafter called the original security) obtain the right, by operation of law or otherwise, to acquire all or any part of a class of another or substitute security of the same or another issuer, or an additional amount of the original security, then:

(i) All or any part of the class of such other or substituted security shall be temporarily exempted from the operation of section 12(a) to the extent necessary to render lawful transactions therein on an issued or "when-issued" basis on any national securities exchange on which the original, the other or the substituted security is lawfully admitted to trading; and

(ii) The additional amount of the original security shall be temporarily exempted from the operation of section 12(a) to the extent necessary to render lawful transactions therein on a "when-issued" basis on any national securities exchange on which the original security is lawfully admitted to trading.

(2) The exemptions provided by paragraph (a)(1) of this rule shall be available only if the following conditions are met:

(i) A registration statement is in effect under the Securities Act of 1933 to the extent required as to the security which is the subject of such exemption, or the terms of any applicable exemption from registration under such Act have been complied with, if required;

(ii) Any stockholder approval necessary to the issuance of the security which is the subject of the exemption, has been obtained; and

1. Copy filed with the Federal Register Division.

(iii) All other necessary official action, other than the filing or recording of charter amendments or other documents with the appropriate state authorities, has been taken to authorize and assure the issuance of the security which is the subject of such exemption.

(b) The exemption provided by this rule shall terminate on the earliest of the following dates:

(1) When registration of the exempt security on the exchange becomes effective;

(2) When the exempt security is granted unlisted trading privileges on the exchange;

(3) The close of business on the tenth day after (i) withdrawal of an application for registration of the exempt security on the exchange; (ii) withdrawal by the exchange of its certification of approval of the exempt security for listing and registration; (iii) withdrawal of an application for admission of the exempt security to unlisted trading privileges on the exchange; or (iv) the sending to the exchange of notice of the entry of an order by the Commission denying an application for admission of the exempt security to unlisted trading privileges on the exchange;

(4) The close of business on the one hundred and twentieth day after the date on which the exempt security was admitted by action of the exchange to trading thereon as a security exempted from the operation of section 12(a) by this rule, unless prior thereto an application for registration of the exempt security or for admission of the exempt security to unlisted trading privileges on the exchange has been filed.

(c) Notwithstanding paragraph (b) of this rule, the Commission, having due regard for the public interest and the protection of investors, may at any time extend the period of exemption of any security by this rule or may sooner terminate the exemption upon notice to the exchange and to the issuer of the extension or termination thereof.

(d) The exchange shall file with the Commission a notification on Form 26[1] promptly after taking action to admit any security to trading under this rule: *Provided, however,* That no notification need be filed under this rule concerning the admission or proposed admission to trading of additional amounts of a class of security admitted to trading on such exchange.

(e) Rule 10b–1 shall be applicable to all securities exempted from the operation of section 12(a) by this rule.

Rule 12a–6. Exemption of securities underlying certain options from Section 12(a)

(a) When used in this rule, the following terms shall have the meanings indicated unless the context otherwise requires:

(1) The term *option* shall include any put, call, spread, straddle, or other option or privilege of buying a security from or selling a security to another without being bound to do so, but such term shall not include any such option where the writer is: the issuer of the security which may be purchased or sold upon exercise of the option, or is a person that directly, or indirectly, through one or more intermediaries, controls, or is controlled by, or is under common control with such issuer;

(2) The term *underlying security* means a security which relates to or is the subject of an option.

(b) Any underlying security shall be exempt from the operation of Section 12(a) of the Act if all of the following terms and conditions are met:

(1) The related option is duly listed and registered on a national securities exchange;

(2) The only transactions on such exchange with respect to such underlying securities consist of the delivery of and payment for such underlying securities pursuant to the terms of such options relating to the exercise thereof; and

(3) Such underlying security is *(i)* duly listed and registered on another national securities exchange at the time the option is issued; or *(ii)* duly quoted on the National Association of Securities Dealers Automated Quotation System ("NASDAQ") at the time the option is issued.

Rule 12a–7. Exemption of stock contained in standardized market baskets from Section 12(a) of the Act

(a) Any component stock of a standardized market basket shall be exempt from the registration requirement of section 12(a) of the Act, solely for the purpose of inclusion in a standardized market basket, provided that all of the following terms and conditions are met:

(1) The standardized market basket has been duly approved by the Commission for listing on a national securities exchange pursuant to the requirements of section 19(b) of the Act; and

(2) The stock is an NMS stock as defined in Rule 600 of Regulation NMS and is either:

(i) Listed and registered for trading on a national securities exchange by the issuer or

(ii) Quoted on the National Association of Securities Dealers Automated Quotation System;

(b) When used in this rule, the term standardized market basket means a group of at least 100 stocks purchased or sold in a single execution and at a single trading location with physical delivery and transfer of ownership of each component stock resulting from such execution.

Rule 12a–8. Exemption of depositary shares

Depositary shares (as that term is defined in Rule 12b–2) registered on Form F–6 (17 CFR 239.36), but not the underlying deposited securities, shall be exempt from the operation of section 12(a) of the Act (15 U.S.C. 78*l*(a)).

Rule 12a–9. Exemption of standardized options from Section 12(a) of the Act

The provisions of section 12(a) of the Act (15 U.S.C. 78*l*(a)) do not apply in respect of any standardized option, as defined by section Rule 9b–1(a)(4), issued by a clearing agency registered under section 17A of the Act (15 U.S.C. 78q–1) and traded on a national securities exchange registered pursuant to section 6(a) of the Act (15 U.S.C. 78f(a)).

Rule 12a–10. Exemption of security-based swaps from Section 12(a) of the Act

The provisions of Section 12(a) of the Act do not apply to any security-based swap that:

(a) Is issued or will be issued by a clearing agency registered as a clearing agency under Section 17A of the Act (15 U.S.C. 78q–1) or exempt from registration under Section 17A of the Act pursuant to a rule, regulation, or order of the Commission, in its function as a central counterparty with respect to the security-based swap;

(b) The Commission has determined is required to be cleared or that is permitted to be cleared pursuant to the clearing agency's rules;

(c) Is sold to an eligible contract participant (as defined in Section 1a(18) of the Commodity Exchange Act (7 U.S.C. 1a(18))) in reliance on Rule 239 under the Securities Act of 1933; and

(d) Is traded on a national securities exchange registered pursuant to Section 6(a) of the Act.

Rule 12a–11. Exemption of security-based swaps sold in reliance on Securities Act of 1933 Rule 240 from Section 12(a) of the Act

(a) The provisions of Section 12(a) of the Act (15 U.S.C. 78l(a)) do not apply to any security-based swap offered and sold in reliance on Rule 240 under the Securities Act of 1933.

(b) This rule will expire on February 11, 2017.

REGULATION 12B. REGISTRATION AND REPORTING

ATTENTION ELECTRONIC FILERS

THIS REGULATION SHOULD BE READ IN CONJUNCTION WITH REGULATION S–T (17 CFR 232), WHICH GOVERNS THE PREPARATION AND SUBMISSION OF DOCUMENTS IN ELECTRONIC FORMAT. MANY PROVISIONS RELATING TO THE PREPARATION AND SUBMISSION OF DOCUMENTS IN PAPER FORMAT CONTAINED IN THIS REGULATION ARE SUPERSEDED BY THE PROVISIONS OF REGULATION S–T FOR DOCUMENTS REQUIRED TO BE FILED IN ELECTRONIC FORMAT.

GENERAL

Rule 12b–1. Scope of regulation

The rules contained in this regulation shall govern all registration statements pursuant to sections 12(b) and 12(g) of the Act and all reports filed pursuant to sections 13 and 15(d) of the Act, including all amendments to such statements and reports, except that any provision in a form covering the same subject matter as any such rule shall be controlling.

Rule 12b–2. Definitions

Unless the context otherwise requires, the following terms, when used in the rules contained in this regulation or in Regulation 13A or 15D or in the forms for statements and reports filed pursuant to section 12, 13 or 15(d) of the Act, shall have the respective meanings indicated in this rule:

Accelerated Filer and Large Accelerated Filer. (1) *Accelerated Filer*. The term *accelerated filer* means an issuer after it first meets the following conditions as of the end of its fiscal year:

(i) The issuer had an aggregate worldwide market value of the voting and non-voting common equity held by its non-affiliates of $75 million or more, but less than $700 million, as of the last business day of the issuer's most recently completed second fiscal quarter;

(ii) The issuer has been subject to the requirements of section 13(a) or 15(d) of the Act (15 U.S.C. 78m or 78o(d)) for a period of at least twelve calendar months; and

(iii) The issuer has filed at least one annual report pursuant to section 13(a) or 15(d) of the Act.

(2) *Large Accelerated Filer*. The term *large accelerated filer* means an issuer after it first meets the following conditions as of the end of its fiscal year:

(i) The issuer had an aggregate worldwide market value of the voting and non-voting common equity held by its non-affiliates of $700 million or more, as of the last business day of the issuer's most recently completed second fiscal quarter;

(ii) The issuer has been subject to the requirements of section 13(a) or 15(d) of the Act for a period of at least twelve calendar months; and

(iii) The issuer has filed at least one annual report pursuant to section 13(a) or 15(d) of the Act.

(3) *Entering and Exiting Accelerated Filer and Large Accelerated Filer Status*. (i) The determination at the end of the issuer's fiscal year for whether a non-accelerated filer becomes an accelerated filer, or whether a non-accelerated filer or accelerated filer becomes a large accelerated filer, governs the deadlines for the annual report to be filed for that fiscal year, the quarterly and annual reports to be filed for the subsequent fiscal year and all annual and quarterly reports to be filed thereafter while the issuer remains an accelerated filer or large accelerated filer.

(ii) Once an issuer becomes an accelerated filer, it will remain an accelerated filer unless the issuer determines at the end of a fiscal year that the aggregate worldwide market value of the voting and non-voting common equity held by non-affiliates of the issuer was less than $50 million, as of the last business day of the issuer's most recently completed second fiscal quarter. An issuer making this determination becomes a non-accelerated filer. The issuer will not become an accelerated filer again unless it subsequently meets the conditions in paragraph (1) of this definition.

(iii) Once an issuer becomes a large accelerated filer, it will remain a large accelerated filer unless the issuer determines at the end of a fiscal year that the aggregate worldwide market value of the voting and non-voting common equity held by non-affiliates of the issuer was less than $500 million, as of the last business day of the issuer's most recently completed second fiscal quarter. If the issuer's aggregate worldwide market value was $50 million or more, but less than $500 million, as of the last business day of the issuer's most recently completed second fiscal quarter, the issuer becomes an accelerated filer. If the issuer's aggregate worldwide market value was less than $50 million, as of the last business day of the issuer's most recently completed second fiscal quarter, the issuer becomes a non-accelerated filer. An issuer will not become a large accelerated filer again unless it subsequently meets the conditions in paragraph (2) of this definition.

(iv) The determination at the end of the issuer's fiscal year for whether an accelerated filer becomes a non-accelerated filer, or a large accelerated filer becomes an accelerated filer or a non-accelerated filer, governs the deadlines for the annual report to be filed for that fiscal year, the quarterly and annual reports to be filed for the subsequent fiscal year and all annual and quarterly reports to be filed thereafter while the issuer remains an accelerated filer or non-accelerated filer.

NOTE TO PARAGRAPHS (1), (2) AND (3): The aggregate worldwide market value of the issuer's outstanding voting and non-voting common equity shall be computed by use of the price at which the common equity was last sold, or the average of the bid and asked prices of such common equity, in the principal market for such common equity.

Affiliate. An "affiliate" of, or a person "affiliated" with, a specified person, is a person that directly, or indirectly through one or more intermediaries, controls, or is controlled by, or is under common control with, the person specified.

Amount. The term "amount," when used in regard to securities, means the principal amount if relating to evidences of indebtedness, the number of shares if relating to shares, and the number of units if relating to any other kind of security.

Associate. The term "associate" used to indicate a relationship with any person, means (1) any corporation or organization (other than the registrant or a majority-owned subsidiary of the registrant) of which such person is an officer or partner or is, directly or indirectly, the beneficial owner of 10 percent or more of any class of equity securities, (2) any trust or other estate in which such person has a substantial beneficial interest or as to which such person serves as trustee or in a similar fiduciary capacity, and (3) any relative or spouse of such person, or any relative of such spouse, who has the same home as such person or who is a director or officer of the registrant or any of its parents or subsidiaries.

Business Combination Related Shell Company: The term "business combination related shell company" means a shell company (as defined in Rule 12b–2) that is:

(1) Formed by an entity that is not a shell company solely for the purpose of changing the corporate domicile of that entity solely within the United States; or

(2) Formed by an entity that is not a shell company solely for the purpose of completing a business combination transaction (as defined in Rule 165(f) under the Securities Act of 1933) among one or more entities other than the shell company, none of which is a shell company.

Certified. The term "certified," when used in regard to financial statements, means examined and reported upon with an opinion expressed by an independent public or certified public accountant.

Charter. The term "charter" includes articles of incorporation, declarations of trust, articles of association or partnership, or any similar instrument, as amended, effecting (either with or without filing with any governmental agency) the organization or creation of an incorporated or unincorporated person.

Common Equity. The term "common equity" means any class of common stock or an equivalent interest, including but not limited to a unit of beneficial interests in a trust or a limited partnership interest.

Control. The term "control" (including the terms "controlling," "controlled by" and "under common control with") means the possession, direct or indirect, of the power to direct or cause the direction of the management and policies of a person, whether through the ownership of voting securities, by contract, or otherwise.

Depositary Share. The term "depositary share" means a security, evidenced by an American Depositary Receipt, that represents a foreign security or a multiple of or fraction thereof deposited with a depositary.

Emerging Growth Company. (1) The term emerging growth company means an issuer that had total annual gross revenues of less than $1,070,000,000 during its most recently completed fiscal year.

(2) An issuer that is an emerging growth company as of the first day of that fiscal year shall continue to be deemed an emerging growth company until the earliest of:

(i) the last day of the fiscal year of the issuer during which it had total annual gross revenues of $1,070,000,000 or more;

(ii) the last day of the fiscal year of the issuer following the fifth anniversary of the date of the first sale of common equity securities of the issuer pursuant to an effective registration statement under the Securities Act of 1933;

(iii) the date on which such issuer has, during the previous three year period, issued more than $1,000,000,000 in non-convertible debt; or

(iv) the date on which such issuer is deemed to be a large accelerated filer, as defined in Rule 12b-2 of the Exchange Act (§240.12b–2 of this chapter), or any successor thereto.

Employee. The term "employee" does not include a director, trustee, or officer.

Fiscal Year. The term "fiscal year" means the annual accounting period or, if no closing date has been adopted, the calendar year ending on December 31.

Majority-Owned Subsidiary. The term "majority-owned subsidiary" means a subsidiary more than 50 percent of whose outstanding securities representing the right, other than as affected by events of default, to vote for the election of directors, is owned by the subsidiary's parent and/or one or more of the parent's other majority-owned subsidiaries.

Managing Underwriter. The term "managing underwriter" includes an underwriter (or underwriters) who, by contract or otherwise, deals with the registrant; organizes the selling effort; receives some benefit directly or indirectly in which all other underwriters similarly situated do not share in proportion to their respective interests in the underwriting; or represents any other underwriters in such matters as maintaining the records of the distribution, arranging the allotments of securities offered or arranging for appropriate stabilization activities, if any.

Material. The term "material," when used to qualify a requirement for the furnishing of information as to any subject, limits the information required to those matters to which there is a substantial likelihood that a reasonable investor would attach importance in determining whether to buy or sell the securities registered.

Material Weakness. The term "material weakness" is a deficiency, or a combination of deficiencies, in internal control over financial reporting such that there is a reasonable possibility that a material misstatement of the registrant's annual or interim financial statements will not be prevented or detected on a timely basis.

Parent. A "parent" of a specified person is an affiliate controlling such person directly, or indirectly through one or more intermediaries.

Predecessor. The term "predecessor" means a person the major portion of the business and assets of which another person acquired in a single succession or in a series of related successions in each of which the acquiring person acquiring the major portion of the business and assets of the acquired person.

Previously Filed or Reported. The terms "previously filed" and "previously reported" mean previously filed with, or reported in, a statement under section 12, a report under section 13 or 15(d), a definitive proxy statement or information statement under section 14 of the Act, or a registration statement under the Securities Act of 1933: *Provided,* That information contained in any such document shall be deemed to have been previously filed with, or reported to, an exchange only if such document is filed with such exchange.

Principal Underwriter. The term "principal underwriter" means an underwriter in privity of contract with the issuer of the securities as to which he is underwriter.

Promoter. (1) The term "promoter" includes:

(i) Any person who, acting along or in conjunction with one or more other persons, directly or indirectly takes initiative in founding and organizing the business or enterprise of an issuer; or

(ii) Any person who, in connection with the founding and organizing of the business or enterprise of an issuer, directly or indirectly receives in consideration of services or property, or both services and property, 10 percent or more of any class of securities of the issuer or 10 percent or more of the proceeds from the sale of any class of such securities. However, a person who receives such securities or proceeds either solely as underwriting commissions or solely in consideration of property shall not be deemed a promoter within the meaning of this paragraph if such person does not otherwise take part in founding and organizing the enterprise.

(2) All persons coming within the definition of "promoter" in paragraph (1) of this definition may be referred to as "founders" or "organizers" or by another term provided that such term is reasonably descriptive of those persons' activities with respect to the issuer.

Prospectus. Unless otherwise specified or the context otherwise requires, the term "prospectus" means a prospectus meeting the requirements of section 10(a) of the Securities Act of 1933 as amended.

Registrant. The term "registrant" means an issuer of securities with respect to which a registration statement or report is to be filed.

Registration Statement. The term "registration statement" or "statement," when used with reference to registration pursuant to section 12 of the Act, includes both an application for registration of securities on a national securities exchange pursuant to section 12(b) of the Act and a registration statement filed pursuant to section 12(g) of the Act.

Share. The term "share" means a share of stock in a corporation or unit of interest in an unincorporated person.

Shell Company: The term "shell company" means a registrant, other than an asset-backed issuer as defined in Item 1101(b) of Regulation AB, that has:

(1) No or nominal operations; and

(2) Either:

(i) No or nominal assets;

(ii) Assets consisting solely of cash and cash equivalents; or

(iii) Assets consisting of any amount of cash and cash equivalents and nominal other assets.

NOTE: For purposes of this definition, the determination of a registrant's assets (including cash and cash equivalents) is based solely on the amount of assets that would be reflected on the registrant's balance sheet prepared in accordance with generally accepted accounting principles on the date of that determination.

Significant Deficiency. The term "significant deficiency" is a deficiency, or a combination of deficiencies, in internal control over financial reporting that is less severe than a material weakness, yet important enough to merit attention by those responsible for oversight of the registrant's financial reporting.

Significant Subsidiary. The term *significant subsidiary* means a subsidiary, including its subsidiaries, which meets any of the following conditions:

(1) The registrant's and its other subsidiaries' investments in and advances to the subsidiary exceed 10 percent of the total assets of the registrant and its subsidiaries consolidated as of the end of the most recently completed fiscal year (for a proposed combination between entities under common control, this condition is also met when the number of common shares exchanged or to be exchanged by the registrant exceeds 10 percent of its total common shares outstanding at the date the combination is initiated); or

(2) The registrant's and its other subsidiaries' proportionate share of the total assets (after intercompany eliminations) of the subsidiary exceeds 10 percent of the total assets of the registrant and its subsidiaries consolidated as of the end of the most recently completed fiscal year; or

(3) The registrant's and its other subsidiaries' equity in the income from continuing operations before income taxes of the subsidiary exclusive of amounts attributable to any noncontrolling interests exceeds 10 percent of such income of the registrant and its subsidiaries consolidated for the most recently completed fiscal year.

NOTE 1: A registrant that files its financial statements in accordance with or provides a reconciliation to U.S. Generally Accepted Accounting Principles shall make the prescribed tests using amounts determined under U.S. Generally Accepted Accounting Principles. A foreign private issuer that files its financial statements in accordance with IFRS as issued by the IASB shall make the prescribed tests using amounts determined under IFRS as issued by the IASB.

COMPUTATIONAL NOTE 1 TO PARAGRAPH (3): For purposes of making the prescribed income test the following guidance should be applied:

1. When a loss exclusive of amounts attributable to any noncontrolling interests has been incurred by either the parent and its subsidiaries consolidated or the tested subsidiary, but not both, the equity in the income or loss of the tested subsidiary exclusive of amounts attributable to any noncontrolling interests should be excluded from such income of the registrant and its subsidiaries consolidated for purposes of the computation.

2. If income of the registrant and its subsidiaries consolidated exclusive of amounts attributable to any noncontrolling interests for the most recent fiscal year is at least 10 percent lower than the average of the income for the last five fiscal years, such average income should be substituted for purposes of the computation. Any loss years should be omitted for purposes of computing average income.

Smaller Reporting Company. As used in this part, the term *smaller reporting company* means an issuer that is not an investment company, an asset-backed issuer (as defined in

Item 1101 of Regulation AB), or a majority-owned subsidiary of a parent that is not a smaller reporting company and that:

(1) Had a public float of less than $250 million; or

(2) Had annual revenues of less than $100 million and either:

(i) No public float; or

(ii) A public float of less than $700 million.

(3) Whether an issuer is a smaller reporting company is determined on an annual basis.

(i) For issuers that are required to file reports under section 13(a) or 15(d) of the Exchange Act:

(A) Public float is measured as of the last business day of the issuer's most recently completed second fiscal quarter and computed by multiplying the aggregate worldwide number of shares of its voting and non-voting common equity held by non-affiliates by the price at which the common equity was last sold, or the average of the bid and asked prices of common equity, in the principal market for the common equity;

(B) Annual revenues are as of the most recently completed fiscal year for which audited financial statements are available; and

(C) An issuer must reflect the determination of whether it came within the definition of smaller reporting company in its quarterly report on Form 10–Q for the first fiscal quarter of the next year, indicating on the cover page of that filing, and in subsequent filings for that fiscal year, whether it is a smaller reporting company, except that, if a determination based on public float indicates that the issuer is newly eligible to be a smaller reporting company, the issuer may choose to reflect this determination beginning with its first quarterly report on Form 10–Q following the determination, rather than waiting until the first fiscal quarter of the next year.

(ii) For determinations based on an initial registration statement under the Securities Act or Exchange Act for shares of its common equity:

(A) Public float is measured as of a date within 30 days of the date of the filing of the registration statement and computed by multiplying the aggregate worldwide number of shares of its voting and non-voting common equity held by non-affiliates before the registration plus, in the case of a Securities Act registration statement, the number of shares of its voting and non-voting common equity included in the registration statement by the estimated public offering price of the shares;

(B) Annual revenues are as of the most recently completed fiscal year for which audited financial statements are available; and

(C) The issuer must reflect the determination of whether it came within the definition of smaller reporting company in the registration statement and must appropriately indicate on the cover page of the filing, and subsequent filings for the fiscal year in which the filing is made, whether it is a smaller reporting company. The issuer must re-determine its status at the end of its second fiscal quarter and then reflect any change in status as provided in paragraph (3)(i)(C) of this definition. In the case of a determination based on an initial Securities Act registration statement, an issuer that was not determined to be a smaller reporting company has the option to re-determine its status at the conclusion of the offering covered by the registration statement based on the actual offering price and number of shares sold.

(iii) Once an issuer determines that it does not qualify for smaller reporting company status because it exceeded one or more of the current thresholds, it will remain unqualified unless when making its annual determination either:

(A) It determines that its public float was less than $200 million; or

(B) It determines that its public float and its annual revenues meet the requirements for subsequent qualification included in the following chart:

Prior Annual Revenues	**Prior Public Float**	
	None or less than $700 million	**$700 million or more**
Less than $100 million	Neither threshold exceeded.	**Public float** Less than $560 million; and **Revenues** Less than $100 million.
$100 million or more	**Public float** None or less than $700 million; and **Revenues** Less than $80 million.	**Public float** Less than $560 million; and **Revenues** Less than 80 million.

Instruction 1 to definition of "smaller reporting company": A registrant that qualifies as a smaller reporting company under the public float thresholds identified in paragraphs (1) and (3)(iii)(A) of this definition will qualify as a smaller reporting company regardless of its revenues.

Subsidiary. A "subsidiary" of a specified person is an affiliate controlled by such person directly, or indirectly through one or more intermediaries. (See also "majority-owned subsidiary," "significant subsidiary," and "totally-held subsidiary.")

Succession. The term "succession" means the direct acquisition of the assets comprising a going business, whether by merger, consolidation, purchase, or other direct transfer; or the acquisition of control of a shell company in a transaction required to be reported on Form 8–K (17 CFR 249.308) in compliance with Item 5.01 of that Form or on Form 20–F (17 CFR 249.220f) in compliance with Rule 13a–19 or Rule 15d–19. Except for an acquisition of control of a shell company, the term does not include the acquisition of control of a business unless followed by the direct acquisition of its assets. The terms *succeed* and *successor* have meanings correlative to the foregoing.

Totally Held Subsidiary. The term "totally held subsidiary" means a subsidiary (1) substantially all of whose outstanding securities are owned by its parent and/or the parent's other totally held subsidiaries, and (2) which is not indebted to any person other than its parent and/or the parent's other totally held subsidiaries in an amount which is material in relation to the particular subsidiary, excepting indebtedness incurred in the ordinary course of business which is not overdue and which matures within one year from the date of its creation, whether evidenced by securities or not.

Voting Securities. The term "voting securities" means securities the holders of which are presently entitled to vote for the election of directors.

Wholly-Owned Subsidiary. The term "wholly-owned subsidiary" means a subsidiary substantially all of whose outstanding voting securities are owned by its parent and/or the parent's other wholly-owned subsidiaries.

Rule 12b–3. Title of securities

Wherever the title of securities is required to be stated there shall be given such information as will indicate the type and general character of the securities, including the following:

(a) In the case of shares, the par or stated value, if any; the rate of dividends, if fixed, and whether cumulative or noncumulative; a brief indication of the preference, if any; and if convertible, a statement to that effect.

(b) In the case of funded debt, the rate of interest; the date of maturity, or if the issue matures serially, a brief indication of the serial maturities, such as "maturing serially from 1950 to 1960"; if the payment of principal or interest is contingent, an appropriate indication of such contingency; a brief indication of the priority of the issue; and if convertible, a statement to that effect.

(c) In the case of any other kind of security, appropriate information of comparable character.

Rule 12b–4. Supplemental information

The Commission or its staff may, where it is deemed appropriate, request supplemental information concerning the registrant, a registration statement or a periodic or other report under the Act. This information shall not be required to be filed with or deemed part of the registration statement or report. The information shall be returned to the registrant upon request, provided that:

(a) Such request is made at the time such information is furnished to the staff;

(b) The return of such information is consistent with the protection of investors; and

(c) The return of such information is consistent with the provisions of the Freedom of Information Act (5 U.S.C. 552).

Rule 12b–5. Determination of affiliates of banks

In determining whether a person is an "affiliate" or "parent" of a bank or whether a bank is a "subsidiary" or "majority-owned subsidiary" of a person, within the meaning of those terms as defined in Rule 12b–2, voting securities of the bank held by a corporation all of the stock of which is directly owned by the United States Government shall not be taken into consideration.

Rule 12b–6. When securities are deemed to be registered

A class of securities with respect to which a registration statement has been filed pursuant to section 12 of the Act shall be deemed to be registered for the purposes of sections 13, 14, 15(d) and 16 of the Act and the rules and regulations thereunder only when such statement has become effective as provided in section 12, and securities of said class shall not be subject to sections 13, 14 and 16 of the Act until such statement has become effective as provided in section 12.

Rule 12b–7. [Reserved]

FORMAL REQUIREMENTS

Rule 12b–10. Requirements as to proper form

Every statement or report shall be on the form prescribed therefor by the Commission, as in effect on the date of filing. Any statement or report shall be deemed to be filed on the proper form unless objection to the form is made by the Commission within thirty days after the date of filing.

Rule 12b–11. Number of copies; signatures; binding

(a) Except as provided in a particular form, three complete copies of each statement or report, including exhibits and all other papers and documents filed as a part thereof, shall be filed with the Commission. At least one complete copy of each statement shall be filed with each exchange on which the securities covered thereby are to be registered. At least one complete copy of each report under section 13 of the

Act shall be filed with each exchange on which the registrant has securities registered.

(b) At least one copy of each statement or report filed with the Commission and one copy thereof filed with each exchange shall be signed in the manner prescribed by the appropriate form.

(c) Each copy of a statement or report filed with the Commission or with an exchange shall be bound in one or more parts. Copies filed with the Commission shall be bound without stiff covers. The statement or report shall be bound on the left side in such a manner as to leave the reading matter legible.

(d) *Signatures.* Where the Act or the rules, forms, reports or schedules thereunder, including paragraph (b) of this rule, require a document filed with or furnished to the Commission to be signed, such document shall be manually signed, or signed using either typed signatures or duplicated or facsimile versions of manual signatures. Where typed, duplicated or facsimile signatures are used, each signatory to the filing shall manually sign a signature page or other document authenticating, acknowledging or otherwise adopting his or her signature that appears in the filing. Such document shall be executed before or at the time the filing is made and shall be retained by the filer for a period of five years. Upon request, the filer shall furnish to the Commission or its staff a copy of any or all documents retained pursuant to this rule.

Rule 12b–12. Requirements as to paper, printing and language

(a) Statements and reports shall be filed on good quality, unglazed white paper, no larger than 8½ x 11 inches in size, insofar as practicable. To the extent that the reduction of larger documents would render them illegible, such documents may be filed on paper larger than 8½ x 11 inches in size.

(b) The statement or report and, insofar as practicable, all papers and documents filed as a part thereof, shall be printed, lithographed, mimeographed, or typewritten. However, the statement or report or any portion thereof may be prepared by any similar process which, in the opinion of the Commission, produces copies suitable for a permanent record and microfilming. Irrespective of the process used, all copies of any such material shall be clear, easily readable and suitable for repeated photocopying. Debits in credit categories and credits in debit categories shall be designated so as to be clearly distinguishable as such on photocopies.

(c) The body of all printed statements and reports and all notes to financial statements and other tabular data included therein shall be in roman type at least as large and as legible as 10-point modern type. However, to the extent necessary for convenient presentation, financial statements and other tabular data, including tabular data in notes, may be in roman type at least as large as and as legible as 8-point modern type. All such type shall be leaded at least 2 points.

(d)(1) All Exchange Act filings and submissions must be in the English language, except as otherwise provided by this rule. If a filing or submission requires the inclusion of a document that is in a foreign language, a party must submit instead a fair and accurate English translation of the entire foreign language document, except as provided by paragraph (d)(3) of this rule.

(2) If a filing or submission subject to review by the Division of Corporation Finance requires the inclusion of a foreign language document as an exhibit or attachment, a party must submit a fair and accurate English translation of the foreign language document if consisting of any of the following, or an amendment of any of the following:

(i) Articles of incorporation, memoranda of association, bylaws, and other comparable documents, whether original or restated;

(ii) Instruments defining the rights of security holders, including indentures qualified or to be qualified under the Trust Indenture Act of 1939;

(iii) Voting agreements, including voting trust agreements;

(iv) Contracts to which directors, officers, promoters, voting trustees or security holders named in a registration statement, report or other document are parties;

(v) Contracts upon which a filer's business is substantially dependent;

(vi) Audited annual and interim consolidated financial information; and

(vii) Any document that is or will be the subject of a confidential treatment request under Rule 24b–2 or Rule 406 under the Securities Act of 1933.

(3)(i) A party may submit an English summary instead of an English translation of a foreign language document as an exhibit or attachment to a filing or submission subject to review by the Division of Corporation Finance, as long as:

(A) The foreign language document does not consist of any of the subject matter enumerated in paragraph (d)(2) of this rule; or

(B) The applicable form permits the use of an English summary.

(ii) Any English summary submitted under paragraph (d)(3) of this rule must:

(A) Fairly and accurately summarize the terms of each material provision of the foreign language document; and

(B) Fairly and accurately describe the terms that have been omitted or abridged.

(4) When submitting an English summary English translation of a foreign language document under this rule, a party must identify the submission as either an English summary or English translation. A party may submit a copy of the unabridged foreign language document when including an English summary or English translation of a foreign language document in a filing or submission. A party must provide a copy of any foreign language document upon the request of Commission staff.

(5) A foreign government or its political subdivision must provide a fair and accurate English translation of its latest annual budget submitted as Exhibit B to Form 18 (17 CFR 249.218) or Exhibit (c) to Form 18–K (17 CFR 249.318) only if one is available. If no English translation is available, a filer must provide a copy of the foreign language version of its latest annual budget as an exhibit.

(6) A Canadian issuer may file an exhibit, attachment or other part of a Form 40–F registration statement or annual report (17 CFR 249.240f), Schedule 13E–4F (17 CFR 240.13e–102), Schedule 14D–1F (17 CFR 240.14d–102), or Schedule 14D–9F (17 CFR 240.14d–103), that contains text in both French and English if the issuer included the French text to comply with the requirements of the Canadian securities administrator or other Canadian authority and, for an electronic filing, if the filing is an HTML document, as defined in Regulation S–T Rule 11.

(e) Where a statement or report is distributed to investors through an electronic medium, issuers may satisfy legibility requirements applicable to printed documents, such as paper size and type size and font, by presenting all required information in a format readily communicated to investors.

Rule 12b–13. Preparation of statement or report

The statement or report shall contain the numbers and captions of all items of the appropriate form, but the text of the items may be omitted provided the answers thereto are so prepared as to indicate to the reader the coverage of the items without the necessity of his referring to the text of the items or instructions thereto. However, where any item requires information to be given in tabular form, it shall be given in substantially the tabular form specified in the item. All instructions, whether appearing under the items of the form or elsewhere therein, are to be omitted. Unless expressly provided otherwise, if any item is inapplicable or the answer thereto is in the negative, an appropriate statement to that effect shall be made.

Rule 12b–14. Riders; inserts

Riders shall not be used. If the statement or report is typed on a printed form, and the space provided for the answer to any given item is insufficient, reference shall be made in such space to a full insert page or pages on which the item number and caption and the complete answer are given.

Rule 12b–15. Amendments

All amendments must be filed under cover of the form amended, marked with the letter "A" to designate the document as an amendment, *e.g.*, "10–K/A," and in compliance with pertinent requirements applicable to statements and reports. Amendments filed pursuant to this section must set forth the complete text of each item as amended. Amendments must be numbered sequentially and be filed separately for each statement or report amended. Amendments to a statement may be filed either before or after registration becomes effective. Amendments must be signed on behalf of the registrant by a duly authorized representative of the registrant. An amendment to any report required to include the certifications as specified in Rule 13a–14(a) or Rule 15d–14(a) must include new certifications by each principal executive and principal financial officer of the registrant, and an amendment to any report required to be accompanied by the certifications as specified in Rule 13a–14(b) or Rule 15d–14(b) must be accompanied by new certifications by each principal executive and principal financial officer of the registrant. An amendment to any report required to include the certifications as specified in Rule 13a–14(d) or Rule 15d–14(d) must include a new certification by an individual specified in Rule 13a–14(e) or Rule 15d–14(e), as applicable. The requirements of the form being amended will govern the number of copies to be filed in connection with a paper format amendment. Electronic filers satisfy the provisions dictating the number of copies by filing one copy of the amendment in electronic format. See Rule 309 of Regulation S–T.

GENERAL REQUIREMENTS AS TO CONTENTS

Rule 12b–20. Additional information

In addition to the information expressly required to be included in a statement or report, there shall be added such further material information, if any, as may be necessary to make the required statements, in the light of the circumstances under which they are made not misleading.

Rule 12b–21. Information unknown or not available

Information required need be given only insofar as it is known or reasonably available to the registrant. If any required information is unknown and not reasonably available to the registrant, either because the obtaining thereof would involve unreasonable effort or expense, or because it rests peculiarly within the knowledge of another person not affiliated with the registrant, the information may be omitted, subject to the following conditions.

(a) The registrant shall give such information on the subject as it possesses or can acquire without unreasonable effort or expense, together with the sources thereof.

(b) The registrant shall include a statement either showing that unreasonable effort or expense would be involved or indicating the absence of any affiliation with the person within whose knowledge the information rests and stating the result of a request made to such person for the information.

Rule 12b–22. Disclaimer of control

If the existence of control is open to reasonable doubt in any instance, the registrant may disclaim the existence of control and any admission thereof; in such case, however, the registrant shall state the material facts pertinent to the possible existence of control.

Rule 12b–23. Incorporation by reference

(a) Except for information filed as an exhibit which is covered by Rule 12b–32, information may be incorporated by reference in answer, or partial answer, to any item of a registration statement or report subject to the following provisions:

(1) Financial statements incorporated by reference shall satisfy the requirements of the form or report in which they are incorporated. Financial statements or other financial data required to be given in comparative form for two or more fiscal years or periods shall not be incorporated by reference unless the material incorporated by reference includes the entire period for which the comparative data is given;

(2) Information in any part of the registration statement or report may be incorporated by reference in answer, or partial answer, to any other item of the registration statement or report; and

(3) Copies of any information or financial statement incorporated into a registration statement or report by reference, or copies of the pertinent pages of the document containing such information or statement, shall be filed as an exhibit to the statement or report, except that:

(i) A proxy or information statement incorporated by reference in response to Part III of Form 10–K (17 CFR 249.310);

(ii) A form of prospectus filed pursuant to 17 CFR 230.424(b) incorporated by reference in response to Item 1 of Form 8–A (17 CFR 249.208a); and

(iii) Information filed on Form 8–K (17 CFR 249.308) need not be filed as an exhibit.

(b) Any incorporation by reference of matter pursuant to this rule shall be subject to the provisions of Item 10(d) of Regulation S–K restricting incorporation by reference of documents that incorporate by reference other information. Material incorporated by reference shall be clearly identified in the reference by page, paragraph, and caption or otherwise. Where only certain pages of a document are incorporated by reference and filed as an exhibit, the document from which the material is taken shall be clearly identified in the reference. An express statement that the specified matter is incorporated by reference shall be made at the particular place in the statement or report where the information is required. Matter shall not be incorporated by reference in any case where such incorporation would render the statement or report incomplete, unclear or confusing.

Rule 12b–24. [Reserved]

Rule 12b–25. Notification of inability to timely file all or any required portion of a Form 10–K, 20–F, 11–K, N–SAR, N–CSR, 10–Q or 10–D

(a) If all or any required portion of an annual or transition report on Form 10–K, 20–F or 11–K (17 CFR 249.310, 249.220f or 249.311), a quarterly or transition report on Form 10–Q (17 CFR 249.308a), or a distribution report on Form 10-D (17 CFR 249.312) required to be filed pursuant to section 13 or 15(d) of the Act (15 U.S.C. 78m or 78o(d)) and rules thereunder, or if all or any required portion of a semi-annual, annual or transition report on Form N–CSR (17 CFR 249.331; 17 CFR 274.128) or Form N–SAR (17 CFR 249.330; 17 CFR 274.101) required to be filed pursuant to section 13 or 15(d) of the Act or section 30 of the Investment Company Act of 1940 (15 U.S.C. 80a–29) and the rules thereunder, is not filed within the time period prescribed for such report, the registrant, no later than one business day after the due date for such report, shall file a Form 12b–25 (17 CFR 249.322) with the Commission which shall contain disclosure of its inability to file the report timely and the reasons therefor in reasonable detail.

(b) With respect to any report or portion of any report described in paragraph (a) of this rule which is not timely filed because the registrant is unable to do so without unreasonable effort or expense, such report shall be deemed to be filed on the prescribed due date for such report if:

(1) The registrant files the Form 12b–25 in compliance with paragraph (a) of this rule and, when applicable, furnishes the exhibit required by paragraph (c) of this rule;

(2) The registrant represents in the Form 12b–25 that:

(i) The reason(s) causing the inability to file timely could not be eliminated by the registrant without unreasonable effort or expense; and

(ii) The subject annual report, semi-annual report or transition report on Form 10–K, 20–F, 11–K, N–SAR, or N–CSR, or portion thereof, will be filed no later than the fifteenth calendar day following the prescribed due date; or the subject quarterly report or transition report on Form 10–Q or distribution report on Form 10–D, or portion thereof, will be filed no later than the fifth calendar day following the prescribed due date; and

(3) The report/portion thereof is actually filed within the period specified by paragraph (b)(2)(ii) of this rule.

(c) If paragraph (b) of this rule is applicable and the reason the subject report/portion thereof cannot be filed timely without unreasonable effort or expense relates to the inability of any person, other than the registrant, to furnish any required opinion, report or certification, the Form 12b–25 shall have attached as an exhibit a statement signed by such person stating the specific reasons why such person is unable to furnish the required opinion, report or certification on or before the date such report must be filed.

(d) Notwithstanding paragraph (b) of this rule, a registrant will not be eligible to use any registration statement form under the Securities Act of 1933 the use of which is predicated on timely filed reports until the subject report is actually filed pursuant to paragraph (b)(3) of this rule.

(e) If a Form 12b–25 filed pursuant to paragraph (a) of this rule relates only to a portion of a subject report, the registrant shall:

(1) File the balance of such report and indicate on the cover page thereof which disclosure items are omitted; and

(2) Include, on the upper right corner of the amendment to the report which includes the previously omitted information, the following statement:

The following items were the subject of a Form 12b–25 and are included herein: (*List Item Numbers*)

(f) The provisions of this rule shall not apply to financial statements to be filed by amendment to a form 10–K and 10–KSB as provided for by paragraph (a) of § 210.3–09 or schedules to be filed by amendment in accordance with General Instruction A to Form 10–K.

(g) *Electronic Filings.* The provisions of this rule shall not apply to reports required to be filed in electronic format if the sole reason the report is not filed within the time period prescribed is that the filer is unable to file the report in electronic format. Filers unable to submit a report in electronic format within the time period prescribed solely due to difficulties with electronic filing should comply with either Rule 201 or 202 of Regulation S–T or apply for an adjustment of filing date pursuant to Rule 13(b) of Regulation S–T.

(h) *Interactive Data Submissions.* The provisions of this rule shall not apply to the submission or posting of an Interactive Data File (Rule 11 of Regulation S–T). Filers unable to submit or post an Interactive Data File within the time period prescribed should comply with either Rule 201 or 202 of Regulation S–T.

EXHIBITS

Rule 12b-30. Additional exhibits

The registrant may file such exhibits as it may desire, in addition to those required by the appropriate form. Such exhibits shall be so marked as to indicate clearly the subject matters to which they refer.

Rule 12b-31. Omission of substantially identical documents

In any case where two or more indentures, contracts, franchises, or other documents required to be filed as exhibits are substantially identical in all material respects except as to the parties thereto, the dates of execution, or other details, the registrant need file a copy of only one of such documents, with a schedule identifying the other documents omitted and setting forth the material details in which such documents differ from the document of which a copy is filed. The Commission may at any time in its discretion require the filing of copies of any document so omitted.

Rule 12b-32. Incorporation of exhibits by reference

(a) Any document or part thereof filed with the Commission pursuant to any act administered by the Commission may, subject to 17 CFR 228.10(f) and Item 10(d) of Regulation S–K, be incorporated by reference as an exhibit to any statement or report filed with the Commission by the same or any other person. Any document or part thereof filed with an exchange pursuant to the Act may be incorporated by reference as an exhibit to any statement or report filed with the exchange by the same or any other person.

(b) If any modification has occurred in the text of any document incorporated by reference since the filing thereof, the registrant shall file with the reference a statement containing the text of any such modification and the date thereof.

Rule 12b-33. Annual reports to other federal agencies

Notwithstanding any rule or other requirement to the contrary, whenever copies of an annual report by a registrant to any other Federal agency are required or permitted to be filed as an exhibit to an application or report filed by such registrant with the Commission or with a securities exchange, only one copy of such annual report need be filed with the Commission and one copy thereof with each such exchange, provided appropriate reference to such copy is made in each copy of the application or report filed with the Commission or with such exchange.

SPECIAL PROVISIONS

Rule 12b-35. [Reserved]

Rule 12b-36. Use of financial statements filed under other acts

Where copies of certified financial statements filed under other acts administered by the Commission are filed with a statement or report, the accountant's certificate shall be manually signed or manually-signed copies of the certificate shall be filed with the financial statements. Where such financial statements are incorporated by reference in a statement or report, the written consent of the accountant to such incorporation by reference shall be filed with the statement or report. Such consent shall be dated and signed manually.

Rule 12b-37. Satisfaction of filing requirements

With regard to issuers eligible to rely on Release No. 34–45589 (March 18, 2002) or Release No. IC–25463 (March 18, 2002) (each of which may be viewed on the Commission's website at *www.sec.gov*), filings made in accordance with the provisions of those Releases shall satisfy the issuer's requirement to make such a filing under Section 13(a), 14 or 15(d) of the Act (15 U.S.C. 77m(a), 78n or 78o(d)), as applicable, and the Commission's rules and regulations thereunder.

CERTIFICATION BY EXCHANGES AND EFFECTIVENESS OF REGISTRATION

Rule 12d1–1. Registration effective as to class or series

(a) An application filed pursuant to section 12(b) and (c) of the Act for registration of a security on a national securities exchange shall be deemed to apply for registration of the entire class of such security. Registration shall become effective, as provided in section 12(d) of the Act, (1) as to the shares or amounts of such class then issued, and (2) without further application for registration, upon issuance as to additional shares or amounts of such class then or thereafter authorized.

(b) This rule shall apply to classes of securities of which a specified number of shares or amounts was registered or registered upon notice of issuance, and to applications for registration filed, prior to the close of business on January 28, 1954, as well as to classes registered, or applications filed, thereafter.

(c) This rule shall not affect the right of a national securities exchange to require the issuer of a registered security to file documents with or pay fees to the exchange in connection with the modification of such security or the issuance of additional shares or amounts.

(d) If a class of security is issuable in two or more series with different terms, each such series shall be deemed a separate class for the purposes of this rule.

Rule 12d1–2. Effectiveness of registration

(a) A request for acceleration of the effective date of registration pursuant to section 12(d) of the Act and Rule 12d1–1 shall be made in writing by either the registrant, the exchange, or both and shall briefly describe the reasons therefor.

(b) A registration statement on Form 8–A (17 CFR 249.208a) for the registration of a class of securities under Section 12(b) of the Act (15 U.S.C. 78*l*(b)) shall become effective:

(1) If a class of securities is not concurrently being registered under the Securities Act of 1933 ("Securities Act"), upon the later of receipt by the Commission of certification from the national securities exchange or the filing of the Form 8–A with the Commission; or

(2) If a class of securities is concurrently being registered under the Securities Act, upon the later of the filing of the Form 8–A with the Commission, receipt by the Commission of certification from the national securities exchange listed on the Form 8–A or effectiveness of the Securities Act registration statement relating to the class of securities.

(c) A registration statement on Form 8–A (17 CFR 249.208a) for the registration of a class of securities under Section 12(g) of the Act (15 U.S.C. 78*l*(g)) shall become effective:

(1) If a class of securities is not concurrently being registered under the Securities Act, upon the filing of the Form 8–A with the Commission; or

(2) If class of securities is concurrently being registered under the Securities Act, upon the later of the filing of the Form 8–A with the Commission or the effectiveness of the Securities Act registration statement relating to the class of securities.

Rule 12d1–3. Requirements as to certification

(a) Certification that a security has been approved by an exchange for listing and registration pursuant to section 12(d) of the Act and Rule 12d1–1 shall be made by the governing committee or other corresponding authority of the exchange.

(b) The certification shall specify (1) the approval of the exchange for listing and registration; (2) the title of the security so approved; (3) the date of filing with the exchange of the application for registration and of any amendments thereto; and (4) any conditions imposed on such certification. The exchange shall promptly notify the Commission of the partial or complete satisfaction of any such conditions.

(c) The certification may be made by telegram but in such case shall be confirmed in writing. All certifications in writing and all amendments thereto shall be filed with the Commission in duplicate and at least one copy shall be manually signed by the appropriate exchange authority.

Rule 12d1–4. Date of receipt of certification by commission

The date of receipt by the Commission of the certification approving a security for listing and registration shall be the date on which the certification is actually received by the Commission or the date on which the application for registration to which the certification relates is actually received by the Commission, whichever date is later.

Rule 12d1–5. Operation of certification on subsequent amendments

If an amendment to the application for registration of a security is filed with the exchange and with the Commission after the receipt by the Commission of the certification of the exchange approving the security for listing and registration, the certification, unless withdrawn, shall be deemed made with reference to the application as amended.

Rule 12d1-6. Withdrawal of certification

An exchange may, by notice to the Commission, withdraw its certification prior to the time that the registration to which it relates first becomes effective pursuant to Rule 12d1-1.

SUSPENSION OF TRADING, WITHDRAWAL, AND STRIKING FROM LISTING AND REGISTRATION

Rule 12d2-1. Suspension of trading

(a) A national securities exchange may suspend from trading a security listed and registered thereon in accordance with its rules. Such exchange shall promptly notify the Commission of any such suspension, the effective date thereof, and the reasons therefor.

(b) Any such suspension may be continued until such time as it shall appear to the Commission that such suspension is designed to evade the provisions of section 12(d) and the rules and regulations thereunder relating to the withdrawal and striking of a security from listing and registration. During the continuance of such suspension the exchange shall notify the Commission promptly of any change in the reasons for the suspension. Upon the restoration to trading of any security suspended under this rule, the exchange shall notify the Commission promptly of the effective date thereof.

(c) Suspension of trading shall not terminate the registration of any security.

Rule 12d2-2. Removal from listing and registration

PRELIMINARY NOTE:

1. The filing of the Form 25 (17 CFR 249.25) by an issuer relates solely to the withdrawal of a class of securities from listing on a national securities exchange and/or from registration under section 12(b) of the Act (15 U.S.C. 78*l*(b)), and shall not affect its obligation to be registered under section 12(g) of the Act and/or reporting obligations under section 15(d) of the Act (15 U.S.C. 78*o*(d)).

2. *Implementation.* The rules of each national securities exchange must be designed to meet the requirements of this rule and must be operative no later than April 24, 2006. Each national securities exchange must submit to the Commission a proposed rule change that complies with section 19(b) of the Act (15 U.S.C. 78s) and Rule 19b-4 thereunder, and this rule no later than October 20, 2005.

(a) A national securities exchange must file with the Commission an application on Form 25 (17 CFR 249.25) to strike a class of securities from listing on a national securities exchange and/or registration under section 12(b) of the Act within a reasonable time after the national securities exchange is reliably informed that any of the following conditions exist with respect to such a security:

(1) The entire class of the security has been called for redemption, maturity or retirement; appropriate notice thereof has been given; funds sufficient for the payment of all such securities have been deposited with an agency authorized to make such payments; and such funds have been made available to security holders.

(2) The entire class of the security has been redeemed or paid at maturity or retirement.

(3) The instruments representing the securities comprising the entire class have come to evidence, by operation of law or otherwise, other securities in substitution therefor and represent no other right, except, if such be the fact, the right to receive an immediate cash payment (the right of dissenters to receive the appraised or fair value of their holdings shall not prevent the application of this provision).

(4) All rights pertaining to the entire class of the security have been extinguished; provided, however, that where such an event occurs as a result of an order of a court or other governmental authority, the order shall be final, all applicable appeal periods shall have expired, and no appeals shall be pending.

EFFECTIVE DATE: Such an application shall be deemed to be granted and shall become effective at the opening of business on such date as the exchange shall specify in said application, but not less than 10 days following the date on which said application is filed with the Commission: *Provided, however,* That in the event removal is being effected under paragraph (a)(3) and the exchange has admitted or intends to admit a successor security to trading under the temporary exemption provided for by Rule 12a-5, such date shall not be earlier than the date on which the successor security is removed from its exempt status.

(b)(1) In cases not provided for in paragraph (a) of this rule, a national securities exchange may file an application on Form 25 to strike a class of securities from listing and/or withdraw the registration of such securities, in accordance with its rules, if the rules of such exchange, at a minimum, provide for:

(i) Notice to the issuer of the exchange's decision to delist its securities;

(ii) An opportunity for appeal to the national securities exchange's board of directors, or to a committee designated by the board; and

(iii) Public notice of the national securities exchange's final determination to remove the security from listing and/or registration, by issuing a press release and posting notice on its website. Public notice under this paragraph shall be disseminated no fewer than 10 days before the delisting becomes effective pursuant to paragraph (d)(1) of this rule, and must remain posted on its website until the delisting is effective.

(2) A national securities exchange must promptly deliver a copy of the application on Form 25 to the issuer.

(c)(1) The issuer of a class of securities listed on a national securities exchange and/or registered under section 12(b) of the Act may file an application on Form 25 to notify the Commission of its withdrawal of such securities from listing on such national securities exchange and its intention to withdraw the securities from registration under section 12(b) of the Act.

(2) An issuer filing Form 25 under this paragraph must satisfy the requirements in paragraph (c)(2) of this rule and represent on the Form 25 that such requirements have been met:

(i) The issuer must comply with all applicable laws in effect in the state in which it is incorporated and with the national securities exchange's rules governing an issuer's voluntary withdrawal of a class of securities from listing and/or registration.

(ii) No fewer than 10 days before the issuer files an application on Form 25 with the Commission, the issuer must provide written notice to the national securities exchange of its determination to withdraw the class of securities from listing and/or registration on such exchange. Such written notice must set forth a description of the security involved, together with a statement of all material facts relating to the reasons for withdrawal from listing and/or registration.

(iii) Contemporaneous with providing written notice to the exchange of its intent to withdraw a class of securities from listing and/or registration, the issuer must publish notice of such intention, along with its reasons for such withdrawal, via a press release and, if it has a publicly accessible Web site, posting such notice on that Web site. Any notice provided on an issuer's Web site under this paragraph shall remain available until the delisting on Form 25 has become effective pursuant to paragraph (d)(1) of this rule. If the issuer has not arranged for listing and/or registration on another national securities exchange or for quotation of its security in a quotation medium (as defined in Rule 15c2–11), then the press release and posting on the Web site must contain this information.

(3) A national securities exchange, that receives, pursuant to paragraph (c)(2)(ii) of this rule, written notice from an issuer that such issuer has determined to withdraw a class of securities from listing and/or registration on such exchange, must provide notice on its Web site of the issuer's intent to delist and/or withdraw from registration its securities by the next business day. Such notice must remain posted on the exchange's Web site until the delisting on Form 25 is effective pursuant to paragraph (d)(1) of this rule.

(d)(1) An application on Form 25 to strike a class of securities from listing on a national securities exchange will be effective 10 days after Form 25 is filed with the Commission.

(2) An application on Form 25 to withdraw the registration of a class of securities under section 12(b) of the Act will be effective 90 days, or such shorter period as the Commission may determine, after filing with the Commission.

(3) Notwithstanding paragraphs (d)(1) and (d)(2) of this rule, the Commission may, by written notice to the exchange and issuer, postpone the effectiveness of an application to delist and/or to deregister to determine whether the application on Form 25 to strike the security from registration under section 12(b) of the Act has been made in accordance with the rules of the exchange, or what terms should be imposed by the Commission for the protection of investors.

(4) Notwithstanding paragraph (d)(2) of this rule, whenever the Commission commences a proceeding against an issuer under section 12 of the Act prior to the withdrawal of the registration of a class of securities, such security will remain registered under section 12(b) of the Act until the final decision of such proceeding or until the Commission otherwise determines to suspend the effective date of, or revoke, the registration of a class of securities.

(5) An issuer's duty to file any reports under section 13(a) of the Act (15 U.S.C. 78m(a)) and the rules and regulations thereunder solely because of such security's registration under section 12(b) of the Act will be suspended upon the effective date for the delisting pursuant to paragraph (d)(1) of this rule. If, following the effective date of delisting on Form 25, the Commission, an exchange, or an issuer delays the withdrawal of a security's registration under section 12(b) of the Act, an issuer shall, within 60 days of such delay, file any reports that would have been required under section 13(a) of the Act and the rules and regulations thereunder, had the Form 25 not been filed. The issuer also shall timely file any subsequent reports required under section 13(a) of the Act for the duration of the delay.

(6) An issuer whose reporting responsibilities under section 13(a) of the Act are suspended for a class of securities under paragraph (d)(5) of this rule is, nevertheless, required to file any reports that an issuer with such a class of securities registered under section 12 of the Act would be required to file under section 13(a) of the Act if such class of securities:

(i) Is registered under section 12(g) of the Act; or

(ii) Would be registered, or would be required to be registered, under section 12(g) of the Act but for the exemption from registration under section 12(g) of the Act provided by section 12(g)(2)(A) of the Act.

(7)(i) An issuer whose reporting responsibilities under section 13(a) of the Act are suspended under paragraph (d)(5) of this rule is, nevertheless, required to file any reports that would be required under section 15(d) of the Act but for the fact that the reporting obligations are:

(A) Suspended for a class of securities under paragraph (d)(5) of this rule; and

(B) Suspended, terminated, or otherwise absent under section 12(g) of the Act.

(ii) The reporting responsibilities of an issuer under section 15(d) of the Act shall continue until the issuer is required to file reports under section 13(a) of the Act or the issuer's reporting responsibilities under section 15(d) of the Act are otherwise suspended.

(8) In the event removal is being effected under paragraph (a)(3) of this rule and the national securities exchange has admitted or intends to admit a successor security to trading under the temporary exemption provided for by Rule 12a–5, the effective date of the Form 25, as set forth in paragraph (d)(1) of this rule, shall not be earlier than the date the successor security is removed from its exempt status.

(e) The following are exempt from section 12(d) of the Act and the provisions of this rule:

(1) Any standardized option, as defined in Rule 9b–1, that is:

(i) Issued by a clearing agency registered under section 17A of the Act (15 U.S.C. 78q–1); and

(ii) Traded on a national securities exchange registered pursuant to section 6(a) of the Act (15 U.S.C. 78f(a)); and

(2) Any security futures product that is:

(i) Traded on a national securities exchange registered under section 6(a) of the Act or on a national securities association registered pursuant to section 15A(a) of the Act (15 U.S.C. 78o–3(a)); and

(ii) Cleared by a clearing agency registered as a clearing agency pursuant to section 17A of the Act or is exempt from registration under section 17A(b)(7) of the Act.

UNLISTED TRADING

Rule 12f–1. Applications for permission to extend unlisted trading privileges

(a) An application to reinstate unlisted trading privileges may be made to the Commission by any national securities exchange for the extension of unlisted trading privileges to any security for which such unlisted trading privileges have been suspended by the Commission, pursuant to section 12(f)(2)(A) of the Act (15 U.S.C. 78*l*(2)(A)). One copy of such application, executed by a duly authorized officer of the exchange, shall be filed and shall set forth:

(1) Name of issuer;

(2) Title of security;

(3) The name of each national securities exchange, if any, on which such security is listed or admitted to unlisted trading privileges;

(4) Whether transaction information concerning such security is reported pursuant to an effective transaction reporting plan contemplated by Rule 601 of Regulation NMS;

(5) The date of the Commission's suspension of unlisted trading privileges in the security on the exchange;

(6) Any other information which is deemed pertinent to the question of whether the reinstatement of unlisted trading privileges in such security is consistent with the maintenance of fair and orderly markets and the protection of investors; and

(7) That a copy of the instant application has been mailed, or otherwise personally provided, to the issuer of the securities for which unlisted trading privileges are sought and to each exchange listed in item (3) of this rule.

Rule 12f-2. Extending unlisted trading privileges to a security that is the subject of an initial public offering

(a) *General Provision.* A national securities exchange may extend unlisted trading privileges to a subject security when at least one transaction in the subject security has been effected on the national securities exchange upon which the security is listed and the transaction has been reported pursuant to an effective transaction reporting plan, as defined in Rule 600 of Regulation NMS.

(b) The extension of unlisted trading privileges pursuant to this rule shall be subject to all the provisions set forth in Section 12(f) of the Act (15 U.S.C. 78*l*(f)), as amended, and any rule or regulation promulgated thereunder, or which may be promulgated thereunder while the extension is in effect.

(c) *Definitions.* For the purposes of this rule:

(1) The term *subject security* shall mean a security that is the subject of an initial public offering, as that term is defined in section 12(f)(1)(G)(i) of the Act (15 U.S.C. 78*l*(f)(1)(G)(i)), and

(2) An *initial public offering commences* at such time as is described in section 12(f)(1)(G)(ii) of the Act (15 U.S.C. 78*l*(f)(1)(G)(ii)).

Rule 12f-3. Termination or suspension of unlisted trading privileges

(a) The issuer of any security for which unlisted trading privileges on any exchange have been continued or extended, or any broker or dealer who makes or creates a market for such security, or any other person having a bona fide interest in the question of termination or suspension of such unlisted trading privileges, may make application to the Commission for the termination or suspension of such unlisted trading privileges. One duly executed copy of such application shall be filed, and it shall contain the following information;

(1) Name and address of applicant;

(2) A brief statement of the applicant's interest in the question of termination or suspension of such unlisted trading privileges;

(3) Title of security;

(4) Name of issuer;

(5) Amount of such security issued and outstanding (number of shares of stock or principal amount of bonds), stating source of information;

(6) Annual volume of public trading in such security (number of shares of stock or principal amount of bonds) on such exchange for each of the three calendar years immediately preceding the date of such application, and monthly volume of trading in such security for each of the twelve calendar months immediately preceding the date of such application;

(7) Price range on such exchange for each of the twelve calendar months immediately preceding the date of such application; and

(8) A brief statement of the information in the applicant's possession, and the sources thereof, with respect to (i) the extent of public trading in such security on such exchange, and (ii) the character of trading in such security on such exchange; and

(9) A brief statement that a copy of the instant application has been mailed, or otherwise personally provided, to the exchange from which the suspension or termination of unlisted trading privileges is sought, and to any other exchange on which such security is listed or traded pursuant to unlisted trading privileges.

(b) Unlisted trading privileges in any security on any national securities exchange may be suspended or terminated by such exchange in accordance with its rules.

Rule 12f-4. Exemption of securities admitted to unlisted trading privileges from Sections 13, 14, and 16

(a) Any security for which unlisted trading privileges on any national securities exchange have been continued or extended pursuant to section 12(f) of the Act shall be exempt from section 13 of the Act unless (1) such security or another security of the same issuer is listed and registered on a national securities exchange or registered pursuant to section 12(g) of the Act, or (2) such issuer would be required to file information, documents and reports pursuant to section 15(d) of the Act but for the fact that securities of the issuer are deemed to be "registered on a national securities exchange" within the meaning of section 12(f)(6) of the Act.

(b) Any security for which unlisted trading privileges on any national securities exchange have been continued or extended pursuant to section 12(f) of the Act shall be exempt from section 14 of the Act unless such security is also listed and registered on a national securities exchange or registered pursuant to section 12(g) of the Act.

(c)(1) Any equity security for which unlisted trading privileges on any national securities exchange have been continued or extended pursuant to section 12(f) of the Act shall be exempt from section 16 of the Act unless such security or another equity security of the same issuer is listed and registered on a national securities exchange or registered pursuant to section 12(g) of the Act.

(2) Any equity security for which unlisted trading privileges on any national securities exchange have been continued or extended pursuant to section 12(f) of the Act and which is not listed and registered on any other such exchange or registered pursuant to rule 12(g) of the Act shall be exempt from section 16 of the Act insofar as that section would otherwise apply to any person who is directly or indirectly the beneficial owner of more than 10 percent of such security, unless another equity security of the issuer of such unlisted security is so listed or registered and such beneficial owner is a director or officer of such issuer or directly or indirectly the beneficial owner of more than 10 percent of any such listed or registered security.

(d) Any reference in this rule to a security registered pursuant to section 12(g) of the Act shall include, and any reference to a security not so registered shall exclude, any security as to which a registration statement pursuant to such section is at the time required to be effective.

Rule 12f-5. Exchange rules for securities to which unlisted trading privileges are extended

A national securities exchange shall not extend unlisted trading privileges to any security unless the national securities exchange has in effect a rule or rules providing for transactions in the class or type of security to which the exchange extends unlisted trading privileges.

Rule 12f-6. [Reserved]

EXTENSIONS AND TEMPORARY EXEMPTIONS; DEFINITIONS

Rule 12g-1. Registration of securities; exemption from section 12(g)

An issuer is not required to register a class of equity securities pursuant to section 12(g)(1) of the Act (15 U.S.C. 78*l*(g)(1)) if on the last day of its most recent fiscal year:

(a) The issuer had total assets not exceeding $10 million; or

(b) (1) The class of equity securities was held of record by fewer than 2,000 persons and fewer than 500 of those persons were not accredited investors (as such term is defined in Rule 501(a) of this chapter, determined as of such day rather than at the time of the sale of the securities); or

(2) The class of equity securities was held of record by fewer than 2,000 persons in the case of a bank; a savings and loan holding company, as such term is defined in section 10 of the Home Owners' Loan Act (12 U.S.C. 1461); or a bank holding company, as such term is defined in section 2 of the Bank Holding Company Act of 1956 (12 U.S.C. 1841).

Rule 12g-2. Securities deemed to be registered pursuant to section 12(g)(1) upon termination of exemption pursuant to section 12(g)(2)(A) or (B)

Any class of securities that would have been required to be registered pursuant to section 12(g)(1) of the Act (15 U.S.C. 78*l*(g)(1)) except for the fact that it was exempt from such registration by section 12(g)(2)(A) of the Act (15 U.S.C. 78*l*(g)(2)(A)) because it was listed and registered on a national securities exchange, or by section 12(g)(2)(B) of the Act

(15 U.S.C. 78*l*(g)(2)(B)) because it was issued by an investment company registered pursuant to section 8 of the Investment Company Act of 1940 (15 U.S.C. 80a- 8), shall upon the termination of the listing and registration of such class or the termination of the registration of such company and without the filing of an additional registration statement be deemed to be registered pursuant to section 12(g)(1) of the Act if at the time of such termination:

(a) The issuer of such class of securities has elected to be regulated as a business development company pursuant to sections 55 through 65 of the Investment Company Act of 1940 (15 U.S.C. 80a-54 through 64) and such election has not been withdrawn; or

(b) Securities of the class are not exempt from such registration pursuant to section 12 of the Act (15 U.S.C. 78*l*) or rules thereunder and all securities of such class are held of record by 300 or more persons, or 1,200 or more persons in the case of a bank; a savings and loan holding company, as such term is defined in section 10 of the Home Owners' Loan Act (12 U.S.C. 1461); or a bank holding company, as such term is defined in section 2 of the Bank Holding Company Act of 1956 (12 U.S.C. 1841).

Rule 12g–3. Registration of securities of successor issuers under Section 12(b) or 12(g)

(a) Where in connection with a succession by merger, consolidation, exchange of securities, acquisition of assets or otherwise, securities of an issuer that are not already registered pursuant to section 12 of the Act (15 U.S.C. 78*l*) are issued to the holders of any class of securities of another issuer that is registered pursuant to either section 12(b) or (g) of the Act (15 U.S.C. 78*l*(b) or (g)), the class of securities so issued shall be deemed to be registered under the same paragraph of section 12 of the Act unless upon consummation of the succession:

(1) Such class is exempt from such registration other than by Rule 12g3–2;

(2) All securities of such class are held of record by fewer than 300 persons, or 1,200 persons in the case of a bank; a savings and loan holding company, as such term is defined in section 10 of the Home Owners' Loan Act (12 U.S.C. 1461); or a bank holding company, as such term is defined in section 2 of the Bank Holding Company Act of 1956 (12 U.S.C. 1841); or

(3) The securities issued in connection with the succession were registered on Form F–8 or Form F–80 (17 CFR 239.38 or 239.41) and following succession the successor would not be required to register such class of securities under section 12 of the Act (15 U.S.C. 78*l*) but for this rule.

(b) Where in connection with a succession by merger, consolidation, exchange of securities, acquisition of assets or otherwise, securities of an issuer that are not already registered pursuant to section 12 of the Act (15 U.S.C. 78*l*) are issued to the holders of any class of securities of another issuer that is required to file a registration statement pursuant to either section 12(b) or (g) of the Act (15 U.S.C. 78*l*(b) or (g)) but has not yet done so, the duty to file such statement shall be deemed to have been assumed by the issuer of the class of securities so issued. The successor issuer shall file a registration statement pursuant to the same paragraph of section 12 of the Act with respect to such class within the period of time the predecessor issuer would have been required to file such a statement unless upon consummation of the succession:

(1) Such class is exempt from such registration other than by Rule 12g3–2;

(2) All securities of such class are held of record by fewer than 300 persons, or 1,200 persons in the case of a bank; a savings and loan holding company, as such term is defined in section 10 of the Home Owners' Loan Act (12 U.S.C. 1461); or a bank holding company, as such term is defined in section 2 of the Bank Holding Company Act of 1956 (12 U.S.C. 1841); or

(3) The securities issued in connection with the succession were registered on Form F–8 or Form F–80 (17 CFR 239.38 or 17 CFR 239.41) and following the succession the successor would not be required to register such class of securities under section 12 of the Act (15 U.S.C. 78*l*) but for this rule.

(c) Where in connection with a succession by merger, consolidation, exchange of securities, acquisition of assets or otherwise, securities of an issuer that are not already registered pursuant to section 12 of the Act (15 U.S.C. 78l) are issued to the holders of classes of securities of two or more other issuers that are each registered pursuant to section 12 of the Act; the class of securities so issued shall be deemed to be registered under section 12 of the Act unless upon consummation of the succession:

(1) Such class is exempt from such registration other than by Rule 12g3–2;

(2) All securities of such class are held of record by fewer than 300 persons, or 1,200

persons in the case of a bank; a savings and loan holding company, as such term is defined in section 10 of the Home Owners' Loan Act (12 U.S.C. 1461); or a bank holding company, as such term is defined in section 2 of the Bank Holding Company Act of 1956 (12 U.S.C. 1841); or

(3) The securities issued in connection with the succession were registered on Form F–8 or Form F–80 (17 CFR 239.38 or 17 CFR 239.41) and following succession the successor would not be required to register such class of securities under section 12 of the Act (15 U.S.C. 78*l*) but for this rule.

(d) If the classes of securities issued by two or more predecessor issuers (as described in paragraph (c) of this rule) are registered under the same paragraph of section 12 of the Act (15 U.S.C. 78*l*), the class of securities issued by the successor issuer shall be deemed registered under the same paragraph of section 12 of the Act. If the classes of securities issued by the predecessor issuers are not registered under the same paragraph of section 12 of the Act, the class of securities issued by the successor issuer shall be deemed registered under section 12(g) of the Act (15 U.S.C. 78*l*(g)).

(e) An issuer that is deemed to have a class of securities registered pursuant to section 12 of the Act (15 U.S.C. 78*l*) according to paragraph (a), (b), (c) or (d) of this rule shall file reports on the same forms and such class of securities shall be subject to the provisions of sections 14 and 16 of the Act (15 U.S.C. 78n and 78p) to the same extent as the predecessor issuers, except as follows:

(1) An issuer that is not a foreign issuer shall not be eligible to file on Form 20–F (17 CFR 249.220f) or to use the exemption in Rule 3a12–3.

(2) A foreign private issuer shall be eligible to file on Form 20–F (17 CFR 249.220f) and to use the exemption in Rule 3a12–3.

(f) An issuer that is deemed to have a class of securities registered pursuant to section 12 of the Act (15 U.S.C. 78*l*) according to paragraphs (a), (b), (c) or (d) of this rule shall indicate in the Form 8–K (17 CFR 249.308) report filed with the Commission in connection with the succession, pursuant to the requirements of Form 8–K, the paragraph of section 12 of the Act under which the class of securities issued by the successor issuer is deemed registered by operation of paragraphs (a), (b), (c) or (d) of this rule. If a successor issuer that is deemed registered under section 12(g) of the Act (15 U.S.C. 78*l*(g)) by paragraph (d) of this rule intends to list a class of securities on a national securities exchange, it must file a registration statement pursuant to section 12(b) of the Act (15 U.S.C. 78*l*(b)) with respect to that class of securities.

(g) An issuer that is deemed to have a class of securities registered pursuant to section 12 of the Act (15 U.S.C. 78*l*) according to paragraph (a), (b), (c) or (d) of this rule shall file an annual report for each fiscal year beginning on or after the date as of which the succession occurred. Annual reports shall be filed within the period specified in the appropriate form. Each such issuer shall file an annual report for each of its predecessors that had securities registered pursuant to section 12 of the Act (15 U.S.C. 78*l*) covering the last full fiscal year of the predecessor before the registrant's succession, unless such report has been filed by the predecessor. Such annual report shall contain information that would be required if filed by the predecessor.

Rule 12g3–2. Exemptions for American Depositary Receipts and certain foreign securities

(a) Securities of any class issued by any foreign private issuer shall be exempt from section 12(g) (15 U.S.C. 78*l*(g)) of the Act if the class has fewer than 300 holders resident in the United States. This exemption shall continue until the next fiscal year end at which the issuer has a class of equity securities held by 300 or more persons resident in the United States. For the purpose of determining whether a security is exempt pursuant to this paragraph:

(1) Securities held of record by persons resident in the United States shall be determined as provided in Rule 12g5–1 except that securities held of record by a broker, dealer, bank or nominee for any of them for the accounts of customers resident in the United States shall be counted as held in the United States by the number of separate accounts for which the securities are held. The issuer may rely in good faith on information as to the number of such separate accounts supplied by all owners of the class of its securities which are brokers, dealers, or banks or a nominee for any of them.

(2) Persons in the United States who hold the security only through a Canadian Retirement Account (as that term is defined in Rule 237(a)(2) under the Securities Act of 1933), shall not be counted as holders resident in the United States.

(b)(1) A foreign private issuer shall be exempt from the requirement to register a class of equity securities under section 12(g) of the Act (15 U.S.C. 78*l*(g)) if:

(i) The issuer is not required to file or furnish reports under section 13(a) of the Act (15 U.S.C. 78m(a)) or section 15(d) of the Act (15 U.S.C. 78o(d));

(ii) The issuer currently maintains a listing of the subject class of securities on one or more exchanges in a foreign jurisdiction that, either singly or together with the trading of the same class of the issuer's securities in another foreign jurisdiction, constitutes the primary trading market for those securities; and

(iii) The issuer has published in English, on its Internet Web site or through an electronic information delivery system generally available to the public in its primary trading market, information that, since the first day of its most recently completed fiscal year, it:

(A) Has made public or been required to make public pursuant to the laws of the country of its incorporation, organization or domicile;

(B) Has filed or been required to file with the principal stock exchange in its primary trading market on which its securities are traded and which has been made public by that exchange; and

(C) Has distributed or been required to distribute to its security holders.

NOTE 1 TO PARAGRAPH (b)(1): For the purpose of paragraph (b) of this rule, *primary trading market* means that at least 55 percent of the trading in the subject class of securities on a worldwide basis took place in, on or through the facilities of a securities market or markets in a single foreign jurisdiction or in no more than two foreign jurisdictions during the issuer's most recently completed fiscal year. If a foreign private issuer aggregates the trading of its subject class of securities in two foreign jurisdictions for the purpose of this paragraph, the trading for the issuer's securities in at least one of the two foreign jurisdictions must be larger than the trading in the United States for the same class of the issuer's securities. When determining an issuer's primary trading market under this paragraph, calculate average daily trading volume in the United States and on a worldwide basis as under Rule 12h–6.

NOTE 2 TO PARAGRAPH (b)(1): Paragraph (b)(1)(iii) of this rule does not apply to an issuer when claiming the exemption under paragraph (b) upon the effectiveness of the termination of its registration of a class of securities under section 12(g) of the Act, or the termination of its obligation to file or furnish reports under section 15(d) of the Act.

NOTE 3 TO PARAGRAPH (b)(1): Compensatory stock options for which the underlying securities are in a class exempt under paragraph (b) of this rule are also exempt under that paragraph.

(2)(i) In order to maintain the exemption under paragraph (b) of this rule, a foreign private issuer shall publish, on an ongoing basis and for each subsequent fiscal year, in English, on its Internet Web site or through an electronic information delivery system generally available to the public in its primary trading market, the information specified in paragraph (b)(1)(iii) of this rule.

(ii) An issuer must electronically publish the information required by paragraph (b)(2) of this rule promptly after the information has been made public.

(3)(i) The information required to be published electronically under paragraph (b) of this rule is information that is material to an investment decision regarding the subject securities, such as information concerning:

(A) Results of operations or financial condition;

(B) Changes in business;

(C) Acquisitions or dispositions of assets;

(D) The issuance, redemption or acquisition of securities;

(E) Changes in management or control;

(F) The granting of options or the payment of other remuneration to directors or officers; and

(G) Transactions with directors, officers or principal security holders.

(ii) At a minimum, a foreign private issuer shall electronically publish English translations of the following documents required to be published under paragraph (b) of this rule if in a foreign language:

(A) Its annual report, including or accompanied by annual financial statements;

(B) Interim reports that include financial statements;

(C) Press releases; and

(D) All other communications and documents distributed directly to security holders of each class of securities to which the exemption relates.

(c) The exemption under paragraph (b) of this rule shall remain in effect until:

(1) The issuer no longer satisfies the electronic publication condition of paragraph (b)(2) of this rule;

(2) The issuer no longer maintains a listing of the subject class of securities on one or more exchanges in a primary trading market, as defined under paragraph (b)(1) of this rule; or

(3) The issuer registers a class of securities under section 12 of the Act or incurs reporting obligations under section 15(d) of the Act.

(d) Depositary shares registered on Form F–6 (17 CFR 239.36), but not the underlying deposited securities, are exempt from section 12(g) of the Act under this paragraph.

Rule 12g–4. Certification of termination of registration under Section 12(g)

(a) Termination of registration of a class of securities under section 12(g) of the Act (15 U.S.C. 78*l*(g)) shall take effect 90 days, or such shorter period as the Commission may determine, after the issuer certifies to the Commission on Form 15 (Rule 323 of this chapter) that the class of securities is held of record by:

(1) Fewer than 300 persons, or in the case of a bank; a savings and loan holding company, as such term is defined in section 10 of the Home Owners' Loan Act (12 U.S.C. 1461); or a bank holding company, as such term is defined in section 2 of the Bank Holding Company Act of 1956 (12 U.S.C. 1841), 1,200 persons; or

(2) Fewer than 500 persons, where the total assets of the issuer have not exceeded $10 million on the last day of each of the issuer's most recent three fiscal years.

(b) The issuer's duty to file any reports required under section 13(a) shall be suspended immediately upon filing a certification on Form 15, *Provided, however,* That if the certification on Form 15 is subsequently withdrawn or denied, the issuer shall, within 60 days after the date of such withdrawal or denial, file with the Commission all reports which would have been required had the certification on Form 15 not been filed. If the suspension resulted from the issuer's merger into, or consolidation with, another issuer or issuers, the certification shall be filed by the successor issuer.

Rule 12g5–1. Definition of securities "held of record"

(a) For the purpose of determining whether an issuer is subject to the provisions of sections 12(g) and 15(d) of the Act, securities shall be deemed to be "held of record" by each person who is identified as the owner of such securities on records of security holders maintained by or on behalf of the issuer, subject to the following:

(1) In any case where the records of security holders have not been maintained in accordance with accepted practice, any additional person who would be identified as such an owner on such records if they had been maintained in accordance with accepted practice shall be included as a holder of record.

(2) Securities identified as held of record by a corporation, a partnership, a trust whether or not the trustees are named, or other organization shall be included as so held by one person.

(3) Securities identified as held of record by one or more persons as trustees, executors, guardians, custodians or in other fiduciary capacities with respect to a single trust, estate or account shall be included as held of record by one person.

(4) Securities held by two or more persons as co-owners shall be included as held by one person.

(5) Each outstanding unregistered or bearer certificate shall be included as held of record by a separate person, except to the extent that the issuer can establish that, if such securities were registered they would be held of record, under the provisions of this rule, by a lesser number of persons.

(6) Securities registered in substantially similar names where the issuer has reason to believe because of the address or other indications that such names represent the same person, may be included as held of record by one person.

(7) Other than when determining compliance with Rule 257(d)(2) of Regulation A (of this chapter), the definition of "held of record" shall not include securities issued in a Tier 2 offering pursuant to Regulation A by an issuer that:

(i) Is required to file reports pursuant to Rule 257(b) of Regulation A (of this chapter);

(ii) Is current in filing annual, semiannual and special financial reports pursuant to such rule as of its most recently completed fiscal year end;

(iii) Has engaged a transfer agent registered pursuant to Section 17A(c) of the Act to perform the function of a transfer agent with respect to such securities; and

(iv) Had a public float of less than $75 million as of the last business day of its most recently completed semiannual period, computed by multiplying the aggregate worldwide number of shares of its common equity securities held by non-affiliates by the price at which such securities were last sold (or the average bid and asked prices of such securities) in the principal market for such securities or, in the event the result of such public float calculation was zero, had annual revenues of less than $50 million as of its most recently completed fiscal year. An issuer that would be required to register a class of securities under Section 12(g) of the Act as a result of exceeding the applicable threshold in this paragraph (a)(7)(iv), may continue to exclude the relevant securities from the definition of "held of record" for a transition period ending on the penultimate day of the fiscal year two years after the date it became ineligible. The transition period terminates immediately upon the failure of an issuer to timely file any periodic report due pursuant to Rule 257 (of this chapter) at which time the issuer must file a registration statement that registers that class of securities under the Act within 120 days.

(8)(i) For purposes of determining whether an issuer is required to register a class of equity securities with the Commission pursuant to section 12(g)(1) of the Act (15 U.S.C. 78*l*(g)(1)), an issuer may exclude securities:

(A) Held by persons who received the securities pursuant to an employee compensation plan in transactions exempt from, or not subject to, the registration requirements of section 5 of the Securities Act of 1933 (15 U.S.C. 77e); and

(B) Held by persons who received the securities in a transaction exempt from, or not subject to, the registration requirements of section 5 of the Securities Act (15 U.S.C. 77e) from the issuer, a predecessor of the issuer or an acquired company in substitution or exchange for excludable securities under paragraph (a)(8)(i)(A) of this section, as long as the persons were eligible to receive securities pursuant to § 230.701(c) of this chapter at the time the excludable securities were originally issued to them.

(ii) As a non-exclusive safe harbor under this paragraph (a)(8):

(A) An issuer may deem a person to have received the securities pursuant to an employee compensation plan if such plan and the person who received the securities pursuant to the plan met the plan and participant conditions of Rule 701(c) of this chapter; and

(B) An issuer may, solely for the purposes of Section 12(g) of the Act (15 U.S.C. 78*l*(g)(1)), deem the securities to have been issued in a transaction exempt from, or not subject to, the registration requirements of Section 5 of the Securities Act (15 U.S.C. 77e) if the issuer had a reasonable belief at the time of the issuance that the securities were issued in such a transaction.

(b) Notwithstanding paragraph (a) of this rule:

(1) Securities held, to the knowledge of the issuer, subject to a voting trust, deposit agreement or similar arrangement shall be included as held of record by the record holders of the voting trust certificates, certificates of deposit, receipts or similar evidences of interest in such securities: *Provided, however,* That the issuer may rely in good faith on such information as is received in response to its request from a non–affiliated issuer of the certificates or evidences of interest.

(2) Whole or fractional securities issued by a savings and loan association, building and loan association, cooperative bank, homestead association, or similar institution for the sole purpose of qualifying a borrower for membership in the issuer, and which are to be redeemed or repurchased by the issuer when the borrower's loan is terminated, shall not be included as held of record by any person.

(3) If the issuer knows or has reason to know that the form of holding securities of record is used primarily to circumvent the provisions of section 12(g) or 15(d) of the Act, the beneficial owners of such securities shall be deemed to be the record owners thereof.

(7) Other than when determining compliance with Rule 257(d)(2) of Regulation A, the definition of "held of record" shall not include securities issued in a Tier 2 offering pursuant to Regulation A by an issuer that:

(i) Is required to file reports pursuant to Rule 257(b) of Regulation A;

(ii) Is current in filing annual, semiannual and special financial reports pursuant to such rule as of its most recently completed fiscal year end;

(iii) Has engaged a transfer agent registered pursuant to Section 17A(c) of the Act to perform the function of a transfer agent with respect to such securities; and

(iv) Had a public float of less than $75 million as of the last business day of its most recently completed semiannual period, computed by multiplying the aggregate worldwide number of shares of its common equity securities held by non-affiliates by the price at which such securities were last sold (or the average bid and asked prices of such securities) in the principal market for such securities or, in the event the result of such public float calculation was zero, had annual revenues of less than $50 million as of its most recently completed fiscal year. An issuer that would be required to register a class of securities under Section 12(g) of the Act as a result of exceeding the applicable threshold in this paragraph (a)(7)(iv), may continue to exclude the relevant securities from the definition of "held of record" for a transition period ending on the penultimate day of the fiscal year two years after the date it became ineligible. The transition period terminates immediately upon the failure of an issuer to timely file any periodic report due pursuant to Rule 257 at which time the issuer must file a registration statement that registers that class of securities under the Act within 120 days.

Rule 12g5–2. Definition of "total assets"

For the purpose of section 12(g)(1) of the Act, the term *total assets* shall mean the total assets as shown on the issuer's balance sheet or the balance sheet of the issuer and its subsidiaries consolidated, whichever is larger, as required to be filed on the form prescribed for registration under this rule and prepared in accordance with the pertinent provisions of Regulation S–X. Where the security is a certificate of deposit, voting trust certificate, or certificate or other evidence of interest in a similar trust or agreement, the "total assets" of the issuer of the security held under the trust or agreement shall be deemed to be the "total assets" of the issuer of such certificate or evidence of interest.

Rule 12h–1. Exemptions from registration under Section 12(g) of the Act

Issuers shall be exempt from the provisions of section 12(g) of the Act with respect to the following securities:

(a) Any interest or participation in an employee stock bonus, stock purchase, profit sharing, pension, retirement, incentive, thrift, savings or similar plan which is not transferable by the holder except in the event of death or mental incompetency, or any security issued solely to fund such plans;

(b) Any interest or participation in any common trust fund or similar fund maintained by a bank exclusively for the collective investment and reinvestment of monies contributed thereto by the bank in its capacity as a trustee, executor, administrator, or guardian. For purposes of this paragraph (b), the term "common trust fund" shall include a common trust fund which is maintained by a bank which is a member of an affiliated group, as defined in section 1504(a) of the Internal Revenue Code of 1954 (26 U.S.C. 1504(a)), and which is maintained exclusively for the investment and reinvestment of monies contributed thereto by one or more bank members of such affiliated group in the capacity of trustee, executor, administrator, or guardian; *Provided*, that:

(1) The common trust fund is operated in compliance with the same state and federal regulatory requirements as would apply if the bank maintaining such fund and any other contributing banks were the same entity; and

(2) The rights of persons for whose benefit a contributing bank acts as trustee, executor, administrator or guardian would not be diminished by reason of the maintenance of such common trust fund by another bank member of the affiliated group;

(c) Any class of equity security which would not be outstanding 60 days after a registration statement would be required to be filed with respect thereto;

(d) Any standardized option, as that term is defined in Rule 9b–1(a)(4), that is issued by a clearing agency registered under section 17A of the Act (15 U.S.C. 78q–1) and traded on a national securities exchange registered pursuant to section 6(a) of the Act (15 U.S.C. 78f(a)) or on a national securities association registered pursuant to section 15A(a) of the Act (15 U.S.C. 78o–3(a));

(e) Any security futures product that is traded on a national securities exchange registered pursuant to section 6 of the Act (15 U.S.C. 78f) or on a national securities association registered pursuant to section 15A(a) of the Act (15 U.S.C. 78o–3(a)) and cleared by a clearing agency that is registered pursuant to section 17A of the Act (15 U.S.C. 78q–1) or is exempt from registration under section 17A(b)(7) of the Act (15 U.S.C. 78q–1(b)(7)).

(f)(1) Stock options issued under written compensatory stock option plans under the following conditions:

(i) The issuer of the equity security underlying the stock options does not have a class of security registered under section 12 of the Act and is not required to file reports pursuant to section 15(d) of the Act;

(ii) The stock options have been issued pursuant to one or more written compensatory stock option plans established by the issuer, its parents, its majority-owned subsidiaries or majority-owned subsidiaries of the issuer's parents;

NOTE TO PARAGRAPH (f)(1)(ii): All stock options issued under all written compensatory stock option plans on the same class of equity security of the issuer will be considered part of the same class of equity security for purposes of the provisions of paragraph (f) of this rule.

(iii) The stock options are held only by those persons described in Rule 701(c) under the Securities Act of 1933 or their permitted transferees as provided in paragraph (f)(1)(iv) of this rule;

(iv) The stock options and, prior to exercise, the shares to be issued on exercise of the stock options are restricted as to transfer by the optionholder other than to persons who are family members (as defined in Rule 701(c)(3) under the Securities Act of 1933) through gifts or domestic relations orders, or to an executor or guardian of the optionholder upon the death or disability of the optionholder until the issuer becomes subject to the reporting requirements of section 13 or 15(d) of the Act or is no longer relying on the exemption pursuant to this rule; provided that the optionholder may transfer the stock options to the issuer, or in connection with a change of control or other acquisition transaction involving the issuer, if after such transaction the stock options no longer will be outstanding and the issuer no longer will be relying on the exemption pursuant to this rule;

NOTE TO PARAGRAPH (f)(1)(iv): For purposes of this rule, optionholders may include any permitted transferee under paragraph (f)(1)(iv) of this rule; provided that such permitted transferees may not further transfer the stock options.

(v) The stock options and the shares issuable upon exercise of such stock options are restricted as to any pledge, hypothecation, or other transfer, including any short position, any "put equivalent position" (as defined in Rule 16a–1(h)), or any "call equivalent position" (as defined in Rule 16a–1(b)) by the optionholder prior to exercise of an option, except in the circumstances permitted in paragraph (f)(1)(iv) of this rule, until the issuer becomes subject to the reporting requirements of section 13 or 15(d) of the Act or is no longer relying on the exemption pursuant paragraph (f)(1) of this rule;

NOTE TO PARAGRAPHS (f)(1)(iv) AND (f)(1)(v): The transferability restrictions in paragraphs (f)(1)(iv) and (f)(1)(v) of this rule must be contained in a written compensatory stock option plan, individual written compensatory stock option agreement, other stock purchase or stockholder agreement to which the issuer and the optionholder are a signatory or party, other enforceable agreement by or against the issuer and the optionholder, or in the issuer's by-laws or certificate or articles of incorporation.

(vi) The issuer has agreed in the written compensatory stock option plan, the individual written compensatory stock option agreement, or another agreement enforceable against the issuer to provide the following information to optionholders once the issuer is relying on the exemption pursuant to paragraph (f)(1) of this rule until the issuer becomes subject to the reporting requirements of section 13 or 15(d) of the Act or is no longer relying on the exemption pursuant paragraph (f)(1) of this rule:

The information described in Rules 701(e)(3), (4), and (5) under the Securities Act, every six months with the financial statements being not more than 180 days old and with such information provided either by physical or electronic delivery to the optionholders or by written notice to the optionholders of the availability of the information on an Internet site that may be password-protected and of any password needed to access the information.

NOTE TO PARAGRAPH (f)(1)(vi): The issuer may request that the optionholder agree to keep the information to be provided pursuant to this rule confidential. If an optionholder does not agree to keep the information to be provided pursuant to this rule confidential, then the issuer is not required to provide the information.

(2) If the exemption provided by paragraph (f)(1) of this rule ceases to be available, the issuer of the stock options that is relying on the exemption provided by this rule must file a registration statement to register the class of stock options under section 12 of the Act within 120 calendar days after the exemption provided by paragraph (f)(1) of this rule ceases to be available; and

(g)(1) Stock options issued under written compensatory stock option plans under the following conditions:

(i) The issuer of the equity security underlying the stock options has registered a class of security under section 12 of the Act or is required to file periodic reports pursuant to section 15(d) of the Act;

(ii) The stock options have been issued pursuant to one or more written compensatory stock option plans established by the issuer, its parents, its majority-owned subsidiaries or majority-owned subsidiaries of the issuer's parents;

NOTE TO PARAGRAPH (g)(1)(ii): All stock options issued under all of the written compensatory stock option plans on the same class of equity security of the issuer will be considered part of the same class of equity security of the issuer for purposes of the provisions of paragraph (g) of this rule; and

(iii) The stock options are held only by those persons described in Rule 701(c) under the Securities Act of 1933 or those persons specified in General Instruction A.1(a) of Form S–8 (17 CFR 239.16b); provided that an issuer can still rely on this exemption if there is an insignificant deviation from satisfaction of the condition in this paragraph (g)(1)(iii) and after December 7, 2007 the issuer has made a good faith and reasonable attempt to comply with the conditions of this paragraph (g)(1)(iii). For purposes of this paragraph (g)(1)(iii), an insignificant deviation exists if the number of optionholders that do not meet the condition in this paragraph (g)(1)(iii) are insignificant both as to the aggregate number of optionholders and number of outstanding stock options.

(2) If the exemption provided by paragraph (g)(1) of this rule ceases to be available, the issuer of the stock options that is relying on the exemption provided by this rule must file a registration statement to register the class of stock options or a class of security under section 12 of the Act within 60 calendar days after the exemption provided in paragraph (g)(1) of this rule ceases to be available.

(h) Any security-based swap that is issued by a clearing agency registered as a clearing agency under Section 17A of the Act or exempt from registration under Section 17A of the Act pursuant to a rule, regulation, or order of the Commission in its function as a central counterparty that the Commission has determined must be cleared or that is permitted to be cleared pursuant to the clearing agency's rules, and that was sold to an eligible contract participant (as defined in Section 1a(18) of the Commodity Exchange Act) in reliance on Rule 239 under the Securities Act of 1933.

(*i*) Any security-based swap offered and sold in reliance on Rule 240 under the Securities Act of 1933. This rule will expire on February 11, 2014.

Rule 12h–2. [Reserved]

Rule 12h–3. Suspension of duty to file reports under Section 15(d)

(a) Subject to paragraphs (c) and (d) of this rule, the duty under section 15(d) to file reports required by section 13(a) of the Act with respect to a class of securities specified in paragraph (b) of this rule shall be suspended for such class of securities immediately upon filing with the Commission a certification on Form 15 (17 CFR 249.323) if the issuer of such class has filed all reports required by section 13(a), without regard to Rule 12b–25 (17 CFR 249.322), for the shorter of its most recent three fiscal years and the portion of the current year preceding the date of filing Form 15, or the period since the issuer became subject to such reporting obligation. If the certification on Form 15 is subsequently withdrawn or denied, the issuer shall, within 60 days, file with the commission all reports which would have been required if such certification had not been filed.

(b) The classes of securities eligible for the suspension provided in paragraph (a) of this rule are:

(1) Any class of securities, other than any class of asset-backed securities, held of record by:

(i) Fewer than 300 persons, or in the case of a bank; a savings and loan holding company, as such term is defined in section 10 of the Home Owners' Loan Act (12 U.S.C. 1461); or a bank holding company, as such term is defined in section 2 of the Bank Holding Company Act of 1956 (12 U.S.C. 1841), 1,200 persons; or

(ii) Fewer than 500 persons, where the total assets of the issuer have not exceeded $10 million on the last day of each of the issuer's three most recent fiscal years; and

(2) Any class of securities deregistered pursuant to section 12(d) of the Act if such class would not thereupon be deemed registered under section 12(g) of the Act or the rules thereunder.

NOTE TO PARAGRAPH (b): The suspension of classes of asset-backed securities is addressed in Rule 15d–22.

(c) This rule shall not be available for any class of securities for a fiscal year in which a registration statement relating to that class becomes effective under the Securities Act of 1933, or is required to be updated pursuant to section 10(a)(3) of the Act, and, in the case of paragraph (b)(1)(ii), the two succeeding fiscal years; *Provided, however,* That this paragraph shall not apply to the duty to file reports which arises solely from a registration statement filed by an issuer with no significant assets, for the reorganization of a non-reporting issuer into a one subsidiary holding company in which equity security holders receive the same proportional interest in the holding company as they held in the non-reporting issuer, except for changes resulting from the exercise of dissenting shareholder rights under state law.

(d) The suspension provided by this rule relates only to the reporting obligation under section 15(d) with respect to a class of securities, does not affect any other duties imposed on that class of securities, and shall continue as long as either criteria (i) or (ii) of paragraph (b)(1) is met on the first day of any subsequent fiscal year; *Provided, however,* That such criteria need not be met if the duty to file reports arises solely from a registration statement filed by an issuer with no significant assets in a reorganization of a non-reporting company into a one subsidiary holding company in which equity security holders receive the same proportional interest in the holding company as they held in the non-reporting issuer except for changes resulting from the exercise of dissenting shareholder rights under state law.

(e) If the suspension provided by this rule is discontinued because a class of securities does not meet the eligibility criteria of paragraph (b) on the first day of an issuer's fiscal year, then the issuer shall resume periodic reporting pursuant to section 15(d) of the Act by filing an annual report on Form 10–K for its preceding fiscal year, not later than 120 days after the end of such fiscal year.

Rule 12h–4. Exemption from duty to file reports under Section 15(d)

An issuer shall be exempt from the duty under section 15(d) of the Act to file reports required by section 13(a) of the Act with respect to securities registered under the Securities Act of 1933 on Form F–7, Form F–8 or Form F–80, provided that the issuer is exempt from the obligations of Section 12(g) of the Act pursuant to Rule 12g3–2(b).

Rule 12h–5. Exemption for subsidiary issuers of guaranteed securities and subsidiary guarantors

(a) Any issuer of a guaranteed security, or guarantor of a security, that is permitted to omit financial statements by Rule 3–10 of Regulation S–X is exempt from the requirements of Section 13(a) or 15(d) of the Act (15 U.S.C. 78m(a) or 78o(d)).

(b) Any issuer of a guaranteed security, or guarantor of a security, that would be permitted to omit financial statements by Rule 3–10 of Regulation S–X, but is required to file financial statements in accordance with the operation of Rule 3–10(g) of Regulation S–X, is exempt from the requirements of Section 13(a) or 15(d) of the Act (15 U.S.C. 78m(a) or 78o(d)).

Rule 12h–6. Certification by a foreign private issuer regarding the termination of registration of a class of securities under Section 12(g) or the duty to file reports under Section 13(a) or Section 15(d)

(a) A foreign private issuer may terminate the registration of a class of securities under section 12(g) of the Act (15 U.S.C. 78l(g)), or terminate the obligation under section 15(d) of the Act (15 U.S.C. 78o(d)) to file or furnish reports required by section 13(a) of the Act (15 U.S.C. 78m(a)) with respect to a class of equity securities, or both, after certifying to the Commission on Form 15F (17 CFR 249.324) that:

(1) The foreign private issuer has had reporting obligations under section 13(a) or section 15(d) of the Act for at least the 12 months preceding the filing of the Form 15F, has filed or furnished all reports required for this period, and has filed at least one annual report pursuant to section 13(a) of the Act;

(2) The foreign private issuer's securities have not been sold in the United States in a registered offering under the Securities Act of 1933 (15 U.S.C. 77a et seq.) during the 12 months preceding the filing of the Form 15F, other than securities issued:

(i) To the issuer's employees;

(ii) By selling security holders in non-underwritten offerings;

(iii) Upon the exercise of outstanding rights granted by the issuer if the rights are granted pro rata to all existing security holders of the class of the issuer's securities to which the rights attach;

(iv) Pursuant to a dividend or interest reinvestment plan; or

(v) Upon the conversion of outstanding convertible securities or upon the exercise of outstanding transferable warrants issued by the issuer;

NOTE TO PARAGRAPH (a)(2): The exceptions in paragraphs (a)(2)(iii)–(v) do not apply to securities issued pursuant to a standby underwritten offering or other similar arrangement in the United States;

(3) The foreign private issuer has maintained a listing of the subject class of securities for at least the 12 months preceding the filing of the Form 15F on one or more exchanges in a foreign jurisdiction that, either singly or together with the trading of the same class of the issuer's securities in another foreign jurisdiction, constitutes the primary trading market for those securities; and

(4)(i) The average daily trading volume of the subject class of securities in the United States for a recent 12–month period has been no greater than 5 percent of the average daily trading volume of that class of securities on a worldwide basis for the same period; or

(ii) On a date within 120 days before the filing date of the Form 15F, a foreign private issuer's subject class of equity securities is either held of record by:

(A) Less than 300 persons on a worldwide basis; or

(B) Less than 300 persons resident in the United States.

NOTE TO PARAGRAPH (a)(4): If an issuer's equity securities trade in the form of American Depositary Receipts in the United States, for purposes of paragraph (a)(4)(i), it must calculate the trading volume of its American Depositary Receipts in terms of the number of securities represented by those American Depositary Receipts.

(b) A foreign private issuer must wait at least 12 months before it may file a Form 15F to terminate its section 13(a) or 15(d) reporting obligations in reliance on paragraph (a)(4)(i) of this rule if:

(1) The issuer has delisted a class of equity securities from a national securities exchange or inter-dealer quotation system in the United States, and at the time of delisting, the average daily trading volume of that class of securities in the United States exceeded 5 percent of the average daily trading volume of that class of securities on a worldwide basis for the preceding 12 months; or

(2) The issuer has terminated a sponsored American Depositary Receipts facility, and at the time of termination the average daily trading volume in the United States of the American Depositary Receipts exceeded 5 percent of the average daily trading volume of the underlying class of securities on a worldwide basis for the preceding 12 months.

(c) A foreign private issuer may terminate its duty to file or furnish reports pursuant to section 13(a) or section 15(d) of the Act with respect to a class of debt securities after certifying to the Commission on Form 15F that:

(1) The foreign private issuer has filed or furnished all reports required by section 13(a) or section 15(d) of the Act, including at least one annual report pursuant to section 13(a) of the Act; and

(2) On a date within 120 days before the filing date of the Form 15F, the class of debt securities is either held of record by:

(i) Less than 300 persons on a worldwide basis; or

(ii) Less than 300 persons resident in the United States.

(d)(1) Following a merger, consolidation, exchange of securities, acquisition of assets or otherwise, a foreign private issuer that has succeeded to the registration of a class of securities under section 12(g) of the Act of another issuer pursuant to Rule 12g–3, or to the reporting obligations of another issuer under section 15(d) of the Act pursuant to Rule 15d–5, may file a Form 15F to terminate that registration or those reporting obligations if:

(i) Regarding a class of equity securities, the successor issuer meets the conditions under paragraph (a) of this rule; or

(ii) Regarding a class of debt securities, the successor issuer meets the conditions under paragraph (c) of this rule.

(2) When determining whether it meets the prior reporting requirement under paragraph (a)(1) or paragraph (c)(1) of this rule, a successor issuer may take into account the reporting history of the issuer whose reporting obligations it has assumed pursuant to Rule 12g–3 or Rule 15d–5.

(e) *Counting Method.* When determining under this rule the number of United States residents holding a foreign private issuer's equity or debt securities:

(1)(i) Use the method for calculating record ownership Rule 12g3–2(a), except that you may limit your inquiry regarding the amount of securities represented by accounts of customers resident in the United States to brokers, dealers, banks and other nominees located in:

(A) The United States;

(B) The foreign private issuer's jurisdiction of incorporation, legal organization or establishment; and

(C) The foreign private issuer's primary trading market, if different from the issuer's jurisdiction of incorporation, legal organization or establishment.

(ii) If you aggregate the trading volume of the issuer's securities in two foreign jurisdictions for the purpose of complying with paragraph (a)(3) of this rule, you must include both of those foreign jurisdictions when conducting your inquiry under paragraph (e)(1)(i) of this rule.

(2) If, after reasonable inquiry, you are unable without unreasonable effort to obtain information about the amount of securities represented by accounts of customers resident in the United States, for purposes of this rule, you may assume that the customers are the residents of the jurisdiction in which the nominee has its principal place of business.

(3) You must count securities as owned by United States holders when publicly filed reports of beneficial ownership or other reliable information that is provided to you indicates that the securities are held by United States residents.

(4) When calculating under this rule the number of your United States resident security holders, you may rely in good faith on the assistance of an independent information services provider that in the regular course of its business assists issuers in determining the number of, and collecting other information concerning, their security holders.

(f) *Definitions.* For the purpose of this rule:

(1) *Debt security* means any security other than an equity security as defined under Rule 3a11–1, including:

(i) Non-participatory preferred stock, which is defined as non-convertible capital stock, the holders of which are entitled to a preference in payment of dividends and in distribution of assets on liquidation, dissolution, or winding up of the issuer, but are not entitled to participate in residual earnings or assets of the issuer; and

(ii) Notwithstanding Rule 3a11–1, any debt security described in paragraph (f)(3)(i) and (ii) of this rule;

(2) *Employee* has the same meaning as the definition of employee provided in Form S–8 (17 CFR 239.16b).

(3) *Equity security* means the same as under Rule 3a11–1, but, for purposes of paragraphs (a)(3) and (a)(4)(i) of this rule, does not include:

(i) Any debt security that is convertible into an equity security, with or without consideration;

(ii) Any debt security that includes a warrant or right to subscribe to or purchase an equity security;

(iii) Any such warrant or right; or

(iv) Any put, call, straddle, or other option or privilege that gives the holder the option of buying or selling a security but does not require the holder to do so.

(4) *Foreign private issuer* has the same meaning as under Rule 3b–4.

(5) *Primary trading market* means that:

(i) At least 55 percent of the trading in a foreign private issuer's class of securities that is the subject of Form 15F took place in, on or through the facilities of a securities market or markets in a single foreign jurisdiction or in no more than two foreign jurisdictions during a recent 12–month period; and

(ii) If a foreign private issuer aggregates the trading of its subject class of securities in two foreign jurisdictions for the purpose of paragraph (a)(3) of this rule, the trading for the issuer's securities in at least one of the two foreign jurisdictions must be larger than the trading in the United States for the same class of the issuer's securities.

(6) *Recent 12–month period* means a 12–calendar-month period that ended no more than 60 days before the filing date of the Form 15F.

(g)(1) Suspension of a foreign private issuer's duty to file reports under section 13(a) or section 15(d) of the Act shall occur immediately upon filing the Form 15F with the Commission if filing pursuant to paragraph (a), (c) or (d) of this rule. If there are no objections from the Commission, 90 days, or such shorter period as the Commission may determine, after the issuer has filed its Form 15F, the effectiveness of any of the following shall occur:

(i) The termination of registration of a class of securities under section 12(g); and

(ii) The termination of a foreign private issuer's duty to file reports under section 13(a) or section 15(d) of the Act.

(2) If the Form 15F is subsequently withdrawn or denied, the issuer shall, within 60 days after the date of the withdrawal or denial, file with or submit to the Commission all reports that would have been required had the issuer not filed the Form 15F.

(h) As a condition to termination of registration or reporting under paragraph (a), (c) or (d) of this rule, a foreign private issuer must, either before or on the date that it files its Form 15F, publish a notice in the United States that discloses its intent to terminate its registration of a class of securities under section 12(g) of the Act, or its reporting obligations under section 13(a) or section 15(d) of the Act, or both. The issuer must publish the notice through a means reasonably designed to provide broad dissemination of the information to the public in the United States. The issuer must also submit a copy of the notice to the Commission, either under cover of a Form 6–K (17 CFR 249.306) before or at the time of filing of the Form 15F, or as an exhibit to the Form 15F.

(i)(1) A foreign private issuer that, before the effective date of this rule, terminated the registration of a class of securities under section 12(g) of the Act or suspended its reporting obligations regarding a class of equity or debt securities under section 15(d) of the Act may file a Form 15F in order to:

(i) Terminate under this rule the registration of a class of equity securities that was the subject of a Form 15 (17 CFR 249.323) filed by the issuer pursuant to Rule 12g–4; or

(ii) Terminate its reporting obligations under section 15(d) of the Act, which had been suspended by the terms of that section or by the issuer's filing of a Form 15 pursuant to Rule 12h–3, regarding a class of equity or debt securities.

(2) In order to be eligible to file a Form 15F under this paragraph:

(i) If a foreign private issuer terminated the registration of a class of securities pursuant to Rule 12g–4 or suspended its reporting obligations pursuant to Rule 12h–3 or section 15(d) of the Act regarding a class of equity securities, the issuer must meet the requirements under paragraph (a)(3) and paragraph (a)(4)(i) or (a)(4)(ii) of this rule; or

(ii) If a foreign private issuer suspended its reporting obligations pursuant to Rule 12h–3 or section 15(d) of the Act regarding a class of debt securities, the issuer must meet the requirements under paragraph (c)(2) of this rule.

(3)(i) If the Commission does not object, 90 days after the filing of a Form 15F under this paragraph, or such shorter period as the Commission may determine, the effectiveness of any of the following shall occur:

(A) The termination under this rule of the registration of a class of equity securities, which was the subject of a Form 15 filed pursuant to Rule 12g–4, and the duty to file reports required by section 13(a) of the Act regarding that class of securities; or

(B) The termination of a foreign private issuer's reporting obligations under section 15(d) of the Act, which had previously been suspended by the terms of that section or by the issuer's filing of a Form 15 pursuant to Rule 12h–3, regarding a class of equity or debt securities.

(ii) If the Form 15F is subsequently withdrawn or denied, the foreign private issuer shall, within 60 days after the date of the withdrawal or denial, file with or submit to the Commission all reports that would have been required had the issuer not filed the Form 15F.

NOTE TO RULE 12h–6: The suspension of classes of asset-backed securities is addressed in Rule 15d–22.

Rule 12h–7. Exemption for issuers of securities that are subject to insurance regulation

An issuer shall be exempt from the duty under section 15(d) of the Act (15 U.S.C. 78o(d)) to file reports required by section 13(a) of the Act (15 U.S.C. 78m(a)) with respect to securities registered under the Securities Act of 1933, provided that:

(a) The issuer is a corporation subject to the supervision of the insurance commissioner, bank commissioner, or any agency or officer performing like functions, of any State;

(b) The securities do not constitute an equity interest in the issuer and are either subject to regulation under the insurance laws of the domiciliary State of the issuer or are guarantees of securities that are subject to regulation under the insurance laws of that jurisdiction;

(c) The issuer files an annual statement of its financial condition with, and is supervised and its financial condition examined periodically by, the insurance commissioner, bank commissioner, or any agency or officer performing like functions, of the issuer's domiciliary State;

(d) The securities are not listed, traded, or quoted on an exchange, alternative trading system (as defined in Rule 300(a) of Regulation ATS), inter-dealer quotation system (as defined in Rule 15c2–11(e)(2)), electronic communications network, or any other similar system, network, or publication for trading or quoting;

(e) The issuer takes steps reasonably designed to ensure that a trading market for the securities does not develop, including, except to the extent prohibited by the law of any State or by action of the insurance commissioner, bank commissioner, or any agency or officer performing like functions of any State, requiring written notice to, and acceptance by, the issuer prior to any assignment or other transfer of the securities and reserving the right to refuse assignments or other transfers at any time on a non-discriminatory basis; and

(f) The prospectus for the securities contains a statement indicating that the issuer is relying on the exemption provided by this rule.

REGULATION 13A. REPORTS OF ISSUERS OF SECURITIES REGISTERED PURSUANT TO SECTION 12

ANNUAL REPORTS

Rule 13a–1. Requirement of annual reports

Every issuer having securities registered pursuant to section 12 of the Act (15 U.S.C. 78*l*) shall file an annual report on the appropriate form authorized or prescribed therefor for each fiscal year after the last full fiscal year for which financial statements were filed in its registration statement. Annual reports shall be filed within the period specified in the appropriate form.

Rule 13a–2. [Reserved]

Rule 13a–3. Reporting by Form 40–F registrant

A registrant that is eligible to use Forms 40–F and 6–K and files reports in accordance therewith shall be deemed to satisfy the requirements of Regulation 13A (Rules 13a–1 through 13a–17).

Rule 13a–10. Transition reports

(a) Every issuer that changes its fiscal closing date shall file a report covering the resulting transition period between the closing date of its most recent fiscal year end and the opening date of its new fiscal year; *Provided, however,* that an issuer shall file an annual report for any fiscal year that ended before the date on which the issuer determined to change its fiscal year end. In no event shall the transition report cover a period of 12 or more months.

(b) The report pursuant to this section shall be filed for the transition period not more than the number of days specified in paragraph (j) of this section after either the close of the transition period or the date of the determination to change the fiscal closing date, whichever is later. The report shall be filed on the form appropriate for annual reports of the issuer, shall cover the period from the close of the last fiscal year end and shall indicate clearly the period covered. The financial statements for the transition period filed therewith shall be audited. Financial statements, which may be unaudited, shall be filed for the comparable period of the prior year, or a footnote, which may be unaudited, shall state for the comparable period of the prior year, revenues, gross profits, income taxes, income or loss from continuing operations and net income or loss. The effects of any discontinued operations as classified under the provisions of generally accepted accounting principles also shall be shown, if applicable. Per share data based upon such income or loss and net income or loss shall be presented in conformity with applicable accounting standards. Where called for by the time span to be covered, the comparable period financial statements or footnote shall be included in subsequent filings.

(c) If the transition period covers a period of less than six months, in lieu of the report required by paragraph (b) of this rule, a report may be filed for the transition period on Form 10–Q (17 CFR 249.308a) not more than the number of days specified in paragraph (j) of this rule after either the close of the transition period or the date of the determination to change the fiscal closing date, whichever is later. The report on Form 10–Q shall cover the period from the close of the last fiscal year end and shall indicate clearly the period covered. The financial statements filed therewith need not be audited but, if they are not audited, the issuer shall file with the first annual report for the newly adopted fiscal year separate audited statements of income and cash flows covering the transition period. The notes to financial statements for the transition period included in such first annual report may be integrated with the notes to financial statements for the full fiscal period. A separate audited balance sheet as of the end of the transition period shall be filed in the annual report only if the audited balance sheet as of the end of the fiscal year prior to the transition period is not filed. Schedules need not be filed in transition reports on Form 10–Q.

(d) Notwithstanding the foregoing in paragraphs (a), (b), and (c) of this rule, if the transition period covers a period of one month or less, the issuer need not file a separate transition report if either:

(1) The first report required to be filed by the issuer for the newly adopted fiscal year after the date of the determination to change the fiscal year end is an annual report, and that report covers the transition period as well as the fiscal year; or

(2)(i) The issuer files with the first annual report for the newly adopted fiscal year separate audited statements of income and cash flows covering the transition period; and

(ii) The first report required to be filed by the issuer for the newly adopted fiscal year after the date of the determination to change the fiscal year end is a quarterly report on Form 10–Q; and

(iii) Information on the transition period is included in the issuer's quarterly report on Form 10–Q for the first quarterly period (except the fourth quarter) of the newly adopted fiscal year that ends after the date of the determination to change the fiscal year. The information covering the transition period required by Part II and Item 2 of Part I may be combined with the information regarding the quarter. However, the financial statements required by Part I, which may be unaudited, shall be furnished separately for the transition period.

(e) Every issuer required to file quarterly reports on Form 10–Q pursuant to Rule 13a–13 that changes its fiscal year end shall:

(1) File a quarterly report on Form 10–Q within the time period specified in General Instruction A.1. to that form for any quarterly period (except the fourth quarter) of the old fiscal year that ends before the date on which the issuer determined to change its fiscal year end, except that the issuer need not file such quarterly report if the date on which the quarterly period ends also is the date on which the transition period ends;

(2) File a quarterly report on Form 10–Q within the time specified in General Instruction A.1. to that form for each quarterly period of the old fiscal year within the transition period. In lieu of a quarterly report for any quarter of the old fiscal year within the transition period, the issuer may file a quarterly report on Form 10–Q for any period of three months within the transition period that coincides with a quarter of the newly adopted fiscal year if the quarterly report is filed within the number of days specified in paragraph (j) of this rule after the end of such three month period, provided the issuer thereafter continues filing quarterly reports on the basis of the quarters of the newly adopted fiscal year;

(3) Commence filing quarterly reports for the quarters of the new fiscal year no later than the quarterly report for the first quarter of the new fiscal year that ends after the date on which the issuer determined to change the fiscal year end; and

(4) Unless such information is or will be included in the transition report, or the first annual report on Form 10–K for the newly adopted fiscal year, include in the initial quarterly report on Form 10–Q for the newly adopted fiscal year information on any period beginning on the first day subsequent to the period covered by the issuer's final quarterly report on Form 10–Q or annual report on Form 10–K for the old fiscal year. The information covering such period required by Part II and Item 2 of Part I may be combined with the information regarding the quarter. However, the financial statements required by Part I, which may be unaudited, shall be furnished separately for such period.

NOTE TO PARAGRAPHS (c) AND (e): If it is not practicable or cannot be cost-justified to furnish in a transition report on Form 10–Q or a quarterly report for the newly adopted fiscal year financial statements for corresponding periods of the prior year where required, financial statements may be furnished for the quarters of the preceding fiscal year that most nearly are comparable if the issuer furnishes an adequate discussion of seasonal and other factors that could affect the comparability of information or trends reflected, an assessment of the comparability of the data, and a representation as to the reason recasting has not been undertaken.

(f) Every successor issuer with securities registered under Section 12 of this Act that has a different fiscal year from that of its predecessor(s) shall file a transition report pursuant to this rule, containing the required information about each predecessor, for the transition period, if any, between the close of the fiscal year covered by the last annual report of each predecessor and the date of succession. The report shall be filed for the transition period on the form appropriate for annual reports of the issuer not more than the number of days specified in paragraph (j) of this rule after the date of the succession, with financial statements in conformity with the requirements set forth in paragraph (b) of this rule. If the transition period covers a period of less than six months, in lieu of a transition report on the form appropriate for the issuer's annual reports, the report may be filed for the transition period on Form 10–Q not more than the number of days specified in paragraph (j) of this rule after the date of the succession, with financial statements in conformity with the requirements set forth in paragraph (c) of this rule. Notwithstanding the foregoing, if the transition period covers a period of one month or less, the successor issuer need not file a separate transition report if the information is reported by the successor issuer in conformity with the requirements set forth in paragraph (d) of this rule.

(g)(1) Paragraphs (a) through (f) of this rule shall not apply to foreign private issuers.

(2) Every foreign private issuer that changes its fiscal closing date shall file a report covering the resulting transition period between the closing date of its most recent fiscal year end and the opening date of its new fiscal year. In no event shall a transition report cover a period longer than 12 months.

(3) The report for the transition period shall be filed on Form 20–F (17 CFR 249.220f of this chapter) responding to all items to which such issuer is required to respond when Form 20–F is used as an annual report. The financial statements for the transition period filed therewith shall be audited. The report shall be filed within four months after either the close of the transition period or the date on which the issuer made the determination to change the fiscal closing date, whichever is later.

(4) If the transition period covers a period of six or fewer months, in lieu of the report required by paragraph (g)(3) of this rule, a report for the transition period may be filed on Form 20–F responding to Items 5, 8.A.7, 13, 14, and 17 or 18 within three months after either the close of the transition period or the date on which the issuer made the determination to change the fiscal closing date, whichever is later. The financial statements required by either Item 17 or Item 18 shall be furnished for the transition period. Such financial statements may be unaudited and condensed as permitted in Article 10 of Regulation S–X, but if the financial statements are unaudited and condensed, the issuer shall file with the first annual report for the newly adopted fiscal year separate audited statements of income and cash flows covering the transition period.

(5) Notwithstanding the foregoing in paragraphs (g)(2), (g)(3), and (g)(4) of this rule, if the transition period covers a period of one month or less, a foreign private issuer need not file a separate transition report if the first annual report for the newly adopted fiscal year covers the transition period as well as the fiscal year.

(h) The provisions of this rule shall not apply to investment companies required to file reports pursuant to Rule 30b1–1 under the Investment Company Act of 1940 (15 U.S.C. 80a–1 *et seq.*).

(i) No filing fee shall be required for a transition report filed pursuant to this rule.

(j)(1) For transition reports to be filed on the form appropriate for annual reports of the issuer, the number of days shall be:

(i) 60 days (75 days for fiscal years ending before December 15, 2006) for large accelerated filers (as defined in Rule 12b–2);

(ii) 75 days for accelerated filers (as defined in Rule 12b–2); and

(iii) 90 days for all other issuers; and

(2) For transition reports to be filed on Form 10–Q (17 CFR 249.308a), the number of days shall be:

(i) 40 days for large accelerated filers and accelerated filers (as defined in Rule 12b–2); and

(ii) 45 days for all other issuers.

(k)(1) Paragraphs (a) through (g) of this rule shall not apply to asset-backed issuers.

(2) Every asset-backed issuer that changes its fiscal closing date shall file a report covering the resulting transition period between the closing date of its most recent fiscal year and the opening date of its new fiscal year. In no event shall a transition report cover a period longer than 12 months.

(3) The report for the transition period shall be filed on Form 10–K (17 CFR 249.310) responding to all items to which such asset-backed issuer is required to respond pursuant to General Instruction J. of Form 10–K. Such report shall be filed within 90 days after the later of either the close of

the transition period or the date on which the issuer made the determination to change the fiscal closing date.

(4) Notwithstanding the foregoing in paragraphs (k)(2) and (k)(3) of this rule, if the transition period covers a period of one month or less, an asset-backed issuer need not file a separate transition report if the first annual report for the newly adopted fiscal year covers the transition period as well as the fiscal year.

(5) Any obligation of the asset-backed issuer to file distribution reports pursuant to Rule 13a–17 will continue to apply regardless of a change in the asset-backed issuer's fiscal closing date.

NOTE 1: In addition to the report or reports required to be filed pursuant to this rule, every issuer, except a foreign private issuer or an investment company required to file reports pursuant to Rule 30b1–1 under the Investment Company Act of 1940, that changes its fiscal closing date is required to file a report on Form 8–K responding to Item 8 thereof within the period specified in General Instruction B.1. to that form.

NOTE 2: The report or reports to be filed pursuant to this rule must include the certification required by Rule 13a–14.

Rule 13a–11. Current reports on Form 8–K

(a) Except as provided in paragraph (b) of this rule, every registrant subject to Rule 13a–11 shall file a current report on Form 8–K within the period specified in that form, unless substantially the same information as that required by Form 8–K has been previously reported by the registrant.

(b) This section shall not apply to foreign governments, foreign private issuers required to make reports on Form 6–K (17 CFR 249.306) pursuant to Rule 13a–16, issuers of American Depositary Receipts for securities of any foreign issuer, or investment companies required to file reports pursuant to Rule 30b1–1 under the Investment Company Act of 1940, except where such an investment company is required to file:

(1) Notice of a blackout period pursuant to Rule 104 of Regulation BTR;

(2) Disclosure pursuant to Instruction 2 to Rule 14a–11(b)(1) of information concerning outstanding shares and voting; or

(3) Disclosure pursuant to Instruction 2 to Rule 14a–11(b)(10) of the date by which a nominating shareholder or nominating shareholder group must submit the notice required pursuant to Rule 14a–11(b)(10).

(c) No failure to file a report on Form 8–K that is required solely pursuant to Item 1.01, 1.02, 2.03, 2.04, 2.05, 2.06, 4.02(a), 5.02 or 6.03 of Form 8–K shall be deemed to be a violation of 15 U.S.C. 78j(b) and Form 10b–5.

Rule 13a–13. Quarterly reports on Form 10–Q

(a) Except as provided in paragraphs (b) and (c) of this rule, every issuer that has securities registered pursuant to section 12 of the Act and is required to file annual reports pursuant to section 13 of the Act, and has filed or intends to file such reports on Form 10–K (17 CFR 249.310), shall file a quarterly report on Form 10–Q (17 CFR 249.308a) within the period specified in General Instruction A.1. to that form for each of the first three quarters of each fiscal year of the issuer, commencing with the first fiscal quarter following the most recent fiscal year for which full financial statements were included in the registration statement, or, if the registration statement included financial statements for an interim period subsequent to the most recent fiscal year end meeting the requirements of Article 10 of Regulation S–X and Rule 8–03 of Regulation S–X for smaller reporting companies, for the first fiscal quarter subsequent to the quarter reported upon in the registration statement. The first quarterly report of the issuer shall be filed either within 45 days after the effective date of the registration statement or on or before the date on which such report would have been required to be filed if the issuer has been required to file reports on 10–Q as of its last fiscal quarter, whichever is later.

(b) The provisions of this rule shall not apply to the following issuers:

(1) Investment companies required to file reports pursuant to Rule 30b1–1; or

(2) Foreign private issuers required to file reports pursuant to Rule 13a–16; and

(3) Asset-backed issuers required to file reports pursuant to Rule 13a–17.

(c) Part I of the quarterly reports on Form 10–Q need not be filed by:

(1) Mutual life insurance companies; or

(2) Mining companies not in the production stage but engaged primarily in the exploration for the development of mineral deposits other than oil, gas or coal, if all of the following conditions are met:

(i) The registrant has not been in production during the current fiscal year or the two years immediately prior thereto; except that being in production for an aggregate period of not more than eight months over the three-year period shall not be a violation of this condition.

(ii) Receipts from the sale of mineral products or from the operations of mineral producing properties by the registrant and its subsidiaries combined have not exceeded $500,000 in any of the most recent six years and have not aggregated more than $1,500,000 in the most recent six fiscal years.

(d) Notwithstanding the foregoing provisions of this rule, the financial information required by Part I of Form 10–Q shall not be deemed to be "filed" for the purpose of section 18 of the Act or otherwise subject to the liabilities of that section of the Act but shall be subject to all other provisions of the Act.

Rule 13a–14. Certification of disclosure in annual and quarterly reports

(a) Each report, including transition reports, filed on Form 10–Q, Form 10–K, Form 20–F or Form 40–F (17 CFR 249.308a, 249.310, 249.220f or 249.240f) under section 13(a) of the Act (15 U.S.C. 78m(a)), other than a report filed by an Asset–Backed Issuer (as defined in Item 1101 of Regulation AB) or a report on Form 20–F filed under Rule 13a–19, must include certifications in the form specified in the applicable exhibit filing requirements of such report and such certifications must be filed as an exhibit to such report. Each principal executive and principal financial officer of the issuer, or persons performing similar functions, at the time of filing of the report must sign a certification. The principal executive and principal financial officers of an issuer may omit the portion of the introductory language in paragraph 4 as well as language in paragraph 4(b) of the certification that refers to the certifying officers' responsibility for designing, establishing and maintaining internal control over financial reporting for the issuer until the issuer becomes subject to the internal control over financial reporting requirements in Rule 13a–15 or Rule 15d–15.

(b) Each periodic report containing financial statements filed by an issuer pursuant to section 13(a) of the Act (15 U.S.C. 78m(a)) must be accompanied by the certifications required by Section 1350 of Chapter 63 of Title 18 of the United States Code (18 U.S.C. 1350) and such certifications must be furnished as an exhibit to such report as specified in the applicable exhibit requirements for such report. Each principal executive and principal financial officer of the issuer (or equivalent thereof) must sign a certification. This requirement may be satisfied by a single certification signed by an issuer's principal executive and principal financial officers.

(c) A person required to provide a certification specified in paragraph (a), (b) or (d) of this rule may not have the certification signed on his or her behalf pursuant to a power of attorney or other form of confirming authority.

(d) Each annual report and transition report filed on Form 10–K (17 CFR 249.310) by an asset-backed issuer under section 13(a) of the Act (15 U.S.C. 78m(a)) must include a certification in the form specified in the applicable exhibit filing requirements of such report and such certification must be filed as an exhibit to such report. Terms used in paragraphs (d) and (e) of this rule have the same meaning as in Item 1101 of Regulation AB.

(e) With respect to asset-backed issuers, the certification required by paragraph (d) of this rule must be signed by either:

(1) The senior officer in charge of securitization of the depositor if the depositor is signing the report; or

(2) The senior officer in charge of the servicing function of the servicer if the servicer is signing the report on behalf of the issuing entity. If multiple servicers are involved in servicing the pool assets, the senior officer in charge of the servicing function of the master servicer (or entity performing the equivalent function) must sign if a representative of the servicer is to sign the report on behalf of the issuing entity.

(f) The certification requirements of this rule do not apply to an Interactive Data File, as defined in Rule 11 of Regulation S–T.

Rule 13a–15. Controls and procedures

(a) Every issuer that has a class of securities registered pursuant to section 12 of the Act (15 U.S.C. 78*l*), other than an Asset–Backed Issuer (as defined in Item 1101 of Regulation AB), a small business investment company registered on Form N–5 (17 CFR 239.24 and 274.5), or a unit investment trust as defined in section 4(2) of the Investment Company Act of 1940 (15 U.S.C. 80a–4(2)), must maintain disclosure controls and procedures (as defined in paragraph (e) of this rule) and, if the issuer either had been required to file an annual report pursuant to section 13(a) or 15(d) of the Act (15 U.S.C. 78m(a) or 78o(d)) for the prior fiscal year or had filed an annual report with the Commission for the prior fiscal year, internal control over financial reporting (as defined in paragraph (f) of this rule).

(b) Each such issuer's management must evaluate, with the participation of the issuer's principal executive and principal financial officers, or persons performing similar functions, the effectiveness of the issuer's disclosure controls and procedures, as of the end of each fiscal quarter, except that management must perform this evaluation:

(1) In the case of a foreign private issuer (as defined in Rule 3b–4) as of the end of each fiscal year; and

(2) In the case of an investment company registered under section 8 of the Investment Company Act of 1940 (15 U.S.C. 80a–8), within the 90-day period prior to the filing date of each report requiring certification under 17 CFR 270.30a–2.

(c) The management of each such issuer, that either had been required to file an annual report pursuant to section 13(a) or 15(d) of the Act (15 U.S.C. 78m(a) or 78o(d)) for the prior fiscal year or previously had filed an annual report with the Commission for the prior fiscal year, other than an investment company registered under section 8 of the Investment Company Act of 1940, must evaluate, with the participation of the issuer's principal executive and principal financial officers, or persons performing similar functions, the effectiveness, as of the end of each fiscal year, of the issuer's internal control over financial reporting. The framework on which management's evaluation of the issuer's internal control over financial reporting is based must be a suitable, recognized control framework that is established by a body or group that has followed due-process procedures, including the broad distribution of the framework for public comment. Although there are many different ways to conduct an evaluation of the effectiveness of internal control over financial reporting to meet the requirements of this paragraph, an evaluation that is conducted in accordance with the interpretive guidance issued by the Commission in Release No. 34–55929 will satisfy the evaluation required by this paragraph.

(d) The management of each such issuer that either had been required to file an annual report pursuant to section 13(a) or 15(d) of the Act (15 U.S.C. 78m(a) or 78o(d)) for the prior fiscal year or had filed an annual report with the Commission for the prior fiscal year, other than an investment company registered under section 8 of the Investment Company Act of 1940 (15 U.S.C. 80a–8), must evaluate, with the participation of the issuer's principal executive and principal financial officers, or persons performing similar functions, any change in the issuer's internal control over financial reporting, that occurred during each of the issuer's fiscal quarters, or fiscal year in the case of a foreign private issuer, that has materially affected, or is reasonably likely to materially affect, the issuer's internal control over financial reporting.

(e) For purposes of this rule, the term *disclosure controls and procedures* means controls and other procedures of an issuer that are designed to ensure that information required to be disclosed by the issuer in the reports that it files or submits under the Act (15 U.S.C. 78a *et seq.*) is recorded, processed, summarized and reported, within the time periods specified in the Commission's rules and forms. Disclosure controls and procedures include, without limitation, controls and procedures designed to ensure that information required to be disclosed by an issuer in the reports that it files or submits under the Act is accumulated and communicated to the issuer's management, including its principal executive and principal financial officers, or persons performing similar functions, as appropriate to allow timely decisions regarding required disclosure.

(f) The term *internal control over financial reporting* is defined as a process designed by, or under the supervision of, the issuer's principal executive and principal financial officers, or persons performing similar functions, and effected by the issuer's board of directors, management and other personnel, to provide reasonable assurance regarding the reliability of financial reporting and the preparation of financial statements for external purposes in accordance with generally accepted accounting principles and includes those policies and procedures that:

(1) Pertain to the maintenance of records that in reasonable detail accurately and fairly reflect the transactions and dispositions of the assets of the issuer;

(2) Provide reasonable assurance that transactions are recorded as necessary to permit preparation of financial statements in accordance with generally accepted accounting principles, and that receipts and expenditures of the issuer are being made only in accordance with authorizations of management and directors of the issuer; and

(3) Provide reasonable assurance regarding prevention or timely detection of unauthorized acquisition, use or disposition of the issuer's assets that could have a material effect on the financial statements.

Rule 13a–16. Reports of foreign private issuers on Form 6–K (17 CFR 249.306)

(a) Every foreign private issuer which is subject to Rule 13a–1 shall make reports on Form 6–K, except that this rule shall not apply to:

(1) Investment companies required to file reports pursuant to Rule 30b1–1; or

(2) issuers of American depositary receipts for securities of any foreign issuer; or

(3) Issuers filing periodic reports on Form 10–K, Form 10–Q and Form 8–K; or

(4) Asset-backed issuers, as defined in Item 1101 of Regulation AB.

(b) Such reports shall be transmitted promptly after the information required by Form 6–K is made public by the issuer, by the country of its domicile or under the laws of which it was incorporated or organized, or by a foreign securities exchange with which the issuer has filed the information.

(c) Reports furnished pursuant to this rule shall not be deemed to be "filed" for the purpose of section 18 of the Act or otherwise subject to the liabilities of that section.

Rule 13a–17. Reports of asset-backed issuers on Form 10–D (17 CFR 249.312)

Every asset-backed issuer subject to Rule 13a–1 shall make reports on Form 10–D (17 CFR 249.312). Such reports shall be filed within the period specified in Form 10-D.

Rule 13a–18. Compliance with servicing criteria for asset-backed securities

(a) This rule applies to every class of asset-backed securities subject to the reporting requirements of section 13(a) of the Act (15 U.S.C. 78m(a)). Terms used in this rule have the same meaning as in Item 1101 of Regulation AB.

(b) *Reports on Assessments of Compliance with Servicing Criteria for Asset-Backed Securities Required.* With regard to a class of asset-backed securities subject to the reporting requirements of section 13(a) of the Act, the annual report on Form 10–K (17 CFR 249.308) for such class must include from each party participating in the servicing function a report regarding its assessment of compliance with the servicing criteria specified in paragraph (d) of Item 1122 of Regulation AB, as of and for the period ending the end of each fiscal year, with respect to asset-backed securities transactions taken as a whole involving the party participating in the servicing function and that are backed by the same asset type backing the class of asset-backed securities (including the asset-backed securities transaction that is to be the subject of the report on Form 10–K for that fiscal year).

(c) *Attestation Reports on Assessments of Compliance with Servicing Criteria for Asset-Backed Securities Required.* With respect to each report included pursuant to paragraph (b) of this rule, the annual report on Form 10–K must also include a report by a registered public accounting firm that attests to, and reports on, the assessment made by the asserting party. The attestation report on assessment of compliance with servicing criteria for asset-backed securities must be made in accordance with standards for attestation engagements issued or adopted by the Public Company Accounting Oversight Board.

NOTE TO RULE 13a–18. If multiple parties are participating in the servicing function, a separate assessment report and attestation report must be included for each party participating in the servicing function. A party participating in the servicing function means any entity (*e.g.*, master servicer, primary servicers, trustees) that is performing activities that address the criteria in paragraph (d) of Item 1122 of Regulation AB, unless such entity's activities relate only to 5% or less of the pool assets.

Rule 13a–19. Reports by shell companies on Form 20–F

Every foreign private issuer that was a shell company, other than a business combination related shell company, immediately before a transaction that causes it to cease to be a shell company shall, within four business days of completion of that transaction, file a report on Form 20–F (17 CFR 249.220f) containing the information that would be required if the issuer were filing a form for registration of securities on Form 20–F to register under the Act all classes of the issuer's securities subject to the reporting requirements of section 13 (15 U.S.C. 78m) or section 15(d) (15 U.S.C. 78o(d)) of the Act upon consummation of the transaction, with such information reflecting the registrant and its securities upon consummation of the transaction.

Rule 13a–20. Plain English presentation of specified information

(a) Any information included or incorporated by reference in a report filed under section 13(a) of the Act (15 U.S.C. 78m(a)) that is required to be disclosed pursuant to Item 402, 403, 404 or 407 of Regulation S–K must be presented in a clear, concise and understandable manner. You must prepare the disclosure using the following standards:

(1) Present information in clear, concise sections, paragraphs and sentences;

(2) Use short sentences;

(3) Use definite, concrete, everyday words;

(4) Use the active voice;

(5) Avoid multiple negatives;

(6) Use descriptive headings and subheadings;

(7) Use a tabular presentation or bullet lists for complex material, wherever possible;

(8) Avoid legal jargon and highly technical business and other terminology;

(9) Avoid frequent reliance on glossaries or defined terms as the primary means of explaining information. Define terms in a glossary or other section of the document only if the meaning is unclear from the context. Use a glossary only if it facilitates understanding of the disclosure; and

(10) In designing the presentation of the information you may include pictures, logos, charts, graphs and other design elements so long as the design is not misleading and the required information is clear. You are encouraged to use tables, schedules, charts and graphic illustrations that present relevant data in an understandable manner, so long as such presentations are consistent with applicable disclosure requirements and consistent with other information in the document. You must draw graphs and charts to scale. Any information you provide must not be misleading.

(b) [Reserved]

NOTE TO RULE 13a-20. In drafting the disclosure to comply with this rule, you should avoid the following:

1. Legalistic or overly complex presentations that make the substance of the disclosure difficult to understand;

2. Vague "boilerplate" explanations that are imprecise and readily subject to different interpretations;

3. Complex information copied directly from legal documents without any clear and concise explanation of the provision(s); and

4. Disclosure repeated in different sections of the document that increases the size of the document but does not enhance the quality of the information.

REGULATION 13B-2. MAINTENANCE OF RECORDS AND PREPARATION OF REQUIRED REPORTS

Rule 13b2-1. Falsification of accounting records

No person shall, directly or indirectly, falsify or cause to be falsified, any book, record or account subject to section 13(b)(2)(A) of the Securities Exchange Act.

Rule 13b2-2. Representations and conduct in connection with the preparation of required reports and documents

(a) No director or officer of an issuer shall, directly or indirectly:

(1) Make or cause to be made a materially false or misleading statement to an accountant in connection with; or

(2) Omit to state, or cause another person to omit to state, any material fact necessary in order to make statements made, in light of the circumstances under which such statements were made, not misleading, to an accountant in connection with:

(i) Any audit, review or examination of the financial statements of the issuer required to be made pursuant to this subpart; or

(ii) The preparation or filing of any document or report required to be filed with the Commission pursuant to this subpart or otherwise.

(b)(1) No officer or director of an issuer, or any other person acting under the direction thereof, shall directly or indirectly take any action to coerce, manipulate, mislead, or fraudulently influence any independent public or certified public accountant engaged in the performance of an audit or review of the financial statements of that issuer that are required to be filed with the Commission pursuant to this subpart or otherwise if that person knew or should have known that such action, if successful, could result in rendering the issuer's financial statements materially misleading.

(2) For purposes of paragraphs (b)(1) and (c)(2) of this rule, actions that, "if successful, could result in rendering the issuer's financial statements materially misleading" include, but are not limited to, actions taken at any time with respect to the professional engagement period to coerce, manipulate, mislead, or fraudulently influence an auditor:

(i) To issue or reissue a report on an issuer's financial statements that is not warranted in the circumstances (due to material violations of generally accepted accounting principles, the standards of the PCAOB, or other professional or regulatory standards);

(ii) Not to perform audit, review or other procedures required by the standards of the PCAOB or other professional standards;

(iii) Not to withdraw an issued report; or

(iv) Not to communicate matters to an issuer's audit committee.

(c) In addition, in the case of an investment company registered under section 8 of the Investment Company Act of 1940 (15 U.S.C. 80a–8), or a business development company as defined in section 2(a)(48) of the Investment Company Act of 1940 (15 U.S.C. 80a–2(a)(48)), no officer or director of the company's investment adviser, sponsor, depositor, trustee, or administrator (or, in the case of paragraph (c)(2) of this rule, any other person acting under the direction thereof) shall, directly or indirectly:

(1)(i) Make or cause to be made a materially false or misleading statement to an accountant in connection with; or

(ii) Omit to state, or cause another person to omit to state, any material fact necessary in order to make statements made, in light of the circumstances under which such statements were made, not misleading to an accountant in connection with:

(A) Any audit, review, or examination of the financial statements of the investment company required to be made pursuant to this subpart; or

(B) The preparation or filing of any document or report required to be filed with the Commission pursuant to this subpart or otherwise; or

(2) Take any action to coerce, manipulate, mislead, or fraudulently influence any independent public or certified public accountant engaged in the performance of an audit or review of the financial statements of that investment company that are required to be filed with the Commission pursuant to this subpart or otherwise if that person knew or should have known that such action, if successful, could result in rendering the investment company's financial statements materially misleading.

REGULATION 13D–G

ATTENTION ELECTRONIC FILERS

THIS REGULATION SHOULD BE READ IN CONJUNCTION WITH REGULATION S–T (17 CFR 232), WHICH GOVERNS THE PREPARATION AND SUBMISSION OF DOCUMENTS IN ELECTRONIC FORMAT. MANY PROVISIONS RELATING TO THE PREPARATION AND SUBMISSION OF DOCUMENTS IN PAPER FORMAT CONTAINED IN THIS REGULATION ARE SUPERSEDED BY THE PROVISIONS OF REGULATION S–T FOR DOCUMENTS REQUIRED TO BE FILED IN ELECTRONIC FORMAT.

Rule 13d–1. Filing of Schedule 13D and 13G

(a) Any person who, after acquiring directly or indirectly the beneficial ownership of any equity security of a class which is specified in paragraph (i) of this rule, is directly or indirectly the beneficial owner of more than five percent of the class shall, within 10 days after the acquisition, file with the Commission, a statement containing the information required by Schedule 13D (Rule 13d–101).

(b)(1) A person who would otherwise be obligated under paragraph (a) of this rule to file a statement on Schedule 13D (Rule 13d–101) may, in lieu thereof, file with the Commission, a short-form statement on Schedule 13G (Rule 13d–102), *Provided,* That:

(i) Such person has acquired such securities in the ordinary course of his business and not with the purpose nor with the effect of changing or influencing the control of the issuer, nor in connection with or as a participant in any transaction having such purpose or effect, including any transaction subject to Rule 13d–3(b), other than activities solely in connection with a nomination under Rule 14a–11; and

(ii) Such person is:

(A) A broker or dealer registered under section 15 of the Act (15 U.S.C. 78o);

(B) A bank as defined in section 3(a)(6) of the Act (15 U.S.C. 78c);

(C) An insurance company as defined in section 3(a)(19) of the Act (15 U.S.C. 78c);

(D) An investment company registered under section 8 of the Investment Company Act of 1940 (15 U.S.C. 80a–8);

(E) Any person registered as an investment adviser under Section 203 of the Investment

Advisers Act of 1940 (15 U.S.C. 80b–3) or under the laws of any state;

(F) An employee benefit plan as defined in Section 3(3) of the Employee Retirement Income Security Act of 1974, as amended, 29 U.S.C. 1001 *et seq.* ("ERISA") that is subject to the provisions of ERISA, or any such plan that is not subject to ERISA that is maintained primarily for the benefit of the employees of a state or local government or instrumentality, or an endowment fund;

(G) A parent holding company or control person, provided the aggregate amount held directly by the parent or control person, and directly and indirectly by their subsidiaries or affiliates that are not persons specified in Rule 13d–1(b)(1)(ii)(A) through (J), does not exceed one percent of the securities of the subject class;

(H) A savings association as defined in Section 3(b) of the Federal Deposit Insurance Act (12 U.S.C. 1813);

(I) A church plan that is excluded from the definition of an investment company under section 3(c)(14) of the Investment Company Act of 1940 (15 U.S.C. 80a–3);

(J) A non-U.S. institution that is the functional equivalent of any of the institutions listed in paragraphs (b)(1)(ii)(A) through (I) of this rule, so long as the non-U.S. institution is subject to a regulatory scheme that is substantially comparable to the regulatory scheme applicable to the equivalent U.S. institution; and

(K) A group, provided that all the members are persons specified in Rule 13d–1(b)(1)(ii)(A) through (J).

(iii) Such person has promptly notified any other person (or group within the meaning of section 13(d)(3) of the Act) on whose behalf it holds, on a discretionary basis, securities exceeding five percent of the class, of any acquisition or transaction on behalf of such other person which might be reportable by that person under section 13(d) of the Act. This paragraph only requires notice to the account owner of information which the filing person reasonably should be expected to know and which would advise the account owner of an obligation he may have to file a statement pursuant to section 13(d) of the Act or an amendment thereto.

Instruction 1 to Paragraph (b)(1). For purposes of paragraph (b)(1)(i) of this section, the exception for activities solely in connection with a nomination under Rule 14a–11 will not be available after the election of directors.

(2) The Schedule 13G filed pursuant to paragraph (b)(1) of this rule shall be filed within 45 days after the end of the calendar year in which the person became obligated under paragraph (b)(1) of this rule to report the person's beneficial ownership as of the last day of the calendar year, *Provided,* That it shall not be necessary to file a Schedule 13G unless the percentage of the class of equity security specified in paragraph (i) of this rule beneficially owned as of the end of the calendar year is more than five percent; *However*, if the person's direct or indirect beneficial ownership exceeds 10 percent of the class of equity securities prior to the end of the calendar year, the initial Schedule 13G shall be filed within 10 days after the end of the first month in which the person's direct or indirect beneficial ownership exceeds 10 percent of the class of equity securities, computed as of the last day of the month.

(c) A person who would otherwise be obligated under paragraph (a) of this rule to file a statement on Schedule 13D (Rule 13d–101) may, in lieu thereof, file with the Commission, within 10 days after an acquisition described in paragraph (a) of this rule, a short-form statement on Schedule 13G (Rule 13d–102). *Provided,* That the person:

(1) Has not acquired the securities with any purpose, or with the effect, of changing or influencing the control of the issuer, or in connection with or as a participant in any transaction having that purpose or effect, including any transaction subject to Rule 13d–3(b), other than activities solely in connection with a nomination under Rule 14a–11;

Instruction 1 to Paragraph (c)(1). For purposes of paragraph (c)(1) of this section, the exception for activities solely in connection with a nomination under Rule 14a–11 will not be available after the election of directors.

(2) Is not a person reporting pursuant to paragraph (b)(1) of this rule; and

(3) Is not directly or indirectly the beneficial owner of 20 percent or more of the class.

(d) Any person who, as of the end of any calendar year, is or becomes directly or indirectly the beneficial owner of more than five percent of any equity security of a class specified in paragraph (i) of this rule and who is not required to file a statement under paragraph (a) of this rule by virtue of the exemption provided by Section 13(d)(6)(A) or (B) of the Act (15

U.S.C. 78m(d)(6)(A) or 78m(d)(6)(B)), or because the beneficial ownership was acquired prior to December 22, 1970, or because the person otherwise (except for the exemption provided by Section 13(d)(6)(C) of the Act (15 U.S.C. 78m(d)(6)(C))) is not required to file a statement, shall file with the Commission, within 45 days after the end of the calendar year in which the person became obligated to report under this paragraph (d), a statement containing the information required by Schedule 13G (Rule 13d–102).

(e)(1) Notwithstanding paragraph (b) and (c) of this rule and Rule 13d–2(b), a person that has reported that it is the beneficial owner of more than five percent of a class of equity securities in a statement on Schedule 13G (Rule 13d–102) pursuant to paragraph (b) or (c) of this rule, or is required to report the acquisition but has not yet filed the schedule, shall immediately become subject to Rules 13d–1(a) and 13d–2(a) and shall file a statement on Schedule 13D (Rule 13d–101) within 10 days if, and shall remain subject to those requirements for so long as, the person:

(i) Has acquired or holds the securities with a purpose or effect of changing or influencing control of the issuer, or in connection with or as a participant in any transaction having that purpose or effect, including any transaction subject to Rule 13d–3(b); and

(ii) Is at that time the beneficial owner of more than five percent of a class of equity securities described in Rule 13d–1(i).

(2) From the time the person has acquired or holds the securities with a purpose or effect of changing or influencing control of the issuer, or in connection with or as a participant in any transaction having that purpose or effect until the expiration of the tenth day from the date of the filing of the Schedule 13D (Rule 13d–101) pursuant to this rule, that person shall not:

(i) Vote or direct the voting of the securities described therein; or

(ii) Acquire an additional beneficial ownership interest in any equity securities of the issuer of the securities, nor of any person controlling the issuer.

(f)(1) Notwithstanding paragraph (c) of this rule and Rule 13d–2(b), persons reporting on Schedule 13G (Rule 13d–102) pursuant to paragraph (c) of this rule shall immediately become subject to Rules 13d–1(a) and 13d–2(a) and shall remain subject to those requirements for so long as, and shall file a statement on Schedule 13D (Rule 13d–101) within 10 days of the date on which, the person's beneficial ownership equals or exceeds 20 percent of the class of equity securities.

(2) From the time of the acquisition of 20 percent or more of the class of equity securities until the expiration of the tenth day from the date of the filing of the Schedule 13D (Rule 13d–101) pursuant to this rule, the person shall not:

(i) Vote or direct the voting of the securities described therein, or

(ii) Acquire an additional beneficial ownership interest in any equity securities of the issuer of the securities, nor of any person controlling the issuer.

(g) Any person who has reported an acquisition of securities in a statement on Schedule 13G (Rule 13d–102) pursuant to paragraph (b) of this rule, or has become obligated to report on the Schedule 13G (Rule 13d–102) but has not yet filed the Schedule, and thereafter ceases to be a person specified in paragraph (b)(1)(ii) of this rule or determines that it no longer has acquired or holds the securities in the ordinary course of business shall immediately become subject to Rule 13d–1(a) or Rule 13d–1(c) (if the person satisfies the requirements specified in Rule 13d–1(c)), and Rule 13d–2(a), (b) or (d), and shall file, within 10 days thereafter, a statement on Schedule 13D (Rule 13d–101) or amendment to Schedule 13G, as applicable, if the person is a beneficial owner at that time of more than five percent of the class of equity securities.

(h) Any person who has filed a Schedule 13D (Rule 13d–101) pursuant to paragraph (e), (f) or (g) of this rule may again report its beneficial ownership on Schedule 13G (Rule 13d–102) pursuant to paragraphs (b) or (c) of this rule provided the person qualifies thereunder, as applicable, by filing a Schedule 13G (Rule 13d–102) once the person determines that the provisions of paragraph (e), (f) or (g) of this rule no longer apply.

(i) For the purpose of this regulation, the term "equity security" means any equity security of a class which is registered pursuant to section 12 of that Act, or any equity security of any insurance company which would have been required to be so registered except for the exemption contained in section 12(g)(2)(G) of the Act, or any equity security issued by a closed-end investment company registered under the Investment Company Act of 1940; *Provided,* Such term shall not include securities of a class of non-voting securities.

(j) For the purpose of sections 13(d) and 13(g), any person, in determining the amount of outstanding securities of a class of equity securities, may rely upon information set forth in the issuer's most recent quarterly or annual report, and any current report subsequent thereto, filed with the Commission pursuant to this Act, unless he knows or has reason to believe that the information contained therein is inaccurate.

(k)(1) Whenever two or more persons are required to file a statement containing the information required by Schedule 13D or Schedule 13G with respect to the same securities, only one statement need be filed: *Provided,* That:

(i) Each person on whose behalf the statement is filed is individually eligible to use the Schedule on which the information is filed;

(ii) Each person on whose behalf the statement is filed is responsible for the timely filing of such statement and any amendments thereto, and for the completeness and accuracy of the information concerning such person contained therein; such person is not responsible for the completeness or accuracy of the information concerning the other persons making the filing, unless such person knows or has reason to believe that such information is inaccurate; and

(iii) Such statement identifies all such persons, contains the required information with regard to each such person, indicates that such statement is filed on behalf of all such persons, and includes, as an exhibit, their agreement in writing that such a statement is filed on behalf of each of them.

(2) A group's filing obligation may be satisfied either by a single joint filing or by each of the group's members making an individual filing. If the group's members elect to make their own filings, each such filing should identify all members of the group but the information provided concerning the other persons making the filing need only reflect information which the filing person knows or has reason to know.

Rule 13d–2. Filing of amendments to Schedules 13D or 13G

(a) If any material change occurs in the facts set forth in the Schedule 13D (Rule 13d–101) required by Rule 13d–1(a), including, but not limited to, any material increase or decrease in the percentage of the class beneficially owned, the person or persons who were required to file the statement shall promptly file or cause to be filed with the Commission an amendment disclosing that change. An acquisition or disposition of beneficial ownership of securities in an amount equal to one percent or more of the class of securities shall be deemed "material" for purposes of this rule; acquisitions or dispositions of less than those amounts may be material, depending upon the facts and circumstances.

(b) Notwithstanding paragraph (a) of this rule, and provided that the person filing a Schedule 13G (Rule 13d–102) pursuant to Rule 13d–1(b) or Rule 13d–1(c) continues to meet the requirements set forth therein, any person who has filed a Schedule 13G (Rule 13d–102) pursuant to Rule 13d–1(b), Rule 13d–1(c) or Rule 13d–1(d) shall amend the statement within forty-five days after the end of each calendar year if, as of the end of the calendar year, there are any changes in the information reported in the previous filing on that Schedule: *Provided, however,* That an amendment need not be filed with respect to a change in the percent of class outstanding previously reported if the change results solely from a change in the aggregate number of securities outstanding. Once an amendment has been filed reflecting beneficial ownership of five percent or less of the class of securities, no additional filings are required unless the person thereafter becomes the beneficial owner of more than five percent of the class and is required to file pursuant to Rule 13d–1.

(c) Any person relying on Rule 13d–1(b) that has filed its initial Schedule 13G (Rule 13d–102) pursuant to that paragraph shall, in addition to filing any amendments pursuant to Rule 13d–2(b), file an amendment on Schedule 13G (Rule 13d–102) within 10 days after the end of the first month in which the person's direct or indirect beneficial ownership, computed as of the last day of the month, exceeds 10 percent of the class of equity securities. Thereafter, that person shall, in addition to filing any amendments pursuant to Rule 13d–2(b), file an amendment on Schedule 13G (Rule 13d–102) within 10 days after the end of the first month in which the person's direct or indirect beneficial ownership, computed as of the last day of the month, increases or decreases by more than five percent of the class of equity securities. Once an amendment has been filed reflecting beneficial ownership of five percent or less of the class of securities, no additional filings are required by this paragraph (c).

(d) Any person relying on Rule 13d–1(c) and has filed its initial Schedule 13G (Rule 13d–102) pursuant to that paragraph shall, in addition to filing any amendments pursuant to Rule 13d–2(b), file an amendment on Schedule 13G (Rule 13d–102) promptly upon acquiring, directly or indirectly, greater than 10 percent of a class of equity securities specified in Rule 13d–1(d), and thereafter promptly upon increasing or decreasing its beneficial ownership by more than five percent of the class of equity securities. Once an amendment has been filed reflecting beneficial ownership of five percent or less of the class of securities, no additional filings are required by this paragraph (d).

(e) The first electronic amendment to a paper format Schedule 13D or Schedule 13G shall restate the entire text of the Schedule 13D or 13G, but previously filed paper exhibits to such Schedules are not required to be restated electronically. See Rule 102 of Regulation S–T regarding amendments to exhibits previously filed in paper format. Notwithstanding the foregoing, if the sole purpose of filing the first electronic Schedule 13D or 13G amendment is to report a change in beneficial ownership that would terminate the filer's obligation to report, the amendment need not include a restatement of the entire text of the Schedule being amended.

NOTE TO RULE 13d–2: For persons filing a short-form statement pursuant to Rule 13d–1(b) or (c), see also Rules 13d–1(e), (f), and (g).

Rule 13d–3. Determination of beneficial owner

(a) For the purposes of section 13(d) and 13(g) of the Act a beneficial owner of a security includes any person who, directly or indirectly, through any contract, arrangement, understanding, relationship, or otherwise has or shares:

(1) Voting power which includes the power to vote, or to direct the voting of, such security; and/or,

(2) Investment power which includes the power to dispose, or to direct the disposition, of such security.

(b) Any person who, directly or indirectly, creates or uses a trust, proxy, power of attorney, pooling arrangement or any other contract, arrangement, or device with the purpose or effect of divesting such person of beneficial ownership of a security or preventing the vesting of such beneficial ownership as part of a plan or scheme to evade the reporting requirements of section 13(d) or 13(g) of the Act shall be deemed for purposes of such section to be the beneficial owner of such security.

(c) All securities of the same class beneficially owned by a person, regardless of the form which such beneficial ownership takes, shall be aggregated in calculating the number of shares beneficially owned by such person.

(d) Notwithstanding the provisions of paragraphs (a) and (c) of this rule:

(1)(i) A person shall be deemed to be the beneficial owner of a security, subject to the provisions of paragraph (b) of this rule, if that person has the right to acquire beneficial ownership of such security, as defined in Rule 13d–3(a) within sixty days, including but not limited to any right to acquire: (A) through the exercise of any option, warrant or right; (B) through the conversion of a security; (C) pursuant to the power to revoke a trust, discretionary account, or similar arrangement; or (D) pursuant to the automatic termination of a trust, discretionary account or similar arrangement; provided, however, any person who acquires a security or power specified in paragraphs (d)(1)(i) (A), (B) or (C), of this rule, with the purpose or effect of changing or influencing the control of the issuer, or in connection with or as a participant in any transaction having such purpose or effect, immediately upon such acquisition shall be deemed to be the beneficial owner of the securities which may be acquired through the exercise or conversion of such security or power. Any securities not outstanding which are subject to such options, warrants, rights or conversion privileges shall be deemed to be outstanding for the purpose of computing the percentage of outstanding securities of the class owned by such person but shall not be deemed to be outstanding for the purpose of computing the percentage of the class by any other person.

(ii) Paragraph (d)(1)(i) of this rule remains applicable for the purpose of determining the obligation to file with respect to the underlying security even though the option, warrant, right or convertible security is of a class of equity security, as defined in Rule 13d–1(i), and may therefore give rise to a separate obligation to file.

(2) A member of a national securities exchange shall not be deemed to be a beneficial owner of securities held directly or indirectly by it on behalf of another person solely because such member is the record holder of such securities and, pursuant to the rules of such exchange, may direct the vote of such securities, without instruction, on other than contested matters or matters that may affect substantially the rights or privileges of the holders of the securities to be voted, but is otherwise precluded by the rules of such exchange from voting without instruction.

(3) A person who in the ordinary course of his business is a pledgee of securities under a written pledge agreement shall not be deemed to be the beneficial owner of such pledged securities until the pledgee has taken all formal steps necessary which are required to declare a default and determines that the power to vote or to direct the vote or to dispose or to direct the disposition of such pledged securities will be exercised, provided that:

(i) The pledgee agreement is bona fide and was not entered into with the purpose nor with the effect of changing or influencing the control of the issuer, nor in connection with any transaction having such purpose or effect, including any transaction subject to Rule 13d–3(b);

(ii) The pledgee is a person specified in Rule 13d–1(b)(ii), including persons meeting the conditions set forth in paragraph (G) thereof; and

(iii) The pledgee agreement, prior to default, does not grant to the pledgee:

(A) The power to vote or to direct the vote of the pledged securities; or

(B) The power to dispose or direct the disposition of the pledged securities, other than the grant of such power(s) pursuant to a pledge agreement under which credit is extended subject to Regulation T and in which the pledgee is a broker or dealer registered under section 15 of the Act.

(4) A person engaged in business as an underwriter of securities who acquires securities through his participation in good faith in a firm commitment underwriting registered under the Securities Act of 1933 shall not be deemed to be the beneficial owner of such securities until the expiration of forty days after the date of such acquisition.

Rule 13d–4. Disclaimer of beneficial ownership

Any person may expressly declare in any statement filed that the filing of such statement shall not be construed as an admission that such person is, for the purposes of section 13(d) or 13(g) of the Act, the beneficial owner of any securities covered by the statement.

Rule 13d–5. Acquisition of securities

(a) A person who becomes a beneficial owner of securities shall be deemed to have acquired such securities for purposes of section 13(d)(1) of the Act, whether such acquisition was through purchase or otherwise. However, executors or administrators of a decedent's estate generally will be presumed not to have acquired beneficial ownership of the securities in the decedent's estate until such time as such executors or administrators are qualified under local law to perform their duties.

(b)(1) When two or more persons agree to act together for the purpose of acquiring, holding, voting or disposing of equity securities of an issuer, the group formed thereby shall be deemed to have acquired beneficial ownership, for purposes of Sections 13(d) and 13(g) of the Act, as of the date of such agreement, of all equity securities of that issuer beneficially owned by any such persons.

(2) Notwithstanding the previous paragraph, a group shall be deemed not to have acquired any equity securities beneficially owned by the other members of the group solely by virtue of their concerted actions relating to the purchase of equity securities directly from an issuer in a transaction not involving a public offering, *Provided*, That:

(i) All the members of the group are persons specified in Rule 13d–1(b)(1)(ii);

(ii) The purchase is in the ordinary course of each member's business and not with the purpose nor with the effect of changing or influencing control of the issuer, nor in connection with or as a participant in any transaction having such purpose or effect, including any transaction subject to Rule 13d–3(b);

(iii) There is no agreement among, or between any members of the group to act together with respect to the issuer or its securities except for the purpose of facilitating the specific purchase involved; and

(iv) The only actions among or between any members of the group with respect to the issuer or its securities subsequent to the closing date of the non-public offering are those which are necessary to conclude ministerial matters directly related to the completion of the offer or sale of the securities.

Rule 13d–6. Exemption of certain acquisitions

The acquisition of securities of an issuer by a person who, prior to such acquisition, was a beneficial owner of more than five percent of the outstanding securities of the same class as those acquired shall be exempt from section 13(d) of the act, *Provided*, That:

(a) The acquisition is made pursuant to preemptive subscription rights in an offering made to all holders of securities of the class to which the preemptive subscription rights pertain;

(b) Such person does not acquire additional securities except through the exercise of his pro rata share of the preemptive subscription rights; and

(c) The acquisition is duly reported, if required, pursuant to section 16(a) of the Act and the rules and regulations thereunder.

Rule 13d–7. Dissemination

One copy of the Schedule filed pursuant to Rules 13d–1 and 13d–2 shall be sent to the issuer of the security at its principal executive office, by registered or certified mail. A copy of Schedules filed pursuant to Rules 13d–1(a) and 13d–2(a) shall also be sent to each national securities exchange where the security is traded.

Rule 13d–101. Schedule 13D—Information to be included in statements filed pursuant to Rule 13d–1(a) and Amendments thereto filed pursuant to Rule 13d–2(a)

SCHEDULE 13D

Under the Securities Exchange Act of 1934

(Amendment No. ______)*

______

(Name of Issuer)

______

(Title of Class of Securities)

______

(CUSIP Number)

______

(Name, Address and Telephone Number of Person Authorized to Receive Notices and Communications)

______

(Date of Event which Requires Filing of this Statement)

If the filing person has previously filed a statement on Schedule 13G to report the acquisition that is the subject of this Schedule 13D, and is filing this schedule because of Rules 13d–1(e), 13d–1(f) or 13d–1(g), check the following box.

NOTE: Schedules filed in paper format shall include a signed original and five copies of the schedule, including all exhibits. See Rule 13d–7 for other parties to whom copies are to be sent.

CUSIP No. ______

(1) Names of Reporting Persons.	
(2) Check the Appropriate Box if a Member of a Group (See Instructions)	(a) ______ (b) ______
(3) SEC Use Only	
(4) Source of Funds (See Instructions)	
(5) Check if Disclosure of Legal Proceedings is Required Pursuant to Items 2(d) or 2(e)	
(6) Citizenship or Place of Organization	
Number of Shares Beneficially Owned by Each Reporting Person With	
(7) Sole Voting Power	
(8) Shared Voting Power	
(9) Sole Dispositive Power	
(10) Shared Dispositive Power	
(11) Aggregate Amount Beneficially Owned by Each Reporting Person	
(12) Check if the Aggregate Amount in Row (11) Excludes Certain Shares (See Instructions)	
(13) Percent of Class Represented by Amount in Row (11)	
(14) Type of Reporting Person (See Instructions)	

* The remainder of this cover page shall be filled out for a reporting person's initial filing on this form with respect to the subject class of securities, and for any subsequent amendment containing information which would alter disclosures provided in a prior cover page.

The information required on the remainder of this cover page shall not be deemed to be "filed" for the purpose of Section 18 of the Securities Exchange Act of 1934 ("Act") or otherwise subject to the liabilities of that section of the Act but shall be subject to all other provisions of the Act (however, see the Notes).

Instructions for Cover Page

(1) *Names of Reporting Persons.* Furnish the full legal name of each person for whom the report is filed—i.e., each person required to sign the schedule itself—including each member of a group. Do not include the name of a person required to be identified in the report but who is not a reporting person.

(2) If any of the shares beneficially owned by a reporting person are held as a member of a group and the membership is expressly affirmed, please check row 2(a). If the reporting person disclaims membership in a group or describes a relationship with other person but does not affirm the existence of a group, please check row 2(b) (unless it is a joint filing pursuant to Rule 13d-1(k)(1) in which case it may not be necessary to check row 2(b)).

(3) The 3rd row is for SEC internal use; please leave blank.

(4) Classify the source of funds or other consideration used or to be used in making the purchases as required to be disclosed pursuant to Item 3 of Schedule 13D and insert the appropriate symbol (or symbols if more than one is necessary) in row (4):

Category of Source	Symbol
Subject Company (Company whose securities are being acquired)	SC
Bank	BK
Affiliate (of reporting person)	AF
Working Capital (of reporting person)	WC
Personal Funds (of reporting person)	PF
Other	OO

(5) If disclosure of legal proceedings or actions is required pursuant to either Items 2(d) or 2(e) of Schedule 13D, row 5 should be checked.

(6) *Citizenship or Place of Organization.* Furnish citizenship if the named reporting person is a natural person. Otherwise, furnish place of organization. (See Item 2 of Schedule 13D).

(7)–(11) [Reserved]

(12) Check if the aggregate amount reported as beneficially owned in row (11) does not include shares which the reporting person discloses in the report but as to which beneficial ownership is disclaimed pursuant to Rule 13d–4 under the Securities Exchange Act of 1934.

(13) *Aggregate Amount Beneficially Owned by Each Reporting Person, etc.* Rows (7) through (11), inclusive, and (13) are to be completed in accordance with the provisions of Item 5 of Schedule 13D. All percentages are to be rounded off to nearest tenth (one place after decimal point).

(14) *Type of Reporting Person.* Please classify each "reporting person" according to the following breakdown and place the appropriate symbol (or symbols, i.e., if more than one is applicable, insert all applicable symbols) on the form:

Category	Symbol
Broker Dealer	BD
Bank	BK
Insurance Company	IC
Investment Company	IV
Investment Adviser	IA
Employee Benefit Plan or Endowment Fund	EP
Parent Holding Company/Control Person	HC
Savings Association	SA
Church Plan	CP
Corporation	CO
Partnership	PN
Individual	IN
Other	OO

NOTES: Attach as many copies of the second part of the cover page as are needed, one reporting person per page.

Filing persons may, in order to avoid unnecessary duplication, answer items on the schedules (Schedule 13D, 13G, or TO) by appropriate cross references to an item or items on the cover page(s). This approach may only be used where the cover page item or items provide all the disclosure required by the schedule item. Moreover, such a use of a cover page item will result in the item becoming a part of the schedule and accordingly being considered as "filed" for purposes of section 18 of the Securities Exchange Act or otherwise subject to the liabilities of that section of the Act.

Reporting persons may comply with their cover page filing requirements by filing either completed copies of the blank forms available from the Commission, printed or typed facsimiles, or computer printed facsimiles, provided the documents filed have identical formats to the forms prescribed in the Commission's regulations and meet existing Securities Exchange Act rules as to such matters as clarity and size (Securities Exchange Act Rule 12b–12).

SPECIAL INSTRUCTIONS FOR COMPLYING WITH SCHEDULE 13D

Under sections 13(d) and 23 of the Securities Exchange Act of 1934 and the rules and regulations thereunder, the Commission is authorized to solicit the information required to be supplied by this schedule by certain security holders of certain issuers.

Disclosure of the information specified in this schedule is mandatory. The information will be used for the primary purpose of determining and disclosing the holdings of certain beneficial owners of certain equity securities. This statement will be made a matter of public record. Therefore, any information given will be available for inspection by any member of the public.

Because of the public nature of the information, the Commission can use it for a variety of purposes, including referral to other governmental authorities or securities self-regulatory organizations for investigatory purposes or in connection with litigation involving the federal securities laws or other civil, criminal or regulatory statutes or provisions.

Failure to disclose the information requested by this schedule, may result in civil or criminal action against the persons involved for violation of the federal securities laws and rules promulgated thereunder.

General Instructions

A. The item number and captions of the items shall be included but the text of the items is to be omitted. The answers to the items shall be so prepared as to indicate clearly the coverage of the items without referring to the text of the items. Answer every item. If an item is inapplicable or the answer is in the negative, so state.

B. Information contained in exhibits to the statement may be incorporated by reference in answer or partial answer to any item or sub-item of the statement unless it would render such answer misleading, incomplete, unclear or confusing. Material incorporated by reference shall be clearly identified in the reference by page, paragraph, caption or otherwise. An express statement that the specified matter is incorporated by reference shall be made at the particular place in the statement where the information is required. A copy of any information or a copy of the pertinent pages of a document containing such information which is incorporated by reference shall be submitted with this statement as an exhibit and shall be deemed to be filed with the Commission for all purposes of the Act.

C. If the statement is filed by a general or limited partnership, syndicate, or other group, the information called for by Items 2–6, inclusive, shall be given with respect to (i) each partner of such general partnership; (ii) each partner who is denominated as a general partner or who functions as a general partner of such limited partnership; (iii) each member of such syndicate or group; and (iv) each person controlling such partner or member. If the statement is filed by a corporation or if a person referred to in (i), (ii), (iii) or (iv) of this Instruction is a corporation, the information called for by the above mentioned items shall be given with respect to (a) each executive officer and director of such corporation; (b) each person controlling such corporation; and (c) each executive officer and director of any corporation or other person ultimately in control of such corporation.

Item 1. Security and Issuer

State the title of the class of equity securities to which this statement relates and the name and address of the principal executive offices of the issuer of such securities.

Item 2. Identity and Background

If the person filing this statement or any person enumerated in Instruction C of this statement is a corporation, general partnership, limited partnership, syndicate or other group of persons, state its name, the state or other place of its organization, its principal business, the address of its principal business, the address of its principal office and the information required by (d) and (e) of this Item. If the person filing this statement or any person enumerated in Instruction C is a natural person, provide the information specified in (a) through (f) of this Item with respect to such person(s).

(a) Name;

(b) Residence or business address;

(c) Present principal occupation or employment and the name, principal business and address of any corporation or other organization in which such employment is conducted;

(d) Whether or not, during the last five years, such person has been convicted in a criminal proceeding (excluding traffic violations or similar misdemeanors) and, if so, give the dates, nature of conviction, name and location of court, any penalty imposed, or other disposition of the case;

(e) Whether or not, during the last five years, such person was a party to a civil proceeding of a judicial or administrative body of competent jurisdiction and as a result of such proceeding was or is subject to a judgment, decree or final order enjoining future violations of, or prohibiting or mandating activities subject to, federal or state securities laws or finding any violation with respect to such laws; and, if so, identify and describe such proceedings and summarize the terms of such judgment, decree or final order; and

(f) Citizenship.

Item 3. Source and Amount of Funds or Other Consideration

State the source and the amount of funds or other consideration used or to be used in making the purchases, and if any part of the purchase price is or will be represented by funds or other consideration borrowed or otherwise obtained for the purpose of acquiring, holding, trading or voting the securities, a description of the transaction and the names of the parties thereto. Where material, such information should also be provided with respect to prior acquisitions not previously reported pursuant to this regulation. If the source of all or any part of the funds is a loan made in the ordinary course of business by a bank, as defined in section 3(a)(6) of the Act, the name of the bank shall not be made available to the public if the person at the time of filing the statement so requests in writing and files such request, naming such bank, with the Secretary of the Commission. If the securities were acquired other than by purchase, describe the method of acquisition.

Item 4. Purpose of Transaction

State the purpose or purposes of the acquisition of securities of the issuer. Describe any plans or proposals which the reporting persons may have which relate to or would result in:

(a) The acquisition by any person of additional securities of the issuer, or the disposition of securities of the issuer;

(b) An extraordinary corporate transaction, such as a merger, reorganization or liquidation, involving the issuer or any of its subsidiaries;

(c) A sale or transfer of a material amount of assets of the issuer or of any of its subsidiaries;

(d) Any change in the present board of directors or management of the issuer, including any plans or proposals to change the number or term of directors or to fill any existing vacancies on the board;

(e) Any material change in the present capitalization or dividend policy of the issuer;

(f) Any other material change in the issuer's business or corporate structure, including but not limited to, if the issuer is a registered closed-end investment company, any plans or proposals to make any changes in its investment policy for which a vote is required by section 13 of the Investment Company Act of 1940;

(g) Changes in the issuer's charter, bylaws or instruments corresponding thereto or other actions which may impede the acquisition of control of the issuer by any person;

(h) Causing a class of securities of the issuer to be delisted from a national securities exchange or to cease to be authorized to be quoted in an inter-dealer quotation system of a registered national securities association;

(i) A class of equity securities of the issuer becoming eligible for termination of registration pursuant to Section 12(g)(4) of the Act; or

(j) Any action similar to any of those enumerated above.

Item 5. Interest in Securities of the Issuer

(a) State the aggregate number and percentage of the class of securities identified pursuant to Item 1 (which may be based on the number of securities outstanding as contained in the most recently available filing with the Commission by the issuer unless the filing person has reason to believe such information is not current) beneficially owned (identifying those shares which there is a right to acquire) by each person named in Item 2. The above mentioned information should also be furnished with respect to persons who, together with any of the persons named in Item 2, comprise a group within the meaning of section 13(d)(3) of the Act;

(b) For each person named in response to paragraph (a), indicate the number of shares as to which there is sole power to vote or to direct the vote, shared power to vote or to direct the vote, sole power to dispose or to direct the disposition. Provide the applicable information required by Item 2 with respect to each person with whom the power to vote or to direct the vote or to dispose or direct the disposition is shared;

(c) Describe any transactions in the class of securities reported on that were effected during the past sixty days or since the most recent filing on Schedule 13D (Rule 13d–101), whichever is less, by the persons named in response to paragraph (a).

Instruction. The description of a transaction required by Item 5(c) shall include, but not necessarily be limited to: (1) the identity of the person covered by Item 5(c) who effected the transaction; (2) the date of the transaction; (3) the amount of securities involved; (4) the price per share or unit; and (5) where and how the transaction was effected.

(d) If any other person is known to have the right to receive or the power to direct the receipt of dividends from, or the proceeds from the sale of, such securities, a statement to that effect should be included in response to this Item and, if such interest relates to more than five percent of the class, such person should be identified. A listing of the shareholders of an investment company registered under the Investment Company Act of 1940 or the beneficiaries of an employee benefit plan, pension fund or endowment fund is not required.

(e) If applicable, state the date on which the reporting person ceased to be the beneficial owner of more than five percent of the class of securities.

Instruction. For computations regarding securities which represent a right to acquire an underlying security, see Rule 13d–3(d)(1) and the note thereto.

Item 6. Contracts, Arrangements, Understandings or Relationships with Respect to Securities of the Issuer

Describe any contracts, arrangements, understandings or relationships (legal or otherwise) among the persons named in Item 2 and between such persons and any person with respect to any securities of the issuer, including but not limited to transfer or voting of any of the securities, finder's fees, joint ventures, loan or option arrangements, puts or calls, guarantees of profits, division of profits or loss, or the giving or withholding of proxies, naming the persons with whom such contracts, arrangements, understandings or relationships have been entered into. Include such information for any of the securities that are pledged or otherwise subject to a contingency the occurrence of which would give another person voting power or investment power over such securities except that disclosure of standard default and similar provisions contained in loan agreements need not be included.

Item 7. Material to Be Filed as Exhibits

The following shall be filed as exhibits: Copies of written agreements relating to the filing of joint acquisition statements as required by Rule 13d–1(k) and copies of all written agreements, contracts, arrangements, understandings, plans, or proposals relating to: (1) The borrowing of funds to finance the acquisition as disclosed in Item 3; (2) the acquisition of issuer control, liquidation, sale of assets, merger, or change in business or corporate structure, or any other matter as disclosed in Item 4; and (3) the transfer or voting of the securities, finder's fees, joint ventures, options, puts, calls, guarantees of loans, guarantees against loss or of profit, or the giving or withholding of any proxy as disclosed in Item 6.

Signature. After reasonable inquiry and to the best of my knowledge and belief, I certify that the information set forth in this statement is true, complete and correct.

____
(Date)

____
(Signature)

____
(Name/Title)

The original statement shall be signed by each person on whose behalf the statement is filed or his authorized representative. If the statement is signed on behalf of a person by his authorized representative (other than an executive officer or general partner of the filing person), evidence of the representative's authority to sign on behalf of such person shall be filed with the statement: *Provided, however,* That a power of attorney for this purpose which is already on file with the Commission may be incorporated by reference. The name of any title of each person who signs the statement shall be typed or printed beneath his signature.

ATTENTION: Intentional misstatements or omissions of fact constitute Federal criminal violations (See 18 U.S.C. 1001). Rule 13d-102 Schedule 13G Information to be included in statements filed pursuant to Rule 13d–1(b) and amendments thereto filed pursuant to Rule 13d–2(b).

Rule 13d–102. Schedule 13G. Information to be included in statements filed pursuant to Rule 13d–1(b), (c) and (d) and Amendments thereto filed pursuant to Rule 13d–2

SCHEDULE 13G

Under the Securities Exchange Act of 1934

(Amendment No.______)*

____
(Name of Issuer)

____
(Title of Class of Securities)

____
(CUSIP Number)

____
(Date of Event Which Requires Filing of this Statement)

* The remainder of this cover page shall be filled out for a reporting person's initial filing on this form with respect to the subject class of securities, and for any subsequent amendment containing information which would alter the disclosures provided in a prior page.

Check the appropriate box to designate the rule pursuant to which this Schedule is filed:

[ ] Rule 13d–1(b)

[ ] Rule 13d–1(c)

[ ] Rule 13d–1(d)

Check the following box if a fee is being paid with this statement. (A fee is not required only if the filing person: (1) has a previous statement on file reporting beneficial ownership of more than five percent of the class of securities described in Item 1; and (2) has filed no amendment subsequent thereto reporting beneficial ownership of five percent or less of such class.) (See Rule 13d–7.)

❑

CUSIP No. ______

(1)	Names of Reporting Persons.	
(2)	Check the Appropriate Box if a Member of a Group (See Instructions)	(a) (b)
(3)	SEC Use Only	
(4)	Citizenship or Place of Organization	
Number of Shares Beneficially Owned by Each Reporting Person With	(5) Sole Voting Power	
	(6) Shared Voting Power	
	(7) Sole Dispositive Power	
	(8) Shared Dispositive Power	
(9)	Aggregate Amount Beneficially Owned by Each Reporting Person	
(10)	Check if the Aggregate Amount in Row (9) Excludes Certain Shares (See Instructions)	
(11)	Percent of Class Represented by Amount in Row (9)	
(12)	Type of Reporting Person (See Instructions)	

Instructions for Cover Page

(1) *Names of Reporting Persons.* Furnish the full legal name of each person for whom the report is

The information required in the remainder of this cover page shall not be deemed to be "filed" for the purpose of Section 18 of the Securities Exchange Act of 1934 ("Act") or otherwise subject to the liabilities of that section of the Act but shall be subject to all other provisions of the Act (however, see Notes).

filed—i.e., each person required to sign the schedule itself—including each member of a group. Do not include the name of a person required to be identified in the report but who is not a reporting person.

(2) If any of the shares beneficially owned by a reporting person are held as a member of a group and that membership is expressly affirmed, please check row 2(a). If the reporting person disclaims membership in a group or describes a relationship with other person but does not affirm the existence of a group, please check row 2(b) [unless it is a joint filing pursuant to Rule 13d–1(k)(1) in which case it may not be necessary to check row 2(b)].

(3) The third row is for SEC internal use; please leave blank.

(4) *Citizenship or Place of Organization.* Furnish citizenship if the named reporting person is a natural person. Otherwise, furnish place of organization.

(5)–(9), (11) *Aggregate Amount Beneficially Owned By Each Reporting Person, etc.* Rows (5) through (9) inclusive, and (11) are to be completed in accordance with the provisions of Item 4 of Schedule 13G. All percentages are to be rounded off to the nearest tenth (one place after decimal point).

(10) Check if the aggregate amount reported as beneficially owned in row (9) does not include shares as to which beneficial ownership is disclaimed pursuant to Rule 13d–4 under the Securities Exchange Act of 1934.

(12) *Type of Reporting Person.* Please classify each "reporting person" according to the following breakdown (see Item 3 of Schedule 13G) and place the appropriate Symbol on the form:

Category	Symbol
Broker Dealer	BD
Bank	BK
Insurance Company	IC
Investment Company	IV
Investment Adviser	IA
Employee Benefit Plan or Endowment Fund	EP
Parent Holding Company/Control Person	HC
Savings Association	SA
Church Plan	CP
Corporation	CO
Partnership	PN
Individual	IN
Non–U.S. Institution	FI
Other	OO

NOTES: Attach as many copies of the second part of the cover page as are needed, one reporting person per page.

Filing persons may, in order to avoid unnecessary duplication, answer items on the schedules (Schedule 13D, 13G or TO) by appropriate cross references to an item or items on the cover page(s). This approach may only be used where the cover page item or items provide all the disclosure required by the schedule item. Moreover, such a use of a cover page item will result in the item becoming a part of the schedule and accordingly being considered as "filed" for purposes of Section 18 of the Securities Exchange Act or otherwise subject to the liabilities of that section of the Act.

Reporting persons may comply with their cover page filing requirements by filing either completed copies of the blank forms available from the Commission, printed or typed facsimiles, or computer printed facsimiles, provided the documents filed have identical formats to the forms prescribed in the Commission's regulations and meet existing Securities Exchange Act rules as to such matters as clarity and size (Securities Exchange Act Rule 12b–12).

SPECIAL INSTRUCTIONS FOR COMPLYING WITH SCHEDULE 13G

Under Sections 13(d), 13(g) and 23 of the Securities Exchange Act of 1934 and the rules and regulations thereunder, the Commission is authorized to solicit the information required to be supplied by this schedule by certain security holders of certain issuers.

Disclosure of the information specified in this schedule is mandatory. The information will be used for the primary purpose of determining and disclosing the holdings of certain beneficial owners of certain equity securities. This statement will be made a matter of public record. Therefore, any information given will be available for inspection by any member of the public.

Because of the public nature of the information, the Commission can use it for a variety of purposes, including referral to other governmental authorities or securities self-regulatory organizations for investigatory purposes or in connection with litigation involving the federal securities laws or other civil, criminal or regulatory statutes or provisions.

Failure to disclose the information requested by this schedule may result in civil or criminal action against the persons involved for violation of the Federal securities laws and rules promulgated thereunder.

General Instructions

A. Statements filed pursuant to Rule 13d–1(b) containing the information required by this schedule shall be filed not later than February 14 following the calendar year covered by the statement or within the time specified in Rules 13d–1(b)(2) and 13d–2(c). Statements filed pursuant to Rule 13d–1(c) shall be filed within the time specified in Rules 13d–1(c), 13d–2(b) and 13d–2(d). Statements filed pursuant to Rule 13d–1(d) shall be filed not later than February 14 following the calendar year covered by the statement pursuant to Rules 13d–1(d) and 13d–2(b).

B. Information contained in a form which is required to be filed by rules under Section 13(f) [15 USC 78m(f)] for the same calendar year as that covered by a statement on this Schedule may be incorporated by reference in response to any of the items of this Schedule. If such information is incorporated by reference in this Schedule, copies of the relevant pages of such form shall be filed as an exhibit to this Schedule.

C. The item numbers and captions of the items shall be included but the text of the items is to be omitted. The answers to the items shall be so prepared as to indicate clearly the coverage of the items without referring to the text of the items. Answer every item. If an item is inapplicable or the answer is in the negative, so state.

Item 1(a). Name of Issuer

______

Item 1(b). Address of Issuer's Principal Executive Offices

______

2(a). Name of Person Filing

______

2(b). Address of Principal Business Office or, if None, Residence

______

2(c). Citizenship

______

2(d). Title of Class of Securities

______

2(e). CUSIP No.

______

Item 3. If This Statement is Filed Pursuant to Rules 13d–1(b) or 13d–2(b) or (c), Check Whether the Person Filing is a:

(a) [ ] Broker or dealer registered under section 15 of the Act (15 U.S.C. 78o);

(b) [ ] Bank as defined in section 3(a)(6) of the Act (15 U.S.C. 78c);

(c) [ ] Insurance company as defined in section 3(a)(19) of the Act (15 U.S.C. 78c);

(d) [ ] Investment company registered under section 8 of the Investment Company Act of 1940 (15 U.S.C. 80a–8);

(e) [ ] An investment adviser in accordance with Rule 13d–1(b)(1)(ii)(E);

(f) [ ] An employee benefit plan or endowment fund in accordance with Rule 13d–1(b)(1)(ii)(F);

(g) [ ] A parent holding company or control person in accordance with Rule 13d–1(b)(1)(ii)(G);

(h) [ ] A savings associations as defined in Section 3(b) of the Federal Deposit Insurance Act (12 U.S.C. 1813);

(i) [ ] A church plan that is excluded from the definition of an investment company under section 3(c)(14) of the Investment Company Act of 1940 (15 U.S.C. 80a–3);

(j) [ ] A non-U.S. institution in accordance with Rule 13d–1(b)(1)(ii)(J);

(k) [ ] Group, in accordance with Rule 13d–1(b)(1)(ii)(K).

If filing as a non-U.S. institution in accordance with Rule 13d–1(b)(1)(ii)(J), please specify the type of institution: ______

Item 4. Ownership

Provide the following information regarding the aggregate number and percentage of the class of securities of the issuer identified in Item 1.

(a) Amount beneficially owned: ______.

(b) Percent of class: ______.

(c) Number of shares as to which the person has:

(i) Sole power to vote or to direct the vote ______.

(ii) Shared power to vote or to direct the vote ______.

(iii) Sole power to dispose or to direct the disposition of ______.

(iv) Shared power to dispose or to direct the disposition of ______.

Instruction. For computations regarding securities which represent a right to acquire an underlying security *see* Rule 13d–3(d)(1).

Item 5. Ownership of Five Percent or Less of a Class

If this statement is being filed to report the fact that as of the date hereof the reporting person has ceased to be the beneficial owner of more than five percent of the class of securities, check the following [].

Instruction. Dissolution of a group requires a response to this item.

Item 6. Ownership of More Than Five Percent on Behalf of Another Person

If any other person is known to have the right to receive or the power to direct the receipt of dividends from, or the proceeds from the sale of, such securities, a statement to that effect should be included in response to this item and, if such interest relates to more than five percent of the class, such person should be identified. A listing of the shareholders of an investment company registered under the Investment Company Act of 1940 or the beneficiaries of employee benefit plan, pension fund or endowment fund is not required.

Item 7. Identification and Classification of the Subsidiary Which Acquired the Security Being Reported on by the Parent Holding Company or Control Person

If a parent holding company or control person has filed this schedule pursuant to Rule 13d–1(b)(1)(ii)(G), so indicate under Item 3(g) and attach an exhibit stating the identity and the Item 3 classification of the relevant subsidiary. If a parent holding company or control person has filed this schedule pursuant to Rule 13d–1(c) or Rule 13d–1(d), attach an exhibit stating the identification of the relevant subsidiary.

Item 8. Identification and Classification of Members of the Group

If a group has filed this schedule pursuant to Rule 13d–1(b)(1)(ii)(J), so indicate under Item 3(j) and attach an exhibit stating the identity and Item 3 classification of each member of the group. If a group has filed this schedule pursuant to Rule 13d–1(c) or Rule 13d–1(d), attach an exhibit stating the identity of each member of the group.

Item 9. Notice of Dissolution of Group

Notice of dissolution of a group may be furnished as an exhibit stating the date of the dissolution and that all further filings with respect to transactions in the security reported on will be filed, if required, by members of the group, in their individual capacity. See Item 5.

Item 10. Certifications

(a) The following certification shall be included if the statement is filed pursuant to Rule13d–1(b):

By signing below I certify that, to the best of my knowledge and belief, the securities referred to above were acquired and are held in the ordinary course of business and were not acquired and are not held for the purpose of or with the effect of changing or influencing the control of the issuer of the securities and were not acquired and are not held in connection with or as a participant in any transaction having that purpose or effect, other than activities solely in connection with a nomination under Rule 14a–11.

(b) The following certification shall be included if the statement is filed pursuant to Rule 13d–1(b)(1)(ii)(J), or if the statement is filed pursuant to Rule 13d–1(b)(1)(ii)(K) and a member of the group is a non-U.S. institution eligible to file pursuant to Rule 13d–1(b)(1)(ii)(J):

By signing below I certify that, to the best of my knowledge and belief, the foreign regulatory scheme applicable to [insert particular category of institutional investor] is substantially comparable to the regulatory scheme applicable to the functionally equivalent U.S. institution(s). I also undertake to furnish to the Commission staff, upon request, information that would otherwise be disclosed in a Schedule 13D.

(c) The following certification shall be included if the statement is filed pursuant to Rule 13d–1(c):

By signing below I certify that, to the best of my knowledge and belief, the securities referred to above were not acquired and are not held for the purpose of or with the effect of changing or influencing the control of the issuer of the securities and were not acquired and are not held in connection with or as a participant in any transaction having that purpose or effect, other than activities solely in connection with a nomination under Rule 14a–11.

Signature. After reasonable inquiry and to the best of my knowledge and belief, I certify that the information set forth in this statement is true, complete and correct.

Dated: _______

____
Signature.

____
Name/Title.

The original statement shall be signed by each person on whose behalf the statement is filed or his authorized representative. If the statement is signed on behalf of a person by his authorized representative other than an executive officer or general partner of the filing person, evidence of the representative's authority to sign on behalf of such person shall be filed with the statement: *Provided, however,* That a power of attorney for this purpose which is already on file with the Commission may be incorporated by reference. The name and any title of each person who signs the statement shall be typed or printed beneath his signature.

* * *

NOTE: Schedules filed in paper format shall include a signed original and five copies of the schedule, including all exhibits. See Rule 13d–7 for other parties for whom copies are to be sent.

ATTENTION: Intentional misstatements or omissions of fact constitute Federal criminal violations (See 18 U.S.C. 1001).

Rule 13e–1. Purchase of securities by the issuer during a third–party tender offer

An issuer that has received notice that it is the subject of a tender offer made under Section 14(d)(1) of the Act (15 U.S.C. 78n), that has commenced under Rule 14d–2 must not purchase any of its equity securities during the tender offer unless the issuer first:

(a) Files a statement with the Commission containing the following information:

(1) The title and number of securities to be purchased;

(2) The names of the persons or classes of persons from whom the issuer will purchase the securities;

(3) The name of any exchange, inter-dealer quotation system or any other market on or through which the securities will be purchased;

(4) The purpose of the purchase;

(5) Whether the issuer will retire the securities, hold the securities in its treasury, or dispose of the securities. If the issuer intends to dispose of the securities, describe how it intends to do so; and

(6) The source and amount of funds or other consideration to be used to make the purchase. If the issuer borrows any funds or other consideration to make the purchase or enters any agreement for the purpose of acquiring, holding, or trading the securities, describe the transaction and agreement and identify the parties; and

(b) Pays the fee required by Rule 0–11 when it files the initial statement.

(c) This section does not apply to periodic repurchases in connection with an employee benefit plan or other similar plan of the issuer so long as the purchases are made in the ordinary course and not in response to the tender offer.

Instruction to Rule 13e–1: File eight copies if paper filing is permitted.

Rule 13e–2. [Reserved]

Rule 13e–3. Going private transactions by certain issuers or their affiliates

(a) *Definitions.* Unless indicated otherwise or the context otherwise requires, all terms used in this rule and in Schedule 13E–3 shall have the same meaning as in the Act or elsewhere in the General Rules and Regulations thereunder. In addition, the following definitions apply:

(1) An *affiliate* of an issuer is a person that directly or indirectly through one or more intermediaries controls, is controlled by, or is under common control with such issuer. For the purposes of this rule only, a person who is not an affiliate of an issuer at the commencement of such person's tender offer for a class of equity securities of such issuer will not be deemed an affiliate of such issuer prior to the stated termination of such tender offer and any extensions thereof;

(2) The term *purchase* means any acquisition for value including, but not limited to, (i) any acquisition pursuant to the dissolution of an issuer subsequent to the sale or other disposition of substantially all the assets of such issuer to its affiliate, (ii) any acquisition pursuant to a merger, (iii) any acquisition of fractional interests in connection with a reverse stock split, and (iv) any acquisition subject to the control of an issuer or an affiliate of such issuer;

(3) A *Rule 13e–3 transaction* is any transaction or series of transactions involving one or more of the transactions described in paragraph (a)(3)(i) of this rule which has either a reasonable likelihood or a purpose of producing, either directly or indirectly, any of the effects described in paragraph (a)(3)(ii) of this rule;

(i) The transactions referred to in paragraph (a)(3) of this rule are:

(A) A purchase of any equity security by the issuer of such security or by an affiliate of such issuer;

(B) A tender offer for or request or invitation for tenders of any equity security made by the issuer of such class of securities or by an affiliate of such issuer; or

(C) A solicitation subject to Regulation 14A (Rules 14a–1 to 14b–1) of any proxy, consent or authorization of, or a distribution subject to Regulation 14C (Rules 14c–1 to 14c–101) of information statements to, any equity security holder by the issuer of the class of securities or by an affiliate of such issuer, in connection with: a merger, consolidation, reclassification, recapitalization, reorganization or similar corporate transaction of an issuer or between an issuer (or its subsidiaries) and its affiliate; a sale of substantially all the assets of an issuer to its affiliate or group of affiliates; or a reverse stock split of any class of equity securities of the issuer involving the purchase of fractional interests.

(ii) The effects referred to in paragraph (a)(3) of this rule are:

(A) Causing any class of equity securities of the issuer which is subject to section 12(g) or section 15(d) of the Act to become eligible for termination of registration under Rule 12g–4 or Rule 12h–6, or causing the reporting obligations with respect to such class to become eligible for termination under Rule 12h–6; or suspension under Rule 12h–3 or section 15(d); or

(B) Causing any class of equity securities of the issuer which is either listed on a national securities exchange or authorized to be quoted in an inter-dealer quotation system of a registered national securities association to be neither listed on any national securities exchange nor authorized to be quoted on an inter-dealer quotation system of any registered national securities association.

(4) An *unaffiliated security holder* is any security holder of an equity security subject to a Rule 13e–3 transaction who is not an affiliate of the issuer of such security.

(b) *Application of Rule to an Issuer (or an Affiliate of Such Issuer) Subject to Section 12 of the Act.*

(1) It shall be a fraudulent, deceptive or manipulative act or practice, in connection with a Rule 13e–3 transaction, for an issuer which has a class of equity securities registered pursuant to section 12 of the Act or which is a closed-end investment company registered under the Investment Company Act of 1940, or an affiliate of such issuer, directly or indirectly

(i) To employ any device, scheme or artifice to defraud any person;

(ii) To make any untrue statement of a material fact or to omit to state a material fact necessary in order to make the statements made, in light of the circumstances under which they were made, not misleading; or

(iii) To engage in any act, practice or course of business which operates or would operate as a fraud or deceit upon any person.

(2) As a means reasonably designed to prevent fraudulent, deceptive or manipulative acts or practices in connection with any Rule 13e–3 transaction, it shall be unlawful for an issuer which has a class of equity securities registered pursuant to Section 12 of the Act, or an affiliate of such issuer, to engage, directly or indirectly, in a Rule 13e–3 transaction unless:

(i) Such issuer or affiliate complies with the requirements of paragraphs (d), (e) and (f) of this rule; and

(ii) The Rule 13e–3 transaction is not in violation of paragraph (b)(1) of this rule.

(c) *Application of Rule to an Issuer (or an Affiliate of Such Issuer) Subject to Section 15(d) of the Act.*

(1) It shall be unlawful as a fraudulent, deceptive or manipulative act or practice for an issuer which is required to file periodic reports pursuant to Section 15(d) of the Act, or an affiliate of such issuer, to engage, directly or indirectly, in a Rule 13e–3 transaction unless such issuer or affiliate complies with the requirements of paragraphs (d), (e) and (f) of this rule.

(2) An issuer or affiliate which is subject to paragraph (c)(1) of this rule and which is soliciting proxies or distributing information statements in connection with a transaction described in paragraph (a)(3)(i)(A) of this rule may elect to use the timing procedures for conducting a solicitation subject to Regulation 14A (Rules 14a–1 to 14b–1) or a distribution subject to Regulation 14C (Rules 14c–1 to 14c–101) in complying with paragraphs (d), (e) and (f) of this rule, provided, that if an election is made, such solicitation or distribution is conducted in accordance with the requirements of the respective regulations, including the filing of preliminary copies of soliciting materials or an information statement at the time specified in Regulation 14A or 14C, respectively.

(d) *Material Required to Be Filed.* The issuer or affiliate engaging in a Rule 13e–3 transaction must file with the Commission:

(1) A Schedule 13E–3 (Rule 13e–100), including all exhibits;

(2) An amendment to Schedule 13E–3 reporting promptly any material changes in the information set forth in the schedule previously filed; and

(3) A final amendment to Schedule 13E–3 reporting promptly the results of the Rule 13e–3 transaction.

(e) *Disclosure of Information to Security Holders.*

(1) In addition to disclosing the information required by any other applicable rule or regulation under the federal securities laws, the issuer or affiliate engaging in a Rule 13e–3 transaction must

disclose to security holders of the class that is the subject of the transaction, as specified in paragraph (f) of this rule, the following:

(i) The information required by Item 1 of Schedule 13E–3 (Rule 13e–100) (Summary Term Sheet);

(ii) The information required by Items 7, 8 and 9 of Schedule 13E–3, which must be prominently disclosed in a "Special Factors" section in the front of the disclosure document;

(iii) A prominent legend on the outside front cover page that indicates that neither the Securities and Exchange Commission nor any state securities commission has: approved or disapproved of the transaction; passed upon the merits or fairness of the transaction; or passed upon the adequacy or accuracy of the disclosure in the document. The legend also must make it clear that any representation to the contrary is a criminal offense;

(iv) The information concerning appraisal rights required by Item 1016 of Regulation M–A; and

(v) The information required by the remaining items of Schedule 13E–3, except for Item 1016 of Regulation M–A (exhibits), or a fair and adequate summary of the information.

Instructions to Paragraph (e)(1):

1. If the Rule 13e–3 transaction also is subject to Regulation 14A (Rules 14a–1 through 14b–2) or 14C (Rules 14c–1 through 14c–101), the registration provisions and rules of the Securities Act of 1933, Regulation 14D or Rule 13e–4, the information required by paragraph (e)(1) of this rule must be combined with the proxy statement, information statement, prospectus or tender offer material sent or given to security holders.

2. If the Rule 13e–3 transaction involves a registered securities offering, the legend required by Item 501(b)(7) of Regulation S–K must be combined with the legend required by paragraph (e)(1)(iii) of this rule.

3. The required legend must be written in clear, plain language.

(2) If there is any material change in the information previously disclosed to security holders, the issuer or affiliate must disclose the change promptly to security holders as specified in paragraph (f)(1)(iii) of this rule.

(f) *Dissemination of Information to Security Holders.*

(1) If the Rule 13e–3 transaction involves a purchase as described in paragraph (a)(3)(i)(A) of this rule or a vote, consent, authorization, or distribution of information statements as described in paragraph (a)(3)(i)(C) of this rule, the issuer or affiliate engaging in the Rule 13e–3 transaction shall:

(i) Provide the information required by paragraph (e) of this rule: (A) in accordance with the provisions of any applicable federal or state law, but in no event later than 20 days prior to: any such purchase; any such vote, consent or authorization; or with respect to the distribution of information statements, the meeting date, or if corporate action is to be taken by means of the written authorization or consent of security holders, the earliest date on which corporate action may be taken: *Provided, however,* That if the purchase subject to this rule is pursuant to a tender offer excepted from Rule 13e–4 by paragraph (g)(5) of Rule 13e–4, the information required by paragraph (e) of this rule shall be disseminated in accordance with paragraph (e) of Rule 13e–4 no later than 10 business days prior to any purchase pursuant to such tender offer, (B) to each person who is a record holder of a class of equity security subject to the Rule 13e–3 transaction as of a date not more than 20 days prior to the date of dissemination of such information.

(ii) If the issuer or affiliate knows that securities of the class of securities subject to the Rule 13e–3 transaction are held of record by a broker, dealer, bank or voting trustee or their nominees, such issuer or affiliate shall (unless Rule 14a–13(a) or 14c–7 is applicable) furnish the number of copies of the information required by paragraph (e) of this rule that are requested by such persons (pursuant to inquiries by or on behalf of the issuer or affiliate), instruct such persons to forward such information to the beneficial owners of such securities in a timely manner and undertake to pay the reasonable expenses incurred by such persons in forwarding such information; and

(iii) Promptly disseminate disclosure of material changes to the information required by paragraph (d) of this rule in a manner reasonably calculated to inform security holders.

(2) If the Rule 13e–3 transaction is a tender offer or a request or invitation for tenders of equity securities which is subject to Regulation 14D or Rule 13e–4, the tender offer containing the information required by paragraph (e) of this rule, and any material change with respect thereto, shall be published, sent or given in accordance with Regu-

lation 14D or Rule 13e–4, respectively, to security holders of the class of securities being sought by the issuer or affiliate.

(g) *Exceptions.* This rule shall not apply to:

(1) Any Rule 13e–3 transaction by or on behalf of a person which occurs within one year of the date of termination of a tender offer in which such person was the bidder and became an affiliate of the issuer as a result of such tender offers *Provided,* That the consideration offered to unaffiliated security holders in such Rule 13e–3 transaction is at least equal to the highest consideration offered during such tender offer and *Provided further,* That:

(i) If such tender offer was made for any or all securities of a class of the issuer;

(A) Such tender offer fully disclosed such person's intention to engage in a Rule 13e–3 transaction, the form and effect of such transaction and, to the extent known, the proposed terms thereof; and

(B) Such Rule 13e–3 transaction is substantially similar to that described in such tender offer; or

(ii) If such tender offer was made for less than all the securities of a class of the issuer:

(A) Such tender offer fully disclosed a plan of merger, a plan of liquidation or a similar binding agreement between such person and the issuer with respect to a Rule 13e–3 transaction; and

(B) Such Rule 13e–3 transaction occurs pursuant to the plan of merger, plan of liquidation or similar binding agreement disclosed in the bidder's tender offer.

(2) Any Rule 13e–3 transaction in which the security holders are offered or receive only an equity security *Provided,* That:

(i) Such equity security has substantially the same rights as the equity security which is the subject of the Rule 13e–3 transaction including, but not limited to, voting, dividends, redemption and liquidation rights except that this requirement shall be deemed to be satisfied if unaffiliated security holders are offered common stock;

(ii) Such equity security is registered pursuant to section 12 of the Act or reports are required to be filed by the issuer thereof pursuant to section 15(d) of the Act; and

(iii) If the security which is the subject of the Rule 13e–3 transaction was either listed on a national securities exchange or authorized to be quoted in an inter-dealer quotation system of a registered national securities association, such equity security is either listed on a national securities exchange or authorized to be quoted in an inter-dealer quotation system of a registered national securities association.

(3) [Reserved]

(4) Redemptions, calls or similar purchases of an equity security by an issuer pursuant to specific provisions set forth in the instrument(s) creating or governing that class of equity securities; or

(5) Any solicitation by an issuer with respect to a plan of reorganization under Chapter XI of the Bankruptcy Act, as amended, if made after the entry of an order approving such plan pursuant to section 1125(b) of that Act and after, or concurrently with, the transmittal of information concerning such plan as required by section 1125(b) of that Act.

(6) Any tender offer or business combination made in compliance with Rule 802 under the Securities Act of 1933, Rule 13e–4(h)(8) or Rule 14d–1(c) or any other kind of transaction that otherwise meets the conditions for reliance on the cross-border exemptions set forth in Rule 13e–4(h)(8), Rule 14d–1(c) or Rule 802 under the Securities Act of 1933 except for the fact that it is not technically subject to those rules.

Instruction to Rule 13e–3(g)(6). To the extent applicable, the acquiror must comply with the conditions set forth in Rule 802 under the Securities Act of 1933, and Rule 13e–4(h)(8) and Rule 14d–1(c). If the acquiror publishes or otherwise disseminates an informational document to the holders of the subject securities in connection with the transaction, the acquiror must furnish an English translation of that informational document, including any amendments thereto, to the Commission under cover of Form CB (17 CFR 239.800) by the first business day after publication or dissemination. If the acquiror is a foreign entity, it must also file a Form F–X (17 CFR 239.42) with the Commission at the same time as the submission of the Form CB to appoint an agent for service in the United States.

Rule 13e–4. Tender offers by issuers

(a) *Definitions.* Unless the context otherwise requires, all terms used in this rule and in Schedule TO shall have the same meaning as in the Act or elsewhere in the General Rules and Regulations thereunder. In addition, the following definitions shall apply:

(1) The term *issuer* means any issuer which has a class of equity security registered pursuant to section 12 of the Act, or which is required to file pe-

riodic reports pursuant to section 15(d) of the Act, or which is a closed-end investment company registered under the Investment Company Act of 1940.

(2) The term *issuer tender offer* refers to a tender offer for, or a request or invitation for tenders of, any class of equity security, made by the issuer of such class of equity security or by an affiliate of such issuer.

(3) As used in this rule and in Schedule TO (Rule 14d–100), the term *business day* means any day, other than Saturday, Sunday or a federal holiday, and shall consist of the time period from 12:01 a.m. through 12:00 midnight Eastern Time. In computing any time period under this rule or Schedule TO, the date of the event that begins the running of such time period shall be included *except that* if such event occurs on other than a business day such period shall begin to run on and shall include the first business day thereafter.

(4) The term *commencement* means 12:01 a.m. on the date that the issuer or affiliate has first published, sent or given the means to tender to security holders. For purposes of this rule, the means to tender includes the transmittal form or a statement regarding how the transmittal form may be obtained.

(5) The term *termination* means the date after which securities may not be tendered pursuant to an issuer tender offer.

(6) The term *security holders* means holders of record and beneficial owners of securities of the class of equity security which is the subject of an issuer tender offer.

(7) The term *security position listing* means, with respect to the securities of any issuer held by a registered clearing agency in the name of the clearing agency or its nominee, a list of those participants in the clearing agency on whose behalf the clearing agency holds the issuer's securities and of the participants' respective positions in such securities as of a specified date.

(b) *Filing, Disclosure and Dissemination.* As soon as practicable on the date of commencement of the issuer tender offer, the issuer or affiliate making the issuer tender offer must comply with:

(1) The filing requirements of paragraph (c)(2) of this rule;

(2) The disclosure requirements of paragraph (d)(1) of this rule; and

(3) The dissemination requirements of paragraph (e) of this rule.

(c) *Material Required to Be Filed.* The issuer or affiliate making the issuer tender offer must file with the Commission:

(1) All written communications made by the issuer or affiliate relating to the issuer tender offer, from and including the first public announcement, as soon as practicable on the date of the communication;

(2) A Schedule TO (Rule 14d–100), including all exhibits;

(3) An amendment to Schedule TO (Rule 14d–100) reporting promptly any material changes in the information set forth in the schedule previously filed; and

(4) A final amendment to Schedule TO (Rule 14d–100) reporting promptly the results of the issuer tender offer.

Instructions to Rule 13e–4(c):

1. Pre-commencement communications must be filed under cover of Schedule TO (Rule 14d–100) and the box on the cover page of the schedule must be marked.

2. Any communications made in connection with an exchange offer registered under the Securities Act of 1933 need only be filed under Rule 425 under the Securities Act of 1933 and will be deemed filed under this rule.

3. Each pre-commencement written communication must include a prominent legend in clear, plain language advising security holders to read the tender offer statement when it is available because it contains important information. The legend also must advise investors that they can get the tender offer statement and other filed documents for free at the Commission's web site and explain which documents are free from the issuer.

4. See Rules 135, 165, and 166 under the Securities Act of 1933 for pre-commencement communications made in connection with registered exchange offers.

5. "Public announcement" is any oral or written communication by the issuer, affiliate or any person authorized to act on their behalf that is reasonably designed to, or has the effect of, informing the public or security holders in general about the issuer tender offer.

(d) *Disclosure of Tender Offer Information to Security Holders.*

(1) The issuer or affiliate making the issuer tender offer must disclose, in a manner prescribed by paragraph (e)(1) of this rule, the following:

(i) The information required by Item 1 of Schedule TO (Rule 14d–100) (summary term sheet); and

(ii) The information required by the remaining items of Schedule TO for issuer tender offers, except for Item 12 (exhibits), or a fair and adequate summary of the information.

(2) If there are any material changes in the information previously disclosed to security holders, the issuer or affiliate must disclose the changes promptly to security holders in a manner specified in paragraph (e)(3) of this rule.

(3) If the issuer or affiliate disseminates the issuer tender offer by means of summary publication as described in paragraph (e)(1)(iii) of this rule, the summary advertisement must not include a transmittal letter that would permit security holders to tender securities sought in the offer and must disclose at least the following information:

(i) The identity of the issuer or affiliate making the issuer tender offer;

(ii) The information required by Items 1004(a)(1) and 1006(a) of Regulation M–A;

(iii) Instructions on how security holders can obtain promptly a copy of the statement required by paragraph (d)(1) of this rule, at the issuer or affiliate's expense; and

(iv) A statement that the information contained in the statement required by paragraph (d)(1) of this rule is incorporated by reference.

(e) *Dissemination of Tender Offers to Security Holders.* An issuer tender offer will be deemed to be published, sent or given to security holders if the issuer or affiliate making the issuer tender offer complies fully with one or more of the methods described in this rule.

(1) For issuer tender offers in which the consideration offered consists solely of cash and/or securities exempt from registration under section 3 of the Securities Act of 1933 (15 U.S.C. 77c):

(i) Dissemination of cash issuer tender offers by long-form publication: By making adequate publication of the information required by paragraph (d)(1) of this rule in a newspaper or newspapers, on the date of commencement of the issuer tender offer.

(ii) Dissemination of any issuer tender offer by use of stockholder and other lists:

(A) By mailing or otherwise furnishing promptly a statement containing the information required by paragraph (d)(1) of this rule to each security holder whose name appears on the most recent stockholder list of the issuer;

(B) By contacting each participant on the most recent security position listing of any clearing agency within the possession or access of the issuer or affiliate making the issuer tender offer, and making inquiry of each participant as to the approximate number of beneficial owners of the securities sought in the offer that are held by the participant;

(C) By furnishing to each participant a sufficient number of copies of the statement required by paragraph (d)(1) of this rule for transmittal to the beneficial owners; and

(D) By agreeing to reimburse each participant promptly for its reasonable expenses incurred in forwarding the statement to beneficial owners.

(iii) Dissemination of certain cash issuer tender offers by summary publication:

(A) If the issuer tender offer is not subject to Rule 13e–3, by making adequate publication of a summary advertisement containing the information required by paragraph (d)(3) of this rule in a newspaper or newspapers, on the date of commencement of the issuer tender offer; and

(B) By mailing or otherwise furnishing promptly the statement required by paragraph (d)(1) of this rule and a transmittal letter to any security holder who requests a copy of the statement or transmittal letter.

Instruction to Paragraph (e)(1): For purposes of paragraphs (e)(1)(i) and (e)(1)(iii) of this rule, adequate publication of the issuer tender offer may require publication in a newspaper with a national circulation, a newspaper with metropolitan or regional circulation, or a combination of the two, depending upon the facts and circumstances involved.

(2) For tender offers in which the consideration consists solely or partially of securities registered under the Securities Act of 1933, a registration statement containing all of the required information, including pricing information, has been filed and a preliminary prospectus or a prospectus that meets the requirements of Section 10(a) of the Securities Act (15 U.S.C. 77j(a)), including a letter of transmittal, is delivered to security holders. However, for going-private transactions (as defined by Rule 13e–3) and roll-up transactions (as described by Item 901 of Regulation S–K), a registration statement registering the securities to be offered must have become effective and only a prospectus that meets the requirements of Section 10(a)

of the Securities Act may be delivered to security holders on the date of commencement.

Instructions to Paragraph (e)(2):

1. If the prospectus is being delivered by mail, mailing on the date of commencement is sufficient.

2. A preliminary prospectus used under this rule may not omit information under Rules 430 or 430A under the Securities Act of 1933.

3. If a preliminary prospectus is used under this rule and the issuer must disseminate material changes, the tender offer must remain open for the period specified in paragraph (e)(3) of this rule.

4. If a preliminary prospectus is used under this rule, tenders may be requested in accordance with Rule 162(a) under the Securities Act of 1933.

(3) If a material change occurs in the information published, sent or given to security holders, the issuer or affiliate must disseminate promptly disclosure of the change in a manner reasonably calculated to inform security holders of the change. In a registered securities offer where the issuer or affiliate disseminates the preliminary prospectus as permitted by paragraph (e)(2) of this rule, the offer must remain open from the date that material changes to the tender offer materials are disseminated to security holders, as follows:

(i) Five business days for a prospectus supplement containing a material change other than price or share levels;

(ii) Ten business days for a prospectus supplement containing a change in price, the amount of securities sought, the dealer's soliciting fee, or other similarly significant change;

(iii) Ten business days for a prospectus supplement included as part of a post-effective amendment; and

(iv) Twenty business days for a revised prospectus when the initial prospectus was materially deficient.

(f) *Manner of Making Tender Offer*.

(1) The issuer tender offer, unless withdrawn, shall remain open until the expiration of:

(i) At least twenty business days from its commencement; and

(ii) At least ten business days from the date that notice of an increase or decrease in the percentage of the class of securities being sought or the consideration offered or the dealer's soliciting fee to be given is first published, sent or given to security holders. *Provided, however,* That, for purposes of this paragraph, the acceptance for payment by the issuer or affiliate of an additional amount of securities not to exceed two percent of the class of securities that is the subject of the tender offer shall not be deemed to be an increase. For purposes of this paragraph, the percentage of a class of securities shall be calculated in accordance with section 14(d)(3) of the Act.

(2) The issuer or affiliate making the issuer tender offer shall permit securities tendered pursuant to the issuer tender offer to be withdrawn:

(i) At any time during the period such issuer tender offer remains open; and

(ii) If not yet accepted for payment, after the expiration of forty business days from the commencement of the issuer tender offer.

(3) If the issuer or affiliate makes a tender offer for less than all of the outstanding equity securities of a class, and if a greater number of securities is tendered pursuant thereto than the issuer or affiliate is bound or willing to take up and pay for, the securities taken up and paid for shall be taken up and paid for as nearly as may be pro rata, disregarding fractions, according to the number of securities tendered by each security holder during the period such offer remains open; *Provided, however,* That this provision shall not prohibit the issuer or affiliate making the issuer tender offer from:

(i) Accepting all securities tendered by persons who own, beneficially or of record, an aggregate of not more than a specified number which is less than one hundred shares of such security and who tender all their securities, before prorating securities tendered by others; or

(ii) Accepting by lot securities tendered by security holders who tender all securities held by them and who, when tendering their securities, elect to have either all or none or at least a minimum amount or none accepted, if the issuer or affiliate first accepts all securities tendered by security holders who do not so elect;

(4) In the event the issuer or affiliate making the issuer tender increases the consideration offered after the issuer tender offer has commenced, such issuer or affiliate shall pay such increased consideration to all security holders whose tendered securities are accepted for payment by such issuer or affiliate.

(5) The issuer or affiliate making the tender offer shall either pay the consideration offered, or return the tendered securities, promptly after the termination or withdrawal of the tender offer.

(6) Until the expiration of at least ten business days after the date of termination of the issuer tender offer, neither the issuer nor any affiliate shall make any purchases, otherwise than pursuant to the tender offer, of:

(i) Any security which is the subject of the issuer tender offer, or any security of the same class and series, or any right to purchase any such securities; and

(ii) In the case of an issuer tender offer which is an exchange offer, any security being offered pursuant to such exchange offer, or any security of the same class and series, or any right to purchase any such security.

(7) The time periods for the minimum offering periods pursuant to this rule shall be computed on a concurrent as opposed to a consecutive basis.

(8) No issuer or affiliate shall make a tender offer unless:

(i) The tender offer is open to all security holders of the class of securities subject to the tender offer; and

(ii) The consideration paid to any security holder for securities tendered in the tender offer is the highest consideration paid to any other security holder for securities tendered in the tender offer.

(9) Paragraph (f)(8)(i) of this rule shall not:

(i) Affect dissemination under paragraph (e) of this rule; or

(ii) Prohibit an issuer or affiliate from making a tender offer excluding all security holders in a state where the issuer or affiliate is prohibited from making the tender offer by administrative or judicial action pursuant to a state statute after a good faith effort by the issuer or affiliate to comply with such statute.

(10) Paragraph (f)(8)(ii) of this rule shall not prohibit the offer of more than one type of consideration in a tender offer, provided that:

(i) Security holders are afforded equal right to elect among each of the types of consideration offered; and

(ii) The highest consideration of each type paid to any security holder is paid to any other security holder receiving that type of consideration.

(11) If the offer and sale of securities constituting consideration offered in an issuer tender offer is prohibited by the appropriate authority of a state after a good faith effort by the issuer or affiliate to register or qualify the offer and sale of such securities in such state:

(i) The issuer or affiliate may offer security holders in such state an alternative form of consideration; and

(ii) Paragraph (f)(10) of this rule shall not operate to require the issuer or affiliate to offer or pay the alternative form of consideration to security holders in any other state.

(12)(i) Paragraph (f)(8)(ii) of this rule shall not prohibit the negotiation, execution or amendment of an employment compensation, severance or other employee benefit arrangement, or payments made or to be made or benefits granted or to be granted according to such an arrangement, with respect to any security holder of the issuer, where the amount payable under the arrangement:

(A) Is being paid or granted as compensation for past services performed, future services to be performed, or future services to be refrained from performing, by the security holder (and matters incidental thereto); and

(B) Is not calculated based on the number of securities tendered or to be tendered in the tender offer by the security holder.

(ii) The provisions of paragraph (f)(12)(i) of this rule shall be satisfied and, therefore, pursuant to this non-exclusive safe harbor, the negotiation, execution or amendment of an arrangement and any payments made or to be made or benefits granted or to be granted according to that arrangement shall not be prohibited by paragraph (f)(8)(ii) of this rule, if the arrangement is approved as an employment compensation, severance or other employee benefit arrangement solely by independent directors as follows:

(A) The compensation committee or a committee of the board of directors that performs functions similar to a compensation committee of the issuer approves the arrangement, regardless of whether the issuer is a party to the arrangement, or, if an affiliate is a party to the arrangement, the compensation committee or a committee of the board of directors that performs functions similar to a compensation committee of the affiliate approves the arrangement; or

(B) If the issuer's or affiliate's board of directors, as applicable, does not have a compensation committee or a committee of the board of directors that performs functions similar to a compensation committee or if none of the members of the issuer's or affiliate's compensation committee or committee that performs functions similar to a compensation committee is independent, a special committee of the board of directors formed to consider and approve the arrangement approves the arrangement; or

(C) If the issuer or affiliate, as applicable, is a foreign private issuer, any or all members of the board of directors or any committee of the board of directors authorized to approve employment compensation, severance or other employee benefit arrangements under the laws or regulations of the home country approves the arrangement.

Instructions to Paragraph (f)(12)(ii): For purposes of determining whether the members of the committee approving an arrangement in accordance with the provisions of paragraph (f)(12)(ii) of this rule are independent, the following provisions shall apply:

1. If the issuer or affiliate, as applicable, is a listed issuer (as defined in Rule 10A–3) whose securities are listed either on a national securities exchange registered pursuant to section 6(a) of the Exchange Act (15 U.S.C. 78f(a)) or in an inter-dealer quotation system of a national securities association registered pursuant to section 15A(a) of the Exchange Act (15 U.S.C. 78o–3(a)) that has independence requirements for compensation committee members that have been approved by the Commission (as those requirements may be modified or supplemented), apply the issuer's or affiliate's definition of independence that it uses for determining that the members of the compensation committee are independent in compliance with the listing standards applicable to compensation committee members of the listed issuer.

2. If the issuer or affiliate, as applicable, is not a listed issuer (as defined in Rule 10A–3), apply the independence requirements for compensation committee members of a national securities exchange registered pursuant to section 6(a) of the Exchange Act (15 U.S.C. 78f(a)) or an inter-dealer quotation system of a national securities association registered pursuant to section 15A(a) of the Exchange Act (15 U.S.C. 78o–3(a)) that have been approved by the Commission (as those requirements may be modified or supplemented). Whatever definition the issuer or affiliate, as applicable, chooses, it must apply that definition consistently to all members of the committee approving the arrangement.

3. Notwithstanding Instructions 1 and 2 to paragraph (f)(12)(ii), if the issuer or affiliate, as applicable, is a closed-end investment company registered under the Investment Company Act of 1940, a director is considered to be independent if the director is not, other than in his or her capacity as a member of the board of directors or any board committee, an "interested person" of the investment company, as defined in section 2(a)(19) of the Investment Company Act of 1940 (15 U.S.C. 80a–2(a)(19)).

4. If the issuer or affiliate, as applicable, is a foreign private issuer, apply either the independence standards set forth in Instructions 1 and 2 to paragraph (f)(12)(ii) or the independence requirements of the laws, regulations, codes or standards of the home country of the issuer or affiliate, as applicable, for members of the board of directors or the committee of the board of directors approving the arrangement.

5. A determination by the issuer's or affiliate's board of directors, as applicable, that the members of the board of directors or the committee of the board of directors, as applicable, approving an arrangement in accordance with the provisions of paragraph (f)(12)(ii) are independent in accordance with the provisions of this instruction to paragraph (f)(12)(ii) shall satisfy the independence requirements of paragraph (f)(12)(ii).

Instruction to Paragraph (f)(12): The fact that the provisions of paragraph (f)(12) of this rule extend only to employment compensation, severance and other employee benefit arrangements and not to other arrangements, such as commercial arrangements, does not raise any inference that a payment under any such other arrangement constitutes consideration paid for securities in a tender offer.

(13) *Electronic Filings.* If the issuer or affiliate is an electronic filer, the minimum offering periods set forth in paragraph (f)(1) of this rule shall be tolled for any period during which it fails to file in electronic format, absent a hardship exemption Rules 201 and 202 of Regulation S–T, Schedule TO, the tender offer material specified in Item 9 1016(a)(1) of Regulation M–A, and any amendments thereto. If such documents were filed in paper pursuant to a hardship exemption (see Rules 201 and 202 of Regulation S–T), the minimum offering periods shall be tolled for any period during which a required confirming electronic copy of such Schedule and tender offer material is delinquent.

(g) The requirements of section 13(e)(1) of the Act and Rule 13e–4 and Schedule TO thereunder shall be deemed satisfied with respect to any issuer tender offer, including any exchange offer, where the issuer is incorporated or organized under the laws of Canada or any Canadian province or territory, is a foreign private issuer, and is not an investment company registered or required to be registered under the Investment Company Act of 1940, if less than 40 percent of the class of securities that is the subject of the tender offer is held by U.S. holders, and the tender offer is subject to, and the issuer complies with, the laws, regulations and policies of Canada and/or any of its provinces or territories governing the conduct of the offer (unless the issuer has received an exemption(s) from, and the issuer tender offer does not comply with, requirements that otherwise would be prescribed by this rule), *provided that:*

(1) Where the consideration for an issuer tender offer subject to this paragraph consists solely of cash, the entire disclosure document or documents required to be furnished to holders of the class of securities to be acquired shall be filed with the Commission on Schedule 13E–4F (Rule 13e–102) and disseminated to shareholders residing in the United States in accordance with such Canadian laws, regulations and policies; or

(2) Where the consideration for an issuer tender offer subject to this paragraph includes securities to be issued pursuant to the offer, any registration statement and/or prospectus relating thereto shall be filed with the Commission along with the Schedule 13E–4F referred to in paragraph (g)(1) of this rule, and shall be disseminated, together with the home jurisdiction document(s) accompanying such Schedule, to shareholders of the issuer residing in the United States in accordance with such Canadian laws, regulations and policies.

NOTE: Notwithstanding the grant of an exemption from one or more of the applicable Canadian regulatory provisions imposing requirements that otherwise would be prescribed by this rule, the issuer tender offer will be eligible to proceed in accordance with the requirements of this rule if the Commission by order determines that the applicable Canadian regulatory provisions are adequate to protect the interest of investors.

(h) This rule shall not apply to:

(1) Calls or redemptions of any security in accordance with the terms and conditions of its governing instruments;

(2) Offers to purchase securities evidenced by a scrip certificate, order form or similar document which represents a fractional interest in a share of stock or similar security;

(3) Offers to purchase securities pursuant to a statutory procedure for the purchase of dissenting security holders' securities;

(4) Any tender offer which is subject to section 14(d) of the Act;

(5) Offers to purchase from security holders who own an aggregate of not more than a specified number of shares that is less than one hundred: *Provided however,* That:

(i) The offer complies with paragraph (f)(8)(i) of this rule with respect to security holders who own a number of shares equal to or less than the specified number of shares, except that an issuer can elect to exclude participants in a plan as that term is defined in Rule 100 of Regulation M, or to exclude security holders who do not own their shares as of a specified date determined by the issuer; and

(ii) The offer complies with paragraph (f)(8)(ii) of this rule or the consideration paid pursuant to the offer is determined on the basis of a uniformly applied formula based on the market price of the subject security;

(6) An issuer tender offer made solely to effect a rescission offer: *Provided, however,* That the offer is registered under the Securities Act of 1933 (15 U.S.C. 77a *et seq.*), and the consideration is equal to the price paid by each security holder, plus legal interest if the issuer elects to or is required to pay legal interest;

(7) Offers by closed-end management investment companies to repurchase equity securities pursuant to 17 CFR 270.23c–3; or

(8) *Cross–Border Tender Offers (Tier I).* Any issuer tender offer (including any exchange offer) where the issuer is a foreign private issuer as defined in Rule 3b–4 if the following conditions are satisfied.

(i) Except in the case of an issuer tender offer that is commenced during the pendency of a tender offer made by a third party in reliance on Rule 14d–1(c), U.S. holders do not hold more than 10 percent of the class of securities sought in the offer (as determined under Instructions 2 or 3 to paragraph (h)(8) and paragraph (i) of this rule); and

(ii) The issuer or affiliate must permit U.S. holders to participate in the offer on terms at least as favorable as those offered any other holder of the same class of securities that is the subject of the offer; however:

(A) *Registered Exchange Offers.* If the issuer or affiliate offers securities registered under the Securities Act of 1933 (15 U.S.C. 77a *et seq.*), the issuer or affiliate need not extend the offer to security holders in those states or jurisdictions that prohibit the offer or sale of the securities after the issuer or affiliate has made a good faith effort to register or qualify the offer and sale of securities in that state or jurisdiction, except that the issuer or affiliate must offer the same cash alternative to security holders in any such state or jurisdiction that it has offered to security holders in any other state or jurisdiction.

(B) *Exempt Exchange Offers.* If the issuer or affiliate offers securities exempt from registration under Rule 802 under the Securities Act of 1933, the issuer or affiliate need not extend the offer to security holders in those states or jurisdictions that require registration or qualification, except that the issuer or affiliate must offer the same cash alternative to security holders in any such state or jurisdiction that it has offered to security holders in any other state or jurisdiction.

(C) *Cash Only Consideration*. The issuer or affiliate may offer U.S. holders cash only consideration for the tender of the subject securities, notwithstanding the fact that the issuer or affiliate is offering security holders outside the United States a consideration that consists in whole or in part of securities of the issuer or affiliate, if the issuer or affiliate has a reasonable basis for believing that the amount of cash is substantially equivalent to the value of the consideration offered to non-U.S. holders, and either of the following conditions are satisfied:

(*1*) The offered security is a "margin security" within the meaning of Regulation T (12 CFR 220.2) and the issuer or affiliate undertakes to provide, upon the request of any U.S. holder or the Commission staff, the closing price and daily trading volume of the security on the principal trading market for the security as of the last trading day of each of the six months preceding the announcement of the offer and each of the trading days thereafter; or

(*2*) If the offered security is not a "margin security" within the meaning of Regulation T (12 CFR 220.2), the issuer or affiliate undertakes to provide, upon the request of any U.S. holder or the Commission staff, an opinion of an independent expert stating that the cash consideration offered to U.S. holders is substantially equivalent to the value of the consideration offered security holders outside the United States.

(D) *Disparate Tax Treatment*. If the issuer or affiliate offers "loan notes" solely to offer sellers tax advantages not available in the United States and these notes are neither listed on any organized securities market nor registered under the Securities Act of 1933 (15 U.S.C. 77a *et seq.*), the loan notes need not be offered to U.S. holders.

(iii) *Informational Documents*. (A) If the issuer or affiliate publishes or otherwise disseminates an informational document to the holders of the securities in connection with the issuer tender offer (including any exchange offer), the issuer or affiliate must furnish that informational document, including any amendments thereto, in English, to the Commission on Form CB (17 CFR 249.480) by the first business day after publication or dissemination. If the issuer or affiliate is a foreign company, it must also file a Form F–X (17 CFR 239.42) with the Commission at the same time as the submission of Form CB to appoint an agent for service in the United States.

(B) The issuer or affiliate must disseminate any informational document to U.S. holders, including any amendments thereto, in English, on a comparable basis to that provided to security holders in the home jurisdiction.

(C) If the issuer or affiliate disseminates by publication in its home jurisdiction, the issuer or affiliate must publish the information in the United States in a manner reasonably calculated to inform U.S. holders of the offer.

(iv) An investment company registered or required to be registered under the Investment Company Act of 1940 (15 U.S.C. 80a–1 *et seq.*), other than a registered closed-end investment company, may not use this paragraph (h)(8); or

(9) Any other transaction or transactions, if the Commission, upon written request or upon its own motion, exempts such transaction or transactions, either unconditionally, or on specified terms and conditions, as not constituting a fraudulent, deceptive or manipulative act or practice comprehended within the purpose of this rule.

(i) *Cross-Border Tender Offers (Tier II)*. Any issuer tender offer (including any exchange offer) that meets the conditions in paragraph (i)(1) of this rule shall be entitled to the exemptive relief specified in paragraph (i)(2) of this rule, provided that such issuer tender offer complies with all the requirements of this rule other than those for which an exemption has been specifically provided in paragraph (i)(2) of this rule. In addition, any issuer tender offer (including any exchange offer) subject only to the requirements of section 14(e) of the Act and Regulation 14E (Rules 14e–1 through 14e–8) thereunder that meets the conditions in paragraph (i)(1) of this rule also shall be entitled to the exemptive relief specified in paragraph (i)(2) of this rule, to the extent needed under the requirements of Regulation 14E, so long as the tender offer complies with all requirements of Regulation 14E other than those for which an exemption has been specifically provided in paragraph (i)(2) of this rule:

(1) Conditions. (i) The issuer is a foreign private issuer as defined in Rule 3b–4 and is not an investment company registered or required to be registered under the Investment Company Act of 1940 (15 U.S.C. 80a–1 *et seq.*), other than a registered closed-end investment company; and

(ii) Except in the case of an issuer tender offer commenced during the pendency of a tender offer made by a third party in reliance on Rule 14d–1(d), U.S. holders do not hold more than 40 percent of the class of securities sought in the offer (as determined in accordance with Instructions 2 or 3 to paragraphs (h)(8) and (i) of this rule).

(2) *Exemptions.* The issuer tender offer shall comply with all requirements of this rule other than the following:

(i) *Equal Treatment—Loan Notes.* If the issuer or affiliate offers loan notes solely to offer sellers tax advantages not available in the United States and these notes are neither listed on any organized securities market nor registered under the Securities Act (15 U.S.C. 77a *et seq.*), the loan notes need not be offered to U.S. holders, notwithstanding paragraph (f)(8) and (h)(9) of this rule.

(ii) *Equal Treatment—Separate U.S. and Foreign Offers.* Notwithstanding the provisions of paragraph (f)(8) of this rule, an issuer or affiliate conducting an issuer tender offer meeting the conditions of paragraph (i)(1) of this rule may separate the offer into multiple offers: one offer made to U.S. holders, which also may include all holders of American Depositary Shares representing interests in the subject securities, and one or more offers made to non-U.S. holders. The U.S. offer must be made on terms at least as favorable as those offered any other holder of the same class of securities that is the subject of the tender offers. U.S. holders may be included in the foreign offer(s) only where the laws of the jurisdiction governing such foreign offer(s) expressly preclude the exclusion of U.S. holders from the foreign offer(s) and where the offer materials distributed to U.S. holders fully and adequately disclose the risks of participating in the foreign offer(s).

(iii) *Notice of Extensions.* Notice of extensions made in accordance with the requirements of the home jurisdiction law or practice will satisfy the requirements of Rule 14e–1(d).

(iv) *Prompt Payment.* Payment made in accordance with the requirements of the home jurisdiction law or practice will satisfy the requirements of Rule 14e–1(c).

(v) *Suspension of Withdrawal Rights During Counting of Tendered Securities.* The issuer or affiliate may suspend withdrawal rights required under paragraph (f)(2) of this rule at the end of the offer and during the period that securities tendered into the offer are being counted, provided that:

(A) The issuer or affiliate has provided an offer period, including withdrawal rights, for a period of at least 20 U.S. business days;

(B) At the time withdrawal rights are suspended, all offer conditions have been satisfied or waived, except to the extent that the issuer or affiliate is in the process of determining whether a minimum acceptance condition included in the terms of the offer has been satisfied by counting tendered securities; and

(C) Withdrawal rights are suspended only during the counting process and are reinstated immediately thereafter, except to the extent that they are terminated through the acceptance of tendered securities.

(vi) *Early Termination of an Initial Offering Period.* An issuer or affiliate conducting an issuer tender offer may terminate an initial offering period, including a voluntary extension of that period, if at the time the initial offering period and withdrawal rights terminate, the following conditions are met:

(A) The initial offering period has been open for at least 20 U.S. business days;

(B) The issuer or affiliate has adequately discussed the possibility of and the impact of the early termination in the original offer materials;

(C) The issuer or affiliate provides a subsequent offering period after the termination of the initial offering period;

(D) All offer conditions are satisfied as of the time when the initial offering period ends; and

(E) The issuer or affiliate does not terminate the initial offering period or any extension of that period during any mandatory extension required under U.S. tender offer rules.

Instructions to Paragraph (h)(8) and (i) of this rule:

1. *Home jurisdiction* means both the jurisdiction of the issuer's incorporation, organization or chartering and the principal foreign market where the issuer's securities are listed or quoted.

2. *U.S. holder* means any security holder resident in the United States. To determine the percentage of outstanding securities held by U.S. holders:

i. Calculate the U.S. ownership as of a date no more than 60 days before and no more than 30 days after the public announcement of the tender offer. If you are unable to calculate as of a date within these time frames, the calculation may be made as of the most recent practicable date before public announcement, but in no event earlier than 120 days before announcement;

ii. Include securities underlying American Depositary Shares convertible or exchangeable into the securities that are the subject of the tender offer when calculating the number of subject securities outstanding, as well as the number held by U.S. holders. Exclude from the calculations other types of securities that are convertible or exchangeable into the securities that are the subject of the tender offer, such as warrants, options and convertible securities;

iii. Use the method of calculating record ownership in Rule 12g3–2(a), except that your inquiry as to the amount of securities represented by accounts of customers resident in the United States may be limited to brokers, dealers, banks and other nominees located in the United States, your jurisdiction of incorporation, and the jurisdiction that is the primary trading market for the subject securities, if different than your jurisdiction of incorporation;

iv. If, after reasonable inquiry, you are unable to obtain information about the amount of securities represented by accounts of customers resident in the United States, you may assume, for purposes of this definition, that the customers are residents of the jurisdiction in which the nominee has its principal place of business; and

v. Count securities as beneficially owned by residents of the United States as reported on reports of beneficial ownership that are provided to you or publicly filed and based on information otherwise provided to you.

3. If you are unable to conduct the analysis of U.S. ownership set forth in Instruction 2 above, U.S. holders will be presumed to hold 10 percent or less of the outstanding subject securities (40 percent for Tier II) so long as there is a primary trading market outside the United States, as defined in Rule 12h–6(f)(5), unless:

i. Average daily trading volume of the subject securities in the United States for a recent twelve-month period ending on a date no more than 60 days before the public announcement of the tender offer exceeds 10 percent (or 40 percent) of the average daily trading volume of that class of securities on a worldwide basis for the same period; or

ii. The most recent annual report or annual information filed or submitted by the issuer with securities regulators of the home jurisdiction or with the Commission or any jurisdiction in which the subject securities trade before the public announcement of the offer indicates that U.S. holders hold more than 10 percent (or 40 percent) of the outstanding subject class of securities; or

iii. You know or have reason to know, before the public announcement of the offer, that the level of U.S. ownership of the subject securities exceeds 10 percent (or 40 percent) of such securities. As an example, you are deemed to know information about U.S. ownership of the subject class of securities that is publicly available and that appears in any filing with the Commission or any regulatory body in the home jurisdiction and, if different, the non-U.S. jurisdiction in which the primary trading market for the subject class of securities is located. You are also deemed to know information obtained or readily available from any other source that is reasonably reliable, including from persons you have retained to advise you about the transaction, as well as from third-party information providers. These examples are not intended to be exclusive.

4. *United States* means the United States of America, its territories and possessions, any State of the United States, and the District of Columbia.

5. The exemptions provided by paragraphs (h)(8) and (i) of this rule are not available for any securities transaction or series of transactions that technically complies with paragraph (h)(8) and (i) of this rule but are part of a plan or scheme to evade the provisions of this rule.

(j)(1) It shall be a fraudulent, deceptive or manipulative act or practice, in connection with an issuer tender offer, for an issuer or an affiliate of such issuer, in connection with an issuer tender offer:

(i) To employ any device, scheme or artifice to defraud any person;

(ii) To make any untrue statement of a material fact or to omit to state a material fact necessary in order to make the statements made, in the light of the circumstances under which they were made, not misleading; or

(iii) To engage in any act, practice or course of business which operates or would operate as a fraud or deceit upon any person.

(2) As a means reasonably designed to prevent fraudulent, deceptive or manipulative acts or practices in connection with any issuer tender offer, it shall be unlawful for an issuer or an affiliate of such issuer to make an issuer tender offer unless:

(i) Such issuer or affiliate complies with the requirements of paragraphs (b), (c), (d), (e), and (f) of this rule; and

(ii) The issuer tender offer is not in violation of paragraph (j)(1) of this rule.

Rule 13e–100. Schedule 13E–3. Transaction statement under Section 13(e) of the Securities Exchange Act of 1934 and Rule 13e–3 thereunder

Securities and Exchange Commission,
Washington, D.C. 20549

Rule 13e–3. Transaction Statement under Section 13(e) of the Securities Exchange Act of 1934 (Amendment No. ___)

____
(Name of the Issuer)

____
(Names of Persons Filing Statement)

____
(Title of Class of Securities)

____

(CUSIP Number of Class of Securities)

____

(Name, Address, and Telephone Numbers of Person Authorized to Receive Notices and Communications on Behalf of the Persons Filing Statement)

This statement is filed in connection with (check the appropriate box):

a. [ ] The filing of solicitation materials or an information statement subject to Regulation 14A (Rules 14a–1 through 14b–2), Regulation 14C (Rules 14c–1 through 14c–101) or Rule 13e–3(c) under the Securities Exchange Act of 1934 ("the Act").

b. [ ] The filing of a registration statement under the Securities Act of 1933.

c. [ ] A tender offer.

d. [ ] None of the above.

Check the following box if the soliciting materials or information statement referred to in checking box (a) are preliminary copies: [ ]

Check the following box if the filing is a final amendment reporting the results of the transaction [ ]

Calculation of Filing Fee

Transaction Valuation *	Amount of Filing Fee

* Set forth the amount on which the filing fee is calculated and state how it was determined.

[ ] Check the box if any part of the fee is offset as provided by Rule 0–11(a)(2) and identify the filing with which the offsetting fee was previously paid. Identify the previous filing by registration statement number, or the Form or Schedule and the date of its filing.

Amount Previously Paid:

Form or Registration No.: ____________

Filing Party: ____________

Date Filed: ____________

General Instructions:

A. File eight copies of the statement, including all exhibits, with the Commission if paper filing is permitted.

B. This filing must be accompanied by a fee payable to the Commission as required by Rule 0–11(b).

C. If the statement is filed by a general or limited partnership, syndicate or other group, the information called for by Items 3, 5, 6, 10 and 11 must be given with respect to: (i) Each partner of the general partnership; (ii) each partner who is, or functions as, a general partner of the limited partnership; (iii) each member of the syndicate or group; and (iv) each person controlling the partner or member. If the statement is filed by a corporation or if a person referred to in (i), (ii), (iii) or (iv) of this Instruction is a corporation, the information called for by the items specified above must be given with respect to: (a) Each executive officer and director of the corporation; (b) each person controlling the corporation; and (c) each executive officer and director of any corporation or other person ultimately in control of the corporation.

D. Depending on the type of Rule 13e–3 transaction (Rule 13e–3(a)(3)), this statement must be filed with the Commission:

1. At the same time as filing preliminary or definitive soliciting materials or an information statement under Regulations 14A or 14C of the Act;

2. At the same time as filing a registration statement under the Securities Act of 1933;

3. As soon as practicable on the date a tender offer is first published, sent or given to security holders; or

4. At least 30 days before any purchase of securities of the class of securities subject to the Rule 13e–3 transaction, if the transaction does not involve a solicitation, an information statement, the registration of securities or a tender offer, as described in paragraphs 1, 2 or 3 of this Instruction; and

5. If the Rule 13e–3 transaction involves a series of transactions, the issuer or affiliate must file this statement at the time indicated in paragraphs 1 through 4 of this Instruction for the first transaction and must amend the schedule promptly with respect to each subsequent transaction.

E. If an item is inapplicable or the answer is in the negative, so state. The statement published, sent or given to security holders may omit negative and not applicable responses, except that responses to Items 7, 8 and 9 of this schedule must be provided in full. If the schedule includes any information that is not published, sent or given to security holders, provide that information or specifically incorporate it by reference under the appropriate item number and heading in the schedule. Do not recite the text of disclosure requirements in the schedule or any document published, sent or given to security holders. Indicate clearly the coverage of the requirements without referring to the text of the items.

F. Information contained in exhibits to the statement may be incorporated by reference in answer or partial answer to any item unless it would render the answer misleading, incomplete, unclear or confusing. A copy of any information that is incorporated by reference or a copy of the pertinent pages of a document containing the information must be submitted with this statement as an exhibit, unless it was previously filed with the Commission electronically on EDGAR. If an exhibit contains information responding to more than one item in the schedule, all information in that exhibit may be incorporated by reference once in response to the several items in the schedule for which it provides an answer. Information incorporated by reference is deemed filed with the Commission for all purposes of the Act.

G. If the Rule 13e–3 transaction also involves a transaction subject to Regulation 14A (Rules 14a–1 through 14b–2) or 14C (Rules 14c–1 through 14c–101) of the Act, the registration of securities under the Securities Act of 1933 and the General Rules and Regulations of that Act, or a tender offer subject to Regulation 14D (Rules 14d–1 through 14d–101) or 13e–4, this statement must incorporate by reference the information contained in the proxy, information, registration or tender offer statement in answer to the items of this statement.

H. The information required by the items of this statement is intended to be in addition to any disclosure requirements of any other form or schedule that may be filed with the Commission in connection with the Rule 13e–3 transaction. If those forms or schedules require less information on any topic than this statement, the requirements of this statement control.

I. If the Rule 13e–3 transaction involves a tender offer, then a combined statement on Schedules 13E–3 and TO may be filed with the Commission under cover of Schedule TO (Rule 14d–100). See Instruction J of Schedule TO (Rule 14d–100).

J. Amendments disclosing a material change in the information set forth in this statement may omit any information previously disclosed in this statement.

Item 1. Summary Term Sheet

Furnish the information required by Item 1001 of Regulation M–A unless information is disclosed to security holders in a prospectus that meets the requirements of Rule 421(d) under the Securities Act of 1933.

Item 2. Subject Company Information

Furnish the information required by Item 1002 of Regulation M–A.

Item 3. Identity and Background of Filing Person

Furnish the information required by Item 1003(a) through (c) of Regulation M–A.

Item 4. Terms of the Transaction

Furnish the information required by Item 1004(a) and (c) through (f) of Regulation M–A.

Item 5. Past Contacts, Transactions, Negotiations and Agreements

Furnish the information required by Item 1005(a) through (c) and (e) of Regulation M–A.

Item 6. Purposes of the Transaction and Plans or Proposals

Furnish the information required by Item 1006(b) and (c)(1) through (8) of Regulation M–A.

Instruction to Item 6: In providing the information specified in Item 1006(c) for this item, discuss any activities or transactions that would occur after the Rule 13e–3 transaction.

Item 7. Purposes, Alternatives, Reasons and Effects

Furnish the information required by Item 1013 of Regulation M–A.

Item 8. Fairness of the Transaction

Furnish the information required by Item 1014 of Regulation M–A.

Item 9. Reports, Opinions, Appraisals and Negotiations

Furnish the information required by Item 1015 of Regulation M–A.

Item 10. Source and Amounts of Funds or Other Consideration

Furnish the information required by Item 1007 of Regulation M–A.

Item 11. Interest in Securities of the Subject Company

Furnish the information required by Item 1008 of Regulation M–A.

Item 12. The Solicitation or Recommendation

Furnish the information required by Item 1012(d) and (e) of Regulation M–A.

Item 13. Financial Statements

Furnish the information required by Item 1010(a) through (b) of Regulation M–A for the issuer of the subject class of securities.

Instructions to Item 13:

1. The disclosure materials disseminated to security holders may contain the summarized financial information required by Item 1010(c) of Regulation M–A instead of the financial information required by Item 1010(a) and (b). In that case, the financial information required by Item 1010(a) and (b) of Regulation M–A must be disclosed directly or incorporated by reference in the statement. If summarized financial information is disseminated to security holders, include appropriate instructions on how more complete financial information can be obtained. If the summarized financial information is prepared on the basis of a comprehensive body of accounting principles other than U.S. GAAP, the summarized financial information must be accompanied by a reconciliation as described in Instruction 2.

2. If the financial statements required by this Item are prepared on the basis of a comprehensive body of accounting principles other than U.S. GAAP, provide a reconciliation to U.S. GAAP in accordance with Item 17 of Form 20–F (17 CFR 249.220f).

3. The filing person may incorporate by reference financial statements contained in any document filed with the Commission, solely for the purposes of this schedule, if: (a) The financial statements substantially meet the requirements of this Item; (b) an express statement is made that the financial statements are incorporated by reference; (c) the matter incorporated by reference is clearly identified by page, paragraph, caption or otherwise; and (d) if the matter incorporated by reference is not filed with this Schedule, an indication is made where the information may be inspected and copies obtained. Financial statements that are required to be presented in comparative form for two or more fiscal years or periods may not be incorporated by reference unless the material incorporated by reference includes the entire period for which the comparative data is required to be given. *See* General Instruction F to this Schedule.

Item 14. Persons/Assets, Retained, Employed, Compensated or Used

Furnish the information required by Item 1009 of Regulation M–A.

Item 15. Additional Information

Furnish the information required by Item 1011(b) and (c) of Regulation M–A.

Item 16. Exhibits

File as an exhibit to the Schedule all documents specified in Item 1016(a) through (d), (f) and (g) of Regulation M–A.

Signature. After due inquiry and to the best of my knowledge and belief, I certify that the information set forth in this statement is true, complete and correct.

(Signature)

(Name and title)

(Date)

Instruction to Signature: The statement must be signed by the filing person or that person's authorized representative. If the statement is signed on behalf of a person by an authorized representative (other than an executive officer of a corporation or general partner of a partnership), evidence of the representative's authority to sign on behalf of the person must be filed with the statement. The name and any title of each person who signs the statement must be typed or printed beneath the signature. See Rule 12b–11 with respect to signature requirements.

(Signature)

(Name and Title)

Rule 13e–101. [Reserved]

Rule 13e–102. Schedule 13E–4F. Tender offer statement pursuant to Section 13(e)(1) of the Securities Exchange Act of 1934 and Rule 13e–4 thereunder

U.S. Securities and Exchange Commission

Washington, D.C. 20549

Schedule 13E–4F

ISSUER TENDER OFFER STATEMENT Pursuant to Section 13(e)(1) of the Securities Exchange Act of 1934

[Amendment No. ____]

(Exact Name of Issuer as specified in its charter)

(Translation of Issuer's Name into English) (if applicable)

(Jurisdiction of Issuer's Incorporation or Organization)

(Name(s) of Person(s) Filing Statement)

(Title of Class of Securities)

(CUSIP Number of Class of Securities) (if applicable)

(Name, address (including zip code) and telephone number (including area code) of person authorized to receive notices and communications on behalf of the person(s) filing statement)

(Date tender offer first published, sent or given to securityholders)

Calculation of Filing Fee

Transaction Valuation *

* Set forth the amount on which the filing fee is calculated and state how it was determined.

Amount of Filing Fee

[] Check box if any part of the fee is offset as provided by Rule 0–11(a)(2) and identify the filing with which the offsetting fee was previously paid. Identify the previous filing by registration statement number, or the Form or Schedule and the date of its filing.

Amount Previously Paid: ____

Registration No. ____

Filing Party: ____

Form: ____

Date Filed: ____

GENERAL INSTRUCTIONS

I. ELIGIBILITY REQUIREMENTS FOR USE OF SCHEDULE 13E–4F

A. Schedule 13E–4F may be used by any foreign private issuer if: (1) the issuer is incorporated or organized under the laws of Canada or any Canadian province or territory; (2) the issuer is making a cash tender or exchange offer for the issuer's own securities; and (3) less than 40 percent of the class of such issuer's securities outstanding that is the subject of the tender offer is held by U.S. holders. The calculation of securities held by U.S. holders shall be made as of the end of the issuer's last quarter or, if such quarter terminated within 60 days of the filing date, as of the end of the issuer's preceding quarter.

Instructions.

1. For purposes of this Schedule, "foreign private issuer" shall be construed in accordance with Rule 405 under the Securities Act.

2. For purposes of this Schedule, the term "U.S. holder" shall mean any person whose address appears on the records of the issuer, any voting trustee, any depositary, any share transfer agent or any person acting in a similar capacity on behalf of the issuer as being located in the United States.

3. If this Schedule is filed during the pendency of one or more ongoing cash tender or exchange offers for securities of the class subject to this offer that was commenced or was eligible to be commenced on Schedule 14D–1F and/or Form F–8 or Form F–80, the date for calculation of U.S. ownership for purposes of this Schedule shall be the same as that date used by the initial bidder or issuer.

4. For purposes of this Schedule, the class of subject securities shall not include any securities that may be converted into or are exchangeable for the subject securities.

B. Any issuer using this Schedule must extend the cash tender or exchange offer to U.S. holders of the class of securities subject to the offer upon terms and conditions not less favorable than those extended to any other holder of the same class of such securities, and must comply with the requirements of any Canadian federal, provincial and/or territorial law, regulation or policy relating to the terms and conditions of the offer.

C. This Schedule shall not be used if the issuer is an investment company registered or required to be registered under the Investment Company Act of 1940.

III. Filing Instructions and Fees

A.(1) The issuer must file this Schedule and any amendment to the Schedule (see Part I, Item 1.(b)), including all exhibits and other documents filed as part of the Schedule or amendment, in electronic format via the Commission's Electronic Data Gathering, Analysis, and Retrieval (EDGAR) system in accordance with the EDGAR rules set forth in Regulation S–T (17 CFR Part 232). For assistance with technical questions about EDGAR or to request an access code, call the EDGAR Filer Support Office at (202) 551–8900. For assistance with the EDGAR rules, call the Office of EDGAR and Information Analysis at (202) 551–3610.

(2) If filing the Schedule in paper under a hardship exemption in Rule 201 or Rule 202 of Regulation S–T, or as otherwise permitted, the issuer must file with the Commission at its principal office five copies of the complete Schedule and any amendment, including exhibits and all other documents filed as a part of the Schedule or amendment. The issuer must bind, staple or otherwise compile each copy in one or more parts without stiff covers. The issuer must further bind the Schedule or amendment on the side or stitching margin in a manner that leaves the reading matter legible. The issuer must provide three additional copies of the Schedule or amendment without exhibits to the Commission.

B. An electronic filer must provide the signatures required for the Schedule or amendment in accordance with Rule 302 of Regulation S–T. An issuer filing in paper must have the original and at least one copy of the Schedule and any amendment signed in accordance with Exchange Act Rule 12b–11(d) by the persons whose signatures are required for this Schedule or amendment. The issuer must also conform the unsigned copies.

C. At the time of filing this Schedule with the Commission, the issuer shall pay to the Commission in accordance with Rule 0–11 of the Exchange Act, a fee in U.S. dollars in the amount prescribed by Section 13(e)(3) of the Exchange Act. See also Rule 0–9 of the Exchange Act.

(1) The value of the securities to be acquired solely for cash shall be the amount of cash to be paid for them, calculated into U.S. dollars.

(2) The value of the securities to be acquired with securities or other non-cash consideration, whether or not in combination with a cash payment for the same securities, shall be based on the market value of the securities to be acquired by the issuer as established in accordance with paragraph (3) of this rule.

(3) When the fee is based upon the market value of the securities, such market value shall be established by either the average of the high and low prices reported on the consolidated reporting system (for exchange-traded securities and last sale reported for over-the-counter securities) or the average of the bid and asked price (for other over-the-counter securities) as of a specified date within 5 business days prior to the date of filing the Schedule. If there is no market for the securities to be acquired by the issuer, the value shall be based upon the book value of such securities computed as of the latest practicable date prior to the date of filing of the Schedule, unless the issuer of the securities is in bankruptcy or receivership or has an accumulated capital deficit, in which case one-third of the principal amount, par value or stated value of such securities shall be used.

D. If at any time after the initial payment of the fee the aggregate consideration offered is increased, an additional filing fee based upon such increase shall be paid with the required amended filing.

E. The issuer must file the Schedule or amendment in electronic format in the English language in accordance with Rule 306 of Regulation S–T. The issuer may file part of the Schedule or amendment, or exhibit or other attachment to the Schedule or amendment, in both French and English if the issuer included the French text to comply with the requirements of the Canadian securities administrator or other Canadian authority and, for an electronic filing, if the filing is an HTML document, as defined in Rule 11 of Regulation S–T. For both an electronic filing and a paper filing, the issuer may provide an English translation or English summary of a foreign language document as an exhibit or other attachment to the Schedule or amendment as permitted by the rules of the applicable Canadian securities administrator.

F. A paper filer must number sequentially the signed original of the Schedule or amendment (in addition to any internal numbering that otherwise may be present) by handwritten, typed, printed or other legible form of notation from the first page through the last page of the Schedule or amendment, including any exhibits or attachments. A paper filer must disclose the total number of pages on the first page of the sequentially numbered Schedule or amendment.

III. Compliance with the Exchange Act

A. Pursuant to Rule 13e–4(g), the issuer shall be deemed to comply with the requirements of Section 13(e)(1) of the Exchange Act and Rule 13e–4 and Schedule TO thereunder in connection with a cash tender or exchange offer for securities that may be made pursuant to this Schedule, provided that, if an exemption has been granted from the requirements of Canadian federal, provincial and/or territorial laws, regulations or policies, and the tender offer does not comply with requirements that otherwise would be prescribed by Rule 13e–4, the issuer (absent an order from the Commission) shall comply with the provisions of Section 13(e)(1) of the Exchange Act and Rule 13e–4 and Schedule 14E–4 thereunder.

B. Any cash tender or exchange offer made pursuant to this Schedule is not exempt from the antifraud provisions of Section 10(b) of the Exchange Act and Rule 10b–5 thereunder, Section 13(e)(1) of the Exchange Act and Rule 13e–4(b)(1) thereunder, and Section 14(e) of the Exchange Act and Rule 14e–3 thereunder, and this Schedule shall be deemed "filed" for purposes of Section 18 of the Exchange Act.

C. The issuer's attention is directed to Regulation M, in the case of an issuer exchange offer, and to Rule 14e–5, in the case of an issuer cash tender offer or issuer exchange offer. [*See* Exchange Act Release No. 29355 (June 21, 1991) containing an exemption from Rule 10b–13, the predecessor to Rule 14e–5.]

PART I. INFORMATION REQUIRED TO BE SENT TO SHAREHOLDERS

Item 1. Home Jurisdiction Documents

(a) This Schedule shall be accompanied by the entire disclosure document or documents required to be delivered to holders of securities to be acquired by the issuer in the proposed transaction pursuant to the laws, regulations or policies of the Canadian jurisdiction in which the issuer is incorporated or organized, and any other Canadian federal, provincial and/or territorial law, regulation or policy relating to the terms and conditions of the offer. The Schedule need not include any documents incorporated by reference into such disclosure document(s) and not distributed to offerees pursuant to any such law, regulation or policy.

(b) Any amendment made by the issuer to a home jurisdiction document or documents shall be filed with the Commission under cover of this Schedule, which must indicate on the cover page the number of the amendment.

(c) In an exchange offer where securities of the issuer have been or are to be offered or cancelled in the transaction, such securities shall be registered on forms promulgated by the Commission under the Securities Act of 1933 including, where available, the Commission's Form F–8 or F–80 providing for inclusion in that registration statement of the home jurisdiction prospectus.

Item 2. Informational Legends

The following legends, to the extent applicable, shall appear on the outside front cover page of the home jurisdiction document(s) in bold-face roman type at least as high as ten-point modern type and at least two-points leaded:

"This tender offer is made by a foreign issuer for its own securities, and while the offer is subject to disclosure requirements of the country in which the issuer is incorporated or organized, investors should be aware that these requirements are different from those of the United States. Financial statements included herein, if any, have been prepared in accordance with foreign generally accepted accounting principles and thus may not be comparable to financial statements of United States companies.

"The enforcement by investors of civil liabilities under the federal securities laws may be affected adversely by the fact that the issuer is located in a foreign country, and that some or all of its officers and directors are residents of a foreign country.

"Investors should be aware that the issuer or its affiliates, directly or indirectly, may bid for or make purchases of the securities of the issuer subject to the offer, or of its related securities, during the period of the issuer tender offer, as permitted by applicable Canadian laws or provincial laws or regulations."

Note to Item 2. If the home jurisdiction document(s) are delivered through an electronic medium, the issuer may satisfy the legibility requirements for the required legends relating to type size and fonts by presenting the legend in any manner reasonably calculated to draw security holder attention to it.

PART II. INFORMATION NOT REQUIRED TO BE SENT TO SHAREHOLDERS

The exhibits specified below shall be filed as part of the Schedule, but are not required to be sent to shareholders unless so required pursuant to the laws, regulations or policies of Canada and/or any of its provinces or territories. Exhibits shall be lettered or numbered appropriately for convenient reference.

(1) File any reports or information that, in accordance with the requirements of the home jurisdiction(s), must be made publicly available by the issuer in connection with the transaction, but need not be disseminated to shareholders.

(2) File copies of any documents incorporated by reference into the home jurisdiction document(s).

(3) If any name is signed to the Schedule pursuant to power of attorney, manually signed copies of any such power of attorney shall be filed. If the name of any officer signing on behalf of the issuer is signed pursuant to a power of attorney, certified copies of a resolution of the issuer's board of directors authorizing such signature also shall be filed.

PART III. UNDERTAKINGS AND CONSENT TO SERVICE OF PROCESS

1. Undertakings

The Schedule shall set forth the following undertakings of the issuer:

(a) The issuer undertakes to make available, in person or by telephone, representatives to respond to inquiries made by the Commission staff, and to furnish promptly, when requested to do so by the Commission staff, information relating to this Schedule or to transactions in said securities.

(b) The issuer also undertakes to disclose in the United States, on the same basis as it is required to make such disclosure pursuant to applicable Canadian federal and/or provincial or territorial laws, regulations or policies, or otherwise discloses, information regarding purchases of the issuer's securities in connection with the cash tender or exchange offer covered by this Schedule. Such information shall be set forth in amendments to this Schedule.

2. Consent to Service of Process

(a) At the time of filing this Schedule, the issuer shall file with the Commission a written irrevocable consent and power of attorney on Form F–X.

(b) Any change to the name or address of a registrant's agent for service shall be communicated promptly to the Commission by amendment to Form F–X referencing the file number of the registrant.

PART IV. SIGNATURES

A. The Schedule shall be signed by each person on whose behalf the Schedule is filed or its authorized representative. If the Schedule is signed on behalf of a person by his authorized representative (other than an executive officer or general partner of the company), evidence of the representative's authority shall be filed with the Schedule.

B. The name of each person who signs the Schedule shall be typed or printed beneath his signature.

C. By signing this Schedule, the person(s) filing the Schedule consents without power of revocation that any administrative subpoena may be served, or any administrative proceeding, civil suit or civil action where the cause of action arises out of or relates to or concerns any offering made or purported to be made in connection with the filing on Schedule 13E–4F or any purchases or sales of any securities in connection therewith, may be commenced against it in any administrative tribunal or in any appropriate court in any place subject to the jurisdiction of any state or of the United States by service of said subpoena or process upon the registrant's designated agent.

After due inquiry and to the best of my knowledge and belief, I certify that the information set forth in this statement is true, complete and correct.

(Signature)

(Name/Title)

(Date)

Rule 13f–1. Reporting by institutional investment managers of information with respect to accounts over which they exercise investment discretion

(a)(1) Every institutional investment manager which exercises investment discretion with respect to accounts holding section 13(f) securities, as defined in paragraph (c) of this rule, having an aggregate fair market value on the last trading day of any month of any calendar year of at least $100,000,000 shall file a report on Form 13F (17 CFR 249.325) with the Commission within 45 days after the last day of such calendar year and within 45 days after the last day of each of the first three calendar quarters of the subsequent calendar year.

(2) An amendment to a Form 13F (17 CFR 249.325) report, other than one reporting only holdings that were not previously reported in a public filing for the same period, must set forth the complete text of the Form 13F. Amendments must be numbered sequentially.

(b) For the purposes of this rule, "investment discretion" has the meaning set forth in section 3(a)(35) of the Act. An institutional investment manager shall also be deemed to exercise "investment discretion" with respect to all accounts over which any person under its control exercises investment discretion.

(c) For purposes of this rule "section 13(f) securities" shall mean equity securities of a class described in section 13(d)(1) of the Act that are admitted to trading on a national securities exchange or quoted on the automated quotation system of a registered securities association. In determining what classes of securities are section 13(f) securities, an institutional investment manager may rely on the most recent list of such securities published by the Commission pursuant to section 13(f)(4) of the Act. Only securities of a class on such list shall be counted in determining whether an institutional investment manager must file a report under this rule (Rule 13f–1(a)) and only those securities shall be reported in such report. Where a person controls the issuer of a class of equity securities which are "section 13(f) securities" as defined in this rule, those securities shall not be deemed to be "section 13(f) securities" with respect to the controlling person, provided that such person does not otherwise exercise investment discretion with respect to accounts with fair market value of at least $100,000,000 within the meaning of paragraph (a) of this rule.

Rule 13h–1. Large trader reporting*

(a) *Definitions*. For purposes of this section:

(1) The term *large trader* means any person that:

(i) Directly or indirectly, including through other persons controlled by such person, exercises investment discretion over one or more accounts and effects transactions for the purchase or sale of any NMS security for or on behalf of such accounts, by or through one or more registered broker-dealers, in an aggregate amount equal to or greater than the identifying activity level; or

(ii) Voluntarily registers as a large trader by filing electronically with the Commission Form 13H (17 CFR 249.327).

* The SEC implemented a two-phased approach to implementation of the recordkeeping, reporting, and monitoring requirements of Rule 13h–1. On April 20, 2012, the SEC issued an Order Temporarily Exempting Broker–Dealers from the Recordkeeping, Reporting, and Monitoring Requirements of Rule 13h–1 under the Securities Exchange Act of 1934 and Granting an Exemption for Certain Securities Transactions as part of the first phase. In Phase One, the SEC provided a temporary exemption to extend the compliance date from April 30, 2012 to May 1, 2013 for the broker-dealer recordkeeping and reporting requirements, except with respect to a clearing broker-dealer for a large trader where the large trader: (1) is a U.S.-registered broker-dealer, or (2) trades through a sponsored access arrangement, for which the temporary exemption was extended only to November 30, 2012. The SEC has fully implemented Phase One and is now focusing its attention on Phase Two. As such, the recent temporary exemption solely applies to the Phase Two broker-dealer recordkeeping, reporting, and monitoring requirements of Rule 13h–1. The SEC release number is 24–69281. The text of the exemption is as follows:

IT IS HEREBY ORDERED, pursuant to Exchange Act Section 13(h)(6) and Rule 13h–1(g) thereunder, that broker-dealers subject to the recordkeeping, reporting, and monitoring requirements of Rule 13h–1 (other than clearing broker-dealers for a large trader that either (1) is a U.S.-registered broker0dealer, or (2) trades through a sponsored access arrangement) are temporarily exempted from those requirements until November 1, 2013.

(2) The term *person* has the same meaning as in Section 13(h)(8)(E) of the Securities Exchange Act of 1934 (15 U.S.C. 78m(h)(8)(E)).

(3) The term *control* (including the terms controlling, controlled by and under common control with) means the possession, direct or indirect, of the power to direct or cause the direction of the management and policies of a person, whether through the ownership of securities, by contract, or otherwise. For purposes of this section only, any person that directly or indirectly has the right to vote or direct the vote of 25% or more of a class of voting securities of an entity or has the power to sell or direct the sale of 25% or more of a class of voting securities of such entity, or in the case of a partnership, has the right to receive, upon dissolution, or has contributed, 25% or more of the capital, is presumed to control that entity.

(4) The term *investment discretion* has the same meaning as in Section 3(a)(35) of the Securities Exchange Act of 1934 (15 U.S.C. 78c(3)(a)(35)). A person's employees who exercise investment discretion within the scope of their employment are deemed to do so on behalf of such person.

(5) The term *NMS security* has the meaning provided for in Rule 600(b)(46) under Regulation NMS.

(6) The term *transaction* or *transactions* means all transactions in NMS securities, excluding the purchase or sale of such securities pursuant to exercises or assignments of option contracts. For the sole purpose of determining whether a person is a large trader, the following transactions are excluded from this definition:

(i) Any journal or bookkeeping entry made to an account in order to record or memorialize the receipt or delivery of funds or securities pursuant to the settlement of a transaction;

(ii) Any transaction that is part of an offering of securities by or on behalf of an issuer, or by an underwriter on behalf of an issuer, or an agent for an issuer, whether or not such offering is subject to registration under the Securities Act of 1933, provided, however, that this exemption shall not include an offering of securities effected through the facilities of a national securities exchange;

(iii) Any transaction that constitutes a gift;

(iv) Any transaction effected by a court appointed executor, administrator, or fiduciary pursuant to the distribution of a decedent's estate;

(v) Any transaction effected pursuant to a court order or judgment;

(vi) Any transaction effected pursuant to a rollover of qualified plan or trust assets subject to Section 402(a)(5) of the Internal Revenue Code (26 U.S.C. 1 *et seq.*);

(vii) Any transaction between an employer and its employees effected pursuant to the award, allocation, sale, grant, or exercise of a NMS security, option or other right to acquire securities at a pre-established price pursuant to a plan which is primarily for the purpose of an issuer benefit plan or compensatory arrangement; or

(viii) Any transaction to effect a business combination, including a reclassification, merger, consolidation, or tender offer subject to Section 14(d) of the Securities Exchange Act of 1934 (15 U.S.C. 78n(d)); an issuer tender offer or other stock buyback by an issuer; or a stock loan or equity repurchase agreement.

(7) The term *identifying activity level* means: aggregate transactions in NMS securities that are equal to or greater than:

(i) During a calendar day, either two million shares or shares with a fair market value of $20 million; or

(ii) During a calendar month, either twenty million shares or shares with a fair market value of $200 million.

(8) The term *reporting activity level* means:

(i) Each transaction in NMS securities, effected in a single account during a calendar day, that is equal to or greater than 100 shares;

(ii) Any transaction in NMS securities for fewer than 100 shares, effected in a single account during a calendar day, that a registered broker-dealer may deem appropriate; or

(iii) Such other amount that may be established by order of the Commission from time to time.

(9) The term *Unidentified Large Trader* means each person who has not complied with the identi-

fication requirements of paragraphs (b)(1) and (b)(2) of this section that a registered broker-dealer knows or has reason to know is a large trader. For purposes of determining under this section whether a registered broker-dealer has reason to know that a person is large trader, a registered broker-dealer need take into account only transactions in NMS securities effected by or through such broker-dealer.

(b) *Identification Requirements for Large Traders.*

(1) *Form 13H.* Except as provided in paragraph (b)(3) of this section, each large trader shall file electronically Form 13H (17 CFR 249.327) with the Commission, in accordance with the instructions contained therein:

(i) Promptly after first effecting aggregate transactions, or after effecting aggregate transactions subsequent to becoming inactive pursuant to paragraph (b)(3) of this section, equal to or greater than the identifying activity level;

(ii) Within 45 days after the end of each full calendar year; and

(iii) Promptly following the end of a calendar quarter in the event that any of the information contained in a Form 13H filing becomes inaccurate for any reason.

(2) *Disclosure of Large Trader Status.* Each large trader shall disclose to the registered broker-dealers effecting transactions on its behalf its large trader identification number and each account to which it applies. A large trader on Inactive Status pursuant to paragraph (b)(3) of this section must notify broker-dealers promptly after filing for reactivated status with the Commission.

(3) *Filing Requirement.*

(i) *Compliance by Controlling Person.* A large trader shall not be required to separately comply with the requirements of this paragraph (b) if a person who controls the large trader complies with all of the requirements under paragraphs (b)(1), (b)(2), and (b)(4) of this section applicable to such large trader with respect to all of its accounts.

(ii) *Compliance by Controlled Person.* A large trader shall not be required to separately comply with the requirements of this paragraph (b) if one or more persons controlled by such large trader collectively comply with all of the requirements under paragraphs (b)(1), (b)(2), and (b)(4) of this section applicable to such large trader with respect to all of its accounts.

(iii) *Inactive Status.* A large trader that has not effected aggregate transactions at any time during the previous full calendar year in an amount equal to or greater than the identifying activity level shall become inactive upon filing a Form 13H (17 CFR 249.327) and thereafter shall not be required to file Form 13H or disclose its large trader status unless and until its transactions again are equal to or greater than the identifying activity level. A large trader that has ceased operations may elect to become inactive by filing an amended Form 13H to indicate its terminated status.

(4) *Other Information.* Upon request, a large trader must promptly provide additional descriptive or clarifying information that would allow the Commission to further identify the large trader and all accounts through which the large trader effects transactions.

(c) *Aggregation.*

(1) *Transactions.* For the purpose of determining whether a person is a large trader, the following shall apply:

(i) The volume or fair market value of transactions in equity securities and the volume or fair market value of the equity securities underlying transactions in options on equity securities, purchased and sold, shall be aggregated;

(ii) The fair market value of transactions in options on a group or index of equity securities (or based on the value thereof), purchased and sold, shall be aggregated; and

(iii) Under no circumstances shall a person subtract, offset, or net purchase and sale transactions, in equity securities or option contracts, and among or within accounts, when aggregating the volume or fair market value of transactions for purposes of this section.

(2) *Accounts.* Under no circumstances shall a person disaggregate accounts to avoid the identification requirements of this section.

(d) *Recordkeeping Requirements for Broker and Dealers.*

(1) *Generally.* Every registered broker-dealer shall maintain records of all information required under paragraphs (d)(2) and (d)(3) of this section

for all transactions effected directly or indirectly by or through:

(i) An account such broker-dealer carries for a large trader or an Unidentified Large Trader, or

(ii) If the broker-dealer is a large trader, any proprietary or other account over which such broker-dealer exercises investment discretion.

(iii) Additionally, where a non-broker-dealer carries an account for a large trader or an Unidentified Large Trader, the broker-dealer effecting transactions directly or indirectly for such large trader or Unidentified Large Trader shall maintain records of all of the information required under paragraphs (d)(2) and (d)(3) of this section for those transactions.

(2) *Information.* The information required to be maintained for all transactions shall include:

(i) The clearing house number or alpha symbol of the broker or dealer submitting the information and the clearing house numbers or alpha symbols of the entities on the opposite side of the transaction;

(ii) Identifying symbol assigned to the security;

(iii) Date transaction was executed;

(iv) The number of shares or option contracts traded in each specific transaction; whether each transaction was a purchase, sale, or short sale; and, if an option contract, whether the transaction was a call or put option, an opening purchase or sale, a closing purchase or sale, or an exercise or assignment;

(v) Transaction price;

(vi) Account number;

(vii) Identity of the exchange or other market center where the transaction was executed.

(viii) A designation of whether the transaction was effected or caused to be effected for the account of a customer of such registered broker-dealer, or was a proprietary transaction effected or caused to be effected for the account of such broker-dealer;

(ix) If part or all of an account's transactions at the registered broker-dealer have been transferred or otherwise forwarded to one or more ccounts at another registered broker-dealer, n identifier for this type of transaction; and if t or all of an account's transactions at the rting broker-dealer have been transferred erwise received from one or more other registered broker-dealers, an identifier for this type of transaction;

(x) If part or all of an account's transactions at the reporting broker-dealer have been transferred or otherwise received from another account at the reporting broker-dealer, an identifier for this type of transaction; and if part or all of an account's transactions at the reporting broker-dealer have been transferred or otherwise forwarded to one or more other accounts at the reporting broker-dealer, an identifier for this type of transaction;

(xi) If a transaction was processed by a depository institution, the identifier assigned to the account by the depository institution;

(xii) The time that the transaction was executed; and

(xiii) The large trader identification number(s) associated with the account, unless the account is for an Unidentified Large Trader.

(3) *Information Relating to Unidentified Large Traders.* With respect to transactions effected directly or indirectly by or through the account of an Unidentified Large Trader, the information required to be maintained for all transactions also shall include such Unidentified Large Trader's name, address, date the account was opened, and tax identification number(s).

(4) *Retention.* The records and information required to be made and kept pursuant to the provisions of this section shall be kept for such periods of time as provided in Rule 17a–4(b).

(5) *Availability of Information.* The records and information required to be made and kept pursuant to the provisions of this rule shall be available on the morning after the day the transactions were effected (including Saturdays and holidays).

(e) *Reporting Requirements for Brokers and Dealers.* Upon the request of the Commission, every registered broker-dealer who is itself a large trader or carries an account for a large trader or an Unidentified Large Trader shall electronically report to the Commission, using the infrastructure supporting Rule 17a–25, in machine-readable form and in accordance with instructions issued by the Commission, all information required under paragraphs (d)(2) and (d)(3) of this section for all transactions effected directly or indirectly by or through accounts carried by such broker-dealer for large traders and Unidentified Large Traders, equal to or greater than the reporting activity level. Additionally, where a non-broker-dealer carries an account for a large trader or an Unidentified Large Trader, the broker-dealer effecting such transactions directly or indirectly for a large trader shall electronically report using the infrastructure supporting Rule 17a–25, in machine-readable form and in accordance with instructions issued by the Commission, all information required under paragraphs (d)(2) and (d)(3) of this section for such transactions equal to or greater than the reporting activity level. Such reports shall be submitted to the Commission no later than the day and time specified in the request for transaction information, which shall be no earlier than the opening of business of the day following such request, unless in unusual circumstances the same-day submission of information is requested.

(f) *Monitoring Safe Harbor*. For the purposes of this rule, a registered broker-dealer shall be deemed not to know or have reason to know that a person is a large trader if it does not have actual knowledge that a person is a large trader and it establishes policies and procedures reasonably designed to:

(1) Identify persons who have not complied with the identification requirements of paragraphs (b)(1) and (b)(2) of this section but whose transactions effected through an account or a group of accounts carried by such broker-dealer or through which such broker-dealer executes transactions, as applicable (and considering account name, tax identification number, or other identifying information available on the books and records of such broker-dealer) equal or exceed the identifying activity level;

(2) Treat any persons identified in paragraph (f)(1) of this section as an Unidentified Large Trader for purposes of this section; and

(3) Inform any person identified in paragraph (f)(1) of this section of its potential obligations under this section.

(g) *Exemptions*. Upon written application or upon its own motion, the Commission may by order exempt, upon specified terms and conditions or for stated periods, any person or class of persons or any transaction or class of transactions from the provisions of this section to the extent that such exemption is consistent with the purposes of the Securities Exchange Act of 1934.

Rule 13k–1. Foreign bank exemption from the insider lending prohibition under Section 13(k)

(a) For the purpose of this rule:

(1) *Foreign bank* means an institution:

(i) The home jurisdiction of which is other than the United States;

(ii) That is regulated as a bank in its home jurisdiction; and

(iii) That engages directly in the business of banking.

(2) *Home jurisdiction* means the country, political subdivision or other place in which a foreign bank is incorporated or organized.

(3) *Engages directly in the business of banking* means that an institution engages directly in banking activities that are usual for the business of banking in its home jurisdiction.

(4) *Affiliate, parent* and *subsidiary* have the same meaning as under Rule 12b–2.

(b) An issuer that is a foreign bank or the parent or other affiliate of a foreign bank is exempt from the prohibition of extending, maintaining, arranging for, or renewing credit in the form of a personal loan to or for any of its directors or executive officers under section 13(k) of the Act (15 U.S.C. 78m(k)) with respect to any such loan made by the foreign bank as long as:

(1) Either:

(i) The laws or regulations of the foreign bank's home jurisdiction require the bank to insure its deposits or be subject to a deposit guarantee or protection scheme; or

(ii) The Board of Governors of the Federal Reserve System has determined that the foreign bank or another bank organized in the foreign bank's home jurisdiction is subject to comprehensive supervision or regulation on a consolidated basis by the bank supervisor in its home jurisdiction under 12 CFR 211.24(c); and

(2) The loan by the foreign bank to any of its directors or executive officers or those of its parent or other affiliate:

(i) Is on substantially the same terms as those prevailing at the time for comparable transactions by the foreign bank with other persons who are not executive officers, directors or employees of the foreign bank, its parent or other affiliate; or

(ii) Is pursuant to a benefit or compensation program that is widely available to the employees of the foreign bank, its parent or other affiliate and does not give preference to any the executive officers or directors of the foreign bank, its parent or other affiliate over any other employees of the foreign bank, its parent or other affiliate; or

(iii) Has received express approval by the bank supervisor in the foreign bank's home jurisdiction.

NOTES TO PARAGRAPH (b):

1. The exemption provided in paragraph (b) of this rule applies to a loan by the subsidiary of a foreign bank to a director or executive officer of the foreign bank, its parent or other affiliate as long as the subsidiary is under the supervision or regulation of the bank supervisor in the foreign bank's home jurisdiction, the subsidiary's loan meets the requirements of paragraph (b)(2) of this rule, and the foreign bank meets the requirements of paragraph (b)(1) of this rule.

2. For the purpose of paragraph (b)(1)(ii) of this rule, a foreign bank may rely on a determination by the Board of Governors of the Federal Reserve System that another bank in the foreign bank's home jurisdiction is subject to comprehensive supervision or regulation on a consolidated basis by the bank supervisor under 12 CFR 211.24(c) as long as the foreign bank is under substantially the same banking supervision or regulation as the other bank in their home jurisdiction.

(c) As used in paragraph (1) of section 13(k) of the Act (15 U.S.C. 78m(k)(1)), issuer does not include a foreign government, as defined under Rule 405 under the Securities Act of 1933, that files a registration statement under the Securities Act of 1933 (15 U.S.C. 77a *et seq.*) on Schedule B.

Rule 13n–1. Registration of security-based swap data repository

(a) *Definitions.* For purposes of this section –

(1) *Non-resident security-based swap data repository* means:

(i) In the case of an individual, one who resides in or has his principal place of business in any place not in the United States;

(ii) In the case of a corporation, one incorporated in or having its principal place of business in any place not in the United States; or

(iii) In the case of a partnership or other unincorporated organization or association, one having its principal place of business in any place not in the United States.

(2) *Tag* (including the term tagged) has the same meaning as set forth in Rule 11 of Regulation S–T.

(b) An application for the registration of a security-based swap data repository and all amendments thereto shall be filed electronically in a tagged data format on Form SDR (17 CFR 249.1500) with the Commission in accordance with the instructions contained therein. As part of the application process, each security-based swap data repository shall provide additional information to any representative of the Commission upon request.

(c) Within 90 days of the date of the publication of notice of the filing of such application (or within such longer period as to which the applicant consents), the Commission shall –

(1) By order grant registration; or

(2) Institute proceedings to determine whether registration should be granted or denied. Such proceedings shall include notice of the issues under consideration and opportunity for hearing on the record and shall be concluded within 180 days of the date of the publication of notice of the filing of the application for registration under paragraph (b) of this section. At the conclusion of such proceedings, the Commission, by order, shall grant or deny such registration. The Commission may extend the time for conclusion of such proceedings for up to 90 days if it finds good cause for such extension and publishes its reasons for so finding or for such longer period as to which the applicant consents.

(3) The Commission shall grant the registration of a security-based swap data repository if the Commission finds that such security-based swap data repository is so organized, and has the capacity, to be able to assure the prompt, accurate, and reliable performance of its functions as a security-based swap data repository, comply with any applicable provision of the federal securities laws and the rules and regulations thereunder, and carry out its functions in a manner consistent with the purposes of section 13(n) of the Act and the rules and regulations thereunder. The Commission shall deny the registration of a security-based swap data repository if it does not make any such finding.

(d) If any information reported in items 1 through 17, 26, and 48 of Form SDR (17 CFR 249.1500) or in any amendment thereto is or becomes inaccurate for any reason, whether before or after the registration has been granted, the security-based swap data repository shall promptly file an amendment on Form SDR updating such information. In addition, the security-based swap data repository shall annually file an amendment on Form SDR within 60 days after the end of each fiscal year of such security-based swap data repository.

(e) Each security-based swap data repository shall designate and authorize on Form SDR an agent in the United States, other than a Commission member, official, or employee, who shall accept any notice or service of process, pleadings, or other documents in any action or proceedings brought against the security-based swap data repository to enforce the federal securities laws and the rules and regulations thereunder.

(f) Any non-resident security-based swap data repository applying for registration pursuant to this section shall:

(1) Certify on Form SDR that the security-based swap data repository can, as a matter of law, and will provide the Commission with prompt access to the books and records of such security-based swap data repository and can, as a matter of law, and will submit to onsite inspection and examination by the Commission, and

(2) Provide an opinion of counsel that the security-based swap data repository can, as a matter of law, provide the Commission with prompt access to the books and records of such security-based swap data repository and can, as a matter of law, submit to onsite inspection and examination by the Commission.

(g) An application for registration or any amendment thereto that is filed pursuant to this section shall be considered a "report" filed with the Commission for purposes of sections 18(a) and 32(a) of the Act and the rules and regulations thereunder and other applicable provisions of the United States Code and the rules and regulations thereunder.

Rule 13n–2. Withdrawal from registration; revocation and cancellation

(a) *Definition. For purposes of this section, tag (including the term tagged) has the same meaning as set forth in Rule 11 of Regulation S–T.*

(b) A registered security-based swap data repository may withdraw from registration by filing a withdrawal from registration on Form SDR (17 CFR 249.1500) electronically in a tagged data format. The security-based swap data repository shall designate on Form SDR a person to serve as the custodian of the security-based swap data repository's books and records. When filing a withdrawal from registration on Form SDR, a security-based swap data repository shall update any inaccurate information.

(c) A withdrawal from registration filed by a security-based swap data repository shall become effective for all matters (except as provided in this paragraph (c)) on the 60th day after the filing thereof with the Commission, within such longer period of time as to which such security-based swap data repository consents or which the Commission, by order, may determine as necessary or appropriate in the public interest or for the protection of investors, or within such shorter period of time as the Commission may determine.

(d) A withdrawal from registration that is filed pursuant to this section shall be considered a "report" filed with the Commission for purposes of sections 18(a) and 32(a) of the Act and the rules and regulations thereunder and other applicable provisions of the United States Code and the rules and regulations thereunder.

(e) If the Commission finds, on the record after notice and opportunity for hearing, that any registered security-based swap data repository has obtained its registration by making any false and misleading statements with respect to any material fact or has violated or failed to comply with any provision of the federal securities laws and the rules and regulations thereunder, the Commission, by order, may revoke the registration. Pending final determination of whether any registration shall be revoked, the Commission, by order, may suspend such registration, if such suspension appears to the Commission, after notice and opportunity for hearing on the record, to be necessary or appropriate in the public interest or for the protection of investors.

(f) If the Commission finds that a registered security-based swap data repository is no longer in existence or has ceased to do business in the capacity specified in its application for registration, the Commission, by order, may cancel the registration.

Rule 13n–3. Registration of successor to registered security-based swap data repository

(a) In the event that a security-based swap data repository succeeds to and continues the business of a security-based swap data repository registered pursuant to section 13(n) of the Act, the registration of the predecessor shall be deemed to remain effective as the registration of the successor if, within 30 days after such succession, the successor files an application for registration on Form SDR (17 CFR 249.1500), and the predecessor files a withdrawal from registration on Form SDR; provided, however, that the registration of the predecessor security-based swap data repository shall cease to be effective 90 days after the publication of notice of the filing of the application for registration on Form SDR filed by the successor security-based swap data repository.

(b) Notwithstanding paragraph (a) of this section, if a security-based swap data repository succeeds to and continues the business of a registered predecessor security-based swap data repository, and the succession is based solely on a change in the predecessor's date or state of incorporation, form of organization, or composition of a partnership, the successor may, within 30 days after the succession, amend the registration of the predecessor security-based swap data repository on Form SDR (17 CFR 249.1500) to reflect these changes. This amendment shall be deemed an application for registration filed by the predecessor and adopted by the successor.

Rule 13n–4. Duties and core principles of security-based swap data repository

(a) *Definitions.* For purposes of this section –

(1) *Affiliate* of a security-based swap data repository means a person that, directly or indirectly, controls, is controlled by, or is under common control with the security-based swap data repository.

(2) *Board* means the board of directors of the security-based swap data repository or a body performing a function similar to the board of directors of the security-based swap data repository.

(3) *Control* (including the terms controlled by and under common control with) means the possession, direct or indirect, of the power to direct or cause the direction of the management and policies of a person, whether through the ownership of voting securities, by contract, or otherwise. A person is presumed to control another person if the person:

(i) Is a director, general partner, or officer exercising executive responsibility (or having similar status or functions);

(ii) Directly or indirectly has the right to vote 25 percent or more of a class of voting securities or has the power to sell or direct the sale of 25 percent or more of a class of voting securities; or

(iii) In the case of a partnership, has the right to receive, upon dissolution, or has contributed, 25 percent or more of the capital.

(4) *Director* means any member of the board.

(5) *Direct electronic access* means access, which shall be in a form and manner acceptable to the Commission, to data stored by a security-based swap data repository in an electronic format and updated at the same time as the security-based swap data repository's data is updated so as to provide the Commission or any of its designees with the ability to query or analyze the data in the same manner that the security-based swap data repository can query or analyze the data.

(6) *Market participant* means any person participating in the security-based swap market, including, but not limited to, security-based swap dealers, major security-based swap participants, and any other counterparties to a security-based swap transaction.

(7) *Nonaffiliated third party of a security-based swap data repository* means any person except:

(i) The security-based swap data repository;

(ii) Any affiliate of the security-based swap data repository; or

(iii) A person employed by a security-based swap data repository and any entity that is not the security-based swap data repository's affiliate (and "nonaffiliated third party" includes such entity that jointly employs the person).

(8) Person associated with a security-based swap data repository means:

(i) Any partner, officer, or director of such security-based swap data repository (or any person occupying a similar status or performing similar functions);

(ii) Any person directly or indirectly controlling, controlled by, or under common control with such security-based swap data repository; or

(iii) Any employee of such security-based swap data repository.

(b) *Duties.* To be registered, and maintain registration, as a security-based swap data repository, a security-based swap data repository shall:

(1) Subject itself to inspection and examination by any representative of the Commission;

(2) Accept data as prescribed in Regulation SBSR (17 CFR 242.900 through 242.909) for each security-based swap;

(3) Confirm, as prescribed in Rule 13n–5, with both counterparties to the security-based swap the accuracy of the data that was submitted;

(4) Maintain, as prescribed in Rule 13n–5, the data described in Regulation SBSR in such form, in such manner, and for such period as provided therein and in the Act and the rules and regulations thereunder;

(5) Provide direct electronic access to the Commission (or any designee of the Commission, including another registered entity);

(6) Provide the information described in Regulation SBSR in such form and at such frequency as prescribed in Regulation SBSR to comply with the public reporting requirements set forth in section 13(m) of the Act and the rules and regulations thereunder;

(7) At such time and in such manner as may be directed by the Commission, establish automated systems for monitoring, screening, and analyzing security-based swap data;

(8) Maintain the privacy of any and all security-based swap transaction information that the security-based swap data repository receives from a security-based swap dealer, counterparty, or any registered entity as prescribed in Rule 13n–9 under the Securities Exchange Act of 1934;

(9) On a confidential basis, pursuant to section 24 of the Act (15 U.S.C. 78x), upon request, and after notifying the Commission of the request in a manner consistent with paragraph (d) of this rule, make available security-based swap data obtained by the security-based swap data repository, including individual counterparty trade and position data, to the following:

(i) The Board of Governors of the Federal Reserve System and any Federal Reserve Bank;

(ii) The Office of the Comptroller of the Currency;

(iii) The Federal Deposit Insurance Corporation;

(iv) The Farm Credit Administration;

(v) The Federal Housing Finance Agency;

(vi) The Financial Stability Oversight Council;

(vii) The Commodity Futures Trading Commission;

(viii) The Department of Justice;

(ix) The Office of Financial Research; and

(x) Any other person that the Commission determines to be appropriate, conditionally or unconditionally, by order, including, but not limited to—

(A) Foreign financial supervisors (including foreign futures authorities);

(B) Foreign central banks;

(C) Foreign ministries; and

(D) Other foreign authorities;

(10) Before sharing information with any entity described in paragraph (b)(9) of this rule, there shall be in effect an arrangement between the Commission and the entity (in the form of a memorandum of understanding or otherwise) to address the confidentiality of the security-based swap information made available to the entity; this arrangement shall be deemed to satisfy the requirement, set forth in section 13(n)(5)(H) of the Act (15 U.S.C. 78m(n)(5)(H)), that the security-based swap data repository receive a written agreement from the entity stating that the entity shall abide by the confidentiality requirements described in section 24 of the Act (15 U.S.C. 78x) relating to the information on security-based swap transactions that is provided; and

(11) Designate an individual to serve as a chief compliance officer.

(c) *Compliance with core principles.* A security-based swap data repository shall comply with the core principles as described in this paragraph.

(1) *Market access to services and data.* Unless necessary or appropriate to achieve the purposes of the Act and the rules and regulations thereunder, the security-based swap data repository shall not adopt any policies or procedures or take any action that results in an unreasonable restraint of trade or impose any material anticompetitive burden on the trading, clearing, or reporting of transactions. To comply with this core principle, each security-based swap data repository shall:

(i) Ensure that any dues, fees, or other charges imposed by, and any discounts or rebates offered by, a security-based swap data repository are fair and reasonable and not unreasonably discriminatory. Such dues, fees, other charges, discounts, or rebates shall be applied consistently across all similarly-situated users of such security-based swap data repository's services, including, but not limited to, market participants, market infrastructures (including central counterparties), venues from which data can be submitted to the security-based swap data repository (including exchanges, security-based swap execution facilities, electronic trading venues, and matching and confirmation platforms), and third party service providers;

(ii) Permit market participants to access specific services offered by the security-based swap data repository separately;

(iii) Establish, monitor on an ongoing basis, and enforce clearly stated objective criteria that would permit fair, open, and not unreasonably discriminatory access to services offered and data maintained by the security-based swap data repository as well as fair, open, and not unreasonably discriminatory participation by market participants, market infrastructures, venues from which data can be submitted to the security-based swap data repository, and third party service providers that seek to connect to or link with the security-based swap data repository; and

(iv) Establish, maintain, and enforce written policies and procedures reasonably designed to review any prohibition or limitation of any person with respect to access to services offered, directly or indirectly, or data maintained by the security-based swap data repository and to grant such person access to such services or data if such person has been discriminated against unfairly.

(2) *Governance arrangements.* Each security-based swap data repository shall establish governance arrangements that are transparent to fulfill public interest requirements under the Act and the rules and regulations thereunder; to carry out functions consistent with the Act, the rules and regulations thereunder, and the purposes of the Act; and to support the objectives of the Federal Government, owners, and participants. To comply with this core principle, each security-based swap data repository shall:

(i) Establish governance arrangements that are well defined and include a clear organizational structure with effective internal controls;

(ii) Establish governance arrangements that provide for fair representation of market participants;

(iii) Provide representatives of market participants, including end-users, with the opportunity to participate in the process for nominating directors and with the right to petition for alternative candidates; and

(iv) Establish, maintain, and enforce written policies and procedures reasonably designed to ensure that the security-based swap data repository's senior management and each member of the board or committee that has the authority to act on behalf of the board possess requisite skills and expertise to fulfill their responsibilities in the management and governance of the security-based swap data repository, have a clear understanding of their responsibilities, and exercise sound judgment about the security-based swap data repository's affairs.

(3) *Conflicts of interest.* Each security-based swap data repository shall establish and enforce written policies and procedures reasonably designed to minimize conflicts of interest in the decision-making process of the security-based swap data repository and establish a process for resolving any such conflicts of interest. Such conflicts of interest include, but are not limited to: conflicts between the commercial interests of a security-based swap data repository and its statutory and regulatory responsibilities; conflicts in connection with the commercial interests of certain market participants or linked market infrastructures, third party service providers, and others; conflicts between, among, or with persons associated with the security-based swap data repository, market participants, affiliates of the security-based swap data repository, and nonaffiliated third parties; and misuse of confidential information, material, nonpublic information, and/or intellectual property. To comply with this core principle, each security-based swap data repository shall:

(i) Establish, maintain, and enforce written policies and procedures reasonably designed to identify and mitigate potential and existing conflicts of interest in the security-based swap data repository's decision-making process on an ongoing basis;

(ii) With respect to the decision-making process for resolving any conflicts of interest, require the recusal of any person involved in such conflict from such decision-making; and

(iii) Establish, maintain, and enforce reasonable written policies and procedures regarding the security-based swap data repository's non-commercial and/or commercial use of the security-based swap transaction information that it receives from a market participant, any registered entity, or any other person.

(d) *Notification requirement compliance.* To satisfy the notification requirement of the data access provisions of paragraph (b)(9) of this rule, a security-based swap data repository shall inform the Commission upon its receipt of the first request for security-based swap data from a particular entity (which may include any request to be provided ongoing online or electronic access to the data), and the repository shall maintain records of all information related to the initial and all subsequent requests for data access from that entity, including records of all instances of online or electronic access, and records of all data provided in connection with such requests or access.

Note to Rule 13n–4: This rule is not intended to limit, or restrict, the applicability of other provisions of the federal securities laws, including, but not limited to, section 13(m) of the Act and the rules and regulations thereunder.

Rule 13n–5. Data collection and maintenance

(a) *Definitions. For purposes of this section –*

(1) *Asset class* means those security-based swaps in a particular broad category, including, but not limited to, credit derivatives and equity derivatives.

(2) *Position* means the gross and net notional amounts of open security-based swap transactions aggregated by one or more attributes, including, but not limited to, the:

(i) Underlying instrument, index, or reference entity;

(ii) Counterparty;

(iii) Asset class;

(iv) Long risk of the underlying instrument, index, or reference entity; and

(v) Short risk of the underlying instrument, index, or reference entity.

(3) *Transaction data* means all information reported to a security-based swap data repository pursuant to the Act and the rules and regulations thereunder, except for information provided pursuant to Rule 906(b) of Regulation SBSR.

(b) *Requirements.* Every security-based swap data repository registered with the Commission shall comply with the following data collection and data maintenance standards:

(1) *Transaction data.* (i) Every security-based swap data repository shall establish, maintain, and enforce written policies and procedures reasonably designed for the reporting of complete and accurate transaction data to the security-based swap data repository and shall accept all transaction data that is reported in accordance with such policies and procedures.

(ii) If a security-based swap data repository accepts any security-based swap in a particular asset class, the security-based swap data repository shall accept all security-based swaps in that asset class that are reported to it in accordance with its policies and procedures required by paragraph (b)(1)(i) of this section.

(iii) Every security-based swap data repository shall establish, maintain, and enforce written policies and procedures reasonably designed to satisfy itself that the transaction data that has been submitted to the security-based swap data repository is complete and accurate, and clearly identifies the source for each trade side and the pairing method (if any) for each transaction in order to identify the level of quality of the transaction data.

(iv) Every security-based swap data repository shall promptly record the transaction data it receives.

(2) *Positions.* Every security-based swap data repository shall establish, maintain, and enforce written policies and procedures reasonably designed to calculate positions for all persons with open security-based swaps for which the security-based swap data repository maintains records.

(3) Every security-based swap data repository shall establish, maintain, and enforce written policies and procedures reasonably designed to ensure that the transaction data and positions that it maintains are complete and accurate.

(4) Every security-based swap data repository shall maintain transaction data and related identifying information for not less than five years after the applicable security-based swap expires and historical positions for not less than five years:

(i) In a place and format that is readily accessible and usable to the Commission and other persons with authority to access or view such information; and

(ii) In an electronic format that is non-rewriteable and non-erasable.

(5) Every security-based swap data repository shall establish, maintain, and enforce written policies and procedures reasonably designed to prevent any provision in a valid security-based swap from being invalidated or modified through the procedures or operations of the security-based swap data repository.

(6) Every security-based swap data repository shall establish procedures and provide facilities reasonably designed to effectively resolve disputes over the accuracy of the transaction data and positions that are recorded in the security-based swap data repository.

(7) If a security-based swap data repository ceases doing business, or ceases to be registered pursuant to section 13(n) of the Act and the rules and regulations thereunder, it must continue to preserve, maintain, and make accessible the transaction data and historical positions required to be collected, maintained, and preserved by this section in the manner required by the Act and the rules and regulations thereunder and for the remainder of the period required by this section.

(8) Every security-based swap data repository shall make and keep current a plan to ensure that the transaction data and positions that are recorded in the security-based swap data repository continue to be maintained in accordance with Rule 13n–5(b)(7), which shall include procedures for transferring the transaction data and positions to the Commission or its designee (including another registered security-based swap data repository).

Rule 13n–6. Automated systems

Every security-based swap data repository, with respect to those systems that support or are integrally related to the performance of its activities, shall establish, maintain, and enforce written policies and procedures reasonably designed to ensure that its systems provide adequate levels of capacity, integrity, resiliency, availability, and security.

Rule 13n–7. Recordkeeping of security-based swap data repository

(a) Every security-based swap data repository shall make and keep current the following books and records relating to its business:

(1) A record for each office listing, by name or title, each person at that office who, without delay, can explain the types of records the security-based swap data repository maintains at that office and the information contained in those records; and

(2) A record listing each officer, manager, or person performing similar functions of the security-based swap data repository responsible for establishing policies and procedures that are reasonably designed to ensure compliance with the Act and the rules and regulations thereunder.

(b) *Recordkeeping rule* for security-based swap data repositories. (1) Every security-based swap data repository shall keep and preserve at least one copy of all documents, including all documents and policies and procedures required by the Act and the rules and regulations thereunder, correspondence, memoranda, papers, books, notices, accounts, and other such records as shall be made or received by it in the course of its business as such.

(2) Every security-based swap data repository shall keep all such documents for a period of not less than five years, the first two years in a place that is immediately available to representatives of the Commission for inspection and examination.

(3) Every security-based swap data repository shall, upon request of any representative of the Commission, promptly furnish to the possession of such representative copies of any documents required to be kept and preserved by it pursuant to paragraphs (a) and (b) of this section.

(c) If a security-based swap data repository ceases doing business, or ceases to be registered pursuant to section 13(n) of the Act and the rules and regulations thereunder, it must continue to preserve, maintain, and make accessible the records and data required to be collected, maintained and preserved by this section in the manner required by this section and for the remainder of the period required by this section.

(d) This section does not apply to transaction data and positions collected and maintained pursuant to Rule 13n–5.

Rule 13n–8. Reports to be provided to the Commission

Every security-based swap data repository shall promptly report to the Commission, in a form and manner acceptable to the Commission, such information as the Commission determines to be necessary or appropriate for the Commission to perform the duties of the Commission under the Act and the rules and regulations thereunder.

Rule 13n–9. Privacy requirements of security-based swap data repository

(a) *Definitions. For purposes of this section –*

(1) *Affiliate of a security-based swap data repository* means a person that, directly or indirectly, controls, is controlled by, or is under common control with the security-based swap data repository.

(2) *Control* (including the terms controlled by and under common control with) means the possession, direct or indirect, of the power to direct or cause the direction of the management and pol-

icies of a person, whether through the ownership of voting securities, by contract, or otherwise. A person is presumed to control another person if the person:

(i) Is a director, general partner, or officer exercising executive responsibility (or having similar status or functions);

(ii) Directly or indirectly has the right to vote 25 percent or more of a class of voting securities or has the power to sell or direct the sale of 25 percent or more of a class of voting securities; or

(iii) In the case of a partnership, has the right to receive, upon dissolution, or has contributed, 25 percent or more of the capital.

(3) *Market participant* means any person participating in the security-based swap market, including, but not limited to, security-based swap dealers, major security-based swap participants, and any other counterparties to a security-based swap transaction.

(4) *Nonaffiliated third party of a security-based swap data repository* means any person except:

(i) The security-based swap data repository;

(ii) The security-based swap data repository's affiliate; or

(iii) A person employed by a security-based swap data repository and any entity that is not the security-based swap data repository's affiliate (and nonaffiliated third party includes such entity that jointly employs the person).

(5) *Nonpublic personal information* means:

(i) Personally identifiable information that is not publicly available information; and

(ii) Any list, description, or other grouping of market participants (and publicly available information pertaining to them) that is derived using personally identifiable information that is not publicly available information.

(6) *Personally identifiable information* means any information:

(i) A market participant provides to a security-based swap data repository to obtain service from the security-based swap data repository;

(ii) About a market participant resulting from any transaction involving a service between the security-based swap data repository and the market participant; or

(iii) The security-based swap data repository obtains about a market participant in connection with providing a service to that market participant.

(7) *Person associated with a security-based swap data repository* means:

(i) Any partner, officer, or director of such security-based swap data repository (or any person occupying a similar status or performing similar functions);

(ii) Any person directly or indirectly controlling, controlled by, or under common control with such security-based swap data repository; or

(iii) Any employee of such security-based swap data repository.

(b) Each security-based swap data repository shall:

(1) Establish, maintain, and enforce written policies and procedures reasonably designed to protect the privacy of any and all security-based swap transaction information that the security-based swap data repository receives from a security-based swap dealer, counterparty, or any registered entity. Such policies and procedures shall include, but are not limited to, policies and procedures to protect the privacy of any and all security-based swap transaction information that the security-based swap data repository shares with affiliates and nonaffiliated third parties; and

(2) Establish and maintain safeguards, policies, and procedures reasonably designed to prevent the misappropriation or misuse, directly or indirectly, of:

(i) Any confidential information received by the security-based swap data repository, including, but not limited to, trade data, position data, and any nonpublic personal information about a market participant or any of its customers;

(ii) Material, nonpublic information; and/or

(iii) Intellectual property, such as trading strategies or portfolio positions,

by the security-based swap data repository or any person associated with the security-based swap data repository for their personal benefit or the benefit of others. Such safeguards, policies, and procedures shall address, without limitation:

(A) Limiting access to such confidential information, material, nonpublic information, and intellectual property;

(B) Standards pertaining to the trading by persons associated with the security-based swap data repository for their personal benefit or the benefit of others; and

(C) Adequate oversight to ensure compliance with this subparagraph.

Rule 13n–10. Disclosure requirements of security-based swap data repository

(a) *Definition.* For purposes of this section, market participant means any person participating in the over-the-counter derivatives market, including, but not limited to, security-based swap dealers, major security-based swap participants, and any other counterparties to a security-based swap transaction.

(b) Before accepting any security-based swap data from a market participant or upon a market participant's request, a security-based swap data repository shall furnish to the market participant a disclosure document that contains the following written information, which must reasonably enable the market participant to identify and evaluate accurately the risks and costs associated with using the services of the security-based swap data repository:

(1) The security-based swap data repository's criteria for providing others with access to services offered and data maintained by the security-based swap data repository;

(2) The security-based swap data repository's criteria for those seeking to connect to or link with the security-based swap data repository;

(3) A description of the security-based swap data repository's policies and procedures regarding its safeguarding of data and operational reliability, as described in Rule 13n–6;

(4) A description of the security-based swap data repository's policies and procedures reasonably designed to protect the privacy of any and all security-based swap transaction information that the security-based swap data repository receives from a security-based swap dealer, counterparty, or any registered entity, as described in Rule 13n–9(b)(1);

(5) A description of the security-based swap data repository's policies and procedures regarding its non-commercial and/or commercial use of the security-based swap transaction information that it receives from a market participant, any registered entity, or any other person;

(6) A description of the security-based swap data repository's dispute resolution procedures involving market participants, as described in Rule 13n–5(b)(6);

(7) A description of all the security-based swap data repository's services, including any ancillary services;

(8) The security-based swap data repository's updated schedule of any dues; unbundled prices, rates, or other fees for all of its services, including any ancillary services; any discounts or rebates offered; and the criteria to benefit from such discounts or rebates; and

(9) A description of the security-based swap data repository's governance arrangements.

Rule 13n–11. Chief compliance officer of security-based swap data repository; compliance reports and financial reports

(a) *In general.* Each security-based swap data repository shall identify on Form SDR (17 CFR 249.1500) a person who has been designated by the board to serve as a chief compliance officer of the security-based swap data repository. The compensation, appointment, and removal of the chief compliance officer shall require the approval of a majority of the security-based swap data repository's board.

(b) *Definitions.* For purposes of this section –

(1) *Board* means the board of directors of the security-based swap data repository or a body performing a function similar to the board of directors of the security-based swap data repository.

(2) *Director* means any member of the board.

(3) *EDGAR Filer Manual* has the same meaning as set forth in Rule 11 of Regulation S–T.

(4) *Interactive Data Financial Report* has the same meaning as set forth in Rule 11 of Regulation S–T.

(5) *Material change* means a change that a chief compliance officer would reasonably need to know in order to oversee compliance of the security-based swap data repository.

(6) *Material compliance matter* means any compliance matter that the board would reasonably need to know to oversee the compliance of the security-based swap data repository and that involves, without limitation:

(i) A violation of the federal securities laws by the security-based swap data repository, its officers, directors, employees, or agents;

(ii) A violation of the policies and procedures of the security-based swap data repository by the security-based swap data repository, its officers, directors, employees, or agents; or

(iii) A weakness in the design or implementation of the policies and procedures of the security-based swap data repository.

(7) *Official filing* has the same meaning as set forth in Rule 11 of Regulation S–T.

(8) Senior officer means the chief executive officer or other equivalent officer.

(9) Tag (including the term tagged) has the same meaning as set forth in Rule 11 of Regulation S–T.

(c) *Duties.* Each chief compliance officer of a security-based swap data repository shall:

(1) Report directly to the board or to the senior officer of the security-based swap data repository;

(2) Review the compliance of the security-based swap data repository with respect to the requirements and core principles described in section 13(n) of the Act and the rules and regulations thereunder;

(3) In consultation with the board or the senior officer of the security-based swap data repository, take reasonable steps to resolve any material conflicts of interest that may arise;

(4) Be responsible for administering each policy and procedure that is required to be established pursuant to section 13 of the Act and the rules and regulations thereunder;

(5) Take reasonable steps to ensure compliance with the Act and the rules and regulations thereunder relating to security-based swaps, including each rule prescribed by the Commission under section 13 of the Act;

(6) Establish procedures for the remediation of noncompliance issues identified by the chief compliance officer through any –

(i) Compliance office review;

(ii) Look-back;

(iii) Internal or external audit finding;

(iv) Self-reported error; or

(v) Validated complaint; and

(7) Establish and follow appropriate procedures for the handling, management response, remediation, retesting, and closing of noncompliance issues.

(d) *Compliance reports*—(1) In general. The chief compliance officer shall annually prepare and sign a report that contains a description of the compliance of the security-based swap data repository with respect to the Act and the rules and regulations thereunder and each policy and procedure of the security-based swap data repository (including the code of ethics and conflicts of interest policies of the security-based swap data repository). Each compliance report shall also contain, at a minimum, a description of:

(i) The security-based swap data repository's enforcement of its policies and procedures;

(ii) Any material changes to the policies and procedures since the date of the preceding compliance report;

(iii) Any recommendation for material changes to the policies and procedures as a result of the annual review, the rationale for such recommendation, and whether such policies and procedures were or will be modified by the security-based swap data repository to incorporate such recommendation; and

(iv) Any material compliance matters identified since the date of the preceding compliance report.

(2) *Requirements.* A financial report of the security-based swap data repository shall be filed with the Commission as described in paragraph (g) of this section and shall accompany a compliance report as described in paragraph (d)(1) of this section. The compliance report shall include a certification by the chief compliance officer that, to the best of his or her knowledge and reasonable belief, and under penalty of law, the compliance report is accurate and complete. The compliance report shall also be filed in a tagged data format in accordance with the instructions contained in the EDGAR Filer Manual, as described in Rule 301 of Regulation S–T.

(e) The chief compliance officer shall submit the annual compliance report to the board for its review prior to the filing of the report with the Commission.

(f) *Financial reports.* Each financial report filed with a compliance report shall:

(1) Be a complete set of financial statements of the security-based swap data repository that are prepared in accordance with U.S. generally accepted accounting principles for the most recent two fiscal years of the security-based swap data repository;

(2) Be audited in accordance with the standards of the Public Company Accounting Oversight Board by a registered public accounting firm that is qualified and independent in accordance with Rule 2–01 of Regulation S–X;

(3) Include a report of the registered public accounting firm that complies with paragraphs (a) through (d) of Rule 2–02 of Regulation S–X;

(4) If the security-based swap data repository's financial statements contain consolidated information of a subsidiary of the security-based swap data repository, provide condensed financial information, in a financial statement footnote, as to the financial position, changes in financial position and results of operations of the security-based swap data repository, as of the same dates and for the same periods for which audited consolidated financial statements are required. Such financial information need not be presented in greater detail than is required for condensed statements by Rules 10–01(a)(2), (3), and (4) of Regulation S–X. Detailed footnote disclosure that would normally be included with complete financial statements may be omitted with the exception of disclosures regarding material contingencies, long-term obligations, and guarantees. Descriptions of significant provisions of the security-based swap data repository's long-term obligations, mandatory dividend or redemption requirements of redeemable stocks, and guarantees of the security-based swap data repository shall be provided along with a five-year schedule of maturities of debt. If the material contingencies, long-term obligations, redeemable stock requirements, and guarantees of the security-based swap data repository have been separately disclosed in the consolidated statements, then they need not be repeated in this schedule; and

(5) Be provided as an official filing in accordance with the EDGAR Filer Manual and include, as part of the official filing, an Interactive Data Financial Report filed in accordance with Rule 407 of Regulation S–T.

(g) Reports filed pursuant to paragraphs (d) and (f) of this section shall be filed within 60 days after the end of the fiscal year covered by such reports.

(h) No officer, director, or employee of a security-based swap data repository may directly or indirectly take any action to coerce, manipulate, mislead, or fraudulently influence the security-based swap data repository's chief compliance officer in the performance of his or her duties under this section.

Rule 13n–12. Exemption from requirements governing security-based swap data repositories for certain non-U.S. persons

(a) *Definitions.* For purposes of this section—

(1) Non-U.S. person means a person that is not a U.S. person.

(2) U.S. person shall have the same meaning as set forth in Rule 3a71–3(a)(4)(i).

(b) A non-U.S. person that performs the functions of a security-based swap data repository within the United States shall be exempt from the registration and other requirements set forth in section 13(n) of the Act, and the rules and regulations thereunder, provided that each regulator with supervisory authority over such non-U.S. person has entered into a memorandum of understanding or other arrangement with the Commission that addresses the confidentiality of data collected and maintained by such non-U.S. person, access by the Commission to such data, and any other matters determined by the Commission.

Rule 13p–1. Requirement of report regarding disclosure of registrant's supply chain information regarding conflict minerals

Every registrant that files reports with the Commission under Sections 13(a) of the Exchange Act, having conflict minerals that are necessary to the functionality or production of a product manufactured or contracted by that registrant to be manufactured, shall file a report on Form SD within the period specified in that Form disclosing the information required by the applicable items of Form SD as specified in that Form (17 CFR 249b.400).

Rule 13q–1. Disclosure of payments made by resource extraction issuers

(a) *Resource extraction issuers.* Every issuer that is required to file an annual report with the Commission pursuant to Section 13 or 15(d) of the Exchange Act (15 U.S.C. 78m or 78o(d)) and engages in the commercial development of oil, natural gas, or minerals must file a report on Form SD (17 CFR 249b.400) within the period specified in that Form disclosing the information required by the applicable items of Form SD as specified in that Form.

(b) *Anti-evasion*. Disclosure is required under this rule in circumstances in which an activity related to the commercial development of oil, natural gas, or minerals, or a payment or series of payments made by a resource extraction issuer to a foreign government or the Federal Government for the purpose of commercial development of oil, natural gas, or minerals is not, in form or characterization, within one of the categories of activities or payments specified in Form SD, but is part of a plan or scheme to evade the disclosure required under this rule.

(c) *Alternative reporting*. An application for recognition of a regime as substantially similar for purposes of alternative reporting must be filed in accordance with the procedures set forth in Rule 0–13 under the Securities Exchange Act of 1934, except that, for purposes of this paragraph (c), applications may be submitted by resource extraction issuers, governments, industry groups, or trade associations.

(d) *Exemptive relief*. An application for exemptive relief under this rule may be filed in accordance with the procedures set forth in Rule 0–12 under the Securities Exchange Act of 1934.

(e) *Public compilation*. To the extent practicable, the staff will periodically make a compilation of the information required to be filed under this rule publicly available online. The staff may determine the form, manner and timing of the compilation, except that no information included therein may be anonymized (whether by redacting the names of the resource extraction issuer or otherwise).

REGULATION 14A. SOLICITATION OF PROXIES

ATTENTION ELECTRONIC FILERS

THIS REGULATION SHOULD BE READ IN CONJUNCTION WITH REGULATION S–T (17 CFR 232), WHICH GOVERNS THE PREPARATION AND SUBMISSION OF DOCUMENTS IN ELECTRONIC FORMAT. MANY PROVISIONS RELATING TO THE PREPARATION AND SUBMISSION OF DOCUMENTS IN PAPER FORMAT CONTAINED IN THIS REGULATION ARE SUPERSEDED BY THE PROVISIONS OF REGULATION S–T FOR DOCUMENTS REQUIRED TO BE FILED IN ELECTRONIC FORMAT.

Rule 14a–1. Definitions

Unless the context otherwise requires, all terms used in this regulation have the same meanings as in the Act or elsewhere in the General Rules and Regulations thereunder. In addition, the following definitions apply unless the context otherwise requires:

(a) *Associate*. The term "associate," used to indicate a relationship with any person, means: (1) Any corporation or organization (other than the registrant or a majority owned subsidiary of the registrant) of which such person is an officer or partner or is, directly or indirectly, the beneficial owner of 10 percent or more of any class of equity securities;

(2) Any trust or other estate in which such person has a substantial beneficial interest or as to which such person serves as trustee or in a similar fiduciary capacity; and

(3) Any relative or spouse of such person, or any relative of such spouse, who has the same home as such person or who is a director or officer of the registrant or any of its parents or subsidiaries.

(b) *Employee Benefit Plan*. For purposes of Rules 14a–13, 14b–1 and 14b–2, the term "employee benefit plan" means any purchase, savings, option, bonus, appreciation, profit sharing, thrift, incentive, pension or similar plan primarily for employees, directors, trustees or officers.

(c) *Entity That Exercises Fiduciary Powers*. The term "entity that exercises fiduciary powers" means any entity that holds securities in nominee name or otherwise on behalf of a beneficial owner but does not include a clearing agency registered pursuant to Section 17A of the Act or a broker or a dealer.

(d) *Exempt Employee Benefit Plan Securities*. For purposes of Rules 14a–13, 14b–1 and 14b–2, the term "exempt employee benefit plan securities" means:

(1) Securities of the registrant held by an employee benefit plan, as defined in paragraph (b) of this rule, where such plan is established by the registrant; or

(2) If notice regarding the current solicitation has been given pursuant to Rule 14a–13(a)(1)(ii)(C) or if notice regarding the current request for a list of names, addresses and securities positions of beneficial owners has been given pursuant to Rule 14a–13(b)(3), securities of the registrant held by

an employee benefit plan, as defined in paragraph (b) of this rule, where such plan is established by an affiliate of the registrant.

(e) *Last Fiscal Year*. The term "last fiscal year" of the registrant means the last fiscal year of the registrant ending prior to the date of the meeting for which proxies are to be solicited or, if the solicitation involves written authorizations or consents in lieu of a meeting, the earliest date they may be used to effect corporate action.

(f) *Proxy*. The term "proxy" includes every proxy, consent or authorization within the meaning of section 14(a) of the Act. The consent or authorization may take the form of failure to object or to dissent.

(g) *Proxy Statement*. The term "proxy statement" means the statement required by Rule 14a–3(a), whether or not contained in a single document.

(h) *Record Date*. The term "record date" means the date as of which the record holders of securities entitled to vote at a meeting or by written consent or authorization shall be determined.

(i) *Record Holder*. For purposes of Rules 14a–13, 14b–1 and 14b–2, the term "record holder" means any broker, dealer, voting trustee, bank, association or other entity that exercises fiduciary powers which holds securities of record in nominee name or otherwise or as a participant in a clearing agency registered pursuant to Section 17A of the Act.

(j) *Registrant*. The term "registrant" means the issuer of the securities in respect of which proxies are to be solicited.

(k) *Respondent Bank*. For purposes of Rules 14a–13, 14b–1 and 14b–2, the term "respondent bank" means any bank, association or other entity that exercises fiduciary powers which holds securities on behalf of beneficial owners and deposits such securities for safekeeping with another bank, association or other entity that exercises fiduciary powers.

(*l*) *Solicitation*. (1) The terms "solicit" and "solicitation" include:

(i) Any request for a proxy whether or not accompanied by or included in a form of proxy;

(ii) Any request to execute or not to execute, or to revoke, a proxy; or

(iii) The furnishing of a form of proxy or other communication to security holders under circumstances reasonably calculated to result in the procurement, withholding or revocation of a proxy.

(2) The terms do not apply, however, to:

(i) The furnishing of a form of proxy to a security holder upon the unsolicited request of such security holder;

(ii) The performance by the registrant of acts required by Rule 14a–7;

(iii) The performance by any person of ministerial acts on behalf of a person soliciting a proxy; or

(iv) A communication by a security holder who does not otherwise engage in a proxy solicitation (other than a solicitation exempt under Rule 14a–2) stating how the security holder intends to vote and the reasons therefor, provided that the communication:

(A) Is made by means of speeches in public forums, press releases, published or broadcast opinions, statements, or advertisements appearing in a broadcast media, or newspaper, magazine or other bona fide publication disseminated on a regular basis,

(B) Is directed to persons to whom the security holder owes a fiduciary duty in connection with the voting of securities of a registrant held by the security holder, or

(C) Is made in response to unsolicited requests for additional information with respect to a prior communication by the security holder made pursuant to this paragraph (*l*)(2)(iv).

Rule 14a–2. Solicitations to which Rules 14a–3 to 14a–15 apply

Rules 14a–3 to 14a–15, except as specified, apply to every solicitation of a proxy with respect to securities registered pursuant to Section 12 of the Act (15 U.S.C. 78*l*), whether or not trading in such securities has been suspended. To the extent specified below certain of these rules also apply to roll-up transactions that do not involve an entity with securities registered pursuant to Section 12 of the Act.

(a) Rules 14a–3 to 14a–15 do not apply to the following:

(1) Any solicitation by a person in respect to securities carried in his name or in the name of his nominee (otherwise than as voting trustee) or held in his custody, if such person—

(i) Receives no commission or remuneration for such solicitation, directly or indirectly, other than reimbursement of reasonable expenses,

(ii) Furnishes promptly to the person solicited (or such person's household in accordance with Rule 14a–3(e)(1)) a copy of all soliciting material with respect to the same subject matter or meeting received from all persons who shall furnish copies thereof for such purpose and who shall, if requested, defray the reasonable expenses to be incurred in forwarding such material, and

(iii) In addition, does no more than impartially instruct the person solicited to forward a proxy to the person, if any, to whom the person solicited desires to give a proxy, or impartially request from the person solicited instructions as to the authority to be conferred by the proxy and state that a proxy will be given if no instructions are received by a certain date.

(2) Any solicitation by a person in respect of securities of which he is the beneficial owner;

(3) Any solicitation involved in the offer and sale of securities registered under the Securities Act of 1933: *Provided,* That this paragraph shall not apply to securities to be issued in any transaction of the character specified in paragraph (a) of Rule 145 under that Act;

(4) Any solicitation with respect to a plan of reorganization under Chapter 11 of the Bankruptcy Reform Act of 1978, as amended, if made after the entry of an order approving the written disclosure statement concerning a plan of reorganization pursuant to section 1125 of said Act and after, or concurrently with, the transmittal of such disclosure statement as required by section 1125 of said Act;

(5) [Reserved]

(6) Any solicitation through the medium of a newspaper advertisement which informs security holders of a source from which they may obtain copies of a proxy statement, form of proxy and any other soliciting material and does no more than:

(i) Name the registrant,

(ii) State the reason for the advertisement, and

(iii) Identify the proposal or proposals to be acted upon by security holders.

(b) Rules 14a–3 to 14a–6 (other than 14a–6(g) and 14a–6(p)), 14a–8, 14a–10, and 14a–12 to 14a–15 do not apply to the following:

(1) Any solicitation by or on behalf of any person who does not, at any time during such solicitation, seek directly or indirectly, either on its own or another's behalf, the power to act as proxy for a security holder and does not furnish or otherwise request, or act on behalf of a person who furnishes or requests, a form of revocation, abstention, consent or authorization. *Provided, however,* That the exemption set forth in this paragraph shall not apply to:

(i) The registrant or an affiliate or associate of the registrant (other than an officer or director or any person serving in a similar capacity);

(ii) An officer or director of the registrant or any person serving in a similar capacity engaging in a solicitation financed directly or indirectly by the registrant;

(iii) An officer, director, affiliate or associate of a person that is ineligible to rely on the exemption set forth in this paragraph (other than persons specified in paragraph (b)(1)(i) of this rule), or any person serving in a similar capacity;

(iv) Any nominee for whose election as a director proxies are solicited;

(v) Any person soliciting in opposition to a merger, recapitalization, reorganization, sale of assets or other extraordinary transaction recommended or approved by the board of directors of the registrant who is proposing or intends to propose an alternative transaction to which such person or one of its affiliates is a party;

(vi) Any person who is required to report beneficial ownership of the registrant's equity securities on a Schedule 13D (Rule 13d–101), unless such person has filed a Schedule 13D and has not disclosed pursuant to Item 4 thereto an intent, or reserved the right, to engage in a control transaction, or any contested solicitation for the election of directors;

(vii) Any person who receives compensation from an ineligible person directly related to the solicitation of proxies, other than pursuant to Rule 14a–13;

(viii) Where the registrant is an investment company registered under the Investment Company Act of 1940 (15 U.S.C. 80–2), an "interested person" of that investment company, as that term is defined in section 2(a)(19) of the Investment Company Act;

(ix) Any person who, because of a substantial interest in the subject matter of the solicitation, is likely to receive a benefit from a successful solicitation that would not be shared pro rata by all other holders of the same class of securities, other than a benefit arising from the person's employment with the registrant; and

(x) Any person acting on behalf of any of the foregoing.

(2) Any solicitation made otherwise than on behalf of the registrant where the total number of persons solicited is not more than ten.

(3) The furnishing of proxy voting advice by any person (the "advisor") to any other person with whom the advisor has a business relationship, if:

(i) The advisor renders financial advice in the ordinary course of his business;

(ii) The advisor discloses to the recipient of the advice any significant relationship with the registrant or any of its affiliates, or a security holder proponent of the matter on which advice is given, as well as any material interest of the advisor in such matter;

(iii) The advisor receives no special commission or remuneration for furnishing the proxy voting advice from any person other than a recipient of the advice and other persons who receive similar advice under this subsection; and

(iv) The proxy voting advice is not furnished on behalf of any person soliciting proxies or on behalf of a participant in an election subject to the provisions of Rule 14a–12(c); and

(4) Any solicitation in connection with a roll-up transaction as defined in Item 901(c) of Regulation S–K in which the holder of a security that is the subject of a proposed roll-up transaction engages in preliminary communications with other holders of securities that are the subject of the same limited partnership roll-up transaction for the purpose of determining whether to solicit proxies, consents, or authorizations in opposition to the proposed limited partnership roll-up transaction; *provided, however,* that:

(i) This exemption shall not apply to a security holder who is an affiliate of the registrant or general partner or sponsor; and

(ii) This exemption shall not apply to a holder of five percent (5%) or more of the outstanding securities of a class that is the subject of the proposed roll-up transaction who engages in the business of buying and selling limited partnership interests in the secondary market unless that holder discloses to the persons to whom the communications are made such ownership interest and any relations of the holder to the parties of the transaction or to the transaction itself, as required by Rule 14a–6(n)(1) and specified in the Notice of Exempt Preliminary Roll-up Communication (Rule 14a–104). If the communication is oral, this disclosure may be provided to the security holder orally. Whether the communication is written or oral, the notice required by Rule 14a–6(n) and Rule 14a–104 shall be furnished to the Commission.

(5) Publication or distribution by a broker or a dealer of a research report in accordance with Rule 138 or Rule 139 under the Securities Act of 1933 during a transaction in which the broker or dealer or its affiliate participates or acts in an advisory role.

(6) Any solicitation by or on behalf of any person who does not seek directly or indirectly, either on its own or another's behalf, the power to act as proxy for a shareholder and does not furnish or otherwise request, or act on behalf of a person who furnishes or requests, a form of revocation, abstention, consent, or authorization in an electronic shareholder forum that is established, maintained or operated pursuant to the provisions of Rule 14a–17, provided that the solicitation is made more than 60 days prior to the date announced by a registrant for its next annual or special meeting of shareholders. If the registrant announces the date of its next annual or special meeting of shareholders less than 60 days before the meeting date, then the solicitation may not be made more than two days following the date of the registrant's announcement of the meeting date. Participation in an electronic shareholder forum does not eliminate a person's eligibility to solicit proxies after the date that this exemption is no longer available, or is no longer being relied upon, provided that any such solicitation is conducted in accordance with this regulation.

(7) Any solicitation by or on behalf of any shareholder in connection with the formation of a nominating shareholder group pursuant to Rule 14a–11, provided that:

(i) The soliciting shareholder is not holding the registrant's securities with the purpose, or with the effect, of changing control of the registrant or to gain a number of seats on the board of directors that exceeds the maximum number of nominees that the registrant could be required to include under Rule 14a-11(d);

(ii) Each written communication includes no more than:

(A) A statement of each soliciting shareholder's intent to form a nominating shareholder group in order to nominate one or more directors under Rule 14a-11;

(B) Identification of, and a brief statement regarding, the potential nominee or nominees or, where no nominee or nominees have been identified, the characteristics of the nominee or nominees that the shareholder intends to nominate, if any;

(C) The percentage of voting power of the registrant's securities that are entitled to be voted on the election of directors that each soliciting shareholder holds or the aggregate percentage held by any group to which the shareholder belongs; and

(D) The means by which shareholders may contact the soliciting party.

(iii) Any written soliciting material published, sent or given to shareholders in accordance with this paragraph must be filed by the shareholder with the Commission, under the registrant's Exchange Act file number, or, in the case of a registrant that is an investment company registered under the Investment Company Act of 1940 (15 U.S.C. 80a-1 et seq.), under the registrant's Investment Company Act file number, no later than the date the material is first published, sent or given to shareholders. Three copies of the material must at the same time be filed with, or mailed for filing to, each national securities exchange upon which any class of securities of the registrant is listed and registered. The soliciting material must include a cover page in the form set forth in Schedule 14N and the appropriate box on the cover page must be marked.

(iv) In the case of an oral solicitation made in accordance with the terms of this section, the nominating shareholder must file a cover page in the form set forth in Schedule 14N, with the appropriate box on the cover page marked, under the registrant's Exchange Act file number (or in the case of an investment company registered under the Investment Company Act of 1940 (15 U.S.C. 80a-1 et seq.), under the registrant's Investment Company Act file number), no later than the date of the first such communication.

Instruction to Paragraph (b)(7): The exemption provided in paragraph (b)(7) of this section shall not apply to a shareholder that subsequently engages in soliciting or other nominating activities outside the scope of Rule 14a-2(b)(8) and 14a-11 in connection with the subject election of directors or is or becomes a member of any other group, as determined under section 13(d)(3) of the Act (15 U.S.C. 78m(d)(3) and Rule 13d-5(b)), or otherwise, with persons engaged in soliciting or other nominating activities in connection with the subject election of directors.

(8) Any solicitation by or on behalf of a nominating shareholder or nominating shareholder group in support of its nominee that is included or that will be included on the registrant's form of proxy in accordance with Rule 14a-11 or for or against the registrant's nominee or nominees, provided that:

(i) The soliciting party does not, at any time during such solicitation, seek directly or indirectly, either on its own or another's behalf, the power to act as proxy for a shareholder and does not furnish or otherwise request, or act on behalf of a person who furnishes or requests, a form of revocation, abstention, consent or authorization;

(ii) Any written communication includes:

(A) The identity of each nominating shareholder and a description of his or her direct or indirect interests, by security holdings or otherwise;

(B) A prominent legend in clear, plain language advising shareholders that a shareholder nominee is or will be included in the registrant's proxy statement and that they should read the registrant's proxy statement when available because it includes important information (or, if the registrant's proxy statement is publicly available, advising shareholders of that fact and encouraging shareholders to read the registrant's proxy statement because it includes important information). The legend also must explain to shareholders that they can find the registrant's proxy statement, other soliciting material, and any other relevant documents at no charge on the Commission's Web site; and

(iii) Any written soliciting material published, sent or given to shareholders in accordance with this paragraph must be filed by the nominating shareholder or nominating shareholder group with the Commission, under the registrant's Exchange Act file number, or, in the case of a registrant that is an investment company registered under the Investment Company Act of 1940, under the registrant's Investment Company Act file number, no later than the date the material is first published, sent or given to shareholders. Three copies of the material must at the same time be filed with, or mailed for filing to, each national securities exchange upon which any class of securities of the registrant is listed and registered. The soliciting material must include a cover page in the form set forth in Schedule 14N and the appropriate box on the cover page must be marked.

Instructions to Paragraph (b)(8).

1. A nominating shareholder or nominating shareholder group may rely on the exemption provided in paragraph (b)(8) of this section only after receiving notice from the registrant in accordance with Rule 14a–11(g)(1) or 14a–11(g)(3)(iv) that the registrant will include the nominating shareholder's or nominating shareholder group's nominee or nominees in its form of proxy.

2. Any solicitation by or on behalf of a nominating shareholder or nominating shareholder group in support of its nominee included or to be included on the registrant's form of proxy in accordance with Rule 14a–11 or for or against the registrant's nominee or nominees must be made in reliance on the exemption provided in paragraph (b)(8) of this section and not on any other exemption.

3. The exemption provided in paragraph (b)(8) of this section shall not apply to a person that subsequently engages in soliciting or other nominating activities outside the scope of Rule 14a–11 in connection with the subject election of directors or is or becomes a member of any other group, as determined under section 13(d)(3) of the Act (15 U.S.C. 78m(d)(3) and Rule 13d–5(b)), or otherwise, with persons engaged in soliciting or other nominating activities in connection with the subject election of directors.

Rule 14a–3. Information to be furnished to security holders

(a) No solicitation subject to this regulation shall be made unless each person solicited is concurrently furnished or has previously been furnished with:

(1) A publicly-filed preliminary or definitive proxy statement, in the form and manner described in Rule 14a–16, containing the information specified in Schedule 14A (Rule 14a–101);

(2) A preliminary or definitive written proxy statement included in a registration statement filed under the Securities Act of 1933 on Form S–4 or F–4 (17 CFR 239.25 or 239.34) or Form N–14 (17 CFR 239.23) and containing the information specified in such Form; or

(3) A publicly-filed preliminary or definitive proxy statement, not in the form and manner described in Rule 14a–16, containing the information specified in Schedule 14A (Rule 14a–101), if:

(i) The solicitation relates to a business combination transaction as defined in Rule 165 under the Securities Act of 1933, as well as transactions for cash consideration requiring disclosure under Item 14 of Schedule 14A; or

(ii) The solicitation may not follow the form and manner described in Rule 14a–16 pursuant to the laws of the state of incorporation of the registrant;

(b) If the solicitation is made on behalf of the registrant, other than an investment company registered under the Investment Company Act of 1940, and relates to an annual (or special meeting in lieu of the annual) meeting of security holders, or written consent in lieu of such meeting, at which directors are to be elected, each proxy statement furnished pursuant to paragraph (a) of this rule shall be accompanied or preceded by an annual report to security holders as follows:

(1) The report shall include, for the registrant and its subsidiaries consolidated and audited balance sheets as of the end of each of the two most recent fiscal years and audited statements of income and cash flows for each of the three most recent fiscal years prepared in accordance with Regulation S–X, except that the provisions of Article 3 (other than Rules 3–03(e), 3–04 and 3–20 of Regulation S–X) and Article 11 shall not apply. Any financial statement schedules or exhibits or separate financial statements which may otherwise be required in filings with the Commission may be omitted. If the financial statements of the registrant and its subsidiaries consolidated in the annual report filed or to be filed with the Commission are not required to be audited, the financial statements required by this paragraph may be unaudited. A smaller reporting company may provide the information in Article 8 of Regulation S–X in lieu of the financial information required by this paragraph 9(b)(1).

Note 1 to Paragraph (b)(1): If the financial statements for a period prior to the most recently completed fiscal year have been examined by a predecessor accountant, the separate report of the predecessor accountant may be omitted in the report to security holders, provided the registrant has obtained from the predecessor accountant a reissued report covering the prior period presented and the successor accountant clearly indicates in the scope paragraph of his or her report (a) that the financial statements of the prior period were examined by other accountants, (b) the date of their report, (c) the type of opinion expressed by the predecessor accountant and (d) the substantive reasons therefore, if it was other than unqualified. It should be noted, however, that the separate report of any predecessor accountant is required in filings with the Commission. If, for instance,

* Appears to be a mistake in Release 34–56994.

the financial statements in the annual report to security holders are incorporated by reference in a Form 10–K, the separate report of a predecessor accountant shall be filed in Part II or in Part IV as a financial statement schedule.

NOTE 2 TO PARAGRAPH (b)(i)*: For purposes of complying with Rule 14a–3, if the registrant, has changed its fiscal closing date, financial statements covering two years and one period of 9 to 12 months shall be deemed to satisfy the requirements for statements of income and cash flows for the three most recent fiscal years.

(2)(i) Financial statements and notes thereto shall be presented in roman type at least as large and as legible as 10-point modern type. If necessary for convenient presentation, the financial statements may be in roman type as large and as legible as 8-point modern type. All type shall be leaded at least 2–points.

(ii) Where the annual report to security holders is delivered through an electronic medium, issuers may satisfy legibility requirements applicable to printed documents, such as type size and font, by presenting all required information in a format readily communicated to investors.

(3) The report shall contain the supplementary financial information required by Item 302 of Regulation S–K.

(4) The report shall contain information concerning changes in and disagreements with accountants on accounting and financial disclosure required by Item 304 of Regulation S–K.

(5)(i) The report shall contain the selected financial data required by Item 301 of Regulation S–K.

(ii) The report shall contain management's discussion and analysis of financial condition and results of operations required by Item 303 of Regulation S–K.

(iii) The report shall contain the quantitative and qualitative disclosures about market risk required by Item 305 of Regulation S–K.

(6) The report shall contain a brief description of the business done by the registrant and its subsidiaries during the most recent fiscal year which will, in the opinion of management, indicate the general nature and scope of the business of the registrant and its subsidiaries.

(7) The report shall contain information relating to the registrant's industry segments, classes of similar products or services, foreign and domestic operations and export sales required by paragraphs (b), (c)(1)(i) and (d) of Item 101 of Regulation S–K.

(8) The report shall identify each of the registrant's directors and executive officers, and shall indicate the principal occupation or employment of each such person and the name and principal business of any organization by which such person is employed.

(9) The report shall contain the market price of and dividends on the registrant's common equity and related security holder matters required by Items 201(a), (b) and (c) of Regulation S–K. If the report precedes or accompanies a proxy statement or information statement relating to an annual meeting of security holders at which directors are to be elected (or special meeting or written consents in lieu of such meeting), furnish the performance graph required by Item 201(e) of Regulation S–K.

(10) The registrant's proxy statement, or the report, shall contain an undertaking in bold face or otherwise reasonably prominent type to provide without charge to each person solicited upon the written request of any such person, a copy of the registrant's annual report on Form 10–K, including the financial statements and the financial statement schedules, required to be filed with the Commission pursuant to Rule 13a–1 under the Act for the registrant's most recent fiscal year, and shall indicate the name and address (including title or department) of the person to whom such a written request is to be directed. In the discretion of management, a registrant need not undertake to furnish without charge copies of all exhibits to its Form 10–K, provided that the copy of the annual report on Form 10–K furnished without charge to requesting security holders is accompanied by a list briefly describing all the exhibits not contained therein and indicating that the registrant will furnish any exhibit upon the payment of a specified reasonable fee, which fee shall be limited to the registrant's reasonable expenses in furnishing such exhibit. If the registrant's annual report to security holders complies with all of the disclosure requirements of Form 10–K and is filed with the Commission in satisfaction of its Form 10–K filing requirements, such registrant need not furnish a separate Form 10–K to security holders who receive a copy of such annual report.

NOTE TO PARAGRAPH (b)(10): Pursuant to the undertaking required by paragraph (b)(10) of this rule, a registrant shall furnish a copy of its annual report on Form 10–K (17 CFR 249.310) to a beneficial owner of its securities upon receipt of a written request from such person. Each request must set forth a good faith representation that, as of the record date for the solicitation requiring the furnishing of the annual report to security holders pursuant to paragraph

(b) of this rule, the person making the request was a beneficial owner of securities entitled to vote.

(11) Subject to the foregoing requirements, the report may be in any form deemed suitable by management and the information required by paragraphs (b)(5) to (b)(10) of this rule may be presented in an appendix or other separate section of the report, provided that the attention of security holders is called to such presentation.

NOTE: Registrants are encouraged to utilize tables, schedules, charts, and graphic illustrations to present financial information in an understandable manner. Any presentation of financial information must be consistent with the data in the financial statements contained in the report and, if appropriate, should refer to relevant portions of the financial statements and notes thereto.

(12) [Reserved]

(13) Paragraph (b) of this rule shall not apply, however, to solicitations made on behalf of the registrant before the financial statements are available if a solicitation is being made at the same time in opposition to the registrant and if the registrant's proxy statement includes an undertaking in bold face type to furnish such annual report to security holders to all persons being solicited at least 20 calendar days before the date of the meeting or, if the solicitation refers to a written consent or authorization in lieu of a meeting, at least 20 calendar days prior to the earliest date on which it may be used to effect corporate action.

(c) Seven copies of the report sent to security holders pursuant to this rule shall be mailed to the Commission, solely for its information, not later than the date on which such report is first sent or given to security holders or the date on which preliminary copies, or definitive copies, if preliminary filing was not required, of solicitation material are filed with the Commission pursuant to Rule 14a–6, whichever date is later. The report is not deemed to be "soliciting material" or to be "filed" with the Commission or subject to this regulation otherwise than as provided in this rule, or to the liabilities of Section 18 of the Act, except to the extent that the registrant specifically requests that it be treated as a part of the proxy soliciting material or incorporates it in the proxy statement or other filed report by reference.

(d) An annual report to security holders prepared on an integrated basis pursuant to General Instruction H to Form 10–K (17 CFR 249.310) may also be submitted in satisfaction of this rule. When filed as the annual report on Form 10–K, responses to the Items of that form are subject to section 18 of the Act notwithstanding paragraph (c) of this rule.

(e)(1)(i) A registrant will be considered to have delivered an annual report to security holders, proxy statement or Notice of Internet Availability of Proxy Materials, as described in Rule 14a–16, to all security holders of record who share an address if:

(A) The registrant delivers one annual report to security holders, proxy statement or Notice of Internet Availability of Proxy Materials, as applicable, to the shared address;

(B) The registrant addresses the annual report to security holders, proxy statement or Notice of Internet Availability of Proxy Materials, as applicable, to the security holders as a group (for example, "ABC Fund [or Corporation] Security Holders," "Jane Doe and Household," "The Smith Family"), to each of the security holders individually (for example, "John Doe and Richard Jones") or to the security holders in a form to which each of the security holders has consented in writing;

NOTE TO PARAGRAPH (e)(1)(i)(B): Unless the registrant addresses the annual report to security holders, proxy statement or Notice of Internet Availability of Proxy Materials to the security holders as a group or to each of the security holders individually, it must obtain, from each security holder to be included in the householded group, a separate affirmative written consent to the specific form of address the registrant will use.

(C) The security holders consent, in accordance with paragraph (e)(1)(ii) of this rule, to delivery of one annual report to security holders or proxy statement, as applicable;

(D) With respect to delivery of the proxy statement or Notice of Internet Availability of Proxy Materials, the registrant delivers, together with or subsequent to delivery of the proxy statement, a separate proxy card for each security holder at the shared address; and

(E) The registrant includes an undertaking in the proxy statement to deliver promptly upon written or oral request a separate copy of the annual report to security holders, proxy statement or Notice of Internet Availability of Proxy Materials, as applicable, to a security holder at a shared address to which a single copy of the document was delivered.

(ii) *Consent*. (A) *Affirmative Written Consent*. Each security holder must affirmatively consent, in writing, to delivery of one annual report to security holders or proxy statement, as applicable. A security holder's affirmative written consent will be considered valid only if the security holder has been informed of:

(*1*) The duration of the consent;

(*2*) The specific types of documents to which the consent will apply;

(*3*) The procedures the security holder must follow to revoke consent; and

(*4*) The registrant's obligation to begin sending individual copies to a security holder within thirty days after the security holder revokes consent.

(B) *Implied Consent.* The registrant need not obtain affirmative written consent from a security holder for purposes of paragraph (e)(1)(ii)(A) of this rule if all of the following conditions are met:

(*1*) The security holder has the same last name as the other security holders at the shared address or the registrant reasonably believes that the security holders are members of the same family;

(*2*) The registrant has sent the security holder a notice at least 60 days before the registrant begins to rely on this rule concerning delivery of annual reports to security holders, proxy statements or Notices of Internet Availability of Proxy Materials to that security holder. The notice must:

(*i*) Be a separate written document;

(*ii*) State that only one annual report to security holders, proxy statement or Notice of Internet Availability of Proxy Materials, as applicable, will be delivered to the shared address unless the registrant receives contrary instructions;

(*iii*) Include a toll-free telephone number, or be accompanied by a reply form that is pre-addressed with postage provided, that the security holder can use to notify the registrant that the security holder wishes to receive a separate annual report to security holders, proxy statement or Notice of Internet Availability of Proxy Materials;

(*iv*) State the duration of the consent;

(*v*) Explain how a security holder can revoke consent;

(*vi*) State that the registrant will begin sending individual copies to a security holder within thirty days after the security holder revokes consent; and

(*vii*) Contain the following prominent statement, or similar clear and understandable statement, in bold-face type: "Important Notice Regarding Delivery of Security Holder Documents." This statement also must appear on the envelope in which the notice is delivered. Alternatively, if the notice is delivered separately from other communications to security holders, this statement may appear either on the notice or on the envelope in which the notice is delivered.

NOTE TO PARAGRAPH (e)(1)(ii)(B)(2): The notice should be written in plain English. See Rule 421(d)(2) under the Securities Act of 1933 for a discussion of plain English principles.

(*3*) The registrant has not received the reply form or other notification indicating that the security holder wishes to continue to receive an individual copy of the annual report to security holders, proxy statement or Notice of Internet Availability of Proxy Materials, as applicable, within 60 days after the registrant sent the notice required by paragraph (e)(1)(ii)(B)(*2*) of this rule; and

(*4*) The registrant delivers the document to a post office box or residential street address.

NOTE TO PARAGRAPH (e)(1)(ii)(B)(4): The registrant can assume that a street address is residential unless the registrant has information that indicates the street address is a business.

(iii) *Revocation of Consent.* If a security holder, orally or in writing, revokes consent to delivery of one annual report to security holders, proxy statement or Notice of Internet Availability of Proxy Materials to a shared address, the registrant must begin sending individual copies to that security holder within 30 days after the registrant receives revocation of the security holder's consent.

(iv) *Definition of Address.* Unless otherwise indicated, for purposes of this rule, address means a street *address,* a post office box number, an electronic mail address, a facsimile telephone number or other similar destination to which paper or electronic documents are delivered, unless otherwise provided in this rule. If the registrant has reason to believe that the

address is a street address of a multi-unit building, the address must include the unit number.

Note to Paragraph (e)(1): A person other than the registrant making a proxy solicitation may deliver a single proxy statement to security holders of record or beneficial owners who have separate accounts and share an address if: (a) the registrant or intermediary has followed the procedures in this rule; and (b) the registrant or intermediary makes available the shared address information to the person in accordance with Rule 14a–7(a)(2)(i) and (ii).

(2) Notwithstanding paragraphs (a) and (b) of this rule, unless state law requires otherwise, a registrant is not required to send an annual report to security holders, proxy statement or Notice of Internet Availability of Proxy Materials to a security holder if:

(i) An annual report to security holders and a proxy statement, or a Notice of Internet of Availability of Proxy Materials, for two consecutive annual meetings; or

(ii) All, and at least two, payments (if sent by first class mail) of dividends or interest on securities, or dividend reinvestment confirmations, during a twelve month period, have been mailed to such security holder's address and have been returned as undeliverable. If any such security holder delivers or causes to be delivered to the registrant written notice setting forth his then current address for security holder communications purposes, the registrant's obligation to deliver an annual report to security holders, a proxy statement or a Notice of Internet Availability of Proxy Materials under this rule is reinstated.

(f) The provisions of paragraph (a) of this rule shall not apply to a communication made by means of speeches in public forums, press releases, published or broadcast opinions, statements, or advertisements appearing in a broadcast media, newspaper, magazine or other bona fide publication disseminated on a regular basis, provided that:

(1) No form of proxy, consent or authorization or means to execute the same is provided to a security holder in connection with the communication; and

(2) At the time the communication is made, a definitive proxy statement is on file with the Commission pursuant to Rule 14a–6(b).

Rule 14a–4. Requirements as to proxy

(a) The form of proxy (1) Shall indicate in boldface type whether or not the proxy is solicited on behalf of the registrant's board of directors or, if provided other than by a majority of the board of directors, shall indicate in bold-face type on whose behalf the solicitation is made;

(2) Shall provide a specifically designated blank space for dating the proxy card; and

(3) Shall identify clearly and impartially each separate matter intended to be acted upon, whether or not related to or conditioned on the approval of other matters, and whether proposed by the registrant or by security holders. No reference need be made, however, to proposals as to which discretionary authority is conferred pursuant to paragraph (c) of this rule.

Note to Paragraph (a)(3) (electronic filers): Electronic filers shall satisfy the filing requirements of Rule 14a–6(a) or (b) with respect to the form of proxy by filing the form of proxy as an appendix at the end of the proxy statement. Forms of proxy shall not be filed as exhibits or separate documents within an electronic submission.

(b)(1) Means shall be provided in the form of proxy whereby the person solicited is afforded an opportunity to specify by boxes a choice between approval or disapproval of, or abstention with respect to, each separate matter referred to therein as intended to be acted upon, other than elections to office and votes to determine the frequency of shareholder votes on executive compensation pursuant to Rule 14a–21(b). A proxy may confer discretionary authority with respect to matters as to which a choice is not specified by the security holder provided that the form of proxy states in bold-face type how it is intended to vote the shares represented by the proxy in each such case.

(2) A form of proxy that provides for the election of directors shall set forth the names of persons nominated for election as directors, including any person whose nomination by a shareholder or shareholder group satisfies the requirements of Rule 14a–11, an applicable state or foreign law provision, or a registrant's governing documents as they relate to the inclusion of shareholder director nominees in the registrant's proxy materials. Such form of proxy shall clearly provide any of the following means for security holders to withhold authority to vote for each nominee:

(i) A box opposite the name of each nominee which may be marked to indicate that authority to vote for such nominee is withheld; or

(ii) An instruction in bold-face type which indicates that the security holder may withhold authority to vote for any nominee by lining through or otherwise striking out the name of any nominee; or

(iii) Designated blank spaces in which the security holder may enter the names of nominees with respect to whom the security holder chooses to withhold authority to vote; or

(iv) Any other similar means, provided that clear instructions are furnished indicating how the security holder may withhold authority to vote for any nominee.

Such form of proxy also may provide a means for the security holder to grant authority to vote for the nominees set forth, as a group, provided that there is a similar means for the security holder to withhold authority to vote for such group of nominees. Any such form of proxy which is executed by the security holder in such manner as not to withhold authority to vote for the election of any nominee shall be deemed to grant such authority, provided that the form of proxy so states in bold-face type. Means to grant authority to vote for any nominees as a group or to withhold authority for any nominees as a group may not be provided if the form of proxy includes one or more shareholder nominees in accordance with Rule 14a–11, an applicable state or foreign law provision, or a registrant's governing documents as they relate to the inclusion of shareholder director nominees in the registrant's proxy materials.

Instructions:

1. Paragraph (2) does not apply in the case of a merger, consolidation or other plan if the election of directors is an integral part of the plan.

2. If applicable state law gives legal effect to votes cast against a nominee, then in lieu of, or in addition to, providing a means for security holders to withhold authority to vote, the registrant should provide a similar means for security holders to vote against each nominee.

(3) A form of proxy which provides for a shareholder vote on the frequency of shareholder votes to approve the compensation of executives required by section 14A(a)(2) of the Securities Exchange Act of 1934 (15 U.S.C. 78n–1(a)(2)) shall provide means whereby the person solicited is afforded an opportunity to specify by boxes a choice among 1, 2 or 3 years, or abstain.

(c) A proxy may confer discretionary authority to vote on any of the following matters:

(1) For an annual meeting of shareholders, if the registrant did not have notice of the matter at least 45 days before the date on which the registrant first sent its proxy materials for the prior year's annual meeting of shareholders (or date specified by an advance notice provision), and a specific statement to that effect is made in the proxy statement or form of proxy. If during the prior year the registrant did not hold an annual meeting, or if the date of the meeting has changed more than 30 days from the prior year, then notice must not have been received a reasonable time before the registrant sends its proxy materials for the current year.

(2) In the case in which the registrant has received timely notice in connection with an annual meeting of shareholders (as determined under paragraph (c)(1) of this rule), if the registrant includes, in the proxy statement, advice on the nature of the matter and how the registrant intends to exercise its discretion to vote on each matter. However, even if the registrant includes this information in its proxy statement, it may not exercise discretionary voting authority on a particular proposal if the proponent:

(i) Provides the registrant with a written statement, within the time-frame determined under paragraph (c)(1) of this rule, that the proponent intends to deliver a proxy statement and form of proxy to holders of at least the percentage of the company's voting shares required under applicable law to carry the proposal;

(ii) Includes the same statement in its proxy materials filed under Rule 14a–6; and

(iii) Immediately after soliciting the percentage of shareholders required to carry the proposal, provides the registrant with a statement from any solicitor or other person with knowledge that the necessary steps have been taken to deliver a proxy statement and form of proxy to holders of at least the percentage of the company's voting shares required under applicable law to carry the proposal.

(3) For solicitations other than for annual meetings or for solicitations by persons other than the registrant, matters which the persons making the solicitation do not know, a reasonable time before the solicitation, are to be presented at the meeting, if a specific statement to that effect is made in the proxy statement or form of proxy.

(4) Approval of the minutes of the prior meeting if such approval does not amount to ratification of the action taken at that meeting;

(5) The election of any person to any office for which a bona fide nominee is named in the proxy statement and such nominee is unable to serve or for good cause will not serve.

(6) Any proposal omitted from the proxy statement and form of proxy pursuant to Rule 14a–8 or 14a–9.

(7) Matters incident to the conduct of the meeting.

(d) No proxy shall confer authority:

(1) To vote for the election of any person to any office for which a bona fide nominee is not named in the proxy statement, or

(2) To vote at any annual meeting other than the next annual meeting (or any adjournment thereof) to be held after the date on which the proxy statement and form of proxy are first sent or given to security holders.

(3) To vote with respect to more than one meeting (and any adjournment thereof) or more than one consent solicitation or

(4) To consent to or authorize any action other than the action proposed to be taken in the proxy statement, or matters referred to in paragraph (c) of this rule. A person shall not be deemed to be a bona fide nominee and he shall not be named as such unless he has consented to being named in the proxy statement and to serve if elected. *Provided, however,* That nothing in this Rule 14a–4 shall prevent any person soliciting in support of nominees who, if elected, would constitute a minority of the board of directors, from seeking authority to vote for nominees named in the registrant's proxy statement, so long as the soliciting party:

(i) Seeks authority to vote in the aggregate for the number of director positions then subject to election;

(ii) Represents that it will vote for all the registrant nominees, other than those registrant nominees specified by the soliciting party;

(iii) Provides the security holder an opportunity to withhold authority with respect to any other registrant nominee by writing the name of that nominee on the form of proxy; and

(iv) States on the form of proxy and in the proxy statement that there is no assurance that the registrant's nominees will serve if elected with any of the soliciting party's nominees.

(e) The proxy statement or form of proxy shall provide, subject to reasonable specified conditions, that the shares represented by the proxy will be voted and that where the person solicited specifies by means of a ballot provided pursuant to paragraph (b) a choice with respect to any matter to be acted upon, the shares will be voted in accordance with the specifications so made.

(f) No person conducting a solicitation subject to this regulation shall deliver a form of proxy, consent or authorization to any security holder unless the security holder concurrently receives, or has previously received, a definitive proxy statement that has been filed with the Commission pursuant to Rule 14a–6(b).

Rule 14a–5. Presentation of information in proxy statement

(a) The information included in the proxy statement shall be clearly presented and the statements made shall be divided into groups according to subject matter and the various groups of statements shall be preceded by appropriate headings. The order of items and sub-items in the schedule need not be followed. Where practicable and appropriate, the information shall be presented in tabular form. All amounts shall be stated in figures. Information required by more than one applicable item need not be repeated. No statement need be made in response to any item or sub-item which is inapplicable.

(b) Any information required to be included in the proxy statement as to terms of securities or other subject matter which from a standpoint of practical necessity must be determined in the future may be stated in terms of present knowledge and intention. To the extent practicable, the authority to be conferred concerning each such matter shall be confined within limits reasonably related to the need for discretionary authority. Subject to the foregoing, information which is not known to the persons on whose behalf the solicitation is to be made and which it is not reasonably within the power of such persons to ascertain or procure may be omitted, if a brief statement of the circumstances rendering such information unavailable is made.

(c) Any information contained in any other proxy soliciting material which has been furnished to each person solicited in connection with the same meeting or subject matter may be omitted from the proxy statement, if a clear reference is made to the particular document containing such information.

(d)(1) All printed proxy statements shall be in roman type at least as large and as legible as 10-point modern type, except that to the extent necessary for convenient presentation financial statements and other tabular data, but not the notes thereto, may be in roman type at least as large and as legible as

8-point modern type. All such type shall be leaded at least 2 points.

(2) Where a proxy statement is delivered through an electronic medium, issuers may satisfy legibility requirements applicable to printed documents, such as type size and font, by presenting all required information in a format readily communicated to investors.

(e) All proxy statements shall disclose, under an appropriate caption, the following dates:

(1) The deadline for submitting shareholder proposals for inclusion in the registrant's proxy statement and form of proxy for the registrant's next annual meeting, calculated in the manner provided in Rule 14a–8(e)(Question 5);

(2) The date after which notice of a shareholder proposal submitted outside the processes of Rule 14a–8 is considered untimely, either calculated in the manner provided by Rule 14a–4(c)(1) or as established by the registrant's advance notice provision, if any, authorized by applicable state law; and

(3) The deadline for submitting nominees for inclusion in the registrant's proxy statement and form of proxy pursuant to Rule 14a–11, an applicable state or foreign law provision, or a registrant's governing documents as they relate to the inclusion of shareholder director nominees in the registrant's proxy materials for the registrant's next annual meeting of shareholders.

(f) If the date of the next annual meeting is subsequently advanced or delayed by more than 30 calendar days from the date of the annual meeting to which the proxy statement relates, the registrant shall, in a timely manner, inform shareholders of such change, and the new dates referred to in paragraphs (e)(1) and (e)(2) of this rule, by including a notice, under Item 5, in its earliest possible quarterly report on Form 10–Q (17 CFR 249.308a) or, in the case of investment companies, in a shareholder report under Rule 30d–1 under the Investment Company Act of 1940, or, if impracticable, any means reasonably calculated to inform shareholders.

Rule 14a–6. Filing requirements

(a) *Preliminary Proxy Statement.* Five preliminary copies of the proxy statement and form of proxy shall be filed with the Commission at least 10 calendar days prior to the date definitive copies of such material are first sent or given to security holders, or such shorter period prior to that date as the Commission may authorize upon a showing of good cause thereunder. A registrant, however, shall not file with the Commission a preliminary proxy statement, form of proxy or other soliciting material to be furnished to security holders concurrently therewith if the solicitation relates to an annual (or special meeting in lieu of the annual) meeting, or for an investment company registered under the Investment Company Act of 1940 (15 U.S.C. 80a–1 *et seq.*) or a business development company, if the solicitation relates to any meeting of security holders at which the only matters to be acted upon are:

(1) The election of directors;

(2) The election, approval or ratification of accountant(s);

(3) A security holder proposal included pursuant to Rule 14a–8;

(4) A shareholder nominee for director included pursuant to Rule 14a–11, an applicable state or foreign law provision, or a registrant's governing documents as they relate to the inclusion of shareholder director nominees in the registrant's proxy materials.

(5) The approval or ratification of a plan as defined in paragraph (a)(6)(ii) of Item 402 of Regulation S–K or amendments to such a plan;

(6) With respect to an investment company registered under the Investment Company Act of 1940 or a business development company, a proposal to continue, without change, any advisory or other contract or agreement that previously has been the subject of a proxy solicitation for which proxy material was filed with the Commission pursuant to this rule;

(7) With respect to an open-end investment company registered under the Investment Company Act of 1940, a proposal to increase the number of shares authorized to be issued and/or;

(8) A vote to approve the compensation of executives as required pursuant to Section 14A(a)(1) of the Securities Exchange Act of 1934 (15 U.S.C. 78n–1(a)(1)) Rule 14a–21(a), or pursuant to section 111(e)(1) of the Emergency Economic Stabilization Act of 2008 (12 U.S.C. 5221(e)(1)) and Rule 14a–20 of this chapter, a vote to determine the frequency of shareholder votes to approve the compensation of executives as required pursuant to Section 14A(a)(2) of the Securities Exchange Act of 1934 (15 U.S.C. 78n–1(a)(2)) and Rule 14a–21(b), or any other shareholder advisory vote on executive compensation.

This exclusion from filing preliminary proxy material does not apply if the registrant comments upon or refers to a solicitation in opposition in connection with the meeting in its proxy material.

NOTE 1 TO PARAGRAPH (a): The filing of revised material does not recommence the ten day time period unless the revised material contains material revisions or material new proposal(s) that constitute a fundamental change in the proxy material.

NOTE 2 TO PARAGRAPH (a): The official responsible for the preparation of the proxy material should make every effort to verify the accuracy and completeness of the information required by the applicable rules. The preliminary material should be filed with the Commission at the earliest practicable date.

NOTE 3 TO PARAGRAPH (a): *Solicitation in Opposition.* For purposes of the exclusion from filing preliminary proxy material, a "solicitation in opposition" includes: (a) Any solicitation opposing a proposal supported by the registrant; and (b) any solicitation supporting a proposal that the registrant does not expressly support, other than a security holder proposal included in the registrant's proxy material pursuant to Rule 14a–8. The inclusion of a security holder proposal in the registrant's proxy material pursuant to Rule 14a–8 does not constitute a "solicitation in opposition," even if the registrant opposes the proposal and/or includes a statement in opposition to the proposal. The inclusion of a shareholder nominee in the registrant's proxy materials pursuant to Rule 14a–11, an applicable state or foreign law provision, or a registrant's governing documents as they relate to the inclusion of shareholder director nominees in the registrant's proxy materials does not constitute a "solicitation in opposition" for purposes of Rule 14a–6(a) even if the registrant opposes the shareholder nominee and solicits against the shareholder nominee and in favor of a registrant nominee.

NOTE 4 TO PARAGRAPH (a): A registrant that is filing proxy material in preliminary form only because the registrant has commented on or referred to a solicitation in opposition should indicate that fact in a transmittal letter when filing the preliminary material with the Commission.

(b) *Definitive Proxy Statement and Other Soliciting Material.* Eight definitive copies of the proxy statement, form of proxy and all other soliciting materials, in the same form as the materials sent to security holders, must be filed with the Commission no later than the date they are first sent or given to security holders. Three copies of these materials also must be filed with, or mailed for filing to, each national securities exchange on which the registrant has a class of securities listed and registered.

(c) *Personal Solicitation Materials.* If part of all of the solicitation involves personal solicitation, then eight copies of all written instructions or other materials that discuss, review or comment on the merits of any matter to be acted on, that are furnished to persons making the actual solicitation for their use directly or indirectly in connection with the solicitation, must be filed with the Commission no later than the date the materials are first sent or given to these persons.

(d) *Release Dates.* All preliminary proxy statements and forms of proxy filed pursuant to paragraph (a) of this rule shall be accompanied by a statement of the date on which definitive copies thereof filed pursuant to paragraph (b) of this rule are intended to be released to security holders. All definitive material filed pursuant to paragraph (b) of this rule shall be accompanied by a statement of the date on which copies of such material were released to security holders, or, if not released, the date on which copies thereof are intended to be released. All material filed pursuant to paragraph (c) of this rule shall be accompanied by a statement of the date on which copies thereof were released to the individual who will make the actual solicitation or if not released, the date on which copies thereof are intended to be released.

(e)(1) *Public Availability of Information.* All copies of preliminary proxy statements and forms of proxy filed pursuant to paragraph (a) of this rule shall be clearly marked "Preliminary Copies," and shall be deemed immediately available for public inspection unless confidential treatment is obtained pursuant to paragraph (e)(2) of this rule.

(2) *Confidential Treatment.* If action will be taken on any matter specified in Item 14 of Schedule 14A (Rule 14a–101), all copies of the preliminary proxy statement and form of proxy filed under paragraph (a) of this rule will be for the information of the Commission only and will not be deemed available for public inspection until filed with the Commission in definitive form so long as:

(i) The proxy statement does not relate to a matter or proposal subject to Rule 13e–3 or a roll-up transaction as defined in Item 901(c) of Regulation S–K;

(ii) Neither the parties to the transaction nor any persons authorized to act on their behalf have made any public communications relating to the transaction except for statements where the content is limited to the information specified in Rule 135 under the Securities Act of 1933; and

(iii) The materials are filed in paper and marked "Confidential, For Use of the Commission Only." In all cases, the materials may be disclosed to any department or agency of the United States Government and to the Congress, and the Commission may make any inquiries or investigation into the materials as may be necessary to conduct an adequate review by the Commission.

Instruction to Paragraph (e)(2): If communications are made publicly that go beyond the information specified in Rule 135 under the Securities Act of 1933, the preliminary proxy materials must be re-filed promptly with the Commission as public materials.

(f) *Communications Not Required to Be Filed.* Copies of replies to inquiries from security holders requesting further information and copies of communications which do no more than request that forms of proxy theretofore solicited be signed and returned need not be filed pursuant to this rule.

(g) *Solicitations Subject to Rule 14a–2(b)(1).*

(1) Any person who:

(i) Engages in a solicitation pursuant to Rule 14a–2(b)(1), and

(ii) At the commencement of that solicitation owns beneficially securities of the class which is the subject of the solicitation with a market value of over $5 million

shall furnish or mail to the Commission, not later than three days after the date the written solicitation is first sent or given to any security holder, five copies of a statement containing the information specified in the Notice of Exempt Solicitation (Rule 14a–103) which statement shall attach as an exhibit all written soliciting materials. Five copies of an amendment to such statement shall be furnished or mailed to the Commission, in connection with dissemination of any additional communications, not later than three days after the date the additional material is first sent or given to any security holder. Three copies of the Notice of Exempt Solicitation and amendments thereto shall, at the same time the materials are furnished or mailed to the Commission, be furnished or mailed to each national securities exchange upon which any class of securities of the registrant is listed and registered.

(2) Notwithstanding paragraph (g)(1) of this rule, no such submission need be made with respect to oral solicitations (other than with respect to scripts used in connection with such oral solicitations), speeches delivered in a public forum, press releases, published or broadcast opinions, statements, and advertisements appearing in a broadcast media, or a newspaper, magazine or other bona fide publication disseminated on a regular basis.

(h) *Revised Material.* Where any proxy statement, form of proxy or other material filed pursuant to this rule is amended or revised, two of the copies of such amended or revised material filed pursuant to this rule (or in the case of investment companies registered under the Investment Company Act of 1940, three of such copies) shall be marked to indicate clearly and precisely the changes effected therein. If the amendment or revision alters the text of the material the changes in such text shall be indicated by means of underscoring or in some other appropriate manner.

(i) *Fees.* At the time of filing the proxy solicitation material, the persons upon whose behalf the solicitation is made, other than investment companies registered under the Investment Company Act of 1940 shall pay to the Commission the following applicable fee:

(1) For preliminary proxy material involving acquisitions, mergers, spinoffs, consolidations or proposed sales or other dispositions of substantially all the assets of the company, a fee established in accordance with Rule 0–11 shall be paid. No refund shall be given.

(2) For all other proxy submissions and submissions made pursuant to Rule 14a–6(g), no fee shall be required.

(j) *Merger Proxy Materials.*

(1) Any proxy statement, form of proxy or other soliciting material required to be filed by this rule that also is either

(i) Included in a registration statement filed under the Securities Act of 1933 on Forms S–4 (17 CFR 239.25), F–4 (17 CFR 239.34) or N–14 (17 CFR 239.23); or

(ii) Filed under Rules 424, 425, or 497 under the Securities Act of 1933 is required to be filed only under the Securities Act, and is deemed filed under this rule.

(2) Under paragraph (j)(1) of this rule, the fee required by paragraph (i) of this rule need not be paid.

(k) *Computing Time Periods.* In computing time periods beginning with the filing date specified in Regulation 14A (Rules 14a–1 to 14b–1), the filing date shall be counted as the first day of the time period and midnight of the last day shall constitute the end of the specified time period.

(*l*) *Roll–Up Transactions.* If a transaction is a roll-up transaction as defined in Item 901(c) of Regulation S–K and is registered (or authorized to be registered) on Form S–4 (17 CFR 229.25) or Form F–4 (17 CFR 229.34), the proxy statement of the sponsor or the general partner as defined in Item 901(d) and Item 901(a), respectively, of Regulation S–K must be distributed to security holders no later than the lesser of 60 calendar days prior to the date on which the meeting of security holders is held or action is taken, or the maximum number of days permitted for giving notice under applicable state law.

(m) *Cover Page.* Proxy materials filed with the Commission shall include a cover page in the form set forth in Schedule 14A. The cover page required by this paragraph need not be distributed to security holders.

(n) *Solicitations Subject to Rule 14a–2(b)(4).* Any person who:

(1) Engages in a solicitation pursuant to Rule 14a–2(b)(4); and

(2) At the commencement of that solicitation both owns five percent (5%) or more of the outstanding securities of a class that is the subject of the proposed roll-up transaction, and engages in the business of buying and selling limited partnership interests in the secondary market, shall furnish or mail to the Commission, not later than three days after the date an oral or written solicitation by that person is first made, sent or provided to any security holder, five copies of a statement containing the information specified in the Notice of Exempt Preliminary Roll-up Communication (Rule 14a–104). Five copies of any amendment to such statement shall be furnished or mailed to the Commission not later than three days after a communication containing revised material is first made, sent or provided to any security holder.

(o) *Solicitations Before Furnishing a Definitive Proxy Statement.* Solicitations that are published, sent or given to security holders before they have been furnished a definitive proxy statement must be made in accordance with Rule 14a–12 unless there is an exemption available under Rule 14a–2.

(p) *Solicitations Subject to Rule 14a–11.* Any soliciting material that is published, sent or given to shareholders in connection with Rule 14a–2(b)(7) or (b)(8) must be filed with the Commission as specified in that section.

Rule 14a–7. Obligations of registrants to provide a list of, or mail soliciting material to, security holders

(a) If the registrant has made or intends to make a proxy solicitation in connection with a security holder meeting or action by consent or authorization, upon the written request by any record or beneficial holder of securities of the class entitled to vote at the meeting or to execute a consent or authorization to provide a list of security holders or to mail the requesting security holder's materials, regardless of whether the request references this rule, the registrant shall:

(1) Deliver to the requesting security holder within five business days after receipt of the request:

(i) Notification as to whether the registrant has elected to mail the security holder's soliciting materials or provide a security holder list if the election under paragraph (b) of this rule is to be made by the registrant;

(ii) A statement of the approximate number of record holders and beneficial holders, separated by type of holder and class, owning securities in the same class or classes as holders which have been or are to be solicited on management's behalf, or any more limited group of such holders designated by the security holder if available or retrievable under the registrant's or its transfer agent's security holder data systems; and

(iii) The estimated cost of mailing a proxy statement, form of proxy or other communication to such holders, including to the extent known or reasonably available, the estimated costs of any bank, broker, and similar person through whom the registrant has solicited or intends to solicit beneficial owners in connection with the security holder meeting or action;

(2) Perform the acts set forth in either paragraphs (a)(2)(i) or (a)(2)(ii) of this rule, at the registrant's or requesting security holder's option, as specified in paragraph (b) of this rule:

(i) Send copies of any proxy statement, form of proxy, or other soliciting material, including a Notice of Internet Availability of Proxy Materials (as described in Rule 14a–16), furnished by the security holder to the record holders, including banks, brokers, and similar entities, designated by the security holder. A sufficient number of copies must be sent to the banks, brokers, and similar entities for distribution to all beneficial owners designated by the security holder. The security holder may designate only record holders and/or beneficial owners who have not requested paper and/or e-mail copies of the proxy statement. If the registrant has received affirmative written or implied consent to deliver a single proxy statement to security holders at a shared address in accordance with the procedures in Rule 14a–3(e)(1), a single copy of the proxy statement or Notice of Internet Availability of Proxy Materials furnished by the security holder shall be sent to that address, provided that if multiple copies of the Notice of Internet Availability of Proxy Materials are furnished by the security holder for that address, the registrant shall deliver those copies in a single envelope to that address. The registrant shall send the security holder material with reasonable promptness after tender of the material to be sent, envelopes or other containers therefore, postage or payment for postage and other reasonable expenses of effecting such distribution. The registrant shall not be responsible for the content of the material; or

(ii) Deliver the following information to the requesting security holder within five business days of receipt of the request:

(A) A reasonably current list of the names, addresses and security positions of the record holders, including banks, brokers and similar entities holding securities in the same class or classes as holders which have been or are to be solicited on management's behalf, or any more limited group of such holders designated by the security holder if available or retrievable under the registrant's or its transfer agent's security holder data systems;

(B) The most recent list of names, addresses and security positions of beneficial owners as specified in Rule 14a–13(b), in the possession, or which subsequently comes into the possession, of the registrant;

(C) The names of security holders at a shared address that have consented to delivery of a single copy of proxy materials to a shared address, if the registrant has received written or implied consent in accordance with Rule 14a–3(e)(1); and

(D) If the registrant has relied on Rule 14a–16, the names of security holders who have requested paper copies of the proxy materials for all meetings and the names of security holders who, as of the date that the registrant receives the request, have requested paper copies of the proxy materials only for the meeting to which the solicitation relates.

(iii) All security holder list information shall be in the form requested by the security holder to the extent that such form is available to the registrant without undue burden or expense. The registrant shall furnish the security holder with updated record holder information on a daily basis or, if not available on a daily basis, at the shortest reasonable intervals; provided, however, the registrant need not provide beneficial or record holder information more current than the record date for the meeting or action.

(b)(1) The requesting security holder shall have the options set forth in paragraph (a)(2) of this rule, and the registrant shall have corresponding obligations, if the registrant or general partner or sponsor is soliciting or intends to solicit with respect to:

(i) A proposal that is subject to Rule 13e–3;

(ii) A roll-up transaction as defined in Item 901(c) of Regulation S–K that involves an entity with securities registered pursuant to Section 12 of the Act (15 U.S.C. 78*l*); or

(iii) A roll-up transaction as defined in Item 901(c) of Regulation S–K that involves a limited partnership, unless the transaction involves only:

(A) Partnerships whose investors will receive new securities or securities in another entity that are not reported under a transaction reporting plan declared effective before December 17, 1993 by the Commission under Section 11A of the Act (15 U.S.C. 78k–1); or

(B) Partnerships whose investors' securities are reported under a transaction reporting plan declared effective before December 17, 1993 by the Commission under Section 11A of the Act (15 U.S.C. 78k–1).

(2) With respect to all other requests pursuant to this rule, the registrant shall have the option to either mail the security holder's material or furnish the security holder list as set forth in this rule.

(c) At the time of a list request, the security holder making the request shall:

(1) If holding the registrant's securities through a nominee, provide the registrant with a statement by the nominee or other independent third party, or a copy of a current filing made with the Commission and furnished to the registrant, confirming such holder's beneficial ownership; and

(2) Provide the registrant with an affidavit, declaration, affirmation or other similar document provided for under applicable state law identifying the proposal or other corporate action that will

be the subject of the security holder's solicitation or communication and attesting that:

(i) The security holder will not use the list information for any purpose other than to solicit security holders with respect to the same meeting or action by consent or authorization for which the registrant is soliciting or intends to solicit or to communicate with security holders with respect to a solicitation commenced by the registrant; and

(ii) The security holder will not disclose such information to any person other than a beneficial owner for whom the request was made and an employee or agent to the extent necessary to effectuate the communication or solicitation.

(d) The security holder shall not use the information furnished by the registrant pursuant to paragraph (a)(2)(ii) of this rule for any purpose other than to solicit security holders with respect to the same meeting or action by consent or authorization for which the registrant is soliciting or intends to solicit or to communicate with security holders with respect to a solicitation commenced by the registrant; or disclose such information to any person other than an employee, agent, or beneficial owner for whom a request was made to the extent necessary to effectuate the communication or solicitation. The security holder shall return the information provided pursuant to paragraph (a)(2)(ii) of this rule and shall not retain any copies thereof or of any information derived from such information after the termination of the solicitation.

(e) The security holder shall reimburse the reasonable expenses incurred by the registrant in performing the acts requested pursuant to paragraph (a) of this rule.

NOTE 1 TO RULE 14a–7. Reasonably prompt methods of distribution to security holders may be used instead of mailing. If an alternative distribution method is chosen, the costs of that method should be considered where necessary rather than the costs of mailing.

NOTE 2 TO RULE 14a–7: When providing the information required by Rule 14a–7(a)(1)(ii), if the registrant has received affirmative written or implied consent to delivery of a single copy of proxy materials to a shared address in accordance with Rule 14a–3(e)(1), it shall exclude from the number of record holders those to whom it does not have to deliver a separate proxy statement.

Rule 14a–8. Shareholder proposals

This rule addresses when a company must include a shareholder's proposal in its proxy statement and identify the proposal in its form of proxy when the company holds an annual or special meeting of shareholders. In summary, in order to have your shareholder proposal included on a company's proxy card, and included along with any supporting statement in its proxy statement, you must be eligible and follow certain procedures. Under a few specific circumstances, the company is permitted to exclude your proposal, but only after submitting its reasons to the Commission. We structured this rule in a question-and-answer format so that it is easier to understand. The references to "you" are to a shareholder seeking to submit the proposal.

(a) *Question 1:* What is a proposal? A shareholder proposal is your recommendation or requirement that the company and/or its board of directors take action, which you intend to present at a meeting of the company's shareholders. Your proposal should state as clearly as possible the course of action that you believe the company should follow. If your proposal is placed on the company's proxy card, the company must also provide in the form of proxy means for shareholders to specify by boxes a choice between approval or disapproval, or abstention. Unless otherwise indicated, the word "proposal" as used in this rule refers both to your proposal, and to your corresponding statement in support of your proposal (if any).

(b) *Question 2:* Who is eligible to submit a proposal, and how do I demonstrate to the company that I am eligible? (1) In order to be eligible to submit a proposal, you must have continuously held at least $2,000 in market value, or 1%, of the company's securities entitled to be voted on the proposal at the meeting for at least one year by the date you submit the proposal. You must continue to hold those securities through the date of the meeting.

(2) If you are the registered holder of your securities, which means that your name appears in the company's records as a shareholder, the company can verify your eligibility on its own, although you will still have to provide the company with a written statement that you intend to continue to hold the securities through the date of the meeting of shareholders. However, if like many shareholders you are not a registered holder, the company likely does not know that you are a shareholder, or how many shares you own. In this case, at the time you submit your proposal, you must prove your eligibility to the company in one of two ways:

(i) The first way is to submit to the company a written statement from the "record" holder of your securities (usually a broker or bank) verifying that, at the time you submitted your proposal, you continuously held the securities for at least one year. You must also include your own written statement that you intend to continue to hold the securities through the date of the meeting of shareholders; or

(ii) The second way to prove ownership applies only if you have filed a Schedule 13D (Rule 13d–101), Schedule 13G (Rule 13d–102), Form 3 (17 CFR 249.103), Form 4 (17 CFR 249.104) and/or Form 5 (17 CFR 249.105), or amendments to those documents or updated forms, reflecting your ownership of the shares as of or before the date on which the one-year eligibility period begins. If you have filed one of these documents with the SEC, you may demonstrate your eligibility by submitting to the company:

(A) A copy of the schedule and/or form, and any subsequent amendments reporting a change in your ownership level;

(B) Your written statement that you continuously held the required number of shares for the one-year period as of the date of the statement; and

(C) Your written statement that you intend to continue ownership of the shares through the date of the company's annual or special meeting.

(c) *Question 3:* How many proposals may I submit? Each shareholder may submit no more than one proposal to a company for a particular shareholders' meeting.

(d) *Question 4:* How long can my proposal be? The proposal, including any accompanying supporting statement, may not exceed 500 words.

(e) *Question 5:* What is the deadline for submitting a proposal? (1) If you are submitting your proposal for the company's annual meeting, you can in most cases find the deadline in last year's proxy statement. However, if the company did not hold an annual meeting last year, or has changed the date of its meeting for this year more than 30 days from last year's meeting, you can usually find the deadline in one of the company's quarterly reports on Form 10–Q (17 CFR 249.308a) or in shareholder reports of investment companies under Rule 30d–1 of the Investment Company Act of 1940. In order to avoid controversy, shareholders should submit their proposals by means, including electronic means, that permit them to prove the date of delivery.

(2) The deadline is calculated in the following manner if the proposal is submitted for a regularly scheduled annual meeting. The proposal must be received at the company's principal executive offices not less than 120 calendar days before the date of the company's proxy statement released to shareholders in connection with the previous year's annual meeting. However, if the company did not hold an annual meeting the previous year, or if the date of this year's annual meeting has been changed by more than 30 days from the date of the previous year's meeting, then the deadline is a reasonable time before the company begins to print and send its proxy materials.

(3) If you are submitting your proposal for a meeting of shareholders other than a regularly scheduled annual meeting, the deadline is a reasonable time before the company begins to print and send its proxy materials.

(f) *Question 6:* What if I fail to follow one of the eligibility or procedural requirements explained in answers to Questions 1 through 4 of this rule? (1) The company may exclude your proposal, but only after it has notified you of the problem, and you have failed adequately to correct it. Within 14 calendar days of receiving your proposal, the company must notify you in writing of any procedural or eligibility deficiencies, as well as of the time frame for your response. Your response must be postmarked, or transmitted electronically, no later than 14 days from the date you received the company's notification. A company need not provide you such notice of a deficiency if the deficiency cannot be remedied, such as if you fail to submit a proposal by the company's properly determined deadline. If the company intends to exclude the proposal, it will later have to make a submission under Rule 14a–8 and provide you with a copy under Question 10 below, Rule 14a–8(j).

(2) If you fail in your promise to hold the required number of securities through the date of the meeting of shareholders, then the company will be permitted to exclude all of your proposals from its proxy materials for any meeting held in the following two calendar years.

(g) *Question 7:* Who has the burden of persuading the Commission or its staff that my proposal can be excluded? Except as otherwise noted, the burden is on the company to demonstrate that it is entitled to exclude a proposal.

(h) *Question 8:* Must I appear personally at the shareholders' meeting to present the proposal? (1) Either you, or your representative who is qualified under state law to present the proposal on your behalf, must attend the meeting to present the proposal. Whether you attend the meeting yourself or send a qualified representative to the meeting in your place, you should make sure that you, or your representative, follow the proper state law procedures for attending the meeting and/or presenting your proposal.

(2) If the company holds its shareholder meeting in whole or in part via electronic media, and the company permits you or your representative to present your proposal via such media, then you may appear through electronic media rather than traveling to the meeting to appear in person.

(3) If you or your qualified representative fail to appear and present the proposal, without good cause, the company will be permitted to exclude all of your proposals from its proxy materials for any meetings held in the following two calendar years.

(i) *Question 9:* If I have complied with the procedural requirements, on what other bases may a company rely to exclude my proposal? (1) Improper under state law: If the proposal is not a proper subject for action by shareholders under the laws of the jurisdiction of the company's organization;

Note to Paragraph (i)(1): Depending on the subject matter, some proposals are not considered proper under state law if they would be binding on the company if approved by shareholders. In our experience, most proposals that are cast as recommendations or requests that the board of directors take specified action are proper under state law. Accordingly, we will assume that a proposal drafted as a recommendation or suggestion is proper unless the company demonstrates otherwise.

(2) *Violation of Law:* If the proposal would, if implemented, cause the company to violate any state, federal, or foreign law to which it is subject;

Note to Paragraph (i)(2): We will not apply this basis for exclusion to permit exclusion of a proposal on grounds that it would violate foreign law if compliance with the foreign law would result in a violation of any state or federal law.

(3) *Violation of Proxy Rules:* If the proposal or supporting statement is contrary to any of the Commission's proxy rules, including Rule 14a–9, which prohibits materially false or misleading statements in proxy soliciting materials;

(4) *Personal Grievance; Special Interest:* If the proposal relates to the redress of a personal claim or grievance against the company or any other person, or if it is designed to result in a benefit to you, or to further a personal interest, which is not shared by the other shareholders at large;

(5) *Relevance:* If the proposal relates to operations which account for less than 5 percent of the company's total assets at the end of its most recent fiscal year, and for less than 5 percent of its net earnings and gross sales for its most recent fiscal year, and is not otherwise significantly related to the company's business;

(6) *Absence of Power/Authority:* If the company would lack the power or authority to implement the proposal;

(7) *Management Functions:* If the proposal deals with a matter relating to the company's ordinary business operations;

(8) *Director Elections*: If the proposal:

(i) Would disqualify a nominee who is standing for election;

(ii) Would remove a director from office before his or her term expired;

(iii) Questions the competence, business judgment, or character of one or more nominees or directors;

(iv) Seeks to include a specific individual in the company's proxy materials for election to the board of directors; or

(v) Otherwise could affect the outcome of the upcoming election of directors.

(9) *Conflicts with Company's Proposal:* If the proposal directly conflicts with one of the company's own proposals to be submitted to shareholders at the same meeting;

Note to Paragraph (i)(9): A company's submission to the Commission under this rule should specify the points of conflict with the company's proposal.

(10) *Substantially Implemented:* If the company has already substantially implemented the proposal;

Note to Paragraph (i)(10): A company may exclude a shareholder proposal that would provide an advisory vote or seek future advisory votes to approve the compensation of executives as disclosed pursuant to Item 402 of Regulation S–K (17 CFR 229.402) or any successor to Item 402 (a "say-on-pay vote") or that relates to the frequency of say-on-pay votes, provided that in the most recent shareholder vote required by Rule 14a–21(b) a single year (*i.e.,* one, two, or three years) received approval of a majority of votes cast on the matter and the company has adopted a policy on the frequency of say-on-pay votes that is consistent with the choice of the majority of votes cast in the most recent shareholder vote required by Rule 14a–21(b).

(11) *Duplication:* If the proposal substantially duplicates another proposal previously submitted to the company by another proponent that will be included in the company's proxy materials for the same meeting;

(12) *Resubmissions:* If the proposal deals with substantially the same subject matter as another proposal or proposals that has or have been previously included in the company's proxy materials within the preceding 5 calendar years, a company may exclude it from its proxy materials for any meeting held within 3 calendar years of the last time it was included if the proposal received:

(i) Less than 3% of the vote if proposed once within the preceding 5 calendar years;

(ii) Less than 6% of the vote on its last submission to shareholders if proposed twice previously within the preceding 5 calendar years; or

(iii) Less than 10% of the vote on its last submission to shareholders if proposed three times or more previously within the preceding 5 calendar years; and

(13) *Specific Amount of Dividends:* If the proposal relates to specific amounts of cash or stock dividends.

(j) *Question 10:* What procedures must the company follow if it intends to exclude my proposal? (1) If the company intends to exclude a proposal from its proxy materials, it must file its reasons with the Commission no later than 80 calendar days before it files its definitive proxy statement and form of proxy with the Commission. The company must simultaneously provide you with a copy of its submission. The Commission staff may permit the company to make its submission later than 80 days before the company files its definitive proxy statement and form of proxy, if the company demonstrates good cause for missing the deadline.

(2) The company must file six paper copies of the following:

(i) The proposal;

(ii) An explanation of why the company believes that it may exclude the proposal, which should, if possible, refer to the most recent applicable authority, such as prior Division letters issued under the rule; and

(iii) A supporting opinion of counsel when such reasons are based on matters of state or foreign law.

(k) *Question 11:* May I submit my own statement to the Commission responding to the company's arguments?

Yes, you may submit a response, but it is not required. You should try to submit any response to us, with a copy to the company, as soon as possible after the company makes its submission. This way, the Commission staff will have time to consider fully your submission before it issues its response. You should submit six paper copies of your response.

(*l*) *Question 12:* If the company includes my shareholder proposal in its proxy materials, what information about me must it include along with the proposal itself?

(1) The company's proxy statement must include your name and address, as well as the number of the company's voting securities that you hold. However, instead of providing that information, the company may instead include a statement that it will provide the information to shareholders promptly upon receiving an oral or written request.

(2) The company is not responsible for the contents of your proposal or supporting statement.

(m) *Question 13:* What can I do if the company includes in its proxy statement reasons why it believes shareholders should not vote in favor of my proposal, and I disagree with some of its statements?

(1) The company may elect to include in its proxy statement reasons why it believes shareholders should vote against your proposal. The company is allowed to make arguments reflecting its own point of view, just as you may express your own point of view in your proposal's supporting statement.

(2) However, if you believe that the company's opposition to your proposal contains materially false or misleading statements that may violate our anti-fraud rule, Rule 14a–9, you should promptly send to the Commission staff and the company a letter explaining the reasons for your view, along with a copy of the company's statements opposing your proposal. To the extent possible, your letter should include specific factual information demonstrating the inaccuracy of the company's claims. Time permitting, you may wish to try to work out your differences with the company by yourself before contacting the Commission staff.

(3) We require the company to send you a copy of its statements opposing your proposal before it sends its proxy materials, so that you may bring to our attention any materially false or misleading statements, under the following timeframes:

(i) If our no-action response requires that you make revisions to your proposal or supporting statement as a condition to requiring the company to include it in its proxy materials, then the company must provide you with a copy of its opposition statements no later than 5 calendar days after the company receives a copy of your revised proposal; or

(ii) In all other cases, the company must provide you with a copy of its opposition statements no later than 30 calendar days before its files definitive copies of its proxy statement and form of proxy under Rule 14a–6.

Rule 14a–9. False or misleading statements

(a) No solicitation subject to this regulation shall be made by means of any proxy statement, form of proxy, notice of meeting or other communication, written or oral, containing any statement which, at the time and in the light of the circumstances under which it is made, is false or misleading with respect to any material fact, or which omits to state any material fact necessary in order to make the statements therein not false or misleading or necessary to correct any statement in any earlier communication with respect to the solicitation of a proxy for the same meeting or subject matter which has become false or misleading.

(b) The fact that a proxy statement, form of proxy or other soliciting material has been filed with or examined by the Commission shall not be deemed a finding by the Commission that such material is accurate or complete or not false or misleading, or that the Commission has passed upon the merits of or approved any statement contained therein or any matter to be acted upon by security holders. No representation contrary to the foregoing shall be made.

(c) No nominee, nominating shareholder or nominating shareholder group, or any member thereof, shall cause to be included in a registrant's proxy materials, either pursuant to the federal proxy rules, an applicable state or foreign law provision, or a registrant's governing documents as they relate to including shareholder nominees for director in a registrant's proxy materials, include in a notice on Schedule 14N (Rule 14n–101), or include in any other related communication, any statement which, at the time and in the light of the circumstances under which it is made, is false or misleading with respect to any material fact, or which omits to state any material fact necessary in order to make the statements therein not false or misleading or necessary to correct any statement in any earlier communication with respect to a solicitation for the same meeting or subject matter which has become false or misleading.

NOTE: The following are some examples of what, depending upon particular facts and circumstances, may be misleading within the meaning of this rule.

(a) Predictions as to specific future market values.

(b) Material which directly or indirectly impugns character, integrity or personal reputation, or directly or indirectly makes charges concerning improper, illegal or immoral conduct or associations, without factual foundation.

(c) Failure to so identify a proxy statement, form of proxy and other soliciting material as to clearly distinguish it from the soliciting material of any other person or persons soliciting for the same meeting or subject matter.

(d) Claims made prior to a meeting regarding the results of a solicitation.

Rule 14a–10. Prohibition of certain solicitations

No person making a solicitation which is subject to Rules 14a–1 to 14a–10 shall solicit—

(a) Any undated or post dated proxy; or

(b) Any proxy which provides that it shall be deemed to be dated as of any date subsequent to the date on which it is signed by the security holder.

Rule 14a–11. [Reserved]

Rule 14a–12. Solicitation before furnishing a proxy statement

(a) Notwithstanding the provisions of Rule 14a–3(a), a solicitation may be made before furnishing security holders with a proxy statement meeting the requirements of Rule 14a–3(a) if:

(1) Each written communication includes:

(i) The identity of the participants in the solicitation (as defined in Instruction 3 to Item 4 of Schedule 14A (Rule 14a–101)) and a description of their direct or indirect interests, by security holdings or otherwise, or a prominent legend in clear, plain language advising security holders where they can obtain that information; and

(ii) A prominent legend in clear, plain language advising security holders to read the proxy statement when it is available because it contains important information. The legend also must explain to investors that they can get the proxy statement, and any other relevant documents, for free at the Commission's web site and describe which documents are available free from the participants; and

(2) A definitive proxy statement meeting the requirements of Rule 14a–3(a) is sent or given to

security holders solicited in reliance on this rule before or at the same time as the forms of proxy, consent or authorization are furnished to or requested from security holders.

(b) Any soliciting material published, sent or given to security holders in accordance with paragraph (a) of this rule must be filed with the Commission no later than the date the material is first published, sent or given to security holders. Three copies of the material must at the same time be filed with, or mailed for filing to, each national securities exchange upon which any class of securities of the registrant is listed and registered. The soliciting material must include a cover page in the form set forth in Schedule 14A and the appropriate box on the cover page must be marked. Soliciting material in connection with a registered offering is required to be filed only under Rule 424 or Rule 425 under the Securities Act of 1933, and will be deemed filed under this rule.

(c) Solicitations by any person or group of persons for the purpose of opposing a solicitation subject to this regulation by any other person or group of persons with respect to the election or removal of directors at any annual or special meeting of security holders also are subject to the following provisions:

(1) *Application of This Rule to Annual Report to Security Holders.* Notwithstanding the provisions of Rule 14a-3(b) and (c), any portion of the annual report to security holders referred to in Rule 14a-3(b) that comments upon or refers to any solicitation subject to this rule, or to any participant in the solicitation, other than the solicitation by the management, must be filed with the Commission as proxy material subject to this regulation. This must be filed in electronic format unless an exemption is available under Rules 201 or 202 of Regulation S-T.

(2) *Use of Reprints or Reproductions.* In any solicitation subject to this Rule 14a-12(c), soliciting material that includes, in whole or part, any reprints or reproductions of any previously published material must:

(i) State the name of the author and publication, the date of prior publication, and identify any person who is quoted without being named in the previously published material.

(ii) Except in the case of a public or official document or statement, state whether or not the consent of the author and publication has been obtained to the use of the previously published material as proxy soliciting material.

(iii) If any participant using the previously published material, or anyone on his or her behalf, paid, directly or indirectly, for the preparation or prior publication of the previously published material, or has made or proposes to make any payments or give any other consideration in connection with the publication or republication of the material, state the circumstances.

Instruction 1 to Rule 14a-12. If paper filing is permitted, file eight copies of the soliciting material with the Commission, except that only three copies of the material specified by Rule 14a-12(c)(1) need be filed.

Instruction 2 to Rule 14a-12. Any communications made under this rule after the definitive proxy statement is on file but before it is disseminated also must specify that the proxy statement is publicly available and the anticipated date of dissemination.

Instruction 3 to Rule 14a-12. Inclusion of a nominee pursuant to Rule 14a-11, an applicable state or foreign law provision, or a registrant's governing documents as they relate to the inclusion of shareholder director nominees in the registrant's proxy materials, or solicitations by a nominating shareholder or nominating shareholder group that are made in connection with that nomination constitute solicitations in opposition subject to Rule 14a-12(c), except for purposes of Rule 14a-6(a).

Rule 14a-13. Obligation of registrants in communicating with beneficial owners

(a) If the registrant knows that securities of any class entitled to vote at a meeting (or by written consents or authorizations if no meeting is held) with respect to which the registrant intends to solicit proxies, consents or authorizations are held of record by a broker, dealer, voting trustee, bank, association, or other entity that exercises fiduciary powers in nominee name or otherwise, the registrant shall:

(1) By first class mail or other equally prompt means:

(i) Inquire of each such record holder:

(A) Whether other persons are the beneficial owners of such securities and if so, the number of copies of the proxy and other soliciting material necessary to supply such material to such beneficial owners;

(B) In the case of an annual (or special meeting in lieu of the annual) meeting, or written consents in lieu of such meeting, at which directors are to be elected, the number of copies of the annual report to security holders necessary to supply such report to beneficial owners to whom such reports are to be distributed by such record holder or its nominee and not by the registrant; and

(C) If the record holder has an obligation under Rules 14b–1(b)(3) or 14b–2(b)(4)(ii) and (iii) and (3), whether an agent has been designated to act on its behalf in fulfilling such obligation and, if so, the name and address of such agent; and

(D) Whether it holds the registrant's securities on behalf of any respondent bank and, if so, the name and address of each such respondent bank; and

(ii) Indicate to each such record holder:

(A) Whether the registrant, pursuant to paragraph (c) of this rule, intends to distribute the annual report to security holders to beneficial owners of its securities whose names, addresses and securities positions are disclosed pursuant to Rules 14b–1(b)(3) and 14(b)–2(b)(4)(ii) and (iii);

(B) The record date; and

(C) At the option of the registrant, any employee benefit plan established by an affiliate of the registrant that holds securities of the registrant that the registrant elects to treat as exempt employee benefit plan securities;

(2) Upon receipt of a record holder's or respondent bank's response indicating, pursuant to Rule 14b–2(b)(1)(i), the names and addresses of its respondent banks, within one business day after the date such response is received, make an inquiry of and give notification to each such respondent bank in the same manner required by paragraph (a)(1) of this rule; *Provided, however,* the inquiry required by paragraphs (a)(1) and (a)(2) of this rule shall not cover beneficial owners of exempt employee benefit plan securities;

(3) Make the inquiry required by paragraph (a)(1) of this section at least 20 business days prior to the record date of the meeting of security holders, or

(i) If such inquiry is impracticable 20 business days prior to the record date of a special meeting, as many days before the record date of such meeting as is practicable or,

(ii) If consents or authorization are solicited, and such inquiry is impracticable 20 business days before the earliest date on which they may be used to effect corporate action, as many days before that date as is practicable, or

(iii) At such later time as the rules of a national securities exchange on which the class of securities in question is listed may permit for good cause shown; *Provided, however,* That if a record holder or respondent bank has informed the registrant that a designated office(s) or department(s) is to receive such inquiries, the inquiry shall be made to such designated office(s) or department(s);

(4) Supply, in a timely manner, each record holder and respondent bank of whom the inquiries required by paragraphs (a)(1) and (a)(2) of this rule are made with copies of the proxy, other proxy soliciting material, and/or the annual report to security holders, in such quantities, assembled in such form and at such place(s), as the record holder or respondent bank may reasonably request in order to send such material to each beneficial owner of securities who is to be furnished with such material by the record holder or respondent bank; and

(5) Upon the request of any record holder or respondent bank that is supplied with proxy soliciting material and/or annual reports to security holders pursuant to paragraph (a)(4) of this rule, pay its reasonable expenses for completing the sending of such material to beneficial owners.

NOTE 1: If the registrant's list of security holders indicates that some of its securities are registered in the name of a clearing agency registered pursuant to section 17A of the Act (*e.g.*, "Cede & Co.," nominee for the Depository Trust Company), the registrant shall make appropriate inquiry of the clearing agency and thereafter of the participants in such clearing agency who may hold on behalf of a beneficial owner, or respondent bank and shall comply with the above paragraph with respect to any such participant (see Rule 14a–1(i)).

NOTE 2: The attention of registrants is called to the fact that each broker, dealer, bank, association and other entity that exercises fiduciary powers has an obligation pursuant to Rule 14b–1(b), and Rule 14b–2(b) (except as provided therein with respect to employee benefit plan securities held in nominee name) and, with respect to brokers and dealers, applicable self-regulatory organization requirements to obtain and forward, within the time periods prescribed therein, (a) proxies (or in lieu thereof requests for voting instructions) and proxy soliciting materials to beneficial owners on whose behalf it holds securities, and (b) annual reports to security holders to beneficial owners on whose behalf it holds securities, unless the registrant has notified the record holder or respondent bank that it has assumed responsibility to send such material to beneficial owners whose names, addresses and securities positions are disclosed pursuant to Rule 14b–1(b)(3) and Rule 14b–2(b)(4)(ii) and (iii).

NOTE 3: The attention of registrants is called to the fact that registrants have an obligation, pursuant to paragraph (d) of this rule, to cause proxies (or in lieu thereof requests for voting instructions), proxy soliciting material and annual reports to security holders to be furnished, in a timely manner, to beneficial owners of exempt employee benefit plan securities.

(b) Any registrant requesting pursuant to Rule 14b–1(b)(3) and Rule 14b–2(b)(4)(ii) and (iii) and (3) a list of names, addresses and securities positions of beneficial owners of its securities who either have consented or have not objected to disclosure of such information shall:

(1) By first class mail or other equally prompt means, inquire of each record holder and each respondent bank identified to the registrant pursuant to Rule 14b–2(b)(4)(i) whether such record holder or respondent bank holds the registrant's securities on behalf of any respondent banks and, if so, the name and address of each such respondent bank;

(2) Request such list to be compiled as of a date no earlier than five business days after the date the registrant's request is received by the record holder or respondent bank; *Provided, however,* That if the record holder or respondent bank has informed the registrant that a designated office(s) or department(s) is to receive such requests, the request shall be made to such designated office(s) or department(s);

(3) Make such request to the following persons that hold the registrant's securities on behalf of beneficial owners: all brokers, dealers, banks, associations and other entities that exercise fiduciary powers; *Provided, however,* such request shall not cover beneficial owners of exempt employee benefit plan securities as defined in Rule 14a–1(d)(1); and, at the option of the registrant, such request may give notice of any employee benefit plan established by an affiliate of the registrant that holds securities of the registrant that the registrant elects to treat as exempt employee benefit plan securities;

(4) Use the information furnished in response to such request exclusively for purposes of corporate communications; and

(5) Upon the request of any record holder or respondent bank to whom such request is made, pay the reasonable expenses, both direct and indirect, of providing beneficial owner information.

NOTE: A registrant will be deemed to have satisfied its obligations under paragraph (b) of this rule by requesting consenting and non-objecting beneficial owner lists from a designated agent acting on behalf of the record holder or respondent bank and paying to that designated agent the reasonable expenses of providing the beneficial owner information.

(c) A registrant, at its option, may mail its annual report to security holders to the beneficial owners whose identifying information is provided by record holders and respondent banks, pursuant to Rule 14b–1(c) and Rule 14b–2(e)(2) and (3), provided that such registrant notifies the record holders and respondent banks, at the time it makes the inquiry required by paragraph (a) of this rule, that the registrant will send the annual report to security holders to the beneficial owners so identified.

(d) If a registrant solicits proxies, consents or authorizations from record holders and respondent banks who hold securities on behalf of beneficial owners, the registrant shall cause proxies (or in lieu thereof requests for voting instructions), proxy soliciting material and annual reports to security holders to be furnished, in a timely manner, to beneficial owners of exempt employee benefit plan securities.

Rule 14a–14. Modified or superseded documents

(a) Any statement contained in a document incorporated or deemed to be incorporated by reference shall be deemed to be modified or superseded, for purposes of the proxy statement, to the extent that a statement contained in the proxy statement or in any other subsequently filed document that also is or is deemed to be incorporated by reference modifies or replaces such statement.

(b) The modifying or superseding statement may but need not, state it has modified or superseded a prior statement or include any other information set forth in the document that is not so modified or superseded. The making of a modifying or superseding statement shall not be deemed an admission that the modified or superseded statement, when made, constituted an untrue statement of a material fact, an omission to state a material fact necessary to make a statement not misleading, or the employment of a manipulative, deceptive, or fraudulent device, contrivance, scheme, transaction, act, practice, course of business or artifice to defraud, as those terms are used in the Securities Act of 1933, the Securities Exchange Act of 1934 ("the Act"), the Investment Company Act of 1940, or the rules and regulations thereunder.

(c) Any statement so modified shall not be deemed in its unmodified form to constitute part of the proxy statement for purposes of the Act. Any statement so superseded shall not be deemed to constitute a part of the proxy statement for purposes of the Act.

Rule 14a–15. Differential and contingent compensation in connection with roll–up transactions

(a) It shall be unlawful for any person to receive compensation for soliciting proxies, consents, or authorizations directly from security holders in connection with a roll-up transaction as provided in paragraph (b) of this rule, if the compensation is:

(1) Based on whether the solicited proxy, consent, or authorization either approves or disapproves the proposed roll-up transaction; or

(2) Contingent on the approval, disapproval, or completion of the roll-up transaction.

(b) This rule is applicable to a roll-up transaction as defined in Item 901(c) of Regulation S–K, except for a transaction involving only:

(1) Finite-life entities that are not limited partnerships;

(2) Partnerships whose investors will receive new securities or securities in another entity that are not reported under a transaction reporting plan declared effective before December 17, 1993 by the Commission under Section 11A of the Act (15 U.S.C. 78k–1); or

(3) Partnerships whose investors' securities are reported under a transaction reporting plan declared effective before December 17, 1993 by the Commission under Section 11A of the Act (15 U.S.C. 78k–1).

Rule 14a–16. Internet availability of proxy materials

(a)(1) A registrant shall furnish a proxy statement pursuant to Rule 14a–3(a), or an annual report to security holders pursuant to Rule 14a–3(b), to a security holder by sending the security holder a Notice of Internet Availability of Proxy Materials, as described in this rule, 40 calendar days or more prior to the security holder meeting date, or if no meeting is to be held, 40 calendar days or more prior to the date the votes, consents or authorizations may be used to effect the corporate action, and complying with all other requirements of this rule.

(2) Unless the registrant chooses to follow the full set delivery option set forth in paragraph (n) of this rule, it must provide the record holder or respondent bank with all information listed in paragraph (d) of this rule in sufficient time for the record holder or respondent bank to prepare, print and send a Notice of Internet Availability of Proxy Materials to beneficial owners at least 40 calendar days before the meeting date.

(b)(1) All materials identified in the Notice of Internet Availability of Proxy Materials must be publicly accessible, free of charge, at the Web site address specified in the notice on or before the time that the notice is sent to the security holder and such materials must remain available on that Web site through the conclusion of the meeting of security holders.

(2) All additional soliciting materials sent to security holders or made public after the Notice of Internet Availability of Proxy Materials has been sent must be made publicly accessible at the specified Web site address no later than the day on which such materials are first sent to security holders or made public.

(3) The Web site address relied upon for compliance under this rule may not be the address of the Commission's electronic filing system.

(4) The registrant must provide security holders with a means to execute a proxy as of the time the Notice of Internet Availability of Proxy Materials is first sent to security holders.

(c) The materials must be presented on the Web site in a format, or formats, convenient for both reading online and printing on paper.

(d) The Notice of Internet Availability of Proxy Materials must contain the following:

(1) A prominent legend in bold-face type that states "Important Notice Regarding the Availability of Proxy Materials for the Shareholder Meeting To Be Held on [insert meeting date]";

(2) An indication that the communication is not a form for voting and presents only an overview of the more complete proxy materials, which contain important information and are available on the Internet or by mail, and encouraging a security holder to access and review the proxy materials before voting;

(3) The Internet Web site address where the proxy materials are available;

(4) Instructions regarding how a security holder may request a paper or e-mail copy of the proxy materials at no charge, including the date by which they should make the request to facilitate timely delivery, and an indication that they will not otherwise receive a paper or e-mail copy;

(5) The date, time, and location of the meeting, or if corporate action is to be taken by written consent, the earliest date on which the corporate action may be effected;

(6) A clear and impartial identification of each separate matter intended to be acted on and the soliciting person's recommendations, if any, re-

garding those matters, but no supporting statements;

(7) A list of the materials being made available at the specified Web site;

(8) A toll-free telephone number, an e-mail address, and an Internet Web site where the security holder can request a copy of the proxy statement, annual report to security holders, and form of proxy, relating to all of the registrant's future security holder meetings and for the particular meeting to which the proxy materials being furnished relate;

(9) Any control/identification numbers that the security holder needs to access his or her form of proxy;

(10) Instructions on how to access the form of proxy, provided that such instructions do not enable a security holder to execute a proxy without having access to the proxy statement and, if required by Rule 14a–3(b), the annual report to security holders; and

(11) Information on how to obtain directions to be able to attend the meeting and vote in person.

(e)(1) The Notice of Internet Availability of Proxy Materials may not be incorporated into, or combined with, another document, except that it may be incorporated into, or combined with, a notice of security holder meeting required under state law, unless state law prohibits such incorporation or combination.

(2) The Notice of Internet Availability of Proxy Materials may contain only the information required by paragraph (d) of this rule and any additional information required to be included in a notice of security holders meeting under state law; provided that:

(i) The registrant must revise the information on the Notice of Internet Availability of Proxy Materials, including any title to the document, to reflect the fact that:

(A) The registrant is conducting a consent solicitation rather than a proxy solicitation; or

(B) The registrant is not soliciting proxy or consent authority, but is furnishing an information statement pursuant to Rule 14c–2; and

(ii) The registrant may include a statement on the Notice to educate security holders that no personal information other than the identification or control number is necessary to execute a proxy.

(f)(1) Except as provided in paragraph (h) of this rule, the Notice of Internet Availability of Proxy Materials must be sent separately from other types of security holder communications and may not accompany any other document or materials, including the form of proxy.

(2) Notwithstanding paragraph (f)(1) of this rule, the registrant may accompany the Notice of Internet Availability of Proxy Materials with:

(i) A pre-addressed, postage-paid reply card for requesting a copy of the proxy materials;

(ii) A copy of any notice of security holder meeting required under state law if that notice is not combined with the Notice of Internet Availability of Proxy Materials;

(iii) In the case of an investment company registered under the Investment Company Act of 1940, the company's prospectus, a summary prospectus that satisfies the requirements of Rule 498(b) of this chapter, or a report that is required to be transmitted to stockholders by section 30(e) of the Investment Company Act (15 U.S.C. 80a–29(e)) and the rules thereunder; and

(iv) An explanation of the reasons for a registrant's use of the rules detailed in this section and the process of receiving and reviewing the proxy materials and voting as detailed in this section.

(g) *Plain English.* (1) To enhance the readability of the Notice of Internet Availability of Proxy Materials, the registrant must use plain English principles in the organization, language, and design of the notice.

(2) The registrant must draft the language in the Notice of Internet Availability of Proxy Materials so that, at a minimum, it substantially complies with each of the following plain English writing principles:

(i) Short sentences;

(ii) Definite, concrete, everyday words;

(iii) Active voice;

(iv) Tabular presentation or bullet lists for complex material, whenever possible;

(v) No legal jargon or highly technical business terms; and

(vi) No multiple negatives.

(3) In designing the Notice of Internet Availability of Proxy Materials, the registrant may include pictures, logos, or similar design elements so long as the design is not misleading and the required information is clear.

(h) The registrant may send a form of proxy to security holders if:

(1) At least 10 calendar days or more have passed since the date it first sent the Notice of Internet Availability of Proxy Materials to security holders and the form of proxy is accompanied by a copy of the Notice of Internet Availability of Proxy Materials; or

(2) The form of proxy is accompanied or preceded by a copy, via the same medium, of the proxy statement and any annual report to security holders that is required by Rule 14a–3(b).

(i) The registrant must file a form of the Notice of Internet Availability of Proxy Materials with the Commission pursuant to Rule 14a–6(b) no later than the date that the registrant first sends the notice to security holders.

(j) *Obligation to Provide Copies.* (1) The registrant must send, at no cost to the record holder or respondent bank and by U.S. first class mail or other reasonably prompt means, a paper copy of the proxy statement, information statement, annual report to security holders, and form of proxy (to the extent each of those documents is applicable) to any record holder or respondent bank requesting such a copy within three business days after receiving a request for a paper copy.

(2) The registrant must send, at no cost to the record holder or respondent bank and via e-mail, an electronic copy of the proxy statement, information statement, annual report to security holders, and form of proxy (to the extent each of those documents is applicable) to any record holder or respondent bank requesting such a copy within three business days after receiving a request for an electronic copy via e-mail.

(3) The registrant must provide copies of the proxy materials for one year after the conclusion of the meeting or corporate action to which the proxy materials relate, provided that, if the registrant receives the request after the conclusion of the meeting or corporate action to which the proxy materials relate, the registrant need not send copies via First Class mail and need not respond to such request within three business days.

(4) The registrant must maintain records of security holder requests to receive materials in paper or via e-mail for future solicitations and must continue to provide copies of the materials to a security holder who has made such a request until the security holder revokes such request.

(k) *Security Holder Information.* (1) A registrant or its agent shall maintain the Internet Web site on which it posts its proxy materials in a manner that does not infringe on the anonymity of a person accessing such Web site.

(2) The registrant and its agents shall not use any e-mail address obtained from a security holder solely for the purpose of requesting a copy of proxy materials pursuant to paragraph (j) of this rule for any purpose other than to send a copy of those materials to that security holder. The registrant shall not disclose such information to any person other than an employee or agent to the extent necessary to send a copy of the proxy materials pursuant to paragraph (j) of this rule.

(*l*) A person other than the registrant may solicit proxies pursuant to the conditions imposed on registrants by this rule, provided that:

(1) A soliciting person other than the registrant is required to provide copies of its proxy materials only to security holders to whom it has sent a Notice of Internet Availability of Proxy Materials; and

(2) A soliciting person other than the registrant must send its Notice of Internet Availability of Proxy Materials by the later of:

(i) 40 calendar days prior to the security holder meeting date or, if no meeting is to be held, 40 calendar days prior to the date the votes, consents, or authorizations may be used to effect the corporate action; or

(ii) The date on which it files its definitive proxy statement with the Commission, provided its preliminary proxy statement is filed no later than 10 calendar days after the date that the registrant files its definitive proxy statement.

(3) *Content of the Soliciting Person's Notice of Internet Availability of Proxy Materials.* (i) If, at the time a soliciting person other than the registrant sends its Notice of Internet Availability of Proxy Materials, the soliciting person is not aware of all matters on the registrant's agenda for the meeting of security holders, the soliciting person's Notice on Internet Availability of Proxy Materials must provide a clear and impartial identification

of each separate matter on the agenda to the extent known by the soliciting person at that time. The soliciting person's notice also must include a clear statement indicating that there may be additional agenda items of which the soliciting person is not aware and that the security holder cannot direct a vote for those items on the soliciting person's proxy card provided at that time.

(ii) If a soliciting person other than the registrant sends a form of proxy not containing all matters intended to be acted upon, the Notice of Internet Availability of Proxy Materials must clearly state whether execution of the form of proxy will invalidate a security holder's prior vote on matters not presented on the form of proxy.

(m) This rule shall not apply to a proxy solicitation in connection with a business combination transaction, as defined in Rule 165 under the Securities Act of 1933, as well as transactions for cash consideration requiring disclosure under Item 14 of Schedule 14A.

(n) *Full Set Delivery Option.*

(1) For purposes of this paragraph (n), the term full set of proxy materials shall include all of the following documents:

(i) A copy of the proxy statement;

(ii) A copy of the annual report to security holders if required by Rule 14a–3(b); and

(iii) A form of proxy.

(2) Notwithstanding paragraphs (e) and (f)(2) of this rule, a registrant or other soliciting person may:

(i) Accompany the Notice of Internet Availability of Proxy Materials with a full set of proxy materials; or

(ii) Send a full set of proxy materials without a Notice of Internet Availability of Proxy Materials if all of the information required in a Notice of Internet Availability of Proxy Materials pursuant to paragraphs (d) and (n)(4) is incorporated in the proxy statement and the form of proxy.

(3) A registrant or other soliciting person that sends a full set of proxy materials to a security holder pursuant to this paragraph (n) need not comply with

(i) The timing provisions of paragraphs (a) and (*l*)(2); and

(ii) The obligation to provide copies pursuant to paragraph (j) of this rule.

(4) A registrant or other soliciting person that sends a full set of proxy materials to a security holder pursuant to this paragraph (n) need not include in its Notice of Internet Availability of Proxy Materials, proxy statement, or form of proxy the following disclosures:

(i) Instructions regarding the nature of the communication pursuant to paragraph (d)(2) of this section;

(ii) Instructions on how to request a copy of the proxy materials; and

(iii) Instructions on how to access the form of proxy pursuant to paragraph (d)(10).

Rule 14a–17. Electronic shareholder forums

(a) A shareholder, registrant, or third party acting on behalf of a shareholder or registrant may establish, maintain, or operate an electronic shareholder forum to facilitate interaction among the registrant's shareholders and between the registrant and its shareholders as the shareholder or registrant deems appropriate. Subject to paragraphs (b) and (c) of this rule, the forum must comply with the federal securities laws, including Section 14(a) of the Act and its associated regulations, other applicable federal laws, applicable state laws, and the registrant's governing documents.

(b) No shareholder, registrant, or third party acting on behalf of a shareholder or registrant, by reason of establishing, maintaining, or operating an electronic shareholder forum, will be liable under the federal securities laws for any statement or information provided by another person to the electronic shareholder forum. Nothing in this rule prevents or alters the application of the federal securities laws, including the provisions for liability for fraud, deception, or manipulation, or other applicable federal and state laws to the person or persons that provide a statement or information to an electronic shareholder forum.

(c) Reliance on the exemption in Rule 14a–2(b)(6) to participate in an electronic shareholder forum does not eliminate a person's eligibility to solicit proxies after the date that the exemption in Rule 14a–2(b)(6) is no longer available, or is no longer being relied upon, provided that any such solicitation is conducted in accordance with this regulation.

Rule 14a–18. Disclosure regarding nominating shareholders and nominees submitted for inclusion in a registrant's proxy materials pursuant to applicable state or foreign law, or a registrant's governing documents

To have a nominee included in a registrant's proxy materials pursuant to a procedure set forth under applicable state or foreign law, or the registrant's governing documents addressing the inclusion of shareholder director nominees in the registrant's proxy materials, the nominating shareholder or nominating shareholder group must provide notice to the registrant of its intent to do so on a Schedule 14N and file that notice, including the required disclosure, with the Commission on the date first transmitted to the registrant. This notice shall be postmarked or transmitted electronically to the registrant by the date specified by the registrant's advance notice provision or, where no such provision is in place, no later than 120 calendar days before the anniversary of the date that the registrant mailed its proxy materials for the prior year's annual meeting, except that, if the registrant did not hold an annual meeting during the prior year, or if the date of the meeting has changed by more than 30 calendar days from the prior year, then the nominating shareholder or nominating shareholder group must provide notice a reasonable time before the registrant mails its proxy materials, as specified by the registrant in a Form 8–K (17 CFR 249.308) filed pursuant to Item 5.08 of Form 8–K.

Instruction to Rule 14a–18: The registrant is not responsible for any information provided in the Schedule 14N by the nominating shareholder or nominating shareholder group, which is submitted as required by this section or otherwise provided by the nominating shareholder or nominating shareholder group that is included in the registrant's proxy materials.

Rule 14a–20. Shareholder approval of executive compensation of TARP recipients

If a solicitation is made by a registrant that is a *TARP recipient*, as defined in section 111(a)(3) of the Emergency Economic Stabilization Act of 2008 (12 U.S.C. 5221(a)(3)), during the period in which any obligation arising from financial assistance provided under the *TARP*, as defined in section 3(8) of the Emergency Economic Stabilization Act of 2008 (12 U.S.C. 5202(8)), remains outstanding and the solicitation relates to an annual (or special meeting in lieu of the annual) meeting of security holders for which proxies will be solicited for the election of directors, as required pursuant to section 111(e)(1) of the Emergency Economic Stabilization Act of 2008 (12 U.S.C. 5221(e)(1)), the registrant shall provide a separate shareholder vote to approve the compensation of executives, as disclosed pursuant to Item 402 of Regulation S–K, including the compensation discussion and analysis, the compensation tables, and any related material.

NOTE TO RULE 14a–20: TARP recipients that are smaller reporting companies entitled to provide scaled disclosure pursuant to Item 402(*l*) of Regulation S–K are not required to include a compensation discussion and analysis in their proxy statements in order to comply with this section. In the case of these smaller reporting companies, the required vote must be to approve the compensation of executives as disclosed pursuant to Item 402(m) through (q) of Regulation S–K.

Rule 14a–21. Shareholder approval of executive compensation, frequency of votes for approval of executive compensation and shareholder approval of golden parachute compensation

(a) If a solicitation is made by a registrant, other than an emerging growth company as defined in Rule 12b–2, and the solicitation relates to an annual or other meeting of shareholders at which directors will be elected and for which the rules of the Commission require executive compensation disclosure pursuant to Item 402 of Regulation S–K, the registrant shall, for the first annual or other meeting of shareholders on or after January 21, 2011, or for the first annual or other meeting of shareholders on or after January 21, 2013 if the registrant is a smaller reporting company, and thereafter no later than the annual or other meeting of shareholders held in the third calendar year after the immediately preceding vote under this subsection, include a separate resolution subject to shareholder advisory vote to approve the compensation of its named executive officers, as disclosed pursuant to Item 402 of Regulation S–K.

Instruction to Rule 14a–21(a):

The registrant's resolution shall indicate that the shareholder advisory vote under this subsection is to approve the compensation of the registrant's named executive officers as disclosed pursuant to Item 402 of Regulation S–K. The following is a non–exclusive example of a resolution that would satisfy the requirements of this subsection: "RESOLVED, that the compensation paid to the company's named executive officers, as disclosed pursuant to Item 402 of Regulation S–K, including the Compensation Discussion and Analysis, compensation tables and narrative discussion is hereby APPROVED."

(b) If a solicitation is made by a registrant, other than an emerging growth company as defined in Rule 12b–2, and the solicitation relates to an annual or other meeting of shareholders at which directors will be elected and for which the rules of the Commission require executive compensation disclosure pursuant to Item 402 of Regulation S–K, the registrant shall, for the first annual or other meeting of shareholders on or after January 21, 2011, or for the first annual or other meeting of shareholders on or after January 21, 2013 if the registrant is a smaller reporting company, and thereafter no later than the annual or other meeting of shareholders held in the sixth calendar year after the immediately preceding vote under this subsection, include a separate resolution subject to shareholder advisory vote as to whether the shareholder vote required by paragraph (a) of this section should occur every 1, 2 or 3 years. Registrants required to provide a separate shareholder vote pursuant to Rule 14a–20 shall include the separate resolution required by this section for the first annual or other meeting of shareholders after the registrant has repaid all obligations arising from financial assistance provided under the TARP, as defined in section 3(8) of the Emergency Economic Stabilization Act of 2008 (12 U.S.C. 5202(8)), and thereafter no later than the annual or other meeting of shareholders held in the sixth calendar year after the immediately preceding vote under this subsection.

(c) If a solicitation is made by a registrant, other than an emerging growth company as defined in Rule 12b–2, for a meeting of shareholders at which shareholders are asked to approve an acquisition, merger, consolidation or proposed sale or other disposition of all or substantially all the assets of the registrant, the registrant shall include a separate resolution subject to shareholder advisory vote to approve any agreements or understandings and compensation disclosed pursuant to Item 402(t) of Regulation S–K, unless such agreements or understandings have been subject to a shareholder advisory vote under paragraph (a) of this section. Consistent with section 14A(b) of the Exchange Act (15 U.S.C. 78n–1(b)), any agreements or understandings between an acquiring company and the named executive officers of the registrant, where the registrant is not the acquiring company, are not required to be subject to the separate shareholder advisory vote under this paragraph.

Instructions to Rule 14a–21:

1. Disclosure relating to the compensation of directors required by Item 402(k) and Item 402(r) of Regulation S–K is not subject to the shareholder vote required by paragraph (a) of this section. If a registrant includes disclosure pursuant to Item 402(s) of Regulation S–K about the registrant's compensation policies and practices as they relate to risk management and risk–taking incentives, these policies and practices would not be subject to the shareholder vote required by paragraph (a) of this section. To the extent that risk considerations are a material aspect of the registrant's compensation policies or decisions for named executive officers, the registrant is required to discuss them as part of its Compensation Discussion and Analysis under 17 CFR 229.402(b), and therefore such disclosure would be considered by shareholders when voting on executive compensation.

2. If a registrant includes disclosure of golden parachute compensation arrangements pursuant to Item 402(t) in an annual meeting proxy statement, such disclosure would be subject to the shareholder advisory vote required by paragraph (a) of this section.

3. Registrants that are smaller reporting companies entitled to provide scaled disclosure in accordance with Item 402(*l*) of Regulation S–K are not required to include a Compensation Discussion and Analysis in their proxy statements in order to comply with this section. For smaller reporting companies, the vote required by paragraph (a) of this section must be to approve the compensation of the named executive officers as disclosed pursuant to Item 402(m) through (q) of Regulation S–K.

4. A registrant that has ceased being an emerging growth company shall include the first separate resolution described under §240.14a-21(a) not later than the end of (i) in the case of a registrant that was an emerging growth company for less than two years after the date of first sale of common equity securities of the registrant pursuant to an effective registration statement under the Securities Act of 1933 (15 U.S.C 77a et seq.), the three-year period beginning on such date; and (ii) in the case of any other registrant, the one-year period beginning on the date the registrant is no longer an emerging growth company.

Rule 14a–101. Schedule 14A—Information required in proxy statement

SCHEDULE 14A INFORMATION

Proxy Statement Pursuant to Section 14(a) of the Securities Exchange Act of 1934

(Amendment No.   )

Filed by the Registrant [ ]

Filed by a party other than the Registrant [ ]

Check the appropriate box:

[ ] Preliminary Proxy Statement

[ ] Confidential, for Use of the Commission Only (as permitted by Rule 14a–6(e)(2))

[ ] Definitive Proxy Statement

[ ] Definitive Additional Materials

[ ] Soliciting Material Under Rule 14a–12

(Name of Registrant as Specified In Its Charter)

(Name(s) of Person(s) Filing Proxy Statement, if other than the Registrant)

Payment of Filing Fee (Check the appropriate box):

[ ] No fee required

[ ] Fee computed on table below per Exchange Act Rules 14a–6(i)(1) and 0–11

(1) Title of each class of securities to which transaction applies:

---

(2) Aggregate number of securities to which transaction applies:

---

(3) Per unit price or other underlying value of transaction computed pursuant to Exchange Act Rule 0–11 (set forth the amount on which the filing fee is calculated and state how it was determined):

---

(4) Proposed maximum aggregate value of transaction:

(5) Total fee paid:

[ ] Fee paid previously with preliminary materials.

[ ] Check box if any part of the fee is offset as provided by Exchange Act Rule 0–11(a)(2) and identify the filing for which the offsetting fee was paid previously. Identify the previous filing by registration statement number, or the Form or Schedule and the date of its filing.

(1) Amount Previously Paid:

---

(2) Form. Schedule or Registration Statement No.:

---

(3) Filing Party:

---

(4) Date Filed:

NOTES: A. Where any item calls for information with respect to any matter to be acted upon and such matter involves other matters with respect to which information is called for by other items of this schedule, the information called for by such other items also shall be given. For example, where a solicitation of security holders is for the purpose of approving the authorization of additional securities which are to be used to acquire another specified company, and the registrants' security holders will not have a separate opportunity to vote upon the transaction, the solicitation to authorize the securities is also a solicitation with respect to the acquisition. Under those facts, information required by Items 11, 13 and 14 shall be furnished.

B. Where any item calls for information with respect to any matter to be acted upon at the meeting, such item need be answered in the registrant's soliciting material only with respect to proposals to be made by or on behalf of the registrant.

C. Except as otherwise specifically provided, where any item calls for information for a specified period with regard to directors, executive officers, officers or other persons holding specified positions or relationships, the information shall be given with regard to any person who held any of the specified positions or relationship at any time during the period. Information, other than information required by Item 404 of Regulation S–K, need not be included for any portion of the period during which such person did not hold any such position or relationship, provided a statement to that effect is made.

D. Information may be incorporated by reference only in the manner and to the extent specifically permitted in the items of this schedule. Where incorporation by reference is used, the following shall apply:

1. Any incorporation by reference of information pursuant to the provisions of this schedule shall be subject to the provisions of Item 10(d) of Regulation S–K restricting incorporation by reference of documents that incorporate by reference other information. A registrant incorporating any documents, or portions of documents, shall include a statement on the last page(s) of the proxy statement as to which documents, or portions of documents, are incorporated by reference. Information shall not be incorporated by reference in any case where such incorporation would render the statement incomplete, unclear or confusing.

2. If a document is incorporated by reference but not delivered to security holders, include an undertaking to provide, without charge, to each person to whom a proxy statement is delivered, upon written or oral request of such person and by first class mail or other equally prompt means within one business day of receipt of such request, a copy of any and all of the information that has been incorporated by reference in the proxy statement (not including exhibits to the information that is incorporated by reference unless such exhibits are specifically incorporated by reference into the information that the proxy statement incorporates), and the address (including title or department) and telephone numbers to which such a request is to be directed. This includes information contained in documents filed subsequent to the date on which definitive copies of the proxy statement are sent or given to security holders, up to the date of responding to the request.

3. If a document or portion of a document other than an annual report sent to security holders pursuant to the requirements of Rule 14a–3 with respect to the same meeting or solicitation of consents or authorizations as that to which the proxy statement relates is incorporated by reference in the manner permitted by Item 13(b) or Item 14(e)(1) of this Schedule, the proxy statement must be sent to security holders no later than 20 business days prior to the date on which the meeting of such security holders is held or, if no meeting is held, at least 20 business days prior to the date the votes, consents or authorizations may be used to effect the corporate action.

4. *Electronic Filings.* If any of the information required by Items 13 or 14 of this Schedule is incorporated by reference from an annual or quarterly report to security holders, such report, or any portion thereof incorporated by reference, shall be filed in electronic format with the proxy statement.

E. In Item 13 of this Schedule, the reference to "meets the requirements of Form S–3" shall refer to a registrant who meets the following requirements:

(1) The registrant meets the requirements of General Instruction I.A. of Form S–3; and

(2) One of the following is met:

(i) The registrant meets the aggregate market value requirement of General Instruction I.B.1 of Form S–3; or

(ii) Action is to be taken as described in Items 11, 12, and 14 of this schedule which concerns non-convertible debt or preferred securities issued by a registrant meeting the requirements of General Instruction I.B.2. of Form S–3 (referenced in 17 CFR 239.13); or

(iii) The registrant is a majority-owned subsidiary and one of the conditions of General Instruction I.C. of Form S–3 is met.

Item 1. Date, Time and Place Information

(a) State the date, time and place of the meeting of security holders, and the complete mailing address, including ZIP Code, of the principal executive offices of the registrant, unless such information is otherwise disclosed in material furnished to security holders with or preceding the proxy statement. If action is to be taken by written consent, state the date by which consents are to be submitted if state law requires that such a date be specified or if the person soliciting intends to set a date.

(b) On the first page of the proxy statement, as delivered to security holders, state the approximate date on which the proxy statement and form of proxy are first sent or given to security holders.

(c) Furnish the information required to be in the proxy statement by Rule 14a–5(e).

Item 2. Revocability of Proxy

State whether or not the person giving the proxy has the power to revoke it. If the right of revocation before the proxy is exercised is limited or is subject to compliance with any formal procedure, briefly describe such limitation or procedure.

Item 3. Dissenters' Right of Appraisal

Outline briefly the rights of appraisal or similar rights of dissenters with respect to any matter to be acted upon and indicate any statutory procedure required to be followed by dissenting security holders in order to perfect such rights. Where such rights may be exercised only within a limited time after the date of adoption of a proposal, the filing of a charter amendment or other similar act, state whether the persons solicited will be notified of such date.

Instructions.

1. Indicate whether a security holder's failure to vote against a proposal will constitute a waiver of his appraisal or similar rights and whether a vote against a proposal will be deemed to satisfy any notice requirements under State law with respect to appraisal rights. If the State law is unclear, state what position will be taken in regard to these matters.

2. Open-end investment companies registered under the Investment Company Act of 1940 are not required to respond to this item.

Item 4. Persons Making the Solicitation

(a) *Solicitations Not Subject to Rule 14a–12(c).* (1) If the solicitation is made by the registrant, so state. Give the name of any director of the registrant who has informed the registrant in writing that he intends to oppose any action intended to be taken by the registrant and indicate the action which he intends to oppose.

(2) If the solicitation is made otherwise than by the registrant, so state and give the names of the participants in the solicitation, as defined in paragraphs (a)(iii), (iv), (v) and (vi) of Instruction 3 to this Item.

(3) If the solicitation is to be made otherwise than by the use of the mails or pursuant to Rule 14a–16, describe the methods to be employed. If the solicitation is to be made by specially engaged employees or paid solicitors, state (i) the material features of any contract or arrangement for such solicitation and identify the parties, and (ii) the cost or anticipated cost thereof.

(4) State the names of the persons by whom the cost of solicitation has been or will be borne, directly or indirectly.

(b) *Solicitations Subject to Rule 14a–12(c).* (1) State by whom the solicitation is made and describe the methods employed and to be employed to solicit security holders.

(2) If regular employees of the registrant or any other participant in a solicitation have been or are to be employed to solicit security holders, describe the class or classes of employees to be so employed, and the manner and nature of their employment for such purpose.

(3) If specially engaged employees, representatives or other persons have been or are to be employed to solicit security holders, state (i) the material features of any contract or arrangement for such solicitation and the identity of the parties, (ii) the cost or anticipated cost thereof, and (iii) the approximate number of such employees or employees of any other person (naming such other person) who will solicit security holders.

(4) State the total amount estimated to be spent and the total expenditures to date for, in further-

ance of, or in connection with the solicitation of security holders.

(5) State by whom the cost of the solicitation will be borne. If such cost is to be borne initially by any person other than the registrant, state whether reimbursement will be sought from the registrant, and, if so, whether the question of such reimbursement will be submitted to a vote of security holders.

(6) If any such solicitation is terminated pursuant to a settlement between the registrant and any other participant in such solicitation, describe the terms of such settlement, including the cost or anticipated cost thereof to the registrant.

Instructions. 1. With respect to solicitations subject to Rule 14a–12(c), costs and expenditures within the meaning of this Item 4 shall include fees for attorneys, accountants, public relations or financial advisers, solicitors, advertising, printing, transportation, litigation and other costs incidental to the solicitation, except that the registrant may exclude the amount of such costs represented by the amount normally expended for a solicitation for an election of directors in the absence of a contest, and costs represented by salaries and wages of regular employees and officers, provided a statement to the effect is included in the proxy statement.

2. The information required pursuant to paragraph (b)(6) of this Item should be included in any amended or revised proxy statement or other soliciting materials relating to the same meeting or subject matter furnished to security holders by the registrant subsequent to the date of settlement.

3. For purposes of this Item 4 and Item 5 of this Schedule 14A:

(a) The terms "participant" and "participant in a solicitation" include the following:

(i) The registrant;

(ii) Any director of the registrant, and any nominee for whose election as a director proxies are solicited;

(iii) Any committee or group which solicits proxies, any member of such committee or group, and any person whether or not named as a member who, acting alone or with one or more other persons, directly or indirectly takes the initiative, or engages, in organizing, directing, or arranging for the financing of any such committee or group;

(iv) Any person who finances or joins with another to finance the solicitation of proxies, except persons who contribute not more than $500 and who are not otherwise participants;

(v) Any person who lends money or furnishes credit or enters into any other arrangements, pursuant to any contract or understanding with a participant, for the purpose of financing or otherwise inducing the purchase, sale, holding or voting of securities of the registrant by any participant or other persons, in support of or in opposition to a participant; except that such terms do not include a bank, broker or dealer who, in the ordinary course of business, lends money or executes orders for the purchase or sale of securities and who is not otherwise a participant; and

(vi) Any person who solicits proxies.

(b) The terms "participant" and "participant in a solicitation" do not include:

(i) Any person or organization retained or employed by a participant to solicit security holders and whose activities are limited to the duties required to be performed in the course of such employment;

(ii) Any person who merely transmits proxy soliciting material or performs other ministerial or clerical duties;

(iii) Any person employed by a participant in the capacity of attorney, accountant, or advertising, public relations or financial adviser, and whose activities are limited to the duties required to be performed in the course of such employment;

(iv) Any person regularly employed as an officer or employee of the registrant or any of its subsidiaries who is not otherwise a participant; or

(v) Any officer or director of, or any person regularly employed by, any other participant, if such officer, director or employee is not otherwise a participant.

Item 5. Interest of Certain Persons in Matters to Be Acted Upon

(a) *Solicitations Not Subject to Rule 14a-12(c).* Describe briefly any substantial interest, direct or indirect, by security holdings or otherwise, of each of the following persons in any matter to be acted upon, other than elections to office:

(1) If the solicitation is made on behalf of the registrant, each person who has been a director or executive officer of the registrant at any time since the beginning of the last fiscal year.

(2) If the solicitation is made otherwise than on behalf of the registrant, each participant in the solicitation, as defined in paragraphs (a)(iii), (iv), (v), and (vi) of Instruction 3 to Item 4 of this Schedule 14A.

(3) Each nominee for election as a director of the registrant.

(4) Each associate of the foregoing persons.

(5) If the solicitation is made on behalf of the registrant, furnish the information required by Item 402(t) of Regulation S–K.

Instruction to Paragraph (a). Except in the case of a solicitation subject to this regulation made in opposition to another solicitation subject to this regulation, this subitem (a) shall not apply to any interest arising from the ownership of securities of the registrant where the security holder receives no extra or special benefit not shared on a pro rata basis by all other holders of the same class.

(b) *Solicitations Subject to Rule 14a–12(c).* (1) Describe briefly any substantial interest, direct or indirect, by security holdings or otherwise, of each participant as defined in paragraphs (a)(ii), (iii), (iv), (v) and (vi) of Instruction 3 to Item 4 of this Schedule 14A, in any matter to be acted upon at the meeting, and include with respect to each participant the following information, or a fair and accurate summary thereof:

(i) Name and business address of the participant.

(ii) The participant's present principal occupation or employment and the name, principal business and address of any corporation or other organization in which such employment is carried on.

(iii) State whether or not, during the past ten years, the participant has been convicted in a criminal proceeding (excluding traffic violations or similar misdemeanors) and, if so, give dates, nature of conviction, name and location of court, and penalty imposed or other disposition of the case. A negative answer need not be included in the proxy statement or other soliciting material.

(iv) State the amount of each class of securities of the registrant which the participant owns beneficially, directly or indirectly.

(v) State the amount of each class of securities of the registrant which the participant owns of record but not beneficially.

(vi) State with respect to all securities of the registrant purchased or sold within the past two years, the dates on which they were purchased or sold and the amount purchased or sold on each such date.

(vii) If any part of the purchase price or market value of any of the shares specified in paragraph (b)(1)(vi) of this Item is represented by funds borrowed or otherwise obtained for the purpose of acquiring or holding such securities, so state and indicate the amount of the indebtedness as of the latest practicable date. If such funds were borrowed or obtained otherwise than pursuant to a margin account or bank loan in the regular course of business of a bank, broker or dealer, briefly describe the transaction, and state the names of the parties.

(viii) State whether or not the participant is, or was within the past year, a party to any contract, arrangements or understandings with any person with respect to any securities of the registrant, including, but not limited to joint ventures, loan or option arrangements, puts or calls, guarantees against loss or guarantees of profit, division of losses or profits, or the giving or withholding of proxies. If so, name the parties to such contracts, arrangements or understandings and give the details thereof.

(ix) State the amount of securities of the registrant owned beneficially, directly or indirectly, by each of the participant's associates and the name and address of each such associate.

(x) State the amount of each class of securities of any parent or subsidiary of the registrant which the participant owns beneficially, directly or indirectly.

(xi) Furnish for the participant and associates of the participant the information required by Item 404(a) of Regulation S–K.

(xii) State whether or not the participant or any associates of the participant have any arrangement or understanding with any person—

(A) with respect to any future employment by the registrant or its affiliates; or

(B) with respect to any future transactions to which the registrant or any of its affiliates will or may be a party.

If so, describe such arrangement or understanding and state the names of the parties thereto.

(2) With respect to any person, other than a director or executive officer of the registrant acting solely in that capacity, who is a party to an arrangement or understanding pursuant to which a nominee for election as director is proposed to be elected, describe any substantial interest, direct or indirect, by security holdings or otherwise, that such person has in any matter to be acted upon at the meeting, and furnish the information called for by paragraphs (b)(1)(xi) and (xii) of this Item.

(3) If the solicitation is made on behalf of the registrant, furnish the information required by Item 402(t) of Regulation S–K.

Instruction to Paragraph (b). For purposes of this Item 5, beneficial ownership shall be determined in accordance with Rule 13d–3 under the Act.

Item 6. Voting Securities and Principal Holders Thereof

(a) As to each class of voting securities of the registrant entitled to be voted at the meeting (or by written consents or authorizations if no meeting is held), state the number of shares outstanding and the number of votes to which each class is entitled.

(b) State the record date, if any, with respect to this solicitation. If the right to vote or give consent is not to be determined, in whole or in part, by reference to a record date, indicate the criteria for the determination of security holders entitled to vote or give consent.

(c) If action is to be taken with respect to the election of directors and if the persons solicited have cumulative voting rights: (1) Make a statement that they have such rights, (2) briefly describe such rights, (3) state briefly the conditions precedent to the exercise thereof, and (4) if discretionary authority to cumulate votes is solicited, so indicate.

(d) Furnish the information required by Item 403 of Regulation S–K to the extent known by the persons on whose behalf the solicitation is made.

(e) If, to the knowledge of the persons on whose behalf the solicitation is made, a change in control of the registrant has occurred since the beginning of its last fiscal year, state the name of the person(s) who acquired such control, the amount and the source of the consideration used by such person or persons; the basis of the control, the date and a description of the transaction(s) which resulted in the change of control and the percentage of voting securities of the registrant now beneficially owned directly or indirectly by the person(s) who acquired control; and the identity of the person(s) from whom control was assumed. If the source of all or any part of the consideration used is a loan made in the ordinary course of business by a bank as defined by section 3(a)(6) of the Act, the identity of such bank shall be omitted provided a request for confidentiality has been made pursuant to section 13(d)(1)(B) of the Act by the person(s) who acquired control. In lieu thereof, the material shall indicate that the identity of the bank has been so omitted and filed separately with the Commission.

Instructions. 1. State the terms of any loans or pledges obtained by the new control group for the purpose of acquiring control, and the names of the lenders or pledgees.

2. Any arrangements or understandings among members of both the former and new control groups and their associates with respect to election of directors or other matters should be described.

Item 7. Directors and Executive Officers

If action is to be taken with respect to the election of directors, furnish the following information in tabular form to the extent practicable. If, however, the solicitation is made on behalf of persons other than the registrant, the information required need be furnished only as to nominees of the persons making the solicitation.

(a) The information required by instruction 4 to Item 103 of Regulation S–K with respect to directors and executive officers.

(b) The information required by Items 401, 404(a) and (b), 405 and 407(d)(4), (d)(5) and (h) of Regulation S–K.

(c) The information required by Item 407(a) of Regulation S–K.

(d) The information required by Item 407(b), (c)(1), (c)(2), (d)(1), (d)(2), (d)(3), (e)(1), (e)(2), (e)(3) and (f) of Regulation S–K.

(e) If a shareholder nominee or nominees are submitted to the registrant for inclusion in the registrant's proxy materials pursuant to Rule 14a–11 and the registrant is not permitted to exclude the nominee or nominees pursuant to the provisions of Rule 14a–11, the registrant must include in its proxy statement the disclosure required from the nominating shareholder or nominating shareholder group under Item 5 of Schedule 14N with regard to the nominee or nominees and the nominating shareholder or nominating shareholder group.

Instruction to Item 7(e): The information disclosed pursuant to paragraph (e) of this Item will not be deemed incorporated by reference into any filing under the Securities Act of 1933 (15 U.S.C. 77a *et seq.*), the Securities Exchange Act of 1934 (15 U.S.C. 78a *et seq.*), or the Investment Company Act of 1940 (15 U.S.C. 80a–1 et seq.), except to the extent that the registrant specifically incorporates that information by reference.

(f) If a registrant is required to include a shareholder nominee or nominees submitted to the registrant for inclusion in the registrant's proxy materials pursuant to a procedure set forth under applicable state or foreign law, or the registrant's governing documents providing for the inclusion of shareholder director nominees in the registrant's proxy materials, the registrant must include in its proxy statement the disclosure required from the nominating shareholder or nominating shareholder group under Item 6 of Schedule 14N with regard to the nominee or nominees and the nominating shareholder or nominating shareholder group.

Instruction to Item 7(f): The information disclosed pursuant to paragraph (f) of this Item will not be deemed incorporated by reference into any filing under the Securities

Act of 1933 (15 U.S.C. 77a *et seq.*), the Securities Exchange Act of 1934 (15 U.S.C. 78a *et seq.*), or the Investment Company Act of 1940 (15 U.S.C. 80a–1 *et seq.*), except to the extent that the registrant specifically incorporates that information by reference.

(g) In lieu of the information required by this Item 7, investment companies registered under the Investment Company Act of 1940 (15 U.S.C. 80a) must furnish the information required by Item 22(b) of this Schedule 14A.

Item 8. Compensation of Directors and Executive Officers

Furnish the information required by Item 402 of Regulation S–K and paragraphs (e)(4) and (e)(5) of Item 407 of Regulation S–K if action is to be taken with regard to:

(a) The election of directors

(b) Any bonus, profit sharing or other compensation plan, contract, or arrangement in which any director, nominee for election as a director, or executive officer of the registrant will participate,

(c) Any pension or retirement plan in which any such person will participate or

(d) The granting or extension to any such person of any options, warrants or rights to purchase any securities, other than warrants or rights issued to security holders as such, on a pro rata basis.

However, if the solicitation is made on behalf of persons other than the registrant, the information required need be furnished only as to nominees of the persons making the solicitation and associates of such nominees. In the case of investment companies registered under the Investment Company Act of 1940 (15 U.S.C. 80a), furnish the information required by Item 22(b)(13) of this Schedule 14A.

Instruction. If an otherwise reportable compensation plan became subject to such requirements because of an acquisition or merger and, within one year of the acquisition or merger, such plan was terminated for purposes of prospective eligibility, the registrant may furnish a description of its obligation to the designated individuals pursuant to the compensation plan. Such description may be furnished in lieu of a description of the compensation plan in the proxy statement.

Item 9. Independent Public Accountants

If the solicitation is made on behalf of the registrant and relates to: (1) The annual (or special meeting in lieu of annual) meeting of security holders at which directors are to be elected, or a solicitation of consents or authorizations in lieu of such meeting or (2) the election, approval or ratification of the registrant's accountant, furnish the following information describing the registrant's relationship with its independent public accountant:

(a) The name of the principal accountant selected or being recommended to security holders for election, approval or ratification for the current year. If no accountant has been selected or recommended, so state and briefly describe the reasons therefor.

(b) The name of the principal accountant for the fiscal year most recently completed if different from the accountant selected or recommended for the current year or if no accountant has yet been selected or recommended for the current year.

(c) The proxy statement shall indicate: (1) Whether or not representatives of the principal accountant for the current year and for the most recently completed fiscal year are expected to be present at the security holders' meeting, (2) whether or not they will have the opportunity to make a statement if they desire to do so and (3) whether or not such representatives are expected to be available to respond to appropriate questions.

(d) If during the registrant's two most recent fiscal years or any subsequent interim period, (1) an independent accountant who was previously engaged as the principal accountant to audit the registrant's financial statements, or an independent accountant on whom the principal accountant expressed reliance in its report regarding a significant subsidiary, has resigned (or indicated it has declined to stand for reelection after the completion of the current audit) or was dismissed, or (2) a new independent accountant has been engaged as either the principal accountant to audit the registrant's financial statements or as an independent accountant on whom the principal accountant has expressed or is expected to express reliance in its report regarding a significant subsidiary, then, notwithstanding any previous disclosure, provide the information required by Item 304(a) of Regulation S–K.

(e)(1) Disclose, under the caption *Audit Fees*, the aggregate fees billed for each of the last two fiscal years for professional services rendered by the principal accountant for the audit of the registrant's annual financial statements and review of financial statements included in the registrant's Form 10–Q (17 CFR 249.308a) or services that are normally provided by the accountant in connection with statutory and regulatory filings or engagements for those fiscal years.

(2) Disclose, under the caption *Audit–Related Fees*, the aggregate fees billed in each of the last two fiscal years for assurance and related services by the principal accountant that are reasonably related to the performance of the audit or review

of the registrant's financial statements and are not reported under paragraph (e)(1) of this Item. Registrants shall describe the nature of the services comprising the fees disclosed under this category.

(3) Disclose, under the caption *Tax Fees*, the aggregate fees billed in each of the last two fiscal years for professional services rendered by the principal accountant for tax compliance, tax advice, and tax planning. Registrants shall describe the nature of the services comprising the fees disclosed under this category.

(4) Disclose, under the caption *All Other Fees*, the aggregate fees billed in each of the last two fiscal years for products and services provided by the principal accountant, other than the services reported in paragraphs (e)(1) through (e)(3) of this Item. Registrants shall describe the nature of the services comprising the fees disclosed under this category.

(5)(i) Disclose the audit committee's pre-approval policies and procedures described in 17 CFR 210.2–01(c)(7)(i).

(ii) Disclose the percentage of services described in each of paragraphs (e)(2) through (e)(4) of this rule that were approved by the audit committee pursuant to Rule 2–01(c)(7)(i)(C) of Regulation S–X.

(6) If greater than 50 percent, disclose the percentage of hours expended on the principal accountant's engagement to audit the registrant's financial statements for the most recent fiscal year that were attributed to work performed by persons other than the principal accountant's full-time, permanent employees.

(7) If the registrant is an investment company, disclose the aggregate non-audit fees billed by the registrant's accountant for services rendered to the registrant, and to the registrant's investment adviser (not including any subadviser whose role is primarily portfolio management and is subcontracted with or overseen by another investment adviser), and any entity controlling, controlled by, or under common control with the adviser that provides ongoing services to the registrant for each of the last two fiscal years of the registrant.

(8) If the registrant is an investment company, disclose whether the audit committee of the board of directors has considered whether the provision of non-audit services that were rendered to the registrant's investment adviser (not including any subadviser whose role is primarily portfolio management and is subcontracted with or overseen by another investment adviser), and any entity controlling, controlled by, or under common control with the investment adviser that provides ongoing services to the registrant that were not pre-approved pursuant to Rule 2–01(c)(7)(ii) of Regulation S–X is compatible with maintaining the principal accountant's independence.

Instruction to Item 9(e).

For purposes of Item 9(e)(2), (3), and (4), registrants that are investment companies must disclose fees billed for services rendered to the registrant and separately, disclose fees required to be approved by the investment company registrant's audit committee pursuant to Rule 2–01(c)(7)(ii) of Regulation S–X. Registered investment companies must also disclose the fee percentages as required by Item 9(e)(5)(ii) for the registrant and separately, disclose the fee percentages as required by Item 9(e)(5)(ii) for the fees required to be approved by the investment company registrant's audit committee pursuant to Rule 2–01(c)(7)(ii) of Regulation S–X.

Item 10. Compensation Plans

If action is to be taken with respect to any plan pursuant to which cash or noncash compensation may be paid or distributed, furnish the following information:

(a) *Plans Subject to Security Holder Action.* (1) Describe briefly the material features of the plan being acted upon, identify each class of persons who will be eligible to participate therein, indicate the approximate number of persons in each such class and state the basis of such participation.

(2)(i) In the tabular format specified below, disclose the benefits or amounts that will be received by or allocated to each of the following under the plan being acted upon, if such benefits or amounts are determinable:

New Plan Benefits

Plan name Name and position	Dollar value ($)	Number of units
CEO		
A		
B		
C		
D		
Executive Group		
Non–Executive Director Group		
Non–Executive Officer Employee Group		

(ii) The table required by paragraph (a)(2)(i) of this Item shall provide information as to the following persons:

(A) Each person (stating name and position) specified in paragraph (a)(3) of Item 402 of Regulation S–K;

Instruction: In the case of investment companies registered under the Investment Company Act of 1940, furnish the information for Compensated Persons as defined in Item 22(b)(13)(i) of this Schedule in lieu of the persons specified in paragraph (a)(3) of Item 402 of Regulation S–K.

(B) All current executive officers as a group;

(C) All current directors who are not executive officers as a group; and

(D) All employees, including all current officers who are not executive officers, as a group.

Instruction to New Plan Benefits Table: Additional columns should be added for each plan with respect to which security holder action is to be taken.

(iii) If the benefits or amounts specified in paragraph (a)(2)(i) of this item are not determinable, state the benefits or amounts which would have been received by or allocated to each of the following for the last completed fiscal year if the plan had been in effect, if such benefits or amounts may be determined, in the table specified in paragraph (a)(2)(i) of this Item:

(A) Each person (stating name and position) specified in paragraph (a)(3) of Item 402 of Regulation S–K;

(B) All current executive officers as a group;

(C) All current directors who are not executive officers as a group; and

(D) All employees, including all current officers who are not executive officers, as a group.

(3) If the plan to be acted upon can be amended, otherwise than by a vote of security holders, to increase the cost thereof to the registrant or to alter the allocation of the benefits as between the persons and groups specified in paragraph (a)(2) of this item, state the nature of the amendments which can be so made.

(b)(1) *Additional Information Regarding Specified Plans Subject to Security Holder Action.* With respect to any pension or retirement plan submitted for security holder action, state:

(i) The approximate total amount necessary to fund the plan with respect to past services, the period over which such amount is to be paid and the estimated annual payments necessary to pay the total amount over such period; and

(ii) The estimated annual payment to be made with respect to current services. In the case of a pension or retirement plan, information called for by paragraph (a)(2) of this Item may be furnished in the format specified by paragraph (h)(2) of Item 402 of Regulation S–K.

Instruction to Paragraph (b)(1)(ii).

In the case of investment companies registered under the Investment Company Act of 1940 (15 U.S.C. 80a), refer to Instruction 4 in Item 22(b)(13)(i) of this Schedule in lieu of paragraph (h)(2) of Item 402 of Regulation S–K.

(2)(i) With respect to any specific grant of or any plan containing options, warrants or rights submitted for security holder action, state:

(A) The title and amount of securities underlying such options, warrants or rights;

(B) The prices, expiration dates and other material conditions upon which the options, warrants or rights may be exercised;

(C) The consideration received or to be received by the registrant or subsidiary for the granting or extension of the options, warrants or rights;

(D) The market value of the securities underlying the options, warrants, or rights as of the latest practicable date; and

(E) In the case of options, the federal income tax consequences of the issuance and exercise of such options to the recipient and the registrant; and

(ii) State separately the amount of such options received or to be received by the following persons if such benefits or amounts are determinable:

(A) Each person (stating name and position) specified in paragraph (a)(3) of Item 402 of Regulation S–K;

(B) All current executive officers as a group;

(C) All current directors who are not executive officers as a group;

(D) Each nominee for election as a director;

(E) Each associate of any of such directors, executive officers or nominees;

(F) Each other person who received or is to receive 5 percent of such options, warrants or rights; and

(G) All employees, including all current officers who are not executive officers, as a group.

Instructions to Item 10.

1. The term *plan* as used in this Item means any plan as defined in paragraph (a)(6)(ii) of Item 402 of Regulation S–K.

2. If action is to be taken with respect to a material amendment or modification of an existing plan, the item shall be answered with respect to the plan as proposed to be amended or modified and shall indicate any material differences from the existing plan.

3. If the plan to be acted upon is set forth in a written document, three copies thereof shall be filed with the Commission at the time copies of the proxy statement and form of proxy are first filed pursuant to paragraph (a) or (b) of Rule 14a–6. Electronic filers shall file with the Commission a copy of such written plan document in electronic format as an appendix to the proxy statement. It need not be provided to security holders unless it is a part of the proxy statement.

4. Paragraph (b)(2)(ii) does not apply to warrants or rights to be issued to security holders as such on a pro rata basis.

5. The Commission shall be informed, as supplemental information, when the proxy statement is first filed, as to when the options, warrants or rights and the shares called for thereby will be registered under the Securities Act or, if such registration is not contemplated, the section of the Securities Act or rule of the Commission under which exemption from such registration is claimed and the facts relied upon to make the exemption available.

Item 11. Authorization or Issuance of Securities Otherwise Than for Exchange

If action is to be taken with respect to the authorization or issuance of any securities otherwise than for exchange for outstanding securities of the registrant, furnish the following information:

(a) State the title and amount of securities to be authorized or issued.

(b) Furnish the information required by Item 202 of Regulation S–K. If the terms of the securities cannot be stated or estimated with respect to any or all of the securities to be authorized, because no offering thereof is contemplated in the proximate future, and if no further authorization by security holders for the issuance thereof is to be obtained, it should be stated that the terms of the securities to be authorized, including dividend or interest rates, conversion prices, voting rights, redemption prices, maturity dates, and similar matters will be determined by the board of directors. If the securities are additional shares of common stock of a class outstanding, the description may be omitted except for a statement of the preemptive rights, if any. Where the statutory provisions with respect to preemptive rights are so indefinite or complex that they cannot be stated in summarized form, it will suffice to make a statement in the form of an opinion of counsel as to the existence and extent of such rights.

(c) Describe briefly the transaction in which the securities are to be issued including a statement as to (1) the nature and approximate amount of consideration received or to be received by the registrant and (2) the approximate amount devoted to each purpose so far as determinable for which the net proceeds have been or are to be used. If it is impracticable to describe the transaction in which the securities are to be issued, state the reason, indicate the purpose of the authorization of the securities, and state whether further authorization for the issuance of the securities by a vote of security holders will be solicited prior to such issuance.

(d) If the securities are to be issued otherwise than in a public offering for cash, state the reasons for the proposed authorization or issuance and the general effect thereof upon the rights of existing security holders.

(e) Furnish the information required by Item 13(a) of this schedule.

Item 12. Modification or Exchange of Securities

If action is to be taken with respect to the modification of any class of securities of the registrant, or the issuance or authorization for issuance of securities of the registrant in exchange for outstanding securities of the registrant, furnish the following information:

(a) If outstanding securities are to be modified, state the title and amount thereof. If securities are to be issued in exchange for outstanding securities, state the title and amount of securities to be so issued, the title and amount of outstanding securities to be exchanged therefor and the basis of the exchange.

(b) Describe any material differences between the outstanding securities and the modified or new securities in respect of any of the matters concerning which information would be required in the description of the securities in Item 202 of Regulation S–K.

(c) State the reasons for the proposed modification or exchange and the general effect thereof upon the rights of existing security holders.

(d) Furnish a brief statement as to arrears in dividends or as to defaults in principal or interest in respect to the outstanding securities which are to be modified or exchanged and such other information as may be appropriate in the particular case to disclose adequately the nature and effect of the proposed action.

(e) Outline briefly any other material features of the proposed modification or exchange. If the plan of proposed action is set forth in a written document, file copies thereof with the Commission in accordance with Rule 14a–6.

(f) Furnish the information required by Item 13(a) of this Schedule.

Instruction. If the existing security is presently listed and registered on a national securities exchange, state whether the registrant intends to apply for listing and registration of the new or reclassified security on such exchange or any other exchange. If the registrant does not intend to make such application, state the effect of the termination of such listing and registration.

Item 13. Financial and Other Information

(*See* Notes D and E at the beginning of this Schedule.)

(a) *Information Required.* If action is to be taken with respect to any matter specified in Item 11 or 12, furnish the following information:

(1) Financial statements meeting the requirements of Regulation S–X, including financial information required by Rule 3–05 and Article 11 of Regulation S–X with respect to transactions other than pursuant to which action is to be taken as described in this proxy statement (A smaller reporting company may provide the information in Rules 8–04 and 8–05 of Regulation S–X in lieu of the financial information required by Rule 3–05 and Article 11 of Regulation S–X);

(2) Item 302 of Regulation S–K, supplementary financial information;

(3) Item 303 of Regulation S–K, management's discussion and analysis of financial condition and results of operations;

(4) Item 304 of Regulation S–K, changes in and disagreements with accountants on accounting and financial disclosure; and

(5) Item 305 of Regulation S–K, quantitative and qualitative disclosures about market risk; and

(6) A statement as to whether or not representatives of the principal accountants for the current year and for the most recently completed fiscal year:

(i) Are expected to be present at the security holders' meeting;

(ii) Will have the opportunity to make a statement if they desire to do so; and

(iii) Are expected to be available to respond to appropriate questions.

(b) *Incorporation by Reference.* The information required pursuant to paragraph (a) of this Item may be incorporated by reference into the proxy statement as follows:

(1) *S–3 Registrants.* If the registrant meets the requirements of Form S–3 (*see* Note E to this Schedule), it may incorporate by reference to previously-filed documents any of the information required by paragraph (a) of this Item, provided that the requirements of paragraph (c) are met. Where the registrant meets the requirements of Form S–3 and has elected to furnish the required information by incorporation by reference, the registrant may elect to update the information so incorporated by reference to information in subsequently-filed documents.

(2) *All Registrants.* The registrant may incorporate by reference any of the information required by paragraph (a) of this Item, provided that the information is contained in an annual report to security holders or a previously-filed statement or report, such report or statement is delivered to security holders with the proxy statement and the requirements of paragraph (c) are met.

(c) *Certain Conditions Applicable to Incorporation by Reference.* Registrants eligible to incorporate by reference into the proxy statement the information required by paragraph (a) of this Item in the manner specified by paragraphs (b)(1) and (b)(2) may do so only if:

(1) The information is not required to be included in the proxy statement pursuant to the requirement of another Item;

(2) The proxy statement identifies on the last page(s) the information incorporated by reference; and

(3) The material incorporated by reference substantially meets the requirements of this Item or the appropriate portions of this Item.

Instructions to Item 13.

1. Notwithstanding the provisions of this Item, any or all of the information required by paragraph (a) of this Item, not material for the exercise of prudent judgment in regard to the matter to be acted upon may be omitted. In the usual case the information is deemed material to the exercise of prudent judgment where the matter to be acted upon is the authorization or issuance of a material amount of senior securities, but the information is not deemed material where the matter to be acted upon is the authorization or issuance of common stock, otherwise than in an exchange, merger, consolidation, acquisition or similar transaction, the authorization of preferred stock without present intent to issue or the authorization of preferred stock for issuance for cash in an amount constituting fair value.

2. In order to facilitate compliance with Rule 2–02(a) of Regulation S–X, one copy of the definitive proxy statement filed with the Commission shall include a manually signed copy of the accountant's report. If the financial statements are incorporated by reference, a manually signed copy of the accountant's report shall be filed with the definitive proxy statement.

3. Notwithstanding the provisions of Regulation S–X, no schedules other than those prepared in accordance with Rules 12–15, 12–28 and 12–29 (or, for management investment companies, Rules 12–12 through 12–14) of that regulation need be furnished in the proxy statement.

4. Unless registered on a national securities exchange or otherwise required to furnish such information, registered investment companies need not furnish the information required by paragraphs (a)(2) or (3) of this Item.

5. If the registrant submits preliminary proxy material incorporating by reference financial statements required by this Item, the registrant should furnish a draft of the financial statements if the document from which they are incorporated has not been filed with or furnished to the Commission.

6. A registered investment company need not comply with items (a)(2), (a)(3), and (a)(5) of this Item 13.

Item 14. Mergers, Consolidations, Acquisitions and Similar Matters

(*See* Notes A and D at the beginning of this Schedule.)

Instructions to Item 14:

1. In transactions in which the consideration offered to security holders consists wholly or in part of securities registered under the Securities Act of 1933, furnish the information required by Form S–4 (17 CFR 239.25), Form F–4 (17 CFR 239.34), or Form N–14 (17 CFR 239.23), as applicable, instead of this Item. Only a Form S–4, Form F–4, or Form N–14 must be filed in accordance with Rule 14a–6(j).

2. (a) In transactions in which the consideration offered to security holders consists wholly of cash, the information required by paragraph (c)(1) of this Item for the acquiring company need not be provided unless the information is material to an informed voting decision (*e.g.*, the security holders of the target company are voting and financing is not assured).

(b) Additionally, if only the security holders of the target company are voting:

i. The financial information in paragraphs (b)(8)—(11) of this Item for the acquiring company and the target need not be provided; and

ii. The information in paragraph (c)(2) of this Item for the target company need not be provided.

If, however, the transaction is a going-private transaction (as defined by Rule 13e–3), then the information required by paragraph (c)(2) of this Item must be provided and to the extent that the going-private rules require the information specified in paragraph (b)(8)—(b)(11) of this Item, that information must be provided as well.

3. In transactions in which the consideration offered to security holders consists wholly of securities exempt from registration under the Securities Act of 1933 or a combination of exempt securities and cash, information about the acquiring company required by paragraph (c)(1) of this Item need not be provided if only the security holders of the acquiring company are voting, unless the information is material to an informed voting decision. If only the security holders of the target company are voting, information about the target company in paragraph (c)(2) of this Item need not be provided. However, the information required by paragraph (c)(2) of this Item must be provided if the transaction is a going-private (as defined by Rule 13e–3) or roll-up (as described by Item 901 of Regulation S–K) transaction.

4. The information required by paragraphs (b)(8)—(11) and (c) need not be provided if the plan being voted on involves only the acquiring company and one or more of its totally held subsidiaries and does not involve a liquidation or a spin-off.

5. To facilitate compliance with Rule 2–02(a) of Regulation S–X (technical requirements relating to accountants' reports), one copy of the definitive proxy statement filed with the Commission must include a signed copy of the accountant's report. If the financial statements are incorporated by reference, a signed copy of the accountant's report must be filed with the definitive proxy statement. Signatures may be typed if the document is filed electronically on EDGAR. See Rule 302 of Regulation S–T.

6. Notwithstanding the provisions of Regulation S–X, no schedules other than those prepared in accordance with Rules 12–15, 12–28 and 12–29 of RegulationS–X (or, for management investment companies, Rules 12–12 through 12–14 of Regulation S–X) of that regulation need be furnished in the proxy statement.

7. If the preliminary proxy material incorporates by reference financial statements required by this Item, a draft of the financial statements must be furnished to the Commission staff upon request if the document from which they are incorporated has not been filed with or furnished to the Commission.

(a) *Applicability.* If action is to be taken with respect to any of the following transactions, provide the information required by this Item:

(1) A merger or consolidation;

(2) An acquisition of securities of another person;

(3) An acquisition of any other going business or the assets of a going business;

(4) A sale or other transfer of all or any substantial part of assets; or

(5) A liquidation or dissolution.

(b) *Transaction Information.* Provide the following information for each of the parties to the transaction unless otherwise specified:

(1) *Summary Term Sheet.* The information required by Item 1001 of Regulation M–A.

(2) *Contact Information.* The name, complete mailing address and telephone number of the principal executive offices.

(3) *Business Conducted.* A brief description of the general nature of the business conducted.

(4) *Terms of the Transaction.* The information required by Item 1004(a)(2) of Regulation M–A.

(5) *Regulatory Approvals.* A statement as to whether any federal or state regulatory requirements must be complied with or approval must be obtained in connection with the transaction and, if so, the status of the compliance or approval.

(6) *Reports, Opinions, Appraisals.* If a report, opinion or appraisal materially relating to the transaction has been received from an outside party, and is referred to in the proxy statement, furnish the information required by Item 1015(b) of Regulation M–A.

(7) *Past Contacts, Transactions or Negotiations.* The information required by Items 1005(b) and 1011(a)(1) of Regulation M–A, for the parties to the transaction and their affiliates during the periods for which financial statements are presented or incorporated by reference under this Item.

(8) *Selected Financial Data.* The selected financial data required by Item 301 of Regulation S–K.

(9) *Pro Forma Selected Financial Data.* If material, the information required by Item 301 of Regulation S–K for the acquiring company, showing the pro forma effect of the transaction.

(10) *Pro Forma Information.* In a table designed to facilitate comparison, historical and pro forma per share data of the acquiring company and historical and equivalent pro forma per share data of the target company for the following Items:

(i) Book value per share as of the date financial data is presented pursuant to Item 301 of Regulation S–K;

(ii) Cash dividends declared per share for the periods for which financial data is presented pursuant to Item 301 of Regulation S–K; and

(iii) Income (loss) per share from continuing operations for the periods for which financial data is presented pursuant to Item 301 of Regulation S–K.

Instructions to Paragraphs (b)(8), (b)(9) and (b)(10):

1. For a business combination, present the financial information required by paragraphs (b)(9) and (b)(10) only for the most recent fiscal year and interim period. For a combination between entities under common control, present the financial information required by paragraphs (b)(9) and (b)(10) (except for information with regard to book value) for the most recent three fiscal years and interim period. For purposes of these paragraphs, book value information need only be provided for the most recent balance sheet date.

2. Calculate the equivalent pro forma per share amounts for one share of the company being acquired by multiplying the exchange ratio times each of:

(i) The pro forma income (loss) per share before non-recurring charges or credits directly attributable to the transaction;

(ii) The pro forma book value per share; and

(iii) The pro forma dividends per share of the acquiring company.

3. Unless registered on a national securities exchange or otherwise required to furnish such information, registered investment companies need not furnish the information required by paragraphs (b)(8) and (b)(9) of this Item.

(11) *Financial Information.* If material, financial information required by Article 11 of Regulation S–X with respect to this transaction.

Instructions to Paragraph (b)(11):

1. Present any Article 11 information required with respect to transactions other than those being voted upon (where not incorporated by reference) together with the pro forma information relating to the transaction being voted upon. In presenting this information, you must clearly distinguish between the transaction being voted upon and any other transaction.

2. If current pro forma financial information with respect to all other transactions is incorporated by reference, you need only present the pro forma effect of this transaction.

(c) *Information About the Parties to the Transaction.* (1) *Acquiring Company.* Furnish the information required by Part B (Registrant Information) of Form S–4 (17 CFR 239.25) or Form F–4 (17 CFR 239.34), as applicable, for the acquiring company. However, financial statements need only be presented for the latest two fiscal years and interim periods.

(2) *Acquired Company.* Furnish the information required by Part C (Information with Respect to the Company Being Acquired) of Form S–4 (17 CFR 239.25) or Form F–4 (17 CFR 239.34), as applicable.

(d) *Information About Parties to the Transaction: Registered Investment Companies and Business Development Companies.* If the acquiring company or the acquired company is an investment company registered under the Investment Company Act of 1940 or a business development company as defined by Section 2(a)(48) of the Investment Company Act of 1940, provide the following information for that company instead of the information specified by Paragraph (c) of this Item:

(1) Information required by Item 101 of Regulation S–K, description of business;

(2) Information required by Item 102 of Regulation S–K, description of property;

(3) Information required by Item 103 of Regulation S–K, legal proceedings;

(4) Information required by Item 201(a), (b) and (c) of Regulation S–K, market price of and dividends on the registrant's common equity and related stockholder matters;

(5) Financial statements meeting the requirements of Regulation S–X, including financial information required by Rule 3–05 and Article 11 of Regulation S–X with respect to transactions other than that as to which action is to be taken as described in this proxy statement;

(6) Information required by Item 301 of Regulation S–K, selected financial data;

(7) Information required by Item 302 of Regulation S–K, supplementary financial information;

(8) Information required by Item 303 of Regulation S–K, management's discussion and analysis of financial condition and results of operations; and

(9) Information required by Item 304 of Regulation S–K, changes in and disagreements with accountants on accounting and financial disclosure.

Instruction to Paragraph (d) of Item 14: Unless registered on a national securities exchange or otherwise required to furnish such information, registered investment companies need not furnish the information required by paragraphs (d)(6), (d)(7) and (d)(8) of this Item.

(e) *Incorporation by Reference.* (1) The information required by paragraph (c) of this rule may be incorporated by reference into the proxy statement to the same extent as would be permitted by Form S–4 (17 CFR 239.25) or Form F–4 (17 CFR 239.34), as applicable.

(2) Alternatively, the registrant may incorporate by reference into the proxy statement the information required by paragraph (c) of this Item if it is contained in an annual report sent to security holders in accordance with Rule 14a–3 with respect to the same meeting or solicitation of consents or authorizations that the proxy statement relates to and the information substantially meets the disclosure requirements of Item 14 or Item 17 of Form S–4 (17 CFR 239.25) or Form F–4 (17 CFR 239.34), as applicable.

Item 15. Acquisition or Disposition of Property

If action is to be taken with respect to the acquisition or disposition of any property, furnish the following information:

(a) Describe briefly the general character and location of the property.

(b) State the nature and amount of consideration to be paid or received by the registrant or any subsidiary. To the extent practicable, outline briefly the facts bearing upon the question of the fairness of the consideration.

(c) State the name and address of the transferer or transferee, as the case may be and the nature of any material relationship of such person to the registrant or any affiliate of the registrant.

(d) Outline briefly any other material features of the contract or transaction.

Item 16. Restatement of Accounts

If action is to be taken with respect to the restatement of any asset, capital, or surplus account of the registrant, furnish the following information:

(a) State the nature of the restatement and the date as of which it is to be effective.

(b) Outline briefly the reasons for the restatement and for the selection of the particular effective date.

(c) State the name and amount of each account (including any reserve accounts) affected by the restatement and the effect of the restatement thereon. Tabular presentation of the amounts shall be made when appropriate, particularly in the case of recapitalizations.

(d) To the extent practicable, state whether and the extent, if any, to which the restatement will, as of the date thereof, alter the amount available for distribution to the holders of equity securities.

Item 17. Action With Respect to Reports

If action is to be taken with respect to any report of the registrant or of its directors, officers or committees or any minutes of a meeting of its security holders furnish the following information:

(a) State whether or not such action is to constitute approval or disapproval of any of the matters referred to in such reports or minutes.

(b) Identify each of such matters which it is intended will be approved or disapproved, and furnish the information required by the appropriate item or items of this schedule with respect to each such matter.

Item 18. Matters Not Required to Be Submitted

If action is to be taken with respect to any matter which is not required to be submitted to a vote of security holders, state the nature of such matter, the reasons for submitting it to a vote of security holders and what action is intended to be taken by the registrant in the event of a negative vote on the matter by the security holders.

Item 19. Amendment of Charter, Bylaws of Other Documents

If action is to be taken with respect to any amendment of the registrant's charter, bylaws or other documents as to which information is not required above, state briefly the reasons for and the general effect of such amendment.

Instructions. 1. Where the matter to be acted upon is the classification of directors, state whether vacancies which occur during the year may be filled by the board of directors to serve only until the next annual meeting or may be so filled for the remainder of the full term.

2. Attention is directed to the discussion of disclosure regarding anti-takeover and similar proposals in Release No. 34–15230 (October 13, 1978).

Item 20. Other Proposed Action

If action is to be taken on any matter not specifically referred to in this Schedule 14A, describe briefly the substance of each such matter in substantially the same degree of detail as is required by Items 5 to 19, inclusive, of this Schedule, and, with respect to investment companies registered under the Investment Company Act of 1940, Item 22 of this Schedule. Registrants required to provide a separate shareholder vote pursuant to section 111(e)(1) of the Emergency Economic Stabilization Act of 2008 (12 U.S.C. 5221(e)(1)) and Rule 14a–20 shall disclose that they are providing such a vote as required pursuant to the Emergency Economic Stabilization Act of 2008, and briefly explain the general effect of the vote, such as whether the vote is non-binding.

Item 21. Voting Procedures

As to each matter which is to be submitted to a vote of security holders, furnish the following information:

(a) State the vote required for approval or election, other than for the approval of auditors.

(b) Disclose the method by which votes will be counted, including the treatment and effect of abstentions and broker non-votes under applicable state law as well as registrant charter and by-law provisions.

Item 22. Information Required in Investment Company Proxy Statement

(a) *General.* (1) *Definitions.* Unless the context otherwise requires, terms used in this Item that are defined in Rule 14a–1 (with respect to proxy soliciting material), in Rule 14c–1 (with respect to information statements), and in the Investment Company Act of 1940 shall have the same meanings provided therein and the following terms shall also apply:

(i) *Administrator.* The term "Administrator" shall mean any person who provides significant administrative or business affairs management services to a Fund.

(ii) *Affiliated Broker.* The term "Affiliated Broker" shall mean any broker:

(A) That is an affiliated person of the Fund;

(B) That is an affiliated person of such person; or

(C) An affiliated person of which is an affiliated person of the Fund, its investment adviser, principal underwriter, or Administrator.

(iii) *Distribution Plan.* The term "Distribution Plan" shall mean a plan adopted pursuant to Rule 12b–1 under the Investment Company Act of 1940 (17 CFR 270.12b–1).

(iv) *Family of Investment Companies.* The term "Family of Investment Companies" shall mean any two or more registered investment companies that:

(A) Share the same investment adviser or principal underwriter; and

(B) Hold themselves out to investors as related companies for purposes of investment and investor services.

(v) *Fund.* The term "Fund" shall mean a Registrant or, where the Registrant is a series company, a separate portfolio of the Registrant.

(vi) *Fund Complex.* The term "Fund Complex" shall mean two or more Funds that:

(A) Hold themselves out to investors as related companies for purposes of investment and investor services; or

(B) Have a common investment adviser or have an investment adviser that is an affiliated person of the investment adviser of any of the other Funds.

(vii) *Immediate Family Member.* The term "Immediate Family Member" shall mean a person's spouse; child residing in the person's household (including step and adoptive children); and any dependent of the person, as defined in section 152 of the Internal Revenue Code (26 U.S.C. 152).

(viii) *Officer.* The term "Officer" shall mean the president, vice-president, secretary, treasurer, controller, or any other officer who performs policy-making functions.

(ix) *Parent*. The term "Parent" shall mean the affiliated person of a specified person who controls the specified person directly or indirectly through one or more intermediaries.

(x) *Registrant*. The term "Registrant" shall mean an investment company registered under the Investment Company Act of 1940 (15 U.S.C. 80a) or a business development company as defined by section 2(a)(48) of the Investment Company Act of 1940 (15 U.S.C. 80a–2(a)(48)).

(xi) *Sponsoring Insurance Company*. The term "Sponsoring Insurance Company" of a Fund that is a separate account shall mean the insurance company that establishes and maintains the separate account and that owns the assets of the separate account.

(xii) *Subsidiary*. The term "Subsidiary" shall mean an affiliated person of a specified person who is controlled by the specified person directly, or indirectly through one or more intermediaries.

(2) [Reserved]

(3) *General Disclosure*. Furnish the following information in the proxy statement of a Fund or Funds:

(i) State the name and address of the Fund's investment adviser, principal underwriter, and Administrator.

(ii) When a Fund proxy statement solicits a vote on proposals affecting more than one Fund or class of securities of a Fund (unless the proposal or proposals are the same and affect all Fund or class shareholders), present a summary of all of the proposals in tabular form on one of the first three pages of the proxy statement and indicate which Fund or class shareholders are solicited with respect to each proposal.

(iii) Unless the proxy statement is accompanied by a copy of the Fund's most recent annual report, state prominently in the proxy statement that the Fund will furnish, without charge, a copy of the annual report and the most recent semi-annual report succeeding the annual report, if any, to a shareholder upon request, providing the name, address, and toll-free telephone number of the person to whom such request shall be directed (or, if no toll-free telephone number is provided, a self-addressed postage paid card for requesting the annual report). The Fund should provide a copy of the annual report and the most recent semi-annual report succeeding the annual report, if any, to the requesting shareholder by first class mail, or other means designed to assure prompt delivery, within three business days of the request.

(iv) If the action to be taken would, directly or indirectly, establish a new fee or expense or increase any existing fee or expense to be paid by the Fund or its shareholders, provide a table showing the current and pro forma fees (with the required examples) using the format prescribed in the appropriate registration statement form under the Investment Company Act of 1940 (for open-end management investment companies, Item 2 of Form N–1A (17 CFR 239.15A); for closed-end management investment companies, Item 3 of Form N–2 (17 CFR 239.14); and for separate accounts that offer variable annuity contracts, Item 3 of Form N–3 (17 CFR 239.17a)).

Instructions. 1. Where approval is sought only for a change in asset breakpoints for a pre-existing fee that would not have increased the fee for the previous year (or have the effect of increasing fees or expenses, but for any other reason would not be reflected in a pro forma fee table), describe the likely effect of the change in lieu of providing pro forma fee information.

2. An action would indirectly establish or increase a fee or expense where, for example, the approval of a new investment advisory contract would result in higher custodial or transfer agency fees.

3. The tables should be prepared in a manner designed to facilitate understanding of the impact of any change in fees or expenses.

4. A Fund that offers its shares exclusively to one or more separate accounts and thus is not required to include a fee table in its prospectus (see Item 3 of Form N–1A (17 CFR 239.15A)) should nonetheless prepare a table showing current and pro forma expenses and disclose that the table does not reflect separate account expenses, including sales load.

(v) If action is to be taken with respect to the election of directors or the approval of an advisory contract, describe any purchases or sales of securities of the investment adviser or its Parents, or Subsidiaries of either, since the beginning of the most recently completed fiscal year by any director or any nominee for election as a director of the Fund.

Instructions. 1. Identify the parties, state the consideration, the terms of payment and describe any arrangement or understanding with respect to the composition of the board of directors of the Fund or of the investment adviser, or with respect to the selection of appointment of any person to any office with either such company.

2. Transactions involving securities in an amount not exceeding one percent of the outstanding securities of any class of the investment adviser or any of its Parents or Subsidiaries may be omitted.

(b) *Election of Directors.* If action is to be taken with respect to the election of directors of a Fund, furnish the following information in the proxy statement in addition to, in the case of business development companies, the information (and in the format) required by Item 7 and Item 8 of this Schedule 14A.

Instructions to Introductory Text of Paragraph (b). 1. Furnish information with respect to a prospective investment adviser to the extent applicable.

2. If the solicitation is made by or on behalf of a person other than the Fund or an investment adviser of the Fund, provide information only as to nominees of the person making the solicitation.

3. When providing information about directors and nominees for election as directors in response to this Item 22(b), furnish information for directors or nominees who are or would be "interested persons" of the Fund within the meaning of section 2(a)(19) of the Investment Company Act of 1940 (15 U.S.C. 80a–2(a)(19)) separately from the information for directors or nominees who are not or would not be interested persons of the Fund. For example, when furnishing information in a table, you should provide separate tables (or separate sections of a single table) for directors and nominees who are or would be interested persons and for directors or nominees who are not or would not be interested persons. When furnishing information in narrative form, indicate by heading or otherwise the directors or nominees who are or would be interested persons and the directors or nominees who are not or would not be interested persons.

4. No information need be given about any director whose term of office as a director will not continue after the meeting to which the proxy statement relates.

(1) Provide the information required by the following table for each director, nominee for election as director, Officer of the Fund, person chosen to become an Officer of the Fund, and, if the Fund has an advisory board, member of the board. Explain in a footnote to the table any family relationship between the persons listed.

(1)	(2)	(3)	(4)	(5)	(6)
Name, Address, and Age.	Position(s) Held with Fund.	Term of Office and Length of Time Served.	Principal Occupation(s) During Past 5 Years.	Number of Portfolios in Fund Complex Overseen by Director or Nominee for Director.	Other Directorships Held by Director or Nominee for Director

Instructions to Paragraph (b)(1). 1. For purposes of this paragraph, the term "family relationship" means any relationship by blood, marriage, or adoption, not more remote than first cousin.

2. No nominee or person chosen to become a director or Officer who has not consented to act as such may be named in response to this Item. In this regard, see Rule 14a–4(d) under the Securities Exchange Act of 1934.

3. If fewer nominees are named than the number fixed by or pursuant to the governing instruments, state the reasons for this procedure and that the proxies cannot be voted for a greater number of persons than the number of nominees named.

4. For each director or nominee for election as director who is or would be an "interested person" of the Fund within the meaning of section 2(a)(19) of the Investment Company Act of 1940 (15 U.S.C. 80a–2(a)(19)), describe, in a footnote or otherwise, the relationship, events, or transactions by reason of which the director or nominee is or would be an interested person.

5. State the principal business of any company listed under column (4) unless the principal business is implicit in its name.

6. Include in column (5) the total number of separate portfolios that a nominee for election as director would oversee if he were elected.

7. Indicate in column (6) directorships not included in column (5) that are held by a director or nominee for election as director in any company with a class of securities registered pursuant to section 12 of the Exchange Act (15 U.S.C. 78l), or subject to the requirements of section 15(d) of the Exchange Act (15 U.S.C. 78o(d)), or any company registered as an investment company under the Investment Company Act of 1940, (15 U.S.C. 80a), as amended, and name the companies in which the directorships are held. Where the other directorships include directorships overseeing two or more portfolios in the same Fund Complex, identify the Fund Complex and provide the number of portfolios overseen as a director in the Fund Complex rather than listing each portfolio separately.

(2) For each individual listed in column (1) of the table required by paragraph (b)(1) of this Item, except for any director or nominee for election as director who is not or would not be an "interested person" of the Fund within the meaning of section 2(a)(19) of the Investment Company Act of 1940 (15 U.S.C. 80a–2(a)(19)), describe any positions, including as an officer, employee, director, or general partner, held with affiliated persons or principal underwriters of the Fund.

Instruction to Paragraph (b)(2). When an individual holds the same position(s) with two or more registered investment companies that are part of the same Fund Complex, identify the Fund Complex and provide the number of registered investment companies for which the position(s) are held rather than listing each registered investment company separately.

(3)(i) For each director or nominee for election as director, briefly discuss the specific experience, qualifications, attributes, or skills that led to the conclusion that the person should serve as a director for the Fund at the time that the disclosure is made in light of the Fund's business and structure. If material, this disclosure should cover more than the past five years, including information about the person's particular areas of expertise or other relevant qualifications.

(ii) Describe briefly any arrangement or understanding between any director, nominee for election as director, Officer, or person chosen to become an Officer, and any other person(s) (naming the person(s)) pursuant to which he was or is to be selected as a director, nominee, or Officer.

Instruction to Paragraph (b)(3)(ii). Do not include arrangements or understandings with directors or Officers acting solely in their capacities as such.

(4)(i) Unless disclosed in the table required by paragraph (b)(1) of this Item, describe any positions, including as an officer, employee, director, or general partner, held by any director or nominee for election as director, who is not or would not be an "interested person" of the Fund within the meaning of section 2(a)(19) of the Investment Company Act of 1940 (15 U.S.C. 80a–2(a)(19)), or Immediate Family Member of the director or nominee, during the past five years, with:

(A) The Fund;

(B) An investment company, or a person that would be an investment company but for the exclusions provided by sections 3(c)(1) and 3(c)(7) of the Investment Company Act of 1940 (15 U.S.C. 80a–3(c)(1) and (c)(7)), having the same investment adviser, principal underwriter, or Sponsoring Insurance Company as the Fund or having an investment adviser, principal underwriter, or Sponsoring Insurance Company that directly or indirectly controls, is controlled by, or is under common control with an investment adviser, principal underwriter, or Sponsoring Insurance Company of the Fund;

(C) An investment adviser, principal underwriter, Sponsoring Insurance Company, or affiliated person of the Fund; or

(D) Any person directly or indirectly controlling, controlled by, or under common control with an investment adviser, principal underwriter, or Sponsoring Insurance Company of the Fund.

(ii) Unless disclosed in the table required by paragraph (b)(1) of this Item or in response to paragraph (b)(4)(i) of this Item, indicate any directorships held during the past five years by each director or nominee for election as director in any company with a class of securities registered pursuant to section 12 of the Exchange Act (15 U.S.C. 78l) or subject to the requirements of section 15(d) of the Exchange Act (15 U.S.C. 78o(d)) or any company registered as an investment company under the Investment Company Act of 1940 (15 U.S.C. 80a–1 et seq.), as amended, and name the companies in which the directorships were held.

Instruction to Paragraph (b)(4). When an individual holds the same position(s) with two or more portfolios that are part of the same Fund Complex, identify the Fund Complex and provide the number of portfolios for which the position(s) are held rather than listing each portfolio separately.

(5) For each director or nominee for election as director, state the dollar range of equity securities beneficially owned by the director or nominee as required by the following table:

(i) In the Fund; and

(ii) On an aggregate basis, in any registered investment companies overseen or to be overseen by the director or nominee within the same Family of Investment Companies as the Fund.

(1)	(2)	(3)
Name of Director or Nominee.	Dollar Range of Equity Securities in the Fund.	Aggregate Dollar Range of Equity Securities in All Funds Overseen or to be Overseen by Director or Nominee in Family of Investment Companies

Instructions to Paragraph (b)(5). 1. Information should be provided as of the most recent practicable date. Specify the valuation date by footnote or otherwise.

2. Determine "beneficial ownership" in accordance with rule 16a–1(a)(2) under the Securities Exchange Act of 1934.

3. If action is to be taken with respect to more than one Fund, disclose in column (2) the dollar range of equity securities beneficially owned by a director or nominee in each such Fund overseen or to be overseen by the director or nominee.

4. In disclosing the dollar range of equity securities beneficially owned by a director or nominee in columns (2) and (3), use the following ranges: none, $1–$10,000, $10,001–$50,000, $50,001–$100,000, or over $100,000.

(6) For each director or nominee for election as director who is not or would not be an "interested person" of the Fund within the meaning of section 2(a)(19) of the Investment Company Act of 1940 (15 U.S.C. 80a–2(a)(19)), and his Immediate Family

Members, furnish the information required by the following table as to each class of securities owned beneficially or of record in:

(i) An investment adviser, principal underwriter, or Sponsoring Insurance Company of the Fund; or

(ii) A person (other than a registered investment company) directly or indirectly controlling, controlled by, or under common control with an investment adviser, principal underwriter, or Sponsoring Insurance Company of the Fund:

(1)	(2)	(3)	(4)	(5)	(6)
Name of Director or Nominee.	Name of Owners and Relationships to Director or Nominee.	Company	Title of Class	Value of Securities	Percent of Class

Instructions to Paragraph (b)(6). 1. Information should be provided as of the most recent practicable date. Specify the valuation date by footnote or otherwise.

2. An individual is a "beneficial owner" of a security if he is a "beneficial owner" under either Rule 13d–3 or Rule 16a–1(a)(2) under the Exchange Act.

3. Identify the company in which the director, nominee, or Immediate Family Member of the director or nominee owns securities in column (3). When the company is a person directly or indirectly controlling, controlled by, or under common control with an investment adviser, principal underwriter, or Sponsoring Insurance Company, describe the company's relationship with the investment adviser, principal underwriter, or Sponsoring Insurance Company.

4. Provide the information required by columns (5) and (6) on an aggregate basis for each director (or nominee) and his Immediate Family Members.

(7) Unless disclosed in response to paragraph (b)(6) of this Item, describe any direct or indirect interest, the value of which exceeds $120,000, of each director or nominee for election as director who is not or would not be an "interested person" of the Fund within the meaning of section 2(a)(19) of the Investment Company Act of 1940 (15 U.S.C. 80a–2(a)(19)), or Immediate Family Member of the director or nominee, during the past five years, in:

(i) An investment adviser, principal underwriter, or Sponsoring Insurance Company of the Fund; or

(ii) A person (other than a registered investment company) directly or indirectly controlling, controlled by, or under common control with an investment adviser, principal underwriter, or Sponsoring Insurance Company of the Fund.

Instructions to Paragraph (b)(7). 1. A director, nominee, or Immediate Family Member has an interest in a company if he is a party to a contract, arrangement, or understanding with respect to any securities of, or interest in, the company.

2. The interest of the director (or nominee) and the interests of his Immediate Family Members should be aggregated in determining whether the value exceeds $120,000.

(8) Describe briefly any material interest, direct or indirect, of any director or nominee for election as director who is not or would not be an "interested person" of the Fund within the meaning of section 2(a)(19) of the Investment Company Act of 1940 (15 U.S.C. 80a–2(a)(19)), or Immediate Family Member of the director or nominee, in any transaction, or series of similar transactions, since the beginning of the last two completed fiscal years of the Fund, or in any currently proposed transaction, or series of similar transactions, in which the amount involved exceeds $120,000 and to which any of the following persons was or is to be a party:

(i) The Fund;

(ii) An Officer of the Fund;

(iii) An investment company, or a person that would be an investment company but for the exclusions provided by sections 3(c)(1) and 3(c)(7) of the Investment Company Act of 1940 (15 U.S.C. 80a–3(c)(1) and (c)(7)), having the same investment adviser, principal underwriter, or Sponsoring Insurance Company as the Fund or having an investment adviser, principal underwriter, or Sponsoring Insurance Company that directly or indirectly controls, is controlled by, or is under common control with an investment adviser, principal underwriter, or Sponsoring Insurance Company of the Fund;

(iv) An Officer of an investment company, or a person that would be an investment company but for the exclusions provided by sections 3(c)(1) and 3(c)(7) of the Investment Company Act of 1940 (15 U.S.C. 80a–3(c)(1) and (c)(7)), having the same investment adviser, principal underwriter, or Sponsoring Insurance Company as the Fund or having an investment adviser, principal underwriter, or Sponsoring Insurance Company that directly or indirectly controls, is controlled by, or is under common control with an investment adviser, principal underwriter, or Sponsoring Insurance Company of the Fund;

(v) An investment adviser, principal underwriter, or Sponsoring Insurance Company of the Fund;

(vi) An Officer of an investment adviser, principal underwriter, or Sponsoring Insurance Company of the Fund;

(vii) A person directly or indirectly controlling, controlled by, or under common control with an investment adviser, principal underwriter, or Sponsoring Insurance Company of the Fund; or

(viii) An Officer of a person directly or indirectly controlling, controlled by, or under common control with an investment adviser, principal underwriter, or Sponsoring Insurance Company of the Fund.

Instructions to Paragraph (b)(8). 1. Include the name of each director, nominee, or Immediate Family Member whose interest in any transaction or series of similar transactions is described and the nature of the circumstances by reason of which the interest is required to be described.

2. State the nature of the interest, the approximate dollar amount involved in the transaction, and, where practicable, the approximate dollar amount of the interest.

3. In computing the amount involved in the transaction or series of similar transactions, include all periodic payments in the case of any lease or other agreement providing for periodic payments.

4. Compute the amount of the interest of any director, nominee, or Immediate Family Member of the director or nominee without regard to the amount of profit or loss involved in the transaction(s).

5. As to any transaction involving the purchase or sale of assets, state the cost of the assets to the purchaser and, if acquired by the seller within two years prior to the transaction, the cost to the seller. Describe the method used in determining the purchase or sale price and the name of the person making the determination.

6. If the proxy statement relates to multiple portfolios of a series Fund with different fiscal years, then, in determining the date that is the beginning of the last two completed fiscal years of the Fund, use the earliest date of any series covered by the proxy statement.

7. Disclose indirect, as well as direct, material interests in transactions. A person who has a position or relationship with, or interest in, a company that engages in a transaction with one of the persons listed in paragraphs (b)(8)(i) through (b)(8)(viii) of this Item may have an indirect interest in the transaction by reason of the position, relationship, or interest. The interest in the transaction, however, will not be deemed "material" within the meaning of paragraph (b)(8) of this Item where the interest of the director, nominee, or Immediate Family Member arises solely from the holding of an equity interest (including a limited partnership interest, but excluding a general partnership interest) or a creditor interest in a company that is a party to the transaction with one of the persons specified in paragraphs (b)(8)(i) through (b)(8)(viii) of this Item, and the transaction is not material to the company.

8. The materiality of any interest is to be determined on the basis of the significance of the information to investors in light of all the circumstances of the particular case. The importance of the interest to the person having the interest, the relationship of the parties to the transaction with each other, and the amount involved in the transaction are among the factors to be considered in determining the significance of the information to investors.

9. No information need be given as to any transaction where the interest of the director, nominee, or Immediate Family Member arises solely from the ownership of securities of a person specified in paragraphs (b)(8)(i) through (b)(8)(viii) of this Item and the director, nominee, or Immediate Family Member receives no extra or special benefit not shared on a pro rata basis by all holders of the class of securities.

10. Transactions include loans, lines of credit, and other indebtedness. For indebtedness, indicate the largest aggregate amount of indebtedness outstanding at any time during the period, the nature of the indebtedness and the transaction in which it was incurred, the amount outstanding as of the latest practicable date, and the rate of interest paid or charged.

11. No information need be given as to any routine, retail transaction. For example, the Fund need not disclose that a director has a credit card, bank or brokerage account, residential mortgage, or insurance policy with a person specified in paragraphs (b)(8)(i) through (b)(8)(viii) of this Item unless the director is accorded special treatment.

(9) Describe briefly any direct or indirect relationship, in which the amount involved exceeds $120,000, of any director or nominee for election as director who is not or would not be an "interested person" of the Fund within the meaning of section 2(a)(19) of the Investment Company Act of 1940 (15 U.S.C. 80a–2(a)(19)), or Immediate Family Member of the director or nominee, that exists, or has existed at any time since the beginning of the last two completed fiscal years of the Fund, or is currently proposed, with any of the persons specified in paragraphs (b)(8)(i) through (b)(8)(viii) of this Item. Relationships include:

(i) Payments for property or services to or from any person specified in paragraphs (b)(8)(i) through (b)(8)(viii) of this Item;

(ii) Provision of legal services to any person specified in paragraphs (b)(8)(i) through (b)(8)(viii) of this Item;

(iii) Provision of investment banking services to any person specified in paragraphs (b)(8)(i) through (b)(8)(viii) of this Item, other than as a participating underwriter in a syndicate; and

(iv) Any consulting or other relationship that is substantially similar in nature and scope to the relationships listed in paragraphs (b)(9)(i) through (b)(9)(iii) of this Item.

Instructions to Paragraph (b)(9). 1. Include the name of each director, nominee, or Immediate Family Member whose relationship is described and the nature of the circumstances by reason of which the relationship is required to be described.

2. State the nature of the relationship and the amount of business conducted between the director, nominee, or Immediate Family Member and the person specified in paragraphs (b)(8)(i) through (b)(8)(viii) of this Item as a result of the relationship since the beginning of the last two completed fiscal years of the Fund or proposed to be done during the Fund's current fiscal year.

3. In computing the amount involved in a relationship, include all periodic payments in the case of any agreement providing for periodic payments.

4. If the proxy statement relates to multiple portfolios of a series Fund with different fiscal years, then, in determining the date that is the beginning of the last two completed fiscal years of the Fund, use the earliest date of any series covered by the proxy statement.

5. Disclose indirect, as well as direct, relationships. A person who has a position or relationship with, or interest in, a company that has a relationship with one of the persons listed in paragraphs (b)(8)(i) through (b)(8)(viii) of this Item may have an indirect relationship by reason of the position, relationship, or interest.

6. In determining whether the amount involved in a relationship exceeds $120,000, amounts involved in a relationship of the director (or nominee) should be aggregated with those of his Immediate Family Members.

7. In the case of an indirect interest, identify the company with which a person specified in paragraphs (b)(8)(i) through (b)(8)(viii) of this Item has a relationship; the name of the director, nominee, or Immediate Family Member affiliated with the company and the nature of the affiliation; and the amount of business conducted between the company and the person specified in paragraphs (b)(8)(i) through (b)(8)(viii) of this Item since the beginning of the last two completed fiscal years of the Fund or proposed to be done during the Fund's current fiscal year.

8. In calculating payments for property and services for purposes of paragraph (b)(9)(i) of this Item, the following may be excluded:

A. Payments where the transaction involves the rendering of services as a common contract carrier, or public utility, at rates or charges fixed in conformity with law or governmental authority; or

B. Payments that arise solely from the ownership of securities of a person specified in paragraphs (b)(8)(i) through (b)(8)(viii) of this Item and no extra or special benefit not shared on a pro rata basis by all holders of the class of securities is received.

9. No information need be given as to any routine, retail relationship. For example, the Fund need not disclose that a director has a credit card, bank or brokerage account, residential mortgage, or insurance policy with a person specified in paragraphs (b)(8)(i) through (b)(8)(viii) of this Item unless the director is accorded special treatment.

(10) If an Officer of an investment adviser, principal underwriter, or Sponsoring Insurance Company of the Fund, or an Officer of a person directly or indirectly controlling, controlled by, or under common control with an investment adviser, principal underwriter, or Sponsoring Insurance Company of the Fund, serves, or has served since the beginning of the last two completed fiscal years of the Fund, on the board of directors of a company where a director of the Fund or nominee for election as director who is not or would not be an "interested person" of the Fund within the meaning of section 2(a)(19) of the Investment Company Act of 1940 (15 U.S.C. 80a–2(a)(19)), or Immediate Family Member of the director or nominee, is, or was since the beginning of the last two completed fiscal years of the Fund, an Officer, identify:

(i) The company;

(ii) The individual who serves or has served as a director of the company and the period of service as director;

(iii) The investment adviser, principal underwriter, or Sponsoring Insurance Company or person controlling, controlled by, or under common control with the investment adviser, principal underwriter, or Sponsoring Insurance Company where the individual named in paragraph (b)(10)(ii) of this Item holds or held office and the office held; and

(iv) The director of the Fund, nominee for election as director, or Immediate Family Member who is or was an Officer of the company; the office held; and the period of holding the office.

Instruction to Paragraph (b)(10). If the proxy statement relates to multiple portfolios of a series Fund with different fiscal years, then, in determining the date that is the beginning of the last two completed fiscal years of the Fund, use the earliest date of any series covered by the proxy statement.

(11) Provide in tabular form, to the extent practicable, the information required by Items 401(f) and (g), 404(a), 405, and 407(h) of Regulation S–K.

Instruction to Paragraph 22(b)(11). Information provided under paragraph (b)(8) of this Item 22 is deemed to satisfy the requirements of Item 404(a) of Regulation S–K for information about directors, nominees for election as directors, and Immediate Family Members of directors and nominees, and need not be provided under this paragraph (b)(11).

(12) Describe briefly any material pending legal proceedings, other than ordinary routine litigation incidental to the Fund's business, to which any director or nominee for director or affiliated person of such director or nominee is a party adverse to the Fund or any of its affiliated persons or has a material interest adverse to the Fund or any of its affiliated persons. Include the name of the court where the case is pending, the date in-

stituted, the principal parties, a description of the factual basis alleged to underlie the proceeding, and the relief sought.

(13) In the case of a Fund that is an investment company registered under the Investment Company Act of 1940 (15 U.S.C. 80a), for all directors, and for each of the three highest-paid Officers that have aggregate compensation from the Fund for the most recently completed fiscal year in excess of $60,000 ("Compensated Persons"):

(i) Furnish the information required by the following table for the last fiscal year:

COMPENSATION TABLE

(1)	(2)	(3)	(4)	(5)
Name of Person, Position.	Aggregate Compensation From Fund.	Pension or Retirement Benefits Accrued as Part of Fund Expenses.	Estimated Annual Benefits Upon Retirement.	Total Compensation From Fund and Complex Paid to Directors

Instructions to Paragraph (b)(13)(i). 1. For column (1), indicate, if necessary, the capacity in which the remuneration is received. For Compensated Persons that are directors of the Fund, compensation is amounts received for service as a director.

2. If the Fund has not completed its first full year since its organization, furnish the information for the current fiscal year, estimating future payments that would be made pursuant to an existing agreement or understanding. Disclose in a footnote to the Compensation Table the period for which the information is furnished.

3. Include in column (2) amounts deferred at the election of the Compensated Person, whether pursuant to a plan established under Section 401(k) of the Internal Revenue Code (26 U.S.C. 401(k)) or otherwise, for the fiscal year in which earned. Disclose in a footnote to the Compensation Table the total amount of deferred compensation (including interest) payable to or accrued for any Compensated Person.

4. Include in columns (3) and (4) all pension or retirement benefits proposed to be paid under any existing plan in the event of retirement at normal retirement date, directly or indirectly, by the Fund or any of its Subsidiaries, or by other companies in the Fund Complex. Omit column (4) where retirement benefits are not determinable.

5. For any defined benefit or actuarial plan under which benefits are determined primarily by final compensation (or average final compensation) and years of service, provide the information required in column (4) in a separate table showing estimated annual benefits payable upon retirement (including amounts attributable to any defined benefit supplementary or excess pension award plans) in specified compensation and years of service classifications. Also provide the estimated credited years of service for each Compensated Person.

6. Include in column (5) only aggregate compensation paid to a director for service on the board and other boards of investment companies in a Fund Complex specifying the number of such other investment companies.

(ii) Describe briefly the material provisions of any pension, retirement, or other plan or any arrangement other than fee arrangements disclosed in paragraph (b)(13)(i) of this Item pursuant to which Compensated Persons are or may be compensated for any services provided, including amounts paid, if any, to the Compensated Person under any such arrangements during the most recently completed fiscal year. Specifically include the criteria used to determine amounts payable under any plan, the length of service or vesting period required by the plan, the retirement age or other event that gives rise to payments under the plan, and whether the payment of benefits is secured or funded by the Fund.

(14) State whether or not the Fund has a separately designated audit committee established in accordance with section 3(a)(58)(A) of the Act (15 U.S.C. 78c(a)(58)(A)). If the entire board of directors is acting as the Fund's audit committee as specified in section 3(a)(58)(B) of the Act (15 U.S.C. 78c(a)(58)(B)), so state. If applicable, provide the disclosure required by Rule 10A–3(d) regarding an exemption from the listing standards for audit committees. Identify the other standing committees of the Fund's board of directors, and provide the following information about each committee, including any separately designated audit committee and any nominating committee:

(i) A concise statement of the functions of the committee;

(ii) The members of the committee and, in the case of a nominating committee, whether or not the members of the committee are "interested persons" of the Fund as defined in section 2(a)(19) of the Investment Company Act of 1940 (15 U.S.C. 80a–2(a)(19)); and

(iii) The number of committee meetings held during the last fiscal year.

Instruction to Paragraph (b)(14): For purposes of Item 22(b)(14), the term "nominating committee" refers not only to nominating committees and committees performing similar functions, but also to groups of directors fulfilling the role of a nominating committee, including the entire board of directors.

(15)(i) Provide the information (and in the format) required by Items 407(b)(1), (b)(2) and (f) of Regulation S–K; and

(ii) Provide the following regarding the requirements for the director nomination process:

(A) The information (and in the format) required by Items 407(c)(1) and (c)(2) of Regulation S–K; and

(B) If the Fund is a listed issuer (as defined in Rule 10A–3) whose securities are listed on a national securities exchange registered pursuant to section 6(a) of the Act (15 U.S.C. 78f(a)) or in an automated inter-dealer quotation system of a national securities association registered pursuant to section 15A of the Act (15 U.S.C. 78o–3(a)) that has independence requirements for nominating committee members, identify each director that is a member of the nominating committee that is not independent under the independence standards described in this paragraph. In determining whether the nominating committee members are independent, use the Fund's definition of independence that it uses for determining if the members of the nominating committee are independent in compliance with the independence standards applicable for the members of the nominating committee in the listing standards applicable to the Fund. If the Fund does not have independence standards for the nominating committee, use the independence standards for the nominating committee in the listing standards applicable to the Fund.

Instruction to Paragraph (b)(15)(ii)(B). If the national securities exchange or inter-dealer quotation system on which the Fund's securities are listed has exemptions to the independence requirements for nominating committee members upon which the Fund relied, disclose the exemption relied upon and explain the basis for the Fund's conclusion that such exemption is applicable.

(16) In the case of a Fund that is a closed-end investment company:

(i) Provide the information (and in the format) required by Item 407(d)(1), (d)(2) and (d)(3) of Regulation S–K; and

(ii) Identify each director that is a member of the Fund's audit committee that is not independent under the independence standards described in this paragraph. If the Fund does not have a separately designated audit committee, or committee performing similar functions, the Fund must provide the disclosure with respect to all members of its board of directors.

(A) If the Fund is a listed issuer (as defined in Rule 10A–3) whose securities are listed on a national securities exchange registered pursuant to section 6(a) of the Act (15 U.S.C. 78f(a)) or in an automated inter-dealer quotation system of a national securities association registered pursuant to section 15A of the Act (15 U.S.C. 78o–3(a)) that has independence requirements for audit committee members, in determining whether the audit committee members are independent, use the Fund's definition of independence that it uses for determining if the members of the audit committee are independent in compliance with the independence standards applicable for the members of the audit committee in the listing standards applicable to the Fund. If the Fund does not have independence standards for the audit committee, use the independence standards for the audit committee in the listing standards applicable to the Fund.

(B) If the Fund is not a listed issuer whose securities are listed on a national securities exchange registered pursuant to section 6(a) of the Act (15 U.S.C. 78f(a)) or in an automated inter-dealer quotation system of a national securities association registered pursuant to section 15A of the Act (15 U.S.C. 78o–3(a)), in determining whether the audit committee members are independent, use a definition of independence of a national securities exchange registered pursuant to section 6(a) of the Act (15 U.S.C. 78f(a)) or an automated inter-dealer quotation system of a national securities association registered pursuant to section 15A of the Act (15 U.S.C. 780–3(a)) which has requirements that a majority of the board of directors be independent and that has been approved by the Commission, and state which definition is used. Whatever such definition the Fund chooses, it must use the same definition with respect to all directors and nominees for director. If the national securities exchange or national securities association whose standards are used has independence standards for the members of the audit committee, use those specific standards.

Instruction to Paragraph (b)(16)(ii). If the national securities exchange or inter-dealer quotation system on which the Fund's securities are listed has exemptions to the independence requirements for nominating committee members upon which the Fund relied, disclose the exemption relied upon and explain the basis for the Fund's conclusion that such exemption is applicable. The same disclosure should be provided if the Fund is not a listed issuer and the national securities exchange or inter-dealer quotation system selected by the Fund has exemptions that are applicable to the Fund.

(17) In the case of a Fund that is an investment company registered under the Investment Company Act of 1940 (15 U.S.C. 80a), if a director has resigned or declined to stand for re-election to the board of directors since the date of the last annual meeting of security holders because of a disagreement with the registrant on any matter relating to the registrant's operations, policies or practices, and if the director has furnished the registrant with a letter describing such disagreement and requesting that the matter be disclosed, the registrant shall state the date of resignation or declination to stand for re-election and summarize the director's description of the disagreement. If the registrant believes that the description provided by the director is incorrect or incomplete, it may include a brief statement presenting its view of the disagreement.

(18) If a shareholder nominee or nominees are submitted to the Fund for inclusion in the Fund's proxy materials pursuant to Rule 14a–11 and the Fund is not permitted to exclude the nominee or nominees pursuant to the provisions of Rule 14a–11, the Fund must include in its proxy statement the disclosure required from the nominating shareholder or nominating shareholder group under Item 5 of Schedule 14N with regard to the nominee or nominees and the nominating shareholder or nominating shareholder group.

Instruction to Paragraph (b)(18): The information disclosed pursuant to paragraph (b)(18) of this Item will not be deemed incorporated by reference into any filing under the Securities Act of 1933 (15 U.S.C. 77a *et seq.*), the Securities Exchange Act of 1934 (15 U.S.C. 78a *et seq.*), or the Investment Company Act of 1940 (15 U.S.C. 80a–1 *et seq.*), except to the extent that the Fund specifically incorporates that information by reference.

(19) If a Fund is required to include a shareholder nominee or nominees submitted to the Fund for inclusion in the Fund's proxy materials pursuant to a procedure set forth under applicable state or foreign law or the Fund's governing documents providing for the inclusion of shareholder director nominees in the Fund's proxy materials, the Fund must include in its proxy statement the disclosure required from the nominating shareholder or nominating shareholder group under Item 6 of Schedule 14N with regard to the nominee or nominees and the nominating shareholder or nominating shareholder group.

Instruction to paragraph (b)(19): The information disclosed pursuant to paragraph (b)(19) of this Item will not be deemed incorporated by reference into any filing under the Securities Act of 1933 (15 U.S.C. 77a *et seq.*), the Securities Exchange Act of 1934 (15 U.S.C. 78a *et seq.*), or the Investment Company Act of 1940 (15 U.S.C. 80a–1 *et seq.*), except to the extent that the Fund specifically incorporates that information by reference.

(c) *Approval of Investment Advisory Contract.* If action is to be taken with respect to an investment advisory contract, include the following information in the proxy statement.

Instruction. Furnish information with respect to a prospective investment adviser to the extent applicable (including the name and address of the prospective investment adviser).

(1) With respect to the existing investment advisory contract:

(i) State the date of the contract and the date on which it was last submitted to a vote of security holders of the Fund, including the purpose of such submission;

(ii) Briefly describe the terms of the contract, including the rate of compensation of the investment adviser;

(iii) State the aggregate amount of the investment adviser's fee and the amount and purpose of any other material payments by the Fund to the investment adviser, or any affiliated person of the investment adviser, during the last fiscal year of the Fund;

(iv) If any person is acting as an investment adviser of the Fund other than pursuant to a written contract that has been approved by the security holders of the company, identify the person and describe the nature of the services and arrangements;

(v) Describe any action taken with respect to the investment advisory contract since the beginning of the Fund's last fiscal year by the board of directors of the Fund (unless described in response to paragraph (c)(1)(vi) of this Item 22); and

(vi) If an investment advisory contract was terminated or not renewed for any reason, state the date of such termination or non-renewal, identify the parties involved, and describe the circumstances of such termination or non-renewal.

(2) State the name, address and principal occupation of the principal executive officer and each director or general partner of the investment adviser.

Instruction. If the investment adviser is a partnership with more than ten general partners, name:

(i) The general partners with the five largest economic interests in the partnership, and, if different, those general partners comprising the management or executive committee of the partnership or exercising similar authority;

(ii) The general partners with significant management responsibilities relating to the fund.

(3) State the names and addresses of all Parents of the investment adviser and show the basis of control of the investment adviser and each Parent by its immediate Parent.

Instructions. 1. If any person named is a corporation, include the percentage of its voting securities owned by its immediate Parent.

2. If any person named is a partnership, name the general partners having the three largest partnership interests (computed by whatever method is appropriate in the particular case).

(4) If the investment adviser is a corporation and if, to the knowledge of the persons making the solicitation or the persons on whose behalf the solicitation is made, any person not named in answer to paragraph (c)(3) of this Item 22 owns, of record or beneficially, ten percent or more of the outstanding voting securities of the investment adviser, indicate that fact and state the name and address of each such person.

(5) Name each officer or director of the Fund who is an officer, employee, director, general partner or shareholder of the investment adviser. As to any officer or director who is not a director or general partner of the investment adviser and who owns securities or has any other material direct or indirect interest in the investment adviser or any other person controlling, controlled by or under common control with the investment adviser, describe the nature of such interest.

(6) Describe briefly and state the approximate amount of, where practicable, any material interest, direct or indirect, of any director of the Fund in any material transactions since the beginning of the most recently completed fiscal year, or in any material proposed transactions, to which the investment adviser of the Fund, any Parent or Subsidiary of the investment adviser (other than another Fund), or any Subsidiary of the Parent of such entities was or is to be a party.

Instructions. 1. Include the name of each person whose interest in any transaction is described and the nature of the relationship by reason of which such interest is required to be described. Where it is not practicable to state the approximate amount of the interest, indicate the approximate amount involved in the transaction.

2. As to any transaction involving the purchase or sale of assets by or to the investment adviser, state the cost of the assets to the purchaser and the cost thereof to the seller if acquired by the seller within two years prior to the transaction.

3. If the interest of any person arises from the position of the person as a partner in a partnership, the proportionate interest of such person in transactions to which the partnership is a party need not be set forth, but state the amount involved in the transaction with the partnership.

4. No information need be given in response to this paragraph (c)(6) of Item 22 with respect to any transaction that is not related to the business or operations of the Fund and to which neither the Fund nor any of its Parents or Subsidiaries is a party.

(7) Disclose any financial condition of the investment adviser that is reasonably likely to impair the financial ability of the adviser to fulfill its commitment to the fund under the proposed investment advisory contract.

(8) Describe the nature of the action to be taken on the investment advisory contract and the reasons therefor, the terms of the contract to be acted upon, and, if the action is an amendment to, or a replacement of, an investment advisory contract, the material differences between the current and proposed contract.

(9) If a change in the investment advisory fee is sought, state:

(i) The aggregate amount of the investment adviser's fee during the last year;

(ii) The amount that the adviser would have received had the proposed fee been in effect; and

(iii) The difference between the aggregate amounts stated in response to paragraphs (c)(9)(i) and (ii) of this Item as a percentage of the amount stated in response to paragraph (c)(9)(i) of this Item.

(10) If the investment adviser acts as such with respect to any other Fund having a similar investment objective, identify and state the size of such other Fund and the rate of the investment adviser's compensation. Also indicate for any Fund identified whether the investment adviser has waived, reduced, or otherwise agreed to reduce its compensation under any applicable contract.

Instruction. Furnish the information in response to this paragraph (c)(10) of Item 22 in tabular form.

(11) Discuss in reasonable detail the material factors and the conclusions with respect thereto that form the basis for the recommendation of the board of directors that the shareholders approve an investment advisory contract. Include the following in the discussion:

(i) Factors relating to both the board's selection of the investment adviser and approval of the advisory fee and any other amounts to be paid by the Fund under the contract. This would include, but not be limited to, a discussion of the nature, extent, and quality of the services to be provided by the investment adviser; the investment performance of the Fund and the investment adviser; the costs of the services to be provided and profits to be realized by the investment adviser and its affiliates from the relationship with the Fund; the extent to which economies of scale would be realized as the Fund grows; and whether fee levels reflect these economies of scale for the benefit of Fund investors. Also indicate in the discussion whether the board relied upon comparisons of the services to be rendered and the amounts to be paid under the contract with those under other investment advisory contracts, such as contracts of the same and other types of clients (*e.g.*, pension funds and other institutional investors). If the board relied upon such comparisons, describe the comparisons that were relied on and how they assisted the board in determining to recommend that the shareholders approve the advisory contract; and

(ii) If applicable, any benefits derived or to be derived by the investment adviser from the relationship with the Fund such as soft dollar arrangements by which brokers provide research to the Fund or its investment adviser in return for allocating Fund brokerage.

Instructions. 1. Conclusory statements or a list of factors will not be considered sufficient disclosure. Relate the factors to the specific circumstances of the Fund and the investment advisory contract for which approval is sought and state how the board evaluated each factor. For example, it is not sufficient to state that the board considered the amount of the investment advisory fee without stating what the board concluded about the amount of the fee and how that affected its determination to recommend approval of the contract.

2. If any factor enumerated in paragraph (c)(11)(i) of this Item 22 is not relevant to the board's evaluation of the investment advisory contract for which approval is sought, not this and explain the reasons why that factor is not relevant.

(12) Describe any arrangement or understanding made in connection with the proposed investment advisory contract with respect to the composition of the board of directors of the Fund or the investment adviser or with respect to the selection or appointment of any person to any office with either such company.

(13) For the most recently completed fiscal year, state:

(i) The aggregate amount of commissions paid to any Affiliated Broker; and

(ii) The percentage of the Fund's aggregate brokerage commissions paid to any such Affiliated Broker.

Instruction. Identify each Affiliated Broker and the relationships that cause the broker to be an Affiliated Broker.

(14) Disclose the amount of any fees paid by the Fund to the investment adviser, its affiliated persons or any affiliated person of such person during the most recent fiscal year for services provided to the Fund (other than under the investment advisory contract or for brokerage commissions). State whether these services will continue to be provided after the investment advisory contract is approved.

(d) *Approval of Distribution Plan.* If action is to be taken with respect to a Distribution Plan, include the following information in the proxy statement.

Instruction. Furnish information on a prospective basis to the extent applicable.

(1) Describe the nature of the action to be taken on the Distribution Plan and the reason therefor, the terms of the Distribution Plan to be acted upon, and, if the action is an amendment to, or a replacement of, a Distribution Plan, the material differences between the current and proposed Distribution Plan.

(2) If the Fund has a Distribution Plan in effect:

(i) Provide the date that the Distribution Plan was adopted and the date of the last amendment, if any;

(ii) Disclose the persons to whom payments may be made under the Distribution Plan, the rate of the distribution fee and the purposes for which such fee may be used;

(iii) Disclose the amount of distribution fees paid by the Fund pursuant to the plan during its most recent fiscal year, both in the aggregate and as a percentage of the Fund's average net assets during the period;

(iv) Disclose the name of, and the amount of any payments made under the Distribution Plan by the Fund during its most recent fiscal year to, any person who is an affiliated person of the Fund, its investment adviser, principal underwriter, or Administrator, an affiliated person of such person, or a person that during the most recent fiscal year received 10% or more of the aggregate amount paid under the Distribution Plan by the Fund;

(v) Describe any action taken with respect to the Distribution Plan since the beginning of the Fund's most recent fiscal year by the board of directors of the Fund; and

(vi) If a Distribution Plan was or is to be terminated or not renewed for any reason, state the date or prospective date of such termination or non-renewal, identify the parties involved, and describe the circumstances of such termination or non-renewal.

(3) Describe briefly and state the approximate amount of, where practicable, any material interest, direct or indirect, of any director or nominee for election as a director of the Fund in any material transactions since the beginning of the most recently completed fiscal year, or in any material proposed transactions, to which any person identified in response to Item 22(d)(2)(iv) was or is to be a party.

Instructions. 1. Include the name of each person whose interest in any transaction is described and the nature of the relationship by reason of which such interest is required to be described. Where it is not practicable to state the approximate amount of the interest, indicate the approximate amount involved in the transaction.

2. As to any transaction involving the purchase or sale of assets, state the cost of the assets to the purchaser and the cost thereof to the seller if acquired by the seller within two years prior to the transaction.

3. If the interest of any person arises from the position of the person as a partner in a partnership, the proportionate interest of such person in transactions to which the partnership is a party need not be set forth but state the amount involved in the transaction with the partnership.

4. No information need be given in response to this paragraph (d)(3) of Item 22 with respect to any transaction that is not related to the business or operations of the Fund and to which neither the Fund nor any of its Parents or Subsidiaries is a party.

(4) Discuss in reasonable detail the material factors and the conclusions with respect thereto which form the basis for the conclusion of the board of directors that there is a reasonable likelihood that the proposed Distribution Plan (or amendment thereto) will benefit the Fund and its shareholders.

Instruction. Conclusory statements or a list of factors will not be considered sufficient disclosure.

Item 23. Delivery of Documents to Security Holders Sharing an Address

If one annual report to security holders, proxy statement, or Notice of Internet Availability of Proxy Materials is being delivered to two or more security holders who share an address in accordance with Rule 14a–3(e)(1), furnish the following information:

(a) State that only one annual report to security holders, proxy statement, or Notice of Internet Availability of Proxy Materials, as applicable, is being delivered to multiple security holders sharing an address unless the registrant has received contrary instructions from one or more of the security holders;

(b) Undertake to deliver promptly upon written or oral request a separate copy of the annual report to security holders, proxy statement, or Notice of Internet Availability of Proxy Materials, as applicable, to a security holder at a shared address to which a single copy of the documents was delivered and provide instructions as to how a security holder can notify the registrant that the security holder wishes to receive a separate copy of an annual report to security holders, proxy statement, or Notice of Internet Availability of Proxy Materials, as applicable;

(c) Provide the phone number and mailing address to which a security holder can direct a notification to the registrant that the security holder wishes to receive a separate annual report to security holders, proxy statement, or Notice of Internet Availability of Proxy Materials, as applicable, in the future; and

(d) Provide instructions how security holders sharing an address can request delivery of a single copy of annual reports to security holders, proxy statements, or Notices of Internet Availability of Proxy Materials if they are receiving multiple copies of annual reports to security holders, proxy statements, or Notices of Internet Availability of Proxy Materials.

Item 24. Shareholder Approval of Executive Compensation.

Registrants required to provide any of the separate shareholder votes pursuant to Rule 14a–21 shall disclose that they are providing each such vote as required pursuant to section 14A of the Securities Exchange Act (15 U.S.C. 78n–1), briefly explain the general effect of each vote, such as whether each such vote is non–binding, and, when applicable, disclose the current frequency of shareholder advisory votes on executive compensation required by Rule 14a–21(a) and when the next such shareholder advisory vote will occur.

Item 25. Exhibits.

Provide the legal opinion required to be filed by Item 402(u)(4)(i) of Regulation S–K (17 CFR 229.402(u)) in an exhibit to this Schedule 14A.

UB UNIVERSAL BUSINESS CORPORATION **Proxy**

270 Universal Center, Horizon, California 91770

This Proxy is Solicited on Behalf of the Board of Directors.

The undersigned hereby appoints John Red, Mary Blue, and Lee White as Proxies, each with the power to appoint his or her substitute, and hereby authorizes them to represent and to vote, as designated below, all the shares of common stock of Universal Business held on record by the undersigned on October 23, 1980, at the annual meeting of shareholders to be held on December 20, 1980 or any adjournment thereof.

1. ELECTION OF DIRECTORS FOR all nominees listed below *(except as marked to the contrary below)* ☐ WITHHOLD AUTHORITY to vote for all nominees listed below ☐

(INSTRUCTION To withhold authority to vote for any individual nominee strike a line through the nominee's name in the list below)

J. Allen, S. Brown, J. Doe, J. Green, G. Johansen, A. Jones, M. Roe, J. Smith and M. Stanton

2. PROPOSAL TO APPROVE THE APPOINTMENT OF DOLLAR AND CENTS as the independent public accountants of the corporation

☐ FOR ☐ AGAINST ☐ ABSTAIN

3. STOCKHOLDER PROPOSAL RELATING TO FORM AND CONTENT OF POST-MEETING REPORTS:

☐ FOR ☐ AGAINST ☐ ABSTAIN

[C6891]

4. In their discretion the Proxies are authorized to vote upon such other business as may properly come before the meeting

This proxy when properly executed will be voted in the manner directed herein by the undersigned stockholder. If no direction is made, this proxy will be voted for Proposals 1, 2, and 3.

Please sign exactly as name appears below. When shares are held by joint tenants, both should sign. When signing as attorney, as executor, administrator, trustee or guardian, please give full title as such. If a corporation, please sign in full corporate name by President or other authorized officer. If a partnership please sign in partnership name by authorized person.

SAMPLE CARD A

DATED ________________ 1980

PLEASE MARK SIGN DATE AND RETURN THE PROXY CARD PROMPTLY USING THE ENCLOSED ENVELOPE

____
Signature

____
Signature if held jointly

[C6892]

UB UNIVERSAL BUSINESS CORPORATION **Proxy**

270 Universal Center, Horizon, California 91770

This Proxy is Solicited on Behalf of the Board of Directors.

The undersigned hereby appoints John Red, Mary Blue, and Lee White as Proxies, each with the power to appoint his or her substitute, and hereby authorizes them to represent and to vote, as designated below, all the shares of common stock of Universal Business held on record by the undersigned on October 23, 1980, at the annual meeting of shareholders to be held on December 20, 1980 or any adjournment thereof.

1. ELECTION OF DIRECTORS FOR all nominees listed below *(except as marked to the contrary below)* ☐ WITHHOLD AUTHORITY to vote for all nominees listed below ☐

(INSTRUCTION To withhold authority to vote for any individual nominee write that nominee's name on the space provided below)

J. Allen, S. Brown, J. Doe, J. Green, G. Johansen, A. Jones, M. Roe, J. Smith and M. Stanton

2. PROPOSAL TO APPROVE THE APPOINTMENT OF DOLLAR AND CENTS as the independent public accountants of the corporation

☐ FOR ☐ AGAINST ☐ ABSTAIN

3. STOCKHOLDER PROPOSAL RELATING TO FORM AND CONTENT OF POST-MEETING REPORTS:

☐ FOR ☐ AGAINST ☐ ABSTAIN

[C6894]

4. In their discretion the Proxies are authorized to vote upon such other business as may properly come before the meeting

This proxy when properly executed will be voted in the manner directed herein by the undersigned stockholder. If no direction is made, this proxy will be voted for Proposals 1, 2, and 3.

Please sign exactly as name appears below. When shares are held by joint tenants, both should sign. When signing as attorney, as executor, administrator, trustee or guardian, please give full title as such. If a corporation, please sign in full corporate name by President or other authorized officer. If a partnership please sign in partnership name by authorized person.

SAMPLE CARD B

DATED ______________ 1980

PLEASE MARK SIGN DATE AND RETURN THE PROXY CARD PROMPTLY USING THE ENCLOSED ENVELOPE

Signature

Signature if held jointly

[C6893]

UB **UNIVERSAL BUSINESS CORPORATION** **Proxy**

270 Universal Center, Horizon, California 91770

This Proxy Is Solicited on Behalf of the Board of Directors.

The undersigned hereby appoints John Red, Mary Blue, and Lee White as Proxies, each with the power to appoint his or her substitute, and hereby authorizes them to represent and to vote, as designated below, all the shares of common stock of Universal Business held on record by the undersigned on October 23, 1980, at the annual meeting of shareholders to be held on December 20, 1980 or any adjournment thereof.

1. ELECTION OF DIRECTORS — FOR all nominees listed below *(except as marked to the contrary below)* ☐ — WITHHOLD AUTHORITY to vote for all nominees listed below ☐

(INSTRUCTION To withhold authority to vote for any individual nominee mark the box next to the nominee's name below)

☐ J. Allen ☐ S. Brown ☐ J. Doe ☐ J. Green ☐ G. Johansen ☐ A. Jones ☐ M. Roe ☐ J. Smith ☐ M. Stanton

2. PROPOSAL TO APPROVE THE APPOINTMENT OF DOLLAR AND CENTS as the independent public accountants of the corporation

☐ FOR ☐ AGAINST ☐ AGAINST

3. STOCKHOLDER PROPOSAL RELATING TO FORM AND CONTENT OF POST-MEETING REPORTS:

☐ FOR ☐ ABSTAIN ☐ ABSTAIN

[C6896]

4. In their discretion the Proxies are authorized to vote upon such other business as may properly come before the meeting.

This proxy when properly executed will be voted in the manner directed herein by the undersigned stockholder. If no direction is made, this proxy will be voted for Proposals 1, 2, and 3.

Please sign exactly as name appears below. When shares are held by joint tenants, both should sign. When signing as attorney, as executor, administrator, trustee or guardian, please give full title as such. If a corporation, please sign in full corporate name by President or other authorized officer. If a partnership please sign in partnership name by authorized person.

SAMPLE CARD C

DATED ______________ 1980

____
Signature

____
Signature if held jointly

PLEASE MARK SIGN DATE AND RETURN THE PROXY CARD PROMPTLY USING THE ENCLOSED ENVELOPE

[C6895]

Rule 14a–102. [Reserved]

Rule 14a–103. Notice of exempt solicitation

U.S. Securities and Exchange Commission
Washington, DC 20549
Notice of Exempt Solicitation

1. Name of the Registrant:

2. Name of person relying on exemption:

3. Address of person relying on exemption:

4. Written materials. Attach written material required to be submitted pursuant to Rule 14a–6(g)(1).

Rule 14a–104. Notice of exempt preliminary roll-up communication. Information regarding ownership interests and any potential conflicts of interest to be included in statements submitted by or on behalf of a person pursuant to Rule 14a–2(b)(4) and Rule 14a–6(n)

United States Securities and Exchange Commission Washington, D.C. 20549
Notice of Exempt Preliminary Roll–Up Communication

1. Name of registrant appearing on Securities Act of 1933 registration statement for the roll-up transaction (or, if registration statement has not been filed, name of entity into which partnerships are to be rolled up):

2. Name of partnership that is the subject of the proposed roll-up transaction:

3. Name of person relying on exemption:

4. Address of person relying on exemption:

5. Ownership interest of security holder in partnership that is the subject of the proposed roll-up transaction:

NOTE: To the extent that the holder owns securities in any other entities involved in this roll-up transaction, disclosure of these interests also should be made.

6. Describe any and all relations of the holder to the parties to the transaction or to the transaction itself:

a. The holder is engaged in the business of buying and selling limited partnership interests in the secondary market would be adversely affected if the roll-up transaction were completed.

b. The holder would suffer direct (or indirect) material financial injury if the roll-up transaction were completed since it is a service provider to an affected limited partnership.

c. The holder is engaged in another transaction that may be competitive with the pending roll-up transaction.

d. Any other relations to the parties involved in the transaction or to the transaction itself, or any benefits enjoyed by the holder not shared on a pro rata basis by all other holders of the same class of securities of the partnership that is the subject of the proposed roll-up transaction.

Rule 14b–1. Obligation of registered brokers and dealers in connection with the prompt forwarding of certain communications to beneficial owners

(a) *Definitions.* Unless the context otherwise requires, all terms used in this rule shall have the same meanings as in the Act and, with respect to proxy soliciting material, as in Rule 14a–1 thereunder and, with respect to information statements, as in Rule 14c–1 thereunder. In addition, as used in this rule, the term "registrant" means:

(1) The issuer of a class of securities registered pursuant to Section 12 of the Act; or

(2) An investment company registered under the Investment Company Act of 1940.

(b) *Dissemination and Beneficial Owner Information Requirements.* A broker or dealer registered under Section 15 of the Act shall comply with the following requirements for disseminating certain communications to beneficial owners and providing beneficial owner information to registrants.

(1) The broker or dealer shall respond, by first class mail or other equally prompt means, directly to the registrant no later than seven business days after the date it receives an inquiry made in accordance with Rule 14a–13(a) or Rule 14c–7(a) by indicating, by means of a search card or otherwise:

(i) The approximate number of customers of the broker or dealer who are beneficial owners of the registrant's securities that are held of record by the broker, dealer, or its nominee;

(ii) The number of customers of the broker or dealer who are beneficial owners of the registrant's securities who have objected to disclosure of their names, addresses, and securities positions if the registrant has indicated, pursuant to Rule 14a–13(a)(1)(ii)(A) or Rule 14c–7(a)(1)(ii)(A), that it will distribute the annual report to security holders to beneficial owners of its securities whose names, addresses and securities positions are disclosed pursuant to paragraph (b)(3) of this rule; and

(iii) The identity of the designated agent of the broker or dealer, if any, acting on its behalf in fulfilling its obligations under paragraph (b)(3) of this rule; *Provided, however,* that if the broker or dealer has informed the registrant that a designated office(s) or department(s) is to receive such inquiries, receipt for purposes of paragraph (b)(1) of this rule shall mean receipt by such designated office(s) or department(s).

(2) The broker or dealer shall, upon receipt of the proxy, other proxy soliciting material, information statement, and/or annual report to security holders from the registrant or other soliciting person, forward such materials to its customers who are beneficial owners of the registrant's securities no later than five business days after receipt of the proxy material, information statement or annual report to security holders.

NOTE TO PARAGRAPH (b)(2): At the request of a registrant, or on its own initiative so long as the registrant does not object, a broker or dealer may, but is not required to, deliver one annual report to security holders, proxy statement, information statement, or Notice of Internet Availability of Proxy Materials to more than one beneficial owner sharing an address if the requirements set forth in Rule 14a–3(e)(1) (with respect to annual reports to security holders, proxy statements, and Notices of Internet Availability of Proxy Materials) and Rule 14c–3(c) (with respect to annual reports to security holders, information statements, and Notices of Internet Availability of Proxy Materials) applicable to registrants, with the exception of Rule 14a–3(e)(1)(i)(E), are satisfied instead by the broker or dealer.

(3) The broker or dealer shall, through its agent or directly:

(i) Provide the registrant, upon the registrant's request, with the names, addresses, and securities positions, compiled as of a date specified in the registrant's request which is no earlier than five business days after the date the registrant's request is received, of its customers who are beneficial owners of the registrant's securities and who have not objected to disclosure of such information; *Provided, however,* that if the broker or dealer has informed the registrant that a designated office(s) or department(s) is to receive such requests, receipt shall mean receipt by such designated office(s) or department(s); and

(ii) Transmit the data specified in paragraph (b)(3)(i) of this rule to the registrant no later than five business days after the record date or other date specified by the registrant.

NOTE 1. Where a broker or dealer employs a designated agent to act on its behalf in performing the obligations imposed on the broker or dealer by paragraph (b)(3) of this rule, the five business day time period for determining the date as of which the beneficial owner information is to be compiled is calculated from the date the designated agent receives the registrant's request. In complying with the registrant's request for beneficial owner information under paragraph (b)(3) of this rule, a broker or dealer need only supply the registrant with the names, addresses and securities positions of non-objecting beneficial owners.

NOTE 2. If a broker or dealer receives a registrant's request less than five business days before the requested compilation date, it must provide a list compiled as of a date that is no more than five business days after receipt and transmit the list within five business days after the compilation date.

(c) *Exceptions to Dissemination and Beneficial Owner Information Requirements.* A broker or dealer registered under Section 15 of the Act shall be subject to the following with respect to its dissemination and beneficial owner information requirements.

(1) With regard to beneficial owners of exempt employee benefit plan securities, the broker or dealer shall:

(i) Not include information in its response pursuant to paragraph (b)(1) of this rule or forward proxies (or in lieu thereof requests for voting instructions), proxy soliciting material, information statements, or annual reports to security holders pursuant to paragraph (b)(2) of this rule to such beneficial owners; and

(ii) Not include in its response, pursuant to paragraph (b)(3) of this rule, data concerning such beneficial owners.

(2) A broker or dealer need not satisfy:

(i) Its obligations under paragraphs (b)(2), (b)(3) and (d) of this rule if the registrant or other soliciting person, as applicable, does not provide assurance of reimbursement of the broker's or dealer's reasonable expenses, both direct and indirect, incurred in connection with performing the obligations imposed by paragraphs (b)(2), (b)(3) and (d) of this rule; or

(ii) Its obligation under paragraph (b)(2) of this rule to forward annual reports to security holders to non-objecting beneficial owners identified by the broker or dealer, through its agent or directly, pursuant to paragraph (b)(3) of this rule if the registrant notifies the broker or dealer pursuant to Rule 14a–13(c) or Rule 14c–7(c) that the registrant will send the annual report to security holders to such non-objecting beneficial owners identified by the broker or dealer and delivered in a list to the registrant pursuant to paragraph (b)(3) of this rule.

(3) In its response pursuant to paragraph (b)(1) of this rule, a broker or dealer shall not include information about annual reports to security holders, proxy statements or information statements that will not be delivered to security holders sharing an address because of the broker or dealer's reliance on the procedures referred to in the Note to paragraph (b)(2) of this rule.

(d) *Compliance with Rule 14a–16.* Upon receipt from the soliciting person of all of the information listed in Rule 14a–16(d), the broker or dealer shall:

(1) Prepare and send a Notice of Internet Availability of Proxy Materials containing the information required in paragraph (e) of this rule to beneficial owners no later than:

(i) With respect to a registrant, 40 calendar days prior to the security holder meeting date or, if no meeting is to be held, 40 calendar days prior to the date the votes, consents, or authorizations may be used to effect the corporate action; and

(ii) With respect to a soliciting person other than the registrant, the later of:

(A) 40 calendar days prior to the security holder meeting date or, if no meeting is to be held, 40 calendar days prior to the date the votes, consents, or authorizations may be used to effect the corporate action; or

(B) 10 calendar days after the date that the registrant first sends its proxy statement or Notice of Internet Availability of Proxy Materials to security holders.

(2) Establish a Web site at which beneficial owners are able to access the broker or dealer's request for voting instructions and, at the broker or dealer's option, establish a Web site at which beneficial owners are able to access the proxy statement and other soliciting materials, provided that such Web sites are maintained in a manner consistent with paragraphs (b), (c), and (k) of Rule 14a–16;

(3) Upon receipt of a request from the registrant or other soliciting person, send to security holders specified by the registrant or other soliciting person a copy of the request for voting instructions accompanied by a copy of the intermediary's Notice of Internet Availability of Proxy Materials 10 calendar days or more after the broker or dealer sends its Notice of Internet Availability of Proxy Materials pursuant to paragraph (d)(1); and

(4) Upon receipt of a request for a copy of the materials from a beneficial owner:

(i) Request a copy of the soliciting materials from the registrant or other soliciting person, in the form requested by the beneficial owner, within three business days after receiving the beneficial owner's request;

(ii) Forward a copy of the soliciting materials to the beneficial owner, in the form requested by the beneficial owner, within three business days after receiving the materials from the registrant or other soliciting person; and

(iii) Maintain records of security holder requests to receive a paper or e-mail copy of the proxy materials in connection with future proxy solicitations and provide copies of the proxy materials to a security holder who has made such a request for all securities held in the account of that security holder until the security holder revokes such request.

(5) Notwithstanding any other provisions in this paragraph (d), if the broker or dealer receives copies of the proxy statement and annual report to security holders (if applicable) from the soliciting

person with instructions to forward such materials to beneficial owners, the broker or dealer:

(i) Shall either:

(A) Prepare a Notice of Internet Availability of Proxy Materials and forward it with the proxy statement and annual report to security holders (if applicable); or

(B) Incorporate any information required in the Notice of Internet Availability of Proxy Materials that does not appear in the proxy statement into the broker or dealer's request for voting instructions to be sent with the proxy statement and annual report (if applicable);

(ii) Need not comply with the following provisions:

(A) The timing provisions of paragraph (d)(1)(ii); and

(B) Paragraph (d)(4); and

(iii) Need not include in its Notice of Internet Availability of Proxy Materials or request for voting instructions the following disclosures:

(A) Legends 1 and 3 in Rule 14a–16(d)(1); and

(B) Instructions on how to request a copy of the proxy materials.

(e) *Content of Notice of Internet Availability of Proxy Materials*. The broker or dealer's Notice of Internet Availability of Proxy Materials shall:

(1) Include all information, as it relates to beneficial owners, required in a registrant's Notice of Internet Availability of Proxy Materials under Rule 14a–16(d), provided that the broker or dealer shall provide its own, or its agent's, toll-free telephone number, an e-mail address, and an Internet Web site to service requests for copies from beneficial owners;

(2) Include a brief description, if applicable, of the rules that permit the broker or dealer to vote the securities if the beneficial owner does not return his or her voting instructions; and

(3) Otherwise be prepared and sent in a manner consistent with paragraphs (e), (f), and (g) of Rule 14a–16.

Rule 14b–2. Obligation of banks, associations and other entities that exercise fiduciary powers in connection with the prompt forwarding of certain communications to beneficial owners

(a) *Definitions.* Unless the context otherwise requires, all terms used in this rule shall have the same meanings as in the Act and, with respect to proxy soliciting material, as in Rule 14a–1 thereunder and, with respect to information statements, as in Rule 14c–1 thereunder. In addition, as used in this rule, the following terms shall apply:

(1) The term *banks* means a bank, association, or other entity that exercises fiduciary powers.

(2) The term *beneficial owner* includes any person who has or shares, pursuant to an instrument, agreement, or otherwise, the power to vote, or to direct the voting of a security.

NOTE 1. If more than one person shares voting power, the provisions of the instrument creating that voting power shall govern with respect to whether consent to disclosure of beneficial owner information has been given.

NOTE 2. If more than one person shares voting power or if the instrument creating that voting power provides that such power shall be exercised by different persons depending on the nature of the corporate action involved, all persons entitled to exercise such power shall be deemed beneficial owners; *Provided, however,* that only one such beneficial owner need be designated among the beneficial owners to receive proxies or requests for voting instructions, other proxy soliciting material, information statements, and/or annual reports to security holders, if the person so designated assumes the obligation to disseminate, in a timely manner, such materials to the other beneficial owners.

(3) The term *registrant* means:

(i) The issuer of a class of securities registered pursuant to Section 12 of the Act; or

(ii) An investment company registered under the Investment Company Act of 1940.

(b) *Dissemination and Beneficial Owner Information Requirements.* A bank shall comply with the following requirements for disseminating certain communications to beneficial owners and providing beneficial owner information to registrants.

(1) The bank shall:

(i) Respond, by first class mail or other equally prompt means, directly to the registrant, no later than one business day after the date it receives an inquiry made in accordance with Rule 14a–13(a) or Rule 14c–7(a) by indicating the name and address of each of its respondent banks that holds the registrant's securities on behalf of beneficial owners, if any; and

(ii) Respond, by first class mail or other equally prompt means, directly to the registrant no later than seven business days after the date it receives an inquiry made in accordance with Rule 14a–13(a) or Rule 14c–7(a) by indicating, by means of a search card or otherwise:

(A) The approximate number of customers of the bank who are beneficial owners of the registrant's securities that are held of record by the bank or its nominee;

(B) If the registrant has indicated, pursuant to Rule 14a–13(a)(1)(ii)(A) or Rule 14c–7(a)(1)(ii)(A), that it will distribute the annual report to security holders to beneficial owners of its securities whose names, addresses, and securities positions are disclosed pursuant to paragraphs (b)(4)(ii) and (iii) of this rule:

(1) With respect to customer accounts opened on or before December 28, 1986, the number of beneficial owners of the registrant's securities who have affirmatively consented to disclosure of their names, addresses, and securities positions; and

(2) With respect to customer accounts opened after December 28, 1986, the number of beneficial owners of the registrant's securities who have not objected to disclosure of their names, addresses, and securities positions; and

(C) The identity of its designated agent, if any, acting on its behalf in fulfilling its obligations under paragraphs (b)(4)(ii) and (iii) of this rule;

Provided, however, that, if the bank or respondent bank has informed the registrant that a designated office(s) or department(s) is to receive such inquiries, receipt for purposes of paragraphs (b)(1)(i) and (ii) of this rule shall mean receipt by such designated office(s) or department(s).

(2) Where proxies are solicited, the bank shall, within five business days after the record date:

(i) Execute an omnibus proxy, including a power of substitution, in favor of its respondent banks and forward such proxy to the registrant; and

(ii) Furnish a notice to each respondent bank in whose favor an omnibus proxy has been executed that it has executed such a proxy, including a power of substitution, in its favor pursuant to paragraph (b)(2)(i) of this rule.

(3) Upon receipt of the proxy, other proxy soliciting material, information statement, and/or annual report to security holders from the registrant or other soliciting person, the bank shall forward such materials to each beneficial owner on whose behalf it holds securities, no later than five business days after the date it receives such material and, where a proxy is solicited, the bank shall forward, with the other proxy soliciting material and/or the annual report to security holders, either:

(i) A properly executed proxy:

(A) Indicating the number of securities held for such beneficial owner;

(B) Bearing the beneficial owner's account number or other form of identification, together with instructions as to the procedures to vote the securities;

(C) Briefly stating which other proxies, if any, are required to permit securities to be voted under the terms of the instrument creating that voting power or applicable state law; and

(D) Being accompanied by an envelope addressed to the registrant or its agent, if not provided by the registrant; or

(ii) A request for voting instructions (for which registrant's form of proxy may be used and which shall be voted by the record holder bank or respondent bank in accordance with the instructions received), together with an envelope addressed to the record holder bank or respondent bank.

Note to Paragraph (b)(3): At the request of a registrant, or on its own initiative so long as the registrant does not object, a bank may, but is not required to, deliver one annual report to security holders, proxy statement, information statement, or Notice of Internet Availability of Proxy Materials to more than one beneficial owner sharing an address if the requirements set forth in Rule 14a–3(e)(1) (with respect to annual reports to security holders, proxy statements, and Notices of Internet Availability of Proxy Materials) and Rule 14c–3(c) (with respect to annual reports to security holders, information statements, and Notices of Internet Availability of Proxy Materials) applicable to registrants, with the exception of Rule 14a–3(e)(1)(i)(E), are satisfied instead by the bank.

(4) The bank shall:

(i) Respond, by first class mail or other equally prompt means, directly to the registrant no later than one business day after the date it receives an inquiry made in accordance with Rule 14a–13(b)(1) or Rule 14c–7(b)(1) by indicating the name and address of each of its respondent banks that holds the registrant's securities on behalf of beneficial owners, if any;

(ii) Through its agent or directly, provide the registrant, upon the registrant's request, and within the time specified in paragraph (b)(4)(iii) of this rule, with the names, addresses, and securities position, compiled as of a date specified in the registrant's request which is no earlier than five business days after the date the registrant's request is received, of:

(A) With respect to customer accounts opened on or before December 28, 1986, beneficial owners of the registrant's securities on whose behalf it holds securities who have consented affirmatively to disclosure of such information, subject to paragraph (b)(5) of this rule; and

(B) With respect to customer accounts opened after December 28, 1986, beneficial owners of the registrant's securities on whose behalf it holds securities who have not objected to disclosure of such information;

Provided, however, that if the record holder bank or respondent bank has informed the registrant that a designated office(s) or department(s) is to receive such requests, receipt for purposes of paragraphs (b)(4)(i) and (ii) of this rule shall mean receipt by such designated office(s) or department(s); and

(iii) Through its agent or directly, transmit the data specified in paragraph (b)(4)(ii) of this rule to the registrant no later than five business days after the date specified by the registrant.

NOTE 1. Where a record holder bank or respondent bank employs a designated agent to act on its behalf in performing the obligations imposed on it by paragraphs (b)(4)(ii) and (iii) of this rule, the five business day time period for determining the date as of which the beneficial owner information is to be compiled is calculated from the date the designated agent receives the registrant's request. In complying with the registrant's request for beneficial owner information under paragraph (b)(4)(ii) and (iii) of this rule, a record holder bank or respondent bank need only supply the registrant with the names, addresses and securities positions of affirmatively consenting and non-objecting beneficial owners.

NOTE 2. If a record holder bank or respondent bank receives a registrant's request less than five business days before the requested compilation date, it must provide a list compiled as of a date that is no more than five business days after receipt and transmit the list within five business days after the compilation date.

(5) For customer accounts opened on or before December 28, 1986, unless the bank has made a good faith effort to obtain affirmative consent to disclosure of beneficial owner information pursuant to paragraph (b)(4)(ii) of this rule, the bank shall provide such information as to beneficial owners who do not object to disclosure of such information. A good faith effort to obtain affirmative consent to disclosure of beneficial owner information shall include, but shall not be limited to, making an inquiry:

(i) Phrased in neutral language, explaining the purpose of the disclosure and the limitations on the registrant's use thereof;

(ii) Either in at least one mailing separate from other account mailings or in repeated mailings; and

(iii) In a mailing that includes a return card, postage paid enclosure.

(c) *Exceptions to Dissemination and Beneficial Owner Information Requirements.* The bank shall be subject to the following with respect to its dissemination and beneficial owner requirements.

(1) With regard to beneficial owners of exempt employee benefit plan securities, the bank shall not:

(i) Include information in its response pursuant to paragraph (b)(1) of this rule; or forward proxies (or in lieu thereof requests for voting instructions), proxy soliciting material, information statements, or annual reports to security holders pursuant to paragraph (b)(3) of this rule to such beneficial owners; or

(ii) Include in its response pursuant to paragraphs (b)(4) and (b)(5) of this rule data concerning such beneficial owners.

(2) The bank need not satisfy:

(i) Its obligations under paragraphs (b)(2), (b)(3), (b)(4) and (d) of this rule if the registrant or other soliciting person, as applicable, does not provide assurance of reimbursement of its reasonable expenses, both direct and indirect, incurred in connection with performing the obligations imposed by paragraphs (b)(2), (b)(3), (b)(4) and (d) of this rule; or

(ii) Its obligation under paragraph (b)(3) of this rule to forward annual reports to security holders to consenting and non-objecting beneficial owners identified pursuant to paragraphs (b)(4)(ii) and (iii) of this rule if the registrant notifies the record holder bank or respondent bank, pursuant to Rule 14a–13(c) or Rule 14c–7(c), that the registrant will send the annual report to security holders to beneficial owners whose names, addresses and securities positions are disclosed pursuant to paragraphs (b)(4)(ii) and (iii) of this rule.

(3) For the purposes of determining the fees which may be charged to registrants pursuant to Rule 14a–13(b)(5), Rule 14c–7(a)(5), and paragraph (c)(2) of this rule for performing obligations under paragraphs (b)(2), (b)(3), and (b)(4) of this rule: an amount no greater than that permitted to be charged by brokers or dealers for reimbursement of their reasonable expenses, both direct and indirect, incurred in connection with performing the obligations imposed by paragraphs (b)(2) and (b)(3) of Rule 14b–1, shall be deemed to be reasonable.

(4) In its response pursuant to paragraph (b)(1)(ii)(A) of this rule, a bank shall not include information about annual reports to security holders, proxy statements or information statements that will not be delivered to security holders sharing an address because of the bank's reliance on the procedures referred to in the Note to paragraph (b)(3) of this rule.

(d) *Compliance with Rule 14a–16.* Upon receipt from the soliciting person of all of the information listed in Rule 14a–16(d) to the bank, the bank shall:

(1) Prepare and send a Notice of Internet Availability of Proxy Materials containing the information required in paragraph (e) of this rule to beneficial owners no later than:

(i) With respect to a registrant, 40 calendar days prior to the security holder meeting date or, if no meeting is to be held, 40 calendar days prior to the date the votes, consents, or authorizations may be used to effect the corporate action; and

(ii) With respect to a soliciting person other than the registrant, the later of:

(A) 40 calendar days prior to the security holder meeting date or, if no meeting is to be held, 40 calendar days prior to the date the votes, consents, or authorizations may be used to effect the corporate action; or

(B) 10 calendar days after the date that the registrant first sends its proxy statement or Notice of Internet Availability of Proxy Materials to security holders.

(2) Establish a Web site at which beneficial owners are able to access the bank's request for voting instructions and, at the bank's option, establish a Web site at which beneficial owners are able to access the proxy statement and other soliciting materials, provided that such Web sites are maintained in a manner consistent with paragraphs (b), (c), and (k) of Rule 14a–16;

(3) Upon receipt of a request from the registrant or other soliciting person, send to security holders specified by the registrant or other soliciting person a copy of the request for voting instructions accompanied by a copy of the intermediary's Notice of Internet Availability of Proxy Materials 10 days or more after the bank sends its Notice of Internet Availability of Proxy Materials pursuant to paragraph (d)(1); and

(4) Upon receipt of a request for a copy of the materials from a beneficial owner:

(i) Request a copy of the soliciting materials from the registrant or other soliciting person, in the form requested by the beneficial owner, within three business days after receiving the beneficial owner's request;

(ii) Forward a copy of the soliciting materials to the beneficial owner, in the form requested by the beneficial owner, within three business days after receiving the materials from the registrant or other soliciting person; and

(iii) Maintain records of security holder requests to receive a paper or e-mail copy of the proxy materials in connection with future proxy solicitations and provide copies of the proxy materials to a security holder who has made such a request for all securities held in the account of that security holder until the security holder revokes such request.

(5) Notwithstanding any other provisions in this paragraph (d), if the bank receives copies of the proxy statement and annual report to security holders (if applicable) from the soliciting person with instructions to forward such materials to beneficial owners, the bank:

(i) Shall either:

(A) Prepare a Notice of Internet Availability of Proxy Materials and forward it with the proxy statement and annual report to security holders (if applicable); or

(B) Incorporate any information required in the Notice of Internet Availability of Proxy Materials that does not appear in the proxy statement into the bank's request for voting instructions to be sent with the proxy statement and annual report (if applicable);

(ii) Need not comply with the following provisions:

(A) The timing provisions of paragraph (d)(1)(ii); and

(B) Paragraph (d)(4); and

(iii) Need not include in its Notice of Internet Availability of Proxy Materials or request for voting instructions the following disclosures:

(A) Legends 1 and 3 in Rule 14a–16(d)(1); and

(B) Instructions on how to request a copy of the proxy materials.

(e) *Content of Notice of Internet Availability of Proxy Materials.* The bank's Notice of Internet Availability of Proxy Materials shall:

(1) Include all information, as it relates to beneficial owners, required in a registrant's Notice of Internet Availability of Proxy Materials under Rule 14a–16(d), provided that the bank shall provide its own, or its agent's, toll-free telephone number, e-mail address, and Internet Web site to service requests for copies from beneficial owners; and

(2) Otherwise be prepared and sent in a manner consistent with paragraphs (e), (f), and (g) of Rule 14a–16.

REGULATION 14C. DISTRIBUTION OF INFORMATION PURSUANT TO SECTION 14(c)

ATTENTION ELECTRONIC FILERS

THIS REGULATION SHOULD BE READ IN CONJUNCTION WITH REGULATION S–T (17 CFR 232), WHICH GOVERNS THE PREPARATION AND SUBMISSION OF DOCUMENTS IN ELECTRONIC FORMAT. MANY PROVISIONS RELATING TO THE PREPARATION AND SUBMISSION OF DOCUMENTS IN PAPER FORMAT CONTAINED IN THIS REGULATION ARE SUPERSEDED BY THE PROVISIONS OF REGULATION S–T FOR DOCUMENTS REQUIRED TO BE FILED IN ELECTRONIC FORMAT.

Rule 14c–1. Definitions

Unless the context otherwise requires, all terms used in this regulation have the same meanings as in the Act or elsewhere in the general rules and regulations thereunder. In addition, the following definitions apply unless the context otherwise requires:

(a) *Associate.* The term "associate" used to indicate a relationship with any person, means:

(1) Any corporation or organization (other than the registrant or a majority-owned subsidiary of the registrant) of which such person is an officer or partner or is, directly or indirectly, the beneficial owner of 10 percent or more of any class of equity securities,

(2) Any trust or other estate in which such person has a substantial beneficial interest or as to which such person serves as trustee or in a similar fiduciary capacity, and

(3) Any relative or spouse of such person, or any relative of such spouse, who has the same home as such person or who is a director or officer of the registrant or any of its parents or subsidiaries.

(b) *Employee Benefit Plan.* For purposes of Rule 14c–7, the term "employee benefit plan" means any purchase, savings, option, bonus, appreciation, profit sharing, thrift, incentive, pension or similar plan primarily for employees, directors, trustees or officers.

(c) *Entity That Exercises Fiduciary Powers.* The term "entity that exercises fiduciary powers" means any entity that holds securities in nominee name or otherwise on behalf of a beneficial owner but does not include a clearing agency registered pursuant to section 17A of the Act, or a broker or a dealer.

(d) *Exempt Employee Benefit Plan Securities.* For purposes of Rule 14c–7, the term "exempt employee benefit plan securities" means:

(1) Securities of the registrant held by an employee benefit plan, as defined in paragraph (b) of this rule, where such plan is established by the registrant; or

(2) If notice regarding the current distribution of information statements has been given pursuant to Rule 14c–7(a)(1)(ii)(C) or if notice regarding the current request for a list of names, addresses and securities positions of beneficial owners has been given pursuant to Rule 14c–7(b)(3), securities of the registrant held by an employee bene-

fit plan, as defined in paragraph (b) of this rule, where such plan is established by an affiliate of the registrant.

(e) *Information Statement.* The term "information statement" means the statement required by Rule 14c–2, whether or not contained in a single document.

(f) *Last Fiscal Year.* The term "last fiscal year" of the registrant means the last fiscal year of the registrant ending prior to the date of the meeting with respect to which an information statement is required to be distributed, or if the information statement involves consents or authorizations in lieu of a meeting, the earliest date on which they may be used to effect corporate action.

(g) *Proxy.* The term "proxy" includes every proxy, consent or authorization within the meaning of Section 14(a) of the Act. The consent or authorization may take the form of failure to object or to dissent.

(h) *Record Date.* The term "record date" means the date as of which the record holders of securities entitled to vote at a meeting or by written consent or authorization shall be determined.

(i) *Record Holder.* For purposes of Rule 14c–7, the term "record holder" means any broker, dealer, voting trustee, bank, association or other entity that exercises fiduciary powers which holds securities of record in nominee name or otherwise or as a participant in a clearing agency registered pursuant to Section 17A of the Act.

(j) *Registrant.* The term "registrant" means:

(1) The issuer of a class of securities registered pursuant to Section 12 of the Act; or

(2) An investment company registered under the Investment Company Act of 1940 that has made a public offering of its securities.

(k) *Respondent Bank.* For purposes of Rule 14c–7, the term "respondent bank" means any bank, association or other entity that exercises fiduciary powers which holds securities on behalf of beneficial owners and deposits such securities for safekeeping with another bank, association or other entity that exercises fiduciary powers.

Rule 14c–2. Distribution of information statement

(a)(1) In connection with every annual or other meeting of the holders of the class of securities registered pursuant to section 12 of the Act or of a class of securities issued by an investment company registered under the Investment Company Act of 1940 that has made a public offering of securities, including the taking of corporate action by the written authorization or consent of security holders, the registrant shall transmit to every security holder of the class that is entitled to vote or give an authorization or consent in regard to any matter to be acted upon and from whom proxy authorization or consent is not solicited on behalf of the registrant pursuant to section 14(a) of the Act:

(i) A written information statement containing the information specified in Schedule 14C (Rule 14c–101);

(ii) A publicly-filed information statement, in the form and manner described in Rule 14c–3(d), containing the information specified in Schedule 14C (Rule 14c–101); or

(iii) A written information statement included in a registration statement filed under the Securities Act of 1933 on Form S–4 or F–4 (17 CFR 239.25 or 17 CFR 239.34) or Form N–14 (17 CFR 239.23) and containing the information specified in such Form.

(2) Notwithstanding paragraph (a)(1) of this rule:

(i) In the case of a class of securities in unregistered or bearer form, such statements need to be transmitted only to those security holders whose names are known to the registrant; and

(ii) No such statements need to be transmitted to a security holder if a registrant would be excused from delivery of an annual report to security holders or a proxy statement under Rule 14a–3(e)(2) if such rule were applicable.

(b) The information statement shall be sent or given at least 20 calendar days prior to the meeting date or, in the case of corporate action taken pursuant to the consents or authorizations of security holders, at least 20 calendar days prior to the earliest date on which the corporate action may be taken.

(c) If a transaction is a roll-up transaction as defined in Item 901(c) of Regulation S–K and is registered (or authorized to be registered) on Form S–4 (17 CFR 229.25) or Form F–4 (17 CFR 229.34), the information statement must be distributed to security holders no later than the lesser of 60 calendar days prior to the date on which the meeting of security holders is held or action is taken, or the maximum number of days permitted for giving notice under applicable state law.

(d) A registrant shall transmit an information statement to security holders pursuant to paragraph (a) of this rule by satisfying the requirements set forth in Rule 14a–16; provided, however, that the registrant shall revise the information required in the Notice of Internet Availability of Proxy Materials, including changing the title of that notice, to reflect the fact that the registrant is not soliciting proxies for the meeting.

Rule 14c–3. Annual report to be furnished security holders

(a) If the information statement relates to an annual (or special meeting in lieu of the annual) meeting, or written consent in lieu of such meeting, of security holders at which directors of the registrant, other than an investment company registered under the Investment Company Act of 1940, are to be elected, it shall be accompanied or preceded by an annual report to security holders:

(1) The annual report to security holders shall contain the information specified in paragraphs (b)(1) through (b)(11) of Rule 14a–3.

(2) [Reserved]

(b) Seven copies of the report sent to security holders pursuant to this rule shall be mailed to the Commission, solely for its information, not later than the date on which such report is first sent or given to security holders or the date on which preliminary copies or definitive copies, if preliminary filing was not required, of the information statement are filed with the Commission pursuant to Rule 14c–5, whichever date is later. The report is not deemed to be "filed" with the Commission or subject to this regulation otherwise than as provided in this rule, or to the liabilities of Section 18 of the Act, except to the extent that the registrant specifically requests that it be treated as a part of the information statement or incorporates it in the information statement or other filed report by reference.

(c) A registrant will be considered to have delivered a Notice of Internet Availability of Proxy Materials, annual report to security holders or information statement to security holders of record who share an address if the requirements set forth in Rule 14a–3(e)(1) are satisfied with respect to the Notice of Internet Availability of Proxy Materials, annual report to security holders or information statement, as applicable.

(d) A registrant shall furnish an annual report to security holders pursuant to paragraph (a) of this rule by satisfying the requirements set forth in Rule 14a–16.

Rule 14c–4. Presentation of information in information statement

(a) The information included in the information statement shall be clearly presented and the statements made shall be divided into groups according to subject matter and the various groups of statements shall be preceded by appropriate headings. The order of items and sub-items in the schedule need not be followed. Where practicable and appropriate, the information shall be presented in tabular form. All amounts shall be stated in figures. Information required by more than one applicable item need not be repeated. No statement need be made in response to any item or sub-item which is inapplicable.

(b) Any information required to be included in the information statement as to terms of securities or other subject matters which from a standpoint of practical necessity must be determined in the future may be stated in terms of present knowledge and intention. Subject to the foregoing, information which is not known to the registrant and which it is not reasonably within the power of the registrant to ascertain or procure may be omitted, if a brief statement of the circumstances rendering such information unavailable is made.

(c) All printed information statements shall be in roman type at least as large and as legible as 10–point modern type except that to the extent necessary for convenient presentation, financial statements and other tabular data, but not the notes thereto, may be in roman type at least as large and as legible as 8–point modern type. All such type shall be leaded at least 2 points.

(d) Where an information statement is delivered through an electronic medium, issuers may satisfy legibility requirements applicable to printed documents, such as type size and font, by presenting all required information in a format readily communicated to investors.

Rule 14c–5. Filing requirements

(a) *Preliminary Information Statement.* Five preliminary copies of the information statement shall be filed with the Commission at least 10 calendar days prior to the date definitive copies of such statement are first sent or given to security holders, or such shorter period prior to that date as the Commission may authorize upon a showing of good cause therefor. In computing the 10–day period, the filing date of the preliminary copies is to be counted as the first day and the 11th day is the date on which definitive copies of the information statement may be sent to security holders. A registrant, however, shall not file with the Commission a preliminary information statement if it relates to an annual (or special meeting in lieu of the annual) meeting, of security holders at which the only matters to be acted upon are:

(1) The election of directors;

(2) The election, approval or ratification of accountant(s);

(3) A security holder proposal identified in the registrant's information statement pursuant to Item 4 of Schedule 14C (Rule 14c–101); and/or

(4) The approval or ratification of a plan as defined in paragraph (a)(6)(ii) of Item 402 of Regulation S–K or amendments to such a plan.

This exclusion from filing a preliminary information statement does not apply if the registrant comments upon or refers to a solicitation in opposition in connection with the meeting in its information statement.

NOTE 1: The filing of revised material does not recommence the ten day time period unless the revised material contains material revisions or material new proposal(s) that constitute a fundamental change in the information statement.

NOTE 2: The officials responsible for the preparation of the information statement should make every effort to verify the accuracy and completeness of the information required by the applicable rules. The preliminary statement should be filed with the Commission at the earliest practicable date.

NOTE 3: *Solicitation in Opposition.* For purposes of the exclusion from filing a preliminary information statement, a "solicitation in opposition" includes: (a) Any solicitation opposing a proposal supported by the registrant; and (b) any solicitation supporting a proposal that the registrant does not expressly support, other than a security holder proposal identified in the registrant's information statement pursuant to Item 4 of Schedule 14C. The identification of a security holder proposal in the registrant's information statement does not constitute a "solicitation in opposition," even if the registrant opposes the proposal and/or includes a statement in opposition to the proposal.

NOTE 4: A registrant that is filing an information statement in preliminary form only because the registrant has commented on or referred to an opposing solicitation should indicate that fact in a transmittal letter when filing the preliminary material with the Commission.

(b) *Definitive Information Statement.* Eight definitive copies of the information statement, in the form in which it is furnished to security holders, must be filed with the Commission no later than the date the information statement is first sent or given to security holders. Three copies of these materials also must be filed with, or mailed for filing to, each national securities exchange on which the registrant has a class of securities listed and registered.

(c) *Release Dates.* All preliminary material filed pursuant to paragraph (a) of this rule shall be accompanied by a statement of the date on which copies thereof filed pursuant to paragraph (b) of this rule are intended to be released to security holders. All definitive material filed pursuant to paragraph (b) of this rule shall be accompanied by a statement of the date on which copies of such material have been released to security holders or, if not released, the date on which copies thereof are intended to be released.

(d)(1) *Public Availability of Information.* All copies of material filed pursuant to paragraph (a) of this rule shall be clearly marked "Preliminary Copies," and shall be deemed immediately available for public inspection unless confidential treatment is obtained pursuant to paragraph (d)(2) of this rule.

(2) *Confidential Treatment.* If action will be taken on any matter specified in Item 14 of Schedule 14A (Rule 14a–101), all copies of the preliminary information statement filed under paragraph (a) of this rule will be for the information of the Commission only and will not be deemed available for public inspection until filed with the Commission in definitive form so long as:

(i) The information statement does not relate to a matter or proposal subject to Rule 13e–3 or a roll-up transaction as defined in Item 901(c) of Regulation S–K;

(ii) Neither the parties to the transaction nor any persons authorized to act on their behalf have made any public communications relating to the transaction except for statements where the content is limited to the information specified in Rule 135 under the Securities Act of 1933; and

(iii) The materials are filed in paper and marked "Confidential, For Use of the Commission Only." In all cases, the materials may be disclosed to any department or agency of the United States Government and to the Congress, and the Commission may make any inquiries or investigation into the materials as may be necessary to conduct an adequate review by the Commission.

Instruction to Paragraph (d)(2): If communications are made publicly that go beyond the information specified in Rule 135 under the Securities Act of 1933, the materials must be re-filed publicly with the Commission.

(e) *Revised Information Statements.* Where any information statement filed pursuant to this section is amended or revised, two of the copies of such amended or revised material filed pursuant to this rule shall be marked to indicate clearly and precisely the changes effected therein. If the amendment or revision alters the text of the material, the changes in such text shall be indicated by means of underscoring or in some other appropriate manner.

(f) *Merger Material.* Notwithstanding the foregoing provisions of this rule, any information statement or other material included in a registration statement filed under the Securities Act of 1933 on Form N–14, S–4, or F–4 (17 CFR 239.23, 17 CFR 239.25 or 17 CFR 239.34) shall be deemed filed both for the purposes of that Act and for the purposes of this rule, but separate copies of such material need not be furnished pursuant to this rule, nor shall any fee be required under paragraph (a) of this rule. However, any additional material used after the effective date of the registration statement on Form N–14, S–4 or F–4 shall be filed in accordance with this rule, unless separate copies of such material are required to be filed as an amendment of such registration statement.

(g) *Fees.* At the time of filing the preliminary information statement regarding an acquisition, merger, spin-off, consolidation or proposed sale or other disposition of substantially all the assets of the company, the registrant shall pay the Commission a fee, no part of which shall be refunded, established in accordance with Rule 0–11.

(h) *Cover Page.* Each information statement filed with the Commission shall include a cover page in the form set forth in Schedule 14C (Rule 14c–101). The cover page required by this paragraph need not be distributed to security holders.

Rule 14c–6. False or misleading statements

(a) No information statement shall contain any statement which, at the time and in the light of the circumstances under which it is made, is false or misleading with respect to any material fact, or which omits to state any material fact necessary in order to make the statements therein not false or misleading or necessary to correct any statement in any earlier communication with respect to the same meeting or subject matter which has become false or misleading.

(b) The fact that an information statement has been filed with or examined by the Commission shall not be deemed a finding by the Commission that such material is accurate or complete or not false or misleading, or that the Commission has passed upon the merits of or approved any statement contained therein or any matter to be acted upon by security holders. No representation contrary to the foregoing shall be made.

Rule 14c–7. Providing copies of material for certain beneficial owners

(a) If the registrant knows that securities of any class entitled to vote at a meeting, or by written authorizations or consents if no meeting is held, are held of record by a broker, dealer, voting trustee, or bank, association, or other entity that exercises fiduciary powers in nominee name or otherwise, the registrant shall:

(1) By first class mail or other equally prompt means:

(i) Inquire of each such record holder:

(A) Whether other persons are the beneficial owners of such securities and, if so, the number of copies of the information statement necessary to supply such material to such beneficial owners;

(B) In the case of an annual (or special meeting in lieu of the annual) meeting, or written consents in lieu of such meeting, at which directors are to be elected, the number of copies of the annual report to security holders, necessary to supply such report to such beneficial owners for whom proxy material has not been and is not to be made available and to whom such reports are to be distributed by such record holder or its nominee and not by the registrant;

(C) If the record holder or respondent bank has an obligation under Rule 14b–1(b)(3) or Rule 14b–2(b)(4)(ii) and (iii), whether an agent has been designated to act on its behalf in fulfilling such obligation, and, if so, the name and address of such agent; and

(D) Whether it holds the registrant's securities on behalf of any respondent bank and, if so, the name and address of each such respondent bank; and

(ii) Indicate to each such record holder:

(A) Whether the registrant pursuant to paragraph (c) of this rule intends to distribute the annual report to security holders to beneficial owners of its securities whose names, addresses and securities positions are disclosed pursuant to Rule 14b–1(b)(3) and Rule 14b–2(b)(4)(ii) and (iii);

(B) The record date; and

(C) At the option of the registrant, any employee benefit plan established by an affiliate of the registrant that holds securities of the registrant that the registrant elects to treat as exempt employee benefit plan securities;

(2) Upon receipt of a record holders's or respondent bank's response indicating, pursuant to Rule 14b–2(b)(1)(i), the names and addresses of its respondent banks, within one business day after the date such response is received, make an inquiry of and give notification to each such respondent bank in the same manner required by paragraph (a)(1) of this rule; *Provided, however,* the inquiry required by paragraphs (a)(1) and (a)(2) of this rule shall not cover beneficial owners of exempt employee benefit plan securities.

(3) Make the inquiry required by paragraph (a)(1) of this rule on the earlier of:

(i) At least 20 business days prior to the record date of the meeting of security holders or the record date of written consents in lieu of a meeting; or

(ii) At least 20 business days prior to the date the information statement is required to be sent or given pursuant to Rule 14c–2(b);

Provided, however, That, if a record holder or respondent bank has informed the registrant that a designated office(s) or department(s) is to receive such inquiries, the inquiry shall be made to such designated office(s) or department(s);

(4) Supply, in a timely manner, each record holder and respondent bank of whom the inquiries required by paragraphs (a)(1) and (a)(2) of this rule are made with copies of the information statement and/or the annual report to security holders, in such quantities, assembled in such form and at such places(s), as the record holder or respondent bank may reasonably request in order to send such material to each beneficial owner of securities who is to be furnished with such material by the record holder or respondent bank; and

(5) Upon the request of any record holder or respondent bank that is supplied with Notices of Internet Availability of Proxy Materials, information statements and/or annual reports to security holders pursuant to paragraph (a)(3) of this rule, pay its reasonable expenses for completing the sending of such material to beneficial owners.

NOTE 1: If the registrant's list of security holders indicates that some of its securities are registered in the name of a clearing agency registered pursuant to section 17A of the Act (*e.g.*, "Cede & Co.," nominee for the Depository Trust Company), the registrant shall make appropriate inquiry of the clearing agency and thereafter of the participants in such a clearing agency who may hold on behalf of a beneficial owner or respondent bank, and shall comply with the above paragraph with respect to any such participant (see Rule 14c–1(h)).

NOTE 2: The attention of registrants is called to the fact that each broker, dealer, bank, association, and other entity that exercises fiduciary powers has an obligation pursuant to Rule 14b–1 and Rule 14b–2 (except as provided therein with respect to exempt employee benefit plan securities held in nominee name) and with respect to brokers and dealers, applicable self-regulatory organization requirements to obtain and forward, within the time periods prescribed therein, (a) information statements to beneficial owners on whose behalf it holds securities, and (b) annual reports to security holders to beneficial owners on whose behalf it holds securities, unless the registrant has notified the record holder or respondent bank that it has assumed responsibility to send such material to beneficial owners whose names, addresses and securities positions are disclosed pursuant to Rule 14b–1(b)(3) and Rule 14b–2(b)(4)(ii) and (iii).

NOTE 3: The attention of registrants is called to the fact that registrants have an obligation, pursuant to paragraph (d) of this rule, to cause information statements and annual reports to security holders to be furnished, in accordance with Rule 14c–2, to beneficial owners of exempt employee benefit plan securities.

(b) Any registrant requesting pursuant to Rule 14b–1(b)(3) and Rule 14b–2(b)(4)(ii) and (iii) a list of names, addresses and securities positions of beneficial owners of its securities who either have consented or have not objected to disclosure of such information shall:

(1) By first class mail or other equally prompt means, inquire of each record holder and each respondent bank identified to the registrant pursuant to Rule 14b–2(e)(1) whether such record holder or respondent bank holds the registrant's securities on behalf of any respondent banks and, if so, the name and address of each such respondent bank;

(2) Request such list be compiled as of a date no earlier than five business days after the date the registrant's request is received by the record holder or respondent bank; *Provided, however,* That if the record holder or respondent bank has informed the registrant that a designated office(s) or department(s) is to receive such requests, the request shall be made to such designated offices(s) or department(s);

(3) Make such request to the following persons that hold the registrant's securities on behalf of

beneficial owners: all brokers, dealers, banks, associations and other entities that exercise fiduciary powers; *Provided, however,* such request shall not cover beneficial owners of exempt employee benefit plan securities as defined in Rule 14a–1(d)(1); and, at the option of the registrant, such request may give notice of any employee benefit plan established by an affiliate of the registrant that holds securities of the registrant that the registrant elects to treat as exempt employee benefit plan securities;

(4) Use the information furnished in response to such request exclusively for purposes of corporate communications; and

(5) Upon the request of any record holder or respondent bank to whom such request is made, pay the reasonable expenses, both direct and indirect, of providing beneficial owner information.

NOTE: A registrant will be deemed to have satisfied its obligations under paragraph (b) of this rule by requesting consenting and non-objecting beneficial owner lists from a designated agent acting on behalf of the record holder or respondent bank and paying to that designated agent the reasonable expenses of providing the beneficial owner information.

(c) A registrant, at its option, may send by mail or other equally prompt means, its annual report to security holders to the beneficial owners whose identifying information is provided by record holders and respondent banks, pursuant to Rule 14b–1(b)(3) and Rule 14b–2(b)(4)(ii) and (iii), provided that such registrant notifies the record holders and respondent banks at the time it makes the inquiry required by paragraph (a) of this rule that the registrant will send the annual report to security holders to the beneficial owners so identified.

(d) If a registrant furnishes information statements to record holders and respondent banks who hold securities on behalf of beneficial owners, the registrant shall cause information statements and annual reports to security holders to be furnished, in accordance with Rule 14c–2, to beneficial owners of exempt employee benefit plan securities.

Rule 14c–101. Schedule 14c—Information required in information statement

SCHEDULE 14C INFORMATION

Information Statement Pursuant to Section 14(c) of the Securities Exchange Act of 1934

(Amendment No.)

Check the appropriate box:

[ ] Preliminary Information Statement

[ ] Confidential, for Use of the Commission Only (as permitted by Rule 14c–5(d)(2))

[ ] Definitive Information Statement

____

(Name of Registrant As Specified In Charter)

Payment of Filing Fee (Check the appropriate box):

[ ] No fee required.

[ ] Fee computed on table below per Exchange Act Rules 14c–5(g) and 0–11

(1) Title of each class of securities to which transaction applies:

____

(2) Aggregate number of securities to which transaction applies:

____

(3) Per unit price or other underlying value of transaction computed pursuant to Exchange Act Rule 0–11 (set forth the amount on which the filing fee is calculated and state how it was determined):

____

(4) Proposed maximum aggregate value of transaction:

____

(5) Total fee paid:

____

[ ] Fee paid previously with preliminary materials.

[ ] Check box if any part of the fee is offset as provided by Exchange Act Rule 0–11(a)(2) and identify the filing for which the offsetting fee was paid previously. Identify the previous filing by registration statement number, or the Form or Schedule and the date of its filing.

(1) Amount Previously Paid:

____

(2) Form, Schedule or Registration Statement No.:

____

(3) Filing Party:

____

(4) Date Filed:

____

NOTE TO COVER PAGE: Where any item, other than Item 4, calls for information with respect to any matter to be acted upon at the meeting or, if no meeting is being held, by written authorization or consent, such item need be answered only with respect to proposals to be made by the registrant. Registrants and acquirees that meet the definition of "smaller reporting company" under Rule 12b–2 under the Securities Exchange Act of 1934 shall refer to the disclosure items in Regulation S–K (Items 10 through 1123) with specific attention to the scaled disclosure requirements for smaller reporting companies, if any. A smaller reporting company may provide the information in Article 8 of Regulation S–X in lieu of any financial statements required by Item 1 of Schedule 14C.

Item 1. Information Required by Items of Schedule 14A (Rule 14a–101)

Furnish the information called for by all of the items of Schedule 14A (Rule 14a–101) (other than Items 1(c), 2, 4 and 5 thereof) which would be applicable to any matter to be acted upon at the meeting if proxies were to be solicited in connection with the meeting. Notes A, C, D and E to Schedule 14A are also applicable to Schedule 14C.

Item 2. Statement That Proxies Are Not Solicited

The following statement shall be set forth on the first page of the information statement in boldface type:

WE ARE NOT ASKING YOU FOR A PROXY AND YOU ARE REQUESTED NOT TO SEND US A PROXY

Item 3. Interest of Certain Persons in or Opposition to Matters to Be Acted Upon

(a) Describe briefly any substantial interest, direct or indirect, by security holdings or otherwise, of each of the following persons in any matter to be acted upon, other than elections to office:

(1) Each person who has been a director or officer of the registrant at any time since the beginning of the last fiscal year;

(2) Each nominee for election as a director of the registrant;

(3) Each associate of the foregoing persons.

(b) Give the name of any director of the registrant who has informed the registrant in writing that he intends to oppose any action to be taken by the registrant at the meeting and indicate the action which he intends to oppose.

(c) Furnish the information required by Item 402(t) of Regulation S–K.

Item 4. Proposals by Security Holders

If any security holder entitled to vote at the meeting or by written authorization or consent has submitted to the registrant a reasonable time before the information statement is to be transmitted to security holders a proposal, other than elections to office, which is accompanied by notice of his intention to present the proposal for action at the meeting the registrant shall, if a meeting is held, make a statement to that effect, identify the proposal and indicate the disposition proposed to be made of the proposal by the registrant at the meeting.

Instructions. 1. This Item need not be answered as to any proposal submitted with respect to an annual meeting if such proposal is submitted less than 60 days in advance of a day corresponding to the date of mailing a proxy statement or information statement in connection with the last annual meeting of security holders.

2. If the registrant intends to rule a proposal out of order, the Commission shall be so advised 20 calendar days prior to the date the definitive copies of the information statement are filed with the Commission, together with a statement of the reasons why the proposal is not deemed to be a proper subject for action by security holders.

Item 5. Delivery of Documents to Security Holders Sharing an Address

If one annual report to security holders, information statement, or Notice of Internet Availability of Proxy Materials is being delivered to two or more security holders who share an address, furnish the following information in accordance with Rule 14a–3(e)(1):

(a) State that only one annual report to security holders, information statement, or Notice of Internet Availability of Proxy Materials, as applicable, is being delivered to multiple security holders sharing an address unless the registrant has received contrary instructions from one or more of the security holders;

(b) Undertake to deliver promptly upon written or oral request a separate copy of the annual report to security holders, information statement, or Notice of Internet Availability of Proxy Materials, as applicable, to a security holder at a shared address to which a single copy of the documents was delivered and provide instructions as to how a security holder can notify the registrant that the security holder wishes to receive a separate copy of an annual report to security holders, information statement, or Notice of Internet Availability of Proxy Materials, as applicable;

(c) Provide the phone number and mailing address to which a security holder can direct a notification to the registrant that the security holder wishes to receive a separate annual report to security holders, information statement, or Notice of Internet Availability of Proxy Materials, as applicable, in the future; and

(d) Provide instructions how security holders sharing an address can request delivery of a single copy of annual reports to security holders, information statements, or Notices of Internet Availability of Proxy Materials if they are receiving multiple copies of annual reports to security holders, information statements, or Notices of Internet Availability of Proxy Materials.

REGULATION 14D

ATTENTION ELECTRONIC FILERS

THIS REGULATION SHOULD BE READ IN CONJUNCTION WITH REGULATIONS S–T (17 CFR 232), WHICH GOVERNS THE PREPARATION AND SUBMISSION OF DOCUMENTS IN ELECTRONIC FORMAT. MANY PROVISIONS RELATING TO THE PREPARATION AND SUBMISSION OF DOCUMENTS IN PAPER FORMAT CONTAINED IN THIS REGULATION ARE SUPERSEDED BY THE PROVISIONS OF REGULATION S–T FOR DOCUMENTS REQUIRED TO BE FILED IN ELECTRONIC FORMAT.

Rule 14d–1. Scope of and definitions applicable to Regulations 14D and 14E

(a) *Scope.* Regulation 14D (Rules 14d–1 through 14d–101) shall apply to any tender offer that is subject to section 14(d)(1) of the Act (15 U.S.C. 78n(d)(1)), including, but not limited to, any tender offer for securities of a class described in that section that is made by an affiliate of the issuer of such class. Regulation 14E (Rules 14e–1 through 14e–8) shall apply to any tender offer for securities (other than exempted securities) unless otherwise noted therein.

(b) The requirements imposed by sections 14(d)(1) through 14(d)(7) of the Act, Regulation 14D and Schedule TO and 14D–9 thereunder, and Rule 14e–1 of Regulation 14E under the Act, shall be deemed satisfied with respect to any tender offer, including any exchange offer, for the securities of an issuer incorporated or organized under the laws of Canada or any Canadian province or territory, if such issuer is a foreign private issuer and is not an investment company registered or required to be registered under the Investment Company Act of 1940, if less than 40 percent of the class of securities outstanding that is the subject of the tender offer is held by U.S. holders, and the tender offer is subject to, and the bidder complies with, the laws, regulations and policies of Canada and/or any of its provinces or territories governing the conduct of the offer (unless the bidder has received an exemption(s) from, and the tender offer does not comply with, requirements that otherwise would be prescribed by Regulation 14D or 14E), *provided that:*

(1) In the case of tender offers subject to section 14(d)(1) of the Act, where the consideration for a tender offer subject to this rule consists solely of cash, the entire disclosure document or documents required to be furnished to holders of the class of securities to be acquired shall be filed with the Commission on Schedule 14D–1F (Rule 14d–102) and disseminated to shareholders of the subject company residing in the United States in accordance with such Canadian laws, regulations and policies; or

(2) Where the consideration for a tender offer subject to this rule includes securities of the bidder to be issued pursuant to the offer, any registration statement and/or prospectus relating thereto shall be filed with the Commission along with the Schedule 14D–1F referred to in paragraph (b)(1) of this rule, and shall be disseminated, together with the home jurisdiction document(s) accompanying such Schedule, to shareholders of the subject company residing in the United States in accordance with such Canadian laws, regulations and policies.

NOTE 1. For purposes of any tender offer, including any exchange offer, otherwise eligible to proceed in accordance with Rule 14d–1(b) under the Act, the issuer of the subject securities will be presumed to be a foreign private issuer and U.S. holders will be presumed to hold less than 40 percent of such outstanding securities, unless (a) the aggregate trading volume of that class on national securities exchanges in the United States and on NASDAQ exceeded its aggregate trading volume on securities exchanges in Canada and on the Canadian Dealing Network, Inc. ("CDN") over the 12 calendar month period prior to commencement of this offer, or if commenced in response to a prior offer, over the 12 calendar month period prior to the commencement of the initial offer (based on volume figures published by such exchanges and NASDAQ and CDN); (b) the most recent annual report or annual information form filed or submitted by the issuer with securities regulators of Ontario, Quebec, British Columbia or Alberta (or, if the issuer of the subject securities is not a reporting issuer in any of such provinces, with any other Canadian securities regulator) or with the Commission indicates that U.S. holders hold 40 percent or more of the outstanding subject class of securities; or (c) the offeror has actual knowledge that the level of U.S. ownership equals or exceeds 40 percent of such securities.

NOTE 2. Notwithstanding the grant of an exemption from one or more of the applicable Canadian regulatory provisions imposing requirements that otherwise would be prescribed by Regulation 14D or 14E, the tender offer will be eligible to proceed in accordance with the requirements of this rule if the Commission by order determines that the applicable Canadian regulatory provisions are adequate to protect the interest of investors.

(c) *Tier I.* Any tender offer for the securities of a foreign private issuer as defined in Rule 3b–4 is exempt from the requirements of sections 14(d)(1) through 14(d)(7) of the Act (15 U.S.C. 78n(d)(1) through 78n(d)(7)), Regulation 14D (Rules 14d–1 through 14d–10) and Schedules TO (Rule 14d–100) and 14D–9 (Rule 14d–101) thereunder, and Rules

14e–1 and 14e–2 of Regulation 14E under the Act if the following conditions are satisfied:

(1) *U.S. Ownership Limitation.* Except the in case of a tender offer that is commenced during the pendency of a tender offer made by a prior bidder in reliance on this paragraph or Rule 13e–4(h)(8), U.S. holders do not hold more than 10 percent of the class of securities sought in the offer (as determined under Instructions 2 or 3 to paragraphs (c) and (d) of this rule).

(2) *Equal Treatment.* The bidder must permit U.S. holders to participate in the offer on terms at least as favorable as those offered any other holder of the same class of securities that is the subject of the tender offer; however:

(i) *Registered Exchange Offers.* If the bidder offers securities registered under the Securities Act of 1933 (15 U.S.C. 77a *et seq.*), the bidder need not extend the offer to security holders in those states or jurisdictions that prohibit the offer or sale of the securities after the bidder has made a good faith effort to register or qualify the offer and sale of securities in that state or jurisdiction, except that the bidder must offer the same cash alternative to security holders in any such state or jurisdiction that it has offered to security holders in any other state or jurisdiction.

(ii) *Exempt Exchange Offers.* If the bidder offers securities exempt from registration under Rule 802 under the Securities Act of 1933, the bidder need not extend the offer to security holders in those states or jurisdictions that require registration or qualification, except that the bidder must offer the same cash alternative to security holders in any such state or jurisdiction that it has offered to security holders in any other state or jurisdiction.

(iii) *Cash Only Consideration.* The bidder may offer U.S. holders only a cash consideration for the tender of the subject securities, notwithstanding the fact that the bidder is offering security holders outside the United States a consideration that consists in whole or in part of securities of the bidder, so long as the bidder has a reasonable basis for believing that the amount of cash is substantially equivalent to the value of the consideration offered to non-U.S. holders, and either of the following conditions are satisfied:

(A) The offered security is a "margin security" within the meaning of Regulation T (12 CFR 220.2) and the issuer undertakes to provide, upon the request of any U.S. holder or the Commission staff, the closing price and daily trading volume of the security on the principal trading market for the security as of the last trading day of each of the six months preceding the announcement of the offer and each of the trading days thereafter; or

(B) If the offered security is not a "margin security" within the meaning of Regulation T (12 CFR 220.2) the issuer undertakes to provide, upon the request of any U.S. holder or the Commission staff, an opinion of an independent expert stating that the cash consideration offered to U.S. holders is substantially equivalent to the value of the consideration offered security holders outside the United States.

(iv) *Disparate Tax Treatment.* If the bidder offers loan notes solely to offer sellers tax advantages not available in the United States and these notes are neither listed on any organized securities market nor registered under the Securities Act of 1933 (15 U.S.C. 77a *et seq.*), the loan notes need not be offered to U.S. holders.

(3) *Informational Documents.* (i) The bidder must disseminate any informational document to U.S. holders, including any amendments thereto, in English, on a comparable basis to that provided to security holders in the home jurisdiction.

(ii) If the bidder disseminates by publication in its home jurisdiction, the bidder must publish the information in the United States in a manner reasonably calculated to inform U.S. holders of the offer.

(iii) In the case of tender offers for securities described in section 14(d)(1) of the Act (15 U.S.C. 78n(d)(1)), if the bidder publishes or otherwise disseminates an informational document to the holders of the securities in connection with the tender offer, the bidder must furnish that informational document, including any amendments thereto, in English, to the Commission on Form CB (17 CFR 249.480) by the first business day after publication or dissemination. If the bidder is a foreign company, it must also file a Form F–X (17 CFR 239.42) with the Commission at the same time as the submission of Form CB to appoint an agent for service in the United States.

(4) *Investment Companies.* The issuer of the securities that are the subject of the tender offer is

not an investment company registered or required to be registered under the Investment Company Act of 1940 (15 U.S.C. 80a–1 *et seq.*), other than a registered closed-end investment company.

(d) *Tier II.* A person conducting a tender offer (including any exchange offer) that meets the conditions in paragraph (d)(1) of this rule shall be entitled to the exemptive relief specified in paragraph (d)(2) of this rule, provided that such tender offer complies with all the requirements of this rule other than those for which an exemption has been specifically provided in paragraph (d)(2) of this rule. In addition, a person conducting a tender offer subject only to the requirements of section 14(e) of the Act (15 U.S.C. 78n(e)) and Regulation 14E thereunder that meets the conditions in paragraph (d)(1) of the rule also shall be entitled to the exemptive relief specified in paragraph (d)(2) of this rule, to the extent needed under the requirements of Regulation 14E, so long as the tender offer complies with all requirements of Regulation 14E other than those for which an exemption has been specifically provided in paragraph (d)(2) of this rule:

(1) *Conditions.* (i) The subject company is a foreign private issuer as defined in Rule 3b–4 and is not an investment company registered or required to be registered under the Investment Company Act of 1940 (15 U.S.C. 80a–1 *et seq.*), other than a registered closed-end investment company;

(ii) Except in the case of a tender offer that is commenced during the pendency of a tender offer made by a prior bidder in reliance on this paragraph or Rule 13e–4(i), U.S. holders do not hold more than 40 percent of the class of securities sought in the offer (as determined under Instructions 2 or 3 to paragraphs (c) and (d) of this rule); and

(iii) The bidder complies with all applicable U.S. tender offer laws and regulations, other than those for which an exemption has been provided for in paragraph (d)(2) of this rule.

(2) *Exemptions.* (i) *Equal Treatment—Loan Notes.* If the bidder offers loan notes solely to offer sellers tax advantages not available in the United States and these notes are neither listed on any organized securities market nor registered under the Securities Act of 1933 (15 U.S.C. 77a *et seq.*), the loan notes need not be offered to U.S. holders, notwithstanding Rule 14d–10.

(ii) *Equal Treatment—Separate U.S. and Foreign Offers.* Notwithstanding the provisions of Rule 14d–10, a bidder conducting a tender offer meeting the conditions of paragraph (d)(1) of this rule may separate the offer into multiple offers: one offer made to U.S. holders, which also may include all holders of American Depositary Shares representing interests in the subject securities, and one or more offers made to non-U.S. holders. The U.S. offer must be made on terms at least as favorable as those offered any other holder of the same class of securities that is the subject of the tender offers. U.S. holders may be included in the foreign offer(s) only where the laws of the jurisdiction governing such foreign offer(s) expressly preclude the exclusion of U.S. holders from the foreign offer(s) and where the offer materials distributed to U.S. holders fully and adequately disclose the risks of participating in the foreign offer(s).

(iii) *Notice of Extensions.* Notice of extensions made in accordance with the requirements of the home jurisdiction law or practice will satisfy the requirements of Rule 14e–1(d).

(iv) *Prompt Payment.* Payment made in accordance with the requirements of the home jurisdiction law or practice will satisfy the requirements of Rule 14e–1(c). Where payment may not be made on a more expedited basis under home jurisdiction law or practice, payment for securities tendered during any subsequent offering period within 20 business days of the date of tender will satisfy the prompt payment requirements of Rule 14d–11(e). For purposes of this paragraph, a business day is determined with reference to the target's home jurisdiction.

(v) *Subsequent Offering Period/Withdrawal Rights.* A bidder will satisfy the announcement and prompt payment requirements of Rule 14d–11(d), if the bidder announces the results of the tender offer, including the approximate number of securities deposited to date, and pays for tendered securities in accordance with the requirements of the home jurisdiction law or practice and the subsequent offering period commences immediately following such announcement. Notwithstanding section 14(d)(5) of the Act (15 U.S.C. 78n(d)(5)), the bidder need not extend withdrawal rights following the close of the offer and prior to the commencement of the subsequent offering period.

(vi) *Payment of Interest on Securities Tendered During Subsequent Offering Period.* Notwithstanding the requirements of Rule 14d–11(f), the bidder may pay interest on securities tendered during a subsequent offering period, if required under applicable foreign law. Paying interest on securities tendered during a subsequent offering period in accordance with this rule will not be deemed to violate Rule 14d–10(a)(2).

(vii) *Suspension of Withdrawal Rights During Counting of Tendered Securities.* The bidder may suspend withdrawal rights required under section 14(d)(5) of the Act (15 U.S.C. 78n(d)(5)) at the end of the offer and during the period that securities tendered into the offer are being counted, provided that:

(A) The bidder has provided an offer period including withdrawal rights for a period of at least 20 U.S. business days;

(B) At the time withdrawal rights are suspended, all offer conditions have been satisfied or waived, except to the extent that the bidder is in the process of determining whether a minimum acceptance condition included in the terms of the offer has been satisfied by counting tendered securities; and

(C) Withdrawal rights are suspended only during the counting process and are reinstated immediately thereafter, except to the extent that they are terminated through the acceptance of tendered securities.

(viii) *Mix and Match Elections and the Subsequent Offering Period.* Notwithstanding the requirements of Rule 14d–11(b), where the bidder offers target security holders a choice between different forms of consideration, it may establish a ceiling on one or more forms of consideration offered. Notwithstanding the requirements of Rule 14d–11(f), a bidder that establishes a ceiling on one or more forms of consideration offered pursuant to this subsection may offset elections of tendering security holders against one another, subject to proration, so that elections are satisfied to the greatest extent possible and pro rated to the extent that they cannot be satisfied in full. Such a bidder also may separately offset and pro rate securities tendered during the initial offering period and those tendered during any subsequent offering period, notwithstanding the requirements of Rule 14d–10(c).

(ix) *Early Termination of an Initial Offering Period.* A bidder may terminate an initial offering period, including a voluntary extension of that period, if at the time the initial offering period and withdrawal rights terminate, the following conditions are met:

(A) The initial offering period has been open for at least 20 U.S. business days;

(B) The bidder has adequately discussed the possibility of and the impact of the early termination in the original offer materials;

(C) The bidder provides a subsequent offering period after the termination of the initial offering period;

(D) All offer conditions are satisfied as of the time when the initial offering period ends; and

(E) The bidder does not terminate the initial offering period or any extension of that period during any mandatory extension required under U.S. tender offer rules.

Instructions to Paragraphs (c) and (d):

1. *Home jurisdiction* means both the jurisdiction of the subject company's incorporation, organization or chartering and the principal foreign market where the subject company's securities are listed or quoted.

2. *U.S. holder* means any security holder resident in the United States. Except as otherwise provided in Instruction 3 below, to determine the percentage of outstanding securities held by U.S. holders:

i. Calculate the U.S. ownership as of a date no more than 60 before and no more than 30 days after public announcement of the tender offer. If you are unable to calculate as of a date within these time frames, the calculation may be made as of the most recent practicable date before public announcement, but in no event earlier than 120 days before announcement;

ii. Include securities underlying American Depositary Shares convertible or exchangeable into the securities that are the subject of the tender offer when calculating the number of subject securities outstanding, as well as the number held by U.S. holders. Exclude from the calculations other types of securities that are convertible or exchangeable into the securities that are the subject of the tender offer, such as warrants, options and convertible securities. Exclude from those calculations securities held by the bidder;

iii. Use the method of calculating record ownership in Rule 12g3–2(a) under the Act, except that your inquiry as to the amount of securities represented by accounts of customers resident in the United States may be limited to brokers, dealers, banks and other nominees located in the United States, the subject company's jurisdiction of incorporation or that of each participant in a business combination, and the jurisdiction that is the primary trading market for the subject securities, if different than the subject company's jurisdiction of incorporation;

iv. If, after reasonable inquiry, you are unable to obtain information about the amount of securities represented by accounts of customers resident in the United States, you may assume, for purposes of this definition, that the customers are residents of the jurisdiction in which the nominee has its principal place of business; and

v. Count securities as beneficially owned by residents of the United States as reported on reports of beneficial ownership that are provided to you or publicly filed and based on information otherwise provided to you.

3. In a tender offer by a bidder other than an affiliate of the issuer of the subject securities that is not made pursuant to an agreement with the issuer of the subject securities, the issuer of the subject securities will be presumed to be a foreign private issuer and U.S. holders will be presumed to hold less than 10 percent (40 percent in the case of paragraph (d) of this rule) of such outstanding securities, unless paragraphs i., ii., or iii. of this instruction indicate otherwise. In addition, where the bidder is unable to conduct the analysis of U.S. ownership set forth in Instruction 2 above, the bidder may presume that the percentage of securities held by U.S. holders is less than 10 percent (40 percent in the case of paragraph (d) of this rule) of the outstanding securities so long as there is a primary trading market for the subject securities outside the U.S., as defined in Rule 12h–6(f)(5), unless:

i. Average daily trading volume of the subject securities in the United States for a recent twelve-month period ending on a date no more than 60 days before the public announcement of the offer exceeds 10 percent (40 percent in the case of paragraph (d) of this rule) of the average daily trading volume of that class of securities on a worldwide basis for the same period; or

ii. The most recent annual report or annual information filed or submitted by the issuer with securities regulators of the home jurisdiction or with the Commission or any jurisdiction in which the subject securities trade before the public announcement of the offer indicates that U.S. holders hold more than 10 percent (40 percent in the case of paragraph (d) of this rule) of the outstanding subject class of securities; or

iii. The bidder knows or has reason to know, before the public announcement of the offer, that the level of U.S. ownership exceeds 10 percent (40 percent in the case of paragraph (d) of this rule) of such securities. As an example, a bidder is deemed to know information about U.S. ownership of the subject class of securities that is publicly available and that appears in any filing with the Commission or any regulatory body in the issuer's jurisdiction of incorporation or (if different) the non-U.S. jurisdiction in which the primary trading market for the subject securities is located. The bidder is deemed to know information about U.S. ownership available from the issuer or obtained or readily available from any other source that is reasonably reliable, including from persons it has retained to advise it about the transaction, as well as from third-party information providers. These examples are not intended to be exclusive.

iv. The bidder knows or has reason to know that the level of U.S. ownership exceeds 10 percent (40 percent in the case of 14d–1(d)) of such securities.

4. *United States* means the United States of America, its territories and possessions, any State of the United States, and the District of Columbia.

5. The exemptions provided by paragraphs (c) and (d) of this rule are not available for any securities transaction or series of transactions that technically complies with paragraph (c) or (d) of this rule but are part of a plan or scheme to evade the provisions of Regulations 14D or 14E.

(e) Notwithstanding paragraph (a) of this rule, the requirements imposed by sections 14(d)(1) through 14(d)(7) of the Act [15 U.S.C. 78n(d)(1) through 78n(d)(7)], Regulation 14D promulgated thereunder (Rules 14d–1 through 14d–10), and Rules 14e–1 and 14e–2 shall not apply by virtue of the fact that a bidder for the securities of a foreign private issuer, as defined in Rule 3b–4, the subject company of such a tender offer, their representatives, or any other person specified in Rule 14d–9(d), provides any journalist with access to its press conferences held outside of the United States, to meetings with its representatives conducted outside of the United States, or to written press-related materials released outside the United States, at or in which a present or proposed tender offer is discussed, if:

(1) Access is provided to both U.S. and foreign journalists; and

(2) With respect to any written press-related materials released by the bidder or its representatives that discuss a present or proposed tender offer for equity securities registered under Section 12 of the Act [15 U.S.C. 78*l*], the written press-related materials must state that these written press-related materials are not an extension of a tender offer in the United States for a class of equity securities of the subject company. If the bidder intends to extend the tender offer in the United States at some future time, a statement regarding this intention, and that the procedural and filing requirements of the Williams Act will be satisfied at that time, also must be included in these written press-related materials. No means to tender securities, or coupons that could be returned to indicate interest in the tender offer, may be provided as part of, or attached to, these written press-related materials.

(f) For the purpose of Rule 14d–1(e), a bidder may presume that a target company qualifies as a foreign private issuer if the target company is a foreign issuer and files registration statements or reports on the disclosure forms specifically designated for foreign private issuers, claims the exemption from registration under the Act pursuant to Rule 12g3–2(b), or is not reporting in the United States.

(g) *Definitions.* Unless the context otherwise requires, all terms used in Regulation 14D and Regulation 14E have the same meaning as in the Act and in Rule 12b–2 promulgated thereunder. In addition, for purposes of sections 14(d) and 14(e) of the Act and Regulations 14D and 14E, the following definitions apply:

(1) The term *beneficial owner* shall have the same meaning as that set forth in Rule 13d–3: *Provided, however,* That, except with respect to Rule 14d–3, Rule 14d–9(d) and Item 6 of Schedule

14D–1, the term shall not include a person who does not have or share investment power or who is deemed to be a beneficial owner by virtue of Rule 13d–3(d)(1);

(2) The term *bidder* means any person who makes a tender offer or on whose behalf a tender offer is made: *Provided, however,* That the term does not include an issuer which makes a tender offer for securities of any class of which it is the issuer;

(3) The term *business day* means any day, other than Saturday, Sunday or a federal holiday, and shall consist of the time period from 12:01 a.m. through 12:00 midnight Eastern time. In computing any time period under section 14(d)(5) or section 14(d)(6) of the Act or under Regulation 14D or Regulation 14E, the date of the event which begins the running of such time period shall be included *except that* if such event occurs on other than a business day such period shall begin to run on and shall include the first business day thereafter; and

(4) The term *initial offering period* means the period from the time the offer commences until all minimum time periods, including extensions, required by Regulations 14D (Rules 14d–1 through 14d–103) and 14E (Rules 14e–1 through 14e–8) have been satisfied and all conditions to the offer have been satisfied or waived within these time periods.

(5) The term *security holders* means holders of record and beneficial owners of securities which are the subject of a tender offer;

(6) The term *security position listing* means, with respect to securities of any issuer held by a registered clearing agency in the name of the clearing agency or its nominee, a list of those participants in the clearing agency on whose behalf the clearing agency holds the issuer's securities and of the participants' respective positions in such securities as of a specified date.

(7) The term *subject company* means any issuer of securities which are sought by a bidder pursuant to a tender offer;

(8) The term *subsequent offering period* means the period immediately following the initial offering period meeting the conditions specified in Rule 14d–11.

(9) The term *tender offer material* means:

(i) The bidder's formal offer, including all the material terms and conditions of the tender offer and all amendments thereto;

(ii) The related transmittal letter (whereby securities of the subject company which are sought in the tender offer may be transmitted to the bidder or its depositary) and all amendments thereto; and

(iii) Press releases, advertisements, letters and other documents published by the bidder or sent or given by the bidder to security holders which, directly or indirectly, solicit, invite or request tenders of the securities being sought in the tender offer;

(h) *Signatures.* Where the Act or the rules, forms, reports or schedules thereunder require a document filed with or furnished to the Commission to be signed, such document shall be manually signed, or signed using either typed signatures or duplicated or facsimile versions of manual signatures. Where typed, duplicated or facsimile signatures are used, each signatory to the filing shall manually sign a signature page or other document authenticating, acknowledging or otherwise adopting his or her signature that appears in the filing. Such document shall be executed before or at the time the filing is made and shall be retained by the filer for a period of five years. Upon request, the filer shall furnish to the Commission or its staff a copy of any or all documents retained pursuant to this rule.

Rule 14d–2. Commencement of a tender offer

(a) *Date of Commencement.* A bidder will have commenced its tender offer for purposes of section 14(d) of the Act (15 U.S.C. 78n) and the rules under that section at 12:01 a.m. on the date when the bidder has first published, sent or given the means to tender to security holders. For purposes of this rule, the means to tender includes the transmittal form or a statement regarding how the transmittal form may be obtained.

(b) *Pre-Commencement Communications.* A communication by the bidder will not be deemed to constitute commencement of a tender offer if:

(1) It does not include the means for security holders to tender their shares into the offer; and

(2) All written communications relating to the tender offer, from and including the first public announcement, are filed under cover of Schedule TO (Rule 14d–100) with the Commission no later than the date of the communication. The bidder also

must deliver to the subject company and any other bidder for the same class of securities the first communication relating to the transaction that is filed, or required to be filed, with the Commission.

Instructions to Paragraph (b)(2):

1. The box on the front of Schedule TO indicating that the filing contains pre-commencement communications must be checked.

2. Any communications made in connection with an exchange offer registered under the Securities Act of 1933 need only be filed under Rule 425 under the Securities Act of 1933 and will be deemed filed under this rule.

3. Each pre-commencement written communication must include a prominent legend in clear, plain language advising security holders to read the tender offer statement when it is available because it contains important information. The legend also must advise investors that they can get the tender offer statement and other filed documents for free at the Commission's web site and explain which documents are free from the offeror.

4. See Rules 135, 165 and 166 under the Securities Act of 1933 for pre-commencement communications made in connection with registered exchange offers.

5. "Public announcement" is any oral or written communication by the bidder, or any person authorized to act on the bidder's behalf, that is reasonably designed to, or has the effect of, informing the public or security holders in general about the tender offer.

(c) *Filing and Other Obligations Triggered By Commencement*. As soon as practicable on the date of commencement, a bidder must comply with the filing requirements of Rule 14d–3(a), the dissemination requirements of Rule 14d–4(a) or (b), and the disclosure requirements of Rule 14d–6(a).

Rule 14d–3. Filing and transmission of tender offer statement

(a) *Filing and Transmittal*. No bidder shall make a tender offer if, after consummation thereof, such bidder would be the beneficial owner of more than 5 percent of the class of the subject company's securities for which the tender offer is made, unless as soon as practicable on the date of the commencement of the tender offer such bidder:

(1) Files with the Commission a Tender Offer Statement on Schedule TO (Rule 14d–100), including all exhibits thereto;

(2) Delivers a copy of such Schedule TO, including all exhibits thereto:

(i) To the subject company at its principal executive office; and

(ii) To any other bidder, which has filed a Schedule TO with the Commission relating to a tender offer which has not yet terminated for the same class of securities of the subject company, at such bidder's principal executive office or at the address of the person authorized to receive notices and communications (which is disclosed on the cover sheet of such other bidder's Schedule TO);

(3) Gives telephonic notice of the information required by Rule 14d–6(d)(2)(i) and (ii) and mails by means of first class mail a copy of such Schedule TO, including all exhibits thereto:

(i) To each national securities exchange where such class of the subject company's securities is registered and listed for trading (which may be based upon information contained in the subject company's most recent Annual Report on Form 10–K (17 CFR 249.310) filed with the Commission unless the bidder has reason to believe that such information is not current), which telephonic notice shall be made when practicable before the opening of each such exchange; and

(ii) To the National Association of Securities Dealers, Inc. ("NASD") if such class of the subject company's securities is authorized for quotation in the NASDAQ interdealer quotation system.

(b) *Post-Commencement Amendments and Additional Materials*. The bidder making the tender offer must file with the Commission:

(1) An amendment to Schedule TO (Rule 14d–100) reporting promptly any material changes in the information set forth in the schedule previously filed and including copies of any additional tender offer materials as exhibits; and

(2) A final amendment to Schedule TO (Rule 14d–100) reporting promptly the results of the tender offer.

Instruction to Paragraph (b): A copy of any additional tender offer materials or amendment filed under this rule must be sent promptly to the subject company and to any exchange and/or NASD, as required by paragraph (a) of this rule, but in no event later than the date the materials are first published, sent or given to security holders.

(c) *Certain Announcements*. Notwithstanding the provisions of paragraph (b) of this rule, if the additional tender offer material or an amendment to Schedule TO discloses only the number of shares deposited to date, and/or announces an extension of the time during which shares may be tendered, then the bidder may file such tender offer material or amendment and send a copy of such tender offer material or amendment to the subject company, any exchange and/or the NASD, as required by paragraph (a) of this rule, promptly after the date such tender offer material is first published or sent or given to security holders.

Rule 14d–4. Dissemination of tender offers to security holders

As soon as practicable on the date of commencement of a tender offer, the bidder must publish, send or give the disclosure required by Rule 14d–6 to security holders of the class of securities that is the subject of the offer, by complying with all of the requirements of any of the following:

(a) *Cash Tender Offers and Exempt Securities Offers.* For tender offers in which the consideration consists solely of cash and/or securities exempt from registration under section 3 of the Securities Act of 1933 (15 U.S.C. 77c):

(1) *Long-Form Publication.* The bidder makes adequate publication in a newspaper or newspapers of long-form publication of the tender offer.

(2) *Summary Publication.* (i) If the tender offer is not subject to Rule 13e–3, the bidder makes adequate publication in a newspaper or newspapers of a summary advertisement of the tender offer; and

(ii) Mails by first class mail or otherwise furnishes with reasonable promptness the bidder's tender offer materials to any security holder who requests such tender offer materials pursuant to the summary advertisement or otherwise.

(3) *Use of Stockholder Lists and Security Position Listings.* Any bidder using stockholder lists and security position listings under Rule 14d–5 must comply with paragraph (a)(1) or (2) of this rule on or before the date of the bidder's request under Rule 14d–5(a).

Instruction to Paragraph (a): Tender offers may be published or sent or given to security holders by other methods, but with respect to summary publication and the use of stockholder lists and security position listings under Rule 14d–5, paragraphs (a)(2) and (a)(3) of this rule are exclusive.

(b) *Registered Securities Offers.* For tender offers in which the consideration consists solely or partially of securities registered under the Securities Act of 1933, a registration statement containing all of the required information, including pricing information, has been filed and a preliminary prospectus or a prospectus that meets the requirements of section 10(a) of the Securities Act (15 U.S.C. 77j(a)), including a letter of transmittal, is delivered to security holders. However, for going-private transactions (as defined by Rule 13e–3) and roll-up transactions (as described by Item 901 of Regulation S–K), a registration statement registering the securities to be offered must have become effective and only a prospectus that meets the requirements of section 10(a) of the Securities Act may be delivered to security holders on the date of commencement.

Instructions to Paragraph (b):

1. If the prospectus is being delivered by mail, mailing on the date of commencement is sufficient.

2. A preliminary prospectus used under this rule may not omit information under Rule 430 or Rule 430A under the Securities Act of 1933.

3. If a preliminary prospectus is used under this section and the bidder must disseminate material changes, the tender offer must remain open for the period specified in paragraph (d)(2) of this rule.

4. If a preliminary prospectus is used under this rule, tenders may be requested in accordance with Rule 162(a) under the Securities Act of 1933.

(c) *Adequate Publication.* Depending on the facts and circumstances involved, adequate publication of a tender offer pursuant to this rule may require publication in a newspaper with a national circulation or may only require publication in a newspaper with metropolitan or regional circulation or may require publication in a combination thereof: *Provided, however,* That publication in all editions of a daily newspaper with a national circulation shall be deemed to constitute adequate publication.

(d) *Publication of Changes and Extension of the Offer.*

(1) If a tender offer has been published or sent or given to security holders by one or more of the methods enumerated in paragraph (a) of this rule, a material change in the information published, sent or given to security holders shall be promptly disseminated to security holders in a manner reasonably designed to inform security holders of such change; *Provided, however,* That if the bidder has elected pursuant to Rule 14d–5(f)(1) to require the subject company to disseminate amendments disclosing material changes to the tender offer materials pursuant to Rule 14d–5, the bidder shall disseminate material changes in the information published or sent or given to security holders at least pursuant to Rule 14d–5.

(2) In a registered securities offer where the bidder disseminates the preliminary prospectus as permitted by paragraph (b) of this rule, the offer must remain open from the date that material changes to the tender offer materials are disseminated to security holders, as follows:

(i) Five business days for a prospectus supplement containing a material change other than price or share levels;

(ii) Ten business days for a prospectus supplement containing a change in price, the amount of securities sought, the dealer's soliciting fee, or other similarly significant change;

(iii) Ten business days for a prospectus supplement included as part of a post-effective amendment; and

(iv) Twenty business days for a revised prospectus when the initial prospectus was materially deficient.

Rule 14d–5. Dissemination of certain tender offers by the use of stockholder lists and security position listings

(a) *Obligations of the Subject Company.* Upon receipt by a subject company at its principal executive offices of a bidder's written request, meeting the requirements of paragraph (e) of this rule, the subject company shall comply with the following sub-paragraphs.

(1) The subject company shall notify promptly transfer agents and any other person who will assist the subject company in complying with the requirements of this rule of the receipt by the subject company of a request by a bidder pursuant to this rule.

(2) The subject company shall promptly ascertain whether the most recently prepared stockholder list, written or otherwise, within the access of the subject company was prepared as of a date earlier than ten business days before the date of the bidder's request and, if so, the subject company shall promptly prepare or cause to be prepared a stockholder list as of the most recent practicable date which shall not be more than ten business days before the date of the bidder's request.

(3) The subject company shall make an election to comply and shall comply with all of the provisions of either paragraph (b) or paragraph (c) of this rule. The subject company's election once made shall not be modified or revoked during the bidder's tender offer and extensions thereof.

(4) No later than the second business day after the date of the bidder's request, the subject company shall orally notify the bidder, which notification shall be confirmed in writing, of the subject company's election made pursuant to paragraph (a)(3) of this rule. Such notification shall indicate (i) the approximate number of security holders of the class of securities being sought by the bidder and, (ii) if the subject company elects to comply with paragraph (b) of this rule, appropriate information concerning the location for delivery of the bidder's tender offer materials and the approximate direct costs incidental to the mailing to security holders of the bidder's paragraph (g)(2) of this rule.

(b) *Mailing of Tender Offer Materials by the Subject Company.* A subject company which elects pursuant to paragraph (a)(3) of this rule to comply with the provisions of this paragraph shall perform the acts prescribed by the following paragraphs.

(1) The subject company shall promptly contact each participant named on the most recent security position listing of any clearing agency within the access of the subject company and make inquiry of each such participant as to the approximate number of beneficial owners of the subject company securities being sought in the tender offer held by each such participant.

(2) No later than the third business day after delivery of the bidder's tender offer materials pursuant to paragraph (g)(1) of this rule, the subject company shall begin to mail or cause to be mailed by means of first class mail a copy of the bidder's tender offer materials to each person whose name appears as a record holder of the class of securities for which the offer is made on the most recent stockholder list referred to in paragraph (a)(2) of this rule. The subject company shall use its best efforts to complete the mailing in a timely manner but in no event shall such mailing be completed in a substantially greater period of time than the subject company would complete a mailing to security holders of its own materials relating to the tender offer.

(3) No later than the third business day after the delivery of the bidder's tender offer materials pursuant to paragraph (g)(1) of this rule, the subject company shall begin to transmit or cause to be transmitted a sufficient number of sets of the bidder's tender offer materials to the participants named on the security position listings described in paragraph (b)(1) of this rule. The subject company shall use its best efforts to complete the transmittal in a timely manner but in no event shall such transmittal be completed in a substantially greater period of time than the subject company would complete a transmittal to such participants pursuant to security position listings of clearing agencies of its own material relating to the tender offer.

(4) The subject company shall promptly give oral notification to the bidder, which notification shall

be confirmed in writing, of the commencement of the mailing pursuant to paragraph (b)(2) of this rule and of the transmittal pursuant to paragraph (b)(3) of this rule.

(5) During the tender offer and any extension thereof the subject company shall use reasonable efforts to update the stockholder list and shall mail or cause to be mailed promptly following each update a copy of the bidder's tender offer materials (to the extent sufficient sets of such materials have been furnished by the bidder) to each person who has become a record holder since the later of (i) the date of preparation of the most recent stockholder list referred to in paragraph (a)(2) of this rule or (ii) the last preceding update.

(6) If the bidder has elected pursuant to paragraph (f)(1) of this rule to require the subject company to disseminate amendments disclosing material changes to the tender offer materials pursuant to this rule, the subject company, promptly following delivery of each such amendment, shall mail or cause to be mailed a copy of each such amendment to each record holder whose name appears on the shareholder list described in paragraphs (a)(2) and (b)(5) of this rule and shall transmit or cause to be transmitted sufficient copies of such amendment to each participant named on security position listings who received sets of the bidder's tender offer materials pursuant to paragraph (b)(3) of this rule.

(7) The subject company shall not include any communication other than the bidder's tender offer materials or amendments thereto in the envelopes or other containers furnished by the bidder.

(8) Promptly following the termination of the tender offer, the subject company shall reimburse the bidder the excess, if any, of the amounts advanced pursuant to paragraph (f)(3)(iii) over the direct costs incidental to compliance by the subject company and its agents in performing the acts required by this rule computed in accordance with paragraph (g)(2) of this rule.

(c) *Delivery of Stockholder Lists and Security Position Listings.* A subject company which elects pursuant to paragraph (a)(3) of this rule to comply with the provisions of this paragraph shall perform the acts prescribed by the following paragraphs.

(1) No later than the third business day after the date of the bidder's request, the subject company must furnish to the bidder at the subject company's principal executive office a copy of the names and addresses of the record holders on the most recent stockholder list referred to in paragraph (a)(2) of this rule; the names and addresses of participants identified on the most recent security position listing of any clearing agency that is within the access of the subject company; and the most recent list of names, addresses and security positions of beneficial owners as specified in Rule 14a–13(b), in the possession of the subject company, or that subsequently comes into its possession. All security holder list information must be in the format requested by the bidder to the extent the format is available to the subject company without undue burden or expense.

(2) If the bidder has elected pursuant to paragraph (f)(1) of this rule to require the subject company to disseminate amendments disclosing material changes to the tender offer materials, the subject company shall update the stockholder list by furnishing the bidder with the name and address of each record holder named on the stockholder list, and not previously furnished to the bidder, promptly after such information becomes available to the subject company during the tender offer and any extensions thereof.

(d) *Liability of Subject Company and Others.* Neither the subject company nor any affiliate or agent of the subject company nor any clearing agency shall be:

(1) Deemed to have made a solicitation or recommendation respecting the tender offer within the meaning of section 14(d)(4) based solely upon the compliance or noncompliance by the subject company or any affiliate or agent of the subject company with one or more requirements of this rule;

(2) Liable under any provision of the Federal securities laws to the bidder or to any security holder based solely upon the inaccuracy of the current names or addresses on the stockholder list or security position listing, unless such inaccuracy results from a lack of reasonable care on the part of the subject company or any affiliate or agent of the subject company;

(3) Deemed to be an "underwriter" within the meaning of section (2)(11) of the Securities Act of 1933 for any purpose of that Act or any rule or regulation promulgated thereunder based solely upon the compliance or noncompliance by the subject company or any affiliate or agent of the subject company with one or more of the requirements of this rule;

(4) Liable under any provision of the Federal securities laws for the disclosure in the bidder's tender offer materials, including any amendment thereto, based solely upon the compliance or non-compliance by the subject company or any affiliate or agent of the subject company with one or more of the requirements of this rule.

(e) *Content of the Bidder's Request.* The bidder's written request referred to in paragraph (a) of this rule shall include the following:

(1) The identity of the bidder;

(2) The title of the class of securities which is the subject of the bidder's tender offer;

(3) A statement that the bidder is making a request to the subject company pursuant to paragraph (a) of this rule for the use of the stockholder list and security position listings for the purpose of disseminating a tender offer to security holders;

(4) A statement that the bidder is aware of and will comply with the provisions of paragraph (f) of this rule;

(5) A statement as to whether or not it has elected pursuant to paragraph (f)(1) of this rule to disseminate amendments disclosing material changes to the tender offer materials pursuant to this rule; and

(6) The name, address and telephone number of the person whom the subject company shall contact pursuant to paragraph (a)(4) of this rule.

(f) *Obligations of the Bidder.* Any bidder who requests that a subject company comply with the provisions of paragraph (a) of this rule shall comply with the following paragraphs.

(1) The bidder shall make an election whether or not to require the subject company to disseminate amendments disclosing material changes to the tender offer materials pursuant to this rule, which election shall be included in the request referred to in paragraph (a) of this rule and shall not be revocable by the bidder during the tender offer and extensions thereof.

(2) With respect to a tender offer subject to section 14(d)(1) of the Act in which the consideration consists solely of cash and/or securities exempt from registration under section 3 of the Securities Act of 1933, the bidder shall comply with the requirements of Rule 14d–4(a)(3).

(3) If the subject company elects to comply with paragraph (b) of this rule,

(i) The bidder shall promptly deliver the tender offer materials after receipt of the notification from the subject company as provided in paragraph (a)(4) of this rule;

(ii) The bidder shall promptly notify the subject company of any amendment to the bidder's tender offer materials requiring compliance by the subject company with paragraph (b)(6) of this rule and shall promptly deliver such amendment to the subject company pursuant to paragraph (g)(1) of this rule;

(iii) The bidder shall advance to the subject company an amount equal to the approximate cost of conducting mailings to security holders computed in accordance with paragraph (g)(2) of this rule;

(iv) The bidder shall promptly reimburse the subject company for the direct costs incidental to compliance by the subject company and its agents in performing the acts required by this rule computed in accordance with paragraph (g)(2) of this rule which are in excess of the amount advanced pursuant to paragraph (f)(2)(iii) of this rule; and

(v) The bidder shall mail by means of first class mail or otherwise furnish with reasonable promptness the tender offer materials to any security holder who requests such materials.

(4) If the subject company elects to comply with paragraph (c) of this rule,

(i) The bidder shall use the stockholder list and security position listings furnished to the bidder pursuant to paragraph (c) of this rule exclusively in the dissemination of tender offer materials to security holders in connection with the bidder's tender offer and extensions thereof;

(ii) The bidder shall return the stockholder lists and security position listings furnished to the bidder pursuant to paragraph (c) of this rule promptly after the termination of the bidder's tender offer;

(iii) The bidder shall accept, handle and return the stockholder lists and security position listings furnished to the bidder pursuant to paragraph (c) of this rule to the subject company on a confidential basis;

(iv) The bidder shall not retain any stockholder list or security position listing furnished by the subject company pursuant to paragraph (c) of this rule, or any copy thereof, nor retain any information derived from any such list or listing or copy thereof after the termination of the bidder's tender offer;

(v) The bidder shall mail by means of first class mail, at its own expense, a copy of its tender offer materials to each person whose identity appears on the stockholder list as furnished and updated by the subject company pursuant to paragraphs (c)(1) and (c)(2) of this rule;

(vi) The bidder shall contact the participants named on the security position listing of any clearing agency, make inquiry of each participant as to the approximate number of sets of tender offer materials required by each such participant, and furnish, at its own expense, sufficient sets of tender offer materials and any amendment thereto to each such participant for subsequent transmission to the beneficial owners of the securities being sought by the bidder;

(vii) The bidder shall mail by means of first class mail or otherwise furnish with reasonable promptness the tender offer materials to any security holder who requests such materials; and

(viii) The bidder shall promptly reimburse the subject company for direct costs incidental to compliance by the subject company and its agents in performing the acts required by this rule computed in accordance with paragraph (g)(2) of this rule.

(g) *Delivery of Materials, Computation of Direct Costs.* (1) Whenever the bidder is required to deliver tender offer materials or amendments to tender offer materials, the bidder shall deliver to the subject company at the location specified by the subject company in its notice given pursuant to paragraph (a)(4) of this rule a number of sets of the materials or of the amendment, as the case may be, at least equal to the approximate number of security holders specified by the subject company in such notice, together with appropriate envelopes or other containers therefor: *Provided, however,* That such delivery shall be deemed not to have been made unless the bidder has complied with paragraph (f)(3)(iii) of this rule at the time the materials or amendments, as the case may be, are delivered.

(2) The approximate direct cost of mailing the bidder's tender offer materials shall be computed by adding (i) the direct cost incidental to the mailing of the subject company's last annual report to shareholders (excluding employee time), less the costs of preparation and printing of the report, and postage, plus (ii) the amount of first class postage required to mail the bidder's tender offer materials. The approximate direct costs incidental to the mailing of the amendments to the bidder's tender offer materials shall be computed by adding (iii) the estimated direct costs of preparing mailing labels, of updating shareholders lists and of third party handling charges plus (iv) the amount of first class postage required to mail the bidder's amendment. Direct costs incidental to the mailing of the bidder's tender offer materials and amendments thereto when finally computed may include all reasonable charges paid by the subject company to third parties for supplies or services, including costs attendant to preparing shareholder lists, mailing labels, handling the bidder's materials, contacting participants named on security position listings and for postage, but shall exclude indirect costs, such as employee time which is devoted to either contesting or supporting the tender offer on behalf of the subject company. The final billing for direct costs shall be accompanied by an appropriate accounting in reasonable detail.

NOTE TO RULE 14d-5. Reasonably prompt methods of distribution to security holders may be used instead of mailing. If alternative methods are chosen, the approximate direct costs of distribution shall be computed by adding the estimated direct costs of preparing the document for distribution through the chosen medium (including updating of shareholder lists) plus the estimated reasonable cost of distribution through that medium. Direct costs incidental to the distribution of tender offer materials and amendments thereto may include all reasonable charges paid by the subject company to third parties for supplies or services, including costs attendant to preparing shareholder lists, handling the bidder's materials, and contacting participants named on security position listings, but shall not include indirect costs, such as employee time which is devoted to either contesting or supporting the tender offer on behalf of the subject company.

Rule 14d-6. Disclosure of tender offer information to security holders

(a) *Information Required on Date of Commencement.* (1) *Long-Form Publication.* If a tender offer is published, sent or given to security holders on the date of commencement by means of long-form publication under Rule 14d-4(a)(1), the long-form publication must include the information required by paragraph (d)(1) of this rule.

(2) *Summary Publication.* If a tender offer is published, sent or given to security holders on the date of commencement by means of summary publication under Rule 14d-4(a)(2):

(i) The summary advertisement must contain at least the information required by paragraph (d)(2) of this rule; and

(ii) The tender offer materials furnished by the bidder upon request of any security holder must include the information required by paragraph (d)(1) of this rule.

(3) *Use of Stockholder Lists and Security Position Listings.* If a tender offer is published, sent or given to security holders on the date of commencement by the use of stockholder lists and security position listings under Rule 14d–4(a)(3):

(i) The summary advertisement must contain at least the information required by paragraph (d)(2) of this rule; and

(ii) The tender offer materials transmitted to security holders pursuant to such lists and security position listings and furnished by the bidder upon the request of any security holder must include the information required by paragraph (d)(1) of this rule.

(4) *Other Tender Offers.* If a tender offer is published or sent or given to security holders other than pursuant to Rule 14d–4(a), the tender offer materials that are published or sent or given to security holders on the date of commencement of such offer must include the information required by paragraph (d)(1) of this rule.

(b) *Information Required in Other Tender Offer Materials Published After Commencement.* Except for tender offer materials described in paragraphs (a)(2)(ii) and (a)(3)(ii) of this rule, additional tender offer materials published, sent or given to security holders after commencement must include:

(1) The identities of the bidder and subject company;

(2) The amount and class of securities being sought;

(3) The type and amount of consideration being offered; and

(4) The scheduled expiration date of the tender offer, whether the tender offer may be extended and, if so, the procedures for extension of the tender offer.

Instruction to Paragraph (b): If the additional tender offer materials are summary advertisements, they also must include the information required by paragraphs (d)(2)(v) of this rule.

(c) *Material Changes.* A material change in the information published or sent or given to security holders must be promptly disclosed to security holders in additional tender offer materials.

(d) *Information to Be Included.* (1) *Tender Offer Materials Other than Summary Publication.* The following information is required by paragraphs (a)(1), (a)(2)(ii), (a)(3)(ii) and (a)(4) of this rule:

(i) The information required by Item 1 of Schedule TO (Rule 14d–100) (Summary Term Sheet); and

(ii) The information required by the remaining items of Schedule TO (Rule 14d–100) for third-party tender offers, except for Item 12 (exhibits) of Schedule TO (Rule 14d–100), or a fair and adequate summary of the information.

(2) *Summary Publication.* The following information is required in a summary advertisement under paragraphs (a)(2)(i) and (a)(3)(i) of this rule:

(i) The identity of the bidder and the subject company;

(ii) The information required by Item 1004(a)(1) of Regulation M–A;

(iii) If the tender offer is for less than all of the outstanding securities of a class of equity securities, a statement as to whether the purpose or one of the purposes of the tender offer is to acquire or influence control of the business of the subject company;

(iv) A statement that the information required by paragraph (d)(1) of this rule is incorporated by reference into the summary advertisement;

(v) Appropriate instructions as to how security holders may obtain promptly, at the bidder's expense, the bidder's tender offer materials; and

(vi) In a tender offer published or sent or given to security holders by use of stockholder lists and security position listings under Rule 14d–4(a)(3), a statement that a request is being made for such lists and listings. The summary publication also must state that tender offer materials will be mailed to record holders and will be furnished to brokers, banks and similar persons whose name appears or whose nominee appears on the list of security holders or, if applicable, who are listed as participants in a clearing agency's security position listing for subsequent transmittal to beneficial owners of such securities. If the list furnished to the bidder also included beneficial owners pursuant to Rule 14d–5(c)(1) and tender offer materials will be mailed directly to beneficial holders, include a statement to that effect.

(3) *No Transmittal Letter.* Neither the initial summary advertisement nor any subsequent summary advertisement may include a transmittal letter (the letter furnished to security holders for transmission of securities sought in the tender offer) or any amendment to the transmittal letter.

Rule 14d–7. Additional withdrawal rights

(a)(1) *Rights.* In addition to the provisions of section 14(d)(5) of the Act, any person who has deposited securities pursuant to a tender offer has the right to withdraw any such securities during the period such offer, request or invitation remains open.

(2) *Exemption During Subsequent Offering Period.* Notwithstanding the provisions of section 14(d)(5) of the Act (15 U.S.C. 78n(d)(5)) and paragraph (a) of this rule, the bidder need not offer withdrawal rights during a subsequent offering period.

(b) *Notice of Withdrawal.* Notice of withdrawal pursuant to this rule shall be deemed to be timely upon the receipt by the bidder's depositary of a written notice of withdrawal specifying the name(s) of the tendering stockholder(s), the number or amount of the securities to be withdrawn and the name(s) in which the certificate(s) is (are) registered, if different from that of the tendering security holder(s). A bidder may impose other reasonable requirements, including certificate numbers and a signed request for withdrawal accompanied by a signature guarantee, as conditions precedent to the physical release of withdrawn securities.

Rule 14d–8. Exemption from statutory pro rata requirements

Notwithstanding the pro rata provisions of Section 14(d)(6) of the Act, if any person makes a tender offer or request or invitation for tenders, for less than all of the outstanding equity securities of a class, and if a greater number of securities are deposited pursuant thereto than such person is bound or willing to take up and pay for, the securities taken up and paid for shall be taken up and paid for as nearly as may be pro rata, disregarding fractions, according to the number of securities deposited by each depositor during the period such offer, request or invitation remains open.

Rule 14d–9. Recommendation or solicitation by the subject company and others

(a) *Pre–Commencement Communications.* A communication by a person described in paragraph (e) of this rule with respect to a tender offer will not be deemed to constitute a recommendation or solicitation under this section if:

(1) The tender offer has not commenced under Rule 14d–2; and

(2) The communication is filed under cover of Schedule 14D–9 (Rule 14d–101) with the Commission no later than the date of the communication.

Instructions to Paragraph (a)(2):

1. The box on the front of Schedule 14D–9 (Rule 14d–101) indicating that the filing contains pre-commencement communications must be checked.

2. Any communications made in connection with an exchange offer registered under the Securities Act of 1933 need only be filed under Rule 425 under the Securities Act of 1933 and will be deemed filed under this rule.

3. Each pre-commencement written communication must include a prominent legend in clear, plain language advising security holders to read the company's solicitation/recommendation statement when it is available because it contains important information. The legend also must advise investors that they can get the recommendation and other filed documents for free at the Commission's web site and explain which documents are free from the filer.

4. See Rules 135, 165 and 166 under the Securities Act of 1933 for pre-commencement communications made in connection with registered exchange offers.

(b) *Post–Commencement Communications.* After commencement by a bidder under Rule 14d–2, no solicitation or recommendation to security holders may be made by any person described in paragraph (e) of this rule with respect to a tender offer for such securities unless as soon as practicable on the date such solicitation or recommendation is first published or sent or given to security holders such person complies with the following:

(1) Such person shall file with the Commission a Tender Offer Solicitation/Recommendation Statement on Schedule 14D–9 (Rule 14d–101), including all exhibits thereto; and

(2) If such person is either the subject company or an affiliate of the subject company,

(i) Such person shall hand deliver a copy of the Schedule 14D–9 to the bidder at its principal office or at the address of the person authorized to receive notices and communications (which is set forth on the cover sheet of the bidder's Schedule TO (Rule 14d–101) filed with the Commission); and

(ii) Such person shall give telephonic notice (which notice to the extent possible shall be given prior to the opening of the market) of the information required by Items 1003(d) and 1012(a) of Regulation M–A and shall mail a copy of the Schedule to each national securities exchange where the class of securities is registered and listed for trading and, if the class is authorized for quotation in the NASDAQ interdealer quotation system, to the National Association of Securities Dealers, Inc. ("NASD").

(3) If such person is neither the subject company nor an affiliate of the subject company.

(i) Such person shall mail a copy of the schedule to the bidder at its principal office or at the address of the person authorized to receive notices and communications (which is set forth on the cover sheet of the bidder's Schedule TO (Rule 14d–100) filed with the Commission); and

(ii) Such person shall mail a copy of the Schedule to the subject company at its principal office.

(c) *Amendments.* If any material change occurs in the information set forth in the Schedule 14D–9 (Rule 14d–101) required by this rule, the person who filed such Schedule 14D–9 shall:

(1) File with the Commission an amendment on Schedule 14D–9 (Rule 14d–101) disclosing such change promptly, but not later than the date such material is first published, sent or given to security holders; and

(2) Promptly deliver copies and give notice of the amendment in the same manner as that specified in paragraph (b)(2) or (3) of this rule, whichever is applicable; and

(3) Promptly disclose and disseminate such change in a manner reasonably designed to inform security holders of such change.

(d) *Information Required in Solicitation or Recommendation.* Any solicitation or recommendation to holders of a class of securities referred to in section 14(d)(1) of the Act with respect to a tender offer for such securities shall include the name of the person making such solicitation or recommendation and the information required by Items 1 through 8 of Schedule 14D–9 (Rule 14d–101) or a fair and adequate summary thereof: *Provided, however,* That such solicitation or recommendation may omit any of such information previously furnished to security holders of such class of securities by such person with respect to such tender offer.

(e) *Applicability.* (1) Except as provided in paragraphs (e)(2) and (f) of this rule, this rule shall only apply to the following persons:

(i) The subject company, any director, officer, employee, affiliate or subsidiary of the subject company;

(ii) Any record holder or beneficial owner of any security issued by the subject company, by the bidder, or by any affiliate of either the subject company or the bidder; and

(iii) Any person who makes a solicitation or recommendation to security holders on behalf of any of the foregoing or on behalf of the bidder other than by means of a solicitation or recommendation to security holders which has been filed with the Commission pursuant to this rule or Rule 14d–3.

(2) Notwithstanding paragraph (e)(1) of this rule, this rule shall not apply to the following persons:

(i) A bidder who has filed a Schedule TO (Rule 14d–101) pursuant to Rule 14d–3;

(ii) Attorneys, banks, brokers, fiduciaries or investment advisers who are not participating in a tender offer in more than a ministerial capacity and who furnish information and/or advice regarding such tender offer to their customers or clients on the unsolicited request of such customers or clients or solely pursuant to a contract or a relationship providing for advice to the customer or client to whom the information and/or advice is given.

(iii) Any person specified in paragraph (d)(1) of this rule if:

(A) The subject company is the subject of a tender offer conducted under Rule 14d–1(c);

(B) Any person specified in paragraph (e)(1) of this rule furnishes to the Commission on Form CB (17 CFR 249.480) the entire informational document it publishes or otherwise disseminates to holders of the class of securities in connection with the tender offer no later than the next business day after publication or dissemination;

(C) Any person specified in paragraph (e)(1) of this rule disseminates any informational document to U.S. holders, including any amendments thereto, in English, on a comparable basis to that provided to security holders in the issuer's home jurisdiction; and

(D) Any person specified in paragraph (e)(1) of this rule disseminates by publication in its home jurisdiction, such person must publish the information in the United States in a manner reasonably calculated to inform U.S. security holders of the offer.

(f) *Stop-Look-and-Listen Communication.* This rule shall not apply to the subject company with respect to a communication by the subject company to its security holders which only:

(1) Identifies the tender offer by the bidder;

(2) States that such tender offer is under consideration by the subject company's board of directors and/or management;

(3) States that on or before a specified date (which shall be no later than 10 business days from the date of commencement of such tender offer) the subject company will advise such security holders of (i) whether the subject company recommends acceptance or rejection of such tender offer; expresses no opinion and remains neutral toward such tender offer; or is unable to take a position with respect to such tender offer and (ii) the reason(s) for the position taken by the subject company with respect to the tender offer (including the inability to take a position); and

(4) Requests such security holders to defer making determination whether to accept or reject such tender offer until they have been advised of the subject company's position with respect thereto pursuant to paragraph (f)(3) of this rule.

(g) *Statement of Management's Position.* A statement by the subject company's of its position with respect to a tender offer which is required to be published or sent or given to security holders pursuant to Rule 14e–2 shall be deemed to constitute a solicitation or recommendation within the meaning of this rule and section 14(d)(4) of the Act.

Rule 14d–10. Equal treatment of security holders

(a) No bidder shall make a tender offer unless:

(1) The tender offer is open to all security holders of the class of securities subject to the tender offer; and

(2) The consideration paid to any security holder for securities tendered in the tender offer is the highest consideration paid to any other security holder for securities tendered in the tender offer.

(b) Paragraph (a)(1) of this rule shall not:

(1) Affect dissemination under Rule 14d–4; or

(2) Prohibit a bidder from making a tender offer excluding all security holders in a state where the bidder is prohibited from making the tender offer by administrative or judicial action pursuant to a state statute after a good faith effort by the bidder to comply with such statute.

(c) Paragraph (a)(2) of this rule shall not prohibit the offer of more than one type of consideration in a tender offer, *Provided,* That:

(1) Security holders are afforded equal right to elect among each of the types of consideration offered; and

(2) The highest consideration of each type paid to any security holder is paid to any other security holder receiving that type of consideration.

(d)(1) Paragraph (a)(2) of this rule shall not prohibit the negotiation, execution or amendment of an employment compensation, severance or other employee benefit arrangement, or payments made or to be made or benefits granted or to be granted according to such an arrangement, with respect to any security holder of the subject company, where the amount payable under the arrangement:

(i) Is being paid or granted as compensation for past services performed, future services to be performed, or future services to be refrained from performing, by the security holder (and matters incidental thereto); and

(ii) Is not calculated based on the number of securities tendered or to be tendered in the tender offer by the security holder.

(2) The provisions of paragraph (d)(1) of this rule shall be satisfied and, therefore, pursuant to this non-exclusive safe harbor, the negotiation, execution or amendment of an arrangement and any payments made or to be made or benefits granted or to be granted according to that arrangement shall not be prohibited by paragraph (a)(2) of this rule, if the arrangement is approved as an employment compensation, severance or other employee benefit arrangement solely by independent directors as follows:

(i) The compensation committee or a committee of the board of directors that performs functions similar to a compensation committee of the subject company approves the arrangement, regardless of whether the subject company is a party to the arrangement, or, if the bidder is a party to the arrangement, the compensation committee or a committee of the board of directors that performs functions similar to a compensation committee of the bidder approves the arrangement; or

(ii) If the subject company's or bidder's board of directors, as applicable, does not have a compensation committee or a committee of the board of directors that performs functions similar to a compensation committee or if none of the members of the subject company's or bidder's compensation committee or committee that performs functions similar to a compensation committee is independent, a special committee of the board of directors formed to consider and approve the arrangement approves the arrangement; or

(iii) If the subject company or bidder, as applicable, is a foreign private issuer, any or all members of the board of directors or any committee of the board of directors authorized to approve employment compensation, severance or other employee benefit arrangements under the laws or regulations of the home country approves the arrangement.

Instructions to Paragraph (d)(2): For purposes of determining whether the members of the committee approving an arrangement in accordance with the provisions of paragraph (d)(2) of this rule are independent, the following provisions shall apply:

1. If the bidder or subject company, as applicable, is a listed issuer (as defined in Rule 10A–3) whose securities are listed either on a national securities exchange registered pursuant to section 6(a) of the Exchange Act (15 U.S.C. 78f(a)) or in an inter-dealer quotation system of a national securities association registered pursuant to section 15A(a) of the Exchange Act (15 U.S.C. 78o–3(a)) that has independence requirements for compensation committee members that have been approved by the Commission (as those requirements may be modified or supplemented), apply the bidder's or subject company's definition of independence that it uses for determining that the members of the compensation committee are independent in compliance with the listing standards applicable to compensation committee members of the listed issuer.

2. If the bidder or subject company, as applicable, is not a listed issuer (as defined in Rule 10A–3), apply the independence requirements for compensation committee members of a national securities exchange registered pursuant to section 6(a) of the Exchange Act (15 U.S.C. 78f(a)) or an inter-dealer quotation system of a national securities association registered pursuant to section 15A(a) of the Exchange Act (15 U.S.C. 78o–3(a)) that have been approved by the Commission (as those requirements may be modified or supplemented). Whatever definition the bidder or subject company, as applicable, chooses, it must apply that definition consistently to all members of the committee approving the arrangement.

3. Notwithstanding Instructions 1 and 2 to paragraph (d)(2), if the bidder or subject company, as applicable, is a closed-end investment company registered under the Investment Company Act of 1940, a director is considered to be independent if the director is not, other than in his or her capacity as a member of the board of directors or any board committee, an "interested person" of the investment company, as defined in section 2(a)(19) of the Investment Company Act of 1940 (15 U.S.C. 80a–2(a)(19)).

4. If the bidder or the subject company, as applicable, is a foreign private issuer, apply either the independence standards set forth in Instructions 1 and 2 to paragraph (d)(2) or the independence requirements of the laws, regulations, codes or standards of the home country of the bidder or subject company, as applicable, for members of the board of directors or the committee of the board of directors approving the arrangement.

5. A determination by the bidder's or the subject company's board of directors, as applicable, that the members of the board of directors or the committee of the board of directors, as applicable, approving an arrangement in accordance with the provisions of paragraph (d)(2) are independent in accordance with the provisions of this instruction to paragraph (d)(2) shall satisfy the independence requirements of paragraph (d)(2).

Instruction to Paragraph (d): The fact that the provisions of paragraph (d) of this rule extend only to employment compensation, severance and other employee benefit arrangements and not to other arrangements, such as commercial arrangements, does not raise any inference that a payment under any such other arrangement constitutes consideration paid for securities in a tender offer.

(e) If the offer and sale of securities constituting consideration offered in a tender offer is prohibited by the appropriate authority of a state after a good faith effort by the bidder to register or qualify the offer and sale of such securities in such state:

(1) The bidder may offer security holders in such state an alternative form of consideration; and

(2) Paragraph (c) of this rule shall not operate to require the bidder to offer or pay the alternative form of consideration to security holders in any other state.

(f) This rule shall not apply to any tender offer with respect to which the Commission, upon written request or upon its own motion, either unconditionally or on specified terms and conditions, determines that compliance with this rule is not necessary or appropriate in the public interest or for the protection of investors.

Rule 14d–11. Subsequent offering period

A bidder may elect to provide a subsequent offering period of at least three business days during which tenders will be accepted if:

(a) The initial offering period of at least 20 business days has expired;

(b) The offer is for all outstanding securities of the class that is the subject of the tender offer, and if the bidder is offering security holders a choice of different forms of consideration, there is no ceiling on any form of consideration offered;

(c) The bidder immediately accepts and promptly pays for all securities tendered during the initial offering period;

(d) The bidder announces the results of the tender offer, including the approximate number and percentage of securities deposited to date, no later than 9:00 a.m. Eastern time on the next business day after the expiration date of the initial offering period and immediately begins the subsequent offering period;

(e) The bidder immediately accepts and promptly pays for all securities as they are tendered during the subsequent offering period; and

(f) The bidder offers the same form and amount of consideration to security holders in both the initial and the subsequent offering period.

NOTE TO RULE 14d-11: No withdrawal rights apply during the subsequent offering period in accordance with Rule 14d-7(a)(2).

Rule 14d-100. Schedule to tender offer statement under Section 14(d)(1) or 13(e)(1) of the Securities Exchange Act of 1934

Securities and Exchange Commission,

Washington, D.C. 20549

Schedule TO

Tender Offer Statement under Section 14(d)(1) or 13(e)(1) of the Securities Exchange Act of 1934

(Amendment No. ________)*

____

(Name of Subject Company (issuer))

____

(Names of Filing Persons (identifying status as offeror, issuer or other person))

____

(Title of Class of Securities)

____

(CUSIP Number of Class of Securities)

(Name, address, and telephone numbers of person authorized to receive notices and communications on behalf of filing persons)

Calculation of Filing Fee

Transaction Valuation *	Amount of Filing Fee

* Set forth the amount on which the filing fee is calculated and state how it was determined.

[ ] Check the box if any part of the fee is offset as provided by Rule 0-11(a)(2) and identify the filing with which the offsetting fee was previously paid. Identify the previous filing by registration statement number, or the Form or Schedule and the date of its filing.

Amount Previously Paid: ________________

Form or Registration No.: ________________

Filing Party: ________________

Date Filed: ________________

[ ] Check the box if the filing relates solely to preliminary communications made before the commencement of a tender offer.

Check the appropriate boxes below to designate any transactions to which the statement relates:

[ ] third-party tender offer subject to Rule 14d-1.

[ ] issuer tender offer subject to Rule 13e-4.

[ ] going-private transaction subject to Rule 13e-3.

[ ] amendment to Schedule 13D under Rule 13d-2.

Check the following box if the filing is a final amendment reporting the results of the tender offer: [ ]

If applicable, check the appropriate box(es) below to designate the appropriate rule provision(s) relied upon:

[ ] Rule 13e-4(i) (Cross-Border Issuer Tender Offer)

[ ] Rule 14d-1(d) (Cross-Border Third-Party Tender Offer)

General Instructions:

A. File eight copies of the statement, including all exhibits, with the Commission if paper filing is permitted.

B. This filing must be accompanied by a fee payable to the Commission as required by Rule 0-11.

C. If the statement is filed by a general or limited partnership, syndicate or other group, the information called for by Items 3 and 5-8 for a third-party tender offer and Items 5-8 for an issuer tender offer must be given with respect to: (i) Each partner of the general partnership; (ii) each partner who is, or functions as, a general partner of the limited partnership; (iii) each member of the syndicate or group; and (iv) each person controlling the partner or member. If the statement is filed by a corporation or if a person referred to in (i), (ii), (iii) or (iv) of this Instruction is a corporation, the information called for by the items specified above must be given with respect to: (a) Each executive officer and director of the corporation; (b) each person controlling the corporation; and (c) each executive officer and director of any corporation or other person ultimately in control of the corporation.

D. If the filing contains only preliminary communications made before the commencement of a tender offer, no signature or filing fee is required. The filer need not respond to the items in the schedule. Any pre-commencement communications that are filed under cover of this schedule need not be incorporated by reference into the schedule.

E. If an item is inapplicable or the answer is in the negative, so state. The statement published, sent or given to security holders may omit negative and not applicable responses. If the schedule includes any information that is not published, sent or given to security holders, provide that information or specifically incorporate it by reference under the appropriate item number and heading in the schedule. Do not recite the text of disclosure requirements in the schedule or any document published, sent or given to security holders. Indicate clearly the coverage of the requirements without referring to the text of the items.

F. Information contained in exhibits to the statement may be incorporated by reference in answer or partial answer to any item unless it would render the answer misleading, incomplete, unclear or confusing. A copy of any information that is incorporated by reference or a copy of the pertinent pages of a document containing the information must be submitted with this statement as an exhibit, unless it was previously filed with the Commission electronically on EDGAR. If an exhibit contains information responding to more than one item in the schedule, all information in that exhibit may be incorporated by reference once in response to the several items in the schedule for which it provides an answer. Information incorporated by reference is deemed filed with the Commission for all purposes of the Act.

G. A filing person may amend its previously filed Schedule 13D (Rule 13d–101) on Schedule TO (Rule 14d–100) if the appropriate box on the cover page is checked to indicate a combined filing and the information called for by the fourteen disclosure items on the cover page of Schedule 13D (Rule 13d–101) is provided on the cover page of the combined filing with respect to each filing person.

H. The final amendment required by Rule 14d–3(b)(2) and Rule 13e–4(c)(4) will satisfy the reporting requirements of section 13(d) of the Act with respect to all securities acquired by the offeror in the tender offer.

I. Amendments disclosing a material change in the information set forth in this statement may omit any information previously disclosed in this statement.

J. If the tender offer disclosed on this statement involves a going-private transaction, a combined Schedule TO (Rule 14d–100) and Schedule 13E–3 (Rule 13e–100) may be filed with the Commission under cover of Schedule TO. The Rule 13e–3 box on the cover page of the Schedule TO must be checked to indicate a combined filing. All information called for by both schedules must be provided except that Items 1–3, 5, 8 and 9 of Schedule TO may be omitted to the extent those items call for information that duplicates the item requirements in Schedule 13E–3.

K. For purposes of this statement, the following definitions apply:

(1) The term *offeror* means any person who makes a tender offer or on whose behalf a tender offer is made;

(2) The term *issuer tender offer* has the same meaning as in Rule 13e–4(a)(2); and

(3) The term *third-party tender offer* means a tender offer that is not an issuer tender offer.

Special Instructions for Complying With Schedule TO

Under Sections 13(e), 14(d) and 23 of the Act and the rules and regulations of the Act, the Commission is authorized to solicit the information required to be supplied by this schedule.

Disclosure of the information specified in this schedule is mandatory. The information will be used for the primary purpose of disclosing tender offer and going-private transactions. This statement will be made a matter of public record. Therefore, any information given will be available for inspection by any member of the public.

Because of the public nature of the information, the Commission can use it for a variety of purposes, including referral to other governmental authorities or securities self-regulatory organizations for investigatory purposes or in connection with litigation involving the Federal securities laws or other civil, criminal or regulatory statutes or provisions.

Failure to disclose the information required by this schedule may result in civil or criminal action against the persons involved for violation of the federal securities laws and rules.

Item 1. Summary Term Sheet

Furnish the information required by Item 1001 of Regulation M–A unless information is disclosed to security holders in a prospectus that meets the requirements of Rule 421(d) under the Securities Act of 1933.

Item 2. Subject Company Information

Furnish the information required by Item 1002(a) through (c) of Regulation M–A.

Item 3. Identity and Background of Filing Person

Furnish the information required by Item 1003(a) through (c) of Regulation M–A for a third-party tender offer and the information required by Item 1003(a) of Regulation M–A for an issuer tender offer.

Item 4. Terms of the Transaction

Furnish the information required by Item 1004(a) of Regulation M–A for a third-party tender offer and the information required by Item 1004(a) through (b) of Regulation M–A for an issuer tender offer.

Item 5. Past Contacts, Transactions, Negotiations and Agreements

Furnish the information required by Item 1005(a) and (b) of Regulation M–A for a third-party tender offer and the information required by Item 1005(e) of Regulation M–A for an issuer tender offer.

Item 6. Purposes of the Transaction and Plans or Proposals

Furnish the information required by Item 1006(a) and (c)(1) through (7) of Regulation M–A for a third-party tender offer and the information required by Item 1006(a) through (c) of Regulation M–A for an issuer tender offer.

Item 7. Source and Amount of Funds or Other Consideration

Furnish the information required by Item 1007(a), (b) and (d) of Regulation M–A.

Item 8. Interest in Securities of the Subject Company

Furnish the information required by Item 1008 of Regulation M–A.

Item 9. Persons/Assets, Retained, Employed, Compensated or Used

Furnish the information required by Item 1009(a) of Regulation M–A.

Item 10. Financial Statements

If material, furnish the information required by Item 1010(a) and (b) of Regulation M–A for the issuer in an issuer tender offer and for the offeror in a third-party tender offer.

Instructions to Item 10:

1. Financial statements must be provided when the offeror's financial condition is material to security holder's decision whether to sell, tender or hold the securities sought. The facts and circumstances of a tender offer, particularly the terms of the tender offer, may influence a determination as to whether financial statements are material, and thus required to be disclosed.

2. Financial statements are *not* considered material when: (a) The consideration offered consists solely of cash; (b) the offer is not subject to any financing condition; *and* either: (c) the offeror is a public reporting company under Section 13(a) or 15(d) of the Act that files reports electronically on EDGAR, or (d) the offer is for all outstanding securities of the subject class. Financial information may be required, however, in a two-tier transaction. *See* Instruction 5 below.

3. The filing person may incorporate by reference financial statements contained in any document filed with the Commission, solely for the purposes of this schedule, if: (a) The financial statements substantially meet the requirements of this item; (b) an express statement is made that the financial statements are incorporated by reference; (c) the information incorporated by reference is clearly identified by page, paragraph, caption or otherwise; and (d) if the information incorporated by reference is not filed with this schedule, an indication is made where the information may be inspected and copies obtained. Financial statements that are required to be presented in comparative form for two or more fiscal years or periods may not be incorporated by reference unless the material incorporated by reference includes the entire period for which the comparative data is required to be given. *See* General Instruction F to this schedule.

4. If the offeror in a third-party tender offer is a natural person, and such person's financial information is material, disclose the net worth of the offeror. If the offeror's net worth is derived from material amounts of assets that are not readily marketable or there are material guarantees and contingencies, disclose the nature and approximate amount of the individual's net worth that consists of illiquid assets and the magnitude of any guarantees or contingencies that may negatively affect the natural person's net worth.

5. Pro forma financial information is required in a negotiated third-party cash tender offer when securities are intended to be offered in a subsequent merger or other transaction in which remaining target securities are acquired and the acquisition of the subject company is significant to the offeror under Rule 11–01(b)(1) of Regulation S–X. The offeror must disclose the financial information specified in Item 3(f) and Item 5 of Form S–4 (17 CFR 239.25) in the schedule filed with the Commission, but may furnish only the summary financial information specified in Item 3(d), (e) and (f) of Form S–4 in the disclosure document sent to security holders. If pro forma financial information is required by this instruction, the historical financial statements specified in Item 1010 of Regulation M–A are required for the bidder.

6. The disclosure materials disseminated to security holders may contain the summarized financial information specified by Item 1010(c) of Regulation M–A instead of the financial information required by Item 1010(a) and (b). In that case, the financial information required by Item 1010(a) and (b) of Regulation M–A must be disclosed in the statement. If summarized financial information is disseminated to security holders, include appropriate instructions on how more complete financial information can be obtained. If the summarized financial information is prepared on the basis of a comprehensive body of accounting principles other than U.S. GAAP, the summarized financial information must be accompanied by a reconciliation as described in Instruction 8 of this Item.

7. If the offeror is not subject to the periodic reporting requirements of the Act, the financial statements required by this Item need not be audited if audited financial statements are not available or obtainable without unreasonable cost or expense. Make a statement to that effect and the reasons for their unavailability.

8. If the financial statements required by this Item are prepared on the basis of a comprehensive body of accounting principles other than U.S. GAAP, provide a reconciliation to U.S. GAAP in accordance with Item 17 of Form 20–F, unless a reconciliation is unavailable or not obtainable without unreasonable cost or expense. At a minimum, however, when financial statements are prepared on a basis other than U.S. GAAP, a narrative description of all material variations in accounting principles, practices and methods used in preparing the non-U.S. GAAP financial statements from those accepted in the U.S. must be presented.

Item 11. Additional Information

Furnish the information required by Item 1011(a) and (c) of Regulation M–A.

Item 12. Exhibits

File as an exhibit to the Schedule all documents specified by Item 1016 (a), (b), (d), (g) and (h) of Regulation M–A.

Item 13. Information Required by Schedule 13E–3

If the Schedule TO is combined with Schedule 13E–3 (Rule 13e–100), set forth the information required by Schedule 13E–3 that is not included or covered by the items in Schedule TO.

Signature. After due inquiry and to the best of my knowledge and belief, I certify that the information set forth in this statement is true, complete and correct.

____

(Signature)

____

(Name and title)

____

(Date)

Instruction to Signature: The statement must be signed by the filing person or that person's authorized representative. If the statement is signed on behalf of a person by an authorized representative (other than an executive officer of a corporation or general partner of a partnership), evidence of the representative's authority to sign on behalf of the person must be filed with the statement. The name and any title of each person who signs the statement must be typed or printed beneath the signature. See Rules 12b–11 and 14d–1(h) with respect to signature requirements.

Rule 14d–101. Schedule 14D–9

Securities and Exchange Commission,

Washington, D.C. 20549

Schedule 14D–9

Solicitation/Recommendation Statement under Section 14(d)(4) of the Securities Exchange Act of 1934

(Amendment No. ___)

___

(Name of Subject Company)

___

(Names of Persons Filing Statement)

___

(Title of Class of Securities)

___

(CUSIP Number of Class of Securities)

___

(Name, address, and telephone numbers of person authorized to receive notices and communications on behalf of the persons filing statement)

[ ] Check the box if the filing relates solely to preliminary communications made before the commencement of a tender offer.

General Instructions:

A. File eight copies of the statement, including all exhibits, with the Commission if paper filing is permitted.

B. If the filing contains only preliminary communications made before the commencement of a tender offer, no signature is required. The filer need not respond to the items in the schedule. Any pre-commencement communications that are filed under cover of this schedule need not be incorporated by reference into the schedule.

C. If an item is inapplicable or the answer is in the negative, so state. The statement published, sent or given to security holders may omit negative and not applicable responses. If the schedule includes any information that is not published, sent or given to security holders, provide that information or specifically incorporate it by reference under the appropriate item number and heading in the schedule. Do not recite the text of disclosure requirements in the schedule or any document published, sent or given to security holders. Indicate clearly the coverage of the requirements without referring to the text of the items.

D. Information contained in exhibits to the statement may be incorporated by reference in answer or partial answer to any item unless it would render the answer misleading, incomplete, unclear or confusing. A copy of any information that is incorporated by reference or a copy of the pertinent pages of a document containing the information must be submitted with this statement as an exhibit, unless it was previously filed with the Commission electronically on EDGAR. If an exhibit contains information responding to more than one item in the schedule, all information in that exhibit may be incorporated by reference once in response to the several items in the schedule for which it provides an answer. Information incorporated by reference is deemed filed with the Commission for all purposes of the Act.

E. Amendments disclosing a material change in the information set forth in this statement may omit any information previously disclosed in this statement.

Item 1. Subject Company Information

Furnish the information required by Item 1002(a) and (b) of Regulation M–A.

Item 2. Identity and Background of Filing Person

Furnish the information required by Item 1003(a) and (d) of Regulation M–A.

Item 3. Past Contacts, Transactions, Negotiations and Agreements

Furnish the information required by Item 1005(d) of Regulation M–A.

Item 4. The Solicitation or Recommendation

Furnish the information required by Item 1012(a) through (c) of Regulation M–A.

Item 5. Person/Assets, Retained, Employed, Compensated or Used

Furnish the information required by Item 1009(a) of Regulation M–A.

Item 6. Interest in Securities of the Subject Company

Furnish the information required by Item 1008(b) of Regulation M–A.

Item 7. Purposes of the Transaction and Plans or Proposals

Furnish the information required by Item 1006(d) of Regulation M–A.

Item 8. Additional Information

Furnish the information required by Item 1011(b) and (c) of Regulation M–A.

Item 9. Exhibits

File as an exhibit to the Schedule all documents specified by Item 1016(a), (e) and (g) of Regulation M–A (17 CFR 229.1016).

Signature. After due inquiry and to the best of my knowledge and belief, I certify that the information set forth in this statement is true, complete and correct.

____
(Signature)

____
(Name and title)

____
(Date)

Instruction to Signature: The statement must be signed by the filing person or that person's authorized representative. If the statement is signed on behalf of a person by an authorized representative (other than an executive officer of a corporation or general partner of a partnership), evidence of the representative's authority to sign on behalf of the person must be filed with the statement. The name and any title of each person who signs the statement must be typed or printed beneath the signature. See Rule 14d–1(h) with respect to signature requirements.

NOTE: For the scope of and definitions applicable to Regulation 14E, refer to Rule 14d–1.

REGULATION 14E

Rule 14e–1. Unlawful tender offer practices

As a means reasonably designed to prevent fraudulent, deceptive or manipulative acts or practices within the meaning of section 14(e) of the Act, no person who makes a tender offer shall:

(a) Hold such tender offer open for less than twenty business days from the date such tender offer is first published or sent to security holders; provided, however, that if the tender offer involves a roll-up transaction as defined in Item 901(c) of Regulation S–K (17 CFR 229.901(c)) and the securities being offered are registered (or authorized to be registered) on Form S–4 (17 CFR 229.25) or Form F–4 (17 CFR 229.31), the offer shall not be open for less than sixty calendar days from the date the tender offer is first published or sent to security holders;

(b) Increase or decrease the percentage of the class of securities being sought or the consideration offered or the dealer's soliciting fee to be given in a tender offer unless such tender offer remains open for at least ten business days from the date that notice of such increase or decrease is first published or sent or given to security holders;

Provided, however, That, for purposes of this paragraph, the acceptance for payment of an additional amount of securities not to exceed two percent of the class of securities that is the subject of the tender offer shall not be deemed to be an increase. For purposes of this paragraph, the percentage of a class of securities shall be calculated in accordance with section 14(d)(3) of the Act.

(c) Fail to pay the consideration offered or return the securities deposited by or on behalf of security holders promptly after the termination or withdrawal of a tender offer. This paragraph does not prohibit a bidder electing to offer a subsequent offering period under Rule 14d–11 from paying for securities during the subsequent offering period in accordance with that rule.

(d) Extend the length of a tender offer without issuing a notice of such extension by press release or other public announcement, which notice shall include disclosure of the approximate number of securities deposited to date and shall be issued no later than the earlier of: (i) 9:00 a.m. Eastern time, on the next business day after the scheduled expiration date of the offer or (ii), if the class of securities which is the subject of the tender offer is registered on one or more national securities exchanges, the first opening of any one of such exchanges on the next business day after the scheduled expiration date of the offer.

(e) The periods of time required by paragraphs (a) and (b) of this rule shall be tolled for any period during which the bidder has failed to file in electronic format, absent a hardship exemption (Rules 201 and 202 of Regulation S–T), the Schedule TO Tender Offer Statement (Rule 14d–100), any tender offer material required to be filed by Item 12 of that Schedule pursuant to paragraph (a) of Item 1016 of Regulation M–A, and any amendments thereto. If such documents were filed in paper pursuant to a hardship exemption (*see* Rules 201 and 202(d) of Regulation S–T), the minimum offering periods shall be tolled for any period during which a required confirming electronic copy of such Schedule and tender offer material is delinquent.

Rule 14e–2. Position of subject company with respect to a tender offer

(a) *Position of Subject Company*. As a means reasonably designed to prevent fraudulent, deceptive or manipulative acts or practices within the meaning of section 14(e) of the Act, the subject company, no later than 10 business days from the date the tender offer is first published or sent or given, shall publish, send or give to security holders a statement disclosing that the subject company:

(1) Recommends acceptance or rejection of the bidder's tender offer;

(2) Expresses no opinion and is remaining neutral toward the bidder's tender offer; or

(3) Is unable to take a position with respect to the bidder's tender offer. Such statement shall also include the reason(s) for the position (including the inability to take a position) disclosed therein.

(b) *Material Change.* If any material change occurs in the disclosure required by paragraph (a) of this rule, the subject company shall promptly publish, send or give a statement disclosing such material charge to security holders.

(c) Any issuer, a class of the securities of which is the subject of a tender offer filed with the Commission on Schedule 14D–1F and conducted in reliance upon and in conformity with Rule 14d–1(b) under the Act, and any director or officer of such issuer where so required by the laws, regulations and policies of Canada and/or any of its provinces or territories, in lieu of the statements called for by paragraph (a) of this rule and Rule 14d–9 under the Act, shall file with the Commission on Schedule 14D–9F the entire disclosure document(s) required to be furnished to holders of securities of the subject issuer by the laws, regulations and policies of Canada and/or any of its provinces or territories governing the conduct of the tender offer, and shall disseminate such document(s) in the United States in accordance with such laws, regulations and policies.

(d) *Exemption for Cross-Border Tender Offers.* The subject company shall be exempt from this rule with respect to a tender offer conducted under Rule 14d–1(c).

Rule 14e–3. Transactions in securities on the basis of material, nonpublic information in the context of tender offers

(a) If any person has taken a substantial step or steps to commence, or has commenced, a tender offer (the "offering person"), it shall constitute a fraudulent, deceptive or manipulative act or practice within the meaning of section 14(e) of the Act for any other person who is in possession of material information relating to such tender offer which information he knows or has reason to know is nonpublic and which he knows or has reason to know has been acquired directly or indirectly from:

(1) The offering person,

(2) The issuer of the securities sought or to be sought by such tender offer, or

(3) Any officer, director, partner or employee or any other person acting on behalf of the offering person or such issuer,

to purchase or sell or cause to be purchased or sold any of such securities or any securities convertible into or exchangeable for any such securities or any option or right to obtain or to dispose of any of the foregoing securities, unless within a reasonable time prior to any purchase or sale such information and its source are publicly disclosed by press release or otherwise.

(b) A person other than a natural person shall not violate paragraph (a) of this rule if such person shows that:

(1) The individual(s) making the investment decision on behalf of such person to purchase or sell any security described in paragraph (a) or to cause any such security to be purchased or sold by or on behalf of others did not know the material, nonpublic information; and

(2) Such person had implemented one or a combination of policies and procedures, reasonable under the circumstances, taking into consideration the nature of the person's business, to ensure that individual(s) making investment decision(s) would not violate paragraph (a), which policies and procedures may include, but are not limited to, (i) those which restrict any purchase, sale and causing any purchase and sale of any such security or (ii) those which prevent such individual(s) from knowing such information.

(c) Notwithstanding anything in paragraph (a) of this rule to the contrary, the following transactions shall not be violations of paragraph (a) of this rule:

(1) Purchase(s) of any security described in paragraph (a) of this rule by a broker or by another agent on behalf of an offering person; or

(2) Sale(s) by any person of any security described in paragraph (a) to the offering person.

(d)(1) As a means reasonably designed to prevent fraudulent, deceptive or manipulative acts or practices within the meaning of section 14(e) of the Act, it shall be unlawful for any person described in paragraph (d)(2) of this rule to communicate material, nonpublic information relating to a tender offer to any other person under circumstances in which it is reasonably foreseeable that such communication is likely to result in a violation of this rule *except* that this paragraph shall not apply to a communication made in good faith.

(i) To the officers, directors, partners or employees of the offering person, to its advisors or to other persons, involved in the planning, financing, preparation or execution of such tender offer;

(ii) To the issuer whose securities are sought or to be sought by such tender offer, to its officers, directors, partners, employees or advisors or to other persons, involved in the planning, financing, preparation or execution of the activities of the issuer with respect to such tender offer; or

(iii) To any person pursuant to a requirement of any statute or rule or regulation promulgated thereunder.

(2) The persons referred to in paragraph (d)(1) of this rule are:

(i) The offering person or its officers, directors, partners, employees or advisors;

(ii) The issuer of the securities sought or to be sought by such tender offer or its officers, directors, partners, employees or advisors;

(iii) Anyone acting on behalf of the persons in paragraph (d)(2)(i) of this rule or the issuer or persons in paragraph (d)(2)(ii) of this rule; and

(iv) Any person in possession of material information relating to a tender offer which information he knows or has reason to know is nonpublic and which he knows or has reason to know has been acquired directly or indirectly from any of the above.

Rule 14e–4. Prohibited transactions in connection with partial tender offers

(a) *Definitions.* For purposes of this rule:

(1) The amount of a person's "net long position" in a subject security shall equal the excess, if any, of such person's "long position" over such person's "short position." For the purposes of determining the net long position as of the end of the proration period and for tendering concurrently to two or more partial tender offers, securities that have been tendered in accordance with the rule and not withdrawn are deemed to be part of the person's long position.

(i) Such person's *long position,* is the amount of subject securities that such person:

(A) Or his agent has title to or would have title to but for having lent such securities; or

(B) Has purchased, or has entered into an unconditional contract, binding on both parties thereto, to purchase but has not yet received; or

(C) Has exercised a standardized call option for; or

(D) Has converted, exchanged, or exercised an equivalent security for; or

(E) Is entitled to receive upon conversion, exchange, or exercise of an equivalent security.

(ii) Such person's *short position,* is the amount of subject securities or subject securities underlying equivalent securities that such person:

(A) Has sold, or has entered into an unconditional contract, binding on both parties thereto, to sell; or

(B) Has borrowed; or

(C) Has written a non-standardized call option, or granted any other right pursuant to which his shares may be tendered by another person; or

(D) Is obligated to deliver upon exercise of a standardized option sold on or after the date that a tender offer is first publicly announced or otherwise made known by the bidder to holders of the security to be acquired, if the exercise price of such option is lower than the highest tender offer price or stated amount of the consideration offered for the subject security. For the purpose of this paragraph, if one or more tender offers for the same security are ongoing on such date, the announcement date shall be that of the first announced offer.

(2) The term *equivalent security* means:

(i) Any security (including any option, warrant, or other right to purchase the subject security), issued by the person whose securities are the subject of the offer, that is immediately convertible into, or exchangeable or exercisable for, a subject security, or

(ii) Any other right or option (other than a standardized call option) that entitles the holder thereto to acquire a subject security, but only if the holder thereof reasonably believes that the maker or writer of the right or option has title to and possession of the subject security and upon exercise will promptly deliver the subject security.

(3) The term *subject security* means a security that is the subject of any tender offer or request or invitation for tenders.

(4) For purposes of this rule, a person shall be deemed to "tender" a security if he:

(i) Delivers a subject security pursuant to an offer,

(ii) Causes such delivery to be made,

(iii) Guarantees delivery of a subject security pursuant to a tender offer,

(iv) Causes a guarantee of such delivery to be given by another person, or

(v) Uses any other method by which acceptance of a tender offer may be made.

(5) The term *partial tender offer* means a tender offer or request or invitation for tenders for less than all of the outstanding securities subject to the offer in which tenders are accepted either by lot or on a *pro rata* basis for a specified period, or a tender offer for all of the outstanding shares that offers a choice of consideration in which tenders for different forms of consideration may be accepted either by lot or on a *pro rata* basis for a specified period.

(6) The term *standardized call option* means any call option that is traded on an exchange, or for which quotation information is disseminated in an electronic interdealer quotation system of a registered national securities association.

(b) It shall be unlawful for any person acting alone or in concert with others, directly or indirectly, to tender any subject security in a partial tender offer:

(1) For his own account unless at the time of tender, and at the end of the proration period or period during which securities are accepted by lot (including any extensions thereof), he has a net long position equal to or greater than the amount tendered in (i) the subject security and will deliver or cause to be delivered such security for the purpose of tender to the person making the offer within the period specified in the offer; or (ii) an equivalent security and, upon the acceptance of his tender will acquire the subject security by conversion, exchange, or exercise of such equivalent security to the extent required by the terms of the offer, and will deliver or cause to be delivered the subject security so acquired for the purpose of tender to the person making the offer within the period specified in the offer; or

(2) For the account of another person unless the person making the tender:

(i) Possesses the subject security or an equivalent security, or

(ii) Has a reasonable belief that, upon information furnished by the person on whose behalf the tender is made, such person owns the subject security or an equivalent security and will promptly deliver the subject security or such equivalent security for the purpose of tender to the person making the tender.

(c) This rule shall not prohibit any transaction or transactions which the Commission, upon written request or upon its own motion, exempts, either unconditionally or on specified terms and conditions.

Rule 14e–5. Prohibiting purchases outside of a tender offer

(a) *Unlawful Activity.* As a means reasonably designed to prevent fraudulent, deceptive or manipulative acts or practices in connection with a tender offer for equity securities, no covered person may directly or indirectly purchase or arrange to purchase any subject securities or any related securities except as part of the tender offer. This prohibition applies from the time of public announcement of the tender offer until the tender offer expires. This prohibition does not apply to any purchases or arrangements to purchase made during the time of any subsequent offering period as provided for in Rule 14d–11 if the consideration paid or to be paid for the purchases or arrangements to purchase is the same in form and amount as the consideration offered in the tender offer.

(b) *Excepted Activity.* The following transactions in subject securities or related securities are not prohibited by paragraph (a) of this rule:

(1) *Exercises of Securities.* Transactions by covered persons to convert, exchange, or exercise related securities into subject securities, if the covered person owned the related securities before public announcement;

(2) *Purchases for Plans.* Purchases or arrangements to purchase by or for a plan that are made by an agent independent of the issuer;

(3) *Purchases During Odd-Lot Offers.* Purchases or arrangements to purchase if the tender offer is excepted under Rule 13e–4(h)(5);

(4) *Purchases as Intermediary.* Purchases by or through a dealer-manager or its affiliates that are

made in the ordinary course of business and made either:

(i) On an agency basis not for a covered person; or

(ii) As principal for its own account if the dealer-manager or its affiliate is not a market maker, and the purchase is made to offset a contemporaneous sale after having received an unsolicited order to buy from a customer who is not a covered person;

(5) *Basket Transactions.* Purchases or arrangements to purchase a basket of securities containing a subject security or a related security if the following conditions are satisfied:

(i) The purchase or arrangement to purchase is made in the ordinary course of business and not to facilitate the tender offer;

(ii) The basket contains 20 or more securities; and

(iii) Covered securities and related securities do not comprise more than 5% of the value of the basket;

(6) *Covering Transactions.* Purchases or arrangements to purchase that are made to satisfy an obligation to deliver a subject security or a related security arising from a short sale or from the exercise of an option by a non-covered person if:

(i) The short sale or option transaction was made in the ordinary course of business and not to facilitate the offer;

(ii) In the case of a short sale, the short sale was entered into before public announcement of the tender offer; and

(iii) In the case of an exercise of an option, the covered person wrote the option before public announcement of the tender offer;

(7) *Purchases Pursuant to Contractual Obligations.* Purchases or arrangements to purchase pursuant to a contract if the following conditions are satisfied:

(i) The contract was entered into before public announcement of the tender offer;

(ii) The contract is unconditional and binding on both parties; and

(iii) The existence of the contract and all material terms including quantity, price and parties are disclosed in the offering materials;

(8) *Purchases or Arrangements to Purchase by an Affiliate of the Dealer-Manager.* Purchases or arrangements to purchase by an affiliate of a dealer-manager if the following conditions are satisfied:

(i) The dealer-manager maintains and enforces written policies and procedures reasonably designed to prevent the flow of information to or from the affiliate that might result in a violation of the federal securities laws and regulations;

(ii) The dealer-manager is registered as a broker or dealer under Section 15(a) of the Act;

(iii) The affiliate has no officers (or persons performing similar functions) or employees (other than clerical, ministerial, or support personnel) in common with the dealer-manager that direct, effect, or recommend transactions in securities; and

(iv) The purchases or arrangements to purchase are not made to facilitate the tender offer;

(9) *Purchases by Connected Exempt Market Makers or Connected Exempt Principal Traders.* Purchases or arrangements to purchase if the following conditions are satisfied:

(i) The issuer of the subject security is a foreign private issuer, as defined in Rule 3b–4(c);

(ii) The tender offer is subject to the United Kingdom's City Code on Takeovers and Mergers;

(iii) The purchase or arrangement to purchase is effected by a connected exempt market maker or a connected exempt principal trader, as those terms are used in the United Kingdom's City Code on Takeovers and Mergers;

(iv) The connected exempt market maker or the connected exempt principal trader complies with the applicable provisions of the United Kingdom's City Code on Takeovers and Mergers; and

(v) The tender offer documents disclose the identity of the connected exempt market maker or the connected exempt principal trader and disclose, or describe how U.S. security holders can obtain, information regarding market making or principal purchases by such market maker or principal trader to the extent that this information is required to be made public in the United Kingdom;

(10) *Purchases During Cross-Border Tender Offers.* Purchases or arrangements to purchase if the following conditions are satisfied:

(i) The tender offer is excepted under Rule 13e–4(h)(8) or Rule 14d–1(c);

(ii) The offering documents furnished to U.S. holders prominently disclose the possibility of any purchases, or arrangements to purchase, or the intent to make such purchases;

(iii) The offering documents disclose the manner in which any information about any such purchases or arrangements to purchase will be disclosed;

(iv) The offeror discloses information in the United States about any such purchases or arrangements to purchase in a manner comparable to the disclosure made in the home jurisdiction, as defined in Rule 13e–4(i)(3); and

(v) The purchases comply with the applicable tender offer laws and regulations of the home jurisdiction; and

(11) *Purchases or Arrangements to Purchase Pursuant to a Foreign Tender Offer(s).* Purchases or arrangements to purchase pursuant to a foreign offer(s) where the offeror seeks to acquire subject securities through a U.S. tender offer and a concurrent or substantially concurrent foreign offer(s), if the following conditions are satisfied:

(i) The U.S. and foreign tender offer(s) meet the conditions for reliance on the Tier II cross-border exemptions set forth in Rule 14d–1(d);

(ii) The economic terms and consideration in the U.S. tender offer and foreign tender offer(s) are the same, provided that any cash consideration to be paid to U.S. security holders may be converted from the currency to be paid in the foreign tender offer(s) to U.S. dollars at an exchange rate disclosed in the U.S. offering documents;

(iii) The procedural terms of the U.S. tender offer are at least as favorable as the terms of the foreign tender offer(s);

(iv) The intention of the offeror to make purchases pursuant to the foreign tender offer(s) is disclosed in the U.S. offering documents; and

(v) Purchases by the offeror in the foreign tender offer(s) are made solely pursuant to the foreign tender offer(s) and not pursuant to an open market transaction(s), a private transaction(s), or other transaction(s); and

(12) *Purchases or Arrangements to Purchase by an Affiliate of the Financial Advisor and an Offeror and Its Affiliates.*

(i) Purchases or arrangements to purchase by an affiliate of a financial advisor and an offeror and its affiliates that are permissible under and will be conducted in accordance with the applicable laws of the subject company's home jurisdiction, if the following conditions are satisfied:

(A) The subject company is a foreign private issuer as defined in Rule 3b–4(c);

(B) The covered person reasonably expects that the tender offer meets the conditions for reliance on the Tier II cross-border exemptions set forth in Rule 14d–1(d);

(C) No purchases or arrangements to purchase otherwise than pursuant to the tender offer are made in the United States;

(D) The United States offering materials disclose prominently the possibility of, or the intention to make, purchases or arrangements to purchase subject securities or related securities outside of the tender offer, and if there will be public disclosure of purchases of subject or related securities, the manner in which information regarding such purchases will be disseminated;

(E) There is public disclosure in the United States, to the extent that such information is made public in the subject company's home jurisdiction, of information regarding all purchases of subject securities and related securities otherwise than pursuant to the tender offer from the time of public announcement of the tender offer until the tender offer expires;

(F) Purchases or arrangements to purchase by an offeror and its affiliates must satisfy the following additional condition: the tender offer price will be increased to match any consideration paid outside of the tender offer that is greater than the tender offer price; and

(G) Purchases or arrangements to purchase by an affiliate of a financial advisor must satisfy the following additional conditions:

(*1*) The financial advisor and the affiliate maintain and enforce written policies and procedures reasonably designed to prevent the transfer of information among the financial advisor and affiliate that might result in a violation of U.S. federal securities laws and regulations through the establishment of information barriers;

(*2*) The financial advisor has an affiliate that is registered as a broker or dealer under section 15(a) of the Act;

(*3*) The affiliate has no officers (or persons performing similar functions) or employees (other than clerical, ministerial, or support personnel) in common with the financial advisor that direct, effect, or recommend transactions in the subject securities or related securities who also will be involved in providing the offeror or subject company with financial advisory services or dealer-manager services; and

(*4*) The purchases or arrangements to purchase are not made to facilitate the tender offer.

(ii) Reserved.

(c) *Definitions*. For purposes of this rule, the term:

(1) *Affiliate* has the same meaning as in Rule 12b–2;

(2) *Agent independent* of the issuer has the same meaning as in Rule 100(b) of Regulation M;

(3) *Covered person* means:

(i) The offeror and its affiliates;

(ii) The offeror's dealer-manager and its affiliates;

(iii) Any advisor to any of the persons specified in paragraph (c)(3)(i) and (ii) of this rule, whose compensation is dependent on the completion of the offer; and

(iv) Any person acting, directly or indirectly, in concert with any of the persons specified in this paragraph (c)(3) in connection with any purchase or arrangement to purchase any subject securities or any related securities;

(4) *Plan* has the same meaning as in Rule 100(b) of Regulation M;

(5) *Public announcement* is any oral or written communication by the offeror or any person authorized to act on the offeror's behalf that is reasonably designed to, or has the effect of, informing the public or security holders in general about the tender offer;

(6) *Related securities* means securities that are immediately convertible into, exchangeable for, or exercisable for subject securities;

(7) *Subject securities* has the same meaning as in Item 1000 of Regulation M–A; and

(8) *Subject company* has the same meaning as in Item 1000 of Regulation M–A; and

(9) *Home jurisdiction* has the same meaning as in the Instructions to paragraphs (c) and (d) of Rule 14d–1.

(d) *Exemptive Authority*. Upon written application or upon its own motion, the Commission may grant an exemption from the provisions of this rule, either unconditionally or on specified terms or conditions, to any transaction or class of transactions or any security or class of security, or any person or class of persons.

Rule 14e–6. Repurchase offers by certain closed-end registered investment companies

Rules 14e–1 and 14e–2 shall not apply to any offer by a closed-end management investment company to repurchase equity securities of which it is the issuer pursuant to Rule 23c–3 under the Investment Company Act of 1940.

Rule 14e–7. Unlawful tender offer practices in connection with roll-ups

In order to implement Section 14(h) of the Act:

(a)(1) It shall be unlawful for any person to receive compensation for soliciting tenders directly from security holders in connection with a roll-up transaction as provided in paragraph (a)(2) of this rule, if the compensation is:

(i) Based on whether the solicited person participates in the tender offer; or

(ii) Contingent on the success of the tender offer.

(2) Paragraph (a)(1) of this rule is applicable to a roll-up transaction as defined in Item 901(c) of Regulation S–K, structured as a tender offer, except for a transaction involving only:

(i) Finite-life entities that are not limited partnerships;

(ii) Partnerships whose investors will receive new securities or securities in another entity that are not reported under a transaction reporting plan declared effective before December 17, 1993 by the Commission under Section 11A of the Act; or

(iii) Partnerships whose investors' securities are reported under a transaction reporting plan declared effective before December 17, 1993 by the Commission under Section 11A of the Act.

(b)(1) It shall be unlawful for any finite-life entity that is the subject of a roll-up transaction as provided in paragraph (b)(2) of this rule to fail to provide a security holder list or mail communications related to a tender offer that is in furtherance of the roll-up transaction, at the option of a requesting security holder, pursuant to the procedures set forth in Rule 14a–7.

(2) Paragraph (b)(1) of this rule is applicable to a roll-up transaction as defined in Item 901(c) of Regulation S–K, structured as a tender offer, that involves:

(i) An entity with securities registered pursuant to Section 12 of the Act; or

(ii) A limited partnership, unless the transaction involves only:

(A) Partnerships whose investors will receive new securities or securities in another entity that are not reported under a transaction reporting plan declared effective before December 17, 1993 by the Commission under Section 11A of the Act; or

(B) Partnerships whose investors' securities are reported under a transaction reporting plan declared effective before December 17, 1993 by the Commission under Section 11A of the Act (15 U.S.C. 78k–1).

Rule 14e–8. Prohibited conduct in connection with pre-commencement communications

It is a fraudulent, deceptive or manipulative act or practice within the meaning of section 14(e) of the Act for any person to publicly announce that the person (or a party on whose behalf the person is acting) plans to make a tender offer that has not yet been commenced, if the person:

(a) Is making the announcement of a potential tender offer without the intention to commence the offer within a reasonable time and complete the offer;

(b) Intends, directly or indirectly, for the announcement to manipulate the market price of the stock of the bidder or subject company; or

(c) Does not have the reasonable belief that the person will have the means to purchase securities to complete the offer.

Rule 14f–1. Change in majority of directors

If, pursuant to any arrangement or understanding with the person or persons acquiring securities in a transaction subject to section 13(d) or 14(d) of the Act, any persons are to be elected or designated as directors of the issuer, otherwise than at a meeting of security holders, and the persons so elected or designated will constitute a majority of the directors of the issuer, then, not less than 10 days prior to the date any such person take office as a director, or such shorter period prior to that date as the Commission may authorize upon a showing of good cause therefor, the issuer shall file with the Commission and transmit to all holders of record of securities of the issuer who would be entitled to vote at a meeting for election of directors, information substantially equivalent to the information which would be required by Items 6(a), (d) and (e), 7 and 8 of Schedule 14A of Regulation 14A (Rule 14a–101) to be transmitted if such person or persons were nominees for election as directors at a meeting of such security holders. Eight copies of such information shall be filed with the Commission.

REGULATION 14N: FILINGS REQUIRED BY CERTAIN NOMINATING SHAREHOLDERS

Rule 14n–1. Filing of Schedule 14N

(a) A shareholder or group of shareholders that submits a nominee or nominees in accordance with Rule 14a–11 or a procedure set forth under applicable state or foreign law, or a registrant's governing documents providing for the inclusion of shareholder director nominees in the registrant's proxy materials shall file with the Commission a statement containing the information required by Schedule 14N and simultaneously provide the notice on Schedule 14N to the registrant.

(b)(1) Whenever two or more persons are required to file a statement containing the information required by Schedule 14N, only one statement need be filed. The statement must identify all such persons, contain the required information with regard to each such person, indicate that the statement is filed on behalf of all such persons, and include, as an appendix, their agreement in writing that the statement is filed on behalf of each of them. Each person on whose behalf the statement is filed is responsible for the timely filing of that statement and any amendments thereto, and for the completeness and accuracy of the information concerning such person contained therein; such person is not responsible for the completeness or accuracy of the information concerning the other persons making the filing.

(2) If the group's members elect to make their own filings, each filing should identify all members of the group but the information provided concerning the other persons making the filing need only reflect information which the filing person knows or has reason to know.

Rule 14n–2. Filing of amendments to Schedule 14N

(a) If any material change occurs with respect to the nomination, or in the disclosure or certifications set forth in the Schedule 14N required by Rule 14n–1(a), the person or persons who were required to file the statement shall promptly file or cause to be filed with the Commission an amendment disclosing that change.

(b) An amendment shall be filed within 10 calendar days of the final results of the election being announced by the registrant stating the nominating shareholder's or the nominating shareholder group's intention with regard to continued ownership of their shares.

Rule 14n–3. Dissemination

One copy of Schedule 14N filed pursuant to Rules 14n–1 and 14n–2 shall be mailed by registered or certified mail or electronically transmitted to the registrant at its principal executive office. Three copies of the material must at the same time be filed with, or mailed for filing to, each national securities exchange upon which any class of securities of the registrant is listed and registered.

Rule 14n–101. Schedule 14N—Information to be included in statements filed pursuant to Rule 14n–1 and amendments thereto filed pursuant to Rule 14n–2

Securities and Exchange Commission, Washington, D.C. 20549

Schedule 14N

Under the Securities Exchange Act of 1934

(Amendment No.)*

____

(Name of Issuer)

____

(Title of Class of Securities)

____

(CUSIP Number)

[ ] Solicitation pursuant to Rule 14a–2(b)(7) under the Securities Exchange Act of 1934

[ ] Solicitation pursuant to Rule14a–2(b)(8) under the Securities Exchange Act of 1934

[ ] Notice of Submission of a Nominee or Nominees in Accordance with Rule 14a–11 under the Securities Exchange Act of 1934

* The remainder of this cover page shall be filled out for a reporting person's initial filing on this form with respect to the subject class of securities, and for any subsequent amendment containing information which would alter disclosures provided in a prior cover page. The information required on the remainder of this cover page shall not be deemed to be "filed" for the purpose of Section 18 of the Securities Exchange Act of 1934 ("Act") or otherwise subject to the liabilities of that section of the Act but shall be subject to all other provisions of the Act (however, see the Notes).

[ ] Notice of Submission of a Nominee or Nominees in Accordance with Procedures Set Forth Under Applicable State or Foreign Law, or the Registrant's Governing Documents

(1) Names of reporting persons: ______

(2) Mailing address and phone number of each reporting person (or, where applicable, the authorized representative): ______

(3) Amount of securities held that are entitled to be voted on the election of directors held by each reporting person (and, where applicable, amount of securities held in the aggregate by the nominating shareholder group), but including loaned securities and net of securities sold short or borrowed for purposes other than a short sale: ______

(4) Number of votes attributable to the securities entitled to be voted on the election of directors represented by amount in Row (3) (and, where applicable, aggregate number of votes attributable to the securities entitled to be voted on the election of directors held by group):

Instructions for Cover Page:

(1) *Names of Reporting Persons*—Furnish the full legal name of each person for whom the report is filed—*i.e.*, each person required to sign the schedule itself—including each member of a group. Do not include the name of a person required to be identified in the report but who is not a reporting person.

(3) and (4) *Amount Held by Each Reporting Person*—Rows (3) and (4) are to be completed in accordance with the provisions of Item 3 of Schedule 14N.

Notes: Attach as many copies of parts one through three of the cover page as are needed, one reporting person per copy.

Filing persons may, in order to avoid unnecessary duplication, answer items on Schedule 14N by appropriate cross references to an item or items on the cover page(s). This approach may only be used where the cover page item or items provide all the disclosure required by the schedule item. Moreover, such a use of a cover page item will result in the item becoming a part of the schedule and accordingly being considered as "filed" for purposes of Section 18 of the Act or otherwise subject to the liabilities of that section of the Act.

Special Instructions for Complying with Schedule 14N

Under Sections 14 and 23 of the Securities Exchange Act of 1934 and the rules and regulations thereunder, the Commission is authorized to solicit the information required to be supplied by this Schedule. The information will be used for the primary purpose of determining and disclosing the holdings and interests of a nominating shareholder or nominating shareholder group. This statement will be made a matter of public record. Therefore, any information given will be available for inspection by any member of the public.

Because of the public nature of the information, the Commission can use it for a variety of purposes, including referral to other governmental authorities or securities self-organizations for investigatory purposes or in connection with litigation involving the Federal securities laws or other civil, criminal or regulatory statutes or provisions. Failure to disclose the information requested by this schedule may result in civil or criminal action against the persons involved for violation of the Federal securities laws and rules promulgated thereunder, or in some cases, exclusion of the nominee from the registrant's proxy materials.

General Instructions to Item Requirements. The item numbers and captions of the items shall be included but the text of the items is to be omitted. The answers to the items shall be prepared so as to indicate clearly the coverage of the items without referring to the text of the items. Answer every item. If an item is inapplicable or the answer is in the negative, so state.

Item 1(a). Name of Registrant

Item 1(b). Address of Registrant's Principal Executive Offices

Item 2(a). Name of Person Filing

Item 2(b). Address or Principal Business Office or, if None, Residence

Item 2(c). Title of Class of Securities

Item 2(d). CUSIP No.

Item 3. Ownership

Provide the following information, in accordance with Instruction 3 to Rule 14a–11(b)(1) under the Securities Exchange Act of 1934:

(a) Amount of securities held and entitled to be voted on the election of directors (and, where applicable, amount of securities held in the aggregate by the nominating shareholder group): ______.

(b) The number of votes attributable to the securities referred to in paragraph (a) of this Item: ______.

(c) The number of votes attributable to securities that have been loaned but which the reporting person:

(i) has the right to recall; and

(ii) will recall upon being notified that any of the nominees will be included in the registrant's proxy statement and proxy card: ______.

(d) The number of votes attributable to securities that have been sold in a short sale that is not closed out, or that have been borrowed for purposes other than a short sale: ______.

(e) The sum of paragraphs (b) and (c), minus paragraph (d) of this Item, divided by the aggregate number of votes derived from all classes of securities of the registrant that are entitled to vote on the election of directors, and expressed as a percentage: ______.

Item 4. Statement of Ownership from a Nominating Shareholder or Each Member of a Nominating Shareholder Group Submitting this Notice Pursuant to Rule 14a–11

(a) If the nominating shareholder, or each member of the nominating shareholder group, is the registered holder of the shares, please so state. Otherwise, attach to the Schedule 14N one or more written statements from the persons (usually brokers or banks) through which the nominating shareholder's securities are held, verifying that, within seven calendar days prior to filing the shareholder notice on Schedule 14N with the Commission and transmitting the notice to the registrant, the nominating shareholder continuously held the amount of securities being used to satisfy the ownership threshold for a period of at least three years. In the alternative, if the nominating shareholder has filed a Schedule 13D, Schedule 13G, Form 3, Form 4, and/or Form 5, or amendments to those documents, reflecting ownership of the securities as of or before the date on which the three-year eligibility period begins, so state and incorporate that filing or amendment by reference.

(b) Provide a written statement that the nominating shareholder, or each member of the nominating shareholder group, intends to continue to hold the amount of securities that are used for purposes of satisfying the minimum ownership requirement of Rule 14a–11(b)(1) through the date of the meeting of shareholders, as required by Rule 14a–11(b)(4). Additionally, provide a written statement from the nominating shareholder or each member of the nominating shareholder group regarding the nominating shareholder's or nominating shareholder group member's intent with respect to continued ownership after the election of directors, as required by Rule 14a–11(b)(5).

Instruction to Item 4: If the nominating shareholder or any member of the nominating shareholder group is not the registered holder of the securities and is not proving ownership for purposes of Rule 14a–11(b)(3) by providing previously filed Schedules 13D or 13G or Forms 3, 4, or 5, and the securities are held in an account with a broker or bank that is a participant in the Depository Trust Company ("DTC") or other clearing agency acting as a securities depository, a written statement or statements from that participant or participants in the following form will satisfy Rule 14a–11(b)(3):

As of [date of this statement], [name of nominating shareholder or member of the nominating shareholder group] held at least [number of securities owned continuously for at least three years] of the [registrant's] [class of securities], and has held at least this amount of such securities continuously for [at least three years]. [Name of clearing agency participant] is a participant in [name of clearing agency] whose nominee name is [nominee name].

[name of clearing agency participant]

By: [name and title of representative]

Date:

If the securities are held through a broker or bank (e.g. in an omnibus account) that is not a participant in a clearing agency acting as a securities depository, the nominating shareholder or member of the nominating shareholder group must (a) obtain and submit a written statement or statements (the "initial broker statement") from the broker or bank with which the nominating shareholder or member of the nominating shareholder group maintains an account that provides the information about securities ownership set forth above and (b) obtain and submit a separate written statement from the clearing agency participant through which the securities of the nominating shareholder or member of the nominating shareholder group are held, that (i) identifies the broker or bank for whom the clearing agency participant holds the securities, and (ii) states that the account of such broker or bank has held, as of the date of the separate written statement, at least the number of securities specified in the initial broker statement, and (iii) states that this account has held at least that amount of securities continuously for at least three years.

If the securities have been held for less than three years at the relevant entity, provide written statements covering a continuous period of three years and modify the language set forth above as appropriate.

For purposes of complying with Rule 14a–11(b)(3), loaned securities may be included in the amount of securities set forth in the written statements.

Item 5. Disclosure Required for Shareholder Nominations Submitted Pursuant to Rule 14a–11

If a nominating shareholder or nominating shareholder group is submitting this notice in connection with the inclusion of a shareholder nominee or nominees for director in the registrant's proxy materials pursuant to Rule 14a–11 under the Securities Exchange Act of 1934, provide the following information:

(a) A statement that the nominee consents to be named in the registrant's proxy statement and form of proxy and, if elected, to serve on the registrant's board of directors;

(b) Disclosure about the nominee as would be provided in response to the disclosure requirements of Items 4(b), 5(b), 7(a), (b) and (c) and, for investment companies, Item 22(b) of Schedule 14A, as applicable;

(c) Disclosure about the nominating shareholder or each member of a nominating shareholder group as would be required of a participant in response to the disclosure requirements of Items 4(b) and 5(b) of Schedule 14A, as applicable;

(d) Disclosure about whether the nominating shareholder or any member of a nominating shareholder group has been involved in any legal proceeding during the past ten years, as specified in Item 401(f) of Regulation S–K.

Disclosure pursuant to this paragraph need not be provided if provided in response to Item 5(c) of this section;

Instruction 1 to Item 5 (c) and (d): Where the nominating shareholder is a general or limited partnership, syndicate or other group, the information called for in paragraphs (c) and (d) of this Item must be given with respect to:

a. Each partner of the general partnership;

b. Each partner who is, or functions as, a general partner of the limited partnership;

c. Each member of the syndicate or group; and

d. Each person controlling the partner or member.

Instruction 2 to Item 5 (c) and (d): If the nominating shareholder is a corporation or if a person referred to in a., b., c. or d. of Instruction 1 to paragraphs (c) and (d) of this Item is a corporation, the information called for in paragraphs (c) and (d) of this Item must be given with respect to:

a. Each executive officer and director of the corporation;

b. Each person controlling the corporation; and

c. Each executive officer and director of any corporation or other person ultimately in control of the corporation.

(e) Disclosure about whether, to the best of the nominating shareholder's or group's knowledge, the nominee meets the director qualifications, if any, set forth in the registrant's governing documents;

(f) A statement that, to the best of the nominating shareholder's or group's knowledge, in the case of a registrant other than an investment company, the nominee meets the objective criteria for "independence" of the national securities exchange or national securities association rules applicable to the registrant, if any, or, in the case of a registrant that is an investment company, the nominee is not an "interested person" of the registrant as defined in section 2(a)(19) of the Investment Company Act of 1940.

Instruction to Item 5(f): For this purpose, the nominee would be required to meet the definition of "independence" that is generally applicable to directors of the registrant and not any particular definition of independence applicable to members of the audit committee of the registrant's board of directors. To the extent a national securities exchange or national securities association rule imposes a standard regarding independence that requires a subjective determination by the board or a group or committee of the board (for example, requiring that the board of directors or any group or committee of the board of directors make a determination regarding the existence of factors material to a determination of a nominee's independence), the nominee would not be required to meet the subjective determination of independence as part of the shareholder nomination process.

(g) The following information regarding the nature and extent of the relationships between the nominating shareholder or nominating shareholder group, the nominee, and/or the registrant or any affiliate of the registrant:

(1) Any direct or indirect material interest in any contract or agreement between the nominating shareholder or any member of the nominating shareholder group, the nominee, and/or the registrant or any affiliate of the registrant (including any employment agreement, collective bargaining agreement, or consulting agreement);

(2) Any material pending or threatened legal proceeding in which the nominating shareholder or any member of the nominating shareholder group and/or the nominee is a party or a material participant, and that involves the registrant, any of its executive officers or directors, or any affiliate of the registrant; and

(3) Any other material relationship between the nominating shareholder or any member of the nominating shareholder group, the nominee, and/or the registrant or any affiliate of the registrant not otherwise disclosed;

Note to Item 5(g)(3): Any other material relationship of the nominating shareholder or any member of the nominating shareholder group or nominee with the registrant or any affiliate of the registrant may include, but is not limited to, whether the nominating shareholder or any member of the nominating shareholder group currently has, or has had in the past, an employment relationship with the registrant or any affiliate of the registrant (including consulting arrangements).

(h) The Web site address on which the nominating shareholder or nominating shareholder group may publish soliciting materials, if any; and

(i) Any statement in support of the shareholder nominee or nominees, which may not exceed 500 words for each nominee, if the nominating shareholder or nominating shareholder group elects to have such statement included in the registrant's proxy materials.

Item 6. Disclosure Required by Rule 14a–18

If a nominating shareholder or nominating shareholder group is submitting this notice in connection with the inclusion of a shareholder nominee or nominees for director in the registrant's proxy materials pursuant to a procedure set forth under applicable state or foreign law, or the registrant's governing documents provide the following disclosure:

(a) A statement that the nominee consents to be named in the registrant's proxy statement and form of proxy and, if elected, to serve on the registrant's board of directors;

(b) Disclosure about the nominee as would be provided in response to the disclosure requirements of Items 4(b), 5(b), 7(a), (b) and (c) and, for investment companies, Item 22(b) of Schedule 14A, as applicable;

(c) Disclosure about the nominating shareholder or each member of a nominating shareholder group as would be required in response to the disclosure requirements of Items 4(b) and 5(b) of Schedule 14A as applicable;

(d) Disclosure about whether the nominating shareholder or any member of a nominating shareholder group has been involved in any legal proceeding during the past ten years, as specified in Item 401(f) of Regulation S–K. Disclosure pursuant to this paragraph need not be provided if provided in response to Item 6(c) of this section;

Instruction 1 to Item 6(c) and (d): Where the nominating shareholder is a general or limited partnership, syndicate or other group, the information called for in paragraphs (c) and (d) of this Item must be given with respect to:

a. Each partner of the general partnership;

b. Each partner who is, or functions as, a general partner of the limited partnership;

c. Each member of the syndicate or group; and

d. Each person controlling the partner or member.

Instruction 2 to Item 6(c) and (d): If the nominating shareholder is a corporation or if a person referred to in a., b., c. or d. of Instruction 1 to paragraphs (c) and (d) of this Item is a corporation, the information called for in paragraphs (c) and (d) of this Item must be given with respect to:

a. Each executive officer and director of the corporation;

b. Each person controlling the corporation; and

c. Each executive officer and director of any corporation or other person ultimately in control of the corporation.

(e) The following information regarding the nature and extent of the relationships between the nominating shareholder or nominating shareholder group, the nominee, and/or the registrant or any affiliate of the registrant:

(1) Any direct or indirect material interest in any contract or agreement between the nominating shareholder or any member of the nominating shareholder group, the nominee, and/or the registrant or any affiliate of the registrant (including any employment agreement, collective bargaining agreement, or consulting agreement);

(2) Any material pending or threatened legal proceeding in which the nominating shareholder or any member of the nominating shareholder group and/or nominee is a party or a material participant, involving the registrant, any of its executive officers or directors, or any affiliate of the registrant; and

(3) Any other material relationship between the nominating shareholder or any member of the nominating shareholder group, the nominee, and/or the registrant or any affiliate of the registrant not otherwise disclosed; and

Instruction to Item 6(e)(3): Any other material relationship of the nominating shareholder or any member of the nominating shareholder group with the registrant or any affiliate of the registrant may include, but is not limited to, whether the nominating shareholder or any member of the nominating shareholder group currently has, or has had in the past, an employment relationship with the registrant or any affiliate of the registrant (including consulting arrangements).

(f) The Web site address on which the nominating shareholder or nominating shareholder group may publish soliciting materials, if any.

Item 7. Notice of Dissolution of Group or Termination of Shareholder Nomination

Notice of dissolution of a nominating shareholder group or the termination of a shareholder nomination shall state the date of the dissolution or termination.

Item 8. Signatures

(a) The following certifications shall be provided by the filing person submitting this notice pursuant to Rule 14a–11, or in the case of a group, each filing person whose securities are being aggregated for purposes of meeting the ownership threshold set out in Rule 14a–11(b)(1) exactly as set forth below:

I, [identify the certifying individual], after reasonable inquiry and to the best of my knowledge and belief, certify that:

(1) I [or if signed by an authorized representative, the name of the nominating shareholder or each member of the nominating shareholder group, as appropriate] am [is] not holding any of the registrant's securities with the purpose, or with the effect, of changing control of the registrant or to gain a number of seats on the board of directors that exceeds the maximum number of nominees that the registrant could be required to include under Rule 14a–11(d);

(2) I [or if signed by an authorized representative, the name of the nominating shareholder or each member of the nominating shareholder group, as appropriate] otherwise satisfy [satisfies] the requirements of Rule 14a–11(b), as applicable;

(3) The nominee or nominees satisfies the requirements of Rule 14a–11(b), as applicable; and

(4) The information set forth in this notice on Schedule 14N is true, complete and correct.

(b) The following certification shall be provided by the filing person or persons submitting this notice in connection with the submission of a nominee or nominees in accordance with procedures set forth under applicable state or foreign law or the registrant's governing documents:

I, [identify the certifying individual], after reasonable inquiry and to the best of my knowledge and belief, certify that the information set forth in this notice on Schedule 14N is true, complete and correct.

Dated: ____________

Signature: ____________

Name/Title: ____________

The original statement shall be signed by each person on whose behalf the statement is filed or his authorized representative. If the statement is signed on behalf of a person by his authorized representative other than an executive officer or general partner of the filing person, evidence of the representative's authority to sign on behalf of such person shall be filed with the statement, *provided, however*, that a power of attorney for this purpose which is already on file with the Commission may be incorporated by reference. The name and any title of each person who signs the statement shall be typed or printed beneath his signature.

Attention: Intentional misstatements or omissions of fact constitute Federal criminal violations (see 18 U.S.C. 1001).

EXEMPTION OF CERTAIN OTC DERIVATIVES DEALERS

Rule 15a–1. Securities activities of OTC derivatives dealers

PRELIMINARY NOTE:

OTC derivatives dealers are a special class of broker-dealers that are exempt from certain broker-dealer requirements, including membership in a self-regulatory organization (Rule 15b9–2), regular broker-dealer margin rules (Rule 36a1–1), and application of the Securities Investor Protection Act of 1970 (Rule 36a1–2). OTC derivative dealers are subject to special requirements, including limitations on the scope of their securities activities (Rule 15a–1), specified internal risk management control systems (Rule 15c3–4), recordkeeping obligations (Rule 17a–3(a)(10)), and reporting responsibilities (Rule 17a–12). They are also subject to alternative net capital treatment (Rule 15c3–1(a)(5)). This rule 15a–1 uses a number of defined terms in setting forth the securities activities in which an OTC derivatives dealer may engage: "OTC derivatives dealer," "eligible OTC derivative instrument," "cash management securities activities," and "ancillary portfolio management securities activities." These terms are defined under Rules 3b–12 through 3b–15.

(a) The securities activities of an OTC derivatives dealer shall:

(1) Be limited to:

(i) Engaging in dealer activities in eligible OTC derivative instruments that are securities;

(ii) Issuing and reacquiring securities that are issued by the dealer, including warrants on securities, hybrid securities, and structured notes;

(iii) Engaging in cash management securities activities;

(iv) Engaging in ancillary portfolio management securities activities; and

(v) Engaging in such other securities activities that the Commission designates by order pursuant to paragraph (b)(1) of this rule; and

(2) Consist primarily of the activities described in paragraphs (a)(1)(i), (a)(1)(ii), and (a)(1)(iii) of this rule; and

(3) Not consist of any other securities activities, including engaging in any transaction in any security that is not an eligible OTC derivative instrument, except as permitted under paragraphs (a)(1)(iii), (a)(1)(iv), and (a)(1)(v) of this rule.

(b) The Commission, by order, entered upon its own initiative or after considering an application for exemptive relief, may clarify or expand the scope of eligible OTC derivative instruments and the scope of permissible securities activities of an OTC derivatives dealer. Such orders may:

(1) Identify other permissible securities activities;

(2) Determine that a class of fungible instruments that are standardized as to their material economic terms is within the scope of eligible OTC derivative instrument;

(3) Clarify whether certain contracts, agreements, or transactions are within the scope of eligible OTC derivative instrument; or

(4) Clarify whether certain securities activities are within the scope of ancillary portfolio management securities activities.

(c) To the extent an OTC derivatives dealer engages in any securities transaction pursuant to paragraphs (a)(1)(i) through (a)(1)(v) of this rule, such transaction shall be effected through a registered broker or dealer (other than an OTC derivatives dealer) that, in the case of any securities transaction pursuant to paragraphs (a)(1)(i), or (a)(1)(iii) through (a)(1)(v) of this rule, is an affiliate of the OTC derivatives dealer, except that this paragraph (c) shall not apply if:

(1) The counterparty to the transaction with the OTC derivatives dealer is acting as principal and is:

(i) A registered broker or dealer;

(ii) A bank acting in a dealer capacity, as permitted by U.S. law;

(iii) A foreign broker or dealer; or

(iv) An affiliate of the OTC derivatives dealer; or

(2) The OTC derivatives dealer is engaging in an ancillary portfolio management securities activity, and the transaction is in a foreign security, and a registered broker or dealer, a bank, or a foreign broker or dealer is acting as agent for the OTC derivatives dealer.

(d) To the extent an OTC derivatives dealer induces or attempts to induce any counterparty to enter into any securities transaction pursuant to paragraphs (a)(1)(i) through (a)(1)(v) of this rule, any communication or contact with the counterparty concerning the transaction (other than clerical and ministerial activities conducted by an associated person of the OTC derivatives dealer) shall be conducted by one or more registered persons that, in the case of any securities transaction pursuant to paragraphs (a)(1)(i), or (a)(1)(iii) through (a)(1)(v) of this rule, is associated with an affiliate of the OTC derivatives dealer, except that this paragraph (d) shall not apply if the counterparty to the transaction with the OTC derivatives dealer is:

(1) A registered broker or dealer;

(2) A bank acting in a dealer capacity, as permitted by U.S. law;

(3) A foreign broker or dealer; or

(4) An affiliate of the OTC derivatives dealer.

(e) For purposes of this rule, the term *hybrid security* means a security that incorporates payment features economically similar to options, forwards, futures, swap agreements,or collars involving currencies, interest or other rates, commodities, securities, indices, quantitative measures, or other financial or economic interests or property of any kind, or any payment or delivery that is dependent on the occurrence or nonoccurrence of any event associated with a potential financial, economic, or commercial consequence (or any combination, permutation, or derivative of such contract or underlying interest).

(f) For purposes of this rule, the term *affiliate* means any organization (whether incorporated or unincorporated) that directly or indirectly controls, is controlled by, or is under common control with, the OTC derivatives dealer.

(g) For purposes of this rule, the term *foreign broker or dealer* means any person not resident in the United States (including any U.S. person engaged in business as a broker or dealer entirely outside the United States, except as otherwise permitted by Rule 15a–6) that is not an office or branch of, or a natural person associated with, a registered broker or dealer, whose securities activities, if conducted in the United States, would be described by the definition of "broker" in section 3(a)(4) of the Act or "dealer" in section 3(a)(5) of the Act.

(h) For purposes of this rule, the term *foreign security* means any security (including a depositary share issued by a United States bank, provided that the depositary share is initially offered and sold outside the United States in accordance with Regulation S under the Securities Act of 1933) issued by a person not organized or incorporated under the laws of the United States, provided the transaction that involves such security is not effected on a national securities exchange or on a market operated by a registered national securities association; or a debt security (including a convertible debt security) issued by an issuer organized or incorporated under the laws of the United States that is initially offered and sold outside the United States in accordance with Regulation S under the Securities Act of 1933.

(i) For purposes of this rule, the term *registered person* is:

(A) A natural person who is associated with a registered broker or dealer and is registered or approved under the rules of a self-regulatory organization of which such broker or dealer is a member; or

(B) If the counterparty to the transaction with the OTC derivatives dealer is a resident of a jurisdiction other than the United States, a natural person who is not resident in the United States and is associated with a broker or dealer that is registered or licensed by a foreign financial regulatory authority in the jurisdiction in which such counterparty is resident or in which such natural person is located, in accordance with applicable legal requirements, if any.

EXEMPTION OF CERTAIN SECURITIES FROM SECTION 15(a)

Rule 15a-2. Exemption of certain securities of cooperative apartment houses from Section 15(a)

Shares of a corporation which represent ownership, or entitle the holders thereof to possession and occupancy, of specific apartment units in property owned by such corporations and organized and operated on a cooperative basis are hereby exempted from the operation of section 15(a) of the Act, when such shares are sold by or through a real estate broker licensed under the laws of the political subdivision in which the property is located.

Rule 15a-3. [Reserved]

Rule 15a-4. Forty-five day exemption from registration for certain members of national securities exchanges

(a) A natural person who is a member of a national securities exchange shall, upon termination of his association with a registered broker-dealer, be exempt, for a period of forty-five days after such termination, from the registration requirement of Section 15(a) of the Act solely for the purpose of continuing to effect transactions on the floor of such exchange if (1) such person has filed with the Commission an application for registration as a broker-dealer and such person complies in all material respects with rules of the Commission applicable to registered brokers and dealers and (2) such exchange has filed with the Commission a statement that it has reviewed such application and that there do not appear to be grounds for its denial.

(b) The exemption from registration provided by this rule shall not be available to any person while there is pending before the Commission any proceeding involving any such person pursuant to Section 15(b)(1)(B) of the Act.

Rule 15a-5. Exemption of certain non-bank lenders

A lender approved under the rules and regulations of the Small Business Administration shall be exempt from the registration requirement of Section 15(a)(1) of the Act if it does not engage in the business of effecting transactions in securities or of buying and selling securities for its own account except in respect of receiving notes evidencing loans to small business concerns and selling the portion of such notes guaranteed by the Small Business Administration through or to a registered broker or dealer or to a bank, a savings institution, an insurance company, or an account over which an investment adviser registered pursuant to the Investment Advisers Act of 1940 exercises investment discretion.

REGISTRATION OF BROKERS AND DEALERS

Rule 15a-6. Exemption of certain foreign brokers and dealers

(a) A foreign broker or dealer shall be exempt from the registration requirements of sections 15(a)(1) and 15B(a)(1) of the Act to the extent that the foreign broker or dealer:

(1) Effects transactions in securities with or for persons that have not been solicited by the foreign broker or dealer; or

(2) Furnishes research reports to major U.S. institutional investors, and effects transactions in the securities discussed in the research reports with or for those major U.S. institutional investors, provided that:

(i) The research reports do not recommend the use of the foreign broker or dealer to effect trades in any security;

(ii) The foreign broker or dealer does not initiate contact with those major U.S. institutional investors to follow up on the research reports, and does not otherwise induce or attempt to induce the purchase or sale of any security by those major U.S. institutional investors;

(iii) If the foreign broker or dealer has a relationship with a registered broker or dealer that satisfies the requirements of paragraph (a)(3) of this rule, any transactions with the foreign broker or dealer in securities discussed in the research reports are effected only through that registered broker or dealer, pursuant to the provisions of paragraph (a)(3) of this rule; and

(iv) The foreign broker or dealer does not provide research to U.S. persons pursuant to any express or implied understanding that those U.S. persons will direct commission income to the foreign broker or dealer; or

(3) Induces or attempts to induce the purchase or sale of any security by a U.S. institutional investor or a major U.S. institutional investor, provided that:

(i) The foreign broker or dealer:

(A) Effects any resulting transactions with or for the U.S. institutional investor or the major U.S. institutional investor through a registered broker or dealer in the manner described by paragraph (a)(3)(iii) of this rule; and

(B) Provides the Commission (upon request or pursuant to agreements reached between any foreign securities authority, including any foreign government, as specified in section 3(a)(50) of the Act, and the Commission or the U.S. Government) with any information or documents within the possession, custody, or control of the foreign broker or dealer, any testimony of foreign associated persons, and any assistance in taking the evidence of other persons, wherever located, that the Commission requests and that relates to transactions under paragraph (a)(3) of this rule, except that if, after the foreign broker or dealer has exercised its best efforts to provide the information, documents, testimony, or assistance, including requesting the appropriate governmental body and, if legally necessary, its customers (with respect to customer information) to permit the foreign broker or dealer to provide the information, documents, testimony, or assistance to the Commission, the foreign broker or dealer is prohibited from providing this information, documents, testimony, or assistance by applicable foreign law or regulations, then this paragraph (a)(3)(i)(B) shall not apply and the foreign broker or dealer will be subject to paragraph (c) of this rule;

(ii) The foreign associated person of the foreign broker or dealer effecting transactions with the U.S. institutional investor or the major U.S. institutional investor:

(A) Conducts all securities activities from outside the U.S., except that the foreign associated persons may conduct visits to U.S. institutional investors and major U.S. institutional investors within the United States, provided that:

(*1*) The foreign associated person is accompanied on these visits by an associated person of a registered broker or dealer that accepts responsibility for the foreign associated person's communications with the U.S. institutional investor or the major U.S. institutional investor; and

(*2*) Transactions in any securities discussed during the visit by the foreign associated person are effected only through the registered broker or dealer, pursuant to paragraph (a)(3) of this rule; and

(B) Is determined by the registered broker or dealer to:

(*1*) Not be subject to a statutory disqualification specified in section 3(a)(39) of the Act, or any substantially equivalent foreign

(*i*) Expulsion or suspension from membership,

(*ii*) Bar or suspension from association,

(*iii*) Denial of trading privileges,

(*iv*) Order denying, suspending, or revoking registration or barring or suspending association, or

(*v*) Finding with respect to causing any such effective foreign suspension, expulsion, or order;

(*2*) Not to have been convicted of any foreign offense, enjoined from any foreign act, conduct, or practice, or found to have committed any foreign act substantially equivalent to any of those listed in section 15(b)(4) (B), (C), (D), or (E) of the Act; and

(*3*) Not to have been found to have made or caused to be made any false foreign statement or omission substantially equivalent to any of those listed in section 3(a)(39)(E) of the Act; and

(iii) The registered broker or dealer through which the transaction with the U.S. institutional investor or the major U.S. institutional investor is effected:

(A) Is responsible for:

(*1*) Effecting the transactions conducted under paragraph (a)(3) of this rule, other than negotiating their terms;

(*2*) Issuing all required confirmations and statements to the U.S. institutional investor or the major U.S. institutional investor;

(*3*) As between the foreign broker or dealer and the registered broker or dealer, extending or arranging for the extension of any credit to the U.S. institutional investor or the major U.S. institutional investor in connection with the transactions;

(*4*) Maintaining required books and records relating to the transactions, including those required by Rules 17a–3 and 17a–4 under the Act;

(*5*) Complying with Rule 15c3–1 under the Act with respect to the transactions; and

(*6*) Receiving, delivering, and safeguarding funds and securities in connection with the transactions on behalf of the U.S. institutional investor or the major U.S. institutional investor in compliance with Rule 15c3–3 under the Act;

(B) Participates through an associated person in all oral communications between the foreign associated person and the U.S. institutional investor, other than a major U.S. institutional investor;

(C) Has obtained from the foreign broker or dealer, with respect to each foreign associated person, the types of information specified in Rule 17a–3(a)(12) under the Act, provided that the information required by paragraph (a)(12)(d) of that rule shall include sanctions imposed by foreign securities authorities, exchanges, or associations, including without limitation those described in paragraph (a)(3)(ii)(B) of this rule;

(D) Has obtained from the foreign broker or dealer and each foreign associated person written consent to service of process for any civil action brought by or proceeding before the Commission or a self-regulatory organization (as defined in section 3(a)(26) of the Act), providing that process may be served on them by service on the registered broker or dealer in the manner set forth on the registered broker's or dealer's current Form BD; and

(E) Maintains a written record of the information and consents required by paragraphs (a)(3)(iii)(C) and (D) of this rule, and all records in connection with trading activities of the U.S. institutional investor or the major U.S. institutional investor involving the foreign broker or dealer conducted under paragraph (a)(3) of this rule, in an office of the registered broker or dealer located in the United States (with respect to nonresident registered brokers or dealers, pursuant to Rule 17a–7(a) under the Act), and makes these records available to the Commission upon request; or

(4) Effects transactions in securities with or for, or induces or attempts to induce the purchase or sale of any security by:

(i) A registered broker or dealer, whether the registered broker or dealer is acting as principal for its own account or as agent for others, or a bank acting pursuant to an exception or exemption from the definition of "broker" or "dealer" in sections 3(a)(4)(B), 3(a)(4)(E), or 3(a)(5)(C) of the Act or the rules thereunder;

(ii) The African Development Bank, the Asian Development Bank, the Inter–American Development Bank, the International Bank for Reconstruction and Development, the International Monetary Fund, the United Nations, and their agencies, affiliates, and pension funds;

(iii) A foreign person temporarily present in the United States, with whom the foreign broker or dealer had a bona fide, pre-existing relationship before the foreign person entered the United States;

(iv) Any agency or branch of a U.S. person permanently located outside the United States, provided that the transactions occur outside the United States; or

(v) U.S. citizens resident outside the United States, provided that the transactions occur outside the United States, and that the foreign broker or dealer does not direct its selling efforts toward identifiable groups of U.S. citizens resident abroad.

(b) When used in this rule,

(1) the term *family of investment companies* shall mean:

(i) Except for insurance company separate accounts, any two or more separately registered investment companies under the Investment Company Act of 1940 that share the same investment adviser or principal underwriter and hold themselves out to investors as related companies for purposes of investment and investor services; and

(ii) With respect to insurance company separate accounts, any two or more separately registered separate accounts under the Investment Company Act of 1940 that share the same investment adviser or principal underwriter and function under operational or accounting or control systems that are substantially similar.

(2) The term *foreign associated person* shall mean any natural person domiciled outside the United States who is an associated person, as defined in section 3(a)(18) of the Act, of the foreign broker or dealer, and who participates in the solicitation of a U.S. institutional investor or a major U.S. institutional investor under paragraph (a)(3) of this rule.

(3) The term *foreign broker or dealer* shall mean any non-U.S. resident person (including any U.S. person engaged in business as a broker or dealer entirely outside the United States, except as otherwise permitted by this rule) that is not an office or branch of, or a natural person associated with, a registered broker or dealer, whose securities activities, if conducted in the United States, would be described by the definition of "broker" or "dealer" in sections 3(a)(4) or 3(a)(5) of the Act.

(4) The term *major U.S. institutional investor* shall mean a person that is:

(i) A U.S. institutional investor that has, or has under management, total assets in excess of $100 million; provided, however, that for purposes of determining the total assets of an investment company under this rule, the investment company may include the assets of any family of investment companies of which it is a part; or

(ii) An investment adviser registered with the Commission under section 203 of the Investment Advisers Act of 1940 that has total assets under management in excess of $100 million.

(5) The term *registered broker or dealer* shall mean a person that is registered with the Commission under sections 15(b), 15B(a)(2), or 15C(a)(2) of the Act.

(6) The term *United States* shall mean the United States of America, including the States and any territories and other areas subject to its jurisdiction.

(7) The term *U.S. institutional investor* shall mean a person that is:

(i) An investment company registered with the Commission under section 8 of the Investment Company Act of 1940; or

(ii) A bank, savings and loan association, insurance company, business development company, small business investment company, or employee benefit plan defined in Rule 501(a)(1) under the Securities Act of 1933; a private business development company defined in Rule 501(a)(2) under the Securities Act of 1933; an organization described in section 501(c)(3) of the Internal Revenue Code, as defined in Rule 501(a)(3) under the Securities Act of 1933; or a trust defined in Rule 501(a)(7) under the Securities Act of 1933.

(c) The Commission, by order after notice and opportunity for hearing, may withdraw the exemption provided in paragraph (a)(3) of this rule with respect to the subsequent activities of a foreign broker or dealer or class of foreign brokers or dealers conducted from a foreign country, if the Commission finds that the laws or regulations of that foreign country have prohibited the foreign broker or dealer, or one of a class of foreign brokers or dealers, from providing, in response to a request from the Commission, information or documents within its possession, custody, or control, testimony of foreign associated persons, or assistance in taking the evidence of other persons, wherever located, related to activities exempted by paragraph (a)(3) of this rule.

Rule 15a–7. [Reserved]

Rule 15a–8. [Reserved]

Rule 15a–9. [Reserved]

Rule 15a–10. Exemption of certain brokers or dealers with respect to security futures products

(a) A broker or dealer that is registered by notice with the Commission pursuant to section 15(b)(11)(A) of the Act and that is not a member of either a national securities exchange registered pursuant to section 6(a) of the Act or a national securities association registered pursuant to section 15A(a) of the Act will be exempt from the registration requirement of section 15(a)(1) of the Act solely to act as a broker or a dealer in security futures products.

(b) A broker or dealer that is registered by notice with the Commission pursuant to section 15(b)(11)(A) of the Act and that is a member of either a national securities exchange registered pursuant to section 6(a) of the Act or a national securities association registered pursuant to section 15A(a) of the Act will be exempt from the registration requirement of section 15(a)(1) of the Act solely to act as a broker or a dealer in security futures products, if:

(1) The rules of any such exchange or association of which the broker or dealer is a member provides specifically for a broker or dealer that is registered by notice with the Commission pursuant to section 15(b)(11)(A) of the Act to become a member of such exchange or association; and

(2) The broker or dealer complies with section 11(a)–(c) of the Act with respect to any transactions in security futures products on a national securities exchange registered pursuant to section 6(a) of the Act of which it is a member, notwithstanding section 15(b)(11)(B)(ii) of the Act.

Rule 15a–11. [Reserved]

Rule 15b1–1. Application for registration of brokers or dealers

(a) An application for registration of a broker or dealer that is filed pursuant to section 15(b) of the Act shall be filed on Form BD (17 CFR 249.501) in accordance with the instructions to the form. A broker or dealer that is an OTC derivatives dealer shall indicate where appropriate on Form BD that the type o business in which it is engaged is that of acting as an OTC derivatives dealer.

(b) Every application for registration of a broker or dealer that is filed on or after January 25, 1993, shall be filed with the Central Registration Depository operated by the Financial Industry Regulations Authority, Inc.

(c) An application for registration that is filed with the Central Registration Depository pursuant to this section shall be considered a "report" filed with the Commission for purposes of Sections 15(b), 17(a), 18(a), 32(a) and other applicable provisions of the Act.

Rule 15b1–2. [Reserved]

Rule 15b1–3. Registration of successor to registered broker or dealer

(a) In the event that a broker or dealer succeeds to and continues the business of a broker or dealer registered pursuant to section 15(b) of the Act, the registration of the predecessor shall be deemed to remain effective as the registration of the successor if the successor, within 30 days after such succession, files an application for registration on Form BD, and the predecessor files a notice of withdrawal from registration on Form BDW; *Provided, however,* That the registration of the predecessor broker or dealer will cease to be effective as the registration of the successor broker or dealer 45 days after the application for registration on Form BD is filed by such successor.

(b) Notwithstanding paragraph (a) of this rule, if a broker or dealer succeeds to and continues the business of a registered predecessor broker or dealer, and the succession is based solely on a change in the predecessor's date or state of incorporation, form of organization, or composition of a partnership, the successor may, within 30 days after the succession, amend the registration of the predecessor broker or dealer on Form BD to reflect these changes. This amendment shall be deemed an application for registration filed by the predecessor and adopted by the successor.

Rule 15b1–4. Registration of fiduciaries

The registration of a broker or dealer shall be deemed to be the registration of any executor, administrator, guardian, conservator, assignee for the benefit of creditors, receiver, trustee in insolvency or bankruptcy, or other fiduciary, appointed or qualified by order, judgment, or decree of a court of competent jurisdiction to continue the business of such registered broker or dealer: *Provided,* That such fiduciary files with the Commission, within 30 days after entering upon the performance of his duties, a statement setting forth as to such fiduciary substantially the information required by Form BD.

Rule 15b1–5. Consent to service of process to be furnished by nonresident brokers or dealers and by nonresident general partners or managing agents of brokers or dealers

(a) Each nonresident broker or dealer registered or applying for registration pursuant to section 15(b) of the Securities Exchange Act of 1934, each nonresident general partner of a broker or dealer partnership which is registered or applying for registration, and each nonresident managing agent of any other unincorporated broker or dealer which is registered or applying for registration, shall furnish to the Commission, in a form prescribed by or acceptable to it, a written irrevocable consent and power of attorney which (1) designates the Securities and Exchange Commission as an agent upon whom may be served any process, pleadings, or other papers in any civil suit or action brought in any appropriate court in any place subject to the jurisdiction of the United States, with respect to any cause of action (i) which accrues during the period beginning when such broker or dealer becomes registered pursuant to section 15 of the Securities Exchange Act of 1934 and the rules and regulations thereunder and ending either when such registration is cancelled or revoked, or when the Commission receives from such broker or dealer a notice to withdraw from such registration, whichever is earlier, (ii) which arises out of any activity, in any place subject to the jurisdiction of the United States, occurring in connection with the conduct of business of a broker or dealer, and (iii) which is founded, directly or indirectly, upon the provisions of the Securities Act of 1933, the Securities Exchange Act of 1934, the Trust Indenture Act of 1939, the Investment Company Act of 1940, the Investment Advisers Act of 1940, or any rule or regulation under any of said Acts; and (2) stipulates and agrees that any such civil suit or action may be commenced by the service of process upon the Commission and the forwarding of a copy thereof as provided in paragraph (c) of this rule, and that the service as aforesaid of any such process, pleadings, or other papers upon the Commission shall be taken and held in all courts to be as valid and binding as if due personal service thereof had been made.

(b) The required consent and power of attorney shall be furnished to the Commission within the following period of time:

(1) Each nonresident broker or dealer registered at the time this rule becomes effective, and each nonresident general partner or managing agent of an unincorporated broker or dealer registered at the time this rule becomes effective, shall furnish such consent and power of attorney within 60 days after such date;

(2) Each broker or dealer applying for registration after the effective date of this rule shall furnish, at the time of filing such application, all the consents and powers of attorney required to be furnished by such broker or dealer and by each general partner or managing agent thereof: *Provided, however,* That where an application for registration of a broker or dealer is pending at the time this rule becomes effective such consents and powers of attorney shall be furnished within 30 days after this rule becomes effective.

(3) Each broker or dealer registered or applying for registration who or which becomes a nonresident broker or dealer after the effective date of this rule, and each general partner or managing agent, of an unincorporated broker or dealer registered or applying for registration, who becomes a nonresident after the effective date of this rule, shall furnish such consent and power of attorney within 30 days thereafter.

(c) Service of any process, pleadings or other papers on the Commission under this rule shall be made by delivering the requisite number of copies thereof to the Secretary of the Commission or to such other person as the Commission may authorize to act in its behalf. Whenever any process, pleadings or other papers as aforesaid are served upon the Commission, it shall promptly forward a copy thereof by registered or certified mail to the appropriate defendants at their last address of record filed with the Commission. The Commission shall be furnished a sufficient number of copies for such purpose, and one copy for its file.

(d) For purposes of this rule the following definitions shall apply:

(1) The term *broker* shall have the meaning set out in section 3(a)(4) of the Securities Exchange Act of 1934.

(2) The term *dealer* shall have the meaning set out in section 3(a)(5) of the Securities Exchange Act of 1934.

(3) The term *managing agent* shall mean any person, including a trustee, who directs or manages or who participates in the directing or managing of the affairs of any unincorporated organization or association which is not a partnership.

(4) The term *nonresident broker or dealer* shall mean (i) in the case of an individual, one who resides in or has his principal place of business in any place not subject to the jurisdiction of the United States; (ii) in the case of a corporation, one incorporated in or having its principal place of business in any place not subject to the jurisdiction of the United States; (iii) in the case of a partnership or other unincorporated organization or association, one having its principal place of business in any place not subject to the jurisdiction of the United States.

(5) A general partner or managing agent of a broker or dealer shall be deemed to be a nonresident if he resides in any place not subject to the jurisdiction of the United States.

Rule 15b1-6. Notice to brokers and dealers of requirements regarding lost securityholders and unresponsive payees

Brokers and dealers are hereby notified of Rule 17Ad-17, which addresses certain requirements with respect to lost securityholders and unresponsive payees that may be applicable to them.

Rule 15b2-1. [Reserved]

Rule 15b2-2. Inspection of newly registered brokers and dealers

(a) *Definition.* For the purpose of this rule the term *applicable financial responsibility rules* shall include:

(1) Any rule adopted by the Commission pursuant to sections 8, 15(c)(3), 17(a), or 17(e)(1)(A) of the Act;

(2) Any rule adopted by the Commission relating to hypothecation or lending of customer securities;

(3) Any other rule adopted by the Commission relating to the protection of funds or securities; and

(4) Any rule adopted by the Secretary of the Treasury pursuant to section 15C(b)(1) of the Act.

(b) Each self-regulatory organization that has responsibility for examining a broker or dealer member (including members that are government securities brokers or government securities dealers registered pursuant to section 15C(a)(1)(A) of the Act) for compliance with applicable financial responsibility rules is authorized and directed to conduct an inspection of the member, within six months of the member's registration with the Commission, to determine whether the member is operating in conformity with applicable financial responsibility rules.

(c) The examining self-regulatory organization is further authorized and directed to conduct an inspection of the member no later than twelve months from the member's registration with the Commission, to determine whether the member is operating in conformity with all other applicable provisions of the Act and rules thereunder.

(d) In each case where the examining self-regulatory organization determines that a broker or dealer member has not commenced actual operations within six months of the member's registration with the Commission, it shall delay the inspection pursuant to this rule until the second six month period from the member's registration with the Commission.

(e) No inspection need be conducted as provided for in paragraphs (b) and (c) of this rule if:

(1) The member was registered with the Commission prior to April 26, 1982;

(2) An inspection of the member has already been conducted by another self-regulatory organization pursuant to this section;

(3) An inspection of the member has already been conducted by the Commission pursuant to section 15(b)(2)(C) of the Act; or

(4) The member is registered with the Commission pursuant to section 15(b)(11)(A) of the Act.

Rule 15b3-1. Amendments to application

(a) If the information contained in any application for registration as a broker or dealer, or in any amendment thereto, is or becomes inaccurate for any reason, the broker or dealer shall promptly file with the Central Registration Depository (operated by the Financial Industry Regulatory Authority, Inc.) an amendment on Form BD correcting such information.

(b) Every amendment filed with the Central Registration Depository pursuant to this rule shall constitute a "report" filed with the Commission within the meaning of Sections 15(b), 17(a), 18(a), 32(a) and other applicable provisions of the Act.

Rule 15b5-1. Extension of registration for purposes of the Securities Investor Protection Act of 1970 after cancellation or revocation

Commission revocation or cancellation of the registration of a broker or dealer pursuant to Section 15(b) of the Act: (i) shall be effective for all purposes, except as hereinafter provided, on the date of the order of revocation or cancellation or, if such order is stayed, on the date the stay is terminated; and (ii) shall be effective six months after the date of the order of revocation or cancellation (or, if such order is stayed, the date the stay is terminated) with respect to a broker's or dealer's registration status as a member within the meaning of Section 3(a)(2) of the Securities Investor Protection Act of 1970 for purposes of the application of Sections 5, 6 and 7 thereof to customer claims arising prior to the date of the order of revocation or cancellation (or, if such order is stayed, the date the stay is terminated).

Rule 15b6-1. Withdrawal from registration

(a) Notice of withdrawal from registration as a broker or dealer pursuant to Section 15(b) of the Act shall be filed on Form BDW (17 CFR 249.501a) in accordance with the instructions contained therein. Every notice of withdrawal from registration as a broker or dealer shall be filed with the Central Registration Depository (operated by the Financial Industry Regulatory Authority, Inc.) in accordance with applicable filing requirements. Prior to filing a notice of withdrawal from registration on Form BDW (17 CFR 249.501a), a broker or dealer shall amend Form BD (17 CFR 249.501) in accordance with Rule 15b3–1(a) to update any inaccurate information.

(b) A notice of withdrawal from registration filed by a broker or dealer pursuant to Section 15(b) of the Act shall become effective for all matters (except as provided in this paragraph (b) and in paragraph (c) of this rule) on the 60th day after the filing thereof with the Commission, within such longer period of time as to which such broker or dealer consents or which the Commission by order may determine as necessary or appropriate in the public interest or for the protection of investors, or within such shorter period of time as the Commission may determine. If a notice of withdrawal from registration is filed with the Commission at any time subsequent to the date of the issuance of a Commission order instituting proceedings pursuant to Section 15(b) of the Act to censure, place limitations on the activities, functions or operations of, or suspend or revoke the registration of, such broker or dealer, or if prior to the effective date of the notice of withdrawal pursuant to this paragraph (b), the Commission institutes such a proceeding or a proceeding to impose terms or conditions upon such withdrawal, the notice of withdrawal shall not become effective pursuant to this paragraph (b) except at such time and upon such terms and conditions as the Commission deems necessary or appropriate in the public interest or for the protection of investors.

(c) With respect to a broker's or dealer's registration status as a member within the meaning of Section 3(a)(2) of the Securities Investor Protection Act of 1970 (15 U.S.C. 78ccc(a)(2)) for purposes of the application of Sections 5, 6, and 7 (15 U.S.C. 78eee, 78fff, and 78fff–1) thereof to customer claims arising prior to the effective date of withdrawal pursuant to paragraph (b) of this rule, the effective date of a broker's or dealer's withdrawal from registration pursuant to this paragraph (c) shall be six months after the effective date of withdrawal pursuant to paragraph (b) of this rule or such shorter period of time as the Commission may determine.

(d) Every notice of withdrawal filed with the Central Registration Depository pursuant to this rule shall constitute a "report" filed with the Commission within the meaning of Sections 15(b), 17(a), 18(a), 32(a) and other applicable provisions of the Act.

(e) The Commission, by order, may exempt any broker or dealer from the filing requirements provided in Form BDW (17 CFR 249.501a) under conditions that differ from the filing instructions contained in Form BDW.

Rule 15b7–1. Compliance with qualification requirements of self-regulatory organizations

No registered broker or dealer shall effect any transaction in, or induce the purchase or sale of, any security unless any natural person associated with such broker or dealer who effects or is involved in effecting such transaction is registered or approved in accordance with the standards of training, experience, competence, and other qualification standards (including but not limited to submitting and maintaining all required forms, paying all required fees, and passing any required examinations) established by the rules of any national securities exchange or national securities association of which such broker or dealer is a member or under the rules of the Municipal Securities Rulemaking Board (if it is subject to the rules of that organization).

Rule 15b9–1. Exemption for certain exchange members

(a) Any broker or dealer required by Section 15(b)(8) of the Act to become a member of a registered national securities association shall be exempt from such requirement if it (1) is a member of a national securities exchange, (2) carries no customer accounts, and (3) has annual gross income derived from purchases and sales of securities otherwise than on a national securities exchange of which it is a member in an amount no greater than $1,000.

(b) The gross income limitation contained in paragraph (a) of this rule, shall not apply to income derived from transactions (1) for the dealer's own account with or through another registered broker or dealer or (2) through the Intermarket Trading System.

(c) For purposes of this rule, the term *Intermarket Trading System* shall mean the intermarket communications linkage operated jointly by certain self-regulatory organizations pursuant to a plan filed with, and approved by, the Commission pursuant to Rule 608 of Regulation NMS.

Rule 15b9–2. Exemption from SRO membership for OTC derivatives dealers

An OTC derivatives dealer, as defined in Rule 3b–12, shall be exempt from any requirement under section 15(b)(8) of the Act to become a member of a registered national securities association.

Rule 15b11–1. Registration by notice of security futures product broker–dealers

(a) A broker or dealer may register by notice pursuant to section 15(b)(11)(A) of the Act if it:

(1) Is registered with the Commodity Futures Trading Commission as a futures commission merchant or an introducing broker, as those terms are defined in the Commodity Exchange Act (7 U.S.C. 1, *et seq.*), respectively;

(2) Is a member of the National Futures Association or another national securities association registered under section 15A(k) of the Act; and

(3) Is not required to register as a broker or dealer in connection with transactions in securities other than security futures products.

(b) A broker or dealer registering by notice pursuant to section 15(b)(11)(A) of the Act must file Form BD–N (17 CFR 249.501b) in accordance with the instructions to the form. A broker or dealer registering by notice pursuant to this rule must indicate where appropriate on Form BD–N that it satisfies all of the conditions in paragraph (a) of this rule.

(c) If the information contained in any notice of registration filed on Form BD–N (17 CFR 249.501b) pursuant to this rule is or becomes inaccurate for any reason, the broker or dealer shall promptly file an amendment on Form BD–N correcting such information.

(d) An application for registration by notice, and any amendments thereto, that are filed on Form BD–N (17 CFR 249.501b) pursuant to this rule will be considered a "report" filed with the Commission for purposes of sections 15(b), 17(a), 18(a), 32(a) and other applicable provisions of the Act.

RULES RELATING TO OVER–THE–COUNTER MARKETS

Rule 15c1–1. Definitions

As used in any rule adopted pursuant to Section 15(c)(1) of the Act:

(a) The term *customer* shall not include a broker or dealer or a municipal securities dealer; provided, however, That the term "customer" shall include a municipal securities dealer (other than a broker or dealer) with respect to transactions in securities other than municipal securities.

(b) The term *the completion of the transaction* means:

(1) In the case of a customer who purchases a security through or from a broker, dealer or municipal securities dealer, except as provided in paragraph (b)(2) of this rule, the time when such customer pays the broker, dealer or municipal securities dealer any part of the purchase price, or, if payment is effected by a bookkeeping entry, the time when such bookkeeping entry is made by the broker, dealer or municipal securities dealer for any part of the purchase price;

(2) In the case of a customer who purchases a security through or from a broker, dealer or municipal securities dealer and who makes payment therefor prior to the time when payment is requested or notification is given that payment is due, the time when such broker, dealer or municipal securities dealer delivers the security to or into the account of such customer;

(3) In the case of a customer who sells a security through or to a broker, dealer or municipal securities dealer except as provided in paragraph (b)(4) of this rule, if the security is not in the custody of the broker, dealer or municipal securities dealer at the time of sale, the time when the security is delivered to the broker, dealer or municipal securities dealer, and if the security is in the custody of the broker, dealer or municipal securities dealer at the time of sale, the time when the broker, dealer or municipal securities dealer transfers the security from the account of such customer;

(4) In the case of a customer who sells a security through or to a broker, dealer or municipal securities dealer and who delivers such security to such broker, dealer or municipal securities dealer prior to the time when delivery is requested or notification is given that delivery is due, the time when such broker, dealer or municipal securities dealer makes payment to or into the account of such customer.

Rule 15c1-2. Fraud and misrepresentation

(a) The term *manipulative, deceptive, or other fraudulent device or contrivance,* as used in section 15(c)(1) of the Act, is hereby defined to include any act, practice, or course of business which operates or would operate as a fraud or deceit upon any person.

(b) The term *manipulative, deceptive or other fraudulent device or contrivance,* as used in section 15(c)(1) of the Act, is hereby defined to include any untrue statement of a material fact and any omission to state a material fact necessary in order to make the statements made, in the light of the circumstances under which they are made, not misleading, which statement or omission is made with knowledge or reasonable grounds to believe that it is untrue or misleading.

(c) The scope of this rule shall not be limited by any specific definitions of the term *manipulative, deceptive, or other fraudulent device or contrivance* contained in other rules adopted pursuant to section 15(c)(1) of the Act.

Rule 15c1-3. Misrepresentation by brokers, dealers and municipal securities dealers as to registration

The term *manipulative, deceptive, or other fraudulent device or contrivance,* as used in Section 15(c)(1) of the Act, is hereby defined to include any representation by a broker or dealer that the registration of a broker or dealer, pursuant to Section 15(b) of the Act, or the registration of a municipal securities dealer pursuant to Section 15B(a) of the Act, or the failure of the Commission to deny or revoke such registration, indicates in any way that the Commission has passed upon or approved the financial standing, business, or conduct of such registered broker, dealer or municipal securities dealer or the merits of any security or any transaction or transactions therein.

Rule 15c1-4. [Reserved]

Rule 15c1-5. Disclosure of control

The term *manipulative, deceptive or other fraudulent device or contrivance,* as used in Section 15(c)(1) of the Act, is hereby defined to include any act of any broker, dealer or municipal securities dealer controlled by, controlling, or under common control with, the issuer of any security, designed to effect with or for the account of a customer any transaction in, or to induce the purchase or sale by such customer of, such security unless such broker, dealer or municipal securities dealer, before entering into any contract with or for such customer for the purchase or sale of such security, discloses to such customer the existence of such control, and unless such disclosure, if not made in writing, is supplemented by the giving or sending of written disclosure at or before the completion of the transaction.

Rule 15c1-6. Disclosure of interest in distributions

The term *manipulative, deceptive, or other fraudulent device or contrivance,* as used in Section 15(c)(1) of the Act, is hereby defined to include any act of any broker who is acting for a customer or for both such customer and some other person, or of any dealer or municipal securities dealer who receives or has promise of receiving a fee from a customer for advising such customer with respect to securities, designed to effect with or for the account of such customer any transaction in, or to induce the purchase or sale by such customer of, any security in the primary or secondary distribution of which such broker, dealer or municipal securities dealer is participating or is otherwise financially interested unless such broker, dealer or municipal securities dealer, at or before the completion of each such transaction gives or sends to such customer written notification of the existence of such participation or interest.

Rule 15c1-7. Discretionary accounts

(a) The term *manipulative, deceptive, or other fraudulent device or contrivance,* as used in Section 15(c) of the Act, is hereby defined to include any act of any broker, dealer or municipal securities dealer designed to effect with or for any customer's account in respect to which such broker, dealer or municipal securities dealer or his agent or employee is vested with any discretionary power any transactions of purchase or sale which are excessive in size or frequency in view of the financial resources and character of such account.

(b) The term *manipulative, deceptive, or other fraudulent device or contrivance,* as used in Section 15(c)(1) of the Act, is hereby defined to include any act of any broker, dealer or municipal securities dealer designed to effect with or for any customer's account in respect to which such broker, dealer or municipal securities dealer or his agent or employee is vested with any discretionary power any transaction of purchase or sale unless immediately after effecting such transaction such broker, dealer or municipal securities dealer makes a record of such transaction which record includes the name of such customer, the name, amount and price of the security, and the date and time when such transaction took place.

Rule 15c1–8. Sales at the market

The term *manipulative, deceptive, or other fraudulent device or contrivance,* as used in Section 15(c) (1) of the Act, is hereby defined to include any representation made to a customer by a broker, dealer or municipal securities dealer who is participating or otherwise financially interested in the primary or secondary distribution of any security which is not admitted to trading on a national securities exchange that such security is being offered to such customer "at the market" or at a price related to the market price unless such broker, dealer or municipal securities dealer knows or has reasonable grounds to believe that a market for such security exists other than that made, created, or controlled by him, or by any person for whom he is acting or with whom he is associated in such distribution, or by any person controlled by, controlling or under common control with him.

Rule 15c1–9. Use of pro forma balance sheets

The term *manipulative, deceptive, or other fraudulent device or contrivance,* as used in section 15(c) (1) of the Act, is hereby defined to include the use of financial statements purporting to give effect to the receipt and application of any part of the proceeds from the sale or exchange of securities, unless the assumptions upon which each such financial statement is based are clearly set forth as part of the caption to each such statement in type at least as large as that used generally in the body of the statement.

Rule 15c2–1. Hypothecation of customers' securities

(a) *General Provisions.* The term *fraudulent, deceptive, or manipulative act or practice,* as used in section 15(c)(2) of the Act, is hereby defined to include the direct or indirect hypothecation by a broker, or dealer, or his arranging for or permitting, directly, or indirectly, the continued hypothecation of any securities carried for the account of any customer under circumstances:

(1) That will permit the commingling of securities carried for the account of any such customer with securities carried for the account of any other customer, without first obtaining the written consent of each such customer to such hypothecation;

(2) That will permit such securities to be commingled with securities carried for the account of any person other than a bona fide customer of such broker or dealer under a lien for a loan made to such broker or dealer; or

(3) That will permit securities carried for the account of customers to be hypothecated, or subjected to any lien or liens or claims or claims of the pledgee or pledgees, for a sum which exceeds the aggregate indebtedness of all customers in respect of securities carried for their accounts; except that this clause shall not be deemed to be violated by reason of an excess arising on any day through the reduction of the aggregate indebtedness of customers on such day: *Provided,* That funds or securities in an amount sufficient to eliminate such excess are paid or placed in transfer to pledgee for the purpose of reducing the sum of the liens or claims to which securities carried for the account of customers are subject as promptly as practicable after such reduction occurs, but before the lapse of one-half hour after the commencement of banking hours on the next banking day at the place where the largest principal amount of loans of such broker or dealer are payable and, in any event, before such broker or dealer on such day has obtained or increased any bank loan collateralized by securities carried for the account of customers.

(b) *Definitions.* For the purposes of this rule:

(1) The term *customer* shall not include any general or special partner or any director or officer of such broker or dealer, or any participant, as such, in any joint, group or syndicate account with such broker or dealer or with any partner, officer or director thereof. The term also shall not include a counterparty who has delivered collateral to an OTC derivatives dealer pursuant to a transaction in an eligible OTC derivative instrument, or pursuant to the OTC derivatives dealer's cash management securities activities or ancillary portfolio management securities activities, and who has received a prominent written notice from the OTC derivatives dealer that:

(i) Except as otherwise agreed in writing by the OTC derivatives dealer and the counterparty, the dealer may repledge or otherwise use the collateral in its business;

(ii) In the event of the OTC derivatives dealer's failure, the counterparty will likely be considered an unsecured creditor of the dealer as to that collateral;

(iii) The Securities Investor Protection Act of 1970 (15 U.S.C 78aaa through 78lll) does not protect the counterparty; and

(iv) The collateral will not be subject to the requirements of Rule 8c–1, Rule 15c2–1, Rule 15c3–2, or Rule 15c3–3;

(2) The term *securities carried for the account of any customer* shall be deemed to mean:

(i) Securities received by or on behalf of such broker or dealer for the account of any customer;

(ii) Securities sold and appropriated by such broker or dealer to a customer, except that if such securities were subject to a lien when appropriated to a customer they shall not be deemed to be "securities carried for the account of any customer" pending their release from such lien as promptly as practicable;

(iii) Securities sold, but not appropriated, by such broker or dealer to a customer who has made any payment therefor, to the extent that such broker or dealer owns and has received delivery of securities of like kind, except that if such securities were subject to a lien when such payment was made they shall not be deemed to be "securities carried for the account of any customer" pending their release from such lien as promptly as practicable;

(3) *Aggregate indebtedness* shall not be deemed to be reduced by reason of uncollected items. In computing aggregate indebtedness, related guaranteed and guarantor accounts shall be treated as a single account and considered on a consolidated basis, and balances in accounts carrying both long and short positions shall be adjusted by treating the market value of the securities required to cover such short positions as though such market value were a debit; and

(4) In computing the sum of the liens or claims to which securities carried for the account of customers of a broker or dealer are subject, any rehypothecation of such securities by another broker or dealer who is subject to this rule or to Rule 8c–1 shall be disregarded.

(c) *Exemption for Cash Accounts.* The provisions of paragraph (a)(1) of this rule shall not apply to any hypothecation of securities carried for the account of a customer in a special cash account within the meaning of section 4(c) of Regulation T of the Board of Governors of the Federal Reserve System: *Provided,* That at or before the completion of the transaction of purchase of such securities for, or of sale of such securities to, such customer, written notice is given or sent to such customer disclosing that such securities are or may be hypothecated under circumstances which will permit the commingling thereof with securities carried for the account of other customers. The term *the completion of the transaction* shall have the meaning given to such term by Rule 15c1–1(b).

(d) *Exemption for Clearing House Liens.* The provisions of paragraphs (a)(2), (a)(3), and (f) of this rule shall not apply to any lien or claim of the clearing corporation, or similar department or association, of a national securities exchange or a registered national securities association, for a loan made and to be repaid on the same calendar day, which is incidental to the clearing of transactions in securities or loans through such corporation, department, or association: *Provided, however,* That for the purpose of paragraph (a)(3) of this rule, "aggregate indebtedness of all customers in respect of securities carried for their accounts" shall not include indebtedness in respect of any securities subject to any lien or claim exempted by this paragraph.

(e) *Exemption for Certain Liens on Securities of Noncustomers.* The provisions of paragraph (a)(2) of this rule hereof shall not be deemed to prevent such broker or dealer from permitting securities not carried for the account of a customer to be subjected (i) to a lien for a loan made against securities carried for the account of customers, or (ii) to a lien for a loan made and to be repaid on the same calendar day. For the purpose of this exemption, a loan shall be deemed to be "made against securities carried for the account of customers" if only securities carried for the account of customers are used to obtain or to increase such loan or as substitutes for other securities carried for the account of customers.

(f) *Notice and Certification Requirements.* No person subject to this rule shall hypothecate any security carried for the account of a customer unless, at or prior to the time of each such hypothecation, he gives written notice to the pledgee that the security pledged is carried for the account of a customer and that such hypothecation does not contravene any provision of this rule, except that in the case of an omnibus account the broker or dealer for whom such account is carried may furnish a signed statement to the person carrying such account that all securities carried therein by such broker or dealer will be securities carried for the account of his customers and that the hypothecation thereof by such broker or dealer will not contravene any provision of this rule. The provisions of this clause shall not apply to any hypothecation of securities under any lien or claim of a pledgee securing a loan made and to be repaid on the same calendar day.

(g) The fact that securities carried for the accounts of customers and securities carried for the accounts of others are represented by one or more certificates in the custody of a clearing corporation or other subsidiary organization of either a national securities exchange or of a registered national securities association, or of a custodian bank, in accordance with a system for the central handling of securities established by a national securities exchange or a registered national securities association, pursuant to which system the hypothecation of such securities is effected by bookkeeping entries without physical delivery of such securities, shall not, in and of itself, result in a commingling of securities, prohibited by paragraph (*a*)(1) or (*a*)(2) hereof, whenever a participating member, broker or dealer hypothecates securities in accordance with such system: *Provided, however,* That (1) any such custodian of any securities held by or for such system shall agree that it will not for any reason, including the assertion of any claim, right or lien of any kind, refuse or refrain from promptly delivering any such securities (other than securities then hypothecated in accordance with such system) to such clearing corporation or other subsidiary organization or as directed by it, except that nothing in such agreement shall be deemed to require the custodian to deliver any securities in contravention of any notice of levy, seizure or similar notice, or order or judgment, issued or directed by a governmental agency or court, or officer thereof, having jurisdiction over such custodian, which on its face affects such securities; (2) such systems shall have safeguards in the handling, transfer and delivery of securities and provisions for fidelity bond coverage of the employees and agents of the clearing corporation or other subsidiary organization and for periodic examinations by independent public accountants; and (3) the provisions of this paragraph (g) shall not be effective with respect to any particular system unless the agreement required by paragraph (g)(1) of this rule and the safeguards and provisions required by paragraph (g)(2) of this rule shall have been deemed adequate by the Commission for the protection of investors, and unless any subsequent amendments to such agreement, safeguards or provisions shall have been deemed adequate by the Commission for the protection of investors.

Rule 15c2–3. [Reserved]

Rule 15c2–4. Transmission or maintenance of payments received in connection with underwritings

It shall constitute a "fraudulent, deceptive, or manipulative act or practice" as used in Section 15(c)(2) of the Act, for any broker, dealer or municipal securities dealer participating in any distribution of securities, other than a firm-commitment underwriting, to accept any part of the sale price of any security being distributed unless:

(a) The money or other consideration received is promptly transmitted to the persons entitled thereto; or

(b) If the distribution is being made on an "all-or-none" basis, or on any other basis which contemplates that payment is not to be made to the person on whose behalf the distribution is being made until some further event or contingency occurs, (1) the money or other consideration received is promptly deposited in a separate bank account, as agent or trustee for the persons who have the beneficial interests therein, until the appropriate event or contingency has occurred, and then the funds are promptly transmitted or returned to the persons entitled thereto, or (2) all such funds are promptly transmitted to a bank which has agreed in writing to hold all such funds in escrow for the persons who have the beneficial interests therein and to transmit or return such funds directly to the persons entitled thereto when the appropriate event or contingency has occurred.

Rule 15c2–5. Disclosure and other requirements when extending or arranging credit in certain transactions

(a) It shall constitute a "fraudulent, deceptive, or manipulative act or practice" as used in section 15(c)(2) of the Act for any broker or dealer to offer or sell any security to, or to attempt to induce the purchase of any security by, any person, in connection with which such broker or dealer, directly or indirectly offers to extend any credit to or to arrange any loan for such person, or extends to or participates in arranging any loan for such person, unless such broker or dealer, before any purchase, loan or other related element of the transaction is entered into:

(1) Delivers to such person a written statement setting forth the exact nature and extent of (i) such person's obligations under the particular loan arrangement, including, among other things, the specific charges which such person will incur under such loan in each period during which the loan may continue or be extended, (ii) the risks and disadvantages which such person will incur in the entire transaction, including the loan arrangement, (iii) all commissions, discounts, and other remuneration received and to be received, in connection with the entire transaction including the loan arrangement, by the broker or dealer,

by any person controlling, controlled by, or under common control with the broker or dealer, and by any other person participating in the transaction; *Provided, however,* That the broker or dealer shall be deemed to be in compliance with this subparagraph if the customer, before any purchase, loan, or other related element of the transaction is entered into in a manner legally binding upon the customer, receives a statement from the lender, or receives a prospectus or offering circular from the broker or dealer, which statement, prospectus or offering circular contains the information required by this paragraph; and

(2) Obtains from such person information concerning his financial situation and needs, reasonably determines that the entire transaction, including the loan arrangement, is suitable for such person, and retains in his files a written statement setting forth the basis upon which the broker or dealer made such determination; *Provided, however,* That the written statement referred to in this subparagraph must be made available to the customer on request.

(b) This rule shall not apply to any credit extended or any loan arranged by any broker or dealer subject to the provisions of Regulation T (12 CFR part 220) if such credit is extended or such loan is arranged, in compliance with the requirements of such regulation, only for the purpose of purchasing or carrying the security offered or sold: *Provided, however,* That notwithstanding this paragraph, the provisions of paragraph (a) shall apply in full force with respect to any transaction involving the extension of or arrangement for credit by a broker or dealer (i) in a special insurance premium funding account within the meaning of Section 4(k) of Regulation T or (ii) in compliance with the terms of Rule 3a12–5.

(c) This rule shall not apply to any offer to extend credit or arrange any loan, or to any credit extended or loan arranged, in connection with any offer or sale, or attempt to induce the purchase, of any municipal security.

(d) This rule shall not apply to a transaction involving the extension of credit by an OTC derivatives dealer, as defined in Rule 3b–12, if the transaction is exempt from the provisions of Section 7(c) of the Act pursuant to Rule 36a1–1.

Rule 15c2–6. [Reserved]

Rule 15c2–7. Identification of quotations

(a) It shall constitute an attempt to induce the purchase or sale of a security by making a "fictitious quotation" within the meaning of Section 15(c)(2) of the Act, for any broker or dealer to furnish or submit, directly or indirectly, any quotation for a security (other than a municipal security) to an inter-dealer quotation system unless:

(1) The inter-dealer-quotation-system is informed, if such is the case, that the quotation is furnished or submitted;

(i) By a correspondent broker or dealer for the account or in behalf of another broker or dealer, and if so, the identity of such other broker or dealer; and/or

(ii) In furtherance of one or more other arrangements (including a joint account, guarantee of profit, guarantee against loss, commission, markup, markdown, indication of interest and accommodation arrangement) between or among brokers or dealers, and if so, the identity of each broker or dealer participating in any such arrangement or arrangements: *Provided, however,* That the provisions of this subparagraph shall not apply if only one of the brokers or dealers participating in any such arrangement or arrangements furnishes or submits a quotation with respect to the security to an inter-dealer-quotation-system.

(2) The inter-dealer-quotation-system to which the quotation is furnished or submitted makes it a general practice to disclose with each published quotation, by appropriate symbol or otherwise, the category or categories (paragraphs (a)(1)(i) and/or (a)(1)(ii) of this rule) in furtherance of which the quotation is submitted, and the identities of all other brokers and dealers referred to in paragraph (a)(1) of this rule where such information is supplied to the inter-dealer-quotation-system under the provisions of paragraph (a)(1) of this rule.

(b) It shall constitute an attempt to induce the purchase or sale of a security by making a "fictitious quotation," within the meaning of section 15(c)(2) of the Act, for a broker or dealer to enter into any correspondent or other arrangement (including a joint account, guarantee of profit, guarantee against loss, commission, markup, markdown, indication of interest and accommodation arrangement) in furtherance of which two or more brokers or dealers furnish or submit quotations with respect to a particular security unless such broker or dealer informs all brokers or dealers furnishing or submitting such quotations of the existence of such correspondent and other arrangements, and the identity of the parties thereto.

(c) For purposes of this rule:

(1) The term *inter-dealer-quotation-system* shall mean any system of general circulation to brokers and dealers which regularly disseminates quotations of identified brokers or dealers but shall not include a quotation sheet prepared and distributed by a broker or dealer in the regular course of his business and containing only quotations of such broker or dealer.

(2) The term *quotation* shall mean any bid or offer, or any indication of interest (such as OW or BW) in any bid or offer.

(3) The term *correspondent* shall mean a broker or dealer who has a direct line of communication to another broker or dealer located in a different city or geographic area.

Rule 15c2–8. Delivery of prospectus

(a) It shall constitute a deceptive act or practice, as those terms are used in section 15(c)(2) of the Act, for a broker or dealer to participate in a distribution of securities with respect to which a registration statement has been filed under the Securities Act of 1933 unless he complies with the requirements set forth in paragraphs (b) through (h) of this rule. For the purposes of this rule, a broker or dealer participating in the distribution shall mean any underwriter and any member or proposed member of the selling group.

(b) In connection with an issue of securities, the issuer of which has not previously been required to file reports pursuant to sections 13(a) or 15(d) of the Securities Exchange Act of 1934, unless such issuer has been exempted from the requirement to file reports thereunder pursuant to section 12(h) of the Act, such broker or dealer shall deliver a copy of the preliminary prospectus to any person who is expected to receive a confirmation of sale at least 48 hours prior to the sending of such confirmation. Provided, however, this paragraph (b) shall apply to all issuances of asset-backed securities (as defined in Item 1101(c) of Regulation AB) regardless of whether the issuer has previously been required to file reports pursuant to sections 13(a) or 15(d) of the Securities Exchange Act of 1934, or exempted from the requirement to file reports thereunder pursuant to section 12(h) of the Act (15 U.S.C. 781).

(c) Such broker or dealer shall take reasonable steps to furnish to any person who makes written request for a preliminary prospectus between the filing date and a reasonable time prior to the effective date of the registration statement to which such prospectus relates, a copy of the latest preliminary prospectus on file with the Commission. Reasonable steps shall include receiving an undertaking by the managing underwriter or underwriters to send such copy to the address given in the requests.

(d) Such broker or dealer shall take reasonable steps to comply promptly with the written request of any person for a copy of the final prospectus relating to such securities during the period between the effective date of the registration statement and the later of either the termination of such distribution, or the expiration of the applicable 40– or 90–day period under section 4(a)(3) of the Securities Act of 1933. Reasonable steps shall include receiving an undertaking by the managing underwriter or underwriters to send such copy to the address given in the requests. (The 40–day and 90–day periods referred to above shall be deemed to apply for purposes of this rule irrespective of the provisions of paragraphs (b) and (d) of Rule 174 under the Securities Act of 1933).

(e) Such broker or dealer shall take reasonable steps (1) to make available a copy of the preliminary prospectus relating to such securities to each of his associated persons who is expected, prior to the effective date, to solicit customers' orders for such securities before the making of any such solicitation by such associated persons and (2) to make available to each such associated person a copy of any amended preliminary prospectus promptly after the filing thereof.

(f) Such broker or dealer shall take reasonable steps to make available a copy of the final prospectus relating to such securities to each of his associated persons who is expected, after the effective date, to solicit customers' orders for such securities prior to the making of any such solicitation by such associated persons, unless a preliminary prospectus which is substantially the same as the final prospectus except for matters relating to the price of the stocks, has been so made available.

(g) If the broker or dealer is a managing underwriter of such distribution, he shall take reasonable steps to see to it that all other brokers or dealers participating in such distribution are promptly furnished with sufficient copies, as requested by them, of each preliminary prospectus, each amended preliminary prospectus and the final prospectus to enable them to comply with paragraphs (b), (c), (d), and (e) of this rule.

(h) If the broker or dealer is a managing underwriter of such distribution, he shall take reasonable steps to see that any broker or dealer participating in the distribution or trading in the registered security is furnished reasonable quantities of the final prospectus relating to such securities, as requested by him, in order to enable him to comply with the prospectus delivery requirements of section 5(b)(1) and (2) of the Securities Act of 1933.

(i) This rule shall not require the furnishing of prospectuses in any state where such furnishing would be unlawful under the laws of such state: *Provided, however,* That this provision is not to be construed to relieve a broker or dealer from complying with the requirements of section 5(b)(1) and (2) of the Securities Act of 1933.

Rule 15c2–11. Initiation or resumption of quotations without specified information

PRELIMINARY NOTE:

Brokers and dealers may wish to refer to Securities Exchange Act Release No. 29094 (April 17, 1991), for a discussion of procedures for gathering and reviewing the information required by this rule and the requirement that a broker or dealer have a reasonable basis for believing that the information is accurate and obtained from reliable sources.

(a) As a means reasonably designed to prevent fraudulent, deceptive, or manipulative acts or practices, it shall be unlawful for a broker or dealer to publish any quotation for a security or, directly or indirectly, to submit any such quotation for publication, in any quotation medium (as defined in this rule) unless such broker or dealer has in its records the documents and information required by this paragraph (for purposes of this rule, "paragraph (a) information"), and, based upon a review of the paragraph (a) information together with any other documents and information required by paragraph (b) of this rule, has a reasonable basis under the circumstances for believing that the paragraph (a) information is accurate in all material respects, and that the sources of the paragraph (a) information are reliable. The information required pursuant to this paragraph is:

(1) A copy of the prospectus specified by section 10(a) of the Securities Act of 1933 for an issuer that has filed a registration statement under the Securities Act of 1933, other than a registration statement on Form F–6, which became effective less than 90 calendar days prior to the day on which such broker or dealer publishes or submits the quotation to the quotation medium, *Provided* That such registration statement has not thereafter been the subject of a stop order which is still in effect when the quotation is published or submitted; or

(2) A copy of the offering circular provided for under Regulation A under the Securities Act of 1933 for an issuer that has filed a notification under Regulation A and was authorized to commence the offering less than 40 calendar days prior to the day on which such broker or dealer publishes or submits the quotation to the quotation medium, *Provided* That the offering circular provided for under Regulation A has not thereafter become the subject of a suspension order which is still in effect when the quotation is published or submitted; or

(3) A copy of the issuer's most recent annual report filed pursuant to section 13 or 15(d) of the Act or pursuant to Regulation A, or a copy of the annual statement referred to in section 12(g)(2)(G)(i) of the Act in the case of an issuer required to file reports pursuant to section 13 or 15(d) of the Act or an issuer of a security covered by section 12(g)(2)(B) or (G) of the Act, together with any semiannual, quarterly and current reports that have been filed under the provisions of the Act or Regulation A by the issuer after such annual report or annual statement; *provided, however,* that until such issuer has filed its first annual report pursuant to section 13 or 15(d) of the Act or pursuant to Regulation A, or annual statement referred to in section 12(g)(2)(G)(i) of the Act, the broker or dealer has in its records a copy of the prospectus specified by section 10(a) of the Securities Act of 1933 included in a registration statement filed by the issuer under the Securities Act of 1933, other than a registration statement on Form F–6, or a copy of the offering circular specified by Regulation A included in an offering statement filed by the issuer under Regulation A, that became effective or was qualified within the prior 16 months, or a copy of any registration statement filed by the issuer under section 12 of the Act that became effective within the prior 16 months, together with any semiannual, quarterly and current reports filed thereafter under section 13 or 15(d) of the Act or Regulation A; and *provided further,* that the broker or dealer has a reasonable basis under the circumstances for believing that the issuer is current in filing annual, semiannual, quarterly, and current reports filed pursuant to section 13 or 15(d) of the Act or Regulation A, or, in the case of an insurance company exempted from section 12(g) of the Act by reason of section 12(g)(2)(G) thereof, the annual statement referred to in section 12(g)(2)(G)(i) of the Act; or

(4) The information that, since the beginning of its last fiscal year, the issuer has published pur-

suant to Rule 12g3–2(b), and which the broker or dealer shall make reasonably available upon the request of a person expressing an interest in a proposed transaction in the issuer's security with the broker or dealer, such as by providing the requesting person with appropriate instructions regarding how to obtain the information electronically; or

(5) The following information, which shall be reasonably current in relation to the day the quotation is submitted and which the broker or dealer shall make reasonably available upon request to any person expressing an interest in a proposed transaction in the security with such broker or dealer:

(i) The exact name of the issuer and its predecessor (if any);

(ii) The address of its principal executive offices;

(iii) The state of incorporation, if it is a corporation;

(iv) The exact title and class of the security;

(v) The par or stated value of the security;

(vi) The number of shares or total amount of the securities outstanding as of the end of the issuer's most recent fiscal year;

(vii) The name and address of the transfer agent;

(viii) The nature of the issuer's business;

(ix) The nature of products or services offered;

(x) The nature and extent of the issuer's facilities;

(xi) The name of the chief executive officer and members of the board of directors;

(xii) The issuer's most recent balance sheet and profit and loss and retained earnings statements;

(xiii) Similar financial information for such part of the 2 preceding fiscal years as the issuer or its predecessor has been in existence;

(xiv) Whether the broker or dealer or any associated person is affiliated, directly or indirectly with the issuer;

(xv) Whether the quotation is being published or submitted on behalf of any other broker or dealer, and, if so, the name of such broker or dealer; and

(xvi) Whether the quotation is being submitted or published directly or indirectly on behalf of the issuer, or any director, officer or any person, directly or indirectly the beneficial owner of more than 10 percent of the outstanding units or shares of any equity security of the issuer, and, if so, the name of such person, and the basis for any exemption under the federal securities laws for any sales of such securities on behalf of such person.

If such information is made available to others upon request pursuant to this paragraph, such delivery, unless otherwise represented, shall not constitute a representation by such broker or dealer that such information is accurate, but shall constitute a representation by such broker or dealer that the information is reasonably current in relation to the day the quotation is submitted, that the broker or dealer has a reasonable basis under the circumstances for believing the information is accurate in all material respects, and that the information was obtained from sources which the broker or dealer has a reasonable basis for believing are reliable. This paragraph (a)(5) shall not apply to any security of an issuer included in paragraph (a)(3) of this rule unless a report or statement of such issuer described in paragraph (a)(3) of this rule is not reasonably available to the broker or dealer. A report or statement of an issuer described in paragraph (a)(3) of this rule shall be "reasonably available" when such report or statement is filed with the Commission.

(b) With respect to any security the quotation of which is within the provisions of this rule, the broker or dealer submitting or publishing such quotation shall have in its records the following documents and information:

(1) A record of the circumstances involved in the submission of publication of such quotation, including the identity of the person or persons for whom the quotation is being submitted or published and any information regarding the transactions provided to the broker or dealer by such person or persons;

(2) A copy of any trading suspension order issued by the Commission pursuant to section 12(k) of the Act respecting any securities of the issuer or its predecessor (if any) during the 12 months preceding the date of the publication or submission of the quotation, or a copy of the public release issued by the Commission announcing such trading suspension order; and

(3) A copy or a written record of any other material information (including adverse information) regarding the issuer which comes to the broker's or dealer's knowledge or possession before the publication or submission of the quotation.

(c) The broker or dealer shall preserve the documents and information required under paragraphs (a) and (b) of this rule for a period of not less than three years, the first two years in an easily accessible place.

(d)(1) For any security of an issuer included in paragraph (a)(5) of this rule, the broker or dealer submitting the quotation shall furnish to the interdealer quotation system (as defined in paragraph (e)(2) of this rule), in such form as such system shall prescribe, at least 3 business days before the quotation is published or submitted, the information regarding the security and the issuer which such broker or dealer is required to maintain pursuant to said paragraph (a)(5) of this rule.

(2) For any security of an issuer included in paragraph (a)(3) of this rule,

(i) A broker-dealer shall be in compliance with the requirement to obtain current reports filed by the issuer if the broker-dealer obtains all current reports filed with the Commission by the issuer as of a date up to five business days in advance of the earlier of the date of submission of the quotation to the quotation medium and the date of submission of the information in paragraph (a) of this section pursuant to the applicable rule of the Financial Industry Regulatory Authority, Inc. or its successor organization; and

(ii) A broker-dealer shall be in compliance with the requirement to obtain the annual, quarterly, and current reports filed by the issuer, if the broker-dealer has made arrangements to receive all such reports when filed by the issuer and it has regularly received reports from the issuer on a timely basis, unless the broker-dealer has a reasonable basis under the circumstances for believing that the issuer has failed to file a required report or has filed a report but has not sent it to the broker-dealer.

(e) For purposes of this rule:

(1) *Quotation medium* shall mean any "interdealer quotation system" or any publication or electronic communications network or other device which is used by brokers or dealers to make known to others their interest in transactions in any security, including offers to buy or sell at a stated price or otherwise, or invitations of offers to buy or sell.

(2) *Interdealer quotation system* shall mean any system of general circulation to brokers or dealers which regularly disseminates quotations of identified brokers or dealers.

(3) Except as otherwise specified in this rule, *quotation* shall mean any bid or offer at a specified price with respect to a security, or any indication of interest by a broker or dealer in receiving bids or offers from others for a security, or any indication by a broker or dealer that he wishes to advertise his general interest in buying or selling a particular security.

(4) *Issuer,* in the case of quotations for American Depositary Receipts, shall mean the issuer of the deposited shares represented by such American Depositary Receipts.

(f) The provisions of this rule shall not apply to:

(1) The publication or submission of a quotation respecting a security admitted to trading on a national securities exchange and which is traded on such an exchange on the same day as, or on the business day next preceding, the day the quotation is published or submitted.

(2) The publication or submission by a broker or dealer, solely on behalf of a customer (other than a person acting as or for a dealer), of a quotation that represents the customer's indication of interest and does not involve the solicitation of the customer's interest; *Provided, however,* That this paragraph (f)(2) shall not apply to a quotation consisting of both a bid and an offer, each of which is at a specified price, unless the quotation medium specifically identifies the quotation as representing such an unsolicited customer interest.

(3)(i) The publication or submission, in an interdealer quotation system that specifically identifies as such unsolicited customer indications of interest of the kind described in paragraph (f)(2) of this rule, of a quotation respecting a security which has been the subject of quotations (exclusive of any identified customer interests) in such a system on each of at least 12 days within the previous 30 calendar days, with no more than 4 business days in succession without a quotation; or

(ii) The publication or submission, in an interdealer quotation system that does not so identify any such unsolicited customer indications of interest, of a quotation respecting a security which has been the subject of both bid and ask quotations in an interdealer quotation system at specified prices on each of at least 12 days within the previous 30 calendar days, with no more than 4 business days in succession without such a two-way quotation;

(iii) A dealer acting in the capacity of market maker, as defined in section 3(a)(38) of the Act, that has published or submitted a quotation respecting a security in an interdealer quotation system and such quotation has qualified for an exception provided in this paragraph (f)(3), may continue to publish or submit quotations for such security in the interdealer quotation system without compliance with this rule unless and until such dealer ceases to submit or publish a quotation or ceases to act in the capacity of market maker respecting such security.

(4) The publication or submission of a quotation respecting a municipal security.

(5) The publication or submission of a quotation respecting a Nasdaq security (as defined in Rule 600 of Regulation NMS), and such security's listing is not suspended, terminated, or prohibited.

(g) The requirement in paragraph (a)(5) of this rule that the information with respect to the issuer be "reasonably current" will be presumed to be satisfied, unless the broker or dealer has information to the contrary, if:

(1) The balance sheet is as of a date less than 16 months before the publication or submission of the quotation, the statements of profit and loss and retained earnings are for the 12 months preceding the date of such balance sheet, and if such balance sheet is not as of a date less than 6 months before the publication or submission of the quotation, it shall be accompanied by additional statements of profit and loss and retained earnings for the period from the date of such balance sheet to a date less than 6 months before the publication or submission of the quotation.

(2) Other information regarding the issuer specified in paragraph (a)(5) of this rule is as of a date within 12 months prior to the publication or submission of the quotation.

(h) This rule shall not prohibit any publication or submission of any quotation if the Commission, upon written request or upon its own motion, exempts such quotation either unconditionally or on specified terms and conditions, as not constituting a fraudulent, manipulative or deceptive practice comprehended within the purpose of this rule.

Rule 15c2–12. Municipal securities disclosure

PRELIMINARY NOTE:

For a discussion of disclosure obligations relating to municipal securities, issuers, brokers, dealers, and municipal securities dealers should refer to Securities Act Release No. 7049, Securities Exchange Act Release No. 33741, FR–42 (March 9, 1994). For a discussion of the obligations of underwriters to have a reasonable basis for recommending municipal securities, brokers, dealers, and municipal securities dealers should refer to Securities Exchange Act Release No. 26100 (Sept. 22, 1988) and Securities Exchange Act Release No. 26985 (June 28, 1989).

(a) *General.* As a means reasonably designed to prevent fraudulent, deceptive, or manipulative acts or practices, it shall be unlawful for any broker, dealer, or municipal securities dealer (a "Participating Underwriter" when used in connection with an Offering) to act as an underwriter in a primary offering of municipal securities with an aggregate principal amount of $1,000,000 or more (an "Offering") unless the Participating Underwriter complies with the requirements of this rule or is exempted from the provisions of this rule.

(b) *Requirements.* (1) Prior to the time the Participating Underwriter bids for, purchases, offers, or sells municipal securities in an Offering, the Participating Underwriter shall obtain and review an official statement that an issuer of such securities deems final as of its date, except for the omission of no more than the following information: the offering price(s), interest rate(s), selling compensation, aggregate principal amount, principal amount per maturity, delivery dates, any other terms or provisions required by an issuer of such securities to be specified in a competitive bid, ratings, other terms of the securities depending on such matters, and the identity of the underwriter(s).

(2) Except in competitively bid offerings, from the time the Participating Underwriter has reached an understanding with an issuer of municipal securities that it will become a Participating Underwriter in an Offering until a final official statement is available, the Participating Underwriter shall send no later than the next business day, by first class mail or other equally prompt means, to any potential customer, on request, a single copy of the most recent preliminary official statement, if any.

(3) The Participating Underwriter shall contract with an issuer of municipal securities or its designated agent to receive, within seven business

days after any final agreement to purchase, offer, or sell the municipal securities in an Offering and in sufficient time to accompany any confirmation that requests payment from any customer, copies of a final official statement in sufficient quantity to comply with paragraph (b)(4) of this rule and the rules of the Municipal Securities Rulemaking Board.

(4) From the time the final official statement becomes available until the earlier of

(i) Ninety days from the end of the underwriting period or

(ii) The time when the official statement is available to any person from the Municipal Securities Rulemaking Board, but in no case less than twenty-five days following the end of the underwriting period, the Participating Underwriter in an Offering shall send no later than the next business day, by first-class mail or other equally prompt means, to any potential customer, on request, a single copy of the final official statement.

(5)(i) A Participating Underwriter shall not purchase or sell municipal securities in connection with an Offering unless the Participating Underwriter has reasonably determined that an issuer of municipal securities, or an obligated person for whom financial or operating data is presented in the final official statement has undertaken, either individually or in combination with other issuers of such municipal securities or obligated persons, in a written agreement or contract for the benefit of holders of such securities, to provide the following to the Municipal Securities Rulemaking Board, either directly or indirectly through an indenture trustee or a designated agent:

(A) Annual financial information for each obligated person for whom financial information or operating data is presented in the final official statement, or, for each obligated person meeting the objective criteria specified in the undertaking and used to select the obligated persons for whom financial information or operating data is presented in the final official statement, except that, in the case of pooled obligations, the undertaking shall specify such objective criteria;

(B) If not submitted as part of the annual financial information, then when and if available, audited financial statements for each obligated person covered by paragraph (b)(5)(i)(A) of this rule;

(C) In a timely manner not in excess of ten business days after the occurrence of the event, notice of any of the following events with respect to the securities being offered in the Offering:

(*1*) Principal and interest payment delinquencies;

(*2*) Non-payment related defaults, if material;

(*3*) Unscheduled draws on debt service reserves reflecting financial difficulties;

(*4*) Unscheduled draws on credit enhancements reflecting financial difficulties;

(*5*) Substitution of credit or liquidity providers, or their failure to perform;

(*6*) Adverse tax opinions, the issuance by the Internal Revenue Service of proposed or final determinations of taxability, Notices of Proposed Issue (IRS Form 5701-TEB) or other material notices or determinations with respect to the tax status of the security, or other material events affecting the tax status of the security;

(*7*) Modifications to rights of security holders, if material;

(*8*) Bond calls, if material, and tender offers;

(*9*) Defeasances;

(*10*) Release, substitution, or sale of property securing repayment of the securities, if material;

(*11*) Rating changes;

(*12*) Bankruptcy, insolvency, receivership or similar event of the obligated person;

NOTE TO PARAGRAPH (b)(5)(i)(C)(12): For the purposes of the event identified in subparagraph (b)(5)(i)(C)(12), the event is considered to occur when any of the following occur: the appointment of a receiver, fiscal agent or similar officer for an obligated person in a proceeding under the U.S. Bankruptcy Code or in any other proceeding under state or federal law in which a court or governmental authority has assumed jurisdiction over substantially all of the assets or business of the obligated person, or if such jurisdiction has been assumed by leaving the existing governing body and officials or officers in possession but subject to the supervision and orders of a court or governmental authority, or the entry of an order confirming a plan of reorganization, arrangement or liquidation by a court or governmental authority having supervision or jurisdiction over substantially all of the assets or business of the obligated person;

(*13*) The consummation of a merger, consolidation, or acquisition involving an obligated person or the sale of all or substantially all of the assets of the obligated person, other than in the ordinary course of business, the entry into a definitive agreement to undertake such an action or the termination of a definitive agreement relating to any such actions, other than pursuant to its terms, if material;

(*14*) Appointment of a successor or additional trustee or the change of name of a trustee, if material;

(*15*) Incurrence of a financial obligation of the obligated person, if material, or agreement to covenants, events of default, remedies, priority rights, or other similar terms of a financial obligation of the obligated person, any of which affect security holders, if material; and

(*16*) Default, event of acceleration, termination event, modification of terms, or other similar events under the terms of a financial obligation of the obligated person, any of which reflect financial difficulties; and

(D) In a timely manner, notice of a failure of any person specified in paragraph (b)(5)(i)(A) of this rule to provide required annual financial information, on or before the date specified in the written agreement or contract.

(ii) The written agreement or contract for the benefit of holders of such securities also shall identify each person for whom annual financial information and notices of material events will be provided, either by name or by the objective criteria used to select such persons, and, for each such person shall:

(A) Specify, in reasonable detail, the type of financial information and operating data to be provided as part of annual financial information;

(B) Specify, in reasonable detail, the accounting principles pursuant to which financial statements will be prepared, and whether the financial statements will be audited; and

(C) Specify the date on which the annual financial information for the preceding fiscal year will be provided, and to whom it will be provided.

(iii) Such written agreement or contract for the benefit of holders of such securities also may provide that the continuing obligation to provide annual financial information and notices of events may be terminated with respect to any obligated person, if and when such obligated person no longer remains an obligated person with respect to such municipal securities.

(iv) Such written agreement or contract for the benefit of holders of such securities also shall provide that all documents provided to the Municipal Securities Rulemaking Board shall be accompanied by identifying information as prescribed by the Municipal Securities Rulemaking Board.

(c) *Recommendations.* As a means reasonably designed to prevent fraudulent, deceptive, or manipulative acts or practices, it shall be unlawful for any broker, dealer, or municipal securities dealer to recommend the purchase or sale of a municipal security unless such broker, dealer, or municipal securities dealer has procedures in place that provide reasonable assurance that it will receive prompt notice of any event disclosed pursuant to paragraph (b)(5)(i)(C), paragraph (b)(5)(i)(D), and paragraph (d)(2)(ii)(B) of this rule with respect to that security.

(d) *Exemptions.* (1) This rule shall not apply to a primary offering of municipal securities in authorized denominations of $100,000 or more, if such securities:

(i) Are sold to no more than thirty-five persons each of whom the Participating Underwriter reasonably believes:

(A) Has such knowledge and experience in financial and business matters that it is capable of evaluating the merits and risks of the prospective investment; and

(B) Is not purchasing for more than one account or with a view to distributing the securities; or

(ii) Have a maturity of nine months or less.

(2) Paragraph (b)(5) of this rule shall not apply to an Offering of municipal securities if, at such time as an issuer of such municipal securities delivers the securities to the Participating Underwriters:

(i) No obligated person will be an obligated person with respect to more than $10,000,000 in aggregate amount of outstanding municipal securities, including the offered securities and excluding municipal securities that were offered in a transaction exempt from this rule pursuant to paragraph (d)(1) of this rule;

(ii) An issuer of municipal securities or obligated person has undertaken, either individually or in combination with other issuers of municipal securities or obligated persons, in a written agreement or contract for the benefit of holders of such municipal securities, to provide the following to the Municipal Securities Rulemaking Board in an electronic format as prescribed by the Municipal Securities Rulemaking Board:

(A) At least annually, financial information or operating data regarding each obligated person for which financial information or operating data is presented in the final official statement, as specified in the undertaking, which financial information and operating data shall include, at a minimum, that financial information and operating data which is customarily prepared by such obligated person and is publicly available; and

(B) In a timely manner not in excess of ten business days after the occurrence of the event, notice of events specified in paragraph (b)(5)(i)(C) of this rule with respect to the securities that are the subject of the Offering; and

(C) Such written agreement or contract for the benefit of holders of such securities also shall provide that all documents provided to the Municipal Securities Rulemaking Board shall be accompanied by identifying information as prescribed by the Municipal Securities Rulemaking Board; and

(iii) The final official statement identifies by name, address, and telephone number the persons from which the foregoing information, data, and notices can be obtained.

(3) The provisions of paragraph (b)(5) of this rule, other than paragraph (b)(5)(i)(C) of this rule, shall not apply to an Offering of municipal securities, if such municipal securities have a stated maturity of 18 months or less.

(4) The provisions of paragraph (c) of this rule shall not apply to municipal securities:

(i) Sold in an Offering to which paragraph (b)(5) of this rule did not apply, other than Offerings exempt under paragraph (d)(2)(ii) of this rule; or

(ii) Sold in an Offering exempt from this section under paragraph (d)(1) of this rule.

(5) With the exception of paragraphs (b)(1) through (b)(4), this rule shall apply to a primary offering of municipal securities in authorized denominations of $100,000 or more if such securities may, at the option of the holder thereof, be tendered to an issuer of such securities or its designated agent for redemption or purchase at par value or more at least as frequently as every nine months until maturity, earlier redemption, or purchase by an issuer or its designated agent; provided, however, that paragraphs (b)(5) and (c) of this rule shall not apply to such securities outstanding on November 30, 2010, for so long as they continuously remain in authorized denominations of $100,000 or more and may, at the option of the holder thereof, be tendered to an issuer of such securities or its designated agent for redemption or purchase at par value or more at least as frequently as every nine months until maturity, earlier redemption, or purchase by an issuer or its designated agent.

(e) *Exemptive Authority.* The Commission, upon written request, or upon its own motion, may exempt any broker, dealer, or municipal securities dealer, whether acting in the capacity of a Participating Underwriter or otherwise, that is a participant in a transaction or class of transactions from any requirement of this rule, either unconditionally or on specified terms and conditions, if the Commission determines that such an exemption is consistent with the public interest and the protection of investors.

(f) *Definitions.* For the purposes of this rule—

(1) The term *authorized denominations of $100,000 or more* means municipal securities with a principal amount of $100,000 or more and with restrictions that prevent the sale or transfer of such securities in principal amounts of less than $100,000 other than through a primary offering; except that, for municipal securities with an original issue discount of 10 percent or more, the term means municipal securities with a minimum purchase price of $100,000 or more and with restrictions that prevent the sale or transfer of such securities, in principal amounts that are less than the original principal amount at the time of the primary offering, other than through a primary offering.

(2) The term *end of the underwriting period* means the later of such time as

(i) The issuer of municipal securities delivers the securities to the Participating Underwriters or

(ii) The Participating Underwriter does not retain, directly or as a member or an underwriting syndicate, an unsold balance of the securities for sale to the public.

(3) The term *final official statement* means a document or set of documents prepared by an issuer of municipal securities or its representatives that is complete as of the date delivered to the Participating Underwriter(s) and that sets forth information concerning the terms of the proposed issue of securities; information, including financial information or operating data, concerning such issuers of municipal securities and those other entities, enterprises, funds, accounts, and other persons material to an evaluation of the Offering; and a description of the undertakings to be provided pursuant to paragraph (b)(5)(i), paragraph (d)(2)(ii), and paragraph (d)(2)(iii) of this rule, if applicable, and of any instances in the previous five years in which each person specified pursuant to paragraph (b)(5)(ii) of this rule failed to comply, in all material respects, with any previous undertakings in a written contract or agreement specified in paragraph (b)(5)(i) of this rule. Financial information or operating data may be set forth in the document or set of documents, or may be included by specific reference to documents available to the public on the Municipal Securities Rulemaking Board's Internet Web site or filed with the Commission.

(4) The term *issuer of municipal securities* means the governmental issuer specified in section 3(a)(29) of the Act and the issuer of any separate security, including a separate security as defined in Rule 3b–5(a) under the Act.

(5) The term *potential customer* means (i) any person contacted by the Participating Underwriter concerning the purchase of municipal securities that are intended to be offered or have been sold in an Offering, (ii) any person who has expressed an interest to the Participating Underwriter in possibly purchasing such municipal securities, and (iii) any person who has a customer account with the Participating Underwriter.

(6) The term *preliminary official statement* means an official statement prepared by or for an issuer of municipal securities for dissemination to potential customers prior to the availability of the final official statement.

(7) The term *primary offering* means an offering of municipal securities directly or indirectly by or on behalf of an issuer of such securities, including any remarketing of municipal securities

(i) That is accompanied by a change in the authorized denomination of such securities from $100,000 or more to less than $100,000, or

(ii) That is accompanied by a change in the period during which such securities may be tendered to an issuer of such securities or its designated agent for redemption or purchase from a period of nine months or less to a period of more than nine months.

(8) The term *underwriter* means any person who has purchased from an issuer of municipal securities with a view to, or offers or sells for an issuer of municipal securities in connection with, the offering of any municipal security, or participates or has a direct or indirect participation in any such undertaking, or participates or has a participation in the direct or indirect underwriting of any such undertaking; except, that such term shall not include a person whose interest is limited to a commission, concession, or allowance from an underwriter, broker, dealer, or municipal securities dealer not in excess of the usual and customary distributors' or sellers' commission, concession, or allowance.

(9) The term *annual financial information* means financial information or operating data, provided at least annually, of the type included in the final official statement with respect to an obligated person, or in the case where no financial information or operating data was provided in the final official statement with respect to such obligated person, of the type included in the final official statement with respect to those obligated persons that meet the objective criteria applied to select the persons for which financial information or operating data will be provided on an annual basis. Financial information or operating data may be set forth in the document or set of documents, or may be included by specific reference to documents available to the public on the Municipal Securities Rulemaking Board's Internet Web site or filed with the Commission.

(10) The term *obligated person* means any person, including an issuer of municipal securities, who is either generally or through an enterprise, fund or account of such person committed by contract or other arrangement to support payment of all, or part of the obligations on the municipal

securities to be sold in the Offering (other than providers of municipal bond insurance, letters of credit, or other liquidity facilities).

(11)(i) The term *financial obligation* means a:

(A) Debt obligation;

(B) Derivative instrument entered into in connection with, or pledged as security or a source of payment for, an existing or planned debt obligation; or

(C) Guarantee of paragraph (f)(11)(i)(A) or (B).

(ii) The term *financial obligation* shall not include municipal securities as to which a final official statement has been provided to the Municipal Securities Rulemaking Board consistent with this rule.

(g) *Transitional Provision.* If on July 28, 1989 a Participating Underwriter was contractually committed to act as underwriter in an Offering of municipal securities originally issued before July 29, 1989, the requirements of paragraphs (b)(3) and (b)(4) shall not apply to the Participating Underwriter in connection with such an Offering. Paragraph (b)(5) of this rule shall not apply to a Participating Underwriter that has contractually committed to act as an underwriter in an Offering of municipal securities before July 3, 1995: *except that* paragraph (b)(5)(i)(A) and paragraph (b)(5)(i)(B) shall not apply with respect to fiscal years ending prior to January 1, 1996. Paragraph (c) shall become effective on January 1, 1996. Paragraph (d)(2)(ii) and paragraph (d)(2)(iii) of this rule shall not apply to an Offering of municipal securities commencing prior to January 1, 1996.

Rule 15c3–1. Net capital requirements for brokers and dealers

(a) Every broker or dealer must at all times have and maintain net capital no less than the greater of the highest minimum requirement applicable to its ratio requirement under paragraph (a)(1) of this section, or to any of its activities under paragraph (a)(2) of this section, and must otherwise not be "insolvent" as that term is defined in paragraph (c)(16) of this section. In lieu of applying paragraphs (a)(1) and (a)(2) of this rule, an OTC derivatives dealer shall maintain net capital pursuant to paragraph (a)(5) of this rule. Each broker or dealer also shall comply with the supplemental requirements of paragraphs (a)(4) and (a)(9) of this rule, to the extent either paragraph is applicable to its activities. In addition, a broker or dealer shall maintain net capital of not less than its own net capital requirement plus the sum of each broker's or dealer's subsidiary or affiliate minimum net capital requirements, which is consolidated pursuant to Appendix C, Rule 15c3–1c.

Ratio Requirements

(1) *Aggregate Indebtedness Standard.* (i) No broker or dealer, other than one that elects the provisions of paragraph (a)(1)(ii) of this rule, shall permit its aggregate indebtedness to all other persons to exceed 1500 percent of its net capital (or 800 percent of its net capital for 12 months after commencing business as a broker or dealer).

(ii) *Alternative Standard.* A broker or dealer may elect not to be subject to the Aggregate Indebtedness Standard of paragraph (a)(1)(i) of this rule. That broker or dealer shall not permit its net capital to be less than the greater of $250,000 or 2 percent of aggregate debit items computed in accordance with the Formula for Determination of Reserve Requirements for Brokers and Dealers (Exhibit A to Rule 15c3–3a). Such broker or dealer shall notify its Examining Authority, in writing, of its election to operate under this paragraph (a)(1)(ii). Once a broker or dealer has notified its Examining Authority, it shall continue to operate under this paragraph unless a change is approved upon application to the Commission. A broker or dealer that elects this standard and is not exempt from Rule 15c3–3 shall:

(A) Make the computation required by Rule 15c3–3(e) and set forth in Exhibit A, Rule 15c3–3a, on a weekly basis and, in lieu of the 1 percent reduction of certain debit items required by Note E(3) in the computation of its Exhibit A requirement, reduce aggregate debit items in such computation by 3 percent;

(B) Include in Items 7 and 8 of Exhibit A, Rule 15c3–3a, the market value of items specified therein more than 7 business days old;

(C) Exclude credit balances in accounts representing amounts payable for securities not yet received from the issuer or its agent which securities are specified in paragraphs (c)(2)(vi)(A) and (E) of this rule and any related debit items from the Exhibit A requirement for 3 business days; and

(D) Deduct from net worth in computing net capital 1 percent of the contract value of all failed to deliver contracts or securities borrowed that were allocated to failed to receive contracts of the same issue and which thereby were excluded from Items 11 or 12 of Exhibit A, Rule 15c3-3a.

(iii) *Futures Commission Merchants.* No broker or dealer registered as a futures commission merchant shall permit its net capital to be less than the greater of its requirement under paragraph (a)(1)(i) or (ii) of this rule, or 4 percent of the funds required to be segregated pursuant to the Commodity Exchange Act and the regulations thereunder (less the market value of commodity options purchased by option customers on or subject to the rules of a contract market, each such deduction not to exceed the amount of funds in the customer's account).

MINIMUM REQUIREMENTS

See Appendix E (Rule 15c3-1E) for temporary minimum requirements.

(2) *Brokers or Dealers That Carry Customer Accounts.* (i) A broker or dealer (other than one described in paragraphs (a)(2)(ii) or (a)(8) of this rule) shall maintain net capital of not less than $250,000 if it carries customer or broker or dealer accounts and receives or holds funds or securities for those persons. A broker or dealer shall be deemed to receive funds, or to carry customer or broker or dealer accounts and to receive funds from those persons if, in connection with its activities as a broker or dealer, it receives checks, drafts, or other evidences of indebtedness made payable to itself or persons other than the requisite registered broker or dealer carrying the account of a customer, escrow agent, issuer, underwriter, sponsor, or other distributor of securities. A broker or dealer shall be deemed to hold securities for, or to carry customer or broker or dealer accounts, and hold securities of, those persons if it does not promptly forward or promptly deliver all of the securities of customers or of other brokers or dealers received by the firm in connection with its activities as a broker or dealer. A broker or dealer, without complying with this paragraph (a)(2)(i), may receive securities only if its activities conform with the provisions of paragraphs (a)(2)(iv) or (v) of this rule, and may receive funds only in connection with the activities described in paragraph (a)(2)(v) of this rule.

(ii) A broker or dealer that is exempt from the provisions of Rule 15c3-3 pursuant to paragraph (k)(2)(i) thereof shall maintain net capital of not less than $100,000.

(iii) *Dealers.* A dealer shall maintain net capital of not less than $100,000. For the purposes of this rule, the term "dealer" includes:

(A) Any broker or dealer that endorses or writes options otherwise than on a registered national securities exchange or a facility of a registered national securities association; and

(B) Any broker or dealer that effects more than ten transactions in any one calendar year for its own investment account. This rule shall not apply to those persons engaging in activities described in paragraphs (a)(2)(v), (a)(2)(vi) or (a)(8) of this rule, or to those persons whose underwriting activities are limited solely to acting as underwriters in best efforts or all or none underwritings in conformity with paragraph (b)(2) of Rule 15c2-4, so long as those persons engage in no other dealer activities.

(iv) *Brokers or Dealers That Introduce Customer Accounts and Receive Securities.* A broker or dealer shall maintain net capital of not less than $50,000 if it introduces transactions and accounts of customers or other brokers or dealers to another registered broker or dealer that carries such accounts on a fully disclosed basis, and if the broker or dealer receives but does not hold customer or other broker or dealer securities. A broker or dealer operating under this paragraph (a)(2)(iv) of this rule may participate in a firm commitment underwriting without being subject to the provisions of paragraph (a)(2)(iii) of this rule, but may not enter into a commitment for the purchase of shares related to that underwriting.

(v) *Brokers or Dealers Engaged in the Sale of Redeemable Shares of Registered Investment Companies and Certain Other Share Accounts.* A broker or dealer shall maintain net capital of not less than $25,000 if it acts as a broker or dealer with respect to the purchase, sale and redemption of redeemable shares of registered investment companies or of interests or participations in an insurance company separate account directly from or to the issuer on other than a subscription way basis. A broker or dealer operating under this rule may sell securities for the account of a customer to obtain funds for the immediate reinvestment in redeemable securities of registered investment companies. A broker or dealer operating under this paragraph (a)(2)(v) must promptly transmit all funds and promptly deliver all securities received in connection with its activities as a broker or dealer, and may not otherwise hold funds or securities for, or owe money or securities to, customers.

(vi) *Other Brokers or Dealers.* A broker or dealer that does not receive, directly or indirectly, or hold funds or securities for, or owe funds or securities to, customers and does not carry accounts of, or for, customers and does not engage in any of the activities described in paragraphs (a)(2)(i) through (v) of this rule shall maintain net capital of not less than $5,000. A broker or dealer operating under this paragraph may engage in the following dealer activities without being subject to the requirements of paragraph (a)(2)(iii) of this rule:

(A) In the case of a buy order, prior to executing such customer's order, it purchases as principal the same number of shares or purchases shares to accumulate the number of shares necessary to complete the order, which shall be cleared through another registered broker or dealer or

(B) In the case of a sell order, prior to executing such customer's order, it sells as principal the same number of shares or a portion thereof, which shall be cleared through another registered broker or dealer.

(3) [Reserved]

(4) *Capital Requirements for Market Makers.* A broker or dealer engaged in activities as a market maker as defined in paragraph (c)(8) of this rule shall maintain net capital in an amount not less than $2,500 for each security in which it makes a market (unless a security in which it makes a market has a market value of $5 or less, in which event the amount of net capital shall be not less than $1,000 for each such security) based on the average number of such markets made by such broker or dealer during the 30 days immediately preceding the computation date. Under no circumstances shall it have net capital less than that required by the provisions of paragraph (a) of this rule, or be required to maintain net capital of more than $1,000,000 unless required by paragraph (a) of this rule.

(5) In accordance with Appendix F to this rule (Rule 15c3–1f), the Commission may grant an application by an OTC derivatives dealer when calculating net capital to use the market risk standards of Appendix F as to some or all of its positions in lieu of the provisions of paragraph (c)(2)(vi) of this rule and the credit risk standards of Appendix F to its receivables (including counterparty net exposure) arising from transactions in eligible OTC derivative instruments in lieu of the requirements of paragraph (c)(2)(iv) of this rule. An OTC derivatives dealer shall at all times maintain tentative net capital of not less than $100 million and net capital of not less than $20 million.

(6) *Market Makers, Specialists and Certain Other Dealers.* (i) A dealer who meet the conditions of paragraph (a)(6)(ii) of this rule may elect to operate under this paragraph (a)(6) and thereby not apply, except to the extent required by this paragraph (a)(6), the provisions of paragraphs (c)(2)(vi) or Appendix A, Rule 15c3–1a, of this rule to market maker and specialist transactions and, in lieu thereof, apply thereto the provisions of paragraph (a)(6)(iii) of this rule.

(ii) This paragraph (a)(6) shall be available to a dealer who does not effect transactions with other than brokers or dealers, who does not carry customer accounts, who does not effect transactions in options not listed on a registered securities exchange or facility of a registered national securities association, and whose market maker or specialist transactions are effected through and carried in a market maker or specialist account cleared by another broker or dealer as provided in paragraph (a)(6)(iv) of this rule.

(iii) A dealer who elects to operate pursuant to this paragraph (a)(6) shall at all times maintain a liquidating equity in respect of securities positions in his market maker or specialist account at least equal to:

(A) An amount equal to 25 percent (5 percent in the case of exempted securities) of the market value of the long positions and 30 percent of the market value of the short positions; provided, however, in the case of long or short positions in options and long or short positions in securities other than options which relate to a bona fide hedged position as defined in paragraph (c)(2)(x)(C) of this rule, such amount shall equal the deductions in respect of such positions specified by Appendix A (Rule 15c3-1a).

(B) Such lesser requirement as may be approved by the Commission under specified terms and conditions upon written application of the dealer and the carrying broker or dealer.

(C) For purposes of this paragraph (a)(6)(iii), equity in such specialist or market maker account shall be computed by (*1*) marking all securities positions long or short in the account to their respective current market values, (*2*) adding (deducting in the case of a debit balance) the credit balance carried in such specialist or market maker account, and (*3*) adding (deducting in the case of short positions) the market value of positions long in such account.

(iv) The dealer shall obtain from the broker or dealer carrying the market maker or specialist account a written undertaking which shall be designated "Notice Pursuant to Section Rule 15c3–1(a)(6) of Intention to Carry Specialist or Market Maker Account." Said undertaking shall contain the representations required by this paragraph (a)(6) and shall be filed with the Commission's Washington, DC Office, the regional office of the Commission for the region in which the broker or dealer has its principal place of business and the Designated Examining Authorities of both firms prior to effecting any transactions in said account. The broker or dealer carrying such account:

(A) Shall mark the account to the market not less than daily and shall issue appropriate calls for additional equity which shall be met by noon of the following business day;

(B) Shall notify by telegraph the Commission and the Designated Examining Authorities pursuant to Rule 17a–11, if the market maker or specialist fails to deposit any required equity within the time prescribed in paragraph (a)(6)(iv)(A) of this rule; said telegraphic notice shall be received by the Commission and the Designated Examining Authorities not later than the close of business on the day said call is not met;

(C) Shall not extend further credit in the account if the equity in the account falls below that prescribed in paragraph (a)(6)(iii) of this rule, and

(D) Shall take steps to liquidate promptly existing positions in the account in the event of a failure to meet a call for equity.

(v) No such carrying broker or dealer shall permit the sum of (A) the deductions required by paragraph (c)(2)(x)(A) of this rule in respect of all transactions in market maker accounts guaranteed, endorsed or carried by such broker or dealer pursuant to paragraph (c)(2)(x) of this rule and (B) the equity required by paragraph (iii) of this paragraph (a)(6) in respect of all transactions in the accounts of specialists or market makers in options carried by such broker or dealer pursuant to this paragraph (a)(6) to exceed 1,000 percent of such broker's or dealer's net capital as defined in paragraph (c)(2) of this rule for any period exceeding five business days; *Provided,* That solely for purposes of this paragraph (a)(6)(v), deductions or equity required in a specialist or market maker account in respect of positions in fully paid securities (other than options), which do not underlie options listed on the national securities exchange or facility of a national securities association of which the specialist or market maker is a member, need not be recognized. *Provided, further,* That if at any time such sum exceeds 1,000 percent of such broker's or dealer's net capital, then the broker or dealer shall immediately transmit telegraphic notice of such event to the principal office of the Commission in Washington, DC, the regional office of the Commission for the region in which the broker or dealer maintains its principal place of business, and such broker's or dealer's Designated Examining Authority. *Provided, further,* That if at any time such sum exceeds 1,000 percent of such broker's or dealer's net capital, then such broker or dealer shall be subject to the prohibitions against withdrawal of equity capital set forth in paragraph (e) of this rule, and to the prohibitions against reduction, prepayment and repayment of subordination agreements set forth in paragraph (b)(11) of Rule 15c3–1d, as if such broker or dealer's net capital were below the minimum standards specified by each of the aforementioned paragraphs.

(7) *Alternative Net Capital Computation for Broker–Dealers that Elect to Be Supervised on a Consolidated Basis.* In accordance with Appendix E to this rule (Rule 15c3–1e), the Commission may approve, in whole or in part, an application or an amendment to an application by a broker or dealer to calculate net capital using the market risk standards of Appendix E to compute a deduction for market risk on some or all of its positions, instead of the provisions of paragraphs (c)(2)(vi) and (c)(2)(vii) of this rule, and using the credit risk standards of Appendix E to compute a deduction for credit risk on certain credit exposures arising from transactions in derivatives instruments, instead of the provisions of paragraph (c)(2)(iv) of

this rule, subject to any conditions or limitations on the broker or dealer the Commission may require as necessary or appropriate in the public interest or for the protection of investors. A broker or dealer that has been approved to calculate its net capital under Appendix E must:

(i) At all times maintain tentative net capital of not less than $1 billion and net capital of not less than $500 million;

(ii) Provide notice that same day in accordance with Rule 17a–11(g) if the broker's or dealer's tentative net capital is less than $5 billion. The Commission may, upon written application, lower the threshold at which notification is necessary under this paragraph (a)(7)(ii), either unconditionally or on specified terms and conditions, if a broker or dealer satisfies the Commission that notification at the $5 billion threshold is unnecessary because of, among other factors, the special nature of its business, its financial position, its internal risk management system, or its compliance history; and

(iii) Comply with Rule 15c3–4 as though it were an OTC derivatives dealer with respect to all of its business activities, except that paragraphs (c)(5)(xiii), (c)(5)(xiv), (d)(8), and (d)(9) of Rule 15c3–4 shall not apply.

(8) *Municipal Securities Brokers' Brokers.* (i) A municipal securities brokers' broker, as defined in subparagraph (ii) of this paragraph (a)(8), may elect not to be subject to the limitations of paragraph (c)(2)(ix) of this rule provided that such brokers' broker complies with the requirements set out in paragraphs (a)(8)(iii), (iv) and (v) of this rule.

(ii) The term municipal securities *brokers' broker* shall mean a municipal securities broker or dealer who acts exclusively as an undisclosed agent in the purchase or sale of municipal securities for a registered broker or dealer or registered municipal securities dealer, who has no "customers" as defined in this rule and who does not have or maintain any municipal securities in its proprietary or other accounts.

(iii) In order to qualify to operate under this paragraph (a)(8), a brokers' broker shall at all times have and maintain net capital of not less than $150,000.

(iv) For purposes of this paragraph (a)(8), a brokers' broker shall deduct from net worth 1% of the contract value of each municipal failed to deliver contract which is outstanding 21 business days or longer. Such deduction shall be increased by any excess of the contract price of the fail to deliver over the market value of the underlying security.

(v) For purposes of this paragraph (a)(8), a brokers' broker may exclude from its aggregate indebtedness computation indebtedness adequately collateralized by municipal securities outstanding for not more than one business day and offset by municipal securities failed to deliver of the same issue and quantity. In no event may a brokers' broker exclude any overnight bank loan attributable to the same municipal securities failed to deliver contract for more than one business day. A brokers' broker need not deduct from net worth the amount by which the market value of securities failed to receive outstanding longer than thirty (30) calendar days exceeds the contract value of those failed to receives as required by Rule 15c3–1(c)(2)(iv)(E).

(9) *Certain Additional Capital Requirements for Brokers or Dealers Engaging in Reverse Repurchase Agreements.* A broker or dealer shall maintain net capital in addition to the amounts required under paragraph (a) of this rule in an amount equal to 10 percent of:

(i) The excess of the market value of United States Treasury Bills, Bonds, and Notes subject to reverse repurchase agreements with any one party over 105 percent of the contract prices (including accrued interest) for reverse repurchase agreements with that party;

(ii) The excess of the market value of securities issued or guaranteed as to principal or interest by an agency of the United States or mortgage related securities as defined in section 3(a)(41) of the Act subject to reverse repurchase agreements with any one party over 110 percent of the contract prices (including accrued interest) for reverse repurchase agreements with that party; and

(iii) The excess of the market value of other securities subject to reverse repurchase agreements with any one party over 120 percent of the contract prices (including accrued interest) for reverse repurchase agreements with that person.

(b) *Exemptions*: (1) The provisions of this rule shall not apply to any specialist:

(i) Whose securities business, except for an occasional non-specialist related securities transaction for its own account, is limited to that of acting as an options market maker on a national securities exchange;

(ii) That is a member in good standing and subject to the capital requirements of a national securities exchange;

(iii) That does not transact a business in securities with other than a broker or dealer registered with the Commission under section 15 or section 15C of the Act or a member of a national securities exchange; and

(iv) That is not a clearing member of The Options Clearing Corporation and whose securities transactions are effected through and carried in an account cleared by another broker or dealer registered with the Commission under section 15 of the Act.

(2) A member in good standing of a national securities exchange who acts as a floor broker (and whose activities do not require compliance with other provisions of this rule), may elect to comply, in lieu of the other provisions of this rule, with the following financial responsibility standard: the value of the exchange membership of the member (based on the lesser of the most recent sale price or current bid price for an exchange membership) is not less than $15,000, or an amount equal to the excess of $15,000 over the value of the exchange membership is held by an independent agent in escrow; *Provided,* That the rules of such exchange require that the proceeds from the sale of the exchange membership of the member and the amount held in escrow pursuant to this paragraph shall be subject to the prior claims of the exchange and its clearing corporation and those arising directly from the closing out of contracts entered into on the floor of such exchange.

(3) The Commission may, upon written application, exempt from the provisions of this rule, either unconditionally or on specified terms and conditions, any broker or dealer who satisfies the Commission that, because of the special nature of its business, its financial position, and the safeguards it has established for the protection of customers' funds and securities, it is not necessary in the public interest or for the protection of investors to subject the particular broker or dealer to the provisions of this rule.

(c) *Definitions.* For the purpose of this rule:

(1) *Aggregate Indebtedness.* The term "aggregate indebtedness" shall be deemed to mean the total money liabilities of a broker or dealer arising in connection with any transaction whatsoever and includes, among other things, money borrowed, money payable against securities loaned and securities "failed to receive," the market value of securities borrowed to the extent to which no equivalent value is paid or credited (other than the market value of margin securities borrowed from customers in accordance with the provisions of Rule 15c3–3 and margin securities borrowed from non-customers), customers' and non-customers' free credit balances, credit balances in customers' and on-customers' accounts having short positions in securities, equities in customers' and non-customers' future commodities accounts and credit balances in customers' and non-customers' commodities accounts, but excluding:

(i) *Exclusions from Aggregate Indebtedness.* Indebtedness adequately collateralized by securities which are carried long by the broker or dealer and which have not been sold or by securities which collateralize a secured demand note pursuant to Appendix (D) to this Rule 15c3–1d; indebtedness adequately collateralized by spot commodities which are carried long by the broker or dealer and which have not been sold; or, until October 1, 1976, indebtedness adequately collateralized by municipal securities outstanding for not more than one business day and offset by municipal securities failed to deliver of the same issue and quantity, where such indebtedness is incurred by a broker or dealer effecting transactions solely in municipal securities who is either registered with the Commission or temporarily exempt from such registration pursuant to Rule 15a–1(T) or Rule 15Ba2–3(T);

(ii) Amounts payable against securities loaned, which securities are carried long by the broker or dealer and which have not been sold or which securities collateralize a secured demand note pursuant to Appendix (D) (Rule 15c);

(iii) Amounts payable against securities failed to receive which securities are carried long by the broker or dealer and which have not been sold or which securities collateralize a secured demand note pursuant to Appendix (D) (Rule 15c3–1d) or amounts payable against securities failed to receive for which the broker or dealer also has a receivable related to securities of the same issue and quantity thereof which are either fails to deliver or securities borrowed by the broker or dealer;

(iv) Credit balances in accounts representing amounts payable for securities or money market instruments not yet received from the issuer or its agent which securities are specified in paragraph (c)(2)(vi)(E) and which amounts are outstanding in such accounts not more than three (3) business days;

(v) Equities in customers' and non-customers' accounts segregated in accordance with the provisions of the Commodity Exchange Act and the rules and regulations thereunder;

(vi) Liability reserves established and maintained for refunds of charges required by section 27(d) of the Investment Company Act of 1940, but only to the extent of amounts on deposit in a segregated trust account in accordance with Rule 27d–1 under the Investment Company Act of 1940;

(vii) Amounts payable to the extent funds and qualified securities are required to be on deposit and are deposited in a "Special Reserve Bank Account for the Exclusive Benefit of Customers" pursuant to Rule 15c3–3;

(viii) Fixed liabilities adequately secured by assets acquired for use in the ordinary course of the trade or business of a broker or dealer but no other fixed liabilities secured by assets of the broker or dealer shall be so excluded unless the sole recourse of the creditor for nonpayment of such liability is to such asset;

(ix) Liabilities on open contractual commitments;

(x) Indebtedness subordinated to the claims of creditors pursuant to a satisfactory subordination agreement, as defined in Appendix (D) (Rule 15c3–1d);

(xi) Liabilities which are effectively subordinated to the claims of creditors (but which are not subject to a satisfactory subordination agreement as defined in Appendix (D) (Rule 15c3–1d)) by non-customers of the broker or dealer prior to such subordination, except such subordinations by customers as may be approved by the Examining Authority for such broker or dealer;

(xii) Credit balances in accounts of general partners;

(xiii) Deferred tax liabilities;

(xiv) Eighty-five percent of amounts payable to a registered investment company related to fail to deliver receivables of the same quantity arising out of purchases of shares of those registered investment companies; and

(xv) Eighty-five percent of amounts payable against securities loaned for which the broker or dealer has receivables related to securities of the same class and issue and quantity that are securities borrowed by the broker or dealer.

(2) *Net Capital.* The term "net capital" shall be deemed to mean the net worth of a broker or dealer, adjusted by:

(i) *Adjustments to Net Worth Related to Unrealized Profit or Loss, Deferred Tax Provisions, and Certain Liabilities.* (A) Adding unrealized profits (or deducting unrealized losses) in the accounts of the broker or dealer;

(B)(*1*) In determining net worth, all long and all short positions in listed options shall be marked to their market value and all long and all short securities and commodities positions shall be marked to their market value.

(*2*) In determining net worth, the value attributed to any unlisted option shall be the difference between the option's exercise value and the market value of the underlying security. In the case of an unlisted call, if the market value of the underlying security is less than the exercise value of such call it shall be given no value and in the case of an unlisted put if the market value of the underlying security is more than the exercise value of the unlisted put it shall be given no value.

(C) Adding to net worth the lesser of any deferred income tax liability related to the items in (*1*), (*2*), and (*3*) below, or the sum of (*1*), (*2*) and (*3*) below;

(*1*) The aggregate amount resulting from applying to the amount of the deductions computed in accordance with paragraph (c)(2)(vi) of this rule and Appendices (A) and (B) (Rules 15c3–1a and 15c3–1b), the appropriate Federal and State tax rate(s) applicable to any unrealized gain on the asset on which the deduction was computed;

(*2*) Any deferred tax liability related to income accrued which is directly related to an asset otherwise deducted pursuant to this rule;

(*3*) Any deferred tax liability related to unrealized appreciation in value of any asset(s) which has been otherwise deducted from net worth in accordance with the provisions of this rule; and,

(D) Adding, in the case of future income tax benefits arising as a result of unrealized losses, the amount of such benefits not to exceed the amount of income tax liabilities accrued on the books and records of the broker or dealer, but only to the extent such benefits could have been applied to reduce accrued tax liabilities on the date of the capital computation, had the related unrealized losses been realized on that date.

(E) Adding to net worth any actual tax liability related to income accrued which is directly related to an asset otherwise deducted pursuant to this rule.

(F) Adding to net worth any liability or expense relating to the business of the broker or dealer for which a third party has assumed the responsibility, unless the broker or dealer can demonstrate that the third party has adequate resources independent of the broker or dealer to pay the liability or expense.

(G) Subtracting from net worth any contribution of capital to the broker or dealer:

(*1*) Under an agreement that provides the investor with the option to withdraw the capital; or

(*2*) That is intended to be withdrawn within a period of one year of contribution. Any withdrawal of capital made within one year of its contribution is deemed to have been intended to be withdrawn within a period of one year, unless the withdrawal has been approved in writing by the Examining Authority for the broker or dealer.

(ii) *Subordinated Liabilities.* Excluding liabilities of the broker or dealer which are subordinated to the claims of creditors pursuant to a satisfactory subordination agreement, as defined in Appendix (D) (Rule 15c3–1d).

(iii) *Sole Proprietors.* Deducting, in the case of a broker or dealer who is a sole proprietor, the excess of liabilities which have not been incurred in the course of business as a broker or dealer over assets not used in the business.

(iv) *Assets Not Readily Convertible Into Cash.* Deducting fixed assets and assets which cannot be readily converted into cash (less any indebtedness excluded in accordance with subdivision (c)(1)(viii) of this rule) including, among other things:

(A) *Fixed Assets and Prepaid Items.* Real estate; furniture and fixtures; exchange memberships; prepaid rent, insurance and other expenses; goodwill, organization expenses;

(B) All unsecured advances and loans; deficits in customers' and non-customers' unsecured and partly secured notes; deficits in omnibus credit accounts maintained in compliance with the requirements of 12 CFR 220.7(f) of Regulation T under the Securities Exchange Act of 1934, or similar accounts carried on behalf of another broker or dealer, after application of calls for margin, marks to the market or other required deposits that are outstanding 5 business days or less; deficits in customers' and non-customers' unsecured and partly secured accounts after application of calls for margin, marks to market or other required deposits that are outstanding 5 business days or less, except deficits in cash accounts as defined in 12 CFR 220.8 of Regulation T under the Securities Exchange Act of 1934 for which not more than one extension respecting a specified securities transaction has been requested and granted, and deducting for securities carried in any of such accounts the percentages specified in paragraph (c)(2)(vi) of this section or Appendix A (Rule 15c3-1a); the market value of stock loaned in excess of the value of any collateral received therefor; receivables arising out of free shipments of securities (other than mutual fund redemptions) in excess of $5,000 per shipment and all free shipments (other than mutual fund redemptions) outstanding more than 7 business days, and mutual fund redemptions outstanding more than 16 business days; and any collateral deficiencies in secured demand notes as defined in Appendix D (Rule 15c3–1d); a broker or dealer that participates in a loan of securities by one party to another party will be deemed a principal for the purpose of the deductions required under this section, unless the broker or dealer has fully disclosed the identity of each party to the other and each party has expressly agreed in writing that the obligations of the broker or dealer do not include a guarantee of performance by the other party and that such party's remedies in the event of a default by the other party do not include a right of setoff against obligations, if any, of the broker or dealer.

(C) Interest receivable, floor brokerage receivable, commissions receivable from other brokers or dealers (other than syndicate profits which shall be treated as required in subparagraph (c)(2)(iv)(E) of this rule), mutual fund concessions receivable and management fees receivable from registered investment companies, all of which receivables are outstanding longer than thirty (30) days from the date they arise; dividends receivable outstanding longer than thirty (30) days from the payable date; good faith deposits arising in connection with a non-municipal securities underwriting, outstanding longer than eleven (11) business days from the settlement of the underwriting with the issuer; receivables due from participation in municipal securities underwriting syndicates and municipal securities joint underwriting accounts which are outstanding longer than sixty (60) days from settlement of the underwriting with the issuer and good faith deposits arising in connection with an underwriting of municipal securities, outstanding longer than sixty (60) days from settlement of the underwriting with the issuer; and receivables due from participation in municipal securities secondary trading joint accounts, which are outstanding longer than sixty (60) days from the date all securities have been delivered by the account manager to the account members;

(D) *Insurance Claims.* Insurance claims which, after seven (7) business days from the date the loss giving rise to the claim is discovered, are not covered by an opinion of outside counsel that the claim is valid and is covered by insurance policies presently in effect; insurance claims which after twenty (20) business days from the date the loss giving rise to the claim is discovered and which are accompanied by an opinion of outside counsel described above, have not been acknowledged in writing by the insurance carrier as due and payable; and insurance claims acknowledged in writing by the carrier as due and payable outstanding longer than twenty (20) business days from the date they are so acknowledged by the carrier; and,

(E) *Other Deductions.* All other unsecured receivables; all assets doubtful of collection less any reserves established therefor; the amount by which the market value of securities failed to receive outstanding longer than thirty (30) calendar days exceeds the contract value of such fails to receive; and the funds on deposit in a "segregated trust account" in accordance with Rule 27d-1 under the Investment Company Act of 1940, but only to the extent that the amount on deposit in such segregated trust account exceeds the amount of liability reserves established and maintained for refunds of charges required by sections 27(d) and 27(f) of the Investment Company Act of 1940; *Provided*, That the following need not be deducted:

(*1*) Any amounts deposited in a Customer Reserve Bank Account or PAB Reserve Bank Account pursuant to Rule 15c3-3(e),

(*2*) Cash and securities held in a securities account at a carrying broker or dealer (except where the account has been subordinated to the claims of creditors of the carrying broker or dealer), and

(*3*) Clearing deposits.

(F)(*1*) For purposes of this paragraph:

(*i*) The term *reverse repurchase agreement deficit* shall mean the difference between the contract price for resale of the securities under a reverse repurchase agreement and the market value of those securities (if less than the contract price).

(*ii*) The term *repurchase agreement deficit* shall mean the difference between the market value of securities subject to the repurchase agreement and the contract price for repurchase of the securities (if less than the market value of the securities).

(*iii*) As used in paragraph (c)(2)(iv)(F)(*1*), the term *contract price* shall include accrued interest.

(*iv*) Reverse repurchase agreement deficits and the repurchase agreement deficits where the counterparty is the Federal Reserve Bank of New York shall be disregarded.

(*2*)(*i*) In the case of a reverse repurchase agreement, the deduction shall be equal to the reverse repurchase agreement deficit.

(*ii*) In determining the required deductions under paragraph (c)(2)(iv)(F)(*2*)(*i*), the broker or dealer may reduce the reverse repurchase agreement deficit by:

(*A*) Any margin or other deposits held by the broker or dealer on account of the reverse repurchase agreement;

(*B*) Any excess market value of the securities over the contract price for resale of those securities under any other reverse repurchase agreement with the same party;

(*C*) The difference between the contract price for resale and the market value of securities subject to repurchase agreements with the same party (if the market value of those securities is less than the contract price); and

(*D*) Calls for margin, marks to the market, or other required deposits which are outstanding one business day or less.

(*3*)(*i*) In the case of repurchase agreements, the deduction shall be:

(*A*) The excess of the repurchase agreement deficit over 5 percent of the contract price for resale of United States Treasury Bills, Notes and Bonds, 10 percent of the contract price for the resale of securities issued or guaranteed as to principal or interest by an agency of the United States or mortgage related securities as defined in section 3(a)(41) of the Act and 20 percent of the contract price for the resale of other securities and;

(*B*) The excess of the aggregate repurchase agreement deficits with any one party over 25 percent of the broker or dealer's net capital before the application of paragraph (c)(2)(vi) of this rule (less any deduction taken with respect to repurchase agreements with that party under paragraph (c)(2)(iv)(F)(*3*)(*i*)(*A*) of this rule) or, if greater;

(*C*) The excess of the aggregate repurchase agreement deficits over 300 percent of the broker or dealer's net capital before the application of paragraph (c)(2)(vi) of this rule.

(*ii*) In determining the required deduction under paragraph (c)(2)(iv)(F)(*3*)(*i*), the broker or dealer may reduce a repurchase agreement deficit by:

(*A*) Any margin or other deposits held by the broker or dealer on account of a reverse repurchase agreement with the same party to the extent not otherwise used to reduce a reverse repurchase deficit;

(*B*) The difference between the contract price and the market value of securities subject to other repurchase agreements with the same party (if the market value of those securities is less than the contract price) not otherwise used to reduce a reverse repurchase agreement deficit; and

(*C*) Calls for margin, marks to the market, or other required deposits which are outstanding one business day or less to the extent not otherwise used to reduce a reverse repurchase agreement deficit.

(G) *Securities Borrowed.* 1 percent of the market value of securities borrowed collateralized by an irrevocable letter of credit.

(H) Any receivable from an affiliate of the broker or dealer (not otherwise deducted from net worth) and the market value of any collateral given to an affiliate (not otherwise deducted from net worth) to secure a liability over the amount of the liability of the broker or dealer unless the books and records of the affiliate are made available for examination when requested by the representatives of the Commission or the Examining Authority for the broker or dealer in order to demonstrate the validity of the receivable or payable. The provisions of this subsection shall not apply where the affiliate is a registered broker or dealer, registered government securities broker or dealer or bank as defined in section 3(a)(6) of the Act or insurance company as defined in section 3(a)(19) of the Act or investment company registered under the Investment Company Act of 1940 or federally insured savings and loan association or futures commission merchant registered pursuant to the Commodity Exchange Act.

(v)(A) *Securities Differences.* Deducting the market value of all short securities differences (which shall include securities positions reflected on the securities record which are not susceptible to either count or confirmation) unresolved after discovery in accordance with the following schedule:

Percentage of Market Value of Short Securities Differences	Numbers of Business Days After Discovery
25 percent	7
50 percent	14
75 percent	21
100 percent	28

(B) Deducting the market value of any long securities differences, where such securities have been sold by the broker or dealer before they are adequately resolved, less any reserves established therefor;

(C) The designated examining authority for a broker or dealer may extend the periods in (v)(A) of this rule for up to 10 business days if it finds that exceptional circumstances warrant an extension.

(vi) *Securities Haircuts.* Deducting the percentages specified in paragraphs (c)(2)(vi) (A) through (M) of this rule (or the deductions prescribed for securities positions set forth in Appendix (A) (Rule 15c3–1a)) of the market value of all securities, money market instruments or options in the proprietary or other accounts of the broker or dealer.

(A)(*1*) In the case of a security issued or guaranteed as to principal or interest by the United States or any agency thereof, the applicable percentages of the market value of the net long or short position in each of the categories specified below are:

CATEGORY 1

(*i*) Less than 3 months to maturity—0 percent.

(*ii*) 3 months but less than 6 months to maturity—1/2 of 1 percent.

(*iii*) 6 months but less than 9 months to maturity—3/4 of 1 percent.

(*iv*) 9 months but less than 12 months to maturity—1 percent.

CATEGORY 2

(*i*) 1 year but less than 2 years to maturity—1 1/2%.

(*ii*) 2 years but less than 3 years to maturity—2%.

CATEGORY 3

(*i*) 3 years but less than 5 years to maturity—3%.

(*ii*) 5 years but less than 10 years to maturity—4%.

CATEGORY 4

(*i*) 10 years but less than 15 years to maturity—4 1/2%.

(*ii*) 15 years but less than 20 years to maturity—5%.

(*iii*) 20 years but less than 25 years to maturity—5 1/2%.

(*iv*) 25 years or more to maturity—6%.

Brokers or dealers shall compute a deduction for each category above as follows: Compute the deductions for the net long or short positions in each subcategory above. The deduction for the category shall be the net of the aggregate deductions on the long positions and the aggregate deductions on short positions in each category plus 50% of the lesser of the aggregate deductions on the long or short positions.

(*2*) A broker or dealer may elect to deduct, in lieu of the computation required under paragraph (c)(2)(vi)(A)(*1*) of this rule, the applicable percentages of the market value of the net long or short positions in each of the subcategories specified in paragraph (c)(2)(vi)(A)(*1*) of this rule.

(*3*) In computing deductions under paragraph (c)(2)(vi)(A)(*1*) of this rule, a broker or dealer may elect to exclude the market value of a long or short security from one category and a security from another category, *Provided,* That:

(*i*) Such securities have maturity dates:

(*A*) Between 9 months and 15 months and within 3 months of one another.

(*B*) Between 2 years and 4 years and within 1 year of one another; or

(*C*) Between 8 years and 12 years and within 2 years of one another.

(*ii*) The net market value of the two excluded securities shall remain in the category of the security with the higher market value.

(*4*) In computing deductions under paragraph (c)(2)(vi)(A)(*1*) of this rule, a broker or dealer may include in the categories specified in paragraph (c)(2)(vi)(A)(*1*) of this rule, long or short positions in securities issued by the United States or any agency thereof that are deliverable against long or short positions in futures contracts relating to Government securities, traded on a recognized contract market approved by the Commodity Futures Trading Commission, which are held in the proprietary or other accounts of the broker or dealer. The value of the long or short positions included in the categories shall be determined by the contract value of the futures contract held in the account. The provisions of Appendix B to Rule 15c3–1 will in any event apply to the positions in futures contracts.

(*5*) In the case of a Government securities dealer that reports to the Federal Reserve System, that transacts business directly with the Federal Reserve System, and which maintains at all times a minimum net capital of at least $50,000,000, before application of the deductions provided for in paragraph (c)(2)(vi) of this rule, the deduction for a security issued or guaranteed as to principal or interest by the United States or any agency thereof shall be 75% of the deduction otherwise computed under paragraph (c)(2)(vi)(A) of this rule.

(B)(*1*) In the case of any municipal security which has a scheduled maturity at date of issue of 731 days or less and which is issued at par value and pays interest at maturity, or which is issued at a discount, and which is not traded flat or in default as to principal or interest, the applicable percentages of the market value on the greater of the long or short position in each of the categories specified below are:

(*i*) Less than 30 days to maturity—0%;

(*ii*) 30 days but less than 91 days to maturity—1/8 of 1%;

(*iii*) 91 days but less than 181 days to maturity—1/4 of 1%;

(*iv*) 181 days but less than 271 days to maturity—3/8 of 1%;

(*v*) 271 days but less than 366 days to maturity—1/2 of 1%;

(*vi*) 366 days but less than 456 days to maturity—3/4 of 1%;

(*vii*) 456 days but less than 732 days to maturity—1%.

(*2*) In the case of any municipal security, other than those specified in paragraph (c)(2)(vi)(B)(*1*), which is not traded flat or in default as to principal or interest, the applicable percentages of the market value of the greater of the long or short position in each of the categories specified below are:

(*i*) Less than 1 year to maturity—1%;

(*ii*) 1 year but less than 2 years to maturity—2%;

(*iii*) 2 years but less than 3 1/2 years to maturity—3%;

(*iv*) 3 1/2 years but less than 5 years to maturity—4%;

(*v*) 5 years but less than 7 years to maturity—5%;

(*vi*) 7 years but less than 10 years to maturity—5 1/2%;

(*vii*) 10 years but less than 15 years to maturity—6%;

(*viii*) 15 years but less than 20 years to maturity—6 1/2%;

(*ix*) 20 years or more to maturity—7%.

(C) *Canadian Debt Obligations.* In the case of any security issued or unconditionally guaranteed as to principal and interest by the Government of Canada, the percentages of market value to be deducted shall be the same as in (A) above.

(D)(*1*) In the case of redeemable securities of an investment company registered under the Investment Company Act of 1940, which assets consist of cash or money market instruments and which is described in Rule 2a-7 of this chapter, the deduction will be 2% of the market value of the greater of the long or short position.

(*2*) In the case of redeemable securities of an investment company registered under the Investment Company Act of 1940, which assets are in the form of cash or securities or money market instruments of any maturity which are described in paragraph (c)(2)(vi)(A) through (C) or (E) of this rule, the deduction shall be 7% of the market value of the greater of the long or short positions.

(*3*) In the case of redeemable securities of an investment company registered under the Investment Company Act of 1940, which assets are in the form of cash or securities or money market instruments which are described in paragraphs (c)(2)(vi)(A) through (C) or (E) and (F) of this rule, the deduction shall be 9% of the market value of the long or short position.

(E) *Commercial paper, bankers' acceptances and certificates of deposit.* In the case of any short term promissory note or evidence of indebtedness which has a fixed rate of interest or is sold at a discount, which has a maturity date at date of issuance not exceeding nine months exclusive of days of grace, or any renewal thereof, the maturity of which is likewise limited and has only a minimal amount of credit risk, or in the case of any negotiable certificates of deposit or bankers' acceptance or similar type of instrument issued or guaranteed by any bank as defined in section 3(a)(6) of the Securities Exchange Act of 1934, the applicable percentage of the market value of the greater of the long or short position in each of the categories specified below are:

(*1*) Less than 30 days to maturity—0 percent;

(*2*) 30 days but less than 91 days to maturity—1/8 of 1 percent;

(*3*) 91 days but less than 181 days to maturity—1/4 of 1 percent;

(*4*) 181 days but less than 271 days to maturity—3/8 of 1 percent;

(*5*) 271 days but less than 1 year to maturity—1/2 of 1 percent; and

(*6*) With respect to any negotiable certificate of deposit or bankers acceptance or similar type of instrument issued or guaranteed by any bank, as defined above, having 1 year or more to maturity, the deduction shall be on the greater of the long or short position and shall be the same percentage as that prescribed in paragraph (c)(2)(vi)(A) of this rule.

(F)(*1*) *Nonconvertible debt securities.* In the case of nonconvertible debt securities having a fixed interest rate and a fixed maturity date, which are not traded flat or in default as to principal or interest and which have only a minimal amount of credit risk, the applicable percentages of the market value of the greater of the long or short position in each of the categories specified below are:

(*i*) Less than 1 year to maturity—2%;

(*ii*) 1 year but less than 2 years to maturity—3%;

(*iii*) 2 years but less than 3 years to maturity—5%;

(*iv*) 3 years but less than 5 years to maturity—6%;

(*v*) 5 years but less than 10 years to maturity—7%;

(*vi*) 10 years but less than 15 years to maturity—71/2%;

(*vii*) 15 years but less than 20 years to maturity—8.0%;

(*viii*) 20 years but less than 25 years to maturity—81/2%;

(*ix*) 25 years or more to maturity—9.0%.

(*2*) A broker or dealer may elect to exclude from the above categories long or short positions that are hedged with short or long positions in securities issued by the United States or any agency thereof or nonconvertible debt securities having a fixed interest rate and a fixed maturity date and which are not traded flat or in default as to principal or interest, and which have only a minimal amount of credit risk if such securities have maturity dates:

(*i*) Less than five years and within 6 months of each other;

(*ii*) Between 5 years and 10 years and within 9 months of each other;

(*iii*) Between 10 years and 15 years and within 2 years of each other; or

(*iv*) 15 years or more and within 10 years of each other.

The broker-dealer shall deduct the amounts specified in paragraphs 4(c)(2)(vi)(F)(*3*) and (*4*) of this rule.

(*3*) With respect to those positions described in paragraph (c)(2)(vi)(F)(*2*) of this rule that include a long or short position in securities issued by the United States or any agency thereof, the broker or dealer shall exclude the hedging short or long United States or agency securities position from the applicable haircut category under paragraph (c)(2)(vi)(A) of this rule. The broker or dealer shall deduct the percentage of the market value of the hedged long or short position in nonconvertible debt securities as specified in each of the categories below:

(*i*) Less than 5 years to maturity—1 1/2%;

(*ii*) 5 years but less than 10 years to maturity—2 1/2%;

(*iii*) 10 years but less than 15 years to maturity—2 3/4%;

(*iv*) 15 years or more to maturity—3%.

(*4*) With respect to those positions described in paragraph (c)(2)(vi)(F)(*2*) of this rule that include offsetting long and short positions in nonconvertible debt securities, the broker or dealer shall deduct a percentage of the market value of the hedged long or short position in nonconvertible debt securities as specified in each of the categories below:

(*i*) Less than 5 years to maturity—1 3/4%;

(*ii*) 5 years but less than 10 years to maturity—3%;

(*iii*) 10 years but less than 15 years to maturity—3 1/4%;

(*iv*) 15 years or more to maturity—3 1/2%.

(*5*) In computing deductions under paragraph (c)(2)(vi)(F)(*3*) of this rule, a broker or dealer may include in the categories specified in paragraph (c)(2)(vi)(F)(*3*) of this rule, long or short positions in securities issued by the United States or any agency thereof that are deliverable against long or short positions in futures contracts relating to Government securities, traded on a recognized contract market approved by the Commodity Futures Trading Commission, which are held in the proprietary or other accounts of the broker or dealer. The value of the long or short positions included in the categories shall be determined by the contract value of the futures contract held in the account.

(*6*) The provisions of Appendix B to Rule 15c3–1 will in any event apply to the positions in futures contracts.

(G) *Convertible Debt Securities.* In the case of a debt security not in default which has a fixed rate of interest and a fixed maturity date and which is convertible into an equity security, the deductions shall be as follows: If the market value is 100 percent or more of the principal amount, the deduction shall be determined as specified in paragraph (c)(2)(vi)(J) below; if the market value is less than the principal amount, the deduction shall be determined as specified in subparagraph (F) of this rule if such securities are rated as required by subparagraph (F) of this rule.

(H) In the case of cumulative, non-convertible preferred stock ranking prior to all other classes of stock of the same issuer, which has only a minimal amount of credit risk and which are not in arrears as to dividends, the deduction shall be 10% of the market value of the greater of the long or short position.

(I) In order to apply a deduction under paragraphs (c)(2)(vi)(E), (c)(2)(vi)(F)(*1*), (c)(2)(vi)(F)(*2*), or (c)(2)(vi)(H) of this section, the broker or dealer must assess the creditworthiness of the security or money market instrument pursuant to policies and procedures for assessing and monitoring creditworthiness that the broker or dealer establishes, documents, maintains, and enforces. The policies and procedures must be reasonably designed for the purpose of determining whether a security or money market instrument has only a minimal amount of credit risk. Policies and procedures that are reasonably designed for this purpose should result in assessments of creditworthiness that typically are consistent with market data. A broker-dealer that opts not to make an assessment of creditworthiness under this paragraph may not apply the deductions under paragraphs (c)(2)(vi)(E), (c)(2)(vi)(F)(*1*), (c)(2)(vi)(F)(*2*), or (c)(2)(vi)(H) of this section.

Note to Paragraph (c)(2)(vi)(I): For a discussion of the "minimal amount of credit risk" standard, *see Removal of Certain References to Credit Ratings Under the Securities Exchange Act of 1934*, Exchange Act Release No. 34-71194 (Dec. 27, 2013).

(J) *All Other Securities.* In the case of all securities or evidences of indebtedness, except those described in Appendix (A), Rule 15c3–

1a, which are not included in any of the percentage categories enumerated in paragraphs (c)(2)(vi)(A) through (H) of this rule or paragraph (c)(2)(vi)(K)(ii) of this rule, the deduction shall be 15 percent of the market value of the greater of the long or short positions and to the extent the market value of the lesser of the long or short positions exceeds 25 percent of the market value of the greater of the long or short positions, the percentage deduction on such excess shall be 15 percent of the market value of such excess. No deduction need be made in the case of:

(*1*) A security that is convertible into or exchangeable for another security within a period of 90 days, subject to no conditions other than the payment of money, and the other securities into which such security is convertible or for which it is exchangeable, are short in the accounts of such broker or dealer; or

(*2*) A security that has been called for redemption and that is redeemable within 90 days.

(K) *Securities with a Limited Market.* In the case of securities (other than exempted securities, nonconvertible debt securities, and cumulative nonconvertible preferred stock) which are not:

(*1*) Traded on a national securities exchange;

(*2*) Designated as "OTC Margin Stock" pursuant to Regulation T under the Securities Exchange Act of 1934;

(*3*) Quoted on "NASDAQ"; or

(*4*) Redeemable shares of investment companies registered under the Investment Company Act of 1940, the deduction shall be as follows:

(*i*) In the case where there are regular quotations in an inter-dealer quotations system for the securities by three or more independent market-makers (exclusive of the computing broker or dealer) and where each such quotation represents a bona fide offer to brokers or dealers to both buy and sell in reasonable quantities at stated prices, or where a ready market as defined in subparagraph (c)(11)(ii) is deemed to exist, the deduction shall be determined in accordance with subparagraph (c)(2)(vi)(J) of this rule;

(*ii*) In the case where there are regular quotations in an inter-dealer quotations system for the securities by only one or two independent market-makers (exclusive of the computing broker or dealer) and where each such quotation represents a bona fide offer to brokers or dealers both to buy and sell in reasonable quantities, at stated prices, the deduction on both the long and short position shall be 40 percent.

(L) Where a broker or dealer demonstrates that there is sufficient liquidity for any securities long or short in the proprietary or other accounts of the broker or dealer which are subject to a deduction required by paragraph (c)(2)(vi)(K) of this rule, such deduction, upon a proper showing to the Examining Authority for the broker or dealer, may be appropriately decreased, but in no case shall such deduction be less than that prescribed in paragraph (c)(2)(vi)(J) of this rule.

(M) *Undue Concentration.* (*1*) In the case of money market instruments, or securities of a single class or series of an issuer, including any option written, endorsed or held to purchase or sell securities of such a single class or series of an issuer (other than "exempted securities" and redeemable securities of an investment company registered pursuant to the Investment Company Act of 1940), and securities underwritten (in which case the deduction provided for herein shall be applied after 11 business days), which are long or short in the proprietary or other accounts of a broker or dealer, including securities that are collateral to secured demand notes defined in Appendix (D), Rule 15c3–1d, and that have a market value of more than 10 percent of the "net capital" of a broker or dealer before the application of paragraph (c)(2)(vi) of this rule or Appendix (A), Rule 15c3–1a, there shall be an additional deduction from net worth and/or the Collateral Value for securities collateralizing a secured demand note defined in Appendix (D), Rule 15c3–1d equal to 50 percent of the percentage deduction otherwise provided by this paragraph (c)(2)(vi) of this rule or Appendix (A), Rule 15c3–1d, on that portion of the securities position in excess of 10 percent of the "net capital" of the broker or dealer before the application of paragraph (c)(2)(vi) of this rule and Appendix (A), Rule 15c3–1a. In the case of securities described in paragraph (c)(2)(vi)(J), the additional deduction required by this paragraph (c)(2)(vi)(M) shall be 15 percent.

(2) This paragraph (c)(2)(vi)(M) shall apply notwithstanding any long or short position exemption provided for in paragraph (c)(2)(vi)(J) of this rule (except for long or short position exemptions arising out of the first proviso to paragraph (c)(2)(vi)(J)) and the deduction on any such exempted position shall be 15 percent of that portion of the securities position in excess of 10 percent of the broker or dealer's net capital before the application of paragraph (c)(2)(vi) of this rule and Appendix A, Rule 15c3–1a.

(3) This paragraph (c)(2)(vi)(M) shall be applied to an issue of equity securities only on the market value of such securities in excess of $10,000 or the market value of 500 shares, whichever is greater, or $25,000 in the case of a debt security.

(4) This paragraph (c)(2)(vi)(M) will be applied to an issue of municipal securities having the same security provisions, date of issue, interest rate, day, month and year of maturity only if such securities have a market value in excess of $500,000 in bonds ($5,000,000 in notes) or 10 percent of tentative net capital, whichever is greater, and are held in position longer than 20 business days from the date the securities are received by the syndicate manager from the issuer.

(5) Any specialist that is subject to a deduction required by this paragraph (c)(2)(vi)(M), respecting its specialty stock, that can demonstrate to the satisfaction of the Examining Authority for such broker or dealer that there is sufficient liquidity for such specialist's specialty stock and that such deduction need not be applied in the public interest for the protection of investors, may upon a proper showing to such Examining Authority have such undue concentration deduction appropriately decreased, but in no case shall the deduction prescribed in paragraph (c)(2)(vi)(J) of this rule above be reduced. Each such Examining Authority shall make and preserve for a period of not less than 3 years a record of each application granted pursuant to this paragraph (c)(2)(vi)(M)(5), which shall contain a summary of the justification for the granting of the application.

(N) Any specialist that limits its securities business to that of a specialist (except for an occasional non-specialist related securities transaction for its own account), that does not transact a business in securities with other than a broker or dealer registered with the Commission under section 15 or 15C of the Act or a member of a national securities exchange, and that is not a clearing member of The Options Clearing Corporation need not deduct from net worth in computing net capital those deductions, as to its specialty securities, set forth in paragraph (c)(2)(vi) of this rule or Appendix A to this rule, except for paragraph (e) of this rule limiting withdrawals of equity capital and Appendix D to this rule relating to satisfactory subordination agreements. As to a specialist that is solely an options specialist, in paragraph (e) the term "net capital" shall be deemed to mean "net capital before the application of paragraph (c)(2)(vi) of this rule or Appendix A to this rule" and "excess net capital" shall be deemed to be the amount of net capital before the application of paragraph (c)(2)(vi) of this rule or Appendix A to this rule in excess of the amount of net capital required under paragraph (a) of this rule. In reports filed pursuant to Rule 17a–5 and in making the record required by Rule 17a–3(a)(11) each specialist shall include the deductions that would otherwise have been required by paragraph (c)(2)(vi) of this rule or Appendix A to this rule in the absence of this paragraph (c)(2)(vi)(N).

(vii) *Non-Marketable Securities.* Deducting 100 percent of the carrying value in the case of securities or evidence of indebtedness in the proprietary or other accounts of the broker or dealer, for which there is no ready market, as defined in paragraph (c)(11) of this rule, and securities, in the proprietary or other accounts of the broker or dealer, which cannot be publicly offered or sold because of statutory, regulatory or contractual arrangements or other restrictions.

(viii) *Open Contractual Commitments.* Deducting, in the case of a broker or dealer that has open contractual commitments (other than those option positions subject to Appendix (A), Rule 15c3–1a) the respective deductions as specified in paragraph (c)(2)(vi) of this rule or Appendix (B), Rule 15c3–1b, from the value (which shall be the market value whenever there is a market) of each net long and each net short position contemplated by any open contractual commitment in the proprietary or other accounts of the broker or dealer.

(A) The deduction for contractual commitments in those securities that are treated in paragraph (c)(2)(vi)(J) of this rule shall be 30 percent unless the class and issue of the securities subject to the open contractual commitment deduction are listed for trading on a national securities exchange or are designated as NASDAQ National Market System Securities.

(B) A broker or dealer that maintains in excess of $250,000 of net capital may add back to net worth up to $150,000 of any deduction computed under this paragraph (c)(2)(viii)(B).

(C) The deduction with respect to any single commitment shall be reduced by the unrealized profit in such commitment, in an amount not greater than the deduction provided for by this paragraph (or increased by the unrealized loss), in such commitment, and in no event shall an unrealized profit on any closed transactions operate to increase net capital.

(ix) Deducting from the contract value of each failed to deliver contract which is outstanding 5 business days or longer (21 business days or longer in the case of municipal securities) the percentages of the market value of the underlying security which would be required by application of the deduction required by paragraph (c)(2)(vi) of this rule. Such deduction, however, shall be increased by any excess of the contract price of the failed to deliver contract over the market value of the underlying security or reduced by any excess of the market value of the underlying security over the contract value of the failed to deliver contract, but not to exceed the amount of such deduction. The designated examining authority for the broker or dealer may, upon application of the broker or dealer, extend for a period up to 5 business days, any period herein specified where it is satisfied that the extension is warranted. The designated examining authority upon expiration of the extension may extend for one additional period of up to 5 business days, any period herein specified when it is satisfied that the extension is warranted.

(x) *Brokers or Dealers Carrying Accounts of Listed Option Specialists.* (A) With respect to any transaction of a specialist in listed options, who is either not otherwise subject to the provisions of this rule or is described in paragraph (c)(2)(vi)(N) of this rule, for whose specialist account a broker or dealer acts as a guarantor, endorser, or carrying broker or dealer, such broker or dealer shall adjust its net worth by deducting as of noon of each business day the amounts computed as of the prior business day pursuant to Rule 15c3–1a. The required deductions may be reduced by any liquidating equity that exists in such specialist's market-maker account as of that time and shall be increased to the extent of any liquidating deficit in such account. Noon shall be determined according to the local time where the broker or dealer is headquartered. In no event shall excess equity in the specialist's market-maker account result in an increase of the net capital of any such guarantor, endorser, or carrying broker or dealer.

(B) *Definitions. (1)* The term *listed option* shall mean any option traded on a registered national securities exchange or automated facility of a registered national securities association.

(2) For purposes of this rule, the equity in an individual specialist's market-maker account shall be computed by:

(i) Marking all securities positions long or short in the account to their respective current market values;

(ii) Adding (deducting in the case of a debit balance) the credit balance carried in such specialist's market-maker account; and

(iii) Adding (deducting in the case of short positions) the market value of positions long in such account.

(C) No guarantor, endorser, or carrying broker or dealer shall permit the sum of the deductions required pursuant to Rule 15c3–1a in respect of all transactions in specialists' market-maker accounts guaranteed, endorsed, or carried by such broker or dealer to exceed 1,000 percent of such broker's or dealer's net capital as defined in Rule 15c3–1(c)(2) for any period exceeding three business days.

If at any time such sum exceeds 1,000 percent of such broker's or dealer's net capital, then the broker or dealer shall:

(1) Immediately transmit telegraphic or facsimile notice of such event to the Division of Market Regulation in the headquarters office of the Commission in Washington, D.C., to the regional office of the Commission for the region in which the broker or dealer maintains its principal place of business, and to its examining authority designated pursuant to Section 17(d) of the Act (15 U.S.C. 78q(d)) ("Designated Examining Authority"); and

(2) Be subject to the prohibitions against withdrawal of equity capital set forth in Rule 15c3–1(e) and to the prohibitions against reduction, prepayment, and repayment of subordination agreements set forth in paragraph (b)(11) of Rule 15c3–1d, as if such broker or dealer's net capital were below the minimum standards specified by each of those paragraphs.

(D) If at any time there is a liquidating deficit in a specialist's market-maker account, then the broker or dealer guaranteeing, endorsing, or carrying listed options transactions in such specialist's market-maker account may not extend any further credit in that account, and shall take steps to liquidate promptly existing positions in the account. This paragraph shall not prevent the broker or dealer from, upon approval by the broker's or dealer's Designated Examining Authority, entering into hedging positions in the specialist's market-maker account. The broker or dealer also shall transmit telegraphic or facsimile notice of the deficit and its amount by the close of business of the following business day to its Designated Examining Authority and the Designated Examining Authority of the specialist, if different from its own.

(E) Upon written application to the Commission by the specialist and the broker or dealer guaranteeing, endorsing, or carrying options transactions in such specialist's market-maker account, the Commission may approve upon specified terms and conditions lesser adjustments to net worth than those specified in Rule 15c3–1a.

(xi) *Brokers or Dealers Carrying Specialists or Market Makers Accounts.* With respect to a broker or dealer who carries a market maker or specialist account, or with respect to any transaction in options listed on a registered national securities exchange for which a broker or dealer acts as a guarantor or endorser of options written by a specialist in a specialist account, the broker or dealer shall deduct, for each account carried or for each class or series of options guaranteed or endorsed, any deficiency in collateral required by paragraph (a)(6) of this rule.

(xii) *Deduction from Net Worth for Certain Undermargined Accounts.* Deducting the amount of cash required in each customer's or non-customer's account to meet the maintenance margin requirements of the Examining Authority for the broker or dealer, after application of calls for margin, marks to the market or other required deposits which are outstanding 5 business days or less.

(xiii) *Deduction from Net Worth for Indebtedness Collateralized by Exempted Securities.* Deducting, at the option of the broker or dealer, in lieu of including such amounts in aggregate indebtedness, 4 percent of the amount of any indebtedness secured by exempted securities or municipal securities if such indebtedness would otherwise be includable in aggregate indebtedness.

(xiv) *Deduction from net worth for excess deductible amounts related to fidelity bond coverage.* Deducting the amount specified by rule of the Examining Authority for the broker or dealer with respect to a requirement to maintain fidelity bond coverage.

(3) *Exempted Securities.* The term "exempted securities" shall mean those securities deemed exempted securities by section 3(a)(12) of the Securities Exchange Act of 1934 and rules thereunder.

(4) *Contractual Commitments.* The term "contractual commitments" shall include underwriting, when issued, when distributed and delayed delivery contracts, the writing or endorsement of puts and calls and combinations thereof, commitments in foreign currencies, and spot (cash) commodities contracts, but shall not include uncleared regular way purchases and sales of securities and contracts in commodities futures. A series of contracts of purchase or sale of the same security conditioned, if at all, only upon issuance may be treated as an individual commitment.

(5) *Adequately Secured.* Indebtedness shall be deemed to be adequately secured within the

meaning of this rule when the excess of the market value of the collateral over the amount of the indebtedness is sufficient to make the loan acceptable as a fully secured loan to banks regularly making secured loans to brokers or dealers.

(6) *Customer*. The term "customer" shall mean any person from whom, or on whose behalf, a broker or dealer has received, acquired or holds funds or securities for the account of such person, but shall not include a broker or dealer or a registered municipal securities dealer, or a general, special or limited partner or director or officer of the broker or dealer, or any person to the extent that such person has a claim for property or funds which by contract, agreement, or understanding, or by operation of law, is part of the capital of the broker or dealer. *Provided, however,* That the term "customer" shall also include a broker or dealer, but only insofar as such broker or dealer maintains a special omnibus account carried with another broker or dealer in compliance with 12 CFR 220.4(b) of Regulation T under the Securities Exchange Act of 1934.

(7) *Non–Customer*. The term "non-customer" means a broker or dealer, registered municipal securities dealer, general partner, limited partner, officer, director and persons to the extent their claims are subordinated to the claims of creditors of the broker or dealer.

(8) *Market Maker*. The term "market maker" shall mean a dealer who, with respect to a particular security, (i) regularly publishes bona fide, competitive bid and offer quotations in a recognized interdealer quotation system; or (ii) furnishes bona fide competitive bid and offer quotations on request; and, (iii) is ready, willing and able to effect transactions in reasonable quantities at his quoted prices with other brokers or dealers.

(9) *Promptly Transmit and Deliver*. A broker or dealer is deemed to "promptly transmit" all funds and to "promptly deliver" all securities within the meaning of subparagraphs (a)(2)(i) and (a)(2)(v) of this rule where such transmission or delivery is made no later than noon of the next business day after the receipt of such funds or securities; provided, however, That such prompt transmission or delivery shall not be required to be effected prior to the settlement date for such transactions.

(10) *Promptly Forward*. A broker or dealer is deemed to "promptly forward" funds or securities within the meaning of paragraph (a)(2)(i) of this rule only when such forwarding occurs no later than noon of the next business day following receipt of such funds or securities.

(11) *Ready Market*. (i) The term "ready market" shall include a recognized established securities market in which there exists independent bona fide offers to buy and sell so that a price reasonably related to the last sales price or current bona fide competitive bid and offer quotations can be determined for a particular security almost instantaneously and where payment will be received in settlement of a sale at such price within a relatively short time conforming to trade custom.

(ii) A "ready market" shall also be deemed to exist where securities have been accepted as collateral for a loan by a bank as defined in Section 3(a)(6) of the Securities Exchange Act of 1934 and where the broker or dealer demonstrates to its Examining Authority that such securities adequately secure such loans as that term is defined in paragraph (c)(5) of this rule.

(12) *Examining Authority*. The term "Examining Authority" of a broker or dealer shall mean for the purposes of Rules 15c3-1 and 15c3-1a–d the national securities exchange or national securities association of which the broker or dealer is a member or, if the broker or dealer is a member of more than one such self-regulatory organization, the organization designated by the Commission as the Examining Authority for such broker or dealer, or if the broker or dealer is not a member of any such self-regulatory organization, the Regional Office of the Commission where such broker or dealer has its principal place of business.

(13) *Entities That Have a Principal Regulator*. (i) For purposes of Rule 15c3-1e and Rule 15c3-1g, the term *entity that has a principal regulator* shall mean a person (other than a natural person) that is not a registered broker or dealer (other than a broker or dealer) registered under section 15(b)(11) of the Act, provided that the person is:

(A) An insured depository institution as defined in section 3(c)(2) of the Federal Deposit Insurance Act (12 U.S.C. 1813(c)(2));

(B) Registered as a futures commission merchant or an introducing broker with the Commodity Futures Trading Commission;

(C) Registered with or licensed by a State insurance regulator and issues any insurance, endowment, or annuity policy or contract;

(D) A foreign bank as defined in section 1(b)(7) of the International Banking Act of 1978

(12 U.S.C. 3101(7)) that has its headquarters in a jurisdiction for which any foreign bank has been approved by the Board of Governors of the Federal Reserve System to conduct business pursuant to the standards set forth in 12 CFR 211.24(c), provided such foreign bank represents to the Commission that it is subject to the same supervisory regime as the foreign bank previously approved by the Board of Governors of the Federal Reserve System;

(E) Not primarily in the securities business, and the person is:

(*1*) A corporation organized under section 25A of the Federal Reserve Act (12 U.S.C. 611 through 633); or

(*2*) A corporation having an agreement or undertaking with the Board of Governors of the Federal Reserve System under section 25 of the Federal Reserve Act (12 U.S.C. 601 through 604a); or

(F) A person that the Commission finds is another entity that is subject to comprehensive supervision, has in place appropriate arrangements so that information that the person provides to the Commission is sufficiently reliable for the purposes of determining compliance with Rule 15c3–1e and Rule 15c3–1g, and it is appropriate to consider the person to be an entity that has a principal regulator considering all relevant circumstances, including the person's mix of business.

(ii) For purposes of Rules 15c3–1e, 15c3–1g, 17h–1T, and 17h2T, the term *ultimate holding company that has a principal regulator* shall mean a person (other than a natural person) that:

(A) Is a financial holding company or a company that is treated as a financial holding company under the Bank Holding Company Act of 1956 (12 U.S.C. 1840 *et seq.*), or

(B) The Commission determines to be an ultimate holding company that has a principal regulator, if that person is subject to consolidated, comprehensive supervision; there are in place appropriate arrangements so that information that the person provides to the Commission is sufficiently reliable for the purposes of determining compliance with Rule 15c3–1e and Rule 15c3–1g; and it is appropriate to consider the person to be an ultimate holding company that has a principal regulator in view of all relevant circumstances, including the person's mix of business.

(14) *Municipal Securities.* The term "municipal securities" shall mean those securities included within the definition of "municipal securities" in section 3(a)(29) of the Securities Exchange of 1934.

(15) The term *tentative net capital* shall mean the net capital of a broker or dealer before deducting the securities haircuts computed pursuant to paragraph (c)(2)(vi) of this section and the charges on inventory computed pursuant to Appendix B to this rule (Rule 15c3–1b). However, for purposes of paragraph (a)(5) of this section, the term *tentative net capital* means the net capital of an OTC derivatives dealer before deducting the charges for market and credit risk as computed pursuant to Appendix F to this rule (Rule 15c3–1f) or paragraph (c)(2)(vi) of this rule, if applicable, and increased by the balance sheet value (including counterparty net exposure) resulting from transactions in eligible OTC derivative instruments which would otherwise be deducted by virtue of paragraph (c)(2)(iv) of this rule. For purposes of paragraph (a)(7) of this rule, the term *tentative net capital* means the net capital of the broker or dealer before deductions for market and credit risk computed pursuant to Rule 15c3–1e or paragraph (c)(2)(vi) of this rule, if applicable, and increased by the balance sheet value (including counterparty net exposure) resulting from transactions in derivative instruments which would otherwise be deducted by virtue of paragraph (c)(2)(iv) of this rule. Tentative net capital shall include securities for which there is no ready market, as defined in paragraph (c)(11) of this rule, if the use of mathematical models has been approved for purposes of calculating deductions from net capital for those securities pursuant to Rule 15c3–1e.

INSOLVENT

(16) For the purposes of this section, a broker or dealer is insolvent if the broker or dealer:

(i) Is the subject of any bankruptcy, equity receivership proceeding or any other proceeding to reorganize, conserve, or liquidate such broker or dealer or its property or is applying for the appointment or election of a receiver, trustee, or liquidator or similar official for such broker or dealer or its property;

(ii) Has made a general assignment for the benefit of creditors;

(iii) Is insolvent within the meaning of section 101 of title 11 of the United States Code, or is unable to meet its obligations as they mature, and has made an admission to such effect in writing or in any court or before any agency of the United States or any State; or

(iv) Is unable to make such computations as may be necessary to establish compliance with this section or with Rule 15c3–3.

(d) *Debt–Equity Requirements.* No broker or dealer shall permit the total of outstanding principal amounts of its satisfactory subordination agreements (other than such agreements which qualify under this paragraph (d) as equity capital) to exceed 70 percent of its debt-equity total, as hereinafter defined, for a period in excess of 90 days or for such longer period which the Commission may, upon application of the broker or dealer, grant in the public interest or for the protection of investors. In the case of a corporation, the debt-equity total shall be the sum of its outstanding principal amounts of satisfactory subordination agreements, par or stated value of capital stock, paid in capital in excess of par, retained earnings, unrealized profit and loss or other capital accounts. In the case of a partnership, the debt-equity total shall be the sum of its outstanding principal amounts of satisfactory subordination agreements, capital accounts of partners (exclusive of such partners' securities accounts) subject to the provisions of paragraph (e) of this rule, and unrealized profit and loss. In the case of a sole proprietorship, the debt-equity total shall include the sum of its outstanding principal amounts of satisfactory subordination agreements, capital accounts of the sole proprietorship and unrealized profit and loss. *Provided, however,* That a satisfactory subordination agreement entered into by a partner or stockholder which has an initial term of at least three years and has a remaining term of not less than 12 months shall be considered equity for the purposes of this paragraph (d) if:

(1) It does not have any of the provisions for accelerated maturity provided for by paragraphs (b)(9)(i), (b)(10)(i) or (b)(10)(ii) of Appendix (D) (Rule 15c3–1d) and is maintained as capital subject to the provisions restricting the withdrawal thereof required by paragraph (e) of this rule or

(2) The partnership agreement provides that capital contributed pursuant to a satisfactory subordination agreement as defined in Appendix (D) (Rule 15c3–1d) shall in all respects be partnership capital subject to the provisions restricting the withdrawal thereof required by paragraph (e) of this rule.

(e)(1) *Notice Provisions Relating to Limitations on the Withdrawal of Equity Capital.* No equity capital of the broker or dealer or a subsidiary or affiliate consolidated pursuant to Appendix C (Rule 15c3–1c) may be withdrawn by action of a stockholder or a partner or by redemption or repurchase of shares of stock by any of the consolidated entities or through the payment of dividends or any similar distribution, nor may any unsecured advance or loan be made to a stockholder, partner, sole proprietor, employee or affiliate without written notice given in accordance with paragraph (e)(1)(iv) of this rule:

(i) Two business days prior to any withdrawals, advances or loans if those withdrawals, advances or loans on a net basis exceed in the aggregate in any 30 calendar day period, 30 percent of the broker or dealer's excess net capital. A broker or dealer, in an emergency situation, may make withdrawals, advances or loans that on a net basis exceed 30 percent of the broker or dealer's excess net capital in any 30 calendar day period without giving the advance notice required by this paragraph, with the prior approval of its Examining Authority. Where a broker or dealer makes a withdrawal with the consent of its Examining Authority, it shall in any event comply with paragraph (e)(1)(ii) of this rule; or

(ii) Two business days after any withdrawals, advances or loans if those withdrawals, advances or loans on a net basis exceed in the aggregate in any 30 calendar day period, 20 percent of the broker or dealer's excess net capital.

(iii) This paragraph (e)(1) does not apply to:

(A) Securities or commodities transactions in the ordinary course of business between a broker or dealer and an affiliate where the broker or dealer makes payment to or on behalf of such affiliate for such transaction and then receives payment from such affiliate for the securities or commodities transaction within two business days from the date of the transaction; or

(B) Withdrawals, advances or loans which in the aggregate in any thirty calendar day period, on a net basis, equal $500,000 or less.

(iv) Each required notice shall be effective when received by the Commission in Washington, DC, the regional office of the Commission for the region in which the broker or dealer has its principal place of business, the broker or dealer's Examining Authority and the Commodity Futures Trading Commission if such broker or dealer is registered with that Commission.

(2) *Limitations on Withdrawal of Equity Capital.* No equity capital of the broker or dealer or a subsidiary or affiliate consolidated pursuant to Appendix C (Rule 15c3–1e) may be withdrawn by action of a stockholder or a partner or by redemption or repurchase of shares of stock by any of the consolidated entities or through the payment of dividends or any similar distribution, nor may any unsecured advance or loan be made to a stockholder, partner, sole proprietor, employee or affiliate, if after giving effect thereto and to any other such withdrawals, advances or loans and any Payments of Payment Obligations (as defined in appendix D (Rule 15c3–1d)) under satisfactory subordination agreements which are scheduled to occur within 180 days following such withdrawal, advance or loan if:

(i) The broker or dealer's net capital would be less than 120 percent of the minimum dollar amount required by paragraph (a) of this rule;

(ii) The broker-dealer is registered as a futures commission merchant, its net capital would be less than 7 percent of the funds required to be segregated pursuant to the Commodity Exchange Act and the regulations thereunder (less the market value of commodity options purchased by option customers on or subject to the rules of a contract market, each such deduction not to exceed the amount of funds in the option customer's account);

(iii) The broker-dealer's net capital would be less than 25 percent of deductions from net worth in computing net capital required by paragraphs (c)(2)(vi), (f) and appendix A of this rule, unless the broker or dealer has the prior approval of the Commission to make such withdrawal;

(iv) The total outstanding principal amounts of satisfactory subordination agreements of the broker or dealer and any subsidiaries or affiliates consolidated pursuant to appendix C (Rule 15c3–1c) (other than such agreements which qualify as equity under paragraph (d) of this rule) would exceed 70% of the debt-equity total as defined in paragraph (d) of this rule;

(v) The broker or dealer is subject to the aggregate indebtedness limitations of paragraph (a), the aggregate indebtedness of any of the consolidated entities exceeds 1,000 percent of its net capital; or

(vi) The broker or dealer is subject to the alternative net capital requirement of paragraph (f) of this rule, its net capital would be less than 5 percent of aggregate debit items computed in accordance with Rule 15c3–3a.

(3)(i) *Temporary restrictions on withdrawal of net capital.* The Commission may by order restrict, for a period of up to twenty business days, any withdrawal by the broker or dealer of equity capital or unsecured loan or advance to a stockholder, partner, sole proprietor, member, employee or affiliate under such terms and conditions as the Commission deems necessary or appropriate in the public interest or consistent with the protection of investors if the Commission, based on the information available, concludes that such withdrawal, advance or loan may be detrimental to the financial integrity of the broker or dealer, or may unduly jeopardize the broker or dealer's ability to repay its customer claims or other liabilities which may cause a significant impact on the markets or expose the customers or creditors of the broker or dealer to loss without taking into account the application of the Securities Investor Protection Act of 1970.

(ii) An order temporarily prohibiting the withdrawal of capital shall be rescinded if the Commission determines that the restriction on capital withdrawal should not remain in effect. A hearing on an order temporarily prohibiting the withdrawal of capital will be held within two business days from the date of the request in writing by the broker or dealer.

(4)(i) *Miscellaneous Provisions.* Excess net capital is that amount in excess of the amount required under paragraph (a) of this rule. For the purposes of paragraphs (e)(1) and (e)(2) of this rule, a broker or dealer may use the amount of excess net capital and deductions required under paragraphs (c)(2)(vi), (f) and appendix A of this rule reported in its most recently required filed Form X–17A–5 for the purposes of calculating the effect of a projected withdrawal, advance or loan relative to excess net capital or deductions. The broker or dealer must assure itself that the excess net capital or the deductions reported on the most recently required filed Form X–17A–5 have not materially changed since the time such report was filed.

(ii) The term equity capital includes capital contributions by partners, par or stated value of capital stock, paid-in capital in excess of par, retained earnings or other capital accounts. The term equity capital does not include securities in the securities accounts of partners and balances in limited partners' capital accounts in excess of their stated capital contributions.

(iii) Paragraphs (e)(1) and (e)(2) of this rule shall not preclude a broker or dealer from making required tax payments or preclude the payment to partners of reasonable compensation, and such payments shall not be included in the calculation of withdrawals, advances, or loans for purposes of paragraphs (e)(1) and (e)(2) of this rule.

(iv) For the purpose of this paragraph (e), any transaction between a broker or dealer and a stockholder, partner, sole proprietor, employee or affiliate that results in a diminution of the broker or dealer's net capital shall be deemed to be an advance or loan of net capital.

Rule 15c3–1a. Options (Appendix A to Rule 15c3–1)

(a) *Definitions.* (1) The term *unlisted option* shall mean any option not included in the definition of listed option provided in paragraph (c)(2)(x) of Rule 15c3–1.

(2) The term *option series* refers to listed option contracts of the same type (either a call or a put) and exercise style, covering the same underlying security with the same exercise price, expiration date, and number of underlying units.

(3) The term *related instrument* within an option class or product group refers to futures contracts and options on futures contracts covering the same underlying instrument. In relation to options on foreign currencies a related instrument within an option class also shall include forward contracts on the same underlying currency.

(4) The term *underlying instrument* refers to long and short positions, as appropriate, covering the same foreign currency, the same security, or a security which is exchangeable for or convertible into the underlying security within a period of 90 days. If the exchange or conversion requires the payment of money or results in a loss upon conversion at the time when the security is deemed an underlying instrument for purposes of this Appendix A, the broker or dealer will deduct from net worth the full amount of the conversion loss. The term underlying instrument shall not be deemed to include securities options, futures contracts, options on futures contracts, qualified stock baskets, or unlisted instruments.

(5) The term *options class* refers to all options contracts covering the same underlying instrument.

(6) The term *product group* refers to two or more option classes, related instruments, underlying instruments, and qualified stock baskets in the same portfolio type (see paragraph (b)(1)(ii) of this rule) for which it has been determined that a percentage of offsetting profits may be applied to losses at the same valuation point.

(b) The deduction under this Appendix A to Rule 15c3–1 shall equal the sum of the deductions specified in paragraph (b)(1)(v)(C) or (b)(2) of this rule.

(1) *Theoretical Pricing Charges.* (i) *Definitions.* (A) The terms *theoretical gains and losses* shall mean the gain and loss in the value of individual option series, the value of underlying instruments, related instruments, and qualified stock baskets within that option's class, at 10 equidistant intervals (valuation points) ranging from an assumed movement (both up and down) in the current market value of the underlying instrument equal to the percentage corresponding to the deductions otherwise required under Rule 15c3–1 for the underlying instrument (see paragraph (a)(1)(iii) of this rule). Theoretical gains and losses shall be calculated using a theoretical options pricing model that satisfies the criteria set forth in paragraph (a)(1)(i)(B) of this rule.

(B) The term *theoretical options pricing model* shall mean any mathematical model, other than a broker-dealer proprietary model, approved by a Designated Examining Authority. Such Designated Examining Authority shall submit the model to the Commission, together with a description of its methods for approving models. Any such model shall calculate theoretical gains and losses as described in paragraph (a)(1)(i)(A) of this rule for all series and issues of equity, index and foreign currency options and related instruments, and shall be made available equally and on the same terms to all registered brokers or dealers. Its procedures shall include the arrangement of the vendor to supply accurate and timely data to each broker-dealer with respect to its services, and the fees for distribution of the services. The data provided to brokers or dealers shall also contain the minimum requirements set forth in paragraph (b)(1)(v)(C) of this rule and the product group offsets set forth in paragraph (b)(1)(v)(B) of this rule. At a minimum, the model shall consider the following factors in pricing the option:

(*1*) The current spot price of the underlying asset;

(*2*) The exercise price of the option;

(*3*) The remaining time until the option's expiration;

(*4*) The volatility of the underlying asset;

(*5*) Any cash flows associated with ownership of the underlying asset that can reasonably be expected to occur during the remaining life of the option; and

(*6*) The current term structure of interest rates.

(C) The term *major market foreign currency* shall mean the currency of a sovereign nation.

(D) The term *qualified stock basket* shall mean a set or basket of stock positions which represents no less than 50% of the capitalization for a high-capitalization or non-high-capitalization diversified market index, or, in the case of a narrow-based index, no less than 95% of the capitalization for such narrow-based index.

(ii) With respect to positions involving listed options in a single specialist's market-maker account, and, separately, with respect to positions involving listed option positions in its proprietary or other account, the broker or dealer shall group long and short positions into the following portfolio types:

(A) Equity options on the same underlying instrument and positions in that underlying instrument;

(B) Options on the same major market foreign currency, positions in that major market foreign currency, and related instruments within those options' classes;

(C) High-capitalization diversified market index options, related instruments within the option's class, and qualified stock baskets in the same index;

(D) Non-high-capitalization diversified index options, related instruments within the index option's class, and qualified stock baskets in the same index; and

(E) Narrow-based index options, related instruments within the index option's class, and qualified stock baskets in the same index.

(iii) Before making the computation, each broker or dealer shall obtain the theoretical gains and losses for each options series and for the related and underlying instruments within those options' class in each specialist's market-maker account guaranteed, endorsed, or carried by a broker or dealer, or in the proprietary or other accounts of that broker or dealer. For each option series, the theoretical options pricing model shall calculate theoretical prices at 10 equidistant valuation points within a range consisting of an increase or a decrease of the following percentages of the daily market price of the underlying instrument:

(A) + (–) 15% for equity securities with a ready market, narrow-based indexes, and non-high-capitalization diversified indexes;

(B) + (–) 6% for major market foreign currencies;

(C) + (–) 20% for all other currencies; and

(D) + (–) 10% for high-capitalization diversified indexes.

(iv) As to non-clearing option specialists and market-makers, the percentages of the daily market price of the underlying instrument shall be:

(A) + (–) 4½% for major market foreign currencies; and

(B) + 6(–) 8% for high-capitalization diversified indexes.

(C) + (–) 10% for a non-clearing market-maker, or specialist in non-high capitalization diversified index product group.

(v)(A) The broker or dealer shall multiply the corresponding theoretical gains and losses at each of the 10 equidistant valuation points by the number of positions held in a particular options series, the related instruments and qualified stock baskets within the option's class, and the positions in the same underlying instrument.

(B) In determining the aggregate profit or loss for each portfolio type, the broker or dealer will be allowed the following offsets in the following order, provided, that in the case of qualified stock baskets, the broker or dealer may elect to net individual stocks between qualified stock baskets and take the appropriate deduction on the remaining, if any, securities:

(*1*) First, a broker or dealer is allowed the following offsets within an option's class:

(*i*) Between options on the same underlying instrument, positions covering the same underlying instrument, and related instruments within the option's class, 100% of a position's gain shall offset another position's loss at the same valuation point;

(*ii*) Between index options, related instruments within the option's class, and qualified stock baskets on the same index, 95%, or such other amount as designated by the Commission, of gains shall offset losses at the same valuation point;

(*2*) Second, a broker-dealer is allowed the following offsets within an index product group;

(*i*) Among positions involving different high-capitalization diversified index option classes within the same product group, 90% of the gain in a high-capitalization diversified market index option, related instruments, and qualified stock baskets within that index option's class shall offset the loss at the same valuation point in a different high-capitalization diversified market index option, related instruments, and qualified stock baskets within that index option's class;

(*ii*) Among positions involving different non-high-capitalization diversified index option classes within the same product group, 75% of the gain in a non-high-capitalization diversified market index option, related instruments, and qualified stock baskets within that index option's class shall offset the loss at the same valuation point in another non-high-capitalization diversified market index option, related instruments, and qualified stock baskets within that index option's class or product group;

(*iii*) Among positions involving different narrow-based index option classes within the same product group, 90% of the gain in a narrow-based market index option, related instruments, and qualified stock baskets within that index option's class shall offset the loss at the same valuation point in another narrow-based market index option, related instruments, and qualified stock baskets within that index option's class or product group;

(*iv*) No qualified stock basket should offset another qualified stock basket; and

(*3*) Third, a broker-dealer is allowed the following offsets between product groups: Among positions involving different diversified index product groups within the same market group, 50% of the gain in a diversified market index option, a related instrument, or a qualified stock basket within that index option's product group shall offset the loss at the same valuation point in another product group;

(C) For each portfolio type, the total deduction shall be the larger of:

(*1*) The amount for any of the 10 equidistant valuation points representing the largest theoretical loss after applying the offsets provided in paragraph (b)(1)(v)(B) of this rule; or

(*2*) A minimum charge equal to 25% times the multiplier for each equity and index option contract and each related instrument within the option's class or product group, or $25 for each option on a major market foreign currency with the minimum charge for futures contracts and options on futures contracts adjusted for contract size differentials, not to exceed market value in the case of long positions in options and options on futures contracts; plus

(*3*) In the case of portfolio types involving index options and related instruments offset by a qualified stock basket, there will be a minimum charge of 5% of the market value of the qualified stock basket for high-capitalization diversified and narrow-based indexes; and

(*4*) In the case of portfolio types involving index options and related instruments offset by a qualified stock basket, there will be a minimum charge of 7½% of the market value of the qualified stock basket for non-high-capitalization diversified indexes.

(2) *Alternative Strategy Based Method.* A broker or dealer may elect to apply the alternative strategy based method in accordance with the provisions of this paragraph (b)(2).

(i) *Definitions.* (A) The term *intrinsic value* or *in-the-money amount* shall mean the amount by which the exercise value, in the case of a call, is less than the current market value of the underlying instrument, and, in the case of a put, is greater than the current market value of the underlying instrument.

(B) The term *out-of-the-money amount* shall mean the amount by which the exercise value, in the case of a call, is greater than the current market value of the underlying instrument, and, in the case of a put, is less than the current market value of the underlying instrument.

(C) The term *term value* shall mean the current market value of an option contract that is in excess of its intrinsic value.

(ii) Every broker or dealer electing to calculate adjustments to net worth in accordance with the provisions of this paragraph (b)(2) must make the following adjustments to net worth:

(A) Add the time value of a short position in a listed option; and

(B) Deduct the time value of a long position in a listed option, which relates to a position in the same underlying instrument or in a related instrument within the option class or product group as recognized in the strategies enumerated in paragraph (b)(2)(iii)(D) of this rule; and

(C) Add the net short market value or deduct the long market value of listed options as recognized in the strategies enumerated in paragraphs (b)(2)(iii)(E)(1) and (2) of this rule.

(iii) In computing net capital after the adjustments provided for in paragraph (b)(2)(ii) of this rule, every broker or dealer shall deduct the percentages specified in this paragraph (b)(2)(iii) for all listed option positions, positions covering the same underlying instrument and related instruments within the options' class or product group.

(A) *Uncovered Calls.* Where a broker or dealer is short a call, deducting the percentage required by paragraphs (c)(2)(vi)(A) through (K) of Rule 15c3–1 of the current market value of the underlying instrument for such option reduced by its out-of-the-money amount, to the extent that such reduction does not operate to increase net capital. In no event shall this deduction be less than the greater of $250 for each short call option contract for 100 shares or 50% of the aforementioned percentage.

(B) *Uncovered Puts.* Where a broker or dealer is short a put, deducting the percentage required by paragraphs (c)(2)(vi)(A) through (K) of Rule 15c3–1 of the current market value of the underlying instrument for such option reduced by its out-of-the-money amount, to the extent that such reduction does not operate to increase net capital. In no event shall the deduction provided by this paragraph be less than the greater of $250 for each short put option contract for 100 shares or 50% of the aforementioned percentage.

(C) *Long Positions.* Where a broker or dealer is long puts or calls, deducting 50 percent of the market value of the net long put and call positions in the same options series.

(D) *Certain Security Positions with Offsetting Options.* (*1*) Where a broker or dealer is long a put for which it has an offsetting long position in the same number of units of the same underlying instrument, deducting the percentage required by paragraphs (c)(2)(vi)(A) through (K) of Rule 15c3–1 of the current market value of the underlying instrument for the long offsetting position, not to exceed the out-of-the-money amount of the option. In no event shall the deduction provided by this paragraph be less than $25 for each option contract for 100 shares, provided that the minimum charge need not exceed the intrinsic value of the option.

(*2*) Where a broker or dealer is long a call for which it has an offsetting short position in the same number of units of the same underlying instrument, deducting the percentage required by paragraphs (c)(2)(vi)(A) through (K) of Rule 15c3–1 of the current market value of the underlying instrument for the short offsetting position, not to exceed the out-of-the-money amount of the option. In no event shall the deduction provided by this paragraph be less than $25 for each option contract for 100 shares, provided that the minimum charge need not exceed the intrinsic value of the option.

(*3*) Where a broker or dealer is short a call for which it has an offsetting long position in the same number of units of the same underlying instrument, deducting the percentage required by paragraphs (c)(2)(vi)(A) through (K) of Rule 15c3-1 of the current market value of the underlying instrument for the offsetting long position reduced by the short call's intrinsic value. In no event shall the deduction provided by this paragraph be less than $25 for each option contract for 100 shares.

(E) *Certain Spread Positions.* (*1*) Where a broker or dealer is short a listed call and is also long a listed call in the same class of options contracts and the long option expires on the same date as or subsequent to the short option, the deduction, after adjustments required in paragraph (b) of this rule, shall be the amount by which the exercise value of the long call exceeds the exercise value of the short call. If the exercise value of the long call is less than or equal to the exercise value of the short call, no deduction is required.

(*2*) Where a broker or dealer is short a listed put and is also long a listed put in the same class of options contracts and the long option expires on the same date as or subsequent to the short option, the deduction, after the adjustments required in paragraph (b) of this rule, shall be the amount by which the exercise value of the short put exceeds the exercise value of the long put. If the exercise value of the long put is equal to or greater than the exercise value of the short put, no deduction is required.

(c) With respect to transactions involving unlisted options, every broker or dealer shall determine the value of unlisted option positions in accordance with the provision of paragraph (c)(2)(i) of Rule 15c3-1, and shall deduct the percentages of all securities positions or unlisted options in the proprietary or other accounts of the broker or dealer specified in this paragraph (c). However, where computing the deduction required for a security position as if the security position had no related unlisted option position and positions in unlisted options as if uncovered would result in a lesser deduction from net worth, the broker or dealer may compute such deductions separately.

(1) *Uncovered Calls.* Where a broker or dealer is short a call, deducting 15 percent (or such other percentage required by paragraphs (c)(2)(vi)(A) through (K) of Rule 15c3-1) of the current market value of the security underlying such option reduced by any excess of the exercise value of the call over the current market value of the underlying security. In no event shall the deduction provided by this paragraph be less than $250 for each option contract for 100 shares.

(2) *Uncovered Puts.* Where a broker or dealer is short a put, deducting 15 percent (or such other percentage required by paragraphs (c)(2)(vi)(A) through (K) of Rule 15c3-1) of the current market value of the security underlying the option reduced by any excess of the market value of the underlying security over the exercise value of the put. In no event shall the deduction provided by this paragraph be less than $250 for each option contract for 100 shares.

(3) *Covered Calls.* Where a broker or dealer is short a call and long equivalent units of the underlying security, deducting 15 percent (or such other percentage required by paragraphs (c)(2)(vi)(A) through (K) of Rule 15c3-1) of the current market value of the underlying security reduced by any excess of the current market value of the underlying security over the exercise value of the call. No reduction under this paragraph shall have the effect of increasing net capital.

(4) *Covered Puts.* Where a broker or dealer is short a put and short equivalent units of the underlying security, deducting 15 percent (or such other percentage required by paragraphs (c)(2)(vi)(A) through (K) of Rule 15c3-1) of the current market value of the underlying security reduced by any excess of the exercise value of the put over the market value of the underlying security. No such reduction shall have the effect of increasing net capital.

(5) *Conversion Accounts.* Where a broker or dealer is long equivalent units of the underlying security, long a put written or endorsed by a broker or dealer and short a call in its proprietary or other accounts, deducting 5 percent (or 50 percent of such other percentage required by paragraphs (c)(2)(vi)(A) through (K) of Rule 15c3-1) of the current market value of the underlying security.

(6) Where a broker or dealer is short equivalent units of the underlying security, long a call written or endorsed by a broker or dealer and short a put in his proprietary or other accounts, deducting

5 percent (or 50 percent of such other percentage required by paragraphs (c)(2)(vi)(A) through (K) of Rule 15c3–1) of the market value of the underlying security.

(7) *Long Options*. Where a broker or dealer is long a put or call endorsed or written by a broker or dealer, deducting 15 percent (or such other percentage required by paragraphs (c)(2)(vi)(A) through (K) of Rule 15c3–1) of the market value of the underlying security, not to exceed any value attributed to such option in paragraph (c)(2)(i) of Rule 15c3–1.

Rule 15c3–1b. Adjustments to net worth and aggregate indebtedness for certain commodities transactions (Appendix B to Rule 15c3–1)

(a) Every broker or dealer in computing net capital pursuant to Rule 15c3–1 shall comply with the following:

(1) Where a broker or dealer has an asset or liability which is treated or defined in paragraph (c) of Rule 15c3–1, the inclusion or exclusion of all or part of such asset or liability for the computation of aggregate indebtedness and net capital shall be in accordance with paragraph (c) of Rule 15c3–1 except as specifically provided otherwise in this Appendix B. Where a commodity related asset or liability is specifically treated or defined in 17 CFR 1.17 and is not generally or specifically treated or defined in Rule 15c3–1 or this Appendix B, the inclusion or exclusion of all or part of such asset or liability for the computation of aggregate indebtedness and net capital shall be in accordance with 17 CFR 1.17.

(2) *Aggregate Indebtedness*. The term *aggregate indebtedness* as defined in paragraph (c)(1) of this rule shall exclude with respect to commodity-related transactions:

(i) Indebtedness arising in connection with an advance to a non-proprietary account when such indebtedness is adequately collateralized by spot commodities eligible for delivery on a contract market and when such spot commodities are covered;

(ii) Advances received by the broker or dealer against bill of lading issued in connection with the shipment of commodities sold by the broker or dealer; and

(iii) Equity balances in the accounts of general partners.

(3) *Net Capital*. In computing net capital as defined in paragraph (c)(2) of this rule, the net worth of a broker or dealer shall be adjusted as follows with respect to commodity-related transactions:

(i) *Unrealized Profit or Loss for Certain Commodities Transactions*. (A) Unrealized profits shall be added and unrealized losses shall be deducted in the commodities accounts of the broker or dealer, including unrealized profits and losses on fixed price commitments and forward contract; and

(B) The value attributed to any commodity option which is not traded on a contract market shall be the difference between the option's strike price and the market value for the physical or futures contract which is the subject of the option. In the case of a long call commodity option, if the market value for the physical or futures contract which is the subject of the option is less than the strike price of the option, it shall be given no value. In the case of a long put commodity option, if the market value for the physical commodity or futures contract which is the subject of the option is more than the striking price of the option, it shall be given no value.

(ii) Deduct any unsecured commodity futures or option account containing a ledger balance and open trades the combination of which liquidates to a deficit or containing a debit ledger balance only: *Provided, however,* Deficits or debit ledger balances in unsecured customers', non-customers' and proprietary accounts, which are the subject of calls for margin or other required deposits need not be deducted until the close of business on the business day following the date on which such deficit or debit ledger balance originated.

(iii) Deduct all unsecured receivables, advances and loans except for:

(A) Management fees receivable from commodity pools outstanding no longer than thirty (30) days from the date they are due;

(B) Receivables from foreign clearing organizations;

(C) Receivables from registered futures commission merchants or brokers, resulting from commodity futures or option transactions, except those specifically excluded under paragraph (3)(ii) of this Appendix B. In the case of an introducing broker or an applicant for registration as an introducing broker, include 50 percent of the value of a guarantee or security deposit with a futures commission merchant which carries or intends to carry accounts for the customers of the introducing broker.

(iv) Deduct all inventories (including work in process, finished goods, raw materials and inventories held for resale) except for readily marketable spot commodities; or spot commodities which adequately collateralize indebtedness under paragraph (c)(7) of 17 CFR 1.17;

(v) Guarantee deposits with commodities clearing organizations are not required to be deducted from net worth;

(vi) Stock in commodities clearing organizations to the extent of its margin value is not required to be deducted from net worth;

(vii) Deduct from net worth the amount by which any advances paid by the broker or dealer on cash commodity contracts and used in computing net capital exceeds 95 percent of the market value of the commodities covered by such contracts;

(viii) Do not include equity in the commodity accounts of partners in net worth.

(ix) In the case of all inventory, fixed price commitments and forward contracts, except for inventory and forward contracts in the inter-bank market in those foreign currencies which are purchased or sold for future delivery on or subject to the rules of a contract market and covered by an open futures contract for which there will be no charge, deduct the applicable percentage of the net position specified below:

(A) Inventory which is currently registered as deliverable on a contract market and covered by an open futures contract or by a commodity option on a physical—No charge.

(B) Inventory which is covered by an open futures contract or commodity option—5% of the market value.

(C) Inventory which is not covered—20% of the market value.

(D) Fixed price commitments (open purchases and sales) and forward contracts which are covered by an open futures contract or commodity option—10% of the market value.

(E) Fixed price commitments (open purchases and sales) and forward contracts which are not covered by an open futures contract or commodity option—20% of the market value.

(x) Deduct 4% of the market value of commodity options granted (sold) by option customers on or subject to the rules of a contract market;

(xi) [Reserved]

(xii) Deduct for undermargined customer commodity futures accounts the amount of funds required in each such account to meet maintenance margin requirements of the applicable board of trade or, if there are no such maintenance margin requirements, clearing organization margin requirements applicable to such positions, after application of calls for margin, or other required deposits which are outstanding three business days or less. If there are no such maintenance margin requirements or clearing organization margin requirements on such accounts, then deduct the amount of funds required to provide margin equal to the amount necessary after application of calls for margin, or other required deposits outstanding three days or less to restore original margin when the original margin has been depleted by 50 percent or more. *Provided,* To the extent a deficit is deducted from net worth in accordance with paragraph (a)(3)(ii) of this Appendix B, such amount shall not also be deducted under this paragraph (a)(3)(xii). In the event that an owner of a customer account has deposited an asset other than cash to margin, guarantee or secure his account, the value attributable to such asset for purposes of this paragraph shall be the lesser of (A) the value attributable to such asset pursuant to the margin rules of the applicable board of trade, or (B) the market value of such asset after application of the percentage deductions specified in paragraph (a)(3)(ix) of this Appendix B or, where appropriate, specified in paragraph (c)(2)(vi) or (c)(2)(vii) of Rule 15c3–1;

(xiii) Deduct for undermargined non-customer and omnibus commodity futures accounts the amount of funds required in each such account to meet maintenance margin requirements of the applicable board of trade or, if there are no such maintenance margin requirements, clearing organization margin requirements applicable to such positions, after application of calls for margin, or other required deposits which are outstanding two business days or less. If there are no such maintenance margin requirements or clearing organization margin requirements, then deduct the amount of funds required to provide margin equal to the amount necessary after application of calls for margin, or other required deposits outstanding two days or less to restore original margin when the original margin has been depleted by 50 percent or more. *Provided,* To the extent a deficit is deducted from net worth in accordance with paragraph (a)(3)(ii) of this Appendix B such amount shall not also be deducted under this paragraph (a)(3)(xiii). In the event that an owner of a non-customer or omnibus account has deposited an asset other than cash to margin, guarantee or secure his account, the value attributable to such asset for purposes of this paragraph shall be the lesser of (A) the value attributable to such asset pursuant to the margin rules of the applicable board of trade, or (B) the market value of such asset after application of the percentage deductions specified in paragraph (a)(3)(ix) of this Appendix B or, where appropriate, specified in paragraph (c)(2)(vi) or (c)(2)(vii) of Rule 15c3–1;

(xiv) In the case of open futures contracts and granted (sold) commodity options held in proprietary accounts carried by the broker or dealer which are not covered by a position held by the broker or dealer or which are not the result of a "changer trade" made in accordance with the rules of a contract market, deduct:

(A) For a broker or dealer which is a clearing member of a contract market for the positions on such contract market cleared by such member, the applicable margin requirement of the applicable clearing organization;

(B) For a broker or dealer which is a member of a self-regulatory organization 150% of the applicable maintenance margin requirement of the applicable board of trade or clearing organization, whichever is greater; or

(C) For all other brokers or dealers, 200% of the applicable maintenance margin requirement of the applicable board of trade or clearing organization, whichever is greater; or

(D) For open contracts or granted (sold) commodity options for which there are no applicable maintenance margin requirements, 200% of the applicable initial margin requirement;

Provided, the equity in any such proprietary account shall reduce the deduction required by this paragraph (a)(3)(xiv) if such equity is not otherwise includable in net capital.

(xv) In the case of a broker or dealer which is a purchaser of a commodity option which is traded on a contract market the deduction shall be the same safety factor as if the broker or dealer were the grantor of such option in accordance with paragraph (3)(xiv), but in no event shall the safety factor be greater than the market value attributed to such option.

(xvi) In the case of a broker or dealer which is a purchaser of a commodity option not traded on a contract market which has value and such value is used to increase net capital, the deduction is ten percent of the market value of the physical or futures contract which is the subject of such option but in no event more than the value attributed to such option.

(xvii) Deduct 5% of all unsecured receivables includable under paragraph (3)(iii)(C) of this Appendix B used by the broker or dealer in computing "net capital" and which are not receivable from (A) a futures commission merchant registered as such with the Commodity Futures Trading Commission, or (B) a broker or dealer which is registered as such with the Securities and Exchange Commission.

(xviii) A loan or advance or any other form of receivable shall not be considered "secured" for the purposes of paragraph (a)(3) of this Appendix B unless the following conditions exist:

(A) The receivable is secured by readily marketable collateral which is otherwise unencumbered and which can be readily converted into cash: *Provided, however,* That the receivable will be considered secured only to the extent of the market value of such collateral after application of the percentage deductions specified in paragraph (a)(3)(ix) of this Appendix B; and

(B)(*1*) The readily marketable collateral is in the possession or control of the broker or dealer; or

(*2*) The broker or dealer has a legally enforceable, written security agreement, signed by the debtor, and has a perfected security interest in the readily marketable collateral within the meaning of the laws of the State in which the readily marketable collateral is located.

(xix) The term *cover* for purposes of this Appendix B shall mean cover as defined in 17 CFR 1.17(j).

(xx) The term *customer* for purposes of this Appendix B shall mean customer as defined in 17 CFR 1.17(b)(2). The term "non-customer" for purposes of this Appendix B shall mean non-customer as defined in 17 CFR 1.17(b)(4).

Rule 15c3–1c. Consolidated computations of net capital and aggregate indebtedness for certain subsidiaries and affiliates (Appendix C to Rule 15c3–1)

(a) *Flow Through Capital Benefits.* Every broker or dealer in computing its net capital and aggregate indebtedness pursuant to Rule 15c3–1 shall, subject to the provisions of paragraphs (b) and (d) of this Appendix, consolidate in a single computation assets and liabilities of any subsidiary or affiliate for which it guarantees, endorses or assumes directly or indirectly the obligations or liabilities. The assets and liabilities of a subsidiary or affiliate whose liabilities and obligations have not been guaranteed, endorsed, or assumed directly or indirectly by the broker or dealer may also be so consolidated if an opinion of counsel is obtained as provided for in paragraph (b) below.

(b) *Required Counsel Opinions.* (1) If the consolidation, provided for in paragraph (a) of this rule, of any such subsidiary or affiliate results in the increase of the broker's or dealer's net capital and/or the decrease of the broker's or dealer's and/or the decrease of the broker's or dealer's minimum net capital requirement paragraph (a) of Rule 15c3–1 and an opinion of counsel described in paragraph (b)(2) of this rule has not been obtained, such benefits shall not be recognized in the broker's or dealer's computation required by this rule.

(2) Except as provided for in paragraph (b)(1) of this rule, consolidation shall be permitted with respect to any subsidiaries or affiliates which are majority owned and controlled by the broker or dealer for which the broker or dealer can demonstrate to the satisfaction of the Commission, through the Examining Authority, by an opinion of counsel that the net asset values, or the portion thereof related to the parent's ownership interest in the subsidiary or affiliate may be caused by the broker or dealer or a trustee appointed pursuant to the Securities Investor Protection Act of 1970 or otherwise, to be distributed to the broker or dealer within 30 calendar days. Such opinion shall also set forth the actions necessary to cause such a distribution to be made, identify the parties having the authority to take such actions, identify and describe the rights of other parties or classes of parties, including but not limited to customers, general creditors, subordinated lenders, minority shareholders, employees, litigants and governmental or regulatory authorities, who may delay or prevent such a distribution and such other assurances as the Commission or the Examining Authority by rule or interpretation may require. Such opinion shall be current and periodically renewed in connection with the broker's or dealer's annual audit pursuant to Rule 17a–5 under the Securities Exchange Act of 1934 or upon any material change in circumstances.

(c) *Principles of Consolidation.* In preparing a consolidated computation of net capital and/or aggregate indebtedness pursuant to this rule, the following minimum and non-exclusive requirements shall be observed:

(1) Consolidated net worth shall be reduced by the estimated amount of any tax reasonably anticipated to be incurred upon distribution of the assets of the subsidiary or affiliate.

(2) Liabilities of a consolidated subsidiary or affiliate which are subordinated to the claims of present and future creditors pursuant to a satisfactory subordination agreement shall not be added to consolidated net worth unless such subordination extends also to the claims of present or future creditors of the parent broker or dealer and all consolidated subsidiaries.

(3) Subordinated liabilities of a consolidated subsidiary or affiliate which are consolidated in accordance with paragraph (c)(2) of this rule may not be prepaid, repaid or accelerated if any of the entities included in such consolidation would otherwise be unable to comply with the provisions of Appendix (D), Rule 15c3–1d.

(4) Each broker or dealer included within the consolidation shall at all times be in compliance with the net capital requirement to which it is subject.

(d) *Certain Precluded Acts.* No broker or dealer shall guarantee, endorse or assume directly or indirectly any obligation or liability of a subsidiary or affiliate unless the obligation or liability is reflected in the computation of net capital and/or aggregate indebtedness pursuant to Rule 15c3–1 or this Appendix (C), except as provided in paragraph (b)(1) of this rule.

Rule 15c3–1d. Satisfactory subordination agreements (Appendix D to Rule 15c3–1)

(a) *Introduction.* (1) This Appendix sets forth minimum and non-exclusive requirements for satisfactory subordination agreements (hereinafter "subordination agreement"). The Examining Authority may require or the broker or dealer may include such other provisions as deemed necessary or appropriate to the extent such provisions do not cause the subordination agreement to fail to meet the minimum requirements of this Appendix (D).

(2) *Certain Definitions.* For purposes of Rule 15c3–1 and this Appendix (D):

(i) A subordination agreement may be either a subordinated loan agreement or a secured demand note agreement.

(ii) The term *subordinated loan agreement* shall mean the agreement or agreements evidencing or governing a subordinated borrowing of cash.

(iii) The term *Collateral Value* of any securities pledged to secure a secured demand note shall mean the market value of such securities after giving effect to the percentage deductions set forth in paragraph (c)(2)(vi) of Rule 15c3–1 except for paragraph (c)(2)(vi)(J). In lieu of the deduction under (c)(2)(vi)(J), the broker or dealer shall reduce the market value of the securities pledged to secure the secured demand note by 30 percent.

(iv) The term *Payment Obligation* shall mean the obligation of a broker or dealer in respect to any subordination agreement (A) to repay cash loaned to the broker or dealer pursuant to a subordinated loan agreement or (B) to return a secured demand note contributed to the broker or dealer or reduce the unpaid principal amount thereof and to return cash or securities pledged as collateral to secure the secured demand note and (C) "Payment" shall mean the performance by a broker or dealer of a Payment Obligation.

(v)(A) The term *secured demand note agreement* shall mean an agreement (including the related secured demand note) evidencing or governing the contribution of a secured demand note to a broker or dealer and the pledge of securities and/or cash with the broker or dealer as collateral to secure payment of such secured demand note. The secured demand note agreement may provide that neither the lender, his heirs, executors, administrators or assigns shall be personally liable on such note and that in the event of default the broker or dealer shall look for payment of such note solely to the collateral then pledged to secure the same.

(B) The secured demand note shall be a promissory note executed by the lender and shall be payable on the demand of the broker or dealer to which it is contributed; provided, however, That the making of such demand may be conditioned upon the occurrence of any of certain events which are acceptable to the Commission and to the Examining Authority for such broker or dealer.

(C) If such note is not paid upon presentment and demand as provided for therein, the broker or dealer shall have the right to liquidate all or any part of the securities then pledged as collateral to secure payment of the same and to apply the net proceeds of such liquidation, together with any cash then included in the collateral, in payment of such note. Subject to the prior rights of the broker or dealer as pledgee, the lender, as defined herein, may retain ownership of the collateral and have the benefit of any increases and bear the risks of any decreases in the value of the collateral and may retain the right to vote securities contained within the collateral and any right to income therefrom or distributions thereon, except the broker or dealer shall have the right to receive and hold as pledgee all dividends payable in securities and all partial and complete liquidating dividends.

(D) Subject to the prior rights of the broker or dealer as pledgee, the lender may have the right to direct the sale of any securities included in the collateral, to direct the purchase of securities with any cash included therein, to withdraw excess collateral or to substitute cash or other securities as collateral, provided that the net proceeds of any such sale and the cash so substituted and the securities so purchased or substituted are held by the broker or dealer, as pledgee, and are included within the collateral to secure payment of the secured demand note, and provided further that no such transaction shall be permitted if, after giving effect thereto, the sum of the amount of any cash, plus the Collateral Value of the securities, then pledged as collateral to secure the secured demand note would be less than the unpaid principal amount of the secured demand note.

(E) Upon payment by the lender, as distinguished from a reduction by the lender which is provided for in (b)(6)(iii) or reduction by the broker or dealer as provided for in subparagraph (b)(7) of this Appendix (D), of all or any part of the unpaid principal amount of the secured demand note, a broker or dealer shall issue to the lender a subordinated loan agreement in the amount of such payment (or in the case of a broker or dealer that is a partnership credit a capital account of the lender) or issue preferred or common stock of the broker or dealer in the amount of such payment, or any combination of the foregoing, as provided for in the secured demand note agreement.

(F) The term *lender* shall mean the person who lends cash to a broker or dealer pursuant to a subordinated loan agreement and the person who contributes a secured demand note to a broker or dealer pursuant to a secured demand note agreement.

(b) *Minimum Requirements for Subordination Agreements.* (1) Subject to paragraph (a) of this rule, a subordination agreement shall mean a written agreement between the broker or dealer and the lender, which (i) has a minimum term of one year, except for temporary subordination agreements provided for in subparagraph (c)(5) of this Appendix (D), and (ii) is a valid and binding obligation enforceable in accordance with its terms (subject as to enforcement to applicable bankruptcy, insolvency, reorganization, moratorium and other similar laws) against the broker or dealer and the lender and their respective heirs, executors, administrators, successors and assigns.

(2) *Specific Amount.* All subordination agreements shall be for a specific dollar amount which shall not be reduced for the duration of the agreement except by installments as specifically provided for therein and except as otherwise provided in this Appendix (D).

(3) *Effective Subordination.* The subordination agreement shall effectively subordinate any right of the lender to receive any Payment with respect thereto, together with accrued interest or compensation, to the prior payment or provision for payment in full of all claims of all present and future creditors of the broker or dealer arising out of any matter occurring prior to the date on which the related Payment Obligation matures consistent with the provisions of Rule 15c3-1 and Rule 15c3-1d, except for claims which are the subject of subordination agreements which rank on the same priority as or junior to the claim of the lender under such subordination agreements.

(4) *Proceeds of Subordinated Loan Agreements.* The subordinated loan agreement shall provide that the cash proceeds thereof shall be used and dealt with by the broker or dealer as part of its capital and shall be subject to the risks of the business.

(5) *Certain Rights of the Broker or Dealer.* The subordination agreement shall provide that the broker or dealer shall have the right to:

(i) Deposit any cash proceeds of a subordinated loan agreement and any cash pledged as collateral to secure a secured demand note in an account or accounts in its own name in any bank or trust company;

(ii) Pledge, repledge, hypothecate and rehypothecate, any or all of the securities pledged as collateral to secure a secured demand note, without notice, separately or in common with other securities or property for the purpose of securing any indebtedness of the broker or dealer; and

(iii) Lend to itself or others any or all of the securities and cash pledged as collateral to secure a secured demand note.

(6) *Collateral for Secured Demand Notes.* Only cash and securities which are fully paid for and which may be publicly offered or sold without registration under the Securities Act of 1933, and the offer, sale and transfer of which are not otherwise restricted, may be pledged as collateral to secure a secured demand note. The secured demand note agreement shall provide that if at any time the sum of the amount of any cash, plus the Collateral Value of any securities, then pledged as collateral to secure the secured demand note is less than the unpaid principal amount of the secured demand note, the broker or dealer must immediately transmit written notice to that effect to the lender and the Examining Authority for such broker or dealer. The secured demand note agreement shall also require that following such transmittal:

(i) The lender, prior to noon of the business day next succeeding the transmittal of such notice, may pledge as collateral additional cash or securities sufficient, after giving effect to such pledge, to bring the sum of the amount of any cash plus the Collateral Value of any securities, then pledged as collateral to secure the secured demand note, up to an amount not less than the unpaid principal amount of the secured demand note; and

(ii) Unless additional cash or securities are pledged by the lender as provided in paragraph (b)(6)(i) of this rule, the broker or dealer at noon on the business day next succeeding the transmittal of notice to the lender must commence sale, for the account of the lender, of such of the securities then pledged as collateral to secure the secured demand note and apply so much of the net proceeds, thereof, together with such of the cash then pledged as collateral to secure the secured demand note as may be necessary to eliminate the unpaid principal amount of the secured demand note; *Provided, however,* That the unpaid principal amount of the secured demand note need not be reduced below the sum of the amount of any remaining cash, plus the Collateral Value of the remaining securities, then pledged as collateral to secure the secured demand note. The broker or dealer may not purchase for its own account any securities subject to such a sale.

(iii) The secured demand note agreement also may provide that, in lieu of the procedures specified in the provisions required by paragraph (b)(6)(ii) of this rule, the lender with the prior written consent of the broker or dealer and the Examining Authority for the broker or dealer may reduce the unpaid principal amount of the secured demand note. After giving effect to such reduction, the aggregate indebtedness of the broker or dealer may not exceed 1000 percent of its net capital or, in the case of a broker or dealer operating pursuant to paragraph (a)(1)(ii) of Rule 15c3–1, net capital may not be less than 5 percent of aggregate debit items computed in accordance with Rule 15c3–3a, or, if registered as a futures commission merchant, 7 percent of the funds required to be segregated pursuant to the Commodity Exchange Act and the regulations thereunder (less the market value of commodity options purchased by option customers subject to the rules of a contract market, each such deduction not to exceed the amount of funds in the option customer's account), if greater. No single secured demand note shall be permitted to be reduced by more than 15 percent of its original principal amount and after such reduction no excess collateral may be withdrawn. No Examining Authority shall consent to a reduction of the principal amount of a secured demand note if, after giving effect to such reduction, net capital would be less than 120 percent of the minimum dollar amount required by Rule 15c3–1.

(7) *Permissive Prepayments.* A broker or dealer at its option but not at the option of the lender may, if the subordination agreement so provides, make a Payment of all or any portion of the Payment Obligation thereunder prior to the scheduled maturity date of such Payment Obligation (hereinafter referred to as a "Prepayment"), but in no event may any Prepayment be made before the expiration of one year from the date such subordination agreement became effective. This restriction shall not apply to temporary subordination agreements that comply with the provisions of paragraph (c)(5) of this Appendix D. No Prepayment shall be made, if, after giving effect thereto (and to all Payments of Payment Obligations under any other subordinated agreements then outstanding the maturity or accelerated maturities of which are scheduled to fall due within six months after the date such Prepayment is to occur pursuant to this provision or on or prior to the date on which the Payment Obligation in respect of such Prepayment is scheduled to mature disregarding this provision, whichever date is earlier) without reference to any projected profit or loss of the broker or dealer, either aggregate indebtedness of the broker or dealer would exceed 1000 percent of its net capital or its net capital would be less than 120 percent of the minimum dollar amount required by Rule 15c3–1 or, in the case of a broker or dealer operating pursuant to paragraph (a)(1)(ii) of Rule 15c3–1, its net capital would be less than 5 percent of its aggregate debit items computed in accordance with Rule 15c3–3a, or if registered as a futures commission merchant, 7 percent of the funds required to be segregated pursuant to the Commodity Exchange Act and the regulations thereunder (less the market value of commodity options purchased by option customers subject to the rules of a contract market, each such deduction not to exceed the amount of funds in the option customer's account), if greater, or its net capital would be less than 120 percent of the minimum dollar amount required by paragraph (a)(1)(ii) of Rule 15c3–1. Notwithstanding the above, no Prepayment shall occur without the prior written approval of the Examining Authority for such broker or dealer.

(8) *Suspended Repayment.* (i) The Payment obligation of the broker or dealer in respect of any

subordination agreement shall be suspended and shall not mature, if, after giving effect to Payment of such Payment Obligation (and to all Payments of Payment Obligations of such broker or dealer under any other subordination agreement(s) then outstanding that are scheduled to mature on or before such Payment Obligation) either (A) the aggregate indebtedness of the broker or dealer would exceed 1200 percent of its net capital or, in the case of a broker or dealer operating pursuant to paragraph (a)(1)(ii) of Rule 15c3–1, its net capital would be less than 5 percent of aggregate debit items computed in accordance with Rule 15c3–3a or, if registered as a futures commission merchant, 6 percent of the funds required to be segregated pursuant to the Commodity Exchange Act and the regulations thereunder (less the market value of commodity options purchased by option customers on or subject to the rules of a contract market, each such deduction not to exceed the amount of funds in the option customer's account) if greater, or (B) its net capital would be less than 120 percent of the minimum dollar amount required by Rule 15c3–1 including paragraph (a)(1)(ii), if applicable. The subordination agreement may provide that if the Payment Obligation of the broker or dealer thereunder does not mature and is suspended as a result of the requirement of this paragraph (b)(8) for a period of not less than six months, the broker or dealer shall thereupon commence the rapid and orderly liquidation of its business but the right of the lender to receive Payment, together with accrued interest or compensation, shall remain subordinate as required by the provisions of Rule 15c3–1 and Rule 15c3–1d.

(9) *Accelerated Maturity-Obligation to Repay to Remain Subordinate.* (i) Subject to the provisions of subparagraph (b)(8) of this Appendix, a subordination agreement may provide that the lender may, upon prior written notice to the broker or dealer and the Examining Authority given not earlier than six months after the effective date of such subordination agreement, accelerate the date on which the Payment Obligation of the broker or dealer, together with accrued interest or compensation, is scheduled to mature to a date not earlier than six months after the giving of such notice, but the right of the lender to receive Payment, together with accrued interest or compensation, shall remain subordinate as required by the provisions of Rule 15c3–1 and Rule 15c3–1d.

(ii) Notwithstanding the provisions of subparagraph (b)(8) of this Appendix, the Payment Obligation of the broker or dealer with respect to a subordination agreement, together with accrued interest and compensation, shall mature in the event of any receivership, insolvency, liquidation pursuant to the Securities Investor Protection Act of 1970 or otherwise, bankruptcy, assignment for the benefit of creditors, reorganization whether or not pursuant to the bankruptcy laws, or any other marshalling of the assets and liabilities of the broker or dealer but the right of the lender to receive Payment, together with accrued interest or compensation, shall remain subordinate as required by the provisions of Rule 15c3–1 and Rule 15c3–1d.

(10)(i) *Accelerated Maturity of Subordination Agreements on Event of Default and Event of Acceleration—Obligation to Repay to Remain Subordinate.* A subordination agreement may provide that the lender may, upon prior written notice to the broker or dealer and the Examining Authority of the broker or dealer of the occurrence of any Event of Acceleration (as hereinafter defined) given no sooner than six months after the effective date of such subordination agreement, accelerate the date on which the Payment Obligation of the broker or dealer, together with accrued interest or compensation, is scheduled to mature, to the last business day of a calendar month which is not less than six months after notice of acceleration is received by the broker or dealer and the Examining Authority for the broker or dealer. Any subordination agreement containing such Events of Acceleration may also provide, that if upon such accelerated maturity date the Payment Obligation of the broker or dealer is suspended as required by subparagraph (b)(8) of this Appendix (D) and liquidation of the broker or dealer has not commenced on or prior to such accelerated maturity date, then notwithstanding subparagraph (b)(8) of this appendix the Payment Obligation of the broker or dealer with respect to such subordination agreement shall mature on the day immediately following such accelerated maturity date and in any such event the Payment Obligations of the broker or dealer with respect to all other subordination agreements then outstanding shall also mature at the same time but the rights of the respective lenders to receive Payment, together with accrued interest or compensation, shall remain subordinate as required by the provisions of this Appendix (D). Events of Acceleration which may be included in a subordination agreement complying with this paragraph (b)(10) shall be limited to:

(A) Failure to pay interest or any installment of principal on a subordination agreement as scheduled;

(B) Failure to pay when due other money obligations of a specified material amount;

(C) Discovery that any material, specified representation or warranty of the broker or dealer which is included in the subordination agreement and on which the subordination agreement was based or continued was inaccurate in a material respect at the time made;

(D) Any specified and clearly measurable event which is included in the subordination agreement and which the lender and the broker or dealer agree (1) is a significant indication that the financial position of the broker or dealer has changed materially and adversely from agreed upon specified norms or (2) could materially and adversely affect the ability of the broker or dealer to conduct its business as conducted on the date the subordination agreement was made; or (3) is a significant change in the senior management of the broker or dealer or in the general business conducted by the broker or dealer from that which obtained on the date the subordination agreement became effective;

(E) Any continued failure to perform agreed covenants included in the subordination agreement relating to the conduct of the business of the broker or dealer or relating to the maintenance and reporting of its financial position; and

(ii) Notwithstanding the provisions of subparagraph (b)(8) of this Appendix, a subordination agreement may, *provide,* That, if liquidation of the business of the broker or dealer has not already commenced, the Payment Obligation of the broker or dealer shall mature, together with accrued interest or compensation, upon the occurrence of an Event of Default (as hereinafter defined). Such agreement may also, provide, that, if liquidation of the business of the broker or dealer has not already commenced, the rapid and orderly liquidation of the business of the broker or dealer shall then commence upon the happening of an Event of Default. Any subordination agreement which so provides for maturity of the Payment Obligation upon the occurrence of an Event of Default shall also, *provide,* That the date on which such Event of Default occurs shall, if liquidation of the broker or dealer has not already commenced, be the date on which the Payment Obligations of the broker or dealer with respect to all other subordination agreements then outstanding shall mature but the rights of the respective lenders to receive Payment, together with accrued interest or compensation, shall remain subordinate as required by the provisions of this Appendix (D). Events of Default which may be included in a subordination agreement shall be limited to:

(A) The making of an application by the Securities Investor Protection Corporation for a decree adjudicating that customers of the broker or dealer are in need of protection under the Securities Investor Protection Act of 1970 and the failure of the broker or dealer to obtain the dismissal of such application within 30 days;

(B) The aggregate indebtedness of the broker or dealer exceeding 1500 percent of its net capital or, in the case of a broker or dealer that has elected to operate under paragraph (a)(1)(ii) of Rule 15c3–1, its net capital computed in accordance therewith is less than 2 percent of its aggregate debit items computed in accordance with Rule 15c3–3a or, if registered as a futures commission merchant, 4 percent of the funds required to be segregated pursuant to the Commodity Exchange Act and the regulations thereunder (less the market value of commodity options purchased by option customers on or subject to the rules of a contract market, each such deduction not to exceed the amount of funds in the option customer's account), if greater, throughout a period of 15 consecutive business days, commencing on the day the broker or dealer first determines and notifies the Examining Authority for the broker or dealer, or the Examining Authority or the Commission first determines and notifies the broker or dealer of such fact;

(C) The Commission shall revoke the registration of the broker or dealer;

(D) The Examining Authority shall suspend (and not reinstate within 10 days) or revoke the broker's or dealer's status as a member thereof;

(E) Any receivership, insolvency, liquidation pursuant to the Securities Investor Protection Act of 1970 or otherwise, bankruptcy, assignment for the benefit of creditors, reorganization whether or not pursuant to bankruptcy laws, or any other marshalling of the assets and liabilities of the broker or dealer.

A subordination agreement which contains any of the provisions permitted by this subparagraph (b)(10) shall not contain the provision otherwise permitted by clause (i) of subparagraph (b)(9).

(11) *Brokers and Dealers Carrying the Accounts of Specialists and Market Makers in Listed Options.* A subordination agreement which becomes effective on or after August 1, 1977 in favor of a broker or dealer who guarantees, endorses, carries or clears specialist or market maker transactions in options listed on a national securities exchange or facility of a national securities association shall provide that reduction, prepayment or repayment of the unpaid principal amount thereof, pursuant to those terms of the agreement required or permitted by paragraphs (b)(6)(iii), (b)(7) or (b)(8)(i) of this rule, shall not occur in contravention of paragraphs (a)(6)(v), (a)(7)(iv) or (c)(2)(x)(B)(1) or Rule 15c3–1 insofar as they apply to such broker or dealer.

(c) *Miscellaneous Provisions.* (1) *Prohibited Cancellation.* The subordination agreement shall not be subject to cancellation by either party; no Payment shall be made with respect thereto and the agreement shall not be terminated, rescinded or modified by mutual consent or otherwise if the effect thereof would be inconsistent with the requirements of Rule 15c3–1 and Rule 15c3–1d.

(2) Every broker or dealer shall immediately notify the Examining Authority for such broker or dealer if, after giving effect to all Payments of Payment Obligations under subordination agreements then outstanding that are then due or mature within the following six months without reference to any projected profit or loss of the broker or dealer, either the aggregate indebtedness of the broker or dealer would exceed 1200 percent of its net capital or its net capital would be less than 120 percent of the minimum dollar amount required by Rule 15c3–1, or, in the case of a broker or dealer operating pursuant to paragraph (a)(1)(ii) of Rule 15c3–1, its net capital would be less than 5 percent of aggregate debit items computed in accordance with Rule 15c3–3a, or, if registered as a futures commission merchant, 6 percent of the funds required to be segregated pursuant to the Commodity Exchange Act and the regulations thereunder (less the market value of commodity options purchased by option customers on or subject to the rules of a contract market, each such deduction not to exceed the amount of funds in the option customer's account) if greater, or less than 120 percent of the minimum dollar amount required by paragraph (a)(1)(ii) of Rule 15c3–1.

(3) *Certain Legends.* If all the provisions of a satisfactory subordination agreement do not appear in a single instrument, then the debenture or other evidence of indebtedness shall bear on its face an appropriate legend stating that it is issued subject to the provisions of a satisfactory subordination agreement which shall be adequately referred to and incorporated by reference.

(4) *Legal Title to Securities.* All securities pledged as collateral to secure a secured demand note must be in bearer form, or registered in the name of the broker or dealer or the name of its nominee or custodian.

(5)(i) *Temporary and Revolving Subordination Agreements.* For the purpose of enabling a broker or dealer to participate as an underwriter of securities or other extraordinary activities in compliance with the net capital requirements of Rule 15c3–1, a broker or dealer shall be permitted, on no more than three occasions in any 12 month period, to enter into a subordination agreement on a temporary basis that has a stated term of no more than 45 days from the date such subordination agreement became effective. This temporary relief shall not apply to a broker or dealer if, within the preceding thirty calendar days, it has given notice pursuant to Rule 17a–11, or if immediately prior to entering into such subordination agreement, either:

(A) The aggregate indebtedness of the broker or dealer exceeds 1000 percent of its net capital or its net capital is less than 120 percent of the minimum dollar amount required by Rule 15c3–1, or

(B) In the case of a broker or dealer operating pursuant to paragraph (a)(1)(ii) of Rule 15c3–1, its net capital is less than 5 percent of aggregated debits computed in accordance with Rule 15c3–3a or, if registered as a futures commission merchant, less than 7 percent of the funds required to be segregated pursuant to the Commodity Exchange Act and the regulations thereunder (less the market value of commodity options purchased by option customers on or subject to the rules of a contract market, each such deduction not to exceed the amount of funds in the option customer's account), if greater, or less than

120 percent of the minimum dollar amount required by paragraph (a)(1)(ii) of this rule, or

(C) The amount of its then outstanding subordination agreements exceeds the limits specified in paragraph (d) of Rule 15c3–1. Such temporary subordination agreement shall be subject to all other provisions this Appendix D.

(ii) A broker or dealer shall be permitted to enter into a revolving subordinated loan agreement which provides for prepayment within less than one year of all or any portion of the Payment Obligation thereunder at the option of the broker or dealer upon the prior written approval of the Examining Authority for the broker or dealer. The Examining Authority, however, shall not approve any prepayment if:

(A) After giving effect thereto (and to all Payments of Payment Obligations under any other subordinated agreements then outstanding, the maturity or accelerated maturities of which are scheduled to fall due within six months after the date such prepayment is to occur pursuant to this provision or on or prior to the date on which the Payment Obligation in respect of such prepayment is scheduled to mature disregarding this provision, whichever date is earlier) without reference to any projected profit or loss of the broker or dealer, either aggregate indebtedness of the broker or dealer would exceed 900 percent of its net capital or its net capital would be less than 200 percent of the minimum dollar amount required by Rule 15c3–1 or, in the case of a broker or dealer operating pursuant to paragraph (a)(1)(ii) of Rule 15c3–1, its net capital would be less than 6 percent of the aggregate debit items computed in accordance with Rule 15c3–3a or, if registered as a futures commission merchant, 10 percent of the funds required to be segregated pursuant to the Commodity Exchange Act and the regulations thereunder (less the market value of commodity options purchased by option customers on or subject to the rules of a contract market, each such deduction not to exceed the amount of funds in the option customer's account), if greater, or its net capital would be less than 200 percent of the minimum dollar amount required by paragraph (a)(1)(ii) of this rule, or

(B) Pre-tax losses during the latest three-month period equalled more than 15 percent of current excess net capital. Any subordination agreement entered into pursuant to this paragraph (c)(5)(ii) shall be subject to all the other provisions of this Appendix D. Any such subordination agreement shall not be considered equity for purposes of subsection (d) of Rule 15c3–1, despite the length of the initial term of the loan.

(6)(i) *Filing.* Two copies of any proposed subordination agreement (including nonconforming subordination agreements) shall be filed at least 10 days prior to the proposed execution date of the agreement with the Commission's Regional Office for the region in which the broker or dealer maintains its principal place of business or at such other time as the Regional Office for good cause shall accept such filing. Copies of the proposed agreement shall also be filed with the Examining Authority in such quantities and at such time as the Examining Authority may require. The broker or dealer shall also file with said parties a statement setting forth the name and address of the lender, the business relationship of the lender to the broker or dealer, and whether the broker or dealer carried funds or securities for the lender at or about the time the proposed agreement was so filed. All agreements shall be examined by the Commission's Regional Office or the Examining Authority with whom such agreement is required to be filed prior to their becoming effective. No proposed agreement shall be a satisfactory subordination agreement for the purposes of this section unless and until the Examining Authority has found the agreement acceptable and such agreement has become effective in the form found acceptable.

(ii) The broker or dealer need not file with the Regional Office for the region in which the broker or dealer maintains its principal place of business (if a Regional Office is not its Examining Authority) copies of any proposed subordination agreement or the statement described above if the Examining Authority for that broker or dealer has consented to file with the Commission periodic reports (not less than monthly) summarizing for the period, on a firm-by-firm basis, the subordination agreements it has approved for that period. Such reports should include at the minimum, the amount of the loan and its duration, the name of the lender and the business relationship of the lender to the broker or dealer.

(7) *Subordination Agreements in Effect Prior to Adoption.* Any subordination agreement which has been entered into prior to December 20, 1978 and which has been deemed to be satisfactorily subordinated pursuant to Rule 15c3–1 as in effect prior to December 20, 1978, shall continue to be deemed a satisfactory subordination agreement until the maturity of such agreement. *Provided,* That no renewal of an agreement which provides for automatic or optional renewal by the broker or dealer or lender shall be deemed to be a satisfactory subordination agreement unless such renewed agreement meets the requirements of this Appendix within 6 months from December 20, 1978. *Provided, further,* That all subordination agreements must meet the requirements of this Appendix within 5 years of December 20, 1978.

Rule 15c3–1e. Deductions for market and credit risk for certain brokers or dealers (Appendix E to Rule 15c3–1)

PRELIMINARY NOTE:

Appendices E and G to the net capital rule set forth a program that allows a broker or dealer to use an alternative approach to computing net capital deductions, subject to the conditions described in the Appendices, including supervision of the broker's or dealer's ultimate holding company under the program. The program is designed to reduce the likelihood that financial and operational weakness in the holding company will destabilize the broker or dealer, or the broader financial system. The focus of this supervision of the ultimate holding company is its financial and operational condition and its risk management controls and methodologies.

(a) *Application.* A broker or dealer may apply to the Commission for authorization to compute deductions for market risk pursuant to this Appendix E in lieu of computing deductions pursuant to Rule 15c3–1(c)(2)(vi) and (c)(2)(vii) and to compute deductions for credit risk pursuant to this Appendix E on credit exposures arising from transactions in derivatives instruments (if this Appendix E is used to calculate deductions for market risk on these instruments) in lieu of computing deductions pursuant to Rule 15c3–1(c)(2)(iv):

(1) A broker-dealer shall submit the following information to the Commission with its application:

(i) An executive summary of the information provided to the Commission with its application and an identification of the ultimate holding company of the broker or dealer;

(ii) A comprehensive description of the internal risk management control system of the broker or dealer and how that system satisfies the requirements set forth in Rule 15c3–4;

(iii) A list of the categories of positions that the broker or dealer holds in its proprietary accounts and a brief description of the methods that the broker or dealer will use to calculate deductions for market and credit risk on those categories of positions;

(iv) A description of the mathematical models to be used to price positions and to compute deductions for market risk, including those portions of the deductions attributable to specific risk, if applicable, and deductions for credit risk; a description of the creation, use, and maintenance of the mathematical models; a description of the broker's or dealer's internal risk management controls over those models, including a description of each category of persons who may input data into the models; if a mathematical model incorporates empirical correlations across risk categories, a description of the process for measuring correlations; a description of the backtesting procedures the broker or dealer will use to backtest the mathematical model used to calculate maximum potential exposure; a description of how each mathematical model satisfies the applicable qualitative and quantitative requirements set forth in paragraph (d) of this Appendix E; and a statement describing the extent to which each mathematical model used to compute deductions for market and credit risk will be used as part of the risk analyses and reports presented to senior management;

(v) If the broker or dealer is applying to the Commission for approval to use scenario analysis to calculate deductions for market risk for certain positions, a list of those types of positions, a description of how those deductions will be calculated using scenario analysis, and an explanation of why each scenario analysis is appropriate to calculate deductions for market risk on those types of positions;

(vi) A description of how the broker or dealer will calculate current exposure;

(vii) A description of how the broker or dealer will determine internal credit ratings of counterparties and internal credit risk weights of counterparties, if applicable;

(viii) A written undertaking by the ultimate holding company of the broker or dealer, if it is not an ultimate holding company that has a principal regulator, in a form acceptable to the Commission, signed by a duly authorized person at the ultimate holding company, to the effect that, as a condition of Commission approval of the application of the broker or dealer to compute deductions for market and credit risk pursuant to this Appendix E, the ultimate holding company agrees to:

(A) Comply with all applicable provisions of this Appendix E;

(B) Comply with all applicable provisions of Rule 15c3–1g;

(C) Comply with the provisions of Rule 15c3–4 with respect to an internal risk management control system for the affiliate group as though it were an OTC derivatives dealer with respect to all of its business activities, except that paragraphs (c)(5)(xiii), (c)(5)(xiv), (d)(8), and (d)(9) of Rule 15c3–4 shall not apply;

(D) As part of the internal risk management control system for the affiliate group, establish, document, and maintain procedures for the detection and prevention of money laundering and terrorist financing;

(E) Permit the Commission to examine the books and records of the ultimate holding company and any of its affiliates, if the affiliate is not an entity that has a principal regulator;

(F) If the disclosure to the Commission of any information required as a condition for the broker or dealer to compute deductions for market and credit risk pursuant to this Appendix E could be prohibited by law or otherwise, cooperate with the Commission, to the extent permissible, including by describing any secrecy laws or other impediments that could restrict the ability of material affiliates to provide information on their operations or activities and by discussing the manner in which the ultimate holding company and the broker or dealer propose to provide the Commission with adequate information or assurances of access to information;

(G) Make available to the Commission information about the ultimate holding company or any of its material affiliates that the Commission finds is necessary to evaluate the financial and operational risk within the ultimate holding company and its material affiliates and to evaluate compliance with the conditions of eligibility of the broker or dealer to compute deductions to net capital under the alternative method of this Appendix E;

(H) Make available examination reports of principal regulators for those affiliates of the ultimate holding company that are not subject to Commission examination; and

(I) Acknowledge that, if the ultimate holding company fails to comply in a material manner with any provision of its undertaking, the Commission may, in addition to any other conditions necessary or appropriate in the public interest or for the protection of investors, increase the multiplication factors the ultimate holding company uses to calculate allowances for market and credit risk, as defined in Rule 15c3–1g(a)(2) and (a)(3) or impose any condition with respect to the broker or dealer listed in paragraph (e) of this Appendix E; and

(ix) A written undertaking by the ultimate holding company of the broker or dealer, if the ultimate holding company has a principal regulator, in a form acceptable to the Commission, signed by a duly authorized person at the ultimate holding company, to the effect that, as a condition of Commission approval of the application of the broker or dealer to compute deductions for market and credit risk pursuant to this Appendix E, the ultimate holding company agrees to:

(A) Comply with all applicable provisions of this Appendix E;

(B) Comply with all applicable provisions of Rule 15c3–1g;

(C) Make available to the Commission information about the ultimate holding company that the Commission finds is necessary to evaluate the financial and operational risk within the ultimate holding company and to evaluate compliance with the conditions of eligibility of the broker or dealer to compute net capital under the alternative method of this Appendix E; and

(D) Acknowledge that if the ultimate holding company fails to comply in a material manner with any provision of its undertaking, the Commission may, in addition to any other conditions necessary or appropriate in the public interest or for the protection of investors, impose any condition with respect to the broker or dealer listed in paragraph (e) of this Appendix E;

(2) As a condition of Commission approval, the ultimate holding company of the broker or dealer, if it is not an ultimate holding company that has a principal regulator, shall include the following information with the application:

(i) A narrative description of the business and organization of the ultimate holding company;

(ii) An alphabetical list of the affiliates of the ultimate holding company (referred to as the "affiliate group," which shall include the ultimate holding company), with an identification of the financial regulator, if any, that regulates the affiliate, and a designation of the members of the affiliate group that are material to the ultimate holding company ("material affiliates");

(iii) An organizational chart that identifies the ultimate holding company, the broker or dealer, and the material affiliates;

(iv) Consolidated and consolidating financial statements of the ultimate holding company as of the end of the quarter preceding the filing of the application;

(v) Sample computations for the ultimate holding company of allowable capital and allowances for market risk, credit risk, and operational risk, determined pursuant to Rule 15c3–1g(a)(1)–(a)(4);

(vi) A list of the categories of positions that the affiliate group holds in its proprietary accounts and a brief description of the method that the ultimate holding company proposes to use to calculate allowances for market and credit risk, pursuant to Rule 15c3–1g(a)(2) and (a)(3), on those categories of positions;

(vii) A description of the mathematical models to be used to price positions and to compute the allowance for market risk, including those portions of the allowance attributable to specific risk, if applicable, and the allowance for credit risk; a description of the creation, use, and maintenance of the mathematical models; a description of the ultimate holding company's internal risk management controls over those models, including a description of each category of persons who may input data into the models; if a mathematical model incorporates empirical correlations across risk categories, a description of the process for measuring correlations; a description of the backtesting procedures the ultimate holding company will use to backtest the mathematical model used to calculate maximum potential exposure; a description of how each mathematical model satisfies the applicable qualitative and quantitative requirements set forth in paragraph (d) of this Appendix E; a statement describing the extent to which each mathematical model used to compute allowances for market and credit risk is used as part of the risk analyses and reports presented to senior management; and a description of any positions for which the ultimate holding company proposes to use a method other than VaR to compute an allowance for market risk and a description of how that allowance would be determined;

(viii) A description of how the ultimate holding company will calculate current exposure;

(ix) A description of how the ultimate holding company will determine the credit risk weights of counterparties and internal credit ratings of counterparties, if applicable;

(x) A description of how the ultimate holding company will calculate an allowance for operational risk under Rule 15c3–1g(a)(4);

(xi) For each instance in which a mathematical model used by the broker or dealer to calculate a deduction for market risk or to calculate maximum potential exposure for a particular product or counterparty differs from the mathematical model used by the ultimate holding company to calculate an allowance for market risk or to calculate maximum potential exposure for that same product or counterparty, a description of the difference(s) between the mathematical models;

(xii) A comprehensive description of the risk management control system for the affiliate group that the ultimate holding company has established to manage affiliate group-wide risk, including market, credit, liquidity and funding, legal and compliance, and operational risks, and how that system satisfies the requirements of Rule 15c3–4; and

(xiii) Sample risk reports that are provided to the persons at the ultimate holding company who are responsible for managing group-wide risk and that will be provided to the Commission pursuant to Rule 15c3–1g(b)(1)(i)(H);

(3) As a condition of Commission approval, the ultimate holding company of the broker or dealer, if the ultimate holding company has a principal regulator, shall include the following information with the broker's or dealer's application:

(i) A narrative description of the business and organization of the ultimate holding company;

(ii) An alphabetical list of the affiliates of the ultimate holding company (referred to as the "affiliate group," which shall include the ultimate holding company), with an identification of the financial regulator, if any, that regulates the affiliate, and a designation of those affiliates that are material to the ultimate holding company ("material affiliates");

(iii) An organizational chart that identifies the ultimate holding company, the broker or dealer, and the material affiliates;

(iv) Consolidated and consolidating financial statements of the ultimate holding company as of the end of the quarter preceding the filing of the application;

(v) The most recent capital measurements of the ultimate holding company, as reported to its principal regulator, calculated in accordance with the standards published by the Basel Committee on Banking Supervision, as amended from time to time;

(vi) For each instance in which a mathematical model to be used by the broker or dealer to calculate a deduction for market risk or to calculate maximum potential exposure for a particular product or counterparty differs from the mathematical model used by the ultimate holding company to calculate an allowance for market risk or to calculate maximum potential exposure for that same product or counterparty, a description of the difference(s) between the mathematical models; and

(vii) Sample risk reports that are provided to the persons at the ultimate holding company who are responsible for managing group-wide risk and that will be provided to the Commission under Rule 15c3–1g(b)(1)(i)(H);

(4) The application of the broker or dealer shall be supplemented by other information relating to the internal risk management control system, mathematical models, and financial position of the broker or dealer or the ultimate holding company of the broker or dealer that the Commission may request to complete its review of the application;

(5) The application shall be considered filed when received at the Commission's principal office in Washington, DC. A person who files an application pursuant to this section for which it seeks confidential treatment may clearly mark each page or segregable portion of each page with the words "Confidential Treatment Requested." All information submitted in connection with the application will be accorded confidential treatment, to the extent permitted by law;

(6) If any of the information filed with the Commission as part of the application of the broker or dealer is found to be or becomes inaccurate before the Commission approves the application, the broker or dealer must notify the Commission promptly and provide the Commission with a description of the circumstances in which the information was found to be or has become inaccurate along with updated, accurate information;

(7) The Commission may approve the application or an amendment to the application, in whole or in part, subject to any conditions or limitations the Commission may require, if the Commission finds the approval to be necessary or appropriate in the public interest or for the protection of investors, after determining, among other things, whether the broker or dealer has met the requirements of this Appendix E and is in compliance with other applicable rules promulgated under the Act and by self-regulatory organizations, and whether the ultimate holding company of the broker or dealer is in compliance with the terms of its undertakings, as provided to the Commission;

(8) A broker or dealer shall amend its application to calculate certain deductions for market and credit risk under this Appendix E and submit the amendment to the Commission for approval before it may change materially a mathematical model used to calculate market or credit risk or before it may change materially its internal risk management control system;

(9) As a condition to the broker's or dealer's calculation of deductions for market and credit risk under this Appendix E, an ultimate holding company that does not have a principal regulator shall submit to the Commission, as an amendment to the broker's or dealer's application, any material changes to a mathematical model or other methods used to calculate allowances for market, credit, and operational risk, and any material changes to the internal risk management control system for the affiliate group. The ultimate holding com-

pany must submit these material changes to the Commission before making them;

(10) As a condition for the broker or dealer to compute deductions for market and credit risk under this Appendix E, the broker or dealer agrees that:

(i) It will notify the Commission 45 days before it ceases to compute deductions for market and credit risk under this Appendix E; and

(ii) The Commission may determine by order that the notice will become effective after a shorter or longer period of time if the broker or dealer consents or if the Commission determines that a shorter or longer period of time is necessary or appropriate in the public interest or for the protection of investors; and

(11) Notwithstanding paragraph (a)(10) of this rule, the Commission, by order, may revoke a broker's or dealer's exemption that allows it to use the market risk standards of this Appendix E to calculate deductions for market risk, instead of the provisions of Rule 15c3–1(c)(2)(vi) and (c)(2)(vii), and the exemption to use the credit risk standards of this Appendix E to calculate deductions for credit risk on certain credit exposures arising from transactions in derivatives instruments, instead of the provisions of Rule 15c3–1(c)(2)(iv), if the Commission finds that such exemption is no longer necessary or appropriate in the public interest or for the protection of investors. In making its finding, the Commission will consider the compliance history of the broker or dealer related to its use of models, the financial and operational strength of the broker or dealer and its ultimate holding company, the broker's or dealer's compliance with its internal risk management controls, and the ultimate holding company's compliance with its undertakings.

(b) *Market Risk.* A broker or dealer whose application, including amendments, has been approved under paragraph (a) of this Appendix E shall compute a deduction for market risk in an amount equal to the sum of the following:

(1) For positions for which the Commission has approved the broker's or dealer's use of value-at-risk ("VaR") models, the VaR of the positions multiplied by the appropriate multiplication factor determined according to paragraph (d)(1)(iii) of this Appendix E, except that the initial multiplication factor shall be three, unless the Commission determines, based on a review of the broker's or dealer's application or an amendment to the application under paragraph (a) of this Appendix E, including a review of its internal risk management control system and practices and VaR models, that another multiplication factor is appropriate;

(2) For positions for which the VaR model does not incorporate specific risk, a deduction for specific risk to be determined by the Commission based on a review of the broker's or dealer's application or an amendment to the application under paragraph (a) of this Appendix E and the positions involved;

(3) For positions for which the Commission has approved the broker's or dealer's application to use scenario analysis, the greatest loss resulting from a range of adverse movements in relevant risk factors, prices, or spreads designed to represent a negative movement greater than, or equal to, the worst ten-day movement over the four years preceding calculation of the greatest loss, or some multiple of the greatest loss based on the liquidity of the positions subject to scenario analysis. If historical data is insufficient, the deduction shall be the largest loss within a three standard deviation movement in those risk factors, prices, or spreads over a ten-day period, multiplied by an appropriate liquidity adjustment factor. Irrespective of the deduction otherwise indicated under scenario analysis, the resulting deduction for market risk must be at least $25 per 100 share equivalent contract for equity positions, or one-half of one percent of the face value of the contract for all other types of contracts, even if the scenario analysis indicates a lower amount. A qualifying scenario must include the following:

(i) A set of pricing equations for the positions based on, for example, arbitrage relations, statistical analysis, historic relationships, merger evaluation, or fundamental valuation of an offering of securities;

(ii) Auxiliary relationships mapping risk factors to prices; and

(iii) Data demonstrating the effectiveness of the scenario in capturing market risk, including specific risk; and

(4) For all remaining positions, the deductions specified in Rule 15c3–1(c)(2)(vi), (c)(2)(vii), and applicable appendices to Rule 15c3–1.

(c) *Credit Risk.* A broker or dealer whose application, including amendments, has been approved under paragraph (a) of this Appendix E shall compute a deduction for credit risk on transactions in derivative instruments (if this Appendix E is used to calculate a deduction for market risk on those instruments) in an amount equal to the sum of the following:

(1) A counterparty exposure charge in an amount equal to the sum of the following:

(i) The net replacement value in the account of each counterparty that is insolvent, or in bankruptcy, or that has senior unsecured long-term debt in default; and

(ii) For a counterparty not otherwise described in paragraph (c)(1)(i) of this Appendix E, the credit equivalent amount of the broker's or dealer's exposure to the counterparty, as defined in paragraph (c)(4)(i) of this Appendix E, multiplied by the credit risk weight of the counterparty, as defined in paragraph (c)(4)(vi) of this Appendix E, multiplied by 8%;

(2) A concentration charge by counterparty in an amount equal to the sum of the following:

(i) For each counterparty with a credit risk weight of 20% or less, 5% of the amount of the current exposure to the counterparty in excess of 5% of the tentative net capital of the broker or dealer;

(ii) For each counterparty with a credit risk weight of greater than 20% but less than 50%, 20% of the amount of the current exposure to the counterparty in excess of 5% of the tentative net capital of the broker or dealer; and

(iii) For each counterparty with a credit risk weight of greater than 50%, 50% of the amount of the current exposure to the counterparty in excess of 5% of the tentative net capital of the broker or dealer; and

(3) A portfolio concentration charge of 100% of the amount of the broker's or dealer's aggregate current exposure for all counterparties in excess of 50% of the tentative net capital of the broker or dealer;

(4) *Terms.* (i) The credit equivalent amount of the broker's or dealer's exposure to a counterparty is the sum of the broker's or dealer's maximum potential exposure to the counterparty, as defined in paragraph (c)(4)(ii) of this Appendix E, multiplied by the appropriate multiplication factor, and the broker's or dealer's current exposure to the counterparty, as defined in paragraph (c)(4)(iii) of this Appendix E. The broker or dealer must use the multiplication factor determined according to paragraph (d)(1)(v) of this Appendix E, except that the initial multiplication factor shall be one, unless the Commission determines, based on a review of the broker's or dealer's application or an amendment to the application approved under paragraph (a) of this Appendix E, including a review of its internal risk management control system and practices and VaR models, that another multiplication factor is appropriate;

(ii) The *maximum potential exposure* is the VaR of the counterparty's positions with the broker or dealer, after applying netting agreements with the counterparty meeting the requirements of paragraph (c)(4)(iv) of this Appendix E, taking into account the value of collateral from the counterparty held by the broker or dealer in accordance with paragraph (c)(4)(v) of this Appendix E, and taking into account the current replacement value of the counterparty's positions with the broker or dealer;

(iii) The *current exposure* of the broker or dealer to a counterparty is the current replacement value of the counterparty's positions with the broker or dealer, after applying netting agreements with the counterparty meeting the requirements of paragraph (c)(4)(iv) of this Appendix E and taking into account the value of collateral from the counterparty held by the broker or dealer in accordance with paragraph (c)(4)(v) of this Appendix E;

(iv) *Netting Agreements.* A broker or dealer may include the effect of a netting agreement that allows the broker or dealer to net gross receivables from and gross payables to a counterparty upon default of the counterparty if:

(A) The netting agreement is legally enforceable in each relevant jurisdiction, including in insolvency proceedings;

(B) The gross receivables and gross payables that are subject to the netting agreement with a counterparty can be determined at any time; and

(C) For internal risk management purposes, the broker-dealer monitors and controls its exposure to the counterparty on a net basis;

(v) *Collateral.* When calculating maximum potential exposure and current exposure to a counterparty, the fair market value of collateral pledged and held may be taken into account provided:

(A) The collateral is marked to market each day and is subject to a daily margin maintenance requirement;

(B) The collateral is subject to the broker's or dealer's physical possession or control;

(C) The collateral is liquid and transferable;

(D) The collateral may be liquidated promptly by the firm without intervention by any other party;

(E) The collateral agreement is legally enforceable by the broker or dealer against the counterparty and any other parties to the agreement;

(F) The collateral does not consist of securities issued by the counterparty or a party related to the broker or dealer or to the counterparty;

(G) The Commission has approved the broker's or dealer's use of a VaR model to calculate deductions for market risk for the type of collateral in accordance with this Appendix E; and

(H) The collateral is not used in determining the credit rating of the counterparty;

(vi) *Credit risk weights of counterparties.* A broker or dealer that computes its deductions for credit risk pursuant to this Appendix E shall apply a credit risk weight for transactions with a counterparty of either 20%, 50%, or 150% based on an internal credit rating the broker or dealer determines for the counterparty.

(A) As part of its initial application or in an amendment, the broker or dealer may request Commission approval to apply a credit risk weight of either 20%, 50%, or 150% based on internal calculations of credit ratings, including internal estimates of the maturity adjustment. Based on the strength of the broker's or dealer's internal credit risk management system, the Commission may approve the application. The broker or dealer must make and keep current a record of the basis for the credit rating of each counterparty;

(B) For the portion of a current exposure covered by a written guarantee where that guarantee is an unconditional and irrevocable guarantee of the due and punctual payment and performance of the obligation and the broker or dealer can demand immediate payment from the guarantor after any payment is missed without having to make collection efforts, the broker or dealer may substitute the credit risk weight of the guarantor for the credit risk weight of the counterparty; and

(C) As part of its initial application or in an amendment, the broker or dealer may request Commission approval to reduce deductions for credit risk through the use of credit derivatives.

(d) *VaR Models.* To be approved, each VaR model must meet the following minimum qualitative and quantitative requirements:

(1) *Qualitative Requirements.* (i) The VaR model used to calculate market or credit risk for a position must be integrated into the daily internal risk management system of the broker or dealer;

(ii) The VaR model must be reviewed both periodically and annually. The periodic review may be conducted by the broker's or dealer's internal audit staff, but the annual review must be conducted by a registered public accounting firm, as that term is defined in section 2(a)(12) of the Sarbanes–Oxley Act of 2002 (15 U.S.C. 7201 *et seq.*); and

(iii) For purposes of computing market risk, the broker or dealer must determine the appropriate multiplication factor as follows:

(A) Beginning three months after the broker or dealer begins using the VaR model to calculate market risk, the broker or dealer must conduct backtesting of the model by comparing its actual daily net trading profit or loss with the corresponding VaR measure generated by the VaR model, using a 99 percent, one-tailed confidence level with price changes equivalent to a one business-day movement in rates and prices, for each of the past 250 business days, or other period as may be appropriate for the first year of its use;

(B) On the last business day of each quarter, the broker or dealer must identify the number of backtesting exceptions of the VaR model, that is, the number of business days in the past 250 business days, or other period as may be appropriate for the first year of its use, for which the actual net trading loss, if any, exceeds the corresponding VaR measure; and

(C) The broker or dealer must use the multiplication factor indicated in Table 1 of this Appendix E in determining its market risk until it obtains the next quarter's backtesting results;

TABLE 1—MULTIPLICATION FACTOR BASED ON THE NUMBER OF BACKTESTING EXCEPTIONS OF THE VAR MODEL

Number of exceptions	Multiplication factor
4 or fewer	3.00
5	3.40
6	3.50
7	3.65
8	3.75
9	3.85
10 or more	4.00

(iv) For purposes of incorporating specific risk into a VaR model, a broker or dealer must demonstrate that it has methodologies in place to capture liquidity, event, and default risk adequately for each position. Furthermore, the models used to calculate deductions for specific risk must:

(A) Explain the historical price variation in the portfolio;

(B) Capture concentration (magnitude and changes in composition);

(C) Be robust to an adverse environment; and

(D) Be validated through backtesting; and

(v) For purposes of computing the credit equivalent amount of the broker's or dealer's exposures to a counterparty, the broker or dealer must determine the appropriate multiplication factor as follows:

(A) Beginning three months after it begins using the VaR model to calculate maximum potential exposure, the broker or dealer must conduct backtesting of the model by comparing, for at least 80 counterparties with widely varying types and sizes of positions with the firm, the ten-business day change in its current exposure to the counterparty based on its positions held at the beginning of the ten-business day period with the corresponding ten-business day maximum potential exposure for the counterparty generated by the VaR model;

(B) As of the last business day of each quarter, the broker or dealer must identify the number of backtesting exceptions of the VaR model, that is, the number of ten-business day periods in the past 250 business days, or other period as may be appropriate for the first year of its use, for which the change in current exposure to a counterparty exceeds the corresponding maximum potential exposure; and

(C) The broker or dealer will propose, as part of its application, a schedule of multiplication factors, which must be approved by the Commission based on the number of backtesting exceptions of the VaR model. The broker or dealer must use the multiplication factor indicated in the approved schedule in determining the credit equivalent amount of its exposures to a counterparty until it obtains the next quarter's backtesting results, unless the Commission determines, based on, among other relevant factors, a review of the broker's or dealer's internal risk management control system, including a review of the VaR model, that a different adjustment or other action is appropriate;

(2) *Quantitative Requirements.* (i) For purposes of determining market risk, the VaR model must use a 99 percent, one-tailed confidence level with price changes equivalent to a ten business-day movement in rates and prices;

(ii) For purposes of determining maximum potential exposure, the VaR model must use a 99 percent, one-tailed confidence level with price changes equivalent to a one-year movement in rates and prices; or based on a review of the broker's or dealer's procedures for managing collateral and if the collateral is marked to market daily and the broker or dealer has the ability to call for additional collateral daily, the Commission may approve a time horizon of not less than ten business days;

(iii) The VaR model must use an effective historical observation period of at least one year. The broker or dealer must consider the effects of market stress in its construction of the model. Historical data sets must be updated at least monthly and reassessed whenever market prices or volatilities change significantly; and

(iv) The VaR model must take into account and incorporate all significant, identifiable market risk factors applicable to positions in the accounts of the broker or dealer, including:

(A) Risks arising from the non-linear price characteristics of derivatives and the sensitivity of the market value of those positions to changes in the volatility of the derivatives' underlying rates and prices;

(B) Empirical correlations with and across risk factors or, alternatively, risk factors sufficient to cover all the market risk inherent in the positions in the proprietary or other trading accounts of the broker or dealer, including interest rate risk, equity price risk, foreign exchange risk, and commodity price risk;

(C) Spread risk, where applicable, and segments of the yield curve sufficient to capture differences in volatility and imperfect correlation of rates along the yield curve for securities and derivatives that are sensitive to different interest rates; and

(D) Specific risk for individual positions.

(e) *Additional Conditions*. As a condition for the broker or dealer to use this Appendix E to calculate certain of its capital charges, the Commission may impose additional conditions on the broker or dealer, which may include, but are not limited to restricting the broker's or dealer's business on a product-specific, category-specific, or general basis; submitting to the Commission a plan to increase the broker's or dealer's net capital or tentative net capital; filing more frequent reports with the Commission; modifying the broker's or dealer's internal risk management control procedures; or computing the broker's or dealer's deductions for market and credit risk in accordance with Rule 15c3–1(c)(2)(vi), (c)(2)(vii), and (c)(2)(iv), as appropriate. If it is not an ultimate holding company that has a principal regulator, the Commission also may require, as a condition of continuation of the exemption, the ultimate holding company of the broker or dealer to file more frequent reports or to modify its group-wide internal risk management control procedures. If the Commission finds it is necessary or appropriate in the public interest or for the protection of investors, the Commission may impose additional conditions on either the broker-dealer, or the ultimate holding company, if it is an ultimate holding company that does not have a principal regulator, if:

(1) The broker or dealer is required by Rule 15c3–1(a)(7)(ii) to provide notice to the Commission that the broker's or dealer's tentative net capital is less than $5 billion;

(2) The broker or dealer or the ultimate holding company of the broker or dealer fails to meet the reporting requirements set forth in Rule 17a–5 or Rule 15c3–1g(b), as applicable;

(3) Any event specified in Rule 17a–11 occurs;

(4) There is a material deficiency in the internal risk management control system or in the mathematical models used to price securities or to calculate deductions for market and credit risk or allowances for market and credit risk, as applicable, of the broker or dealer or the ultimate holding company of the broker or dealer;

(5) The ultimate holding company of the broker or dealer fails to comply with its undertakings that the broker or dealer has filed with its application pursuant to paragraph (a)(1)(viii) or (a)(1)(ix) of this Appendix E;

(6) The broker or dealer fails to comply with this Appendix E; or

(7) The Commission finds that imposition of other conditions is necessary or appropriate in the public interest or for the protection of investors.

Rule 15c3–1f. Optional market and credit risk requirements for OTC derivatives dealers (Appendix F to Rule 15c3–1)

(a) *Application Requirements*. An OTC derivatives dealer may apply to the Commission for authorization to compute capital charges for market and credit risk pursuant to this Appendix F in lieu of computing securities haircuts pursuant to Rule 15c3–1(c)(2)(vi).

(1) An OTC derivatives dealer's application shall contain the following information:

(i) *Executive Summary*. An OTC derivatives dealer shall include in its application an Executive Summary of information provided to the Commission.

(ii) *Description of Methods for Computing Market Risk Charges*. An OTC derivatives dealer shall provide a description of all statistical models used for pricing OTC derivative instruments and for computing value-at-risk ("VAR"), a description of the applicant's controls over those models, and a statement regarding whether the firm has developed its own internal VAR models. If the OTC derivatives dealer's VAR model incorporates empirical correlations across risk categories, the dealer shall describe its process for measuring correlations and describe the qualitative and quantitative aspects of the model which at a minimum must adhere to the criteria set forth in paragraph (e) of this Appendix F. The application shall further state whether the OTC derivatives dealer intends to use an alternative method for computing its market risk charge for equity instruments and, if applicable, a description of how its own theoretical pricing model contains the minimum pricing factors set forth in Appendix A (Rule 15c3–1a). The application shall also describe any category of securities having no ready market or any category of debt securities which are below investment grade for which the OTC derivatives dealer wishes to use its VAR model to calculate its market risk charge or for which it wishes to use an alternative method for computing this charge and a description of how those charges would be determined.

(iii) *Internal Risk Management Control Systems.* An OTC derivatives dealer shall provide a comprehensive description of its internal risk management control systems and how those systems adhere to the requirements set forth in Rule 15c3–4(a) through (d).

(2) The Commission may approve the application after reviewing the application to determine whether the OTC derivatives dealer:

(i) Has adopted internal risk management control systems that meet the requirements set forth in Rule 15c3–4; and

(ii) Has adopted a VAR model that meets the requirements set forth in paragraphs (e)(1) and (e)(2) of this Appendix F.

(3) If the OTC derivatives dealer materially amends its VAR model or internal risk management control systems as described in its application, including any material change in the categories of non-marketable securities that it wishes to include in its VAR model, the dealer shall file an application describing the changes which must be approved by the Commission before the changes may be implemented. After reviewing the application for changes to the dealer's VAR model or internal risk management control systems to determine whether, with the changes, the OTC derivatives dealer's VAR model and internal risk management control systems would meet the requirements set forth in this Appendix F and Rule 15c3–4, the Commission may approve the application.

(4) The applications provided for in this paragraph (a) shall be considered filed when received at the Commission's principal office in Washington, DC. All applications filed pursuant to this paragraph (a) shall be deemed to be confidential.

(b) *Compliance with Rule 15c3–4.* An OTC derivatives dealer must be in compliance in all material respects with Rule 15c3–4 regarding its internal risk management control systems in order to be in compliance with Rule 15c3–1.

(c) *Market Risk.* An OTC derivatives dealer electing to apply this Appendix F shall compute a capital charge for market risk which shall be the aggregate of the charges computed below:

(1) *Value-at-Risk.* An OTC derivatives dealer shall deduct from net worth an amount for market risk for eligible OTC derivative instruments and other positions in its proprietary or other accounts equal to the VAR of these positions obtained from its proprietary VAR model, multiplied by the appropriate multiplication factor in paragraph (e)(1)(iv)(C) of this Appendix F. The OTC derivatives dealer may not elect to calculate its capital charges under this paragraph (c)(1) until its application to use the VAR model has been approved by the Commission.

(2) *Alternative Method for Equities.* An OTC derivatives dealer may elect to use this alternative method to calculate its market risk for equity instruments, including OTC options, upon approval by the Commission on application by the dealer. Under this alternative method, the deduction for market risk must be the amount computed pursuant to Appendix A to Rule 15c3–1. In this computation, the OTC derivatives dealer may use its own theoretical pricing model provided that it contains the minimum pricing factors set forth in Appendix A.

(3) *Non–Marketable Securities.* An OTC derivatives dealer may not use a VAR model to determine a capital charge for any category of securities having no ready market or any category of debt securities which are below investment grade or any derivative instrument based on the value of these categories of securities, unless the Commission has granted, pursuant to paragraph (a)(1) of this Appendix F, its application to use its VAR model for any such category of securities. The dealer in any event may apply, pursuant to paragraph (a)(1) of this Appendix F, for an alternative treatment for any such category of securities, rather than calculate the market risk capital charge for such category of securities under Rule 15c3–1(c)(2)(vi) and (vii).

(4) *Residual Positions.* To the extent that a position has not been included in the calculation of the market risk charge in paragraphs (c)(1) through (c)(3) of this rule, the market risk charge for the

position shall be computed under Rule 15c3–1(c)(2)(vi).

(d) *Credit Risk.* The capital charge for credit risk arising from an OTC derivatives dealer's transactions in eligible OTC derivative instruments shall be:

(1) The net replacement value in the account of a counterparty (including the effect of legally enforceable netting agreements and the application of liquid collateral) that is insolvent, or in bankruptcy, or that has senior unsecured long-term debt in default;

(2) As to a counterparty not otherwise described in paragraph (d)(1) of this rule, the net replacement value in the account of the counterparty (including the effect of legally enforceable netting agreements and the application of liquid collateral) multiplied by 8%, and further multiplied by a counterparty factor of 20%, 50%, or 100% based on an internal credit rating the OTC derivatives dealer determines for the counterparty; and

(3) A concentration charge where the net replacement value in the account of any one counterparty (other than a counterparty described in paragraph (d)(1) of this section) exceeds 25% of the OTC derivatives dealer's tentative net capital, calculated as follows:

(i) For counterparties for which an OTC derivatives dealer assigns an internal rating for senior unsecured long-term debt or commercial paper that would apply a 20% counterparty factor under (d)(2) of this section, 5% of the amount of the net replacement value in excess of 25% of the OTC derivatives dealer's tentative net capital;

(ii) For counterparties for which an OTC derivatives dealer assigns an internal rating for senior unsecured long-term debt that would apply a 50% counterparty factor under (d)(2) of this section, 20% of the amount of the net replacement value in excess of 25% of the OTC derivatives dealer's tentative net capital;

(iii) For counterparties for which an OTC derivatives dealer assigns an internal rating for senior unsecured long-term debt that would apply a 100% counterparty factor under (d)(2) of this section, 50% of the amount of the net replacement value in excess of 25% of the OTC derivatives dealer's tentative net capital.

(4) Counterparties may be rated by the OTC derivatives dealer, or by an affiliated bank or affiliated broker-dealer of the OTC derivatives dealer, upon approval by the Commission on application by the OTC derivatives dealer. Based on the strength of the OTC derivatives dealer's internal credit risk management system, the Commission may approve the application. The OTC derivatives dealer must make and keep current a record of the basis for the credit rating for each counterparty.

(e) *VAR Models.* An OTC derivatives dealer's VAR model must meet the following qualitative and quantitative requirements:

(1) *Qualitative Requirements.* An OTC derivatives dealer applying this Appendix F must have a VAR model that meets the following minimum qualitative requirements:

(i) The OTC derivatives dealer's VAR model must be integrated into the firm's daily risk management process;

(ii) The OTC derivatives dealer must conduct appropriate stress tests of the VAR model, and develop appropriate procedures to follow in response to the results of such tests;

(iii) The OTC derivatives dealer must conduct periodic reviews (which may be performed by internal audit staff) of its VAR model. The OTC derivatives dealer's VAR model also must be subject to annual reviews conducted by independent public accountants; and

(iv) The OTC derivatives dealer must conduct backtesting of the VAR model pursuant to the following procedures:

(A) Beginning one year after the OTC derivatives dealer begins using its VAR model to calculate its net capital, the OTC derivatives dealer must conduct backtesting by comparing each of its most recent 250 business days' actual net trading profit or loss with the corresponding daily VAR measures generated for determining market risk capital charges and calibrated to a one-day holding period and a 99 percent, one-tailed confidence level;

(B) Once each quarter, the OTC derivatives dealer must identify the number of exceptions, that is, the number of business days for which the actual daily net trading loss, if any, exceeded the corresponding daily VAR measure; and

(C) An OTC derivatives dealer must use the multiplication factor indicated in Table 1 of this Appendix F in determining its capital charge for market risk until it obtains the next quarter's backtesting results, unless the Commission determines that a different adjustment or other action is appropriate.

TABLE 5—MULTIPLICATION FACTOR BASED ON RESULTS OF BACKTESTING

Number of exceptions	Multiplication factor
4 or fewer	3.00
5	3.40
6	3.50
7	3.65
8	3.75
9	3.85
10 or more	4.00

(2) *Quantitative Requirements.* An OTC derivatives dealer applying this Appendix F must have a VAR model that meets the following minimum quantitative requirements:

(i) The VAR measures must be calculated on a daily basis using a 99 percent, one-tailed confidence level with a price change equivalent to a ten-business day movement in rates and prices;

(ii) The effective historical observation period for VAR measures must be at least one year, and the weighted average time lag of the individual observations cannot be less than six months. Historical data sets must be updated at least every three months and reassessed whenever market prices or volatilities are subject to large changes;

(iii) The VAR measures must include the risks arising from the non-linear price characteristics of options positions and the sensitivity of the market value of the positions to changes in the volatility of the underlying rates or prices. An OTC derivatives dealer must measure the volatility of options positions by different maturities;

(iv) The VAR measures may incorporate empirical correlations within and across risk categories, provided that the OTC derivatives dealer has described its process for measuring correlations in its application to apply this Appendix F and the Commission has approved its application. In the event that the VAR measures do not incorporate empirical correlations across risk categories, the OTC derivatives dealer must add the separate VAR measures for the four major risk categories in paragraph (e)(2)(v) of this Appendix F to determine its aggregate VAR measure; and

(v) The OTC derivatives dealer's VAR model must use risk factors sufficient to measure the market risk inherent in all covered positions. The risk factors must address, at a minimum, the following major risk categories: interest rate risk, equity price risk, foreign exchange rate risk, and commodity price risk. For material exposures in the major currencies and markets, modeling techniques must capture, at a minimum, spread risk and must incorporate enough segments of the yield curve to capture differences in volatility and less-than-perfect correlation of rates along the yield curve. An OTC derivatives dealer must provide the Commission with evidence that the OTC derivatives dealer's VAR model takes account of specific risk in positions, including specific equity risk, if the OTC derivatives dealer intends to utilize its VAR model to compute capital charges for equity price risk.

Rule 15c3–1g. Conditions for ultimate holding companies of certain brokers or dealers (Appendix G to Rule 15c3–1)

As a condition for a broker or dealer to compute certain of its deductions to capital in accordance with Rule 15c3–1e, pursuant to its undertaking, the ultimate holding company of the broker or dealer shall:

(a) *Conditions Regarding Computation of Allowable Capital and Risk Allowances.* If it is not an ultimate holding company that has a principal regulator, as that term is defined in Rule 15c3–1(c)(13), calculate allowable capital and allowances for market, credit, and operational risk on a consolidated basis as follows:

(1) *Allowable Capital.* The ultimate holding company must compute allowable capital as the sum of:

(i) Common shareholders' equity on the consolidated balance sheet of the holding company less:

(A) Goodwill;

(B) Deferred tax assets, except those permitted for inclusion in Tier 1 capital by the Board of Governors of the Federal Reserve System ("Federal Reserve") (12 CFR 225, Appendix A);

(C) Other intangible assets; and

(D) Other deductions from common stockholders' equity as required by the Federal Reserve in calculating Tier 1 capital (as defined in 12 CFR 225, Appendix A);

(ii) Cumulative and non-cumulative preferred stock, except that the amount of cumulative preferred stock may not exceed 33% of the items included in allowable capital pursuant to paragraph (a)(1)(i) of this Appendix G, excluding cumulative preferred stock, provided that:

(A) The stock does not have a maturity date;

(B) The stock cannot be redeemed at the option of the holder of the instrument;

(C) The stock has no other provisions that will require future redemption of the issue; and

(D) The issuer of the stock can defer or eliminate dividends;

(iii) The sum of the following items on the consolidated balance sheet, to the extent that the sum does not exceed the sum of the items included in allowable capital pursuant to paragraphs (a)(1)(i) and (ii) of this Appendix G:

(A) Cumulative preferred stock in excess of the 33% limit specified in paragraph (a)(1)(ii) of this Appendix G and subject to the conditions of paragraphs (a)(1)(ii)(A) through (D) of this Appendix G;

(B) Subordinated debt if the original weighted average maturity of the subordinated debt is at least five years; each subordinated debt instrument states clearly on its face that repayment of the debt is not protected by any Federal agency or the Securities Investor Protection Corporation; the subordinated debt is unsecured and subordinated in right of payment to all senior indebtedness of the ultimate holding company; and the subordinated debt instrument permits acceleration only in the event of bankruptcy or reorganization of the ultimate holding company under Chapters 7 (liquidation) and 11 (reorganization) of the U.S. Bankruptcy Code; and

(C) As part of the broker's or dealer's application to calculate deductions for market and credit risk under Rule 15c3-1e, an ultimate holding company may request to include, for a period of three years after adoption of this Appendix G, long-term debt that has an original weighted average maturity of at least five years and that cannot be accelerated, except upon the occurrence of certain events as the Commission may approve. As part of a subsequent amendment to the broker's or dealer's application, the broker or dealer may request permission for the ultimate holding company to include long-term debt that meets these criteria in allowable capital for up to an additional two years; and

(iv) Hybrid capital instruments that are permitted for inclusion in Tier 2 capital by the Federal Reserve (as defined in 12 CFR 225, Appendix A);

(2) *Allowance for Market Risk.* The ultimate holding company shall compute an allowance for market risk for all proprietary positions, including debt instruments, equity instruments, commodity instruments, foreign exchange contracts, and derivative contracts, as the aggregate of the following:

(i) *Value at Risk.* The VaR of its positions, multiplied by the appropriate multiplication factor as set forth in Rule 15c3-1e(d). The VaR of the positions must be obtained using approved VaR models meeting the applicable qualitative and quantitative requirements of Rule 15c3-1e(d); and

(ii) *Alternative Method.* For positions for which there does not exist adequate historical data to support a VaR model, the ultimate holding company must propose a model that produces a suitable allowance for market risk for those positions;

(3) *Allowance for Credit Risk.* The ultimate holding company shall compute an allowance for credit risk for certain assets on the consolidated balance sheet and certain off-balance sheet items, including loans and loan commitments, exposures due to derivatives contracts, structured financial products, and other extensions of credit, and credit substitutes as follows:

(i) By multiplying the credit equivalent amount of the ultimate holding company's exposure to the counterparty, as defined in paragraphs (a)(3)(i)(A), (B) and (C) of this Appendix G, by the appropriate credit risk weight, as defined in paragraph (a)(3)(i)(F) of this Appendix G, of the asset, off-balance sheet item, or counterparty, then multiplying that product by 8%, in accordance with the following:

(A) For certain loans and loan commitments, the credit equivalent amount is determined by multiplying the nominal amount of the contract by the following credit conversion factors:

(1) 0% credit conversion factor for loan commitments that:

(i) May be unconditionally cancelled by the lender; or

(ii) May be cancelled by the lender due to credit deterioration of the borrower;

(2) 20% credit conversion factor for:

(i) Loan commitments of less than one year; or

(ii) Short-term self-liquidating trade related contingencies, including letters of credit;

(3) 50% credit conversion factor for loan commitments with an original maturity of greater than one year that contain transaction contingencies, including performance bonds, revolving underwriting facilities, note issuance facilities and bid bonds; and

(4) 100% credit conversion factor for bankers' acceptances, stand-by letters of credit, and forward purchases of assets, and similar direct credit substitutes;

(B) For derivatives contracts and for repurchase agreements, reverse repurchase agreements, stock lending and borrowing, and similar collateralized transactions, the credit equivalent amount is the sum of the ultimate holding company's maximum potential exposure to the counterparty, as defined in paragraph (a)(3)(i)(E) of this Appendix G, multiplied by the appropriate multiplication factor, and the ultimate holding company's current exposure to the counterparty, as defined in paragraph (a)(3)(i)(D) of this Appendix G. The ultimate holding company must use the multiplication factor determined according to Rule 15c3–1e(d)(1)(v), except that the initial multiplication factor shall be one, unless the Commission determines, based on a review of the group-wide internal risk management control system and practices, including a review of the VaR models, that another multiplication factor is appropriate;

(C) The credit equivalent amount for other assets shall be the asset's book value on the ultimate holding company's consolidated balance sheet or other amount as determined according to the standards published by the Basel Committee on Banking Supervision, as amended from time to time;

(D) The current exposure is the current replacement value of a counterparty's positions, after applying netting agreements with that counterparty meeting the requirements of Rule 15c3–1e(c)(4)(iv) and taking into account the value of collateral from the counterparty in accordance with Rule 15c3–1e(c)(4)(v);

(E) The *maximum potential exposure* is the VaR of the counterparty's positions with the member of the affiliate group, after applying netting agreements with the counterparty meeting the requirements of paragraph (c)(4)(iv) of Rule 15c3–1e, taking into account the value of collateral from the counterparty held by the member of the affiliate in accordance with paragraph (c)(4)(v) of Rule 15c3–1e, and taking into account the current replacement value of the counterparty's positions with the member of the affiliate group, except that for repurchase agreements, reverse repurchase agreements, stock lending and borrowing, and similar collateralized transactions, maximum potential exposure must be calculated using a time horizon of not less than five days;

(F) Credit ratings and credit risk weights shall be determined according to the provisions of paragraphs (c)(4)(vi)(A) and (c)(4)(vi)(B) of Rule 15c3–1e, respectively;

(G) As part of the broker's or dealer's initial application or in an amendment, the ultimate holding company may request Commission approval to reduce allowances for credit risk through the use of credit derivatives;

(H) For the portion of a current exposure covered by a written guarantee, where that guarantee is an unconditional and irrevocable guarantee of the due and punctual payment and performance of the obligation and the ultimate holding company or member of the affiliate group can demand payment after any payment is missed without having to make collection efforts, the ultimate holding company or member of the affiliate group may substitute the credit risk weight of the guarantor for the credit risk weight of the counterparty; or

(ii) As part of the broker's or dealer's initial application or in an amendment to the application, the ultimate holding company may request Commission approval to use a method of calculating credit risk that is consistent with standards published by the Basel Committee on Banking Supervision in International Convergence of Capital Measurement and Capital Standards (July 1988), as amended from time to time; and

(4) Allowance for operational risk. The ultimate holding company shall compute an allowance for operational risk in accordance with the standards published by the Basel Committee on Banking Supervision, as amended from time to time.

(b) *Conditions Regarding Reporting Requirements.* File reports with the Commission in accordance with the following:

(1) If it is not an ultimate holding company that has a principal regulator, as that term is defined in Rule 15c3–1(c)(13), the ultimate holding company shall file with the Commission:

(i) A report as of the end of each month, filed not later than 30 calendar days after the end of the month. A monthly report need not be filed for a month-end that coincides with a fiscal quarter-end. The monthly report shall include:

(A) A consolidated balance sheet and income statement (including notes to the financial statements) for the ultimate holding company and statements of allowable capital and allowances for market, credit, and operational risk computed pursuant to paragraph (a) of this appendix G, except that the consolidated balance sheet and income statement for the first month of the fiscal year may be filed at a later time to which the Commission agrees (when reviewing the affiliated broker's or dealer's application under Rule 15c3–1e(a)). A statement of comprehensive income (as defined in Rule 1–02 of Regulation S–X) shall be included in place of an income statement, if required by the applicable generally accepted accounting principles.

(B) A graph reflecting, for each business line, the daily intra-month VaR;

(C) Consolidated credit risk information, including aggregate current exposure and current exposures (including commitments) listed by counterparty for the 15 largest exposures;

(D) The 10 largest commitments listed by counterparty;

(E) Maximum potential exposure listed by counterparty for the 15 largest exposures;

(F) The aggregate maximum potential exposure;

(G) A summary report reflecting the geographic distribution of the ultimate holding company's exposures on a consolidated basis for each of the top ten countries to which it is exposed (by residence of the main operating group of the counterparty); and

(H) Certain regular risk reports provided to the persons responsible for managing group-wide risk as the Commission may request from time to time;

(ii) A quarterly report as of the end of each fiscal quarter, filed not later than 35 calendar days after the end of the quarter. The quarterly report shall include, in addition to the information contained in the monthly report as required by paragraph (b)(1)(i) of this Appendix G, the following:

(A) Consolidating balance sheets and income statements for the ultimate holding company. The consolidating balance sheet must provide information regarding each material affiliate of the ultimate holding company in a separate column, but may aggregate information regarding members of the affiliate group that are not material affiliates into one column. Statements of comprehensive income (as defined in Rule 1–02 of Regulation S–X) shall be included in place of an income statement, if required by the applicable generally accepted accounting principles;

(B) The results of backtesting of all internal models used to compute allowable capital and allowances for market and credit risk indicating, for each model, the number of backtesting exceptions;

(C) A description of all material pending legal or arbitration proceedings, involving either the ultimate holding company or any of its affiliates, that are required to be disclosed by the ultimate holding company under generally accepted accounting principles;

(D) The aggregate amount of unsecured borrowings and lines of credit, segregated into categories, scheduled to mature within twelve months from the most recent fiscal quarter as to each material affiliate; and

(E) For a quarter-end that coincides with the ultimate holding company's fiscal year-end, the ultimate holding company need not include consolidated and consolidating balance sheets and income statements (or statements of comprehensive income, as applicable) in its quarterly reports. The consolidating balance sheet and income statement (or statement of comprehensive income, as applicable) for the quarter-end that coincides with the fiscal year-end may be filed at a later time to which the Commission agrees (when reviewing the affiliated broker's or dealer's application under Rule 15c3–1e(a));

(iii) An annual audited report as of the end of the ultimate holding company's fiscal year, filed not later than 65 calendar days after the end of the fiscal year. The annual report shall include:

(A) Consolidated financial statements for the ultimate holding company audited by a registered public accounting firm, as that term is defined in section 2(a)(12) of the Sarbanes–Oxley Act of 2002 (15 U.S.C. 7201 *et seq.*). The audit shall be made in accordance with the rules promulgated by the Public Company Accounting Oversight Board. The audited financial statements must include a supporting schedule containing statements of allowable capital and allowances for market, credit, and operational risk computed pursuant to paragraph (a) of this Appendix G; and

(B) A supplemental report entitled "Accountant's Report on Internal Risk Management Control System" prepared by a registered public accounting firm, as that term is defined in section 2(a)(12) of the Sarbanes–Oxley Act of 2002 (15 U.S.C. 7201 *et seq.*), indicating the results of the registered public accounting firm's review of the ultimate holding company's compliance with Rule 15c3–4. The procedures are to be performed and the report is to be prepared in accordance with procedures agreed upon by the ultimate holding company and the registered public accounting firm conducting the review. The agreed-upon procedures are to be performed and the report is to be prepared in accordance with rules promulgated by the Public Company Accounting Oversight Board. The ultimate holding company must file, before commencement of the initial review, the procedures agreed upon by the ultimate holding company and the registered public accounting firm with the Division of Market Regulation, Office of Financial Responsibility, at Commission's principal office in Washington, DC. Before commencement of each subsequent review, the ultimate holding company must notify the Commission of any changes in the procedures;

(iv) An organizational chart, as of the ultimate holding company's fiscal year-end, concurrently with its quarterly report for the quarter-end that coincides with its fiscal year-end. The ultimate holding company must provide quarterly updates of the organizational chart if a material change in the information provided to the Commission has occurred;

(2) If the ultimate holding company is an entity that has a principal regulator, as that term is defined in Rule 15c3–1(c)(13), the ultimate holding company must file with the Commission:

(i) A quarterly report as of the end of each fiscal quarter, filed not later than 35 calendar days after the end of the quarter, or a later time to which the Commission may agree upon application. The quarterly report shall include:

(A) Consolidated (including notes to the financial statements) and consolidating balance sheets and income statements for the ultimate holding company. Statements of comprehensive income (as defined in Rule 1–02 of Regulation S–X) shall be included in place of income statements, if required by the applicable generally accepted accounting principles;

(B) Its most recent capital measurements computed in accordance with the standards published by the Basel Committee on Banking Supervision, as amended from time to time, as reported to its principal regulator;

(C) Certain regular risk reports provided to the persons responsible for managing group-wide risk as the Commission may request from time to time; and

(D) For a quarter-end that coincides with the ultimate holding company's fiscal year-end, the ultimate holding company need not include consolidated and consolidating balance sheets and income statements (or statements of comprehensive income, as applicable) in its quarterly reports. The consolidating balance sheet and income statement (or statement of comprehensive income, as applicable) for the quarter-end that coincides with the fiscal year- end may be filed at a later time to which the Commission agrees (when reviewing the affiliated broker's or dealer's application under Rule 15c3–1e(a)).

(ii) An annual audited report as of the end of the ultimate holding company's fiscal year, filed with the Commission when required to be filed by any regulator;

(3) The reports that the ultimate holding company must file in accordance with paragraph (b) of this Appendix G will be considered filed when two copies are received at the Commission's principal office in Washington, DC. A person who files reports pursuant to this section for which he or she seeks confidential treatment may clearly mark each page or segregable portion of each page with the words "Confidential Treatment Requested." The copies shall be addressed to the Division of Market Regulation, Risk Assessment Group; and

(4) The reports that the ultimate holding company must file with the Commission in accordance with paragraph (b) of this Appendix G will be accorded confidential treatment to the extent permitted by law.

(c) *Conditions Regarding Records To Be Made.* If it is not an ultimate holding company that has a principal regulator, make and keep current the following records:

(1) A record of the results of funding and liquidity stress tests that the ultimate holding company has conducted in response to the following events at least once each quarter and a record of the contingency plan to respond to each of these events:

(i) A credit rating downgrade of the ultimate holding company;

(ii) An inability of the ultimate holding company to access capital markets for unsecured short-term funding;

(iii) An inability of the ultimate holding company to access liquid assets in regulated entities across international borders when the events described in paragraphs (c)(1)(i) or (ii) of this Appendix G occur; and

(iv) An inability of the ultimate holding company to access credit or assets held at a particular institution when the events described in paragraphs (c)(1)(i) or (ii) of this Appendix G occur;

(2) A record of the basis for the determination of credit risk weights for each counterparty;

(3) A record of the basis for the determination of internal credit ratings for each counterparty; and

(4) A record of the calculations of allowable capital and allowances for market, credit and operational risk computed currently at least once per month on a consolidated basis.

(d) *Conditions Regarding Preservation of Records.* (1) Must preserve the following information, documents, and reports for a period of not less than three years in an easily accessible place using any media acceptable under Rule 17a–4(f):

(i) The documents created in accordance with paragraph (c) of this Appendix G;

(ii) Any application or documents filed with the Commission pursuant to Rule 15c3–1e and this Appendix G and any written responses received from the Commission;

(iii) All reports and notices filed with the Commission pursuant to Rule 15c3–1e and this Appendix G; and

(iv) If the ultimate holding company does not have a principal regulator, all written policies and procedures concerning the group-wide internal risk management control system established pursuant to Rule 15c3–1e(a)(1)(viii)(C); and

(2) The ultimate holding company may maintain the records referred to in paragraph (d)(1) of this Appendix G either at the ultimate holding company, at an affiliate, or at a records storage facility, provided that the records are located within the United States. If the records are maintained by an entity other than the ultimate holding company, the ultimate holding company shall obtain and file with the Commission a written undertaking by the entity maintaining the records, in a form acceptable to the Commission, signed by a duly authorized person at the entity maintaining the records, to the effect that the records will be treated as if the ultimate holding company were maintaining the records pursuant to this section and that the entity maintaining the records will permit examination of such records at any time or from time to time during business hours by representatives or designees of the Commission and will promptly furnish the Commission or its designee a true, legible, complete, and current paper copy of any or all or any part of such records. The election to operate pursuant to the provisions of this paragraph shall not relieve the ultimate holding company that is required to maintain and preserve such records from any of its reporting or recordkeeping responsibilities under this rule.

(e) *Conditions Regarding Notification.* The ultimate holding company of a broker or dealer that computes certain of its capital charges in accordance with Rule 15c3–1e shall:

(1) Send notice promptly (but within 24 hours) after the occurrence of the following events:

(i) The early warning indications of low capital as the Commission may agree;

(ii) The ultimate holding company files a Form 8–K (17 CFR 249.308) with the Commission; and

(iii) A material affiliate declares bankruptcy or otherwise becomes insolvent; and

(2) If it is not an ultimate holding company that has a principal regulator, as defined in Rule 15c3–1(c)(13), send notice promptly (but within 24 hours) after the occurrence of the following events:

(i) The ultimate holding company becomes aware that an NRSRO has determined to reduce materially its assessment of the creditworthiness of a material affiliate or the credit rating(s) assigned to one or more outstanding short or long-term obligations of a material affiliate;

(ii) The ultimate holding company becomes aware that any financial regulatory agency or self-regulatory organization has taken significant enforcement or regulatory action against a material affiliate; and

(iii) The occurrence of any backtesting exception under Rule 15c3–1e(d)(1)(iii) or (iv) that would require that the ultimate holding company use a higher multiplication factor in the calculation of its allowances for market or credit risk;

(3) Every notice given or transmitted by paragraph (e) of this Appendix G will be given or transmitted to the Division of Market Regulation, Office of Financial Responsibility, at the principal office of the Commission in Washington, DC. A person who files notification pursuant to this section for which he or she seeks confidential treatment may clearly mark each page or segregable portion of each page with the words "Confidential Treatment Request." For the purposes of this Appendix G, "notice" shall be given or transmitted by telegraphic notice or facsimile transmission. The notice described by paragraph (e)(2) of this Appendix G may be transmitted by overnight delivery. Notices filed pursuant to this paragraph will be accorded confidential treatment to the extent permitted by law; and

(4) Upon the written request of the ultimate holding company, or upon its own motion, the Commission may grant an extension of time or an exemption from any of the requirements of this paragraph (e) either unconditionally or on specified terms and conditions as are necessary or appropriate in the public interest or for the protection of investors.

Rule 15c3–2. [Reserved]

Rule 15c3–3. Customer protection—reserves and custody of securities

(a) *Definitions.* For the purpose of this rule:

(1) The term *customer* shall mean any person from whom or on whose behalf a broker or dealer has received or acquired or holds funds or securities for the account of that person. The term shall not include a broker or dealer, a municipal securities dealer, or a government securities broker or government securities dealer. The term shall, however, include another broker or dealer to the extent that broker or dealer maintains an omnibus account for the account of customers with the broker or dealer in compliance with Regulation T (12 CFR 220.1 through 220.12). The term shall not include a general partner or director or principal officer of the broker or dealer or any other person to the extent that person has a claim for property or funds which by contract, agreement or understanding, or by operation of law, is part of the capital of the broker or dealer or is subordinated to the claims of creditors of the broker or dealer. In addition, the term shall not include a person to the extent that the person has a claim for security futures products held in a futures account, or any security futures product and any futures product held in a "proprietary account" as defined by the Commodity Futures Trading Commission in § 1.3(y). The term also shall not include a counterparty who has delivered collateral to an OTC derivatives dealer pursuant to a transaction in an eligible OTC derivative instrument, or pursuant to the OTC derivatives dealer's cash management securities activities or ancillary portfolio management securities activities, and who has received a prominent written notice from the OTC derivatives dealer that:

(i) Except as otherwise agreed in writing by the OTC derivatives dealer and the counterparty, the dealer may repledge or otherwise use the collateral in its business;

(ii) In the event of the OTC derivatives dealer's failure, the counterparty will likely be considered an unsecured creditor of the dealer as to that collateral;

(iii) The Securities Investor Protection Act of 1970 (15 U.S.C. 78aaa *et seq.*) (SIPA) does not protect the counterparty; and

(iv) The collateral will not be subject to the requirements of Rule 8c–1, Rule 15c2–1, Rule 15c3–2, or Rule 15c3–3.

(2) The term *securities carried for the account of a customer* (hereinafter also "customer securities") shall mean:

(i) Securities received by or on behalf of a broker or dealer for the account of any customer and securities carried long by a broker or dealer for the account of any customer; and

(ii) Securities sold to, or bought for, a customer by a broker or dealer.

(3) The term *fully paid securities* means all securities carried for the account of a customer in a cash account as defined in Regulation T (12 CFR 220.1 *et seq.*), as well as securities carried for the account of a customer in a margin account or any special account under Regulation T that have no loan value for margin purposes, and all margin equity securities in such accounts if they are fully paid: *Provided, however*, that the term *fully paid securities* does not apply to any securities purchased in transactions for which the customer has not made full payment.

(4) The term *margin securities* means those securities carried for the account of a customer in a margin account as defined in section 4 of Regulation T (12 CFR 220.4), as well as securities carried in any other account (such accounts hereinafter referred to as "margin accounts") other than the securities referred to in paragraph (a)(3) of this section.

(5) The term *excess margin securities* shall mean those securities referred to in paragraph (a)(4) of this rule carried for the account of a customer having a market value in excess of 140 percent of the total of the debit balances in the customer's account or accounts encompassed by paragraph (a)(4) of this rule which the broker or dealer identifies as not constituting margin securities.

(6) The term *qualified security* shall mean a security issued by the United States or a security in respect of which the principal and interest are guaranteed by the United States.

(7) The term *bank* means a bank as defined in section 3(a)(6) of the Act and will also mean any building and loan, savings and loan or similar banking institution subject to supervision by a Federal banking authority. With respect to a broker or dealer that maintains its principal place of business in Canada, the term "bank" also means a Canadian bank subject to supervision by a Canadian authority.

(8) The term *free credit balances* means liabilities of a broker or dealer to customers which are subject to immediate cash payment to customers on demand, whether resulting from sales of securities, dividends, interest, deposits or otherwise, excluding, however, funds in commodity accounts which are segregated in accordance with the Commodity Exchange Act or in a similar manner, or which are funds carried in a proprietary account as that term is defined in regulations under the Commodity Exchange Act. The term "free credit balances" also includes, if subject to immediate cash payment to customers on demand, funds carried in a securities account pursuant to a self-regulatory organization portfolio margining rule approved by the Commission under section 19(b) under the Securities Exchange Act of 1934 ("SRO portfolio margining rule"), including variation margin or initial margin, marks to market, and proceeds resulting from margin paid or released in connection with closing out, settling or exercising futures contracts and options thereon.

(9) The term *other credit balances* means cash liabilities of a broker or dealer to customers other than free credit balances and funds in commodity accounts which are segregated in accordance with the Commodity Exchange Act or in a similar manner, or funds carried in a proprietary account as that term is defined in regulations under the Commodity Exchange Act. The term "other credit balances" also includes funds that are cash liabilities of a broker or dealer to customers other than free credit balances and are carried in a securities account pursuant to an SRO portfolio margining rule, including variation margin or initial margin, marks to market, and proceeds resulting from margin paid or released in connection with closing out, settling or exercising futures contracts and options thereon.

(10) The term *funds carried for the account of any customer* (hereinafter also "customer funds") shall mean all free credit and other credit balances carried for the account of the customer.

(11) The term *principal officer* shall mean the president, executive vice president, treasurer, secretary or any other person performing a similar function with the broker or dealer.

(12) The term *household members and other persons related to principals* includes husbands or wives, children, sons-in-law or daughters-in-law and any household relative to whose support a principal contributes directly or indirectly. For purposes of this paragraph (a)(12), a principal shall be deemed to be a director, general partner, or principal officer of the broker or dealer.

(13) The term *affiliated person* includes any person who directly or indirectly controls a broker or dealer or any person who is directly or indirectly controlled by or under common control with the broker or dealer. Ownership of 10% or more of the common stock of the relevant entity will be deemed prima facie control of that entity for purposes of this paragraph.

(14) The term *securities account* shall mean an account that is maintained in accordance with the requirements of section 15(c)(3) of the Act and Rule 15c3-3.

(15) The term *futures account* (also referred to as "commodity account") shall mean an account that is maintained in accordance with the segregation requirements of section 4d of the Commodity Exchange Act (7 U.S.C. 6d) and the rules thereunder.

(16) The term *PAB account* means a proprietary securities account of a broker or dealer (which includes a foreign broker or dealer, or a foreign bank acting as a broker or dealer) other than a delivery-versus-payment account or a receipt-versus-payment account. The term does not include an account that has been subordinated to the claims of creditors of the carrying broker or dealer.

(17) The term *Sweep Program* means a service provided by a broker or dealer where it offers to its customer the option to automatically transfer free credit balances in the securities account of the customer to either a money market mutual fund product as described in Rule 2a-7 of this chapter or an account at a bank whose deposits are insured by the Federal Deposit Insurance Corporation.

(b) *Physical Possession or Control of Securities.* (1) A broker or dealer shall promptly obtain and shall thereafter maintain the physical possession or control of all fully paid securities and excess margin securities carried by a broker or dealer for the account of customers.

(2) A broker or dealer shall not be deemed to be in violation of the provisions of paragraph (b)(1) of this rule regarding physical possession or control of customers' securities if, solely as the result of normal business operations, temporary lags occur between the time when a security is required to be in the possession or control of the broker or dealer and the time that it is placed in the broker's or dealer's physical possession or under its control, provided that the broker or dealer takes timely steps in good faith to establish prompt physical possession or control. The burden of proof shall be on the broker or dealer to establish that the failure to obtain physical possession or control of securities carried for the account of customers as required by paragraph (b)(1) of this rule is merely temporary and solely the result of normal business operations including same day receipt and redelivery (turnaround), and to establish that it has taken timely steps in good faith to place them in its physical possession or control.

(3) A broker or dealer shall not be deemed to be in violation of the provisions of paragraph (b)(1) of this rule regarding physical possession or control of fully-paid or excess margin securities borrowed from any person, provided that the broker or dealer and the lender, at or before the time of the loan, enter into a written agreement that, at a minimum;

(i) Sets forth in a separate schedule or schedules the basis of compensation for any loan and generally the rights and liabilities of the parties as to the borrowed securities;

(ii) Provides that the lender will be given a schedule of the securities actually borrowed at the time of the borrowing of the securities;

(iii) Specifies that the broker or dealer:

(A) Must provide to the lender, upon the execution of the agreement or by the close of the business day of the loan if the loan occurs subsequent to the execution of the agreement, collateral, which fully secures the loan of securities, consisting exclusively of cash or United States Treasury bills and Treasury notes or an irrevocable letter of credit issued by a bank as defined in section 3(a)(6)(A)–(C) of the Act or such other collateral as the Commission designates as permissible by order as necessary or appropriate in the public interest and consistent with the protection of investors after giving consideration to the collateral's liquidity, volatility, market depth and location, and the issuer's creditworthiness; and

(B) Must mark the loan to the market not less than daily and, in the event that the market value of all the outstanding securities loaned at the close of trading at the end of the business day exceeds 100 percent of the collateral then held by the lender, the borrowing broker or dealer must provide additional collateral of the type described in paragraph (b)(3)(iii)(A) of this rule to the lender by the close of the next business day as necessary to equal, together with the collateral then held by the lender, not less than 100 percent of the market value of the securities loaned; and

(iv) Contains a prominent notice that the provisions of SIPA may not protect the lender with respect to the securities loan transaction and that, therefore, the collateral delivered to the lender may constitute the only source of satisfaction of the broker's or dealer's obligation in the event the broker or dealer fails to return the securities.

(4)(i) Notwithstanding paragraph (k)(2)(i) of this rule, a broker or dealer that retains custody of securities that are the subject of a repurchase agreement between the broker or dealer and a counterparty shall:

(A) Obtain the repurchase agreement in writing;

(B) Confirm in writing the specific securities that are the subject of a repurchase transaction pursuant to such agreement at the end of the trading day on which the transaction is initiated and at the end of any other day during which other securities are substituted if the substitution results in a change to issuer, maturity date par amount or coupon rate as specified in the previous confirmation;

(C) Advise the counterparty in the repurchase agreement that the Securities Investor Protection Corporation has taken the position that the provisions of SIPA do not protect the counterparty with respect to the repurchase agreement; and,

(D) Maintain possession or control of securities that are the subject of the agreement.

(ii) For purposes of this paragraph (b)(4), securities are in the broker's or dealer's control only if they are in the control of the broker or dealer within the meaning of Rule 15c3-3(c)(1), (c)(3), (c)(5) or (c)(6) of this rule.

(iii) A broker or dealer shall not be in violation of the requirement to maintain possession or control pursuant to paragraph (b)(4)(i)(D) during the trading day if:

(A) In the written repurchase agreement, the counterparty grants the broker or dealer the right to substitute other securities for those subject to the agreement; and

(B) The provision in the written repurchase agreement governing the right, if any, to substitute is immediately preceded by the following disclosure statement, which must be prominently displayed:

REQUIRED DISCLOSURE

The [seller] is not permitted to substitute other securities for those subject to this agreement and therefore must keep the [buyer's] securities segregated at all times, unless in this agreement the [buyer grants the [seller]] the right to substitute other securities. If the buyer grants the right to substitute, this means that the [buyer's] securities will likely be commingled with the [seller's] own securities during the trading day. The [buyer] is advised that, during any trading day that the [buyer's] securities are commingled with the [seller's] securities, they will be subject to liens granted by the [seller] to its clearing bank and may be used by the [seller] for deliveries on other securities transactions. Whenever the securities are commingled, the [seller's] ability to resegregate substitute securities for the [buyer] will be subject to the [seller's] ability to satisfy the clearing lien or to obtain substitute securities.

(iv) A confirmation issued in accordance with paragraph (b)(4)(i)(B) of this rule shall specify the issuer, maturity date, coupon rate, par amount and market value of the security and shall further identify a CUSIP or mortgage-backed security pool number, as appropriate, except that a CUSIP or a pool number is not required on the confirmation if it is identified in internal records of the broker or dealer that designate the specific security of the counterparty. For purposes of this paragraph (b)(4)(iv), the market value of any security that is the subject of the repurchase transaction shall be the most recently available bid price plus accrued interest, obtained by any reasonable and consistent methodology.

(v) This paragraph (b)(4) shall not apply to a repurchase agreement between the broker or dealer and another broker or dealer (including a government securities broker or dealer), a registered municipal securities dealer, or a general partner or director or principal officer of the broker or dealer or any person to the extent that the person's claim is explicitly subordinated to the claims of creditors of the broker or dealer.

(5) A broker or dealer is required to obtain and thereafter maintain the physical possession or control of securities carried for a PAB account, unless the broker or dealer has provided written notice to the account holder that the securities may be used in the ordinary course of its securities business, and has provided an opportunity for the account holder to object.

(c) *Control of Securities.* Securities under the control of a broker or dealer shall be deemed to be securities which:

(1) Are represented by one or more certificates in the custody or control of a clearing corporation or other subsidiary organization of either national securities exchanges or of a registered national securities association, or of a custodian bank in accordance with a system for the central handling of securities complying with the provisions of Rule 8c–1(g) and Rule 15c2–1(g), the delivery of which certificates to the broker or dealer does not require the payment of money or value, and if the books or records of the broker or dealer identify the customers entitled to receive specified quantities or units of the securities so held for such customers collectively; or

(2) Are carried for the account of any customer by a broker or dealer and are carried in an omnibus credit account in the name of such broker or dealer with another broker or dealer in compliance with the requirements of section 7(f) of Regulation T (12 CFR 220.7(f)), such securities being deemed to be under the control of such broker or dealer to the extent that it has instructed such carrying broker or dealer to maintain physical possession or control of them free of any charge, lien, or claim of any kind in favor of such carrying broker or dealer or any persons claiming through such carrying broker or dealer; or

(3) Are the subject of bona fide items of transfer; provided that securities shall be deemed not to be the subject of bona fide items of transfer if, within 40 calendar days after they have been transmitted for transfer by the broker or dealer to the issuer or its transfer agent, new certificates conforming to the instructions of the broker or dealer have not been received by the broker or dealer, the broker or dealer has not received a written statement by the issuer or its transfer agent acknowledging the transfer instructions and the possession of the securities or the broker or dealer has not obtained a revalidation of a window ticket from a transfer agent with respect to the certificate delivered for transfer; or

(4) Are in the custody of a foreign depository, foreign clearing agency or foreign custodian bank which the Commission upon application from a broker or dealer or upon its own motion shall designate as a satisfactory control location for securities; or

(5) Are in the custody or control of a bank as defined in section 3(a)(6) of the Act, the delivery of which securities to the broker or dealer does not require the payment of money or value and the bank having acknowledged in writing that the securities in its custody or control are not subject to any right, charge, security interest, lien or claim of any kind in favor of a bank or any person claiming through the bank; or

(6)(i) Are held in or are in transit between offices of the broker or dealer; or (ii) are held by a corporate subsidiary if the broker or dealer owns and exercises a majority of the voting rights of all of the voting securities of such subsidiary, assumes or guarantees all of the subsidiary's obligations and liabilities, operates the subsidiary as a branch office of the broker or dealer, and assumes full responsibility for compliance by the subsidiary and all of its associated persons with the provisions of the federal securities laws as well as for all of the other acts of the subsidiary and such associated persons; or

(7) Are held in such other locations as the Commission shall upon application from a broker or dealer find and designate to be adequate for the protection of customer securities.

(d) *Requirement to Reduce Securities to Possession or Control.* Not later than the next business day, a broker or dealer, as of the close of the preceding business day, shall determine from its books or records the quantity of fully paid securities and excess margin securities in its possession or control and the quantity of fully paid securities and excess margin securities not in its possession or control. In making this daily determination inactive margin accounts (accounts having no activity by reason of purchase or sale of securities, receipt or delivery of cash or securities or similar type events) may be computed not less than once weekly. If such books or records indicate, as of such close of the business day, that such broker or dealer has not obtained physical possession or control of all fully paid and excess margin securities as required by this section and there are securities of the same issue and class in any of the following noncontrol locations:

(1) Securities subject to a lien securing moneys borrowed by the broker or dealer or securities loaned to another broker or dealer or clearing corporation, then the broker or dealer shall, not later than the business day following the day on which such determination is made, issue instructions for the release of such securities from the lien or return of such loaned securities and shall obtain physical possession or control of such securities within two business days following the date of issuance of the instructions in the case of securities subject to lien securing borrowed moneys and within five business days following the date of issuance of instructions in the case of securities loaned; or

(2) Securities included on the broker's or dealer's books or records as failed to receive more than 30 calendar days, then the broker or dealer shall, not later than the business day following the day on which such determination is made, take prompt steps to obtain physical possession or control of securities so failed to receive through a buy-in procedure or otherwise; or

(3) Securities receivable by the broker or dealer as a security dividend receivable, stock split or similar distribution for more than 45 calendar days, then the broker or dealer shall, not later than the business day following the day on which such determination is made, take prompt steps to obtain physical possession or control of securities so receivable through a buy-in procedure or otherwise; or

(4) Securities included on the broker's or dealer's books or records that allocate to a short position of the broker or dealer or a short position for another person, excluding positions covered by paragraph (m) of this section, for more than 30 calendar days, then the broker or dealer must, not later than the business day following the day on which the determination is made, take prompt steps to obtain physical possession or control of such securities. For the purposes of this paragraph (d)(4), the 30 day time period will not begin to run with respect to a syndicate short position established in connection with an offering of securities until the completion of the underwriter's participation in the distribution as determined pursuant to Rule 100(b) of Regulation M of this chapter (17 CFR 242.100 through 242.105); or

(5) A broker or dealer which is subject to the requirements of Rule 15c3-3 with respect to physical possession or control of fully paid and excess margin securities shall prepare and maintain a current and detailed description of the procedures which it utilizes to comply with the possession or control requirements set forth in this section. The records required herein shall be made available upon request to the Commission and to the designated examining authority for such broker or dealer.

(e) *Special reserve bank accounts for the exclusive benefit of customers and PAB accounts.* (1) Every broker or dealer must maintain with a bank or banks at all times when deposits are required or hereinafter specified a "Special Reserve Bank Account for the Exclusive Benefit of Customers" (hereinafter referred to as the *Customer Reserve Bank Account*) and a "Special Reserve Bank Account for Brokers and Dealers" (hereinafter referred to as the *PAB Reserve Bank Account*), each of which will be separate from the other and from any other bank account of the broker or dealer. Such broker or dealer must at all times maintain in the Customer Reserve Bank Account and the PAB Reserve Bank Account, through deposits made therein, cash and/or qualified securities in amounts computed in accordance with the formula attached as Exhibit A (17 CFR 240.15c3-3a), as applied to customer and PAB accounts respectively.

(2) With respect to each computation required pursuant to paragraph (e)(1) of this section, a broker or dealer must not accept or use any of the amounts under items comprising Total Credits under the formula referred to in paragraph (e)(1) of this section except for the specified purposes indicated under items comprising Total Debits under the formula, and, to the extent Total Credits exceed Total Debits, at least the net amount thereof must be maintained in the Customer Reserve Bank Account and PAB Reserve Bank Account pursuant to paragraph (e)(1) of this section.

(3) *Reserve Bank Account Computations.*

(i) Computations necessary to determine the amount required to be deposited in the Customer Reserve Bank Account and PAB Reserve Bank Account as specified in paragraph (e)(1) of this section must be made weekly, as of the close of the last business day of the week, and the deposit so computed must be made no later than one hour after the opening of banking business on the second following business day; *provided, however,* a broker or dealer which has aggregate indebtedness not exceeding 800 percent of net capital (as defined in Rule 15c3–1) and which carries aggregate customer funds (as defined in paragraph (a)(10) of this section), as computed at the last required computation pursuant to this section, not exceeding $1,000,000, may in the alternative make the Customer Reserve Bank Account computation monthly, as of the close of the last business day of the month, and, in such event, must deposit not less than 105 percent of the amount so computed no later than one hour after the opening of banking business on the second following business day.

(ii) If a broker or dealer, computing on a monthly basis, has, at the time of any required computation, aggregate indebtedness in excess of 800 percent of net capital, such broker or dealer must thereafter compute weekly as aforesaid until four successive weekly Customer Reserve Bank Account computations are made, none of which were made at a time when its aggregate indebtedness exceeded 800 percent of its net capital.

(iii) A broker or dealer that does not carry the accounts of a "customer" as defined by this section or conduct a proprietary trading business may make the computation to be performed with respect to PAB accounts under paragraph (e)(1) of this section monthly rather than weekly. If a broker or dealer performing the computation with respect to PAB accounts under paragraph (e)(1) of this section on a monthly basis is, at the time of any required computation, required to deposit additional cash or qualified securities in the PAB Reserve Bank Account, the broker or dealer must thereafter perform the computation required with respect to PAB accounts under paragraph (e)(1) of this section weekly until four successive weekly computations are made, none of which is made at a time when the broker or dealer was required to deposit additional cash or qualified securities in the PAB Reserve Bank Account.

(iv) Computations in addition to the computations required in this paragraph (e)(3), may be made as of the close of any business day, and the deposits so computed must be made no later than one hour after the opening of banking business on the second following business day.

(v) The broker or dealer must make and maintain a record of each such computation made pursuant to this paragraph (e)(3) or otherwise and preserve each such record in accordance with Rule 17a–4.

(4) If the computation performed under paragraph (e)(3) of this section with respect to PAB accounts results in a deposit requirement, the requirement may be satisfied to the extent of any excess debit in the computation performed under paragraph (e)(3) of this section with respect to customer accounts of the same date. However, a deposit requirement resulting from the computation performed under paragraph (e)(3) of this section with respect to customer accounts cannot be satisfied with excess debits from the computation performed under paragraph (e)(3) of this section with respect to PAB accounts.

(5) In determining whether a broker or dealer maintains the minimum deposits required under this section, the broker or dealer must exclude the total amount of any cash deposited with an affiliated bank. The broker or dealer also must exclude cash deposited with a non-affiliated bank to the extent that the amount of the deposit exceeds 15% of the bank's equity capital as reported by the bank in its most recent Call Report or any successor form the bank is required to file by its appropriate Federal banking agency (as defined by section 3 of the Federal Deposit Insurance Act).

(f) *Notification of banks.* A broker or dealer required to maintain a Customer Reserve Bank Account and PAB Reserve Bank Account prescribed by paragraph (e)(1) of this section or who maintains a Special Account referred to in paragraph (k) of this section must obtain and preserve in accordance with Rule 17a–4 a written notification from each bank with which it maintains a Customer Reserve Bank Account, a PAB Reserve Bank Account, or a Special Account that the bank was informed that all cash and/or qualified securities deposited therein are being held by the bank for the exclusive benefit of the customers and account holders of the broker or dealer in accordance with the regulations of the Commission, and are being kept separate from any other accounts maintained by the broker or dealer with the bank, and the broker or dealer must have a written contract with the bank which provides that the cash and/or qualified securities will at no time be used directly or indirectly as security for a loan to the broker or dealer by the bank and will not be subject to any right, charge, security interest, lien, or claim of any kind in favor of the bank or any person claiming through the bank.

(g) *Withdrawals from the reserve bank accounts.* A broker or dealer may make withdrawals from a Customer Reserve Bank Account and a PAB Reserve Bank Account if and to the extent that at the time of the withdrawal the amount remaining in the Customer Reserve Bank Account and PAB Reserve Bank Account is not less than the amount then required by paragraph (e) of this section. A bank may presume that any request for withdrawal from a Reserve Bank Account is in conformity and compliance with this paragraph (g). On any business day on which a withdrawal is made, the broker or dealer shall make a record of the computation on the basis of which he makes such withdrawal, and he shall preserve such computation in accordance with Rule 17a–4.

(h) *Buy–In of Short Security Differences.* A broker or dealer shall within 45 calendar days after the date of the examination, count, verification and comparison of securities pursuant to Rule 17a–13 or otherwise or to the annual report of financial condition in accordance with Rule 17a–5 or 17a–12, buy-in all short security differences which are not resolved during the 45-day period.

(i) *Notification in the Event of Failure to Make a Required Deposit.* If a broker or dealer shall fail to make in its Customer Reserve Bank Account, PAB Reserve Bank Account or special account a deposit, as required by this rule, the broker or dealer shall by telegram immediately notify the Commission and the regulatory authority for the broker or dealer, which examines such broker or dealer as to financial responsibility and shall promptly thereafter confirm such notification in writing.

(j) *Treatment of free credit balances.* (1) A broker or dealer must not accept or use any free credit balance carried for the account of any customer of the broker or dealer unless such broker or dealer has established adequate procedures pursuant to which each customer for whom a free credit balance is carried will be given or sent, together with or as part of the customer's statement of account, whenever sent but not less frequently than once every three months, a written statement informing the customer of the amount due to the customer by the broker or dealer on the date of the statement, and that the funds are payable on demand of the customer.

(2) A broker or dealer must not convert, invest, or transfer to another account or institution, credit balances held in a customer's account except as provided in paragraphs (j)(2)(i) and (ii) of this section.

(i) A broker or dealer is permitted to invest or transfer to another account or institution, free credit balances in a customer's account only upon a specific order, authorization, or draft from the customer, and only in the manner, and under the terms and conditions, specified in the order, authorization, or draft.

(ii) A broker or dealer is permitted to transfer free credit balances held in a customer's securities account to a product in its Sweep Program or to transfer a customer's interest in one product in a Sweep Program to another product in a Sweep Program, *provided*:

(A) For an account opened on or after the effective date of this paragraph (j)(2)(ii), the customer gives prior written affirmative consent to having free credit balances in the customer's securities account included in the Sweep Program after being notified:

(*1*) Of the general terms and conditions of the products available through the Sweep Program; and

(*2*) That the broker or dealer may change the products available under the Sweep Program.

(B) For any account:

(*1*) The broker or dealer provides the customer with the disclosures and notices regarding the Sweep Program required by each self-regulatory organization of which the broker or dealer is a member;

(*2*) The broker or dealer provides notice to the customer, as part of the customer's quarterly statement of account, that the balance in the bank deposit account or shares of the money market mutual fund in which the customer has a beneficial interest can be liquidated on the customer's order and the proceeds returned to the securities account or remitted to the customer; and

(*3*)(*i*) The broker or dealer provides the customer with written notice at least 30 calendar days before:

(*A*) Making changes to the terms and conditions of the Sweep Program;

(*B*) Making changes to the terms and conditions of a product currently available through the Sweep Program;

(*C*) Changing, adding or deleting products available through the Sweep Program; or

(*D*) Changing the customer's investment through the Sweep Program from one product to another.

(*ii*) The notice must describe the new terms and conditions of the Sweep Program or product or the new product, and the options available to the customer if the customer does not accept the new terms and conditions or product.

(k) *Exemptions.* (1) The provisions of this rule shall not be applicable to a broker or dealer meeting all of the following conditions:

(i) The broker's or dealer's transactions as dealer (as principal for its own account) are limited to the purchase, sale, and redemption of redeemable securities of registered investment companies or of interests or participations in an insurance company separate account, whether or not registered as an investment company; except that a broker or dealer transacting business as a sole proprietor may also effect occasional transactions in other securities for its own account with or through another registered broker or dealer;

(ii) The broker's or dealer's transactions as broker (agent) are limited to: (a) The sale and redemption of redeemable securities of registered investment companies or of interests or participations in an insurance company separate account, whether or not registered as an investment company; (b) the solicitation of share accounts for savings and loan associations insured by an instrumentality of the United States; and (c) the sale of securities for the account of a customer to obtain funds for immediate reinvestment in redeemable securities of registered investment companies; and

(iii) The broker or dealer promptly transmits all funds and delivers all securities received in connection with its activities as a broker or dealer, and does not otherwise hold funds or securities for, or owe money or securities to, customers.

(iv) Notwithstanding the foregoing, this section shall not apply to any insurance company which is a registered broker-dealer, and which otherwise meets all of the conditions in paragraphs (k)(1)(i), (ii), and (iii) of this rule, solely by reason of its participation in transactions that are a part of the business of insurance, including the purchasing, selling, or holding of securities for or on behalf of such company's general and separate accounts.

(2) The provisions of this rule shall not be applicable to a broker or dealer:

(i) Who carries no margin accounts, promptly transmits all customer funds and delivers all securities received in connection with its activities as a broker or dealer, does not otherwise hold funds or securities for, or owe money or securities to, customers and effectuates all financial transactions between the broker or dealer and its customers through one or more bank accounts, each to be designated as "Special Account for the Exclusive Benefit of Customers of (name of the broker or dealer)"; or

(ii) Who, as an introducing broker or dealer, clears all transactions with and for customers on a fully disclosed basis with a clearing broker or dealer, and who promptly transmits all customer funds and securities to the clearing broker or dealer which carries all of the accounts of such customers and maintains and preserves such books and records pertaining thereto pursuant to the requirements of Rule 17a–3 and Rule 17a–4, as are customarily made and kept by a clearing broker or dealer.

(3) Upon written application by a broker or dealer, the Commission may exempt such broker or dealer from the provisions of this section, either unconditionally or on specified terms and conditions, if the Commission finds that the broker or dealer has established safeguards for the protection of funds and securities of customers comparable with those provided for by this section and that it is not necessary in the public interest or for the protection of investors to subject the particular broker or dealer to the provisions of this rule.

(*l*) *Delivery of Securities.* Nothing stated in this rule shall be construed as affecting the absolute right of a customer of a broker or dealer to receive in the course of normal business operations following demand made on the broker or dealer, the physical delivery of certificates for:

(1) Fully paid securities to which he is entitled and,

(2) Margin securities upon full payment by such customer to the broker or dealer of the customer's indebtedness to the broker or dealer; and, subject to the right of the broker or dealer under Regulation T to retain collateral for its own protection beyond the requirements of Regulation T, excess

margin securities not reasonably required to collateralize such customer's indebtedness to the broker or dealer.

(m) *Completion of Sell Orders on Behalf of Customers.* If a broker or dealer executes a sell order of a customer (other than an order to execute a sale of securities which the seller does not own) and if for any reason whatever the broker or dealer has not obtained possession of the securities from the customer within 10 business days after the settlement date, the broker or dealer shall immediately thereafter close the transaction with the customer by purchasing securities of like kind and quantity: Provided, however, The term customer for the purpose of this paragraph (m) shall not include a broker or dealer who maintains an omnibus credit with another broker or dealer in compliance with Rule 7(f) of Regulation T.

NOTE TO PARAGRAPH (m): See 38 FR 12103, May 9, 1973 for an order suspending indefinitely the operation of paragraph (m) as to sell orders for exempted securities (e.g., U.S. Government and municipal obligations).

[Paragraph (m) is suspended with respect to exempted securities by virtue of SEC Exchange Act Release No. 10093 (Apr. 10, 1973).]

(n) *Extensions of Time.* If a registered national securities exchange or a registered national securities association is satisfied that a broker or dealer is acting in good faith in making the application and that exceptional circumstances warrant such action, such exchange or association, on application of the broker or dealer, may extend any period specified in paragraphs (d)(2), (3) and (4), paragraph (h) and paragraph (m) of this rule, relating to the requirement that such broker or dealer take action within a designated period of time to buy-in in a security, for one or more limited periods commensurate with the circumstances. Each such exchange or association shall make and preserve for a period of not less than 3 years a record of each extension granted pursuant to this paragraph (n) of this rule which shall contain a summary of the justification for the granting of the extension.

(*o*) *Security Futures Products.* (1) Where Security Futures Products Shall Be Held. A broker or dealer registered with the Commission pursuant to section 15(b)(1) of the Act that is also a futures commission merchant registered with the Commodity Futures Trading Commission pursuant to section 4f(a)(1) of the Commodity Exchange Act:

(i) Shall hold a customer's security futures products in either a securities account or a futures account; and

(ii) Shall establish written policies or procedures for determining whether customer security futures products will be placed in a securities account or a futures account and, if applicable, the process by which a customer may elect the type or types of account in which security futures products will be held (including the procedure to be followed if a customer fails to make an election of account type).

(2) *Disclosure and Record Requirements.* (i) Except as provided in paragraph (*o*)(2)(ii), before a broker or dealer registered with the Commission pursuant to section 15(b)(1) of the Act accepts the first order for a security futures product from or on behalf of a customer, the broker or dealer shall furnish the customer with a disclosure document containing the following information:

(A) A description of the protections provided by the requirements set forth under this section and SIPA applicable to a securities account;

(B) A description of the protections provided by the requirements set forth under section 4d of the Commodity Exchange Act (7 U.S.C. 6d) applicable to a futures account;

(C) A statement indicating whether the customer's security futures products will be held in a securities account or a futures account, or whether the firm permits customers to make or change an election of account type; and

(D) A statement that, with respect to holding the customer's security futures products in a securities account or a futures account, the alternative regulatory scheme is not available to the customer with relation to that account.

(ii) Where a customer account containing an open security futures product position is transferred to a broker or dealer registered with the Commission pursuant to section 15(b)(1) of the Act, that broker or dealer may instead provide the statements described in paragraphs (*o*)(2)(i)(C) and (*o*)(2)(i)(D) of this section no later than ten business days after the date the account is received.

(3) *Changes in Account Type.* A broker or dealer registered with the Commission pursuant to section 15(b)(1) of the Act that is also a futures commission merchant registered pursuant to section 4f(a)(1) of the Commodity Exchange Act (7 U.S.C. 6f(a)(1)) may change the type of account in

which a customer's security futures products will be held; *provided* that:

(i) The broker or dealer creates a record of each change in account type, including the name of the customer, the account number, the date the broker or dealer received the customer's request to change the account type, if applicable, and the date the change in account type became effective; and

(ii) The broker or dealer, at least ten days before the customer's account type is changed:

(A) Notifies the customer in writing of the date that the change will become effective; and

(B) Provides the customer with the disclosures described in paragraph (*o*)(2)(i) of this rule.

Rule 15c3–3a. Exhibit A–Formula for determination of customer and PAB account reserve requirements of brokers and dealers under Rule 15c3–3

	Credits	**Debits**
1. Free credit balances and other credit balances in customers' security accounts. (See NOTE A)	$XXX	
2. Monies borrowed collateralized by securities carried for the accounts of customers (See NOTE B)	XXX	...
3. Monies payable against customers' securities loaned (See NOTE C)	XXX	...
4. Customers' securities failed to receive (See NOTE D)	XXX	...
5. Credit balances in firm accounts which are attributable to principal sales to customers.	XXX	...
6. Market value of stock dividends, stock splits and similar distributions receivable outstanding over 30 calendar days	XXX	...
7. Market value of short security count differences over 30 calendar days old	XXX	...
8. Market value of short securities and credits (not to be offset by longs or by debits) in all suspense accounts over 30 calendar days	XXX	...
9. Market value of securities which are in transfer in excess of 40 calendar days and have not been confirmed to be in transfer by the transfer agent or the issuer during the 40 days	XXX	...
10. Debit balances in customers' cash and margin accounts excluding unsecured accounts and accounts doubtful of collection. (See NOTE E)	...	XXX
11. Securities borrowed to effectuate short sales by customers and securities borrowed to make delivery on customers' securities failed to deliver	...	XXX
12. Failed to deliver of customers' securities not older than 30 calendar days	...	XXX
13. Margin required and on deposit with the Options Clearing Corporation for all option contracts written or purchased in customer accounts. (See NOTE F)	...	XXX
14. Margin required and on deposit with a clearing agency registered with the Commission under section 17A of the Securities Exchange Act of 1934 (15 U.S.C. 78q–1) or a derivatives clearing organization registered with the Commodity Futures Trading Commission under section 5b of the Commodity Exchange Act (7 U.S.C. 7a–1) related to the following types of positions written, purchased or sold in customer accounts: (1) security futures products and (2) futures contracts (and options thereon) carried in a securities account pursuant to an SRO portfolio margining rule (See NOTE G)	...	XXX
Total credits	...	
Total debits	...	...
15. Excess of total credits (sum of items 1-9) over total debits (sum of items 10-14) required to be on deposit in the "Reserve Bank Account" (Rule 15c3–3(e)). If the computation is made monthly as permitted by this section, the deposit must be not less than 105% of the excess of total credits over total debits.	...	XXX

Notes Regarding the Customer Reserve Bank Account Computation

NOTE A. Item 1 must include all outstanding drafts payable to customers which have been applied against free credit balances or other credit balances and must also include checks drawn in excess of bank balances per the records of the broker or dealer.

NOTE B. Item 2 must include the amount of options-related or security futures product-related Letters of Credit obtained by a member of a registered clearing agency or a derivatives clearing organization which are collateralized by customers' securities, to the extent of the member's margin requirement at the registered clearing agency or derivatives clearing organization. Item 2 must also include the amount of Letters of Credit which are collateralized by customers' securities and related to other futures contracts (and options thereon) carried in a securities account pursuant to an SRO portfolio margining rule.

NOTE C. Item 3 must include in addition to monies payable against customers' securities loaned the amount by which the market value of securities loaned exceeds the collateral value received from the lending of such securities.

NOTE D. Item 4 must include in addition to customers' securities failed to receive the amount by which the market value of securities failed to receive and outstanding more than thirty (30) calendar days exceeds their contract value.

NOTE E. (1) Debit balances in margin accounts must be reduced by the amount by which a specific security (other than an exempted security) which is collateral for margin accounts exceeds in aggregate value 15 percent of the aggregate value of all securities which collateralize all margin accounts receivable; provided, however, the required reduction must not be in excess of the amounts of the debit balance required to be excluded because of this concentration rule. A specified security is deemed to be collateral for a margin account only to the extent it represents in value not more than 140 percent of the customer debit balance in a margin account.

(2) Debit balances in special omnibus accounts, maintained in compliance with the requirements of Section 7(f) of Regulation T (12 CFR 220.7(f)) or similar accounts carried on behalf of another broker or dealer, must be reduced by any deficits in such accounts (or if a credit, such credit must be increased) less any calls for margin, mark to the market, or other required deposits which are outstanding 5 business days or less.

(3) Debit balances in customers' cash and margin accounts included in the formula under Item 10 must be reduced by an amount equal to 1 percent of their aggregate value.

(4) Debit balances in cash and margin accounts of household members and other persons related to principals of a broker or dealer and debit balances in cash and margin accounts of affiliated persons of a broker or dealer must be excluded from the Reserve Formula, unless the broker or dealer can demonstrate that such debit balances are directly related to credit items in the formula.

(5) Debit balances in margin accounts (other than omnibus accounts) must be reduced by the amount by which any single customer's debit balance exceeds 25% (to the extent such amount is greater than $50,000) of the broker-dealer's tentative net capital (i.e., net capital prior to securities haircuts) unless the broker or dealer can demonstrate that the debit balance is directly related to credit items in the Reserve Formula. Related accounts (e.g., the separate accounts of an individual, accounts under common control or subject to cross guarantees) will be deemed to be a single customer's accounts for purposes of this provision.

If the registered national securities exchange or the registered national securities association having responsibility for examining the broker or dealer ("designated examining authority") is satisfied, after taking into account the circumstances of the concentrated account including the quality, diversity, and marketability of the collateral securing the debit balances or margin accounts subject to this provision, that the concentration of debit balances is appropriate, then such designated examining authority may grant a partial or plenary exception from this provision. The debit balance may be included in the reserve formula computation for five business days from the day the request is made.

(6) Debit balances in joint accounts, custodian accounts, participation in hedge funds or limited partnerships or similar type accounts or arrangements that include both assets of a person or persons who would be excluded from the definition of customer ("noncustomer") and assets of a person or persons who would be included in the definition of customer must be included in the Reserve Formula in the following manner: if the percentage ownership of the non-customer is less than 5 percent then the entire debit balance shall be included in the formula; if such percentage ownership is between 5 percent and 50 percent then the portion of the debit balance attributable to the non-customer must be excluded from the formula unless the broker or dealer can demonstrate that the debit balance is directly related to credit items in the formula; or if such percentage ownership is greater than 50 percent, then the entire debit balance must be excluded from the formula unless the broker or dealer can demonstrate that the debit balance is directly related to credit items in the formula.

NOTE F. Item 13 must include the amount of margin required and on deposit with the Options Clearing Corporation to the extent such margin is represented by cash, proprietary qualified securities and letters of credit collateralized by customers' securities.

NOTE G. (a) Item 14 must include the amount of margin required and on deposit with a clearing agency registered with the Commission under section 17A of the Securities Exchange Act of 1934 (15 U.S.C. 78q–1) or a derivatives clearing organization registered with the Commodity Futures Trading Commission under section 5b of the Commodity Exchange Act (7 U.S.C. 7a–1) for customer accounts to the extent that the margin is represented by cash, proprietary qualified securities, and letters of credit collateralized by customers' securities.

(b) Item 14 will apply only if the broker or dealer has the margin related to security futures products, or futures (and options thereon) carried in a securities account pursuant to an approved SRO portfolio margining program on deposit with:

(1) A registered clearing agency or derivatives clearing organization that:

(i) Maintains security deposits from clearing members in connection with regulated options or futures transactions and assessment power over member firms that equal a combined total of at least $2 billion, at least $500 million of which must be in the form of security deposits. For the purposes of this NOTE G, the term "security deposits" refers to a general fund, other than margin deposits or their equivalent, that consists of cash or securities held by a registered clearing agency or derivative clearing organization; or

(ii) Maintains at least $3 billion in margin deposits; or

(iii) Does not meet the requirements of paragraphs (b)(1)(i) through (b)(1)(iii) of this NOTE G, if the Commission has determined, upon a written request for exemption by or for the benefit of the broker or dealer, that the broker or dealer may utilize such a registered clearing agency or derivatives clearing organization. The Commission may, in its sole discretion, grant such an exemption subject to such conditions as are appropriate under the circumstances, if the Commission determines that such conditional or unconditional exemption is necessary or appropriate in the public interest, and is consistent with the protection of investors; and

(2) A registered clearing agency or derivatives clearing organization that, if it holds funds or securities deposited as margin for security futures products or futures in a portfolio margin account in a bank, as defined in section 3(a)(6) of the Securities Exchange Act of 1934 (15 U.S.C. 78c(a)(6)), obtains and preserves written

notification from the bank at which it holds such funds and securities or at which such funds and securities are held on its behalf. The written notification will state that all funds and/or securities deposited with the bank as margin (including customer security futures products and futures in a portfolio margin account), or held by the bank and pledged to such registered clearing agency or derivatives clearing agency as margin, are being held by the bank for the exclusive benefit of clearing members of the registered clearing agency or derivatives clearing organization (subject to the interest of such registered clearing agency or derivatives clearing organization therein), and are being kept separate from any other accounts maintained by the registered clearing agency or derivatives clearing organization with the bank. The written notification also will provide that such funds and/or securities will at no time be used directly or indirectly as security for a loan to the registered clearing agency or derivatives clearing organization by the bank, and will be subject to no right, charge, security interest, lien, or claim of any kind in favor of the bank or any person claiming through the bank. This provision, however, will not prohibit a registered clearing agency or derivatives clearing organization from pledging customer funds or securities as collateral to a bank for any purpose that the rules of the Commission or the registered clearing agency or derivatives clearing organization otherwise permit; and

(3) A registered clearing agency or derivatives clearing organization establishes, documents, and maintains:

(i) Safeguards in the handling, transfer, and delivery of cash and securities;

(ii) Fidelity bond coverage for its employees and agents who handle customer funds or securities. In the case of agents of a registered clearing agency or derivatives clearing organization, the agent may provide the fidelity bond coverage; and

(iii) Provisions for periodic examination by independent public accountants; and

(iv) A derivatives clearing organization that, if it is not otherwise registered with the Commission, has provided the Commission with a written undertaking, in a form acceptable to the Commission, executed by a duly authorized person at the derivatives clearing organization, to the effect that, with respect to the clearance and settlement of the customer security futures products and futures in a portfolio margin account of the broker or dealer, the derivatives clearing organization will permit the Commission to examine the books and records of the derivatives clearing organization for compliance with the requirements set forth in Rule 15c3–3a, NOTE G (b)(1) through (3).

(c) Item 14 will apply only if a broker or dealer determines, at least annually, that the registered clearing agency or derivatives clearing organization with which the broker or dealer has on deposit margin related to securities future products or futures in a portfolio margin account meets the conditions of this NOTE G.

Notes Regarding the PAB Reserve Bank Account Computation

NOTE 1. Broker-dealers should use the formula in Exhibit A for the purposes of computing the PAB reserve requirement, except that references to "accounts," "customer accounts, or "customers" will be treated as references to PAB accounts.

NOTE 2. Any credit (including a credit applied to reduce a debit) that is included in the computation required by Rule 15c3-3 with respect to customer accounts (the "customer reserve computation") may not be included as a credit in the computation required by Rule 15c3–3 with respect to PAB accounts (the "PAB reserve computation").

NOTE 3. Note E(1) to Rule 15c3–3a does not apply to the PAB reserve computation.

NOTE 4. Note E(3) to Rule 15c3–3a which reduces debit balances by 1% does not apply to the PAB reserve computation.

NOTE 5. Interest receivable, floor brokerage, and commissions receivable of another broker or dealer from the broker or dealer (excluding clearing deposits) that are otherwise allowable assets under Rule 15c3–1 need not be included in the PAB reserve computation, provided the amounts have been clearly identified as payables on the books of the broker or dealer. Commissions receivable and other receivables of another broker or dealer from the broker or dealer that are otherwise non-allowable assets under Rule 15c3–1 and clearing deposits of another broker or dealer may be included as "credit balances" for purposes of the PAB reserve computation, provided the commissions receivable and other receivables are subject to immediate cash payment to the other broker or dealer and the clearing deposit is subject to payment within 30 days.

NOTE 6. Credits included in the PAB reserve computation that result from the use of securities held for a PAB account ("PAB securities") that are pledged to meet intra-day margin calls in a cross-margin account established between the Options Clearing Corporation and any regulated derivatives clearing organization may be reduced to the extent that the excess margin held by the other clearing corporation in the cross-margin relationship is used the following business day to replace the PAB securities that were previously pledged. In addition, balances resulting from a portfolio margin account that are segregated pursuant to Commodity Futures Trading Commission regulations need not be included in the PAB Reserve Bank Account computation.

NOTE 7. Deposits received prior to a transaction pending settlement which are \$5 million or greater for any single transaction or \$10 million in aggregate may be excluded as credits from the PAB reserve computation if such balances are placed and maintained in a separate PAB Reserve Bank Account by 12 p.m. Eastern Time on the following business day. Thereafter, the money representing any such deposits may be withdrawn to complete the related transactions without performing a new PAB reserve computation.

NOTE 8. A credit balance resulting from a PAB reserve computation may be reduced by the amount that items representing such credits are swept into money market funds or mutual funds of an investment company registered under the Investment Company Act of 1940 on or prior to 10 a.m. Eastern Time on the deposit date provided that the credits swept into any such fund are not subject to any right, charge, security interest, lien, or claim of any kind in favor of the investment company or the broker or dealer. Any credits that have been swept into money market funds or mutual funds must be maintained in the name of a particular broker or for the benefit of another broker.

NOTE 9. Clearing deposits required to be maintained at registered clearing agencies may be included as debits in the PAB reserve computation to the extent the percentage of the deposit, which is based upon the clearing agency's aggregate deposit requirements (e.g., dollar trading volume), that relates to the proprietary business of other brokers and dealers can be identified.

NOTE 10. A broker or dealer that clears PAB accounts through an affiliate or third party clearing broker must include these PAB account balances and the omnibus PAB account balance in its PAB reserve computation.

Rule 15c3–4. Internal risk management control systems for OTC derivatives dealers

(a) An OTC derivatives dealer shall establish, document, and maintain a system of internal risk management controls to assist it in managing the risks associated with its business activities, including market, credit, leverage, liquidity, legal, and operational risks.

(b) An OTC derivatives dealer shall consider the following when adopting its internal control system guidelines, policies, and procedures:

(1) The ownership and governance structure of the OTC derivatives dealer;

(2) The composition of the governing body of the OTC derivatives dealer;

(3) The management philosophy of the OTC derivatives dealer;

(4) The scope and nature of established risk management guidelines;

(5) The scope and nature of the permissible OTC derivatives activities;

(6) The sophistication and experience of relevant trading, risk management, and internal audit personnel;

(7) The sophistication and functionality of information and reporting systems; and

(8) The scope and frequency of monitoring, reporting, and auditing activities.

(c) An OTC derivatives dealer's internal risk management control system shall include the following elements:

(1) A risk control unit that reports directly to senior management and is independent from business trading units;

(2) Separation of duties between personnel responsible for entering into a transaction and those responsible for recording the transaction in the books and records of the OTC derivatives dealer;

(3) Periodic reviews (which may be performed by internal audit staff) and annual reviews (which must be conducted by independent certified public accountants) of the OTC derivatives dealer's risk management systems;

(4) Definitions of risk, risk monitoring, and risk management; and

(5) Written guidelines, approved by the OTC derivatives dealer's governing body, that include and discuss the following:

(i) The OTC derivatives dealer's consideration of the elements in paragraph (b) of this section;

(ii) The scope, and the procedures for determining the scope, of authorized activities or any nonquantitative limitation on the scope of authorized activities;

(iii) Quantitative guidelines for managing the OTC derivatives dealer's overall risk exposure;

(iv) The type, scope, and frequency of reporting by management on risk exposures;

(v) The procedures for and the timing of the governing body's periodic review of the risk monitoring and risk management written guidelines, systems, and processes;

(vi) The process for monitoring risk independent of the business or trading units whose activities create the risks being monitored;

(vii) The performance of the risk management function by persons independent from or senior to the business or trading units whose activities create the risks;

(viii) The authority and resources of the groups or persons performing the risk monitoring and risk management functions;

(ix) The appropriate response by management when internal risk management guidelines have been exceeded;

(x) The procedures to monitor and address the risk that an OTC derivatives transaction contract will be unenforceable;

(xi) The procedures requiring the documentation of the principal terms of OTC derivatives transactions and other relevant information regarding such transactions;

(xii) The procedures authorizing specified employees to commit the OTC derivatives dealer to particular types of transactions;

(xiii) The procedures to prevent the OTC derivatives dealer from engaging in any securities transaction that is not permitted under Rule 15a–1; and

(xiv) The procedures to prevent the OTC derivatives dealer from improperly relying on the exceptions to Rule 15a–1(c) and Rule 15a–1(d), including the procedures to determine whether a counterparty is acting in the capacity of principal or agent.

(d) Management must periodically review, in accordance with written procedures, the OTC derivatives dealer's business activities for consistency with risk management guidelines including that:

(1) Risks arising from the OTC derivatives dealer's OTC derivatives activities are consistent with prescribed guidelines;

(2) Risk exposure guidelines for each business unit are appropriate for the business unit;

(3) The data necessary to conduct the risk monitoring and risk management function as well as the valuation process over the OTC derivatives dealer's portfolio of products is accessible on a timely basis and information systems are available to capture, monitor, analyze, and report relevant data;

(4) Procedures are in place to enable management to take action when internal risk management guidelines have been exceeded;

(5) Procedures are in place to monitor and address the risk that an OTC derivatives transaction contract will be unenforceable;

(6) Procedures are in place to identify and address any deficiencies in the operating systems and to contain the extent of losses arising from unidentified deficiencies;

(7) Procedures are in place to authorize specified employees to commit the OTC derivatives dealer to particular types of transactions, to specify any quantitative limits on such authority, and to provide for the oversight of their exercise of such authority;

(8) Procedures are in place to prevent the OTC derivatives dealer from engaging in any securities transaction that is not permitted under Rule 15a–1;

(9) Procedures are in place to prevent the OTC derivatives dealer from improperly relying on the exceptions to Rule 15a–1(c) and Rule 15a–1(d), including procedures to determine whether a counterparty is acting in the capacity of principal or agent;

(10) Procedures are in place to provide for adequate documentation of the principal terms of OTC derivatives transactions and other relevant information regarding such transactions;

(11) Personnel resources with appropriate expertise are committed to implementing the risk monitoring and risk management systems and processes; and

(12) Procedures are in place for the periodic internal and external review of the risk monitoring and risk management functions.

Rule 15c3–5. Risk management controls for brokers or dealers with market access

(a) For the purpose of this section:

(1) The term *market access* shall mean (i) access to trading in securities on an exchange or alternative trading system as a result of being a member or subscriber of the exchange or alternative trading system, respectively; or (ii) access to trading in securities on an alternative trading system provided by a broker–dealer operator of an alternative trading system to a non–broker–dealer.

(2) The term *regulatory requirements* shall mean all federal securities laws, rules and regulations, and rules of self–regulatory organizations, that are applicable in connection with market access.

(b) A broker or dealer with market access, or that provides a customer or any other person with access to an exchange or alternative trading system through use of its market participant identifier or otherwise, shall establish, document, and maintain a system of risk management controls and supervisory procedures reasonably designed to manage the financial, regulatory, and other risks of this business activity. Such broker or dealer shall preserve a copy of its supervisory procedures and a written description of its risk management controls as part of its books and records in a manner consistent with Rule 17a–4(e)(7). A broker–dealer that routes orders on behalf of an exchange or alternative trading system for the purpose of accessing other trading centers with protected quotations in compliance with Rule 611 of Regulation NMS (17 CFR 242.611) for NMS stocks, or in compliance with a national market system plan for listed options, shall not be required to comply with this rule with regard to such routing services, except with regard to paragraph (c)(1)(ii) of this section.

(c) The risk management controls and supervisory procedures required by paragraph (b) of this section shall include the following elements:

(1) *Financial Risk Management Controls and Supervisory Procedures.* The risk management controls and supervisory procedures shall be reasonably designed to systematically limit the finan-

cial exposure of the broker or dealer that could arise as a result of market access, including being reasonably designed to:

(i) Prevent the entry of orders that exceed appropriate pre-set credit or capital thresholds in the aggregate for each customer and the broker or dealer and, where appropriate, more finely-tuned by sector, security, or otherwise by rejecting orders if such orders would exceed the applicable credit or capital thresholds; and

(ii) Prevent the entry of erroneous orders, by rejecting orders that exceed appropriate price or size parameters, on an order-by-order basis or over a short period of time, or that indicate duplicative orders.

(2) *Regulatory Risk Management Controls and Supervisory Procedures.* The risk management controls and supervisory procedures shall be reasonably designed to ensure compliance with all regulatory requirements, including being reasonably designed to:

(i) Prevent the entry of orders unless there has been compliance with all regulatory requirements that must be satisfied on a pre-order entry basis;

(ii) Prevent the entry of orders for securities for a broker or dealer, customer, or other person if such person is restricted from trading those securities;

(iii) Restrict access to trading systems and technology that provide market access to persons and accounts pre-approved and authorized by the broker or dealer; and

(iv) Assure that appropriate surveillance personnel receive immediate post-trade execution reports that result from market access.

(d) The financial and regulatory risk management controls and supervisory procedures described in paragraph (c) of this section shall be under the direct and exclusive control of the broker or dealer that is subject to paragraph (b) of this section.

(1) Notwithstanding the foregoing, a broker or dealer that is subject to paragraph (b) of this section may reasonably allocate, by written contract, after a thorough due diligence review, control over specific regulatory risk management controls and supervisory procedures described in paragraph (c)(2) of this section to a customer that is a registered broker or dealer, provided that such broker or dealer subject to paragraph (b) of this section has a reasonable basis for determining that such customer, based on its position in the transaction and relationship with an ultimate customer, has better access than the broker or dealer to that ultimate customer and its trading information such that it can more effectively implement the specified controls or procedures.

(2) Any allocation of control pursuant to paragraph (d)(1) of this section shall not relieve a broker or dealer that is subject to paragraph (b) of this section from any obligation under this section, including the overall responsibility to establish, document, and maintain a system of risk management controls and supervisory procedures reasonably designed to manage the financial, regulatory, and other risks of market access.

(e) A broker or dealer that is subject to paragraph (b) of this section shall establish, document, and maintain a system for regularly reviewing the effectiveness of the risk management controls and supervisory procedures required by paragraphs (b) and (c) of this section and for promptly addressing any issues.

(1) Among other things, the broker or dealer shall review, no less frequently than annually, the business activity of the broker or dealer in connection with market access to assure the overall effectiveness of such risk management controls and supervisory procedures. Such review shall be conducted in accordance with written procedures and shall be documented. The broker or dealer shall preserve a copy of such written procedures, and documentation of each such review, as part of its books and records in a manner consistent with Rule 17a–4(e)(7) and Rule 17a–4(b), respectively.

(2) The Chief Executive Officer (or equivalent officer) of the broker or dealer shall, on an annual basis, certify that such risk management controls and supervisory procedures comply with paragraphs (b) and (c) of this section, and that the broker or dealer conducted such review, and such certifications shall be preserved by the broker or dealer as part of its books and records in a manner consistent with Rule 17a–4(b).

(f) The Commission, by order, may exempt from the provisions of this section, either unconditionally or on specified terms and conditions, any broker or dealer, if the Commission determines that such exemption is necessary or appropriate in the public interest consistent with the protection of investors.

Rule 15c6–1. Settlement cycle

(a) Except as provided in paragraphs (b), (c), and (d) of this section, a broker or dealer shall not effect or enter into a contract for the purchase or sale of a security (other than an exempted security, government security, municipal security, commercial paper, bankers' acceptances, or commercial bills) that provides for payment of funds and delivery of securities later than the second business day after the date of the contract unless otherwise expressly agreed to by the parties at the time of the transaction.

(b) Paragraphs (a) and (c) of this rule shall not apply to contracts:

(1) For the purchase or sale of limited partnership interests that are not listed on an exchange or for which quotations are not disseminated through an automated quotation system of a registered securities association;

(2) For the purchase or sale of securities that the Commission may from time to time, taking into account then existing market practices, exempt by order from the requirements of paragraph (a) of this rule, either unconditionally or on specified terms and conditions, if the Commission determines that such exemption is consistent with the public interest and the protection of investors.

(c) Paragraph (a) of this rule shall not apply to contracts for the sale for cash of securities that are priced after 4:30 p.m. Eastern time on the date such securities are priced and that are sold by an issuer to an underwriter pursuant to a firm commitment underwritten offering registered under the Securities Act of 1933 or sold to an initial purchaser by a broker-dealer participating in such offering provided that a broker or dealer shall not effect or enter into a contract for the purchase or sale of such securities that provides for payment of funds and delivery of securities later than the fourth business day after the date of the contract unless otherwise expressly agreed to by the parties at the time of the transaction.

(d) For purposes of paragraphs (a) and (c) of this rule, the parties to a contract shall be deemed to have expressly agreed to an alternate date for payment of funds and delivery of securities at the time of the transaction for a contract for the sale for cash of securities pursuant to a firm commitment offering if the managing underwriter and the issuer have agreed to such date for all securities sold pursuant to such offering and the parties to the contract have not expressly agreed to another date for payment of funds and delivery of securities at the time of the transaction.

REGULATION 15d: REPORTS OF REGISTRANTS UNDER THE SECURITIES ACT OF 1933

ANNUAL REPORTS

Rule 15d–1. Requirement of annual reports

Every registrant under the Securities Act of 1933 shall file an annual report, on the appropriate form authorized or prescribed therefor, for the fiscal year in which the registration statement under the Securities Act of 1933 became effective and for each fiscal year thereafter, unless the registrant is exempt from such filing by section 15(d) of the Act or rules thereunder. Annual reports shall be filed within the period specified in the appropriate report form.

Rule 15d–2. Special financial report

(a) If the registration statement under the Securities Act of 1933 did not contain certified financial statements for the registrant's last full fiscal year (or for the life of the registrant if less than a full fiscal year) preceding the fiscal year in which the registration statement became effective, the registrant shall, within 90 days after the effective date of the registration statement, file a special report furnishing certified financial statements for such last full fiscal year or other period, as the case may be, meeting the requirements of the form appropriate for annual reports of the registrant. If the registrant is a foreign private issuer as defined in Rule 405 under the Securities Act of 1933, then the special financial report shall be filed on the appropriate form for annual reports of the registrant and shall be filed by the later of 90 days after the date on which the registration statement became effective, or four months following the end of the registrant's latest full fiscal year.

(b) The report shall be filed under cover of the facing sheet of the form appropriate for annual reports of the registrant, shall indicate on the facing sheet that it contains only financial statements for the fiscal year in question, and shall be signed in accordance with the requirements of the annual report form.

Rule 15d–3. Reports for depositary shares registered on Form F-6

Annual and other reports are not required with respect to Depositary Shares registered on Form F–6 (Rule 36 under the Securities Act of 1933). The exemption in this section does not apply to any deposited securities registered on any other form under the Securities Act of 1933.

Rule 15d–4. Reporting by Form 40–F registrants

A registrant that is eligible to use Forms 40–F and 6–K and files reports in accordance therewith shall be deemed to satisfy the requirements of Regulation 15d (Rules 15d–1 through 15d–2).

Rule 15d–5. Reporting by successor issuers

(a) Where in connection with a succession by merger, consolidation, exchange of securities, acquisition of assets or otherwise, securities of any issuer that is not required to file reports pursuant to section 15(d) of the Act are issued to the holders of any class of securities of another issuer that is required to file such reports, the duty to file reports pursuant to such section shall be deemed to have been assumed by the issuer of the class of securities so issued. The successor issuer shall, after the consummation of the succession, file reports in accordance with section 15(d) of the Act and the rules and regulations thereunder, unless that issuer is exempt from filing such reports or the duty to file such reports is suspended under section 15(d) of the Act.

(b) An issuer that is deemed to be a successor issuer according to paragraph (a) of this rule shall file reports on the same forms as the predecessor issuer except as follows:

(1) An issuer that is not a foreign issuer shall not be eligible to file on Form 20–F (17 CFR 249.220F).

(2) A foreign private issuer shall be eligible to file on Form 20–F.

(c) The provisions of paragraph (a) of this rule shall not apply to an issuer of securities in connection with a succession that was registered on Form F–8 (17 CFR 239.38) or Form F–10 (17 CFR 239.40) or Form F–80 (17 CFR 239.41).

Rule 15d–6. Suspension of duty to file reports

If the duty of an issuer to file reports pursuant to section 15(d) of the Act as to any fiscal year is suspended as provided in section 15(d) of the Act, such issuer shall, within 30 days after the beginning of the first fiscal year, file a notice on Form 15 informing the Commission of such suspension unless Form 15 has already been filed pursuant to Rule 12h–3. If the suspension resulted from the issuer's merger into, or consolidation with, another issuer or issuers, the notice shall be filed by the successor issuer.

OTHER REPORTS

Rule 15d–10. Transition reports

(a) Every issuer that changes its fiscal closing date shall file a report covering the resulting transition period between the closing date of its most recent fiscal year and the opening date of its new fiscal year; *Provided, however,* that an issuer shall file an annual report for any fiscal year that ended before the date on which the issuer determined to change its fiscal year end. In no event shall the transition report cover a period of 12 or more months.

(b) The report pursuant to this section shall be filed for the transition period not more than the number of days specified in paragraph (j) of this section after either the close of the transition period or the date of the determination to change the fiscal closing date, whichever is later. The report shall be filed on the form appropriate for annual reports of the issuer, shall cover the period from the close of the last fiscal year end and shall indicate clearly the period covered. The financial statements for the transition period filed therewith shall be audited. Financial statements, which may be unaudited, shall be filed for the comparable period of the prior year, or a footnote, which may be unaudited, shall state for the comparable period of the prior year, revenues, gross profits, income taxes, income or loss from continuing operations and net income or loss. The effects of any discontinued operations as classified under the provisions of generally accepted accounting principles also shall be shown, if applicable. Per share data based upon such income or loss and net income or loss shall be presented in conformity with applicable accounting standards. Where called for by the time span to be covered, the comparable period financial statements or footnote shall be included in subsequent filings.

(c) If the transition period covers a period of less than six months, in lieu of the report required by paragraph (b) of this rule, a report may be filed for the transition period on Form 10–Q (17 CFR 249.308) not more than the number of days specified in paragraph (j) of this rule after either the close of the transition period or the date of the determination to change the fiscal closing date, whichever is later. The report on Form 10–Q shall cover the period from the close of the last fiscal year end and shall indicate clearly the period covered. The financial statements filed therewith need not be audited but, if they are not audited, the issuer shall file with the first annual report for the newly adopted fiscal year separate audited statements of income and cash flows covering the transition period. The notes to financial statements for the transition period included in such first annual report may be integrated with the notes to financial statements for the full fiscal period. A separate audited balance sheet as of the end of the transition period shall be filed in the annual report only if the audited balance sheet as of the end of the fiscal year before the transition period is not filed. Schedules need not be filed in transition reports on Form 10–Q.

(d) Notwithstanding the foregoing in paragraphs (a), (b), and (c) of this rule, if the transition period covers a period of one month or less, the issuer need not file a separate transition report if either:

(1) the first report required to be filed by the issuer for the newly adopted fiscal year after the date of the determination to change the fiscal year end is an annual report, and that report covers the transition period as well as the fiscal year; or

(2)(i) The issuer files with the first annual report for the newly adopted fiscal year separate audited statements of income and cash flows covering the transition period; and

(ii) The first report required to be filed by the issuer for the newly adopted fiscal year after the date of the determination to change the fiscal year end is a quarterly report on Form 10–Q; and

(iii) Information on the transition period is included in the issuer's quarterly report on Form 10–Q for the first quarterly period (except the fourth quarter) of the newly adopted fiscal year that ends after the date of the determination to change the fiscal year. The information covering the transition period required by Part II and Item 2 of Part I may be combined with the information regarding the quarter. However, the financial statements required by Part I, which may be unaudited, shall be furnished separately for the transition period.

(e) Every issuer required to file quarterly reports on Form 10–Q pursuant to Rule 15d–13 that changes its fiscal year end shall:

(1) File a quarterly report on Form 10–Q within the time period specified in General Instruction A.1. to that form for any quarterly period (except the fourth quarter) of the old fiscal year that ends before the date on which the issuer determined to change its fiscal year end, except that the issuer need not file such quarterly report if the date on which the quarterly period ends also is the date on which the transition period ends;

(2) File a quarterly report on Form 10–Q within the time specified in General Instruction A.1. to that form for each quarterly period of the old fiscal year within the transition period. In lieu of a quarterly report for any quarter of the old fiscal year within the transition period, the issuer may file a quarterly report on Form 10–Q for any period of three months within the transition period that coincides with a quarter of the newly adopted fiscal year if the quarterly report is filed within the number of days specified in paragraph (j) of this rule after the end of such three month period, provided the issuer thereafter continues filing quarterly reports on the basis of the quarters of the newly adopted fiscal year;

(3) Commence filing quarterly reports for the quarters of the new fiscal year no later than the quarterly report for the first quarter of the new fiscal year that ends after the date on which the issuer determined to change the fiscal year end; and

(4) Unless such information is or will be included in the transition report, or the first annual report on Form 10–K for the newly adopted fiscal year, include in the initial quarterly report on Form 10–Q for the newly adopted fiscal year information on any period beginning on the first day after the period covered by the issuer's final quarterly report on Form 10–Q or annual report on Form 10–K for the old fiscal year. The information covering such period required by Part II and Item 2 of Part I may be combined with the information regarding the quarter. However, the financial statements required by Part I, which may be unaudited, shall be furnished separately for such period.

NOTE TO PARAGRAPHS (c) AND (e): If it is not practicable or cannot be cost-justified to furnish in a transition report on Form 10–Q or a quarterly report for the newly adopted fiscal year financial statements for corresponding periods of the prior year where required, financial statements may be furnished for the quarters of the preceding fiscal year that most nearly are comparable if the issuer furnishes an adequate discussion of seasonal and other factors that could affect the comparability of information or trends reflected, an assessment of the comparability of the data, and a representation as to the reason recasting has not been undertaken.

(f) Every successor issuer that has a different fiscal year from that of its predecessor(s) shall file a transition report pursuant to this rule, containing the required information about each predecessor, for the transition period, if any, between the close of the fiscal year covered by the last annual report of each predecessor and the date of succession. The report shall be filed for the transition period on the form appropriate for annual reports of the issuer not more than the number of days specified in paragraph (j) of this rule after the date of the succession, with financial statements in conformity with the requirements set forth in paragraph (b) of this rule. If the transition period covers a period of less than six months, in lieu of a transition report on the form appropriate for the issuer's annual reports, the report may be filed for the transition period on Form 10–Q not more than the number of days specified in paragraph (j) of this rule after the date of the succession, with financial statements in conformity with the requirements set forth in paragraph (c) of this rule. Notwithstanding the foregoing, if the transition period covers a period of one month or less, the successor issuer need not file a separate transition report if the information is reported by the successor issuer in conformity with the requirements set forth in paragraph (d) of this rule.

(g)(1) Paragraphs (a) through (f) of this rule shall not apply to foreign private issuers.

(2) Every foreign private issuer that changes its fiscal closing date shall file a report covering the resulting transition period between the closing date of its most recent year and the opening date of its new fiscal year. In no event shall a transition report cover a period longer than 12 months.

(3) The report for the transition period shall be filed on Form 20–F (17 CFR 249.220f of this chapter) responding to all items to which such issuer is required to respond when Form 20–F is used as an annual report. The financial statements for the transition period filed therewith shall be audited. The report shall be filed within four months after either the close of the transition period or the date on which the issuer made the determination to change the fiscal closing date, whichever is later.

(4) If the transition period covers a period of six or fewer months, in lieu of the report required by paragraph (g)(3) of this rule, a report for the transition period may be filed on Form 20–F responding to Items 5, 8.A.7., 13, 14, and 17 or 18 within three months after either the close of the transition period or the date on which the issuer made the determination to change the fiscal closing date, whichever is later. The financial statements required by either Item 17 or Item 18 shall be furnished for the transition period. Such financial statements may be unaudited and condensed as permitted in Article 10 of Regulation S–X, but if the financial statements are unaudited and condensed, the issuer shall file with the first annual report for the newly adopted fiscal year separate audited statements of income and cash flows covering the transition period.

(5) Notwithstanding the foregoing in paragraphs (g)(2), (g)(3), and (g)(4) of this rule, if the transition period covers a period of one month or less, a foreign private issuer need not file a separate transition report if the first annual report for the newly adopted fiscal year covers the transition period as well as the fiscal year.

(h) The provisions of this rule shall not apply to investment companies required to file reports pursuant to Rule 30b1–1 under the Investment Company Act of 1940.

(i) No filing fee shall be required for a transition report filed pursuant to this rule.

(j)(1) For transition reports to be filed on the form appropriate for annual reports of the issuer, the number of days shall be:

(i) 60 days (75 days for fiscal years ending before December 15, 2006) for large accelerated filers (as defined in Rule 12b–2);

(ii) 75 days for accelerated filers (as defined in Rule 12b–2); and

(iii) 90 days for all other issuers; and

(2) For transition reports to be filed on Form 10–Q (17 CFR 249.308), the number of days shall be:

(i) 40 days for large accelerated filers and accelerated filers (as defined in Rule 12b–2); and

(ii) 45 days for all other issuers.

(k)(1) Paragraphs (a) through (g) of this rule shall not apply to asset-backed issuers.

(2) Every asset-backed issuer that changes its fiscal closing date shall file a report covering the resulting transition period between the closing date of its most recent fiscal year and the opening date of its new fiscal year. In no event shall a transition report cover a period longer than 12 months.

(3) The report for the transition period shall be filed on Form 10–K (17 CFR 249.310) responding to all items to which such asset-backed issuer is required to respond pursuant to General Instruction J. of Form 10–K. Such report shall be filed within 90 days after the later of either the close of the transition period or the date on which the issuer made the determination to change the fiscal closing date.

(4) Notwithstanding the foregoing in paragraphs (k)(2) and (k)(3) of this rule, if the transition period covers a period of one month or less, an asset-backed issuer need not file a separate transition report if the first annual report for the newly adopted fiscal year covers the transition period as well as the fiscal year.

(5) Any obligation of the asset-backed issuer to file distribution reports pursuant to Rule 15d–17 will continue to apply regardless of a change in the asset-backed issuer's fiscal closing date.

NOTE 1: In addition to the report or reports required to be filed pursuant to this section, every issuer, except a foreign private issuer or an investment company required to file reports pursuant to Rule 30b1–1 under the Investment Company Act of 1940, that changes its fiscal closing date is required to file a Form 8–K (17 CFR 249.308) report that includes the information required by Item 5.03 of Form 8–K within the period specified in General Instruction B.1. to that form.

NOTE 2: The report or reports to be filed pursuant to this section must include the certification required by Rule 15d–14.

Rule 15d–11. Current reports on Form 8–K (17 CFR 249.308)

(a) Except as provided in paragraph (b) of this rule, every registrant subject to Rule 15d–1 shall file a current report on Form 8–K within the period specified in that form unless substantially the same information as that required by Form 8–K has been previously reported by the registrant.

(b) This section shall not apply to foreign governments, foreign private issuers required to make reports on Form 6–K (17 CFR 249.306) pursuant to Rule 15d–16, issuers of American Depositary Receipts for securities of any foreign issuer, or investment companies required to file reports pursuant to Rule 30b(1)–1 under the Investment Company Act of 1940, except where such an investment company is required to file:

(1) Notice of a blackout period pursuant to Rule 104 of Regulation BTR;

(2) Disclosure pursuant to Instruction 2 to Rule 14a–11(b)(1) of information concerning outstanding shares and voting; or

(3) Disclosure pursuant to Instruction 2 to Rule 14a–11(b)(10) of the date by which a nominating shareholder or nominating shareholder group must submit the notice required pursuant to Rule 14a–11(b)(10).

(c) No failure to file a report on Form 8–K that is required solely pursuant to Item 1.01, 1.02, 2.03, 2.04, 2.05, 2.06, 4.02(a), 5.02(e) or 6.03 of Form 8–K shall be deemed to be a violation of 15 U.S.C. 78j(b) and Rule 10b–5.

Rule 15d–13. Quarterly reports on Form 10–Q (17 CFR 249.308a)

(a) Except as provided in paragraphs (b) and (c) of this rule, every issuer that has securities registered pursuant to the Securities Act and is required to file annual reports pursuant to section 15(d) of the Act on Form 10–K (17 CFR 249.310) shall file a quarterly report on Form 10–Q (17 CFR 249.308) within the period specified in General Instruction A.1 to that form for each of the first three quarters of each fiscal year of the issuer, commencing with the first fiscal quarter following the most recent fiscal year for which full financial statements were included in the registration statement, or, if the registration statement included financial statements for an interim period after the most recent fiscal year end meeting the requirements of Article 10 of Regulation S–X, or Rule 8–03 of Regulation S–X for smaller reporting companies, for the first fiscal quarter after the quarter reported upon in the registration statement. The first quarterly report of the issuer shall be filed either within 45 days after the effective date of the registration statement or on or before the date on which such report would have been required to be filed if the issuer had been required to file reports on Form 10–Q as of its last fiscal quarter, whichever is later.

(b) The provisions of this rule shall not apply to the following issuers:

(1) Investment companies required to file reports pursuant to Rule 30b1–1;

(2) Foreign private issuers required to file reports pursuant to Rule 15d–16; and

(3) Asset-backed issuers required to file reports pursuant to Rule 15d–17.

(c) Part I of the quarterly reports on Form 10–Q need not be filed by:

(1) Mutual life insurance companies; or

(2) Mining companies not in the production stage but engaged primarily in the exploration for the development of mineral deposits other than oil, gas or coal, if all of the following conditions are met:

(i) The registrant has not been in production during the current fiscal year or the two years immediately prior thereto; except that being in production for an aggregate period of not more than eight months over the three-year period shall not be a violation of this condition.

(ii) Receipts from the sale of mineral products or from the operations of mineral producing properties by the registrant and its subsidiaries combined have not exceeded $500,000 in any of the most recent six years and have not aggregated more than $1,500,000 in the most recent six fiscal years;

(d) Notwithstanding the foregoing provisions of this rule, the financial information required by Part I of Form 10–Q shall not be deemed to be "filed" for the purpose of section 18 of the Act or otherwise subject to the liabilities of that section of the Act, but shall be subject to all other provisions of the Act.

(e) Notwithstanding the foregoing provisions of this rule, the financial information required by Part I of Form 10–Q, or financial information submitted in lieu thereof pursuant to paragraph (d) of this rule, shall not be deemed to be "filed" for the purpose of section 18 of the Act or otherwise subject to the liabilities of that section of the Act but shall be subject to all other provisions of the Act.

Rule 15d–14. Certification of disclosure in annual and quarterly reports

(a) Each report, including transition reports, filed on Form 10–Q, Form 10–K, Form 20–F or Form 40–F (17 CFR 249.308a, 249.310, 249.220f or 249.240f) under section 15(d) of the Act, other than a report filed by an Asset–Backed Issuer (as defined in Item 1101 of Regulation AB) or a report on Form 20–F filed under Rule 15d–19, must include certifications in the form specified in the applicable exhibit filing requirements of such report and such certifications must be filed as an exhibit to such report. Each principal executive and principal financial officer of the issuer, or persons performing similar functions, at the time of filing of the report must sign a certification. The principal executive and principal financial officers of an issuer may omit the portion of the introductory language in paragraph 4 as well as language in paragraph 4(b) of the certification that refers to the certifying officers' responsibility for designing, establishing and maintaining internal control over financial reporting for the issuer until the issuer becomes subject to the internal control over financial reporting requirements in Rule 13a–15 or Rule 15d–15.

(b) Each periodic report containing financial statements filed by an issuer pursuant to section 15(d) of the Act must be accompanied by the certifications required by Section 1350 of Chapter 63 of Title 18 of the United States Code (18 U.S.C. 1350) and such certifications must be furnished as an exhibit to such report as specified in the applicable exhibit requirements for such report. Each principal executive and principal financial officer of the issuer (or equivalent thereof) must sign a certification. This requirement may be satisfied by a single certification signed by an issuer's principal executive and principal financial officers.

(c) A person required to provide a certification specified in paragraph (a), (b) or (d) of this rule may not have the certification signed on his or her behalf pursuant to a power of attorney or other form of confirming authority.

(d) Each annual report and transition report filed on Form 10–K (17 CFR 249.310) by an asset-backed issuer under section 15(d) of the Act must include a certification in the form specified in the applicable exhibit filing requirements of such report and such certification must be filed as an exhibit to such report. Terms used in paragraphs (d) and (e) of this rule have the same meaning as in Item 1101 of Regulation AB.

(e) With respect to asset-backed issuers, the certification required by paragraph (d) of this rule must be signed by either:

(1) The senior officer in charge of securitization of the depositor if the depositor is signing the report; or

(2) The senior officer in charge of the servicing function of the servicer if the servicer is signing the report on behalf of the issuing entity. If multiple servicers are involved in servicing the pool assets, the senior officer in charge of the servicing function of the master servicer (or entity performing the equivalent function) must sign if a repre-

sentative of the servicer is to sign the report on behalf of the issuing entity.

(f) The certification requirements of this rule do not apply to an Interactive Data File, as defined in Rule 11 of Regulation S–T.

Rule 15d–15. Controls and procedures

(a) Every issuer that files reports under section 15(d) of the Act, other than an Asset Backed Issuer (as defined in Item 1101 of Regulation AB), a small business investment company registered on Form N–5 (17 CFR 239.24 and 274.5), or a unit investment trust as defined in section 4(2) of the Investment Company Act of 1940 (15 U.S.C. 80a–4(2)), must maintain disclosure controls and procedures (as defined in paragraph (e) of this rule) and, if the issuer either had been required to file an annual report pursuant to section 13(a) or 15(d) of the Act for the prior fiscal year or had filed an annual report with the Commission for the prior fiscal year, internal control over financial reporting (as defined in paragraph (f) of this rule).

(b) Each such issuer's management must evaluate, with the participation of the issuer's principal executive and principal financial officers, or persons performing similar functions, the effectiveness of the issuer's disclosure controls and procedures, as of the end of each fiscal quarter, except that management must perform this evaluation:

(1) In the case of a foreign private issuer (as defined in Rule 3b–4) as of the end of each fiscal year; and

(2) In the case of an investment company registered under section 8 of the Investment Company Act of 1940 (15 U.S.C. 80a–8), within the 90-day period prior to the filing date of each report requiring certification under Rule 30a–2.

(c) The management of each such issuer, that either had been required to file an annual report pursuant to section 13(a) or 15(d) of the Act for the prior fiscal year or previously had filed an annual report with the Commission for the prior fiscal year, other than an investment company registered under section 8 of the Investment Company Act of 1940, must evaluate, with the participation of the issuer's principal executive and principal financial officers, or persons performing similar functions, the effectiveness, as of the end of each fiscal year, of the issuer's internal control over financial reporting. The framework on which management's evaluation of the issuer's internal control over financial reporting is based must be a suitable, recognized control framework that is established by a body or group that has followed due-process procedures, including the broad distribution of the framework for public comment. Although there are many different ways to conduct an evaluation of the effectiveness of internal control over financial reporting to meet the requirements of this paragraph, an evaluation that is conducted in accordance with the interpretive guidance issued by the Commission in Release No. 34–55929 will satisfy the evaluation required by this paragraph.

(d) The management of each such issuer that previously either had been required to file an annual report pursuant to section 13(a) or 15(d) of the Act for the prior fiscal year or previously had filed an annual report with the Commission for the prior fiscal year, other than an investment company registered under section 8 of the Investment Company Act of 1940 (15 U.S.C. 80a–8), must evaluate, with the participation of the issuer's principal executive and principal financial officers, or persons performing similar functions, any change in the issuer's internal control over financial reporting, that occurred during each of the issuer's fiscal quarters, or fiscal year in the case of a foreign private issuer, that has materially affected, or is reasonably likely to materially affect, the issuer's internal control over financial reporting.

(e) For purposes of this section, the term disclosure controls and procedures means controls and other procedures of an issuer that are designed to ensure that information required to be disclosed by the issuer in the reports that it files or submits under the Act is recorded, processed, summarized and reported, within the time periods specified in the Commission's rules and forms. Disclosure controls and procedures include, without limitation, controls and procedures designed to ensure that information required to be disclosed by an issuer in the reports that it files or submits under the Act is accumulated and communicated to the issuer's management, including its principal executive and principal financial officers, or persons performing similar functions, as appropriate to allow timely decisions regarding required disclosure.

(f) The term *internal control over financial reporting* is defined as a process designed by, or under the supervision of, the issuer's principal executive and principal financial officers, or persons performing similar functions, and effected by the issuer's board of directors, management and other personnel, to provide reasonable assurance regarding the reliability of financial reporting and the preparation of financial statements for external purposes in accordance with generally accepted accounting principles and includes those policies and procedures that:

(1) Pertain to the maintenance of records that in reasonable detail accurately and fairly reflect the transactions and dispositions of the assets of the issuer;

(2) Provide reasonable assurance that transactions are recorded as necessary to permit preparation of financial statements in accordance with generally accepted accounting principles, and that receipts and expenditures of the issuer are being made only in accordance with authorizations of management and directors of the issuer; and

(3) Provide reasonable assurance regarding prevention or timely detection of unauthorized acquisition, use or disposition of the issuer's assets that could have a material effect on the financial statements.

Rule 15d–16. Reports of foreign private issuers on Form 6–K (17 CFR 249.306)

(a) Every foreign private issuer which is subject to Rule 15d–1 shall make reports on Form 6–K, except that this rule shall not apply to:

(1) Investment companies required to file reports pursuant to Rule 30b1–1;

(2) Issuers of American depositary receipts for securities of any foreign issuer; and

(3) Asset-backed issuers, as defined in Item 1101 of Regulation AB.

(b) Such reports shall be transmitted promptly after the information required by Form 6–K is made public by the issuer, by the country of its domicile or under the laws of which it was incorporated or organized or by a foreign securities exchange with which the issuer has filed the information.

(c) Reports furnished pursuant to this rule shall not be deemed to be "filed" for the purpose of section 18 of the Act or otherwise subject to the liabilities of that section.

Rule 15d–17. Reports of asset-backed issuers on Form 10–D (17 CFR 249.312)

Every asset-backed issuer subject to Rule 15d–1 shall make reports on Form 10–D (17 CFR 249.312). Such reports shall be filed within the period specified in Form 10–D.

Rule 15d–18. Compliance with servicing criteria for asset-backed securities

(a) This section applies to every class of asset-backed securities subject to the reporting requirements of section 15(d) of the Act. Terms used in this section have the same meaning as in Item 1101 of Regulation AB.

(b) Reports on assessments of compliance with servicing criteria for asset-backed securities required. With regard to a class of asset-backed securities subject to the reporting requirements of section 15(d) of the Act, the annual report on Form 10–K (17 CFR 249.308) for such class must include from each party participating in the servicing function a report regarding its assessment of compliance with the servicing criteria specified in paragraph (d) of Item 1122 of Regulation AB, as of and for the period ending the end of each fiscal year, with respect to asset-backed securities transactions taken as a whole involving the party participating in the servicing function and that are backed by the same asset type backing the class of asset-backed securities (including the asset-backed securities transaction that is to be the subject of the report on Form 10–K for that fiscal year).

(c) *Attestation Reports on Assessments of Compliance with Servicing Criteria for Asset-Backed Securities Required.* With respect to each report included pursuant to paragraph (b) of this rule, the annual report on Form 10–K must also include a report by a registered public accounting firm that attests to, and reports on, the assessment made by the asserting party. The attestation report on assessment of compliance with servicing criteria for asset-backed securities must be made in accordance with standards for attestation engagements issued or adopted by the Public Company Accounting Oversight Board.

NOTE TO RULE 15d–18: If multiple parties are participating in the servicing function, a separate assessment report and attestation report must be included for each party participating in the servicing function. A party participating in the servicing function means any entity (*e.g.*, master servicer, primary servicers, trustees) that is performing activities that address the criteria in paragraph (d) of Item 1122 of Regulation AB, unless such entity's activities relate only to 5% or less of the pool assets.

Rule 15d–19. Reports by shell companies on Form 20–F

Every foreign private issuer that was a shell company, other than a business combination related shell company, immediately before a transaction that causes it to cease to be a shell company shall, within four business days of completion of that transaction, file a report on Form 20–F (17 CFR 249.220f) containing the information that would be required if the issuer were filing a form for registration of securities on Form 20–F to register under the Act all classes of the issuer's securities subject to the reporting requirements of section 13 or section 15(d) of the Act upon consummation of the transaction, with such information reflecting the registrant and its securities upon consummation of the transaction.

Rule 15d–20. Plain English presentation of specified information

(a) Any information included or incorporated by reference in a report filed under section 15(d) of the Act that is required to be disclosed pursuant to Item 402, 403, 404 or 407 of Regulation S–K must be presented in a clear, concise and understandable manner. You must prepare the disclosure using the following standards:

(1) Present information in clear, concise sections, paragraphs and sentences;

(2) Use short sentences;

(3) Use definite, concrete, everyday words;

(4) Use the active voice;

(5) Avoid multiple negatives;

(6) Use descriptive headings and subheadings;

(7) Use a tabular presentation or bullet lists for complex material, wherever possible;

(8) Avoid legal jargon and highly technical business and other terminology;

(9) Avoid frequent reliance on glossaries or defined terms as the primary means of explaining information. Define terms in a glossary or other section of the document only if the meaning is unclear from the context. Use a glossary only if it facilitates understanding of the disclosure; and

(10) In designing the presentation of the information you may include pictures, logos, charts, graphs and other design elements so long as the design is not misleading and the required information is clear. You are encouraged to use tables, schedules, charts and graphic illustrations that present relevant data in an understandable manner, so long as such presentations are consistent with applicable disclosure requirements and consistent with other information in the document. You must draw graphs and charts to scale. Any information you provide must not be misleading.

(b) [Reserved]

NOTE TO RULE 15d–20: In drafting the disclosure to comply with this section, you should avoid the following:

1. Legalistic or overly complex presentations that make the substance of the disclosure difficult to understand;

2. Vague "boilerplate" explanations that are imprecise and readily subject to different interpretations;

3. Complex information copied directly from legal documents without any clear and concise explanation of the provision(s); and

4. Disclosure repeated in different sections of the document that increases the size of the document but does not enhance the quality of the information.

EXEMPTION OF CERTAIN ISSUERS FROM SECTION 15(d) OF THE ACT

Rule 15d–21. Reports for employee stock purchase, savings and similar plans

(a) Separate annual and other reports need not be filed pursuant to section 15(d) of the Act with respect to any employee stock purchase, savings or similar plan: *Provided*,

(1) The issuer of the stock or other securities offered to employees through their participation in the plan files annual reports on Form 10–K (17 CFR 249.310); and

(2) Such issuer furnishes, as a part of its annual report on such form or as an amendment thereto, the financial statements required by Form 11–K with respect to the plan.

(b) If the procedure permitted by this Rule is followed, the financial statements required by Form 11–K with respect to the plan shall be filed within 120 days after the end of the fiscal year of the plan, either as a part of or as an amendment to the annual report of the issuer for its last fiscal year, *provided that* if the fiscal year of the plan ends within 62 days prior to the end of the fiscal year of the issuer, such information, financial statements and exhibits may be furnished as a part of the issuer's next annual report. If a plan subject to the Employee Retirement Income Security Act of 1974 uses the procedure permitted by this Rule, the financial statements required by Form 11–K shall be filed within 180 days after the plan's fiscal year end.

Rule 15d–22. Reporting regarding asset-backed securities under Section 15(d) of the Act

(a) With respect to an offering of asset-backed securities registered pursuant to Rule 415(a)(1)(vii) or Rule 415(a)(1)(xii) under the Securities Act of 1933:

(1) Annual and other reports need not be filed pursuant to section 15(d) of the Act regarding

any class of securities to which such registration statement relates until the first bona fide sale in a takedown of securities under the registration statement; and

(2) The starting and suspension dates for any reporting obligation under section 15(d) of the Act with respect to a takedown of any class of asset-backed securities are determined separately for each takedown of securities under the registration statement.

(b) The duty to file annual and other reports pursuant to section 15(d) of the Act regarding any class of asset-backed securities is suspended:

(1) As to any semi-annual fiscal period, if, at the beginning of the semi-annual fiscal period, other than a period in the fiscal year within which the registration statement became effective, or, for offerings conducted pursuant to Rule 415(a)(1)(vii) or Rule 415(a)(1)(xii) under the Securities Act of 1933, the takedown for the offering occurred, there are no asset-backed securities of such class that were sold in a registered transaction held by non-affiliates of the depositor and a certification on Form 15 (17 CFR 249.323) has been filed; or

(2) When there are no asset-backed securities of such class that were sold in a registered transaction still outstanding, immediately upon filing with the Commission a certification on Form 15 (17 CFR 249.323) if the issuer of such class has filed all reports required by Section 13(a), without regard to Rule 12b–25 (17 CFR 249.322), for the shorter of its most recent three fiscal years and the portion of the current year preceding the date of filing Form 15, or the period since the issuer became subject to such reporting obligation. If the certification on Form 15 is subsequently withdrawn or denied, the issuer shall, within 60 days, file with the Commission all reports which would have been required if such certification had not been filed.

NOTE 1 TO PARAGRAPH (b): Securities held of record by a broker, dealer, bank or nominee for any of them for the accounts of customers shall be considered as held by the separate accounts for which the securities are held.

NOTE 2 TO PARAGRAPH (b): An issuer may not suspend reporting if the issuer and its affiliates acquire and resell securities as part of a plan or scheme to evade the reporting obligations of Section 15(d).

(c) This section does not affect any other reporting obligation applicable with respect to any classes of securities from additional takedowns under the same or different registration statements or any reporting obligation that may be applicable pursuant to section 12 of the Act.

Rule 15d–23. Reporting regarding certain securities underlying asset-backed securities under Section 15(d) of the Act

(a) Regarding a class of asset-backed securities, if the asset pool for the asset-backed securities includes a pool asset representing an interest in or the right to the payments or cash flows of another asset pool, then no separate annual and other reports need be filed pursuant to section 15(d) of the Act because of the separate registration of the distribution of the pool asset under the Securities Act (15 U.S.C. 77a *et seq.*), if the following conditions are met:

(1) Both the issuing entity for the asset-backed securities and the entity that issued the pool asset were established under the direction of the same sponsor and depositor;

(2) The pool asset was created solely to satisfy legal requirements or otherwise facilitate the structuring of the asset-backed securities transaction;

(3) The pool asset is not part of a scheme to avoid the registration or reporting requirements of the Act;

(4) The pool asset is held by the issuing entity and is a part of the asset pool for the asset-backed securities; and

(5) The offering of the asset-backed securities and the offering of the pool asset were both registered under the Securities Act (15 U.S.C. 77a *et seq.*).

(b) Paragraph (a) of this section does not affect any reporting obligation applicable with respect to the asset-backed securities or any other reporting obligation that may be applicable with respect to the pool asset or any other securities by the issuer of that pool asset pursuant to section 12 or 15(d) of the Act.

(c) This section does not affect any obligation to provide information regarding the pool asset or the asset pool underlying the pool asset in a filing with respect to the asset-backed securities. See Item 1100(d) of Regulation AB.

(d) Terms used in this section have the same meaning as in Item 1101 of Regulation AB.

PENNY STOCKS

Rule 15g–1. Exemptions for certain transactions

The following transactions shall be exempt from Rules 15g–2, 15g–3, 15g–4, 15g–5, and 15g–6:

(a) Transactions by a broker or dealer:

(1) Whose commissions, commission equivalents, mark-ups, and mark-downs from transactions in penny stocks during each of the immediately preceding three months and during eleven or more of the preceding twelve months, or during the immediately preceding six months, did not exceed five percent of its total commissions, commission equivalents, mark-ups, and mark-downs from transactions in securities during those months; and

(2) Who has not been a market maker in the penny stock that is the subject of the transaction in the immediately preceding twelve months.

NOTE: Prior to April 28, 1993, commissions, commission equivalents, mark-ups, and mark-downs from transactions in designated securities, as defined in Rule 15c2–6(d)(2) as of April 15, 1992, may be considered to be commissions, commission equivalents, mark-ups, and mark-downs from transactions in penny stocks for purposes of paragraph (a)(1) of this rule.

(b) Transactions in which the customer is an institutional accredited investor, as defined in Rules 501(a) (1), (2), (3), (7), or (8).

(c) Transactions that meet the requirements of Regulation D, or transactions with an issuer not involving any public offering pursuant to section 4(a)(2) of the Securities Act of 1933.

(d) Transactions in which the customer is the issuer, or a director, officer, general partner, or direct or indirect beneficial owner of more than five percent of any class of equity security of the issuer, of the penny stock that is the subject of the transaction.

(e) Transactions that are not recommended by the broker or dealer.

(f) Any other transaction or class of transactions or persons or class of persons that, upon prior written request or upon its own motion, the Commission conditionally or unconditionally exempts by order as consistent with the public interest and the protection of investors.

Rule 15g–2. Penny stock disclosure document relating to the penny stock market

(a) It shall be unlawful for a broker or dealer to effect a transaction in any penny stock for or with the account of a customer unless, prior to effecting such transaction, the broker or dealer has furnished to the customer a document containing the information set forth in Schedule 15G, Rule 15g–100, and has obtained from the customer a signed and dated acknowledgement of receipt of the document.

(b) Regardless of the form of acknowledgement used to satisfy the requirements of paragraph (a) of this rule, it shall be unlawful for a broker or dealer to effect a transaction in any penny stock for or with the account of a customer less than two business days after the broker or dealer sends such document.

(c) The broker or dealer shall preserve, as part of its records, a copy of the written acknowledgment required by paragraph (a) of this rule for the period specified in Rule 17a–4(b).

(d) Upon request of the customer, the broker or dealer shall furnish the customer with a copy of the information set forth on the Commission's Web site at *http://www.sec.gov/investor/pubs/microcapstock.htm.*

Rule 15g–3. Broker or dealer disclosure of quotations and other information relating to the penny stock market

(a) *Requirement.* It shall be unlawful for a broker or dealer to effect a transaction in any penny stock with or for the account of a customer unless such broker or dealer discloses to such customer, within the time periods and in the manner required by paragraph (b) of this rule, the following information:

(1) The inside bid quotation and the inside offer quotation for the penny stock.

(2) If paragraph (a)(1) of this rule does not apply because of the absence of an inside bid quotation and an inside offer quotation:

(i) With respect to a transaction effected with or for a customer on a principal basis (other than as provided in paragraph (a)(2)(ii) of this rule):

(A) The dealer shall disclose its offer price for the security:

(1) If during the previous five days the dealer has effected no fewer than three *bona fide* sales to other dealers consistently at its offer price for the security current at the time of those sales, and

(2) If the dealer reasonably believes in good faith at the time of the transaction

with the customer that its offer price accurately reflects the price at which it is willing to sell one or more round lots to another dealer. For purposes of paragraph (a)(2)(i)(A) of this rule, "consistently" shall constitute, at a minimum, seventy-five percent of the dealer's *bona fide* interdealer sales during the previous five-day period, and, if the dealer has effected only three *bona fide* inter-dealer sales during such period, all three of such sales.

(B) The dealer shall disclose its bid price for the security:

(1) If during the previous five days the dealer has effected no fewer than three *bona fide* purchases from other dealers consistently at its bid price for the security current at the time of those purchases, and

(2) If the dealer reasonably believes in good faith at the time of the transaction with the customer that its bid price accurately reflects the price at which it is willing to buy one or more round lots from another dealer. For purposes of paragraph (a)(2)(i)(B) of this rule, "consistently" shall constitute, at a minimum, seventy-five percent of the dealer's *bona fide* interdealer purchases during the previous five-day period, and, if the dealer has effected only three *bona fide* inter-dealer purchases during such period, all three of such purchases.

(C) If the dealer's bid or offer prices to the customer do not satisfy the criteria of paragraphs (a)(2)(i)(A) or (a)(2)(i)(B) of this rule, the dealer shall disclose to the customer:

(1) That it has not effected inter-dealer purchases or sales of the penny stock consistently at its bid or offer price, and

(2) The price at which it last purchased the penny stock from, or sold the penny stock to, respectively, another dealer in a *bona fide* transaction.

(ii) With respect to transactions effected by a broker or dealer with or for the account of the customer:

(A) On an agency basis or

(B) On a basis other than as a market maker in the security, where, after having received an order from the customer to purchase a penny stock, the dealer effects the purchase from another person to offset a contemporaneous sale of the penny stock to such customer, or, after having received an order from the customer to sell the penny stock, the dealer effects the sale to another person to offset a contemporaneous purchase from such customer, the broker or dealer shall disclose the best independent inter-dealer bid and offer prices for the penny stock that the broker or dealer obtains through reasonable diligence. A broker-dealer shall be deemed to have exercised reasonable diligence if it obtains quotations from three market makers in the security (or all known market makers if there are fewer than three).

(3) With respect to bid or offer prices and transaction prices disclosed pursuant to paragraph (a) of this rule, the broker or dealer shall disclose the number of shares to which the bid and offer prices apply.

(b) *Timing.* (1) The information described in paragraph (a) of this rule:

(i) Shall be provided to the customer orally or in writing prior to effecting any transaction with or for the customer for the purchase or sale of such penny stock; and

(ii) Shall be given or sent to the customer in writing, at or prior to the time that any written confirmation of the transaction is given or sent to the customer pursuant to Rule 10b–10.

(2) A broker or dealer, at the time of making the disclosure pursuant to paragraph (b)(1)(i) of this rule, shall make and preserve as part of its records, a record of such disclosure for the period specified in Rule 17a–4(b).

(c) *Definitions.* For purposes of this rule:

(1) The term *bid price* shall mean the price most recently communicated by the dealer to another broker or dealer at which the dealer is willing to purchase one or more round lots of the penny stock, and shall not include indications of interest.

(2) The term *offer price* shall mean the price most recently communicated by the dealer to another broker or dealer at which the dealer is willing to sell one or more round lots of the penny stock and shall not include indications of interest.

(3) The term *inside bid quotation* for a security shall mean the highest bid quotation for the security displayed by a market maker in the security on a Qualifying Electronic Quotation System, at

any time in which at least two market makers are contemporaneously displaying on such system bid and offer quotations for the security at specified prices.

(4) The term *inside offer quotation* for a security shall mean the lowest offer quotation for the security displayed by a market maker in the security on a Qualifying Electronic Quotation System, at any time in which at least two market makers are contemporaneously displaying on such system bid and offer quotations for the security at specified prices.

(5) The term *Qualifying Electronic Quotation System* shall mean an automated inter-dealer quotation system that has the characteristics set forth in section 17B(b)(2) of the Act, or such other automated inter-dealer quotation system designated by the Commission for purposes of this rule.

Rule 15g–4. Disclosure of compensation to brokers or dealers

PRELIMINARY NOTE

Brokers and dealers may wish to refer to Securities Exchange Act Release No. 30608 (April 20, 1992) for a discussion of the procedures for computing compensation in active and competitive markets, inactive and competitive markets, and dominated and controlled markets.

(a) *Disclosure Requirement.* It shall be unlawful for any broker or dealer to effect a transaction in any penny stock for or with the account of a customer unless such broker or dealer discloses to such customer, within the time periods and in the manner required by paragraph (b) of this rule, the aggregate amount of any compensation received by such broker or dealer in connection with such transaction.

(b) *Timing.* (1) The information described in paragraph (a) of this rule:

(i) Shall be provided to the customer orally or in writing prior to effecting any transaction with or for the customer for the purchase or sale of such penny stock; and

(ii) Shall be given or sent to the customer in writing, at or prior to the time that any written confirmation of the transaction is given or sent to the customer pursuant to Rule 10b–10.

(2) A broker or dealer, at the time of making the disclosure pursuant to paragraph (b)(1)(i) of this rule, shall make and preserve as part of the records, a record of each disclosure for the period specified in Rule 17a–4(b).

(c) *Definition of Compensation.* For purposes of this rule, *compensation* means, with respect to a transaction in a penny stock:

(1) If a broker is acting as agent for a customer, the amount of any remuneration received or to be received by it from such customer in connection with such transaction;

(2) If, after having received a buy order from a customer, a dealer other than a market maker purchased the penny stock as principal from another person to offset a contemporaneous sale to such customer or, after having received a sell order from a customer, sold the penny stock as principal to another person to offset a contemporaneous purchase from such customer, the difference between the price to the customer and such contemporaneous purchase or sale price; or

(3) If the dealer otherwise is acting as principal for its own account, the difference between the price to the customer and the prevailing market price.

(d) *Active and Competitive Market.* For purposes of this rule only, a market may be deemed to be "active and competitive" in determining the prevailing market price with respect to a transaction by a market maker in a penny stock if the aggregate number of transactions effected by such market maker in the penny stock in the five business days preceding such transaction is less than twenty percent of the aggregate number of all transactions in the penny stock reported on a Qualifying Electronic Quotation System (as defined in Rule 15g–3(c)(5)) during such five-day period. No presumption shall arise that a market is not "active and competitive" solely by reason of a market maker not meeting the conditions specified in this paragraph.

Rule 15g–5. Disclosure of compensation of associated persons in connection with penny stock transactions

(a) *General.* It shall be unlawful for a broker or dealer to effect a transaction in any penny stock for or with the account of a customer unless the broker or dealer discloses to such customer, within the time periods and in the manner required by paragraph (b) of this rule, the aggregate amount of cash compensation that any associated person of the broker or dealer who is a natural person and has communicated with the customer concerning the transaction at or prior to receipt of the customer's transaction order, other than any person whose function is solely clerical or ministerial, has received or will receive from any source in connection with the transaction and that is determined at or prior to the time of the transaction, including separate disclosure, if applicable, of the source and amount of such compensation that is not paid by the broker or dealer.

(b) *Timing.* (1) The information described in paragraph (a) of this rule:

(i) Shall be provided to the customer orally or in writing prior to effecting any transaction with or for the customer for the purchase or sale of such penny stock; and

(ii) Shall be given or sent to the customer in writing at or prior to the time that any written confirmation of the transaction is given or sent to the customer pursuant to Rule 10b–10.

(2) A broker or dealer, at the time of making the disclosure pursuant to paragraph (b)(1)(i) of this rule, shall make and preserve as part of its records, a record of such disclosure for the period specified in Rule 17a–4(b).

(c) *Contingent Compensation Arrangements.* Where a portion or all of the cash or other compensation that the associated person may receive in connection with the transaction may be determined and paid following the transaction based on aggregate sales volume levels or other contingencies, the written disclosure required by paragraph (b)(1)(ii) of this rule shall state that fact and describe the basis upon which such compensation is determined.

Rule 15g–6. Account statements for penny stock customers

(a) *Requirement.* It shall be unlawful for any broker or dealer that has effected the sale to any customer, other than in a transaction that is exempt pursuant to Rule 15g–1, of any security that is a penny stock on the last trading day of any calendar month, or any successor of such broker or dealer, to fail to give or send to such customer a written statement containing the information described in paragraphs (c) and (d) of this rule with respect to each such month in which such security is held for the customer's account with the broker or dealer, within ten days following the end of such month.

(b) *Exemptions.* A broker or dealer shall be exempted from the requirement of paragraph (a) of this rule under either of the following circumstances:

(1) If the broker or dealer does not effect any transactions in penny stocks for or with the account of the customer during a period of six consecutive calendar months, then the broker or dealer shall not be required to provide monthly statements for each quarterly period that is immediately subsequent to such six-month period and in which the broker or dealer does not effect any transaction in penny stocks for or with the account of the customer, *provided* that the broker or dealer gives or sends to the customer written statements containing the information described in paragraphs (d) and (e) of this rule on a quarterly basis, within ten days following the end of each such quarterly period.

(2) If, on all but five or fewer trading days of any quarterly period, a security has a price of five dollars or more, the broker or dealer shall not be required to provide a monthly statement covering the security for subsequent quarterly periods, until the end of any such subsequent quarterly period on the last trading day of which the price of the security is less than five dollars.

(c) *Price Determinations.* For purposes of paragraphs (a) and (b) of this rule, the price of a security on any trading day shall be determined at the close of business in accordance with the provisions of Rule 3a51–1(d)(1).

(d) *Market and Price Information.* The statement required by paragraph (a) of this rule shall contain at least the following information with respect to each penny stock covered by paragraph (a) of this rule, as of the last trading day of the period to which the statement relates:

(1) The identity and number of shares or units of each such security held for the customer's account; and

(2) The estimated market value of the security, to the extent that such estimated market value can be determined in accordance with the following provisions:

(i) The highest inside bid quotation for the security on the last trading day of the period to which the statement relates, multiplied by the number of shares or units of the security held for the customer's account; or

(ii) If paragraph (d)(2)(i) of this rule is not applicable because of the absence of an inside bid quotation, and if the broker or dealer furnishing the statement has effected at least ten separate Qualifying Purchases in the security during the last five trading days of the period to which the statement relates, the weighted average price per share paid by the broker or dealer in all Qualifying Purchases effected during such five-day period, multiplied by the number of shares or units of the security held for the customer's account; or

(iii) If neither of paragraphs (d)(2)(i) nor (d)(2)(ii) of this rule is applicable, a statement that there is "no estimated market value" with respect to the security.

(e) *Legend.* In addition to the information required by paragraph (d) of this rule, the written statement required by paragraph (a) of this rule shall include a conspicuous legend that is identified with the penny stocks described in the statement and that contains the following language:

If this statement contains an estimated value, you should be aware that this value may be based on a limited number of trades or quotes. Therefore, you may not be able to sell these securities at a price equal or near to the value shown. However, the broker-dealer furnishing this statement may not refuse to accept your order to sell these securities. Also, the amount you receive from a sale generally will be reduced by the amount of any commissions or similar charges. If an estimated value is not shown for a security, a value could not be determined because of a lack of information.

(f) *Preservation of Records.* Any broker or dealer subject to this rule shall preserve, as part of its records, copies of the written statements required by paragraph (a) of this rule and keep such records for the periods specified in Rule 17a–4(b).

(g) *Definitions.* For purposes of this rule:

(1) The term *Quarterly period* shall mean any period of three consecutive full calendar months.

(2) The *inside bid quotation* for a security shall mean the highest bid quotation for the security displayed by a market maker in the security on a Qualifying Electronic Quotation System, at any time in which at least two market makers are contemporaneously displaying on such system bid and offer quotations for the security at specified prices.

(3) The term *Qualifying Electronic Quotation System* shall mean an automated inter-dealer quotation system that has the characteristics set forth in Section 17B(b)(2) of the Act, or such other automated inter-dealer quotation system designated by the Commission for purposes of this rule.

(4) The term *Qualifying Purchases* shall mean *bona fide* purchases by a broker or dealer of a penny stock for its own account, each of which involves at least 100 shares, but excluding any block purchase involving more than one percent of the outstanding shares or units of the security.

Rule 15g–8. Sales of escrowed securities of blank check companies

As a means reasonably designed to prevent fraudulent, deceptive, or manipulative acts or practices, it shall be unlawful for any person to sell or offer to sell any security that is deposited and held in an escrow or trust account pursuant to Rule 419 under the Securities Act of 1933, or any interest in or related to such security, other than pursuant to a qualified domestic relations order as defined by the Internal Revenue Code of 1986, as amended (26 U.S.C. 1 *et seq.*), or Title I of the Employee Retirement Income Security Act (29 U.S.C. 1001 *et seq.*), or the rules thereunder.

Rule 15g–9. Sales practice requirements for certain low–priced securities

(a) As a means reasonably designed to prevent fraudulent, deceptive, or manipulative acts or practices, it shall be unlawful for a broker or dealer to sell a penny stock to, or to effect the purchase of a penny stock by, any person unless:

(1) The transaction is exempt under paragraph (c) of this rule; or

(2) Prior to the transaction:

(i) The broker or dealer has approved the person's account for transactions in penny stocks in accordance with the procedures set forth in paragraph (b) of this rule; and

(ii)(A) The broker or dealer has received from the person an agreement to the transaction setting forth the identity and quantity of the penny stock to be purchased; and

(B) Regardless of the form of agreement used to satisfy the requirements of paragraph (a)(2)(ii)(A) of this rule, it shall be unlawful for such broker or dealer to sell a penny stock to, or to effect the purchase of a penny stock by, for or with the account of a customer less than two business days after the broker or dealer sends such agreement.

(b) In order to approve a person's account for transactions in penny stocks, the broker or dealer must:

(1) Obtain from the person information concerning the person's financial situation, investment experience, and investment objectives;

(2) Reasonably determine, based on the information required by paragraph (b)(1) of this rule and any other information known by the broker-dealer, that transactions in penny stocks are

suitable for the person, and that the person (or the person's independent adviser in these transactions) has sufficient knowledge and experience in financial matters that the person (or the person's independent adviser in these transactions) reasonably may be expected to be capable of evaluating the risks of transactions in penny stocks;

(3) Deliver to the person a written statement:

(i) Setting forth the basis on which the broker or dealer made the determination required by paragraph (b)(2) of this rule;

(ii) Stating in a highlighted format that it is unlawful for the broker or dealer to effect a transaction in a penny stock subject to the provisions of paragraph (a)(2) of this rule unless the broker or dealer has received, prior to the transaction, a written agreement to the transaction from the person; and

(iii) Stating in a highlighted format immediately preceding the customer signature line that:

(A) The broker or dealer is required by this rule to provide the person with the written statement; and

(B) The person should not sign and return the written statement to the broker or dealer if it does not accurately reflect the person's financial situation, investment experience, and investment objectives; and

(4)(i) Obtain from the person a signed and dated copy of the statement required by paragraph (b)(3) of this rule; and

(ii) Regardless of the form of statement used to satisfy the requirements of paragraph (b)(4)(i) of this rule, it shall be unlawful for such broker or dealer to sell a penny stock to, or to effect the purchase of a penny stock by, for or with the account of a customer less than two business days after the broker or dealer sends such statement.

(c) For purposes of this rule, the following transactions shall be exempt:

(1) Transactions that are exempt under Rule 15g–1(a), (b), (d), (e), and (f).

(2) Transactions that meet the requirements of Rule 506 of the Securities Act of 1933 (including, where applicable, the requirements of Rule 501 through Rule 503, and Rule 507 through Rule 508), or transactions with an issuer not involving any public offering pursuant to section 4(a)(2) of the Securities Act of 1933.

(3) Transactions in which the purchaser is an established customer of the broker or dealer.

(d) For purposes of this rule:

(1) The term *penny stock* shall have the same meaning as in Rule 3a51–1.

(2) The term *established customer* shall mean any person for whom the broker or dealer, or a clearing broker on behalf of such broker or dealer, carries an account, and who in such account:

(i) Has effected a securities transaction, or made a deposit of funds or securities, more than one year previously; or

(ii) Has made three purchases of penny stocks that occurred on separate days and involved different issuers.

Rule 15g–100. Schedule 15G—Information to be included in the document distributed pursuant to Rule 15g–2

SECURITIES AND EXCHANGE COMMISSION
Washington, DC 20549

SCHEDULE 15G

Under the Securities Exchange Act of 1934

Instructions to Schedule 15G

A. Schedule 15G (Schedule) may be provided to customers in its entirety either on paper or electronically. It may also be provided to customers electronically through a link to the SEC's Web site.

1. *If the Schedule is sent in paper form*, the format and typeface of the Schedule must be reproduced exactly as presented. For example, words that are capitalized must remain capitalized, and words that are underlined or bold must remain underlined or bold. The typeface must be clear and easy to read. The Schedule may be reproduced either by photocopy or by printing.

2. *If the Schedule is sent electronically*, the e-mail containing the Schedule must have as a subject line "Important Information on Penny Stocks." The Schedule reproduced in the text of the e-mail must be clear, easy-to-read type presented in a manner reasonably calculated to draw the customer's attention to the language in the document, especially words that are capitalized, underlined or in bold.

3. *If the Schedule is sent electronically using a hyperlink to the SEC Website*, the e-mail contain-

ing the hyperlink must have as a subject line: "Important Information on Penny Stocks." Immediately before the hyperlink, the text of the e-mail must reproduce the following statement in clear, easy-to-read type presented in a manner reasonably calculated to draw the customer's attention to the words: "We are required by the U.S. Securities and Exchange Commission to give you the following disclosure statement: *http://www.sec.gov/investor/schedule15g.htm*. It explains some of the risks of investing in penny stocks. Please read it carefully before you agree to purchase or sell a penny stock."

B. Regardless of how the Schedule is provided to the customer, the communication must also provide the name, address, telephone number and e-mail address of the broker. E-mail messages may also include any privacy or confidentiality information that the broker routinely includes in e-mail messages sent to customers. No other information may be included in these communications, other than instructions on how to provide a signed and dated acknowledgement of receipt of the Schedule.

C. The document entitled "Important Information on Penny Stocks" must be distributed as Schedule 15G and must be no more than two pages in length if provided in paper form.

D. The disclosures made through the Schedule are in addition to any other disclosures that are required under the Federal securities laws.

E. Recipients of the document must not be charged any fee for the document.

F. The content of the Schedule is as follows:

Important Information on Penny Stocks

The U.S. Securities and Exchange Commission (SEC) requires your broker to give this statement to you, and to obtain your signature to show that you have received it, before your first trade in a penny stock. This statement contains important information—and you should read it carefully before you sign it, and before you decide to purchase or sell a penny stock.

In addition to obtaining your signature, the SEC requires your broker to wait at least two business days after sending you this statement before executing your first trade to give you time to carefully consider your trade.

Penny Stocks Can Be Very Risky

Penny stocks are low-priced shares of small companies. Penny stocks may trade infrequently—which means that it may be difficult to sell penny stock shares once you have them. Because it may also be difficult to find quotations for penny stocks, they may be impossible to accurately price. Investors in penny stock should be prepared for the possibility that they may lose their whole investment.

While penny stocks generally trade over-the-counter, they may also trade on U.S. securities exchanges, facilities of U.S. exchanges, or foreign exchanges. You should learn about the market in which the penny stock trades to determine how much demand there is for this stock and how difficult it will be to sell. Be especially careful if your broker is offering to sell you newly issued penny stock that has no established trading market.

The securities you are considering have not been approved or disapproved by the SEC. Moreover, the SEC has not passed upon the fairness or the merits of this transaction nor upon the accuracy or adequacy of the information contained in any prospectus or any other information provided by an issuer or a broker or dealer.

Information You Should Get

In addition to this statement, your broker is required to give you a statement of your financial situation and investment goals explaining why his or her firm has determined that penny stocks are a suitable investment for you. In addition, your broker is required to obtain your agreement to the proposed penny stock transaction.

Before you buy penny stock, Federal law requires your salesperson to tell you the "*offer*" and the "*bid*" on the stock, and the "*compensation*" the salesperson and the firm receive for the trade. The firm also must send a confirmation of these prices to you after the trade. You will need this price information to determine what profit or loss, if any, you will have when you sell your stock.

The offer price is the wholesale price at which the dealer is willing to sell stock to other dealers. The bid price is the wholesale price at which the dealer is willing to buy the stock from other dealers. In its trade with you, the dealer may add a retail charge to these wholesale prices as compensation (called a "markup" or "markdown").

The difference between the bid and the offer price is the dealer's "*spread.*" A spread that is large compared with the purchase price can make a resale of a stock very costly. To be profitable when you sell, the bid price of your stock must rise above the amount of this spread *and* the compensation charged by both your selling and purchasing dealers. *Remember that if the dealer has no bid price, you may not be able to sell the stock after you buy it, and may lose your whole investment.*

After you buy penny stock, your brokerage firm must send you a monthly account statement that gives an estimate of the value of each penny stock in your account, if there is enough information to make an estimate. If the firm has not bought or sold any penny stocks for your account for six months, it can provide these statements every three months.

Additional information about low-priced securities—including penny stocks—is available on the SEC's Web site at *http://www.sec.gov/investor/pubs/microcapstock.htm*. In addition, your broker will send you a copy of this information upon request. The SEC encourages you to learn all you can before making this investment.

Brokers' Duties and Customers' Rights and Remedies

Remember that your salesperson is not an impartial advisor—he or she is being paid to sell you stock. Do not rely only on the salesperson, but seek outside advice before you buy any stock. You can get the disciplinary history of a salesperson or firm from NASD at 1–800–289–9999 or contact NASD via the Internet at *http://www.nasd.com*. You can also get additional information from your state securities official. The North American Securities Administrators Association, Inc. can give you contact information for your state. You can reach NASAA at (202) 737–0900 or via the Internet at *www.nasaa.org*.

If you have problems with a salesperson, contact the firm's compliance officer. You can also contact the securities regulators listed above. Finally, if you are a victim of fraud, you may have rights and remedies under state and Federal law. In addition to the regulators listed above, you also may contact the SEC with complaints at (800) SEC-0330 or via the Internet at *help@sec.gov*.

NATIONAL AND AFFILIATED SECURITIES ASSOCIATIONS

Rule 15Aa–1. Registration of a national or an affiliated securities association

Any application for registration of an association as a national, or as an affiliated securities association shall be made in triplicate on Form X–15AA–1 accompanied by three copies of the exhibits prescribed by the Commission to be filed in connection therewith.

Rule 15Aj–1. Amendments and supplements to registration statements of securities associations

Every association applying for registration or registered as a national securities association or as an affiliated securities association shall keep its registration statement up to date in the manner prescribed below:

(a) *Amendments.* Promptly after the discovery of any inaccuracy in the registration statement or in any amendment or supplement thereto the association shall file with the Commission an amendment correcting such inaccuracy.

(b) *Current Supplements.* Promptly after any change which renders no longer accurate any information contained or incorporated in the registration statement or in any amendment or supplement thereto the association shall file with the Commission a current supplement setting forth such change, except that:

(1) Supplements setting forth changes in the information called for in Exhibit C need not be filed until 10 days after the calendar month in which the changes occur.

(2) No current supplements need be filed with respect to changes in the information called for in Exhibit B.

(3) If changes in the information called for in items (1) and (2) of Exhibit C are reported in any record which is published at least once a month by the association and promptly filed in triplicate with the Commission, no current supplement need be filed with respect thereto.

(c) *Annual Supplements.* (1) Promptly after March 1 of each year, the association shall file with the Commission an annual consolidated supplement as of such date on Form X–15AJ–2 (17 CFR 249.803) except that:

(i) If the securities association publishes or cooperates in the publication of the information required in Items 6(a) and 6(b) of Form X–15AJ–2 on an annual or more frequent basis, in lieu of filing such an item the securities association may:

(A) Identify the publication in which such information is available, the name, address, and telephone number of the person from whom such publication may be obtained, and the price thereof; and

(B) Certify to the accuracy of such information as of its date.

(ii) Promptly after March 1, 1995, and every three years thereafter each association shall file complete Exhibit A to Form X-15AJ-2. The information contained in this exhibit shall be up to date as of the latest practicable date within 3 months of the date on which these exhibits are filed. If the association publishes or cooperates in the publication of the information required in this exhibit on an annual or more frequent basis, in lieu of filing such exhibit the association may:

(A) Identify the publication in which such information is available, the name, address, and telephone number of the person from whom such publication may be obtained, and the price thereof; and

(B) Certify to the accuracy of such information as of its date. If a securities association keeps the information required in this exhibit up to date and makes it available to the Commission and the public upon request, in lieu of filing such an exhibit a securities association may certify that the information is kept up to date and is available to the Commission and the public upon request.

(2) Promptly after the close of each fiscal year of the association, it shall file with the Commission a supplement setting forth its balance sheet as of the close of such year and its income and expense statement for such year.

(d) *Filing, Dating, Etc.* Each amendment or supplement shall be filed in triplicate, at least one of which must be signed and attested, in the same manner as required in the case of the original registration statement, and must conform to the requirements of Form X-15AJ-1, except that the annual consolidated supplement shall be filed on Form X-15AJ-2. All amendments and supplements shall be dated and numbered in order of filing. One amendment or supplement may include any number of changes. In addition to the formal filing of amendments and supplements above described, each association shall send to the Commission three copies of any notices, reports, circulars, loose-leaf insertions, riders, new additions, lists, or other records of changes covered by amendments or supplements when, as, and if such records are made available to members of the association.

Rule 15A*l*2-1. [Reserved]

Rule 15Ba2-1. Application for registration of municipal securities dealers which are banks or separately identifiable departments or divisions of banks

(a) An application for registration, pursuant to Section 15B(a) of the Act, of a municipal securities dealer which is a bank (as defined in section 3(a)(6) of the Act) or a separately identifiable department or division of a bank (as defined by the Municipal Securities Rulemaking Board), shall be filed with the Commission on Form MSD (17 CFR 249.950), in accordance with the instructions contained therein.

(b) If the information contained in any application for registration pursuant to paragraph (a) of this rule, or in any amendment to such application, is or becomes inaccurate for any reason, applicant shall promptly file an amendment on Form MSD (17 CFR 249.950) correcting such information.

(c) Every amendment filed pursuant to this rule shall constitute a "report" within the meaning of sections 17 and 32(a) of the Act.

Rule 15Ba2-2. Application for registration of non-bank municipal securities dealers whose business is exclusively intrastate

(a) An application for registration, pursuant to section 15B(a) of the Act, of a municipal securities dealer who is not subject to the requirements of Rule 15Ba2-1, that is filed on or after January 25, 1993, shall be filed with the Central Registration Depository (operated by the Financial Industry Regulatory Authority, Inc.) on Form BD in accordance with the instructions contained therein.

(b) Every applicant shall file with its application for registration a statement that such applicant is filing for registration as an intrastate dealer in accordance with the requirements of this rule. Such statement shall be deemed a part of the application for registration.

(c) If the information contained in any application for registration filed pursuant to paragraph (a) of this rule, or in any amendment to such application, is or becomes inaccurate for any reason, the dealer shall promptly file with the Central Registration Depository an amendment on Form BD correcting such information.

(d) Every application or amendment filed with the Central Registration Depository pursuant to this section shall constitute a "report" filed with the Commission within the meaning of Sections 15(b), 15B(c), 17(a), 18(a), 32(a) and other applicable provisions of the Act.

Rule 15Ba2–4. Registration of successor to registered municipal securities dealer

(a) In the event that a municipal securities dealer succeeds to and continues the business of a registered municipal securities dealer, the registration of the predecessor shall be deemed to remain effective as the registration of the successor if the successor, within 30 days after such succession, files an application for registration on Form MSD, in the case of a municipal securities dealer that is a bank or a separately identifiable department or division of a bank, or Form BD, in the case of any other municipal securities dealer, and the predecessor files a notice of withdrawal from registration on Form MSDW or Form BDW, as the case may be; *Provided, however,* That the registration of the predecessor dealer will cease to be effective as the registration of the successor dealer 45 days after the application for registration on Form MSD or Form BD is filed by such successor.

(b) Notwithstanding paragraph (a) of this rule, if a municipal securities dealer succeeds to and continues the business of a registered predecessor municipal securities dealer, and the succession is based solely on a change in the predecessor's date or state of incorporation, form of organization, or composition of a partnership, the successor may, within 30 days after the succession, amend the registration of the predecessor dealer on Form MSD, in the case of a predecessor municipal securities dealer that is a bank or a separately identifiable department or division of a bank, or on Form BD, in the case of any other municipal securities dealer, to reflect these changes. This amendment shall be deemed an application for registration filed by the predecessor and adopted by the successor.

Rule 15Ba2–5. Registration of fiduciaries

The registration of a municipal securities dealer shall be deemed to be the registration of any executor, administrator, guardian, conservator, assignee for the benefit of creditors, receiver, trustee in insolvency or bankruptcy, or other fiduciary, appointed or qualified by order, judgment, or decree of a court of competent jurisdiction to continue the business of such registered municipal securities dealer; provided, that such fiduciary files with the Commission, within 30 days after entering upon the performance of his duties, a statement setting forth as to such fiduciary substantially the information required by Form MSD, if the municipal securities dealer is a bank or a separately identifiable department of a bank, or Form BD, if the municipal securities dealer is other than a bank or a separately identifiable department or division of a bank.

Rule 15Bc3–1. Withdrawal from registration of municipal securities dealers

(a) Notice of withdrawal from registration as a municipal securities dealer pursuant to Section 15B(c) shall be filed on Form MSDW (17 CFR 249.1110), in the case of a municipal securities dealer which is a bank or a separately identifiable department or division of a bank, or Form BDW (17 CFR 249.501a), in the case of any other municipal securities dealer, in accordance with the instructions contained therein. Prior to filing a notice of withdrawal from registration on Form MSDW (17 CFR 249.1110) or Form BDW (17 CFR 249.501a), a municipal securities dealer shall amend Form MSD (17 CFR 249.1100) in accordance with Rule 15Ba2–1(b) or amend Form BD (17 CFR 249.501) in accordance with Rule 15Ba2–2(c) to update any inaccurate information.

(b) Every notice of withdrawal from registration as a municipal securities dealer that is filed on Form BDW (17 CFR 249.501a) shall be filed with the Central Registration Depository (operated by the Financial Industry Regulatory Authority, Inc.) in accordance with applicable filing requirements. Every notice of withdrawal of Form MSDW (17 CFR 249.1110) shall be filed with the Commission.

(c) A notice of withdrawal from registration filed by a municipal securities dealer pursuant to Section 15B(c) shall become effective for all matters on the 60th day after the filing thereof with the Commission, within such longer period of time as to which such municipal securities dealer consents or which the Commission by order may determine as necessary or appropriate in the public interest or for the protection of investors, or within such shorter period of time as the Commission may determine. If a notice of withdrawal from registration is filed with the Commission at any time subsequent to the date of the issuance of a Commission order instituting proceedings pursuant to Section 15B(c) to censure, place limitations on the activities, functions or operations of, or suspend or revoke the registration of, such municipal securities dealer, or if prior to the effective date of the notice of withdrawal pursuant to this paragraph (c), the Commission institutes such a proceeding or a proceeding to impose terms or conditions upon such withdrawal, the notice of withdrawal shall not become effective pursuant to this paragraph (c) except at such time and upon such terms and conditions as the Commission deems necessary or appropriate in the public interest or for the protection of investors.

(d) Every notice of withdrawal filed with the Central Registration Depository pursuant to this section shall constitute a "report" filed with the Commission within the meaning of Sections 15B(c), 17(a), 18(a), 32(a) and other applicable provisions of the Act.

(e) The Commission, by order, may exempt any broker or dealer from the filing requirements provided in Form BDW (17 CFR 249.501a) under conditions that differ from the filing instructions contained in Form BDW.

Rule 15Bc7–1. Availability of examination reports

(a) Upon written request, copies of any report of an examination of a municipal securities dealer made by the Commission or furnished to it by an appropriate regulatory agency pursuant to section 17(c)(3) of the Act or by a registered securities association pursuant to section 15B(c)(7)(B) of the Act shall be made available to the Municipal Securities Rulemaking Board (the "Board") by the Commission, subject to the following limitations:

(1) The Board shall establish by rule and shall maintain adequate procedures for ensuring the confidentiality of any information made available to it by the Commission pursuant to section 15B(c)(7)(B) of the Act;

(2) Information made available to the Board shall not identify any municipal securities broker, municipal securities dealer, or associated person that is the subject of a non-public examination report.

(b) If information to be made available to the Board is furnished to the Commission on a separate form prepared by an appropriate regulatory agency other than the Commission or by a registered securities association, that form, rather than a copy of any report of an examination, will be made available to the Board, provided that the conditions set forth in this paragraph are satisfied. Within sixty days of every six month period ending May 31 and November 30, each appropriate regulatory agency or registered securities association making available information on a separate form shall furnish to the Commission two copies of a form containing the information set forth in paragraphs (b)(1) through (b)(8) of this rule. The Commission shall make one copy of the form promptly available to the Board. Copies of any forms furnished pursuant to this paragraph shall not identify any municipal securities broker, municipal securities dealer, or associated person that is the subject of an examination from which information was derived for the form; however, the Commission may obtain for its own use, upon request, the identity of any such examinee or the full examination reports. Furnished forms shall include the following information:

(1) The report period.

(2)(i) With respect to a registered securities association, the number of examinations that formed the basis of the report and, of these examinations, the number that were routine, special, and financial/operational. (ii) With respect to an appropriate regulatory agency that is a bank agency, the number of examinations that formed the basis of the report and, of these examinations, the number that were routine, special, and financial/operational. The number of examinations that formed the basis of the report of bank dealers and the number of examinations of separately identifiable departments or divisions of banks effecting municipal securities transactions.

(3) Indications of the violations of each Board rule found in examinations that formed the basis for the report.

(4) Copies of public notices issued during the report period of any formal actions and non-public information regarding any actions taken on violations of Board rules.

(5) Any comments concerning any questionable practices relating to municipal securities activities, whether or not covered by provisions of the Act and the rules and regulations thereunder, including the rules of the Board.

(6) Descriptions of any significant or recurring customer complaints relating to municipal securities activities received by the appropriate regulatory agency or registered securities association during the report period or by municipal securities dealers during the 12 month period preceding the examination.

(7) Description of any novel issues or interpretations arising under the Board's rules.

(8) Description of any changes to existing Board rules or additional rules that would improve the regulatory scheme for municipal securities profes-

sionals or assist in the enforcement of the Board's rules.

(c) Copies of any report of an examination of a municipal securities broker or municipal securities dealer made by the Commission or furnished to it pursuant to section 15B(c)(7)(B) or 17(c)(3) of the Act, or separate forms made available to the Commission pursuant to paragraph (b) of this rule, will be maintained in a non-public file.

REGISTRATION OF GOVERNMENT SECURITIES BROKERS AND GOVERNMENT SECURITIES DEALERS

Rule 15Ca1–1. Notice of government securities broker-dealer activities

(a) Every government securities broker or government securities dealer that is a broker or dealer registered pursuant to section 15 or 15B of the Act (other than a financial institution as defined in section 3(a)(46) of the Act) shall file with the Commission written notice on Form BD (17 CFR 249.501) in accordance with the instructions contained therein that it is a government securities broker or government securities dealer. After July 25, 1987, every broker or dealer subject to this paragraph shall file notice that it is a government securities broker or government securities dealer prior to or on the date it begins acting as a government securities broker or government securities dealer.

(b) Every government securities broker or government securities dealer required to file notice under paragraph (a) of this rule shall file with the Commission written notice on Form BD in accordance with the instructions contained therein when it ceases to be a government securities broker or government securities dealer. Notice shall be filed within 30 days after the date the broker or dealer has ceased acting as a government securities broker or a government securities dealer.

(c) Any notice required pursuant to this section shall be considered filed with the Commission if it is filed with the Central Registration Depository (operated by the Financial Industry Regulatory Authority, Inc.) in accordance with applicable filing requirements.

Rule 15Ca2–1. Application for registration as a government securities broker or government securities dealer

(a) An application for registration pursuant to Section 15C(a)(1)(A) of the Act, of a government securities broker or government securities dealer that is filed on or after January 25, 1993, shall be filed with the Central Registration Depository (operated by the Financial Industry Regulatory Authority, Inc.) on Form BD in accordance with the instructions contained therein.

(b) Every application or amendment filed pursuant to this rule shall constitute a "report" filed with the Commission within the meaning of Sections 15, 15C, 17(a), 18, 32(a), and other applicable provisions of the Act.

Rule 15Ca2–2. [Reserved]

Rule 15Ca2–3. Registration of successor to registered government securities broker or government securities dealer

(a) In the event that a government securities broker or government securities dealer succeeds to and continues the business of a government securities broker or government securities dealer registered pursuant to section 15C(a)(1)(A) of the Act, the registration of the predecessor shall be deemed to remain effective as the registration of the successor if the successor, within 30 days after such succession, files an application for registration on Form BD, and the predecessor files a notice of withdrawal from registration on Form BDW; *Provided, however,* That the registration of the predecessor government securities broker or government securities dealer will cease to be effective as the registration of the successor government securities broker or government securities dealer 45 days after the application for registration on Form BD is filed by such successor.

(b) Notwithstanding paragraph (a) of this rule, if a government securities broker or government securities dealer succeeds to and continues the business of a predecessor government securities broker or government securities dealer that is registered pursuant to section 15C(a)(1)(A) of the Act, and the succession is based solely on a change in the predecessor's date or state of incorporation, form of organization, or composition of a partnership, the successor may, within 30 days after the succession, amend the registration of the predecessor broker or dealer on Form BD to reflect these changes. This amendment shall be deemed an application for registration filed by the predecessor and adopted by the successor.

Rule 15Ca2–4. Registration of fiduciaries

The registration of a government securities broker or government securities dealer pursuant to section 15C of the Act shall be deemed to be the registration of any executor, administrator, guardian, conservator, assignee for the benefit of creditors, receiver, trustee in insolvency or bankruptcy, or other fiduciary, appointed or qualified by order, judgment, or decree of a court of competent jurisdiction to continue the business of such registered government securities broker or government securities dealer, provided that such fiduciary files with the Commission, no more than 30 days after entering upon the performance of its duties, a statement setting forth as to such fiduciary substantially the information required by Form BD.

Rule 15Ca2–5. Consent to service of process to be furnished by non-resident government securities brokers or government securities dealers and by non-resident general partners or managing agents of government securities brokers or government securities dealers

(a) Each non-resident government securities broker or government securities dealer applying for registration pursuant to section 15C(a)(1)(A) of the Act, each non-resident general partner of a government securities broker or government securities dealer partnership that is applying for such registration, and each non-resident managing agent of any other unincorporated government securities broker or government securities dealer that is applying for registration, shall furnish to the Commission, in a form acceptable to the Commission, a written irrevocable consent and power of attorney that—

(1) Designates the Securities and Exchange Commission as an agent of such government securities broker or government securities dealer upon whom may be served any process, pleadings, or other papers in any civil suit or action brought in any appropriate court in any place subject to the jurisdiction of the United States, with respect to any cause of action,

(i) That accrues during the period beginning when such government securities broker or government securities dealer becomes registered pursuant to section 15C(a)(1)(A) of the Act and ending either when such registration is cancelled or revoked, or when a notice filed by such government securities broker or government securities dealer to withdraw from such registration becomes effective, whichever is earlier,

(ii) That arises out of any activity, in any place subject to the jurisdiction of the United States, occurring in connection with the conduct of the business of such government securities broker or government securities dealer, and

(iii) That is founded, directly or indirectly, upon the Securities Act of 1933, the Securities Exchange Act of 1934, the Trust Indenture Act of 1939, the Investment Company Act of 1940, the Investment Advisers Act of 1940, or any rule or regulation under any of those Acts, and

(2) Stipulates and agrees that any such civil suit or action may be commenced against such government securities broker or government securities dealer by the service of process upon the Commission and the forwarding of a copy thereof as provided in paragraph (c) of this rule and that the service as aforesaid of any such process, pleadings, or other papers upon the Commission shall be taken and held in all courts to be as valid and binding as if due process service thereof had been made.

(b) Each government securities broker or government securities dealer registered pursuant to section 15C(a)(1)(A) of the Act that becomes a non-resident government securities broker or government securities dealer, and each general partner or managing agent of an unincorporated government securities broker or government securities dealer registered or applying for registration pursuant to section 15C(a)(1)(A) of the Act who becomes a non-resident after such registration or filing of an application for such registration, shall furnish such consent and power of attorney no more than 30 days thereafter.

(c) Service of any process, pleadings or other papers on the Commission under this rule shall be made by delivering the requisite number of copies thereof to the Secretary of the Commission or to such other person as the Commission may authorize to act in its behalf. Whenever any process, pleadings, or other papers as aforesaid are served upon the Commission, it shall promptly forward a copy thereof by registered or certified mail to the appropriate defendants at their last address of record filed with the Commission; but any failure by the Commission to forward such a copy shall have no effect on the validity of the service made upon the Commission. The Commission shall be furnished a sufficient number of copies for such purpose, and one copy for its file.

(d) For purposes of this rule the following definitions shall apply:

(1) The term *managing agent* shall mean any person, including a trustee, who directs or manages or who participates in the directing or managing of the affairs of any unincorporated organization or association that is not a partnership.

(2) The term *non-resident government securities broker or government securities dealer* shall mean (i) in the case of an individual, one who is domiciled in or has his principal place of business in any place not subject to the jurisdiction of the United States, (ii) in the case of a corporation, one incorporated in or having its principal place of business in any place not subject to the jurisdiction of the United States; (iii) in the case of a partnership or other unincorporated organization or association, one having its principal place of business in any place not subject to the jurisdiction of the United States.

(3) A general partner or managing agent of a government securities broker or government securities dealer shall be deemed to be a non-resident if he is domiciled in any place not subject to the jurisdiction of the United States.

Rule 15Cc1–1. Withdrawal from registration of government securities brokers or government securities dealers

(a) Notice of withdrawal from registration as a government securities broker or government securities dealer pursuant to Section 15C(a)(1)(A) of the Act shall be filed on Form BDW (17 CFR 249.501a) in accordance with the instructions contained therein. Every notice of withdrawal from registration as a government securities broker or dealer shall be filed with the Central Registration Depository (operated by the Financial Industry Regulatory Authority, Inc.) in accordance with applicable filing requirements. Prior to filing a notice of withdrawal from registration on Form BDW (17 CFR 249.501a), a government securities broker or government securities dealer shall amend Form BD (17 CFR 249.501) in accordance with 17 CFR 400.5(a) to update any inaccurate information.

(b) A notice of withdrawal from registration filed by a government securities broker or government securities dealer shall become effective for all matters on the 60th day after the filing thereof with the Commission, within such longer period of time as to which such government securities broker or government securities dealer consents or the Commission by order may determine as necessary or appropriate in the public interest or for the protection of investors, or within such shorter period of time as the Commission may determine. If a notice of withdrawal from registration is filed with the Commission at any time subsequent to the date of the issuance of a Commission order instituting proceedings pursuant to Section 15C(c) to censure, place limitations on the activities, functions or operations of, or suspend or revoke the registration of such government securities broker or government securities dealer, or if prior to the effective date of the notice of withdrawal pursuant to this paragraph (b), the Commission institutes such a proceeding or a proceeding to impose terms or conditions upon such withdrawal, the notice of withdrawal shall not become effective pursuant to this paragraph (b) except at such time and upon such terms and conditions as the Commission deems necessary or appropriate in the public interest or for the protection of investors.

(c) Every notice of withdrawal filed with the Central Registration Depository pursuant to this section shall constitute a "report" filed with the Commission within the meaning of Sections 15(b), 15C(c), 17(a), 18(a), 32(a) and other applicable provisions of the Act.

(d) The Commission, by order, may exempt any broker or dealer from the filing requirements provided in Form BDW (17 CFR 249.501a) under conditions that differ from the filing instructions contained in Form BDW.

REGISTRATION AND REGULATION OF SECURITY-BASED SWAP DEALERS AND MAJOR SECURITY-BASED SWAP PARTICIPANTS

Rule 15Fb1-1. Signatures

(a) Required signatures to, or within, any electronic submission (including, without limitation, signatories within the forms and certifications required by Rule 15Fb2-1, Rule 15Fb2-4 and Rule 15Fb6-2) must be in typed form rather than manual format. Signatures in an HTML, XML or XBRL document that are not required may, but are not required to, be presented in a graphic or image file within the electronic filing. When used in connection with an electronic filing, the term "signature" means an electronic entry in the form of a magnetic impulse or other form of computer data compilation of any letters or series of letters or characters comprising a name, executed, adopted or authorized as a signature.

(b) Each signatory to an electronic filing (including, without limitation, each signatory to the forms and certifications required by Rules 15Fb2-1, 15Fb2-4 and 15Fb6-2) shall manually sign a signature page or other document authenticating, acknowledging or otherwise adopting his or her signature that appears in typed form within the electronic filing. Such document shall be executed before or at the time the electronic filing is made. Upon request, the security-based swap dealer or major security-based swap participant shall furnish to the Commission or its staff a copy of any or all documents retained pursuant to this paragraph (b).

(c) A person required to provide a signature on an electronic submission (including, without limitation, each signatory to the forms and certifications required by Rules 15Fb2-1, 15Fb2-4, and 15Fb6-2) may not have the form or certification signed on his or her behalf pursuant to a power of attorney or other form of confirming authority.

(d) Each manually signed signature page or other document authenticating, acknowledging or otherwise adopting his or her signature that appears in typed form within the electronic filing –

(1) on Schedule F to Form SBSE (§249.1600 of this chapter), SBSE-A (§249.1600a of this chapter), or SBSE-BD (§249.1600b of this chapter), as appropriate, shall be retained by the filer until at least three years after the form or certification has been replaced or is no longer effective;

(2) on Form SBSE-C (§249.1600c of this chapter) shall be retained by the filer until at least three years after the Form was filed with the Commission.

Rule 15Fb2-1. Registration of security-based swap dealers and major security-based swap participants

(a) *Application.* An application for registration of a security-based swap dealer or a major security-based swap participant that is filed pursuant to Section 15F(b) of the Securities Exchange Act of 1934 (15 U.S.C. 78o-10(b)) shall be filed on Form SBSE (§249.1600 of this chapter) or Form SBSE-A (§249.1600a of this chapter) or Form SBSE-BD (§249.1600b of this chapter), as appropriate, in accordance with paragraph (c) and the instructions to the forms. Applicants shall also file as part of their application the required certifications on Form SBSE-C (§249.1600c of this chapter).

(b) *Senior Officer Certification.* A senior officer shall certify on Form SBSE–C (§ 249.1600c of this chapter) that;

(1) after due inquiry, he or she has reasonably determined that the security-based swap dealer or major security-based swap participant has developed and implemented written policies and procedures reasonably designed to prevent violation of federal securities laws and the rules thereunder, and

(2) he or she has documented the process by which he or she reached such determination.

(c) *Filing.*

(1) *Electronic filing.* Every application for registration of a security-based swap dealer or major security-based swap participant and any additional registration documents shall be filed electronically with the Commission through the Commission's EDGAR system.

(2) *Filing date.* An application of a security-based swap dealer or a major security-based swap participant submitted pursuant to paragraph (a) of this section shall be considered filed when an applicant has submitted a complete Form SBSE-C (§249.1600c of this chapter) and a complete Form SBSE (§249.1600 of this chapter), Form SBSE-A (§249.1600a of this chapter), or Form SBSE-BD (§249.1600b of this chapter), as appropriate, and all required additional documents electronically with the Commission.

(d) *Conditional registration.* An applicant that has submitted a complete Form SBSE-C (§249.1600c of this chapter) and a complete Form SBSE (§249.1600 of this chapter) or Form SBSE-A (§249.1600a of this chapter) or Form SBSE-BD (§249.1600b of this chapter), as applicable, in accordance with paragraph (b) within the time periods set forth in Rule 3a67-8 (if the person is a major security-based swap participant) or Rule 3a71-2(b) (if the person is a security- based swap dealer), and has not withdrawn its registration shall be conditionally registered.

(e) *Commission decision.* The Commission may deny or grant ongoing registration to a security-based swap dealer or major security-based swap participant based on a security-based swap dealer's or major security-based swap participant's application, filed pursuant to paragraph (a) of this section. The Commission will grant ongoing registration if it finds that the requirements of Section 15F(b) of the Securities Exchange Act of 1934 (15 U.S.C. 78o-10(b)) are satisfied. The Commission may institute proceedings to determine whether ongoing registration should be denied if it does not or cannot make such finding or if the applicant is subject to a statutory disqualification (as described in Sections 3(a)(39)(A) through (F) of the Securities Exchange Act of 1934 (15 U.S.C. 78c(a)(39)(A) – (F)), or the Commission is aware of inaccurate statements in the application. Such proceedings shall include notice of the grounds for denial under consideration and opportunity for hearing. At the conclusion of such proceedings, the Commission shall grant or deny such registration.

Rule 15Fb2-3. Amendments to Form SBSE, Form SBSE-A, and Form SBSE-BD

If a security-based swap dealer or a major security-based swap participant finds that the information contained in its Form SBSE (§249.1600 of this chapter), Form SBSE-A (§249.1600a of this chapter), or Form SBSE-BD (§249.1600b of this chapter), as appropriate, or in any amendment thereto, is or has become inaccurate for any reason, the security-based swap dealer or a major security-based swap participant shall promptly file an amendment electronically with the Commission through the Commission's EDGAR system on the appropriate Form to correct such information.

Rule 15Fb2-4. Nonresident security-based swap dealers and major security-based swap participants

(a) *Definition.* For purposes of this section, the terms *nonresident security-based swap dealer* and *nonresident major security-based swap participant* shall mean:

(1) In the case of an individual, one who resides, or has his or her principal place of business, in any place not in the United States;

(2) In the case of a corporation, one incorporated in or having its principal place of business in any place not in the United States; or

(3) In the case of a partnership or other unincorporated organization or association, one having its principal place of business in any place not in the United States.

(b) *Power of attorney.*

(1) Each nonresident security-based swap dealer and nonresident major security-based swap participant registered or applying for registration pursuant to Section 15F(b) of the Securities Exchange Act of 1934 (15 U.S.C. 78o-10(b)) shall obtain a written irrevocable consent and power of attorney appointing an agent in the United States, other than the Commission or a Commission member, official or employee, upon whom may be served any process, pleadings, or other papers in any action brought against the nonresident security-based swap dealer or nonresident major security-based swap participant to enforce the Securities Exchange Act of 1934 (15 U.S.C. 78a et seq.). This consent and power of attorney must be signed by the nonresident security-based swap dealer or nonresident major security-based swap participant and the named agent(s) for service of process.

(2) Each nonresident security-based swap dealer and nonresident major security-based swap participant registered or applying for registration pursuant to section 15F(b) of the Securities Exchange Act of 1934 (15 U.S.C. 78o-10(b)) shall, at the time of filing its application on Form SBSE (§249.1600 of this chapter), Form SBSE-A (§249.1600a of this chapter), or Form SBSE-BD (§249.1600b of this chapter), as appropriate, furnish to the Commission the name and address of its United States agent for service of process on Schedule F to the appropriate form.

(3) Any change of a nonresident security-based swap dealer's and nonresident major security-based swap participant's agent for service of process and any change of name or address of a nonresident security-based swap dealer's and nonresident major security-based swap participant's existing agent for service of process shall be communicated promptly to the Commission through amendment of the Schedule F of Form SBSE (§249.1600 of this chapter), Form SBSE-A (§249.1600a of this chapter), or Form SBSE-BD (§249.1600b of this chapter), as appropriate.

(4) Each nonresident security-based swap dealer and nonresident major security-based swap participant must promptly appoint a successor agent for service of process, consistent with the process described in paragraph (b)(1), if the nonresident security-based swap dealer and nonresident major security-based swap participant discharges its identified agent for service of process or if its agent for service of process is unwilling or unable to accept service on behalf of the nonresident security-based swap dealer or nonresident major security-based swap participant.

(5) Each nonresident security-based swap dealer and nonresident major security-based swap participant must maintain, as part of its books and records, the agreement identified in para-

graphs (b)(1) and (b)(4) of this section for at least three years after the agreement is terminated.

(c) *Access to books and records.*

(1) *Certification and opinion of counsel.* Each nonresident security-based swap dealer and nonresident major security-based swap participant applying for registration pursuant to Section 15F(b) of the Securities Exchange Act of 1934 (15 U.S.C. 78o-10(b) shall:

(i) certify on Schedule F of Form SBSE (§249.1600 of this chapter), Form SBSE-A (§249.1600a of this chapter), or Form SBSE-BD (§249.1600b of this chapter), as appropriate, that the nonresident security-based swap dealer and nonresident major security-based swap participant can, as a matter of law, and will provide the Commission with prompt access to the books and records of such nonresident security-based swap dealer and nonresident major security-based swap participant, and can, as a matter of law, and will submit to onsite inspection and examination by the Commission; and

(ii) provide an opinion of counsel that the nonresident security-based swap dealer and nonresident major security-based swap participant can, as a matter of law, provide the Commission with prompt access to the books and records of such nonresident security-based swap dealer and nonresident major security-based swap participant, and can, as a matter of law, submit to onsite inspection and examination by the Commission.

(2) *Amendments.* Each nonresident security-based swap dealer and nonresident major security-based swap participant shall re-certify, on Schedule F to Form SBSE (§249.1600 of this chapter), Form SBSE-A (§249.1600a of this chapter), or Form SBSE-BD (§249.1600b of this chapter), as applicable, within 90 days after any changes in the legal or regulatory framework that would impact the nonresident security-based swap dealer's or nonresident major security-based swap participant's ability to provide, or the manner in which it provides the Commission with prompt access to its books and records, or would impact the Commission's ability to inspect and examine the nonresident security-based swap dealer or nonresident major security-based swap participant. The re-certification shall be accompanied by a revised opinion of counsel describing how, as a matter of law, the nonresident security-based swap dealer or nonresident major security- based swap participant will continue to meet its obligations to provide the Commission with prompt access to its books and records and to be subject to Commission inspection and examination under the new regulatory regime.

Rule 15Fb2-5. Registration of successor to registered security-based swap dealer or a major security-based swap participant

(a) In the event that a security-based swap dealer or major security-based swap participant succeeds to and continues the business of a security-based swap dealer or major security-based swap participant registered pursuant to Section 15F(b) of the Securities Exchange Act of 1934 (15 U.S.C. 78o-10(b)), the registration of the predecessor shall be deemed to remain effective as the registration of the successor if the successor, within 30 days after such succession, files an application for registration in accordance with §240.15Fb2-1, and the predecessor files a notice of withdrawal from registration on Form SBSE-W (§249.1601 of this chapter).

(b) Notwithstanding paragraph (a) of this section, if a security-based swap dealer or major security-based swap participant succeeds to and continues the business of a registered predecessor security-based swap dealer or major security-based swap participant, and the succession is based solely on a change in the predecessor's date or state of incorporation, form of organization, or composition of a partnership, the successor may, within 30 days after the succession, amend the registration of the predecessor security-based swap dealer or major security-based swap participant on Form SBSE (§249.1600 of this chapter), Form SBSE-A (§249.1600a of this chapter), or Form SBSE-BD (§249.1600b of this chapter), as appropriate, to reflect these changes. This amendment shall be deemed an application for registration filed by the predecessor and adopted by the successor.

Rule 15Fb2-6. Registration of fiduciaries

The registration of a security-based swap dealer or a major security-based swap participant shall be deemed to be the registration of any executor, administrator, guardian, conservator, assignee for the benefit of creditors, receiver, trustee in insolvency or bankruptcy, or other fiduciary, appointed or qualified by order, judgment, or decree of a court of competent jurisdiction to continue the business of such registered security-based swap dealer or a major security-based swap participant; Provided, that such fiduciary files with the Commission, within 30 days after entering upon the performance of his or her duties, an amended Form SBSE (§249.1600 of this chapter), Form SBSE-A (§249.1600a of this chapter), or Form SBSE-BD (§249.1600b of this chapter), as appropriate, indicating the fiduciary's position with respect to management of the firm and, as an additional document, a copy of the order, judgment, decree, or other document appointing the fiduciary.

Rule 15Fb3-1. Duration of registration

(a) *General.* A person registered as a security-based swap dealer or major security-based swap participant in accordance with §240.15Fb2-1 will continue to be so registered until the effective date of any cancellation, revocation or withdrawal of such registration.

(b) *Conditional registration.* Notwithstanding paragraph (a) of this section, conditional registration shall expire on the date the registrant withdraws from registration or the Commission grants or denies the person's ongoing registration in accordance with Rule 15Fb2-1(e).

Rule 15Fb3-2. Withdrawal from registration

(a) Notice of withdrawal from registration as a security-based swap dealer or major security- based swap participant pursuant to Section 15F(b) of the Securities Exchange Act of 1934 (15 U.S.C. 78o-10(b)) shall be filed on Form SBSE-W (§249.1601 of this chapter) in accordance with the instructions contained therein. Every notice of withdrawal from registration as a security-based swap dealer or major security-based swap participant shall be filed electronically with the Commission through the Commission's EDGAR system. Prior to filing a notice of withdrawal from registration on Form SBSE-W, a security-based swap dealer or major security-based swap participant shall amend its Form SBSE (§249.1600 of this chapter), Form SBSE-A (§249.1600a of this chapter) or Form SBSE-BD (§249.1600b of this chapter), as appropriate, in accordance with Rule 15Fb2-3(a) to update any inaccurate information.

(b) A notice of withdrawal from registration filed by a security-based swap dealer or major security-based swap participant pursuant to Section 15F(b) of the Securities Exchange Act of 1934 (15 U.S.C. 78o-10(b)) shall become effective for all matters (except as provided in this paragraph (b)) on the 60th day after the filing thereof with the Commission or its designee, within such longer period of time as to which such security-based swap dealer or major security-based swap participant consents or which the Commission by order may determine as necessary or appropriate in the public interest or for the protection of investors, or within such shorter period of time as the Commission may determine. If a notice of withdrawal from registration is filed with the Commission at any time subsequent to the date of the issuance of a Commission order instituting proceedings to censure, place limitations on the activities, functions or operations of, or suspend or revoke the registration of, such security-based swap dealer or major security-based swap participant, or if prior to the effective date of the notice of withdrawal pursuant to this paragraph (b), the Commission institutes such a proceeding or a proceeding to impose terms or conditions upon such withdrawal, the notice of withdrawal shall not become effective pursuant to this paragraph (b) except at such time and upon such terms and conditions as the Commission deems necessary or appropriate in the public interest or for the protection of investors.

Rule 15Fb3-3. Cancellation and revocation of registration

(a) *Cancellation.* If the Commission finds that any person registered pursuant to Rule 15Fb2-1 is no longer in existence or has ceased to do business as a security-based swap dealer or major security-based swap participant, the Commission shall by order cancel the registration of such person.

(b) *Revocation.* The Commission, by order, shall censure, place limitations on the activities, functions, or operations of, or revoke the registration of any security-based swap dealer or major security-based swap participant that has registered with the Commission if it makes a finding as specified in Section 15F(*l*)(2) of the Securities Exchange Act of 1934 (15 U.S.C. 78o-10(*l*)(2)).

Rule 15Fb6-1. Associated persons

Unless otherwise ordered by the Commission, when it files an application to register with the Commission as a security-based swap dealer or major security-based swap participant, a security-based swap dealer or a major security-based swap participant may permit a person that is associated with such security-based swap dealer or major security-based swap participant that is not a natural person and that is subject to statutory disqualification to effect or be involved in effecting security-based swaps on its behalf, provided that the statutory disqualification(s), described in Sections 3(a)(39)(A) through (F) of the Securities Exchange Act of 1934 (15 U.S.C. 78c(a)(39)(A) – (F)), occurred prior to the compliance date of this rule, and provided that it identifies each such associated person on Schedule C of Form SBSE (§249.1600 of this chapter), Form SBSE-A (§249.1600a of this chapter), or Form SBSE-BD (§249.1600b of this chapter), as appropriate.

Rule 15Fb6-2. Associated person certification

(a) *Certification.* No registered security-based swap dealer or major security-based swap participant shall act as a security-based swap dealer or major security-based swap participant unless it has certified electronically on Form SBSE-C (Section 249.1600c of this chapter) that it neither knows, nor in the exercise of reasonable care should have known, that any person associated with such security-based swap dealer or major security-based swap participant who effects or is involved in effecting security-based swaps on behalf of the security-based swap dealer or major security- based swap participant is subject to a statutory disqualification, as described in Sections 3(a)(39)(A) through (F) of the Securities Exchange Act of 1934 (15 U.S.C. 78c(a)(39)(A) – (F)), unless otherwise specifically provided by rule, regulation or order of the Commission.

(b) To support the certification required by paragraph (a) of this section, the security-based swap dealer's or major security-based swap participant's Chief Compliance Officer, or his or her designee, shall review and sign the questionnaire or application for employment, which the security-based swap dealer or major security-based swap participant is required to obtain pursuant to the relevant recordkeeping rule applicable to such security-based swap dealer or major security-based swap participant, executed by each associated person who is a natural person and who effects or is involved in effecting security based swaps on the security-based swap dealer's or major security-based swap participant's behalf. The questionnaire or application shall serve as a basis for a background check of the associated person to verify that the person is not subject to statutory disqualification.

BUSINESS CONDUCT STANDARDS FOR SECURITY-BASED SWAP DEALERS AND MAJOR SECURITY-BASED SWAP PARTICIPANTS

Rule 15Fh-1. Scope and reliance on representations

(a) *Scope.* Rules 15Fh-1 through 15Fh-6, and Rule 15Fk-1 are not intended to limit, or restrict, the applicability of other provisions of the federal securities laws, including but not limited to section 17(a) of the Securities Act of 1933 and sections 9 and 10(b) of the Act, and rules and regulations thereunder, or other applicable laws and rules and regulations. Rules 15Fh-1 through 15Fh-6, and Rule 15Fk-1 apply, as relevant, in connection with entering into security-based swaps and continue to apply, as appropriate, over the term of executed security-based swaps. Rules 15Fh-3(a) through 15Fh-3(f), Rule 15Fh-4(b) and Rule 15Fh-5 are not applicable to security-based swaps that security-based swap dealers or major security- based swap participants enter into with their majority-owned affiliates. For these purposes the counterparties to a security-based swap are majority-owned affiliates if one counterparty directly or indirectly owns a majority interest in the other, or if a third party directly or indirectly owns a majority interest in both counterparties to the security-based swap, where "majority interest" is the right to vote or direct the vote of a majority of a class of voting securities of an entity, the power to sell or direct the sale of a majority of a class of voting securities of an entity, or the right to receive upon dissolution or the contribution of a majority of the capital of a partnership.

(b) *Reliance on representations.* A security-based swap dealer or major security-based swap participant may rely on written representations from the counterparty or its representative to satisfy its due diligence requirements under §240.15Fh, unless it has information that would cause a reasonable person to question the accuracy of the representation.

Rule 15Fh-2. Definitions

As used in Rules 15Fh-1 through 15Fh-6:

(a) *Act as an advisor to a special entity.* A security-based swap dealer *acts as an advisor to a special entity* when it recommends a security-based swap or a trading strategy that involves the use of a security-based swap to the special entity, unless:

(1) With respect to a special entity as defined in Rule 15Fh-2(d)(3):

(i) The special entity represents in writing that it has a fiduciary as defined in section 3 of the Employee Retirement Income Security Act of 1974 (29 U.S.C. 1002) that is responsible for representing the special entity in connection with the security-based swap;

(ii) The fiduciary represents in writing that it acknowledges that the security- based swap dealer is not acting as an advisor; and

(iii)The special entity represents in writing:

(A) That it will comply in good faith with written policies and procedures reasonably designed to ensure that any recommendation the special entity receives from the security-based swap dealer involving a security-based swap transaction is evaluated by a fiduciary before the transaction is entered into; or

(B) That any recommendation the special entity receives from the security- based swap dealer involving a security-based swap transaction will be evaluated by a fiduciary before the transaction is entered into.

(2) With respect to any special entity:

(i) The special entity represents in writing that:

(A) It acknowledges that the security-based swap dealer is not acting as an advisor; and

(B) The special entity will rely on advice from a qualified independent representative as defined in Rule 15Fh-5(a); and

(ii) The security-based swap dealer discloses to the special entity that it is not undertaking to act in the best interest of the special entity, as otherwise required by section 15F(h)(4) of the Act.

(b) *Eligible contract participant* means any person as defined in section 3(a)(65) of the Act and the rules and regulations thereunder and in section 1a of the Commodity Exchange Act (7 U.S.C. 1a) and the rules and regulations thereunder.

(c) *Security-based swap dealer or major security-based swap participant* includes, where relevant, an associated person of the security-based swap dealer or major security- based swap participant.

(d) *Special entity means*:

(1) A Federal agency;

(2) A State, State agency, city, county, municipality, other political subdivision of a State, or any instrumentality, department, or a corporation of or established by a State or political subdivision of a State;

(3) Any employee benefit plan, subject to Title I of the Employee Retirement Income Security Act of 1974 (29 U.S.C. 1002);

(4) Any employee benefit plan defined in section 3 of the Employee Retirement Income Security Act of 1974 (29 U.S.C. 1002) and not otherwise defined as a special entity, unless such employee benefit plan elects not to be a special entity by notifying a security-based swap dealer or major security-based swap participant of its election prior to entering into a security-based swap with the particular security-based swap dealer or major security-based swap participant;

(5) Any governmental plan, as defined in section 3(32) of the Employee Retirement Income Security Act of 1974 (29 U.S.C. 1002(32)); or

(6) Any endowment, including an endowment that is an organization described in section 501(c)(3) of the Internal Revenue Code of 1986.

(e) A person is subject to a statutory disqualification for purposes of Rule 15Fh-5 if that person would be subject to a statutory disqualification, as described in section 3(a)(39)(A)-(F) of the Act.

Rule 15Fh-3. Business conduct requirements

(a) *Counterparty status*—(1) *Eligible contract participant.* A security-based swap dealer or a major security-based swap participant shall verify that a counterparty meets the eligibility standards for an eligible contract participant before entering into a security- based swap with that counterparty, provided that the requirements of this paragraph (a)(1) shall not apply to a transaction executed on a registered national securities exchange.

(2) *Special entity.* A security-based swap dealer or a major security-based swap participant shall verify whether a counterparty is a special entity before entering into a security-based swap with that counterparty, unless the transaction is executed on a registered or exempt security-based swap execution facility or registered national securities exchange, and the security-based swap dealer or major security-based swap participant does not know the identity of the counterparty at a reasonably sufficient time prior to execution of the transaction to permit the security-based swap dealer or major security-based swap participant to comply with the obligations of paragraph (a) of this section.

(3) *Special entity election.* In verifying the special entity status of a counterparty pursuant to Rule 15Fh-3(a)(2), a security-based swap dealer or major security- based swap participant shall verify whether a counterparty is eligible to elect not to be a special entity under Rule 15Fh-2(d)(4) and, if so, notify such counterparty of its right to make such an election.

(b) *Disclosure.* At a reasonably sufficient time prior to entering into a security-based swap, a security-based swap dealer or major security-based swap participant shall disclose to a counterparty, other than a security-based swap dealer, major security-based swap participant, swap dealer or major swap participant, material information concerning the security-based swap in a manner reasonably designed to allow the counterparty to assess the material risks and characteristics and material incentives or conflicts of interest, as described below, so long as the identity of the counterparty is known to the security-based swap dealer or major security-based swap participant at a reasonably sufficient time prior to execution of the transaction to permit the security- based swap dealer or major security-based swap participant to comply with the obligations of paragraph (b) of this section.

(1) *Material risks and characteristics* means the material risks and characteristics of the particular security-based swap, which may include:

(i) Market, credit, liquidity, foreign currency, legal, operational, and any other applicable risks; and

(ii) The material economic terms of the security-based swap, the terms relating to the operation of the security-based swap, and the rights and obligations of the parties during the term of the security-based swap.

(2) *Material incentives or conflicts of interest* means any material incentives or conflicts of interest that the security-based swap dealer or major security-based swap participant may have in connection with the security-based swap, including any compensation or other incentives from any source other than the counterparty in connection with the security-based swap to be entered into with the counterparty.

(3) *Record.* The security-based swap dealer or major security-based swap participant shall make a written record of the non-written disclosures made pursuant to this paragraph (b), and provide a written version of these disclosures to its counterparties in a timely manner, but in any case no later than the delivery of the trade acknowledgement of the particular transaction pursuant to Rule 15Fi-1.

(c) *Daily mark.* A security-based swap dealer or major security-based swap participant shall disclose the daily mark to the counterparty, other than a security-based swap dealer, major security-based swap participant, swap dealer or major swap participant, which shall be:

(1) For a cleared security-based swap, upon request of the counterparty, the daily mark that the security-based swap dealer or major security-based swap participant receives from the appropriate clearing agency;

(2) For an uncleared security-based swap, the midpoint between the bid and offer, or the calculated equivalent thereof, as of the close of business, unless the parties agree in writing otherwise to a different time, on each business day during the term of the security-based swap. The daily mark may be based on market quotations for comparable security-based swaps, mathematical models or a combination thereof. The security-based swap dealer or major security-based swap participant shall also disclose its data sources and a description of the methodology and assumptions used to prepare the daily mark, and promptly disclose any material changes to such data sources, methodology and assumptions during the term of the security-based swap; and

(3) The security-based swap dealer or major security-based swap participant shall provide the daily mark without charge to the counterparty and without restrictions on the internal use of the daily mark by the counterparty.

(d) *Disclosure regarding clearing rights.* A security-based swap dealer or major security-based swap participant shall disclose the following information to a counterparty, other than a security-based swap dealer, major security-based swap participant, swap dealer or major swap participant, so long as the identity of the counterparty is known to the security-based swap dealer or major security-based swap participant at a reasonably sufficient time prior to execution of the transaction to permit the security-based swap dealer or major security-based swap participant to comply with the obligations of paragraph (d) of this section:

(1) *For security-based swaps subject to clearing requirement.* Before entering into a security-based swap subject to the clearing requirement under section 3C(a) of the Act, a security-based swap

dealer or major security-based swap participant shall:

(i) Disclose to the counterparty the names of the clearing agencies that accept the security-based swap for clearing, and through which of those clearing agencies the security-based swap dealer or major security-based swap participant is authorized or permitted, directly or through a designated clearing member, to clear the security-based swap; and

(ii) Notify the counterparty that it shall have the sole right to select which of the clearing agencies described in paragraph (d)(1)(i) of this section shall be used to clear the security-based swap subject to section 3C(g)(5) of the Act.

(2) *For security-based swaps not subject to clearing requirement.* Before entering into a security-based swap not subject to the clearing requirement under section 3C(a) of the Act, a security-based swap dealer or major security-based swap participant shall:

(i) Determine whether the security-based swap is accepted for clearing by one or more clearing agencies;

(ii) Disclose to the counterparty the names of the clearing agencies that accept the security-based swap for clearing, and whether the security-based swap dealer or major security-based swap participant is authorized or permitted, directly or through a designated clearing member, to clear the security-based swap through such clearing agencies; and

(iii)Notify the counterparty that it may elect to require clearing of the security- based swap and shall have the sole right to select the clearing agency at which the security-based swap will be cleared, provided it is a clearing agency at which the security-based swap dealer or major security-based swap participant is authorized or permitted, directly or through a designated clearing member, to clear the security-based swap.

(3) *Record.* The security-based swap dealer or major security-based swap participant shall make a written record of the non-written disclosures made pursuant to this paragraph (d), and provide a written version of these disclosures to its counterparties in a timely manner, but in any case no later than the delivery of the trade acknowledgement of the particular transaction pursuant to §240.15Fi-1.

(e) *Know your counterparty.* Each security-based swap dealer shall establish, maintain and enforce written policies and procedures reasonably designed to obtain and retain a record of the essential facts concerning each counterparty whose identity is known to the security-based swap dealer that are necessary for conducting business with such counterparty. For purposes of paragraph (e) of this section, the *essential facts concerning a counterparty* are:

(1) Facts required to comply with applicable laws, regulations and rules;

(2) Facts required to implement the security-based swap dealer's credit and operational risk management policies in connection with transactions entered into with such counterparty; and

(3) Information regarding the authority of any person acting for such counterparty.

(f) *Recommendations of security-based swaps or trading strategies.*

(1) A security- based swap dealer that recommends a security-based swap or trading strategy involving a security-based swap to a counterparty, other than a security-based swap dealer, major security-based swap participant, swap dealer, or major swap participant, must:

(i) Under take reasonable diligence to understand the potential risks and rewards associated with the recommended security-based swap or trading strategy involving a security-based swap; and

(ii) Have a reasonable basis to believe that a recommended security-based swap or trading strategy involving a security-based swap is suitable for the counterparty. To establish a reasonable basis for a recommendation, a security-based swap dealer must have or obtain relevant information regarding the counterparty, including the counterparty's investment profile, trading objectives, and its ability to absorb potential losses associated with the recommended security-based swap or trading strategy involving a security- based swap.

(2) A security-based swap dealer may also fulfill its obligations under paragraph (f)(1)(ii) of this section with respect to an institutional counterparty, if:

(i) The security-based swap dealer reasonably determines that the counterparty, or an agent to which the counterparty has delegated decision-making authority, is capable of independently evaluating investment risks with regard to the relevant security-based swap or trading strategy involving a security- based swap;

(ii) The counterparty or its agent affirmatively represents in writing that it is exercising independent judgment in evaluating the recommendations of the security-based swap dealer with regard to the relevant security-based swap or trading strategy involving a security-based swap; and

(iii) The security-based swap dealer discloses that it is acting in its capacity as a counterparty, and is not undertaking to assess the suitability of the security- based swap or trading strategy for the counterparty.

(3) A security-based swap dealer will be deemed to have satisfied its obligations under paragraph (f)(2)(i) of this section if it receives written representations, as provided in Rule 15Fh-1(b), that:

(i) In the case of a counterparty that is not a special entity, the counterparty has complied in good faith with written policies and procedures that are reasonably designed to ensure that the persons responsible for evaluating the recommendation and making trading decisions on behalf of the counterparty are capable of doing so; or

(ii) In the case of a counterparty that is a special entity, satisfy the terms of the safe harbor in Rule15Fh-5(b).

(4) For purposes of paragraph (f)(2) of this section, an institutional counterparty is a counterparty that is an eligible contract participant as defined in clauses (A)(i), (ii), (iii), (iv), (viii), (ix) or (x), or clause (B)(ii) (other than a person described in clause (A)(v)) of section 1a(18) of the Commodity Exchange Act (7 U.S.C. 1(a)(18)) and the rules and regulations thereunder, or any person (whether a natural person, corporation, partnership, trust or otherwise) with total assets of at least $50 million.

(g) *Fair and balanced communications.* A security-based swap dealer or major security- based swap participant shall communicate with counterparties in a fair and balanced manner based on principles of fair dealing and good faith. In particular:

(1) Communications must provide a sound basis for evaluating the facts with regard to any particular security-based swap or trading strategy involving a security- based swap;

(2) Communications may not imply that past performance will recur or make any exaggerated or unwarranted claim, opinion or forecast; and

(3) Any statement referring to the potential opportunities or advantages presented by a security-based swap shall be balanced by an equally detailed statement of the corresponding risks.

(h) *Supervision*—(1) *In general.* A security-based swap dealer or major security-based swap participant shall establish and maintain a system to supervise, and shall diligently supervise, its business and the activities of its associated persons. Such a system shall be reasonably designed to prevent violations of the provisions of applicable federal securities laws and the rules and regulations thereunder relating to its business as a security-based swap dealer or major security-based swap participant, respectively

(2) *Minimum requirements.* The system required by paragraph (h)(1) of this section shall, at a minimum, provide for:

(i) The designation of at least one person with authority to carry out the supervisory responsibilities of the security-based swap dealer or major security-based swap participant for each type of business in which it engages for which registration as a security-based swap dealer or major security-based swap participant is required;

(ii) The use of reasonable efforts to determine that all supervisors are qualified, either by virtue of experience or training, to carry out their assigned responsibilities; and

(iii) Establishment, maintenance and enforcement of written policies and procedures addressing the supervision of the types of security-based swap business in which the security-based swap dealer or major security-based swap participant is engaged and the activities of its associated persons that are reasonably designed to prevent violations of applicable federal securities laws and the rules and regulations thereunder, and that include, at a minimum:

(A) Procedures for the review by a supervisor of transactions for which registration as a security-based swap dealer or major security-based swap participant is required;

(B) Procedures for the review by a supervisor of incoming and outgoing written (including electronic) correspondence with counterparties or potential counterparties and internal written communications relating to the security-based swap dealer's or major security-based swap participant's business involving security-based swaps;

(C) Procedures for a periodic review, at least annually, of the security-based swap business in which the security-based swap dealer or major security- based swap participant engages that is reasonably designed to assist in detecting and preventing violations of applicable federal securities laws and the rules and regulations thereunder;

(D) Procedures to conduct a reasonable investigation regarding the good character, business repute, qualifications, and experience of any person prior to that person's association with the security-based swap dealer or major security-based swap participant;

(E) Procedures to consider whether to permit an associated person to establish or maintain a securities or commodities account or a trading relationship in the name of, or for the benefit of such associated person, at another security-based swap dealer, broker, dealer, investment adviser, or other financial institution; and if permitted, procedures to supervise the trading at the other security-based swap dealer, broker, dealer, investment adviser, or financial institution;

(F) A description of the supervisory system, including the titles, qualifications and locations of supervisory persons and the responsibilities of each supervisory person with respect to the types of business in which the security-based swap dealer or major security-based swap participant is engaged;

(G) Procedures prohibiting an associated person who performs a supervisory function from supervising his or her own activities or reporting to, or having his or her compensation or continued employment determined by, a person or persons he or she is supervising; provided, however, that if the security-based swap dealer or major security-based swap participant determines, with respect to any of its supervisory personnel, that compliance with this requirement is not possible because of the firm's size or a supervisory person's position within the firm, the security-based swap dealer or major security-based swap participant must document the factors used to reach such determination and how the supervisory arrangement with respect to such supervisory personnel otherwise complies with paragraph (h)(1) of this section, and include a summary of such determination in the annual compliance report prepared by the security- based swap dealer's or major security-based swap participant's chief compliance officer pursuant to Rule 15Fk-1(c);

(H) Procedures reasonably designed to prevent the supervisory system required by paragraph (h)(1) of this section from being compromised due to the conflicts of interest that may be present with respect to the associated person being supervised, including the position of such person, the revenue such person generates for the security-based swap dealer or major security-based swap participant, or any compensation that the associated person conducting the supervision may derive from the associated person being supervised; and

(I) Procedures reasonably designed, taking into consideration the nature of such security-based swap dealer's or major security-based swap participant's business, to comply with the duties set forth in section 15F(j) of the Act.

(3) *Failure to supervise.* A security-based swap dealer or major security-based swap participant or an associated person of a security-based swap dealer or major security-based swap participant shall not be deemed to have failed to diligently supervise any other person, if such other person is not subject to his or her supervision, or if:

(i) The security-based swap dealer or major security-based swap participant has established and maintained written policies and procedures as required in Rule 15Fh-3(h)(2)(iii), and a documented system for applying those policies and procedures, that would reasonably be expected to prevent and detect, insofar as practicable, any violation of the federal securities laws and the rules and regulations thereunder relating to security-based swaps; and

(ii) The security-based swap dealer or major security-based swap participant, or associated person of the security-based swap dealer or major security-based swap participant, has reasonably discharged the duties and obligations required by such written policies and procedures and documented system and did not have a reasonable basis to believe that such written policies and procedures and documented system were not being followed.

(4) *Maintenance of written supervisory procedures.* A security-based swap dealer or major security-based swap participant shall:

(i) Promptly amend its written supervisory procedures as appropriate when material changes occur in applicable securities laws or rules or regulations thereunder, and when material changes occur in its business or supervisory system; and

(ii) Promptly communicate any material amendments to its supervisory procedures to all associated persons to whom such amendments are relevant based on their activities and responsibilities.

Rule 15Fh-4. Antifraud provisions for security-based swap dealers and major security-based swap participants; special requirements for security-based swap dealers acting as advisors to special entities

(a) *Antifraud provisions.* It shall be unlawful for a security-based swap dealer or major security-based swap participant:

(1) To employ any device, scheme, or artifice to defraud any special entity or prospective customer who is a special entity;

(2) To engage in any transaction, practice, or course of business that operates as a fraud or deceit on any special entity or prospective customer who is a special entity; or

(3) To engage in any act, practice, or course of business that is fraudulent, deceptive, or manipulative.

(b) *Special requirements for security-based swap dealers acting as advisors to special entities.* A security-based swap dealer that acts as an advisor to a special entity regarding a security-based swap shall comply with the following requirements:

(1) *Duty.* The security-based swap dealer shall have a duty to make a reasonable determination that any security-based swap or trading strategy involving a security-based swap recommended by the security-based swap dealer is in the best interests of the special entity.

(2) *Reasonable efforts.* The security-based swap dealer shall make reasonable efforts to obtain such information that the security-based swap dealer considers necessary to make a reasonable determination that a security-based swap or trading strategy involving a security-based swap is in the best interests of the special entity. This information shall include, but not be limited to:

(i) The authority of the special entity to enter into a security-based swap;

(ii) The financial status of the special entity, as well as future funding needs;

(iii) The tax status of the special entity;

(iv) The hedging, investment, financing or other objectives of the special entity;

(v) The experience of the special entity with respect to entering into security-based swaps, generally, and security-based swaps of the type and complexity being recommended;

(vi) Whether the special entity has the financial capability to withstand changes in market conditions during the term of the security-based swap; and

(vii) Such other information as is relevant to the particular facts and circumstances of the special entity, market conditions and the type of security-based swap or trading strategy involving a security-based swap being recommended.

(3) *Exception.* The requirements of this paragraph (b) shall not apply with respect to a security-based swap if:

(i) The transaction is executed on a registered or exempt security-based swap execution facility or registered national securities exchange; and

(ii) The security-based swap dealer does not know the identity of the counterparty at a reasonably sufficient time prior to execution of the transaction to permit the security-based swap dealer to comply with the obligations of paragraph (b) of this section.

Rule 15Fh-5. Special requirements for security-based swap dealers and major security-based swap participants acting as counterparties to special entities

(a)(1) A security-based swap dealer or major security-based swap participant that offers to enter into or enters into a security-based swap with a special entity, other than a special entity defined in Rule 15Fh-2(d)(3), must have a reasonable basis to believe that the special entity has a qualified independent representative. For these purposes, a qualified independent representative is a representative that:

(i) Has sufficient knowledge to evaluate the transaction and risks;

(ii) Is not subject to a statutory disqualification;

(iii) Undertakes a duty to act in the best interests of the special entity;

(iv) Makes appropriate and timely disclosures to the special entity of material information concerning the security-based swap;

(v) Evaluates, consistent with any guidelines provided by the special entity, the fair pricing and the appropriateness of the security-based swap;

(vi) In the case of a special entity defined in Rules 15Fh-2(d)(2) or (5), is a person that is subject to rules of the Commission, the Commodity Futures Trading Commission or a self-regulatory organization subject to the jurisdiction of the Commission or the Commodity Futures Trading Commission prohibiting it from engaging in specified activities if certain political contributions have been made, provided that this paragraph (a)(1)(vi) shall not apply if the independent representative is an employee of the special entity; and

(vii) Is independent of the security-based swap dealer or major security-based swap participant.

(A) A representative of a special entity is independent of a security-based swap dealer or major security-based swap participant if the representative does not have a relationship with the security-based swap dealer or major security-based swap participant, whether compensatory or otherwise, that reasonably could affect the independent judgment or decision-making of the representative.

(B) A representative of a special entity will be deemed to be independent of a security-based swap dealer or major security-based swap participant if:

(*1*) The representative is not and, within one year of representing the special entity in connection with the security-based swap, was not an associated person of the security-based swap dealer or major security-based swap participant;

(*2*) The representative provides timely disclosures to the special entity of all material conflicts of interest that could reasonably affect the judgment or decision making of the representative with respect to its obligations to the special entity and complies with policies and procedures reasonably designed to manage and mitigate such material conflicts of interest; and

(*3*) The security-based swap dealer or major security-based swap participant did not refer, recommend, or introduce the representative to the special entity within one year of the representative's representation of the special entity in connection with the security-based swap.

(2) A security-based swap dealer or major security-based swap participant that offers to enter into or enters into a security-based swap with a special entity as defined in Rule 15Fh-2(d)(3) must have a reasonable basis to believe that the special entity has a representative that is a fiduciary as defined in section 3 of the Employee Retirement Income Security Act of 1974 (29 U.S.C. 1002).

(b) *Safe harbor*. (1) A security-based swap dealer or major security-based swap participant shall be deemed to have a reasonable basis to believe that the special entity, other than a special entity defined in Rule 15Fh-2(d)(3), has a representative that satisfies the applicable requirements of paragraph (a)(1) of this section, provided that:

(i) The special entity represents in writing to the security-based swap dealer or major security-based swap participant that it has complied in good faith with written policies and procedures reasonably designed to ensure that it has selected a representative that satisfies the applicable requirements of paragraph (a)(1) of this section, and that such policies and procedures provide for ongoing monitoring of the performance of such representative consistent with the requirements of paragraph (a)(1) of this section; and

(ii) The representative represents in writing to the special entity and security- based swap dealer or major security-based swap participant that the representative:

(A) Has policies and procedures reasonably designed to ensure that it satisfies the applicable requirements of paragraph (a)(1) of this section;

(B) Meets the independence test in paragraph (a)(1)(vii) of this section; has the knowledge required under paragraph (a)(1)

(i) of this section; is not subject to a statutory disqualification under paragraph (a)(1)(ii) of this section; undertakes a duty to act in the best interests of the special entity as required under paragraph (a)(1)(iii) of this section; and is subject to the requirements regarding political contributions, as applicable, under paragraph (a)(1)(vi) of this section; and

(C) Is legally obligated to comply with the applicable requirements of paragraph (a)(1) of this section by agreement, condition of employment, law, rule, regulation, or other enforceable duty.

(2) A security-based swap dealer or major security-based swap participant shall be deemed to have a reasonable basis to believe that a special entity defined in Rule 15Fh-2(d)(3) of this section has a representative that satisfies the applicable requirements in paragraph (a)(2) of this section, provided that the special entity provides in writing to the security-based swap dealer or major security-based swap participant the representative's name and contact information, and represents in writing that the representative is a fiduciary as defined in section 3 of the Employee Retirement Income Security Act of 1974 (29 U.S.C. 1002).

(c) Before initiation of a security-based swap with a special entity, a security-based swap dealer shall disclose to the special entity in writing the capacity in which the security- based swap dealer is acting in connection with the security-based swap and, if the security-based swap dealer engages in business with the counterparty in more than one capacity, the security-based swap dealer shall disclose the material differences between such capacities and any other financial transaction or service involving the counterparty.

(d) The requirements of this section shall not apply with respect to a security-based swap if:

(1) The transaction is executed on a registered or exempt security-based swap execution facility or registered national securities exchange; and

(2) The security-based swap dealer or major security-based swap participant does not know the identity of the counterparty at a reasonably sufficient time prior to execution of the transaction to permit the security-based swap dealer or major security-based swap participant to comply with the obligations of paragraphs (a) through (c) of this section.

Rule 15Fh-6. Political contributions by certain security-based swap dealers

(a) *Definitions*. For the purposes of this section:

(1) The term *contribution* means any gift, subscription, loan, advance, or deposit of money or anything of value made:

(i) For the purpose of influencing any election for federal, state or local office;

(ii) For payment of debt incurred in connection with any such election; or

(iii)For transition or inaugural expenses incurred by the successful candidate for state or local office.

(2) The term *covered associate* means:

(i) Any general partner, managing member or executive officer, or other person with a similar status or function;

(ii) Any employee who solicits a municipal entity to enter into a security-based swap with the security-based swap dealer and any person who supervises, directly or indirectly, such employee; and

(iii) A political action committee controlled by the security-based swap dealer or by a person described in paragraphs (a)(2)(i) and (ii) of this section.

(3) The term *executive officer of a security-based swap dealer* means:

(i) The president;

(ii) Any vice president in charge of a principal business unit, division or function (such as sales, administration or finance);

(iii) Any other officer of the security-based swap dealer who performs a policy-making function; or

(iv) Any other person who performs similar policy-making functions for the security-based swap dealer.

(4) The term *municipal entity* is defined in section 15B(e)(8) of the Act.

(5) The term *official of a municipal entity* means any person (including any election committee for such person) who was, at the time of the contribution, an incumbent, candidate or successful candidate for elective office of a municipal entity, if the office:

(i) Is directly or indirectly responsible for, or can influence the outcome of, the selection of a security-based swap dealer by a municipal entity; or

(ii) Has authority to appoint any person who is directly or indirectly responsible for, or can influence the outcome of, the selection of a security-based swap dealer by a municipal entity.

(6) The term *payment* means any gift, subscription, loan, advance, or deposit of money or anything of value.

(7) The term *regulated person* means:

(i) A person that is subject to rules of the Commission, the Commodity Futures Trading Commission or a self-regulatory organization subject to the jurisdiction of the Commission or the Commodity Futures Trading Commission prohibiting it from engaging in specified activities if certain political contributions have been made, or its officers or employees;

(ii) A general partner, managing member or executive officer of such person, or other individual with a similar status or function; or

(iii) An employee of such person who solicits a municipal entity for the security- based swap dealer and any person who supervises, directly or indirectly, such employee.

(8) The term *solicit* means a direct or indirect communication by any person with a municipal entity for the purpose of obtaining or retaining an engagement related to a security-based swap.

(b) *Prohibitions and exceptions.* (1) It shall be unlawful for a security-based swap dealer to offer to enter into, or enter into, a security-based swap, or a trading strategy involving a security-based swap, with a municipal entity within two years after any contribution to an official of such municipal entity was made by the security-based swap dealer, or by any covered associate of the security-based swap dealer.

(2) The prohibition in paragraph (b)(1) of this section does not apply:

(i) If the only contributions made by the security-based swap dealer to an official of such municipal entity were made by a covered associate, if a natural person:

(A) To officials for whom the covered associate was entitled to vote at the time of the contributions, *if* the contributions in the aggregate do not exceed $350 to any one official per election; or

(B) To officials for whom the covered associate was not entitled to vote at the time of the contributions, *if* the contributions in the aggregate do not exceed $150 to any one official, per election;

(ii) To a security-based swap dealer as a result of a contribution made by a natural person more than six months prior to becoming a covered associate of the security-based swap dealer, *however*, this exclusion shall not apply if the natural person, after becoming a covered associate, solicits the municipal entity on behalf of the security-based swap dealer to offer to enter into, or to enter into, security-based swap, or a trading strategy involving a security- based swap; or

(iii) With respect to a security-based swap that is executed on a registered national securities exchange or registered or exempt security-based swap execution facility where the security-based swap dealer does not know the identity of the counterparty to the transaction at a reasonably sufficient time prior to execution of the transaction to permit the security-based swap dealer to comply with the obligations of paragraph (b)(1) of this section.

(3) No security-based swap dealer or any covered associate of the security-based swap dealer shall:

(i) Provide or agree to provide, directly or indirectly, payment to any person to solicit a municipal entity to offer to enter into, or to enter into, a security- based swap or any trading strategy involving a security-based swap with that security-based swap dealer unless such person is a regulated person; or

(ii) Coordinate, or solicit any person or political action committee to make, any:

(A) Contribution to an official of a municipal entity with which the security- based swap dealer is offering to enter into, or has entered into, a security- based swap or a trading strategy involving a security-based swap; or

(B) Payment to a political party of a state or locality with which the security- based swap dealer is offering to enter into, or has entered into, a security- based swap or a trading strategy involving a security-based swap.

(c) *Circumvention of rule.* No security-based swap dealer shall, directly or indirectly, through or by any other person or means, do any act that would result in a violation of paragraph (a) or (b) of this section.

(d) *Requests for exemption.* The Commission, upon application, may conditionally or unconditionally exempt a security-based swap dealer from the prohibition under paragraph (b)(1) of this section. In determining whether to grant an exemption, the Commission will consider, among other factors:

(1) Whether the exemption is necessary or appropriate in the public interest and consistent with the protection of investors and the purposes of the Act;

(2) Whether the security-based swap dealer:

(i) Before the contribution resulting in the prohibition was made, adopted and implemented policies and procedures reasonably designed to prevent violations of this section;

(ii) Prior to or at the time the contribution which resulted in such prohibition was made, had no actual knowledge of the contribution; and

(iii) After learning of the contribution:

(A) Has taken all available steps to cause the contributor involved in making the contribution which resulted in such prohibition to obtain a return of the contribution; and

(B) Has taken such other remedial or preventive measures as may be appropriate under the circumstances;

(3) Whether, at the time of the contribution, the contributor was a covered associate or otherwise an employee of the security-based swap dealer, or was seeking such employment;

(4) The timing and amount of the contribution which resulted in the prohibition;

(5) The nature of the election (*e.g.*, federal, state or local); and

(6) The contributor's apparent intent or motive in making the contribution that resulted in the prohibition, as evidenced by the facts and circumstances surrounding the contribution.

(e) *Prohibitions inapplicable.* (1) The prohibitions under paragraph (b) of this section shall not apply to a contribution made by a covered associate of the security-based swap dealer if:

(i) The security-based swap dealer discovered the contribution within 120 calendar days of the date of such contribution;

(ii) The contribution did not exceed $350; and

(iii) The covered associate obtained a return of the contribution within 60 calendar days of the date of discovery of the contribution by the security-based swap dealer.

(2) A security-based swap dealer that has more than 50 covered associates may not rely on paragraph (e)(1) of this section more than three times in any 12-month period, while a security-based swap dealer that has 50 or fewer covered associates may not rely on paragraph (e)(1) of this section more than twice in any 12-month period.

(3) A security-based swap dealer may not rely on paragraph (e)(1) of this section more than once for any covered associate, regardless of the time between contributions.

Rule 15Fi-1. Definitions

For the purposes of Rules 15Fi-1 and 15Fi-2:

(a) The term *business day* means any day other than a Saturday, Sunday, or legal holiday.

(b) The term *clearing agency* means a clearing agency as defined in section 3(a)(23) of the Securities Exchange Act of 1934 (15 U.S.C. 78c(a)(23)) that is registered pursuant to section 17A of the Securities Exchange Act of 1934 (15 U.S.C. 78q-1) and provides central counterparty services for security-based swap transactions.

(c) The term *clearing transaction* means a security-based swap that has a clearing agency as a direct counterparty.

(d) The term *day of execution* means the calendar day of the counterparty to the security- based swap transaction that ends the latest, provided that if a security-based swap transaction is

(1) Entered into after 4:00 p.m. in the place of a counterparty; or

(2) Entered into on a day that is not a business day in the place of a counterparty, then such security-based swap transaction shall be deemed to have been entered into by that counterparty on the immediately succeeding business day of that counterparty, and the day of execution shall be determined with reference to such business day.

(e) The term *execution* means the point at which the counterparties become irrevocably bound to a transaction under applicable law.

(f) The term *security-based swap execution facility* means a security-based swap execution facility as defined in section 3(a)(77) of the Securities Exchange Act of 1934 (15 U.S.C. 78c(a)(77)) that is registered pursuant to section 3D of the Securities Exchange Act of 1934 (15 U.S.C. 78c-4).

(g) The term *national securities exchange* means an exchange as defined in section 3(a)(1) of the Securities Exchange Act of 1934 (15 U.S.C. 78c(a)(1)) that is registered pursuant to section 6 of the Securities Exchange Act of 1934 (15 U.S.C. 78f).

(h) The term *trade acknowledgment* means a written or electronic record of a security- based swap transaction sent by one counterparty of the security-based swap transaction to the other.

(i) The term *verification* means the process by which a trade acknowledgment has been manually, electronically, or by some other legally equivalent means, signed by the receiving counterparty.

Rule 15Fi-2. Acknowledgment and verification of security-based swap transactions

(a) *Trade acknowledgment requirement.* In any transaction in which a security-based swap dealer or major security-based swap participant purchases from or sells to any counterparty a security-based swap, a trade acknowledgment must be provided by:

(1) The security-based swap dealer, if the transaction is between a security-based swap dealer and a major security-based swap participant;

(2) The security-based swap dealer or major security-based swap participant, if only one counterparty in the transaction is a security-based swap dealer or major security-based swap participant; or

(3) The counterparty that the counterparties have agreed will provide the trade acknowledgment in any transaction other than one described by paragraph (a)(1) or (a)(2) of this section.

(b) *Prescribed time.* Any trade acknowledgment required by paragraph (a) of this section must be provided promptly, but in any event by the end of the first business day following the day of execution.

(c) *Form and content of trade acknowledgment.* Any trade acknowledgment required by paragraph (a) of this section must be provided through electronic means that provide reasonable assurance of delivery and a record of transmittal, and must disclose all the terms of the security- based swap transaction.

(d) *Trade verification.* (1) A security-based swap dealer or major security-based swap participant must establish, maintain, and enforce written policies and procedures that are reasonably designed to obtain prompt verification of the terms of a trade acknowledgment provided pursuant to paragraph (a) of this section.

(2) A security-based swap dealer or major security-based swap participant must promptly verify the accuracy of, or dispute with its counterparty, the terms of a trade acknowledgment it receives pursuant to paragraph (a) of this section.

(e) *Exception for clearing transactions.* A security-based swap dealer or major security- based swap participant is excepted from the requirements of this section with respect to any clearing transaction.

(f) Exception for transactions executed on a security-based swap execution facility or national securities exchange or accepted for clearing by a clearing agency.

(1) A security-based swap dealer or major security-based swap participant is excepted from the requirements of this subsection with respect to any security-based swap transaction executed on a security-based swap execution facility or national securities exchange, provided that the rules, procedures or processes of the security-based swap execution facility or national securities exchange provide for the acknowledgment and verification of all terms of the security-based swap transaction no later than the time required by paragraphs (b) and (d)(2) of this section.

(2) A security-based swap dealer or major security-based swap participant is excepted from the requirements of this subsection with respect to any security-based swap transaction that is submitted for clearing to a clearing agency, provided that:

(i) The security-based swap transaction is submitted for clearing as soon as technologically practicable, but in any event no later than the time established for providing a trade acknowledgment under paragraph (b) of this section; and

(ii) The rules, procedures or processes of the clearing agency provide for the acknowledgment and verification of all terms of the security-based swap transaction prior to or at the same time that the security-based swap transaction is accepted for clearing.

(3) If a security-based swap dealer or major security-based swap participant receives notice that a security-based swap transaction has not been

acknowledged and verified pursuant to the rules, procedures or processes of a security-based swap execution facility or a national securities exchange, or accepted for clearing by a clearing agency, the security-based swap dealer or major security-based swap participant shall comply with the requirements of this section with respect to such security-based swap transaction as if such security-based swap transaction were executed at the time the security-based swap dealer or major security-based swap participant receives such notice.

(g) *Exemption from Rule 10b-10.* A security-based swap dealer or major security-based swap participant that is also a broker or dealer, is purchasing from or selling to any counterparty, and that complies with paragraph (a) or (d)(2) of this section with respect to the security-based swap transaction, is exempt from the requirements of Rule 10b-10 with respect to the security-based swap transaction.

Rule 15Fk-1. Designation of chief compliance officer for security-based swap dealers and major security-based swap participants

(a) In general. A security-based swap dealer and major security-based swap participant shall designate an individual to serve as a chief compliance officer on its registration form.

(b) *Duties.* The chief compliance officer shall:

(1) Report directly to the board of directors or to the senior officer of the security- based swap dealer or major security-based swap participant; and

(2) Take reasonable steps to ensure that the registrant establishes, maintains and reviews written policies and procedures reasonably designed to achieve compliance with the Act and the rules and regulations thereunder relating to its business as a security-based swap dealer or major security-based swap participant by:

(i) Reviewing the compliance of the security-based swap dealer or major security-based swap participant with respect to the security-based swap dealer and major security-based swap participant requirements described in section 15F of the Act, and the rules and regulations thereunder, where the review shall involve preparing the registrant's annual assessment of its written policies and procedures reasonably designed to achieve compliance with section 15F of the Act, and the rules and regulations thereunder, by the security-based swap dealer or major security-based swap participant;

(ii) Taking reasonable steps to ensure that the registrant establishes, maintains and reviews policies and procedures reasonably designed to remediate non-compliance issues identified by the chief compliance officer through any means, including any:

(A) Compliance office review;

(B) Look-back;

(C) Internal or external audit finding;

(D) Self-reporting to the Commission and other appropriate authorities; or

(E) Complaint that can be validated; and

(iii) Taking reasonable steps to ensure that the registrant establishes and follows procedures reasonably designed for the handling, management response, remediation, retesting, and resolution of non-compliance issues;

(3) In consultation with the board of directors or the senior officer of the security- based swap dealer or major security-based swap participant, take reasonable steps to resolve any material conflicts of interest that may arise; and

(4) Administer each policy and procedure that is required to be established pursuant to section 15F of the Act and the rules and regulations thereunder.

(c) *Annual reports*—(1) *In general.* The chief compliance officer shall annually prepare and sign a compliance report that contains a description of the written policies and procedures of the security-based swap dealer or major security-based swap participant described in paragraph (b) of this section (including the code of ethics and conflict of interest policies).

(2) *Requirements.* (i) Each compliance report shall also contain, at a minimum, a description of:

(A) The security-based swap dealer or major security-based swap participant's assessment of the effectiveness of its policies and procedures relating to its business as a security-based swap dealer or major security-based participant;

(B) Any material changes to the registrant's policies and procedures since the date of the preceding compliance report;

(C) Any areas for improvement, and recommended potential or prospective changes or improvements to its compliance program and resources devoted to compliance;

(D) Any material non-compliance matters identified; and

(E) The financial, managerial, operational, and staffing resources set aside for compliance with the Act and the rules and regulations thereunder relating to its business as a security-based swap dealer or major security-based swap participant, including any material deficiencies in such resources.

(ii) A compliance report under paragraph (c)(1) of this section also shall:

(A) Be submitted to the Commission within 30 days following the deadline for filing the security-based swap dealer's or major security-based swap participant's annual financial report with the Commission pursuant to section 15F of the Act and rules and regulations thereunder;

(B) Be submitted to the board of directors and audit committee (or equivalent bodies) and the senior officer of the security-based swap dealer or major security-based swap participant prior to submission to the Commission;

(C) Be discussed in one or more meetings conducted by the senior officer with the chief compliance officer(s) in the preceding 12 months, the subject of which addresses the obligations in this section; and

(D) Include a certification by the chief compliance officer or senior officer that, to the best of his or her knowledge and reasonable belief and under penalty of law, the information contained in the compliance report is accurate and complete in all material respects.

(iii) *Extensions of time.* A security-based swap dealer or major security-based swap participant may request from the Commission an extension of time to submit its compliance report, provided the registrant's failure to timely submit the report could not be eliminated by the registrant without unreasonable effort or expense. Extensions of the deadline will be granted at the discretion of the Commission.

(iv) *Incorporation by reference.* A security-based swap dealer or major security- based swap participant may incorporate by reference sections of a compliance report that have been submitted within the current or immediately preceding reporting period to the Commission.

(v) *Amendments.* A security-based swap dealer or major security-based swap participant shall promptly submit an amended compliance report if material errors or omissions in the report are identified. An amendment must contain the certification required under paragraph (c)(2)(ii)(D) of this section.

(d) *Compensation and removal.* The compensation and removal of the chief compliance officer shall require the approval of a majority of the board of directors of the security-based swap dealer or major security-based swap participant.

(e) *Definitions.* For purposes of this section, references to:

(1) The *board* or *board of directors* shall include a body performing a function similar to the board of directors.

(2) The *senior officer* shall include the chief executive officer or other equivalent officer.

(3) *Complaint that can be validated* shall include any written complaint by a counterparty involving the security-based swap dealer or major security-based swap participant or associated person of a security-based swap dealer or major security-based swap participant that can be supported upon reasonable investigation.

(4) A *material non-compliance matter* means any non-compliance matter about which the board of directors of the security-based swap dealer or major security-based swap participant would reasonably need to know to oversee the compliance of the security-based swap dealer or major security-based swap participant, and that involves, without limitation:

(i) A violation of the federal securities laws relating to its business as a security-based swap dealer or major security-based swap participant by the firm or its officers, directors, employees or agents;

(ii) A violation of the policies and procedures relating to its business as a security-based swap dealer or major security-based swap participant by the firm or its officers, directors, employees or agents; or

(iii) A weakness in the design or implementation of the policies and procedures relating to its business as a security-based swap dealer or major security-based swap participant.

DISCLOSURE FOR ASSET-BACKED SECURITIES

Rule 15Ga-1. Repurchases and replacements relating to asset-backed securities

(a) *General.* With respect to any asset-backed security (as that term is defined in Section 3(a)(79) of the Securities Exchange Act of 1934) for which the underlying transaction agreements contain a covenant to repurchase or replace an underlying asset for breach of a representation or warranty, a securitizer (as that term is defined in Section 15G(a) of the Securities Exchange Act of 1934) shall disclose fulfilled and unfulfilled repurchase requests across all trusts by providing the information required in paragraph (1) concerning all assets securitized by the securitizer that were the subject of a demand to repurchase or replace for breach of the representations and warranties concerning the pool assets for all asset-backed securities held by non-affiliates of the securitizer during the reporting period.

Name of Issuing Entity	Check if Regis-tered	Name of Originator	Total Assets in ABS by Originator			Assets That Were Subject of Demand			Assets That Were Repurchased or Replaced			Assets Pending Repurchase or Replacement (within cure period)			Demand in Dispute			Demand Withdrawn			Demand Rejected		
			(#)	($)	(% of principal balance)	(#)	($)	(% of principal balance)	(#)	($)	(% of principal balance)	(#)	($)	(% of principal balance)	(#)	($)	(% of principal balance)	(#)	($)	(% of principal balance)	(#)	($)	(% of principal balance)
(a)	(b)	(c)	(d)	(e)	(f)	(g)	(h)	(i)	(j)	(k)	(l)	(m)	(n)	(o)	(p)	(q)	(r)	(s)	(t)	(u)	(v)	(w)	(x)
Asset Class X																							
Issuing Entity A CIK #	X	Originator 1																					
		Originator 2																					
Total			#	$		#	$		#	$		#	$		#	$		#	$		#	$	
Asset Class Y																							
Issuing Entity B		Originator 3																					
Total			#	$		#	$		#	$		#	$		#	$		#	$		#	$	
Total			#	$		#	$		#	$		#	$		#	$		#	$		#	$	

(1) The table shall:

(i) Disclose the asset class and group the issuing entities by asset class (column (a)).

(ii) Disclose the name of the issuing entity (as that term is defined in Item 1101(f) of Regulation AB of the asset-backed securities. List the issuing entities in order of the date of formation (column (a)).

Instruction to Paragraph (a)(1)(ii): Include all issuing entities with outstanding asset-backed securities during the reporting period.

(iii) For each named issuing entity, indicate by check mark whether the transaction was registered under the Securities Act of 1933 (column (b)) and disclose the CIK number of the issuing entity (column (a)).

(iv) Disclose the name of the originator of the underlying assets (column (c)).

Instruction to Paragraph (a)(1)(iv): Include all originators that originated assets in the asset pool for each issuing entity.

(v) Disclose the number, outstanding principal balance and percentage by principal balance of assets at the time of securitization (columns (d) through (f)).

(vi) Disclose the number, outstanding principal balance and percentage by principal balance of assets that were subject of a demand to repurchase or replace for breach of representations and warranties (columns (g) through (i)).

(vii) Disclose the number, outstanding principal balance and percentage by principal balance of assets that were repurchased or replaced for breach of representations and warranties (columns (j) through (*l*)).

(viii) Disclose the number, outstanding principal balance and percentage by principal balance of assets that are pending repurchase or replacement for breach of representations and warranties due to the expiration of a cure period (columns (m) through (*o*)).

(ix) Disclose the number, outstanding principal balance and percentage by principal balance of assets that are pending repurchase or replacement for breach of representations and warranties because the demand is currently in dispute (columns (p) through (r)).

(x) Disclose the number, outstanding principal balance and percentage by principal balance of assets that were not repurchased or replaced because the demand was withdrawn (columns (s) through (u)).

(xi) Disclose the number, outstanding principal balance and percentage by principal balance of assets that were not repurchased or replaced because the demand was rejected (columns (v) through (x)).

Instruction to Paragraphs (a)(1)(vi) through (xi): For purposes of these paragraphs (a)(1)(vi) through (xi) the outstanding principal balance shall be the principal balance as of the reporting period end date and the percentage by principal balance shall be the outstanding principal balance of an asset divided by the outstanding principal balance of the asset pool as of the reporting period end date.

(xii) Provide totals by asset class, issuing entity and for all issuing entities for columns that require number of assets and principal amounts (columns (d), (e), (g), (h), (j), (k), (m), (n) (p), (q), (s), (t), (v) and (w)).

Instruction 1 to Paragraph (a)(1): The table should include any activity during the reporting period, including activity related to assets subject to demands made prior to the beginning of the reporting period.

Instruction 2 to Paragraph (a)(1): Indicate by footnote and provide narrative disclosure in order to further explain the information presented in the table, as appropriate.

(2) If any of the information required by this paragraph (a) is unknown and not available to the securitizer without unreasonable effort or expense, such information may be omitted, provided the securitizer provides the information it possesses or can acquire without unreasonable effort or expense, and the securitizer includes a statement showing that unreasonable effort or expense would be involved in obtaining the omitted information. Further, if a securitizer requested and was unable to obtain all information with respect to investor demands upon a trustee that occurred prior to July 22, 2010, so state by footnote. In this case, also state that the disclosures do not contain investor demands upon a trustee made prior to July 22, 2010.

(b) In the case of multiple affiliated securitizers for a single asset-backed securities transaction, if one securitizer has filed all the disclosures required in order to meet the obligations under paragraph (a) of this section, other affiliated securitizers shall not be required to separately provide and file the same disclosures related to the same asset-backed security.

(c) The disclosures in paragraph (a) of this section shall be provided by a securitizer:

(1) For the three year period ended December 31, 2011, by any securitizer that issued an asset-backed security during the period, or organized and initiated an asset-backed securities transaction during the period, by securitizing an asset, either directly or indirectly, including through an affiliate, in each case, if the underlying transaction agreements provide a covenant to repurchase or replace an underlying asset for breach of a representation or warranty and the securitizer has asset-backed securities, containing such a covenant, outstanding and held by non-affiliates as of the end of the three year period. If a securitizer has no activity to report, it shall indicate by checking the appropriate box on Form ABS–15G (17 CFR 249.1400). The requirement of this paragraph (c)(1) applies to all issuances of asset-backed securities whether or not publicly registered under the provisions of the Securities Act of 1933. The disclosures required by this paragraph (c)(1) shall be filed no later than February 14, 2012.

Instruction to Paragraph (c)(1): For demands made prior to January 1, 2009, the disclosure should include any related activity subsequent to January 1, 2009 associated with such demand.

(2) For each calendar quarter, by any securitizer that issued an asset-backed security during the period, or organized and initiated an asset-backed securities transaction by securitizing an asset, either directly or indirectly, including through an affiliate, or had outstanding asset-backed securities held by non-affiliates during the period, in each case, if the underlying transaction agreements provide a covenant to repurchase or replace an underlying asset for breach of a representation or warranty. The disclosures required by this paragraph (c)(2) shall be filed no later than 45 calendar days after the end of such calendar quarter:

(i) Except that, a securitizer may suspend its duty to provide periodic quarterly disclosures if no activity occurred during the initial filing period in paragraph (c)(1) of this section or during a calendar quarter that is required to be reported under paragraph (a) of this section. A securitizer shall indicate that it has no activity to report by checking the appropriate box on Form ABS–15G (17 CFR 249.1400). Thereafter, a periodic quarterly report required by this paragraph (c)(2) will only be required if a change in the demand, repurchase or replacement activity occurs that is required to be reported under paragraph (a) of this section during a calendar quarter; and

(ii) Except that, annually, any securitizer that has suspended its duty to provide quarterly disclosures pursuant to paragraph (c)(2)(i) of this section must confirm that no activity occurred during the previous calendar year by checking the appropriate box on Form ABS–15G (17 CFR 249.1400). The confirmation required by this paragraph (c)(2)(ii) shall be filed no later than 45 days after each calendar year.

(3) Except that, if a securitizer has no asset-backed securities outstanding held by non-affiliates, the duty under paragraph (c)(2) of this section to file periodically the disclosures required by paragraph (a) of this section shall be terminated immediately upon filing a notice on Form ABS–15G (17 CFR 249.1400).

Rule 15Ga–2. Findings and conclusions of third-party due diligence reports

(a) The issuer or underwriter of an offering of any asset-backed security (as that term is defined in Section 3(a)(79) of the Act) that is to be rated by a nationally recognized statistical rating organization must furnish Form ABS–15G to the Commission containing the findings and conclusions of any third-party due diligence report obtained by the issuer or underwriter at least five business days prior to the first sale in the offering.

Instruction to paragraph (a): Disclosure of the findings and conclusions includes, but is not limited to, disclosure of the criteria against which the loans were evaluated, and how the evaluated loans compared to those criteria along with the basis for including any loans not meeting those criteria. This disclosure is only required for an initial rating and does not need to be furnished in connection with any subsequent rating actions. For purposes of this rule, the date of first sale is the date on which the first investor is irrevocably contractually committed to invest, which, depending on the terms and conditions of the contract, could be the date on which the issuer receives the investor's subscription agreement or check.

(b) In the case where the issuer and one or more underwriters have obtained the same third-party due diligence report related to a particular asset-backed securities transaction, if any one such party has furnished all the disclosures required in order to meet the obligations under paragraph (a) of this section, the other party or parties are not required to separately furnish the same disclosures related to such third-party due diligence report.

(c) If the disclosure required by this rule has been made in the prospectus (including an attribution to the third-party that provided the third-party due diligence report), the issuer or underwriter may refer to that section of the prospectus in Form ABS–15G rather than providing the findings and conclusions itself directly in Form ABS–15G.

(d) For purposes of paragraphs (a) and (b) of this section, *issuer* is defined in Rule 17g–10(d)(2) and *third-party due diligence report* means any report containing findings and conclusions of any *due diligence services* as defined in Rule 17g–10(d)(1) performed by a third party.

(e) The requirements of this rule would not apply to an offering of an asset-backed security if certain conditions are met, including:

(i) The offering is not required to be, and is not, registered under the Securities Act of 1933;

(ii) The issuer of the rated security is not a U.S. person (as defined under Securities Act Rule 902(k)); and

(iii) the security issued by the issuer will be offered and sold upon issuance, and any underwriter or arranger linked to the security will effect transactions of the security after issuance, only in transactions that occur outside the United States.

(f) The requirements of this rule would not apply to an offering of an asset-backed security if certain conditions are met, including:

(i) The issuer of the rated security is a municipal issuer; and

(ii) The offering is not required to be, and is not, registered under the Securities Act of 1933.

(g) For purposes of paragraph (f) of this section, a municipal issuer is an issuer (as that term is defined in Rule 17g–10(d)(2)) that is any State or Territory of the United States, the District of Columbia, any political subdivision of any State, Territory or the District of Columbia, or any public instrumentality of one or more States, Territories or the District of Columbia.

(h) An offering of an asset-backed security that is exempted from the requirements of this rule pursuant to paragraph (f) of this section remains subject to the requirements of Section 15E(s)(4)(A) of the Act, which requires that the issuer or underwriter of any asset-backed security shall make publicly available the findings and conclusions of any third-party due diligence report obtained by the issuer or underwriter.

REPORTS OF DIRECTORS, OFFICERS, AND PRINCIPAL SHAREHOLDERS

Rule 16a–1. Definition of terms

Terms defined in this Rule shall apply solely to section 16 of the Act and the rules thereunder. These terms shall not be limited to section 16(a) of the Act but also shall apply to all other subsections under section 16 of the Act.

(a) The term *beneficial owner* shall have the following applications:

(1) Solely for purposes of determining whether a person is a beneficial owner of more than ten percent of any class of equity securities registered pursuant to section 12 of the Act, the term "beneficial owner" shall mean any person who is deemed a beneficial owner pursuant to section 13(d) of the Act and the rules thereunder; *provided, however,* that the following institutions or persons shall not be deemed the beneficial owner of securities of such class held for the benefit of third parties or in customer or fiduciary accounts in the ordinary course of business (or in the case of an employee benefit plan specified in paragraph (a)(1)(vi) of this rule, of securities of such class allocated to plan participants where participants have voting power) as long as such shares are acquired by such institutions or persons without the purpose or effect of changing or influencing control of the issuer or engaging in any arrangement subject to Rule 13d–3(b):

(i) A broker or dealer registered under section 15 of the Act;

(ii) A bank as defined in section 3(a)(6) of the Act;

(iii) An insurance company as defined in section 3(a)(19) of the Act;

(iv) An investment company registered under section 8 of the Investment Company Act of 1940 (15 U.S.C. 80a–8);

(v) Any person registered as an investment adviser under Section 203 of the Investment Advisers Act of 1940 (15 U.S.C. 80b–3) or under the laws of any state;

(vi) An employee benefit plan as defined in Section 3(3) of the Employee Retirement Income Security Act of 1974, as amended, 29 U.S.C. 1001 *et seq.* ("ERISA") that is subject to the provisions of ERISA, or any such plan that is not subject to ERISA that is maintained primarily for the benefit of the employees of a state or local government or instrumentality, or an endowment fund;

(vii) A parent holding company or control person, provided the aggregate amount held directly by the parent or control person, and directly and indirectly by their subsidiaries or affiliates that are not persons specified in paragraphs (a)(1)(i) through (x), does not exceed one percent of the securities of the subject class;

(viii) A savings association as defined in Section 3(b) of the Federal Deposit Insurance Act (12 U.S.C. 1813);

(ix) A church plan that is excluded from the definition of an investment company under section 3(c)(14) of the Investment Company Act of 1940 (15 U.S.C. 80a–3);

(x) A non-U.S. institution that is the functional equivalent of any of the institutions listed in paragraphs (a)(1)(i) through (ix) of this rule, so long as the non-U.S. institution is subject to a regulatory scheme that is substantially comparable to the regulatory scheme applicable to the equivalent U.S. institution and the non-U.S. institution is eligible to file a Schedule 13G pursuant to Rule 13d–1(b)(1)(ii)(J); and

(xi) A group, provided that all the members are persons specified in Rule 16a–1(a)(1)(i) through (x).

NOTE TO PARAGRAPH (a): Pursuant to this rule, a person deemed a beneficial owner of more than ten percent of any class of equity securities registered under section 12 of the Act would file a Form 3, but the securities holdings disclosed on Form 3, and changes in beneficial ownership reported on subsequent Forms 4 (17 CFR 249.104) or 5 (17 CFR 249.105), would be determined by the definition of "beneficial owner" in paragraph (a)(2) of this rule.

(2) Other than for purposes of determining whether a person is a beneficial owner of more than ten percent of any class of equity securities registered under Section 12 of the Act, the term *beneficial owner* shall mean any person who, directly or indirectly, through any contract, arrangement, understanding, relationship or otherwise, has or shares a direct or indirect pecuniary interest in the equity securities, subject to the following:

(i) The term *pecuniary interest* in any class of equity securities shall mean the opportunity, directly or indirectly, to profit or share in any profit derived from a transaction in the subject securities.

(ii) The term *indirect pecuniary interest* in any class of equity securities shall include, but not be limited to:

(A) Securities held by members of a person's immediate family sharing the same household; provided, however, that the presumption of such beneficial ownership may be rebutted; *see also* Rule 16a–1(a)(4);

(B) A general partner's proportionate interest in the portfolio securities held by a general or limited partnership. The general partner's proportionate interest, as evidenced by the partnership agreement in effect at the time of the transaction and the partnership's most recent financial statements, shall be the greater of:

(*1*) The general partner's share of the partnership's profits, including profits attributed to any limited partnership interests held by the general partner and any other interests in profits that arise from the purchase and sale of the partnership's portfolio securities; or

(*2*) The general partner's share of the partnership capital account, including the share attributable to any limited partnership interest held by the general partner.

(C) A performance-related fee, other than an asset-based fee, received by any broker, dealer, bank, insurance company, investment company, investment adviser, investment manager, trustee or person or entity performing a similar function; *provided, however,* that no pecuniary interest shall be present where:

(*1*) The performance-related fee, regardless of when payable, is calculated based upon net capital gains and/or net capital appreciation generated from the portfolio or from the fiduciary's overall performance over a period of one year or more; and

(*2*) Equity securities of the issuer do not account for more than ten percent of the market value of the portfolio. A right to a nonperformance-related fee alone shall not represent a pecuniary interest in the securities;

(D) A person's right to dividends that is separated or separable from the underlying securities. Otherwise, a right to dividends alone shall not represent a pecuniary interest in the securities;

(E) A person's interest in securities held by a trust, as specified in Rule 16a–8(b); and

(F) A person's right to acquire equity securities through the exercise or conversion of any derivative security, whether or not presently exercisable.

(iii) A shareholder shall not be deemed to have a pecuniary interest in the portfolio securities held by a corporation or similar entity in which the person owns securities if the shareholder is not a controlling shareholder of the entity and does not have or share investment control over the entity's portfolio.

(3) Where more than one person subject to section 16 of the Act is deemed to be a beneficial owner of the same equity securities, all such persons must report as beneficial owners of the securities, either separately or jointly, as provided in Rule 16a–3(j). In such cases, the amount of short-swing profit recoverable shall not be increased above the amount recoverable if there were only one beneficial owner.

(4) Any person filing a statement pursuant to section 16(a) of the Act may state that the filing shall not be deemed an admission that such person is, for purposes of section 16 of the Act or otherwise, the beneficial owner of any equity securities covered by the statement.

(5) The following interests are deemed not to confer beneficial ownership for purposes of section 16 of the Act:

(i) Interests in portfolio securities held by any investment company registered under the Investment Company Act of 1940; and

(ii) Interests in securities comprising part of a broad-based, publicly traded market basket or index of stocks, approved for trading by the appropriate federal governmental authority.

(b) The term *call equivalent position* shall mean a derivative security position that increases in value as the value of the underlying equity increases, including, but not limited to, a long convertible security, a long call option, and a short put option position.

(c) The term *derivative securities* shall mean any option, warrant, convertible security, stock appreciation right, or similar right with an exercise or conversion privilege at a price related to an equity security, or similar securities with a value derived from the value of an equity security, but shall not include:

(1) Rights of a pledgee of securities to sell the pledged securities;

(2) Rights of all holders of a class of securities of an issuer to receive securities pro rata, or obligations to dispose of securities, as a result of a merger, exchange offer, or consolidation involving the issuer of the securities;

(3) Rights or obligations to surrender a security, or have a security withheld, upon the receipt or exercise of a derivative security or the receipt or vesting of equity securities, in order to satisfy the exercise price or the tax withholding consequences of receipt, exercise or vesting;

(4) Interests in broad-based index options, broad-based index futures, and broad-based publicly traded market baskets of stocks approved for trading by the appropriate federal governmental authority;

(5) Interests or rights to participate in employee benefit plans of the issuer;

(6) Rights with an exercise or conversion privilege at a price that is not fixed; or

(7) Options granted to an underwriter in a registered public offering for the purpose of satisfying over-allotments in such offering.

(d) The term "equity security of such issuer" shall mean any equity security or derivative security relating to an issuer, whether or not issued by that issuer.

(e) The term "immediate family" shall mean any child, stepchild, grandchild, parent, stepparent, grandparent, spouse, sibling, mother-in-law, father-in-law, son-in-law, daughter-in-law, brother-in-law, or sister-in-law, and shall include adoptive relationships.

(f) The term "officer" shall mean an issuer's president, principal financial officer, principal accounting officer (or, if there is no such accounting officer, the controller), any vice-president of the issuer in charge of a principal business unit, division or function (such as sales, administration or finance), any other officer who performs a policy-making function, or any other person who performs similar policy-making functions for the issuer. Officers of the issuer's parent(s) or subsidiaries shall be deemed officers of the issuer if they perform such policy-making functions for the issuer. In addition, when the issuer is a limited partnership, officers or employees of the general partner(s) who perform policy-making functions for the limited partnership are deemed officers of the limited partnership. When the issuer is a trust, officers or employees of the trustee(s) who perform policy-making functions for the trust are deemed officers of the trust.

NOTE: "Policy-making function" is not intended to include policy-making functions that are not significant. If pursuant to Item 401(b) of Regulation S–K the issuer identifies a person as an "executive officer," it is presumed that the Board of Directors has made that judgment and that the persons so identified are the officers for purposes of Section 16 of the Act, as are such other persons enumerated in this paragraph (f) but not in Item 401(b).

(g) The term *portfolio securities* shall mean all securities owned by an entity, other than securities issued by the entity.

(h) The term *put equivalent position* shall mean a derivative security position that increases in value as the value of the underlying equity decreases, including, but not limited to, a long put option and a short call option position.

Rule 16a–2. Persons and transactions subject to Section 16

Any person who is the beneficial owner, directly or indirectly, of more than ten percent of any class of equity securities ("ten percent beneficial owner") registered pursuant to section 12 of the Act, any director or officer of the issuer of such securities, and any person specified in section 30(h) of the Investment Company Act of 1940 (15 U.S.C. 80a–29(h)), including any person specified in Rule 16a–8, shall be subject to the provisions of section 16 of the Act. The rules under section 16 of the Act apply to any class of equity securities of an issuer whether or not registered under section 12 of the Act. The rules under section 16 of the Act also apply to non-equity securities as provided by the Investment Company Act of 1940. With respect to transactions by persons subject to section 16 of the Act:

(a) A transaction(s) carried out by a director or officer in the six months prior to the director or officer becoming subject to section 16 of the Act shall be subject to section 16 of the Act and reported on the first required Form 4 only if the transaction(s) occurred within six months of the transaction giving rise to the Form 4 filing obligation and the director or officer became subject to section 16 of the Act solely as a result of the issuer registering a class of equity securities pursuant to section 12 of the Act.

(b) A transaction(s) following the cessation of director or officer status shall be subject to section 16 of the Act only if:

(1) Executed within a period of less than six months of an opposite transaction subject to section 16(b) of the Act that occurred while that person was a director or officer; and

(2) Not otherwise exempted from section 16(b) of the Act pursuant to the provisions of this chapter.

NOTE TO PARAGRAPH (b): For purposes of this paragraph, an acquisition and a disposition each shall be an opposite transaction with respect to the other.

(c) The transaction that results in a person becoming a ten percent beneficial owner is not subject to section 16 of the Act unless the person otherwise is subject to section 16 of the Act. A ten percent beneficial owner not otherwise subject to section 16 of the Act must report only those transactions conducted while the beneficial owner of more than ten percent of a class of equity securities of the issuer registered pursuant to section 12 of the Act.

(d)(1) Transactions by a person or entity shall be exempt from the provisions of section 16 of the Act for the 12 months following appointment and qualification, to the extent such person or entity is acting as:

(i) Executor or administrator of the estate of a decedent;

(ii) Guardian or member of a committee for an incompetent;

(iii) Receiver, trustee in bankruptcy, assignee for the benefit of creditors, conservator, liquidating agent, or other similar person duly authorized by law to administer the estate or assets of another person; or

(iv) Fiduciary in a similar capacity.

(2) Transactions by such person or entity acting in a capacity specified in paragraph (d)(1) of this rule after the period specified in that paragraph shall be subject to section 16 of the Act only where the estate, trust or other entity is a beneficial owner of more than ten percent of any class of equity security registered pursuant to section 12 of the Act.

Rule 16a–3. Reporting transactions and holdings

(a) Initial statements of beneficial ownership of equity securities required by section 16(a) of the Act shall be filed on Form 3. Statements of changes in beneficial ownership required by that section shall be filed on Form 4. Annual statements shall be filed on Form 5. At the election of the reporting person, any transaction required to be reported on Form 5 may be reported on an earlier filed Form 4. All such statements shall be prepared and filed in accordance with the requirements of the applicable form.

(b) A person filing statements pursuant to section 16(a) of the Act with respect to any class of equity securities registered pursuant to section 12 of the Act need not file an additional statement on Form 3:

(1) When an additional class of equity securities of the same issuer becomes registered pursuant to section 12 of the Act; or

(2) When such person assumes a different or an additional relationship to the same issuer (for example, when an officer becomes a director).

(c) Any issuer that has equity securities listed on more than one national securities exchange may designate one exchange as the only exchange with which reports pursuant to section 16(a) of the Act need be filed. Such designation shall be made in writing and shall be filed with the Commission and with each national securities exchange on which any equity security of the issuer is listed at the time of such election. The reporting person's obligation to file reports with each national securities exchange on which any equity security of the issuer is listed shall be satisfied by filing with the exchange so designated.

(d) Any person required to file a statement with respect to securities of a single issuer under both section 16(a) of the Act (15 U.S.C. 78p(a)) and section 30(h) of the Investment Company Act of 1940 may file a single statement containing the required information, which will be deemed to be filed under both Acts.

(e) Any person required to file a statement under section 16(a) of the Act shall, not later than the time the statement is transmitted for filing with the Commission, send or deliver a duplicate to the person designated by the issuer to receive such statements, or, in the absence of such a designation, to the issuer's corporate secretary or person performing equivalent functions.

(f)(1) A Form 5 shall be filed by every person who at any time during the issuer's fiscal year was subject to section 16 of the Act with respect to such issuer, except as provided in paragraph (f)(2) of this rule. The Form shall be filed within 45 days after the issuer's fiscal year end, and shall disclose the following holdings and transactions not reported previously on Forms 3, 4 or 5:

(i) All transactions during the most recent fiscal year that were exempt from Section 16(b) of the Act, except:

(A) Exercises and conversions of derivative securities exempt under either Rule 16b–3 or Rule 16b–6(b), and any transaction exempt under Rule 16b–3(d), Rule 16b–3(e), or Rule 16b–3(f) (these are required to be reported on Form 4);

(B) Transactions exempt from section 16(b) of the Act pursuant to Rule 16b–3(c), which shall be exempt from section 16(a) of the Act; and

(C) Transactions exempt from section 16(a) of the Act pursuant to another rule;

(ii) Transactions that constituted small acquisitions pursuant to Rule 16a–6(a);

(iii) all holdings and transactions that should have been reported during the most recent fiscal year, but were not; and

(iv) with respect to the first Form 5 requirement for a reporting person, all holdings and transactions that should have been reported in each of the issuer's last two fiscal years but were not, based on the reporting person's reasonable belief in good faith in the completeness and accuracy of the information.

(2) Notwithstanding the above, no Form 5 shall be required where all transactions otherwise required to be reported on the Form 5 have been reported before the due date of the Form 5.

Persons no longer subject to Section 16 of the Act, but who were subject to the Section at any time during the issuer's fiscal year, must file a Form 5 unless paragraph (f)(2) is satisfied. *See also* Rule 16a–2(b) regarding the reporting obligations of persons ceasing to be officers or directors.

(g)(1) A Form 4 must be filed to report: All transactions not exempt from section 16(b) of the Act; All transactions exempt from section 16(b) of the Act pursuant to Rule 16b–3(d), Rule 16b–3(e), or Rule 16b–(f); and all exercises and conversions of derivative securities, regardless of whether exempt from section 16(b) of the Act. Form 4 must be filed before the end of the second business day following the day on which the subject transaction has been executed.

(2) Solely for purposes of section 16(a)(2)(C) of the Act and paragraph (g)(1) of this rule, the date on which the executing broker, dealer or plan administrator notifies the reporting person of the execution of the transaction is deemed the date of execution for a transaction where the following conditions are satisfied:

(i) the transaction is pursuant to a contract, instruction or written plan for the purchase or sale of equity securities of the issuer (as defined in Rule 16a–1(d)) that satisfies the affirmative defense conditions of Rule 10b5–1(c); and

(ii) the reporting person does not select the date of execution.

(3) Solely for purposes of section 16(a)(2)(C) of the Act and paragraph (g)(1) of this rule, the date on which the plan administrator notifies the reporting person that the transaction has been executed is deemed the date of execution for a discretionary transaction (as defined in Rule 16b–3(b)(1)) for which the reporting person does not select the date of execution.

(4) In the case of the transactions described in paragraphs (g)(2) and (g)(3) of this rule, if the notification date is later than the third business day following the trade date of the transaction, the date of execution is deemed to be the third business day following the trade date of the transaction.

(5) At the option of the reporting person, transactions that are reportable on Form 5 may be reported on Form 4, so long as the Form 4 is filed no later than the due date of the Form 5 on which the transaction is otherwise required to be reported.

(h) The date of filing with the Commission shall be the date of receipt by the Commission.

(i) *Signatures.* Where Section 16 of the Act, or the rules or forms thereunder, require a document filed with or furnished to the Commission to be signed, such document shall be manually signed, or signed using either typed signatures or duplicated or facsimile versions of manual signatures. Where typed, duplicated or facsimile signatures are used, each signatory to the filing shall manually sign a signature page or other document authenticating, acknowledging or otherwise adopting his or her signature that appears in the filing. Such document shall be executed before or at the time the filing is made and shall be retained by the filer for a period of five years. Upon request, the filer shall furnish to the Commission or its staff a copy of any or all documents retained pursuant to this rule.

(j) Where more than one person subject to section 16 of the Act is deemed to be a beneficial owner of the same equity securities, all such persons must report as beneficial owners of the securities, either separately or jointly. Where persons in a group are deemed to be beneficial owners of equity securities pursuant to Rule 16a–1(a)(1) due to the aggregation of holdings, a single Form 3, 4 or 5 may be filed on behalf of all persons in the group. Joint and group filings must include all required information for each beneficial owner, and such filings must be signed by each beneficial owner, or on behalf of such owner by an authorized person.

(k) Any issuer that maintains a corporate Web site shall post on that Web site by the end of the business day after filing any Form 3, 4, or 5 filed under section 16(a) of the Act as to the equity securities of that issuer. Each such form shall remain accessible on such issuer's Web site for at least a 12-month period. In the case of an issuer that is an investment company and that does not maintain its own Web site, if any of the issuer's investment adviser, sponsor, depositor, trustee, administrator, principal underwriter, or any affiliated person of the investment company maintains a Web site that includes the name of the issuer, the issuer shall comply with the posting requirements by posting the forms on one such Web site.

Rule 16a–4. Derivative securities

(a) For purposes of section 16 of the Act, both derivative securities and the underlying securities to which they relate shall be deemed to be the same class of equity securities, *except that* the acquisition or disposition of any derivative security shall be separately reported.

(b) The exercise or conversion of a call equivalent position shall be reported on Form 4 and treated for reporting purposes as:

(1) A purchase of the underlying security; and

(2) A closing of the derivative security position.

(c) The exercise or conversion of a put equivalent position shall be reported on Form 4 and treated for reporting purposes as:

(1) A sale of the underlying security; and

(2) A closing of the derivative security position.

(d) The disposition or closing of a long derivative security position, as a result of cancellation or expiration, shall be exempt from section 16(a) of the Act if exempt from section 16(b) of the Act pursuant to Rule 16b–6(d).

NOTE TO RULE 16a–4: A purchase or sale resulting from an exercise or conversion of a derivative security may be exempt from section 16(b) of the Act pursuant to Rule 16b–3 or Rule 16b–6(b).

Rule 16a–5. Odd–lot dealers

Transactions by an odd-lot dealer (a) in odd-lots as reasonably necessary to carry on odd-lot transactions, or (b) in round lots to offset odd-lot transactions previously or simultaneously executed or reasonably anticipated in the usual course of business, shall be exempt from the provisions of section 16(a) of the Act with respect to participation by such odd-lot dealer in such transaction.

Rule 16a–6. Small acquisitions

(a) Any acquisition of an equity security or the right to acquire such securities, other than an acquisition from the issuer (including an employee benefit plan sponsored by the issuer), not exceeding $10,000 in market value shall be reported on Form 5, subject to the following conditions:

(1) Such acquisition, when aggregated with other acquisitions of securities of the same class (including securities underlying derivative securities, but excluding acquisitions exempted by rule from section 16(b) or previously reported on Form 4 or Form 5) within the prior six months, does not exceed a total of $10,000 in market value; and

(2) The person making the acquisition does not within six months thereafter make any disposition, other than by a transaction exempt from section 16(b) of the Act.

(b) If an acquisition no longer qualifies for the reporting deferral in paragraph (a) of this rule, all such acquisitions that have not yet been reported must be reported on Form 4 before the end of the second business day following the day on which the conditions of paragraph (a) of this rule are no longer met.

Rule 16a–7. Transactions effected in connection with a distribution

(a) Any purchase and sale, or sale and purchase, of a security that is made in connection with the distribution of a substantial block of securities shall be exempt from the provisions of section 16(a) of the

Act, to the extent specified in this Rule, subject to the following conditions:

(1) The person effecting the transaction is engaged in the business of distributing securities and is participating in good faith, in the ordinary course of such business, in the distribution of such block of securities; and

(2) The security involved in the transaction is:

(i) Part of such block of securities and is acquired by the person effecting the transaction, with a view to distribution thereof, from the issuer or other person on whose behalf such securities are being distributed or from a person who is participating in good faith in the distribution of such block of securities; or

(ii) A security purchased in good faith by or for the account of the person effecting the transaction for the purpose of stabilizing the market price of securities of the class being distributed or to cover an over-allotment or other short position created in connection with such distribution.

(b) Each person participating in the transaction must qualify on an individual basis for an exemption pursuant to this rule.

Rule 16a–8. Trusts

(a) *Persons Subject to Section 16.* (1) *Trusts.* A trust shall be subject to section 16 of the Act with respect to securities of the issuer if the trust is a beneficial owner, pursuant to Rule 16a–1(a)(1), of more than ten percent of any class of equity securities of the issuer registered pursuant to section 12 of the Act ("ten percent beneficial owner").

(2) *Trustees, Beneficiaries, and Settlors.* In determining whether a trustee, beneficiary, or settlor is a ten percent beneficial owner with respect to the issuer:

(i) Such persons shall be deemed the beneficial owner of the issuer's securities held by the trust, to the extent specified by Rule 16a–1(a)(1); and

(ii) Settlors shall be deemed the beneficial owner of the issuer's securities held by the trust where they have the power to revoke the trust without the consent of another person.

(b) *Trust Holdings and Transactions.* Holdings and transactions in the issuer's securities held by a trust shall be reported by the trustee on behalf of the trust, if the trust is subject to section 16 of the Act, except as provided below. Holdings and transactions in the issuer's securities held by a trust (whether or not subject to section 16 of the Act) may be reportable by other parties as follows:

(1) *Trusts.* The trust need not report holdings and transactions in the issuer's securities held by the trust in an employee benefit plan subject to the Employee Retirement Income Security Act over which no trustee exercises investment control.

(2) *Trustees.* If, as provided by Rule 16a–1(a)(2), a trustee subject to Section 16 of the Act has a pecuniary interest in any holding or transaction in the issuer's securities held by the trust, such holding or transaction shall be attributed to the trustee and shall be reported by the trustee in the trustee's individual capacity, as well as on behalf of the trust. With respect to performance fees and holdings of the trustee's immediate family, trustees shall be deemed to have a pecuniary interest in the trust holdings and transactions in the following circumstances:

(i) A performance fee is received that does not meet the proviso of Rule 16a–1(a)(2)(ii)(C); or

(ii) at least one beneficiary of the trust is a member of the trustee's immediate family. The pecuniary interest of the immediate family member(s) shall be attributed to and reported by the trustee.

(3) *Beneficiaries.* A beneficiary subject to section 16 of the Act shall have or share reporting obligations with respect to transactions in the issuer's securities held by the trust, if the beneficiary is a beneficial owner of the securities pursuant to Rule 16a–1(a)(2), as follows:

(i) If a beneficiary shares investment control with the trustee with respect to a trust transaction, the transaction shall be attributed to and reported by both the beneficiary and the trust;

(ii) If a beneficiary has investment control with respect to a trust transaction without consultation with the trustee, the transaction shall be attributed to and reported by the beneficiary only; and

(iii) In making a determination as to whether a beneficiary is the beneficial owner of the securities pursuant to Rule 16a–1(a)(2), beneficiaries shall be deemed to have a pecuniary interest in the issuer's securities held by the trust to the extent of their pro rata interest in the trust where the trustee does not exercise exclusive investment control.

NOTE TO PARAGRAPH (b)(3): Transactions and holdings attributed to a trust beneficiary may be reported by the trustee on behalf of the beneficiary, provided that the report is signed by the beneficiary or other authorized person. Where the transactions and holdings are attributed both to the trustee and trust beneficiary, a joint report may be filed in accordance with Rule 16a–3(j).

(4) *Settlors.* If a settlor subject to section 16 of the Act reserves the right to revoke the trust without the consent of another person, the trust holdings and transactions shall be attributed to and reported by the settlor instead of the trust; *Provided, however,* That if the settlor does not exercise or share investment control over the issuer's securities held by the trust, the trust holdings and transactions shall be attributed to and reported by the trust instead of the settlor.

(c) *Remainder Interests.* Remainder interests in a trust are deemed not to confer beneficial ownership for purposes of section 16 of the Act, provided that the persons with the remainder interests have no power, directly or indirectly, to exercise or share investment control over the trust.

(d) A trust, trustee, beneficiary or settlor becoming subject to section 16(a) of the Act pursuant to this Rule also shall be subject to sections 16(b) and 16(c) of the Act.

Rule 16a–9. Stock splits, stock dividends, and pro rata rights

The following shall be exempt from section 16 of the Act:

(a) The increase or decrease in the number of securities held as a result of a stock split or stock dividend applying equally to all securities of a class, including a stock dividend in which equity securities of a different issuer are distributed; and

(b) The acquisition of rights, such as shareholder or pre-emptive rights, pursuant to a pro rata grant to all holders of the same class of equity securities registered under section 12 of the Act.

NOTE: The exercise or sale of a pro rata right shall be reported pursuant to Rule 16a–4 and the exercise shall be eligible for exemption from section 16(b) of the Act pursuant to Rule 16b–6(b).

Rule 16a–10. Exemptions under Section 16(a)

Except as provided in Rule 16a–6, any transaction exempted from the requirements of section 16(a) of the Act, insofar as it is otherwise subject to the provisions of section 16(b), shall be likewise exempt from section 16(b) of the Act.

Rule 16a–11. Dividend or interest reinvestment plans

Any acquisition of securities resulting from the reinvestment of dividends or interest on securities of the same issuer shall be exempt from section 16 of the Act if the acquisition is made pursuant to a plan providing for the regular reinvestment of dividends or interest and the plan provides for broad-based participation, does not discriminate in favor of employees of the issuer, and operates on substantially the same terms for all plan participants.

Rule 16a–12. Domestic relations orders

The acquisition or disposition of equity securities pursuant to a domestic relations order, as defined in the Internal Revenue Code or Title I of the Employee Retirement Income Security Act, or the rules thereunder, shall be exempt from section 16 of the Act.

Rule 16a–13. Change in form of beneficial ownership

A transaction, other than the exercise or conversion of a derivative security or deposit into or withdrawal from a voting trust, that effects only a change in the form of beneficial ownership without changing a person's pecuniary interest in the subject equity securities shall be exempt from section 16 of the Act.

EXEMPTION OF CERTAIN TRANSACTIONS FROM SECTION 16(b)

Rule 16b–1. Transactions approved by a regulatory authority

Any purchase and sale, or sale and purchase, of a security shall be exempt from section 16(b) of the Act, if the transaction is effected by an investment company registered under the Investment Company Act of 1940 (15 U.S.C. 80a–1 *et seq.*) and both the purchase and sale of such security have been exempted from the provisions of section 17(a) (15 U.S.C. 80a–17(a)) of the Investment Company Act of 1940, by rule or order of the Commission.

Rule 16b–2. [Reserved]

Rule 16b–3. Transactions between an issuer and its officers or directors

(a) *General.* A transaction between the issuer (including an employee benefit plan sponsored by the issuer) and an officer or director of the issuer that involves issuer equity securities shall be exempt from section 16(b) of the Act if the transaction satisfies the applicable conditions set forth in this section.

(b) *Definitions.* (1) A *Discretionary Transaction* shall mean a transaction pursuant to an employee benefit plan that:

(i) Is at the volition of a plan participant;

(ii) Is not made in connection with the participant's death, disability, retirement or termination of employment;

(iii) Is not required to be made available to a plan participant pursuant to a provision of the Internal Revenue Code; and

(iv) Results in either an intra-plan transfer involving an issuer equity securities fund, or a cash distribution funded by a volitional disposition of an issuer equity security.

(2) An *Excess Benefit Plan* shall mean an employee benefit plan that is operated in conjunction with a Qualified Plan, and provides only the benefits or contributions that would be provided under a Qualified Plan but for any benefit or contribution limitations set forth in the Internal Revenue Code of 1986, or any successor provisions thereof.

(3)(i) A *Non-Employee Director* shall mean a director who:

(A) Is not currently an officer (as defined in Rule 16a–1(f)) of the issuer or a parent or subsidiary of the issuer, or otherwise currently employed by the issuer or a parent or subsidiary of the issuer;

(B) Does not receive compensation, either directly or indirectly, from the issuer or a parent or subsidiary of the issuer, for services rendered as a consultant or in any capacity other than as a director, except for an amount that does not exceed the dollar amount for which disclosure would be required pursuant to Item 404(a) of Regulation S–K; and

(C) Does not possess an interest in any other transaction for which disclosure would be required pursuant to Item 404(a) of Regulation S–K.

(ii) Notwithstanding paragraph (b)(3)(i) of this section, a *Non–Employee Director* of a closed-end investment company shall mean a director who is not an "interested person" of the issuer, as that term is defined in section 2(a)(19) of the Investment Company Act of 1940.

(4) A *Qualified Plan* shall mean an employee benefit plan that satisfies the coverage and participation requirements of Sections 410 and 401(a)(26) of the Internal Revenue Code of 1986, or any successor provisions thereof.

(5) A *Stock Purchase Plan* shall mean an employee benefit plan that satisfies the coverage and participation requirements of sections 423(b)(3) and 423(b)(5), or section 410, of the Internal Revenue Code of 1986, or any successor provisions thereof.

(c) *Tax-Conditioned Plans.* Any transaction (other than a Discretionary Transaction) pursuant to a Qualified Plan, an Excess Benefit Plan, or a Stock Purchase Plan shall be exempt without condition.

(d) *Acquisitions from the Issuer.* Any transaction, other than a Discretionary Transaction, involving an acquisition from the issuer (including without limitation a grant or award), whether or not intended for a compensatory or other particular purpose, shall be exempt if:

(1) The transaction is approved by the board of directors of the issuer, or a committee of the board of directors that is composed solely of two or more Non-Employee Directors;

(2) The transaction is approved or ratified, in compliance with Section 14 of the Act, by either: the affirmative votes of the holders of a majority of the securities of the issuer present, or represented, and entitled to vote at a meeting duly held in accordance with the applicable laws of the state or other jurisdiction in which the issuer is incorporated; or the written consent of the holders of a majority of the securities of the issuer entitled to vote; *provided that* such ratification occurs no later than the date of the next annual meeting of shareholders; or

(3) The issuer equity securities so acquired are held by the officer or director for a period of six months following the date of such acquisition, *provided that* this condition shall be satisfied with respect to a derivative security if at least six months elapse from the date of acquisition of the derivative security to the date of disposition of the derivative security (other than upon exercise or conversion) or its underlying equity security.

(e) *Dispositions to the Issuer*. Any transaction, other than a Discretionary Transaction, involving the disposition to the issuer of issuer equity securities, whether or not intended for a compensatory or other particular purpose, shall be exempt, provided that the terms of such disposition are approved in advance in the manner prescribed by either paragraph (d)(1) or paragraph (d)(2) of this rule.

(f) *Discretionary Transactions.* A Discretionary Transaction shall be exempt only if effected pursuant to an election made at least six months following the date of the most recent election, with respect to any plan of the issuer, that effected a Discretionary Transaction that was:

(1) An acquisition, if the transaction to be exempted would be a disposition; or

(2) A disposition, if the transaction to be exempted would be an acquisition.

NOTES TO RULE 16B–3

NOTE (1): The exercise or conversion of a derivative security that does not satisfy the conditions of this section is eligible for exemption from section 16(b) of the Act to the extent that the conditions of Rule 16b–6(b) are satisfied.

NOTE (2): Section 16(a) reporting requirements applicable to transactions exempt pursuant to this section are set forth in Rule 16a–3(f) and (g) and Rule 16a–4.

NOTE (3): The approval conditions of paragraphs (d)(1), (d)(2) or (e) of this rule require the approval of each specific transaction, and are not satisfied by approval of a plan in its entirety except for the approval of a plan pursuant to which the terms and conditions of each transaction are fixed in advance, such as a formula plan. Where the terms of a subsequent transaction (such as the exercise price of an option, or the provision of an exercise or tax withholding right) are provided for in a transaction as initially approved pursuant to paragraphs (d)(1), (d)(2) and (e), such subsequent transaction shall not require further specific approval.

NOTE (4): For purposes of determining a director's status under those portions of paragraph (b)(3)(i) that reference Item 404(a) of Regulation S–K, an issuer may rely on the disclosure provided under Item 404(a) of Regulation S–K for the issuer's most recent fiscal year contained in the most recent filing in which disclosure required under Item 404(a) is presented. Where a transaction disclosed in that filing was terminated before the director's proposed service as a Non-Employee Director, that transaction will not bar such service. The issuer must believe in good faith that any current or contemplated transaction in which the director participates will not be required to be disclosed under Item 404(a) of Regulation S–K, based on information readily available to the issuer and the director at the time such director proposes to act as a Non-Employee Director. At such time as the issuer believes in good faith, based on readily available information, that a current or contemplated transaction with a director will be required to be disclosed under Item 404(a) of Regulation S–K in a future filing, the director no longer is eligible to serve as a Non-Employee Director; *provided, however,* that this determination does not result in retroactive loss of a Rule 16b–3 exemption for a transaction previously approved by the director while serving as a Non-Employee Director consistent with this note. In making the determinations specified in this Note, the issuer may rely on information it obtains from the director, for example, pursuant to a response to an inquiry.

Rule 16b–4. [Reserved]

Rule 16b–5. Bona fide gifts and inheritance

Both the acquisition and the disposition of equity securities shall be exempt from the operation of section 16(b) of the Act if they are: (a) bona fide gifts; or (b) transfers of securities by will or the laws of descent and distribution.

Rule 16b–6. Derivative securities

(a) The establishment of or increase in a call equivalent position or liquidation of or decrease in a put equivalent position shall be deemed a purchase of the underlying security for purposes of section 16(b) of the Act, and the establishment of or increase in a put equivalent position or liquidation of or decrease in a call equivalent position shall be deemed a sale of the underlying securities for purposes of section 16(b) of the Act; *Provided, however,* That if the increase or decrease occurs as a result of the fixing of the exercise price of a right initially issued without a fixed price, where the date the price is fixed is not known in advance and is outside the control of the recipient, the increase or decrease shall be exempt from section 16(b) of the Act with respect to any offsetting transaction within the six months prior to the date the price is fixed.

(b) The closing of a derivative security position as a result of its exercise or conversion shall be exempt from the operation of section 16(b) of the Act, and the acquisition of underlying securities at a fixed exercise price due to the exercise or conversion of a call equivalent position or the disposition of underlying securities at a fixed exercise price due to the exercise of a put equivalent position shall be exempt from the operation of section 16(b) of the Act; *Provided, however,* That the acquisition of underlying securities from the exercise of an out-of-the-money option, warrant, or right shall not be exempt unless the exercise is necessary to comport with the sequential exercise provisions of the Internal Revenue Code (26 U.S.C. 422A).

NOTE TO PARAGRAPH (b): The exercise or conversion of a derivative security that does not satisfy the conditions of this section is eligible for exemption from section 16(b) of the Act to the extent that the conditions of Rule 16b–3 are satisfied.

(c) In determining the short-swing profit recoverable pursuant to section 16(b) of the Act from transactions involving the purchase and sale or sale and purchase of derivative and other securities, the following rules apply:

(1) Short-swing profits in transactions involving the purchase and sale or sale and purchase of de-

rivative securities that have identical characteristics (*e.g.*, purchases and sales of call options of the same strike price and expiration date, or purchases and sales of the same series of convertible debentures) shall be measured by the actual prices paid or received in the short-swing transactions.

(2) Short-swing profits in transactions involving the purchase and sale or sale and purchase of derivative securities having different characteristics but related to the same underlying security (*e.g.*, the purchase of a call option and the sale of a convertible debenture) or derivative securities and underlying securities shall not exceed the difference in price of the underlying security on the date of purchase or sale and the date of sale or purchase. Such profits may be measured by calculating the short-swing profits that would have been realized had the subject transactions involved purchases and sales solely of the derivative security that was purchased or solely of the derivative security that was sold, valued as of the time of the matching purchase or sale, and calculated for the lesser of the number of underlying securities actually purchased or sold.

(d) Upon cancellation or expiration of an option within six months of the writing of the option, any profit derived from writing the option shall be recoverable under section 16(b) of the Act. The profit shall not exceed the premium received for writing the option. The disposition or closing of a long derivative security position, as a result of cancellation or expiration, shall be exempt from section 16(b) of the Act where no value is received from the cancellation or expiration.

Rule 16b–7. Mergers, reclassifications, and consolidations

(a) The following transactions shall be exempt from the provisions of section 16(b) of the Act:

(1) The acquisition of a security of a company, pursuant to a merger, reclassification or consolidation, in exchange for a security of a company that before the merger, reclassification or consolidation, owned 85 percent or more of either:

(i) The equity securities of all other companies involved in the merger, reclassification or consolidation, or in the case of a consolidation, the resulting company; or

(ii) The combined assets of all the companies involved in the merger, reclassification or consolidation, computed according to their book values before the merger, reclassification or consolidation as determined by reference to their most recent available financial statements for a 12 month period before the merger, reclassification or consolidation, or such shorter time as the company has been in existence.

(2) The disposition of a security, pursuant to a merger, reclassification or consolidation, of a company that before the merger, reclassification or consolidation, owned 85 percent or more of either:

(i) The equity securities of all other companies involved in the merger, reclassification or consolidation or, in the case of a consolidation, the resulting company; or

(ii) The combined assets of all the companies undergoing merger, reclassification or consolidation, computed according to their book values before the merger, reclassification or consolidation as determined by reference to their most recent available financial statements for a 12 month period before the merger, reclassification or consolidation.

(b) A merger within the meaning of this rule shall include the sale or purchase of substantially all the assets of one company by another in exchange for equity securities which are then distributed to the security holders of the company that sold its assets.

(c) The exemption provided by this rule applies to any securities transaction that satisfies the conditions specified in this rule and is not conditioned on the transaction satisfying any other conditions.

(d) Notwithstanding the foregoing, if a person subject to section 16 of the Act makes any non-exempt purchase of a security in any company involved in the merger, reclassification or consolidation and any non-exempt sale of a security in any company involved in the merger, reclassification or consolidation within any period of less than six months during which the merger, reclassification or consolidation took place, the exemption provided by this rule shall be unavailable to the extent of such purchase and sale.

Rule 16b–8. Voting trusts

Any acquisition or disposition of an equity security or certificate representing equity securities involved in the deposit or withdrawal from a voting trust or deposit agreement shall be exempt from section 16(b) of the Act if substantially all of the assets held under the voting trust or deposit agreement immediately after the deposit or immediately prior to the withdrawal consisted of equity securities of the same class as the security deposited or withdrawn;

Provided, however, That this exemption shall not apply if there is a non-exempt purchase or sale of an equity security of the class deposited within six months (including the date of withdrawal or deposit) of a non-exempt sale or purchase, respectively, of any certificate representing such equity security (other than the actual deposit or withdrawal).

EXEMPTION OF CERTAIN TRANSACTIONS FROM SECTION 16(c)

Rule 16c–1. Brokers

Any transaction shall be exempt from section 16(c) of the Act to the extent necessary to render lawful the execution by a broker of an order for an account in which the broker has no direct or indirect interest.

Rule 16c–2. Transactions effected in connection with a distribution

Any transaction shall be exempt from section 16(c) of the Act to the extent necessary to render lawful any sale made by or on behalf of a dealer in connection with a distribution of a substantial block of securities, where the sale is represented by an over-allotment in which the dealer is participating as a member of an underwriting group, or the dealer or a person acting on the dealer's behalf intends in good faith to offset such sale with a security to be acquired by or on behalf of the dealer as a participant in an underwriting, selling, or soliciting-dealer group of which the dealer is a member at the time of the sale, whether or not the security to be acquired is subject to a prior offering to existing security holders or some other class of persons.

Rule 16c–3. Exemption of sales of securities to be acquired

(a) Whenever any person is entitled, incident to ownership of an issued security and without the payment of consideration, to receive another security "when issued" or "when distributed," the sale of the security to be acquired shall be exempt from the operation of section 16(c) of the Act; *Provided*, That:

(1) The sale is made subject to the same conditions as those attaching to the right of acquisition;

(2) Such person exercises reasonable diligence to deliver such security to the purchaser promptly after the right of acquisition matures; and

(3) Such person reports the sale on the appropriate form for reporting transactions by persons subject to Section 16(a) of the Act.

(b) This rule shall not exempt transactions involving both a sale of the issued security and a sale of a security "when issued" or "when distributed" if the combined transactions result in a sale of more securities than the aggregate of issued securities owned by the seller plus those to be received for the other security "when issued" or "when distributed."

Rule 16c–4. Derivative securities

Establishing or increasing a put equivalent position shall be exempt from Section 16(c) of the Act, so long as the amount of securities underlying the put equivalent position does not exceed the amount of underlying securities otherwise owned.

ARBITRAGE TRANSACTIONS

Rule 16e–1. Arbitrage transactions under Section 16

It shall be unlawful for any director or officer of an issuer of an equity security which is registered pursuant to section 12 of the Act to effect any foreign or domestic arbitrage transaction in any equity security of such issuer, whether registered or not, unless he shall include such transaction in the statements required by section 16(a) and shall account to such issuer for the profits arising from such transaction, as provided in section 16(b). The provision of section 16(c) shall not apply to such arbitrage transactions. The provisions of section 16 shall not apply to any bona fide foreign or domestic arbitrage transaction insofar as it is effected by any person other than such director or officer of the issuer of such security.

PRESERVATION OF RECORDS AND REPORTS OF CERTAIN STABILIZING ACTIVITIES

Rule 17a-1. Recordkeeping rule for national securities exchanges, national securities associations, registered clearing agencies and the Municipal Securities Rulemaking Board

(a) Every national securities exchange, national securities association, registered clearing agency and the Municipal Securities Rulemaking Board shall keep and preserve at least one copy of all documents, including all correspondence, memoranda, papers, books, notices, accounts, and other such records as shall be made or received by it in the course of its business as such and in the conduct of its self-regulatory activity.

(b) Every national securities exchange, national securities association, registered clearing agency and the Municipal Securities Rulemaking Board shall keep all such documents for a period of not less than five years, the first two years in an easily accessible place, subject to the destruction and disposition provisions of Rule 17a-6.

(c) Every national securities exchange, registered securities association, registered clearing agency and the Municipal Securities Rulemaking Board shall, upon request of any representative of the Commission, promptly furnish to the possession of such representative copies of any documents required to be kept and preserved by it pursuant to paragraphs (a) and (b) of this rule.

Rule 17a-2. Recordkeeping requirements relating to stabilizing activities

(a) *Scope of Rule.* This rule shall apply to any person who effects any purchase of a security subject to Rule 104 of Regulation M for the purpose of, or who participates in a syndicate or group that engages in, "stabilizing," as defined in Rule 100 of Regulation M, the price of any security; or effects a purchase that is a "syndicate covering transaction," as defined in Rule 100 of Regulation M; or imposes a "penalty bid," as defined in Rule 100 of Regulation M:

(1) With respect to which a registration statement has been, or is to be, filed pursuant to the Securities Act of 1933; or

(2) Which is being, or is to be, offered pursuant to an exemption from registration under Regulation A (Rules 251 through 263 under the Securities Act of 1933) adopted under the Securities Act of 1933; or

(3) Which is being, or is to be, otherwise offered, if the aggregate offering price of the securities being offered exceeds $5,000,000.

(b) *Definitions.* For purposes of this rule, the following definitions shall apply:

(1) The term *manager* shall mean the person stabilizing or effecting syndicate covering transactions or imposing a penalty bid for its sole account or for the account of a syndicate or group in which it is a participant, and who, by contract or otherwise, deals with the issuer, organizes the selling effort, receives some benefit from the underwriting that is not shared by other underwriters, or represents any other underwriters in such matters as maintaining the records of the distribution and arranging for allotments of the securities offered.

(2) The term *exempted security* means an exempted security as defined in section 3(a)(12) of the Act, including securities issued, or guaranteed both as to principal and interest, by the International Bank for Reconstruction and Development.

(c) *Records Relating to Stabilizing, Syndicate Covering Transactions, and Penalty Bids Required to Be Maintained by Manager.* Any person subject to this section who acts as a manager and stabilizes or effects syndicate covering transactions or imposes a penalty bid shall:

(1) Promptly record and maintain the following separately retrievable information, for a period of not less than three years, the first two years in an easily accessible place; *Provided, however,* That if the information is in a record required to be made pursuant to Rule 17a-3 or Rule 17a-4, or otherwise preserved, such information need not be maintained in a separate file if the person can sort promptly and retrieve the information as if it had been kept in a separate file as a record made pursuant to, and preserves the information in accordance with the time periods specified in, this paragraph (c)(1):

(i) The name and class of any security stabilized or any security in which syndicate covering transactions have been effected or a penalty bid has been imposed;

(ii) The price, date, and time at which each stabilizing purchase or syndicate covering transaction was effected by the manager or by any participant in the syndicate or group, and whether any penalties were assessed;

(iii) The names and the addresses of the members of the syndicate or group;

(iv) Their respective commitments, or, in the case of a standby or contingent underwriting, the percentage participation of each member of the syndicate or group therein; and

(v) The dates when any penalty bid was in effect.

(2) Promptly furnish to each of the members of the syndicate or group the name and class of any security being stabilized, and the date and time at which the first stabilizing purchase was effected by the manager or by any participant in the syndicate or group; and

(3) Promptly notify each of the members of such syndicate or group of the date and time when stabilizing was terminated.

(d) *Notification to Manager*. Any person who has a participation in a syndicate account but who is not a manager of such account, and who effects one or more stabilizing purchases or syndicate covering transactions for its sole account or for the account of a syndicate or group, shall within three business days following such purchase notify the manager of the price, date, and time at which such stabilizing purchase or syndicate covering transaction was effected, and shall in addition notify the manager of the date and time when such stabilizing purchase or syndicate covering transaction was terminated. The manager shall maintain such notifications in a separate file, together with the information required by paragraph (c)(1) of this rule, for a period of not less than three years, the first two years in an easily accessible place.

Rule 17a–3. Records to be made by certain exchange members, brokers, and dealers

(a) Every member of a national securities exchange who transacts a business in securities directly with others than members of a national securities exchange, and every broker or dealer who transacts a business in securities through the medium of any such member, and every broker or dealer registered pursuant to section 15 of the Securities Exchange Act of 1934, as amended, (15 U.S.C. 78*o*) shall make and keep current the following books and records relating to its business:

(1) Blotters (or other records of original entry) containing an itemized daily record of all purchases and sales of securities, all receipts and deliveries of securities (including certificate numbers), all receipts and disbursements of cash and all other debits and credits. Such records shall show the account for which each such transaction was effected, the name and amount of securities, the unit and aggregate purchase or sale price (if any), the trade date, and the name or other designation of the person from whom purchased or received or to whom sold or delivered.

(2) Ledgers (or other records) reflecting all assets and liabilities, income and expense and capital accounts.

(3) Ledger accounts (or other records) itemizing separately as to each cash and margin account of every customer and of such member, broker or dealer and partners thereof, all purchases, sales, receipts, and deliveries of securities and commodities for such account and all other debits and credits to such account.

(4) Ledgers (or other records) reflecting the following:

(i) Securities in transfer;

(ii) Dividends and interest received;

(iii) Securities borrowed and securities loaned;

(iv) Moneys borrowed and moneys loaned (together with a record of the collateral therefor and any substitutions in such collateral);

(v) Securities failed to receive and failed to deliver;

(vi) All long and all short securities record differences arising from the examination, count, verification and comparison pursuant to Rule 17a–5, Rule 17a–12, and Rule 17a–13 (by date of examination, count, verification and comparison showing for each security the number of long or short count differences);

(vii) Repurchase and reverse repurchase agreements;

(5) A securities record or ledger reflecting separately for each security as of the clearance dates all "long" or "short" positions (including securities in safekeeping and securities that are the subjects of repurchase or reverse repurchase agreements) carried by such member, broker or dealer

for its account of for the account of its customers or partners or others and showing the location of all securities long and the offsetting position to all securities short, including long security count differences and short security count differences classified by the date of the physical count and verification in which they were discovered, and in all cases the name or designation of the account in which each position is carried.

(6)(i) A memorandum of each brokerage order, and of any other instruction, given or received for the purchase or sale of securities, whether executed or unexecuted. The memorandum shall show the terms and conditions of the order or instructions and of any modification or cancellation thereof; the account for which entered; the time the order was received; the time of entry; the price at which executed; the identity of each associated person, if any, responsible for the account; the identity of any other person who entered or accepted the order on behalf of the customer or, if a customer entered the order on an electronic system, a notation of that entry; and, to the extent feasible, the time of execution or cancellation. The memorandum need not show the identity of any person, other than the associated person responsible for the account, who may have entered or accepted the order if the order is entered into an electronic system that generates the memorandum and if that system is not capable of receiving an entry of the identity of any person other than the responsible associated person; in that circumstance, the member, broker or dealer shall produce upon request by a representative of a securities regulatory authority a separate record which identifies each other person. An order entered pursuant to the exercise of discretionary authority by the member, broker or dealer, or associated person thereof, shall be so designated. The term *instruction* shall include instructions between partners and employees of a member, broker or dealer. The term *time of entry* shall mean the time when the member, broker or dealer transmits the order or instruction for execution.

(ii) This memorandum need not be made as to a purchase, sale or redemption of a security on a subscription way basis directly from or to the issuer, if the member, broker or dealer maintains a copy of the customer's subscription agreement regarding a purchase, or a copy of any other document required by the issuer regarding a sale or redemption.

(7) A memorandum of each purchase and sale for the account of the member, broker, or dealer showing the price and, to the extent feasible, the time of execution; and, in addition, where the purchase or sale is with a customer other than a broker or dealer, a memorandum of each order received, showing the time of receipt; the terms and conditions of the order and of any modification thereof; the account for which it was entered; the identity of each associated person, if any, responsible for the account; the identity of any other person who entered or accepted the order on behalf of the customer or, if a customer entered the order on an electronic system, a notation of that entry. The memorandum need not show the identity of any person other than the associated person responsible for the account who may have entered the order if the order is entered into an electronic system that generates the memorandum and if that system is not capable of receiving an entry of the identity of any person other than the responsible associated person: in that circumstance, the member, broker or dealer shall produce upon request by a representative of a securities regulatory authority a separate record which identifies each other person. An order with a customer other than a member, broker or dealer entered pursuant to the exercise of discretionary authority by the member, broker or dealer, or associated person thereof, shall be so designated.

(8) Copies of confirmations of all purchases and sales of securities, including all repurchase and reverse repurchase agreements, and copies of notices of all other debits and credits for securities, cash and other items for the account of customers and partners of such member, broker or dealer.

(9) A record in respect of each cash and margin account with such member, broker or dealer indicating (i) the name and address of the beneficial owner of such account, and (ii) except with respect to exempt employee benefit plan securities as defined in Rule 14a–1(d), but only to the extent such securities are held by employee benefit plans established by the issuer of the securities, whether not the beneficial owner of securities registered in the name of such members, brokers or dealers, or a registered clearing agency or its nominee objects to disclosure of his or her identity, address and securities positions to issuers, and (iii) in the case of a margin account, the signature of such owner, *Provided*, That, in the case of a joint account or an account of a corporation, such records are required

only in respect of the person or persons authorized to transact business for such account.

(10) A record of all puts, calls, spreads, straddles, and other options in which such member, broker, or dealer has any direct or indirect interest or which such member, broker, or dealer has granted or guaranteed, containing, at least, an identification of the security and the number of units involved. An OTC derivatives dealer shall also keep a record of all eligible OTC derivative instruments as defined in Rule 3b–13 in which the OTC derivatives dealer has any direct or indirect interest or which it has written or guaranteed, containing, at a minimum, an identification of the security or other instrument, the number of units involved, and the identity of the counterparty.

(11) A record of the proof of money balances of all ledger accounts in the form of trial balances, and a record of the computation of aggregate indebtedness and net capital, as of the trial balance date, pursuant to Rule 15c3–1: *Provided, however,* (i) That such computation need not be made by any member, broker or dealer unconditionally exempt form Rule 15c3–1 by paragraph (b)(1) or (b)(3), thereof; and (ii) that any member of an exchange whose members are exempt from Rule 15c3–1 by paragraph (b)(2) thereof shall make a record of the computation of aggregate indebtedness and net capital as of the trial balance date in accordance with the capital rules of at least one of the exchanges therein listed of which it is a member. Such trial balances and computations shall be prepared currently at least once a month.

(12)(i) A questionnaire or application for employment executed by each "associated person" (as defined in paragraph (h)(4) of this rule) of the member, broker or dealer, which questionnaire or application shall be approved in writing by an authorized representative of the member, broker or dealer and shall contain at least the following information with respect to the associated person:

(A) The associated person's name, address, social security number, and the starting date of the associated person's employment or other association with the member, broker or dealer;

(B) The associated person's date of birth;

(C) A complete, consecutive statement of all the associated person's business connections for at least the preceding ten years, including whether the employment was part-time or full-time.

(D) A record of any denial of membership or registration, and of any disciplinary action taken, or sanction imposed, upon the associated person by any Federal or State agency, or by any national securities exchange or national securities association, including any finding that the associated person was a cause of any disciplinary action or had violated any law;

(E) A record of any denial, suspension, expulsion or revocation of membership or registration of any member, broker or dealer with which the associated person was associated in any capacity when such action was taken;

(F) A record of any permanent or temporary injunction entered against the associated person or any member, broker or dealer with which the associated person was associated in any capacity at the time such injunction was entered;

(G) A record of any arrest or indictment for any felony, or any misdemeanor pertaining to securities, commodities, banking, insurance or real estate (including, but not limited to, acting or being associated with a broker-dealer, investment company, investment adviser, futures sponsor, bank, or savings and loan association), fraud, false statements or omissions, wrongful taking of property or bribery, forgery, counterfeiting or extortion, and the disposition of the foregoing.

(H) A record of any other name or names by which the associated person has been known or which the associated person has used;

Provided, however, That if such associated person has been registered as a registered representative of such member, broker or dealer with, or the associated person's employment has been approved by, the Financial Industry Regulatory Authority, Inc., or the American Stock Exchange LLC, the Boston Stock Exchange, Inc., the Chicago Stock Exchange, Inc., New York Stock Exchange LLC, NYSE Arca, Inc., the Philadelphia Stock Exchange, Inc., the Chicago Board Options Exchange, Incorporated, the National Stock Exchange, Inc. or the International Securities Exchange, LLC, then retention of a full, correct, and complete copy of any and all applications for such registration or approval shall be deemed to satisfy the requirements of this paragraph.

(ii) A record listing every associated person of the member, broker or dealer which shows, for each associated person, every office of the member, broker or dealer where the associated person regularly conducts the business of handling funds or securities or effecting any transactions in, or inducing or attempting to induce the purchase or sale of any security for the member, broker or dealer, and the Central Registration Depository number, if any, and every internal identification number or code assigned to that person by the member, broker or dealer.

(13) Records required to be maintained pursuant to paragraph (d) of Rule 17f–2.

(14) Copies of all Forms X–17F–1A filed pursuant to Rule 17f–1, all agreements between reporting institutions regarding registration or other aspects of Rule 17f–1, and all confirmations or other information received from the Commission or its designee as a result of inquiry.

(15) Records required to be maintained pursuant to paragraph (e) of Rule 17f–2.

(16)(i) The following records regarding any internal broker-dealer system of which such a broker or dealer is the sponsor:

(A) A record of the broker's or dealer's customers that have access to an internal broker-dealer system sponsored by such broker or dealer (identifying any affiliations between such customers and the broker or dealer);

(B) Daily summaries of trading in the internal broker-dealer system, including:

(*1*) Securities for which transactions have been executed through use of such system; and

(*2*) Transaction volume (separately stated for trading occurring during hours when consolidated trade reporting facilities are and are not in operation):

(*i*) With respect to equity securities, stated in number of trades, number of shares, and total U.S. dollar value;

(*ii*) With respect to debt securities, stated in total settlement value in U.S. dollars; and

(*iii*) With respect to other securities, stated in number of trades, number of units of securities, and in dollar value, or other appropriate commonly used measure of value of such securities; and

(C) Time-sequenced records of each transaction effected through the internal broker-dealer system, including date and time executed, price, size, security traded, counterparty identification information, and method of execution (if internal broker-dealer system allows alternative means or locations for execution, such as routing to another market, matching with limit orders, or executing against the quotations of the broker or dealer sponsoring the system).

(ii) For purposes of paragraph (a) of this rule, the term:

(A) *Internal Broker-Dealer System* shall mean any facility, other than a national securities exchange, an exchange exempt from registration based on limited volume, or an alternative trading system as defined in Regulation ATS, Rule 300 through Rule 303, that provides a mechanism, automated in full or in part, for collecting, receiving, disseminating, or displaying system orders and facilitating agreement to the basic terms of a purchase or sale of a security between a customer and the sponsor, or between two-customers of the sponsor, through use of the internal broker-dealer system or through the broker or dealer sponsor of such system;

(B) *Sponsor* shall mean any broker or dealer that organizes, operates, administers, or otherwise directly controls an internal broker-dealer trading system or, if the operator of the internal broker-dealer system is not a registered broker or dealer, any broker or dealer that, pursuant to contract, affiliation, or other agreement with the system operator, is involved on a regular basis with executing transactions in connection with use of the internal broker-dealer system, other than solely for its own account or as a customer with access to the internal broker-dealer system; and

(C) *System order* means any order or other communication or indication submitted by any customer with access to the internal broker-dealer system for entry into a trading system announcing an interest in purchasing or selling a security. The term "system order" does not include inquiries or indications of interest that are not entered into the internal broker-dealer system.

(17) For each account with a natural person as a customer or owner:

(i)(A) An account record including the customer's or owner's name, tax identification number, address, telephone number, date of birth, employment status (including occupation and whether the customer is an associated person of a member, broker or dealer), annual income, net worth (excluding value of primary residence), and the account's investment objectives. In the case of a joint account, the account record must include personal information for each joint owner who is a natural person; however, financial information for the individual joint owners may be combined. The account record shall indicate whether it has been signed by the associated person responsible for the account, if any, and approved or accepted by a principal of the member, broker or dealer. For accounts in existence on the effective date of this rule, the member, broker or dealer must obtain this information within three years of the effective date of the rule.

(B) A record indicating that:

(*1*) The member, broker or dealer has furnished to each customer or owner within three years of the effective date of this section, and to each customer or owner who opened an account after the effective date of this section within thirty days of the opening of the account, and thereafter at intervals no greater than thirty-six months, a copy of the account record or an alternate document with all information required by paragraph (a)(17)(i)(A) of this rule. The member, broker or dealer may elect to send this notification with the next statement mailed to the customer or owner after the opening of the account. The member, broker or dealer may choose to exclude any tax identification number and date of birth from the account record or alternative document furnished to the customer or owner. The member, broker or dealer shall include with the account record or alternative document provided to each customer or owner an explanation of any terms regarding investment objectives. The account record or alternate document furnished to the customer or owner shall include or be accompanied by prominent statements that the customer or owner should mark any corrections and return the account record or alternate document to the member, broker or dealer, and that the customer or owner should notify the member, broker or dealer of any future changes to information contained in the account record.

(*2*) For each account record updated to reflect a change in the name or address of the customer or owner, the member, broker or dealer furnished a notification of that change to the customer's old address, or to each joint owner, and the associated person, if any, responsible for that account, on or before the 30th day after the date the member, broker or dealer received notice of the change.

(*3*) For each change in the account's investment objectives the member, broker or dealer has furnished to each customer or owner, and the associated person, if any, responsible for that account a copy of the updated customer account record or alternative document with all information required to be furnished by paragraph (a)(17)(i)(B)(*1*) of this rule, on or before the 30th day after the date the member, broker or dealer received notice of any change, or, if the account was updated for some reason other than the firm receiving notice of a change, after the date the account record was updated. The member, broker or dealer may elect to send this notification with the next statement scheduled to be mailed to the customer or owner.

(C) For purposes of this paragraph (a)(17), the neglect, refusal, or inability of a customer or owner to provide or update any account record information required under paragraph (a)(17)(i)(A) of this rule shall excuse the member, broker or dealer from obtaining that required information.

(D) The account record requirements in paragraph (a)(17)(i)(A) of this rule shall only apply to accounts for which the member, broker or dealer is, or has within the past 36 months been, required to make a suitability determination under the federal securities laws or under the requirements of a self-regulatory organization of which it is a member. Additionally, the furnishing requirement in paragraph (a)(17)(i)(B)(*1*) of this rule shall not be applicable to an account for which, within the last 36 months, the member, broker or dealer has not been required to make a suitability determination under the federal securities laws or under the requirements of a self-regulatory organization of which it is a member. This paragraph (a)(17)(i)(D) does not relieve a member, broker or dealer from any obligation arising from the rules of a self-regulatory organization of which it is a member regarding the collection of information from a customer or owner.

(ii) If an account is a discretionary account, a record containing the dated signature of each customer or owner granting the authority and the dated signature of each natural person to whom discretionary authority was granted.

(iii) A record for each account indicating that each customer or owner was furnished with a copy of each written agreement entered into on or after the effective date of this paragraph pertaining to that account and that, if requested by the customer or owner, the customer or owner was furnished with a fully executed copy of each agreement.

(18) A record:

(i) As to each associated person of each written customer complaint received by the member, broker or dealer concerning that associated person. The record shall include the complainant's name, address, and account number; the date the complaint was received; the name of any other associated person identified in the complaint; a description of the nature of the complaint; and the disposition of the complaint. Instead of the record, a member, broker or dealer may maintain a copy of each original complaint in a separate file by the associated person named in the complaint along with a record of the disposition of the complaint.

(ii) Indicating that each customer of the member, broker or dealer has been provided with a notice containing the address and telephone number of the department of the member, broker or dealer to which any complaints as to the account may be directed.

(19) A record:

(i) As to each associated person listing each purchase and sale of a security attributable, for compensation purposes, to that associated person. The record shall include the amount of compensation if monetary and a description of the compensation if nonmonetary. In lieu of making this record, a member, broker or dealer may elect to produce the required information promptly upon request of a representative of a securities regulatory authority.

(ii) Of all agreements pertaining to the relationship between each associated person and the member, broker or dealer including a summary of each associated person's compensation arrangement or plan with the member, broker or dealer, including commission and concession schedules and, to the extent that compensation is based on factors other than remuneration per trade, the method by which the compensation is determined.

(20) A record, which need not be separate from the advertisements, sales literature, or communications, documenting that the member, broker or dealer has complied with, or adopted policies and procedures reasonably designed to establish compliance with, applicable federal requirements and rules of a self-regulatory organization of which the member, broker or dealer is a member which require that advertisements, sales literature, or any other communications with the public by a member, broker or dealer or its associated persons be approved by a principal.

(21) A record for each office listing, by name or title, each person at that office who, without delay, can explain the types of records the firm maintains at that office and the information contained in those records.

(22) A record listing each principal of a member, broker or dealer responsible for establishing policies and procedures that are reasonably designed to ensure compliance with any applicable federal requirements or rules of a self-regulatory organization of which the member, broker or dealer is a member that require acceptance or approval of a record by a principal.

(23) A record documenting the credit, market, and liquidity risk management controls established and maintained by the broker or dealer to assist it in analyzing and managing the risks associated with its business activities, *Provided*, that the records required by this paragraph (a)(23) need only be made if the broker or dealer has more than:

(i) $1,000,000 in aggregate credit items as computed under Rule 15c3-3a; or

(ii) $20,000,000 in capital, which includes debt subordinated in accordance with Rule 15c3-1d.

(b)(1) This rule shall not be deemed to require a member of a national securities exchange, a broker, or dealer who transacts a business in securities through the medium of any such member, or a broker or dealer registered pursuant to section 15 of the Act, to make or keep such records of transactions cleared for such member, broker, or dealer as are customarily made and kept by a clearing broker or dealer pursuant to the requirements of Rule 17a–3 and Rule 17a–4: *Provided,* That the clearing broker or dealer has and maintains net capital of not less than $25,000 and is otherwise in compliance with Rule 15c3–1 or the capital rules of the exchange of which such clearing broker or dealer is a member if the members of such exchange are exempt from Rule 15c3–1 by paragraph (b)(2) thereof.

(2) This rule shall not be deemed to require a member of a national securities exchange, a broker, or dealer who transacts a business in securities through the medium of any such member, or a broker or dealer registered pursuant to section 15 of the Act, to make or keep such records of transactions cleared for such member, broker or dealer by a bank as are customarily made and kept by a clearing broker or dealer pursuant to the requirements of Rule 17a–3 and Rule 17a–4: *Provided,* That such member, broker, or dealer obtains from such bank an agreement in writing to the effect that the records made and kept by such bank are the property of the member, broker, or dealer: *And provided further,* That such bank files with the Commission a written undertaking in form acceptable to the Commission and signed by a duly authorized person, that such books and records are available for examination by representatives of the Commission as specified in section 17(a) of the Act, and that it will furnish to the Commission, upon demand, at its principal office in Washington, D.C., or at any regional office of the Commission designated in such demand, true, correct, complete, and current copies of any or all of such records. Such undertaking shall include the following provisions:

The undersigned hereby undertakes to maintain and preserve on behalf of [*BD*] the books and records required to be maintained and preserved by [*BD*] pursuant to Rules 17a–3 and 17a–4 under the Securities Exchange Act of 1934 and to permit examination of such books and records at any time or from time to time during business hours by examiners or other representatives of the Securities and Exchange Commission, and to furnish to said Commission at its principal office in Washington, D.C., or at any regional office of said Commission specified in a demand made by or on behalf of said Commission for copies of books and records, true, correct, complete, and current copies of any or all, or any part, of such books and records. This undertaking shall be binding upon the undersigned, and the successors and assigns of the undersigned.

Nothing herein contained shall be deemed to relieve such member, broker, or dealer from the responsibility that such books and records be accurately maintained and preserved as specified in Rules 17a–3 and 17a–4.

(c) This rule shall not be deemed to require a member of a national securities exchange, or a broker or dealer registered pursuant to section 15 of the Securities Exchange Act of 1934, as amended, to make or keep such records as are required by paragraph (a) reflecting the sale of United States Tax Savings Notes, United States Defense Savings Stamps, or United States Defense Savings Bonds, Series E, F, and G.

(d) The records specified in paragraph (a) of this rule shall not be required with respect to any cash transaction of $100 or less involving only subscription rights or warrants which by their terms expire within 90 days after the issuance thereof.

(e) For purposes of transactions in municipal securities by municipal securities brokers and municipal securities dealers, compliance with Rule G–8 of the Municipal Securities Rulemaking Board will be deemed to be in compliance with this rule.

(f) *Security Futures Products.* The provisions of this section shall not apply to security futures product transactions and positions in a futures account (as that term is defined in Rule 15c3–3(a)(15)); *provided,* that the Commodity Futures Trading Commission's recordkeeping rules apply to those transactions and positions.

(g) Every member, broker or dealer shall make and keep current, as to each office, the books and records described in paragraphs (a)(1), (a)(6), (a)(7), (a)(12), (a)(17), (a)(18)(i), (a)(19), (a)(20), (a)(21), and (a)(22) of this rule.

(h) When used in this rule:

(1) The term *office* means any location where one or more associated persons regularly conduct the business of handling funds or securities or effecting any transactions in, or inducing or attempting to induce the purchase or sale of, any security.

(2) The term *principal* means any individual registered with a registered national securities association as a principal or branch manager of a member, broker or dealer or any other person who has been delegated supervisory responsibility over associated persons by the member, broker or dealer.

(3) The term *securities regulatory authority* means the Commission, any self-regulatory organization, or any securities commission (or any agency or office performing like functions) of the States.

(4) The term *associated person* means an "associated person of a member" or "associated person of a broker or dealer" as defined in sections 3(a)(21) and 3(a)(18) of the Act respectively, but shall not include persons whose functions are solely clerical or ministerial.

Rule 17a–4. Records to be preserved by certain exchange members, brokers, and dealers

(a) Every member, broker and dealer subject to Rule 17a–3 shall preserve for a period of not less than six years, the first two years in an easily accessible place, all records required to be made pursuant to paragraphs (a)(1), (a)(2), (a)(3), (a)(5), (a)(21), (a)(22) of Rule 17a–3, and analogous records created pursuant to paragraph (f) of Rule 17a–3.

(b) Every member, broker and dealer subject to Rule 17a–3 shall preserve for a period of not less than three years, the first two years in an easily accessible place:

(1) All records required to be made pursuant to Rule 17a–3(a)(4), (a)(6), (a)(7), (a)(8), (a)(9), (a)(10), (a)(16), (a)(18), (a)(19), (a)(20), and analogous records created pursuant to Rule 17a–3(g).

(2) All check books, bank statements, canceled checks, and cash reconciliations.

(3) All bills receivable or payable (or copies thereof), paid or unpaid, relating to the business of such member, broker, or dealer, as such.

(4) Originals of all communications received and copies of all communications sent (and any approvals thereof) by the member, broker or dealer (including inter-office memoranda and communications) relating to its business as such, including all communications which are subject to rules of a self-regulatory organization of which the member, broker or dealer is a member regarding communications with the public. As used in this paragraph (b)(4), the term communications includes sales scripts.

(5) All trial balances, computations of aggregate indebtedness and net capital (and working papers in connection therewith), financial statements, branch office reconciliations, and internal audit working papers, relating to the business of such member, broker, or dealer, as such.

(6) All guarantees of accounts and all powers of attorney and other evidence of the granting of any discretionary authority given in respect of any account, and copies of resolutions empowering an agent to act on behalf of a corporation.

(7) All written agreements (or copies thereof) entered into by such member, broker, or dealer relating to its business as such, including agreements with respect to any account.

(8) Records which contain the following information in support of amounts included in the report prepared as of the audit date on Form X–17A–5 (17 CFR 249.617), Part II or Part IIA or Part IIB and in annual audited financial statements required by Rule 17a–5(d) and Rule 17a–12(b):

(i) Money balance position, long or short, including description, quantity, price and valuation of each security including contractual commitments in customers' accounts, in cash and fully secured accounts, partly secured accounts, unsecured accounts and in securities accounts payable to customers;

(ii) Money balance and position, long or short, including description, quantity, price and valuation of each security including contractual commitments in non-customers' accounts, in cash and fully secured accounts, partly secured and unsecured accounts, and in securities accounts payable to non-customers;

(iii) Position, long or short, including description, quantity, price and valuation of each security including contractual commitments included in the Computation of Net Capital as commitments, securities owned, securities owned not readily marketable, and other investments owned not readily marketable;

(iv) Amount of secured demand note, description of collateral securing such secured demand note including quantity, price and valuation of each security and cash balance securing such secured demand note;

(v) Description of futures commodity contracts, contract value on trade date, market value, gain or loss, and liquidating equity or deficit in customers' and non-customers' accounts;

(vi) Description of futures commodity contracts, contract value on trade date, market value, gain or loss and liquidating equity or deficit in trading and investment accounts;

(vii) Description, money balance, quantity, price and valuation of each spot commodity position or commitments in customers' and non-customers' accounts;

(viii) Description, money balance, quantity, price and valuation of each spot commodity position or commitments in trading and investment accounts;

(ix) Number of shares, description of security, exercise price, cost and market value of put and call options including short out of the money options having no market or exercise value, showing listed and unlisted put and call options separately;

(x) Quantity, price, and valuation of each security underlying the haircut for undue concentration made in the Computation for Net Capital;

(xi) Description, quantity, price and valuation of each security and commodity position or contractual commitment, long or short, in each joint account in which the broker or dealer has an interest, including each participant's interest and margin deposit;

(xii) Description, settlement date, contract amount, quantity, market price, and valuation for each aged failed to deliver requiring a charge in the Computation of Net Capital pursuant to Rule 15c3–1;

(xiii) Detail relating to information for possession or control requirements under Rule 15c3–3 and reported on the schedule in Part II or IIA of Form X–17A–5 (17 CFR 249.617);

(xiv) Detail of all items, not otherwise substantiated, which are charged or credited in the Computation of Net Capital pursuant to Rule 15c3–1, such as cash margin deficiencies, deductions related to securities values and undue concentration, aged securities differences and insurance claims receivable; and

(xv) Other schedules which are specifically prescribed by the Commission as necessary to support information reported as required by Rule 17a–5 and Rule 17a–12.

(9) The records required to be made pursuant to Rules 15c3–3(d)(5) and (*o*).

(10) The records required to be made pursuant to Rule 15c3–4 and the results of the periodic reviews conducted pursuant to Rule 15c3–4(d).

(11) All notices relating to an internal broker-dealer system provided to the customers of the broker or dealer that sponsors such internal broker-dealer system, as defined in paragraph (a)(16)(ii)(A) of Rule 17a–3. Notices, whether written or communicated through the internal broker-dealer trading system or other automated means, shall be preserved under this paragraph (b)(11) if they are provided to all customers with access to an internal broker-dealer system, or to one or more classes of customers. Examples of notices to be preserved under this paragraph (b)(11) include, but are not limited to, notices addressing hours of system operations, system malfunctions, changes to system procedures, maintenance of hardware and software, and instructions pertaining to access to the internal broker-dealer system.

(12) The records required to be made pursuant to Rule 15c3–1e(c)(4)(vi).

(13) The written policies and procedures the broker-dealer establishes, documents, maintains, and enforces to assess creditworthiness for the purpose of Rule 15c3–1 paragraphs (c)(2)(vi)(E), (F)(*1*), (F)(*2*), and (H).

(c) Every member, broker and dealer subject to Rule 17a–3 shall preserve for a period of not less than six years after the closing of any customer's account any account cards or records which relate to the terms and conditions with respect to the opening and maintenance of the account.

(d) Every member, broker and dealer subject to Rule 17a–3 shall preserve during the life of the enterprise and of any successor enterprise all partnership articles or, in the case of a corporation, all articles of incorporation or charter, minute books and stock certificate books (or, in the case of any other form of legal entity, all records such as articles of organization or formation, and minute books used for a purpose similar to those records required for corporations or partnerships), all Forms BD (17 CFR 249.501), all Forms BDW (17 CFR 249.501a), all amendments to these forms, all licenses or other documentation showing the registration of the member, broker or dealer with any securities regulatory authority.

(e) Every member, broker and dealer subject to Rule 17a–3 shall maintain and preserve in an easily accessible place:

(1) All records required under paragraph (a)(12) of Rule 17a–3 until at least three years after the associated person's employment and any other connection with the member, broker or dealer has terminated.

(2) All records required under paragraph (a)(13) of Rule 17a–3 until at least three years after the termination of employment or association of those persons required by Rule 17f–2 to be fingerprinted; and

(3) All records required pursuant to paragraph (a)(15) of Rule 17a–3 for the life of the enterprise.

(4) All records required pursuant to paragraph (a)(14) of Rule 17a–3 for three years.

(5) All account record information required pursuant to Rule 17a–3(a)(17) until at least six years after the earlier of the date the account was closed or the date on which the information was replaced or updated.

(6) Each report which a securities regulatory authority has requested or required the member, broker or dealer to make and furnish to it pursuant to an order or settlement, and each securities regulatory authority examination report until three years after the date of the report.

(7) Each compliance, supervisory, and procedures manual, including any updates, modifications, and revisions to the manual, describing the policies and practices of the member, broker or dealer with respect to compliance with applicable laws and rules, and supervision of the activities of each natural person associated with the member, broker or dealer until three years after the termination of the use of the manual.

(8) All reports produced to review for unusual activity in customer accounts until eighteen months after the date the report was generated. In lieu of maintaining the reports, a member, broker or dealer may produce promptly the reports upon request by a representative of a securities regulatory authority. If a report was generated in a computer system that has been changed in the most recent eighteen month period in a manner such that the report cannot be reproduced using historical data in the same format as it was originally generated, the report may be produced by using the historical data in the current system, but must be accompanied by a record explaining each system change which affected the reports. If a report is generated in a computer system that has been changed in the most recent eighteen month period in a manner such that the report cannot be reproduced in any format using historical data, the member, broker or dealer shall promptly produce upon request a record of the parameters that were used to generate the report at the time specified by a representative of a securities regulatory authority, including a record of the frequency with which the reports were generated.

(9) All records required pursuant to Rule 17a–3(a)(23) until three years after the termination of the use of the risk management controls documented therein.

(f) The records required to be maintained and preserved pursuant to Rules 17a–3 and 17a–4 may be immediately produced or reproduced on "micrographic media" (as defined in this rule) or by means of "electronic storage media" (as defined in this rule) that meet the conditions set forth in this paragraph and be maintained and preserved for the required time in that form.

(1) For purposes of this rule:

(i) The term *micrographic media* means microfilm or microfiche, or any similar medium; and

(ii) The term *electronic storage media* means any digital storage medium or system and, in the case of both paragraphs (f)(1)(i) and (f)(1)(ii) of this rule, that meets the applicable conditions set forth in this paragraph (f).

(2) If electronic storage media is used by a member, broker, or dealer, it shall comply with the following requirements:

(i) The member, broker, or dealer must notify its examining authority designated pursuant to section 17(d) of the Act prior to employing electronic storage media. If employing any electronic storage media other than optical disk technology (including CD-ROM), the member, broker, or dealer must notify its designated examining authority at least 90 days prior to employing such storage media. In either case, the member, broker, or dealer must provide its own representation or one from the storage medium vendor or other third party with appropriate expertise that the selected storage media meets the conditions set forth in this paragraph (f)(2).

(ii) The electronic storage media must:

(A) Preserve the records exclusively in a non-rewriteable, non-erasable format;

(B) Verify automatically the quality and accuracy of the storage media recording process;

(C) Serialize the original and, if applicable, duplicate units of storage media, and time-date for the required period of retention the information placed on such electronic storage media; and

(D) Have the capacity to readily download indexes and records preserved on the electronic storage media to any medium acceptable under this paragraph (f) as required by the Commission or the self-regulatory organizations of which the member, broker, or dealer is a member.

(3) If a member, broker, or dealer uses micrographic media or electronic storage media, it shall:

(i) At all times have available, for examination by the staffs of the Commission and self-regulatory organizations of which it is a member, facilities for immediate, easily readable projection or production of micrographic media or electronic storage media images and for producing easily readable images.

(ii) Be ready at all times to provide, and immediately provide, any facsimile enlargement which the staffs of the Commission, any self-regulatory organization of which it is a member, or any State securities regulator having jurisdiction over the member, broker or dealer may request.

(iii) Store separately from the original, a duplicate copy of the record stored on any medium acceptable under Rule 17a–4 for the time required.

(iv) Organize and index accurately all information maintained on both original and any duplicate storage media.

(A) At all times, a member, broker, or dealer must be able to have such indexes available for examination by the staffs of the Commission and the self-regulatory organizations of which the broker or dealer is a member.

(B) Each index must be duplicated and the duplicate copies must be stored separately from the original copy of each index.

(C) Original and duplicate indexes must be preserved for the time required for the indexed records.

(v) The member, broker, or dealer must have in place an audit system providing for accountability regarding inputting of records required to be maintained and preserved pursuant to Rules 17a–3 and 17a–4 to electronic storage media and inputting of any changes made to every original and duplicate record maintained and preserved thereby.

(A) At all times, a member, broker, or dealer must be able to have the results of such audit system available for examination by the staffs of the Commission and the self-regulatory organizations of which the broker or dealer is a member.

(B) The audit results must be preserved for the time required for the audited records.

(vi) The member, broker, or dealer must maintain, keep current, and provide promptly upon request by the staffs of the Commission or the self-regulatory organizations of which the member, broker, or broker-dealer is a member all information necessary to access records and indexes stored on the electronic storage media; or place in escrow and keep current a copy of the physical and logical file format of the electronic storage media, the field format of all different information types written on the electronic storage media and the source code, together with the appropriate documentation and information necessary to access records and indexes.

(vii) For every member, broker, or dealer exclusively using electronic storage media for some or all of its record preservation under this section, at least one third party ("the undersigned"), who has access to and the ability to download information from the member's, broker's, or dealer's electronic storage media to any acceptable medium under this section, shall file with the designated examining authority for the member, broker, or dealer the following undertakings with respect to such records:

The undersigned hereby undertakes to furnish promptly to the U.S. Securities and Exchange Commission ("Commission"), its designees or representatives, any self-regulatory organization of which it is a member, or any State securities regulator having jurisdiction over the member, broker or dealer, upon reasonable request, such information as is deemed necessary by the staffs of the Commission, any self-regulatory organization of which it is a member, or any State securities regulator having jurisdiction over the member, broker or dealer to download information kept on the broker's or dealer's electronic storage media to any medium acceptable under Rule 17a–4.

Furthermore, the undersigned hereby undertakes to take reasonable steps to provide access to information contained on the broker's or dealer's electronic storage media, including, as appropriate, arrangements for the downloading of any record required to be maintained and preserved by the broker or dealer pursuant to Rules 17a–3 and 17a–4 under the Securities Exchange Act of 1934 in a format acceptable to the staffs of the Commission, any self-regulatory organization of which it is a member, or any State securities regulator having jurisdiction over the member, broker or dealer. Such arrangements will provide specifically that in the event of a failure on the part of a broker or dealer to download the record into a readable format and after reasonable notice to the broker or dealer, upon being provided with the appropriate electronic storage medium, the undersigned will undertake to do so, as the staffs of the Commission, any self-regulatory organization of which it is a member, or any State securities regulator having jurisdiction over the member, broker or dealer may request.

(g) If a person who has been subject to Rule 17a–3 ceases to transact a business in securities directly with others than members of a national securities exchange, or ceases to transact a business in securities through the medium of a member of a national securities exchange, or ceases to be registered pursuant to section 15 of the Securities Exchange Act of 1934, as amended, such person shall, for the remainder of the periods of time specified in this rule, continue to preserve the records which he theretofore preserved pursuant to this rule.

(h) For purposes of transactions in municipal securities by municipal securities brokers and municipal securities dealers, compliance with Rule G–9 of the Municipal Securities Rulemaking Board will be deemed to be compliance with this section.

(i) If the records required to be maintained and preserved pursuant to the provisions of Rule 17a–3 and Rule 17a–4 are prepared or maintained by an outside service bureau, depository, bank which does not operate pursuant to Rule 17a–3(b)(2), or other record keeping service on behalf of the member, broker or dealer required to maintain and preserve such records, such outside entity shall file with the Commission a written undertaking in form acceptable to the Commission, signed by a duly authorized person, to the effect that such records are the property of the member, broker or dealer required to maintain and preserve such records and will be surrendered promptly on request of the member, broker or dealer and including the following provision:

> With respect to any books and records maintained or preserved on behalf of [BD], the undersigned hereby undertakes to permit examination of such books and records at any time or from time to time during business hours by representatives or designees of the Securities and Exchange Commission, and to promptly furnish to said Commission or its designee true, correct, complete and current hard copy of any or all or any part of such books and records.

Agreement with an outside entity shall not relieve such member, broker or dealer from the responsibility to prepare and maintain records as specified in this rule or in Rule 17a–3.

(j) Every member, broker and dealer subject to this section shall furnish promptly to a representative of the Commission legible, true, complete, and current copies of those records of the member, broker or dealer that are required to be preserved under this section, or any other records of the member, broker or dealer subject to examination under section 17(b) of the Act that are requested by the representative of the Commission.

(k) *Exchanges of Futures for Physical.* (1) Except as provided in paragraph (k)(2) of this rule, upon request of any designee or representative of the Commission or of any self-regulatory organization of which it is a member, every member, broker or dealer subject to this section shall request and obtain from its customers documentation regarding an exchange of security futures products for physical securities, including documentation of underlying cash transactions and exchanges. Upon receipt of such documentation, the member, broker or dealer shall promptly provide that documentation to the requesting designee or representative.

(2) This paragraph (k) does not apply to an underlying cash transaction(s) or exchange(s) that was effected through a member, broker or dealer registered with the Commission and is of a type required to be recorded pursuant to Rule 17a–3.

(*l*) Records for the most recent two year period required to be made pursuant to Rule 17a–3(g) and paragraphs (b)(4) and (e)(7) of this rule which relate to an office shall be maintained at the office to which they relate. If an office is a private residence where only one associated person (or multiple associated persons who reside at that location and are members of the same immediate family) regularly conducts business, and it is not held out to the public as an office nor are funds or securities of any customer of the member, broker or dealer handled there, the member, broker or dealer need not maintain records at that office, but the records must be maintained at another location within the same State as the member, broker or dealer may select. Rather than maintain the records at each office, the member, broker or dealer may choose to produce the records promptly at the request of a representative of a securities regulatory authority at the office to which they relate or at another location agreed to by the representative.

(m) When used in this rule:

(1) The term *office* shall have the meaning set forth in Rule 17a–3(h)(1).

(2) The term *principal* shall have the meaning set forth in Rule 17a–3(h)(2).

(3) The term *securities regulatory authority* shall have the meaning set forth in Rule 17a–3(h)(3).

(4) The term *associated person* shall have the meaning set forth in Rule 17a–3(h)(4).

Rule 17a–5. Reports to be made by certain brokers and dealers

(a) *Filing of Monthly and Quarterly Reports.*

(1) This paragraph (a) shall apply to every broker or dealer registered pursuant to section 15 of the Act.

(2)(i) Every broker or dealer subject to this paragraph (a) who clears transactions or carries customer accounts must file with the Commission Part I of Form X–17A–5 (17 CFR 249.617) within 10 business days after the end of each month.

(ii) Every broker or dealer subject to this paragraph (a) who clears transactions or carries customer accounts must file with the Commission Part II of Form X–17A–5 (17 CFR 249.617) within 17 business days after the end of the calendar quarter and within 17 business days after the end of the fiscal year of the broker or dealer where that date is not the end of a calendar quarter. Certain of such brokers or dealers must file with the Commission Part IIA in lieu thereof if the nature of their business is limited as described in the instructions to Part II of Form X–17A–5 (17 CFR 249.617).

(iii) Every broker or dealer that neither clears transactions nor carries customer accounts must file with the Commission Part IIA of Form X–17A–5 (17 CFR 249.617) within 17 business days after the end of each calendar quarter and within 17 business days after the end of the fiscal year of the broker or dealer where that date is not the end of the calendar quarter.

(iv) Upon receiving written notice from the Commission or the examining authority designated pursuant to section 17(d) of the Act ("designated examining authority"), a broker or dealer who receives such notice must file with the Commission monthly, or at such times as shall be specified, Part II or Part IIA of Form X–17A–5 (17 CFR 249.617) and such other financial or operational information as shall be required by the Commission or the designated examining authority.

(3) The reports provided for in this paragraph (a) that must be filed with the Commission shall be considered filed when received at the Commission's principal office in Washington, DC and the regional office of the Commission for the region in which the broker or dealer has its principal place of business. All reports filed pursuant to this paragraph (a) shall be deemed to be confidential.

(4) The provisions of paragraphs (a)(2) and (3) of this rule shall not apply to a member of a national securities exchange or a registered national securities association if said exchange or association maintains records containing the information required by Part I, Part II or Part IIA of Form X–17A–5 (17 CFR 249.617) as to such member, and transmits to the Commission a copy of the applicable parts of Form X–17A–5 (17 CFR 249.617) as to such member, pursuant to a plan, the procedures and provisions of which have been submitted to and declared effective by the Commission. Any such plan filed by a national securities exchange or a registered national securities association may provide that when a member is also a member of one or more national securities exchanges, or of one or more national securities exchanges and a registered national securities association, the information required to be submitted with respect to any such member may be submitted by only one specified national securities exchange or registered national securities association. For the purposes of this rule, a plan filed with the Commission by a national securities exchange or a registered national securities association shall not become effective unless the Commission, having due regard for the fulfillment of the Commission's duties and responsibilities under the provisions of the Act, declares the plan to be effective. Further, the Commission, in declaring any such plan effective, may impose such terms and conditions relating to the provisions of the plan and the period of its effectiveness as may be deemed necessary or appropriate in the public

interest, for the protection of investors, or to carry out the Commission's duties and responsibilities under the Act.

(5) Every broker or dealer subject to this paragraph (a) must file Form Custody (17 CFR 249.639) with its designated examining authority within 17 business days after the end of each calendar quarter and within 17 business days after the end of the fiscal year of the broker or dealer where that date is not the end of a calendar quarter. The designated examining authority must maintain the information obtained through the filing of Form Custody and transmit the information to the Commission, at such time as it transmits the applicable part of Form X–17A–5 (17 CFR 249.617) as required in paragraph (a)(4) of this section.

(6) Each broker or dealer that computes certain of its capital charges in accordance with Rule 15c3–1e must file the following additional reports:

(i) Within 17 business days after the end of each month that is not a quarter, as of month-end:

(A) For each product for which the broker or dealer calculates a deduction for market risk other than in accordance with Rule 15c3–1e(b)(1) or (b)(3), the product category and the amount of the deduction for market risk;

(B) A graph reflecting, for each business line, the daily intra-month VaR;

(C) The aggregate value at risk for the broker or dealer;

(D) For each product for which the broker or dealer uses scenario analysis, the product category and the deduction for market risk;

(E) Credit risk information on derivatives exposures, including:

(*1*) Overall current exposure;

(*2*) Current exposure (including commitments) listed by counterparty for the 15 largest exposures;

(*3*) The 10 largest commitments listed by counterparty;

(*4*) The broker or dealer's maximum potential exposure listed by counterparty for the 15 largest exposures;

(*5*) The broker or dealer's aggregate maximum potential exposure;

(*6*) A summary report reflecting the broker or dealer's current and maximum potential exposures by credit rating category; and

(*7*) A summary report reflecting the broker or dealer's current exposure for each of the top ten countries to which the broker or dealer is exposed (by residence of the main operating group of the counterparty); and

(F) Regular risk reports supplied to the broker's or dealer's senior management in the format described in the application; and

(ii) Within 17 business days after the end of each quarter:

(A) Each of the reports required to be filed in paragraph (a)(6)(i) of this rule;

(B) A report identifying the number of business days for which the actual daily net trading loss exceeded the corresponding daily VaR; and

(C) The results of backtesting of all internal models used to compute allowable capital, including VaR and credit risk models, indicating the number of backtesting exceptions.

(7) Upon written application by a broker or dealer to its designated examining authority, the designated examining authority may extend the time for filing the information required by this paragraph (a). The designated examining authority for the broker or dealer shall maintain, in the manner prescribed in Rule 17a–1, a record of each extension granted.

(b) *Report Filed upon Termination of Membership Interest.* (1) If a broker or dealer holding any membership interest in a national securities exchange or registered national securities association ceases to be a member in good standing of such exchange or association, such broker or dealer shall, within two business days after such event, file with the Commission Part II or Part IIA of Form X–17A–5 (17 CFR 249.617) as determined by the standards set forth in paragraphs (a)(2)(ii) and (iii) of this rule as of the date of such event. The report shall be filed at the Commission's principal office in Washington, DC, and with the regional office of the Commission for the region in which the broker or dealer has its principal place of business: *Provided, however,* That such report need not be made or filed if the Commission, upon written request or upon its own motion, exempts such broker or dealer, either unconditionally or on specified terms and conditions, from such requirement: *Provided, further,* That the Commission may, upon request of the broker or dealer, grant extensions of time for filing the report specified herein for good cause shown.

(2) The broker or dealer must attach to the report required by paragraph (b)(1) of this section an oath or affirmation that to the best knowledge and belief of the person making the oath or affirmation the information contained in the report is true and correct. The oath or affirmation must be made before a person duly authorized to administer such oaths or affirmations. If the broker or dealer is a sole proprietorship, the oath or affirmation must be made by the proprietor; if a partnership, by a general partner; if a corporation, by a duly authorized officer; or if a limited liability company or limited liability partnership, by the chief executive officer, chief financial officer, manager, managing member, or those members vested with management authority for the limited liability company or limited liability partnership.

(3) For the purposes of this paragraph (b) "membership interest" shall include the following: full membership, allied membership, associated membership, floor privileges, and any other interest that entitles a broker or dealer to the exercise of any privilege on an exchange or with an association.

(4) For the purposes of this paragraph (b), any broker or dealer shall be deemed to have ceased to be a member in good standing of such exchange or association when the broker or dealer has resigned, withdrawn, or been suspended or expelled from a membership interest in such exchange or association, or has directly or through any associated person sold or entered into an agreement for the sale of a membership interest which would on consummation thereof result in the termination of the broker's or dealer's membership interest in such exchange or association.

(5) Whenever any national securities exchange or registered national securities association takes any action which causes any broker or dealer which is a member of such exchange or association to cease to be a member in good standing of such exchange or association or when such exchange or association learns of any action by such member of any other person which causes such broker or dealer to cease to be a member in good standing of such exchange or association, such exchange or association shall report such action promptly to the Commission, furnishing information as to the circumstances surrounding the event, and shall send a copy of such notification to the broker or dealer and notify such broker or dealer of its responsibilities under this paragraph (b).

(c) *Customer Statements.* (1) *Who Must Furnish the Statements.* Every broker or dealer shall file with the Commission at its principal office in Washington, DC, with the regional office of the Commission for the region in which the broker or dealer has its principal place of business, and with each national securities exchange and registered national securities association of which it is a member, and shall send to its customers the statements prescribed by paragraphs (c)(2) and (3) of this rule, except as provided in paragraph (c)(5) of this rule or if the activities of such broker or dealer are limited to any one or combination of the following and are conducted in the manner prescribed herein:

(i) As introducing broker or dealer, the forwarding of all the transactions of customers of the introducing broker or dealer to a clearing broker or dealer on a fully disclosed basis: *Provided,* That such clearing broker or dealer reflects such transactions on its books and records in accounts it carries in the names of such customers and that the introducing broker or dealer does not hold funds or securities for, or owe funds or securities to, customers other than funds and securities promptly forwarded to the clearing broker or dealer or to customers;

(ii) The prompt forwarding of subscriptions for securities to the issuer, underwriter or other distributor of such securities and of receiving checks, drafts, notes, or other evidences of indebtedness payable solely to the issuer, underwriter or other distributor who delivers the security directly to the subscriber or to a custodian bank, if the broker or dealer does not otherwise hold funds or securities for, or owe money or securities to, customers;

(iii) The sale and redemption of redeemable shares of registered investment companies or the solicitation of share accounts of savings and loan associations and otherwise qualified to maintain net capital of no less than what is required under Rule 240.15c3-1(a)(2)(iv) or the offering to extend any credit to or participate in arranging a loan for a customer to purchase insurance in connection with the sale of redeemable shares of registered investment companies; or

(iv) Conduct which would exempt the broker or dealer from the provisions of Rule 17a–13 by reason of the provisions of paragraph (a) of that rule.

(2) *Audited Statements to Be Furnished.* Audited statements shall be furnished within 105 days after the end of the fiscal year of the broker or dealer. The statements may be furnished 30 days after that time limit has expired if the broker or dealer sends them with the next mailing of the broker's or dealer's quarterly customer statements of account. In that case, the broker or dealer must include a statement in that mailing of the amount of the broker's or dealer's net capital and its required net capital in accordance with Rule 15c3–1, as of a fiscal month end that is within the 75-day period immediately preceding the date the statements are sent to customers. The audited statements shall include the following:

(i) A Statement of Financial Condition with appropriate notes prepared in accordance with U.S. generally accepted accounting principles which shall be audited if the financial statements furnished in accordance with paragraph (d) of this rule are required to be certified;

(ii) A footnote containing a statement of the amount of the broker's or dealer's net capital and its required net capital, computed in accordance with Rule 15c3–1. Such statement shall include summary financial statements of subsidiaries consolidated pursuant to Appendix C of Rule 15c3–1, where material, and the effect thereof on the net capital and required net capital of the broker or dealer;

(iii) A statement indicating that the Statement of Financial Condition of the most recent financial report of the broker or dealer under paragraph (d)(1)(i)(A) of this section is available for examination at the principal office of the broker or dealer, and at the regional office of the Commission for the region in which the broker or dealer has its principal place of business.

(iv) If, in connection with the most recent annual reports required under paragraph (d) of this section, the report of the independent public accountant required under paragraph (d)(1)(i)(C) of this section covering the report of the broker or dealer required under paragraph (d)(1)(i)(B)(*1*) of this section identifies one or more *material weaknesses*, a statement by the broker or dealer that one or more *material weaknesses* have been identified and that a copy of the report of the independent public accountant required under paragraph (d)(1)(i)(C) of this section is currently available for the customer's inspection at the principal office of the Commission in Washington, DC, and the regional office of the Commission for the region in which the broker or dealer has its principal place of business.

(3) *Unaudited Statements to Be Furnished.* Unaudited statements dated 6 months from the date of the audited statements required to be furnished by paragraphs (c)(1) and (2) of this rule shall be furnished within 65 days after the date of the unaudited statements. The unaudited statements may be furnished 70 days after that time limit has expired if the broker or dealer sends them with the next mailing of the broker's or dealer's quarterly customer statements of account. In that case, the broker or dealer must include a statement in that mailing of the amount of the broker's or dealer's net capital and its required net capital in accordance with Rule 15c3–1, as of a fiscal month end that is within the 75–day period immediately preceding the date the statements are sent to customers. The unaudited statements shall contain the information specified in paragraphs (c)(2)(i) and (ii) of this rule.

(4) *Definition of "Customer."* For purposes of this paragraph (c), the term "*customer*" includes any person other than:

(i) Another broker or dealer who is exempted by paragraph (c)(1) of this rule;

(ii) A general, special or limited partner or director or officer of a broker or dealer; or

(iii) Any person to the extent that such person has a claim for property or funds which by contract, agreement or understanding, or by operation of law, is part of the capital of the broker or dealer or is subordinated to the claims of creditors of the broker or dealer, for or with whom a broker or dealer has effected a securities transaction in a particular month, which month shall be either the month preceding the balance sheet date or the month following the balance sheet date in which the statement is sent.

The term "customer" also includes any person for whom the broker or dealer holds securities for safekeeping or as collateral or for whom the broker or dealer carries a free credit balance in the month in which customers are determined for purposes of this paragraph (c).

(5) *Exemption from Sending Certain Financial Information to Customers.* A broker or dealer is not required to send to its customers the statements prescribed by paragraphs (c)(2) and (c)(3) of this section if the following conditions are met:

(i) The broker or dealer semi-annually sends its customers, at the times it otherwise is required to send its customers the statements prescribed by paragraphs (c)(2) and (c)(3) of this rule, a financial disclosure statement that includes:

(A) The amount of the broker's or dealer's net capital and its required net capital in accordance with Rule 15c3–1, as of the date of the statements prescribed by paragraphs (c)(2) and (c)(3) of this rule;

(B) To the extent required under paragraph (c)(2)(ii) of this rule, a description of the effect on the broker's or dealer's net capital and required net capital of the consolidation of the assets and liabilities of subsidiaries or affiliates consolidated pursuant to Appendix C of Rule 15c3–1; and

(C) Any statements otherwise required by paragraphs (c)(2)(iii) and (iv) of this rule.

(ii) The financial disclosure statement is given prominence in the materials delivered to customers of the broker or dealer and includes an appropriate caption stating that customers may obtain the statements prescribed by paragraphs (c)(2) and (c)(3) of this rule, at no cost, by:

(A) Accessing the broker's or dealer's website at the specified Internet Uniform Resource Locator (URL); or

(B) Calling the broker's or dealer's specified toll-free telephone number.

(iii) Not later than 90 days after the date of the audited statements prescribed by paragraph (c)(2) of this rule and not later than 75 days after the date of the unaudited statements prescribed by paragraph (c)(3) of this rule, the broker or dealer publishes the statements on its website, accessible by hyperlinks in either textual or button format, which are separate, prominent links, are clearly visible, and are placed in each of the following locations:

(A) On the broker's or dealer's website home page; and

(B) On each page at which a customer can enter or log on to the broker's or dealer's website; and

(C) If the websites for two or more brokers or dealers can be accessed from the same Home page, on the Home page of the website of each broker or dealer.

(iv) The broker or dealer maintains a toll-free telephone number that customers can call to request a copy of the statements prescribed by paragraphs (c)(2) and (c)(3) of this rule.

(v) If a customer requests a copy of the statements prescribed by paragraphs (c)(2) and (c)(3) of this rule, the broker or dealer sends it promptly at no cost to the customer.

(d) *Annual reports.* (1)(i) Except as provided in paragraphs (d)(1)(iii) and (d)(1)(iv) of this section, every broker or dealer registered under section 15 of the Act must file annually:

(A) A financial report as described in paragraph (d)(2) of this section; and

(B)(*1*) If the broker or dealer did not claim it was exempt from Rule 15c3–3 throughout the most recent fiscal year, a compliance report as described in paragraph (d)(3) of this section executed by the person who makes the oath or affirmation under paragraph (e)(2) of this section; or

(*2*) If the broker or dealer did claim that it was exempt from Rule 15c3–3 throughout the most recent fiscal year, an exemption report as described in paragraph (d)(4) of this section executed by the person who makes the oath or affirmation under paragraph (e)(2) of this section;

(C) Except as provided in paragraph (e)(1)(i) of this section, a report prepared by an independent public accountant, under the engagement provisions in paragraph (g) of this section, covering each report required to be filed under paragraphs (d)(1)(i)(A) and (B) of this section.

(ii) The reports required to be filed under this paragraph (d) must be as of the same fiscal year end each year, unless a change is approved in writing by the designated examining authority for the broker or dealer under paragraph (n) of this section. A copy of the written approval must be sent to the Commission's principal office in Washington, DC, and the regional office of the

Commission for the region in which the broker or dealer has its principal place of business.

(iii) A broker or dealer succeeding to and continuing the business of another broker or dealer need not file the reports under this paragraph (d) as of a date in the fiscal year in which the succession occurs if the predecessor broker or dealer has filed reports in compliance with this paragraph (d) as of a date in such fiscal year.

(iv) A broker or dealer that is a member of a national securities exchange, has transacted a business in securities solely with or for other members of a national securities exchange, and has not carried any margin account, credit balance, or security for any person who is defined as a *customer* in paragraph (c)(4) of this section, is not required to file reports under this paragraph (d).

(2) *Financial report*. The financial report must contain:

(i) A Statement of Financial Condition, a Statement of Income, a Statement of Cash Flows, a Statement of Changes in Stockholders' or Partners' or Sole Proprietor's Equity, and a Statement of Changes in Liabilities Subordinated to Claims of General Creditors. The statements must be prepared in accordance with U.S. generally accepted accounting principles and must be in a format that is consistent with the statements contained in Form X–17A–5 (17 CFR 249.617) Part II or Part IIA. If the Statement of Financial Condition filed in accordance with instructions to Form X–17A–5, Part II or Part IIA, is not consolidated, a summary of financial data, including the assets, liabilities, and net worth or stockholders' equity, for subsidiaries not consolidated in the Part II or Part IIA Statement of Financial Condition as filed by the broker or dealer must be included in the notes to the financial statements reported on by the independent public accountant.

NOTE 1 TO PARAGRAPH (d)(2)(i). If there is other comprehensive income in the period(s)presented, the financial report must contain a Statement of Comprehensive Income (as defined in Rule 1–02 of Regulation S–X) in place of a Statement of Income.

(ii) Supporting schedules that include, from Part II or Part IIA of Form X–17A–5 (17 CFR 249.617), a Computation of Net Capital Under Rule 15c3–1, a Computation for Determination of the Reserve Requirements under Exhibit A of Rule 15c3–3, and Information Relating to the Possession or Control Requirements Under Rule 15c3–3.

(iii) If either the Computation of Net Capital under Rule 15c3–1 or the Computation for Determination of the Reserve Requirements Under Exhibit A of Rule 15c3–3 in the financial report is materially different from the corresponding computation in the most recent Part II or Part IIA of Form X–17A–5 (17 CFR 249.617) filed by the broker or dealer pursuant to paragraph (a) of this section, a reconciliation, including appropriate explanations, between the computation in the financial report and the computation in the most recent Part II or Part IIA of Form X–17A–5 filed by the broker or dealer. If no material differences exist, a statement so indicating must be included in the financial report.

(3) *Compliance report*. (i) The compliance report must contain:

(A) Statements as to whether:

(*1*) The broker or dealer has established and maintained *Internal Control Over Compliance* as that term is defined in paragraph (d)(3)(ii) of this section;

(*2*) The Internal Control Over Compliance of the broker or dealer was effective during the most recent fiscal year;

(*3*) The Internal Control Over Compliance of the broker or dealer was effective as of the end of the most recent fiscal year;

(*4*) The broker or dealer was in compliance with Rule 15c3–1 and Rule 15c3–3(e) as of the end of the most recent fiscal year; and

(*5*) The information the broker or dealer used to state whether it was in compliance with Rule 15c3–1 and Rule 15c3–3(e) was derived from the books and records of the broker or dealer.

(B) If applicable, a description of each material weakness in the Internal Control Over Compliance of the broker or dealer during the most recent fiscal year.

(C) If applicable, a description of any instance of non-compliance with Rule 15c3–1 or Rule 15c3-3(e) as of the end of the most recent fiscal year.

(ii) The term *Internal Control Over Compliance* means internal controls that have the objective of providing the broker or dealer with reasonable assurance that non-compliance with Rule 15c3–1, Rule 15c3–3, Rule 17a–13, or any rule of the designated examining authority of the broker or dealer that requires account statements to be sent to the customers of the broker or dealer (an "Account Statement Rule") will be prevented or detected on a timely basis.

(iii) The broker or dealer is not permitted to conclude that its Internal Control Over Compliance was effective during the most recent fiscal year if there were one or more material weaknesses in its Internal Control Over Compliance during the most recent fiscal year. The broker or dealer is not permitted to conclude that its Internal Control Over Compliance was effective as of the end of the most recent fiscal year if there were one or more material weaknesses in its internal control as of the end of the most recent fiscal year. A *material weakness* is a deficiency, or a combination of deficiencies, in Internal Control Over Compliance such that there is a reasonable possibility that non-compliance with Rule 15c3–1 or Rule 15c3–3(e) will not be prevented or detected on a timely basis or that non-compliance to a material extent with Rule 15c3–3, except for paragraph (e), Rule 17a–13, or any Account Statement Rule will not be prevented or detected on a timely basis. A *deficiency in Internal Control Over Compliance* exists when the design or operation of a control does not allow the management or employees of the broker or dealer, in the normal course of performing their assigned functions, to prevent or detect on a timely basis non-compliance with Rule 15c3–1, Rule 15c3–3, Rule 17a–13, or any Account Statement Rule.

(4) *Exemption report*. The exemption report must contain the following statements made to the best knowledge and belief of the broker or dealer:

(i) A statement that identifies the provisions in Rule 15c3–3(k) under which the broker or dealer claimed an exemption from Rule 15c3–3;

(ii) A statement that the broker or dealer met the identified exemption provisions in Rule 15c3–3(k) throughout the most recent fiscal year without exception or that it met the identified exemption provisions in Rule 15c3–3(k) throughout the most recent fiscal year except as described under paragraph (d)(4)(iii) of this section; and

(iii) If applicable, a statement that identifies each exception during the most recent fiscal year in meeting the identified exemption provisions in Rule 15c3–3(k) and that briefly describes the nature of each exception and the approximate date(s) on which the exception existed.

(5) The annual reports must be filed not more than sixty (60) calendar days after the end of the fiscal year of the broker or dealer.

(6) The annual reports must be filed at the regional office of the Commission for the region in which the broker or dealer has its principal place of business, the Commission's principal office in Washington, DC, the principal office of the designated examining authority for the broker or dealer, and with the Securities Investor Protection Corporation ("SIPC") if the broker or dealer is a member of SIPC. Copies of the reports must be provided to all self-regulatory organizations of which the broker or dealer is a member, unless the self-regulatory organization by rule waives this requirement.

(e) *Nature and Form of Reports*. The annual reports filed pursuant to paragraph (d) of this rule must be prepared and filed in accordance with the following requirements:

(1)(i) The broker or dealer is not required to engage an independent public accountant to provide the reports required under paragraph (d)(1)(i)(C) of this section if, since the date of the registration of the broker or dealer under section 15 of the Act or of the previous annual reports filed under paragraph (d) of this section:

(A) The securities business of the broker or dealer has been limited to acting as broker (agent) for the issuer in soliciting subscriptions for securities of the issuer, the broker has promptly transmitted to the issuer all funds and promptly delivered to the subscriber all securities received in connection with the transaction, and the broker has not otherwise held funds or securities for or owed money or securities to customers; or

(B) The securities business of the broker or dealer has been limited to buying and selling evidences of indebtedness secured by mortgage, deed of trust, or other lien upon real estate or leasehold interests, and the broker or dealer has not carried any margin account, credit balance, or security for any securities customer.

(ii) A broker or dealer that files annual reports under paragraph (d) of this section that are not covered by reports prepared by an independent public accountant must include in the oath or affirmation required by paragraph (e)(2) of this section a statement of the facts and circumstances relied upon as a basis for exemption from the requirement that the annual reports filed under paragraph (d) of this section be covered by reports prepared by an independent public accountant.

(2) The broker or dealer must attach to the financial report an oath or affirmation that, to the best knowledge and belief of the person making the oath or affirmation,

(i) The financial report is true and correct; and

(ii) Neither the broker or dealer, nor any partner, officer, director, or equivalent person, as the case may be, has any proprietary interest in any account classified solely as that of a customer.

The oath or affirmation must be made before a person duly authorized to administer such oaths or affirmations. If the broker or dealer is a sole proprietorship, the oath or affirmation must be made by the proprietor; if a partnership, by a general partner; if a corporation, by a duly authorized officer; or if a limited liability company or limited liability partnership, by the chief executive officer, chief financial officer, manager, managing member, or those members vested with management authority for the limited liability company or limited liability partnership.

(3) The annual reports filed under paragraph (d) of this section are not confidential, except that, if the Statement of Financial Condition in a format that is consistent with Form X–17A–5 (17 CFR 249.617), Part II, or Part IIA, is bound separately from the balance of the annual reports filed under paragraph (d) of this section, and each page of the balance of the annual reports is stamped "confidential," then the balance of the annual reports shall be deemed confidential to the extent permitted by law. However, the annual reports, including the confidential portions, will be available for official use by any official or employee of the U.S. or any State, by national securities exchanges and registered national securities associations of which the broker or dealer filing such a report is a member, by the Public Company Accounting Oversight Board, and by any other person if the Commission authorizes disclosure of the annual reports to that person as being in the public interest. Nothing contained in this paragraph may be construed to be in derogation of the rules of any registered national securities association or national securities exchange that give to customers of a member broker or dealer the right, upon request to the member broker or dealer, to obtain information relative to its financial condition.

(4)(i) The broker or dealer must file with SIPC a report on the SIPC annual general assessment reconciliation or exclusion from membership forms that contains such information and is in such format as determined by SIPC by rule and approved by the Commission.

(ii) Until the earlier of two years after the date paragraph (e)(4)(i) of this section is effective or SIPC adopts a rule under paragraph (e)(4)(i) of this section and the rule is approved by the Commission, the broker or dealer must file with SIPC a supplemental report on the status of the membership of the broker or dealer in SIPC if, under paragraph (d)(1)(i)(C) of this section, the broker or dealer is required to file reports prepared by an independent public accountant. The supplemental report must include the independent public accountant's report on applying agreed-upon procedures based on the performance of the procedures enumerated in paragraph (e)(4)(ii)(C) of this section. The supplemental report must cover the SIPC annual general assessment reconciliation or exclusion from membership forms not previously reported on under this paragraph (e)(4) that were required to be filed on or prior to the date of the annual reports required by paragraph (d) of this section: Provided, that the broker or dealer is not required to file the supplemental report on the SIPC annual general assessment reconciliation or exclusion from membership form for any period during which the SIPC assessment is a specified dollar value as provided for in section 4(d)(1)(c) of the Securities Investor Protection Act of 1970, as amended. The supplemental report must be filed with the regional office of the Commission for the region in which the broker or dealer has its principal place of business, the Commission's principal office in Washington, DC, the principal office of the designated examining authority for the broker or dealer, and the principal office of SIPC. The supplemental report must include the following:

(A) A schedule of assessment payments showing any overpayments applied and overpayments carried forward including: payment dates, amounts, and name of SIPC collection agent to whom mailed; or

(B) If exclusion from membership was claimed, a statement that the broker or dealer qualified for exclusion from membership under the Securities Investor Protection Act of 1970, as amended; and

(C) *An independent public accountant's report.* The independent public accountant must be engaged to perform the following procedures:

(*1*) Comparison of listed assessment payments with respective cash disbursements record entries;

(*2*) For all or any portion of a fiscal year, comparison of amounts reflected in the annual reports required by paragraph (d) of this section with amounts reported in the Annual General Assessment Reconciliation (Form SIPC–7);

(*3*) Comparison of adjustments reported in Form SIPC–7 with supporting schedules and working papers supporting the adjustments;

(*4*) Proof of the arithmetical accuracy of the calculations reflected in Form SIPC–7 and in the schedules and working papers supporting any adjustments; and

(*5*) Comparison of the amount of any overpayment applied with the Form SIPC–7 on which it was computed; or

(*6*) If exclusion from membership is claimed, a comparison of the income or loss reported in the financial report required by paragraph (d)(2) of this section with the Certification of Exclusion from Membership (Form SIPC–3).

(f)(1) *Qualifications of independent public accountant.* The independent public accountant must be qualified and independent in accordance with 17 CFR 210.2-01 of this chapter and the independent public accountant must be registered with the Public Company Accounting Oversight Board if required by the Sarbanes–Oxley Act of 2002.

(2) *Statement regarding independent public accountant.* (i) Every broker or dealer that is required to file annual reports under paragraph (d) of this section must file no later than December 10 of each year (or 30 calendar days after the effective date of its registration as a broker or dealer, if earlier) a statement as prescribed in paragraph (f)(2)(ii) of this section with the Commission's principal office in Washington, DC, the regional office of the Commission for the region in which its principal place of business is located, and the principal office of the designated examining authority for the broker or dealer. The statement must be dated no later than December 1 (or 20 calendar days after the effective date of its registration as a broker or dealer, if earlier). If the engagement of an independent public accountant is of a continuing nature, providing for successive engagements, no further filing is required. If the engagement is for a single year, or if the most recent engagement has been terminated or amended, a new statement must be filed by the required date.

(ii) The statement must be headed "Statement regarding independent public accountant under Rule 17a–5(f)(2)" and must contain the following information and representations:

(A) Name, address, telephone number, and registration number of the broker or dealer.

(B) Name, address, and telephone number of the independent public accountant.

(C) The date of the fiscal year of the annual reports of the broker or dealer covered by the engagement.

(D) Whether the engagement is for a single year or is of a continuing nature.

(E) A representation that the independent public accountant has undertaken the items enumerated in paragraphs (g)(1) and (2) of this section.

(F) Except as provided in paragraph (f)(2)(iii) of this section, a representation that the broker or dealer agrees to allow representatives of the Commission or its designated examining authority, if requested in writing for purposes of an examination of the broker or dealer, to review the audit documentation associated with the reports of the independent public accountant filed under paragraph (d)(1)(i)(C) of this section. For purposes of this paragraph, "audit documentation" has the meaning provided in standards of the Public Company Accounting Oversight Board. The Commission anticipates that, if requested, it will accord confidential treatment to all documents it may obtain from an independent public accountant under this paragraph to the extent permitted by law.

(G) Except as provided in paragraph (f)(2)(iii) of this section, a representation that the broker or dealer agrees to allow the independent public accountant to discuss with representatives of the Commission and its designated examining authority, if requested in writing for purposes of an examination of the broker or dealer, the findings associated with the reports of the independent public accountant filed under paragraph (d)(1)(i)(C) of this section.

(iii) If a broker or dealer neither clears transactions nor carries customer accounts, the broker or dealer is not required to include the representations in paragraphs (f)(2)(ii)(F) and (G) of this section.

(iv) Any broker or dealer that is not required to file reports prepared by an independent public accountant under paragraph (d)(1)(i)(C) of this section must file a statement required under paragraph (f)(2)(i) of this section indicating the date as of which the unaudited reports will be prepared.

(3) *Replacement of accountant*. A broker or dealer must file a notice that must be received by the Commission's principal office in Washington, DC, the regional office of the Commission for the region in which its principal place of business is located, and the principal office of the designated examining authority for the broker or dealer not more than 15 business days after:

(i) The broker or dealer has notified the independent public accountant that provided the reports the broker or dealer filed under paragraph (d)(1)(i)(C) of this section for the most recent fiscal year that the independent public accountant's services will not be used in future engagements; or

(ii) The broker or dealer has notified an independent public accountant that was engaged to provide the reports required under paragraph (d)(1)(i)(C) of this section that the engagement has been terminated; or

(iii) An independent public accountant has notified the broker or dealer that the independent public accountant would not continue under an engagement to provide the reports required under paragraph (d)(1)(i)(C) of this section; or

(iv) A new independent public accountant has been engaged to provide the reports required under paragraph (d)(1)(i)(C) of this section without any notice of termination having been given to or by the previously engaged independent public accountant.

(v) The notice must include:

(A) The date of notification of the termination of the engagement or of the engagement of the new independent public accountant, as applicable; and

(B) The details of any issues arising during the 24 months (or the period of the engagement, if less than 24 months) preceding the termination or new engagement relating to any matter of accounting principles or practices, financial statement disclosure, auditing scope or procedure, or compliance with applicable rules of the Commission, which issues, if not resolved to the satisfaction of the former independent public accountant, would have caused the independent public accountant to make reference to them in the report of the independent public accountant. The issues required to be reported include both those resolved to the former independent public accountant's satisfaction and those not resolved to the former accountant's satisfaction. Issues contemplated by this section are those that occur at the decision-making level – that is, between principal financial officers of the broker or dealer and personnel of the accounting firm responsible for rendering its report. The notice must also state whether the accountant's report filed under paragraph (d)(1)(i)(C) of this section for any of the past two fiscal years contained an adverse opinion or a disclaimer of opinion or was qualified as to uncertainties, audit scope, or accounting principles, and must describe the nature of each such adverse opinion, disclaimer of opinion, or qualification. The broker or dealer must also request the former independent public accountant to furnish the broker or dealer with a letter addressed to the Commission stating whether the independent public accountant agrees with the statements contained in the notice of the broker or dealer and, if not, stating the respects in which independent public accountant does not agree. The broker or dealer must file three copies of the notice and the accountant's letter, one copy of which must be manually signed by the sole proprietor, a general partner, or a duly authorized corporate, limited liability company, or limited liability partnership officer or member, as appropriate, and by the independent public accountant, respectively.

(g) *Engagement of independent public accountant.* The independent public accountant engaged by the broker or dealer to provide the reports required under paragraph (d)(1)(i)(C) of this section must, as part of the engagement, undertake the following, as applicable:

(1) To prepare an independent public accountant's report based on an examination of the financial report required to be filed by the broker or dealer under paragraph (d)(1)(i)(A) of this section in accordance with standards of the Public Company Accounting Oversight Board; and

(2)(i) To prepare an independent public accountant's report based on an examination of the statements required under paragraphs (d)(3)(i)(A)(*2*) through (*5*) of this section in the compliance report required to be filed by the broker or dealer under paragraph (d)(1)(i)(B)(*1*) of this section in accordance with standards of the Public Company Accounting Oversight Board; or

(ii) To prepare an independent public accountant's report based on a review of the statements required under paragraphs (d)(4)(i) through (iii) of this section in the exemption report required to be filed by the broker or dealer under paragraph (d)(1)(i)(B)(*2*) of this section in accordance with standards of the Public Company Accounting Oversight Board.

(h) *Notification of non-compliance or material weakness.* If, during the course of preparing the independent public accountant's reports required under paragraph (d)(1)(i)(C) of this section, the independent public accountant determines that the broker or dealer is not in compliance with Rule 15c3–1, Rule 15c3–3, or Rule 17a–13 or any rule of the designated examining authority of the broker or dealer that requires account statements to be sent to the customers of the broker or dealer, as applicable, or the independent public accountant determines that any material weaknesses (as defined in paragraph (d)(3)(iii) of this section) exist, the independent public accountant must immediately notify the chief financial officer of the broker or dealer of the nature of the non-compliance or material weakness. If the notice from the accountant concerns an instance of non-compliance that would require a broker or dealer to provide a notification under Rule 15c3–1, Rule 15c3–3, or Rule 17a–11, or if the notice concerns a material weakness, the broker or dealer must provide a notification in accordance with Rule 15c3–1, Rule 15c3–3, or Rule 17a–11, as applicable, and provide a copy of the notification to the independent public accountant. If the independent public accountant does not receive the notification within one business day, or if the independent public accountant does not agree with the statements in the notification, then the independent public accountant must notify the Commission and the designated examining authority within one business day. The report from the accountant must, if the broker or dealer failed to file a notification, describe any instances of non-compliance that required a notification under Rule 15c3–1, Rule 15c3–3, or Rule 17a–11, or any material weaknesses. If the broker or dealer filed a notification, the report from the accountant must detail the aspects of the notification of the broker or dealer with which the accountant does not agree.

NOTE TO PARAGRAPH (h): The attention of the broker or dealer and the independent public accountant is called to the fact that under Rule 17a–11(b)(1), among other things, a broker or dealer whose net capital declines below the minimum required pursuant to Rule 15c3–1 shall give notice of such deficiency that same day in accordance with Rule 17a–11(g) and the notice shall specify the broker or dealer's net capital requirement and its current amount of net capital. The attention of the broker or dealer and accountant also is called to the fact that under Rule 15c3–3(i), if a broker or dealer shall fail to make a reserve bank account or special account deposit, as required by Rule 15c3–3, the broker or dealer shall by telegram immediately notify the Commission and the regulatory authority for the broker or dealer, which examines such broker or dealer as to financial responsibility and shall promptly thereafter confirm such notification in writing.

(i) *Reports of the independent public accountant required under paragraph (d)(1)(i)(C) of this section*—(1) *Technical requirements.* The independent public accountant's reports must:

(i) Be dated;

(ii) Be signed manually;

(iii) Indicate the city and state where issued; and

(iv) Identify without detailed enumeration the items covered by the reports.

(2) Representations. The independent public accountant's reports must:

(i) State whether the examinations or review, as applicable, were made in accordance with standards of the Public Company Accounting Oversight Board;

(ii) Identify any examination and, if applicable, review procedures deemed necessary by the independent public accountant under the circumstances of the particular case that have been omitted and the reason for their omission.

(iii) Nothing in this section may be construed to imply authority for the omission of any procedure that independent public accountants would ordinarily employ in the course of an examination or review made for the purpose of expressing the opinions or conclusions required under this section.

(3) Opinion or conclusion to be expressed. The independent public accountant's reports must state clearly:

(i) The opinion of the independent public accountant with respect to the financial report required under paragraph (d)(1)(i)(A) of this section and the accounting principles and practices reflected in that report;

(ii) The opinion of the independent public accountant with respect to the financial report required under paragraph (d)(1)(i)(A) of this section, as to the consistency of the application of the accounting principles, or as to any changes in those principles, that have a material effect on the financial statements; and

(iii)(A) The opinion of the independent public accountant with respect to the statements required under paragraphs (d)(3)(i)(A)(*2*) through (*5*) of this section in the compliance report required under paragraph (d)(1)(i)(B)(*1*) of this section; or

(B) The conclusion of the independent public accountant with respect to the statements required under paragraphs (d)(4)(i) through (iii) of this section in the exemption report required under paragraph (d)(1)(i)(B)(*2*) of this section.

(4) Exceptions. Any matters to which the independent public accountant takes exception must be clearly identified, the exceptions must be specifically and clearly stated, and, to the extent practicable, the effect of each such exception on any related items contained in the annual reports required under paragraph (d) of this section must be given.

(j) [Reserved]

(k) *Supplemental Reports.* Each broker or dealer that computes certain of its capital charges in accordance with Rule 15c3–1e shall file concurrently with the annual audit report a supplemental report on management controls, which shall be prepared by a registered public accounting firm (as that term is defined in section 2(a)(12) of the Sarbanes–Oxley Act of 2002 (15 U.S.C. 7201 *et seq.*)). The supplemental report shall indicate the results of the accountant's review of the internal risk management control system established and documented by the broker or dealer in accordance with Rule 15c3–4. This review shall be conducted in accordance with procedures agreed upon by the broker or dealer and the registered public accounting firm conducting the review. The agreed upon procedures are to be performed and the report is to be prepared in accordance with the rules promulgated by the Public Company Accounting Oversight Board. The purpose of the review is to confirm that the broker or dealer has established, documented, and is in compliance with the internal risk management controls established in accordance with Rule 15c3–4. Before commencement of the review and no later than December 10 of each year, the broker or dealer shall file a statement with the Division of Market Regulation, Office of Financial Responsibility, at the Commission's principal office in Washington, DC that includes:

(1) A description of the agreed-upon procedures agreed to by the broker or dealer and the registered public accounting firm; and

(2) A notice describing changes in those agreed-upon procedures, if any. If there are no changes, the broker or dealer should so indicate.

(*l*) *Use of Certain Statements Filed With the Securities and Exchange Commission.* At the request of any broker or dealer who is (1) an investment company registered under the Investment Company Act of 1940, or (2) a sponsor or depositor of such a registered investment company who effects transactions in securities only with, or on behalf of, such registered investment company, the Commission will accept the financial statements filed pursuant to section 13 or 15(d) of the Securities Exchange Act of 1934 or section 30 of the Investment Company Act of 1940 and the rules and regulations promulgated thereunder as a filing pursuant to paragraph (d) of this rule. Such a filing shall be deemed to satisfy the requirements of this rule for any calendar year in which such financial statements are filed, provided that the statements so filed meet the requirements of the other rules under which they are filed with respect to time of filing and content.

(m) *Extensions and Exemptions.* (1) A broker's or dealer's designated examining authority may extend the period under paragraph (d) of this rule for filing annual reports. The designated examining authority for the broker or dealer shall maintain, in the manner prescribed in Rule 17a–1, a record of each extension granted.

(2) Any "bank" as defined in section 3(a)(6) of the Act and any "insurance company" as defined in Section 3(a)(19) of the Act registered as a broker or dealer to sell variable contracts but exempt from Rule 15c3–1 shall be exempt from the provisions of this rule.

(3) On written request of any national securities exchange, registered national securities association, broker or dealer, or on its own motion, the Commission may grant an extension of time or an exemption from any of the requirements of this rule either unconditionally or on specified terms and conditions.

(4) The provisions of Rule 17a–5 shall not apply to a broker or dealer registered pursuant to section 15(b)(11)(A) of the Act that is not a member of either a national securities exchange pursuant to section 6(a) of the Act or a national securities association registered pursuant to section 15A(a) of the Act.

(n) *Notification of Change of Fiscal Year.* (1) In the event any broker or dealer finds it necessary to change its fiscal year, it must file, with the Commission's principal office in Washington, DC, the regional office of the Commission for the region in which the broker or dealer has its principal place of business and the principal office of the designated examining authority for such broker or dealer, a notice of such change.

(2) Such notice shall contain a detailed explanation of the reasons for the change. Any change in the filing period for the annual reports must be approved in writing by the designated examining authority of the broker or dealer.

(o) *Filing Requirements.* For purposes of filing requirements as described in Rule 17a–5, such filing shall be deemed to have been accomplished upon receipt at the Commission's principal office in Washington, DC, with duplicate originals simultaneously filed at the locations prescribed in the particular paragraph of Rule 17a–5 which is applicable.

(p) *Compliance with Rule 17a–12.* An OTC derivatives dealer may comply with Rule 17a–5 by complying with the provisions of Rule 17a–12.

Rule 17a–6. Right of national securities exchange, national securities association, registered clearing agency or the Municipal Securities Rulemaking Board to destroy or dispose of documents

(a) Any document kept by or on file with a national securities exchange, national securities association, registered clearing agency or the Municipal Securities Rulemaking Board pursuant to the Act or any rule or regulation thereunder may be destroyed or otherwise disposed of by such exchange, association, clearing agency or the Municipal Securities Rulemaking Board at the end of five years or at such earlier date as is specified in a plan for the destruction or disposition of any such documents if such plan has been filed with the Commission by such exchange, association, clearing agency or the Municipal Securities Rulemaking Board and has been declared effective by the Commission.

(b) Such plan may provide that any such document may be transferred to microfilm or other recording medium after such time as specified in the plan and thereafter be maintained and preserved in that form. If a national securities exchange, association, clearing agency or the Municipal Securities Rulemaking Board uses microfilm or other recording medium it shall:

(1) Be ready at all times to provide, and immediately provide, easily readable projection of the microfilm or other recording medium and easily readable hard copy thereof;

(2) Provide indexes permitting the immediate location of any such document on the microfilm or other recording medium; and

(3) In the case of microfilm, store a duplicate copy of the microfilm separately from the original microfilm for the time required.

(c) For the purposes of this rule a plan filed with the Commission by a national securities exchange, association, clearing agency or the Municipal Securities Rulemaking Board shall not become effective unless the Commission, having due regard for the public interest and for the protection of investors, declares the plan to be effective. The Commission in its declaration may limit the applications, reports, and documents as to which it shall apply, and may impose any other terms and conditions to the plan and to the period of its effectiveness which it deems necessary or appropriate in the public interest or for the protection of investors.

Rule 17a–7. Records of non–resident brokers and dealers

(a)(1) Except as provided in paragraphs (b) and (c) of this rule, each non-resident broker or dealer registered or applying for registration pursuant to section 15 of the Act shall keep, maintain, and preserve, at a place within the United States designated in a notice from him as provided in paragraph (a)(2) of this rule, true, correct, complete and current copies of the books and records which he is required to make, keep current, maintain or preserve pursuant to any provision of any rule or regulation of the Commission adopted under the act.

(2) Except as provided in paragraph (b) each non-resident broker or dealer subject to this rule shall furnish to the Commission a written notice specifying the address of the place within the United States where the copies of the books and records required to be kept and preserved by him pursuant to paragraph (a)(1) of this rule are located. Each non-resident broker or dealer registered or applying for registration when this rule becomes effective shall file such notice within 30 days after such rule becomes effective. Each non-resident broker or dealer who files an application for registration after this rule becomes effective shall file such notice with such application for registration.

(b) Notwithstanding the provisions of paragraph (a) of this rule, a non-resident broker or dealer subject to this rule need not keep or preserve within the United States copies of the books and records referred to in said paragraph (a), if:

(1) Such broker or dealer files with the Commission, at the time or within the period provided by paragraph (a)(2) of this rule, a written undertaking in form acceptable to the Commission and signed by a person thereunto duly authorized, to furnish to the Commission, upon demand, at its principal office in Washington, DC, or at any Regional Office of the Commission designated in such demand, true, correct, complete and current copies of any or all of the books and records which he is required to make, keep current, maintain or preserve pursuant to any provision of any rule or regulation of the Commission adopted under the act, or any part of such books and records which may be specified in such demand. Such undertaking shall be in substantially the following form:

> The undersigned hereby undertakes to furnish at his own expense to the Securities and Exchange Commission at its principal office in Washington, DC, or at any Regional Office of said Commission specified in a demand for copies of books and records made by or on behalf of said Commission, true, correct, complete and current copies of any or all, or any part, of the books and records which the undersigned is required to make, keep current or preserve pursuant to any provision of any rule or regulation of the Securities and Exchange Commission under the Securities Exchange Act of 1934. This undertaking shall be suspended during any period when the undersigned is making, keeping current, and preserving copies of all of said books and records at a place within the United States in compliance with Rule 17a–7 under the Securities Exchange Act of 1934. This undertaking shall be binding upon the undersigned and the heirs, successors and assigns of the undersigned, and the written irrevocable consents and powers of attorney of the undersigned, its general partners and managing agents filed with the Securities and Exchange Commission shall extend to and cover any action to enforce same; and

(2) Such broker or dealer furnishes to the Commission at his own expense within 14 days after written demand therefor forwarded to him by registered mail at his last address of record filed with the Commission and signed by the Secretary of the Commission or such other person as the Commission may authorize to act in its behalf, true, correct, complete and current copies of any or all books and records which such broker or dealer is required to make, keep current or preserve pursuant to any provision of any rule or regulation of the Commission adopted under the Act, or any part of such books and records which may be specified in said written demand. Such copies shall be furnished to the Commission at its principal office in Washington, DC, or at any Regional Office of the Commission which may be specified in said written demand.

(c) The provisions of this rule shall not apply to a broker or dealer registered pursuant to section 15(b)(11)(A) of the Act that is not a member of either a national securities exchange pursuant to section 6(a) of the Act or a national securities association registered pursuant to section 15A(a) of the Act.

(d) For purposes of this rule the following definitions shall apply:

(1) The term *broker* shall have the meaning set out in section 3(a)(4) of the Act;

(2) The term *dealer* shall have the meaning set out in section 3(a)(5) of the Act;

(3) The term *non-resident broker or dealer* shall mean (i) in the case of an individual, one who resides in or has his principal place of business in any place not subject to the jurisdiction of the United States; (ii) in the case of a corporation, one incorporated in or having its principal place of business in any place not subject to the juris-

diction of the United States; (iii) in the case of a partnership or other unincorporated organization or association, one having its principal place of business in any place not subject to the jurisdiction of the United States.

Rule 17a–8. Financial recordkeeping and reporting of currency and foreign transactions

Every registered broker or dealer who is subject to the requirements of the Currency and Foreign Transactions Reporting Act of 1970 shall comply with the reporting, recordkeeping and record retention requirements of Chapter X of title 31 of the Code of Federal Regulations. Where Chapter X of title 31 of the Code of Federal Regulations and Rule 17a–4 require the same records or reports to be preserved for different periods of time, such records or reports shall be preserved for the longer period of time.

Rule 17a–10. Report of revenue and expenses

(a)(1) Every broker or dealer exempted from the filing requirements of paragraph (a) of Rule 17a–5 shall, not later than 17 business days after the close of each calendar year, file the Facing Page, a Statement of Income (Loss) and balance sheet from Part IIA of Form X–17A–5 (17 CFR 249.617) and Schedule I of Form X–17A–5 (17 CFR 249.617) for such calendar year.

(2) Every broker or dealer subject to the filing requirements of paragraph (a) of Rule 17a–5 shall submit Schedule I of Form X–17A–5 (17 CFR 249.617) with its Form X–17A–5 (17 CFR 249.617) for the calendar quarter ending December 31 of each year.

(b) The provisions of paragraph (a) of this rule shall not apply to a member of a national securities exchange or a registered national securities association which maintains records containing the information required by Form X–17A–5 (17 CFR 249.617) as to each of its members, and which transmits to the Commission a copy of the record as to each such member pursuant to a plan, the procedures and provisions of which have been submitted to and declared effective by the Commission. Any such plan filed by a national securities exchange or a registered national securities association may provide that when a member is also a member of one or more national securities exchanges, or of one or more national securities exchanges and a registered national securities association, the information required to be submitted with respect to any such member may be transmitted by only one specified national securities exchange or registered national securities association. For the purpose of this rule, a plan filed with the Commission by a national securities exchange or a registered national securities association shall not become effective unless the Commission, having due regard for the public interest, for the protection of investors, and for the fulfillment of the Commission's functions under the provisions of the Act, declares the plan to be effective. Further, the Commission, in declaring any such plan effective, may impose such terms and conditions relating to the provisions of the plan and the period of its effectiveness as may be deemed necessary or appropriate in the public interest, for the protection of investors, or to carry out the Commission's duties under the Act.

(c) Individual reports filed by, or on behalf of, brokers, dealers or members of national securities exchanges pursuant to this rule are to be considered nonpublic information, except in cases where the Commission determines that it is in the public interest to direct otherwise.

(d) In the event any broker or dealer finds that it cannot file the annual report required by paragraph (a) of this rule within the time specified without undue hardship, it may file with the Commission's principal office in Washington, DC, prior to the date upon which the report is due, an application for an extension of time to a specified date which shall not be later than 60 days after the close of the calendar year for which the report is to be made. The application shall state the reasons for the requested extension and shall contain an agreement to file the report on or before the specified date.

Rule 17a–11. Notification provisions for brokers and dealers

(a) This rule shall apply to every broker or dealer registered with the Commission pursuant to section 15 of the Act.

(b)(1) Every broker or dealer whose net capital declines below the minimum amount required pursuant to Rule 15c3–1, or is insolvent as that term is defined in Rule 15c3–1(c)(16), must give notice of such deficiency that same day in accordance with paragraph (g) of this section. The notice shall specify the broker or dealer's net capital requirement and its current amount of net capital. If a broker or dealer is informed by its designated examining authority or the Commission that it is, or has been, in violation of Rule 15c3–1 and the broker or dealer has not given notice of the capital deficiency under this Rule 17a–11, the broker or dealer, even if it does not agree that it is, or has been, in violation of Rule

15c3–1, shall give notice of the claimed deficiency, which notice may specify the broker's or dealer's reasons for its disagreement.

(2) In addition to the requirements of paragraph (b)(1) of this rule, an OTC derivatives dealer or broker or dealer permitted to compute net capital pursuant to the alternative method of Rule 15c3–1e shall also provide notice if its tentative net capital falls below the minimum amount required pursuant to Rule 15c3–1. The notice shall specify the tentative net capital requirements, and current amount of net capital and tentative net capital, of the OTC derivatives dealer or the broker or dealer permitted to compute net capital pursuant to the alternative method of Rule 15c3–1e.

(c) Every broker or dealer shall send notice promptly (but within 24 hours) after the occurrence of the events specified in paragraphs (c)(1), (c)(2), (c)(3), (c)(4) or (c)(5) of this rule in accordance with paragraph (g) of this rule:

(1) If a computation made by a broker or dealer subject to the aggregate indebtedness standard of Rule 15c3–1 shows that its aggregate indebtedness is in excess of 1,200 percent of its net capital; or

(2) If a computation made by a broker or dealer, which has elected the alternative standard of Rule 15c3–1, shows that its net capital is less than 5 percent of aggregate debit items computed in accordance with Rule 15c3–3a Exhibit A: Formula for Determination Reserve Requirement of Brokers and Dealers under Rule 15c3–3; or

(3) If a computation made by a broker or dealer pursuant to Rule 15c3–1 shows that its total net capital is less than 120 percent of the broker's or dealer's required minimum net capital, or if a computation made by an OTC derivatives dealer pursuant to Rule 15c3–1 shows that its total tentative net capital is less than 120 percent of the dealer's required minimum tentative net capital.

(4) The occurrence of the fourth and each subsequent backtesting exception under Rule 15c3–1f(e)(1)(iv) during any 250 business day measurement period.

(5) If a computation made by a broker or dealer pursuant to Rule 15c3–1 shows that the total amount of money payable against all securities loaned or subject to a repurchase agreement or the total contract value of all securities borrowed or subject to a reverse repurchase agreement is in excess of 2500 percent of its tentative net capital; *provided*, however, that for purposes of this leverage test transactions involving government securities, as defined in section 3(a)(42) of the Securities Exchange Act of 1934, must be excluded from the calculation; *provided* further, however, that a broker or dealer will not be required to send the notice required by this paragraph (c)(5) if it reports monthly its securities lending and borrowing and repurchase and reverse repurchase activity (including the total amount of money payable against securities loaned or subject to a repurchase agreement and the total contract value of securities borrowed or subject to a reverse repurchase agreement) to its designated examining authority in a form acceptable to its designated examining authority.

(d) Every broker or dealer who fails to make and keep current the books and records required by Rule 17a–3, shall give notice of this fact that same day in accordance with paragraph (g) of this rule, specifying the books and records which have not been made or which are not current. The broker or dealer shall also transmit a report in accordance with paragraph (g) of this rule within 48 hours of the notice stating what the broker or dealer has done or is doing to correct the situation.

(e) Whenever any broker or dealer discovers, or is notified by an independent public accountant under Rule 17a–12(i)(2), of the existence of any material inadequacy as defined in Rule 17a–12(h)(2), or whenever any broker or dealer discovers, or is notified by an independent public accountant under Rule 17a–5(h), of the existence of any material weakness as defined in Rule 17a–5(d)(3)(iii), the broker or dealer must:

(1) Give notice, in accordance with paragraph (g) of this section, of the material inadequacy or material weakness within 24 hours of the discovery or notification of the material inadequacy or the material weakness; and

(2) Transmit a report, in accordance with paragraph (g) of this section, within 48 hours of the notice stating what the broker or dealer has done or is doing to correct the situation.

(f) Every national securities exchange or national securities association that learns that a member broker or dealer has failed to send notice or transmit a report as required by paragraphs (b), (c), (d), or (e) of this rule, even after being advised by the securities exchange or the national securities association to send notice or transmit a report, shall immediately give notice of such failure in accordance with paragraph (g) of this rule.

(g) Every notice or report required to be given or transmitted by this section shall be given or transmitted to the principal office of the Commission in Washington, DC, the regional office of the Commission for the region in which the broker or dealer has its principal place of business, the designated examining authority of which such broker or dealer is a member, and the Commodity Futures Trading Commission if the broker or dealer is registered as a futures commission merchant with such Commission. For the purposes of this section, "notice" shall be given or transmitted by telegraphic notice or facsimile transmission. The report required by paragraphs (d) or (e)(2) of this rule may be transmitted by overnight delivery.

(h) Other notice provisions relating to the Commission's financial responsibility or reporting rules are contained in Rule 15c3–1(a)(6)(iv)(B), Rule 15c3–1(a)(6)(v), Rule 15c3–1(a)(7)(ii), Rule 15c3–1(a)(7)(iii), Rule 15c3–1(c)(2)(x)(B)(1), Rule 15c3–1(c)(2)(x)(F)(3), Rule 15c3–1(e), Rule 15c3–1d(c)(2), Rule 15c3–3(i), Rule 17a–5(h) and Rule 17a–12(i)(2).

(i) The provisions of this rule shall not apply to a broker or dealer registered pursuant to section 15(b)(11)(A) of the Act that is not a member of either a national securities exchange pursuant to section 6(a) of the Act or a national securities association registered pursuant to section 15A(a) of the Act.

Rule 17a–12. Reports to be made by certain OTC derivatives dealers

(a) *Filing of Quarterly Reports.* (1) This paragraph (a) shall apply to every OTC derivatives dealer registered pursuant to Section 15 of the Act.

(i) Every OTC derivatives dealer shall file Part IIB of Form X–17A–5 (17 CFR 249.617) within 17 business days after the end of each calendar quarter and within 17 business days after the date selected for the annual audit of financial statements where said date is other than the end of the calendar quarter.

(ii) Upon receiving from the Commission written notice that additional reporting is required, an OTC derivatives dealer shall file monthly, or at such times as shall be specified, Part IIB of Form X–17A–5 (17 CFR 249.617) and such other financial or operational information as shall be required by the Commission.

(2) The reports provided for in this paragraph (a) shall be considered filed when received at the Commission's principal office in Washington, DC. All reports filed pursuant to this paragraph (a) shall be deemed to be confidential.

(3) Upon written application by an OTC derivatives dealer to the Commission, the Commission may extend the time for filing the information required by this paragraph (a). The written application shall be filed with the Commission at its principal office in Washington DC.

(b) *Annual Filing of Audited Financial Statements.* (1)(i) Every OTC derivatives dealer registered pursuant to Section 15 of the Act shall file annually, on a calendar or fiscal year basis, a report which shall be audited by a certified public accountant. Reports filed pursuant to this paragraph (b) shall be as of the same fixed or determinable date each year, unless a change is approved in writing by the Commission.

(ii) An OTC derivatives dealer succeeding to and continuing the business of another OTC derivatives dealer need not file a report under this paragraph (b) as of a date in the fiscal or calendar year in which the succession occurs if the predecessor OTC derivatives dealer has filed a report in compliance with this paragraph (b) as of a date in such fiscal or calendar year.

(2) The annual audit report shall contain a Statement of Financial Condition (in a format and on a basis which is consistent with the total reported on the Statement of Financial Condition contained in Form X–17A–5 (17 CFR 249.617)), Part IIB, a Statement of Income, a Statement of Cash Flows, a Statement of Changes in Stockholders' or Partners' or Sole Proprietor's Equity, and a Statement of Changes in Liabilities Subordinated to Claims of General Creditors. Such statements shall be in a format which is consistent with such statements as contained in Form X–17A–5 (17 CFR 249.617), Part IIB. If the Statement of Financial Condition filed in accordance with instructions to Form X–17A–5 (17 CFR 249.617), Part IIB, is not consolidated, a summary of financial data for subsidiaries not consolidated in the Part IIB Statement of Financial Condition as filed by the OTC derivatives dealer shall be included in the notes to the consolidated statement of financial condition reported on by the certified public accountant. The summary financial data shall include the assets, liabilities, and net worth or stockholders' equity of the unconsolidated subsidiaries.

NOTE 1 TO PARAGRAPH (b)(2). If there is other comprehensive income in the period(s) presented, the financial report must contain a Statement of Comprehensive Income (as defined in Rule 1–02 of Regulation S–X of this chapter) in place of a Statement of Income.

(3) Supporting schedules shall include, from Part IIB of Form X–17A–5 (17 CFR 249.617), a Computation of Net Capital under Rule 15c3–1.

(4) A reconciliation, including appropriate explanations, of the Computation of Net Capital under Rule 15c3–1 contained in the audit report with the broker's or dealer's corresponding unaudited most recent. Part IIB filing shall be filed with the report when material differences exist. If no material differences exist, a statement so indicating shall be filed.

(5) The annual audit report shall be filed not more than sixty days after the date of the financial statements.

(6) Two copies of the annual audit report shall be filed at the Commission's principal office in Washington, DC.

(c) *Nature and Form of Reports.* The financial statements filed pursuant to paragraph (b) of this rule shall be prepared and filed in accordance with the following requirements:

(1) An audit shall be conducted by a certified public accountant who shall be in fact independent as defined in paragraph (f) of this section, and it shall give an opinion covering the statements filed pursuant to paragraph (b) of this rule.

(2) Attached to the report shall be an oath or affirmation that, to the best knowledge and belief of the person making such oath or affirmation, the financial statements and schedules are true and correct and neither the OTC derivatives dealer, nor any partner, officer, or director, as the case may be, has any significant interest in any counterparty or in any account classified solely as that of a counterparty. The oath or affirmation shall be made before a person duly authorized to administer such oaths or affirmations. If the OTC derivatives dealer is a sole proprietorship, the oath or affirmation shall be made by the proprietor; if a partnership, by a general partner; or if a corporation, by a duly authorized officer.

(3) All of the statements filed pursuant to paragraph (b) of this rule shall be confidential except that they shall be available for use by any official or employee of the United States or by any other person to whom the Commission authorizes disclosure of such information as being in the public interest.

(d) *Qualification of Accountants.* The Commission will not recognize any person as a certified public accountant who is not duly registered and in good standing as such under the laws of the State of his principal office.

(e) *Designation of Accountant.* (1) Every OTC derivatives dealer shall file no later than December 10 of each year with the Commission's principal office in Washington, DC a statement indicating the existence of an agreement, dated no later than December 1 of that year, with a certified public accountant covering a contractual commitment to conduct the OTC derivatives dealer's annual audit during the following calendar year.

(2) If the agreement is of a continuing nature, providing for successive yearly audits, no further filing is required. If the agreement is for a single audit, or if the continuing agreement previously filed has been terminated or amended, a new statement must be filed by the required date.

(3) The statement shall be headed "Notice pursuant to Rule 17a–12(e)" and shall contain the following information:

(i) Name, address, telephone number, and registration number of the OTC derivatives dealer;

(ii) Name, address, and telephone number of the certified public accounting firm; and

(iii) The audit date of the OTC derivatives dealer for the year covered by the agreement.

(4) Notwithstanding the date of filing specified in paragraph (e)(1) of this rule, every OTC derivatives dealer shall file the notice provided for in paragraph (e) of this rule within 30 days following the effective date of registration as an OTC derivatives dealer.

(f) *Independence of Accountant.* A certified public accountant shall be independent in accordance with the provisions of Rule 2–01(b) and (c) of Regulation S–X.

(g) *Replacement of Accountant.* (1) An OTC derivatives dealer shall file a notice that must be received by the Commission's principal office in Washington, DC not more than 15 business days after:

(i) The OTC derivatives dealer has notified the certified public accountant whose opinion covered the most recent financial statements filed under paragraph (b) of this rule that the certified public accountant's services will not be utilized in future engagements; or

(ii) The OTC derivatives dealer has notified a certified public accountant who was engaged to give an opinion covering the financial statements to be filed under paragraph (b) of this section that the engagement has been terminated; or

(iii) A certified public accountant has notified the OTC derivatives dealer that it will not continue under an engagement or give an opinion covering the financial statements to be filed under paragraph (b) of this rule; or

(iv) A new certified public accountant has been engaged to give an opinion covering the financial statements to be filed under paragraph (b) of this rule without any notice of termination having been given to or by the previously engaged certified public accountant.

(2) Such notice shall state the date of notification of the termination of the engagement of the former certified public accountant or the engagement of the new certified public accountant, as applicable, and the details of any disagreements existing during the 24 months (or the period of the engagement, if less) preceding such termination or new engagement relating to any matter of accounting principles or practices, financial statement disclosure, auditing scope or procedure, or compliance with applicable rules of the Commission, which disagreements, if not resolved to the satisfaction of the former certified public accountant, would have caused the former certified public accountant to make reference to them in connection with the report on the subject matter of the disagreements. The disagreements required to be reported in response to the preceding sentence include both those resolved to the former certified public accountant's satisfaction and those not resolved to the former certified public accountant's satisfaction. Disagreements contemplated by this section are those that occur at the decision-making level (*i.e.,* between principal financial officers of the OTC derivatives dealer and personnel of the certified public accounting firm responsible for rendering its report). The notice shall also state whether the certified public accountant's report on the financial statements for any of the past two years contained an adverse opinion or a disclaimer of opinion or was qualified as to uncertainties, audit scope, or accounting principles, and describe the nature of each such adverse opinion, disclaimer of opinion, or qualification. The OTC derivatives dealer shall also request the former certified public accountant to furnish the OTC derivatives dealer with a letter addressed to the Commission stating whether the former certified public accountant agrees with the statements contained in the notice of the OTC derivatives dealer and, if not, stating the respects in which the former certified public accountant does not agree. The OTC derivatives dealer shall file three copies of the notice and the certified public accountant's letter, one copy of which shall be manually signed by the sole proprietor, or a general partner or a duly authorized corporate officer, as appropriate, and by the certified public accountant.

(h) *Audit Objectives.* (1) The audit shall be made in accordance with U.S. Generally Accepted Auditing Standards and shall include a review of the accounting system, the internal accounting controls, and procedures for safeguarding securities including appropriate tests thereof for the period since the date of the prior audited financial statements. The audit shall include all procedures necessary under the circumstances to enable the certified public accountant to express an opinion on the statement of financial condition, results of operations, cash flows, and the Computation of Net Capital under Rule 15c3–1. The scope of the audit and review of the accounting system, the internal accounting controls, and procedures for safeguarding securities shall be sufficient to provide reasonable assurance that any material inadequacies existing at the date of the examination in the following are disclosed:

(i) The accounting system;

(ii) The internal accounting controls; and

(iii) The procedures for safeguarding securities.

(2) A material inadequacy in the accounting system, internal accounting controls, procedures for safeguarding securities, and practices and procedures referred to in paragraph (h)(1) of this rule that must be reported under these audit objectives includes any condition which has contributed substantially to or, if appropriate corrective action is not taken, could reasonably be expected to:

(i) Inhibit an OTC derivatives dealer from promptly completing securities transactions or promptly discharging its responsibilities to counterparties, other brokers and dealers, or creditors;

(ii) Result in material financial loss;

(iii) Result in material misstatements of the OTC derivatives dealer's financial statements; or

(iv) Result in violations of the Commission's recordkeeping or financial responsibility rules to an extent that could reasonably be expected to result in the conditions described in paragraphs (h)(2)(i), (ii), or (iii) of this rule.

(i) *Extent and Timing of Audit Procedures.* (1) The extent and timing of audit procedures are matters for the certified public accountant to determine on the basis of its review and evaluation of existing internal controls and other audit procedures performed in accordance with U.S. Generally Accepted Auditing Standards and the audit objectives set forth in paragraph (h) of this rule.

(2) If, during the course of the audit or interim work, the certified public accountant determines that any material inadequacies exist in the accounting system, internal accounting controls, procedures for safeguarding securities, or as otherwise defined in paragraph (h)(2) of this rule, then the certified public accountant shall call it to the attention of the chief financial officer of the OTC derivatives dealer, who shall inform the Commission by telegraphic or facsimile notice within 24 hours thereafter as set forth in Rule 17a–11(e) and (g). The OTC derivatives dealer shall also furnish the certified public accountant with a copy of said notice to the Commission by telegram or facsimile within the same 24 hour period. If the certified public accountant fails to receive such notice from the OTC derivatives dealer within that 24 hour period, or if the certified public accountant disagrees with the statements contained in the notice of the OTC derivatives dealer, the certified public accountant shall inform the Commission by report of material inadequacy within 24 hours thereafter as set forth in Rule 17a–11(g). Such report from the certified public accountant shall, if the OTC derivatives dealer failed to file a notice, describe any material inadequacies found to exist. If the OTC derivatives dealer filed a notice, the certified public accountant shall file a report detailing the aspects, if any, of the OTC derivatives dealer's notice with which the certified public accountant does not agree.

(j) *Accountant's Report, General Provisions.* (1) *Technical Requirements.* The certified public accountant's report shall be dated; be signed manually; indicate the city and state where issued; and identify without detailed enumeration the financial statements and schedules covered by the report.

(2) *Representations as to the Audit.* The certified public accountant's report shall state that the audit was made in accordance with U.S. Generally Accepted Auditing Standards; state whether the certified public accountant reviewed the procedures followed for safeguarding securities; and designate any auditing procedures deemed necessary by the certified public accountant under the circumstances of the particular case that have been omitted, and the reason for their omission. Nothing in this section shall be construed to imply authority for the omission of any procedure which certified public accountants would ordinarily employ in the course of an audit made for the purpose of expressing the opinions required under this rule.

(3) *Opinion to Be Expressed.* The certified public accountant's report shall state clearly the opinion of the certified public accountant:

(i) In respect of the financial statements and schedules covered by the report and the accounting principles and practices reflected therein; and

(ii) As to the consistency of the application of the accounting principles, or as to any changes in such principles which have a material effect on the financial statements.

(4) *Exceptions.* Any matters to which the certified public accountant takes exception shall be clearly identified, explained, and, to the extent practicable, the effect of each such exception on the related financial statements shall be provided.

(5) *Definitions.* For the purpose of this section, the terms *audit* (or *examination*), *accountant's report,* and *certified* shall have the meanings given in Rule 1–02 of Regulation S–X.

(k) *Accountant's Report on Material Inadequacies and Reportable Conditions.* The OTC derivatives dealer shall file concurrently with the annual audit report a supplemental report by the certified public accountant describing any material inadequacies or any matter that would be deemed to be a reportable condition under U.S. Generally Accepted Auditing Standards that are unresolved as of the date of the certified public accountant's report. The report shall also describe any material inadequacies found to have existed since the date of the previous audit. The supplemental report shall indicate any corrective action taken or proposed by the OTC derivatives dealer with regard to any identified material inadequacies or reportable conditions. If the audit did not disclose any material inadequacies or reportable conditions, the supplemental report shall so state.

(*l*) *Accountant's Report on Management Controls.* (1) The OTC derivatives dealer shall file concurrently with the annual audit report a supplemental report by the certified public accountant indicating the results of the certified public accountant's review of the OTC derivatives dealer's internal risk management control system with respect to the requirements of Rule 15c3–4. This review shall be conducted in accordance with procedures agreed to by the OTC derivatives dealer and the certified public accountant conducting the review. The purpose of the review is to confirm that the OTC derivatives dealer has established, documented, and maintained an internal risk management control system in accordance with Rule 15c3–4, and is in compliance with that internal risk management control system.

(2) The agreed-upon procedures are to be performed, and the report is to be prepared, in accordance with U.S. Generally Accepted Attestation Standards.

(3) Prior to the commencement of the initial review, every OTC derivatives dealer shall file the procedures to be performed pursuant to paragraph (*l*)(1) of this rule with the Commission's principal office in Washington, DC. Prior to the commencement of any subsequent review, every OTC derivatives dealer shall file with the Commission's principal office in Washington, DC a notice of changes to the agreed-upon procedures.

(m) *Accountant's Report on Inventory Pricing and Modeling.* (1) The OTC derivatives dealer shall file concurrently with the annual audit report a supplemental report by the certified public accountant indicating the results of the certified public accountant's review of the broker's or dealer's inventory pricing and modeling procedures. This review shall be conducted in accordance with procedures agreed to by the OTC derivatives dealer and by the certified public accountant conducting the review. The purpose of the review is to confirm that the pricing and modeling procedures relied upon by the OTC derivatives dealer conform to the procedures submitted to the Commission as part of its OTC derivatives dealer application, and that the procedures comply with the qualitative and quantitative standards set forth in Rule 15c3–1f.

(2) The agreed-upon procedures are to be performed and the report is to be prepared in accordance with U.S. Generally Accepted Attestation Standards.

(3) Every OTC derivatives dealer shall file prior to the commencement of the initial review, the procedures to be performed pursuant to paragraph (m)(1) of this rule with the Commission's principal office in Washington, DC. Prior to the commencement of each subsequent review, every OTC derivatives dealer shall file with the Commission's principal office in Washington, DC notice of changes in the agreed-upon procedures.

(n) *Extensions and Exemptions.* Upon the written request of the OTC derivatives dealer, or on its own motion, the Commission may grant an extension of time or an exemption from any of the requirements of this section either unconditionally or on specified terms and conditions.

(o) *Notification of Change of Fiscal Year.* (1) In the event any OTC derivatives dealer finds it necessary to change its fiscal year, it must file a notice of such change with the Commission's principal office in Washington, DC.

(2) Such notice shall contain a detailed explanation of the reasons for the change. Any change in the filing period for the audit report must be approved by the Commission.

(p) *Filing Requirements.* For purposes of filing requirements as described in Rule 17a–12, these filings shall be deemed to have been accomplished upon receipt at the Commission's principal office in Washington, DC.

Rule 17a–13. Quarterly security counts to be made by certain exchange members, brokers and dealers

(a) This rule shall apply to every member of a national securities exchange who transacts a business in securities directly with or for others than members of a national securities exchange, every broker or dealer (other than a member) who transacts a business in securities through the medium of any member of a national securities exchange, and every broker or dealer registered pursuant to section 15 of the Act; except that a broker or dealer meeting all of the following conditions shall be exempt from the provisions of this rule:

(1) His dealer transactions (as principal for his own account) are limited to the purchase, sale, and redemption of redeemable shares of registered investment companies or of interests or participations in an insurance company separate account, whether or not registered as an investment company; except that a broker or dealer transacting business as a sole proprietor may also effect occasional transactions in other securities for his

own account with or through another registered broker-dealer;

(2) His transactions as broker (agent) are limited to:

(i) The sale and redemption of redeemable securities of registered investment companies or of interests or participations in an insurance company separate account, whether or not registered as an investment company;

(ii) The solicitation of share accounts for savings and loan associations insured by an instrumentality of the United States; and

(iii) The sale of securities for the account of a customer to obtain funds for immediate reinvestment in redeemable securities of registered investment companies; and

(3) He promptly transmits all funds and delivers all securities received in connection with his activities as a broker or dealer, and does not otherwise hold funds or securities for or owe money or securities to customers.

Notwithstanding the foregoing, this rule shall not apply to any insurance company which is a registered broker-dealer, and which otherwise meets all of the conditions in paragraphs (a)(1), (2), and (3) of this rule solely by reason of its participation in transactions that are a part of the business of insurance, including the purchasing, selling, or holding of securities for or on behalf of such company's general and separate accounts.

(b) Any member, broker, or dealer who is subject to the provisions of this rule shall at least once in each calendar quarter-year:

(1) Physically examine and count all securities held including securities that are the subjects of repurchase or reverse repurchase agreements;

(2) Account for all securities in transfer, in transit, pledged, loaned, borrowed, deposited, failed to receive, failed to deliver, subject to repurchase or reverse repurchase agreements or otherwise subject to his control or direction but not in his physical possession by examination and comparison of the supporting detail records with the appropriate ledger control accounts;

(3) Verify all securities in transfer, in transit, pledged, loaned, borrowed, deposited, failed to receive, failed to deliver, subject to repurchase or reverse repurchase agreements or otherwise subject to his control or direction but not in his physical possession, where such securities have been in said status for longer than thirty days;

(4) Compare the results of the count and verification with his records; and

(5) Record on the books and records of the member, broker, or dealer all unresolved differences setting forth the security involved and date of comparison in a security count difference account no later than 7 business days after the date of each required quarterly security examination, count, and verification in accordance with the requirements provided in paragraph (c) of this rule. *Provided, however,* That no examination, count, verification, and comparison for the purpose of this section shall be within 2 months of or more than 4 months following a prior examination, count, verification, and comparison made hereunder.

(c) The examination, count, verification, and comparison may be made either as of a date certain or on a cyclical basis covering the entire list of securities. In either case the recordation shall be effected within 7 business days subsequent to the examination, count, verification, and comparison of a particular security. In the event that an examination, count, verification, and comparison is made on a cyclical basis, it shall not extend over more than 1 calendar quarter-year, and no security shall be examined, counted, verified, or compared for the purpose of this rule less than 2 months or more than 4 months after a prior examination, count, verification, and comparison.

(d) The examination, count, verification, and comparison shall be made or supervised by persons whose regular duties do not require them to have direct responsibility for the proper care and protection of the securities or the making or preservation of the subject records.

(e) The provisions of this section shall not apply to a broker or dealer registered pursuant to section 15(b)(11)(A) of the Act that is not a member of either a national securities exchange pursuant to section 6(a) of the Act or a national securities association registered pursuant to section 15A(a) of the Act.

(f) The Commission may, upon written request, exempt from the provisions of this rule, either unconditionally or on specified terms and conditions, any member, broker, or dealer who satisfies the Commission that it is not necessary in the public interest and for the protection of investors to subject the particular member, broker, or dealer to certain or all of the provisions of this rule, because of the special nature of his business, the safeguards he has established for the protection of customers' funds and securities, or such other reason as the Commission deems appropriate.

Rule 17a–18. [Reserved]

Rule 17a–19. Form X–17A–19. Report by national securities exchanges and registered national securities associations of changes in the membership status of any of their members

Every national securities exchange and every registered national securities association shall file with the Commission at its principal office in Washington, DC, and with the Securities Investor Protection Corporation such information as is required by 17 CFR 249.635 on Form X–17A–19 within 5 business days of the occurrence of the initiation of the membership of any person or the suspension or termination of the membership of any member. Nothing in this rule shall be deemed to relieve a national securities exchange or a registered national securities association of its responsibilities under Rule 17a–5(b)(5) except that, to the extent a national securities exchange or a registered national securities association promptly files a report on Form X–17A–19 including therewith, inter alia, information sufficient to satisfy the requirements of Rule 17a–5(b)(5), it shall not be required to file a report pursuant to Rule 17a–5(b). Upon the occurrence of the events described in this paragraph, every national securities exchange and every registered national securities association shall notify in writing such member of its responsibilities under Rule 17a–5(b).

Rule 17a–21. Reports of the Municipal Securities Rulemaking Board

(a) *Annual Report of the Municipal Securities Rulemaking Board.* The Municipal Securities Rulemaking Board shall file annual reports with the Commission as follows:

(1) Prior to October 1, 1976, the Municipal Securities Rulemaking Board shall file with the Commission an annual report for the period from its formation until June 30, 1976 and shall include whatever information, data and recommendations it considers advisable with regard to matters within its jurisdiction.

(2) Prior to December 1, 1977, the Municipal Securities Rulemaking Board shall file with the Commission an annual report for the period from July 1, 1976 until September 30, 1977 and shall include whatever information, data and recommendations it considers advisable with regard to matters within its jurisdiction.

(3) Prior to December 1 of each year beginning in 1978, the Municipal Securities Rulemaking Board shall file with the Commission an annual report for the twelve months immediately preceding October 1 of that year and shall include whatever information, data and recommendations it considers advisable with regard to matters within its jurisdiction.

(4) The Municipal Securities Rulemaking Board shall include in its annual report a statement and an analysis of its expenses and operations including:

(i) A balance sheet as of the end of the period covered by the report and a statement of revenues and expenses for the Board for that period;

(ii) The rules of the Board including any written interpretations of the rules or staff interpretive letters, except that this information may be included in the annual report once every three years and shall be up to date as of the latest practicable date within 3 months of the date on which this information is filed. If the Board publishes or cooperates in the publication of this information on an annual or more frequent basis, in lieu of including such information in the annual report the Board may:

(A) Identify the publication in which such information is available, the name, address, and telephone number of the person from whom such publication may be obtained, and the price thereof; and

(B) Certify to the accuracy of such information as of its date. If the Board keeps this information up to date and makes it available to the Commission and the public upon request, in lieu of filing such information the Board may certify that the information is kept up to date and is available to the Commission and the public upon request;

(iii) The following information concerning members of the Board:

(A) Name;

(B) Dates of commencement and termination of present term of office;

(C) Length of time each member has held such office;

(D) Name of principal organization with which connected;

(E) Title; and

(F) City wherein the principal office of such organization is located;

(iv) Address of the Board, the name and address of each person authorized to receive notices on behalf of the Board from the Commission, and the name and address of counsel to the Board, if any; and

(v) A list, including addresses, as of the latest practicable date, alphabetically arranged, of all municipal securities brokers and municipal securities dealers which have paid to the Board fees and charges to defray the costs and expenses of operating the Board.

(5) Within 10 days after the discovery of any material inaccuracy in its annual report or in any amendment thereto the Municipal Securities Rulemaking Board shall file with the Commission an amendment correcting such inaccuracy.

(b) *Supplemental Reports of the Municipal Securities Rulemaking Board.* The Municipal Securities Rulemaking Board shall file supplemental reports to the Commission as follows:

(1) Within 10 days after issuing or making generally available to municipal securities brokers and municipal securities dealers any materials (including notices, circulars, bulletins, lists, periodicals, etc.), the Municipal Securities Rulemaking Board shall file with the Commission three copies of such material (unless such material is filed with the Commission pursuant to Rule 19b–4).

(2) Within 10 days after any action is taken which renders no longer accurate any of the information required by paragraphs (a)(3)(iii), (iv), (v), and (vi) of this rule to be contained in the annual report of the Municipal Securities Rulemaking Board (except action reported to the Commission pursuant to Rule 19b–4), the Board shall file with the Commission written notification in triplicate setting forth the nature of such action and the effective date thereof. Such notice may be filed either in the form of a letter or in the form of a notice made generally available to municipal securities brokers and municipal securities dealers.

Rule 17a–22. Supplemental material of registered clearing agencies

Within ten days after issuing, or making generally available, to its participants or to other entities with whom it has a significant relationship, such as pledgees, transfer agents, or self-regulatory organizations, any material (including, for example, manuals, notices, circulars, bulletins, lists, or periodicals), a registered clearing agency shall file three copies of such material with the Commission. A registered clearing agency for which the Commission is not the appropriate regulatory agency shall at the same time file one copy of such material with its appropriate regulatory agency.

Rule 17a–23. [Reserved]

Rule 17a–25. Electronic submission of securities transaction information by exchange members, brokers, and dealers

(a) Every member, broker, or dealer subject to Rule 17a–3 shall, upon request, electronically submit to the Commission the securities transaction information as required in this rule:

(1) If the transaction was a proprietary transaction effected or caused to be effected by the member, broker, or dealer for any account in which such member, broker, or dealer, or person associated with the member, broker, or dealer, is directly or indirectly interested, such member, broker or dealer shall submit the following information:

(i) Clearing house number, or alpha symbol of the member, broker, or dealer submitting the information;

(ii) Clearing house number(s), or alpha symbol(s) of the member(s), broker(s) or dealer(s) on the opposite side of the transaction;

(iii) Identifying symbol assigned to the security;

(iv) Date transaction was executed;

(v) Number of shares, or quantity of bonds or options contracts, for each specific transaction; whether each transaction was a purchase, sale, or short sale; and, if an options contract, whether open long or short or close long or short;

(vi) Transaction price;

(vii) Account number; and

(viii) The identity of the exchange or other market where the transaction was executed.

(2) If the transaction was effected or caused to be effected by the member, broker, or dealer for any customer account, such member, broker, or dealer shall submit the following information:

(i) Information contained in paragraphs (a)(1)(i) through (a)(1)(viii) of this rule;

(ii) Customer name, address(es), branch office number, registered representative number, whether the order was solicited or unsolicited, date account opened, and the customer's tax identification number(s); and

(iii) If the transaction was effected for a customer of another member, broker, or dealer, whether the other member, broker, or dealer was acting as principal or agent on the transaction.

(b) In addition to the information in paragraph (a) of this rule, a member, broker, or dealer shall, upon request, electronically submit to the Commission the following securities transaction information for transactions involving entities that trade using multiple accounts:

(1)(i) If part or all of an account's transactions at the reporting member, broker, or dealer have been transferred or otherwise forwarded to one or more accounts at another member, broker, or dealer, an identifier for this type of transaction; and

(ii) If part or all of an account's transactions at the reporting member, broker, or dealer have been transferred or otherwise received from one or more other members, brokers, or dealers, an identifier for this type of transaction.

(2)(i) If part or all of an account's transactions at the reporting member, broker, or dealer have been transferred or otherwise received from another account at the reporting member, broker, or dealer, an identifier for this type of transaction; and

(ii) If part or all of an account's transactions at the reporting member, broker, or dealer have been transferred or otherwise forwarded to one or more other accounts at the reporting member, broker, or dealer, an identifier for this type of transaction.

(3) If an account's transaction was processed by a depository institution, the identifier assigned to the account by the depository institution.

(c) Every member, broker, or dealer shall, upon request, submit to the Commission and, keep current, information containing the full name, title, address, telephone number(s), facsimile number(s); and electronic-mail address(es) for each person designated by the member, broker, or dealer as responsible for processing securities transaction information requests from the Commission.

(d) The member, broker, or dealer should comply with the format for the electronic submission of the securities transaction information described in paragraphs (a) and (b) of this rule as specified by the member, broker, or dealer's designated self-regulatory organization under Rule 17d–1, unless otherwise specified by Commission rule.

Rule 17d–1. Examination for compliance with applicable financial responsibility rules

(a) Where a member of SIPC is a member of more than one self-regulatory organization, the Commission shall designate by written notice to one of such organizations responsibility for examining such member for compliance with applicable financial responsibility rules. In making such designations the Commission shall take into consideration the regulatory capabilities and procedures of the self-regulatory organizations, availability of staff, convenience of location, unnecessary regulatory duplication, and such other factors as the Commission may consider germane to the protection of investors, the cooperation and coordination among self-regulatory organizations, and the development of a national market system and a national system for the clearance and settlement of securities transactions.

(b) Upon designation of responsibility pursuant to paragraph (a) of this rule, all other self-regulatory organizations of which such person is a member shall be relieved of such responsibility to the extent specified.

(c) After the Commission has acted pursuant to paragraphs (a) and (b) of this rule, any self-regulatory organization relieved of responsibility with respect to a member may notify customers of, and persons doing business with, such member of the limited nature of its responsibility for such member's compliance with applicable financial responsibility rules.

Rule 17d–2. Program for allocation of regulatory responsibility

(a) Any two or more self-regulatory organizations may file with the Commission within ninety (90) days of the effective date of this rule, and thereafter as changes in designation are necessary or appropriate, a plan for allocating among the self-regulatory organizations the responsibility to receive regulatory reports from persons who are members or participants of more than one of such self-regulatory organizations to examine such persons for compliance, or to enforce compliance by such persons, with specified provisions of the Securities Exchange Act of 1934, the rules and regulations thereunder, and the rules of such self-regulatory organizations, or to carry out other specified regulatory functions with respect to such persons.

(b) Any plan filed hereunder may contain provisions for the allocation among the parties of expenses reasonably incurred by the self-regulatory organization having regulatory responsibilities under the plan.

(c) After appropriate notice and opportunity for comment, the Commission may, by written notice, declare such a plan, or any part of the plan, effective if it finds the plan, or any part thereof, necessary or appropriate in the public interest and for the protection of investors, to foster cooperation and coordination among self-regulatory organizations, or to remove impediments to and foster the development of the national market system and a national system for the clearance and settlement of securities transactions and in conformity with the factors set forth in section 17(d) of the Securities Exchange Act of 1934.

(d) Upon the effectiveness of such a plan or part thereof, any self-regulatory organization which is a party to the plan shall be relieved of responsibility as to any person for whom such responsibility is allocated under the plan to another self-regulatory organization to the extent of such allocation.

(e) Nothing herein shall preclude any self-regulatory organization from entering into more than one plan filed hereunder.

(f) After the Commission has declared a plan or part thereof effective pursuant to paragraph (c) of this rule or acted pursuant to paragraph (g) of this rule, a self-regulatory organization relieved of responsibility may notify customers of, and persons doing business with, such member or participant of the limited nature of its responsibility for such member's or participant's acts, practices, and course of business.

(g) In the event that plans declared effective pursuant to paragraph (c) of this rule do not provide for all members or participants or do not allocate all regulatory responsibilities, the Commission may, after due consideration of the factors enumerated in section 17(d)(1) and notice and opportunity for comment, designate one or more of the self-regulatory organizations responsible for specified regulatory responsibilities with respect to such members or participants.

Rule 17f–1. Requirements for reporting and inquiry with respect to missing, lost, counterfeit or stolen securities

(a) *Definitions.* For purposes of this rule:

(1) The term *reporting institution* shall include every national securities exchange, member thereof, registered securities association, broker, dealer, municipal securities dealer, government securities broker, government securities dealer, registered transfer agent, registered clearing agency, participant therein, member of the Federal Reserve System and bank whose deposits are insured by the Federal Deposit Insurance Corporation;

(2) The term *uncertificated security* shall mean a security not represented by an instrument and the transfer of which is registered upon books maintained for that purpose by or on behalf of the issuer;

(3) The term *global certificate securities issue* shall mean a securities issue for which a single master certificate representing the entire issue is registered in the nominee name of a registered clearing agency and for which beneficial owners cannot receive negotiable securities certificates;

(4) The term *customer* shall mean any person with whom the reporting institution has entered into at least one prior securities-related transaction; and

(5) The term *securities-related transaction* shall mean a purchase, sale or pledge of investment securities, or a custodial arrangement for investment securities.

(6) The term *securities certificate* means any physical instrument that represents or purports to represent ownership in a security that was printed by or on behalf of the issuer thereof and shall include any such instrument that is or was:

(i) Printed but not issued;

(ii) Issued and outstanding, including treasury securities;

(iii) Cancelled, which for this purpose means either or both of the procedures set forth in Rule 17Ad–19(a)(1); or

(iv) Counterfeit or reasonably believed to be counterfeit.

(7) The term *issuer* shall include an issuer's:

(i) Transfer agent(s), paying agent(s), tender agent(s), and person(s) providing similar services; and

(ii) Corporate predecessor(s) and successor(s).

(8) The term *missing* shall include any securities certificate that:

(i) Cannot be located or accounted for, but is not believed to be lost or stolen; or

(ii) A transfer agent claims or believes was destroyed in any manner other than by the transfer agent's own certificate destruction procedures as provided in Rule 17Ad–19.

(b) Every reporting institution shall register with the Commission or its designee in accordance with instructions issued by the Commission except:

(1) A member of a national securities exchange who effects securities transactions through the trading facilities of the exchange and has not received or held customer securities within the last six months;

(2) A reporting institution that, within the last six months, limited its securities activities exclusively to uncertificated securities, global securities issues or any securities issue for which neither record nor beneficial owners can obtain a negotiable securities certificate; or

(3) A reporting institution whose business activities, within the last six months, did not involve the handling of securities certificates.

(c) *Reporting Requirements.* (1) *Stolen Securities.* (i) Every reporting institution shall report to the Commission or its designee, and to a registered transfer agent for the issue, the discovery of the theft or loss of any securities certificates where there is substantial basis for believing that criminal activity was involved. Such report shall be made within one business day of the discovery and, if the certificate numbers of the securities cannot be ascertained at that time, they shall be reported as soon thereafter as possible.

(ii) Every reporting institution shall promptly report to the Federal Bureau of Investigation upon the discovery of the theft or loss of any securities certificate where there is substantial basis for believing that criminal activity was involved.

(2) *Missing or Lost Securities.* Every reporting institution shall report to the Commission or its designee, and to a registered transfer agent for the issue, the discovery of the loss of any securities certificate where criminal actions are not suspected when the securities certificate has been missing or lost for a period of two business days. Such report shall be made within one business day of the end of such period except that:

(i) Securities certificates lost, missing, or stolen while in transit to customers, transfer agents, banks, brokers or dealers shall be reported by the delivering institution by the later of two business days after notice of non-receipt or as soon after such notice as the certificate numbers of the securities can be ascertained.

(ii) Where a shipment of retired securities certificates is in transit between any transfer agents, banks, brokers, dealers, or other reporting institutions, with no affiliation existing between such entities, and the delivering institution fails to receive notice of receipt or non-receipt of the certificates, the delivering institution shall act to determine the facts. In the event of non-delivery where the certificates are not recovered by the delivering institution, the delivering institution shall report the certificates as lost, stolen, or missing to the Commission or its designee within a reasonable time under the circumstances but in any event within twenty business days from the date of shipment.

(iii) Securities certificates considered lost or missing as a result of securities counts or verifications required by rule, regulation or otherwise (*e.g.*, dividend record date verification made as a result of firm policy or internal audit function report) shall be reported by the later of ten business days after completion of such securities count or verification or as soon after such count or verification as the certificate numbers of the securities can be ascertained.

(iv) Securities certificates not received during the completion of delivery, deposit or withdrawal shall be reported in the following manner:

(A) Where delivery of the securities certificates is through a clearing agency, the delivering institution shall supply to the receiving institution the certificate number of the security within two business days from the date of request from the receiving institution. The receiving institution shall report within one business day of notification of the certificate number;

(B) Where the delivery of securities certificates is in person and where the delivering institution has a receipt, the delivering institution shall supply the receiving institution the certificate numbers of the securities within two business days from the date of request from the receiving institution. The receiving institution shall report within one business day of notification of the certificate number;

(C) Where the delivery of securities certificates is in person and where the delivering institution has no receipt, the delivering institution shall report within two business days of notification of non-receipt by the receiving institution; or

(D) Where delivery of securities certificates is made by mail or via draft, if payment is not received within ten business days, the delivering institution shall confirm with the receiving institution the failure to receive such delivery; if confirmation shows non-receipt, the delivering institution shall report within two business days of such confirmation.

(3) *Counterfeit Securities.* Every reporting institution shall report the discovery of any counterfeit securities certificate to the Commission or its designee, to a registered transfer agent for the issue, and to the Federal Bureau of Investigation within one business day of such discovery.

(4) *Transfer Agent Reporting Obligations.* Every transfer agent shall make the reports required above only if it receives notification of the loss, theft or counterfeiting from a non-reporting institution or if it receives notification other than on a Form X–17F–1A or if the certificate was in its possession at the time of the loss.

(5) *Recovery.* Every reporting institution that originally reported a lost, missing or stolen securities certificate pursuant to this rule shall report recovery of that securities certificate to the Commission or its designee and to a registered transfer agent for the issue within one business day of such recovery or finding. Every reporting institution that originally made a report in which criminality was indicated also shall notify the Federal Bureau of Investigation that the securities certificate has been recovered.

(6) *Information to Be Reported.* All reports made pursuant to this rule shall include, if applicable or available, the following information with respect to each securities certificate:

(i) Issuer;

(ii) Type of security and series;

(iii) Date of issue;

(iv) Maturity date;

(v) Denomination;

(vi) Interest rate;

(vii) Certificate number, including alphabetical prefix or suffix;

(viii) Name in which registered;

(ix) Distinguishing characteristics, if counterfeit;

(x) Date of discovery of loss or recovery;

(xi) CUSIP number;

(xii) Financial Industry Numbering System ("FINS") Number; and

(xiii) Type of loss.

(7) *Forms.* Reporting institutions shall make all reports to the Commission or its designee and to a registered transfer agent for the issue pursuant to this section on Form X–17F–1A. Reporting institutions shall make reports to the Federal Bureau of Investigation pursuant to this Section on Form X–17F–1A, unless the reporting institution is a member of the Federal Reserve System or a bank whose deposits are insured by the Federal Deposit Insurance Corporation, in which case reports may be made on the form required by the institution's appropriate regulatory agency for reports to the Federal Bureau of Investigation.

(d) *Required Inquiries.* (1) Every reporting institution (except a reporting institution that, acting in its capacity as transfer agent, paying agent, exchange agent or tender agent for an equity issue, or registrar for a bond or other debt issue, compares all transactions against a shareholder or bondholder list and a current list of stop transfers) shall inquire of the Commission or its designee with respect to every securities certificate which comes into its possession or keeping, whether by pledge, transfer or otherwise, to ascertain whether such securities certificate has been reported as missing, lost, counterfeit or stolen, unless:

(i) The securities certificate is received directly from the issuer or issuing agent at issuance;

(ii) The securities certificate is received from another reporting institution or from a Federal Reserve Bank or Branch;

(iii) The securities certificate is received from a customer of the reporting institution; and

(A) Is registered in the name of such customer or its nominee; or

(B) Was previously sold to such customer, as verified by the internal records of the reporting institution;

(iv) The securities certificate is received as part of a transaction which has an aggregate face value of $10,000 or less in the case of bonds, or market value of $10,000 or less in the case of stocks; or

(v) The securities certificate is received directly from a drop which is affiliated with a reporting institution for the purposes of receiving or delivering certificates on behalf of the reporting institution.

(2) *Form of Inquiry.* Inquiries shall be made in such manner as prescribed by the Commission or its designee.

(3) A reporting institution shall make required inquiries by the end of the fifth business day after a securities certificate comes into its possession or keeping, provided that such inquiries shall be made before the certificate is sold, used as collateral, or sent to another reporting institution.

(e) *Permissive Reports and Inquiries.* Every reporting institution may report to or inquire of the Commission or its designee with respect to any securities certificate not otherwise required by this rule to be the subject of a report or inquiry. The Commission on written request or upon its own motion may permit reports to and inquiries of the system by any other person or entity upon such terms and conditions as it deems appropriate and necessary in the public interest and for the protection of investors.

(f) *Exemptions.* The following types of securities are not subject to paragraphs (c) and (d) of this rule:

(1) Security issues not assigned CUSIP number;

(2) Bond coupons;

(3) Uncertificated securities;

(4) Global securities issues; and

(5) Any securities issue for which neither record nor beneficial owners can obtain a negotiable securities certificate.

(g) *Recordkeeping.* Every reporting institution shall maintain and preserve in an easily accessible place for three years copies of all Forms X–17F–1A filed pursuant to this section, all agreements between reporting institutions regarding registration or other aspects of this section, and all confirmations or other information received from the Commission or its designee as a result of inquiry.

Rule 17f–2. Fingerprinting of securities industry personnel

(a) *Exemptions for the Fingerprinting Requirement.* Except as otherwise provided in paragraph (a)(1) or (2) of this rule, every member of a national securities exchange, broker, dealer, registered transfer agent and registered clearing agency shall require that each of its partners, directors, officers and employees be fingerprinted and shall submit, or cause to be submitted, the fingerprints of such persons to the Attorney General of the United States or its designee for identification and appropriate processing.

(1) *Permissive Exemptions.* Every member of a national securities exchange, broker, dealer, registered transfer agent and registered clearing agency may claim one or more of the exemptions in paragraph (a)(1)(i), (ii), (iii) or (iv) of this rule; *Provided,* That all the requirements of paragraph (e) of this rule are also satisfied.

(i) *Member of a National Securities Exchange, Broker, Dealer or Registered Clearing Agency.* Every person who is a partner, director, officer or employee of a member of a national securities exchange, broker, dealer, or registered clearing agency shall be exempt if that person:

(A) Is not engaged in the sale of securities;

(B) Does not regularly have access to the keeping, handling or processing of (*1*) securities, (*2*) monies, or (*3*) the original books and records relating to the securities or the monies; and

(C) Does not have direct supervisory responsibility over persons engaged in the activities referred to in paragraphs (a)(1)(i)(A) and (B) of this rule.

(ii) *Registered Transfer Agents.* Every person who is a partner, director, officer or employee of a registered transfer agent shall be exempt if that person:

(A) Is not engaged in transfer agent functions (as defined in section 3(a)(25) of the Securities Exchange Act of 1934) or activities incidental thereto; or

(B) Meets the conditions in paragraphs (a)(1)(i)(B) and (C) of this rule.

(iii) *Registered Broker-Dealers Engaged in Sales of Certain Securities.* Every partner, director, officer and employee of a registered broker or dealer who satisfies paragraph (a)(1)(i)

(B) of this rule shall be exempt if that broker or dealer:

(A) Is engaged exclusively in the sale of shares of registered open-end management investment companies, variable contracts, or interests in limited partnerships, unit investment trusts or real estate investment trusts; *Provided*, That those securities ordinarily are not evidenced by certificates;

(B) Is current in its continuing obligation under Rules 15b1–1 and 15b3–1(b) to update Item 10 of Form BD to disclose the existence of any statutory disqualification set forth in sections 3(a)(39), 15(b)(4) and 15(b)(6) of the Securities Exchange Act of 1934;

(C) Has insurance or bonding indemnifying it for losses to customers caused by the fraudulent or criminal acts of any of its partners, directors, officers or employees for whom an exemption is being claimed under paragraph (a)(1)(iii) of this rule; and

(D) Is subject to the jurisdiction of a state insurance department with respect to its sale of variable contracts.

(iv) *Illegible Fingerprint Cards.* Every person who is a partner, director, officer or employee shall be exempt if that member of a national securities exchange, broker, dealer, registered transfer agent or registered clearing agency, on at least three occasions:

(A) Attempts in good faith to obtain from such person a complete set of fingerprints acceptable to the Attorney General or its designee for identification and appropriate processing by requiring that person to be fingerprinted, by having that person's fingerprints rolled by a person competent to do so and by submitting the fingerprint cards for the person to the Attorney General of the United States or its designee in accordance with proper procedures;

(B) Has that person's fingerprint cards returned to it by the Attorney General of the United States or its designee without that person's fingerprints having been identified because the fingerprints were illegible; and

(C) Retains the returned fingerprint cards and any other required records in accordance with paragraph (d) of this rule and Rules 17a–3(a)(13), 17a–4(e)(2) and 17Ad–7(e)(1) under the Securities Exchange Act of 1934.

(2) *Other Exemptions by Application to the Commission.* The Commission, upon specified terms, conditions and periods, may grant exemptions to any class of partners, directors, officers or employees of any member of a national securities exchange, broker, dealer, registered transfer agent or registered clearing agency, if the Commission finds that such action is not inconsistent with the public interest or the protection of investors.

(b) *Fingerprinting Pursuant to Other Law.* Every member of a national securities exchange, broker, dealer, registered transfer agent and registered clearing agency may satisfy the fingerprinting requirement of section 17(f)(2) of the Securities Exchange Act of 1934 as to any partner, director, officer or employee, if:

(1) The person, in connection with his or her present employment with such organization, has been fingerprinted pursuant to any other law, statute, rule or regulation of any state or federal government or agency thereof;

(2) The fingerprint cards for that person are submitted, or are caused to be submitted, to the Attorney General of the United States or its designee for identification and appropriate processing, and the Attorney General or its designee has processed those fingerprint cards; and

(3) The processed fingerprint cards or any substitute records, together with any information received from the Attorney General or its designee, are maintained in accordance with paragraph (d) of this rule.

(c) *Fingerprinting Plans of Self-Regulatory Organizations.* The fingerprinting requirement of section 17(f)(2) of the Securities Exchange Act of 1934 may be satisfied by submitting appropriate and complete fingerprint cards to a registered national securities exchange or to a registered national securities association which, pursuant to a plan filed with, and declared effective by, the Commission, forwards such fingerprint cards to the Attorney General of the United States or its designee for identification and appropriate processing. Any plan filed by a registered national securities exchange or a registered national securities association shall not become effective, unless declared effective by the Commission as not inconsistent with the public interest or the protection of investors; and, in declaring any such plan effective, the Commission may impose any terms and conditions relating to the provisions of the plan and the period of its effectiveness as it may deem necessary or appropriate in the public interest, for the protection of investors, or otherwise in furtherance of the purposes of the Securities Exchange Act of 1934.

(d) *Record Maintenance.* (1) Every member of a national securities exchange, broker, dealer, registered transfer agent and registered clearing agency shall maintain the processed fingerprint card or any substitute record when such card is not returned after processing, together with any information received from the Attorney General or its designee, for every person required to be fingerprinted under section 17(f)(2) of the Securities Exchange Act of 1934 and for persons who have complied with this section pursuant to paragraph (b) or (c) of this rule. Every substitute record shall state the name of the person whose fingerprint card was submitted to the Attorney General of the United States, the name of the member of a national securities exchange, broker, dealer, registered transfer agent or registered clearing agency that submitted the fingerprint card, the name of the person or organization that rolled the fingerprints, the date on which the fingerprints were rolled, and the date the fingerprint card was submitted to the Attorney General of the United States. The processed fingerprint card and every other substitute record containing the information required by this paragraph, together with any information received from the Attorney General of the United States, shall be kept in an easily accessible place at the organization's principal office and shall be made available upon request to the Commission, the appropriate regulatory agency (if not the Commission) or other designated examining authority. The organization's principal office must provide to the regional, branch or satellite office actually employing the person written evidence that the person's fingerprints have been processed by the FBI, and must provide to that office a copy of any criminal history record information received from the FBI. All fingerprint cards, records, and information required to be maintained under this paragraph shall be retained for a period of not less than three years after termination of that person's employment or relationship with the organization.

(2) *Record Maintenance by Designated Examining Authorities.* The records required to be maintained and preserved by a member of a national securities exchange, broker, or dealer pursuant to the requirements of paragraph (d)(1) of this rule may be maintained and preserved on behalf of that member, broker or dealer by a self-regulatory organization that is also the designated examining authority for that member, broker or dealer, *Provided* That the self-regulatory organization has filed in accordance with Rule 17f–2(c) a fingerprinting plan or amendments to an existing plan concerning the storage and maintenance of records and that plan, as amended, has been declared effective by the Commission, and *Provided Further* That:

(i) Such records are subject at any time, or from time to time, to reasonable periodic, special or other examinations by representatives of the Commission; and

(ii) The self-regulatory organization furnishes to the Commission, upon demand, at either the principal office or at the regional office complete, correct and current hard copies of any and all such records.

(3) *Reproduction of Records on Microfilm.* The records required to be maintained pursuant to paragraph (d)(1) of this rule may be produced or reproduced on microfilm and preserved in that form. If such microfilm substitution for hard copy is made by a member of a national securities exchange, broker, dealer, registered transfer agent or registered clearing agency, or by a self-regulatory organization maintaining and storing records pursuant to paragraph (d)(2) of this rule, it shall at all times:

(i) Have available for examination by the Commission, the appropriate regulatory agency (if not the Commission) or other designated examining authority, facilities for the immediate, easily readable projection of the microfilm and for the production of easily readable and legible facsimile enlargements;

(ii) File and index the films in such a manner as to permit the immediate location and retrieval of any particular record;

(iii) Be ready to provide, and immediately provide, any facsimile enlargement which the Commission, the appropriate regulatory agency (if not the Commission) or other designated examining authority by their examiners or other representatives may request; and

(iv) For the period for which the microfilm records are required to be maintained, store separately from the original microfilm records a copy of the microfilm records.

(e) *Notice Requirement.* Every member of a national securities exchange, broker, dealer, registered transfer agent and registered clearing agency that claims one or more of the exemptions in paragraph (a)(1) of this rule shall make and keep current a statement entitled "Notice Pursuant to Rule 17f–2" containing the information specified in paragraph (e)(1) of this rule.

(1) *Contents of Statement.* The Notice required by paragraph (e) of this rule shall:

(i) State the name of the organization and state whether it is a member of a national securities exchange, broker, dealer, registered transfer agent, or registered clearing agency;

(ii) Identify by division, department, class, or name and position within the organization all persons who are claimed to have satisfied the fingerprinting requirement of section 17(f)(2) of the Securities Exchange Act of 1934 pursuant to paragraph (b) of this rule;

(iii) Identify by division, department, class, title or position within the organization all persons claimed to be exempt under paragraphs (a)(1)(i) through (iii) of this rule, and identify by name all persons claimed to be exempt under paragraph (a)(1)(iv). Persons identified under this paragraph (e)(1)(iii) shall be exempt from the requirement of section 17(f)(2) of the Securities Exchange Act of 1934 unless notified to the contrary by the Commission;

(iv) Describe, in generic terms, the nature of the duties of the person or classes of persons, and the nature of the functions and operations of the divisions and departments, identified as exempt in paragraph (e)(1)(iii) of this rule; and

(v) Describe the security measures utilized to ensure that only those persons who have been fingerprinted in accordance with the fingerprinting requirement of section 17(f)(2) of the Securities Exchange Act of 1934 or who are exempt under paragraph (a)(1)(iv) of this rule have access to the keeping, handling or processing of securities or monies or the original books and records relating thereto.

(2) *Record Maintenance.* A copy of the Notice required to be made and kept current under paragraph (e) of this rule shall be kept in an easily accessible place at the organization's principal office and at the office employing the persons for whom exemptions are claimed and shall be made available upon request for inspection by the Commission, appropriate regulatory agency (if not the Commission) or other designated examining authority.

(3) *Exemption from the Notice Requirement.* A registered transfer agent that performs transfer agent functions only on behalf of itself as an issuer and that receives fewer than 500 items for transfer and fewer than 500 items for processing during any six consecutive months shall be exempt from the Notice requirement of paragraph (c) of this rule.

NATIONALLY RECOGNIZED STATISTICAL RATING ORGANIZATIONS

Rule 17g–1. Application for registration as a nationally recognized statistical rating organization

(a) *Initial Application.* A credit rating agency applying to the Commission to be registered under section 15E of the Act as a nationally recognized statistical rating organization must file with the Commission two paper copies of an initial application on Form NRSRO (17 CFR 249b.300) that follows all applicable instructions for the Form.

(b) *Application to Register for an Additional Class of Credit Ratings.* A nationally recognized statistical rating organization applying to register for an additional class of the credit ratings described in section 3(a)(62)(B) of the Act must file with the Commission two paper copies of an application to add a class of credit ratings on Form NRSRO that follows all applicable instructions for the Form. The application will be subject to the requirements of section 15E(a)(2) of the Act.

(c) *Supplementing an Application Prior to Final Action by the Commission.* An applicant must promptly file with the Commission two paper copies of a written notice if information submitted to the Commission in an initial application to be registered as a nationally recognized statistical rating organization or in an application to register for an additional class of credit ratings is found to be or becomes materially inaccurate prior to the date of a Commission order granting or denying the application. The notice must identify the information that was found to be materially inaccurate. The applicant also must promptly file with the Commission two paper copies of an application supplement on Form NRSRO that follows all applicable instructions for the Form.

(d) *Withdrawing an Application.* An applicant may withdraw an initial application to be registered as a nationally recognized statistical rating organization or an application to register for an additional class of credit ratings prior to the date of a Commission order granting or denying the application. To withdraw the application, the applicant must furnish the Commission with a written notice of withdrawal executed by a duly authorized person.

(e) *Update of registration.* A nationally recognized statistical rating organization amending materially inaccurate information in its application for registration pursuant to section 15E(b)(1) of the Act must promptly file with the Commission an update of its registration on Form NRSRO that follows all applicable instructions for the Form. A Form NRSRO and the information and documents in Exhibits 2 through 9 to Form NRSRO, as applicable, filed under this paragraph must be filed electronically with the Commission on EDGAR as a PDF document in the format required by the EDGAR Filer Manual, as defined in Rule 11 of Regulation S–T.

(f) *Annual certification.* A nationally recognized statistical rating organization amending its application for registration pursuant to section 15E(b)(2) of the Act must file with the Commission an annual certification on Form NRSRO that follows all applicable instructions for the Form not later than 90 days after the end of each calendar year. A Form NRSRO and the information and documents in Exhibits 1 through 9 to Form NRSRO filed under this paragraph must be filed electronically with the Commission on EDGAR as a PDF document in the format required by the EDGAR Filer Manual, as defined in Rule 11 of Regulation S–T.

(g) *Withdrawal from registration.* A nationally recognized statistical rating organization withdrawing from registration pursuant to section 15E(e)(1) of the Act must furnish the Commission with a notice of withdrawal from registration on Form NRSRO that follows all applicable instructions for the Form. The withdrawal from registration will become effective 45 calendar days after the notice is furnished to the Commission upon such terms and conditions as the Commission may establish as necessary in the public interest or for the protection of investors. A Form NRSRO furnished under this paragraph must be furnished electronically with the Commission on EDGAR as a PDF document in the format required by the EDGAR Filer Manual, as defined in Rule 11 of Regulation S–T.

(h) *Filing or furnishing Form NRSRO.* A Form NRSRO filed or furnished, as applicable, under any paragraph of this section will be considered filed with or furnished to the Commission on the date the Commission receives a complete and properly executed Form NRSRO that follows all applicable instructions for the Form. Information filed or furnished, as applicable, on a confidential basis and for which confidential treatment has been requested pursuant to applicable Commission rules will be accorded confidential treatment to the extent permitted by law.

(i) Public availability of Form NRSRO. A nationally recognized statistical rating organization must make its current Form NRSRO and information and documents in Exhibits 1 through 9 to Form NRSRO publicly and freely available on an easily accessible portion of its corporate Internet website within 10 business days after the date of the Commission order granting an initial application for registration as a nationally recognized statistical rating organization or an application to register for an additional class of credit ratings and within 10 business days after filing with or furnishing to, as applicable, the Commission a Form NRSRO under paragraph (e), (f), or (g) of this section. In addition, a nationally recognized statistical rating organization must make its most recently filed Exhibit 1 to Form NRSRO freely available in writing to any individual who requests a copy of the Exhibit.

Rule 17g–2. Records to be made and retained by nationally recognized statistical rating organizations

(a) *Records Required to Be Made and Retained.* A nationally recognized statistical rating organization must make and retain the following books and records, which must be complete and current:

(1) Records of original entry into the accounting system of the nationally recognized statistical rating organization and records reflecting entries to and balances in all general ledger accounts of the nationally recognized statistical rating organization for each fiscal year.

(2) Records with respect to each current credit rating of the nationally recognized statistical rating organization indicating (as applicable):

(i) The identity of any credit analyst(s) that participated in determining the credit rating;

(ii) The identity of the person(s) that approved the credit rating before it was issued;

(iii) If a quantitative model was a substantial component in the process of determining the credit rating of a security or money market instrument issued by an asset pool or as part of any asset-backed securities transaction, a record of the rationale for any material difference between the credit rating implied by the model and the final credit rating issued; and

(iv) Whether the credit rating was solicited or unsolicited.

(3) An account record for each person (for example, an obligor, issuer, underwriter, or other user) that has paid the nationally recognized statistical rating organization for the issuance or maintenance of a credit rating indicating:

(i) The identity and address of the person; and

(ii) The credit rating(s) determined or maintained for the person.

(4) An account record for each subscriber to the credit ratings and/or credit analysis reports of the nationally recognized statistical rating organization indicating the identity and address of the subscriber.

(5) A record listing the general types of services and products offered by the nationally recognized statistical rating organization.

(6) A record documenting the established procedures and methodologies used by the nationally recognized statistical rating organization to determine credit ratings.

(7) A record that lists each security and money market instrument and its corresponding credit rating issued by an asset pool or as part of any asset-backed securities transaction where the nationally recognized statistical rating organization, in determining the credit rating for the security or money market instrument, treats assets within such pool or as a part of such transaction that are not subject to a credit rating of the nationally recognized statistical rating organization by any or a combination of the following methods:

(i) Determining credit ratings for the unrated assets;

(ii) Performing credit assessments or determining private credit ratings for the unrated assets;

(iii) Determining credit ratings or private credit ratings, or performing credit assessments for the unrated assets by taking into consideration the internal credit analysis of another person; or

(iv) Determining credit ratings or private credit ratings, or performing credit assessments for the unrated assets by taking into consideration (but not necessarily adopting) the credit ratings of another nationally recognized statistical rating organization.

(8) For each outstanding credit rating, a record showing all rating actions and the date of such actions from the initial credit rating to the current credit rating identified by the name of the rated security or obligor and, if applicable, the CUSIP of the rated security or the Central Index Key (CIK) number of the rated obligor.

(9) A record documenting the policies and procedures the nationally recognized statistical rating organization is required to establish, maintain, and enforce pursuant to section 15E(h)(4)(A) of the Act Rule 17g–8(c).

(b) *Records Required to Be Retained.* A nationally recognized statistical rating organization must retain the following books and records (excluding drafts of documents) that relate to its business as a credit rating agency:

(1) Significant records (for example, bank statements, invoices, and trial balances) underlying the information included in the annual financial reports the nationally recognized statistical rating organization filed with or furnished to, as applicable, the Commission pursuant to Rule 17g–3.

(2) Internal records, including nonpublic information and work papers, used to form the basis of a credit rating issued by the nationally recognized statistical rating organization.

(3) Credit analysis reports, credit assessment reports, and private credit rating reports of the nationally recognized statistical rating organization and internal records, including nonpublic information and work papers, used to form the basis for the opinions expressed in these reports.

(4) Compliance reports and compliance exception reports.

(5) Internal audit plans, internal audit reports, documents relating to internal audit follow-up measures, and all records identified by the internal auditors of the nationally recognized statistical rating organization as necessary to perform the audit of an activity that relates to its business as a credit rating agency.

(6) Marketing materials of the nationally recognized statistical rating organization that are published or otherwise made available to persons that are not associated with the nationally recognized statistical rating organization.

(7) External and internal communications, including electronic communications, received and sent by the nationally recognized statistical rating organization and its employees that relate to initiating, determining, maintaining, monitoring, changing, or withdrawing a credit rating.

(8) Any written communications received from persons not associated with the nationally recognized statistical rating organization that contain complaints about the performance of a credit analyst in initiating, determining, maintaining, monitoring, changing, or withdrawing a credit rating.

(9) Internal documents that contain information, analysis, or statistics that were used to develop a procedure or methodology to treat the credit ratings of another nationally recognized statistical rating organization for the purpose of determining a credit rating for a security or money market instrument issued by an asset pool or part of any asset-backed securities transaction.

(10) For each security or money market instrument identified in the record required to be made and retained under paragraph (a)(7) of this rule, any document that contains a description of how assets within such pool or as a part of such transaction not rated by the nationally recognized statistical rating organization but rated by another nationally recognized statistical rating organization were treated for the purpose of determining the credit rating of the security or money market instrument.

(11) Forms NRSRO (including Exhibits and accompanying information and documents) the nationally recognized statistical rating organization filed with or furnished to, as applicable, the Commission.

(12) The internal control structure the nationally recognized statistical rating organization is required to establish, maintain, enforce, and document pursuant to section 15E(c)(3)(A) of the Act.

(13) The policies and procedures the nationally recognized statistical rating organization is required to establish, maintain, enforce, and document pursuant to Rule 17g–8(a).

(14) The policies and procedures the nationally recognized statistical rating organization is required to establish, maintain, enforce, and document pursuant to Rule 17g–8(b).

(15) The standards of training, experience, and competence for credit analysts the nationally recognized statistical rating organization is required to establish, maintain, enforce, and document pursuant to Rule 17g–9.

(c) *Record retention periods.* The records required to be retained pursuant to paragraphs (a) and (b) of this section must be retained for three years after the date the record is made or received, except that a record identified in paragraph (a)(9), (b)(12), (b)(13), (b)(14), or (b)(15) of this section must be retained until three years after the date the record is replaced with an updated record.

(d) *Manner of Retention.* An original, or a true and complete copy of the original, of each record required to be retained pursuant to paragraphs (a) and (b) of this section must be maintained in a manner that, for the applicable retention period specified in paragraph (c) of this section, makes the original record or copy easily accessible to the principal office of the nationally recognized statistical rating organization and to any other office that conducted activities causing the record to be made or received.

(e) *Third–Party Record Custodian.* The records required to be retained pursuant to paragraphs (a) and (b) of this rule may be made or retained by a third-party record custodian, provided the nationally recognized statistical rating organization furnishes the Commission at its principal office in Washington, DC with a written undertaking of the custodian executed by a duly authorized person. The undertaking must be in substantially the following form:

> The undersigned acknowledges that books and records it has made or is retaining for [the nationally recognized statistical rating organization] are the exclusive property of [the nationally recognized statistical rating organization]. The undersigned undertakes that upon the request of [the nationally recognized statistical rating organization] it will promptly provide the books and records to [the nationally recognized statistical rating organization] or the U.S. Securities and Exchange Commission ("Commission") or its representatives and that upon the request of the Commission it will promptly permit examination by the Commission or its representatives of the records at any time or from time to time during business hours and promptly furnish to the Commission or its representatives a true and complete copy of any or all or any part of such books and records.

A nationally recognized statistical rating organization that engages a third-party record custodian remains responsible for complying with every provision of this rule.

(f) A nationally recognized statistical rating organization must promptly furnish the Commission or its representatives with legible, complete, and current copies, and, if specifically requested, English translations of those records of the nationally recognized statistical rating organization required to be retained pursuant to paragraphs (a) and (b) this rule, or any other records of the nationally recognized statistical rating organization subject to examination under section 17(b) of the Act (15 U.S.C. 78q(b)) that are requested by the Commission or its representatives.

Rule 17g–3. Annual financial and other reports to be filed or furnished by nationally recognized statistical rating organizations

(a) A nationally recognized statistical rating organization must annually, not more than 90 calendar days after the end of its fiscal year (as indicated on its current Form NRSRO):

(1) File with the Commission a financial report, as of the end of the fiscal year, containing audited financial statements of the nationally recognized statistical rating organization or audited consolidated financial statements of its parent if the nationally recognized statistical rating organization is a separately identifiable division or department of the parent. The audited financial statements must:

(i) Include a balance sheet, an income statement (or a statement of comprehensive income, as defined in Rule 1–02 of Regulation S–X, if required by the applicable generally accepted accounting principles noted in paragraph (a)(1)(ii) of this section) and statement of cash flows, and a statement of changes in ownership equity;

(ii) Be prepared in accordance with generally accepted accounting principles in the jurisdiction in which the nationally recognized statistical rating organization or its parent is incorporated, organized, or has its principal office; and

(iii) Be certified by an accountant who is qualified and independent in accordance with paragraphs (a), (b), and (c)(1), (2), (3), (4), (5) and (8) of Rule 2–01 of Regulation S–X. The accountant must give an opinion on the financial statements in accordance with paragraphs (a) through (d) of Rule 2–02 of Regulation S–X.

(2) File with the Commission a financial report, as of the end of the fiscal year, containing, if applicable, unaudited consolidating financial statements of the parent of the nationally recognized statistical rating organization that include the nationally recognized statistical rating organization.

NOTE TO PARAGRAPH (a)(2): This financial report must be filed only if the audited financial statements provided pursuant to paragraph (a)(1) of this rule are consolidated financial statements of the parent of the nationally recognized statistical rating organization.

(3) File with the Commission an unaudited financial report, as of the end of the fiscal year, providing information concerning the revenue of the nationally recognized statistical rating organization in each of the following categories (as applicable) for the fiscal year:*

(i) Revenue from determining and maintaining credit ratings;

(ii) Revenue from subscribers;

(iii) Revenue from granting licenses or rights to publish credit ratings; and

(iv) Revenue from all other services and products (include descriptions of any major sources of revenue).

(4) File with the Commission an unaudited financial report, as of the end of the fiscal year, providing the total aggregate and median annual compensation of the credit analysts of the nationally recognized statistical rating organization for the fiscal year.*

NOTE TO PARAGRAPH (a)(4): In calculating total and median annual compensation, the nationally recognized statistical rating organization may exclude deferred compensation, provided such exclusion is noted in the report.

(5) File with the Commission an unaudited financial report, as of the end of the fiscal year, listing the 20 largest issuers and subscribers that used credit rating services provided by the nationally recognized statistical rating organization by amount of net revenue attributable to the issuer or subscriber during the fiscal year. Additionally, include on the list any obligor or underwriter that used the credit rating services provided by the nationally recognized statistical rating organization if the net revenue attributable to the obligor or underwriter during the fiscal year equaled or exceeded the net revenue attributable to the 20th largest issuer or subscriber. Include the net revenue amount for each person on the list.*

* 17g–3(a)(3), (a)(4), (a)(5), and (a)(6) have been altered by the editors for grammar.

NOTE TO PARAGRAPH (a)(5): A person is deemed to have "used the credit rating services" of the nationally recognized statistical rating organization if the person is any of the following: an obligor that is rated by the nationally recognized statistical rating organization (regardless of whether the obligor paid for the credit rating); an issuer that has securities or money market instruments subject to a credit rating of the nationally recognized statistical rating organization (regardless of whether the issuer paid for the credit rating); any other person that has paid the nationally recognized statistical rating organization to determine a credit rating with respect to a specific obligor, security, or money market instrument; or a subscriber to the credit ratings, credit ratings data, or credit analysis of the nationally recognized statistical rating organization. In calculating net revenue attributable to a person, the nationally recognized statistical rating organization should include all revenue earned by the nationally recognized statistical rating organization for any type of service or product, regardless of whether related to credit rating services, and net of any rebates and allowances paid or owed to the person by the nationally recognized statistical rating organization.

(6) Furnish the Commission with an unaudited report, as of the end of the fiscal year, of the number of credit ratings actions (upgrades, downgrades, placements on credit watch, and withdrawals) taken during the fiscal year in each class of credit ratings identified in section 3(a)(62)(B) of the Act for which the nationally recognized statistical rating organization is registered with the Commission.*

NOTE TO PARAGRAPH (a)(6): A nationally recognized statistical rating organization registered in the class of credit ratings described in section 3(a)(62)(B)(iv) of the Act must include credit ratings actions taken on credit ratings of any security or money market instrument issued by an asset pool or as part of any asset-backed or mortgage-backed securities transaction for purposes of reporting the number of credit ratings actions in this class.

(7)(i) File with the Commission an unaudited report containing an assessment by management of the effectiveness during the fiscal year of the internal control structure governing the implementation of and adherence to policies, procedures, and methodologies for determining credit ratings the nationally recognized statistical rating organization is required to establish, maintain, enforce, and document pursuant to section 15E(c)(3)(A) of the Act that includes:

(A) A description of the responsibility of management in establishing and maintaining an effective internal control structure;

(B) A description of each material weakness in the internal control structure identified during the fiscal year, if any, and a description, if applicable, of how each identified material weakness was addressed; and

(C) A statement as to whether the internal control structure was effective as of the end of the fiscal year.

(ii) Management is not permitted to conclude that the internal control structure of the nationally recognized statistical rating organization was effective as of the end of the fiscal year if there were one or more material weaknesses in the internal control structure as of the end of the fiscal year.

(iii) For purposes of this paragraph (a)(7), a deficiency in the internal control structure exists when the design or operation of a control does not allow management or employees, in the normal course of performing their assigned functions, to prevent or detect a failure of the nationally recognized statistical rating organization to:

(A) Implement a policy, procedure, or methodology for determining credit ratings in accordance with the policies and procedures of the nationally recognized statistical rating organization; or

(B) Adhere to an implemented policy, procedure, or methodology for determining credit ratings.

(iv) For purposes of this paragraph (a)(7), a material weakness exists if a deficiency, or a combination of deficiencies, in the design or operation of the internal control structure creates a reasonable possibility that a failure identified in paragraph (a)(7)(iii) of this section that is material will not be prevented or detected on a timely basis.

(8) File with the Commission an unaudited annual report on the compliance of the nationally recognized statistical rating organization with the securities laws and the policies and procedures of the nationally recognized statistical rating organization pursuant to section 15E(j)(5)(B) of the Act.

(b)(1) The nationally recognized statistical rating organization must attach to the reports filed or furnished, as applicable, pursuant to paragraphs (a)(1) through (6) of this section a signed statement by a duly authorized person associated with the nationally recognized statistical rating organization stating that the person has responsibility for the reports and, to the best knowledge of the person, the reports fairly present, in all material respects, the financial condition, results of operations, cash flows, revenues, analyst compensation, and credit rating actions of the nationally recognized statistical rating organization for the period presented; and

(2) The nationally recognized statistical rating organization must attach to the report filed pursuant to paragraph (a)(7) of this section a signed statement by the chief executive officer of the nationally recognized statistical rating organization or, if the nationally recognized statistical rating organization does not have a chief executive officer, an individual performing similar functions, stating that the chief executive officer or equivalent individual has responsibility for the report and, to the best knowledge of the chief executive officer or equivalent individual, the report fairly presents, in all material respects: an assessment by management of the effectiveness of the internal control structure during the fiscal year that includes a description of the responsibility of management in establishing and maintaining an effective internal control structure; a description of each material weakness in the internal control structure identified during the fiscal year, if any, and a description, if applicable, of how each identified material weakness was addressed; and an assessment by management of the effectiveness of the internal control structure as of the end of the fiscal year.

(c) The Commission may grant an extension of time or an exemption with respect to any requirements in this rule either unconditionally or on specified terms and conditions on the written request of a nationally recognized statistical rating organization if the Commission finds that such extension or exemption is necessary or appropriate in the public interest and consistent with the protection of investors.

(d) *Electronic filing.* The reports must be filed with or furnished to, as applicable, the Commission electronically on EDGAR as PDF documents in the format required by the EDGAR Filer Manual, as defined in Rule 11 of Regulation S–T.

(e) *Confidential treatment.* Information in a report filed or furnished, as applicable, on a confidential basis and for which confidential treatment has been requested pursuant to applicable Commission rules will be accorded confidential treatment to the extent permitted by law. Confidential treatment may be requested by marking each page "Confidential Treatment Requested" and by complying with Commission rules governing confidential treatment.

Rule 17g–4. Prevention of misuse of material nonpublic information

(a) The written policies and procedures a nationally recognized statistical rating organization establishes, maintains, and enforces to prevent the misuse of material, nonpublic information pursuant to section 15E(g)(1) of the Act (15 U.S.C. 78o–7(g)(1)) must include policies and procedures reasonably designed to prevent:

(1) The inappropriate dissemination within and outside the nationally recognized statistical rating organization of material nonpublic information obtained in connection with the performance of credit rating services;

(2) A person within the nationally recognized statistical rating organization from purchasing, selling, or otherwise benefiting from any transaction in securities or money market instruments when the person is aware of material nonpublic information obtained in connection with the performance of credit rating services that affects the securities or money market instruments; and

(3) The inappropriate dissemination within and outside the nationally recognized statistical rating organization of a pending credit rating action before issuing the credit rating on the Internet or through another readily accessible means.

(b) For the purposes of this rule, the term *person within a nationally recognized statistical rating organization* means a nationally recognized statistical rating organization, its credit rating affiliates identified on Form NRSRO, and any partner, officer, director, branch manager, and employee of the nationally recognized statistical rating organization or its credit rating affiliates (or any person occupying a similar status or performing similar functions).

Rule 17g–5. Conflicts of interest*

(a) A person within a nationally recognized statistical rating organization is prohibited from having a conflict of interest relating to the issuance or main-

* On November 22, 2011, the SEC issued an Order Extending Temporary Conditional Exemption for Nationally Recognized Statistical Rating Organizations from Requirements of Rule 17g–5 under the Securities Exchange Act Of 1934. Pursuant to the Order, an NRSRO is not required to comply with Rule Rule 17g–5(a)(3) until December 2, 2014 with respect to credit ratings where: (1) The issuer of the security or money market instrument is not a U.S. person; and (2) The NRSRO has a reasonable basis to conclude that the structured finance product will be offered and sold upon issuance, and that any arranger linked to the structured finance product will effect transactions of the structured finance product after issuance, only in transactions that occur outside the U.S. The SEC release number is 34–70919.

tenance of a credit rating identified in paragraph (b) of this rule, unless:

(1) The nationally recognized statistical rating organization has disclosed the type of conflict of interest in Exhibit 6 to Form NRSRO in accordance with section 15E(a)(1)(B)(vi) of the Act (15 U.S.C. 78o–7(a)(1)(B)(vi)) and Rule 17g–1;

(2) The nationally recognized statistical rating organization has established and is maintaining and enforcing written policies and procedures to address and manage conflicts of interest in accordance with section 15E(h) of the Act (15 U.S.C. 78o–7(h)); and

(3) In the case of the conflict of interest identified in paragraph (b)(9) of this section relating to issuing or maintaining a credit rating for a security or money market instrument issued by an asset pool or as part of any asset-backed securities transaction, the nationally recognized statistical rating organization:

(i) Maintains on a password-protected Internet website a list of each such security or money market instrument for which it is currently in the process of determining an initial credit rating in chronological order and identifying the type of security or money market instrument, the name of the issuer, the date the rating process was initiated, and the Internet website address where the issuer, sponsor, or underwriter of the security or money market instrument represents that the information described in paragraphs (a)(3)(iii)(C) through E of this section can be accessed;

(ii) Provides free and unlimited access to such password-protected Internet website during the applicable calendar year to any nationally recognized statistical rating organization that provides it with a copy of the certification described in paragraph (e) of this section that covers that calendar year, provided that such certification indicates that the nationally recognized statistical rating organization providing the certification either:

(A) Determined and maintained credit ratings for at least 10% of the issued securities and money market instruments for which it accessed information pursuant to Rule 17g–5(a)(3)(iii) in the calendar year prior to the year covered by the certification, if it accessed such information for 10 or more issued securities or money market instruments; or

(B) Has not accessed information pursuant to Rule 17g–5(a)(3) 10 or more times during the most recently ended calendar year; and

(iii) Obtains from the issuer, sponsor, or underwriter of each such security or money market instrument a written representation that can reasonably be relied upon that the issuer, sponsor, or underwriter will:

(A) Maintain the information described in paragraphs (a)(3)(iii)(C) through E of this section available at an identified password-protected Internet website that presents the information in a manner indicating which information currently should be relied on to determine or monitor the credit rating;

(B) Provide access to such password-protected Internet website during the applicable calendar year to any nationally recognized statistical rating organization that provides it with a copy of the certification described in paragraph (e) of this section that covers that calendar year, provided that such certification indicates that the nationally recognized statistical rating organization providing the certification either:

(*1*) determined and maintained credit ratings for at least 10% of the issued securities and money market instruments for which it accessed information pursuant to Rule 17g–5(a)(3)(iii) in the calendar year prior to the year covered by the certification, if it accessed such information for 10 or more issued securities or money market instruments; or

(*2*) has not accessed information pursuant to Rule 17g–5(a)(3) 10 or more times during the most recently ended calendar year.

(C) Post on such password-protected Internet website all information the issuer, sponsor, or underwriter provides to the nationally recognized statistical rating organization, or contracts with a third party to provide to the nationally recognized statistical rating organization, for the purpose of determining the initial credit rating for the security or money market instrument, including information about the characteristics of the assets underlying or referenced by the security or money market instrument, and the legal structure of the security or money market instrument, at the same time such information is provided to the nationally recognized statistical rating organization; and

(D) Post on such password-protected Internet website all information the issuer, sponsor, or underwriter provides to the nationally recognized statistical rating organization, or contracts with a third party to provide to the nationally recognized statistical rating organization, for the purpose of undertaking credit rating surveillance on the security or money market instrument, including information about the characteristics and performance of the assets underlying or referenced by the security or money market instrument at the same time such information is provided to the nationally recognized statistical rating organization.

(E) Post on such password-protected Internet website, promptly after receipt, any executed Form ABS Due Diligence–15E (17 CFR 249b.500) containing information about the security or money market instrument delivered by a person employed to provide third-party due diligence services with respect to the security or money market instrument.

(b) *Conflicts of Interest.* For purposes of this rule, each of the following is a conflict of interest:

(1) Being paid by issuers or underwriters to determine credit ratings with respect to securities or money market instruments they issue or underwrite.

(2) Being paid by obligors to determine credit ratings with respect to the obligors.

(3) Being paid for services in addition to determining credit ratings by issuers, underwriters, or obligors that have paid the nationally recognized statistical rating organization to determine a credit rating.

(4) Being paid by persons for subscriptions to receive or access the credit ratings of the nationally recognized statistical rating organization and/or for other services offered by the nationally recognized statistical rating organization where such persons may use the credit ratings of the nationally recognized statistical rating organization to comply with, and obtain benefits or relief under, statutes and regulations using the term *nationally recognized statistical rating organization.*

(5) Being paid by persons for subscriptions to receive or access the credit ratings of the nationally recognized statistical rating organization and/or for other services offered by the nationally recognized statistical rating organization where such persons also may own investments or have entered into transactions that could be favorably or adversely impacted by a credit rating issued by the nationally recognized statistical rating organization.

(6) Allowing persons within the nationally recognized statistical rating organization to directly own securities or money market instruments of, or having other direct ownership interests in, issuers or obligors subject to a credit rating determined by the nationally recognized statistical rating organization.

(7) Allowing persons within the nationally recognized statistical rating organization to have a business relationship that is more than an arms length ordinary course of business relationship with issuers or obligors subject to a credit rating determined by the nationally recognized statistical rating organization.

(8) Having a person associated with the nationally recognized statistical rating organization that is a broker or dealer engaged in the business of underwriting securities or money market instruments.

(9) Issuing or maintaining a credit rating for a security or money market instrument issued by an asset pool or as part of any asset-backed securities transaction that was paid for by the issuer, sponsor, or underwriter of the security or money market instrument;

(10) Any other type of conflict of interest relating to the issuance of credit ratings by the nationally recognized statistical rating organization that is material to the nationally recognized statistical rating organization and that is identified by the nationally recognized statistical rating organization in Exhibit 6 to Form NRSRO in accordance with section 15E(a)(1)(B)(vi) of the Act and Rule 17g–1.

(c) *Prohibited Conflicts.* A nationally recognized statistical rating organization is prohibited from having the following conflicts of interest relating to the issuance or maintenance of a credit rating as a credit rating agency:

(1) The nationally recognized statistical rating organization issues or maintains a credit rating solicited by a person that, in the most recently ended fiscal year, provided the nationally recog-

nized statistical rating organization with net revenue (as reported under Rule 17g–3) equaling or exceeding 10% of the total net revenue of the nationally recognized statistical rating organization for the fiscal year;

(2) The nationally recognized statistical rating organization issues or maintains a credit rating with respect to a person (excluding a sovereign nation or an agency of a sovereign nation) where the nationally recognized statistical rating organization, a credit analyst that participated in determining the credit rating, or a person responsible for approving the credit rating, directly owns securities of, or has any other direct ownership interest in, the person that is subject to the credit rating;

(3) The nationally recognized statistical rating organization issues or maintains a credit rating with respect to a person associated with the nationally recognized statistical rating organization;

(4) The nationally recognized statistical rating organization issues or maintains a credit rating where a credit analyst who participated in determining the credit rating, or a person responsible for approving the credit rating, is an officer or director of the person that is subject to the credit rating;

(5) The nationally recognized statistical rating organization issues or maintains a credit rating with respect to an obligor or security where the nationally recognized statistical rating organization or a person associated with the nationally recognized statistical rating organization made recommendations to the obligor or the issuer, underwriter, or sponsor of the security about the corporate or legal structure, assets, liabilities, or activities of the obligor or issuer of the security;

(6) The nationally recognized statistical rating organization issues or maintains a credit rating where the fee paid for the rating was negotiated, discussed, or arranged by a person within the nationally recognized statistical rating organization who has responsibility for participating in determining credit ratings or for developing or approving procedures or methodologies used for determining credit ratings, including qualitative and quantitative models;

(7) The nationally recognized statistical rating organization issues or maintains a credit rating where a credit analyst who participated in determining or monitoring the credit rating, or a person responsible for approving the credit rating received gifts, including entertainment, from the obligor being rated, or from the issuer, underwriter, or sponsor of the securities being rated, other than items provided in the context of normal business activities such as meetings that have an aggregate value of no more than $25; or

(8) The nationally recognized statistical rating organization issues or maintains a credit rating where a person within the nationally recognized statistical rating organization who participates in determining or monitoring the credit rating, or developing or approving procedures or methodologies used for determining the credit rating, including qualitative and quantitative models, also:

(i) Participates in sales or marketing of a product or service of the nationally recognized statistical rating organization or a product or service of an affiliate of the nationally recognized statistical rating organization; or

(ii) Is influenced by sales or marketing considerations.

(d) For the purposes of this rule, the term *person within a nationally recognized statistical rating organization* means a nationally recognized statistical rating organization, its credit rating affiliates identified on Form NRSRO, and any partner, officer, director, branch manager, and employee of the nationally recognized statistical rating organization or its credit rating affiliates (or any person occupying a similar status or performing similar functions).

(e) *Certification.* In order to access a password-protected Internet website described in paragraph (a)(3) of this section, a nationally recognized statistical rating organization must furnish to the Commission, for each calendar year for which it is requesting a password, the following certification, signed by a person duly authorized by the certifying entity:

The undersigned hereby certifies that it will access the Internet websites described in Rule 17g–5(a)(3) solely for the purpose of determining or monitoring credit ratings. Further, the undersigned certifies that it will keep the information it accesses pursuant to Rule 17g–5(a)(3) confidential and treat it as material nonpublic information subject to its written policies and procedures established, maintained, and enforced pursuant to section 15E(g)(1) of the Act and Rule 17g–4. Further, the undersigned certifies that it will determine and maintain credit ratings for at least 10% of the issued securities and money market instruments for which it accesses information pursuant to Rule

17g–5(a)(3)(iii), if it accesses such information for 10 or more issued securities or money market instruments in the calendar year covered by the certification. Further, the undersigned certifies one of the following as applicable: (1) In the most recent calendar year during which it accessed information pursuant Rule 17g–5(a)(3), the undersigned accessed information for [Insert Number] issued securities and money market instruments through Internet websites described in Rule 17g–5(a)(3) and determined and maintained credit ratings for [Insert Number] of such securities and money market instruments; or (2) The undersigned previously has not accessed information pursuant to Rule 17g–5(a)(3) 10 or more times during the most recently ended calendar year.

(f) Upon written application by a nationally recognized statistical rating organization, the Commission may exempt, either unconditionally or on specified terms and conditions, such nationally recognized statistical rating organization from the provisions of paragraph (c)(8) of this section if the Commission finds that due to the small size of the nationally recognized statistical rating organization it is not appropriate to require the separation within the nationally recognized statistical rating organization of the production of credit ratings from sales and marketing activities and such exemption is in the public interest.

(g) In a proceeding pursuant to section 15E(d)(1) of the Act, the Commission shall suspend or revoke the registration of a nationally recognized statistical rating organization if the Commission finds, in lieu of a finding specified under sections 15E(d)(1)(A), (B), (C), (D), (E), or (F) of the Act, that the nationally recognized statistical rating organization has violated a rule issued under section 15E(h) of the Act and that the violation affected a credit rating.

Rule 17g–6. Prohibited acts and practices

(a) *Prohibitions.* A nationally recognized statistical rating organization is prohibited from engaging in any of the following unfair, coercive, or abusive practices:

(1) Conditioning or threatening to condition the issuance of a credit rating on the purchase by an obligor or issuer, or an affiliate of the obligor or issuer, of any other services or products, including pre-credit rating assessment products, of the nationally recognized statistical rating organization or any person associated with the nationally recognized statistical rating organization.

(2) Issuing, or offering or threatening to issue, a credit rating that is not determined in accordance with the nationally recognized statistical rating organization's established procedures and methodologies for determining credit ratings, based on whether the rated person, or an affiliate of the rated person, purchases or will purchase the credit rating or any other service or product of the nationally recognized statistical rating organization or any person associated with the nationally recognized statistical rating organization.

(3) Modifying, or offering or threatening to modify, a credit rating in a manner that is contrary to the nationally recognized statistical rating organization's established procedures and methodologies for modifying credit ratings based on whether the rated person, or an affiliate of the rated person, purchases or will purchase the credit rating or any other service or product of the nationally recognized statistical rating organization or any person associated with the nationally recognized statistical rating organization.

(4) Issuing or threatening to issue a lower credit rating, lowering or threatening to lower an existing credit rating, refusing to issue a credit rating, or withdrawing or threatening to withdraw a credit rating, with respect to securities or money market instruments issued by an asset pool or as part of any asset-backed or mortgage-backed securities transaction, unless all or a portion of the assets within such pool or part of such transaction also are rated by the nationally recognized statistical rating organization, where such practice is engaged in by the nationally recognized statistical rating organization for an anticompetitive purpose.

Rule 17g–7. Disclosure requirements

(a) *Disclosures to be made when taking a rating action.* Except as provided in paragraph (a)(3) of this section, a nationally recognized statistical rating organization must publish the items described in paragraphs (a)(1) and (2) of this section, as applicable, when taking a rating action with respect to a credit rating assigned to an obligor, security, or money market instrument in a class of credit ratings for which the nationally recognized statistical rating organization is registered. For purposes of this section, the term *rating action* means any of the following: the publication of an expected or preliminary credit rating assigned to an obligor, security, or money market instrument before the publication of an initial credit rating; an initial credit rating; an upgrade or downgrade of an existing credit rating (including a downgrade to, or assignment of, default); and an affirmation or withdrawal of an existing credit rating if the affirmation or withdrawal is the result of a review of the credit rating assigned to the obligor, security, or money market instrument by the nationally recognized statistical rating organization using applicable procedures and methodologies for determining credit ratings. The items described in paragraphs (a)(1) and (2) of this section must be published in the same manner as the credit rating that is the result or subject of the rating action and made available to the same persons who can receive or access the credit rating that is the result or subject of the rating action.

(1) *Information disclosure form.* A form generated by the nationally recognized statistical rating organization that meets the requirements of paragraphs (a)(1)(i) through (iii) of this section.

(i) *Format.* The form generated by the nationally recognized statistical rating organization must be in a format that:

(A) Organizes the information into numbered items that are identified by the type of information being disclosed and a reference to the paragraph in this section that specifies the disclosure of the information, and are in the order that the paragraphs specifying the information to be disclosed are codified in this section;

NOTE TO PARAGRAPH (a)(1)(i)(A): A given item in the form should be identified by a title that identifies the type of information and references paragraph (a)(1)(ii)(A) , (B), (C), (D), (E), (F), (G), (H), (I), (J), (K), (L), (M), (N), or (a)(2) of this section based on the information being disclosed in the item. For example, the information specified in paragraph (a)(1)(ii)(C) of this section should be identified with the caption "Main Assumptions and Principles Used to Construct the Rating Methodology used to Determine the Credit Rating as required by Paragraph (a)(1)(ii)(C) of Rule 17g–7"). The form must organize the items of information in the following order: items 1 through 14 must contain the information specified in paragraphs (a)(1)(ii)(A) through (N) of this section, respectively, and item 15 must contain the certifications specified in paragraph (a)(2) of this section (the information specified in each paragraph comprising a separate item). For example, item 3 must contain the information specified in paragraph (a)(1)(ii)(C) of this section.

(B) Is easy to use and helpful for users of credit ratings to understand the information contained in the form; and

(C) Provides the content described in paragraphs (a)(1)(ii)(K) through (M) of this section in a manner that is directly comparable across types of obligors, securities, and money market instruments.

(ii) *Content.* The form generated by the nationally recognized statistical rating organization must contain the following information about the credit rating:

(A) The symbol, number, or score in the rating scale used by the nationally recognized statistical rating organization to denote credit rating categories and notches within categories assigned to the obligor, security, or money market instrument that is the subject of the credit rating and, as applicable, the identity of the obligor or the identity and a description of the security or money market instrument;

(B) The version of the procedure or methodology used to determine the credit rating;

(C) The main assumptions and principles used in constructing the procedures and methodologies used to determine the credit rating, including qualitative methodologies and quantitative inputs, and, if the credit rating is for a structured finance product, assumptions about the correlation of defaults across the underlying assets;

(D) The potential limitations of the credit rating, including the types of risks excluded from the credit rating that the nationally recognized statistical rating organization does not comment on, including, as applicable, liquidity, market, and other risks;

(E) Information on the uncertainty of the credit rating including:

(*1*) Information on the reliability, accuracy, and quality of the data relied on in determining the credit rating; and

(*2*) A statement relating to the extent to which data essential to the determination of the credit rating were reliable or limited, including:

(*i*) Any limits on the scope of historical data; and

(*ii*) Any limits on accessibility to certain documents or other types of information that would have better informed the credit rating;

(F) Whether and to what extent the nationally recognized statistical rating organization used due diligence services of a third party in taking the rating action, and, if the nationally recognized statistical rating organization used such services, either:

(*1*) A description of the information that the third party reviewed in conducting the due diligence services and a summary of the findings and conclusions of the third party; or

(*2*) A cross-reference to a Form ABS Due Diligence–15E executed by the third party that is published with the form, provided the cross-referenced Form ABS Due Diligence–15E (§ 249b.500 of this chapter) contains a description of the information that the third party reviewed in conducting the due diligence services and a summary of the findings and conclusions of the third party;

(G) If applicable, how servicer or remittance reports were used, and with what frequency, to conduct surveillance of the credit rating;

(H) A description of the types of data about any obligor, issuer, security, or money market instrument that were relied upon for the purpose of determining the credit rating;

(I) A statement containing an overall assessment of the quality of information available and considered in determining the credit rating for the obligor, security, or money market instrument, in relation to the quality of information available to the nationally recognized statistical rating organization in rating similar obligors, securities, or money market instruments;

(J) Information relating to conflicts of interest of the nationally recognized statistical rating organization, which must include:

(*1*) As applicable, a statement that the nationally recognized statistical rating organization was:

(*i*) Paid to determine the credit rating by the obligor being rated or the issuer, underwriter, depositor, or sponsor of the security or money market instrument being rated;

(*ii*) Paid to determine the credit rating by a person other than the obligor being rated or the issuer, underwriter, depositor, or sponsor of the security or money market instrument being rated; or

(*iii*) Not paid to determine the credit rating;

(*2*) If applicable, in a statement required under paragraph (a)(1)(ii)(J)(*1*)(*i*) or (*ii*) of this section, a statement that the nationally recognized statistical rating organization also was paid for services other than determining credit ratings during the most recently ended fiscal year by the person that paid the nationally recognized statistical rating organization to determine the credit rating; and

(*3*) If the rating action results from a review conducted pursuant to section 15E(h)(4)(A) of the Act and Rule 17g–8(c), the following information (as applicable):

(*i*) If the rating action is a revision of a credit rating pursuant to Rule 17g–8(c)(2)(i)(A), an explanation that the reason for the action is the discovery that a credit rating assigned to the obligor, security, or money market instrument in one or more prior rating actions was influenced by a conflict of interest, including a description of the nature of the conflict, the date and associated credit rating of each prior rating action that the nationally recognized statistical rating organization has determined was influenced by the conflict, and a description of the impact the conflict had on the prior rating action or actions; or

(*ii*) If the rating action is an affirmation of a credit rating pursuant to Rule 17g–8(c)(2)(i)(B), an explanation that the reason for the action is the discovery that a credit rating assigned to the obligor, security, or money market instrument in one or more prior rating actions was influenced by a conflict of interest, including a description of the nature of the conflict, an explanation of why no rating action was taken to revise the credit rating notwithstanding the presence of the conflict, the date and associated credit rating of each prior rating action the nationally recognized statistical rating organization has determined was influenced by the conflict, and a description of the impact the conflict had on the prior rating action or actions.

(K) An explanation or measure of the potential volatility of the credit rating, including:

(*1*) Any factors that are reasonably likely to lead to a change in the credit rating; and

(*2*) The magnitude of the change that could occur under different market conditions determined by the nationally recognized statistical rating organization to be relevant to the rating;

(L) Information on the content of the credit rating, including:

(*1*) If applicable, the historical performance of the credit rating; and

(*2*) The expected probability of default and the expected loss in the event of default;

(M) Information on the sensitivity of the credit rating to assumptions made by the nationally recognized statistical rating organization, including:

(*1*) Five assumptions made in the ratings process that, without accounting for any other factor, would have the greatest impact on the credit rating if the assumptions were proven false or inaccurate; provided that, if the nationally recognized statistical rating organization has made fewer than five such assumptions, it need only disclose information on the assumptions that would have an impact on the credit rating; and

(*2*) An analysis, using specific examples, of how each of the assumptions identified in paragraph (a)(1)(ii)(M)(1) of this section impacts the credit rating;

(N)(*1*) If the credit rating is assigned to an asset-backed security as defined in section 3(a)(79) of the Act, information on:

(*i*) The representations, warranties, and enforcement mechanisms available to investors which were disclosed in the prospectus, private placement memorandum or other offering documents for the asset-backed security and that relate to the asset pool underlying the asset-backed security; and

(*ii*) How they differ from the representations, warranties, and enforcement mechanisms in issuances of similar securities;

(*2*) A nationally recognized statistical rating organization must include the information required under paragraph (a)(1)(ii)(N)(1) of this section only if the rating action is a preliminary credit rating, an initial credit rating, or, in the case of a rating action other than a preliminary credit rating or initial credit rating, the rating action is the first rating action taken after a material change in the representations, warranties, or enforcement mechanisms described in paragraph (a)(1)(ii)(N)(1) of this section and the rating action involves an asset-backed security that was initially rated by the nationally recognized statistical rating organization on or after September 26, 2011.

(iii) *Attestation.* The nationally recognized statistical rating organization must attach to the form a signed statement by a person within the nationally recognized statistical rating organization stating that the person has responsibility for the rating action and, to the best knowledge of the person:

(A) No part of the credit rating was influenced by any other business activities;

(B) The credit rating was based solely upon the merits of the obligor, security, or money market instrument being rated; and

(C) The credit rating was an independent evaluation of the credit risk of the obligor, security, or money market instrument.

(2) *Third-party due diligence certification.* Any executed Form ABS Due Diligence–15E (§ 249b.500 of this chapter) containing information about the security or money market instrument subject to the rating action that is received by the nationally recognized statistical rating organization or obtained by the nationally recognized statistical rating organization through an Internet website maintained by the issuer, sponsor, or underwriter of the security or money market instrument pursuant to Rule 17g–5(a)(3).

(3) *Exemption.* The provisions of paragraphs (a)(1) and (a)(2) do not apply to a rating action if:

(i) The rated obligor or issuer of the rated security or money market instrument is not a U.S. person (as defined in § 230.902(k) of this chapter); and

(ii) The nationally recognized statistical rating organization has a reasonable basis to conclude that a security or money market instrument issued by the rated obligor or the issuer will be offered and sold upon issuance, and that any underwriter or arranger linked to the security or money market instrument will effect transactions in the security or money market instrument after issuance, only in transactions that occur outside the United States.

(b) *Disclosure of credit rating histories*—(1) *Credit ratings subject to the disclosure requirement.* A nationally recognized statistical rating organization must publicly disclose for free on an easily accessible portion of its corporate Internet website:

(i) For a class of credit rating in which the nationally recognized statistical rating organization is registered with the Commission as of the effective date of paragraph (b) of this section, the credit rating assigned to each obligor, security, and money market instrument in the class that was outstanding as of, or initially determined on or after, the date three years prior to the effective date of this rule, and any subsequent upgrade or downgrade of the credit rating (including a downgrade to, or assignment of, default), and a withdrawal of the credit rating; and

(ii) For a class of credit rating in which the nationally recognized statistical rating organization is registered with the Commission after the effective date of paragraph (b) of this section, the credit rating assigned to each obligor, security, and money market instrument in the class that was outstanding as of, or initially determined on or after, the date three years prior to the date the nationally recognized statistical rating organization is registered in the class, and any subsequent upgrade or downgrade of the credit rating (including a downgrade to, or assignment of, default), and a withdrawal of the credit rating.

(2) Information. A nationally recognized statistical rating organization must include, at a minimum, the following information with each credit rating disclosed pursuant to paragraph (b)(1) of this section:

(i) The identity of the nationally recognized statistical rating organization disclosing the rating action;

(ii) The date of the rating action;

(iii) If the rating action is taken with respect to a credit rating of an obligor as an entity, the following identifying information about the obligor, as applicable:

(A) The Legal Entity Identifier issued by a utility endorsed or otherwise governed by the Global LEI Regulatory Oversight Committee or the Global LEI Foundation (LEI) of the obligor, if available, or, if an LEI is not available, the Central Index Key (CIK) number of the obligor, if available; and

(B) The name of the obligor.

(iv) If the rating action is taken with respect to a credit rating of a security or money market instrument, as applicable:

(A) The LEI of the issuer of the security or money market instrument, if available, or, if an LEI is not available, the CIK number of the issuer of the security or money market instrument, if available;

(B) The name of the issuer of the security or money market instrument; and

(C) The CUSIP of the security or money market instrument;

(v) A classification of the rating action as either:

(A) An addition to the rating history disclosure because the credit rating was outstanding as of the date three years prior to the effective date of the requirements in paragraph (b) of this section or because the credit rating was outstanding as of the date three years prior to the nationally recognized statistical rating organization becoming registered in the class of credit ratings;

(B) An initial credit rating;

(C) An upgrade of an existing credit rating;

(D) A downgrade of an existing credit rating, which would include classifying the obligor, security, or money market instrument as in default, if applicable; or

(E) A withdrawal of an existing credit rating and, if the classification is withdrawal, the nationally recognized statistical rating organization also must classify the reason for the withdrawal as either:

(*1*) The obligor defaulted, or the security or money market instrument went into default;

(*2*) The obligation subject to the credit rating was extinguished by payment in full of all outstanding principal and interest due on the obligation according to the terms of the obligation; or

(*3*) The credit rating was withdrawn for reasons other than those set forth in paragraph (b)(2)(v)(E)(1) or (2) of this section; and

(vi) The classification of the class or subclass that applies to the credit rating as either:

(A) Financial institutions, brokers, or dealers;

(B) Insurance companies;

(C) Corporate issuers; or

(D) Issuers of structured finance products in one of the following subclasses:

(*1*) Residential mortgage backed securities ("RMBS") (for purposes of this subclass, RMBS means a securitization primarily of residential mortgages);

(*2*) Commercial mortgage backed securities ("CMBS") (for purposes of this subclass, CMBS means a securitization primarily of commercial mortgages);

(*3*) Collateralized loan obligations ("CLOs") (for purposes of this subclass, a CLO means a securitization primarily of commercial loans);

(*4*) Collateralized debt obligations ("CDOs") (for purposes of this subclass, a CDO means a securitization primarily of other debt instruments such as RMBS, CMBS, CLOs, CDOs, other asset backed securities, and corporate bonds);

(*5*) Asset-backed commercial paper conduits ("ABCP") (for purposes of this subclass, ABCP means short term notes issued by a structure that securitizes a variety of financial assets, such as trade receivables or credit card receivables, which secure the notes);

(*6*) Other asset-backed securities ("other ABS") (for purposes of this subclass, other ABS means a securitization primarily of auto loans, auto leases, floor plans, credit card receivables, student loans, consumer loans, or equipment leases); or

(*7*) Other structured finance products ("other SFPs") (for purposes of this subclass, other SFPs means any structured finance product not identified in paragraphs (b)(2)(iv)(D)(1) through (6)) of this section; or

(E) Issuers of government securities, municipal securities, or securities issued by a foreign government in one of the following subclasses:

(*1*) Sovereign issuers;

(*2*) U.S. public finance; or

(*3*) International public finance; and

(vii) The credit rating symbol, number, or score in the applicable rating scale of the nationally recognized statistical rating organization assigned to the obligor, security, or money market instrument as a result of the rating action or, if the credit rating remained unchanged as a result of the action, the credit rating symbol, number, or score in the applicable rating scale of the nationally recognized statistical rating organization assigned to the obligor, security, or money market instrument as of the date of the rating action (in either case, include a credit rating in a default category, if applicable).

(3) *Format and frequency of updating.* The information identified in paragraph (b)(2) of this section must be disclosed in an interactive data file that uses an XBRL (eXtensible Business Reporting Language) format and the List of XBRL Tags for nationally recognized statistical rating organizations as published on the Internet website of the Commission, and must be updated no less frequently than monthly.

(4) *Timing.* The nationally recognized statistical rating organization must disclose the information required in paragraph (b)(2) of this section:

(i) Within twelve months from the date the rating action is taken, if the credit rating subject to the action was paid for by the obligor being rated or by the issuer, underwriter, depositor, or sponsor of the security being rated; or

(ii) Within twenty-four months from the date the rating action is taken, if the credit rating subject to the action is not a credit rating described in paragraph (b)(4)(i) of this section.

(5) *Removal of a credit rating history.* The nationally recognized statistical rating organization may cease disclosing a rating history of an obligor, security, or money market instrument if at least 15 years have elapsed since a rating action classified as a withdrawal of a credit rating pursuant to paragraph (b)(2)(v)(E) of this section was disclosed in the rating history of the obligor, security, or money market instrument.

Rule 17g–8. Policies, procedures, and internal controls

(a) *Policies and procedures with respect to the procedures and methodologies used to determine credit ratings.* A nationally recognized statistical rating organization must establish, maintain, enforce, and document policies and procedures reasonably designed to ensure:

(1) That the procedures and methodologies, including qualitative and quantitative data and models, the nationally recognized statistical rating organization uses to determine credit ratings are approved by its board of directors or a body performing a function similar to that of a board of directors.

(2) That the procedures and methodologies, including qualitative and quantitative data and models, the nationally recognized statistical rating organization uses to determine credit ratings are developed and modified in accordance with the policies and procedures of the nationally recognized statistical rating organization.

(3) That material changes to the procedures and methodologies, including changes to qualitative and quantitative data and models, the nationally recognized statistical rating organization uses to determine credit ratings are:

(i) Applied consistently to all current and future credit ratings to which the changed procedures or methodologies apply; and

(ii) To the extent that the changes are to surveillance or monitoring procedures and methodologies, applied to current credit ratings to which the changed procedures or methodologies apply within a reasonable period of time, taking into consideration the number of credit ratings impacted, the complexity of the procedures and methodologies used to determine the credit ratings, and the type of obligor, security, or money market instrument being rated.

(4) That the nationally recognized statistical rating organization promptly publishes on an easily accessible portion of its corporate Internet website:

(i) Material changes to the procedures and methodologies, including to qualitative models or quantitative inputs, the nationally recognized statistical rating organization uses to determine credit ratings, the reason for the changes, and the likelihood the changes will result in changes to any current credit ratings; and

(ii) Notice of the existence of a significant error identified in a procedure or methodology, including a qualitative or quantitative model, the nationally recognized statistical rating organization uses to determine credit ratings that may result in a change to current credit ratings.

(5) That the nationally recognized statistical rating organization discloses the version of a credit rating procedure or methodology, including the qualitative methodology or quantitative inputs, used with respect to a particular credit rating.

(b) *Policies and procedures with respect to credit rating symbols, numbers, or scores.* A nationally recognized statistical rating organization must establish, maintain, enforce, and document policies and procedures that are reasonably designed to:

(1) Assess the probability that an issuer of a security or money market instrument will default, fail to make timely payments, or otherwise not make payments to investors in accordance with the terms of the security or money market instrument.

(2) Clearly define each symbol, number, or score in the rating scale used by the nationally recognized statistical rating organization to denote a credit rating category and notches within a category for each class of credit ratings for which the nationally recognized statistical rating organization is registered (including subclasses within each class) and to include such definitions in Exhibit 1 to Form NRSRO (§ 249b.300 of this chapter).

(3) Apply any symbol, number, or score defined pursuant to paragraph (b)(2) of this section in a manner that is consistent for all types of obligors, securities, and money market instruments for which the symbol, number, or score is used.

(c) *Policies and procedures with respect to look-back reviews.* The policies and procedures a nationally recognized statistical rating organization is required to establish, maintain, and enforce pursuant to section 15E(h)(4)(A) of the Act must address instances in which a review conducted pursuant to those policies and procedures determines that a conflict of interest influenced a credit rating assigned to an obligor, security, or money market instrument by including, at a minimum, procedures that are reasonably designed to ensure that the nationally recognized statistical rating organization will:

(1) Promptly determine whether the current credit rating assigned to the obligor, security, or money market instrument must be revised so that it no longer is influenced by a conflict of interest and is solely a product of the documented procedures and methodologies the nationally recognized statistical rating organization uses to determine credit ratings; and

(2)(i) Promptly publish, based on the determination of whether a current credit rating referred to in paragraph (c)(1) of this section must be revised (as applicable):

(A) A revised credit rating, if appropriate, and include with the publication of the revised credit rating the information required by Rule 17g–7(a)(1)(ii)(J)(*3*)(*i*); or

(B) An affirmation of the credit rating, if appropriate, and include with the publication of the affirmation the information required by Rule 17g–7(a)(1)(ii)(J)(*3*)(*ii*).

(ii) If the credit rating is not revised or affirmed pursuant to paragraph (c)(2)(i) of this section within fifteen calendar days of the date of the discovery that the credit rating was influenced by a conflict of interest, publish a rating action placing the credit rating on watch or review and include with the publication an explanation that the reason for the action is the discovery that the credit rating was influenced by a conflict of interest.

(d) *Internal control structures.* A nationally recognized statistical rating organization must take into consideration the factors identified in paragraphs (d)(1) through (4) of this section when establishing, maintaining, enforcing, and documenting an effective internal control structure governing the implementation of and adherence to policies, procedures, and methodologies for determining credit ratings pursuant to section 15E(c)(3)(A) of the Act.

(1) With respect to establishing the internal control structure, the nationally recognized statistical rating organization must take into consideration:

(i) Controls reasonably designed to ensure that a newly developed methodology or proposed update to an in-use methodology for determining credit ratings is subject to an appropriate review process (for example, by persons who are independent from the persons that developed the methodology or methodology update) and to management approval prior to the new or updated methodology being employed by the nationally recognized statistical rating organization to determine credit ratings;

(ii) Controls reasonably designed to ensure that a newly developed methodology or update to an in-use methodology for determining credit ratings is disclosed to the public for consultation prior to the new or updated methodology being employed by the nationally recognized statistical rating organization to determine credit ratings, that the nationally recognized statistical rating organization makes comments received as part of the consultation publicly available, and that the nationally recognized statistical rating organization considers the comments before implementing the methodology;

(iii) Controls reasonably designed to ensure that in-use methodologies for determining credit ratings are periodically reviewed (for example, by persons who are independent from the persons who developed and/or use the methodology) in order to analyze whether the methodology should be updated;

(iv) Controls reasonably designed to ensure that market participants have an opportunity to provide comment on whether in-use methodologies for determining credit ratings should be updated, that the nationally recognized statistical rating organization makes any such comments received publicly available, and that the nationally recognized statistical rating organization considers the comments;

(v) Controls reasonably designed to ensure that newly developed or updated quantitative models proposed to be incorporated into a credit rating methodology are evaluated and validated prior to being put into use;

(vi) Controls reasonably designed to ensure that quantitative models incorporated into in-use credit rating methodologies are periodically reviewed and back-tested;

(vii) Controls reasonably designed to ensure that a nationally recognized statistical rating organization engages in analysis before commencing the rating of a class of obligors, securities, or money market instruments the nationally recognized statistical rating organization has not previously rated to determine whether the nationally recognized statistical rating organization has sufficient competency, access to necessary information, and resources to rate the type of obligor, security, or money market instrument;

(viii) Controls reasonably designed to ensure that a nationally recognized statistical rating organization engages in analysis before commencing the rating of an "exotic" or "bespoke" type of obligor, security, or money market instrument to review the feasibility of determining a credit rating;

(ix) Controls reasonably designed to ensure that measures (for example, statistics) are used to evaluate the performance of credit ratings as part of the review of in-use methodologies for determining credit ratings to analyze whether the methodologies should be updated or the work of the analysts employing the methodologies should be reviewed;

(x) Controls reasonably designed to ensure that, with respect to determining credit ratings, the work and conclusions of the lead credit analyst developing an initial credit rating or conducting surveillance on an existing credit rating is reviewed by other analysts, supervisors, or senior managers before a rating action is formally taken (for example, having the work reviewed through a rating committee process);

(xi) Controls reasonably designed to ensure that a credit analyst documents the steps taken in developing an initial credit rating or conducting surveillance on an existing credit rating with sufficient detail to permit an after-the-fact review or internal audit of the rating file to analyze whether the analyst adhered to the nationally recognized statistical rating organization's procedures and methodologies for determining credit ratings;

(xii) Controls reasonably designed to ensure that the nationally recognized statistical rating organization conducts periodic reviews or internal audits of rating files to analyze whether analysts adhere to the nationally recognized statistical rating organization's procedures and methodologies for determining credit ratings; and

(xiii) Any other controls necessary to establish an effective internal control structure taking into consideration the nature of the business of the nationally recognized statistical rating organization, including its size, activities, organizational structure, and business model.

(2) With respect to maintaining the internal control structure, the nationally recognized statistical rating organization must take into consideration:

(i) Controls reasonably designed to ensure that the nationally recognized statistical rating organization conducts periodic reviews of whether it has devoted sufficient resources to implement and operate the documented internal control structure as designed;

(ii) Controls reasonably designed to ensure that the nationally recognized statistical rating organization conducts periodic reviews or ongoing monitoring to evaluate the effectiveness of the internal control structure and whether it should be updated;

(iii) Controls reasonably designed to ensure that any identified deficiencies in the internal control structure are assessed and addressed on a timely basis;

(iv) Any other controls necessary to maintain an effective internal control structure taking into consideration the nature of the business of the nationally recognized statistical rating organization, including its size, activities, organizational structure, and business model.

(3) With respect to enforcing the internal control structure, the nationally recognized statistical rating organization must take into consideration:

(i) Controls designed to ensure that additional training is provided or discipline taken with respect to employees who fail to adhere to requirements imposed by the internal control structure;

(ii) Controls designed to ensure that a process is in place for employees to report failures to adhere to the internal control structure; and

(iii) Any other controls necessary to enforce an effective internal control structure taking into consideration the nature of the business of the nationally recognized statistical rating organization, including its size, activities, organizational structure, and business model.

(4) With respect to documenting the internal control structure, the nationally recognized statistical rating organization must take into consideration any controls necessary to document an effective internal control structure taking into consideration the nature of the business of the nationally recognized statistical rating organization,

including its size, activities, organizational structure, and business model.

Rule 17g–9. Standards of training, experience, and competence for credit analysts

(a) A nationally recognized statistical rating organization must establish, maintain, enforce, and document standards of training, experience, and competence for the individuals it employs to participate in the determination of credit ratings that are reasonably designed to achieve the objective that the nationally recognized statistical rating organization produces accurate credit ratings in the classes of credit ratings for which the nationally recognized statistical rating organization is registered.

(b) The nationally recognized statistical rating organization must consider the following when establishing the standards required under paragraph (a) of this section:

(1) If the credit rating procedures and methodologies used by the individual involve qualitative analysis, the knowledge necessary to effectively evaluate and process the data relevant to the creditworthiness of the obligor being rated or the issuer of the securities or money market instruments being rated;

(2) If the credit rating procedures and methodologies used by the individual involve quantitative analysis, the technical expertise necessary to understand any models and model inputs that are a part of the procedures and methodologies;

(3) The classes and subclasses of credit ratings for which the individual participates in determining credit ratings and the factors relevant to such classes and subclasses, including the geographic location, sector, industry, regulatory and legal framework, and underlying assets, applicable to the obligors or issuers in the classes and subclasses; and

(4) The complexity of the obligors, securities, or money market instruments for which the individual participates in determining credit ratings.

(c) The nationally recognized statistical rating organization must include the following in the standards required under paragraph (a) of this section:

(1) A requirement for periodic testing of the individuals employed by the nationally recognized statistical rating organization to participate in the determination of credit ratings on their knowledge of the procedures and methodologies used by the nationally recognized statistical rating organization to determine credit ratings in the classes and subclasses of credit ratings for which the individual participates in determining credit ratings; and

(2) A requirement that at least one individual with an appropriate level of experience in performing credit analysis, but not less than three years, participates in the determination of a credit rating.

Rule 17g–10. Certification of providers of third-party due diligence services in connection with asset-backed securities

(a) The written certification that a person employed to provide third-party due diligence services is required to provide to a nationally recognized statistical rating organization pursuant to section 15E(s)(4)(B) of the Act must be on Form ABS Due Diligence–15E (§ 249b.500 of this chapter).

(b) The written certification must be signed by an individual who is duly authorized by the person providing the third-party due diligence services to make such a certification.

(c) A person employed to provide third-party due diligence services will be deemed to have satisfied its obligations under section 15E(s)(4)(B) of the Act if the person promptly delivers an executed Form ABS Due Diligence–15E (§ 249b.500 of this chapter) after completion of the due diligence services to:

(1) A nationally recognized statistical rating organization that provided a written request for the Form prior to the completion of the due diligence services stating that the services relate to a credit rating the nationally recognized statistical rating organization is producing;

(2) A nationally recognized statistical rating organization that provides a written request for the Form after the completion of the due diligence services stating that the services relate to a credit rating the nationally recognized statistical rating organization is producing; and

(3) The issuer or underwriter of the asset-backed security for which the due diligence services relate that maintains the Internet website with respect to the asset-backed security pursuant to Rule 17g–5(a)(3).

(d) For purposes of section 15E(s)(4)(B) of the Act and this section:

(1) The term *due diligence services* means a review of the assets underlying an asset-backed se-

curity, as defined in section 3(a)(79) of the Act for the purpose of making findings with respect to:

(i) The accuracy of the information or data about the assets provided, directly or indirectly, by the securitizer or originator of the assets;

(ii) Whether the origination of the assets conformed to, or deviated from, stated underwriting or credit extension guidelines, standards, criteria, or other requirements;

(iii) The value of collateral securing the assets;

(iv) Whether the originator of the assets complied with federal, state, or local laws or regulations; or

(v) Any other factor or characteristic of the assets that would be material to the likelihood that the issuer of the asset-backed security will pay interest and principal in accordance with applicable terms and conditions.

(2) The term *issuer* includes a sponsor, as defined in § 229.1101 of this chapter, or depositor, as defined in § 229.1101 of this chapter, that participates in the issuance of an asset-backed security, as defined in section 3(a)(79) of the Act.

(3) The term *originator* has the same meaning as in section 15G(a)(4) of the Act.

(4) The term *securitizer* has the same meaning as in section 15G(a)(3) of the Act.

Rule 17h–1T. Risk assessment recordkeeping requirements for associated persons of brokers and dealers

(a) *Requirement to Maintain and Preserve Information.* (1) Every broker or dealer registered with the Commission pursuant to section 15 of the Act, and every municipal securities dealer registered pursuant to Section 15B of the Act for which the Commission is the appropriate regulatory agency, unless exempt pursuant to paragraph (d) of this rule, shall maintain and preserve the following information:

(i) An organizational chart which includes the broker or dealer and all its associated persons. Included in the organizational chart shall be a designation of which associated persons are Material Associated Persons as that term is used in paragraph (a)(2) of this rule;

(ii) Written policies, procedures, or systems concerning the broker or dealer's:

(A) Method(s) for monitoring and controlling financial and operational risks to it resulting from the activities of any of its associated persons, other than a natural person;

(B) Financing and capital adequacy, including information regarding sources of funding, together with a narrative discussion by management of the liquidity of the material assets, the structure of debt capital, and sources of alternative funding; and

(C) Trading positions and risks, such as records regarding reporting responsibilities for trading activities, policies relating to restrictions or limitations on trading securities and financial instruments or products, and a description of the types of reviews conducted to monitor existing positions, and limitations or restrictions on trading activities.

(iii) A description of all material pending legal or arbitration proceedings involving a Material Associated Person or the broker or dealer that are required to be disclosed by the ultimate holding company under generally accepted accounting principles on a consolidated basis;

(iv) Consolidated and consolidating balance sheets, prepared in accordance with generally accepted accounting principles, which may be unaudited and which shall include the notes to the financial statements, as of quarter end for the broker or dealer and its ultimate holding company;

(v) Quarterly consolidated and consolidating income statements and consolidated cash flow statements, prepared in accordance with generally accepted accounting principles, which may be unaudited and which shall include the notes to the financial statements, for the broker or dealer and its ultimate holding company;

NOTE 1 TO PARAGRAPH (a)(1)(v). Statements of comprehensive income (as defined in Rule 1–02 of Regulation S–X) must be included in place of income statements, if required by the applicable generally accepted accounting principles.

(vi) The amount as of quarter end, and at month end if greater than quarter end, of the aggregate long and short securities and commodities positions held by each Material Associated Person, including a separate listing of each single unhedged securities or commodities position, other than U.S. government or agency securities, that exceeds the Materiality Threshold at any month end;

(vii) The notional or contractual amounts, and in the case of options, the value of the underlying instruments, as of quarter end, of financial instruments with off-balance sheet risk and financial instruments with concentrations of credit risk (defined as the possibility that a loss may occur from the failure of another party to perform according to the terms of a contract) where the Material Associated Person operates a trading book, with a separate entry of each commitment where the credit risk (defined as the possibility that a loss may occur from the failure of another party to perform according to the terms of a contract) with respect to a counterparty exceeds the Materiality Threshold at quarter end;

(viii) The aggregate amount as of quarter end, and the amount at month end if greater than quarter end, of all bridge loans and those other material unsecured extensions of credit (not including intra-group receivables) with an initial or remaining maturity of less than one year by each Material Associated Person, together with the allowance for losses for such transactions, including a specific description of any extensions of credit to a single borrower exceeding the Materiality Threshold at any month end;

(ix) The aggregate amount as of quarter end, and the amount at month end if greater than quarter end, of commercial paper, secured and other unsecured borrowing, bank loans, lines of credit, or any other borrowings, and the principal installments of long-term or medium-term debt, scheduled to mature within twelve months from the most recent fiscal quarter for the broker or dealer and each Material Associated Person; and

(x) Data relating to real estate activities, including mortgage loans and investments in real estate, but not including trading positions in whole loans, conducted by each Material Associated Person, including:

(A) Real estate loans and investments by type of property, such as construction and development, residential, commercial and industrial or farmland;

(B) The geographic distribution, as of quarter end, by type of loan or investment where the amount exceeds the Materiality Threshold at quarter end;

(C) The aggregate carrying value of loans which each Material Associated Person deems to be not current as to interest or principal, together with the Material Associated Person's criteria for the determination of which loans are not current, or which are in the process of foreclosure or that have been restructured;

(D) The allowance for losses on loans and on investment real estate by type of loan or investment, and the activity in the allowance for losses account; and

(E) Information about risk concentration in the real estate investment and loan portfolio, including information about risk concentration to a single borrower or location of property if the risk concentration exceeds the Materiality Threshold at quarter end.

(2) The determination of whether an associated person of a broker or dealer is a Material Associated Person shall involve consideration of all aspects of the activities of, and the relationship between, both entities, including without limitation, the following factors:

(i) The legal relationship between the broker or dealer and the associated person;

(ii) The overall financing requirements of the broker or dealer and the associated person, and the degree, if any, to which the broker or dealer and the associated person are financially dependent on each other;

(iii) The degree, if any, to which the broker or dealer or its customers rely on the associated person for operational support or services in connection with the broker's or dealer's business;

(iv) The level of risk present in the activities of the broker's or dealer's associated persons; and

(v) The extent to which the associated person has the authority or the ability to cause a withdrawal of capital from the broker or dealer.

(3) The information, reports and records required by the provisions of this rule shall be maintained and preserved in accordance with the provisions of Rule 17a–4 and shall be kept for a period of not less than three years in an easily accessible place.

(4) For the purposes of this rule and Rule 17h–2T, the term "Materiality Threshold" shall mean the greater of:

(i) $100 million; or

(ii) 10 percent of the broker or dealer's tentative net capital based on the most recently filed Form X–17A–5 or 10 percent of the Material Associated Person's tangible net worth, whichever is greater.

(b) *Special Provisions with Respect to Material Associated Persons Subject to the Supervision of Certain Domestic Regulators.* A broker or dealer shall be deemed to be in compliance with the recordkeeping requirements of paragraph (a) of this rule with respect to a Material Associated Person if:

(1) Such Material Associated Person is subject to examination by, or the reporting requirements of, a Federal banking agency and the broker or dealer maintains in accordance with the provisions of this rule copies of all reports submitted by such Material Associated Person with the Federal banking agency pursuant to section 5211 of the Revised Statutes, section 9 of the Federal Reserve Act, section 7(a) of the Federal Deposit Insurance Act, section 10(b) of the Home Owners' Loan Act, or section 5 of the Bank Holding Company Act of 1956 other than the Form FR 2068; or

(2) If such Material Associated Person is subject to the supervision of an insurance commissioner or other similar official or agency of a state, and the broker or dealer maintains in accordance with the provisions of this rule copies of the Annual and Quarterly Statements with Schedules and Exhibits prepared by the insurance company on forms prescribed by the National Association of Insurance Commissioners; or

(3) In the event an insurance company is not required to prepare Quarterly Statements on forms prescribed by the National Association of Insurance Commissioners, the broker or dealer must maintain and preserve the records required by paragraph (a) of this rule on a quarterly basis; or

(4) In the case of a Material Associated Person that is subject to the supervision of the Commodity Futures Trading Commission, the broker or dealer maintains in accordance with the provisions of this rule copies of the reports filed on Forms 1 FR–FCM or 1 FR–IB by such Material Associated Person with the Commodity Futures Trading Commission.

(c) *Special Provisions with Respect to Material Associated Persons Subject to the Supervision of a Foreign Financial Regulatory Authority.* A broker or dealer shall be deemed to be in compliance with the recordkeeping requirements of paragraph (a) of this rule with respect to a Material Associated Person if such broker or dealer maintains in accordance with the provisions of this rule copies of the reports filed by such Material Associated Persons with a Foreign Financial Regulatory Authority. The broker or dealer shall maintain a copy of the original report and a copy translated into the English language. For the purposes of this rule, the term Foreign Financial Regulatory Authority shall have the meaning set forth in section 3(a)(51) of the Act.

(d) *Exemptions.* (1) The provisions of this rule shall not apply to any broker or dealer which is exempt from the provisions of Rule 15c3–3:

(i) Pursuant to paragraph (k)(1) of Rule 15c3–3; or

(ii) Pursuant to paragraph (k)(2) of Rule 15c3–3; or

(iii) If the broker or dealer does not qualify for an exemption from the provisions of Rule 15c3–3 and such broker or dealer does not hold funds or securities for, or owe money or securities to, customers and does not carry the accounts of or for customers; unless

(iv) In the case of paragraphs (d)(1)(ii) or (d)(1)(iii) of this rule, the broker or dealer maintains capital including debt subordinated in accordance with appendix D of Rule 15c3–1 equal to or greater than $20,000,000.

(2) The provisions of this rule shall not apply to any broker or dealer which maintains capital including debt subordinated in accordance with appendix D of Rule 15c3–1 of less than $250,000, even if the broker or dealer hold funds or securities for, or owes money or securities to, customers or carries the accounts of or for customers.

(3) In calculating capital for the purposes of this paragraph, a broker or dealer shall include the equity capital and subordinated debt of any other registered brokers or dealers that are associated with the broker or dealer and are not otherwise exempt from the provisions pursuant to paragraph (d)(1)(i) of this rule.

(4) The provisions of this rule shall not apply to a broker or dealer that computes certain of its capital charges in accordance with Rule 15c3–1e if that broker or dealer is affiliated with an ultimate holding company that is not an ultimate holding company that has a principal regulator, as defined in Rule 15c3–1(c)(13).

(5) The Commission may, upon written application by a Reporting Broker or Dealer, exempt from

the provisions of this rule, either unconditionally or on specified terms and conditions, any brokers or dealers associated with such Reporting Broker or Dealer. The term "Reporting Broker or Dealer" shall mean, in the case of a broker or dealer that is associated with other registered brokers or dealers, the broker or dealer which maintains the greatest amount of net capital as reported on its most recently fixed Form X–17A–5. In granting exemptions under this rule, the Commission shall consider, among other factors, whether the records and other information required to be maintained pursuant to this rule concerning the Material Associated Persons of the broker or dealer associated with the Reporting Broker or Dealer will be available to the Commission pursuant to Rule 17h–2T.

(e) *Location of Records.* A broker or dealer required to maintain records concerning a Material Associated Person pursuant to this rule may maintain those records either at the Material Associated Person or at a records storage facility provided that the records are located within the boundaries of the United States and the records are kept in an easily accessible place, as that term is used in Rule 17a–4. In order to operate pursuant to the provisions of this paragraph, the Material Associated Person or other entity maintaining the records shall file with the Commission a written undertaking in form acceptable to the Commission, signed by a duly authorized person, to the effect that the records will be treated as if the broker or dealer was maintaining the records pursuant to this rule and that the entity maintaining the records undertakes to permit examination of such records at any time or from time to time during business hours by representatives or designees of the Commission and to promptly furnish the Commission or its designee true, correct, complete and current hard copy of any or all or any part of such records. The election to operate pursuant to the provisions of this paragraph shall not relieve the broker or dealer required to maintain and preserve such records from any of its responsibilities under this rule or Rule 17h–2T.

(f) *Confidentiality.* All information obtained by the Commission pursuant to the provisions of this rule from a broker or dealer concerning a Material Associated Person shall be deemed confidential information for the purposes of section 24(b) of the Act.

(g) *Temporary Implementation Schedule.* Every broker or dealer subject to the requirements of this rule shall maintain and preserve the information required by paragraphs (a)(1)(i), (ii), and (iii) of this rule commencing September 30, 1992. Commencing December 31, 1992, the provisions of this rule shall apply in their entirety.

Rule 17h–2T. Risk assessment reporting requirements for brokers and dealers

(a) *Reporting Requirements of Risk Assessment Information Required to Be Maintained By Rule 17h–1T.* (1) Every broker or dealer registered with the Commission pursuant to section 15 of the Act, and every municipal securities dealer registered pursuant to section 15B of the Act for which the Commission is the appropriate regulatory agency, unless exempt pursuant to paragraph (b) of this rule, shall file a Form 17–H within 60 calendar days after the end of each fiscal quarter. The Form 17–H for the fourth fiscal quarter shall be filed within 60 calendar days of the end of the fiscal year. The cumulative year-end financial statements required by Rule 17h–1T may be filed separately within 105 calendar days of the end of the fiscal year.

(2) The reports required to be filed pursuant to paragraph (a)(1) of this rule shall be considered filed when received at the Commission's principal office in Washington, DC.

(3) For the purposes of this rule, the term Material Associated Person shall have the meaning used in Rule 17h–1T.

(b) *Exemptions.* (1) The provisions of this rule shall not apply to any broker or dealer which is exempt from the provisions of Rule 15c3–3:

(i) Pursuant to paragraph (k)(1) of Rule 15c3–3; or

(ii) Pursuant to paragraph (k)(2) of Rule 15c3–3; or

(iii) If the broker or dealer does not qualify for an exemption from the provisions of Rule 15c3–3 and such broker or dealer does not hold funds or securities for, or owe money or securities to, customers and does not carry the accounts of or for customers; unless

(iv) In the case of paragraphs (b)(1)(ii) or (b)(1)(iii) of this rule, the broker or dealer maintains capital including debt subordinated in accordance with appendix D of Rule 15c3–1 equal to or greater than $20,000,000.

(2) The provisions of this rule shall not apply to any broker or dealer which maintains capital including debt subordinated in accordance with appendix D of Rule 15c3–1 of less than $250,000, even if the broker or dealer hold funds or securi-

ties for, or owes money or securities to, customers or carries the accounts of or for customers.

(3) In calculating capital and subordinated debt for the purposes of this rule, a broker or dealer shall include the equity capital and subordinated debt of any other registered brokers or dealers that are associated with the broker or dealer and are not otherwise exempt from the provisions pursuant to paragraph (b)(1)(i) of this rule.

(4) The provisions of this rule shall not apply to a broker or dealer that computes certain of its capital charges in accordance with Rule 15c3–1e if that broker or dealer is affiliated with an ultimate holding company that is not an ultimate holding company that has a principal regulator, as defined in Rule 15c3–1(c)(13).

(5) The Commission may, upon written application by a Reporting Broker or Dealer, exempt from the provisions of this rule, either unconditionally or on specified terms and conditions, any brokers or dealers associated with the Reporting Broker or Dealer. The term "Reporting Broker or Dealer" shall mean, in the case of a broker or dealer that is associated with other registered brokers or dealers, the broker or dealer which maintains the greatest amount of net capital as reported on its most recently filed Form X–17A–5. In granting exemptions under this rule, the Commission shall consider, among other factors, whether the records and other information required to be maintained pursuant to Rule 17h–1T concerning the Material Associated Persons of the broker or dealer associated with the Reporting Broker or Dealer will be available to the Commission pursuant to the provisions of this rule.

(c) *Special Provisions with Respect to Material Associated Persons Subject to the Supervision of Certain Domestic Regulators.* A broker or dealer shall be deemed to be in compliance with the reporting requirements of paragraph (a) of this rule with respect to a Material Associated Person if:

(1) Such Material Associated Person is subject to examination by or the reporting requirements of a Federal banking agency and the broker or dealer or such Material Associated Person furnishes in accordance with paragraph (a) of this rule copies of reports filed on Form FR Y–9C, Form FR Y–6, Form FR Y–7, and Form FR 2068 by the Material Associated Person with the Federal banking agency pursuant to section 5211 of the Revised Statutes, section 9 of the Federal Reserve Act, section 7(a) of the Federal Deposit Insurance Act, section 10(b) of the Home Owners' Loan Act, or section 5 of the Bank Holding Company Act of 1956; or

(2) If the Material Associated Person is subject to the supervision of an insurance commissioner or other similar official agency of a state; and

(i) In the case of a Material Associated Person organized as a public stock company, the broker or dealer furnishes in accordance with the provisions of this rule copies of the filings made by the insurance company pursuant to sections 13 or 15 of the Act and the Investment Company Act of 1940; or

(ii) In the case of Material Associated Person organized as a mutual insurance company or a non-public stock company, the broker or dealer furnishes in accordance with the provisions of this rule copies of the Annual and Quarterly Statements prepared by the insurance company on forms prescribed by the National Association of Insurance Commissioners. The Annual Statement furnished to the Commission pursuant to this rule shall include: The classification (distribution by state) section from the schedule of real estate; distribution by state, the interest overdue (more than three months), in process of foreclosure, and foreclosed properties transferred to real estate during the year sections from the schedule of mortgages; and the quality and maturity distribution of all bonds at statement values and by major types of issues section from the schedule of bonds and stocks. All other Schedules and Exhibits to such Annual and Quarterly Statements shall be maintained at the broker-dealer pursuant to the provisions of Rule 17h–1T but not furnished to the Commission.

(iii) In the event an insurance company organized as a stock or mutual company is not required to prepare Quarterly Statements, the broker or dealer must file with the Commission a Form 17–H in accordance with the provisions of this rule on a quarterly basis.

(3) In the case of a Material Associated Person that is subject to the supervision of the Commodity Futures Trading Commission, the broker or dealer furnishes in accordance with the provisions of this rule copies of the reports filed by the Material Associated Person with the Commodity Futures Trading Commission on Forms 1 FR–FCM or 1 FR–IB.

(4) No broker or dealer shall be required to furnish to the Commission any examination report

of any Federal banking agency or any supervisory recommendations or analyses contained therein with respect to a Material Associated Person that is subject to the regulation of a Federal banking agency. All information received by the Commission pursuant to this rule concerning a Material Associated Person that is subject to examination by or the reporting requirements of a Federal banking agency shall be deemed confidential for the purposes of section 24(b) of the Act.

(5) The furnishing of any information or documents by a broker or dealer pursuant to this rule shall not constitute an admission for any purpose that a Material Associated Person is otherwise subject to the Act. Any documents or information furnished to the Commission by a broker or dealer pursuant to this rule shall not be deemed to be "filed" for the purposes of the liabilities set forth in section 18 of the Act.

(d) *Special Provisions with Respect to Material Associated Persons Subject to the Supervision of a Foreign Financial Regulatory Authority.* A broker or dealer shall be deemed to be in compliance with the reporting requirements of this rule with respect to a Material Associated Person if such broker or dealer furnishes in accordance with the provisions of this rule copies of the reports filed by such Material Associated Person with a Foreign Financial Regulatory Authority. The broker or dealer shall file a copy of the original report and a copy translated into the English language. For the purposes of this rule, the term Foreign Financial Regulatory Authority shall have the meaning set forth in section 3(a)(51) of the Act.

(e) *Confidentiality.* All information obtained by the Commission pursuant to the provisions of this rule from a broker or dealer concerning a Material Associated Person shall be deemed confidential information for the purposes of section 24(b) of the Act.

(f) *Temporary Implementation Schedule.* Every broker or dealer subject to the requirements of this rule shall file the information required by Items 1, 2 and 3 of Form 17-H by October 31, 1992. Commencing December 31, 1992, the provisions of this rule shall apply in their entirety.

Rule 17Ab2-1. Registration of clearing agencies

(a) An application for registration or for exemption from registration as a clearing agency, as defined in section 3(a)(23) of the Act, or an amendment to any such application shall be filed with the Commission on Form CA-1, in accordance with the instructions thereto.

(b) Any applicant for registration or for exemption from registration as a clearing agency whose application is filed with the Commission on or before November 24, 1975, on and in accordance with the instructions to Form CA-1, with respect to the clearing agency activities described in the application shall, during the period from December 1, 1975 until the Commission grants registration, denies registration or grants an exemption from registration, be exempt from the registration provisions of section 17A(b) of the Act and the rules and regulations thereunder and, unless the Commission shall otherwise provide by rule or by order, the provisions of the Act and the rules and regulations thereunder which would be applicable to clearing agencies as a result of registration under the Act.

(c)(1) The Commission, upon the request of a clearing agency, may grant registration of the clearing agency in accordance with sections 17A(b) and 19(a)(1) of the Act but exempt the registrant from one or more of the requirements as to which the Commission is directed to make a determination pursuant to paragraphs (A) through (I) of section 17A(b)(3) of the Act, Provided that any such registration shall be effective only for eighteen months from the date the registration is made effective (or such longer period as the Commission may provide by order).

(2) In the case of any clearing agency registered in accordance with paragraph (c)(1) of this rule, not later than nine months from the date such registration is made effective the Commission either will grant registration in accordance with sections 17A(b) and 19(a)(1) of the Act, without exempting the registrant from one or more of the requirements as to which the Commission is directed to make a determination pursuant to subparagraphs (A) through (I) of section 17A(b)(3) of the Act, or will institute proceedings in accordance with section 19(a)(1)(B) of the Act to determine whether registration should be denied at the expiration of the registration granted in accordance with paragraph (1) of this rule.

(d) The filing of an amendment to an application for registration or for exemption from registration as a clearing agency, which registration or exemption has not been granted, or the filing of additional information or documents prior to the granting of registration or an exemption from registration shall extend to ninety days from the date such filing is made (or to such longer period as to which the applicant consents) the period within which the Commission shall grant registration, institute proceedings to determine whether such registration shall be denied, or conditionally or unconditionally exempt registrant from the registration and other provisions of Section 17A of the Act or the rules or regulations thereunder.

(e) If any information reported at items 1–3 of Form CA–1 is or becomes inaccurate, misleading or incomplete for any reason, whether before or after registration or an exemption from registration has been granted, the registrant shall file promptly an amendment on Form CA–1 correcting the inaccurate, misleading or incomplete information.

(f) Every application for registration or for exemption from registration as a clearing agency or amendment to, or additional information or document filed in connection with, any such application shall constitute a "report" or "application" within the meaning of sections 17, 17A, 19 and 32(a) of the Act.

Rule 17Ab2–2. Determinations affecting covered clearing agencies

(a) The Commission may, if it deems appropriate, upon application by any clearing agency or member of a clearing agency, or on its own initiative, determine whether a covered clearing agency is systemically important in multiple jurisdictions. In determining whether a covered clearing agency is systemically important in multiple jurisdictions, the Commission may consider:

(1) Whether the covered clearing agency is a designated clearing agency; and

(2) Whether the clearing agency has been determined to be systemically important by one or more jurisdictions other than the United States through a process that includes consideration of whether the foreseeable effects of a failure or disruption of the designated clearing agency could threaten the stability of each relevant jurisdiction's financial system.

(b) The Commission may, if it deems appropriate, determine whether any of the activities of a clearing agency providing central counterparty services, in addition to clearing agencies registered with the Commission for the purpose of clearing security-based swaps, have a more complex risk profile. In determining whether a clearing agency's activity has a more complex risk profile, the Commission may consider whether the clearing agency clears financial instruments that are characterized by discrete jump-to-default price changes or that are highly correlated with potential participant defaults.

(c) The Commission may, if it deems appropriate, upon application by any clearing agency or member of a clearing agency, or on its own initiative, determine whether to rescind any determination made pursuant to paragraph (a) or (b) of this rule. In determining whether to rescind any such determination, the Commission may consider a change in circumstances such that the covered clearing agency no longer meets the criteria supporting the determination in effect.

(d) The Commission shall publish notice of its intention to consider making a determination under paragraph (a), (b), or (c) of this rule, together with a brief statement of the grounds under consideration therefor, and provide at least a 30-day public comment period prior to any such determination, giving all interested persons an opportunity to submit written data, views, and arguments concerning such proposed determination. The Commission may provide the clearing agency subject to the proposed determination opportunity for hearing regarding the proposed determination.

(e) Notice of determinations under paragraph (a), (b), or (c) of this rule shall be given by prompt publication thereof, together with a statement of written reasons therefor.

(f) For purposes of this rule, the terms covered clearing agency, designated clearing agency, and systemically important in multiple jurisdictions shall have the meanings set forth in Rule 17Ad–22(a).

Rule 17Ac2–1. Application for registration of transfer agents

(a) An application for registration, pursuant to section 17A(c) of the Act, of a transfer agent for which the Commission is the appropriate regulatory agency, as defined in section 3(a)(34)(B) of the Act, shall be filed with the Commission on Form TA–1, in accordance with the instructions contained therein and shall become effective on the thirtieth day following the date on which the application is filed, unless the Commission takes affirmative action to accelerate, deny or postpone such registration in accordance with the provisions of section 17A(c) of the Act.

(b) The filing of any amendment to an application for registration as a transfer agent pursuant to paragraph (a) of this rule, which registration has not become effective, shall postpone the effective date of the registration until the thirtieth day following the date on which the amendment is filed, unless the Commission takes affirmative action to accelerate, deny or postpone the registration in accordance with the provisions of section 17A(c) of the Act.

(c) If any of the information reported on Form TA–1 (17 CFR 249b.100) becomes inaccurate, misleading, or incomplete, the registrant shall correct the information by filing an amendment within sixty days following the date on which the information becomes inaccurate, misleading, or incomplete.

(d) Every registration and amendment filed pursuant to this rule shall be filed with the Commission electronically in the Commission's EDGAR system. Transfer agents should refer to Form TA–1 and the instructions to the form (17 CFR 249b.100) and to the EDGAR Filer Manual (17 CFR 232.301) for the technical requirements and instructions for electronic filing. Transfer agents that have previously filed a Form TA–1 with the Commission must refile the information on their Form TA–1, as amended, in electronic format in EDGAR as an amended Form TA–1.

(e) Every registration and amendment filed pursuant to this rule shall constitute a "report" or "application" within the meaning of sections 17, 17A(c), and 32(a) of the Act.

Rule 17Ac2–2. Annual reporting requirement for registered transfer agents

(a) Every transfer agent registered on December 31 must file a report covering the reporting period on Form TA–2 (17 CFR 249b.102) by March 31 following the end of the reporting period. Form TA–2 must be completed in accordance with the instructions contained in the Form. A transfer agent may file an amendment to Form TA–2 pursuant to the instructions on the form to correct information that has become inaccurate, incomplete, or misleading. A transfer agent may file an amendment at any time; however, in order to be timely filed, all required portions of the form must be completed and filed in accordance with this rule and the instructions to the form by the date the form is required to be filed with the Commission.

(1) A registered transfer agent that received fewer than 1,000 items for transfer in the reporting period and that did not maintain master securityholder files for more than 1,000 individual securityholder accounts as of December 31 of the reporting period must complete Questions 1 through 5, 11, and the signature section of Form TA–2.

(2) A named transfer agent that engaged a service company to perform all of its transfer agent functions during the reporting period must complete Questions 1 through 3 and the signature section of Form TA–2.

(3) A named transfer agent that engaged a service company to perform some but not all of its transfer agent functions during the reporting period must complete all of Form TA–2 but should enter zero (0) for those questions that relate to transfer agent functions performed by the service company on behalf of the named transfer agent.

(b) For purposes of this rule, the term *reporting period* shall mean the calendar year ending December 31 for which Form TA–2 is being filed. The term *named transfer agent* shall have the same meaning as defined in Rule 17Ad–9(j). The term *service company* shall have the same meaning as defined in Rule 17Ad–9(k).

(c) Every annual report and amendment filed pursuant to this rule shall be filed with the Commission electronically in the Commission's EDGAR system. Transfer agents should refer to Form TA–2 and the instructions to the form (17 CFR 249b.102) and the EDGAR Filer Manual (17 CFR 232.301) for further information regarding electronic filing. Every registered transfer agent must file an electronic Form TA–1 with the Commission, or an electronic amendment to its Form TA–1 if the transfer agent previously filed a paper Form TA–1 with the Commission, before it may file an electronic Form TA–2 or Form TA–W with the Commission.

Rule 17Ac3–1. Withdrawal from registration with the commission

(a) Notice of withdrawal from registration as a transfer agent with the Commission pursuant to section 17A(c)(4) of the Act shall be filed on Form TA–W in accordance with the instructions contained thereon.

(b) Except as hereinafter provided, a notice to withdraw from registration filed by a transfer agent pursuant to section 17A(c)(4) of the Act shall become effective on the sixtieth day after the filing thereof with the Commission or within such shorter period of time as the Commission may determine. If a notice to withdraw from registration is filed with the Commission at any time subsequent to the date of issuance of a Commission order instituting proceedings pursuant to section 17A(c)(3) of the Act, or if prior to the effective date of the notice of withdrawal the Commission institutes such a proceeding or a proceeding to impose terms and conditions upon such withdrawal, the notice of withdrawal shall not become effective except at such time and upon such terms and conditions as the Commission deems necessary or appropriate in the public interest, for the protection of investors, or in furtherance of the purposes of section 17A.

(c) Every withdrawal from registration filed pursuant to this rule shall be filed with the Commission electronically in the Commission's EDGAR system. Transfer agents should refer to Form TA–W and the instructions to the form (17 CFR 249b.101) and the EDGAR Filer Manual (17 CFR 232.301) for further information regarding electronic filing.

(d) Every notice of withdrawal filed pursuant to this rule shall constitute a "report" within the meaning of sections 17 and 32(a) of the Act.

Rule 17Ad–1. Definitions

As used in this rule and Rules 17Ad–2, 17Ad–3, 17Ad–4, 17Ad–5, 17Ad–6 and 17Ad–7:

(a)(1) The term *item* means:

(i) A certificate or certificates of the same issue of securities covered by one ticket (or, if there is no ticket, presented by one presentor) presented for transfer, or an instruction to a transfer agent which holds securities registered in the name of the presentor to transfer or to make available all or a portion of those securities;

(ii) Each line on a "deposit shipment control list" or a "withdrawal shipment control list" submitted by a registered clearing agency; or

(iii) In the case of an outside registrar, each certificate to be countersigned.

(2) If a "deposit shipment control list" or "withdrawal shipment control list" contains both routine and non-routine transfer instructions, a registered transfer agent shall at its option:

(i) Retain all transfer instructions listed on the shipment control list and treat each line on the shipment control list as a routine item; or

(ii) Return promptly to the registered clearing agency a shipment control list line containing non-routine transfer instructions (together with a copy of the shipment control list, an explanation for the returned instructions and all routine transfer instructions reflected on the same line) and treat each line on the shipment control list that reflects retained transfer instructions as a routine item.

(3) A *deposit shipment control list* means a list of transfer instructions that accompanies certificates to be cancelled and reissued in the nominee name of a registered clearing agency.

(4) A *withdrawal shipment control list* means a list of instructions (either in paper or electronic medium) that:

(i) Directs issuance of certificates in the names of persons or entities other than the registered clearing agency; and

(ii) Accompanies certificates to be cancelled which are registered in the nominee name of a registered clearing agency, or directs the transfer agent to reduce certificate or position balances maintained by the transfer agent on behalf of a registered clearing agency under that clearing agency's transfer agent custody program.

(b) The term *outside registrar* with respect to a transfer item means a transfer agent which performs only the registrar function for the certificate or certificates presented for transfer and includes the persons performing similar functions with respect to debt issues.

(c) An item is *made available* when

(1) In the case of an item for which the services of an outside registrar are not required, or which has been received from an outside registrar after processing, the transfer agent dispatches or mails the item to, or the item is awaiting pick-up by, the presentor or a person designated by the presentor, or

(2) In the case of an item for which the services of an outside registrar are required, the transfer agent dispatches or mails the item to, or the item is awaiting pick-up by, the outside registrar, or

(3) In the case of an item for which an outside registrar has completed processing, the outside registrar dispatches or mails the item to, or the item is awaiting pick-up by, the presenting transfer agent.

(d) The *transfer* of an item is accomplished when, in accordance with the presentor's instructions, all acts necessary to cancel the certificate or certificates presented for transfer and to issue a new certificate or certificates, including the performance of the registrar function, are completed and the item is made available to the presentor by the transfer agent, or when, in accordance with the presentor's instructions, a transfer agent which holds securities registered in the name of the presentor completes all acts necessary to issue a new certificate or certificates representing all or a portion of those securities and makes available the new certificate or certificates to the presentor or a person designated by the presentor or, with respect to those transfers of record ownership to be accomplished without the physical issuance of certificates, completes registration of change in ownership of all or a portion of those securities.

(e) The *turnaround* of an item is completed when transfer is accomplished or, when an outside registrar is involved, the transfer agent in accordance with the presentor's instructions completes all acts necessary to cancel the certificate or certificates presented for transfer and to issue a new certificate or certificates, and the item is made available to an outside registrar.

(f) The term *process* means the accomplishing by an outside registrar of all acts necessary to perform the registrar function and to make available to the presenting transfer agent the completed certificate or certificates or to advise the presenting transfer agent, orally or in writing, why performance of the registrar function is delayed or may not be completed.

(g) The *receipt* of an item or a written inquiry or request occurs when the item or written inquiry or request arrives at the premises at which the transfer agent performs transfer agent functions, as defined in Section 3(a)(25) of the Act.

(h) A *business day* is any day during which the transfer agent is normally open for business and excludes Saturdays, Sundays and legal holidays or other holidays normally observed by the transfer agent.

(i) An item is *routine* if it does not (1) require requisitioning certificates of an issue for which the transfer agent, under the terms of its agency, does not maintain a supply of certificates; (2) include a certificate as to which the transfer agent has received notice of a stop order, adverse claim or any other restriction on transfer; (3) require any additional certificates, documentation, instructions, assignments, guarantees, endorsements, explanations or opinions of counsel before transfer may be effected; (4) require review of supporting documentation other than assignments, endorsements or stock powers, certified corporate resolutions, signature or other common and ordinary guarantees or appropriate tax or tax waivers; (5) involve a transfer in connection with a reorganization, tender offer, exchange, redemption or liquidation; (6) include a warrant, right or convertible security presented for transfer of record ownership within five business days before any day upon which exercise or conversion privileges lapse or change; (7) include a warrant, right or convertible security presented for exercise or conversion; or (8) include a security of an issue which within the previous 15 business days was offered to the public, pursuant to a registration statement effective under the Securities Act of 1933, in an offering not of a continuing nature.

(j) The term *depository-eligible securities issue* means an issue of securities that is eligible for deposit at any securities depository that is registered with the Commission under the Securities Exchange Act of 1934 as a clearing agency.

Rule 17Ad–2. Turnaround, processing and forwarding of items

(a) Every registered transfer agent (except when acting as an outside registrar) shall turnaround within three business days of receipt at least 90 percent of all routine items received for transfer during a month. For the purposes of this paragraph, items received at or before noon on a business day shall be deemed to have been received at noon on that day, and items received after noon on a business day or received on a day not a business day shall be deemed to have been received at noon on the next business day.

(b) Every registered transfer agent acting as an outside registrar shall process at least 90 percent of all items received during a month (1) by the opening of business on the next business day, in the case of items received at or before noon on a business day, and (2) by noon of the next business day, in the case of items received after noon on a business day. For the purposes of paragraphs (b) and (d) of this rule, "items received" shall not include any item enumerated in Rule 17Ad–1(i)(5), (6), (7) or (8) or any item which is not accompanied by a debit or cancelled certificate. For the purposes of this paragraph, items received on a day not a business day shall be deemed to have been received before noon on the next business day.

(c) Any registered transfer agent which fails to comply with paragraph (a) of this rule with respect to any month shall, within ten business days following the end of such month, file with the Commission and the transfer agent's appropriate regulatory agency, if it is not the Commission, a written notice in accordance with paragraph (h) of this rule. Such notice shall state the number of routine items and the number of non-routine items received for transfer during the month, the number of routine items which the registered transfer agent failed to turnaround in accordance with the requirements of paragraph (a) of this rule, the percentage that such routine items represent of all routine items received during the month, the reasons for such failure, the steps which have been taken, are being taken or will be taken to prevent a future failure and the number of routine items, aged in increments of one business day, which as of the close of business on the last business day of the month have been in its possession for more than four business days and have not been turned around.

(d) Any registered transfer agent which fails to comply with paragraph (b) of this rule with respect to any month shall, within ten business days following the end of such month, file with the Commission and the transfer agent's appropriate regulatory agency, if it is not the Commission, a written notice in accordance with paragraph (h) of this rule. Such notice shall state the number of items received for processing during the month, the number of items which the registered transfer agent failed to process in accordance with the requirements of paragraph (b) of this rule, the percentage that such items represent of all items received during the month, the reasons for such failure and the steps which have been taken, are being taken or will be taken to prevent a future failure, and the number of items which as of the close of business on the last business day of the month have been in the transfer agent's possession for more than the time allowed for processing and have not been processed.

(e)(1) Except as provided in paragraph (e)(2) of this rule, all routine items not turned around within three business days of receipt as required by paragraph (a) of this rule and all items not processed within the periods required by paragraph (b) of this rule shall be turned around promptly, and all non-routine items shall receive diligent and continuous attention and shall be turned around as soon as possible.

(2) A transfer agent that is exempt under Rule 17Ad–4(b) and that has received 30 days notice of depository-eligibility of an issue for which it performs transfer agent functions shall turnaround ninety percent of all routine items received during a month within five business days of receipt. Such transfer agent shall devote diligent and continuous attention to the remaining ten percent of routine items and shall turnaround these items as soon as possible.

(f) A registered transfer agent which receives items at locations other than the premises at which it performs transfer agent functions shall have appropriate procedures to assure, and shall assure, that items are forwarded to such premises promptly.

(g) A registered transfer agent which receives processed items from an outside registrar shall have appropriate procedures to assure, and shall assure, that such items are made available promptly to the presentor.

(h) Any notice required by this rule or Rule 17Ad–4 shall be filed as follows:

(1) Any notice required to be filed with the Commission shall be filed in triplicate with the principal office of the Commission in Washington, DC 20549 and, in the case of a registered transfer agent for which the Commission is the appropriate regulatory agency, an additional copy shall be filed with the Regional Office of the Commission for the region in which the registered transfer agent has its principal office for transfer agent activities.

(2) Any notice required to be filed with the Comptroller of the Currency shall be filed with the Office of the Comptroller of the Currency, Administrator of National Banks, Washington, DC 20219.

(3) Any notice required to be filed with the Board of Governors of the Federal Reserve System shall be filed with the Board of Governors of the Federal Reserve System, Washington, DC 20251 and with the Federal Reserve Bank of the district in which the registered transfer agent's principal banking operations are conducted.

(4) Any notice required to be filed with the Federal Deposit Insurance Corporation shall be filed with the Federal Deposit Insurance Corporation, Washington, DC 20429.

Rule 17Ad–3. Limitations on expansion

(a) Any registered transfer agent which is required to file any notice pursuant to Rule 17Ad–2(c) or (d) for each of three consecutive months shall not, from the fifth business day after the end of the third such month until the end of the next following period of three successive months during which no such notices have been required:

(1) Initiate the performance of any transfer agent function or activity for an issue for which the transfer agent does not perform, or is not under agreement to perform, transfer agent functions prior to such fifth business day; and

(2) with respect to an issue for which transfer agent functions are being performed on such fifth business day, initiate for that issue the performance of an additional transfer agent function

or activity which the transfer agent does not perform, or is not under agreement to perform, prior to such fifth business day.

(b) Any registered transfer agent which for each of two consecutive months fails to turnaround at least 75% of all routine items in accordance with the requirements of Rule 17Ad–2(a) or to process at least 75% of all items in accordance with the requirements of Rule 17Ad–2(b) shall be subject to the limitations imposed by paragraph (a) of this rule and further shall, within twenty business days after the close of the second such month, send to the chief executive officer of each issuer for which such registered transfer agent acts a copy of the written notice filed pursuant to Rule 17Ad–2(c) or (d) with respect to the second such month.

Rule 17Ad–4. Applicability of Rules 17Ad–2, 17Ad–3 and 17Ad–6(a) (1) through (7) and (11)

(a) Rules 17Ad–2, 17Ad–3 and 17Ad–6(a)(1) through (7) and (11) shall not apply to interests in limited partnerships, to redeemable securities of investment companies registered under section 8 of the Investment Company Act of 1940, or to interests in dividend reinvestment programs.

(b)(1) For purposes of this rule, *exempt transfer agent* means a transfer agent that during any six consecutive months shall have received fewer than 500 items for transfer and fewer than 500 items for processing.

(2) Except as provided in paragraph (c) of this rule, an exempt transfer agent that satisfies the requirements of paragraph (b)(3) shall be exempt from the provisions of Rules 17Ad–2(a), (b), (c), (d) and (h), Rule 17Ad–3 and Rules 17Ad–6(a)(2) through (7) and (11).

(3) Within ten business days following the close of the sixth consecutive month described in paragraph (b)(1) of this rule, an exempt transfer agent shall:

(i) If its appropriate regulatory agency is either the Commission or the Office of the Comptroller of the Currency, prepare and maintain in its possession a document certifying that the transfer agent qualifies as exempt under paragraph (b)(1) of this rule; or

(ii) If its appropriate regulatory agency is either the Board of Governors of the Federal Reserve System or the Federal Deposit Insurance Corporation, file with the appropriate regulatory agency a notice certifying that it qualifies as exempt under paragraph (b)(1) of this rule.

(c) Within five business days following the close of each month, every exempt transfer agent shall calculate the number of items which it received during the preceding six months. Whenever any exempt transfer agent no longer qualifies as such under paragraph (b)(1), within ten business days after the end of such month: (1) It shall prepare and maintain in its possession a document so stating, if subject to paragraph (b)(3)(i) of this rule; or (2) It shall file with its appropriate regulatory agency a notice to that effect, if subject to paragraph (b)(3)(ii) of this rule. Thereafter, beginning with the first month following the month in which such document is required to be prepared or such notice is required to be filed, the registered transfer agent no longer shall be exempt under paragraph (b) of this rule. Any registered transfer agent which has ceased to be an exempt transfer agent under this paragraph shall not qualify again for exemption until it has conducted its transfer agent operations pursuant to the foregoing rule for six consecutive months following the month in which it was required to prepare the document or prepare and file the notice specified in this paragraph.

Rule 17Ad–5. Written inquiries and requests

(a) When any person makes a written inquiry to a registered transfer agent concerning the status of an item presented for transfer during the preceding six months by such person or anyone acting on his behalf, which inquiry identifies the issue, the number of shares (or principal amount of debt securities or number of units if relating to any other kind of security) presented, the approximate date of presentment and the name in which it is registered, the registered transfer agent shall, within five business days following receipt of the inquiry, respond, stating whether the item has been received; if received, whether it has been transferred; if received and not transferred, the reason for the delay and what additional matter, if any, is necessary before transfer may be effected; and, if received and transferred, the date and manner in which the completed item was made available, the addressee and address to which it was made available and the number of any new certificate which was registered and the name in which it was registered. If a new certificate is dispatched or mailed to the presentor within five business days following receipt of an inquiry pertaining to that certificate, no further response to the inquiry shall be required pursuant to this paragraph.

(b) When any broker-dealer requests in writing that a registered transfer agent acknowledge the transfer instructions and the possession of a security presented for transfer by such broker-dealer or revalidate a window ticket with respect to such security and the request identifies the issue, the number of shares (or principal amount of debt securities or number of units if relating to any other kind of security), the approximate date of presentment, the certificate number and the name in which it is registered, every registered transfer agent shall, within five business days following receipt of the request, in writing, confirm or deny possession of the security, and, if the registered transfer agent has possession, (1) acknowledge the transfer instructions or (2) revalidate the window ticket. If a new certificate is dispatched or mailed to the presentor within five business days following receipt of a request pertaining to that certificate, no further response to the inquiry shall be required pursuant to this paragraph.

(c) When any person, or anyone acting under his authority, requests in writing that a transfer agent confirm possession as of a given date of a certificate presented by such person during the 30 days before the date the inquiry is received and the request identifies the issue, the number of shares (or principal amount of debt securities or number of units if relating to any other kind of security), the approximate date of presentment, the certificate number and the name in which the certificate was registered, every registered transfer agent shall, within ten business days following receipt of the request and upon assurance of payment of a reasonable fee if required by such transfer agent, make available a written response to such person, or anyone acting under his authority, confirming or denying possession of such security as of such given date.

(d) When any person requests in writing a transcript of such person's account with respect to a particular issue, either as the account appears currently or as it appeared on a specific date not more than six months prior to the date the registered transfer agent receives the request, every registered transfer agent shall, within twenty business days following receipt of the request and upon assurance of payment of a reasonable fee if required by such transfer agent, make available to such person a transcript, ledger or statement of account in sufficient detail to permit reconstruction of such account as of the date for which the transcript was requested.

(e)(1) *Response to Written Inquiries Concerning Dividend and Interest Payments.* A registered transfer agent shall respond, within ten business days of receipt, to current claims that contain sufficient detail. A registered transfer agent shall respond, within twenty business days of receipt, to aged claims that contain sufficient detail. The response shall indicate in writing that the inquiry has been received, whether the claim requires further research and, if so, a reasonable estimate of how long that research may take. If no further research is required, the response shall indicate whether that claim is being or will be paid and, if not, the reason for not paying the claim. A registered transfer agent shall devote diligent attention to unresolved inquiries and shall resolve all inquiries as soon as possible.

(2) *Misdirected Written Inquiries Concerning Dividend and Interest Payments.* In the event that a transfer agent is not the dividend disbursing or interest paying agent for an issue that is the subject of a claim under this rule, but performed those or any transfer agent services for that issue within the preceding three years, the transfer agent shall provide in writing to the inquirer, within ten business days of receipt of the inquiry, the name and address of the current dividend disbursing or interest paying agent. If the transfer agent did not perform those or other transfer agent services for the issue within the preceding three years, the transfer agent must respond to the inquiry and may respond by returning the inquiry with a statement that the transfer agent is not the current dividend disbursing or interest paying agent and that it does not know the name and address of the current dividend disbursing or interest paying agent.

(3) As used in this paragraph:

(i) A *current claim* means a written inquiry concerning non-payment or incorrect payment of dividends or interest, the payment date for which occurred within the preceding six months.

(ii) An *aged claim* means a written inquiry concerning non-payment or incorrect payment of dividends or interest, the payment date for which occurred more than six months before the inquiry.

(iii) *sufficient detail* means a written inquiry or request that identifies: the issue; the name(s) in which the securities are registered; the number of shares (or principal amount of debt securities or number of units for any other kind of security) involved; the approximate record date(s) or payment date(s) relating to the claim; and, with respect to registered broker-dealers, registered clearing agencies, or banks, certificate numbers.

(f) *Telephone Response*. (1) A transfer agent may satisfy the written response requirements of this rule by a telephone response to the inquirer if:

(i) The telephone response resolves that inquiry; and

(ii) The inquirer does not request a written response.

(2) When any person makes a written inquiry or request that would qualify under paragraph (e) of this rule except that it fails to provide sufficient detail as specified in paragraph (e)(3)(iii) of this rule, a registered transfer agent may telephone the inquirer to obtain the necessary additional detail within the time periods specified in paragraph (e)(1) of this rule. If the transfer agent does not receive the additional detail within ten business days, the transfer agent immediately shall make a written request for the additional information.

(g)(1) When any person makes a written inquiry or request which would qualify under paragraph (a), (b), (c) or (d) of this rule except that it fails to provide all of the information specified in those paragraphs, or requests information which refers to a time earlier than the time periods specified in those paragraphs, a registered transfer agent shall confirm promptly receipt of the inquiry or request and respond to it as soon as possible.

(2) When any person makes a written inquiry or request which would qualify under paragraph (e) of this rule except that it fails to provide sufficient detail as specified in paragraph (e)(3)(iii) of this rule, a registered transfer agent must respond to the inquiry within the time periods specified in paragraph (e)(1) of this rule. A registered transfer agent may respond to such an inquiry in accordance with paragraph (e)(1) as though sufficient detail had been provided, or may return it to the inquirer, requesting the additional necessary details.

Rule 17Ad–6. Recordkeeping

(a) Every registered transfer agent shall make and keep current the following:

(1) A receipt, ticket, schedule, log or other record showing the business day each routine item and each non-routine item is (i) received from the presentor and, if applicable, from the outside registrar and (ii) made available to the presentor and, if applicable, to the outside registrar;

(2) A log, tally, journal, schedule or other record showing for each month:

(i) The number of routine items received;

(ii) The number of routine items received during the month that were turned around within three business days of receipt;

(iii) The number of routine items received during the month that were not turned around within three business days of receipt;

(iv) The number of non-routine items received during the month;

(v) The number of non-routine items received during the month that were turned around;

(vi) The number of routine items that, as of the close of business on the last business day of each month, have been in such registered transfer agent's possession for more than four business days, aged in increments of one business day (beginning on the fifth business day); and

(vii) The number of non-routine items in such registered transfer agent's possession as of the close of business on the last business day of each month;

(3) With respect to items for which the registered transfer agent acts as an outside registrar:

(i) A receipt, ticket, schedule, log or other record showing the date and time:

(A) Each item is (1) received from the presenting transfer agent and (2) made available to the presenting transfer agent;

(B) Each written or oral notice of refusal to perform the registrar function is made available to the presenting transfer agent (and the substance of the notice); and

(ii) A log, tally, journal, schedule or other record showing for each month:

(A) The number of items received;

(B) The number of items processed within the time required by Rule 17Ad–2(b); and

(C) The number of items not processed within the time required by Rule 17Ad–2(b);

(4) A record of calculations demonstrating the registered transfer agent's monitoring of its performance under Rule 17Ad–2(a) and (b);

(5) A copy of any written notice filed pursuant to Rule 17Ad–2;

(6) Any written inquiry or request, including those not subject to the requirements of Rule 17Ad–5, concerning an item, showing the date

received; a copy of any written response to an inquiry or request, showing the date dispatched or mailed to the presentor; if no response to an inquiry or request was made, the date the certificate involved was made available to the presentor; or, in the case of an inquiry or request under Rule 17Ad–5(a) responded to by telephone, a telephone log or memorandum showing the date and substance of any telephone response to the inquiry;

(7) A log, journal, schedule or other record showing the number of inquiries subject to Rule 17Ad–5(a), (b), (c) and (d) received during each month but not responded to within the required time frames and the number of such inquiries pending as of the close of business on the last business day of each month;

(8) Any document, resolution, contract, appointment or other writing, and any supporting document, concerning the appointment and the termination of such appointment of such registered transfer agent to act in any capacity for any issue on behalf of the issuer, on behalf of itself as the issuer or on behalf of any person who was engaged by the issuer to act on behalf of the issuer;

(9) Any record of an active (i.e., unreleased) stop order, notice of adverse claim or any other restriction on transfer;

(10) A copy of any transfer journal and registrar journal prepared by such registered transfer agent; and

(11) Any document upon which the transfer agent bases its determination that an item received for transfer was received in connection with a reorganization, tender offer, exchange, redemption, liquidation, conversion or the sale of securities registered pursuant to the Securities Act of 1933 and, accordingly, was not routine under Rule 17Ad–1(i)(5) or (8).

(b) Every registered transfer agent which, under the terms of its agency, maintains security holder records for an issue or which acts as a registrar for an issue shall, with respect to such issue, obtain from the issuer or its transfer agent and retain documentation setting forth the total number of shares or principal amount of debt securities or total number of units if relating to any other kind of security authorized and the total issued and outstanding pursuant to issuer authorization.

(c) Every registered transfer agent which, under the terms of its agency, maintains security holder records for an issue shall, with respect to such issue, retain each cancelled registered bond, debenture, share, warrant or right, other registered evidence of indebtedness, or other certificate of ownership and all accompanying documentation, except legal papers returned to the presentor.

Rule 17Ad–7. Record retention

(a) The records required by Rule 17Ad–6(a)(1), (3)(i), (6) or (11) shall be maintained for a period of not less than two years, the first six months in an easily accessible place.

(b) The records required by Rule 17Ad–6(a)(2), (3)(ii), (4), (5) or (7) shall be maintained for a period of not less than two years, the first year in an easily accessible place.

(c) The records required by Rule 17Ad–6(a)(8), (9) and (10) and (b) shall be maintained in an easily accessible place during the continuance of the transfer agency and shall be maintained for one year after termination of the transfer agency.

(d) The records required by Rule 17Ad–6(c) shall be maintained for a period of not less than six years, the first six months in an easily accessible place.

(e) Every registered transfer agent shall maintain in an easily accessible place:

(1) All records required under Rule 17f–2(d) until at least three years after the termination of employment of those persons required by Rule 17f–2 to be fingerprinted; and

(2) All records required pursuant to Rule 17f–2(e).

(f) Subject to the conditions set forth in this rule, the records required to be maintained pursuant to Rule 17Ad–6 may be retained using electronic or micrographic media and may be preserved in those formats for the time required by Rule 17Ad–7. Records stored electronically or micrographically in accordance with this paragraph may serve as a substitute for the hard copy records required to be maintained pursuant to Rule 17Ad–6.

(1) For purposes of this rule:

(i) The term *micrographic media* means microfilm or microfiche or any similar medium.

(ii) The term *electronic storage media* means any digital storage medium or system.

(iii) The term *ARA* means your appropriate regulatory agency as that term is defined in 15 U.S.C. 78c(a)(34).

(2) If you as a registered transfer agent use electronic storage media or micrographic media to store your records, you must:

(i) Have available at all times for examination by the staffs of the Commission and of your ARA facilities to project or produce immediately easily readable images of such records;

(ii) Be ready at all times to provide such records that the staffs of the Commission and your ARA or their representatives may request;

(iii) Create an accurate index of such records, store the index with those records, and have the index available at all times for examination by the staffs of the Commission and your ARA;

(iv) Have quality assurance procedures to verify the quality and accuracy of the electronic or micrographic recording process; and

(v) Maintain separately from the originals duplicates of the records and the index that you store on electronic storage media or micrographic media. You may store the duplicates of the indexed records on any medium permitted by this rule. You must preserve the duplicate records and index for the same time that is required by this rule for the indexed records, and you must have them available at all times for examination by the staffs of the Commission and your ARA.

(3) Any electronic storage media that you use to store your records must:

(i) Ensure the security and integrity of the records by means of manual and automated controls that assure the authenticity and quality of the electronic facsimile, detect attempts to alter or remove the records, and provide means to recover altered, damaged, or lost records resulting from any cause;

(ii) Externally label all removable units of storage media using a unique identifier that allows the manual association of that removable storage unit with its place and order in the recordkeeping system; and

(iii) Uniquely identify files and internally label each file with its unique name, the date and time of file creation, the date and time of last modification or extension, and a file sequence number when the file spans more than one volume.

(4) If you use electronic storage media or micrographic media to store your records, you must establish an audit system that accounts for the inputting of and any changes to every record that is stored on electronic storage media or micrographic media. The results of such audit system must:

(i) Be available at all times for examination by the staffs of the Commission and your ARA; and

(ii) Be preserved for the same time that is required by this rule for the underlying records.

(5) If you use electronic storage media or micrographic media to store your records, you must:

(i) Maintain, keep current, and provide promptly upon request by the staffs of the Commission and your ARA all information necessary to access the records and indexes stored on electronic storage media or micrographic media; and

(ii) Place, or have a third party place on your behalf, in escrow with an independent third party and keep current a copy of the physical and logical format of the electronic storage or micrographic media, the field format of all different information types written on the electronic storage media and source code, and the appropriate documentation and information necessary to access records and indexes. The independent escrow agent must file an undertaking signed by a duly authorized person with the Commission and your ARA stating that:

"[Name of Third Party] hereby undertakes to furnish promptly upon request to the U.S. Securities and Exchange Commission, its designees, or representatives, upon reasonable request, a current copy of the physical and logical format of the electronic storage or micrographic media, the field format of all different information types written on the electronic storage media and source code, and the appropriate documentation and information necessary to access the records and indexes of [Name of Transfer Agent]'s electronic records management system."

(6)(i) If you use a third party to maintain or preserve some or all of the required records using electronic storage media or micrographic media, such third party shall file a written undertaking signed by a duly authorized person with the Commission and your ARA stating that:

"With respect to any books and records maintained or preserved on behalf of [Name of Transfer Agent], [Name of Third Party] hereby undertakes to permit examination of such books and records at any time or from time to time during business hours by representatives or designees of the U.S. Securities and Exchange Commission, and to promptly furnish to said Commission or its designee true, correct, complete, and current hard copies of any or all or any part of such books and records."

(ii) Agreement with a third party to maintain your records shall not relieve you from the responsibility to prepare and maintain records as specified in this rule or in Rule 17Ad–6.

(g) If the records required to be maintained and preserved by a registered transfer agent pursuant to the requirements of Rules 17Ad–6 and 17Ad–7 are maintained and preserved on behalf of the registered transfer agent by an outside service bureau, other recordkeeping service or the issuer, the registered transfer agent shall obtain, from such outside service bureau, other recordkeeping service or the issuer, an agreement, in writing, to the effect that:

(1) Such records are subject at any time, or from time to time, to reasonable periodic, special, or other examinations by representatives of the Commission and the appropriate regulatory agency for such registered transfer agent, if it is not the Commission; and

(2) The outside service bureau, recordkeeping service, or issuer will furnish to the Commission and the appropriate regulatory agency, upon demand, at either the principal office or at any regional office, complete, correct and current hard copies of any and all such records.

(h) When a registered transfer agent ceases to perform transfer agent functions for an issue, the responsibility of such transfer agent under Rule 17Ad–7 to retain the records required to be made and keep current under Rule 17Ad–6(a)(1), (6), (9), (10) and (11), (b) and (c) shall end upon the delivery of such records to the successor transfer agent.

(i) The records required by Rules 17Ad–17(d) and 17Ad–19(c) shall be maintained for a period of not less than three years, the first year in an easily accessible place.

Rule 17Ad–8. Securities position listings

(a) For purposes of this rule, the term *securities position listing* means, with respect to the securities of any issuer held by a registered clearing agency in the name of the clearing agency or its nominee, a list of those participants in the clearing agency on whose behalf the clearing agency holds the issuer's securities and of the participants' respective positions in such securities as of a specified date.

(b) Upon request, a registered clearing agency shall furnish a securities position listing promptly to each issuer whose securities are held in the name of the clearing agency or its nominee. A registered clearing agency may charge issuers requesting securities position listings a fee designed to recover the reasonable costs of providing the securities position listing to the issuer.

Rule 17Ad–9. Definitions

As used in this rule and Rules 17Ad–10, 17Ad–11, 17Ad–12 and 17Ad–13:

(a) *Certificate detail,* with respect to certificated securities, includes, at a minimum, all of the following, and with respect to uncertificated securities, includes items (2) through (8):

(1) The certificate number;

(2) The number of shares for equity securities or the principal dollar amount for debt securities;

(3) The securityholder's registration;

(4) The address of the registered securityholder;

(5) The issue date of the security;

(6) The cancellation date of the security;

(7) In the case of redeemable securities of investment companies, an appropriate description of each debit and credit (i.e., designation indicating purchase, redemption, or transfer); and

(8) Any other identifying information about securities and securityholders the transfer agent reasonably deems essential to its recordkeeping system for the efficient and effective research of record differences.

(b) *Master securityholder file* is the official list of individual securityholder accounts. With respect to uncertified securities of companies registered under the Investment Company Act of 1940, the master securityholder file may consist of multiple, but linked, automated files.

(c) A *subsidiary file* is any list or record of accounts, securityholders, or certificates that evidences debits or credits that have not been posted to the master securityholder file.

(d) A *control book* is the record or other document that shows the total number of shares (in the case of equity securities) or the principal dollar amount (in the case of debt securities) authorized and issued by the issuer.

(e) A *credit* is an addition of appropriate certificate detail to the master securityholder file.

(f) A *debit* is a cancellation of appropriate certificate detail from the master securityholder file.

(g) A *record difference* occurs when either:

(1) The total number of shares or total principal dollar amount of securities in the master securityholder file does not equal the number of shares or principal dollar amount in the control book; or

(2) The security transferred or redeemed contains certificate detail different from the certificate detail currently on the master securityholder file, which difference cannot be immediately resolved.

(h) A *recordkeeping transfer agent* is the registered transfer agent that maintains and updates the master securityholder file.

(i) A *co-transfer agent* is the registered transfer agent that transfers securities but does not maintain and update the master securityholder file.

(j) A *named transfer agent* is the registered transfer agent that is engaged by an issuer to perform transfer agent functions for an issue of securities but has engaged a service company to perform some or all of those functions.

(k) A *service company* is the registered transfer agent engaged by a named transfer agent to perform transfer agent functions for that named transfer agent.

(*l*) A *file* includes automated and manual records.

Rule 17Ad–10. Prompt posting of certificate detail to master securityholder files, maintenance of accurate securityholder files, communications between co-transfer agents and recordkeeping transfer agents, maintenance of current control book, retention of certificate detail and "buy–in" of physical over-issuance

(a)(1) Every recordkeeping transfer agent shall promptly and accurately post to the master securityholder file debits and credits containing minimum and appropriate certificate detail representing every security transferred, purchased, redeemed or issued; *Provided, however,* That if a security transferred or redeemed contains certificate detail different from that currently posted to the master securityholder file, the credit shall be posted to the master securityholder file and the debit and related certificate detail shall be maintained in a subsidiary file until resolved. The recordkeeping transfer agent shall exercise diligent and continuous attention to resolve the resulting record difference and, once resolved, shall post to the master securityholder file the debit maintained in the subsidiary file. Postings of certificate detail shall remain on the master securityholder file until a debit to a securityholder account is appropriate.

(2) As used in this paragraph, the term *promptly* means the following number of days after issuance, purchase, transfer, or redemption of a security:

(i) With respect to recordkeeping transfer agents (other than transfer agents that perform transfer agent functions with respect to redeemable securities issued by investment companies registered under section 8 of the Investment Company Act of 1940) that are exempt transfer agents under Rule 17Ad–4(b), 30 calendar days;

(ii) With respect to recordkeeping transfer agents (other than transfer agents that perform transfer agent functions with respect to redeemable securities issued by investment companies registered under section 8 of the Investment Company Act of 1940) that:

(A) Perform transfer agent functions solely for their own or their affiliated companies' securities issues, and

(B) Employ batch posting systems, ten business days; and

(iii) With respect to all other recordkeeping transfer agents, five business days;

Provided, however, That all securities transferred, purchased, redeemed or issued prior to record date, but posted subsequent thereto, shall be posted as of the record date.

(3) With respect to posting certificate detail from transfer journals received by the recordkeeping transfer agent from a co-transfer agent, the time frames set forth in paragraph (a)(2) shall commence upon receipt of those journals by the recordkeeping transfer agent.

(b) Every recordkeeping transfer agent shall maintain and keep current an accurate master securityholder file and subsidiary files. If such transfer agent has any record difference, its master securityholder file and subsidiary files must accurately represent all relevant debits and credits until the record difference is resolved. The recordkeeping transfer agent shall exercise diligent and continuous attention to resolve all record differences.

(c)(1) Every co-transfer agent shall dispatch or mail promptly to the recordkeeping transfer agent a record of debits and credits for every security transferred or issued. For the purposes of this paragraph, "promptly" means within two business days following transfer of each security, and, with respect to transfers occurring within five business days of record date, daily.

(2) Within three business days following the end of each month, every co-transfer agent shall mail to the recordkeeping transfer agent for each issue of securities for which it acts as a co-transfer agent, a report setting forth:

(i) The principal dollar amount of debt securities or the number of shares and related market value of equity securities comprising any buy-in executed by the co-transfer agent during the preceding month pursuant to paragraph (g) of this rule; and

(ii) The reason for the buy-in.

(d) Every co-transfer agent shall respond promptly to all inquiries from the recordkeeping transfer agent regarding records required to be dispatched or mailed by the co-transfer agent pursuant to Rule 17Ad–10(c). For the purposes of this paragraph, "promptly" means within five business days of receipt of an inquiry from a recordkeeping transfer agent.

(e) Every recordkeeping transfer agent shall maintain and keep current an accurate control book for each issue of securities. A change in the control book shall not be made except upon written authorization from a duly authorized agent of the issuer.

(f) Every recordkeeping transfer agent shall retain a record of all certificate detail deleted from the master securityholder file for a period of six years from the date of deletion. In lieu of maintaining a hard copy, a recordkeeping transfer agent may comply with this paragraph by complying with Rule 17Ad–7(f) or Rule 17Ad–7(g).

(g)(1) A registered transfer agent, in the event of any actual physical overissuance that such transfer agent caused and of which it has knowledge, shall, within 60 days of the discovery of such overissuance, buy in securities equal to the number of shares in the case of equity securities or the principal dollar amount in the case of debt securities. During the sixty–day period, the registered transfer agent shall devote diligent attention to resolving the overissuance and recovering the certificates. This paragraph requires a buy-in only by the transfer agent that erroneously issued the certificate(s) giving rise to the physical overissuance, and applies only to those physical overissuances created by transfers or issuances subsequent to September 30, 1983.

(2) If a transfer agent obtains a letter from the party holding the overissued certificates that confirms that the overissued certificate(s) will be returned to the transfer agent not later than thirty days after the expiration of the sixty-day period, the transfer agent need not buy in securities by the sixtieth day. If, however, the certificate(s) are not returned to the transfer agent within the additional thirty-day period, the transfer agent immediately must execute the buy-in in accordance with paragraph (g)(1) of this rule.

(3) If the certificates involved are covered by a surety bond indemnifying the transfer agent for all expenses incurred as a result of actual overissuance, the transfer agent need not buy in the securities. The transfer agent, however, shall devote diligent attention to resolving the overissuance and recovering the certificates.

(4) For purposes of this paragraph, "discovery of the overissuance" occurs when the transfer agent identifies the erroneously issued certificate(s) and the registered securityholder(s).

(h) Subsequent to the effective date of this rule, registered transfer agents that:

(1) Assume the maintenance and updating of master securityholder files from predecessor transfer agents,

(2) Establish a new master securityholder file for a particular issue, or

(3) Convert from manual to automated systems, must carry over any existing certificate detail required by this rule on the master securityholder file. A recordkeeping transfer agent shall not be required to add certificate detail to the master securityholder file respecting certificates issued prior to the effective date of this rule.

Rule 17Ad–11. Reports regarding aged record differences, buy–ins and failure to post certificate detail to master securityholder and subsidiary files

(a) *Definitions.* (1) *Issuer capitalization* means the market value of the issuer's authorized and outstanding equity securities or, with respect to a municipal securities issuer, the market value of all debt issues for which the transfer agent performs recordkeeping functions on behalf of that issuer, determined by reference to the control book and current market prices.

(2) An *aged record difference* is a record difference that has existed for more than thirty calendar days.

(b) *Reports to Issuers.* (1) Within ten business days following the end of each month, every recordkeeping transfer agent shall report the information specified in paragraph (d)(1) of this rule to the persons specified in paragraph (b)(3) of this rule, when the aggregate market value of aged record differences in all equity securities issues or debt securities issues maintained on behalf of a particular issuer exceeds the thresholds set forth in the table below.

Issuer Capitalization	Aggregate Market Value of Aged Record Differences Exceeds: For equity securities	For debt securities
1) $5 million or less	$ 50,000	$ 100,000
2) Greater than $5 million but less than $50 million	$ 250,000	$ 500,000
3) Greater than $50 million but less than $150 million	$ 500,000	$1,000,000
4) Greater than $150 million	$1,000,000	$2,000,000

(2) Within ten business days following the end of each month (or within ten days thereafter in the case of a named transfer agent that receives a report from a service company pursuant to paragraph (b)(3)(i)(C)), every recordkeeping transfer agent shall report the information specified in paragraph (d)(2) of this rule to the persons specified in paragraph (b)(3) of this rule, with respect to each issue of securities for which it acts as recordkeeping transfer agent, concerning any securities bought-in pursuant to Rule 17Ad–10(g) or reported as bought-in pursuant to Rule 17Ad–10(c) during the preceding month.

(3) The report shall be sent:

(i) By every recordkeeping transfer agent (other than a recordkeeping transfer agent that performs transfer agent functions solely for its own securities):

(A) To the official performing corporate secretary functions for the issuer of the securities for which the aged record difference exists or for which the buy-in occurred;

(B) With respect to an issue of municipal securities, to the chief financial officer of the issuer of the securities for which the aged record difference exists or for which the buy-in occurred; or

(C) If it acts as a service company, to the named transfer agent; and

(ii) By every named transfer agent that is engaged by an issuer to maintain and update the master securityholder file:

(A) To the official performing corporate secretary functions for the issuer of the securities for which the aged record difference exists or for which the buy-in occurred; or

(B) With respect to an issue of municipal securities, to the chief financial officer of the issuer of the securities for which the aged record difference exists or for which the buy-in occurred.

(c) *Reports to Appropriate Regulatory Agencies.* (1) Within ten business days following the end of each calendar quarter, every recordkeeping transfer agent shall report the information specified in paragraph (d)(1) of this rule to its appropriate regulatory agency in accordance with Rule 17Ad–2(h), when the aggregate market value of aged record differences for all issues for which it performs recordkeeping functions exceeds the thresholds specified below:

(i) $300,000 if it is a recordkeeping transfer agent for 5 or fewer issues;

(ii) $500,000 for 6–24 issues;

(iii) $800,000 for 25–49 issues;

(iv) $1 million for 50–74 issues;

(v) $1.2 million for 75–99 issues;

(vi) $1.4 million for 100–499 issues;

(vii) $1.6 million for 500–999 issues;

(viii) $2.6 million for 1000–1999 issues; and

(ix) An additional $1 million for each additional 1000 issues.

(2) Within ten business days following the end of each calendar quarter, every recordkeeping transfer agent shall report the information specified in paragraph (d)(2) of this rule to its appropriate regulatory agency in accordance with Rule 17Ad–2(h), concerning buy-ins of all issues for which it acts as recordkeeping transfer agent, when the aggregate market value of all buy-ins executed pursuant to Rule 17Ad–10(g) during that calendar quarter exceeds $100,000.

(3) When the recordkeeping transfer agent has any debits or credits for securities transferred, purchased, redeemed or issued that are unposted to the master securityholder and/or subsidiary files for more than five business days after debits and credits are required to be posted to the mas-

ter securityholder file or subsidiary files pursuant to Rule 17Ad–10, it shall immediately report such fact to its appropriate regulatory agency in accordance with Rule 17Ad–2(h) and shall state in that report what steps have been, and are being, taken to correct the situation.

(d) *Content of Reports.* (1) Each report pursuant to paragraphs (b)(1) and (c)(1) of this rule shall set forth with respect to each issue of securities:

(i) The principal dollar amount and related market value of debt securities or the number of shares and related market value of equity securities comprising the aged record difference (including information concerning aged record differences existing as of the effective date of this rule);

(ii) The reasons for the aged record difference; and

(iii) The steps being taken or to be taken to resolve the aged record difference.

(2) Each report pursuant to paragraphs (b)(2) and (c)(2) of this rule shall set forth with respect to each issue of securities:

(i) The principal dollar amount of debt securities and related market value or the number of shares and related market value of equity securities comprising any buy-in executed pursuant to Rule 17Ad–10(g);

(ii) The party that executed the buy-in; and

(iii) The reason for the buy-in.

(e) For purposes of this rule, the market value of an issue shall be determined as of the last business day on which market value information is available during the reporting period.

(f) A copy of any report required under this section shall be retained by the reporting transfer agent for a period of not less than three years, the first year in an easily accessible place.

Rule 17Ad–12. Safeguarding of funds and securities

(a) Any registered transfer agent that has custody or possession of any funds or securities related to its transfer agent activities shall assure that:

(1) All such securities are held in safekeeping and are handled, in light of all facts and circumstances, in a manner reasonably free from risk of theft, loss or destruction (other than by a transfer agent's certificate destruction procedures pursuant to Rule 17Ad–19) and

(2) All such funds are protected, in light of all facts and circumstances, against misuse. In evaluating which particular safeguards and procedures must be employed, the cost of the various safeguards and procedures as well as the nature and degree of potential financial exposure are two relevant factors.

(b) For purposes of this rule, the term *securities* shall have the same meaning as the term *securities certificate* as defined in Rule 17f–1(a)(6).

Rule 17Ad–13. Annual study and evaluation of internal accounting control

(a) *Accountant's Report.* Every registered transfer agent, except as provided in paragraph (d) of this rule, shall file annually with the Commission and the transfer agent's appropriate regulatory agency in accordance with Rule 17Ad–2(h), a report specified in paragraph (a)(1) of this rule prepared by an independent accountant concerning the transfer agent's system of internal accounting control and related procedures for the transfer of record ownership and the safeguarding of related securities and funds. That report shall be filed within 90 calendar days of the date of the study and evaluation set forth in paragraph (a)(1).

(1) The accountant's report shall:

(i) State whether the study and evaluation was made in accordance with generally accepted auditing standards using the criteria set forth in paragraph (a)(3) of this rule;

(ii) Describe any material inadequacies found to exist as of the date of the study and evaluation and any corrective action taken, or if no material inadequacy existed, the report shall so state;

(iii) Comment on the current status of any material inadequacy described in the immediately preceding report; and

(iv) Indicate the date of the study and evaluation.

(2) The study and evaluation of the transfer agent's system of internal accounting control for the transfer of record ownership and the safeguarding of related securities and funds shall cover the following:

(i) Transferring securities related to changes of ownership (*i.e.*, cancellation of certificates or other instruments evidencing prior ownership and issuance of certificates or instruments evidencing current ownership);

(ii) Registering changes of ownership on the books and records of the issuer;

(iii) Transferring record ownership as a result of corporate actions (*e.g.*, issuance, retirement, redemption, liquidation, conversion, exchange, tender offer or other types of reorganization);

(iv) Dividend disbursement or interest paying-agent activities;

(v) Administering dividend reinvestment programs; and

(vi) Distributing statements respecting initial offerings of securities.

(3) For purposes of this report, the objectives of a transfer agent's system of internal accounting control for the transfer of record ownership and the safeguarding of related securities and funds should be to provide reasonable, but not absolute, assurance that securities and funds are safeguarded against loss from unauthorized use or disposition and that transfer agent activities are performed promptly and accurately. For purposes of this report, a material inadequacy is a condition for which the independent accountant believes that the prescribed procedures or the degree of compliance with them do not reduce to a relatively low level the risk that errors or irregularities, in amounts that would have a significant adverse effect on the transfer agent's ability promptly and accurately to transfer record ownership and safeguard related securities and funds, would occur or not be detected within a timely period by employees in the normal course of performing their assigned functions. Occurrence of errors or irregularities more frequently than in isolated instances may be evidence that the system has a material inadequacy. A significant adverse effect on a transfer agent's ability promptly and accurately to transfer record ownership and safeguard related securities and funds could result from any condition or conditions that individually, or taken as a whole, would reasonably be expected to:

(i) Inhibit the transfer agent from promptly and accurately discharging its responsibilities under its contractual agreement with the issuer;

(ii) Result in material financial loss to the transfer agent; or

(iii) Result in a violation of Rules 17Ad-2, 17Ad-10 or 17Ad-12(a).

(b) *Notice of Corrective Action.* If the accountant's report describes any material inadequacy, the transfer agent shall, within sixty calendar days after receipt of the report, notify the Commission and its appropriate regulatory agency in writing regarding the corrective action taken or proposed to be taken.

(c) *Record Retention.* The accountant's report and any documents required by paragraph (b) of this rule shall be maintained by the transfer agent for at least three years, the first year in an easily accessible place.

(d) *Exemptions.* The requirements of Rule 17Ad-13 shall not apply to registered transfer agents that qualify for exemptions pursuant to this paragraph, 17Ad-13(d).

(1) A registered transfer agent shall be exempt if it performs transfer agent functions solely for:

(i) Its own securities;

(ii) Securities issued by a subsidiary in which it owns 51% or more of the subsidiary's capital stock; and

(iii) Securities issued by another corporation that owns 51% or more of the capital stock of the registered transfer agent.

(2) A registered transfer agent shall be exempt if it:

(i) Is an exempt transfer agent pursuant to Rule 17Ad-4(b); and

(ii) In the case of a transfer agent that performs transfer agent functions for redeemable securities issued by companies registered under section 8 of the Investment Company Act of 1940, maintains master securityholder files consisting of fewer than 1000 shareholder accounts, in the aggregate, for each of such issues for which it performs transfer agent functions.

(3) A registered transfer agent shall be exempt if it is a bank or financial institution subject to regulation by the Board of Governors of the Federal Reserve System, the Office of the Comptroller of the Currency or the Federal Deposit Insurance Corporation, provided that it is not notified to the contrary by its appropriate regulatory agency and provided that a report similar in scope to the requirements of Rule 17Ad-13(a) is prepared for either the bank's board of directors or an audit committee of the board of directors.

Rule 17Ad–14. Tender agents

(a) *Establishing Book–Entry Depository Accounts.* When securities of a subject company have been declared eligible by one or more qualified registered securities depositories for the services of those depositories at the time a tender or exchange offer is commenced, no registered transfer agent shall act on behalf of the bidder as a depositary, in the case of a tender offer, or an exchange agent, in the case of an exchange offer, in connection with a tender or exchange offer, unless that transfer agent has established, within two business days after commencement of the offer, specially designated accounts. These accounts shall be maintained throughout the duration of the offer, including protection periods, with all qualified registered securities depositories holding the subject company's securities, for purposes of receiving from depository participants securities being tendered to the bidder by book-entry delivery pursuant to transmittal letters and other documentation and for purposes of allowing tender agents to return to depository participants by book-entry movement securities withdrawn from the offer.

(b) *Exclusions.* The rule shall not apply to tender or exchange offers (1) that are made for a class of securities of a subject company that has fewer than (i) 500 security holders of record for that class, or (ii) 500,000 shares of that class outstanding; or (2) that are made exclusively to security holders of fewer than 100 shares of a class of securities.

(c) *Definitions.* For purposes of this rule, (1) the terms *subject company, business day, security holders,* and *transmittal letter* shall be given the meanings provided in Rule 14d–1(b); (2) unless the context otherwise requires, a tender or exchange offer shall be deemed to have commenced as specified in Rule 14d–2; (3) the term *bidder* shall mean any person who makes a tender or exchange offer or on whose behalf a tender or exchange offer is made; (4) a *qualified registered securities depository* shall mean a registered clearing agency having rules and procedures approved by the Commission pursuant to section 19 of the Securities Exchange Act of 1934 to enable book-entry delivery of the securities of the subject company to, and return of those securities from, the transfer agent through the facilities of that securities depository; and (5) the term *depositary* refers to that agent of the bidder receiving securities from tendering depository participants and paying those participants for shares tendered. The term *exchange agent* refers to the agent performing like functions in connection with an exchange offer.

(d) *Exemptions.* The Commission may exempt from the provisions of this rule, either unconditionally or on specified terms and conditions, any registered transfer agent, tender or exchange offer, or class of tender or exchange offers, if the Commission determines that an exemption is consistent with the public interest, the protection of investors, the prompt and accurate clearance and settlement of securities transactions, the maintenance of fair and orderly markets, or the removal of impediments to a national clearance and settlement system.

Rule 17Ad–15. Signature guarantees

(a) *Definitions.* For purposes of this rule, the following terms shall mean:

(1) *Act* means the Securities Exchange Act of 1934;

(2) *Eligible Guarantor Institution* means:

(i) Banks (as that term is defined in Section 3(a) of the Federal Deposit Insurance Act [12 U.S.C. 1813(a)]);

(ii) Brokers, dealers, municipal securities dealers, municipal securities brokers, government securities dealers, and government securities brokers, as those terms are defined under the Act;

(iii) Credit unions (as that term is defined in Section 19(b)(1)(A) of the Federal Reserve Act [12 U.S.C. 461(b)]);

(iv) National securities exchanges, registered securities associations, clearing agencies, as those terms are used under the Act; and

(v) Savings associations (as that term is defined in section 3(b) of the Federal Deposit Insurance Act [12 U.S.C. 1813(b)]).

(3) *Guarantee* means a guarantee of the signature of the person endorsing a certificated security, or originating an instruction to transfer ownership of a security or instructions concerning transfer of securities.

(b) *Acceptance of Signature Guarantees.* A registered transfer agent shall not, directly or indirectly, engage in any activity in connection with a guarantee, including the acceptance or rejection of such guarantee, that results in the inequitable treatment of any eligible guarantor institution or a class of institutions.

(c) *Transfer Agent's Standards and Procedures.* Every registered transfer agent shall establish:

(1) written standards for the acceptance of guarantees of securities transfers from eligible guarantor institutions; and

(2) procedures, including written guidelines where appropriate to ensure that those standards are used in determining whether to accept or reject guarantees from eligible guarantor institutions. Such standards and procedures shall not establish terms and conditions (including those pertaining to financial condition) that, as written or applied, treat different classes of eligible guarantor institutions inequitably, or result in the rejection of a guarantee from an eligible guarantor institution solely because the guarantor institution is of a particular type specified in paragraphs (a)(2)(i)—(a)(2)(iv) of this rule.

(d) *Rejection of Items Presented for Transfer.* (1) No registered transfer agent shall reject a request for transfer of a certificated or uncertificated security because the certificate, instruction, or documents accompanying the certificate or instruction includes an unacceptable guarantee, unless the transfer agent determines that the guarantor, if it is an eligible guarantor institution, does not satisfy the transfer agent's written standards or procedures.

(2) A registered transfer agent shall notify the guarantor and the presentor of the rejection and the reasons for the rejection within two business days after rejecting a transfer request because of a determination that the guarantor does not satisfy the transfer agent's written standards or procedures. Notification to the presentor may be accomplished by making the rejected item available to the presentor. Notification to the guarantor may be accomplished by telephone, facsimile, or ordinary mail.

(e) *Record Retention.* (1) Every registered transfer agent shall maintain a copy of the standards and procedures specified in paragraph (c) of this rule in an easily accessible place.

(2) Every registered transfer agent shall make available a copy of the standards and procedures specified in paragraph (c) of this rule to any person requesting a copy of such standards and procedures. The registered transfer agent shall respond within three days of a request for such standards and procedures by sending the requesting party a copy of the requested transfer agent's standards and procedures.

(3) Every registered transfer agent shall maintain, for a period of three years following the date of the rejection, a record of transfers rejected, including the reason for the rejection, who the guarantor was and whether the guarantor failed to meet the transfer agent's guarantee standards.

(f) *Exclusions.* Nothing in this rule shall prohibit a transfer agent from rejecting a request for transfer of a certificated or uncertificated security;

(1) For reasons unrelated to acceptance of the guarantor institution;

(2) Because the person acting on behalf of the guarantor institution is not authorized by that institution to act on its behalf, provided that the transfer agent maintains a list of people authorized to act on behalf of that guarantor institution; or

(3) Because the eligible guarantor institution of a type specified in paragraph (a)(2)(ii) of this rule is neither a member of a clearing corporation nor maintains net capital of at least $100,000.

(g) *Signature Guarantee Program.* (1) A registered transfer agent shall be deemed to comply with paragraph (c) of this rule if its standards and procedures include:

(i) Rejecting a request for transfer because the guarantor is neither a member of nor a participant in a signature guarantee program; or

(ii) Accepting a guarantee from an eligible guarantor institution who, at the time of issuing the guarantee, is a member of or participant in a signature guarantee program.

(2) Within the first six months after revising its standards and procedures to include a signature guarantee program, the transfer agent shall not reject a request for transfer because the guarantor is neither a member of nor participant in a signature guarantee program, unless the transfer agent has given that guarantor ninety days written notice of the transfer agent's intent to reject transfers with guarantees from written notice of the transfer agents intent to reject transfers with guarantees from non-participating or non-member guarantors.

(3) For purposes of paragraph (g) of this rule the term "signature guarantee program," means a program, the terms and conditions of which the transfer agent reasonably determines:

(i) To facilitate the equitable treatment of eligible guarantor institutions; and

(ii) To promote the prompt, accurate and safe transfer of securities by providing:

(A) Adequate protection to the transfer agent against risk of financial loss in the event persons have no recourse against the eligible guarantor institution; and

(B) Adequate protection to the transfer agent against the issuance of unauthorized guarantees.

Rule 17Ad–16. Notice of assumption or termination of transfer agent services

(a) A registered transfer agent that ceases to perform transfer agent services on behalf of an issuer of securities, including a registered transfer agent that ceases to perform transfer agent services on behalf of an issuer of securities because of a merger or acquisition by another transfer agent, shall send written notice of such termination to the appropriate qualified registered securities depository on or before the later of ten calendar days prior to the effective date of such termination or the day the transfer agent is notified of the effective date of such termination. Such notice shall include the full name, address, telephone number, and Financial Industry Number Standard ("FINS") number of the transfer agent ceasing to perform the transfer agent services for the issuer; the issuer's name; the issue or issues handled and their CUSIP number(s); and if known, the name, address, and telephone number of the transfer agent that thereafter will provide transfer services for the issuer. If no successor transfer agent is known, the notice shall include the name and address of a contact person at the issuer.

(b) A registered transfer agent that changes its name or address or that assumes transfer agent services on behalf of an issuer of securities, including a transfer agent that assumes transfer agent services on behalf of an issuer of securities because of a merger or acquisition of another transfer agent, shall send written notice of such to the appropriate qualified registered securities depository on or before the later of ten calendar days prior to the effective date of such change in status or the day the transfer agent is notified of the effective date of such change in status. A notice regarding a change of name or address shall include the full name, address, telephone number, and FINS number of the transfer agent and the location where certificates are received for transfer. A notice regarding the assumption of transfer agent services on behalf of an issuer of securities, including assumption of transfer agent services resulting from the merger or acquisition of another transfer agent, shall include the full name, address, telephone number, and FINS number of the transfer agent assuming the transfer agent services for the issuer; the issuer's name; and the issue or issues handled and their CUSIP number(s).

(c) The notice described in paragraphs (a) and (b) of this rule shall be delivered by means of secure communication. For purposes of this rule, secure communication shall include telegraph, overnight mail, facsimile, or any other form of secure communication.

(d)(1) The appropriate qualified registered securities depository that receives notices pursuant to paragraphs (a) and (b) of this rule shall deliver within 24 hours a copy of such notices to each qualified registered securities depository. A qualified registered securities depository that receives notice pursuant to this rule shall deliver a copy of such notices to its own participants within 24 hours.

(2) A qualified registered securities depository may comply with its notice requirements under paragraph (d)(1) of this rule by making available the notice of all material information from the notice within 24 hours in a manner set forth in the rules of the qualified registered securities depository.

(3) A qualified registered securities depository shall maintain such notices for a period of not less than two years, the first six months in an easily accessible place. Such notice shall be made available to the Commission or other persons as the Commission may designate by order.

(4) A registered transfer agent that provides notice pursuant to paragraphs (a) and (b) of this rule shall maintain such notice for a period of not less than two years, the first six months in an easily accessible place.

(e) For purposes of this rule, a *qualified registered securities depository* shall mean a clearing agency registered under section 17A of the Act (15 U.S.C. 78q–1) that performs clearing agency functions as described in Section 3(a)(23)(A)(i) of the Act (15 U.S.C. 78c(a)(23)(A)(i)) and that has rules and procedures concerning its responsibility for maintaining, updating, and providing appropriate access to the information it receives pursuant to this rule.

(f) For purposes of this rule, an *appropriate qualified registered securities depository* shall mean the qualified registered securities depository that the Commission so designates by order or, in the absence of such designation, the qualified registered securities depository that is the largest holder of record of all qualified registered securities depositories as of the most recent record date.

Rule 17Ad–17. Lost securityholders and unresponsive payees

(a)(1) Every recordkeeping transfer agent whose master securityholder file includes accounts of lost securityholders and every broker or dealer that has customer security accounts that include accounts of lost securityholders shall exercise reasonable care to ascertain the correct addresses of such securityholders. In exercising reasonable care to ascertain such lost securityholders' correct addresses, each such recordkeeping transfer agent and each such broker or dealer shall conduct two database searches using at least one information database service. The transfer agent, broker, or dealer shall search by taxpayer identification number or by name if a search based on taxpayer identification number is not reasonably likely to locate the securityholder. Such database searches must be conducted without charge to a lost securityholder and with the following frequency:

(i) Between three and twelve months of such securityholder becoming a lost securityholder; and

(ii) Between six and twelve months after the first search for such lost securityholder by the transfer agent, broker, or dealer.

(2) A transfer agent, broker, or dealer may not use a search method or service to establish contact with lost securityholders that results in a charge to a lost securityholder prior to completing the searches set forth in paragraph (a)(1) of this section.

(3) A transfer agent, broker, or dealer need not conduct the searches set forth in paragraph (a)(1) of this section for a lost securityholder if:

(i) It has received documentation that such securityholder is deceased; or

(ii) The aggregate value of assets listed in the lost securityholder's account, including all dividend, interest, and other payments due to the lost securityholder and all securities owned by the lost securityholder as recorded in the master securityholder files of the transfer agent or in the customer security account records of the broker or dealer, is less than $25; or

(iii) The securityholder is not a natural person.

(b) For purposes of this section:

(1) *Information data base service* means either:

(i) Any automated data base service that contains addresses from the entire United States geographic area, contains the names of at least 50% of the United States adult population, is indexed by taxpayer identification number or name, and is updated at least four times a year; or

(ii) Any service or combination of services which produces results comparable to those of the service described in paragraph (b)(1)(i) of this rule in locating lost securityholders.

(2) *Lost securityholder* means a securityholder:

(i) To whom an item of correspondence that was sent to the securityholder at the address contained in the transfer agent's master securityholder file or in the customer security account records of the broker or dealer has been returned as undeliverable; provided, however, that if such item is re-sent within one month to the lost securityholder, the transfer agent, broker, or dealer may deem the securityholder to be a lost securityholder as of the day the re-sent item is returned as undeliverable; and

(ii) For whom the transfer agent, broker, or dealer has not received information regarding the securityholder's new address.

(c)(1) The paying agent, as defined in paragraph (c)(2) of this section, shall provide not less than one written notification to each unresponsive payee, as defined in paragraph (c)(3) of this section, stating that such unresponsive payee has been sent a check that has not yet been negotiated. Such notification may be sent with a check or other mailing subsequently sent to the unresponsive payee but must be provided no later than seven (7) months (or 210 days) after the sending of the not yet negotiated check. The paying agent shall not be required to send a written notice to an unresponsive payee if such unresponsive payee would be considered a lost securityholder by a transfer agent, broker, or dealer.

(2) The term *paying agent* shall include any issuer, transfer agent, broker, dealer, investment adviser, indenture trustee, custodian, or any other person that accepts payments from the issuer of a security and distributes the payments to the holders of the security.

(3) A securityholder shall be considered an *unresponsive payee* if a check is sent to the securityholder by the paying agent and the check is not negotiated before the earlier of the paying agent's sending the next regularly scheduled check or the elapsing of six (6) months (or 180 days) after the sending of the not yet negotiated check. A secu-

rityholder shall no longer be considered an *unresponsive payee* when the securityholder negotiates the check or checks that caused the securityholder to be considered an *unresponsive payee.*

(4) A paying agent shall be excluded from the requirements of paragraph (c)(1) of this section where the value of the not yet negotiated check is less than $25.

(5) The requirements of paragraph (c)(1) of this section shall have no effect on state escheatment laws.

(d) Every recordkeeping transfer agent, every broker or dealer that has customer security accounts, and every paying agent shall maintain records to demonstrate compliance with the requirements set forth in this section, which records shall include written procedures that describe the transfer agent's, broker's, dealer's, or paying agent's methodology for complying with this section, and shall retain such records in accordance with Rule 17Ad–7(*i*).

Rule 17Ad–19. Requirements for cancellation, processing, storage, transportation, and destruction or other disposition of securities certificates

(a) *Definitions.* For purposes of this rule:

(1) The terms *cancelled* or *cancellation* means the process in which a securities certificate:

(i) Is physically marked to clearly indicate that it no longer represents a claim against the issuer; and

(ii) Is voided on the records of the transfer agent.

(2) The term *cancelled certificate facility* means any location where securities certificates are cancelled and thereafter processed, stored, transported, destroyed or otherwise disposed of.

(3) The term *certificate number* means a unique identification or serial number that is assigned and affixed by an issuer or transfer agent to each securities certificate.

(4) The term *controlled access* means the practice of permitting the entry of only authorized personnel to areas where securities certificates are cancelled and thereafter processed, stored, transported, destroyed or otherwise disposed of.

(5) The term *CUSIP number* means the unique identification number that is assigned to each securities issue.

(6) The term *destruction* means the physical ruination of a securities certificate by a transfer agent as part of the certificate destruction procedures that make the reconstruction of the certificate impossible.

(7) The term *otherwise disposed of* means any disposition other than by destruction.

(8) The term *securities certificate* has the same meaning that it has in Rule 17f–1(a)(6).

(b) *Required Procedures for the Cancellation, Storage, Transportation, Destruction, or Other Disposition of Securities Certificates.* Every transfer agent involved in the handling, processing, or storage of securities certificates shall establish and implement written procedures for the cancellation, storage, transportation, destruction, or other disposition of securities certificates. This requirement applies to any agent that the transfer agent uses to perform any of these activities.

(c) *Written Procedures.* The written procedures required by paragraph (b) of this rule at a minimum shall provide that:

(1) There is controlled access to any cancelled certificate facility;

(2) Each cancelled certificate be marked with the word "CANCELLED" by stamp or perforation on the face of the certificate unless the transfer agent has procedures adopted pursuant to this rule for the destruction of cancelled certificates within three business days of their cancellation;

(3) A record that is indexed and retrievable by CUSIP and certificate number that contains the CUSIP number, certificate number with any prefix or suffix, denomination, registration, issue date, and cancellation date of each cancelled certificate;

(4) A record that is indexed and retrievable by CUSIP and certificate number of each destroyed securities certificate or securities certificate otherwise disposed of, the records must contain for each destroyed or otherwise disposed of certificate the CUSIP number, certificate number with any prefix or suffix, denomination, registration, issue date, and cancellation date, and additionally for any certificate otherwise disposed of a record of how it was disposed of, the name and address of the party to whom it was disposed, and the date of disposition;

(5) The physical transportation of cancelled certificates be made in a secure manner and that

the transfer agent maintain separately a record of the CUSIP number and certificate number of each certificate in transit;

(6) Authorized personnel of the transfer agent or its designee supervise and witness the intentional destruction of any cancelled certificate and retain copies of all records relating to certificates which were destroyed; and

(7) Reports to the Lost and Stolen Securities Program be effected in a timely and complete manner, as provided in Rule 17f–1 of any cancelled certificate that is lost, stolen, missing, or counterfeit.

(d) *Recordkeeping*. Every transfer agent subject to this rule shall maintain records that demonstrate compliance with the requirements set forth in this rule and that describe the transfer agent's methodology for complying with this rule for three years, the first year in an easily accessible place.

(e) *Exemptive Authority*. Upon written application or upon its own motion, the Commission may grant an exemption from any of the provisions of this rule, either unconditionally or on specific terms and conditions, to any transfer agent or any class of transfer agents and to any securities certificate or any class of securities certificates.

Rule 17Ad–20. Issuer restrictions or prohibitions on ownership by securities intermediaries

(a) Except as provided in paragraph (c) of this rule, no registered transfer agent shall transfer any equity security registered pursuant to section 12 or any equity security that subjects an issuer to reporting under section 15(d) of the Act (15 U.S.C. 78l or 15 U.S.C. 78o(d)) if such security is subject to any restriction or prohibition on transfer to or from a securities intermediary in its capacity as such.

(b) The term *securities intermediary* means a clearing agency registered under section 17A of the Act (15 U.S.C. 78q–1) or a person, including a bank, broker, or dealer, that in the ordinary course of its business maintains securities accounts for others in its capacity as such.

(c) The provisions of this rule shall not apply to any equity security issued by a partnership as defined in Rule 901(b) of Regulation S–K (17 CFR 229.901(b)).

Rule 17Ad–22. Standards for clearing agencies

(a) *Definitions*. For purposes of this section:

(1) *Backtesting* means an ex-post comparison of actual outcomes with expected outcomes derived from the use of margin models.

(2) *Central counterparty* means a clearing agency that interposes itself between the counterparties to securities transactions, acting functionally as the buyer to every seller and the seller to every buyer.

(3) *Central securities depository services* means services of a clearing agency that is a securities depository as described in Section 3(a)(23)(A) of the Act (15 U.S.C. 78c(a)(23)(A)).

(4) *Clearing agency involved in activities with a more complex risk profile* means a clearing agency registered with the Commission under Section 17A of the Act (15 U.S.C. 78q–1) that:

(i) Provides central counterparty services for security-based swaps;

(ii) Has been determined by the Commission to be involved in activities with a more complex risk profile at the time of its initial registration; or

(iii) Is subsequently determined by the Commission to be involved in activities with a more complex risk profile pursuant to Rule 17Ab2–2(b).

(5) *Covered clearing agency* means a designated clearing agency or a clearing agency involved in activities with a more complex risk profile for which the Commodity Futures Trading Commission is not the Supervisory Agency as defined in Section 803(8) of the Payment, Clearing, and Settlement Supervision Act of 2010 (12 U.S.C. 5461 *et seq.*).

(6) *Designated clearing agency* means a clearing agency registered with the Commission under Section 17A of the Exchange Act (15 U.S.C. 78q–1) that is designated systemically important by the Financial Stability Oversight Council pursuant to the Payment, Clearing, and Settlement Supervision Act of 2010 (12 U.S.C. 5461 *et seq.*) and for which the Commission is the supervisory agency as defined in Section 803(8) of the Payment, Clearing, and Settlement Supervision Act of 2010 (12 U.S.C. 5461 *et seq.*).

(7) *Financial market utility* has the same meaning as defined in Section 803(6) of the Payment, Clearing, and Settlement Supervision Act of 2010 (12 U.S.C. 5462(6)).

(8) *Link* means, for purposes of paragraph (e)(20) of this section, a set of contractual and operational arrangements between two or more clearing agencies, financial market utilities, or trading markets that connect them directly or indirectly for the purposes of participating in settlement, cross margining, expanding their services to additional instruments or participants, or for any other purposes material to their business.

(9) *Model validation* means an evaluation of the performance of each material risk management model used by a covered clearing agency (and the related parameters and assumptions associated with such models), including initial margin models, liquidity risk models, and models used to generate clearing or guaranty fund requirements, performed by a qualified person who is free from influence from the persons responsible for the development or operation of the models or policies being validated.

(10) *Net capital* as used in paragraph (b)(7) of this section means net capital as defined in Rule 15c3–1 for broker-dealers or any similar risk adjusted capital calculation for all other prospective clearing members.

(11) *Normal market conditions* as used in paragraphs (b)(1) and (2) of this section means conditions in which the expected movement of the price of cleared securities would produce changes in a clearing agency's exposures to its participants that would be expected to breach margin requirements or other risk control mechanisms only one percent of the time.

(12) *Participant family* means that if a participant directly, or indirectly through one or more intermediaries, controls, is controlled by, or is under common control with, another participant then the affiliated participants shall be collectively deemed to be a single participant family for purposes of paragraphs (b)(3), (d)(14), (e)(4), and (e)(7) of this section.

(13) *Potential future exposure* means the maximum exposure estimated to occur at a future point in time with an established single-tailed confidence level of at least 99 percent with respect to the estimated distribution of future exposure.

(14) *Qualifying liquid resources* means, for any covered clearing agency, the following, in each relevant currency:

(i) Cash held either at the central bank of issue or at creditworthy commercial banks;

(ii) Assets that are readily available and convertible into cash through prearranged funding arrangements, such as:

(A) Committed arrangements without material adverse change provisions, including:

(1) Lines of credit;

(2) Foreign exchange swaps; and

(3) Repurchase agreements; or

(B) Other prearranged funding arrangements determined to be highly reliable even in extreme but plausible market conditions by the board of directors of the covered clearing agency following a review conducted for this purpose not less than annually; and

(iii) Other assets that are readily available and eligible for pledging to (or conducting other appropriate forms of transactions with) a relevant central bank, if the covered clearing agency has access to routine credit at such central bank in a jurisdiction that permits said pledges or other transactions by the covered clearing agency.

(15) *Security-based swap* means a security-based swap as defined in Section 3(a)(68) of the Act (15 U.S.C. 78c(a)(68)).

(16) *Sensitivity analysis* means an analysis that involves analyzing the sensitivity of a model to its assumptions, parameters, and inputs that:

(i) Considers the impact on the model of both moderate and extreme changes in a wide range of inputs, parameters, and assumptions, including correlations of price movements or returns if relevant, which reflect a variety of historical and hypothetical market conditions. Sensitivity analysis must use actual portfolios and, where applicable, hypothetical portfolios that reflect the characteristics of proprietary positions and customer positions;

(ii) When performed by or on behalf of a covered clearing agency involved in activities with a more complex risk profile, considers the most volatile relevant periods, where practical, that have been experienced by the markets served by the clearing agency; and

(iii) Tests the sensitivity of the model to stressed market conditions, including the market conditions that may ensue after the default of a member and other extreme but plausible conditions as defined in a covered clearing agency's risk policies.

(17) *Stress testing* means the estimation of credit or liquidity exposures that would result from the realization of potential stress scenarios, such as extreme price changes, multiple defaults, or changes in other valuation inputs and assumptions.

(18) *Systemically important in multiple jurisdictions* means, with respect to a covered clearing agency, a covered clearing agency that has been determined by the Commission to be systemically important in more than one jurisdiction pursuant to Rule 17Ab2–2.

(19) *Transparent* means, for the purposes of paragraphs (e)(1), (2), and (10) of this section, to the extent consistent with other statutory and Commission requirements on confidentiality and disclosure, that documentation required under paragraphs (e)(1), (2), and (10) is disclosed to the Commission and, as appropriate, to other relevant authorities, to clearing members and to customers of clearing members, to the owners of the covered clearing agency, and to the public.

(b) A registered clearing agency that performs central counterparty services shall establish, implement, maintain and enforce written policies and procedures reasonably designed to:

(1) Measure its credit exposures to its participants at least once a day and limit its exposures to potential losses from defaults by its participants under normal market conditions so that the operations of the clearing agency would not be disrupted and non-defaulting participants would not be exposed to losses that they cannot anticipate or control.

(2) Use margin requirements to limit its credit exposures to participants under normal market conditions and use risk-based models and parameters to set margin requirements and review such margin requirements and the related risk-based models and parameters at least monthly.

(3) Maintain sufficient financial resources to withstand, at a minimum, a default by the participant family to which it has the largest exposure in extreme but plausible market conditions; provided that a registered clearing agency acting as a central counterparty for security-based swaps shall maintain additional financial resources sufficient to withstand, at a minimum, a default by the two participant families to which it has the largest exposures in extreme but plausible market conditions, in its capacity as a central counterparty for security based swaps. Such policies and procedures may provide that the additional financial resources may be maintained by the security-based swap clearing agency generally or in separately maintained funds.

(4) Provide for an annual model validation consisting of evaluating the performance of the clearing agency's margin models and the related parameters and assumptions associated with such models by a qualified person who is free from influence from the persons responsible for the development or operation of the models being validated.

(5) Provide the opportunity for a person that does not perform any dealer or security based swap dealer services to obtain membership on fair and reasonable terms at the clearing agency to clear securities for itself or on behalf of other persons.

(6) Have membership standards that do not require that participants maintain a portfolio of any minimum size or that participants maintain a minimum transaction volume.

(7) Provide a person that maintains net capital equal to or greater than $50 million with the ability to obtain membership at the clearing agency, provided that such persons are able to comply with other reasonable membership standards, with any net capital requirements being scalable so that they are proportional to the risks posed by the participant's activities to the clearing agency; provided, however, that the clearing agency may provide for a higher net capital requirement as a condition for membership at the clearing agency if the clearing agency demonstrates to the Commission that such a requirement is necessary to mitigate risks that could not otherwise be effectively managed by other measures and the Commission approves the higher net capital requirement as part of a rule filing or clearing agency registration application.

(c) *Record of financial resources and annual audited financial statements.* (1) Each fiscal quarter (based on calculations made as of the last business day of the clearing agency's fiscal quarter), or at any time upon Commission request, a registered clearing agency that performs central counterparty services shall calculate and maintain a record, in accordance with Rule 17a–1, of the financial and qualifying liquid resources necessary to meet the requirements, as applicable, of paragraphs (b)(3), (e)(4), and (e)(7) of this section, and sufficient documentation to explain the methodology it uses to compute such financial resources or qualifying liquid resources requirement.

(2) Within 60 days after the end of its fiscal year, each registered clearing agency shall post on its website its annual audited financial statements. Such financial statements shall:

(i) Include, for the clearing agency and its subsidiaries, consolidated balance sheets as of the end of the two most recent fiscal years and statements of income, changes in stockholders' equity and other comprehensive income and cash flows for each of the two most recent fiscal years;

(ii) Be prepared in accordance with U.S. generally accepted accounting principles, except that for a clearing agency that is a corporation or other organization incorporated or organized under the laws of any foreign country the consolidated financial statements may be prepared in accordance with U.S. generally accepted accounting principles or International Financial Reporting Standards as issued by the International Accounting Standards Board;

(iii) Be audited in accordance with standards of the Public Company Accounting Oversight Board by a registered public accounting firm that is qualified and independent in accordance with Rule 2–01 of Regulation S–X; and

(iv) Include a report of the registered public accounting firm that complies with paragraphs (a) through (d) of Rule 2–02 of Regulation S–X.

(d) Each registered clearing agency that is not a covered clearing agency shall establish, implement, maintain and enforce written policies and procedures reasonably designed to, as applicable:

(1) Provide for a well-founded, transparent, and enforceable legal framework for each aspect of its activities in all relevant jurisdictions.

(2) Require participants to have sufficient financial resources and robust operational capacity to meet obligations arising from participation in the clearing agency; have procedures in place to monitor that participation requirements are met on an ongoing basis; and have participation requirements that are objective and publicly disclosed, and permit fair and open access.

(3) Hold assets in a manner that minimizes risk of loss or of delay in its access to them; and invest assets in instruments with minimal credit, market and liquidity risks.

(4) Identify sources of operational risk and minimize them through the development of appropriate systems, controls, and procedures; implement systems that are reliable, resilient and secure, and have adequate, scalable capacity; and have business continuity plans that allow for timely recovery of operations and fulfillment of a clearing agency's obligations.

(5) Employ money settlement arrangements that eliminate or strictly limit the clearing agency's settlement bank risks, that is, its credit and liquidity risks from the use of banks to effect money settlements with its participants; and require funds transfers to the clearing agency to be final when effected.

(6) Be cost-effective in meeting the requirements of participants while maintaining safe and secure operations.

(7) Evaluate the potential sources of risks that can arise when the clearing agency establishes links either cross-border or domestically to clear or settle trades, and ensure that the risks are managed prudently on an ongoing basis.

(8) Have governance arrangements that are clear and transparent to fulfill the public interest requirements in Section 17A of the Act applicable to clearing agencies, to support the objectives of owners and participants, and to promote the effectiveness of the clearing agency's risk management procedures.

(9) Provide market participants with sufficient information for them to identify and evaluate the risks and costs associated with using its services.

(10) Immobilize or dematerialize securities certificates and transfer them by book entry to the greatest extent possible when the clearing agency provides central securities depository services.

(11) Make key aspects of the clearing agency's default procedures publicly available and establish default procedures that ensure that the clearing agency can take timely action to contain losses and liquidity pressures and to continue meeting its obligations in the event of a participant default.

(12) Ensure that final settlement occurs no later than the end of the settlement day; and require that intraday or real-time finality be provided where necessary to reduce risks.

(13) Eliminate principal risk by linking securities transfers to funds transfers in a way that achieves delivery versus payment.

(14) Institute risk controls, including collateral requirements and limits to cover the clearing agency's credit exposure to each participant family exposure fully, that ensure timely settlement in the event that the participant with the largest payment obligation is unable to settle when the clearing agency provides central securities depository services and extends intraday credit to participants.

(15) State to its participants the clearing agency's obligations with respect to physical deliveries and identify and manage the risks from these obligations.

(e) Each covered clearing agency shall establish, implement, maintain and enforce written policies and procedures reasonably designed to, as applicable:

(1) Provide for a well-founded, clear, transparent, and enforceable legal basis for each aspect of its activities in all relevant jurisdictions.

(2) Provide for governance arrangements that:

(i) Are clear and transparent;

(ii) Clearly prioritize the safety and efficiency of the covered clearing agency;

(iii) Support the public interest requirements in Section 17A of the Act (15 U.S.C. 78q–1) applicable to clearing agencies, and the objectives of owners and participants;

(iv) Establish that the board of directors and senior management have appropriate experience and skills to discharge their duties and responsibilities;

(v) Specify clear and direct lines of responsibility; and

(vi) Consider the interests of participants' customers, securities issuers and holders, and other relevant stakeholders of the covered clearing agency.

(3) Maintain a sound risk management framework for comprehensively managing legal, credit, liquidity, operational, general business, investment, custody, and other risks that arise in or are borne by the covered clearing agency, which:

(i) Includes risk management policies, procedures, and systems designed to identify, measure, monitor, and manage the range of risks that arise in or are borne by the covered clearing agency, that are subject to review on a specified periodic basis and approved by the board of directors annually;

(ii) Includes plans for the recovery and orderly wind-down of the covered clearing agency necessitated by credit losses, liquidity shortfalls, losses from general business risk, or any other losses;

(iii) Provides risk management and internal audit personnel with sufficient authority, resources, independence from management, and access to the board of directors;

(iv) Provides risk management and internal audit personnel with a direct reporting line to, and oversight by, a risk management committee and an independent audit committee of the board of directors, respectively; and

(v) Provides for an independent audit committee.

(4) Effectively identify, measure, monitor, and manage its credit exposures to participants and those arising from its payment, clearing, and settlement processes, including by:

(i) Maintaining sufficient financial resources to cover its credit exposure to each participant fully with a high degree of confidence;

(ii) To the extent not already maintained pursuant to paragraph (e)(4)(i) of this section, for a covered clearing agency providing central counterparty services that is either systemically important in multiple jurisdictions or a clearing agency involved in activities with a more complex risk profile, maintaining additional financial resources at the minimum to enable it to cover a wide range of foreseeable stress scenarios that include, but are not limited to, the default of the two participant families that would potentially cause the largest aggregate credit exposure for the covered clearing agency in extreme but plausible market conditions;

(iii) To the extent not already maintained pursuant to paragraph (e)(4)(i) of this section, for a covered clearing agency not subject to paragraph (e)(4)(ii) of this rule, maintaining additional financial resources at the minimum to enable it to cover a wide range of foreseeable stress scenarios that include, but are not limited to, the default of the participant family that would potentially cause the largest aggregate credit exposure for the covered clearing agency in extreme but plausible market conditions;

(iv) Including prefunded financial resources, exclusive of assessments for additional guaranty fund contributions or other resources that are not prefunded, when calculating the financial resources available to meet the standards under paragraphs (e)(4)(i) through (iii) of this section, as applicable;

(v) Maintaining the financial resources required under paragraphs (e)(4)(ii) and (iii) of this section, as applicable, in combined or separately maintained clearing or guaranty funds;

(vi) Testing the sufficiency of its total financial resources available to meet the minimum financial resource requirements under paragraphs (e)(4)(i) through (iii) of this section, as applicable, by:

(A) Conducting stress testing of its total financial resources once each day using standard predetermined parameters and assumptions;

(B) Conducting a comprehensive analysis on at least a monthly basis of the existing stress testing scenarios, models, and underlying parameters and assumptions, and considering modifications to ensure they are appropriate for determining the covered clearing agency's required level of default protection in light of current and evolving market conditions;

(C) Conducting a comprehensive analysis of stress testing scenarios, models, and underlying parameters and assumptions more frequently than monthly when the products cleared or markets served display high volatility or become less liquid, or when the size or concentration of positions held by the covered clearing agency's participants increases significantly; and

(D) Reporting the results of its analyses under paragraphs (e)(4)(vi)(B) and (C) of this section to appropriate decision makers at the covered clearing agency, including but not limited to, its risk management committee or board of directors, and using these results to evaluate the adequacy of and adjust its margin methodology, model parameters, models used to generate clearing or guaranty fund requirements, and any other relevant aspects of its credit risk management framework, in supporting compliance with the minimum financial resources requirements set forth in paragraphs (e)(4)(i) through (iii) of this section;

(vii) Performing a model validation for its credit risk models not less than annually or more frequently as may be contemplated by the covered clearing agency's risk management framework established pursuant to paragraph (e)(3) of this section;

(viii) Addressing allocation of credit losses the covered clearing agency may face if its collateral and other resources are insufficient to fully cover its credit exposures, including the repayment of any funds the covered clearing agency may borrow from liquidity providers; and

(ix) Describing the covered clearing agency's process to replenish any financial resources it may use following a default or other event in which use of such resources is contemplated.

(5) Limit the assets it accepts as collateral to those with low credit, liquidity, and market risks, and set and enforce appropriately conservative haircuts and concentration limits if the covered clearing agency requires collateral to manage its or its participants' credit exposure; and require a review of the sufficiency of its collateral haircuts and concentration limits to be performed not less than annually.

(6) Cover, if the covered clearing agency provides central counterparty services, its credit exposures to its participants by establishing a risk-based margin system that, at a minimum:

(i) Considers, and produces margin levels commensurate with, the risks and particular attributes of each relevant product, portfolio, and market;

(ii) Marks participant positions to market and collects margin, including variation margin or equivalent charges if relevant, at least daily and includes the authority and operational capacity to make intraday margin calls in defined circumstances;

(iii) Calculates margin sufficient to cover its potential future exposure to participants in the interval between the last margin collection and the close out of positions following a participant default;

(iv) Uses reliable sources of timely price data and uses procedures and sound valuation models for addressing circumstances in which pricing data are not readily available or reliable;

(v) Uses an appropriate method for measuring credit exposure that accounts for relevant product risk factors and portfolio effects across products;

(vi) Is monitored by management on an ongoing basis and is regularly reviewed, tested, and verified by:

(A) Conducting backtests of its margin model at least once each day using standard predetermined parameters and assumptions;

(B) Conducting a sensitivity analysis of its margin model and a review of its parameters and assumptions for backtesting on at least a monthly basis, and considering modifications to ensure the backtesting practices are appropriate for determining the adequacy of the covered clearing agency's margin resources;

(C) Conducting a sensitivity analysis of its margin model and a review of its parameters and assumptions for backtesting more frequently than monthly during periods of time when the products cleared or markets served display high volatility or become less liquid, or when the size or concentration of positions held by the covered clearing agency's participants increases or decreases significantly; and

(D) Reporting the results of its analyses under paragraphs (e)(6)(vi)(B) and (C) of this section to appropriate decision makers at the covered clearing agency, including but not limited to, its risk management committee or board of directors, and using these results to evaluate the adequacy of and adjust its margin methodology, model parameters, and any other relevant aspects of its credit risk management framework; and

(vii) Requires a model validation for the covered clearing agency's margin system and related models to be performed not less than annually, or more frequently as may be contemplated by the covered clearing agency's risk management framework established pursuant to paragraph (e)(3) of this section.

(7) Effectively measure, monitor, and manage the liquidity risk that arises in or is borne by the covered clearing agency, including measuring, monitoring, and managing its settlement and funding flows on an ongoing and timely basis, and its use of intraday liquidity by, at a minimum, doing the following:

(i) Maintaining sufficient liquid resources at the minimum in all relevant currencies to effect same-day and, where appropriate, intraday and multiday settlement of payment obligations with a high degree of confidence under a wide range of foreseeable stress scenarios that includes, but is not limited to, the default of the participant family that would generate the largest aggregate payment obligation for the covered clearing agency in extreme but plausible market conditions;

(ii) Holding qualifying liquid resources sufficient to meet the minimum liquidity resource requirement under paragraph (e)(7)(i) of this section in each relevant currency for which the covered clearing agency has payment obligations owed to clearing members;

(iii) Using the access to accounts and services at a Federal Reserve Bank, pursuant to Section 806(a) of the Payment, Clearing, and Settlement Supervision Act of 2010 (12 U.S.C. 5465(a)), or other relevant central bank, when available and where determined to be practical by the board of directors of the covered clearing agency, to enhance its management of liquidity risk;

(iv) Undertaking due diligence to confirm that it has a reasonable basis to believe each of its liquidity providers, whether or not such liquidity provider is a clearing member, has:

(A) Sufficient information to understand and manage the liquidity provider's liquidity risks; and

(B) The capacity to perform as required under its commitments to provide liquidity to the covered clearing agency;

(v) Maintaining and testing with each liquidity provider, to the extent practicable, the covered clearing agency's procedures and operational capacity for accessing each type of relevant liquidity resource under paragraph (e)(7)(i) of this section at least annually;

(vi) Determining the amount and regularly testing the sufficiency of the liquid resources held for purposes of meeting the minimum liquid resource requirement under paragraph (e)(7)(i) of this section by, at a minimum:

(A) Conducting stress testing of its liquidity resources at least once each day using standard and predetermined parameters and assumptions;

(B) Conducting a comprehensive analysis on at least a monthly basis of the existing stress testing scenarios, models, and underlying parameters and assumptions used in evaluating liquidity needs and resources, and considering modifications to ensure they are appropriate for determining the clearing agency's identified liquidity needs and resources in light of current and evolving market conditions;

(C) Conducting a comprehensive analysis of the scenarios, models, and underlying parameters and assumptions used in evaluating liquidity needs and resources more frequently than monthly when the products cleared or markets served display high volatility or become less liquid, when the size or concentration of positions held by the clearing agency's participants increases significantly, or in other appropriate circumstances described in such policies and procedures; and

(D) Reporting the results of its analyses under paragraphs (e)(7)(vi)(B) and (C) of this section to appropriate decision makers at the covered clearing agency, including but not limited to, its risk management committee or board of directors, and using these results to evaluate the adequacy of and adjust its liquidity risk management methodology, model parameters, and any other relevant aspects of its liquidity risk management framework;

(vii) Performing a model validation of its liquidity risk models not less than annually or more frequently as may be contemplated by the covered clearing agency's risk management framework established pursuant to paragraph (e)(3) of this section;

(viii) Addressing foreseeable liquidity shortfalls that would not be covered by the covered clearing agency's liquid resources and seek to avoid unwinding, revoking, or delaying the same-day settlement of payment obligations;

(ix) Describing the covered clearing agency's process to replenish any liquid resources that the clearing agency may employ during a stress event; and

(x) Undertaking an analysis at least once a year that evaluates the feasibility of maintaining sufficient liquid resources at a minimum in all relevant currencies to effect same-day and, where appropriate, intraday and multiday settlement of payment obligations with a high degree of confidence under a wide range of foreseeable stress scenarios that includes, but is not limited to, the default of the two participant families that would potentially cause the largest aggregate payment obligation for the covered clearing agency in extreme but plausible market conditions if the covered clearing agency provides central counterparty services and is either systemically important in multiple jurisdictions or a clearing agency involved in activities with a more complex risk profile.

(8) Define the point at which settlement is final to be no later than the end of the day on which the payment or obligation is due and, where necessary or appropriate, intraday or in real time.

(9) Conduct its money settlements in central bank money, where available and determined to be practical by the board of directors of the covered clearing agency, and minimize and manage credit and liquidity risk arising from conducting its money settlements in commercial bank money if central bank money is not used by the covered clearing agency.

(10) Establish and maintain transparent written standards that state its obligations with respect to the delivery of physical instruments, and establish and maintain operational practices that identify, monitor, and manage the risks associated with such physical deliveries.

(11) When the covered clearing agency provides central securities depository services:

(i) Maintain securities in an immobilized or dematerialized form for their transfer by book entry, ensure the integrity of securities issues, and minimize and manage the risks associated with the safekeeping and transfer of securities;

(ii) Implement internal auditing and other controls to safeguard the rights of securities issuers and holders and prevent the unauthorized creation or deletion of securities, and conduct periodic and at least daily reconciliation of securities issues it maintains; and

(iii) Protect assets against custody risk through appropriate rules and procedures consistent with relevant laws, rules, and regulations in jurisdictions where it operates.

(12) Eliminate principal risk by conditioning the final settlement of one obligation upon the final settlement of the other, regardless of whether the covered clearing agency settles on a gross or net basis and when finality occurs if the covered clearing agency settles transactions that involve the settlement of two linked obligations.

(13) Ensure the covered clearing agency has the authority and operational capacity to take timely action to contain losses and liquidity demands and continue to meet its obligations by, at a minimum, requiring the covered clearing agency's participants and, when practicable, other stakeholders to participate in the testing and review of its default procedures, including any close-out procedures, at least annually and following material changes thereto.

(14) Enable, when the covered clearing agency provides central counterparty services for security-based swaps or engages in activities that the Commission has determined to have a more complex risk profile, the segregation and portability of positions of a participant's customers and the collateral provided to the covered clearing agency with respect to those positions and effectively protect such positions and related collateral from the default or insolvency of that participant.

(15) Identify, monitor, and manage the covered clearing agency's general business risk and hold sufficient liquid net assets funded by equity to cover potential general business losses so that the covered clearing agency can continue operations and services as a going concern if those losses materialize, including by:

(i) Determining the amount of liquid net assets funded by equity based upon its general business risk profile and the length of time required to achieve a recovery or orderly wind-down, as appropriate, of its critical operations and services if such action is taken;

(ii) Holding liquid net assets funded by equity equal to the greater of either (x) six months of the covered clearing agency's current operating expenses, or (y) the amount determined by the board of directors to be sufficient to ensure a recovery or orderly wind-down of critical operations and services of the covered clearing agency, as contemplated by the plans established under paragraph (e)(3)(ii) of this section, and which:

(A) Shall be in addition to resources held to cover participant defaults or other risks covered under the credit risk standard in paragraph (b)(3) or paragraphs (e)(4)(i) through (iii) of this section, as applicable, and the liquidity risk standard in paragraphs (e)(7)(i) and (ii) of this section; and

(B) Shall be of high quality and sufficiently liquid to allow the covered clearing agency to meet its current and projected operating expenses under a range of scenarios, including in adverse market conditions; and

(iii) Maintaining a viable plan, approved by the board of directors and updated at least annually, for raising additional equity should its equity fall close to or below the amount required under paragraph (e)(15)(ii) of this section.

(16) Safeguard the covered clearing agency's own and its participants' assets, minimize the risk of loss and delay in access to these assets, and invest such assets in instruments with minimal credit, market, and liquidity risks.

(17) Manage the covered clearing agency's operational risks by:

(i) Identifying the plausible sources of operational risk, both internal and external, and mitigating their impact through the use of appropriate systems, policies, procedures, and controls;

(ii) Ensuring that systems have a high degree of security, resiliency, operational reliability, and adequate, scalable capacity; and

(iii) Establishing and maintaining a business continuity plan that addresses events posing a significant risk of disrupting operations.

(18) Establish objective, risk-based, and publicly disclosed criteria for participation, which permit fair and open access by direct and, where relevant, indirect participants and other financial market utilities, require participants to have sufficient financial resources and robust operational capacity to meet obligations arising from participation in the clearing agency, and monitor compliance with such participation requirements on an ongoing basis.

(19) Identify, monitor, and manage the material risks to the covered clearing agency arising from arrangements in which firms that are indirect participants in the covered clearing agency rely on the services provided by direct participants to access the covered clearing agency's payment, clearing, or settlement facilities.

(20) Identify, monitor, and manage risks related to any link the covered clearing agency establishes with one or more other clearing agencies, financial market utilities, or trading markets.

(21) Be efficient and effective in meeting the requirements of its participants and the markets it serves, and have the covered clearing agency's management regularly review the efficiency and effectiveness of its:

(i) Clearing and settlement arrangements;

(ii) Operating structure, including risk management policies, procedures, and systems;

(iii) Scope of products cleared or settled; and

(iv) Use of technology and communication procedures.

(22) Use, or at a minimum accommodate, relevant internationally accepted communication procedures and standards in order to facilitate efficient payment, clearing, and settlement.

(23) Provide for the following:

(i) Publicly disclosing all relevant rules and material procedures, including key aspects of its default rules and procedures;

(ii) Providing sufficient information to enable participants to identify and evaluate the risks, fees, and other material costs they incur by participating in the covered clearing agency;

(iii) Publicly disclosing relevant basic data on transaction volume and values;

(iv) A comprehensive public disclosure that describes its material rules, policies, and procedures regarding its legal, governance, risk management, and operating framework, accurate in all material respects at the time of publication, that includes:

(A) Executive summary. An executive summary of the key points from paragraphs (e)(23)(iv)(B), (C), and (D) of this section;

(B) Summary of material changes since the last update of the disclosure. A summary of the material changes since the last update of paragraph (e)(23)(iv)(C) or (D) of this section;

(C) General background on the covered clearing agency. A description of:

(*1*) The covered clearing agency's function and the markets it serves;

(*2*) Basic data and performance statistics on the covered clearing agency's services and operations, such as basic volume and value statistics by product type, average aggregate intraday exposures to its participants, and statistics on the covered clearing agency's operational reliability; and

(*3*) The covered clearing agency's general organization, legal and regulatory framework, and system design and operations; and

(D) Standard-by-standard summary narrative. A comprehensive narrative disclosure for each applicable standard set forth in paragraphs (e)(1) through (23) of this section with sufficient detail and context to enable a reader to understand the covered clearing agency's approach to controlling the risks and addressing the requirements in each standard; and

(v) Updating the public disclosure under paragraph (e)(23)(iv) of this section every two years, or more frequently following changes to its system or the environment in which it operates to the extent necessary to ensure statements previously provided under paragraph (e)(23)(iv) of this section remain accurate in all material respects.

(f) For purposes of enforcing the Payment, Clearing, and Settlement Supervision Act of 2010 (12 U.S.C. 5461 et seq.), a designated clearing agency for which the Commission acts as supervisory agency shall be subject to, and the Commission shall have the authority under, the provisions of paragraphs (b) through (n) of Section 8 of the Federal Deposit Insurance Act (12 U.S.C. 1818) in the same manner and to the same extent as if such designated clearing agency were an insured depository institution and the Commission were the appropriate Federal banking agency for such insured depository institution.

SUSPENSION AND EXPULSION OF EXCHANGE MEMBERS

Rule 19a3–1. [Reserved]

Rule 19b–3. [Reserved]

Rule 19b–4. Filings with respect to proposed rule changes by self-regulatory organizations

A self-regulatory organization also must refer to Form 19b–4 (17 CFR 249.819) for further requirements with respect to the filing of proposed rule changes.

(a) *Definitions*. As used in this section:

(1) The term *advance notice* means a notice required to be made by a designated clearing agency pursuant to Section 806(e) of the Payment, Clearing and Settlement Supervision Act (12 U.S.C. 5465(e));

(2) The term *designated clearing agency* means a clearing agency that is registered with the Commission, and for which the Commission is the Supervisory Agency (as determined in accordance

with section 803(8) of the Payment, Clearing and Settlement Supervision Act (12 U.S.C. 5462(8)), that has been designated by the Financial Stability Oversight Council pursuant to section 804 of the Payment, Clearing and Settlement Supervision Act (12 U.S.C. 5463) as systemically important or likely to become systemically important;

(3) The term *Payment, Clearing and Settlement Supervision Act* means Title VIII of the Dodd–Frank Wall Street Reform and Consumer Protection Act (124 Stat. 1802, 1803, 1807, 1809, 1811, 1814, 1816, 1818, 1820, 1821; 12 U.S.C. 5461 et seq.);

(4) The term *proposed rule change* has the meaning set forth in Section 19(b)(1) of the Act (15 U.S.C. 78s(b)(1));

(5) The term *security-based swap submission* means a submission of identifying information required to be made by a clearing agency pursuant to section 3C(b)(2) of the Act (15 U.S.C. 78c–3(b)(2)) for each security-based swap, or any group, category, type or class of security-based swaps, that such clearing agency plans to accept for clearing;

(6) The term *stated policy, practice, or interpretation* means:

(i) Any material aspect of the operation of the facilities of the self-regulatory organization; or

(ii) Any statement made generally available to the membership of, to all participants in, or to persons having or seeking access (including, in the case of national securities exchanges or registered securities associations, through a member) to facilities of, the self-regulatory organization ("specified persons"), or to a group or category of specified persons, that establishes or changes any standard, limit, or guideline with respect to:

(A) The rights, obligations, or privileges of specified persons or, in the case of national securities exchanges or registered securities associations, persons associated with specified persons; or

(B) The meaning, administration, or enforcement of an existing rule.

(b)(1) Filings with respect to proposed rule changes by a self-regulatory organization, except filings with respect to proposed rules changes by self-regulatory organizations submitted pursuant to section 19(b)(7) of the Act (15 U.S.C. 78s(b)(7)), shall be made electronically on Form 19b–4 (17 CFR 249.819).

(2) For purposes of Section 19(b) of the Act and this rule, a "business day" is any day other than a Saturday, Sunday, Federal holiday, a day that the Office of Personnel Management has announced that Federal agencies in the Washington, DC area are closed to the public, a day on which the Commission is subject to a Federal government shutdown or a day on which the Commission's Washington, DC office is otherwise not open for regular business.

(c) A stated policy, practice, or interpretation of the self-regulatory organization shall be deemed to be a proposed rule change unless (1) it is reasonably and fairly implied by an existing rule of the self-regulatory organization or (2) it is concerned solely with the administration of the self-regulatory organization and is not a stated policy, practice, or interpretation with respect to the meaning, administration, or enforcement of an existing rule of the self-regulatory organization.

(d) Regardless of whether it is made generally available, an interpretation of an existing rule of the self-regulatory organization shall be deemed to be a proposed rule change if (1) it is approved or ratified by the governing body of the self-regulatory organization and (2) it is not reasonably and fairly implied by that rule.

(e) For the purposes of this paragraph, *new derivative securities product* means any type of option, warrant, hybrid securities product or any other security, other than a single equity option or a security futures product, whose value is based, in whole or in part, upon the performance of, or interest in, an underlying instrument.

(1) The listing and trading of a new derivative securities product by a self-regulatory organization shall not be deemed a proposed rule change, pursuant to paragraph (c)(1) of this rule, if the Commission has approved, pursuant to section 19(b) of the Act (15 U.S.C. 78s(b)), the self-regulatory organization's trading rules, procedures and listing standards for the product class that would include the new derivative securities product and the self-regulatory organization has a surveillance program for the product class.

(2) Recordkeeping and reporting:

(i) Self-regulatory organizations shall retain at their principal place of business a file, available to Commission staff for inspection, of all relevant records and information pertaining to each new derivative securities product traded pursuant to this paragraph (e) for a period of not less than five years, the first two years in an easily accessible place, as prescribed in Rule 17a–1.

(ii) When relying on this paragraph (e), a self-regulatory organization shall submit Form 19b–4(e) (17 CFR 249.820) to the Commission within five business days after commencement of trading a new derivative securities product.

(f) A proposed rule change may take effect upon filing with the Commission pursuant to Section 19(b)(3)(A) of the Act, 15 U.S.C. 78s(b)(3)(A), if properly designated by the self-regulatory organization as:

(1) Constituting a stated policy, practice, or interpretation with respect to the meaning, administration, or enforcement of an existing rule;

(2) Establishing or changing a due, fee, or other charge applicable only to a member;

(3) Concerned solely with the administration of the self-regulatory organization;

(4) Effecting a change in an existing service of a registered clearing agency that either:

(i)(A) Does not adversely affect the safeguarding of securities or funds in the custody or control of the clearing agency or for which it is responsible; and

(B) Does not significantly affect the respective rights or obligations of the clearing agency or persons using the service; or

(ii)(A) Primarily affects the clearing operations of the clearing agency with respect to products that are not securities, including futures that are not security futures, swaps that are not security-based swaps or mixed swaps, and forwards that are not security forwards; and

(B) Either

(*1*) Does not significantly affect any securities clearing operations of the clearing agency or any rights or obligations of the clearing agency with respect to securities clearing or persons using such securities-clearing service, or

(*2*) Does significantly affect any securities clearing operations of the clearing agency or the rights or obligations of the clearing agency with respect to securities clearing or persons using such securities-clearing service, but is necessary to maintain fair and orderly markets for products that are not securities, including futures that are not security futures, swaps that are not security-based swaps or mixed swaps, and forwards that are not security forwards. Proposed rule changes filed pursuant to this subparagraph II must also be filed in accordance with the procedures of Section 19(b)(1) for approval pursuant to Section 19(b)(2) and the regulations thereunder within fifteen days of being filed under Section 19(b)(3)(A).

(5) Effecting a change in an existing order-entry or trading system of a self-regulatory organization that:

(i) Does not significantly affect the protection of investors or the public interest;

(ii) Does not impose any significant burden on competition; and

(iii) Does not have the effect of limiting the access to or availability of the system; or

(6) Effecting a change that:

(i) Does not significantly affect the protection of investors or the public interest;

(ii) Does not impose any significant burden on competition; and

(iii) By its terms, does not become operative for 30 days after the date of the filing, or such shorter time as the Commission may designate if consistent with the protection of investors and the public interest; provided that the self-regulatory organization has given the Commission written notice of its intent to file the proposed rule change, along with a brief description and text of the proposed rule change, at least five business days prior to the date of filing of the proposed rule change, or such shorter time as designated by the Commission.

(g) Proceedings to determine whether a proposed rule change should be disapproved will be conducted pursuant to 17 CFR 21.700–701 (Initiation of Proceedings for SRO Proposed Rule Changes)

(h) Notice of orders issued pursuant to section 19(b) of the Act will be given by prompt publication thereof, together with a statement of written reasons therefor.

(i) Self-regulatory organizations shall retain at their principal place of business a file, available to interested persons for public inspection and copying, of all filings notice or submission, made pursuant to this rule and all correspondence and other communications reduced to writing (including comment letters) to and from such self-regulatory organization concerning any such filing notices or submissions, whether such correspondence and communications are received or prepared before or after the filing, notice or submission of the proposed rule change, advance notice or security-based swap submission, as applicable.

(j) Filings by a self-regulatory organization submitted on Form 19b–4 (17 CFR 249.819) electronically shall contain an electronic signature. For the purposes of this rule, the term electronic signature means an electronic entry in the form of a magnetic impulse or other form of computer data compilation of any letter or series of letters or characters comprising a name, executed, adopted or authorized as a signature. The signatory to an electronically submitted rule filing shall manually sign a signature page or other document, in the manner prescribed by Form 19b–4, authenticating, acknowledging or otherwise adopting his or her signature that appears in typed form within the electronic filing. Such document shall be executed before or at the time the rule filing is electronically submitted and shall be retained by the filer in accordance with Rule 17a–1.

(k) If the conditions of this rule and Form 19b–4 (17 CFR 249.819) are otherwise satisfied, all filings submitted electronically on or before 5:30 p.m. Eastern Standard Time or Eastern Daylight Saving Time, whichever is currently in effect, on a business day, shall be deemed filed on that business day, and all filings submitted after 5:30 p.m. Eastern Standard Time or Eastern Daylight Saving Time, whichever is currently in effect, shall be deemed filed on the next business day.

(*l*) The self-regulatory organization shall post each proposed rule change, and any amendments thereto, on its website within two business days after the filing of the proposed rule change, and any amendments thereto, with the Commission. If a self-regulatory organization does not post a proposed rule change on its website on the same day that it filed the proposal with the Commission, then the self-regulatory organization shall inform the Commission of the date on which it posted such proposal on its website. Such proposed rule change and amendments shall be maintained on the self-regulatory organization's website until:

(1) In the case of a proposed rule change filed under section 19(b)(2) of the Act (15 U.S.C. 78s(b)(2)), the Commission approves or disapproves the proposed rule change or the self–regulatory organization withdraws the proposed rule change, or any amendments, or is notified that the proposed rule change is not properly filed; or

(2) In the case of a proposed rule change filed under section 19(b)(3)(A) of the Act (15 U.S.C. 78s(b)(3)(A)), or any amendment thereto, 60 days after the date of filing, unless the self–regulatory organization withdraws the proposed rule change or is notified that the proposed rule change is not properly filed; and

(3) In the case of proposed rule changes approved by the Commission pursuant to section 19(b)(2) of the Act (15 U.S.C. 78s(b)(2)) or noticed by the Commission pursuant to section 19(b)(3)(A) of the Act (15 U.S.C. 78s(b)(3)(A)), the self–regulatory organization updates its rule text as required by paragraph (m) of this rule; and

(4) In the case of a proposed rule change, or any amendment thereto, that has been disapproved, withdrawn or not properly filed, the self–regulatory organization shall remove the proposed rule change, or any amendment, from its website within two business days of notification of disapproval, improper filing, or withdrawal by the SRO of the proposed rule change.

(m)(1) Each self-regulatory organization shall post and maintain a current and complete version of its rules on its website.

(2) A self-regulatory organization, other than a self-regulatory organization that is registered with the Commission under section 6(g) of the Act (15 U.S.C. 78f(g)) or pursuant to section 15A(k) of the Act (15 U.S.C. 78o–1(k)), shall update its website to reflect rule changes filed pursuant to section 19(b)(2) of the Act (15 U.S.C. 78s(b)(2)) within two business days after it has been notified of the Commission's approval of a proposed rule change, and to reflect rule changes filed pursuant to section 19(b)(3)(A) of the Act (15 U.S.C. 78s(b)(3)(A)) within two business days of the Commission's notice of such proposed rule change.

(3) A self-regulatory organization that is registered with the Commission under section 6(g) of the Act (15 U.S.C. 78f(g)) or pursuant to section 15A(k) of the Act (15 U.S.C. 78o–1(k)), shall update its website to reflect rule changes filed pursuant to section 19(b)(2) of the Act by two business days after the later of:

(A) Notification that the Commission has approved a proposed rule change; and

(B)(i) The filing of a written certification with the Commodity Futures Trading Commission under section 5c(c) of the Commodity Exchange Act (7 U.S.C. 7a–2(c));

(ii) Receipt of notice from the Commodity Futures Trading Commission that it has determined that review of the proposed rule change is not necessary; or

(iii) Receipt of notice from the Commodity Futures Trading Commission that it has approved the proposed rule change.

(4) If a rule change is not effective for a certain period, the self-regulatory organization shall clearly indicate the effective date in the relevant rule text.

(n)(1)(i) A designated clearing agency shall provide an advance notice to the Commission of any proposed change to its rules, procedures, or operations that could materially affect the nature or level of risks presented by such designated clearing agency. Except as provided in paragraph (n)(1)(ii) of this section, such advance notice shall be submitted to the Commission electronically on Form 19b–4 (referenced in 17 CFR 249.819). The Commission shall, upon the filing of any advance notice, provide for prompt publication thereof.

(ii) Any designated clearing agency that files an advance notice with the Commission prior to December 10, 2013, shall file such advance notice in electronic format to a dedicated email address to be established by the Commission. The contents of an advance notice filed pursuant to this paragraph (n)(1)(ii) shall contain the information required to be included for advance notices in the General Instructions for Form 19b–4 (referenced in 17 CFR 249.819).

(2)(i) For purposes of this paragraph (n), the *phrase materially affect the nature or level of risks presented*, when used to qualify determinations on a change to rules, procedures, or operations at the designated clearing agency, means matters as to which there is a reasonable possibility that the change could affect the performance of essential clearing and settlement functions or the overall nature or level of risk presented by the designated clearing agency.

(ii) Changes to rules, procedures, or operations that could materially affect the nature or level of risks presented by a designated clearing agency may include, but are not limited to, changes that materially affect participant and product eligibility, risk management, daily or intraday settlement procedures, default procedures, system safeguards, governance or financial resources of the designated clearing agency.

(iii) Changes to rules, procedures, or operations that may not materially affect the nature or level of risks presented by a designated clearing agency include, but are not limited to:

(A) Changes to an existing procedure, control, or service that do not modify the rights or obligations of the designated clearing agency or persons using its payment, clearing, or settlement services and that do not adversely affect the safeguarding of securities, collateral, or funds in the custody or control of the designated clearing agency or for which it is responsible; or

(B) Changes concerned solely with the administration of the designated clearing agency or related to the routine, daily administration, direction, and control of employees;

(3) The designated clearing agency shall post the advance notice, and any amendments thereto, on its website within two business days after the filing of the advance notice, and any amendments thereto, with the Commission. Such advance notice and amendments shall be maintained on the designated clearing agency's website until the earlier of:

(i) The date the designated clearing agency withdraws the advance notice or is notified that the advance notice is not properly filed; or

(ii) The date the designated clearing agency posts a notice of effectiveness as required by paragraph (n)(4)(ii) of this section.

(4)(i) The designated clearing agency shall post a notice on its website within two business days of the date that any change to its rules, procedures, or operations referred to in an advance notice has been permitted to take effect as such date is determined in accordance with Section 806(e) of the Payment, Clearing and Settlement Supervision Act (12 U.S.C. 5465).

(ii) The designated clearing agency shall post a notice on its website within two business days of the effectiveness of any change to its rules, procedures, or operations referred to in an advance notice.

(5) A designated clearing agency shall provide copies of all materials submitted to the Commission relating to an advance notice with the Board of Governors of the Federal Reserve System contemporaneously with such submission to the Commission.

(6) The publication and website posting requirements contained in paragraphs (n)(1), (n)(3), and (n)(4) of this section do not apply to any information contained in an advance notice for which a designated clearing agency has requested confidential treatment following the procedures set forth in Rule 24b–2.

(*o*)(1) Every clearing agency that is registered with the Commission that plans to accept a security-based swap, or any group, category, type or class of security-based swaps for clearing shall submit to the Commission a security-based swap submission and provide notice to its members of such security-based swap submission.

(2)(i) Except as provided in paragraph (*o*)(2)(ii) of this section, a clearing agency shall submit each security-based swap submission to the Commission electronically on Form 19b–4 (referenced in 17 CFR 249.819) with the information required to be submitted for a security-based swap submission, as provided in Rule 19b–4 and Form 19b–4. Any information submitted to the Commission electronically on Form 19b–4 that is not complete or otherwise in compliance with this section and Form 19b–4 shall not be considered a security-based swap submission and the Commission shall so inform the clearing agency within twenty-one business days of the submission on Form 19b–4 (referenced in 17 CFR 249.819).

(ii) Any clearing agency that files a security-based swap submission with the Commission prior to December 10, 2013, shall file such security-based swap submission in electronic format to a dedicated email address to be established by the Commission. The contents of a security-based swap submission filed pursuant to this paragraph (*o*)(2)(ii) shall contain the information required to be included for security-based swap submissions in the General Instructions for Form 19b–4.

(3) A security-based swap submission submitted by a clearing agency to the Commission shall include a statement that includes, but is not limited to:

(i) How the security-based swap submission is consistent with Section 17A of the Act (15 U.S.C. 78q–1);

(ii) Information that will assist the Commission in the quantitative and qualitative assessment of the factors specified in Section 3C of the Act (15 U.S.C. 78c–3), including, but not limited to:

(A) The existence of significant outstanding notional exposures, trading liquidity and adequate pricing data;

(B) The availability of a rule framework, capacity, operational expertise and resources, and credit support infrastructure to clear the contract on terms that are consistent with the material terms and trading conventions on which the contract is then traded;

(C) The effect on the mitigation of systemic risk, taking into account the size of the market for such contract and the resources of the clearing agency available to clear the contract;

(D) The effect on competition, including appropriate fees and charges applied to clearing; and

(E) The existence of reasonable legal certainty in the event of the insolvency of the relevant clearing agency or one or more of its clearing members with regard to the treatment of customer and security-based swap counterparty positions, funds, and property;

(iii) A description of how the rules of the clearing agency prescribe that all security-based swaps submitted to the clearing agency with the same terms and conditions are economically equivalent within the clearing agency and may be offset with each other within the clearing agency, as applicable to the security-based swaps described in the security-based swap submission; and

(iv) A description of how the rules of the clearing agency provide for nondiscriminatory clearing of a security-based swap executed bilaterally or on or through the rules of an unaffiliated national securities exchange or security-based swap execution facility, as applicable to the security-based swaps described in the security-based swap submission.

(4) A clearing agency shall submit security-based swaps to the Commission for review by

group, category, type or class of security-based swaps, to the extent reasonable and practicable to do so.

(5) A clearing agency shall post each security-based swap submission, and any amendments thereto, on its website within two business days after the submission of the security-based swap submission, and any amendments thereto, with the Commission. Such security-based swap submission and amendments shall be maintained on the clearing agency's website until the Commission makes a determination regarding the security-based swap submission or the clearing agency withdraws the security-based swap submission, or is notified that the security-based swap submission is not properly filed.

(6) In connection with any security-based swap submission that is submitted by a clearing agency to the Commission, the clearing agency shall provide any additional information requested by the Commission as necessary to assess any of the factors it determines to be appropriate in order to make the determination of whether the clearing requirement applies.

(7) Notices of orders issued pursuant to Section 3C of the Act (15 U.S.C. 78c–3), regarding security-based swap submissions will be given by prompt publication thereof, together with a statement of written reasons therefor.

Rule 19b–5. Temporary exemption from the filing requirements of Section 19(b) of the Act

Preliminary Notes

1. The following rule provides for a temporary exemption from the rule filing requirement for self-regulatory organizations that file proposed rule changes concerning the operation of a pilot trading system pursuant to section 19(b) of the Act (15 U.S.C. 78s(b), as amended). All other requirements under the Act that are applicable to self-regulatory organizations continue to apply.

2. The disclosures made pursuant to the provisions of this rule are in addition to any other applicable disclosure requirements under the federal securities laws.

(a) For purposes of this rule, the term *specialist* means any member subject to a requirement of a self-regulatory organization that such member regularly maintain a market in a particular security.

(b) For purposes of this rule, the term *trading system* means the rules of a self-regulatory organization that:

(1) Determine how the orders of multiple buyers and sellers are brought together; and

(2) Establish non-discretionary methods under which such orders interact with each other and under which the buyers and sellers entering such orders agree to the terms of trade.

(c) For purposes of this rule, the term *pilot trading system* shall mean a trading system operated by a self-regulatory organization that is not substantially similar to any trading system or pilot trading system operated by such self-regulatory organization at any time during the preceding year, and that:

(1)(i) Has been in operation for less than two years;

(ii) Is independent of any other trading system operated by such self-regulatory organization that has been approved by the Commission pursuant to section 19(b) of the Act, (15 U.S.C. 78s(b));

(iii) With respect to each security traded on such pilot trading system, during at least two of the last four consecutive calendar months, has traded no more than 5 percent of the average daily trading volume of such security in the United States; and

(iv) With respect to all securities traded on such pilot trading system, during at least two of the last four consecutive calendar months, has traded no more than 20 percent of the average daily trading volume of all trading systems operated by such self-regulatory organization; or

(2)(i) Has been in operation for less than two years;

(ii) With respect to each security traded on such pilot trading system, during at least two of the last four consecutive calendar months, has traded no more than 1 percent of the average daily trading volume of such security in the United States; and

(iii) With respect to all securities traded on such pilot trading system, during at least two of the last four consecutive calendar months, has traded no more than 20 percent of the average daily trading volume of all trading systems operated by such self-regulatory organization; or

(3)(i) Has been in operation for less than two years; and

(ii)(A) Satisfied the definition of *pilot trading system* under paragraph (c)(1) of this rule no more than 60 days ago, and continues to be independent of any other trading system operated by such self-regulatory organization that has been approved by the Commission pursuant to section 19(b) of the Act, (15 U.S.C. 78s(b)); or

(B) Satisfied the definition of *pilot trading system* under paragraph (c)(2) of this rule no more than 60 days ago.

(d) A pilot trading system shall be deemed *independent* of any other trading system operated by a self-regulatory organization if:

(1) Such pilot trading system trades securities other than the issues of securities that trade on any other trading system operated by such self-regulatory organization that has been approved by the Commission pursuant to section 19(b) of the Act, (15 U.S.C. 78s(b));

(2) Such pilot trading system does not operate during the same trading hours as any other trading system operated by such self-regulatory organization that has been approved by the Commission pursuant to section 19(b) of the Act, (15 U.S.C. 78s(b)); or

(3) No specialist or market maker on any other trading system operated by such self-regulatory organization that has been approved by the Commission pursuant to section 19(b) of the Act, (15 U.S.C. 78s(b)), is permitted to effect transactions on the pilot trading system in securities in which they are a specialist or market maker.

(e) A self-regulatory organization shall be exempt temporarily from the requirement under section 19(b) of the Act, (15 U.S.C. 78s(b)), to submit on Form 19b–4, 17 CFR 249.819, proposed rule changes for establishing a pilot trading system, if the self-regulatory organization complies with the following requirements:

(1) *Form PILOT*. The self-regulatory organization:

(i) Files Part I of Form PILOT, 17 CFR 249.821, in accordance with the instructions therein, at least 20 days prior to commencing operation of the pilot trading system;

(ii) Files an amendment on Part I of Form PILOT at least 20 days prior to implementing a material change to the operation of the pilot trading system; and

(iii) Files a quarterly report on Part II of Form PILOT within 30 calendar days after the end of each calendar quarter in which the market has operated after the effective date of this rule.

(2) *Fair Access*. (i) The self-regulatory organization has in place written rules to ensure that all members of the self-regulatory organization have fair access to the pilot trading system, and that information regarding orders on the pilot trading system is equally available to all members of the self-regulatory organization with access to such pilot trading system.

(ii) Notwithstanding the requirement in paragraph (e)(2)(i) of this rule, a specialist on the pilot trading system may have preferred access to information regarding orders that it represents in its capacity as specialist.

(iii) The rules established by a self-regulatory organization pursuant to paragraph (e)(2)(i) of this rule will be considered rules governing the pilot trading system for purposes of the temporary exemption under this rule.

(3) *Trading Rules and Procedures and Listing Standards*. (i) The self-regulatory organization has in place written trading rules and procedures and listing standards necessary to operate the pilot trading system.

(ii) The rules established by a self-regulatory organization pursuant to paragraph (e)(3)(i) of this rule will be considered rules governing the pilot trading system for purposes of the temporary exemption under this rule.

(4) *Surveillance*. The self-regulatory organization establishes internal procedures for the effective surveillance of trading activity on the self-regulatory organization's pilot trading system.

(5) *Clearance and Settlement*. The self-regulatory organization establishes reasonable clearance and settlement procedures for transactions effected on the self-regulatory organizations pilot trading system.

(6) *Types of Securities*. The self-regulatory organization permits to trade on the pilot trading system only securities registered under section 12 of the Act, (15 U.S.C. 78*l*).

(7) *Activities of Specialists*. (i) The self-regulatory organization does not permit any member to be a specialist in a security on the pilot trading system and a specialist in a security on a trading system operated by such self-regulatory organization that has been approved by the Commission pursuant to section 19(b) of the Act, (15 U.S.C. 78s(b)), or on another pilot trading system operated by such self-regulatory organization, if such securities are related securities, except that a member

may be a specialist in related securities that the Commission, upon application by the self-regulatory organization, later determines is necessary or appropriate in the public interest and consistent with the protection of investors;

(ii) Notwithstanding paragraph (e)(7)(i) of this rule, a self-regulatory organization may permit a member to be a specialist in any security on a pilot trading system, if the pilot trading system is operated during trading hours different from the trading hours of the trading system in which such member is a specialist.

(iii) For purposes of paragraph (e)(7) of this rule, the term *related securities* means any two securities in which:

(A) The value of one security is determined, in whole or significant part, by the performance of the other security; or

(B) The value of both securities is determined, in whole or significant part, by the performance of a third security, combination of securities, index, indicator, interest rate or other common factor.

(8) *Examinations, Inspections, and Investigations.* The self-regulatory organization cooperates with the examination, inspection, or investigation by the Commission of transactions effected on the pilot trading system.

(9) *Recordkeeping.* The self-regulatory organization shall retain at its principal place of business and make available to Commission staff for inspection, all the rules and procedures relating to each pilot trading system operating pursuant to this rule for a period of not less than five years, the first two years in an easily accessible place, as prescribed in Rule 17a–1.

(10) *Public Availability of Pilot Trading System Rules.* The self-regulatory organization makes publicly available all trading rules and procedures, including those established under paragraphs (e)(2) and (e)(3) of this rule.

(11) Every notice or amendment filed pursuant to this paragraph (e) shall constitute a "report" within the meaning of sections 11A, 17(a), 18(a), and 32(a), (15 U.S.C. 78k–1, 78q(a), 78r(a), and 78ff(a)), and any other applicable provisions of the Act. All notices or reports filed pursuant to this paragraph (e) shall be deemed to be confidential until the pilot trading system commences operation.

(f)(1) A self-regulatory organization shall request Commission approval, pursuant to section 19(b)(2) of the Act, (15 U.S.C. 78s(b)(2)), for any rule change relating to the operation of a pilot trading system by submitting Form 19b–4, 17 CFR 249.819, no later than two years after the commencement of operation of such pilot trading system, or shall cease operation of the pilot trading system.

(2) Simultaneous with a request for Commission approval pursuant to section 19(b)(2) of the Act, (15 U.S.C. 78s(b)(2)), a self-regulatory organization may request Commission approval pursuant to section 19(b)(3)(A) of the Act, (15 U.S.C. 78s(b)(3)(A)), for any rule change relating to the operation of a pilot trading system by submitting Form 19b–4, 17 CFR 249.819, effective immediate upon filing, to continue operations of such trading system for a period not to exceed six months.

(g) Notwithstanding paragraph (e) of this rule, rule changes with respect to pilot trading systems operated by a self-regulatory organization shall not be exempt from the rule filing requirements of section 19(b)(2) of the Act, (15 U.S.C. 78s(b)(2)), if the Commission determines, after notice to the SRO and opportunity for the SRO to respond, that exemption of such rule changes is not necessary or appropriate in the public interest or consistent with the protection of investors.

Rule 19b–7. Filings with respect to proposed rule changes submitted pursuant to Section 19(b)(7) of the Act

Preliminary Note to Rule 19b–7

A self-regulatory organization also must refer to Form 19b–7 (17 CFR 249.822) for further requirements with respect to the filing of proposed rule changes.

(a) Filings with respect to proposed rule changes by a self-regulatory organization submitted pursuant to Section 19(b)(7) of the Act (15 U.S.C. 78s(b)(7)) shall be made electronically on Form 19b–7 (17 CFR 249.822).

(b) A proposed rule change will not be deemed filed on the date it is received by the Commission unless:

(1) A completed Form 19b–7 (17 CFR 249.822) is submitted electronically; and

(2) In order to elicit meaningful comment, it is accompanied by:

(i) A clear and accurate statement of the basis and purpose of such rule change, including the impact on competition or efficiency, if any; and

(ii) A summary of any written comments (including e-mail) received by the self-regulatory organization on the proposed rule change.

(c) Self-regulatory organizations shall retain at their principle place of business a file, available to interested persons for public inspection and copying, of all filings made pursuant to this rule and all correspondence and other communications reduced to writing (including comment letters) to and from such self-regulatory organization concerning such filing, whether such correspondence and communications are received or prepared before or after the filing of the proposed rule change.

(d) Filings with respect to proposed rule changes by a self-regulatory organization submitted on Form 19b–7 (17 CFR 249.822) electronically shall contain an electronic signature. For the purposes of this rule, the term electronic signature means an electronic entry in the form of a magnetic impulse or other form of computer data compilation of any letter or series of letters or characters comprising a name, executed, adopted or authorized as a signature. The signatory to an electronically submitted rule filing shall manually sign a signature page or other document, in the manner prescribed by Form 19b–7, authenticating, acknowledging or otherwise adopting his or her signature that appears in typed form within the electronic filing. Such document shall be executed before or at the time the rule filing is electronically submitted and shall be retained by the filer in accordance with Rule 17a–1.

(e) If the conditions of this rule and Form 19b–7 (17 CFR 249.822) are otherwise satisfied, all filings submitted electronically on or before 5:30 p.m. Eastern Standard Time or Eastern Daylight Saving Time, whichever is currently in effect, on a business day, shall be deemed filed on that business day, and all filings submitted after 5:30 p.m. Eastern Standard Time or Eastern Daylight Saving Time, whichever is currently in effect, shall be deemed filed on the next business day.

(f) The self-regulatory organization shall post the proposed rule change, and any amendments thereto, submitted on Form 19b–7 (17 CFR 249.822), on its website within two business days after the filing of the proposed rule change, and any amendments thereto, with the Commission. Unless the self-regulatory organization withdraws the proposed rule change or is notified that the proposed rule change is not properly filed, such proposed rule change and amendments shall be maintained on the self-regulatory organization's website until 60 days after:

(1) The filing of a written certification with the Commodity Futures Trading Commission under section 5c(c) of the Commodity Exchange Act (7 U.S.C. 7a–2(c));

(2) The Commodity Futures Trading Commission determines that review of the proposed rule change is not necessary; or

(3) The Commodity Futures Trading Commission approves the proposed rule change; and

(4) In the case of a proposed rule change, or any amendment thereto, that has been withdrawn or not properly filed, the self-regulatory organization shall remove the proposed rule change, or any amendment, from its website within two business days of notification of improper filing or withdrawal by the self-regulatory organization of the proposed rule change.

(g)(1) Each self-regulatory organization shall post and maintain a current and complete version of its rules on its website.

(2) The self-regulatory organization shall update its website to reflect rule changes filed pursuant to section 19(b)(7) of the Act (15 U.S.C. 78s(b)(7)), by two business days after the later of:

(A) The Commission's notice of such proposed rule change; and

(B)(i) The filing of a written certification with the Commodity Futures Trading Commission under section 5c(c) of the Commodity Exchange Act (7 U.S.C. 7a–2(c));

(ii) Receipt of notice from the Commodity Futures Trading Commission that it has determined that review of the proposed rule change is not necessary; or

(iii) Receipt of notice from the Commodity Futures Trading Commission that it has approved the proposed rule change.

(3) If a rule change is not effective for a certain period, the self-regulatory organization shall clearly indicate the effective date in the relevant rule text.

Rule 19c–1. Governing certain off–board agency transactions by members of national securities exchanges

The rules of each national securities exchange shall provide as follows:

No rule, stated policy or practice of this exchange shall prohibit or condition, or be construed to prohibit or condition or otherwise limit, directly or indirectly, the ability of any member acting as agent to effect any transaction otherwise than on this exchange with another person (except when such member also is acting as agent for such other person in such transaction) in any equity security listed on this exchange or to which unlisted trading privileges on this exchange have been extended.

Rule 19c–3. Governing off–board trading by members of national securities exchanges

The rules of each national securities exchange shall provide as follows:

(a) No rule, stated policy or practice of this exchange shall prohibit or condition, or be construed to prohibit, condition or otherwise limit, directly or indirectly, the ability of any member to effect any transaction otherwise than on this exchange in any reported security listed and registered on this exchange or as to which unlisted trading privileges on this exchange have been extended (other than a put option or call option issued by the Options Clearing Corporation) which is not a covered security.

(b) For purposes of this rule,

(1) The term *Act* shall mean the Securities Exchange Act of 1934, as amended.

(2) The term *exchange* shall mean a national securities exchange registered as such with the Securities and Exchange Commission pursuant to section 6 of the Act.

(3) The term *covered security* shall mean (i) Any equity security or class of equity securities which

(A) Was listed and registered on an exchange on April 26, 1979, and

(B) Remains listed and registered on at least one exchange continuously thereafter;

(ii) Any equity security or class of equity securities which

(A) Was traded on one or more exchanges on April 26, 1979, pursuant to unlisted trading privileges permitted by section 12(f)(1)(A) of the Act, and

(B) Remains traded on any such exchange pursuant to such unlisted trading privileges continuously thereafter; and

(iii) Any equity security or class of equity securities which

(A) Is issued in connection with a statutory merger, consolidation or similar plan or reorganization (including a reincorporation or change of domicile) in exchange for an equity security or class of equity securities described in paragraph (b)(3)(i) or (ii) of this rule,

(B) Is listed and registered on an exchange after April 26, 1979, and

(C) Remains listed and registered on at least one exchange continuously thereafter.

(4) The term *reported security* shall mean any security or class of securities for which transaction reports are collected, processed and made available pursuant to an effective transaction reporting plan.

(5) The term *transaction report* shall mean a report containing the price and volume associated with a completed transaction involving the purchase or sale of a security.

(6) The term *effective transaction reporting plan* shall mean any plan approved by the Commission pursuant to Rule 601 of Regulation NMS for collecting, processing, and making available transaction reports with respect to transactions in an equity security or class of equity securities.

Rule 19c–4. Governing certain listing or authorization determinations by national securities exchanges and associations

(a) The rules of each exchange shall provide as follows: No rule, stated policy, practice, or interpretation of this exchange shall permit the listing, or the continuance of the listing, of any common stock or other equity security of a domestic issuer, if the issuer of such security issues any class of security, or takes other corporate action, with the effect of nullifying, restricting or disparately reducing the per share voting rights of holders of an outstanding class or classes of common stock of such issuer registered pursuant to section 12 of the Act.

(b) The rules of each association shall provide as follows: No rule, stated policy, practice, or interpretation of this association shall permit the authorization for quotation and/or transaction reporting through an automated inter-dealer quotation system ("authorization"), or the continuance of authorization, of any common stock or other equity security of a domestic issuer, if the issuer of such security issues any class of security, or takes other corporate action, with the effect of nullifying, restricting, or disparately reducing the per share voting rights of holders of an outstanding class or classes of common stock of such issuer registered pursuant to section 12 of the Act.

(c) For the purposes of paragraphs (a) and (b) of this rule, the following shall be presumed to have the effect of nullifying, restricting, or disparately reducing the per share voting rights of an outstanding class or classes of common stock:

(1) Corporate action to impose any restriction on the voting power of shares of the common stock of the issuer held by a beneficial or record holder based on the number of shares held by such beneficial or record holder;

(2) Corporate action to impose any restriction on the voting power of shares of the common stock of the issuer held by a beneficial or record holder based on the length of time such shares have been held by such beneficial or record holder;

(3) Any issuance of securities through an exchange offer by the issuer for shares of an outstanding class of the common stock of the issuer, in which the securities issued have voting rights greater than or less than the per share voting rights of any outstanding class of the common stock of the issuer;

(4) Any issuance of securities pursuant to a stock dividend, or any other type of distribution of stock, in which the securities issued have voting rights greater than the per share voting rights of any outstanding class of the common stock of the issuer.

(d) For the purpose of paragraphs (a) and (b) of this rule, the following, standing alone, shall be presumed not to have the effect of nullifying, restricting, or disparately reducing the per share voting rights of holders of an outstanding class or classes of common stock:

(1) The issuance of securities pursuant to an initial registered public offering;

(2) The issuance of any class of securities, through a registered public offering, with voting rights not greater than the per share voting rights of any outstanding class of the common stock of the issuer;

(3) The issuance of any class of securities to effect a bona fide merger or acquisition, with voting rights not greater than the per share voting rights of any outstanding class of the common stock of the issuer;

(4) Corporate action taken pursuant to state law requiring a state's domestic corporation to condition the voting rights of a beneficial or record holder of a specified threshold percentage of the corporation's voting stock on the approval of the corporation's independent shareholders.

(e) *Definitions.* The following terms shall have the following meanings for purposes of this rule and the rules of each exchange and association shall include such definitions for the purposes of the prohibition in paragraphs (a) and (b), respectively, of this rule:

(1) The term *Act* shall mean the Securities Exchange Act of 1934, as amended.

(2) The term *common stock* shall include any security of an issuer designated as common stock and any security of an issuer, however designated, which, by statute or by its terms, is a common stock (*e.g.*, a security which entitles the holders thereof to vote generally on matters submitted to the issuer's security holders for a vote).

(3) The term *equity security* shall include any equity security defined as such pursuant to Rule 3a11–1 under the Act.

(4) The term *domestic issuer* shall mean an issuer that is not a "foreign private issuer" as defined in Rule 3b–4 under the Act.

(5) The term *security* shall include any security defined as such pursuant to Section 3(a)(10) of the Act, but shall exclude any class of security having a preference or priority over the issuer's common stock as to dividends, interest payments, redemption or payments in liquidation, if the voting rights of such securities only become effective as a result of specified events, not relating to an acquisition of the common stock of the issuer, which reasonably can be expected to jeopardize the issuer's financial ability to meet its payment obligations to the holders of that class of securities.

(6) The term *exchange* shall mean a national securities exchange, registered as such with the Securities and Exchange Commission pursuant to section 6 of the Act (15 U.S.C. 78f), which makes transaction reports available pursuant to Rule 601 of Regulation NMS; and

(7) The term *association* shall mean a national securities association registered as such with the Securities and Exchange Commission pursuant to Section 15A of the Act.

(f) An exchange or association may adopt a rule, stated policy, practice, or interpretation, subject to the procedures specified by section 19(b) of the Act, specifying what types of securities issuances and other corporate actions are covered by, or excluded from, the prohibition in paragraphs (a) and (b) of this rule, respectively, if such rule, stated policy, practice, or interpretation is consistent with the protection of investors and the public interest, and otherwise in furtherance of the purposes of the Act and this rule.

Rule 19c–5. Governing the multiple listing of options on national securities exchanges

(a) The rules of each national securities exchange that provides a trading market in standardized put or call options shall provide as follows:

(1) On and after January 22, 1990, but not before, no rule, stated policy, practice, or interpretation of this exchange shall prohibit or condition, or be construed to prohibit or condition or otherwise limit, directly or indirectly, the ability of this exchange to list any stock options class first listed on an exchange on or after January 22, 1990, because that options class is listed on another options exchange.

(2) During the period from January 22, 1990, to January 21, 1991, but not before, no rule, stated policy, practice, or interpretation of this exchange shall prohibit or condition, or be construed to prohibit or condition or otherwise limit, directly or indirectly, the ability of this exchange to list up to ten classes of standardized stock options overlying exchange-listed stocks that were listed on another options exchange before January 22, 1990. These ten classes shall be in addition to any option on an exchange-listed stock trading on this exchange that was traded on more than one options exchange before January 22, 1990.

(3) On and after January 21, 1991, but not before, no rule, stated policy, practice, or interpretation of this exchange shall prohibit or condition, or be construed to prohibit or condition or otherwise limit, directly or indirectly, the ability of this exchange to list any stock options class because that options class is listed on another options exchange.

(b) For purposes of paragraph (a)(2) of this rule, if any options class is delisted from an options exchange as a result of a merger of the equity security underlying the option or a failure of the underlying security to satisfy that exchange's options listing standards, then the exchange is permitted to select a replacement option from among those standardized options overlying exchange-listed stocks that were listed on another options exchange before January 22, 1990.

(c) For purposes of this rule, the term *exchange* shall mean a national securities exchange, registered as such with the Commission pursuant to Section 6 of the Securities Exchange Act of 1934, as amended.

(d) For purposes of this rule, the term *standardized option* shall have the same meaning as that term is defined in Rule 9b–1 under the Securities Exchange Act of 1934.

(e) For purposes of this rule, the term *options class* shall have the same meaning as that term is defined in Rule 9b–1 under the Securities Exchange Act of 1934.

Rule 19d–1. Notices by self-regulatory organizations of final disciplinary actions, denials, bars, or limitations respecting membership, association, participation, or access to services, and summary suspensions

(a) *General.* If any self-regulatory organization for which the Commission is the appropriate regulatory agency takes any action described in this rule to which the person affected thereby has consented and such action

(1) Conditions or limits membership or participation in, association with a member of, or access to services offered by, such organization or a member thereof and

(2) Is based upon a statutory disqualification defined in section 3(a)(39) of the Act,

notice thereof shall be filed under Rule 19h–1 and not under this rule.

(b) The notice requirement of section 19(d)(1) of the Act, concerning an action subject to such section taken by a self-regulatory organization for which the Commission is the appropriate regulatory agency, shall be satisfied by any notice with respect to such action (including a notice filed pursuant to this rule) which contains the information required in the statement supporting the organization's determination required by section 6(d)(1) or (2), section 15A(h)(1) or (2), or section 17A(b)(5)(A) or (B) of the Act, as appropriate.

(c)(1) Any self-regulatory organization for which the Commission is the appropriate regulatory agency that takes any final disciplinary action with respect to any person shall promptly file a notice thereof with the Commission in accordance with paragraph (d) of this rule. For the purposes of this rule, a "final disciplinary action" shall mean the imposition of any final disciplinary sanction pursuant to section 6(b)(6), 15A(b)(7), or 17A(b)(3)(G) of the Act or other action of a self-regulatory organization which, after notice and opportunity for hearing, results in any final disposition of charges of:

(i) One or more violations of—

(A) The rules of such organization;

(B) The provisions of the Act or rules thereunder; or

(C) In the case of a municipal securities broker or dealer, the rules of the Municipal Securities Rulemaking Board;

(ii) Acts or practices constituting a statutory disqualification of a type defined in subparagraph (D) or (E) (except prior convictions) of Section 3(a)(39) of the Act; or

(iii) In the case of a proceeding by a national securities exchange or registered securities association based on section 6(c)(3)(A)(ii), 6(c)(3)(B)(ii), 15A(g)(3)(A)(ii) or 15A(g)(3)(B)(ii) of the Act, acts or practices inconsistent with just and equitable principles of trade.

Provided, however, That in the case of a disciplinary action in which a national securities exchange imposes a fine not exceeding $1,000 or suspends floor privileges of a clerical employee for not more than five days for violation of any of its regulations concerning personal decorum on a trading floor, the disposition shall not be considered "final" for purposes of this paragraph if the sanctioned person has not sought an adjudication, including a hearing, or otherwise exhausted his administrative remedies at the exchange with respect to the matter. *Provided further,* That this exemption from the notice requirement of this paragraph shall not be available where a decorum sanction is imposed at, or results from, a hearing on the matter.

(2) Any disciplinary action, other than a decorum sanction not deemed "final" under paragraph (c)(1) of this rule, taken by a self-regulatory organization for which the Commission is the appropriate regulatory agency against any person for violation of a rule of the self-regulatory organization which has been designated as a minor rule violation pursuant to a plan or any amendment thereto filed with and declared effective by the Commission under this paragraph, shall not be considered "final" for purposes of paragraph (c)(1) of this rule if the sanction imposed consists of a fine not exceeding $2500 and the sanctioned person has not sought an adjudication, including a hearing, or otherwise exhausted his administrative remedies at the self-regulatory organization with respect to the matter. After appropriate notice of the terms of substance of the filing or a description of the subjects and issues involved and opportunity for interested persons to submit written comment, the Commission may, by order, declare such plan or amendment effective if it finds that such plan or amendment is consistent with the public interest, the protection of investors, or otherwise in furtherance of the purposes of the Act. The Commission in its order may restrict the categories of violations to be designated as minor rule violations and may impose any other terms or conditions to the plan (including abbreviated reporting of selected minor rule violations) and to the period of its effectiveness which it deems necessary or appropriate in the public interest, for the protection of investors or otherwise in furtherance of the purposes of the Act.

(d) *Contents of Notice Required by Paragraph (c)(1).* Any notice filed pursuant to paragraph (c)(1) of this rule shall consist of the following, as appropriate:

(1) The name of the respondent concerned together with his last known place of residence or business as reflected on the records of the self-regulatory organization and the name of the person, committee, or other organizational unit which brought the charges involved; except that, as to any respondent who has been found not to have violated a provision covered by a charge, identifying information with respect to such person may be deleted insofar as the notice reports the disposition of that charge, unless, prior to the filing of the notice, the respondent requests otherwise;

(2) A statement describing the investigative or other origin of the action;

(3) As charged in the proceeding, the specific provisions of the Act, the rules or regulations thereunder, the rules of the organization, and, in the case of a registered securities association, the rules of the Municipal Securities Rulemaking Board, and, in the event a violation of other statutes or rules constitutes a violation of any rule of the organization, such other statutes or rules; and a statement describing the answer of the respondent to the charges;

(4) A statement setting forth findings of fact with respect to any act or practice which such respondent was charged with having engaged in or omitted; the conclusion of the organization as to whether such respondent is deemed to have violated any provision covered by the charges; and a statement of the organization in support of the resolution of the principal issues raised in the proceedings;

(5) A statement describing any sanction imposed, the reasons therefor, and the date upon which such sanction has or will become effective, together with a finding, if appropriate, as to

whether such respondent was a cause of any sanction imposed upon any other person; and

(6) Such other matters as the organization may deem relevant.

(e) *Notice of Final Denial, Bar, Prohibition, Termination or Limitation Based on Qualification or Administrative Rules.* Any final action of a self-regulatory organization for which the Commission is the appropriate regulatory agency that is taken with respect to any person constituting a denial, bar, prohibition, or limitation of membership, participation or association with a member, or of access to services offered by a self-regulatory organization or a member thereof, and which is based on an alleged failure of any person to:

(1) Pass any test or examination required by the rules of the Commission or such organization;

(2) Comply with other qualification standards established by rules of the Commission or such organization; or

(3) Comply with any administrative requirements of such organization (including failure to pay entry or other dues or fees or to file prescribed forms or reports) not involving charges of violations which may lead to a disciplinary sanction

Shall not be considered a "disciplinary action" for purposes of paragraph (c) of this rule; but notice thereof shall be promptly filed with the Commission in accordance with paragraph (f) of this rule, *Provided, however,* That no disposition of a matter shall be considered "final" pursuant to this paragraph which results merely from a notice of such failure to the person affected, if such person has not sought an adjudication, including a hearing, or otherwise exhausted his administrative remedies within such organization with respect to such a matter.

(f) *Contents of Notice Required by Paragraph (e).* Any notice filed pursuant to paragraph (e) of this rule shall consist of the following, as appropriate:

(1) The name of each person concerned together with his last known place of residence or business as reflected on the records of the organization;

(2) The specific provisions of the Act, the rules or regulations thereunder, the rules of the organization, and, in the case of a registered securities association, the rules of the Municipal Securities Rulemaking Board, upon which the action of the organization was based, and a statement describing the answer of the person concerned;

(3) A statement setting forth findings of fact and conclusions as to each alleged failure of the person to pass any required examination, comply with other qualification standards, or comply with administrative obligations, and a statement of the organization in support of the resolution of the principal issues raised in the proceeding;

(4) The date upon which such action has or will become effective; and

(5) Such other matters as the organization may deem relevant.

(g) *Notice of Final Action Based upon Prior Adjudicated Statutory Disqualifications.* Any self-regulatory organization for which the Commission is the appropriate regulatory agency that takes any final action with respect to any person which:

(1) Denies or conditions membership or participation in, or association with a member of, such organization or prohibits or limits access to services offered by such organization or a member thereof; and

(2) Is based upon a statutory disqualification of a type defined in subparagraph (A), (B), or (C) of section 3(a)(39) of the Act or consisting of a prior conviction, as described in subparagraph (E) of said section 3(a)(39), shall promptly file a notice of such action with the Commission in accordance with paragraph (h) of this rule, *provided, however,* That no disposition of a matter shall be considered "final" pursuant to this paragraph where such person has not sought an adjudication, including a hearing, or otherwise exhausted his administrative remedies within such organization with respect to such a matter.

(h) *Contents of Notice Required by Paragraph (g).* Any notice filed pursuant to paragraph (g) of this rule shall consist of the following, as appropriate:

(1) The name of the person concerned together with his last known place of residence or business as reflected on the record of the organization;

(2) A statement setting forth the principal issues raised, the answer of any person concerned, and a statement of the organization in support of the resolution of the principal issues raised in the proceeding;

(3) Any description furnished by or on behalf of the person concerned of the activities engaged in by the person since the adjudication upon which the disqualification is based;

(4) Any description furnished by or on behalf of the person concerned of the prospective business or employment in which the person plans to engage and the manner and extent of supervision to be exercised over and by such person;

(5) A copy of the order or decision of the court, the Commission or the self-regulatory organization which adjudicated the matter giving rise to such statutory disqualification;

(6) The nature of the action taken and the date upon which such action is to be made effective; and

(7) Such other matters as the organization deems relevant.

(i) *Notice of Summary Suspension of Membership, Participation, or Association, or Summary Limitation or Prohibition of Access to Services.* If any self-regulatory organization for which the Commission is the appropriate regulatory agency summarily suspends a member, participant, or person associated with a member, or summarily limits or prohibits any person with respect to access to or services offered by the organization or (in the case of a national securities exchange or a registered securities association) a member thereof pursuant to the provisions of section 6(d)(3), 15A(h)(3) or 17A(b)(5)(C) of the Act, such organization shall, within 24 hours of the effectiveness of such summary suspension, limitation or prohibition notify the Commission of such action, which notice shall contain at least the following information:

(1) The name of the person concerned together with his last known place of residence or business as reflected on the records of the organization;

(2) The date upon which such summary action has or will become effective;

(3) If such summary action is based upon the provisions of section 6(d)(3)(A), 15A(h)(3)(A), or 17A(b)(5)(C)(i) of the Act, a copy of the relevant order or decision of the self-regulatory organization;

(4) If such summary action is based upon the provisions of section 6(d)(3)(B) or (C), 15A(h)(3)(B) or (C), or 17A(b)(5)(C)(ii) or (iii) of the Act, a statement describing, as appropriate:

(i) The financial or operating difficulty of the member or participant upon which such organization determined the member or participant could not be permitted to continue to do business with safety to investors, creditors, other members or participants, or the organization;

(ii) The pertinent failure to meet qualification requirements or other prerequisites for access and the basis upon which such organization determined that the person concerned could not be permitted to have access with safety to investors, creditors, other members, or the organization; or

(iii) The default of any delivery of funds or securities to a clearing agency by a participant.

(5) The nature and effective date of the suspension, limitation or prohibition; and

(6) Such other matters as the organization deems relevant.

(j) *Notice of Limitation or Prohibition of Access to Services by Delisting of Security.* Any national securities exchange for which the Commission is the appropriate regulatory agency that delists a security pursuant to section 12(d) of the Act, and Rule 12d2–2 must file a notice with the Commission in accordance with paragraph (k) of this rule.

(k) *Contents of Notice Required by Paragraph (j) of this Rule.* The national securities exchange shall file notice pursuant to paragraph (j) of this rule on Form 25 (17 CFR 249.25). Form 25 shall serve as notification to the Commission of such limitation or prohibition of access to services. The national securities exchange must attach a copy of its delisting determination to Form 25 and file Form 25 with the attachment on EDGAR.

Rule 19d–2. Applications for stays of disciplinary sanctions or summary suspensions by a self-regulatory organization

If any self-regulatory organization imposes any final disciplinary sanction as to which a notice is required to be filed with the Commission pursuant to Section 19(d)(1) of the Exchange Act, 15 U.S.C. 78s(d)(1), pursuant to Section 6(b)(6), 15A(b)(7) or 17A(b)(3)(G) of the Act, or summarily suspends or limits or prohibits access pursuant to Section 6(d)(3), 15A(h)(3) or 17A(b)(5)(C) of the Act, any person aggrieved thereby for which the Commission is the appropriate regulatory agency may file with the Commission a written motion for a stay of imposition of such action pursuant to Rule 401 of the Commission's Rules of Practice, 17 CFR 201.401.

Rule 19d–3. Applications for review of final disciplinary sanctions, denials of membership, participation or association, or prohibitions or limitations of access to services imposed by self-regulatory organizations

Applications to the Commission for review of any final disciplinary sanction, denial or conditioning of membership, participation, bar from association, or prohibition or limitation with respect to access to services offered by a self-regulatory organization or a member thereof by any such organization shall be made pursuant to Rule 420 of the Commission's Rules of Practice, 17 CFR 201.420.

Rule 19d–4. Notice by the Public Company Accounting Oversight Board of disapproval of registration or of disciplinary action

(a) *Definitions.* (1) *Board* means the Public Company Accounting Oversight Board.

(2) *Public accounting firm* shall have the meaning set forth in 15 U.S.C. 7201(a)(11).

(3) *Registered public accounting firm* shall have the meaning set forth in 15 U.S.C. 7201(a)(12).

(4) *Associated person* shall mean a person associated with a registered public accounting firm as defined in 15 U.S.C. 7201(a)(9).

(b)(1) *Notice of Disapproval of Registration.* If the Board disapproves a completed application for registration by a public accounting firm, the Board shall file a notice of its disapproval with the Commission within 30 days and serve a copy on the public accounting firm.

(2) *Contents of the Notice.* The notice required by paragraph (b)(1) of this rule shall provide the following information:

(i) The name of the public accounting firm and the public accounting firm's last known address as reflected in the Board's records;

(ii) The basis for the Board's disapproval, and a copy of the Board's written notice of disapproval; and

(iii) Such other information as the Board may deem relevant.

(c)(1) *Notice of Disciplinary Action.* If the Board imposes any final disciplinary sanction on any registered public accounting firm or any associated person of a registered public accounting firm under 15 U.S.C. 7215(b)(3) or 7215(c), the Board shall file a notice of the disciplinary sanction with the Commission within 30 days and serve a copy on the person sanctioned.

(2) *Contents of the Notice.* The notice required by paragraph (c)(1) of this rule shall provide the following information:

(i) The name of the registered public accounting firm or the associated person, together with the firm's or the person's last known address as reflected in the Board's records;

(ii) A description of the acts or practices, or omissions to act, upon which the sanction is based;

(iii) A statement of the sanction imposed, the reasons therefor, or a copy of the Board's statement justifying the sanction, and the effective date of such sanction; and

(iv) Such other information as the Board may deem relevant.

Rule 19g2–1. Enforcement of compliance by national securities exchanges and registered securities associations with the Act and rules and regulations thereunder

(a) In enforcing compliance, within the meaning of section 19(g) of the Act, with the Act and the rules and regulations thereunder by its members and persons associated with its members, a national securities exchange or registered securities association is not required:

(1) To enforce compliance with sections 12 (other than sections 12(j) and 12(k)), 13, 14 (other than section 14(b)), 15(d) and 16 and the rules thereunder except to the extent of any action normally taken with respect to any person which is not a member or a person associated with a member;

(2) To enforce compliance with respect to persons associated with a member, other than securities persons or persons who control a member; and

(3) To conduct examinations as to qualifications of, require filing of periodic reports by, or conduct regular inspections (including examinations of books and records) of, persons associated with a member, other than securities persons whose functions are not solely clerical or ministerial.

(b) For the purpose of this rule:

(1) A *securities person* is a person who is a general partner or officer (or person occupying a similar status or performing similar functions) or

employee of a member; *Provided, however,* That a registered broker or dealer which controls, is controlled by, or is under common control with, the member and the general partners and officers (and persons occupying similar status or performing similar functions) and employees of such a registered broker or dealer shall be securities persons if they effect, directly or indirectly, transactions in securities through the member by use of facilities maintained or supervised by such exchange or association; and

(2) *Control* means the power to direct or cause the direction of the management or policies of a company whether through ownership of securities, by contract or otherwise; *Provided, however,* That:

(i) Any person who, directly or indirectly, (A) has the right to vote 25 percent or more of the voting securities, (B) is entitled to receive 25 percent or more of the net profits, or (C) is a director (or person occupying a similar status or performing similar functions) of a company shall be presumed to be a person who controls such company;

(ii) Any person not covered by paragraph (b)(2)(i) of this rule shall be presumed not to be a person who controls such company; and

(iii) Any presumption may be rebutted on an appropriate showing.

Rule 19h–1. Notice by a self-regulatory organization of proposed admission to or continuance in membership or participation or association with a member of any person subject to a statutory disqualification, and applications to the Commission for relief therefrom

(a) *Notice of Admission or Continuance Notwithstanding a Statutory Disqualification.* (1) Any self-regulatory organization proposing, conditionally or unconditionally, to admit to, or continue any person in, membership or participation or (in the case of a national securities exchange or registered securities exchange or registered securities association) association with a member, notwithstanding a statutory disqualification, as defined in section 3(a)(39) of the Act, with respect to such person, shall file a notice with the Commission of such proposed admission or continuance. If such disqualified person has not consented to the terms of such proposal, notice of the organization's action shall be filed pursuant to rule 19d–1 under the Act and not this rule.

(2) With respect to a person associated with a member of a national securities exchange or registered securities association, notices need be filed with the Commission pursuant to this rule only if such person:

(i) Controls such member, is a general partner or officer (or person occupying a similar status or performing similar functions) of such member, is an employee who, on behalf of such member, is engaged in securities advertising, public relations, research, sales, trading, or training or supervision of other employees who engage or propose to engage in such activities, except clerical and ministerial persons engaged in such activities, or is an employee with access to funds, securities or books and records, or

(ii) Is a broker or dealer not registered with the Commission, or controls such (unregistered) broker or dealer or is a general partner or officer (or person occupying a similar status or performing similar functions) of such broker or dealer.

(3) A notice need not be filed with the Commission pursuant to this rule if:

(i) The person subject to the statutory disqualification is already a participant in, a member of, or a person associated with a member of, a self-regulatory organization, and the terms and conditions of the proposed admission by another self-regulatory organization are the same in all material respects as those imposed or not disapproved in connection with such person's prior admission or continuance pursuant to an order of the Commission under paragraph (d) of this rule or other substantially equivalent written communication.

(ii) The self-regulatory organization finds, after reasonable inquiry, that except for the identity of the employer concerned, the terms and conditions of the proposed admission or continuance are the same in all material respects as those imposed or not disapproved in connection with a prior admission or continuance of the person subject to the statutory disqualification pursuant to an order of the Commission under paragraph (d) of this rule or other substantially equivalent written communication and that there is no intervening conduct or other circumstance that would cause the employment to be inconsistent with the public interest or the protection of investors;

(iii) The disqualification consists of (A) an injunction from engaging in any action, conduct, or practice specified in section 15(b)(4)(C) of the Act, which injunction was entered 10 or more years prior to the proposed admission or continuance—*Provided, however,* That in the case of a final or permanent injunction which was preceded by a preliminary injunction against the same person in the same court proceeding, such ten-year period shall begin to run from the date of such preliminary injunction—and/or (B) a finding by the Commission or a self-regulatory organization of a willful violation of the Act, the Securities Act of 1933, the Investment Advisers Act of 1940, the Investment Company Act of 1940, or a rule or regulation under one or more of such Acts and the sanction for such violation is no longer in effect;

(iv) The disqualification previously (A) was a basis for the institution of an administrative proceeding pursuant to a provision of the federal securities laws, and (B) was considered by the Commission in determining a sanction against such person in the proceeding; and the Commission concluded in such proceeding that it would not restrict or limit the future securities activities of such person in the capacity now proposed or, if it imposed any such restrictions or limitations for a specified time period, such time period has elapsed;

(v) The disqualification consists of a court order or judgment of injunction or conviction, and such order or judgment (A) expressly includes a provision that, on the basis of such order or judgment, the Commission will not institute a proceeding against such person pursuant to section 15(b) or 15B of the Act or that the future securities activities of such persons in the capacity now proposed will not be restricted or limited or (B) includes such restrictions or limitations for a specified time period and such time period has elapsed; or

(vi) In the case of a person seeking to become associated with a broker or dealer or municipal securities dealer, the Commission has previously consented to such proposed association pursuant to section 15(b)(6) or 15B(c)(4) of the Act.

In the case of an admission to membership, participation, or association, if an exception provided for in this paragraph (a)(3) is applicable, the self-regulatory organization shall, pursuant to its rules, determine when the admission to membership, participation, or association shall become effective.

(4) If a self-regulatory organization determines to admit to, or continue any person in, membership, participation, or association with a member pursuant to an exception from the notice requirements provided in paragraph (a)(3)(ii), (iv) or (v) of this rule, such organization shall, within 14 calendar days of its making of such determination, furnish to the Commission, by letter, a notification setting forth, as appropriate:

(i) The name of the person subject to the statutory disqualification;

(ii) The name of the person's prospective and immediately preceding employers who are (were) brokers or dealers or municipal securities dealers;

(iii) The name of the person's prospective supervisor(s);

(iv) The respective places of such employments as reflected on the records of the self-regulatory organization;

(v) If applicable, the findings of the self-regulatory organization referred to in paragraph (a)(3)(ii) of this rule and the nature (including relevant dates) of the previous Commission or court determination referred to in paragraph (a)(3)(iv) or (v) of this rule; and

(vi) An identification of any other self-regulatory organization which has indicated its agreement with the terms and conditions of the proposed admission or continuance;

(5) If a notice or notification has been previously filed or furnished pursuant to this rule by a self-regulatory organization, any other such organization need not file or furnish a separate notice or notification pursuant to this rule with respect to the same matter if such other organization agrees with the terms and conditions of the membership, participation or association reflected in the notice or notification so filed or furnished, and such agreement is set forth in the notice or notification.

(6) The notice requirements of sections 6(c)(2), 15A(g)(2), and 17A(b)(4)(A) of the Act concerning an action of a self-regulatory organization subject to one (or more) of such sections and this paragraph (a) shall be satisfied by a notice with respect to such action filed in accordance with paragraph (c) of this rule.

(7) The Commission, by written notice to a self-regulatory organization on or before the thirtieth day after receipt of a notice under this Rule, may direct that such organization not admit to membership, participation, or association with a member any person who is subject to a statutory disqualification for a period not to exceed an additional 60 days beyond the initial 30 day notice period in order that the Commission may extend its consideration of the proposal; *Provided, however,* That during such extended period of consideration, the Commission will not direct the self-regulatory organization to bar the proposed admission to membership, participation or association with a member pursuant to section 6(c)(2), 15A(g)(2), or 17A(b)(4)(A) of the Act, and the Commission will not institute proceedings pursuant to section 15(b) or 15B of the Act on the basis of such disqualification if the self-regulatory organization has permitted the admission to membership, participation or association with a member, on a temporary basis, pending a final Commission determination.

(b) *Preliminary Notifications.* Promptly after receiving an application for admission to, or continuance in, participation or membership in, or association with a member of, a self-regulatory organization which would be required to file with the Commission a notice thereof pursuant to paragraph (a) of this rule if such admission or continuance is ultimately proposed by such organization, the organization shall file with the Commission a notification of such receipt. Such notification shall include, as appropriate:

(1) The date of such receipt;

(2) The names of the person subject to the statutory disqualification and the prospective employer concerned together with their respective last known places of residence or business as reflected on the records of the organization;

(3) The basis for any such disqualification including (if based on a prior adjudication) a copy of the order or decision of the court, the Commission, or the self-regulatory organization which adjudicated the matter giving rise to the disqualification; and

(4) The capacity in which the person concerned is proposed to be employed.

(c) *Contents of Notice of Admission or Continuance.* A notice filed with the Commission pursuant to paragraph (a) of this rule shall contain the following, as appropriate:

(1) The name of the person concerned together with his last known place of residence or business as reflected on the records of the self-regulatory organization;

(2) The basis for any such disqualification from membership, participation or association including (if based on a prior adjudication) a copy of the order or decision of the court, the Commission or the self-regulatory organization which adjudicated the matter giving rise to such disqualification;

(3) In the case of an admission, the date upon which it is proposed by the organization that such membership, participation or association shall become effective, which shall be not less than 30 days from the date upon which the Commission receives the notice;

(4) A description by or on behalf of the person concerned of the activities engaged in by the person since the disqualification arose, the prospective business or employment in which the person plans to engage and the manner and extent of supervision to be exercised over and by such person. This description shall be accompanied by a written statement submitted to the self-regulatory organization by the proposed employer setting forth the terms and conditions of such employment and supervision. The description also shall include (i) the qualifications, experience and disciplinary records of the proposed supervisors of the person and their family relationship (if any) to that person; (ii) the findings and results of all examinations conducted, during the two years preceding the filing of the notice, by self-regulatory organizations of the main office of the proposed employer and of the branch office(s) in which the employment will occur to be subject to supervisory controls; (iii) a copy of a completed Form U–4 with respect to the proposed association of such person and a certification by the self-regulatory organization that such person is fully qualified under all applicable requirements to engage in the proposed activities; and (iv) the name and place of employment of any other associated person of the proposed employer who is subject to a statutory disqualification (other than a disqualification specified in paragraph (a)(3)(iii) of this rule);

(5) If a hearing on the matter has been held by the organization, a certified record of the hearing together with copies of any exhibits introduced therein;

(6) All written submissions not included in a certified oral hearing record which were considered by the organization in its disposition of the matter;

(7) An identification of any other self-regulatory organization which has indicated its agreement

with the terms and conditions of the proposed admission or continuance;

(8) All information furnished in writing to the self-regulatory organization by the staff of the Commission for consideration by the organization in its disposition of the matter or the incorporation by reference of such information, and a statement of the organization's views thereon; and

(9) Such other matters as the organization or person deems relevant.

If the notice contains assertions of material facts not a matter of record before the self-regulatory organization, such facts shall be sworn to by affidavit of the person or organization offering such facts for Commission consideration. The notice may be accompanied by a brief.

(d) *Application to the Commission for Relief from Certain Statutory Disqualifications.* The filing of a notice pursuant to paragraph (a) of this rule shall neither affect nor foreclose any action which the Commission may take with respect to such person pursuant to the provisions of section 15(b), 15B or 19(h) of the Act or any rule thereunder. Accordingly, a notice filed pursuant to paragraph (a) of this rule with respect to the membership, participation, or association of any person subject to an "applicable disqualification," as defined in paragraph (f) of this rule, may be accompanied by an application by or on behalf of the person concerned to the Commission for an order declaring, as applicable, that notwithstanding such disqualification, the Commission:

(1) Will not institute proceedings pursuant to section 15(b)(1)(B), 15(b)(4), 15(b)(6), 15B(a)(2), 15B(c)(2), 19(h)(2) or 19(h)(3) of the Act if such person seeks to obtain or continue registration as a broker or dealer or municipal securities dealer or association with a broker or dealer or municipal securities dealer so registered, or membership or participation in a self-regulatory organization;

(2) Will not direct otherwise, as provided in section 6(c)(2), 15A(g)(2), or 17A(b)(4)(A) of the Act; and

(3) Will deem such person qualified pursuant to Rule G–4 of the Municipal Securities Rulemaking Board under the Act.

If a Commission consent is required in order to render a proposed association lawful under section 15(b)(6) or 15B(c)(4) of the Act, an application by or on behalf of the person seeking such consent shall accompany the notice of the proposed association filed pursuant to paragraph (a) of this rule. The Commission may, in its discretion and subject to such terms and conditions as it deems necessary, issue such an order and consent should the Commission determine not to object to the position of the self-regulatory organization set forth in the notice or application; *Provided, however,* That nothing herein shall foreclose the right of any person, at his election, to apply directly to the Commission for such consent, if he makes such application pursuant to the terms of an existing order of the Commission under section 15(b)(6) or 15B(c)(4) of the Act limiting his association with a broker or dealer or municipal securities dealer but explicitly granting him such a right to apply for entry or reentry at a later time.

(e) *Contents of Application to the Commission.* An application to the Commission pursuant to paragraph (d) of this rule shall consist of the following, as appropriate:

(1) The name of the person subject to the disqualification together with his last known place of residence or business as reflected on the records of the self-regulatory organization;

(2) A copy of the order or decision of the court, the Commission or the self-regulatory organization which adjudicated the matter giving rise to such "applicable disqualification";

(3) The nature of the relief sought and the reasons therefor;

(4) A description of the activities engaged in by the person since the disqualification arose;

(5) A description of the prospective business or employment in which the person plans to engage and the manner and extent of supervision to be exercised over and by such person. This description shall be accompanied by a written statement submitted to the self-regulatory organization by the proposed employer setting forth the terms and conditions of such employment and supervision. The description also shall include (i) the qualifications, experience, and disciplinary records of the proposed supervisors of the person and their family relationship (if any) to that person; (ii) the findings and results of all examinations conducted, during the two years preceding the filing of the application, by self-regulatory organizations of the main office of the proposed employer and of the branch office(s) in which the employment will occur or be subject to supervisory controls; (iii) a copy of a completed Form U–4 with respect to the proposed association of such person and a certification by the self-regulatory organization that such person is fully qualified under all applicable requirements to engage in the proposed activities;

and (iv) the name and place of employment of any other associated person of the proposed employer who is subject to a statutory disqualification (other than a disqualification specified in paragraph (a)(3)(iii) of this rule);

(6) If a hearing on the matter has been held by the organization, a certified copy of the hearing record, together with copies of any exhibits introduced therein;

(7) All written submissions not included in a certified oral hearing record which were considered by the organization in its disposition of the matter;

(8) All information furnished in writing to the self-regulatory organization by the staff of the Commission for consideration by the organization in its disposition of the matter or the incorporation by reference of such information, and a statement of the organization's views thereon; and

(9) Such other matters as the organization or person deems relevant.

If the application contains assertions of material facts not a matter of record before the organization, such facts shall be sworn to by affidavit of the person or organization offering such facts for Commission consideration.

(f) *Definitions.* For purposes of this rule:

(1) The term *applicable disqualification* shall mean:

(i) Any effective order of the Commission pursuant to section 15(b)(4) or (6), 15B(c)(2) or (4) or 19(h)(2) or (3) of the Act—

(A) Revoking, suspending or placing limitations on the registration, activities, functions, or operations of a broker or dealer;

(B) Suspending, barring, or placing limitations on the association, activities, or functions of an associated person of a broker or dealer;

(C) Suspending or expelling any person from membership or participation in a self-regulatory organization; or

(D) Suspending or barring any person from being associated with a member of a national securities exchange or registered securities association;

(ii) Any conviction or injunction of a type described in section 15(b)(4)(B) or (C) of the Act; or

(iii) A failure under the provisions of Rule G–4 of the Municipal Securities Rulemaking Board under the Act, to meet qualifications standards, and such failure may be remedied by a finding or determination by the Commission pursuant to such rule(s) that the person affected nevertheless meets such standards.

(2) The term *control* shall mean the power to direct or cause the direction of the management or policies of a company whether through ownership of securities, by contract or otherwise; *Provided, however,* That

(i) Any person who, directly or indirectly, (A) has the right to vote 10 percent or more of the voting securities, (B) is entitled to receive 10 percent or more of the net profits, or (C) is a director (or person occupying a similar status or performing similar functions) of a company shall be presumed to be a person who controls such company;

(ii) Any person not covered by paragraph (i) shall be presumed not to be a person who controls such company; and

(iii) Any presumption may be rebutted on an appropriate showing.

(g) Where it deems appropriate to do so, the Commission may determine whether to (1) direct, pursuant to section 6(c)(2), 15A(g)(2) or 17A(b)(4)(A) of the Act, that a proposed admission covered by a notice filed pursuant to paragraph (a) of this rule shall be denied or an order barring a proposed association issued or (2) grant or deny an application filed pursuant to paragraph (d) of this rule on the basis of the notice or application filed by the self-regulatory organization, the person subject to the disqualification, or other applicant (such as the proposed employer) on behalf of such person, without oral hearing. Any request for oral hearing or argument should be submitted with the notice or application.

(h) The Rules of Practice (17 CFR Part 201) shall apply to proceedings under this rule to the extent that they are not inconsistent with this rule.

IMPLEMENTATION OF THE WHISTLEBLOWER PROVISIONS OF SECTION 21F OF THE SECURITIES EXCHANGE ACT OF 1934

Rule 21F–1. General

Section 21F of the Securities Exchange Act of 1934, entitled Securities Whistleblower Incentives and Protection, requires the Securities and Exchange Commission (Commission) to pay awards, subject to certain limitations and conditions, to whistleblowers who provide the Commission with original information about violations of the federal securities laws. These rules describe the whistleblower program that the Commission has established to implement the provisions of Section 21F, and explain the procedures you will need to follow in order to be eligible for an award. You should read these procedures carefully because the failure to take certain required steps within the time frames described in these rules may disqualify you from receiving an award for which you otherwise may be eligible. Unless expressly provided for in these rules, no person is authorized to make any offer or promise, or otherwise to bind the Commission with respect to the payment of any award or the amount thereof. The Securities and Exchange Commission's Office of the Whistleblower administers our whistleblower program. Questions about the program or these rules should be directed to the SEC Office of the Whistleblower, 100 F Street, N.E., Washington, DC 20549–5631.

Rule 21F–2. Whistleblower status and retaliation protection

(a) *Definition of a Whistleblower*.

(1) You are a whistleblower if, alone or jointly with others, you provide the Commission with information pursuant to the procedures set forth in Rule 21F–9(a), and the information relates to a possible violation of the federal securities laws (including any rules or regulations thereunder) that has occurred, is ongoing, or is about to occur. A whistleblower must be an individual. A company or another entity is not eligible to be a whistleblower.

(2) To be eligible for an award, you must submit original information to the Commission in accordance with the procedures and conditions described in Rules 21F–4, 21F–8, and 21F–9.

(b) *Prohibition Against Retaliation*:

(1) For purposes of the anti-retaliation protections afforded by Section 21F(h)(1) of the Exchange Act, you are a whistleblower if:

(i) You possess a reasonable belief that the information you are providing relates to a possible securities law violation (or, where applicable, to a possible violation of the provisions set forth in 18 U.S.C. 1514A(a)) that has occurred, is ongoing, or is about to occur, and;

(ii) You provide that information in a manner described in Section 21F(h)(1)(A) of the Exchange Act.

(iii) The anti-retaliation protections apply whether or not you satisfy the requirements, procedures and conditions to qualify for an award.

(2) Section 21F(h)(1) of the Exchange Act, including any rules promulgated thereunder, shall be enforceable in an action or proceeding brought by the Commission.

Rule 21F–3. Payment of awards

(a) *Commission Actions*: Subject to the eligibility requirements described in Rules 21F–2, 21F–8, and 21F–16, the Commission will pay an award or awards to one or more whistleblowers who:

(1) Voluntarily provide the Commission

(2) With original information

(3) That leads to the successful enforcement by the Commission of a federal court or administrative action

(4) In which the Commission obtains monetary sanctions totaling more than $1,000,000.

Note to Paragraph (a): The terms *voluntarily, original information, leads to successful enforcement, action,* and *monetary sanctions* are defined in Rule 21F–4.

(b) *Related Actions*: The Commission will also pay an award based on amounts collected in certain related actions.

(1) A *related action* is a judicial or administrative action that is brought by:

(i) The Attorney General of the United States;

(ii) An appropriate regulatory authority;

(iii) A self-regulatory organization; or

(iv) A state attorney general in a criminal case, and is based on the same original information that the whistleblower voluntarily provided to the Commission, and that led the Commission to obtain monetary sanctions totaling more than $1,000,000.

NOTE TO PARAGRAPH (b): The terms *appropriate regulatory authority* and *self-regulatory organization* are defined in Rule 21F–4 of this chapter.

(2) In order for the Commission to make an award in connection with a related action, the Commission must determine that the same original information that the whistleblower gave to the Commission also led to the successful enforcement of the related action under the same criteria described in these rules for awards made in connection with Commission actions. The Commission may seek assistance and confirmation from the authority bringing the related action in making this determination. The Commission will deny an award in connection with the related action if:

(i) The Commission determines that the criteria for an award are not satisfied; or

(ii) The Commission is unable to make a determination because the Office of the Whistleblower could not obtain sufficient and reliable information that could be used as the basis for an award determination pursuant to Rule 21F–12(a) of this chapter. Additional procedures apply to the payment of awards in related actions. These procedures are described in Rules 21F–11 and 21F–14.

(3) The Commission will not make an award to you for a related action if you have already been granted an award by the Commodity Futures Trading Commission (CFTC) for that same action pursuant to its whistleblower award program under Section 23 of the Commodity Exchange Act (7 U.S.C. 26). Similarly, if the CFTC has previously denied an award to you in a related action, you will be precluded from relitigating any issues before the Commission that the CFTC resolved against you as part of the award denial.

Rule 21F–4. Other definitions

(a) *Voluntary Submission of Information.*

(1) Your submission of information is made voluntarily within the meaning of Rule 21F–1 through 21F–17 if you provide your submission before a request, inquiry, or demand that relates to the subject matter of your submission is directed to you or anyone representing you (such as an attorney):

(i) By the Commission;

(ii) In connection with an investigation, inspection, or examination by the Public Company Accounting Oversight Board, or any self-regulatory organization; or

(iii) In connection with an investigation by Congress, any other authority of the federal government, or a state Attorney General or securities regulatory authority.

(2) If the Commission or any of these other authorities direct a request, inquiry, or demand as described in paragraph (1) of this section to you or your representative first, your submission will not be considered voluntary, and you will not be eligible for an award, even if your response is not compelled by subpoena or other applicable law. However, your submission of information to the Commission will be considered voluntary if you voluntarily provided the same information to one of the other authorities identified above prior to receiving a request, inquiry, or demand from the Commission.

(3) In addition, your submission will not be considered voluntary if you are required to report your original information to the Commission as a result of a pre-existing legal duty, a contractual duty that is owed to the Commission or to one of the other authorities set forth in paragraph (1) of this section, or a duty that arises out of a judicial or administrative order.

(b) *Original Information.*

(1) In order for your whistleblower submission to be considered *original information*, it must be:

(i) Derived from your independent knowledge or independent analysis;

(ii) Not already known to the Commission from any other source, unless you are the original source of the information;

(iii) Not exclusively derived from an allegation made in a judicial or administrative hearing, in a governmental report, hearing, audit, or investigation, or from the news media, unless you are a source of the information; and

(iv) Provided to the Commission for the first time after July 21, 2010 (the date of enactment of the Dodd–Frank Wall Street Reform and Consumer Protection Act).

(2) *Independent knowledge* means factual information in your possession that is not derived from

publicly available sources. You may gain independent knowledge from your experiences, communications and observations in your business or social interactions.

(3) *Independent analysis* means your own analysis, whether done alone or in combination with others. Analysis means your examination and evaluation of information that may be publicly available, but which reveals information that is not generally known or available to the public.

(4) The Commission will not consider information to be derived from your independent knowledge or independent analysis in any of the following circumstances:

(i) If you obtained the information through a communication that was subject to the attorney-client privilege, unless disclosure of that information would otherwise be permitted by an attorney pursuant to 17 CFR 205.3(d)(2), the applicable state attorney conduct rules, or otherwise;

(ii) If you obtained the information in connection with the legal representation of a client on whose behalf you or your employer or firm are providing services, and you seek to use the information to make a whistleblower submission for your own benefit, unless disclosure would otherwise be permitted by an attorney pursuant to 17 CFR 205.3(d)(2), the applicable state attorney conduct rules, or otherwise; or

(iii) In circumstances not covered by paragraphs (b)(4)(i) or (b)(4)(ii) of this section, if you obtained the information because you were:

(A) An officer, director, trustee, or partner of an entity and another person informed you of allegations of misconduct, or you learned the information in connection with the entity's processes for identifying, reporting, and addressing possible violations of law;

(B) An employee whose principal duties involve compliance or internal audit responsibilities, or you were employed by or otherwise associated with a firm retained to perform compliance or internal audit functions for an entity;

(C) Employed by or otherwise associated with a firm retained to conduct an inquiry or investigation into possible violations of law; or

(D) An employee of, or other person associated with, a public accounting firm, if you obtained the information through the performance of an engagement required of an independent public accountant under the federal securities laws (other than an audit subject to Rule 21F-8(c)(4)), and that information related to a violation by the engagement client or the client's directors, officers or other employees.

(iv) If you obtained the information by a means or in a manner that is determined by a United States court to violate applicable federal or state criminal law; or

(v) *Exceptions*. Paragraph (b)(4)(iii) of this section shall not apply if:

(A) You have a reasonable basis to believe that disclosure of the information to the Commission is necessary to prevent the relevant entity from engaging in conduct that is likely to cause substantial injury to the financial interest or property of the entity or investors;

(B) You have a reasonable basis to believe that the relevant entity is engaging in conduct that will impede an investigation of the misconduct; or

(C) At least 120 days have elapsed since you provided the information to the relevant entity's audit committee, chief legal officer, chief compliance officer (or their equivalents), or your supervisor, or since you received the information, if you received it under circumstances indicating that the entity's audit committee, chief legal officer, chief compliance officer (or their equivalents), or your supervisor was already aware of the information.

(vi) If you obtained the information from a person who is subject to this section, unless the information is not excluded from that person's use pursuant to this section, or you are providing the Commission with information about possible violations involving that person.

(5) The Commission will consider you to be an *original source* of the same information that we obtain from another source if the information satisfies the definition of original information and the other source obtained the information from you or your representative. In order to be considered an original source of information that the Commission receives from Congress, any other author-

ity of the federal government, a state Attorney General or securities regulatory authority, any self-regulatory organization, or the Public Company Accounting Oversight Board, you must have voluntarily given such authorities the information within the meaning of these rules. You must establish your status as the original source of information to the Commission's satisfaction. In determining whether you are the original source of information, the Commission may seek assistance and confirmation from one of the other authorities described above, or from another entity (including your employer), in the event that you claim to be the original source of information that an authority or another entity provided to the Commission.

(6) If the Commission already knows some information about a matter from other sources at the time you make your submission, and you are not an original source of that information under paragraph (b)(5) of this section, the Commission will consider you an original source of any information you provide that is derived from your independent knowledge or analysis and that materially adds to the information that the Commission already possesses.

(7) If you provide information to the Congress, any other authority of the federal government, a state Attorney General or securities regulatory authority, any self–regulatory organization, or the Public Company Accounting Oversight Board, or to an entity's internal whistleblower, legal, or compliance procedures for reporting allegations of possible violations of law, and you, within 120 days, submit the same information to the Commission pursuant to Rule 21F–9, as you must do in order for you to be eligible to be considered for an award, then, for purposes of evaluating your claim to an award under Rules 21F–10 and 21F–11, the Commission will consider that you provided information as of the date of your original disclosure, report or submission to one of these other authorities or persons. You must establish the effective date of any prior disclosure, report, or submission, to the Commission's satisfaction. The Commission may seek assistance and confirmation from the other authority or person in making this determination.

(c) *Information that Leads to Successful Enforcement*. The Commission will consider that you provided original information that led to the successful enforcement of a judicial or administrative action in any of the following circumstances:

(1) You gave the Commission original information that was sufficiently specific, credible, and timely to cause the staff to commence an examination, open an investigation, reopen an investigation that the Commission had closed, or to inquire concerning different conduct as part of a current examination or investigation, and the Commission brought a successful judicial or administrative action based in whole or in part on conduct that was the subject of your original information; or

(2) You gave the Commission original information about conduct that was already under examination or investigation by the Commission, the Congress, any other authority of the federal government, a state Attorney General or securities regulatory authority, any self-regulatory organization, or the PCAOB (except in cases where you were an original source of this information as defined in paragraph (b)(4) of this section), and your submission significantly contributed to the success of the action.

(3) You reported original information through an entity's internal whistleblower, legal, or compliance procedures for reporting allegations of possible violations of law before or at the same time you reported them to the Commission; the entity later provided your information to the Commission, or provided results of an audit or investigation initiated in whole or in part in response to information you reported to the entity; and the information the entity provided to the Commission satisfies either paragraph (c)(1) or (c)(2) of this section. Under this paragraph (c)(3), you must also submit the same information to the Commission in accordance with the procedures set forth in Rule 21F–9 within 120 days of providing it to the entity.

(d) An *action* generally means a single captioned judicial or administrative proceeding brought by the Commission. Notwithstanding the foregoing:

(1) For purposes of making an award under Rule 21F–10, the Commission will treat as a Commission action two or more administrative or judicial proceedings brought by the Commission if these proceedings arise out of the same nucleus of operative facts; or

(2) For purposes of determining the payment on an award under Rule 21F–14, the Commission will deem as part of the Commission action upon which the award was based any subsequent Com-

mission proceeding that, individually, results in a monetary sanction of $1,000,000 or less, and that arises out of the same nucleus of operative facts.

(e) *Monetary sanctions* means any money, including penalties, disgorgement, and interest, ordered to be paid and any money deposited into a disgorgement fund or other fund pursuant to Section 308(b) of the Sarbanes–Oxley Act of 2002 (15 U.S.C. 7246(b)) as a result of a Commission action or a related action.

(f) *Appropriate regulatory agency* means the Commission, the Comptroller of the Currency, the Board of Governors of the Federal Reserve System, the Federal Deposit Insurance Corporation, the Office of Thrift Supervision, and any other agencies that may be defined as appropriate regulatory agencies under Section 3(a)(34) of the Exchange Act.

(g) *Appropriate regulatory authority* means an appropriate regulatory agency other than the Commission.

(h) *Self-regulatory organization* means any national securities exchange, registered securities association, registered clearing agency, the Municipal Securities Rulemaking Board, and any other organizations that may be defined as self-regulatory organizations under Section 3(a)(26) of the Exchange Act.

Rule 21F–5. Amount of award

(a) The determination of the amount of an award is in the discretion of the Commission.

(b) If all of the conditions are met for a whistleblower award in connection with a Commission action or a related action, the Commission will then decide the percentage amount of the award applying the criteria set forth in Rule 21F–6 and pursuant to the procedures set forth in Rules 21F–10 and 21F–11. The amount will be at least 10 percent and no more than 30 percent of the monetary sanctions that the Commission and the other authorities are able to collect. The percentage awarded in connection with a Commission action may differ from the percentage awarded in connection with a related action.

(c) If the Commission makes awards to more than one whistleblower in connection with the same action or related action, the Commission will determine an individual percentage award for each whistleblower, but in no event will the total amount awarded to all whistleblowers in the aggregate be less than 10 percent or greater than 30 percent of the amount the Commission or the other authorities collect.

Rule 21F–6. Criteria for determining amount of award

In exercising its discretion to determine the appropriate award percentage, the Commission may consider the following factors in relation to the unique facts and circumstances of each case, and may increase or decrease the award percentage based on its analysis of these factors. In the event that awards are determined for multiple whistleblowers in connection an action, these factors will be used to determine the relative allocation of awards among the whistleblowers.

(a) *Factors that May Increase the Amount of a Whistleblower's Award.* In determining whether to increase the amount of an award, the Commission will consider the following factors, which are not listed in order of importance.

(1) *Significance of the Information Provided by the Whistleblower.* The Commission will assess the significance of the information provided by a whistleblower to the success of the Commission action or related action. In considering this factor, the Commission may take into account, among other things:

(i) The nature of the information provided by the whistleblower and how it related to the successful enforcement action, including whether the reliability and completeness of the information provided to the Commission by the whistleblower resulted in the conservation of Commission resources;

(ii) The degree to which the information provided by the whistleblower supported one or more successful claims brought in the Commission or related action.

(2) *Assistance Provided by the Whistleblower.* The Commission will assess the degree of assistance provided by the whistleblower and any legal representative of the whistleblower in the Commission action or related action. In considering this factor, the Commission may take into account, among other things:

(i) Whether the whistleblower provided ongoing, extensive, and timely cooperation and assistance by, for example, helping to explain complex transactions, interpreting key evidence, or identifying new and productive lines of inquiry;

(ii) The timeliness of the whistleblower's initial report to the Commission or to an internal compliance or reporting system of business organizations committing, or impacted by, the securities violations, where appropriate;

(iii) The resources conserved as a result of the whistleblower's assistance;

(iv) Whether the whistleblower appropriately encouraged or authorized others to assist the staff of the Commission who might otherwise not have participated in the investigation or related action;

(v) The efforts undertaken by the whistleblower to remediate the harm caused by the violations, including assisting the authorities in the recovery of the fruits and instrumentalities of the violations; and

(vi) Any unique hardships experienced by the whistleblower as a result of his or her reporting and assisting in the enforcement action.

(3) *Law Enforcement Interest.* The Commission will assess its programmatic interest in deterring violations of the securities laws by making awards to whistleblowers who provide information that leads to the successful enforcement of such laws. In considering this factor, the Commission may take into account, among other things:

(i) The degree to which an award enhances the Commission's ability to enforce the federal securities laws and protect investors; and

(ii) The degree to which an award encourages the submission of high quality information from whistleblowers by appropriately rewarding whistleblowers' submission of significant information and assistance, even in cases where the monetary sanctions available for collection are limited or potential monetary sanctions were reduced or eliminated by the Commission because an entity self-reported a securities violation following the whistleblower's related internal disclosure, report, or submission.

(iii) Whether the subject matter of the action is a Commission priority, whether the reported misconduct involves regulated entities or fiduciaries, whether the whistleblower exposed an industry-wide practice, the type and severity of the securities violations, the age and duration of misconduct, the number of violations, and the isolated, repetitive, or ongoing nature of the violations; and

(iv) The dangers to investors or others presented by the underlying violations involved in the enforcement action, including the amount of harm or potential harm caused by the underlying violations, the type of harm resulting from or threatened by the underlying violations, and the number of individuals or entities harmed.

(4) *Participation in Internal Compliance Systems.* The Commission will assess whether, and the extent to which, the whistleblower and any legal representative of the whistleblower participated in internal compliance systems. In considering this factor, the Commission may take into account, among other things:

(i) Whether, and the extent to which, a whistleblower reported the possible securities violations through internal whistleblower, legal or compliance procedures before, or at the same time as, reporting them to the Commission; and

(ii) Whether, and the extent to which, a whistleblower assisted any internal investigation or inquiry concerning the reported securities violations.

(b) *Factors that may Decrease the Amount of a Whistleblower's Award.* In determining whether to decrease the amount of an award, the Commission will consider the following factors, which are not listed in order of importance.

(1) *Culpability.* The Commission will assess the culpability or involvement of the whistleblower in matters associated with the Commission's action or related actions. In considering this factor, the Commission may take into account, among other things:

(i) The whistleblower's role in the securities violations;

(ii) The whistleblower's education, training, experience, and position of responsibility at the time the violations occurred;

(iii) Whether the whistleblower acted with scienter, both generally and in relation to others who participated in the violations;

(iv) Whether the whistleblower financially benefitted from the violations;

(v) Whether the whistleblower is a recidivist;

(vi) The egregiousness of the underlying fraud committed by the whistleblower; and

(vii) Whether the whistleblower knowingly interfered with the Commission's investigation of the violations or related enforcement actions.

(2) *Unreasonable Reporting Delay.* The Commission will assess whether the whistleblower unreasonably delayed reporting the securities violations. In considering this factor, the Commission may take into account, among other things:

(i) Whether the whistleblower was aware of the relevant facts but failed to take reasonable steps to report or prevent the violations from occurring or continuing;

(ii) Whether the whistleblower was aware of the relevant facts but only reported them after learning about a related inquiry, investigation, or enforcement action; and

(iii) Whether there was a legitimate reason for the whistleblower to delay reporting the violations.

(3) *Interference with Internal Compliance and Reporting Systems.* The Commission will assess, in cases where the whistleblower interacted with his or her entity's internal compliance or reporting system, whether the whistleblower undermined the integrity of such system. In considering this factor, the Commission will take into account whether there is evidence provided to the Commission that the whistleblower knowingly:

(i) Interfered with an entity's established legal, compliance, or audit procedures to prevent or delay detection of the reported securities violation;

(ii) Made any material false, fictitious, or fraudulent statements or representations that hindered an entity's efforts to detect, investigate, or remediate the reported securities violations; and

(iii) Provided any false writing or document knowing the writing or document contained any false, fictitious or fraudulent statements or entries that hindered an entity's efforts to detect, investigate, or remediate the reported securities violations.

Rule 21F–7. Confidentiality of submissions

(a) Section 21F(h)(2) of the Exchange Act requires that the Commission not disclose information that could reasonably be expected to reveal the identity of a whistleblower, except that the Commission may disclose such information in the following circumstances:

(1) When disclosure is required to a defendant or respondent in connection with a federal court or administrative action that the Commission files or in another public action or proceeding that is filed by an authority to which we provide the information, as described below;

(2) When the Commission determines that it is necessary to accomplish the purposes of the Exchange Act and to protect investors, it may provide your information to the Department of Justice, an appropriate regulatory authority, a self regulatory organization, a state attorney general in connection with a criminal investigation, any appropriate state regulatory authority, the Public Company Accounting Oversight Board, or foreign securities and law enforcement authorities. Each of these entities other than foreign securities and law enforcement authorities is subject to the confidentiality requirements set forth in Section 21F(h) of the Exchange Act. The Commission will determine what assurances of confidentiality it deems appropriate in providing such information to foreign securities and law enforcement authorities. (3) The Commission may make disclosures in accordance with the Privacy Act of 1974 (5 U.S.C. 552a).

(b) You may submit information to the Commission anonymously. If you do so, however, you must also do the following:

(1) You must have an attorney represent you in connection with both your submission of information and your claim for an award, and your attorney's name and contact information must be provided to the Commission at the time you submit your information;

(2) You and your attorney must follow the procedures set forth in Rule 21F–9 for submitting original information anonymously; and

(3) Before the Commission will pay any award to you, you must disclose your identity to the Commission and your identity must be verified by the Commission as set forth in Rule 21F–10.

Rule 21F–8. Eligibility

(a) To be eligible for a whistleblower award, you must give the Commission information in the form and manner that the Commission requires. The procedures for submitting information and making a claim for an award are described in Rules 21F–9 through 21F–11. You should read these procedures carefully because you need to follow them in order to be eligible for an award, except that the Commission may, in its sole discretion, waive any of these procedures based upon a showing of extraordinary circumstances.

(b) In addition to any forms required by these rules, the Commission may also require that you provide certain additional information. You may be required to:

(1) Provide explanations and other assistance in order that the staff may evaluate and use the information that you submitted;

(2) Provide all additional information in your possession that is related to the subject matter of your submission in a complete and truthful manner, through follow-up meetings, or in other forms that our staff may agree to;

(3) Provide testimony or other evidence acceptable to the staff relating to whether you are eligible, or otherwise satisfy any of the conditions, for an award; and

(4) Enter into a confidentiality agreement in a form acceptable to the Office of the Whistleblower, covering any non-public information that the Commission provides to you, and including a provision that a violation of the agreement may lead to your ineligibility to receive an award.

(c) You are not eligible to be considered for an award if you do not satisfy the requirements of paragraphs (a) and (b) of this section. In addition, you are not eligible if:

(1) You are, or were at the time you acquired the original information provided to the Commission, a member, officer, or employee of the Commission, the Department of Justice, an appropriate regulatory agency, a self-regulatory organization, the Public Company Accounting Oversight Board, or any law enforcement organization;

(2) You are, or were at the time you acquired the original information provided to the Commission, a member, officer, or employee of a foreign government, any political subdivision, department, agency, or instrumentality of a foreign government, or any other foreign financial regulatory authority as that term is defined in Section 3(a)(52) of the Exchange Act;

(3) You are convicted of a criminal violation that is related to the Commission action or to a related action (as defined in Rule 21F–4) for which you otherwise could receive an award;

(4) You obtained the original information that you gave the Commission through an audit of a company's financial statements, and making a whistleblower submission would be contrary to requirements of Section 10A of the Exchange Act.

(5) You are the spouse, parent, child, or sibling of a member or employee of the Commission, or you reside in the same household as a member or employee of the Commission;

(6) You acquired the original information you gave the Commission from a person:

(i) Who is subject to paragraph (c)(4) of this section, unless the information is not excluded from that person's use, or you are providing the Commission with information about possible violations involving that person; or

(ii) With the intent to evade any provision of these rules; or

(7) In your whistleblower submission, your other dealings with the Commission, or your dealings with another authority in connection with a related action, you knowingly and willfully make any false, fictitious, or fraudulent statement or representation, or use any false writing or document knowing that it contains any false, fictitious, or fraudulent statement or entry with intent to mislead or otherwise hinder the Commission or another authority.

Rule 21F–9. Procedures for submitting original information

(a) To be considered a whistleblower under Section 21F of the Exchange Act, you must submit your information about a possible securities law violation by either of these methods:

(1) Online, through the Commission's website located at www.sec.gov; or

(2) By mailing or faxing a Form TCR (Tip, Complaint or Referral) (17 CFR 249.1800) to the SEC Office of the Whistleblower, 100 F Street NE, Washington, DC 20549–5631, Fax (703) 813–9322.

(b) Further, to be eligible for an award, you must declare under penalty of perjury at the time you submit your information pursuant to paragraph (a)(1) or (2) of this section that your information is true and correct to the best of your knowledge and belief.

(c) Notwithstanding paragraphs (a) and (b) of this section, if you are providing your original information to the Commission anonymously, then your attorney must submit your information on your behalf pursuant to the procedures specified in paragraph (a) of this section. Prior to your attorney's submission, you must provide your attorney with a completed Form TCR (17 CFR 249.1800) that you have signed under penalty of perjury. When your attorney makes her submission on your behalf, your attorney will be required to certify that he or she:

(1) Has verified your identity;

(2) Has reviewed your completed and signed Form TCR (17 CFR 249.1800) for completeness and accuracy and that the information contained therein is true, correct and complete to the best of the attorney's knowledge, information and belief;

(3) Has obtained your non-waivable consent to provide the Commission with your original completed and signed Form TCR (17 CFR 249.1800) in the event that the Commission requests it due to concerns that you may have knowingly and willfully made false, fictitious, or fraudulent statements or representations, or used any false writing or document knowing that the writing or document contains any false fictitious or fraudulent statement or entry; and

(4) Consents to be legally obligated to provide the signed Form TCR (17 CFR 249.1800) within seven (7) calendar days of receiving such request from the Commission.

(d) If you submitted original information in writing to the Commission after July 21, 2010 (the date of enactment of the Dodd–Frank Wall Street Reform and Consumer Protection Act) but before the effective date of these rules, your submission will be deemed to satisfy the requirements set forth in paragraphs (a) and (b) of this section. If you were an anonymous whistleblower, however, you must provide your attorney with a completed and signed copy of Form TCR (17 CFR 249.1800) within 60 days of the effective date of these rules, your attorney must retain the signed form in his or her records, and you must provide of copy of the signed form to the Commission staff upon request by Commission staff prior to any payment of an award to you in connection with your submission. Notwithstanding the foregoing, you must follow the procedures and conditions for making a claim for a whistleblower award described in Rules 21F–10 and 21F–11.

Rule 21F–10. Procedures for making a claim for a whistleblower award in SEC actions that result in monetary sanctions in excess of $1,000,000

(a) Whenever a Commission action results in monetary sanctions totaling more than $1,000,000, the Office of the Whistleblower will cause to be published on the Commission's website a Notice of Covered Action. Such Notice will be published subsequent to the entry of a final judgment or order that alone, or collectively with other judgments or orders previously entered in the Commission action, exceeds $1,000,000; or, in the absence of such judgment or order subsequent to the deposit of monetary sanctions exceeding $1,000,000 into a disgorgement or other fund pursuant to Section 308(b) of the Sarbanes–Oxley Act of 2002. A claimant will have ninety (90) days from the date of the Notice of Covered Action to file a claim for an award based on that action, or the claim will be barred.

(b) To file a claim for a whistleblower award, you must file Form WB–APP, *Application for Award for Original Information Provided Pursuant to Section 21F of the Securities Exchange Act of 1934* (17 CFR 249.1801). You must sign this form as the claimant and submit it to the Office of the Whistleblower by mail or fax. All claim forms, including any attachments, must be received by the Office of the Whistleblower within ninety (90) calendar days of the date of the Notice of Covered Action in order to be considered for an award.

(c) If you provided your original information to the Commission anonymously, you must disclose your identity on the Form WB–APP (17 CFR 249.1801), and your identity must be verified in a form and manner that is acceptable to the Office of the Whistleblower prior to the payment of any award.

(d) Once the time for filing any appeals of the Commission's judicial or administrative action has expired, or where an appeal has been filed, after all appeals in the action have been concluded, the staff designated by the Director of the Division of Enforcement (Claims Review Staff) will evaluate all timely whistleblower award claims submitted on Form WB–APP (17 CFR 249.1801) in accordance with the criteria set forth in these rules. In connection with this process, the Office of the Whistleblower may require that you provide additional information relating to your eligibility for an award or satisfaction of any of the conditions for an award, as set forth in Rule 21F–(8)(b). Following that evaluation, the Office of the Whistleblower will send you a Preliminary Determination setting forth a preliminary assessment as to whether the claim should be allowed or denied and, if allowed, setting forth the proposed award percentage amount.

(e) You may contest the Preliminary Determination made by the Claims Review Staff by submitting a written response to the Office of the Whistleblower setting forth the grounds for your objection to either the denial of an award or the proposed amount of an award. The response must be in the form and manner that the Office of the Whistleblower shall require. You may also include documentation or other evidentiary support for the grounds advanced in your response.

(1) Before determining whether to contest a Preliminary Determination, you may:

(i) Within thirty (30) days of the date of the Preliminary Determination, request that the Office of the Whistleblower make available for your review the materials from among those set forth in Rule 21F–12(a) that formed the basis of the Claims Review Staff's Preliminary Determination.

(ii) Within thirty (30) calendar days of the date of the Preliminary Determination, request a meeting with the Office of the Whistleblower; however, such meetings are not required and the office may in its sole discretion decline the request.

(2) If you decide to contest the Preliminary Determination, you must submit your written response and supporting materials within sixty (60) calendar days of the date of the Preliminary Determination, or if a request to review materials is made pursuant to paragraph (e)(1) of this section, then within sixty (60) calendar days of the Office of the Whistleblower making those materials available for your review.

(f) If you fail to submit a timely response pursuant to paragraph (e) of this section, then the Preliminary Determination will become the Final Order of the Commission (except where the Preliminary Determination recommended an award, in which case the Preliminary Determination will be deemed a Proposed Final Determination for purposes of paragraph (h) of this section). Your failure to submit a timely response contesting a Preliminary Determination will constitute a failure to exhaust administrative remedies, and you will be prohibited from pursuing an appeal pursuant to Rule 21F–13.

(g) If you submit a timely response pursuant to paragraph (e) of this section, then the Claims Review Staff will consider the issues and grounds advanced in your response, along with any supporting documentation you provided, and will make its Proposed Final Determination.

(h) The Office of the Whistleblower will then notify the Commission of each Proposed Final Determination. Within thirty 30 days thereafter, any Commissioner may request that the Proposed Final Determination be reviewed by the Commission. If no Commissioner requests such a review within the 30–day period, then the Proposed Final Determination will become the Final Order of the Commission. In the event a Commissioner requests a review, the Commission will review the record that the staff relied upon in making its determinations, including your previous submissions to the Office of the Whistleblower, and issue its Final Order.

(i) The Office of the Whistleblower will provide you with the Final Order of the Commission.

Rule 21F–11. Procedures for determining awards based upon a related action

(a) If you are eligible to receive an award following a Commission action that results in monetary sanctions totaling more than $1,000,000, you also may be eligible to receive an award based on the monetary sanctions that are collected from a related action (as defined in Rule 21F–3).

(b) You must also use Form WB–APP (17 CFR 249.1801) to submit a claim for an award in a related action. You must sign this form as the claimant and submit it to the Office of the Whistleblower by mail or fax as follows:

(1) If a final order imposing monetary sanctions has been entered in a related action at the time you submit your claim for an award in connection with a Commission action, you must submit your claim for an award in that related action on the same Form WB–APP (referenced in 17 CFR 249.1801) that you use for the Commission action.

(2) If a final order imposing monetary sanctions in a related action has not been entered at the time you submit your claim for an award in

connection with a Commission action, you must submit your claim on Form WB–APP (referenced in 17 CFR 249.1801) within ninety (90) days of the issuance of a final order imposing sanctions in the related action.

(c) The Office of the Whistleblower may request additional information from you in connection with your claim for an award in a related action to demonstrate that you directly (or through the Commission) voluntarily provided the governmental agency, regulatory authority or self-regulatory organization the same original information that led to the Commission's successful covered action, and that this information led to the successful enforcement of the related action. The Office of the Whistleblower may, in its discretion, seek assistance and confirmation from the other agency in making this determination.

(d) Once the time for filing any appeals of the final judgment or order in a related action has expired, or if an appeal has been filed, after all appeals in the action have been concluded, the Claims Review Staff will evaluate all timely whistleblower award claims submitted on Form WB–APP (referenced in 17 CFR 249.1801) in connection with the related action. The evaluation will be undertaken pursuant to the criteria set forth in these rules. In connection with this process, the Office of the Whistleblower may require that you provide additional information relating to your eligibility for an award or satisfaction of any of the conditions for an award, as set forth Rule 21F–(8)(b). Following this evaluation, the Office of the Whistleblower will send you a Preliminary Determination setting forth a preliminary assessment as to whether the claim should be allowed or denied and, if allowed, setting forth the proposed award percentage amount.

(e) You may contest the Preliminary Determination made by the Claims Review Staff by submitting a written response to the Office of the Whistleblower setting forth the grounds for your objection to either the denial of an award or the proposed amount of an award. The response must be in the form and manner that the Office of the Whistleblower shall require. You may also include documentation or other evidentiary support for the grounds advanced in your response.

(1) Before determining whether to contest a Preliminary Determination, you may:

(i) Within thirty (30) days of the date of the Preliminary Determination, request that the Office of the Whistleblower make available for your review the materials from among those set forth in Rule 21F–12(a) of this chapter that formed the basis of the Claims Review Staff's Preliminary Determination.

(ii) Within thirty (30) days of the date of the Preliminary Determination, request a meeting with the Office of the Whistleblower; however, such meetings are not required and the office may in its sole discretion decline the request.

(2) If you decide to contest the Preliminary Determination, you must submit your written response and supporting materials within sixty (60) calendar days of the date of the Preliminary Determination, or if a request to review materials is made pursuant to paragraph (e)(1)(i) of this section, then within sixty (60) calendar days of the Office of the Whistleblower making those materials available for your review.

(f) If you fail to submit a timely response pursuant to paragraph (e) of this section, then the Preliminary Determination will become the Final Order of the Commission (except where the Preliminary Determination recommended an award, in which case the Preliminary Determination will be deemed a Proposed Final Determination for purposes of paragraph (h) of this section). Your failure to submit a timely response contesting a Preliminary Determination will constitute a failure to exhaust administrative remedies, and you will be prohibited from pursuing an appeal pursuant to Rule 21F–13.

(g) If you submit a timely response pursuant to paragraph (e) of this section, then the Claims Review Staff will consider the issues and grounds that you advanced in your response, along with any supporting documentation you provided, and will make its Proposed Final Determination.

(h) The Office of the Whistleblower will notify the Commission of each Proposed Final Determination. Within thirty 30 days thereafter, any Commissioner may request that the Proposed Final Determination be reviewed by the Commission. If no Commissioner requests such a review within the 30–day period, then the Proposed Final Determination will become the Final Order of the Commission. In the event a Commissioner requests a review, the Commission will review the record that the staff relied upon in making its determinations, including your previous submissions to the Office of the Whistleblower, and issue its Final Order.

(i) The Office of the Whistleblower will provide you with the Final Order of the Commission.

Rule 21F–12. Materials that may form the basis of an award determination and that may comprise the record on appeal

(a) The following items constitute the materials that the Commission and the Claims Review Staff may rely upon to make an award determination pursuant to Rules 21F–10 and 21F–11:

(1) Any publicly available materials from the covered action or related action, including:

(i) The complaint, notice of hearing, answers and any amendments thereto;

(ii) The final judgment, consent order, or final administrative order;

(iii) Any transcripts of the proceedings, including any exhibits;

(iv) Any items that appear on the docket; and

(v) Any appellate decisions or orders.

(2) The whistleblower's Form TCR (referenced in 17 CFR 249.1800), including attachments, and other related materials provided by the whistleblower to assist the Commission with the investigation or examination;

(3) The whistleblower's Form WB–APP (referenced in 17 CFR 249.1800), including attachments, and any other filings or submissions from the whistleblower in support of the award application;

(4) Sworn declarations (including attachments) from the Commission staff regarding any matters relevant to the award determination;

(5) With respect to an award claim involving a related action, any statements or other information that the entity provides or identifies in connection with an award determination, provided the entity has authorized the Commission to share the information with the claimant. (Neither the Commission nor the Claims Review Staff may rely upon information that the entity has not authorized the Commission to share with the claimant); and

(6) Any other documents or materials including sworn declarations from third-parties that are received or obtained by the Office of the Whistleblower to assist the Commission resolve the claimant's award application, including information related to the claimant's eligibility. (Neither the Commission nor the Claims Review Staff may rely upon information that the entity has not authorized the Commission to share with the claimant).

(b) These rules do not entitle claimants to obtain from the Commission any materials (including any pre-decisional or internal deliberative process materials that are prepared exclusively to assist the Commission in deciding the claim) other than those listed in paragraph (a) of this section. Moreover, the Office of the Whistleblower may make redactions as necessary to comply with any statutory restrictions, to protect the Commission's law enforcement and regulatory functions, and to comply with requests for confidential treatment from other law enforcement and regulatory authorities. The Office of the Whistleblower may also require you to sign a confidentiality agreement, as set forth in Rule 21F–(8)(b)(4), before providing these materials.

Rule 21F–13. Appeals

(a) Section 21F of the Exchange Act commits determinations of whether, to whom, and in what amount to make awards to the Commission's discretion. A determination of whether or to whom to make an award may be appealed within 30 days after the Commission issues its final decision to the United States Court of Appeals for the District of Columbia Circuit, or to the circuit where the aggrieved person resides or has his principal place of business. Where the Commission makes an award based on the factors set forth in Rule 21F–6 of not less than 10 percent and not more than 30 percent of the monetary sanctions collected in the Commission or related action, the Commission's determination regarding the amount of an award (including the allocation of an award as between multiple whistleblowers, and any factual findings, legal conclusions, policy judgments, or discretionary assessments involving the Commission's consideration of the factors in Rule 21F–6) is not appealable.

(b) The record on appeal shall consist of the Preliminary Determination, the Final Order of the Commission, and any other items from those set forth in Rule 21F–12(a) of this chapter that either the claimant or the Commission identifies for inclusion in the record. The record on appeal shall not include any pre-decisional or internal deliberative process materials that are prepared exclusively to assist the Commission in deciding the claim (including the staff's Draft Final Determination in the event that the Commissioners reviewed the claim and issued the Final Order).

Rule 21F–14. Procedures applicable to the payment of awards

(a) Any award made pursuant to these rules will be paid from the Securities and Exchange Commission Investor Protection Fund (the Fund).

(b) A recipient of a whistleblower award is entitled to payment on the award only to the extent that a monetary sanction is collected in the Commission action or in a related action upon which the award is based.

(c) Payment of a whistleblower award for a monetary sanction collected in a Commission action or related action shall be made following the later of:

(1) The date on which the monetary sanction is collected; or

(2) The completion of the appeals process for all whistleblower award claims arising from:

(i) The Notice of Covered Action, in the case of any payment of an award for a monetary sanction collected in a Commission action; or

(ii) The related action, in the case of any payment of an award for a monetary sanction collected in a related action.

(d) If there are insufficient amounts available in the Fund to pay the entire amount of an award payment within a reasonable period of time from the time for payment specified by paragraph (c) of this section, then subject to the following terms, the balance of the payment shall be paid when amounts become available in the Fund, as follows:

(1) Where multiple whistleblowers are owed payments from the Fund based on awards that do not arise from the same Notice of Covered Action (or related action), priority in making these payments will be determined based upon the date that the collections for which the whistleblowers are owed payments occurred. If two or more of these collections occur on the same date, those whistleblowers owed payments based on these collections will be paid on a pro rata basis until sufficient amounts become available in the Fund to pay their entire payments.

(2) Where multiple whistleblowers are owed payments from the Fund based on awards that arise from the same Notice of Covered Action (or related action), they will share the same payment priority and will be paid on a pro rata basis until sufficient amounts become available in the Fund to pay their entire payments.

Rule 21F–15. No amnesty

The Securities Whistleblower Incentives and Protection provisions do not provide amnesty to individuals who provide information to the Commission. The fact that you may become a whistleblower and assist in Commission investigations and enforcement actions does not preclude the Commission from bringing an action against you based upon your own conduct in connection with violations of the federal securities laws. If such an action is determined to be appropriate, however, the Commission will take your cooperation into consideration in accordance with its Policy Statement Concerning Cooperation by Individuals in Investigations and Related Enforcement Actions (17 CFR 202.12).

Rule 21F–16. Awards to whistleblowers who engage in culpable conduct

In determining whether the required $1,000,000 threshold has been satisfied (this threshold is further explained in Rule 21F–10) for purposes of making any award, the Commission will not take into account any monetary sanctions that the whistleblower is ordered to pay, or that are ordered against any entity whose liability is based substantially on conduct that the whistleblower directed, planned, or initiated. Similarly, if the Commission determines that a whistleblower is eligible for an award, any amounts that the whistleblower or such an entity pay in sanctions as a result of the action or related actions will not be included within the calculation of the amounts collected for purposes of making payments.

Rule 21F–17. Staff communications with individuals reporting possible securities law violations

(a) No person may take any action to impede an individual from communicating directly with the Commission staff about a possible securities law violation, including enforcing, or threatening to enforce, a confidentiality agreement (other than agreements dealing with information covered by Rules 21F–4(b)(4)(i) and 21F–4(b)(4)(ii) of this chapter related to the legal representation of a client) with respect to such communications.

(b) If you are a director, officer, member, agent, or employee of an entity that has counsel, and you have initiated communication with the Commission relating to a possible securities law violation, the staff is authorized to communicate directly with you regarding the possible securities law violation without seeking the consent of the entity's counsel.

INSPECTION AND PUBLICATION OF INFORMATION FILED UNDER THE ACT

Rule 24b–1. Documents to be kept public by exchanges

Upon action of the Commission granting an exchange's application for registration or exemption, the exchange shall make available to public inspection at its offices during reasonable office hours a copy of the statement and exhibits filed with the Commission (including any amendments thereto) except those portions thereof to the disclosure of which the exchange shall have filed objection pursuant to Rule 24b–2 which objection shall not have been overruled by the Commission pursuant to section 24(b) of the Act.

Rule 24b–2. Nondisclosure of information filed with the Commission and with any exchange

PRELIMINARY NOTE

Except as otherwise provided in this rule confidential treatment requests shall be submitted in paper format only, whether or not the filer is required to submit a filing in electronic format.

(a) Any person filing any registration statement, report, application, statement, correspondence, notice or other document (herein referred to as the material filed) pursuant to the Act may make written objection to the public disclosure of any information contained therein in accordance with the procedure set forth below. The procedure provided in this rule shall be the exclusive means of requesting confidential treatment of information required to be filed under the Act.

(b) Except as otherwise provided in paragraphs (g) and (h), the person shall omit from material filed the portion thereof which it desires to keep undisclosed (hereinafter called the confidential portion). In lieu thereof, it shall indicate at the appropriate place in the material filed that the confidential portion has been so omitted and filed separately with the Commission. The person shall file with the copies of the material filed with the Commission:

(1) One copy of the confidential portion, marked "Confidential Treatment," of the material filed with the Commission. The copy shall contain an appropriate identification of the item or other requirement involved and, notwithstanding that the confidential portion does not constitute the whole of the answer, the entire answer thereto; except that in the case where the confidential portion is part of a financial statement or schedule, only the particular financial statement or schedule need be included. The copy of the confidential portion shall be in the same form as the remainder of the material filed;

(2) An application making objection to the disclosure of the confidential portion. Such application shall be on a sheet or sheets separate from the confidential portion, and shall contain (i) an identification of the portion; (ii) a statement of the grounds of objection referring to, and containing an analysis of the applicable exemption(s) from disclosure under the Commission's rules and regulations adopted under the Freedom of Information Act (17 CFR 200.80), and a justification of the period of time for which confidential treatment is sought; (iii) a written consent to the furnishing of the confidential portion to other government agencies, offices or bodies and to the Congress; and (iv) the name of each exchange, if any, with which the material is filed.

(3) The copy of the confidential portion and the application filed in accordance with this paragraph (b) shall be enclosed in a separate envelope marked "Confidential Treatment" and addressed to The Secretary, Securities and Exchange Commission, Washington, DC 20549.

(c) Pending a determination as to the objection filed the material for which confidential treatment has been applied will not be made available to the public.

(d)(1) If it is determined that the objection should be sustained, a notation to that effect will be made at the appropriate place in the material filed. Such a determination will not preclude reconsideration whenever appropriate, such as upon receipt of any subsequent request under the Freedom of Information Act (5 U.S.C. Section 552) and, if appropriate, revocation of the confidential status of all or a portion of the information in question. Where an initial determination has been made under this rule to sustain objections to disclosure, the Commission will attempt to give the person requesting confidential treatment advance notice, wherever possible, if confidential treatment is revoked.

(2) In any case where an objection to disclosure has been disallowed or where a prior grant of confidential treatment has been revoked, the person who requested such treatment will be so informed by registered or certified mail to the person or his agent for service. Pursuant to Rule 431 of the Commission's Rules of Practice, persons making objections to disclosure may petition the Commission for review of a determination by the Division disallowing objections or revoking confidential treatment.

(e) The confidential portion shall be made available to the public at the time and according to the conditions specified in paragraphs (d)(1) and (2) of this rule:

(1) Upon the lapse of five days after the dispatch of notice by registered or certified mail of a determination disallowing an objection, if prior to the lapse of such five days the person shall not have communicated to the Secretary of the Commission his intention to seek review by the Commission under Rule 431 of the Commission's Rules of Practice of the determination made by the Division; or

(2) If such a petition for review shall have been filed under Rule 431 of the Commission's Rules of Practice, upon final disposition thereof adverse to the petitioner.

(f) If the confidential portion is made available to the public, one copy thereof shall be attached to each copy of the material filed with the Commission and with each exchange.

(g) An SCI entity (as defined in Rule 1000) shall not omit the confidential portion from the material filed in electronic format on Form SCI pursuant to Regulation SCI, § 242.1000 et. seq., and, in lieu of the procedures described in paragraph (b) of this section, may request confidential treatment of all information provided on Form SCI by completing Section IV of Form SCI.

(h) A security-based swap data repository shall not omit the confidential portion from the material filed in electronic format pursuant to section 13(n) of the Act (15 U.S.C. 78m(n)) and the rules and regulations thereunder. In lieu of the procedures described in paragraph (b) of this section, a security-based swap data repository shall request confidential treatment electronically for any material filed in electronic format pursuant to section 13(n) of the Act (15 U.S.C. 78m(n)) and the rules and regulations thereunder.

Rule 24b–3. Information filed by issuers and others under Sections 12, 13, 14, and 16

(a) Except as otherwise provided in this rule and in Rule 17a–6, each exchange shall keep available to the public, under reasonable regulations as to the manner of inspection, during reasonable office hours, all information regarding a security registered on such exchange which is filed with it pursuant to section 12, 13, 14, or 16 or any rules or regulations thereunder. This requirement shall not apply to any information to the disclosure of which objection has been filed pursuant to Rule 24b–2, which objection shall not have been overruled by the Commission pursuant to section 24(b). The making of such information available pursuant to this rule shall not be deemed a representation by any exchange as to the accuracy, completeness, or genuineness thereof.

(b) In the case of an application for registration of a security pursuant to section 12 an exchange may delay making available the information contained therein until it has certified to the Commission its approval of such security for listing and registration.

Rule 24c–1. Access to nonpublic information

(a) For purposes of this rule, the term "nonpublic information" means records, as defined in Section 24(a) of the Act, and other information in the Commission's possession, which are not available for public inspection and copying.

(b) The Commission may, in its discretion and upon a showing that such information is needed, provide nonpublic information in its possession to any of the following persons if the person receiving such nonpublic information provides such assurances of confidentiality as the Commission deems appropriate:

(1) A federal, state, local or foreign government or any political subdivision, authority, agency or instrumentality of such government;

(2) A self-regulatory organization as defined in Section 3(a)(26) of the Act, or any similar organization empowered with self-regulatory responsibilities under the federal securities laws (as defined in Section 3(a)(47) of the Act), the Commodity Ex-

change Act (7 U.S.C. 1, *et seq.*), or any substantially equivalent foreign statute or regulation;

(3) A foreign financial regulatory authority as defined in Section 3(a)(51) of the Act;

(4) The Securities Investor Protection Corporation or any trustee or counsel for a trustee appointed pursuant to Section 5(b) of the Securities Investor Protection Act of 1970;

(5) A trustee in bankruptcy;

(6) A trustee, receiver, master, special counsel or other person that is appointed by a court of competent jurisdiction or as a result of an agreement between the parties in connection with litigation or an administrative proceeding involving allegations of violations of the securities laws (as defined in Section 3(a)(47) of the Act) or the Commission's Rules of Practice, 17 CFR Part 201, or otherwise, where such trustee, receiver, master, special counsel or other person is specifically designated to perform particular functions with respect to, or as a result of, the litigation or proceeding or in connection with the administration and enforcement by the Commission of the federal securities laws or the Commission's Rules of Practice;

(7) A bar association, state accountancy board or other federal, state, local or foreign licensing or oversight authority, or a professional association or self-regulatory authority to the extent that it performs similar functions; or

(8) A duly authorized agent, employee or representative of any of the above persons.

(c) Nothing contained in this rule shall affect:

(1) The Commission's authority or discretion to provide or refuse to provide access to, or copies of, nonpublic information in its possession in accordance with such other authority or discretion as the Commission possesses by statute, rule or regulation; or

(2) The Commission's responsibilities under the Privacy Act of 1974 (5 U.S.C. 552a), or the Right to Financial Privacy Act of 1978 (12 U.S.C. 3401–22) as limited by section 21(h) of the Act.

Rule 31. Section 31 transaction fees

(a) *Definitions.* For the purpose of this rule, the following definitions shall apply:

(1) *Assessment charge* means the amount owed by a covered SRO for a covered round turn transaction pursuant to section 31(d) of the Act.

(2) *Billing period* means, for a single calendar year:

(i) January 1 through August 31 ("billing period 1"); or

(ii) September 1 through December 31 ("billing period 2").

(3) *Charge date* means the date on which a covered sale or covered round turn transaction occurs for purposes of determining the liability of a covered SRO pursuant to section 31 of the Act. The charge date is:

(i) The settlement date, with respect to any covered sale (other than a covered sale resulting from the exercise of an option settled by physical delivery or from the maturation of a security future settled by physical delivery) or covered round turn transaction that a covered SRO is required to report to the Commission based on data that the covered SRO receives from a designated clearing agency;

(ii) The exercise date, with respect to a covered sale resulting from the exercise of an option settled by physical delivery;

(iii) The maturity date, with respect to a covered sale resulting from the maturation of a security future settled by physical delivery; and

(iv) The trade date, with respect to all other covered sales and covered round turn transactions.

(4) *Covered association* means any national securities association by or through any member of which covered sales or covered round turn transactions occur otherwise than on a national securities exchange.

(5) *Covered exchange* means any national securities exchange on which covered sales or covered round turn transactions occur.

(6) *Covered sale* means a sale of a security, other than an exempt sale or a sale of a security future, occurring on a national securities exchange or by or through any member of a national securities association otherwise than on a national securities exchange.

(7) *Covered round turn transaction* means a round turn transaction in a security future, other than a round turn transaction in a future on a narrow-based security index, occurring on a national securities exchange or by or through a member of a national securities association otherwise than on a national securities exchange.

(8) *Covered SRO* means a covered exchange or covered association.

(9) *Designated clearing agency* means a clearing agency registered under section 17A of the Act that clears and settles covered sales or covered round turn transactions.

(10) *Due date* means:

(i) March 15, with respect to the amounts owed by covered SROs under section 31 of the Act for covered sales and covered round turn transactions having a charge date in billing period 2; and

(ii) September 30, with respect to the amounts owed by covered SROs under section 31 of the Act for covered sales and covered round turn transactions having a charge date in billing period 1.

(11) *Exempt sale* means:

(i) Any sale of a security offered pursuant to an effective registration statement under the Securities Act of 1933 (except a sale of a put or call option issued by the Options Clearing Corporation) or offered in accordance with an exemption from registration afforded by section 3(a) or 3(b) of the Securities Act of 1933, or a rule thereunder;

(ii) Any sale of a security by an issuer not involving any public offering within the meaning of section 4(a)(2) of the Securities Act of 1933;

(iii) Any sale of a security pursuant to and in consummation of a tender or exchange offer;

(iv) Any sale of a security upon the exercise of a warrant or right (except a put or call), or upon the conversion of a convertible security;

(v) Any sale of a security that is executed outside the United States and is not reported, or required to be reported, to a transaction reporting association as defined in Rule 600 of Regulation NMS and any approved plan filed thereunder;

(vi) Any sale of an option on a security index (including both a narrow-based security index and a non-narrow-based security index);

(vii) Any sale of a bond, debenture, or other evidence of indebtedness; and

(viii) Any recognized riskless principal sale.

(12) *Fee rate* means the fee rate applicable to covered sales under section 31(b) or (c) of the Act, as adjusted from time to time by the Commission pursuant to section 31(j) of the Act.

(13) *Narrow-based security index* means the same as in section 3(a)(55)(B) and (C) of the Act.

(14) *Recognized riskless principal sale* means a sale of a security where all of the following conditions are satisfied:

(i) A broker-dealer receives from a customer an order to buy (sell) a security;

(ii) The broker-dealer engages in two contemporaneous offsetting transactions as principal, one in which the broker-dealer buys (sells) the security from (to) a third party and the other in which the broker-dealer sells (buys) the security to (from) the customer; and

(iii) The Commission, pursuant to section 19(b)(2) of the Act, has approved a proposed rule change submitted by the covered SRO on which the second of the two contemporaneous offsetting transactions occurs that permits that transaction to be reported as riskless.

(15) *Round turn transaction in a security future* means one purchase and one sale of a contract of sale for future delivery.

(16) *Physical delivery exchange-traded option* means a securities option that is listed and registered on a national securities exchange and settled by the physical delivery of the underlying securities.

(17) *Section 31 bill* means the bill sent by the Commission to a covered SRO pursuant to section 31 of the Act showing the total amount due from the covered SRO for the billing period, as calculated by the Commission based on the data submitted by the covered SRO in its Form R31 (17 CFR 249.11) submissions for the months of the billing period.

(18) *Trade reporting system* means an automated facility operated by a covered SRO used to collect or compare trade data.

(b) *Reporting of covered sales and covered round turn transactions.* (1) Each covered SRO shall submit a completed Form R31 (17 CFR 249.11) to the Commission within ten business days after the end of each month.

(2) A covered exchange shall provide on Form R31 the following data on covered sales and covered round turn transactions occurring on that exchange and having a charge date in that month:

(i) The aggregate dollar amount of covered sales that it reported to a designated clearing agency, as reflected in the data provided by the designated clearing agency;

(ii) The aggregate dollar amount of covered sales resulting from the exercise of physical delivery exchange-traded options or from matured security futures, as reflected in the data provided by a designated clearing agency that clears and settles options or security futures;

(iii) The aggregate dollar amount of covered sales that it captured in a trade reporting system but did not report to a designated clearing agency;

(iv) The aggregate dollar amount of covered sales that it neither captured in a trade reporting system nor reported to a designated clearing agency; and

(v) The total number of covered round turn transactions that it reported to a designated clearing agency, as reflected in the data provided by the designated clearing agency.

(3) A covered association shall provide on Form R31 the following data on covered sales and covered round turn transactions occurring by or through any member of such association otherwise than on a national securities exchange and having a charge date in that month:

(i) The aggregate dollar amount of covered sales that it captured in a trade reporting system;

(ii) The aggregate dollar amount of covered sales that it did not capture in a trade reporting system; and

(iii) The total number of covered round turn transactions that it reported to a designated clearing agency, as reflected in the data provided by the designated clearing agency.

(4) *Duties of Designated Clearing Agency.* (i) A designated clearing agency shall provide a covered SRO, upon request, the data in its possession needed by the covered SRO to complete Part I of Form R31 (17 CFR 249.11).

(ii) If a covered exchange trades physical delivery exchange-traded options or security futures that settle by physical delivery of the underlying securities, the designated clearing agency that clears and settles such transactions shall provide that covered exchange with the data in its possession relating to the covered sales resulting from the exercise of such options or from the matured security futures. If, during a particular month, the designated clearing agency cannot determine the covered exchange on which the options or security futures originally were traded, the designated clearing agency shall assign covered sales resulting from exercises or maturations as follows. To provide Form R31 data to the covered exchange for a particular month, the designated clearing agency shall:

(A) Calculate the aggregate dollar amount of all covered sales in the previous calendar month resulting from exercises and maturations, respectively, occurring on all covered exchanges for which it clears and settles transactions;

(B) Calculate, for the previous calendar month, the aggregate dollar amount of covered sales of physical delivery exchange-traded options occurring on each covered exchange for which it clears and settles transactions, and the aggregate dollar amount of covered sales of physical delivery exchange-traded options occurring on all such exchanges collectively;

(C) Calculate, for the previous calendar month, the total number of covered round turn transactions in security futures that settle by physical delivery that occurred on each covered exchange for which it clears and settles transactions, and the total number of covered round turn transactions in security futures that settle by physical delivery that occurred on all such exchanges collectively;

(D) Determine for the previous calendar month each covered exchange's percentage of the total dollar volume of physical delivery exchange-traded options ("exercise percentage") and each covered exchange's percentage of the total number of covered round turn transactions in security futures that settle by physical delivery ("maturation percentage"); and

(E) In the current month, assign to each covered exchange for which it clears and settles covered sales the exercise percentage of the aggregate dollar amount of covered sales on all covered exchanges resulting from the exercise of physical delivery exchange-traded options and the maturation percentage of all covered sales on all covered exchanges resulting from the maturation of security futures that settle by physical delivery.

(5) A covered SRO shall provide in Part I of Form R31 only the data supplied to it by a designated clearing agency.

(c) *Calculation and Billing of Section 31 Fees.* (1) The amount due from a covered SRO for a billing period, as reflected in its Section 31 bill, shall be the sum of the monthly amounts due for each month in the billing period.

(2) The monthly amount due from a covered SRO shall equal:

(i) The aggregate dollar amount of its covered sales that have a charge date in that month, times the fee rate; plus

(ii) The total number of its covered round turn transactions that have a charge date in that month, times the assessment charge.

(3) By the due date, each covered SRO shall pay the Commission, either directly or through a designated clearing agency acting as agent, the entire amount due for the billing period, as reflected in its Section 31 bill.

Rule 36a1–1. Exemption from Section 7 for OTC derivatives dealers

PRELIMINARY NOTE

OTC derivatives dealers are a special class of broker-dealers that are exempt from certain broker-dealer requirements, including membership in a self-regulatory organization (Rule 15b9–2), regular broker-dealer margin rules (Rule 36a1–1), and application of the Securities Investor Protection Act of 1970 (Rule 36a1–2). OTC derivative dealers are subject to special requirements, including limitations on the scope of their securities activities (Rule 15a–1), specified internal risk management control systems (Rule 15c3–4), recordkeeping obligations (Rule 17a–3(a)(10)), and reporting responsibilities (Rule 17a–12). They are also subject to alternative net capital treatment (Rule 15c3–1(a)(5)).

(a) Except as otherwise provided in paragraph (b) of this rule, transactions involving the extension of credit by an OTC derivatives dealer shall be exempt from the provisions of section 7(c) of the Act, provided that the OTC derivatives dealer complies with Section 7(d) of the Act.

(b) The exemption provided under paragraph (a) of this rule shall not apply to extensions of credit made directly by a registered broker or dealer (other than an OTC derivatives dealer) in connection with transactions in eligible OTC derivative instruments for which an OTC derivatives dealer acts as counterparty.

Rule 36a1–2. Exemption from SIPA for OTC derivatives dealers

PRELIMINARY NOTE

OTC derivatives dealers are a special class of broker-dealers that are exempt from certain broker-dealer requirements, including membership in a self-regulatory organization (Rule 15b9–2), regular broker-dealer margin rules (Rule 36a1–1), and application of the Securities Investor Protection Act of 1970 (Rule 36a1–2). OTC derivative dealers are subject to special requirements, including limitations on the scope of their securities activities (Rule 15a–1), specified internal risk management control systems (Rule 15c3–4), recordkeeping obligations (Rule 17a–3(a)(10)), and reporting responsibilities (Rule 17a–12). They are also subject to alternative net capital treatment (Rule 15c3–1(a)(5)).

OTC derivatives dealers, as defined in Rule 3b–12, shall be exempt from the provisions of the Securities Investor Protection Act of 1970 (15 U.S.C. 78aaa through 78lll).

REGULATION M

(Cite as 17 CFR § 242.___)

Rule 100. Preliminary note; Definitions

(a) *Preliminary Note:* Any transaction or series of transactions, whether or not effected pursuant to the provisions of Regulation M (Rule 100 through 105), remain subject to the antifraud and antimanipulation provisions of the securities laws, including, without limitation, Section 17(a) of the Securities Act of 1933 and Sections 9, 10(b), and 15(c) of the Securities Exchange Act of 1934.

(b) For purposes of Regulation M (Rules 100 through 105) the following definitions shall apply:

ADTV means the worldwide average daily trading volume during the two full calendar months immediately preceding, or any 60 consecutive calendar days ending within the 10 calendar days preceding, the filing of the registration statement; or, if there is no registration statement or if the distribution involves the sale of securities on a delayed basis pursuant to Rule 415 under the Securities Act of 1933, two full calendar months immediately preceding, or any consecutive 60 calendar days ending within the 10 calendar days preceding, the determination of the offering price.

Affiliated purchaser means:

(1) A person acting, directly or indirectly, in concert with a distribution participant, issuer, or selling security holder in connection with the acquisition or distribution of any covered security; or

(2) An affiliate, which may be a separately identifiable department or division of a distribution participant, issuer, or selling security holder, that, directly or indirectly, controls the purchases of any covered security by a distribution participant, issuer, or selling security holder, whose purchases are controlled by any such person, or whose purchases are under common control with any such person; or

(3) An affiliate, which may be a separately identifiable department or division of a distribution participant, issuer, or selling security holder, that regularly purchases securities for its own account or for the account of others, or that recommends or exercises investment discretion with respect to the purchase or sale of securities; *Provided, however,* That this paragraph (3) shall not apply to such affiliate if the following conditions are satisfied:

(i) The distribution participant, issuer, or selling security holder:

(A) Maintains and enforces written policies and procedures reasonably designed to prevent the flow of information to or from the affiliate that might result in a violation of Rules 101, 102, and 104; and

(B) Obtains an annual, independent assessment of the operation of such policies and procedures; and

(ii) The affiliate has no officers (or persons performing similar functions) or employees (other than clerical, ministerial, or support personnel) in common with the distribution participant, issuer, or selling security holder that direct, effect, or recommend transactions in securities; and

(iii) The affiliate does not, during the applicable restricted period, act as a market maker (other than as a specialist in compliance with the rules of a national securities exchange), or engage, as a broker or a dealer, in solicited transactions or proprietary trading, in covered securities.

Agent independent of the issuer means a trustee or other person who is independent of the issuer. The agent shall be deemed to be independent of the issuer only if:

(1) The agent is not an affiliate of the issuer; and

(2) Neither the issuer nor any affiliate of the issuer exercises any direct or indirect control or influence over the prices or amounts of the securities to be purchased, the timing of, or the manner in which, the securities are to be purchased, or the selection of a broker or dealer (other than the independent agent itself) through which purchases may be executed; *Provided, however,* That the issuer or its affiliate will not be deemed to have such control or influence solely because it revises not more than once in any three-month period the source of the shares to fund the plan, the basis for determining the amount of its contributions to a plan, or the basis for determining the frequency of its allocations to a plan, or any formula specified in a plan that determines the amount or timing of securities to be purchased by the agent.

Asset-backed security has the meaning contained in Item 1101 of Regulation AB.

At-the-market offering means an offering of securities at other than a fixed price.

Business day refers to a 24 hour period determined with reference to the principal market for the securities to be distributed, and that includes a complete trading session for that market.

Completion of participation in a distribution. Securities acquired in the distribution for investment by any person participating in a distribution, or any affiliated purchaser of such person, shall be deemed to be distributed. A person shall be deemed to have completed its participation in a distribution as follows:

(1) An issuer or selling security holder, when the distribution is completed;

(2) An underwriter, when such person's participation has been distributed, including all other securities of the same class that are acquired in connection with the distribution, and any stabilization arrangements and trading restrictions in connection with the distribution have been terminated; *Provided, however,* That an underwriter's participation will not be deemed to have been completed if a syndicate overallotment option is exercised in an amount that exceeds the net syndicate short position at the time of such exercise; and

(3) Any other person participating in the distribution, when such person's participation has been distributed.

Covered security means any security that is the subject of a distribution, or any reference security.

Current exchange rate means the current rate of exchange between two currencies, which is obtained from at least one independent entity that provides or disseminates foreign exchange quotations in the ordinary course of its business.

Distribution means an offering of securities, whether or not subject to registration under the Securities Act, that is distinguished from ordinary trading transactions by the magnitude of the offering and the presence of special selling efforts and selling methods.

Distribution participant means an underwriter, prospective underwriter, broker, dealer, or other person who has agreed to participate or is participating in a distribution.

Electronic communications network has the meaning provided in Rule 600.

Employee has the meaning contained in Form S–8 (17 CFR 239.16b) relating to employee benefit plans.

Exchange Act means the Securities Exchange Act of 1934.

Independent bid means a bid by a person who is not a distribution participant, issuer, selling security holder, or affiliated purchaser.

NASD means the National Association of Securities Dealers, Inc. or any of its subsidiaries.

Nasdaq means the electronic dealer quotation system owned and operated by The Nasdaq Stock Market, Inc.

Nasdaq security means a security that is authorized for quotation on Nasdaq, and such authorization is not suspended, terminated, or prohibited.

Net purchases means the amount by which a passive market maker's purchases exceed its sales.

Offering price means the price at which the security is to be or is being distributed.

Passive market maker means a market maker that effects bids or purchases in accordance with the provisions of Rule 103.

Penalty bid means an arrangement that permits the managing underwriter to reclaim a selling concession from a syndicate member in connection with an offering when the securities originally sold by the syndicate member are purchased in syndicate covering transactions.

Plan means any bonus, profit-sharing, pension, retirement, thrift, savings, incentive, stock purchase, stock option, stock ownership, stock appreciation, dividend reinvestment, or similar plan; or any dividend or interest reinvestment plan or employee benefit plan as defined in Rule 405 under the Securities Act of 1933.

Principal market means the single securities market with the largest aggregate reported trading volume for the class of securities during the 12 full calendar months immediately preceding the filing of the registration statement; or, if there is no registration statement or if the distribution involves the sale of securities on a delayed basis pursuant to Rule 415 under the Securities Act of 1933, during the 12 full calendar months immediately preceding the determination of the offering price. For the purpose of determining the aggregate trading volume in a security, the trading volume of depositary shares representing such security shall be included, and shall be multiplied by the multiple or fraction of the security represented by the depositary share. For purposes of this paragraph, depositary share means a security, evidenced by a depositary receipt, that represents another security, or a multiple or fraction thereof, deposited with a depositary.

Prospective underwriter means a person:

(1) Who has submitted a bid to the issuer or selling security holder, and who knows or is reasonably certain that such bid will be accepted, whether or not the terms and conditions of the underwriting have been agreed upon; or

(2) Who has reached, or is reasonably certain to reach, an understanding with the issuer or selling security holder, or managing underwriter that such person will become an underwriter, whether or not the terms and conditions of the underwriting have been agreed upon.

Public float value shall be determined in the manner set forth on the front page of Form 10–K (17 CFR 249.310), even if the issuer of such securities is not required to file Form 10–K, relating to the aggregate market value of common equity securities held by non-affiliates of the issuer.

Reference period means the two full calendar months immediately preceding the filing of the registration statement or, if there is no registration statement or if the distribution involves the sale of securities on a delayed basis pursuant to Rule 415 under the Securities Act of 1933, the two full calendar months immediately preceding the determination of the offering price.

Reference security means a security into which a security that is the subject of a distribution ("subject security") may be converted, exchanged, or exercised or which, under the terms of the subject security, may in whole or in significant part determine the value of the subject security.

Restricted period means:

(1) For any security with an ADTV value of $100,000 or more of an issuer whose common equity securities have a public float value of $25 million or more, the period beginning on the later of one business day prior to the determination of the offering price or such time that a person becomes a distribution participant, and ending upon such person's completion of participation in the distribution; and

(2) For all other securities, the period beginning on the later of five business days prior to the determination of the offering price or such time that a person becomes a distribution participant, and ending upon such person's completion of participation in the distribution.

(3) In the case of a distribution involving a merger, acquisition, or exchange offer, the period beginning on the day proxy solicitation or offering materials are first disseminated to security holders, and ending upon the completion of the distribution.

Securities Act means the Securities Act of 1933.

Selling security holder means any person on whose behalf a distribution is made, other than an issuer.

Stabilize or stabilizing means the placing of any bid, or the effecting of any purchase, for the purpose of pegging, fixing, or maintaining the price of a security.

Syndicate covering transaction means the placing of any bid or the effecting of any purchase on behalf of the sole distributor or the underwriting syndicate or group to reduce a short position created in connection with the offering.

30% ADTV limitation means 30 percent of the market maker's ADTV in a covered security during the reference period, as obtained from the NASD.

Underwriter means a person who has agreed with an issuer or selling security holder:

(1) To purchase securities for distribution; or

(2) To distribute securities for or on behalf of such issuer or selling security holder; or

(3) To manage or supervise a distribution of securities for or on behalf of such issuer or selling security holder.

Rule 101. Activities by distribution participants

(a) *Unlawful Activity.* In connection with a distribution of securities, it shall be unlawful for a distribution participant or an affiliated purchaser of such person, directly or indirectly, to bid for, purchase, or attempt to induce any person to bid for or purchase, a covered security during the applicable restricted period; *Provided, however,* That if a distribution participant or affiliated purchaser is the issuer or selling security holder of the securities subject to the distribution, such person shall be subject to the provisions of Rule 102, rather than this rule.

(b) *Excepted Activity.* The following activities shall not be prohibited by paragraph (a) of this rule:

(1) *Research.* The publication or dissemination of any information, opinion, or recommendation, if the conditions of Rule 138 or Rule 139 under the Securities Act of 1933 are met; or

(2) *Transactions Complying with Certain Other Rules.* Transactions complying with Rule 103 or Rule 104; or

(3) *Odd-Lot Transactions.* Transactions in odd-lots; or transactions to offset odd-lots in connection with an odd-lot tender offer conducted pursuant to Rule 13e–4(h)(5); or

(4) *Exercises of Securities.* The exercise of any option, warrant, right, or any conversion privilege set forth in the instrument governing a security; or

(5) *Unsolicited Transactions.* Unsolicited brokerage transactions; or unsolicited purchases that are not effected from or through a broker or dealer, on a securities exchange, or through an inter-dealer quotation system or electronic communications network; or

(6) *Basket Transactions.* (i) Bids or purchases, in the ordinary course of business, in connection with a basket of 20 or more securities in which a covered security does not comprise more than 5% of the value of the basket purchased; or

(ii) Adjustments to such a basket in the ordinary course of business as a result of a change in the composition of a standardized index; or

(7) *De Minimis Transactions.* Purchases during the restricted period, other than by a passive market maker, that total less than 2% of the ADTV of the security being purchased, or unaccepted bids; *Provided, however,* That the person making such bid or purchase has maintained and enforces written policies and procedures reasonably designed to achieve compliance with the other provisions of this rule; or

(8) *Transactions in Connection with a Distribution.* Transactions among distribution participants in connection with a distribution, and purchases of securities from an issuer or selling security holder in connection with a distribution, that are not effected on a securities exchange, or through an inter-dealer quotation system or electronic communications network; or

(9) *Offers to Sell or the Solicitation of Offers to Buy.* Offers to sell or the solicitation of offers to buy the securities being distributed (including securities acquired in stabilizing), or securities offered as principal by the person making such offer or solicitation; or

(10) *Transactions in Rule 144A Securities.* Transactions in securities eligible for resale under Rule 144A(d)(3) under the Securities Act of 1933, or any reference security, if the Rule 144A securities are sold in the United States solely to:

(i) Qualified institutional buyers, as defined in Rule 144A(a)(1) under the Securities Act of 1933, or to purchasers that the seller and any person acting on behalf of the seller reasonably believes are qualified institutional buyers, in transactions exempt from registration under Section 4(a)(2) of the Securities Act (15 U.S.C. 77d(2)) or Rules 144A or 500 through 508 under the Securities Act of 1933; or

(ii) Persons not deemed to be "U.S. persons" for purposes of Rule 902(o)(2) or Rule 902(o)(7) under the Securities Act of 1933, during a distribution qualifying under paragraph (b)(10)(i) of this rule.

(c) *Excepted Securities.* The provisions of this rule shall not apply to any of the following securities:

(1) *Actively-Traded Securities.* Securities that have an ADTV value of at least $1 million and are issued by an issuer whose common equity securities have a public float value of at least $150 million; *Provided, however,* That such securities are not issued by the distribution participant or an affiliate of the distribution participant; or

(2) *Investment Grade Nonconvertible and Asset-Backed Securities.* Nonconvertible debt securities, nonconvertible preferred securities, and asset-backed securities, that are rated by at least one nationally recognized statistical rating organization, as that term is used in Rule 15c3–1 under the Securities Exchange Act of 1934, in one of its generic rating categories that signifies investment grade; or

(3) *Exempted Securities.* "Exempted securities" as defined in section 3(a)(12) of the Exchange Act; or

(4) *Face-Amount Certificates or Securities Issued by an Open-End Management Investment Company or Unit Investment Trust.* Face-amount certificates issued by a face-amount certificate company, or redeemable securities issued by an open-end management investment company or a unit investment trust. Any terms used in this paragraph

(c)(4) that are defined in the Investment Company Act of 1940 (15 U.S.C. 80a–1 *et seq.*) shall have the meanings specified in such Act.

(d) *Exemptive Authority.* Upon written application or upon its own motion, the Commission may grant an exemption from the provisions of this rule, either unconditionally or on specified terms and conditions, to any transaction or class of transactions, or to any security or class of securities.

Rule 102. Activities by issuers and selling security holders during a distribution

(a) *Unlawful Activity.* In connection with a distribution of securities effected by or on behalf of an issuer or selling security holder, it shall be unlawful for such person, or any affiliated purchaser of such person, directly or indirectly, to bid for, purchase, or attempt to induce any person to bid for or purchase, a covered security during the applicable restricted period; *Except that* if an affiliated purchaser is a distribution participant, such affiliated purchaser may comply with Rule 101, rather than this rule.

(b) *Excepted Activity.* The following activities shall not be prohibited by paragraph (a) of this rule:

(1) *Odd-Lot Transactions.* Transactions in odd-lots, or transactions to offset odd-lots in connection with an odd-lot tender offer conducted pursuant to Rule 13e–4(h)(5); or

(2) *Transactions by Closed-End Investment Companies.* (i) Transactions complying with Rule 23c–3 under the Investment Company Act of 1940; or

(ii) Periodic tender offers of securities, at net asset value, conducted pursuant to Rule 13e–4 by a closed-end investment company that engages in a continuous offering of its securities pursuant to Rule 415 under the Securities Act of 1933; *Provided, however,* That such securities are not traded on a securities exchange or through an inter-dealer quotation system or electronic communications network; or

(3) *Redemptions by Commodity Pools or Limited Partnerships.* Redemptions by commodity pools or limited partnerships, at a price based on net asset value, which are effected in accordance with the terms and conditions of the instruments governing the securities; *Provided, however,* That such securities are not traded on a securities exchange; or through an inter-dealer quotation system or electronic communications network; or

(4) *Exercises of Securities.* The exercise of any option, warrant, right, or any conversion privilege set forth in the instrument governing a security; or

(5) *Offers to Sell or the Solicitation of Offers to Buy.* Offers to sell or the solicitation of offers to buy the securities being distributed; or

(6) *Unsolicited Purchases.* Unsolicited purchases that are not effected from or through a broker or dealer, on a securities exchange, or through an inter-dealer quotation system or electronic communications network; or

(7) *Transactions in Rule 144A Securities.* Transactions in securities eligible for resale under Rule 144A(d)(3) under the Securities Act of 1933, or any reference security, if the Rule 144A securities are sold in the United States solely to:

(i) Qualified institutional buyers, as defined in Rule 144A(a)(1) under the Securities Act of 1933, or to purchasers that the seller and any person acting on behalf of the seller reasonably believes are qualified institutional buyers, in transactions exempt from registration under section 4(a)(2) of the Securities Act or Rule 144A or Rule 500 through Rule 508 under the Securities Act of 1933; or

(ii) Persons not deemed to be "U.S. persons" for purposes of Rule 902(*o*)(2) or Rule 902(*o*)(7) under the Securities Act of 1933, during a distribution qualifying under paragraph (b)(7)(i) of this rule.

(c) *Plans.* (1) Paragraph (a) of this rule shall not apply to distributions of securities pursuant to a plan which are made:

(i) Solely to employees or security holders of an issuer or its subsidiaries, or to a trustee or other person acquiring such securities for the accounts of such persons; or

(ii) To persons other than employees or security holders, if bids for or purchases of securities pursuant to the plan are effected solely by an agent independent of the issuer and the securities are from a source other than the issuer or an affiliated purchaser of the issuer.

(2) Bids for or purchases of any security made or effected by or for a plan shall be deemed to be a purchase by the issuer unless the bid is made, or the purchase is effected, by an agent independent of the issuer.

(d) *Excepted Securities.* The provisions of this rule shall not apply to any of the following securities:

(1) *Actively-Traded Reference Securities.* Reference securities with an ADTV value of at least $1 million that are issued by an issuer whose common equity securities have a public float value of at least $150 million; *Provided, however,* That such securities are not issued by the issuer, or any affiliate of the issuer, of the security in distribution.

(2) *Investment Grade Nonconvertible and Asset-Backed Securities.* Nonconvertible debt securities, nonconvertible preferred securities, and asset-backed securities, that are rated by at least one nationally recognized statistical rating organization, as that term is used in Rule 15c3–1 under the Securities Act of 1933, in one of its generic rating categories that signifies investment grade; or

(3) *Exempted Securities.* "Exempted securities" as defined in section 3(a)(12) of the Exchange Act (15 U.S.C. 78c(a)(12)); or

(4) *Face-Amount Certificates or Securities Issued by an Open-End Management Investment Company or Unit Investment Trust.* Face-amount certificates issued by a face-amount certificate company, or redeemable securities issued by an open-end management investment company or a unit investment trust. Any terms used in this paragraph (d)(4) that are defined in the Investment Company Act of 1940 (15 U.S.C. 80a–1 *et seq.*) shall have the meanings specified in such Act.

(e) *Exemptive Authority.* Upon written application or upon its own motion, the Commission may grant an exemption from the provisions of this rule, either unconditionally or on specified terms and conditions, to any transaction or class of transactions, or to any security or class of securities.

Rule 103. NASDAQ passive market making

(a) *Scope of Rule.* This rule permits broker-dealers to engage in market making transactions in covered securities that are Nasdaq securities without violating the provisions of Rule 101; *Except That* this rule shall not apply to any security for which a stabilizing bid subject to Rule 104 is in effect, or during any at-the-market offering or best efforts offering.

(b) *Conditions to Be Met.* (1) *General Limitations.* A passive market maker must effect all transactions in the capacity of a registered market maker on Nasdaq. A passive market maker shall not bid for or purchase a covered security at a price that exceeds the highest independent bid for the covered security at the time of the transaction, except as permitted by paragraph (b)(3) of this rule or required by a rule promulgated by the Commission or the NASD governing the handling of customer orders.

(2) *Purchase Limitation.* On each day of the restricted period, a passive market maker's net purchases shall not exceed the greater of its 30% ADTV limitation or 200 shares (together, "purchase limitation"); *Provided, however,* That a passive market maker may purchase all of the securities that are part of a single order that, when executed, results in its purchase limitation being equalled or exceeded. If a passive market maker's net purchases equal or exceed its purchase limitation, it shall withdraw promptly its quotations from Nasdaq. If a passive market maker withdraws its quotations pursuant to this paragraph, it may not effect any bid or purchase in the covered security for the remainder of that day, irrespective of any later sales during that day, unless otherwise permitted by Rule 101.

(3) *Requirement to Lower the Bid.* If all independent bids for a covered security are reduced to a price below the passive market maker's bid, the passive market maker must lower its bid promptly to a level not higher than the then highest independent bid; *Provided, however,* That a passive market maker may continue to bid and effect purchases at its bid at a price exceeding the then highest independent bid until the passive market maker purchases an aggregate amount of the covered security that equals or, through the purchase of all securities that are part of a single order, exceeds the lesser of two times the minimum quotation size for the security, as determined by NASD rules, or the passive market maker's remaining purchasing capacity under paragraph (b)(2) of this rule.

(4) *Limitation on Displayed Size.* At all times, the passive market maker's displayed bid size may not exceed the lesser of the minimum quotation size for the covered security, or the passive market maker's remaining purchasing capacity under paragraph (b)(2) of this rule; *Provided, however,* That a passive market maker whose purchasing capacity at any time is between one and 99 shares may display a bid size of 100 shares.

(5) *Identification of a Passive Market Making Bid.* The bid displayed by a passive market maker shall be designated as such.

(6) *Notification and Reporting to the NASD.* A passive market maker shall notify the NASD in advance of its intention to engage in passive market making, and shall submit to the NASD information regarding passive market making purchases, in such form as the NASD shall prescribe.

(7) *Prospectus Disclosure:* The prospectus for any registered offering in which any passive market maker intends to effect transactions in any covered security shall contain the information required in Items 502 and 508 of Regulation S–B and Items 502 and 508 of Regulation S–K.

(c) *Transactions at Prices Resulting from Unlawful Activity.* No transaction shall be made at a price that the passive market maker knows or has reason to know is the result of activity that is fraudulent, manipulative, or deceptive under the securities laws, or any rule or regulation thereunder.

Rule 104. Stabilizing and other activities in connection with an offering

(a) *Unlawful Activity.* It shall be unlawful for any person, directly or indirectly, to stabilize, to effect any syndicate covering transaction, or to impose a penalty bid, in connection with an offering of any security, in contravention of the provisions of this rule. No stabilizing shall be effected at a price that the person stabilizing knows or has reason to know is in contravention of this rule, or is the result of activity that is fraudulent, manipulative, or deceptive under the securities laws, or any rule or regulation thereunder.

(b) *Purpose.* Stabilizing is prohibited except for the purpose of preventing or retarding a decline in the market price of a security.

(c) *Priority.* To the extent permitted or required by the market where stabilizing occurs, any person stabilizing shall grant priority to any independent bid at the same price irrespective of the size of such independent bid at the time that it is entered.

(d) *Control of Stabilizing.* No sole distributor or syndicate or group stabilizing the price of a security or any member or members of such syndicate or group shall maintain more than one stabilizing bid in any one market at the same price at the same time.

(e) *At-the-Market Offerings.* Stabilizing is prohibited in an at-the-market offering.

(f) *Stabilizing Levels.* (1) *Maximum Stabilizing Bid.* Notwithstanding the other provisions of this paragraph (f), no stabilizing shall be made at a price higher than the lower of the offering price or the stabilizing bid for the security in the principal market (or, if the principal market is closed, the stabilizing bid in the principal market at its previous close).

(2) *Initiating Stabilizing.* (i) *Initiating Stabilizing When the Principal Market is Open.* After the opening of quotations for the security in the principal market, stabilizing may be initiated in any market at a price no higher than the last independent transaction price for the security in the principal market if the security has traded in the principal market on the day stabilizing is initiated or on the most recent prior day of trading in the principal market and the current asked price in the principal market is equal to or greater than the last independent transaction price. If both conditions of the preceding sentence are not satisfied, stabilizing may be initiated in any market after the opening of quotations in the principal market at a price no higher than the highest current independent bid for the security in the principal market.

(ii) *Initiating Stabilizing When the Principal Market is Closed.* (A) When the principal market for the security is closed, but immediately before the opening of quotations for the security in the market where stabilizing will be initiated, stabilizing may be initiated at a price no higher than the lower of:

(1) The price at which stabilizing could have been initiated in the principal market for the security at its previous close; or

(2) The most recent price at which an independent transaction in the security has been effected in any market since the close of the principal market, if the person stabilizing knows or has reason to know of such transaction.

(B) When the principal market for the security is closed, but after the opening of quotations in the market where stabilizing will be initiated, stabilizing may be initiated at a price no higher than the lower of:

(1) The price at which stabilization could have been initiated in the principal market for the security at its previous close; or

(2) The last independent transaction price for the security in that market if the security has traded in that market on the day stabilizing is initiated or on the last preceding business day and the current asked price in

that market is equal to or greater than the last independent transaction price. If both conditions of the preceding sentence are not satisfied, under this paragraph (f)(2)(ii)(B)(*2*), stabilizing may be initiated at a price no higher than the highest current independent bid for the security in that market.

(iii) *Initiating Stabilizing When There is No Market for the Security or Before the Offering Price is Determined.* If no *bona fide* market for the security being distributed exists at the time stabilizing is initiated, no stabilizing shall be initiated at a price in excess of the offering price. If stabilizing is initiated before the offering price is determined, then stabilizing may be continued after determination of the offering price at the price at which stabilizing then could be initiated.

(3) *Maintaining or Carrying Over a Stabilizing Bid.* A stabilizing bid initiated pursuant to paragraph (f)(2) of this rule, which has not been discontinued, may be maintained, or carried over into another market, irrespective of changes in the independent bids or transaction prices for the security.

(4) *Increasing or Reducing a Stabilizing Bid.* A stabilizing bid may be increased to a price no higher than the highest current independent bid for the security in the principal market if the principal market is open, or, if the principal market is closed, to a price no higher than the highest independent bid in the principal market at the previous close thereof. A stabilizing bid may be reduced, or carried over into another market at a reduced price, irrespective of changes in the independent bids or transaction prices for the security. If stabilizing is discontinued, it shall not be resumed at a price higher than the price at which stabilizing then could be initiated.

(5) *Initiating, Maintaining, or Adjusting a Stabilizing Bid to Reflect the Current Exchange Rate.* If a stabilizing bid is expressed in a currency other than the currency of the principal market for the security, such bid may be initiated, maintained, or adjusted to reflect the current exchange rate, consistent with the provisions of this rule. If, in initiating, maintaining, or adjusting a stabilizing bid pursuant to this paragraph (f)(5), the bid would be at or below the midpoint between two trading differentials, such stabilizing bid shall be adjusted downward to the lower differential.

(6) *Adjustments to Stabilizing Bid.* If a security goes ex-dividend, ex-rights, or ex-distribution, the stabilizing bid shall be reduced by an amount equal to the value of the dividend, right, or distribution. If, in reducing a stabilizing bid pursuant to this paragraph (f)(6), the bid would be at or below the midpoint between two trading differentials, such stabilizing bid shall be adjusted downward to the lower differential.

(7) *Stabilizing of Components.* When two or more securities are being offered as a unit, the component securities shall not be stabilized at prices the sum of which exceeds the then permissible stabilizing price for the unit.

(8) *Special Prices.* Any stabilizing price that otherwise meets the requirements of this rule need not be adjusted to reflect special prices available to any group or class of persons (including employees or holders of warrants or rights).

(g) *Offerings with No U.S. Stabilizing Activities.* (1) Stabilizing to facilitate an offering of a security in the United States shall not be deemed to be in violation of this rule if all of the following conditions are satisfied:

(i) No stabilizing is made in the United States;

(ii) Stabilizing outside the United States is made in a jurisdiction with statutory or regulatory provisions governing stabilizing that are comparable to the provisions of this rule; and

(iii) No stabilizing is made at a price above the offering price in the United States, except as permitted by paragraph (f)(5) of this rule.

(2) For purposes of this paragraph (g), the Commission by rule, regulation, or order may determine whether a foreign statute or regulation is comparable to this rule considering, among other things, whether such foreign statute or regulation: specifies appropriate purposes for which stabilizing is permitted; provides for disclosure and control of stabilizing activities; places limitations on stabilizing levels; requires appropriate recordkeeping; provides other protections comparable to the provisions of this rule; and whether procedures exist to enable the Commission to obtain information concerning any foreign stabilizing transactions.

(h) *Disclosure and Notification.* (1) Any person displaying or transmitting a bid that such person knows is for the purpose of stabilizing shall provide prior notice to the market on which such stabilizing will be effected, and shall disclose its purpose to the person with whom the bid is entered.

(2) Any person effecting a syndicate covering transaction or imposing a penalty bid shall provide prior notice to the self-regulatory organization with direct authority over the principal market in the United States for the security for which the syndicate covering transaction is effected or the penalty bid is imposed.

(3) Any person subject to this rule who sells to, or purchases for the account of, any person any security where the price of such security may be or has been stabilized, shall send to the purchaser at or before the completion of the transaction, a prospectus, offering circular, confirmation, or other document containing a statement similar to that comprising the statement provided for in Item 502(d) of Regulation S–B or Item 502(d) of Regulation S–K.

(i) *Recordkeeping Requirements.* A person subject to this section shall keep the information and make the notification required by Rule 17a–2.

(j) *Excepted Securities.* The provisions of this section shall not apply to:

(1) *Exempted Securities.* "Exempted securities," as defined in Section 3(a)(12) of the Exchange Act; or

(2) *Transactions of Rule 144A Securities.* Transactions in securities eligible for resale under Rule 144A(d)(3) under the Securities Act of 1933, if such securities are sold in the United States solely to:

(i) Qualified institutional buyers, as defined in Rule 144A(a)(1) under the Securities Act of 1933, or to purchasers that the seller and any person acting on behalf of the seller reasonably believes are qualified institutional buyers, in transactions exempt from registration under section 4(a)(2) of the Securities Act or Rule 144A or Rule 500 through Rule 508 under the Securities Act of 1933; or

(ii) Persons not deemed to be "U.S. persons" for purposes of Rule 902(*o*)(2) or Rule 902(*o*)(7) under the Securities Act of 1933, during a distribution qualifying under paragraph (j)(2)(i) of this rule.

(k) *Exemptive Authority.* Upon written application or upon its own motion, the Commission may grant an exemption from the provisions of this rule, either unconditionally or on specified terms and conditions, to any transaction or class of transactions, or to any security or class of securities.

Rule 105. Short selling in connection with a public offering

(a) *Unlawful Activity.* In connection with an offering of equity securities for cash pursuant to a registration statement or a notification on Form 1–A (17 CFR 239.90) or Form 1–E (Item 200 of 17 CFR 239) filed under the Securities Act of 1933 ("offered securities"), it shall be unlawful for any person to sell short (as defined in Rule 200(a) of Regulation SHO) the security that is the subject of the offering and purchase the offered securities from an underwriter or broker or dealer participating in the offering if such short sale was effected during the period ("Rule 105 restricted period") that is the shorter of the period:

(1) Beginning five business days before the pricing of the offered securities and ending with such pricing; or

(2) Beginning with the initial filing of such registration statement or notification on Form 1–A or Form 1–E and ending with the pricing.

(b) *Excepted Activity.* (1) *Bona Fide Purchase.* It shall not be prohibited for such person to purchase the offered securities as provided in paragraph (a) of this rule if:

(i) Such person makes a bona fide purchase(s) of the security that is the subject of the offering that is:

(A) At least equivalent in quantity to the entire amount of the Rule 105 restricted period short sale(s);

(B) Effected during regular trading hours;

(C) Reported to an "effective transaction reporting plan" (as defined in Rule 600(b)(22) of Regulation NMS); and

(D) Effected after the last Rule 105 restricted period short sale, and no later than the business day prior to the day of pricing; and

(ii) Such person did not effect a short sale, that is reported to an effective transaction reporting plan, within the 30 minutes prior to the close of regular trading hours (as defined in Rule 600(b)(64) of Regulation NMS) on the business day prior to the day of pricing.

(2) *Separate Accounts.* Paragraph (a) of this rule shall not prohibit the purchase of the offered security in an account of a person where such person

sold short during the Rule 105 restricted period in a separate account, if decisions regarding securities transactions for each account are made separately and without coordination of trading or cooperation among or between the accounts.

(3) *Investment Companies.* Paragraph (a) of this rule shall not prohibit an investment company (as defined by Section 3 of the Investment Company Act) that is registered under Section 8 of the Investment Company Act, or a series of such company (investment company) from purchasing an offered security where any of the following sold the offered security short during the Rule 105 restricted period:

(i) An affiliated investment company, or any series of such a company; or

(ii) A separate series of the investment company.

(c) *Excepted Offerings.* This rule shall not apply to offerings that are not conducted on a firm commitment basis.

(d) *Exemptive Authority.* Upon written application or upon its own motion, the Commission may grant an exemption from the provisions of this section, either unconditionally or on specified terms and conditions, to any transaction or class of transactions, or to any security or class of securities by the Commission.

REGULATION SHO—REGULATION OF SHORT SALES

(Cite as 17 CFR § 242.___)

Rule 200. Definition of "short sale" and marking requirements

(a) The term *short sale* shall mean any sale of a security which the seller does not own or any sale which is consummated by the delivery of a security borrowed by, or for the account of, the seller.

(b) A person shall be deemed to own a security if:

(1) The person or his agent has title to it; or

(2) The person has purchased, or has entered into an unconditional contract, binding on both parties thereto, to purchase it, but has not yet received it; or

(3) The person owns a security convertible into or exchangeable for it and has tendered such security for conversion or exchange; or

(4) The person has an option to purchase or acquire it and has exercised such option; or

(5) The person has rights or warrants to subscribe to it and has exercised such rights or warrants; or

(6) The person holds a security futures contract to purchase it and has received notice that the position will be physically settled and is irrevocably bound to receive the underlying security.

(c) A person shall be deemed to own securities only to the extent that he has a net long position in such securities.

(d) A broker or dealer shall be deemed to own a security, even if it is not net long, if:

(1) The broker or dealer acquired that security while acting in the capacity of a block positioner; and

(2) If and to the extent that the broker or dealer's short position in the security is the subject of offsetting positions created in the course of bona fide arbitrage, risk arbitrage, or bona fide hedge activities.

(e) A broker-dealer shall be deemed to own a security even if it is not net long, if:

(1) The broker-dealer is unwinding index arbitrage position involving a long basket of stock and one or more short index futures traded on a board of trade or one or more standardized options contracts as defined in Rule 9b–1(a)(4); and

(2) If and to the extent that the broker-dealer's short position in the security is the subject of offsetting positions created and maintained in the course of bona fide arbitrage, risk arbitrage, or bona fide hedge activities; and

(3) The sale does not occur during a period commencing at the time that the NYSE Composite Index has declined by two percent or more from its closing value on the previous day and terminating upon the end of the trading day. The two percent shall be calculated at the beginning of each calendar quarter and shall be two percent, rounded down to the nearest 10 points, of the average closing value of the NYSE Composite Index for the last month of the previous quarter.

(f) In order to determine its net position, a broker or dealer shall aggregate all of its positions in a security unless it qualifies for independent trading unit aggregation, in which case each independent trading unit shall aggregate all of its positions in a security to determine its net position. Independent trading unit aggregation is available only if:

(1) The broker or dealer has a written plan of organization that identifies each aggregation unit, specifies its trading objective(s), and supports its independent identity;

(2) Each aggregation unit within the firm determines, at the time of each sale, its net position for every security that it trades;

(3) All traders in an aggregation unit pursue only the particular trading objective(s) or strategy(s) of that aggregation unit and do not coordinate that strategy with any other aggregation unit; and

(4) Individual traders are assigned to only one aggregation unit at any time.

(g) A broker or dealer must mark all sell orders of any equity security as "long" or "short," or "short exempt."

(1) An order to sell shall be marked "long" only if the seller is deemed to own the security being sold pursuant to paragraphs (a) through (f) of this rule and either:

(i) The security to be delivered is in the physical possession or control of the broker or dealer; or

(ii) It is reasonably expected that the security will be in the physical possession or control of the broker or dealer no later than the settlement of the transaction.

(2) A sale order shall be marked "short exempt" only if the provisions of Rule 201(c) or (d) are met.

(h) Upon written application or upon its own motion, the Commission may grant an exemption from the provisions of this rule, either unconditionally or on specified terms and conditions, to any transaction or class of transactions, or to any security or class of securities, or to any person or class of persons.

Rule 201. Circuit breaker

(a) *Definitions.* For the purposes of this section:

(1) The term *covered security* shall mean any NMS stock as defined in Rule 600(b)(47).

(2) The term *effective transaction reporting* plan for a covered security shall have the same meaning as in Rule 600(b)(22).

(3) The term *listing market* shall have the same meaning as the term "listing market" as defined in the effective transaction reporting plan for the covered security.

(4) The term *national best bid* shall have the same meaning as in Rule 600(b)(42).

(5) The term *odd lot* shall have the same meaning as in Rule 600(b)(49).

(6) The term *plan processor* shall have the same meaning as in Rule 600(b)(55).

(7) The term *regular trading hours* shall have the same meaning as in Rule 600(b)(64).

(8) The term *riskless principal* shall mean a transaction in which a broker or dealer, after having received an order to buy a security, purchases the security as principal at the same price to satisfy the order to buy, exclusive of any explicitly disclosed markup or markdown, commission equivalent, or other fee, or, after having received an order to sell, sells the security as principal at the same price to satisfy the order to sell, exclusive of any explicitly disclosed markup or markdown, commission equivalent, or other fee.

(9) The term *trading center* shall have the same meaning as in Rule 600(b)(78).

(b)(1) A trading center shall establish, maintain, and enforce written policies and procedures reasonably designed to:

(i) Prevent the execution or display of a short sale order of a covered security at a price that is less than or equal to the current national best bid if the price of that covered security decreases by 10% or more from the covered security's closing price as determined by the listing market for the covered security as of the end of regular trading hours on the prior day; and

(ii) Impose the requirements of paragraph (b)(1)(i) of this section for the remainder of the day and the following day when a national best bid for the covered security is calculated and disseminated on a current and continuing basis by a plan processor pursuant to an effective national market system plan.

(iii) *Provided, however,* that the policies and procedures must be reasonably designed to permit:

(A) The execution of a displayed short sale order of a covered security by a trading center if, at the time of initial display of the short sale order, the order was at a price above the current national best bid; and

(B) The execution or display of a short sale order of a covered security marked "short exempt" without regard to whether the order is at a price that is less than or equal to the current national best bid.

(2) A trading center shall regularly surveil to ascertain the effectiveness of the policies and procedures required by paragraph (b)(1) of this section and shall take prompt action to remedy deficiencies in such policies and procedures.

(3) The determination regarding whether the price of a covered security has decreased by 10% or more from the covered security's closing price as determined by the listing market for the covered security as of the end of regular trading hours on the prior day shall be made by the listing market for the covered security and, if such decrease has occurred, the listing market shall immediately notify the single plan processor responsible for consolidation of information for the covered security pursuant to Rule 603(b). The single plan processor must then disseminate this information.

(c) Following any determination and notification pursuant to paragraph (b)(3) of this section with respect to a covered security, a broker or dealer submitting a short sale order of the covered security in question to a trading center may mark the order "short exempt" if the broker or dealer identifies the order as being at a price above the current national best bid at the time of submission; *provided, however*:

(1) The broker or dealer that identifies a short sale order of a covered security as "short exempt" in accordance with this paragraph (c) must establish, maintain, and enforce written policies and procedures reasonably designed to prevent incorrect identification of orders for purposes of this paragraph; and

(2) The broker or dealer shall regularly surveil to ascertain the effectiveness of the policies and procedures required by paragraph (c)(1) of this section and shall take prompt action to remedy deficiencies in such policies and procedures.

(d) Following any determination and notification pursuant to paragraph (b)(3) of this section with respect to a covered security, a broker or dealer may mark a short sale order of a covered security "short exempt" if the broker or dealer has a reasonable basis to believe that:

(1) The short sale order of a covered security is by a person that is deemed to own the covered security pursuant to Rule 200, provided that the person intends to deliver the security as soon as all restrictions on delivery have been removed.

(2) The short sale order of a covered security is by a market maker to offset customer odd-lot orders or to liquidate an odd–lot position that changes such broker's or dealer's position by no more than a unit of trading.

(3) The short sale order of a covered security is for a good faith account of a person who then owns another security by virtue of which he is, or presently will be, entitled to acquire an equivalent number of securities of the same class as the securities sold; provided such sale, or the purchase which such sale offsets, is effected for the bona fide purpose of profiting from a current difference between the price of the security sold and the security owned and that such right of acquisition was originally attached to or represented by another security or was issued to all the holders of any such securities of the issuer.

(4) The short sale order of a covered security is for a good faith account and submitted to profit from a current price difference between a security on a foreign securities market and a security on a securities market subject to the jurisdiction of the United States, provided that the short seller has an offer to buy on a foreign market that allows the seller to immediately cover the short sale at the time it was made. For the purposes of this paragraph (d)(4), a depository receipt of a security shall be deemed to be the same security as the security represented by such receipt.

(5)(i) The short sale order of a covered security is by an underwriter or member of a syndicate or group participating in the distribution of a security in connection with an over–allotment of securities; or

(ii) The short sale order of a covered security is for purposes of a lay-off sale by an underwriter or member of a syndicate or group in connection with a distribution of securities through a rights or standby underwriting commitment.

(6) The short sale order of a covered security is by a broker or dealer effecting the execution of a customer purchase or the execution of a cus-

tomer "long" sale on a riskless principal basis. In addition, for purposes of this paragraph (d)(6), a broker or dealer must have written policies and procedures in place to assure that, at a minimum:

(i) The customer order was received prior to the offsetting transaction;

(ii) The offsetting transaction is allocated to a riskless principal or customer account within 60 seconds of execution; and

(iii) The broker or dealer has supervisory systems in place to produce records that enable the broker or dealer to accurately and readily reconstruct, in a time-sequenced manner, all orders on which a broker or dealer relies pursuant to this exception.

(7) The short sale order is for the sale of a covered security at the volume weighted average price (VWAP) that meets the following criteria:

(i) The VWAP for the covered security is calculated by:

(A) Calculating the values for every regular way trade reported in the consolidated system for the security during the regular trading session, by multiplying each such price by the total number of shares traded at that price;

(B) Compiling an aggregate sum of all values; and

(C) Dividing the aggregate sum by the total number of reported shares for that day in the security.

(ii) The transactions are reported using a special VWAP trade modifier.

(iii) The VWAP matched security:

(A) Qualifies as an "actively-traded security" pursuant to Rule 101 and Rule 102; or

(B) The proposed short sale transaction is being conducted as part of a basket transaction of twenty or more securities in which the subject security does not comprise more than 5% of the value of the basket traded.

(iv) The transaction is not effected for the purpose of creating actual, or apparent, active trading in or otherwise affecting the price of any security.

(v) A broker or dealer shall be permitted to act as principal on the contra-side to fill customer short sale orders only if the broker's or dealer's position in the covered security, as committed by the broker or dealer during the pre-opening period of a trading day and aggregated across all of its customers who propose to sell short the same security on a VWAP basis, does not exceed 10% of the covered security's relevant average daily trading volume.

(e) No self-regulatory organization shall have any rule that is not in conformity with, or conflicts with, this section.

(f) Upon written application or upon its own motion, the Commission may grant an exemption from the provisions of this section, either unconditionally or on specified terms and conditions, to any person or class of persons, to any transaction or class of transactions, or to any security or class of securities to the extent that such exemption is necessary or appropriate, in the public interest, and is consistent with the protection of investors.

Rule 203. Borrowing and delivery requirements

(a) *Long Sales.* (1) If a broker or dealer knows or has reasonable grounds to believe that the sale of an equity security was or will be effected pursuant to an order marked "long," such broker or dealer shall not lend or arrange for the loan of any security for delivery to the purchaser's broker after the sale, or fail to deliver a security on the date delivery is due.

(2) The provisions of paragraph (a)(1) of this rule shall not apply:

(i) To the loan of any security by a broker or dealer through the medium of a loan to another broker or dealer;

(ii) If the broker or dealer knows, or has been reasonably informed by the seller, that the seller owns the security, and that the seller would deliver the security to the broker or dealer prior to the scheduled settlement of the transaction, but the seller failed to do so; or

(iii) If, prior to any loan or arrangement to loan any security for delivery, or failure to deliver, a national securities exchange, in the case of a sale effected thereon, or a national securities association, in the case of a sale not effected on an exchange, finds:

(A) That such sale resulted from a mistake made in good faith;

(B) That due diligence was used to ascertain that the circumstances specified in Rule 200(g) existed; and

(C) Either that the condition of the market at the time the mistake was discovered was such that undue hardship would result from covering the transaction by a "purchase for cash" or that the mistake was made by the seller's broker and the sale was at a permissible price under any applicable short sale price test.

(b) *Short Sales.* (1) A broker or dealer may not accept a short sale order in an equity security from another person, or effect a short sale in an equity security for its own account, unless the broker or dealer has:

(i) Borrowed the security, or entered into a bona-fide arrangement to borrow the security; or

(ii) Reasonable grounds to believe that the security can be borrowed so that it can be delivered on the date delivery is due; and

(iii) Documented compliance with this paragraph (b)(1).

(2) The provisions of paragraph (b)(1) of this rule shall not apply to:

(i) A broker or dealer that has accepted a short sale order from another registered broker or dealer that is required to comply with paragraph (b)(1) of this rule, unless the broker or dealer relying on this exception contractually undertook responsibility for compliance with paragraph (b)(1) of this rule;

(ii) Any sale of a security that a person is deemed to own pursuant to Rule 200, provided that the broker or dealer has been reasonably informed that the person intends to deliver such security as soon as all restrictions on delivery have been removed. If the person has not delivered such security within 35 days after the trade date, the broker-dealer that effected the sale must borrow securities or close out the short position by purchasing securities of like kind and quantity;

(iii) Short sales effected by a market maker in connection with bona-fide market making activities in the security for which this exception is claimed; and

(iv) Transactions in security futures.

(3) If a participant of a registered clearing agency has a fail to deliver position at a registered clearing agency in a threshold security for thirteen consecutive settlement days, the participant shall immediately thereafter close out the fail to deliver position by purchasing securities of like kind and quantity:

(i) *Provided, however,* that a participant of a registered clearing agency that has a fail to deliver position at a registered clearing agency in a threshold security on the effective date of this amendment and which, prior to the effective date of this amendment, had been previously grandfathered from the close-out requirement in this paragraph (b)(3) (*i.e.,* because the participant of a registered clearing agency had a fail to deliver position at a registered clearing agency on the settlement day preceding the day that the security became a threshold security), shall close out that fail to deliver position within thirty-five consecutive settlement days of the effective date of this amendment by purchasing securities of like kind and quantity;

(ii) *Provided, however,* that if a participant of a registered clearing agency has a fail to deliver position at a registered clearing agency in a threshold security that was sold pursuant to Rule 144 under the Securities Act of 1933 for thirty-five consecutive settlement days, the participant shall immediately thereafter close out the fail to deliver position in the security by purchasing securities of like kind and quantity;

(iii) *Provided, however,* that a participant of a registered clearing agency that has a fail to deliver position at a registered clearing agency in a threshold security on the effective date of this amendment and which, prior to the effective date of this amendment, had been previously excepted from the close-out requirement in paragraph (b)(3) of this rule (*i.e.,* because the participant of a registered clearing agency had a fail to deliver position in the threshold security that is attributed to short sales effected by a registered options market maker to establish or maintain a hedge on options positions that were created before the security became a threshold security), shall immediately close out that fail to deliver position, including any adjustments to the fail to deliver position, within 35 consecutive settlement days of the effective date of this amendment by purchasing securities of like kind and quantity;

(iv) If a participant of a registered clearing agency has a fail to deliver position at a registered clearing agency in a threshold security for thirteen consecutive settlement days, the participant and any broker or dealer for which it clears transactions, including any market maker that would otherwise be entitled to rely on the exception provided in paragraph (b)(2)(iii) of this rule, may not accept a short sale order in the threshold security from another person, or effect a short sale in the threshold security for its own account, without borrowing the security or entering into a bona-fide arrangement to borrow the security, until the participant closes out the fail to deliver position by purchasing securities of like kind and quantity;

(v) If a participant of a registered clearing agency entitled to rely on the 35 consecutive settlement day close-out requirement contained in paragraph (b)(3)(i), (b)(3)(ii), or (b)(3)(iii) of this rule has a fail to deliver position at a registered clearing agency in the threshold security for 35 consecutive settlement days, the participant and any broker or dealer for which it clears transactions, including any market maker, that would otherwise be entitled to rely on the exception provided in paragraph (b)(2)(ii) of this rule, may not accept a short sale order in the threshold security from another person, or effect a short sale in the threshold security for its own account, without borrowing the security or entering into a bona-fide arrangement to borrow the security, until the participant closes out the fail to deliver position by purchasing securities of like kind and quantity;

(vi) If a participant of a registered clearing agency reasonably allocates a portion of a fail to deliver position to another registered broker or dealer for which it clears trades or for which it is responsible for settlement, based on such broker or dealer's short position, then the provisions of this paragraph (b)(3) relating to such fail to deliver position shall apply to the portion of such registered broker or dealer that was allocated the fail to deliver position, and not to the participant; and

(vii) A participant of a registered clearing agency shall not be deemed to have fulfilled the requirements of this paragraph (b)(3) where the participant enters into an arrangement with another person to purchase securities as required by this paragraph (b)(3), and the participant knows or has reason to know that the other person will not deliver securities in settlement of the purchase.

(c) *Definitions.* (1) For purposes of this rule, the term *market maker* has the same meaning as in section 3(a)(38) of the Securities Exchange Act of 1934.

(2) For purposes of this rule, the term *participant* has the same meaning as in section 3(a)(24) of the Exchange Act.

(3) For purposes of this rule, the term *registered clearing agency* means a clearing agency, as defined in section 3(a)(23)(A) of the Exchange Act (15 U.S.C. 78c(a)(23)(A)), that is registered with the Commission pursuant to section 17A of the Exchange Act.

(4) For purposes of this rule, the term *security future* has the same meaning as in section 3(a)(55) of the Exchange Act.

(5) For purposes of this rule, the term *settlement day* means any business day on which deliveries of securities and payments of money may be made through the facilities of a registered clearing agency.

(6) For purposes of this rule, the term *threshold security* means any equity security of an issuer that is registered pursuant to section 12 of the Exchange Act or for which the issuer is required to file reports pursuant to section 15(d) of the Exchange Act:

(i) For which there is an aggregate fail to deliver position for five consecutive settlement days at a registered clearing agency of 10,000 shares or more, and that is equal to at least 0.5% of the issue's total shares outstanding;

(ii) Is included on a list disseminated to its members by a self-regulatory organization; and

(iii) *Provided, however,* that a security shall cease to be a threshold security if the aggregate fail to deliver position at a registered clearing agency does not exceed the level specified in paragraph (c)(6)(i) of this rule for five consecutive settlement days.

(d) *Exemptive Authority.* Upon written application or upon its own motion, the Commission may grant an exemption from the provisions of this rule, either unconditionally or on specified terms and conditions, to any transaction or class of transactions, or to any security or class of securities, or to any person or class of persons.

Rule 204. Close–out requirement

(a) A participant of a registered clearing agency must deliver securities to a registered clearing agency for clearance and settlement on a long or short sale in any equity security by settlement date, or if a participant of a registered clearing agency has a fail to deliver position at a registered clearing agency in any equity security for a long or short sale transaction in that equity security, the participant shall, by no later than the beginning of regular trading hours on the settlement day following the settlement date, immediately close out its fail to deliver position by borrowing or purchasing securities of like kind and quantity; *Provided, however*:

(1) If a participant of a registered clearing agency has a fail to deliver position at a registered clearing agency in any equity security and the participant can demonstrate on its books and records that such fail to deliver position resulted from a long sale, the participant shall by no later than the beginning of regular trading hours on the third consecutive settlement day following the settlement date, immediately close out the fail to deliver position by purchasing or borrowing securities of like kind and quantity;

(2) If a participant of a registered clearing agency has a fail to deliver position at a registered clearing agency in any equity security resulting from a sale of a security that a person is deemed to own pursuant to Rule 200 and that such person intends to deliver as soon as all restrictions on delivery have been removed, the participant shall, by no later than the beginning of regular trading hours on the thirty-fifth consecutive calendar day following the trade date for the transaction, immediately close out the fail to deliver position by purchasing securities of like kind and quantity; or

(3) If a participant of a registered clearing agency has a fail to deliver position at a registered clearing agency in any equity security that is attributable to bona fide market making activities by a registered market maker, options market maker, or other market maker obligated to quote in the over-the-counter market, the participant shall by no later than the beginning of regular trading hours on the third consecutive settlement day following the settlement date, immediately close out the fail to deliver position by purchasing or borrowing securities of like kind and quantity.

(b) If a participant of a registered clearing agency has a fail to deliver position in any equity security at a registered clearing agency and does not close out such fail to deliver position in accordance with the requirements of paragraph (a) of this section, the participant and any broker or dealer from which it receives trades for clearance and settlement, including any market maker that would otherwise be entitled to rely on the exception provided in Rule 203(b)(2)(iii), may not accept a short sale order in the equity security from another person, or effect a short sale in the equity security for its own account, to the extent that the broker or dealer submits its short sales to that participant for clearance and settlement, without first borrowing the security, or entering into a bona fide arrangement to borrow the security, until the participant closes out the fail to deliver position by purchasing securities of like kind and quantity and that purchase has cleared and settled at a registered clearing agency; *Provided, however*: A broker or dealer shall not be subject to the requirements of this paragraph if the broker or dealer timely certifies to the participant of a registered clearing agency that it has not incurred a fail to deliver position on settlement date for a long or short sale in an equity security for which the participant has a fail to deliver position at a registered clearing agency or that the broker or dealer is in compliance with paragraph (e) of this section.

(c) The participant must notify any broker or dealer from which it receives trades for clearance and settlement, including any market maker that would otherwise be entitled to rely on the exception provided in Rule 203(b)(2)(iii):

(1) That the participant has a fail to deliver position in an equity security at a registered clearing agency that has not been closed out in accordance with the requirements of paragraph (a) of this section; and

(2) When the purchase that the participant has made to close out the fail to deliver position has cleared and settled at a registered clearing agency.

(d) If a participant of a registered clearing agency reasonably allocates a portion of a fail to deliver position to another registered broker or dealer for which it clears trades or from which it receives trades for settlement, based on such broker's or dealer's short position, the provisions of paragraphs (a) and (b) of this section relating to such fail to deliver position shall apply to such registered broker or dealer that was allocated the fail to deliver position, and not to the participant. A broker or dealer that has been allocated a portion of a fail to deliver position that does not comply with the provisions of paragraph (a) of this section must immediately notify the participant that it has become subject to the requirements of paragraph (b) of this section.

(e) Even if a participant of a registered clearing agency has not closed out a fail to deliver position at a registered clearing agency in accordance with paragraph (a) of this section, or has not allocated a fail to deliver position to a broker or dealer in accordance with paragraph (d) of this section, a broker or dealer shall not be subject to the requirements of paragraph (a) or (b) of this section if the broker or dealer purchases or borrows the securities, and if:

(1) The purchase or borrow is bona fide;

(2) The purchase or borrow is executed after trade date but by no later than the end of regular trading hours on settlement date for the transaction;

(3) The purchase or borrow is of a quantity of securities sufficient to cover the entire amount of that broker's or dealer's fail to deliver position at a registered clearing agency in that security; and

(4) The broker or dealer can demonstrate that it has a net flat or net long position on its books and records on the day of the purchase or borrow.

(f) A participant of a registered clearing agency shall not be deemed to have fulfilled the requirements of this section where the participant enters into an arrangement with another person to purchase or borrow securities as required by this section, and the participant knows or has reason to know that the other person will not deliver securities in settlement of the purchase or borrow.

(g) *Definitions*. (1) For purposes of this section, the term *settlement date* shall mean the business day on which delivery of a security and payment of money is to be made through the facilities of a registered clearing agency in connection with the sale of a security.

(2) For purposes of this section, the term *regular trading hours* has the same meaning as in Rule 600(b)(64) of Regulation NMS.

REGULATION ATS—ALTERNATIVE TRADING SYSTEMS

(Cite as 17 CFR § 242.___)

PRELIMINARY NOTES

1. An alternative trading system is required to comply with the requirements in this Regulation ATS, unless such alternative trading system:

(a) Is registered as a national securities exchange;

(b) Is exempt from registration as a national securities exchange based on the limited volume of transactions effected on the alternative trading system; or

(c) Trades only government securities and certain other related instruments.

All alternative trading systems must comply with the antifraud, antimanipulation, and other applicable provisions of the federal securities laws.

2. The requirements imposed upon an alternative trading system by Regulation ATS are in addition to any requirements applicable to broker-dealers registered under section 15 of the Act.

3. An alternative trading system must comply with any applicable state law relating to the offer or sale of securities or the registration or regulation of persons or entities effecting transactions in securities.

4. The disclosures made pursuant to the provisions of this rule are in addition to any other disclosure requirements under the federal securities laws.

Rule 300. Definitions

For purposes of this rule, the following definitions shall apply:

(a) *Alternative trading system* means any organization, association, person, group of persons, or system:

(1) That constitutes, maintains, or provides a market place or facilities for bringing together purchasers and sellers of securities or for otherwise performing with respect to securities the functions commonly performed by a stock exchange within the meaning of Rule 3b–16; and

(2) That does not:

(i) Set rules governing the conduct of subscribers other than the conduct of such subscribers' trading on such organization, association, person, group of persons, or system; or

(ii) Discipline subscribers other than by exclusion from trading.

(b) *Subscriber* means any person that has entered into a contractual agreement with an alternative trading system to access such alternative trading system for the purpose of effecting transactions in securities or submitting, disseminating, or displaying orders on such alternative trading system, including a customer, member, user, or participant in an alternative trading system. A subscriber, however, shall not include a national securities exchange or national securities association.

(c) *Affiliate of a Subscriber* means any person that, directly or indirectly, controls, is under common control with, or is controlled by, the subscriber, including any employee.

(d) *Debt security* shall mean any security other than an equity security, as defined in Rule 3a11–1 under the Securities Exchange Act of 1934, as well as non-participatory preferred stock.

(e) *Order* means any firm indication of a willingness to buy or sell a security, as either principal or agent, including any bid or offer quotation, market order, limit order, or other priced order.

(f) *Control* means the power, directly or indirectly, to direct the management or policies of the broker-dealer of an alternative trading system, whether through ownership of securities, by contract, or otherwise. A person is presumed to control the broker-dealer of an alternative trading system, if that person:

(1) Is a director, general partner, or officer exercising executive responsibility (or having similar status or performing similar functions);

(2) Directly or indirectly has the right to vote 25 percent or more of a class of voting security or has the power to sell or direct the sale of 25 percent or more of a class of voting securities of the broker-dealer of the alternative trading system; or

(3) In the case of a partnership, has contributed, or has the right to receive upon dissolution, 25 percent or more of the capital of the broker-dealer of the alternative trading system.

(g) *NMS stock* shall have the meaning provided in Rule 600 of Regulation NMS; *provided, however,* that a debt or convertible debt security shall not be deemed an NMS stock for purposes of this Regulation ATS.

(h) *Effective transaction reporting plan* shall have the meaning provided in Rule 600 of Regulation NMS.

(i) *Corporate Debt Security* shall mean any security that:

(1) Evidences a liability of the issuer of such security;

(2) Has a fixed maturity date that is at least one year following the date of issuance; and

(3) Is not an exempted security, as defined in section 3(a)(12) of the Act.

(j) *Commercial Paper* shall mean any note, draft, or bill of exchange which arises out of a current transaction or the proceeds of which have been or are to be used for current trans-actions, and which has a maturity at the time of issuance of not exceeding nine months, exclusive of days of grace, or any renewal thereof the maturity of which is likewise limited.

(k) *NMS Stock ATS* means an alternative trading system, as defined in paragraph (a) of this section, that trades NMS stocks, as defined in paragraph (g) of this section.

Rule 301. Requirements for alternative trading systems

(a) *Scope of Rule.* An alternative trading system shall comply with the requirements in paragraph (b) of this rule, unless such alternative trading system:

(1) Is registered as an exchange under section 6 of the Act;

(2) Is exempted by the Commission from registration as an exchange based on the limited volume of transactions effected;

(3) Is operated by a national securities association;

(4)(i) Is registered as a broker-dealer under sections 15(b) or 15C of the Act, and 78o–5), or is a bank, and

(ii) Limits its securities activities to the following instruments:

(A) Government securities, as defined in section 3(a)(42) of the Act;

(B) Repurchase and reverse repurchase agreements solely involving securities included within paragraph (a)(4)(ii)(A) of this rule;

(C) Any put, call, straddle, option, or privilege on a government security, other than a put, call, straddle, option, or privilege that:

(*1*) Is traded on one or more national securities exchanges; or

(*2*) For which quotations are disseminated through an automated quotation system operated by a registered securities association; and

(D) Commercial paper.

(5) Is exempted, conditionally or unconditionally, by Commission order, after application by such alternative trading system, from one or more of the requirements of paragraph (b) of this rule or Rule 304. The Commission will grant such exemption only after determining that such an order is consistent with the public interest, the protection of investors, and the removal of impediments to, and perfection of the mechanisms of, a national market system.

(b) *Requirements.* Every alternative trading system subject to this Regulation ATS, pursuant to paragraph (a) of this rule, shall comply with the requirements in this paragraph (b).

(1) *Broker-Dealer Registration.* The alternative trading system shall register as a broker-dealer under section 15 of the Act.

(2) *Notice.* (i) The alternative trading system shall file an initial operation report on Form ATS, 17 CFR 249.637, in accordance with the instructions therein, at least 20 days prior to commencing operation as an alternative trading system.

(ii) The alternative trading system shall file an amendment on Form ATS at least 20 calendar days prior to implementing a material change to the operation of the alternative trading system.

(iii) If any information contained in the initial operation report filed under paragraph (b)(2)(i) of this rule becomes inaccurate for any reason and has not been previously reported to the Commission as an amendment on Form ATS, the alternative trading system shall file an amendment on Form ATS correcting such information within 30 calendar days after the end of each calendar quarter in which the alternative trading system has operated.

(iv) The alternative trading system shall promptly file an amendment on Form ATS correcting information previously reported on Form ATS after discovery that any information filed under paragraphs (b)(2)(i), (ii) or (iii) of this rule was inaccurate when filed.

(v) The alternative trading system shall promptly file a cessation of operations report on Form ATS in accordance with the instructions therein upon ceasing to operate as an alternative trading system.

(vi) Every notice or amendment filed pursuant to this paragraph (b)(2) shall constitute a "report" within the meaning of sections 11A, 17(a), 18(a), and 32(a), and any other applicable provisions of the Act.

(vii) The reports provided for in paragraph (b)(2) of this rule shall be considered filed upon receipt by the Division of Trading and Markets, at the Commission's principal office in Washington, DC. Duplicate originals of the reports provided for in paragraphs (b)(2)(i) through (v) of this rule must be filed with surveillance personnel designated as such by any self-regulatory organization that is the designated examining authority for the alternative trading system pursuant to Rule 17d–1 simultaneously with filing with the Commission. Duplicates of the reports required by paragraph (b)(9) of this rule shall be provided to surveillance personnel of such self-regulatory authority upon request. All reports filed pursuant to this paragraph (b)(2) and paragraph (b)(9) of this rule shall be deemed confidential when filed.

(viii) An NMS Stock ATS that is operating pursuant to an initial operation report on Form ATS on file with the Commission as of January 7, 2019 ("Legacy NMS Stock ATS") shall be subject to the requirements of paragraphs (b)(2)(i) through (vii) of this section until that ATS files an initial Form ATS–N with the Commission pursuant to paragraph (a)(1)(iv)(A) of Rule 304. Thereafter, the Legacy NMS Stock ATS shall file reports pursuant to Rule 304. An alternative trading system that trades NMS stocks and securities other than NMS stocks shall be subject to the requirements of 17 CFR 242.304 with respect to NMS stocks and paragraph (b)(2) of this section with respect to non-NMS stocks. As of January 7, 2019, an entity seeking to operate as an NMS Stock ATS shall not be subject to the requirements of paragraphs (b)(2)(i) through (vii) of this section and shall file reports pursuant to Rule 304.

(3) *Order Display and Execution Access.* (i) An alternative trading system shall comply with the requirements set forth in paragraph (b)(3)(ii) of this rule, with respect to any NMS stock in which the alternative trading system:

(A) Displays subscriber orders to any person (other than alternative trading system employees); and

(B) During at least 4 of the preceding 6 calendar months, had an average daily trading volume of 5 percent or more of the aggregate average daily share volume for such NMS stock as reported by an effective transaction reporting plan.

(ii) Such alternative trading system shall provide to a national securities exchange or national securities association the prices and sizes of the orders at the highest buy price and the lowest sell price for such NMS stock, displayed to more than one person in the alternative trading system, for inclusion in the quotation data made available by the national securities exchange or national securities association to vendors pursuant to Rule 602.

(iii) With respect to any order displayed pursuant to paragraph (b)(3)(ii) of this rule, an alternative trading system shall provide to any broker-dealer that has access to the national securities exchange or national securities association to which the alternative trading system provides the prices and sizes of displayed orders pursuant to paragraph (b)(3)(ii) of this rule, the ability to effect a transaction with such orders that is:

(A) Equivalent to the ability of such broker-dealer to effect a transaction with other orders displayed on the exchange or by the association; and

(B) At the price of the highest priced buy order or lowest priced sell order displayed for the lesser of the cumulative size of such priced orders entered therein at such price, or the size of the execution sought by such broker-dealer

(4) *Fees.* The alternative trading system shall not charge any fee to broker-dealers that access the alternative trading system through a national securities exchange or national securities association, that is inconsistent with equivalent access to the alternative trading system required by paragraph (b)(3)(iii) of this rule. In addition, if the national securities exchange or national securities association to which an alternative trading system provides the prices and sizes of orders under paragraphs (b)(3)(ii) and (b)(3)(iii) of this rule establishes rules designed to assure consistency with standards for access to quotations dis-

played on such national securities exchange, or the market operated by such national securities association, the alternative trading system shall not charge any fee to members that is contrary to, that is not disclosed in the manner required by, or that is inconsistent with any standard of equivalent access established by such rules.

(5) *Fair Access.* (i) An alternative trading system shall comply with the requirements in paragraph (b)(5)(ii) of this rule, if during at least 4 of the preceding 6 calendar months, such alternative trading system had:

(A) With respect to any NMS stock, 5 percent or more of the average daily volume in that security reported by an effective transaction reporting plan;

(B) With respect to an equity security that is not an NMS stock and for which transactions are reported to a self-regulatory organization, 5 percent or more of the average daily trading volume in that security as calculated by the self-regulatory organization to which such transactions are reported;

(C) With respect to municipal securities, 5 percent or more of the average daily volume traded in the United States; or

(D) With respect to corporate debt securities, 5 percent or more of the average daily volume traded in the United States.

(ii) An alternative trading system shall:

(A) Establish written standards for granting access to trading on its system;

(B) Not unreasonably prohibit or limit any person in respect to access to services offered by such alternative trading system by applying the standards established under paragraph (b)(5)(ii)(A) of this rule in an unfair or discriminatory manner;

(C) Make and keep records of:

(1) All grants of access including, for all subscribers, the reasons for granting such access; and

(2) All denials or limitations of access and reasons, for each applicant, for denying or limiting access; and

(D) Report the information required on Form ATS–R (17 CFR 249.638) regarding grants, denials, and limitations of access.

(iii) Notwithstanding paragraph (b)(5)(i) of this rule, an alternative trading system shall not be required to comply with the requirements in paragraph (b)(5)(ii) of this rule, if such alternative trading system:

(A) Matches customer orders for a security with other customer orders;

(B) Such customers' orders are not displayed to any person, other than employees of the alternative trading system; and

(C) Such orders are executed at a price for such security disseminated by an effective transaction reporting plan, or derived from such prices.

(6) *Capacity, Integrity, and Security of Automated Systems.* (i) The alternative trading system shall comply with the requirements in paragraph (b)(6)(ii) of this rule, if during at least 4 of the preceding 6 calendar months, such alternative trading system had:

(A) With respect to municipal securities, 20 percent or more of the average daily volume traded in the United States; or

(B) With respect to corporate debt securities, 20 percent or more of the average daily volume traded in the United States.

(ii) With respect to those systems that support order entry, order routing, order execution, transaction reporting, and trade comparison, the alternative trading system shall:

(A) Establish reasonable current and future capacity estimates;

(B) Conduct periodic capacity stress tests of critical systems to determine such system's ability to process transactions in an accurate, timely, and efficient manner;

(C) Develop and implement reasonable procedures to review and keep current its system development and testing methodology;

(D) Review the vulnerability of its systems and data center computer operations to internal and external threats, physical hazards, and natural disasters;

(E) Establish adequate contingency and disaster recovery plans;

(F) On an annual basis, perform an independent review, in accordance with established audit procedures and standards, of such alternative trading system's controls for ensuring that paragraphs (b)(6)(ii)(A) through (E) of this rule are met, and conduct a review by senior management of a report containing the recommendations and conclusions of the independent review; and

(G) Promptly notify the Commission staff of material systems outages and significant systems changes.

(iii) Notwithstanding paragraph (b)(6)(i) of this rule, an alternative trading system shall not be required to comply with the requirements in paragraph (b)(6)(ii) of this rule, if such alternative trading system:

(A) Matches customer orders for a security with other customer orders;

(B) Such customers' orders are not displayed to any person, other than employees of the alternative trading system; and

(C) Such orders are executed at a price for such security disseminated by an effective transaction reporting plan, or derived from such prices.

(7) *Examinations, Inspections, and Investigations.* The alternative trading system shall permit the examination and inspection of its premises, systems, and records, and cooperate with the examination, inspection, or investigation of subscribers, whether such examination is being conducted by the Commission or by a self-regulatory organization of which such subscriber is a member.

(8) *Recordkeeping.* The alternative trading system shall:

(i) Make and keep current the records specified in Rule 302; and

(ii) Preserve the records specified in Rule 303.

(9) *Reporting.* The alternative trading system shall:

(i) Separately file the information required by Form ATS–R (17 CFR 249.638) for transactions in NMS stocks, as defined in paragraph (g) of this section, and transactions in securities other than NMS stocks within 30 calendar days after the end of each calendar quarter in which the market has operated after the effective date of this rule; and

(ii) Separately file the information required by Form ATS–R for transactions in NMS stocks and transactions in securities other than NMS stocks within 10 calendar days after an alternative trading system ceases to operate.

(10) *Written procedures to Ensure the Confidential Treatment of Trading Information.* (i) The alternative trading system shall establish adequate written safeguards and written procedures to protect subscribers' confidential trading information. Such written safeguards and written procedures shall include:

(A) Limiting access to the confidential trading information of subscribers to those employees of the alternative trading system who are operating the system or responsible for its compliance with these or any other applicable rules;

(B) Implementing standards controlling employees of the alternative trading system trading for their own accounts; and

(ii) The alternative trading system shall adopt and implement adequate written oversight procedures to ensure that the written safeguards and procedures established pursuant to paragraph (b)(10)(i) of this rule are followed.

(11) *Name.* The alternative trading system shall not use in its name the word "exchange," or derivations of the word "exchange," such as the term "stock market."

Rule 302. Recordkeeping requirements for alternative trading systems

To comply with the condition set forth in paragraph (b)(8) of Rule 301, an alternative trading system shall make and keep current the following records:

(a) A record of subscribers to such alternative trading system (identifying any affiliations between the alternative trading system and subscribers to the alternative trading system, including common directors, officers, or owners);

(b) Daily summaries of trading in the alternative trading system including:

(1) Securities for which transactions have been executed;

(2) Transaction volume, expressed with respect to equity securities in:

(i) Number of trades;

(ii) Number of shares traded; and

(iii) Total settlement value in terms of U.S. dollars; and

(3) Transaction volume, expressed with respect to debt securities in:

(i) Number of trades; and

(ii) Total U.S. dollar value; and

(c) Time-sequenced records of order information in the alternative trading system, including:

(1) Date and time (expressed in terms of hours, minutes, and seconds) that the order was received;

(2) Identity of the security;

(3) The number of shares, or principal amount of bonds, to which the order applies;

(4) An identification of the order as related to a program trade or an index arbitrage trade as defined in New York Stock Exchange Rule 80A;

(5) The designation of the order as a buy or sell order;

(6) The designation of the order as a short sale order;

(7) The designation of the order as a market order, limit order, stop order, stop limit order, or other type or order;

(8) Any limit or stop price prescribed by the order;

(9) The date on which the order expires and, if the time in force is less than one day, the time when the order expires;

(10) The time limit during which the order is in force;

(11) Any instructions to modify or cancel the order;

(12) The type of account, *i.e.*, retail, wholesale, employee, proprietary, or any other type of account designated by the alternative trading system, for which the order is submitted;

(13) Date and time (expressed in terms of hours, minutes, and seconds) that the order was executed;

(14) Price at which the order was executed;

(15) Size of the order executed (expressed in number of shares or units or principal amount); and

(16) Identity of the parties to the transaction.

Rule 303. Record preservation requirements for alternative trading systems

(a) To comply with the condition set forth in paragraph (b)(8) of Rule 301, an alternative trading system shall preserve the following records:

(1) For a period of not less than three years, the first two years in an easily accessible place, an alternative trading system shall preserve:

(i) All records required to be made pursuant to Rule 302;

(ii) All notices provided by such alternative trading system to subscribers generally, whether written or communicated through automated means, including, but not limited to, notices addressing hours of system operations, system malfunctions, changes to system procedures, maintenance of hardware and software, instructions pertaining to access to the market and denials of, or limitations on, access to the alternative trading system;

(iii) If subject to paragraph (b)(5)(ii) of Rule 301, at least one copy of such alternative trading system's standards for access to trading, all documents relevant to the alternative trading systems decision to grant, deny, or limit access to any person, and all other documents made or received by the alternative trading system in the course of complying with paragraph (b)(5) of Rule 301; and

(iv) At least one copy of all documents made or received by the alternative trading system in the course of complying with paragraph (b)(6) of Rule 301, including all correspondence, memoranda, papers, books, notices, accounts, reports, test scripts, test results, and other similar records.

(v) At least one copy of the written safeguards and written procedures to protect subscribers' confidential trading information and the written oversight procedures created in the course of complying with paragraph (b)(10) of Rule 301.

(2) During the life of the enterprise and of any successor enterprise, an alternative trading system shall preserve:

(i) All partnership articles or, in the case of a corporation, all articles of incorporation or charter, minute books and stock certificate books; and

(ii) Copies of reports filed pursuant to paragraph (b)(2) of Rule 301 or Rule 304 and records made pursuant to paragraph (b)(5) of Rule 301.

(b) The records required to be maintained and preserved pursuant to paragraph (a) of this rule must be produced, reproduced, and maintained in paper form or in any of the forms permitted under Rule 17a–4(f).

(c) Alternative trading systems must comply with any other applicable recordkeeping or reporting requirement in the Act, and the rules and regulations thereunder. If the information in a record required to be made pursuant to this section is preserved in a record made pursuant to Rule 17a–3 or Rule 17a–4, or otherwise preserved by the alternative trading system (whether in summary or some other form), this rule shall not require the sponsor to maintain such information in a separate file, provided that the sponsor can promptly sort and retrieve the information as if it had been kept in a separate file as a record made pursuant to this section, and preserves the information in accordance with the time periods specified in paragraph (a) of this rule.

(d) The records required to be maintained and preserved pursuant to this section may be prepared or maintained by a service bureau, depository, or other recordkeeping service on behalf of the alternative trading system. An agreement with a service bureau, depository, or other recordkeeping service shall not relieve the alternative trading system from the responsibility to prepare and maintain records as specified in this section. The service bureau, depository, or other recordkeeping service shall file with the Commission a written undertaking in a form acceptable to the Commission, signed by a duly authorized person, to the effect that such records are the property of the alternative trading system required to be maintained and preserved and will be surrendered promptly on request of the alternative trading system, and shall include the following provision: With respect to any books and records maintained or preserved on behalf of (name of alternative trading system), the undersigned hereby undertakes to permit examination of such books and records at any time, or from time to time, during business hours by the staff of the Securities and Exchange Commission, any self-regulatory organization of which the alternative trading system is a member, or any State securities regulator having jurisdiction over the alternative trading system, and to promptly furnish to the Commission, self-regulatory organization of which the alternative trading system is a member, or any State securities regulator having jurisdiction over the alternative trading system a true, correct, complete and current hard copy of any, all, or any part of, such books and records.

(e) Every alternative trading system shall furnish to any representative of the Commission promptly upon request, legible, true, and complete copies of those records that are required to be preserved under this rule.

Rule 304. NMS Stock ATSs

(a) *Conditions to the exemption.* Unless not required to comply with Regulation ATS pursuant to paragraph (a) of Rule 301, an NMS Stock ATS must comply with Rule 300 through Rule 304 (except paragraph (b)(2)(i) through (vii) of Rule 301) to be exempt pursuant to paragraph (a)(2) of Rule3a1–1.

(1) *Initial Form ATS–N.* (i) *Filing and effectiveness requirement.* No exemption is available to an NMS Stock ATS pursuant to paragraph (a)(2) of Rule 3a1–1unless the NMS Stock ATS files with the Commission an initial Form ATS–N, in accordance with the conditions of this section, and the initial Form ATS–N is effective pursuant to paragraph (a)(1)(iii) or (a)(1)(iv)(A) of this section.

(ii) *Commission review period.* (A) The Commission may, by order, as provided in paragraph (a)(1)(iii) of this section, declare an initial Form ATS–N filed by an NMS Stock ATS ineffective no later than 120 calendar days from the date of filing with the Commission, or, if applicable, the end of the extended review period. The Commission may extend the initial Form ATS–N review period for:

(*1*) An additional 90 calendar days, if the Form ATS–N is unusually lengthy or raises novel or complex issues that require additional time for review, in which case the Commission will notify the NMS Stock ATS in writing within the initial 120-calendar day review period and will briefly describe the reason for the determination for which additional time for review is required; or

(*2*) Any extended review period to which a duly authorized representative of the NMS Stock ATS agrees in writing.

(B) During review by the Commission of the initial Form ATS-N, the NMS Stock ATS shall amend its initial Form ATS–N pursuant to the requirements of paragraphs (a)(2)(i)(B) and (C) of this section. To make material changes to its initial Form ATS–N during the Commission review period, the NMS Stock

ATS shall withdraw its filed initial Form ATS–N and may refile an initial Form ATS–N pursuant to paragraph (a)(1) of this section.

(iii) *Effectiveness; Ineffectiveness determination.* (A) An initial Form ATS–N, as amended, filed by an NMS Stock ATS will become effective, unless declared ineffective, upon the earlier of:

(*1*) The completion of review by the Commission and publication pursuant to paragraph (b)(2)(i) of this section; or

(*2*) The expiration of the review period, or, if applicable, the end of the extended review period, pursuant to paragraph (a)(1)(ii) of this section.

(B) The Commission will, by order, declare an initial Form ATS–N ineffective if it finds, after notice and opportunity for hearing, that such action is necessary or appropriate in the public interest, and is consistent with the protection of investors. If the Commission declares an initial Form ATS–N ineffective, the NMS Stock ATS shall be prohibited from operating as an NMS Stock ATS pursuant to paragraph (a)(2) of Rule 3a1–1. An initial Form ATS–N declared ineffective does not prevent the NMS Stock ATS from subsequently filing a new Form ATS–N.

(iv) *Transition for Legacy NMS Stock ATSs. (A) Initial Form ATS–N filing requirements.* A Legacy NMS Stock ATS shall file with the Commission an initial Form ATS–N, in accordance with the conditions of this section, no earlier than January 7, 2019, and no later than February 8, 2019. An initial Form ATS–N filed by a Legacy NMS Stock ATS shall supersede and replace for purposes of the exemption the previously filed Form ATS of the Legacy NMS Stock ATS. The Legacy NMS Stock ATS may operate, on a provisional basis, pursuant to the filed initial Form ATS–N, and any amendments thereto, during the review of the initial Form ATS–N by the Commission. An initial Form ATS–N filed by a Legacy NMS Stock ATS, as amended, will become effective, unless declared ineffective, upon the earlier of:

(*1*) The completion of review by the Commission and publication pursuant to paragraph (b)(2)(i) of this section; or

(*2*) The expiration of the review period, or, if applicable, the end of the extended review period, pursuant to paragraph (a)(1)(iv)(B) of this section.

(B) *Commission review period; Ineffectiveness determination.* The Commission may, by order, as provided in paragraph (a)(1)(iii) of this section, declare an initial Form ATS–N filed by a Legacy NMS Stock ATS ineffective no later than 120 calendar days from the date of filing with the Commission, or, if applicable, the end of the extended review period. The Commission may extend the initial Form ATS–N review period for a Legacy NMS Stock ATS for:

(*1*) An additional 120 calendar days if the initial Form ATS–N is unusually lengthy or raises novel or complex issues that require additional time for review, in which case the Commission will notify the Legacy NMS Stock ATS in writing within the initial 120-calendar day review period and will briefly describe the reason for the determination for which additional time for review is required; or

(*2*) Any extended review period to which a duly-authorized representative of the Legacy NMS Stock ATS agrees in writing.

(C) *Amendments to initial Form ATS–N.* During review by the Commission of the initial Form ATS–N filed by a Legacy NMS Stock ATS, the Legacy NMS Stock ATS shall amend its initial Form ATS–N pursuant to the requirements of paragraphs (a)(2)(i)(A) through (D) of this section.

(2) *Form ATS–N amendment.* (i) Filing requirements. An NMS Stock ATS shall amend a Form ATS–N, in accordance with the conditions of this section:

(A) At least 30 calendar days, except as provided by paragraph (a)(2)(i)(D) of this section, prior to the date of implementation of a material change to the operations of the NMS Stock ATS or to the activities of the broker-dealer operator or its affiliates that are subject to disclosure on Form ATS–N ("Material Amendment");

(B) No later than 30 calendar days after the end of each calendar quarter to correct information that has become inaccurate or incomplete for any reason and was not required to be reported to the Commission as a Form ATS–N amendment pursuant to paragraphs (a)(2)(i)(A), (C), or (D) of this section ("Updating Amendment");

(C) Promptly, to correct information in any previous disclosure on Form ATS–N, after discovery that any information previously filed on Form ATS–N was materially inaccurate or incomplete when filed ("Correcting Amendment"); or

(D) No later than seven calendar days after information required to be disclosed in Part III, Items 24 and 25 on Form ATS–N has become inaccurate or incomplete ("Order Display and Fair Access Amendment").

(ii) *Commission review period; Ineffectiveness determination*. The Commission will, by order, declare ineffective any Form ATS–N amendment filed pursuant to paragraphs (a)(2)(i)(A) through (D) of this section, no later than 30 calendar days from filing with the Commission, if the Commission finds that such action is necessary or appropriate in the public interest, and is consistent with the protection of investors. A Form ATS–N amendment declared ineffective shall prohibit the NMS Stock ATS from operating pursuant to the ineffective Form ATS–N amendment. A Form ATS–N amendment declared ineffective does not prevent the NMS Stock ATS from subsequently filing a new Form ATS–N amendment. During review by the Commission of a Material Amendment, the NMS Stock ATS shall amend the Material Amendment pursuant to the requirements of paragraphs (a)(2)(i)(B) through (C) of this section. To make material changes to a filed Material Amendment during the Commission review period, an NMS Stock ATS shall withdraw its filed Material Amendment and must file the new Material Amendment pursuant to (a)(2)(i)(A) of this section.

(3) *Notice of cessation*. An NMS Stock ATS shall notice its cessation of operations on Form ATS–N at least 10 business days prior to the date the NMS Stock ATS will cease to operate as an NMS Stock ATS. The notice of cessation shall cause the Form ATS–N to become ineffective on the date designated by the NMS Stock ATS.

(4) *Suspension, limitation, and revocation of the exemption from the definition of exchange*. (i) The Commission will, by order, if it finds, after notice and opportunity for hearing, that such action is necessary or appropriate in the public interest, and is consistent with the protection of investors, suspend for a period not exceeding twelve months, limit, or revoke the exemption for an NMS Stock ATS pursuant to paragraph (a)(2) of 17 CFR 240.3a1–1.

(ii) If the exemption for an NMS Stock ATS is suspended or revoked pursuant to paragraph (a)(4)(i) of this section, the NMS Stock ATS shall be prohibited from operating pursuant to the exemption pursuant to paragraph (a)(2) of 17 CFR 240.3a1–1. If the exemption for an NMS Stock ATS is limited pursuant to paragraph (a)(4)(i) of this section, the NMS Stock ATS shall be prohibited from operating in a manner otherwise inconsistent with the terms and conditions of the Commission order.

(b) *Public disclosures*. (1) Every Form ATS–N filed pursuant to this section shall constitute a "report" within the meaning of sections 11A, 17(a), 18(a), and 32(a) (15 U.S.C. 78k- 1, 78q(a), 78r(a), and 78ff(a)), and any other applicable provisions of the Act.

(2) The Commission will make public via posting on the Commission's website, each:

(i) Effective initial Form ATS–N, as amended;

(ii) Order of ineffective initial Form ATS–N;

(iii) Form ATS–N amendment to an effective Form ATS–N:

(A) *Material Amendments*: The cover page of the Material Amendment will be made public by the Commission upon filing and, unless the Commission declares the Material Amendment ineffective, the entirety of the Material Amendment, as amended, will be made public by the Commission following the expiration of the review period pursuant to paragraph (a)(2)(ii) of this section.

(B) *Updating, Correcting, and Order Display and Fair Access Amendments*: The entirety of Updating, Correcting, and Order Display and Fair Access Amendments will be made public by the Commission upon filing. Notwithstanding the foregoing, an Updating or Correcting Amendment filed to a Material Amendment will be made public by the Commission following the expiration of the review period for such Material Amendment pursuant to paragraph (a)(2)(ii) of this section.

(iv) Order of ineffective Form ATS–N amendment;

(v) Notice of cessation; and

(vi) Order suspending, limiting, or revoking the exemption for an NMS Stock ATS from the definition of an "exchange" pursuant to paragraph (a)(2) of 17 CFR 240.3a1–1.

(3) Each NMS Stock ATS shall make public via posting on its website a direct URL hyperlink to the Commission's website that contains the documents enumerated in paragraph (b)(2) of this section.

(c) *Form ATS–N disclosure requirements.* (1) An NMS Stock ATS must file a Form ATS–N in accordance with the instructions therein.

(2) Any report required to be filed with the Commission under this section shall be filed on Form ATS-N, and include all information as prescribed in Form ATS–N and the instructions thereto. Such document shall be executed at, or prior to, the time Form ATS–N is filed and shall be retained by the NMS Stock ATS in accordance with 17 CFR 242.303 and 232.302, and the instructions in Form ATS–N.

CUSTOMER MARGIN REQUIREMENTS FOR SECURITY FUTURES

(Cite as 17 CFR § 242.___)

Rule 400. Customer margin requirements for security futures—authority, purpose, interpretation, and scope

(a) *Authority and Purpose.* Rules 400 through 406 and 17 CFR 41.42 through 41.49 ("this Regulation, Rules 400 through 406") are issued by the Securities and Exchange Commission ("Commission") jointly with the Commodity Futures Trading Commission ("CFTC"), pursuant to authority delegated by the Board of Governors of the Federal Reserve System under section 7(c)(2)(A) of the Securities Exchange Act of 1934. The principal purpose of this Regulation (Rules 400 through 406) is to regulate customer margin collected by brokers, dealers, and members of national securities exchanges, including futures commission merchants required to register as brokers or dealers under section 15(b)(11) of the Act, relating to security futures.

(b) *Interpretation.* This Regulation (Rules 400 through 406) shall be jointly interpreted by the Commission and the CFTC, consistent with the criteria set forth in clauses (i) through (iv) of section 7(c)(2)(B) of the Act and the provisions of Regulation T (12 CFR part 220).

(c) *Scope.* (1) This Regulation (Rules 400 through 406) does not preclude a self-regulatory authority, under rules that are effective in accordance with section 19(b)(2) of the Act or section 19(b)(7) of the Act and, as applicable, section 5c(c) of the Commodity Exchange Act ("CEA") (7 U.S.C. 7a–2(c)), or a security futures intermediary from imposing additional margin requirements on security futures, including higher initial or maintenance margin levels, consistent with this Regulation (Rules 400 through 406), or from taking appropriate action to preserve its financial integrity.

(2) This Regulation (Rules 400 through 406) does not apply to:

(i) Financial relations between a customer and a security futures intermediary to the extent that they comply with a portfolio margining system under rules that meet the criteria set forth in section 7(c)(2)(B) of the Act and that are effective in accordance with section 19(b)(2) of the Act;

(ii) Financial relations between a security futures intermediary and a foreign person involving security futures traded on or subject to the rules of a foreign board of trade;

(iii) Margin requirements that clearing agencies registered under section 17A of the Exchange Act or derivatives clearing organizations registered under section 5b of the CEA (7 U.S.C. 7a–1) impose on their members;

(iv) Financial relations between a security futures intermediary and a person based on a good faith determination by the security futures intermediary that such person is an exempted person; and

(v) Financial relations between a security futures intermediary and, or arranged by a security futures intermediary for, a person relating to trading in security futures by such person for its own account, if such person:

(A) Is a member of a national securities exchange or national securities association registered pursuant to section 15A(a) of the Act; and

(B) Is registered with such exchange or such association as a security futures dealer pursuant to rules that are effective in accordance with section 19(b)(2) of the Act and, as applicable, section 5c(c) of the CEA (7 U.S.C. 7a–2(c)), that:

(*1*) Require such member to be registered as a floor trader or a floor broker with the CFTC under Section 4f(a)(1) of the CEA (7 U.S.C. 6f(a)(1)), or as a dealer with the Commission under section 15(b) of the Act (15 U.S.C. 78o(b));

(*2*) Require such member to maintain records sufficient to prove compliance with this paragraph (c)(2)(v) and the rules of the exchange or association of which it is a member;

(*3*) Require such member to hold itself out as being willing to buy and sell security futures for its own account on a regular or continuous basis; and

(*4*) Provide for disciplinary action, including revocation of such member's registration as a security futures dealer, for such member's failure to comply with this Regulation (Rules 400 through 406) or the rules of the exchange or association.

(d) *Exemption.* The Commission may exempt, either unconditionally or on specified terms and conditions, financial relations involving any security futures intermediary, customer, position, or transaction, or any class of security futures intermediaries, customers, positions, or transactions, from one or more requirements of this Regulation (Rules 400 through 406), if the Commission determines that such exemption is necessary or appropriate in the public interest and consistent with the protection of investors. An exemption granted pursuant to this paragraph shall not operate as an exemption from any CFTC rules. Any exemption that may be required from such rules must be obtained separately from the CFTC.

Rule 401. Definitions

(a) For purposes of this Regulation (Rules 400 through 406) only, the following terms shall have the meanings set forth in this rule.

(1) *Applicable margin rules* and *margin rules applicable to an account* mean the rules and regulations applicable to financial relations between a security futures intermediary and a customer with respect to security futures and related positions carried in a securities account or futures account as provided in Rule 402(a) of this Regulation (Rule 400 through 406).

(2) *Broker* shall have the meaning provided in section 3(a)(4) of the Act.

(3) *Contract multiplier* means the number of units of a narrow-based security index expressed as a dollar amount, in accordance with the terms of the security future contract.

(4) *Current market value* means, on any day:

(i) With respect to a security future:

(A) If the instrument underlying such security future is a stock, the product of the daily settlement price of such security future as shown by any regularly published reporting or quotation service, and the applicable number of shares per contract; or

(B) If the instrument underlying such security future is a narrow-based security index, as defined in section 3(a)(55)(B) of the Act, the product of the daily settlement price of such security future as shown by any regularly published reporting or quotation service, and the applicable contract multiplier.

(ii) With respect to a security other than a security future, the most recent closing sale price of the security, as shown by any regularly published reporting or quotation service. If there is no recent closing sale price, the security futures intermediary may use any reasonable estimate of the market value of the security as of the most recent close of business.

(5) *Customer* excludes an exempted person and includes:

(i) Any person or persons acting jointly:

(A) On whose behalf a security futures intermediary effects a security futures transaction or carries a security futures position; or

(B) Who would be considered a customer of the security futures intermediary according to the ordinary usage of the trade;

(ii) Any partner in a security futures intermediary that is organized as a partnership who would be considered a customer of the security futures intermediary absent the partnership relationship; and

(iii) Any joint venture in which a security futures intermediary participates and which would be considered a customer of the security futures intermediary if the security futures intermediary were not a participant.

(6) *Daily settlement price* means, with respect to a security future, the settlement price of such security future determined at the close of trading each day, under the rules of the applicable exchange, clearing agency, or derivatives clearing organization.

(7) *Dealer* shall have the meaning provided in section 3(a)(5) of the Act.

(8) *Equity* means the equity or margin equity in a securities or futures account, as computed in accordance with the margin rules applicable to the account and subject to adjustment under Rule 404(c), (d) and (e) of this Regulation (Rules 400 through 406).

(9) *Exempted person* means:

(i) A member of a national securities exchange, a registered broker or dealer, or a registered futures commission merchant, a substantial portion of whose business consists of transactions in securities, commodity futures, or commodity options with persons other than brokers, dealers, futures commission merchants, floor brokers, or floor traders, and includes a person who:

(A) Maintains at least 1000 active accounts on an annual basis for persons other than brokers, dealers, persons associated with a broker or dealer, futures commission merchants, floor brokers, floor traders, and persons affiliated with a futures commission merchant, floor broker, or floor trader that are effecting transactions in securities, commodity futures, or commodity options;

(B) Earns at least $10 million in gross revenues on an annual basis from transactions in securities, commodity futures, or commodity options with persons other than brokers, dealers, persons associated with a broker or dealer, futures commission merchants, floor brokers, floor traders, and persons affiliated with a futures commission merchant, floor broker, or floor trader; or

(C) Earns at least 10 percent of its gross revenues on an annual basis from transactions in securities, commodity futures, or commodity options with persons other than brokers, dealers, persons associated with a broker or dealer, futures commission merchants, floor brokers, floor traders, and persons affiliated with a futures commission merchant, floor broker, or floor trader.

(ii) For purposes of paragraph (a)(9)(i) of this rule only, persons affiliated with a futures commission merchant, floor broker, or floor trader means any partner, officer, director, or branch manager of such futures commission merchant, floor broker, or floor trader (or any person occupying a similar status or performing similar functions), any person directly or indirectly controlling, controlled by, or under common control with such futures commission merchant, floor broker, or floor trader, or any employee of such a futures commission merchant, floor broker, or floor trader.

(iii) A member of a national securities exchange, a registered broker or dealer, or a registered futures commission merchant that has been in existence for less than one year may meet the definition of exempted person based on a six-month period.

(10) *Exempted security* shall have the meaning provided in section 3(a)(12) of the Act.

(11) *Floor broker* shall have the meaning provided in Section 1a(16) of the CEA (7 U.S.C. 1a(16)).

(12) *Floor trader* shall have the meaning provided in Section 1a(17) of the CEA (7 U.S.C. 1a(17)).

(13) *Futures account* shall have the meaning provided in Rule 15c3–3(a) under the Securities Exchange Act of 1934.

(14) *Futures commission merchant* shall have the meaning provided in Section 1a of the CEA (7 U.S.C. 1a).

(15) *Good faith*, with respect to making a determination or accepting a statement concerning financial relations with a person, means that the security futures intermediary is alert to the circumstances surrounding such financial relations, and if in possession of information that would cause a prudent person not to make the determination or accept the notice or certification without inquiry, investigates and is satisfied that it is correct.

(16) *Listed option* means a put or call option that is:

(i) Issued by a clearing agency that is registered under section 17A of the Act (15 U.S.C. 17q–1) or cleared and guaranteed by a derivatives clearing organization that is registered under Section 5b of the CEA (7 U.S.C. 7a–1); and

(ii) Traded on or subject to the rules of a self-regulatory authority.

(17) *Margin call* means a demand by a security futures intermediary to a customer for a deposit of cash, securities or other assets to satisfy the required margin for security futures or related positions or a special margin requirement.

(18) *Margin deficiency* means the amount by which the required margin in an account is not satisfied by the equity in the account, as computed in accordance with Rule 404 of this Regulation (Rules 400 through 406).

(19) *Margin equity security* shall have the meaning provided in Regulation T.

(20) *Margin security* shall have the meaning provided in Regulation T.

(21) *Member* shall have the meaning provided in section 3(a)(3) of the Act, and shall include persons registered under section 15(b)(11) of the Act that are permitted to effect transactions on a na-

tional securities exchange without the services of another person acting as executing broker.

(22) *Money market mutual fund* means any security issued by an investment company registered under section 8 of the Investment Company Act of 1940 (15 U.S.C. 80a–8) that is considered a money market fund under Rule 2a–7 under the Investment Company Act of 1940.

(23) *Persons associated with a broker or dealer* shall have the meaning provided in section 3(a)(18) of the Act.

(24) *Regulation T* means Regulation T promulgated by the Board of Governors of the Federal Reserve System, 12 CFR part 220, as amended from time to time.

(25) *Regulation T collateral value*, with respect to a security, means the current market value of the security reduced by the percentage of required margin for a position in the security held in a margin account under Regulation T.

(26) *Related position*, with respect to a security future, means any position in an account that is combined with the security future to create an offsetting position as provided in Rule 403(b)(2) of this Regulation (Rules 400 through 406).

(27) *Related transaction*, with respect to a position or transaction in a security future, means:

(i) Any transaction that creates, eliminates, increases or reduces an offsetting position involving a security future and a related position, as provided in Rule 403(b)(2) of this Regulation (Rules 400 through 406); or

(ii) Any deposit or withdrawal of margin for the security future or a related position, except as provided in Rules 405(b) of this Regulation (Rules 400 through 406).

(28) *Securities account* shall have the meaning provided in Rule 15c3–3(a) under the Securities Exchange Act of 1934.

(29) *Security futures intermediary* means any creditor as defined in Regulation T with respect to its financial relations with any person involving security futures.

(30) *Self-regulatory authority* means a national securities exchange registered under section 6 of the Act, a national securities association registered under section 15A of the Act, a contract market registered under Section 5 of the CEA (7 U.S.C. 7) or Section 5f of the CEA (7 U.S.C. 7b–1), or a derivatives transaction execution facility registered under Section 5a of the CEA (7 U.S.C. 7a).

(31) *Special margin requirement* shall have the meaning provided in Rule 404(e)(1)(ii) of this Regulation (Rules 400 through 406).

(32) *Variation settlement* means any credit or debit to a customer account, made on a daily or intraday basis, for the purpose of marking to market a security future or any other contract that is:

(i) Issued by a clearing agency that is registered under section 17A of the Act or cleared and guaranteed by a derivatives clearing organization that is registered under Section 5b of the CEA (7 U.S.C. 7a–1); and

(ii) Traded on or subject to the rules of a self-regulatory authority.

(b) Terms used in this Regulation (Rules 400 through 406) and not otherwise defined in this section shall have the meaning set forth in the margin rules applicable to the account.

(c) Terms used in this Regulation (Rules 400 through 406) and not otherwise defined in this section or in the margin rules applicable to the account shall have the meaning set forth in the Act and the CEA; if the definitions of a term in the Act and the CEA are inconsistent as applied in particular circumstances, such term shall have the meaning set forth in rules, regulations, or interpretations jointly promulgated by the Commission and the CFTC.

Rule 402. General provisions

(a) *Applicable Margin Rules.* Except to the extent inconsistent with this Regulation (Rules 400 through 406):

(1) A security futures intermediary that carries a security future on behalf of a customer in a securities account shall record and conduct all financial relations with respect to such security future and related positions in accordance with Regulation T and the margin rules of the self-regulatory authorities of which the security futures intermediary is a member.

(2) A security futures intermediary that carries a security future on behalf of a customer in a futures account shall record and conduct all financial relations with respect to such security future and related positions in accordance with the margin rules of the self-regulatory authorities of which the security futures intermediary is a member.

(b) *Separation and Consolidation of Accounts.* (1) The requirements for security futures and related positions in one account may not be met by considering items in any other account, except as permitted or required under paragraph (b)(2) of this rule or applicable margin rules. If withdrawals of cash, securities or other assets deposited as margin are permitted under this Regulation (Rules 400 through 406), bookkeeping entries shall be made when such cash, securities, or assets are used for purposes of meeting requirements in another account.

(2) Notwithstanding paragraph (b)(1) of this rule, the security futures intermediary shall consider all futures accounts in which security futures and related positions are held that are within the same regulatory classification or account type and are owned by the same customer to be a single account for purposes of this Regulation (Rules 400 through 406). The security futures intermediary may combine such accounts with other futures accounts that are within the same regulatory classification or account type and are owned by the same customer for purposes of computing a customer's overall margin requirement, as permitted or required by applicable margin rules.

(c) *Accounts of Partners.* If a partner of the security futures intermediary has an account with the security futures intermediary in which security futures or related positions are held, the security futures intermediary shall disregard the partner's financial relations with the firm (as shown in the partner's capital and ordinary drawing accounts) in calculating the margin or equity of any such account.

(d) *Contribution to Joint Venture.* If an account in which security futures or related positions are held is the account of a joint venture in which the security futures intermediary participates, any interest of the security futures intermediary in the joint account in excess of the interest which the security futures intermediary would have on the basis of its right to share in the profits shall be margined in accordance with this Regulation (Rules 400 through 406).

(e) *Extensions of Credit.* (1) No security futures intermediary may extend or maintain credit to or for any customer for the purpose of evading or circumventing any requirement under this Regulation (Rules 400 through 406).

(2) A security futures intermediary may arrange for the extension or maintenance of credit to or for any customer by any person, provided that the security futures intermediary does not willfully arrange credit that would constitute a violation of Regulation T, U or X of the Board of Governors of the Federal Reserve System (12 CFR parts 220, 221, and 224) by such person.

(f) *Change in Exempted Person Status.* Once a person ceases to qualify as an exempted person, it shall notify the security futures intermediary of this fact before entering into any new security futures transaction or related transaction that would require additional margin to be deposited under this Regulation (Rules 400 through 406). Financial relations with respect to any such transactions shall be subject to the provisions of this Regulation (Rules 400 through 406).

Rule 403. Required margin

(a) *Applicability.* Each security futures intermediary shall determine the required margin for the security futures and related positions held on behalf of a customer in a securities account or futures account as set forth in this rule.

(b) *Required Margin.* (1) *General Rule.* The required margin for each long or short position n a security future shall be twenty (20) percent of the current market value of such security future.

(2) *Offsetting Positions.* Notwithstanding the margin levels specified in paragraph (b)(1) of this rule, a self-regulatory authority may set the required initial or maintenance margin level for an offsetting position involving security futures and related positions at a level lower than the level that would be required under paragraph (b)(1) of this rule if such positions were margined separately, pursuant to rules that meet the criteria set forth in section 7(c)(2)(B) of the Act and are effective in accordance with section 19(b)(2) of the Act and, as applicable, Section 5c(c) of the CEA (7 U.S.C. 7a–2(c)).

(c) *Procedures for Certain Margin Level Adjustments.* An exchange registered under section 6(g) of the Act, or a national securities association registered under section 15A(k) of the Act, may raise or lower the required margin level for a security future to a level not lower than that specified in this section, in accordance with section 19(b)(7) of the Act.

Rule 404. Type, form and use of margin

(a) *When Margin is Required.* Margin is required to be deposited whenever the required margin for security futures and related positions in an account is not satisfied by the equity in the account, subject to adjustment under paragraph (c) of this rule.

(b) *Acceptable Margin Deposits.* (1) The required margin may be satisfied by a deposit of cash, margin securities (subject to paragraph (b)(2) of this rule), exempted securities, any other asset permitted under Regulation T to satisfy a margin deficiency in a securities margin account, or any combination thereof, each as valued in accordance with paragraph (c) of this rule.

(2) Shares of a money market mutual fund may be accepted as a margin deposit for purposes of this Regulation (Rules 400 through 406), *provided that:*

(i) The customer waives any right to redeem the shares without the consent of the security futures intermediary and instructs the fund or its transfer agent accordingly;

(ii) The security futures intermediary (or clearing agency or derivatives clearing organization with which the shares are deposited as margin) obtains the right to redeem the shares in cash, promptly upon request; and

(iii) The fund agrees to satisfy any conditions necessary or appropriate to ensure that the shares may be redeemed in cash, promptly upon request.

(c) *Adjustments.* (1) *Futures Accounts.* For purposes of this rule, the equity in a futures account shall be computed in accordance with the margin rules applicable to the account, subject to the following:

(i) A security future shall have no value;

(ii) Each net long or short position in a listed option on a contract for future delivery shall be valued in accordance with the margin rules applicable to the account;

(iii) Except as permitted in paragraph (e) of this rule, each margin equity security shall be valued at an amount no greater than its Regulation T collateral value;

(iv) Each other security shall be valued at an amount no greater than its current market value reduced by the percentage specified for such security in Rule 15c3–1(c)(2)(vi) under the Securities Exchange Act of 1934;

(v) Freely convertible foreign currency may be valued at an amount no greater than its daily marked-to-market U.S. dollar equivalent;

(vi) Variation settlement receivable (or payable) by an account at the close of trading on any day shall be treated as a credit (or debit) to the account on that day; and

(vii) Each other acceptable margin deposit or component of equity shall be valued at an amount no greater than its value under Regulation T.

(2) *Securities Accounts.* For purposes of this rule, the equity in a securities account shall be computed in accordance with the margin rules applicable to the account, subject to the following:

(i) A security future shall have no value;

(ii) Freely convertible foreign currency may be valued at an amount no greater than its daily mark-to-market U.S. dollar equivalent; and

(iii) Variation settlement receivable (or payable) to an account at the close of trading on any day shall be treated as a credit (or debit) by the account on that day.

(d) *Satisfaction Restriction.* Any transaction, position or deposit that is used to satisfy the required margin for security futures or related positions under this Regulation (Rules 400 through 406), including a related position, shall be unavailable to satisfy the required margin for any other position or transaction or any other requirement.

(e) *Alternative Collateral Valuation for Margin Equity Securities in a Futures Account.* (1) Notwithstanding paragraph (c)(1)(iii) of this rule, a security futures intermediary need not value a margin equity security at its Regulation T collateral value when determining whether the required margin for the security futures and related positions in a futures account is satisfied, *provided that:*

(i) The margin equity security is valued at an amount no greater than the current market value of the security reduced by the lowest percentage level of margin required for a long position in the security held in a margin account under the rules of a national securities exchange registered pursuant to section 6(a) of the Act;

(ii) Additional margin is required to be deposited on any day when the day's security futures transactions and related transactions would create or increase a margin deficiency in the account if the margin equity securities were valued at their Regulation T collateral value, and shall be for the amount of the margin deficiency so created or increased (a "special margin requirement"); and

(iii) Cash, securities, or other assets deposited as margin for the positions in an account are not permitted to be withdrawn from the account at any time that:

(A) Additional cash, securities, or other assets are required to be deposited as margin under this section for a transaction in the account on the same or a previous day; or

(B) The withdrawal, together with other transactions, deposits, and withdrawals on the same day, would create or increase a margin deficiency if the margin equity securities were valued at their Regulation T collateral value.

(2) All security futures transactions and related transactions on any day shall be combined to determine the amount of a special margin requirement. Additional margin deposited to satisfy a special margin requirement shall be valued at an amount no greater than its Regulation T collateral value.

(3) If the alternative collateral valuation method set forth in paragraph (e) of this rule is used with respect to an account in which security futures or related positions are carried:

(i) An account that is transferred from one security futures intermediary to another may be treated as if it had been maintained by the transferee from the date of its origin, if the transferee accepts, in good faith, a signed statement of the transferor (or, if that is not practicable, of the customer), that any margin call issued under this Regulation (Rules 400 through 406) has been satisfied; and

(ii) An account that is transferred from one customer to another as part of a transaction, not undertaken to avoid the requirements of this Regulation (Rules 400 through 406), may be treated as if it had been maintained for the transferee from the date of its origin, if the security futures intermediary accepts in good faith and keeps with the transferee account a signed statement of the transferor describing the circumstances for the transfer.

(f) *Guarantee of Accounts.* No guarantee of a customer's account shall be given any effect for purposes of determining whether the required margin in an account is satisfied, except as permitted under applicable margin rules.

Rule 405. Withdrawal of Margin

(a) *By the Customer.* Except as otherwise provided in Rule 404(e)(1)(ii) of this Regulation (Rules 400 through 406), cash, securities, or other assets deposited as margin for positions in an account may be withdrawn, provided that the equity in the account after such withdrawal is sufficient to satisfy the required margin for the security futures and related positions in the account under this Regulation (Rules 400 through 406).

(b) *By the Security Futures Intermediary.* Notwithstanding paragraph (a) of this rule, the security futures intermediary, in its usual practice, may deduct the following items from an account in which security futures or related positions are held if they are considered in computing the balance of such account:

(1) Variation settlement payable, directly or indirectly, to a clearing agency that is registered under section 17A of the Act or a derivatives clearing organization that is registered under section 5b of the CEA (7 U.S.C. 7a–1);

(2) Interest charged on credit maintained in the account;

(3) Communication or shipping charges with respect to transactions in the account;

(4) Payment of commissions, brokerage, taxes, storage and other charges lawfully accruing in connection with the positions and transactions in the account;

(5) Any service charges that the security futures intermediary may impose; or

(6) Any other withdrawals that are permitted from a securities margin account under Regulation T, to the extent permitted under applicable margin rules.

Rule 406. Undermargined accounts

(a) *Failure to Satisfy Margin Call.* If any margin call required by this Regulation (Rules 400 through 406) is not met in full, the security futures intermediary shall take the deduction required with respect to an undermargined account in computing its net capital under Commission or CFTC rules.

(b) *Accounts that Liquidate to a Deficit.* If at any time there is a liquidating deficit in an account in which security futures are held, the security futures intermediary shall take steps to liquidate positions in the account promptly and in an orderly manner.

(c) *Liquidation of Undermargined Accounts not Required.* Notwithstanding Section 402(a) of this Regulation (Rules 400 through 406), section 220.4(d) of Regulation T (12 CFR 220.4(d)) respecting liquidation of positions in lieu of deposit shall not apply with respect to security futures carried in a securities account.

REGULATION AC—ANALYST CERTIFICATION

(Cite as 17 CFR § 242.___)

Rule 500. Definitions

For purposes of Regulation AC (Rules 500 through 505) the term:

Covered person of a broker or dealer means an associated person of that broker or dealer but does not include:

(1) An associated person:

(i) If the associated person has no officers (or persons performing similar functions) or employees in common with the broker or dealer who can influence the activities of research analysts or the content of research reports; and

(ii) If the broker or dealer maintains and enforces written policies and procedures reasonably designed to prevent the broker or dealer, any controlling persons, officers (or persons performing similar functions), and employees of the broker or dealer from influencing the activities of research analysts and the content of research reports prepared by the associated person.

(2) An associated person who is an investment adviser:

(i) Not registered with the Commission as an investment adviser because of the prohibition of section 203A of the Investment Advisers Act of 1940 (15 U.S.C. 80b–3a); and

(ii) Not registered or required to be registered with the Commission as a broker or dealer.

Note to Definition of Covered Person: An associated person of a broker or dealer who is not a covered person continues to be subject to the federal securities laws, including the anti-fraud provisions of the federal securities laws.

Foreign person means any person who is not a U.S. person.

Foreign security means a security issued by a foreign issuer for which a U.S. market is not the principal trading market.

Public appearance means any participation by a research analyst in a seminar, forum (including an interactive electronic forum), or radio or television or other interview, in which the research analyst makes a specific recommendation or provides information reasonably sufficient upon which to base an investment decision about a security or an issuer.

Registered broker or dealer means a broker or dealer registered or required to register pursuant to section 15 or section 15B of the Securities Exchange Act of 1934 or a government securities broker or government securities dealer registered or required to register pursuant to section 15C(a)(1)(A) of the Securities Exchange Act of 1934.

Research analyst means any natural person who is primarily responsible for the preparation of the content of a research report.

Research report means a written communication (including an electronic communication) that includes an analysis of a security or an issuer and provides information reasonably sufficient upon which to base an investment decision.

Third party research analyst means:

(1) With respect to a broker or dealer, any research analyst not employed by that broker or dealer or any associated person of that broker or dealer; and

(2) With respect to a covered person of a broker or dealer, any research analyst not employed by that covered person, by the broker or dealer with whom that covered person is associated, or by any other associated person of the broker or dealer with whom that covered person is associated.

United States has the meaning contained in Rule 902(*l*) under the Securities Act of 1933.

U.S. person has the meaning contained in Rule 902(k) under the Securities Act of 1933.

Rule 501. Certifications in connection with research reports

(a) A broker or dealer or covered person that publishes, circulates, or provides a research report prepared by a research analyst to a U.S. person in the United States shall include in that research report a clear and prominent certification by the research analyst containing the following:

(1) A statement attesting that all of the views expressed in the research report accurately reflect the research analyst's personal views about any and all of the subject securities or issuers; and

(2)(i) A statement attesting that no part of the research analyst's compensation was, is, or will be, directly or indirectly, related to the specific recommendations or views expressed by the research analyst in the research report; or

(ii) A statement:

(A) Attesting that part or all of the research analyst's compensation was, is, or will be, directly or indirectly, related to the specific recommendations or views expressed by the research analyst in the research report;

(B) Identifying the source, amount, and purpose of such compensation; and

(C) Further disclosing that the compensation could influence the recommendations or views expressed in the research report.

(b) A broker or dealer or covered person that publishes, circulates, or provides a research report prepared by a third party research analyst to a U.S. person in the United States shall be exempt from the requirements of this section with respect to such research report if the following conditions are satisfied:

(1) The employer of the third party research analyst has no officers (or persons performing similar functions) or employees in common with the broker or dealer or covered person; and

(2) The broker or dealer (or, with respect to a covered person, the broker or dealer with whom the covered person is associated) maintains and enforces written policies and procedures reasonably designed to prevent the broker or dealer, any controlling persons, officers (or persons performing similar functions), and employees of the broker or dealer from influencing the activities of the third party research analyst and the content of research reports prepared by the third party research analyst.

Rule 502. Certifications in connection with public appearances

(a) If a broker or dealer publishes, circulates, or provides a research report prepared by a research analyst employed by the broker or dealer or covered person to a U.S. person in the United States, the broker or dealer must make a record within 30 days after any calendar quarter in which the research analyst made a public appearance that contains the following:

(1) A statement by the research analyst attesting that the views expressed by the research analyst in all public appearances during the calendar quarter accurately reflected the research analyst's personal views at that time about any and all of the subject securities or issuers; and

(2) A statement by the research analyst attesting that no part of the research analyst's compensation was, is, or will be, directly or indirectly, related to the specific recommendations or views expressed by the research analyst in such public appearances.

(b) If the broker or dealer does not obtain a statement by the research analyst in accordance with paragraph (a) of this rule:

(1) The broker or dealer shall promptly notify in writing its examining authority, designated pursuant to section 17(d) of the Securities Exchange Act of 1934 and Rule 17d–2 under the Securities Exchange Act of 1934, that the research analyst did not provide the certifications specified in paragraph (a) of this rule; and

(2) For 120 days following notification pursuant to paragraph (b)(1) of this rule, the broker or dealer shall disclose in any research report prepared by the research analyst and published, circulated, or provided to a U.S. person in the United States that the research analyst did not provide the certifications specified in paragraph (a) of this rule.

(c) In the case of a research analyst who is employed outside the United States by a foreign person located outside the United States, this rule shall only apply to a public appearance while the research analyst is physically present in the United States.

(d) A broker or dealer shall preserve the records specified in paragraphs (a) and (b) of this rule in accordance with Rule 17a–4 under the Securities Exchange Act of 1934 and for a period of not less than 3 years, the first 2 years in an accessible place.

Rule 503. Certain foreign research reports

A foreign person, located outside the United States and not associated with a registered broker or dealer, who prepares a research report concerning a foreign security and provides it to a U.S. person in the United States in accordance with the provisions of Rule 15a–6(a)(2) under the Securities Exchange Act of 1934 shall be exempt from the requirements of this regulation.

Rule 504. Notification to associated persons

A broker or dealer shall notify any person with whom that broker or dealer is associated who publishes, circulates, or provides research reports:

(a) Whether the broker or dealer maintains and enforces written policies and procedures reasonably designed to prevent the broker or dealer, any controlling persons, officers (or persons performing similar functions), or employees of the broker or dealer from influencing the activities of research analysts and the content of research reports prepared by the associated person; and

(b) Whether the associated person has any officers (or persons performing similar functions) or employees in common with the broker or dealer who can influence the activities of research analysts or the content of research reports and, if so, the identity of those persons.

Rule 505. Exclusion for news media

No provision of this Regulation AC shall apply to any person who:

(a) Is the publisher of any bona fide newspaper, news magazine or business or financial publication of general and regular circulation; and

(b) Is not registered or required to be registered with the Commission as a broker or dealer or investment adviser.

REGULATION NMS—REGULATION OF THE NATIONAL MARKET SYSTEM

(Cite as 17 CFR § 242.___)

Rule 600. NMS security designation and definitions

(a) The term *national market system security* as used in section 11A(a)(2) of the Act shall mean any NMS security as defined in paragraph (b) of this rule.

(b) For purposes of Regulation NMS (Rules 600 through 612), the following definitions shall apply:

(1) *Aggregate quotation size* means the sum of the quotation sizes of all responsible brokers or dealers who have communicated on any national securities exchange bids or offers for an NMS security at the same price.

(2) *Alternative trading system* has the meaning provided in Rule 300(a) of Regulation ATS.

(3) *Automated quotation* means a quotation displayed by a trading center that:

(i) Permits an incoming order to be marked as immediate-or-cancel;

(ii) Immediately and automatically executes an order marked as immediate-or-cancel against the displayed quotation up to its full size;

(iii) Immediately and automatically cancels any unexecuted portion of an order marked as immediate-or-cancel without routing the order elsewhere;

(iv) Immediately and automatically transmits a response to the sender of an order marked as immediate-or-cancel indicating the action taken with respect to such order; and

(v) Immediately and automatically displays information that updates the displayed quotation to reflect any change to its material terms.

(4) *Automated trading center* means a trading center that:

(i) Has implemented such systems, procedures, and rules as are necessary to render it capable of displaying quotations that meet the requirements for an automated quotation set forth in paragraph (b)(3) of this rule;

(ii) Identifies all quotations other than automated quotations as manual quotations;

(iii) Immediately identifies its quotations as manual quotations whenever it has reason to believe that it is not capable of displaying automated quotations; and

(iv) Has adopted reasonable standards limiting when its quotations change from automated quotations to manual quotations, and vice versa, to specifically defined circumstances that promote fair and efficient access to its automated quotations and are consistent with the maintenance of fair and orderly markets.

(5) *Average effective spread* means the share-weighted average of effective spreads for order executions calculated, for buy orders, as double the amount of difference between the execution price and the midpoint of the national best bid and national best offer at the time of order receipt and, for sell orders, as double the amount of difference between the midpoint of the national best bid and national best offer at the time of order receipt and the execution price.

(6) *Average realized spread* means the share-weighted average of realized spreads for order executions calculated, for buy orders, as double the amount of difference between the execution price and the midpoint of the national best bid and national best offer five minutes after the time of order execution and, for sell orders, as double the amount of difference between the midpoint of the national best bid and national best offer five minutes after the time of order execution and the execution price; *provided, however*, that the midpoint of the final national best bid and national best offer disseminated for regular trading hours shall be used to calculate a realized spread if it is disseminated less than five minutes after the time of order execution.

(7) *Best bid and best offer* mean the highest priced bid and the lowest priced offer.

(8) *Bid* or *offer* means the bid price or the offer price communicated by a member of a national securities exchange or member of a national securities association to any broker or dealer, or to any customer, at which it is willing to buy or sell one or more round lots of an NMS security, as either principal or agent, but shall not include indications of interest.

(9) *Block size with respect to* an order means it is:

(i) Of at least 10,000 shares; or

(ii) For a quantity of stock having a market value of at least $200,000.

(10) *Categorized by order size* means dividing orders into separate categories for sizes from 100 to 499 shares, from 500 to 1999 shares, from 2000 to 4999 shares, and 5000 or greater shares.

(11) *Categorized by order type* means dividing orders into separate categories for market orders, marketable limit orders, inside-the-quote limit orders, at-the-quote limit orders, and near-the-quote limit orders.

(12) *Categorized by security* means dividing orders into separate categories for each NMS stock that is included in a report.

(13) *Consolidated display* means:

(i) The prices, sizes, and market identifications of the national best bid and national best offer for a security; and

(ii) Consolidated last sale information for a security.

(14) *Consolidated last sale information* means the price, volume, and market identification of the most recent transaction report for a security that is disseminated pursuant to an effective national market system plan.

(15) *Covered order* means any market order or any limit order (including immediate-or-cancel orders) received by a market center during regular trading hours at a time when a national best bid and national best offer is being disseminated, and, if executed, is executed during regular trading hours, but shall exclude any order for which the customer requests special handling for execution, including, but not limited to, orders to be executed at a market opening price or a market closing price, orders submitted with stop prices, orders to be executed only at their full size, orders to be executed on a particular type of tick or bid, orders submitted on a "not held" basis, orders for other than regular settlement, and orders to be executed at prices unrelated to the market price of the security at the time of execution.

(16) *Customer* means any person that is not a broker or dealer.

(17) *Customer limit order* means an order to buy or sell an NMS stock at a specified price that is not for the account of either a broker or dealer; *provided, however,* that the term *customer limit order* shall include an order transmitted by a broker or dealer on behalf of a customer.

(18) *Customer order* means an order to buy or sell an NMS security that is not for the account of a broker or dealer, but shall not include any order for a quantity of a security having a market value of at least $50,000 for an NMS security that is an option contract and a market value of at least $200,000 for any other NMS security.

(19) *Directed order* means a customer order that the customer specifically instructed the broker or dealer to route to a particular venue for execution.

(20) *Dynamic market monitoring device* means any service provided by a vendor on an interrogation device or other display that:

(i) Permits real-time monitoring, on a dynamic basis, of transaction reports, last sale data, or quotations with respect to a particular security; and

(ii) Displays the most recent transaction report, last sale data, or quotation with respect to that security until such report, data, or quotation has been superseded or supplemented by the display of a new transaction report, last sale data, or quotation reflecting the next reported transaction or quotation in that security.

(21) *Effective national market system plan* means any national market system plan approved by the Commission (either temporarily or on a permanent basis) pursuant to Rule 608.

(22) *Effective transaction reporting plan* means any transaction reporting plan approved by the Commission pursuant to Rule 601.

(23) *Electronic communications network* means, for the purposes of Rule 602(b)(5), any electronic system that widely disseminates to third parties orders entered therein by an exchange market maker or OTC market maker, and permits such orders to be executed against in whole or in part; except that the term *electronic communications network* shall not include:

(i) Any system that crosses multiple orders at one or more specified times at a single price set by the system (by algorithm or by any derivative pricing mechanism) and does not allow orders to be crossed or executed against directly by participants outside of such times; or

(ii) Any system operated by, or on behalf of, an OTC market maker or exchange market maker that executes customer orders primarily against the account of such market maker as principal, other than riskless principal.

(24) *Exchange market maker* means any member of a national securities exchange that is registered as a specialist or market maker pursuant to the rules of such exchange.

(25) *Exchange-traded security* means any NMS security or class of NMS securities listed and registered, or admitted to unlisted trading privileges, on a national securities exchange; *provided, however,* that securities not listed on any national securities exchange that are traded pursuant to unlisted trading privileges are excluded.

(26) *Executed at the quote* means, for buy orders, execution at a price equal to the national best offer at the time of order receipt and, for sell orders, execution at a price equal to the national best bid at the time of order receipt.

(27) *Executed outside the quote* means, for buy orders, execution at a price higher than the national best offer at the time of order receipt and, for sell orders, execution at a price lower than the national best bid at the time of order receipt.

(28) *Executed with price improvement* means, for buy orders, execution at a price lower than the national best offer at the time of order receipt and, for sell orders, execution at a price higher than the national best bid at the time of order receipt.

(29) *Inside-the-quote limit order, at-the-quote limit order*, and *near-the-quote limit order* mean non-marketable buy orders with limit prices that are, respectively, higher than, equal to, and lower by $0.10 or less than the national best bid at the time of order receipt, and non-marketable sell orders with limit prices that are, respectively, lower than, equal to, and higher by $0.10 or less than the national best offer at the time of order receipt.

(30) *Intermarket sweep order* means a limit order for an NMS stock that meets the following requirements:

(i) When routed to a trading center, the limit order is identified as an intermarket sweep order; and

(ii) Simultaneously with the routing of the limit order identified as an intermarket sweep order, one or more additional limit orders, as necessary, are routed to execute against the full displayed size of any protected bid, in the case of a limit order to sell, or the full displayed size of any protected offer, in the case of a limit order to buy, for the NMS stock with a price that is superior to the limit price of the limit order identified as an intermarket sweep order. These additional routed orders also must be marked as intermarket sweep orders.

(31) *Interrogation device* means any securities information retrieval system capable of displaying transaction reports, last sale data, or quotations upon inquiry, on a current basis on a terminal or other device.

(32) *Joint self-regulatory organization plan* means a plan as to which two or more self-regulatory organizations, acting jointly, are sponsors.

(33) *Last sale data* means any price or volume data associated with a transaction.

(34) *Listed equity security* means any equity security listed and registered, or admitted to unlisted trading privileges, on a national securities exchange.

(35) *Listed option* means any option traded on a registered national securities exchange or automated facility of a national securities association.

(36) *Make publicly available* means posting on an Internet Web site that is free and readily accessible to the public, furnishing a written copy to customers on request without charge, and notifying customers at least annually in writing that a written copy will be furnished on request.

(37) *Manual quotation* means any quotation other than an automated quotation.

(38) *Market center* means any exchange market maker, OTC market maker, alternative trading system, national securities exchange, or national securities association.

(39) *Marketable limit order* means any buy order with a limit price equal to or greater than the national best offer at the time of order receipt, or any sell order with a limit price equal to or less than the national best bid at the time of order receipt.

(40) *Moving ticker* means any continuous real-time moving display of transaction reports or last sale data (other than a dynamic market monitoring device) provided on an interrogation or other display device.

(41) *Nasdaq security* means any registered security listed on The Nasdaq Stock Market, Inc.

(42) *National best bid and national best offer* means, with respect to quotations for an NMS security, the best bid and best offer for such security that are calculated and disseminated on a current and continuing basis by a plan processor pursuant to an effective national market system plan; *provided,* that in the event two or more market centers transmit to the plan processor pursuant to such plan identical bids or offers for an NMS security, the best bid or best offer (as the case may be) shall be determined by ranking all such identical bids or offers (as the case may be) first by size (giving the highest ranking to the bid or offer associated with the largest size), and then by time (giving the highest ranking to the bid or offer received first in time).

(43) *National market system plan* means any joint self-regulatory organization plan in connection with:

(i) The planning, development, operation or regulation of a national market system (or a subsystem thereof) or one or more facilities thereof; or

(ii) The development and implementation of procedures and/or facilities designed to achieve compliance by self-regulatory organizations and their members with any section of this Regulation NMS and part 240, subpart A promulgated pursuant to section 11A of the Act.

(44) *National securities association* means any association of brokers and dealers registered pursuant to section 15A of the Act.

(45) *National securities exchange* means any exchange registered pursuant to section 6 of the Act.

(46) *NMS security* means any security or class of securities for which transaction reports are collected, processed, and made available pursuant to an effective transaction reporting plan, or an effective national market system plan for reporting transactions in listed options.

(47) *NMS stock* means any NMS security other than an option.

(48) *Non-directed order* means any customer order other than a directed order.

(49) *Odd-lot* means an order for the purchase or sale of an NMS stock in an amount less than a round lot.

(50) *Options class* means all of the put option or call option series overlying a security, as defined in section 3(a)(10) of the Act.

(51) *Options series* means the contracts in an options class that have the same unit of trade, expiration date, and exercise price, and other terms or conditions.

(52) *OTC market maker* means any dealer that holds itself out as being willing to buy from and sell to its customers, or others, in the United States, an NMS stock for its own account on a regular or continuous basis otherwise than on a national securities exchange in amounts of less than block size.

(53) *Participants,* when used in connection with a national market system plan, means any self-regulatory organization which has agreed to act in accordance with the terms of the plan but which is not a signatory of such plan.

(54) *Payment for order flow* has the meaning provided in Rule 10b–10 under the Securities Exchange Act of 1934.

(55) *Plan processor* means any self-regulatory organization or securities information processor acting as an exclusive processor in connection with the development, implementation and/or operation of any facility contemplated by an effective national market system plan.

(56) *Profit-sharing relationship* means any ownership or other type of affiliation under which the broker or dealer, directly or indirectly, may share in any profits that may be derived from the execution of non-directed orders.

(57) *Protected bid* or *protected offer* means a quotation in an NMS stock that:

(i) Is displayed by an automated trading center;

(ii) Is disseminated pursuant to an effective national market system plan; and

(iii) Is an automated quotation that is the best bid or best offer of a national securities exchange, the best bid or best offer of The Nasdaq Stock Market, Inc., or the best bid or best offer of a national securities association other than the best bid or best offer of The Nasdaq Stock Market, Inc.(58) *Protected quotation* means a protected bid or a protected offer.

(59) *Published aggregate quotation size* means the aggregate quotation size calculated by a na-

tional securities exchange and displayed by a vendor on a terminal or other display device at the time an order is presented for execution to a responsible broker or dealer.

(60) *Published bid and published offer* means the bid or offer of a responsible broker or dealer for an NMS security communicated by it to its national securities exchange or association pursuant to Rule 602 and displayed by a vendor on a terminal or other display device at the time an order is presented for execution to such responsible broker or dealer.

(61) *Published quotation size* means the quotation size of a responsible broker or dealer communicated by it to its national securities exchange or association pursuant to Rule 602 and displayed by a vendor on a terminal or other display device at the time an order is presented for execution to such responsible broker or dealer.

(62) *Quotation* means a bid or an offer.

(63) *Quotation size*, when used with respect to a responsible broker's or dealer's bid or offer for an NMS security, means:

(i) The number of shares (or units of trading) of that security which such responsible broker or dealer has specified, for purposes of dissemination to vendors, that it is willing to buy at the bid price or sell at the offer price comprising its bid or offer, as either principal or agent; or

(ii) In the event such responsible broker or dealer has not so specified, a normal unit of trading for that NMS security.

(64) *Regular trading hours* means the time between 9:30 a.m. and 4:00 p.m. Eastern Time, or such other time as is set forth in the procedures established pursuant to Rule 605(a)(2).

(65) *Responsible broker or dealer* means:

(i) When used with respect to bids or offers communicated on a national securities exchange, any member of such national securities exchange who communicates to another member on such national securities exchange, at the location (or locations) or through the facility or facilities designated by such national securities exchange for trading in an NMS security a bid or offer for such NMS security, as either principal or agent; *provided, however,* that, in the event two or more members of a national securities exchange have communicated on or through such national securities exchange bids or offers for an NMS security at the same price, each such member shall be considered a *responsible broker or dealer* for that bid or offer, subject to the rules of priority and precedence then in effect on that national securities exchange; and further *provided,* that for a bid or offer which is transmitted from one member of a national securities exchange to another member who undertakes to represent such bid or offer on such national securities exchange as agent, only the last member who undertakes to represent such bid or offer as agent shall be considered the *responsible broker or dealer* for that bid or offer; and

(ii) When used with respect to bids and offers communicated by a member of an association to a broker or dealer or a customer, the member communicating the bid or offer (regardless of whether such bid or offer is for its own account or on behalf of another person).

(66) *Revised bid or offer* means a market maker's bid or offer which supersedes its published bid or published offer

(67) *Revised quotation size* means a market maker's quotation size which supersedes its published quotation size.

(68) *Self-regulatory organization* means any national securities exchange or national securities association.

(69) *Specified persons*, when used in connection with any notification required to be provided pursuant to Rule 602(a)(3) and any election (or withdrawal thereof) permitted under Rule 602(a)(5), means:

(i) Each vendor;

(ii) Each plan processor; and

(iii) The processor for the Options Price Reporting Authority (in the case of a notification for a subject security which is a class of securities underlying options admitted to trading on any national securities exchange).

(70) *Sponsor*, when used in connection with a national market system plan, means any self-regulatory organization which is a signatory to such plan and has agreed to act in accordance with the terms of the plan.

(71) *SRO display-only facility* means a facility operated by or on behalf of a national securities exchange or national securities association that displays quotations in a security, but does not ex-

ecute orders against such quotations or present orders to members for execution.

(72) *SRO trading facility* means a facility operated by or on behalf of a national securities exchange or a national securities association that executes orders in a security or presents orders to members for execution.

(73) *Subject security* means:

(i) With respect to a national securities exchange:

(A) Any exchange-traded security other than a security for which the executed volume of such exchange, during the most recent calendar quarter, comprised one percent or less of the aggregate trading volume for such security as reported pursuant to an effective transaction reporting plan or effective national market system plan; and

(B) Any other NMS security for which such exchange has in effect an election, pursuant to Rule 602(a)(5)(i), to collect, process, and make available to a vendor bids, offers, quotation sizes, and aggregate quotation sizes communicated on such exchange; and

(ii) With respect to a member of a national securities association:

(A) Any exchange-traded security for which such member acts in the capacity of an OTC market maker unless the executed volume of such member, during the most recent calendar quarter, comprised one percent or less of the aggregate trading volume for such security as reported pursuant to an effective transaction reporting plan or effective national market system plan; and

(B) Any other NMS security for which such member acts in the capacity of an OTC market maker and has in effect an election, pursuant to Rule 602(a)(5)(ii), to communicate to its association bids, offers, and quotation sizes for the purpose of making such bids, offers, and quotation sizes available to a vendor.

(74) *Time of order execution* means the time (to the second) that an order was executed at any venue.

(75) *Time of order receipt* means the time (to the second) that an order was received by a market center for execution.

(76) *Time of the transaction* has the meaning provided in Rule 10b–10 under the Securities Exchange Act of 1934.

(77) *Trade-through* means the purchase or sale of an NMS stock during regular trading hours, either as principal or agent, at a price that is lower than a protected bid or higher than a protected offer.

(78) *Trading center* means a national securities exchange or national securities association that operates an SRO trading facility, an alternative trading system, an exchange market maker, an OTC market maker, or any other broker or dealer that executes orders internally by trading as principal or crossing orders as agent.

(79) *Trading rotation* means, with respect to an options class, the time period on a national securities exchange during which:

(i) Opening, re-opening, or closing transactions in options series in such options class are not yet completed; and

(ii) Continuous trading has not yet commenced or has not yet ended for the day in options series in such options class.

(80) *Transaction report* means a report containing the price and volume associated with a transaction involving the purchase or sale of one or more round lots of a security.

(81) *Transaction reporting association* means any person authorized to implement or administer any transaction reporting plan on behalf of persons acting jointly under Rule 601(a).

(82) *Transaction reporting plan* means any plan for collecting, processing, making available or disseminating transaction reports with respect to transactions in securities filed with the Commission pursuant to, and meeting the requirements of, Rule 601.

(83) *Vendor* means any securities information processor engaged in the business of disseminating transaction reports, last sale data, or quotations with respect to NMS securities to brokers, dealers, or investors on a real-time or other current and continuing basis, whether through an electronic communications network, moving ticker, or interrogation device.

Rule 601. Dissemination of transaction reports and last sale data with respect to transactions in NMS stocks

(a) *Filing and Effectiveness of Transaction Reporting Plans.* (1) Every national securities exchange shall file a transaction reporting plan regarding transactions in listed equity and Nasdaq securities executed through its facilities, and every national securities association shall file a transaction reporting plan regarding transactions in listed equity and Nasdaq securities executed by its members otherwise than on a national securities exchange.

(2) Any transaction reporting plan, or any amendment thereto, filed pursuant to this section shall be filed with the Commission, and considered for approval, in accordance with the procedures set forth in Rule 608(a) and (b). Any such plan, or amendment thereto, shall specify, at a minimum:

(i) The listed equity and Nasdaq securities or classes of such securities for which transaction reports shall be required by the plan;

(ii) Reporting requirements with respect to transactions in listed equity securities and Nasdaq securities, for any broker or dealer subject to the plan;

(iii) The manner of collecting, processing, sequencing, making available and disseminating transaction reports and last sale data reported pursuant to such plan;

(iv) The manner in which such transaction reports reported pursuant to such plan are to be consolidated with transaction reports from national securities exchanges and national securities associations reported pursuant to any other effective transaction reporting plan;

(v) The applicable standards and methods which will be utilized to ensure promptness of reporting, and accuracy and completeness of transaction reports;

(vi) Any rules or procedures which may be adopted to ensure that transaction reports or last sale data will not be disseminated in a fraudulent or manipulative manner;

(vii) Specific terms of access to transaction reports made available or disseminated pursuant to the plan; and

(viii) That transaction reports or last sale data made available to any vendor for display on an interrogation device identify the marketplace where each transaction was executed.

(3) No transaction reporting plan filed pursuant to this section, or any amendment to an effective transaction reporting plan, shall become effective unless approved by the Commission or otherwise permitted in accordance with the procedures set forth in Rule 608.

(b) *Prohibitions and Reporting Requirements.* (1) No broker or dealer may execute any transaction in, or induce or attempt to induce the purchase or sale of, any NMS stock:

(i) On or through the facilities of a national securities exchange unless there is an effective transaction reporting plan with respect to transactions in such security executed on or through such exchange facilities; or

(ii) Otherwise than on a national securities exchange unless there is an effective transaction reporting plan with respect to transactions in such security executed otherwise than on a national securities exchange by such broker or dealer.

(2) Every broker or dealer who is a member of a national securities exchange or national securities association shall promptly transmit to the exchange or association of which it is a member all information required by any effective transaction reporting plan filed by such exchange or association (either individually or jointly with other exchanges and/or associations).

(c) *Retransmission of Transaction Reports or Last Sale Data.* Notwithstanding any provision of any effective transaction reporting plan, no national securities exchange or national securities association may, either individually or jointly, by rule, stated policy or practice, transaction reporting plan or otherwise, prohibit, condition or otherwise limit, directly or indirectly, the ability of any vendor to retransmit, for display in moving tickers, transaction reports or last sale data made available pursuant to any effective transaction reporting plan; *provided, however,* that a national securities exchange or national securities association may, by means of an effective transaction reporting plan, condition such retransmission upon appropriate undertakings to ensure that any charges for the distribution of transaction reports or last sale data in moving tickers permitted by paragraph (d) of this rule are collected.

(d) *Charges.* Nothing in this rule shall preclude any national securities exchange or national securities association, separately or jointly, pursuant to the terms of an effective transaction reporting plan, from imposing reasonable, uniform charges (irrespective of geographic location) for distribution of transaction reports or last sale data.

(e) *Appeals*. The Commission may, in its discretion, entertain appeals in connection with the implementation or operation of any effective transaction reporting plan in accordance with the provisions of Rule 608(d).

(f) *Exemptions*. The Commission may exempt from the provisions of this rule, either unconditionally or on specified terms and conditions, any national securities exchange, national securities association, broker, dealer, or specified security if the Commission determines that such exemption is consistent with the public interest, the protection of investors and the removal of impediments to, and perfection of the mechanisms of, a national market system.

Rule 602. Dissemination of quotations in NMS securities

(a) *Dissemination Requirements for National Securities Exchanges and National Securities Associations*. (1) Every national securities exchange and national securities association shall establish and maintain procedures and mechanisms for collecting bids, offers, quotation sizes, and aggregate quotation sizes from responsible brokers or dealers who are members of such exchange or association, processing such bids, offers, and sizes, and making such bids, offers, and sizes available to vendors, as follows:

(i) Each national securities exchange shall at all times such exchange is open for trading, collect, process, and make available to vendors the best bid, the best offer, and aggregate quotation sizes for each subject security listed or admitted to unlisted trading privileges which is communicated on any national securities exchange by any responsible broker or dealer, but shall not include:

(A) Any bid or offer executed immediately after communication and any bid or offer communicated by a responsible broker or dealer other than an exchange market maker which is cancelled or withdrawn if not executed immediately after communication; and

(B) Any bid or offer communicated during a period when trading in that security has been suspended or halted, or prior to the commencement of trading in that security on any trading day, on that exchange.

(ii) Each national securities association shall, at all times that last sale information with respect to NMS securities is reported pursuant to an effective transaction reporting plan, collect, process, and make available to vendors the best bid, best offer, and quotation sizes communicated otherwise than on an exchange by each member of such association acting in the capacity of an OTC market maker for each subject security and the identity of that member (excluding any bid or offer executed immediately after communication), except during any period when over-the-counter trading in that security has been suspended.

(2) Each national securities exchange shall, with respect to each published bid and published offer representing a bid or offer of a member for a subject security, establish and maintain procedures for ascertaining and disclosing to other members of that exchange, upon presentation of orders sought to be executed by them in reliance upon paragraph (b)(2) of this rule, the identity of the responsible broker or dealer who made such bid or offer and the quotation size associated with it.

(3)(i) If, at any time a national securities exchange is open for trading, such exchange determines, pursuant to rules approved by the Commission pursuant to section 19(b)(2) of the Act (15 U.S.C. 78s(b)(2)), that the level of trading activities or the existence of unusual market conditions is such that the exchange is incapable of collecting, processing, and making available to vendors the data for a subject security required to be made available pursuant to paragraph (a)(1) of this rule in a manner that accurately reflects the current state of the market on such exchange, such exchange shall immediately notify all specified persons of that determination. Upon such notification, responsible brokers or dealers that are members of that exchange shall be relieved of their obligation under paragraphs (b)(2) and (c)(3) of this rule and such exchange shall be relieved of its obligations under paragraphs (a)(1) and (2) of this rule for that security; *provided, however,* that such exchange will continue, to the maximum extent practicable under the circumstances, to collect, process, and make available to vendors data for that security in accordance with paragraph (a)(1) of this rule.

(ii) During any period a national securities exchange, or any responsible broker or dealer that is a member of that exchange, is relieved of any obligation imposed by this section for any subject security by virtue of a notification made pursuant to paragraph (a)(3)(i) of this rule, such exchange shall monitor the activity or conditions which formed the basis for such notification and shall immediately renotify all specified persons when that exchange is once again capable of collecting, processing, and making available to vendors the data for that security required to be made available pursuant to paragraph (a)(1) of this rule in a manner that accurately reflects the current state of the market on such exchange. Upon such renotification, any exchange or responsible broker or dealer which had been relieved of any obligation imposed by this section as a consequence of the prior notification shall again be subject to such obligation.

(4) Nothing in this rule shall preclude any national securities exchange or national securities association from making available to vendors indications of interest or bids and offers for a subject security at any time such exchange or association is not required to do so pursuant to paragraph (a)(1) of this rule.

(5)(i) Any national securities exchange may make an election for purposes of the definition of *subject security* in Rule 600(b)(73) for any NMS security, by collecting, processing, and making available bids, offers, quotation sizes, and aggregate quotation sizes in that security; except that for any NMS security previously listed or admitted to unlisted trading privileges on only one exchange and not traded by any OTC market maker, such election shall be made by notifying all specified persons, and shall be effective at the opening of trading on the business day following notification.

(ii) Any member of a national securities association acting in the capacity of an OTC market maker may make an election for purposes of the definition of *subject security* in Rule 600(b)(73) for any NMS security, by communicating to its association bids, offers, and quotation sizes in that security; except that for any other NMS security listed or admitted to unlisted trading privileges on only one exchange and not traded by any other OTC market maker, such election shall be made by notifying its association and all specified persons, and shall be effective at the opening of trading on the business day following notification.

(iii) The election of a national securities exchange or member of a national securities association for any NMS security pursuant to this paragraph (a)(5) shall cease to be in effect if such exchange or member ceases to make available or communicate bids, offers, and quotation sizes in such security.

(b) *Obligations of Responsible Brokers and Dealers.* (1) Each responsible broker or dealer shall promptly communicate to its national securities exchange or national securities association, pursuant to the procedures established by that exchange or association, its best bids, best offers, and quotation sizes for any subject security.

(2) Subject to the provisions of paragraph (b)(3) of this rule, each responsible broker or dealer shall be obligated to execute any order to buy or sell a subject security, other than an odd-lot order, presented to it by another broker or dealer, or any other person belonging to a category of persons with whom such responsible broker or dealer customarily deals, at a price at least as favorable to such buyer or seller as the responsible broker's or dealer's published bid or published offer (exclusive of any commission, commission equivalent or differential customarily charged by such responsible broker or dealer in connection with execution of any such order) in any amount up to its published quotation size.

(3)(i) No responsible broker or dealer shall be obligated to execute a transaction for any subject security as provided in paragraph (b)(2) of this rule to purchase or sell that subject security in an amount greater than such revised quotation size if:

(A) Prior to the presentation of an order for the purchase or sale of a subject security, a responsible broker or dealer has communicated to its exchange or association, pursuant to paragraph (b)(1) of this rule, a revised quotation size; or

(B) At the time an order for the purchase or sale of a subject security is presented, a responsible broker or dealer is in the process of effecting a transaction in such subject security, and immediately after the completion of such transaction, it communicates to its exchange or association a revised quotation size, such responsible broker or dealer shall not be obligated by paragraph (b)(2) of this rule to purchase or sell that subject security in an amount greater than such revised quotation size.

(ii) No responsible broker or dealer shall be obligated to execute a transaction for any subject security as provided in paragraph (b)(2) of this rule if:

(A) Before the order sought to be executed is presented, such responsible broker or dealer has communicated to its exchange or association pursuant to paragraph (b)(1) of this rule, a revised bid or offer; or

(B) At the time the order sought to be executed is presented, such responsible broker or dealer is in the process of effecting a transaction in such subject security, and, immediately after the completion of such transaction, such responsible broker or dealer communicates to its exchange or association pursuant to paragraph (b)(1) of this rule, a revised bid or offer; *provided, however,* that such responsible broker or dealer shall nonetheless be obligated to execute any such order in such subject security as provided in paragraph (b)(2) of this rule at its revised bid or offer in any amount up to its published quotation size or revised quotation size.

(4) Subject to the provisions of paragraph (a)(4) of this rule:

(i) No national securities exchange or OTC market maker may make available, disseminate or otherwise communicate to any vendor, directly or indirectly, for display on a terminal or other display device any bid, offer, quotation size, or aggregate quotation size for any NMS security which is not a subject security with respect to such exchange or OTC market maker; and

(ii) No vendor may disseminate or display on a terminal or other display device any bid, offer, quotation size, or aggregate quotation size from any national securities exchange or OTC market maker for any NMS security which is not a subject security with respect to such exchange or OTC market maker.

(5)(i) Entry of any priced order for an NMS security by an exchange market maker or OTC market maker in that security into an electronic communications network that widely disseminates such order shall be deemed to be:

(A) A bid or offer under this rule, to be communicated to the market maker's exchange or association pursuant to this paragraph (b) for at least the minimum quotation size that is required by the rules of the market maker's exchange or association if the priced order is for the account of a market maker, or the actual size of the order up to the minimum quotation size required if the priced order is for the account of a customer; and

(B) A communication of a bid or offer to a vendor for display on a display device for purposes of paragraph (b)(4) of this rule.

(ii) An exchange market maker or OTC market maker that has entered a priced order for an NMS security into an electronic communications network that widely disseminates such order shall be deemed to be in compliance with paragraph (b)(5)(i)(A) of this rule if the electronic communications network:

(A)(*1*) Provides to a national securities exchange or national securities association (or an exclusive processor acting on behalf of one or more exchanges or associations) the prices and sizes of the orders at the highest buy price and the lowest sell price for such security entered in, and widely disseminated by, the electronic communications network by exchange market makers and OTC market makers for the NMS security, and such prices and sizes are included in the quotation data made available by such exchange, association, or exclusive processor to vendors pursuant to this rule; and

(*2*) Provides, to any broker or dealer, the ability to effect a transaction with a priced order widely disseminated by the electronic communications network entered therein by an exchange market maker or OTC market maker that is:

(*i*) Equivalent to the ability of any broker or dealer to effect a transaction with an exchange market maker or OTC market maker pursuant to the rules of the national securities exchange or national securities association to which the electronic communications network supplies such bids and offers; and

(*ii*) At the price of the highest priced buy order or lowest priced sell order, or better, for the lesser of the cumulative size of such priced orders entered therein by exchange market makers or OTC market makers at such price, or the size of the execution sought by the broker or dealer, for such security; or

(B) Is an alternative trading system that:

(*1*) Displays orders and provides the ability to effect transactions with such orders under Rule 301(b)(3); and

(*2*) Otherwise is in compliance with Regulation ATS (Rule 300 through 303).

(c) *Transactions in Listed Options.* (1) A national securities exchange or national securities association:

(i) Shall not be required, under paragraph (a) of this rule, to collect from responsible brokers or dealers who are members of such exchange or association, or to make available to vendors, the quotation sizes and aggregate quotation sizes for listed options, if such exchange or association establishes by rule and periodically publishes the quotation size for which such responsible brokers or dealers are obligated to execute an order to buy or sell an options series that is a subject security at its published bid or offer under paragraph (b)(2) of this rule;

(ii) May establish by rule and periodically publish a quotation size, which shall not be for less than one contract, for which responsible brokers or dealers who are members of such exchange or association are obligated under paragraph (b)(2) of this rule to execute an order to buy or sell a listed option for the account of a broker or dealer that is in an amount different from the quotation size for which it is obligated to execute an order for the account of a customer; and

(iii) May establish and maintain procedures and mechanisms for collecting from responsible brokers and dealers who are members of such exchange or association, and making available to vendors, the quotation sizes and aggregate quotation sizes in listed options for which such responsible broker or dealer will be obligated under paragraph (b)(2) of this rule to execute an order from a customer to buy or sell a listed option and establish by rule and periodically publish the size, which shall not be less than one contract, for which such responsible brokers or dealers are obligated to execute an order for the account of a broker or dealer.

(2) If, pursuant to paragraph (c)(1) of this rule, the rules of a national securities exchange or national securities association do not require its members to communicate to it their quotation sizes for listed options, a responsible broker or dealer that is a member of such exchange or association shall:

(i) Be relieved of its obligations under paragraph (b)(1) of this rule to communicate to such exchange or association its quotation sizes for any listed option; and

(ii) Comply with its obligations under paragraph (b)(2) of this rule by executing any order to buy or sell a listed option, in an amount up to the size established by such exchange's or association's rules under paragraph (c)(1) of this rule.

(3) *Thirty Second Response.* Each responsible broker or dealer, within thirty seconds of receiving an order to buy or sell a listed option in an amount greater than the quotation size established by a national securities exchange's or national securities association's rules pursuant to paragraph (c)(1) of this rule, or its published quotation size must:

(i) Execute the entire order; or

(ii)(A) Execute that portion of the order equal to at least:

(*1*) The quotation size established by a national securities exchange's or national securities association's rules, pursuant to paragraph (c)(1) of this rule, to the extent that such exchange or association does not collect and make available to vendors quotation size and aggregate quotation size under paragraph (a) of this rule; or

(*2*) Its published quotation size; and

(B) Revise its bid or offer.

(4) Notwithstanding paragraph (c)(3) of this rule, no responsible broker or dealer shall be obligated to execute a transaction for any listed option as provided in paragraph (b)(2) of this rule if:

(i) Any of the circumstances in paragraph (b)(3) of this rule exist; or

(ii) The order for the purchase or sale of a listed option is presented during a trading rotation in that listed option.

(d) *Exemptions.* The Commission may exempt from the provisions of this section, either unconditionally or on specified terms and conditions, any responsible broker or dealer, electronic communications network, national securities exchange, or national securities association if the Commission determines that such exemption is consistent with the public interest, the protection of investors and the removal of impediments to and perfection of the mechanism of a national market system.

Rule 603. Distribution, consolidation, and display of information with respect to quotations for and transactions in NMS Stocks

(a) *Distribution of Information.* (1) Any exclusive processor, or any broker or dealer with respect to information for which it is the exclusive source, that distributes information with respect to quotations for or transactions in an NMS stock to a securities information processor shall do so on terms that are fair and reasonable.

(2) Any national securities exchange, national securities association, broker, or dealer that distributes information with respect to quotations for or transactions in an NMS stock to a securities information processor, broker, dealer, or other persons shall do so on terms that are not unreasonably discriminatory.

(b) *Consolidation of Information.* Every national securities exchange on which an NMS stock is traded and national securities association shall act jointly pursuant to one or more effective national market system plans to disseminate consolidated information, including a national best bid and national best offer, on quotations for and transactions in NMS stocks. Such plan or plans shall provide for the dissemination of all consolidated information for an individual NMS stock through a single plan processor.

(c) *Display of Information.* (1) No securities information processor, broker, or dealer shall provide, in a context in which a trading or order-routing decision can be implemented, a display of any information with respect to quotations for or transactions in an NMS stock without also providing, in an equivalent manner, a consolidated display for such stock.

(2) The provisions of paragraph (c)(1) of this rule shall not apply to a display of information on the trading floor or through the facilities of a national securities exchange or to a display in connection with the operation of a market linkage system implemented in accordance with an effective national market system plan.

(d) *Exemptions.* The Commission, by order, may exempt from the provisions of this rule, either unconditionally or on specified terms and conditions, any person, security, or item of information, or any class or classes of persons, securities, or items of information, if the Commission determines that such exemption is necessary or appropriate in the public interest, and is consistent with the protection of investors.

Rule 604. Display of customer limit orders

(a) *Specialists and OTC Market Makers.* For all NMS stocks:

(1) Each member of a national securities exchange that is registered by that exchange as a specialist, or is authorized by that exchange to perform functions substantially similar to that of a specialist, shall publish immediately a bid or offer that reflects:

(i) The price and the full size of each customer limit order held by the specialist that is at a price that would improve the bid or offer of such specialist in such security; and

(ii) The full size of each customer limit order held by the specialist that:

(A) Is priced equal to the bid or offer of such specialist for such security;

(B) Is priced equal to the national best bid or national best offer; and

(C) Represents more than a *de minimis* change in relation to the size associated with the specialist's bid or offer.

(2) Each registered broker or dealer that acts as an OTC market maker shall publish immediately a bid or offer that reflects:

(i) The price and the full size of each customer limit order held by the OTC market maker that is at a price that would improve the bid or offer of such OTC market maker in such security; and

(ii) The full size of each customer limit order held by the OTC market maker that:

(A) Is priced equal to the bid or offer of such OTC market maker for such security;

(B) Is priced equal to the national best bid or national best offer; and

(C) Represents more than a *de minimis* change in relation to the size associated with the OTC market maker's bid or offer.

(b) *Exceptions.* The requirements in paragraph (a) of this rule shall not apply to any customer limit order:

(1) That is executed upon receipt of the order.

(2) That is placed by a customer who expressly requests, either at the time that the order is placed or prior thereto pursuant to an individu-

ally negotiated agreement with respect to such customer's orders, that the order not be displayed.

(3) That is an odd-lot order.

(4) That is a block size order, unless a customer placing such order requests that the order be displayed.

(5) That is delivered immediately upon receipt to a national securities exchange or national securities association-sponsored system, or an electronic communications network that complies with the requirements of Rule 602(b)(5)(ii) with respect to that order.

(6) That is delivered immediately upon receipt to another exchange member or OTC market maker that complies with the requirements of this rule with respect to that order.

(7) That is an "all or none" order.

(c) *Exemptions.* The Commission may exempt from the provisions of this rule, either unconditionally or on specified terms and conditions, any responsible broker or dealer, electronic communications network, national securities exchange, or national securities association if the Commission determines that such exemption is consistent with the public interest, the protection of investors and the removal of impediments to and perfection of the mechanism of a national market system.

Rule 605. Disclosure of order execution information

PRELIMINARY NOTE:

Rule 605 requires market centers to make available standardized, monthly reports of statistical information concerning their order executions. This information is presented in accordance with uniform standards that are based on broad assumptions about order execution and routing practices. The information will provide a starting point to promote visibility and competition on the part of market centers and broker-dealers, particularly on the factors of execution price and speed. The disclosures required by this rule do not encompass all of the factors that may be important to investors in evaluating the order routing services of a broker-dealer. In addition, any particular market center's statistics will encompass varying types of orders routed by different broker-dealers on behalf of customers with a wide range of objectives. Accordingly, the statistical information required by this rule alone does not create a reliable basis to address whether any particular broker-dealer failed to obtain the most favorable terms reasonably available under the circumstances for customer orders.

(a) *Monthly Electronic Reports by Market Centers.* (1) Every market center shall make available for each calendar month, in accordance with the procedures established pursuant to paragraph (a)(2) of this rule, a report on the covered orders in NMS stocks that it received for execution from any person. Such report shall be in electronic form; shall be categorized by security, order type, and order size; and shall include the following columns of information:

(i) For market orders, marketable limit orders, inside-the-quote limit orders, at-the-quote limit orders, and near-the-quote limit orders:

(A) The number of covered orders;

(B) The cumulative number of shares of covered orders;

(C) The cumulative number of shares of covered orders cancelled prior to execution;

(D) The cumulative number of shares of covered orders executed at the receiving market center;

(E) The cumulative number of shares of covered orders executed at any other venue;

(F) The cumulative number of shares of covered orders executed from 0 to 9 seconds after the time of order receipt;

(G) The cumulative number of shares of covered orders executed from 10 to 29 seconds after the time of order receipt;

(H) The cumulative number of shares of covered orders executed from 30 seconds to 59 seconds after the time of order receipt;

(I) The cumulative number of shares of covered orders executed from 60 seconds to 299 seconds after the time of order receipt;

(J) The cumulative number of shares of covered orders executed from 5 minutes to 30 minutes after the time of order receipt; and

(K) The average realized spread for executions of covered orders; and

(ii) For market orders and marketable limit orders:

(A) The average effective spread for executions of covered orders;

(B) The cumulative number of shares of covered orders executed with price improvement;

(C) For shares executed with price improvement, the share-weighted average amount per share that prices were improved;

(D) For shares executed with price improvement, the share-weighted average period from the time of order receipt to the time of order execution;

(E) The cumulative number of shares of covered orders executed at the quote;

(F) For shares executed at the quote, the share-weighted average period from the time of order receipt to the time of order execution;

(G) The cumulative number of shares of covered orders executed outside the quote;

(H) For shares executed outside the quote, the share-weighted average amount per share that prices were outside the quote; and

(I) For shares executed outside the quote, the share-weighted average period from the time of order receipt to the time of order execution.

(2) Every national securities exchange on which NMS stocks are traded and each national securities association shall act jointly in establishing procedures for market centers to follow in making available to the public the reports required by paragraph (a)(1) of this rule in a uniform, readily accessible, and usable electronic form. In the event there is no effective national market system plan establishing such procedures, market centers shall prepare their reports in a consistent, usable, and machine-readable electronic format, and make such reports available for downloading from an Internet Web site that is free and readily accessible to the public.

(3) A market center shall make available the report required by paragraph (a)(1) of this rule within one month after the end of the month addressed in the report.

(b) *Exemptions*. The Commission may, by order upon application, conditionally or unconditionally exempt any person, security, or transaction, or any class or classes of persons, securities, or transactions, from any provision or provisions of this rule, if the Commission determines that such exemption is necessary or appropriate in the public interest, and is consistent with the protection of investors.

Rule 606. Disclosure of order routing information

(a) *Quarterly Report on Order Routing*. (1) Every broker or dealer shall make publicly available for each calendar quarter a report on its routing of non-directed orders in NMS securities during that quarter. For NMS stocks, such report shall be divided into three separate sections for securities that are listed on the New York Stock Exchange, Inc., securities that are qualified for inclusion in The Nasdaq Stock Market, Inc., and securities that are listed on the American Stock Exchange LLC or any other national securities exchange. Such report also shall include a separate section for NMS securities that are option contracts. Each of the four sections in a report shall include the following information:

(i) The percentage of total customer orders for the section that were non-directed orders, and the percentages of total non-directed orders for the section that were market orders, limit orders, and other orders;

(ii) The identity of the ten venues to which the largest number of total non-directed orders for the section were routed for execution and of any venue to which five percent or more of non-directed orders were routed for execution, the percentage of total non-directed orders for the section routed to the venue, and the percentages of total non-directed market orders, total non-directed limit orders, and total non-directed other orders for the section that were routed to the venue; and

(iii) A discussion of the material aspects of the broker's or dealer's relationship with each venue identified pursuant to paragraph (a)(1)(ii) of this rule, including a description of any arrangement for payment for order flow and any profit-sharing relationship.

(2) A broker or dealer shall make the report required by paragraph (a)(1) of this rule publicly available within one month after the end of the quarter addressed in the report.

(b) *Customer Requests for Information on Order Routing*. (1) Every broker or dealer shall, on request of a customer, disclose to its customer the identity of the venue to which the customer's orders were routed for execution in the six months prior to the request, whether the orders were directed orders or non-directed orders, and the time of the transactions, if any, that resulted from such orders.

(2) A broker or dealer shall notify customers in writing at least annually of the availability on request of the information specified in paragraph (b)(1) of this rule.

(c) *Exemptions*. The Commission may, by order upon application, conditionally or unconditionally exempt any person, security, or transaction, or any class or classes of persons, securities, or transactions, from any provision or provisions of this rule, if the Commission determines that such exemption is necessary or appropriate in the public interest, and is consistent with the protection of investors.

Rule 607. Customer account statements

(a) No broker or dealer acting as agent for a customer may effect any transaction in, induce or attempt to induce the purchase or sale of, or direct orders for purchase or sale of, any NMS stock or a security authorized for quotation on an automated inter-dealer quotation system that has the characteristics set forth in section 17B of the Act, unless such broker or dealer informs such customer, in writing, upon opening a new account and on an annual basis thereafter, of the following:

(1) The broker's or dealer's policies regarding receipt of payment for order flow from any broker or dealer, national securities exchange, national securities association, or exchange member to which it routes customers' orders for execution, including a statement as to whether any payment for order flow is received for routing customer orders and a detailed description of the nature of the compensation received; and

(2) The broker's or dealer's policies for determining where to route customer orders that are the subject of payment for order flow absent specific instructions from customers, including a description of the extent to which orders can be executed at prices superior to the national best bid and national best offer.

(b) *Exemptions.* The Commission, upon request or upon its own motion, may exempt by rule or by order, any broker or dealer or any class of brokers or dealers, security or class of securities from the requirements of paragraph (a) of this rule with respect to any transaction or class of transactions, either unconditionally or on specified terms and conditions, if the Commission determines that such exemption is consistent with the public interest and the protection of investors.

Rule 608. Filing and amendment of national market system plans

(a) *Filing of National Market System Plans and Amendments Thereto.* (1) Any two or more self-regulatory organizations, acting jointly, may file a national market system plan or may propose an amendment to an effective national market system plan ("proposed amendment") by submitting the text of the plan or amendment to the Secretary of the Commission, together with a statement of the purpose of such plan or amendment and, to the extent applicable, the documents and information required by paragraphs (a)(4) and (5) of this rule.

(2) The Commission may propose amendments to any effective national market system plan by publishing the text thereof, together with a statement of the purpose of such amendment, in accordance with the provisions of paragraph (b) of this rule.

(3) Self-regulatory organizations are authorized to act jointly in:

(i) Planning, developing, and operating any national market subsystem or facility contemplated by a national market system plan;

(ii) Preparing and filing a national market system plan or any amendment thereto; or

(iii) Implementing or administering an effective national market system plan.

(4) Every national market system plan filed pursuant to this section, or any amendment thereto, shall be accompanied by:

(i) Copies of all governing or constituent documents relating to any person (other than a self-regulatory organization) authorized to implement or administer such plan on behalf of its sponsors; and

(ii) To the extent applicable:

(A) A detailed description of the manner in which the plan or amendment, and any facility or procedure contemplated by the plan or amendment, will be implemented;

(B) A listing of all significant phases of development and implementation (including any pilot phase) contemplated by the plan or amendment, together with the projected date of completion of each phase;

(C) An analysis of the impact on competition of implementation of the plan or amendment or of any facility contemplated by the plan or amendment;

(D) A description of any written understandings or agreements between or among plan sponsors or participants relating to interpretations of the plan or conditions for becoming a sponsor or participant in the plan; and

(E) In the case of a proposed amendment, a statement that such amendment has been approved by the sponsors in accordance with the terms of the plan.

(5) Every national market system plan, or any amendment thereto, filed pursuant to this section shall include a description of the manner in which any facility contemplated by the plan or amendment will be operated. Such description shall include, to the extent applicable:

(i) The terms and conditions under which brokers, dealers, and/or self-regulatory organizations will be granted or denied access (including specific procedures and standards governing the granting or denial of access);

(ii) The method by which any fees or charges collected on behalf of all of the sponsors and/or participants in connection with access to, or use of, any facility contemplated by the plan or amendment will be determined and imposed (including any provision for distribution of any net proceeds from such fees or charges to the sponsors and/or participants) and the amount of such fees or charges;

(iii) The method by which, and the frequency with which, the performance of any person acting as plan processor with respect to the implementation and/or operation of the plan will be evaluated; and

(iv) The method by which disputes arising in connection with the operation of the plan will be resolved.

(6) In connection with the selection of any person to act as plan processor with respect to any facility contemplated by a national market system plan (including renewal of any contract for any person to so act), the sponsors shall file with the Commission a statement identifying the person selected, describing the material terms under which such person is to serve as plan processor, and indicating the solicitation efforts, if any, for alternative plan processors, the alternatives considered and the reasons for selection of such person.

(7) Any national market system plan (or any amendment thereto) which is intended by the sponsors to satisfy a plan filing requirement contained in any other section of this Regulation NMS and part 240, subpart A shall, in addition to compliance with this rule, also comply with the requirements of such other rule.

(8)(i) A participant in an effective national market system plan shall ensure that a current and complete version of the plan is posted on a plan Web site or on a Web site designated by plan participants within two business days after notification by the Commission of effectiveness of the plan. Each participant in an effective national market system plan shall ensure that such Web site is updated to reflect amendments to such plan within two business days after the plan participants have been notified by the Commission of its approval of a proposed amendment pursuant to paragraph (b) of this rule. If the amendment is not effective for a certain period, the plan participants shall clearly indicate the effective date in the relevant text of the plan. Each plan participant also shall provide a link on its own Web site to the Web site with the current version of the plan.

(ii) The plan participants shall ensure that any proposed amendments filed pursuant to paragraph (a) of this rule are posted on a plan Web site or a designated Web site no later than two business days after the filing of the proposed amendments with the Commission. The plan participants shall maintain any proposed amendment to the plan on a plan Web site or a designated Web site until the Commission approves the plan amendment and the plan participants update the Web site to reflect such amendment or the plan participants withdraw the proposed amendment. If the plan participants withdraw proposed amendments, the plan participants shall remove such amendments from the plan Web site or designated Web site within two business days of withdrawal. Each plan participant shall provide a link to the Web site with the current version of the plan.

(b) *Effectiveness of National Market System Plans.* (1) The Commission shall publish notice of the filing of any national market system plan, or any proposed amendment to any effective national market system plan (including any amendment initiated by the Commission), together with the terms of substance of the filing or a description of the subjects and issues involved, and shall provide interested persons an opportunity to submit written comments. No national market system plan, or any amendment thereto, shall become effective unless approved by the Commission or otherwise permitted in accordance with paragraph (b)(3) of this rule.

(2) Within 120 days of the date of publication of notice of filing of a national market system plan or an amendment to an effective national market system plan, or within such longer period as the Commission may designate up to 180 days of such date if it finds such longer period to be appropriate and publishes its reasons for so finding or as to which the sponsors consent, the Commission

shall approve such plan or amendment, with such changes or subject to such conditions as the Commission may deem necessary or appropriate, if it finds that such plan or amendment is necessary or appropriate in the public interest, for the protection of investors and the maintenance of fair and orderly markets, to remove impediments to, and perfect the mechanisms of, a national market system, or otherwise in furtherance of the purposes of the Act. Approval of a national market system plan, or an amendment to an effective national market system plan (other than an amendment initiated by the Commission), shall be by order. Promulgation of an amendment to an effective national market system plan initiated by the Commission shall be by rule.

(3) A proposed amendment may be put into effect upon filing with the Commission if designated by the sponsors as:

(i) Establishing or changing a fee or other charge collected on behalf of all of the sponsors and/or participants in connection with access to, or use of, any facility contemplated by the plan or amendment (including changes in any provision with respect to distribution of any net proceeds from such fees or other charges to the sponsors and/or participants);

(ii) Concerned solely with the administration of the plan, or involving the governing or constituent documents relating to any person (other than a self-regulatory organization) authorized to implement or administer such plan on behalf of its sponsors; or

(iii) Involving solely technical or ministerial matters. At any time within 60 days of the filing of any such amendment, the Commission may summarily abrogate the amendment and require that such amendment be refiled in accordance with paragraph (a)(1) of this rule and reviewed in accordance with paragraph (b)(2) of this rule, if it appears to the Commission that such action is necessary or appropriate in the public interest, for the protection of investors, or the maintenance of fair and orderly markets, to remove impediments to, and perfect the mechanisms of, a national market system or otherwise in furtherance of the purposes of the Act.

(4) Notwithstanding the provisions of paragraph (b)(1) of this rule, a proposed amendment may be put into effect summarily upon publication of notice of such amendment, on a temporary basis not to exceed 120 days, if the Commission finds that such action is necessary or appropriate in the public interest, for the protection of investors or the maintenance of fair and orderly markets, to remove impediments to, and perfect the mechanisms of, a national market system or otherwise in furtherance of the purposes of the Act.

(5) Any plan (or amendment thereto) in connection with:

(i) The planning, development, operation, or regulation of a national market system (or a subsystem thereof) or one or more facilities thereof; or

(ii) The development and implementation of procedures and/or facilities designed to achieve compliance by self-regulatory organizations and/or their members of any section of this Regulation NMS (Rules 600 through 612) and part 240, subpart A promulgated pursuant to section 11A of the Act, approved by the Commission pursuant to section 11A of the Act (or pursuant to any rule or regulation thereunder) prior to the effective date of this rule (either temporarily or permanently) shall be deemed to have been filed and approved pursuant to this rule and no additional filing need be made by the sponsors with respect to such plan or amendment; *provided, however,* that all terms and conditions associated with any such approval (including time limitations) shall continue to be applicable; *provided, further,* that any amendment to such plan filed with or approved by the Commission on or after the effective date of this rule shall be subject to the provisions of, and considered in accordance with the procedures specified in, this rule.

(c) *Compliance with Terms of National Market System Plans.* Each self-regulatory organization shall comply with the terms of any effective national market system plan of which it is a sponsor or a participant. Each self-regulatory organization also shall, absent reasonable justification or excuse, enforce compliance with any such plan by its members and persons associated with its members.

(d) *Appeals.* The Commission may, in its discretion, entertain appeals in connection with the implementation or operation of any effective national market system plan as follows:

(1) Any action taken or failure to act by any person in connection with an effective national market system plan (other than a prohibition or limitation of access reviewable by the Commission pursuant to section 11A(b)(5) or section 19(d) of

the Act shall be subject to review by the Commission, on its own motion or upon application by any person aggrieved thereby (including, but not limited to, self-regulatory organizations, brokers, dealers, issuers, and vendors), filed not later than 30 days after notice of such action or failure to act or within such longer period as the Commission may determine.

(2) Application to the Commission for review, or the institution of review by the Commission on its own motion, shall not operate as a stay of any such action unless the Commission determines otherwise, after notice and opportunity for hearing on the question of a stay (which hearing may consist only of affidavits or oral arguments).

(3) In any proceedings for review, if the Commission, after appropriate notice and opportunity for hearing (which hearing may consist solely of consideration of the record of any proceedings conducted in connection with such action or failure to act and an opportunity for the presentation of reasons supporting or opposing such action or failure to act) and upon consideration of such other data, views, and arguments as it deems relevant, finds that the action or failure to act is in accordance with the applicable provisions of such plan and that the applicable provisions are, and were, applied in a manner consistent with the public interest, the protection of investors, the maintenance of fair and orderly markets, and the removal of impediments to, and the perfection of the mechanisms of a national market system, the Commission, by order, shall dismiss the proceeding. If the Commission does not make any such finding, or if it finds that such action or failure to act imposes any burden on competition not necessary or appropriate in furtherance of the purposes of the Act, the Commission, by order, shall set aside such action and/or require such action with respect to the matter reviewed as the Commission deems necessary or appropriate in the public interest, for the protection of investors, and the maintenance of fair and orderly markets, or to remove impediments to, and perfect the mechanisms of, a national market system.

(e) *Exemptions.* The Commission may exempt from the provisions of this rule, either unconditionally or on specified terms and conditions, any self-regulatory organization, member thereof, or specified security, if the Commission determines that such exemption is consistent with the public interest, the protection of investors, the maintenance of fair and orderly markets and the removal of impediments to, and perfection of the mechanisms of, a national market system.

Rule 609. Registration of securities information processors: form of application and amendments

(a) An application for the registration of a securities information processor shall be filed on Form SIP (17 CFR 249.1001) in accordance with the instructions contained therein.

(b) If any information reported in items 1–13 or item 21 of Form SIP or in any amendment thereto is or becomes inaccurate for any reason, whether before or after the registration has been granted, the securities information processor shall promptly file an amendment on Form SIP correcting such information.

(c) The Commission, upon its own motion or upon application by any securities information processor, may conditionally or unconditionally exempt any securities information processor from any provision of the rules or regulations adopted under section 11A(b) of the Act.

(d) Every amendment filed pursuant to this section shall constitute a "report" within the meaning of sections 17(a), 18(a) and 32(a) of the Act (15 U.S.C. 78q(a), 78r(a), and 78ff(a)).

Rule 610. Access to quotations

(a) *Quotations of SRO Trading Facility.* A national securities exchange or national securities association shall not impose unfairly discriminatory terms that prevent or inhibit any person from obtaining efficient access through a member of the national securities exchange or national securities association to the quotations in an NMS stock displayed through its SRO trading facility.

(b) *Quotations of SRO Display–Only Facility.* (1) Any trading center that displays quotations in an NMS stock through an SRO display-only facility shall provide a level and cost of access to such quotations that is substantially equivalent to the level and cost of access to quotations displayed by SRO trading facilities in that stock.

(2) Any trading center that displays quotations in an NMS stock through an SRO display-only facility shall not impose unfairly discriminatory terms that prevent or inhibit any person from obtaining efficient access to such quotations through a member, subscriber, or customer of the trading center.

(c) *Fees for Access to Quotations.* A trading center shall not impose, nor permit to be imposed, any fee or fees for the execution of an order against a protected quotation of the trading center or against any other quotation of the trading center that is the best bid or best offer of a national securities exchange, the best bid or best offer of The Nasdaq Stock Market, Inc., or the best bid or best offer of a national securities association other than the best bid or best offer of The Nasdaq Stock Market, Inc. in an NMS stock that exceed or accumulate to more than the following limits:

(1) If the price of a protected quotation or other quotation is $1.00 or more, the fee or fees cannot exceed or accumulate to more than $0.003 per share; or

(2) If the price of a protected quotation or other quotation is less than $1.00, the fee or fees cannot exceed or accumulate to more than 0.3% of the quotation price per share.

(d) *Locking or Crossing Quotations.* Each national securities exchange and national securities association shall establish, maintain, and enforce written rules that:

(1) Require its members reasonably to avoid:

(i) Displaying quotations that lock or cross any protected quotation in an NMS stock; and

(ii) Displaying manual quotations that lock or cross any quotation in an NMS stock disseminated pursuant to an effective national market system plan;

(2) Are reasonably designed to assure the reconciliation of locked or crossed quotations in an NMS stock; and

(3) Prohibit its members from engaging in a pattern or practice of displaying quotations that lock or cross any protected quotation in an NMS stock, or of displaying manual quotations that lock or cross any quotation in an NMS stock disseminated pursuant to an effective national market system plan, other than displaying quotations that lock or cross any protected or other quotation as permitted by an exception contained in its rules established pursuant to paragraph (d)(1) of this rule.

(e) *Exemptions.* The Commission, by order, may exempt from the provisions of this rule, either unconditionally or on specified terms and conditions, any person, security, quotations, orders, or fees, or any class or classes of persons, securities, quotations, orders, or fees, if the Commission determines that such exemption is necessary or appropriate in the public interest, and is consistent with the protection of investors.

Rule 611. Order protection rule

(a) *Reasonable Policies and Procedures.* (1) A trading center shall establish, maintain, and enforce written policies and procedures that are reasonably designed to prevent trade-throughs on that trading center of protected quotations in NMS stocks that do not fall within an exception set forth in paragraph (b) of this rule and, if relying on such an exception, that are reasonably designed to assure compliance with the terms of the exception.

(2) A trading center shall regularly surveil to ascertain the effectiveness of the policies and procedures required by paragraph (a)(1) of this rule and shall take prompt action to remedy deficiencies in such policies and procedures.

(b) *Exceptions.* (1) The transaction that constituted the trade-through was effected when the trading center displaying the protected quotation that was traded through was experiencing a failure, material delay, or malfunction of its systems or equipment.

(2) The transaction that constituted the trade-through was not a "regular way" contract.

(3) The transaction that constituted the trade-through was a single-priced opening, reopening, or closing transaction by the trading center.

(4) The transaction that constituted the trade-through was executed at a time when a protected bid was priced higher than a protected offer in the NMS stock.

(5) The transaction that constituted the trade-through was the execution of an order identified as an intermarket sweep order.

(6) The transaction that constituted the trade-through was effected by a trading center that simultaneously routed an intermarket sweep order to execute against the full displayed size of any protected quotation in the NMS stock that was traded through.

(7) The transaction that constituted the trade-through was the execution of an order at a price that was not based, directly or indirectly, on the quoted price of the NMS stock at the time of execution and for which the material terms were not reasonably determinable at the time the commitment to execute the order was made.

(8) The trading center displaying the protected quotation that was traded through had displayed, within one second prior to execution of the transaction that constituted the trade-through, a best bid or best offer, as applicable, for the NMS stock with a price that was equal or inferior to the price of the trade-through transaction.

(9) The transaction that constituted the trade-through was the execution by a trading center of an order for which, at the time of receipt of the order, the trading center had guaranteed an execution at no worse than a specified price (a "stopped order"), where:

(i) The stopped order was for the account of a customer;

(ii) The customer agreed to the specified price on an order-by-order basis; and

(iii) The price of the trade-through transaction was, for a stopped buy order, lower than the national best bid in the NMS stock at the time of execution or, for a stopped sell order, higher than the national best offer in the NMS stock at the time of execution.

(c) *Intermarket Sweep Orders*. The trading center, broker, or dealer responsible for the routing of an intermarket sweep order shall take reasonable steps to establish that such order meets the requirements set forth in Rule 600(b)(30).

(d) *Exemptions*. The Commission, by order, may exempt from the provisions of this rule, either unconditionally or on specified terms and conditions, any person, security, transaction, quotation, or order, or any class or classes of persons, securities, quotations, or orders, if the Commission determines that such exemption is necessary or appropriate in the public interest, and is consistent with the protection of investors.

Rule 612. Minimum pricing increment

(a) No national securities exchange, national securities association, alternative trading system, vendor, or broker or dealer shall display, rank, or accept from any person a bid or offer, an order, or an indication of interest in any NMS stock priced in an increment smaller than $0.01 if that bid or offer, order, or indication of interest is priced equal to or greater than $1.00 per share.

(b) No national securities exchange, national securities association, alternative trading system, vendor, or broker or dealer shall display, rank, or accept from any person a bid or offer, an order, or an indication of interest in any NMS stock priced in an increment smaller than $0.0001 if that bid or offer, order, or indication of interest is priced less than $1.00 per share.

(c) The Commission, by order, may exempt from the provisions of this rule, either unconditionally or on specified terms and conditions, any person, security, quotation, or order, or any class or classes of persons, securities, quotations, or orders, if the Commission determines that such exemption is necessary or appropriate in the public interest, and is consistent with the protection of investors.

Rule 613. Consolidated audit trail

(a) *Creation of a National Market System Plan Governing a Consolidated Audit Trail.*

(1)* Each national securities exchange and national securities association shall jointly file on or before 270 days from the date of publication of the Adopting Release in the *Federal Register* a national market system plan to govern the creation, implementation, and maintenance of a consolidated audit trail and central repository as required by this section. The national market system plan shall discuss the following considerations:

(i) The method(s) by which data will be reported to the central repository including, but not limited to, the sources of such data and the manner in which the central repository will receive, extract, transform, load, and retain such data; and the basis for selecting such method(s);

(ii) The time and method by which the data in the central repository will be made available to regulators, in accordance with paragraph (e)(1) of this section, to perform surveillance or analyses, or for other purposes as part of their regulatory and oversight responsibilities;

(iii) The reliability and accuracy of the data reported to and maintained by the central repository throughout its lifecycle, including transmission and receipt from market participants; data extraction, transformation and loading at the central repository; data maintenance and

* On March 7, 2013, the SEC issued an Order Granting a Temporary Exemption Pursuant to Section 36(a)(1) of the Securities Exchange Act of 1934 from the Filing Deadline Specified in Rule 613(a)(1) of the Exchange Act. This order grants a temporary exemption to SROs from the deadline for submitting the NMS plan to govern the creation, implementation, and maintenance of a consolidated audit trail and central repository contained in Rule 613(a)(1) until December 6, 2013. The SEC release number is 34–69060.

management at the central repository; and data access by regulators;

(iv) The security and confidentiality of the information reported to the central repository;

(v) The flexibility and scalability of the systems used by the central repository to collect, consolidate and store consolidated audit trail data, including the capacity of the consolidated audit trail to efficiently incorporate, in a cost-effective manner, improvements in technology, additional capacity, additional order data, information about additional securities or transactions, changes in regulatory requirements, and other developments;

(vi) The feasibility, benefits, and costs of broker-dealers reporting to the consolidated audit trail in a timely manner:

(A) The identity of all market participants (including broker-dealers and customers) that are allocated NMS securities, directly or indirectly, in a primary market transaction;

(B) The number of such securities each such market participant is allocated; and

(C) The identity of the broker-dealer making each such allocation;

(vii) The detailed estimated costs for creating, implementing, and maintaining the consolidated audit trail as contemplated by the national market system plan, which estimated costs should specify:

(A) An estimate of the costs to the plan sponsors for establishing and maintaining the central repository;

(B) An estimate of the costs to members of the plan sponsors, initially and on an ongoing basis, for reporting the data required by the national market system plan;

(C) An estimate of the costs to the plan sponsors, initially and on an ongoing basis, for reporting the data required by the national market system plan; and

(D) How the plan sponsors propose to fund the creation, implementation, and maintenance of the consolidated audit trail, including the proposed allocation of such estimated costs among the plan sponsors, and between the plan sponsors and members of the plan sponsors;

(viii) An analysis of the impact on competition, efficiency and capital formation of creating, implementing, and maintaining of the national market system plan;

(ix) A plan to eliminate existing rules and systems (or components thereof) that will be rendered duplicative by the consolidated audit trail, including identification of such rules and systems (or components thereof); to the extent that any existing rules or systems related to monitoring quotes, orders, and executions provide information that is not rendered duplicative by the consolidated audit trail, an analysis of:

(A) Whether the collection of such information remains appropriate;

(B) If still appropriate, whether such information should continue to be separately collected or should instead be incorporated into the consolidated audit trail; and

(C) If no longer appropriate, how the collection of such information could be efficiently terminated; the steps the plan sponsors propose to take to seek Commission approval for the elimination of such rules and systems (or components thereof); and a timetable for such elimination, including a description of how the plan sponsors propose to phase in the consolidated audit trail and phase out such existing rules and systems (or components thereof);

(x) Objective milestones to assess progress toward the implementation of the national market system plan;

(xi) The process by which the plan sponsors solicited views of their members and other appropriate parties regarding the creation, implementation, and maintenance of the consolidated audit trail, a summary of the views of such members and other parties, and how the plan sponsors took such views into account in preparing the national market system plan; and

(xii) Any reasonable alternative approaches to creating, implementing, and maintaining a consolidated audit trail that the plan sponsors considered in developing the national market system plan including, but not limited to, a description of any such alternative approach; the relative advantages and disadvantages of each such alternative, including an assessment of the alternative's costs and benefits; and the basis upon which the plan sponsors selected the approach reflected in the national market system plan.

(2) The national market system plan, or any amendment thereto, filed pursuant to this section shall comply with the requirements in Rule 608(a), if applicable, and be filed with the Commission pursuant to Rule 608.

(3) The national market system plan submitted pursuant to this section shall require each national securities exchange and national securities association to:

(i) Within two months after effectiveness of the national market system plan jointly (or under the governance structure described in the plan) select a person to be the plan processor;

(ii) Within four months after effectiveness of the national market system plan synchronize their business clocks and require members of each such exchange and association to synchronize their business clocks in accordance with paragraph (d) of this section;

(iii) Within one year after effectiveness of the national market system plan provide to the central repository the data specified in paragraph (c) of this section;

(iv) Within fourteen months after effectiveness of the national market system plan implement a new or enhanced surveillance system(s) as required by paragraph (f) of this section;

(v) Within two years after effectiveness of the national market system plan require members of each such exchange and association, except those members that qualify as small broker-dealers as defined in Rule 0–10(c) under the Securities Exchange Act of 1934, to provide to the central repository the data specified in paragraph (c) of this section; and

(vi) Within three years after effectiveness of the national market system plan require members of each such exchange and association that qualify as small broker-dealers as defined in Rule 0–10(c) under the Securities Exchange Act of 1934 to provide to the central repository the data specified in paragraph (c) of this section.

(4) Each national securities exchange and national securities association shall be a sponsor of the national market system plan submitted pursuant to this section and approved by the Commission.

(5) No national market system plan filed pursuant to this section, or any amendment thereto, shall become effective unless approved by the Commission or otherwise permitted in accordance with the procedures set forth in Rule 608. In determining whether to approve the national market system plan, or any amendment thereto, and whether the national market system plan or any amendment thereto is in the public interest under Rule 608(b)(2), the Commission shall consider the impact of the national market system plan or amendment, as applicable, on efficiency, competition, and capital formation.

(b) *Operation and Administration of the National Market System Plan.*

(1) The national market system plan submitted pursuant to this section shall include a governance structure to ensure fair representation of the plan sponsors, and administration of the central repository, including the selection of the plan processor.

(2) The national market system plan submitted pursuant to this section shall include a provision addressing the requirements for the admission of new sponsors of the plan and the withdrawal of existing sponsors from the plan.

(3) The national market system plan submitted pursuant to this section shall include a provision addressing the percentage of votes required by the plan sponsors to effectuate amendments to the plan.

(4) The national market system plan submitted pursuant to this section shall include a provision addressing the manner in which the costs of operating the central repository will be allocated among the national securities exchanges and national securities associations that are sponsors of the plan, including a provision addressing the manner in which costs will be allocated to new sponsors to the plan.

(5) The national market system plan submitted pursuant to this section shall require the appointment of a Chief Compliance Officer to regularly review the operation of the central repository to assure its continued effectiveness in light of market and technological developments, and make any appropriate recommendations for enhancements to the nature of the information collected and the manner in which it is processed.

(6) The national market system plan submitted pursuant to this section shall include a provision requiring the plan sponsors to provide to

the Commission, at least every two years after effectiveness of the national market system plan, a written assessment of the operation of the consolidated audit trail. Such document shall include, at a minimum:

(i) An evaluation of the performance of the consolidated audit trail including, at a minimum, with respect to data accuracy (consistent with paragraph (e)(6) of this section), timeliness of reporting, comprehensiveness of data elements, efficiency of regulatory access, system speed, system downtime, system security (consistent with paragraph (e)(4) of this section), and other performance metrics to be determined by the Chief Compliance Officer, along with a description of such metrics;

(ii) A detailed plan, based on such evaluation, for any potential improvements to the performance of the consolidated audit trail with respect to any of the following: improving data accuracy; shortening reporting timeframes; expanding data elements; adding granularity and details regarding the scope and nature of Customer–IDs; expanding the scope of the national market system plan to include new instruments and new types of trading and order activities; improving the efficiency of regulatory access; increasing system speed; reducing system downtime; and improving performance under other metrics to be determined by the Chief Compliance Officer;

(iii) An estimate of the costs associated with any such potential improvements to the performance of the consolidated audit trail, including an assessment of the potential impact on competition, efficiency, and capital formation; and

(iv) An estimated implementation timeline for any such potential improvements, if applicable.

(7) The national market system plan submitted pursuant to this section shall include an Advisory Committee which shall function in accordance with the provisions set forth in this paragraph (b)(7). The purpose of the Advisory Committee shall be to advise the plan sponsors on the implementation, operation, and administration of the central repository.

(i) The national market system plan submitted pursuant to this section shall set forth the term and composition of the Advisory Committee, which composition shall include representatives of the member firms of the plan sponsors.

(ii) Members of the Advisory Committee shall have the right to attend any meetings of the plan sponsors, to receive information concerning the operation of the central repository, and to provide their views to the plan sponsors; provided, however, that the plan sponsors may meet without the Advisory Committee members in executive session if, by affirmative vote of a majority of the plan sponsors, the plan sponsors determine that such an executive session is required.

(c) *Data Recording and Reporting.*

(1) The national market system plan submitted pursuant to this section shall provide for an accurate, time-sequenced record of orders beginning with the receipt or origination of an order by a member of a national securities exchange or national securities association, and further documenting the life of the order through the process of routing, modification, cancellation, and execution (in whole or in part) of the order.

(2) The national market system plan submitted pursuant to this section shall require each national securities exchange, national securities association, and member to report to the central repository the information required by paragraph (c)(7) of this section in a uniform electronic format, or in a manner that would allow the central repository to convert the data to a uniform electronic format, for consolidation and storage.

(3) The national market system plan submitted pursuant to this section shall require each national securities exchange, national securities association, and member to record the information required by paragraphs (c)(7)(i) through (v) of this section contemporaneously with the reportable event. The national market system plan shall require that information recorded pursuant to paragraphs (c)(7)(i) through (v) of this section must be reported to the central repository by 8:00 a.m. Eastern Time on the trading day following the day such information has been recorded by the national securities exchange, national securities association, or member. The national market system plan may accommodate voluntary reporting prior to 8:00 a.m. Eastern Time, but shall not impose an earlier reporting deadline on the reporting parties.

(4) The national market system plan submitted pursuant to this section shall require each member of a national securities exchange or national securities association to record and report to the

central repository the information required by paragraphs (c)(7)(vi) through (viii) of this section by 8:00 a.m. Eastern Time on the trading day following the day the member receives such information. The national market system plan may accommodate voluntary reporting prior to 8:00 a.m. Eastern Time, but shall not impose an earlier reporting deadline on the reporting parties.

(5) The national market system plan submitted pursuant to this section shall require each national securities exchange and its members to record and report to the central repository the information required by paragraph (c)(7) of this section for each NMS security registered or listed for trading on such exchange or admitted to unlisted trading privileges on such exchange.

(6) The national market system plan submitted pursuant to this section shall require each national securities association and its members to record and report to the central repository the information required by paragraph (c)(7) of this section for each NMS security for which transaction reports are required to be submitted to the association.

(7) The national market system plan submitted pursuant to this section shall require each national securities exchange, national securities association, and any member of such exchange or association to record and electronically report to the central repository details for each order and each reportable event, including, but not limited to, the following information:

(i) For original receipt or origination of an order:

(A) Customer–ID(s) for each customer;

(B) The CAT–Order–ID;

(C) The CAT–Reporter–ID of the broker-dealer receiving or originating the order;

(D) Date of order receipt or origination;

(E) Time of order receipt or origination (using time stamps pursuant to paragraph (d)(3) of this section); and

(F) Material terms of the order.

(ii) For the routing of an order, the following information:

(A) The CAT–Order–ID;

(B) Date on which the order is routed;

(C) Time at which the order is routed (using time stamps pursuant to paragraph (d)(3) of this section);

(D) The CAT–Reporter–ID of the broker-dealer or national securities exchange routing the order;

(E) The CAT–Reporter–ID of the broker-dealer, national securities exchange, or national securities association to which the order is being routed;

(F) If routed internally at the broker-dealer, the identity and nature of the department or desk to which an order is routed; and

(G) Material terms of the order.

(iii) For the receipt of an order that has been routed, the following information:

(A) The CAT–Order–ID;

(B) Date on which the order is received;

(C) Time at which the order is received (using time stamps pursuant to paragraph (d)(3) of this section);

(D) The CAT–Reporter–ID of the broker-dealer, national securities exchange, or national securities association receiving the order;

(E) The CAT–Reporter–ID of the broker-dealer or national securities exchange routing the order; and

(F) Material terms of the order.

(iv) If the order is modified or cancelled, the following information:

(A) The CAT–Order–ID;

(B) Date the modification or cancellation is received or originated;

(C) Time the modification or cancellation is received or originated (using time stamps pursuant to paragraph (d)(3) of this section);

(D) Price and remaining size of the order, if modified;

(E) Other changes in material terms of the order, if modified; and

(F) The CAT–Reporter–ID of the broker-dealer or Customer–ID of the person giving the modification or cancellation instruction.

(v) If the order is executed, in whole or part, the following information:

(A) The CAT–Order–ID;

(B) Date of execution;

(C) Time of execution (using time stamps pursuant to paragraph (d)(3) of this section);

(D) Execution capacity (principal, agency, riskless principal);

(E) Execution price and size;

(F) The CAT–Reporter–ID of the national securities exchange or broker-dealer executing the order; and

(G) Whether the execution was reported pursuant to an effective transaction reporting plan or the Plan for Reporting of Consolidated Options Last Sale Reports and Quotation Information.

(vi) If the order is executed, in whole or part, the following information:

(A) The account number for any subaccounts to which the execution is allocated (in whole or part);

(B) The CAT–Reporter–ID of the clearing broker or prime broker, if applicable; and

(C) The CAT–Order–ID of any contra-side order(s).

(vii) If the trade is cancelled, a cancelled trade indicator.

(viii) For original receipt or origination of an order, the following information:

(A) Information of sufficient detail to identify the customer; and

(B) Customer account information.

(8) All plan sponsors and their members shall use the same Customer–ID and CAT–Reporter–ID for each customer and broker-dealer.

(d) *Clock Synchronization and Time Stamps.* The national market system plan submitted pursuant to this section shall require:

(1) Each national securities exchange, national securities association, and member of such exchange or association to synchronize its business clocks that are used for the purposes of recording the date and time of any reportable event that must be reported pursuant to this section to the time maintained by the National Institute of Standards and Technology, consistent with industry standards;

(2) Each national securities exchange and national securities association to evaluate annually the clock synchronization standard to determine whether it should be shortened, consistent with changes in industry standards; and

(3) Each national securities exchange, national securities association, and member of such exchange or association to utilize the time stamps required by paragraph (c)(7) of this section, with at minimum the granularity set forth in the national market system plan submitted pursuant to this section, which shall reflect current industry standards and be at least to the millisecond. To the extent that the relevant order handling and execution systems of any national securities exchange, national securities association, or member of such exchange or association utilize time stamps in increments finer than the minimum required by the national market system plan, the plan shall require such national securities exchange, national securities association, or member to utilize time stamps in such finer increments when providing data to the central repository, so that all reportable events reported to the central repository by any national securities exchange, national securities association, or member can be accurately sequenced. The national market system plan shall require the sponsors of the national market system plan to annually evaluate whether industry standards have evolved such that the required time stamp standard should be in finer increments.

(e) *Central Repository.*

(1) The national market system plan submitted pursuant to this section shall provide for the creation and maintenance of a central repository. Such central repository shall be responsible for the receipt, consolidation, and retention of all information reported pursuant to paragraph (c)(7) of this section. The central repository shall store and make available to regulators data in a uniform electronic format, and in a form in which all events pertaining to the same originating order are linked together in a manner that ensures timely and accurate retrieval of the information required by paragraph (c)(7) of this section for all reportable events for that order.

(2) Each national securities exchange, national securities association, and the Commission shall have access to the central repository, including all

systems operated by the central repository, and access to and use of the data reported to and consolidated by the central repository under paragraph (c) of this section, for the purpose of performing its respective regulatory and oversight responsibilities pursuant to the federal securities laws, rules, and regulations. The national market system plan submitted pursuant to this section shall provide that such access to and use of such data by each national securities exchange, national securities association, and the Commission for the purpose of performing its regulatory and oversight responsibilities pursuant to the federal securities laws, rules, and regulations shall not be limited.

(3) The national market system plan submitted pursuant to this section shall include a provision requiring the creation and maintenance by the plan processor of a method of access to the consolidated data stored in the central repository that includes the ability to run searches and generate reports.

(4) The national market system plan submitted pursuant to this section shall include policies and procedures, including standards, to be used by the plan processor to:

(i) Ensure the security and confidentiality of all information reported to the central repository by requiring that:

(A) All plan sponsors and their employees, as well as all employees of the central repository, agree to use appropriate safeguards to ensure the confidentiality of such data and agree not to use such data for any purpose other than surveillance and regulatory purposes, provided that nothing in this paragraph (A) shall be construed to prevent a plan sponsor from using the data that it reports to the central repository for regulatory, surveillance, commercial, or other purposes as otherwise permitted by applicable law, rule, or regulation;

(B) Each plan sponsor adopt and enforce rules that:

(1) Require information barriers between regulatory staff and non-regulatory staff with regard to access and use of data in the central repository; and

(2) Permit only persons designated by plan sponsors to have access to the data in the central repository;

(C) The plan processor:

(1) Develop and maintain a comprehensive information security program for the central repository, with dedicated staff, that is subject to regular reviews by the Chief Compliance Officer;

(2) Have a mechanism to confirm the identity of all persons permitted to access the data; and

(3) Maintain a record of all instances where such persons access the data; and

(D) The plan sponsors adopt penalties for non-compliance with any policies and procedures of the plan sponsors or central repository with respect to information security.

(ii) Ensure the timeliness, accuracy, integrity, and completeness of the data provided to the central repository pursuant to paragraph (c) of this section; and

(iii) Ensure the accuracy of the consolidation by the plan processor of the data provided to the central repository pursuant to paragraph (c) of this section.

(5) The national market system plan submitted pursuant to this section shall address whether there will be an annual independent evaluation of the security of the central repository and:

(i) If so, provide a description of the scope of such planned evaluation; and

(ii) If not, provide a detailed explanation of the alternative measures for evaluating the security of the central repository that are planned instead.

(6) The national market system plan submitted pursuant to this section shall:

(i) Specify a maximum error rate to be tolerated by the central repository for any data reported pursuant to paragraphs (c)(3) and (c)(4) of this section; describe the basis for selecting such maximum error rate; explain how the plan sponsors will seek to reduce such maximum error rate over time; describe how the plan will seek to ensure compliance with such maximum error rate and, in the event of noncompliance, will promptly remedy the causes thereof;

(ii) Require the central repository to measure the error rate each business day and promptly take appropriate remedial action, at a minimum, if the error rate exceeds the maximum error rate specified in the plan;

(iii) Specify a process for identifying and correcting errors in the data reported to the central repository pursuant to paragraphs (c)(3) and (c)(4) of this section, including the process for notifying the national securities exchanges, national securities association, and members who reported erroneous data to the central repository of such errors, to help ensure that such errors are promptly corrected by the reporting entity, and for disciplining those who repeatedly report erroneous data; and

(iv) Specify the time by which data that has been corrected will be made available to regulators.

(7) The national market system plan submitted pursuant to this section shall require the central repository to collect and retain on a current and continuing basis and in a format compatible with the information consolidated and stored pursuant to paragraph (c)(7) of this section:

(i) Information, including the size and quote condition, on the national best bid and national best offer for each NMS security;

(ii) Transaction reports reported pursuant to an effective transaction reporting plan filed with the Commission pursuant to, and meeting the requirements of, Rule 601; and

(iii) Last sale reports reported pursuant to the Plan for Reporting of Consolidated Options Last Sale Reports and Quotation Information filed with the Commission pursuant to, and meeting the requirements of, Rule 608.

(8) The national market system plan submitted pursuant to this section shall require the central repository to retain the information collected pursuant to paragraphs (c)(7) and (e)(7) of this section in a convenient and usable standard electronic data format that is directly available and searchable electronically without any manual intervention for a period of not less than five years.

(f) *Surveillance.* Every national securities exchange and national securities association subject to this section shall develop and implement a surveillance system, or enhance existing surveillance systems, reasonably designed to make use of the consolidated information contained in the consolidated audit trail.

(g) *Compliance by Members.*

(1) Each national securities exchange and national securities association shall file with the Commission pursuant to section 19(b)(2) of the Act and Rule 19b–4 under the Securities Exchange Act of 1934 on or before 60 days from approval of the national market system plan a proposed rule change to require its members to comply with the requirements of this section and the national market system plan approved by the Commission.

(2) Each member of a national securities exchange or national securities association shall comply with all the provisions of any approved national market system plan applicable to members.

(3) The national market system plan submitted pursuant to this section shall include a provision requiring each national securities exchange and national securities association to agree to enforce compliance by its members with the provisions of any approved plan.

(4) The national market system plan submitted pursuant to this section shall include a mechanism to ensure compliance with the requirements of any approved plan by the members of a national securities exchange or national securities association.

(h) *Compliance by National Securities Exchanges and National Securities Associations.*

(1) Each national securities exchange and national securities association shall comply with the provisions of the national market system plan approved by the Commission.

(2) Any failure by a national securities exchange or national securities association to comply with the provisions of the national market system plan approved by the Commission shall be considered a violation of this section.

(3) The national market system plan submitted pursuant to this section shall include a mechanism to ensure compliance by the sponsors of the plan with the requirements of any approved plan. Such enforcement mechanism may include penalties where appropriate.

(i) *Other Securities and Other Types of Transactions.* The national market system plan submitted pursuant to this section shall include a provision requiring each national securities exchange and national securities association to jointly provide to the Commission within six months after effectiveness of the national market system plan a document outlining how such exchanges and associations could incorporate into the consolidated audit trail information with respect to equity securities that are not NMS securities, debt securities, primary market transactions in equity securities that are not NMS securities, and primary market transactions in debt securities, including details for each order and reportable event that may be required to be provided, which market participants may be required to provide the data, an implementation timeline, and a cost estimate.

(j) *Definitions.*

(1) The term *CAT-Order–ID* shall mean a unique order identifier or series of unique order identifiers that allows the central repository to efficiently and accurately link all reportable events for an order, and all orders that result from the aggregation or disaggregation of such order.

(2) The term *CAT-Reporter–ID* shall mean, with respect to each national securities exchange, national securities association, and member of a national securities exchange or national securities association, a code that uniquely and consistently identifies such person for purposes of providing data to the central repository.

(3) The term *customer* shall mean:

(i) The account holder(s) of the account at a registered broker-dealer originating the order; and

(ii) Any person from whom the broker-dealer is authorized to accept trading instructions for such account, if different from the account holder(s).

(4) The term *customer account information* shall include, but not be limited to, account number, account type, customer type, date account opened, and large trader identifier (if applicable).

(5) The term *Customer-ID* shall mean, with respect to a customer, a code that uniquely and consistently identifies such customer for purposes of providing data to the central repository.

(6) The term *error rate* shall mean the percentage of reportable events collected by the central repository in which the data reported does not fully and accurately reflect the order event that occurred in the market.

(7) The term *material terms of the order* shall include, but not be limited to, the NMS security symbol; security type; price (if applicable); size (displayed and non-displayed); side (buy/sell); order type; if a sell order, whether the order is long, short, short exempt; open/close indicator; time in force (if applicable); if the order is for a listed option, option type (put/call), option symbol or root symbol, underlying symbol, strike price, expiration date, and open/close; and any special handling instructions.

(8) The term *order* shall include:

(i) Any order received by a member of a national securities exchange or national securities association from any person;

(ii) Any order originated by a member of a national securities exchange or national securities association; or

(iii) Any bid or offer.

(9) The term *reportable event* shall include, but not be limited to, the original receipt or origination, modification, cancellation, routing, and execution (in whole or in part) of an order, and receipt of a routed order.

REGULATION SBSR—REGULATORY REPORTING AND PUBLIC DISSEMINATION OF SECURITY-BASED SWAP INFORMATION

(Cite as 17 CFR § 242.___)

Rule 900. Definitions

Terms used in Rules 900 through 909 that appear in Section 3 of the Exchange Act have the same meaning as in Section 3 of the Exchange Act and the rules or regulations thereunder. In addition, for purposes of Regulation SBSR (Rules 900 through 909), the following definitions shall apply:

(a) *Affiliate* means any person that, directly or indirectly, controls, is controlled by, or is under common control with, a person.

(b) *Asset class* means those security-based swaps in a particular broad category, including, but not limited to, credit derivatives and equity derivatives.

(c) [Reserved].

(d) *Branch ID* means the UIC assigned to a branch or other unincorporated office of a participant.

(e) *Broker ID* means the UIC assigned to a person acting as a broker for a participant.

(f) *Business day* means a day, based on U.S. Eastern Time, other than a Saturday, Sunday, or a U.S. federal holiday.

(g) *Clearing transaction* means a security-based swap that has a registered clearing agency as a direct counterparty.

(h) *Control* means, for purposes of Rules 900 through 909, the possession, direct or indirect, of the power to direct or cause the direction of the management and policies of a person, whether through the ownership of voting securities, by contract, or otherwise. A person is presumed to control another person if the person:

(1) Is a director, general partner or officer exercising executive responsibility (or having similar status or functions);

(2) Directly or indirectly has the right to vote 25 percent or more of a class of voting securities or has the power to sell or direct the sale of 25 percent or more of a class of voting securities; or

(3) In the case of a partnership, has the right to receive, upon dissolution, or has contributed, 25 percent or more of the capital.

(i) *Counterparty* means a person that is a direct counterparty or indirect counterparty of a security-based swap.

(j) *Counterparty ID* means the UIC assigned to a counterparty to a security-based swap.

(k) *Direct counterparty* means a person that is a primary obligor on a security-based swap.

(*l*) *Direct electronic access* has the same meaning as in Rule 13n–4(a)(5).

(m) *Exchange Act* means the Securities Exchange Act of 1934, as amended.

(n) *Execution agent ID* means the UIC assigned to any person other than a broker or trader that facilitates the execution of a security-based swap on behalf of a direct counterparty.

(*o*) *Foreign branch* has the same meaning as in Rule 3a71–3(a)(1).

(p) *Indirect counterparty* means a guarantor of a direct counterparty's performance of any obligation under a security-based swap such that the direct counterparty on the other side can exercise rights of recourse against the indirect counterparty in connection with the security-based swap; for these purposes a direct counterparty has rights of recourse against a guarantor on the other side if the direct counterparty has a conditional or unconditional legally enforceable right, in whole or in part, to receive payments from, or otherwise collect from, the guarantor in connection with the security-based swap.

(q) *Life cycle event* means, with respect to a security-based swap, any event that would result in a change in the information reported to a registered security-based swap data repository under Rule 901(c), (d), or (i), including: an assignment or novation of the security-based swap; a partial or full termination of the security-based swap; a change in the cash flows originally reported; for a security-based swap that is not a clearing transaction, any change to the title or date of any master agreement, collateral agreement, margin agreement, or any other agreement incorporated by reference into the security-based swap contract; or a corporate action affecting a security or securities on which the security-based swap is based (e.g., a merger, dividend, stock split, or bankruptcy). Notwithstanding the above, a life cycle event shall not include the scheduled expiration of the security-based swap, a previously described and anticipated interest rate adjustment (such as a quarterly interest rate adjustment), or other event that does not result in any change to the contractual terms of the security-based swap.

(r) *Non-mandatory report* means any information provided to a registered security-based swap data repository by or on behalf of a counterparty other than as required by Rules 900 through 909.

(s) *Non-U.S. person* means a person that is not a U.S. person.

(t) *Parent* means a legal person that controls a participant.

(u) *Participant*, with respect to a registered security-based swap data repository, means:

(1) A counterparty, that meets the criteria of Rule 908(b), of a security-based swap that is reported to that registered security-based swap data repository to satisfy an obligation under Rule 901(a);

(2) A platform that reports a security-based swap to that registered security-based swap data repository to satisfy an obligation under Rule 901(a);

(3) A registered clearing agency that is required to report to that registered security-based swap data repository whether or not it has accepted a security-based swap for clearing pursuant to Rule 901(e)(1)(ii); or

(4) A registered broker-dealer (including a registered security-based swap execution facility) that is required to report a security-based swap to that registered security-based swap data repository by Rule 901(a).

(v) *Platform* means a national securities exchange or security-based swap execution facility that is registered or exempt from registration.

(w) *Platform ID* means the UIC assigned to a platform on which a security-based swap is executed.

(x) *Post-trade processor* means any person that provides affirmation, confirmation, matching, reporting, or clearing services for a security-based swap transaction.

(y) *Pre-enactment security-based swap* means any security-based swap executed before July 21, 2010 (the date of enactment of the Dodd–Frank Act (Pub. L. No. 111-203, H.R. 4173)), the terms of which had not expired as of that date.

(z) *Price* means the price of a security-based swap transaction, expressed in terms of the commercial conventions used in that asset class.

(aa) *Product* means a group of security-based swap contracts each having the same material economic terms except those relating to price and size.

(bb) *Product ID* means the UIC assigned to a product.

(cc) *Publicly disseminate* means to make available through the Internet or other electronic data feed that is widely accessible and in machine-readable electronic format.

(dd) [Reserved].

(ee) *Registered clearing agency* means a person that is registered with the Commission as a clearing agency pursuant to section 17A of the Exchange Act and any rules or regulations thereunder.

(ff) *Registered security-based swap data repository* means a person that is registered with the Commission as a security-based swap data repository pursuant to section 13(n) of the Exchange Act and any rules or regulations thereunder.

(gg) *Reporting side* means the side of a security-based swap identified by Rule 901(a)(2).

(hh) *Side* means a direct counterparty and any guarantor of that direct counterparty's performance who meets the definition of indirect counterparty in connection with the security-based swap.

(ii) *Time of execution* means the point at which the counterparties to a security-based swap become irrevocably bound under applicable law.

(jj) *Trader ID* means the UIC assigned to a natural person who executes one or more security-based swaps on behalf of a direct counterparty.

(kk) *Trading desk* means, with respect to a counterparty, the smallest discrete unit of organization of the participant that purchases or sells security-based swaps for the account of the participant or an affiliate thereof.

(ll) *Trading desk ID* means the UIC assigned to the trading desk of a participant.

(mm) *Transaction ID* means the UIC assigned to a specific security-based swap transaction.

(nn) *Transitional security-based swap* means a security-based swap executed on or after July 21, 2010, and before the first date on which trade-by-trade reporting of security-based swaps in that asset class to a registered security-based swap data repository is required pursuant to Rules 900 through 909.

(oo) *Ultimate parent* means a legal person that controls a participant and that itself has no parent.

(pp) *Ultimate parent ID* means the UIC assigned to an ultimate parent of a participant.

(qq) *Unique Identification Code* or *UIC* means a unique identification code assigned to a person, unit of a person, product, or transaction.

(rr) *United States* has the same meaning as in Rule 3a71–3(a)(5).

(ss) *U.S. person* has the same meaning as in Rule 3a71–3(a)(4).

(tt) *Widely accessible*, as used in paragraph (cc) of this rule, means widely available to users of the information on a non-fee basis.

Rule 901. Reporting obligations

(a) *Assigning reporting duties.* A security-based swap, including a security-based swap that results from the allocation, termination, novation, or assignment of another security-based swap, shall be reported as follows:

(1) *Platform-executed security-based swaps that will be submitted to clearing.* If a security-based swap is executed on a platform and will be submitted to clearing, the platform on which the transaction was executed shall report to a registered security-based swap data repository the counterparty ID or the execution agent ID of each direct counterparty, as applicable, and the information set forth in paragraph (c) of this rule (except that, with respect to paragraph (c)(5) of this rule, the platform need indicate only if both direct counterparties are registered security-based swap dealers), and paragraphs (d)(9) and (10) of this rule.

(2) *All other security-based swaps.* For all security-based swaps other than platform-executed security-based swaps that will be submitted to clearing, the reporting side shall provide the information required by Rules 900 through 909 to a registered security-based swap data repository. The reporting side shall be determined as follows:

(i) *Clearing transactions.* For a clearing transaction, the reporting side is the registered clearing agency that is a counterparty to the transaction.

(ii) *Security-based swaps other than clearing transactions.* (A) If both sides of the security-based swap include a registered security-based swap dealer, the sides shall select the reporting side.

(B) If only one side of the security-based swap includes a registered security-based swap dealer, that side shall be the reporting side.

(C) If both sides of the security-based swap include a registered major security-based swap participant, the sides shall select the reporting side.

(D) If one side of the security-based swap includes a registered major security-based swap participant and the other side includes neither a registered security-based swap dealer nor a registered major security-based swap participant, the side including the registered major security-based swap participant shall be the reporting side.

(E) If neither side of the security-based swap includes a registered security-based swap dealer or registered major security-based swap participant:

(*1*) If both sides include a U.S. person, the sides shall select the reporting side.

(*2*) If one side includes a non-U.S. person that falls within Rule 908(b)(5) or a U.S. person and the other side includes a non-U.S. person that falls within Rule 908(b)(5), the sides shall select the reporting side.

(*3*) If one side includes only non-U.S. persons that do not fall within Rule 908(b)(5) and the other side includes a non-U.S. person that falls within Rule 908(b)(5) or a U.S. person, the side including a non-U.S. person that falls within Rule 908(b)(5) or a U.S. person shall be the reporting side.

(*4*) If neither side includes a U.S. person and neither side includes a non-U.S. person that falls within Rule 908(b)(5) but the security-based swap is effected by or through a registered broker-dealer (including a registered security-based swap execution facility), the registered broker-dealer (including a registered security-based swap execution facility) shall report the counterparty ID or the execution agent ID of each direct counterparty, as applicable, and the information set forth in paragraph (c) of this rule (except that, with respect to paragraph (c)(5) of this rule, the registered broker-dealer (including a registered security-based swap execution facility) need indicate only if both direct counterparties are registered security-based swap dealers) and paragraphs (d)(9) and (10) of this rule.

(3) *Notification to registered clearing agency.* A person who, under paragraph (a)(1) or (a)(2)(ii) of this rule, has a duty to report a security-based swap that has been submitted to clearing at a registered clearing agency shall promptly provide that registered clearing agency with the transaction ID of the submitted security-based swap and the identity of the registered security based swap data repository to which the transaction will be reported or has been reported.

(b) *Alternate recipient of security-based swap information.* If there is no registered security-based swap data repository that will accept the report required by Rule 901(a), the person required to make such report shall instead provide the required information to the Commission.

(c) *Primary trade information.* The reporting side shall report the following information within the timeframe specified in paragraph (j) of this section:

(1) The product ID, if available. If the security-based swap has no product ID, or if the product ID does not include the following information, the reporting side shall report:

(i) Information that identifies the security-based swap, including the asset class of the security-based swap and the specific underlying reference asset(s), reference issuer(s), or reference index;

(ii) The effective date;

(iii) The scheduled termination date;

(iv) The terms of any standardized fixed or floating rate payments, and the frequency of any such payments; and

(v) If the security-based swap is customized to the extent that the information provided in paragraphs (c)(1)(i) through (iv) of this section does not provide all of the material information necessary to identify such customized security-based swap or does not contain the data elements necessary to calculate the price, a flag to that effect;

(2) The date and time, to the second, of execution, expressed using Coordinated Universal Time (UTC);

(3) The price, including the currency in which the price is expressed and the amount(s) and currenc(ies) of any up-front payments;

(4) The notional amount(s) and the currenc(ies) in which the notional amount(s) is expressed;

(5) If both sides of the security-based swap include a registered security-based swap dealer, an indication to that effect;

(6) Whether the direct counterparties intend that the security-based swap will be submitted to clearing; and

(7) If applicable, any flags pertaining to the transaction that are specified in the policies and procedures of the registered security-based swap data repository to which the transaction will be reported.

(d) *Secondary trade information.* In addition to the information required under paragraph (c) of this rule, for each security-based swap for which it is the reporting side, the reporting side shall report the following information within the timeframe specified in paragraph (j) of this rule:

(1) The counterparty ID or the execution agent ID of each counterparty, as applicable;

(2) As applicable, the branch ID, broker ID, execution agent ID, trader ID, and trading desk ID of the direct counterparty on the reporting side;

(3) To the extent not provided pursuant to paragraph (c)(1) of this rule, the terms of any fixed or floating rate payments, or otherwise customized or non-standard payment streams, including the frequency and contingencies of any such payments;

(4) For a security-based swap that is not a clearing transaction and that will not be allocated after execution, the title and date of any master agreement, collateral agreement, margin agreement, or any other agreement incorporated by reference into the security-based swap contract;

(5) To the extent not provided pursuant to paragraph (c) of this rule or other provisions of this paragraph (d), any additional data elements included in the agreement between the counterparties that are necessary for a person to determine the market value of the transaction;

(6) If applicable, and to the extent not provided pursuant to paragraph (c) of this rule, the name of the clearing agency to which the security-based swap will be submitted for clearing;

(7) If the direct counterparties do not intend to submit the security-based swap to clearing, whether they have invoked the exception in Section 3C(g) of the Exchange Act (15 U.S.C. 78c–3(g));

(8) To the extent not provided pursuant to the other provisions of this paragraph (d), if the direct counterparties do not submit the security-based swap to clearing, a description of the settlement terms, including whether the security-based swap is cash-settled or physically settled, and the method for determining the settlement value;

(9) The platform ID, if applicable, or if a registered broker-dealer (including a registered security-based swap execution facility) is required to report the security-based swap by Rule 901(a)(2)(ii)(E)(4), the broker ID of that registered broker-dealer (including a registered security-based swap execution facility); and

(10) If the security-based swap arises from the allocation, termination, novation, or assignment of one or more existing security-based swaps, the transaction ID of the allocated, terminated, assigned, or novated security-based swap(s), except in the case of a clearing transaction that results from the netting or compression of other clearing transactions.

(e) *Reporting of life cycle events.* (1)(i) Generally. A life cycle event, and any adjustment due to a life cycle event, that results in a change to information previously reported pursuant to paragraph (c), (d), or (i) of this rule shall be reported by the reporting side, except that the reporting side shall not report whether or not a security-based swap has been accepted for clearing.

(ii) *Acceptance for clearing.* A registered clearing agency shall report whether or not it has accepted a security-based swap for clearing.

(2) All reports of life cycle events and adjustments due to life cycle events shall, within the timeframe specified in paragraph (j) of this rule, be reported to the entity to which the original security-based swap transaction will be reported or has been reported and shall include the transaction ID of the original transaction.

(f) *Time stamping incoming information.* A registered security-based swap data repository shall time stamp, to the second, its receipt of any information submitted to it pursuant to paragraph (c), (d), (e), or (i) of this rule.

(g) *Assigning transaction ID.* A registered security-based swap data repository shall assign a transaction ID to each security-based swap, or establish or endorse a methodology for transaction IDs to be assigned by third parties.

(h) *Format of reported information.* A person having a duty to report shall electronically transmit the information required under this rule in a format required by the registered security-based swap data repository to which it reports.

(i) *Reporting of pre-enactment and transitional security-based swaps.* With respect to any pre-enactment security-based swap or transitional security-based swap in a particular asset class, and to the extent that information about such transaction is available, the reporting side shall report all of the information required by paragraphs (c) and (d) of this rule to a registered security-based swap data repository that accepts security-based swaps in that asset class and indicate whether the security-based swap was open as of the date of such report.

(j) *Interim timeframe for reporting.* The reporting timeframe for paragraphs (c) and (d) of this rule shall be 24 hours after the time of execution (or acceptance for clearing in the case of a security-based swap that is subject to regulatory reporting and public dissemination solely by operation of Rule 908(a)(1)(ii)), or, if 24 hours after the time of execution or acceptance, as applicable, would fall on a day that is not a business day, by the same time on the next day that is a business day. The reporting timeframe for paragraph (e) of this rule shall be 24 hours after the occurrence of the life cycle event or the adjustment due to the life cycle event.

Appendix to Rule 901. Reports regarding the establishment of block thresholds and reporting delays for regulatory reporting of security-based swap transaction data

This appendix sets forth guidelines applicable to reports that the Commission has directed its staff to make in connection with the determination of block thresholds and reporting delays for security-based swap transaction data. The Commission intends to use these reports to inform its specification of the criteria for determining what constitutes a large notional security-based swap transaction (block trade) for particular markets and contracts; and the appropriate time delay for reporting large notional security-based swap transactions (block trades) to the public in order to implement regulatory requirements under Section 13 of the Act. In producing these reports, the staff shall consider security-based swap data collected by the Commission pursuant to other Title VII rules, as well as any other applicable information as the staff may determine to be appropriate for its analysis.

(a) *Report topics.* As appropriate, based on the availability of data and information, the reports should address the following topics for each asset class:

(1) *Price impact.* In connection with the Commission's obligation to specify criteria for determining what constitutes a block trade and the appropriate reporting delay for block trades, the report generally should assess the effect of notional amount and observed reporting delay on price impact of trades in the security-based swap market.

(2) *Hedging.* In connection with the Commission's obligation to specify criteria for determining what constitutes a block trade and the appropriate reporting delay for block trades, the report generally should consider potential relationships between observed reporting delays and the incidence and cost of hedging large trades in the security-based swap market, and whether these relationships differ for interdealer trades and dealer to customer trades.

(3) *Price efficiency.* In connection with the Commission's obligation to specify criteria for determining what constitutes a block trade and the appropriate reporting delay for block trades, the report generally should assess the relationship between reporting delays and the speed with which transaction information is impounded into market

prices, estimating this relationship for trades of different notional amounts.

(4) *Other topics*. Any other analysis of security-based swap data and information, such as security-based swap market liquidity and price volatility, that the Commission or the staff deem relevant to the specification of:

(i) The criteria for determining what constitutes a large notional security-based swap transaction (block trade) for particular markets and contracts; and

(ii) The appropriate time delay for reporting large notional security-based swap transactions (block trades).

(b) *Timing of reports*. Each report shall be complete no later than two years following the initiation of public dissemination of security-based swap transaction data by the first registered SDR in that asset class.

(c) *Public comment on the report*. Following completion of the report, the report shall be published in the Federal Register for public comment.

Rule 902. Public dissemination of transaction reports

(a) *General*. Except as provided in paragraph (c) of this rule, a registered security-based swap data repository shall publicly disseminate a transaction report of a security-based swap, or a life cycle event or adjustment due to a life cycle event, immediately upon receipt of information about the security-based swap, or upon re-opening following a period when the registered security-based swap data repository was closed. The transaction report shall consist of all the information reported pursuant to Rule 901(c), plus any condition flags contemplated by the registered security-based swap data repository's policies and procedures that are required by Rule 907.

(b) [Reserved]

(c) *Non-disseminated information*. A registered security-based swap data repository shall not disseminate:

(1) The identity of any counterparty to a security-based swap;

(2) With respect to a security-based swap that is not cleared at a registered clearing agency and that is reported to the registered security-based swap data repository, any information disclosing the business transactions and market positions of any person;

(3) Any information regarding a security-based swap reported pursuant to Rule 901(i);

(4) Any non-mandatory report;

(5) Any information regarding a security-based swap that is required to be reported pursuant to Rules 901 and 908(a)(1) but is not required to be publicly disseminated pursuant to Rule 908(a)(2);

(6) Any information regarding a clearing transaction that arises from the acceptance of a security-based swap for clearing by a registered clearing agency or that results from netting other clearing transactions;

(7) Any information regarding the allocation of a security-based swap; or

(8) Any information regarding a security-based swap that has been rejected from clearing or rejected by a prime broker if the original transaction report has not yet been publicly disseminated.

(d) *Temporary restriction on other market data sources*. No person shall make available to one or more persons (other than a counterparty or a post-trade processor) transaction information relating to a security-based swap before the primary trade information about the security-based swap is sent to a registered security-based swap data repository.

Rule 903. Coded information

(a) If an internationally recognized standards-setting system that imposes fees and usage restrictions on persons that obtain UICs for their own usage that are fair and reasonable and not unreasonably discriminatory and that meets the criteria of paragraph (b) of this section is recognized by the Commission and has assigned a UIC to a person, unit of a person, or product (or has endorsed a methodology for assigning transaction IDs), the registered security-based swap data repository shall employ that UIC (or methodology for assigning transaction IDs). If no such system has been recognized by the Commission, or a recognized system has not assigned a UIC to a particular person, unit of a person, or product (or has not endorsed a methodology for assigning transaction IDs), the registered security-based swap data repository shall assign a UIC to that person, unit of person, or product using its own methodology (or endorse a methodology for assigning transaction IDs). If the Commission has recognized such a system that assigns UICs to persons, each participant of a registered security-based swap data repository shall obtain a UIC from or through that system for identifying itself, and each participant that acts as a guarantor of a direct counterparty's performance of any obligation under a security-based swap that is subject to Rule 908(a) shall, if the direct counterparty has not already done so, obtain a UIC for identifying the direct counterparty from or through that system, if that system permits third-party registration without a requirement to obtain prior permission of the direct counterparty.

(b) A registered security-based swap data repository may permit information to be reported pursuant to Rule 901, and may publicly disseminate that information pursuant to Rule 902, using codes in place of certain data elements, provided that the information necessary to interpret such codes is widely available to users of the information on a non-fee basis.

Rule 904. Operating hours of registered security-based swap data repositories

A registered security-based swap data repository shall have systems in place to continuously receive and disseminate information regarding security-based swaps pursuant to Rule 900 through Rule 909, subject to the following exceptions:

(a) A registered security-based swap data repository may establish normal closing hours during periods when, in its estimation, the U.S. market and major foreign markets are inactive. A registered security-based swap data repository shall provide reasonable advance notice to participants and to the public of its normal closing hours.

(b) A registered security-based swap data repository may declare, on an ad hoc basis, special closing hours to perform system maintenance that cannot wait until normal closing hours. A registered security-based swap data repository shall, to the extent reasonably possible under the circumstances, avoid scheduling special closing hours during periods when, in its estimation, the U.S. market and major foreign markets are most active; and provide reasonable advance notice of its special closing hours to participants and to the public.

(c) During normal closing hours, and to the extent reasonably practicable during special closing hours, a registered security-based swap data repository shall have the capability to receive and hold in queue information regarding security-based swaps that has been reported pursuant to Rules 900 through 909.

(d) When a registered security-based swap data repository re-opens following normal closing hours or special closing hours, it shall disseminate transaction reports of security-based swaps held in queue, in accordance with the requirements of Rule 902.

(e) If a registered security-based swap data repository could not receive and hold in queue transaction information that was required to be reported pursuant to Rule 900 through Rule 909, it must immediately upon re-opening send a message to all participants that it has resumed normal operations. Thereafter, any participant that had an obligation to report information to the registered security-based swap data repository pursuant to Rule 900 through Rule 909, but could not do so because of the registered security-based swap data repository's inability to receive and hold in queue data, must promptly report the information to the registered security-based swap data repository.

Rule 905. Correction of errors in security-based swap information

(a) *Duty to correct.* Any counterparty or other person having a duty to report a security-based swap that discovers an error in information previously reported pursuant to Rules 900 through 909 shall correct such error in accordance with the following procedures:

(1) If a person that was not the reporting side for a security-based swap transaction discovers an error in the information reported with respect to such security-based swap, that person shall promptly notify the person having the duty to report the security-based swap of the error; and

(2) If the person having the duty to report a security-based swap transaction discovers an error in the information reported with respect to a security-based swap, or receives notification from a counterparty of an error, such person shall promptly submit to the entity to which the security-based swap was originally reported an amended report pertaining to the original transaction report. If the person having the duty to report reported the initial transaction to a registered security-based swap data repository, such person shall submit an amended report to the registered security-based swap data repository in a manner consistent with the policies and procedures contemplated by Rule 907(a)(3).

(b) *Duty of security-based swap data repository to correct.* A registered security-based swap data repository shall:

(1) Upon discovery of an error or receipt of a notice of an error, verify the accuracy of the terms of the security-based swap and, following such verification, promptly correct the erroneous information regarding such security-based swap contained in its system; and

(2) If such erroneous information relates to a security-based swap that the registered security-based swap data repository previously disseminated and falls into any of the categories of information enumerated in Rule 901(c), publicly disseminate a corrected transaction report of the security-based swap promptly following verification of the trade by the counterparties to the security-based swap, with an indication that the report relates to a previously disseminated transaction.

Rule 906. Other duties of participants

(a) *Identifying missing UIC information.* A registered security-based swap data repository shall identify any security-based swap reported to it for which the registered security-based swap data repository does not have the counterparty ID and (if applicable) the broker ID, branch ID, execution agent ID, trading desk ID, and trader ID of each direct counterparty. Once a day, the registered security-based swap data repository shall send a report to each participant of the registered security-based swap data repository or, if applicable, an execution agent, identifying, for each security-based swap to which that participant is a counterparty, the security based swap(s) for which the registered security-based swap data repository lacks counterparty ID and (if applicable) broker ID, branch ID, execution agent ID, trading desk ID, and trader ID. A participant of a registered security-based swap data repository that receives such a report shall provide the missing information with respect to its side of each security-based swap referenced in the report to the registered security-based swap data repository within 24 hours.

(b) *Duty to provide ultimate parent and affiliate information.* Each participant of a registered security-based swap data repository that is not a platform, a registered clearing agency, an externally managed investment vehicle, or a registered broker-dealer (including a registered security-based swap execution facility) that becomes a participant solely as a result of making a report to satisfy an obligation under Rule 901(a)(2)(ii)(E)(4) shall provide to the registered security-based swap data repository information sufficient to identify its ultimate parent(s) and any affiliate(s) of the participant that also are participants of the registered security based swap data repository, using ultimate parent IDs and counterparty IDs. Any such participant shall promptly notify the registered security-based swap data repository of any changes to that information.

(c) *Policies and procedures to support reporting compliance.* Each participant of a registered security-based swap data repository that is a registered security-based swap dealer, registered major security-based swap participant, registered clearing agency, platform, or registered broker-dealer (including a registered security-based swap execution facility) that becomes a participant solely as a result of making a report to satisfy an obligation under Rule 901(a)(2)(ii)(E)(4) shall establish, maintain, and enforce written policies and procedures that are reasonably designed to ensure that it complies with any obligations to report information to a registered security-based swap data repository in a manner consistent with Rules 900 through 909. Each such participant shall review and update its policies and procedures at least annually.

Rule 907. Policies and procedures of registered security-based swap data repositories

(a) *General policies and procedures.* With respect to the receipt, reporting, and dissemination of data pursuant to Rules 900 through 909, a registered security-based swap data repository shall establish and maintain written policies and procedures:

(1) That enumerate the specific data elements of a security-based swap that must be reported, which shall include, at a minimum, the data elements specified in Rule 901(c) and (d);

(2) That specify one or more acceptable data formats (each of which must be an open-source structured data format that is widely used by participants), connectivity requirements, and other protocols for submitting information;

(3) For specifying procedures for reporting life cycle events and corrections to previously submitted information, making corresponding updates or corrections to transaction records, and applying an appropriate flag to the transaction report to indicate that the report is an error correction required to be disseminated by Rule 905(b)(2), or is a life cycle event, or any adjustment due to a life cycle event, required to be disseminated by Rule 902(a);

(4) For:

(i) Identifying characteristic(s) of a security-based swap, or circumstances associated with the execution or reporting of the security-based swap, that could, in the fair and reasonable estimation of the registered security-based swap data repository, cause a person without knowledge of these characteristic(s) or circumstance(s), to receive a distorted view of the market;

(ii) Establishing flags to denote such characteristic(s) or circumstance(s);

(iii) Directing participants that report security-based swaps to apply such flags, as appropriate, in their reports to the registered security-based swap data repository; and

(iv) Applying such flags:

(A) To disseminated reports to help to prevent a distorted view of the market; or

(B) In the case of a transaction referenced in Rule 902(c), to suppress the report from public dissemination entirely, as appropriate;

(5) For assigning UICs in a manner consistent with Rule 903; and

(6) For periodically obtaining from each participant other than a platform, registered clearing agency, externally managed investment vehicle, or registered broker-dealer (including a registered security-based swap execution facility) that becomes a participant solely as a result of making a report to satisfy an obligation under Rule 901(a)(2)(ii)(E)(4) information that identifies the participant's ultimate parent(s) and any participant(s) with which the participant is affiliated, using ultimate parent IDs and counterparty IDs.

(b) [Reserved].

(c) *Public availability of policies and procedures.* A registered security-based swap data repository shall make the policies and procedures required by Rules 900 through 909 publicly available on its website.

(d) *Updating of policies and procedures.* A registered security-based swap data repository shall review, and update as necessary, the policies and procedures required by Rules 900 through 909 at least annually. Such policies and procedures shall indicate the date on which they were last reviewed.

(e) A registered security-based swap data repository shall provide to the Commission, upon request, information or reports related to the timeliness, accuracy, and completeness of data reported to it pursuant to Rules 900 through 909 and the registered security-based swap data repository's policies and procedures thereunder.

Rule 908. Cross-border matters

(a) *Application of Regulation SBSR to cross-border transactions.* (1) A security-based swap shall be subject to regulatory reporting and public dissemination if:

(i) There is a direct or indirect counterparty that is a U.S. person on either or both sides of the transaction;

(ii) The security-based swap is accepted for clearing by a clearing agency having its principal place of business in the United States;

(iii) The security-based swap is executed on a platform having its principal place of business in the United States;

(iv) The security-based swap is effected by or through a registered broker-dealer (including a registered security-based swap execution facility); or

(v) The transaction is connected with a non-U.S. person's security-based swap dealing activity and is arranged, negotiated, or executed by personnel of such non-U.S. person located in a U.S. branch or office, or by personnel of an agent of such non-U.S. person located in a U.S. branch or office.

(2) A security-based swap that is not included within paragraph (a)(1) of this rule shall be subject to regulatory reporting but not public dissemination if there is a direct or indirect counterparty on either or both sides of the transaction that is a registered security-based swap dealer or a registered major security-based swap participant.

(b) *Limitation on obligations.* Notwithstanding any other provision of Rules 900 through 909, a person shall not incur any obligation under Rules 900 through 909 unless it is:

(1) A U.S. person;

(2) A registered security-based swap dealer or registered major security-based swap participant;

(3) A platform;

(4) A registered clearing agency; or

(5) A non-U.S. person that, in connection with such person's security-based swap dealing activity, arranged, negotiated, or executed the security-based swap using its personnel located in a U.S. branch or office, or using personnel of an agent located in a U.S. branch or office.

(c) *Substituted compliance*—(1) *General.* Compliance with the regulatory reporting and public dissemination requirements in sections 13(m) and 13A of the Act and the rules and regulations thereunder, may be satisfied by compliance with the rules of a foreign jurisdiction that is the subject of a Commission order described in paragraph (c)(2) of this section, provided that at least one of the direct counterparties to the security-based swap is either a non-U.S. person or a foreign branch.

(2) *Procedure.* (i) The Commission may, conditionally or unconditionally, by order, make a substituted compliance determination regarding regulatory reporting and public dissemination of security-based swaps with respect to a foreign jurisdiction if that jurisdiction's requirements for the regulatory reporting and public dissemination of security-based swaps are comparable to otherwise applicable requirements. The Commission may, conditionally or unconditionally, by order, make a substituted compliance determination regarding regulatory reporting of security-based swaps that are subject to Rule 908(a)(2) with respect to a foreign jurisdiction if that jurisdiction's requirements for the regulatory reporting of security-based swaps are comparable to otherwise applicable requirements.

(ii) A party that potentially would comply with requirements under Rules 900 through 909 pursuant to a substituted compliance order or any foreign financial regulatory authority or authorities supervising such a person's security-based swap activities may file an application, pursuant to the procedures set forth in Rule 0–13 of this chapter, requesting that the Commission make a substituted compliance determination regarding regulatory reporting and public dissemination with respect to a foreign jurisdiction the rules of which also would require reporting and public dissemination of those security-based swaps.

(iii) In making such a substituted compliance determination, the Commission shall take into account such factors as the Commission determines are appropriate, such as the scope and objectives of the relevant foreign regulatory requirements, as well as the effectiveness of the supervisory compliance program administered, and the enforcement authority exercised, by the foreign financial regulatory authority to support oversight of its regulatory reporting and public dissemination system for security-based swaps. The Commission shall not make such a substituted compliance determination unless it finds that:

(A) The data elements that are required to be reported pursuant to the rules of the foreign jurisdiction are comparable to those required to be reported pursuant to Rule 901;

(B) The rules of the foreign jurisdiction require the security-based swap to be reported and publicly disseminated in a manner and a timeframe comparable to those required by Rules 900 through 909 (or, in the case of transactions that are subject to Rule 908(a)(2) but not to Rule 908(a)(1), the rules of the foreign jurisdiction require the security-based swap to be reported in a manner and a timeframe comparable to those required by Rules 900 through 909);

(C) The Commission has direct electronic access to the security-based swap data held by a trade repository or foreign regulatory authority to which security-based swaps are reported pursuant to the rules of that foreign jurisdiction; and

(D) Any trade repository or foreign regulatory authority in the foreign jurisdiction that receives and maintains required transaction reports of security-based swaps pursuant to the laws of that foreign jurisdiction is subject to requirements regarding data collection and maintenance; systems capacity, integrity, resiliency, availability, and security; and recordkeeping that are comparable to the requirements imposed on security-based swap data repositories by the Commission's rules and regulations.

(iv) Before issuing a substituted compliance order pursuant to this section, the Commission shall have entered into memoranda of understanding and/or other arrangements with the relevant foreign financial regulatory authority or authorities under such foreign financial regulatory system addressing supervisory and enforcement cooperation and other matters arising under the substituted compliance determination.

(v) The Commission may, on its own initiative, modify or withdraw such order at any time, after appropriate notice and opportunity for comment.

Rule 909. Registration of security-based swap data repository as a securities information processor

A registered security-based swap data repository shall also register with the Commission as a securities information processor on Form SDR (Rule 1500).

REGULATION SCI—SYSTEMS COMPLIANCE AND INTEGRITY

(Cite as 17 CFR § 242.___)

Rule 1000. Definitions

For purposes of Regulation SCI (Rules 1000 through 1007), the following definitions shall apply:

Critical SCI systems means any SCI systems of, or operated by or on behalf of, an SCI entity that:

(1) Directly support functionality relating to:

(i) Clearance and settlement systems of clearing agencies;

(ii) Openings, reopenings, and closings on the primary listing market;

(iii) Trading halts;

(iv) Initial public offerings;

(v) The provision of consolidated market data; or

(vi) Exclusively-listed securities; or

(2) Provide functionality to the securities markets for which the availability of alternatives is significantly limited or nonexistent and without which there would be a material impact on fair and orderly markets.

Electronic signature has the meaning set forth in Rule 19b-4(j) of the Exchange Act.

Exempt clearing agency subject to ARP means an entity that has received from the Commission an exemption from registration as a clearing agency under Section 17A of the Act, and whose exemption contains conditions that relate to the Commission's Automation Review Policies (ARP), or any Commission regulation that supersedes or replaces such policies.

Indirect SCI systems means any systems of, or operated by or on behalf of, an SCI entity that, if breached, would be reasonably likely to pose a security threat to SCI systems.

Major SCI event means an SCI event that has had, or the SCI entity reasonably estimates would have:

(1) Any impact on a critical SCI system; or

(2) A significant impact on the SCI entity's operations or on market participants.

Plan processor has the meaning set forth in Rule 600(b)(55).

Responsible SCI personnel means, for a particular SCI system or indirect SCI system impacted by an SCI event, such senior manager(s) of the SCI entity having responsibility for such system, and their designee(s).

SCI alternative trading system or *SCI ATS* means an alternative trading system, as defined in Rule 300(a) of Regulation ATS, which during at least four of the preceding six calendar months:

(1) Had with respect to NMS stocks:

(i) Five percent (5%) or more in any single NMS stock, and one-quarter percent (0.25%) or more in all NMS stocks, of the average daily dollar volume reported by applicable transaction reporting plans; or

(ii) One percent (1%) or more in all NMS stocks of the average daily dollar volume reported by applicable transaction reporting plans; or

(2) Had with respect to equity securities that are not NMS stocks and for which transactions are reported to a self-regulatory organization, five percent (5%) or more of the average daily dollar volume as calculated by the self-regulatory organization to which such transactions are reported;

(3) Provided, however, that such SCI ATS shall not be required to comply with the requirements of Regulation SCI until six months after satisfying any of paragraphs (1) or (2) of this section, as applicable, for the first time.

SCI entity means an SCI self-regulatory organization, SCI alternative trading system, plan processor, or exempt clearing agency subject to ARP.

SCI event means an event at an SCI entity that constitutes:

(1) A systems disruption;

(2) A systems compliance issue; or

(3) A systems intrusion.

SCI review means a review, following established procedures and standards, that is performed by objective personnel having appropriate experience to conduct reviews of SCI systems and indirect SCI systems, and which review contains:

(1) A risk assessment with respect to such systems of an SCI entity; and

(2) An assessment of internal control design and effectiveness of its SCI systems and indirect SCI

systems to include logical and physical security controls, development processes, and information technology governance, consistent with industry standards.

SCI self-regulatory organization or *SCI SRO* means any national securities exchange, registered securities association, or registered clearing agency, or the Municipal Securities Rulemaking Board; *provided however*, that for purposes of this section, the term SCI self-regulatory organization shall not include an exchange that is notice registered with the Commission pursuant to 15 U.S.C. 78f(g) or a limited purpose national securities association registered with the Commission pursuant to 15 U.S.C. 78*o*-3(k).

SCI systems means all computer, network, electronic, technical, automated, or similar systems of, or operated by or on behalf of, an SCI entity that, with respect to securities, directly support trading, clearance and settlement, order routing, market data, market regulation, or market surveillance.

Senior management means, for purposes of Rule 1003(b), an SCI entity's Chief Executive Officer, Chief Technology Officer, Chief Information Officer, General Counsel, and Chief Compliance Officer, or the equivalent of such employees or officers of an SCI entity.

Systems compliance issue means an event at an SCI entity that has caused any SCI system of such entity to operate in a manner that does not comply with the Act and the rules and regulations thereunder or the entity's rules or governing documents, as applicable.

Systems disruption means an event in an SCI entity's SCI systems that disrupts, or significantly degrades, the normal operation of an SCI system.

Systems intrusion means any unauthorized entry into the SCI systems or indirect SCI systems of an SCI entity.

Rule 1001. Obligations related to policies and procedures of SCI entities

(a) *Capacity, integrity, resiliency, availability, and security*. (1) Each SCI entity shall establish, maintain, and enforce written policies and procedures reasonably designed to ensure that its SCI systems and, for purposes of security standards, indirect SCI systems, have levels of capacity, integrity, resiliency, availability, and security, adequate to maintain the SCI entity's operational capability and promote the maintenance of fair and orderly markets.

(2) Policies and procedures required by paragraph (a)(1) of this section shall include, at a minimum:

(i) The establishment of reasonable current and future technological infrastructure capacity planning estimates;

(ii) Periodic capacity stress tests of such systems to determine their ability to process transactions in an accurate, timely, and efficient manner;

(iii) A program to review and keep current systems development and testing methodology for such systems;

(iv) Regular reviews and testing, as applicable, of such systems, including backup systems, to identify vulnerabilities pertaining to internal and external threats, physical hazards, and natural or manmade disasters;

(v) Business continuity and disaster recovery plans that include maintaining backup and recovery capabilities sufficiently resilient and geographically diverse and that are reasonably designed to achieve next business day resumption of trading and two-hour resumption of critical SCI systems following a wide-scale disruption;

(vi) Standards that result in such systems being designed, developed, tested, maintained, operated, and surveilled in a manner that facilitates the successful collection, processing, and dissemination of market data; and

(vii) Monitoring of such systems to identify potential SCI events.

(3) Each SCI entity shall periodically review the effectiveness of the policies and procedures required by this paragraph (a), and take prompt action to remedy deficiencies in such policies and procedures.

(4) For purposes of this paragraph (a), such policies and procedures shall be deemed to be reasonably designed if they are consistent with current SCI industry standards, which shall be comprised of information technology practices that are widely available to information technology professionals in the financial sector and issued by an authoritative body that is a U.S. governmental entity or agency, association of U.S. governmental entities or agencies, or widely recognized organization. Compliance with such current SCI industry standards, however, shall not be the exclusive means

to comply with the requirements of this paragraph (a).

(b) *Systems compliance.* (1) Each SCI entity shall establish, maintain, and enforce written policies and procedures reasonably designed to ensure that its SCI systems operate in a manner that complies with the Act and the rules and regulations thereunder and the entity's rules and governing documents, as applicable.

(2) Policies and procedures required by paragraph (b)(1) of this section shall include, at a minimum:

(i) Testing of all SCI systems and any changes to SCI systems prior to implementation;

(ii) A system of internal controls over changes to SCI systems;

(iii) A plan for assessments of the functionality of SCI systems designed to detect systems compliance issues, including by responsible SCI personnel and by personnel familiar with applicable provisions of the Act and the rules and regulations thereunder and the SCI entity's rules and governing documents; and

(iv) A plan of coordination and communication between regulatory and other personnel of the SCI entity, including by responsible SCI personnel, regarding SCI systems design, changes, testing, and controls designed to detect and prevent systems compliance issues.

(3) Each SCI entity shall periodically review the effectiveness of the policies and procedures required by this paragraph (b), and take prompt action to remedy deficiencies in such policies and procedures.

(4) Safe harbor from liability for individuals. Personnel of an SCI entity shall be deemed not to have aided, abetted, counseled, commanded, caused, induced, or procured the violation by an SCI entity of this paragraph (b) if the person:

(i) Has reasonably discharged the duties and obligations incumbent upon such person by the SCI entity's policies and procedures; and

(ii) Was without reasonable cause to believe that the policies and procedures relating to an SCI system for which such person was responsible, or had supervisory responsibility, were not established, maintained, or enforced in accordance with this paragraph (b) in any material respect.

(c) *Responsible SCI personnel.* (1) Each SCI entity shall establish, maintain, and enforce reasonably designed written policies and procedures that include the criteria for identifying responsible SCI personnel, the designation and documentation of responsible SCI personnel, and escalation procedures to quickly inform responsible SCI personnel of potential SCI events.

(2) Each SCI entity shall periodically review the effectiveness of the policies and procedures required by paragraph (c)(1) of this section, and take prompt action to remedy deficiencies in such policies and procedures.

Rule 1002. Obligations related to SCI events

(a) *Corrective action.* Upon any responsible SCI personnel having a reasonable basis to conclude that an SCI event has occurred, each SCI entity shall begin to take appropriate corrective action which shall include, at a minimum, mitigating potential harm to investors and market integrity resulting from the SCI event and devoting adequate resources to remedy the SCI event as soon as reasonably practicable.

(b) *Commission notification and recordkeeping of SCI events.* Each SCI entity shall:

(1) Upon any responsible SCI personnel having a reasonable basis to conclude that an SCI event has occurred, notify the Commission of such SCI event immediately;

(2) Within 24 hours of any responsible SCI personnel having a reasonable basis to conclude that the SCI event has occurred, submit a written notification pertaining to such SCI event to the Commission, which shall be made on a good faith, best efforts basis and include:

(i) A description of the SCI event, including the system(s) affected; and

(ii) To the extent available as of the time of the notification: the SCI entity's current assessment of the types and number of market participants potentially affected by the SCI event; the potential impact of the SCI event on the market; a description of the steps the SCI entity has taken, is taking, or plans to take, with respect to the SCI event; the time the SCI event was resolved or timeframe within which the SCI event is expected to be resolved; and any other pertinent information known by the SCI entity about the SCI event;

(3) Until such time as the SCI event is resolved and the SCI entity's investigation of the SCI event is closed, provide updates pertaining to such SCI event to the Commission on a regular basis, or at such frequency as reasonably requested by a representative of the Commission, to correct any materially incorrect information previously provided, or when new material information is discovered, including but not limited to, any of the information listed in paragraph (b)(2)(ii) of this section;

(4)(i)(A) If an SCI event is resolved and the SCI entity's investigation of the SCI event is closed within 30 calendar days of the occurrence of the SCI event, then within five business days after the resolution of the SCI event and closure of the investigation regarding the SCI event, submit a final written notification pertaining to such SCI event to the Commission containing the information required in paragraph (b)(4)(ii) of this section.

(B)(*1*) If an SCI event is not resolved or the SCI entity's investigation of the SCI event is not closed within 30 calendar days of the occurrence of the SCI event, then submit an interim written notification pertaining to such SCI event to the Commission within 30 calendar days after the occurrence of the SCI event containing the information required in paragraph (b)(4)(ii) of this section, to the extent known at the time.

(*2*) Within five business days after the resolution of such SCI event and closure of the investigation regarding such SCI event, submit a final written notification pertaining to such SCI event to the Commission containing the information required in paragraph (b)(4)(ii) of this section.

(ii) Written notifications required by paragraph (b)(4)(i) of this section shall include:

(A) A detailed description of: the SCI entity's assessment of the types and number of market participants affected by the SCI event; the SCI entity's assessment of the impact of the SCI event on the market; the steps the SCI entity has taken, is taking, or plans to take, with respect to the SCI event; the time the SCI event was resolved; the SCI entity's rule(s) and/or governing document(s), as applicable, that relate to the SCI event; and any other pertinent information known by the SCI entity about the SCI event;

(B) A copy of any information disseminated pursuant to paragraph (c) of this section by the SCI entity to date regarding the SCI event to any of its members or participants; and

(C) An analysis of parties that may have experienced a loss, whether monetary or otherwise, due to the SCI event, the number of such parties, and an estimate of the aggregate amount of such loss.

(5) The requirements of paragraphs (b)(1) through (4) of this section shall not apply to any SCI event that has had, or the SCI entity reasonably estimates would have, no or a de minimis impact on the SCI entity's operations or on market participants. For such events, each SCI entity shall:

(i) Make, keep, and preserve records relating to all such SCI events; and

(ii) Submit to the Commission a report, within 30 calendar days after the end of each calendar quarter, containing a summary description of such systems disruptions and systems intrusions, including the SCI systems and, for systems intrusions, indirect SCI systems, affected by such systems disruptions and systems intrusions during the applicable calendar quarter.

(c) *Dissemination of SCI events.* (1) Each SCI entity shall:

(i) Promptly after any responsible SCI personnel has a reasonable basis to conclude that an SCI event that is a systems disruption or systems compliance issue has occurred, disseminate the following information about such SCI event:

(A) The system(s) affected by the SCI event; and

(B) A summary description of the SCI event; and

(ii) When known, promptly further disseminate the following information about such SCI event:

(A) A detailed description of the SCI event;

(B) The SCI entity's current assessment of the types and number of market participants potentially affected by the SCI event; and

(C) A description of the progress of its corrective action for the SCI event and when the SCI event has been or is expected to be resolved; and

(iii) Until resolved, provide regular updates of any information required to be disseminated under paragraphs (c)(1)(i) and (ii) of this section.

(2) Each SCI entity shall, promptly after any responsible SCI personnel has a reasonable basis to conclude that a SCI event that is a systems intrusion has occurred, disseminate a summary description of the systems intrusion, including a description of the corrective action taken by the SCI entity and when the systems intrusion has been or is expected to be resolved, unless the SCI entity determines that dissemination of such information would likely compromise the security of the SCI entity's SCI systems or indirect SCI systems, or an investigation of the systems intrusion, and documents the reasons for such determination.

(3) The information required to be disseminated under paragraphs (c)(1) and (2) of this section promptly after any responsible SCI personnel has a reasonable basis to conclude that an SCI event has occurred, shall be promptly disseminated by the SCI entity to those members or participants of the SCI entity that any responsible SCI personnel has reasonably estimated may have been affected by the SCI event, and promptly disseminated to any additional members or participants that any responsible SCI personnel subsequently reasonably estimates may have been affected by the SCI event; provided, however, that for major SCI events, the information required to be disseminated under paragraphs (c)(1) and (2) of this section shall be promptly disseminated by the SCI entity to all of its members or participants.

(4) The requirements of paragraphs (c)(1) through (3) of this section shall not apply to:

(i) SCI events to the extent they relate to market regulation or market surveillance systems; or

(ii) Any SCI event that has had, or the SCI entity reasonably estimates would have, no or a de minimis impact on the SCI entity's operations or on market participants.

Rule 1003. Obligations related to systems changes; SCI review

(a) *Systems changes*. Each SCI entity shall:

(1) Within 30 calendar days after the end of each calendar quarter, submit to the Commission a report describing completed, ongoing, and planned material changes to its SCI systems and the security of indirect SCI systems, during the prior, current, and subsequent calendar quarters, including the dates or expected dates of commencement and completion. An SCI entity shall establish reasonable written criteria for identifying a change to its SCI systems and the security of indirect SCI systems as material and report such changes in accordance with such criteria.

(2) Promptly submit a supplemental report notifying the Commission of a material error in or material omission from a report previously submitted under this paragraph (a).

(b) *SCI review*. Each SCI entity shall:

(1) Conduct an SCI review of the SCI entity's compliance with Regulation SCI not less than once each calendar year; *provided, however*, that:

(i) Penetration test reviews of the network, firewalls, and production systems shall be conducted at a frequency of not less than once every three years; and

(ii) Assessments of SCI systems directly supporting market regulation or market surveillance shall be conducted at a frequency based upon the risk assessment conducted as part of the SCI review, but in no case less than once every three years; and

(2) Submit a report of the SCI review required by paragraph (b)(1) of this section to senior management of the SCI entity for review no more than 30 calendar days after completion of such SCI review; and

(3) Submit to the Commission, and to the board of directors of the SCI entity or the equivalent of such board, a report of the SCI review required by paragraph (b)(1) of this section, together with any response by senior management, within 60 calendar days after its submission to senior management of the SCI entity.

Rule 1004. SCI entity business continuity and disaster recovery plans testing requirements for members or participants

With respect to an SCI entity's business continuity and disaster recovery plans, including its backup systems, each SCI entity shall:

(a) Establish standards for the designation of those members or participants that the SCI entity reasonably determines are, taken as a whole, the minimum necessary for the maintenance of fair and orderly markets in the event of the activation of such plans;

(b) Designate members or participants pursuant to the standards established in paragraph (a) of this section and require participation by such designated members or participants in scheduled functional and performance testing of the operation of such plans, in the manner and frequency specified by the SCI entity, provided that such frequency shall not be less than once every 12 months; and

(c) Coordinate the testing of such plans on an industry- or sector-wide basis with other SCI entities.

Rule 1005. Recordkeeping requirements related to compliance with Regulation SCI

(a) An SCI SRO shall make, keep, and preserve all documents relating to its compliance with Regulation SCI as prescribed in Rule 17a–1.

(b) An SCI entity that is not an SCI SRO shall:

(1) Make, keep, and preserve at least one copy of all documents, including correspondence, memoranda, papers, books, notices, accounts, and other such records, relating to its compliance with Regulation SCI, including, but not limited to, records relating to any changes to its SCI systems and indirect SCI systems;

(2) Keep all such documents for a period of not less than five years, the first two years in a place that is readily accessible to the Commission or its representatives for inspection and examination; and

(3) Upon request of any representative of the Commission, promptly furnish to the possession of such representative copies of any documents required to be kept and preserved by it pursuant to paragraphs (b)(1) and (2) of this section.

(c) Upon or immediately prior to ceasing to do business or ceasing to be registered under the Securities Exchange Act of 1934, an SCI entity shall take all necessary action to ensure that the records required to be made, kept, and preserved by this section shall be accessible to the Commission and its representatives in the manner required by this section and for the remainder of the period required by this section.

Rule 1006. Electronic filing and submission

(a) Except with respect to notifications to the Commission made pursuant to Rule 1002(b)(1) or updates to the Commission made pursuant to Rule 1002(b)(3), any notification, review, description, analysis, or report to the Commission required to be submitted under Regulation SCI shall be filed electronically on Form SCI (17 CFR § 249.1900), include all information as prescribed in Form SCI and the instructions thereto, and contain an electronic signature; and

(b) The signatory to an electronically filed Form SCI shall manually sign a signature page or document, in the manner prescribed by Form SCI, authenticating, acknowledging, or otherwise adopting his or her signature that appears in typed form within the electronic filing. Such document shall be executed before or at the time Form SCI is electronically filed and shall be retained by the SCI entity in accordance with Rule 1005.

Rule 1007. Requirements for service bureaus

If records required to be filed or kept by an SCI entity under Regulation SCI are prepared or maintained by a service bureau or other recordkeeping service on behalf of the SCI entity, the SCI entity shall ensure that the records are available for review by the Commission and its representatives by submitting a written undertaking, in a form acceptable to the Commission, by such service bureau or other recordkeeping service, signed by a duly authorized person at such service bureau or other recordkeeping service. Such a written undertaking shall include an agreement by the service bureau to permit the Commission and its representatives to examine such records at any time or from time to time during business hours, and to promptly furnish to the Commission and its representatives true, correct, and current electronic files in a form acceptable to the Commission or its representatives or hard copies of any or all or any part of such records, upon request, periodically, or continuously and, in any case, within the same time periods as would apply to the SCI entity for such records. The preparation or maintenance of records by a service bureau or other recordkeeping service shall not relieve an SCI entity from its obligation to prepare, maintain, and provide the Commission and its representatives access to such records.

REGULATION FD

(Cite as 17 CFR § 243.___)

Rule 100. General rule regarding selective disclosure

(a) Whenever an issuer, or any person acting on its behalf, discloses any material nonpublic information regarding that issuer or its securities to any person described in paragraph (b)(1) of this rule, the issuer shall make public disclosure of that information as provided in Rule 101(e):

(1) Simultaneously, in the case of an intentional disclosure; and

(2) Promptly, in the case of a non-intentional disclosure.

(b)(1) Except as provided in paragraph (b)(2) of this rule, paragraph (a) of this rule shall apply to a disclosure made to any person outside the issuer:

(i) Who is a broker or dealer, or a person associated with a broker or dealer, as those terms are defined in Section 3(a) of the Securities Exchange Act of 1934;

(ii) Who is an investment adviser, as that term is defined in Section 202(a)(11) of the Investment Advisers Act of 1940; an institutional investment manager, as that term is defined in Section 13(f)(6) of the Securities Exchange Act of 1934, that filed a report on Form 13F (17 CFR 249.325) with the Commission for the most recent quarter ended prior to the date of the disclosure; or a person associated with either of the foregoing. For purposes of this paragraph, a "person associated with an investment adviser or institutional investment manager" has the meaning set forth in Section 202(a)(17) of the Investment Advisers Act of 1940 (15 U.S.C. 80b–2(a)(17)), assuming for these purposes that an institutional investment manager is an investment adviser;

(iii) Who is an investment company, as defined in Section 3 of the Investment Company Act of 1940 (15 U.S.C. 80a–23), or who would be an investment company but for Section 3(c)(1) (15 U.S.C. 80a–3(c)(1)) or Section 3(c)(7) (15 U.S.C. 80a–3(c)(7)) thereof, or an affiliated person of either of the foregoing. For purposes of this paragraph, "affiliated person" means only those persons described in Section 2(a)(3)(C), (D), (E), and (F) of the Investment Company Act of 1940 (15 U.S.C. 80a–2(a)(3)(C), (D), (E), and (F)), assuming for these purposes that a person who would be an investment company but for Section 3(c)(1) (15 U.S.C. 80a–3(c)(1)) or Section 3(c)(7) (15 U.S.C. 80a–3(c)(7)) of the Investment Company Act of 1940 is an investment company; or

(iv) Who is a holder of the issuer's securities, under circumstances in which it is reasonably foreseeable that the person will purchase or sell the issuer's securities on the basis of the information.

(2) Paragraph (a) of this rule shall not apply to a disclosure made:

(i) To a person who owes a duty of trust or confidence to the issuer (such as an attorney, investment banker, or accountant);

(ii) To a person who expressly agrees to maintain the disclosed information in confidence;

(iii) In connection with a securities offering registered under the Securities Act, other than an offering of the type described in any of Rule 415(a)(1)(i) through (vi) under the Securities Act (except an offering of the type described in Rule 415(a)(1)(i) under the Securities Act also involving a registered offering, whether or not underwritten, for capital formation purposes for the account of the issuer (unless the issuer's offering is being registered for the purpose of evading the requirements of this section)), if the disclosure is by any of the following means:

(A) A registration statement filed under the Securities Act, including a prospectus contained therein;

(B) A free writing prospectus used after filing of the registration statement for the offering or a communication falling within the exception to the definition of prospectus contained in clause (a) of section 2(a)(10) of the Securities Act;

(C) Any other Section 10(b) prospectus;

(D) A notice permitted by Rule 135 under the Securities Act;

(E) A communication permitted by Rule 134 under the Securities Act; or

(F) An oral communication made in connection with the registered securities offering after filing of the registration statement for the offering under the Securities Act.

Rule 101. Definitions

This section defines certain terms as used in Regulation FD (Rules 100–103).

(a) *Intentional.* A selective disclosure of material nonpublic information is "intentional" when the person making the disclosure either knows, or is reckless in not knowing, that the information he or she is communicating is both material and nonpublic.

(b) *Issuer.* An "issuer" subject to this regulation is one that has a class of securities registered under Section 12 of the Securities Exchange Act of 1934, or is required to file reports under Section 15(d) of the Securities Exchange Act of 1934, including any closed-end investment company (as defined in Section 5(a)(2) of the Investment Company Act of 1940) (15 U.S.C. 80a–5(a)(2)), but not including any other investment company or any foreign government or foreign private issuer, as those terms are defined in Rule 405 under the Securities Act.

(c) *Person Acting on Behalf of an Issuer.* "Person acting on behalf of an issuer" means any senior official of the issuer (or, in the case of a closed-end investment company, a senior official of the issuer's investment adviser), or any other officer, employee, or agent of an issuer who regularly communicates with any person described in Rule 100(b)(1)(i), (ii), or (iii), or with holders of the issuer's securities. An officer, director, employee, or agent of an issuer who discloses material nonpublic information in breach of a duty of trust or confidence to the issuer shall not be considered to be acting on behalf of the issuer.

(d) *Promptly.* "Promptly" means as soon as reasonably practicable (but in no event after the later of 24 hours or the commencement of the next day's trading on the New York Stock Exchange) after a senior official of the issuer (or, in the case of a closed-end investment company, a senior official of the issuer's investment adviser) learns that there has been a non-intentional disclosure by the issuer or person acting on behalf of the issuer of information that the senior official knows, or is reckless in not knowing, is both material and nonpublic.

(e) *Public Disclosure.* (1) Except as provided in paragraph (e)(2) of this rule, an issuer shall make the "public disclosure" of information required by Rule 100(a) by furnishing to or filing with the Commission a Form 8–K (17 CFR 249.308) disclosing that information.

(2) An issuer shall be exempt from the requirement to furnish or file a Form 8–K if it instead disseminates the information through another method (or combination of methods) of disclosure that is reasonably designed to provide broad, non-exclusionary distribution of the information to the public.

(f) *Senior Official.* "Senior official" means any director, executive officer (as defined in Rule 3b–7), investor relations or public relations officer, or other person with similar functions.

(g) *Securities Offering.* For purposes of Rule 100(b)(2)(iv):

(1) *Underwritten Offerings.* A securities offering that is underwritten commences when the issuer reaches an understanding with the broker-dealer that is to act as managing underwriter and continues until the later of the end of the period during which a dealer must deliver a prospectus or the sale of the securities (unless the offering is sooner terminated);

(2) *Non-Underwritten Offerings.* A securities offering that is not underwritten:

(i) If covered by Rule 415(a)(1)(x) under the Securities Act of 1933, commences when the issuer makes its first bona fide offer in a takedown of securities and continues until the later of the end of the period during which each dealer must deliver a prospectus or the sale of the securities in that takedown (unless the takedown is sooner terminated);

(ii) If a business combination as defined in Rule 165(f)(1) under the Securities Act of 1933, commences when the first public announcement of the transaction is made and continues until the completion of the vote or the expiration of the tender offer, as applicable (unless the transaction is sooner terminated);

(iii) If an offering other than those specified in paragraphs (a) and (b) of this rule, commences when the issuer files a registration statement and continues until the later of the end of the period during which each dealer must deliver a prospectus or the sale of the securities (unless the offering is sooner terminated).

Rule 102. No effect on antifraud liability

No failure to make a public disclosure required solely by Rule 100 shall be deemed to be a violation of Rule 10b–5 under the Securities Exchange Act.

Rule 103. No effect on Exchange Act reporting status

A failure to make a public disclosure required solely by Rule 100 shall not affect whether:

(a) For purposes of Forms S–2 (17 CFR 239.12), S–3 (17 CFR 239.13) and S–8 (17 CFR 239.16b), SF–3 (17 CFR 239.45) under the Securities Act, an issuer is deemed to have filed all the material required to be filed pursuant to Section 13 or 15(d) of the Securities Exchange Act of 1934 or, where applicable, has made those filings in a timely manner; or

(b) There is adequate current public information about the issuer for purposes of Rule 144(c) under the Securities Act of 1933.

REGULATION BTR—BLACKOUT TRADING RESTRICTION

(Cite as 17 CFR § 245.___)

Rule 100. Definitions

As used in Regulation BTR (Rules 100 through 104), unless the context otherwise requires:

(a) The term *acquired in connection with service or employment as a director or executive officer*, when applied to a director or executive officer, means that he or she acquired, directly or indirectly, an equity security:

(1) At a time when he or she was a director or executive officer, under a compensatory plan, contract, authorization or arrangement, including, but not limited to, an option, warrants or rights plan, a pension, retirement or deferred compensation plan or a bonus, incentive or profit-sharing plan (whether or not set forth in any formal plan document), including a compensatory plan, contract, authorization or arrangement with a parent, subsidiary or affiliate;

(2) At a time when he or she was a director or executive officer, as a result of any transaction or business relationship described in paragraph (a) of Item 404 of Regulation S–K or, in the case of a foreign private issuer, Item 7.B of Form 20–F (but without application of the disclosure thresholds of such provisions), to the extent that he or she has a pecuniary interest (as defined in paragraph (*l*) of this rule) in the equity securities;

(3) At a time when he or she was a director or executive officer, as directors' qualifying shares or other securities that he or she must hold to satisfy minimum ownership requirements or guidelines for directors or executive officers;

(4) Prior to becoming, or while, a director or executive officer where the equity security was acquired as a direct or indirect inducement to service or employment as a director or executive officer; or

(5) Prior to becoming, or while, a director or executive officer where the equity security was received as a result of a business combination in respect of an equity security of an entity involved in the business combination that he or she had acquired in connection with service or employment as a director or executive officer of such entity.

(b) Except as provided in Rule 102, the term *blackout period*:

(1) With respect to the equity securities of any issuer (other than a foreign private issuer), means any period of more than three consecutive business days during which the ability to purchase, sell or otherwise acquire or transfer an interest in any equity security of such issuer held in an individual account plan is temporarily suspended by the issuer or by a fiduciary of the plan with respect to not fewer than 50% of the participants or beneficiaries located in the United States and its territories and possessions under all individual account plans (as defined in paragraph (j) of this rule) maintained by the issuer that permit participants or beneficiaries to acquire or hold equity securities of the issuer;

(2) With respect to the equity securities of any foreign private issuer (as defined in Rule 3b–4(c) under the Securities Exchange Act of 1934), means any period of more than three consecutive business days during which both:

(i) The conditions of paragraph (b)(1) of this rule are met; and

(ii)(A) The number of participants and beneficiaries located in the United States and its territories and possessions subject to the temporary suspension exceeds 15% of the total number of employees of the issuer and its consolidated subsidiaries; or

(B) More than 50,000 participants and beneficiaries located in the United States and its territories and possessions are subject to the temporary suspension.

(3) In determining the individual account plans (as defined in paragraph (j) of this rule) maintained by an issuer for purposes of this paragraph (b):

(i) The rules under section 414(b), (c), (m) and (*o*) of the Internal Revenue Code (26 U.S.C. 414(b), (c), (m) and (*o*)) are to be applied; and

(ii) An individual account plan that is maintained outside of the United States primarily for the benefit of persons substantially all of whom are nonresident aliens (within the meaning of section 104(b)(4) of the Employee Retirement Income Security Act of 1974 (29 U.S.C. 1003(b)(4))) is not to be considered.

(4) In determining the number of participants and beneficiaries in an individual account plan (as defined in paragraph (j) of this rule) maintained by an issuer:

(i) The determination may be made as of any date within the 12-month period preceding the beginning date of the temporary suspension in question; provided that if there has been a significant change in the number of participants or beneficiaries in an individual account plan since the date selected, the determination for such plan must be made as of the most recent practicable date that reflects such change; and

(ii) The determination may be made without regard to overlapping plan participation.

(c)(1) The term *director* has, except as provided in paragraph (c)(2) of this rule, the meaning set forth in section 3(a)(7) of the Exchange Act.

(2) In the case of a foreign private issuer (as defined in Rule 3b–4(c) under the Securities Exchange Act of 1934), the term *director* means an individual within the definition set forth in section 3(a)(7) of the Exchange Act who is a management employee of the issuer.

(d) The term *derivative security* has the meaning set forth in Rule 16a–1(c) under the Securities Exchange Act of 1934.

(e) The term *equity security* has the meaning set forth in section 3(a)(11) of the Exchange Act and Rule 3a11–1.

(f) The term *equity security of the issuer* means any equity security or derivative security relating to an issuer, whether or not issued by that issuer.

(g) The term *Exchange Act* means the Securities Exchange Act of 1934.

(h)(1) The term *executive officer* has, except as provided in paragraph (h)(2) of this rule, the meaning set forth in Rule 16a–1(f) under the Securities Exchange Act of 1934.

(2) In the case of a foreign private issuer (as defined in Rule 3b–4(c) under the Securities Exchange Act of 1934), the term *executive officer* means the principal executive officer or officers, the principal financial officer or officers and the principal accounting officer or officers of the issuer.

(i) The term *exempt security* has the meaning set forth in section 3(a)(12) of the Exchange Act.

(j) The term *individual account plan* means a pension plan which provides for an individual account for each participant and for benefits based solely upon the amount contributed to the participant's account, and any income, expenses, gains and losses, and any forfeitures of accounts of other participants which may be allocated to such participant's account, except that such term does not include a one-participant retirement plan (within the meaning of section 101(i)(8)(B) of the Employee Retirement Income Security Act of 1974 (29 U.S.C. 1021(i)(8)(B))), nor does it include a pension plan in which participation is limited to directors of the issuer.

(k) The term *issuer* means an issuer (as defined in section 3(a)(8) of the Exchange Act, the securities of which are registered under section 12 of the Exchange Act or that is required to file reports under section 15(d) of the Exchange Act or that files or has filed a registration statement that has not yet become effective under the Securities Act of 1933 and that it has not withdrawn.

(*l*) The term *pecuniary interest* has the meaning set forth in Rule 16a–1(a)(2)(i) of this chapter and the term *indirect pecuniary interest* has the meaning set forth in Rule 16a–1(a)(2)(ii) under the Securities Exchange Act of 1934. Rule 16a–1(a)(2)(iii) under the Securities Exchange Act of 1934 also shall apply to determine pecuniary interest for purposes of this regulation.

Rule 101. Prohibition of insider trading during pension fund blackout periods

(a) Except to the extent otherwise provided in paragraph (c) of this rule, it is unlawful under section 306(a)(1) of the Sarbanes–Oxley Act of 2002 (15 U.S.C. 7244(a)(1)) for any director or executive officer of an issuer of any equity security (other than an exempt security), directly or indirectly, to purchase, sell or otherwise acquire or transfer any equity security of the issuer (other than an exempt security) during any blackout period with respect to such equity security, if such director or executive officer acquires or previously acquired such equity security in connection with his or her service or employment as a director or executive officer.

(b) For purposes of section 306(a)(1) of the Sarbanes–Oxley Act of 2002, any sale or other transfer of an equity security of the issuer during a blackout period will be treated as a transaction involving an equity security "acquired in connection with service or employment as a director or executive officer" (as defined in Rule 100(a)) to the extent that the director or executive officer has a pecuniary interest (as defined in Rule 100(*l*)) in such equity security, unless the director or executive officer establishes by specific identification of securities that the transaction did not involve an equity security "acquired in connection with service or employment as a director or executive officer." To establish that the equity security was not so acquired, a director or executive officer must identify the source of the equity securities and demonstrate that he or she has utilized the same specific identification for any purpose related to the transaction (such as tax reporting and any applicable disclosure and reporting requirements).

(c) The following transactions are exempt from section 306(a)(1) of the Sarbanes–Oxley Act of 2002:

(1) Any acquisition of equity securities resulting from the reinvestment of dividends in, or interest on, equity securities of the same issuer if the acquisition is made pursuant to a plan providing for the regular reinvestment of dividends or interest and the plan provides for broad-based participation, does not discriminate in favor of employees of the issuer and operates on substantially the same terms for all plan participants;

(2) Any purchase or sale of equity securities of the issuer pursuant to a contract, instruction or written plan entered into by the director or executive officer that satisfies the affirmative defense conditions of Rule 10b5–1(c) under the Securities Exchange Act of 1934; provided that the director or executive officer did not enter into or modify the contract, instruction or written plan during the blackout period (as defined in Rule 100(b)) in question, or while aware of the actual or approximate beginning or ending dates of that blackout period (whether or not the director or executive officer received notice of the blackout period as required by Section 306(a)(6) of the Sarbanes–Oxley Act of 2002 (15 U.S.C. 7244(a)(6)));

(3) Any purchase or sale of equity securities, other than a Discretionary Transaction (as defined in Rule 16b–3(b)(1) under the Securities Exchange Act of 1934), pursuant to a Qualified Plan (as defined in Rule 16b–3(b)(4)), an Excess Benefit Plan (as defined in Rule 16b–3(b)(2) under the Securities Exchange Act of 1934) or a Stock Purchase Plan (as defined in Rule 16b–3(b)(5) under the Securities Exchange Act of 1934) (or, in the case of a foreign private issuer, pursuant to an employee benefit plan that either (i) has been approved by the taxing authority of a foreign jurisdiction, or (ii) is eligible for preferential treatment under the tax laws of a foreign jurisdiction because the plan provides for broad-based employee participation); provided that a Discretionary Transaction that meets the conditions of paragraph (c)(2) of this rule also shall be exempt;

(4) Any grant or award of an option, stock appreciation right or other equity compensation pursuant to a plan that, by its terms:

(i) Permits directors or executive officers to receive grants or awards; and

(ii) Either:

(A) States the amount and price of securities to be awarded to designated directors and executive officers or categories of directors and executive officers (though not necessarily to others who may participate in the plan) and specifies the timing of awards to directors and executive officers; or

(B) Sets forth a formula that determines the amount, price and timing, using objective criteria (such as earnings of the issuer, value of the securities, years of service, job classification, and compensation levels);

(5) Any exercise, conversion or termination of a derivative security that the director or executive officer did not write or acquire during the blackout period (as defined in Rule 100(b)) in question, or while aware of the actual or approximate beginning or ending dates of that blackout period (whether or not the director or executive officer received notice of the blackout period as required by Section 306(a)(6) of the Sarbanes–Oxley Act of 2002); and either:

(i) The derivative security, by its terms, may be exercised, converted or terminated only on a fixed date, with no discretionary provision for earlier exercise, conversion or termination; or

(ii) The derivative security is exercised, converted or terminated by a counterparty and the director or executive officer does not exercise any influence on the counterparty with respect to whether or when to exercise, convert or terminate the derivative security;

(6) Any acquisition or disposition of equity securities involving a bona fide gift or a transfer by will or the laws of descent and distribution;

(7) Any acquisition or disposition of equity securities pursuant to a domestic relations order, as defined in the Internal Revenue Code or Title I of the Employment Retirement Income Security Act of 1974, or the rules thereunder;

(8) Any sale or other disposition of equity securities compelled by the laws or other requirements of an applicable jurisdiction;

(9) Any acquisition or disposition of equity securities in connection with a merger, acquisition, divestiture or similar transaction occurring by operation of law;

(10) The increase or decrease in the number of equity securities held as a result of a stock split or stock dividend applying equally to all securities of that class, including a stock dividend in which equity securities of a different issuer are distributed; and the acquisition of rights, such as shareholder or pre-emptive rights, pursuant to a pro rata grant to all holders of the same class of equity securities; and

(11) Any acquisition or disposition of an asset-backed security, as defined in Item 1101 of Regulation AB.

Rule 102. Exceptions to definition of blackout period

The term "blackout period," as defined in Rule 100(b), does not include:

(a) A regularly scheduled period in which participants and beneficiaries may not purchase, sell or otherwise acquire or transfer an interest in any equity security of an issuer, if a description of such period, including its frequency and duration and the plan transactions to be suspended or otherwise affected, is:

(1) Incorporated into the individual account plan or included in the documents or instruments under which the plan operates; and

(2) Disclosed to an employee before he or she formally enrolls, or within 30 days following formal enrollment, as a participant under the individual account plan or within 30 days after the adoption of an amendment to the plan. For purposes of this paragraph (a)(2), the disclosure may be provided in any graphic form that is reasonably accessible to the employee; or

(b) Any trading suspension described in Rule 100(b) that is imposed in connection with a corporate merger, acquisition, divestiture or similar transaction involving the plan or plan sponsor, the principal purpose of which is to permit persons affiliated with the acquired or divested entity to become participants or beneficiaries, or to cease to be participants or beneficiaries, in an individual account plan; provided that the persons who become participants or beneficiaries in an individual account plan are not able to participate in the same class of equity securities after the merger, acquisition, divestiture or similar transaction as before the transaction.

Rule 103. Issuer right of recovery; right of action by equity security owner

(a) *Recovery of Profits.* Section 306(a)(2) of the Sarbanes–Oxley Act of 2002 (15 U.S.C. 7244(a)(2)) provides that any profit realized by a director or executive officer from any purchase, sale or other acquisition or transfer of any equity security of an issuer in violation of section 306(a)(1) of that Act (15 U.S.C. 7244(a)(1)) will inure to and be recoverable by the issuer, regardless of any intention on the part of the director or executive officer in entering into the transaction.

(b) *Actions to Recover Profit.* Section 306(a)(2) of the Sarbanes–Oxley Act of 2002 provides that an action to recover profit may be instituted at law or in equity in any court of competent jurisdiction by the issuer, or by the owner of any equity security of the issuer in the name and on behalf of the issuer if the issuer fails or refuses to bring such action within 60 days after the date of request, or fails diligently to prosecute the action thereafter, except that no such suit may be brought more than two years after the date on which such profit was realized.

(c) *Measurement of Profit.* (1) In determining the profit recoverable in an action undertaken pursuant to section 306(a)(2) of the Sarbanes–Oxley Act of 2002 from a transaction that involves a purchase, sale or other acquisition or transfer (other than a grant, exercise, conversion or termination of a derivative security) in violation of section 306(a)(1) of that Act of an equity security of an issuer that is registered pursuant to section 12(b) or 12(g) of the Exchange Act and listed on a national securities exchange or listed in an automated inter-dealer quotation system of a national securities association, profit (including any loss avoided) may be measured by comparing the difference between the amount paid or received for the equity security on the date of the transaction during the blackout period and the average market price of the equity security calculated over the first three trading days after the ending date of the blackout period.

(2) In determining the profit recoverable in an action undertaken pursuant to section 306(a)(2) of the Sarbanes–Oxley Act of 2002 from a transaction that is not described in paragraph (c)(1) of this rule, profit (including any loss avoided) may

be measured in a manner that is consistent with the objective of identifying the amount of any gain realized or loss avoided by a director or executive officer as a result of a transaction taking place in violation of section 306(a)(1) of that Act during the blackout period as opposed to taking place outside of such blackout period.

(3) The terms of this rule do not limit in any respect the authority of the Commission to seek or determine remedies as the result of a transaction taking place in violation of section 306(a)(1) of the Sarbanes–Oxley Act.

Rule 104. Notice

(a) In any case in which a director or executive officer is subject to section 306(a)(1) of the Sarbanes–Oxley Act of 2002 (15 U.S.C. 7244(a)(1)) in connection with a blackout period (as defined in Rule 100(b)) with respect to any equity security, the issuer of the equity security must timely notify each director or officer and the Commission of the blackout period.

(b) For purposes of this rule:

(1) The notice must include:

(i) The reason or reasons for the blackout period;

(ii) A description of the plan transactions to be suspended during, or otherwise affected by, the blackout period;

(iii) A description of the class of equity securities subject to the blackout period;

(iv) The length of the blackout period by reference to:

(A) The actual or expected beginning date and ending date of the blackout period; or

(B) The calendar week during which the blackout period is expected to begin and the calendar week during which the blackout period is expected to end, provided that the notice to directors and executive officers describes how, during such week or weeks, a director or executive officer may obtain, without charge, information as to whether the blackout period has begun or ended; and provided further that the notice to the Commission describes how, during the blackout period and for a period of two years after the ending date of the blackout period, a security holder or other interested person may obtain, without charge, the actual beginning and ending dates of the blackout period.

(C) For purposes of this paragraph (b)(1)(iv), a *calendar week* means a seven-day period beginning on Sunday and ending on Saturday; and

(v) The name, address and telephone number of the person designated by the issuer to respond to inquiries about the blackout period, or, in the absence of such a designation, the issuer's human resources director or person performing equivalent functions.

(2) (i) Notice to an affected director or executive officer will be considered timely if the notice described in paragraph (b)(1) of this rule is provided (in graphic form that is reasonably accessible to the recipient):

(A) No later than five business days after the issuer receives the notice required by section 101(i)(2)(E) of the Employment Retirement Income Security Act of 1974 (29 U.S.C. 1021(i)(2)(E)); or

(B) If no such notice is received by the issuer, a date that is at least 15 calendar days before the actual or expected beginning date of the blackout period.

(ii) Notwithstanding paragraph (b)(2)(i) of this rule, the requirement to give advance notice will not apply in any case in which the inability to provide advance notice of the blackout period is due to events that were unforeseeable to, or circumstances that were beyond the reasonable control of, the issuer, and the issuer reasonably so determines in writing. Determinations described in the preceding sentence must be dated and signed by an authorized representative of the issuer. In any case in which this exception to the advance notice requirement applies, the issuer must provide the notice described in paragraph (b)(1) of this rule, as well as a copy of the written determination, to all affected directors and executive officers as soon as reasonably practicable.

(iii) If there is a subsequent change in the beginning or ending dates of the blackout period as provided in the notice to directors and executive officers under paragraph (b)(2)(i) of this rule, an issuer must provide directors and executive officers with an updated notice explaining the reasons for the change in the date or dates and identifying all material changes in the information contained in the prior notice. The updated notice is required to be provided as soon as reasonably practicable, unless such notice in advance of the termination of a blackout period is impracticable.

(3) Notice to the Commission will be considered timely if:

(i) The issuer, except as provided in paragraph (b)(3)(ii) of this rule, files a current report on Form 8–K (17 CFR 249.308) within the time prescribed for filing the report under the instructions for the form; or

(ii) In the case of a foreign private issuer (as defined in Rule 3b–4(c)), the issuer includes the information set forth in paragraph (b)(1) of this section in the first annual report on Form 20–F (17 CFR 249.220f) or 40–F (17 CFR 249.240f) required to be filed after the receipt of the notice of a blackout period required by 29 CFR 2520.101–3(c) within the time prescribed for filing the report under the instructions for the form or in an earlier filed report on Form 6–K (17 CFR 249.306).

(iii) If there is a subsequent change in the beginning or ending dates of the blackout period as provided in the notice to the Commission under paragraph (b)(3)(i) of this rule, an issuer must file a current report on Form 8–K containing the updated beginning or ending dates of the blackout period, explaining the reasons for the change in the date or dates and identifying all material changes in the information contained in the prior report. The updated notice is required to be provided as soon as reasonably practicable.

FORMS UNDER THE SECURITIES EXCHANGE ACT OF 1934

UNITED STATES SECURITIES AND EXCHANGE COMMISSION

Washington, D.C. 20549

FORM 3

INITIAL STATEMENT OF BENEFICIAL OWNERSHIP OF SECURITIES

The Commission is authorized to solicit the information required by this form pursuant to sections 16(a) and 23(a) of the Securities Exchange Act of 1934; and sections 30(h) and 38 of the Investment Company Act of 1940, and the rules and regulations thereunder.

Disclosure of information specified on this form is mandatory. The information will be used for the primary purpose of disclosing the holdings of directors, officers, and beneficial owners of registered companies. Information disclosed will be a matter of public record and available for inspection by members of the public. The Commission can use it in investigations or litigation involving the federal securities laws or other civil, criminal, or regulatory statutes or provisions, as well as for referral to other governmental authorities and self–regulatory organizations. Failure to disclose required information may result in civil or criminal action against persons involved for violations of the federal securities laws and rules.

GENERAL INSTRUCTIONS

1. Who Must File

(a) This Form must be filed by the following persons ("reporting person"):

(i) any director or officer of an issuer with a class of equity securities registered pursuant to Section 12 of the Securities Exchange Act of 1934 ("Exchange Act"); (*Note:* Title is not determinative for purposes of determining "officer" status. *See* Rule 16a–1(f) for the definition of "officer");

(ii) any beneficial owner of greater than 10% of a class of equity securities registered under Section 12 of the Exchange Act, as determined by voting or investment control over the securities pursuant to Rule 16a–1(a)(1) ("ten percent holder");

(iii) [Reserved].

(iv) any officer, director, member of an advisory board, investment adviser, affiliated person of an investment adviser or beneficial owner of more than 10% of any class of outstanding securities (other than short-term paper) of a registered closed-end investment company, under Section 30(f) of the Investment Company Act of 1940; and

(v) any trust, trustee, beneficiary or settlor required to report pursuant to Rule 16a–8.

(b) If a reporting person is not an officer, director, or ten percent holder, the person should check "other" in Item 5 (Relationship of Reporting Person to Issuer) and describe the reason for reporting status in the space provided.

(c) If a person described above does not beneficially own any securities required to be reported (*See* Rule 16a–1 and Instruction 5), the person is required to file this Form and state that no securities are beneficially owned.

2. When Form Must Be Filed Form 3

(a) This Form must be filed within 10 days after the event by which the person becomes a reporting person (*i.e.*, officer, director, ten percent holder or other person). This Form and any amendment is deemed filed with the Commission or the Exchange on the date it is received by the Commission or the Exchange, respectively. *See*, however, Rule 16a–3(h) regarding delivery to a third party business that guarantees delivery of the filing no later than the specified due date.

(b) A reporting person of an issuer that is registering securities for the first time under Section 12 of the Exchange Act must file this Form no later than the effective date of the registration statement.

(c) A separate Form shall be filed to reflect beneficial ownership of securities of each issuer.

3. Where Form Must Be Filed

(a) A reporting person must file this Form in electronic format via the Commission's Electronic Data Gathering Analysis and Retrieval System (EDGAR) in accordance with EDGAR rules set forth in Regulation S–T, except that a filing person that has obtained a hardship exception under Regulation S–T Rule 202 may file the Form in paper. For assistance with technical questions about EDGAR or to request an access code, call the EDGAR Filer Support Office at (202) 942–2900. For assistance with questions about the EDGAR rules, call the Office of EDGAR and Information Analysis at (202) 942–2940.

(b) At the time this Form or any amendment is filed with the Commission, file one copy with each Exchange on which any class of securities of the issuer is registered. If the issuer has designated a single Exchange to receive Section 16 filings, the copy shall be filed with that Exchange only.

(c) Any person required to file this Form or amendment shall, not later than the time the Form or amendment is transmitted for filing with the Commission, send or deliver a copy to the person designated by the issuer to receive the copy or, if no person is so designated, the issuer's corporate secretary (or person performing similar functions) in accordance with Rule 16a–3(e).

NOTE: If filing pursuant to a hardship exception under Regulation S–T Rule 202, file three copies of this Form or any amendment, at least one of which is signed, with the Securities and Exchange Commission, 450 5th Street, NW, Washington, DC 20549. (Acknowledgement of receipt by the Commission may be obtained by enclosing a self-addressed stamped postcard identifying the Form or amendment filed.)

4. Class of Securities Reported

(a)(i) Persons reporting pursuant to Section 16(a) of the Exchange Act shall include information as to their beneficial ownership of any class of equity securities of the issuer, even though one or more of such classes may not be registered pursuant to Section 12 of the Act.

(ii) [Reserved].

(iii) Persons reporting pursuant to Section 30(f) of the Investment Company Act of 1940 shall include information as to their beneficial ownership of any class of securities (equity or debt) of the registered closed-end investment company (other than "short-term paper" as defined in Section 2(a)(38) of the Investment Company Act).

(b) The title of the security should clearly identify the class, even if the issuer has only one class of securities outstanding; for example, "Common Stock," "Class A Common Stock," "Class B Convertible Preferred Stock," etc.

(c) The amount of securities beneficially owned should state the face amount of debt securities (U.S. Dollars) or the number of equity securities, whichever is appropriate.

5. Holdings Required to Be Reported

(a) *General Requirements*. Report holdings of each class of securities of the issuer beneficially owned as of the date of the event requiring the filing of this Form. *See* Instruction 4 as to securities required to be reported.

(b) *Beneficial Ownership Reported (Pecuniary Interest)*. (i) Although for purposes of determining status as a ten percent holder, a person is deemed to beneficially own securities over which that person has voting or investment control (*see* Rule 16a–1(a)(1)), for reporting purposes, a person is deemed to be the beneficial owner of securities if that person has or shares the opportunity, directly or indirectly, to profit or share in any profit derived from a transaction in the securities ("pecuniary interest"). *See* Rule 16a–1(a)(2). *See also* Rule 16a–8 for the application of the beneficial ownership definition to trust holdings and transactions.

(ii) Both direct and indirect beneficial ownership of securities shall be reported. Securities beneficially owned directly are those held in the reporting person's name or in the name of a bank, broker or nominee for the account of the reporting person. In addition, securities held as joint tenants, tenants in common, tenants by the entirety, or as community property are to be reported as held directly. If a person has a pecuniary interest, by reason of any contract understanding or relationship (including a family relationship or arrangement) in securities held in the name of another person, that person is an indirect beneficial owner of those securities. *See* Rule 16a–1(a)(2)(ii) for certain indirect beneficial ownerships.

(iii) Report securities beneficially owned directly on a separate line from those beneficially owned indirectly. Report different forms of indirect ownership on separate lines. The nature of indirect ownership shall be stated as specifically as possible; for example, "By Self as Trustee for X," "By Spouse," "By X Trust," "By Y Corporation," etc.

(iv) In stating the amount of securities owned indirectly through a partnership, corporation, trust, or other entity, report the number of securities representing the reporting person's proportionate interest in securities beneficially owned by that entity. Alternatively, at the option of the reporting person, the entire amount of the entity's interest may be reported. *See* Rule 16a–1(a)(2)(ii)(B) and Rule 16a–1(a)(2)(iii).

(v) Where more than one person beneficially owns the same equity securities, such owners may file Form 3 individually or jointly. Joint and group filings may be made by any designated beneficial owner. Holdings of securities owned separately by any joint or group filer are permitted to be included in the joint filing. Indicate only the name and address of the designated filer in Item 1 of Form 3 and attach a list of the names and addresses of each other reporting person. Joint and group filings must include all required information for each beneficial owner, and such filings must be signed by each beneficial owner, or on behalf of such owner by an authorized person.

If this Form is being filed in paper pursuant to a hardship exemption and the space provided for signatures is insufficient, attach a signature page. If this Form is being filed in paper, submit any attached listing of names or signatures on another Form 3, copy of Form 3 or separate page of 8½ by 11 inch white paper, indicate the number of pages comprising the report (Form plus attachments) at the bottom of each report page (*e.g.*, 1 of 3, 2 of 3, 3 of 3), and include the name of the designated filer and information required by Items 2 and 3 of the Form on the attachment.

See Rule 16a–3(i) regarding signatures.

(c) *Non-Derivative and Derivative Securities.*

(i) Report non-derivative securities beneficially owned in Table I and derivative securities (*e.g.*, puts, calls, options, warrants, convertible securities, or other rights or obligations to buy or sell securities) beneficially owned in Table II. Derivative securities beneficially owned that are both equity securities and convertible or exchangeable for other equity securities (*e.g.*, convertible preferred securities) should be reported only on Table II.

(ii) The title of a derivative security and the title of the equity security underlying the derivative security should be shown separately in the appropriate columns in Table II. The "puts" and "calls" reported in Table II include, in addition to separate puts and calls, any combination of the two, such as spreads and straddles. In reporting an option in Table II, state whether it represents a right to buy, a right to sell, an obligation to buy, or an obligation to sell the equity securities subject to the options.

(iii) Describe in the appropriate columns in Table II characteristics of derivative securities, including title, exercise or conversion price, date exercisable, expiration date, and the title and amount of securities underlying the derivative security.

(iv) Securities constituting components of a unit shall be reported separately on the applicable table (*e.g.*, if a unit has a non-derivative security component and a derivative security component, the non-derivative security component shall be reported in Table I and the derivative security component shall be reported in Table II). The relationship between individual securities comprising the unit shall be indicated in the space provided for explanation of responses.

6. Additional Information

(a) If the space provided in the line items on the Electronic Form is insufficient, use the space provided for footnotes. If the space provided for footnotes is insufficient, create a footnote that refers to an exhibit to the form that contains the additional information.

(b) If the space provided in the line items of this Form or space provided for additional comments is insufficient, attach another Form 3, copy of Form 3 or a separate page of 8½ by 11 inch white paper to Form 3, completed as appropriate to include the additional comments. Each attached page must include information required in Items 1, 2 and 3 of the Form. The number of pages comprising the report (Form plus attachments) shall be indicated at the bottom of each report page (*e.g.*, 1 of 3, 2 of 3, 3 of 3).

(c) If one or more exhibits are included, whether due to a lack of space or because the exhibit is, by nature, a separate document (e.g., a power of attorney), provide a sequentially numbered list of the exhibits in the Form. Use the number "24" for any power of attorney and the number "99" for any other exhibit. If there is more than one of either such exhibit, then use numerical subparts. If the exhibit is being filed as a confirming electronic copy under Regulation S–T Rule 202(d), then place the designation "CE" (confirming exhibit) next to the name of the exhibit in the exhibit list. If the exhibit is being filed in paper pursuant to a hardship exception under Regulation S–T Rule 202, then place the designation "P" (paper) next to the name of the exhibit in the exhibit list.

(d) If additional information is not reported as provided in paragraph (a), (b) or (c) of this instruction, whichever apply, it will be assumed that no additional information was provided.

7. Signature

(a) If the Form is filed for an individual, it shall be signed by that person or specifically on behalf of the individual by a person authorized to sign for the individual. If signed on behalf of the individual by another person, the authority of such person to sign the Form shall be confirmed to the Commission in writing in an attachment to the Form or as soon as practicable in an amendment by the individual for whom the Form is filed, unless such a confirmation still in effect is on file with the Commission. The confirming statement need only indicate that the reporting person authorizes and designates the named person or persons to file the Form on the reporting person's behalf, and state the duration of the authorization.

(b) If the Form is filed for a corporation, partnership, trust, or other entity, the capacity in which the individual signed shall be set forth (*e.g.*, John Smith, Secretary, on behalf of X Corporation).

8. Amendments

(a) If this Form is filed as an amendment in order to add one or more lines of ownership information to Table I or Table II of the Form being amended, provide each line being added, together with one or more footnotes, as necessary, to explain the addition of the line or lines. Do not repeat lines of ownership information that were disclosed in the original Form and are not being amended.

(b) If this Form is filed as an amendment in order to amend one or more lines of ownership information that already were disclosed in Table I or Table II of the Form being amended, provide the complete line or lines being amended, as amended, together with one or more footnotes, as necessary, to explain the amendment of the line or lines. Do not repeat lines of ownership information that were disclosed in the original Form and are not being amended.

(c) If this Form is filed as an amendment for any purpose other than or in addition to the purposes described in paragraphs (a) and (b) of this General Instruction 8, provide one or more footnotes, as necessary, to explain the amendment.

FORM 3

UNITED STATES SECURITIES AND EXCHANGE COMMISSION
Washington, D.C. 20549
Form 3

INITIAL STATEMENT OF BENEFICIAL OWNERSHIP OF SECURITIES

OMB APPROVAL	
OMB Number:	3235-0104
Expires:	February 28, 2011
Estimated average burden hours per response.	0.5

Filed pursuant to Section 16(a) of the Securities Exchange Act of 1934, Section 17(a) of the Public Utility Holding Company Act of 1935 or Section 30(h) of the Investment Company Act of 1940

(Print or Type Responses)

1. Name and Address of Reporting Person*	2. Date of Event Requiring Statement (Month/Day/Year)	3. Issuer Name and Ticker or Trading Symbol	
(Last) (First) (Middle)		4. Relationship of Reporting Person(s) to Issuer (Check all applicable) ____ Director ____ 10% Owner ____ Officer (give title below) ____ Other (specify below)	5. If Amendment, Date Original Filed (Month/Day/Year)
(Street)			6. Individual or Joint/Group Filing (Check Applicable Line) __ Form filed by One Reporting Person __ Form filed by More than One Reporting Person
(City) (State) (Zip)			

Table I — Non-Derivative Securities Beneficially Owned

1. Title of Security (Instr. 4)	2. Amount of Securities Beneficially Owned (Instr. 4)	3. Ownership Form: Direct (D) or Indirect (I) (Instr. 5)	4. Nature of Indirect Beneficial Ownership (Instr. 5)

Reminder: Report on a separate line for each class of securities beneficially owned directly or indirectly.
* If the form is filed by more than one reporting person, *see* Instruction 5(b)(v).

Potential persons who are to respond to the collection of information contained in this form are not required to respond unless the form displays a currently valid OMB control number.

(Over)
SEC 1473 (1-05)

FORM 3 (continued) **Table II — Derivative Securities Beneficially Owned (*e.g.*, puts, calls, warrants, options, convertible securities)**

1. Title of Derivative Security (Instr. 4)	2. Date Exercisable and Expiration Date (Month/Day/Year)		3. Title and Amount of Securities Underlying Derivative Security (Instr. 4)		4. Conversion or Exercise Price of Derivative Security	5. Ownership Form of Derivative Security: Direct (D) or Indirect (I) (Instr. 5)	6. Nature of Indirect Beneficial Ownership (Instr. 5)
	Date Exercisable	Expiration Date	Title	Amount or Number of Shares			

Explanation of Responses:

****Signature of Reporting Person** **Date**

**** Intentional misstatements or omissions of facts constitute Federal Criminal Violations.** ***See* 18 U.S.C. 1001 and 15 U.S.C. 78ff(a).**

Note: File three copies of this Form, one of which must be manually signed. If space is insufficient, *See* Instruction 6 for procedure.

Potential persons who are to respond to the collection of information contained in this form are not required to respond unless the form displays a currently valid OMB Number.

Page 2

UNITED STATES
SECURITIES AND EXCHANGE COMMISSION
Washington, D.C. 20549

FORM 4

STATEMENT OF CHANGES IN BENEFICIAL OWNERSHIP OF SECURITIES

The Commission is authorized to solicit the information required by this Form pursuant to Sections 16(a) and 23(a) of the Securities Exchange Act of 1934, and sections 30(h) and 38 of the Investment Company Act of 1940, and the rules and regulations thereunder.

Disclosure of information specified on this form is mandatory. The information will be used for the primary purpose of disclosing the transactions and holdings of directors, officers, and beneficial owners of registered companies. Information disclosed will be a matter of public record and available for inspection by members of the public. The Commission can use it in investigations or litigation involving the federal securities laws or other civil, criminal, or regulatory statutes or provisions, as well as for referral to other governmental authorities and self-regulatory organizations. Failure to disclose required information may result in civil or criminal action against persons involved for violations of the federal securities laws and rules.

GENERAL INSTRUCTIONS

1. When Form Must Be Filed Form 4

(a) This Form must be filed before the end of the second business day following the day on which a transaction resulting in a change in beneficial ownership has been executed (see Rule 16a–1(a)(2) and Instruction 4 regarding the meaning of "beneficial owner," and Rule 16a–3(g) regarding determination of the date of execution for specified transactions). This Form and any amendment is deemed filed with the Commission or the Exchange on the date it is received by the Commission or Exchange, respectively. *See*, however, Rule 16a–3(h) regarding delivery to a third party business that guarantees delivery of the filing no later than the specified due date.

(b) A reporting person no longer subject to Section 16 of the Securities Exchange Act of 1934 ("Exchange Act") must check the exit box appearing on this Form. However, Form 4 and 5 obligations may continue to be applicable. *See* Rule 16a–3(f); *see also* Rule 16a–2(b) (transactions after termination of insider status). Form 5 transactions to date may be included on this Form and subsequent Form 5 transactions may be reported on a later Form 4 or Form 5, provided all transactions are reported by the required date.

(c) A separate Form shall be filed to reflect beneficial ownership of securities of each issuer.

(d) If a reporting person is not an officer, director, or ten percent holder, the person should check "other" in Item 6 (Relationship of Reporting Person to Issuer) and describe the reason for reporting status in the space provided.

2. Where Form Must be Filed

(a) A reporting person must file this Form in electronic format via the Commission's Electronic Data Gathering Analysis and Retrieval System (EDGAR) in accordance with EDGAR rules set forth in Regulation S–T, except that a filing person that has obtained a hardship exception under Regulation S–T Rule 202 may file the Form in paper. For assistance with technical questions about EDGAR or to request an access code, call the EDGAR Filer Support Office at (202) 942–8900. For assistance with questions about the EDGAR rules, call the Office of EDGAR and Information Analysis at (202) 942–2940.

(b) At the time this Form or any amendment is filed with the Commission, file one copy with each Exchange on which any class of securities of the issuer is registered. If the issuer has designated a single Exchange to receive Section 16 filings, the copy shall be filed with that Exchange only.

(c) Any person required to file this Form or amendment shall, not later than the time the Form or amendment is transmitted for filing with the Commission, send or deliver a copy to the person designated by the issuer to receive the copy or, if no person is so designated, the issuer's corporate secretary (or person performing similar functions) in accordance with Rule 16a–3(e).

NOTE: If filing pursuant to a hardship exception under Regulation S–T Rule 202, file three copies of this Form or any amendment, at least one of which is signed, with the Securities and Exchange Commission, 450 5th Street, NW, Washington, DC 20549. (Acknowledgement of receipt by the Commission may be obtained by enclosing a self-addressed stamped postcard identifying the Form or amendment filed.)

3. Class of Securities Reported

(a)(i) Persons reporting pursuant to Section 16(a) of the Exchange Act must report each transaction resulting in a change in beneficial ownership of any class of equity securities of the issuer and the beneficial ownership of that class of securities following the reported transaction(s) even though one or more of such classes may not be registered pursuant to Section 12 of the Exchange Act.

(ii) [Reserved].

(iii) Persons reporting pursuant to Section 30(f) of the Investment Company Act of 1940 shall report each transaction resulting in a change in beneficial ownership of any class of securities (equity or debt) of the registered closed-end investment company (other than "short-term paper" as defined in Section 2(a)(38) of the Investment Company Act) and the beneficial ownership of that class of securities following the reported transaction(s).

(b) The title of the security should clearly identify the class, even if the issuer has only one class of securities outstanding; for example, "Common Stock," "Class A Common Stock," "Class B Convertible Preferred Stock," etc.

(c) The amount of securities beneficially owned should state the face amount of debt securities (U.S. Dollars) or the number of equity securities, whichever is appropriate.

4. Transactions and Holdings Required to be Reported

(a) *General Requirements*

(i) Report, in accordance with Rule 16a–3(g):

(1) all transactions not exempt from section 16(b);

(2) all transactions exempt from Section 16(b) pursuant to Rules 16b–3, 16b–3(e), or 16b–3(f); and

(3) all exercises and conversions of derivative securities, regardless of whether exempt from Section 16(b) of the Act.

Every transaction must be reported even though acquisitions and dispositions are equal. Report total beneficial ownership following the reported transaction(s) for each class of securities in which a transaction was reported.

NOTE: The amount of securities beneficially owned following the reported transaction(s) specified in Column 5 of Table I and Column 9 of Table II should reflect those holdings reported or required to be reported by the date of the Form. Transactions and holdings eligible for deferred reporting on Form 5 need not be reflected in the month end total unless the transactions were reported earlier or are included on this Form.

(ii) Each transaction should be reported on a separate line. Transaction codes specified in Item 8 should be used to identify the nature of the transaction resulting in an acquisition or disposition of a security. A deemed execution date must be reported in Column 2A of Table I or Column 3A of Table II only if the execution date for the transaction is calculated pursuant to Rule 16a–3(g)(2) or 16a–3(g)(3).

NOTE: Transactions reportable on Form 5 may, at the option of the reporting person, be reported on a Form 4 filed before the due date of the Form 5. (*See* Instruction 8 for the code for voluntarily reported transactions.)

(b) *Beneficial Ownership Reported (Pecuniary Interest).*

(i) Although for purposes of determining status as a ten percent holder, a person is deemed to beneficially own securities over which that person exercises voting or investment control (*see* Rule 16a–1(a)(1)), for reporting transactions and holdings, a person is deemed to be the beneficial owner of securities if that person has the opportunity, directly or indirectly, to profit or share in any profit derived from a transaction in the securities ("pecuniary interest"). *See* Rule 16a–1(a)(2). *See also* Rule 16a–8 for the application of the beneficial ownership definition to trust holdings and transactions.

(ii) Both direct and indirect beneficial ownership of securities shall be reported. Securities beneficially owned directly are those held in the reporting person's name or in the name of a bank, broker or nominee for the account of the reporting person. In addition, securities held as joint tenants, tenants in common, tenants by the entirety, or as community property are to be reported as held directly. If a person has a pecuniary interest, by reason of any contract, understanding or relationship (including a family relationship or arrangement), in securities held in the name of another person, that person is an indirect beneficial owner of the securities. *See* Rule 16a–1(a)(2)(ii) for certain indirect beneficial ownerships.

(iii) Report transactions in securities beneficially owned directly on a separate line from those beneficially owned indirectly. Report different forms of indirect ownership on separate lines. The nature of indirect ownership shall be stated as specifically as possible; for example, "By Self as Trustee for X," "By Spouse," "By X Trust," "By Y Corporation," etc.

(iv) In stating the amount of securities acquired, disposed of, or beneficially owned indirectly through a partnership, corporation, trust, or other entity, report the number of securities representing the reporting person's proportionate interest in transactions conducted by that entity or holdings of that entity. Alternatively, at the option of the reporting person, the entire amount of the entity's interest may be reported. *See* Rule 16a–1(a)(2)(ii)(B) and Rule 16a–1(a)(2)(iii).

(v) Where more than one beneficial owner of the same equity securities must report the same transaction on Form 4, such owners may file Form 4 individually or jointly. Joint and group filings may be made by any designated beneficial owner. Transactions with respect to securities owned separately by any joint or group filer are permitted to be included in the joint filing. Indicate only the name and address of the designated filer in Item 1 of Form 4 and attach a list of the names and addresses of each other reporting person. Joint and group filings must include all required information for each beneficial owner, and such filings must be signed by each beneficial owner, or on behalf of such owner by an authorized person. If this Form is being filed in paper pursuant to a hardship exemption and the space provided for signatures is insufficient, attach a signature page. If this Form is being filed in paper, submit any attached listing of names or signatures on another Form 4, copy of Form 4 or separate page of 8½ by 11 inch white paper, indicate the number of pages comprising the report (Form plus attachments) at the bottom of each report page (*e.g.*, 1 of 3, 2 of 3, 3 of 3), and include the name of the designated filer and information required by Items 2 and 3 of the Form on the attachment.

See Rule 16a–3(i) regarding signatures.

(c) *Non-Derivative and Derivative Securities.*

(i) Report acquisitions or dispositions and holdings of non-derivative securities in Table I. Report acquisitions or dispositions and holdings of derivative securities (*e.g.*, puts, calls, options, warrants, convertible securities, or other rights or obligations to buy or sell securities) in Table II. Report the exercise or conversion of a derivative security in Table II (as a disposition of the derivative security) and report in Table I the holdings of the underlying security. Report acquisitions or dispositions and holdings of derivative securities that are both equity securities and convertible or exchangeable for other equity securities (*e.g.*, convertible preferred securities) only in Table II.

(ii) The title of a derivative security and the title of the equity security underlying the derivative security should be shown separately in the appropriate columns in Table II. The "puts" and "calls" reported in Table II include, in addition to separate puts and calls, any combination of the two, such as spreads and straddles. In reporting an option in Table II, state whether it represents a right to buy, a right to sell, an obligation to buy, or an obligation to sell the equity securities subject to the option.

(iii) Describe in the appropriate columns in Table II characteristics of derivative securities, including title, exercise or conversion price, date exercisable, expiration date, and the title and amount of securities underlying the derivative security. If the transaction reported is a purchase or a sale of a derivative security, the purchase or sale price of that derivative security shall be reported in column 8. If the transaction is the exercise or conversion of a derivative security, leave column 8 blank and report the exercise or conversion price of the derivative security in column 2.

(iv) Securities constituting components of a unit shall be reported separately on the applicable table (*e.g.*, if a unit has a non-derivative security component and a derivative security component, the non-derivative security component shall be reported in Table I and the derivative security component shall be reported in Table II). The relationship between individual securities comprising the unit shall be indicated in the space provided for explanation of responses. When securities are purchased or sold as a unit, state the purchase or sale price per unit and other required information regarding the unit securities.

5. Price of Securities

(a) Prices of securities shall be reported in U.S. dollars on a per share basis, not an aggregate basis, except that the aggregate price of debt shall be stated. Amounts reported shall exclude brokerage commissions and other costs of execution.

(b) If consideration other than cash was paid for the security, describe the consideration, including the value of the consideration, in the space provided for explanation of responses.

6. Additional Information

(a) If the space provided in the line items on the electronic Form is insufficient, use the space provided for footnotes. If the space provided for footnotes is insufficient, create a footnote that refers to an exhibit to the form that contains the additional information.

(b) If the space provided in the line items on the paper Form or space provided for additional comments is insufficient, attach another Form 4, copy of Form 4 or separate 8½ by 11 inch white paper to Form 4, completed as appropriate to include the additional comments. Each attached page must include information required in Items 1, 2 and 3 of the Form. The number of pages comprising the report (Form plus attachments) shall be indicated at the bottom of each report page (*e.g.*, 1 of 3, 2 of 3, 3 of 3).

(c) If one or more exhibits are included, whether due to a lack of space or because the exhibit is, by nature, a separate document (*e.g.*, a power of attorney), provide a sequentially numbered list of the exhibits in the Form. Use the number "24" for any power of attorney and the number "99" for any other exhibit. If there is more than one of either such exhibit, then use numerical subparts. If the exhibit is being filed as a confirming electronic copy under Regulation S–T Rule 202(d), then place the designation "CE" (confirming exhibit) next to the name of the exhibit in the exhibit list. If the exhibit is being filed in paper pursuant to a hardship exception under Regulation S-T Rule 202, then place the designation "P" (paper) next to the name of the exhibit in the exhibit list.

(d) If additional information is not reported as provided in paragraph (a), (b) or (c) of this instruction, whichever apply, it will be assumed that no additional information was provided.

7. Signature

(a) If the Form is filed for an individual, it shall be signed by that person or specifically on behalf of the individual by a person authorized to sign for the individual. If signed on behalf of the individual by another person, the authority of such person to sign the Form shall be confirmed to the Commission in writing in an attachment to the Form or as soon as practicable in an amendment by the individual for whom the Form is filed, unless such a confirmation still in effect is on file with the Commission. The confirming statement need only indicate that the reporting person authorizes and designates the named person or persons to file the Form on the reporting person's behalf, and state the duration of the authorization.

(b) If the Form is filed for a corporation, partnership, trust, or other entity, the capacity in which the individual signed shall be set forth (*e.g.*, John Smith, Secretary, on behalf of X Corporation).

8. Transaction Codes

Use the codes listed below to indicate in Table I, Column 3 and Table II, Column 4 the character of the transaction reported. Use the code that most appropriately describes the transaction. If the transaction is not specifically listed, use transaction code "J" and describe the nature of the transaction in the space for explanation of responses. If a transaction is voluntarily reported earlier than required, place "V" in the appropriate column to so indicate; otherwise, the column should be left blank. If a transaction involves an equity swap or instrument with similar characteristics, use transaction Code "K" in addition to the code(s) that most appropriately describes the transaction, *e.g.*, "S/K" or "P/K."

General Transaction Codes

P—Open market or private purchase of non-derivative or derivative security

S—Open market or private sale of non-derivative or derivative security

V—Transaction voluntarily reported earlier than required

Rule 16b–3 Transaction Codes

A—Grant, award or other acquisition pursuant to Rule 16b–3(d)

D—Disposition to the issuer of issuer equity securities pursuant to Rule 16b–3(e)

F—Payment of exercise price or tax liability by delivering or withholding securities incident to the receipt, exercise or vesting of a security issued in accordance with Rule 16b–3

I—Discretionary transaction in accordance with Rule 16b–3(f) resulting in acquisition or disposition of issuer securities

M—Exercise or conversion of derivative security exempted pursuant to Rule 16b–3

Derivative Securities Codes (Except for transactions exempted pursuant to Rule 16b–3)

C—Conversion of derivative security

E—Expiration of short derivative position

H—Expiration (or cancellation) of long derivative position with value received

O—Exercise of out-of-the-money derivative security

X—Exercise of in-the-money or at-the-money derivative security

Other Section 16(b) Exempt Transaction and Small Acquisition Codes (Except for Rule 16b–3 Codes Above)

G—Bona fide gift

L—Small acquisition under Rule 16a–6

W—Acquisition or disposition by will or the laws of descent and distribution

Z—Deposit into or withdrawal from voting trust

Other Transaction Codes

J—Other acquisition or disposition (describe transaction)

K—Transaction in equity swap or instrument with similar characteristics

U—Disposition pursuant to a tender of shares in a change of control transaction

9. Amendments

(a) If this Form is filed as an amendment in order to add one or more lines of transaction information to Table I or Table II of the Form being amended, provide each line being added, together with one or more footnotes, as necessary, to explain the addition of the line or lines. Do not repeat lines of transaction information that were disclosed in the original Form and are not being amended.

(b) If this Form is filed as an amendment in order to amend one or more lines of transaction information that already were disclosed in Table I or Table II of the Form being amended, provide the complete line or lines being amended, as amended, together with one or more footnotes, as necessary, to explain the amendment of the line or lines. Do not repeat lines of transaction information that were disclosed in the original Form and are not being amended.

(c) If this Form is filed as an amendment for any purpose other than or in addition to the purposes described in paragraphs (a) and (b) of this General Instruction 9, provide one or more footnotes, as necessary, to explain the amendment.

FORM 4

☐ **Check this box if no longer subject to Section 16. Form 4 or Form 5 obligations may continue. *See* Instruction 1(b).**

UNITED STATES SECURITIES AND EXCHANGE COMMISSION
Washington, D.C. 20549

STATEMENT OF CHANGES IN BENEFICIAL OWNERSHIP

Filed pursuant to Section 16(a) of the Securities Exchange Act of 1934, Section 17(a) of the Public Utility Holding Company Act of 1935 or Section 30(h) of the Investment Company Act of 1940

OMB APPROVAL	
OMB Number:	3235-0287
Expires:	February 28, 2011
Estimated average burden hours per response.	0.5

(Print or Type Responses)

1. Name and Address of Reporting Person*	2. Issuer Name and Ticker or Trading Symbol	5. Relationship of Reporting Person(s) to Issuer (Check all applicable) ____ Director ____ 10% Owner ____ Officer (give title below) ____ Other (specify below) ____
(Last) (First) (Middle)	3. Date of Earliest Transcaction Required to be Reported (Month/Day/Year) / 4. If Amendment, Date Original Filed(Month/Day/Year)	
(Street)		6. Individual or Joint/Group Filing (Check Applicable Line) ___Form filed by One Reporting Person ___Form filed by More than One Reporting Person
(City) (State) (Zip)	**Table I — Non-Derivative Securities Acquired, Disposed of, or Beneficially Owned**	

1. Title of Security (Instr. 3)	2. Transaction Date (Month/Day/Year)	2A. Deemed Execution Date, if any (Month/Day/Year)	3. Transaction Code (Instr. 8)		4. Securities Acquired (A) or Disposed of (D) (Instr. 3, 4 and 5)			5. Amount of Securities Beneficially Owned Following Reported Transaction (s) (Instr. 3 and 4)	6. Ownership Form: Direct (D) or Indirect (I) (Instr. 4)	7. Nature of Indirect Beneficial Ownership (Instr. 4)
			Code	V	Amount	(A) or (D)	Price			

Reminder: Report on a separate line for each class of securities beneficially owned directly or indirectly.
* If the form is filed by more than one reporting person, *see* Instruction 4(b)(v).

Potential persons who are to respond to the collection of information contained in this form are not required to respond unless the form displays a currently valid OMB control number.

(Over)
SEC 1474 (01-05)

FORM 4 (continued)

Table II — Derivative Securities Acquired, Disposed of, or Beneficially Owned
(*e.g.*, puts, calls, warrants, options, convertible securities)

1. Title of Derivative Security (Instr. 3)	2. Conversion or Exercise Price of Derivative Security	3. Transaction Date (Month/Day/Year)	3A. Deemed Execution Date, if any (Month/Day/Year)	4. Transaction Code (Instr. 8)		5. Number of Derivative Securities Acquired (A) or Disposed of (D) (Instr. 3, 4, and 5)		6. Date Exercisable and Expiration Date (Month/Day/Year)		7. Title and Amount of Underlying Securities (Instr. 3 and 4)		8. Price of Derivative Security (Instr. 5)	9. Number of derivative Securities Beneficially Owned following Reported Transaction(s) (Instr. 4)	10. Ownership Form of Derivative Security: Direct (D) or Indirect (I) (Instr. 4)	11. Nature of Indirect Beneficial Ownership (Instr. 4)
				Code	V	(A)	(D)	Date Exercisable	Expiration Date	Title	Amount or Number of Shares				

Explanation of Responses:

** Intentional misstatements or omissions of facts constitute Federal Criminal Violations.
See 18 U.S.C. 1001 and 15 U.S.C. 78ff(a).

______________________________ ______________
Signature of Reporting Person **Date

Note: File three copies of this Form, one of which must be manually signed. If space is insufficient, *see* Instruction 6 for procedure.

Potential persons who are to respond to the collection of information contained in this form are not required to respond unless the form displays a currently valid OMB Number.

Page 2

UNITED STATES
SECURITIES AND EXCHANGE COMMISSION
Washington, D.C. 20549

FORM 5

ANNUAL STATEMENT OF BENEFICIAL OWNERSHIP OF SECURITIES

The Commission is authorized to solicit the information required by this Form pursuant to Sections 16(a) and 23(a) of the Securities Exchange Act of 1934, and sections 30(h) and 38 of the Investment Company Act of 1940, and the rules and regulations thereunder.

Disclosure of information specified on this form is mandatory. The information will be used for the primary purpose of disclosing the transactions and holdings of directors, officers, and beneficial owners of registered companies. Information disclosed will be a matter of public record and available for inspection by members of the public. The Commission can use it in investigations or litigation involving the federal securities laws or other civil, criminal, or regulatory statutes or provisions, as well as for referral to other governmental authorities and self–regulatory organizations. Failure to disclose required information may result in civil or criminal action against persons involved for violations of the federal securities laws and rules.

GENERAL INSTRUCTIONS

1. When Form Must Be Filed Form 5

(a) This Form must be filed on or before the 45th day after the end of the issuer's fiscal year in accordance with Rule 16a–3(f). This Form and any amendment is deemed filed with the Commission or the Exchange on the date it is received by the Commission or the Exchange, respectively. *See,* however, Rule 16a–3(h) regarding delivery to a third party business that guarantees delivery of the filing no later than the specified due date.

(b) A reporting person no longer subject to Section 16 of the Securities Exchange Act of 1934 ("Exchange Act") must check the exit box appearing on this Form. Transactions and holdings previously reported are not required to be included on this Form. Form 4 or Form 5 obligations may continue to be applicable. *See* Rules 16a–3(f); *see also* Rule 16a–2(b) (transactions after termination of insider status).

(c) A separate Form shall be filed to reflect beneficial ownership of securities of each issuer.

(d) If a reporting person is not an officer, director, or ten percent holder, the person should check "other" in Item 6 (Relationship of Reporting Person to Issuer) and describe the reason for reporting status in the space provided.

2. Where Form Must Be Filed

(a) A reporting person must file this Form in electronic format via the Commission's Electronic Data Gathering Analysis and Retrieval System (EDGAR) in accordance with EDGAR rules set forth in Regulation S–T, except that a filing person that has obtained a hardship exception under Regulation S–T Rule 202 may file the Form in paper. For assistance with technical questions about EDGAR or to request an access code, call the EDGAR Filer Support Office at (202) 942–8900. For assistance with questions about the EDGAR rules, call the Office of EDGAR and Information Analysis at (202) 942–2940.

(b) At the time this Form or any amendment is filed with the Commission, file one copy with each Exchange on which any class of securities of the issuer is registered. If the issuer has designated a single Exchange to receive Section 16 filings, the copy shall be filed with that Exchange only.

(c) Any person required to file this Form or amendment shall, not later than the time the Form or amendment is transmitted for filing with the Commission, send or deliver a copy to the person designated by the issuer to receive the copy or, if no person is so designated, the issuer's corporate secretary (or person performing similar functions) in accordance with Rule 16a–3(e).

NOTE: If filing pursuant to a hardship exception under Regulation S–T Rule 202, file three copies of this Form or any amendment, at least one of which is signed, with the Securities and Exchange Commission, 450 5th Street, NW, Washington, DC

20549. (Acknowledgement of receipt by the Commission may be obtained by enclosing a self-addressed stamped postcard identifying the Form or amendment filed.)

3. Class of Securities Reported

(a)(i) Persons reporting pursuant to Section 16(a) of the Exchange Act shall include information as to transactions and holdings required to be reported in any class of equity securities of the issuer and the beneficial ownership at the end of the year of that class of equity securities, even though one or more of such classes may not be registered pursuant to Section 12 of the Exchange Act.

(ii) [Reserved].

(iii) Persons reporting pursuant to Section 30(h) of the Investment Company Act of 1940 shall include transactions and holdings required to be reported in any class of securities (equity or debt) of the registered closed-end investment company (other than "short-term paper" as defined in Section 2(a)(38) of the Investment Company Act) and the beneficial ownership at the end of the year of that class of securities.

(b) The title of the security should clearly identify the class, even if the issuer has only one class of securities outstanding; for example, "Common Stock," "Class A Common Stock," "Class B Convertible Preferred Stock," etc.

(c) The amount of securities beneficially owned should state the face amount of debt securities (U.S. Dollars) or the number of equity securities, whichever is appropriate.

4. Transactions and Holdings Required to be Reported

(a) *General Requirements*

(i) Pursuant to Rule 16a–3(f), if not previously reported, the following transactions, and total beneficial ownership as of the end of the issuer's fiscal year (or the earlier date applicable to a person ceasing to be an insider during the fiscal year) for any class of securities for which a transaction is reported, shall be reported:

(A) any transaction during the issuer's most recent fiscal year that was exempt from Section 16(b) of the Act, except: (1) any transaction exempt from Section 16(b) pursuant to Rules 16b–3, 16b–3(e), or 16b–3(f) (these are required to be reported in Form 4); (2) any exercise or conversion of derivative securities exempt under either Rule 16b–3 or 16b–6(b) (these are required to be reported on Form 4); (3) any transaction exempt from Section 16(b) of the Act pursuant to Rule 16b–3(c), which is exempt from Section 16(a) of the Act; and (4) any transaction exempt from Section 16 of the Act pursuant to another Section 16(a) rule;

(B) any small acquisition or series of acquisitions in a six month period during the issuer's fiscal year not exceeding $10,000 in market value (*see* Rule 16a–6);

(C) any transactions or holdings that should have been reported during the issuer's fiscal year on a Form 3 or Form 4, but were not reported. The first Form 5 filing obligation shall include all holdings and transactions that should have been reported in each of the issuer's last two fiscal years but were not. *See* Instruction 8 for the code to identify delinquent Form 3 holdings or Form 4 transactions reported on this Form 5.

NOTE: A required Form 3 or Form 4 must be filed within the time specified by the Form. Form 3 holdings or Form 4 transactions reported on Form 5 represent delinquent Form 3 and Form 4 filings.

(ii) Each transaction should be reported on a separate line. Transaction codes specified in Instruction 8 should be used to identify the nature of the transaction resulting in an acquisition or disposition of a security. A deemed execution date must be reported in Column 2A of Table I or Column 3A of Table II only if the execution date for the transaction is calculated pursuant to Rule 16a–3(g)(2) or 16a–3(g)(3).

(iii) Every transaction shall be reported even though acquisitions and dispositions with respect to a class of securities are equal. Report total beneficial ownership as of the end of the issuer's fiscal year for all classes of securities in which a transaction was reported.

(b) *Beneficial Ownership Reported (Pecuniary Interest)*

(i) Although, for purposes of determining status as a ten percent holder, a person is deemed to beneficially own securities over which that person has voting or investment control (*see* Rule 16a–1(a)(1)), for reporting transactions and holdings, a person is deemed to be the beneficial owner of securities if that person has or shares the opportunity, directly or indirectly, to profit or share in any profit derived from a transaction in the securities ("pecuniary interest"). *See* Rule 16a–1(a)(2). *See also* Rule 16a–8 for the application of the beneficial ownership definition to trust holdings and transactions.

(ii) Both direct and indirect beneficial ownership of securities shall be reported. Securities beneficially owned directly are those held in the reporting person's name or in the name of a bank, broker or nominee for the account of the reporting person. In addition, securities held as joint tenants, tenants in common, tenants by the entirety, or as community property are to be reported as held directly. If a person has a pecuniary interest, by reason of any contract, understanding, or relationship (including a family relationship or arrangement) in securities held in the name of another person, that person is an indirect beneficial owner of the securities. *See* Rule 16a–1(a)(2)(ii) for certain indirect beneficial ownerships.

(iii) Report transactions in securities beneficially owned directly on separate lines from those beneficially owned indirectly. Report different forms of indirect ownership on separate lines. The nature of indirect ownership shall be stated as specifically as possible; for example, "By Self as Trustee for X," "By Spouse," "By X Trust," "By Y Corporation," etc.

(iv) In stating the amount of securities acquired, disposed of, or beneficially owned indirectly through a partnership, corporation, trust, or other entity, report the number of securities representing the reporting person's proportionate interest in transactions conducted by that entity or holdings of that entity. Alternatively, at the option of the reporting person, the entire amount of the entity's interest may be reported. *See* Rule 16a–1(a)(2)(ii)(B) and Rule 16a–1(a)(2)(iii).

(v) Where more than one beneficial owner of the same equity securities must report on Form 5, such owners may file Form 5 individually or jointly. Joint and group filings may be made by any designated beneficial owner. Transactions and holdings with respect to securities owned separately by any joint or group filer are permitted to be included in the joint filing. Indicate only the name and address of the designated filer in Item 1 of Form 5 and attach a list of the names and addresses of each other reporting person. Joint and group filings must include all required information for each beneficial owner, and such filings must be signed by each beneficial owner, or on behalf of such owner by an authorized person.

If this Form is being filed in paper pursuant to a hardship exemption and the space provided for signatures is insufficient, attach a signature page. If this form is being filed on paper, submit any attached listing of names or signatures on another Form 5, copy of Form 5 or separate page of 8½ by 11 inch white paper, indicate the number of pages comprising the report (Form plus attachments) at the bottom of each report page (*e.g.,* 1 of 3, 2 of 3, 3 of 3), and include the name of the designated filer and information required by Items 2 and 3 of the Form on the attachment.

See Rule 16a–23(i) regarding signatures.

(c) *Non–Derivative and Derivative Securities*

(i) Report acquisitions or dispositions and holdings of non-derivative securities in Table I. Report acquisitions or dispositions and holdings of derivative securities (*e.g.,* puts, calls, options, warrants, convertible securities, or other rights or obligations to buy or sell securities) in Table II. Report the exercise or conversion of a derivative security in Table II (as a disposition of the derivative security) and report in Table I the holdings of the underlying security. Report acquisitions or dispositions and holdings of derivative securities that are both equity securities and convertible or exchangeable for other equity securities (*e.g.,* convertible preferred securities) only in Table II.

(ii) The title of a derivative security and the title of the equity security underlying the derivative security should be shown separately in the appropriate columns in Table II. The "puts" and "calls" reported in Table II include, in addition to separate puts and calls, any combination of the two, such as spreads and straddles. In reporting an option in Table II, state whether it represents a right to buy, a right to sell, an obligation to buy, or an obligation to sell the equity securities subject to the option.

(iii) Describe in the appropriate columns in Table II characteristics of derivative securities, including title, exercise or conversion price, date exercisable, expiration date, and the title and amount of securities underlying the derivative security. If the transaction reported is a purchase or sale of a derivative security, the purchase or sale price of that derivative security shall be reported in column 8. If the transaction is the exercise or conversion of a derivative security, leave column 8 blank and report the exercise or conversion price of the derivative security in column 2.

(iv) Securities constituting components of a unit shall be reported separately on the applicable table (*e.g.,* if a unit has a non-derivative security component and a derivative security component, the non-derivative security component shall be reported in Table I and the derivative security component shall be reported in Table II). The relationship between individual securities comprising the unit shall be indicated in the space provided for explanation of responses. When securities are purchased or sold as a unit, state the purchase or sale price per unit and other required information regarding the unit securities.

5. Price of Securities

(a) Prices of securities shall be reported in U.S. dollars and on a per share basis, not an aggregate basis, except that the aggregate price of debt shall be stated. Amounts reported shall exclude brokerage commissions and other costs of execution.

(b) If consideration other than cash was paid for the security, describe the consideration, including the value of the consideration, in the space provided for explanation of responses.

6. Additional Information

(a) If the space provided in the line items on the electronic Form is insufficient, use the space provided for footnotes. If the space provided for footnotes is insufficient, create a footnote that refers to an exhibit to the form that contains the additional information.

(b) If the space provided in the line items on the paper Form or space provided for additional comments is insufficient, attach another Form 5, copy of Form 5 or separate 8 1/2 by 11 inch white paper to Form 5, completed as appropriate to include the additional comments. Each attached page must include information required in Items 1, 2 and 3 of the Form. The number of pages comprising the report (Form plus attachments) shall be indicated at the bottom of each report page (*e.g.*, 1 of 3, 2 of 3, 3 of 3).

(c) If one or more exhibits are included, whether due to a lack of space or because the exhibit is, by nature, a separate document (*e.g.*, a power of attorney), provide a sequentially numbered list of the exhibits in the Form. Use the number "24" for any power of attorney and the number "99" for any other exhibit. If there is more than one of either such exhibit, then use numerical subparts. If the exhibit is being filed as a confirming electronic copy under Regulation S–T Rule 202(d), then place the designation "CE" (confirming exhibit) next to the name of the exhibit in the exhibit list. If the exhibit is being filed in paper pursuant to a hardship exception under Regulation S–T Rule 202, then place the designation "P" (paper) next to the name of the exhibit in the exhibit list.

(d) If additional information is not reported as provided in paragraph (a), (b) or (c) of this instruction, whichever apply, it will be assumed that no additional information was provided.

7. Signature

(a) If the Form is filed for an individual, it shall be signed by that person or specifically on behalf of the individual by a person authorized to sign for the individual. If signed on behalf of the individual by another person, the authority of such person to sign the Form shall be confirmed to the Commission in writing in an attachment to the Form or as soon as practicable in an amendment by the individual for whom the Form is filed, unless such a confirmation still in effect is on file with the Commission. The confirming statement need only indicate that the reporting person authorizes and designates the named person or persons to file the Form on the reporting person's behalf, and state the duration of the authorization.

(b) If the Form is filed for a corporation, partnership, trust, or other entity, the capacity in which the individual signed shall be set forth (*e.g.*, John Smith, Secretary, on behalf of X Corporation).

8. Transaction Codes

Use the codes listed below to indicate in Table I, Column 3 and Table II, Column 4 the character of the transaction reported. Use the code that most appropriately describes the transaction. If the transaction is not specifically listed, use transaction code "J" and describe the nature of the transaction in the space for explanation of responses. If a transaction involves an equity swap or instrument with similar characteristics, use transaction code "K" in addition to the code(s) that most appropriately describes the transaction, *e.g.*, "S/K" or "P/K."

General Transaction Codes

P—Open market or private purchase of non-derivative or derivative security

S—Open market or private sale of non-derivative or derivative security

Rule 16b–3 Transaction Codes

A—Grant, award or other acquisition pursuant to Rule 16b–3(d)

D—Disposition to the issuer of issuer equity securities pursuant to Rule 16b–3(e)

F—Payment of exercise price or tax liability by delivering or withholding securities incident to the receipt, exercise or vesting of a security issued in accordance with Rule 16b–3

I—Discretionary transaction in accordance with Rule 16b–3(f) resulting in acquisition or disposition of issuer securities

M—Exercise or conversion of derivative security exempted pursuant to Rule 16b–3

Derivative Securities Codes (Except for Transactions Exempted Pursuant to Rule 16b–3)

C—Conversion of derivative security

E—Expiration of short derivative position

H—Expiration (or cancellation) of long derivative position with value received

O—Exercise of out-of-the-money derivative security

X—Exercise of in-the-money or at-the-money derivative security

Other Section 16(b) Exempt Transaction and Small Acquisition Codes (Except for Rule 16b–3 Codes Above)

G—Bona fide gift

L—Small acquisition under Rule 16a–6

W—Acquisition or disposition by will or the laws of descent and distribution

Z—Deposit into or withdrawal from voting trust

Other Transaction Codes

J—Other acquisition or disposition (describe transaction)

K—Transaction in equity swap or instrument with similar characteristics

U—Disposition pursuant to a tender of shares in a change of control transaction

Form 3, 4 or 5 Holdings or Transactions Not Previously Reported

To indicate that a holding should have been reported previously on Form 3, place a "3" in Table I, column 3 or Table II, column 4, as appropriate. Indicate in the space provided for explanation of responses the event triggering the Form 3 filing obligation. To indicate that a transaction should have been reported previously on Form 4, place a "4" next to the transaction code reported in Table I, column 3 or Table II, column 4 (e.g., an open market purchase of a non-derivative security that should have been reported previously on Form 4 should be designated as "P4"). To indicate that a transaction should have been reported on previous Form 5, place a "5" in Table I, column 3 or Table II, column 4, as appropriate. In addition, the appropriate box on the front page of the Form should be checked.

9. Amendments

(a) If this Form is filed as an amendment in order to add one or more lines of transaction or ownership information to Table I or Table II of the Form being amended, provide each line being added, together with one or more footnotes, as necessary, to explain the addition of the line or lines. Do not repeat lines of transaction or ownership information that were disclosed in the original Form and are not being amended.

(b) If this Form is filed as an amendment in order to amend one or more lines of transaction or ownership information that already were disclosed in Table I or Table II of the Form being amended, provide the complete line or lines being amended, as amended, together with one or more footnotes, as necessary, to explain the amendment of the line or lines. Do not repeat lines of transaction or ownership information that were disclosed in the original Form and are not being amended.

(c) If this Form is filed as an amendment for any purpose other than or in addition to the purposes described in paragraphs (a) and (b) of this General Instruction 9, provide one or more footnotes, as necessary, to explain the amendment.

FORM 5

☐ Check box if no longer subject to Section 16. Form 4 or Form 5 obligations may continue. *See* Instruction 1(b).
☐ Form 3 Holdings Reported
☐ Form 4 Transactions Reported

UNITED STATES SECURITIES AND EXCHANGE COMMISSION
Washington, D.C. 20549

ANNUAL STATEMENT OF CHANGES IN BENEFICIAL OWNERSHIP OF SECURITIES

Filed pursuant to Section 16(a) of the Securities Exchange Act of 1934, Section 17(a) of the Public Utility Holding Company Act of 1935 or Section 30(h) of the Investment Company Act of 1940

OMB APPROVAL	
OMB Number:	3235-0362
Expires:	February 28, 2011
Estimated average burden hours per response.	1.0

1. Name and Address of Reporting Person*

(Last) (First) (Middle)

(Street)

(City) (State) (Zip)

2. Issuer Name and Ticker or Trading Symbol

3. Statement for Issuer's Fiscal Year Ended (Month//Day/Year)

4. If Amendment, Date Original Filed (Month/Day/Year)

5. Relationship of Reporting Person(s) to Issuer (Check all applicable)
_____ Director _____ 10% Owner
_____ Officer (give title below) _____ Other (specify below)
____

6. Individual or Joint/Group Reporting (check applicable line)
_____ Form Filed by One Reporting Person
_____ Form Filed by More than One Reporting Person

Table I — Non-Derivative Securities Acquired, Disposed of, or Beneficially Owned

1. Title of Security (Instr. 3)	2. Transaction Date (Month/ Day/ Year)	2A. Deemed Execution Date, if any (Month/ Day/ Year)	3. Transaction Code (Instr. 8)	4. Securities Acquired (A) or Disposed of (D) (Instr. 3, 4 and 5)			5. Amount of Securities Beneficially Owned at end of Issuer's Fiscal Year (Instr. 3 and 4)	6. Ownership Form: Direct (D) or Indirect (I) (Instr. 4)	7. Nature of Indirect Beneficial Ownership (Instr. 4)
				Amount	(A) or (D)	Price			

Reminder: Report on a separate line for each class of securities beneficially owned directly or indirectly.
* If the form is filed by more than one reporting person, see instruction 4(b)(v).

(Over)
SEC 2270 (1-05)

Potential persons who are to respond to the collection of information contained in this form are not required to respond unless the form displays a currently valid OMB control number.

FORM 5 (continued)

Table II — Derivative Securities Acquired, Disposed of, or Beneficially Owned
(*e.g.*, puts, calls, warrants, options, convertible securities)

1. Title of Derivative Security (Instr. 3)	2. Conversion or Exercise Price of Derivative Security	3. Transaction Date (Month/Day/Year)	3A Deemed Execution Date, if any (Month/Day/Year)	4. Transaction Code (Instr. 8)	5. Number of Derivative Securities Acquired (A) or Disposed of (D) (Instr. 3, 4, and 5)		6. Date Exercisable and Expiration Date (Month/Day/Year)		7. Title and Amount of Underlying Securities (Instr. 3 and 4)		8. Price of Derivative Security (Instr. 5)	9. Number of Derivative Securities Beneficially Owned at End of Issuer's Fiscal Year (Instr. 4)	10. Ownership Form of Derivative Securities: Direct (D) or Indirect (I) (Instr. 4)	11. Nature of Indirect Beneficial Ownership (Instr. 4)
					(A)	(D)	Date Exercisable	Expiration Date	Title	Amount or Number of Shares				

Explanation of Responses:

** Signature of Reporting Person — Date

**** Intentional misstatements or omissions of facts constitute Federal Criminal Violations.**
***See* 18 U.S.C. 1001 and 15 U.S.C. 78ff(a).**

Note: File three copies of this Form, one of which must be manually signed.
If space provided is insufficient, *see* Instruction 6 for procedure.

Potential persons who are to respond to the collection of information contained in this form are not required to respond unless the form displays a currently valid OMB number.

Page 2

UNITED STATES
SECURITIES AND EXCHANGE COMMISSION

Washington, D.C. 20549

FORM 10

GENERAL FORM FOR REGISTRATION OF SECURITIES PURSUANT TO SECTION 12(b) OR (g) OF THE SECURITIES EXCHANGE ACT OF 1934

GENERAL INSTRUCTIONS

A. Rule as to Use of Form 10 Form 10

Form 10 shall be used for registration pursuant to Section 12(b) or (g) of the Securities Exchange Act of 1934 of classes of securities of issuers for which no other form is prescribed.

B. Application of General Rules and Regulations

(a) The General Rules and Regulations under the Act contain certain general requirements which are applicable to registration on any form. These general requirements should be carefully read and observed in the preparation and filing of registration statements on this form.

(b) Particular attention is directed to Regulation 12B [17 CFR 240.12b–1—240.12b–36] which contains general requirements regarding matters such as the kind and size of paper to be used, the legibility of the registration statement, the information to be given whenever the title of securities is required to be stated, and the filing of the registration statement. The definitions contained in Rule 12b–2 [17 CFR 240.12b–2] should be especially noted.

C. Preparation of Registration Statement

(a) This form is not to be used as a blank form to be filled in, but only as a guide in the preparation of the registration statement on paper meeting the requirements of Rule 12b–12 [17 CFR 240.12b–12]. The registration statement shall contain the item numbers and captions, but the text of the items may be omitted. The answers to the items shall be prepared in the manner specified in Rule 12b–13 [17 CFR 240.12b–13].

(b) Unless otherwise stated, the information required shall be given as of a date reasonably close to the date of filing the registration statement.

(c) Attention is directed to Rule 12b–20 [17 CFR 240.12b–20] which states: "In addition to the information expressly required to be included in a statement or report, there shall be added such further material information, if any, as may be necessary to make the required statements, in light of the circumstances under which they are made, not misleading."

D. Signature and Filing of Registration Statement

Three complete copies of the registration statement, including financial statements, exhibits and all other papers and documents filed as a part thereof, and five additional copies which need not include exhibits, shall be filed with the Commission. At least one complete copy of the registration statement, including financial statements, exhibits and all other papers and documents filed as a part thereof, shall be filed with each exchange on which any class of securities is to be registered. At least one complete copy of the registration statement filed with the Commission and one such copy filed with each exchange shall be manually signed. Copies not manually signed shall bear typed or printed signatures.

E. Omission of Information Regarding Foreign Subsidiaries

Information required by any item or other requirement of this form with respect to any foreign subsidiary may be omitted to the extent that the required disclosure would be detrimental to the registrant. However, financial statements, otherwise required, shall not be omitted pursuant to this instruction. Where information is omitted pursuant to this instruction, a statement shall be made that such information has been omitted and the names of the subsidiaries involved shall be separately furnished to the Commission. The Commission may, in its discretion, call for justification that the required disclosure would be detrimental.

F. Incorporation by Reference

Attention is directed to Rule 12b–23 [17 CFR 240.12b–23] which provides for the incorporation by reference of information contained in certain documents in answer or partial answer to any item of a registration statement.

UNITED STATES
SECURITIES AND EXCHANGE COMMISSION
Washington, D.C. 20549

FORM 10

GENERAL FORM FOR REGISTRATION OF SECURITIES PURSUANT TO SECTION 12(b) OR (g) OF THE SECURITIES EXCHANGE ACT OF 1934

____
(Exact name of registrant as specified in its charter)

____
(State or other jurisdiction of incorporation or organization) (I.R.S. Employer Identification No.)

____
(Address of principal executive offices) (Zip Code)

Registrant's telephone number, including area code ______________

Securities to be registered pursuant to Section 12(b) of the Act:

Title of each class to be so registered	Name of each exchange on which each class is to be registered

Securities to be registered pursuant to Section 12(g) of the Act:

____
(Title of class)

____
(Title of class)

SEC1396 (11–06)

Indicate by check mark whether the registrant is a large accelerated filer, an accelerated filer, a non-accelerated filer, a smaller reporting company, or an emerging growth company. See the definitions of "large accelerated filer," "accelerated filer," "smaller reporting company," and "emerging growth company" in Rule 12b–2 of the Exchange Act.

Large accelerated filer ❑
Accelerated filer ❑
Non-accelerated filer ❑
Smaller reporting company ❑
Emerging growth company ❑

If an emerging growth company, indicate by check mark if the registrant has elected not to use the extended transition period for complying with any new or revised financial accounting standards provided pursuant to Section 13(a) of the Securities Act. ❑

INFORMATION REQUIRED IN REGISTRATION STATEMENT

Item 1. Business

Furnish the information required by Item 101 of Regulation S–K (17 CFR 229.101).

Item 1A. Risk Factors

Set forth, under the caption "Risk Factors," where appropriate, the risk factors described in Item 503(c) of Regulation S–K (17 CFR 229.503(c)) applicable to the registrant. Provide any discussion of risk factors in plain English in accordance with Rule 421(d) of the Securities Act of 1933 (17 CFR 230.421(d)). Smaller reporting companies are not required to provide the information required by this item.

Item 2. Financial Information

Furnish the information required by Items 301, 303, and 305 of Regulation S–K (17 CFR 229.301, 229.303, and 229.305).

Item 3. Properties

Furnish the information required by Item 102 of Regulation S–K (17 CFR 229.102).

Item 4. Security Ownership of Certain Beneficial Owners and Management

Furnish the information required by Item 403 of Regulation S–K (17 CFR 229.403).

Item 5. Directors and Executive Officers

Furnish the information required by Item 401 of Regulation S–K (17 CFR 229.401).

Item 6. Executive Compensation

Furnish the information required by Item 402 of Regulation S–K (17 CFR 229.402).

Item 7. Certain Relationships and Related Transactions, and Director Independence

Furnish the information required by Item 404 of Regulation S–K (17 CFR 229.404).

Item 8. Legal Proceedings

Furnish the information required by Item 103 of Regulation S–K (17 CFR 229.103).

Item 9. Market Price of and Dividends on the Registrant's Common Equity and Related Stockholder Matters

Furnish the information required by Item 201 of Regulation S–K (17 CFR 229.201).

Item 10. Recent Sales of Unregistered Securities

Furnish the information required by Item 701 of Regulation S–K (17 CFR 229.701).

Item 11. Description of Registrant's Securities to be Registered

Furnish the information required by Item 202 of Regulation S–K (17 CFR 229.202). If the class of securities to be registered will trade in the form of American Depositary Receipts, furnish Item 202(f) disclosure for such American Depositary Receipts as well.

Item 12. Indemnification of Directors and Officers

Furnish the information required by Item 702 of Regulation S–K (17 CFR 229.702).

Item 13. Financial Statements and Supplementary Data

Furnish all financial statements required by Regulation S–X and the supplementary financial information required by Item 302 of Regulation S–K (17 CFR 229.302). Smaller reporting companies may provide the financial information required by Article 8 of Regulation S–X in lieu of the information required in other parts of Regulation S–X.

Item 14. Changes in and Disagreements with Accountants on Accounting and Financial Disclosure

Furnish the information required by Item 304 of Regulation S–K (17 CFR 229.304).

Item 15. Financial Statements and Exhibits

(a) List separately all financial statements filed as part of the registration statement.

(b) Furnish the exhibits required by Item 601 of Regulation S–K (17 CFR 229.601).

SIGNATURES

Pursuant to the requirements of Section 12 of the Securities Exchange Act of 1934, the registrant has duly caused this registration statement to be signed on its behalf by the undersigned, thereunto duly authorized.

____
(Registrant)
Date ____________________
By ____________________
(Signature)*

* Print name and title of the signing officer under his signature.

UNITED STATES
SECURITIES AND EXCHANGE COMMISSION

Washington, D.C. 20549

FORM 10–Q

GENERAL INSTRUCTIONS

A. Rule as to Use of Form 10–Q

1. Form 10–Q shall be used for quarterly reports under Section 13 or 15(d) of the Securities Exchange Act of 1934, filed pursuant to Rule 13a–13 or Rule 15d–13. A quarterly report on this form pursuant to Rule 13a–13 or Rule 15d–13 shall be filed within the following period after the end of each of the first three fiscal quarters of each fiscal year, but no report need be filed for the fourth quarter of any fiscal year:

a. 40 days after the end of the fiscal quarter for large accelerated filers and accelerated filers (as defined in Rule 126–2); and

b. 45 days after the end of the fiscal quarter for all other registrants.

B. Application of General Rules and Regulations

1. The General Rules and Regulations under the Act contain certain general requirements which are applicable to reports on any form. These general requirements should be carefully read and observed in the preparation and filing of reports on this form.

2. Particular attention is directed to Regulation 12B which contains general requirements regarding matters such as the kind and size of paper to be used, the legibility of the report, the information to be given whenever the title of securities is required to be stated, and the filing of the report. The definitions contained in Rule 12b–2 should be especially noted. See also Regulations 13A and 15D.

C. Preparation of Report

1. This is not a blank form to be filled in. It is a guide copy to be used in preparing the report in accordance with Rules 12b–11 and 12b–12. The Commission does not furnish blank copies of this form to be filled in for filing.

2. These general instructions are not to be filed with the report. The instructions to the various captions on the form are also to be omitted from the report as filed.

D. Incorporation by Reference

1. If the registrant makes available to its stockholders or otherwise publishes, within the period prescribed for filing the report, a document or statement containing information meeting some or all of the requirements of Part I of this form, the information called for may be incorporated by reference from such published document or statement, in answer or partial answer to any item or items of Part I of this form, provided copies thereof are filed as an exhibit to Part I of the report on this form.

2. Other information may be incorporated by reference in answer or partial answer to any item or items of Part II of this form in accordance with the provisions of Rule 12b–23.

3. If any information required by Part I or Part II is incorporated by reference into an electronic format document from the quarterly report to security holders as provided in General Instruction D, any portion of the quarterly report to security holders incorporated by reference shall be filed as an exhibit in electronic format, as required by Item 601(b)(13) of Regulation S–K.

E. Integrated Reports to Security Holders

Quarterly reports to security holders may be combined with the required information of Form 10–Q and will be suitable for filing with the Commission if the following conditions are satisfied:

1. The combined report contains full and complete answers to all items required by Part I of this form. When responses to a certain item of required disclosure are separated within the combined report, an appropriate cross-reference should be made.

2. If not included in the combined report, the cover page, appropriate responses to Part II, and the required signatures shall be included in the Form 10–Q. Additionally, as appropriate, a cross-reference sheet should be filed indicating the location of information required by the items of the form.

3. If an electronic filer files any portion of a quarterly report to security holders in combination with the required information of Form 10–Q, as provided in this instruction, only such portions filed in satisfaction of the Form 10–Q requirements shall be filed in electronic format.

F. Filed Status of Information Presented

1. Pursuant to Rule 13a–13(d) and Rule 15d–13(d), the information presented in satisfaction of the requirements of Items 1, 2 and 3 of Part I of this form, whether included directly in a report on this form, incorporated therein by reference from a report, document or statement filed as an exhibit to Part I of this form pursuant to Instruction D(1) above, included in an integrated report pursuant to Instruction E above, or contained in a statement regarding computation of per share earnings or a letter regarding a change in accounting principles filed as an exhibit to Part I pursuant to Item 601 of Regulation S–K (§ 229.601 of this chapter), except as provided by Instruction F(2) below, shall not be deemed filed for the purpose of Section 18 of the Act or otherwise subject to the liabilities of that section of the Act but shall be subject to the other provisions of the Act.

2. Information presented in satisfaction of the requirements of this form other than those of items 1, 2 and 3 of Part I shall be deemed filed for the purpose of Section 18 of the Act; except that, where information presented in response to Item 1 or 2 of Part I (or as an exhibit thereto) is also used to satisfy Part II requirements through incorporation by reference, only that portion of Part I (or exhibit thereto) consisting of the information required by Part II shall be deemed so filed.

G. Signature and Filing of Report

If the report is filed in paper pursuant to a hardship exemption from electronic filing (see Item 201 et seq. of Regulation S–T, three complete copies of the report, including any financial statements, exhibits or other papers or documents filed as a part thereof, and five additional copies which need not include exhibits must be filed with the Commission. At least one complete copy of the report, including any financial statements, exhibits or other papers or documents filed as a part thereof, must be filed with each exchange on which any class of securities of the registrant is registered. At least one complete copy of the report filed with the Commission and one such copy filed with each exchange must be manually signed on the registrant's behalf by a duly authorized officer of the registrant and by the principal financial or chief accounting officer of the registrant. (*See* Rule 12b–11(d).)) Copies not manually signed must bear typed or printed signatures. In the case where the principal executive officer, principal financial officer or chief accounting officer is also duly authorized to sign on behalf of the registrant, one signature is acceptable provided that the registrant clearly indicates the dual responsibilities of the signatory.

H. Omission of Information by Certain Wholly-Owned Subsidiaries

If on the date of the filing of its report on Form 10–Q, the registrant meets the conditions specified in paragraph (1) below, then such registrant may omit the information called for in the items specified in paragraph (2) below.

1. Conditions for availability of the relief specified in paragraph (2) below:

a. All of the registrant's equity securities are owned, either directly or indirectly, by a single person which is a reporting company under the Act and which has filed all the material required to be filed pursuant to section 13, 14 or 15(d) thereof, as applicable;

b. During the preceding thirty-six calendar months and any subsequent period of days, there has not been any material default in the payment of principal, interest, a sinking or purchase fund installment, or any other material default not cured within thirty days, with respect to any indebtedness of the registrant or its subsidiaries, and there has not been any material default in the payment of rentals under material long-term leases; and

c. There is prominently set forth, on the cover page of the Form 10–Q, a statement that the registrant meets the conditions set forth in General Instruction H(1)(a) and (b) of Form 10–Q and is therefore filing this Form with the reduced disclosure format.

2. Registrants meeting the conditions specified in paragraph (1) above are entitled to the following relief:

a. Such registrants may omit the information called for by Item 2 of Part I, Management's Discussion and Analysis of Financial Condition and Results of Operations, provided that the registrant includes in the Form 10–Q a management's narrative analysis of the results of operations explaining the reasons for material changes in the amount of revenue and expense items between the most recent fiscal year-to-date period presented and the corresponding year-to-date period in the preceding fiscal year. Explanations of material changes should include, but not be limited to, changes in the various elements which determine revenue and expense levels such as unit sales volume, prices charged and paid, production levels, production cost variances, labor costs and discretionary spending programs. In addition, the analysis should include an explanation of the effect of any changes in accounting principles and practices or method of application that have a material effect on net income as reported.

b. Such registrants may omit the information called for in the following Part II Items: Item 2, Changes in Securities; Item 3, Defaults Upon Senior Securities.

c. Such registrants may omit the information called for by Item 3 of Part I, Quantitative and Qualitative Disclosures About Market Risk.

UNITED STATES
SECURITIES AND EXCHANGE COMMISSION

Washington, D.C. 20549

FORM 10–Q

(Mark One)

[ ] **QUARTERLY REPORT PURSUANT TO SECTION 13 OR 15(d) OF THE SECURITIES EXCHANGE ACT OF 1934**

For the quarterly period ended ______________________________

or

[ ] **TRANSITION REPORT PURSUANT TO SECTION 13 OR 15(d) OF THE SECURITIES EXCHANGE ACT OF 1934**

For the transition period from ______________ to ______________

Commission File Number ______________________________

____
(Exact name of registrant as specified in its charter)

______________________________ ______________________________
(State or other jurisdiction of incorporation or organization) (I.R.S. Employer Identification No.)

______________________________ ______________________________
(Address of principal executive offices) (Zip Code)

____
(Registrant's telephone number, including area code)

____
(Former name, former address and former fiscal year, if changed since last report.)

Indicate by check mark whether the registrant (1) has filed all reports required to be filed by Section 13 or 15(d) of the Securities Exchange Act of 1934 during the preceding 12 months (or for such shorter period that the registrant was required to file such reports), and (2) has been subject to such filing requirements for the past 90 days.

Yes ❑ No ❑

Indicate by check mark whether the registrant has submitted electronically every Interactive Data File required to be submitted pursuant to Rule 405 of Regulation S–T during the preceding 12 months (or for such shorter period that the registrant was required to submit such files).

Yes ❑ No ❑

Indicate by check mark whether the registrant is a large accelerated filer, an accelerated filer, a non-accelerated filer, a smaller reporting company, or an emerging growth company. See the definitions of "large accelerated filer," "accelerated filer," "smaller reporting company," and "emerging growth company" in Rule 12b–2 of the Exchange Act.

Large accelerated filer ❑
Accelerated filer ❑
Non-accelerated filer ❑
Smaller reporting company ❑
Emerging growth company ❑

If an emerging growth company, indicate by check mark if the registrant has elected not to use the extended transition period for complying with any new or revised financial accounting standards provided pursuant to Section 13(a) of the Securities Act. ❑

Indicate by check mark whether the registrant is a shell company (as defined in Rule 12b–2 of the Exchange Act) (Check One).

Yes ❑ No ❑

APPLICABLE ONLY TO ISSUERS INVOLVED IN BANKRUPTCY PROCEEDINGS DURING THE PRECEDING FIVE YEARS:

Indicate by check mark whether the registrant has filed all documents and reports required to be filed by Sections 12, 13 or 15(d) of the Securities Exchange Act of 1934 subsequent to the distribution of securities under a plan confirmed by a court.

Yes ❑ No ❑

APPLICABLE ONLY TO CORPORATE ISSUERS:

Indicate the number of shares outstanding of each of the issuer's classes of common stock, as of the latest practicable date.

PART I—FINANCIAL INFORMATION

Item 1. Financial Statements.

Provide the information required by Rule 10–01 of Regulation S–X (17 CFR 210). A smaller reporting company, defined in Rule 12b–2 may provide the information required by Article 8–03 of Regulation S–X (17 CFR 210.8–03).

Item 2. Management's Discussion and Analysis of Financial Condition and Results of Operations.

Furnish the information required by Item 303 of Regulation S–K.

Item 3. Quantitative and Qualitative Disclosures About Market Risk.

Furnish the information required by Item 305 of Regulation S–K.

Item 4. Controls and Procedures.

Furnish the information required by Item 307 of Regulation S–K and Item 308(c) of Regulation S–K.

PART II—OTHER INFORMATION

Instruction.

The report shall contain the item numbers and captions of all applicable items of Part II, but the text of such items may be omitted provided the responses clearly indicate the coverage of the item. Any item which is inapplicable or to which the answer is negative may be omitted and no reference thereto need be made in the report. If substantially the same information has been previously reported by the registrant, an additional report of the information on this form need not be made. The term "previously reported" is defined in Rule 12b–2. A separate response need not be presented in Part II where information called for is already disclosed in the financial information provided in Part I and is incorporated by reference into Part II of the report by means of a statement to that effect in Part II which specifically identifies the incorporated information.

Item 1. Legal Proceedings.

Furnish the information required by Item 103 of Regulation S–K. As to such proceedings which have been terminated during the period covered by the report, provide similar information, including the date of termination and a description of the disposition thereof with respect to the registrant and its subsidiaries.

Instruction.

A legal proceeding need only be reported in the 10–Q filed for the quarter in which it first became a reportable event and in subsequent quarters in which there have been material developments. Subsequent Form 10–Q filings in the same fiscal year in which a legal proceeding or a material development is reported should reference any previous reports in that year.

Item 1A. Risk Factors.

Set forth any material changes from risk factors as previously disclosed in the registrant's Form 10–K (17 CFR 249.310) in response to Item 1A. to Part 1 of Form 10–K. Smaller reporting companies are not required to provide the information required by this item.

Item 2. Unregistered Sales of Equity Securities and Use of Proceeds.

(a) Furnish the information required by Item 701 of Regulation S–K as to all equity securities of the registrant sold by the registrant during the period covered by the report that were not registered under the Securities Act. If the Item 701 information previously has been included in a Current Report on Form 8–K, however, it need not be furnished.

(b) If required pursuant to Rule 463 of the Securities Act of 1933, furnish the information required by Item 701(f) of Regulation S–K.

(c) Furnish the information required by Item 703 of Regulation S–K for any purchase made in the quarter covered by the report. Provide disclosures covering repurchases made on a monthly basis. For example, if the quarter began on January 16 and ended on April 15, the chart would show repurchases for the months from January 16 through February 15, February 16 through March 15, and March 16 through April 15.

Instruction: Working capital restrictions and other limitations upon the payment of dividends are to be reported hereunder.

Item 3. Defaults Upon Senior Securities.

(a) If there has been any material default in the payment of principal, interest, a sinking or purchase fund installment, or any other material default not cured within 30 days, with respect to any indebtedness of the registrant or any of its significant subsidiaries exceeding 5 percent of the total assets of the registrant and its consolidated subsidiaries, identify the indebtedness and state the nature of the default. In the case of such a default in the payment of principal, interest, or a sinking or purchase fund installment, state the amount of the default and the total arrearage on the date of filing this report.

Instruction: This paragraph refers only to events which have become defaults under the governing instruments, i.e., after the expiration of any period of grace and compliance with any notice requirements.

(b) If any material arrearage in the payment of dividends has occurred or if there has been any other material delinquency not cured within 30 days, with respect to any class of preferred stock of the registrant which is registered or which ranks prior to any class of registered securities, or with respect to any class of preferred stock of any significant subsidiary of the registrant, give the title of the class and state the nature of the arrearage or delinquency. In the case of an arrearage in the payment of dividends, state the amount and the total arrearage on the date of filing this report.

Instructions to Item 3:

1. Item 3 need not be answered as to any default or arrearage with respect to any class of securities all of which is held by, or for the account of, the registrant or its totally held subsidiaries.

2. The information required by Item 3 need not be made if previously disclosed on a report on Form 8–K (17 CFR 249.308).

Item 4. Mine Safety Disclosures.

If applicable, provide a statement that the information concerning mine safety violations or other regulatory matters required by Section 1503(a) of the Dodd–Frank Wall Street Reform and Consumer Protection Act and Item 104 of Regulations S–K is included in exhibit 95 to the quarterly report.

Item 5. Other Information.

(a) The registrant must disclose under this item any information required to be disclosed in a report on Form 8–K during the period covered by this Form 10–Q, but not reported, whether or not otherwise required by this Form 10–Q. If disclosure of such information is made under this term, it need not be repeated in a report on Form 8–K which would otherwise be required to be filed with respect to such information or in a subsequent report on Form 10–Q; and

(b) Furnish the information required by Item 407(c)(3) of Regulation S–K.

Item 6. Exhibits.

Furnish the exhibits required by Item 601 of Regulation S–K.

SIGNATURES*

Pursuant to the requirements of the Securities Exchange Act of 1934, the registrant has duly caused this report to be signed on its behalf by the undersigned thereunto duly authorized.

____
(Registrant)

Date ____________________
(Signature)**

Date ____________________
(Signature)**

* See General Instruction G.

** Print name and title of the signing officer under his signature.

UNITED STATES
SECURITIES AND EXCHANGE COMMISSION
Washington, D.C. 20549

FORM 10–K

ANNUAL REPORT PURSUANT TO SECTION 13 OR 15(d) OF THE SECURITIES EXCHANGE ACT OF 1934

GENERAL INSTRUCTIONS

A. Rule as to Use of Form 10–K.

(1) This Form shall be used for annual reports pursuant to Section 13 or 15(d) of the Securities Exchange Act of 1934 (the "Act") for which no other form is prescribed. This Form also shall be used for transition reports filed pursuant to Section 13 or 15(d) of the Act.

(2) Annual reports on this Form shall be filed within the following period:

(a) 60 days after the end of the fiscal year covered by the report (75 days for fiscal years ending before December 15, 2006) for large accelerated filers (as defined in Rule 12b–2):

(b) 75 days after the end of the fiscal year covered by the report for accelerated filers (as defined in Rule 12b–2); and

(c) 90 days after the end of the fiscal year covered by the report for all other registrants.

(3) Transition reports on this Form shall be filed in accordance with the requirements set forth in Rule 13a–10 or Rule 15d–10 applicable when the registrant changes its fiscal year end.

(4) Notwithstanding paragraphs (2) and (3) of this General Instruction A., all schedules required by Article 12 of Regulation S–X (17 CFR 210.12–01—210.12–29) may, at the option of the registrant, be filed as an amendment to the report not later than 30 days after the applicable due date of the report.

B. Application of General Rules and Regulations.

(1) The General Rules and Regulations under the Act contain certain general requirements which are applicable to reports on any form. These general requirements should be carefully read and observed in the preparation and filing of reports on this Form.

(2) Particular attention is directed to Regulation 12B which contains general requirements regarding matters such as the kind and size of paper to be used, the legibility of the report, the information to be given whenever the title of securities is required to be stated, and the filing of the report. The definitions contained in Rule 12b–2 should be especially noted. *See also* Regulations 13A and 15D.

C. Preparation of Report.

(1) This form is not to be used as a blank form to be filled in, but only as a guide in the preparation of the report on paper meeting the requirements of Rule 12b–12. Except as provided in General Instruction G, the answers to the items shall be prepared in the manner specified in Rule 12b–13.

(2) Except where information is required to be given for the fiscal year or as of a specified date, it shall be given as of the latest practicable date.

(3) Attention is directed to Rule 12b–20, which states: "In addition to the information expressly required to be included in a statement or report, there shall be added such further material information, if any, as may be necessary to make the required statements, in the light of the circumstances under which they are made, not misleading."

D. Signature and Filing of Report.

(1) Three complete copies of the report, including financial statements, financial statement schedules, exhibits, and all other papers and documents filed as a part thereof, and five additional copies which need not include exhibits, shall be filed with the Commission. At least one complete copy of the report, including financial statements, financial statement schedules, exhibits, and all other papers and documents filed as a part thereof, shall be filed with each exchange on which any class of securities of the registrant is registered. At least one complete copy of the report filed with the Commission and one such copy filed with each exchange shall be manually signed. Copies not manually signed shall bear typed or printed signatures.

(2)(a) The report must be signed by the registrant, and on behalf of the registrant by its principal executive officer or officers, its principal financial officer or officers, its controller or principal accounting officer, and by at least the majority of the board of directors or persons performing similar functions. Where the registrant is a limited partnership, the report must be signed by the majority of the board of directors of any corporate general partner who signs the report.

(b) The name of each person who signs the report shall be typed or printed beneath his signature. Any person who occupies more than one of the specified positions shall indicate each capacity in which he signs the report. Attention is directed to Rule 12b–11 concerning manual signatures and signatures pursuant to powers of attorney.

(3) Registrants are requested to indicate in a transmittal letter with the Form 10–K whether the financial statements in the report reflect a change from the preceding year in any accounting principles or practices, or in the method of applying any such principles or practices.

E. Disclosure with Respect to Foreign Subsidiaries.

Information required by any item or other requirement of this form with respect to any foreign subsidiary may be omitted to the extent that the required disclosure would be detrimental to the registrant. However, financial statements and financial statement schedules, otherwise required, shall not be omitted pursuant to this Instruction. Where information is omitted pursuant to this Instruction, a statement shall be made that such information has been omitted and the names of the subsidiaries involved shall be separately furnished to the Commission. The Commission may, in its discretion, call for justification that the required disclosure would be detrimental.

F. Information as to Employee Stock Purchase, Savings and Similar Plans.

Attention is directed to Rule 15d–21 which provides that separate annual and other reports need not be filed pursuant to Section 15(d) of the Act with respect to any employee stock purchase, savings or similar plan if the issuer of the stock or other securities offered to employees pursuant to the plan furnishes to the Commission the information and documents specified in the Rule.

G. Information to Be Incorporated by Reference.

(1) Attention is directed to Rule 12b–23 which provides for the incorporation by reference of information contained in certain documents in answer or partial answer to any item of a report.

(2) The information called for by Parts I and II of this form (Items 1 through 9A or any portion thereof) may, at the registrant's option, be incorporated by reference from the registrant's annual report to security holders furnished to the Commission pursuant to Rule 14a–3(b) or Rule 14c–3(a) or from the registrant's annual report to security holders, even if not furnished to the Commission pursuant to Rule 14a–3(b) or Rule 14c–3(a), provided such annual report contains the information required by Rule 14a–3.

NOTE 1: In order to fulfill the requirements of Part I of Form 10–K, the incorporated portion of the annual report to security holders must contain the information required by Items 1–3 of Form 10–K, to the extent applicable.

NOTE 2: If any information required by Part I or Part II is incorporated by reference into an electronic format document from the annual report to security holders as provided in General Instruction G, any portion of the annual report to security holders incorporated by reference shall be filed as an exhibit in electronic format, as required by Item 601(b)(13) of Regulation S–K.

(3) The information required by Part III (Items 10, 11, 12, 13 and 14) may be incorporated by reference from the registrant's definitive proxy statement (filed or required to be filed pursuant to Regulation 14A) or definitive information statement (filed or to be filed pursuant to Regulation 14C) which involves the election of directors, if such definitive proxy statement or information statement is filed with the Commission not later than 120 days after the end of the fiscal year covered by the Form 10–K. However, if such definitive proxy statement or information statement is not filed with the Commission in the 120–day period or is not required to be filed with the Commission by virtue of Rule 3a12–3(b) under the Exchange Act, the Items comprising the Part III information must be filed as part of the Form 10–K, or as an amendment to the Form 10–K, not later than the end of the 120–day period. It should be noted that the information regarding executive officers required by Item 401 of Regulation S–K may be included in Part I of Form 10–K under an appropriate caption. See Instruction 3 to Item 401(b) of Regulation S–K.

(4) No item numbers of captions of items need be contained in the material incorporated by reference into the report. However, the registrant's attention is directed to Rule 12b–23(e) regarding the specific disclosure required in the report concerning information incorporated by reference. When the registrant combines all of the information in Parts I and II of this Form (Items 1 through 9A) by incorpora-

tion by reference from the registrant's annual report to security holders and all of the information in Part III of this Form (Items 10 through 14) by incorporating by reference from a definitive proxy statement or information statement involving the election of directors, then, notwithstanding General Instruction C(1), this Form shall consist of the facing or cover page, those sections incorporated from the annual report to security holders, the proxy or information statement, and the information, if any, required by Part IV of this Form, signatures, and a cross-reference sheet setting forth the item numbers and captions in Parts I, II and III of this Form and the page and/or pages in the referenced materials where the corresponding information appears.

H. Integrated Reports to Security Holders.

Annual reports to security holders may be combined with the required information of Form 10–K and will be suitable for filing with the Commission if the following conditions are satisfied:

(1) The combined report contains full and complete answers to all items required by Form 10–K. When responses to a certain item of required disclosure are separated within the combined report, an appropriate cross-reference should be made. If the information required by Part III of Form 10–K is omitted by virtue of General Instruction G, a definitive proxy or information statement shall be filed.

(2) The cover page and the required signatures are included. As appropriate, a cross-reference sheet should be filed indicating the location of information required by the items of the Form.

(3) If an electronic filer files any portion of an annual report to security holders in combination with the required information of Form 10–K, as provided in this instruction, only such portions filed in satisfaction of the Form 10–K requirements shall be filed in electronic format.

I. Omission of Information by Certain Wholly-Owned Subsidiaries.

If, on the date of the filing of its report on Form 10–K, the registrant meets the conditions specified in paragraph (1) below, then such registrant may furnish the abbreviated narrative disclosure specified in paragraph (2) below.

(1) Conditions for availability of the relief specified in paragraph (2) below.

(a) All of the registrant's equity securities are owned, either directly or indirectly, by a single person which is a reporting company under the Act and which has filed all the material required to be filed pursuant to section 13, 14, or 15(d) thereof, as applicable, and which is named in conjunction with the registrant's description of its business;

(b) During the preceding thirty-six calendar months and any subsequent period of days, there has not been any material default in the payment of principal, interest, a sinking or purchase fund installment, or any other material default not cured within thirty days, with respect to any indebtedness of the registrant or its subsidiaries, and there has not been any material default in the payment of rentals under material long-term leases;

(c) There is prominently set forth, on the cover page of the Form 10–K, a statement that the registrant meets the conditions set forth in General Instruction (I)(1)(a) and (b) of Form 10–K and is therefore filing this Form with the reduced disclosure format; and

(d) The registrant is not an asset-backed issuer, as defined in Item 1101 of Regulation AB (17.

(2) Registrants meeting the conditions specified in paragraph (1) above are entitled to the following relief:

(a) Such registrants may omit the information called for by Item 6, Selected Financial Data, and Item 7, Management's Discussion and Analysis of Financial Condition and Results of Operations provided that the registrant includes in the Form 10–K a management's narrative analysis of the results of operations explaining the reasons for material changes in the amount of revenue and expense items between the most recent fiscal year presented and the fiscal year immediately preceding it. Explanations of material changes should include, but not be limited to, changes in the various elements which determine revenue and expense levels such as unit sales volume, prices charged and paid, production levels, production cost variances, labor costs and discretionary spending programs. In addition, the analysis should include an explanation of the effect of any changes in accounting principles and practices or method of application that have a material effect on net income as reported.

(b) Such registrants may omit the list of subsidiaries exhibit required by Item 601 of Regulation S–K.

(c) Such registrants may omit the information called for by the following otherwise required Items: Item 10, Directors and Executive Officers of the Registrant; Item 11, Executive Compensation; Item 12, Security Ownership of Certain Beneficial Owners and Management; and Item 13, Certain Relationships and Related Transactions.

(d) In response to Item 1, Business, such registrant only need furnish a brief description of the business done by the registrant and its subsidiaries during the most recent fiscal year which will, in the opinion of management, indicate the general nature and scope of the business of the registrant and its subsidiaries, and in response to Item 2, Properties, such registrant only need furnish a brief description of the material properties of the registrant and its subsidiaries to the extent, in the opinion of the management, necessary to an understanding of the business done by the registrant and its subsidiaries.

J. Use of This Form by Asset-Backed Issuers.

The following applies to registrants that are asset-backed issuers. Terms used in this General Instruction J. have the same meaning as in Item 1101 of Regulation AB.

(1) *Items That May Be Omitted*. Such registrants may omit the information called for by the following otherwise required Items:

(a) Item 1, Business;

(b) Item 1A. Risk Factors;

(c) Item 2, Properties;

(d) Item 3, Legal Proceedings;

(e) [Reserved];

(f) Item 5, Market for Registrant's Common Equity and Related Stockholder Matters;

(g) Item 6, Selected Financial Data;

(h) Item 7, Management's Discussion and Analysis of Financial Condition and Results of Operations;

(i) Item 7A, Quantitative and Qualitative Disclosures About Market Risk;

(j) Item 8, Financial Statements and Supplementary Data;

(k) Item 9, Changes in and Disagreements With Accountants on Accounting and Financial Disclosure;

(*l*) Item 9A, Controls and Procedures;

(m) If the issuing entity does not have any executive officers or directors, Item 10, Directors and Executive Officers of the Registrant, Item 11, Executive Compensation, Item 12, Security Ownership of Certain Beneficial Owners and Management, and Item 13, Certain Relationships and Related Transactions; and

(n) Item 14, Principal Accountant Fees and Services.

(2) *Substitute Information to Be Included*. In addition to the Items that are otherwise required by this Form, the registrant must furnish in the Form 10–K the following information:

(a) Immediately after the name of the issuing entity on the cover page of the Form 10–K, as separate line items, the exact name of the depositor as specified in its charter and the exact name of the sponsor as specified in its charter. Include a Central Index Key number for the depositor and the issuing entity, and if available, the sponsor.

(b) Item 1112(b) of Regulation AB;

(c) Items 1114(b)(2) and 1115(b) of Regulation AB;

(d) Item 1117 of Regulation AB;

(e) Item 1119 of Regulation AB;

(f) Item 1122 of Regulation AB; and

(g) Item 1123 of Regulation AB.

(3) *Signatures*. The Form 10–K must be signed either:

(a) On behalf of the depositor by the senior officer in charge of securitization of the depositor; or

(b) On behalf of the issuing entity by the senior officer in charge of the servicing function of the servicer. If multiple servicers are involved in servicing the pool assets, the senior officer in charge of the servicing function of the master servicer (or entity performing the equivalent function) must sign if a representative of the servicer is to sign the report on behalf of the issuing entity.

UNITED STATES
SECURITIES AND EXCHANGE COMMISSION

Washington, D.C. 20549

(Mark One)

FORM 10–K

[ ] ANNUAL REPORT PURSUANT TO SECTION 13 OR 15(d) OF THE SECURITIES EXCHANGE ACT OF 1934

For the fiscal year ended ______________________________

or

[ ] TRANSITION REPORT PURSUANT TO SECTION 13 OR 15(d) OF THE SECURITIES EXCHANGE ACT OF 1934

For the transition period from ______________ to ______________

Commission file number ______________________________

____
(Exact name of registrant as specified in its charter)

______________________________ ______________________________
(State or other jurisdiction of incorporation or organization) (I.R.S. Employer Identification No.)

______________________________ ______________________________
(Address of principal executive offices) (Zip Code)

____
(Registrant's telephone number, including area code)

____

Registrant's telephone number, including area code ______________________________

Securities registered pursuant to Section 12(b) of the Act:

Title of each class	Name of each exchange on which registered

Securities to be registered pursuant to Section 12(g) of the Act:

____
(Title of class)

____
(Title of class)

Indicate by check mark if the registrant is a well-known seasoned issuer, as defined in Rule 405 of the Securities Act.

Yes ❑ No ❑

Indicate by check mark if the registrant is not required to file reports pursuant to Section 13 or Section 15(d) of the Act.

Yes ❑ No ❑

Note—Checking the box above will not relieve any registrant required to file reports pursuant to Section 13 or 15(d) of the Exchange Act from their obligations under those Sections.

Indicate by check mark whether the registrant (1) has filed all reports required to be filed by Section 13 or 15(d) of the Securities Exchange Act of 1934 during the preceding 12 months (or for such shorter period that the registrant was required to file such reports), and (2) has been subject to such filing requirements for the past 90 days.

Yes ❑ No ❑

Indicate by check mark whether the registrant has submitted electronically every Interactive Data File required to be submitted pursuant to Rule 405 of Regulation S–T during the preceding 12 months (or for such shorter period that the registrant was required to submit such files).

Yes ❑ No ❑

Indicate by check mark if disclosure of delinquent filers pursuant to Item 405 of Regulation S–K (17 CFR 229.405) is not contained herein, and will not be contained, to the best of registrant's knowledge, in definitive proxy or information statements incorporated by reference in Part III of this Form 10–K or any amendment to this Form 10–K.

❑

Indicate by check mark whether the registrant is a large accelerated filer, an accelerated filer, a non-accelerated filer, a smaller reporting company, or an emerging growth company. See the definitions of "large accelerated filer," "accelerated filer," "smaller reporting company," and "emerging growth company" in Rule 12b–2 of the Exchange Act.

Large accelerated filer ❑
Accelerated filer ❑
Non-accelerated filer ❑
Smaller reporting company ❑
Emerging growth company ❑

If an emerging growth company, indicate by check mark if the registrant has elected not to use the extended transition period for complying with any new or revised financial accounting standards provided pursuant to Section 13(a) of the Securities Act. ❑

Indicate by check mark whether the registrant is a shell company (as defined in Rule 12b–2 of the Act).

Yes ❑ No ❑

State the aggregate market value of the voting and non-voting common equity held by non-affiliates computed by reference to the price at which the common equity was last sold, or the average bid and asked price of such common equity, as of the last business day of the registrant's most recently completed second fiscal quarter.

Note. If a determination as to whether a particular person or entity is an affiliate cannot be made without involving unreasonable effort and expense, the aggregate market value of the common stock held by non-affiliates may be calculated on the basis of assumptions reasonable under the circumstances, provided that the assumptions are set forth in this Form.

APPLICABLE ONLY TO REGISTRANTS INVOLVED IN BANKRUPTCY PROCEEDINGS DURING THE PRECEDING FIVE YEARS:

Indicate by check mark whether the registrant has filed all documents and reports required to be filed by Section 12, 13 or 15(d) of the Securities Exchange Act of 1934 subsequent to the distribution of securities under a plan confirmed by a court.

Yes ❑ No ❑

(APPLICABLE ONLY TO CORPORATE REGISTRANTS)

Indicate the number of shares outstanding of each of the registrant's classes of common stock, as of the latest practicable date.

DOCUMENTS INCORPORATED BY REFERENCE

List hereunder the following documents if incorporated by reference and the Part of the Form 10–K (e.g., Part I, Part II, etc.) into which the document is incorporated: (1) Any annual report to security holders; (2) Any proxy or information statement; and (3) Any prospectus filed pursuant to Rule 424(b) or (c) under the Securities Act of 1933. The listed documents should be clearly described for identification purposes (e.g., annual report to security holders for fiscal year ended December 24, 1980).

PART I

[See General Instruction G(2)]

Item 1. Business.

Furnish the information required by Item 101 of Regulation S–K (17 CFR 229.101) except that the discussion of the development of the registrant's business need only include developments since the beginning of the fiscal year for which this report is filed.

Item 1A. Risk Factors.

Set forth, under the caption "Risk Factors," where appropriate, the risk factors described in Item 503(c) of Regulation S–K (17 CFR 229.503(c)) applicable to the registrant. Provide any discussion of risk factors in plain English in accordance with Rule 421(d) of the Securities Act of 1933. Smaller reporting companies are not required to provide the information required by this item.

Item 1B. Unresolved Staff Comments.

If the registrant is an accelerated filer or a large accelerated filer, as defined in Rule 12b–2 under the Securities Exchange Act of 1934 (17 CFR 240.12b–2), or is a well-known seasoned issuer as defined in Rule 405 under the Securities Act of 1933 (17 CFR 230.405) and has received written comments from the Commission staff regarding its periodic or current reports under the Act not less than 180 days before the end of its fiscal year to which the annual report relates, and such comments remain unresolved, disclose the substance of any such unresolved comments that the registrant believes are material. Such disclosure may provide other information including the position of the registrant with respect to any such comment.

Item 2. Properties.

Furnish the information required by Item 102 of Regulation S–K (17 CFR 229.102).

Item 3. Legal Proceedings.

(a) Furnish the information required by Item 103 of Regulation S–K (17 CFR 229.103).

(b) As to any proceeding that was terminated during the fourth quarter of the fiscal year covered by this report, furnish information similar to that required by Item 103 of Regulation S–K (17 CFR 229.103), including the date of termination and a description of the disposition thereof with respect to the registrant and its subsidiaries.

Item 4. Mine Safety Disclosures.

If applicable, provide a statement that the information concerning mine safety violations or other regulatory matters required by Section 1503(a) of the Dodd–Frank Wall Street Reform and Consumer Protection Act and Item 104 of Regulation S–K (17 CFR 229.104) is included in exhibit 95 to the annual report.

PART II

[See General Instruction G(2)]

Item 5. Market for Registrant's Common Equity, Related Stockholder Matters and Issuer Purchases of Equity Securities.

(a) Furnish the information required by Item 201 of Regulation S–K (17 CFR 229.201) and Item 701 of Regulation S–K (17 CFR 229.701) as to all equity securities of the registrant sold by the registrant during the period covered by the report that were not registered under the Securities Act. If the Item 701 information previously has been included in a Quarterly Report on Form 10–Q, or in a Current Report on Form 8–K (17 CFR 249.308), it need not be furnished.

(b) If required pursuant to Rule 463 (17 CFR 230.463) of the Securities Act of 1933, furnish the information required by Item 701(f) of Regulation S–K (17 CFR 229.701(f)).

(c) Furnish the information required by Item 703 of Regulation S–K (17 CFR 229.703) for any repurchase made in a month within the fourth quarter of the fiscal year covered by the report. Provide disclosures covering repurchases made on a monthly basis. For example, if the fourth quarter began on January 16 and ended on April 15, the chart would show repurchases for the months from January 16 through February 15, February 16 through March 15, and March 16 through April 15.

Item 6. Selected Financial Data.

Furnish the information required by Item 301 of Regulation S–K (17 CFR 229.301).

Item 7. Management's Discussion and Analysis of Financial Condition and Results of Operation.

Furnish the information required by Item 303 of Regulation S–K (17 CFR 229.303).

Item 7A. Quantitative and Qualitative Disclosures About Market Risk.

Furnish the information required by Item 305 of Regulation S–K (17 CFR 229.305).

Item 8. Financial Statements and Supplementary Data.

(a) Furnish financial statements meeting the requirements of Regulation S–X (17 CFR Part 210), except Rule 3–05 of Regulation S–X and Article 11 thereof, and the supplementary financial information required by Item 302 of Regulation S–K (17 CFR 229.302). Financial statements of the registrant and its subsidiaries consolidated (as required by Rule 14a–3(b)) shall be filed under this item. Other financial statements and schedules required under Regulation S–X may be filed as "Financial Statement Schedules" pursuant to Item 15, Exhibits, Financial Statement Schedules, and Reports on Form 8–K, of this form.

(b) A smaller reporting company may provide the information required by Article 8 of Regulation S–X in lieu of any financial statements required by Item 8 of this Form.

Item 9. Changes in and Disagreements with Accountants on Accounting and Financial Disclosure.

Furnish the information required by Item 304(b) of Regulation S–K (17 CFR 229.304(b)).

Item 9A. Controls and Procedures.

Furnish the information required by Item 307 and 308 of Regulation S–K (17 CFR 229.307 and 229.308).

Item 9B. Other Information.

The registrant must disclose under this item any information required to be disclosed in a report on Form 8–K during the fourth quarter of the year covered by this Form 10–K, but not reported, whether or not otherwise required by this Form 10–K. If disclosure of such information is made under this item, it need not be repeated in a report on Form 8–K which would otherwise be required to be filed with respect to such information or in a subsequent report on Form 10–K.

PART III

[See General Instruction G(3)]

Item 10. Directors, Executive Officers and Corporate Governance.

Furnish the information required by Items 401, 405, 406, and 407(c)(3), (d)(4) and (d)(5) of Regulation S–K (17 CFR 229.401, 229.405, 229.406 and 229.407(c)(3), (d)(4) and (d)(5)).

Instruction:

Checking the box provided on the cover page of this Form to indicate that Item 405 disclosure of delinquent Form 3, 4, or 5 filers is not contained herein is intended to facilitate Form processing and review. Failure to provide such indication will not create liability for violation of the federal securities laws. The space should be checked only if there is no disclosure in this Form of reporting person delinquencies in response to Item 405 and the registrant, at the time of filing the Form 10–K, has reviewed the information necessary to ascertain, and has determined that, Item 405 disclosure is not expected to be contained in Part III of the Form 10–K or incorporated by reference.

Item 11. Executive Compensation.

Furnish the information required by Item 402 of Regulation S–K (17 CFR 229.402) and paragraphs (e)(4) and (e)(5) of Item 407 of Regulation S–K (17 CFR 229.407(e)(4)).

Item 12. Security Ownership of Certain Beneficial Owners and Management and Related Stockholder Matters.

Furnish the information required by Item 201(d) of Regulation S–K (17 CFR 229.201(d) of this chapter) and by Item 403 of Regulation S–K (17 CFR 229.403 of this chapter).

Item 13. Certain Relationships and Related Transactions, and Director Independence.

Furnish the information required by Item 404 of Regulation S–K (17 CFR 229.404) and Item 407(a) of Regulation S–K (17 CFR 229.407(a)).

Item 14. Principal Accountant Fees and Services.

Furnish the information required by Item 9(e) of Schedule 14A (17 CFR 240.14a–101).

(1) Disclose, under the caption *Audit Fees,* the aggregate fees billed for each of the last two fiscal years for professional services rendered by the principal accountant or the audit of the registrant's annual financial statements and review of financial statements included in the registrant's Form 10–Q (17 CFR 249.308a) or services that are normally provided by the accountant in connection with statutory and regulatory filings or engagements for those fiscal years.

(2) Disclose, under the caption *Audit–Related Fees,* the aggregate fees billed in each of the last two fiscal years for assurance and related services by the principal accountant that are reasonably related to the performance of the audit or review of the registrant's financial statements and are not reported under Item 9(e)(1) of Schedule 14A. Registrants shall describe the nature of the services comprising the fees disclosed under this category.

(3) Disclose, under the caption *Tax Fees,* the aggregate fees billed in each of the last two fiscal years for professional services rendered by the principal accountant for tax compliance, tax advice, and tax planning. Registrants shall describe the nature of the services comprising the fees disclosed under this category.

(4) Disclose, under the caption *All Other Fees,* the aggregate fees billed in each of the last two fiscal years for products and services provided by the principal accountant, other than the services reported in Items 9(e)(1) through 9(e)(3) of Schedule 14A. Registrants shall describe the nature of the services comprising the fees disclosed under this category.

(5)(i) Disclose the audit committee's pre-approval policies and procedures described in paragraph (c)(7)(i) of Rule 2–01 of Regulation S–X.

(ii) Disclose the percentage of services described in each of Items 9(e)(2) through 9(e)(4) of Schedule 14A that were approved by the audit committee pursuant to paragraph (c)(7)(i)(C) of Rule 2–01 of Regulation S–X.

(6) If greater than 50 percent, disclose the percentage of hours expended on the principal accountant's engagement to audit the registrant's financial statements for the most recent fiscal year that were attributed to work performed by persons other than the principal accountant's full-time, permanent employees.

PART IV

Item 15. Exhibits and Financial Statement Schedules.

(a) List the following documents filed as a part of the report:

1. All financial statements;

2. Those financial statement schedules required to be filed by Item 8 of this Form, and by paragraph (d) below.

3. Those exhibits required by Item 601 of Regulation S–K (17 CFR 229.601) and by paragraph (b) below. Identify in the list each management contract or compensatory plan or arrangement required to be filed as an exhibit to this form pursuant to Item 15(b) of this report.

(b) Registrants shall file, as exhibits to this form, the exhibits required by Item 601 of Regulation S–K (17 CFR 229.601).

(c) Registrants shall file, as financial statement schedules to this form, the financial statements required by Regulation S–X (17 CFR 210) which are excluded from the annual report to shareholders by Rule 14a–3(b), including (1) separate financial statements of subsidiaries not consolidated and fifty percent or less owned persons; (2) separate financial statements of affiliates whose securities are pledged as collateral; and (3) schedules.

SIGNATURES

[See General Instruction D]

Pursuant to the requirements of Section 13 or 15(d) of the Securities Exchange Act of 1934, the registrant has duly caused this report to be signed on its behalf by the undersigned, thereunto duly authorized.

(Registrant) ______________________________

By (Signature and Title)* ______________________________

Date ______________________________

Pursuant to the requirements of the Securities Exchange Act of 1934, this report has been signed below by the following persons on behalf of the registrant and in the capacities and on the dates indicated.

By (Signature and Title)* ______________________________

Date ______________________________

By (Signature and Title)* ______________________________

Date ______________________________

Supplemental Information to be Furnished with Reports Filed Pursuant to Section 15(d) of the Act by Registrants Which Have Not Registered Securities Pursuant to Section 12 of the Act.

(a) Except to the extent that the materials enumerated in (1) and/or (2) below are specifically incorporated into this Form by reference (in which case *see* Rule 12b–23(b)), every registrant which files an annual report on this Form pursuant to Section 15(d) of the Act shall furnish to the Commission for its information, at the time of filing its report on this Form, four copies of the following:

(1) Any annual report to security holders covering the registrant's last fiscal year; and

(2) Every proxy statement, form of proxy or other proxy soliciting material sent to more than ten of the registrant's security holders with respect to any annual or other meeting of security holders.

(b) The foregoing material shall not be deemed to be "filed" with the Commission or otherwise subject to the liabilities of Section 18 of the Act, except to the extent that the registrant specifically incorporates it in its annual report on this Form by reference.

(c) If no such annual report or proxy material has been sent to security holders, a statement to that effect shall be included under this caption. If such report or proxy material is to be furnished to security holders subsequent to the filing of the annual report of this Form, the registrant shall so state under this caption and shall furnish copies of such material to the Commission when it is sent to security holders.

UNITED STATES SECURITIES AND EXCHANGE COMMISSION

Washington, D.C. 20549

FORM 8–K

CURRENT REPORT

PURSUANT TO SECTION 13 OR 15(d) OF THE SECURITIES EXCHANGE ACT OF 1934

Date of Report (Date of earliest event reported) ____________

____
(Exact name of registrant as specified in its charter)

____________ ____________ ____________
(State or other jurisdiction of incorporation) (Commission File Number) (IRS Employer Identification No.)

____________ ____________
(Address of principal executive offices) (Zip Code)

Registrant's telephone number, including area code ____________

____
(Former name or former address, if changed since last report.)

Check the appropriate box below if the Form 8–K filing is intended to simultaneously satisfy the filing obligation of the registrant under any of the following provisions (see General Instruction A.2. below):

[ ] Written communications pursuant to Rule 425 under the Securities Act (17 CFR 230.425)

[ ] Soliciting material pursuant to Rule 14a–12 under the Exchange Act (17 CFR 240.14a–12)

[ ] Pre-commencement communications pursuant to Rule 14d–2(b) under the Exchange Act (17 CFR 240.14d–2(b))

[ ] Pre-commencement communications pursuant to Rule 13c–4(c) under the Exchange Act (17 CFR 240.13c–4(c))

Indicate by check mark whether the registrant is an emerging growth company as defined in as defined in Rule 405 of the Securities Act of 1933 (§230.405 of this chapter) or Rule 12b-2 of the Securities Exchange Act of 1934 (§240.12b-2 of this chapter).

Emerging growth company ❑

If an emerging growth company, indicate by check mark if the registrant has elected not to use the extended transition period for complying with any new or revised financial accounting standards provided pursuant to Section 13(a) of the Exchange Act. ❑

GENERAL INSTRUCTIONS

A. Rules as to Use of Form 8–K.

1. Form 8–K shall be used for current reports under Section 13 or 15(d) of the Securities Exchange Act of 1934, filed pursuant to Rule 13a–11 or Rule 15d–11 and for reports of nonpublic information required to be disclosed by Regulation FD (17 CFR 243.100 and 243.101).

2. Form 8–K may be used by a registrant to satisfy its filing obligations pursuant to Rule 425 under the Securities Act, regarding written communications related to business combination transactions, or Rules 14a–12(b) or Rule 14d–2(b) under the Exchange Act, relating to soliciting materials and pre-commencement communications pursuant to tender offers, respectively, provided that the Form 8–K filing satisfies all the substantive requirements of those rules (other

than the Rule 425(c) requirement to include certain specified information in any prospectus filed pursuant to such rule). Such filing is also deemed to be filed pursuant to any rule for which the box is checked. A registrant is not required to check the box in connection with Rule 14a–12(b) or Rule 14d–2(b) if the communication is filed pursuant to Rule 425. Communications filed pursuant to Rule 425 are deemed filed under the other applicable sections. See Note 2 to Rule 425, Rule 14a–12(b) and Instruction 2 to Rule 14d–2(b)(2).

B. Events to be Reported and Time for Filing of Reports.

1. A report on this form is required to be filed or furnished, as applicable, upon the occurrence of any one or more of the events specified in the items in Sections 1–6 and 9 of this form. Unless otherwise specified, a report is to be filed or furnished within four business days after occurrence of the event. If the event occurs on a Saturday, Sunday or holiday on which the Commission is not open for business, then the four business day period shall begin to run on, and include, the first business day thereafter. A registrant either furnishing a report on this form under Item 7.01 (Regulation FD Disclosure) or electing to file a report on this form under Item 8.01 (Other Events) solely to satisfy its obligations under Regulation FD (17 CFR 243.100 and 243.101) must furnish such report or make such filing, as applicable, in accordance with the requirements of Rule 100(a) of Regulation FD, including the deadline for furnishing or filing such report. A report pursuant to Item 5.08 is to be filed within four business days after the registrant determines the anticipated meeting date.

2. The information in a report furnished pursuant to Item 2.02 (Results of Operations and Financial Condition) or Item 7.01 (Regulation FD Disclosure) shall not be deemed to be "filed" for purposes of Section 18 of the Exchange Act or otherwise subject to the liabilities of that section, unless the registrant specifically states that the information is to be considered "filed" under the Exchange Act or incorporates it by reference into a filing under the Securities Act or the Exchange Act. If a report on Form 8–K contains disclosures under Item 2.02 or Item 7.01, whether or not the report contains disclosures regarding other items, all exhibits to such report relating to Item 2.02 or Item 7.01 will be deemed furnished, and not filed, unless the registrant specifies, under Item 9.01 (Financial Statements and Exhibits), which exhibits, or portions of exhibits, are intended to be deemed filed rather than furnished pursuant to this instruction.

3. If the registrant previously has reported substantially the same information as required by this form, the registrant need not make an additional report of the information on this form. To the extent that an item calls for disclosure of developments concerning a *previously reported* event or transaction, any information required in the new report or amendment about the previously reported event or transaction may be provided by incorporation by reference to the previously filed report. The term previously reported is defined in Rule 12b–2.

4. Copies of agreements, amendments or other documents or instruments required to be filed pursuant to Form 8–K are not required to be filed or furnished as exhibits to the Form 8–K unless specifically required to be filed or furnished by the applicable Item. This instruction does not affect the requirement to otherwise file such agreements, amendments or other documents or instruments, including as exhibits to registration statements and periodic reports pursuant to the requirements of Item 601 of Regulation S–K.

5. When considering current reporting on this form, particularly of other events of material importance pursuant to Item 7.01 (Regulation FD Disclosure) and Item 8.01 (Other Events), registrants should have due regard for the accuracy, completeness and currency of the information in registration statements filed under the Securities Act which incorporate by reference information in reports filed pursuant to the Exchange Act, including reports on this form.

6. A registrant's report under Item 7.01 (Regulation FD Disclosure) or Item 8.01 (Other Events) will not be deemed an admission as to the materiality of any information in the report that is required to be disclosed solely by Regulation FD.

C. Application of General Rules and Regulations.

1. The General Rules and Regulations under the Act contain certain general requirements which are applicable to reports on any form. These general requirements should be carefully read and observed in the preparation and filing of reports on this form.

2. Particular attention is directed to Regulation 12B (17 CFR 240.12b–1 et seq.) which contains general requirements regarding matters such as the kind and size of paper to be used, the legibility of the report, the information to be given whenever the title of securities is required to be stated, and the filing of the report. The definitions contained in Rule 12b–2 should be especially noted. See also Regulations 13A (17 CFR 240.13a–1 et seq.) and 15D (17 CFR 240.15d–1 et seq.).

D. Preparation of Report.

This form is not to be used as a blank form to be filled in, but only as a guide in the preparation of the report on paper meeting the requirements of Rule 12b–12. The report shall contain the number and caption of the applicable item, but the text of such item may be omitted, provided the answers thereto are prepared in the manner specified in Rule 12b–13. To the extent that Item 1.01 and one or more other items of the form are applicable, registrants need not provide the number and caption of Item 1.01 so long as the substantive disclosure required by Item 1.01 is disclosed in the report and the number and caption of the other applicable item(s) are provided. All items that are not required to be answered in a particular report may be omitted and no reference thereto need be made in the report. All instructions should also be omitted.

E. Signature and Filing of Report.

Three complete copies of the report, including any financial statements, exhibits or other papers or documents filed as a part thereof, and five additional copies which need not include exhibits, shall be filed with the Commission. At least one complete copy of the report, including any financial statements, exhibits or other papers or documents filed as a part thereof, shall be filed, with each exchange on which any class of securities of the registrant is registered. At least one complete copy of the report filed with the Commission and one such copy filed with each exchange shall be manually signed. Copies not manually signed shall bear typed or printed signatures.

F. Incorporation by Reference.

If the registrant makes available to its stockholders or otherwise publishes, within the period prescribed for filing the report, a press release or other document or statement containing information meeting some or all of the requirements of this form, the information called for may be incorporated by reference to such published document or statement, in answer or partial answer to any item or items of this form, provided copies thereof are filed as an exhibit to the report on this form.

G. Use of this Form by Asset–Backed Issuers.

The following applies to registrants that are asset-backed issuers. Terms used in this General Instruction G. have the same meaning as in Item 1101 of Regulation AB (17 CFR 229.1101).

1. *Reportable Events That May Be Omitted.*

The registrant need not file a report on this Form upon the occurrence of any one or more of the events specified in the following:

(a) Item 2.01, Completion of Acquisition or Disposition of Assets;

(b) Item 2.02, Results of Operations and Financial Condition;

(c) Item 2.03, Creation of a Direct Financial Obligation or an Obligation under an Off–Balance Sheet Arrangement of a Registrant;

(d) Item 2.05, Costs Associated with Exit or Disposal Activities;

(e) Item 2.06, Material Impairments;

(f) Item 3.01, Notice of Delisting or Failure to Satisfy a Continued Listing Rule or Standard; Transfer of Listing;

(g) Item 3.02, Unregistered Sales of Equity Securities;

(h) Item 4.01, Changes in Registrant's Certifying Accountant;

(i) Item 4.02, Non–Reliance on Previously Issued Financial Statements or a Related Audit Report or Completed Interim Review;

(j) Item 5.01, Changes in Control of Registrant;

(k) Item 5.02, Departure of Directors or Principal Officers; Election of Directors; Appointment of Principal Officers;

(*l*) Item 5.04, Temporary Suspension of Trading Under Registrant's Employee Benefit Plans; and

(m) Item 5.05, Amendments to the Registrant's Code of Ethics, or Waiver of a Provision of the Code of Ethics.

2. *Additional Disclosure for the Form 8–K Cover Page.*

Immediately after the name of the issuing entity on the cover page of the Form 8–K, as separate line items, identify the exact name of the depositor as specified in its charter and the exact name of the sponsor as specified in its charter. Include a Central Index Key number for the depositor and the issuing entity, and if available, the sponsor.

3. *Signatures.*

The Form 8–K must be signed by the depositor. In the alternative, the Form 8–K may be signed on behalf of the issuing entity by a duly authorized representative of the servicer. If multiple servicers are involved in servicing the pool assets, a duly authorized representative of the master servicer (or entity performing the equivalent function) must sign if a representative of the servicer is to sign the report on behalf of the issuing entity.

INFORMATION TO BE INCLUDED IN THE REPORT

Section 1. Registrant's Business and Operations

Item 1.01 Entry into a Material Definitive Agreement.

(a) If the registrant has entered into a material definitive agreement not made in the ordinary course of business of the registrant, or into any amendment of such agreement that is material to the registrant, disclose the following information:

(1) the date on which the agreement was entered into or amended, the identity of the parties to the agreement or amendment and a brief description of any material relationship between the registrant or its affiliates and any of the parties, other than in respect of the material definitive agreement or amendment; and

(2) a brief description of the terms and conditions of the agreement or amendment that are material to the registrant.

(b) For purposes of this Item 1.01, a *material definitive agreement* means an agreement that provides for obligations that are material to and enforceable against the registrant, or rights that are material to the registrant and enforceable by the registrant against one or more other parties to the agreement, in each case whether or not subject to conditions.

Instructions:

1. Any material definitive agreement of the registrant not made in the ordinary course of the registrant's business must be disclosed under this Item 1.01. An agreement is deemed to be not made in the ordinary course of a registrant's business even if the agreement is such as ordinarily accompanies the kind of business conducted by the registrant if it involves the subject matter identified in Item 601(b)(10)(ii)(A)–(D) of Regulation S–K. An agreement involving the subject matter identified in Item 601(b)(10)(iii)(A) or (B) need not be disclosed under this Item.

2. A registrant must provide disclosure under this Item 1.01 if the registrant succeeds as a party to the agreement or amendment to the agreement by assumption or assignment (other than in connection with a merger or acquisition or similar transaction).

3. With respect to asset-backed securities, as defined in Item 1101 of Regulation AB, disclosure is required under this Item 1.01 regarding the entry into or an amendment to a definitive agreement that is material to the asset-backed securities transaction, even if the registrant is not a party to such agreement (*e.g.*, a servicing agreement with a servicer contemplated by Item 1108(a)(3) of Regulation AB).

Item 1.02 Termination of a Material Definitive Agreement.

(a) If a material definitive agreement which was not made in the ordinary course of business of the registrant and to which the registrant is a party is terminated otherwise than by expiration of the agreement on its stated termination date, or as a result of all parties completing their obligations under such agreement, and such termination of the agreement is material to the registrant, disclose the following information:

(1) the date of the termination of the material definitive agreement, the identity of the parties to the agreement and a brief description of any material relationship between the registrant or its affiliates and any of the parties other than in respect of the material definitive agreement;

(2) a brief description of the terms and conditions of the agreement that are material to the registrant;

(3) a brief description of the material circumstances surrounding the termination; and

(4) any material early termination penalties incurred by the registrant.

(b) For purposes of this Item 1.02, the term *material definitive agreement* shall have the same meaning as set forth in Item 1.01(b).

Instructions:

1. No disclosure is required solely by reason of this Item 1.02 during negotiations or discussions regarding termination of a material definitive agreement unless and until the agreement has been terminated.

2. No disclosure is required solely by reason of this Item 1.02 if the registrant believes in good faith that the material definitive agreement has not been terminated, unless the registrant has received a notice of termination pursuant to the terms of agreement.

3. With respect to asset-backed securities, as defined in Item 1101 of Regulation AB (17 CFR 229.1101), disclosure is required under this Item 1.02 regarding the termination of a definitive agreement that is material to the asset-backed securities transaction (otherwise than by expiration of the agreement on its stated termination date or as a result of all parties completing their obligations under such agreement), even if the registrant is not a party to such agreement (*e.g.*, a servicing agreement with a servicer contemplated by Item 1108(a)(3) of Regulation AB).

Item 1.03 Bankruptcy or Receivership.

(a) If a receiver, fiscal agent or similar officer has been appointed for a registrant or its parent, in a proceeding under the U.S. Bankruptcy Code or in any other proceeding under state or federal law in which a court or governmental authority has assumed jurisdiction over substantially all of the assets or business of the registrant or its parent, or if such jurisdiction has been assumed by leaving the existing directors and officers in possession but subject to the supervision and orders of a court or governmental authority, disclose the following information:

(1) the name or other identification of the proceeding;

(2) the identity of the court or governmental authority;

(3) the date that jurisdiction was assumed; and

(4) the identity of the receiver, fiscal agent or similar officer and the date of his or her appointment.

(b) If an order confirming a plan of reorganization, arrangement or liquidation has been entered by a court or governmental authority having supervision or jurisdiction over substantially all of the assets or business of the registrant or its parent, disclose the following;

(1) the identity of the court or governmental authority;

(2) the date that the order confirming the plan was entered by the court or governmental authority;

(3) a summary of the material features of the plan and, pursuant to Item 9.01 (Financial Statements and Exhibits), a copy of the plan as confirmed;

(4) the number of shares or other units of the registrant or its parent issued and outstanding, the number reserved for future issuance in respect of claims and interests filed and allowed under the plan, and the aggregate total of such numbers; and

(5) information as to the assets and liabilities of the registrant or its parent as of the date that the order confirming the plan was entered, or a date as close thereto as practicable.

Instructions:

(1) The information called for in paragraph (b)(5) of this Item 1.03 may be presented in the form in which it was furnished to the court or governmental authority.

(2) With respect to asset-backed securities, disclosure also is required under this Item 1.03 if the depositor (or servicer if the servicer signs the report on Form 10–K (17 CFR 249.310) of the issuing entity) becomes aware of any instances described in paragraph (a) or (b) of this Item with respect to the sponsor, depositor, servicer contemplated by Item 1108(a)(3) of Regulation AB, trustee, significant obligor, enhancement or support provider contemplated by Items 1114(b) or 1115 of Regulation AB or other material party contemplated by Item 1101(d)(1) of Regulation AB. Terms used in this Instruction 2 have the same meaning as in Item 1101 of Regulation AB.

Item 1.04 Mine Safety–Reporting of Shutdowns and Patterns of Violations.

(a) If the registrant or a subsidiary of the registrant has received, with a respect to a coal or other mine of which the registrant or a subsidiary of the registrant is an operator

- an imminent danger order issued under section 107(a) of the Federal Mine Safety and Health Act of 1977 (30 U.S.C. 817(a));
- a written notice from the Mine Safety and Health Administration that the coal or other mine has a pattern of violations of mandatory health or safety standards that are of such nature as could have significantly contributed to the cause and effect of coal or other mine health or safety hazards under section 104(e) of such Act (30 U.S.C. 814(e)); or
- a written notice from the Mine Safety and Health Administration that the coal or other mine has the potential to have such a pattern,

disclose the following information:

(1) The date of receipt by the issuer or a subsidiary of such order or notice.

(2) The category of the order or notice.

(3) The name and location of the mine involved.

Instructions:

1. The term "coal or other mine" means a coal or other mine, as defined in section 3 of the Federal Mine Safety and Health Act of 1977 (30 U.S.C. 802), that is subject to the provisions of such Act (30 U.S.C. 801 et seq.).

2. The term "operator" has the meaning given the term in section 3 of the Federal Mine Safety and Health Act of 1977 (30 U.S.C. 802).

Section 2. Financial Information

Item 2.01 Completion of Acquisition or Disposition of Assets.

If the registrant or any of its majority-owned subsidiaries has completed the acquisition or disposition of a significant amount of assets, otherwise than in the ordinary course of business, disclose the following information:

(a) the date of completion of the transaction;

(b) a brief description of the assets involved;

(c) the identity of the person(s) from whom the assets were acquired or to whom they were sold and the nature of any material relationship, other than in respect of the transaction, between such person(s) and the registrant or any of its affiliates, or any director or officer of the registrant, or any associate of any such director or officer;

(d) the nature and amount of consideration given or received for the assets and, if any material relationship is disclosed pursuant to paragraph (c) of this Item 2.01, the formula or principle followed in determining the amount of such consideration;

(e) if the transaction being reported is an acquisition and if a material relationship exists between the registrant or any of its affiliates and the source(s) of the funds used in the acquisition, the identity of the source(s) of the funds unless all or any part of the consideration used is a loan made in the ordinary course of business by a bank as defined by Section 3(a)(6) of the Act, in which case the identity of such bank may be omitted provided the registrant:

(1) has made a request for confidentiality pursuant to Section 13(d)(1)(B) of the Act; and

(2) states in the report that the identity of the bank has been so omitted and filed separately with the Commission; and

(f) If the registrant was a shell company, other than a business combination related shell company, as those terms are defined in Rule 12b–2 under the Exchange Act, immediately before the transaction, the information that would be required if the registrant were filing a general form for registration of securities on Form 10 under the Exchange Act reflecting all classes of the registrant's securities subject to the reporting requirements of Section 13 (15 U.S.C. 78m) or Section 15(d) (15 U.S.C. 78o(d)) of such Act upon consummation of the transaction, with such information reflecting the registrant and its securities upon consummation of the transaction. Notwithstanding General Instruction B.3. to Form 8–K, if any disclosure required by this Item 2.01(f) is previously reported, as that term is defined in Rule 12b–2 under the Exchange Act (17 CFR 240.12b–2), the registrant may identify the filing in which that disclosure is included instead of including that disclosure in this report.

Instructions:

1. No information need be given as to:

(i) any transaction between any person and any wholly-owned subsidiary of such person;

(ii) any transaction between two or more wholly-owned subsidiaries of any person; or

(iii) the redemption or other acquisition of securities from the public, or the sale or other disposition of securities to the public, by the issuer of such securities or by a wholly-owned subsidiary of that issuer.

2. The term *acquisition* includes every purchase, acquisition by lease, exchange, merger, consolidation, succession or other acquisition, except that the term does not include the construction or development of property by or for the registrant or its subsidiaries or the acquisition of materials for such purpose. The term *disposition* includes every sale, disposition by lease, exchange, merger, consolidation, mortgage, assignment or hypothecation of assets, whether for the benefit of creditors or otherwise, abandonment, destruction, or other disposition.

3. The information called for by this Item 2.01 is to be given as to each transaction or series of related transactions of the size indicated. The acquisition or disposition of securities is deemed the indirect acquisition or disposition of the assets represented by such securities if it results in the acquisition or disposition of control of such assets.

4. An acquisition or disposition shall be deemed to involve a significant amount of assets:

(i) if the registrant's and its other subsidiaries' equity in the net book value of such assets or the amount paid or received for the assets upon such acquisition or disposition exceeded 10% of the total assets of the registrant and its consolidated subsidiaries; or

(ii) if it involved a business (see 17 CFR 210.11–01(d)) that is significant (see 17 CFR 210.11–01(b)).

Acquisitions of individually insignificant businesses are not required to be reported pursuant to this Item 2.01 unless they are related businesses (see 17 CFR 210.3–05(a)(3)) and are significant in the aggregate.

5. Attention is directed to the requirements in Item 9.01 (Financial Statements and Exhibits) with respect to the filing of:

(i) financial statements of businesses acquired;

(ii) *pro forma* financial information; and

(iii) copies of the plans of acquisition or disposition as exhibits to the report.

Item 2.02 Results of Operations and Financial Condition.

(a) If a registrant, or any person acting on its behalf, makes any public announcement or release (including any update of an earlier announcement or release) disclosing material non-public information regarding the registrant's results of operations or financial condition for a completed quarterly or annual fiscal period, the registrant shall disclose the date of the announcement or release, briefly identify the announcement or release and include the text of that announcement or release as an exhibit.

(b) A Form 8–K is not required to be furnished to the Commission under this Item 2.02 in the case of disclosure of material non-public information that is disclosed orally, telephonically, by webcast, by broadcast, or by similar means if:

(1) the information is provided as part of a presentation that is complementary to, and initially occurs within 48 hours after, a related, written announce-

ment or release that has been furnished on Form 8–K pursuant to this Item 2.02 prior to the presentation;

(2) the presentation is broadly accessible to the public by dial-in conference call, by webcast, by broadcast or by similar means;

(3) the financial and other statistical information contained in the presentation is provided on the registrant's website, together with any information that would be required under 17 CFR 244.100; and

(4) the presentation was announced by a widely disseminated press release, that included instructions as to when and how to access the presentation and the location on the registrant's website where the information would be available.

Instructions:

1. The requirements of this Item 2.02 are triggered by the disclosure of material non-public information regarding a completed fiscal year or quarter. Release of additional or updated material non-public information regarding a completed fiscal year or quarter would trigger an additional Item 2.02 requirement.

2. The requirements of paragraph (e)(1)(i) of Item 10 of Regulation S–K shall apply to disclosures under this Item 2.02.

3. Issuers that make earnings announcements or other disclosures of material non-public information regarding a completed fiscal year or quarter in an interim or annual report to shareholders are permitted to specify which portion of the report contains the information required to be furnished under this Item 2.02.

4. This Item 2.02 does not apply in the case of a disclosure that is made in a quarterly report filed with the Commission on Form 10–Q (17 CFR 249.308a) or an annual report filed with the Commission on Form 10–K (17 CFR 249.310).

Item 2.03 Creation of a Direct Financial Obligation or an Obligation under an Off–Balance Sheet Arrangement of a Registrant.

(a) If the registrant becomes obligated on a direct financial obligation that is material to the registrant, disclose the following information:

(1) the date on which the registrant becomes obligated on the direct financial obligation and a brief description of the transaction or agreement creating the obligation;

(2) the amount of the obligation, including the terms of its payment and, if applicable, a brief description of the material terms under which it may be accelerated or increased and the nature of any recourse provisions that would enable the registrant to recover from third parties; and

(3) a brief description of the other terms and conditions of the transaction or agreement that are material to the registrant.

(b) If the registrant becomes directly or contingently liable for an obligation that is material to the registrant arising out of an off-balance sheet arrangement, disclose the following information:

(1) the date on which the registrant becomes directly or contingently liable on the obligation and a brief description of the transaction or agreement creating the arrangement and obligation;

(2) a brief description of the nature and amount of the obligation of the registrant under the arrangement, including the material terms whereby it may become a direct obligation, if applicable, or may be accelerated or increased and the nature of any recourse provisions that would enable the registrant to recover from third parties;

(3) the maximum potential amount of future payments (undiscounted) that the registrant may be required to make, if different; and

(4) a brief description of the other terms and conditions of the obligation or arrangement that are material to the registrant.

(c) For purposes of this Item 2.03, *direct financial obligation* means any of the following:

(1) a long-term debt obligation, as defined in Item 303(a)(5)(ii)(A) of Regulation S–K;

(2) a capital lease obligation, as defined in Item 303(a)(5)(ii)(B) of Regulation S–K;

(3) an operating lease obligation, as defined in Item 303(a)(5)(ii)(C) of Regulation S–K; or

(4) a short-term debt obligation that arises other than in the ordinary course of business.

(d) For purposes of this Item 2.03, *off-balance sheet arrangement* has the meaning set forth in Item 303(a)(4)(ii) of Regulation S–K.

(e) For purposes of this Item 2.03, short-term debt obligation means a payment obligation under a borrowing arrangement that is scheduled to mature within one year, or, for those registrants that use the operating cycle concept of working capital, within a registrant's operating cycle that is longer than one year, as discussed in FASB ASC paragraph 210–10–45–3 (Balance Sheet Topic).

Instructions:

1. A registrant has no obligation to disclose information under this Item 2.03 until the registrant enters into an agreement enforceable against the registrant, whether or not subject to conditions, under which the direct financial

obligation will arise or be created or issued. If there is no such agreement, the registrant must provide the disclosure within four business days after the occurrence of the closing or settlement of the transaction or arrangement under which the direct financial obligation arises or is created.

2. A registrant must provide the disclosure required by paragraph (b) of this Item 2.03 whether or not the registrant is also a party to the transaction or agreement creating the contingent obligation arising under the off-balance sheet arrangement. In the event that neither the registrant nor any affiliate of the registrant is also a party to the transaction or agreement creating the contingent obligation arising under the off-balance sheet arrangement in question, the four business day period for reporting the event under this Item 2.03 shall begin on the earlier of (i) the fourth business day after the contingent obligation is created or arises, and (ii) the day on which an executive officer, as defined in 17 CFR 240.3b–7, of the registrant becomes aware of the contingent obligation.

3. In the event that an agreement, transaction or arrangement requiring disclosure under this Item 2.03 comprises a facility, program or similar arrangement that creates or may give rise to direct financial obligations of the registrant in connection with multiple transactions, the registrant shall:

(i) disclose the entering into of the facility, program or similar arrangement if the entering into of the facility is material to the registrant; and

(ii) as direct financial obligations arise or are created under the facility or program, disclose the required information under this Item 2.03 to the extent that the obligations are material to the registrant (including when a series of previously undisclosed individually immaterial obligations become material in the aggregate).

4. For purposes of Item 2.03(b)(3), the maximum amount of future payments shall not be reduced by the effect of any amounts that may possibly be recovered by the registrant under recourse or collateralization provisions in any guarantee agreement, transaction or arrangement.

5. If the obligation required to be disclosed under this Item 2.03 is a security, or a term of a security, that has been or will be sold pursuant to an effective registration statement of the registrant, the registrant is not required to file a Form 8–K pursuant to this Item 2.03, *provided* that the prospectus relating to that sale contains the information required by this Item 2.03 and is filed within the required time period under Securities Act Rule 424.

Item 2.04 Triggering Events That Accelerate or Increase a Direct Financial Obligation or an Obligation under an Off–Balance Sheet Arrangement.

(a) If a triggering event causing the increase or acceleration of a direct financial obligation of the registrant occurs and the consequences of the event, taking into account those described in paragraph (a)(4) of this Item 2.04, are material to the registrant, disclose the following information:

(1) the date of the triggering event and a brief description of the agreement or transaction under which the direct financial obligation was created and is increased or accelerated;

(2) a brief description of the triggering event;

(3) the amount of the direct financial obligation, as increased if applicable, and the terms of payment or acceleration that apply; and

(4) any other material obligations of the registrant that may arise, increase, be accelerated or become direct financial obligations as a result of the triggering event or the increase or acceleration of the direct financial obligation.

(b) If a triggering event occurs causing an obligation of the registrant under an off-balance sheet arrangement to increase or be accelerated, or causing a contingent obligation of the registrant under an off-balance sheet arrangement to become a direct financial obligation of the registrant, and the consequences of the event, taking into account those described in paragraph (b)(4) of this Item 2.04, are material to the registrant, disclose the following information:

(1) The date of the triggering event and a brief description of the off-balance sheet arrangement;

(2) A brief description of the triggering event;

(3) The nature and amount of the obligation, as increased if applicable, and the terms of payment or acceleration that apply; and

(4) Any other material obligations of the registrant that may arise, increase, be accelerated or become direct financial obligations as a result of the triggering event or the increase or acceleration of the obligation under the off-balance sheet arrangement or its becoming a direct financial obligation of the registrant.

(c) For purposes of this Item 2.04, the term direct financial obligation has the meaning provided in Item 2.03 of this form, but shall also include an obligation arising out of an off-balance sheet arrangement that is accrued under FASB ASC Section 450–20–25, *Contingencies—Loss Contingencies—Recognition*, as a probable loss contingency.

(d) For purposes of this Item 2.04, the term *off-balance sheet arrangement* has the meaning provided in Item 2.03 of this form.

(e) For purposes of this Item 2.04, a *triggering event* is an event, including an event of default, event of acceleration or similar event, as a result of which a direct financial obligation of the registrant or an obligation of the registrant arising under an off-balance sheet arrangement is increased or becomes accelerated or as a result of which a contingent obligation of the registrant arising out of an off-balance sheet arrangement becomes a direct financial obligation of the registrant.

Instructions:

1. Disclosure is required if a triggering event occurs in respect of an obligation of the registrant under an off-balance sheet arrangement and the consequences are material to the registrant, whether or not the registrant is also a party to the transaction or agreement under which the triggering event occurs.

2. No disclosure is required under this Item 2.04 unless and until a triggering event has occurred in accordance with the terms of the relevant agreement, transaction or arrangement, including, if required, the sending to the registrant of notice of the occurrence of a triggering event pursuant to the terms of the agreement, transaction or arrangement and the satisfaction of all conditions to such occurrence, except the passage of time.

3. No disclosure is required solely by reason of this Item 2.04 if the registrant believes in good faith that no triggering event has occurred, unless the registrant has received a notice described in Instruction 2 to this Item 2.04.

4. Where a registrant is subject to an obligation arising out of an off-balance sheet arrangement, whether or not disclosed pursuant to Item 2.03 of this form, if a triggering event occurs as a result of which under that obligation an accrual for a probable loss is required under FASB ASC Section 450–20–25, the obligation arising out of the off-balance sheet arrangement becomes a direct financial obligation as defined in this Item 2.04. In that situation, if the consequences as determined under Item 2.04(b) are material to the registrant, disclosure is required under this Item 2.04.

5. With respect to asset-backed securities, as defined in 17 CFR 229.1101, disclosure also is required under this Item 2.04 if an early amortization, performance trigger or other event, including an event of default, has occurred under the transaction agreements for the asset-backed securities that would materially alter the payment priority or distribution of cash flows regarding the asset-backed securities or the amortization schedule for the asset-backed securities. In providing the disclosure required by this Item, identify the changes to the payment priorities, flow of funds or asset-backed securities as a result. Disclosure is required under this Item whether or not the registrant is a party to the transaction agreement that results in the occurrence identified.

Item 2.05 Costs Associated with Exit or Disposal Activities.

If the registrant's board of directors, a committee of the board of directors or the officer or officers of the registrant authorized to take such action if board action is not required, commits the registrant to an exit or disposal plan, or otherwise disposes of a long-lived asset or terminates employees under a plan of termination described in FASB ASC paragraph 420–10–25–4 (Exit or Disposal Cost Obligations Topic), under which material charges will be incurred under generally accepted accounting principles applicable to the registrant, disclose the following information:

(a) the date of the commitment to the course of action and a description of the course of action, including the facts and circumstances leading to the expected action and the expected completion date;

(b) for each major type of cost associated with the course of action (for example, one-time termination benefits, contract termination costs and other associated costs), an estimate of the total amount or range of amounts expected to be incurred in connection with the action;

(c) an estimate of the total amount or range of amounts expected to be incurred in connection with the action; and

(d) the registrant's estimate of the amount or range of amounts of the charge that will result in future cash expenditures, *provided, however*, that if the registrant determines that at the time of filing it is unable in good faith to make a determination of an estimate required by paragraphs (b), (c) or (d) of this Item 2.05, no disclosure of such estimate shall be required; *provided further, however*, that in any such event, the registrant shall file an amended report on Form 8–K under this Item 2.05 within four business days after it makes a determination of such an estimate or range of estimates.

Item 2.06 Material Impairments.

If the registrant's board of directors, a committee of the board of directors or the officer or officers of the registrant authorized to take such action if board action is not required, concludes that a material charge for impairment to one or more of its assets, including, without limitation, impairments of securities or goodwill, is required under generally accepted accounting principles applicable to the registrant, disclose the following information:

(a) the date of the conclusion that a material charge is required and a description of the impaired asset or assets and the facts and circumstances leading to the conclusion that the charge for impairment is required;

(b) the registrant's estimate of the amount or range of amounts of the impairment charge; and

(c) the registrant's estimate of the amount or range of amounts of the impairment charge that will result in future cash expenditures, *provided, however*, that if the registrant determines that at the time of filing it is unable in good faith to make a determination of an estimate required by paragraphs (b) or (c) of this Item 2.06, no disclosure of such estimate shall be required; *provided further, however*, that in any such event, the registrant shall file an amended report on Form 8–K under this Item 2.06 within four business days after it makes a determination of such an estimate or range of estimates.

Instruction:

No filing is required under this Item 2.06 if the conclusion is made in connection with the preparation, review or audit of financial statements required to be included in the next periodic report due to be filed under the Exchange Act, the periodic report is filed on a timely basis and such conclusion is disclosed in the report.

Section 3. Securities and Trading Markets

Item 3.01 Notice of Delisting or Failure to Satisfy a Continued Listing Rule or Standard; Transfer of Listing.

(a) If the registrant has received notice from the national securities exchange or national securities association (or a facility thereof) that maintains the principal listing for any class of the registrant's common equity (as defined in Exchange Act Rule 12b–2) that:

- The registrant or such class of the registrant's securities does not satisfy a rule or standard for continued listing on the exchange or association;
- The exchange has submitted an application under Exchange Act Rule 12d2–2 to the Commission to delist such class of the registrant's securities; or
- The association has taken all necessary steps under its rules to delist the security from its automated inter-dealer quotation system,

the registrant must disclose:

(i) The date that the registrant received the notice;

(ii) The a rule or standard for continued listing on the national securities exchange or national securities association that the registrant fails, or has failed to, satisfy; and

(iii) Any action or response that, at the time of filing, the registrant has determined to take in response to the notice.

(b) If the registrant has notified the national securities exchange or national securities association (or a facility thereof) that maintains the principal listing for any class of the registrant's common equity (as defined in Exchange Act Rule 12b–2) that the registrant is aware of any material noncompliance with a rule or standard for continued listing on the exchange or association, the registrant must disclose:

(i) The date that the registrant provided such notice to the exchange or association;

(ii) The rule or standard for continued listing on the exchange or association that the registrant fails, or has failed, to satisfy; and

(iii) Any action or response that, at the time of filing, the registrant has determined to take regarding its noncompliance.

(c) If the national securities exchange or national securities association (or a facility thereof) that maintains the principal listing for any class of the registrant's common equity (as defined in Exchange Act Rule 12b–2), in lieu of suspending trading in or delisting such class of the registrant's securities, issues a public reprimand letter or similar communication indicating that the registrant has violated a rule or standard for continued listing on the exchange or association, the registrant must state the date, and summarize the contents of the letter or communication.

(d) If the registrant's board of directors, a committee of the board of directors or the officer or officers of the registrant authorized to take such action if board action is not required, has taken definitive action to cause the listing of a class of its common equity to be withdrawn from the national securities exchange, or terminated from the automated inter-dealer quotation system of a registered national securities association, where such exchange or association maintains the principal listing for such class of securities, including by reason of a transfer of the listing or quotation to another securities exchange or quotation system, describe the action taken and state the date of the action.

Instructions:

1. The registrant is not required to disclose any information required by paragraph (a) of this Item 3.01 where the delisting is a result of one of the following:

- The entire class of the security has been called for redemption, maturity or retirement; appropriate notice thereof has been given; if required by the terms of the securities, funds sufficient for the payment of all such securities have been deposited with an agency authorized to make such payments; and such funds have been made available to security holders;
- The entire class of the security has been redeemed or paid at maturity or retirement;
- The instruments representing the entire class of securities have come to evidence, by operation of law or otherwise, other securities in substitution therefor and represent no other right, except, if true, the right to receive an immediate cash payment (the right of dissenters to receive the appraised or fair value of their holdings shall not prevent the application of this provision); or
- All rights pertaining to the entire class of the security have been extinguished; provided, however, that where such an event occurs as the result of an order of a court or other governmental authority, the order shall be final, all applicable appeal periods shall have expired and no appeals shall be pending.

2. A registrant must provide the disclosure required by paragraph (a) or (b) of this Item 3.01, as applicable, regarding any failure to satisfy a rule or standard for continued listing on the national securities exchange or national securities association (or a facility thereof) that maintains the principal listing for any class of the registrant's common

equity (as defined in Exchange Act Rule 12b–2 (17 CFR 240.12b–2)) even if the registrant has the benefit of a grace period or similar extension period during which it may cure the deficiency that triggers the disclosure requirement.

3. Notices or other communications subsequent to an initial notice sent to, or by, a registrant under Item 3.01(a), (b) or (c) that continue to indicate that the registrant does not comply with the same rule or standard for continued listing that was the subject of the initial notice are not required to be filed, but may be filed voluntarily.

4. Registrants whose securities are quoted exclusively (i.e., the securities are not otherwise listed on an exchange or association) on automated inter-dealer quotation systems are not subject to this Item 3.01 and such registrants are thus not required to file a Form 8–K pursuant to this Item 3.01 if the securities are no longer quoted on such quotation system. If a security is listed on an exchange or association and is also quoted on an automated inter-dealer quotation system, the registrant is subject to the disclosure obligations of Item 3.01 if any of the events specified in Item 3.01 occur.

Item 3.02 Unregistered Sales of Equity Securities.

(a) If a registrant sells equity securities in a transaction that is not registered under the Securities Act, furnish the information set forth in paragraphs (a) and (c) through (e) of Item 701 of Regulation S–K. For purposes of determining the required filing date for the Form 8–K under this Item 3.02(a), the registrant has no obligation to disclose information under this Item 3.02 until the registrant enters into an agreement enforceable against the registrant, whether or not subject to conditions, under which the equity securities are to be sold. If there is no such agreement, the registrant must provide the disclosure within four business days after the occurrence of the closing or settlement of the transaction or arrangement under which the equity securities are to be sold.

(b) No report need be filed under this Item 3.02 if the equity securities sold, in the aggregate since its last report filed under this Item 3.02 or its last periodic report, whichever is more recent, constitute less than 1% of the number of shares outstanding of the class of equity securities sold. In the case of a smaller reporting company, no report need be filed if the equity securities sold, in the aggregate since its last report filed under this Item 3.02 or its last periodic report, whichever is more recent, constitute less than 5% of the number of shares outstanding of the class of equity securities sold.

Instructions:

1. For purposes of this Item 3.02, "the number of shares outstanding" refers to the actual number of shares of equity securities of the class outstanding and does not include outstanding securities convertible into or exchangeable for such equity securities.

2. A smaller reporting company is defined in Item 10(f)(1) of Regulation S–K.

Item 3.03 Material Modification to Rights of Security Holders.

(a) If the constituent instruments defining the rights of the holders of any class of registered securities of the registrant have been materially modified, disclose the date of the modification, the title of the class of securities involved and briefly describe the general effect of such modification upon the rights of holders of such securities.

(b) If the rights evidenced by any class of registered securities have been materially limited or qualified by the issuance or modification of any other class of securities by the registrant, briefly disclose the date of the issuance or modification, the general effect of the issuance or modification of such other class of securities upon the rights of the holders of the registered securities.

Instruction:

Working capital restrictions and other limitations upon the payment of dividends must be reported pursuant to this Item 3.03.

Section 4. Matters Related to Accountants and Financial Statements

Item 4.01 Changes in Registrant's Certifying Accountant.

(a) If an independent accountant who was previously engaged as the principal accountant to audit the registrant's financial statements, or an independent accountant upon whom the principal accountant expressed reliance in its report regarding a significant subsidiary, resigns (or indicates that it declines to stand for re-appointment after completion of the current audit) or is dismissed, disclose the information required by Item 304(a)(1) of Regulation S–K including compliance with Item 304(a)(3) of Regulation S–K.

(b) If a new independent accountant has been engaged as either the principal accountant to audit the registrant's financial statements or as an independent accountant on whom the principal accountant is expected to express reliance in its report regarding a significant subsidiary, the registrant must disclose the information required by Item 304(a)(2) of Regulation S–K.

Instruction:

The resignation or dismissal of an independent accountant, or its refusal to stand for re-appointment, is a reportable event separate from the engagement of a new independent accountant. On some occasions, two reports on Form 8–K are required for a single change in accountants, the first on the resignation (or refusal to stand for re-appointment) or dismissal of the former accountant and the second when the new accountant is engaged. Information required in the second Form 8–K in such situations need not be provided to the extent that it has been reported previously in the first Form 8–K.

Item 4.02 Non–Reliance on Previously Issued Financial Statements or a Related Audit Report or Completed Interim Review.

(a) If the registrant's board of directors, a committee of the board of directors or the officer or officers of the registrant authorized to take such action if board action is not required, concludes that any previously issued financial statements, covering one or more years or interim periods for which the registrant is required to provide financial statements under Regulation S–X (17 CFR 210), should no longer be relied upon because of an error in such financial statements as addressed in FASB ASC Topic 250, *Accounting Changes and Error Corrections*, as may be modified, supplemented or succeeded, disclose the following information:

(1) the date of the conclusion regarding the non-reliance and an identification of the financial statements and years or periods covered that should no longer be relied upon;

(2) a brief description of the facts underlying the conclusion to the extent known to the registrant at the time of filing; and

(3) a statement of whether the audit committee, or the board of directors in the absence of an audit committee, or authorized officer or officers, discussed with the registrant's independent accountant the matters disclosed in the filing pursuant to this Item 4.02(a).

(b) If the registrant is advised by, or receives notice from, its independent accountant that disclosure should be made or action should be taken to prevent future reliance on a previously issued audit report or completed interim review related to previously issued financial statements, disclose the following information:

(1) the date on which the registrant was so advised or notified;

(2) identification of the financial statements that should no longer be relied upon;

(3) a brief description of the information provided by the accountant; and

(4) a statement of whether the audit committee, or the board of directors in the absence of an audit committee, or authorized officer or officers, discussed with the independent accountant the matters disclosed in the filing pursuant to this Item 4.02(b).

(c) If the registrant receives advisement or notice from its independent accountant requiring disclosure under paragraph (b) of this Item 4.02, the registrant must:

(1) provide the independent accountant with a copy of the disclosures it is making in response to this Item 4.02 that the independent accountant shall receive no later than the day that the disclosures are filed with the Commission;

(2) request the independent accountant to furnish to the registrant as promptly as possible a letter addressed to the Commission stating whether the independent accountant agrees with the statements made by the registrant in response to this Item 4.02 and, if not, stating the respects in which it does not agree; and

(3) amend the registrant's previously filed Form 8–K by filing the independent accountant's letter as an exhibit to the filed Form 8–K no later than two business days after the registrant's receipt of the letter.

Section 5. Corporate Governance and Management

Item 5.01 Changes in Control of Registrant.

(a) If, to the knowledge of the registrant's board of directors, a committee of the board of directors or authorized officer or officers of the registrant, a change in control of the registrant has occurred, furnish the following information:

(1) the identity of the person(s) who acquired such control;

(2) the date and a description of the transaction(s) which resulted in the change in control;

(3) the basis of the control, including the percentage of voting securities of the registrant now beneficially owned directly or indirectly by the person(s) who acquired control;

(4) the amount of the consideration used by such person(s);

(5) the source(s) of funds used by the person(s), *unless* all or any part of the consideration used is a loan made in the ordinary course of business by a bank as defined by Section 3(a)(6) of the Act, in which case the identity of such bank may be omitted provided the person who acquired control:

(i) has made a request for confidentiality pursuant to Section 13(d)(1)(B) of the Act; and

(ii) states in the report that the identity of the bank has been so omitted and filed separately with the Commission.

(6) the identity of the person(s) from whom control was assumed;

(7) any arrangements or understandings among members of both the former and new control groups and their associates with respect to election of directors or other matters; and

(8) if the registrant was a shell company, other than a business combination related shell company, as those terms are defined in Rule 12b–2 under the Exchange Act, immediately before the change in control, the information that would be required if the registrant were filing a general form for registration of securities on Form 10 under the Exchange Act reflecting all classes of the registrant's securities subject to the reporting requirements of Section 13 or Section 15(d) of such Act upon consummation of the change in control, with such information reflecting the registrant and its securities upon consummation of the transaction. Notwithstanding General Instruction B.3. to Form 8–K, if any disclosure required by this Item 5.01(a)(8) is previously reported, as that term is defined in Rule 12b–2 under the Exchange Act (17 CFR 240.12b–2), the registrant may identify the filing in which that disclosure is included instead of including that disclosure in this report.

(b) Furnish the information required by Item 403(c) of Regulation S–K or Item 403(c).

Item 5.02 Departure of Directors or Certain Officers; Election of Directors; Appointment of Certain Officers; Compensatory Arrangements of Certain Officers.

(a)(1) If a director has resigned or refuses to stand for re-election to the board of directors since the date of the last annual meeting of shareholders because of a disagreement with the registrant, known to an executive officer of the registrant, as defined in Rule 3b–7, on any matter relating to the registrant's operations, policies or practices, or if a director has been removed for cause from the board of directors, disclose the following information:

(i) the date of such resignation, refusal to stand for re-election or removal;

(ii) any positions held by the director on any committee of the board of directors at the time of the director's resignation, refusal to stand for re-election or removal; and

(iii) a brief description of the circumstances representing the disagreement that the registrant believes caused, in whole or in part, the director's resignation, refusal to stand for re-election or removal.

(2) If the director has furnished the registrant with any written correspondence concerning the circumstances surrounding his or her resignation, refusal or removal, the registrant shall file a copy of the document as an exhibit to the report on Form 8–K.

(3) The registrant also must:

(i) provide the director with a copy of the disclosures it is making in response to this Item 5.02 no later than the day the registrant file the disclosures with the Commission;

(ii) provide the director with the opportunity to furnish the registrant as promptly as possible with a letter addressed to the registrant stating whether he or she agrees with the statements made by the registrant in response to this Item 5.02 and, if not, stating the respects in which he or she does not agree; and

(iii) file any letter received by the registrant from the director with the Commission as an exhibit by an amendment to the previously filed Form 8–K within two business days after receipt by the registrant.

(b) If the registrant's principal executive officer, president, principal financial officer, principal accounting officer, principal operating officer, or any person performing similar functions, or any named executive officer, retires, resigns or is terminated from that position, or if a director retires, resigns, is removed, or refuses to stand for re-election (except in circumstances described in paragraph (a) of this Item 5.02), disclose the fact that the event has occurred and the date of the event.

(c) If the registrant appoints a new principal executive officer, president, principal financial officer, principal accounting officer, principal operating officer, or person performing similar functions, disclose the following information with respect to the newly appointed officer:

(1) the name and position of the newly appointed officer and the date of the appointment;

(2) the information required by Items 401(b), (d), (e) and Item 404(a) of Regulation S–K; and

(3) a brief description of any material plan, contract or arrangement (whether or not written) to

which a covered officer is a party or in which he or she participates that is entered into or material amendment in connection with the triggering event or any grant or award to any such covered person or modification thereto, under any such plan, contract or arrangement in connection with any such event.

Instruction to paragraph (c):

If the registrant intends to make a public announcement of the appointment other than by means of a report on Form 8–K, the registrant may delay filing the Form 8–K containing the disclosures required by this Item 5.02(c) until the day on which the registrant otherwise makes public announcement of the appointment of such officer.

(d) If the registrant elects a new director, except by a vote of security holders at an annual meeting or special meeting convened for such purpose, disclose the following information:

(1) the name of the newly elected director and the date of election;

(2) a brief description of any arrangement or understanding between the new director and any other persons, naming such persons, pursuant to which such director was selected as a director;

(3) the committees of the board of directors to which the new director has been, or at the time of this disclosure is expected to be, named; and

(4) the information required by Item 404(a) of Regulation S–K.

(5) a brief description of any material plan, contract or arrangement (whether or not written) to which the director is a party or in which he or she participates that is entered into or material amendment in connection with the triggering event or any grant or award to any such covered person or modification thereto, under any such plan, contract or arrangement in connection with any such event.

(e) If the registrant enters into, adopts, or otherwise commences a material compensatory plan, contract or arrangement (whether or not written), as to which the registrant's principal executive officer, principal financial officer, or a named executive officer participates or is a party, or such compensatory plan, contract or arrangement is materially amended or modified, or a material grant or award under any such plan, contract or arrangement to any such person is made or materially modified, then the registrant shall provide a brief description of the terms and conditions of the plan, contract or arrangement and the amounts payable to the officer thereunder.

Instructions to Paragraph (e):

1. Disclosure under this Item 5.02(e) shall be required whether or not the specified event is in connection with events otherwise triggering disclosure pursuant to this Item 5.02.

2. Grants or awards (or modifications thereto) made pursuant to a plan, contract or arrangement (whether involving cash or equity), that are materially consistent with the previously disclosed terms of such plan, contract or arrangement, need not be disclosed under this Item 5.02(e), provided the registrant has previously disclosed such terms and the grant, award or modification is disclosed when Item 402 of Regulation S–K requires such disclosure.

(f)(1) If the salary or bonus of a named executive officer cannot be calculated as of the most recent practicable date and is omitted from the Summary Compensation Table as specified in Instruction 1 to Item 402(b)(2)(iii) of Regulation S–K, disclose the appropriate information under this Item 5.02(f) when there is a payment, grant, award, decision or other occurrence as a result of which such amounts become calculable in whole or part. Disclosure under this Item 5.02(f) shall include a new total compensation figure for the named executive officer, using the new salary or bonus information to recalculate the information that was previously provided with respect to the named executive officer in the registrant's Summary Compensation Table for which the salary and bonus information was omitted in reliance on Instruction 1 to Item 402(b)(2)(iii) and (iv) of Regulation S–K.

(2) As specified in Instruction 6 to Item 402(u) of Regulation S-K (17 CFR 229.402(u)), disclosure under this Item 5.02(f) with respect to the salary or bonus of a principal executive officer shall include pay ratio disclosure pursuant to Item 402(u) of Regulation S-K calculated using the new total compensation figure for the principal executive officer. Pay ratio disclosure is not required under this Item 5.02(f) until the omitted salary or bonus amounts for such principal executive officer become calculable in whole.

Instructions to Item 5.02:

1. The disclosure requirements of this Item 5.02 do not apply to a registrant that is a wholly-owned subsidiary of an issuer with a class of securities registered under Section 12 of the Exchange Act, or that is required to file reports under Section 15(d) of the Exchange Act.

2. To the extent that any information called for in Item 5.02(c)(3) or Item 5.02(d)(3) or Item 5.02(d)(4) is not determined or is unavailable at the time of the required filing, the registrant shall include a statement this effect in the filing and then must file an amendment to its Form 8–K filing under this Item 5.02 containing such information within four business days after the information is determined or becomes available.

3. The registrant need not provide information with respect to plans, contracts, and arrangements to the extent they do not discriminate in scope, terms or operation, in favor of executive officers or directors of the registrant and that are available generally to all salaried employees.

4. For purposes of this Item, the term "named executive officer" shall refer to those executive officers for whom disclosure was required in the registrant's most recent filing with the Commission under the Securities Act or Exchange Act that required disclosure pursuant to Item 402(c) of Regulation S–K.

Item 5.03 Amendments to Articles of Incorporation or Bylaws; Change in Fiscal Year.

(a) If a registrant with a class of equity securities registered under Section 12 of the Exchange Act amends its articles of incorporation or bylaws and a proposal for the amendment was not disclosed in a proxy statement or information statement filed by the registrant, disclose the following information:

(1) The effective date of the amendment; and

(2) A description of the provision adopted or changed by amendment and, if applicable, the previous provision.

(b) If the registrant determines to change the fiscal year from that used in its most recent filing with the Commission other than by means of:

(1) a submission to a vote of security holders through the solicitation of proxies or otherwise; or

(2) an amendment to its articles of incorporation or bylaws,

disclose the date of such determination, the date of the new fiscal year end and the form (for example, Form 10–K or Form 10–Q) on which the report covering the transition period will be filed.

Instructions to Item 5.03:

(1) Refer to Item 601(b)(3) of Regulation S–K, regarding the filing of exhibits to this Item 5.03.

(2) With respect to asset-backed securities, as defined in Item 1101 of Regulation AB, disclosure is required under this Item 5.03 regarding any amendment to the governing documents of the issuing entity, regardless of whether the class of asset-backed securities is reporting under Section 13 or 15(d) of the Exchange Act.

Item 5.04 Temporary Suspension of Trading Under Registrant's Employee Benefit Plans.

(a) No later than the fourth business day after which the registrant receives the notice required by section 101(i)(2)(E) of the Employment Retirement Income Security Act of 1974 (29 U.S.C. 1021(i)(2)(E)), or, if such notice is not received by the registrant, on the same date by which the registrant transmits a timely notice to an affected officer or director within the time period prescribed by Rule 104(b)(2)(i)(B) or 104(b)(2)(ii) of Regulation BTR (17 CFR 245.104(b)(2)(i)(B) or 17 CFR 245.104(b)(2)(ii)), provide the information specified in Rule 104(b) (17 CFR 245.104(b)) and the date the registrant received the notice required by section 101(i)(2)(E) of the Employment Retirement Income Security Act of 1974 (29 U.S.C. 1021(i)(2)(E)), if applicable.

(b) On the same date by which the registrant transmits a timely updated notice to an affected officer or director, as required by the time period under Rule 104(b)(2)(iii) of Regulation BTR (17 CFR 245.104(b)(2)(iii)), provide the information specified in Rule 104(b)(3)(iii) (17 CFR 245.104(b)(2)(iii)).

Item 5.05 Amendments to the Registrant's Code of Ethics, or Waiver of a Provision of the Code of Ethics.

(a) Briefly describe the date and nature of any amendment to a provision of the registrant's code of ethics that applies to the registrant's principal executive officer, principal financial officer, principal accounting officer or controller or persons performing similar functions and that relates to any element of the code of ethics definition enumerated in Item 406(b) of Regulations S–K.

(b) If the registrant has granted a waiver, including an implicit waiver, from a provision of the code of ethics to an officer or person described in paragraph (a) of this Item 5.05, and the waiver relates to one or more of the elements of the code of ethics definition referred to in paragraph (a) of this Item 5.05, briefly describe the nature of the waiver, the name of the person to whom the waiver was granted, and the date of the waiver.

(c) The registrant does not need to provide any information pursuant to this Item 5.05 if it discloses the required information on its Internet website within four business days following the date of the amendment or waiver and the registrant has disclosed in its most recently filed annual report its Internet address and intention to provide disclosure in this manner. If the registrant elects to disclose the information required by this Item 5.05 through its website, such information must remain available on the website for at least a 12-month period. Following the 12-month period, the registrant must retain the information for a period of not less than five years. Upon request, the registrant must furnish to the Commission or its staff a copy of any or all information retained pursuant to this requirement.

Instructions:

1. The registrant does not need to disclose technical, administrative or other non-substantive amendments to its code of ethics.

2. For purposes of this Item 5.05:

(i) The term *waiver* means the approval by the registrant of a material departure from a provision of the code of ethics; and

(ii) The term *implicit waiver* means the registrant's failure to take action within a reasonable period of time regarding a material departure from a provision of the code of ethics that has been made known to an executive officer, as defined in Rule 3b–7 of the registrant.

Item 5.06 Change in Shell Company Status.

If a registrant that was a shell company, other than a business combination related shell company, as those terms are defined in Rule 12b–2 under the Exchange Act, has completed a transaction that has the effect of causing it to cease being a shell company, as defined in Rule 12b–2, disclose the material terms of the transaction. Notwithstanding General Instruction B.3. to Form 8–K, if any disclosure required by this Item 5.06 is previously reported, as that term is defined in Rule 12b–2 under the Exchange Act, the registrant may identify the filing in which that disclosure is included instead of including that disclosure in this report.

Item 5.07 Submission of Matters to a Vote of Security Holders.

If any matter was submitted to a vote of security holders, through the solicitation of proxies or otherwise, provide the following information:

(a) The date of the meeting and whether it was an annual or special meeting. This information must be provided only if a meeting of security holders was held.

(b) If the meeting involved the election of directors, the name of each director elected at the meeting, as well as a brief description of each other matter voted upon at the meeting; and state the number of votes cast for, against or withheld, as well as the number of abstentions and broker non-votes as to each such matter, including a separate tabulation with respect to each nominee for office. For the vote on the frequency of shareholder advisory votes on executive compensation required by section 14A(a)(2) of the Securities Exchange Act of 1934 and Rule 14a–21(b), state the number of votes cast for each of 1 year, 2 years, and 3 years, as well as the number of abstentions.

(c) A description of the terms of any settlement between the registrant and any other participant (as defined in Instruction 3 to Item 4 of Schedule 14A (Rule 14a–101)) terminating any solicitation subject to Rule 14a–12(c), including the cost or anticipated cost to the registrant.

(d) No later than one hundred fifty calendar days after the end of the annual or other meeting of shareholders at which shareholders voted on the frequency of shareholder votes on the compensation of executives as required by section 14A(a)(2) of the Securities Exchange Act of 1934, but in no event later than sixty calendar days prior to the deadline for submission of shareholder proposals under Rule 14a-8, as disclosed in the registrant's most recent proxy statement for an annual or other meeting of shareholders relating to the election of directors at which shareholders voted on the frequency of shareholder votes on the compensation of executives as required by section 14A(a)(2) of the Securities Exchange Act of 1934, by amendment to the most recent Form 8–K filed pursuant to (b) of this Item, disclose the company's decision in light of such vote as to how frequently the company will include a shareholder vote on the compensation of executives in its proxy materials until the next required vote on the frequency of shareholder votes on the compensation of executives.

Instructions to Item 5.07:

(1) The four business day period for reporting the event under this Item 5.07, other than with respect to Item 5.07(d), shall begin to run on the day on which the meeting ended.

(2) If any matter has been submitted to a vote of security holders otherwise than at a meeting of such security holders, corresponding information with respect to such submission shall be provided. The solicitation of any authorization or consent (other than a proxy to vote at a stockholders' meeting) with respect to any matter shall be deemed a submission of such matter to a vote of security holders within the meaning of this item.

(3) If the registrant did not solicit proxies and the board of directors as previously reported to the Commission was re-elected in its entirety, a statement to that effect in answer to paragraph (b) will suffice as an answer thereto regarding the election of directors.

(4) If the registrant has furnished to its security holders proxy soliciting material containing the information called for by paragraph (c), the paragraph may be answered by reference to the information contained in such material.

(5) A registrant may omit the information called for by this Item 5.07 if, on the date of the filing of its report on Form 8–K, the registrant meets the following conditions:

1. All of the registrant's equity securities are owned, either directly or indirectly, by a single person which is a reporting company under the Exchange Act and which has filed all the material required to be filed pursuant to Section 13, 14 or 15(d) thereof, as applicable; and

2. During the preceding thirty-six calendar months and any subsequent period of days, there has not been any material default in the payment of principal, interest, a sinking or purchase fund installment, or any other material default not cured within thirty days, with respect to any indebtedness of the registrant or its subsidiaries, and there has not been any material default in the payment of rentals under material long-term leases.

Item 5.08 Shareholder Director Nominations.

(a) If the registrant did not hold an annual meeting the previous year, or if the date of this year's annual meeting has been changed by more than 30 calendar days from the date of the previous year's meeting, then the registrant is required to disclose the date by which a nominating shareholder or nominating shareholder group must submit the notice on Schedule 14N required pursuant to Rule 14a–11(b)(10), which date shall be a reasonable time before the registrant mails its proxy materials for the meeting. Where a registrant is required to include shareholder director nominees in the registrant's proxy materials pursuant to either an applicable state or foreign law provision, or a provision in the registrant's governing documents, then the registrant is required to disclose the date by which a nominating shareholder or nominating shareholder group must submit the notice on Schedule 14N required pursuant to Rule 14a–18.

(b) If the registrant is a series company as defined in Rule 18f–2(a) under the Investment Company Act of 1940, then the registrant is required to disclose in connection with the election of directors at an annual meeting of shareholders (or, in lieu of such an annual meeting, a special meeting of shareholders) the total number of shares of the registrant outstanding and entitled to be voted (or if the votes are to be cast on a basis other than one vote per share, then the total number of votes entitled to be voted and the basis for allocating such votes) on the election of directors at such meeting of shareholders as of the end of the most recent calendar quarter.

Section 6. Asset-Backed Securities

The Items in this Section 6 apply only to asset-backed securities. Terms used in this Section 6 have the same meaning as in Item 1101 of Regulation AB.

Item 6.01 ABS Informational and Computational Material.

Report under this Item any ABS informational and computational material filed in, or as an exhibit to, this report.

Item 6.02 Change of Servicer or Trustee.

If a servicer contemplated by Item 1108(a)(2) of Regulation AB or a trustee has resigned or has been removed, replaced or substituted, or if a new servicer contemplated by Item 1108(a)(2) of Regulation AB or trustee has been appointed, state the date the event occurred and the circumstances surrounding the change. In addition, provide the disclosure required by Item 1108(d) of Regulation AB, as applicable, regarding the servicer or trustee change. If a new servicer contemplated by Item 1108(a)(3) of this Regulation AB or a new trustee has been appointed, provide the information required by Item 1108(b) through (d) of Regulation AB regarding such servicer or Item 1109 of Regulation AB regarding such trustee, as applicable.

Instruction:

To the extent that any information called for by this Item regarding such servicer or trustee is not determined or is unavailable at the time of the required filing, the registrant shall include a statement to this effect in the filing and then must file an amendment to its Form 8–K filing under this Item 6.02 containing such information within four business days after the information is determined or becomes available.

Item 6.03 Change in Credit Enhancement or Other External Support.

(a) *Loss of existing enhancement or support.* If the depositor (or servicer if the servicer signs the report on Form 10–K (17 CFR 249.310) of the issuing entity) becomes aware that any material enhancement or support specified in Item 1114(a)(1) through (3) of Regulation AB or Item 1115 of Regulation AB that was previously applicable regarding one or more classes of the asset-backed securities has terminated other than by expiration of the contract on its stated termination date or as a result of all parties completing their obligations under such agreement, then disclose:

(1) the date of the termination of the enhancement;

(2) the identity of the parties to the agreement relating to the enhancement or support;

(3) a brief description of the terms and conditions of the enhancement or support that are material to security holders;

(4) a brief description of the material circumstances surrounding the termination; and

(5) any material early termination penalties paid or to be paid out of the cash flows backing the asset-backed securities.

(b) *Addition of New Enhancement or Support.* If the depositor (or servicer if the servicer signs the report on Form 10–K (17 CFR 249.310) of the issuing entity) becomes aware that any material enhancement specified in Item 1114(a)(1) through (3) of Regulation AB or Item 1115 of Regulation AB has been added with respect to one or more classes of the asset-backed securities, then provide the date of addition of the new enhancement or support and the disclosure required by Items 1114 or 1115 of Regulation AB, as applicable, with respect to such new enhancement or support.

(c) *Material Change to Enhancement or Support.* If the depositor (or servicer if the servicer signs the report on Form 10–K (17 CFR 249.310) of the issuing entity) becomes aware that any existing material enhancement or support specified in Item 1114(a)(1) through (3) of Regulation AB or Item 1115 of Regulation AB with respect to one or more classes of the asset-backed securities has been materially amended or modified, disclose:

(1) the date on which the agreement or agreements relating to the enhancement or support was amended or modified;

(2) the identity of the parties to the agreement or agreements relating to the amendment or modification; and

(3) a brief description of the material terms and conditions of the amendment or modification.

Instructions:

1. Disclosure is required under this Item whether or not the registrant is a party to any agreement regarding the enhancement or support if the loss, addition or modification of such enhancement or support materially affects, directly or indirectly, the asset-backed securities, the pool assets or the cash flow underlying the asset-backed securities.

2. To the extent that any information called for by this Item regarding the enhancement or support is not determined or is unavailable at the time of the required filing, the registrant shall include a statement to this effect in the filing and then must file an amendment to its Form 8–K filing under this Item 6.03 containing such information within four business days after the information is determined or becomes available.

3. The instructions to Items 1.01 and 1.02 of this Form apply to this Item.

4. Notwithstanding Items 1.01 and 1.02 of this Form, disclosure regarding changes to material enhancement or support is to be reported under this Item 6.03 in lieu of those Items.

Item 6.04 Failure to Make a Required Distribution.

If a required distribution to holders of the asset-backed securities is not made as of the required distribution date under the transaction documents, and such failure is material, identify the failure and state the nature of the failure to make the timely distribution.

Item 6.05 Securities Act Updating Disclosure.

Regarding an offering of asset-backed securities registered on Form SF–3 (17 CFR 239.45), if any material pool characteristic of the actual asset pool at the time of issuance of the asset-backed securities differs by 5% or more (other than as a result of the pool assets converting into cash in accordance with their terms) from the description of the asset pool in the prospectus filed for the offering pursuant to Securities Act Rule 424, disclose the information required by Items 1111 and 1112 of Regulation AB regarding the characteristics of the actual asset pool. If applicable, also provide information required by Items 1108 and 1110 of Regulation AB regarding any new servicers or originators that would be required to be disclosed under those items regarding the pool assets.

Instruction:

No report is required under this Item if substantially the same information is provided in a post-effective amendment to the Securities Act registration statement or in a subsequent prospectus filed pursuant to Securities Act Rule 424.

Item 6.06 Static Pool

Regarding an offering of asset-backed securities registered on Form SF–1 (17 CFR 239.44) or Form SF–3 (17 CFR 239.45), in lieu of providing the static pool information as required by Item 1105 of Regulation AB in a form of prospectus or prospectus, an issuer may file the required information in this report or as an exhibit to this report. The static pool disclosure must be filed by the time of effectiveness of a registration statement on Form SF–1, by the same date of the filing of a form of prospectus, as required by Rule 424(h), and by the same date of the filing of a final prospectus meeting the requirements of section 10(a) of the Securities Act filed in accordance with Rule 424(b).

Instructions:

1. Refer to Item 601(b)(106) of Regulation S–K regarding the filing of exhibits to this Item 6.06.

2. Refer to Item 10 of Form SF–1 (17 CFR 239.44) or Item 10 of Form SF–3 (17 CFR 239.45) regarding incorporation by reference.

Section 7. Regulation FD

Item 7.01 Regulation FD Disclosure.

Unless filed under Item 8.01, disclose under this item only information that the registrant elects to disclose through Form 8–K pursuant to Regulation FD (17 CFR 243.100 through 243.103).

Section 8. Other Events

Item 8.01 Other Events.

The registrant may, at its option, disclose under this Item 8.01 any events, with respect to which information is not otherwise called for by this form, that the registrant deems of importance to security holders. The registrant may, at its option, file a report under this Item 8.01 disclosing the nonpublic information required to be disclosed by Regulation FD (17 CFR 243.100 through 243.103).

Section 9. Financial Statements and Exhibits

Item 9.01 Financial Statements and Exhibits.

List below the financial statements, pro forma financial information and exhibits, if any, filed as a part of this report.

(a) *Financial Statements of Businesses Acquired.*

(1) For any business acquisition required to be described in answer to Item 2.01 of this form, financial statements of the business acquired shall be filed for the periods specified in Rule 3–05(b) of Regulation S–X or Rule 8–04(b) of Regulation S–X for smaller reporting companies.

(2) The financial statements shall be prepared pursuant to Regulation S–X except that supporting schedules need not be filed. A manually signed accountant's report should be provided pursuant to Rule 2–02 of Regulation S–X.

(3) With regard to the acquisition of one or more real estate properties, the financial statements and any additional information specified by Rules 3–14 or Rule 8–06 of Regulation S–X for smaller reporting companies.

(4) Financial statements required by this item may be filed with the initial report, or by amendment not later than 71 calendar days after the date that the initial report on Form 8–K must be filed. If the financial statements are not included in the initial report, the registrant should so indicate in the Form 8–K report and state when the required financial statements will be filed. The registrant may, at its option, include unaudited financial statements in the initial report on Form 8–K.

(b) *Pro Forma Financial Information.*

(1) For any transaction required to be described in answer to Item 2.01 of this form, furnish any pro forma financial information that would be required pursuant to Article 11 of Regulation S–X (17 CFR 210) or Rule 8–05 of Regulation S–X for smaller reporting companies.

(2) The provisions of paragraph (a)(4) of this Item 9.01 shall also apply to pro forma financial information relative to the acquired business.

(c) *Shell Company Transactions.* The provisions of paragraph (a)(4) and (b)(2) of this Item shall not apply to the financial statements or pro forma financial information required to be filed under this Item with regard to any transaction required to be described in answer to Item 2.01 of this Form by a registrant that was a shell company, other than a business combination related shell company, as those terms are defined in Rule 12b–2 under the Exchange Act immediately before that transaction. Accordingly, with regard to any transaction required to be described in answer to Item 2.01 of this Form by a registrant that was a shell company, other than a business combination related shell company, immediately before that transaction, the financial statements and pro forma financial information required by this Item must be filed in the initial report. Notwithstanding General Instruction B.3. to Form 8–K, if any financial statement or any financial information required to be filed in the initial report by this Item 9.01(c) is previously reported, as that term is defined in Rule 12b–2 under the Exchange Act, the registrant may identify the filing in which that disclosure is included instead of including that disclosure in the initial report.

(d) *Exhibits.* The exhibits shall be deemed to be filed or furnished, depending upon the relevant item requiring such exhibit, in accordance with the provisions of Item 601 of Regulation S–K and Instruction B.2 to this form.

Instruction:

During the period after a registrant has reported a business combination pursuant to Item 2.01 of this form, until the date on which the financial statements specified by this Item 9.01 must be filed, the registrant will be deemed current for purposes of its reporting obligations under Section 13(a) or 15(d) of the Exchange Act. With respect to filings under the Securities Act, however, registration statements will not be declared effective and post-effective amendments to registrations statements will not be declared effective unless financial statements meeting the requirements of Rule 3–05 of Regulation S–X are provided. In addition, offerings should not be made pursuant to effective registration statements, or pursuant to Rule 506 of Regulation D where any purchasers are not accredited investors under Rule 501(a) of that Regulation, until the audited financial statements required by Rule 3–05 of Regulation S–X are filed; *provided, however*, that the following offerings or sales of securities may proceed notwithstanding that financial statements of the acquired business have not been filed:

(a) offerings or sales of securities upon the conversion of outstanding convertible securities or upon the exercise of outstanding warrants or rights;

(b) dividend or interest reinvestment plans;

(c) employee benefit plans;

(d) transactions involving secondary offerings; or

(e) sales of securities pursuant to Rule 144 (17 CFR 230.144).

SIGNATURES

Pursuant to the requirements of the Securities Exchange Act of 1934, the registrant has duly caused this report to be signed on its behalf by the undersigned hereunto duly authorized.

_______________________________ _______________________________

(Registrant) Date

____

(Signature)*

* Print name and title of the signing officer under his signature.

UNITED STATES
SECURITIES AND EXCHANGE COMMISSION
Washington, DC 20549

FORM TCR

TIP, COMPLAINT OR REFERRAL

A. INFORMATION ABOUT YOU

COMPLAINANT 1: 1. Last Name		First	M.I.
2. Street Address			Apartment/ Unit #
City	State/ Province	ZIP/ Postal Code	Country
3. Telephone	Alt. Phone	E-mail Address	Preferred method of communication
4. Occupation			
COMPLAINANT 2: 1. Last Name		First	M.I.
2. Street Address			Apartment/ Unit #
City	State/ Province	ZIP/ Postal Code	Country
3. Telephone	Alt. Phone	E-mail Address	Preferred method of communication
4. Occupation			

B. ATTORNEY'S INFORMATION (If Applicable - See Instructions)

1. Attorney's Name			
2. Firm Name			
3. Street Address			
City	State/ Province	ZIP/ Postal Code	Country
4. Telephone	Fax	E-mail Address	

C. TELL US ABOUT THE INDIVIDUAL OR ENTITY YOU HAVE A COMPLAINT AGAINST

INDIVIDUAL/ENTITY 1:

1. Type: ☐ Individual ☐ Entity

If an individual, specify profession:

If an entity, specify type:

2. Name

3. Street Address | Apartment/ Unit #

City | State/ Province | ZIP/ Postal Code | Country

4. Phone | E-mail Address | Internet address

INDIVIDUAL/ENTITY 2:

1. Type: ☐ Individual ☐ Entity

If an individual, specify profession:

If an entity, specify type:

2. Name

3. Street Address | Apartment/ Unit #

City | State/ Province | ZIP/ Postal Code | Country

4. Phone | E-mail Address | Internet Address

D. TELL US ABOUT YOUR COMPLAINT

1. Occurrence Date (mm/dd/yyyy): / /

2. Nature of complaint:

3a. Has the complainant or counsel had any prior communication(s) with the SEC concerning this matter? YES ☐ NO ☐

3b. If the answer to 3a is "Yes," name of SEC staff member with whom the complainant or counsel communicated

4a. Has the complainant or counsel provided the information to any other agency or organization, or has any other agency or organization requested the information or related information from you?

YES ☐ NO ☐

4b. If the answer to 4a is "Yes," please provide details. Use additional sheets if necessary.

4c. Name and contact information for point of contact at agency or organization, if known

5a. Does this complaint relate to an entity of which the complainant is or was an officer, director, counsel, employee, consultant or contractor?
YES ☐ NO ☐

5b. If the answer to question 5a is "yes," has the complainant reported this violation to his or her supervisor, compliance office, whistleblower hotline, ombudsman, or any other available mechanism at the entity for reporting violations? YES ☐ NO ☐

5c. If the answer to question 5b is "yes," please provide details. Use additional sheets if necessary.

5d. Date on which the complainant took the action(s) described in question 5b (mm/dd/yyyy): / /

6a. Has the complainant taken any other action regarding your complaint? YES ☐ NO ☐

6b. If the answer to question 6a is "yes," please provide details. Use additional sheets if necessary.

7a. Type of security or investment, if relevant

7b. Name of issuer or security, if relevant

7c. Security/ Ticker Symbol or CUSIP no.

8. State in detail all facts pertinent to the alleged violation. Explain why the complainant believes the acts described constitute a violation of the federal securities laws. Use additional sheets if necessary.

9. Describe all supporting materials in the complainant's possession and the availability and location of any additional supporting materials not in complainant's possession. Use additional sheets, if necessary.

10. Describe how and from whom the complainant obtained the information that supports this claim. If any information was obtained from an attorney or in a communication where an attorney was present, identify such information with as much particularity as possible. In addition, if any information was obtained from a public source, identify the source with as much particularity as possible. Attach additional sheets if necessary.

11. Identify with particularity any documents or other information in your submission that you believe could reasonably be expected to reveal your identity and explain the basis for your belief that your identity would be revealed if the documents were disclosed to a third party.

12. Provide any additional information you think may be relevant.

E. ELIGIBILITY REQUIREMENTS AND OTHER INFORMATION

1. Are you, or were you at the time you acquired the original information you are submitting to us, a member, officer or employee of the Department of Justice, the Securities and Exchange Commission, the Comptroller of the Currency, the Board of Governors of the Federal Reserve System, the Federal Deposit Insurance Corporation, the Office of Thrift Supervision; the Public Company Accounting Oversight Board; any law enforcement organization; or any national securities exchange, registered securities association, registered clearing agency, or the Municipal Securities Rulemaking Board?

YES ☐ NO ☐

2. Are you, or were you at the time you acquired the original information you are submitting to us, a member, officer or employee of a foreign government, any political subdivision, department, agency, or instrumentality of a foreign government, or any other foreign financial regulatory authority as that term is defined in Section 3(a)(52) of the Securities Exchange Act of 1934 (15 U.S.C. §78c(a)(52))?

YES ☐ NO ☐

3. Did you acquire the information being provided to us through the performance of an engagement required under the federal securities laws by an independent public accountant?

YES ☐ NO ☐

4. Are you providing this information pursuant to a cooperation agreement with the SEC or another agency or organization?

YES ☐ NO ☐

5. Are you a spouse, parent, child, or sibling of a member or employee of the SEC, or do you reside in the same household as a member or employee of the SEC?

YES ☐ NO ☐

6. Are you providing this information before you (or anyone representing you) received any request, inquiry or demand that relates to the subject matter of your submission (i) from the SEC, (ii) in connection with an investigation, inspection or examination by the Public Company Accounting Oversight Board, or any self-regulatory organization; or (iii) in connection with an investigation by the Congress, any other authority of the federal government, or a state Attorney General or securities regulatory authority?

YES ☐ NO ☐

7. Are you currently a subject or target of a criminal investigation, or have you been convicted of a criminal violation, in connection with the information you are submitting to the SEC?

YES ☐ NO ☐

8. Did you acquire the information being provided to us from any person described in questions E1 through E7?

YES ☐ NO ☐

9. Use this space to provide additional details relating to your responses to questions 1 through 8. Use additional sheets if necessary.

F. WHISTLEBLOWER'S DECLARATION

I declare under penalty of perjury under the laws of the United States that the information contained herein is true, correct and complete to the best of my knowledge, information and belief. I fully understand that I may be subject to prosecution and ineligible for a whistleblower award if, in my submission of information, my other dealings with the SEC, or my dealings with another authority in connection with a related action, I knowingly and willfully make any false, fictitious, or fraudulent statements or representations, or use any false writing or document knowing that the writing or document contains any false, fictitious, or fraudulent statement or entry.

Print name	
Signature	Date

G. COUNSEL CERTIFICATION

I certify that I have reviewed this form for completeness and accuracy and that the information contained herein is true, correct and complete to the best of my knowledge, information and belief. I further certify that I have verified the identity of the whistleblower on whose behalf this form is being submitted by viewing the whistleblower's valid, unexpired government issued identification (*e.g.*, driver's license, passport) and will retain an original, signed copy of this form, with Section F signed by the whistleblower, in my records. I further certify that I have obtained the whistleblower's non-waiveable consent to provide the Commission with his or her original signed Form TCR upon request in the event that the Commission requests it due to concerns that the whistleblower may have knowingly and willfully made false, fictitious, or fraudulent statements or representations, or used any false writing or document knowing that the writing or document contains any false fictitious or fraudulent statement or entry; and that I consent to be legally obligated to do so within 7 calendar days of receiving such a request from the Commission.

Signature	Date

SUBMISSION PROCEDURES

• After manually completing this Form TCR, please send it by mail or delivery to the SEC Office of the Whistleblower, 100 F. Street, NE, Washington, DC 20549, or by facsimile to (703) 813–9322.

• You have the right to submit information anonymously. If you are submitting anonymously and you want to be considered for a whistleblower award, however, you *must* be represented by an attorney in this matter and Section B of this form must be completed. Otherwise, you may, but are not required, to have an attorney. If you are not represented by an attorney in this matter, you may leave Section B blank.

• If you are submitting information for the SEC's whistleblower award program, you *must* submit your information either using this Form TCR or electronically through the SEC's Electronic Data Collection System, available on the SEC web site at [insert link].

INSTRUCTIONS FOR COMPLETING FORM TCR:

Section A: Information about You

Questions 1–3: Please provide the following information about yourself:

- Last name, first name, and middle initial
- Complete address, including city, state and zip code
- Telephone number and, if available, an alternate number where you can be reached
- Your e-mail address (to facilitate communications, we strongly encourage you to provide your email address),
- Your preferred method of communication; and
- Your occupation

Section B: Information about Your Attorney. Complete this section only if you are represented by an attorney in this matter. You must be represented by an attorney, and this section must be completed, if you are submitting your information anonymously and you want to be considered for the SEC's whistleblower award program.

Questions 1–4: Provide the following information about the attorney representing you in this matter:

- Attorney's name
- Firm name
- Complete address, including city, state and zip code
- Telephone number and fax number, and
- E-mail address

Section C: Tell Us about the Individual and/or Entity You Have a Complaint Against. If your complaint relates to more than two individuals and/or entities, you may attach additional sheets.

Question 1: Choose one of the following that best describes the individual or entity to which your complaint relates:

• **For Individuals**: accountant, analyst, attorney, auditor, broker, compliance officer, employee, executive officer or director, financial planner, fund manager, investment advisor representative, stock promoter, trustee, unknown, or other (specify).

• **For Entity**: bank, broker-dealer, clearing agency, day trading firm, exchange, Financial Industry Regulatory Authority, insurance company, investment advisor, investment advisor representative, investment company, Individual Retirement Account or 401(k) custodian/administrator, market maker, municipal securities dealers, mutual fund, newsletter company/investment publication company, on-line trading firm, private fund company (including hedge fund, private equity fund, venture capital fund, or real estate fund), private/closely held company, publicly held company, transfer agent/paying agent/registrar, underwriter, unknown, or other (specify).

Questions 2–4: For each subject, provide the following information, if known:

- Full name
- Complete address, including city, state and zip code
- Telephone number,
- E-mail address, and
- Internet address, if applicable

Section D: Tell Us about Your Complaint

Question 1: State the date (mm/dd/yyyy) that the alleged conduct began.

Question 2: Choose the option that you believe best describes the nature of your complaint. If you are alleging more than one violation, please list all that you believe may apply. Use additional sheets if necessary.

• Theft/misappropriation (advance fee fraud; lost or stolen securities; hacking of account)

• Misrepresentation/omission (false/misleading marketing/sales literature; inaccurate, misleading or non-disclosure by Broker–Dealer, Investment Adviser and Associated Person; false/material misstatements in firm research that were basis of transaction)

• Offering fraud (Ponzi/pyramid scheme; other offering fraud)

• Registration violations (unregistered securities offering)

• Trading (after hours trading; algorithmic trading; front-running; insider trading, manipulation of securities/prices; market timing; inaccurate quotes/pricing information; program trading; short selling; trading suspensions; volatility)

• Fees/mark-ups/commissions (excessive or unnecessary administrative fees; excessive commissions or sales fees; failure to disclose fees; insufficient notice of change in fees; negotiated fee problems; excessive mark-ups/markdowns; excessive or otherwise improper spreads)

• Corporate disclosure/reporting/other issuer matter (audit; corporate governance; conflicts of interest by management; executive compensation; failure to notify shareholders of corporate events; false/misleading financial statements, offering documents, press releases, proxy materials; failure to file reports; financial fraud; Foreign Corrupt Practices Act violations; going private transactions; mergers and acquisitions; restrictive legends, including 144 issues; reverse stock splits; selective disclosure—Regulation FD, 17 CFR 243; shareholder proposals; stock options for employees; stock splits; tender offers)

• Sales and advisory practices (background information on past violations/integrity; breach of fiduciary duty/responsibility (IA); failure to disclose breakpoints; churning/excessive trading; cold calling; conflict of interest; abuse of authority in discretionary trading; failure to respond to investor; guarantee against loss/promise to buy back shares; high pressure sales techniques; instructions by client not followed; investment objectives not followed; margin; poor investment advice; Regulation E (Electronic Transfer Act); Regulation S–P, 17 CFR 248, (privacy issues); solicitation methods (non-cold calling; seminars); suitability; unauthorized transactions)

• Operational (bond call; bond default); difficulty buying/selling securities; confirmations/statements; proxy materials/prospectus; delivery of funds/proceeds; dividend and interest problems; exchanges/switches of mutual funds with fund family; margin (illegal extension of margin credit, Regulation T restrictions, unauthorized margin transactions); online issues (trading system operation); settlement (including T+1 or T=3 concerns); stock certificates; spam; tax reporting problems; titling securities (difficulty titling ownership); trade execution.

• Customer accounts (abandoned or inactive accounts; account administration and processing; identity theft affecting account; IPOs: problems with IPO allocation or eligibility; inaccurate valuation of Net Asset Value; transfer of account)

• Comments/complaints about SEC, Self–Regulatory Organization, and Securities Investor Protection Corporation processes & programs (arbitration: bias by arbitrators/forum, failure to pay/comply with award, mandatory arbitration requirements, procedural problems or delays); SEC: complaints about enforcement actions, complaints about rulemaking, failure to act; Self–Regulatory Organization: failure to act; Investor Protection: inadequacy of laws or rules; SIPC: customer protection, proceedings and Broker-Dealer liquidations;

• Other (analyst complaints; market maker activities; employer/employee disputes; specify other).

Question 3a: State whether you or your counsel have had any prior communications with the SEC concerning this matter.

Question 3b: If the answer to question 3a is yes, provide the name of the SEC staff member with whom you or your counsel communicated.

Question 4a: Indicate whether you or your counsel have provided the information you are providing to the SEC to any other agency or organization.

Question 4b: If the answer to question 4a is yes, provide details.

Question 4c: Provide the name and contact information of the point of contact at the other agency or organization, if known.

Question 5a: Indicate whether your complaint relates to an entity of which you are, or were in the past, an officer, director, counsel, employee, consultant, or contractor.

Question 5b: If the answer to question 5a is yes, state whether you have reported this violation to your supervisor, compliance office, whistleblower hotline, ombudsman, or any other available mechanism at the entity for reporting violations.

Question 5c: If the answer to question 5b is yes, provide details.

Question 5d: Provide the date on which you took the actions described in questions 5a and 5b.

Question 6a: Indicate whether you have taken any other action regarding your complaint, including whether you complained to the SEC, another regulator, a law enforcement agency, or any other agency or organization; initiated legal action, mediation or arbitration, or initiated any other action.

Question 6b: If you answered yes to question 6a, provide details, including the date on which you took the action(s) described, the name of the person or entity to whom you directed any report or complaint and contact information for the person or entity, if known, and the complete case name, case number, and forum of any legal action you have taken. Use additional sheets if necessary.

Question 7a: Choose from the following the option that you believe best describes the type of security or investment at issue, if applicable:

• 1031 exchanges

• 529 plans

• American Depositary Receipts

• Annuities (equity-indexed annuities, fixed annuities, variable annuities)

• Asset-backed securities

• Auction rate securities

• Banking products (including credit cards)

• Certificates of deposit (CDs)

• Closed-end funds

• Coins and precious metals (gold, silver, etc.)

• Collateralized mortgage obligations (CMOs)

• Commercial paper

• Commodities (currency transactions, futures, stock index options)

• Convertible securities

• Debt (corporate, lower-rated or "junk," municipal)

• Equities (exchange-traded, foreign, Over-the-Counter, unregistered, linked notes)

• Exchange Traded Funds

• Franchises or business ventures

• Hedge funds

• Insurance contracts (not annuities)

• Money-market funds

• Mortgage-backed securities (mortgages, reverse mortgages)

• Mutual funds

- Options (commodity options, index options)
- Partnerships
- Preferred shares
- Prime bank securities/high yield programs
- Promissory notes
- Real estate (real estate investment trusts (REITs))
- Retirement plans (401(k), IRAs)
- Rights and warrants
- Structured note products
- Subprime issues
- Treasury securities
- U.S. government agency securities
- Unit investment trusts (UIT)
- Viaticals and life settlements
- Wrap accounts
- Separately Managed Accounts (SMAs)
- Unknown
- Other (specify)

Question 7b: Provide the name of the issuer or security, if applicable.

Question 7c: Provide the ticker symbol or CUSIP number of the security, if applicable.

Question 8: State in detail all the facts pertinent to the alleged violation. Explain why you believe the facts described constitute a violation of the federal securities laws. Attach additional sheets if necessary.

Question 9: Describe all supporting materials in your possession and the availability and location of additional supporting materials not in your possession. Attach additional sheets if necessary.

Question 10: Describe how you obtained the information that supports your allegation. If any information was obtained from an attorney or in a communication where an attorney was present, identify such information with as much particularity as possible. In addition, if any information was obtained from a public source, identify the source with as much particularity as possible. Attach additional sheets if necessary.

Question 11: You may use this space to identify any documents or other information in your submission that you believe could reasonably be expected to reveal your identity. Explain the basis for your belief that your identity would be revealed if the documents or information were disclosed to a third party.

Question 12: Provide any additional information you think may be relevant.

Section E: Eligibility Requirements

Question 1: State whether you are currently, or were at the time you acquired the original information that you are submitting to the SEC, a member, officer, or employee of the Department of Justice; the Securities and Exchange Commission; the Comptroller of the Currency, the Board of Governors of the Federal Reserve System, the Federal Deposit Insurance Corporation, the Office of Thrift Supervision; the Public Company Accounting Oversight Board; any law enforcement organization; or any national securities exchange, registered securities association, registered clearing agency, the Municipal Securities Rulemaking Board.

Question 2: State whether you are, or were you at the time you acquired the original information you are submitting to the SEC, a member, officer or employee of a foreign government, any political subdivision, department, agency, or instrumentality of a foreign government, or any other foreign financial regulatory authority as that term is defined in Section 3(a)(52) of the Securities Exchange Act of 1934.

- Section 3(a)(52) of the Exchange Act currently defines "foreign financial regulatory authority" as "any (A) foreign securities authority, (B) other governmental body or foreign equivalent of a self-regulatory organization empowered by a foreign government to administer or enforce its laws relating to the regulation of fiduciaries, trusts, commercial lending, insurance, trading in contracts of sale of a commodity for future delivery, or other instruments traded on or subject to the rules of a contract market, board of trade, or foreign equivalent, or other financial activities, or (C) membership organization a function of which is to regulate participation of its members in activities listed above."

Question 3: State whether you acquired the information you are providing to the SEC through the performance of an engagement required under the securities laws by an independent public accountant.

Question 4: State whether you are providing the information pursuant to a cooperation agreement with the SEC or with any other agency or organization.

Question 5: State whether you are a spouse, parent, child or sibling of a member or employee of the SEC, or whether you reside in the same household as a member or employee of the SEC.

Question 6: State whether you acquired the information you are providing to the SEC from any individual described in Question 1 through 5 of this Section.

Question 7: If you answered "yes" to questions 1 though 6, please provide details.

Question 8a: State whether you are providing the information you are submitting to the SEC before you (or anyone representing you) received any request, inquiry or demand that relates to the subject matter of your submission in connection with: (i) an investigation, inspection or examination by the SEC, the Public Company Accounting Oversight Board, or any self-regulatory organization; or (ii) an investigation by Congress, or any other authority of the federal government, or a state Attorney General or securities regulatory authority?

Question 8b: If you answered "no" to questions 8a, please provide details. Use additional sheets if necessary.

Question 9a: State whether you are the subject or target of a criminal investigation or have been convicted of a criminal violation in connection with the information you are submitting to the SEC.

Question 9b: If you answered "yes" to question 9a, please provide details, including the name of the agency or organization that conducted the investigation or initiated the action against you, the name and telephone number of your point of contact at the agency or organization, if available and the investigation/case name and number, if applicable. Use additional sheets, if necessary.

Section F: Whistleblower's Declaration

You must sign this Declaration if you are submitting this information pursuant to the SEC whistleblower program and wish to be considered for an award. If you are submitting your information anonymously, you must still sign this Declaration, and you must provide your attorney with the original of this signed form.

If you are not submitting your information pursuant to the SEC whistleblower program, you do not need to sign this Declaration.

Section G: Counsel Certification

If you are submitting this information pursuant to the SEC whistleblower program and are doing so anonymously, your attorney must sign the Counsel Certification section.

If you are represented in this matter but you are not submitting your information pursuant to the SEC whistleblower program, your attorney does not need to sign the Counsel Certification Section.

UNITED STATES
SECURITIES AND EXCHANGE COMMISSION
Washington, DC 20549

FORM WB–APP

APPLICATION FOR AWARD FOR ORIGINAL INFORMATION SUBMITTED PURSUANT TO SECTION 21F OF THE SECURITIES EXCHANGE ACT OF 1934

A. APPLICANT'S INFORMATION (REQUIRED FOR ALL SUBMISSIONS)

1. Last Name	First	M.I.	Social Security No.
2. Street Address			Apartment/ Unit #
City	State/ Province	ZIP Code	Country
3. Telephone	Alt. Phone	E-mail Address	

B. ATTORNEY'S INFORMATION (IF APPLICABLE – SEE INSTRUCTIONS)

1. Attorney's name			
2. Firm Name			
3. Street Address			
City	State/ Province	ZIP Code	Country
4. Telephone	Fax	E-mail Address	

C. TIP/COMPLAINT DETAILS

1. Manner in which original information was submitted to SEC:	SEC website ☐ Mail ☐ Fax ☐ Other ☐ ________
2a. Tip, Complaint or Referral number	2b. Date TCR referred to in 2a submitted to SEC / /
2c. Subject(s) of the Tip, Complaint or Referral:	

D. NOTICE OF COVERED ACTION

1. Date of Notice of Covered Action to which claim relates: / /	2. Notice Number:
3a. Case Name	3b. Case Number

E. CLAIMS PERTAINING TO RELATED ACTIONS

1. Name of agency or organization to which you provided your information	
2. Name and contact information for point of contact at agency or organization, if known.	
3a. Date you provided your information / /	3b. Date action filed by agency/organization / /
4a. Case Name	4b. Case number

F. ELIGIBILITY REQUIREMENTS AND OTHER INFORMATION

1. Are you, or were you at the time you acquired the original information you submitted to us, a member, officer or employee of the Department of Justice, the Securities and Exchange Commission, the Comptroller of the Currency, the Board of Governors of the Federal Reserve System, the Federal Deposit Insurance Corporation, the Office of Thrift Supervision; the Public Company Accounting Oversight Board; any law enforcement organization; or any national securities exchange, registered securities association, registered clearing agency, the Municipal Securities Rulemaking Board?

YES ☐ NO ☐

2. Are you, or were you at the time you acquired the original information you submitted to us, a member, officer or employee of a foreign government, any political subdivision, department, agency, or instrumentality of a foreign government, or any other foreign financial regulatory authority as that term is defined in Section 3(a)(52) of the Securities Exchange Act of 1934 (15 U.S.C. §78c(a)(52))?	YES ☐ NO ☐
3. Did you obtain the information you are providing to us through the performance of an engagement required under the federal securities laws by an independent public accountant?	YES ☐ NO ☐
4. Did you provide the information identified in Section C above pursuant to a cooperation agreement with the SEC or another agency or organization?	YES ☐ NO ☐
5. Are you a spouse, parent, child, or sibling of a member or employee of the Commission, or do you reside in the same household as a member or employee of the Commission?	YES ☐ NO ☐
6. Did you acquire the information you are providing to us from any person described in questions F1 through F5?	YES ☐ NO ☐
7. If you answered "yes" to any of questions 1 through 6 above, please provide details. Use additional sheets if necessary.	
8a. Did you provide the information identified in Section C above before you (or anyone representing you) received any request, inquiry or demand that relates to the subject matter of your submission (i) from the SEC, (ii) in connection with an investigation, inspection or examination by the Public Company Accounting Oversight Board, or any self-regulatory organization; or (iii) in connection with an investigation by the Congress, any other authority of the federal government, or a state Attorney General or securities regulatory authority?	YES ☐ NO ☐
8b. If you answered "yes" to question 8a, please provide details. Use additional sheets if necessary.	
9a. Are you currently a subject or target of a criminal investigation, or have you been convicted of a criminal violation, in connection with the information upon which your application for an award is based?	YES ☐ NO ☐
9b. If you answered "Yes" to question 9a, please provide details. Use additional sheets if necessary.	

G. ENTITLEMENT TO AWARD

Explain the basis for your belief that you are entitled to an award in connection with your submission of information to us, or to another agency in a related action. Provide any additional information you think may be relevant in light of the criteria for determining the amount of an award set forth in Rule 21F-6 under the Securities Exchange Act of 1934. Include any supporting documents in your possession or control, and attach additional sheets, if necessary.

H. DECLARATION

I declare under penalty of perjury under the laws of the United States that the information contained herein is true, correct and complete to the best of my knowledge, information and belief. I fully understand that I may be subject to prosecution and ineligible for a whistleblower award if, in my submission of information, my other dealings with the SEC, or my dealings with another authority in connection with a related action, I knowingly and willfully make any false, fictitious, or fraudulent statements or representations, or use any false writing or document knowing that the writing or document contains any false, fictitious, or fraudulent statement or entry.

Signature	Date

GENERAL

• This form should be used by persons making a claim for a whistleblower award in connection with information provided to the SEC or to another agency in a related action. In order to be deemed eligible for an award, you must meet all the requirements set forth in Section 21F of the Securities Exchange Act of 1934 and the rules thereunder.

• You must sign the Form WB–APP as the claimant. If you provided your information to the SEC anonymously, you must now disclose your identity on this form and your identity must be verified in a form and manner that is acceptable to the Office of the Whistleblower prior to the payment of any award.

○ If you are filing your claim in connection with information that you provided to the SEC, then your Form WB–APP, and any attachments thereto, **must be received by the SEC Office of the Whistleblower within sixty (60) days of the date of the Notice of Covered Action to which the claim relates.**

○ If you are filing your claim in connection with information you provided to another agency in a related action, then your Form WB–APP, and any attachments there to, must be received by the SEC Office of the Whistleblower as follows:

• If a final order imposing monetary sanctions has been entered in a related action at the time you submit your claim for an award in connection with a Commission action, **you must submit your claim for an award in that related action on the same Form WB–APP that you use for the Commission action.**

• If a final order imposing monetary sanctions in a related action has not been entered at the time you submit your claim for an award in connection with a Commission action, **you must submit your claim on Form WB–APP within sixty (60) days of the issuance of a final order imposing sanctions in the related action.**

• You must submit your Form WB–APP to us in one of the following two ways:

○ By mailing or delivering the signed form to the SEC Office of the Whistleblower, 100 F Street NE, Washington, DC 20549–5631; or

○ By faxing the signed form to (703) 813–9322.

Instructions for Completing Form WB–APP

Section A: Applicant's Information

Questions 1–3: Provide the following information about yourself:

- First and last name, and middle initial
- Complete address, including city, state and zip code
- Telephone number and, if available, an alternate number where you can be reached
- E-mail address

Section B: Attorney's Information

If you are represented by an attorney in this matter, provide the information requested. If you are not representing an attorney in this matter, leave this Section blank.

Questions 1–4: Provide the following information about the attorney representing you in this matter:

- Attorney's name
- Firm name
- Complete address, including city, state and zip code
- Telephone number and fax number, and
- E-mail address.

Section C: Tip/Complaint Details

Question 1: Indicate the manner in which your original information was submitted to the SEC.

Question 2a: Include the TCR (Tip, Complaint or Referral) number to which this claim relates.

Question 2b: Provide the date on which you submitted your information to the SEC.

Question 2c: Provide the name of the individual(s) or entity(s) to which your complaint related.

Section D: Notice of Covered Action

The process for making a claim for a whistleblower award begins with the publication of a "Notice of a Covered Action" on the Commission's website. This notice is published whenever a judicial or administrative action brought by the Commission results in the imposition of monetary sanctions exceeding $1,000,000. The Notice is published on the Commission's website subsequent to the entry of a final judgment or order in the action that by itself, or collectively with other judgments or orders previously entered in the action, exceeds the $1,000,000 threshold.

Question 1: Provide the date of the Notice of Covered Action to which this claim relates.

Question 2: Provide the notice number of the Notice of Covered Action.

Question 3a: Provide the case name referenced in Notice of Covered Action.

Question 3b: Provide the case number referenced in Notice of Covered Action.

Section E: Claims Pertaining to Related Actions

Question 1: Provide the name of the agency or organization to which you provided your information.

Question 2: Provide the name and contact information for your point of contact at the agency or organization, if known.

Question 3a: Provide the date on which that you provided your information to the agency or organization referenced in question E1.

Question 3b: Provide the date on which the agency or organization referenced in question E1 filed the related action that was based upon the information you provided.

Question 4a: Provide the case name of the related action.

Question 4b: Provide the case number of the related action.

Section F: Eligibility Requirements

Question 1: State whether you are currently, or were at the time you acquired the original information that you submitted to the SEC a member, officer, or employee of the Department of Justice; the Securities and Exchange Commission; the Comptroller of the Currency, the Board of Governors of the Federal Reserve System, the Federal Deposit Insurance Corporation, the Office of Thrift Supervision; the Public Company Accounting Oversight Board; any law enforcement organization; or any national securities exchange, registered securities association, registered clearing agency, the Municipal Securities Rulemaking Board Congress, or any other federal, state or local authority, or any self regulatory organization, or the Public Company Accounting Oversight Board about a matter to which the information your submission was relevant.

Question 2: State whether you are, or were you at the time you acquired the original information you submitted to the SEC, a member, officer or employee of a foreign government, any political subdivision, department, agency, or instrumentality of a foreign government, or any other foreign financial regulatory authority as that term is defined in Section 3(a)(52) of the Securities Exchange Act of 1934.

- Section 3(a)(52) of the Exchange Act currently defines "foreign financial regulatory authority" as "any (A) foreign securities authority, (B) other governmental body or foreign equivalent of a self-regulatory organization empowered by a foreign government to administer or enforce its laws relating to the regulation of fiduciaries, trusts, commercial lending, insurance, trading in contracts of sale of a commodity for future delivery, or other instruments traded on or subject to the rules of a contract market, board of trade, or foreign equivalent, or other financial activities, or (C) membership organization a function of which is to regulate participation of its members in activities listed above."

Question 3: Indicate whether you acquired the information you provided to the SEC through the performance of an engagement required under the securities laws by an independent public accountant.

Question 4: State whether you provided the information submitted to the SEC pursuant to a cooperation agreement with the SEC or with any other agency or organization.

Question 5: State whether you are a spouse, parent, child or sibling of a member or employee of the Commission, or whether you reside in the same household as a member or employee of the Commission.

Question 6: State whether you acquired the information you are providing to the SEC from any individual described in Question 1 through 5 of this Section.

Question 7: If you answered "yes" to questions 1 though 6, please provide details.

Question 8a: State whether you provided the information identified submitted to the SEC before you (or anyone representing you) received any request, inquiry or demand from the SEC.

Question 8b: If you answered "no" to questions 8a, please provide details. Use additional sheets if necessary.

Question 9a: State whether you are the subject or target of a criminal investigation or have been convicted of a criminal violation in connection with the information upon which your application for award is based.

Question 9b: If you answered "yes" to question 9a, please provide details, including the name of the agency or organization that conducted the investigation or initiated the action against you, the name and telephone number of your point of contact at the agency or organization, if available and the investigation/case name and number, if applicable. Use additional sheets, if necessary. If you previously provided this information on Form WB–DEC, you may leave this question blank, unless your response has changed since the time you submitted your Form WB–DEC.

Section G: Entitlement to Award

This section is optional. Use this section to explain the basis for your belief that you are entitled to an award in connection with your submission of information to us or to another agency in connection with a related action. Specifically address how you believe you voluntarily provided the Commission with original information that led to the successful enforcement of a judicial or administrative action filed by the Commission, or a related action. Refer to Rules 21F–3 and 21F–4 under the Exchange Act for further information concerning the relevant award criteria. You may attach additional sheets, if necessary. Rule 21F–6 under the Exchange Act provides that in determining the amount of an award, the Commission will evaluate the following factors: (a) the significance of the information provided by a whistleblower to the success of the Commission action or related action; (b) the degree of assistance provided by the whistleblower and any legal representative of the whistleblower in the Commission action or related action; (c) the programmatic interest of the Commission in deterring violations of the securities laws by making awards to whistleblowers who provide information that leads to the successful enforcement of such laws; and (d) whether the award otherwise enhances the Commission's ability to enforce the federal securities laws, protect investors, and encourage the submission of high quality information from whistleblowers. Address these factors in your response as well. Additional information about the criteria the Commission may consider in determining the amount of an award is available on the Commission's website at [insert WBO web page address]

Section H: Declaration

This section must be signed by the claimant.

C. INVESTMENT COMPANY ACT OF 1940

15 U.S.C. § 80a–1 et seq.

Section Act	15 U.S.C.	
1	80a–1	Findings and Declaration of Policy
2	80a–2	Definitions
3	80a–3	Definition of Investment Company
4	80a–4	Classification of Investment Companies
5	80a–5	Subclassification of Management Companies
6	80a–6	Exemptions
7	80a–7	Transactions by Unregistered Investment Companies
8	80a–8	Registration of Investment Companies
9	80a–9	Ineligibility of Certain Affiliated Persons and Underwriters
10	80a–10	Affiliations or Interest of Directors, Officers, and Employees
11	80a–11	Offers to Exchange Securities
12	80a–12	Functions and Activities of Investment Companies
13	80a–13	Changes in Investment Policy
14	80a–14	Size of Investment Companies
15	80a–15	Contracts of Advisers and Underwriters
16	80a–16	Board of Directors
17	80a–17	Transactions of Certain Affiliated Persons and Underwriters
18	80a–18	Capital Structure of Investment Companies
19	80a–19	Payments or Distributions
20	80a–20	Proxies; Voting Trusts; Circular Ownership
21	80a–21	Loans by Management Companies
22	80a–22	Distribution, Redemption, and Repurchase of Securities; Regulations by Securities Associations
23	80a–23	Closed-End Companies
24	80a–24	Registration of Securities Under Securities Act of 1933
25	80a–25	Reorganization Plans; Reports by Commission
26	80a–26	Unit Investment Trusts
27	80a–27	Periodic Payment Plans
28	80a–28	Face-Amount Certificate Companies
29		[Repealed]
30	80a–29	Reports and Financial Statements of Investment Companies and Affiliated Persons
31	80a–30	Accounts and Records
32	80a–31	Accountants and Auditors
33	80a–32	Filing of Documents with Commission in Civil Actions
34	80a–33	Destruction and Falsification of Reports and Records
35	80a–34	Unlawful Representations and Names
36	80a–35	Breach of Fiduciary Duty
37	80a–36	Larceny and Embezzlement
38	80a–37	Rules, Regulations, and Orders
39	80a–38	Procedure for Issuance of Rules and Regulations
40	80a–39	Procedure for Issuance of Orders
41	80a–40	Hearings by Commission
42	80a–41	Enforcement of Title
43	80a–42	Court Review of Orders
44	80a–43	Jurisdiction of Offenses and Suits
45	80a–44	Disclosure of Information Filed with Commission; Copies
46	80a–45	Reports by Commission; Hiring and Leasing Authority
47	80a–46	Validity of Contracts
48	80a–47	Violation of Title
49	80a–48	Penalties
50	80a–49	Construction with Other Laws

Section Act	**15 U.S.C.**	
51	80a–50	Separability
52	80a–51	Short Title
53	80a–52	Effective Date
54	80a–53	Election to Be Regulated as Business Development Company
55	80a–54	Acquisitions of Assets by Business Development Companies
56	80a–55	Qualifications of Directors
57	80a–56	Transactions with Certain Affiliates
58	80a–57	Changes in Investment Policy
59	80a–58	Incorporation of Title Provisions
60	80a–59	Functions and Activities of Business Development Companies
61	80a–60	Capital Structure
62	80a–61	Loans
63	80a–62	Distribution and Repurchase of Securities
64	80a–63	Accounts and Records
65	80a–64	Preventing Compliance with Title; Liability of Controlling Persons

INVESTMENT COMPANY ACT OF 1940

15 U.S.C. § 80–1 et seq.

Findings and Declaration of Policy

Sec. 1. (a) Upon the basis of facts disclosed by the record and reports of the Securities and Exchange Commission made pursuant to section 30 of the Public Utility Holding Company Act of 1935, and facts otherwise disclosed and ascertained, it is hereby found that investment companies are affected with a national public interest in that, among other things—

(1) the securities issued by such companies, which constitute a substantial part of all securities publicly offered, are distributed, purchased, paid for, exchanged, transferred, redeemed, and repurchased by use of the mails and means and instrumentalities of interstate commerce, and in the case of the numerous companies which issue redeemable securities this process of distribution and redemption is continuous;

(2) the principal activities of such companies—investing, reinvesting, and trading in securities—are conducted by use of the mails and means and instrumentalities of interstate commerce, including the facilities of national securities exchanges, and constitute a substantial part of all transactions effected in the securities markets of the Nation;

(3) such companies customarily invest and trade in securities issued by, and may dominate and control or otherwise affect the policies and management of, companies engaged in business in interstate commerce;

(4) such companies are media for the investment in the national economy of a substantial part of the national savings and may have a vital effect upon the flow of such savings into the capital markets; and

(5) the activities of such companies, extending over many States, their use of the instrumentalities of interstate commerce and the wide geographic distribution of their security holders, make difficult, if not impossible, effective State regulation of such companies in the interest of investors.

(b) Upon the basis of facts disclosed by the record and reports of the Securities and Exchange Commission made pursuant to section 30 of the Public Utility Holding Company Act of 1935, and facts otherwise disclosed and ascertained, it is hereby declared that the national public interest and the interest of investors are adversely affected—

(1) when investors purchase, pay for, exchange, receive dividends upon, vote, refrain from voting, sell, or surrender securities issued by investment companies without adequate, accurate, and explicit information, fairly presented, concerning the character of such securities and the circumstances, policies, and financial responsibility of such companies and their management;

(2) when investment companies are organized, operated, managed, or their portfolio securities are selected, in the interest of directors, officers, investment advisers, depositors, or other affiliated persons thereof, in the interest of underwriters, brokers, or dealers, in the interest of special classes of their security holders, or in the interest of other investment companies or persons engaged in other lines of business, rather than in the interest of all classes of such companies' security holders;

(3) when investment companies issue securities containing inequitable or discriminatory provisions, or fail to protect the preferences and privileges of the holders of their outstanding securities;

(4) when the control of investment companies is unduly concentrated through pyramiding or inequitable methods of control, or is inequitably distributed, or when investment companies are managed by irresponsible persons;

(5) when investment companies, in keeping their accounts, in maintaining reserves, and in computing their earnings and the asset value of their outstanding securities, employ unsound or misleading methods, or are not subjected to adequate independent scrutiny;

(6) when investment companies are reorganized, become inactive, or change the character of their business, or when the control or management thereof is transferred, without the consent of their security holders;

(7) when investment companies by excessive borrowing and the issuance of excessive amounts of senior securities increase unduly the speculative character of their junior securities; or

(8) when investment companies operate without adequate assets or reserves.

It is hereby declared that the policy and purposes of this title, in accordance with which the provisions of this title shall be interpreted, are to mitigate and, so far as is feasible, to eliminate the conditions enumerated in this section which adversely affect the national public interest and the interest of investors.

Definitions

Sec. 2. (a) When used in this subchapter, unless the context otherwise requires—

(1) "Advisory board" means a board, whether elected or appointed, which is distinct from the board of directors or board of trustees, of an investment company, and which is composed solely of persons who do not serve such company in any other capacity, whether or not the functions of such board are such as to render its members "directors" within the definition of that term, which board has advisory functions as to investments but has no power to determine that any security or other investment shall be purchased or sold by such company.

(2) "Affiliated company" means a company which is an affiliated person.

(3) "Affiliated person" of another person means (A) any person directly or indirectly owning, controlling, or holding with power to vote, 5 per centum or more of the outstanding voting securities of such other person; (B) any person 5 per centum or more of whose outstanding voting securities are directly or indirectly owned, controlled, or held with power to vote, by such other person; (C) any person directly or indirectly controlling, controlled by, or under common control with, such other person; (D) any officer, director, partner, copartner, or employee of such other person; (E) if such other person is an investment company, any investment adviser thereof or any member of an advisory board thereof; and (F) if such other person is an unincorporated investment company not having a board of directors, the depositor thereof.

(4) "Assignment" includes any direct or indirect transfer or hypothecation of a contract or chose in action by the assignor, or of a controlling block of the assignor's outstanding voting securities by a security holder of the assignor; but does not include an assignment of partnership interests incidental to the death or withdrawal of a minority of the members of the partnership having only a minority interest in the partnership business or to the admission to the partnership of one or more members who, after such admission, shall be only a minority of the members and shall have only a minority interest in the business.

(5) "Bank" means (A) a depository institution (as defined in section 3 of the Federal Deposit Insurance Act) or a branch or agency of a foreign bank (as such terms are defined in section 1(b) of the International Banking Act of 1978), (B) a member bank of the Federal Reserve System, (C) any other banking institution or trust company, whether incorporated or not, doing business under the laws of any State or of the United States, a substantial portion of the business of which consists of receiving deposits or exercising fiduciary powers similar to those permitted to national banks under the authority of the Comptroller of the Currency, and which is supervised and examined by State or Federal authority having supervision over banks, and which is not operated for the purpose of evading the provisions of this title, and (D) a receiver, conservator, or other liquidating agent of any institution or firm included in clauses (A), (B), or (C) of this paragraph.

(6) The term "broker" has the same meaning as given in section 3 of the Securities Exchange Act of 1934, except that such term does not include any person solely by reason of the fact that such person is an underwriter for one or more investment companies.

(7) "Commission" means the Securities and Exchange Commission.

(8) "Company" means a corporation, a partnership, an association, a joint-stock company, a trust, a fund, or any organized group of persons whether incorporated or not; or any receiver, trustee in a case under title 11 of the United States Code or similar official or any liquidating agent for any of the foregoing, in his capacity as such.

(9) "Control" means the power to exercise a controlling influence over the management or policies of a company, unless such power is solely the result of an official position with such company.

Any person who owns beneficially, either directly or through one or more controlled companies, more than 25 per centum of the voting securities of a company shall be presumed to control such company. Any person who does not so own more than 25 per centum of the voting securities of any company shall be presumed not to control such company. A natural person shall be presumed not to be a controlled person within the meaning of this title. Any such presumption may be rebutted by evidence, but except as hereinafter provided, shall continue until a determination to the contrary made by the Commission by order either on its own motion or on application by an interested person. If an application filed hereunder is not granted or denied by the Commission within sixty days after filing thereof, the determination sought by the application shall be deemed to have been temporarily granted pending final determination of the Commission thereon. The Commission, upon its own motion or upon application, may by order revoke or modify any order issued under this paragraph whenever it shall find that the determination embraced in such original order is no longer consistent with the facts.

(10) "Convicted" includes a verdict, judgment, or plea of guilty, or a finding of guilt on a plea of nolo contendere, if such verdict, judgment, plea, or finding has not been reversed, set aside, or withdrawn, whether or not sentence has been imposed.

(11) The term "dealer" has the same meaning as given in the Securities Exchange Act of 1934, but does not include an insurance company or investment company.

(12) "Director" means any director of a corporation or any person performing similar functions with respect to any organization, whether incorporated or unincorporated, including any natural person who is a member of a board of trustees of a management company created as a common-law trust.

(13) "Employees' securities company" means any investment company or similar issuer all of the outstanding securities of which (other than short-term paper) are beneficially owned (A) by the employees or persons on retainer of a single employer or of two or more employers each of which is an affiliated company of the other, (B) by former employees of such employer or employers, (C) by members of the immediate family of such employees, persons on retainer, or former employees, (D) by any two or more of the foregoing classes of persons, or (E) by such employer or employers together with any one or more of the foregoing classes of persons.

(14) "Exchange" means any organization, association, or group of persons, whether incorporated or unincorporated, which constitutes, maintains, or provides a market place or facilities for bringing together purchasers and sellers of securities or for otherwise performing with respect to securities the functions commonly performed by a stock exchange as that term is generally understood, and includes the market place and the market facilities maintained by such exchange.

(15) "Face-amount certificate" means any certificate, investment contract, or other security which represents an obligation on the part of its issuer to pay a stated or determinable sum or sums at a fixed or determinable date or dates more than twenty-four months after the date of issuance, in consideration of the payment of periodic installments of a stated or determinable amount (which security shall be known as a face-amount certificate of the "installment type"); or any security which represents a similar obligation on the part of a face-amount certificate company, the consideration for which is the payment of a single lump sum (which security shall be known as a "fully paid" face-amount certificate).

(16) "Government security" means any security issued or guaranteed as to principal or interest by the United States, or by a person controlled or supervised by and acting as an instrumentality of the Government of the United States pursuant to authority granted by the Congress of the United States; or any certificate of deposit for any of the foregoing.

(17) "Insurance company" means a company which is organized as an insurance company, whose primary and predominant business activity is the writing of insurance or the reinsuring of risks underwritten by insurance companies, and which is subject to supervision by the insurance commissioner or a similar official or agency of a State; or any receiver or similar official or any liquidating agent for such a company, in his capacity as such.

(18) "Interstate commerce" means trade, commerce, transportation, or communication among the several States, or between any foreign country and any State, or between any State and any place or ship outside thereof.

(19) "Interested person" of another person means—

(A) when used with respect to an investment company—

(i) any affiliated person of such company,

(ii) any member of the immediate family of any natural person who is an affiliated person of such company,

(iii) any interested person of any investment adviser of or principal underwriter for such company,

(iv) any person or partner or employee of any person who at any time since the beginning of the last two completed fiscal years of such company has acted as legal counsel for such company,

(v) any person or any affiliated person of a person (other than a registered investment company) that, at any time during the 6–month period preceding the date of the determination of whether that person or affiliated person is an interested person, has executed any portfolio transactions for, engaged in any principal transactions with, or distributed shares for—

(I) the investment company;

(II) any other investment company having the same investment adviser as such investment company or holding itself out to investors as a related company for purposes of investment or investor services; or

(III) any account over which the investment company's investment adviser has brokerage placement discretion,

(vi) any person or any affiliated person of a person (other than a registered investment company) that, at any time during the 6–month period preceding the date of the determination of whether that person or affiliated person is an interested person, has loaned money or other property to—

(I) the investment company;

(II) any other investment company having the same investment adviser as such investment company or holding itself out to investors as a related company for purposes of investment or investor services; or

(III) any account for which the investment company's investment adviser has borrowing authority, and

(vii) any natural person whom the Commission by order shall have determined to be an interested person by reason of having had, at any time since the beginning of the last two completed fiscal years of such company, a material business or professional relationship with such company or with the principal executive officer of such company or with any other investment company having the same investment adviser or principal underwriter or with the principal executive officer of such other investment company:

Provided, That no person shall be deemed to be an interested person of an investment company solely by reason of (aa) his being a member of its board of directors or advisory board or an owner of its securities, or (bb) his membership in the immediate family of any person specified in clause (aa) of this proviso; and

(B) when used with respect to an investment adviser of or principal underwriter for any investment company—

(i) any affiliated person of such investment adviser or principal underwriter,

(ii) any member of the immediate family of any natural person who is an affiliated person of such investment adviser or principal underwriter,

(iii) any person who knowingly has any direct or indirect beneficial interest in, or who is designated as trustee, executor, or guardian of any legal interest in, any security issued either by such investment adviser or principal underwriter or by a controlling person of such investment adviser or principal underwriter,

(iv) any person or partner or employee of any person who at any time since the beginning of the last two completed fiscal years of such investment company has acted as legal counsel for such investment adviser or principal underwriter,

(v) any person or any affiliated person of a person (other than a registered investment company) that, at any time during the 6–month period preceding the date of the determination of whether that person or affiliated person is an interested person, has executed any portfolio transactions for, engaged in any principal transactions with, or distributed shares for—

(I) any investment company for which the investment adviser or principal underwriter serves as such;

(II) any investment company holding itself out to investors, for purposes of investment or investor services, as a company related to any investment company for which the investment adviser or principal underwriter serves as such; or

(III) any account over which the investment adviser has brokerage placement discretion,

(vi) any person or any affiliated person of a person (other than a registered investment company) that, at any time during the 6–month period preceding the date of the determination of whether that person or affiliated person is an interested person, has loaned money or other property to—

(I) any investment company for which the investment adviser or principal underwriter serves as such;

(II) any investment company holding itself out to investors, for purposes of investment or investor services, as a company related to any investment company for which the investment adviser or principal underwriter serves as such; or

(III) any account for which the investment adviser has borrowing authority, and

(vii) any natural person whom the Commission by order shall have determined to be an interested person by reason of having had at any time since the beginning of the last two completed fiscal years of such investment company a material business or professional relationship with such investment adviser or principal underwriter or with the principal executive officer or any controlling person of such investment adviser or principal underwriter.

For the purposes of this paragraph (19), "member of the immediate family" means any parent, spouse of a parent, child, spouse of a child, spouse, brother, or sister, and includes step and adoptive relationships. The Commission may modify or revoke any order issued under clause (vii) of subparagraph (A) or (B) of this paragraph whenever it finds that such order is no longer consistent with the facts. No order issued pursuant to clause (vii) of subparagraph (A) or (B) of this paragraph shall become effective until at least sixty days after the entry thereof, and no such order shall affect the status of any person for the purposes of this title or for any other purpose for any period prior to the effective date of such order.

(20) "Investment adviser" of an investment company means (A) any person (other than a bona fide officer, director, trustee, member of an advisory board, or employee of such company, as such) who pursuant to contract with such company regularly furnishes advice to such company with respect to the desirability of investing in, purchasing or selling securities or other property, or is empowered to determine what securities or other property shall be purchased or sold by such company, and (B) any other person who pursuant to contract with a person described in clause (A) regularly performs substantially all of the duties undertaken by such person described in said clause (A); but does not include (i) a person whose advice is furnished solely through uniform publications distributed to subscribers thereto, (ii) a person who furnishes only statistical and other factual information, advice regarding economic factors and trends, or advice as to occasional transactions in specific securities, but without generally furnishing advice or making recommendations regarding the purchase or sale of securities, (iii) a company furnishing such services at cost to one or more investment companies, insurance companies, or other financial institutions, (iv) any person the character and amount of whose compensation for such services must be approved by a court, or (v) such other persons as the Commission may by rules and regulations or order determine not to be within the intent of this definition.

(21) "Investment banker" means any person engaged in the business of underwriting securities issued by other persons, but does not include an investment company, any person who acts as an underwriter in isolated transactions but not as a part of a regular business, or any person solely by reason of the fact that such person is an underwriter for one or more investment companies.

(22) "Issuer" means every person who issues or proposes to issue any security, or has outstanding any security which it has issued.

(23) "Lend" includes a purchase coupled with an agreement by the vendor to repurchase; "borrow" includes a sale coupled with a similar agreement.

(24) "Majority-owned subsidiary" of a person means a company 50 per centum or more of the outstanding voting securities of which are owned by such person, or by a company which, within the meaning of this paragraph, is a majority-owned subsidiary of such person.

(25) "Means or instrumentality of interstate commerce" includes any facility of a national securities exchange.

(26) "National securities exchange" means an exchange registered under section 6 of the Securities Exchange Act of 1934.

(27) "Periodic payment plan certificate" means (A) any certificate, investment contract, or other security providing for a series of periodic payments by the holder, and representing an undivided interest in certain specified securities or in a unit or fund of securities purchased wholly or partly with the proceeds of such payments, and (B) any security the issuer of which is also issuing securities of the character described in clause (A) of this paragraph and the holder of which has substantially the same rights and privileges as those which holders of securities of the character described in said clause (A) have upon completing the periodic payments for which such securities provide.

(28) "Person" means a natural person or a company.

(29) "Principal underwriter" of or for any investment company other than a closed-end company, or of any security issued by such a company, means any underwriter who as principal purchases from such company, or pursuant to contract has the right (whether absolute or conditional) from time to time to purchase from such company, any such security for distribution, or who as agent for such company sells or has the right to sell any such security to a dealer or to the public or both, but does not include a dealer who purchases from such company through a principal underwriter acting as agent for such company. "Principal underwriter" of or for a closed-end company or any issuer which is not an investment company, or of any security issued by such a company or issuer, means any underwriter who, in connection with a primary distribution of securities, (A) is in privity of contract with the issuer or an affiliated person of the issuer; (B) acting alone or in concert with one or more other persons, initiates or directs the formation of an underwriting syndicate; or (C) is allowed a rate of gross commission, spread, or other profit greater than the rate allowed another underwriter participating in the distribution.

(30) "Promoter" of a company or a proposed company means a person who, acting alone or in concert with other persons, is initiating or directing, or has within one year initiated or directed, the organization of such company.

(31) "Prospectus", as used in section 22, means a written prospectus intended to meet the requirements of section 10(a) of the Securities Act of 1933 and currently in use. As used elsewhere, "prospectus" means a prospectus as defined in the Securities Act of 1933.

(32) "Redeemable security" means any security, other than short-term paper, under the terms of which the holder, upon its presentation to the issuer or to a person designated by the issuer, is entitled (whether absolutely or only out of surplus) to receive approximately his proportionate share of the issuer's current net assets, or the cash equivalent thereof.

(33) "Reorganization" means (A) a reorganization under the supervision of a court of competent jurisdiction; (B) a merger or consolidation; (C) a sale of 75 per centum or more in value of the assets of a company; (D) a restatement of the capital of a company, or an exchange of securities issued by a company for any of its own outstanding securities; (E) a voluntary dissolution or liquidation of a company; (F) a recapitalization or other procedure or transaction which has for its purpose the alteration, modification, or elimination of any of the rights, preferences, or privileges of any class of securities issued by a company, as provided in its charter or other instrument creating or defining such rights, preferences, and privileges; (G) an exchange of securities issued by a company for outstanding securities issued by another company or companies, preliminary to and for the purpose of effecting or consummating any of the foregoing; or (H) any exchange of securities by a company which is not an investment company for securities issued by a registered investment company.

(34) "Sale", "sell", "offer to sell", or "offer for sale" includes every contract of sale or disposition of, attempt or offer to dispose of, or solicitation of an offer to buy, a security or interest in a security, for value. Any security given or delivered with, or as a bonus on account of, any purchase of securities or any other thing, shall be conclusively presumed to constitute a part of the subject of such purchase and to have been sold for value.

(35) "Sales load" means the difference between the price of a security to the public and that portion of the proceeds from its sale which is received and invested or held for investment by the issuer (or in the case of a unit investment trust, by

the depositor or trustee), less any portion of such difference deducted for trustee's or custodian's fees, insurance premiums, issue taxes, or administrative expenses or fees which are not properly chargeable to sales or promotional activities. In the case of a periodic payment plan certificate, "sales load" includes the sales load on any investment company securities in which the payments made on such certificate are invested, as well as the sales load on the certificate itself.

(36) "Security" means any note, stock, treasury stock, security future, bond, debenture, evidence of indebtedness, certificate of interest or participation in any profit-sharing agreement, collateral-trust certificate, preorganization certificate or subscription, transferable share, investment contract, voting-trust certificate, certificate of deposit for a security, fractional undivided interest in oil, gas, or other mineral rights, any put, call, straddle, option, or privilege on any security (including a certificate of deposit) or on any group or index of securities (including any interest therein or based on the value thereof), or any put, call, straddle, option, or privilege entered into on a national securities exchange relating to foreign currency, or, in general, any interest or instrument commonly known as a "security", or any certificate of interest or participation in, temporary or interim certificate for, receipt for, guarantee of, or warrant or right to subscribe to or purchase, any of the foregoing.

(37) "Separate account" means an account established and maintained by an insurance company pursuant to the laws of any State or territory of the United States, or of Canada or any province thereof, under which income, gains and losses, whether or not realized, from assets allocated to such account, are, in accordance with the applicable contract, credited to or charged against such account without regard to other income, gains, or losses of the insurance company.

(38) "Short-term paper" means any note, draft, bill of exchange, or banker's acceptance payable on demand or having a maturity at the time of issuance of not exceeding nine months, exclusive of days of grace, or any renewal thereof payable on demand or having a maturity likewise limited; and such other classes of securities, of a commercial rather than an investment character, as the Commission may designate by rules and regulations.

(39) "State" means any State of the United States, the District of Columbia, Puerto Rico, the Virgin Islands, or any other possession of the United States.

(40) "Underwriter" means any person who has purchased from an issuer with a view to, or sells for an issuer in connection with, the distribution of any security, or participates or has a direct or indirect participation in any such undertaking, or participates or has a participation in the direct or indirect underwriting of any such undertaking; but such term shall not include a person whose interest is limited to a commission from an underwriter or dealer not in excess of the usual and customary distributor's or seller's commission. As used in this paragraph the term "issuer" shall include, in addition to an issuer, any person directly or indirectly controlling or controlled by the issuer, or any person under direct or indirect common control with the issuer. When the distribution of the securities in respect of which any person is an underwriter is completed such person shall cease to be an underwriter in respect of such securities or the issuer thereof.

(41) "Value", with respect to assets of registered investment companies, except as provided in subsection (b) of section 28 of this title, means—

(A) as used in sections 3, 5, and 12 of this title, (i) with respect to securities owned at the end of the last preceding fiscal quarter for which market quotations are readily available, the market value at the end of such quarter; (ii) with respect to other securities and assets owned at the end of the last preceding fiscal quarter, fair value at the end of such quarter, as determined in good faith by the board of directors; and (iii) with respect to securities and other assets acquired after the end of the last preceding fiscal quarter, the cost thereof; and

(B) as used elsewhere in this title, (i) with respect to securities for which market quotations are readily available, the market value of such securities; and (ii) with respect to other securities and assets, fair value as determined in good faith by the board of directors;

in each case as of such time or times as determined pursuant to this title, and the rules and regulations issued by the Commission hereunder. Notwithstanding the fact that market quotations for securities issued by controlled companies are available, the board of directors may in good faith determine the value of such securities: *Provided*,

That the value so determined is not in excess of the higher of market value or asset value of such securities in the case of majority-owned subsidiaries, and is not in excess of market value in the case of other controlled companies.

For purposes of the valuation of those assets of a registered diversified company which are not subject to the limitations provided for in section 5(b)(1), the Commission may, by rules and regulations or orders, permit any security to be carried at cost, if it shall determine that such procedure is consistent with the general intent and purposes of this title. For purposes of sections 5 and 12 in lieu of values determined as provided in clause (A) above, the Commission shall by rules and regulations permit valuation of securities at cost or other basis in cases where it may be more convenient for such company to make its computations on such basis by reason of the necessity or desirability of complying with the provisions of any United States revenue laws or rules and regulations issued thereunder, or the laws or the rules and regulations issued thereunder of any State in which the securities of such company may be qualified for sale.

The foregoing definition shall not derogate from the authority of the Commission with respect to the reports, information, and documents to be filed with the Commission by any registered company, or with respect to the accounting policies and principles to be followed by any such company, as provided in sections 8, 30, and 31 of this title.

(42) "Voting security" means any security presently entitling the owner or holder thereof to vote for the election of directors of a company. A specified percentage of the outstanding voting securities of a company means such amount of its outstanding voting securities as entitles the holder or holders thereof to cast said specified percentage of the aggregate votes which the holders of all the outstanding voting securities of such company are entitled to cast. The vote of a majority of the outstanding voting securities of a company means the vote, at the annual or a special meeting of the security holders of such company duly called, (A) of 67 per centum or more of the voting securities present at such meeting, if the holders of more than 50 per centum of the outstanding voting securities of such company are present or represented by proxy; or (B) of more than 50 per centum of the outstanding voting securities of such company, whichever is the less.

(43) "Wholly-owned subsidiary" of a person means a company 95 per centum or more of the outstanding voting securities of which are owned by such person, or by a company which, within the meaning of this paragraph, is a wholly-owned subsidiary of such person.

(44) "Securities Act of 1933", "Securities Exchange Act of 1934", and "Trust Indenture Act of 1939" mean those Acts, respectively, as heretofore or hereafter amended.

(45) "Savings and loan association" means a savings and loan association, building and loan association, cooperative bank, homestead association, or similar institution, which is supervised and examined by State or Federal authority having supervision over any such institution, and a receiver, conservator, or other liquidating agent of any such institution.

(46) "Eligible portfolio company" means any issuer which—

(A) is organized under the laws of, and has its principal place of business in, any State or States;

(B) is neither an investment company as defined in section 3 (other than a small business investment company which is licensed by the Small Business Administration to operate under the Small Business Investment Act of 1958 and which is a wholly-owned subsidiary of the business development company) nor a company which would be an investment company except for the exclusion from the definition of investment company in section 3(c); and

(C) satisfies one of the following:

(i) it does not have any class of securities with respect to which a member of a national securities exchange, broker, or dealer may extend or maintain credit to or for a customer pursuant to rules or regulations adopted by the Board of Governors of the Federal Reserve System under section 7 of the Securities Exchange Act of 1934;

(ii) it is controlled by a business development company, either alone or as part of a group acting together, and such business development company in fact exercises a controlling influence over the management or policies of such eligible portfolio company and, as a result of such control, has an affiliated person who is a director of such eligible portfolio company;

(iii) it has total assets of not more than $4,000,000, and capital and surplus (shareholders' equity less retained earnings) of not less than $2,000,000, except that the Commission may adjust such amounts by rule, regulation, or order to reflect changes in 1 or more generally accepted indices or other indicators for small businesses; or

(iv) it meets such other criteria as the Commission may, by rule, establish as consistent with the public interest, the protection of investors, and the purposes fairly intended by the policy and provisions of this title.

(47) "Making available significant managerial assistance" by a business development company means—

(A) any arrangement whereby a business development company, through its directors, officers, employees, or general partners, offers to provide, and, if accepted, does so provide, significant guidance and counsel concerning the management, operations, or business objectives and policies of a portfolio company;

(B) the exercise by a business development company of a controlling influence over the management or policies of a portfolio company by the business development company acting individually or as part of a group acting together which controls such portfolio company; or

(C) with respect to a small business investment company licensed by the Small Business Administration to operate under the Small Business Investment Act of 1958, the making of loans to a portfolio company.

For purposes of subparagraph (A), the requirement that a business development company make available significant managerial assistance shall be deemed to be satisfied with respect to any particular portfolio company where the business development company purchases securities of such portfolio company in conjunction with one or more other persons acting together, and at least one of the persons in the group makes available significant managerial assistance to such portfolio company, except that such requirement will not be deemed to be satisfied if the business development company, in all cases, makes available significant managerial assistance solely in the manner described in this sentence.

(48) "Business development company" means any closed-end company which—

(A) is organized under the laws of, and has its principal place of business in, any State or States;

(B) is operated for the purpose of making investments in securities described in paragraphs (1) through (3) of section 55(a), and makes available significant managerial assistance with respect to the issuers of such securities, provided that a business development company must make available significant managerial assistance only with respect to the companies which are treated by such business development company as satisfying the 70 per centum of the value of its total assets condition of section 55, and provided further that a business development company need not make available significant managerial assistance with respect to any company described in paragraph (46)(C)(iii), or with respect to any other company that meets such criteria as the Commission may by rule, regulation, or order permit, as consistent with the public interest, the protection of investors, and the purposes of this subchapter; and

(C) has elected pursuant to section 54(a) to be subject to the provisions of sections 55 through 65.

(49) "Foreign securities authority" means any foreign government or any governmental body or regulatory organization empowered by a foreign government to administer or enforce its laws as they relate to securities matters.

(50) "Foreign financial regulatory authority" means any (A) foreign securities authority, (B) other governmental body or foreign equivalent of a self-regulatory organization empowered by a foreign government to administer or enforce its laws relating to the regulation of fiduciaries, trusts, commercial lending, insurance, trading in contracts of sale of a commodity for future delivery, or other instruments traded on or subject to the rules of a contract market, board of trade or foreign equivalent, or other financial activities, or (C) membership organization a function of which is to regulate the participation of its members in activities listed above.

(51)(A) "Qualified purchaser" means—

(i) any natural person (including any person who holds a joint, community property, or other similar shared ownership interest in an issuer that is excepted under section 3(c)(7) with that person's qualified purchaser spouse) who owns not less than $5,000,000 in investments, as defined by the Commission;

(ii) any company that owns not less than $5,000,000 in investments and that is owned directly or indirectly by or for 2 or more natural persons who are related as siblings or spouse (including former spouses), or direct lineal descendants by birth or adoption, spouses of such persons, the estates of such persons, or foundations, charitable organizations, or trusts established by or for the benefit of such persons;

(iii) any trust that is not covered by clause (ii) and that was not formed for the specific purpose of acquiring the securities offered, as to which the trustee or other person authorized to make decisions with respect to the trust, and each settlor or other person who has contributed assets to the trust, is a person described in clause (i), (ii), or (iv); or

(iv) any person, acting for its own account or the accounts of other qualified purchasers, who in the aggregate owns and invests on a discretionary basis, not less than $25,000,000 in investments.

(B) The Commission may adopt such rules and regulations applicable to the persons and trusts specified in clauses (i) through (iv) of subparagraph (A) as it determines are necessary or appropriate in the public interest or for the protection of investors.

(C) The term "qualified purchaser" does not include a company that, but for the exceptions provided for in paragraph (1) or (7) of section 3(c), would be an investment company (hereafter in this paragraph referred to as an "excepted investment company"), unless all beneficial owners of its outstanding securities (other than short-term paper), determined in accordance with section 3(c)(1)(A), that acquired such securities on or before April 30, 1996 (hereafter in this paragraph referred to as "pre-amendment beneficial owners"), and all pre-amendment beneficial owners of the outstanding securities (other than short-term paper) of any excepted investment company that, directly or indirectly, owns any outstanding securities of such excepted investment company, have consented to its treatment as a qualified purchaser. Unanimous consent of all trustees, directors, or general partners of a company or trust referred to in clause (ii) or (iii) of subparagraph (A) shall constitute consent for purposes of this subparagraph.

(52) The terms "security future" and "narrow-based security index" have the same meanings as provided in section 3(a)(55) of the Securities Exchange Act of 1934.

(53) The term "credit rating agency" has the same meaning as in section 3 of the Securities Exchange Act of 1934.

(54) The terms "commodity pool", "commodity pool operator", "commodity trading advisor", "major swap participant", "swap", "swap dealer", and "swap execution facility" have the same meanings as in section 1a of the Commodity Exchange Act.

(b) No provision in this title shall apply to, or be deemed to include, the United States, a State, or any political subdivision of a State, or any agency, authority, or instrumentality of any one or more of the foregoing, or any corporation which is wholly owned directly or indirectly by any one or more of the foregoing, or any officer, agent, or employee of any of the foregoing acting as such in the course of his official duty, unless such provision makes specific reference thereto.

(c) *Consideration of Promotion of Efficiency, Competition, and Capital Formation.* Whenever pursuant to this title the Commission is engaged in rulemaking and is required to consider or determine whether an action is consistent with the public interest, the Commission shall also consider, in addition to the protection of investors, whether the action will promote efficiency, competition, and capital formation.

Definition of Investment Company

Sec. 3. (a) *Definitions.* (1) When used in this title, "investment company" means any issuer which—

(A) is or holds itself out as being engaged primarily, or proposes to engage primarily, in the business of investing, reinvesting, or trading in securities;

(B) is engaged or proposes to engage in the business of issuing face-amount certificates of the installment type, or has been engaged in such business and has any such certificates outstanding; or

(C) is engaged or proposes to engage in the business of investing, reinvesting, owning, holding, or trading in securities, and owns or proposes to acquire investment securities having a value exceeding 40 per centum of the value of such issuer's total assets (exclusive of Government securities and cash items) on an unconsolidated basis.

(2) As used in this section, "investment securities" includes all securities except (A) Government securities, (B) securities issued by employees' securities companies, and (C) securities issued by majority-owned subsidiaries of the owner which are (i) not investment companies, and (ii) are not relying on the exception from the definition of investment company in paragraph (1) or (7) of subsection (c).

(b) *Exemptions from Provisions.* Notwithstanding paragraph (1)(C) of subsection (a), none of the following persons is an investment company within the meaning of this title:

(1) Any issuer primarily engaged, directly or through a wholly-owned subsidiary or subsidiaries, in a business or businesses other than that of investing, reinvesting, owning, holding, or trading in securities.

(2) Any issuer which the Commission, upon application by such issuer, finds and by order declares to be primarily engaged in a business or businesses other than that of investing, reinvesting, owning, holding, or trading in securities either directly or (A) through majority-owned subsidiaries or (B) through controlled companies conducting similar types of businesses. The filing of an application under this paragraph in good faith by an issuer other than a registered investment company shall exempt the applicant for a period of sixty days from all provisions of this title applicable to investment companies as such. For cause shown, the Commission by order may extend such period of exemption for an additional period or periods. Whenever the Commission, upon its own motion or upon application, finds that the circumstances which gave rise to the issuance of an order granting an application under this paragraph no longer exist, the Commission shall by order revoke such order.

(3) Any issuer all the outstanding securities of which (other than short-term paper and directors' qualifying shares) are directly or indirectly owned by a company excepted from the definition of investment company by paragraph (1) or (2) of this subsection.

(c) *Further Exemptions.* Notwithstanding subsection (a), none of the following persons is an investment company within the meaning of this title:

(1) Any issuer whose outstanding securities (other than short-term paper) are beneficially owned by not more than one hundred persons and which is not making and does not presently propose to make a public offering of its securities. Such issuer shall be deemed to be an investment company for purposes of the limitations set forth in subparagraphs (A)(i) and (B)(i) of section 12(d)(1) governing the purchase or other acquisition by such issuer of any security issued by any registered investment company and the sale of any security issued by any registered open-end investment company to any such issuer. For purposes of this paragraph:

(A) Beneficial ownership by a company shall be deemed to be beneficial ownership by one person, except that, if the company owns 10 per centum or more of the outstanding voting securities of the issuer, and is or, but for the exception provided for in this paragraph or paragraph (7), would be an investment company, the beneficial ownership shall be deemed to be that of the holders of such company's outstanding securities (other than short-term paper).

(B) Beneficial ownership by any person who acquires securities or interests in securities of an issuer described in the first sentence of this paragraph shall be deemed to be beneficial ownership by the person from whom such transfer was made, pursuant to such rules and regulations as the Commission shall prescribe as necessary or appropriate in the public interest and consistent with the protection of investors and the purposes fairly intended by the policy and provisions of this title, where the transfer was caused by legal separation, divorce, death, or other involuntary event.

(2)(A) Any person primarily engaged in the business of underwriting and distributing securities issued by other persons, selling securities to customers, acting as broker, and acting as market intermediary, or any one or more of such activities, whose gross income normally is derived principally from such business and related activities.

(B) For purposes of this paragraph—

(i) the term "market intermediary" means any person that regularly holds itself out as being willing contemporaneously to engage in, and that is regularly engaged in, the business of entering into transactions on both sides of the market for a financial contract or one or more such financial contracts; and

(ii) the term "financial contract" means any arrangement that—

(I) takes the form of an individually negotiated contract, agreement, or option to buy, sell, lend, swap, or repurchase, or other similar individually negotiated transaction commonly entered into by participants in the financial markets;

(II) is in respect of securities, commodities, currencies, interest or other rates, other measures of value, or any other financial or economic interest similar in purpose or function to any of the foregoing; and

(III) is entered into in response to a request from a counter party for a quotation, or is otherwise entered into and structured to accommodate the objectives of the counter party to such arrangement.

(3) Any bank or insurance company; any savings and loan association, building and loan association, cooperative bank, homestead association, or similar institution, or any receiver, conservator, liquidator, liquidating agent, or similar official or person thereof or therefor; or any common trust fund or similar fund maintained by a bank exclusively for the collective investment and reinvestment of moneys contributed thereto by the bank in its capacity as a trustee, executor, administrator, or guardian, if—

(A) such fund is employed by the bank solely as an aid to the administration of trusts, estates, or other accounts created and maintained for a fiduciary purpose;

(B) except in connection with the ordinary advertising of the bank's fiduciary services, interests in such fund are not—

(i) advertised; or

(ii) offered for sale to the general public; and

(C) fees and expenses charged by such fund are not in contravention of fiduciary principles established under applicable Federal or State law.

(4) Any person substantially all of whose business is confined to making small loans, industrial banking, or similar businesses.

(5) Any person who is not engaged in the business of issuing redeemable securities, face-amount certificates of the installment type or periodic payment plan certificates, and who is primarily engaged in one or more of the following businesses: (A) Purchasing or otherwise acquiring notes, drafts, acceptances, open accounts receivable, and other obligations representing part or all of the sales price of merchandise, insurance, and services; (B) making loans to manufacturers, wholesalers, and retailers of, and to prospective purchasers of, specified merchandise, insurance, and services; and (C) purchasing or otherwise acquiring mortgages and other liens on and interests in real estate.

(6) Any company primarily engaged, directly or through majority-owned subsidiaries, in one or more of the businesses described in paragraphs (3) (4), and (5), or in one or more of such businesses (from which not less than 25 per centum of such company's gross income during its last fiscal year was derived) together with an additional business or businesses other than investing, reinvesting, owning, holding, or trading in securities.

(7)(A) Any issuer, the outstanding securities of which are owned exclusively by persons who, at the time of acquisition of such securities, are qualified purchasers, and which is not making and does not at that time propose to make a public offering of such securities. Securities that are owned by persons who received the securities from a qualified purchaser as a gift or bequest, or in a case in which the transfer was caused by legal separation, divorce, death, or other involuntary event, shall be deemed to be owned by a qualified purchaser, subject to such rules, regulations, and orders as the Commission may prescribe as necessary or appropriate in the public interest or for the protection of investors.

(B) Notwithstanding subparagraph (A), an issuer is within the exception provided by this paragraph if—

(i) in addition to qualified purchasers, outstanding securities of that issuer are beneficially owned by not more than 100 persons who are not qualified purchasers, if—

(I) such persons acquired any portion of the securities of such issuer on or before September 1, 1996; and

(II) at the time at which such persons initially acquired the securities of such issuer, the issuer was excepted by paragraph (1); and

(ii) prior to availing itself of the exception provided by this paragraph—

(I) such issuer has disclosed to each beneficial owner, as determined under paragraph (1), that future investors will be limited to qualified purchasers, and that ownership in such issuer is no longer limited to not more than 100 persons; and

(II) concurrently with or after such disclosure, such issuer has provided each beneficial owner, as determined under paragraph (1), with a reasonable opportunity to redeem any part or all of their interests in the issuer, notwithstanding any agreement to the contrary between the issuer and such persons, for that person's proportionate share of the issuer's net assets.

(C) Each person that elects to redeem under subparagraph (B)(ii)(II) shall receive an amount in cash equal to that person's proportionate share of the issuer's net assets, unless the issuer elects to provide such person with the option of receiving, and such person agrees to receive, all or a portion of such person's share in assets of the issuer. If the issuer elects to provide such persons with such an opportunity, disclosure concerning such opportunity shall be made in the disclosure required by subparagraph (B)(ii)(I).

(D) An issuer that is excepted under this paragraph shall nonetheless be deemed to be an investment company for purposes of the limitations set forth in subparagraphs (A)(i) and (B)(i) of section 12(d)(1) relating to the purchase or other acquisition by such issuer of any security issued by any registered investment company and the sale of any security issued by any registered open-end investment company to any such issuer.

(E) For purposes of determining compliance with this paragraph and paragraph (1), an issuer that is otherwise excepted under this paragraph and an issuer that is otherwise excepted under paragraph (1) shall not be treated by the Commission as being a single issuer for purposes of determining whether the outstanding securities of the issuer excepted under paragraph (1) are beneficially owned by not more than 100 persons or whether the outstanding securities of the issuer excepted under this paragraph are owned by persons that are not qualified purchasers. Nothing in this subparagraph shall be construed to establish that a person is a bona fide qualified purchaser for purposes of this paragraph or a bona fide beneficial owner for purposes of paragraph (1).

(8) [Repealed].

(9) Any person substantially all of whose business consists of owning or holding oil, gas, or other mineral royalties or leases, or fractional interests therein, or certificates of interest or participation in or investment contracts relative to such royalties, leases, or fractional interests.

(10)(A) Any company organized and operated exclusively for religious, educational, benevolent, fraternal, charitable, or reformatory purposes—

(i) no part of the net earnings of which inures to the benefit of any private shareholder or individual: or

(ii) which is or maintains a fund described in subparagraph (B).

(B) For the purposes of subparagraph (A)(ii), a fund is described in this subparagraph if such fund is a pooled income fund, collective trust fund, collective investment fund, or similar fund maintained by a charitable organization exclusively for the collective investment and reinvestment of one or more of the following:

(i) assets of the general endowment fund or other funds of one or more charitable organizations;

(ii) assets of a pooled income fund;

(iii) assets contributed to a charitable organization in exchange for the issuance of charitable gift annuities;

(iv) assets of a charitable remainder trust or of any other trust, the remainder interests of which are irrevocably dedicated to any charitable organization;

(v) assets of a charitable lead trust;

(vi) assets of a trust, the remainder interests of which are revocably dedicated to or for the benefit of 1 or more charitable organizations, if the ability to revoke the dedication is limited to circumstances involving—

(I) an adverse change in the financial circumstances of a settlor or an income beneficiary of the trust;

(II) a change in the identity of the charitable organization or organizations having the remainder interest, provided that the new beneficiary is also a charitable organization; or

(III) both the changes described in subclauses (I) and (II);

(vii) assets of a trust not described in clauses (i) through (v), the remainder interests of which are revocably dedicated to a charitable organization, subject to subparagraph (C); or

(viii) such assets as the Commission may prescribe by rule, regulation, or order in accordance with section 6(c).

(C) A fund that contains assets described in clause (vii) of subparagraph (B) shall be excluded from the definition of an investment company for a period of 3 years after the date of enactment of this subparagraph, but only if—

(i) such assets were contributed before the date which is 60 days after the date of enactment of this subparagraph; and

(ii) such assets are commingled in the fund with assets described in one or more of clauses (i) through (vi) and (viii) of subparagraph (B).

(D) For purposes of this paragraph—

(i) a trust or fund is "maintained" by a charitable organization if the organization serves as a trustee or administrator of the trust or fund or has the power to remove the trustees or administrators of the trust or fund and to designate new trustees or administrators;

(ii) the term "pooled income fund" has the same meaning as in section 642(c)(5) of the Internal Revenue Code of 1986;

(iii) the term "charitable organization" means an organization described in paragraphs (1) through (5) of section 170(c) or section 501(c)(3) of the Internal Revenue Code of 1986;

(iv) the term "charitable lead trust" means a trust described in section 170(f)(2)(B), 2055(e)(2)(B), or 2522(c)(2)(B) of the Internal Revenue Code of 1986;

(v) the term "charitable remainder trust" means a charitable remainder annuity trust or a charitable remainder unitrust, as those terms are defined in section 664(d) of the Internal Revenue Code of 1986; and

(vi) the term "charitable gift annuity" means an annuity issued by a charitable organization that is described in section 501(m)(5) of the Internal Revenue Code of 1986.

(11) Any employee's stock bonus, pension, or profit-sharing trust which meets the requirements for qualification under section 401 of the Internal Revenue Code of 1986; or any governmental plan described in section 3(a)(2)(C) of the Securities Act of 1933; or any collective trust fund maintained by a bank consisting solely of assets of one or more of such trusts, governmental plans, or church plans, companies or accounts that are excluded from the definition of an investment company under paragraph (14) of this subsection; or any separate account the assets of which are derived solely from (A) contributions under pension or profit-sharing plans which meet the requirements of section 401 of the Internal Revenue Code of 1986 or the requirements for deduction of the employer's contribution under section 404(a)(2) of such Code, (B) contributions under governmental plans in connection with which interests, participations, or securities are exempted from the registration provisions of section 5 of the Securities Act of 1933 by section 3(a)(2)(C) of such Act, and (C) advances made by an insurance company in connection with the operation of such separate account.

(12) Any voting trust the assets of which consist exclusively of securities of a single issuer which is not an investment company.

(13) Any security holders' protective committee or similar issuer having outstanding and issuing no securities other than certificates of deposit and short-term paper.

(14) Any church plan described in section 414(e) of the Internal Revenue Code of 1986, if, under any such plan, no part of the assets may be used for, or diverted to, purposes other than the exclusive benefit of plan participants or beneficiaries, or any company or account that is—

(A) established by a person that is eligible to establish and maintain such a plan under section 414(e) of the Internal Revenue Code of 1986; and

(B) substantially all of the activities of which consist of—

(i) managing or holding assets contributed to such church plans or other assets which are permitted to be commingled with the assets of church plans under the Internal Revenue Code of 1986; or

(ii) administering or providing benefits pursuant to church plans.

Classification of Investment Companies

Sec. 4. For the purposes of this title, investment companies are divided into three principal classes, defined as follows:

(1) "Face-amount certificate company" means an investment company which is engaged or proposes to engage in the business of issuing face-amount certificates of the installment type, or which has been engaged in such business and has any such certificate outstanding.

(2) "Unit investment trust" means an investment company which (A) is organized under a trust indenture, contract of custodianship or agency, or similar instrument, (B) does not have a board of directors, and (C) issues only redeemable securities, each of which represents an undivided interest in a unit of specified securities; but does not include a voting trust.

(3) "Management company" means any investment company other than a face-amount certificate company or a unit investment trust.

Subclassification of Management Companies

Sec. 5. (a) *Open-End and Closed-End Companies.* For the purpose of this title, management companies are divided into open-end and closed-end companies, defined as follows:

(1) "Open-end company" means a management company which is offering for sale or has outstanding any redeemable security of which it is the issuer.

(2) "Closed-end company" means any management company other than an open-end company.

(b) *Diversified and Non-Diversified Companies.* Management companies are further divided into diversified companies and non-diversified companies, defined as follows:

(1) "Diversified company" means a management company which meets the following requirements: At least 75 per centum of the value of its total assets is represented by cash and cash items (including receivables), Government securities, securities of other investment companies, and other securities for the purposes of this calculation limited in respect of any one issuer to an amount not greater in value than 5 per centum of the value of the total assets of such management company and to not more than 10 per centum of the outstanding voting securities of such issuer.

(2) "Non-diversified company" means any management company other than a diversified company.

(c) *Loss of Status as Diversified Company.* A registered diversified company which at the time of its qualification as such meets the requirements of paragraph (1) of subsection (b) shall not lose its status as a diversified company because of any subsequent discrepancy between the value of its various investments and the requirements of said paragraph, so long as any such discrepancy existing immediately after its acquisition of any security or other property is neither wholly nor partly the result of such acquisition.

Exemptions

Sec. 6. (a) *Exemption of Specified Investment Companies.* The following investment companies are exempt from the provisions of this title:

(1) Any company organized or otherwise created under the laws of and having its principal office and place of business in Puerto Rico, the Virgin Islands, or any other possession of the United States; but such exemption shall terminate if any security of which such company is the issuer is offered for sale or sold after the effective date of this title, by such company or an underwriter therefor to a resident of any State other than the State in which such company is organized.

(2) Any company which since the effective date of this title or within five years prior to such date has been reorganized under the supervision of a court of competent jurisdiction, if (A) such company was not an investment company at the commencement of such reorganization proceedings, (B) at the conclusion of such proceedings all outstanding securities of such company were owned by creditors of such company or by persons to whom such securities were issued on account of creditors' claims, and (C) more than 50 per centum of the voting securities of such company, and securities representing more than 50 per centum of the net asset value of such company, are currently owned beneficially by not more than twenty-five persons; but such exemption shall terminate if any security of which such company is the issuer is offered for sale or sold to the public after the conclusion of such proceedings by the issuer or by or through any underwriter. For the purposes of this paragraph, any new company organized as part of the reorganization shall be deemed the same company as its predecessor; and beneficial

ownership shall be determined in the manner provided in section 3(c)(1).

(3) Any issuer as to which there is outstanding a writing filed with the Commission by the Federal Savings and Loan Insurance Corporation stating that exemption of such issuer from the provisions of this title is consistent with the public interest and the protection of investors and is necessary or appropriate by reason of the fact that such issuer holds or proposes to acquire any assets or any product of any assets which have been segregated (A) from assets of any company which at the filing of such writing is an insured institution within the meaning of section 401(a) of the National Housing Act, as heretofore or hereafter amended, or (B) as a part of or in connection with any plan for or condition to the insurance of accounts of any company by said corporation or the conversion of any company into a Federal savings and loan association. Any such writing shall expire when canceled by a writing similarly filed or at the expiration of two years after the date of its filing, whichever first occurs; but said corporation may, nevertheless, before, at, or after the expiration of any such writing file another writing or writings with respect to such issuer.

(4) Any company which prior to March 15, 1940, was and now is a wholly-owned subsidiary of a registered face-amount certificate company and was prior to said date and now is organized and operating under the insurance laws of any State and subject to supervision and examination by the insurance commissioner thereof, and which prior to March 15, 1940, was and now is engaged, subject to such laws, in business substantially all of which consists of issuing and selling only to residents of such State and investing the proceeds from, securities providing for or representing participations or interests in intangible assets consisting of mortgages or other liens on real estate or notes or bonds secured thereby or in a fund or deposit of mortgages or other liens on real estate or notes or bonds secured thereby or having outstanding such securities so issued and sold.

(5)(A) Any company that is not engaged in the business of issuing redeemable securities, the operations of which are subject to regulation by the State in which the company is organized under a statute governing entities that provide financial or managerial assistance to enterprises doing business, or proposing to do business, in that State if—

(i) the organizational documents of the company state that the activities of the company are limited to the promotion of economic, business, or industrial development in the State through the provision of financial or managerial assistance to enterprises doing business, or proposing to do business, in that State, and such other activities that are incidental or necessary to carry out that purpose;

(ii) immediately following each sale of the securities of the company by the company or any underwriter for the company, not less than 80 percent of the securities of the company being offered in such sale, on a class-by-class basis, are held by persons who reside or who have a substantial business presence in that State;

(iii) the securities of the company are sold, or proposed to be sold, by the company or by any underwriter for the company, solely to accredited investors, as that term is defined in section 2(a)(15) of the Securities Act of 1933, or to such other persons that the Commission, as necessary or appropriate in the public interest and consistent with the protection of investors, may permit by rule, regulation, or order; and

(iv) the company does not purchase any security issued by an investment company or by any company that would be an investment company except for the exclusions from the definition of the term "investment company" under paragraph (1) or (7) of section 3(c), other than—

(I) any debt security that meets such standards of credit-worthiness as the Commission shall adopt; or

(II) any security issued by a registered open-end investment company that is required by its investment policies to invest not less than 65 percent of its total assets in securities described in subclause (I) or securities that are determined by such registered open-end investment company to be comparable in quality to securities described in subclause (I).

(B) Notwithstanding the exemption provided by this paragraph, section 9 (and, to the extent necessary to enforce section 9, sections 38 through 51) shall apply to a company described in this paragraph as if the company were an investment company registered under this title.

(C) Any company proposing to rely on the exemption provided by this paragraph shall file with the Commission a notification stating that the company intends to do so, in such form and manner as the Commission may prescribe by rule.

(D) Any company meeting the requirements of this paragraph may rely on the exemption provided by this paragraph upon filing with the Commission the notification required by subparagraph (C), until such time as the Commission determines by order that such reliance is not in the public interest or is not consistent with the protection of investors.

(E) The exemption provided by this paragraph may be subject to such additional terms and conditions as the Commission may by rule, regulation, or order determine are necessary or appropriate in the public interest or for the protection of investors.

(b) *Exemption of Employees' Security Company upon Application; Matters Considered.* Upon application by any employees' security company, the Commission shall by order exempt such company from the provisions of this title and of the rules and regulations hereunder, if and to the extent that such exemption is consistent with the protection of investors. In determining the provisions to which such an order of exemption shall apply, the Commission shall give due weight, among other things, to the form of organization and the capital structure of such company, the persons by whom its voting securities, evidences of indebtedness, and other securities are owned and controlled, the prices at which securities issued by such company are sold and the sales load thereon, the disposition of the proceeds of such sales, the character of the securities in which such proceeds are invested, and any relationship between such company and the issuer of any such security.

(c) *Exemption of Persons, Securities or Any Class or Classes of Persons as Necessary and Appropriate in Public Interest.* The Commission, by rules and regulations upon its own motion, or by order upon application, may conditionally or unconditionally exempt any person, security, or transaction, or any class or classes of persons, securities, or transactions, from any provision or provisions of this title or of any rule or regulation thereunder, if and to the extent that such exemption is necessary or appropriate in the public interest and consistent with the protection of investors and the purposes fairly intended by the policy and provisions of this title.

(d) *Exemption of Closed-End Investment Companies.* The Commission, by rules and regulations or order, shall exempt a closed-end investment company from any or all provisions of this title, but subject to such terms and conditions as may be necessary or appropriate in the public interest or for the protection of investors, if—

(1) the aggregate sums received by such company from the sale of all its outstanding securities, plus the aggregate offering price of all securities of which such company is the issuer and which it proposes to offer for sale, do not exceed $10,000,000, or such other amount as the Commission may set by rule, regulation, or order.

(2) no security of which such company is the issuer has been or is proposed to be sold by such company or any underwriter therefor, in connection with a public offering, to any person who is not a resident of the State under the laws of which such company is organized or otherwise created; and

(3) such exemption is not contrary to the public interest or inconsistent with the protection of investors.

(e) *Application of Certain Specified Provisions of Subtitle to Otherwise Exempt Companies.* If, in connection with any rule, regulation, or order under this section exempting any investment company from any provision of section 7, the Commission deems it necessary or appropriate in the public interest or for the protection of investors that certain specified provisions of this title pertaining to registered investment companies shall be applicable in respect of such company, the provisions so specified shall apply to such company, and to other persons in their transactions and relations with such company, as though such company were a registered investment company.

(f) *Exemption of Closed-End Company Treated as Business Development Company.* Any closed-end company which—

(1) elects to be treated as a business development company pursuant to section 54; or

(2) would be excluded from the definition of an investment company by section 3(c)(1), except that it presently proposes to make a public offering of its securities as a business development company, and has notified the Commission, in a form and manner which the Commission may, by

rule, prescribe, that it intends in good faith to file, within 90 days, a notification of election to become subject to the provisions of sections 55 through 65,

shall be exempt from sections 1 through 53, except to the extent provided in sections 59 through 65.

Transactions by Unregistered Investment Companies

Sec. 7. (a) *Prohibition of Transactions in Interstate Commerce by Companies.* No investment company organized or otherwise created under the laws of the United States or of a State and having a board of directors, unless registered under section 8, shall directly or indirectly—

(1) offer for sale, sell, or deliver after sale, by the use of the mails or any means or instrumentality of interstate commerce, any security or any interest in a security, whether the issuer of such security is such investment company or another person; or offer for sale, sell, or deliver after sale any such security or interest, having reason to believe that such security or interest will be made the subject of a public offering by use of the mails or any means or instrumentality of interstate commerce;

(2) purchase, redeem, retire, or otherwise acquire or attempt to acquire, by use of the mails or any means or instrumentality of interstate commerce, any security or any interest in a security, whether the issuer of such security is such investment company or another person;

(3) control any investment company which does any of the acts enumerated in paragraphs (1) and (2);

(4) engage in any business in interstate commerce; or

(5) control any company which is engaged in any business in interstate commerce.

The provisions of this subsection (a) shall not apply to transactions of an investment company which are merely incidental to its dissolution.

(b) *Prohibition of Transaction in Interstate Commerce by Depositors or Trustees of Companies.* No depositor or trustee of or underwriter for any investment company, organized or otherwise created under the laws of the United States or of a State and not having a board of directors, unless such company is registered under section 8 or exempt under section 6, shall directly or indirectly—

(1) offer for sale, sell, or deliver after sale, by use of the mails or any means or instrumentality of interstate commerce, any security or any interest in a security of which such company is the issuer; or offer for sale, sell, or deliver after sale any such security or interest, having reason to believe that such security or interest will be made the subject of a public offering by use of the mails or any means or instrumentality of interstate commerce;

(2) purchase, redeem, or otherwise acquire or attempt to acquire, by use of the mails or any means or instrumentality of interstate commerce, any security or any interest in a security of which such company is the issuer; or

(3) sell or purchase for the account of such company, by use of the mails or any means or instrumentality of interstate commerce, any security or interest in a security, by whomever issued.

The provisions of this subsection (b) shall not apply to transactions which are merely incidental to the dissolution of an investment company.

(c) *Prohibitions of Transactions in Interstate Commerce by Promoters of Proposed Investment Companies.* No promoter of a proposed investment company, and no underwriter for such a promoter, shall make use of the mails or any means or instrumentality of interstate commerce, directly or indirectly, to offer for sale, sell, or deliver after sale, in connection with a public offering, any preorganization certificate or subscription for such a company.

(d) *Prohibition of Transactions in Interstate Commerce by Companies Not Organized Under Laws of the United States or a State; Exceptions.* No investment company, unless organized or otherwise created under the laws of the United States or of a State, and no depositor or trustee of or underwriter for such a company not so organized or created, shall make use of the mails or any means or instrumentality of interstate commerce, directly or indirectly, to offer for sale, sell, or deliver after sale, in connection with a public offering, any security of which such company is the issuer. Notwithstanding the provisions of this subsection and of section 8(a), the Commission is authorized, upon application by an investment company organized or otherwise created under the laws of a foreign country, to issue a conditional or unconditional order permitting such company to register under this title and to make a public offering of its securities by use of the mails and means or instrumentalities of interstate commerce, if the Commission finds that, by reason of special circumstances or arrangements, it is both legally and practically feasible effectively to enforce the provisions of this title against such company and that the issuance of such order is otherwise consistent with the public interest and the protection of investors.

(e) *Disclosure by Exempt Charitable Organizations.* Each fund that is excluded from the definition of an investment company under section 3(c)(10)(B) of this Act shall provide, to each donor to such fund, at the time of the donation or within 90 days after the date of enactment of this subsection, whichever is later, written information describing the material terms of the operation of such fund.

Registration of Investment Companies

Sec. 8. (a) *Notification of Registration; Effective Date of Registration.* Any investment company organized or otherwise created under the laws of the United States or of a State may register for the purposes of this title by filing with the Commission a notification of registration in such form as the Commission shall by rules and regulations prescribe as necessary or appropriate in the public interest or for the protection of investors. An investment company shall be deemed to be registered upon receipt by the Commission of such notification of registration.

(b) *Registration Statements; Contents.* Every registered investment company shall file with the Commission, within such reasonable time after registration as the Commission shall fix by rules and regulations, an original and such copies of a registration statement, in such form and containing such of the following information and documents as the Commission shall by rules and regulations prescribe as necessary or appropriate in the public interest or for the protection of investors:

(1) a recital of the policy of the registrant in respect of each of the following types of activities, such recital consisting in each case of a statement whether the registrant reserves freedom of action to engage in activities of such type, and if such freedom of action is reserved, a statement briefly indicating, insofar as is practicable, the extent to which the registrant intends to engage therein: (A) the classification and subclassifications, as defined in sections 4 and 5, within which the registrant proposes to operate; (B) borrowing money; (C) the issuance of senior securities; (D) engaging in the business of underwriting securities issued by other persons; (E) concentrating investments in a particular industry or group of industries; (F) the purchase and sale of real estate and commodities, or either of them; (G) making loans to other persons; and (H) portfolio turn-over (including a statement showing the aggregate dollar amount of purchases and sales of portfolio securities, other than Government securities, in each of the last three full fiscal years preceding the filing of such registration statement);

(2) a recital of all investment policies of the registrant, not enumerated in paragraph (1), which are changeable only if authorized by shareholder vote;

(3) a recital of all policies of the registrant, not enumerated in paragraphs (1) and (2), in respect of matters which the registrant deems matters of fundamental policy;

(4) the name and address of each affiliated person of the registrant; the name and principal address of every company, other than the registrant, of which each such person is an officer, director, or partner; a brief statement of the business experience for the preceding five years of each officer and director of the registrant; and

(5) the information and documents which would be required to be filed in order to register under the Securities Act of 1933 and the Securities Exchange Act of 1934 all securities (other than short-term paper) which the registrant has outstanding or proposes to issue.

(c) *Alternative Information.* The Commission shall make provision, by permissive rules and regulations or order, for the filing of the following, or so much of the following as the Commission may designate, in lieu of the information and documents required pursuant to subsection (b):

(1) copies of the most recent registration statement filed by the registrant under the Securities Act of 1933 and currently effective under such Act, or if the registrant has not filed such a statement, copies of a registration statement filed by the registrant under the Securities Exchange Act of 1934 and currently effective under such Act;

(2) copies of any reports filed by the registrant pursuant to section 13 or 15(d) of the Securities Exchange Act of 1934; and

(3) a report containing reasonably current information regarding the matters included in copies filed pursuant to paragraphs (1) and (2), and such further information regarding matters not included in such copies as the Commission is authorized to require under subsection (b).

(d) *Registration of Unit Investment Trusts.* If the registrant is a unit investment trust substantially all of the assets of which are securities issued by another registered investment company, the Commission is authorized to prescribe for the registrant, by rules and regulations or order, a registration statement which eliminates inappropriate duplication of information contained in the registration statement filed under this section by such other investment company.

(e) *Failure to File Registration Statement or Omission of Material Fact.* If it appears to the Commission that a registered investment company has failed to file the registration statement required by this section or a report required pursuant to section 30(a) or (b), or has filed such a registration statement or report but omitted therefrom material facts required to be stated therein, or has filed such a registration statement or report in violation of section 34(b), the Commission shall notify such company by registered mail or certified mail of the failure to file such registration statement or report, or of the respects in which such registration statement or report appears to be materially incomplete or misleading, as the case may be, and shall fix a date (in no event earlier than thirty days after the mailing of such notice) prior to which such company may file such registration statement or report or correct the same. If such registration statement or report is not filed or corrected within the time so fixed by the Commission or any extension thereof, the Commission, after appropriate notice and opportunity for hearing, and upon such conditions and with such exemptions as it deems appropriate for the protection of investors, may by order suspend the registration of such company until such statement or report is filed or corrected, or may by order revoke such registration, if the evidence establishes—

(1) that such company has failed to file a registration statement required by this section or a report required pursuant to section 30(a) or (b), or has filed such a registration statement or report but omitted therefrom material facts required to be stated therein, or has filed such a registration statement or report in violation of section 34(b); and

(2) that such suspension or revocation is in the public interest.

(f) *Cessation of Existence as Investment Company.* Whenever the Commission, on its own motion or upon application, finds that a registered investment company has ceased to be an investment company, it shall so declare by order and upon the taking effect of such order the registration of such company shall cease to be in effect. If necessary for the protection of investors, an order under this subsection may be made upon appropriate conditions. The Commission's denial of any application under this subsection shall be by order.

Ineligibility of Certain Affiliated Persons and Underwriters

Sec. 9. (a) *Persons Deemed Ineligible for Service with Investment Companies, Etc.; Investment Adviser.* It shall be unlawful for any of the following persons to serve or act in the capacity of employee, officer, director, member of an advisory board, investment adviser, or depositor of any registered investment company, or principal underwriter for any registered open-end company, registered unit investment trust, or registered face-amount certificate company:

(1) any person who within 10 years has been convicted of any felony or misdemeanor involving the purchase or sale of any security or arising out of such person's conduct as an underwriter, broker, dealer, investment adviser, municipal securities dealer, government securities broker, government securities dealer, bank, transfer agent, credit rating agency, or entity or person required to be registered under the Commodity Exchange Act, or as an affiliated person, salesman, or employee of any investment company, bank, insurance company, or entity or person required to be registered under the Commodity Exchange Act;

(2) any person who, by reason of any misconduct, is permanently or temporarily enjoined by order, judgment, or decree of any court of competent jurisdiction from acting as an underwriter, broker, dealer, investment adviser, municipal securities dealer, government securities broker, government securities dealer, bank, transfer agent, credit rating agency, or entity or person required to be registered under the Commodity Exchange Act, or as an affiliated person, salesman, or employee of any investment company, bank, insurance company, or entity or person required to be registered under the Commodity Exchange Act, or from engaging in or continuing any conduct or practice in connection with any such activity or in connection with the purchase or sale of any security; or

(3) a company any affiliated person of which is ineligible, by reason of paragraph (1) or (2), to serve or act in the foregoing capacities.

For the purposes of paragraphs (1), (2), and (3) of this subsection, the term "investment adviser" shall include an investment adviser as defined in title II of this Act.

(b) *Certain Persons Serving Investment Companies; Administrative Action of Commission.* The Commission may, after notice and opportunity for hearing, by order prohibit, conditionally or unconditionally, either permanently or for such period of time as it in its discretion shall deem appropriate in the public interest, any person from serving or acting as an employee, officer, director, member of an advisory board, investment adviser or depositor of, or principal underwriter for, a registered investment company or affiliated person of such investment adviser, depositor, or principal underwriter, if such person—

(1) has willfully made or caused to be made in any registration statement, application or report filed with the Commission under this title any statement which was at the time and in the light of the circumstances under which it was made false or misleading with respect to any material fact, or has omitted to state in any such registration statement, application, or report any material fact which was required to be stated therein;

(2) has willfully violated any provision of the Securities Act of 1933, or of the Securities Exchange Act of 1934, or of title II of this Act, or of this title, or of the Commodity Exchange Act, or of any rule or regulation under any of such statutes;

(3) has willfully aided, abetted, counseled, commanded, induced, or procured the violation by any other person of the Securities Act of 1933, or of the Securities Exchange Act of 1934, or of title II of this Act, or of this title, or of the Commodity Exchange Act, or of any rule or regulation under any of such statutes;

(4) has been found by a foreign financial regulatory authority to have—

(A) made or caused to be made in any application for registration or report required to be filed with a foreign securities authority, or in any proceeding before a foreign securities authority with respect to registration, any statement that was at the time and in light of the circumstances under which it was made false or misleading with respect to any material fact, or has omitted to state in any application or report to a foreign securities authority any material fact that is required to be stated therein;

(B) violated any foreign statute or regulation regarding transactions in securities or contracts of sale of a commodity for future delivery traded on or subject to the rules of a contract market or any board of trade; or

(C) aided, abetted, counseled, commanded, induced, or procured the violation by any other person of any foreign statute or regulation regarding transactions in securities or contracts of sale of a commodity for future delivery traded on or subject to the rules of a contract market or any board of trade;

(5) within 10 years has been convicted by a foreign court of competent jurisdiction of a crime, however denominated by the laws of the relevant foreign government, that is substantially equivalent to an offense set forth in paragraph (1) of subsection (a); or

(6) by reason of any misconduct, is temporarily or permanently enjoined by any foreign court of competent jurisdiction from acting in any of the capacities, set forth in paragraph (2) of subsection (a), or a substantially equivalent foreign capacity, or from engaging in or continuing any conduct or practice in connection with any such activity or in connection with the purchase or sale of any security.

(c) *Application of Ineligible Person for Exemption.* Any person who is ineligible, by reason of subsection (a), to serve or act in the capacities enumerated in that subsection, may file with the Commission an application for an exemption from the provisions of that subsection. The Commission shall by order grant such application, either unconditionally or on an appropriate temporary or other conditional basis, if it is established that the prohibitions of subsection (a) as applied to such person, are unduly or disproportionately severe or that the conduct of such person has been such as not to make it against the public interest or protection of investors to grant such application.

(d) *Money Penalties in Administrative Proceedings.*

(1) *Authority of Commission.*

(A) *In General.* In any proceeding instituted pursuant to subsection (b) of this section against any person, the Commission may impose a civil penalty if it finds, on the record after notice and opportunity for hearing, that such penalty is in the public interest, and that such person—

(i) has willfully violated any provision of the Securities Act of 1933, the Securities Exchange Act of 1934, subchapter II of this chapter, or this subchapter, or the rules or regulations thereunder;

(ii) has willfully aided, abetted, counseled, commanded, induced, or procured such a violation by any other person; or

(iii) has willfully made or caused to be made in any registration statement, application, or report required to be filed with the Commission under this subchapter, any statement which was, at the time and in the light of the circumstances under which it was made, false or misleading with respect to any material fact, or has omitted to state in any such registration statement, application, or report any material fact which was required to be stated therein;

(B) *Cease-and-Desist Proceedings.* In any proceeding instituted pursuant to subsection (f) against any person, the Commission may impose a civil penalty if the Commission finds, on the record, after notice and opportunity for hearing, that such person—

(i) is violating or has violated any provision of this title, or any rule or regulation issued under this title; or

(ii) is or was a cause of the violation of any provision of this title, or any rule or regulation issued under this title.

(2) *Maximum Amount of Penalty.*

(A) *First Tier.* The maximum amount of penalty for each act or omission described in paragraph (1) shall be $5,000 for a natural person or $50,000 for any other person.

(B) *Second Tier.* Notwithstanding subparagraph (A), the maximum amount of penalty for each such act or omission shall be $50,000 for a natural person or $250,000 for any other person if the act or omission described in paragraph (1) involved fraud, deceit, manipulation, or deliberate or reckless disregard of a regulatory requirement.

(C) *Third Tier.* Notwithstanding subparagraphs (A) and (B), the maximum amount of penalty for each such act or omission shall be $100,000 for a natural person or $500,000 for any other person if—

(i) the act or omission described in paragraph (1) involved fraud, deceit, manipulation, or deliberate or reckless disregard of a regulatory requirement; and

(ii) such act or omission directly or indirectly resulted in substantial losses or created a significant risk of substantial losses to other persons or resulted in substantial pecuniary gain to the person who committed the act or omission.

(3) *Determination of Public Interest.* In considering under this section whether a penalty is in the public interest, the Commission may consider—

(A) whether the act or omission for which such penalty is assessed involved fraud, deceit, manipulation, or deliberate or reckless disregard of a regulatory requirement;

(B) the harm to other persons resulting either directly or indirectly from such act or omission;

(C) the extent to which any person was unjustly enriched, taking into account any restitution made to persons injured by such behavior;

(D) whether such person previously has been found by the Commission, another appropriate regulatory agency, or a self-regulatory organization to have violated the Federal securities laws, State securities laws, or the rules of a self-regulatory organization, has been enjoined by a court of competent jurisdiction from violations of such laws or rules, or has been convicted by a court of competent jurisdiction of violations of such laws or of any felony or misdemeanor described in section 203(e)(2) of the Investment Advisers Act of 1940;

(E) the need to deter such person and other persons from committing such acts or omissions; and

(F) such other matters as justice may require.

(4) *Evidence Concerning Ability to Pay.* In any proceeding in which the Commission may impose a penalty under this section, a respondent may present evidence of the respondent's ability to pay such penalty. The Commission may, in its discretion, consider such evidence in determining whether such penalty is in the public interest. Such evidence may relate to the extent of such person's ability to continue in business and the collectability of a penalty, taking into account any other claims of the United States or third parties upon such person's assets and the amount of such person's assets.

(e) *Authority to Enter an Order Requiring an Accounting and Disgorgement.* In any proceeding in which the Commission may impose a penalty under this section, the Commission may enter an order requiring accounting and disgorgement, including reasonable interest. The Commission is authorized to adopt rules, regulations, and orders concerning payments to investors, rates of interest, periods of accrual, and such other matters as it deems appropriate to implement this subsection.

(f) *Cease-and-Desist Proceedings.*

(1) *Authority of the Commission.* If the Commission finds, after notice and opportunity for hearing, that any person is violating, has violated, or is about to violate any provision of this title, or any rule or regulation thereunder, the Commission may publish its findings and enter an order requiring such person, and any other person that is, was, or would be a cause of the violation, due to an act or omission the person knew or should have known would contribute to such violation, to cease and desist from committing or causing such violation and any future violation of the same provision, rule, or regulation. Such order may, in addition to requiring a person to cease and desist from committing or causing a violation, require such person to comply, or to take steps to effect compliance, with such provision, rule, or regulation, upon such terms and conditions and within such time as the Commission may specify in such order. Any such order may, as the Commission deems appropriate, require future compliance or steps to effect future compliance, either permanently or for such period of time as the Commission may specify, with such provision, rule, or regulation with respect to any security, any issuer, or any other person.

(2) *Hearing.* The notice instituting proceedings pursuant to paragraph (1) shall fix a hearing date not earlier than 30 days nor later than 60 days after service of the notice unless an earlier or a later date is set by the Commission with the consent of any respondent so served.

(3) *Temporary Order.*

(A) *In General.* Whenever the Commission determines that the alleged violation or threatened violation specified in the notice instituting proceedings pursuant to paragraph (1), or the continuation thereof, is likely to result in significant dissipation or conversion of assets, significant harm to investors, or substantial harm to the public interest, including, but not limited to, losses to the Securities Investor Protection Corporation, prior to the completion of the proceeding, the Commission may enter a temporary order requiring the respondent to cease and desist from the violation or threatened violation and to take such action to prevent the violation or threatened violation and to prevent dissipation or conversion of assets, significant harm to investors, or substantial harm to the public interest as the Commission deems appropriate pending completion of such proceedings. Such an order shall be entered only after notice and opportunity for a hearing, unless the Commission, notwithstanding section 40(a) of this title, determines that notice and hearing prior to entry would be impracticable or contrary to the public interest. A temporary order shall become effective upon service upon the respondent and, unless set aside, limited, or suspended by the Commission or a court of competent jurisdiction, shall remain effective and enforceable pending the completion of the proceedings.

(B) *Applicability.* This paragraph shall apply only to a respondent that acts, or, at the time of the alleged misconduct acted, as a broker, dealer, investment adviser, investment company, municipal securities dealer, government securities broker, government securities dealer, or transfer agent, or is, or was at the time of the alleged misconduct, an associated person of, or a person seeking to become associated with, any of the foregoing.

(4) *Review of Temporary Orders.*

(A) *Commission Review.* At any time after the respondent has been served with a temporary cease-and-desist order pursuant to paragraph (3), the respondent may apply to the Commission to have the order set aside, limited, or suspended. If the respondent has been served with a temporary cease-and-desist order entered without a prior Commission hearing, the respondent may, within 10 days after the date on which the order was served, request a hearing on such application and the Commission shall hold a hearing and render a decision on such application at the earliest possible time.

(B) *Judicial Review.* Within—

(i) 10 days after the date the respondent was served with a temporary cease-and-desist order entered with a prior Commission hearing, or

(ii) 10 days after the Commission renders a decision on an application and hearing under subparagraph (A), with respect to any temporary cease-and-desist order entered without a prior Commission hearing, the respondent may apply to the United States district court for the district in which the respondent resides or has its principal place of business, or for the District of Columbia, for an order setting aside, limiting, or suspending the effectiveness or enforcement of the order, and the court shall have jurisdiction to enter such an order. A respondent served with a temporary cease-and-desist order entered without a prior Commission hearing may not apply to the court except after hearing and decision by the Commission on the respondent's application under subparagraph (A) of this paragraph.

(C) *No Automatic Stay of Temporary Order.* The commencement of proceedings under subparagraph (B) of this paragraph shall not, unless specifically ordered by the court, operate as a stay of the Commission's order.

(D) *Exclusive Review.* Section 43 of this title shall not apply to a temporary order entered pursuant to this section.

(5) *Authority to Enter an order Requiring an Accounting and Disgorgement.* In any cease-and-desist proceeding under subsection (f)(1), the Commission may enter an order requiring accounting and disgorgement, including reasonable interest. The Commission is authorized to adopt rules, regulations, and orders concerning payments to investors, rates of interest, periods of accrual, and such other matters as it deems appropriate to implement this subsection.

(g) *Corporate or Other Trustees Performing Functions of Investment Advisers.* For the purposes of this section, the term "investment adviser" includes a corporate or other trustee performing the functions of an investment adviser.

Affiliations or Interest of Directors, Officers, and Employees

Sec. 10. (a) *Interested Persons of Company Who May Serve on Board of Directors.* No registered investment company shall have a board of directors more than 60 per centum of the members of which are persons who are interested persons of such registered company.

(b) *Employment and Use of Directors, Officers, Etc., as Regular Broker, Principal Underwriter, or Investment Banker.* No registered investment company shall—

(1) employ as regular broker any director, officer, or employee of such registered company, or any person of which any such director, officer, or employee is an affiliated person, unless a majority of the board of directors of such registered company shall be persons who are not such brokers or affiliated persons of any of such brokers;

(2) use as a principal underwriter of securities issued by it any director, officer, or employee of such registered company or any person of which any such director, officer, or employee is an interested person, unless a majority of the board of directors of such registered company shall be persons who are not such principal underwriters or interested persons of any of such principal underwriters; or

(3) have as director, officer, or employee any investment banker, or any affiliated person of an investment banker, unless a majority of the board of directors of such registered company shall be persons who are not investment bankers or affiliated persons of any investment banker. For the purposes of this paragraph, a person shall not be deemed an affiliated person of an investment banker solely by reason of the fact that he is an affiliated person of a company of the character described in section 12(d)(3)(A) and (B).

(c) *Officers, Directors, or Employees of One Bank or Bank Holding Company as Majority of Board of Directors of Company; Exceptions.* No registered investment company shall have a majority of its board of directors consisting of persons who are officers, directors, or employees of any one bank (together with its affiliates and subsidiaries) or any one bank holding company (together with its affiliates and subsidiaries) (as such terms are defined in section 2 of the Bank Holding Company Act of 1956) or any one savings and loan holding company, together with its affiliates and subsidiaries (as such terms are defined in section 10 of the Home Owners' Loan Act), except that, if on March 15, 1940, any registered investment company had a majority of its directors consisting of persons who are directors, officers, or employees of any one bank, such company may continue to have the same percentage of its board of directors consisting of persons who are directors, officers, or employees of such bank.

(d) *Exception to Limitation of Number of Interested Persons Who May Serve on Board of Directors.* Notwithstanding subsections (a) and (b)(2) of this section, a registered investment company may have a board of directors all the members of which, except one, are interested persons of the investment adviser of such company, or are officers or employees of such company, if—

(1) such investment company is an open-end company;

(2) such investment adviser is registered under title II of this Act and is engaged principally in the business of rendering investment supervisory services as defined in title II;

(3) no sales load is charged on securities issued by such investment company;

(4) any premium over net asset value charged by such company upon the issuance of any such security, plus any discount from net asset value charged on redemption thereof, shall not in the aggregate exceed 2 per centum;

(5) no sales or promotion expenses are incurred by such registered company; but expenses incurred in complying with laws regulating the issue or sale of securities shall not be deemed sales or promotion expenses;

(6) such investment adviser is the only investment adviser to such investment company, and such investment adviser does not receive a management fee exceeding 1 per centum per annum of the value of such company's net assets averaged over the year or taken as of a definite date or dates within the year;

(7) all executive salaries and executive expenses and office rent of such investment company are paid by such investment adviser; and

(8) such investment company has only one class of securities outstanding, each unit of which has equal voting rights with every other unit.

(e) *Death, Disqualification, or Resignation of Directors as Suspension of Limitation Provisions.* If by reason of the death, disqualification, or bona fide resignation of any director or directors, the requirements of the foregoing provisions of this section or of section 15(f)(1) in respect of directors shall not be met by a registered investment company, the operation of such provision shall be suspended as to such registered company—

(1) for a period of thirty days if the vacancy or vacancies may be filled by action of the board of directors;

(2) for a period of sixty days if a vote of stockholders is required to fill the vacancy or vacancies; or

(3) for such longer period as the Commission may prescribe, by rules and regulations upon its own motion or by order upon application, as not inconsistent with the protection of investors.

(f) *Officer, Director, Etc., of Company Acting as Principal Underwriter of Security Acquired by Company.* No registered investment company shall knowingly purchase or otherwise acquire, during the existence of any underwriting or selling syndicate, any security (except a security of which such company is the issuer) a principal underwriter of which is an officer, director, member of an advisory board, investment adviser, or employee of such registered company, or is a person (other than a company of the character described in section 12(d)(3)(A) and (B)) of which any such officer, director, member of an advisory board, investment adviser, or employee is an affiliated person, unless in acquiring such security such registered company is itself acting as a principal underwriter for the issuer. The Commission, by rules and regulations upon its own motion or by order upon application, may conditionally or unconditionally exempt any transaction or classes of transactions from any of the provisions of this subsection, if and to the extent that such exemption is consistent with the protection of investors.

(g) *Advisory Boards; Restrictions on Membership.* In the case of a registered investment company which has an advisory board, such board, as a distinct entity, shall be subject to the same restrictions as to its membership as are imposed upon a board of directors by this section.

(h) *Application of Section to Unincorporated Registered Management Companies.* In the case of a registered management company which is an unincorporated company not having a board of directors, the provisions of this section shall apply as follows:

(1) the provisions of subsection (a), as modified by subsection (e), shall apply to the board of directors of the depositor of such company;

(2) the provisions of subsections (b) and (c), as modified by subsection (e), shall apply to the board of directors of the depositor and of every investment adviser of such company; and

(3) the provisions of subsection (f) shall apply to purchases and other acquisitions for the account of such company of securities a principal underwriter of which is the depositor or an investment adviser of such company, or an affiliated person of such depositor or investment adviser.

Offers to Exchange Securities

Sec. 11. (a) *Approval by Commission for Exchanges of Securities on Basis Other than Relative Net Asset Value.* It shall be unlawful for any registered open-end company or any principal underwriter for such a company to make or cause to be made an offer to the holder of a security of such company or of any other open-end investment company to exchange his security for a security in the same or another such company on any basis other than the relative net asset values of the respective securities to be exchanged, unless the terms of the offer have first been submitted to and approved by the Commission or are in accordance with such rules and regulations as the Commission may have prescribed in respect of such offers which are in effect at the time such offer is made. For the purposes of this section, (A) an offer by a principal underwriter means an offer communicated to holders of securities of a class or series but does not include an offer made by such principal underwriter to an individual investor in the course of a retail business conducted by such principal underwriter, and (B) the net asset value means the net asset value which is in effect for the purpose of determining the price at which the securities, or class or series of securities involved, are offered for sale to the public either (1) at the time of the receipt by the offeror of the acceptance of the offer or (2) at such later times as is specified in the offer.

(b) *Application of Section to Offers Pursuant to Plan of Reorganization.* The provisions of this section shall not apply to any offer made pursuant to any plan of reorganization, which is submitted to and requires the approval of the holders of at least a majority of the outstanding shares of the class or series to which the security owned by the offeree belongs.

(c) *Application of Section to Specific Exchange Offers.* The provisions of subsection (a) shall be applicable, irrespective of the basis of exchange, (1) to any offer of exchange of any security of a registered open-end company for a security of a registered unit investment trust or registered face-amount certificate company; and (2) to any type of offer of exchange of the securities of registered unit investment trusts or registered face-amount certificate companies for the securities of any other investment company.

Functions and Activities of Investment Companies

Sec. 12. (a) *Purchase of Securities on Margin; Joint Trading Accounts; Short Sales of Securities; Exceptions.* It shall be unlawful for any registered investment company, in contravention of such rules and regulations or orders as the Commission may prescribe as necessary or appropriate in the public interest or for the protection of investors—

(1) to purchase any security on margin, except such short-term credits as are necessary for the clearance of transactions;

(2) to participate on a joint or a joint and several basis in any trading account in securities, except in connection with an underwriting in which such registered company is a participant; or

(3) to effect a short sale of any security, except in connection with an underwriting in which such registered company is a participant.

(b) *Distribution by Investment Company of Securities of Which It Is Issuer.* It shall be unlawful for any registered open-end company (other than a company complying with the provisions of section 10(d)) to act as a distributor of securities of which it is the issuer, except through an underwriter, in contravention of such rules and regulations as the Commission may prescribe as necessary or appropriate in the public interest or for the protection of investors.

(c) *Limitations on Commitments as Underwriter.* It shall be unlawful for any registered diversified company to make any commitment as underwriter, if immediately thereafter the amount of its outstanding underwriting commitments, plus the value of its investments in securities of issuers (other than investment companies) of which it owns more than 10 per centum of the outstanding voting securities, exceeds 25 per centum of the value of its total assets.

(d) *Limitations on Acquisition by Investment Companies of Securities of Other Specific Businesses.*

(1)(A) It shall be unlawful for any registered investment company (the "acquiring company") and any company or companies controlled by such acquiring company to purchase or otherwise acquire any security issued by any other investment company (the "acquired company"), and for any investment company (the "acquiring company") and any company or companies controlled by such acquiring company to purchase or otherwise acquire any security issued by any registered investment company (the "acquired company"), if the acquiring company and any company or companies controlled by it immediately after such purchase or acquisition own in the aggregate—

(i) more than 3 per centum of the total outstanding voting stock of the acquired company;

(ii) securities issued by the acquired company having an aggregate value in excess of 5 per centum of the value of the total assets of the acquiring company; or

(iii) securities issued by the acquired company and all other investment companies (other than Treasury stock of the acquiring company) having an aggregate value in excess of 10 per centum of the value of the total assets of the acquiring company.

(B) It shall be unlawful for any registered open-end investment company (the "acquired company"), any principal underwriter therefor, or any broker or dealer registered under the Securities Exchange Act of 1934, knowingly to sell or otherwise dispose of any security issued by the acquired company to any other investment company (the "acquiring company") or any company or companies controlled by the acquiring company, if immediately after such sale or disposition—

(i) more than 3 per centum of the total outstanding voting stock of the acquired company is owned by the acquiring company and any company or companies controlled by it; or

(ii) more than 10 per centum of the total outstanding voting stock of the acquired company is owned by the acquiring company and other investment companies and companies controlled by them.

(C) It shall be unlawful for any investment company (the "acquiring company") and any company or companies controlled by the acquiring company to purchase or otherwise acquire any security issued by a registered closed-end investment company, if immediately after such purchase or acquisition the acquiring company, other investment companies having the same investment adviser, and companies controlled by such investment companies, own more than 10 per centum of the total outstanding voting stock of such closed-end company.

(D) The provisions of this paragraph shall not apply to a security received as a dividend or as a result of an offer of exchange approved pursuant to section 11 or of a plan of reorganization of any company (other than a plan devised for the purpose of evading the foregoing provisions).

(E) The provisions of this paragraph shall not apply to a security (or securities) purchased or acquired by an investment company if—

(i) the depositor of, or principal underwriter for, such investment company is a broker or dealer registered under the Securities Exchange Act of 1934, or a person controlled by such a broker or dealer;

(ii) such security is the only investment security held by such investment company (or such securities are the only investment securities held by such investment company, if such investment company is a registered unit investment trust that issues two or more classes or series of securities, each of which provides for the accumulation of shares of a different investment company); and

(iii) the purchase or acquisition is made pursuant to an arrangement with the issuer of, or principal underwriter for the issuer of, the security whereby such investment company is obligated—

(aa) either to seek instructions from its security holders with regard to the voting of all proxies with respect to such security and to vote such proxies only in accordance with such instructions, or to vote the shares held by it in the same proportion as the vote of all other holders of such security, and

(bb) in the event that such investment company is not a registered investment company, to refrain from substituting such security unless the Commission shall have approved such substitution in the manner provided in section 26 of this Act.

(F) The provisions of this paragraph shall not apply to securities purchased or otherwise acquired by a registered investment company if—

(i) immediately after such purchase or acquisition not more than 3 per centum of the total outstanding stock of such issuer is owned by such registered investment company and all affiliated persons of such registered investment company; and

(ii) such registered investment company has not offered or sold after January 1, 1971, and is not proposing to offer or sell any security issued by it through a principal underwriter or otherwise at a public offering price which includes a sales load of more than 1/2 per centum.

No issuer of any security purchased or acquired by a registered investment company pursuant to this subparagraph shall be obligated to redeem such security in an amount exceeding 1 per centum of such issuer's total outstanding securities during any period of less than thirty days. Such investment company shall exercise voting rights by proxy or otherwise with respect to any security purchased or acquired pursuant to this subparagraph in the manner prescribed by subparagraph (E) of this subsection.

(G)(i) This paragraph does not apply to securities of a registered open-end investment company or a registered unit investment trust (hereafter in this subparagraph referred to as the "acquired company") purchased or otherwise acquired by a registered open-end investment company or a registered unit investment trust (hereafter in this subparagraph referred to as the "acquiring company") if—

(I) the acquired company and the acquiring company are part of the same group of investment companies;

(II) the securities of the acquired company, securities of other registered open-end investment companies and registered unit investment trusts that are part of the same group of investment companies, Government securities, and short-term paper are the only investments held by the acquiring company;

(III) with respect to—

(aa) securities of the acquired company, the acquiring company does not pay and is not assessed any charges or fees for distribution-related activities, unless the acquiring company does not charge a sales load or other fees or charges for distribution-related activities; or

(bb) securities of the acquiring company, any sales loads and other distribution-related fees charged, when aggregated with any sales load and distribution-related fees paid by the acquiring company with respect to securities of the acquired company, are not excessive under rules adopted pursuant to section 22(b) or section 22(c) by a securities association registered under section 15A of the Securities Exchange Act of 1934, or the Commission;

(IV) the acquired company has a policy that prohibits it from acquiring any securities of registered open-end investment companies or registered unit investment trusts in reliance on this subparagraph or subparagraph (F); and

(V) such acquisition is not in contravention of such rules and regulations as the Commission may from time to time prescribe with respect to acquisitions in accordance with this subparagraph, as necessary and appropriate for the protection of investors.

(ii) For purposes of this subparagraph, the term "group of investment companies" means any 2 or more registered investment companies that hold themselves out to investors as related companies for purposes of investment and investor services.

(H) For the purposes of this paragraph, the value of an investment company's total assets shall be computed as of the time of a purchase or acquisition or as closely thereto as is reasonably possible.

(I) In any action brought to enforce the provisions of this paragraph, the Commission may join as a party the issuer of any security purchased or otherwise acquired in violation of this paragraph, and the court may issue any order with respect to such issuer as may be necessary or appropriate for the enforcement of the provisions of this paragraph.

(J) The Commission, by rule or regulation, upon its own motion or by order upon application, may conditionally or unconditionally exempt any person, security, or transaction, or any class or classes of persons, securities, or transactions from any provision of this paragraph, if and to the extent that such exemption is consistent with the public interest and the protection of investors.

(2) It shall be unlawful for any registered investment company and any company or companies controlled by such registered investment company to purchase or otherwise acquire any security (except a security received as a dividend or as a result of a plan of reorganization of any company, other than a plan devised for the purpose of evading the provisions of this paragraph) issued by any insurance company of which such registered investment company and any company or companies controlled by such registered company do not, at the time of such purchase or acquisition, own in the aggregate at least 25 per centum of the total outstanding voting stock, if such registered com-

pany and any company or companies controlled by it own in the aggregate, or as a result of such purchase or acquisition will own in the aggregate, more than 10 per centum of the total outstanding voting stock of such insurance company.

(3) It shall be unlawful for any registered investment company and any company or companies controlled by such registered investment company to purchase or otherwise acquire any security issued by or any other interest in the business of any person who is a broker, a dealer, is engaged in the business of underwriting, or is either an investment adviser of an investment company or an investment adviser registered under title II of this Act, unless (A) such person is a corporation all the outstanding securities of which (other than short-term paper, securities representing bank loans, and directors' qualifying shares) are, or after such acquisition will be, owned by one or more registered investment companies; and (B) such person is primarily engaged in the business of underwriting and distributing securities issued by other persons, selling securities to customers, or any one or more of such or related activities, and the gross income of such person normally is derived principally from such business or related activities.

(e) *Acquisition of Securities Issued by Corporations in Business of Underwriting, Furnishing Capital to Industry, Etc.* Notwithstanding any provisions of this title, any registered investment company may hereafter purchase or otherwise acquire any security issued by any one corporation engaged or proposing to engage in the business of underwriting, furnishing capital to industry, financing promotional enterprises, purchasing securities of issuers for which no ready market is in existence, and reorganizing companies or similar activities; provided—

(1) That the securities issued by such corporation (other than short-term paper and securities representing bank loans) shall consist solely of one class of common stock and shall have been originally issued or sold for investment to registered investment companies only;

(2) That the aggregate cost of the securities of such corporation purchased by such registered investment company does not exceed 5 per centum of the value of the total assets of such registered company at the time of any purchase or acquisition of such securities; and

(3) That the aggregate paid-in capital and surplus of such corporation does not exceed $100,000,000.

For the purpose of paragraph (1) of section 5(b) any investment in any such corporation shall be deemed to be an investment in an investment company.

(f) *Organization and Ownership by One Registered Face-Amount Certificate Company of All or Part of Capital Stock of Not More than Two Other Face-Amount Certificate Companies; Limitations.* Notwithstanding any provisions of this Act, any registered face-amount certificate company may organize not more than two face-amount certificate companies and acquire and own all or any part of the capital stock thereof only if such stock is acquired and held for investment: *Provided,* That the aggregate cost to such registered company of all such stock so acquired shall not exceed six times the amount of the minimum capital stock requirement provided in subdivision (1) of subsection (a) of section 28 for a face-amount company organized on or after March 15, 1940: *And provided further,* That the aggregate cost to such registered company of all such capital stock issued by face-amount certificate companies organized or otherwise created under laws other than the laws of the United States or any State thereof shall not exceed twice the amount of the minimum capital stock requirement provided in subdivision (1) of subsection (a) of section 28 for a company organized on or after March 15, 1940. Nothing contained in this subsection shall be deemed to prevent the sale of any such stock to any other person if the original purchase was made by such registered face-amount certificate company in good faith for investment and not for resale.

(g) *Exceptions to Limitation on Ownership by Investment Company of Securities of Insurance Company.* Notwithstanding the provisions of this section any registered investment company and any company or companies controlled by such registered company may purchase or otherwise acquire from another investment company or any company or companies controlled by such registered company more than 10 per centum of the total outstanding voting stock of any insurance company owned by any such company or companies, or may acquire the securities of any insurance company if the Commission by order determines that such acquisition is in the public interest because the financial condition of such insurance company will be improved as a result of such acquisition or any plan contemplated as a result thereof. This section shall not be deemed to prohibit the promotion of a new insurance company or the acquisition of the securities of any newly created insurance company by a registered investment company, alone or with other persons. Nothing contained in this section shall in any way affect or derogate from the powers of any insurance commissioner or similar official or agency of the United States or any State, or to affect the right under State law of any insurance company to acquire securities of any other insurance company or insurance companies.

Changes in Investment Policy

Sec. 13. (a) No registered investment company shall, unless authorized by the vote of a majority of its outstanding voting securities—

(1) change its subclassification as defined in section 5(a)(1) and (2) of this title or its subclassification from a diversified to a non-diversified company;

(2) borrow money, issue senior securities, underwrite securities issued by other persons, purchase or sell real estate or commodities or make loans to other persons, except in each case in accordance with the recitals of policy contained in its registration statement in respect thereto;

(3) deviate from its policy in respect of concentration of investments in any particular industry or group of industries as recited in its registration statement, deviate from any investment policy which is changeable only if authorized by shareholder vote, or deviate from any policy recited in its registration statement pursuant to section 8(b)(3); or

(4) change the nature of its business so as to cease to be an investment company.

(b) In the case of a common-law trust of the character described in section 16(c), either written approval by holders of a majority of the outstanding shares of beneficial interest or the vote of a majority of such outstanding shares cast in person or by proxy at a meeting called for the purpose shall for the purposes of subsection (a) be deemed the equivalent of the vote of a majority of the outstanding voting securities, and the provisions of paragraph (42) of section 2(a) as to a majority shall be applicable to the votes casts at such a meeting.

(c) *Limitation on Actions.*

(1) *In General.* Notwithstanding any other provision of Federal or State law, no person may bring any civil, criminal, or administrative action against any registered investment company, or any employee, officer, director, or investment adviser thereof, based solely upon the investment company divesting from, or avoiding investing in, securities issued by persons that the investment company determines, using credible information available to the public—

[*This subparagraph terminates 30 days after the date on which the President certifies to Congress that the Government of Sudan has honored specified commitments, see P.L. 110–174, § 12, set out as a note under 50 USCS § 1701.*]

(A) conduct or have direct investments in business operations in Sudan described in section 3(d) of the Sudan Accountability and Divestment Act of 2007; or

[*This subparagraph ceases to be effective 30 days after President's certification regarding cessation of certain actions by the Government of Iran, pursuant to § 401(a) of Act July 1, 2010, P.L. 111–195, which appears as 22 USCS § 8551(a).*]

(B) engage in investment activities in Iran described in section 8532(c) of Title 22.

(2) *Applicability.*

(A) *Rule of Construction.* Nothing in paragraph (1) shall be construed to create, imply, diminish, change, or affect in any way whether or not a private right of action exists under subsection (a) or any other provision of this subchapter.

(B) *Disclosures.* Paragraph (1) shall not apply to a registered investment company, or any employee, officer, director, or investment adviser thereof, unless the investment company makes disclosures in accordance with regulations prescribed by the Commission.

(3) *Person Defined.* For purposes of this subsection the term "person" includes the Federal Government and any State or political subdivision of a State.

Size of Investment Companies

Sec. 14. (a) *Public Offerings.* No registered investment company organized after the date of enactment of this title, and no principal underwriter for such a company, shall make a public offering of securities of which such company is the issuer, unless—

(1) such company has a net worth of at least $100,000;

(2) such company has previously made a public offering of its securities, and at the time of such offering had a net worth of at least $100,000; or

(3) provision is made in connection with and as a condition of the registration of such securities under the Securities Act of 1933 which in the opinion of the Commission adequately insures (A) that after the effective date of such registration statement such company will not issue any security or receive any proceeds of any subscription for any security until firm agreements have been made with such company by not more than twenty-five responsible persons to purchase from it securities to be issued by it for an aggregate net amount which plus the then net worth of the company, if any, will equal at least $100,000; (B) that said aggregate net amount will be paid in to such company before any subscriptions for such securities will be accepted from any persons in excess of twenty-five; (C) that arrangements will be made whereby any proceeds so paid in, as well as any sales load, will be refunded to any subscriber on demand without any deduction, in the event that the net proceeds so received by the company do not result in the company having a net worth of at least $100,000 within ninety days after such registration statement becomes effective.

At any time after the occurrence of the event specified in clause (C) of paragraph (3) of this subsection the Commission may issue a stop order suspending the effectiveness of the registration statement of such securities under the Securities Act of 1933 and may suspend or revoke the registration of such company under this title.

(b) The Commission is authorized, at such times as it deems that any substantial further increase in size of investment companies creates any problem involving the protection of investors or the public interest, to make a study and investigation of the effects of size on the investment policy of investment companies and on security markets, on concentration of control of wealth and industry, and on companies in which investment companies are interested, and from time to time to report the results of its studies and investigations and its recommendations to the Congress.

Contracts of Advisers and Underwriters

Sec. 15. (a) *Written Contract to Serve or Act as Investment Adviser; Contents.* It shall be unlawful for any person to serve or act as investment adviser of a registered investment company, except pursuant to a written contract, which contract, whether with such registered company or with an investment adviser of such registered company, has been approved by the vote of a majority of the outstanding voting securities of such registered company, and—

(1) precisely describes all compensation to be paid thereunder;

(2) shall continue in effect for a period more than two years from the date of its execution, only so long as such continuance is specifically approved at least annually by the board of directors or by vote of a majority of the outstanding voting securities of such company;

(3) provides, in substance, that it may be terminated at any time, without the payment of any penalty, by the board of directors of such registered company or by vote of a majority of the outstanding voting securities of such company on not more than sixty days' written notice to the investment adviser; and

(4) provides, in substance, for its automatic termination in the event of its assignment.

(b) *Written Contract with Company for Sale by Principal Underwriter of Security of Which Company Is Issuer; Contents.* It shall be unlawful for any principal underwriter for a registered open-end company to offer for sale, sell, or deliver after sale any security of which such company is the issuer, except pursuant to a written contract with such company, which contract—

(1) shall continue in effect for a period more than two years from the date of its execution, only so long as such continuance is specifically approved at least annually by the board of directors or by vote of a majority of the outstanding voting securities of such company; and

(2) provides, in substance, for its automatic termination in the event of its assignment.

(c) *Approval of Contract to Undertake Service as Investment Adviser or Principal Underwriter by Majority of Noninterested Directors.* In addition to the requirements of subsection (a) and (b) of this section, it shall be unlawful for any registered investment company having a board of directors to enter into, renew, or perform any contract or agreement, written or oral, whereby a person undertakes regularly to serve or act as investment adviser of or principal underwriter for such company unless the terms of such contract or agreement and any renewal thereof have been approved by the vote of a majority of directors, who are not parties to such contract or agreement or interested persons of any such party, cast in person at a meeting called for the purpose of voting on such approval. It shall be the duty of the directors of a registered investment company to request and evaluate, and the duty of an investment adviser to such company to furnish, such information as may reasonably be necessary to evaluate the terms of any contract whereby a person undertakes regularly to serve or act as investment adviser of such company. It shall be unlawful for the directors of a registered investment company, in connection with their evaluation of the terms of any contract whereby a person undertakes regularly to serve or act as investment adviser of such company, to take into account the purchase price or other consideration any person may have paid in connection with a transaction of the type referred to in paragraph (1), (3), or (4) of subsection (f).

(d) *Equivalent of Vote of Majority of Outstanding Voting Securities in Case of Common–Law Trust.* In the case of a common-law trust of the character described in section 16(c), either written approval by holders of a majority of the outstanding shares of beneficial interest or the vote of a majority of such outstanding shares cast in person or by proxy at a meeting called for the purpose shall for the purposes of this section be deemed the equivalent of the vote of a majority of the outstanding voting securities, and the provisions of paragraph (42) of section 2(a) as to a majority shall be applicable to the vote cast at such a meeting.

(e) *Exemption of Advisory Boards or Members from Provisions of This Section.* Nothing contained in this section shall be deemed to require or contemplate any action by an advisory board of any registered company or by any of the members of such a board.

(f) *Receipt of Benefits by Investment Adviser from Sale of Securities or Other Interest in Such Investment Adviser Resulting in Assignment of Investment Advisory Contract.*

(1) An investment adviser, or a corporate trustee performing the functions of an investment adviser, of a registered investment company or an affiliated person of such investment adviser or corporate trustee may receive any amount or benefit in connection with a sale of securities of, or a sale of any other interest in, such investment adviser or corporate trustee which results in an assignment of an investment advisory contract with such company or the change in control of or identity of such corporate trustee, if—

(A) for a period of three years after the time of such action, at least 75 per centum of the members of the board of directors of such registered company or such corporate trustee (or successor thereto, by reorganization or otherwise) are not (i) interested persons of the investment adviser of such company or such corporate trustee, or (ii) interested persons of the predecessor investment adviser or such corporate trustee; and

(B) there is not imposed an unfair burden on such company as a result of such transactions or any express or implied terms, conditions, or understandings applicable thereto.

(2)(A) For the purpose of paragraph (1)(A) of this subsection, interested persons of a corporate trustee shall be determined in accordance with section 2(a)(19)(B): *Provided,* That no person shall be deemed to be an interested person of a corporate trustee solely by reason of (i) his being a member of its board of directors or advisory board or (ii) his membership in the immediate family of any person specified in clause (i) of this subparagraph.

(B) For the purpose of paragraph (1)(B) of this subsection, an unfair burden on a registered investment company includes any arrangement, during the two-year period after the date on which any such transaction occurs, whereby the investment adviser or corporate trustee or predecessor or successor investment advisers or corporate trustee or any interested person of any such adviser or any such corporate trustee receives or is entitled to receive any compensation directly or indirectly (i) from any person in connection with the purchase or sale of securities or other property to, from, or on behalf of such company, other than bona fide ordinary compensation as principal underwriter for such company, or (ii) from such company or its security holders for other than bona fide investment advisory or other services.

(3) If—

(A) an assignment of an investment advisory contract with a registered investment company results in a successor investment adviser to such company, or if there is a change in control of or identity of a corporate trustee of a registered investment company, and such adviser or trustee is then an investment adviser or corporate trustee with respect to other assets substantially greater in amount than the amount of assets of such company, or

(B) as a result of a merger of, or a sale of substantially all the assets by, a registered investment company with or to another registered investment company with assets substantially greater in amount, a transaction occurs which would be subject to paragraph (1)(A) of this subsection,

such discrepancy in size of assets shall be considered by the Commission in determining whether or to what extent an application under section 6(c) for exemption from the provisions of paragraph (1)(A) should be granted.

(4) Paragraph (1)(A) of this section shall not apply to a transaction in which a controlling block of outstanding voting securities of an investment adviser to a registered investment company or of a corporate trustee performing the functions of an investment adviser to a registered investment company is—

(A) distributed to the public and in which there is, in fact, no change in the identity of the persons who control such investment adviser or corporate trustee, or

(B) transferred to the investment adviser or the corporate trustee, or an affiliated person or persons of such investment adviser or corporate trustee, or is transferred from the investment adviser or corporate trustee to an affiliated person or persons of the investment adviser or corporate trustee: *Provided,* That (i) each transferee (other than such adviser or trustee) is a natural person and (ii) the transferees (other than such adviser or trustee) owned in the aggregate more than 25 per centum of such voting securities for a period of at least six months prior to such transfer.

Board of Directors

Sec. 16. (a) *Election of Directors.* No person shall serve as a director of a registered investment company unless elected to that office by the holders of the outstanding voting securities of such company, at an annual or a special meeting duly called for that purpose; except that vacancies occurring between such meetings may be filled in any otherwise legal manner if immediately after filling any such vacancy at least two-thirds of the directors then holding office shall have been elected to such office by the holders of the outstanding voting securities of the company at such an annual or special meeting. In the event that at any time less than a majority of the directors of such company holding office at that time were so elected by the holders of the outstanding voting securities, the board of directors or proper officer of such company shall forthwith cause to be held as promptly as possible and in any event within sixty days a meeting of such holders for the purpose of electing directors to fill any existing vacancies in the board of directors unless the Commission shall by order extend such period. The foregoing provisions of this subsection shall not apply to members of an advisory board.

Nothing herein shall, however, preclude a registered investment company from dividing its directors into classes if its charter, certificate of incorporation, articles of association, by-laws, trust indenture, or other instrument or the law under which it is organized, so provides and prescribes the tenure of office of the several classes: *Provided,* That no class shall be elected for a shorter period than one year or for a longer period than five years and the term of office of at least one class shall expire each year.

(b) *Term Vacancies.* Any vacancy on the board of directors of a registered investment company which occurs in connection with compliance with section 15(f)(1)(A) and which must be filled by a person who is not an interested person of either party to a transaction subject to section 15(f)(1)(A) shall be filled only by a person (1) who has been selected and proposed for election by a majority of the directors of such company who are not such interested persons, and (2) who has been elected by the holders of the outstanding voting securities of such company, except that in the case of the death, disqualification, or bona fide resignation of a director selected and elected pursuant to clauses (1) and (2) of this subsection (b), the vacancy created thereby may be filled as provided in subsection (a).

(c) *Trustees of Common-Law Trusts.* The foregoing provisions of this section shall not apply to a common-law trust existing on the date of enactment of this title under an indenture of trust which does not provide for the election of trustees by the shareholders. No natural person shall serve as trustee of such a trust, which is registered as an investment company, after the holders of record of not less than two-thirds of the outstanding shares of beneficial interest in such trust have declared that he be removed from that office either by declaration in writing filed with the custodian of the securities of the trust or by votes cast in person or by proxy at a meeting called for the purpose. Solicitation of such a declaration shall be deemed a solicitation of a proxy within the meaning of section 20(a).

The trustees of such a trust shall promptly call a meeting of shareholders for the purpose of voting upon the question of removal of any such trustee or trustees when requested in writing so to do by the record holders of not less than 10 per centum of the outstanding shares.

Whenever ten or more shareholders of record who have been such for at least six months preceding the date of application, and who hold in the aggregate either shares having a net asset value of at least $25,000 or at least 1 per centum of the outstanding shares, whichever is less, shall apply to the trustees in writing, stating that they wish to communicate with other shareholders with a view to obtaining signatures to a request for a meeting pursuant to this subsection (c) and accompanied by a form of communication and request which they wish to transmit, the trustees shall within five business days after receipt of such application either—

(1) afford to such applicants access to a list of the names and addresses of all shareholders as recorded on the books of the trust; or

(2) inform such applicants as to the approximate number of shareholders of record, and the approximate cost of mailing to them the proposed communication and form of request.

If the trustees elect to follow the course specified in paragraph (2) of this subsection (b) the trustees, upon the written request of such applicants, accompanied by a tender of the material to be mailed and of the reasonable expenses of mailing, shall, with reasonable promptness, mail such material to all shareholders of record at their addresses as recorded on the books, unless within five business days after such tender the trustees shall mail to such applicants and file with the Commission, together with a copy of the material to be mailed, a written statement signed by at least a majority of the trustees to the effect that in their opinion either such material contains untrue statements of fact or omits to state facts necessary to make the statements contained therein not misleading, or would be in violation of applicable law, and specifying the basis of such opinion.

After opportunity for hearing upon the objections specified in the written statement so filed, the Commission may, and if demanded by the trustees or by such applicants shall, enter an order either sustaining one or more of such objections or refusing to sustain any of them. If the Commission shall enter an order refusing to sustain any of such objections, or if, after the entry of an order sustaining one or more of such objections, the Commission shall find, after notice and opportunity for hearing, that all objections so sustained have been met, and shall enter an order so declaring, the trustees shall mail copies of such material to all shareholders with reasonable promptness after the entry of such order and the renewal of such tender.

Transactions of Certain Affiliated Persons and Underwriters

Sec. 17. (a) *Prohibited Transactions.* It shall be unlawful for any affiliated person or promoter of or principal underwriter for a registered investment company (other than a company of the character described in sections 12(d)(3)(A) and (B)), or any affiliated person of such a person, promoter, or principal underwriter, acting as principal—

(1) knowingly to sell any security or other property to such registered company or to any company controlled by such registered company, unless such sale involves solely (A) securities of which the buyer is the issuer, (B) securities of which the seller is the issuer and which are part of a general offering to the holders of a class of its securities, or (C) securities deposited with the trustee of a unit investment trust or periodic payment plan by the depositor thereof;

(2) knowingly to purchase from such registered company, or from any company controlled by such registered company, any security or other property (except securities of which the seller is the issuer);

(3) to borrow money or other property from such registered company or from any company controlled by such registered company (unless the borrower is controlled by the lender) except as permitted in section 21(b); or

(4) to loan money or other property to such registered company, or to any company controlled by such registered company, in contravention of such rules, regulations, or orders as the Commission may, after consultation with and taking into consideration the views of the Federal banking agencies (as defined in section 3 of the Federal Deposit Insurance Act), prescribe or issue consistent with the protection of investors.

(b) *Application for Exemption of Proposed Transaction from Certain Restrictions.* Notwithstanding subsection (a), any person may file with the Commission an application for an order exempting a proposed transaction of the applicant from one or more provisions of that subsection. The Commission shall grant such application and issue such order of exemption if evidence establishes that—

(1) the terms of the proposed transaction, including the consideration to be paid or received, are reasonable and fair and do not involve overreaching on the part of any person concerned;

(2) the proposed transaction is consistent with the policy of each registered investment company concerned, as recited in its registration statement and reports filed under this title; and

(3) the proposed transaction is consistent with the general purposes of this title.

(c) *Sale or Purchase of Merchandise from Any Company or Furnishing of Services Incident to Lessor-Lessee Relationship.* Notwithstanding subsection (a), a person may, in the ordinary course of business, sell to or purchase from any company merchandise or may enter into a lessor-lessee relationship with any person and furnish the services incident thereto.

(d) *Joint or Joint and Several Participation with Company in Transactions.* It shall be unlawful for any affiliated person of or principal underwriter for a registered investment company (other than a company of the character described in section 12(d)(3)(A) and (B)), or any affiliated person of such a person or principal underwriter, acting as principal to effect any transaction in which such registered company, or a company controlled by such registered company, is a joint or a joint and several participant with such person, principal underwriter, or affiliated person, in contravention of such rules and regulations as the Commission may prescribe for the purpose of limiting or preventing participation by such registered or controlled company on a basis different from or less advantageous than that of such other participant. Nothing contained in this subsection shall be deemed to preclude any affiliated person from acting as manager of any underwriting syndicate or other group in which such registered or controlled company is a participant and receiving compensation therefor.

(e) *Acceptance of Compensation, Commissions, Fees, Etc.* It shall be unlawful for any affiliated person of a registered investment company, or any affiliated person of such person—

(1) acting as agent, to accept from any source any compensation (other than a regular salary or wages from such registered company) for the purchase or sale of any property to or for such registered company or any controlled company thereof, except in the course of such person's business as an underwriter or broker; or

(2) acting as broker, in connection with the sale of securities to or by such registered company or any controlled company thereof, to receive from any source a commission, fee, or other remuneration for effecting such transaction which exceeds (A) the usual and customary broker's commission if the sale is effected on a securities exchange, or (B) 2 per centum of the sales price if the sale is effected in connection with a secondary distribution of such securities, or (C) 1 per centum of the purchase or sale price of such securities if the sale is otherwise effected unless the Commission shall, by rules and regulations or order in the public interest and consistent with the protection of investors, permit a larger commission.

(f) *Custody of Securities.*

(1) Every registered management company shall place and maintain its securities and similar investments in the custody of (A) a bank or banks having the qualifications prescribed in paragraph (1) of section 26(a) of this title for the trustees of unit investment trusts; or (B) a company which is a member of a national securities exchange as defined in the Securities Exchange Act of 1934, subject to such rules and regulations as the Commission may from time to time prescribe for the protection of investors; or (C) such registered company, but only in accordance with such rules and regulations or orders as the Commission may from time to time prescribe for the protection of investors.

(2) Subject to such rules, regulations, and orders as the Commission may adopt as necessary or appropriate for the protection of investors, a registered management company or any such custodian, with the consent of the registered management company for which it acts as custodian, may deposit all or any part of the securities owned by such registered management company in a system for the central handling of securities established by a national securities exchange or national securities association registered with the Commission under the Securities Exchange Act of 1934, or such other person as may be permitted by the Commission, pursuant to which system all securities of any particular class or series of any issuer deposited within the system are treated as fungible and may be transferred or pledged by bookkeeping entry without physical delivery of such securities.

(3) Rules, regulations, and orders of the Commission under this subsection, among other

things, may make appropriate provision with respect to such matters as the earmarking, segregation, and hypothecation of such securities and investments, and may provide for or require periodic or other inspections by any or all of the following: Independent public accountants, employees and agents of the Commission, and such other persons as the Commission may designate.

(4) No member of a national securities exchange which trades in securities for its own account may act as custodian except in accordance with rules and regulations prescribed by the Commission for the protection of investors.

(5) If a registered company maintains its securities and similar investments in the custody of a qualified bank or banks, the cash proceeds from the sale of such securities and similar investments and other cash assets of the company shall likewise be kept in the custody of such a bank or banks, or in accordance with such rules and regulations or orders as the Commission may from time to time prescribe for the protection of investors, except that such a registered company may maintain a checking account in a bank or banks having the qualifications prescribed in paragraph (1) of section 26(a) of this title for the trustee of unit investment trusts with the balance of such account or the aggregate balances of such accounts at no time in excess of the amount of the fidelity bond, maintained pursuant to section 17(g) of this title, covering the officers or employees authorized to draw on such account or accounts.

(6) The Commission may, after consultation with and taking into consideration the views of the Federal banking agencies (as defined in section 3 of the Federal Deposit Insurance Act), adopt rules and regulations, and issue orders, consistent with the protection of investors, prescribing the conditions under which a bank, or an affiliated person of a bank, either of which is an affiliated person, promoter, organizer, or sponsor of, or principal underwriter for, a registered management company, may serve as custodian of that registered management company.

(g) *Bonding of Officers and Employees Having Access to Securities or Funds.* The Commission is authorized to require by rules and regulations or orders for the protection of investors that any officer or employee of a registered management investment company who may singly, or jointly with others, have access to securities or funds of any registered company, either directly or through authority to draw upon such funds or to direct generally the disposition of such securities (unless the officer or employee has such access solely through his position as an officer or employee of a bank) be bonded by a reputable fidelity insurance company against larceny and embezzlement in such reasonable minimum amounts as the Commission may prescribe.

(h) *Provisions in Charter, By-Laws, Etc., Protecting Against Liability for Willful Misfeasance, Etc.* After one year from the effective date of this title, neither the charter, certificate of incorporation, articles of association, indenture of trust, nor the bylaws of any registered investment company, nor any other instrument pursuant to which such a company is organized or administered, shall contain any provision which protects or purports to protect any director or officer of such company against any liability to the company or to its security holders to which he would otherwise be subject by reason of willful misfeasance, bad faith, gross negligence or reckless disregard of the duties involved in the conduct of his office.

(i) *Provisions in Contracts Protecting Against Willful Misfeasance, Etc.* After one year from the effective date of this title no contract or agreement under which any person undertakes to act as investment adviser of, or principal underwriter for, a registered investment company shall contain any provision which protects or purports to protect such person against any liability to such company or its security holders to which he would otherwise be subject by reason of willful misfeasance, bad faith, or gross negligence, in the performance of his duties, or by reason of his reckless disregard of his obligations and duties under such contract or agreement.

(j) *Rules and Regulations Prohibiting Fraudulent, Deceptive or Manipulative Courses of Conduct.* It shall be unlawful for any affiliated person of or principal underwriter for a registered investment company or any affiliated person of an investment adviser of or principal underwriter for a registered investment company, to engage in any act, practice, or course of business in connection with the purchase or sale, directly or indirectly, by such person of any security held or to be acquired by such registered investment company in contravention of such rules and regulations as the Commission may adopt to define, and prescribe means reasonably necessary to prevent, such acts, practices, or courses of business as are fraudulent, deceptive or manipulative. Such rules and regulations may include requirements for the adoption of codes of ethics by registered investment companies and investment advisers of, and principal underwriters for, such investment companies establishing such standards as are reasonably necessary to prevent such acts, practices, or courses of business.

Capital Structure of Investment Companies

Sec. 18. (a) *Qualifications on Issuance of Senior Securities.* It shall be unlawful for any registered closed-end company to issue any class of senior security, or to sell any such security of which it is the issuer, unless—

(1) if such class of senior security represents an indebtedness—

(A) immediately after such issuance or sale, it will have an asset coverage of at least 300 per centum;

(B) provision is made to prohibit the declaration of any dividend (except a dividend payable in stock of the issuer), or the declaration of any other distribution, upon any class of the capital stock of such investment company, or the purchase of any such capital stock, unless, in every such case, such class of senior securities has at the time of the declaration of any such dividend or distribution or at the time of any such purchase an asset coverage of at least 300 per centum after deducting the amount of such dividend, distribution, or purchase price, as the case may be, except that dividends may be declared upon any preferred stock if such senior security representing indebtedness has an asset coverage of at least 200 per centum at the time of declaration thereof after deducting the amount of such dividend; and

(C) provision is made either—

(i) that, if on the last business day of each of twelve consecutive calendar months such class of senior securities shall have an asset coverage of less than 100 per centum, the holders of such securities voting as a class shall be entitled to elect at least a majority of the members of the board of directors of such registered company, such voting right to continue until such class of senior security shall have an asset coverage of 110 per centum or more on the last business day of each of three consecutive calendar months, or

(ii) that, if on the last business day of each of twenty-four consecutive calendar months such class of senior securities shall have an asset coverage of less than 100 per centum, an event of default shall be deemed to have occurred;

(2) if such class of senior security is a stock—

(A) immediately after such issuance or sale it will have an asset coverage of at least 200 per centum;

(B) provision is made to prohibit the declaration of any dividend (except a dividend payable in common stock of the issuer), or the declaration of any other distribution, upon the common stock of such investment company, or the purchase of any such common stock, unless in every such case such class of senior security has at the time of the declaration of any such dividend or distribution or at the time of any such purchase an asset coverage of at least 200 per centum after deducting the amount of such dividend, distribution or purchase price, as the case may be;

(C) provision is made to entitle the holders of such senior securities, voting as a class, to elect at least two directors at all times, and, subject to the prior rights, if any, of the holders of any other class of senior securities outstanding, to elect a majority of the directors if at any time dividends on such class of securities shall be unpaid in an amount equal to two full years' dividends on such securities, and to continue to be so represented until all dividends in arrears shall have been paid or otherwise provided for;

(D) provision is made requiring approval by the vote of a majority of such securities, voting as a class, of any plan of reorganization adversely affecting such securities or of any action requiring a vote of security holders as in section 13(a) provided; and

(E) such class of stock shall have complete priority over any other class as to distribution of assets and payment of dividends, which dividends shall be cumulative.

(b) *Asset Coverage in Respect of Senior Securities.* The asset coverage in respect of a senior security provided for in subsection (a) may be determined on the basis of values calculated as of a time within forty-eight hours (not including Sundays or holidays) next preceding the time of such determination. The time of issue or sale shall, in the case of an offering of such securities to existing stockholders of the issuer, be deemed to be the first date on which such offering is made, and in all other cases shall be deemed to be the time as of which a firm commitment to issue or sell and to take or purchase such securities shall be made.

(c) *Prohibitions Relating to Issuance of Senior Securities.* Notwithstanding the provisions of subsection (a) it shall be unlawful for any registered closed-end investment company to issue or sell any senior security representing indebtedness if immediately thereafter such company will have outstanding more than one class of senior security representing indebtedness, or to issue or sell any senior security which is a stock if immediately thereafter such company will have outstanding more than one class of senior security which is a stock, except that (1) any such class of indebtedness or stock may be issued in one or more series: *Provided,* That no such series shall have a preference or priority over any other series upon the distribution of the assets of such registered closed-end company or in respect of the payment of interest or dividends, and (2) promissory notes or other evidences of indebtedness issued in consideration of any loan, extension, or renewal thereof, made by a bank or other person and privately arranged, and not intended to be publicly distributed, shall not be deemed to be a separate class of senior securities representing indebtedness within the meaning of this subsection (c).

(d) *Warrants and Rights to Subscription.* It shall be unlawful for any registered management company to issue any warrant or right to subscribe to or purchase a security of which such company is the issuer, except in the form of warrants or rights to subscribe expiring not later than one hundred and twenty days after their issuance and issued exclusively and ratably to a class or classes of such company's security holders; except that any warrant may be issued in exchange for outstanding warrants in connection with a plan of reorganization.

(e) *Application of Section to Specific Senior Securities.* The provisions of this section 18 shall not apply to any senior securities issued or sold by any registered closed-end company—

(1) for the purpose of refunding through payment, purchase, redemption, retirement, or exchange, any senior security of such registered investment company except that no senior security representing indebtedness shall be so issued or sold for the purpose of refunding any senior security which is a stock; or

(2) pursuant to any plan of reorganization (other than for refunding as referred to in paragraph (1) of this subsection), provided—

(A) that such senior securities are issued or sold for the purpose of substituting or exchanging such senior securities for outstanding senior securities, and if such senior securities represent indebtedness they are issued or sold for the purpose of substituting or exchanging such senior securities for outstanding senior securities representing indebtedness, of any registered investment company which is a party to such plan of reorganization; or

(B) that the total amount of such senior securities so issued or sold pursuant to such plan does not exceed the total amount of senior securities of all the companies which are parties to such plan, and the total amount of senior securities representing indebtedness so issued or sold pursuant to such plan does not exceed the total amount of senior securities representing indebtedness of all such companies, or, alternatively, the total amount of such senior securities so issued or sold pursuant to such plan does not have the effect of increasing the ratio of senior securities representing indebtedness to the securities representing stock or the ratio of senior securities representing stock to securities junior thereto when compared with such ratios as they existed before such reorganization.

(f) *Senior Securities Securing Loans from Bank; Securities Not Included in "Senior Security."*

(1) It shall be unlawful for any registered open-end company to issue any class of senior security or to sell any senior security of which it is the issuer, except that any such registered company shall be permitted to borrow from any bank: *Provided,* That immediately after any such borrowing there is an asset coverage of at least 300 per centum for all borrowings of such registered company: *And provided further,* That in the event that such asset coverage shall at any time fall below 300 per centum such registered company shall, within three days thereafter (not including Sundays and holidays) or such longer period as the Commission may prescribe by rules and regulations, reduce the amount of its borrowings to an extent that the asset coverage of such borrowings shall be at least 300 per centum.

(2) "Senior security" shall not, in the case of a registered open-end company, include a class or classes or a number of series of preferred or special stock each of which is preferred over all other classes or series in respect of assets specifically allocated to that class or series: *Provided,* That (A)

such company has outstanding no class or series of stock which is not so preferred over all other classes or series, or (B) the only other outstanding class of the issuer's stock consists of a common stock upon which no dividend (other than a liquidating dividend) is permitted to be paid and which in the aggregate represents not more than one-half of 1 per centum of the issuer's outstanding voting securities. For the purpose of insuring fair and equitable treatment of the holders of the outstanding voting securities of each class or series of stock of such company, the Commission may by rule, regulation, or order direct that any matter required to be submitted to the holders of the outstanding voting securities of such company shall not be deemed to have been effectively acted upon unless approved by the holders of such percentage (not exceeding a majority) of the outstanding voting securities of each class or series of stock affected by such matter as shall be prescribed in such rule, regulation, or order.

(g) *"Senior Security" Defined.* Unless otherwise provided: "Senior security" means any bond, debenture, note, or similar obligation or instrument constituting a security and evidencing indebtedness, and any stock of a class having priority over any other class as to distribution of assets or payment of dividends; and "senior security representing indebtedness" means any senior security other than stock.

The term "senior security", when used in subparagraphs (B) and (C) of paragraph (1) of subsection (a), shall not include any promissory note or other evidence of indebtedness issued in consideration of any loan, extension, or renewal thereof, made by a bank or other person and privately arranged, and not intended to be publicly distributed; nor shall such term, when used in this section 18, include any such promissory note or other evidence of indebtedness in any case where such a loan is for temporary purposes only and in an amount not exceeding 5 per centum of the value of the total assets of the issuer at the time when the loan is made. A loan shall be presumed to be for temporary purposes if it is repaid within sixty days and is not extended or renewed; otherwise it shall be presumed not to be for temporary purposes. Any such presumption may be rebutted by evidence.

(h) *"Asset Coverage" Defined.* "Asset coverage" of a class of senior security representing an indebtedness of an issuer means the ratio which the value of the total assets of such issuer, less all liabilities and indebtedness not represented by senior securities, bears to the aggregate amount of senior securities representing indebtedness of such issuer. "Asset coverage" of a class of senior security of an issuer which is a stock means the ratio which the value of the total assets of such issuer, less all liabilities and indebtedness not represented by senior securities, bears to the aggregate amount of senior securities representing indebtedness of such issuer plus the aggregate of the involuntary liquidation preference of such class of senior security which is a stock. The involuntary liquidation preference of a class of senior security which is a stock shall be deemed to mean the amount to which such class of senior security would be entitled on involuntary liquidation of the issuer in preference to a security junior to it.

(i) *Future Issuance of Stock as Voting Stock; Exceptions.* Except as provided in subsection (a) of this section, or as otherwise required by law, every share of stock hereafter issued by a registered management company (except a common-law trust of the character described in section 16(c)) shall be a voting stock and have equal voting rights with every other outstanding voting stock: *Provided,* That this subsection shall not apply to shares issued pursuant to the terms of any warrant or subscription right outstanding on March 15, 1940, or any firm contract entered into before March 15, 1940, to purchase such securities from such company nor to shares issued in accordance with any rules, regulations, or orders which the Commission may make permitting such issue.

(j) *Securities Issued by Registered Face-Amount Certificate Company.* Notwithstanding any provision of this title, it shall be unlawful, after the date of enactment of this title, for any registered face-amount certificate company—

(1) to issue, except in accordance with such rules, regulations, or orders as the Commission may prescribe in the public interest or as necessary or appropriate for the protection of investors, any security other than (A) a face-amount certificate; (B) a common stock having a par value and being without preference as to dividends or distributions and having at least equal voting rights with any outstanding security of such company; or (C) short-term payment or promissory notes or other indebtedness issued in consideration of any loan, extension, or renewal thereof, made by a bank or other person and privately arranged and not intended to be publicly offered;

(2) if such company has outstanding any security, other than such face-amount certificates, common stock, promissory notes, or other evidence of indebtedness, to make any distribution or declare

or pay any dividend on any capital security in contravention of such rules and regulations or orders as the Commission may prescribe in the public interest or as necessary or appropriate for the protection of investors or to insure the financial integrity of such company, to prevent the impairment of the company's ability to meet its obligations upon its face-amount certificates; or

(3) to issue any of its securities except for cash or securities including securities of which such company is the issuer.

(k) *Application of Section to Companies Operating Under Small Business of Investment Act Provisions.* The provisions of subparagraphs (A) and (B) of paragraph (1) of subsection (a) of this section shall not apply to investment companies operating under the Small Business Investment Act of 1958, and the provisions of paragraph (2) of said subsection shall not apply to such companies so long as such class of senior security shall be held or guaranteed by the Small Business Administration.

Payments or Distributions

Sec. 19. (a) *Dividends; Restriction; Exception.* It shall be unlawful for any registered investment company to pay any dividend, or to make any distribution in the nature of a dividend payment, wholly or partly from any source other than—

(1) such company's accumulated undistributed net income, determined in accordance with good accounting practice and not including profits or losses realized upon the sale of securities or other properties; or

(2) such company's net income so determined for the current or preceding fiscal year;

unless such payment is accompanied by a written statement which adequately discloses the source or sources of such payment. The Commission may prescribe the form of such statement by rules and regulations in the public interest and for the protection of investors.

(b) *Long-Term Capital Gains; Limitation.* It shall be unlawful in contravention of such rules, regulations, or orders as the Commission may prescribe as necessary or appropriate in the public interest or for the protection of investors for any registered investment company to distribute long-term capital gains, as defined in the Internal Revenue Code of 1954, more often than once every twelve months.

Proxies; Voting Trusts; Circular Ownership

Sec. 20. (a) *Prohibition on Use of Means of Interstate Commerce for Solicitation of Proxies.* It shall be unlawful for any person, by use of the mails or any means or instrumentality of interstate commerce or otherwise, to solicit or to permit the use of his name to solicit any proxy or consent or authorization in respect of any security of which a registered investment company is the issuer in contravention of such rules and regulations as the Commission may prescribe as necessary or appropriate in the public interest or for the protection of investors.

(b) *Prohibition on Use of Means of Interstate Commerce for Sale of Voting-Trust Certificates.* It shall be unlawful for any registered investment company or affiliated person thereof, any issuer of a voting-trust certificate relating to any security of a registered investment company, or any underwriter of such a certificate, by use of the mails or any means or instrumentality of interstate commerce, or otherwise, to offer for sale, sell, or deliver after sale, in connection with a public offering, any such voting-trust certificate.

(c) *Prohibition on Purchase of Securities Knowingly Resulting in Cross-Ownership or Circular Ownership.* No registered investment company shall purchase any voting security if, to the knowledge of such registered company, cross-ownership or circular ownership exists, or after such acquisition will exist, between such registered company and the issuer of such security. Cross-ownership shall be deemed to exist between two companies when each of such companies beneficially owns more than 3 per centum of the outstanding voting securities of the other company. Circular ownership shall be deemed to exist between two companies if such companies are included within a group of three or more companies, each of which—

(1) beneficially owns more than 3 per centum of the outstanding voting securities of one or more other companies of the group; and

(2) has more than 3 per centum of its own outstanding voting securities beneficially owned by another company, or by each of two or more other companies, of the group.

(d) *Duty to Eliminate Existing Cross-Ownership or Circular Ownership.* If cross-ownership or circular ownership between a registered investment company and any other company or companies comes into existence upon the purchase by a registered investment company of the securities of another company, it shall be the duty of such registered company, within one year after it first knows of the existence of such cross-ownership or circular ownership, to eliminate the same.

Loans by Management Companies

Sec. 21. It shall be unlawful for any registered management company to lend money or property to any person, directly or indirectly if—

(a) the investment policies of such registered company, as recited in its registration statement and reports filed under this title, do not permit such a loan; or

(b) such person controls or is under common control with such registered company; except that the provisions of this paragraph shall not apply to any loan from a registered company to a company which owns all of the outstanding securities of such registered company, except directors' qualifying shares.

Distribution, Redemption, and Repurchase of Securities; Regulations by Securities Associations

Sec. 22. (a) *Rules Relating to Minimum Prices for Purchase and Sale of Securities from Investment Company; Time for Resale and Redemption.* A securities association registered under section 15A of the Securities Exchange Act of 1934 may prescribe, by rules adopted and in effect in accordance with said section and subject to all provisions of said section applicable to the rules of such an association—

(1) a method or methods for computing the minimum price at which a member thereof may purchase from any investment company any redeemable security issued by such company and the maximum price at which a member may sell to such company any redeemable security issued by it or which he may receive for such security upon redemption, so that the price in each case will bear such relation to the current net asset value of such security computed as of such time as the rules may prescribe; and

(2) a minimum period of time which must elapse after the sale or issue of such security before any resale to such company by a member or its redemption upon surrender by a member;

in each case for the purpose of eliminating or reducing so far as reasonably practicable any dilution of the value of other outstanding securities of such company or any other result of such purchase, redemption, or sale which is unfair to holders of such other outstanding securities; and said rules may prohibit the members of the association from purchasing, selling, or surrendering for redemption any such redeemable securities in contravention of said rules.

(b) *Rules Relating to Purchase of Securities by Members from Issuer Investment Company.*

(1) Such a securities association may also, by rules adopted and in effect in accordance with said section 15A, and notwithstanding the provisions of subsection (b)(6) thereof but subject to all other provisions of said section applicable to the rules of such an association, prohibit its members from purchasing, in connection with a primary distribution of redeemable securities of which any registered investment company is the issuer, any such security from the issuer or from any principal underwriter except at a price equal to the price at which such security is then offered to the public less a commission, discount, or spread which is computed in conformity with a method or methods, and within such limitations as to the relation thereof to said public offering price, as such rules may prescribe in order that the price at which such security is offered or sold to the public shall not include an excessive sales load but shall allow for reasonable compensation for sales personnel, broker-dealers, and underwriters, and for reasonable sales loads to investors. The Commission shall on application or otherwise, if it appears that smaller companies are subject to relatively higher operating costs, make due allowance therefor by granting any such company or class of companies appropriate qualified exemptions from the provisions of this section.

(2) At any time after the expiration of eighteen months from the date of enactment of the Investment Company Amendments Act of 1970 (or, if earlier, after a securities association has adopted for purposes of paragraph (1) any rule respecting excessive sales loads), the Commission may alter or supplement the rules of any securities association as may be necessary to effectuate the purposes of this subsection in the manner provided by section 19(c) of the Securities Exchange Act of 1934.

(3) If any provision of this subsection is in conflict with any provision of any law of the United States in effect on the date this subsection takes effect, the provisions of this subsection shall prevail.

(c) *Conflicting Rules of Commission and Associations.* The Commission may make rules and regulations applicable to registered investment companies and to principal underwriters of, and dealers in, the redeemable securities of any registered investment company, whether or not members of any securities association, to the same extent, covering the same subject matter, and for the accomplishment of the same ends as are prescribed in subsection (a) of this section in respect of the rules which may be made by a registered securities association governing its members. Any rules and regulations so made by the Commission, to the extent that they may be inconsistent with the rules of any such association, shall so long as they remain in force supersede the rules of the association and be binding upon its members as well as all other underwriters and dealers to whom they may be applicable.

(d) *Sale of Securities Except to or Through Principal Underwriter; Price of Securities.* No registered investment company shall sell any redeemable security issued by it to any person except either to or through a principal underwriter for distribution or at a current public offering price described in the prospectus, and, if such class of security is being currently offered to the public by or through an underwriter, no principal underwriter of such security and no dealer shall sell any such security to any person except a dealer, a principal underwriter, or the issuer, except at a current public offering price described in the prospectus. Nothing in this subsection shall prevent a sale made (i) pursuant to an offer of exchange permitted by section 11 including any offer made pursuant to section 11(b); (ii) pursuant to an offer made solely to all registered holders of the securities, or of a particular class or series of securities issued by the company proportionate to their holdings or proportionate to any cash distribution made to them by the company (subject to appropriate qualifications designed solely to avoid issuance of fractional securities); or (iii) in accordance with rules and regulations of the Commission made pursuant to subsection (b) of section 12.

(e) *Suspension of Right of Redemption or Postponement of Date of Payment.* No registered investment company shall suspend the right of redemption, or postpone the date of payment or satisfaction upon redemption of any redeemable security in accordance with its terms for more than seven days after the tender of such security to the company or its agent designated for that purpose for redemption, except—

(1) for any period (A) during which the New York Stock Exchange is closed other than customary week-end and holiday closings or (B) during which trading on the New York Stock Exchange is restricted;

(2) for any period during which an emergency exists as a result of which (A) disposal by the company of securities owned by it is not reasonably practicable or (B) it is not reasonably practicable for such company fairly to determine the value of its net assets; or

(3) for such other periods as the Commission may by order permit for the protection of security holders of the company.

The Commission shall by rules and regulations determine the conditions under which (i) trading shall be deemed to be restricted and (ii) an emergency shall be deemed to exist within the meaning of this subsection.

(f) *Restrictions on Transferability or Negotiability of Securities.* No registered open-end company shall restrict the transferability or negotiability of any security of which it is the issuer except in conformity with the statements with respect thereto contained in its registration statement nor in contravention of such rules and regulations as the Commission may prescribe in the interests of the holders of all of the outstanding securities of such investment company.

(g) *Issuance of Securities for Services or Property Other than Cash.* No registered open-end company shall issue any of its securities (1) for services; or (2) for property other than cash or securities (including securities of which such registered company is the issuer), except as a dividend or distribution to its security holders or in connection with a reorganization.

Closed–End Companies

Sec. 23. (a) *Issuance of Securities.* No registered closed-end company shall issue any of its securities (1) for services; or (2) for property other than cash or securities (including securities of which such registered company is the issuer), except as a dividend or distribution to its security holders or in connection with a reorganization.

(b) *Sale of Common Stock at Price Below Current Net Asset Value.* No registered closed-end company shall sell any common stock of which it is the issuer at a price below the current net asset value of such stock, exclusive of any distributing commission or discount (which net asset value shall be determined as of a time within forty-eight hours, excluding Sundays and holidays, next preceding the time of such determination), except (1) in connection with an offering to the holders of one or more classes of its capital stock; (2) with the consent of a majority of its common stockholders; (3) upon conversion of a convertible security in accordance with its terms; (4) upon the exercise of any warrant outstanding on the date of enactment of this Act or issued in accordance with the provisions of section 18(d); or (5) under such other circumstances as the Commission may permit by rules and regulations or orders for the protection of investors.

(c) *Purchase of Securities of Which It Is Issuer; Exceptions.* No registered closed-end company shall purchase any securities of any class of which it is the issuer except—

(1) on a securities exchange or such other open market as the Commission may designate by rules and regulations or orders: *Provided,* That if such securities are stock, such registered company shall, within the preceding six months, have informed stockholders of its intention to purchase stock of such class by letter or report addressed to stockholders of such class; or

(2) pursuant to tenders, after reasonable opportunity to submit tenders given to all holders of securities of the class to be purchased; or

(3) under such other circumstances as the Commission may permit by rules and regulations or orders for the protection of investors in order to insure that such purchases are made in a manner or on a basis which does not unfairly discriminate against any holders of the class or classes of securities to be purchased.

Registration of Securities Under Securities Act of 1933

Sec. 24. (a) *Registration Statements; Contents.* In registering under the Securities Act of 1933 any security of which it is the issuer, a registered investment company, in lieu of furnishing a registration statement containing the information and documents specified in schedule A of said Act, may file a registration statement containing the following information and documents:

(1) such copies of the registration statement filed by such company under this title, and of such reports filed by such company pursuant to section 30 or such copies of portions of such registration statement and reports, as the Commission shall designate by rules and regulations; and

(2) such additional information and documents (including a prospectus) as the Commission shall prescribe by rules and regulations as necessary or appropriate in the public interest or for the protection of investors.

(b) *Filing of Three Copies of Advertisement, Pamphlet, Etc. in Connection with Public Offering; Time of Filing.* It shall be unlawful for any of the following companies, or for any underwriter for such a company, in connection with a public offering of any security of which such company is the issuer, to make use of the mails or any means or instrumentalities of interstate commerce to transmit any advertisement, pamphlet, circular, form letter, or other sales literature addressed to or intended for distribution to prospective investors unless three copies of the full text thereof have been filed with the Commission or are filed with the Commission within ten days thereafter:

(1) any registered open-end company;

(2) any registered unit investment trust; or

(3) any registered face-amount certificate company.

(c) *Additional Requirement for Prospectuses Relating to Periodic Payment Plan Certificates or Face-Amount Certificate.* In addition to the powers relative to prospectuses granted the Commission by section 10 of the Securities Act of 1933, the Commission is authorized to require, by rules and regulations or order, that the information contained in any prospectus relating to any periodic payment plan certificate or face-amount certificate registered under the Securities Act of 1933 on or after the effective date of this title be presented in such form and order of items, and such prospectus contain such summaries of any portion of such information, as are necessary or appropriate in the public interest or for the protection of investors.

(d) *Application of Other Provisions to Securities Investment Companies, Face-Amount Certificate Companies, and Open-End Companies or Unit Investment Trusts.* The exemption provided by paragraph (8) of section 3(a) of the Securities Act of 1933 shall not apply to any security of which an investment company is the issuer. The exemption provided by paragraph (11) of said section 3(a) shall not apply to any security of which a registered investment company is the issuer. The exemption provided by the third clause of section 4(a)(3) of the Securities Act of 1933, as amended, shall not apply to any transaction in a security issued by a face-amount certificate company or in a redeemable security issued by an open-end management company or unit investment trust, if any other security of the same class is currently being offered or sold by the issuer or by or through an underwriter in a distribution which is not exempted from section 5 of said Act, except to such extent and subject to such terms and conditions as the Commission, having due regard for the public interest and the protection of investors, may prescribe by rules or regulations with respect to any class of persons, securities, or transactions.

(e) *Amendment of Registration Statements Relating to Securities Issued by Face-Amount Certificate Companies, Open-End Management Companies or Unit Investment Trusts.* For the purposes of section 11 of the Securities Act of 1933, as amended, the effective date of the latest amendment filed shall be deemed the effective date of the registration statement with respect to securities sold after such amendment shall have become effective. For the purposes of section 13 of the Securities Act of 1933, as amended, no such security shall be deemed to have been bona fide offered to the public prior to the effective date of the latest amendment filed pursuant to this subsection. Except to the extent the Commission otherwise provides by rules or regulations as appropriate in the public interest or for the protection of investors, no prospectus relating to a security issued by a face-amount certificate company or a redeemable security issued by an open-end management company or unit investment trust which varies for the purposes of subsection (a)(3) of section 10 of the Securities Act of 1933 from the latest prospectus filed as a part of the registration statement shall be deemed to meet the requirements of said section 10 unless filed as part of an amendment to the registration statement under said Act and such amendment has become effective.

(f) *Registration of Indefinite Amount of Securities.*

(1) *Registration of Securities.* Upon the effective date of its registration statement, as provided by section 8 of the Securities Act of 1933, a face-amount certificate company, open-end management company, or unit investment trust, shall be deemed to have registered an indefinite amount of securities.

(2) *Payment of Registration Fees.* Not later than 90 days after the end of the fiscal year of a company or trust referred to in paragraph (1), the company or trust, as applicable, shall pay a registration fee to the Commission, calculated in the manner specified in section 6(b) of the Securities Act of 1933, based on the aggregate sales price for which its securities (including, for purposes of this paragraph, all securities issued pursuant to a dividend reinvestment plan) were sold pursuant to a registration of an indefinite amount of securities under this subsection during the previous fiscal year of the company or trust, reduced by—

(A) the aggregate redemption or repurchase price of the securities of the company or trust during that year; and

(B) the aggregate redemption or repurchase price of the securities of the company or trust during any prior fiscal year ending not more than 1 year before the date of enactment of the Investment Company Act Amendments of 1996, that were not used previously by the company or trust to reduce fees payable under this section.

(3) *Interest Due on Late Payment.* A company or trust paying the fee required by this subsection or any portion thereof more than 90 days after the end of the fiscal year of the company or trust shall pay to the Commission interest on unpaid amounts, at the average investment rate for Treasury tax and loan accounts published by the Secretary of the Treasury pursuant to section 3717(a) of title 31, United States Code. The payment of interest pursuant to this paragraph shall not preclude the Commission from bringing an action to enforce the requirements of paragraph (2).

(4) *Rulemaking Authority.* The Commission may adopt rules and regulations to implement this subsection.

(g) *Additional Prospectuses.* In addition to any prospectus permitted or required by section 10(a) of the Securities Act of 1933, the Commission shall permit, by rules or regulations deemed necessary or appropriate in the public interest or for the protection of investors, the use of a prospectus for purposes of section 5(b)(1) of that Act with respect to securities issued by a registered investment company. Such a prospectus, which may include information the substance of which is not included in the prospectus specified in section 10(a) of the Securities Act of 1933, shall be deemed to be permitted by section 10(b) of that Act.

Reorganization Plans; Reports by Commission

Sec. 25. (a) *Filing of Reorganization Plan and Other Information with Commission.* Any person who, by use of the mails or any means or instrumentality of interstate commerce or otherwise, solicits or permits the use of his name to solicit any proxy, consent, authorization, power of attorney, ratification, deposit, or dissent in respect of any plan of reorganization of any registered investment company shall file with, or mail to, the Commission for its information, within twenty-four hours after the commencement of any such solicitation, a copy of such plan and any deposit agreement relating thereto and of any proxy, consent, authorization, power of attorney, ratification, instrument of deposit, or instrument of dissent in respect thereto, if or to the extent that such documents shall not already have been filed with the Commission.

(b) *Advisory Report by Commission at Request of Shareholders.* The Commission is authorized, if so requested, prior to any solicitation of security holders with respect to any plan of reorganization, by any registered investment company which is, or any of the securities of which are, the subject of or is a participant in any such plan, or if so requested by the holders of 25 per centum of any class of its outstanding securities, to render an advisory report in respect of the fairness of any such plan and its effect upon any class or classes of security holders. In such event any registered investment company, in respect of which the Commission shall have rendered any such advisory report, shall mail promptly a copy of such advisory report to all its security holders affected by any such plan: *Provided,* That such advisory report shall have been received by it at least forty-eight hours (not including Sundays and holidays) before final action is taken in relation to such plan at any meeting of security holders called to act in relation thereto, or any adjournment of any such meeting, or if no meeting be called, then prior to the final date of acceptance of such plan by security holders. In respect of securities not registered as to ownership, in lieu of mailing a copy of such advisory report, such registered company shall publish promptly a statement of the existence of such advisory report in a newspaper of general circulation in its principal place of business and shall make available copies of such advisory report upon request. Notwithstanding the provision of this section the Commission shall not render such advisory report although so requested by any such investment company or such security holders if the fairness or feasibility of said plan is in issue in any proceeding pending in any court of competent jurisdiction unless such plan is submitted to the Commission for that purpose by such court.

(c) *Enjoinder of Plan of Reorganization.* Any district court of the United States in the State of incorporation of a registered investment company, or any such court for the district in which such company maintains its principal place of business, is authorized to enjoin the consummation of any plan of reorganization of such registered investment company upon proceedings instituted by the Commission (which is authorized so to proceed upon behalf of security holders of such registered company, or any class thereof), if such court shall determine that any such plan is not fair and equitable to all security holders.

(d) *Application of Section to Reorganizations Under Title 11.* Nothing contained in this section shall in any way affect or derogate from the powers of the courts of the United States and the Commission with reference to reorganizations contained in Title 11 of the United States Code.

Unit Investment Trusts

Sec. 26. (a) *Custody and Sale of Securities.* No principal underwriter for or depositor of a registered unit investment trust shall sell, except by surrender to the trustee for redemption, any security of which such trust is the issuer (other than short-term paper), unless the trust indenture, agreement of custodianship, or other instrument pursuant to which such security is issued—

(1) designates one or more trustees or custodians, each of which is a bank, and provides that each such trustee or custodian shall have at all times an aggregate capital, surplus, and undivided profits of a specified minimum amount, which shall not be less than $500,000 (but may also provide, if such trustee or custodian publishes reports of condition at least annually, pursuant to law or to the requirements of its supervising or examining authority, that for the purposes of this paragraph the aggregate capital, surplus, and undivided profits of such trustee or custodian shall be deemed to be its aggregate capital, surplus, and undivided profits as set forth in its most recent report of condition so published);

(2) provides, in substance, (A) that during the life of the trust the trustee or custodian, if not otherwise remunerated, may charge against and collect from the income of the trust, and from the corpus thereof if no income is available, such fees for its services and such reimbursement for its expenses as are provided for in such instrument; (B) that no such charge or collection shall be made except for services theretofore performed or expenses theretofore incurred; (C) that no payment to the depositor of or a principal underwriter for such trust, or to any affiliated person or agent of such depositor or underwriter, shall be allowed

the trustee or custodian as an expense (except that provision may be made for the payment to any such person of a fee, not exceeding such reasonable amount as the Commission may prescribe as compensation for performing bookkeeping and other administrative services, of a character normally performed by the trustee or custodian itself); and (D) that the trustee or custodian shall have possession of all securities and other property in which the funds of the trust are invested, all funds held for such investment, all equalization, redemption, and other special funds of the trust, and all income upon, accretions to, and proceeds of such property and funds, and shall segregate and hold the same in trust (subject only to the charges and collections allowed under clauses (A), (B), and (C)) until distribution thereof to the security holders of the trust;

(3) provides, in substance, that the trustee or custodian shall not resign until either (A) the trust has been completely liquidated and the proceeds of the liquidation distributed to the security holders of the trust, or (B) a successor trustee or custodian, having the qualifications prescribed in paragraph (1), has been designated and has accepted such trusteeship or custodianship; and

(4) provides, in substance, (A) that a record will be kept by the depositor or an agent of the depositor of the name and address of, and the shares issued by the trust and held by, every holder of any security issued pursuant to such instrument, insofar as such information is known to the depositor or agent; and (B) that whenever a security is deposited with the trustee in substitution for any security in which such security holder has an undivided interest, the depositor or the agent of the depositor will, within five days after such substitution, either deliver or mail to such security holder a notice of substitution, including an identification of the securities eliminated and the securities substituted, and a specification of the shares of such security holder affected by the substitution.

(b) *Bank or Affiliated Person of Bank as Trustee or Custodian.* The Commission may, after consultation with and taking into consideration the views of the Federal banking agencies (as defined in section 3 of the Federal Deposit Insurance Act), adopt rules and regulations, and issue orders, consistent with the protection of investors, prescribing the conditions under which a bank, or an affiliated person of a bank, either of which is an affiliated person of a principal underwriter for, or depositor of, a registered unit investment trust, may serve as trustee or custodian under subsection (a)(1).

(c) *Substitution of Securities.* It shall be unlawful for any depositor or trustee of a registered unit investment trust holding the security of a single issuer to substitute another security for such security unless the Commission shall have approved the substitution. The Commission shall issue an order approving such substitution if the evidence establishes that it is consistent with the protection of investors and the purposes fairly intended by the policy and provisions of this title.

(d) *Binding Contract or Agreement Embodying Applicable Provisions Deemed to Qualify Non–Complying Instrument by Which Securities Were Issued.* In the event that a trust indenture, agreement of custodianship, or other instrument pursuant to which securities of a registered unit investment trust are issued does not comply with the requirements of subsection (a) of this section, such instrument will be deemed to meet such requirements if a written contract or agreement binding on the parties and embodying such requirements has been executed by the depositor on the one part and the trustee or custodian on the other part, and three copies of such contract or agreement have been filed with the Commission.

(e) *Liquidation of Unit Investment Trust.* Whenever the Commission has reason to believe that a unit investment trust is inactive and that its liquidation is in the interest of the security holders of such trust, the Commission may file a complaint seeking the liquidation of such trust in the district court of the United States in any district wherein any trustee of such trust resides or has its principal place of business. A copy of such complaint shall be served on every trustee of such trust, and notice of the proceeding shall be given such other interested persons in such manner and at such times as the court may direct. If the court determines that such liquidation is in the interest of the security holders of such trust, the court shall order such liquidation and, after payment of necessary expenses, the distribution of the proceeds to the security holders of the trust in such manner and on such terms as may to the court appear equitable.

(f) *Exemption.*

(1) *In General.* Subsection (a) does not apply to any registered separate account funding variable insurance contracts, or to the sponsoring insurance company and principal underwriter of such account.

(2) *Limitation on Sales.* It shall be unlawful for any registered separate account funding variable insurance contracts, or for the sponsoring insurance company of such account, to sell any such contract—

(A) unless the fees and charges deducted under the contract, in the aggregate, are reasonable in relation to the services rendered, the expenses expected to be incurred, and the risks assumed by the insurance company, and, beginning on the earlier of August 1, 1997, or the earliest effective date of any registration statement or amendment thereto for such contract following the date of enactment of this subsection, the insurance company so represents in the registration statement for the contract; and

(B) unless the insurance company—

(i) complies with all other applicable provisions of this section, as if it were a trustee or custodian of the registered separate account;

(ii) files with the insurance regulatory authority of the State which is the domiciliary State of the insurance company, an annual statement of its financial condition, which most recent statement indicates that the insurance company has a combined capital and surplus, if a stock company, or an unassigned surplus, if a mutual company, of not less than $1,000,000, or such other amount as the Commission may from time to time prescribe by rule, as necessary or appropriate in the public interest or for the protection of investors; and

(iii) together with its registered separate accounts, is supervised and examined periodically by the insurance authority of such State.

(3) *Fees and Charges.* For purposes of paragraph (2), the fees and charges deducted under the contract shall include all fees and charges imposed for any purpose and in any manner.

(4) *Regulatory Authority.* The Commission may issue such rules and regulations to carry out paragraph (2)(A) as it determines are necessary or appropriate in the public interest or for the protection of investors.

Periodic Payment Plans

Sec. 27. (a) *Sale of Certificates; Restrictions.* It shall be unlawful for any registered investment company issuing periodic payment plan certificates, or for any depositor of or underwriter for such company, to sell any such certificate, if—

(1) the sales load on such certificate exceeds 9 per centum of the total payments to be made thereon;

(2) more than one-half of any of the first twelve monthly payments thereon, or their equivalent, is deducted for sales load;

(3) the amount of sales load deducted from any one of such first payments exceeds proportionately the amount deducted from any other such payment, or the amount deducted from any subsequent payment exceeds proportionately the amount deducted from any other subsequent payment;

(4) the first payment on such certificate is less than $20, or any subsequent payment is less than $10;

(5) if such registered company is a management company, the proceeds of such certificate or the securities in which such proceeds are invested are subject to management fees (other than fees for administrative services of the character described in clause (C), paragraph (2), of section 26(a)) exceeding such reasonable amount as the Commission may prescribe, whether such fees are payable to such company or to investment advisers thereof; or

(6) if such registered company is a unit investment trust the assets of which are securities issued by a management company, the depositor of or principal underwriter for such trust, or any affiliated person of such depositor or underwriter, is to receive from such management company or any affiliated person thereof any fee or payment on account of payments on such certificate exceeding such reasonable amount as the Commission may prescribe.

(b) *Exemptions.* If it appears to the Commission, upon application or otherwise, that smaller companies are subjected to relatively higher operating costs and that in order to make due allowance therefor it is necessary or appropriate in the public interest and consistent with the protection of investors that a provision or provisions of paragraph (1), (2), or (3) of subsection (a) relative to sales load be relaxed in the case of certain registered investment companies issuing periodic payment plan certificates, or certain specified classes of such companies, the Commission is authorized by rules and regulations or order to grant any such company or class of companies appropriate qualified exemptions from the provisions of said paragraphs.

(c) *Sale of Certificates; Requirements.* It shall be unlawful for any registered investment company issuing periodic payment plan certificates, or for any depositor of or underwriter for such company, to sell any such certificate, unless—

(1) such certificate is a redeemable security; and

(2) the proceeds of all payments on such certificate (except such amounts as are deducted for sales load) are deposited with a trustee or custodian having the qualifications prescribed in paragraph (1) of section 26(a) for the trustees of unit investment trusts, and are held by such trustee or custodian under an indenture or agreement containing, in substance, the provisions required by paragraphs (2) and (3) of section 26(a) for the trust indentures of unit investment trusts.

(d) *Surrender of Certificates; Regulations.* Notwithstanding subsection (a) of this section, it shall be unlawful for any registered investment company issuing periodic payment plan certificates, or for any depositor of or underwriter for such company, to sell any such certificate unless the certificate provides that the holder thereof may surrender the certificate at any time within the first eighteen months after the issuance of the certificate and receive in payment thereof, in cash, the sum of (1) the value of his account, and (2) an amount, from such underwriter or depositor, equal to that part of the excess paid for sales loading which is over 15 per centum of the gross payments made by the certificate holder. The Commission may make rules and regulations applicable to such underwriters and depositors specifying such reserve requirements as it deems necessary or appropriate in order for such underwriters and depositors to carry out the obligations to refund sales charges required by this subsection.

(e) *Refund Privileges; Notice; Rules.* With respect to any periodic payment plan certificate sold subject to the provisions of subsection (d) of this section, the registered investment company issuing such periodic payment plan certificate, or any depositor of or underwriter for such company, shall in writing (1) inform each certificate holder who has missed three payments or more, within thirty days following the expiration of fifteen months after the issuance of the certificate, or, if any such holder has missed one payment or more after such period of fifteen months but prior to the expiration of eighteen months after the issuance of the certificate, at any time prior to the expiration of such eighteen-month period, of his right to surrender his certificate as specified in subsection (d) of this section, and (2) inform the certificate holder of (A) the value of the holder's account as of the time the written notice was given to such holder, and (B) the amount to which he is entitled as specified in subsection (d) of this section. The Commission may make rules specifying the method, form, and contents of the notice required by this subsection.

(f) *Charges, Statement; Rules; Surrender of Certificates; Regulations.* With respect to any periodic payment plan (other than a plan under which the amount of sales load deducted from any payment thereon does not exceed 9 per centum of such payment), the custodian bank for such plan shall mail to each certificate holder, within sixty days after the issuance of the certificate, a statement of charges to be deducted from the projected payments on the certificate and a notice of his right of withdrawal as specified in this section. The Commission may make rules specifying the method, form, and contents of the notice required by this subsection. The certificate holder may within forty-five days of the mailing of the notice specified in this subsection surrender his certificate and receive in payment thereof, in cash, the sum of (1) the value of his account, and (2) an amount, from the underwriter or depositor, equal to the difference between the gross payments made and the net amount invested. The Commission may make rules and regulations applicable to underwriters and depositors of companies issuing any such certificate specifying such reserve requirements as it deems necessary or appropriate in order for such underwriters and depositors to carry out the obligations to refund sales charges required by this subsection.

(g) *Governing Provisions; Election.* Notwithstanding the provisions of subsections (a) and (d), a registered investment company issuing periodic payment plan certificates may elect, by written notice to the Commission, to be governed by the provisions of subsection (h) rather than the provisions of subsections (a) and (d).

(h) *Sale of Certificates; Restrictions.* Upon making the election specified in subsection (g), it shall be unlawful for any such electing registered investment company issuing periodic payment plan certificates, or for any depositor of or underwriter for such company, to sell any such certificate, if—

(1) the sales load on such certificate exceeds 9 per centum of the total payments to be made thereon;

(2) more than 20 per centum of any payment thereon is deducted for sales load, or an average

of more than 16 per centum is deducted for sales load from the first forty-eight monthly payments thereon, or their equivalent;

(3) the amount of sales load deducted from any one of the first twelve monthly payments, the thirteenth through twenty-fourth monthly payments, the twenty-fifth through thirty-sixth monthly payments, or the thirty-seventh through forty-eighth monthly payments, or their equivalents, respectively, exceeds proportionately the amount deducted from any other such payment, or the amount deducted from any subsequent payment exceeds proportionately the amount deducted from any other subsequent payment;

(4) the deduction for sales load on the excess of the payment or payments in any month over the minimum monthly payment, or its equivalent, to be made on the certificate exceeds the sales load applicable to payments subsequent to the first forty-eight monthly payments or their equivalent;

(5) the first payment on such certificate is less than $20, or any subsequent payment is less than $10;

(6) if such registered company is a management company, the proceeds of such certificate or the securities in which such proceeds are invested are subject to management fees (other than fees for administrative services of the character described in clause (C) of paragraph (2) of section 26(a)) exceeding such reasonable amount as the Commission may prescribe, whether such fees are payable to such company or to investment advisers thereof; or

(7) if such registered company is a unit investment trust the assets of which are securities issued by a management company, the depositor of or principal underwriter for such trust, or any affiliated person of such depositor or underwriter, is to receive from such management company or any affiliated person thereof any fee or payment on account of payments on such certificate exceeding such reasonable amount as the Commission may prescribe.

(i) *Applicability to Registered Separate Account Funding Variable Insurance Contracts.*

(1) This section does not apply to any registered separate account funding variable insurance contracts, or to the sponsoring insurance company and principal underwriter of such account, except as provided in paragraph (2).

(2) It shall be unlawful for any registered separate account funding variable insurance contracts, or for the sponsoring insurance company of such account, to sell any such contract unless—

(A) such contract is a redeemable security; and

(B) the insurance company complies with section 26(f) and any rules or regulations issued by the Commission under section 26(f).

(j) *Termination of Sales.*

(1) *Termination.* Effective 30 days after the date of enactment of the Military Personnel Financial Services Protection Act [September 29, 2006], it shall be unlawful, subject to subsection (i)—

(A) for any registered investment company to issue any periodic payment plan certificate; or

(B) for such company, or any depositor of or underwriter for any such company, or any other person, to sell such a certificate.

(2) *No Invalidation of Existing Certificates.* Paragraph (1) shall not be construed to alter, invalidate, or otherwise affect any rights or obligations, including rights of redemption, under any periodic payment plan certificate issued and sold before 30 days after such date of enactment.

Face-Amount Certificate Companies

Sec. 28. (a) *Issuance or Sale of Certificate.* It shall be unlawful for any registered face-amount certificate company to issue or sell any face-amount certificate, or to collect or accept any payment on any such certificate issued by such company on or after the effective date of this title, unless—

(1) such company, if organized before March 15, 1940, was actively and continuously engaged in selling face-amount certificates on and before that date, and has outstanding capital stock worth upon a fair valuation of assets not less than $50,000; or if organized on or after March 15, 1940, has capital stock in an amount not less than $250,000 which has been bona fide subscribed and paid for in cash; and

(2) such company maintains at all times minimum certificate reserves on all its outstanding face-amount certificates in an aggregate amount calculated and adjusted as follows:

(A) the reserves for each certificate of the installment type shall be based on assumed annual, semi-annual, quarterly, or monthly reserve payments according to the manner in which gross payments for any certificate year are made by the holder, which reserve payments shall be sufficient in amount, as and when accumulated at a rate not to exceed 3½ per centum per annum compounded annually, to provide the minimum maturity or face amount of the certificate when due. Such reserve payments may be graduated according to certificate years so that the reserve payment or payments for the first certificate year shall amount to at least 50 per centum of the required gross annual payment for such year and the reserve payment or payments for each of the second to fifth certificate years inclusive shall amount to at least 93 per centum of each such year's required gross annual payment and for the sixth and each subsequent certificate year the reserve payment or payments shall amount to at least 96 per centum of each such year's required gross annual payment: *Provided*, That such aggregate reserve payments shall amount to at least 93 per centum of the aggregate gross annual payments required to be made by the holder to obtain the maturity of the certificate. The company may at its option take as loading from the gross payment or payments for a certificate year, as and when made by the certificate holder, an amount or amounts equal in the aggregate for such year to not more than the excess, if any, of the gross payment or payments required to be made by the holder for such year, over and above the percentage of the gross annual payment required herein for such year for reserve purposes. Such loading may be taken by the company prior to or after the setting up of the reserve payment or payments for such year and the reserve payment or payments for such year may be graduated and adjusted to correspond with the amount of the gross payment or payments made by the certificate holder for such year less the loading so taken;

(B) if the foregoing minimum percentages of the gross annual payments required under the provisions of such certificate should produce reserve payments larger than are necessary at 3½ per centum per annum compounded annually to provide the minimum maturity or face amount of the certificate when due, the reserve shall be based upon reserve payments accumulated as provided under preceding subparagraph (A) of this paragraph except that in lieu of the 3½ per centum rate specified therein, such rate shall be lowered to the minimum rate, expressed in multiples of one-eighth of 1 per centum, which will accumulate such reserve payments to the maturity value when due;

(C) if the actual annual gross payment to be made by the certificate holder on any certificate issued prior to or after the effective date of this Act is less than the amount of any assumed reserve payment or payments for a certificate year, such company shall maintain as a part of such minimum certificate reserves a deficiency reserve equal to the total present value of future deficiencies in the gross payments, calculated at a rate not to exceed 3½ per centum per annum compounded annually;

(D) for each certificate of the installment type the amount of the reserve shall at any time be at least equal to (1) the then amount of the reserve payments set up under section 28(a)(2)(A) or (B); (2) the accumulations on such reserve payments as computed under subparagraphs (A) or (B) of this paragraph (2); (3) the amount of any deficiency reserve required under subparagraph (C) hereof; and (4) such amount as shall have been credited to the account of each certificate holder in the form of any credit, or any dividend, or any interest in addition to the minimum maturity amount specified in such certificate, plus any accumulations on any amount or amounts so credited, at a rate not exceeding 3½ per centum per annum compounded annually;

(E) for each certificate which is fully paid, including any fully paid obligations resulting from or effected upon the maturity of the previously issued certificate, and for each paid-up certificate issued as provided in subsection (f) of this section prior to maturity, the amount of the reserve shall at any time be at least equal to (1) such amount as and when accumulated at a rate not to exceed 3½ per centum per annum compounded annually, will provide the amount or amounts payable when due and (2) such amount as shall have been credited to the account of each such certificate holder in the form of any credit, or any dividend, or any interest in addition to the minimum maturity amount specified in the certificate, plus any accumulations on any amount or amounts so credited, at a rate not exceeding 3½ per centum per annum compounded annually;

(F) for each certificate of the installment type under which gross payments have been made by or credited to the holder thereof covering a payment period or periods or any part thereof beyond the then current payment period as defined by the terms of such certificate, and for which period or periods no reserve has been set up under subparagraph (A) or (B) hereof, an advance payment reserve shall be set up and maintained in the amount of the present value of any such unapplied advance gross payments, computed at a rate not to exceed 3½ per centum per annum compounded annually;

(G) such appropriate contingency reserves for death and disability benefits and for reinstatement rights on any such certificate providing for such benefits or rights as the Commission shall prescribe by rule, regulation, or order based upon the experience of face-amount companies in relation to such contingencies.

At no time shall the aggregate certificate reserves herein required by subparagraphs (A) to (F), inclusive, be less than the aggregate surrender values and other amounts to which all certificate holders may be then entitled.

For the purpose of this subsection (a), no certificate of the installment type shall be deemed to be outstanding if before a surrender value has been attained the holder thereof has been in continuous default in making his payments thereon for a period of one year.

(b) *Asset Requirements Prior to Sale of Certificates.* It shall be unlawful for any registered face-amount certificate company to issue or sell any face-amount certificate, or to collect or accept any payment on any such certificate issued by such company on or after the effective date of this title, unless such company has, in cash or qualified investments, assets having a value not less than the aggregate amount of the capital stock requirement and certificate reserves as computed under the provisions of subsection (a) hereof. As used in this subsection, "qualified investments" means investments of a kind which life-insurance companies are permitted to invest in or hold under the provisions of the Code of the District of Columbia as heretofore or hereafter amended, and such other investments as the Commission shall by rule, regulation, or order authorize as qualified investments. Such investments shall be valued in accordance with the provisions of said Code where such provisions are applicable. Investments to which such provisions do not apply shall be valued in accordance with such rules, regulations, or orders as the Commission shall prescribe for the protection of investors.

(c) *Certificate Reserve Requirements.* The Commission shall by rule, regulation, or order, in the public interest or for the protection of investors, require a registered face-amount certificate company to deposit and maintain, upon such terms and conditions as the Commission shall prescribe and as are appropriate for the protection of investors, with one or more institutions having the qualifications required by paragraph (1) of section 26(a) for a trustee of a unit investment trust, all or any part of the investments maintained by such company as certificate reserve requirements under the provisions of subsection (b) hereof: *Provided, however,* That where qualified investments are maintained on deposit by such company in respect of its liabilities under certificates issued to or held by residents of any State as required by the statute of such State or by any order, regulation, or requirement of such State or any official or agency thereof, the amount so on deposit, but not to exceed the amount of reserves required by subsection (a) hereof for the certificates so issued or held, shall be deducted from the amount of qualified investments that may be required to be deposited hereunder.

Assets which are qualified investments under subsection (b) and which are deposited under or as permitted by this subsection (c), may be used and shall be considered as a part of the assets required to be maintained under the provisions of said subsection (b).

(d) *Provisions Required in Certificate.* It shall be unlawful for any registered face-amount certificate company to issue or sell any face-amount certificate, or to collect or accept any payment on any such certificate issued by such company on or after the effective date of this title, unless such certificate contains a provision or provisions to the effect—

(1) that, in respect of any certificate of the installment type, during the first certificate year the holder of the certificate, upon surrender thereof, shall be entitled to a value payable in cash not less than the reserve payments as specified in subparagraph (A) or (B) of paragraph (2) of subsection (a) and at the end of such certificate year, a value payable in cash at least equal to 50 per centum of the amount of the gross annual payment required thereby for such year;

(2) that, in respect of any certificate of the installment type, at any time after the expiration of the first certificate year and prior to maturity, the holder of the certificate, upon surrender thereof, shall be entitled to a value payable in cash not

less than the then amount of the reserve for such certificate required by numbered items (1) and (2) of subparagraph (D) of paragraph (2) of subsection (a) hereof, less a surrender charge that shall not exceed 2 per centum of the face or maturity amount of the certificate, or 15 per centum of the amount of such reserve, whichever is the lesser, but in no event shall such value be less than 50 per centum of the amount of such reserve. The amount of the surrender value for the end of each certificate year shall be set out in the certificate;

(3) that, in respect of any certificate of the installment type, the holder of the certificate, upon surrender thereof for cash or upon receipt of a paid-up certificate as provided in subsection (f) hereof, shall be entitled to a value payable in cash equal to the then amount of any advance payment reserve under such certificate required by subparagraph (F) of paragraph (2) of subsection (a) hereof in addition to any other amounts due the holder hereunder;

(4) that at any time prior to maturity, in respect of any certificate which is fully paid, the holder of the certificate, upon surrender thereof, shall be entitled to a value payable in cash not less than the then amount of the reserve for such certificate required by item (1) of subparagraph (E) of paragraph (2) of subsection (a) hereof, less a surrender charge that shall not exceed 2 per centum of the face or maturity amount of the certificate, or 15 per centum of the amount of such reserve, whichever is the lesser: *Provided, however,* That such surrender charge shall not apply as to any obligations of a fully paid type resulting from the maturity of a previously issued certificate. The amount of the surrender value for the end of each certificate year shall be set out in the certificate;

(5) that in respect of any certificate, the holder of the certificate, upon maturity, upon surrender thereof for cash or upon receipt of a paid-up certificate as provided in subsection (f) hereof, shall be entitled to a value payable in cash equal to the then amount of the reserve, if any, for such certificate required by item (4) of subparagraph (D) of paragraph (2) of subsection (a) hereof or item (2) of subparagraph (E) of paragraph (2) of subsection (a) hereof in addition to any other amounts due the holder hereunder.

The term "certificate year" as used in this section in respect of any certificate of the installment type means a period or periods for which one year's payment or payments as provided by the certificate have been made thereon by the holder and the certificate maintained in force by such payments for the time for which the same have been made, and in respect of any certificate which is fully paid or paid-up means any year ending on the anniversary of the date of issuance of the certificate.

Any certificate may provide for loans or advances by the company to the certificate holder on the security of such certificate upon terms prescribed therein but at an interest rate not exceeding 6 per centum per annum. The amount of the required reserves, deposits, and the surrender values thereof available to the holder may be adjusted to take into account any unpaid balance on such loans or advances and interest thereon, for the purposes of this subsection and subsections (b) and (c) hereof.

Any certificate may provide that the company at its option may, prior to the maturity thereof, defer any payment or payments to the certificate holder to which he may be entitled under this subsection (d), for a period of not more than thirty days: *Provided,* That in the event such option is exercised by the company, interest shall accrue on any payment or payments due to the holder, for the period of such deferment at a rate equal to that used in accumulating the reserves for such certificate: *And provided further,* That the Commission may, by rules and regulations or orders in the public interest or for the protection of investors, make provision for any other deferment upon such terms and conditions as it shall prescribe.

(e) *Liability of Holder to Legal Action for Unpaid Amount of Certificate.* It shall be unlawful for any registered face-amount certificate company to issue or sell any face-amount certificate, or to collect or accept any payment on any such certificate issued by such company on or after the effective date of this title, which certificate makes the holder liable to any legal action or proceeding for any unpaid amount on such certificate.

(f) *Optional Right to Paid Up Certificate in Lieu of Cash Surrender Value.* It shall be unlawful for any registered face-amount certificate company to issue or sell any face-amount certificate, or to collect or accept any payment on any such certificate issued by such company on or after the effective date of this title, (1) unless such face-amount certificate contains a provision or provisions to the effect that the holder shall have an optional right to receive a paid-up certificate in lieu of the then attained cash surrender value provided therein and in the amount of such value plus accumulations thereon at a rate to be specified in the paid-up certificate equal to that used in computing the reserve on the original certificate under subparagraph (A) or (B) of paragraph (2) of subsection (a) of this section, such paid-up certificate to become due and payable at the end of a period equal to the balance of the term of such original certificate before maturity; and during the period prior to maturity such paid-up certificate shall have a cash value upon surrender thereof equal to the then amount of the reserve therefor; and (2) unless such face-amount certificate contains a further provision or provisions to the effect that if the holder be in continuous default in his payments on such certificate for a period of six months without having exercised his option to receive a paid-up certificate, as herein provided, the company at the expiration of such six months shall pay the surrender value in cash if such value is less than $100 or if such value is $100 or more shall issue such paid-up certificate to such holder and such payment or issuance, plus the payment of all other amounts to which he may be then entitled under the original certificate, shall operate to cancel his original certificate: *Provided,* That in lieu of the issuance of a new paid-up certificate the original certificate may be converted into a paid-up certificate with the same effect; and (3) unless, where such certificate provides, in the event of default, for the deferment of payments thereon by the holder or of the due dates of such payments or of the maturity date of the certificate, it shall also provide in effect for the right of reinstatement by the holder of the certificate after default and for an option in the holder, at the time of reinstatement, to make up the payment or payments for the default period next preceding such reinstatement with interest thereon not exceeding 6 per centum per annum, with the same effect as if no such default in making such payments had occurred.

The term "default" as used in this subsection (f) shall, without restricting its usual meaning, include a failure to make a payment or payments as and when provided by the certificate.

(g) *Application of Section to Company Issuing Certificates Only to Holders of Previously Issued Certificates.* The foregoing provisions of this section shall not apply to a face-amount certificate company which on or before the effective date of this Act has discontinued the offering of face-amount certificates to the public and issues face-amount certificates only to the holders of certificates previously issued pursuant to an obligation expressed or implied in such certificates.

(h) *Declaration or Payment of Dividends.* It shall be unlawful for any registered face-amount certificate company which does not maintain the minimum certificate reserve on all its outstanding face-amount certificates issued prior to the effective date of this Act, in an aggregate amount calculated and adjusted as provided in section 28, to declare or pay any dividends on the shares of such company for or during any calendar year which shall exceed one-third of the net earnings for the next preceding calendar year or which shall exceed 10 per centum of the aggregate net earnings for the next preceding five calendar years, whichever is the lesser amount, or any dividend which shall have been forbidden by the Commission pursuant to the provision of the next sentence of this paragraph. At least thirty days before such company shall declare, pay, or distribute any dividend, it shall give the Commission written notice of its intention to declare, pay, or distribute the same; and if at any time it shall appear to the Commission that the declaration, payment or distribution of any dividend for or during any calendar year might impair the financial integrity of such company or its ability to meet its liabilities under its outstanding face-amount certificates, it may by order forbid the declaration, distribution, or payment of any such dividend.

(i) *Application of Section to Certificates Issued Prior to Effective Date of Section.* The foregoing provisions of this section shall apply to all face-amount certificates issued prior to the effective date of this subsection; to the collection or acceptance of any payment on such certificates; to the issuance of face-amount certificates to the holders of such certificates pursuant to an obligation expressed or implied in such certificates; to the provisions of such certificates; to the minimum certificate reserves and deposits maintained with respect thereto; and to the assets that the issuer of such certificate was and is required to have with respect to such certificates. With respect to all face-amount certificates issued after the effective date of this subsection, the provisions of this section shall apply except as hereinafter provided.

(1) Notwithstanding subparagraph (A) of paragraph (2) of subsection (a), the reserves for each certificate of the installment type shall be based on assumed annual, semiannual, quarterly, or monthly reserve payments according to the manner in which gross payments for any certificate year are made by the holder, which reserve payments shall be sufficient in amount, as and when accumulated at a rate not to exceed 3½ per cen-

tum per annum compounded annually, to provide the minimum maturity or face amount of the certificate when due. Such reserve payments may be graduated according to certificate years so that the reserve payment or payments for the first three certificate years shall amount to at least 80 per centum of the required gross annual payment for such years; the reserve payment or payments for the fourth certificate year shall amount to at least 90 per centum of such year's required gross annual payment; the reserve payment or payments for the fifth certificate year shall amount to at least 93 per centum of such year's gross annual payment; and for the sixth and each subsequent certificate year the reserve payment or payments shall amount to at least 96 per centum of each such year's required gross annual payment: *Provided,* That such aggregate reserve payments shall amount to at least 93 per centum of the aggregate gross annual payments required to be made by the holder to obtain the maturity of the certificate. The company may at its option take as loading from the gross payment or payments for a certificate year, as and when made by the certificate holder, an amount or amounts equal in the aggregate for such year to not more than the excess, if any, of the gross payment or payments required to be made by the holder for such year, over and above the percentage of the gross annual payment required herein for such year for reserve purposes. Such loading may be taken by the company prior to or after the setting up of the reserve payment or payments for such year and the reserve payment or payments for such year may be graduated and adjusted to correspond with the amount of the gross payment or payments made by the certificate holder for such year less the loading so taken.

(2) Notwithstanding paragraphs (1) and (2) of subsection (d), (A) in respect of any certificate of the installment type, during the first certificate year, the holder of the certificate, upon surrender thereof, shall be entitled to a value payable in cash not less than 80 per centum of the amount of the gross payments made on the certificate; and (B) in respect of any certificate of the installment type, at any time after the expiration of the first certificate year and prior to maturity, the holder of the certificate, upon surrender thereof, shall be entitled to a value payable in cash not less than the then amount of the reserve for such certificate required by clauses (1) and (2) of subparagraph (D) of paragraph (2) of subsection (a), less a surrender charge that shall not exceed 2 per centum of the face or maturity amount of the certificate, or 15 per centum of the amount of such reserve, whichever is lesser, but in no event shall such value be less than 80 per centum of the gross payments made on the certificate. The amount of the surrender value for the end of each certificate year shall be set out in the certificate.

Sec. 29. [Repealed]

Reports and Financial Statements of Investment Companies and Affiliated Persons

Sec. 30. (a) *Annual Report by Company.* Every registered investment company shall file annually with the Commission such information, documents, and reports as investment companies having securities registered on a national securities exchange are required to file annually pursuant to section 13(a) of the Securities Exchange Act of 1934 and the rules and regulations issued thereunder.

(b) *Semi-Annual or Quarterly Filing of Information; Copies of Periodic or Interim Reports Sent to Security Holders.* Every registered investment company shall file with the Commission—

(1) such information, documents, and reports (other than financial statements), as the Commission may require to keep reasonably current the information and documents contained in the registration statement of such company filed under this title; and

(2) copies of every periodic or interim report or similar communication containing financial statements and transmitted to any class of such company's security holders, such copies to be filed not later than ten days after such transmission.

Any information or documents contained in a report or other communication to security holders filed pursuant to paragraph (2) may be incorporated by reference in any report subsequently or concurrently filed pursuant to paragraph (1).

(c) *Minimizing Reporting Burdens.*

(1) The Commission shall take such action as it deems necessary or appropriate, consistent with the public interest and the protection of investors, to avoid unnecessary reporting by, and minimize the compliance burdens on, registered investment companies and their affiliated persons in exercising its authority—

(A) under subsection (f); and

(B) under subsection (b)(1), if the Commission requires the filing of information, documents, and reports under that subsection on a basis more frequently than semiannually.

(2) Action taken by the Commission under paragraph (1) shall include considering, and requesting public comment on—

(A) feasible alternatives that minimize the reporting burdens on registered investment companies; and

(B) the utility of such information, documents, and reports to the Commission in relation to the costs to registered investment companies and their affiliated persons of providing such information, documents, and reports.

(d) *Reports Under This Section in Lieu of Reports Under Other Provisions of Law.* The Commission shall issue rules and regulations permitting the filing with the Commission, and with any national securities exchange concerned, of copies of periodic reports, or of extracts therefrom, filed by any registered investment company pursuant to subsections (a) and (b), in lieu of any reports and documents required of such company under section 13 or 15(d) of the Securities Exchange Act of 1934.

(e) *Semi-Annual Reports to Stockholders.* Every registered investment company shall transmit to its stockholders, at least semiannually, reports containing such of the following information and financial statements or their equivalent, as of a reasonably current date, as the Commission may prescribe by rules and regulations for the protection of investors, which reports shall not be misleading in any material respect in the light of the reports required to be filed pursuant to subsections (a) and (b):

(1) a balance sheet accompanied by a statement of the aggregate value of investments on the date of such balance sheet;

(2) a list showing the amounts and values of securities owned on the date of such balance sheet;

(3) a statement of income, for the period covered by the report, which shall be itemized at least with respect to each category of income and expense representing more than 5 per centum of total income or expense;

(4) a statement of surplus, which shall be itemized at least with respect to each charge or credit to the surplus account which represents more than 5 per centum of the total charges or credits during the period covered by the report;

(5) a statement of the aggregate remuneration paid by the company during the period covered by the report (A) to all directors and to all members of any advisory board for regular compensation; (B) to each director and to each member of an advisory board for special compensation; (C) to all officers; and (D) to each person of whom any officer or director of the company is an affiliated person; and

(6) a statement of the aggregate dollar amount of purchases and sales of investment securities, other than Government securities made during the period covered by the report:

Provided, That if in the judgment of the Commission any item required under this subsection is inapplicable or inappropriate to any specified type or types of investment company, the Commission may by rules and regulations permit in lieu thereof the inclusion of such item of a comparable character as it may deem applicable or appropriate to such type or types of investment company.

(f) *Additional Information.* The Commission may, by rule, require that semiannual reports containing the information set forth in subsection (e) include such other information as the Commission deems necessary or appropriate in the public interest or for the protection of investors.

(g) *Certificate of Independent Public Accountants.* Financial statements contained in annual reports required pursuant to subsections (a) and (e), if required by the rules and regulations of the Commission, shall be accompanied by a certificate of independent public accountants. The certificate of such independent public accountants shall be based upon an audit not less in scope or procedures followed than that which independent public accountants would ordinarily make for the purpose of presenting comprehensive and dependable financial statements, and shall contain such information as the Commission may prescribe, by rules and regulations in the public interest or for the protection of investors, as to the nature and scope of the audit and the findings and opinion of the accountants. Each such report shall state that such independent public accountants have verified securities owned, either by actual examination, or by receipt of a certificate from the custodian, as the Commission may prescribe by rules and regulations.

(h) *Duties and Liabilities of Affiliated Persons.* Every person who is directly or indirectly the beneficial owner of more than 10 per centum of any class of outstanding securities (other than short-term paper) of which a registered closed-end company is the issuer or who is an officer, director, member of an advisory board, investment adviser, or affiliated person of an investment adviser of such a company shall in respect of his transactions in any securities of such company (other than short-term paper) be subject to the same duties and liabilities as those imposed by section 16 of the Securities Exchange Act of 1934 upon certain beneficial owners, directors, and officers in respect of their transactions in certain equity securities.

(i) *Disclosure to Church Plan Participants.* A person that maintains a church plan that is excluded from the definition of an investment company solely by reason of section 3(c)(14) shall provide disclosure to plan participants, in writing, and not less frequently than annually, and for new participants joining such a plan after May 31, 1996, as soon as is practicable after joining such plan, that—

(1) the plan, or any company or account maintained to manage or hold plan assets and interests in such plan, company, or account, are not subject to registration, regulation, or reporting under this title, the Securities Act of 1933, the Securities Exchange Act of 1934, or State securities laws; and

(2) plan participants and beneficiaries therefore will not be afforded the protections of those provisions.

(j) *Notice to Commission.* The Commission may issue rules and regulations to require any person that maintains a church plan that is excluded from the definition of an investment company solely by reason of section 3(c)(14) to file a notice with the Commission containing such information and in such form as the Commission may prescribe as necessary or appropriate in the public interest or consistent with the protection of investors.

Accounts and Records

Sec. 31. (a) *Maintenance of Records.*

(1) *In General.* Each registered investment company, and each underwriter, broker, dealer, or investment adviser that is a majority-owned subsidiary of such a company, shall maintain and preserve such records (as defined in section 3(a)(37) of the Securities Exchange Act of 1934) for such period or periods as the Commission, by rules and regulations, may prescribe as necessary or appropriate in the public interest or for the protection of investors. Each investment adviser that is not a majority-owned subsidiary of, and each depositor of any registered investment company, and each principal underwriter for any registered investment company other than a closed-end company, shall maintain and preserve for such period or periods as the Commission shall prescribe by rules and regulations, such records as are necessary or appropriate to record such person's transactions with such registered company. Each person having custody or use of the securities, deposits, or credits of a registered investment company shall maintain and preserve all records that relate to the custody or use by such person of the securities, deposits, or credits of the registered investment company for such period or periods as the Commission, by rule or regulation, may prescribe, as necessary or appropriate in the public interest or for the protection of investors.

(2) *Minimizing Compliance Burden.* In exercising its authority under this subsection, the Commission shall take such steps as it deems necessary or appropriate, consistent with the public interest and for the protection of investors, to avoid unnecessary recordkeeping by, and minimize the compliance burden on, persons required to maintain records under this subsection (hereafter in this section referred to as "subject persons"). Such steps shall include considering, and requesting public comment on—

(A) feasible alternatives that minimize the recordkeeping burdens on subject persons;

(B) the necessity of such records in view of the public benefits derived from the independent scrutiny of such records through Commission examination;

(C) the costs associated with maintaining the information that would be required to be reflected in such records; and

(D) the effects that a proposed recordkeeping requirement would have on internal compliance, policies and procedures.

(b) *Examinations of Records.*

(1) *In General.* All records required to be maintained and preserved in accordance with subsection (a) shall be subject at any time and from time to time to such reasonable periodic, special, and other examinations by the Commission, or any member or representative thereof, as the Commission may prescribe.

(2) *Availability.* For purposes of examinations referred to in paragraph (1), any subject person shall make available to the Commission or its representatives any copies or extracts from such

records as may be prepared without undue effort, expense, or delay as the Commission or its representatives may reasonably request.

(3) *Commission Action.* The Commission shall exercise its authority under this subsection with due regard for the benefits of internal compliance policies and procedures and the effective implementation and operation thereof.

(4) *Records of Persons With Custody or Use.*

(A) *In General.* Records of persons having custody or use of the securities, deposits, or credits of a registered investment company that relate to such custody or use, are subject at any time, or from time to time, to such reasonable periodic, special, or other examinations and other information and document requests by representatives of the Commission, as the Commission deems necessary or appropriate in the public interest or for the protection of investors.

(B) *Certain Persons Subject to Other Regulation.* Any person that is subject to regulation and examination by a Federal financial institution regulatory agency (as such term is defined under section 212(c)(2) of title 18, United States Code) may satisfy any examination request, information request, or document request described under subparagraph (A), by providing to the Commission a detailed listing, in writing, of the securities, deposits, or credits of the registered investment company within the custody or use of such person.

(c) *Regulatory Authority.* The Commission may, in the public interest or for the protection of investors, issue rules and regulations providing for a reasonable degree of uniformity in the accounting policies and principles to be followed by registered investment companies in maintaining their accounting records and in preparing financial statements required pursuant to this title.

(d) *Exemption Authority.* The Commission, upon application made by any registered investment company, may by order exempt a specific transaction or transactions from the provisions of any rule or regulation made pursuant to subsection (e),* if the Commission finds that such rule or regulation should not reasonably be applied to such transaction.

Accountants and Auditors

Sec. 32. (a) *Selection of Accountant.* It shall be unlawful for any registered management company or registered face-amount certificate company to file with the Commission any financial statement signed or certified by an independent public accountant, unless—

(1) such accountant shall have been selected at a meeting held within thirty days before or after the beginning of the fiscal year or before the annual meeting of stockholders in that year by the vote, cast in person, of a majority of those members of the board of directors who are not interested persons of such registered company;

(2) such selection shall have been submitted for ratification or rejection at the next succeeding annual meeting of stockholders if such meeting be held, except that any vacancy occurring between annual meetings, due to the death or resignation of the accountant, may be filled by the vote of a majority of those members of the board of directors who are not interested persons of such registered company, cast in person at a meeting called for the purpose of voting on such action;

(3) the employment of such accountant shall have been conditioned upon the right of the company by vote of a majority of the outstanding voting securities at any meeting called for the purpose to terminate such employment forthwith without any penalty; and

(4) such certificate or report of such accountant shall be addressed both to the board of directors of such registered company and to the security holders thereof.

If the selection of an accountant has been rejected pursuant to paragraph (2) or his employment terminated pursuant to paragraph (3), the vacancy so occurring may be filled by a vote of a majority of the outstanding voting securities, either at the meeting at which the rejection or termination occurred or, if not so filled, at a subsequent meeting which shall be called for the purpose. In the case of a common-law trust of the character described in section 16(c), no ratification of the employment of such accountant shall be required but such employment may be terminated and such accountant removed by action of the holders of record of a majority of the outstanding shares of beneficial interest in such trust in the same manner as is provided in section 16(c) in respect of the removal of a trustee, and all the provisions therein contained as to the calling of a meeting shall be applicable. In the event of such termination and removal, the vacancy so occurring may be filled by action of the holders of record of a majority of the shares of beneficial interest either

* (e), (f) [redesignated].

at the meeting, if any, at which such termination and removal occurs, or by instruments in writing filed with the custodian, or if not so filed within a reasonable time then at a subsequent meeting which shall be called by the trustees for the purpose. The provisions of paragraph (42) of section 2(a) as to a majority shall be applicable to the vote cast at any meeting of the shareholders of such a trust held pursuant to this subsection.

(b) *Selection of Controller or Other Principal Accounting Officer*. No registered management company or registered face-amount certificate company shall file with the Commission any financial statement in the preparation of which the controller or other principal accounting officer or employee of such company participated, unless such controller, officer or employee was selected, either by vote of the holders of such company's voting securities at the last annual meeting of such security holders, or by the board of directors of such company.

(c) *Reports of Accountants and Auditors*. The Commission is authorized, by rules and regulations or order in the public interest or for the protection of investors, to require accountants and auditors to keep reports, work sheets, and other documents and papers relating to registered investment companies for such period or periods as the Commission may prescribe, and to make the same available for inspection by the Commission or any member or representative thereof.

Filing of Documents with Commission in Civil Actions

Sec. 33. Every registered investment company which is a party and every affiliated person of such company who is a party defendant to any action or claim by a registered investment company or a security holder thereof in a derivative or representative capacity against an officer, director, investment adviser, trustee, or depositor of such company, shall file with the Commission, unless already so filed, (1) a copy of all pleadings, verdicts, or judgments filed with the court or served in connection with such action or claim, (2) a copy of any proposed settlement, compromise, or discontinuance of such action, and (3) a copy of such motions, transcripts, or other documents filed in or issued by the court or served in connection with such action or claim as may be requested in writing by the Commission. If any document referred to in clause (1) or (2)—

(A) is delivered to such company or party defendant, such document shall be filed with the Commission not later than ten days after the receipt thereof; or

(B) is filed in such court or delivered by such company or party defendant, such document shall be filed with the Commission not later than five days after such filing or delivery.

Destruction and Falsification of Reports and Records

Sec. 34. (a) *Willful Destruction*. It shall be unlawful for any person, except as permitted by rule, regulation, or order of the Commission, willfully to destroy, mutilate, or alter any account, book, or other document the preservation of which has been required pursuant to section 31(a) or 32(c).

(b) *Untrue Statements or Omissions*. It shall be unlawful for any person to make any untrue statement of a material fact in any registration statement, application, report, account, record, or other document filed or transmitted pursuant to this title or the keeping of which is required pursuant to section 31(a). It shall be unlawful for any person so filing, transmitting, or keeping any such document to omit to state therein any fact necessary in order to prevent the statements made therein, in the light of the circumstances under which they were made, from being materially misleading. For the purposes of this subsection, any part of any such document which is signed or certified by an accountant or auditor in his capacity as such shall be deemed to be made, filed, transmitted, or kept by such accountant or auditor, as well as by the person filing, transmitting, or keeping the complete document.

Unlawful Representations and Names

Sec. 35. (a) *Misrepresentation of Guarantees*.

(1) *In General*. It shall be unlawful for any person, issuing or selling any security of which a registered investment company is the issuer, to represent or imply in any manner whatsoever that such security or company—

(A) has been guaranteed, sponsored, recommended, or approved by the United States, or any agency, instrumentality or officer of the United States;

(B) has been insured by the Federal Deposit Insurance Corporation; or

(C) is guaranteed by or is otherwise an obligation of any bank or insured depository institution.

(2) *Disclosures.* Any person issuing or selling the securities of a registered investment company that is advised by, or sold through, a bank shall prominently disclose that an investment in the company is not insured by the Federal Deposit Insurance Corporation or any other government agency. The Commission may, after consultation with and taking into consideration the views of the Federal banking agencies (as defined in section 3 of the Federal Deposit Insurance Act), adopt rules and regulations, and issue orders, consistent with the protection of investors, prescribing the manner in which the disclosure under this paragraph shall be provided.

(3) *Definitions.* The terms "insured depository institution" and "appropriate Federal banking agency" have the same meanings as given in section 3 of the Federal Deposit Insurance Act.

(b) *Unlawful Representation of Sponsorship by United States or Agency Thereof.* It shall be unlawful for any person registered under any section of this title to represent or imply in any manner whatsoever that such person has been sponsored, recommended, or approved, or that his abilities or qualifications have in any respect been passed upon by the United States or any agency or officer thereof.

(c) *Statement of Registration Under Securities Provisions.* No provision of subsection (a) or (b) shall be construed to prohibit a statement that a person or security is registered under this Act, the Securities Act of 1933, or the Securities Exchange Act of 1934, if such statement is true in fact and if the effect of such registration is not misrepresented.

(d) *Deceptive or Misleading Names.* It shall be unlawful for any registered investment company to adopt as a part of the name or title of such company, or of any securities of which it is the issuer, any word or words that the Commission finds are materially deceptive or misleading. The Commission is authorized, by rule, regulation, or order, to define such names or titles as are materially deceptive or misleading.

Breach of Fiduciary Duty

Sec. 36. (a) *Civil Actions by Commission; Jurisdiction; Allegations; Injunctive or Other Relief.* The Commission is authorized to bring an action in the proper district court of the United States, or in the United States court of any territory or other place subject to the jurisdiction of the United States, alleging that a person who is, or at the time of the alleged misconduct was, serving or acting in one or more of the following capacities has engaged within five years of the commencement of the action or is about to engage in any act or practice constituting a breach of fiduciary duty involving personal misconduct in respect of any registered investment company for which such person so serves or acts, or at the time of the alleged misconduct, so served or acted—

(1) as officer, director, member of any advisory board, investment adviser, or depositor; or

(2) as principal underwriter, if such registered company is an open-end company, unit investment trust, or face-amount certificate company.

If such allegations are established, the court may enjoin such persons from acting in any or all such capacities either permanently or temporarily and award such injunctive or other relief against such person as may be reasonable and appropriate in the circumstances, having due regard to the protection of investors and to the effectuation of the policies declared in section 1(b) of this title.

(b) *Compensation or Payments as Basis of Fiduciary Duty; Civil Actions by Commission or Security Holder; Burden of Proof; Judicial Consideration of Director or Shareholder Approval; Persons Liable; Extent of Liability; Exempted Transactions; Jurisdiction; Finding Restriction.* For the purposes of this subsection, the investment adviser of a registered investment company shall be deemed to have a fiduciary duty with respect to the receipt of compensation for services, or of payments of a material nature, paid by such registered investment company, or by the security holders thereof, to such investment adviser or any affiliated person of such investment adviser. An action may be brought under this subsection by the Commission, or by a security holder of such registered investment company on behalf of such company, against such investment adviser, or any affiliated person of such investment adviser, or any other person enumerated in subsection (a) of this section who has a fiduciary duty concerning such compensation or payments, for breach of fiduciary duty in respect of such compensation or payments paid by such registered investment company or by the security holders thereof to such investment adviser or person. With respect to any such action the following provisions shall apply:

(1) It shall not be necessary to allege or prove that any defendant engaged in personal misconduct, and the plaintiff shall have the burden of proving a breach of fiduciary duty.

(2) In any such action approval by the board of directors of such investment company of such compensation or payments, or of contracts or other arrangements providing for such compensation or payments, and ratification or approval of such compensation or payments, or of contracts or other arrangements providing for such compensation or payments, by the shareholders of such investment company, shall be given such consideration by the court as is deemed appropriate under all the circumstances.

(3) No such action shall be brought or maintained against any person other than the recipient of such compensation or payments, and no damages or other relief shall be granted against any person other than the recipient of such compensation or payments. No award of damages shall be recoverable for any period prior to one year before the action was instituted. Any award of damages against such recipient shall be limited to the actual damages resulting from the breach of fiduciary duty and shall in no event exceed the amount of compensation or payments received from such investment company, or the security holders thereof, by such recipient.

(4) This subsection shall not apply to compensation or payments made in connection with transactions subject to section 17 of this title, or rules, regulations, or orders thereunder, or to sales loads for the acquisition of any security issued by a registered investment company.

(5) Any action pursuant to this subsection may be brought only in an appropriate district court of the United States.

(6) No finding by a court with respect to a breach of fiduciary duty under this subsection shall be made a basis (A) for a finding of a violation of this title for the purposes of sections 9 and 49 of this title, section 15 of the Securities Exchange Act of 1934, or section 203 of title II of this Act, or (B) for an injunction to prohibit any person from serving in any of the capacities enumerated in subsection (a) of this section.

(c) *Corporate or Other Trustees Performing Functions of Investment Advisers.* For the purposes of subsections (a) and (b) the term "investment adviser" includes a corporate or other trustee performing the functions of an investment adviser.

Larceny and Embezzlement

Sec. 37. Whoever steals, unlawfully abstracts, unlawfully and willfully converts to his own use or to the use of another, or embezzles any of the moneys, funds, securities, credits, property, or assets of any registered investment company shall be deemed guilty of a crime, and upon conviction thereof shall be subject to the penalties provided in section 49. A judgment of conviction or acquittal on the merits under the laws of any State shall be a bar to any prosecution under this section for the same act or acts.

Rules, Regulations, and Orders

Sec. 38. (a) *Powers of Commission.* The Commission shall have authority from time to time to make, issue, amend, and rescind such rules and regulations and such orders as are necessary or appropriate to the exercise of the powers conferred upon the Commission elsewhere in this title, including rules and regulations defining accounting, technical, and trade terms used in this title, and prescribing the form or forms in which information required in registration statements, applications, and reports to the Commission shall be set forth. For the purposes of its rules or regulations the Commission may classify persons, securities, and other matters within its jurisdiction and prescribe different requirements for different classes of persons, securities, or matters.

(b) *Filing Information and Documents.* The Commission, by such rules and regulations or order as it deems necessary or appropriate in the public interest or for the protection of investors, may authorize the filing of any information or documents required to be filed with the Commission under this title, title II of this Act, the Securities Act of 1933, the Securities Exchange Act of 1934, or the Trust Indenture Act of 1939, by incorporating by reference any information or documents theretofore or concurrently filed with the Commission under this title or any of such Acts.

(c) *Good Faith Conformance with Rules, Regulations, and Orders.* No provision of this title imposing any liability shall apply to any act done or omitted in good faith in conformity with any rule, regulation, or order of the Commission, notwithstanding that such rule, regulation, or order may, after such act or omission, be amended or rescinded or be determined by judicial or other authority to be invalid for any reason.

Procedure for Issuance of Rules and Regulations

Sec. 39. Subject to the provisions of the Federal Register Act and regulations prescribed under the authority thereof, the rules and regulations of the Commission under this title, and amendments thereof, shall be effective upon publication in the manner which the Commission shall prescribe, or upon such later date as may be provided in such rules and regulations.

Procedure for Issuance of Orders

Sec. 40. (a) *Notice and Hearing.* Orders of the Commission under this title shall be issued only after appropriate notice and opportunity for hearing. Notice to the parties to a proceeding before the Commission shall be given by personal service upon each party or by registered mail or certified mail or confirmed telegraphic notice to the party's last known business address. Notice to interested persons, if any, other than parties may be given in the same manner or by publication in the Federal Register.

(b) *Application Verified Under Oath Admission as Evidence.* The Commission may provide, by appropriate rules or regulations, that an application verified under oath may be admissible in evidence in a proceeding before the Commission and that the record in such a proceeding may consist, in whole or in part, of such application.

(c) *Parties.* In any proceeding before the Commission, the Commission, in accordance with such rules and regulations as it may prescribe, shall admit as a party any interested State or State agency, and may admit as a party any representative of interested security holders, or any other person whose participation in the proceeding may be in the public interest or for the protection of investors.

Hearings by Commission

Sec. 41. Hearings may be public and may be held before the Commission, any member or members thereof, or any officer or officers of the Commission designated by it, and appropriate records thereof shall be kept.

Enforcement of Title

Sec. 42. (a) *Investigation.* The Commission may make such investigations as it deems necessary to determine whether any person has violated or is about to violate any provision of this title or of any rule, regulation, or order hereunder, or to determine whether any action in any court or any proceeding before the Commission shall be instituted under this title against a particular person or persons, or with respect to a particular transaction or transactions. The Commission shall permit any person to file with it a statement in writing, under oath or otherwise as the Commission shall determine, as to all the facts and circumstances concerning the matter to be investigated.

(b) *Administration of Oaths and Affirmations, Subpoena of Witnesses, Etc.* For the purpose of any investigation or any other proceeding under this title, any member of the Commission, or any officer thereof designated by it, is empowered to administer oaths and affirmations, subpena witnesses, compel their attendance, take evidence, and require the production of any books, papers, correspondence, memoranda, contracts, agreements, or other records which are relevant or material to the inquiry. Such attendance of witnesses and the production of any such records may be required from any place in any State or in any Territory or other place subject to the jurisdiction of the United States at any designated place of hearing.

(c) *Jurisdiction of Courts of United States.* In case of contumacy by, or refusal to obey a subpena issued to, any person, the Commission may invoke the aid of any court of the United States within the jurisdiction of which such investigation or proceeding is carried on, or where such person resides or carries on business, in requiring the attendance and testimony of witnesses and the production of books, papers, correspondence, memoranda, contracts, agreements, and other records. And such court may issue an order requiring such person to appear before the Commission or member or officer designated by the Commission, there to produce records, if so ordered, or to give testimony touching the matter under investigation or in question; any failure to obey such order of the court may be punished by such court as a contempt thereof. All process in any such case may be served in the judicial district whereof such person is an inhabitant or wherever he may be found. Any person who without just cause shall fail or refuse to attend and testify or to answer any lawful inquiry or to produce books, papers, correspondence, memoranda, contracts, agreements, or other records, if in his or its power so to do, in obedience to the subpena of the Commission, shall be guilty of a misdemeanor, and upon conviction shall be subject to a fine of not more than $1,000 or to imprisonment for a term of not more than one year, or both.

(d) *Action for Injunction.* Whenever it shall appear to the Commission that any person has engaged or is about to engage in any act or practice constituting a violation of any provision of this title, or of any rule, regulation, or order hereunder, it may in its discretion bring an action in the proper district court of the United States, or the proper United States court of any Territory or other place subject to the jurisdiction of the United States, to enjoin such acts or practices and to enforce compliance with this title or any rule, regulation, or order hereunder. Upon a showing that such person has engaged or is about to engage in any such act or practice, a permanent or temporary injunction or decree or restraining order shall be granted without bond. In any proceeding under this subsection to enforce compliance with section 7, the court as a court of equity may, to the extent it deems necessary or appropriate, take exclusive jurisdiction and possession of the investment company or companies involved and the books, records, and assets thereof, wherever located; and the court shall have jurisdiction to appoint a trustee, who with the approval of the court shall have power to dispose of any or all of such assets, subject to such terms and conditions as the court may prescribe. The Commission may transmit such evidence as may be available concerning any violation of the provisions of this title, or of any rule, regulation, or order thereunder, to the Attorney General, who, in his discretion, may institute the appropriate criminal proceedings under this title.

(e) *Money Penalties in Civil Actions.*

(1) *Authority of Commission.* Whenever it shall appear to the Commission that any person has violated any provision of this title, the rules or regulations thereunder, or a cease-and-desist order entered by the Commission pursuant to section 9(f) of this title, the Commission may bring an action in a United States district court to seek, and the court shall have jurisdiction to impose, upon a proper showing, a civil penalty to be paid by the person who committed such violation.

(2) *Amount of Penalty.*

(A) *First Tier.* The amount of the penalty shall be determined by the court in light of the facts and circumstances. For each violation, the amount of the penalty shall not exceed the greater of (i) $5,000 for a natural person or $50,000 for any other person, or (ii) the gross amount of pecuniary gain to such defendant as a result of the violation.

(B) *Second Tier.* Notwithstanding subparagraph (A), the amount of penalty for each such violation shall not exceed the greater of (i) $50,000 for a natural person or $250,000 for any other person, or (ii) the gross amount of pecuniary gain to such defendant as a result of the violation, if the violation described in paragraph (1) involved fraud, deceit, manipulation, or deliberate or reckless disregard of a regulatory requirement.

(C) *Third Tier.* Notwithstanding subparagraphs (A) and (B), the amount of penalty for each such violation shall not exceed the greater of (i) $100,000 for a natural person or $500,000 for any other person, or (ii) the gross amount of pecuniary gain to such defendant as a result of the violation, if—

(I) the violation described in paragraph (1) involved fraud, deceit, manipulation, or deliberate or reckless disregard of a regulatory requirement; and

(II) such violation directly or indirectly resulted in substantial losses or created a significant risk of substantial losses to other persons.

(3) *Procedures for Collection.*

(A) *Payment of Penalty to Treasury.* A penalty imposed under this section shall be payable into the Treasury of the United States, except as otherwise provided in section 308 of the Sarbanes–Oxley Act of 2002 and section 21F of the Securities Exchange Act of 1934.

(B) *Collection of Penalties.* If a person upon whom such a penalty is imposed shall fail to pay such penalty within the time prescribed in the court's order, the Commission may refer the matter to the Attorney General who shall recover such penalty by action in the appropriate United States district court.

(C) *Remedy Not Exclusive.* The actions authorized by this subsection may be brought in addition to any other action that the Commission or the Attorney General is entitled to bring.

(D) *Jurisdiction and Venue.* For purposes of section 44 of this title, actions under this paragraph shall be actions to enforce a liability or a duty created by this title.

(4) *Special Provisions Relating to a Violation of a Cease-and-Desist Order.* In an action to enforce a cease-and-desist order entered by the Commission pursuant to section 9(f), each separate violation of such order shall be a separate offense, except that in the case of a violation through a continuing failure to comply with the order, each day of the failure to comply shall be deemed a separate offense.

Court Review of Orders

Sec. 43. (a) Any person or party aggrieved by an order issued by the Commission under this title may obtain a review of such order in the court of appeals of the United States within any circuit wherein such person resides or has his principal place of business, or in the United States Court of Appeals for the District of Columbia, by filing in such court, within sixty days after the entry of such order, a written petition praying that the order of the Commission be modified or set aside in whole or in part. A copy of such petition shall be forthwith transmitted by the clerk of the court to any member of the Commission, or any officer thereof designated by the Commission for that purpose, and thereupon the Commission shall file in the court the record upon which the order complained of was entered, as provided in section 2112 of title 28, United States Code. Upon the filing of such petition such court shall have jurisdiction, which upon the filing of the record shall be exclusive, to affirm, modify, or set aside such order, in whole or in part. No objection to the order of the Commission shall be considered by the court unless such objection shall have been urged before the Commission or unless there were reasonable grounds for failure so to do. The findings of the Commission as to the facts, if supported by substantial evidence, shall be conclusive. If application is made to the court for leave to adduce additional evidence, and it is shown to the satisfaction of the court that such additional evidence is material and that there were reasonable grounds for failure to adduce such evidence in the proceeding before the Commission, the court may order such additional evidence to be taken before the Commission and to be adduced upon the hearing in such manner and upon such terms and conditions as to the court may seem proper. The Commission may modify its findings as to the facts by reason of the additional evidence so taken, and it shall file with the court such modified or new findings, which, if supported by substantial evidence, shall be conclusive, and its recommendation, if any, for the modification or setting aside of the original order. The judgment and decree of the court affirming, modifying, or setting aside, in whole or in part, any such order of the Commission shall be final, subject to review by the Supreme Court of the United States upon certiorari or certification as provided in section 1254 of title 28, United States Code.

(b) The commencement of proceedings under subsection (a) to review an order of the Commission issued under section 8(e) shall operate as a stay of the Commission's order unless the court otherwise orders. The commencement of proceedings under subsection (a) to review an order of the Commission issued under any provision of this title other than section 8(e) shall not operate as a stay of the Commission's order unless the court specifically so orders.

Jurisdiction of Offenses and Suits

Sec. 44. The district courts of the United States and the United States courts of any Territory or other place subject to the jurisdiction of the United States shall have jurisdiction of violations of this subchapter or the rules, regulations, or orders thereunder, and, concurrently with State and Territorial courts, of all suits in equity and actions at law brought to enforce any liability or duty created by, or to enjoin any violation of, this subchapter or the rules, regulations, or orders thereunder. Any criminal proceeding may be brought in the district wherein any act or transaction constituting the violation occurred. A criminal proceeding based upon a violation of section 34, or upon a failure to file a report or other document required to be filed under this subchapter, may be brought in the district wherein the defendant is an inhabitant or maintains his principal office or place of business. Any suit or action to enforce any liability or duty created by, or to enjoin any violation of, this subchapter or rules, regulations, or orders thereunder, may be brought in any such district or in the district wherein the defendant is an inhabitant or transacts business, and process in such cases may be served in any district of which the defendant is an inhabitant or transacts business or wherever the defendant may be found. In any action or proceeding instituted by the Commission under this subchapter in a United States district court for any judicial district, a subpoena issued to compel the attendance of a witness or the production of documents or tangible things (or both) at a hearing or trial may be served at any place within the United States. Rule 45(c)(3)(A)(ii) of the Federal Rules of Civil Procedure shall not apply to a subpoena issued under the preceding sentence. Judgments and decrees so rendered shall be subject to review as provided in sections 1254, 1291, 1292, and 1294 of Title 28. No costs shall be assessed for or against the Commission in any proceeding under this subchapter brought by or against the Commission in any court. The Commission may intervene as a party in any action or suit to enforce any liability or duty created by, or to enjoin any noncompliance with, section 36(b) at any stage of such action or suit prior to final judgment therein.

Disclosure of Information Filed with Commission; Copies

Sec. 45. (a) The information contained in any registration statement, application, report, or other document filed with the Commission pursuant to any provision of this title or of any rule or regulation thereunder (as distinguished from any information or document transmitted to the Commission) shall be made available to the public, unless and except insofar as the Commission, by rules and regulations upon its own motion, or by order upon application, finds that public disclosure is neither necessary nor appropriate in the public interest or for the protection of investors. Except as provided in section 24(c) of the Securities Exchange Act of 1934, it shall be unlawful for any member, officer, or employee of the Commission to use for personal benefit, or to disclose to any person other than an official or employee of the United States or of a State, for official use, or for any such official or employee to use for personal benefit, any information contained in any document so filed or transmitted, if such information is not available to the public.

(b) Photostatic or other copies of information contained in documents filed with the Commission under this title and made available to the public shall be furnished any person at such reasonable charge and under such reasonable limitations as the Commission shall prescribe.

Reports by Commission; Hiring and Leasing Authority

Sec. 46. (a) *Omitted.*

(b) *Hiring and Leasing Authority.* The provisions of section 4(b) of the Securities Exchange Act of 1934 shall be applicable with respect to the power of the Commission—

(1) to appoint and fix the compensation of such employees as may be necessary for carrying out its functions under this title, and

(2) to lease and allocate such real property as may be necessary for carrying out its functions under this title.

Validity of Contracts

Sec. 47. (a) Any condition, stipulation, or provision binding any person to waive compliance with any provision of this title or with any rule, regulation, or order thereunder shall be void.

(b) *Equitable Results; Rescission; Severance.*

(1) A contract that is made, or whose performance involves a violation of this title, or of any rule, regulation, or order thereunder, is unenforceable by either party (or by a nonparty to the contract who acquired a right under the contract with knowledge of the facts by reason of which the making or performance violated or would violate any provision of this title or of any rule, regulation, or order thereunder) unless a court finds that under the circumstances enforcement would produce a more equitable result than nonenforcement and would not be inconsistent with the purposes of this title.

(2) To the extent that a contract described in paragraph (1) has been performed, a court may not deny rescission at the instance of any party unless such court finds that under the circumstances the denial of rescission would produce a more equitable result than its grant and would not be inconsistent with the purposes of this title.

(3) This subsection shall not apply (A) to the lawful portion of a contract to the extent that it may be severed from the unlawful portion of the contract, or (B) to preclude recovery against any person for unjust enrichment.

Violation of Title

Sec. 48. (a) *Procurement.* It shall be unlawful for any person, directly or indirectly, to cause to be done any act or thing through or by means of any other person which it would be unlawful for such person to do under the provisions of this title or any rule, regulation, or order thereunder.

(b) For purposes of any action brought by the Commission under subsection (d) or (e) of section 42, any person that knowingly or recklessly provides substantial assistance to another person in violation of a provision of this Act, or of any rule or regulation issued under this Act, shall be deemed to be in violation of such provision to the same extent as the person to whom such assistance is provided.

(c) *Obstructing Compliance.* It shall be unlawful for any person without just cause to hinder, delay, or obstruct the making, filing, or keeping of any information, document, report, record, or account required to be made, filed, or kept under any provision of this title or any rule, regulation, or order thereunder.

Penalties

Sec. 49. Any person who willfully violates any provision of this title or of any rule, regulation, or order hereunder, or any person who willfully in any registration statement, application, report, account, record, or other document filed or transmitted pursuant to this title or the keeping of which is required pursuant to section 31(a) makes any untrue statement of a material fact or omits to state any material fact necessary in order to prevent the statements made therein from being materially misleading in the light of the circumstances under which they were made, shall upon conviction be fined not more than $10,000 or imprisoned not more than five years, or both; but no person shall be convicted under this section for the violation of any rule, regulation, or order if he proves that he had no actual knowledge of such rule, regulation, or order.

Construction with Other Laws

Sec. 50. Except where specific provision is made to the contrary, nothing in this title shall affect (1) the jurisdiction of the Commission under the Securities Act of 1933, the Securities Exchange Act of 1934, the Trust Indenture Act of 1939, or title II of this Act, over any person, security, or transaction, or (2) the rights, obligations, duties, or liabilities of any person under such Acts; nor shall anything in this title affect the jurisdiction of any other commission, board, agency, or officer of the United States or of any State or political subdivision of any State, over any person, security, or transaction, insofar as such jurisdiction does not conflict with any provision of this title or of any rule, regulation, or order hereunder.

Separability

Sec. 51. If any provision of this title or any provision incorporated in this title by reference, or the application of any such provision to any person or circumstances, shall be held invalid, the remainder of this title and the application of any such provision to person or circumstances other than those as to which it is held invalid shall not be affected thereby.

Short Title

Sec. 52. This title may be cited as the "Investment Company Act of 1940."

Effective Date

Sec. 53. The effective date of the provisions of this title, so far as the same relate to face-amount certificates or to face-amount certificate companies, is January 1, 1941. The effective date of provisions hereof insofar as the same do not apply to face-amount certificates or face-amount certificate companies is November 1, 1940. Except as herein otherwise provided, every provision of this title shall take effect on November 1, 1940.

Election to Be Regulated as Business Development Company

Sec. 54. (a) *Eligibility.* Any company defined in section 2(a)(48)(A) and (B) may elect to be subject to the provisions of sections 55 through 65 by filing with the Commission a notification of election, if such company—

(1) has a class of its equity securities registered under section 12 of the Securities Exchange Act of 1934; or

(2) has filed a registration statement pursuant to section 12 of the Securities Exchange Act of 1934 for a class of its equity securities.

(b) *Form and Manner of Notification; Effect.* The Commission may, by rule, prescribe the form and manner in which notification of election under this section shall be given. A business development company shall be deemed to be subject to sections 55 through 65 upon receipt by the Commission of such notification of election.

(c) *Revocation or Withdrawal of Election.* Whenever the Commission finds, on its own motion or upon application, that a business development company which has filed a notification of election pursuant to subsection (a) of this section has ceased to engage in business, the Commission shall so declare by order revoking such company's election. Any business development company may voluntarily withdraw its election under subsection (a) by filing a notice of withdrawal of election with the Commission, in a form and manner which the Commission may, by rule, prescribe. Such withdrawal shall be effective immediately upon receipt by the Commission.

Acquisition of Assets by Business Development Companies

Sec. 55. (a) *Permissible Assets; Percentage.* It shall be unlawful for a business development company to acquire any assets (other than those described in paragraphs (1) through (7) of this subsection) unless, at the time the acquisition is made, assets described in paragraphs (1) through (6) below represent at least 70 per centum of the value of its total assets (other than assets described in paragraph (7) below):

(1) securities purchased, in transactions not involving any public offering or in such other transactions as the Commission may, by rule, prescribe if it finds that enforcement of this title and of the Securities Act of 1933 with respect to such trans-

actions is not necessary in the public interest or for the protection of investors by reason of the small amount, or the limited nature of the public offering, involved in such transactions—

(A) from the issuer of such securities, which issuer is an eligible portfolio company, from any person who is, or who within the preceding thirteen months has been, an affiliated person of such eligible portfolio company, or from any other person, subject to such rules and regulations as the Commission may prescribe as necessary or appropriate in the public interest or for the protection of investors; or

(B) from the issuer of such securities, which issuer is described in section 2(a)(46)(A) and (B) but is not an eligible portfolio company because it has issued a class of securities with respect to which a member of a national securities exchange, broker, or dealer may extend or maintain credit to or for a customer pursuant to rules or regulations adopted by the Board of Governors of the Federal Reserve System under section 7 of the Securities Exchange Act of 1934, or from any person who is an officer or employee of such issuer, if—

(i) at the time of the purchase, the business development company owns at least 50 per centum of—

(I) the greatest number of equity securities of such issuer and securities convertible into or exchangeable for such securities; and

(II) the greatest amount of debt securities of such issuer,

held by such business development company at any point in time during the period when such issuer was an eligible portfolio company, except that options, warrants, and similar securities which have by their terms expired and debt securities which have been converted, or repaid or prepaid in the ordinary course of business or incident to a public offering of securities of such issuer, shall not be considered to have been held by such business development company for purposes of this requirement; and

(ii) the business development company is one of the 20 largest holders of record of such issuer's outstanding voting securities;

(2) securities of any eligible portfolio company with respect to which the business development company satisfies the requirements of section 2(a)(46)(C)(ii);

(3) securities purchased in transactions not involving any public offering from an issuer described in sections 2(a)(46)(A) and (B) or from a person who is, or who within the preceding thirteen months has been, an affiliated person of such issuer, or from any person in transactions incident thereto, if such securities were—

(A) issued by an issuer that is, or was immediately prior to the purchase of its securities by the business development company, in bankruptcy proceedings, subject to reorganization under the supervision of a court of competent jurisdiction, or subject to a plan or arrangement resulting from such bankruptcy proceedings or reorganization;

(B) issued by an issuer pursuant to or in consummation of such a plan or arrangement; or

(C) issued by an issuer that, immediately prior to the purchase of such issuer's securities by the business development company, was not in bankruptcy proceedings but was unable to meet its obligations as they came due without material assistance other than conventional lending or financing arrangements;

(4) securities of eligible portfolio companies purchased from any person in transactions not involving any public offering, if there is no ready market for such securities and if immediately prior to such purchase the business development company owns at least 60 per centum of the outstanding equity securities of such issuer (giving effect to all securities presently convertible into or exchangeable for equity securities of such issuer as if such securities were so converted or exchanged);

(5) securities received in exchange for or distributed on or with respect to securities described in paragraphs (1) through (4) of this subsection, or pursuant to the exercise of options, warrants, or rights relating to securities described in such paragraphs;

(6) cash, cash items, Government securities, or high quality debt securities maturing in one year or less from the time of investment in such high quality debt securities; and

(7) office furniture and equipment, interests in real estate and leasehold improvements and facilities maintained to conduct the business operations of the business development company, deferred organization and operating expenses, and other

noninvestment assets necessary and appropriate to its operations as a business development company, including notes of indebtedness of directors, officers, employees, and general partners held by a business development company as payment for securities of such company issued in connection with an executive compensation plan described in section 57(j).

(b) *Valuation of Assets.* For purposes of this section, the value of a business development company's assets shall be determined as of the date of the most recent financial statements filed by such company with the Commission pursuant to section 13 of the Securities Exchange Act of 1934, and shall be determined no less frequently than annually.

Qualifications of Directors

Sec. 56. (a) *Non-Interested Persons.* A majority of a business development company's directors or general partners shall be persons who are not interested persons of such company.

(b) *Vacancies; Suspension of Provisions.* If, by reason of the death, disqualification, or bona fide resignation of any director or general partner, a business development company does not meet the requirements of subsection (a) of this section, or the requirements of section 15(f)(1) of this title with respect to directors, the operation of such provisions shall be suspended for a period of 90 days or for such longer period as the Commission may prescribe, upon its own motion or by order upon application, as not inconsistent with the protection of investors.

Transactions With Certain Affiliates

Sec. 57. (a) *Transactions Involving Controlling or Closely Affiliated Persons.* It shall be unlawful for any person who is related to a business development company in a manner described in subsection (b) of this section, acting as principal—

(1) knowingly to sell any security or other property to such business development company or to any company controlled by such business development company, unless such sale involves solely (A) securities of which the buyer is the issuer, or (B) the securities of which the seller is the issuer and which are part of a general offering to the holders of a class of its securities;

(2) knowingly to purchase from such business development company or from any company controlled by such business development company, any security or other property (except securities of which the seller is the issuer);

(3) knowingly to borrow money or other property from such business development company or from any company controlled by such business development company (unless the borrower is controlled by the lender), except as permitted in section 21(b) or section 62; or

(4) knowingly to effect any transaction in which such business development company or a company controlled by such business development company is a joint or a joint and several participant with such person in contravention of such rules and regulations as the Commission may prescribe for the purpose of limiting or preventing participation by such business development company or controlled company on a basis less advantageous than that of such person, except that nothing contained in this paragraph shall be deemed to preclude any person from acting as manager of any underwriting syndicate or other group in which such business development company or controlled company is a participant and receiving compensation therefor.

(b) *Controlling or Closely Affiliated Persons.* The provisions of subsection (a) of this section shall apply to the following persons:

(1) Any director, officer, employee, or member of an advisory board of a business development company or any person (other than the business development company itself) who is, within the meaning of section 2(a)(3)(C) of this title, an affiliated person of any such person specified in this paragraph.

(2) Any investment adviser or promoter of, general partner in, principal underwriter for, or person directly or indirectly either controlling, controlled by, or under common control with, a business development company (except the business development company itself and any person who, if it were not directly or indirectly controlled by the business development company, would not be directly or indirectly under the control of a person who controls the business development company), or any person who is, within the meaning of section 2(a)(3)(C) or (D), an affiliated person of any such person specified in this paragraph.

(c) *Exemption Orders.* Notwithstanding paragraphs (1), (2), and (3) of subsection (a), any person may file with the Commission an application for an order exempting a proposed transaction of the applicant from one or more provisions of such paragraphs. The Commission shall grant such application and issue such order of exemption if evidence establishes that—

(1) the terms of the proposed transaction, including the consideration to be paid or received, are reasonable and fair and do not involve overreaching of the business development company or its shareholders or partners on the part of any person concerned;

(2) the proposed transaction is consistent with the policy of the business development company as recited in the filings made by such company with the Commission under the Securities Act of 1933, its registration statement and reports filed under the Securities Exchange Act of 1934, and its reports to shareholders or partners; and

(3) the proposed transaction is consistent with the general purposes of this title.

(d) *Transactions Involving Noncontrolling Shareholders or Affiliated Persons.* It shall be unlawful for any person who is related to a business development company in the manner described in subsection (e) of this section and who is not subject to the prohibitions of subsection (a) of this section, acting as principal—

(1) knowingly to sell any security or other property to such business development company or to any company controlled by such business development company, unless such sale involves solely (A) securities of which the buyer is the issuer, or (B) securities of which the seller is the issuer and which are part of a general offering to the holders of a class of its securities;

(2) knowingly to purchase from such business development company or from any company controlled by such business development company, any security or other property (except securities of which the seller is the issuer);

(3) knowingly to borrow money or other property from such business development company or from any company controlled by such business development company (unless the borrower is controlled by the lender), except as permitted in section 21(b); or

(4) knowingly to effect any transaction in which such business development company or a company controlled by such business development company is a joint or a joint and several participant with such affiliated person in contravention of such rules and regulations as the Commission may prescribe for the purpose of limiting or preventing participation by such business development company or controlled company on a basis less advantageous than that of such affiliated person, except that nothing contained in this paragraph shall be deemed to preclude any person from acting as manager of any underwriting syndicate or other group in which such business development company or controlled company is a participant and receiving compensation therefor.

(e) *Noncontrolling Shareholders or Affiliated Persons; Executive Officers.* The provisions of subsection (d) of this section shall apply to the following persons:

(1) Any person (A) who is, within the meaning of section 2(a)(3)(A), an affiliated person of a business development company, (B) who is an executive officer or a director of, or general partner in, any such affiliated person, or (C) who directly or indirectly either controls, is controlled by, or is under common control with, such affiliated person.

(2) Any person who is an affiliated person of a director, officer, employee, investment adviser, member of an advisory board or promoter of, principal underwriter for, general partner in, or an affiliated person of any person directly or indirectly either controlling or under common control with a business development company (except the business development company itself and any person who, if it were not directly or indirectly controlled by the business development company, would not be directly or indirectly under the control of a person who controls the business development company).

For purposes of this subsection, the term "executive officer" means the president, secretary, treasurer, any vice president in charge of a principal business function, and any other person who performs similar policymaking functions.

(f) *Approval of Proposed Transactions.* Notwithstanding subsection (d) of this section, a person described in subsection (e) may engage in a proposed transaction described in subsection (d) if such proposed transaction is approved by the required majority (as defined in subsection (*o*)) of the directors of or general partners in the business development company on the basis that—

(1) the terms thereof, including the consideration to be paid or received, are reasonable and fair to the shareholders or partners of the busi-

ness development company and do not involve overreaching of such company or its shareholders or partners on the part of any person concerned;

(2) the proposed transaction is consistent with the interests of the shareholders or partners of the business development company and is consistent with the policy of such company as recited in filings made by such company with the Commission under the Securities Act of 1933, its registration statement and reports filed under the Securities Exchange Act of 1934, and its reports to shareholders or partners; and

(3) the directors or general partners record in their minutes and preserve in their records, for such periods as if such records were required to be maintained pursuant to section 31(a), a description of such transaction, their findings, the information or materials upon which their findings were based, and the basis therefor.

(g) *Transactions in the Ordinary Course of Business.* Notwithstanding subsection (a) or (d), a person may, in the ordinary course of business, sell to or purchase from any company merchandise or may enter into a lessor-lessee relationship with any person and furnish the services incident thereto.

(h) *Inquiry Procedures.* The directors of or general partners in any business development company shall adopt, and periodically review and update as appropriate, procedures reasonably designed to ensure that reasonable inquiry is made, prior to the consummation of any transaction in which such business development company or a company controlled by such business development company proposes to participate, with respect to the possible involvement in the transaction of persons described in subsections (b) and (e) of this section.

(i) *Rules and Regulations of Commission.* Until the adoption by the Commission of rules or regulations under subsections (a) and (d) of this section, the rules and regulations of the Commission under subsections (a) and (d) of section 17 applicable to registered closed-end investment companies shall be deemed to apply to transactions subject to subsections (a) and (d) of this section. Any rules or regulations adopted by the Commission to implement this section shall be no more restrictive than the rules or regulations adopted by the Commission under subsections (a) and (d) of section 17 that are applicable to all registered closed-end investment companies.

(j) *Warrants, Options, and Rights to Purchase Voting Securities; Loans to Facilitate Executive Compensation Plans.* Notwithstanding subsections (a) and (d) of this section, any director, officer, or employee of, or general partner in, a business development company may—

(1) acquire warrants, options, and rights to purchase voting securities of such business development company, and securities issued upon the exercise or conversion thereof, pursuant to an executive compensation plan offered by such company which meets the requirements of section 61(a)(3)(B); and

(2) borrow money from such business development company for the purpose of purchasing securities issued by such company pursuant to an executive compensation plan, if each such loan—

(A) has a term of not more than ten years;

(B) becomes due within a reasonable time, not to exceed sixty days, after the termination of such person's employment or service;

(C) bears interest at no less than the prevailing rate applicable to 90-day United States Treasury bills at the time the loan is made;

(D) at all times is fully collateralized (such collateral may include any securities issued by such business development company); and

(E)(i) in the case of a loan to any officer or employee of such business development company (including any officer or employee who is also a director of such company), is approved by the required majority (as defined in subsection (*o*)) of the directors of or general partners in such company on the basis that the loan is in the best interests of such company and its shareholders or partners; or

(ii) in the case of a loan to any director of such business development company who is not also an officer or employee of such company, or to any general partner in such company, is approved by order of the Commission, upon application, on the basis that the terms of the loan are fair and reasonable and do not involve overreaching of such company or its shareholders or partners.

(k) *Restriction on Brokerage Commissions.* It shall be unlawful for any person described in subsection (*l*)—

(1) acting as agent, to accept from any source any compensation (other than a regular salary or wages from the business development company) for the purchase or sale of any property to or for such business development company or any controlled company thereof, except in the course of such person's business as an underwriter or broker; or

(2) acting as broker, in connection with the sale of securities to or by the business development company or any controlled company thereof, to receive from any source a commission, fee, or other remuneration for effecting such transaction which exceeds—

(A) the usual and customary broker's commission if the sale is effected on a securities exchange;

(B) 2 per centum of the sales price if the sale is effected in connection with a secondary distribution of such securities; or

(C) 1 per centum of the purchase or sale price of such securities if the sale is otherwise effected,

unless the Commission, by rules and regulations or order in the public interest and consistent with the protection of investors, permits a larger commission.

(*l*) *Persons Subject to Brokerage Commission Restrictions.* The provisions of subsection (k) of this section shall apply to the following persons:

(1) Any affiliated person of a business development company.

(2)(A) Any person who is, within the meaning of section 2(a)(3)(B), (C), or (D), an affiliated person of any director, officer, employee, or member of an advisory board of the business development company.

(B) Any person who is, within the meaning of section 2(a)(3)(A), (B), (C), or (D), an affiliated person of any investment adviser of, general partner in, or person directly or indirectly either controlling, controlled by, or under common control with, the business development company.

(C) Any person who is, within the meaning of section 2(a)(3)(C), an affiliated person of any person who is an affiliated person of the business development company within the meaning of section 2(a)(3)(A).

(m) *Receipt of Fee or Salary from Transaction Participant.* For purposes of subsections (a) and (d), a person who is a director, officer, or employee of a party to a transaction and who receives his usual and ordinary fee or salary for usual and customary services as a director, officer, or employee from such party shall not be deemed to have a financial interest or to participate in the transaction solely by reason of his receipt of such fee or salary.

(n) *Profit–Sharing Plans.*

(1) Notwithstanding subsection (a)(4) of this section, a business development company may establish and maintain a profit-sharing plan for its directors, officers, employees, and general partners and such directors, officers, employees and general partners may participate in such profit-sharing plan, if—

(A)(i) in the case of a profit-sharing plan for officers and employees of the business development company (including any officer or employee who is also a director of such company), such profit-sharing plan is approved by the required majority (as defined in subsection (*o*)) of the directors of or general partners in such company on the basis that such plan is reasonable and fair to the shareholders or partners of such company, does not involve overreaching of such company or its shareholders or partners on the part of any person concerned, and is consistent with the interests of the shareholders or partners of such company; or

(ii) in the case of a profit-sharing plan which includes one or more directors of the business development company who are not also officers or employees of such company, or one or more general partners in such company, such profit-sharing plan is approved by order of the Commission, upon application, on the basis that such plan is reasonable and fair to the shareholders or partners of such company, does not involve overreaching of such company or its shareholders or partners on the part of any person concerned, and is consistent with the interests of the shareholders or partners of such company; and

(B) the aggregate amount of benefits which would be paid or accrued under such plan shall not exceed 20 per centum of the business development company's net income after taxes in any fiscal year.

(2) This subsection may not be used where the business development company has outstanding any stock option, warrant, or right issued as part of an executive compensation plan, including a plan pursuant to section 61(a)(3)(B), or has an investment adviser registered or required to be registered under title II of this Act.

(*o*) *Required Majority for Approval of Proposed Transactions.* The term "required majority", when used with respect to the approval of a proposed transaction, plan or arrangement, means both a majority of a business development company's directors or general partners who have no financial interest in such transaction, plan, or arrangement and a majority of such directors or general partners who are not interested persons of such company.

Changes in Investment Policy

Sec. 58. No business development company shall, unless authorized by the vote of a majority of its outstanding voting securities or partnership interests, change the nature of its business so as to cease to be, or to withdraw its election as, a business development company.

Incorporation of Title Provisions

Sec. 59. Notwithstanding the exemption set forth in section 6(f), sections 1, 2, 3, 4, 5, 6, 9, 10(f), 15(a), (c), and (f), 16(b), 17(f) through (j), 19(a), 20(b), 32(a) and (c), 33 through 47, and 49 through 53 of this title shall apply to a business development company to the same extent as if it were a registered closed-end investment company.

Functions and Activities of Business Development Companies

Sec. 60. Notwithstanding the exemption set forth in section 6(f), section 12 shall apply to a business development company to the same extent as if it were a registered closed-end investment company, except that the Commission shall not prescribe any rule, regulation, or order pursuant to section 12(a)(1) governing the circumstances in which a business development company may borrow from a bank in order to purchase any security.

Capital Structure

Sec. 61. (a) *Exceptions for Business Development Company.* Notwithstanding the exemption set forth in section 6(f), section 18 shall apply to a business development company to the same extent as if it were a registered closed-end investment company, except as follows:

(1) The asset coverage requirements of section 18(a)(1)(A) and (B) applicable to business development companies shall be 200 per centum.

(2) Notwithstanding section 18(c), a business development company may issue more than one class of senior security representing indebtedness.

(3) Notwithstanding section 18(d)—

(A) a business development company may issue warrants, options, or rights to subscribe or convert to voting securities of such company, accompanied by securities if—

(i) such warrants, options, or rights expire by their terms within ten years;

(ii) such warrants, options, or rights are not separately transferable unless no class of such warrants, options, or rights and the securities accompanying them has been publicly distributed;

(iii) the exercise or conversion price is not less than the current market value at the date of issuance, or if no such market value exists, the current net asset value of such voting securities; and

(iv) the proposal to issue such securities is authorized by the shareholders or partners of such business development company, and such issuance is approved by the required majority (as defined in section 57(*o*)) of the directors of or general partners in such company on the basis that such issuance is in the best interests of such company and its shareholders or partners;

(B) a business development company may issue, to its directors, officers, employees, and general partners, warrants, options, and rights to purchase voting securities of such company pursuant to an executive compensation plan, if—

(i)(I) in the case of warrants, options, or rights issued to any officer or employee of such business development company (including any officer or employee who is also a director of such company), such securities satisfy the conditions in clauses (i), (iii), and (iv) of subparagraph (A); or (II) in the case of warrants, options, or rights issued to any director of such business development company who is not also an officer or employee of such company, or to any general partner in such company, the proposal to issue such securities satisfies the conditions in clauses (i) and (iii) of subparagraph (A), is authorized by the shareholders or partners of such company, and is approved by order of the Commission, upon application, on the basis that the terms of the proposal are fair and reasonable and do not involve overreaching of such company or its shareholders or partners;

(ii) such securities are not transferable except for disposition by gift, will, or intestacy;

(iii) no investment adviser of such business development company receives any compensation described in section 205(a)(1) of title II of this Act, except to the extent permitted by paragraph (1) or (2) of section 205(b); and

(iv) such business development company does not have a profit-sharing plan described in section 57(n); and

(C) a business development company may issue warrants, options, or rights to subscribe to, convert to, or purchase voting securities not accompanied by securities, if—

(i) such warrants, options, or rights satisfy the conditions in clauses (i) and (iii) of subparagraph (A); and

(ii) the proposal to issue such warrants, options, or rights is authorized by the shareholders or partners of such business development company, and such issuance is approved by the required majority (as defined in section 57(*o*)) of the directors of or general partners in such company on the basis that such issuance is in the best interests of the company and its shareholders or partners.

Notwithstanding this paragraph, the amount of voting securities that would result from the exercise of all outstanding warrants, options, and rights at the time of issuance shall not exceed 25 per centum of the outstanding voting securities of the business development company, except that if the amount of voting securities that would result from the exercise of all outstanding warrants, options, and rights issued to such company's directors, officers, employees, and general partners pursuant to any executive compensation plan meeting the requirements of subparagraph (B) of this paragraph would exceed 15 per centum of the outstanding voting securities of such company, then the total amount of voting securities that would result from the exercise of all outstanding warrants, options, and rights at the time of issuance shall not exceed 20 per centum of the outstanding voting securities of such company.

(4) For purposes of measuring the asset coverage requirements of section 18(a), a senior security created by the guarantee by a business development company of indebtedness issued by another company shall be the amount of the maximum potential liability less the fair market value of the net unencumbered assets (plus the indebtedness which has been guaranteed) available in the borrowing company whose debts have been guaranteed, except that a guarantee issued by a business development company of indebtedness issued by a company which is a wholly-owned subsidiary of the business development company and is licensed as a small business investment company under the Small Business Investment Act of 1958 shall not be deemed to be a senior security of such business development company for purposes of section 18(a) if the amount of the indebtedness at the time of its issuance by the borrowing company is itself taken fully into account as a liability by such business development company, as if it were issued by such business development company, in determining whether such business development company, at that time, satisfies the asset coverage requirements of section 18(a).

(b) *Compliance.* A business development company shall comply with the provisions of this section at the time it becomes subject to sections 55 through 65, as if it were issuing a security of each class which it has outstanding at such time.

Loans

Sec. 62. Notwithstanding the exemption set forth in section 6(f), section 21 shall apply to a business development company to the same extent as if it were a registered closed-end investment company, except that nothing in that section shall be deemed to prohibit—

(1) any loan to a director, officer, or employee of, or general partner in, a business development company for the purpose of purchasing securities of such company as part of an executive compensation plan, if such loan meets the requirements of section 57(j); or

(2) any loan to a company controlled by a business development company, which companies

could be deemed to be under common control solely because a third person controls such business development company.

Distribution and Repurchase of Securities

Sec. 63. Notwithstanding the exemption set forth in section 6(f), section 23 shall apply to a business development company to the same extent as if it were a registered closed-end investment company, except as follows:

(1) The prohibitions of section 23(a)(2) shall not apply to any company which (A) is a wholly-owned subsidiary of, or directly or indirectly controlled by, a business development company, and (B) immediately after the issuance of any of its securities for property other than cash or securities, will not be an investment company within the meaning of section 3(a).

(2) Notwithstanding the provisions of section 23(b), a business development company may sell any common stock of which it is the issuer at a price below the current net asset value of such stock, and may sell warrants, options, or rights to acquire any such common stock at a price below the current net asset value of such stock, if—

(A) the holders of a majority of such business development company's outstanding voting securities, and the holders of a majority of such company's outstanding voting securities that are not affiliated persons of such company, approved such company's policy and practice of making such sales of securities at the last annual meeting of shareholders or partners within one year immediately prior to any such sale, except that the shareholder approval requirements of this subparagraph shall not apply to the initial public offering by a business development company of its securities;

(B) a required majority (as defined in section 57(*o*)) of the directors of or general partners in such business development company have determined that any such sale would be in the best interests of such company and its shareholders or partners; and

(C) a required majority (as defined in section 57(*o*)) of the directors of or general partners in such business development company, in consultation with the underwriter or underwriters of the offering if it is to be underwritten, have determined in good faith, and as of a time immediately prior to the first solicitation by or on behalf of such company of firm commitments to purchase such securities or immediately prior to the issuance of such securities, that the price at which such securities are to be sold is not less than a price which closely approximates the market value of those securities, less any distributing commission or discount.

(3) A business development company may sell any common stock of which it is the issuer at a price below the current net asset value of such stock upon the exercise of any warrant, option, or right issued in accordance with section 61(a)(3).

Accounts and Records

Sec. 64. (a) *Exception for Business Development Company.* Notwithstanding the exemption set forth in section 6(f), section 31 shall apply to a business development company to the same extent as if it were a registered closed-end investment company, except that the reference to the financial statements required to be filed pursuant to section 30 shall be construed to refer to the financial statements required to be filed by such business development company pursuant to section 13 of the Securities Exchange Act of 1934.

(b) *Risk Factors Statement; Availability.*

(1) In addition to the requirements of subsection (a), a business development company shall file with the Commission and supply annually to its shareholders a written statement, in such form and manner as the Commission may, by rule, prescribe, describing the risk factors involved in an investment in the securities of a business development company due to the nature of such company's investment portfolio and capital structure, and shall supply copies of such statement to any registered broker or dealer upon request.

(2) If the Commission finds it is necessary or appropriate in the public interest and consistent with the protection of investors and the purposes fairly intended by the policy and provisions of this title, the Commission may also require, by rule, any person who, acting as principal or agent, sells a security of a business development company to inform the purchaser of such securities, at or before the time of sale, of the existence of the risk statement prepared by such business development company pursuant to this subsection, and make such risk statement available on request. The Commission, in making such rules and regulations, shall consider, among other matters, whether any such rule or regulation would impose any unreasonable burdens on such brokers or

dealers or unreasonably impair the maintenance of fair and orderly markets.

Preventing Compliance with Title Liability of Controlling Persons

Sec. 65. Notwithstanding the exemption set forth in section 6(f), section 48 shall apply to a business development company to the same extent as if it were a registered closed-end investment company, except that the provisions of section 48(a) shall not be construed to require any company which is not an investment company within the meaning of section 3(a) to comply with the provisions of this title which are applicable to a business development company solely because such company is a wholly-owned subsidiary of, or directly or indirectly controlled by, a business development company.

PART 270—RULES AND REGULATIONS, INVESTMENT COMPANY ACT OF 1940

(Cite as 17 CFR § 270.__)

Rule

ATTENTION ELECTRONIC FILERS

THIS REGULATION SHOULD BE READ IN CONJUNCTION WITH REGULATION S–T (17 CFR 232), WHICH GOVERNS THE PREPARATION AND SUBMISSION OF DOCUMENTS IN ELECTRONIC FORMAT MANY PROVISIONS RELATING TO THE PREPARATION AND SUBMISSION OF DOCUMENTS IN PAPER FORMAT CONTAINED IN THIS REGULATION ARE SUPERSEDED BY THE PROVISIONS OF REGULATION S–T FOR DOCUMENTS REQUIRED TO BE FILED IN ELECTRONIC FORMAT.

Rule 0–1. Definition of terms used in this part

(a) As used in the rules and regulations prescribed by the Commission pursuant to the Investment Company Act of 1940, unless the context otherwise requires:

(1) The term *Commission* means the Securities and Exchange Commission.

(2) The term *act* means the Investment Company Act of 1940.

(3) The term *section* refers to a section of the act.

(4) The terms *rule* and *regulations* refer to the rules and regulations adopted by the Commission pursuant to the Act, including the forms for registration and reports and the accompanying instructions thereto.

(5) The term *administrator* means any person who provides significant administrative or business affairs management services to an investment company.

(6)(i) A person is an *independent legal counsel* with respect to the directors who are not interested persons of an investment company ("disinterested directors") if:

(A) A majority of the disinterested directors reasonably determine in the exercise of their judgment (and record the basis for that determination in the minutes of their meeting) that any representation by the person of the company's investment adviser, principal underwriter, administrator ("management organizations"), or any of their control persons, since the beginning of the fund's last two completed fiscal years, is or was sufficiently limited that it is unlikely to adversely affect the professional judgment of the person in providing legal representation to the disinterested directors; and

(B) The disinterested directors have obtained an undertaking from such person to provide them with information necessary to make their determination and to update promptly that information when the person begins to represent, or materially increases his representation of, a management organization or control person.

(ii) The disinterested directors are entitled to rely on the information obtained from the person, unless they know or have reason to believe that the information is materially false or incomplete. The disinterested directors must re-evaluate their determination no less frequently than annually (and record the basis accordingly), except as provided in paragraph (iii) of this rule.

(iii) After the disinterested directors obtain information that the person has begun to represent, or has materially increased his representation of, a management organization (or any of its control persons), the person may continue to be an independent legal counsel, for purposes of paragraph (a)(6)(i) of this rule, for no longer than three months unless during that period the disinterested directors make a new determination under that paragraph.

(iv) For purposes of paragraphs (a)(6)(i)–(iii) of this rule:

(A) The term *person* has the same meaning as in section 2(a)(28) of the Act and, in addition, includes a partner, co-member, or employee of any person; and

(B) The term *control person* means any person (other than an investment company) directly or indirectly controlling, controlled by, or under common control with any of the investment company's management organizations.

(7) Fund governance standards. The board of directors of an investment company ("fund") satisfies the fund governance standards if:

(i) At least seventy-five percent of the directors of the fund are not interested persons of the fund ("disinterested directors") or, if the fund has three directors, all but one are disinterested directors;

(ii) The disinterested directors of the fund select and nominate any other disinterested director of the fund;

(iii) Any person who acts as legal counsel for the disinterested directors of the fund is an independent legal counsel as defined in paragraph (a)(6) of this rule;

(iv) A disinterested director serves as chairman of the board of directors of the fund, presides over meetings of the board of directors and has substantially the same responsibilities as would a chairman of a board of directors;

(v) The board of directors evaluates at least once annually the performance of the board of directors and the committees of the board of directors, which evaluation must include a consideration of the effectiveness of the committee structure of the fund board and the number of funds on whose boards each director serves;

(vi) The disinterested directors meet at least once quarterly in a session at which no directors who are interested persons of the fund are present; and

(vii) The disinterested directors have been authorized to hire employees and to retain advisers and experts necessary to carry out their duties.

(b) Unless otherwise specifically provided, the terms used in the rules and regulations in this part shall have the meaning defined in the Act. The terms "EDGAR," "EDGAR Filer Manual," "electronic filer," "electronic filing," "electronic format," "electronic submission," "paper format," and "signature" shall have the meanings assigned to such terms in Regulation S–T—General Rules for Electronic Filings (Part 232).

(c) A rule or regulation which defines a term without express reference to the act or to the rules and regulations, or to a portion thereof, defines such terms for all purposes as used both in the Act and in the rules and regulations in this part, unless the context otherwise requires.

(d) Unless otherwise specified or the context otherwise requires, the term "prospectus" means a prospectus meeting the requirements of section 10(a) of the Securities Act of 1933 as amended.

(e) Definition of separate account and conditions for availability of exemption under Rules 6c–6, 6c–7, 6c–8, 11a–2, 14a–2, 15a–3, 16a–1, 22d–3, 22e–1, 26a–1, 26a–2, 27a–1, 27a–2, 27a–3, 27c–1, and 32a–2.

(1) As used in the rules and regulations prescribed by the Commission pursuant to the Investment Company Act of 1940, unless otherwise specified or the context otherwise requires, the term "separate account" shall mean an account established and maintained by an insurance company pursuant to the laws of any state or territory of the United States, or of Canada or any province thereof, under which income, gains and losses, whether or not realized, from assets allocated to such account, are, in accordance with the applicable contract, credited to or charged against such account without regard to other income, gains or losses of the insurance company and the term "variable annuity contract" shall mean any accumulation or annuity contract, any portion thereof, or any unit of interest or participation therein pursuant to which the value of the contract, either prior or subsequent to annuitization, or both, varies according to the investment experience of the separate account in which the contract participates.

(2) As conditions to the availability of exemptive Rules 6c–6, 6c–7, 6c–8, 11a–2, 14a–2, 15a–3, 16a–1, 22c–1, 22d–3, 22e–1, 26a–1, 26a–2, 27a–1, 27a–2, 27a–3, 27c–1, and 32a–2, the separate account shall be legally segregated, the assets of the separate account shall, at the time during the year that adjustments in the reserves are made, have a value at least equal to the reserves and other contract liabilities with respect to such account, and at all other times, shall have a value approximately equal to or in excess of such reserves and liabilities; and that portion of such assets having a value equal to, or approximately equal to, such reserves and contract liabilities shall not be charge-

able with liabilities arising out of any other business which the insurance company may conduct.

Rule 0–2. General requirements of papers and applications

(a) *Filing of Papers.* All papers required to be filed with the Commission pursuant to the Act or the rules and regulations thereunder shall, unless otherwise provided by the rules and regulations in this part, be delivered through the mails or otherwise to the Securities and Exchange Commission, Washington, D.C. 20549. Except as otherwise provided by the rules and regulations, the date on which papers are actually received by the Commission shall be the date of filing thereof. If the last day for the timely filing of such papers falls on a Saturday, Sunday, or holiday, such papers may be filed on the first business day following.

(b) *Formal Specifications Respecting Applications.* Every application for an order under any provision of the Act, for which a form with instructions is not specifically prescribed, and every amendment to such application shall be filed in quintuplicate. One copy shall be signed by the applicant but the other four copies may have facsimile or typed signatures. Such applications should be on paper no larger than 8½ x 11 inches in size. To the extent that the reduction of larger documents would render them illegible, such documents may be filed on paper larger than 8½ x 11 inches in size. The left margin should be at least 1½ inches wide and, if the application is bound, it should be bound on the left side. The application must be typed, printed, copied or prepared by any process which, in the opinion of the Commission, produces copies suitable for microfilming. All typewritten or printed matter (including deficits in financial statements) should be set forth in black so as to permit photocopying.

(c) *Authorizations Respecting Applications.* (1) Every application for an order under any provision of the Act, for which a form with instructions is not specifically prescribed and which is executed by a corporation, partnership, or other company and filed with the Commission, shall contain a concise statement of the applicable provisions of the articles of incorporation, bylaws, or similar documents, relating to the right of the person signing and filing such application to take such action on behalf of the applicant, and a statement that all such requirements have been complied with and that the person signing and filing the same is fully authorized to do so. If such authorization is dependent on resolutions of stockholders, directors, or other bodies, such resolutions shall be attached as an exhibit to, or the pertinent provisions thereof shall be quoted in, the application.

(2) If an amendment to any such application shall be filed, such amendment shall contain a similar statement or, in lieu thereof, shall state that the authorization described in the original application is applicable to the individual who signs such amendment and that such authorization still remains in effect.

(3) When any such application or amendment is signed by an agent or attorney, the power of attorney evidencing his authority to sign shall contain similar statements and shall be filed with the Commission.

(d) *Verification of Applications and Statements of Fact.* Every application for an order under any provision of the Act, for which a form with instructions is not specifically prescribed and every amendment to such application, and every statement of fact formally filed in support of, or in opposition to, any application or declaration shall be verified by the person executing the same. An instrument executed on behalf of a corporation shall be verified in substantially the following form, but suitable changes may be made in such form for other kinds of companies and for individuals:

The undersigned states that he or she has duly executed the attached _______ dated _______, 20___ for and on behalf of ____________________; that he or she is

(Name of Company)

____________________ of such company; and

(Title of Officer)

that all action by stockholders, directors, and other bodies necessary to authorize the undersigned to execute and file such instrument has been taken. The undersigned further states that he or she is familiar with such instrument, and the contents thereof, and that the facts therein set forth are true to the best of his or her knowledge, information and belief.

____

(Signature)

(e) *Statement of Grounds for Application.* Each application should contain a brief statement of the reasons why the applicant is deemed to be entitled to the action requested with a reference to the provisions of the act and of the rules and regulations under which application is made.

(f) *Name and Address.* Every application shall contain the name and address of each applicant and the name and address of any person to whom any applicant wishes any question regarding the application to be directed.

(g) The manually signed original (or in the case of duplicate originals, one duplicate original) of all registrations, applications, statements, reports, or other documents filed under the Investment Company Act of 1940, as amended, shall be numbered sequentially (in addition to any internal numbering which otherwise may be present) by handwritten, typed, printed, or other legible form of notation from the facing page of the document through the last page of that document and any exhibits or attachments thereto. Further, the total number of pages contained in a numbered original shall be set forth on the first page of the document.

Rule 0–3. Amendments to registration statements and reports

Registration statements filed with the Commission pursuant to section 8 and reports filed with the Commission pursuant to section 30 may be amended in the following manner:

(a) Each amendment shall conform to the requirements for the registration statement or report it amends with regard to filing, number of copies filed, size, paper, ink, margins, binding, and similar formal matters.

(b) Each amendment to a particular statement or report shall have a facing sheet as follows:

SECURITIES AND EXCHANGE COMMISSION

Washington, DC 20549

Amendment No. ____

to

Form ____

File No. ____

(*Describe the nature of the statement or report*)

Dated ______, 19__,

Pursuant to Section ______ of the Investment Company Act of 1940

____
Name of Registrant

____
Address of Principal Office of Registrant

The facing sheet shall contain in addition any other information required on the facing sheet of the form for the statement or report which is being amended. Amendments to a particular statement or report which is being consecutively in the order in which filed with the Commission.

(c) Each amendment shall contain in the manner required in the original statement or report the text of every item to which it relates and shall set out a complete amended answer to each such item. However, amendments to financial statements may contain only the particular statements or schedules in fact amended.

(d) Each amendment shall have a signature sheet containing the form of signature required in the statement or report it amends.

Rule 0–4. Incorporation by reference

(a) A registered investment company may, subject to the limitations of 17 CFR 228.10(f) and Item 10(d) of Regulation S–K, incorporate by reference as an exhibit, in any registration statement, application or report filed with the Commission, any document or part thereof previously or concurrently filed with the Commission pursuant to any act administered by the Commission. The incorporation may be made whether the matter incorporated was filed by such registered company or any other person. If any modification has occurred in the text of any such document since the filing thereof, the company shall file with the reference a statement containing the text of any such modification and the date thereof. If the number of copies of any document previously or concurrently filed with the Commission is less than the number required to be filed with the registration statement, application or report which incorporates such document, the company shall file therewith as many additional copies of the document as may be necessary to meet the requirements of the registration statement, application or report.

(b) A registered investment company may, subject to the limitations of Rule 24 of Regulation S–X, incorporate by reference, in any registration statement, application or report filed with the Commission any financial statement or part thereof previously or concurrently filed with the Commission pursuant to any act administered by the Commission, if it substantially conforms to the requirements of the form on which such registration statement, application or report is filed. The incorporation may be made whether the matter incorporated was filed by such registered company or any other person. If a certificate of an independent public accountant or accountants is required to accompany a financial statement in any registration statement, application or report, the incorporation by reference of a certificate previously or concurrently filed will not be deemed a compliance with such requirements unless the written consent of the accountant or accountants to such incorporation is filed with the registration statement, application or report.

(c) In each case of incorporation, by reference, the matter incorporated shall be clearly identified in the reference. An express statement shall be made to the effect that the specified matter is incorporated in the registration statement, application, or report at the particular place where the information is required.

(d) Notwithstanding any particular provision permitting incorporation by reference, no registration statement, application or report shall incorporate by reference any exhibit or financial statement which: (1) Has been withdrawn, or (2) Was filed in connection with a registration statement under the Act, or a registration on a national securities exchange, which has ceased to be effective, or (3) Is contained in a registration statement or report subject, at the time of the incorporation by reference, to pending proceedings under section 8(b) or 8(d) of the Securities Act of 1933, section 8(e) of the Act, or to an order entered under any of those sections, or (4) If it is a document that has been filed in paper with respect to an electronic filer under a temporary hardship exemption (Rule 201 of Regulation S–T) and an electronic format copy has not been submitted.

(e) Notwithstanding any particular provision permitting incorporation by reference, the Commission may refuse to permit such incorporation in any case in which in its judgment such incorporation would render the registration statement application, or report incomplete, unclear, or confusing.

Rule 0–5. Procedure with respect to applications and other matters

The procedure herein below set forth will be followed with respect to any proceeding initiated by the filing of an application, or upon the Commission's own motion, pursuant to any section of the Act or any rule or regulation thereunder, unless in the particular case a different procedure is provided:

(a) Notice of the initiation of the proceeding will be published in the Federal Register and will indicate the earliest date upon which an order disposing of the matter may be entered. The notice will also provide that any interested person may, within the period of time specified therein, submit to the Commission in writing any facts bearing upon the desirability of a hearing on the matter and may request that a hearing be held, stating his reasons therefor and the nature of his interest in the matter.

(b) An order disposing of the matter will be issued as of course, following the expiration of the period of time referred to in paragraph (a) of this section, unless the Commission thereafter orders a hearing on the matter.

(c) The Commission will order a hearing on the matter, if it appears that a hearing is necessary or appropriate in the public interest or for the protection of investors, (1) upon the request of an interested person or (2) upon its own motion.

Rule 0–8. Payment of fees

All payment of fees shall be made by wire transfer, or by certified check, bank cashier's check, United States postal money order, or bank money order payable to the Securities and Exchange Commission, omitting the name or title of any official of the Commission. Payment of fees required by this rule shall be made in accordance with the directions set forth in 17 CFR 202.3a.

Rule 0–9. [Reserved]

Rule 0–10. Small entities under the investment company act for purposes of the Regulatory Flexibility Act

(a) *General.* For purposes of Commission rulemaking in accordance with the provisions of Chapter Six of the Administrative Procedure Act (5 U.S.C. 601 *et seq.*) and unless otherwise defined for purposes of a particular rulemaking, the term *small business* or *small organization* for purposes of the Investment Company Act of 1940 shall mean an investment company that, together with other investment companies in the same group of related investment companies, has net assets of $50 million or less as of the end of its most recent fiscal year. For purposes of this section:

(1) In the case of a management company, the term *group of related investment companies* shall mean two or more management companies (including series thereof) that:

(i) Hold themselves out to investors as related companies for purposes of investment and investor services; and

(ii) Either:

(A) Have a common investment adviser or have investment advisers that are affiliated persons of each other; or

(B) Have a common administrator; and

(2) In the case of a unit investment trust, the term *group of related investment companies* shall mean two or more unit investment trusts (including series thereof) that have a common sponsor.

(b) *Special rule for insurance company separate accounts.* In determining whether an insurance company separate account is a *small business* or *small entity* pursuant to paragraph (a) of this rule, the assets of the separate account shall be cumulated with the assets of the general account and all other separate accounts of the insurance company.

(c) *Determination of net assets.* The Commission may calculate its determination of the net assets of a group of related investment companies based on the net assets of each investment company in the group as of the end of such company's fiscal year.

Rule 0–11. Customer identification programs

Each registered open-end company is subject to the requirements of 31 U.S.C. 5318(*l*) and the implementing regulation at 31 CFR 103.131, which requires a customer identification program to be implemented as part of the anti-money laundering program required under subchapter II of chapter 53 of title 31, United States Code and the implementing regulations issued by the Department of the Treasury at 31 CFR part 103. Where 31 CFR 103.131 and this chapter use different definitions for the same term, the definition in 31 CFR 103.131 shall be used for the purpose of compliance with 31 CFR 103.131. Where 31 CFR 103.131 and this chapter require the same records to be preserved for different periods of time, such records shall be preserved for the longer period of time.

Rule 2a–1. Valuation of portfolio securities in special cases

(a) Any investment company whose securities are qualified for sale, or for whose securities application for such qualification has been made, in any State in which the securities owned by such company are required by applicable State law or regulations to be valued at cost or on some other basis different from that prescribed by clause (A) of section 2(a)(41) of the Act for the purpose of determining the percentage of its assets invested in any particular type or classification of securities or in the securities of any one issuer, may, in valuing its securities for the purposes of sections 5 and 12 of the Act, use the same basis of valuation as that used in complying with such State law or regulations in lieu of the method of valuation prescribed by clause (A) of section 2(a)(41) of the Act.

(b) Any open-end company which has heretofore valued its securities at cost for the purpose of qualifying as a "mutual investment company" under the Internal Revenue Code, prior to its amendment by the Revenue Act of 1942, shall henceforth, for the purposes of sections 5 and 12 of the Act, value its securities in accordance with the method prescribed in clause (A) of section 2(a)(41) of the Act unless such company is permitted under paragraph (a) of this section to use a different method of valuation.

(c) A registered investment company which has adopted for the purposes of sections 5 and 12 of the Act a method of valuation permitted by paragraph (a) of this rule, shall state in its registration statement filed pursuant to section 8 of the Act, or in a report filed pursuant to section 30 of the Act, the method of valuation adopted and the facts which justify the adoption of such method. A registered investment company which has adopted for the purposes of sections 5 and 12 of the Act a method of valuation permitted by paragraph (a) of this rule, unless it shall have adopted such method for the purpose or partly for the purpose of qualifying as a "mutual investment company" under the Internal Revenue Code, shall continue to use that method until it has notified the Commission of its desire to use a different method, and has received from the Commission permission for such change. Such permission may be made effective on a fixed date or within such reasonable time thereafter as may be deemed advisable under the circumstances.

(d) If at any time it appears that the method of valuation adopted by any company pursuant to paragraph (a) of this rule is no longer justified by the facts, the Commission may require a change in the method of valuation within a reasonable period of time either to the method prescribed in clause (A) of section 2(a)(41) of the Act or to some other method permitted by paragraph (a) of this rule which is justified by the existing facts.

Rule 2a–2. Effect of eliminations upon valuation of portfolio securities

During any fiscal quarter in which elimination of securities from the portfolio of an investment company occur, the securities remaining in the portfolio shall, for the purpose of sections 5 and 12 of the Act, be so valued as to give effect to the eliminations in accordance with one of the following methods: (a) Specific certificate, (b) first in—first out, (c) last in—first out, or (d) average value. For these purposes, a single method of elimination shall be used consistently with respect to all portfolio securities. In giving effect to eliminations pursuant to this section values shall be computed in accordance with section 2(a)(41)(A) of the Act.

Rule 2a3–1. Investment company limited partners not deemed affiliated persons

PRELIMINARY NOTE TO RULE 2A3–1

This Rule 2a3–1 excepts from the definition of affiliated person in section 2(a)(3) those limited partners of investment companies organized in limited partnership form that are affiliated persons solely because they are partners under section 2(a)(3)(D). Reliance on this Rule 2a3–1 does not except a limited partner that is an affiliated person by virtue of any other provision.

No limited partner of a registered management company or a business development company, organized as a limited partnership and relying on Rule 2a19–2, shall be deemed to be an affiliated person of such company, or any other partner of such company, solely by reason of being a limited partner of such company.

Rule 2a–4. Definition of "current net asset value" for use in computing periodically the current price of redeemable security

(a) The current net asset value of any redeemable security issued by a registered investment company used in computing periodically the current price for the purpose of distribution, redemption, and repurchase means an amount which reflects calculations, whether or not recorded in the books of account, made substantially in accordance with the following, with estimates used where necessary or appropriate.

(1) Portfolio securities with respect to which market quotations are readily available shall be valued at current market value, and other securities and assets shall be valued at fair value as determined in good faith by the board of directors of the registered company.

(2) Changes in holdings of portfolio securities shall be reflected no later than in the first calculation on the first business day following the trade date.

(3) Changes in the number of outstanding shares of the registered company resulting from distributions, redemptions, and repurchases shall be reflected no later than in the first calculation on the first business day following such change.

(4) Expenses, including any investment advisory fees, shall be included to date of calculation. Appropriate provision shall be made for Federal income taxes if required. Investment companies which retain realized capital gains designated as a distribution to shareholders shall comply with paragraph (h) of Rule 6–03 Regulation S–X.

(5) Dividends receivable shall be included to date of calculation either at ex-dividend dates or record dates, as appropriate.

(6) Interest income and other income shall be included to date of calculation.

(b) The items which would otherwise be required to be reflected by paragraphs (a)(4) and (6) of this section need not be so reflected if cumulatively, when netted, they do not amount to as much as one cent per outstanding share.

(c) Notwithstanding the requirements of paragraph (a) of this rule, any interim determination of current net asset value between calculations made as of the close of the New York Stock Exchange on the preceding business day and the current business day may be estimated so as to reflect any change in current net asset value since the closing calculation on the preceding business day.

Rule 2a–6. Certain transactions not deemed assignments

A transaction which does not result in a change of actual control or management of the investment adviser to, or principal underwriter of, an investment company is not an assignment for purposes of section 15(a)(4) or section 15(b)(2) of the Act, respectively.

Rule 2a–7. Money market funds

(a) *Definitions.* (1) *Acquisition (or acquire)* means any purchase or subsequent rollover (but does not include the failure to exercise a demand feature).

(2) *Amortized cost method of valuation* means the method of calculating an investment company's net asset value whereby portfolio securities are valued at the fund's Acquisition cost as adjusted for amortization of premium or accretion of discount rather than at their value based on current market factors.

(3) *Asset-backed security* means a fixed income security (other than a Government Security) issued by a Special Purpose Entity (as defined in this paragraph), substantially all of the assets of which consist of qualifying assets (as defined in this paragraph). *Special purpose entity* means a trust, corporation, partnership or other entity organized for the sole purpose of issuing securities that entitle their holders to receive payments that depend primarily on the cash flow from Qualifying Assets, but does not include a registered investment company. *Qualifying assets* means fi-

nancial assets, either fixed or revolving, that by their terms convert into cash within a finite time period, plus any rights or other assets designed to assure the servicing or timely distribution of proceeds to security holders.

(4) *Business day* means any day, other than Saturday, Sunday, or any customary business holiday.

(5) *Collateralized fully* has the same meaning as defined in Rule 5b–3(c)(1) except that Rule 5b–3(c)(1)(iv)(C) shall not apply.

(6) *Conditional demand feature* means a demand feature that is not an unconditional demand feature. A conditional demand feature is not a guarantee.

(7) *Conduit security* means a security issued by a municipal issuer (as defined in this paragraph) involving an arrangement or agreement entered into, directly or indirectly, with a person other than a municipal issuer, which arrangement or agreement provides for or secures repayment of the security. *Municipal issuer* means a state or territory of the United States (including the District of Columbia), or any political subdivision or public instrumentality of a state or territory of the United States. A conduit security does not include a security that is:

(i) Fully and unconditionally guaranteed by a municipal issuer;

(ii) Payable from the general revenues of the municipal issuer or other municipal issuers (other than those revenues derived from an agreement or arrangement with a person who is not a municipal issuer that provides for or secures repayment of the security issued by the municipal issuer);

(iii) Related to a project owned and operated by a municipal issuer; or

(iv) Related to a facility leased to and under the control of an industrial or commercial enterprise that is part of a public project which, as a whole, is owned and under the control of a municipal issuer.

(8) *Daily liquid assets* means:

(i) Cash;

(ii) Direct obligations of the U.S. Government;

(iii) Securities that will mature, as determined without reference to the exceptions in paragraph (i) of this section regarding interest rate readjustments, or are subject to a demand feature that is exercisable and payable, within one business day; or

(iv) Amounts receivable and due unconditionally within one business day on pending sales of portfolio securities.

(9) *Demand feature* means a feature permitting the holder of a security to sell the security at an exercise price equal to the approximate amortized cost of the security plus accrued interest, if any, at the later of the time of exercise or the settlement of the transaction, paid within 397 calendar days of exercise.

(10) *Demand feature issued by a non-controlled person* means a demand feature issued by:

(i) A person that, directly or indirectly, does not control, and is not controlled by or under common control with the issuer of the security subject to the demand feature (*control* means "control" as defined in section 2(a)(9) of the Act); or

(ii) A sponsor of a special purpose entity with respect to an asset-backed security.

(11) *Eligible security* means a security:

(i) With a remaining maturity of 397 calendar days or less that the fund's board of directors determines presents minimal credit risks to the fund, which determination must include an analysis of the capacity of the security's issuer or guarantor (including for this paragraph the provider of a conditional demand feature, when applicable) to meet its financial obligations, and such analysis must include, to the extent appropriate, consideration of the following factors with respect to the security's issuer or guarantor:

(A) Financial condition; (B) Sources of liquidity; (C) Ability to react to future market-wide and issuer- or guarantor-specific events, including ability to repay debt in a highly adverse situation; and (D) Strength of the issuer or guarantor's industry within the economy and relative to economic trends, and issuer or guarantor's competitive position within its industry.

(ii) That is issued by a registered investment company that is a money market fund; or

(iii) That is a government security.

NOTE to paragraph (a)(11): For a discussion of additional factors that may be relevant in evaluating certain specific asset types see Investment Company Act Release No. IC-31828 (9/16/15).

(12) *Event of insolvency* has the same meaning as defined in Rule 5b–3(c)(2).

(13) *Floating rate security* means a security the terms of which provide for the adjustment of its interest rate whenever a specified interest rate changes and that, at any time until the final maturity of the instrument or the period remaining until the principal amount can be recovered through demand, can reasonably be expected to have a market value that approximates its amortized cost.

(14) *Government money market fund* means a money market fund that invests 99.5 percent or more of its total assets in cash, government securities, and/or repurchase agreements that are collateralized fully.

(15) *Government security* has the same meaning as defined in Rule 2(a)(16).

(16) *Guarantee*:

(i) Means an unconditional obligation of a person other than the issuer of the security to undertake to pay, upon presentment by the holder of the guarantee (if required), the principal amount of the underlying security plus accrued interest when due or upon default, or, in the case of an Unconditional demand feature, an obligation that entitles the holder to receive upon the later of exercise or the settlement of the transaction the approximate amortized cost of the underlying security or securities, plus accrued interest, if any. A guarantee includes a letter of credit, financial guaranty (bond) insurance, and an unconditional demand feature (other than an unconditional demand feature provided by the issuer of the security).

(ii) The sponsor of a special purpose entity with respect to an asset-backed security shall be deemed to have provided a guarantee with respect to the entire principal amount of the asset-backed security for purposes of this section, except paragraphs (a)(11) (definition of eligible security), (d)(2)(ii) (credit substitution), (d)(3)(iv)(A) (fractional guarantees) and (e) (guarantees not relied on) of this section, unless the money market fund's board of directors has determined that the fund is not relying on the sponsor's financial strength or its ability or willingness to provide liquidity, credit or other support to determine the quality (pursuant to paragraph (d)(2) of this section) or liquidity (pursuant to paragraph (d)(4) of this section) of the asset-backed security, and maintains a record of this determination (pursuant to paragraphs (g)(7) and (h)(6) of this section).

(17) *Guarantee issued by a non-controlled person* means a guarantee issued by:

(i) A person that, directly or indirectly, does not control, and is not controlled by or under common control with the issuer of the security subject to the guarantee (*control* means "control" as defined in Rule 2(a)(9), or

(ii) A sponsor of a special purpose entity with respect to an asset-backed security.

(18) *Illiquid security* means a security that cannot be sold or disposed of in the ordinary course of business within seven calendar days at approximately the value ascribed to it by the fund.

(19) *Penny-rounding method* of pricing means the method of computing an investment company's price per share for purposes of distribution, redemption and repurchase whereby the current net asset value per share is rounded to the nearest one percent.

(20) *Refunded security* has the same meaning as defined in Rule 5b–3(c)(4).

(21) *Retail money market fund* means a money market fund that has policies and procedures reasonably designed to limit all beneficial owners of the fund to natural persons.

(22) *Single state fund* means a tax exempt fund that holds itself out as seeking to maximize the amount of its distributed income that is exempt from the income taxes or other taxes on investments of a particular state and, where applicable, subdivisions thereof.

(23) *Tax exempt fund* means any money market fund that holds itself out as distributing income exempt from regular federal income tax.

(24) *Total assets* means, with respect to a money market fund using the Amortized Cost Method, the total amortized cost of its assets and, with respect to any other money market fund, means the total value of the money market fund's assets, as defined in Rule 2(a)(41) and the rules thereunder.

(25) *Unconditional demand feature* means a demand feature that by its terms would be readily exercisable in the event of a default in payment

of principal or interest on the underlying security or securities.

(26) *United States dollar-denominated* means, with reference to a security, that all principal and interest payments on such security are payable to security holders in United States dollars under all circumstances and that the interest rate of, the principal amount to be repaid, and the timing of payments related to such security do not vary or float with the value of a foreign currency, the rate of interest payable on foreign currency borrowings, or with any other interest rate or index expressed in a currency other than United States dollars.

(27) *Variable rate security* means a security the terms of which provide for the adjustment of its interest rate on set dates (such as the last day of a month or calendar quarter) and that, upon each adjustment until the final maturity of the instrument or the period remaining until the principal amount can be recovered through demand, can reasonably be expected to have a market value that approximates its amortized cost.

(28) *Weekly liquid assets* means:

(i) Cash;

(ii) Direct obligations of the U.S. Government;

(iii) Government securities that are issued by a person controlled or supervised by and acting as an instrumentality of the government of the United States pursuant to authority granted by the Congress of the United States that:

(A) Are issued at a discount to the principal amount to be repaid at maturity without provision for the payment of interest; and

(B) Have a remaining maturity date of 60 days or less.

(iv) Securities that will mature, as determined without reference to the exceptions in paragraph (i) of this section regarding interest rate readjustments, or are subject to a demand feature that is exercisable and payable, within five business days; or

(v) Amounts receivable and due unconditionally within five business days on pending sales of portfolio securities.

(b) *Holding Out and Use of Names and Titles*

(1) *Holding Out.* It shall be an untrue statement of material fact within the meaning of section 34(b) of the Act for a registered investment company, in any registration statement, application, report, account, record, or other document filed or transmitted pursuant to the Act, including any advertisement, pamphlet, circular, form letter, or other sales literature addressed to or intended for distribution to prospective investors that is required to be filed with the Commission by section 24(b) of the Act, to hold itself out to investors as a money market fund or the equivalent of a money market fund, unless such registered investment company complies with this section.

(2) *Names.* It shall constitute the use of a materially deceptive or misleading name or title within the meaning of section 35(d) of the Act for a registered investment company to adopt the term "money market" as part of its name or title or the name or title of any redeemable securities of which it is the issuer, or to adopt a name that suggests that it is a money market fund or the equivalent of a money market fund, unless such registered investment company complies with this section.

(3) *Titles.* For purposes of paragraph (b)(2) of this section, a name that suggests that a registered investment company is a money market fund or the equivalent thereof includes one that uses such terms as "cash," "liquid," "money," "ready assets" or similar terms.

(c) *Pricing and Redeeming Shares*

(1) *Share Price Calculation.*

(i) The current price per share, for purposes of distribution, redemption and repurchase, of any redeemable security issued by a government money market fund or retail money market fund, notwithstanding the requirements of section 2(a)(41) of the Act and of Rules 2a–4 and 22c–1 thereunder, may be computed by use of the amortized cost method and/or the penny-rounding method. To use these methods, the board of directors of the government or retail money market fund must determine, in good faith, that it is in the best interests of the fund and its shareholders to maintain a stable net asset value per share or stable price per share, by virtue of either the amortized cost method and/or the penny-rounding method. The government or retail money market fund may continue to use such methods only so long as the board of directors believes that they fairly reflect the market-based net asset value per share and the fund complies with the other requirements of this section.

(ii) Any money market fund that is not a government money market fund or a retail money market fund must compute its price per share for purposes of distribution, redemption and repurchase by rounding the fund's current net asset value per share to a minimum of the fourth decimal place in the case of a fund with a $1.0000 share price or an equivalent or more precise level of accuracy for money market funds with a different share price (*e.g.* $10.000 per share, or $100.00 per share).

(2) *Liquidity Fees and Temporary Suspensions of Redemptions.* Except as provided in paragraphs (c)(2)(iii) and (v) of this section, and notwithstanding sections 22(e) and 27(i) of the Act and Rule 22c–1:

(i) *Discretionary Liquidity Fees and Temporary Suspensions of Redemptions.* If, at any time, the money market fund has invested less than thirty percent of its total assets in weekly liquid assets, the fund may institute a liquidity fee (not to exceed two percent of the value of the shares redeemed) or suspend the right of redemption temporarily, subject to paragraphs (c)(2)(i)(A) and (B) of this section, if the fund's board of directors, including a majority of the directors who are not interested persons of the fund, determines that the fee or suspension of redemptions is in the best interests of the fund.

(A) *Duration and Application of Discretionary Liquidity Fee.* Once imposed, a discretionary liquidity fee must be applied to all shares redeemed and must remain in effect until the money market fund's board of directors, including a majority of the directors who are not interested persons of the fund, determines that imposing such liquidity fee is no longer in the best interests of the fund. Provided however, that if, at the end of a business day, the money market fund has invested thirty percent or more of its total assets in weekly liquid assets, the fund must cease charging the liquidity fee, effective as of the beginning of the next business day.

(B) *Duration of Temporary Suspension of Redemptions.* The temporary suspension of redemptions must apply to all shares and must remain in effect until the fund's board of directors, including a majority of the directors who are not interested persons of the fund, determines that the temporary suspension of redemptions is no longer in the best interests of the fund. Provided, however, that the fund must restore the right of redemption on the earlier of:

(1) The beginning of the next business day following a business day that ended with the money market fund having invested thirty percent or more of its total assets in weekly liquid assets; or

(2) The beginning of the next business day following ten business days after suspending redemptions. The money market fund may not suspend the right of redemption pursuant to this section for more than ten business days in any rolling ninety calendar day period.

(ii) *Default Liquidity Fees.* If, at the end of a business day, the money market fund has invested less than ten percent of its total assets in weekly liquid assets, the fund must institute a liquidity fee, effective as of the beginning of the next business day, as described in paragraphs (c)(2)(ii)(A) and (B) of this section, unless the fund's board of directors, including a majority of the directors who are not interested persons of the fund, determines that imposing the fee is not in the best interests of the fund.

(A) *Amount of Default Liquidity Fees.* The default liquidity fee shall be one percent of the value of shares redeemed unless the money market fund's board of directors, including a majority of the directors who are not interested persons of the fund, determines, at the time of initial imposition or later, that a higher or lower fee level is in the best interests of the fund. A liquidity fee may not exceed two percent of the value of the shares redeemed.

(B) *Duration and Application of Default Liquidity Fee.* Once imposed, the default liquidity fee must be applied to all shares redeemed and shall remain in effect until the money market fund's board of directors, including a majority of the directors who are not interested persons of the fund, determines that imposing such liquidity fee is not in the best interests of the fund. Provided however, that if, at the end of a business day, the money market fund has invested thirty percent or more of its total assets in weekly liquid assets, the fund must cease charging the liquidity fee, effective as of the beginning of the next business day.

(iii) *Government Money Market Funds.* The requirements of paragraphs (c)(2)(i) and (ii) of this section shall not apply to a government money market fund. A government money market fund may, however, choose to rely on the ability to impose liquidity fees and suspend redemptions consistent with the requirements of paragraph (c)(2)(i) and/or (ii) of this section and any other requirements that apply to liquidity fees and temporary suspensions of redemptions (*e.g.*, Item 4(b)(1)(ii) of Form N–1A.

(iv) *Variable Contracts.* Notwithstanding section 27(i) of the Act, a variable insurance contract issued by a registered separate account funding variable insurance contracts or the sponsoring insurance company of such separate account may apply a liquidity fee or temporary suspension of redemptions pursuant to paragraph (c)(2) of this section to contract owners who allocate all or a portion of their contract value to a subaccount of the separate account that is either a money market fund or that invests all of its assets in shares of a money market fund.

(v) *Master Feeder Funds.* Any money market fund (a "feeder fund") that owns, pursuant to section 12(d)(1)(E) of the Act, shares of another money market fund (a "master fund") may not impose liquidity fees or temporary suspensions of redemptions under paragraphs (c)(2)(i) and (ii) of this section, provided however, that if a master fund, in which the feeder fund invests, imposes a liquidity fee or temporary suspension of redemptions pursuant to paragraphs (c)(2)(i) and (ii) of this section, then the feeder fund shall pass through to its investors the fee or redemption suspension on the same terms and conditions as imposed by the master fund.

(d) *Risk-Limiting Conditions*

(1) *Portfolio Maturity.* The money market fund must maintain a dollar-weighted average portfolio maturity appropriate to its investment objective; provided, however, that the money market fund must not:

(i) Acquire any instrument with a remaining maturity of greater than 397 calendar days;

(ii) Maintain a dollar-weighted average portfolio maturity ("WAM") that exceeds 60 calendar days; or

(iii) Maintain a dollar-weighted average portfolio maturity that exceeds 120 calendar days, determined without reference to the exceptions in paragraph (i) of this section regarding interest rate readjustments ("WAL").

(2) *Portfolio quality.*

(i) *General.* The money market fund must limit its portfolio investments to those United States dollar-denominated securities that at the time of acquisition are eligible securities.

(ii) *Securities subject to guarantees.* A security that is subject to a guarantee may be determined to be an eligible security based solely on whether the guarantee is an eligible security, provided however, that the issuer of the guarantee, or another institution, has undertaken to promptly notify the holder of the security in the event the guarantee is substituted with another guarantee (if such substitution is permissible under the terms of the guarantee).

(iii) *Securities subject to conditional demand features.* A security that is subject to a conditional demand feature ("underlying security") may be determined to be an eligible security only if:

(A) The conditional demand feature is an eligible security;

(B) The underlying security or any guarantee of such security is an eligible security, except that the underlying security or guarantee may have a remaining maturity of more than 397 calendar days.

(C) At the time of the acquisition of the underlying security, the money market fund's board of directors has determined that there is minimal risk that the circumstances that would result in the conditional demand feature not being exercisable will occur; and

(1) The conditions limiting exercise either can be monitored readily by the fund or relate to the taxability, under federal, state or local law, of the interest payments on the security; or

(2) The terms of the conditional demand feature require that the fund will receive notice of the occurrence of the condition and the opportunity to exercise the demand feature in accordance with its terms; and

(D) The issuer of the conditional demand feature, or another institution, has undertaken to promptly notify the holder of the security in the event the conditional demand feature is substituted with another conditional demand feature (if such substitution is permissible under the terms of the conditional demand feature).

(3) *Portfolio Diversification*

(i) *Issuer diversification*. The money market fund must be diversified with respect to issuers of securities acquired by the fund as provided in paragraphs (d)(3)(i) and (d)(3)(ii) of this section, other than with respect to government securities.

(A) *Taxable and national funds*. Immediately after the acquisition of any security, a money market fund other than a single state fund must not have invested more than:

(1) Five percent of its total assets in securities issued by the issuer of the security, provided, however, that with respect to paragraph (d)(3)(i)(A) of this section, such a fund may invest up to twenty-five percent of its total assets in the securities of a single issuer for a period of up to three business days after the acquisition thereof; provided, further, that the fund may not invest in the securities of more than one issuer in accordance with the foregoing proviso in this paragraph at any time; and

(2) Ten percent of its total assets in securities issued by or subject to demand features or guarantees from the institution that issued the demand feature or guarantee, provided, however, that a tax exempt fund need only comply with this paragraph with respect to eighty-five percent of its total assets, subject to paragraph (d)(3)(iii) of this section.

(B) *Single state funds*. Immediately after the acquisition of any security, a single state fund must not have invested:

(1) With respect to seventy-five percent of its total assets, more than five percent of its total assets in securities issued by the issuer of the security; and

(2) With respect to seventy-five percent of its total assets, more than ten percent of its total assets in securities issued by or subject to demand features or guarantees from the institution that issued the demand feature or guarantee, subject to paragraph (d)(3)(iii) of this section.

(ii) *Issuer Diversification Calculations*. For purposes of making calculations under paragraph (d)(3)(i) of this section:

(A) *Repurchase Agreements*. The acquisition of a repurchase agreement may be deemed to be an acquisition of the underlying securities, provided the obligation of the seller to repurchase the securities from the money market fund is collateralized fully and the fund's board of directors has evaluated the seller's creditworthiness.

(B) *Refunded Securities*. The acquisition of a refunded security shall be deemed to be an acquisition of the escrowed government securities.

(C) *Conduit Securities*. A conduit security shall be deemed to be issued by the person (other than the municipal issuer) ultimately responsible for payments of interest and principal on the security.

(D) *Asset-Backed Securities*

(1) General. An asset-backed security acquired by a fund ("primary ABS") shall be deemed to be issued by the special purpose entity that issued the asset-backed security, provided, however:

(i) Holdings of Primary ABS. Any person whose obligations constitute ten percent or more of the principal amount of the qualifying assets of the primary ABS ("ten percent obligor") shall be deemed to be an issuer of the portion of the primary ABS such obligations represent; and

(ii) Holdings of Secondary ABS. If a ten percent obligor of a primary ABS is itself a special purpose entity issuing asset-backed securities ("secondary ABS"), any ten percent obligor of such secondary ABS also shall be deemed to be an issuer of the portion of the primary ABS that such ten percent obligor represents.

(2) Restricted Special Purpose Entities. A ten percent obligor with respect to a primary or secondary ABS shall not be deemed to have issued any portion of the assets of a primary ABS as provided in paragraph (d)(3)(ii)(D)(1) of this section if that ten percent obligor is itself a special purpose entity issuing asset-backed securities ("restricted special purpose entity"), and the securities that it issues (other than securities issued

to a company that controls, or is controlled by or under common control with, the restricted special purpose entity and which is not itself a special purpose entity issuing asset-backed securities) are held by only one other special purpose entity.

(3) Demand Features and Guarantees. In the case of a ten percent obligor deemed to be an issuer, the fund must satisfy the diversification requirements of paragraph (d)(3)(iii) of this section with respect to any demand feature or guarantee to which the ten percent obligor's obligations are subject.

(E) *Shares of Other Money Market Funds.* A money market fund that acquires shares issued by another money market fund in an amount that would otherwise be prohibited by paragraph (d)(3)(i) of this section shall nonetheless be deemed in compliance with this section if the board of directors of the acquiring money market fund reasonably believes that the fund in which it has invested is in compliance with this section.

(F) *Treatment of Certain Affiliated Entities*

(1) General. The money market fund, when calculating the amount of its total assets invested in securities issued by any particular issuer for purposes of paragraph (d)(3)(i) of this section, must treat as a single issuer two or more issuers of securities owned by the money market fund if one issuer controls the other, is controlled by the other issuer, or is under common control with the other issuer, provided that "control" for this purpose means ownership of more than 50 percent of the issuer's voting securities.

(2) Equity Owners of Asset-Backed Commercial Paper Special Purpose Entities. The money market fund is not required to aggregate an asset-backed commercial paper special purpose entity and its equity owners under paragraph (d)(3)(ii)(F)*(1)* of this section provided that a primary line of business of its equity owners is owning equity interests in special purpose entities and providing services to special purpose entities, the independent equity owners' activities with respect to the SPEs are limited to providing management or administrative services, and no qualifying assets of the special purpose entity were originated by the equity owners.

(3) Ten Percent Obligors. For purposes of determining ten percent obligors pursuant to paragraph (d)(3)(ii)(D)*(1)*(i) of this section, the money market fund must treat as a single person two or more persons whose obligations in the aggregate constitute ten percent or more of the principal amount of the qualifying assets of the primary ABS if one person controls the other, is controlled by the other person, or is under common control with the person, provided that "control" for this purpose means ownership of more than 50 percent of the person's voting securities.

(iii) *Diversification Rules for Demand Features and Guarantees.* The money market fund must be diversified with respect to demand features and guarantees acquired by the fund as provided in paragraphs (d)(3)(i), (d)(3)(iii), and (d)(3)(iv) of this section, other than with respect to a demand feature issued by the same institution that issued the underlying security, or with respect to a guarantee or demand feature that is itself a government security.

(A) *General.* Immediately after the acquisition of any demand feature or guarantee, any security subject to a demand feature or guarantee, or a security directly issued by the issuer of a demand feature or guarantee, a money market fund must not have invested more than ten percent of its total assets in securities issued by or subject to demand features or guarantees from the institution that issued the demand feature or guarantee, subject to paragraphs (d)(3)(i) and (d)(3)(iii)(B) of this section.

(B) *Tax Exempt Funds.* Immediately after the acquisition of any demand feature or guarantee, any security subject to a demand feature or guarantee, or a security directly issued by the issuer of a demand feature or guarantee (any such acquisition, a "demand feature or guarantee acquisition"), a tax exempt fund, with respect to eighty-five percent of its total assets, must not have invested more than ten percent of its total assets in securities issued by or subject to demand features or guarantees from the institution that issued the demand feature or guarantee; provided that any demand feature or guarantee acquisition in excess of ten percent of the fund's total assets in accordance with this paragraph must be a demand feature or guarantee issued by a non-controlled person.

(iv) *Demand Feature and Guarantee Diversification Calculations*

(A) *Fractional Demand Features or Guarantees*. In the case of a security subject to a demand feature or guarantee from an institution by which the institution guarantees a specified portion of the value of the security, the institution shall be deemed to guarantee the specified portion thereof.

(B) *Layered Demand Features or Guarantees*. In the case of a security subject to demand features or guarantees from multiple institutions that have not limited the extent of their obligations as described in paragraph (d)(3)(iv)(A) of this section, each institution shall be deemed to have provided the demand feature or guarantee with respect to the entire principal amount of the security.

(v) *Diversification Safe Harbor*. A money market fund that satisfies the applicable diversification requirements of paragraphs (d)(3) and (e) of this section shall be deemed to have satisfied the diversification requirements of section 5(b)(1) of the Act and the rules adopted thereunder.

(4) *Portfolio Liquidity*. The money market fund must hold securities that are sufficiently liquid to meet reasonably foreseeable shareholder redemptions in light of the fund's obligations under section 22(e) of the Act and any commitments the fund has made to shareholders; provided, however, that:

(i) *Illiquid Securities*. The money market fund may not acquire any illiquid security if, immediately after the acquisition, the money market fund would have invested more than five percent of its total assets in illiquid securities.

(ii) *Minimum Daily Liquidity Requirement*. The money market fund may not acquire any security other than a daily liquid asset if, immediately after the acquisition, the fund would have invested less than ten percent of its total assets in daily liquid assets. This provision does not apply to tax exempt funds.

(iii) *Minimum Weekly Liquidity Requirement*. The money market fund may not acquire any security other than a weekly liquid asset if, immediately after the acquisition, the fund would have invested less than thirty percent of its total assets in weekly liquid assets.

(e) *Demand Features and Guarantees Not Relied Upon*. If the fund's board of directors has determined that the fund is not relying on a demand feature or guarantee to determine the quality (pursuant to paragraph (d)(2) of this section), or maturity (pursuant to paragraph (i) of this section), or liquidity of a portfolio security (pursuant to paragraph (d)(4) of this section), and maintains a record of this determination (pursuant to paragraphs (g)(3) and (h)(7) of this section), then the fund may disregard such demand feature or guarantee for all purposes of this section.

(f) *Defaults and other events*.

(1) *Adverse events*. Upon the occurrence of any of the events specified in paragraphs (f)(1)(i) through (iii) of this section with respect to a portfolio security, the money market fund shall dispose of such security as soon as practicable consistent with achieving an orderly disposition of the security, by sale, exercise of any demand feature or otherwise, absent a finding by the board of directors that disposal of the portfolio security would not be in the best interests of the money market fund (which determination may take into account, among other factors, market conditions that could affect the orderly disposition of the portfolio security):

(i) The default with respect to a portfolio security (other than an immaterial default unrelated to the financial condition of the issuer);

(ii) A portfolio security ceases to be an eligible security (*e.g.*, no longer presents minimal credit risks); or

(iii) An event of insolvency occurs with respect to the issuer of a portfolio security or the provider of any demand feature or guarantee.

(2) *Notice to the Commission*. The money market fund must notify the Commission of the occurrence of certain material events, as specified in Form N-CR (§ 274.222 of this chapter).

(3) *Defaults for purposes of paragraphs (f)(1) and (2) of this section*. For purposes of paragraphs (f)(1) and (2) of this section, an instrument subject to a demand feature or guarantee shall not be deemed to be in default (and an event of insolvency with respect to the security shall not be deemed to have occurred) if:

(i) In the case of an instrument subject to a demand feature, the demand feature has been exercised and the fund has recovered either the principal amount or the amortized cost of the instrument, plus accrued interest;

(ii) The provider of the guarantee is continuing, without protest, to make payments as due on the instrument; or

(iii) The provider of a guarantee with respect to an asset-backed security pursuant to paragraph (a)(16)(ii) of this section is continuing, without protest, to provide credit, liquidity or other support as necessary to permit the asset-backed security to make payments as due.

(g) *Required Procedures.* The money market fund's board of directors must adopt written procedures including the following:

(1) *Funds Using Amortized Cost.* In the case of a government or retail money market fund that uses the amortized cost method of valuation, in supervising the money market fund's operations and delegating special responsibilities involving portfolio management to the money market fund's investment adviser, the money market fund's board of directors, as a particular responsibility within the overall duty of care owed to its shareholders, shall establish written procedures reasonably designed, taking into account current market conditions and the money market fund's investment objectives, to stabilize the money market fund's net asset value per share, as computed for the purpose of distribution, redemption and repurchase, at a single value.

(i) *Specific Procedures.* Included within the procedures adopted by the board of directors shall be the following:

(A) *Shadow Pricing.* Written procedures shall provide:

(1) That the extent of deviation, if any, of the current net asset value per share calculated using available market quotations (or an appropriate substitute that reflects current market conditions) from the money market fund's amortized cost price per share, shall be calculated at least daily, and at such other intervals that the board of directors determines appropriate and reasonable in light of current market conditions;

(2) For the periodic review by the board of directors of the amount of the deviation as well as the methods used to calculate the deviation; and

(3) For the maintenance of records of the determination of deviation and the board's review thereof.

(B) *Prompt Consideration of Deviation.* In the event such deviation from the money market fund's amortized cost price per share exceeds ½ of 1 percent, the board of directors shall promptly consider what action, if any, should be initiated by the board of directors.

(C) *Material Dilution or Unfair Results.* Where the board of directors believes the extent of any deviation from the money market fund's amortized cost price per share may result in material dilution or other unfair results to investors or existing shareholders, it shall cause the fund to take such action as it deems appropriate to eliminate or reduce to the extent reasonably practicable such dilution or unfair results.

(2) *Funds Using Penny Rounding.* In the case of a government or retail money market fund that uses the penny rounding method of pricing, in supervising the money market fund's operations and delegating special responsibilities involving portfolio management to the money market fund's investment adviser, the money market fund's board of directors, as a particular responsibility within the overall duty of care owed to its shareholders, must establish written procedures reasonably designed, taking into account current market conditions and the money market fund's investment objectives, to assure to the extent reasonably practicable that the money market fund's price per share as computed for the purpose of distribution, redemption and repurchase, rounded to the nearest one percent, will not deviate from the single price established by the board of directors.

(3) *Ongoing Review of Credit Risks.* The written procedures must require the adviser to provide ongoing review of whether each security (other than a government security) continues to present minimal credit risks. The review must:

(i) Include an assessment of each security's credit quality, including the capacity of the issuer or guarantor (including conditional demand feature provider, when applicable) to meet its financial obligations; and

(ii) Be based on, among other things, financial data of the issuer of the portfolio security or provider of the guarantee or demand feature, as the case may be, and in the case of a security subject to a conditional demand feature, the issuer of the security whose financial condition must be monitored under paragraph (d)(2)(iii) of this section, whether such data is publicly available or provided under the terms of the security's governing documents.

(4) *Securities Subject to Demand Features or Guarantees.* In the case of a security subject to one or more demand features or guarantees that the fund's board of directors has determined that the fund is not relying on to determine the quality (pursuant to paragraph (d)(2) of this section), maturity (pursuant to paragraph (i) of this section) or liquidity (pursuant to paragraph (d)(4) of this section) of the security subject to the demand feature or guarantee, written procedures must require periodic evaluation of such determination.

(5) *Adjustable Rate Securities Without Demand Features.* In the case of a variable rate or floating rate security that is not subject to a demand feature and for which maturity is determined pursuant to paragraph (i)(1), (i)(2) or (i)(4) of this section, written procedures shall require periodic review of whether the interest rate formula, upon readjustment of its interest rate, can reasonably be expected to cause the security to have a market value that approximates its amortized cost value.

(6) *Ten Percent Obligors of Asset-Backed Securities.* In the case of an asset-backed security, written procedures must require the fund to periodically determine the number of ten percent obligors (as that term is used in paragraph (d)(3)(ii)(D) of this section) deemed to be the issuers of all or a portion of the asset-backed security for purposes of paragraph (d)(3)(ii)(D) of this section; provided, however, written procedures need not require periodic determinations with respect to any asset-backed security that a fund's board of directors has determined, at the time of acquisition, will not have, or is unlikely to have, ten percent obligors that are deemed to be issuers of all or a portion of that asset-backed security for purposes of paragraph (d)(3)(ii)(D) of this section, and maintains a record of this determination.

(7) *Asset-Backed Securities Not Subject to Guarantees.* In the case of an asset-backed security for which the fund's board of directors has determined that the fund is not relying on the sponsor's financial strength or its ability or willingness to provide liquidity, credit or other support in connection with the asset-backed security to determine the quality (pursuant to paragraph (d)(2) of this section) or liquidity (pursuant to paragraph (d)(4) of this section) of the asset-backed security, written procedures must require periodic evaluation of such determination.

(8) *Stress Testing.* Written procedures must provide for:

(i) *General.* The periodic stress testing, at such intervals as the board of directors determines appropriate and reasonable in light of current market conditions, of the money market fund's ability to have invested at least ten percent of its total assets in weekly liquid assets, and the fund's ability to minimize principal volatility (and, in the case of a money market fund using the amortized cost method of valuation or penny rounding method of pricing as provided in paragraph (c)(1) of this section, the fund's ability to maintain the stable price per share established by the board of directors for the purpose of distribution, redemption and repurchase), based upon specified hypothetical events that include, but are not limited to:

(A) Increases in the general level of short-term interest rates, in combination with various levels of an increase in shareholder redemptions;

(B) An event indicating or evidencing credit deterioration, such as a downgrade or default of particular portfolio security positions, each representing various portions of the fund's portfolio (with varying assumptions about the resulting loss in the value of the security), in combination with various levels of an increase in shareholder redemptions;

(C) A widening of spreads compared to the indexes to which portfolio securities are tied in various sectors in the fund's portfolio (in which a sector is a logically related subset of portfolio securities, such as securities of issuers in similar or related industries or geographic region or securities of a similar security type), in combination with various levels of an increase in shareholder redemptions; and

(D) Any additional combinations of events that the adviser deems relevant.

(ii) A report on the results of such testing to be provided to the board of directors at its next regularly scheduled meeting (or sooner, if appropriate in light of the results), which report must include:

(A) The date(s) on which the testing was performed and an assessment of the money market fund's ability to have invested at least ten percent of its total assets in weekly liquid assets and to minimize principal volatility (and, in the case of a money market fund using the amortized cost method of valuation or penny rounding method of pricing as provided in paragraph (c)(1) of this section to maintain the stable price per share established by the board of directors); and

(B) An assessment by the fund's adviser of the fund's ability to withstand the events (and concurrent occurrences of those events) that are reasonably likely to occur within the following year, including such information as may reasonably be necessary for the board of directors to evaluate the stress testing conducted by the adviser and the results of the testing. The fund adviser must include a summary of the significant assumptions made when performing the stress tests.

(h) *Record Keeping and Reporting*

(1) *Written Procedures.* For a period of not less than six years following the replacement of existing procedures with new procedures (the first two years in an easily accessible place), a written copy of the procedures (and any modifications thereto) described in this section must be maintained and preserved.

(2) *Board Considerations and Actions.* For a period of not less than six years (the first two years in an easily accessible place) a written record must be maintained and preserved of the board of directors' considerations and actions taken in connection with the discharge of its responsibilities, as set forth in this section, to be included in the minutes of the board of directors' meetings.

(3) *Credit risk analysis.* For a period of not less than three years from the date that the credit risks of a portfolio security were most recently reviewed, a written record must be maintained and preserved in an easily accessible place of the determination that a portfolio security is an eligible security, including the determination that it presents minimal credit risks at the time the fund acquires the security, or at such later times (or upon such events) that the board of directors determines that the investment adviser must reassess whether the security presents minimal credit risks.

(4) *Determinations with Respect to Adjustable Rate Securities.* For a period of not less than three years from the date when the assessment was most recently made, a written record must be preserved and maintained, in an easily accessible place, of the determination required by paragraph (g)(5) of this section (that a variable rate or floating rate security that is not subject to a demand feature and for which maturity is determined pursuant to paragraph (i)(1), (i)(2) or (i)(4) of this section can reasonably be expected, upon readjustment of its interest rate at all times during the life of the instrument, to have a market value that approximates its amortized cost).

(5) *Determinations with Respect to Asset-Backed Securities.* For a period of not less than three years from the date when the determination was most recently made, a written record must be preserved and maintained, in an easily accessible place, of the determinations required by paragraph (g)(6) of this section (the number of ten percent obligors (as that term is used in paragraph (d)(3)(ii)(D) of this section) deemed to be the issuers of all or a portion of the asset-backed security for purposes of paragraph (d)(3)(ii)(D) of this section). The written record must include:

(i) The identities of the ten percent obligors (as that term is used in paragraph (d)(3)(ii)(D) of this section), the percentage of the qualifying assets constituted by the securities of each ten percent obligor and the percentage of the fund's total assets that are invested in securities of each ten percent obligor; and

(ii) Any determination that an asset-backed security will not have, or is unlikely to have, ten percent obligors deemed to be issuers of all or a portion of that asset-backed security for purposes of paragraph (d)(3)(ii)(D) of this section.

(6) *Evaluations with Respect to Asset-Backed Securities Not Subject to Guarantees.* For a period of not less than three years from the date when the evaluation was most recently made, a written record must be preserved and maintained, in an easily accessible place, of the evaluation required by paragraph (g)(7) of this section (regarding asset-backed securities not subject to guarantees).

(7) *Evaluations with Respect to Securities Subject to Demand Features or Guarantees.* For a period of not less than three years from the date when the evaluation was most recently made, a written record must be preserved and maintained, in an easily accessible place, of the evaluation required

by paragraph (g)(4) of this section (regarding securities subject to one or more demand features or guarantees).

(8) *Reports with Respect to Stress Testing.* For a period of not less than six years (the first two years in an easily accessible place), a written copy of the report required under paragraph (g)(8)(ii) of this section must be maintained and preserved.

(9) *Inspection of Records.* The documents preserved pursuant to paragraph (h) of this section are subject to inspection by the Commission in accordance with Rule 31(b) as if such documents were records required to be maintained pursuant to rules adopted under Rule 31(a).

(10) *Website Disclosure of Portfolio Holdings and Other Fund Information.* The money market fund must post prominently on its website the following information:

(i) For a period of not less than six months, beginning no later than the fifth business day of the month, a schedule of its investments, as of the last Business Day or subsequent calendar day of the preceding month, that includes the following information:

(A) With respect to the money market fund and each class of redeemable shares thereof:

(1) The WAM; and

(2) The WAL.

(B) With respect to each security held by the money market fund:

(1) Name of the issuer;

(2) Category of investment (indicate the category that identifies the instrument from among the following: U.S. Treasury Debt; U.S. Government Agency Debt; Non-U.S. Sovereign, Sub-Sovereign and Supra-National debt; Certificate of Deposit; Non-Negotiable Time Deposit; Variable Rate Demand Note; Other Municipal Security; Asset Backed Commercial Paper; Other Asset Backed Securities; U.S. Treasury Repurchase Agreement, if collateralized only by U.S. Treasuries (including Strips) and cash; U.S. Government Agency Repurchase Agreement, collateralized only by U.S. Government Agency securities, U.S. Treasuries, and cash; Other Repurchase Agreement, if any collateral falls outside Treasury, Government Agency and cash; Insurance Company Funding Agreement; Investment Company; Financial Company Commercial Paper; and Non-Financial Company Commercial Paper. If Other Instrument, include a brief description);

(3) CUSIP number (if any);

(4) Principal amount;

(5) The maturity date determined by taking into account the maturity shortening provisions in paragraph (i) of this section (*i.e.*, the maturity date used to calculate WAM under paragraph (d)(1)(ii) of this section);

(6) The maturity date determined without reference to the exceptions in paragraph (i) of this section regarding interest rate readjustments (*i.e.*, the maturity used to calculate WAL under paragraph (d)(1)(iii) of this section);

(7) Coupon or yield; and

(8) Value.

(ii) A schedule, chart, graph, or other depiction, which must be updated each business day as of the end of the preceding business day, showing, as of the end of each business day during the preceding six months:

(A) The percentage of the money market fund's total assets invested in daily liquid assets;

(B) The percentage of the money market fund's total assets invested in weekly liquid assets; and

(C) The money market fund's net inflows or outflows.

(iii) A schedule, chart, graph, or other depiction showing the money market fund's net asset value per share (which the fund must calculate based on current market factors before applying the amortized cost or penny-rounding method, if used), rounded to the fourth decimal place in the case of funds with a $1.000 share price or an equivalent level of accuracy for funds with a different share price (*e.g.*, $10.00 per share), as of the end of each business day during the preceding six months, which must be updated each business day as of the end of the preceding business day.

(iv) A link to a website of the Securities and Exchange Commission where a user may obtain the most recent 12 months of publicly available information filed by the money market fund pursuant to Rule 30b1–7.

(v) For a period of not less than one year, beginning no later than the same business day on which the money market fund files an initial report on Form N–CR in response to the occurrence of any event specified in Parts C, E, F, or G of Form N–CR, the same information that the money market fund is required to report to the Commission on Part C (Items C.1, C.2, C.3, C.4, C.5, C.6, and C.7), Part E (Items E.1, E.2, E.3, and E.4), Part F (Items F.1 and F.2), or Part G of Form N–CR concerning such event, along with the following statement: "The Fund was required to disclose additional information about this event [or "these events," as appropriate] on Form N–CR and to file this form with the Securities and Exchange Commission. Any Form N–CR filing submitted by the Fund is available on the EDGAR Database on the Securities and Exchange Commission's Internet site at *http://www.sec.gov*."

(11) *Processing of Transactions.* A government money market fund and a retail money market fund (or its transfer agent) must have the capacity to redeem and sell securities issued by the fund at a price based on the current net asset value per share pursuant to Rule 22c–1. Such capacity must include the ability to redeem and sell securities at prices that do not correspond to a stable price per share.

(i) *Maturity of Portfolio Securities.* For purposes of this section, the maturity of a portfolio security shall be deemed to be the period remaining (calculated from the trade date or such other date on which the fund's interest in the security is subject to market action) until the date on which, in accordance with the terms of the security, the principal amount must unconditionally be paid, or in the case of a security called for redemption, the date on which the redemption payment must be made, except as provided in paragraphs (i)(1) through (i)(8) of this section:

(1) *Adjustable Rate Government Securities.* A government security that is a variable rate security where the variable rate of interest is readjusted no less frequently than every 397 calendar days shall be deemed to have a maturity equal to the period remaining until the next readjustment of the interest rate. A government security that is a floating rate security shall be deemed to have a remaining maturity of one day.

(2) *Short-Term Variable Rate Securities.* A variable rate security, the principal amount of which, in accordance with the terms of the security, must unconditionally be paid in 397 calendar days or less shall be deemed to have a maturity equal to the earlier of the period remaining until the next readjustment of the interest rate or the period remaining until the principal amount can be recovered through demand.

(3) *Long-Term Variable Rate Securities.* A variable rate security, the principal amount of which is scheduled to be paid in more than 397 calendar days, that is subject to a demand feature, shall be deemed to have a maturity equal to the longer of the period remaining until the next readjustment of the interest rate or the period remaining until the principal amount can be recovered through demand.

(4) *Short-Term Floating Rate Securities.* A floating rate security, the principal amount of which, in accordance with the terms of the security, must unconditionally be paid in 397 calendar days or less shall be deemed to have a maturity of one day, except for purposes of determining WAL under paragraph (d)(1)(iii) of this section, in which case it shall be deemed to have a maturity equal to the period remaining until the principal amount can be recovered through demand.

(5) *Long-Term Floating Rate Securities.* A floating rate security, the principal amount of which is scheduled to be paid in more than 397 calendar days, that is subject to a demand feature, shall be deemed to have a maturity equal to the period remaining until the principal amount can be recovered through demand.

(6) *Repurchase Agreements.* A repurchase agreement shall be deemed to have a maturity equal to the period remaining until the date on which the repurchase of the underlying securities is scheduled to occur, or, where the agreement is subject to demand, the notice period applicable to a demand for the repurchase of the securities.

(7) *Portfolio Lending Agreements.* A portfolio lending agreement shall be treated as having a maturity equal to the period remaining until the date on which the loaned securities are scheduled to be returned, or where the agreement is subject to demand, the notice period applicable to a demand for the return of the loaned securities.

(8) *Money Market Fund Securities.* An investment in a money market fund shall be treated as having a maturity equal to the period of time

within which the acquired money market fund is required to make payment upon redemption, unless the acquired money market fund has agreed in writing to provide redemption proceeds to the investing money market fund within a shorter time period, in which case the maturity of such investment shall be deemed to be the shorter period.

(j) *Delegation*. The money market fund's board of directors may delegate to the fund's investment adviser or officers the responsibility to make any determination required to be made by the board of directors under this section other than the determinations required by paragraphs (c)(1) (board findings), (c)(2)(i) and (ii) (determinations related to liquidity fees and temporary suspensions of redemptions), (f)(1) (adverse events), (g)(1) and (g)(2) (amortized cost and penny rounding procedures), and (g)(8) (stress testing procedures) of this section.

(1) *Written guidelines*. The board of directors must establish and periodically review written guidelines (including guidelines for determining whether securities present minimal credit risks as required in paragraphs (d)(2) and (g)(3) of this section) and procedures under which the delegate makes such determinations.

(2) *Oversight*. The board of directors must take any measures reasonably necessary (through periodic reviews of fund investments and the delegate's procedures in connection with investment decisions and prompt review of the adviser's actions in the event of the default of a security or event of insolvency with respect to the issuer of the security or any guarantee or demand feature to which it is subject that requires notification of the Commission under paragraph (f)(2) of this section by reference to Form N-CR (§ 274.222 of this chapter)) to assure that the guidelines and procedures are being followed.

Rule 2a–46. Certain issuers as eligible portfolio companies

The term *eligible portfolio company* shall include any issuer that meets the requirements set forth in paragraphs (A) and (B) of section 2(a)(46) of the Act and that:

(a) Does not have any class of securities listed on a national securities exchange; or

(b) Has a class of securities listed on a national securities exchange, but has an aggregate market value of outstanding voting and non-voting common equity of less than $250 million. For purposes of this paragraph:

(1) The aggregate market value of an issuer's outstanding voting and non-voting common equity shall be computed by use of the price at which the common equity was last sold, or the average of the bid and asked prices of such common equity, in the principal market for such common equity as of a date within 60 days prior to the date of acquisition of its securities by a business development company; and

(2) *Common equity* has the same meaning as in Rule 405 under the Securities Act of 1933.

Rule 2a19–2. Investment company general partners not deemed interested persons

PRELIMINARY NOTE TO RULE 2A19–2

This Rule 2a19–2 conditionally excepts from the definition of interested person in section 2(a)(19) general partners of investment companies organized in limited partnership form. Compliance with the conditions of this Rule 2a19–2 does not relieve an investment company of any other requirement of this Act, or except a general partner that is an interested person by virtue of any other provision.

(a) *Director General Partners Not Deemed Interested Persons*. A general partner serving as a director of a limited partnership investment company shall not be deemed to be an interested person of such company, or of any investment adviser of, or principal underwriter for, such company, solely by reason of being a partner of the limited partnership investment company, or a copartner in the limited partnership investment company with any investment adviser of, or principal underwriter for, the company, *provided* that the Limited Partnership Agreement contains in substance the following:

(1) Only general partners who are natural persons shall serve as, and perform the functions of, directors of the limited partnership investment company, except that any general partner may act as provided in paragraph (a)(2)(iii) of this rule.

(2) A general partner shall not have the authority to act individually on behalf of, or to bind, the Limited Partnership Investment Company, except:

(i) In such person's capacity as investment adviser, principal underwriter, or administrator;

(ii) Within the scope of such person's authority as delegated by the board of directors; or

(iii) In the event that no director of the company remains, to the extent necessary to continue the Limited Partnership Investment Company, for such limited periods as are permitted under the Act to fill director vacancies.

(3) Limited partners shall have all of the rights afforded shareholders under the Act. If a limited partnership interest is transferred in a manner that is effective under the Partnership Agreement, the transferee shall have all of the rights afforded shareholders under the Act.

(4) A general partner shall not withdraw from the Limited Partnership Investment Company or reduce its Federal Tax Status Contribution without giving at least one year's prior written notice to the Limited Partnership Investment Company, if such withdrawal or reduction is likely to cause the company to lose its partnership tax classification. This paragraph (a)(4) shall not apply to an investment adviser general partner if the company terminates its advisory agreement with such general partner.

(b) *Definitions.* (1) *Federal Tax Status Contribution* shall mean the interest (including limited partnership interest) in each material item of partnership income, gain, loss, deduction, or credit, and other contributions, required to be held or made by general partners, pursuant to section 4 of Internal Revenue Service Revenue Procedure 89–12, or any successor provisions thereto.

(2) *Limited Partnership Investment Company* shall mean a registered management company or a business development company that is organized as a limited partnership under state law.

(3) *Partnership Agreement* shall mean the agreement of the partners of the Limited Partnership Investment Company as to the affairs of the limited partnership and the conduct of its business.

Rule 2a19–3. Certain investment company directors not considered interested persons because of ownership of index fund securities

If a director of a registered investment company ("Fund") owns shares of a registered investment company (including the Fund) with an investment objective to replicate the performance of one or more broad-based securities indices ("Index Fund"), ownership of the Index Fund shares will not cause the director to be considered an "interested person" of the Fund or of the Fund's investment adviser or principal underwriter (as defined by section 2(a)(19)(A)(iii) and (B)(iii) of the Act.

Rule 2a41–1. Valuation of standby commitments by registered investment companies

(a) A standby commitment means a right to sell a specified underlying security or securities within a specified period of time and at an exercise price equal to the amortized cost of the underlying security or securities plus accrued interest, if any, at the time of exercise, that may be sold, transferred or assigned only with the underlying security or securities. A standby commitment entitles the holder to receive same day settlement, and will be considered to be from the party to whom the investment company will look for payment of the exercise price. A standby commitment may be assigned a fair value of zero, Provided, That:

(1) The standby commitment is not used to affect the company's valuation of the security or securities underlying the standby commitment; and

(2) Any consideration paid by the company for the standby commitment, whether paid in cash or by paying a premium for the underlying security or securities, is accounted for by the company as unrealized depreciation until the standby commitment is exercised or expires.

Rule 2a51–1. Definition of investments for purposes of Section 2(a)(51) (definition of "qualified purchaser"); certain calculations

(a) *Definitions.* As used in this section:

(1) The term *Commodity Interests* means commodity futures contracts, options on commodity futures contracts, and options on physical commodities traded on or subject to the rules of:

(i) Any contract market designated for trading such transactions under the Commodity Exchange Act and the rules thereunder; or

(ii) Any board of trade or exchange outside the United States, as contemplated in Part 30 of the rules under the Commodity Exchange Act [17 CFR 30.1 through 30.11].

(2) The term *Family Company* means a company described in paragraph (A)(ii) of section 2(a)(51) of the Act.

(3) The term *Investment Vehicle* means an investment company, a company that would be an investment company but for the exclusions provided by sections 3(c)(1) through 3(c)(9) of the Act or the exemptions provided by Rules 3a–6 or 3a–7, or a commodity pool.

(4) The term *Investments* has the meaning set forth in paragraph (b) of this rule.

(5) The term *Physical Commodity* means any physical commodity with respect to which a Commodity Interest is traded on a market specified in paragraph (a)(1) of this rule.

(6) The term *Prospective Qualified Purchaser* means a person seeking to purchase a security of a Section 3(c)(7) Company.

(7) The term *Public Company* means a company that:

(i) Files reports pursuant to section 13 or 15(d) of the Securities Exchange Act of 1934; or

(ii) Has a class of securities that are listed on a "designated offshore securities market" as such term is defined by Regulation S under the Securities Act of 1933.

(8) The term *Related Person* means a person who is related to a Prospective Qualified Purchaser as a sibling, spouse or former spouse, or is a direct lineal descendant or ancestor by birth or adoption of the Prospective Qualified Purchaser, or is a spouse of such descendant or ancestor, provided that, in the case of a Family Company, a Related Person includes any owner of the Family Company and any person who is a Related Person of such owner.

(9) The term *Relying Person* means a Section 3(c)(7) Company or a person acting on its behalf.

(10) The term *Section 3(c)(7) Company* means a company that would be an investment company but for the exclusion provided by section 3(c)(7) of the Act.

(b) *Types of Investments*. For purposes of section 2(a)(51) of the Act [15 U.S.C. 80a–2(a)(51)], the term *Investments* means:

(1) Securities (as defined by section 2(a)(1) of the Securities Act of 1933), other than securities of an issuer that controls, is controlled by, or is under common control with, the Prospective Qualified Purchaser that owns such securities, unless the issuer of such securities is:

(i) An Investment Vehicle;

(ii) A Public Company; or

(iii) A company with shareholders' equity of not less than $50 million (determined in accordance with generally accepted accounting principles) as reflected on the company's most recent financial statements, provided that such financial statements present the information as of a date within 16 months preceding the date on which the Prospective Qualified Purchaser acquires the securities of a Section 3(c)(7) Company;

(2) Real estate held for investment purposes;

(3) Commodity Interests held for investment purposes;

(4) Physical Commodities held for investment purposes;

(5) To the extent not securities, financial contracts (as such term is defined in section 3(c)(2)(B)(ii) of the Act) entered into for investment purposes;

(6) In the case of a Prospective Qualified Purchaser that is a Section 3(c)(7) Company, a company that would be an investment company but for the exclusion provided by section 3(c)(1) of the Act, or a commodity pool, any amounts payable to such Prospective Qualified Purchaser pursuant to a firm agreement or similar binding commitment pursuant to which a person has agreed to acquire an interest in, or make capital contributions to, the Prospective Qualified Purchaser upon the demand of the Prospective Qualified Purchaser; and

(7) Cash and cash equivalents (including foreign currencies) held for investment purposes. For purposes of this section, cash and cash equivalents include:

(i) Bank deposits, certificates of deposit, bankers acceptances and similar bank instruments held for investment purposes; and

(ii) The net cash surrender value of an insurance policy.

(c) *Investment Purposes*. For purposes of this section:

(1) Real estate shall not be considered to be held for investment purposes by a Prospective Qualified Purchaser if it is used by the Prospective Qualified Purchaser or a Related Person for personal purposes or as a place of business, or in connection with the conduct of the trade or business of the Prospective Qualified Purchaser or a Related Person, provided that real estate owned by a Prospective Qualified Purchaser who is engaged primarily in the business of investing, trading or developing real estate in connection with such business may be deemed to be held for investment purposes. Residential real estate shall not be deemed to be used for personal purposes if

deductions with respect to such real estate are not disallowed by section 280A of the Internal Revenue Code [26 U.S.C. 280A].

(2) A Commodity Interest or Physical Commodity owned, or a financial contract entered into, by the Prospective Qualified Purchaser who is engaged primarily in the business of investing, reinvesting, or trading in Commodity Interests, Physical Commodities or financial contracts in connection with such business may be deemed to be held for investment purposes.

(d) *Valuation.* For purposes of determining whether a Prospective Qualified Purchaser is a qualified purchaser, the aggregate amount of Investments owned and invested on a discretionary basis by the Prospective Qualified Purchaser shall be the Investments' fair market value on the most recent practicable date or their cost, provided that:

(1) In the case of Commodity Interests, the amount of Investments shall be the value of the initial margin or option premium deposited in connection with such Commodity Interests; and

(2) In each case, there shall be deducted from the amount of Investments owned by the Prospective Qualified Purchaser the amounts specified in paragraphs (e) and (f) of this rule, as applicable.

(e) *Deductions.* In determining whether any person is a qualified purchaser there shall be deducted from the amount of such person's Investments the amount of any outstanding indebtedness incurred to acquire or for the purpose of acquiring the Investments owned by such person.

(f) *Deductions: Family Companies.* In determining whether a Family Company is a qualified purchaser, in addition to the amounts specified in paragraph (e) of this rule, there shall be deducted from the value of such Family Company's Investments any outstanding indebtedness incurred by an owner of the Family Company to acquire such Investments.

(g) *Special Rules for Certain Prospective Qualified Purchasers.* (1) *Qualified Institutional Buyers.* Any Prospective Qualified Purchaser who is, or who a Relying Person reasonably believes is, a qualified institutional buyer as defined in paragraph (a) of Rule 144A under the Securities Act of 1933, acting for its own account, the account of another qualified institutional buyer, or the account of a qualified purchaser, shall be deemed to be a qualified purchaser provided:

(i) That a dealer described in paragraph (a)(1)(ii) of Rule 144A under the Securities Act of 1933 shall own and invest on a discretionary basis at least $25 million in securities of issuers that are not affiliated persons of the dealer; and

(ii) That a plan referred to in paragraph (a)(1)(i)(D) or (a)(1)(i)(E) of Rule 144A under the Securities Act of 1933, or a trust fund referred to in paragraph (a)(1)(i)(F) of Rule 144A under the Securities Act of 1933 that holds the assets of such a plan, will not be deemed to be acting for its own account if investment decisions with respect to the plan are made by the beneficiaries of the plan, except with respect to investment decisions made solely by the fiduciary, trustee or sponsor of such plan.

(2) *Joint Investments.* In determining whether a natural person is a qualified purchaser, there may be included in the amount of such person's Investments any Investments held jointly with such person's spouse, or Investments in which such person shares with such person's spouse a community property or similar shared ownership interest. In determining whether spouses who are making a joint investment in a Section 3(c)(7) Company are qualified purchasers, there may be included in the amount of each spouse's Investments any Investments owned by the other spouse (whether or not such Investments are held jointly). In each case, there shall be deducted from the amount of any such Investments the amounts specified in paragraph (e) of this rule incurred by each spouse.

(3) *Investments by Subsidiaries.* For purposes of determining the amount of Investments owned by a company under section 2(a)(51)(A)(iv) of the Act, there may be included Investments owned by majority-owned subsidiaries of the company and Investments owned by a company ("Parent Company") of which the company is a majority-owned subsidiary, or by a majority-owned subsidiary of the company and other majority-owned subsidiaries of the Parent Company.

(4) *Certain Retirement Plans and Trusts.* In determining whether a natural person is a qualified purchaser, there may be included in the amount of such person's Investments any Investments held in an individual retirement account or similar account the Investments of which are directed by and held for the benefit of such person.

(h) *Reasonable Belief.* The term "qualified purchaser" as used in section 3(c)(7) of the Act means any person that meets the definition of qualified purchaser in section 2(a)(51)(A) of the Act and the rules thereunder, or that a Relying Person reasonably believes meets such definition.

Rule 2a51–2. Definitions of beneficial owner for certain purposes under Sections 2(a)(51) and 3(c)(7) and determining indirect ownership interests

(a) *Beneficial Ownership: General.* Except as set forth in this rule, for purposes of sections 2(a)(51)(C) and 3(c)(7)(B)(ii) of the Act, the beneficial owners of securities of an excepted investment company (as defined in section 2(a)(51)(C) of the Act shall be determined in accordance with section 3(c)(1) of the Act).

(b) *Beneficial Ownership: Grandfather Provision.* For purposes of section 3(c)(7)(B)(ii) of the Act, securities of an issuer beneficially owned by a company (without giving effect to section 3(c)(1)(A) of the Act ("owning company") shall be deemed to be beneficially owned by one person unless):

(1) The owning company is an investment company or an excepted investment company;

(2) The owning company, directly or indirectly, controls, is controlled by, or is under common control with, the issuer; and

(3) On October 11, 1996, under section 3(c)(1)(A) of the Act as then in effect, the voting securities of the issuer were deemed to be beneficially owned by the holders of the owning company's outstanding securities (other than short-term paper), in which case, such holders shall be deemed to be beneficial owners of the issuer's outstanding voting securities.

(c) *Beneficial Ownership: Consent Provision.* For purposes of section 2(a)(51)(C) of the Act, securities of an excepted investment company beneficially owned by a company (without giving effect to section 3(c)(1)(A) of the Act ("owning company") shall be deemed to be beneficially owned by one person unless):

(1) The owning company is an excepted investment company;

(2) The owning company directly or indirectly controls, is controlled by, or is under common control with the excepted investment company or the company with respect to which the excepted investment company is, or will be, a qualified purchaser; and

(3) On April 30, 1996, under section 3(c)(1)(A) of the Act as then in effect, the voting securities of the excepted investment company were deemed to be beneficially owned by the holders of the owning company's outstanding securities (other than short-term paper), in which case the holders of such excepted company's securities shall be deemed to be beneficial owners of the excepted investment company's outstanding voting securities.

(d) *Indirect Ownership: Consent Provision.* For purposes of section 2(a)(51)(C) of the Act, an excepted investment company shall not be deemed to indirectly own the securities of an excepted investment company seeking a consent to be treated as a qualified purchaser ("qualified purchaser company") unless such excepted investment company, directly or indirectly, controls, is controlled by, or is under common control with, the qualified purchaser company or a company with respect to which the qualified purchaser company is or will be a qualified purchaser.

(e) *Required Consent: Consent Provision.* For purposes of section 2(a)(51)(C) of the Act, the consent of the beneficial owners of an excepted investment company ("owning company") that beneficially owns securities of an excepted investment company that is seeking the consents required by section 2(a)(51)(C) ("consent company") shall not be required unless the owning company directly or indirectly controls, is controlled by, or is under common control with the consent company or the company with respect to which the consent company is, or will be, a qualified purchaser.

NOTES TO RULE 2A51–2:

1. On both April 30, 1996 and October 11, 1996, section 3(c)(1)(A) of the Act as then in effect provided that: (A) Beneficial ownership by a company shall be deemed to be beneficial ownership by one person, except that, if the company owns 10 per centum or more of the outstanding voting securities of the issuer, the beneficial ownership shall be deemed to be that of the holders of such company's outstanding securities (other than short-term paper) unless, as of the date of the most recent acquisition by such company of securities of that issuer, the value of all securities owned by such company of all issuers which are or would, but for the exception set forth in this subparagraph, be excluded from the definition of investment company solely by this paragraph, does not exceed 10 per centum of the value of the company's total assets. Such issuer nonetheless is deemed to be an investment company for purposes of section 12(d)(1).

2. Issuers seeking the consent required by section 2(a)(51)(C) of the Act should note that section 2(a)(51)(C) requires an issuer to obtain the consent of the beneficial owners of its securities and the beneficial owners of securities of any "excepted investment company" that directly or indirectly owns the securities of the issuer. Except as set forth in paragraphs (d) (with respect to indirect owners) and (e) (with respect to direct owners) of this rule, nothing in this section is designed to limit this consent requirement.

Rule 2a51–3. Certain companies as qualified purchasers

(a) For purposes of section 2(a)(51)(A)(ii) and (iv) of the Act, a company shall not be deemed to be a qualified purchaser if it was formed for the specific purpose of acquiring the securities offered by a company excluded from the definition of investment company by section 3(c)(7) of the Act unless each beneficial owner of the company's securities is a qualified purchaser.

(b) For purposes of section 2(a)(51) of the Act, a company may be deemed to be a qualified purchaser if each beneficial owner of the company's securities is a qualified purchaser.

Rule 3a–1. Certain prima facie investment companies

Notwithstanding section 3(a)(1)(C) of the Act, an issuer will be deemed not to be an investment company under the Act; *Provided,* That:

(a) No more than 45 percent of the value (as defined in section 2(a)(41) of the Act) of such issuer's total assets (exclusive of Government securities and cash items) consists of, and no more than 45 percent of such issuer's net income after taxes (for the last four fiscal quarters combined) is derived from, securities other than:

(1) Government securities;

(2) Securities issued by employees' securities companies;

(3) Securities issued by majority-owned subsidiaries of the issuer (other than subsidiaries relying on the exclusion from the definition of investment company in section 3(b)(3) or section 3(c)(1) of the Act) which are not investment companies; and

(4) Securities issued by companies;

(i) Which are controlled primarily by such issuer;

(ii) Through which such issuer engages in a business other than that of investing, reinvesting, owning, holding or trading in securities; and

(iii) Which are not investment companies;

(b) The issuer is not an investment company as defined in section 3(a)(1)(A) or 3(a)(1)(B) of the Act and is not a special situation investment company; and

(c) The percentages described in paragraph (a) of this section are determined on an unconsolidated basis, except that the issuer shall consolidate its financial statements with the financial statements of any wholly-owned subsidiaries.

Rule 3a–2. Transient investment companies

(a) For purposes of sections 3(a)(1)(A) and 3(a)(1)(C) of the Act, an issuer is deemed not to be engaged in the business of investing, reinvesting, owning, holding or trading in securities during a period of time not to exceed one year; *Provided,* That the issuer has a *bona fide* intent to be engaged primarily, as soon as is reasonably possible (in any event by the termination of such period of time), in a business other than that of investing, reinvesting, owning, holding or trading in securities, such intent to be evidenced by:

(1) The issuer's business activities; and

(2) An appropriate resolution of the issuer's board of directors, or by an appropriate action of the person or persons performing similar functions for any issuer not having a board of directors, which resolution or action has been recorded contemporaneously in its minute books or comparable documents.

(b) For purposes of this rule, the period of time described in paragraph (a) shall commence on the earlier of:

(1) The date on which an issuer owns securities and/or cash having a value exceeding 50 percent of the value of such issuer's total assets on either a consolidated or unconsolidated basis; or

(2) The date on which an issuer owns or proposes to acquire investment securities (as defined in section 3(a) of the Act) having a value exceeding 40 per centum of the value of such issuer's total assets (exclusive of Government securities and cash items) on an unconsolidated basis.

(c) No issuer may rely on this section more frequently than once during any three-year period.

Rule 3a–3. Certain investment companies owned by companies which are not investment companies

Notwithstanding section 3(a)(1)(A) or section 3(a)(1)(C) of the Act, an issuer will be deemed not to be an investment company for purposes of the Act; *Provided,* That all of the outstanding securities of the issuer (other than short-term paper, directors' qualifying shares, and debt securities owned by the Small Business Administration) are directly or indirectly owned by a company which satisfies the conditions of Rule 3a–1(a) and which is:

(a) A company that is not an investment company as defined in section 3(a) of the Act;

(b) A company that is an investment company as defined in section 3(a)(1)(C) of the Act, but which is excluded from the definition of the term "investment company" by section 3(b)(1) or 3(b)(2) of the Act; or

(c) A company that is deemed not to be an investment company for purposes of the Act by Rule 3a–1.

Rule 3a–4. Status of investment advisory programs

NOTE: This rule is a nonexclusive safe harbor from the definition of investment company for programs that provide discretionary investment advisory services to clients. There is no registration requirement under section 5 of the Securities Act of 1933 [15 U.S.C. 77e] with respect to programs that are organized and operated in the manner described in Rule 3a–4. The rule is not intended, however, to create any presumption about a program that is not organized and operated in the manner contemplated by the rule.

(a) Any program under which discretionary investment advisory services are provided to clients that has the following characteristics will not be deemed to be an investment company within the meaning of the Act:

(1) Each client's account in the program is managed on the basis of the client's financial situation and investment objectives and in accordance with any reasonable restrictions imposed by the client on the management of the account.

(2)(i) At the opening of the account, the sponsor or another person designated by the sponsor obtains information from the client regarding the client's financial situation and investment objectives, and gives the client the opportunity to impose reasonable restrictions on the management of the account;

(ii) At least annually, the sponsor or another person designated by the sponsor contacts the client to determine whether there have been any changes in the client's financial situation or investment objectives, and whether the client wishes to impose any reasonable restrictions on the management of the account or reasonably modify existing restrictions;

(iii) At least quarterly, the sponsor or another person designated by the sponsor notifies the client in writing to contact the sponsor or such other person if there have been any changes in the client's financial situation or investment objectives, or if the client wishes to impose any reasonable restrictions on the management of the client's account or reasonably modify existing restrictions, and provides the client with a means through which such contact may be made; and

(iv) The sponsor and personnel of the manager of the client's account who are knowledgeable about the account and its management are reasonably available to the client for consultation.

(3) Each client has the ability to impose reasonable restrictions on the management of the client's account, including the designation of particular securities or types of securities that should not be purchased for the account, or that should be sold if held in the account; *Provided, however,* that nothing in this section requires that a client have the ability to require that particular securities or types of securities be purchased for the account.

(4) The sponsor or person designated by the sponsor provides each client with a statement, at least quarterly, containing a description of all activity in the client's account during the preceding period, including all transactions made on behalf of the account, all contributions and withdrawals made by the client, all fees and expenses charged to the account, and the value of the account at the beginning and end of the period.

(5) Each client retains, with respect to all securities and funds in the account, to the same extent as if the client held the securities and funds outside the program, the right to:

(i) Withdraw securities or cash;

(ii) Vote securities, or delegate the authority to vote securities to another person;

(iii) Be provided in a timely manner with a written confirmation or other notification of each securities transaction, and all other documents required by law to be provided to security holders; and

(iv) Proceed directly as a security holder against the issuer of any security in the client's account and not be obligated to join any person involved in the operation of the program, or any other client of the program, as a condition precedent to initiating such proceeding.

(b) As used in this section, the term sponsor refers to any person who receives compensation for sponsoring, organizing or administering the program, or for selecting, or providing advice to clients regarding the selection of, persons responsible for managing the client's account in the program. If a program has more than one sponsor, one person shall be designated the principal sponsor, and such person shall be considered the sponsor of the program under this section.

Rule 3a–5. Exemption for subsidiaries organized to finance the operations of domestic or foreign companies

(a) A finance subsidiary will not be considered an investment company under section 3(a) of the Act and securities of a finance subsidiary held by the parent company or a company controlled by the parent company will not be considered "investment securities" under section 3(a)(1)(C) of the Act; *Provided,* That:

(1) Any debt securities of the finance subsidiary issued to or held by the public are unconditionally guaranteed by the parent company as to the payment of principal, interest, and premium, if any (except that the guarantee may be subordinated in right of payment to other debt of the parent company);

(2) Any non-voting preferred stock of the finance subsidiary issued to or held by the public is unconditionally guaranteed by the parent company as to payment of dividends, payment of the liquidation preference in the event of liquidation, and payments to be made under a sinking fund, if a sinking fund is to be provided (except that the guarantee may be subordinated in right of payment to other debt of the parent company);

(3) The parent company's guarantee provides that in the event of a default in payment of principal, interest, premium, dividends, liquidation preference or payments made under a sinking fund on any debt securities or non-voting preferred stock issued by the finance subsidiary, the holders of those securities may institute legal proceedings directly against the parent company (or, in the case of a partnership or joint venture, against the partners or participants in the joint venture) to enforce the guarantee without first proceeding against the finance subsidiary;

(4) Any securities issued by the finance subsidiary which are convertible or exchangeable are convertible or exchangeable only for securities issued by the parent company (and, in the case of a partnership or joint venture, for securities issued by the partners or participants in the joint venture) or for debt securities or non-voting preferred stock issued by the finance subsidiary meeting the applicable requirements of paragraphs (a)(1) through (a)(3);

(5) The finance subsidiary invests in or loans to its parent company or a company controlled by its parent company at least 85% of any cash or cash equivalents raised by the finance subsidiary through an offering of its debt securities or non-voting preferred stock or through other borrowings as soon as practicable, but in no event later than six months after the finance subsidiary's receipt of such cash or cash equivalents;

(6) The finance subsidiary does not invest in, reinvest in, own, hold or trade in securities other than Government securities, securities of its parent company or a company controlled by its parent company (or in the case of a partnership or joint venture, the securities of the partners or participants in the joint venture) or debt securities (including repurchase agreements) which are exempted from the provisions of the Securities Act of 1933 by section 3(a)(3) of that Act; and

(7) Where the parent company is a foreign bank as the term is used in rule 3a–6, the parent company may, in lieu of the guaranty required by paragraph (a)(1) or (a)(2) of this rule, issue, in favor of the holders of the finance subsidiary's debt securities or non-voting preferred stock, as the case may be, an irrevocable letter of credit in an amount sufficient to fund all of the amounts required to be guaranteed by paragraphs (a)(1) and (a)(2) of this rule, *provided,* that:

(i) payment on such letter of credit shall be conditional only upon the presentation of customary documentation, and

(ii) the beneficiary of such letter of credit is not required by either the letter of credit or applicable law to institute proceedings against the finance subsidiary before enforcing its remedies under the letter of credit.

(b) For purposes of this rule,

(1) A *finance subsidiary* shall mean any corporation—

(i) All of whose securities other than debt securities or non-voting preferred stock meeting the applicable requirements of paragraphs (a)(1) through (a)(3) or directors' qualifying shares are owned by its parent company or a company controlled by its parent company; and

(ii) The primary purpose of which is to finance the business operations of its parent company or companies controlled by its parent company;

(2) A *parent company* shall mean any corporation, partnership or joint venture—

(i) That is not considered an investment company under section 3(a) or that is excepted or exempted by order from the definition of investment company by section 3(b) or by the rules or regulations under section 3(a);

(ii) That is organized or formed under the laws of the United States or of a state or that is a foreign private issuer, or that is a foreign bank or foreign insurance company as those terms are used in Rule 3a–6; and

(iii) In the case of a partnership or joint venture, each partner or participant in the joint venture meets the requirements of paragraphs (b)(2)(i) and (ii).

(3) A *company controlled by the parent company* shall mean any corporation, partnership or joint venture—

(i) That is not considered an investment company under section 3(a) or that is excepted or exempted by order from the definition of investment company by section 3(b) or by the rules or regulations under section 3(a);

(ii) That is either organized or formed under the laws of the United States or of a state or that is a foreign private issuer, or that is a foreign bank or foreign insurance company as those terms are used in Rule 3a–6; and

(iii) In the case of a corporation, more than 25 percent of whose outstanding voting securities are beneficially owned directly or indirectly by the parent company; or

(iv) In the case of a partnership or joint venture, each partner or participant in the joint venture meets the requirements of paragraphs (b)(3) (i) and (ii), and the parent company has the power to exercise a controlling influence over the management or policies of the partnership or joint venture.

(4) A *foreign private issuer* shall mean any issuer which is incorporated or organized under the laws of a foreign country, but not a foreign government or political subdivision of a foreign government.

Rule 3a–6. Foreign banks and foreign insurance companies

(a) Notwithstanding section 3(a)(1)(A) or section 3(a)(1)(C) of the Act, a foreign bank or foreign insurance company shall not be considered an investment company for purposes of the Act.

(b) For purposes of this rule:

(1)(i) *Foreign bank* means a banking institution incorporated or organized under the laws of a country other than the United States, or a political subdivision of a country other than the United States, that is:

(A) Regulated as such by that country's or subdivision's government or any agency thereof;

(B) Engaged substantially in commercial banking activity; and

(C) Not operated for the purpose of evading the provisions of the Act;

(ii) The term *foreign bank* shall also include:

(A) A trust company or loan company that is:

(*1*) Organized or incorporated under the laws of Canada or a political subdivision thereof;

(*2*) Regulated as a trust company or a loan company by that country's or subdivision's government or any agency thereof; and

(*3*) Not operated for the purpose of evading the provisions of the Act; and

(B) A building society that is:

(*1*) Organized under the laws of the United Kingdom or a political subdivision thereof;

(*2*) Regulated as a building society by the country's or subdivision's government or any agency thereof; and

(*3*) Not operated for the purpose of evading the provisions of the Act.

(iii) Nothing in this rule shall be construed to include within the definition of *foreign bank* a common or collective trust or other separate pool of assets organized in the form of a trust or otherwise in which interests are separately offered.

(2) *Engaged substantially in commercial banking activity* means engaged regularly in, and deriving a substantial portion of its business from, extending commercial and other types of credit, and accepting demand and other types of deposits, that are customary for commercial banks in the country in which the head office of the banking institution is located.

(3) *Foreign insurance company* means an insurance company incorporated or organized under the laws of a country other than the United

States, or a political subdivision of a country other than the United States, that is:

(i) Regulated as such by that country's or subdivision's government or any agency thereof;

(ii) Engaged primarily and predominantly in:

(A) The writing of insurance agreements of the type specified in section 3(a)(8) of the Securities Act of 1933, except for the substitution of supervision by foreign government insurance regulators for the regulators referred to in that section; or

(B) The reinsurance of risks on such agreements underwritten by insurance companies; and

(iii) Not operated for the purpose of evading the provisions of the Act. Nothing in this rule shall be construed to include within the definition of "foreign insurance company" a separate account or other pool of assets organized in the form of a trust or otherwise in which interests are separately offered.

NOTE: Foreign banks and foreign insurance companies (and certain of their finance subsidiaries and holding companies) relying on Rule 3a–6 for exemption from the Act may be required by Rule 489 under the Securities Act of 1933 to file Form F–N with the Commission in connection with the filing of a registration statement under the Securities Act of 1933.

Rule 3a–7. Issuers of asset–backed securities

(a) Notwithstanding section 3(a) of the Act, any issuer who is engaged in the business of purchasing, or otherwise acquiring, and holding eligible assets (and in activities related or incidental thereto), and who does not issue redeemable securities will not be deemed to be an investment company; *Provided that:*

(1) The issuer issues fixed-income securities or other securities which entitle their holders to receive payments that depend primarily on the cash flow from eligible assets;

(2) Securities sold by the issuer or any underwriter thereof are fixed-income securities rated, at the time of initial sale, in one of the four highest categories assigned long-term debt or in an equivalent short-term category (within either of which there may be sub-categories or gradations indicating relative standing) by at least one nationally recognized statistical rating organization that is not an affiliated person of the issuer or of any person involved in the organization or operation of the issuer, except that:

(i) Any fixed-income securities may be sold to accredited investors as defined in paragraphs (1), (2), (3), and (7) of Rule 501(a) under the Securities Act of 1933 and any entity in which all of the equity owners come within such paragraphs; and

(ii) Any securities may be sold to qualified institutional buyers as defined in Rule 144A under the Securities Act and to persons (other than any rating organization rating the issuer's securities) involved in the organization or operation of the issuer or an affiliate, as defined in Rule 405 under the Securities Act, of such a person;

Provided, That the issuer or any underwriter thereof effecting such sale exercises reasonable care to ensure that such securities are sold and will be resold to persons specified in paragraphs (a)(2) (i) and (ii) of this rule;

(3) The issuer acquires additional eligible assets, or disposes of eligible assets, only if:

(i) The assets are acquired or disposed of in accordance with the terms and conditions set forth in the agreements, indentures, or other instruments pursuant to which the issuer's securities are issued;

(ii) The acquisition or disposition of the assets does not result in a downgrading in the rating of the issuer's outstanding fixed-income securities; and

(iii) The assets are not acquired or disposed of for the primary purpose of recognizing gains or decreasing losses resulting from market value changes; and

(4) If the issuer issues any securities other than securities exempted from the Securities Act by section 3(a)(3) thereof, the issuer:

(i) Appoints a trustee that meets the requirements of section 26(a)(1) of the Act and that is not affiliated, as that term is defined in Rule 405 under the Securities Act, with the issuer or with any person involved in the organization or operation of the issuer, which does not offer or provide credit or credit enhancement to the issuer, and that executes an agreement or instrument concerning the issuer's securities containing provisions to the effect set forth in section 26(a)(3) of the Act;

(ii) Takes reasonable steps to cause the trustee to have a perfected security interest or ownership interest valid against third parties in those eligible assets that principally generate the cash flow needed to pay the fixed-income security holders, provided that such assets otherwise required to be held by the trustee may be released to the extent needed at the time for the operation of the issuer; and

(iii) Takes actions necessary for the cash flows derived from eligible assets for the benefit of the holders of fixed-income securities to be deposited periodically in a segregated account that is maintained or controlled by the trustee consistent with the rating of the outstanding fixed-income securities.

(b) For purposes of this section:

(1) *Eligible assets* means financial assets, either fixed or revolving, that by their terms convert into cash within a finite time period plus any rights or other assets designed to assure the servicing or timely distribution of proceeds to security holders.

(2) *Fixed-income securities* means any securities that entitle the holder to receive:

(i) A stated principal amount; or

(ii) Interest on a principal amount (which may be a notional principal amount) calculated by reference to a fixed rate or to a standard or formula which does not reference any change in the market value or fair value of eligible assets; or

(iii) Interest on a principal amount (which may be a notional principal amount) calculated by reference to auctions among holders and prospective holders, or through remarketing of the security; or

(iv) An amount equal to specified fixed or variable portions of the interest received on the assets held by the issuer; or

(v) Any combination of amounts described in paragraphs (b)(2) (i), (ii), (iii), and (iv) of this section;

Provided, That substantially all of the payments to which the holders of such securities are entitled consist of the foregoing amounts.

Rule 3a–8. Certain research and development companies

(a) Notwithstanding sections 3(a)(1)(A) and 3(a)(1)(C) of the Act, an issuer will be deemed not to be an investment company if:

(1) Its research and development expenses, for the last four fiscal quarters combined, are a substantial percentage of its total expense for the same period;

(2) Its net income derived from investments in securities, for the last four fiscal quarters combined, does not exceed twice the amount of its research and development expenses for the same period;

(3) Its expenses for investment advisory and management activities, investment research and custody, for the last four fiscal quarters, combined, do not exceed five percent of its total expenses for the same period;

(4) Its investments in securities are capital preservation investments, except that:

(i) No more than 10 percent of the issuer's total assets may consist of other investments, or

(ii) No more than 25 percent of the issuer's total assets may consist of other investments, provided that at least 75 percent of such other investments are investments made pursuant to a collaborative research and development arrangement;

(5) It does not hold itself out as being engaged in the business of investing, reinvesting or trading in securities, and it is not a special situation investment company;

(6) It is primarily engaged, directly, through majority-owned subsidiaries, or through companies which it controls primarily, in a business or businesses other than that of investing, reinvesting, owning, holding, or trading in securities, as evidenced by:

(i) The activities of its officers, directors and employees;

(ii) Its public representations of policies;

(iii) Its historical development; and

(iv) An appropriate resolution of its board of directors, which resolution or action has been recorded contemporaneously in its minute books or comparable documents; and

(7) Its board of directors has adopted a written investment policy with respect to the issuer's capital preservation investments.

(b) For purposes of this rule:

(1) All assets shall be valued in accordance with section 2(a)(41)(A) of the Act;

(2) The percentages described in this section are determined on an unconsolidated basis, except that the issuer shall consolidate its financial statements with the financial statements of any wholly-owned subsidiaries;

(3) *Board of directors* means the issuer's board of directors or an appropriate person or persons performing similar functions for any issuer not having a board of directors;

(4) *Capital preservation investment* means an investment that is made to conserve capital and liquidity until the funds are used in the issuer's primary business or businesses;

(5) *Controlled primarily* means controlled within the meaning of section 2(a)(9) of the Act with a degree of control that is greater than that of any other person;

(6) *Investment made pursuant to a collaborative research and development arrangement* means an investment in an investee made pursuant to a business relationship which:

(i) Is designed to achieve narrowly focused goals that are directly related to, and an integral part of, the issue's research and development activities;

(ii) Calls for the issuer to conduct joint research and development activities with the investee or a company controlled primarily by, or which controls primarily, the investee; and

(iii) Is not entered into for the purpose of avoiding regulation under the Act;

(7) *Investments in securities* means all securities other than securities issued by majority-owned subsidiaries and companies controlled primarily by the issuer that conduct similar types of businesses, through which the issuer is engaged primarily in a business other than that of investing, reinvesting, owning, holding, or trading in securities;

(8) *Other investment* means an investment in securities that is not a capital preservation investment; and

(9) *Research and development expenses* means research and development costs as defined in FASB ASC Topic 730, *Research and Development*, as currently in effect or as it may be subsequently revised.

Rule 3c–1. Definition of beneficial ownership for certain Section 3(c)(1) funds

(a) As used in this rule:

(1) The term *Covered Company* means a company that is an investment company, a Section 3(c)(1) Company or a Section 3(c)(7) Company.

(2) The term *Section 3(c)(1) Company* means a company that would be an investment company but for the exclusion provided by section 3(c)(1) of the Act.

(3) The term *Section 3(c)(7) Company* means a company that would be an investment company but for the exclusion provided by section 3(c)(7) of the Act.

(b) For purposes of section 3(c)(1)(A) of the Act, beneficial ownership by a Covered Company owning 10 percent or more of the outstanding voting securities of a Section 3(c)(1) Company shall be deemed to be beneficial ownership by one person, provided that:

(1) On April 1, 1997, the Covered Company owned 10 percent or more of the outstanding voting securities of the Section 3(c)(1) Company or non-voting securities that, on such date and in accordance with the terms of such securities, were convertible into or exchangeable for voting securities that, if converted or exchanged on or after such date, would have constituted 10 percent or more of the outstanding voting securities of the Section 3(c)(1) Company; and

(2) On the date of any acquisition of securities of the Section 3(c)(1) Company by the Covered Company, the value of all securities owned by the Covered Company of all issuers that are Section 3(c)(1) or Section 3(c)(7) Companies does not exceed 10 percent of the value of the Covered Company's total assets.

Rule 3c–2. Definition of beneficial ownership in small business investment companies

For the purpose of section 3(c)(1) of the Act, beneficial ownership by a company owning 10 per centum or more of the outstanding voting securities of any issuer which is a small business investment company licensed to operate under the Small Business Investment Act of 1958, or which has received from the Small Business Administration notice to proceed to qualify for a license, which notice or license has not been revoked, shall be deemed to be beneficial ownership by one person (a) if and so long as the value of all securities of small business investments companies owned by such company does not exceed 5 per centum of the value of its total assets; or (b) if and so long as such stock of the small business investment company shall be owned by a state development corporation which has been created by or pursuant to an act of the State legislature to promote and assist the growth and development of the economy within such State on a state-wide basis: *Provided,* That such State development corporation is not, or as a result of its investment in the small business investment company (considering such investment as an investment security) would not be, an investment company as defined in section 3 of the Act.

Rule 3c–3. Definition of certain terms used in Section 3(c)(1) of the Act with respect to certain debt securities offered by small business investment companies

The term *public offering* as used in section 3(c)(1) of the Act shall not be deemed to include the offer and sale by a small business investment company, licensed under the Small Business Investment Act of 1958, of any debt security issued by it which is (a) not convertible into, exchangeable for, or accompanied by any equity security, and (b) guaranteed as to timely payment of principal and interest by the Small Business Administration and backed by the full faith and credit of the United States. The holders of any securities offered and sold as described in this section shall be counted, in the aggregate, as one person for purposes of section 3(c)(1) of the Act.

Rule 3c–4. Definition of "common trust fund" as used in Section 3(c)(3) of the Act

The term *common trust fund* as used in section 3(c)(3) of the Act shall include a common trust fund which is maintained by a bank which is a member of an affiliated group, as defined in section 1504(a) of the Internal Revenue Code of 1954, and which is maintained exclusively for the collective investment and reinvestment of monies contributed thereto by one or more bank members of such affiliated group in the capacity of trustee, executor, administrator, or guardian; provided that:

(a) The common trust fund is operated in compliance with the same State and Federal regulatory requirements as would apply if the bank maintaining such fund and any other contributing banks were the same entity; and

(b) The rights of persons for whose benefit a contributing bank acts as trustee, executor, administrator, or guardian would not be diminished by reason of the maintenance of such common trust fund by another bank member of the affiliated group.

Rule 3c–5. Beneficial ownership by knowledgeable employees and certain other persons

(a) As used in this rule:

(1) The term *Affiliated Management Person* means an affiliated person, as such term is defined in section 2(a)(3) of the Act, that manages the investment activities of a Covered Company. For purposes of this definition, the term "investment company" as used in section 2(a)(3) of the Act includes a Covered Company.

(2) The term *Covered Company* means a Section 3(c)(1) Company or a Section 3(c)(7) Company.

(3) The term *Executive Officer* means the president, any vice president in charge of a principal business unit, division or function (such as sales, administration or finance), any other officer who performs a policy-making function, or any other person who performs similar policy-making functions, for a Covered Company or for an Affiliated Management Person of the Covered Company.

(4) The term *Knowledgeable Employee* with respect to any Covered Company means any natural person who is:

(i) An Executive Officer, director, trustee, general partner, advisory board member, or person serving in a similar capacity, of the Covered Company or an Affiliated Management Person of the Covered Company; or

(ii) An employee of the Covered Company or an Affiliated Management Person of the Covered Company (other than an employee performing solely clerical, secretarial or administrative functions with regard to such company or its investments) who, in connection with his or her regular functions or duties, participates in the investment activities of such Covered Company, other Covered Companies, or investment companies the investment activities of which are managed by such Affiliated Management Person of the Covered Company, provided that such employee has been performing such functions and duties for or on behalf of the Covered Company or the Affiliated Management Person of the Covered Company, or substantially similar functions or duties for or on behalf of another company for at least 12 months.

(5) The term *Section 3(c)(1) Company* means a company that would be an investment company but for the exclusion provided by section 3(c)(1) of the Act.

(6) The term *Section 3(c)(7) Company* means a company that would be an investment company but for the exclusion provided by section 3(c)(7) of the Act.

(b) For purposes of determining the number of beneficial owners of a Section 3(c)(1) Company, and whether the outstanding securities of a Section 3(c)(7) Company are owned exclusively by qualified purchasers, there shall be excluded securities beneficially owned by:

(1) A person who at the time such securities were acquired was a Knowledgeable Employee of such Company;

(2) A company owned exclusively by Knowledgeable Employees;

(3) Any person who acquires securities originally acquired by a Knowledgeable Employee in accordance with this rule, provided that such securities were acquired by such person in accordance with Rule 3c–6.

Rule 3c–6. Certain transfers of interests in Section 3(c)(1) and Section 3(c)(7) funds

(a) As used in this section:

(1) The term *Donee* means a person who acquires a security of a Covered Company (or a security or other interest in a company referred to in paragraph (b)(3) of this rule) as a gift or bequest or pursuant to an agreement relating to a legal separation or divorce.

(2) The term *Section 3(c)(1) Company* means a company that would be an investment company but for the exclusion provided by section 3(c)(1) of the Act.

(3) The term *Section 3(c)(7) Company* means a company that would be an investment company but for the exclusion provided by section 3(c)(7) of the Act.

(4) The term *Transferee* means a Section 3(c)(1) Transferee or a Qualified Purchaser Transferee, in each case as defined in paragraph (b) of this rule.

(5) The term *Transferor* means a Section 3(c)(1) Transferor or a Qualified Purchaser Transferor, in each case as defined in paragraph (b) of this rule.

(b) Beneficial ownership by any person ("Section 3(c)(1) Transferee") who acquires securities or interests in securities of a Section 3(c)(1) Company from a person other than the Section 3(c)(1) Company shall be deemed to be beneficial ownership by the person from whom such transfer was made ("Section 3(c)(1) Transferor"), and securities of a Section 3(c)(7) Company that are owned by persons who received the securities from a qualified purchaser other than the Section 3(c)(7) Company ("Qualified Purchaser Transferor") or a person deemed to be a qualified purchaser by this section shall be deemed to be acquired by a qualified purchaser ("Qualified Purchaser Transferee"), provided that the Transferee is:

(1) The estate of the Transferor;

(2) A Donee; or

(3) A company established by the Transferor exclusively for the benefit of (or owned exclusively by) the Transferor and the persons specified in paragraphs (b)(1) and (b)(2) of this rule.

Rule 5b–1. Definition of "total assets"

The term *total assets,* when used in computing values for the purposes of sections 5 and 12 of the Act, shall mean the gross assets of the company with respect to which the computation is made, taken as of the end of the fiscal quarter of the company last preceding the date of computation. This section shall not apply to any company which has adopted either of the alternative methods of valuation permitted by Rule 2a–1.

Rule 5b–2. Exclusion of certain guarantees as securities of the guarantor

(a) For the purposes of section 5 of the Act, a guarantee of a security shall not be deemed to be a security issued by the guarantor: *Provided,* That the value of all securities issued or guaranteed by the guarantor, and owned by the management company, does not exceed 10 percent of the value of the total assets of such management company.

(b) Notwithstanding paragraph (a) of this rule, for the purposes of section 5 of the act, a guarantee by a railroad company of a security issued by a terminal company, warehouse company, switching company, or bridge company, shall not be deemed to be a security issued by such railroad company: *Provided:*

(1) The security is guaranteed jointly or severally by more than one railroad company; and

(2) No one of such guaranteeing railroad companies directly or indirectly controls all of its co-guarantors.

(c) For the purposes of section 5 of the Act, a lease or other arrangement whereby a railroad company is or becomes obligated to pay a stipulated annual sum of rental either to another railroad company or to the security holders of such other railroad company shall not be deemed in itself a guarantee.

Rule 5b-3. Acquisition of repurchase agreement or refunded security treated as acquisition of underlying securities

(a) *Repurchase Agreements.* For purposes of sections 5 and 12(d)(3) of the Act, the acquisition of a repurchase agreement may be deemed to be an acquisition of the underlying securities, provided the obligation of the seller to repurchase the securities from the investment company is Collateralized Fully.

(b) *Refunded Securities.* For purposes of section 5 of the Act, the acquisition of a Refunded Security is deemed to be an acquisition of the escrowed Government Securities.

(c) *Definitions.* As used in this rule:

(1) *Collateralized Fully* in the case of a repurchase agreement means that:

(i) The value of the securities collateralizing the repurchase agreement (reduced by the transaction costs (including loss of interest) that the investment company reasonably could expect to incur if the seller defaults) is, and during the entire term of the repurchase agreement remains, at least equal to the Resale Price provided in the agreement;

(ii) The investment company has perfected its security interest in the collateral;

(iii) The collateral is maintained in an account of the investment company with its custodian or a third party that qualifies as a custodian under the Act;

(iv) The collateral consists entirely of:

(A) Cash items;

(B) Government Securities; or

(C) Securities that the investment company's board of directors, or its delegate, determines at the time the repurchase agreement is entered into:

(1) Each issuer of which has an exceptionally strong capacity to meet its financial obligations; and

NOTE TO PARAGRAPH (c)(1)(iv)(C)*(1)*: For a discussion of the phrase "exceptionally strong capacity to meet its financial obligations" see Investment Company Act Release No. 30847, (December 27, 2013).

(2) Are sufficiently liquid that they can be sold at approximately their carrying value in the ordinary course of business within seven calendar days; and

(v) Upon an Event of Insolvency with respect to the seller, the repurchase agreement would qualify under a provision of applicable insolvency law providing an exclusion from any automatic stay of creditors' rights against the seller.

(2) *Event of Insolvency* means, with respect to a person:

(i) An admission of insolvency, the application by the person for the appointment of a trustee, receiver, rehabilitator, or similar officer for all or substantially all of its assets, a general assignment for the benefit of creditors, the filing by the person of a voluntary petition in bankruptcy or application for reorganization or an arrangement with creditors; or

(ii) The institution of similar proceedings by another person which proceedings are not contested by the person; or

(iii) The institution of similar proceedings by a government agency responsible for regulating the activities of the person, whether or not contested by the person.

(3) *Government Security* means any "Government Security" as defined in section 2(a)(16) of the Act.

(4) *Issuer*, as used in paragraph (c)(1)(iv)(C)*(1)* of this section, means the issuer of a collateral security or the issuer of an unconditional obligation of a person other than the issuer of the collateral security to undertake to pay, upon presentment by the holder of the obligation (if required), the principal amount of the underlying collateral security plus accrued interest when due or upon default.

(5) *Refunded Security* means a debt security the principal and interest payments of which are to be paid by Government Securities ("deposited securities") that have been irrevocably placed in an escrow account pursuant to an agreement between the issuer of the debt security and an escrow agent that is not an "affiliated person," as defined in section 2(a)(3)(C) of the Act, of the issuer of the debt security, and, in accordance with such escrow agreement, are pledged only to the payment of the debt security and, to the extent that excess proceeds are available after all payments of principal, interest, and applicable premiums on the Refunded Securities, the expenses of

the escrow agent and, thereafter, to the issuer or another party; *provided* that:

(i) The deposited securities are not redeemable prior to their final maturity;

(ii) The escrow agreement prohibits the substitution of the deposited securities unless the substituted securities are Government Securities; and

(iii) At the time the deposited securities are placed in the escrow account, or at the time a substitution of the deposited securities is made, an independent certified public accountant has certified to the escrow agent that the deposited securities will satisfy all scheduled payments of principal, interest and applicable premiums on the Refunded Securities.

(6) *Resale Price* means the acquisition price paid to the seller of the securities plus the accrued resale premium on such acquisition price. The accrued resale premium is the amount specified in the repurchase agreement or the daily amortization of the difference between the acquisition price and the resale price specified in the repurchase agreement.

Rule 6a–5. Purchase of certain debt securities by companies relying on Section 6(a)(5) of the Act

For purposes of reliance on the exemption for certain companies under section 6(a)(5)(A) of the Act, a company shall be deemed to have met the requirement for credit-worthiness of certain debt securities under section 6(a)(5)(A)(iv)(I) of the Investment Company Act if, at the time of purchase, the board of directors (or its delegate) determines or members of the company (or their delegate) determine that the debt security is:

(a) Subject to no greater than moderate credit risk; and

(b) Sufficiently liquid that it can be sold at or near its carrying value within a reasonably short period of time.

Rule 6b–1. Exemption of employees' securities company pending determination of application

Any employees' securities company which files an application for an order of exemption under section 6(b) of the Act (54 Stat. 801; 15 U.S.C. 80a–6) shall be exempt, pending final determination of such application by the Commission, from all provisions of the act applicable to investment companies as such.

Rule 6c–3. Exemptions for certain registered variable life insurance separate accounts

A separate account which meets the requirements of paragraph (a) of Rule 6e–2 or paragraph (a) of Rule 6e–3(T) and registers as an investment company under section 8(a) of the Act, and the investment adviser, principal underwriter and depositor of such separate account, shall be exempt from the provisions of the Act specified in paragraph (b) of Rule 6e–2 or paragraph (b) of Rule 6e–3(T), except for sections 7 and 8(a) of the Act, under the same terms and conditions as a separate account claiming exemption under Rule 6e–2 or Rule 6e–2(T).

Rule 6c–6. Exemption for certain registered separate accounts and other persons

(a) As used in this rule,

(1) *Revenue Ruling* shall mean Revenue Ruling 81–225, 1981–41 I.R.B. (October 13, 1981), issued by the Internal Revenue Service on September 25, 1981.

(2) *Existing separate account* shall mean a separate account which is, or is a part of, a unit investment trust registered under the Act, engaged in a continuous offering of its securities on September 25, 1981.

(3) *Existing portfolio company* shall mean a registered open-end management investment company, engaged in a continuous offering of its securities on September 25, 1981, all or part of whose securities were owned by an existing separate account on September 25, 1981.

(4) *New portfolio company* shall mean any registered open-end management investment company the shares of which will be sold to one or more registered separate accounts for the purpose of minimizing the impact of the Revenue Ruling on the contractowners of an existing separate account, which new portfolio company has the same

(i) Investment objectives,

(ii) Fundamental policies, and

(iii) Voting rights as the existing portfolio company and has an advisory fee schedule, including expenses assumed by the adviser, that is at least as advantageous to the new portfolio company as was the fee schedule of the existing portfolio company.

(5) *New separate account* shall mean a separate account which

(i) Is, or is a part of, a unit investment trust registered under the Act;

(ii) Is intended to minimize the impact of the Revenue Ruling on the contract-owners of an existing separate account;

(iii) Invests solely in one or more new portfolio companies;

(iv) Has the same

(A) Sales loads,

(B) Depositor, and

(C) Custodial arrangements

As the existing separate account; and

(v) Has

(A) Asset charges,

(B) Administrative fees, and

(C) Any other fees and charges (not including taxes) that correspond only to fees of the existing separate account and are no greater than those corresponding fees.

(b) Any order of the Commission under the Act, granted to an existing separate account on or before September 25, 1981, shall remain in full force and effect notwithstanding that the existing separate account invests in one or more new portfolio companies in lieu of, or in addition to, investing in one or more existing portfolio companies; *Provided,* That:

(1) No material changes in the facts upon which the order was based have occurred;

(2) All representations, undertakings, and conditions made or agreed to by the existing separate account, and any other person or persons, other than any existing portfolio company, in connection with the issuance of the order are, and continue to be, applicable to the existing separate account and any such other person or persons, unless modified in accordance with this rule;

(3) All representations, undertakings, and conditions made or agreed to by the existing portfolio company in connection with the issuance of the order are made or agreed to by the new portfolio company, unless modified in accordance with this rule; and

(4) Part II of the Registration Statement under the Securities Act of 1933 of the existing separate account

(i) Indicates that the existing separate account is relying upon paragraph (b) of this rule,

(ii) Lists the Investment Company Act release numbers of any orders upon which the existing separate account intends to rely, and

(iii) Contains a representation that the provisions of this paragraph (b) have been complied with.

(c) Any order of the Commission under the Act, granted to an existing separate account on or before September 25, 1981, shall apply with full force and effect to a new separate account and the depositor of and principal underwriter for the new separate account notwithstanding that the new separate account invests in one or more new portfolio companies; *Provided,* That:

(1) No material changes in the facts upon which the order was based have occurred;

(2) All representations, undertakings, and conditions made or agreed to by the depositor, principal underwriter, and any other person or persons other than the existing separate account or any existing portfolio companies, in connection with the issuance of the order are, and continue to be, applicable to such depositor, principal underwriter, and other person or persons, unless modified in accordance with this rule;

(3) All representations, undertakings, and conditions made or agreed to by the existing separate account in connection with the issuance of the order are made or agreed to by the new separate account, unless modified in accordance with this rule;

(4) All representations, undertakings, and conditions made or agreed to by an existing portfolio company in connection with the issuance of the order are made or agreed to by the new portfolio company, unless modified in accordance with this rule; and

(5) Part II of the Registration Statement under the Securities Act of 1933 of the new separate account

(i) Indicates that the new separate account is relying upon paragraph (c) of this rule,

(ii) Lists the Investment Company Act release numbers of any orders upon which the new separate account intends to rely, and

(iii) Contains a representation that the provisions of this paragraph (c) have been complied with.

(d) Any affiliated person or depositor of or principal underwriter for a new or existing separate account or any affiliated person of or principal underwriter for a new or existing portfolio company, and any affiliated person of such persons, principal underwriters, or depositor shall be exempt from section 17(d) of the Act and Rule 17d–1 thereunder to the extent necessary to permit the organization of one or more new portfolio companies; *Provided,* That, any expenses borne by the existing portfolio company or the new portfolio company in connection with such organization are necessary and appropriate and are allocated in a manner that is fair and reasonable to all of the shareholders of these companies.

(e) Any affiliated person or depositor of or principal underwriter for a new or existing separate account and any affiliated persons of such a person, principal underwriter, or depositor shall be exempt from section 17(d) of the Act and Rule 17d–1 thereunder to the extent necessary to permit such person to bear any reasonable expenses arising out of the organization of one or more new portfolio companies or the new separate account.

(f) Any affiliated persons or depositor of or principal underwriter for a new or existing separate account or any affiliated person of or principal underwriter for a new or existing portfolio company, and any affiliated person of such persons, principal underwriters, or depositor shall be exempt from section 17(a) and any existing portfolio company which has made an election pursuant to Rule 18f–1 shall be permitted to revoke that election to the extent necessary to permit transactions involving the transfer of assets from the existing portfolio company to a new portfolio company; *Provided,* That:

(1) Such assets are transferred without the imposition of any fees or charges;

(2) The board of directors of the existing portfolio company, including a majority of the directors of the company who are not interested persons of such company, determines that the transfer of assets is fair and reasonable to all shareholders of the company and such determination, and the basis upon which it was made, is recorded in the minute book of the existing portfolio company;

(3) Any securities involved are valued by the existing portfolio company for purposes of the transfer in accordance with its valuation practices for determining net asset value per share; and

(4) With respect to Rule 18f–1, the existing separate account requests that the existing portfolio company redeem in kind the shares of the portfolio company held by the separate account.

(g) The new portfolio company shall be exempt from section 2(a)(41) of the Act and Rules 2a–4 and 22c–1 under the Act to the extent necessary to permit it to use the same method of valuation for the purpose of pricing its shares for sale, redemption, and repurchase, as the existing portfolio company; *Provided,* That:

(1) The existing portfolio company had on September 25, 1981, an order of the Commission exempting it, for the purposes of pricing its shares for sale, redemption, and repurchase, from

(i) Section 2(a)(41) of the Act and Rules 2a–4 and 22c–1 under the Act to the extent necessary to permit it to use the amortized cost valuation method or

(ii) Rules 2a–4 and 22c–1 under the Act to the extent necessary to permit it to calculate its net asset value per share to the nearest one cent on share values of $1.00;

(2) All representations, undertakings, and conditions made or agreed to by the existing portfolio company in connection with the order are made or agreed to by the new portfolio company unless modified in accordance with this rule; and

(3) Part II of the Registration Statement under the Securities Act of 1933 of the new portfolio company

(i) Indicates that the new portfolio company is relying upon paragraph (g) of this rule,

(ii) Lists the Investment Company Act release numbers of any orders upon which the new portfolio company intends to rely, and

(iii) Contains a representation that the provisions of paragraph (g) have been complied with.

(h) The depositor or trustee of an existing separate account shall be exempt from section 26(c) of the Act to the extent necessary to permit the substitution of securities of the new portfolio company for securities of the existing portfolio company; *Provided,* That, within thirty days of such substitution:

(1) The existing separate account notifies all contractowners of the substitution of securities and any determinations of the board of directors of the new portfolio company required by paragraph (d) of this rule;

(2) The existing separate account delivers a copy of the prospectus of the new portfolio company to all contractowners; and

(3) The existing separate account, concurrently with the notification referred to in paragraph (h)(1) of this rule or the delivery of the prospectus of the new portfolio company referred to in paragraph (h)(2) of this rule, whichever is later, offers to those contractowners who would otherwise have surrender rights under their contracts the right, for a period of at least thirty days from the receipt of this offer, to surrender their contracts without the imposition of any withdrawal charge or contingent deferred sales load, and any surrendering contractowner receives the price next determined after the request for surrender is received by the insurance company.

(i) The existing separate account shall be exempt from section 22(d) of the Act to the extent necessary to permit it to comply with paragraph (h) of this rule and the principal underwriter for or depositor of the existing separate account shall be exempt from section 26(a)(4)(B) of the Act to the extent necessary to permit them to rely on paragraph (h) of this rule.

(j) Notwithstanding section 11 of the Act, the existing separate account or any principal underwriter for the existing separate account may make or cause to be made to the contract-owners of the existing separate account an offer to exchange a security funded by an existing portfolio company for a security funded by a new portfolio company without the terms of that offer having first been submitted to and approved by the Commission; *Provided,* That the exchange is to be made on the basis of the relative net asset values of the securities to be exchanged without the imposition of any fees or charges.

(k) Notwithstanding section 11 of the Act, the new separate account or any principal underwriter for the new separate account may make or cause to be made an offer to the contractowners of the existing separate account to exchange their securities for securities of the new separate account without the terms of that offer having first been submitted to and approved by the Commission; *Provided,* That:

(1) The exchange is to be made on the basis of the relative net asset values of the securities to be exchanged without the imposition of any fees or charges; and

(2) If the new separate account imposes a contingent deferred sales load ("sales load") on the securities to be acquired in the exchange

(i) At the time this sales load is imposed, it is calculated as if

(A) The contractowner had been a contractowner of the new separate account from the date on which he became a contractowner of the existing separate account, in the case of a sales load based on the amount of time the contractowner has been invested in the new separate account, and

(B) Amounts attributable to purchase payments made to the existing separate account had been made to the new separate account on the date on which they were made to the existing separate account, in the case of a sales load based on the amount of time purchased payments have been invested in the new separate account, and

(ii) The total sales load imposed does not exceed 9 percent of the sum of the purchase payments made to the new separate account and that portion of purchase payments made to the existing separate account attributable to the securities exchanged.

(*l*) Notwithstanding the foregoing, the provisions of this rule will be available to a new separate account or new portfolio company, or to any affiliated person or depositor of or principal underwriter for such a new separate account, to any affiliated person of or principal underwriter for such a new portfolio company, to any affiliated person of such persons, depositor, or principal underwriters, or to any substitution of securities effected in reliance on this section, only if such new separate account or new portfolio company is registered under the Act or such substitution is effected prior to September 21, 1983.

Rule 6c–7. Exemptions from certain provisions of Sections 22(e) and 27 for registered separate accounts offering variable annuity contracts to participants in the Texas Optional Retirement Program

A registered separate account, and any depositor of or underwriter for such account, shall be exempt from the provisions of sections 22(e), 27(c)(1), and 27(d) of the Act with respect to any variable annuity contract participating in such account to the extent necessary to permit compliance with the Texas Optional Retirement Program ("Program"), *Provided,* That the separate account, depositor, or underwriter for such account:

(a) Includes appropriate disclosure regarding the restrictions on redemption imposed by the Program in each registration statement, including the prospectus, used in connection with the Program;

(b) Includes appropriate disclosure regarding the restrictions on redemption imposed by the Program in any sales literature used in connection with the offer of annuity contracts to potential Program participants;

(c) Instructs salespeople who solicit Program participants to purchase annuity contracts specifically to bring the restrictions on redemption imposed by the Program to the attention of potential Program participants;

(d) Obtains from each Program participant who purchases an annuity contract in connection with the Program, prior to or at the time of such purchase, a signed statement acknowledging the restrictions on redemption imposed by the Program; and

(e) Includes in Part II of the separate account's registration statement under the Securities Act of 1933 a representation that this section is being relied upon and that the provisions of paragraphs (a)–(d) of this rule have been complied with.

Rule 6c–8. Exemptions for registered separate accounts to impose a deferred sales load and to deduct certain administrative charges

(a) As used in this rule *Deferred sales load* shall mean any sales load, including a contingent deferred sales load, that is deducted upon redemption or annuitization of amounts representing all or a portion of a securityholder's interest in a registered separate account.

(b) A registered separate account, and any depositor of or principal underwriter for such account, shall be exempt from the provisions of sections 2(a)(32), 2(a)(35), 22(c), 26(a)(2)(C), 27(c)(1), 27(c)(2), and 27(d) of the Act and rule 22c–1 under the Act to the extent necessary to permit them to impose a deferred sales load on any variable annuity contract participating in such account, *Provided,* That:

(1) The amount of any such sales load imposed, when added to any sales load previously paid on such contract, shall not exceed 9 percent of purchase payments made to date for such contract; and

(2) The terms of any offer to exchange another contract for the contract are in compliance with the requirements of paragraph (d) or (e) of Rule 11a–2 under the Act.

(c) A registered separate account, and any depositor of or principal underwriter for such account, shall be exempt from sections 2(a)(32), 22(c), 27(c)(1), and 27(d) of the Act and Rule 22c–1 under the Act to the extent necessary to permit them to deduct from the value of any variable annuity contract participating in such account, upon total redemption of the contract prior to the last day of the year, the full annual fee for administrative services that otherwise would have been deducted on that date.

Rule 6c–10. Exemption for certain open-end management investment companies to impose deferred sales loads

(a) A company and any exempted person shall be exempt from the provisions of sections 2(a)(32), 2(a)(35), and 22(d) of the Act and Rule 22c–1 to the extent necessary to permit a deferred sales load to be imposed on shares issued by the company, *Provided,* That:

(1) The amount of the deferred sales load does not exceed a specified percentage of the net asset value or the offering price at the time of purchase;

(2) The terms of the deferred sales load are covered by the provisions of Rule 2830 of the Conduct Rules of the National Association of Securities Dealers, Inc.; and

(3) The same deferred sales load is imposed on all shareholders, except that scheduled variations in or elimination of a deferred sales load may be offered to a particular class of shareholders or transactions, *Provided,* that the conditions in Rule 22d–1 are satisfied. Nothing in this paragraph (a) shall prevent a company from offering to existing shareholders a new scheduled variation that would waive or reduce the amount of a deferred sales load not yet paid.

(b) For purposes of this rule:

(1) *Company* means a registered open-end management investment company, other than a registered separate account, and includes a separate series of the company;

(2) *Exempted person* means any principal underwriter of, dealer in, and any other person authorized to consummate transactions in, securities issued by a company; and

(3) *Deferred sales load* means any amount properly chargeable to sales or promotional expenses that is paid by a shareholder after purchase but before or upon redemption.

Rule 6d–1. Exemption for certain closed-end investment companies

(a) An application under section 6(d) of the Act shall contain the following information:

(1) A brief description of the character of the business and investment policy of the applicant.

(2) The information relied upon by the applicant to satisfy the conditions of paragraphs (1) and (2) of section 6(d) of the Act.

(3) The number of holders of each class of the applicant's outstanding securities.

(4) An unconsolidated balance sheet as of a date not earlier than the end of the applicant's first fiscal year, together with a schedule specifying the title, the amount, the book value and, if determinable, the market value of each security in the applicant's portfolio.

(5) An unconsolidated profit and loss statement for the applicant's last fiscal year.

(6) A statement of each provision of the act from which the applicant seeks exemption, together with a statement of the facts by reason of which, in the applicant's opinion, such exemption is not contrary to the public interest or inconsistent with the protection of investors.

(b) There shall be attached to each copy of the application a copy of Form N–8A. The form need not be executed, but it shall be clearly marked on its facing page as an exhibit to the application. The filing of Form N–8A in this manner shall not be construed as the filing of a notification of registration under section 8(a) of the act.

(c) The application may contain any additional information which the applicant desires to submit.

Rule 6e–2. Exemptions for certain variable life insurance separate accounts

(a) A separate account, and the investment adviser, principal underwriter and depositor of such separate account, shall, except for the exemptions provided in paragraph (b) of this Rule 6e–2, be subject to all provisions of the Act and rules and regulations promulgated thereunder as though such separate account were a registered investment company issuing periodic payment plan certificates if:

(1) Such separate account is established and maintained by a life insurance company pursuant to the insurance laws or code of (i) any state or territory of the United States or the District of Columbia, or (ii) Canada or any province thereof, if it complies to the extent necessary with Rule 7d–1 under the Act;

(2) The assets of the separate account are derived solely from the sale of variable life insurance contracts as defined in paragraph (c)(1) of this Rule 6e–2, and advances made by the life insurance company which established and maintains the separate account ("life insurer") in connection with the operation of such separate account;

(3) The separate account is not used for variable annuity contracts or for funds corresponding to dividend accumulations or other contract liabilities not involving life contingencies;

(4) The income, gains and losses, whether or not realized, from assets allocated to such separate account, are, in accordance with the applicable variable life insurance contract, credited to or charged against such account without regard to other income, gains or losses of the life insurer;

(5) The separate account is legally segregated, and that portion of its assets having a value equal to, or approximately equal to, the reserves and other contract liabilities with respect to such separate account are not chargeable with liabilities arising out of any other business that the life insurer may conduct;

(6) The assets of the separate account have, at each time during the year that adjustments in the reserves are made, a value at least equal to the reserves and other contract liabilities with respect to such separate account, and at all other times, except pursuant to an order of the Commission, have a value approximately equal to or in excess of such reserves and liabilities; and

(7) The investment adviser of the separate account is registered under the Investment Advisers Act of 1940.

(b) If a separate account meets the requirements of paragraph (a) of this section, then such separate account and the other persons described in paragraph (a) of this section shall be exempt from the provisions of the Act as follows:

(1) Section 2(a)(35): *Provided, however,* That the term "sales load," as used in the Act and rules and regulations thereunder, shall have the meaning set forth in paragraph (c)(4) of this rule.

(2) Section 7.

(3) Section 8 to the extent that:

(i) For purposes of paragraph (a) of section 8, the separate account shall file with the Commission a notification on Form N–6EI–1 which identifies such separate account; and

(ii) For purposes of paragraph (b) of section 8, the separate account shall file with the Commission a form to be designated by the Commission within ninety days after filing the notification on Form N–6EI–1: *Provided, however,* That if the fiscal year of the separate account ends within this ninety day period the form may be filed within ninety days after the end of such fiscal year.

(4) Section 9 to the extent that:

(i) The eligibility restrictions of section 9(a) of the Act shall not be applicable to those persons who are officers, directors and employees of the life insurer or its affiliates who do not participate directly in the management or administration of the separate account or in the sale of variable life insurance contracts funded by such separate account; and

(ii) A life insurer shall be ineligible pursuant to paragraph (3) of section 9(a) of the Act to serve as investment adviser, depositor of or principal underwriter for a variable life insurance separate account only if an affiliated person of such life insurer, ineligible by reason of paragraph (1) or (2) of section 9(a), participates directly in the management or administration of the separate account or in the sale of variable life insurance contracts funded by such separate account.

(5) Section 13(a) to the extent that:

(i) An insurance regulatory authority may require pursuant to insurance law or regulation that the separate account make (or refrain from making) certain investments which would result in changes in the sub-classification or investment policies of the separate account;

(ii) Changes in the investment policy of the separate account initiated by contractholders or the board of directors of the separate account may be disapproved by the life insurer, provided that such disapproval is reasonable and is based upon a determination by the life insurer in good faith that:

(A) Such change would be contrary to state law; or

(B) Such change would be inconsistent with the investment objectives of the separate account or would result in the purchase of securities for the separate account which vary from the general quality and nature of investments and investment techniques utilized by other separate accounts of the life insurer or of an affiliated life insurance company, which separate accounts have investment objectives similar to the separate account;

(iii) Any action taken in accordance with paragraph (b)(5)(i) or (ii) of this section and the reasons therefor shall be disclosed in the proxy statement for the next meeting of variable life insurance contractholders of the separate account.

(6) Section 14(a): *Provided,* That until the separate account has total assets of at least $100,000 the life insurer shall have (i) a combined capital and surplus, if a stock company, or (ii) an unassigned surplus, if a mutual company, of not less than $1,000,000 as set forth in the balance sheet of such life insurer contained in the registration statement, or any amendment thereto, relating to variable life insurance contracts funded by such separate account filed pursuant to the Securities Act of 1933, as amended.

(7)(i) Section 15(a) to the extent this section requires that the initial written contract pursuant to which the investment adviser serves or acts shall have been approved by the vote of a majority of the outstanding voting securities of the registered company: *Provided,* That:

(A) Such investment adviser is selected and a written contract is entered into before the effective date of the registration statement under the Securities Act of 1933, as amended, for variable life insurance contracts which are funded by the separate account, and that the terms of the contract are fully disclosed in such registration statement, and

(B) A written contract is submitted to a vote of variable life insurance contractholders at their first meeting after the effective date of the registration statement under the Securities Act of 1933, as amended, on condition that such meeting shall take place within one year after such effective date, unless the time for the holding of such meeting shall be extended by the Commission upon written request for good cause shown;

(ii) Sections 15(a), (b) and (c) to the extent that:

(A) An insurance regulatory authority may disapprove pursuant to insurance law or regulation any contract between the separate account and an investment adviser or principal underwriter;

(B) Changes in the principal underwriter for the separate account initiated by contractholders or the board of directors of the separate account may be disapproved by the life insurer: *Provided,* That such disapproval is reasonable;

(C) Changes in the investment adviser of the separate account initiated by contractholders or the board of directors of the separate account may be disapproved by the life insurer: *Provided,* That such disapproval is reasonable and is based upon a determination by the life insurer in good faith that:

(*1*) The rate of the proposed investment advisory fee will exceed the maximum rate that is permitted to be charged against the assets of the separate account for such services as specified by any variable life insurance contract funded by such separate account; or

(*2*) The proposed investment adviser may be expected to employ investment techniques which vary from the general techniques utilized by the current investment adviser to the separate account, or advise the purchase or sale of securities which would be inconsistent with the investment objectives of the separate account, or which would vary from the quality and nature of investments made by other separate accounts of the life insurer or of an affiliated life insurance company, which separate accounts have investment objectives similar to the separate account;

(D) Any action taken in accordance with paragraph (b)(7)(ii)(A), (B) or (C) of this rule and the reasons therefor shall be disclosed in the proxy statement for the next meeting of variable life insurance contractholders of the separate account.

(8) Section 16(a) to the extent that:

(i) Persons serving as directors of the separate account prior to the first meeting of such account's variable life insurance contractholders are exempt from the requirement of section 16(a) of the Act that such persons be elected by the holders of outstanding voting securities of such account at an annual or special meeting called for that purpose, *Provided,* That:

(A) Such persons have been appointed directors of such account by the life insurer before the effective date of the registration statement under the Securities Act of 1933, as amended, for variable life insurance contracts which are funded by the separate account and are identified in such registration statement (or are replacements appointed by the life insurer for any such persons who have become unable to serve as directors), and

(B) An election of directors for such account shall be held at the first meeting of variable life insurance contractholders after the effective date of the registration statement under the Securities Act of 1933, as amended, relating to contracts funded by such account, which meeting shall take place within one year after such effective date, unless the time for holding such meeting shall be extended by the Commission upon written request for good cause shown;

(ii) A member of the board of directors of such separate account may be disapproved or removed by the appropriate insurance regulatory authority if such person is ineligible to serve as a director of the separate account pursuant to insurance law or regulation of the jurisdiction in which the life insurer is domiciled.

(9) Section 17(f) to the extent that the securities and similar investments of the separate account may be maintained in the custody of the life insurer or an insurance company which is an affiliated person of such life insurer: *Provided,* That:

(i) The securities and similar investments allocated to such separate account are clearly identified as to ownership by such account, and such securities and similar investments are maintained in the vault of an insurance company which meets the qualifications set forth in paragraph (b)(9)(ii) of this rule, and whose procedures and activities with respect to such safekeeping function are supervised by the insurance regulatory authorities of the jurisdiction in which the securities and similar investments will be held;

(ii) The insurance company maintaining such investments must file with an insurance regulatory authority of a state or territory of the United States or the District of Columbia an annual statement of its financial condition in the form prescribed by the National Association of Insurance Commissioners, must be subject to supervision and inspection by such authority and must be examined periodically as to its financial condition and other affairs by such authority, must hold the securities and similar investments of the separate account in its vault, which vault must be equivalent to that of a bank which is a member of the Federal Reserve System, and must have a combined capital and surplus, if a stock company, or an unassigned surplus, if a mutual company, of not less than $1,000,000 as set forth in its most recent annual statement filed with such authority;

(iii) Access to such securities and similar investments shall be limited to employees of or agents authorized by the Commission, representatives of insurance regulatory authorities, independent public accountants for the separate account, accountants for the life insurer and to no more than 20 persons authorized pursuant to a resolution of the board of directors of the separate account, which persons shall be directors of the separate account, officers and responsible employees of the life insurer or officers and responsible employees of the affiliated insurance company in whose vault such investments are maintained (if applicable), and access to such securities and similar investments shall be had only by two or more such persons jointly, at least one of whom shall be a director of the separate account or officer of the life insurer;

(iv) The requirement in paragraph (b)(9)(i) of this rule that the securities and similar investments of the separate account be maintained in the vault of a qualified insurance company shall not apply to securities deposited with insurance regulatory authorities or deposited in a system for the central handling of securities established by a national securities exchange or national securities association registered with the Commission under the Securities Exchange Act of 1934, as amended, or such person as may be permitted by the Commission, or to securities on loan which are collateralized to the extent of their full market value, or to securities hypothecated, pledged, or placed in escrow for the account of such separate account in connection with a loan or other transaction authorized by specific resolution of the board of directors of the separate account, or to securities in transit in connection with the sale, exchange, redemption, maturity or conversion, the exercise of warrants or rights, assents to changes in terms of the securities, or to other transactions necessary or appropriate in the ordinary course of business relating to the management of securities;

(v) Each person when depositing such securities or similar investments in or withdrawing them from the depository or when ordering their withdrawal and delivery from the custody of the life insurer or affiliated insurance company, shall sign a notation in respect of such deposit, withdrawal or order which shall show (A) the date and time of the deposit, withdrawal or order, (B) the title and amount of the securities or other investments deposited, withdrawn or ordered to be withdrawn, and an identification thereof by certificate numbers or otherwise, (C) the manner of acquisition of the securities or similar investments deposited or the purpose for which they have been withdrawn, or ordered to be withdrawn, and (D) if withdrawn and delivered to another person the name of such person. Such notation shall be transmitted promptly to an officer or director of the separate account or the life insurer designated by the board of directors of the separate account who shall not be a person designated for the purpose of paragraph (b)(9)(iii) of this rule. Such notation shall be on serially numbered forms and shall be preserved for at least one year;

(vi) Such securities and similar investments shall be verified by complete examination by an independent public accountant retained by the separate account at least three times during each fiscal year, at least two of which shall be chosen by such accountant without prior notice to such separate account. A certificate of such accountant stating that he has made an examination of such securities and investments and describing the nature and extent of the examination shall be transmitted to the Commission by the accountant promptly after each examination;

(vii) Securities and similar investments of a separate account maintained with a bank or other company whose functions and physical facilities are supervised by federal or state authorities pursuant to any arrangement whereby the directors, officers, employees or agents of the separate account or the life insurer are authorized or permitted to withdraw such investments upon their mere receipt are deemed to be in the custody of the life insurer and shall be exempt from the requirements of section 17(f) so long as the arrangement complies with all provisions of this paragraph (b)(9), except that such securities will be maintained in the vault of a bank or other company rather than the vault of an insurance company.

(10) Section 18(i) to the extent that:

(i) For the purposes of any section of the Act which provides for the vote of securityholders on matters relating to the investment company:

(A) Variable life insurance contractholders shall have one vote for each $100 of cash value funded by the separate account, with fractional votes allocated for amounts less than $100;

(B) The life insurer shall have one vote for each $100 of assets of the separate account not otherwise attributable to contractholders pursuant to paragraph (b)(10)(i)(A) of this section, with fractional votes allocated for amounts less than $100: *Provided,* That after the commencement of sales of variable life insurance contracts funded by the separate account, the life insurer shall cast its votes for and against each matter which may be voted upon by contractholders in the same proportion as the votes cast by contractholders; and

(C) The number of votes to be allocated shall be determined as of a record date not more than 90 days prior to any meeting at which such vote is held: *Provided,* That if a quorum is not present at the meeting, the meeting may be adjourned for up to 60 days without fixing a new record date;

(ii) The requirement of this section that every share of stock issued by a registered management investment company (except a common-law trust of the character described in section 16(b)) shall be a voting stock and have equal voting rights with every other outstanding voting stock shall not be deemed to be violated by actions specifically permitted by any provision of this rule.

(11) Section 19 to the extent that the provisions of this section shall not be applicable to any dividend or similar distribution paid or payable pursuant to provisions of participating variable life insurance contracts.

(12) Sections 22(d), 22(e), and 27(c)(1) and Rule 22c–1 promulgated under section 22(c) to the extent:

(i) That the amount payable on death and the cash surrender value of each variable life insurance contract shall be determined on each day during which the New York Stock Exchange is open for trading, not less frequently than once daily as of the time of the close of trading on such exchange: *Provided,* That the amount payable on death need not be determined more than once each contract month if such determination does not reduce the participation of the contract in the investment experience of the separate account: *Provided further, however,* That if the net valuation premium for such contract is transferred at least annually, then the amount payable on death need be determined only when such net premium is transferred;

(ii) Necessary for compliance with this Rule 6e–2 or with insurance laws and regulations and established administrative procedures of the life insurer with respect to issuance, transfer and redemption procedures for variable life insurance contracts funded by the separate account including, but not limited to, premium rate structure and premium processing, insurance underwriting standards, and the particular benefit afforded by the contract: *Provided, however,* That any procedure or action shall be reasonable, fair and not discriminatory to the interests of the affected contractholder and to all other holders of contracts of the same class or series funded by the separate account: *And, further provided,* That any such action shall be disclosed in the form required to be filed by the separate account with the Commission pursuant to paragraph (b)(3)(ii) of this Rule 6e–2.

(13) Section 27 to the following extent:

(i) Sections 27(a)(1) and 27(h)(1) to the extent that the sales load, as defined in paragraph (c)(4) of this section, on any variable life insurance contract which is funded by the separate account shall not exceed 9 per centum of the payments to be made thereon during the period equal to the lesser of 20 years or the anticipated life expectancy of the insured named in the contract based on the 1958 Commissioners Standard Ordinary Mortality Table;

(ii) Sections 27(a)(3) and 27(h)(3): *Provided,* That the proportionate amount of sales load deducted from any payment during the contract period shall not exceed the proportionate amount deducted from any prior payment during the contract period except that such amount may exceed the amount deducted from a prior payment if the increase is caused by the grading of cash values into reserves or reductions in the annual cost of insurance;

(iii) Sections 27(c)(2), 26(a)(1) and 26(a)(2): *Provided,* That the life insurer complies, to the extent applicable, with all other provisions of section 26 as if it were a trustee, depositor or custodian for the separate account, and:

(A) Files with the insurance regulatory authority of a state or territory of the United States or of the District of Columbia an annual statement of its financial condition in the form prescribed by the National Association of Insurance Commissioners, which most recent statement indicates that it has a combined capital and surplus, if a stock company, or an unassigned surplus, if a mutual company, of not less than $1,000,000;

(B) Is examined from time to time by the insurance regulatory authority of such state, territory or District of Columbia as to its financial condition and other affairs and is subject to supervision and inspection with respect to its separate account operations; and

(C) Limits the fees for administrative services to amounts that are reasonable in relation to services rendered and expenses incurred. The Commission shall retain jurisdiction regarding the determination of such fees;

(iv) Section 27(c)(1) and section 27(d), to the extent that such sections require that the variable life insurance contract be redeemable or provide for a refund in cash: *Provided,* That such contract provides for election by the contractholder of a cash surrender value or certain non-forfeiture and settlement options which are required or permitted by the insurance law or regulation of the jurisdiction in which the contract is offered: *And further provided,* That unless required by the insurance law or regulation of the jurisdiction in which the contract is offered or unless elected by the contractholder, such contract shall not provide for the automatic imposition of any option, including, but not limited to, an automatic premium loan, which would involve the accrual or payment of an interest or similar charge;

(v) Section 27(d): *Provided,* That the variable life insurance contract gives the holder thereof the right to:

(A) Surrender the contract at any time during the first 24 months after issuance and receive in cash an amount not less than the sum of the present value of his contract which is the cash surrender value next computed after receipt by the life insurer of the request for surrender in proper form, plus, depending upon the period over which such contract has been retained by the contractholder, an amount which is a refund of any excess paid for sales loading prior to surrender: *Provided, however,* That if payments for the contract have not been duly paid on the date the request for surrender is received by the life insurer, and if the sum of the cash surrender value and the amount of any excess sales loading which would otherwise be refundable in cash were applied to provide (without sales loading) a non-forfeiture benefit in accordance with the contract, then the contractholder shall be entitled to receive in cash the present value, next computed after receipt by the life insurer of the request for surrender in proper form, of any non-forfeiture benefit then in force. The amount of sales loading to be refunded shall be equal to that part of the excess paid for sales loading which is over the sum of 30 per centum of payments made for the first contract year plus 10 per centum of the payments made for the second contract year; and

(B) Convert the contract at any time during the first 24 months after issuance so long as payments are duly made to a life insurance policy on the life of the insured which provides for fixed death benefits and cash surrender values pursuant to a plan of insurance specified in the contract issued by the life insurer, or by a life insurance company affiliated with such insurer, which provides for the same initial amount of insurance as the variable life insurance contract and premiums which are based on the same issue age and risk classification of the insured as the variable life insurance contract, which conversion shall be subject to an equitable adjustment in payments and cash values to reflect variances, if any, in the payments and cash values under the original contract and the new policy: *Provided,* That the method of computing such adjustment shall be filed with the Commission as an exhibit to the form required pursuant to paragraph (b)(3)(ii) of this rule;

(vi) A depositor or principal underwriter for a variable life insurance contract sold subject to section 27(d) or section 27(f) of the Act, or both, shall be exempt from the requirements of Rule 27d–1 if an insurance company undertakes in writing to guarantee the performance of all obligations of such depositor or principal underwriter under sections 27(d) and 27(f) of the Act to refund charges and such insurance company, depositor and principal underwriter comply with all provisions of Rule 27d–2;

(vii) Section 27(e) and Rule 27e–1 thereunder to the extent that the separate account and the depositor and principal underwriter therefor, when such persons are subject to paragraph (b)(13)(v) of this rule, are required to provide a notice of right of withdrawal and refund to holders of variable life insurance contracts, if the life insurer or a duly authorized agent provides a notice of withdrawal and refund rights on Form N–27I–1, to the holder of any variable life insurance contract under which a refund may be available, provided that such notice shall be sent by first class mail to the contractholder:

(A) At issuance of the variable life insurance contract, which notice may be sent together with the issued variable life insurance contract and an illustration, in a form appropriate for inclusion in the prospectus for the variable life insurance contract, of gross annual payments, death benefits and cash surrender values applicable to the age, sex and underwriting classification of the insured; and

(B) If the contractholder has failed to make a payment prior to the expiration of the refund right provided by paragraph (b)(13)(v) of this rule and the contract has not been reinstated within 30 days following the expiration of the grace period provided in the variable life insurance contract for making of any payment due: *Provided, however,* In any event, if a payment is not made when due such notice shall be sent not less than 15 days prior to the expiration of the refund right, which notice may be sent together with a notification that the payment is overdue or an offer to reinstate the contract;

(viii) Section 27(f) and Rule 27f–1: *Provided,* That:

(A) The contractholder may elect to return the contract within 45 days of the date of the execution of the application for insurance or within 10 days after receipt of the issued contract by the contractholder, or within 10 days after mailing of the notice of the right of withdrawal, whichever is later, and receive a refund of all payments made for such contract;

(B) A refund of all payments to redeeming contractholders will not in any way affect the interests in the separate account or the benefits of other variable life insurance contractholders;

(C) Notice of such withdrawal right and a statement of charges on Form N–27I–2 is sent by first class mail to the contractholder, which notice and statement may be accompanied by the variable life insurance contract and an illustration, in a form appropriate for inclusion in the prospectus for the variable life insurance contract, of payments, death benefits and cash surrender values applicable to the age, sex and underwriting classification of the insured;

(D) The contractholder, in conjunction with the notice of withdrawal right referred to in paragraph (b)(13)(viii)(C) of this rule, is provided with a form of request for refund of payments made, which form shall set forth;

(*1*) Instructions as to the manner in which a refund may be obtained including the address to which the request form should be mailed; and

(*2*) Spaces necessary to indicate the date of such request, the contract number and the signature of the contractholder; and

(E) Within 7 days from the receipt of such duly executed timely request for refund, the life insurer will refund in cash to the contractholder the entire amount of payments made on the contract;

(ix) Solely for purposes of paragraphs (b)(13)(v) and (b)(13)(viii) of this rule, the postmark date on the envelope containing the variable life insurance contract shall determine whether such contract has been submitted for surrender or conversion within the designated period.

(14) Section 32(a)(2): *Provided,* That:

(i) The independent public accountant is selected before the effective date of the registration statement under the Securities Act of 1933, as amended, for variable life insurance contracts which are funded by the separate account, and the identity of such accountant is disclosed in such registration statement, and

(ii) The selection of such accountant is submitted for ratification or rejection to variable life insurance contractholders at their first meeting after the effective date of the registration statement under the Securities Act of 1933, as amended, on condition that such meeting shall take place within one year after such effective date, unless the time for the holding of such meeting shall be extended by the Commission upon written request for good cause shown.

(15) If the separate account is organized as a unit investment trust, all the assets of which consist of the shares of one or more registered management investment companies which offer their shares exclusively to variable life insurance separate accounts of the life insurer or of any affiliated life insurance company:

(i) The eligibility restrictions of section 9(a) of the Act shall not be applicable to those persons who are officers, directors and employees of the life insurer or its affiliates who do not participate directly in the management or administration of any registered management investment company described above;

(ii) The life insurer shall be ineligible pursuant to paragraph (3) of section 9(a) of the Act to serve as investment adviser of or principal underwriter for any registered management investment company described in this paragraph (b)(15) only if an affiliated person of such life insurer, ineligible by reason of paragraphs (1) or (2) of section 9(a), participates in the management or administration of such company;

(iii) The life insurer may vote shares of the registered management investment companies held by the separate account without regard to instructions from contractholders of the separate account if such instructions would require such shares to be voted:

(A) To cause such companies to make (or refrain from making) certain investments which would result in changes in the sub-classification or investment objectives of such companies or to approve or disapprove any contract between such companies and an investment adviser when required to do so by an insurance regulatory authority subject to the provisions of paragraphs (b)(5)(i) and (b)(7)(ii)(A) of this rule; or

(B) In favor of changes in investment objectives, investment adviser of or principal underwriter for such companies subject to the provisions of paragraphs (b)(5)(ii) and (b)(7)(ii)(B) and (C) of this rule;

(iv) Any action taken in accordance with paragraph (b)(15)(iii)(A) or (B) of this section and the reasons therefor shall be disclosed in the next report to contractholders made pursuant to section 30(e) and Rule 30e–2;

(v) Any registered management investment company established by the insurer and described in this paragraph (b)(15) shall be exempt from Section 14(a) provided that until such company has total assets of at least $100,000 the life insurer shall have at least the minimum net worth prescribed in paragraph (b)(6) in this rule; and

(vi) Any registered management investment company established by the insurer and described in this paragraph (b)(15) shall be exempt from Sections 15(a), 16(a), and 32(a)(2) of the Act, to the extent prescribed by paragraphs (b)(7)(i), (b)(8)(i), and (b)(14), provided that such company complies with the conditions set forth in those paragraphs as if it were a separate account.

(c) When used in this rule:

(1) *Variable life insurance contract* means a contract of life insurance, subject to regulation under the insurance laws or code of every jurisdiction in which it is offered, funded by a separate account of a life insurer, which contract, so long as payments are duly paid in accordance with its terms, provides for:

(i) A death benefit and cash surrender value which vary to reflect the investment experience of the separate account;

(ii) An initial stated dollar amount of death benefit, and payment of a death benefit guaranteed by the life insurer to be at least equal to such stated amount; and

(iii) Assumption of the mortality and expense risks thereunder by the life insurer for which a charge against the assets of the separate account may be assessed. Such charge shall be disclosed in the prospectus and shall not be less than fifty per centum of the maximum charge for risk assumption as disclosed in the prospectus and as provided for in the contract.

(2) *Incidental insurance benefits* means insurance benefits provided pursuant to the variable life insurance contract, other than the minimum and variable death benefit, which do not vary in amount or duration in accordance with the investment performance of the separate account, and include, but are not limited to, accidental death and dismemberment benefits, disability income benefits, guaranteed insurability options, and family income or fixed benefit term riders.

(3) *Minimum death benefit* is the amount guaranteed by the life insurer to be paid pursuant to a variable life insurance contract in the event of the death of the insured without regard to the investment performance of the separate account funding the variable life insurance contract, if payments are duly made and if there are no outstanding loans, partial withdrawals or partial surrenders, but does not include any incidental insurance benefits.

(4) *Sales load* charged on any payment is the excess of the payment over the sum of the following:

(i) The amount of the cash value for the first contract year, if any, and the amount of the increase in the cash value for each subsequent contract year, that is attributable to payments made and not attributable to investment earnings;

(ii) The cost of insurance for the period for which the payment is made based on the 1958 Commissioners Standard Ordinary Mortality Table and the assumed investment rate specified in the contract;

(iii) A reasonable charge necessary to cover the risk assumed by the life insurer that the variable death benefit will be less than the guaranteed minimum death benefit;

(iv) Any administrative expenses or fees which are reasonable and in amounts not exceeding anticipated administrative expenses and fees not properly chargeable to sales or promotional activities;

(v) A deduction approximately equal to state premium taxes;

(vi) Any additional charge assessed if the insured does not meet standard underwriting requirements;

(vii) Any additional charge assessed specifically for any incidental insurance benefits which do not vary in relation to the performance of the separate account;

(viii) Any additional charge, in the nature of an interest or service charge or administrative fee, assessed when payments are made more frequently than annually;

(ix) For a participating variable life insurance contract, a deduction for dividends to be paid or credited in accordance with the dividend scale in effect on the issue date of the contract assuming a gross annual investment return for the separate account which funds such contract of 4 percent after deduction for any Federal income taxes, which deduction may be determined pursuant to either of the following methods, provided that the same method must be applied with respect to each payment under the contract:

(A) The actuarial level annual equivalent of dividends to be paid or credited over the period described in paragraph (b)(13)(i) of this rule, based upon the mortality, interest and lapse assumptions used in computing the dividend scale for such contract multiplied by the fraction of the contract year for which the payment is made; or

(B) That portion of the dividend to be paid for the contract year which does not depend on the making of additional payments.

(5) *Assumed investment rate* is the rate of investment return specified in the contract which would be required to be credited to a variable life insurance contract, after deduction of charges for Federal income taxes, investment management fees, portfolio transaction expenses and mortality and expense guarantees, to maintain the variable death benefit equal at all times to the amount of death benefit, other than incidental insurance benefits, which would be payable pursuant to the variable life insurance contract if the death benefit did not vary according to the investment experience of the separate account.

(6) *Variable death benefit* is the amount of death benefit, other than incidental insurance benefits, payable under a variable life insurance contract which varies to reflect the investment performance of the separate account, and which would be payable in the absence of the minimum death benefit.

(7) *Payment,* as used in paragraphs (b)(13)(i), (b)(13)(ii) and (b)(13)(v)(A) of this rule and in sections 27(a)(2) and 27(h)(2) solely with respect to

variable life insurance contracts, means the gross premium payment made less any portion of such gross premium charged for or attributable to the items specified in paragraphs (c)(4)(vi), (c)(4)(vii) and (c)(4)(viii) of this rule. "Payment," as used in any other section of the Rule, means the gross premiums paid or payable for the variable life insurance contract.

Rule 6e–3(T). Temporary exemptions for flexible premium variable life insurance separate accounts

(a) A separate account, and its investment adviser, principal underwriter and depositor, shall, except as provided in paragraph (b) of this rule, comply with all provisions of the Investment Company Act of 1940 and the rules under it that apply to a registered investment company issuing periodic payment play certificates if:

(1) It is a separate account within the meaning of section 2(a)(37) of the Act and is established and maintained by a life insurance company pursuant to the insurance laws or code of (i) any state or territory of the United States or the District of Columbia, or (ii) Canada or any province thereof, if it complies with Rule 7d–1 under the Act (the "life insurer");

(2) The assets of the separate account are derived solely from (i) the sale of flexible premium variable life insurance contracts ("flexible contracts") as defined in paragraph (c)(1) of this rule, (ii) the sale of scheduled premium variable life insurance contracts ("scheduled contracts") as defined in paragraph (c)(1) of Rule 6e–2 under the Act, (iii) funds corresponding to dividend accumulations with respect to such contracts, and (iv) advances made by the life insurer in connection with the operation of such separate account;

(3) The separate account is not used for variable annuity contracts or other contract liabilities not involving life contingencies;

(4) The separate account is legally segregated, and that part of its assets with a value approximately equal to the reserves and other contract liabilities for such separate account are not chargeable with liabilities arising from any other business of the life insurer;

(5) The value of the assets of the separate account, each time adjustments in the reserves are made, is at least equal to the reserves and other contract liabilities of the separate account, and at all other times approximately equals or exceeds the reserves and liabilities; and

(6) The investment adviser of the separate account is registered under the Investment Advisers Act of 1940.

(b) A separate account that meets the requirements of paragraph (a) of this rule, and its investment adviser, principal underwriter and depositor shall be exempt with respect to flexible contracts funded by the separate account from the following provisions of the Act:

(1) Section 2(a)(35), *Provided, however,* That the term "sales load," as used in the Act and rules under it, shall have the meaning set forth in paragraph (c)(4) of this rule. *And provided further,* That in connection with any sales load deducted pursuant to paragraph (d)(1) of this rule, the separate account and other persons shall be exempt from sections 2(a)(32), 12(b), 22(c), 26(a), 27(c)(1), 27(c)(2), and 27(d), and Rules 12b–1 and 22c–1.

(2) Section 7.

(3) Section 8, to the extent that:

(i) For purposes of paragraph (a) of section 8, the separate account filed with the Commission a notification on Form N–6EI–1 which identifies the separate account; and

(ii) For purposes of paragraph (b) of section 8, the separate account shall file with the Commission the form designated by the Commission within ninety days after filing the notification on Form N–6EI–1, *Provided, however,* That if the fiscal year of the separate account end within this ninety day period, the form may be filed within ninety days after the end of such fiscal year.

(4) Section 9, to the extent that:

(i) The eligibility restrictions of section 9(a) shall not apply to persons who are officers, directors or employees of the life insurer or its affiliates and who do not participate directly in the management or administration of the separate account or in the sale of flexible contracts; and

(ii) A life insurer shall be ineligible under paragraph (3) of section 9(a) to serve as investment adviser, depositor of or principal underwriter for the separate account only if an affiliated person of such life insurer, ineligible by reason of paragraphs (1) or (2) of section 9(a), participates directly in the management or administration of the separate account or in the sale of flexible contracts.

(5) Section 13(a), to the extent that:

(i) An insurance regulatory authority may require pursuant to insurance law or regulation that the separate account make (or refrain from making) certain investments which would result in changes in the sub-classification or investment policies of the separate account;

(ii) Changes in the investment policy of the separate account initiated by its contractholders or board of directors may be disapproved by the life insurer, if the disapproval is reasonable and is based on a good faith determination by the life insurer that:

(A) The change would violate state law; or

(B) The change would not be consistent with the investment objectives of the separate account or would result in the purchase of securities for the separate account which vary from the general quality and nature of investments and investment techniques used by other separate accounts of the life insurer or of an affiliated life insurance company with similar investment objectives;

(iii) Any action described in paragraph (b)(5)(i) or (ii) of this rule and the reasons for it shall be disclosed in the next communication to contractholders, but in no case, later than twelve months from the date of such action.

(6) Section 14(a), *Provided,* That until the separate account has total assets of at least $100,000, the life insurer shall have (i) a combined capital and surplus, if a stock company, or (ii) an unassigned surplus, if a mutual company, of not less than $1,000,000 as set forth in the balance sheet of such life insurer contained in the registration statement for flexible contracts filed under the Securities Act of 1933.

(7)(i) Section 15(a), to the extent it requires that the initial written contract with the investment adviser shall have been approved by the vote of a majority of the outstanding voting securities of the registered investment company, *Provided,* That:

(A) The investment adviser is selected and a written contract is entered into before the effective date of the 1933 Act registration statement for flexible contracts, and that the terms of the contract are fully disclosed in the registration statement, and

(B) A written contract is submitted to a vote of contractholders at their first meeting and within one year after the effective date of the 1933 Act registration statement, unless the Commission upon written request and for good cause shown extends the time for the holding of such meeting;

(ii) Sections 15(a), (b) and (c), to the extent that:

(A) An insurance regulatory authority may disapprove pursuant to insurance law or regulation any contract between the separate account and an investment adviser or principal underwriter;

(B) Changes in the principal underwriter for the separate account initiated by contractholders or the board of directors of the separate account may be disapproved by the life insurer, *Provided,* That such disapproval is reasonable;

(C) Changes in the investment adviser of the separate account initiated by contractholders or the board of directors of the separate account may be disapproved by the life insurer, *Provided,* That such disapproval is reasonable and is based on a good faith determination by the life insurer that:

(*1*) The proposed investment advisory fee will exceed the maximum rate specified in any flexible contract that may be charged against the assets of the separate account for such services; or

(*2*) The proposed investment adviser may be expected to employ investment techniques which vary from the general techniques used by the current investment adviser to the separate account, or advise the purchase or sale of securities which would not be consistent with the investment objectives of the separate account, or which would vary from the quality and nature of investments made by other separate accounts with similar investment objectives of the life insurer or an affiliated life insurance company;

(D) Any action described in paragraph (b)(7)(ii) (A), (B) or (C) of this rule and the reasons for it shall be disclosed in the next communication to contractholders, but in no case, later than twelve months from the date of such action.

(8) Section 16(a), to the extent that:

(i) Directors of the separate account serving before the first meeting of the account's contractholders are exempt from the requirement of section 16(a) that they be elected by the holders of outstanding voting securities of the account at an annual or special meeting called for that purpose, *Provided,* That:

(A) Such persons were appointed directors of the account by the life insurer before the effective date of the 1933 Act registration statement for flexible contracts and are identified in the registration statement (or are replacements appointed by the life insurer for any such persons who have become unable to serve as directors), and

(B) An election of directors for the account is held at the first meeting of contractholders and within one year after the effective date of the 1933 Act registration statement for flexible contracts, unless the time for holding the meeting is extended by the Commission upon written request and for good cause shown;

(ii) A member of the board of directors of the separate account may be disapproved or removed by an insurance regulatory authority if the person is not eligible to be a director of the separate account under the law of the life insurer's domicile.

(9) Section 17(f), to the extent that the securities and similar investments of a separate account organized as a management investment company may be maintained in the custody of the life insurer or of an affiliated life insurance company, *Provided,* That:

(i) The securities and similar investments allocated to the separate account are clearly identified as owned by the account, and the securities and similar investments are kept in the vault of an insurance company which meets the qualifications in paragraph (b)(9)(ii) of this rule, and whose safekeeping function is supervised by the insurance regulatory authorities of the jurisdiction in which the securities and similar investments will be held;

(ii) The insurance company maintaining such investments must file with an insurance regulatory authority of a state or territory of the United States or the District of Columbia an annual statement of its financial condition in the form prescribed by the National Association of Insurance Commissioners, must be subject to supervision and inspection by such authority and must be examined periodically as to its financial condition and other affairs by such authority, must hold the securities and similar investments of the separate account in its vault, which vault must be equivalent to that of a bank which is a member of the Federal Reserve System, and must have a combined capital and surplus, if a stock company, or an unassigned surplus, if a mutual company, of not less than $1,000,000 as set forth in its most recent annual statement filed with such authority;

(iii) Access to such securities and similar investments shall be limited to employees of the Commission, representatives of insurance regulatory authorities, independent public accountants retained by the separate account (or on its behalf by the life insurer), accountants for the life insurer, and to no more than 20 persons authorized by a resolution of the board of directors of the separate account, which persons shall be directors of the separate account, officers and responsible employees of the life insurer or officers and responsible employees of the affiliated life insurance company in whose vault the investments are kept (if applicable), and access to such securities and similar investments shall be had only by two or more such persons jointly, at least one of whom shall be a director of the separate account or officer of the life insurer;

(iv) The requirement in paragraph (b)(9)(i) of this rule that the securities and similar investments of the separate account be maintained in the vault of a qualified insurance company shall not apply to securities deposited with insurance regulatory authorities or deposited in accordance with any rule under section 17(f), or to securities on loan which are collateralized to the extent of their full market value, or to securities hypothecated, pledged, or placed in escrow for the account of such separate account in connection with a loan or other transaction authorized by specific resolution of the board of directors of the separate account, or to securities in transit in connection with the sale, exchange, redemption, maturity or conversion, the exercise of warrants or rights, assents to changes in terms of the securities, or to other transactions necessary or appropriate in the ordinary course of business relating to the management of securities;

(v) Each person when depositing such securities or similar investments in or withdrawing them from the depository or when ordering their withdrawal and delivery from the custody of the life insurer or affiliated life insurance company, shall sign a notation showing (A) the date and time of the deposit, withdrawal or order, (B) the title and amount of the securities or other investments deposited, withdrawn or ordered to be withdrawn, and an identification thereof by certificate numbers or otherwise, (C) the manner of acquisition of the securities or similar investments deposited or the purpose for which they have been withdrawn, or ordered to be withdrawn, and (D) if withdrawn and delivered to another person, the name of such person. The notation shall be sent promptly to an officer or director of the separate account or the life insurer designated by the board of directors of the separate account who is not himself permitted to have access to the securities or investments under paragraph (b)(9)(iii) of this rule. The notation shall be on serially numbered forms and shall be kept for at least one year;

(vi) The securities and similar investments shall be verified by complete examination by an independent public accountant retained by the separate account (or on its behalf by the life insurer) at least three times each fiscal year, at least two of which shall be chosen by the accountant without prior notice to the separate account. A certificate of the accountant stating that he has made an examination of such securities and investments and describing the nature and extent of the examination shall be sent to the Commission by the accountant promptly after each examination;

(vii) Securities and similar investments of a separate account maintained with a bank or other company whose functions and physical facilities are supervised by federal or state authorities under any arrangement whereby the directors, officers, employees or agents of the separate account or the life insurer are authorized or permitted to withdraw such investments upon their mere receipt are deemed to be in the custody of the life insurer and shall be exempt from the requirements of section 17(f) so long as the arrangement complies with all provisions of this paragraph (b)(9), except that such securities will be maintained in the vault of a bank or other company rather than the vault of an insurance company.

(10) Section 18(i), to the extent that:

(i) For the purposes of any section of the Act which provides for the vote of securityholders on matters relating to the investment company:

(A) Flexible contractholders shall have one vote for each $100 of cash value funded by the separate account, with fractional votes allocated for amounts less than $100;

(B) The life insurer shall have one vote for each $100 of assets of the separate account not otherwise attributable to contractholders under paragraph (b)(10)(i)(A) of this rule, with fractional votes allocated for amounts less than $100, *Provided,* That after the commencement of sales of flexible contracts, the life insurer shall cast its votes for and against each matter which may be voted upon by contractholders in the same proportion as the votes cast by contractholders; and

(C) The number of votes to be allocated shall be determined as of a record date not more than 90 days before any meeting at which such vote is held, *Provided,* That if a quorum is not present at the meeting, the meeting may be adjourned for up to 60 days without fixing a new record date;

(ii) The requirement of this section that every share of stock issued by a registered management investment company (except a common-law trust of the character described in section 16(c)) shall be a voting stock and have equal voting rights with every other outstanding voting stock shall not be deemed to be violated by actions specifically permitted by any provisions of this rule.

(11) Section 19, to the extent that the provisions of this section shall not apply to any dividend or similar distribution paid or payable under provisions of participating flexible contracts.

(12) Sections 22(c), 22(d), 22(e), and 27(c)(1) and Rule 22c–1 to the extent:

(i) The cash value of each flexible contract shall be computed in accordance with Rule 22c–1(b) under the Act; *Provided, however,* That where actual computation is not necessary for the operation of a particular contract, then the cash value of that contract must only be capable of computation; *And provided further,* That to the extent the calculation of the cash value reflects deductions for the cost of insurance and other insurance benefits or administrative expenses and fees or sales loads, such deductions need only be made at such times as specified in the contract or as necessary for compliance with insurance laws and regulations; and

(ii) The death benefit, unless required by insurance laws and regulations, shall be computed on any day that the investment experience of the separate account would affect the death benefit under the terms of the contract provided that such terms are reasonable, fair, and nondiscriminatory;

(iii) Necessary to comply with this Rule or with insurance laws and regulations and established administrative procedures of the life insurer for issuance, increases in or additions of insurance benefits, transfer and redemption of flexible contracts, including, but not limited to, premium rate structure and premium processing, insurance underwriting standards, and the particular benefit afforded by the contract, *Provided, however,* That any procedure or action shall be reasonable, fair and not discriminatory to the interests of the affected contractholders and to all other holders of contracts of the same class or series funded by the separate account, *And provided further,* That any such action shall be disclosed in the form filed by the separate account with the Commission under paragraph (b)(3)(ii) of this rule.

(13) Section 27, to the following extent:

(i) Sections 27(a)(1), 27(h)(1), and 27(h)(4), to the extent that sales load, as defined in paragraph (c)(4) of this rule, deducted does not exceed that permitted by either subparagraph (A) or (B) below:

(A) 9 per centum of the sum of the guideline annual premiums that would be paid during the period equal to the lesser of 20 years or the anticipated life expectancy of the insured named in the contract based on the 1980 Commissioners Standard Ordinary Mortality Table, *Provided,* That this subparagraph (b)(13)(i)(A) shall not prohibit deduction of sales load, in any manner permitted by this rule, from payments made in excess of the sum of the guideline annual premiums that would be paid during the lesser of 20 years or the anticipated life expectancy of the insured based on the 1980 Commissioners Standard Ordinary Mortality Table; or

(B) 9 per centum of payments made thereon; *Provided,* That the separate account elects by written notice to the Commission to be governed (with respect to each class of flexible contract offered) by either subparagraph (b)(13)(i)(A) or (B); *Provided, however,* That for each class of flexible contract that requires more than four guideline annual premiums within the first two contract periods following issuance of the contract or of an increase in or addition of insurance benefits (within the meaning of paragraph (d)(2) of this rule), the separate account must elect to be governed by subparagraph (b)(13)(i)(B).

(ii) Sections 27(a)(3) and 27(h)(3), *Provided,* That the proportionate amount of sales load deducted from any payment shall not exceed the proportionate amount deducted from any prior payment unless an increase is caused by reductions in the annual cost of insurance, or a reduction in the sales load deducted from amounts transferred to a flexible contract from another plan of insurance;

(iii) Sections 27(c)(2), 26(a)(1), and 26(a)(2), to the extent necessary to permit the actions described in paragraphs (A) through (F) of this section, *Provided,* That the life insurer complies with all other applicable provisions of section 26 as if it were a trustee, depositor or custodian for the separate account; files with the insurance regulatory authority of a state or territory of the United States or of the District of Columbia an annual statement of its financial condition in the form prescribed by the National Association of Insurance Commissioners, which most recent statement indicates that it has a combined capital and surplus, if a stock company, or an unassigned surplus, if a mutual company, of not less than $1,000,000; and is examined from time to time by the insurance regulatory authority of such state, territory or District of Columbia as to its financial condition and other affairs and is subject to supervision and inspection with respect to its separate account operations.

(A) Payment of a fee to the life insurer, or to any affiliated person or agent of the insurer, for bookkeeping or other administrative services provided to the separate account, or for administrative services or expenses incurred in underwriting, issuing, and maintaining flexible contracts, *Provided,* That the fee is not greater than the expenses, without profit:

(*1*) Actually paid by the life insurer for the services provided; and

(*2*) Increased by the value of any services provided directly by the life insurer, as determined in accordance with generally accepted accounting principles consistently applied.

The standard set forth in this paragraph shall be applied as follows: if the separate account reserves the right to increase the fee, the fee shall not exceed the cost of the services to be provided for one year; or if the fee is guaranteed not to increase for a specified period of time, the fee shall not exceed the average expected cost of the services to be provided during the period of the guarantee;

(B) The holding of the assets of the separate account by the life insurer without a trust indenture or other such instrument;

(C) When the separate account is organized as a unit investment trust, the holding of the securities of any registered management investment company which offers its shares to the separate account in uncertificated form;

(D) When the separate account is organized as a management investment company, the holding of its assets in any manner permitted by paragraph (b)(9) of this rule or by section 17(f) or the rules under it;

(E) The deduction of premium or other taxes imposed by any state or other governmental entity, the cost of insurance, charges assessed for incidental insurance benefits or if the insured does not meet standard underwriting requirements, and, if the separate account is organized as a management investment company, an investment advisory fee;

(F) The deduction of a charge for mortality, expense, and any guaranteed death benefit risks assumed by the life insurer under the flexible contracts (collectively, a "risk charge"), *Provided,* That the registration statement under the 1933 Act for flexible contracts includes:

(*1*) A representation that this paragraph is being relied upon;

(*2*) A representation that the level of the risk charge either is:

(*i*) Within the range of industry practice for comparable flexible or scheduled contracts, or

(*ii*) Reasonable in relation to the risks assumed by the life insurer under the contracts;

(*3*) A brief description of the methodology used to support the representation made in response to paragraph (b)(13)(iii)(F)(*2*) of this rule and an undertaking to keep and make available to the Commission upon request the documents used to support that representation;

(*4*) A representation that either:

(*i*) The proceeds from explicit sales loads will be sufficient to cover the expected costs of distributing the flexible contracts; or

(*ii*)(*A*) The life insurer has concluded that there is a reasonable likelihood that the distribution financing arrangement of the separate account will benefit the separate account and contractholders and will keep and make available to the Commission on request a memorandum setting forth the basis for this representation; and

(*B*) If the separate account is organized as a management investment company, a representation that the account will have a board of directors, a majority of whom are not interested persons of the separate account, formulate and approve any plan under Rule 12b–1 to finance distribution expenses. If the separate account is organized as a unit investment trust, a representation that the account will invest only in management investment companies which have undertaken to have a board of directors, a majority of whom are not interested persons of the company, formulate and approve any plan under Rule 12b–1 to finance distribution expenses.

Notwithstanding the provisions of this paragraph (b)(13)(iii)(F), no risk charge may be deducted in reliance thereupon if the registration statement or amendment thereto which initially sets forth the deduction of such charge or its increase becomes effective by lapse of time pursuant to section 8(a) of the 1933 Act or Rule 485 thereunder. Such charge shall be disclosed in the prospectus and shall not be less than fifty per centum of the maximum charge for risk assumption as disclosed in the prospectus and as provided for in the contract. Any separate account organized under the Act as a management investment company and deducting a risk charge pursuant to this section shall be exempt from section 12(b) and Rule 12b–1 thereunder to the extent that monies derived from the risk charge may be used to finance distribution of the flexible contracts;

(iv) Sections 27(c)(1) and 27(d), and sections 2(a)(32) and 22(c) and Rule 22c–1 thereunder, to the extent that:

(A) Such sections require that the flexible contract be redeemable or provide for a refund in cash, *Provided,* That the contract provides for election by the contractholder of a cash surrender value or certain non-forfeiture and settlement options which are required or permitted by the insurance law or regulation of the jurisdiction in which the contract is offered, *And provided further*, That unless required by the insurance law or regulation of the jurisdiction in which the contract is offered or unless elected by the contractholder, the contract shall not provide for the automatic imposition of any option, including, but not limited to, an automatic premium loan, which would involve the accrual or payment of an interest or similar charge.

(B) Notwithstanding the provisions of paragraph (b)(13)(iv)(A) of this rule, if the amounts available under the contract to pay the charges due under the contract on any contract processing day are less than such charges due, the contract may provide that the cash surrender value (and any excess paid for sales loading not used to keep the contract in force pursuant to paragraph (b)(13)(iv)(B)(*2*) of this rule) shall be applied to purchase a non-forfeiture option specified by the life insurer in such contract, *Provided,* That the contract also provides that:

(*1*) Contract processing days occur not less frequently than monthly, and

(*2*) The amount of any excess paid for sales loading (as provided in paragraph (b)(13)(v)(A) of this rule) shall first be applied to keep the contract in force, *Provided, however*, That if the contractholder subsequently makes a payment, the life insurer may recover such excess loading;

(C) Subject to other provisions of this Rule, sales loads and administrative expenses or fees may be deducted upon redemption.

(v) Section 27(d), *Provided,* That the flexible contract gives the holder thereof the right to:

(A) Surrender the contract at any time during the first 24 months after issuance and receive in cash an amount not less than the sum of the present value of his contract which is the cash surrender value next computed after receipt by the life insurer of the request for surrender in proper form, plus, an amount which is a refund of any excess paid for sales loading prior to or in connection with the surrender. The amount of sales loading to be refunded shall be equal to that part of the sales loading in excess of (*1*) the sum of 30 per centum of payments in aggregate amount less than or equal to one guideline annual premium, plus 10 per centum of payments in aggregate amount greater than one guideline annual premium but not more than two guideline annual premiums, and (*2*) 9 per centum of each payment made in excess of two guideline annual premiums;

(B) Convert the contract at any time during the first 24 months after issuance, so long as the contract is in force, to a life insurance policy on the life of the insured under a plan of insurance (other than a plan involving a flexible contract as defined in paragraph (c)(1) of this rule or a scheduled contract as defined in paragraph (c)(1) of Rule 6e–2) specified in the contract, issued by the life insurer or by an affiliated life insurance company, which provides for (*1*) at the election of the contractholder, either the same death benefit or the same net amount at risk as the flexible contract at the time of conversion and (*2*) premiums (or cost of insurance or other charges, ("charges") if such plan of insurance provides for flexible premiums) which are based on the same issue age and risk classification of the insured as the flexible contract. The conversion shall be subject to an equitable adjustment in payments and cash values to reflect variances, if any, in the payments (or charges), dividends, and cash values under the flexible contract and the new policy. The method of computing such adjustment shall be filed with the Commission as an exhibit to the form required under paragraph (b)(3)(ii) of this rule;

(vi) A depositor or principal underwriter for a flexible contract sold subject to section 27(d) or section 27(f), or both, shall be exempt from the requirements of Rule 27d–1 if an insurance company undertakes in writing to guarantee the performance of all obligations of such depositor or principal underwriter under sections 27(d) and 27(f) to refund charges, and such insurance company, depositor and principal underwriter comply with all provisions of Rule 27d–2;

(vii) Section 27(e) and Rule 27e–1 thereunder, to the extent that the separate account and the depositor and principal underwriter therefor, when such persons are subject to paragraph (b)(13)(v)(A) of this rule, are required to provide a notice of right of surrender and refund to holders of flexible contracts, if the life insurer or a duly authorized agent provides a notice of surrender and refund rights on a written document containing information comparable to that required by Form N–27I–1 to the holder of any flexible contract under which a refund may be available, *Provided,* That such notice shall be sent by first class mail or personal delivery to the contractholder:

(A) Upon issuance of the flexible contract, which notice may be sent together with the issued contract and an illustration, in a form appropriate for inclusion in the prospectus for the flexible contract, of guideline annual premiums, death benefits and cash surrender values applicable to the age, sex and underwriting classification of the insured; and

(B) On any contract processing day, prior to the expiration of the surrender and refund right provided in paragraph (b)(13)(v)(A) of this rule, on which the amounts available under the contract on such day to pay the charges authorized by the contract are less than the amount necessary to keep the contract in force until the next following contract processing day. This notice may be sent together with any notice required by applicable state authority to be sent in these circumstances; *Provided, however,* That the right of surrender and refund provided by paragraph (b)(13)(v)(A) of this rule shall not expire until not less than 15 days after the mailing or receipt, if personally delivered, of the last notice referred to in this paragraph (b)(13)(vii)(B) of this rule;

(viii) Section 27(f) and Rule 27f–1 thereunder, *Provided,* That:

(A) The contractholder may elect to return the contract within 45 days of the date of the execution of the application for insurance, or within 10 days after receipt of the issued contract by the contractholder, or within 10 days after mailing or personal delivery of the notice of the right of withdrawal referred to in paragraph (b)(13)(viii)(C) of this rule, whichever is later, and receive a refund equal to the sum of (*1*) the difference between the payments made, including any contract fees or other charges, and the amounts allocated to the separate account under the contract, (*2*) the value of the amounts allocated to the separate account under the contract on the date the returned contract is received by the insurer or its agent, and (*3*) any contract fees and other changes imposed on the amounts allocated to such separate account, *Provided, however,* That if state law or the contract so require, the redeeming contractholder shall receive a refund of all payments made for such contract;

(B) A refund in accordance with paragraph (b)(13)(viii)(A) of this rule to redeeming contractholders will not in any way affect the interests in the separate account or the benefits of other flexible or scheduled contractholders;

(C) Notice of such withdrawal right and a statement of contract fees and other charges on a written document containing information comparable to that required by Form N–27I–2 is sent by first class mail or personal delivery to the contractholder, which notice and statement may be accompanied by the flexible contract, and an illustration, in a form appropriate for inclusion in the prospectus for the flexible contract, of guideline annual premiums (or, if the contract is subject to paragraph (b)(13)(i)(B), payments), death benefits and cash surrender values applicable to the age, sex and underwriting classification of the insured;

(D) The contractholder, in conjunction with the notice of withdrawal right referred to in paragraph (b)(13)(viii)(C), is provided with a form of request for refund of the amount computed in accordance with paragraph (b)(13)(viii)(A), which form shall set forth:

(*1*) Instructions as to the manner in which a refund may be obtained, including the address to which the request form should be mailed; and

(*2*) Spaces necessary to indicate the date of such request, the contract number and the signature of the contractholder; and

(E) Within 7 days from the receipt of such duly executed timely request for refund, the life insurer will refund in cash to the contractholder the amount computed in accordance with paragraph (b)(13)(viii)(A) of this rule; and

(ix) Solely for purposes of paragraphs (b)(13)(v) and (b)(13)(viii) of this rule, the postmark date on the envelope containing the flexible contract shall determine whether such contract has been submitted for surrender, conversion, or withdrawal within the designated period.

(14) Section 32(a)(2), *Provided,* That:

(i) The independent public accountant is selected before the effective date of the 1933 Act registration statement for flexible contracts, and the identity of the accountant is disclosed in the registration statement, and

(ii) The selection of the accountant is submitted for ratification or rejection to flexible contractholders at their first meeting and within one year after the effective date of the 1933 Act registration statement for flexible contracts, unless the time for holding the meeting is extended by order of the Commission.

(15) If the separate account is organized as a unit investment trust, all the assets of which consist of the shares of one or more registered management investment companies which offer their shares exclusively to separate accounts of the life insurer, or of any affiliated life insurance company, offering either scheduled contracts or flexible contracts, or both; or which also offer their shares to variable annuity separate accounts of the life insurer or of an affiliated life insurance company, or which offer their shares to any such life insurance company in consideration solely for advances made by the life insurer in connection with the operation of the separate account; *Provided,* That: the board of directors of each investment company, constituted with a majority of disinterested directors, will monitor such company for the existence of any material irreconcilable conflict between the interests of variable annuity contractholders and scheduled or flexible contractholders investing in such company; the life insurer agrees that it will be responsible for reporting any potential or existing conflicts to the directors; and if a conflict arises, the life insurer will, at its own cost, remedy such conflict up to and including establishing a new registered management investment company and segregating the assets underlying the variable annuity contracts and the scheduled or flexible contracts; Then:

(i) The eligibility restrictions of section 9(a) shall not apply to those persons who are officers, directors or employees of the life insurer or its affiliates who do not participate directly in the management or administration of any registered management investment company described in this paragraph (b)(15);

(ii) The life insurer shall be ineligible under paragraph (3) of section 9(a) to serve as investment adviser of or principal underwriter for any registered management investment company described in this paragraph (b)(15) only if an affiliated person of such life insurer, ineligible by reason of paragraphs (1) or (2) of section 9(a), participates in the management or administration of such company;

(iii) For purposes of any section of the Act which provides for the vote of securityholders on matters relating to the separate account or the underlying registered investment company, the voting provisions of paragraph (b)(10)(i) and (ii) of this rule apply, *Provided,* That:

(A) The life insurer may vote shares of the registered management investment companies held by the separate account without regard to instructions from contractholders of the separate account if such instructions would require such shares to be voted:

(*1*) To cause such companies to make (or refrain from making) certain investments which would result in changes in the sub-classification or investment objectives of such companies or to approve or disapprove any contract between such companies and an investment adviser when required to do so by an insurance regulatory authority subject to the provisions of paragraphs (b)(5)(i) and (b)(7)(ii)(A) of this rule; or

(*2*) In favor of changes in investment objectives, investment adviser of or principal underwriter for such companies subject to the provisions of paragraphs (b)(5)(ii) and (b)(7)(ii) (B) and (C) of this rule;

(B) Any action taken in accordance with paragraph (b)(15)(iii)(A)(1) or (2) of this section and the reasons therefor shall be disclosed in the next report contractholders made under section 30(e) (15 U.S.C. 80a–29(e)) and Rule 30e–2;

(iv) Any registered management investment company established by the life insurer and described in this paragraph (b)(15) shall be exempt from section 14(a), *Provided,* That until the company has total assets of at least $100,000, the life insurer shall have at least the minimum net worth prescribed in paragraph (b)(6) of this rule; and

(v) Any registered management investment company established by the life insurer and described in this paragraph (b)(15) shall be exempt from sections 15(a), 16(a), and 32(a)(2), to the extent prescribed by paragraphs (b)(7)(i), (b)(8)(i), and (b)(14) of this rule, *Provided,* That the company complies with the conditions set forth in those paragraphs as if it were a separate account.

(c) When used in this rule:

(1) *Flexible premium variable life insurance contract* means a contract of life insurance, subject to regulation under the insurance laws or code of every jurisdiction in which it is offered, funded by a separate account of a life insurer, which contract provides for:

(i) Payments which are not fixed by the life insurer as to both timing and amount: *Provided, however,* That the life insurer may fix the timing and minimum amount of payments for the first two contract periods following issuance of the contract or of an increase in or addition of insurance benefits (within the meaning of paragraph (d)(2)), and may prescribe a reasonable minimum amount for any additional payment;

(ii) A death benefit the amount or duration of which may vary to reflect the investment experience of the separate account;

(iii) A cash value which varies to reflect the investment experience of the separate account; and

(iv) There is a reasonable expectation that subsequent payments will be made.

(2) *Incidental insurance benefits* means insurance benefits provided pursuant to the flexible contract, other than any guaranteed and variable death benefit, which do not have discrete cash values that may vary in amount in accordance with the investment experience of the separate account, and include, but are not limited to, accidental death and dismemberment benefits, disability income benefits, guaranteed insurability options, and family income or fixed benefit term riders.

(3) *Guaranteed death benefit* is any amount guaranteed by the life insurer to be paid pursuant to a flexible contract in the event of the death of the insured without regard to the investment experience of the separate account, if there are no outstanding loans or partial surrenders, but does not include any incidental insurance benefits.

(4) *Sales load* charged during a contract period is the excess of any payments made during the period over the sum of the following:

(i) The amount of the change (whether it is an increase or decrease) in the cash value for the period that is not attributable to net investment earnings or to dividends for a participating flexible contract for the period;

(ii) The cost of insurance for the period based on:

(A) For a flexible contract subject to paragraph (b)(13)(i)(A), the 1980 Commissioners Standard Ordinary Mortality Table and net interest at the annual effective rate specified for purposes of paragraph (c)(8)(i)(B) of this rule; or

(B) For a flexible contract subject to paragraph (b)(13)(i)(B), either the 1980 Commissioners Standard Ordinary Mortality Table or the 1958 Commissioners Ordinary Mortality Table (whichever relates to rates guaranteed by the contract) and the assumed investment rate specified in the contract, *Provided, however,* That the 1958 Commissioners Ordinary Mortality Table may only be used for those contracts issued before 1990, or such earlier mandatory date for implementation of the 1980 Commissioners Standard Ordinary Mortality Table under the applicable Standard Nonforfeiture Law for life insurance;

(iii) A reasonable charge necessary to cover the risk assumed by the life insurer that the variable death benefit will be less than any guaranteed death benefit;

(iv) Any administrative expenses or fees which are deducted pursuant to paragraph (b)(13)(iii)(A) of this rule;

(v) A deduction for and approximately equal to state premium taxes;

(vi) Any additional charge assessed if the insured does not meet standard underwriting requirements, including, but not limited to, any additional cost of insurance charge for a contract purchased on a simplified underwriting or guaranteed issue basis;

(vii) Any additional charge assessed specifically for any incidental insurance benefits;

(viii) Any additional charge, the nature of an interest charge, assessed when payments are made more frequently than annually, but only to the extent that such payments are made to fulfill a minimum payment requirement imposed pursuant to paragraph (c)(1)(i) of this rule;

(ix) Any amounts redeemed by the contractholder or paid out to the beneficiary upon the death of the insured which are not attributable to net investment earnings for the period; and

(x) For a participating flexible contract, a deduction for dividends to be paid or credited in accordance with the dividend scale in effect on the issue date of the contract assuming a net annual investment return for the separate account which funds the contract of 5 per centum. The deduction may be determined by either of the following methods, but the same method must be used for each contract period:

(A) The actuarial level annual equivalent of dividends to be paid or credited over the contract periods described in paragraph (b)(13)(i) of this rule, based upon the mortality, interest and lapse assumptions used in computing the dividend scale for the contract (and, if the contract is subject to paragraph (b)(13)(i)(A), the assumption that the guideline annual premium will be paid in each contract period) multiplied by the fraction of the contract year represented by the contract period; or

(B) That portion of the dividend to be paid for the contract year which does not depend on the making of payments in addition to those made during the period.

(5) *Contract period* means the period from a contract issue or anniversary date to the earlier of the next following anniversary date (or, if later, the last day of any grace period commencing before such next following anniversary date) or the termination date of the contract.

(6) *Variable death benefit* is the amount of death benefit, other than incidental insurance benefits, payable under a flexible contract which varies to reflect the investment experience of the separate account and which would be payable in the absence of any guaranteed death benefit.

(7) *Payment,* as used in paragraphs (b)(13)(i), (b)(13)(ii), and (b)(13)(v)(A) of this rule and in sections 27(a)(2) and 27(h)(2) solely with respect to flexible contracts, means for a contract period the gross premiums paid less any portion of such gross premiums charged for the items specified in paragraphs (c)(4)(vi), (c)(4)(vii), and (c)(4)(viii) of this rule. "Payment," as used in any other section of this rule, means the gross premiums paid or payable for the flexible contract, *Except,* That "Payment" shall not include any amount deducted by the life insurer to recover excess sales loading previously applied to keep the contract in force pursuant to paragraph (b)(13)(iv)(B)(*2*) of this rule.

(8)(i) *Guideline annual premium* means the level annual amount that would be payable through the maturity date specified in paragraph (c)(8)(ii)(B) of this rule for the future benefits under the contract if, subject to the provisions of paragraph (c)(8)(ii) of this rule:

(A) The payments were fixed by the life insurer as to both timing and amount, and

(B) The payments were based on the 1980 Commissioners Standard Ordinary Mortality Table, net investment earnings at the greater of an annual effective rate of 5 per centum or rate or rates guaranteed at issuance of the flexible contract, the sales load under the contract, and the fees and charges associated with the contract specified in paragraphs (c)(4)(iii), (c)(4)(iv), (c)(4)(v), (c)(4)(vi), (c)(4)(vii), (c)(4)(viii) (for the first two contract periods as permitted by paragraph (c)(1)(i)), and (c)(4)(x) of this rule.

(ii) In computing the future benefits under the flexible contract for determining the guideline annual premium:

(A) The excess of the amount payable by reason of the death of the insured (determined without regard to any incidental insurance benefits) over the cash value of the contract shall be deemed to be not greater than such excess at the time the contract was issued,

(B) The maturity date shall be the latest maturity date permitted under the contract but not less than 20 years after the date of issue or (if earlier) age 95, and

(C) The amount of any endowment benefit (or sum of endowment benefits) shall be deemed not to exceed the least amount payable by reason of the death of the insured (determined without regard to any incidental insurance benefits) at any time under the contract.

(9) *Cash value* means the amount that would be available in cash upon voluntary termination of a contract by its owner before it becomes payable by death or maturity, without regard to any charges that may be assessed upon such termination and before deduction of any outstanding contract loan.

(10) *Cash surrender value* means the amount available in cash upon voluntary termination of a contract by its owner before it becomes payable by death or maturity, after any charges assessed in connection with the termination have been deducted and before deduction of any outstanding contract loan.

(11) *Net investment earnings* means investment earnings in the separate account after deduction of any asset charges, including but not limited to, such charges for income tax; brokerage and other investment expenses; mortality, expense, and guaranteed death benefit risks; and an investment advisory fee, but not including deductions for sales load. However, "net investment earnings" as used in paragraph (c)(4)(i) of this rule shall not include any amount deducted pursuant to subparagraphs (ii) through (viii) of paragraph (c)(4).

(12) *Contract processing day* means any day on which charges under the contract are deducted from the separate account.

(d) The following computational rules shall be used in applying this rule:

(1) Paragraphs (b)(13)(i) and (b)(13)(ii) of this rule shall be deemed to be satisfied with respect to any flexible contract under which sales load is deducted other than from payments prior to the allocation of net payments to the separate account if:

(i) from issuance of the contract through each contract period, the aggregate amount of sales load deducted is not more than the aggregate amount of sales load that could be deducted under an otherwise identical flexible contract that deducted sales load only from payments prior to their allocation to the separate account; and

(ii)(A) the amount of sales load deducted pursuant to any method permitted under this paragraph (other than asset-based sales loads) does not exceed the proportionate amount of sales load deducted prior thereto pursuant to the same method, unless an increase in such proportionate amount is caused by reductions in the annual cost of insurance, or a reduction in the sales load deducted from amounts transferred to a flexible contract from another plan of insurance; or

(B) for asset-based sales load structures, the percentage of assets taken as sales load does not exceed any of the percentages previously taken pursuant to the same method, unless an increase in such percentage is caused by a reduction in the percentage taken on amounts transferred to a flexible contract from another plan of insurance.

(2)(i) Solely with respect to increases in or additions of insurance benefits requested by a contractholder after issuance of a flexible contract, the contract shall be deemed to satisfy paragraphs (b)(13)(i)(A), (b)(13)(ii), (b)(13)(v), (b)(13)(viii), and (d)(1)(ii) of this rule, *Provided,* That from issuance of the contract through each contract period the aggregate amount of sales load imposed is not more than the aggregate amount of sales load that would be permissible under the base test contract, as defined in paragraph (d)(2)(iii)(B) of this rule, and the incremental test contract, as defined in paragraph (d)(2)(iii)(C) of this rule.

(ii) The following procedures shall be used in applying paragraph (d)(2)(i) of this rule:

(A) Payments for the actual contract, as defined in paragraph (d)(2)(iii)(A) of this rule, and the base and incremental test contracts shall, for purposes of demonstrating compliance with the sales load provisions of this rule, be deemed paid in the following proportionate amounts: level annual payments for the base test contract equal to the guideline annual premium for the contract, commencing upon issuance; level annual payments for the incremental test contract equal to the difference between the guideline annual premium for the actual contract after the increase in or addition of insurance benefits and before such increase or addition, commencing upon such increase or addition; and level annual payments for the actual contract equal to the guideline annual premium for such contract, commencing upon issuance and adjusted for such increase or addition as of the date of such increase or addition, *provided*, That the guideline annual premium used is that defined in paragraph (c)(8) of this rule;

(B) To the extent that the increases in, or additions of, insurance benefits are funded out of cash value, such cash value shall be proportionately allocated between the base test contract and incremental test contract according to the ratio of their respective guideline annual payments, as described in (d)(2)(ii)(A); and

(C) It is assumed that no redemptions are made under the actual and test contracts.

(D) An incremental test contract may deduct, in any manner permitted by this rule, not more than 50 per centum of the sales load which would otherwise be permitted under the base test contract, and not be subject to the surrender, conversion, and withdrawal provisions set forth in paragraphs (b)(13)(v)(A) and (B) and (b)(13)(viii) of this rule, *Provided, however,* That the increased or added benefit will be subject to the surrender, conversion, and withdrawal provisions referenced above if more than such 50 per centum of sales load is assessed.

(iii) For purposes of this paragraph (d)(2):

(A) *Actual contract* shall mean the flexible contract issued to the contractholder, and adjusted for the increase in or addition of insurance benefits, as of the date of the increase or addition;

(B) *Base test contract* shall mean the actual contract had the increase or addition not occurred;

(C) *Incremental test contract* shall mean a flexible contract that, (*1*) is issued on the date of the increase or addition, and (*2*) provides insurance benefits identical to the incremental change in insurance benefits under the actual contract upon such increase or addition; and

(D) Any change in insurance benefits which would occur automatically under a contract, with or without the opportunity for contractholder disapproval, or any change in death benefit operation shall not be considered an "increase in or addition of insurance benefits requested by a contractholder" for purposes of imposing additional sales load.

Rule 7d–1. Specification of conditions and arrangements for Canadian management investment companies requesting order permitting registration

(a) A management investment company organized under the laws of Canada or any province thereof may obtain an order pursuant to section 7(d) permitting its registration under the act and the public offering of its securities, if otherwise appropriate, upon the filing of an application complying with paragraph (b) of this section. All such applications will be considered by the Commission pursuant to the procedure set forth in Rule 0–5 and other applicable rules. Conditions and arrangements proposed by investment companies organized under the laws of other countries will be considered by the Commission in the light of the special circumstances and local laws involved in each case.

(b) An application filed pursuant to this section shall contain, inter alia, the following undertakings and agreements of the applicant:

(1) Applicant will cause each present and future officer, director, investment adviser, principal underwriter and custodian of the applicant to enter into an agreement, to be filed by applicant with the Commission upon the filing of its registration statement or upon the assumption of such office by such person which will provide, among other things, that each such person agrees (i) to comply with the applicant's Letters Patent (Charter) and By Laws, the act and the rules thereunder, and the undertakings and agreements contained in said application insofar as applicable to such person; (ii) to do nothing inconsistent with the applicant's undertakings and agreements required by this section; (iii) that the undertakings enumerated as subdivisions (i) and (ii) of this subparagraph constitute representations and inducements to the Commission to issue its order in the premises and continue the same in effect, as the case may be; (iv) that each such agreement constitutes a contract between such person and the applicant and its shareholders with the intent that applicant's shareholders shall be beneficiaries of and shall have the status of parties to such agreement so as to enable them to maintain actions at law or in equity within the United States and Canada for any violation thereof. In addition the agreement

of each officer and director will contain provisions similar to those contained in paragraph (B)(6) of this rule.

(2) That every agreement and undertaking of the applicant, its officers, directors, investment adviser, principal underwriter and custodian required by this rule (i) constitute inducements to the Commission for the issuance and continuance in effect of, and conditions to, the Commission's order to be entered under this rule; (ii) constitute a contract among applicant and applicant's shareholders with the same intent as set forth in subparagraph (1)(iv) of this paragraph; and (iii) failure by the applicant or any of the above enumerated persons to comply with any such agreement and undertaking, unless permitted by the Commission, shall constitute a violation of the order entered under this rule.

(3) That the Commission, in its discretion, may revoke its order permitting registration of the applicant and the public offering of its securities if it shall find after notice and opportunity for hearing that there shall have been a violation of such order or the act and may determine whether distribution of applicant's assets is necessary or appropriate in the interests of investors and may so direct.

(4) That applicant will perform every action and thing necessary to cause and assist the custodian of its assets to distribute the same, or the proceeds thereof, if the Commission or a court of competent jurisdiction, shall have so directed by a final order.

(5) That any shareholder of the applicant or the Commission on its own motion or on request of shareholders shall have the right to initiate a proceeding (i) before the Commission for the revocation of the order permitting registration of the applicant or (ii) before a court of competent jurisdiction for the liquidation of applicant and a distribution of its assets to its shareholders and creditors. Such court may enter such order in the event that it shall find, after notice and opportunity for hearing that applicant, its officers, directors, investment adviser, principal underwriter or custodian shall have violated any provision of the act or the Commission's order of registration of the applicant.

A court of competent jurisdiction for the purpose of subparagraphs (4) and (5) of this paragraph means the District Court of the United States of the district in which the assets of the applicant are maintained.

(6) That any shareholder of the applicant shall have the right to bring suit at law or in equity, in any court of the United States or Canada having jurisdiction over applicant, its assets or any of its officers or directors to enforce compliance by applicant, its officers and directors with any provision of applicant's Charter or By Laws, the act and the rules thereunder, or undertakings and agreements required by this section, insofar as applicable to such persons. That such court may appoint a trustee or receiver of the applicant with all powers necessary to implement the purposes of such suit, including the administration of the estate, the collection of corporate property including choses-in-action, and distribution of applicant's assets to its creditors and shareholders. That applicant and its officers and directors waive any objection they may be entitled to raise and any right they may have to object to the power and right of any shareholder of the applicant to bring such suit, reserving, however, their right to maintain that they have complied with the aforesaid provisions, undertakings and agreements, and otherwise to dispute such suit on its merits. Applicant, its officers and directors also agree that any final judgment or decree of any United States court as aforesaid, may be granted full faith and credit by a court of competent jurisdiction of Canada and consent that such Canadian court may enter judgment or decree thereon at the instance of any shareholder, receiver or trustee of the applicant.

(7) Applicant will file, and will cause each of its present or future directors, officers, or investment advisers who is not a resident of the United States to file with the Commission irrevocable designation of the applicant's custodian as an agent in the United States to accept service of process in any suit, action or proceeding before the Commission or any appropriate court to enforce the provisions of the acts administered by the Commission, or to enforce any right or liability based upon applicant's Charter, By Laws, contracts, or the respective undertakings and agreements of any such person required by this section, or which alleges a liability on the part of any such persons arising out of their service, acts of transactions relating to the applicant.

(8) Applicant's Charter and By Laws, taken together, will contain, so long as applicant is registered under the act in substance the following:

(i) The provisions of the Act as follows: Section 2(a): *Provided,* That the term "government securities" defined in section 2(a)(16) may include securities issued or guaranteed by Canada or any instrumentality of the government of Canada; the term "value" defined in section 2(a)(41) may be defined solely for the purposes of sections 5 and 12 in accordance with the provisions of Rule 2a-1 if the same shall be necessary or desirable to comply with Canadian regulatory or revenue laws or rules or regulations thereunder; the term "bank" defined in section 2(a)(5) shall be defined solely for the purposes of section 9 and 10, as any banking institution; section 4; section 5; section 6(c); section 9; section 10(a), (b), (c), (e), (f) and (g): *Provided,* That the provisions of section 10(d) may be substituted for the provisions of section 10(a) and 10(b)(2) if applicable; section 11; section 12(a), (b), (c), and (d); section 13(a); section 15(a), (b), and (c); section 16(a); sections 17, 18, 19, 20 and 21; section 22(d); section 22(e): *Provided,* That the Toronto Stock Exchange or the Montreal Stock Exchange or both may be included in addition to the New York Stock Exchange; section 22(f); section 22(g); section 23; section 25(a) and (b); section 30(a), (b), (d), (e), and (f); section 31; section 32(a): *Provided,* That provision may be made for the selection and termination of employment of the accountant in compliance with The Companies Act of Canada; section 32(b). Where a provision of the act prohibits or directs action by an investment company, or its directors, officers or employees, the Charter or By Laws shall state that the applicant of its directors, officers or employees shall or shall not act, as the case may be, in conformity with the intent of the statute; where the provision applies to others, such as principal underwriters, investment advisers, controlled companies and affiliated persons, the Charter or By Laws shall also state that the applicant will not permit the prohibited conduct or will obtain the required action. Any of the provisions of sections 11, 12, 15, 18, 22, 23, 30, and 31 may be omitted if not applicable to a company of applicant's classification or sub-classification as defined in section 4 or 5 of the act or if not applicable because the subject matter of such provisions is prohibited by the Charter or By Laws. Other provisions of the act not specified above may be incorporated in the applicant's Charter or By Laws at its option.

(ii) Any question of interpretation of any term or provision of the Charter or By Laws having a counterpart in or otherwise derived from a term or provision of the act shall be resolved by reference to interpretations, if any, of the corresponding term or provision of the act by the courts of the United States of America or, in the absence of any controlling decision of any such court, by rules, regulations, orders or interpretations of the Commission.

(iii) Applicant will maintain the original or duplicate copies of its books and records at the office of its custodian or other office located within the United States.

(iv) At least a majority of the directors and of the officers of the applicant will be United States citizens of whom a majority will be resident in the United States.

(v) Except as provided in Rule 17f-5 and Rule 17f-7, applicant will appoint, by contract, a bank, as defined in section 2(a)(5) of the Act and having the qualification described in section 26(a)(1) of the Act, to act as trustee of, and maintain in its sole custody in the United States, all of applicant's securities and cash, other than cash necessary to meet applicant's current administrative expenses. The contract will provide, *inter alia,* that the custodian will:

(A) consummate all purchases and sales of securities by applicant, other than purchases and sales on an established securities exchange, through the delivery of securities and receipt of cash, or *vice versa* as the case may be, within the United States, and (B) redeem in the United States such of applicant's shares as shall be surrendered therefor, and (C) distribute applicant's assets, or the proceeds thereof, to applicant's assets, or the proceeds thereof, to applicant's creditors and shareholders, upon service upon the custodian of an order of the Commission or court directing such distribution as provided in paragraphs (b) (3) and (5) of this section.

(vi) Applicant's principal underwriter for the sale of its shares will be a citizen and resident of the United States or a corporation organized under the laws of a state of the United States, and having its principal place of business therein, and if redeemable shares are offered, also a member in good standing of a securities association registered under section 15A of the Securities Exchange Act of 1934.

(vii) Applicant will appoint an accountant, qualified to act as an independent public accountant for the applicant under the act and the rules thereunder, who maintains a permanent office and place of business in the United States.

(viii) Any contract entered into between the applicant and its investment adviser and principal underwriter will contain provisions in compliance with the requirements of sections 15, 17(i) and 31 and the rules thereunder, and require that the investment adviser maintain in the United States its books and records or duplicate copies thereof relating to applicant.

(ix) Applicant's Charter and By Laws will not be changed in any manner inconsistent with this paragraph or the act and the rules thereunder unless authorized by the Commission.

(9) Contracts of the applicant, other than those executed on an established securities exchange which do not involve affiliated persons, will provide that:

(i) Such contracts, irrespective of the place of their execution or performance, will be performed in accordance with the requirements of the Act, the Securities Act of 1933, and the Securities Exchange Act of 1934, if the subject matter of such contracts is within the purview of such acts; and

(ii) In effecting the purchase or sale of assets the parties thereto will utilize the United States mails or means of interstate commerce.

(10) Applicant will furnish to the Commission with its registration statement filed under the act a list of persons affiliated with it and with its investment adviser and principal underwriter and will furnish revisions of such list, if any, concurrently with the filing of periodic reports required to be filed under the Act.

Rule 7d–2. Definition of "public offering" as used in Section 7(d) of the Act with respect to certain Canadian tax-deferred retirement savings accounts

(a) *Definitions.* As used in this rule:

(1) *Canadian law* means the federal laws of Canada, the laws of any province or territory of Canada, and the rules or regulations of any federal, provincial, or territorial regulatory authority, or any self-regulatory authority, of Canada.

(2) *Canadian Retirement Account* means a trust or other arrangement, including, but not limited to, a "Registered Retirement Savings Plan" or "Registered Retirement Income Fund" administered under Canadian law, that is managed by the Participant and:

(i) Operated to provide retirement benefits to a Participant; and

(ii) Established in Canada, administered under Canadian law, and qualified for tax-deferred treatment under Canadian law.

(3) *Eligible Security* means a security issued by a Qualified Company that:

(i) Is offered to a Participant, or sold to his or her Canadian Retirement Account, in reliance on this rule; and

(ii) May also be purchased by Canadians other than Participants.

(4) *Foreign Government* means the government of any foreign country or of any political subdivision of a foreign country.

(5) *Foreign Issuer* means any issuer that is a Foreign Government, a national of any foreign country or a corporation or other organization incorporated or organized under the laws of any foreign country, except an issuer meeting the following conditions:

(i) More than 50 percent of the outstanding voting securities of the issuer are held of record either directly or through voting trust certificates or depositary receipts by residents of the United States; and

(ii) Any of the following:

(A) The majority of the executive officers or directors are United States citizens or residents;

(B) More than 50 percent of the assets of the issuer are located in the United States; or

(C) The business of the issuer is administered principally in the United States.

(iii) For purposes of this definition, the term *resident,* as applied to security holders, means any person whose address appears on the records of the issuer, the voting trustee, or the depositary as being located in the United States.

(6) *Participant* means a natural person who is a resident of the United States, or is temporarily present in the United States, and who contributes to, or is or will be entitled to receive the income and assets from, a Canadian Retirement Account.

(7) *Qualified Company* means a Foreign Issuer whose securities are qualified for investment on a

tax-deferred basis by a Canadian Retirement Account under Canadian law.

(8) *United States* means the United States of America, its territories and possessions, any State of the United States, and the District of Columbia.

(b) *Public Offering.* For purposes of section 7(d) of the Act, the term "public offering" does not include the offer to a Participant, or the sale to his or her Canadian Retirement Account, of Eligible Securities issued by a Qualified Company, if the Qualified Company:

(1) Includes in any written offering materials delivered to a Participant, or to his or her Canadian Retirement Account, a prominent statement that the Eligible Security, and the Qualified Company that issued the Eligible Security, are not registered with the U.S. Securities and Exchange Commission, and that the Eligible Security and the Qualified Company are relying on exemptions from registration.

(2) Has not asserted that Canadian law, or the jurisdiction of the courts of Canada, does not apply in a proceeding involving an Eligible Security.

Rule 8b–1. Scope of Rules 8b–1 through 8b–32

The rules contained in Rules 8b–1 through 8b–32 shall govern all registration statements pursuant to section 8 of the Act, including notifications of registration pursuant to section 8(a), and all reports pursuant to section 30(a) or (b) of the Act, including all amendments to such statements and reports, except that any provision in a form covering the same subject matter as any such rule shall be controlling.

Rule 8b–2. Definitions

Unless the context otherwise requires, the terms in paragraphs (a) through (m) of this rule, when used in the rules contained in Rules 8b–1 through 8b–32, in the rules under section 30(a) or (b) of the Act or in the forms for registration statements and reports pursuant to section 8 or 30(a) or (b) of the Act, shall have the respective meanings indicated in this section. The terms "EDGAR," "EDGAR Filer Manual," "electronic filer," "electronic filing," "electronic format," "electronic submission," "paper format," and "signature" shall have the meanings assigned to such terms in Regulation S–T—General Rules for Electronic Filings (17 CFR 232).

(a) *Amount.* The term "amount", when used in regard to securities, means the principal amount if relating to evidences of indebtedness, the number of shares if relating to shares, and the number of units if relating to any other kind of security.

(b) *Certified.* The term "certified", when used in regard to financial statements, means certified by an independent public or independent certified public accountant or accountants.

(c) *Charter.* The term "charter" includes articles of incorporation, declaration of trust, articles of association or partnership, or any similar instrument, as amended, effecting (either with or without filing with any governmental agency) the organization or creation of an incorporated or unincorporated person.

(d) *Employee.* The term "employee" does not include a director, trustee, officer or member of the advisory board.

(e) *Fiscal Year.* The term "fiscal year" means the annual accounting period or, if no closing date has been adopted, the calendar year ending on December 31.

(f) *Investment Income.* The term "investment income" means the aggregate of net operating income or loss from real estate and gross income from interest, dividends and all other sources, exclusive of profit or loss on sales of securities or other properties.

(g) *Material.* The term "material", when used to qualify a requirement for the furnishing of information as to any subject, limits the information required to those matters as to which an average prudent investor ought reasonably to be informed before buying or selling any security of the particular company.

(h) *Parent.* A "parent" of a specified person is an affiliated person who controls the specified person directly or indirectly through one or more intermediaries.

(i) *Previously Filed or Reported.* The terms "previously filed" and "previously reported" mean previously filed with, or reported in, a registration statement filed under section 8 of the act or under the Securities Act of 1933, a report filed under section 30 of the act or section 13 or 15(d) of the Securities Exchange Act of 1934, a definitive proxy statement filed under section 20 of the act or section 14 of the Securities Exchange Act of 1934, or a prospectus filed under the Securities Act of 1933: *Provided,* That information contained in any such document shall be deemed to have been previously filed with, or reported to, an exchange only if such document is filed with such exchange.

(j) *Share.* The term "share" means a share of stock in a corporation or unit of interest in an unincorporated person.

(k) *Significant Subsidiary.* The term "significant subsidiary" means a subsidiary meeting any one of the following conditions:

(1) The value of the investments in and advances to the subsidiary by its parent and the parent's other subsidiaries, if any exceed 10 percent of the value of the assets of the parent or, if a consolidated balance sheet is filed, the value of the assets of the parent and its consolidated subsidiaries.

(2) The total investment income of the subsidiary or, in the case of a noninvestment company subsidiary, the net income exceeds 10 percent of the total investment income of the parent or, if consolidated statements are filed, 10 percent of the total investment income of the parent and its consolidated subsidiaries.

(3) The subsidiary is the parent of one or more subsidiaries and, together with such subsidiaries would, if considered in the aggregate, constitute a significant subsidiary.

(*l*) *Subsidiary.* A "subsidiary" of a specified person is an affiliated person who is controlled by the specified person, directly or indirectly, through one or more intermediaries.

(m) *Totally-Held Subsidiary.* The term "totally-held subsidiary" means a subsidiary (1) substantially all of whose outstanding securities are owned by its parent and/or the parent's other totally-held subsidiaries, and (2) which is not indebted to any person other than its parent and/or the parent's other totally-held subsidiaries in an amount which is material in relation to the particular subsidiary, excepting indebtedness incurred in the ordinary course of business which is not over-due and which matures within one year from the date of its creation, whether evidenced by securities or not.

Rule 8b–3. Title of securities

Wherever the title of securities is required to be stated, there shall be given such information as will indicate the type and general character of the securities, including the following:

(a) In the case of shares, the par or stated value, if any; the rate of dividends, if fixed, and whether cumulative or noncumulative; a brief indication of the preference, if any; and if convertible, a statement to that effect.

(b) In the case of funded debt, the rate of interest; the date of maturity, or if the issue matures serially, a brief indication of the serial maturities, such as "maturing serially from 1950 to 1960"; if the payment of principal or interest is contingent, an appropriate indication of such contingency; a brief indication of the priority of the issue; and if convertible, a statement to that effect.

(c) In the case of any other kind of security, appropriate information of comparable character.

Rule 8b–4. Interpretation of requirements

Unless the context clearly shows otherwise:

(a) The forms require information only as to the company filing the registration statement or report.

(b) Whenever any fixed period of time in the past is indicated, such period shall be computed from the date of filing.

(c) Whenever words relate to the future, they have reference solely to present intention.

(d) Any words indicating the holder of a position or office include persons, by whatever titles designated, whose duties are those ordinarily performed by holders of such positions or offices.

Rule 8b–5. Time of filing original registration statement

An investment company shall file a registration statement with the Commission on the appropriate form within three months after the filing of notification of registration under section 8(a) of the Act, provided that if the fiscal year of the company ends within the three months period, its registration statement may be filed within three months after the end of such fiscal year.

Rule 8b–10. Requirements as to proper form

Every registration statement or report shall be prepared in accordance with the form prescribed therefor by the Commission, as in effect on the date of filing. Any such statement or report shall be deemed to be filed on the proper form unless objection to the form is made by the Commission within thirty days after the date of filing.

Rule 8b–11. Number of copies; signatures; binding

(a) Three complete copies of each registration statement or report, including exhibits and all other papers and documents filed as a part thereof, shall be filed with the Commission.

(b) In the case of a registration statement filed on Form N–1A (17 CFR 239.15A and 274.11A), Form N–2 (17 CFR 239.14 and 274.11a–1), Form N–3 (17 CFR 239.17a and 274.11b), Form N–4 (17 CFR 239.17b and 274), or Form N–6 (17 CFR 239.17c and 274.11d), three complete copies of each part of the registration statement (including, if applicable, exhibits and all other papers and documents filed as part of Part C of the registration statement) shall be filed with the Commission.

(c) At least one copy of the registration statement or report shall be signed in the manner prescribed by the appropriate form. Unsigned copies shall be conformed. If the signature of any person is affixed pursuant to a power of attorney or other similar authority, a copy of such power of attorney or other authority shall also be filed with the registration statement or report.

(d) Each copy of a registration statement or report filed with the Commission shall be bound in one or more parts without stiff covers. The bindings shall be made on the left-hand side and in such manner as to leave the reading matter legible.

(e) Duplicated or facsimile versions of manual signatures of persons required to sign any registration statement or report, including all amendments and exhibits to such statements or reports, that are filed or submitted to the Commission under the Act, shall be considered manual signatures for the purposes of the Act and the rules and regulations thereunder; provided that, the original signed document is retained by the filer for a period of five years and, upon request, the filer furnishes to the Commission or the staff the original manually signed document.

Rule 8b–12. Requirements as to paper, printing and language

(a) Registration statements and reports shall be filed on good quality, unglazed, white paper, no larger than 8½ x 11 inches in size, insofar as practicable. To the extent that the reduction of larger documents would render them illegible, such documents may be filed on paper larger than 8½ x 11 inches in size.

(b) In the case of a registration statement filed on Form N–1A (17 CFR 239.15A and 274.11A), Form N–2 (17 CFR 239.14 and 274.11a–1 of this chapter), Form N–3 (17 CFR 239.17a and 17 CFR 274.11b), or Form N–4 (17 CFR 239.17b and 274.11c), or Form N–6 (17 CFR 239.17c and 274.11d of this chapter), Part C of the registration statement shall be filed on good quality, unglazed, white paper, no larger than 8½ x 11 inches in size, insofar as practicable. The prospectus and, if applicable, the Statement of Additional Information, however, may be filed on smaller-sized paper provided that the size of paper used in each document is uniform.

(c) The registration statement or report and, insofar as practicable, all papers and documents filed as a part thereof, shall be printed, lithographed, mimeographed, or typewritten. However, the registration statement or report or any portion thereof may be prepared by any similar process which, in the opinion of the Commission, produces copies suitable for permanent record. Irrespective of the process used, all copies of any such material shall be clear, easily readable and suitable for repeated photocopying. Debits in credit categories and credits in debit categories shall be designated so as to be clearly distinguishable as such on photocopies.

(d) The body of all printed registration statements and reports and all notes to financial statements and other tabular data included therein shall be in roman type at least as large as 10–point modern type. However, to the extent necessary for convenient presentation, financial statements and other statistical or tabular data, including tabular data in notes, may be set in type at least as large and as legible as 8–point modern type. All types shall be leaded at least 2 points.

(e) Registration statements and reports shall be in the English language. If any exhibit or other paper or document filed with a registration statement or report is in a foreign language, it shall be accompanied by a translation into the English language.

(f) Where a registration statement or report is distributed through an electronic medium, issuers may satisfy legibility requirements applicable to printed documents, such as paper size, type size and font, bold-face type, italics and red ink, by presenting all required information in a format readily communicated to investors, and where indicated, in a manner reasonably calculated to draw investor attention to specific information.

Rule 8b–13. Preparation of registration statement or report

The registration statement or report shall contain the numbers and captions of all items of the appropriate form, but the text of the items may be omitted provided the answers thereto are so prepared as to indicate to the reader the coverage of the items without the necessity of his referring to the text of the items or instructions thereto. However, where any item requires information to be given in tabular form, it shall be given in substantially the tabular form specified in the item. All instructions, whether appearing under the items of the form or elsewhere therein, are to be omitted from the registration statement or report. Unless expressly provided otherwise, if any item is inapplicable or the answer thereto is in the negative, an appropriate statement to that effect shall be made.

Rule 8b–14. Riders; inserts

Riders shall not be used. If the registration statement or report is typed on a printed form, and the space provided for the answer to any given item is insufficient, reference shall be made in such space to a full insert page or pages on which the item number and caption and the complete answer are given.

Rule 8b–15. Amendments

All amendments shall be filed under cover of the facing sheet of the appropriate form, shall be clearly identified as amendments, and shall comply with all pertinent requirements applicable to registration statements and reports. Amendments shall be filed separately for each separate registration or report amended. Except as permitted under Rule 102(b) of Regulation S–T, any amendment filed under this section shall state the complete text of each item amended. An amendment to any report required to include the certifications as specified in Rule 30a–2(a) must include new certifications by each principal executive and principal financial officer of the registrant, and an amendment to any report required to be accompanied by the certifications as specified in Rule 13a–14(b) or Rule 15d–14(b) under the Securities Exchange Act of 1934 and Rule 30a–2(b) must be accompanied by new certifications by each principal executive and principal financial officer to the registrant.

Rule 8b–16. Amendments to registration statements

(a) Every registered management investment company which is required to file a semi-annual report on Form N–SAR, as prescribed by Rule 30b1–1 shall amend the registration statement required pursuant to section 8(b) by filing, not more than 120 days after the close of each fiscal year ending on or after the date upon which such registration statement was filed, the appropriate form prescribed for such amendments.

(b) Paragraph (a) of this rule shall not apply to a registered closed-end management investment company whose registration statement was filed on Form N–2; provided that the following information is transmitted to shareholders in its annual report to shareholders:

(1) If the company offers a dividend reinvestment plan to shareholders, information about the plan required to be disclosed in the company's prospectus by Item 10.1.e of Form N–2 (17 CFR 274.11a–1);

(2) Any material changes in the company's investment objectives or policies (described in Item 8.2 of Form N–2) that have not been approved by shareholders;

(3) Any changes in the company's charter or by-laws that would delay or prevent a change of control of the company (described in Item 10.1.f of Form N–2) that have not been approved by shareholders;

(4) Any material changes in the principal risk factors associated with investment in the company (described in Item 8.3 of Form N–2); and

(5) Any changes in the persons who are primarily responsible for the day-to-day management of the company's portfolio (described in Item 9.1.c of Form N–2), including any new person's business experience during the past five years and the length of time he or she has been responsible for the management of the portfolio.

(c) In lieu of including a description of the dividend reinvestment plan in its annual report, a company may comply with the disclosure requirement of paragraph (b)(1) of this rule concerning a company's dividend reinvestment plan by delivering to each shareholder annually a separate document containing the information about the plan required to be disclosed in the company's prospectus by Item 10.1.e of Form N–2. Any such document shall be deemed to be a record or document subject to the record-keeping requirements of section 31 and the rules adopted thereunder (17 CFR 31a–1 et seq.).

(d) The changes required to be disclosed by paragraphs (b)(2) through (b)(5) of this rule are those that occurred since the later of either the effective date of the company's registration statement relating to its initial offering of securities under the Securities Act of 1933 (or the most recent post-effective amendment thereto) or the close of the period covered by the previously transmitted annual shareholder report.

Rule 8b–20. Additional information

In addition to the information expressly required to be included in a registration statement or report, there shall be added such further material information, if any, as may be necessary to make the required statements, in the light of the circumstances under which they are made, not misleading.

Rule 8b-21. Information unknown or not available

Information required need be given only insofar as it is known or reasonably available to the registrant. If any required information is unknown and not reasonably available to the registrant, either because the obtaining thereof would involve unreasonable effort or expense, or because it rests peculiarly within the knowledge of another person not affiliated with the registrant, the information may be omitted subject to the following conditions:

(a) The registrant shall give such information on the subject as it possesses or can acquire without unreasonable effort or expense, together with the sources thereof.

(b) The registrant shall include a statement either showing that unreasonable effort or expense would be involved or indicating the absence of any affiliation with the person within whose knowledge the information rests and stating the result of a request made to such person for the information.

Rule 8b-22. Disclaimer of control

If the existence of control is open to reasonable doubt in any instance, the registrant may disclaim the existence of control and any admission thereof; in such case, however, the registrant shall state the material facts pertinent to the possible existence of control.

Rule 8b-23. Incorporation by reference

(a) Any registrant may incorporate by reference, in answer or partial answer to any item of a registration statement or report, any information contained elsewhere in the statement or report or any information contained in any other statement, report or prospectus filed with the Commission under any Act administered by it, so long as a copy of the other statement, report or prospectus is filed with each copy of the registration statement or report in which it is incorporated by reference. In the case of a registration statement, report, or prospectus filed in electronic format, the registrant need not file a copy of the document incorporated by reference if that document also was filed in electronic format. A registrant may incorporate by reference matter contained in an exhibit, however, only to the extent permitted by Rules 8b-24 and 8b-32.

(b) Any financial statement filed with the Commission pursuant to any act administered by the Commission may be incorporated by reference in a registration statement or report, filed with the Commission by the same or any other person, if it substantially conforms to the requirements of the form on which the statement or report is filed.

(c) Material incorporated by reference shall be clearly identified in the reference. An express statement that the specified matter is incorporated by reference shall be made at the particular place in the registration statement or report where the information is required. Matter shall not be incorporated by reference in any case where such incorporation would render the statement incomplete, unclear or confusing.

Rule 8b-24. Summaries or outlines of documents

Where an item requires a summary or outline of the provisions of any document, only a brief statement shall be made, in succinct and condensed form, as to the most important provisions of the document. In addition to such statement, the summary or outline may incorporate by reference particular items, sections, or paragraphs of any exhibit and may be qualified in its entirety by such reference. Matter contained in an exhibit may be incorporated by reference in answer to an item only to the extent permitted by this section.

Rule 8b-25. Extension of time for furnishing information

(a) Subject to paragraph (b) of this rule, if it is impractical to furnish any required information, document or report at the time it is required to be filed, there may be filed with the Commission as a separate document an application (a) identifying the information, document or report in question, (b) stating why the filing thereof at the time required is impracticable, and (c) requesting an extension of time for filing the information, document or report to a specified date not more than 60 days after the date it would otherwise have to be filed. The application shall be deemed granted unless the Commission, within 10 days after receipt thereof, shall enter an order denying the application. Rule 0-5 shall not apply to such applications.

(b) If it is impracticable to furnish any document or report required to be filed in electronic format at the time it is required to be filed, the electronic filer may file under the temporary hardship provision of Rule 201 of Regulation S-T (17 CFR 232.201) or may submit a written application for a continuing hardship exemption, in accordance with Rule 202 of Regulation S-T. Applications for such exemptions shall be considered in accordance with the provisions of those sections and paragraphs (h) and (i) of 17 CFR 200.30–5.

Rule 8b–30. Additional exhibits

A company may file such exhibits as it may desire, in addition to those required by the appropriate form. Such exhibits shall be so marked as to indicate clearly the subject matters to which they refer.

Rule 8b–31. Omission of substantially identical documents

In any case where two or more indentures, contracts, franchises, or other documents required to be filed as exhibits are substantially identical in all material respects except as to the parties thereto, the dates of execution, or other details, copies of only one of such documents need be filed, with a schedule identifying the other documents omitted and setting forth the material details in which such documents differ from the documents filed. The Commission may at any time in its discretion require the filing of copies of any documents so omitted.

Rule 8b–32. Incorporation of exhibits by reference

(a) Except as provided in paragraph (c) of this rule, any document or part thereof filed with the Commission pursuant to any Act administered by the Commission may, subject to the limitations of 17 CFR 228.10(f) and Item 10(d) of Regulation S–K, be incorporated by reference as an exhibit to any registration statement or report filed with the Commission by the same or any other person.

(b) If any modification has occurred in the text of any document incorporated by reference since the filing thereof, a statement containing the text of such modification and the date thereof shall be filed with the reference.

(c) *Electronic Filings.* A registrant may incorporate by reference into a registration statement or report required to be filed electronically only exhibits that have been filed in electronic format, unless the exhibit has been filed in paper under a hardship exemption (Rule 201 or 202 of Regulation S–T) and any required confirming copy has been submitted.

Rule 8f–1. Deregistration of certain registered investment companies

A registered investment company that seeks a Commission order declaring that it is no longer an investment company may file an application with the Commission on Form N–8F (17 CFR 274.218) if the investment company:

(a) Has sold substantially all of its assets to another registered investment company or merged into or consolidated with another registered investment company;

(b) Has distributed substantially all of its assets to its shareholders and has completed, or is in the process of, winding up its affairs;

(c) Qualifies for an exclusion from the definition of "investment company" under section 3(c)(1) or section 3(c)(7) of the Act; or

(d) Has become a business development company.

Rule 10b–1. Definition of regular broker or dealer

The term *regular broker or dealer* of an investment company shall mean:

(a) One of the ten brokers or dealers that received the greatest dollar amount of brokerage commissions by virtue of direct or indirect participation in the company's portfolio transactions during the company's most recent fiscal year;

(b) One of the ten brokers or dealers that engaged as principal in the largest dollar amount of portfolio transactions of the investment company during the company's most recent fiscal year; or

(c) One of the ten brokers or dealers that sold the largest dollar amount of securities of the investment company during the company's most recent fiscal year.

Rule 10e–1. Death, disqualification, or bona fide resignation of directors

If a registered investment company, by reason of the death, disqualification, or bona fide resignation of any director, does not meet any requirement of the Act or any rule or regulation thereunder regarding the composition of the company's board of directors, the operation of the relevant subsection of the Act, rule, or regulation will be suspended as to the company:

(a) For 90 days if the vacancy may be filled by action of the board of directors; or

(b) For 150 days if a vote of stockholders is required to fill the vacancy.

Rule 10f–1. Conditional exemption of certain underwriting transactions

Any purchase or other acquisition by a registered management company acting, pursuant to a written agreement, as an underwriter of securities of an issuer which is not an investment company shall be exempt from the provisions of section 10(f) upon the following conditions:

(a) The party to such agreement other than such registered company is a principal underwriter of such securities, which principal underwriter (1) is a person primarily engaged in the business of underwriting and distributing securities issued by other persons, selling securities to customers, or related activities, whose gross income normally is derived principally from such business or related activities, and (2) does not control or is not under common control with such registered company.

(b) No public offering of the securities underwritten by such agreement has been made prior to the execution thereof.

(c) Such securities have been effectively registered pursuant to the Securities Act of 1933 prior to the execution of such agreement.

(d) In regard to any securities underwritten, whether or not purchased, by the registered company pursuant to such agreement, such company shall be allowed a rate of gross commission, spread, concession or other profit not less than the amount allowed to such principal underwriter, exclusive of any amounts received by such principal underwriter as a management fee from other principal underwriters.

(e) Such agreement is authorized by resolution adopted by a vote of not less than a majority of the board of directors of such registered company, none of which majority is an affiliated person of such principal underwriter, of the issuer of the securities underwritten pursuant to such agreement or of any person engaged in a business described in paragraph (a)(1) of this rule.

(f) The resolution required in paragraph (e) of this section shall state that it has been adopted pursuant to this rule, and shall incorporate the terms of the proposed agreement by attaching a copy thereof as an exhibit or otherwise.

(g) A copy of the resolution required in paragraph (e) of this rule, signed by each member of the board of directors of the registered company who voted in favor of its adoption, shall be transmitted to the Commission not later than the fifth day succeeding the date on which such agreement is executed.

Rule 10f–2. Exercise of warrants or rights received on portfolio securities

Any purchase or other acquisition of securities by a registered investment company pursuant to the exercise of warrants or rights to subscribe to or to purchase securities shall be exempt from the provisions of section 10(f) of the Act, *Provided,* That the warrants or rights so exercised (a) were offered or issued to such company as a security holder on the same basis as all other holders of the class or classes of securities to whom such warrants or rights were offered or issued, and (b) do not exceed 5 percent of the total amount of such warrants or rights so issued.

Rule 10f–3. Exemption for the acquisition of securities during the existence of an underwriting or selling syndicate

(a) *Definitions.* (1) *Domestic Issuer* means any issuer other than a foreign government, a national of any foreign country, or a corporation or other organization incorporated or organized under the laws of any foreign country.

(2) *Eligible Foreign Offering* means a public offering of securities, conducted under the laws of a country other than the United States, that meets the following conditions:

(i) The offering is subject to regulation by a "foreign financial regulatory authority," as defined in section 2(a)(50) of the Act, in such country;

(ii) The securities are offered at a fixed price to all purchasers in the offering (except for any rights to purchase securities that are required by law to be granted to existing security holders of the issuer);

(iii) Financial statements, prepared and audited in accordance with standards required or permitted by the appropriate foreign financial regulatory authority in such country, for the two years prior to the offering, are made available to the public and prospective purchasers in connection with the offering; and

(iv) If the issuer is a Domestic Issuer, it meets the following conditions:

(A) It has a class of securities registered pursuant to section 12(b) or 12(g) of the Securities Exchange Act of 1934 or is required to file reports pursuant to section 15(d) of the Securities Exchange Act of 1934; and

(B) It has filed all the material required to be filed pursuant to section 13(a) or 15(d) of the Securities Exchange Act of 1934 for a period of at least twelve months immediately preceding the sale of securities made in reliance upon this (or for such shorter period that the issuer was required to file such material).

(3) *Eligible Municipal Securities* means "municipal securities," as defined in section 3(a)(29) of the Securities Exchange Act of 1934, that are sufficiently liquid that they can be sold at or near their carrying value within a reasonably short period of time and either:

(i) Are subject to no greater than moderate credit risk; or

(ii) If the issuer of the municipal securities, or the entity supplying the revenues or other payments from which the issue is to be paid, has been in continuous operation for less than three years, including the operation of any predecessors, the securities are subject to a minimal or low amount of credit risk.

(4) *Eligible Rule 144A Offering* means an offering of securities that meets the following conditions:

(i) The securities are offered or sold in transactions exempt from registration under section 4(a)(2) of the Securities Act of 1933, Rule 144A thereunder, or rules 501–508 thereunder;

(ii) The securities are sold to persons that the seller and any person acting on behalf of the seller reasonably believe to include qualified institutional buyers, as defined in Rule 144A(a)(1); and

(iii) The seller and any person acting on behalf of the seller reasonably believe that the securities are eligible for resale to other qualified institutional buyers pursuant to Rule 144A.

(5) *Managed portion* of a portfolio of a registered investment company means a discrete portion of a portfolio of a registered investment company for which a subadviser is responsible for providing investment advice, provided that:

(i) The subadviser is not an affiliated person of any investment adviser, promoter, underwriter, officer, director, member of an advisory board, or employee of the registered investment company; and

(ii) The subadviser's advisory contract:

(A) Prohibits it from consulting with any subadviser of the investment company that is a principal underwriter or an affiliated person of a principal underwriter concerning transactions of the investment company in securities or other assets; and

(B) Limits its responsibility in providing advice to providing advice with respect to such portion.

(6) *Series of a series company* means any class or series of a registered investment company that issues two or more classes or series of preferred or special stock, each of which is preferred over all other classes or series with respect to assets specifically allocated to that class or series.

(7) *Subadviser* means an investment adviser as defined in section 2(a)(20)(B) of the Act.

(b) *Exemption for Purchases by Series Companies and Investment Companies with Managed Portions.* For purposes of this section and section 10(f) of the Act, each Series of a Series Company, and each Managed Portion of a registered investment company, is deemed to be a separate investment company. Therefore, a purchase or acquisition of a security by a registered investment company is exempt from the prohibitions of section 10(f) of the Act if section 10(f) of the Act would not prohibit such purchase if each Series and each Managed Portion of the company were a separately registered investment company.

(c) *Exemptions for Other Purchases.* Any purchase of securities by a registered investment company prohibited by section 10(f) of the Act shall be exempt from the provisions of such section if the following conditions are met:

(1) *Type of Security.* The securities to be purchased are:

(i) Part of an issue registered under the Securities Act of 1933 that is being offered to the public;

(ii) Part of an issue of government securities, as defined in section 2(a)(16) of the Act;

(iii) Eligible Municipal Securities;

(iv) Securities sold in an Eligible Foreign Offering; or

(v) Securities sold in an Eligible Rule 144A Offering.

(2) *Timing and Price.* (i) The securities are purchased prior to the end of the first day on which any sales are made, at a price that is not more than the price paid by each other purchaser of securities in that offering or in any concurrent offering of the securities (except, in the case of an Eligible Foreign Offering, for any rights to purchase

that are required by law to be granted to existing security holders of the issuer); and

(ii) If the securities are offered for subscription upon exercise of rights, the securities shall be purchased on or before the fourth day preceding the day on which the rights offering terminates.

(3) *Reasonable Reliance*. For purposes of determining compliance with paragraphs (c)(1)(v) and (c)(2)(i) of this rule, an investment company may reasonably rely upon written statements made by the issuer or a syndicate manager, or by an underwriter or seller of the securities through which such investment company purchases the securities.

(4) *Continuous Operation*. If the securities to be purchased are part of an issue registered under the Securities Act of 1933 that is being offered to the public, are government securities (as defined in section 2(a)(16) of the Act), or are purchased pursuant to an Eligible Foreign Offering or an Eligible Rule 144A Offering, the issuer of the securities must have been in continuous operation for not less than three years, including the operations of any predecessors.

(5) *Firm Commitment Underwriting*. The securities are offered pursuant to an underwriting or similar agreement under which the underwriters are committed to purchase all of the securities being offered, except those purchased by others pursuant to a rights offering, if the underwriters purchase any of the securities.

(6) *Reasonable Commission*. The commission, spread or profit received or to be received by the principal underwriters is reasonable and fair compared to the commission, spread or profit received by other such persons in connection with the underwriting of similar securities being sold during a comparable period of time.

(7) *Percentage Limit*. (i) *Generally*. The amount of securities of any class of such issue to be purchased by the investment company, aggregated with purchases by any other investment company advised by the investment company's investment adviser, and any purchases by another account with respect to which the investment adviser has investment discretion if the investment adviser exercised such investment discretion with respect to the purchase, does not exceed the following limits:

(A) If purchased in an offering other than an Eligible Rule 144A Offering, 25 percent of the principal amount of the offering of such class; or

(B) If purchased in an Eligible Rule 144A Offering, 25 percent of the total of:

(*1*) The principal amount of the offering of such class sold by underwriters or members of the selling syndicate to qualified institutional buyers, as defined in Rule 144A(a)(1) under the Securities Act of 1933; plus

(*2*) The principal amount of the offering of such class in any concurrent public offering.

(ii) Exemption from Percentage Limit. The requirement in paragraph (c)(7)(i) of this rule applies only if the investment adviser of the investment company is, or is an affiliated person of, a principal underwriter of the security; and

(iii) Separate Aggregation. The requirement in paragraph (c)(7)(i) of this rule applies independently with respect to each investment adviser of the investment company that is, or is an affiliated person of, a principal underwriter of the security.

(8) *Prohibition of Certain Affiliate Transactions*. Such investment company does not purchase the securities being offered directly or indirectly from an officer, director, member of an advisory board, investment adviser or employee of such investment company or from a person of which any such officer, director, member of an advisory board, investment adviser or employee is an affiliated person; provided, that a purchase from a syndicate manager shall not be deemed to be a purchase from a specific underwriter if:

(i) Such underwriter does not benefit directly or indirectly from the transaction; or

(ii) In respect to the purchase of Eligible Municipal Securities, such purchase is not designated as a group sale or otherwise allocated to the account of any person from whom this paragraph prohibits the purchase.

(9) *Periodic Reporting*. The existence of any transactions effected pursuant to this section shall be reported on the Form N–SAR [17 CFR 274.101] of the investment company and a written record of each such transaction, setting forth from whom the securities were acquired, the identity of the underwriting syndicate's members, the terms of the transaction, and the information or mate-

rials upon which the determination described in paragraph (c)(10)(iii) of this rule was made shall be attached thereto.

(10) *Board Review.* The board of directors of the investment company, including a majority of the directors who are not interested persons of the investment company:

(i) Has approved procedures, pursuant to which such purchases may be effected for the company, that are reasonably designed to provide that the purchases comply with all the conditions of this rule;

(ii) Approves such changes to the procedures as the board deems necessary; and

(iii) Determines no less frequently than quarterly that all purchases made during the preceding quarter were effected in compliance with such procedures.

(11) *Board Composition.* The board of directors of the investment company satisfies the fund governance standards defined in Rule 0–1(a)(7).

(12) *Maintenance of Records.* The investment company:

(i) Shall maintain and preserve permanently in an easily accessible place a written copy of the procedures, and any modification thereto, described in paragraphs (c)(10)(i) and (c)(10)(ii) of this rule; and

(ii) Shall maintain and preserve for a period not less than six years from the end of the fiscal year in which any transactions occurred, the first two years in an easily accessible place, a written record of each such transaction, setting forth from whom the securities were acquired, the identity of the underwriting syndicate's members, the terms of the transaction, and the information or materials upon which the determination described in paragraph (c)(10)(iii) of this rule was made.

Rule 11a–1. Definition of "exchange" for purposes of Section 11 of the Act

(a) For the purposes of section 11 of the Act, the term *exchange* as used therein shall include the issuance of any security by a registered investment company in an amount equal to the proceeds, or any portion of the proceeds, paid or payable—

(1) Upon the repurchase, by or at the instance of such issuer, of an outstanding security the terms of which provide for its termination, retirement or cancellation, or

(2) Upon the termination, retirement or cancellation of an outstanding security of such issuer in accordance with the terms thereof.

(b) A security shall not be deemed to have been repurchased by or at the instance of the issuer, or terminated, retired or canceled in accordance with the terms of the security if—

(1) The security was redeemed or repurchased at the instance of the holder; or

(2) A security holder's account was closed for failure to make payments as prescribed in the security or instruments pursuant to which the security was issued, and notice of intention to close the account was mailed to the security holder, and he had a reasonable time in which to meet the deficiency; or

(3) Sale of the security was restricted to a specified, limited group of persons and, in accordance with the terms of the security or the instruments pursuant to which the security was issued, upon its being transferred by the holder to a person not a member of the group eligible to purchase the security, the issuer required the surrender of the security and paid the redemption price thereof.

(c) The provisions of paragraph (a) of this rule shall not apply if, following the repurchase of an outstanding security by or at the instance of the issuer or the termination, retirement or cancellation of an outstanding security in accordance with the terms thereof—

(1) The proceeds are actually paid to the security holder by or on behalf of the issuer within 7 days, and

(2) No sale and no offer (other than by way of exchange) of any security of the issuer is made by or on behalf of the issuer to the person to whom such proceeds were paid, within 60 days after such payment.

(d) The provisions of paragraph (a) of this rule shall not apply to the repurchase, termination, retirement, or cancellation of a security outstanding on the effective date of this section or issued pursuant to a subscription agreement or other plan of acquisition in effect on such date.

Rule 11a–2. Offers of exchange by certain registered separate accounts or others the terms of which do not require prior Commission approval

(a) As used in this rule:

(1) *Deferred sales load* shall mean any sales load, including a contingent deferred sales load, that is deducted upon redemption or annuitization of amounts representing all or a portion of a securityholder's interest in a separate account;

(2) *Exchanged security* shall include not only the security or securities (or portion[s] thereof) of a security holder actually exchanged pursuant to an exchange offer but also any security or securities (or portion[s] thereof) of the securityholder previously exchanged for the exchanged security or its predecessors;

(3) *Front-end sales load* shall mean any sales load that is deducted from one or more purchase payments made by a securityholder before they are invested in a separate account; and

(4) *Purchase payments made for the acquired security,* as used in paragraphs (c)(2) and (d)(2) of this rule, shall not include any purchase payments made for the exchanged security or any appreciation attributable to those purchase payments that are transferred to the offering account in connection with an exchange.

(b) Notwithstanding section 11 of the Act, any registered separate account or any principal underwriter for such an account (collectively, the "offering account") may make or cause to be made an offer to the holder of a security of the offering account, or of any other registered separate account having the same insurance company depositor or sponsor as the offering account or having an insurance company depositor or sponsor that is an affiliate of the offering account's depositor or sponsor, to exchange his security (or portion thereof) (the "exchanged security") for a security (or portion thereof) of the offering account (the "acquired security") without the terms of such exchange offer first having been submitted to and approved by the Commission, as provided below:

(1) If the securities (or portions thereof) involved are variable annuity contracts, then

(i) The exchange must be made on the basis of the relative net asset values of the securities to be exchanged, except that the offering account may deduct at the time of the exchange

(A) An administrative fee which is disclosed in the part of the offering account's registration statement under the Securities Act of 1933 relating to the prospectus, and

(B) Any front-end sales load permitted by paragraph (c) of this section, and

(ii) Any deferred sales load imposed on the acquired security by the offering account shall be calculated in the manner prescribed by paragraph (d) or (e) of this rule; or

(2) If the securities (or portions thereof) involved are variable life insurance contracts offered by a separate account registered under the Act as a unit investment trust, then the exchange must be made on the basis of the relative net asset values of the securities to be exchanged, except that the offering account may deduct at the time of the exchange an administrative fee which is disclosed in the part of the offering account's registration statement under the Securities Act of 1933 relating to the prospectus.

(c) If the offering account imposes a front-end sales load on the acquired security, then such sales load

(1) Shall be a percentage that is no greater than the excess of the rate of the front-end sales load otherwise applicable to that security over the rate of any front-end sales load previously paid on the exchanged security, and

(2) Shall not exceed 9 percent of the sum of the purchase payments made for the acquired security and the exchanged security.

(d) If the offering account imposes a deferred sales load on the acquired security and the exchanged security was also subject to a deferred sales load, then any deferred sales load imposed on the acquired security:

(1) Shall be calculated as if

(i) The holder of the acquired security had been the holder of that security from the date on which he became the holder of the exchanged security and

(ii) Purchase payments made for the exchanged security had been made for the acquired security on the date on which they were made for the exchanged security; and

(2) Shall not exceed 9 percent of the sum of the purchase payments made for the acquired security and the exchanged security.

(e) If the offering account imposes a deferred sales load on the acquired security and a front-end sales load was paid on the exchanged security, then any deferred sales load imposed on the acquired security may not be imposed on purchase payments made for the exchanged security or any appreciation attributable to purchase payments made for the exchanged security that are transferred in connection with the exchange.

(f) Notwithstanding the foregoing, no offer of exchange shall be made in reliance on this section if both a front-end sales load and a deferred sales load are to be imposed on the acquired security or if both such sales loads are imposed on the exchanged security.

Rule 11a–3. Offers of exchange by open–end investment companies other than separate accounts

(a) For purposes of this rule:

(1) *Acquired security* means the security held by a securityholder after completing an exchange pursuant to an exchange offer;

(2) *Administrative fee* means any fee, other than a sales load, deferred sales load or redemption fee, that is

(i) Reasonably intended to cover the costs incurred in processing exchanges of the type for which the fee is charged, *Provided*, That: the offering company will maintain and preserve records of any determination of the costs incurred in connection with exchanges for a period of not less than six years, the first two years in an easily accessible place. The records preserved under this provision shall be subject to inspection by the Commission in accordance with section 31(b) of the Act as if such records were records required to be maintained under rules adopted under section 31(a) of the Act; or

(ii) A nominal fee as defined in paragraph (a)(8) of this rule;

(3) *Deferred sales load* means any amount properly chargeable to sales or promotional expenses that is paid by a shareholder after purchase but before or upon redemption;

(4) *Exchanged security* means

(i) The security actually exchanged pursuant to an exchange offer, and

(ii) Any security previously exchanged for such security or for any of its predecessors;

(5) *Group of investment companies* means any two or more registered open-end investment companies that hold themselves out to investors as related companies for purposes of investment and investor services, and

(i) That have a common investment adviser or principal underwriter, or

(ii) The investment adviser or principal underwriter of one of the companies is an affiliated person as defined in section 2(a)(3) of the Act of the investment adviser or principal underwriter of each of the other companies;

(6) *Offering company* means a registered open-end investment company (other than a registered separate account) or any principal underwriter thereof that makes an offer (an "exchange offer") to the holder of a security of that company, or of another open-end investment company within the same group of investment companies as the offering company, to exchange that security for a security of the offering company;

(7) *Redemption fee* means a fee that is imposed by the fund pursuant to Rule 22c–2; and

(8) *Nominal fee* means a slight or *de minimis* fee.

(b) Notwithstanding section 11(a) of the Act and except as provided in paragraphs (d) and (e) of this rule, in connection with an exchange offer an offering company may cause a securityholder to be charged a sales load on the acquired security, a redemption fee, an administrative fee, or any combination of the foregoing,

Provided, That:

(1) Any administrative fee or scheduled variation thereof is applied uniformly to all securityholders of the class specified;

(2) Any redemption fee charged with respect to the exchanged security or any scheduled variation thereof

(i) Is applied uniformly to all securityholders of the class specified, and

(ii) Does not exceed the redemption fee applicable to a redemption of the exchanged security in the absence of an exchange.

Any scheduled variation of a redemption fee must be reasonably related to the costs to the fund of processing the type of redemptions for which the fee is charged;

(3) No deferred sales load is imposed on the exchanged security at the time of an exchange;

(4) Any sales load charged with respect to the acquired security is a percentage that is no greater than the excess, if any, of the rate of the sales load applicable to that security in the absence of an exchange over the sum of the rates of all sales loads previously paid on the exchanged security,

Provided, That:

(i) The percentage rate of any sales load charged when the acquired security is redeemed, that is solely the result of a deferred sales load imposed on the exchanged security, may be no greater than the excess, if any, of the applicable rate of such sales load, calculated in accordance with paragraph (b)(5) of this rule, over the sum of the rates of all sales loads previously paid on the acquired security, and

(ii) In no event may the sum of the rates of all sales loads imposed prior to and at the time the acquired security is redeemed, including any sales load paid or to be paid with respect to the exchanged security, exceed the maximum sales load rate, calculated in accordance with paragraph (b)(5) of this rule, that would be applicable in the absence of an exchange to the security (exchanged or acquired) with the highest such rate;

(5) Any deferred sales load charged at the time the acquired security is redeemed is calculated as if the holder of the acquired security had held that security from the date on which he became the holder of the exchanged security, *Provided*, That:

(i) The time period during which the acquired security is held need not be included when the amount of the deferred sales load is calculated, if the deferred sales load is

(A) Reduced by the amount of any fees collected on the acquired security under the terms of any plan of distribution adopted in accordance with rule 12b–1 under the Act (a "12b–1 plan"), and

(B) Solely the result of a sales load imposed on the exchanged security, and no other sales loads, including deferred sales loads, are imposed with respect to the acquired security,

(ii) The time period during which the exchanged security is held need not be included when the amount of the deferred sales load on the acquired security is calculated, if

(A) The deferred sales load is reduced by the amount of any fees previously collected on the exchanged security under the terms of any 12b–1 plan, and

(B) The exchanged security was not subject to any sales load, and

(iii) The holding periods in this subsection may be computed as of the end of the calendar month in which a security was purchased or redeemed;

(6) The prospectus of the offering company discloses

(i) The amount of any administrative or redemption fee imposed on an exchange transaction for its securities, as well as the amount of any administrative or redemption fee imposed on its securityholders to acquire the securities of other investment companies in an exchange transaction, and

(ii) If the offering company reserves the right to change the terms of or terminate an exchange offer, that the exchange offer is subject to termination and its terms are subject to change;

(7) Any sales literature or advertising that mentions the existence of the exchange offer also discloses

(i) The existence of any administrative fee or redemption fee that would be imposed at the time of an exchange; and

(ii) If the offering company reserves the right to change the terms of or terminate the exchange offer, that the exchange offer is subject to termination and its terms are subject to change;

(8) Whenever an exchange offer is to be terminated or its terms are to be amended materially, any holder of a security subject to that offer shall be given prominent notice of the impending termination or amendment at least 60 days prior to the date of termination or the effective date of the amendment,

Provided, That:

(i) No such notice need be given if the only material effect of an amendment is to reduce or eliminate an administrative fee, sales load or redemption fee payable at the time of an exchange, and

(ii) No notice need be given if, under extraordinary circumstances, either

(A) There is a suspension of the redemption of the exchanged security under section 22(e) of the Act and the rules and regulations thereunder, or

(B) The offering company temporarily delays or ceases the sale of the acquired security because it is unable to invest amounts effectively in accordance with applicable investment objectives, policies and restrictions; and

(9) In calculating any sales load charged with respect to the acquired security:

(i) If a securityholder exchanges less than all of his securities, the security upon which the highest sales load rate was previously paid is deemed exchanged first; and

(ii) If the exchanged security was acquired through reinvestment of dividends or capital gains distributions, that security is deemed to have been sold with a sales load rate equal to the sales load rate previously paid on the security on which the dividend was paid or distribution made.

(c) If either no sales load is imposed on the acquired security or the sales load imposed is less than the maximum allowed by paragraph (b)(4) of this rule, the offering company may require the exchanging securityholder to have held the exchanged security for a minimum period of time previously established by the offering company and applied uniformly to all securityholders of the class specified.

(d) Any offering company that has previously made an offer of exchange may continue to impose fees or sales loads permitted by an order under section 11(a) of the Act upon shares purchased before the earlier of (1) One year after the effective date of this section, or (2) When the offer has been brought into compliance with the terms of this rule, and upon shares acquired through reinvestment of dividends or capital gains distributions based on such shares, until such shares are redeemed.

(e) Any offering company that has previously made an offer of exchange cannot rely on this rule to amend such prior offer unless

(1) The offering company's prospectus disclosed, during at least the two year period prior to the amendment of the offer (or, if the fund is less than two years old, at all times the offer has been outstanding) that the terms of the offer were subject to change, or

(2) The only effect of such change is to reduce or eliminate an administrative fee, sales load or redemption fee payable at the time of an exchange.

[The Appendix containing illustrations of the sales load provisions of Rule 11a–3 which appears at 54 F.R. 35187 is omitted.]

Rule 12b–1. Distribution of shares by registered open–end management investment company

(a)(1) Except as provided in this rule, it shall be unlawful for any registered open-end management investment company (other than a company complying with the provisions of section 10(d) of the Act) to act as a distributor of securities of which it is the issuer, except through an underwriter;

(2) For purposes of this rule, such a company will be deemed to be acting as a distributor of securities of which it is the issuer, other than through an underwriter, if it engages directly or indirectly in financing any activity which is primarily intended to result in the sale of shares issued by such company, including, but not necessarily limited to, advertising, compensation of underwriters, dealers, and sales personnel, the printing and mailing of prospectuses to other than current shareholders, and the printing and mailing of sales literature;

(b) A registered, open-end management investment company ("Company") may act as a distributor of securities of which it is the issuer: *Provided,* That any payments made by such company in connection with such distribution are made pursuant to a written plan describing all material aspects of the proposed financing of distribution and that all agreements with any person relating to implementation of the plan are in writing: *And further provided,* That:

(1) Such plan has been approved by a vote of at least a majority of the outstanding voting securities of such company, if adopted after any public offering of the company's voting securities or the sale of such securities to persons who are not affiliated persons of the company, affiliated persons of such persons, promoters of the company, or affiliated persons of such promoters;

(2) Such plan, together with any related agreements, has been approved by a vote of the board of directors of such company, and of the directors who are not interested persons of the company and have no direct or indirect financial interest in the operation of the plan or in any agreements related to the plan, cast in person at a meeting called for the purpose of voting on such plan or agreements;

(3) Such plan or agreement provides, in substance:

(i) That it shall continue in effect for a period of more than one year from the date of its execution or adoption only so long as such continuance is specifically approved at least annually in the manner described in paragraph (b)(2) of this rule;

(ii) That any person authorized to direct the disposition of monies paid or payable by such company pursuant to the plan or any related agreement shall provide to the company's board of directors, and the directors shall review, at least quarterly, a written report of the amounts so expended and the purposes for which such expenditures were made; and

(iii) In the case of a plan, that it may be terminated at any time by vote of a majority of the members of the board of directors of the company who are not interested persons of the company and have no direct or indirect financial interest in the operation of the plan or in any agreements related to the plan or by vote of a majority of the outstanding voting securities of such company;

(iv) In the case of an agreement related to a plan:

(A) That it may be terminated at any time, without the payment of any penalty, by vote of a majority of the members of the board of directors of such company who are not interested persons of the company and have no direct or indirect financial interest in the operation of the plan or in any agreements related to the plan or by vote of a majority of the outstanding voting securities of such company on not more than sixty days' written notice to any other party to the agreement, and

(B) For its automatic termination in the event of its assignment;

(4) Such plan provides that it may not be amended to increase materially the amount to be spent for distribution without shareholder approval and that all material amendments of the plan must be approved in the manner described in paragraph (b)(2) of this rule; and

(5) Such plan is implemented and continued in a manner consistent with the provisions of paragraphs (c), (d), and (e) of this rule;

(c) A registered open-end management investment company may rely on the provisions of paragraph (b) of this section only if its board of directors satisfies the fund governance standards as defined in Rule 0–1(a)(7);

(d) In considering whether a registered open-end management investment company should implement or continue a plan in reliance on paragraph (b) of this rule, the directors of such company shall have a duty to request and evaluate, and any person who is a party to any agreement with such company relating to such plan shall have a duty to furnish, such information as may reasonably be necessary to an informed determination of whether such plan should be implemented or continued; in fulfilling their duties under this paragraph the directors should consider and give appropriate weight to all pertinent factors, and minutes describing the factors considered and the basis for the decision to use company assets for distribution must be made and preserved in accordance with paragraph (f) of this rule;

NOTE: For a discussion of factors which may be relevant to a decision to use company assets for distribution, see Investment Company Act Releases Nos. 10862, September 7, 1979, and 11414, October 28, 1980.

(e) A registered open-end management investment company may implement or continue a plan pursuant to paragraph (b) of this rule only if the directors who vote to approve such implementation or continuation conclude, in the exercise of reasonable business judgment and in light of their fiduciary duties under state law and under sections 36(a) and (b) [15 U.S.C. 80a–35(a) and (b)] of the Act, that there is a reasonable likelihood that the plan will benefit the company and its shareholders;

(f) A registered open-end management investment company must preserve copies of any plan, agreement or report made pursuant to this rule for a period of not less than six years from the date of such plan, agreement or report, the first two years in an easily accessible place;

(g) If a plan covers more than one series or class of shares, the provisions of the plan must be severable for each series or class, and whenever this rule provides for any action to be taken with respect to a plan, that action must be taken separately for each series or class affected by the matter. Nothing in this paragraph (g) shall affect the rights of any purchase class under Rule 18f–3(f)(2)(iii); and

(h) Notwithstanding any other provision of this section, a company may not:

(1) Compensate a broker or dealer for any promotion or sale of shares issued by that company by directing to the broker or dealer:

(i) The company's portfolio securities transactions; or

(ii) Any remuneration, including but not limited to any commission, mark-up, mark-down, or other fee (or portion thereof) received or to be received from the company's portfolio transactions effected through any other broker (including a government securities broker) or dealer (including a municipal securities dealer or a government securities dealer); and

(2) Direct its portfolio securities transactions to a broker or dealer that promotes or sells shares issued by the company, unless the company (or its investment adviser):

(i) Is in compliance with the provisions of paragraph (h)(1) of this rule with respect to that broker or dealer; and

(ii) Has implemented, and the company's board of directors (including a majority of directors who are not interested persons of the company) has approved, policies and procedures reasonably designed to prevent:

(A) The persons responsible for selecting brokers and dealers to effect the company's portfolio securities transactions from taking into account the brokers' and dealers' promotion or sale of shares issued by the company or any other registered investment company; and

(B) The company, and any investment adviser and principal underwriter of the company, from entering into any agreement (whether oral or written) or other understanding under which the company directs, or is expected to direct, portfolio securities transactions, or any remuneration described in paragraph (h)(1)(ii) of this rule, to a broker (including a government securities broker) or dealer (including a municipal securities dealer or a government securities dealer) in consideration for the promotion or sale of shares issued by the company or any other registered investment company.

Rule 12d1–1. Exemptions for investments in money market funds

(a) *Exemptions for Acquisition of Money Market Fund Shares.* If the conditions of paragraph (b) of this rule are satisfied, notwithstanding sections 12(d)(1)(A), 12(d)(1)(B), 17(a), and 57 of the Act, and Rule 17d–1:

(1) An investment company ("acquiring fund") may purchase and redeem shares issued by a money market fund; and

(2) A money market fund, any principal underwriter thereof, and a broker or a dealer may sell or otherwise dispose of shares issued by the money market fund to an acquiring fund.

(b) *Conditions.* (1) *Fees.* The acquiring fund pays no sales charge, as defined in Rule 2830(b)(8) of the Conduct Rules of the NASD ("sales charge"), or service fee, as defined in Rule 2830(b)(9) of the Conduct Rules of the NASD, charged in connection with the purchase, sale, or redemption of securities issued by a money market fund ("service fee"); or the acquiring fund's investment adviser waives its advisory fee in an amount necessary to offset any sales charge or service fee.

(2) *Unregistered Money Market Funds.* If the money market fund is not an investment company registered under the Act:

(i) The acquiring fund reasonably believes that the money market fund satisfies the following conditions as if it were a registered open-end investment company:

(A) Operates in compliance with Rule 2a–7;

(B) Complies with sections 17(a), (d), (e), 18, and 22(e) of the Act;

(C) Has adopted procedures designed to ensure that it complies with sections 17(a), (d), (e), 18, and 22(e) of the Act, periodically reviews and updates those procedures, and maintains books and records describing those procedures;

(D) Maintains the records required by Rules 31a–1(b)(1), 31a–1(b)(2)(ii), 31a–1(b)(2)(iv), and 31a–1(b)(9); and

(E) Preserves permanently, the first two years in an easily accessible place, all books and records required to be made under paragraphs (b)(2)(i)(C) and (D) of this rule, and makes those records available for examination on request by the Commission or its staff; and

(ii) The adviser to the money market fund is registered with the Commission as an investment adviser under section 203 of the Investment Advisers Act of 1940.

(c) *Exemption from Certain Monitoring and Recordkeeping Requirements Under Rule 17e–1.* Notwithstanding the requirements of Rules 17e–1(b)(3) and 17e–1(d)(2), the payment of a commission, fee, or other remuneration to a broker shall be deemed as not exceeding the usual and customary broker's commission for purposes of section 17(e)(2)(A) of the Act if:

(1) The commission, fee, or other remuneration is paid in connection with the sale of securities to or by an acquiring fund;

(2) The broker and the acquiring fund are affiliated persons because each is an affiliated person of the same money market fund; and

(3) The acquiring fund is an affiliated person of the money market fund solely because the acquiring fund owns, controls, or holds with power to vote five percent or more of the outstanding securities of the money market fund.

(d) *Definitions.* (1) *Investment company* includes a company that would be an investment company under section 3(a) of the Act (15 U.S.C. 80a–3(a)) but for the exceptions to that definition provided for in sections 3(c)(1) and 3(c)(7) of the Act.

(2) *Money market fund* means:

(i) An open-end management investment company registered under the Act that is regulated as a money market fund under Rule 2a–7; or

(ii) A company that would be an investment company under section 3(a) of the Act but for the exceptions to that definition provided for in sections 3(c)(1) and 3(c)(7) of the Act and that:

(A) Is limited to investing in the types of securities and other investments in which a money market fund may invest under Rule 2a–7; and

(B) Undertakes to comply with all the other requirements of Rule 2a–7, except that, if the company has no board of directors, the company's investment adviser performs the duties of the board of directors.

Rule 12d1–2. Exemptions for investment companies relying on Section 12(d)(1)(G) of the Act

(a) *Exemption to Acquire Other Securities.* Notwithstanding section 12(d)(1)(G)(i)(II) of the Act, a registered open-end investment company or a registered unit investment trust that relies on section 12(d)(1)(G) of the Act to acquire securities issued by another registered investment company that is in the same group of investment companies may acquire, in addition to Government securities and short-term paper:

(1) Securities issued by an investment company, other than securities issued by another registered investment company that is in the same group of investment companies, when the acquisition is in reliance on section 12(d)(1)(A) or 12(d)(1)(F) of the Act;

(2) Securities (other than securities issued by an investment company); and

(3) Securities issued by a money market fund, when the acquisition is in reliance on Rule 12d1–1.

(b) *Definitions.* For purposes of this section, *money market fund* has the same meaning as in Rule 12d1–1(d)(2).

Rule 12d1–3. Exemptions for investment companies relying on Section 12(d)(1)(F) of the Act

(a) *Exemption from Sales Charge Limits.* A registered investment company ("acquiring fund") that relies on section 12(d)(1)(F) of the Act to acquire securities issued by an investment company ("acquired fund") may offer or sell any security it issues through a principal underwriter or otherwise at a public offering price that includes a sales load of more than 1½ percent if any sales charges and service fees charged with respect to the acquiring fund's securities do not exceed the limits set forth in Rule 2830 of the Conduct Rules of the NASD applicable to a fund of funds.

(b) *Definitions.* For purposes of this section, the terms *fund of funds, sales charge,* and *service fee* have the same meanings as in Rule 2830(b) of the Conduct Rules of the NASD.

Rule 12d2–1. Definition of insurance company for purposes of Sections 12(d)(2) and 12(g) of the Act

For purposes of sections 12(d)(2) and 12(g) of the Act, *insurance company* shall include a foreign insurance company as that term is used in Rule 3a–6 under the Act.

Rule 12d3–1. Exemption of acquisitions of securities issued by persons engaged in securities related businesses

(a) Notwithstanding section 12(d)(3) of the Act, a registered investment company, or any company or companies controlled by such registered investment company ("acquiring company") may acquire any security issued by any person, that, in its most recent fiscal year, derived 15 percent or less of its gross revenues from securities related activities unless the acquiring company would control such person after the acquisition.

(b) Notwithstanding section 12(d)(3) of the Act, an acquiring company may acquire any security issued by a person that, in its most recent fiscal year, derived more than 15 percent of its gross revenues from securities related activities, *Provided*, That:

(1) Immediately after the acquisition of any equity security, the acquiring company owns not more than five percent of the outstanding securities of that class of the issuer's equity securities;

(2) Immediately after the acquisition of any debt security, the acquiring company owns not more than ten percent of the outstanding principal amount of the issuer's debt securities; and

(3) Immediately after any such acquisition, the acquiring company has invested not more than five percent of the value of its total assets in the securities of the issuer.

(c) Notwithstanding paragraphs (a) and (b) of this rule, this rule does not exempt the acquisition of:

(1) A general partnership interest; or

(2) A security issued by the acquiring company's promoter, principal underwriter, or any affiliated person of such promoter, or principal underwriter; or

(3) A security issued by the acquiring company's investment adviser, or an affiliated person of the acquiring company's investment adviser, other than a security issued by a subadviser or an affiliated person of a subadviser of the acquiring company provided that:

(i) *Prohibited Relationships*. The subadviser that is (or whose affiliated person is) the issuer is not, and is not an affiliated person of, an investment adviser responsible for providing advice with respect to the portion of the acquiring company that is acquiring the securities, or of any promoter, underwriter, officer, director, member of an advisory board, or employee of the acquiring company;

(ii) *Advisory Contract*. The advisory contracts of the Subadviser that is (or whose affiliated person is) the issuer, and any Subadviser that is advising the portion of the acquiring company that is purchasing the securities:

(A) Prohibit them from consulting with each other concerning transactions of the acquiring company in securities or other assets, other than for purposes of complying with the conditions of paragraphs (a) and (b) of this rule; and

(B) Limit their responsibility in providing advice to providing advice with respect to a discrete portion of the acquiring company's portfolio.

(d) For purposes of this section:

(1) *Securities related activities* are a person's activities as a broker, a dealer, an underwriter, an investment adviser registered under the Investment Advisers Act of 1940, as amended, or as an investment adviser to a registered investment company.

(2) An issuer's gross revenues from its own securities related activities and from its ratable share of the securities related activities of enterprises of which it owns 20 percent or more of the voting or equity interest should be considered in determining the degree to which an issuer is engaged in securities related activities. Such information may be obtained from the issuer's annual report to shareholders, the issuer's annual reports or registration statement filed with the Commission, or the issuer's chief financial officer.

(3) *Equity security* is as defined in Rule 3a–11 under the Securities Exchange Act of 1934.

(4) *Debt security* includes all securities other than equity securities.

(5) Determination of the percentage of an acquiring company's ownership of any class of outstanding equity securities of an issuer shall be made in accordance with the procedures described in the rules under Rule 16 under the Securities Exchange Act of 1934.

(6) Where an acquiring company is considering acquiring or has acquired options, warrants, rights, or convertible securities of a securities related business, the determination required by paragraph (b) of this rule shall be made as though such options, warrants, rights, or conversion privileges had been exercised.

(7) The following transactions will not be deemed to be an acquisition of securities of a securities related business:

(i) Receipt of stock dividends on securities acquired in compliance with this section;

(ii) Receipt of securities arising from a stock-for-stock split on securities acquired in compliance with this section;

(iii) Exercise of options, warrants, or rights acquired in compliance with this section;

(iv) Conversion of convertible securities acquired in compliance with this section; and

(v) Acquisition of Demand Features or Guarantees, as these terms are defined in Rule 2a–7(a)(9) and Rule 2a–7(a)(16) respectively, provided that, immediately after the acquisition of any Demand Feature or Guarantee, the company will not, with respect to 75 percent of the total value of its assets, have invested more than ten percent of the total value of its assets in securities underlying Demand Features or Guarantees from the same institution. For the purposes of this rule, a Demand Feature or Guarantee will be considered to be from the party to whom the company will look for a payment of the exercise price.

(8) Any class or series of an investment company that issues two or more classes or series of preferred or special stock, each of which is preferred over all other classes or series with respect to assets specifically allocated to that class or series, shall be treated as if it is a registered investment company.

(9) *Subadviser* means an investment adviser as defined in section 2(a)(20)(B) of the Act.

Rule 13a–1. Exemption for change of status by temporarily diversified company

A change of its subclassification by a registered management company from that of a diversified company to that of a nondiversified company shall be exempt from the provisions of section 13(a)(1) of the Act, if such change occurs under the following circumstances:

(a) Such company was a nondiversified company at the time of its registration pursuant to section 8(a) or thereafter legally became a nondiversified company.

(b) After its registration and within 3 years prior to such change, such company became a diversified company.

(c) At the time such company became a diversified company, its registration statement filed pursuant to section 8(b) as supplemented and modified by any amendments and reports theretofore filed, did not state that the registrant proposed to become a diversified company.

Rule 14a–1. Use of notification pursuant to Regulation E under the Securities Act of 1933

For the purposes of section 14(a)(3) of the Act, registration of securities under the Securities Act of 1933 by a small business investment company operating under the Small Business Investment Act of 1958 shall be deemed to include the filing of a notification under Rule 604 of Regulation E promulgated under said Act if provision is made in connection with such notification which in the opinion of the Commission adequately insures (a) that after the effective date of such notification such company will not issue any security or receive any proceeds of any subscription for any security until firm agreements have been made with such company by not more than twenty-five responsible persons to purchase from it securities to be issued by it for an aggregate net amount which plus the then net worth of the company, if any, will equal at least $100,000; (b) that said aggregate net amount will be paid into such company before any subscriptions for such securities will be accepted from any persons in excess of twenty-five; (c) that arrangements will be made whereby any proceeds so paid in, as well as any sales load, will be refunded to any subscriber on demand without any deduction, in the event that the net proceeds so received by the company do not result in the company having a net worth of at least $100,000 within ninety days after such notification becomes effective.

Rule 14a–2. Exemption from Section 14(a) of the Act for certain registered separate accounts and their principal underwriters

(a) A registered separate account, and any principal underwriter for such account, shall be exempt from section 14(a) of the Act with respect to a public offering of variable annuity contracts participating in such account if, at the commencement of such offering, the insurance company establishing and maintaining such separate account shall have (1) a combined capital and surplus, if a stock company, or (2) an unassigned surplus, if a mutual company, of not less than $1,000,000 as set forth in the balance sheet of such insurance company contained in the registration statement or any amendment thereto relating to such contracts filed pursuant to the Securities Act of 1933.

(b) Any registered management investment company which has as a promoter an insurance company meeting the requirements of paragraph (a) of this rule and which offers its securities to separate accounts of such insurance company registered under the Act as unit investment trusts ("trust accounts"), and any principal underwriter for such investment company, shall be exempt from section 14(a) with respect to such offering and to the offering of such securities to trust accounts of other insurance companies meeting the requirements of paragraph (a) of this rule.

(c) Any registered management investment company exempt from section 14(a) of the Act pursuant to paragraph (b) of this section shall be exempt from sections 15(a), 16(a), and 32(a)(2) of the Act, to the extent prescribed in Rules 15a–3, 16a–1, and 32a–2 under the Act, provided that such investment company complies with the conditions set forth in those rules as if it were a separate account.

Rule 14a–3. Exemption from Section 14(a) for certain registered unit investment trusts and their principal underwriters

(a) A registered unit investment trust (hereinafter referred to as the "Trust") engaged exclusively in the business of investing in eligible trust securities, and any principal underwriter for the Trust, shall be exempt from section 14(a) of the Act with respect to a public offering of Trust units: *Provided,* That:

(1) At the commencement of such offering the Trust holds at least $100,000 principal amount of eligible trust securities (or delivery statements relating to contracts for the purchase of any such securities which, together with cash or an irrevocable letter of credit issued by a bank in the amount required for their purchase, are held by the Trust for purchase of the securities);

(2) If, within ninety days from the time that the Trust's registration statement has become effective under the Securities Act of 1933 the net worth of the Trust declines to less than $100,000 or the Trust is terminated, the sponsor for the Trust shall—

(i) refund, on demand and without deduction, all sales charges to any unitholders who purchased Trust units from the sponsor (or from any underwriter or dealer participating in the distribution), and

(ii) liquidate the eligible trust securities held by the Trust and distribute the proceeds thereof to the unitholders of the Trust;

(3) The sponsor instructs the trustee when the eligible trust securities are deposited in the Trust that, in the event that redemptions by the sponsor or any underwriter of units constituting a part of the unsold units results in the Trust having a net worth of less than 40 percent of the principal amount of the eligible trust securities (or delivery statements relating to contracts for the purchase of any such securities which, together with cash or an irrevocable letter of credit issued by a bank in the amount required for their purchase, are held by the Trust for purchase of the securities) initially deposited in the Trust—

(i) the trustee shall terminate the Trust and distribute the assets thereof to the unitholders of the Trust, and

(ii) the sponsor for the Trust shall refund, on demand and without deduction, all sales charges to any unitholder who purchased Trust units from the sponsor or from any underwriter or dealer participating in the distribution.

(b) For the purposes of determining the availability of the exemption provided by the foregoing subsection, the term "eligible trust securities" shall mean:

(1) Securities (other than convertible securities) which are issued by a corporation and which have their interest or dividend rate fixed at the time they are issued;

(2) Interest bearing obligations issued by a state, or by any agency, instrumentality, authority or political subdivision thereof;

(3) Government securities; and)

(4) Units of a previously issued series of the Trust: *Provided,* That:

(i) the aggregate principal amount of units of existing series so deposited shall not exceed 10% of the aggregate principal amount of the portfolio of the new series;

(ii) the aggregate principal amount of units of any particular existing series so deposited shall not exceed 5% of the aggregate principal amount of the portfolio of the new series;

(iii) no units shall be so deposited which do not substantially meet investment quality criteria at least as high as those applicable to the new series in which such units are deposited;

(iv) the value of the eligible trust securities underlying units of an existing series deposited in a new series shall not, by reason of maturity of such securities according to their terms within ten years following the date of deposit, be reduced sufficiently for such existing series to be voluntarily terminated;

(v) units of existing series so deposited shall constitute units purchased by the sponsor as market maker and not remaining unsold units from the original distribution of such units; and

(vi) the sponsor shall deposit units of existing series in the new series without a sales charge.

Rule 15a–1. Exemption from stockholders' approval of certain small investment advisory contracts

An investment adviser of a registered investment company shall be exempt from the requirement of sections 15(a) and 15(e) of the act that the written contract pursuant to which he acts shall have been approved by the vote of a majority of the outstanding voting securities of such company, if the following conditions are met:

(a) Such investment adviser is not an affiliated person of such company (except as investment adviser) nor of any principal underwriter for such company.

(b) His compensation as investment adviser of such company in any fiscal year of the company during which any such contract is in effect either (1) is not more than $100 or (2) is not more than $2,500 and not more than 1/40 of 1 percent of the value of the company's net assets averaged over the year or taken as of a definite date or dates within the year.

(c) The aggregate compensation of all investment advisers of such company exempted pursuant to this section in any fiscal year of the company either (1) is not more than $200 or (2) is not more than 1/20 of 1 percent of the value of the company's net assets averaged over the year or taken as of a definite date or dates within the year.

Rule 15a–2. Annual continuance of contracts

(a) For purposes of sections 15(a) and 15(b) of the Act, the continuance of a contract for a period more than two years after the date of its execution shall be deemed to have been specifically approved at least annually by the board of directors or by a vote of a majority of the outstanding voting securities of a registered investment company if such approval occurs:

(1) With respect to the first continuance of a contract, during the 90 days prior to and including the earlier of (i) the date specified in such contract for its termination in the absence of such approval, or (ii) the second anniversary of the date upon which such contract was executed; or

(2) With respect to any subsequent continuance of a contract, during the 90 days prior to and including the first anniversary of the date upon which the most recent previous annual continuance of such contract became effective.

(b) The provisions of paragraph (a) of this rule shall not apply to any continuance of a contract which shall have been approved not later than 90 days after the date of adoption of this section, provided that such contract shall expire, by its terms, not later than 17 months from the date of adoption of this section.

NOTE: This rule does not establish the exclusive method of complying with the Act. It provides one procedure by which a registered investment company may comply with the applicable provisions of sections 15(a) and 15(b) of the Act; it does not preclude any other appropriate procedure. Any annual continuance of a contract approved in accordance with the provisions of paragraphs (a)(1) or (a)(2) of Rule 15A–2 will constitute a renewal of such contract for the purposes of section 15(c) of the Act, and therefore such renewal must be approved by the disinterested directors within the times specified in the section for a continuance.

Rule 15a–3. Exemption for initial period of investment adviser of certain registered separate accounts from requirement of security holder approval of investment advisory contract

(a) An investment adviser of a registered separate account shall be exempt from the requirement under section 15(a) of the Act that the initial written contract pursuant to which the investment adviser serves or acts shall have been approved by the vote of a majority of the outstanding voting securities of such registered separate account, subject to the following conditions:

(1) Such registered separate account qualifies for exemption from section 14(a) of the Act pursuant to Rule 14a–2, or is exempt therefrom by order of the Commission upon application; and

(2) Such written contract shall be submitted to a vote of variable annuity contract owners at their first meeting after the effective date of the registration statement under the Securities Act of 1933, as amended relating to variable annuity contracts participating in such account: *Provided,* That such meeting shall take place within 1 year after such effective date, unless the time for the holding of such meeting shall be extended by the Commission upon written request showing good cause therefor.

Rule 15a–4. Temporary exemption for certain investment advisers*

(a) For purposes of this rule:

(1) *Fund* means an investment company, and includes a separate series of the company.

(2) *Interim contract* means a written investment advisory contract:

(i) That has not been approved by a majority of the fund's outstanding voting securities; and

(ii) That has a duration no greater than 150 days following the date on which the previous contract terminates.

(3) *Previous contract* means an investment advisory contract that has been approved by a majority of the fund's outstanding voting securities and has been terminated.

(b) Notwithstanding section 15(a) of the Act, a person may act as investment adviser for a fund under an interim contract after the termination of a previous contract as provided in paragraphs (b)(1) or (b)(2) of this rule:

(1) In the case of a previous contract terminated by an event described in section 15(a)(3) of the Act, by the failure to renew the previous contract, or by an assignment (other than an assignment by an investment adviser or a controlling person of the investment adviser in connection with which assignment the investment adviser or a controlling person directly or indirectly receives money or other benefit):

(i) The compensation to be received under the interim contract is no greater than the compensation the adviser would have received under the previous contract; and

(ii) The fund's board of directors, including a majority of the directors who are not interested persons of the fund, has approved the interim contract within 10 business days after the termination, at a meeting in which directors may participate by any means of communication that allows all directors participating to hear each other simultaneously during the meeting.

(2) In the case of a previous contract terminated by an assignment by an investment adviser or a controlling person of the investment adviser in connection with which assignment the investment adviser or a controlling person directly or indirectly receives money or other benefit:

(i) The compensation to be received under the interim contract is no greater than the compensation the adviser would have received under the previous contract;

(ii) The board of directors, including a majority of the directors who are not interested persons of the fund, has voted in person to approve the interim contract before the previous contract is terminated;

(iii) The board of directors, including a majority of the directors who are not interested persons of the fund, determines that the scope and quality of services to be provided to the fund under the interim contract will be at least equivalent to the scope and quality of services provided under the previous contract;

(iv) The interim contract provides that the fund's board of directors or a majority of the fund's outstanding voting securities may terminate the contract at any time, without the payment of any penalty, on not more than 10 calendar days' written notice to the investment adviser;

(v) The interim contract contains the same terms and conditions as the previous contract, with the exception of its effective and termination dates, provisions governed by paragraphs (b)(2)(i), (b)(2)(iv), and (b)(2)(vi) of this rule, and any other differences in terms and conditions that the board of directors, including a majority of the directors who are not interested persons of the fund, finds to be immaterial;

(vi) The interim contract contains the following provisions:

(A) The compensation earned under the contract will be held in an interest-bearing escrow account with the fund's custodian or a bank;

(B) If a majority of the fund's outstanding voting securities approve a contract with the investment adviser by the end of the 150–day period, the amount in the escrow account (including interest earned) will be paid to the investment adviser; and

(C) If a majority of the fund's outstanding voting securities do not approve a contract with the investment adviser, the investment adviser will be paid, out of the escrow account, the lesser of:

(*1*) Any costs incurred in performing the interim contract (plus interest earned on that amount while in escrow); or

(*2*) The total amount in the escrow account (plus interest earned); and

(vii) The board of directors of the investment company satisfies the fund governance standards defined in Rule 0–1(a)(7).

Rule 16a–1. Exemption for initial period of directors of certain registered accounts from requirement of election by security holders

(a) Persons serving as the directors of a registered separate account shall, prior to the first meeting of such account's variable annuity contract owners, be exempt from the requirement of section 16(a) of the Act that such persons be elected by the holders of outstanding voting securities of such account at an annual or special meeting called for that purpose, subject to the following conditions:

(1) Such registered separate account qualifies for exemption from section 14(a) of the Act pursuant to Rule 14a–1 or is exempt therefrom by order of the Commission upon application; and

(2) Such persons have been appointed directors of such account by the establishing insurance company; and

(3) An election of directors for such account shall be held at the first meeting of variable annuity contract owners after the effective date of the registration statement under the Securities Act of 1933, as amended, relating to contracts participating in such account: *Provided,* That such meeting shall take place within 1 year after such effective date, unless the time for the holding of such meeting shall be extended by the Commission upon written request showing good cause therefor.

Rule 17a–1. Exemption of certain underwriting transactions exempted by Rule 10f–1

Any transaction exempted pursuant to Rule 10f–1 shall be exempt from the provisions of section 17(a)(1) of the Act.

Rule 17a–2. Exemption of certain purchase, sale or borrowing transactions

Purchase, sale or borrowing transactions occurring in the usual course of business between affiliated persons of registered investment companies shall be exempt from section 17(a) of the act provided (a) the transactions involve notes, drafts, time payment contracts, bills of exchange, acceptance or other property of a commercial character rather than of an investment character; (b) the buyer or lender is a bank; and (c) the seller or borrower is a bank or is engaged principally in the business of installment financing.

Rule 17a–3. Exemption of transactions with fully owned subsidiaries

(a) The following transactions shall be exempt from section 17(a) of the Act:

(1) Transactions solely between a registered investment company and one or more of its fully owned subsidiaries or solely between two or more fully owned subsidiaries of such company.

(2) Transactions solely between any subsidiary of a registered investment company and one or more fully owned subsidiaries of such subsidiary or solely between two or more fully owned subsidiaries of such subsidiary.

(b) The term "fully owned subsidiary" as used in this section, means a subsidiary (1) all of whose outstanding securities, other than directors' qualifying shares, are owned by its parent and/or the parent's other fully owned subsidiaries, and (2) which is not indebted to any person other than its parent and/or the parent's other fully owned subsidiaries in an amount which is material in relation to the particular subsidiary, excepting (i) indebtedness incurred in the ordinary course of business which is not overdue and which matures within one year from the date of its creation, whether evidenced by securities or not, and (ii) any other indebtedness to one or more banks or insurance companies.

Rule 17a–4. Exemption of transactions pursuant to certain contracts

Transactions pursuant to a contract shall be exempt from section 17(a) of the Act if at the time of the making of the contract and for a period of at least six months prior thereto no affiliation or other relationship existed which would operate to make such contract or the subsequent performance thereof subject to the provisions of said section 17(a).

Rule 17a–5. Pro rata distribution neither "sale" nor "purchase"

When a company makes a pro rata distribution in cash or in kind among its common stockholders without giving any election to any stockholder as to the specific assets which such stockholders shall receive, such distribution shall not be deemed to involve a sale to or a purchase from such distributing company as those terms are used in section 17(a) of the Act.

Rule 17a–6. Exemption for transactions with portfolio affiliates

(a) *Exemption for Transactions with Portfolio Affiliates.* A transaction to which a fund, or a company controlled by a fund, and a portfolio affiliate of the fund are parties is exempt from the provisions of section 17(a) of the Act, provided that none of the following persons is a party to the transaction, or has a direct or indirect financial interest in a party to the transaction other than the fund:

(1) An officer, director, employee, investment adviser, member of an advisory board, depositor, promoter of or principal underwriter for the fund;

(2) A person directly or indirectly controlling the fund;

(3) A person directly or indirectly *owning, controlling or holding* with power to vote five percent or more of the outstanding voting securities of the fund;

(4) A person directly or indirectly under common control with the fund, other than:

(i) A portfolio affiliate of the fund; or

(ii) A fund whose sole interest in the transaction or a party to the transaction is an interest in the portfolio affiliate; or

(5) An affiliated person of any of the persons mentioned in paragraphs (a)(1)–(4) of this rule, other than the fund or a portfolio affiliate of the fund.

(b) *Definitions.* (1) *Financial Interest.* (i) The term *financial interest* as used in this section does not include:

(A) Any interest through ownership of securities issued by the fund;

(B) Any interest of a wholly-owned subsidiary of a fund;

(C) Usual and ordinary fees for services as a director;

(D) An interest of a non-executive employee;

(E) An interest of an insurance company arising from a loan or policy made or issued by it in the ordinary course of business to a natural person;

(F) An interest of a bank arising from a loan or account made or maintained by it in the ordinary course of business to or with a natural person, unless it arises from a loan to a person who is an officer, director or executive of a company which is a party to the transaction, or from a loan to a person who directly or indirectly owns, controls, or holds with power to vote, five percent or more of the outstanding voting securities of a company which is a party to the transaction;

(G) An interest acquired in a transaction described in paragraph (d)(3) of Rule 17d–1; or

(H) Any other interest that the board of directors of the fund, including a majority of the directors who are not interested persons of the fund, finds to be not material, provided that the directors record the basis for that finding in the minutes of their meeting.

(ii) A person has a financial interest in any party in which it has a financial interest, in which it had a financial interest within six months prior to the transaction, or in which it will acquire a financial interest pursuant to an arrangement in existence at the time of the transaction.

(2) *Fund* means a registered investment company or separate series of a registered investment company.

(3) *Portfolio affiliate of a fund* means a person that is an affiliated person (or an affiliated person of an affiliated person) of a fund solely because the fund, a fund under common control with the fund, or both:

(i) Controls such person (or an affiliated person of such person); or

(ii) Owns, controls, or holds with power to vote five percent or more of the outstanding voting securities of such person (or an affiliated person of such person).

Rule 17a–7. Exemption of certain purchase or sale transactions between an investment company and certain affiliated persons thereof

A purchase or sale transaction between registered investment companies or separate series of registered investment companies, which are affiliated persons, or affiliated persons of affiliated persons, of each other, between separate series of a registered investment company, or between a registered investment company or a separate series of a registered investment company and a person which is an affiliated person of such registered investment company (or affiliated person of such person) solely by reason of having a common investment adviser or investment advisers which are affiliated persons of each other, common directors, and/or common officers, is exempt from section 17(a) of the Act; *Provided,* That:

(a) The transaction is a purchase or sale, for no consideration other than cash payment against prompt delivery of a security for which market quotations are readily available;

(b) The transaction is effected at the independent current market price of the security. For purposes of this paragraph the "current market price" shall be:

(1) If the security is an "NMS stock" as that term is defined in 17 CFR 242.600, the last sale price with respect to such security reported in the consolidated transaction reporting system ("consolidated system") or the average of the highest current independent bid and lowest current independent offer for such security (reported pursuant to 17 CFR 242.602) if there are no reported transactions in the consolidated system that day; or

(2) If the security is not a reported security, and the principal market for such security is an exchange, then the last sale on such exchange or the average of the highest current independent bid and lowest current independent offer on such exchange if there are no reported transactions on such exchange that day; or

(3) If the security is not a reported security and is quoted in the NASDAQ System, then the average of the highest current independent bid and lowest current independent offer reported on Level 1 of NASDAQ; or

(4) For all other securities, the average of the highest current independent bid and lowest current independent offer determined on the basis of reasonable inquiry;

(c) The transaction is consistent with the policy of each registered investment company and separate series of a registered investment company participating in the transaction, as recited in its registration statement and reports filed under the Act;

(d) No brokerage commission, fee (except for customary transfer fees), or other remuneration is paid in connection with the transaction;

(e) The board of directors of the investment company, including a majority of the directors who are not interested persons of such investment company,

(1) adopts procedures pursuant to which such purchase or sale transactions may be effected for the company, which are reasonably designed to provide that all of the conditions of this section in paragraphs (a) through (d) have been complied with,

(2) makes and approves such changes as the board deems necessary, and

(3) determines no less frequently than quarterly that all such purchases or sales made during the preceding quarter were effected in compliance with such procedures;

(f) The board of directors of the investment company satisfies the fund governance standards defined in Rule 0–1(a)(7).

(g) The investment company (1) maintains and preserves permanently in an easily accessible place a written copy of the procedures (and any modifications thereto) described in paragraph (e) of this section, and (2) maintains and preserves for a period not less than six years from the end of the fiscal year in which any transactions occurred, the first two years in an easily accessible place, a written record of each such transaction setting forth a description of the security purchased or sold, the identity of the person on the other side of the transaction, the terms of the purchase or sale transaction, and the information or materials upon which the determinations described in paragraph (e)(3) of this rule were made.

Rule 17a–8. Mergers of affiliated companies

(a) *Exemption of Affiliated Mergers.* A Merger of a registered investment company (or a series thereof) and one or more other registered investment companies (or series thereof) or Eligible Unregistered Funds is exempt from sections 17(a)(1) and (2) of the Act if:

(1) *Surviving Company.* The Surviving Company is a registered investment company (or a series thereof).

(2) *Board Determinations.* As to any registered investment company (or series thereof) participating in the Merger ("Merging Company"):

(i) The board of directors, including a majority of the directors who are not interested persons of the Merging Company or of any other company or series participating in the Merger, determines that:

(A) Participation in the Merger is in the best interests of the Merging Company; and

(B) The interests of the Merging Company's existing shareholders will not be diluted as a result of the Merger.

NOTE TO PARAGRAPH (a)(2)(i): For a discussion of factors that may be relevant to the determinations in paragraph (a)(2)(i) of this section, see Investment Company Act Release No. 25666, July 18, 2002.

(ii) The directors have requested and evaluated such information as may reasonably be necessary to their determinations in paragraph (a)(2)(i) of this rule, and have considered and given appropriate weight to all pertinent factors.

(iii) The directors, in making the determination in paragraph (a)(2)(i)(B) of this rule, have approved procedures for the valuation of assets to be conveyed by each Eligible Unregistered Fund participating in the Merger. The approved procedures provide for the preparation of a report by an Independent Evaluator, to be considered in assessing the value of any securities (or other assets) for which market quotations are not readily available, that sets forth the fair value of each such asset as of the date of the Merger.

(iv) The determinations required in paragraph (a)(2)(i) of this rule and the bases thereof, including the factors considered by the directors pursuant to paragraph (a)(2)(ii) of this rule, are recorded fully in the minute books of the Merging Company.

(3) *Shareholder Approval.* Participation in the Merger is approved by the vote of a majority of the outstanding voting securities (as provided in section 2(a)(42) of the Act) of any Merging Company that is not a Surviving Company, unless—

(i) No policy of the Merging Company that under section 13 of the Act could not be changed without a vote of a majority of its outstanding voting securities, is materially different from a policy of the Surviving Company;

(ii) No advisory contract between the Merging Company and any investment adviser thereof is materially different from an advisory contract between the Surviving Company and any investment adviser thereof, except for the identity of the investment companies as a party to the contract;

(iii) Directors of the Merging Company who are not interested persons of the Merging Company and who were elected by its shareholders, will comprise a majority of the directors of the Surviving Company who are not interested persons of the Surviving Company; and

(iv) Any distribution fees (as a percentage of the fund's average net assets) authorized to be paid by the Surviving Company pursuant to a plan adopted in accordance with Rule 12b–1 are no greater than the distribution fees (as a percentage of the fund's average net assets) authorized to be paid by the Merging Company pursuant to such a plan.

(4) *Board Composition.* The board of directors of the Merging Company satisfies the fund governance standards defined in Rule 0–1(a)(7).

(5) *Merger Records.* Any Surviving Company preserves written records that describe the Merger and its terms for six years after the Merger (and for the first two years in an easily accessible place).

(b) *Definitions.* For purposes of this rule:

(1) *Merger* means the merger, consolidation, or purchase or sale of substantially all of the assets between a registered investment company (or a series thereof) and another company;

(2) *Eligible Unregistered Fund* means:

(i) A collective trust fund, as described in section 3(c)(11) of the Act;

(ii) A common trust fund or similar fund, as described in section 3(c)(3) of the Act; or

(iii) A separate account, as described in section 2(a)(37) of the Act, that is neither registered under section 8 of the Act, nor required to be so registered;

(3) *Independent Evaluator* means a person who has expertise in the valuation of securities and other financial assets and who is not an interested person, as defined in section 2(a)(19) of the Act, of the Eligible Unregistered Fund or any affiliate thereof except the Merging Company; and

(4) *Surviving Company* means a company in which shareholders of a Merging Company will obtain an interest as a result of a Merger.

Rule 17a–9. Purchase of certain securities from a money market fund by an affiliate, or an affiliate of an affiliate

The purchase of a security from the portfolio of an open-end investment company holding itself out as a money market fund by any affiliated person or promoter of or principal underwriter for the money market fund or any affiliated person of such person shall be exempt from section 17(a) of the Act (15 U.S.C. 80a–17(a)); provided that:

(a) In the case of a portfolio security that has ceased to be an Eligible Security (as defined in Rule 2a–7(a)(12)), or has defaulted (other than an immaterial default unrelated to the financial condition of the issuer):

(1) The purchase price is paid in cash; and

(2) The purchase price is equal to the greater of the amortized cost of the security or its market price (in each case, including accrued interest).

(b) In the case of any other portfolio security:

(1) The purchase price meets the requirements of paragraph (a)(1) and (2) of this section; and

(2) In the event that the purchaser thereafter sells the security for a higher price than the purchase price paid to the money market fund, the purchaser shall promptly pay to the fund the amount by which the subsequent sale price exceeds the purchase price paid to the fund.

Rule 17a-10. Exemption for transactions with certain subadvisory affiliates

(a) *Exemption.* A person that is prohibited by section 17(a) of the Act from entering into a transaction with a fund solely because such person is, or is an affiliated person of, a subadviser of the fund, or a subadviser of a fund that is under common control with the fund, may nonetheless enter into such transaction, if:

(1) *Prohibited Relationship.* The person is not, and is not an affiliated person of, an investment adviser responsible for providing advice with respect to the portion of the fund for which the transaction is entered into, or of any promoter, underwriter, officer, director, member of an advisory board, or employee of the fund.

(2) *Prohibited Conduct.* The advisory contracts of the subadviser that is (or whose affiliated person is) entering into the transaction, and any subadviser that is advising the fund (or portion of the fund) entering into the transaction:

(i) Prohibit them from consulting with each other concerning transactions for the fund in securities or other assets; and

(ii) If both such subadvisers are responsible for providing investment advice to the fund, limit the subadvisers' responsibility in providing advice with respect to a discrete portion of the fund's portfolio.

(b) *Definitions.* (1) *Fund* means a registered investment company and includes a separate series of a registered investment company.

(2) *Subadviser* means an investment adviser as defined in section 2(a)(20)(B) of the Act.

Rule 17d-1. Applications regarding joint enterprises or arrangements and certain profit-sharing plans

(a) No affiliated person of or principal underwriter for any registered investment company (other than a company of the character described in section 12(d)(3)(A) and (B) of the Act) and no affiliated person of such a person or principal underwriter, acting as principal, shall participate in, or effect any transaction in connection with, any joint enterprise or other joint arrangement or profit-sharing plan in which any such registered company, or a company controlled by such registered company, is a participant, and which is entered into, adopted or modified subsequent to the effective date of this rule, unless an application regarding such joint enterprise, arrangement or profit-sharing plan has been filed with the Commission and has been granted by an order entered prior to the submission of such plan or modification to security holders for approval, or prior to such adoption or modification if not so submitted, except that the provisions of this rule shall not preclude any affiliated person from acting as manager of any underwriting syndicate or other group in which such registered or controlled company is a participant and receiving compensation therefor.

(b) In passing upon such applications, the Commission will consider whether the participation of such registered or controlled company in such joint enterprise, joint arrangement or profit-sharing plan on the basis proposed is consistent with the provisions, policies and purposes of the Act and the extent to which such participation is on a basis different from or less advantageous than that of other participants.

(c) "Joint enterprise or other joint arrangement or profit-sharing plan" as used in this rule shall mean any written or oral plan, contract, authorization or arrangement, or any practice or understanding concerning an enterprise or undertaking whereby a registered investment company or a controlled company thereof and any affiliated person of or a principal underwriter for such registered investment company, or any affiliated person of such a person or principal underwriter, have a joint or a joint and several participation, or share in the profits of such enterprise or undertaking, including, but not limited to, any stock option or stock purchase plan, but shall not include an investment advisory contract subject to section 15 of the Act.

(d) Notwithstanding the requirements of paragraph (a) of this rule, no application need be filed pursuant to this rule with respect to any of the following:

(1) Any profit-sharing, stock option or stock purchase plan provided by any controlled company which is not an investment company for its officers, directors or employees, or the purchase of stock or the granting, modification or exercise of options pursuant to such a plan, *provided*:

(i) No individual participates therein who is either: (*A*) An affiliated person of any investment company which is an affiliated person of such controlled company; or (*B*) an affiliated person of the investment adviser or principal underwriter of such investment company; and

(ii) No participant has been an affiliated person of such investment company, its investment adviser or principal underwriter during the life of the plan and for six months prior to, as the case may be: (*A*) Institution of the profit-sharing plan; (*B*) the purchase of stock pursuant to a stock purchase plan; or (*C*) the granting of any options pursuant to a stock option plan.

(2) Any plan provided by any registered investment company or any controlled company for its officers or employees if such plan has been qualified under section 401 of the Internal Revenue Code of 1954 and all contributions paid under said plan by the employer qualify as deductible under section 404 of said Code.

(3) Any loan or advance of credit to, or acquisition of securities or other property of, a small business concern, or any agreement to do any of the foregoing ("Investments"), made by a bank and a small business investment company (SBIC) licensed under the Small Business Investment Act of 1958, whether such transactions are contemporaneous or separated in time, where the bank is an affiliated person of either (i) the SBIC or (ii) an affiliated person of the SBIC; but reports containing pertinent details as to Investments and transactions relating thereto shall be made at such time, on such forms and by such persons as the Commission may from time to time prescribe.

(4) The issuance by a registered investment company which is licensed by the Small Business Administration pursuant to the Small Business Investment Act of 1958 of stock options which qualify under section 422 of the Internal Revenue Code, as amended, and which conform to § 107.805(b) of Chapter I of Title 13 of the Code of Federal Regulations.

(5) Any joint enterprise or other joint arrangement or profit-sharing plan ("joint enterprise") in which a registered investment company or a company controlled by such a company, is a participant, and in which a portfolio affiliate (as defined in Rule 17a–6(b)(3)) of such registered investment company is also a participant, provided that:

(i) None of the persons identified in Rule 17a–6(a) is a participant in the joint enterprise, or has a direct or indirect financial interest in a participant in the joint enterprise (other than the registered investment company);

(ii) *Financial Interest.* (A) The term *financial interest* as used in this rule does not include:

(*1*) Any interest through ownership of securities issued by the registered investment company;

(*2*) Any interest of a wholly owned subsidiary of the registered investment company;

(*3*) Usual and ordinary fees for services as a director;

(*4*) An interest of a non-executive employee;

(*5*) An interest of an insurance company arising from a loan or policy made or issued by it in the ordinary course of business to a natural person;

(*6*) An interest of a bank arising from a loan to a person who is an officer, director, or executive of a company which is a participant in the joint transaction or from a loan to a person who directly or indirectly owns, controls, or holds with power to vote, five percent or more of the outstanding voting securities of a company which is a participant in the joint transaction;

(*7*) An interest acquired in a transaction described in paragraph (d)(3) of this rule; or

(*8*) Any other interest that the board of directors of the investment company, including a majority of the directors who are not interested persons of the investment company, finds to be not material, provided that the directors record the basis for that finding in the minutes of their meeting.

(B) A person has a financial interest in any party in which it has a financial interest, in which it had a financial interest within six months prior to the investment company's participation in the enterprise, or in which it will acquire a financial interest pursuant to an arrangement in existence at the time of the investment company's participation in the enterprise.

(6) The receipt of securities and/or cash by an investment company or a controlled company thereof and an affiliated person of such investment company or an affiliated person of such person pursuant to a plan of reorganization: *Provided,* That no person identified in Rule 17a–6(a)(1) or any company in which such a person has a direct or indirect financial interest (as defined in paragraph (d)(5)(ii) of this rule):

(i) Has a direct or indirect financial interest in the corporation under reorganization, except owning securities of each class or classes owned by such investment company or controlled company;

(ii) Receives pursuant to such plan any securities or other property, except securities of the same class and subject to the same terms as the securities received by such investment company or controlled company, and/or cash in the same proportion as is received by the investment company or controlled company based on securities of the company under reorganization owned by such persons; and

(iii) Is, or has a direct or indirect financial interest in any person (other than such investment company or controlled company) who is:

(A) Purchasing assets from the company under reorganization; or

(B) Exchanging shares with such person in a transaction not in compliance with the standards described in this paragraph (d)(6).

(7) Any arrangement regarding liability insurance policies (other than a bond required pursuant to Rule 17g–1 under the Act); *Provided,* That

(i) The investment company's participation in the joint liability insurance policy is in the best interests of the investment company;

(ii) The proposed premium for the joint liability insurance policy to be allocated to the investment company, based upon its proportionate share of the sum of the premiums that would have been paid if such insurance coverage were purchased separately by the insured parties, is fair and reasonable to the investment company;

(iii) The joint liability insurance policy does not exclude coverage for bona fide claims made against any director who is not an interested person of the investment company, or against the investment company if it is a co-defendant in the claim with the disinterested director, by another person insured under the joint liability insurance policy;

(iv) The board of directors of the investment company, including a majority of the directors who are not interested persons with respect thereto, determine no less frequently than annually that the standards described in paragraphs (i) and (ii) have been satisfied; and

(v) The board of directors of the investment company satisfies the fund governance standards defined in Rule 0–1(a)(7).

(8) An investment adviser's bearing expenses in connection with a merger, consolidation or purchase or sale of substantially all of the assets of a company which involves a registered investment company of which it is an affiliated person.

Rule 17d–2. Form for report by small business investment company and affiliated bank

Form N–17D–1 is hereby prescribed as the form for reports required by paragraph (d)(3) of Rule 17d–1.

Rule 17d–3. Exemption relating to certain joint enterprises or arrangements concerning payment for distribution of shares of a registered open-end management investment company

An affiliated person of, or principal underwriter for, a registered open-end management investment company and an affiliated person of such a person or principal underwriter shall be exempt from section 17(d) of the Act and Rule 17d–1 thereunder, to the extent necessary to permit any such person or principal underwriter to enter into a written agreement with such company whereby the company will make payments in connection with the distribution of its shares,

Provided, That:

(a) Such agreement is made in compliance with the provisions of Rule 12b–1 of this part; and

(b) No other registered management investment company which is either an affiliated person of such company or an affiliated person of such a person is a party to such agreement.

Rule 17e–1. Brokerage transactions on a securities exchange

For purposes of section 17(e)(2)(A) of the Act, a commission, fee or other remuneration shall be deemed as not exceeding the usual and customary broker's commission, if:

(a) The commission, fee, or other remuneration received or to be received is reasonable and fair compared to the commission, fee or other remuneration received by other brokers in connection with comparable transactions involving similar securities being purchased or sold on a securities exchange during a comparable period of time;

(b) The board of directors, including a majority of the directors of the investment company who are not interested persons thereof:

(1) Has adopted procedures which are reasonably designed to provide that such commission, fee, or other remuneration is consistent with the standard described in paragraph (a) of this rule;

(2) Makes and approves such changes as the board deems necessary; and

(3) Determines no less frequently than quarterly that all transactions effected pursuant to this section during the preceding quarter (other than transactions in which the person acting as broker is a person permitted to enter into a transaction with the investment company by Rule 17a–10) were effected in compliance with such procedures;

(c) The board of directors of the investment company satisfies the fund governance standards defined in Rule 0–1(a)(7); and

(d) The investment company:

(1) Shall maintain and preserve permanently in an easily accessible place a copy of the procedures (and any modification thereto) described in paragraph (b)(1) of this rule; and

(2) Shall maintain and preserve for a period not less than six years from the end of the fiscal year in which any transactions occurred, the first two years in an easily accessible place, a record of each such transaction (other than any transaction in which the person acting as broker is a person permitted to enter into a transaction with the investment company by Rule 17a–10) setting forth the amount and source of the commission, fee or other remuneration received or to be received, the identity of the person acting as broker, the terms of the transaction, and the information or materials upon which the findings described in paragraph (b)(3) of this rule were made.

Rule 17f–1. Custody of securities with members of national securities exchanges

(a) No registered management investment company shall place or maintain any of its securities or similar investments in the custody of a company which is a member of a national securities exchange as defined in the Securities Exchange Act of 1934 (whether or not such company trades in securities for its own account) except pursuant to a written contract which shall have been approved, or if executed before January 1, 1941, shall have been ratified not later than that date, by a majority of the board of directors of such investment company.

(b) The contract shall require, and the securities and investments shall be maintained in accordance with the following:

(1) The securities and similar investments held in such custody shall at all times be individually segregated from the securities and investments of any other person and marked in such manner as to clearly identify them as the property of such registered management company, both upon physical inspection thereof and upon examination of the books of the custodian. The physical segregation and marking of such securities and investments may be accomplished by putting them in separate containers bearing the name of such registered management investment company or by attaching tags or labels to such securities and investments.

(2) The custodian shall have no power or authority to assign, hypothecate, pledge or otherwise to dispose of any such securities and investments, except pursuant to the direction of such registered management company and only for the account of such registered investment company.

(3) Such securities and investments shall be subject to no lien or charge of any kind in favor of the custodian or any persons claiming through the custodian.

(4) Such securities and investment shall be verified by actual examination at the end of each annual and semi-annual fiscal period by an independent public accountant retained by the investment company, and shall be examined by such accountant at least one other time, chosen by the accountant during each fiscal year. A certificate of such accountant stating that an examination of such securities has been made, and describing

the nature and extent of the examination, shall be attached to a completed Form N-17f-1 and transmitted to the Commission promptly after each examination.

(5) Such securities and investments shall, at all times, be subject to inspection by the Commission through its employees or agents.

(6) The provisions of paragraphs (b)(1), (2) and (3) of this rule shall not apply to securities and similar investment company for or sold to such investment company by the company which is custodian until the securities have been reduced to the physical possession of the custodian and have been paid for by such investment company: *Provided,* That the company which is custodian shall take possession of such securities at the earliest practicable time. Nothing in this subparagraph shall be construed to relieve any company which is a member of a national securities exchange of any obligation under existing law or under the rules of any national securities exchange.

(c) A copy of any contract executed or ratified pursuant to paragraph (a) of this rule shall be transmitted to the Commission promptly after execution or ratification unless it has been previously transmitted.

(d) Any contract executed or ratified pursuant to paragraph (a) of this rule shall be ratified by the board of directors of the registered management investment company at least annually thereafter.

Rule 17f-2. Custody of investments by registered management investment company

(a) The securities and similar investments of a registered management investment company may be maintained in the custody of such company only in accordance with the provisions of this section. Investments maintained by such a company with a bank or other company whose functions and physical facilities are supervised by Federal or State authority under any arrangement whereunder the directors, officers, employees or agents of such company are authorized or permitted to withdraw such investments upon their mere receipt are deemed to be in the custody of such company and may be so maintained only upon compliance with the provisions of this rule.

(b) Except as provided in paragraph (c) of this section, all such securities and similar investments shall be deposited in the safekeeping of, or in a vault or other depository maintained by, a bank or other company whose functions and physical facilities are supervised by Federal or State authority. Investments so deposited shall be physically segregated at all times from those of any other person and shall be withdrawn only in connection with transactions of the character described in paragraph (c) of this rule.

(c) The first sentence of paragraph (b) of this rule shall not apply to securities on loan which are collateralized to the extent of their full market value, or to securities hypothecated, pledged, or placed in escrow for the account of such investment company in connection with a loan or other transaction authorized by specific resolution of its board of directors, or to securities in transit in connection with the sale, exchange, redemption, maturity or conversion, the exercise of warrants or rights, assents to changes in terms of the securities, or other transactions necessary or appropriate in the ordinary course of business relating to the management of securities.

(d) Except as otherwise provided by law, no person shall be authorized or permitted to have access to the securities and similar investments deposited in accordance with paragraph (b) of this rule except pursuant to a resolution of the board of directors of such investment company. Each such resolution shall designate not more than five persons who shall be either officers or responsible employees of such company and shall provide that access to such investments shall be had only by two or more such persons jointly, at least one of whom shall be an officer; except that access to such investments shall be permitted (1) to properly authorized officers and employees of the bank or other company in whose safekeeping the investments are placed and (2) for the purpose of paragraph (f) of this rule to the independent public accountant jointly with any two persons so designated or with such officer or employee of such bank or such other company. Such investments shall at all times be subject to inspection by the Commission through its authorized employees or agents accompanied, unless otherwise directed by order of the Commission, by one or more of the persons designated pursuant to this paragraph.

(e) Each person when depositing such securities or similar investments in or withdrawing them from the depository or when ordering their withdrawal and delivery from the safekeeping of the bank or other company, shall sign a notation in respect of such deposit, withdrawal or order which shall show (1) the date and time of the deposit, withdrawal or order, (2) the title and amount of the securities or other investments deposited, withdrawn or ordered to be withdrawn, and an identification thereof by certificate numbers or otherwise, (3) the manner of acquisition of the securities or similar investments deposited or the purpose for which they have been withdrawn, or ordered to be withdrawn, and (4) if withdrawn and delivered to another person the name of such person. Such notation shall be transmitted promptly to an officer or director of the investment company designated by its board of directors who shall not be a person designated for the purpose of paragraph (d) of this rule. Such notation shall be on serially numbered forms and shall be preserved for at least one year.

(f) Such securities and similar investments shall be verified by actual examination by an independent public accountant retained by the investment company at least three times during each fiscal year, at least two of which shall be chosen by such accountant without prior notice to such company. A certificate of such accountant, stating that an examination of such securities and investments has been made and describing the nature and extent of the examination shall be attached to a completed Form N–17f–2 and transmitted to the Commission promptly after each examination.

Rule 17f–3. Free cash accounts for investment companies with bank custodians

No registered investment company having a bank custodian shall hold free cash except, upon resolution of its board or directors, a petty cash account may be maintained in an amount not to exceed $500: *Provided,* That such account is operated under the imprest system and is maintained subject to adequate controls approved by the board of directors over disbursements and reimbursements including, but not limited to fidelity bond coverage of persons having access to such funds.

Rule 17f–4. Custody of investment company assets with a securities depository

(a) *Custody Arrangement with a Securities Depository.* A fund's custodian may place and maintain financial assets, corresponding to the fund's security entitlements, with a securities depository or intermediary custodian, if the custodian:

(1) Is at a minimum obligated to exercise due care in accordance with reasonable commercial standards in discharging its duty as a securities intermediary to obtain and thereafter maintain such financial assets;

(2) Is required to provide, promptly upon request by the fund, such reports as are available concerning the internal accounting controls and financial strength of the custodian; and

(3) Requires any intermediary custodian at a minimum to exercise due care in accordance with reasonable commercial standards in discharging its duty as a securities intermediary to obtain and thereafter maintain financial assets corresponding to the security entitlements of its entitlement holders.

(b) *Direct Dealings with Securities Depository.* A fund may place and maintain financial assets, corresponding to the fund's security entitlements, directly with a securities depository, if:

(1) The fund's contract with the securities depository or the securities depository's written rules for its participants:

(i) Obligate the securities depository at a minimum to exercise due care in accordance with reasonable commercial standards in discharging its duty as a securities intermediary to obtain and thereafter maintain financial assets corresponding to the fund's security entitlements; and

(ii) Requires the securities depository to provide, promptly upon request by the fund, such reports as are available concerning the internal accounting controls and financial strength of the securities depository; and

(2) The fund has implemented internal control systems reasonably designed to prevent unauthorized officer's instructions (by providing at least for the form, content and means of giving, recording and reviewing all officer's instructions).

(c) *Definitions.* For purposes of this rule the terms:

(1) *Clearing corporation, financial asset, securities intermediary, and security entitlement* have the same meanings as is attributed to those terms in § 8–102, § 8–103, and §§ 8–501 through 8–511 of the Uniform Commercial Code, 2002 Official Text and Comments, which are incorporated by reference in this section pursuant to 5 U.S.C. 552(a) and 1 CFR part 51. The Director of the Federal Register has approved this incorporation by reference in accordance with 5 U.S.C. 552(a) and 1 CFR part 51. You may obtain a copy of the Uniform Commercial Code from the National Conference of Commissioners on Uniform State Laws, 211 East Ontario Street, Suite 1300, Chicago, Il 60611. You may inspect a copy at the following addresses: Louis Loss Library, U.S. Securities and Exchange Commission, 100 F Street, NE., Washington, DC 20549, and Office of the Federal Register, National Archives and Records Adminis-

tration, 800 North Capitol Street, NW, Suite 700, Washington, DC.

(2) *Custodian* means a bank or other person authorized to hold assets for the fund under section 17(f) of the Act or Commission rules in this chapter, but does not include a fund itself, a foreign custodian whose use is governed by Rule 17f–5 or Rule 17f–7, or a vault, safe deposit box, or other repository for safekeeping maintained by a bank or other company whose functions and physical facilities are supervised by a federal or state authority if the fund maintains its own assets there in accordance with Rule 17f–2.

(3) *Fund* means an investment company registered under the Act and, where the context so requires with respect to a fund that is a unit investment trust or a face-amount certificate company, includes the fund's trustee.

(4) *Intermediary custodian* means any subcustodian that is a securities intermediary and is qualified to act as a custodian.

(5) *Officer's instruction* means a request or direction to a securities depository or its operator, or to a registered transfer agent, in the name of the fund by one or more persons authorized by the fund's board of directors (or by the fund's trustee, if the fund is a unit investment trust or a face-amount certificate company) to give the request or direction.

(6) *Securities depository* means a clearing corporation that is:

(i) Registered with the Commission as a clearing agency under section 17A of the Securities Exchange Act of 1934; or

(ii) A Federal Reserve Bank or other person authorized to operate the federal book entry system described in the regulations of the Department of Treasury codified at 31 CFR 357, Subpart B, or book-entry systems operated pursuant to comparable regulations of other federal agencies.

Rule 17f–5. Custody of investment company assets outside the United States

(a) *Definitions.* For purposes of this rule:

(1) *Eligible Foreign Custodian* means an entity that is incorporated or organized under the laws of a country other than the United States and that is a Qualified Foreign Bank or a majority-owned direct or indirect subsidiary of a U.S. Bank or bank-holding company.

(2) *Foreign Assets* means any investments (including foreign currencies) for which the primary market is outside the United States, and any cash and cash equivalents that are reasonably necessary to effect the Fund's transactions in those investments.

(3) *Foreign Custody Manager* means a Fund's or a Registered Canadian Fund's board of directors or any person serving as the board's delegate under paragraphs (b) or (d) of this rule.

(4) *Fund* means a management investment company registered under the Act and incorporated or organized under the laws of the United States or of a state.

(5) *Qualified Foreign Bank* means a banking institution or trust company, incorporated or organized under the laws of a country other than the United States, that is regulated as such by the country's government or an agency of the country's government.

(6) *Registered Canadian Fund* means a management investment company incorporated or organized under the laws of Canada and registered under the Act pursuant to the conditions of Rule 7d–1.

(7) *U.S. Bank* means an entity that is:

(i) A banking institution organized under the laws of the United States;

(ii) A member bank of the Federal Reserve System;

(iii) Any other banking institution or trust company organized under the laws of any state or of the United States, whether incorporated or not, doing business under the laws of any state or of the United States, a substantial portion of the business of which consists of receiving deposits or exercising fiduciary powers similar to those permitted to national banks under the authority of the Comptroller of the Currency, and which is supervised and examined by state or federal authority having supervision over banks, and which is not operated for the purpose of evading the provisions of this rule; or

(iv) A receiver, conservator, or other liquidating agent of any institution or firm included in paragraphs (a)(7)(i), (ii), or (iii) of this rule.

(b) *Delegation.* A Fund's board of directors may delegate to the Fund's investment adviser or officers or to a U.S. Bank or to a Qualified Foreign Bank the responsibilities set forth in paragraphs (c)(1), (c)(2), or (c)(3) of this rule, *provided that:*

(1) *Reasonable Reliance.* The board determines that it is reasonable to rely on the delegate to perform the delegated responsibilities;

(2) *Reporting.* The board requires the delegate to provide written reports notifying the board of the placement of Foreign Assets with a particular custodian and of any material change in the Fund's foreign custody arrangements, with the reports to be provided to the board at such times as the board deems reasonable and appropriate based on the circumstances of the Fund's arrangements; and

(3) *Exercise of Care.* The delegate agrees to exercise reasonable care, prudence and diligence such as a person having responsibility for the safekeeping of the Fund's Foreign Assets would exercise, or to adhere to a higher standard of care, in performing the delegated responsibilities.

(c) *Maintaining Assets with an Eligible Foreign Custodian.* A Fund or its Foreign Custody Manager may place and maintain the Fund's Foreign Assets in the care of an Eligible Foreign Custodian, *provided that:*

(1) *General Standard.* The Foreign Custody Manager determines that the Foreign Assets will be subject to reasonable care, based on the standards applicable to custodians in the relevant market, if maintained with the Eligible Foreign Custodian, after considering all factors relevant to the safekeeping of the Foreign Assets, including, without limitation:

(i) The Eligible Foreign Custodian's practices, procedures, and internal controls, including, but not limited to, the physical protections available for certificated securities (if applicable), the method of keeping custodial records, and the security and data protection practices;

(ii) Whether the Eligible Foreign Custodian has the requisite financial strength to provide reasonable care for Foreign Assets;

(iii) The Eligible Foreign Custodian's general reputation and standing; and

(iv) Whether the Fund will have jurisdiction over and be able to enforce judgments against the Eligible Foreign Custodian, such as by virtue of the existence of offices in the United States or consent to service of process in the United States.

(2) *Contract.* The arrangement with the Eligible Foreign Custodian is governed by a written contract that the Foreign Custody Manager has determined will provide reasonable care for Foreign Assets based on the standards specified in paragraph (c)(1) of this rule.

(i) The contract must provide:

(A) For indemnification or insurance arrangements (or any combination) that will adequately protect the Fund against the risk of loss of Foreign Assets held in accordance with the contract;

(B) That the Foreign Assets will not be subject to any right, charge, security interest, lien or claim of any kind in favor of the Eligible Foreign Custodian or its creditors, except a claim of payment for their safe custody or administration or, in the case of cash deposits, liens or rights in favor of creditors of the custodian arising under bankruptcy, insolvency, or similar laws;

(C) That beneficial ownership of the Foreign Assets will be freely transferable without the payment of money or value other than for safe custody or administration;

(D) That adequate records will be maintained identifying the Foreign Assets as belonging to the Fund or as being held by a third party for the benefit of the Fund;

(E) That the Fund's independent public accountants will be given access to those records or confirmation of the contents of those records; and

(F) That the Fund will receive periodic reports with respect to the safekeeping of the Foreign Assets, including, but not limited to, notification of any transfer to or from the Fund's account or a third party account containing assets held for the benefit of the Fund.

(ii) The contract may contain, in lieu of any or all of the provisions specified in paragraph (c)(2)(i) of this rule, other provisions that the Foreign Custody Manager determines will provide, in their entirety, the same or a greater level of care and protection for the Foreign Assets as the specified provisions, in their entirety.

(3)(i) *Monitoring the Foreign Custody Arrangements.* The Foreign Custody Manager has established a system to monitor the appropriateness of maintaining the Foreign Assets with a particular custodian under paragraph (c)(1) of this rule, and to monitor performance of the contract under paragraph (c)(2) of this rule.

(ii) If an arrangement with an Eligible Foreign Custodian no longer meets the requirements of this section, the Fund must withdraw the Foreign Assets from the Eligible Foreign Custodian as soon as reasonably practicable.

(d) *Registered Canadian Funds.* Any Registered Canadian Fund may place and maintain its Foreign Assets outside the United States in accordance with the requirements of this rule, *provided that:*

(1) The Foreign Assets are placed in the care of an overseas branch of a U.S. Bank that has aggregate capital, surplus, and undivided profits of a specified amount, which must not be less than $500,000; and

(2) The Foreign Custody Manager is the Fund's board of directors, its investment adviser or officers, or a U.S. Bank.

NOTE TO RULE 17f–5: When a Fund's (or its custodian's) custody arrangement with an Eligible Securities Depository (as defined in Rule 17f–7) involves one or more Eligible Foreign Custodians through which assets are maintained with the Eligible Securities Depository, Rule 17f–5 will govern the Fund's (or its custodian's) use of each Eligible Foreign Custodian, while Rule 17f–7 will govern an Eligible Foreign Custodian's use of the Eligible Securities Depository.

Rule 17f-6. Custody of investment company assets with futures commission merchants and commodity clearing organizations

(a) A Fund may place and maintain cash, securities, and similar investments with a Futures Commission Merchant in amounts necessary to effect the Fund's transactions in Exchange–Traded Futures Contracts and Commodity Options, *Provided that:*

(1) The manner in which the Futures Commission Merchant maintains the Fund's assets shall be governed by a written contract, which provides that:

(i) The Futures Commission Merchant shall comply with the segregation requirements of section 4d(2) of the Commodity Exchange Act (7 U.S.C. 6d(2)) and the rules thereunder (17 CFR Chapter I) or, if applicable, the secured amount requirements of rule 30.7 under the Commodity Exchange Act (17 CFR 30.7);

(ii) The Futures Commission Merchant, as appropriate to the Fund's transactions and in accordance with the Commodity Exchange Act (7 U.S.C. 1 through 25) and the rules and regulations thereunder (including 17 CFR part 30), may place and maintain the Fund's assets to effect the Fund's transactions with another Futures Commission Merchant, a Clearing Organization, a U.S. or Foreign Bank, or a member of a foreign board of trade, and shall obtain an acknowledgement, as required under Rules 1.20(a) or 30.7(c) under the Commodity Exchange Act, as applicable, that such assets are held on behalf of the Futures Commission Merchant's customers in accordance with the provisions of the Commodity Exchange Act; and

(iii) The Futures Commission Merchant shall promptly furnish copies of or extracts from the Futures Commission Merchant's records or such other information pertaining to the Fund's assets as the Commission through its employees or agents may request.

(2) Any gains on the Fund's transactions, other than de minimis amounts, may be maintained with the Futures Commission Merchant only until the next business day following receipt.

(3) If the custodial arrangement no longer meets the requirements of this section, the Fund shall withdraw its assets from the Futures Commission Merchant as soon as reasonably practicable.

(b) For purposes of this rule:

(1) *Clearing Organization* means a clearing organization as defined in Rule 1.3(d) under the Commodity Exchange Act and includes a clearing organization for a foreign board of trade.

(2) *Exchange-Traded Futures Contracts and Commodity Options* means commodity futures contracts, options on commodity futures contracts, and options on physical commodities traded on or subject to the rules of:

(i) Any contract market designated for trading such transactions under the Commodity Exchange Act and the rules thereunder; or

(ii) Any board of trade or exchange outside the United States, as contemplated in Part 30 under the Commodity Exchange Act.

(3) *Fund* means an investment company registered under the Act.

(4) *Futures Commission Merchant* means any person that is registered as a futures commission merchant under the Commodity Exchange Act and that is not an affiliated person of the Fund or an affiliated person of such person.

(5) *U.S. or Foreign Bank* means a bank, as defined in section 2(a)(5) of the Act, or a banking institution or trust company that is incorporated or organized under the laws of a country other than the United States and that is regulated as such by the country's government or an agency thereof.

Rule 17f–7. Custody of investment company assets with a foreign securities depository

(a) *Custody Arrangement with an Eligible Securities Depository.* A Fund, including a Registered Canadian Fund, may place and maintain its Foreign Assets with an Eligible Securities Depository, *provided that:*

(1) *Risk-Limiting Safeguards.* The custody arrangement provides reasonable safeguards against the custody risks associated with maintaining assets with the Eligible Securities Depository, including:

(i) *Risk Analysis and Monitoring.* (A) The fund or its investment adviser has received from the Primary Custodian (or its agent) an analysis of the custody risks associated with maintaining assets with the Eligible Securities Depository; and

(B) The contract between the Fund and the Primary Custodian requires the Primary Custodian (or its agent) to monitor the custody risks associated with maintaining assets with the Eligible Securities Depository on a continuing basis, and promptly notify the Fund or its investment adviser of any material change in these risks.

(ii) *Exercise of Care.* The contract between the Fund and the Primary Custodian states that the Primary Custodian will agree to exercise reasonable care, prudence, and diligence in performing the requirements of paragraphs (a)(1)(i)(A) and (B) of this rule, or adhere to a higher standard of care.

(2) *Withdrawal of Assets from Eligible Securities Depository.* If a custody arrangement with an Eligible Securities Depository no longer meets the requirements of this section, the Fund's Foreign Assets must be withdrawn from the depository as soon as reasonably practicable.

(b) *Definitions.* The terms *Foreign Assets, Fund, Qualified Foreign Bank, Registered Canadian Fund,* and *U.S. Bank* have the same meanings as in Rule 17f–5. In addition:

(1) *Eligible Securities Depository* means a system for the central handling of securities as defined in Rule 17f–4 that:

(i) Acts as or operates a system for the central handling of securities or equivalent book-entries in the country where it is incorporated, or a transnational system for the central handling of securities or equivalent book-entries;

(ii) Is regulated by a foreign financial regulatory authority as defined under section 2(a)(50) of the Act;

(iii) Holds assets for the custodian that participates in the system on behalf of the Fund under safekeeping conditions no less favorable than the conditions that apply to other participants;

(iv) Maintains records that identify the assets of each participant and segregate the system's own assets from the assets of participants;

(v) Provides periodic reports to its participants with respect to its safekeeping of assets, including notices of transfers to or from any participant's account; and

(vi) Is subject to periodic examination by regulatory authorities or independent accountants.

(2) *Primary Custodian* means a U.S. Bank or Qualified Foreign Bank that contracts directly with a Fund to provide custodial services related to maintaining the Fund's assets outside the United States.

NOTE TO RULE 17f–7: When a Fund's (or its custodian's) custody arrangement with an Eligible Securities Depository involves one or more Eligible Foreign Custodians (as defined in Rule 17f–5) through which assets are maintained with the Eligible Securities Depository, Rule 17f–5 will govern the Fund's (or its custodian's) use of each Eligible Foreign Custodian, while Rule 17f–7 will govern an Eligible Foreign Custodian's use of the Eligible Securities Depository.

Rule 17g–1. Bonding of officers and employees of registered management investment companies

(a) Each registered management investment company shall provide and maintain a bond which shall be issued by a reputable fidelity insurance company, authorized to do business in the place where the bond is issued, against larceny and embezzlement, covering each officer and employee of the investment company, who may singly, or jointly with others, have access to securities or funds of the investment company, either directly or through authority to draw upon such funds or to direct generally the disposition of such securities, unless the officer or employee has such access solely through his position as an officer or employee of a bank (hereinafter referred to as "covered persons").

(b) The bond may be in the form of (1) an individual bond for each covered person or a schedule or blanket bond covering such persons, (2) a blanket bond which names the registered management investment company as the only insured (hereinafter referred to as "single insured bond") or (3) a bond which names the registered management investment company and one or more other parties as insureds (hereinafter referred to as a "joint insured bond"), such other insured parties being limited to (i) persons engaged in the management or distribution of the shares of the registered investment company, (ii) other registered investment companies which are managed and/or whose shares are distributed by the same persons (or affiliates of such persons), (iii) persons who are engaged in the management and/or distribution of shares of companies included in paragraph (b)(3)(ii) of this rule, (iv) affiliated persons of any registered management investment company named in the bond or of any person included in paragraph (b)(3)(i) or (b)(3)(iii) of this rule hereinabove who are engaged in the administration of any registered management investment company named as insured in the bond, and (v) any trust, pension, profit-sharing or other benefit plan for officers, directors or employees of persons named in the bond.

(c) A bond of the type described in paragraphs (b)(1) or (b)(2) of this rule shall provide that it shall not be cancelled, terminated or modified except after written notice shall have been given by the acting party to the affected party and to the Commission not less than sixty days prior to the effective date of cancellation, termination or modification. A joint insured bond described in paragraph (b)(3) of this rule shall provide, that (1) it shall not be cancelled, terminated or modified except after written notice shall have been given by the acting party to the affected party and by the fidelity insurance company to all registered investment companies named as insureds and to the Commission, not less than sixty days prior to the effective date of cancellation, termination, or modification and (2) the fidelity insurance company shall furnish each registered management investment company named as an insured with (i) a copy of the bond and any amendment thereto promptly after the execution thereof, (ii) a copy of each formal filing of a claim under the bond by any other named insured promptly after the receipt thereof, and (iii) notification of the terms of the settlement of each such claim prior to the execution of the settlement.

(d) The bond shall be in such reasonable form and amount as a majority of the board of directors of the registered management investment company who are not "interested persons" of such investment company as defined by section 2(a)(19) of the Act shall approve as often as their fiduciary duties require, but not less than once every twelve months, with due consideration to all relevant factors including, but not limited to, the value of the aggregate assets of the registered management investment company to which any covered person may have access, the type and terms of the arrangements made for the custody and safekeeping of such assets, and the nature of the securities in the company's portfolio: *Provided, however,* That (1) the amount of a single insured bond shall be at least equal to an amount computed in accordance with the following schedule:

Amount of Registered Management Investment Company Gross Assets—at the End of the Most Recent Fiscal Quarter Prior to Date of Determination (In Dollars)	Minimum Amount of Bond (In Dollars)
Up to 500,000	50,000.
500,000 to 1,000,000	75,000.
1,000,000 to 2,500,000	100,000.
2,500,000 to 5,000,000	125,000.
5,000,000 to 7,500,000	150,000.
7,500,000 to 10,000,000	175,000.
10,000,000 to 15,000,000	200,000.
15,000,000 to 20,000,000	225,000.
20,000,000 to 25,000,000	250,000.
25,000,000 to 35,000,000	300,000.
35,000,000 to 50,000,000	350,000.
50,000,000 to 75,000,000	400,000.
75,000,000 to 100,000,000	450,000.
100,000,000 to 150,000,000	525,000.
150,000,000 to 250,000,000	600,000.
250,000,000 to 500,000,000	750,000.

500,000,000 to 750,000,000	900,000.
750,000,000 to 1,000,000,000	1,000,000.
1,000,000,000 to 1,500,000,000	1,250,000.
1,500,000,000 to 2,000,000,000	1,500,000.
Over 2,000,000,000	1,500,000 plus 200,000 for each 500,000,000 of gross assets up to a maximum bond of 2,500,000.

(2) A joint insured bond shall be in an amount at least equal to the sum of (i) the total amount of coverage which each registered management investment company named as an insured would have been required to provide and maintain individually pursuant to the schedule hereinabove had each such registered management investment company not been named under a joint insured bond, plus (ii) the amount of each bond which each named insured other than a registered management investment company would have been required to provide and maintain pursuant to federal statutes or regulations had it not been named as an insured under a joint insured bond.

(e) No premium may be paid for any joint insured bond or any amendment thereto unless a majority of the board of directors of each registered management investment company named as an insured therein who are not "interested persons" of such company shall approve the portion of the premium to be paid by such company, taking all relevant factors into consideration including, but not limited to, the number of the other parties named as insured, the nature of the business activities of such other parties, the amount of the joint insured bond, and the amount of the premium for such bond, the ratable allocation of the premium among all parties named as insureds, and the extent to which the share of the premium allocated to the investment company is less than the premium such company would have had to pay if it had provided and maintained a single insured bond.

(f) Each registered management investment company named as an insured in a joint insured bond shall enter into an agreement with all of the other named insureds providing that in the event recovery is received under the bond as a result of a loss sustained by the registered management investment company and one or more other named insureds, the registered management investment company shall receive an equitable and proportionate share of the recovery, but at least equal to the amount which it would have received had it provided and maintained a single insured bond with the minimum coverage required by paragraph (d)(1) of this rule.

(g) Each registered management investment company shall:

(1) File with the Commission (i) within 10 days after receipt of an executed bond of the type described in paragraphs (b)(1) or (b)(2) of this rule or any amendment thereof, (*a*) a copy of the bond, (*b*) a copy of the resolution of a majority of the board of directors who are not "interested persons" of the registered management investment company approving the form and amount of the bond, and (*c*) a statement as to the period for which premiums have been paid; (ii) within 10 days after receipt of an executed joint insured bond, or any amendment thereof, (*a*) a copy of the bond, (*b*) a copy of the resolution of a majority of the board of directors who are not "interested persons" of the registered management investment company approving the amount, type, form and coverage of the bond and the portion of the premium to be paid by such company, (*c*) a statement showing the amount of the single insured bond which the investment company would have provided and maintained had it not been named as an insured under a joint insured bond, (*d*) a statement as to the period for which premiums have been paid, and (*e*) a copy of each agreement between the investment company and all of the other named insureds entered into pursuant to paragraph (f) of this rule, and (iii) a copy of any amendment to the agreement entered into pursuant to paragraph (f) of this rule within 10 days, after the execution of such amendment,

(2) File with the Commission, in writing, within five days after the making of any claim under the bond by the investment company, a statement of the nature and amount of the claim,

(3) File with the Commission, within five days of the receipt thereof, a copy of the terms of the settlement of any claim made under the bond by the investment company, and

(4) Notify by registered mail each member of the board of directors of the investment company at his last known residence address of (i) any cancellation, termination or modification of the bond, not less than forty-five days prior to the effective

date of the cancellation or termination or modification, (ii) the filing and of the settlement of any claim under the bond by the investment company, at the time the filings required by paragraph (g)(2) and (3) of this rule are made with the Commission, and (iii) the filing and of the proposed terms of settlement of any claim under the bond by any other named insured, within five days of the receipt of a notice from the fidelity insurance company.

(h) Each registered management investment company shall designate an officer thereof who shall make the filings and give the notices required by paragraph (g) of this rule.

(i) Where the registered management investment company is an unincorporated company managed by a depositor, trustee or investment adviser, the terms "officer" and "employee" shall include for the purposes of this rule, the officers and employees of the depositor, trustee, or investment adviser.

(j) Any joint insured bond provided and maintained by a registered management investment company and one or more other parties shall be a transaction exempt from the provisions of section 17(d) of the Act and the rules thereunder, if:

(1) The terms and provisions of the bond comply with the provisions of this rule;

(2) The terms and provisions of any agreement required by paragraph (f) of this rule comply with the provisions of that paragraph; and

(3) The board of directors of the investment company satisfies the fund governance standards defined in Rule 0–1(a)(7).

(k) At the next anniversary date of an existing fidelity bond, but not later than one year from the effective date of this rule, arrangements between registered management investment companies and fidelity insurance companies and arrangements between registered management investment companies and other parties named as insureds under joint insured bonds which would not permit compliance with the provisions of this rule shall be modified by the parties so as to effect such compliance.

Rule 17j–1. Personal investment activities of investment company personnel

(a) *Definitions.* For purposes of this rule:

(1) *Access Person* means:

(i) Any Advisory Person of a Fund or of a Fund's investment adviser. If an investment adviser's primary business is advising Funds or other advisory clients, all of the investment adviser's directors, officers, and general partners are presumed to be Access Persons of any Fund advised by the investment adviser. All of a Fund's directors, officers, and general partners are presumed to be Access Persons of the Fund.

(A) If an investment adviser is primarily engaged in a business or businesses other than advising Funds or other advisory clients, the term Access Person means any director, officer, general partner or Advisory Person of the investment adviser who, with respect to any Fund, makes any recommendation, participates in the determination of which recommendation will be made, or whose principal function or duties relate to the determination of which recommendation will be made, or who, in connection with his or her duties, obtains any information concerning recommendations on Covered Securities being made by the investment adviser to any Fund.

(B) An investment adviser is "primarily engaged in a business or businesses other than advising Funds or other advisory clients" if, for each of its most recent three fiscal years or for the period of time since its organization, whichever is less, the investment adviser derived, on an unconsolidated basis, more than 50 percent of its total sales and revenues and more than 50 percent of its income (or loss), before income taxes and extraordinary items, from the other business or businesses.

(ii) Any director, officer or general partner of a principal underwriter who, in the ordinary course of business, makes, participates in or obtains information regarding, the purchase or sale of Covered Securities by the Fund for which the principal underwriter acts, or whose functions or duties in the ordinary course of business relate to the making of any recommendation to the Fund regarding the purchase or sale of Covered Securities.

(2) *Advisory Person* of a Fund or of a Fund's investment adviser means:

(i) Any director, officer, general partner or employee of the Fund or investment adviser (or of any company in a control relationship to the Fund or investment adviser) who, in connection with his or her regular functions or duties, makes, participates in, or obtains information regarding, the purchase or sale of Covered Securities by a Fund, or whose functions relate to the making of any recommendations with respect to such purchases or sales; and

(ii) Any natural person in a control relationship to the Fund or investment adviser who obtains information concerning recommendations made to the Fund with regard to the purchase or sale of Covered Securities by the Fund.

(3) *Control* has the same meaning as in section 2(a)(9) of the Act.

(4) *Covered Security* means a security as defined in section 2(a)(36) of the Act [15 U.S.C. 80a–2(a)(36)], except that it does not include:

(i) Direct obligations of the Government of the United States;

(ii) Bankers' acceptances, bank certificates of deposit, commercial paper and high quality short-term debt instruments, including repurchase agreements; and

(iii) Shares issued by open-end Funds.

(5) *Fund* means an investment company registered under the Investment Company Act.

(6) An *Initial Public Offering* means an offering of securities registered under the Securities Act of 1933, the issuer of which, immediately before the registration, was not subject to the reporting requirements of sections 13 or 15(d) of the Securities Exchange Act of 1934.

(7) *Investment Personnel* of a Fund or of a Fund's investment adviser means:

(i) Any employee of the Fund or investment adviser (or of any company in a control relationship to the Fund or investment adviser) who, in connection with his or her regular functions or duties, makes or participates in making recommendations regarding the purchase or sale of securities by the Fund.

(ii) Any natural person who controls the Fund or investment adviser and who obtains information concerning recommendations made to the Fund regarding the purchase or sale of securities by the Fund.

(8) *A Limited Offering* means an offering that is exempt from registration under the Securities Act of 1933 pursuant to section 4(a)(2) or section 4(a)(5) or pursuant to Rule 504 or Rule 506 under the Securities Act of 1933.

(9) *Purchase or sale of a Covered Security* includes, among other things, the writing of an option to purchase or sell a Covered Security.

(10) *Security Held or to Be Acquired by a Fund* means:

(i) Any Covered Security which, within the most recent 15 days:

(A) Is or has been held by the Fund; or

(B) Is being or has been considered by the Fund or its investment adviser for purchase by the Fund; and

(ii) Any option to purchase or sell, and any security convertible into or exchangeable for, a Covered Security described in paragraph (a)(10)(i) of this rule.

(iii) Any director, officer, general partner or employee of the Fund or investment adviser (or of any company in a control relationship to the Fund or investment adviser) who, in connection with his or her regular functions or duties, makes, participates in, or obtains information regarding, the purchase or sale of Covered Securities by a Fund, or whose functions relate to the making of any recommendations with respect to such purchases or sales; and

(11) *Automatic Investment Plan* means a program in which regular periodic purchases (or withdrawals) are made automatically in (or from) investment accounts in accordance with a predetermined schedule and allocation. An Automatic Investment Plan includes a dividend reinvestment plan.

(b) *Unlawful Actions.* It is unlawful for any affiliated person of or principal underwriter for a Fund, or any affiliated person of an investment adviser of or principal underwriter for a Fund, in connection with the purchase or sale, directly or indirectly, by the person of a Security Held or to be Acquired by the Fund:

(1) To employ any device, scheme or artifice to defraud the Fund;

(2) To make any untrue statement of a material fact to the Fund or omit to state a material fact necessary in order to make the statements made to the Fund, in light of the circumstances under which they are made, not misleading;

(3) To engage in any act, practice or course of business that operates or would operate as a fraud or deceit on the Fund; or

(4) To engage in any manipulative practice with respect to the Fund.

(c) *Code of Ethics.* (1) *Adoption and Approval of Code of Ethics.*

(i) Every Fund (other than a money market fund or a Fund that does not invest in Covered Securities) and each investment adviser of and principal underwriter for the Fund, must adopt a written code of ethics containing provisions reasonably necessary to prevent its Access Persons from engaging in any conduct prohibited by paragraph (b) of this rule.

(ii) The board of directors of a Fund, including a majority of directors who are not interested persons, must approve the code of ethics of the Fund, the code of ethics of each investment adviser and principal underwriter of the Fund, and any material changes to these codes. The board must base its approval of a code and any material changes to the code on a determination that the code contains provisions reasonably necessary to prevent Access Persons from engaging in any conduct prohibited by paragraph (b) of this section. Before approving a code of a Fund, investment adviser or principal underwriter or any amendment to the code, the board of directors must receive a certification from the Fund, investment adviser or principal underwriter that it has adopted procedures reasonably necessary to prevent Access Persons from violating the Fund's, investment adviser's, or principal underwriter's code of ethics. The Fund's board must approve the code of an investment adviser or principal underwriter before initially retaining the services of the investment adviser or principal underwriter. The Fund's board must approve a material change to a code no later than six months after adoption of the material change.

(iii) If a Fund is a unit investment trust, the Fund's principal underwriter or depositor must approve the Fund's code of ethics, as required by paragraph (c)(1)(ii) of this rule. If the Fund has more than one principal underwriter or depositor, the principal underwriters and depositors may designate, in writing, which principal underwriter or depositor must conduct the approval required by paragraph (c)(1)(ii) of this rule, if they obtain written consent from the designated principal underwriter or depositor.

(2) *Administration of Code of Ethics.* (i) The Fund, investment adviser and principal underwriter must use reasonable diligence and institute procedures reasonably necessary to prevent violations of its code of ethics.

(ii) No less frequently than annually, every Fund (other than a unit investment trust) and its investment advisers and principal underwriters must furnish to the Fund's board of directors, and the board of directors must consider, a written report that:

(A) Describes any issues arising under the code of ethics or procedures since the last report to the board of directors, including, but not limited to, information about material violations of the code or procedures and sanctions imposed in response to the material violations; and

(B) Certifies that the Fund, investment adviser or principal underwriter, as applicable, has adopted procedures reasonably necessary to prevent Access Persons from violating the code.

(3) *Exception for Principal Underwriters.* The requirements of paragraphs (c)(1) and (c)(2) of this rule do not apply to any principal underwriter unless:

(i) The principal underwriter is an affiliated person of the Fund or of the Fund's investment adviser; or

(ii) An officer, director or general partner of the principal underwriter serves as an officer, director or general partner of the Fund or of the Fund's investment adviser.

(d) *Reporting Requirements of Access Persons.* (1) *Reports Required.* Unless excepted by paragraph (d)(2) of this rule, every Access Person of a Fund (other than a money market fund or a Fund that does not invest in Covered Securities) and every Access Person of an investment adviser of or principal underwriter for the Fund, must report to that Fund, investment adviser or principal underwriter:

(i) *Initial Holdings Reports.* No later than 10 days after the person becomes an Access Person (which information must be current as of a date no more than 45 days prior to the date the person becomes an Access Person):

(A) The title, number of shares and principal amount of each Covered Security in which the Access Person had any direct or indirect beneficial ownership when the person became an Access Person;

(B) The name of any broker, dealer or bank with whom the Access Person maintained an account in which any securities were held for the direct or indirect benefit of the Access

Person as of the date the person became an Access Person; and

(C) The date that the report is submitted by the Access Person.

(ii) *Quarterly Transaction Reports.* No later than 30 days after the end of a calendar quarter, the following information:

(A) With respect to any transaction during the quarter in a Covered Security in which the Access Person had any direct or indirect beneficial ownership:

(*1*) The date of the transaction, the title, the interest rate and maturity date (if applicable), the number of shares and the principal amount of each Covered Security involved;

(*2*) The nature of the transaction (i.e., purchase, sale or any other type of acquisition or disposition);

(*3*) The price of the Covered Security at which the transaction was effected;

(*4*) The name of the broker, dealer or bank with or through which the transaction was effected; and

(*5*) The date that the report is submitted by the Access Person.

(B) With respect to any account established by the Access Person in which any securities were held during the quarter for the direct or indirect benefit of the Access Person:

(*1*) The name of the broker, dealer or bank with whom the Access Person established the account;

(*2*) The date the account was established; and

(*3*) The date that the report is submitted by the Access Person.

(iii) *Annual Holdings Reports.* Annually, the following information (which information must be current as of a date no more than 45 days before the report is submitted):

(A) The title, number of shares and principal amount of each Covered Security in which the Access Person had any direct or indirect beneficial ownership;

(B) The name of any broker, dealer or bank with whom the Access Person maintains an account in which any securities are held for the direct or indirect benefit of the Access Person; and

(C) The date that the report is submitted by the Access Person.

(2) *Exceptions from Reporting Requirements.* (i) A person need not make a report under paragraph (d)(1) of this rule with respect to transactions effected for, and Covered Securities held in, any account over which the person has no direct or indirect influence or control.

(ii) A director of a Fund who is not an "interested person" of the Fund within the meaning of section 2(a)(19) of the Act, and who would be required to make a report solely by reason of being a Fund director, need not make:

(A) An initial holdings report under paragraph (d)(1)(i) of this rule and an annual holdings report under paragraph (d)(1)(iii) of this rule; and

(B) A quarterly transaction report under paragraph (d)(1)(ii) of this rule, unless the director knew or, in the ordinary course of fulfilling his or her official duties as a Fund director, should have known that during the 15-day period immediately before or after the director's transaction in a Covered Security, the Fund purchased or sold the Covered Security, or the Fund or its investment adviser considered purchasing or selling the Covered Security.

(iii) An Access Person to a Fund's principal underwriter need not make a report to the principal underwriter under paragraph (d)(1) of this rule if:

(A) The principal underwriter is not an affiliated person of the Fund (unless the Fund is a unit investment trust) or any investment adviser of the Fund; and

(B) The principal underwriter has no officer, director or general partner who serves as an officer, director or general partner of the Fund or of any investment adviser of the Fund.

(iv) An Access Person to an investment adviser need not make a separate report to the investment adviser under paragraph (d)(1) of this rule to the extent the information in the report would duplicate information required to be recorded under Rule 204–2(a)(13) under the Investment Advisers Act of 1940.

(v) An Access Person need not make a quarterly transaction report under paragraph (d)(1)(ii) of this rule if the report would duplicate information contained in broker trade confirmations or account statements received by the Fund, investment adviser or principal underwriter with respect to the Access Person in the time period required by paragraph (d)(1)(ii), if all of the information required by that paragraph is contained in the broker trade confirmations or account statements, or in the records of the Fund, investment adviser or principal underwriter.

(vi) An Access Person need not make a quarterly transaction report under paragraph (d)(1)(ii) of this rule with respect to transactions effected pursuant to an Automatic Investment Plan.

(3) *Review of Reports.* Each Fund, investment adviser and principal underwriter to which reports are required to be made by paragraph (d)(1) of this rule must institute procedures by which appropriate management or compliance personnel review these reports.

(4) *Notification of Reporting Obligation.* Each Fund, investment adviser and principal underwriter to which reports are required to be made by paragraph (d)(1) of this rule must identify all Access Persons who are required to make these reports and must inform those Access Persons of their reporting obligation.

(5) *Beneficial Ownership.* For purposes of this section, beneficial ownership is interpreted in the same manner as it would be under Rule 16a–1(a)(2) under the Securities Exchange Act of 1934 in determining whether a person is the beneficial owner of a security for purposes of section 16 of the Securities Exchange Act of 1934 and the rules and regulations thereunder. Any report required by paragraph (d) of this rule may contain a statement that the report will not be construed as an admission that the person making the report has any direct or indirect beneficial ownership in the Covered Security to which the report relates.

(e) *Pre–Approval of Investments in IPOs and Limited Offerings.* Investment Personnel of a Fund or its investment adviser must obtain approval from the Fund or the Fund's investment adviser before directly or indirectly acquiring beneficial ownership in any securities in an Initial Public Offering or in a Limited Offering.

(f) *Recordkeeping Requirements.* (1) Each Fund, investment adviser and principal underwriter that is required to adopt a code of ethics or to which reports are required to be made by Access Persons must, at its principal place of business, maintain records in the manner and to the extent set out in this paragraph (f), and must make these records available to the Commission or any representative of the Commission at any time and from time to time for reasonable periodic, special or other examination:

(A) A copy of each code of ethics for the organization that is in effect, or at any time within the past five years was in effect, must be maintained in an easily accessible place;

(B) A record of any violation of the code of ethics, and of any action taken as a result of the violation, must be maintained in an easily accessible place for at least five years after the end of the fiscal year in which the violation occurs;

(C) A copy of each report made by an Access Person as required by this section, including any information provided in lieu of the reports under paragraph (d)(2)(v) of this rule, must be maintained for at least five years after the end of the fiscal year in which the report is made or the information is provided, the first two years in an easily accessible place;

(D) A record of all persons, currently or within the past five years, who are or were required to make reports under paragraph (d) of this rule, or who are or were responsible for reviewing these reports, must be maintained in an easily accessible place; and

(E) A copy of each report required by paragraph (c)(2)(ii) of this rule must be maintained for at least five years after the end of the fiscal year in which it is made, the first two years in an easily accessible place.

(2) A Fund or investment adviser must maintain a record of any decision, and the reasons supporting the decision, to approve the acquisition by investment personnel of securities under paragraph (e), for at least five years after the end of the fiscal year in which the approval is granted.

Rule 18c–1. Exemption of privately held indebtedness

The issuance or sale of more than one class of senior securities representing indebtedness by a small business investment company, licensed under the Small Business Investment Act of 1958, shall not be prohibited by section 18(c) so long as such small business investment company does not have outstanding any publicly held indebtedness, and all securities of any such class are (a) privately held by the Small Business Administration, or banks, insurance companies or other institutional investors, (b) not intended to be publicly distributed, and (c) not convertible into, exchangeable for, or accompanied by any option to acquire, any equity security.

Rule 18c–2. Exemptions of certain debentures issued by small business investment companies

(a) The issuance or sale of any class of senior security representing indebtedness by a small business investment company licensed under the Small Business Investment Act of 1958 shall not be prohibited by section 18(c) of the Act provided such senior security representing indebtedness is (1) not convertible into, exchangeable for, or accompanied by an option to acquire any equity security; (2) fully guaranteed as to timely payment of all principal and interest by the Small Business Administration and backed by the full faith and credit of the United States; and (3) subordinated to any other debt securities not issued pursuant to this rule or, if such security is not so subordinated, that such security, according to its own terms, will not be preferred over any other unsecured debt securities in the payment of principal and interest: *And further provided*, That all other debt securities then outstanding issued by such small business investment company were issued as permitted by Rule 18c–1 or this rule.

(b) Any security issued and sold as permitted by paragraph (a) of this rule shall be deemed for purposes of Rule 18c–1 to be privately held by the Small Business Administration and for purposes of Rule 18c–1 shall not be deemed to be publicly held outstanding indebtedness.

(c) The issuance or sale of any security as permitted by paragraph (a) of this rule shall not be deemed to be a sale to any person other than the Small Business Administration by any small business investment company licensed under the Small Business Investment Company Act of 1958 which is exempt from any provision of the Investment Company Act, if such exemption is conditioned on such company not offering or selling its securities to any person other than the Small Business Administration.

Rule 18f–1. Exemption from certain requirements of Section 18(f)(1) (of the Act) for registered open-end investment companies which have the right to redeem in kind

(a) A registered open-end investment company which has the right to redeem securities of which it is the issuer in assets other than cash may file with the Commission at any time a notification of election on Form N–18F–1 committing itself to pay in cash all requests for redemption by any shareholder of record, limited in amount with respect to each shareholder during any ninety-day period to the lesser of

(1) $250,000 or

(2) 1 percent of the net asset value of such company at the beginning of such period.

(b) An election pursuant to paragraph (a):

(1) Shall be described in either the prospectus or the Statement of Additional Information, at the discretion of the investment company, and

(2) Shall be irrevocable while this rule is in effect unless the Commission by order upon application permits the withdrawal of such notification of election as being appropriate in the public interest and consistent with the protection of investors.

(c) Upon making the election described in paragraph (a) of this rule, an investment company shall be exempt from the requirements of section 18(f)(1) (of the Act) to the extent necessary for such company to effectuate redemptions in the manner set forth in such paragraph.

Rule 18f–2. Fair and equitable treatment for holders of each class or series of stock of series investment companies

(a) For purposes of this Rule 18f–2 a series company is a registered open-end investment company which, in accordance with the provisions of section 18(f)(2) of the Act, issues two or more classes or series of preferred or special stock each of which is preferred over all other classes or series in respect of assets specifically allocated to that class or series. Any matter required to be submitted by the provisions of the Act or of applicable State law, or otherwise, to the holders of the outstanding voting securities of a series company shall not be deemed to have been effectively acted upon [un]less approved by the holders of a majority of the outstanding voting securities of each class or series of stock affected by such matter.

(b) For the purposes of paragraph (a) of this Rule 18f–2, a class or series of stock will be deemed to be affected by such a matter, unless (1) the interests of each class or series in the matter are substantially identical, or (2) the matter does not affect any interest of such class or series.

(c)(1) With respect to the submission of an investment advisory contract to the holders of the outstanding voting securities of a series company for the approval required by section 15(a) of the Act, such matter shall be deemed to be effectively acted upon with respect to any class or series of securities of such company if a majority of the outstanding voting securities of such class or series vote for the approval of such matter, notwithstanding (i) that such matter has not been approved by the holders of a majority of the outstanding voting securities of any other class or series affected by such matter, and (ii) that such matter has not been approved by the vote of a majority of the outstanding voting securities of such company, provided that if such a majority is required by State law or otherwise, such requirement shall apply.

(2) If any class or series of securities of a series company fails to approve an investment advisory contract in the manner required by paragraph (c)(1) of this rule, the investment adviser of such company may continue to serve or act in such capacity for the period of time pending such required approval of such contract, of a new contract with the same or different adviser, or other definitive action: *Provided*, That the compensation received by such investment adviser during such period is equal to no more than its actual costs incurred in furnishing investment advisory services to such class or series or the amount it would have received under the advisory contract, whichever is less.

(d) With respect to the submission of a change in investment policy to the holders of the outstanding voting securities of a series company for the approval required by section 13 of the Act, such matter shall be deemed to have been effectively acted upon with respect to any class or series of such company if a majority of the outstanding voting securities of such class or series vote for the approval of such matter, notwithstanding (1) that such matter has not been approved by the holders of a majority of the outstanding voting securities of any other class or series affected by such matter, and (2) that such matter has not been approved by the vote of a majority of the outstanding voting securities of such company: *Provided,* That if such a majority is required by State law or otherwise, such requirement shall apply.

(e) The submission to shareholders of the selection of the independent public accountant of a series company required by section 32(a) (of the Act) shall be exempt from the separate voting requirements of paragraph (a) of this Rule 18f–2.

(f) The submission to shareholders of a contract with a principal underwriter of a series company required by section 15(b) of the Act shall be exempt from the separate voting requirements of paragraph (a) of this Rule 18f–2.

(g) The submission to shareholders of nominees for election as directors required by section 16(a) of the Act shall be exempt from the separate voting requirements of paragraph (a) of this Rule 18f–2.

(h) For the purposes of this Rule 18f–2 a "majority of the outstanding voting securities" of a class or series, (1) when used with respect to a matter required by any provision of the Act to be submitted to the outstanding voting securities of a series company, shall have the same meaning as a "majority of the outstanding voting securities of a company" as defined in section 2(a)(42) of the Act; and (2) when used with respect to any other matter required to be submitted to the outstanding voting securities of a series company, shall mean the lesser of (i) the minimum vote of the outstanding voting securities of a company required by applicable State law or other applicable requirement, or (ii) the minimum vote specified by paragraph (1) of this paragraph (h), unless State law requires approval of such matters by a specified percentage of the outstanding voting securities of a particular class or series, in which case, State law shall apply.

Rule 18f–3. Multiple class companies

Notwithstanding sections 18(f)(1) and 18(i) of the Act, a registered open-end management investment company or series or class thereof established in accordance with section 18(f)(2) of the Act whose shares are registered on Form N–1A [Item 15A of 17 CFR 239 and 274.11A] ("company") may issue more than one class of voting stock, *provided* that:

(a) Each class:

(1)(i) Shall have a different arrangement for shareholder services or the distribution of securities or both, and shall pay all of the expenses of that arrangement;

(ii) May pay a different share of other expenses, not including advisory or custodial fees or other expenses related to the management of the company's assets, if these expenses are actually incurred in a different amount by that class, or if the class receives services of a different kind or to a different degree than other classes; and

(iii) May pay a different advisory fee to the extent that any difference in amount paid is the result of the application of the same performance fee provisions in the advisory contract of the company to the different investment performance of each class;

(2) Shall have exclusive voting rights on any matter submitted to shareholders that relates solely to its arrangement;

(3) Shall have separate voting rights on any matter submitted to shareholders in which the interests of one class differ from the interests of any other class; and

(4) Shall have in all other respects the same rights and obligations as each other class.

(b) Expenses may be waived or reimbursed by the company's adviser, underwriter, or any other provider of services to the company.

(c)(1) Income, realized gains and losses, unrealized appreciation and depreciation, and Fundwide Expenses shall be allocated based on one of the following methods (which method shall be applied on a consistent basis):

(i) To each class based on the net assets of that class in relation to the net assets of the company ("relative net assets");

(ii) To each class based on the Simultaneous Equations Method;

(iii) To each class based on the Settled Shares Method, provided that the company is a Daily Dividend Fund (such a company may allocate income and Fundwide Expenses based on the Settled Shares Method and realized gains and losses and unrealized appreciation and depreciation based on relative net assets);

(iv) To each share without regard to class, provided that the company is a Daily Dividend Fund that maintains the same net asset value per share in each class; that the company has received undertakings from its adviser, underwriter, or any other provider of services to the company, agreeing to waive or reimburse the company for payments to such service provider by one or more classes, as allocated under paragraph (a)(1) of this rule, to the extent necessary to assure that all classes of the company maintain the same net asset value per share; and that payments waived or reimbursed under such an undertaking may not be carried forward or recouped at a future date; or

(v) To each class based on any other appropriate method, provided that a majority of the directors of the company, and a majority of the directors who are not interested persons of the company, determine that the method is fair to the shareholders of each class and that the annualized rate of return of each class will generally differ from that of the other classes only by the expense differentials among the classes.

(2) For purposes of this rule:

(i) Daily Dividend Fund means any company that has a policy of declaring distributions of net investment income daily, including any money market fund that operates in compliance with Rule 2a–7;

(ii) Fundwide Expenses means expenses of the company not allocated to a particular class under paragraph (a)(1) of this rule;

(iii) The Settled Shares Method means allocating to each class based on relative net assets, excluding the value of subscriptions receivable; and

(iv) The Simultaneous Equations Method means the simultaneous allocation to each class of each day's income, realized gains and losses, unrealized appreciation and depreciation, and Fundwide Expenses and reallocation to each class of undistributed net investment income, undistributed realized gains or losses, and unrealized appreciation or depreciation, based on the operating results of the company, changes in ownership interests of each class, and expense differentials between the classes, so that the annualized rate of return of each class generally differs from that of the other classes only by the expense differentials among the classes.

(d) Any payments made under paragraph (a) of this rule shall be made pursuant to a written plan setting forth the separate arrangement and expense allocation of each class, and any related conversion features or exchange privileges. Before the first issuance of a share of any class in reliance upon this section, and before any material amendment of a plan, a majority of the directors of the company, and a majority of the directors who are not interested persons of the company, shall find that the plan as proposed to be adopted or amended, including the expense allocation, is in the best interests of each class individually and the company as a whole; initial board approval of a plan under this paragraph (d) is not required, however, if the plan does not make any change in the arrangements and expense allocations previously approved by the board under an existing order of exemption. Before any vote on the plan, the directors shall request and evaluate, and any agreement relating to a class arrangement shall require the parties thereto to furnish, such information as may be reasonably necessary to evaluate the plan.

(e)(1) The board of directors of the investment company satisfies the fund governance standards defined in Rule 0–1(a)(7).

(f) Nothing in this section prohibits a company from offering any class with:

(1) An exchange privilege providing that securities of the class may be exchanged for certain securities of another company; or

(2) A conversion feature providing that shares of one class of the company (the "purchase class") will be exchanged automatically for shares of another class of the company (the "target class") after a specified period of time, *Provided,* That:

(i) The conversion is effected on the basis of the relative net asset values of the two classes without the imposition of any sales load, fee, or other charge;

(ii) The expenses, including payments authorized under a plan adopted pursuant to Rule 12b–1 ("rule 12b–1 plan"), for the target class are not higher than the expenses, including payments authorized under a rule 12b–1 plan, for the purchase class; and

(iii) If the shareholders of the target class approve any increase in expenses allocated to the target class under paragraphs (a)(1)(i) and (a)(1)(ii) of this rule, and the purchase class shareholders do not approve the increase, the company will establish a new target class for the purchase class on the same terms as applied to the target class before that increase.

(3) A conversion feature providing that shares of a class in which an investor is no longer eligible to participate may be converted to shares of a class in which that investor is eligible to participate, *Provided,* That:

(i) The investor is given prior notice of the proposed conversion; and

(ii) The conversion is effected on the basis of the relative net asset values of the two classes without the imposition of any sales load, fee, or other charge.

Rule 19a–1. Written statement to accompany dividend payments by management companies

(a) Every written statement made pursuant to section 19 by or on behalf of a management company shall be made on a separate paper and shall clearly indicate what portion of the payment per share is made from the following sources:

(1) Net income for the current or preceding fiscal year, or accumulated undistributed net income, or both, not including in either case profits or losses from the sale of securities or other properties.

(2) Accumulated undistributed net profits from the sale of securities or other properties (except that an open-end company may treat as a separate source its net profits from such sales during its current fiscal year).

(3) Paid-in surplus or other capital source. To the extent that a payment is properly designated as being made from a source specified in paragraph (1) or (2) of this rule, it need not be designated as having been made from a source specified in this subparagraph.

(b) If the payment is made in whole or in part from a source specified in paragraph (a)(2) of this rule the written statement shall indicate, after giving effect to the part of such payment so specified, the deficit, if any, in the aggregate of (1) accumulated undistributed realized profits less losses on the sale of securities or other properties and (2) the net unrealized appreciation or depreciation of portfolio securities, all as of a date reasonably close to the end of the period as of which the dividend is paid. Any statement made pursuant to the preceding sentence shall specify the amount, if any, of such deficit which represents unrealized depreciation of portfolio securities.

(c) Accumulated undistributed net income and accumulated undistributed net profits from the sale of securities or other properties shall be determined, at the option of the company, either (1) from the date of the organization of the company, (2) from the date of a reorganization, as defined in clause (A) or (B) of section 2(a)(33) of the Act, (3) from the date as of which a write-down of portfolio securities was made in connection with a corporate readjustment, approved by stockholders, of the type known as "quasi-reorganization," or (4) from January 1, 1925, to the close of the period as of which the dividend is paid, without giving effect to such payment.

(d) For the purpose of this rule, open-end companies which upon the sale of their shares allocate to undistributed income or other similar account that portion of the consideration received which represents the approximate per share amount of undistributed net income included in the sales price, and make a corresponding deduction from undistributed net income upon the purchase or redemption of shares need not treat the amounts so allocated as paid-in surplus or other capital source.

(e) For the purpose of this rule, the source or sources from which a dividend is paid shall be determined (or reasonably estimated) to the close of the period as of which it is paid without giving effect to such payment. If any such estimate is subsequently ascertained to be inaccurate in a significant amount, a correction thereof shall be made by a written statement pursuant to section 19(a) of the Act or in the first report to stockholders following discovery of the inaccuracy.

(f) Insofar as a written statement made pursuant to section 19(a) of the Act relates to a dividend on preferred stock paid for a period of less than a year, a company may elect to indicate only that portion of the payment which is made from sources specified in paragraph (a)(1) of this rule, and need not specify the sources from which the remainder was paid. Every company which in any fiscal year elects to make a statement pursuant to the preceding sentence shall transmit to the holders of such preferred stock, at a date reasonably near the end of the last dividend period in such fiscal year, a statement meeting the requirements of paragraph (a) of this rule on an annual basis.

(g) The purpose of this rule, in the light of which it shall be construed, is to afford security holders adequate disclosure of the sources from which dividend payments are made. Nothing in this rule shall be construed to prohibit the inclusion in any written statement of additional information in explanation of the information required by this rule. Nothing in this rule shall be construed to permit a dividend payment in violation of any State law or to prevent compliance with any requirement of State law regarding dividends consistent with this rule.

Rule 19b–1. Frequency of distribution of capital gains

(a) No registered investment company which is a "regulated investment company" as defined in section 851 of the Internal Revenue Code of 1986 ("Code") shall distribute more than one capital gain dividend ("distribution"), as defined in section 852(b)(3)(C) of the Code, with respect to any one taxable year of the company, other than a distribution otherwise permitted by this rule or made pursuant to section 855 of the Code which is supplemental to the prior distribution with respect to the same taxable year of the company and which does not exceed 10% of the aggregate amount distributed for such taxable year.

(b) No registered investment company which is not a "regulated investment company" as defined in section 851 of the Code shall make more than one distribution of long-term capital gains, as defined in the Code, in any one taxable year of the company: *Provided,* That a unit investment trust may distribute capital gain dividends received from a "regulated investment company" within a reasonable time after receipt.

(c) The provisions of this rule shall not apply to a unit investment trust (hereinafter referred to as the "Trust") engaged exclusively in the business of investing in eligible trust securities (as defined in Rule 14a–3(b) under this Act); *Provided,* That:

(1) The capital gain distribution is a result of:

(i) an issuer's calling or redeeming an eligible trust debt security held by the Trust,

(ii) the sale of an eligible trust security by the Trust to provide funds for redemption of Trust units when the amount received by the Trust for such sale exceeds the amount required to satisfy the redemption distribution,

(iii) the sale of an eligible trust security to maintain qualification of the Trust as a "regulated investment company" under section 851 of the Code,

(iv) regular distributions of principal and prepayment of principal on eligible trust securities, or

(v) the sale of an eligible trust security in order to maintain the investment stability of the Trust; and

(2) Capital gains distributions are clearly described as such in a report to the unitholder which accompanies each such distribution.

(d) For purposes of paragraph (c) of this rule, sales made to maintain the investment stability of the Trust means sales made to prevent deterioration of the value of the eligible trust securities held in the

Trust portfolio when one or more of the following factors exist:

(1) A default in the payment of principal or interest on an eligible trust security;

(2) An action involving the issuer of an eligible trust security which adversely affects the ability of such issuer to continue payment of principal or interest on its eligible trust securities; or

(3) A change in market, revenue or credit factors which adversely affects the ability of such issuer to continue payment of principal or interest on its eligible trust securities.

(e) If a registered investment company because of unforeseen circumstances in a particular taxable year proposes to make a distribution which would be prohibited by the provisions of this section, it may file a request with the Commission for authorization to make such a distribution. Such request shall comply with the requirements of Rule 0–2 and shall set forth the pertinent facts and explain the circumstances which the company believes justify such distribution. The request shall be deemed granted unless the Commission within 15 days after receipt thereof shall deny such request as not being necessary or appropriate in the public interest or for the protection of investors and notify the company in writing of such denial.

(f) A registered investment company may make one additional distribution of long-term capital gains, as defined in the Code, with respect to any one taxable year of the company, which distribution is made, in whole or in part, for the purpose of not incurring any tax under section 4982 of the Code. Such additional distribution may be made prior or subsequent to any distribution otherwise permitted by paragraph (a) of this rule.

Rule 20a–1. Solicitation of proxies, consents and authorizations

(a) No person shall solicit or permit the use of his or her name to solicit any proxy, consent, or authorization with respect to any security issued by a registered Fund, except upon compliance with Regulation 14A (Rule 14a–1 under the Securities Exchange Act of 1934), Schedule 14A (17 CFR 240.14a–101), and all other rules and regulations adopted pursuant to section 14(a) of the Securities Exchange Act of 1934 that would be applicable to such solicitation if it were made in respect of a security registered pursuant to section 12 of the Securities Exchange Act of 1934. Unless the solicitation is made in respect of a security registered on a national securities exchange, none of the soliciting material need be filed with such exchange.

(b) If the solicitation is made by or on behalf of the management of the investment company, then the investment adviser or any prospective investment adviser and any affiliated person thereof as to whom information is required in the solicitation shall upon request of the investment company promptly transmit to the investment company all information necessary to enable the management of such company to comply with the rules and regulations applicable to such solicitation. If the solicitation is made by any person other than the management of the investment company, on behalf of and with the consent of the investment adviser or prospective investment adviser, then the investment adviser or prospective investment adviser and any affiliated person thereof as to whom information is required in the solicitation shall upon request of the person making the solicitation promptly transmit to such person all information necessary to enable such person to comply with the rules and regulations applicable to the solicitation.

Instruction. Registrants that have made a public offering of securities and that hold security holder votes for which proxies, consents, or authorizations are not being solicited pursuant to the requirements of this rule should refer to section 14(c) of the Securities Exchange Act of 1934 and the information statement requirements set forth in the rules thereunder.

Rule 22c–1. Pricing of redeemable securities for distribution, redemption and repurchase

(a) No registered investment company issuing any redeemable security, no person designated in such issuer's prospectus as authorized to consummate transactions in any such security, and no principal underwriter of, or dealer in any such security shall sell, redeem, or repurchase any such security except at a price based on the current net asset value of such security which is next computed after receipt of a tender of such security for redemption or of an order to purchase or sell such security; *Provided,* That:

(1) This paragraph shall not prevent a sponsor of a unit investment trust (hereinafter referred to as the "Trust") engaged exclusively in the business of investing in eligible trust securities (as defined in Rule 14a–3(b)) from selling or repurchasing Trust units in a secondary market at a price based on the offering side evaluation of the eligible trust securities in the Trust's portfolio, determined at any time on the last business day of each week, effective for all sales made during the following week, if on the days that such sales or repurchases are

made the sponsor receives a letter from a qualified evaluator stating, in its opinion, that:

(i) in the case of repurchases, the current bid price is not higher than the offering side evaluation, computed on the last business day of the previous week; and

(ii) in the case of resales, the offering side evaluation, computed as of the last business day of the previous week, is not more than one-half of one percent ($5.00 on a unit representing $1,000 principal amount of eligible trust securities) greater than the current offering price.

(2) This paragraph shall not prevent any registered investment company from adjusting the price of its redeemable securities sold pursuant to a merger, consolidation or purchase of substantially all of the assets of a company which meets the conditions specified in Rule 17a–8.

(b) For the purposes of this rule:

(1) the current net asset value of any such security shall be computed no less frequently than once daily, Monday through Friday, at the specific time or times during the day that the board of directors of the investment company sets, in accordance with paragraph (e) of this rule, except on

(i) days on which changes in the value of the investment company's portfolio securities will not materially affect the current net asset value of the investment company's redeemable securities,

(ii) days during which no security is tendered for redemption and no order to purchase or sell such security is received by the investment company; or

(iii) customary national business holidays described or listed in the prospectus and local and regional business holidays listed in the prospectus; and

(2) a "qualified evaluator" shall mean any evaluator which represents it is in a position to determine, on the basis of an informal evaluation of the eligible trust securities held in the Trust's portfolio, whether—

(i) the current bid price is higher than the offering side evaluation, computed on the last business day of the previous week, and

(ii) the offering side evaluation, computed as of the last business day of the previous week, is more than one-half of one percent ($5.00 on a unit representing $1,000 principal amount of eligible trust securities) greater than the current offering price.

(c) Notwithstanding the provisions above, any registered separate account offering variable annuity contracts, any person designated in such account's prospectus as authorized to consummate transactions in such contracts, and any principal underwriter of or dealer in such contracts shall be permitted to apply the initial purchase payment for any such contract at a price based on the current net asset value of such contract which is next computed:

(1) Not later than two business days after receipt of the order to purchase by the insurance company sponsoring the separate account ("insurer"), if the contract application and other information necessary for processing the order to purchase (collectively, "application") are complete upon receipt; or

(2) Not later than two business days after an application which is incomplete upon receipt by the insurer is made complete, *Provided,* That, if an incomplete application is not made complete within five business days after receipt,

(i) The prospective purchaser shall be informed of the reasons for the delay, and

(ii) The initial purchase payment shall be returned immediately and in full, unless the prospective purchaser specifically consents to the insurer retaining the purchase payment until the application is made complete.

(3) As used in this rule:

(i) "Prospective Purchaser" shall mean either an individual contractowner or an individual participant in a group contract.

(ii) "Initial Purchase Payment" shall refer to the first purchase payment submitted to the insurer by, or on behalf of, a prospective purchaser.

(d) The board of directors shall initially set the time or times during the day that the current net asset value shall be computed, and shall make and approve such changes as the board deems necessary.

Rule 22c–2. Redemption fees for redeemable securities

(a) *Redemption Fee.* It is unlawful for any fund issuing redeemable securities, its principal underwriter, or any dealer in such securities, to redeem a redeemable security issued by the fund within seven calendar days after the security was purchased, unless it complies with the following requirements:

(1) *Board Determination.* The fund's board of directors, including a majority of directors who are not interested persons of the fund, must either:

(i) Approve a redemption fee, in an amount (but no more than two percent of the value of shares redeemed) and on shares redeemed within a time period (but no less than seven calendar days), that in its judgment is necessary or appropriate to recoup for the fund the costs it may incur as a result of those redemptions or to otherwise eliminate or reduce so far as practicable any dilution of the value of the outstanding securities issued by the fund, the proceeds of which fee will be retained by the fund; or

(ii) Determine that imposition of a redemption fee is either not necessary or not appropriate.

(2) *Shareholder Information.* With respect to each financial intermediary that submits orders, itself or through its agent, to purchase or redeem shares directly to the fund, its principal underwriter or transfer agent, or to a registered clearing agency, the fund (or on the fund's behalf, the principal underwriter or transfer agent) must either:

(i) Enter into a shareholder information agreement with the financial intermediary (or its agent); or

(ii) Prohibit the financial intermediary from purchasing in nominee name on behalf of other persons, securities issued by the fund. For purposes of this paragraph, "purchasing" does not include the automatic reinvestment of dividends.

(3) *Recordkeeping.* The fund must maintain a copy of the written agreement under paragraph (a)(2)(i) of this rule that is in effect, or at any time within the past six years was in effect, in an easily accessible place.

(b) *Excepted Funds.* The requirements of paragraph (a) of this rule do not apply to the following funds, unless they elect to impose a redemption fee pursuant to paragraph (a)(1) of this rule:

(1) Money market funds;

(2) Any fund that issues securities that are listed on a national securities exchange; and

(3) Any fund that affirmatively permits short-term trading of its securities, if its prospectus clearly and prominently discloses that the fund permits short-term trading of its securities and that such trading may result in additional costs for the fund.

(c) *Definitions.* For the purposes of this rule:

(1) *Financial intermediary* means:

(i) Any broker, dealer, bank, or other person that holds securities issued by the fund, in nominee name;

(ii) A unit investment trust or fund that invests in the fund in reliance on section 12(d)(1)(E) of the Act; and

(iii) In the case of a participant-directed employee benefit plan that owns the securities issued by the fund, a retirement plan's administrator under section 3(16)(A) of the Employee Retirement Income Security Act of 1974 (29 U.S.C. 1002(16)(A)) or any person that maintains the plan's participant records.

(iv) *Financial intermediary* does not include any person that the fund treats as an individual investor with respect to the fund's policies established for the purpose of eliminating or reducing any dilution of the value of the outstanding securities issued by the fund.

(2) *Fund* means an open-end management investment company that is registered or required to register under section 8 of the Act, and includes a separate series of such an investment company.

(3) *Money market fund* means an open-end management investment company that is registered under the Act and is regulated as a money market fund under Rule 2a–7.

(4) *Shareholder* includes a beneficial owner of securities held in nominee name, a participant in a participant-directed employee benefit plan, and a holder of interests in a fund or unit investment trust that has invested in the fund in reliance on section 12(d)(1)(E) of the Act. A shareholder does not include a fund investing pursuant to section 12(d)(1)(G) of the Act, a trust established pursuant to section 529 of the Internal Revenue Code (26 U.S.C. 529), or a holder of an interest in such a trust.

(5) *Shareholder information agreement* means a written agreement under which a financial intermediary agrees to:

(i) Provide, promptly upon request by a fund, the Taxpayer Identification Number (or in the case of non U.S. shareholders, if the Taxpayer Identification Number is unavailable, the International Taxpayer Identification Number or other government issued identifier) of all shareholders who have purchased, redeemed, transferred, or exchanged fund shares held through an account with the financial intermediary, and the amount and dates of such shareholder purchases, redemptions, transfers, and exchanges;

(ii) Execute any instructions from the fund to restrict or prohibit further purchases or exchanges of fund shares by a shareholder who has been identified by the fund as having engaged in transactions of fund shares (directly or indirectly through the intermediary's account) that violate policies established by the fund for the purpose of eliminating or reducing any dilution of the value of the outstanding securities issued by the fund; and

(iii) Use best efforts to determine, promptly upon request of the fund, whether any specific person about whom it has received the identification and transaction information set forth in paragraph (c)(5)(i) of this rule, is itself a financial intermediary ("indirect intermediary") and, upon further request by the fund:

(A) Provide (or arrange to have provided) the identification and transaction information set forth in paragraph (c)(5)(i) of this rule regarding shareholders who hold an account with an indirect intermediary; or

(B) Restrict or prohibit the indirect intermediary from purchasing, in nominee name on behalf of other persons, securities issued by the fund.

Rule 22d–1. Exemption from Section 22(d) to permit sales of redeemable securities at prices which reflect sales loads set pursuant to a schedule

A registered investment company that is the issuer of redeemable securities, a principal underwriter of such securities or a dealer therein shall be exempt from the provisions of section 22(d) to the extent necessary to permit the sale of such securities at prices that reflect scheduled variations in, or elimination of, the sales load. These price schedules may offer such variations in or elimination of the sales load to particular classes of investors or transactions, *Provided,* That:

(a) The company, the principal underwriter and dealers in the company's shares apply any scheduled variation uniformly to all offerees in the class specified;

(b) The company furnishes to existing shareholders and prospective investors adequate information concerning any scheduled variation, as prescribed in applicable registration statement form requirements;

(c) Before making any new sales load variation available to purchasers of the company's shares, the company revises its prospectus and statement of additional information to describe that new variation; and

(d) The company advises existing shareholders of any new sales load variation within one year of the date when that variation is first made available to purchasers of the company's shares.

Rule 22d–2. Exemption from Section 22(d) for certain registered separate accounts

A registered separate account, any principal underwriter for such account, any dealer in contracts or units of interest or participations in such contracts issued by such account and any insurance company maintaining such account shall, with respect to any variable annuity contracts, units, or participations therein issued by such account, be exempted from section 22(d) to the extent necessary to permit the sale of such contracts, units or participations by such persons at prices which reflect variations in the sales load or in any administrative charge or other deductions from the purchase payments; *Provided, however,* That (a) the prospectus discloses as precisely as possible the amount of the variations and the circumstances, if any, in which such variations shall be available or describes the basis for such variations and the manner in which entitlement shall be determined, and (b) any such variations reflect differences in costs or services and are not unfairly discriminatory against any person.

Rule 22e–1. Exemption from Section 22(e) of the Act during annuity payment period of variable annuity contracts participating in certain registered separate accounts

(a) A registered separate account shall during the annuity payment period of variable annuity contracts participating in such account, be exempt from the provisions of section 22(e) of the Act prohibiting the suspension of the right of redemption or postponement of the date of payment or satisfaction upon redemption of any redeemable security, with respect to such contracts under which payments are being made based upon life contingencies.

Rule 22e–2. Pricing of redemption in accordance with Rule 22c–1

An investment company shall not be deemed to have suspended the right of redemption if it prices a redemption request by computing the net asset value of the investment company's redeemable securities in accordance with the provisions of Rule 22c–1.

Rule 22e–3. Exemption for liquidation of money market funds

(a) *Exemption.* A registered open-end management investment company or series thereof ("fund") that is regulated as a money market fund under Rule 2a–7 is exempt from the requirements of section 22(e) of the Act if:

(1) The fund, at the end of a business day, has invested less than ten percent of its total assets in weekly liquid assets or, in the case of a fund that is a government money market fund, as defined in Rule 2a–7(a)(16) or a retail money market fund, as defined in Rule 2a–7(a)(25), the fund's price per share as computed for the purpose of distribution, redemption and repurchase, rounded to the nearest one percent, has deviated from the stable price established by the board of directors or the fund's board of directors, including a majority of directors who are not interested personas of the fund, determines that such a deviation is likely to occur;

(2) The fund's board of directors, including a majority of directors who are not interested persons of the fund, irrevocably has approved the liquidation of the fund; and

(3) The fund, prior to suspending redemptions, notifies the Commission of its decision to liquidate and suspend redemptions by electronic mail directed to the attention of the Director of the Division of Investment Management or the Director's designee.

(b) *Conduits.* Any registered investment company, or series thereof, that owns, pursuant to section 12(d)(1)(E) of the Act, shares of a money market fund that has suspended redemptions of shares pursuant to paragraph (a) of this section also is exempt from the requirements of section 22(e) of the Act. A registered investment company relying on the exemption provided in this paragraph must promptly notify the Commission that it has suspended redemptions in reliance on this section. Notification under this paragraph shall be made by electronic mail directed to the attention of the Director of the Division of Investment Management or the Director's designee.

(c) *Commission Orders.* For the protection of shareholders, the Commission may issue an order to rescind or modify the exemption provided by this section, after appropriate notice and opportunity for hearing in accordance with section 40 of the Act.

(d) *Definitions.* Each of the terms *business day, total assets,* and *weekly liquid assets* has the same meaning as defined in Rule 2a–7.

Rule 22e–4. Liquidity risk management programs

(a) *Definitions.* For purposes of this section:

(1) *Acquisition (or acquire)* means any purchase or subsequent rollover.

(2) *Business day* means any day, other than Saturday, Sunday, or any customary business holiday.

(3) *Convertible to cash* means the ability to be sold, with the sale settled.

(4) *Exchange-traded fund* or ETF means an open-end management investment company (or series or class thereof), the shares of which are listed and traded on a national securities exchange, and that has formed and operates under an exemptive order under the Act granted by the Commission or in reliance on an exemptive rule adopted by the Commission.

(5) *Fund* means an open-end management investment company that is registered or required to register under section 8 of the Act (15 U.S.C. 80a–8) and includes a separate series of such an investment company, but does not include a registered open-end management investment company that is regulated as a money market fund under Rule 2a–7 or an In-Kind ETF.

(6) *Highly liquid investment* means any cash held by a fund and any investment that the fund reasonably expects to be convertible into cash in current market conditions in three business days or less without the conversion to cash significantly changing the market value of the investment, as determined pursuant to the provisions of paragraph (b)(1)(ii) of this section.

(7) *Highly liquid investment minimum* means the percentage of the fund's net assets that the fund invests in highly liquid investments that are assets pursuant to paragraph (b)(1)(iii) of this section.

(8) *Illiquid investment* means any investment that the fund reasonably expects cannot be sold or disposed of in current market conditions in seven calendar days or less without the sale or disposition significantly changing the market value of the investment, as determined pursuant to the provisions of paragraph (b)(1)(ii) of this section.

(9) *In-Kind Exchange Traded Fund* or In-Kind ETF means an ETF that meets redemptions through in-kind transfers of securities, positions, and assets other than a de minimis amount of cash and that publishes its portfolio holdings daily.

(10) *Less liquid investment* means any investment that the fund reasonably expects to be able to sell or dispose of in current market conditions in seven calendar days or less without the sale or disposition significantly changing the market value of the investment, as determined pursuant to the provisions of paragraph (b)(1)(ii) of this section, but where the sale or disposition is reasonably expected to settle in more than seven calendar days.

(11) *Liquidity risk* means the risk that the fund could not meet requests to redeem shares issued by the fund without significant dilution of remaining investors' interests in the fund.

(12) *Moderately liquid investment* means any investment that the fund reasonably expects to be convertible into cash in current market conditions in more than three calendar days but in seven calendar days or less, without the conversion to cash significantly changing the market value of the investment, as determined pursuant to the provisions of paragraph (b)(1)(ii) of this section.

(13) *Person(s) designated to administer the program* means the fund or In-Kind ETF's investment adviser, officer, or officers (which may not be solely portfolio managers of the fund or In-Kind ETF) responsible for administering the program and its policies and procedures pursuant to paragraph (b)(2)(ii) of this section.

(14) *Unit Investment Trust or UIT* means a unit investment trust as defined in section 4(2) of the Act (15 U.S.C. 80a–4).

(b) *Liquidity Risk Management Program*. Each fund and In-Kind ETF must adopt and implement a written liquidity risk management program ("program") that is reasonably designed to assess and manage its liquidity risk.

(1) *Required program elements*. The program must include policies and procedures reasonably designed to incorporate the following elements:

(i) *Assessment, management, and periodic review of liquidity risk*. Each fund and In-Kind ETF must assess, manage, and periodically review (with such review occurring no less frequently than annually) its liquidity risk, which must include consideration of the following factors, as applicable:

(A) The fund or In-Kind ETF's investment strategy and liquidity of portfolio investments during both normal and reasonably foreseeable stressed conditions, including whether the investment strategy is appropriate for an open-end fund, the extent to which the strategy involves a relatively concentrated portfolio or large positions in particular issuers, and the use of borrowings for investment purposes and derivatives;

(B) Short-term and long-term cash flow projections during both normal and reasonably foreseeable stressed conditions;

(C) Holdings of cash and cash equivalents, as well as borrowing arrangements and other funding sources; and

(D) For an ETF:

(*1*) The relationship between the ETF's portfolio liquidity and the way in which, and the prices and spreads at which, ETF shares trade, including, the efficiency of the arbitrage function and the level of active participation by market participants (including authorized participants); and

(*2*) The effect of the composition of baskets on the overall liquidity of the ETF's portfolio.

(ii) *Classification*. Each fund must, using information obtained after reasonable inquiry and taking into account relevant market, trading, and investment-specific considerations, classify each of the fund's portfolio investments (including each of the fund's derivatives transactions) as a highly liquid investment, moderately liquid investment, less liquid investment, or illiquid investment. A fund must review its portfolio investments' classifications, at least monthly in connection with reporting the liquidity classification for each portfolio investment on Form N–PORT in accordance with Rule 30b1–9, and more frequently if changes in relevant market, trading, and investment-specific considerations are reasonably expected to materially affect one or more of its investments' classifications.

NOTE TO PARAGRAPH (b)(1)(ii) INTRODUCTORY TEXT: If an investment could be viewed as either a highly liquid investment or a moderately liquid investment, because the period to convert the investment to cash depends on the calendar or business day convention used, a fund should classify the investment as a highly liquid investment. For a discussion of considerations that may be relevant in classifying the liquidity of the fund's portfolio investments, see Investment Company Act Release No. IC-32315 (Oct. 13, 2016).

(A) The fund may generally classify and review its portfolio investments (including the fund's derivatives transactions) according to their asset class, provided, however, that the fund must separately classify and review any investment within an asset class if the fund or its adviser has information about any market, trading, or investment-specific considerations that are reasonably expected to significantly affect the liquidity characteristics of that investment as compared to the fund's other portfolio holdings within that asset class.

(B) In classifying and reviewing its portfolio investments or asset classes (as applicable), the fund must determine whether trading varying portions of a position in a particular portfolio investment or asset class, in sizes that the fund would reasonably anticipate trading, is reasonably expected to significantly affect its liquidity, and if so, the fund must take this determination into account when classifying the liquidity of that investment or asset class.

(C) For derivatives transactions that the fund has classified as moderately liquid investments, less liquid investments, and illiquid investments, identify the percentage of the fund's highly liquid investments that it has segregated to cover, or pledged to satisfy margin requirements in connection with, derivatives transactions in each of these classification categories.

NOTE TO PARAGRAPH (b)(1)(ii)(C): For purposes of calculating these percentages, a fund that has segregated or pledged highly liquid investments and non-highly liquid investments to cover derivatives transactions classified as moderately liquid, less liquid, or illiquid investments first should apply segregated or pledged assets that are highly liquid investments to cover these transactions, unless it has specifically identified segregated non-highly liquid investments as covering such derivatives transactions.

(iii) *Highly liquid investment minimum*.

(A) Any fund that does not primarily hold assets that are highly liquid investments must:

(*1*) Determine a highly liquid investment minimum, considering the factors specified in paragraphs (b)(1)(i)(A) through (D) of this section, as applicable (but considering those factors specified in paragraphs (b)(1)(i)(A) and (B) only as they apply during normal conditions, and during stressed conditions only to the extent they are reasonably foreseeable during the period until the next review of the highly liquid investment minimum). The highly liquid investment minimum determined pursuant to this paragraph may not be changed during any period of time that a fund's assets that are highly liquid investments are below the determined minimum without approval from the fund's board of directors, including a majority of directors who are not interested persons of the fund;

(*2*) Periodically review, no less frequently than annually, the highly liquid investment minimum; and

(*3*) Adopt and implement policies and procedures for responding to a shortfall of the fund's highly liquid investments below its highly liquid investment minimum, which must include requiring the person(s) designated to administer the program to report to the fund's board of directors no later than its next regularly scheduled meeting with a brief explanation of the causes of the shortfall, the extent of the shortfall, and any actions taken in response, and if the shortfall lasts more than 7 consecutive calendar days, must include requiring the person(s) designated to administer the program to report to the board within one business day thereafter with an explanation of how the fund plans to restore its minimum within a reasonable period of time.

(B) For purposes of determining whether a fund primarily holds assets that are highly liquid investments, a fund must exclude from its calculations the percentage of the fund's assets that are highly liquid investments that it has segregated to cover all derivatives transactions that the fund has classified as moderately liquid investments, less liquid investments, and illiquid investments, or pledged to satisfy margin requirements in connection with those derivatives transactions, as determined pursuant to paragraph (b)(1)(ii)(C) of this section.

(iv) *Illiquid investments*. No fund or In-Kind ETF may acquire any illiquid investment if, immediately after the acquisition, the fund or In-Kind ETF would have invested more than 15% of its net assets in illiquid investments that are assets. If a fund or In-Kind ETF holds more than 15% of its net assets in illiquid investments that are assets:

(A) It must cause the person(s) designated to administer the program to report such an occurrence to the fund's or In-Kind ETF's board of directors within one business day of the occurrence, with an explanation of the extent and causes of the occurrence, and how the fund or In-Kind ETF plans to bring its illiquid investments that are assets to or below 15% of its net assets within a reasonable period of time; and

(B) If the amount of the fund's or In-Kind ETF's illiquid investments that are assets is still above 15% of its net assets 30 days from the occurrence (and at each consecutive 30 day period thereafter), the fund or In-Kind ETF's board of directors, including a majority of directors who are not interested persons of the fund or In-Kind ETF, must assess whether the plan presented to it pursuant to paragraph (b)(1)(iv)(A) continues to be in the best interest of the fund or In-Kind ETF.

(v) *Redemptions in Kind.* A fund that engages in, or reserves the right to engage in, redemptions in kind and any In-Kind ETF must establish policies and procedures regarding how and when it will engage in such redemptions in kind.

(2) *Board oversight.* A fund or In-Kind ETF's board of directors, including a majority of directors who are not interested persons of the fund or In-Kind ETF, must:

(i) Initially approve the liquidity risk management program;

(ii) Approve the designation of the person(s) designated to administer the program; and

(iii) Review, no less frequently than annually, a written report prepared by the person(s) designated to administer the program that addresses the operation of the program and assesses its adequacy and effectiveness of implementation, including, if applicable, the operation of the highly liquid investment minimum, and any material changes to the program.

(3) *Recordkeeping.* The fund or In-Kind ETF must maintain:

(i) A written copy of the program and any associated policies and procedures adopted pursuant to paragraphs (b)(1) through (b)(2) of this section that are in effect, or at any time within the past five years were in effect, in an easily accessible place;

(ii) Copies of any materials provided to the board of directors in connection with its approval under paragraph (b)(2)(i) of this section, and materials provided to the board of directors under paragraph (b)(2)(iii) of this section, for at least five years after the end of the fiscal year in which the documents were provided, the first two years in an easily accessible place; and

(iii) If applicable, a written record of the policies and procedures related to how the highly liquid investment minimum, and any adjustments thereto, were determined, including assessment of the factors incorporated in paragraphs (b)(1)(iii)(A) through (B) of this section and any materials provided to the board pursuant to paragraph (b)(1)(iii)(A)(3) of this section, for a period of not less than five years (the first two years in an easily accessible place) following the determination of, and each change to, the highly liquid investment minimum.

(c) *UIT Liquidity.* On or before the date of initial deposit of portfolio securities into a registered UIT, the UIT's principal underwriter or depositor must determine that the portion of the illiquid investments that the UIT holds or will hold at the date of deposit that are assets is consistent with the redeemable nature of the securities it issues, and must maintain a record of that determination for the life of the UIT and for five years thereafter.

Rule 23c–1. Repurchase of securities by closed-end companies

(a) A registered closed-end company may purchase for cash a security of which it is the issuer, subject to the following conditions:

(1) If the security is a stock entitled to cumulative dividends, such dividends are not in arrears.

(2) If the security is a stock not entitled to cumulative dividends, at least 90 percent of the net income of the issuer for the last preceding fiscal year, determined in accordance with good accounting practice and not including profits or losses realized from the sale of securities or other properties was distributed to its shareholders during such fiscal year or within 60 days after the close of such fiscal year.

(3) If the security to be purchased is junior to any class of outstanding security of the issuer representing indebtedness (except notes or other evidences of indebtedness held by a bank or other person, the issuance of which did not involve a public offering) all securities of such class shall

have an asset coverage of at least 300 percent immediately after such purchase; and if the security to be purchased is junior to any class of outstanding senior security of the issuer which is a stock, all securities of such class shall have an asset coverage of at least 200 percent immediately after such purchase and shall not be in arrears as to dividends.

(4) The seller of the security is not to the knowledge of the issuer an affiliated person of the issuer.

(5) Payment of the purchase price is accompanied or preceded by a written confirmation of the purchase.

(6) The purchase is made at a price not above the market value, if any, or the asset value of such security, whichever is lower, at the time of such purchase.

(7) The issuer discloses to the seller or, if the seller is acting through a broker, to the seller's broker, either prior to or at the time of purchase the approximate or estimated asset coverage per unit of the security to be purchased.

(8) No brokerage commission is paid by the issuer to any affiliated person of the issuer in connection with the purchase.

(9) The purchase is not made in a manner or on a basis which discriminates unfairly against any holders of the class of securities purchased.

(10) If the security is a stock, the issuer has, within the preceding six months, informed stockholders of its intention to purchase stock of such class by letter or report addressed to all the stockholders of such class.

(11) The issuer files with the Commission, as an exhibit to Form N–CSR (17 CFR 249.331 and 274.128), a copy of any written solicitation to purchase securities under this section sent or given during the period covered by the report by or on behalf of the issuer to 10 or more persons.

(b) Notwithstanding the conditions of paragraph (a) of this section, a closed-end company may purchase fractional interests in, or fractional rights to receive, any security of which it is the issuer.

(c) This rule does not apply to purchase of securities made pursuant to section 23(c)(1) or (2) of the Act. A registered closed-end company may file an application with the Commission for an order under section 23(c)(3) of the Act permitting the purchase of any security of which it is the issuer which does not meet the conditions of this rule and which is not to be made pursuant to section 23(c)(1) or (2) of the Act.

(d) This rule relates exclusively to the requirements of section 23(c) of the Act, and the provisions hereof shall not be construed to authorize any action which contravenes any other applicable law, statutory or otherwise, or the provision of any indenture or other instrument pursuant to which securities of the issuer were issued.

Rule 23c–2. Call and redemption of securities issued by registered closed-end companies

(a) notwithstanding the provisions of Rule 23c–1, a registered closed-end investment company may call or redeem any securities of which it is the issuer, in accordance with the terms of such securities or the charter, indenture or other instrument pursuant to which such securities were issued: *Provided*, That, if less than all the outstanding securities of a class or series are to be called or redeemed the call or redemption shall be made by lot, on a pro rata basis, or in such other manner as will not discriminate unfairly against any holder of the securities of such class or series.

(b) A registered closed-end investment company which proposes to call or redeem any securities of which it is the issuer shall file with the Commission notice of its intention to call or redeem such securities at least 30 days prior to the date set for the call or redemption; *Provided, however,* That if notice of the call or the redemption is required to be published in a newspaper or otherwise, notice shall be given to the Commission at least 10 days in advance of the date of publication. Such notice shall be filed in triplicate and shall include (1) the title of the class of securities to be called or redeemed, (2) the date on which the securities are to be called or redeemed, (3) the applicable provisions of the governing instrument pursuant to which the securities are to be called or redeemed and, (4) if less than all the outstanding securities of a class or series are to be called or redeemed, the principal amount or number of shares and the basis upon which the securities to be called or redeemed are to be selected.

Rule 23c–3. Repurchase offers by closed-end companies

(a) *Definitions.* For purposes of this rule:

(1) *Periodic interval* shall mean an interval of three, six, or twelve months.

(2) *Repurchase offer* shall mean an offer pursuant to this section by an investment company to repurchase common stock of which it is the issuer.

(3) *Repurchase offer amount* shall mean the amount of common stock that is the subject of a repurchase offer, expressed as a percentage of such stock outstanding on the repurchase request deadline, that an investment company offers to repurchase in a repurchase offer. The repurchase offer amount shall not be less than five percent nor more than twenty-five percent of the common stock outstanding on a repurchase request deadline. Before each repurchase offer, the repurchase offer amount for that repurchase offer shall be determined by the directors of the company.

(4) *Repurchase payment deadline* with respect to a tender of common stock shall mean the date by which an investment company must pay securities holders for any stock repurchased. A repurchase payment deadline shall occur seven days after the repurchase pricing date applicable to such tender.

(5) *Repurchase pricing date* with respect to a tender of common stock shall mean the date on which an investment company determines the net asset value applicable to the repurchase of the securities. A repurchase pricing date shall occur no later than the fourteenth day after a repurchase request deadline, or the next business day if the fourteenth day is not a business day. In no event shall an investment company determine the net asset value applicable to the repurchase of the stock before the close of business on the repurchase request deadline.

(i) For an investment company making a repurchase offer pursuant to paragraph (b) of this section, the number of days between the repurchase request deadline and the repurchase pricing date for a repurchase offer shall be the maximum number specified by the company pursuant to paragraph (b)(2)(i)(D) of this rule.

(ii) For an investment company making a repurchase offer pursuant to paragraph (c) of this rule, the repurchase pricing date shall be such date as the company shall disclose to security holders in the notification pursuant to paragraph (b)(4) of this rule with respect to such offer.

(iii) For purposes of paragraph (b)(1) of this rule, a repurchase pricing date may be a date earlier than the date determined pursuant to paragraph (a)(5)(i) or (ii) of this rule if, on or immediately following the repurchase request deadline, it appears that the use of an earlier repurchase pricing date is not likely to result in significant dilution of the net asset value of either stock that is tendered for repurchase or stock that is not tendered.

(6) *Repurchase request* shall mean the tender of common stock in response to a repurchase offer.

(7) *Repurchase request deadline* with respect to a repurchase offer shall mean the date by which an investment company must receive repurchase requests submitted by security holders in response to that offer or withdrawals or modifications of previously submitted repurchase requests. The first repurchase request deadline after the effective date of the registration statement for the common stock that is the subject of a repurchase offer, or after a shareholder vote adopting the fundamental policy specifying a company's periodic interval, whichever is later, shall occur no later than two periodic intervals thereafter.

(b) *Periodic Repurchase Offers.* A registered closed-end company or a business development company may repurchase common stock of which it is the issuer from the holders of the stock at periodic intervals, pursuant to repurchase offers made to all holders of the stock, *Provided* that:

(1) The company shall repurchase the stock for cash at the net asset value determined on the repurchase pricing date and shall pay the holders of the stock by the repurchase payment deadline except as provided in paragraph (b)(3) of this rule. The company may deduct from the repurchase proceeds only a repurchase fee, not to exceed two percent of the proceeds, that is paid to the company and is reasonably intended to compensate the company for expenses directly related to the repurchase. A company may not condition a repurchase offer upon the tender of any minimum amount of shares.

(2)(i) The company shall repurchase the security pursuant to a fundamental policy, changeable only by a majority vote of the outstanding voting securities of the company, stating:

(A) That the company will make repurchase offers at periodic intervals pursuant to this rule, as this rule may be amended from time to time;

(B) The periodic intervals between repurchase request deadlines;

(C) The dates of repurchase request deadlines or the means of determining the repurchase request deadlines; and

(D) The maximum number of days between each repurchase request deadline and the next repurchase pricing date.

(ii) The company shall include a statement in its annual report to shareholders of the following:

(A) Its policy under paragraph (b)(2)(i) of this rule; and

(B) With respect to repurchase offers by the company during the period covered by the annual report, the number of repurchase offers, the repurchase offer amount and the amount tendered in each repurchase offer, and the extent to which in any repurchase offer the company repurchased stock pursuant to the procedures in paragraph (b)(5) of this rule.

(iii) A company shall be deemed to be making repurchase offers pursuant to a policy within paragraph (b)(2)(i) of this rule if:

(A) The company makes repurchase offers to its security holders at periodic intervals and, before May 14, 1993, has disclosed in its registration statement its intention to make or consider making such repurchase offers; and

(B) The company's board of directors adopts a policy specifying the matters required by paragraph (b)(2)(i) of this rule, and the periodic interval specified therein conforms generally to the frequency of the company's prior repurchase offers.

(3)(i) The company shall not suspend or postpone a repurchase offer except pursuant to a vote of a majority of the directors, including a majority of the directors who are not interested persons of the company, and only:

(A) If the repurchase would cause the company to lose its status as a regulated investment company under Subchapter M of the Internal Revenue Code [26 U.S.C. 851–860];

(B) If the repurchase would cause the stock that is the subject of the offer that is either listed on a national securities exchange or quoted in an inter-dealer quotation system of a national securities association to be neither listed on any national securities exchange nor quoted on any inter-dealer quotation system of a national securities association;

(C) For any period during which the New York Stock Exchange or any other market in which the securities owned by the company are principally traded is closed, other than customary week-end and holiday closings, or during which trading in such market is restricted;

(D) For any period during which an emergency exists as a result of which disposal by the company of securities owned by it is not reasonably practicable, or during which it is not reasonably practicable for the company fairly to determine the value of its net assets; or

(E) For such other periods as the Commission may by order permit for the protection of security holders of the company.

(ii) If a repurchase offer is suspended or postponed, the company shall provide notice to security holders of such suspension or postponement. If the company renews the repurchase offer, the company shall send a new notification to security holders satisfying the requirements of paragraph (b)(4) of this rule.

(4)(i) No less than twenty-one and no more than forty-two days before each repurchase request deadline, the company shall send to each holder of record and to each beneficial owner of the stock that is the subject of the repurchase offer a notification providing the following information:

(A) A statement that the company is offering to repurchase its securities from security holders at net asset value;

(B) Any fees applicable to such repurchase;

(C) The repurchase offer amount;

(D) The dates of the repurchase request deadline, repurchase pricing date, and repurchase payment deadline, the risk of fluctuation in net asset value between the repurchase request deadline and the repurchase pricing date, and the possibility that the company may use an earlier repurchase pricing date pursuant to paragraph (a)(5)(iii) of this rule;

(E) The procedures for security holders to tender their shares and the right of the security holders to withdraw or modify their tenders until the repurchase request deadline;

(F) The procedures under which the company may repurchase such shares on a pro rata basis pursuant to paragraph (b)(5) of this rule;

(G) The circumstances in which the company may suspend or postpone a repurchase offer pursuant to paragraph (b)(3) of this rule;

(H) The net asset value of the common stock computed no more than seven days before the date of the notification and the means by which security holders may ascertain the net asset value thereafter; and

(I) The market price, if any, of the common stock on the date on which such net asset value was computed, and the means by which security holders may ascertain the market price thereafter.

(ii) The company shall file three copies of the notification with the Commission within three business days after sending the notification to security holders. Those copies shall be accompanied by copies of Form N–23c–3 (17 CFR 274.221) ("Notification of Repurchase Offer"). The format of the copies shall comply with the requirements for registration statements and reports under Rule 8b–12.

(iii) For purposes of sending a notification to a beneficial owner pursuant to paragraph (b)(4)(i) of this rule, where the company knows that shares of common stock that is the subject of a repurchase offer are held of record by a broker, dealer, voting trustee, bank, association or other entity that exercises fiduciary powers in nominee name or otherwise, the company shall follow the procedures for transmitting materials to beneficial owners of securities that are set forth in Rule 14a–13 under the Securities Exchange Act of 1934.

(5) If security holders tender more than the repurchase offer amount, the company may repurchase an additional amount of stock not to exceed two percent of the common stock outstanding on the repurchase request deadline. If the company determines not to repurchase more than the repurchase offer amount, or if security holders tender stock in an amount exceeding the repurchase offer amount plus two percent of the common stock outstanding on the repurchase request deadline, the company shall repurchase the shares tendered on a pro rata basis; *Provided, however,* That this provision shall not prohibit the company from:

(i) Accepting all stock tendered by persons who own, beneficially or of record, an aggregate of not more than a specified number which is less than one hundred shares and who tender all of their stock, before prorating stock tendered by others; or

(ii) Accepting by lot stock tendered by security holders who tender all stock held by them and who, when tendering their stock, elect to have either all or none or at least a minimum amount or none accepted, if the company first accepts all stock tendered by security holders who do not so elect.

(6) The company shall permit tenders of stock for repurchase to be withdrawn or modified at any time until the repurchase request deadline but shall not permit tenders to be withdrawn or modified thereafter.

(7)(i) The current net asset value of the company's common stock shall be computed no less frequently than weekly on such day and at such specific time or times during the day that the board of directors of the company shall set.

(ii) The current net asset value of the company's common stock shall be computed daily on the five business days preceding a repurchase request deadline at such specific time or times during the day that the board of directors of the company shall set.

(iii) For purposes of section 23(b), the current net asset value applicable to a sale of common stock by the company shall be the net asset value next determined after receipt of an order to purchase such stock. During any period when the company is offering its common stock, the current net asset value of the common stock shall be computed no less frequently than once daily, Monday through Friday, at the specific time or times during the day that the board of directors of the company shall set, except on:

(A) Days on which changes in the value of the company's portfolio securities will not materially affect the current net asset value of the common stock;

(B) Days during which no order to purchase its common stock is received, other than days when the net asset value would otherwise be computed pursuant to paragraph (b)(7)(i) of this rule; or

(C) Customary national, local, and regional business holidays described or listed in the prospectus.

(8) The board of directors of the investment company satisfies the fund governance standards defined in Rule 0–1(a)(7).

(9) Any senior security issued by the company or other indebtedness contracted by the company either shall mature by the next repurchase pricing date or shall provide for the redemption or call of such security or the repayment of such indebtedness by the company by the next repurchase pricing date, either in whole or in part, without penalty or premium, as necessary to permit the company to repurchase securities in such repurchase offer amount as the directors of the company shall determine in compliance with the asset coverage requirements of section 18 or 61, as applicable.

(10)(i) From the time a company sends a notification to shareholders pursuant to paragraph (b)(4) of this rule until the repurchase pricing date, a percentage of the company's assets equal to at least 100 percent of the repurchase offer amount shall consist of assets that can be sold or disposed of in the ordinary course of business, at approximately the price at which the company has valued the investment, within a period equal to the period between a repurchase request deadline and the repurchase payment deadline, or of assets that mature by the next repurchase payment deadline.

(ii) In the event that the company's assets fail to comply with the requirements in paragraph (b)(10)(i) of this rule, the board of directors shall cause the company to take such action as it deems appropriate to ensure compliance.

(iii) In supervising the company's operations and portfolio management by the investment adviser, the company's board of directors shall adopt written procedures reasonably designed, taking into account current market conditions and the company's investment objectives, to ensure that the company's portfolio assets are sufficiently liquid so that the company can comply with its fundamental policy on repurchases, and comply with the liquidity requirements of paragraph (b)(10)(i) of this rule. The board of directors shall review the overall composition of the portfolio and make and approve such changes to the procedures as the board deems necessary.

(c) *Discretionary Repurchase Offers.* A registered closed-end company or a business development company may repurchase common stock of which it is the issuer from the holders of the stock pursuant to a repurchase offer that is not made pursuant to a fundamental policy and that is made to all holders of the stock not earlier than two years after another offer pursuant to this paragraph (c) if the company complies with the requirements of paragraphs (b)(1), (3), (4), (5), (6), (7)(ii), (8), (10)(i), and (10)(ii) of this rule.

(d) *Exemption from the Definition of Redeemable Security.* A company that makes repurchase offers pursuant to paragraph (b) or (c) of this rule shall not be deemed thereby to be an issuer of redeemable securities within section 2(a)(32).

Rule 24b–1. Definitions

(a) The term *form letter* as used in section 24(b) of the Act includes (1) one of a series of identical sales letters, and (2) any sales letter a substantial portion of which consists of a statement which is in essence identical with similar statements in sales letters sent to 25 or more persons within any period of 90 consecutive days.

(b) The term *distribution* as used in section 24(b) of the Act includes the distribution or redistribution to prospective investors of the content of any written sales literature, whether such distribution or redistribution is effected by means of written or oral representations or statements.

(c) The term *rules and regulations* as used in section 24(a) and (c) of the Act shall include the forms for registration of securities under the Securities Act of 1933 and the related instructions thereto.

Rule 24b–2. Filing copies of sales literature

Copies of material filed with the Commission for the sole purpose of complying with section 24(b) of the Act either shall be accompanied by a letter of 52 transmittal which makes appropriate references to said section or shall make such appropriate reference on the face of the material.

Rule 24b–3. Sales literature deemed filed

Any advertisement, pamphlet, circular, form letter or other sales literature addressed to or intended for distribution to prospective investors shall be deemed filed with the Commission for purposes of section 24(b) of the Act upon filing with a national securities association registered under Section 15A of the Securities Exchange Act of 1934 that has adopted rules providing standards for the investment company advertising practices of its members and has established and implemented procedures to review that advertising.

Rule 24e–1. Filing of certain prospectuses as post-effective amendments to registration statements under the Securities Act of 1933

Section 24(e) of the Act requires that when a prospectus is revised so that it may be available for use in compliance with section 10(a)(3) of the Securities Act of 1933 for a period extending beyond the time when the previous prospectus would have ceased to be available for such use, such revised prospectus, in order to meet the requirements of section 10 of said Act, must be filed as an amendment to the registration statement under said Act and such amendment must have become effective prior to the use of the revised prospectus. Except as hereinabove provided, section 24(e) of the Act shall not be deemed to govern the times and conditions under which post-effective amendments shall be filed to registration statements under the Securities Act of 1933.

Rule 24f–2. Registration under the Securities Act of 1933 of an indefinite number of certain investment company securities

(a) *General.* Any face-amount certificate company, open-end management company or unit investment trust ("issuer") that is deemed to have registered an indefinite amount of securities pursuant to section 24(f) of the Act must, not later than 90 days after the end of any fiscal year during which it has publicly offered such securities, file Form 24F–2 with the Commission. Form 24F–2 must be prepared in accordance with the requirements of that form, and must be accompanied by the payment of a registration fee with respect to the securities sold during the fiscal year in reliance upon registration pursuant to section 24(f) of the Act calculated in the manner specified in section 24(f) of the Act and in the Form. An issuer that pays the registration fee more than 90 days after the end of its fiscal year must pay interest in the manner specified in section 24(f) of the Act and in Form 24F–2.

(b) *Issuer Ceasing Operations; Mergers and Other Transactions.* For purposes of this section, if an issuer ceases operations, the date the issuer ceases operations will be deemed to be the end of its fiscal year. In the case of a liquidation, merger, or sale of all or substantially all of the assets ("merger") of the issuer, the issuer will be deemed to have ceased operations for the purposes of this section on the date the merger is consummated; provided, however, that in the case of a merger of an issuer or a series of an issuer ("Predecessor Issuer") with another issuer or a series of an issuer ("Successor Issuer"), the Predecessor Issuer will not be deemed to have ceased operations and the Successor Issuer will assume the obligations, fees, and redemption credits of the Predecessor Issuer incurred pursuant to section 24(f) of the Act and Rule 24e–2 (as in effect prior to October 11, 1997; see 17 CFR part 240 to end, revised as of April 1, 1997) if the Successor Issuer:

(1) Had no assets or liabilities, other than nominal assets or liabilities, and no operating history immediately prior to the merger;

(2) Acquired substantially all of the assets and assumed substantially all of the liabilities and obligations of the Predecessor Issuer; and

(3) The merger is not designed to result in the Predecessor Issuer merging with, or substantially all of its assets being acquired by, an issuer (or a series of an issuer) that would not meet the conditions of paragraph (b)(1) of this rule.

(c) *Counting Days.* To determine the date on which Form 24F–2 must be filed with the Commission under paragraph (a) of this rule, the first day of the 90–day period is the first calendar day of the fiscal year following the fiscal year for which the Form is to be filed. If the last day of the 90–day period falls on a Saturday, Sunday or federal holiday, the period ends on the first business day thereafter.

NOTE TO PARAGRAPH (c): For example, a Form 24F–2 for a fiscal year ending on June 30 must be filed no later than September 28. If September 28 falls on a Saturday or Sunday, the Form must be filed on the following Monday.

Rule 26a–1. Payment of administrative fees to the depositor or principal underwriter of a unit investment trust; exemptive relief for separate accounts

(a) For purposes of section 26(a)(2)(C) of the Act, payment of a fee to the depositor of or a principal underwriter for a registered unit investment trust, or to any affiliated person or agent of such depositor or underwriter (collectively, "depositor"), for bookkeeping or other administrative services provided to the trust shall be allowed the custodian or trustee ("trustee") as an expense, *Provided,* That such fee is an amount not greater than the expenses, without profit: (1) actually paid by such depositor directly attributable to the services provided and (2) increased by the services provided directly by such depositor, as determined in accordance with generally accepted accounting principles consistently applied.

(b) A registered separate account, and any depositor of or principal underwriter for such account, shall be exempt from the provisions of sections 26(a) and 27(c)(2) of the Act with respect to any variable annuity contract participating in such account to the extent necessary to permit the deduction of any fee that would be allowed a trustee as an expense as provided in paragraph (a) of this rule, *Provided,* That the standard used in paragraph (a) of this rule shall be applied as follows: if the separate account reserves the right to increase the fee, the fee shall not be greater than the cost of the services to be provided for one year; if the fee is guaranteed not to increase for a specified period of time, the fee shall not be greater than the average expected cost of the services to be provided during the period of the guarantee.

Rule 26a–2. Exemptions from certain provisions of Sections 26 and 27 for registered separate accounts and others regarding custodianship of and deduction of certain fees and charges from the assets of such accounts

A registered separate account, and any depositor of or principal underwriter for such account, shall be exempt from the provisions of sections 26(a) and 27(c)(2) of the Act with respect to any variable annuity contract participating in such account to the extent necessary:

(a) To permit the insurance company that sponsors such account to hold the assets of the separate account and to hold such assets not pursuant to a trust indenture or other such instrument;

(b) To permit any separate account registered under the Act as a unit investment trust to hold the securities of any underlying portfolio companies in uncertificated form;

(c) To permit any separate account registered under the Act as a management investment company to hold its assets in any manner permitted by section 17(f) of the Act or any rules thereunder; and

(d) To permit the deduction from the assets of the separate account of amounts for premium taxes imposed by any State or other governmental entity and, if the separate account is registered under the Act as an open-end management investment company, and investment advisory fee.

Rule 27a–1. Conditions for compliance with and exemptions from certain provisions of Section 27(a)(1) and Section 27(h)(1) of the Act for certain registered separate accounts

(a) A registered separate account, and any depositor of or underwriter for such account, shall with respect to any variable annuity contract participating in such account, be deemed to satisfy the requirements of section 27(a)(1) and section 27(h)(1) of the Act if such contract provides for a sales load which will not exceed 9 per centum of the total payments to be made thereon as of a date not later than the end of the 12th year of such payments: *Provided,* That if a contract be issued for any stipulated shorter payment period the sales load under such contract shall not exceed 9 per centum of the total payments thereunder for such period.

Rule 27a–2. Exemption from Section 27(a)(3) and Section 27(h)(3) of the Act for certain registered separate accounts

(a) A registered separate account, and any depositor of or underwriter for such account, shall be exempt from paragraph (3) of section 27(a) and paragraph (3) of section 27(h) of the Act: *Provided,* That with respect to any variable annuity contract participating in such account the proportionate amount of sales load deducted from any payment during the contract period shall not exceed the proportionate amount deducted from any prior payment during the contract period.

Rule 27a–3. Exemption from Section 27(a)(4) and Section 27(h)(5) of the Act for certain registered separate accounts

(a) A registered separate account, and any depositor of or underwriter for such account, shall be exempt from paragraph (4) of section 27(a) of the Act and paragraph (5) of section 27(h) of the Act as to payments under any variable annuity contract participating in such account which (1) is purchased in connection with a plan which meets the requirements for qualification under section 401 of the Internal Revenue Code of 1954, as amended (Code), or the requirements for deduction of the employer's contributions under section 404(a)(2) of the Code, or (2) meets the requirements of section 403(b) of the Code, but such exemptions shall apply only to contributions or payments within the exclusion allowance for any employee under section 403(b) except as clause (3) hereof applies, or (3) permits no sales load deduction from any payment in excess of 9 per centum of such payment.

Rule 27c–1. Exemption from Section 27(c) (1) and Section 27(d) of the Act during annuity payment period of variable annuity contracts participating in certain registered separate accounts

A registered separate account, and any depositor of or underwriter for such account, shall, during the annuity payment period of variable annuity contracts participating in such account, be exempt from the requirement of paragraph (1) of section 27(c) of the Act that a periodic payment plan certificate be a redeemable security and from section 27(d) of the Act with respect to such contracts under which payments are being made based upon life contingencies.

Rule 27d–1. Reserve requirements for principal underwriters and depositors to carry out the obligations to refund charges required by Section 27(d) and Section 27(f) of the Act

(a)(1) Every depositor of or principal underwriter for the issuer of a periodic payment plan certificate sold subject to section 27(d) or section 27(f) of the Act or both, shall deposit and maintain funds in a segregated trust account as a reserve and as security for the purpose of assuring the refund of charges required by sections 27(d) and 27(f) of the Act.

(2) The assets of such trust account may be held as cash or invested only in one or more of (i) government securities as defined in section 2(a)(16) of the Act (except equity securities) or (ii) negotiable certificates of deposit issued by a bank, as defined in section 2(a)(5) of the Act and having capital and surplus of at least $10 million: *Provided*, That no such investment may have a maturity of more than 5 years, no more than 50 percent of the assets may be invested in obligations having a maturity of more than 1 year, and certificates of deposit of a single issuer may not constitute more than 10 percent of the value of the assets in the account.

(3) Any income, gains, or losses from assets allocated to such account, whether or not realized, shall be credited to or charged against such account without regard to other income, gains, or losses of the depositor or principal underwriter.

(4) The assets of such trust account may be withdrawn only as permitted by paragraph (f) of this rule and shall in no event be chargeable with liabilities arising out of any aspect of the business of the depositor or principal underwriter other than assuring the ability of the depositor or principal underwriter to refund the amounts required by such sections.

(b) For purposes of this rule:

(1) "Excess sales load" on any payment is that portion of the sales load in excess of 15 percent of that payment.

(2) "Monthly payment" shall be the amount of the smallest monthly installment scheduled to be paid during the life of the plan. If payments are required or permitted to be made on a basis less frequently than monthly, an equivalent monthly payment shall be the amount determined by dividing the smallest minimum payment required or permitted in a payment period by the number of months included in such period.

(3) The assets in the segregated trust account shall be valued as follows: (i) With respect to securities for which market quotations are readily available, the market value of such securities; and (ii) with respect to other securities, fair value as determined in good faith by the depositor or principal underwriter.

(c) For every periodic payment plan certificate governed by section 27(d), the depositor or principal underwriter shall deposit into the segregated trust account not less than 45 percent of the excess sales load on each of the first six monthly payments or their equivalent.

(d) For all periodic payment plan certificates governed by section 27(d) which have not been surrendered in accordance with their terms, and for which the depositor or principal underwriter may be liable for the refund of any sales load, the depositor or principal underwriter shall maintain in the segregated trust account an amount equal to not less than 15% of the total refundable sales load on the payments made on those certificates. The depositor or principal underwriter shall also maintain in the segregated trust account such additional amounts as the Commission by order may require for the depositor or principal underwriter to carry out refund obligations pursuant to sections 27(d) and 27(f) of the Act.

(e) For every periodic payment plan certificate governed by section 27(f) of the Act, and for which the depositor or principal underwriter has no obligation to refund any excess sales load pursuant to section 27(d) of the Act, the depositor or principal underwriter shall deposit and maintain during the refund period, at least the following amounts in the segregated trust account:

(1) For certificates that require monthly payments of $100 or less, 20 percent of the difference between the gross payments made and the net amount invested;

(2) For certificates that require monthly payments in excess of $100 and for single payment plan certificates, 30 percent of the difference between the gross payments made and the net amount invested;

(3) For certificates with respect to which the holder is entitled to receive the greater of the refund provided by section 27(f) (of the Act) or a refund of total payments and upon which a total of at least $1,000 has been paid, 100 percent of the difference between the gross payments made and net amount invested; and

(4) Such additional amounts as the Commission by order may require to carry out the obligation to refund charges pursuant to section 27(f) of the Act.

(f) Assets may be withdrawn from the segregated trust account by each depositor or principal underwriter:

(1) To refund excess sales load to a certificate holder exercising the right of surrender specified in section 27(d) of the Act; or

(2) To refund to a certificate holder exercising the right of withdrawal specified in section 27(f) of the Act the difference between the amount of his gross payments and the net amount invested; or

(3) For any other purpose: *Provided, however,* That such withdrawal shall not reduce the segregated trust account to an amount less than the sum of (i) 130 percent of the amount required to be maintained by paragraph (d) of this section, if any, and (ii) 100 percent of that amount required to be maintained by paragraph (e) of this rule, if any.

(g) The minimum amounts required to be maintained by paragraphs (d) and (e) of this rule shall be computed at least monthly. Any additional deposits required by paragraphs (d) or (e) of this rule shall be made immediately after such computation, and any withdrawals permitted by paragraph (f)(3) of this rule may be made only at such time.

(h) Nothing in this section shall be construed to prohibit a depositor or principal underwriter, acting as such for two or more registered investment companies issuing periodic payment plan certificates, from combining in a single segregated trust account the reserves for such companies required by this rule.

(i) The refunds required to be made to certificate holders pursuant to sections 27(d) and 27(f) (of the Act) shall be paid in cash not more than 7 days from the date the certificate is received in proper form by the custodian bank or such other paying agent as may be designated under the periodic payment plan.

(j) Each depositor or principal underwriter shall file with the Commission, within the appropriate period of time specified, an Accounting of Segregated Trust Account. Form N–27D–1 (17 CFR 274.127d–1) is hereby prescribed as such accounting form.

Rule 27d–2. Insurance company undertaking in lieu of segregated trust account

(a) Any depositor of or principal underwriter for the issuer of a periodic payment plan certificate sold subject to section 27(d) or section 27(f) of the Act, or both, shall be exempt from the requirements of Rule 27d–1 if an insurance company (as defined in section 2(a)(17) of the Act) undertakes in writing to guarantee the performance of all obligations of such depositor or principal underwriter to refund charges under sections 27(d) and 27(f) of the Act and paragraph (b) of this rule: *Provided, however,* That:

(1) Such insurance company at all times shall have (i) combined capital paid-up, gross paid in and contributed surplus and unassigned surplus, if a stock company, or (ii) unassigned surplus, if a mutual company, at least equal to the larger of (*A*) $1 million or (*B*) 200 percent of the amount of the total refund obligation of the depositor or underwriter pursuant to sections 27(d) and 27(f) (of the Act) less any liability reserve established by such insurance company to meet such obligations; and

(2) Such depositor or underwriter shall file or cause to be filed with the Commission as an exhibit to the registration statement or any amendment thereto pursuant to the Securities Act of 1933 of the registered investment company issuing periodic payment plan certificates (i) a copy of such written undertaking, and any amendment thereto, (ii) an annual statement certified by a responsible officer of the insurance company indicating that at least on a monthly basis throughout its fiscal year the insurance company has met the requirements of the proviso in paragraph (a)(1) of this rule, and (iii) a Statement of Financial Condition (Balance Sheet) of the insurance company certified by an independent public accountant. Such balance sheet shall be filed at least annual-

ly, within 90 days after the close of the insurance company's fiscal year.

(b) The refunds required to be made to certificate holders pursuant to sections 27(d) and 27(f) (of the Act) shall be paid in cash not more than 7 days from the date the certificate is received in proper form by the custodian bank or such other paying agent as may be designated under the periodic payment plan.

Rule 27e-1. Requirements for notice to be mailed to certain purchasers of periodic payment plan certificates sold subject to Section 27(d) of the Act

(a) The notice required by section 27(e) of the Act shall be sent by first class mail and shall be accompanied by a written instruction sheet and a return form to be used in connection with the exercise of the surrender right described in the notice. No other written or graphic material may be included with such notice.

(b) In the event that regular payments throughout the first 18 months of the plan are required less frequently than monthly, such a notice shall be mailed to any certificate holder who has missed any payment or payments equal to or greater in amount than the amount of payments which, if missed, would have required the mailing of a notice if equal monthly payments had been required during such 15- or 18-month periods.

(c) Any payment not made within 31 days after it is due shall be deemed a missed payment whether or not an equivalent payment is made subsequently by the certificate holder.

(d) In the event any such notice is not mailed prior to 15 days before the expiration of the 18th month, the certificate holder shall have 15 days from the date such notice is mailed within which to exercise the right of surrender described therein. Nothing herein contained shall require a second notice to be mailed to any certificate holder who has been mailed a notice within 30 days following 15 months after the issuance of his certificate.

(e) Notwithstanding the requirements of section 27(e) of the Act, no notice need be mailed to a certificate holder if, at the time such notice would be required to be mailed, he would not be entitled to receive any refund of sales loading upon surrender of his certificate.

(f) Form N-27E-1 is hereby prescribed to inform certificate holders of their right to surrender their certificates pursuant to section 27(d) of the Act.

[Form N-27E-1 is omitted.]

Rule 27f-1. Notice of right of withdrawal required to be mailed to periodic payment plan certificate holders and exemption from Section 27(f) for certain periodic payment plan certificates

(a) The notice and statement of charges (notice) required by section 27(f) of the Act shall be sent by first-class mail and shall be accompanied by a written instruction sheet and a return form to be used in connection with the exercise of the right of withdrawal described in the notice. Except for a confirmation slip, the plan certificate, and any notice required by applicable State law, no other written or graphic material may be included with such notice.

(b) The notice may be mailed by the issuer, the principal underwriter for, or the depositor of, the issuer or a recordkeeping agent for the issuer if the custodian bank has delegated the mailing of the notice to any of them or the issuer has been permitted to operate without a custodian bank by Commission order.

(c) Solely for purposes of section 27(f) of the Act, the postmark date on the envelope containing the certificate shall determine whether a certificate has been surrendered within the 45-day period.

(d) Form N-27F-1 is hereby prescribed to inform certificate holders, other than holders of plans upon which the amount of sales loan deducted from any payment does not exceed 9 percent of any payment and variable annuity contracts, of their withdrawal right pursuant to section 27(f) of the Act.

[Form N-27F-1 is omitted.]

Rule 27g-1. Election to be governed by Section 27(h)

(a) If any registered investment company which issues or intends to issue a periodic payment plan certificate chooses to be governed by the provisions of section 27(h) (of the Act) rather than the provisions of sections 27 (a) and (d) (of the Act), it shall signify such choice by filing with the Commission as an exhibit to its registration statement filed under the Securities Act of 1933 a written Notice of Election to be so governed.

(b) Any registered investment company issuing periodic payment plan certificates which has elected, in accordance with paragraph (a) of this section, to be governed by the provisions of section 27(h) of the Act may thereafter withdraw such election by filing with the Commission, in the manner specified for filing a Notice of Election, a written Notice of Withdrawal of Election: *Provided, however,* That no such withdrawal of election shall be made within 12 months of an election by such company under paragraph (a) of this rule and, provided further that such company may not thereafter elect to be governed by the provisions of section 27(h) (of the Act) until an additional 12-month period has elapsed.

Rule 27h–1. Exemptions from Section 27(h)(4) for certain payments

(a) For purposes of this section and section 27(h)(4) of the Act (1) "minimum monthly payment, or its equivalent," shall be the amount of the smallest monthly installment scheduled to be made during the life of the plan; and (2) "quarter" shall be the 3–month period which commences on the date a periodic payment plan is issued and each 3–month period thereafter.

(b) The provisions of section 27(h)(4) (of the Act) shall not apply to:

(1) That portion of the first payment on a periodic payment plan certificate which equals the amount of five minimum monthly payments: *Provided, however,* That the deduction for sales load on any other payments received during the first quarter after the issuance of the certificate may not exceed the sales load applicable to payments subsequent to the first 48 monthly payments or their equivalent;

(2) A payment or payments received in any subsequent quarter which equals the amount of three minimum monthly payments: *Provided, however,* That after an amount equivalent to three minimum monthly payments (not including payments of arrears) is received in any such subsequent quarter the deduction for sales load on any additional payments received in such quarter may not exceed the sales load applicable to payments subsequent to the first 48 monthly payments or their equivalent;

(3) Payments of arrears by a certificate holder who is delinquent in his payments; and

(4) Any payments made on a periodic payment plan certificate out of the proceeds of completion insurance received upon the death of the certificate holder.

Rule 28b–1. Investment in loans partially or wholly guaranteed under the Servicemen's Readjustment Act of 1944, as amended

(a) The term *qualified investments* as used in section 28(b) of the Investment Company Act of 1940 shall include:

(1) Any loan, any portion of which is guaranteed under Title III of the Servicemen's Readjustment Act of 1944, as amended, and which is secured by a first lien on real estate: *Provided,* The amount of the loan not so guaranteed does not exceed 66⅔ percent of the reasonable value of such real estate as determined by proper appraisal made by an appraiser designated by the Administrator of Veterans' Affairs;

(2) Any secondary loan the full amount of which is guaranteed under section 505(a) of Title III of the above mentioned act and which is secured by a second lien on real estate: *Provided, however,* That any such loan shall be deemed a qualified investment only so long as (i) insurance policies are required to be procured and maintained in an amount sufficient to protect the security against the risks or hazards to which it may be subjected to the extent customary in the locality, and (ii) the loan shall remain guaranteed under Title III of the Servicemen's Readjustment Act of 1944, as amended, to the extent specified in paragraph (a)(1) or (2) of this rule, as the case may be.

(b) Loans made pursuant to this section shall be valued at the original principal amount of the loan less all payments made thereon which have been applied to the reduction of such principal amount.

Rule 30a–1. Annual reports for unit investment trusts

Every registered unit investment trust shall file an annual report on Form N–SAR with respect to each calendar year not more than sixty calendar days after the close of each year. A registered unit investment trust that has filed a registration statement with the Commission registering its securities for the first time under the Securities Act of 1933 is relieved of this reporting obligation with respect to any reporting period or portion thereof prior to the date on which that registration statement becomes effective or is withdrawn.

Rule 30a–2. Certification of Form N–CSR

(a) Each report filed on Form N–CSR (17 CFR 249.331 and 274.128) or Form N–Q (17 CFR 249.332 and 274.130) by a registered management investment company must include certifications in the form specified in Item 12(a)(2) of Form N–CSR or Item 3 of Form N–Q, as applicable, and such certifications must be filed as an exhibit to such report. Each principal executive and principal financial officer of the investment company, or persons performing similar functions, at the time of filing of the report must sign a certification.

(b) Each report on Form N–CSR filed by a registered management investment company under section 13(a) or 15(d) of the Securities Exchange Act of 1934 (15 U.S.C. 78m(a) or 78o(d)) and that contains financial statements must be accompanied by the certifications required by section 1350 of Chapter 63 of Title 18 of the United States Code (18 U.S.C. 1350) and such certifications must be furnished as an exhibit to such report as specified in Item 12(b) of Form N–CSR. Each principal executive and principal financial officer of the investment company (or equivalent thereof) must sign a certification. This requirement may be satisfied by a single certification signed by an investment company's principal executive and principal financial officers.

(c) A person required to provide a certification specified in paragraph (a) or (b) of this rule may not have the certification signed on his or her behalf pursuant to a power of attorney or other form of confirming authority.

Rule 30a–3. Disclosure controls and procedures related to preparation of required filings

(a) Every registered management investment company, other than a small business investment company registered on Form N–5 (17 CFR 239.24 and 274.5), must maintain disclosure controls and procedures (as defined in paragraph (c) of this rule) and internal control over financial reporting (as defined in paragraph (d) of this rule).

(b) Each such registered management investment company's management must evaluate, with the participation of the company's principal executive and principal financial officers, or persons performing similar functions, the effectiveness of the company's disclosure controls and procedures, within the 90-day period prior to the filing date of each report on Form N–CSR (17 CFR 249.331 and 274.128) and Form N–Q (17 CFR 249.332 and 274.130).

(c) For purposes of this rule, the term *disclosure controls and procedures* means controls and other procedures of a registered management investment company that are designed to ensure that information required to be disclosed by the investment company on Form N–CSR (17 CFR 249.331 and 274.128) and Form N–Q (17 CFR 249.332 and 274.130) is recorded, processed, summarized, and reported within the time periods specified in the Commission's rules and forms. Disclosure controls and procedures include, without limitation, controls and procedures designed to ensure that information required to be disclosed by an investment company in the reports that it files or submits on Form N–CSR and Form N–Q is accumulated and communicated to the investment company's management, including its principal executive and principal financial officers, or persons performing similar functions, as appropriate to allow timely decisions regarding required disclosure.

(d) The term *internal control over financial reporting* is defined as a process designed by, or under the supervision of, the registered management investment company's principal executive and principal financial officers, or persons performing similar functions, and effected by the company's board of directors, management, and other personnel, to provide reasonable assurance regarding the reliability of financial reporting and the preparation of financial statements for external purposes in accordance with generally accepted accounting principles and includes those policies and procedures that:

(1) Pertain to the maintenance of records that in reasonable detail accurately and fairly reflect the transactions and dispositions of the assets of the investment company;

(2) Provide reasonable assurance that transactions are recorded as necessary to permit preparation of financial statements in accordance with generally accepted accounting principles, and that receipts and expenditures of the investment company are being made only in accordance with authorizations of management and directors of the investment company; and

(3) Provide reasonable assurance regarding prevention or timely detection of unauthorized acquisition, use, or disposition of the investment company's assets that could have a material effect on the financial statements.

Rule 30b1–1. Semi–annual report for registered management investment companies

Every registered management investment company shall file a semi-annual report on Form N–SAR (17 CFR 274.101) not more than sixty calendar days after the close of each fiscal year and fiscal second quarter. A registered management investment company that has filed a registration statement with the Commission registering its securities for the first time under the Securities Act of 1933 is relieved of this reporting obligation with respect to any reporting period or portion thereof prior to the date on which that registration statement becomes effective or is withdrawn.

Rule 30b1–2. Semi–annual report for totally–owned registered management investment company subsidiary of registered management investment company

Notwithstanding the provisions of rules 30a–1 and 30b1–1, a registered investment company that is a totally-owned subsidiary of a registered management investment company need not file a semi-annual report on Form N–SAR if financial information with respect to that subsidiary is reported in the parent's semi-annual report on Form N–SAR.

Rule 30b1–3. Transition reports

Every registered management investment company filing reports on Form N–SAR that changes its fiscal year end shall file a report on Form N–SAR not more than 60 calendar days after the later of either the close of the transition period or the date of the determination to change the fiscal year end which report shall not cover a period longer than six months.

Rule 30b1–4. Report of proxy voting record

Every registered management investment company, other than a small business investment company registered on Form N-5 (17 CFR 239.24 and 274.5), shall file an annual report on Form N–PX (17 CFR 274.129) not later than August 31 of each year, containing the registrant's proxy voting record for the most recent twelve-month period ended June 30.

Rule 30b1–5. Quarterly report

Every registered management investment company, other than a small business investment company registered on Form N–5 (17 CFR 239.24 and 274.5), shall file a quarterly report on Form N–Q (17 CFR 249.332 and 274.130) not more than 60 days after the close of the first and third quarters of each fiscal year. A registered management investment company that has filed a registration statement with the Commission registering its securities for the first time under the Securities Act of 1933 is relieved of this reporting obligation with respect to any reporting period or portion thereof prior to the date on which that registration statement becomes effective or is withdrawn.

Rule 30b1–7. Monthly report for money market funds

Every registered open-end management investment company, or series thereof, that is regulated as a money market fund under Rule 2a–7 must file with the Commission a monthly report of portfolio holdings on Form N–MFP, current as of the last business day or any subsequent calendar day of the preceding month, no later than the fifth business day of each month.

Rule 30b1–8. Current report for money market funds

Every registered open-end management investment company, or series thereof, that is regulated as a money market fund under Rule 2a–7, that experiences any of the events specified on Form N–CR, must file with the Commission a current report on Form N–CR within the period specified in that form.

Rule 30b1–9. Monthly report

Each registered management investment company or exchange-traded fund organized as a unit investment trust, or series thereof, other than a registered open-end management investment company that is regulated as a money market fund under Rule 2a–7 or a small business investment company registered on Form N–5 (17 CFR 239.24 and 17 CFR 274.5), must file a monthly report of portfolio holdings on Form N–PORT (17 CFR 274.150), current as of the last business day, or last calendar day, of the month. A registered investment company that has filed a registration statement with the Commission registering its securities for the first time under the Securities Act of 1933 is relieved of this reporting obligation with respect to any reporting period or portion thereof prior to the date on which that registration statement becomes effective or is withdrawn. Reports on Form N–PORT must be filed with the Commission no later than 30 days after the end of each month.

Rule 30b1–9(T). Temporary rule regarding monthly report

(a) Until April 1, 2019, each registered management investment company subject to 17 CFR 270.30b1–9 must satisfy its reporting obligation under that section by maintaining in its records the information that is required to be included in Form N–PORT (17 CFR 274.150).

(b) The information maintained in the registered management investment company's records under paragraph (a) of this section shall be treated as a record under section 31(a)(1) of the Act [15 U.S.C. 80a–30(a)(1)] and 17 CFR 270.31a–1(b) of this chapter subject to the requirements of 17 CFR 270.31a–2(a)(2).

(c) This section will expire and no longer be effective on March 31, 2026.

Rule 30b1–10. Current report for open-end management investment companies

Every registered open-end management investment company, or series thereof but not a fund that is regulated as a money market fund under Rule 2a–7, that experiences any event specified on Form N–LIQUID, must file with the Commission a current report on Form N–LIQUID within the period specified in that form.

Rule 30b2–1. Filing of reports to stockholders

(a) Every registered management investment company shall file a report on Form N–CSR (17 CFR 249.331 and 274.128) not later than 10 days after the transmission to stockholders of any report that is required to be transmitted to stockholders under Rule 30e–1.

(b) A registered investment company shall file with the Commission a copy of every periodic or interim report or similar communication containing financial statements that is transmitted by or on behalf of such registered investment company to any class of such company's security holders and that is not required to be filed with the Commission under paragraph (a) of this rule. The filing shall be made not later than 10 days after the transmission to security holders.

Rule 30d–1. Filing of copies of reports to shareholders

A registered management investment company, other than a small business investment company registered on Form N–5 (17 CFR 239.24 and 274.5), that is required to file annual and quarterly reports pursuant to section 13(a) or 15(d) of the Securities Exchange Act of 1934 shall satisfy its requirement to file such reports by the filing, in accordance with the rules and procedures specified therefor, of reports on Form N–CSR (17 CFR 249.331 and 274.128) and Form N–Q (17 CFR 249.332 and 274.130). A registered unit investment trust or a small business investment company registered on Form N–5 that is required to file annual and quarterly reports pursuant to section 13(a) or 15(d) of the Securities Exchange Act of 1934 shall satisfy its requirement to file such reports by the filing, in accordance with the rules and procedures specified therefor, of reports on Form N–SAR (17 CFR 249.330 and 274.101).

Rule 30e–1. Reports to stockholders of management companies

(a) Every registered management company shall transmit to each stockholder of record, at least semi-annually, a report containing the information required to be included in such reports by the company's registration statement form under the 1940 Act, except that the initial report of a newly registered company shall be made as of a date not later than the close of the fiscal year or half-year occurring on or after the date on which the company's notification of registration under the 1940 Act is filed with the Commission.

(b) If any matter was submitted during the period covered by the shareholder report to a vote of shareholders, through the solicitation of proxies or otherwise, furnish the following information:

(1) The date of the meeting and whether it was an annual or special meeting.

(2) If the meeting involved the election of directors, the name of each director elected at the meeting and the name of each other director whose term of office as a director continued after the meeting.

(3) A brief description of each matter voted upon at the meeting and the number of votes cast for, against or withheld, as well as the number of abstentions and broker non-votes as to each such matter, including a separate tabulation with respect to each matter or nominee for office.

Instruction. The solicitation of any authorization or consent (other than a proxy to vote at a shareholders' meeting) with respect to any matter shall be deemed a submission of such matter to a vote of shareholders within the meaning of this paragraph (b).

(c) Each report shall be transmitted within 60 days after the close of the period for which such report is being made.

(d) An open-end company may transmit a copy of its currently effective prospectus or Statement of Additional Information, or both, under the Securities Act, in place of any report required to be transmitted to shareholders by this section, provided that the prospectus or Statement of Additional Information, or both, include all the information that would otherwise be required to be contained in the report by this section. Such prospectus or Statement of Additional Information, or both, shall be transmitted within 60 days after the close of the period for which the report is being made.

(e) The period of time within which any report prescribed by this rule shall be transmitted may be extended by the Commission upon written request showing good cause therefor. Section 0–5 shall not apply to such requests.

(f)(1) A company will be considered to have transmitted a report to shareholders who share an address if:

(i) The company transmits a report to the shared address;

(ii) The company addresses the report to the shareholders as a group (for example, "ABC Fund [or Corporation] Shareholders," "Jane Doe and Household," "The Smith Family") or to each of the shareholders individually (for example, "John Doe and Richard Jones"); and

(iii) The shareholders consent in writing to delivery of one report.

(2) The company need not obtain written consent from a shareholder under paragraph (f)(1)(iii) of this section if all of the following conditions are met:

(i) The shareholder has the same last name as the other shareholders, or the company reasonably believes that the shareholders are members of the same family;

(ii) The company has transmitted a notice to the shareholder at least 60 days before the company begins to rely on this section concerning transmission of reports to that shareholder. The notice must be a separate written statement and:

(A) State that only one report will be delivered to the shared address unless the company receives contrary instructions;

(B) Include a toll-free telephone number or be accompanied by a reply form that is pre-addressed with postage provided, that the shareholder can use to notify the company that he or she wishes to receive a separate report;

(C) State the duration of the consent;

(D) Explain how a shareholder can revoke consent;

(E) State that the company will begin sending individual copies to a shareholder within 30 days after the company receives revocation of the shareholder's consent; and

(F) Contain the following prominent statement, or similar clear and understandable statement, in bold-face type: "Important Notice Regarding Delivery of Shareholder Documents." This statement also must appear on the envelope in which the notice is delivered. Alternatively, if the notice is delivered separately from other communications to investors, this statement may appear either on the notice or on the envelope in which the notice is delivered;

NOTE TO PARAGRAPH (f)(2)(ii): The notice should be written in plain English. See Rule 421(d)(2) under the Securities Act of 1933 for a discussion of plain English principles.

(iii) The company has not received the reply form or other notification indicating that the shareholder wishes to continue to receive an individual copy of the report, within 60 days after the company sent the notice; and

(iv) The company transmits the report to a post office box or to a residential street address. The company can assume a street address is a residence unless it has information that indicates it is a business.

(3) At least once a year, the company must explain to shareholders who have consented under paragraph (f)(1)(iii) or paragraph (f)(2) of this rule how they can revoke their consent. The explanation must be reasonably designed to reach these investors. If a shareholder, orally or in writing, revokes consent to delivery of one report to a shared address, the company must begin sending individual copies to that shareholder within 30 days after the company receives the revocation.

(4) For purposes of this rule, *address* means a street address, a post office box number, an electronic mail address, a facsimile telephone number, or other similar destination to which paper or electronic documents are transmitted, unless otherwise provided in this rule. If the company has reason to believe that the address is a street address of a multi-unit building, the address must include the unit number.

Rule 30e–2. Reports to shareholders of unit investment trusts

(a) At least semiannually every registered unit investment trust substantially all the assets of which consist of securities issued by a management company must transmit to each shareholder of record (including record holders of periodic payment plan certificates), a report containing all the applicable information and financial statements or their equivalent, required by Rule 30e–1 to be included in reports of the management company for the same fiscal period. Each of these reports must be transmitted within the period allowed the management company by Rule 30e–1 for transmitting reports to its shareholders.

(b) Any report required by this rule will be considered transmitted to a shareholder of record if the unit investment trust satisfies the conditions set forth in Rule 30e–1(f) with respect to that shareholder.

Rule 30h–1. Applicability of Section 16 of the Exchange Act to Section 30(h)

(a) The filing of any statement prescribed under section 16(a) of the Securities Exchange Act of 1934 shall satisfy the corresponding requirements of section 30(h) of the Act.

(b) The rules under section 16 of the Securities Exchange Act of 1934 shall apply to any duty, liability or prohibition imposed with respect to a transaction involving any security of a registered closed-end company under section 30(h) of the Act.

(c) No statements need be filed pursuant to section 30(h) of the Act by an affiliated person of an investment adviser in his or her capacity as such if such person is solely an employee, other than an officer, of such investment adviser.

Rule 31a–1. Records to be maintained by registered investment companies, certain majority-owned subsidiaries thereof, and other persons having transactions with registered investment companies

(a) Every registered investment company, and every underwriter, broker, dealer, or investment adviser which is a majority-owned subsidiary of such a company, shall maintain and keep current the accounts, books, and other documents relating to its business which constitute the record forming the basis for financial statements required to be filed pursuant to section 30 of the Investment Company Act of 1940 and of the auditor's certificates relating thereto.

(b) Every registered investment company shall maintain and keep current the following books, accounts, and other documents:

(1) Journals (or other records of original entry) containing an itemized daily record in detail of all purchases and sales of securities (including sales and redemptions of its own securities), all receipts and deliveries of securities (including certificate numbers if such detail is not recorded by custodian or transfer agent), all receipts and disbursements of cash and all other debits and credits. Such records shall show for each such transaction the name and quantity of securities, the unit and aggregate purchase or sale price, commission paid, the market on which effected, the trade date, the settlement date, and the name of the person through or from whom purchased or received or to whom sold or delivered. In the case of a money market fund, also identify the provider of any Demand Feature or Guarantee (as defined in Rule 2a–7(a)(9) or Rule 2a–7(a)(16) respectively) and give a brief description of the nature of the Demand Feature or Guarantee (e.g., unconditional demand feature, conditional demand feature, letter of credit, or bond insurance) and, in a subsidiary portfolio investment record, provide the complete legal name and accounting and other information (including sufficient information to calculate coupons, accruals, maturities, puts, and calls) necessary to identify, value, and account for each investment.

(2) General and auxiliary ledgers (or other records) reflecting all assets, liability, reserve, capital, income and expense accounts, including:

(i) Separate ledger accounts (or other records) reflecting the following:

(*A*) Securities in transfer;

(*B*) Securities in physical possession;

(*C*) Securities borrowed and securities loaned;

(*D*) Monies borrowed and monies loaned (together with a record of the collateral therefor and substitutions in such collateral);

(*E*) Dividends and interest received;

(*F*) Dividends receivable and interest accrued.

Instruction. (*a*) and (*b*) of this subdivision shall be stated in terms of securities quantities only; (*c*) and (*d*) of this subdivision shall be stated in dollar amounts and securities quantities as appropriate; (*e*) and (*f*) of this subdivision shall be stated in dollar amounts only.

(ii) Separate ledger accounts (or other records) for each portfolio security, showing (as of trade dates) (*A*) the quantity and unit and aggregate price for each purchase, sale, receipt, and delivery of securities and commodities for such accounts, and (*B*) all other debits and credits for such accounts. Securities positions and money balances in such ledger accounts (or other records) shall be brought forward periodically but not less frequently than at the end of fiscal quarters. Any portfolio security, the salability of which is conditioned, shall be so noted. A memorandum record shall be available setting forth, with respect to each portfolio security account, the amount and declaration ex-dividend, and payment dates of each dividend declared thereon.

(iii) Separate ledger accounts (or other records) for each broker-dealer bank or other person with or through which transactions in portfolio securities are effected, showing each purchase or sale of securities with or through such persons, including details as to the date of the purchase or sale, the quantity and unit and aggregate price of such securities, and the commissions or other compensation paid to such persons. Purchases or sales effected during the same day at the same price may be aggregated.

(iv) Separate ledger accounts (or other records), which may be maintained by a transfer agent or registrar, showing for each shareholder of record of the investment company the number of shares of capital stock of the company held. In respect of share accumulation accounts (arising from periodic investment plans, dividend reinvestment plans, deposit of issued shares by the owner thereof, etc.), details shall be available as to the dates and number of shares of each accumulation, and except with respect to already issued shares deposited by the owner thereof, prices of each such accumulation.

(3) A securities record or ledger reflecting separately for each portfolio security as of trade date all "long" and "short" positions carried by the investment company for its own account and showing the location of all securities long and the off-setting position to all securities short. The record called for by this paragraph shall not be required in circumstances under which all portfolio securities are maintained by a bank or banks or a member or members of a national securities exchange as custodian under a custody agreement or as agent for such custodian.

(4) Corporate charters, certificates of incorporation or trust agreements, and by-laws, and minute books of stockholders' and directors' or trustees' meetings; and minute books of directors' or trustees' committee and advisory board or advisory committee meetings.

(5) A record of each brokerage order given by or in behalf of the investment company for, or in connection with, the purchase or sale of securities, whether executed or unexecuted. Such record shall include the name of the broker, the terms and conditions of the order and of any modification or cancellation thereof, the time of entry or cancellation, the price at which executed, and the time of receipt of report of execution. The record shall indicate the name of the person who placed the order in behalf of the investment company.

(6) A record of all other portfolio purchases or sales showing details comparable to those prescribed in paragraph (5) of this rule.

(7) A record of all puts, calls, spreads, straddles, and other options in which the investment company has any direct or indirect interest or which the investment company has granted or guaranteed; and a record of any contractual commitments to purchase, sell, receive or deliver securities or other property (but not including open orders placed with broker-dealers for the purchase or sale of securities, which may be cancelled by the company on notices without penalty or cost of any kind); containing, at least, an identification of the security, the number of units involved, the option price, the date of maturity, the date of issuance, and the person to whom issued.

(8) A record of the proof of money balances in all ledger accounts (except shareholder accounts), in the form of trial balances. Such trial balances shall be prepared currently at least once a month.

(9) A record for each fiscal quarter, which shall be completed within ten days after the end of such quarter, showing specifically the basis or bases upon which the allocation of orders for the purchase and sale of portfolio securities to named brokers or dealers and the division of brokerage commissions or other compensation on such purchase and sale orders among named persons were made during such quarter. The record shall indicate the consideration given to (i) sales of shares of the investment company by brokers or dealers, (ii) the supplying of services or benefits by brokers or dealers to the investment company, its investment adviser or principal underwriter or any persons affiliated therewith, and (iii) any other considerations other than the technical qualifications of the brokers and dealers as such. The record shall show the nature of the services or benefits made available, and shall describe in detail the application of any general or specific formula or other determinant used in arriving at such allocation of purchase and sale orders and such division of brokerage commissions or other compensation. The record shall also include the identities of the persons responsible for the determination of such allocation and such division of brokerage commissions or other compensation.

(10) A record in the form of an appropriate memorandum identifying the person or persons, committees, or groups authorizing the purchase or sale of portfolio securities. Where an authorization is made by a committee or group, a record shall be kept of the names of its members who participated in the authorization. There shall be retained as part of the record required by this paragraph any memorandum, recommendation, or instruction supporting or authorizing the purchase or sale of portfolio securities. The requirements of this paragraph are applicable to the extent they are not met by compliance with the requirements of paragraph (4) of this rule.

(11) Files of all advisory material received from the investment adviser, any advisory board or advisory committee, or any other persons from whom the investment company accepts investment advice, other than material which is furnished solely through uniform publications distributed generally.

(12) The term "other records" as used in the expressions "journals (or other records of original entry)" and "ledger accounts (or other records)" shall be construed to include, where appropriate, copies of voucher checks, confirmations, or similar documents which reflect the information required by the applicable rule or rules in appropriate sequence and in permanent form, including similar records developed by the use of automatic data processing systems.

(c) Every underwriter, broker, or dealer which is a majority-owned subsidiary of a registered investment company shall maintain in the form prescribed therein such accounts, books and other documents as are required to be maintained by brokers and dealers by rule adopted under section 17 of the Securities Exchange Act of 1934.

(d) Every depositor of any registered investment company, and every principal underwriter for any registered investment company other than a closed-end investment company, shall maintain such accounts, books and other documents as are required to be maintained by brokers and dealers by the rule adopted under section 17 of the Securities Exchange Act of 1934, to the extent such records are necessary or appropriate to record such person's transactions with such registered investment company.

(e) Every investment adviser which is a majority-owned subsidiary of a registered investment company shall maintain in the form prescribed therein such accounts, books and other documents as are required to be maintained by registered investment advisers by rule adopted under section 204 of the Investment Advisers Act of 1940.

(f) Every investment adviser not a majority-owned subsidiary of a registered investment company shall maintain such accounts, books and other documents as are required to be maintained by registered investment advisers by rule adopted under section 204 of the Investment Advisers Act of 1940, to the extent such records are necessary or appropriate to record such person's transactions with such registered investment company.

Rule 31a–2. Records to be preserved by registered investment companies, certain majority-owned subsidiaries thereof, and other persons having transactions with registered investment companies

(a) Every registered investment company shall:

(1) Preserve permanently, the first two years in an easily accessible place, all books and records required to be made pursuant to paragraphs (1) through (4) of Rule 31a–1(b);

(2) Preserve for a period not less than six years from the end of the fiscal year in which any transactions occurred, the first two years in an easily accessible place, all books and records required to be made pursuant to subparagraphs (5) through (12) or Rule 31a–1(b) and all vouchers, memoranda, correspondence, checkbooks, bank statements, cancelled checks, cash reconciliations, cancelled stock certificates, and all schedules evidencing and supporting each computation of net asset value of the investment company shares, and other documents required to be maintained by Rule 31a–1(a) and not enumerated in Rule 31a–1(b).

(3) Preserve for a period not less than 6 years from the end of the fiscal year last used, the first 2 years in an easily accessible place, any advertisement, pamphlet, circular, form letter or other sales literature addressed to or intended for distribution to prospective investors;

(4) Preserve for a period not less than six years, the first two years in an easily accessible place, any record of the initial determination that a director is not an interested person of the investment company, and each subsequent determination that the director is not an interested person of the investment company. These records must include any questionnaire and any other docu-

ment used to determine that a director is not an interested person of the company;

(5) Preserve for a period not less than six years, the first two years in an easily accessible place, any materials used by the disinterested directors of an investment company to determine that a person who is acting as legal counsel to those directors is an independent legal counsel; and

(6) Preserve for a period not less than six years, the first two years in an easily accessible place, any documents or other written information considered by the directors of the investment company pursuant to section 15(c) of the Act in approving the terms or renewal of a contract or agreement between the company and an investment adviser.

(b) Every underwriter, broker, or dealer which is a majority-owned subsidiary of a registered investment company shall preserve for the periods prescribed therein such accounts, books and other documents as are required to be preserved by brokers and dealers by rule adopted under section 17 of the Securities Exchange Act of 1934.

(c) Every depositor of any registered investment company, and every principal underwriter for any registered investment company other than a closed-end company, shall preserve for a period of not less than six years such accounts, books and other documents as are required to be maintained by brokers and dealers by rule adopted under section 17 of the Securities Exchange Act of 1934, to the extent such records are necessary or appropriate to record such person's transactions with such registered investment company.

(d) Every investment adviser which is a majority-owned subsidiary of a registered investment company shall preserve for the periods prescribed therein such accounts, books and other documents as are required to be preserved by investment advisers by rule adopted under section 204 of the Investment Advisers Act of 1940.

(e) Every investment adviser not a majority-owned subsidiary of a registered investment company shall preserve for a period of not less than six years such accounts, books and other documents as are required to be maintained by registered investment advisers by rule adopted under section 204 of the Investment Advisers Act of 1940, to the extent such records are necessary or appropriate to record such person's transactions with such registered investment company.

(f) *Micrographic and Electronic Storage Permitted.* (1) *General.* The records required to be maintained and preserved under this part may be maintained and preserved for the required time by, or on behalf of, an investment company on:

(i) Micrographic media, including microfilm, microfiche, or any similar medium; or

(ii) Electronic storage media, including any digital storage medium or system that meets the terms of this section.

(2) *General Requirements.* The investment company, or person that maintains and preserves records on its behalf, must:

(i) Arrange and index the records in a way that permits easy location, access, and retrieval of any particular record;

(ii) Provide promptly any of the following that the Commission (by its examiners or other representatives) or the directors of the company may request:

(A) A legible, true, and complete copy of the record in the medium and format in which it is stored;

(B) A legible, true, and complete printout of the record; and

(C) Means to access, view, and print the records; and

(iii) Separately store, for the time required for preservation of the original record, a duplicate copy of the record on any medium allowed by this section.

(3) *Special Requirements for Electronic Storage Media.* In the case of records on electronic storage media, the investment company, or person that maintains and preserves records on its behalf, must establish and maintain procedures:

(i) To maintain and preserve the records, so as to reasonably safeguard them from loss, alteration, or destruction;

(ii) To limit access to the records to properly authorized personnel, the directors of the investment company, and the Commission (including its examiners and other representatives); and

(iii) To reasonably ensure that any reproduction of a non-electronic original record on electronic storage media is complete, true, and legible when retrieved.

(4) Notwithstanding the provisions of paragraphs (a) through (e) of this rule, any record, book or other document may be destroyed in accordance with a plan previously submitted to and approved by the Commission. A plan shall be deemed to have been approved by the Commission if notice to the contrary has not been received within 90 days after submission of the plan to the Commission.

Rule 31a–3. Records prepared or maintained by other than person required to maintain and preserve them

(a) If the records required to be maintained and preserved pursuant to the provisions of Rules 31a–1 and 31a–2 are prepared or maintained by others on behalf of the person required to maintain and preserve such records, the person required to maintain and preserve such records shall obtain from such other person an agreement in writing to the effect that such records are the property of the person required to maintain and preserve such records and will be surrendered promptly on request.

(b) In cases where a bank or member of a national securities exchange acts as custodian, transfer agent, or dividend disbursing agent, compliance with this section shall be considered to have been met if such bank or exchange member agrees in writing to make any records relating to such service available upon request and to preserve for the periods prescribed in Rule 31a–2 any such records as are required to be maintained by Rule 31a–1.

Rule 32a–1. Exemption of certain companies from affiliation provisions of Section 32(a)

A registered investment company shall be exempt from the provisions of paragraph (1) of section 32(a) of the act, insofar as said paragraph requires that independent public accountants for such company be selected by a majority of certain members of the board of directors, if:

(a) Such company meets the conditions of paragraphs (1) to (8), inclusive, of section 10(d) of the act; and

(b) Such accountants are selected by a majority of all the members of the board of directors.

Rule 32a–2. Exemption for initial period from vote of security holders on independent public accountant for certain registered separate accounts

(a) A registered separate account shall be exempt from the requirement under paragraph (2) of section 32(a) of the Act that selection of an independent public accountant shall have been submitted for ratification or rejection at the next succeeding annual meeting of security owners, subject to the following conditions:

(1) Such registered separate account qualifies for exemption from section 14(a) of the Act pursuant to Rule 14a–2, or is exempt therefrom by order of the Commission upon application; and

(2) The selection of such accountant shall be submitted for ratification or rejection to variable annuity contract owners at their first meeting after the effective date of the registration statement under the Securities Act of 1933, as amended, relating to contracts participating in such account: *Provided,* That such meeting shall take place within 1 year after such effective date, unless the time for the holding of such meeting shall be extended by the Commission upon written request showing good cause therefor.

Rule 32a–3. Exemption from provision of Section 32(a)(1) regarding the time period during which a registered management investment company must select an independent public accountant

(a) A registered management investment company ("company") organized in a jurisdiction that does not require it to hold regular annual meetings of its stockholders, and which does not hold a regular annual stockholders' meeting in a given fiscal year, shall be exempt in that fiscal year from the requirement of section 32(a)(1) of the Act that the independent public accountant ("accountant") be selected at a board of directors meeting held within 30 days before or after the beginning of the fiscal year or before the annual meeting of stockholders in that year, *Provided,* That such company is either:

(1) In a set of investment companies as defined in paragraph (b) of this rule, if not all the members of such set have an identical fiscal year end and if such company selects an accountant at a board of directors meeting held within 90 days before or after the beginning of that fiscal year; or

(2) Not in a set of investment companies, or is in a set, each of whose members has the same fiscal year end, and if such company selects an accountant at a board of directors meeting held within 30 days before or 90 days after the beginning of that fiscal year.

(b) For purposes of this rule, "set of investment companies" means any two or more registered management investment companies that hold themselves out to investors as related companies for purposes of investment and investor services, and

(1) That have a common investment adviser or principal underwriter, or

(2) If the investment adviser or principal underwriter of one of the companies is an affiliated person as defined in section 2(a)(3)(C) of the Act of the investment adviser or principal underwriter of each of the other companies.

Rule 32a–4. Independent audit committees

A registered management investment company or a registered face-amount certificate company is exempt from the requirement of section 32(a)(2) of the Act that the selection of the company's independent public accountant be submitted for ratification or rejection at the next succeeding annual meeting of shareholders, if:

(a) The company's board of directors has established a committee, composed solely of directors who are not interested persons of the company, that has responsibility for overseeing the fund's accounting and auditing processes ("audit committee");

(b) The company's board of directors has adopted a charter for the audit committee setting forth the committee's structure, duties, powers, and methods of operation or set forth such provisions in the fund's charter or bylaws; and

(c) The company maintains and preserves permanently in an easily accessible place a copy of the audit committee's charter and any modification to the charter.

Rule 34b–1. Sales literature deemed to be misleading

Any advertisement, pamphlet, circular, form letter, or other sales literature addressed to or intended for distribution to prospective investors that is required to be filed with the Commission by section 24(b) of the Act ("sales literature") shall have omitted to state a fact necessary in order to make the statements made therein not materially misleading unless the sales literature includes the information specified in paragraphs (a) and (b) of this rule.

NOTE TO INTRODUCTORY TEXT OF RULE 34b–1: The fact that the sales literature includes the information specified in paragraphs (a) and (b) of this section does not relieve the investment company, underwriter, or dealer of any obligations with respect to the sales literature under the antifraud provisions of the federal securities laws. For guidance about factors to be weighed in determining whether statements, representations, illustrations, and descriptions contained in investment company sales literature are misleading, *see* Rule 15b under the Securities Act of 1933.

(a) Sales literature for a money market fund shall contain the information required by paragraph (b)(4) of Rule 482 under the Securities Act of 1933, presented in the manner required by paragraph (b)(5) of Rule 482 under the Securities Act of 1933.

(b)(1) Except as provided in paragraph (b)(3) of this rule:

(i) In any sales literature that contains performance data for an investment company, include the disclosure required by paragraph (b)(3) of Rule 482 under the Securities Act of 1933, presented in the manner required by paragraph (b)(5) of Rule 482 under the Securities Act of 1933.

(ii) In any sales literature for a money market fund:

(A) Accompany any quotation of yield or similar quotation purporting to demonstrate the income earned or distributions made by the money market fund with a quotation of current yield specified by paragraph (e)(1)(i) of Rule 482 under the Securities Act of 1933;

(B) Accompany any quotation of the money market fund's tax equivalent yield or tax equivalent effective yield with a quotation of current yield as specified in Rule 482(e)(1)(iii) under the Securities Act of 1933; and

(C) Accompany any quotation of the money market fund's total return with a quotation of the money market fund's current yield specified in paragraph (e)(1)(i) of Rule 482 under the Securities Act of 1933. Place the quotations of total return and current yield next to each other, in the same size print, and if there is a material difference between the quoted total return and the quoted current yield, include a statement that the yield quotation more closely reflects the current earnings of the money market fund than the total return quotation.

(iii) In any sales literature for an investment company other than a money market fund that contains performance data:

(A) Include the total return information required by paragraph (d)(3) of Rule 482 under the Securities Act of 1933;

(B) Accompany any quotation of performance adjusted to reflect the effect of taxes (not including a quotation of tax equivalent yield or other similar quotation purporting to demonstrate the tax equivalent yield earned or distributions made by the company) with the quotations of total return specified by paragraph (d)(4) of Rule 482 under the Securities Act of 1933;

(C) If the sales literature (other than sales literature for a company that is permitted under Rule 35d–1(a)(4) to use a name suggesting that the company's distributions are exempt from federal income tax or from both federal and state income tax) represents or implies that the company is managed to limit or control the effect of taxes on company performance, include the quotations of total return specified by paragraph (d)(4) of Rule 482 under the Securities Act of 1933;

(D) Accompany any quotation of yield or similar quotation purporting to demonstrate the income earned or distributions made by the company with a quotation of current yield specified by paragraph (d)(1) of Rule 482 under the Securities Act of 1933; and

(E) Accompany any quotation of tax equivalent yield or other similar quotation purporting to demonstrate the tax equivalent yield earned or distributions made by the company with a quotation of tax equivalent yield specified in paragraph (d)(2) and current yield specified by paragraph (d)(1) of Rule 482 under the Securities Act of 1933.

(2) Any performance data included in sales literature under paragraphs (b)(1)(ii) or (iii) of this rule must meet the currentness requirements of paragraph (g) of Rule 482 under the Securities Act of 1933.

(3) The requirements specified in paragraph (b)(1) of this rule shall not apply to any quarterly, semi-annual, or annual report to shareholders under Section 30 of the Act (15 U.S.C. 80a–29) containing performance data for a period commencing no earlier than the first day of the period covered by the report; nor shall the requirements of paragraphs (d)(3)(ii), (d)(4)(ii), and (g) of Rule 482 under the Securities Act of 1933 apply to any such periodic report containing any other performance data.

NOTE: Sales literature (except that of a money market fund) containing a quotation of yield or tax equivalent yield must also contain the total return information. In the case of sales literature, the currentness provisions apply from the date of distribution and not the date of submission for publication.

Rule 35d–1. Investment company names

(a) For purposes of section 35(d) of the Act, a materially deceptive and misleading name of a Fund includes:

(1) *Names Suggesting Guarantee or Approval by the United States Government.* A name suggesting that the Fund or the securities issued by it are guaranteed, sponsored, recommended, or approved by the United States government or any United States government agency or instrumentality, including any name that uses the words "guaranteed" or "insured" or similar terms in conjunction with the words "United States" or "U.S. government."

(2) *Names Suggesting Investment in Certain Investments or Industries.* A name suggesting that the Fund focuses its investments in a particular type of investment or investments, or in investments in a particular industry or group of industries, unless:

(i) The Fund has adopted a policy to invest, under normal circumstances, at least 80% of the value of its Assets in the particular type of investments, or in investments in the particular industry or industries, suggested by the Fund's name; and

(ii) Either the policy described in paragraph (a)(2)(i) of this section is a fundamental policy under section 8(b)(3) of the Act, or the Fund has adopted a policy to provide the Fund's shareholders with at least 60 days prior notice of any change in the policy described in paragraph (a)(2)(i) of this rule that meets the requirements of paragraph (c) of this rule.

(3) *Names Suggesting Investment in Certain Countries or Geographic Regions.* A name suggesting that the Fund focuses its investments in a particular country or geographic region, unless:

(i) The Fund has adopted a policy to invest, under normal circumstances, at least 80% of the value of its Assets in investments that are tied economically to the particular country or geographic region suggested by its name;

(ii) The Fund discloses in its prospectus the specific criteria used by the Fund to select these investments; and

(iii) Either the policy described in paragraph (a)(3)(i) of this rule is a fundamental policy under rule 8(b)(3) of the Act, or the Fund has adopted a policy to provide the Fund's shareholders with at least 60 days prior notice of any change in the policy described in paragraph (a)(3)(i) of this rule that meets the requirements of paragraph (c) of this rule.

(4) *Tax–Exempt Funds.* A name suggesting that the Fund's distributions are exempt from federal income tax or from both federal and state income tax, unless the Fund has adopted a fundamental policy under section 8(b)(3) of the Act:

(i) To invest, under normal circumstances, at least 80% of the value of its Assets in investments the income from which is exempt, as applicable, from federal income tax or from both federal and state income tax; or

(ii) To invest, under normal circumstances, its Assets so that at least 80% of the income that it distributes will be exempt, as applicable, from federal income tax or from both federal and state income tax.

(b) The requirements of paragraphs (a)(2) through (a)(4) of this rule apply at the time a Fund invests its Assets, except that these requirements shall not apply to any unit investment trust (as defined in section 4(2) of the Act that has made an initial deposit of securities prior to July 31, 2002). If, subsequent to an investment, these requirements are no longer met, the Fund's future investments must be made in a manner that will bring the Fund into compliance with those paragraphs.

(c) A policy to provide a Fund's shareholders with notice of a change in a Fund's investment policy as described in paragraphs (a)(2)(ii) and (a)(3)(iii) of this rule must provide that:

(1) The notice will be provided in plain English in a separate written document;

(2) The notice will contain the following prominent statement, or similar clear and understandable statement, in bold-face type: "Important Notice Regarding Change in Investment Policy"; and

(3) The statement contained in paragraph (c)(2) of this rule also will appear on the envelope in which the notice is delivered or, if the notice is delivered separately from other communications to investors, that the statement will appear either on the notice or on the envelope in which the notice is delivered.

(d) For purposes of this rule:

(1) *Fund* means a registered investment company and any series of the investment company.

(2) *Assets* means net assets, plus the amount of any borrowings for investment purposes.

Rule 38a–1. Compliance procedures and practices of certain investment companies

(a) Each registered investment company and business development company ("fund") must:

(1) *Policies and Procedures.* Adopt and implement written policies and procedures reasonably designed to prevent violation of the Federal Securities Laws by the fund, including policies and procedures that provide for the oversight of compliance by each investment adviser, principal underwriter, administrator, and transfer agent of the fund;

(2) *Board Approval.* Obtain the approval of the fund's board of directors, including a majority of directors who are not interested persons of the fund, of the fund's policies and procedures and those of each investment adviser, principal underwriter, administrator, and transfer agent of the fund, which approval must be based on a finding by the board that the policies and procedures are reasonably designed to prevent violation of the Federal Securities Laws by the fund, and by each investment adviser, principal underwriter, administrator, and transfer agent of the fund;

(3) *Annual Review.* Review, no less frequently than annually, the adequacy of the policies and procedures of the fund and of each investment adviser, principal underwriter, administrator, and transfer agent and the effectiveness of their implementation;

(4) *Chief Compliance Officer.* Designate one individual responsible for administering the fund's policies and procedures adopted under paragraph (a)(1):

(i) Whose designation and compensation must be approved by the fund's board of directors, including a majority of the directors who are not interested persons of the fund;

(ii) Who may be removed from his or her responsibilities by action of (and only with the approval of) the fund's board of directors, including a majority of the directors who are not interested persons of the fund;

(iii) Who must, no less frequently than annually, provide a written report to the board that, at a minimum, addresses:

(A) The operation of the policies and procedures of the fund and each investment adviser, principal underwriter, administrator, and transfer agent of the fund, any material changes made to those policies and procedures since the date of the last report, and any material changes to the policies and procedures recommended as a result of the annual review conducted pursuant to paragraph (a)(3) of this rule; and

(B) Each Material Compliance Matter that occurred since the date of the last report; and

(iv) Who must, no less frequently than annually, meet separately with the fund's independent directors.

(b) *Unit Investment Trusts.* If the fund is a unit investment trust, the fund's principal underwriter or depositor must approve the fund's policies and procedures and chief compliance officer, must receive all annual reports, and must approve the removal of the chief compliance officer from his or her responsibilities.

(c) *Undue Influence Prohibited.* No officer, director, or employee of the fund, its investment adviser, or principal underwriter, or any person acting under such person's direction may directly or indirectly take any action to coerce, manipulate, mislead, or fraudulently influence the fund's chief compliance officer in the performance of his or her duties under this rule.

(d) *Recordkeeping.* The fund must maintain:

(1) A copy of the policies and procedures adopted by the fund under paragraph (a)(1) that are in effect, or at any time within the past five years were in effect, in an easily accessible place; and

(2) Copies of materials provided to the board of directors in connection with their approval under paragraph (a)(2) of this rule, and written reports provided to the board of directors pursuant to paragraph (a)(4)(iii) of this rule (or, if the fund is a unit investment trust, to the fund's principal underwriter or depositor, pursuant to paragraph (b) of this rule) for at least five years after the end of the fiscal year in which the documents were provided, the first two years in an easily accessible place; and

(3) Any records documenting the fund's annual review pursuant to paragraph (a)(3) of this rule for at least five years after the end of the fiscal year in which the annual review was conducted, the first two years in an easily accessible place.

(e) *Definitions.* For purposes of this rule:

(1) *Federal Securities Laws* means the Securities Act of 1933 (15 U.S.C. 77a–aa), the Securities Exchange Act of 1934 (15 U.S.C. 78a–mm), the Sarbanes–Oxley Act of 2002 (Pub. L. 107–204, 116 Stat. 745 (2002)), the Investment Company Act of 1940 (15 U.S.C. 80a), the Investment Advisers Act of 1940 (15 U.S.C. 80b), Title V of the Gramm–Leach–Bliley Act (Pub. L. No. 106–102, 113 Stat. 1338 (1999)), any rules adopted by the Commission under any of these statutes, the Bank Secrecy Act (31 U.S.C. 5311–5314; 5316–5332) as it applies to funds, and any rules adopted thereunder by the Commission or the Department of the Treasury.

(2) *A Material Compliance Matter* means any compliance matter about which the fund's board of directors would reasonably need to know to oversee fund compliance, and that involves, without limitation:

(i) A violation of the Federal Securities Laws by the fund, its investment adviser, principal underwriter, administrator or transfer agent (or officers, directors, employees or agents thereof),

(ii) A violation of the policies and procedures of the fund, its investment adviser, principal underwriter, administrator or transfer agent, or

(iii) A weakness in the design or implementation of the policies and procedures of the fund, its investment adviser, principal underwriter, administrator or transfer agent.

Rule 45a–1. Confidential treatment of names and addresses of dealers of registered investment company securities

(a) Exhibits calling for the names and addresses of dealers to or through whom principal underwriters of registered investment companies are currently offering securities and which are required to be furnished with registration statements filed pursuant to section 8(b) of the Act, or periodic reports filed pursuant to section 30(a) or section 30(b)(1) of the Act, shall be the subject of confidential treatment and shall not be made available to the public, except that the Commission may by order make such exhibits available to the public if, after appropriate notice and opportunity for hearing, it finds that public disclosure of such material is necessary or appropriate in the public interest or for the protection of investors.

(b) The exhibits referred to in paragraph (a) of this rule shall be filed in quadruplicate with the Commission at the time the registration statement or periodic report is filed. Such exhibits shall be enclosed in a separate envelope marked "Confidential Treatment" and addressed to the Chairman, Securities and Executive Commission, Washington, D.C. Confidential treatment requests shall be submitted in paper only, whether or not the registrant is required to file in electronic format.

Rule 55a–1. Investment activities of business development companies

Notwithstanding section 55(a) of the Act, a business development company may acquire securities purchased in transactions not involving any public offering from an issuer, or from any person who is an officer or employee of the issuer, if the issuer meets the requirements of sections 2(a)(46)(A) and (B) of the Act, but the issuer is not an eligible portfolio company because it does not meet the requirements of Rule 2a–46, and the business development company meets the requirements of paragraphs (i) and (ii) of section 55(a)(1)(B) of the Act.

Rule 57b–1. Exemption for downstream affiliates of business development companies

Notwithstanding subsection (b)(2) of section 57 of the Act, the provisions of subsection (a) of that section shall not apply to any person (a) solely because that person is directly or indirectly controlled by a business development company or (b) solely because that person is, within the meaning of section 2(a)(3)(C) or (D) of the Act, an affiliated person of a person described in (a) of this rule.

Rule 60a–1. Exemption for certain business development companies

Section 12(d)(1)(A) and (C) of the Act shall not apply to the acquisition by a business development company of the outstanding voting securities of a small business investment company licensed to do business under the Small Business Investment Act of 1958 which is operated as a wholly-owned subsidiary of the business development company.

D. INVESTMENT ADVISERS ACT OF 1940

15 U.S.C. § 80b–1 et seq.

Findings

Sec. 201. Upon the basis of facts disclosed by the record and report of the Securities and Exchange Commission made pursuant to section 30 of the Public Utility Holding Company Act of 1935, and facts otherwise disclosed and ascertained, it is found that investment advisers are of national concern, in that, among other things—

(1) their advice, counsel, publications, writings, analyses, and reports are furnished and distributed, and their contracts, subscription agreements, and other arrangements with clients are negotiated and performed, by the use of the mails and means and instrumentalities of interstate commerce;

(2) their advice, counsel, publications, writings, analyses, and reports customarily relate to the purchase and sale of securities traded on national securities exchanges and in interstate over-the-counter markets, securities issued by companies engaged in business in interstate commerce, and securities issued by national banks and member banks of the Federal Reserve System; and

(3) the foregoing transactions occur in such volume as substantially to affect interstate commerce, national securities exchanges, and other securities markets, the national banking system and the national economy.

Definitions

Sec. 202. (a) When used in this title, unless the context otherwise requires, the following definitions shall apply:

(1) "Assignment" includes any direct or indirect transfer or hypothecation of an investment adviso-

ry contract by the assignor or of a controlling block of the assignor's outstanding voting securities by a security holder of the assignor; but if the investment adviser is a partnership, no assignment of an investment advisory contract shall be deemed to result from the death or withdrawal of a minority of the members of the investment adviser having only a minority interest in the business of the investment adviser, or from the admission to the investment adviser of one or more members who, after such admission, shall be only a minority of the members and shall have only a minority interest in the business.

(2) "Bank" means (A) a banking institution organized under the laws of the United States or a Federal savings association, as defined in section 2(5) of the Home Owners' Loan Act, (B) a member bank of the Federal Reserve System, (C) any other banking institution, savings association, as defined in section 2(4) of the Home Owners' Loan Act, or trust company, whether incorporated or not, doing business under the laws of any State or of the United States, a substantial portion of the business of which consists of receiving deposits or exercising fiduciary powers similar to those permitted to national banks under the authority of the Comptroller of the Currency, and which is supervised and examined by State or Federal authority having supervision over banks or savings associations, and which is not operated for the purpose of evading the provisions of this subchapter, and (D) a receiver, conservator, or other liquidating agent of any institution or firm included in clauses (A), (B), or (C) of this paragraph.

(3) The term "broker" has the same meaning as given in section 3 of the Securities Exchange Act of 1934.

(4) "Commission" means the Securities and Exchange Commission.

(5) "Company" means a corporation, a partnership, an association, a joint-stock company, a trust, or any organized group of persons, whether incorporated or not; or any receiver, trustee in a case under title 11 of the United States Code, or similar official, or any liquidating agent for any of the foregoing, in his capacity as such.

(6) "Convicted" includes a verdict, judgment, or plea of guilty, or a finding of guilt on a plea of nolo contendere, if such verdict, judgment, plea, or finding has not been reversed, set aside, or withdrawn, whether or not sentence has been imposed.

(7) The term "dealer" has the same meaning as given in section 3 of the Securities Exchange Act of 1934, but does not include an insurance company or investment company.

(8) "Director" means any director of a corporation or any person performing similar functions with respect to any organization, whether incorporated or unincorporated.

(9) "Exchange" means any organization, association, or group of persons, whether incorporated or unincorporated, which constitutes, maintains, or provides a market place or facilities for bringing together purchasers and sellers of securities or for otherwise performing with respect to securities the functions commonly performed by a stock exchange as that term is generally understood, and includes the market place and the market facilities maintained by such exchange.

(10) "Interstate commerce" means trade, commerce, transportation, or communication among the several States, or between any foreign country and any State, or between any State and any place or ship outside thereof.

(11) "Investment adviser" means any person who, for compensation, engages in the business of advising others, either directly or through publications or writings, as to the value of securities or as to the advisability of investing in, purchasing, or selling securities, or who, for compensation and as part of a regular business, issues or promulgates analyses or reports concerning securities; but does not include (A) a bank, or any bank holding company as defined in the Bank Holding Company Act of 1956 which is not an investment company, except that the term "investment adviser" includes any bank or bank holding company to the extent that such bank or bank holding company serves or acts as an investment adviser to a registered investment company, but if, in the case of a bank, such services or actions are performed through a separately identifiable department or division, the department or division, and not the bank itself, shall be deemed to be the investment adviser; (B) any lawyer, accountant, engineer, or teacher whose performance of such services is solely incidental to the practice of his profession; (C) any broker or dealer whose performance of such services is solely incidental to the conduct of his business as a broker or dealer and who receives no special compensation therefor; (D) the publisher of any bona fide newspaper, news magazine or business or financial publication of general and

regular circulation; (E) any person whose advice, analyses, or reports relate to no securities other than securities which are direct obligations of or obligations guaranteed as to principal or interest by the United States, or securities issued or guaranteed by corporations in which the United States has a direct or indirect interest which shall have been designated by the Secretary of the Treasury, pursuant to section 3(a)(12) of the Securities Exchange Act of 1934, as exempted securities for the purposes of that Act; (F) any nationally recognized statistical rating organization, as that term is defined in section 3(a)(62) of the Securities Exchange Act of 1934, unless such organization engages in issuing recommendations as to purchasing, selling, or holding securities or in managing assets, consisting in whole or in part of securities, on behalf of others; (G) any family office, as defined by rule, regulation, or order of the Commission, in accordance with the purposes of this title; or (H) such other persons not within the intent of this paragraph, as the Commission may designate by rules and regulations or order.

(12) "Investment company", affiliated person, and "insurance company" have the same meanings as in the Investment Company Act of 1940. "Control" means the power to exercise a controlling influence over the management or policies of a company, unless such power is solely the result of an official position with such company.

(13) "Investment supervisory services" means the giving of continuous advice as to the investment of funds on the basis of the individual needs of each client.

(14) "Means or instrumentality of interstate commerce" includes any facility of a national securities exchange.

(15) "National securities exchange" means an exchange registered under section 6 of the Securities Exchange Act of 1934.

(16) "Person" means a natural person or a company.

(17) The term "person associated with an investment adviser" means any partner, officer, or director of such investment adviser (or any person performing similar functions), or any person directly or indirectly controlling or controlled by such investment adviser, including any employee of such investment adviser, except that for the purposes of section 203 (other than subsection (f) thereof), persons associated with an investment adviser whose functions are clerical or ministerial shall not be included in the meaning of such term. The Commission may by rules and regulations classify, for the purposes of any portion or portions of this subchapter, persons, including employees controlled by an investment adviser.

(18) "Security" means any note, stock, treasury stock, security future, bond, debenture, evidence of indebtedness, certificate of interest or participation in any profit-sharing agreement, collateral-trust certificate, preorganization certificate or subscription, transferable share, investment contract, voting-trust certificate, certificate of deposit for a security, fractional undivided interest in oil, gas, or other mineral rights, any put, call, straddle, option, or privilege on any security (including a certificate of deposit) or on any group or index of securities (including any interest therein or based on the value thereof), or any put, call, straddle, option, or privilege entered into on a national securities exchange relating to foreign currency, or, in general, any interest or instrument commonly known as a "security", or any certificate of interest or participation in, temporary or interim certificate for, receipt for, guaranty of, or warrant or right to subscribe to or purchase any of the foregoing.

(19) "State" means any State of the United States, the District of Columbia, Puerto Rico, the Virgin Islands, or any other possession of the United States.

(20) "Underwriter" means any person who has purchased from an issuer with a view to, or sells for an issuer in connection with, the distribution of any security, or participates or has a direct or indirect participation in any such undertaking, or participates or has a participation in the direct or indirect underwriting of any such undertaking; but such term shall not include a person whose interest is limited to a commission from an underwriter or dealer not in excess of the usual and customary distributor's or seller's commission. As used in this paragraph the term "issuer" shall include in addition to an issuer, any person directly or indirectly controlling or controlled by the issuer, or any person under direct or indirect common control with the issuer.

(21) "Securities Act of 1933", "Securities Exchange Act of 1934", and "Trust Indenture Act of 1939", mean those Acts, respectively, as heretofore or hereafter amended.

(22) "Business development company" means any company which is a business development

company as defined in section 2(a)(48) of title I of this Act and which complies with section 55 of title I of this Act, except that—

(A) the 70 per centum of the value of the total assets condition referred to in sections 2(a)(48) and 55 of title I of this Act shall be 60 per centum for purposes of determining compliance therewith;

(B) such company need not be a closed-end company and need not elect to be subject to the provisions of sections 55 through 65 of title I of this Act; and

(C) the securities which may be purchased pursuant to section 55(a) of title I of this Act may be purchased from any person.

For purposes of this paragraph, all terms in sections 2(a)(48) and 55 of title I of this Act shall have the same meaning set forth in such title as if such company were a registered closed-end investment company, except that the value of the assets of a business development company which is not subject to the provisions of sections 55 through 65 of title I of this Act shall be determined as of the date of the most recent financial statements which it furnished to all holders of its securities, and shall be determined no less frequently than annually.

(23) "Foreign securities authority" means any foreign government, or any governmental body or regulatory organization empowered by a foreign government to administer or enforce its laws as they relate to securities matters.

(24) "Foreign financial regulatory authority" means any (A) foreign securities authority, (B) other governmental body or foreign equivalent of a self-regulatory organization empowered by a foreign government to administer or enforce its laws relating to the regulation of fiduciaries, trusts, commercial lending, insurance, trading in contracts of sale of a commodity for future delivery, or other instruments traded on or subject to the rules of a contract market, board of trade or foreign equivalent, or other financial activities, or (C) membership organization a function of which is to regulate the participation of its members in activities listed above.

(25) "Supervised person" means any partner, officer, director (or other person occupying a similar status or performing similar functions), or employee of an investment adviser, or other person who provides investment advice on behalf of the investment adviser and is subject to the supervision and control of the investment adviser.

(26) The term "separately identifiable department or division" of a bank means a unit—

(A) that is under the direct supervision of an officer or officers designated by the board of directors of the bank as responsible for the day-to-day conduct of the bank's investment adviser activities for one or more investment companies, including the supervision of all bank employees engaged in the performance of such activities; and

(B) for which all of the records relating to its investment adviser activities are separately maintained in or extractable from such unit's own facilities or the facilities of the bank, and such records are so maintained or otherwise accessible as to permit independent examination and enforcement by the Commission of this Act or the Investment Company Act of 1940 and rules and regulations promulgated under this Act or the Investment Company Act of 1940.

(27) The terms "security future" and "narrow-based security index" have the same meanings as provided in section 3(a)(55) of the Securities Exchange Act of 1934.

(28) The term "credit rating agency" has the same meaning as in section 3 of the Securities Exchange Act of 1934.

(29) The terms "commodity pool", "commodity pool operator", "commodity trading advisor", "major swap participant", "swap", "swap dealer", and "swap execution facility" have the same meanings as in section 1a of the Commodity Exchange Act.

(29) The term "private fund" means an issuer that would be an investment company, as defined in section 3 of the Investment Company Act of 1940, but for section 3(c)(1) or 3(c)(7) of that Act.*

(30) The term "foreign private adviser" means any investment adviser who—

(A) has no place of business in the United States;

(B) has, in total, fewer than 15 clients and investors in the United States in private funds advised by the investment adviser;

(C) has aggregate assets under management attributable to clients in the United States and investors in the United States in private funds advised by the investment adviser of less than

* Dodd–Frank created two (29)'s.

$25,000,000, or such higher amount as the Commission may, by rule, deem appropriate in accordance with the purposes of this title; and

(D) neither—

(i) holds itself out generally to the public in the United States as an investment adviser; nor

(ii) acts as

(I) an investment adviser to any investment company registered under the Investment Company Act of 1940; or

(II) a company that has elected to be a business development company pursuant to section 54 of the Investment Company Act of 1940, and has not withdrawn its election

(b) *Applicability to Federal or State Government Agency, or Instrumentality, or to Officers, Agents, or Employees Thereof.* No provision in this title shall apply to, or be deemed to include, the United States, a State, or any political subdivision of a State, or any agency, authority, or instrumentality of any one or more of the foregoing, or any corporation which is wholly owned directly or indirectly by any one or more of the foregoing, or any officer, agent, or employee of any of the foregoing acting as such in the course of his official duty, unless such provision makes specific reference thereto.

(c) *Consideration of Promotion of Efficiency, Competition, and Capital Formation.* Whenever pursuant to this title the Commission is engaged in rulemaking and is required to consider or determine whether an action is necessary or appropriate in the public interest, the Commission shall also consider, in addition to the protection of investors, whether the action will promote efficiency, competition, and capital formation.

Registration of Investment Advisers

Sec. 203. (a) *Necessity of Registration.* Except as provided in subsection (b) and section 203A, it shall be unlawful for any investment adviser, unless registered under this section, to make use of the mails or any means or instrumentality of interstate commerce in connection with his or its business as an investment adviser.

(b) *Investment Advisers Who Need Not Be Registered.* The provisions of subsection (a) of this section shall not apply to—

(1) any investment adviser, other than an investment adviser who acts as an investment adviser to any private fund, all of whose clients are residents of the State within which such investment adviser maintains his or its principal office and place of business, and who does not furnish advice or issue analyses or reports with respect to securities listed or admitted to unlisted trading privileges on any national securities exchange;

(2) any investment adviser whose only clients are insurance companies;

(3) any investment adviser that is a foreign private adviser;

(4) any investment adviser that is a charitable organization, as defined in section 3(c)(10)(D) of the Investment Company Act of 1940, or is a trustee, director, officer, employee, or volunteer of such a charitable organization acting within the scope of such person's employment or duties with such organization, whose advice, analyses, or reports are provided only to one or more of the following:

(A) any such charitable organization;

(B) a fund that is excluded from the definition of an investment company under section 3(c)(10)(B) of the Investment Company Act of 1940; or

(C) a trust or other donative instrument described in section 3(c)(10)(B) of the Investment Company Act of 1940, or the trustees, administrators, settlors (or potential settlors), or beneficiaries of any such trust or other instrument;

(5) any plan described in section 414(e) of the Internal Revenue Code of 1986, any person or entity eligible to establish and maintain such a plan under the Internal Revenue Code of 1986, or any trustee, director, officer, or employee of or volunteer for any such plan or person, if such person or entity, acting in such capacity, provides investment advice exclusively to, or with respect to, any plan, person, or entity or any company, account, or fund that is excluded from the definition of an investment company under section 3(c)(14) of the Investment Company Act of 1940;

(6)(A) any investment adviser that is registered with the Commodity Futures Trading Commission as a commodity trading advisor whose business does not consist primarily of acting as an investment adviser, as defined in section 202(a)(11), and that does not act as an investment adviser to—

(i) an investment company registered under title I of this Act; or

(ii) a company which has elected to be a business development company pursuant to section 54 of title I of this Act and has not withdrawn its election or

(B) any investment adviser that is registered with the Commodity Futures Trading Commission as a commodity trading advisor and advises a private fund, provided that, if after the date of enactment of the Private Fund Investment Advisers Registration Act of 2010, the business of the advisor should become predominately the provision of securities–related advice, then such adviser shall register with the Commission.

(7) any investment adviser, other than any entity that has elected to be regulated or is regulated as a business development company pursuant to section 54 of the Investment Company Act of 1940, who solely advises—

(A) small business investment companies that are licensees under the Small Business Investment Act of 1958;

(B) entities that have received from the Small Business Administration notice to proceed to qualify for a license as a small business investment company under the Small Business Investment Act of 1958, which notice or license has not been revoked; or

(C) applicants that are affiliated with 1 or more licensed small business investment companies described in subparagraph (A) and that have applied for another license under the Small Business Investment Act of 1958, which application remains pending.

(c) *Procedure for Registration; Filing of Application; Effective Date of Registration; Amendment of Registration.*

(1) An investment adviser, or any person who presently contemplates becoming an investment adviser, may be registered by filing with the Commission an application for registration in such form and containing such of the following information and documents as the Commission, by rule, may prescribe as necessary or appropriate in the public interest or for the protection of investors:

(A) the name and form of organization under which the investment adviser engages or intends to engage in business; the name of the State or other sovereign power under which such investment adviser is organized; the location of his or its principal office, principal place of business, and branch offices, if any; the names and addresses of his or its partners, officers, directors, and persons performing similar functions or, if such an investment adviser be an individual, of such individual; and the number of his or its employees;

(B) the education, the business affiliations for the past ten years, and the present business affiliations of such investment adviser and of his or its partners, officers, directors, and persons performing similar functions and of any controlling person thereof;

(C) the nature of the business of such investment adviser, including the manner of giving advice and rendering analyses or reports;

(D) a balance sheet certified by an independent public accountant and other financial statements (which shall, as the Commission specifies, be certified);

(E) the nature and scope of the authority of such investment adviser with respect to clients' funds and accounts;

(F) the basis or bases upon which such investment adviser is compensated;

(G) whether such investment adviser, or any person associated with such investment adviser, is subject to any disqualification which would be a basis for denial, suspension, or revocation of registration of such investment adviser under the provisions of subsection (e) of this section; and

(H) a statement as to whether the principal business of such investment adviser consists or is to consist of acting as investment adviser and a statement as to whether a substantial part of the business of such investment adviser, consists or is to consist of rendering investment supervisory services.

(2) Within forty-five days of the date of the filing of such application (or within such longer period as to which the applicant consents) the Commission shall—

(A) by order grant such registration; or

(B) institute proceedings to determine whether registration should be denied. Such proceedings shall include notice of the grounds for denial under consideration and opportunity for hearing and shall be concluded within one hundred twenty days of the date of the filing of the application for registration. At the conclusion of such proceedings the Commission, by order, shall grant or deny such registration. The Commission may extend the time for conclusion of such proceedings for up to ninety days if it finds good cause for such extension and publishes its reasons for so finding or for such longer period as to which the applicant consents.

The Commission shall grant such registration if the Commission finds that the requirements of this section are satisfied and that the applicant is not prohibited from registering as an investment advisor under section 203A. The Commission shall deny such registration if it does not make such a finding or if it finds that if the applicant were so registered, its registration would be subject to suspension or revocation under subsection (e) of this section.

(d) *Other Acts Prohibited by Title.* Any provision of this title (other than subsection (a) of this section) which prohibits any act, practice, or course of business if the mails or any means or instrumentality of interstate commerce are used in connection therewith shall also prohibit any such act, practice, or course of business by any investment adviser registered pursuant to this section or any person acting on behalf of such an investment adviser, irrespective of any use of the mails or any means or instrumentality of interstate commerce in connection therewith.

(e) *Censure, Denial, or Suspension of Registration; Notice and Hearing.* The Commission, by order, shall censure, place limitations on the activities, functions, or operations of, suspend for a period not exceeding twelve months, or revoke the registration of any investment adviser if it finds, on the record after notice and opportunity for hearing, that such censure, placing of limitations, suspension, or revocation is in the public interest and that such investment adviser, or any person associated with such investment adviser, whether prior to or subsequent to becoming so associated—

(1) has willfully made or caused to be made in any application for registration or report required to be filed with the Commission under this title, or in any proceeding before the Commission with respect to registration, any statement which was at the time and in the light of the circumstances under which it was made false or misleading with respect to any material fact, or has omitted to state in any such application or report any material fact which is required to be stated therein.

(2) has been convicted within ten years preceding the filing of any application for registration or at any time thereafter of any felony or misdemeanor or of a substantially equivalent crime by a foreign court of competent jurisdiction which the Commission finds—

(A) involves the purchase or sale of any security, the taking of a false oath, the making of a false report, bribery, perjury, burglary, any substantially equivalent activity however denominated by the laws of the relevant foreign government, or conspiracy to commit any such offense;

(B) arises out of the conduct of the business of a broker, dealer, municipal securities dealer, investment adviser, bank, insurance company, government securities broker, government securities dealer, fiduciary, transfer agent, credit rating agency, foreign person performing a function substantially equivalent to any of the above, or entity or person required to be registered under the Commodity Exchange Act or any substantially equivalent statute or regulation;

(C) involves the larceny, theft, robbery, extortion, forgery, counterfeiting, fraudulent concealment, embezzlement, fraudulent conversion, or misappropriation of funds or securities or substantially equivalent activity however denominated by the laws of the relevant foreign government; or

(D) involves the violation of section 152, 1341, 1342, or 1343 or chapter 25 or 47 of title 18, United States Code, or a violation of substantially equivalent foreign statute.

(3) has been convicted during the 10-year period preceding the date of filing of any application for registration, or at any time thereafter, of—

(A) any crime that is punishable by imprisonment for 1 or more years, and that is not described in paragraph (2); or

(B) a substantially equivalent crime by a foreign court of competent jurisdiction.

(4) is permanently or temporarily enjoined by order, judgment, or decree of any court of competent jurisdiction, including any foreign court of competent jurisdiction, from acting as an investment adviser, underwriter, broker, dealer, municipal securities dealer, government securities broker, government securities dealer, transfer agent, credit rating agency, foreign person performing a function substantially equivalent to any of the above, or entity or person required to be registered under the Commodity Exchange Act or any substantially equivalent statute or regulation, or as

an affiliated person or employee of any investment company, bank, insurance company, foreign entity substantially equivalent to any of the above, or entity or person required to be registered under the Commodity Exchange Act or any substantially equivalent statute or regulation, or from engaging in or continuing any conduct or practice in connection with any such activity, or in connection with the purchase or sale of any security.

(5) has willfully violated any provision of the Securities Act of 1933, the Securities Exchange Act of 1934, the Investment Company Act of 1940, this title, the Commodity Exchange Act, or the rules or regulations under any such statutes or any rule of the Municipal Securities Rulemaking Board, or is unable to comply with any such provision.

(6) has willfully aided, abetted, counseled, commanded, induced, or procured the violation by any other person of any provision of the Securities Act of 1933, the Securities Exchange Act of 1934, the Investment Company Act of 1940, this title, the Commodity Exchange Act, the rules or regulations under any of such statutes, or the rules of the Municipal Securities Rulemaking Board, or has failed reasonably to supervise, with a view to preventing violations of the provisions of such statutes, rules, and regulations, another person who commits such a violation, if such other person is subject to his supervision. For the purposes of this paragraph no person shall be deemed to have failed reasonably to supervise any person, if—

(A) there have been established procedures, and a system for applying such procedures, which would reasonably be expected to prevent and detect, insofar as practicable, any such violation by such other person, and

(B) such person has reasonably discharged the duties and obligations incumbent upon him by reason of such procedures and system without reasonable cause to believe that such procedures and system were not being complied with.

(7) is subject to any order of the Commission barring or suspending the right of the person to be associated with an investment adviser;

(8) has been found by a foreign financial regulatory authority to have—

(A) made or caused to be made in any application for registration or report required to be filed with a foreign securities authority, or in any proceeding before a foreign securities authority with respect to registration, any statement that was at the time and in light of the circumstances under which it was made false or misleading with respect to any material fact, or has omitted to state in any application or report to a foreign securities authority any material fact that is required to be stated therein;

(B) violated any foreign statute or regulation regarding transactions in securities or contracts of sale of a commodity for future delivery traded on or subject to the rules of a contract market or any board of trade; or

(C) aided, abetted, counseled, commanded, induced, or procured the violation by any other person of any foreign statute or regulation regarding transactions in securities or contracts of sale of a commodity for future delivery traded on or subject to the rules of a contract market or any board of trade, or has been found, by the foreign financial regulatory authority, to have failed reasonably to supervise, with a view to preventing violations of statutory provisions, and rules and regulations promulgated thereunder, another person who commits such a violation, if such other person is subject to his supervision; or

(9) is subject to any final order of a State securities commission (or any agency or officer performing like functions), State authority that supervises or examines banks, savings associations, or credit unions, State insurance commission (or any agency or office performing like functions), an appropriate Federal banking agency (as defined in section 3 of the Federal Deposit Insurance Act), or the National Credit Union Administration, that—

(A) bars such person from association with an entity regulated by such commission, authority, agency, or officer, or from engaging in the business of securities, insurance, banking, savings association activities, or credit union activities; or

(B) constitutes a final order based on violations of any laws or regulations that prohibit fraudulent, manipulative, or deceptive conduct.

(f) *Bar or Suspension from Association with Investment Adviser; Notice and Hearing.* The Commission, by order, shall censure or place limitations on the activities of any person associated, seeking to become associated, or, at the time of the alleged misconduct, associated or seeking to become associated with an investment adviser, or suspend for a period not exceeding 12 months or bar any such person from being associated with an investment adviser, broker, dealer, municipal securities dealer, municipal advisor, transfer agent, or nationally recognized statistical rating organization, if the Commission finds, on the record after notice and opportunity for hearing, that such censure, placing of limitations, suspension, or bar is in the public interest and that such person has committed or omitted any act or omission enumerated in paragraph (1), (5), (6), (8), or (9) of subsection (e) of this section or has been convicted of any offense specified in paragraph (2) or (3) of subsection (e) of this section within ten years of the commencement of the proceedings under this subsection, or is enjoined from any action, conduct, or practice specified in paragraph (4) of subsection (e) of this section. It shall be unlawful for any person as to whom such an order suspending or barring him from being associated with an investment adviser is in effect willfully to become, or to be, associated with an investment adviser without the consent of the Commission, and it shall be unlawful for any investment adviser to permit such a person to become, or remain, a person associated with him without the consent of the Commission, if such investment adviser knew, or in the exercise of reasonable care, should have known, of such order.

(g) *Registration of Successor to Business of Investment Adviser*. Any successor to the business of an investment adviser registered under this section shall be deemed likewise registered hereunder, if within thirty days from its succession to such business it shall file an application for registration under this section, unless and until the Commission, pursuant to subsection (c) or subsection (e) of this section, shall deny registration to or revoke or suspend the registration of such successor.

(h) *Withdrawal of Registration*. Any person registered under this section may, upon such terms and conditions as the Commission finds necessary in the public interest or for the protection of investors, withdraw from registration by filing a written notice of withdrawal with the Commission. If the Commission finds that any person registered under this section, or who has pending an application for registration filed under this section, is no longer in existence, is not engaged in business as an investment adviser or is prohibited from registering as an investment adviser under section 203A, the Commission shall by order cancel the registration of such person.

(i) *Money Penalties in Administrative Proceedings*.

(1) *Authority of Commission*.

(A) *In General*. In any proceeding instituted pursuant to subsection (e) or (f) against any person, the Commission may impose a civil penalty if it finds, on the record after notice and opportunity for hearing, that such penalty is in the public interest and that such person—

(i) has willfully violated any provision of the Securities Act of 1933, the Securities Exchange Act of 1934, the Investment Company Act of 1940, or this title, or the rules or regulations thereunder;

(ii) has willfully aided, abetted, counseled, commanded, induced, or procured such a violation by any other person;

(iii) has willfully made or caused to be made in any application for registration or report required to be filed with the Commission under this title, or in any proceeding before the Commission with respect to registration, any statement which was, at the time and in the light of the circumstances under which it was made, false or misleading with respect to any material fact, or has omitted to state in any such application or report any material fact which was required to be stated therein; or

(iv) has failed reasonably to supervise, within the meaning of subsection (e)(6), with a view to preventing violations of the provisions of this title and the rules and regulations thereunder, another person who commits such a violation, if such other person is subject to his supervision;

(B) *Cease-and-Desist Proceedings*. In any proceeding instituted pursuant to subsection (k) against any person, the Commission may impose a civil penalty if the Commission finds, on the record, after notice and opportunity for hearing, that such person—

(i) is violating or has violated any provision of this title, or any rule or regulation issued under this title; or

(ii) is or was a cause of the violation of any provision of this title, or any rule or regulation issued under this title.

(2) *Maximum Amount of Penalty*.

(A) *First Tier*. The maximum amount of penalty for each act or omission described in paragraph (1) shall be $5,000 for a natural person or $50,000 for any other person.

(B) *Second Tier*. Notwithstanding subparagraph (A), the maximum amount of penalty for each such act or omission shall be $50,000 for a natural person or $250,000 for any other person if the act or omission described in paragraph (1) involved fraud, deceit, manipulation, or deliberate or reckless disregard of a regulatory requirement.

(C) *Third Tier.* Notwithstanding subparagraphs (A) and (B), the maximum amount of penalty for each such act or omission shall be $100,000 for a natural person or $500,000 for any other person if—

(i) the act or omission described in paragraph (1) involved fraud, deceit, manipulation, or deliberate or reckless disregard of a regulatory requirement; and

(ii) such act or omission directly or indirectly resulted in substantial losses or created a significant risk of substantial losses to other persons or resulted in substantial pecuniary gain to the person who committed the act or omission.

(3) *Determination of Public Interest.* In considering under this section whether a penalty is in the public interest, the Commission may consider—

(A) whether the act or omission for which such penalty is assessed involved fraud, deceit, manipulation, or deliberate or reckless disregard of a regulatory requirement;

(B) the harm to other persons resulting either directly or indirectly from such act or omission;

(C) the extent to which any person was unjustly enriched, taking into account any restitution made to persons injured by such behavior;

(D) whether such person previously has been found by the Commission, another appropriate regulatory agency, or a self-regulatory organization to have violated the Federal securities laws, State securities laws, or the rules of a self-regulatory organization, has been enjoined by a court of competent jurisdiction from violations of such laws or rules, or has been convicted by a court of competent jurisdiction of violations of such laws or of any felony or misdemeanor described in subsection (e)(2) of this section;

(E) the need to deter such person and other persons from committing such acts or omissions; and

(F) such other matters as justice may require.

(4) *Evidence Concerning Ability to Pay.* In any proceeding in which the Commission may impose a penalty under this section, a respondent may present evidence of the respondent's ability to pay such penalty. The Commission may, in its discretion, consider such evidence in determining whether such penalty is in the public interest. Such evidence may relate to the extent of such person's ability to continue in business and the collectability of a penalty, taking into account any other claims of the United States or third parties upon such person's assets and the amount of such person's assets.

(j) *Authority to Enter Order Requiring Accounting and Disgorgement.* In any proceeding in which the Commission may impose a penalty under this section, the Commission may enter an order requiring accounting and disgorgement, including reasonable interest. The Commission is authorized to adopt rules, regulations, and orders concerning payments to investors, rates of interest, periods of accrual, and such other matters as it deems appropriate to implement this subsection.

(k) *Cease-and-Desist Proceedings.*

(1) *Authority of Commission.* If the Commission finds, after notice and opportunity for hearing, that any person is violating, has violated, or is about to violate any provision of this title, or any rule or regulation thereunder, the Commission may publish its findings and enter an order requiring such person, and any other person that is, was, or would be a cause of the violation, due to an act or omission the person knew or should have known would contribute to such violation, to cease and desist from committing or causing such violation and any future violation of the same provision, rule, or regulation. Such order may, in addition to requiring a person to cease and desist from committing or causing a violation, require such person to comply, or to take steps to effect compliance, with such provision, rule, or regulation, upon such terms and conditions and within such time as the Commission may specify in such order. Any such order may, as the Commission deems appropriate, require future compliance or steps to effect future compliance, either permanently or for such period of time as the Commission may specify, with such provision, rule, or regulation with respect to any security, any issuer, or any other person.

(2) *Hearing.* The notice instituting proceedings pursuant to paragraph (1) shall fix a hearing date not earlier than 30 days nor later than 60 days after service of the notice unless an earlier or a later

date is set by the Commission with the consent of any respondent so served.

(3) *Temporary Order.*

(A) *In General.* Whenever the Commission determines that the alleged violation or threatened violation specified in the notice instituting proceedings pursuant to paragraph (1), or the continuation thereof, is likely to result in significant dissipation or conversion of assets, significant harm to investors, or substantial harm to the public interest, including, but not limited to, losses to the Securities Investor Protection Corporation, prior to the completion of the proceedings, the Commission may enter a temporary order requiring the respondent to cease and desist from the violation or threatened violation and to take such action to prevent the violation or threatened violation and to prevent dissipation or conversion of assets, significant harm to investors, or substantial harm to the public interest as the Commission deems appropriate pending completion of such proceedings. Such an order shall be entered only after notice and opportunity for a hearing, unless the Commission, notwithstanding section 211(c), determines that notice and hearing prior to entry would be impracticable or contrary to the public interest. A temporary order shall become effective upon service upon the respondent and, unless set aside, limited, or suspended by the Commission or a court of competent jurisdiction, shall remain effective and enforceable pending the completion of the proceedings.

(B) *Applicability.* This paragraph shall apply only to a respondent that acts, or, at the time of the alleged misconduct acted, as a broker, dealer, investment adviser, investment company, municipal securities dealer, government securities broker, government securities dealer, or transfer agent, or is, or was at the time of the alleged misconduct, an associated person of, or a person seeking to become associated with, any of the foregoing.

(4) *Review of Temporary Orders.*

(A) *Commission Review.* At any time after the respondent has been served with a temporary cease-and-desist order pursuant to paragraph (3), the respondent may apply to the Commission to have the order set aside, limited, or suspended. If the respondent has been served with a temporary cease-and-desist order entered without a prior Commission hearing, the respondent may, within 10 days after the date on which the order was served, request a hearing on such application and the Commission shall hold a hearing and render a decision on such application at the earliest possible time.

(B) *Judicial Review.* Within—

(i) 10 days after the date the respondent was served with a temporary cease-and-desist order entered with a prior Commission hearing, or

(ii) 10 days after the Commission renders a decision on an application and hearing under subparagraph (A), with respect to any temporary cease-and-desist order entered without a prior Commission hearing,

the respondent may apply to the United States district court for the district in which the respondent resides or has its principal office or place of business, or for the District of Columbia, for an order setting aside, limiting, or suspending the effectiveness or enforcement of the order, and the court shall have jurisdiction to enter such an order. A respondent served with a temporary cease-and-desist order entered without a prior Commission hearing may not apply to the court except after hearing and decision by the Commission on the respondent's application under subparagraph (A) of this paragraph.

(C) *No Automatic Stay of Temporary Order.* The commencement of proceedings under subparagraph (B) of this paragraph shall not, unless specifically ordered by the court, operate as a stay of the Commission's order.

(D) *Exclusive Review.* Section 213 of this title shall not apply to a temporary order entered pursuant to this section.

(5) *Authority to Enter Order Requiring Accounting and Disgorgement.* In any cease-and-desist proceeding under paragraph (1), the Commission may enter an order requiring accounting and disgorgement, including reasonable interest. The Commission is authorized to adopt rules, regulations, and orders concerning payments to investors, rates of interest, periods of accrual, and such other matters as it deems appropriate to implement this subsection.

(*l*) *Exemption of Venture Capital Fund Advisers.*

(1) *In General.* No investment adviser that acts as an investment adviser solely to 1 or more venture capital funds shall be subject to the regis-

tration requirements of this title with respect to the provision of investment advice relating to a venture capital fund. Not later than 1 year after the date of enactment of this subsection [July 21, 2010], the Commission shall issue final rules to define the term "venture capital fund" for purposes of this subsection. The Commission shall require such advisers to maintain such records and provide to the Commission such annual or other reports as the Commission determines necessary or appropriate in the public interest or for the protection of investors.

(2) *Advisers of SBICS.* For purposes of this subsection, a venture capital fund includes an entity described in subparagraph (A), (B), or (C) of subsection (b)(7) (other than an entity that has elected to be regulated or is regulated as a business development company pursuant to section 54 of the Investment Company Act of 1940).

(m) *Exemption of and Reporting by Certain Private Fund Advisers.*

(1) *In General.* The Commission shall provide an exemption from the registration requirements under this section to any investment adviser of private funds, if each of such investment adviser acts solely as an adviser to private funds and has assets under management in the United States of less than $150,000,000.

(2) *Reporting.* The Commission shall require investment advisers exempted by reason of this subsection to maintain such records and provide to the Commission such annual or other reports as the Commission determines necessary or appropriate in the public interest or for the protection of investors.

(3) *Advisers of SBICS.* For purposes of this subsection, the assets under management of a private fund that is an entity described in subparagraph (A), (B), or (C) of subsection (b)(7) (other than an entity that has elected to be regulated or is regulated as a business development company pursuant to section 54 of the Investment Company Act of 1940) shall be excluded from the limit set forth in paragraph (1).

(n) *Registration and Examination of Mid-Sized Fund Advisers.* In prescribing regulations to carry out the requirements of this section with respect to investment advisers acting as investment advisers to mid–sized private funds, the Commission shall take into account the size, governance, and investment strategy of such funds to determine whether they pose systemic risk, and shall provide for registration and examination procedures with respect to the investment advisers of such funds which reflect the level of systemic risk posed by such funds.

State and Federal Responsibilities

Sec. 203A. (a) *Advisers Subject to State Authorities.*

(1) *In General.* No investment adviser that is regulated or required to be regulated as an investment adviser in the State in which it maintains its principal office and place of business shall register under section 203, unless the investment adviser—

(A) has assets under management of not less than $25,000,000, or such higher amount as the Commission may, by rule, deem appropriate in accordance with the purposes of this title; or

(B) is an adviser to an investment company registered under title I of this Act.

(2) *Treatment of Mid-Sized Investment Advisers.*

(A) *In General.* No investment adviser described in subparagraph (B) shall register under section 203, unless the investment adviser is an adviser to an investment company registered under the Investment Company Act of 1940, or a company which has elected to be a business development company pursuant to section 54 of the Investment Company Act of 1940, and has not withdrawn the election, except that, if by effect of this paragraph an investment adviser would be required to register with 15 or more States, then the adviser may register under section 203.

(B) *Covered Persons.* An investment adviser described in this subparagraph is an investment adviser that—

(i) is required to be registered as an investment adviser with the securities commissioner (or any agency or office performing like functions) of the State in which it maintains its principal office and place of business and, if registered, would be subject to examination as an investment adviser by any such commissioner, agency, or office; and

(ii) has assets under management between—

(I) the amount specified under subparagraph (A) of paragraph (1), as such amount may have been adjusted by the Commission pursuant to that subparagraph; and

(II) $100,000,000, or such higher amount as the Commission may, by rule, deem appropriate in accordance with the purposes of this title.

(3) *Definition.* For purposes of this subsection, the term "assets under management" means the securities portfolios with respect to which an investment adviser provides continuous and regular supervisory or management services.

(b) *Advisors Subject to Commission Authority.*

(1) *In General.* No law of any State or political subdivision thereof requiring the registration, licensing, or qualification as an investment adviser or supervised person of an investment adviser shall apply to any person—

(A) that is registered under section 203 as an investment adviser, or that is a supervised person of such person, except that a State may license, register, or otherwise qualify any investment adviser representative who has a place of business located within that State;

(B) that is not registered under section 203 because that person is excepted from the definition of an investment adviser under section 202(a)(11); or

(C) that is not registered under section 203 because that person is exempt from registration as provided in subsection (b)(7) of such section, or is a supervised person of such person.

(2) *Limitation.* Nothing in this subsection shall prohibit the securities commission (or any agency or office performing like functions) of any State from investigating and bringing enforcement actions with respect to fraud or deceit against an investment adviser or person associated with an investment adviser.

(c) *Exemptions.* Notwithstanding subsection (a) of this section, the Commission, by rule or regulation upon its own motion, or by order upon application, may permit the registration with the Commission of any person or class of persons to which the application of subsection (a) of this section would be unfair, a burden on interstate commerce, or otherwise inconsistent with the purposes of this section.

(d) *State Assistance.* Upon request of the securities commissioner (or any agency or officer performing like functions) of any State, the Commission may provide such training, technical assistance, or other reasonable assistance in connection with the regulation of investment advisers by the State.

Reports by Investment Advisers

Sec. 204. (a) *In General.* Every investment adviser who makes use of the mails or of any means or instrumentality of interstate commerce in connection with his or its business as an investment adviser (other than one specifically exempted from registration pursuant to section 203(b) of this title), shall make and keep for prescribed periods such records (as defined in section 3(a)(37) of the Securities Exchange Act of 1934), furnish such copies thereof, and make and disseminate such reports as the Commission, by rule, may prescribe as necessary or appropriate in the public interest or for the protection of investors. All records (as so defined) of such investment advisers are subject at any time, or from time to time, to such reasonable periodic, special, or other examinations by representatives of the Commission as the Commission deems necessary or appropriate in the public interest or for the protection of investors.

(b) *Records and Reports of Private Funds.*

(1) *In General.* The Commission may require any investment adviser registered under this title—

(A) to maintain such records of, and file with the Commission such reports regarding, private funds advised by the investment adviser, as necessary and appropriate in the public interest and for the protection of investors, or for the assessment of systemic risk by the Financial Stability Oversight Council (in this subsection referred to as the "Council"); and

(B) to provide or make available to the Council those reports or records or the information contained therein.

(2) *Treatment of Records.* The records and reports of any private fund to which an investment adviser registered under this title provides investment advice shall be deemed to be the records and reports of the investment adviser.

(3) *Required Information.* The records and reports required to be maintained by an investment adviser and subject to inspection by the Commission under this subsection shall include, for each private fund advised by the investment adviser, a description of—

(A) the amount of assets under management and use of leverage, including off-balance-sheet leverage;

(B) counterparty credit risk exposure;

(C) trading and investment positions;

(D) valuation policies and practices of the fund;

(E) types of assets held;

(F) side arrangements or side letters, whereby certain investors in a fund obtain more favorable rights or entitlements than other investors;

(G) trading practices; and

(H) such other information as the Commission, in consultation with the Council, determines is necessary and appropriate in the public interest and for the protection of investors or for the assessment of systemic risk, which may include the establishment of different reporting requirements for different classes of fund advisers, based on the type or size of private fund being advised.

(4) *Maintenance of Records.* An investment adviser registered under this title shall maintain such records of private funds advised by the investment adviser for such period or periods as the Commission, by rule, may prescribe as necessary and appropriate in the public interest and for the protection of investors, or for the assessment of systemic risk.

(5) *Filing of Records.* The Commission shall issue rules requiring each investment adviser to a private fund to file reports containing such information as the Commission deems necessary and appropriate in the public interest and for the protection of investors or for the assessment of systemic risk.

(6) *Examination of Records.*

(A) *Periodic and Special Examinations.* The Commission—

(i) shall conduct periodic inspections of the records of private funds maintained by an investment adviser registered under this title in accordance with a schedule established by the Commission; and

(ii) may conduct at any time and from time to time such additional, special, and other examinations as the Commission may prescribe as necessary and appropriate in the public interest and for the protection of investors, or for the assessment of systemic risk.

(B) *Availability of Records.* An investment adviser registered under this title shall make available to the Commission any copies or extracts from such records as may be prepared without undue effort, expense, or delay, as the Commission or its representatives may reasonably request.

(7) *Information Sharing.*

(A) *In General.* The Commission shall make available to the Council copies of all reports, documents, records, and information filed with or provided to the Commission by an investment adviser under this subsection as the Council may consider necessary for the purpose of assessing the systemic risk posed by a private fund.

(B) *Confidentiality.* The Council shall maintain the confidentiality of information received under this paragraph in all such reports, documents, records, and information, in a manner consistent with the level of confidentiality established for the Commission pursuant to paragraph (8). The Council shall be exempt from section 552 of title 5, United States Code, with respect to any information in any report, document, record, or information made available, to the Council under this subsection.

(8) *Commission Confidentiality of Reports.* Notwithstanding any other provision of law, the Commission may not be compelled to disclose any report or information contained therein required to be filed with the Commission under this subsection, except that nothing in this subsection authorizes the Commission—

(A) to withhold information from Congress, upon an agreement of confidentiality; or

(B) prevent the Commission from complying with

(i) a request for information from any other Federal department or agency or any self-regulatory organization requesting the report or information for purposes within the scope of its jurisdiction; or

(ii) an order of a court of the United States in an action brought by the United States or the Commission.

(9) *Other Recipients Confidentiality.* Any department, agency, or self-regulatory organization that receives reports or information from the Commission under this subsection shall maintain the confidentiality of such reports, documents, records, and information in a manner consistent with the level of confidentiality established for the Commission under paragraph (8).

(10) *Public Information Exception.*

(A) *In General.* The Commission, the Council, and any other department, agency, or self-regulatory organization that receives information, reports, documents, records, or information from the Commission under this subsection, shall be exempt from the provisions of section 552 of title 5, United States Code, with respect to any such report, document, record, or information. Any proprietary information of an investment adviser ascertained by the Commission from any report required to be filed with the Commission pursuant to this subsection shall be subject to the same limitations on public disclosure as any facts ascertained during an examination, as provided by section 210(b) of this title.

(B) *Proprietary Information.* For purposes of this paragraph, proprietary information includes sensitive, non-public information regarding—

(i) the investment or trading strategies of the investment adviser;

(ii) analytical or research methodologies;

(iii) trading data;

(iv) computer hardware or software containing intellectual property; and

(v) any additional information that the Commission determines to be proprietary.

(11) *Annual Report to Congress.* The Commission shall report annually to Congress on how the Commission has used the data collected pursuant to this subsection to monitor the markets for the protection of investors and the integrity of the markets.

(c) *Filing Depositories.* The Commission may, by rule, require an investment adviser—

(1) to file with the Commission any fee, application, report, or notice required to be filed by this subchapter or the rules issued under this subchapter through any entity designated by the Commission for that purpose; and

(2) to pay the reasonable costs associated with such filing and the establishment and maintenance of the systems required by subsection (c).*

(d) *Access to Disciplinary and Other Information.*

(1) *Maintenance of System to Respond to Inquiries.*

(A) *In General.* The Commission shall require the entity designated by the Commission under subsection (b)(1) of this section to establish and maintain a toll-free telephone listing, or a readily accessible electronic or other process, to receive and promptly respond to inquiries regarding registration information (including disciplinary actions, regulatory, judicial, and arbitration proceedings, and other information required by law or rule to be reported) involving investment advisers and persons associated with investment advisers.

(B) *Applicability.* This subsection shall apply to any investment adviser (and the persons associated with that adviser), whether the investment adviser is registered with the Commission under section 203 or regulated solely by a State, as described in section 203A.

(2) *Recovery of Costs.* An entity designated by the Commission under subsection (b)(1) of this section may charge persons making inquiries, other than individual investors, reasonable fees for responses to inquiries described in paragraph (1).

(3) *Limitation on Liability.* An entity designated by the Commission under subsection (b)(1) of this section shall not have any liability to any person for any actions taken or omitted in good faith under this subsection.

(d) *Records of Persons With Custody or Use.***

(1) *In General.* Records of persons having custody or use of the securities, deposits, or credits of a client, that relate to such custody or use, are subject at any time, or from time to time, to such reasonable periodic, special, or other examinations and other information and document requests by representatives of the Commission, as the Commission deems necessary or appropriate in the public interest or for the protection of investors.

(2) *Certain Persons Subject to Other Regulation.* Any person that is subject to regulation and examination by a Federal financial institution regulatory agency (as such term is defined under section 212(c)(2) of title 18, United States Code) may satisfy any examination request, information request, or document request described under paragraph (1), by providing the Commission with a detailed listing, in writing, of the securities, deposits, or credits of the client within the custody or use of such person.

* Editors Note. Probably should be (d).

** Editors Note. Dodd–Frank created two subsection (d)'s.

Prevention of Misuse of Nonpublic Information

Sec. 204A. Every investment adviser subject to section 204 of this title shall establish, maintain, and enforce written policies and procedures reasonably designed, taking into consideration the nature of such investment adviser's business, to prevent the misuse in violation of this Act or the Securities Exchange Act of 1934, or the rules or regulations thereunder, of material, nonpublic information by such investment adviser or any person associated with such investment adviser. The Commission, as it deems necessary or appropriate in the public interest or for the protection of investors, shall adopt rules or regulations to require specific policies or procedures reasonably designed to prevent misuse in violation of this Act or the Securities Exchange Act of 1934 (or the rules or regulations thereunder) of material, nonpublic information.

Investment Advisory Contracts

Sec. 205. (a) *Compensation Assignment and Partnership-Membership Provisions.* No investment adviser registered or required to be registered with the Commission shall enter into, extend, or renew any investment advisory contract, or in any way perform any investment advisory contract entered into, extended, or renewed on or after the effective date of this title, if such contract—

(1) provides for compensation to the investment adviser on the basis of a share of capital gains upon or capital appreciation of the funds or any portion of the funds of the client;

(2) fails to provide, in substance, that no assignment of such contract shall be made by the investment adviser without the consent of the other party to the contract; or

(3) fails to provide, in substance, that the investment adviser, if a partnership, will notify the other party to the contract of any change in the membership of such partnership within a reasonable time after such change.

(b) *Compensation Prohibition Inapplicable to Certain Compensation Computations.* Paragraph (1) of subsection (a) shall not—

(1) be construed to prohibit an investment advisory contract which provides for compensation based upon the total value of a fund averaged over a definite period, or as of definite dates, or taken as of a definite date;

(2) apply to an investment advisory contract with—

(A) an investment company registered under title I of this Act, or

(B) any other person (except a trust, governmental plan, collective trust fund, or separate account referred to in section 3(c)(11) of title I of this Act), provided that the contract relates to the investment of assets in excess of $1 million, if the contract provides for compensation based on the asset value of the company or fund under management averaged over a specified period and increasing and decreasing proportionately with the investment performance of the company or fund over a specified period in relation to the investment record of an appropriate index of securities prices or such other measure of investment performance as the Commission by rule, regulation, or order may specify;

(3) apply with respect to any investment advisory contract between an investment adviser and a business development company, as defined in this title, if (A) the compensation provided for in such contract does not exceed 20 per centum of the realized capital gains upon the funds of the business development company over a specified period or as of definite dates, computed net of all realized capital losses and unrealized capital depreciation, and the condition of section 61(a)(3)(B)(iii) of title I of this Act is satisfied, and (B) the business development company does not have outstanding any option, warrant, or right issued pursuant to section 61(a)(3)(B) of title I of this Act and does not have a profit-sharing plan described in section 57(n) of title I of this Act;

(4) apply to an investment advisory contract with a company excepted from the definition of an investment company under section 3(c)(7) of title I of this Act; or

(5) apply to an investment advisory contract with a person who is not a resident of the United States.

(c) *Measurement of Changes in Compensation.* For purposes of paragraph (2) of subsection (b), the point from which increases and decreases in compensation are measured shall be the fee which is paid or earned when the investment performance of such company or fund is equivalent to that of the index or other measure of performance, and an index of securities prices shall be deemed appropriate unless the Commission by order shall determine otherwise.

(d) *"Investment Advisory Contract" Defined.* As used in paragraphs (2) and (3) of subsection (a), "investment advisory contract" means any contract or agreement whereby a person agrees to act as investment adviser to or to manage any investment or trading account of another person other than an investment company registered under title I of this Act.

(e) *Exempt Persons and Transactions.* The Commission, by rule or regulation, upon its own motion, or by order upon application, may conditionally or unconditionally exempt any person or transaction, or any class or classes of persons or transactions, from subsection (a)(1), if and to the extent that the exemption relates to an investment advisory contract with any person that the Commission determines does not need the protections of subsection (a)(1), on the basis of such factors as financial sophistication, net worth, knowledge of and experience in financial matters, amount of assets under management, relationship with a registered investment adviser, and such other factors as the Commission determines are consistent with this section. With respect to any factor used in any rule or regulation by the Commission in making a determination under this subsection, if the Commission uses a dollar amount test in connection with such factor, such as a net asset threshold, the Commission shall, by order, not later than 1 year after the date of enactment of the Private Fund Investment Advisers Registration Act of 2010, and every 5 years thereafter, adjust for the effects of inflation on such test. Any such adjustment that is not a multiple of $100,000 shall be rounded to the nearest multiple of $100,000.

(f) *Authority To Restrict Mandatory Pre–Dispute Arbitration.* The Commission, by rule, may prohibit, or impose conditions or limitations on the use of, agreements that require customers or clients of any investment adviser to arbitrate any future dispute between them arising under the Federal securities laws, the rules and regulations thereunder, or the rules of a self-regulatory organization if it finds that such prohibition, imposition of conditions, or limitations are in the public interest and for the protection of investors.

Prohibited Transactions by Investment Advisers

Sec. 206. It shall be unlawful for any investment adviser, by use of the mails or any means or instrumentality of interstate commerce, directly or indirectly—

(1) to employ any device, scheme, or artifice to defraud any client or prospective client;

(2) to engage in any transaction, practice, or course of business which operates as a fraud or deceit upon any client or prospective client;

(3) acting as principal for his own account, knowingly to sell any security to or purchase any security from a client, or acting as broker for a person other than such client, knowingly to effect any sale or purchase of any security for the account of such client, without disclosing to such client in writing before the completion of such transaction the capacity in which he is acting and obtaining the consent of the client to such transaction. The prohibitions of this paragraph shall not apply to any transaction with a customer of a broker or dealer if such broker or dealer is not acting as an investment adviser in relation to such transaction; or

(4) to engage in any act, practice, or course of business which is fraudulent, deceptive, or manipulative. The Commission shall, for the purposes of this paragraph (4) by rules and regulations define, and prescribe means reasonably designed to prevent, such acts, practices, and courses of business as are fraudulent, deceptive, or manipulative.

Exemptions

Sec. 206A. The Commission, by rules and regulations, upon its own motion, or by order upon application, may conditionally or unconditionally exempt any person or transaction, or any class or classes of persons, or transactions, from any provision or provisions of this title or of any rule or regulation thereunder, if and to the extent that such exemption is necessary or appropriate in the public interest and consistent with the protection of investors and the purposes fairly intended by the policy and provisions of this title.

Material Misstatements

Sec. 207. It shall be unlawful for any person willfully to make any untrue statement of a material fact in any registration application or report filed with the Commission under section 203, or 204, or willfully to omit to state in any such application or report any material fact which is required to be stated therein.

General Prohibitions

Sec. 208. (a) *Representations of Sponsorship by United States or Agency Thereof.* It shall be unlawful for any person registered under section 203 to represent or imply in any manner whatsoever that such person has been sponsored, recommended, or approved, or that his abilities or qualifications have in any respect been passed upon by the United States or any agency or any officer thereof.

(b) *Statement of Registration Under Securities Exchange Act of 1934 Provisions.* No provision of subsection (a) shall be construed to prohibit a statement that a person is registered under this title or under the Securities Exchange Act of 1934, if such statement is true in fact and if the effect of such registration is not misrepresented.

(c) *Use of Name "Investment Counsel" as Descriptive of Business.* It shall be unlawful for any person registered under section 203 to represent that he is an investment counsel or to use the name "investment counsel" as descriptive of his business unless (1) his or its principal business consists of acting as investment adviser, and (2) a substantial part of his or its business consists of rendering investment supervisory services.

(d) *Use of Indirect Means to Do Prohibited Act.* It shall be unlawful for any person indirectly, or through or by any other person, to do any act or thing which it would be unlawful for such person to do directly under the provisions of this title or any rule or regulation thereunder.

Enforcement of Title

Sec. 209. (a) *Investigation.* Whenever it shall appear to the Commission, either upon complaint or otherwise, that the provisions of this title or of any rule or regulation prescribed under the authority thereof, have been or are about to be violated by any person, it may in its discretion require, and in any event shall permit, such person to file with it a statement in writing, under oath or otherwise, as to all the facts and circumstances relevant to such violation, and may otherwise investigate all such facts and circumstances.

(b) *Administration of Oaths and Affirmations, Subpoena of Witnesses, Etc.* For the purposes of any investigation or any proceeding under this title, any member of the Commission or any officer thereof designated by it is empowered to administer oaths and affirmations, subpena witnesses, compel their attendance, take evidence, and require the production of any books, papers, correspondence, memoranda, contracts, agreements, or other records which are relevant or material to the inquiry. Such attendance of witnesses and the production of any such records may be required from any place in any State or in any Territory or other place subject to the jurisdiction of the United States at any designated place of hearing.

(c) *Jurisdiction of Courts of United States.* In case of contumacy by, or refusal to obey a subpena issued to, any person, the Commission may invoke the aid of any court of the United States within the jurisdiction of which such investigation or proceeding is carried on, or where such person resides or carries on business, in requiring the attendance and testimony of witnesses and the production of books, papers, correspondence, memoranda, contracts, agreements, and other records. And such court may issue an order requiring such person to appear before the Commission or member or officer designated by the Commission, there to produce records, if so ordered, or to give testimony touching the matter under investigation or in question; and any failure to obey such order of the court may be punished by such court as a contempt thereof. All process in any such case may be served in the judicial district whereof such person is an inhabitant or wherever he may be found. Any person who without just cause shall fail or refuse to attend and testify or to answer any lawful inquiry or to produce books, papers, correspondence, memoranda, contracts, agreements, or other records, if in his or its power so to do, in obedience to the subpena of the Commission, shall be guilty of a misdemeanor, and upon conviction shall be subject to a fine of not more than $1,000 or to imprisonment for a term of not more than one year, or both.

(d) *Action for Injunction.* Whenever it shall appear to the Commission that any person has engaged, is engaged, or is about to engage in any act or practice constituting a violation of any provision of this title, or of any rule, regulation, or order hereunder, or that any person has aided, abetted, counseled, commanded, induced, or procured, is aiding, abetting, counseling, commanding, inducing, or procuring, or is about to aid, abet, counsel, command, induce, or procure such a violation, it may in its discretion bring an action in the proper district court of the United States, or the proper United States court of any Territory or other place subject to the jurisdiction of the United States, to enjoin such acts or practices and to enforce compliance with this title or any rule, regulation, or order hereunder. Upon a showing that such person has engaged, is engaged, or is about to engage in any such act or practice, or in aiding, abetting, counseling, commanding, inducing, or procuring any such act or practice, a permanent or temporary injunction or decree or restraining order shall be granted without bond. The Commission may transmit such evidence as may be available concerning any violation of the provisions of this subchapter, or of any rule, regulation, or order thereunder, to the Attorney General, who, in his discretion, may institute the appropriate criminal proceedings under this title.

(e) *Money Penalties in Civil Actions.*

(1) *Authority of Commission.* Whenever it shall appear to the Commission that any person has violated any provision of this title, the rules or regulations thereunder, or a cease-and-desist order entered by the Commission pursuant to section 203(k), the Commission may bring an action in a United States district court to seek, and the court shall have jurisdiction to impose, upon a proper showing, a civil penalty to be paid by the person who committed such violation.

(2) *Amount of Penalty.*

(A) *First Tier.* The amount of the penalty shall be determined by the court in light of the facts and circumstances. For each violation, the amount of the penalty shall not exceed the greater of (i) $5,000 for a natural person or $50,000 for any other person, or (ii) the gross amount of pecuniary gain to such defendant as a result of the violation.

(B) *Second Tier.* Notwithstanding subparagraph (A), the amount of penalty for each such violation shall not exceed the greater of (i) $50,000 for a natural person or $250,000 for any other person, or (ii) the gross amount of pecuniary gain to such defendant as a result of the violation, if the violation described in paragraph (1) involved fraud, deceit, manipulation, or deliberate or reckless disregard of a regulatory requirement.

(C) *Third Tier.* Notwithstanding subparagraphs (A) and (B), the amount of penalty for each such violation shall not exceed the greater of (i) $100,000 for a natural person or $500,000 for any other person, or (ii) the gross amount of pecuniary gain to such defendant as a result of the violation, if—

(I) the violation described in paragraph (1) involved fraud, deceit, manipulation, or deliberate or reckless disregard of a regulatory requirement; and

(II) such violation directly or indirectly resulted in substantial losses or created a significant risk of substantial losses to other persons.

(3) *Procedures for Collection.*

(A) *Payment of Penalty to Treasury.* A penalty imposed under this section shall be payable into the Treasury of the United States, except as otherwise provided in section 308 of the Sarbanes–Oxley Act of 2002 and section 21F of the Securities Exchange Act of 1934.

(B) *Collection of Penalties.* If a person upon whom such a penalty is imposed shall fail to pay such penalty within the time prescribed in the court's order, the Commission may refer the matter to the Attorney General who shall recover such penalty by action in the appropriate United States district court.

(C) *Remedy Not Exclusive.* The actions authorized by this subsection may be brought in addition to any other action that the Commission or the Attorney General is entitled to bring.

(D) *Jurisdiction and Venue.* For purposes of section 214, actions under this paragraph shall be actions to enforce a liability or a duty created by this title.

(4) *Special Provisions Relating to a Violation of a Cease-and-Desist Order.* In an action to enforce a cease-and-desist order entered by the Commission pursuant to section 203(k), each separate violation of such order shall be a separate offense, except that in the case of a violation through a continuing failure to comply with the order, each day of the failure to comply shall be deemed a separate offense.

(f) *Aiding and Abetting.* For purposes of any action brought by the Commission under subsection (e), any person that knowingly or recklessly has aided, abetted, counseled, commanded, induced, or procured a violation of any provision of this Act, or of any rule, regulation, or order hereunder, shall be deemed to be in violation of such provision, rule, regulation, or order to the same extent as the person that committed such violation.

Disclosure of Information by Commission

Sec. 210. (a) *Information Available to Public.* The information contained in any registration application or report or amendment thereto filed with the Commission pursuant to any provision of this title shall be made available to the public, unless and except insofar as the Commission, by rules and regulations upon its own motion, or by order upon application, finds that public disclosure is neither necessary nor appropriate in the public interest or for the protection of investors. Photostatic or other copies of information contained in documents filed with the Commission under this title and made available to the public shall be furnished to any person at such reasonable charge and under such reasonable limitations as the Commission shall prescribe.

(b) *Disclosure of Fact of Examination or Investigation; Exceptions.* Subject to the provisions of subsections (c) and (d) of section 209 of this title and section 24(c) of the Securities Exchange Act of 1934 the Commission, or any member, officer, or employee thereof, shall not make public the fact that any examination or investigation under this title is being conducted, or the results of or any facts ascertained during any such examination or investigation; and no member, officer, or employee of the Commission shall disclose to any person other than a member, officer, or employee of the Commission any information obtained as a result of any such examination or investigation except with the approval of the Commission. The provisions of this subsection shall not apply—

(1) in the case of any hearing which is public under the provisions of section 212; or

(2) in the case of a resolution or request from either House of Congress.

(c) *Disclosure by Investment Adviser of Identity of Clients.* No provision of this title shall be construed to require, or to authorize the Commission to require any investment adviser engaged in rendering investment supervisory services to disclose the identity, investments, or affairs of any client of such investment adviser, except insofar as such disclosure may be necessary or appropriate in a particular proceeding or investigation having as its object the enforcement of a provision or provisions of this title or for purposes of assessment of potential systemic risk.

Consultation

Sec. 210A. (a) *Examination Results and Other Information.*

(1) The appropriate Federal banking agency shall provide the Commission upon request the results of any examination, reports, records, or other information to which such agency may have access—

(A) with respect to the investment advisory activities of any—

(i) bank holding company or savings and loan holding company;

(ii) bank; or

(iii) separately identifiable department or division of a bank,

that is registered under section 203 of this title; and

(B) in the case of a bank holding company or savings and loan holding company or bank that has a subsidiary or a separately identifiable department or division registered under that section, with respect to the investment advisory activities of such bank or bank holding company or savings and loan holding company.

(2) The Commission shall provide to the appropriate Federal banking agency upon request the results of any examination, reports, records, or other information with respect to the investment advisory activities of any bank holding company or savings and loan holding company, bank, or separately identifiable department or division of a bank, which is registered under section 203 of this title.

(3) Notwithstanding any other provision of law, the Commission and the appropriate Federal banking agencies shall not be compelled to disclose any information provided under paragraph (1) or (2). Nothing in this paragraph shall authorize the Commission or such agencies to withhold information from Congress, or prevent the Commission or such agencies from complying with a request for information from any other Federal department or agency or any self-regulatory organization requesting the information for purposes within the scope of its jurisdiction, or complying with an order of a court of the United States in an action brought by the United States, the Commission, or such agencies. For purposes of section 552 of title 5, United States Code, this paragraph shall be considered a statute described in subsection (b)(3)(B) of such section 552.

(b) *Effect on Other Authority.* Nothing in this section shall limit in any respect the authority of the appropriate Federal banking agency with respect to such bank holding company or savings and loan holding company (or affiliates or subsidiaries thereof), bank, or subsidiary, department, or division or a bank under any other provision of law.

(c) *Definition.* For purposes of this section, the term "appropriate Federal banking agency" shall have the same meaning as given in section 3 of the Federal Deposit Insurance Act.

Rules, Regulations, and Orders of Commission

Sec. 211. (a) *Power of Commission.* The Commission shall have authority from time to time to make, issue, amend, and rescind such rules and regulations and such orders as are necessary or appropriate to the exercise of the functions and powers conferred upon the Commission elsewhere in this title, including rules and regulations defining technical, trade, and other terms used in this title, except that the Commission may not define the term "client" for purposes of paragraphs (1) and (2) of section 206 to include an investor in a private fund managed by an investment adviser, if such private fund has entered into an advisory contract with such adviser. For the purposes of its rules or regulations the Commission may classify persons and matters within its jurisdiction and prescribe different requirements for different classes of persons or matters.

(b) *Effective Date of Regulations.* Subject to the provisions of chapter 15 of title 44, United States Code, and regulations prescribed under the authority thereof, the rules and regulations of the Commission under this title, and amendments thereof, shall be effective upon publication in the manner which the Commission shall prescribe, or upon such later date as may be provided in such rules and regulations.

(c) *Orders of Commission After Notice and Hearing; Type of Notice.* Orders of the Commission under this title shall be issued only after appropriate notice and opportunity for hearing. Notice to the parties to a proceeding before the Commission shall be given by personal service upon each party or by registered mail or certified mail or confirmed telegraphic notice to the party's last known business address. Notice to interested persons, if any, other than parties may be given in the same manner or by publication in the Federal Register.

(d) *Good Faith Compliance with Rules and Regulations.* No provision of this title imposing any liability shall apply to any act done or omitted in good faith in conformity with any rule, regulation, or order of the Commission, notwithstanding that such rule, regulation, or order may, after such act or omission, be amended or rescinded or be determined by judicial or other authority to be invalid for any reason.

(e) *Disclosure Rules on Private Funds.* The Commission and the Commodity Futures Trading Commission shall, after consultation with the Council but not later than 12 months after the date of enactment of the Private Fund Investment Advisers Registration Act of 2010, jointly promulgate rules to establish the form and content of the reports required to be filed with the Commission under subsection 204(b) and with the Commodity Futures Trading Commission by investment advisers that are registered both under this title and the Commodity Exchange Act.*

(g) *Standard of Conduct.*

(1) *In General.* The Commission may promulgate rules to provide that the standard of conduct for all brokers, dealers, and investment advisers, when providing personalized investment advice about securities to retail customers (and such other customers as the Commission may by rule provide), shall be to act in the best interest of the customer without regard to the financial or other interest of the broker, dealer, or investment adviser providing the advice. In accordance with such rules, any material conflicts of interest shall be disclosed and may be consented to by the customer. Such rules shall provide that such standard of conduct shall be no less stringent than the standard applicable to investment advisers under section 206(1) and (2) of this Act when providing personalized investment advice about securities, except the Commission shall not ascribe a meaning to the term "customer" that would include an investor in a private fund managed by an investment adviser, where such private fund has entered into an advisory contract with such adviser. The receipt of compensation based on commission or fees shall not, in and of itself, be considered a violation of such standard applied to a broker, dealer, or investment adviser.

(2) *Retail Customer Defined.* For purposes of this subsection, the term "retail customer" means a natural person, or the legal representative of such natural person, who—

(A) receives personalized investment advice about securities from a broker, dealer, or investment adviser; and

(B) uses such advice primarily for personal, family, or household purposes.

* The Dodd–Frank Amendments skipped subsection (f).

(h) *Other Matters*. The Commission shall—

(1) facilitate the provision of simple and clear disclosures to investors regarding the terms of their relationships with brokers, dealers, and investment advisers, including any material conflicts of interest; and

(2) examine and, where appropriate, promulgate rules prohibiting or restricting certain sales practices, conflicts of interest, and compensation schemes for brokers, dealers, and investment advisers that the Commission deems contrary to the public interest and the protection of investors.

(i) *Harmonization of Enforcement*. The enforcement authority of the Commission with respect to violations of the standard of conduct applicable to an investment adviser shall include—

(1) the enforcement authority of the Commission with respect to such violations provided under this subchapter; and

(2) the enforcement authority of the Commission with respect to violations of the standard of conduct applicable to a broker or dealer providing personalized investment advice about securities to a retail customer under the Securities Exchange Act of 1934, including the authority to impose sanctions for such violations, and

the Commission shall seek to prosecute and sanction violators of the standard of conduct applicable to an investment adviser under this Act to same extent as the Commission prosecutes and sanctions violators of the standard of conduct applicable to a broker or dealer providing personalized investment advice about securities to a retail customer under the Securities Exchange Act of 1934.

Hearings

Sec. 212. Hearings may be public and may be held before the Commission, any member or members thereof, or any officer or officers of the Commission designated by it, and appropriate records thereof shall be kept.

Court Review of Orders

Sec. 213. (a) *Petition; Jurisdictions; Findings of Commission; Additional Evidence; Finality*. Any person or party aggrieved by an order issued by the Commission under this title may obtain a review of such order in the United States court of appeals within any circuit wherein such person resides or has his principal office or place of business, or in the United States Court of Appeals for the District of Columbia, by filing in such court, within sixty days after the entry of such order, a written petition praying that the order of the Commission be modified or set aside in whole or in part. A copy of such petition shall be forthwith transmitted by the clerk of the court to any member of the Commission, or any officer thereof designated by the Commission for that purpose, and thereupon the Commission shall file in the court the record upon which the order complained of was entered, as provided in section 2112 of Title 28, United States Code. Upon the filing of such petition such court shall have jurisdiction, which upon the filing of the record shall be exclusive, to affirm, modify, or set aside such order, in whole or in part. No objection to the order of the Commission shall be considered by the court unless such objection shall have been urged before the Commission or unless there were reasonable grounds for failure so to do. The findings of the Commission as to the facts, if supported by substantial evidence, shall be conclusive. If application is made to the court for leave to adduce additional evidence, and it is shown to the satisfaction of the court that such additional evidence is material and that there were reasonable grounds for failure to adduce such evidence in the proceeding before the Commission, the court may order such additional evidence to be taken before the Commission and to be adduced upon the hearing in such manner and upon such terms and conditions as to the court may seem proper. The Commission may modify its findings as to the facts by reason of the additional evidence so taken, and it shall file with the court such modified or new findings, which, if supported by substantial evidence, shall be conclusive, and its recommendation, if any, for the modification or setting aside of the original order. The judgment and decree of the court affirming, modifying, or setting aside, in whole or in part, any such order of the Commission shall be final, subject to review by the Supreme Court of the United States upon certiorari or certification as provided in section 1254 of title 28, United States Code.

(b) *Stay of Commissions Order*. The commencement of proceedings under subsection (a) shall not, unless specifically ordered by the court, operate as a stay of the Commission's order.

Jurisdiction of Offenses and Suits

Sec. 214. (a) *In General*. The district courts of the United States and the United States courts of any Territory or other place subject to the jurisdiction of the United States shall have jurisdiction of violations of this title or the rules, regulations, or orders thereunder, and, concurrently with State and Territorial courts, of all suits in equity and actions at law brought to enforce any liability or duty created by, or to enjoin any violation of this title or the rules, regulations, or orders thereunder. Any criminal proceeding may be brought in the district wherein any act or transaction constituting the violation occurred. Any suit or action to enforce any liability or duty created by, or to enjoin any violation of this title or rules, regulations, or orders thereunder, may be brought in any such district or in the district wherein the defendant is an inhabitant or transacts business, and process in such cases may be served in any district of which the defendant is an inhabitant or transacts business or wherever the defendant may be found. In any action or proceeding instituted by the Commission under this title in a United States district court for any judicial district, a subpoena issued to compel the attendance of a witness or the production of documents or tangible things (or both) at a hearing or trial may be served at any place within the United States. Rule 45(c)(3)(A)(ii) of the Federal Rules of Civil Procedure shall not apply to a subpoena issued under the preceding sentence. Judgments and decrees so rendered shall be subject to review as provided in sections 1254, 1291, 1292, and 1294 of title 28, United States Code. No costs shall be assessed for or against the Commission in any proceeding under this title brought by or against the Commission in any court.

(b) *Extraterritorial Jurisdiction.* The district courts of the United States and the United States courts of any Territory shall have jurisdiction of an action or proceeding brought or instituted by the Commission or the United States alleging a violation of section 206 involving—

(1) conduct within the United States that constitutes significant steps in furtherance of the violation, even if the violation is committed by a foreign adviser and involves only foreign investors; or

(2) conduct occurring outside the United States that has a foreseeable substantial effect within the United States.

Validity of Contracts

Sec. 215. (a) *Waiver of Compliance as Void.* Any condition, stipulation, or provision binding any person to waive compliance with any provision of this title or with any rule, regulation, or order thereunder shall be void.

(b) *Rights Affected by Invalidity.* Every contract made in violation of any provision of this title and every contract heretofore or hereafter made, the performance of which involves the violation of, or the continuance of any relationship or practice in violation of any provision of this title, or any rule, regulation, or order thereunder, shall be void (1) as regards the rights of any person who, in violation of any such provision, rule, regulation, or order, shall have made or engaged in the performance of any such contract, and (2) as regards the rights of any person who, not being a party to such contract, shall have acquired any right thereunder with actual knowledge of the facts by reason of which the making or performance of such contract was in violation of any such provision.

Sec. 216. [Omitted]. This section terminated, effective May 15, 2000, pursuant to § 3003 of Act Dec. 21, 1995, P.L. 104–66. It provided for an annual report to Congress on the work of the Securities and Exchange Commission.

Penalties

Sec. 217. Any person who willfully violates any provision of this title, or any rule, regulation, or order promulgated by the Commission under authority thereof, shall, upon conviction, be fined not more than $10,000, imprisoned for not more than five years, or both.

Hiring and Leasing Authority of the Commission

Sec. 218. The provisions of section 4(b) of the Securities Exchange Act of 1934 shall be applicable with respect to the power of the Commission—

(1) to appoint and fix the compensation of such other employees as may be necessary for carrying out its functions under this title, and

(2) to lease and allocate such real property as may be necessary for carrying out its functions under this title.

Separability of Provisions

Sec. 219. If any provision of this title or the application of such provision to any person or circumstances shall be held invalid, the remainder of the title and the application of such provision to persons or circumstances other than those as to which it is held invalid shall not be affected thereby.

Short Title

Sec. 220. This title may be cited as the "Investment Advisers Act of 1940".

Effective Date

Sec. 221. This title shall become effective on November 1, 1940.

State Regulation of Investment Advisers

Sec. 222. (a) *Jurisdiction of State Regulators.* Nothing in this subchapter shall affect the jurisdiction of the securities commissioner (or any agency or officer performing like functions) of any State over any security or any person insofar as it does not conflict with the provisions of this subchapter or the rules and regulations thereunder.

(b) *Dual Compliance Purposes.* No State may enforce any law or regulation that would require an investment adviser to maintain any books or records in addition to those required under the laws of the State in which it maintains its principal office and place of business, if the investment adviser—

(1) is registered or licensed as such in the State in which it maintains its principal office and place of business; and

(2) is in compliance with the applicable books and records requirements of the State in which it maintains its principal office and place of business.

(c) *Limitation on Capital and Bond Requirements.* No State may enforce any law or regulation that would require an investment adviser to maintain a higher minimum net capital or to post any bond in addition to any that is required under the laws of the State in which it maintains its principal office and place of business, if the investment adviser—

(1) is registered or licensed as such in the State in which it maintains its principal office and place of business; and

(2) is in compliance with the applicable net capital or bonding requirements of the State in which it maintains its principal office and place of business.

(d) *National De Minimis Standard.* No law of any State or political subdivision thereof requiring the registration, licensing, or qualification as an investment adviser shall require an investment adviser to register with the securities commissioner of the State (or any agency or officer performing like functions) or to comply with such law (other than any provision thereof prohibiting fraudulent conduct) if the investment adviser—

(1) does not have a place of business located within the State; and

(2) during the preceding 12–month period, has had fewer than 6 clients who are residents of that State.

Custody of Client Accounts

Sec. 223. An investment adviser registered under this title shall take such steps to safeguard client assets over which such adviser has custody, including, without limitation, verification of such assets by an independent public accountant, as the Commission may, by rule, prescribe.

Rule of Construction Relating to the Commodities Exchange Act

Sec. 224. Nothing in this title shall relieve any person of any obligation or duty, or affect the availability of any right or remedy available to the Commodity Futures Trading Commission or any private party, arising under the Commodity Exchange Act governing commodity pools, commodity pool operators, or commodity trading advisors.

RULES AND REGULATIONS, INVESTMENT ADVISERS ACT OF 1940

(Cite as 17 CFR § 275.__)

Rule 0–2. General procedures for serving non–residents

(a) *General Procedures for Serving Process, Pleadings, or Other Papers on Non-Resident Investment Advisers, General Partners and Managing Agents.* Under Forms ADV and ADV–NR [17 CFR 279.1 and 279.4], a person may serve process, pleadings, or other papers on a non-resident investment adviser, or on a non-resident general partner or non-resident managing agent of an investment adviser by serving any or all of its appointed agents:

(1) A person may serve a non-resident investment adviser, non-resident general partner, or non-resident managing agent by furnishing the Commission with one copy of the process, pleadings, or papers, for each named party, and one additional copy for the Commission's records.

(2) If process, pleadings, or other papers are served on the Commission as described in this section, the Secretary of the Commission (Secretary) will promptly forward a copy to each named party by registered or certified mail at that party's last address filed with the Commission.

(3) If the Secretary certifies that the Commission was served with process, pleadings, or other papers pursuant to paragraph (a)(1) of this rule and forwarded these documents to a named party pursuant to paragraph (a)(2) of this rule, this certification constitutes evidence of service upon that party.

(b) *Definitions.* For purposes of this rule:

(1) "Managing Agent" means any person, including a trustee, who directs or manages, or who participates in directing or managing, the affairs of any unincorporated organization or association other than a partnership.

(2) "Non-resident" means:

(i) An individual who resides in any place not subject to the jurisdiction of the United States;

(ii) A corporation that is incorporated in or that has its principal office and place of business in any place not subject to the jurisdiction of the United States; and

(iii) A partnership or other unincorporated organization or association that has its principal office and place of business in any place not subject to the jurisdiction of the United States.

(3) "Principal office and place of business" has the same meaning as in Rule 203A–3(c) of this chapter.

Rule 0–3. References to rules and regulations

The term "rules and regulations" refers to all rules and regulations adopted by the Commission pursuant to the Act, including the forms for registration and reports and the accompanying instructions thereto.

Rule 0–4. General requirements of papers and applications

(a) *Filings.* (1) All papers required to be filed with the Commission shall, unless otherwise provided by the rules and regulations, be delivered through the mails or otherwise to the Securities and Exchange Commission, Washington, DC 20549. Except as otherwise provided by the rules and regulations, such papers shall be deemed to have been filed with the Commission on the date when they are actually received by it.

(2) All filings required to be made electronically with the Investment Adviser Registration Depository ("IARD") shall, unless otherwise provided by the rules and regulations in this part, be deemed to have been filed with the Commission upon acceptance by the IARD. Filings required to be made through the IARD on a day that the IARD is closed shall be considered timely filed with the Commission if filed with the IARD no later than the following business day.

(3) Filings required to be made through the IARD during the period in December of each year that the IARD is not available for submission of filings shall be considered timely filed with the Commission if filed with the IARD no later than the following January 7.

NOTE TO PARAGRAPH (a)(3): Each year the IARD shuts down to filers for several days during the end of December to process renewals of state notice filings and registrations. During this period, advisers are not able to submit filings through the IARD. Check the Commission's Web site at *http://www.sec.gov/iard* for the dates of the annual IARD shutdown.

(b) *Formal Specifications Respecting Applications.* Every application for an order under any provision of the Act, for which a form with instructions is not specifically prescribed, and every amendment to such application, shall be filed in quintuplicate. One copy shall be signed by the applicant, but the other four copies may have facsimile or typed signatures. Such applications shall be on paper no larger than $8^1/_2$ x 11 inches in size. To the extent that the reduction of larger documents would render them illegible, those documents may be filed on paper larger than $8^1/_2$ x 11 inches in size. The left margin should be at least $1\frac{1}{2}$ inches wide and, if the application is bound, it should be bound on the left side. All typewritten or printed matter (including deficits in financial statements) should be set forth in black so as to permit photocopying and microfilming.

(c) *Authorization Respecting Applications.* (1) Every application for an order under any provision of the Act, for which a form with instructions is not specifically prescribed and which is executed by a corporation, partnership, or other company and filed with the Commission, shall contain a concise statement of the applicable provisions of the articles of incorporation, bylaws, or similar documents, relating to the right of the person signing and filing such application to take such action on behalf of the applicant, and a statement that all such requirements have been complied with and that the person signing and filing the same is fully authorized to do so. If such authorization is dependent on resolutions of stockholders, directors, or other bodies, such resolutions shall be attached as an exhibit to, or the pertinent provisions thereof shall be quoted in, the application.

(2) If an amendment to any such application shall be filed, such amendment shall contain a similar statement or, in lieu thereof, shall state that the authorization described in the original application is applicable to the individual who signs such amendment and that such authorization still remains in effect.

(3) When any such application or amendment is signed by an agent or attorney, the power of attorney evidencing his authority to sign shall contain similar statements and shall be filed with the Commission.

(d) *Verification of Applications and Statements of Fact.* Every application for an order under any provision of the Act, for which a form with instructions is not specifically prescribed and every amendment to such application, and every statement of fact formally filed in support of, or in opposition to, any application or declaration shall be verified by the person executing the same. An instrument executed on behalf of a corporation shall be verified in substantially the following form, but suitable changes may be made in such form for other kinds of companies and for individuals:

State of ________)
) ss.
County of ________)

The undersigned being duly sworn deposes and says that he has duly executed the attached ________ dated ________, 19__, for and on behalf of ________; that he is the

(Name of company)

________ of such company; and that all

(Title of officer)

action by stockholders, directors, and other bodies necessary to authorize deponent to execute and file such instrument has been taken. Deponent further says that he is familiar with such instrument, and the contents thereof, and that the facts therein set forth are true to the best of his knowledge, information and belief.

____
(Signature)

____
(Type or print name beneath)

Subscribed and sworn to before me a ________ this ________ day of ________, 19__.

(Title of Officer)

[Official Seal] ________

My commission expires

(e) *Statement of Grounds for Application.* Each application should contain a brief statement of the reasons why the applicant is deemed to be entitled to the action requested with a reference to the provisions of the Act and of the rules and regulations under which application is made.

(f) *Name and Address.* Every application shall contain the name and address of each applicant and the name and address of any person to whom any applicant wishes any question regarding the application to be directed.

(g) *Proposed Notice.* A proposed notice of the proceeding initiated by the filing of the application shall accompany each application as an exhibit thereto and, if necessary, shall be modified to reflect any amendments to such application.

(h) *Definition of Application.* For purposes of this rule, an "application" means any application for an order of the Commission under the Act other than an application for registration as an investment adviser.

(i) The manually signed original (or in the case of duplicate originals, one duplicate original) of all registrations, applications, statements, reports, or other documents filed under the Investment Advisers Act of 1940, as amended, shall be numbered sequentially (in addition to any internal numbering which otherwise may be present) by handwritten, typed, printed, or other legible form of notation from the facing page of the document through the last page of that document and any exhibits or attachments thereto. Further, the total number of pages contained in a numbered original shall be set forth on the first page of the document.

Rule 0–5. Procedure with respect to applications and other matters

The procedure hereinbelow set forth will be followed with respect to any proceeding initiated by the filing of an application, or upon the Commission's own motion, pursuant to any section of the Act or any rule or regulation thereunder, unless in the particular case a different procedure is provided:

(a) Notice of the initiation of the proceeding will be published in the Federal Register and will indicate the earliest date upon which an order disposing of the matter may be entered. The notice will also provide that any interested person may, within the period of time specified therein, submit to the Commission in writing any facts bearing upon the desirability of a hearing on the matter and may request that a hearing be held, stating his reasons therefor and the nature of his interest in the matter.

(b) An order disposing of the matter will be issued as of course following the expiration of the period of time referred to in paragraph (a), unless the Commission thereafter orders a hearing on the matter.

(c) The Commission will order a hearing on the matter, if it appears that a hearing is necessary or appropriate in the public interest or for the protection of investors, (1) upon the request of any interested person or (2) upon its own motion.

(d) *Definition of Application.* For purposes of this rule, an "application" means any application for an order of the Commission under the Act other than an application for registration as an investment adviser.

Rule 0–6. Incorporation by reference in applications

(a) A person filing an application may, subject to the limitations of 17 CFR 228.10(f) and Item 10(d) of Regulation S–K (17 CFR 229.10(d)), incorporate by reference as an exhibit to such application any document or part thereof, including any financial statement or part thereof, previously or concurrently filed with the Commission pursuant to any act administered by the Commission. The incorporation may be made whether the matter incorporated was filed by such applicant or any other person. If any modification has occurred in the text of any such document since the filing thereof, the applicant shall file with the reference a statement containing the text of any such modification and the date thereof. If the number of copies of any document previously or concurrently filed with the Commission is less than the number required to be filed with the application which incorporates such document, the applicant shall file therewith as many additional copies of the document as may be necessary to meet the requirements of the application.

(b) Notwithstanding paragraph (a) of this rule, a certificate of an independent public accountant or accountants previously or concurrently filed may not be incorporated by reference in any application unless the written consent of the accountant or accountants to such incorporation is filed with the application.

(c) In each case of incorporation by reference, the matter incorporated shall be clearly identified in the reference. An express statement shall be made to the effect that the specified matter is incorporated in the application at the particular place where the information is required.

(d) Notwithstanding paragraph (a) of this rule, no application shall incorporate by reference any exhibit or financial statement which (1) has been withdrawn, or (2) was filed under any act administered by the Commission in connection with a registration which has ceased to be effective, or (3) is contained in an application for registration, registration statement, or report subject, at the time of the incorporation by reference, to pending proceedings under Section 8(b) or 8(d) of the Securities Act of 1933, Section 8(e) of the Investment Company Act of 1940, Section 15(b)(4)(A) of the Securities Exchange Act of 1934, Section 203(e)(1) of the Act, or to an order entered under any of those Sections.

(e) Notwithstanding paragraph (a) of this rule, the Commission may refuse to permit incorporation by reference in any case in which in its judgment such incorporation would render an application incomplete, unclear, or confusing.

(f) *Definition of Application.* For purposes of this rule, an "application" means any application for an order of the Commission under the Act other than an application for registration as an investment adviser.

NOTE: Prior to incorporating by reference any document as an exhibit to an application, applicants are advised to review 17 CFR 228.10(f) and Item 10(d) of Regulation S–K (17 CFR 229.10(d)) as in effect at the time the application is filed to determine whether such incorporation by reference would be permissible under that rule.

Rule 0–7. Small entities under the Investment Advisers Act for purposes of the Regulatory Flexibility Act

(a) For purposes of Commission rulemaking in accordance with the provisions of Chapter Six of the Administrative Procedure Act [5 U.S.C. 601] and unless otherwise defined for purposes of a particular rulemaking proceeding, the term "small business" or "small organization" for purposes of the Investment Advisers Act of 1940 means an investment adviser that:

(1) Has assets under management, as defined under Section 203A(a)(3) of the Act (15 U.S.C. 80b–3a(a)(3)) and reported on its annual updating amendment to Form ADV [17 CFR 279.1], of less than $25 million, or such higher amount as the Commission may by rule deem appropriate under Section 203A(a)(1)(A) of the Act (15 U.S.C. 80b–3a(a)(1)(A));

(2) Did not have total assets of $5 million or more on the last day of the most recent fiscal year; and

(3) Does not control, is not controlled by, and is not under common control with another investment adviser that has assets under management of $25 million or more (or such higher amount as the Commission may deem appropriate), or any person (other than a natural person) that had total assets of $5 million or more on the last day of the most recent fiscal year.

(b) For purposes of this rule:

(1) *Control* means the power, directly or indirectly, to direct the management or policies of a person, whether through ownership of securities, by contract, or otherwise.

(i) A person is presumed to control a corporation if the person:

(A) Directly or indirectly has the right to vote 25 percent or more of the corporation's voting securities; or

(B) Has the power to sell or direct the sale of 25 percent or more of a class of the corporation's voting securities.

(ii) A person is presumed to control a partnership if the person has the right to receive upon dissolution, or has contributed, 25 percent or more of the capital of the partnership.

(iii) A person is presumed to control a limited liability company (LLC) if the person:

(A) Directly or indirectly has the right to vote 25 percent or more of a class of the interests of the LLC;

(B) Has the right to receive upon dissolution, or has contributed 25 percent or more of the capital of the LLC; or

(C) Is an elected manager of the LLC.

(iv) A person is presumed to control a trust if the person is a trustee or managing agent of the trust.

(2) *Total assets* means the total assets as shown on the balance sheet of the investment adviser or other person described above under paragraph (a)(3) of this rule, or the balance sheet of the investment adviser or such other person with its subsidiaries consolidated, whichever is larger.

Rule 202(a)(1)–1. Certain transactions not deemed assignments

A transaction which does not result in a change of actual control or management of an investment adviser is not an assignment for purposes of section 205(a)(2) of the Act.

Rule 202(a)(11)(G)–1. Family offices

(a) *Exclusion*. A family office, as defined in this section, shall not be considered to be an investment adviser for purpose of the Act.

(b) *Family Office*. A family office is a company (including its directors, partners, members, managers, trustees, and employees acting within the scope of their position or employment) that:

(1) Has no clients other than family clients; provided that if a person that is not a family client becomes a client of the family office as a result of the death of a family member or key employee or other involuntary transfer from a family member or key employee, that person shall be deemed to be a family client for purposes of this rule 202(a)(11)(G)–1 for one year following the completion of the transfer of legal title to the assets resulting from the involuntary event;

(2) Is wholly owned by family clients and is exclusively controlled (directly or indirectly) by one or more family members and/or family entities; and

(3) Does not hold itself out to the public as an investment adviser.

(c) *Grandfathering.* A family office as defined in paragraph (a) above shall not exclude any person, who was not registered or required to be registered under the Act on January 1, 2010, solely because such person provides investment advice to, and was engaged before January 1, 2010, in providing investment advice to:

(1) Natural persons who, at the time of their applicable investment, are officers, directors, or employees of the family office who have invested with the family office before January 1, 2010, and are accredited investors, as defined in Regulation D under the Securities Act of 1933;

(2) Any company owned exclusively and controlled by one or more family members; or

(3) Any investment adviser registered under the Act that provides investment advice to the family office and who identifies investment opportunities to the family office, and invests in such transactions on substantially the same terms as the family office invests, but does not invest in other funds advised by the family office, and whose assets as to which the family office directly or indirectly provides investment advice represents, in the aggregate, not more than 5 percent of the value of the total assets as to which the family office provides investment advice; provided that a family office that would not be a family office but for this subsection (c) shall be deemed to be an investment adviser for purposes of paragraphs (1), (2) and (4) of section 206 of the Act.

(d) *Definitions.* For purposes of this section:

(1) *Affiliated family office* means a family office wholly owned by family clients of another family office and that is controlled (directly or indirectly) by one or more family members of such other family office and/or family entities affiliated with such other family office and has no clients other than family clients of such other family office.

(2) *Control* means the power to exercise a controlling influence over the management or policies of a company, unless such power is solely the result of being an officer of such company.

(3) *Executive officer* means the president, any vice president in charge of a principal business unit, division or function (such as administration or finance), any other officer who performs a policy-making function, or any other person who performs similar policy-making functions, for the family office.

(4) *Family client* means:

(i) Any family member;

(ii) Any former family member;

(iii) Any key employee;

(iv) Any former key employee, provided that upon the end of such individual's employment by the family office, the former key employee shall not receive investment advice from the family office (or invest additional assets with a family office-advised trust, foundation or entity) other than with respect to assets advised (directly or indirectly) by the family office immediately prior to the end of such individual's employment, except that a former key employee shall be permitted to receive investment advice from the family office with respect to additional investments that the former key employee was contractually obligated to make, and that relate to a family-office advised investment existing, in each case prior to the time the person became a former key employee.

(v) Any non-profit organization, charitable foundation, charitable trust (including charitable lead trusts and charitable remainder trusts whose only current beneficiaries are other family clients and charitable or non-profit organizations), or other charitable organization, in each case for which all the funding such foundation, trust or organization holds came exclusively from one or more other family clients;

(vi) Any estate of a family member, former family member, key employee, or, subject to the condition contained in paragraph (d)(4)(iv) of this section, former key employee;

(vii) Any irrevocable trust in which one or more other family clients are the only current beneficiaries;

(viii) Any irrevocable trust funded exclusively by one or more other family clients in which other family clients and non-profit organizations, charitable foundations, charitable trusts, or other charitable organizations are the only current beneficiaries;

(ix) Any revocable trust of which one or more other family clients are the sole grantor;

(x) Any trust of which: (A) each trustee or other person authorized to make decisions with respect to the trust is a key employee; and (B) each settlor or other person who has contributed assets to the trust is a key employee or the key employee's current and/or former spouse or spousal equivalent who, at the time of contribution, holds a joint, community property, or other similar shared ownership interest with the key employee; or

(xi) Any company wholly owned (directly or indirectly) exclusively by, and operated for the sole benefit of, one or more other family clients; provided that if any such entity is a pooled investment vehicle, it is excepted from the definition of "investment company" under the Investment Company Act of 1940.

(5) *Family entity* means any of the trusts, estates, companies or other entities set forth in paragraphs (v), (vi), (vii), (viii), (ix), or (xi) of subsection (d)(4) of this section, but excluding key employees and their trusts from the definition of family client solely for purposes of this definition.

(6) *Family member* means all lineal descendants (including by adoption, stepchildren, foster children, and individuals that were a minor when another family member became a legal guardian of that individual) of a common ancestor (who may be living or deceased), and such lineal descendants' spouses or spousal equivalents; provided that the common ancestor is no more than 10 generations removed from the youngest generation of family members.

(7) *Former family member* means a spouse, spousal equivalent, or stepchild that was a family member but is no longer a family member due to a divorce or other similar event.

(8) *Key employee* means any natural person (including any key employee's spouse or spouse equivalent who holds a joint, community property, or other similar shared ownership interest with that key employee) who is an executive officer, director, trustee, general partner, or person serving in a similar capacity of the family office or its affiliated family office or any employee of the family office or its affiliated family office (other than an employee performing solely clerical, secretarial, or administrative functions with regard to the family office) who, in connection with his or her regular functions or duties, participates in the investment activities of the family office or affiliated family office, provided that such employee has been performing such functions and duties for or on behalf of the family office or affiliated family office, or substantially similar functions or duties for or on behalf of another company, for at least 12 months.

(9) *Spousal equivalent* means a cohabitant occupying a relationship generally equivalent to that of a spouse.

Rule 202(a)(30)-1. Foreign private advisers

(a) *Client*. You may deem the following to be a single client for purposes of section 202(a)(30) of the Act (15 U.S.C. 80b-2(a)(30)):

(1) A natural person, and:

(i) Any minor child of the natural person;

(ii) Any relative, spouse, spousal equivalent, or relative of the spouse or of the spousal equivalent of the natural person who has the same principal residence;

(iii) All accounts of which the natural person and/or the persons referred to in this paragraph (a)(1) are the only primary beneficiaries; and

(iv) All trusts of which the natural person and/or the persons referred to in this paragraph (a)(1) are the only primary beneficiaries;

(2)(i) A corporation, general partnership, limited partnership, limited liability company, trust (other than a trust referred to in paragraph (a)(1)(iv) of this section), or other legal organization (any of which are referred to hereinafter as a "legal organization") to which you provide investment advice based on its investment objectives rather than the individual investment objectives of its shareholders, partners, limited partners, members, or beneficiaries (any of which are referred to hereinafter as an "owner"); and

(ii) Two or more legal organizations referred to in paragraph (a)(2)(i) of this section that have identical owners.

(b) *Special Rules Regarding Clients*. For purposes of this section:

(1) You must count an owner as a client if you provide investment advisory services to the owner separate and apart from the investment advisory services you provide to the legal organization, provided, however, that the determination that an owner is a client will not affect the applicability of this section with regard to any other owner;

(2) You are not required to count an owner as a client solely because you, on behalf of the legal organization, offer, promote, or sell interests in the legal organization to the owner, or report periodi-

cally to the owners as a group solely with respect to the performance of or plans for the legal organization's assets or similar matters;

(3) A limited partnership or limited liability company is a client of any general partner, managing member or other person acting as investment adviser to the partnership or limited liability company;

(4) You are not required to count a private fund as a client if you count any investor, as that term is defined in paragraph (c)(2) of this section, in that private fund as an investor in the United States in that private fund; and

(5) You are not required to count a person as an investor, as that term is defined in paragraph (c)(2) of this section, in a private fund you advise if you count such person as a client in the United States.

NOTE TO PARAGRAPHS (a) AND (b): These paragraphs are a safe harbor and are not intended to specify the exclusive method for determining who may be deemed a single client for purposes of section 202(a)(30) of the Act (15 U.S.C. 80b–2(a)(30)).

(c) *Definitions.* For purposes of section 202(a)(30) of the Act (15 U.S.C. 80b–2(a)(30)):

(1) *Assets under management* means the regulatory assets under management as determined under Item 5.F of Form ADV (17 CFR 279.1).

(2) *Investor* means:

(i) Any person who would be included in determining the number of beneficial owners of the outstanding securities of a private fund under section 3(c)(1) of the Investment Company Act of 1940 (15 U.S.C. 80a–3(c)(1)), or whether the outstanding securities of a private fund are owned exclusively by qualified purchasers under section 3(c)(7) of that Act (15 U.S.C. 80a–3(c)(7)); and

(ii) Any beneficial owner of any outstanding short-term paper, as defined in section 2(a)(38) of the Investment Company Act of 1940 (15 U.S.C. 80a–2(a)(38)), issued by the private fund.

NOTE TO PARAGRAPH (c)(2): You may treat as a single investor any person who is an investor in two or more private funds you advise.

(3) *In the United States* means with respect to:

(i) Any client or investor, any person who is a U.S. person as defined in Rule 902(k) under the Securities Act of 1933, except that any discretionary account or similar account that is held for the benefit of a person in the United States by a dealer or other professional fiduciary is in the United States if the dealer or professional fiduciary is a related person, as defined in Rule 206(4)–2(d)(7), of the investment adviser relying on this section and is not organized, incorporated, or (if an individual) resident in the United States.

NOTE TO PARAGRAPH (c)(3)(i): A person who is in the United States may be treated as not being in the United States if such person was not in the United States at the time of becoming a client or, in the case of an investor in a private fund, each time the investor acquires securities issued by the fund.

(ii) Any place of business, in the United States, as that term is defined in Rule 902(*l*) under the Securities Act of 1933; and

(iii) The public, in the United States, as that term is defined in Rule 902(*l*) under the Securities Act of 1933.

(4) *Place of business* has the same meaning as in Rule 222–1(a).

(5) *Spousal equivalent* has the same meaning as in Rule 202(a)(11)(G)–1(d)(9).

(d) *Holding Out.* If you are relying on this section, you shall not be deemed to be holding yourself out generally to the public in the United States as an investment adviser, within the meaning of section 202(a)(30) of the Act (15 U.S.C. 80b–2(a)(30)), solely because you participate in a non-public offering in the United States of securities issued by a private fund under the Securities Act of 1933 (15 U.S.C. 77a).

Rule 203–1. Application for investment adviser registration

(a) *Form ADV.* To apply for registration with the Commission as an investment adviser, you must complete Form ADV [17 CFR 279.1] by following the instructions in the form and you must file Part 1A of Form ADV and the firm brochure(s) required by Part 2A of Form ADV electronically with the Investment Adviser Registration Depository (IARD) unless you have received a hardship exemption under Rule 203–3. You are not required to file with the Commission the brochure supplements required by Part 2B of Form ADV.

NOTE TO PARAGRAPH (a): Information on how to file with the IARD is available on the Commission's website *at www.sec.gov/iard*. If you are not required to deliver a brochure to any clients, you are not required to prepare or file a brochure with the Commission. If you are not required to deliver a brochure supplement to any clients for any particular supervised person, you are not required to prepare a brochure supplement for that supervised person.

(b) *When Filed.* Each Form ADV is considered filed with the Commission upon acceptance by the IARD.

(c) *Filing Fees.* You must pay FINRA (the operator of the IARD) a filing fee. The Commission has approved the amount of the filing fee. No portion of the filing fee is refundable. Your completed application for registration will not be accepted by FINRA, and thus will not be considered filed with the Commission, until you have paid the filing fee.

Rule 203–2. Withdrawal from investment adviser registration

(a) *Form ADV–W.* You must file Form ADV–W [17 CFR 279.2] to withdraw from investment adviser registration with the Commission (or to withdraw a pending registration application).

(b) *Electronic Filing.* Once you have filed your Form ADV [17 CFR 279.1] (or any amendments to Form ADV) electronically with the investment Adviser Registration Depository (IARD), any Form ADV–W you file must be filed with the IARD, unless you have received a hardship exemption under Rule 203–3.

(c) *Effective Date—Upon Filing.* Each Form ADV–W filed under this section is effective upon acceptance by the IARD, provided however that your investment adviser registration will continue for a period of sixty days after acceptance solely for the purpose of commencing a proceeding under section 203(e) of the Act.

(d) *Filing Fees.* You do not have to pay a fee to file Form ADV–W through the IARD.

(e) *Form ADV–W Is a Report.* Each Form ADV–W required to be filed under this section is a "report" within the meaning of sections 204 and 207 of the Act.

Rule 203–3. Hardship exemptions

This section provides two "hardship exemptions" from the requirement to make Advisers Act filings electronically with the Investment Adviser Registration Depository (IARD).

(a) *Temporary Hardship Exemption.* (1) *Eligibility for Exemption.* If you are registered with the Commission as an investment adviser and submit electronic filings on the Investment Adviser Registration Depository (IARD) system, but have unanticipated technical difficulties that prevent you from submitting a filing to the IARD system, you may request a temporary hardship exemption from the requirements of this chapter to file electronically.

(2) *Application Procedures.* To request a temporary hardship exemption, you must:

(i) File Form ADV–H [17 CFR 279.3] in paper format with NASD no later than one business day after the filing that is the subject of the ADV–H was due; and

(ii) Submit the filing that is the subject of the Form ADV–H in electronic format with the IARD no later than seven business days after the filing was due.

(3) *Effective Date—Upon Filing.* The temporary hardship exemption will be granted when you file a completed Form ADV–H with NASD.

(b) *Continuing Hardship Exemption.* (1) *Eligibility for Exemption.* If you are a "small business" (as described in paragraph (b)(5) of this rule), you may apply for a continuing hardship exemption. The period of the exemption may be no longer than one year after the date on which you apply for the exemption.

(2) *Application Procedures.* To apply for a continuing hardship exemption, you must file Form ADV–H with NASD at least ten business days before a filing is due. The Commission will grant or deny your application within ten business days after you file Form ADV–H.

(3) *Effective Date—Upon Approval.* You are not exempt from the electronic filing requirements until and unless the Commission approves your application. If the Commission approves your application, you may submit your filings to FINRA in paper format for the period of time for which the exemption is granted.

(4) *Criteria for Exemption.* Your application will be granted only if you are able to demonstrate that the electronic filing requirements of this chapter are prohibitively burdensome or expensive.

(5) *Small Business.* You are a "small business" for purposes of this rule if you are required to answer Item 12 of Form ADV [17 CFR 279.1] and checked "no" to each question in Item 12 that you were required to answer.

NOTE TO PARAGRAPH (b): FINRA will charge you an additional fee covering its cost to convert to electronic format a filing made in reliance on a continuing hardship exemption.

Rule 203(*l*)–1. Venture capital fund defined

(a) *Venture capital fund defined.* For purposes of section 203(l) of the Act (15. U.S.C. 80b–3(l)), a venture capital fund is any entity described in subparagraph (A), (B), or (C) of section 203(b)(7) of the Act (15 U.S.C. 80b–3(b)(7)) (other than an entity that has elected to be regulated or is regulated as a business development company pursuant to section 54 of the Investment Company Act of 1940 (15 U.S.C. 80a–53)) or any private fund that:

(1) Represents to investors and potential investors that it pursues a venture capital strategy;

(2) Immediately after the acquisition of any asset, other than qualifying investments or short-term holdings, holds no more than 20 percent of the amount of the fund's aggregate capital contributions and uncalled committed capital in assets (other than short-term holdings) that are not qualifying investments, valued at cost or fair value, consistently applied by the fund;

(3) Does not borrow, issue debt obligations, provide guarantees or otherwise incur leverage, in excess of 15 percent of the private fund's aggregate capital contributions and uncalled committed capital, and any such borrowing, indebtedness, guarantee or leverage is for a non-renewable term of no longer than 120 calendar days, except that any guarantee by the private fund of a qualifying portfolio company's obligations up to the amount of the value of the private fund's investment in the qualifying portfolio company is not subject to the 120 calendar day limit;

(4) Only issues securities the terms of which do not provide a holder with any right, except in extraordinary circumstances, to withdraw, redeem or require the repurchase of such securities but may entitle holders to receive distributions made to all holders pro rata; and

(5) Is not registered under section 8 of the Investment Company Act of 1940 (15 U.S.C. 80a–8), and has not elected to be treated as a business development company pursuant to section 54 of that Act (15 U.S.C. 80a–53).

(b) *Certain Pre–Existing Venture Capital Funds.* For purposes of section 203(*l*) of the Act (15 U.S.C. 80b–3(*l*)) and in addition to any venture capital fund as set forth in paragraph (a) of this section, a venture capital fund also includes any private fund that:

(1) Has represented to investors and potential investors at the time of the offering of the private fund's securities that it pursues a venture capital strategy;

(2) Prior to December 31, 2010, has sold securities to one or more investors that are not related persons, as defined in Rule 206(4)–2(d)(7), of any investment adviser of the private fund; and

(3) Does not sell any securities to (including accepting any committed capital from) any person after July 21, 2011.

(c) *Definitions.* For purposes of this section:

(1) *Committed capital* means any commitment pursuant to which a person is obligated to:

(i) Acquire an interest in the private fund; or

(ii) Make capital contributions to the private fund.

(2) *Equity security* has the same meaning as in section 3(a)(11) of the Securities Exchange Act of 1934 (15 U.S.C. 78c(a)(11)) and Rule 3a11–1 under the Securities Exchange Act of 1934.

(3) *Qualifying investment* means:

(i) An equity security issued by a qualifying portfolio company that has been acquired directly by the private fund from the qualifying portfolio company;

(ii) Any equity security issued by a qualifying portfolio company in exchange for an equity security issued by the qualifying portfolio company described in paragraph (c)(3)(i) of this section; or

(iii) Any equity security issued by a company of which a qualifying portfolio company is a majority-owned subsidiary, as defined in section 2(a)(24) of the Investment Company Act of 1940 (15 U.S.C. 80a–2(a)(24)), or a predecessor, and is acquired by the private fund in exchange for an equity security described in paragraph (c)(3)(i) or (c)(3)(ii) of this section.

(4) *Qualifying portfolio company* means any company that:

(i) At the time of any investment by the private fund, is not reporting or foreign traded and does not control, is not controlled by or under common control with another company, directly or indirectly, that is reporting or foreign traded;

(ii) Does not borrow or issue debt obligations in connection with the private fund's investment in such company and distribute to the private fund the proceeds of such borrowing or issuance in exchange for the private fund's investment; and

(iii) Is not an investment company, a private fund, an issuer that would be an investment company but for the exemption provided by Rule 3a–7 of Investment Company Act, or a commodity pool.

(5) *Reporting or foreign traded* means, with respect to a company, being subject to the reporting requirements under section 13 or 15(d) of the Securities Exchange Act of 1934 (15 U.S.C. 78m or 78o(d)), or having a security listed or traded on any exchange or organized market operating in a foreign jurisdiction.

(6) *Short-term holdings* means cash and cash equivalents, as defined in Rule 2a51–1(b)(7)(i) under the Investment Company Act, U.S. Treasuries with a remaining maturity of 60 days or less, and shares of an open-end management investment company registered under section 8 of the Investment Company Act of 1940 (15 U.S.C. 80a–8) that is regulated as a money market fund under Rule 2a–7 under the Investment Company Act of 1940.

NOTE: For purposes of this section, an investment adviser may treat as a private fund any issuer formed under the laws of a jurisdiction other than the United States that has not offered or sold its securities in the United States or to U.S. persons in a manner inconsistent with being a private fund, provided that the adviser treats the issuer as a private fund under the Act (15 U.S.C. 80b) and the rules thereunder for all purposes.

Rule 203(m)–1. Private fund adviser exemption

(a) *United States Investment Advisers.* For purposes of section 203(m) of the Act (15 U.S.C. 80b–3(m)), an investment adviser with its principal office and place of business in the United States is exempt from the requirement to register under section 203 of the Act if the investment adviser:

(1) Acts solely as an investment adviser to one or more qualifying private funds; and

(2) Manages private fund assets of less than $150 million.

(b) *Non-United States Investment Advisers.* For purposes of section 203(m) of the Act (15 U.S.C. 80b–3(m)), an investment adviser with its principal office and place of business outside of the United States is exempt from the requirement to register under section 203 of the Act if:

(1) The investment adviser has no client that is a United States person except for one or more qualifying private funds; and

(2) All assets managed by the investment adviser at a place of business in the United States are solely attributable to private fund assets, the total value of which is less than $150 million.

(c) *Frequency of Calculations.* For purposes of this section, calculate private fund assets annually, in accordance with General Instruction 15 to Form ADV (17 CFR 279.1).

(d) *Definitions.* For purposes of this section:

(1) *Assets under management* means the regulatory assets under management as determined under Item 5.F of Form ADV (17 CFR 279.1) except that the regulatory assets under management attributable to a private fund that is an entity described in subparagraph (A), (B), or (C) of section 203(b)(7) of the Act (15 U.S.C. 80b–3(b)(7)) (other than an entity that has elected to be regulated or is regulated as a business development company pursuant to section 54 of the Investment Company Act of 1940 (15 U.S.C. 80a–53)) shall be excluded from the definition of assets under management for purposes of this section.

(2) *Place of business* has the same meaning as in Rule 222–1(a).

(3) *Principal office and place of business* of an investment adviser means the executive office of the investment adviser from which the officers, partners, or managers of the investment adviser direct, control, and coordinate the activities of the investment adviser.

(4) *Private fund assets* means the investment adviser's assets under management attributable to a qualifying private fund.

(5) *Qualifying private fund* means any private fund that is not registered under section 8 of the Investment Company Act of 1940 (15 U.S.C. 80a–8) and has not elected to be treated as a business development company pursuant to section 54 of that Act (15 U.S.C. 80a–53). For purposes of this section, an investment adviser may treat as a private fund an issuer that qualifies for an exclusion from the definition of an "investment company," as defined in section 3 of the Investment Company Act of 1940 (15 U.S.C. 80a–3), in addition to those provided by section 3(c)(1) or 3(c)(7) of that Act (15 U.S.C. 80a–3(c)(1) or 15 U.S.C. 80a–3(c)(7)), provided that the investment adviser treats the issuer as a private fund under the Act (15 U.S.C. 80b) and the rules thereunder for all purposes.

(6) *Related person* has the same meaning as in Rule 206(4)–2(d)(7).

(7) *United States* has the same meaning as in Rule 902(*l*) under the Securities Act of 1933.

(8) *United States person* means any person that is a U.S. person as defined in Rule 902(k) under the Securities Act of 1933, except that any discre-

tionary account or similar account that is held for the benefit of a United States person by a dealer or other professional fiduciary is a United States person if the dealer or professional fiduciary is a related person of the investment adviser relying on this section and is not organized, incorporated, or (if an individual) resident in the United States.

NOTE TO PARAGRAPH (d)(8): A client will not be considered a United States person if the client was not a United States person at the time of becoming a client.

Rule 203A–1. Eligibility for SEC registration: switching to or from SEC registration

(a) *Eligibility for SEC Registration of Mid-Sized Investment Advisers*. If you are an investment adviser described in section 203A(a)(2)(B) of the Act (15 U.S.C. 80b–3a(a)(2)(B)):

(1) *Threshold for SEC Registration and Registration Buffer*. You may, but are not required to register with the Commission if you have assets under management of at least $100,000,000 but less than $110,000,000, and you need not withdraw your registration unless you have less than $90,000,000 of assets under management.

(2) *Exceptions*. This paragraph (a) does not apply if:

(i) You are an investment adviser to an investment company registered under the Investment Company Act of 1940 (15 U.S.C. 80a) or to a company which has elected to be a business development company pursuant to section 54 of the Investment Company Act of 1940 (15 U.S.C. 80a–54), and has not withdrawn the election; or

(ii) You are eligible for an exemption described in Rule 203A–2.

(b) *Switching to or from SEC Registration*—

(1) State-Registered Advisers—Switching to SEC Registration. If you are registered with a state securities authority, you must apply for registration with the Commission within 90 days of filing an annual updating amendment to your Form ADV reporting that you are eligible for SEC registration and are not relying on an exemption from registration under sections 203(*l*) or 203(m) of the Act (15 U.S.C. 80b–3(*l*), (m)).

(2) *SEC-Registered Advisers—Switching to State Registration*. If you are registered with the Commission and file an annual updating amendment to your Form ADV reporting that you are not eligible for SEC registration and are not relying on an exemption from registration under sections 203(*l*) or 203(m) of the Act (15 U.S.C. 80b–3(*l*), (m)), you must file Form ADV–W (17 CFR 279.2) to withdraw your SEC registration within 180 days of your fiscal year end (unless you then are eligible for SEC registration). During this period while you are registered with both the Commission and one or more state securities authorities, the Act and applicable State law will apply to your advisory activities.

Rule 203A–2. Exemptions from prohibition on SEC Registration

The prohibition of section 203A(a) of the Act does not apply to:

(a) *Pension Consultants*.

(1) An investment adviser that is a "pension consultant," as defined in this rule, with respect to assets of plans having an aggregate value of at least $200,000,000.

(2) An investment adviser is a pension consultant, for purposes of paragraph (a) of this rule, if the investment adviser provides investment advice to:

(i) Any employee benefit plan described in section 3(3) of the Employee Retirement Income Security Act of 1974 ("ERISA") (29 U.S.C. 1002(3));

(ii) Any governmental plan described in section 3(32) of ERISA (29 U.S.C. 1002(32)); or

(iii) Any church plan described in section 3(33) of ERISA (29 U.S.C. 1002(33));

(3) In determining the aggregate value of assets of plans, include only that portion of a plan's assets for which the investment adviser provided investment advise (including any advice with respect to the selection of an investment adviser to manage such assets). Determine the aggregate value of assets by cumulating the value of assets of plans with respect to which the investment adviser was last employed or retained by contract to provide investment advice during a 12–month period ended within 90 days of filing Schedule I to Form ADV (17 CFR 279.1).

(b) *Investment Advisers Controlling, Controlled by, or Under Common Control with an Investment Adviser Registered with the Commission*. An investment adviser that controls, is controlled by, or is under common control with, an investment adviser eligible to register and registered with, the Commission ("registered adviser"), provided that the principal office and place of business of the investment adviser is the same as that of the registered adviser. For purposes of this paragraph, control means the power to direct or cause the direction of the management or policies of an investment adviser, whether through ownership of securities, by contract, or otherwise. Any person that directly or indirectly has the right to vote 25 percent or more of the voting securities, or is entitled to 25 percent or more of the profits, of an investment adviser is presumed to control that investment adviser.

(c) *Investment Advisers Expecting to be Eligible for SEC Registration Within 120 Days.* An investment adviser that:

(1) Immediately before it registers with the Commission, is not registered or required to be registered with the Commission or a state securities authority of any State and has a reasonable expectation that it would be eligible to register with the Commission within 120 days after the date the investment adviser's registration with the Commission becomes effective;

(2) Indicates on Schedule D of its Form ADV [17 CFR 279.1] that it will withdraw from registration with the Commission if, on the 120th day after the date the investment adviser's registration with the Commission becomes effective, the investment adviser would be prohibited by section 203A(a) of the Act [15 U.S.C. 80b–3a(a)] from registering with the Commission; and

(3) Notwithstanding Rule 203A–1(b)(2) of this chapter, files a completed Form ADV–W [17 CFR 279.2] withdrawing from registration with the Commission within 120 days after the date the investment adviser's registration with the Commission becomes effective.

(d) *Multi-State Investment Advisers.* An investment adviser that:

(1) Upon submission of its application for registration with the Commission, is required by the laws of 15 or more States to register as an investment adviser with the state securities authority in the respective States, and thereafter would, but for this section, be required by the laws of at least 15 States to register as an investment adviser with the state securities authority in the respective States;

(2) Elects to rely on paragraph (d) of this section by:

(i) Indicating on Schedule D of its Form ADV that the investment adviser has reviewed the applicable State and federal laws and has concluded that, in the case of an application for registration with the Commission, it is required by the laws of 15 or more States to register as an investment adviser with the state securities authorities in the respective States or, in the case of an amendment to Form ADV, it would be required by the laws of at least 15 States to register as an investment adviser with the state securities authorities in the respective States, within 90 days prior to the date of filing Form ADV; and

(ii) Undertaking on Schedule D of its Form ADV to withdraw from registration with the Commission if the adviser indicates on an annual updating amendment to Form ADV that the investment adviser would be required by the laws of fewer than 15 States to register as an investment adviser with the state securities authority in the respective States, and that the investment adviser would be prohibited by section 203A(a) of the Act (15 U.S.C. 80b–3a(a)) from registering with the Commission, by filing a completed Form ADV–W within 180 days of the adviser's fiscal year end (unless the adviser then is eligible for SEC registration); and

(3) Maintains in an easily accessible place a record of the States in which the investment adviser has determined it would, but for the exemption, be required to register for a period of not less than five years from the filing of a Form ADV that includes a representation that is based on such record.

(e) *Internet Investment Advisers.*

(1) An investment adviser that:

(i) Provides investment advice to all of its clients exclusively through an interactive website, except that the investment adviser may provide investment advice to fewer than 15 clients through other means during the preceding twelve months;

(ii) Maintains, in an easily accessible place, for a period of not less than five years from the filing of a Form ADV that includes a representation that the adviser is eligible to register with the Commission under paragraph (e) of this rule, a record demonstrating that it provides investment advise to it clients exclusively through an interactive website in accordance with the limits in paragraph (e)(1)(i) of this rule; and

(iii) Does not control, is not controlled by, and is not under common control with, another investment adviser that registers with the Commission under paragraph (b) of this rule solely in reliance on the adviser registered under paragraph (e) of this rule as its registered adviser.

(2) For purposes of paragraph (e) of this rule, interactive website means a website in which computer software-based models or applications provide investment advice to clients based on personal information each client supplies through the website.

(3) An investment adviser may rely on the definition of client in Rule 202(a)(30)–1 in determining whether it provides investment advice to fewer than 15 clients under paragraph (e)(1)(i) of this rule.

Rule 203A–3. Definitions

For purposes of section 203A of the Act (15 U.S.C. 80b–3a) and the rules thereunder:

(a)(1) *Investment Adviser Representative.* "Investment Adviser Representative" of an investment adviser means a supervised person of the investment adviser:

(i) Who has more than five clients who are natural persons (other than excepted persons described in paragraph (a)(3)(i) of this rule); and

(ii) More than ten percent of whose clients are natural persons (other than excepted persons described in paragraph (a)(3)(i) of this rule).

(2) Notwithstanding paragraph (a)(1) of this rule, a supervised person is not an investment adviser representative if the supervised person:

(i) Does not on a regular basis solicit, meet with, or otherwise communicate with clients of the investment adviser; or

(ii) Provides only impersonal investment advice.

(3) For purposes of this rule:

(i) "Excepted person" means a natural person who is a qualified client as described in Rule 205–3(d)(1).

(ii) "Impersonal investment advice" means investment advisory services provided by means of written material or oral statements that do not purport to meet the objectives or needs of specific individuals or accounts.

(4) Supervised persons may rely on the definition of "client" in Rule 202(a)(30)–1 to identify clients for purposes of paragraph (a)(1) of this section, except that supervised persons need not count clients that are not residents of the United States.

(b) *Place of Business.* "Place of business" of an investment adviser representative means:

(1) An office at which the investment adviser representative regularly provides investment advisory services, solicits, meets with, or otherwise communicates with clients; and

(2) Any other location that is held out to the general public as a location at which the investment adviser representative provides investment advisory services, solicits, meets with, or otherwise communicates with clients.

(c) *Principal Office and Place of Business.* "Principal office and place of business" of an investment adviser means the executive office of the investment adviser from which the officers, partners, or managers of the investment adviser direct, control, and coordinate the activities of the investment adviser.

(d) *Assets under Management.* Determine "assets under management" by calculating the securities portfolios with respect to which an investment adviser provides continuous and regular supervisory or management services as reported on the investment adviser's Form ADV (17 CFR 279.1).

(e) *State Securities Authority.* "State securities authority" means the securities commissioner or commission (or any agency, office or officer performing like functions) of any State.

Rule 203A–4. [Reserved]

Rule 203A–5. [Reserved]

Rule 204–1. Amendments to Form ADV

(a) *When Amendment Is Required.* You must amend your Form ADV [17 CFR 279.1]:

(1) At least annually, within 90 days of the end of your fiscal year; and

(2) More frequently, if required by the instructions to Form ADV.

(b) *Electronic Filing of Amendments.*

(1) You must file all amendments to Part 1A of Form ADV and Part 2A of Form ADV electronically with the IARD, unless you have received a continuing hardship exemption under Rule 203–3. You are not required to file with the Commission amendments to brochure supplements required by Part 2B of Form ADV.

(2) If you have received a continuing hardship exemption under Rule 203–3, you must, when you are required to amend your Form ADV, file a completed Part 1A and Part 2A of Form ADV on paper with the SEC by mailing it to FINRA.

NOTE TO PARAGRAPHS (a) AND (b): Information on how to file with the IARD is available on our website at www.sec.gov/iard. For the annual updating amendment: summaries of material changes that are not included in the adviser's brochure must be filed with the Commission as an exhibit to Part 2A in the same electronic file; and if you are not required to prepare a brochure, a summary of material changes, or an annual updating amendment to your brochure, you are not required to file them with the Commission. See the instructions for Part 2A of Form ADV.

(c) *Filing Fees.* You must pay FINRA (the operator of the IARD) an initial filing fee when you first electronically file Part 1A of Form ADV. After you pay the initial filing fee, you must pay an annual filing fee each time you file your annual updating amendment. No portion of either fee is refundable. The Commission has approved the filing fees. Your amended Form ADV will not be accepted by FINRA, and thus will not be considered filed with the Commission, until you have paid the filing fee.

(d) *Amendments to Form ADV Are Reports.* Each amendment required to be filed under this section is a "report" within the meaning of sections 204 and 207 of the Act.

Rule 204–2. Books and records to be maintained by investment advisers

(a) Every investment adviser registered or required to be registered under section 203 of the Act (15 U.S.C. 80b–3) shall make and keep true, accurate and current the following books and records relating to its investment advisory business:

(1) A journal or journals, including cash receipts and disbursements, records, and any other records of original entry forming the basis of entries in any ledger.

(2) General and auxiliary ledgers (or other comparable records) reflecting asset, liability, reserve, capital, income and expense accounts.

(3) A memorandum of each order given by the investment adviser for the purchase or sale of any security, of any instruction received by the investment adviser concerning the purchase, sale, receipt or delivery of a particular security, and of any modification or cancellation of any such order or instruction. Such memoranda shall show the terms and conditions of the order, instruction, modification or cancellation; shall identify the person connected with the investment adviser who recommended the transaction to the client and the person who placed such order; and shall show the account for which entered, the date of entry, and the bank, broker or dealer by or through whom executed where appropriate. Orders entered pursuant to the exercise of discretionary power shall be so designated.

(4) All check books, bank statements, cancelled checks and cash reconciliations of the investment adviser.

(5) All bills or statements (or copies thereof), paid or unpaid, relating to the business of the investment adviser as such.

(6) All trial balances, financial statements, and internal audit working papers relating to the business of such investment adviser.

(7) Originals of all written communications received and copies of all written communications sent by such investment adviser relating to:

(i) Any recommendation made or proposed to be made and any advice given or proposed to be given;

(ii) Any receipt, disbursement or delivery of funds or securities;

(iii) The placing or execution of any order to purchase or sell any security;

(iv) The performance or rate of return of any or all managed accounts or securities recommendations: *Provided, however*:

(A) That the investment adviser shall not be required to keep any unsolicited market letters and other similar communications of general public distribution not prepared by or for the investment adviser, and

(B) That if the investment adviser sends any notice, circular or other advertisement offering any report, analysis, publication or other investment advisory service to more than 10 persons, the investment adviser shall not be required to keep a record of the names and addresses of the persons to whom it was sent; except that if such notice, circular or advertisement is distributed to persons named on any list, the investment adviser shall retain with the copy of such notice, circular or advertisement a memorandum describing the list and the source thereof.

(8) A list or other record of all accounts in which the investment adviser is vested with any discretionary power with respect to the funds, securities or transactions of any client.

(9) All powers of attorney and other evidences of the granting of any discretionary authority by any client to the investment adviser, or copies thereof.

(10) All written agreements (or copies thereof) entered into by the investment adviser with any client or otherwise relating to the business of such investment adviser as such.

(11) A copy of each notice, circular, advertisement, newspaper article, investment letter, bulletin or other communication that the investment adviser circulates or distributes, directly or indirectly, to 10 or more persons (other than persons connected with such investment adviser), and if such notice, circular, advertisement, newspaper article, investment letter, bulletin, or other communication recommends the purchase or sale of a specific security and does not state the reasons for such recommendation, a memorandum of the investment adviser indicating the reasons therefor.

(12)(i) A copy of the investment adviser's code of ethics adopted and implemented pursuant to Rule 204A–1 that is in effect, or at any time within the past five years was in effect;

(ii) A record of any violation of the code of ethics, and of any action taken as a result of the violation; and

(iii) A record of all written acknowledgments as required by Rule 204A–1(a)(5) for each person who is currently, or within the past five years was, a supervised person of the investment adviser.

(13)(i) A record of each report made by an access person as required by Rule 204A–1(b), including any information provided under paragraph (b)(3)(iii) of that rule in lieu of such reports;

(ii) A record of the names of persons who are currently, or within the past five years were, access persons of the investment adviser; and

(iii) A record of any decision, and the reasons supporting the decision, to approve the acquisition of securities by access persons under Rule 204A–1(c), for at least five years after the end of the fiscal year in which the approval is granted.

(14)(i) A copy of each brochure and brochure supplement, and each amendment or revision to the brochure and brochure supplement, that satisfies the requirements of Part 2 of Form ADV (17 CFR 279.1); any summary of material changes that satisfies the requirements of Part 2 of Form ADV but is not contained in the brochure; and a record of the dates that each brochure and brochure supplement, each amendment or revision thereto, and each summary of material changes not contained in a brochure was given to any client or to any prospective client who subsequently becomes a client.

(ii) Documentation describing the method used to compute managed assets for purposes of Item 4.E of Part 2A of Form ADV, if the method differs from the method used to compute regulatory assets under management in Item 5.F of Part 1A of Form ADV.

(iii) A memorandum describing any legal or disciplinary event listed in Item 9 of Part 2A or Item 3 of Part 2B (Disciplinary Information) and presumed to be material, if the event involved the investment adviser or any of its supervised persons and is not disclosed in the brochure or brochure supplement described in paragraph (a)(14)(i) of this section. The memorandum must explain the investment adviser's determination that the described in Item 9 of Part 2A of Form ADV or Item 3 of Part 2B of Form ADV.

(15) All written acknowledgements of receipt obtained from clients pursuant to Rule 206(4)–3(a)(2)(iii)(B) and copies of the disclosure documents delivered to clients by solicitors pursuant to Rule 206(4)–3.

(16) All accounts, books, internal working papers, and any other records or documents that are necessary to form the basis for or demonstrate the calculation of the performance or rate of return of any or all managed accounts or securities recommendations in any notice, circular, advertisement, newspaper article, investment letter, bulletin or other communication that the investment adviser circulates or distributes, directly or indirectly, to any person. (other than persons connected with such investment adviser); provided, however, that, with respect to the performance of managed accounts, the retention of all account statements, if they reflect all debits, credits, and other transactions in a client's account for the period of the statement, and all worksheets necessary to demonstrate the calculation of the performance or rate of return of all managed accounts shall be deemed to satisfy the requirements of this paragraph.

(17)(i) A copy of the investment adviser's policies and procedures formulated pursuant to Rule 206(4)–7(a) that are in effect, or at any time within the past five years were in effect;

(ii) Any records documenting the investment adviser's annual review of those policies and procedures conducted pursuant to Rule 206(4)–7(b) of this chapter;

(iii) A copy of any internal control report obtained or received pursuant to Rule 206(4)–2.

(18)(i) Books and records that pertain to Rule 206(4)–5 containing a list or other record of:

(A) The names, titles and business and residence addresses of all covered associates of the investment adviser;

(B) All government entities to which the investment adviser provides or has provided investment advisory services, or which are or were investors in any covered investment pool to which the investment adviser provides or has provided investment advisory services, as applicable, in the past five years, but not prior to September 13, 2010;

(C) All direct or indirect contributions made by the investment adviser or any of its covered associates to an official of a government entity, or direct or indirect payments to a political party of a state or political subdivision thereof, or to a political action committee; and

(D) The name and business address of each regulated person to whom the investment adviser provides or agrees to provide, directly or indirectly, payment to solicit a government entity for investment advisory services on its behalf, in accordance with Rule 206(4)–5(a)(2).

(ii) Records relating to the contributions and payments referred to in paragraph (a)(18)(i)(C) of this section must be listed in chronological order and indicate:

(A) The name and title of each contributor;

(B) The name and title (including any city/county/state or other political subdivision) of each recipient of a contribution or payment;

(C) The amount and date of each contribution or payment; and

(D) Whether any such contribution was the subject of the exception for certain returned contributions pursuant to Rule 206(4)–5(b)(2).

(iii) An investment adviser is only required to make and keep current the records referred to in paragraphs (a)(18)(i)(A) and (C) of this section if it provides investment advisory services to a government entity or a government entity is an investor in any covered investment pool to which the investment adviser provides investment advisory services.

(iv) For purposes of this section, the terms "contribution," "covered associate," "covered investment pool," "government entity," "official," "payment," "regulated person," and "solicit" have the same meanings as set forth in Rule 206(4)–5.

(b) If an investment adviser subject to paragraph (a) of this rule has custody or possession of securities or funds of any client, the records required to be made and kept under paragraph (a) of this rule shall include:

(1) A journal or other record showing all purchases, sales, receipts and deliveries of securities (including certificate numbers) for such accounts and all other debits and credits to such accounts.

(2) A separate ledger account for each such client showing all purchases, sales, receipts and deliveries of securities, the date and price of each purchase and sale, and all debits and credits.

(3) Copies of confirmations of all transactions effected by or for the account of any such client.

(4) A record for each security in which any such client has a position, which record shall show the name of each such client having any interest in such security, the amount or interest of each such client, and the location of each such security.

(5) A memorandum describing the basis upon which you have determined that the presumption that any related person is not operationally independent under Rule 206(4)–2(d)(5) has been overcome.

(c)(1) Every investment adviser subject to paragraph (a) of this rule who renders any investment supervisory or management service to any client shall, with respect to the portfolio being supervised or managed and to the extent that the information is reasonably available to or obtainable by the investment adviser, make and keep true, accurate and current:

(i) Records showing separately for each such client the securities purchased and sold, and the date, amount and price of each such purchase and sale.

(ii) For each security in which any such client has a current position, information from which the investment adviser can promptly furnish the name of each such client, and the current amount or interest of such client.

(2) Every investment adviser subject to paragraph (a) of this rule that exercises voting authority with respect to client securities shall, with respect to those clients, make and retain the following:

(i) Copies of all policies and procedures by Rule 206(4)–6.

(ii) A copy of each proxy statement that the investment adviser receives regarding client securities. An investment adviser may satisfy this requirement by relying on a third party to make and retain, on the investment adviser's behalf, a copy of a proxy statement (provided that the adviser has obtained an undertaking from the third party to provide a copy of the proxy statement promptly upon request) or may rely on obtaining a copy of a proxy statement from the Commission's Electronic Data Gathering, Analysis, and Retrieval (EDGAR) system.

(iii) A record of each vote cast by the investment adviser on behalf of a client. An investment adviser may satisfy this requirement by relying on a third party to make and retain, on the investment adviser's behalf, a record of the vote cast (provided that the adviser has obtained an undertaking from the third party to provide a copy of the record promptly upon request).

(iv) A copy of any document created by the adviser that was material to making a decision how to vote proxies on behalf of a client or that memorializes the basis for that decision.

(v) A copy of each written client request for information on how the adviser voted proxies on behalf of the client, and a copy of any written response by the investment adviser to any (written or oral) client request for information on how the adviser voted proxies on behalf of the requesting client.

(d) Any books or records required by this section may be maintained by the investment adviser in such manner that the identity of any client to whom such investment adviser renders investment supervisory services is indicated by numerical or alphabetical code or some similar designation.

(e)(1) All books and records required to be made under the provisions of paragraphs (a) to (c)(1)(i), inclusive, and (c)(2) of this rule (except for books and records required to be made under the provisions of paragraphs (a)(11), (a)(12)(i), (a)(12)(iii), (a)(13)(ii), (a)(13)(iii), (a)(16), and (a)(17)(i) of this rule), shall be maintained and preserved in an easily accessible place for a period of not less than five years from the end of the fiscal year during which the last entry was made on such record, the first two years in an appropriate office of the investment adviser.

(2) Partnership articles and any amendments thereto, articles of incorporation, charters, minute books, and stock certificate books of the investment adviser and of any predecessor, shall be maintained in the principal office of the investment adviser and preserved until at least three years after termination of the enterprise.

(3)(i) Books and records required to be made under the provisions of paragraphs (a)(11) and (a)(16) of this rule shall be maintained and preserved in an easily accessible place for a period of not less than five years, the first two years in an appropriate office of the investment adviser, from the end of the fiscal year during which the investment adviser last published or otherwise disseminated, directly or indirectly, the notice, circular, advertisement, newspaper article, investment letter, bulletin or other communication.

(ii) *Transition Rule.* If you are an investment adviser that was, prior to July 21, 2011, exempt from registration under section 203(b)(3) of the Act (15 U.S.C. 80b–3(b)(3)), as in effect on July 20, 2011, paragraph (e)(3)(i) of this section does not require you to maintain or preserve books and records that would otherwise be required to be maintained or preserved under the provisions of paragraph (a)(16) of this section to the extent those books and records pertain to the performance or rate of return of such private fund (as defined in section 202(a)(29) of the Act (15 U.S.C. 80b–2(a)(29)), or other account you advise for any period ended prior to your registration, provided that you continue to preserve any books and records in your possession that pertain to the performance or rate of return of such private fund or other account for such period).

(f) An investment adviser subject to paragraph (a) of this rule, before ceasing to conduct or discontinuing business as an investment adviser shall arrange for and be responsible for the preservation of the books and records required to be maintained and preserved under this section for the remainder of the period specified in this section, and shall notify the Commission in writing, at its principal office, Washington, D.C., 20549, of the exact address where such books and records will be maintained during such period.

(g) *Micrographic and Electronic Storage Permitted.* (1) *General.* The records required to be maintained and preserved pursuant to this part may be maintained and preserved for the required time by an investment adviser on:

(i) Micrographic media, including microfilm, microfiche, or any similar medium; or

(ii) Electronic storage media, including any digital storage medium or system that meets the terms of this section.

(2) *General Requirements.* The investment adviser must:

(i) Arrange and index the records in a way that permits easy location, access, and retrieval of any particular record;

(ii) Provide promptly any of the following that the Commission (by its examiners or other representatives) may request:

(A) A legible, true, and complete copy of the record in the medium and format in which it is stored;

(B) A legible, true, and complete printout of the record; and

(C) Means to access, view, and print the records; and

(iii) Separately store, for the time required for preservation of the original record, a duplicate copy of the record on any medium allowed by this rule.

(3) *Special Requirements for Electronic Storage Media.* In the case of records on electronic storage media, the investment adviser must establish and maintain procedures:

(i) To maintain and preserve the records, so as to reasonably safeguard them from loss, alteration, or destruction;

(ii) To limit access to the records to properly authorized personnel and the Commission (including its examiners and other representatives); and

(iii) To reasonably ensure that any reproduction of a non-electronic original record on electronic storage media is complete, true, and legible when retrieved.

(h)(1) Any book or other record made, kept, maintained and preserved in compliance with Rules 17a–3 and 17a–4 under the Securities Exchange Act of 1934, with rules adopted by the Municipal Securities Rulemaking Board, which is substantially the same as the book or other record required to be made, kept, maintained and preserved under this section, shall be deemed to be made, kept, maintained and preserved in compliance with this section.

(2) A record made and kept pursuant to any provision of paragraph (a) of this rule, which contains all the information required under any other provision of paragraph (a) of this section, need not be maintained in duplicate in order to meet the requirements of the other provision of paragraph (a) of this rule.

(i) As used in this rule the term "discretionary power" shall not include discretion as to the price at which or the time when a transaction is or is to be effected, if, before the order is given by the investment adviser, the client has directed or approved the purchase or sale of a definite amount of the particular security.

(j)(1) Except as provided in paragraph (j)(3) hereof, each non-resident investment adviser registered or applying for registration pursuant to Section 203 of the Act shall keep, maintain and preserve, at a place within the United States designated in a notice from him as provided in paragraph (j)(2) of this rule true, correct, complete and current copies of books and records which he is required to make, keep current, maintain or preserve pursuant to any provision of any rule or regulation of the Commission adopted under the Act.

(2) Except as provided in paragraph (j)(3) of this rule, each nonresident investment adviser subject to this paragraph (j) shall furnish to the Commission a written notice specifying the address of the place within the United States where the copies of the books and records required to be kept and preserved by him pursuant to paragraph (j)(1) hereof are located. Each non-resident investment adviser registered or applying for registration when this paragraph becomes effective shall file such notice within 30 days after such rule becomes effective. Each non-resident investment adviser who files an application for registration after this paragraph becomes effective shall file such notice with such application for registration.

(3) Notwithstanding the provisions of paragraphs (j)(1) and (j)(2) of this rule, a non-resident investment adviser need not keep or preserve within the United States copies of the books and

records referred to in said paragraphs (j)(1) and (j)(2), if:

(i) Such non-resident investment adviser files with the Commission, at the time or within the period provided by paragraph (j)(2) of this rule, a written undertaking, in form acceptable to the Commission and signed by a duly authorized person, to furnish to the Commission, upon demand, at its principal office in Washington, D.C., or at any Regional Office of the Commission designated in such demand, true, correct, complete and current copies of any or all of the books and records which he is required to make, keep current, maintain or preserve pursuant to any provision of any rule or regulation of the Commission adopted under the Act, or any part of such books and records which may be specified in such demand. Such undertaking shall be in substantially the following form:

> The undersigned hereby undertakes to furnish at its own expense to the Securities and Exchange Commission at its principal office in Washington, D.C. or at any Regional Office of said Commission specified in a demand for copies of books and records made by or on behalf of said Commission, true, correct, complete and current copies of any or all, or any part, of the books and records which the undersigned is required to make, keep current or preserve pursuant to any provision of any rule or regulation of the Securities and Exchange Commission under the Investment Advisers Act of 1940. This undertaking shall be suspended during any period when the undersigned is making, keeping current, and preserving copies of all of said books and records at a place within the United States in compliance with Rule 204–2(j) under the Investment Advisers Act of 1940. This undertaking shall be binding upon the undersigned and the heirs, successors and assigns of the undersigned, and the written irrevocable consents and powers of attorney of the undersigned, its general partners and managing agents filed with the Securities and Exchange Commission shall extend to and cover any action to enforce same.

and

(ii) Such non-resident investment adviser furnishes to the Commission, at his own expense 14 days after written demand therefor forwarded to him by registered mail at his last address of record filed with the Commission and signed by the Secretary of the Commission or such person as the Commission may authorize to act in its behalf, true, correct, complete and current copies of any or all books and records which such investment adviser is required to make, keep current or preserve pursuant to any provision of any rule or regulation of the Commission adopted under the Act, or any part of such books and records which may be specified in said written demand. Such copies shall be furnished to the Commission at its principal office in Washington, D.C., or at any Regional Office of the Commission which may be specified in said written demand.

(4) For purposes of this rule the term "non-resident investment adviser" shall have the meaning set out in Rule 0–2(d)(3) under the Act.

(k) Every investment adviser that registers under section 203 of the Act (15 U.S.C. 80b–3) after July 8, 1997 shall be required to preserve in accordance with this section the books and records the investment adviser had been required to maintain by the State in which the investment adviser had its principal office and place of business prior to registering with the Commission.

Rule 204–3. Delivery of brochures and brochure supplements

(a) *General Requirements.* If you are registered under the Act as an investment adviser, you must deliver a brochure and one or more brochure supplements to each client or prospective client that contains all information required by Part 2 of Form ADV [17 CFR 279.1].

(b) *Delivery Requirements.* Subject to paragraph (g), you (or a supervised person acting on your behalf) must:

(1) Deliver to a client or prospective client your current brochure before or at the time you enter into an investment advisory contract with that client.

(2) Deliver to each client, annually within 120 days after the end of your fiscal year and without charge, if there are material changes in your brochure since your last annual updating amendment:

(i) A current brochure, or

(ii) The summary of material changes to the brochure as required by Item 2 of Form ADV, Part 2A that offers to provide your current brochure without charge, accompanied by the website address (if available) and an e–mail address (if available) and telephone number by which a client may obtain the current brochure from you, and the website address for obtaining information about you through the Investment Adviser Public Disclosure (IAPD) system.

(3) Deliver to each client or prospective client a current brochure supplement for a supervised person before or at the time that supervised person begins to provide advisory services to the client; provided, however, that if investment advice for a client is provided by a team comprised of more than five supervised persons, a current brochure supplement need only be delivered to that client for the five supervised persons with the most significant responsibility for the day–to–day advice provided to that client. For purposes of this section, a supervised person will provide advisory services to a client if that supervised person will:

(i) Formulate investment advice for the client and have direct client contact; or

(ii) Make discretionary investment decisions for the client, even if the supervised person will have no direct client contact.

(4) Deliver the following to each client promptly after you create an amended brochure or brochure supplement, as applicable, if the amendment adds disclosure of an event, or materially revises information already disclosed about an event, in response to Item 9 of Part 2A of Form ADV or Item 3 of Part 2B of Form ADV (Disciplinary Information), respectively, (i) the amended brochure or brochure supplement, as applicable, along with a statement describing the material facts relating to the change in disciplinary information, or (ii) a statement describing the material facts relating to the change in disciplinary information.

(c) *Exceptions to Delivery Requirement.*

(1) You are not required to deliver a brochure to a client:

(i) That is an investment company registered under the Investment Company Act of 1940 [15 U.S.C. 80a–1 to 80a–64] or a business development company as defined in that Act, provided that the advisory contract with that client meets the requirements of section 15(c) of that Act [15 U.S.C. 80a–15(c)]; or

(ii) Who receives only impersonal investment advice for which you charge less than $500 per year.

(2) You are not required to deliver a brochure supplement to a client:

(i) To whom you are not required to deliver a brochure under subparagraph (c)(1) of this section;

(ii) Who receives only impersonal investment advice; or

(iii) Who is an officer, employee, or other person related to the adviser that would be a "qualified client" of your firm under Rule 205–3(d)(1)(iii).

(d) *Wrap Fee Program Brochures.*

(1) If you are a sponsor of a wrap fee program, then the brochure that paragraph (b) of this section requires you to deliver to a client or prospective client of the wrap fee program must be a wrap fee program brochure containing all the information required by Part 2A, Appendix 1 of Form ADV. Any additional information in a wrap fee program brochure must be limited to information applicable to wrap fee programs that you sponsor.

(2) You do not have to deliver a wrap fee program brochure if another sponsor of the wrap fee program delivers, to the client or prospective client of the wrap fee program, a wrap fee program brochure containing all the information required by Part 2A, Appendix 1 of Form ADV.

NOTE TO PARAGRAPH (d): A wrap fee program brochure does not take the place of any brochure supplements that you are required to deliver under paragraph (b) of this section.

(e) *Multiple Brochures.* If you provide substantially different advisory services to different clients, you may provide them with different brochures, so long as each client receives all information about the services and fees that are applicable to that client. The brochure you deliver to a client may omit any information required by Part 2A of Form ADV if the information does not apply to the advisory services or fees that you will provide or charge, or that you propose to provide or charge, to that client.

(f) *Other Disclosure Obligations.* Delivering a brochure or brochure supplement in compliance with this section does not relieve you of any other disclosure obligations you have to your advisory clients or prospective clients under any federal or state laws or regulations.

(g) *Definitions.* For purposes of this section:

(1) *Impersonal investment advice* means investment advisory services that do not purport to meet the objectives or needs of specific individuals or accounts.

(2) *Current brochure* and *current brochure supplement* mean the most recent revision of the brochure or brochure supplement, including all amendments to date.

(3) *Sponsor* of a wrap fee program means an investment adviser that is compensated under a wrap fee program for sponsoring, organizing, or administering the program, or for selecting, or providing advice to clients regarding the selection of, other investment advisers in the program.

(4) *Supervised person* means any of your officers, partners or directors (or other persons occupying a similar status or performing similar functions) or employees, or any other person who provides investment advice on your behalf.

(5) *Wrap fee program* means an advisory program under which a specified fee or fees not based directly upon transactions in a client's account is charged for investment advisory services (which may include portfolio management or advice concerning the selection of other investment advisers) and the execution of client transactions.

Rule 204-4. Reporting by exempt reporting advisers

(a) *Exempt Reporting Advisers.* If you are an investment adviser relying on the exemption from registering with the Commission under section 203(*l*) or (m) of the Act (15 U.S.C. 80b-3(*l*) or 80b-3(m)), you must complete and file reports on Form ADV (17 CFR 279.1) by following the instructions in the Form, which specify the information that an exempt reporting adviser must provide.

(b) *Electronic Filing.* You must file Form ADV electronically with the Investment Adviser Registration Depository (IARD) unless you have received a hardship exemption under paragraph (e) of this section.

Note to Paragraph (b): Information on how to file with the IARD is available on the Commission's website at *http://www.sec.gov/iard.*

(c) *When Filed.* Each Form ADV is considered filed with the Commission upon acceptance by the IARD.

(d) *Filing Fees.* You must pay FINRA (the operator of the IARD) a filing fee. The Commission has approved the amount of the filing fee. No portion of the filing fee is refundable. Your completed Form ADV will not be accepted by FINRA, and thus will not be considered filed with the Commission, until you have paid the filing fee.

(e) *Temporary Hardship Exemption.*

(1) *Eligibility for Exemption.* If you have unanticipated technical difficulties that prevent submission of a filing to the IARD, you may request a temporary hardship exemption from the requirements of this chapter to file electronically.

(2) *Application Procedures.* To request a temporary hardship exemption, you must:

(i) File Form ADV-H (17 CFR 279.3) in paper format no later than one business day after the filing that is the subject of the ADV-H was due; and

(ii) Submit the filing that is the subject of the Form ADV-H in electronic format with the IARD no later than seven business days after the filing was due.

(3) *Effective Date-Upon Filing.* The temporary hardship exemption will be granted when you file a completed Form ADV-H.

(f) *Final Report.* You must file a final report in accordance with instructions in Form ADV when:

(1) You cease operation as an investment adviser;

(2) You no longer meet the definition of exempt reporting adviser under paragraph (a); or

(3) You apply for registration with the Commission.

Note to Paragraph (f): You do not have to pay a filing fee to file a final report on Form ADV through the IARD.

Rule 204A-1. Investment adviser codes of ethics

(a) *Adoption of Code of Ethics.* If you are an investment adviser registered or required to be registered under section 203 of the Act (15 U.S.C. 80b-3), you must establish, maintain and enforce a written code of ethics that, at a minimum, includes:

(1) A standard (or standards) of business conduct that you require of your supervised persons, which standard must reflect your fiduciary obligations and those of your supervised persons;

(2) Provisions requiring your supervised persons to comply with applicable Federal securities laws;

(3) Provisions that require all of your access persons to report, and you to review, their personal securities transactions and holdings periodically as provided below;

(4) Provisions requiring supervised persons to report any violations of your code of ethics prompt-

ly to your chief compliance officer or, provided your chief compliance officer also receives reports of all violations, to other persons you designate in your code of ethics; and

(5) Provisions requiring you to provide each of your supervised persons with a copy of your code of ethics and any amendments, and requiring your supervised persons to provide you with a written acknowledgment of their receipt of the code and any amendments.

(b) *Reporting Requirements.* (1) *Holdings Reports.* The code of ethics must require your access persons to submit to your chief compliance officer or other persons you designate in your code of ethics a report of the access person's current securities holdings that meets the following requirements:

(i) *Content of Holdings Reports.* Each holdings report must contain, at a minimum:

(A) The title and type of security, and as applicable the exchange ticker symbol or CUSIP number, number of shares, and principal amount of each reportable security in which the access person has any direct or indirect beneficial ownership;

(B) The name of any broker, dealer or bank with which the access person maintains an account in which any securities are held for the access person's direct or indirect benefit; and

(C) The date the access person submits the report.

(ii) *Timing of Holdings Reports.* Your access persons must each submit a holdings report:

(A) No later than 10 days after the person becomes an access person, and the information must be current as of a date no more than 45 days prior to the date the person becomes an access person.

(B) At least once each 12–month period thereafter on a date you select, and the information must be current as of a date no more than 45 days prior to the date the report was submitted.

(2) *Transaction Reports.* The code of ethics must require access persons to submit to your chief compliance officer or other persons you designate in your code of ethics quarterly securities transactions reports that meet the following requirements:

(i) *Content of Transaction Reports.* Each transaction report must contain, at a minimum, the following information about each transaction involving a reportable security in which the access person had, or as a result of the transaction acquired, any direct or indirect beneficial ownership:

(A) The date of the transaction, the title, and as applicable the exchange ticker symbol or CUSIP number, interest rate and maturity date, number of shares, and principal amount of each reportable security involved;

(B) The nature of the transaction (i.e., purchase, sale or any other type of acquisition or disposition);

(C) The price of the security at which the transaction was effected;

(D) The name of the broker, dealer or bank with or through which the transaction was effected; and (E) The date the access person submits the report.

(ii) *Timing of Transaction Reports.* Each access person must submit a transaction report no later than 30 days after the end of each calendar quarter, which report must cover, at a minimum, all transactions during the quarter.

(3) *Exceptions from Reporting Requirements.* Your code of ethics need not require an access person to submit:

(i) Any report with respect to securities held in accounts over which the access person had no direct or indirect influence or control;

(ii) A transaction report with respect to transactions effected pursuant to an automatic investment plan;

(iii) A transaction report if the report would duplicate information contained in broker trade confirmations or account statements that you hold in your records so long as you receive the confirmations or statements no later than 30 days after the end of the applicable calendar quarter.

(c) *Pre-Approval of Certain Investments.* Your code of ethics must require your access persons to obtain your approval before they directly or indirectly acquire beneficial ownership in any security in an initial public offering or in a limited offering.

(d) *Small Advisers.* If you have only one access person (i.e., yourself), you are not required to submit reports to yourself or to obtain your own approval for investments in any security in an initial public offering or in a limited offering, if you maintain records of all of your holdings and transactions that this section would otherwise require you to report.

(e) *Definitions.* For the purpose of this rule:

(1) *Access person* means:

(i) Any of your supervised persons:

(A) Who has access to nonpublic information regarding any clients' purchase or sale of securities, or nonpublic information regarding the portfolio holdings of any reportable fund, or

(B) Who is involved in making securities recommendations to clients, or who has access to such recommendations that are nonpublic.

(ii) If providing investment advice is your primary business, all of your directors, officers and partners are presumed to be access persons.

(2) *Automatic investment plan* means a program in which regular periodic purchases (or withdrawals) are made automatically in (or from) investment accounts in accordance with a predetermined schedule and allocation. An automatic investment plan includes a dividend reinvestment plan.

(3) *Beneficial ownership* is interpreted in the same manner as it would be under Rule 16a–1(a)(2) under the Securities Exchange Act of 1934 in determining whether a person has beneficial ownership of a security for purposes of section 16 of the Securities Exchange Act of 1934 (15 U.S.C. 78p) and the rules and regulations thereunder. Any report required by paragraph (b) of this rule may contain a statement that the report will not be construed as an admission that the person making the report has any direct or indirect beneficial ownership in the security to which the report relates.

(4) *Federal securities laws* means the Securities Act of 1933 (15 U.S.C. 77a–aa), the Securities Exchange Act of 1934 (15 U.S.C. 78a–mm), the Sarbanes–Oxley Act of 2002 (Pub.L. 107–204, 116 Stat. 745 (2002)), the Investment Company Act of 1940 (15 U.S.C. 80a), the Investment Advisers Act of 1940 (15 U.S.C. 80b), title V of the Gramm–Leach–Bliley Act (Pub.L. 106–102, 113 Stat. 1338 (1999)), any rules adopted by the Commission under any of these statutes, the Bank Secrecy Act (31 U.S.C. 5311–5314; 5316–5332) as it applies to funds and investment advisers, and any rules adopted thereunder by the Commission or the Department of the Treasury.

(5) *Fund* means an investment company registered under the Investment Company Act.

(6) *Initial public offering* means an offering of securities registered under the Securities Act of 1933 (15 U.S.C. 77a), the issuer of which, immediately before the registration, was not subject to the reporting requirements of sections 13 or 15(d) of the Securities Exchange Act of 1934 (15 U.S.C. 78m or 78o(d)).

(7) *Limited offering* means an offering that is exempt from registration under the Securities Act of 1933 pursuant to section 4(a)(2) or section 4(a)(5) (15 U.S.C. 77d(a)(2) or 77d(a)(5)) or pursuant to Rules 504 or 506 under the Securities Act of 1933.

(8) *Purchase or sale of a security* includes, among other things, the writing of an option to purchase or sell a security.

(9) *Reportable fund* means:

(i) Any fund for which you serve as an investment adviser as defined in section 2(a)(20) of the Investment Company Act of 1940 (15 U.S.C. 80a–2(a)(20)) (i.e., in most cases you must be approved by the fund's board of directors before you can serve); or

(ii) Any fund whose investment adviser or principal underwriter controls you, is controlled by you, or is under common control with you. For purposes of this rule, *control* has the same meaning as it does in section 2(a)(9) of the Investment Company Act of 1940 (15 U.S.C. 80a–2(a)(9)).

(10) *Reportable security* means a security as defined in section 202(a)(18) of the Act (15 U.S.C. 80b–2(a)(18)), except that it does not include:

(i) Direct obligations of the Government of the United States;

(ii) Bankers' acceptances, bank certificates of deposit, commercial paper and high quality short-term debt instruments, including repurchase agreements;

(iii) Shares issued by money market funds;

(iv) Shares issued by open-end funds other than reportable funds; and

(v) Shares issued by unit investment trusts that are invested exclusively in one or more open-end funds, none of which are reportable funds.

Rule 204(b)-1. Reporting by investment advisers to private funds

(a) *Reporting by Investment Advisers to Private Funds on Form PF.* If you are an investment adviser registered or required to be registered under section 203 of the Act (15 U.S.C. 80b-3), you act as an investment adviser to one or more private funds and, as of the end of your most recently completed fiscal year, you managed private fund assets of at least $150 million, you must complete and file a report on Form PF (17 CFR 279.9) by following the instructions in the Form, which specify the information that an investment adviser must provide. Your initial report on Form PF is due no later than the last day on which your next update would be timely in accordance with paragraph (e) if you had previously filed the Form; provided that you are not required to file Form PF with respect to any fiscal quarter or fiscal year ending prior to the date on which your resignation becomes effective.

(b) *Electronic Filing.* You must file form PF electronically with the Form PF filing system on the Investment Adviser Registration Depository (IARD).

Note to Paragraph (b): Information on how to file Form PF is available on the Commission's website at *http://www.sec.gov/iard.*

(c) *When Filed.* Each Form PF is considered filed with the Commission upon acceptance by the Form PF filing system.

(d) *Filing Fees.* You must pay the operator of the Form PF filing system a filing fee as required by the instructions to Form PF. The Commission has approved the amount of the filing fee. No portion of the filing fee is refundable. Your completed Form PF will not be accepted by the operator of the Form PF filing system, and thus will not be considered filed with the Commission, until you have paid the filing fee.

(e) *Updates to Form PF.* You must file an updated Form PF:

(1) At least annually, no later than the date specified in the instructions to Form PF; and

(2) More frequently, if required by the instructions to Form PF. You must file all updated reports electronically with the Form PF filing system.

(f) *Temporary Hardship Exemption.*

(1) If you have unanticipated technical difficulties that prevent you from submitting Form PF on a timely basis through the Form PF filing system, you may request a temporary hardship exemption from the requirements of this section to file electronically.

(2) To request a temporary hardship exemption, you must:

(i) Complete and file in paper format, in accordance with the instructions to Form PF, Item A of Section 1a and Section 5 of Form PF, checking the box in Section 1a indicating that you are requesting a temporary hardship exemption, no later than one business day after the electronic Form PF filing was due; and

(ii) Submit the filing fee that is the subject of the Form PF paper filing in electronic format with the Form PF filing system no later than seven business days after the filing was due.

(3) The temporary hardship exemption will be granted when you file Item A of Section 1a and Section 5 of Form PF, checking the box in Section 1a indicating that you are requesting a temporary hardship exemption

(4) The hardship exemptions made available under Rule 203-3 do not apply to Form PF.

(g) *Definitions.* For purposes of this section:

(1) *Assets under management* means the regulatory assets under management as determined under Item 5.F of Form ADV (17 CFR 279.1).

(2) *Private fund assets* means the investment adviser's assets under management attributable to private funds.

Rule 205-1. Definition of "investment performance" of an investment company and "investment record" of an appropriate index of securities prices

(a) *Investment performance* of an investment company for any period shall mean the sum of:

(1) The change in its net asset value per share during such period;

(2) The value of its cash distributions per share accumulated to the end of such period; and

(3) The value of capital gains taxes per share paid or payable on undistributed realized long-term capital gains accumulated to the end of such period;

expressed as a percentage of its net asset value per share at the beginning of such period. For this purpose, the value of distributions per share of realized capital gains, of dividends per share paid from investment income and of capital gains taxes per share paid or payable on undistributed realized long-term capital gains shall be treated as reinvested in shares of the investment company at the net asset value per share in effect at the close of business on the record date for the payment of such distributions and dividends and the date on which provision is made for such taxes, after giving effect to such distributions, dividends and taxes.

(b) *Investment record* of an appropriate index of securities prices for any period shall mean the sum of:

(1) The change in the level of the index during such period; and

(2) The value, computed consistently with the index, of cash distributions made by companies whose securities comprise the index accumulated to the end of such period;

expressed as a percentage of the index level at the beginning of such period. For this purpose cash distributions on the securities which comprise the index shall be treated as reinvested in the index at least as frequently as the end of each calendar quarter following the payment of the dividend.

Rule 205–2. Definition of "specified period" over which the asset value of the company or fund under management is averaged

(a) For purposes of this rule:

(1) *Fulcrum fee* shall mean the fee which is paid or earned when the investment company's performance is equivalent to that of the index or other measure of performance.

(2) *Rolling period* shall mean a period consisting of a specified number of subperiods of definite length in which the most recent subperiod is substituted for the earliest subperiod as time passes.

(b) The specified period over which the asset value of the company or fund under management is averaged shall mean the period over which the investment performance of the company or fund and the investment record of an appropriate index of securities prices or such other measure of investment performance are computed.

(c) Notwithstanding paragraph (b) of this rule, the specified period over which the asset value of the company or fund is averaged for the purpose of computing the fulcrum fee may differ from the period over which the asset value is averaged for computing the performance related portion of the fee, only if

(1) The performance related portion of the fee is computed over a rolling period and the total fee is payable at the end of each subperiod of the rolling period; and

(2) The fulcrum fee is computed on the basis of the asset value averaged over the most recent subperiod or subperiods of the rolling period.

Rule 205–3. Exemption from the compensation prohibition of Section 205(a)(1) for investment advisers

(a) *General.* The provisions of section 205(a)(1) of the Act (15 U.S.C. 80b–5(a)(1)) will not be deemed to prohibit an investment adviser from entering into, performing, renewing or extending an investment advisory contract that provides for compensation to the investment adviser on the basis of a share of the capital gains upon, or the capital appreciation of, the funds, or any portion of the funds, of a client, *Provided*, That the client entering into the contract subject to this section is a qualified client, as defined in paragraph (d)(1) of this rule.

(b) *Identification of the Client.* In the case of a private investment company, as defined in paragraph (d)(3) of this rule, an investment company registered under the Investment Company Act of 1940, or a business development company, as defined in section 202(a)(22) of the Act (15 U.S.C. 80b–2(a)(22)), each equity owner of any such company (except for the investment adviser entering into the contract and any other equity owners not charged a fee on the basis of a share of capital gains or capital appreciation) will be considered a client for purposes of paragraph (a) of this rule.

(c) *Transition Rules.* (1) *Registered Investment Advisers.* If a registered investment adviser entered into a contract and satisfied the conditions of this section that were in effect when the contract was entered into, the adviser will be considered to satisfy the conditions of this section; *Provided*, however, that if a natural person or company who was not a party to the contract becomes a party (including an equity owner of a private investment company advised by the adviser), the conditions of this section in effect at that time will apply with regard to that person or company.

(2) *Registered Investment Advisers that were Previously not Registered.* If an investment adviser was not required to register with the Commission pursuant to section 203 of the Act (15 U.S.C.

80b–3) and was not registered, section 205(a)(1) of the Act will not apply to an advisory contract entered into when the adviser was not required to register and was not registered, or to an account of an equity owner of a private investment company advised by the adviser if the account was established when the adviser was not required to register and was not registered; *Provided, however*, that section 205(a)(1) of the Act will apply with regard to a natural person or company who was not a party to the contract and becomes a party (including an equity owner of a private investment company advised by the adviser) when the adviser is required to register.

(3) *Certain Transfers of Interests.* Solely for purposes of paragraphs (c)(1) and (c)(2) of this section, a transfer of an equity ownership interest in a private investment company by gift or bequest, or pursuant to an agreement related to a legal separation or divorce, will not cause the transferee to "become a party" to the contract and will not cause section 205(a)(1) of the Act to apply to such transferee.

(d) *Definitions.* For the purposes of this rule:

(1) The term *qualified client* means:

(i) A natural person who, or a company that, immediately after entering into the contract has at least $1,000,000 under the management of the investment adviser;

(ii) A natural person who, or a company that, the investment adviser entering into the contract (and any person acting on his behalf) reasonably believes, immediately prior to entering into the contract, either:

(A) Has a net worth (together, in the case of a natural person, with assets held jointly with a spouse) of more than $2,000,000. For purposes of calculating a natural person's net worth:

(*1*) The person's primary residence must not be included as an asset;

(*2*) Indebtedness secured by the person's primary residence, up to the estimated fair market value of the primary residence at the time the investment advisory contract is entered into may not be included as a liability (except that if the amount of such indebtedness outstanding at the time of calculation exceeds the amount outstanding 60 days before such time, other than as a result of the acquisition of the primary residence, the amount of such excess must be included as a liability); and

(*3*) Indebtedness that is secured by the person's primary residence in excess of the estimated fair market value of the residence must be included as a liability; or

(B) Is a qualified purchaser as defined in section 2(a)(51)(A) under the Investment Company Act of 1940 (15 U.S.C. 80a–2(a)(51)(A)) at the time the contract is entered into; or

(iii) A natural person who immediately prior to entering into the contract is:

(A) An executive officer, director, trustee, general partner, or person serving in a similar capacity, of the investment adviser; or

(B) An employee of the investment adviser (other than an employee performing solely clerical, secretarial or administrative functions with regard to the investment adviser) who, in connection with his or her regular functions or duties, participates in the investment activities of such investment adviser, provided that such employee has been performing such functions and duties for or on behalf of the investment adviser, or substantially similar functions or duties for or on behalf of another company for at least 12 months.

(2) The term *company* has the same meaning as in section 202(a)(5) of the Act (15 U.S.C. 80b–2(a)(5)), but does not include a company that is required to be registered under the Investment Company Act of 1940 but is not registered.

(3) The term *private investment company* means a company that would be defined as an investment company under section 3(a) of the Investment Company Act of 1940 (15 U.S.C. 80a–3(a)) but for the exception provided from that definition by section 3(c)(1) of such Act (15 U.S.C. 80a–3(c)(1)).

(4) The term *executive officer* means the president, any vice president in charge of a principal business unit, division or function (such as sales, administration or finance), any other officer who performs a policy-making function, or any other person who performs similar policy-making functions, for the investment adviser.

(e) *Inflation Adjustments.* Pursuant to section 205(e) of the Act, the dollar amounts specified in paragraphs (d)(1)(i) and (d)(1)(ii)(A) of this section shall be adjusted by order of the Commission, on or about May 1, 2016 and issued approximately every five years thereafter. The adjusted dollar amounts established in such orders shall be computed by:

(1) Dividing the year-end value of the Personal Consumption Expenditures Chain–Type Price Index (or any successor index thereto), as published by the United States Department of Commerce, for the calendar year preceding the calendar year in which the order is being issued, by the year-end value of such index (or successor) for the calendar year 1997;

(2) For the dollar amount in paragraph (d)(1)(i) of this section, multiplying $750,000 times the quotient obtained in paragraph (e)(1) of this section and rounding the product to the nearest multiple of $100,000; and

(3) For the dollar amount in paragraph (d)(1)(ii)(A) of this section, multiplying $1,500,000 times the quotient obtained in paragraph (e)(1) of this section and rounding the product to the nearest multiple of $100,000.

Rule 206(3)–1. Exemption of investment advisers registered as broker–dealers in connection with the provision of certain investment advisory services

(a) An investment adviser which is a broker or dealer registered pursuant to Section 15 of the Securities Exchange Act of 1934 shall be exempt from Section 206(3) in connection with any transaction in relation to which such broker or dealer is acting as an investment adviser solely (1) by means of publicly distributed written materials or publicly made oral statements; (2) by means of written materials or oral statements which do not purport to meet the objectives or needs of specific individuals or accounts; (3) through the issuance of statistical information containing no expressions of opinion as to the investment merits of a particular security; or (4) any combination of the foregoing services: *Provided, however,* That such materials and oral statements include a statement that if the purchaser of the advisory communication uses the services of the adviser in connection with a sale or purchase of a security which is a subject of such communication, the adviser may act as principal for its own account or as agent for another person.

(b) For the purpose of this rule, publicly distributed written materials are those which are distributed to 35 or more persons who pay for such materials, and publicly made oral statements are those made simultaneously to 35 or more persons who pay for access to such statements.

NOTE: The requirement that the investment adviser disclose that it may act as principal or agent for another person in the sale or purchase of a security that is the subject of investment advice does not relieve the investment adviser of any disclosure obligation which, depending upon the nature of the relationship between the investment adviser and the client, may be imposed by subparagraphs (1) or (2) of Section 206 or the other provisions of the federal securities laws.

Rule 206(3)–2. Agency cross transactions for advisory clients

(a) An investment adviser, or a person registered as a broker-dealer under section 15 of the Securities Exchange Act of 1934 (15 U.S.C. 78o) and controlling, controlled by, or under common control with an investment adviser, shall be deemed in compliance with the provisions of sections 206(3) of the Act (15 U.S.C. 80b–6(3)) in effecting an agency cross transaction for an advisory client, if:

(1) The advisory client has executed a written consent prospectively authorizing the investment adviser, or any other person relying on this rule, to effect agency cross transactions for such advisory client, provided that such written consent is obtained after full written disclosure that with respect to agency cross transactions the investment adviser or such other person will act as broker for, receive commissions from, and have a potentially conflicting division of loyalties and responsibilities regarding, both parties to such transaction;

(2) The investment adviser, or any other person relying on this rule, sends to each such client a written confirmation at or before the completion of each such transaction, which confirmation includes (i) a statement of the nature of such transaction, (ii) the date such transaction took place, (iii) an offer to furnish upon request, the time when such transaction took place, and (iv) the source and amount of any other remuneration received or to be received by the investment adviser and any other person relying on this rule in connection with the transaction, *Provided, however,* That if, in the case of a purchase, neither the investment adviser nor any other person relying on this rule was participating in a distribution, or in the case of a sale, neither the investment adviser nor any other person relying on this rule was participating in a tender offer, the written confirmation may state whether any other remuneration has been or will be received and that the source and amount of such other remuneration will be furnished upon written request of such customer;

(3) The investment adviser, or any other person relying on this rule, sends to each client, at least

annually, and with or as part of any written statement or summary of such account from the investment adviser or such other person, a written disclosure statement identifying the total number of such transactions during the period since the date of the last such statement or summary, and the total amount of all commissions or other remuneration received or to be received by the investment adviser or any other person relying on this rule in connection with such transactions during such period;

(4) Each written disclosure and confirmation required by this rule includes a conspicuous statement that the written consent referred to in paragraph (a)(1) of this rule may be revoked at any time by written notice to the investment adviser, or to any other person relying on this rule, from the advisory client; and

(5) No such transaction is effected in which the same investment adviser or an investment adviser and any person controlling, controlled by or under common control with such investment adviser recommended the transaction to both any seller and any purchaser.

(b) For purposes of this rule the term *agency cross transaction for an advisory client* shall mean a transaction in which a person acts as an investment adviser in relation to a transaction in which such investment adviser, or any person controlling, controlled by or under common control with such investment adviser, acts as broker for both such advisory client and for another person on the other side of the transaction.

(c) This rule shall not be construed as relieving in any way the investment adviser or another person relying on this rule from acting in the best interests of the advisory client, including fulfilling the duty with respect to the best price and execution for the particular transaction for the advisory client; nor shall it relieve such person or persons from any disclosure obligation which may be imposed by subparagraphs (1) or (2) of Section 206 of the Act or by other applicable provisions of the federal securities laws.

Rule 206(3)–3T. Temporary rule for principal trades with certain advisory clients

(a) An investment adviser shall be deemed in compliance with the provisions of section 206(3) of the Advisers Act (15 U.S.C. 80b–6(3)) when the adviser directly or indirectly, acting as principal for its own account, sells to or purchases from an advisory client any security if:

(1) The investment adviser exercises no "investment discretion" (as such term is defined in section 3(a)(35) of the Securities Exchange Act of 1934 ("Exchange Act") (15 U.S.C. 78c(a)(35))), except investment discretion granted by the advisory client on a temporary or limited basis, with respect to the client's account;

(2) Neither the investment adviser nor any person controlling, controlled by, or under common control with the investment adviser is the issuer of, or, at the time of the sale, an underwriter (as defined in section 202(a)(20) of the Advisers Act (15 U.S.C. 80b–2(a)(20))) of, the security; *except that* the investment adviser or a person controlling, controlled by, or under common control with the investment adviser may be an underwriter of an investment grade debt security (as defined in paragraph (c) of this rule);

(3) The advisory client has executed a written, revocable consent prospectively authorizing the investment adviser directly or indirectly to act as principal for its own account in selling any security to or purchasing any security from the advisory client, so long as such written consent is obtained after written disclosure to the advisory client explaining:

(i) The circumstances under which the investment adviser directly or indirectly may engage in principal transactions;

(ii) The nature and significance of conflicts with its client's interests as a result of the transactions; and

(iii) How the investment adviser addresses those conflicts;

(4) The investment adviser, prior to the execution of each principal transaction:

(i) Informs the advisory client, orally or in writing, of the capacity in which it may act with respect to such transaction; and

(ii) Obtains consent from the advisory client, orally or in writing, to act as principal for its own account with respect to such transaction;

(5) The investment adviser sends a written confirmation at or before completion of each such transaction that includes, in addition to the information required by Rule 10b–10 under the Securities Exchange Act of 1934, a conspicuous, plain

English statement informing the advisory client that the investment adviser:

(i) Disclosed to the client prior to the execution of the transaction that the adviser may be acting in a principal capacity in connection with the transaction and the client authorized the transaction; and

(ii) Sold the security to, or bought the security from, the client for its own account;

(6) The investment adviser sends to the client, no less frequently than annually, written disclosure containing a list of all transactions that were executed in the client's account in reliance upon this rule, and the date and price of such transactions;

(7) The investment adviser is a broker-dealer registered under section 15 of the Exchange Act (15 U.S.C. 78o) and each account for which the investment adviser relies on this rule is a brokerage account subject to the Exchange Act, and the rules thereunder, and the rules of the self-regulatory organization(s) of which it is a member; and

(8) Each written disclosure required by this rule includes a conspicuous, plain English statement that the client may revoke the written consent referred to in paragraph (a)(3) of this rule without penalty at any time by written notice to the investment adviser.

(b) This rule shall not be construed as relieving in any way an investment adviser from acting in the best interests of an advisory client, including fulfilling the duty with respect to the best price and execution for the particular transaction for the advisory client; nor shall it relieve such person or persons from any obligation that may be imposed by sections 206(1) or (2) of the Advisers Act or by other applicable provisions of the federal securities laws.

(c) For purposes of paragraph (a)(2) of this rule, an *investment grade debt security* means a non-convertible debt security that, at the time of sale, is rated in one of the four highest rating categories of at least two nationally recognized statistical rating organizations (as defined in section 3(a)(62) of the Exchange Act (15 U.S.C. 78c(a)(62))).

(d) This rule will expire and no longer be effective on December 31, 2016.

Rule 206(4)–1. Advertisements by investment advisers

(a) It shall constitute a fraudulent, deceptive, or manipulative act, practice, or course of business within the meaning of section 206(4) of the Act (15 U.S.C. 80b–6(4)) for any investment adviser registered or required to be registered under section 203 of the Act (15 U.S.C. 80b–3), directly or indirectly, to publish, circulate, or distribute any advertisement:

(1) Which refers, directly or indirectly, to any testimonial of any kind concerning the investment adviser or concerning any advice, analysis, report or other service rendered by such investment adviser; or

(2) Which refers, directly or indirectly, to past specific recommendations of such investment adviser which were or would have been profitable to any person: *Provided, however,* That this shall not prohibit an advertisement which sets out or offers to furnish a list of all recommendations made by such investment adviser within the immediately preceding period of not less than one year if such advertisement, and such list if it is furnished separately: (i) State the name of each such security recommended, the date and nature of each such recommendation (e.g., whether to buy, sell or hold), the market price at that time, the price at which the recommendation was to be acted upon, and the market price of each such security as of the most recent practicable date, and (ii) contain the following cautionary legend on the first page thereof in print or type as large as the largest print or type used in the body or text thereof: "it should not be assumed that recommendations made in the future will be profitable or will equal the performance of the securities in this list"; or

(3) Which represents, directly or indirectly, that any graph, chart, formula or other device being offered can in and of itself be used to determine which securities to buy or sell, or when to buy or sell them; or which represents directly or indirectly, that any graph, chart, formula or other device being offered will assist any person in making his own decisions as to which securities to buy, sell, or when to buy or sell them, without prominently disclosing in such advertisement the limitations thereof and the difficulties with respect to its use; or

(4) Which contains any statement to the effect that any report, analysis, or other service will be furnished free or without charge, unless such report, analysis or other service actually is or will be furnished entirely free and without any condition or obligation, directly or indirectly; or

(5) Which contains any untrue statement of a material fact, or which is otherwise false or misleading.

(b) For the purposes of this rule the term *advertisement* shall include any notice, circular, letter or other written communication addressed to more than one person, or any notice or other announcement in any publication or by radio or television, which offers (1) any analysis, report, or publication concerning securities, or which is to be used in making any determination as to when to buy or sell any security, or which security to buy or sell, or (2) any graph, chart, formula, or other device to be used in making any determination as to when to buy or sell any security, or which security to buy or sell, or (3) any other investment advisory service with regard to securities.

Rule 206(4)–2. Custody of funds or securities of clients by investment advisers

(a) *Safekeeping Required.* If you are an investment adviser registered or required to be registered under section 203 of the Act (15 U.S.C. 80b–3), it is a fraudulent, deceptive, or manipulative act, practice or course of business within the meaning of section 206(4) of the Act (15 U.S.C. 80b–6(4)) for you to have custody of client funds or securities unless:

(1) *Qualified Custodian.* A qualified custodian maintains those funds and securities:

(i) In a separate account for each client under that client's name; or

(ii) In accounts that contain only your clients' funds and securities, under your name as agent or trustee for the clients.

(2) *Notice to Clients.* If you open an account with a qualified custodian on your client's behalf, either under the client's name or under your name as agent, you notify the client in writing of the qualified custodian's name, address, and the manner in which the funds or securities are maintained, promptly when the account is opened and following any changes to this information. If you send account statements to a client to which you are required to provide this notice, include in the notification provided to that client and in any subsequent account statement you send that client a statement urging the client to compare the account statements from the custodian with those from the adviser.

(3) *Account Statements to Clients.* You have a reasonable basis, after due inquiry, for believing that the qualified custodian sends an account statement, at least quarterly, to each of your clients for which it maintains funds or securities, identifying the amount of funds and of each security in the account at the end of the period and setting forth all transactions in the account during that period.

(4) *Independent Verification.* The client funds and securities of which you have custody are verified by actual examination at least once during each calendar year, except as provided below, by an independent public accountant, pursuant to a written agreement between you and the accountant, at a time that is chosen by the accountant without prior notice or announcement to you and that is irregular from year to year. The written agreement must provide for the first examination to occur within six months of becoming subject to this paragraph, except that, if you maintain client funds or securities pursuant to this section as a qualified custodian, the agreement must provide for the first examination to occur no later than six months after obtaining the internal control report. The written agreement must require the accountant to:

(i) File a certificate on Form ADV–E (17 CFR 279.8) with the Commission within 120 days of the time chosen by the accountant in paragraph (a)(4) of this section, stating that it has examined the funds and securities and describing the nature and extent of the examination;

(ii) Upon finding any material discrepancies during the course of the examination, notify the Commission within one business day of the finding, by means of a facsimile transmission or electronic mail, followed by first class mail, directed to the attention of the Director of the Office of Compliance Inspections and Examinations; and

(iii) Upon resignation or dismissal from, or other termination of, the engagement, or upon removing itself or being removed from consideration for being reappointed, file within four business days Form ADV–E accompanied by a statement that includes:

(A) The date of such resignation, dismissal, removal, or other termination, and the name, address, and contact information of the accountant; and

(B) An explanation of any problems relating to examination scope or procedure that contributed to such resignation, dismissal, removal, or other termination.

(5) *Special Rule for Limited Partnerships and Limited Liability Companies.* If you or a related person is a general partner of a limited partnership (or managing member of a limited liability company, or hold a comparable position for another type of pooled investment vehicle), the account statements required under paragraph (a)(3) of this section must be sent to each limited partner (or member or other beneficial owner).

(6) *Investment Advisers Acting as Qualified Custodians.* If you maintain, or if you have custody because a related person maintains, client funds or securities pursuant to this section as a qualified custodian in connection with advisory services you provide to clients:

(i) The independent public accountant you retain to perform the independent verification required by paragraph (a)(4) of this section must be registered with, and subject to regular inspection as of the commencement of the professional engagement period, and as of each calendar year-end, by, the Public Company Accounting Oversight Board in accordance with its rules; and

(ii) You must obtain, or receive from your related person, within six months of becoming subject to this paragraph and thereafter no less frequently than once each calendar year a written internal control report prepared by an independent public accountant:

(A) The internal control report must include an opinion of an independent public accountant as to whether controls have been placed in operation as of a specific date, and are suitably designed and are operating effectively to meet control objectives relating to custodial services, including the safeguarding of funds and securities held by either you or a related person on behalf of your advisory clients, during the year;

(B) The independent public accountant must verify that the funds and securities are reconciled to a custodian other than you or your related person; and

(C) The independent public accountant must be registered with, and subject to regular inspection as of the commencement of the professional engagement period, and as of each calendar year-end, by, the Public Company Accounting Oversight Board in accordance with its rules.

(7) *Independent Representatives.* A client may designate an independent representative to receive, on his behalf, notices and account statements as required under paragraphs (a)(2) and (a)(3) of this section.

(b) *Exceptions.* (1) *Shares of Mutual Funds.* With respect to shares of an open-end company as defined in section 5(a)(1) of the Investment Company Act of 1940 (15 U.S.C. 80a–5(a)(1)) ("mutual fund"), you may use the mutual fund's transfer agent in lieu of a qualified custodian for purposes of complying with paragraph (a) of this section.

(2) *Certain Privately Offered Securities.* (i) You are not required to comply with paragraph (a)(1) of this section with respect to securities that are:

(A) Acquired from the issuer in a transaction or chain of transactions not involving any public offering;

(B) Uncertificated, and ownership thereof is recorded only on the books of the issuer or its transfer agent in the name of the client; and

(C) Transferable only with prior consent of the issuer or holders of the outstanding securities of the issuer.

(ii) Notwithstanding paragraph (b)(2)(i) of this section, the provisions of this paragraph (b)(2) are available with respect to securities held for the account of a limited partnership (or a limited liability company, or other type of pooled investment vehicle) only if the limited partnership is audited, and the audited financial statements are distributed, as described in paragraph (b)(4) of this section.

(3) *Fee Deduction.* Notwithstanding paragraph (a)(4) of this section, you are not required to obtain an independent verification of client funds and securities maintained by a qualified custodian if:

(i) you have custody of the funds and securities solely as a consequence of your authority to make withdrawals from client accounts to pay your advisory fee; and

(ii) if the qualified custodian is a related person, you can rely on paragraph (b)(6) of this section.

(4) *Limited Partnerships Subject to Annual Audit.* You are not required to comply with paragraphs (a)(2) and (a)(3) of this section and you shall be deemed to have complied with paragraph (a)(4) of this section with respect to the account of a limited partnership (or limited liability company, or another type of pooled investment vehicle)

that is subject to audit (as defined in Rule 1–02(d) of Regulation S–X (17 CFR 210.1–02(d))):

(i) At least annually and distributes its audited financial statements prepared in accordance with generally accepted accounting principles to all limited partners (or members or other beneficial owners) within 120 days of the end of its fiscal year;

(ii) By an independent public accountant that is registered with, and subject to regular inspection as of the commencement of the professional engagement period, and as of each calendar year-end, by, the Public Company Accounting Oversight Board in accordance with its rules; and

(iii) Upon liquidation and distributes its audited financial statements prepared in accordance with generally accepted accounting principles to all limited partners (or members or other beneficial owners) promptly after the completion of such audit.

(5) *Registered Investment Companies*. You are not required to comply with this section (Rule 206(4)–2) with respect to the account of an investment company registered under the Investment Company Act of 1940 (15 U.S.C. 80a–1 to 80a–64).

(6) *Certain Related Persons*. Notwithstanding paragraph (a)(4) of this section, you are not required to obtain an independent verification of client funds and securities if:

(i) you have custody under this rule solely because a related person holds, directly or indirectly, client funds or securities, or has any authority to obtain possession of them, in connection with advisory services you provide to clients; and

(ii) your related person is operationally independent of you.

(c) *Delivery to Related Person*. Sending an account statement under paragraph (a)(5) of this section or distributing audited financial statements under paragraph (b)(4) of this section shall not satisfy the requirements of this section if such account statements or financial statements are sent solely to limited partners (or members or other beneficial owners) that themselves are limited partnerships (or limited liability companies, or another type of pooled investment vehicle) and are your related persons.

(d) *Definitions*. For the purposes of this section:

(1) *Control* means the power, directly or indirectly, to direct the management or policies of a person, whether through ownership of securities, by contract, or otherwise. Control includes:

(i) Each of your firm's officers, partners, or directors exercising executive responsibility (or persons having similar status or functions) is presumed to control your firm;

(ii) A person is presumed to control a corporation if the person:

(A) Directly or indirectly has the right to vote 25 percent or more of a class of the corporation's voting securities; or

(B) Has the power to sell or direct the sale of 25 percent or more of a class of the corporation's voting securities;

(iii) A person is presumed to control a partnership if the person has the right to receive upon dissolution, or has contributed, 25 percent or more of the capital of the partnership;

(iv) A person is presumed to control a limited liability company if the person:

(A) Directly or indirectly has the right to vote 25 percent or more of a class of the interests of the limited liability company;

(B) Has the right to receive upon dissolution, or has contributed, 25 percent or more of the capital of the limited liability company; or

(C) Is an elected manager of the limited liability company; or

(v) A person is presumed to control a trust if the person is a trustee or managing agent of the trust.

(2) *Custody* means holding, directly or indirectly, client funds or securities, or having any authority to obtain possession of them. You have custody if a related person holds, directly or indirectly, client funds or securities, or has any authority to obtain possession of them, in connection with advisory services you provide to clients. Custody includes:

(i) Possession of client funds or securities (but not of checks drawn by clients and made payable to third parties) unless you receive them inadvertently and you return them to the sender promptly but in any case within three business days of receiving them;

(ii) Any arrangement (including a general power of attorney) under which you are authorized or permitted to withdraw client funds or securities maintained with a custodian upon your instruction to the custodian; and

(iii) Any capacity (such as general partner of a limited partnership, managing member of a limited liability company or a comparable position for another type of pooled investment vehicle, or trustee of a trust) that gives you or your supervised person legal ownership of or access to client funds or securities.

(3) *Independent public accountant* means a public accountant that meets the standards of independence described in rule 2–01(b) and (c) of Regulation S–X (17 CFR 210.2–01(b) and (c)).

(4) *Independent representative* means a person that:

(i) Acts as agent for an advisory client, including in the case of a pooled investment vehicle, for limited partners of a limited partnership (or members of a limited liability company, or other beneficial owners of another type of pooled investment vehicle) and by law or contract is obliged to act in the best interest of the advisory client or the limited partners (or members, or other beneficial owners);

(ii) Does not control, is not controlled by, and is not under common control with you; and

(iii) Does not have, and has not had within the past two years, a material business relationship with you.

(5) *Operationally Independent*: for purposes of paragraph (b)(6) of this section, a related person is presumed not to be operationally independent unless each of the following conditions is met and no other circumstances can reasonably be expected to compromise the operational independence of the related person: (i) client assets in the custody of the related person are not subject to claims of the adviser's creditors; (ii) advisory personnel do not have custody or possession of, or direct or indirect access to client assets of which the related person has custody, or the power to control the disposition of such client assets to third parties for the benefit of the adviser or its related persons, or otherwise have the opportunity to misappropriate such client assets; (iii) advisory personnel and personnel of the related person who have access to advisory client assets are not under common supervision; and (iv) advisory personnel do not hold any position with the related person or share premises with the related person.

(6) *Qualified custodian* means:

(i) A bank as defined in section 202(a)(2) of the Advisers Act (15 U.S.C. 80b–2(a)(2)) or a savings association as defined in section 3(b)(1) of the Federal Deposit Insurance Act (12 U.S.C. 1813(b)(1)) that has deposits insured by the Federal Deposit Insurance Corporation under the Federal Deposit Insurance Act (12 U.S.C. 1811);

(ii) A broker-dealer registered under section 15(b)(1) of the Securities Exchange Act of 1934 (15 U.S.C. 78o(b)(1)), holding the client assets in customer accounts;

(iii) A futures commission merchant registered under section 4f(a) of the Commodity Exchange Act (7 U.S.C. 6f(a)), holding the client assets in customer accounts, but only with respect to clients' funds and security futures, or other securities incidental to transactions in contracts for the purchase or sale of a commodity for future delivery and options thereon; and

(iv) A foreign financial institution that customarily holds financial assets for its customers, provided that the foreign financial institution keeps the advisory clients' assets in customer accounts segregated from its proprietary assets.

(7) *Related person* means any person, directly or indirectly, controlling or controlled by you, and any person that is under common control with you.

Rule 206(4)–3. Cash payments for client solicitations

(a) It shall be unlawful for any investment adviser required to be registered pursuant to Section 203 of the Act to pay a cash fee, directly or indirectly, to a solicitor with respect to solicitation activities unless:

(1)(i) The investment adviser is registered under the Act;

(ii) The solicitor is not a person (A) subject to a Commission order issued under Section 203(f) of the Act, or (B) convicted within the previous ten years of any felony or misdemeanor involving conduct described in Section 203(e)(2)(A)–(D) of the Act or (C) who has been found by the Commission to have engaged, or has been convicted of engaging, in any of the conduct specified in paragraphs (1), (5) or (6) of Section 203(e) of the Act, or (D) is subject to an order, judgment or decree described in Section 203(e)(4) or the Act; and

(iii) Such cash fee is paid pursuant to a written agreement to which the adviser is a party; and

NOTE: The investment adviser shall retain a copy of each written agreement required by this paragraph as part of the records required to be kept under Rule 204–2(a)(10) of this chapter.

(2) Such cash fee is paid to a solicitor:

(i) With respect to solicitation activities for the provision of impersonal advisory services only; or

(ii) Who is (A) a partner, officer, director or employee of such investment advisor or (B) a partner, officer, director or employee of a person which controls, is controlled by, or is under common control with such investment adviser; *provided* that that status of such solicitor as a partner, officer, director or employee of such investment adviser or other person, and any affiliation between the investment adviser and such other person, is disclosed to the client at the time of the solicitation or referral; or

(iii) Other than a solicitor specified in paragraph (a)(2)(i) or (ii) above if all of the following conditions are met:

(A) The written agreement required by paragraph (a)(1)(iii) of this rule: (*1*) describes the solicitation activities to be engaged in by the solicitor on behalf of the investment adviser and the compensation to be received therefore; (*2*) contains an undertaking by the solicitor to perform his duties under the agreement in a manner consistent with the instructions of the investment adviser and the provisions of the Act and the rules thereunder; (*3*) requires that the solicitor, at the time of any solicitation activities for which compensation is paid or to be paid by the investment adviser, provide the client with a current copy of the investment adviser's written disclosure statement required by Rule 204–3 of this chapter ("brochure rule") and a separate written disclosure document described in paragraph (b) of this rule.

(B) The investment adviser receives from the client, prior to, or at the time of, entering into any written or oral investment advisory contract with such client, a signed and dated acknowledgement of receipt of the investment adviser's written disclosure statement and the solicitor's written disclosure document.

NOTE: The investment adviser shall retain a copy of each such acknowledgement and solicitor disclosure document as part of the records required to be kept under Rule 204–2(a)(15) of this chapter.

(C) The investment adviser makes a bona fide effort to ascertain whether the solicitor has complied with the agreement, and has a reasonable basis for believing that the solicitor has so complied.

(b) The separate written disclosure document required to be furnished by the solicitor to the client pursuant to this section shall contain the following information:

(1) The name of the solicitor;

(2) The name of the investment adviser;

(3) The nature of the relationship, including any affiliation, between the solicitor and the investment adviser;

(4) A statement that the solicitor will be compensated for his solicitation services by the investment adviser;

(5) The terms of such compensation arrangement, including a description of the compensation paid or to be paid to the solicitor, and

(6) The amount, if any, for the cost of obtaining his account the client will be charged in addition to the advisory fee, and the differential, if any, among clients with respect to the amount or level of advisory fees charged by the investment adviser if such differential is attributable to the existence of any arrangement pursuant to which the investment adviser has agreed to compensate the solicitor for soliciting clients for, or referring clients to, the investment adviser.

(c) Nothing in this section shall be deemed to relieve any person of any fiduciary or other obligation to which such person may be subject under the law.

(d) For purposes of this rule,

(1) *Solicitor* means any person who, directly or indirectly, solicits any client for, or refer any client to, an investment adviser.

(2) *Client* includes any prospective client.

(3) *Impersonal advisory services* means investment advisory services provided solely by means of (i) written materials or oral statements which do not purport to meet the objectives or needs of the specific client, (ii) statistical information containing no expressions of opinions as to the investment merits of particular securities, or (iii) any combination of the foregoing services.

(e) *Special Rule for Solicitation of Government Entity Clients.* Solicitation activities involving a government entity, as defined in Rule 206(4)–5, shall be subject to the additional limitations set forth in that section.

Rule 206(4)–4. [Reserved]

Rule 206(4)–5. Political contributions by certain investment advisers*

(a) *Prohibitions.* As a means reasonably designed to prevent fraudulent, deceptive or manipulative acts, practices, or courses of business within the meaning of section 206(4) of the Act (15 U.S.C. 80b–6(4)), it shall be unlawful:

(1) For any investment adviser registered (or required to be registered) with the Commission, or unregistered in reliance on the exemption available under section 203(b)(3) of the Investment Advisers Act (15 U.S.C. 80b–3(b)(3)), or that is an exempt reporting adviser, as defined in Rule 204–4(a), to provide investment advisory services for compensation to a government entity within two years after a contribution to an official of the government entity is made by the investment adviser or any covered associate of the investment adviser (including a person who becomes a covered associate within two years after the contribution is made); and

(2) For any investment adviser registered (or required to be registered) with the Commission, or unregistered in reliance on the exemption available under section 203(b)(3) of the Investment Advisers Act, or that is an exempt reporting adviser, or any of the investment adviser's covered associates:

(i) To provide or agree to provide, directly or indirectly, payment to any person to solicit a government entity for investment advisory services on behalf of such investment adviser unless such person is:

(A) A regulated person; or

(B) An executive officer, general partner, managing member (or, in each case, a person with a similar status or function), or employee of the investment adviser; and

(ii) To coordinate, or to solicit any person or political action committee to make, any:

(A) Contribution to an official of a government entity to which the investment adviser is providing or seeking to provide investment advisory services; or

(B) Payment to a political party of a state or locality where the investment adviser is providing or seeking to provide investment advisory services to a government entity.

(b) *Exceptions.*

(1) *De minimis Exception.* Paragraph (a)(1) of this section does not apply to contributions made by a covered associate, if a natural person, to officials for whom the covered associate was entitled to vote at the time of the contributions and which in the aggregate do not exceed $350 to any one official, per election, or to officials for whom the covered associate was not entitled to vote at the time of the contributions and which in the aggregate do not exceed $150 to any one official, per election.

(2) *Exception for Certain New Covered Associates.* The prohibitions of paragraph (a)(1) of this section shall not apply to an investment adviser as a result of a contribution made by a natural person more than six months prior to becoming a covered associate of the investment adviser unless such person, after becoming a covered associate, solicits clients on behalf of the investment adviser.

(3) *Exception for Certain Returned Contributions.*

(i) An investment adviser that is prohibited from providing investment advisory services for compensation pursuant to paragraph (a)(1) of this section as a result of a contribution made by a covered associate of the investment adviser is excepted from such prohibition, subject to paragraphs (b)(3)(ii) and (b)(3)(iii) of this section, upon satisfaction of the following requirements:

(A) The investment adviser must have discovered the contribution which resulted in the prohibition within four months of the date of such contribution;

(B) Such contribution must not have exceeded $350; and

(C) The contributor must obtain a return of the contribution within 60 calendar days of the date of discovery of such contribution by the investment adviser.

(ii) In any calendar year, an investment adviser that has reported on its annual updating amendment to Form ADV (17 CFR 279.1) that it has more than 50 employees is entitled to no

* Effective June 11, 2012 the Commission extended the compliance date for the ban on third-party solicitation until nine months after the compliance date of a final rule requiring municipal advisor firms to register under the Securities Exchange Act of 1934. See SEC Release no. IA–3418 (June 8, 2012).

more than three exceptions pursuant to paragraph (b)(3)(i) of this section, and an investment adviser that has reported on its annual updating amendment to Form ADV that it has 50 or fewer employees is entitled to no more than two exceptions pursuant to paragraph (b)(3)(i) of this section.

(iii) An investment adviser may not rely on the exception provided in paragraph (b)(3)(i) of this section more than once with respect to contributions by the same covered associate of the investment adviser regardless of the time period.

(c) *Prohibitions as Applied to Covered Investment Pools.* For purposes of this section, an investment adviser to a covered investment pool in which a government entity invests or is solicited to invest shall be treated as though that investment adviser were providing or seeking to provide investment advisory services directly to the government entity.

(d) *Further Prohibition.* As a means reasonably designed to prevent fraudulent, deceptive or manipulative acts, practices, or courses of business within the meaning of section 206(4) of the Investment Advisers Act, it shall be unlawful for any investment adviser registered (or required to be registered) with the Commission, or unregistered in reliance on the exemption available under section 203(b)(3) of the Investment Advisers Act, or that is an exempt reporting adviser, or any of the investment adviser's covered associates to do anything indirectly which, if done directly, would result in a violation of this section.

(e) *Exemptions.* The Commission, upon application, may conditionally or unconditionally exempt an investment adviser from the prohibition under paragraph (a)(1) of this section. In determining whether to grant an exemption, the Commission will consider, among other factors:

(1) Whether the exemption is necessary or appropriate in the public interest and consistent with the protection of investors and the purposes fairly intended by the policy and provisions of the Investment Advisers Act (15 U.S.C. 80b);

(2) Whether the investment adviser:

(i) Before the contribution resulting in the prohibition was made, adopted and implemented policies and procedures reasonably designed to prevent violations of this section; and

(ii) Prior to or at the time the contribution which resulted in such prohibition was made, had no actual knowledge of the contribution; and

(iii) After learning of the contribution:

(A) Has taken all available steps to cause the contributor involved in making the contribution which resulted in such prohibition to obtain a return of the contribution; and

(B) Has taken such other remedial or preventive measures as may be appropriate under the circumstances;

(3) Whether, at the time of the contribution, the contributor was a covered associate or otherwise an employee of the investment adviser, or was seeking such employment;

(4) The timing and amount of the contribution which resulted in the prohibition;

(5) The nature of the election (e.g, federal, state or local); and

(6) The contributor's apparent intent or motive in making the contribution which resulted in the prohibition, as evidenced by the facts and circumstances surrounding such contribution.

(f) *Definitions.* For purposes of this section:

(1) *Contribution* means any gift, subscription, loan, advance, or deposit of money or anything of value made for:

(i) The purpose of influencing any election for federal, state or local office;

(ii) Payment of debt incurred in connection with any such election; or

(iii) Transition or inaugural expenses of the successful candidate for state or local office.

(2) *Covered associate* of an investment adviser means:

(i) Any general partner, managing member or executive officer, or other individual with a similar status or function;

(ii) Any employee who solicits a government entity for the investment adviser and any person who supervises, directly or indirectly, such employee; and

(iii) Any political action committee controlled by the investment adviser or by any person described in paragraphs (f)(2)(i) and (f)(2)(ii) of this section.

(3) *Covered investment* pool means:

(i) An investment company registered under the Investment Company Act of 1940 (15 U.S.C. 80a) that is an investment option of a plan or program of a government entity; or

(ii) Any company that would be an investment company under section 3(a) of the Investment Company Act of 1940 (15 U.S.C. 80a–3(a)), but for the exclusion provided from that definition by either section 3(c)(1), section 3(c)(7) or section 3(c)(11) of that Act (15 U.S.C. 80a–3(c)(1), (c)(7) or (c)(11)).

(4) *Executive officer* of an investment adviser means:

(i) The president;

(ii) Any vice president in charge of a principal business unit, division or function (such as sales, administration or finance);

(iii) Any other officer of the investment adviser who performs a policy–making function; or

(iv) Any other person who performs similar policy–making functions for the investment adviser.

(5) *Government entity* means any state or political subdivision of a state, including:

(i) Any agency, authority, or instrumentality of the state or political subdivision;

(ii) A pool of assets sponsored or established by the state or political subdivision or any agency, authority or instrumentality thereof, including, but not limited to a "defined benefit plan" as defined in section 414(j) of the Internal Revenue Code (26 U.S.C. 414(j)), or a state general fund;

(iii) A plan or program of a government entity; and

(iv) Officers, agents, or employees of the state or political subdivision or any agency, authority or instrumentality thereof, acting in their official capacity.

(6) *Official* means any person (including any election committee for the person) who was, at the time of the contribution, an incumbent, candidate or successful candidate for elective office of a government entity, if the office:

(i) Is directly or indirectly responsible for, or can influence the outcome of, the hiring of an investment adviser by a government entity; or

(ii) Has authority to appoint any person who is directly or indirectly responsible for, or can influence the outcome of, the hiring of an investment adviser by a government entity.

(7) *Payment* means any gift, subscription, loan, advance, or deposit of money or anything of value.

(8) *Plan or program of a government entity* means any participant–directed investment program or plan sponsored or established by a state or political subdivision or any agency, authority or instrumentality thereof, including, but not limited to, a "qualified tuition plan" authorized by section 529 of the Internal Revenue Code (26 U.S.C. 529), a retirement plan authorized by section 403(b) or 457 of the Internal Revenue Code (26 U.S.C. 403(b) or 457), or any similar program or plan.

(9) *Regulated person* means:

(i) An investment adviser registered with the Commission that has not, and whose covered associates have not, within two years of soliciting a government entity:

(A) Made a contribution to an official of that government entity, other than as described in paragraph (b)(1) of this section; and

(B) Coordinated or solicited any person or political action committee to make any contribution or payment described in paragraphs (a)(2)(ii)(A) and (B) of this section;

(ii) A "broker," as defined in section 3(a)(4) of the Securities Exchange Act of 1934 (15 U.S.C. 78c(a)(4)) or a "dealer," as defined in section 3(a)(5) of that Act (15 U.S.C. 78c(a)(5)), that is registered with the Commission, and is a member of a national securities association registered under 15A of that Act (15 U.S.C. 78o–3), provided that:

(A) The rules of the association prohibit members from engaging in distribution or solicitation activities if certain political contributions have been made; and

(B) The Commission, by order, finds that such rules impose substantially equivalent or more stringent restrictions on broker-dealers than this section imposes on investment advisers and that such rules are consistent with the objectives of this section; and

(iii) A "municipal advisor" registered with the Commission under section 15B of the Exchange Act and subject to rules of the Municipal Securities Rulemaking Board, provided that:

(A) Such rules prohibit municipal advisors from engaging in distribution or solicitation activities if certain political contributions have been made; and

(B) The Commission, by order, finds that such rules impose substantially equivalent or more stringent restrictions on municipal advisors than this section imposes on investment advisers and that such rules are consistent with the objectives of this section.

(10) *Solicit* means:

(i) With respect to investment advisory services, to communicate, directly or indirectly, for the purpose of obtaining or retaining a client for, or referring a client to, an investment adviser; and

(ii) With respect to a contribution or payment, to communicate, directly or indirectly, for the purpose of obtaining or arranging a contribution or payment.

Rule 206(4)–6. Proxy voting

If you are an investment adviser registered or required to be registered under section 203 of the Act (15 U.S.C. 80b–3), it is fraudulent, deceptive, or manipulative act, practice or course of business within the meaning of section 206(4) of the Act (15 U.S.C. 80b–6(4)), for you to exercise voting authority with respect to client securities, unless you:

(a) Adopt and implement written policies and procedures that are reasonably designed to ensure that you vote client securities in the best interest of clients, which procedures must include how you address material conflicts that may arise between your interests and those of your clients;

(b) Disclose to clients how they may obtain information from you about how you voted with respect to their securities; and

(c) Describe to clients your proxy voting policies and procedures and, upon request, furnish a copy of the policies and procedures to the requesting client.

Rule 206(4)–7. Compliance procedures and practices

If you are an investment adviser registered or required to be registered under section 203 of the Investment Advisers Act of 1940 (15 U.S.C. 80b–3), it shall be unlawful within the meaning of section 206 of the Act (15 U.S.C. 80b–6) for you to provide investment advice to clients unless you:

(a) *Policies and Procedures.* Adopt and implement written policies and procedures reasonably designed to prevent violation, by you and your supervised persons, of the Act and the rules that the Commission has adopted under the Act;

(b) *Annual Review.* Review, no less frequently than annually, the adequacy of the policies and procedures established pursuant to this section and the effectiveness of their implementation; and

(c) *Chief Compliance Officer.* Designate an individual (who is a supervised person) responsible for administering the policies and procedures that you adopt under paragraph (a) of this rule

Rule 206(4)–8. Pooled investment vehicles

(a) *Prohibition.* It shall constitute a fraudulent, deceptive, or manipulative act, practice, or course of business within the meaning of section 206(4) of the Act (15 U.S.C. 80b–6(4)) for any investment adviser to a pooled investment vehicle to:

(1) Make any untrue statement of a material fact or to omit to state a material fact necessary to make the statements made, in the light of the circumstances under which they were made, not misleading, to any investor or prospective investor in the pooled investment vehicle; or

(2) Otherwise engage in any act, practice, or course of business that is fraudulent, deceptive, or manipulative with respect to any investor or prospective investor in the pooled investment vehicle.

(b) *Definition.* For purposes of this rule *pooled investment vehicle* means any investment company as defined in section 3(a) of the Investment Company Act of 1940 (15 U.S.C. 80a–3(a)) or any company that would be an investment company under section 3(a) of that Act but for the exclusion provided from that definition by either section 3(c)(1) or section 3(c)(7) of that Act (15 U.S.C. 80a–3(c)(1) or (7)).

Rule 222–1. Definitions

For purposes of section 222 (15 U.S.C. 80b–18a) of the Act:

(a) *Place of Business.* "Place of business" of an investment adviser means:

(1) An office at which the investment adviser regularly provides investment advisory services, solicits, meets with, or otherwise communicates with clients; and

(2) Any other location that is held out to the general public as a location at which the investment adviser provides investment advisory services,

solicits, meets with, or otherwise communicates with clients.

(b) *Principal Office and Place of Business.* "Principal office and place of business" of an investment adviser means the executive office of the investment adviser from which the officers, partners, or managers of the investment adviser direct, control, and coordinate the activities of the investment adviser.

Rule 222–2. Definition of "client" for purposes of the national de minimis standard

For purposes of section 222(d)(2) of the Act (15 U.S.C. 80b–18a(d)(2)), an investment adviser may rely upon the definition of "client" provided by Rule 202(a)(30)–1, without giving regard to paragraph (b)(4) of that section.

E. SEC RULES OF PRACTICE

(Cite as 17 CFR § 201.___)

GENERAL RULES

INITIATION OF PROCEEDINGS AND PREHEARING RULES

RULES REGARDING HEARINGS

INFORMAL PROCEDURES AND SUPPLEMENTARY INFORMATION CONCERNING ADJUDICATORY PROCEEDINGS

SUBPART E—ADJUSTMENT OF CIVIL MONETARY PENALTIES

GENERAL RULES

Rule 100. Scope of the rules of practice

(a) Unless provided otherwise, these Rules of Practice govern proceedings before the Commission under the statutes that it administers.

(b) These rules do not apply to:

(1) Investigations, except where made specifically applicable by the Rules Relating to Investigations, part 203 of this chapter; or

(2) Actions taken by the duty officer pursuant to delegated authority under 17 CFR 200.43.

(3) Initiation of proceedings for SRO proposed rule changes under Rules 700–701, except where made specifically applicable therein.

(c) The Commission, upon its determination that to do so would serve the interests of justice and not result in prejudice to the parties to the proceeding, may by order direct, in a particular proceeding, that an alternative procedure shall apply or that compliance with an otherwise applicable rule is unnecessary.

Rule 101. Definitions

(a) For purposes of these Rules of Practice, unless explicitly stated to the contrary:

(1) *Commission* means the United States Securities and Exchange Commission, or a panel of Commissioners constituting a quorum of the Commission, or a single Commissioner acting as duty officer pursuant to 17 CFR 200.43;

(2) *Counsel* means any attorney representing a party or any other person representing a party pursuant to Rule 102(b);

(3) *Disciplinary proceeding* means an action pursuant to Rule 102(e);

(4) *Enforcement proceeding* means an action, initiated by an order instituting proceedings, held for the purpose of determining whether or not a person is about to violate, has violated, has caused a violation of, or has aided or abetted a violation of any statute or rule administered by the Commission, or whether to impose a sanction as defined in Section 551(10) of the Administrative Procedure Act, 5 U.S.C. 551(10);

(5) *Hearing officer* means an administrative law judge, a panel of Commissioners constituting less than a quorum of the Commission, an individual Commissioner, or any other person duly authorized to preside at a hearing;

(6) *Interested division* means a division or an office assigned primary responsibility by the Commission to participate in a particular proceeding;

(7) *Order instituting proceedings* means an order issued by the Commission commencing a proceeding or an order issued by the Commission to hold a hearing;

(8) *Party* means the interested division, any person named as a respondent in an order instituting proceedings, any applicant named in the caption of any order, persons entitled to notice in a stop order proceeding as set forth in Rule 200(a)(2) or any person seeking Commission review of a decision;

(9) *Proceeding* means any agency process initiated:

(i) By an order instituting proceedings; or

(ii) By the filing, pursuant to Rule 410, of a petition for review of an initial decision by a hearing officer; or

(iii) By the filing, pursuant to Rule 420, of an application for review of a self-regulatory organization determination; or

(iv) By the filing, pursuant to Rule 430, of a notice of intention to file a petition for review of a determination made pursuant to delegated authority; or

(v) By the filing, pursuant to Rule 440, of an application for review of a determination by the Public Company Accounting Oversight Board; or

(vi) By the filing, pursuant to Rule 601 of Regulation NMS, of an application for review of an action or failure to act in connection with the implementation or operation of any effective transaction reporting plan; or

(vii) By the filing, pursuant to Rule 608 of Regulation NMS, of an application for review of an action taken or failure to act in connection with the implementation or operation of any effective national market system plan; or

(viii) By the filing, pursuant to Section 11A(b)(5) of the Securities Exchange Act of 1934, of an application for review of a determination of a registered securities information processor;

(10) *Secretary* means the Secretary of the Commission;

(11) *Temporary sanction* means a temporary cease-and-desist order or a temporary suspension of the registration of a broker, dealer, municipal securities dealer, government securities broker, government securities dealer, or transfer agent pending final determination whether the registration shall be revoked, and

(12) *Board* means the Public Company Accounting Oversight Board.

(b) [Reserved]

Rule 102. Appearance and practice before the Commission

A person shall not be represented before the Commission or a hearing officer except as stated in paragraphs (a) and (b) of this rule or as otherwise permitted by the Commission or a hearing officer.

(a) *Representing Oneself.* In any proceeding, an individual may appear on his or her own behalf.

(b) *Representing Others.* In any proceeding, a person may be represented by an attorney at law admitted to practice before the Supreme Court of the United States or the highest court of any State (as defined in Section 3(a)(16) of the Exchange Act, 15 U.S.C. 78c(a)(16)); a member of a partnership may represent the partnership; a bona fide officer of a corporation, trust or association may represent the corporation, trust or association; and an officer or employee of a state commission or of a department or political subdivision of a state may represent the state commission or the department or political subdivision of the state.

(c) *Former Commission Employees.* Former employees of the Commission must comply with the restrictions on practice contained in the Commission's Conduct Regulation, Subpart M, 17 CFR 200.735.

(d) *Designation of Address for Service; Notice of Appearance; Power of Attorney; Withdrawal.* (1) *Representing Oneself.* When an individual first makes any filing or otherwise appears on his or her own behalf before the Commission or a hearing officer in a proceeding as defined in Rule 101(a), he or she shall file with the Commission, or otherwise state on the record, and keep current, an address at which any notice or other written communication required to be served upon him or her or furnished to him or her may be sent and a telephone number where he or she may be reached during business hours.

(2) *Representing Others.* When a person first makes any filing or otherwise appears in a representative capacity before the Commission or a hearing officer in a proceeding as defined in Rule 101(a), that person shall file with the Commission, and keep current, a written notice stating the name of the proceeding; the representative's name, business address and telephone number; and the name and address of the person or persons represented.

(3) *Power of Attorney.* Any individual appearing or practicing before the Commission in a representative capacity may be required to file a power of attorney with the Commission showing his or her authority to act in such capacity.

(4) *Withdrawal.* Any person seeking to withdraw his or her appearance in a representative capacity shall file a notice of withdrawal with the Commission or the hearing officer. The notice shall state the name, address, and telephone number of the withdrawing representative; the name, address, and telephone number of the person for whom the appearance was made; and the effective date of the withdrawal. If the person seeking to withdraw knows the name, address, and telephone number of the new representative, or knows that the person for whom the appearance was made intends to represent him- or herself, that information shall be included in the notice. The notice must be served on the parties in accordance with Rule 150. The notice shall be filed at least five days before the proposed effective date of the withdrawal.

(e) *Suspension and Disbarment.* (1) *Generally.* The Commission may censure a person or deny, temporarily or permanently, the privilege of appearing or practicing before it in any way to any person who is found by the Commission after notice and opportunity for hearing in the matter:

(i) Not to possess the requisite qualifications to represent others; or

(ii) To be lacking in character or integrity or to have engaged in unethical or improper professional conduct; or

(iii) To have willfully violated, or willfully aided and abetted the violation of any provision of the Federal securities laws or the rules and regulations thereunder.

(iv) With respect to persons licensed to practice as accountants, "improper professional conduct" under Rule 102(e)(1)(ii) means:

(A) Intentional or knowing conduct, including reckless conduct, that results in a violation of applicable professional standards; or

(B) Either of the following two types of negligent conduct:

(*1*) A single instance of highly unreasonable conduct that results in a violation of applicable professional standards in circumstances in which an accountant knows, or should know, that heightened scrutiny is warranted.

(*2*) Repeated instances of unreasonable conduct, each resulting in a violation of applicable professional standards, that indicate a lack of competence to practice before the Commission.

(2) *Certain Professionals and Convicted Persons.* Any attorney who has been suspended or disbarred by a court of the United States or of any State; or any person whose license to practice as an accountant, engineer, or other professional or expert has been revoked or suspended in any State; or any person who has been convicted of a felony or a misdemeanor involving moral turpitude shall be forthwith suspended from appearing or practicing before the Commission. A disbarment, suspension, revocation or conviction within the meaning of this section shall be deemed to have occurred when the disbarring, suspending, revoking or convicting agency or tribunal enters its judgment or order, including a judgment or order on a plea of nolo contendere, regardless of whether an appeal of such judgment or order is pending or could be taken.

(3) *Temporary Suspensions.* An order of temporary suspension shall become effective upon service on the respondent. No order of temporary suspension shall be entered by the Commission pursuant to paragraph (e)(3)(i) of this section more than 90 days after the date on which the final judgment or order entered in a judicial or administrative proceeding described in paragraph (e)(3)(i)(A) or (e)(3)(i)(B) of this rule has become effective, whether upon completion of review or appeal procedures or because further review or appeal procedures are no longer available.

(i) The Commission, with due regard to the public interest and without preliminary hearing, may, by order, temporarily suspend from appearing or practicing before it any attorney, accountant, engineer, or other professional or expert who has been by name:

(A) Permanently enjoined by any court of competent jurisdiction, by reason of his or her misconduct in an action brought by the Commission, from violating or aiding and abetting the violation of any provision of the Federal securities laws or of the rules and regulations thereunder; or

(B) Found by any court of competent jurisdiction in an action brought by the Commission to which he or she is a party or found by the Commission in any administrative proceeding to which he or she is a party to have violated (unless the violation was found not to have been willful) or aided and abetted the violation of any provision of the Federal securities laws or of the rules and regulations thereunder.

(ii) Any person temporarily suspended from appearing and practicing before the Commission in accordance with paragraph (e)(3)(i) of this rule may, within 30 days after service upon him or her of the order of temporary suspension, petition the Commission to lift the temporary suspension. If no petition has been received by the Commission within 30 days after service of the order, the suspension shall become permanent.

(iii) Within 30 days after the filing of a petition in accordance with paragraph (e)(3)(ii) of this rule, the Commission shall either lift the temporary suspension, or set the matter down for hearing at a time and place designated by the Commission, or both, and, after opportunity for hearing, may censure the petitioner or disqualify the petitioner from appearing or practicing before the Commission for a period of time or permanently. In every case in which the temporary suspension has not been lifted, every hearing held and other action taken pursuant to this paragraph (e)(3) shall be expedited in accordance with Rule 500. If the hearing is held before a hearing officer, the time limits set forth in Rule 540 will govern review of the hearing officer's initial decision.

(iv) In any hearing held on a petition filed in accordance with paragraph (e)(3)(ii) of this rule, the staff of the Commission shall show either that the petitioner has been enjoined as described in paragraph (e)(3)(i)(A) of this rule or that the petitioner has been found to have committed or aided and abetted violations as described in paragraph (e)(3)(i)(B) of this rule and that showing, without more, may be the basis for censure or disqualification. Once that showing has been made, the burden shall be upon the petitioner to show cause why he or she should not be censured or temporarily or permanently disqualified from appearing and practicing before the Commission. In any such hearing, the petitioner may not contest any finding made against him or her or fact admitted by him or her in the judicial or administrative proceeding upon which the proceeding under this paragraph (e)(3) is predicated. A person who has consented to the entry of a permanent injunction as described in paragraph (e)(3)(i)(A) of this rule without admitting the facts set forth in the complaint shall be presumed for all purposes under this paragraph (e)(3) to have been enjoined by reason of the misconduct alleged in the complaint.

(4) *Filing of Prior Orders.* Any person appearing or practicing before the Commission who has been the subject of an order, judgment, decree, or finding as set forth in paragraph (e)(3) of this rule shall promptly file with the Secretary a copy thereof (together with any related opinion or statement of the agency or tribunal involved). Failure to file any such paper, order, judgment, decree or finding shall not impair the operation of any other provision of this section.

(5) *Reinstatement.* (i) An application for reinstatement of a person permanently suspended or disqualified under paragraph (e)(1) or (e)(3) of this rule may be made at any time, and the applicant may, in the Commission's discretion, be afforded a hearing; however, the suspension or disqualification shall continue unless and until the applicant has been reinstated by the Commission for good cause shown.

(ii) Any person suspended under paragraph (e)(2) of this rule shall be reinstated by the Commission, upon appropriate application, if all the grounds for application of the provisions of that paragraph are subsequently removed by a reversal of the conviction or termination of the suspension, disbarment, or revocation. An application for reinstatement on any other grounds by any person suspended under paragraph (e)(2) of this rule may be filed at any time and the applicant shall be accorded an opportunity for a hearing in the matter; however, such suspension shall continue unless and until the applicant has been reinstated by order of the Commission for good cause shown.

(6) *Other Proceedings Not Precluded.* A proceeding brought under paragraph (e)(1), (e)(2) or (e)(3) of this rule shall not preclude another proceeding brought under these same paragraphs.

(7) *Public Hearings.* All hearings held under this paragraph (e) shall be public unless otherwise ordered by the Commission on its own motion or after considering the motion of a party.

(f) *Practice Defined.* For the purposes of these Rules of Practice, practicing before the Commission shall include, but shall not be limited to:

(1) Transacting any business with the Commission; and

(2) The preparation of any statement, opinion or other paper by any attorney, accountant, engineer or other professional or expert, filed with the Commission in any registration statement, notification, application, report or other document with the consent of such attorney, accountant, engineer or other professional or expert.

Rule 103. Construction of rules

(a) The Rules of Practice shall be construed and administered to secure the just, speedy, and inexpensive determination of every proceeding.

(b) In any particular proceeding, to the extent that there is a conflict between these rules and a procedural requirement contained in any statute, or any rule or form adopted thereunder, the latter shall control.

(c) For purposes of these rules:

(1) Any term in the singular includes the plural, and any term in the plural includes the singular, if such use would be appropriate;

(2) Any use of a masculine, feminine, or neuter gender encompasses such other genders as would be appropriate; and

(3) Unless the context requires otherwise, counsel for a party may take any action required or permitted to be taken by such party.

Rule 104. Business hours

The Headquarters office of the Commission, at 100 F Street, NE, Washington, DC 20549, is open each day, except Saturdays, Sundays, and Federal legal holidays, from 9 a.m. to 5:30 p.m., Eastern Standard Time or Eastern Daylight Saving Time, whichever is currently in effect in Washington, D.C. Federal legal holidays consist of New Year's Day; Birthday of Martin Luther King, Jr.; Presidents Day; Memorial Day; Independence Day; Labor Day; Columbus Day; Veterans Day; Thanksgiving Day; Christmas Day; and any other day appointed as a holiday in Washington, D.C. by the President or the Congress of the United States.

Rule 110. Presiding officer

All proceedings shall be presided over by the Commission or, if the Commission so orders, by a hearing officer. When the Commission designates that the hearing officer shall be an administrative law judge, the Chief Administrative Law Judge shall select, pursuant to 17 CFR 200.30–10, the administrative law judge to preside.

Rule 111. Hearing officer: authority

The hearing officer shall have the authority to do all things necessary and appropriate to discharge his or her duties. No provision of these Rules of Practice shall be construed to limit the powers of the hearing officer provided by the Administrative Procedure Act, 5 U.S.C. 556, 557. The powers of the hearing officer include, but are not limited to, the following:

(a) Administering oaths and affirmations;

(b) Issuing subpoenas authorized by law and revoking, quashing, or modifying any such subpoena;

(c) Receiving relevant evidence and ruling upon the admission of evidence and offers of proof;

(d) Regulating the course of a proceeding and the conduct of the parties and their counsel;

(e) Holding prehearing and other conferences as set forth in Rule 221 and requiring the attendance at any such conference of at least one representative of each party who has authority to negotiate concerning the resolution of issues in controversy;

(f) Recusing himself or herself upon motion made by a party or upon his or her own motion;

(g) Ordering, in his or her discretion, in a proceeding involving more than one respondent, that the interested division indicate, on the record, at least one day prior to the presentation of any evidence, each respondent against whom that evidence will be offered;

(h) Subject to any limitations set forth elsewhere in these Rules of Practice, considering and ruling upon all procedural and other motions, including a motion to correct a manifest error of fact in the initial decision. A motion to correct is properly filed under this Rule only if the basis for the motion is a patent misstatement of fact in the initial decision. Any motion to correct must be filed within ten days of the initial decision. A brief in opposition may be filed within five days of a motion to correct. The hearing officer shall have 20 days from the date of filing of any brief in opposition filed to rule on a motion to correct;

(i) Preparing an initial decision as provided in Rule 360;

(j) Upon notice to all parties, reopening any hearing prior to the filing of an initial decision therein, or, if no initial decision is to be filed, prior to the time fixed for the filing of final briefs with the Commission; and

(k) Informing the parties as to the availability of one or more alternative means of dispute resolution, and encouraging the use of such methods.

Rule 112. Hearing officer: disqualification and withdrawal

(a) *Notice of Disqualification.* At any time a hearing officer believes himself or herself to be disqualified from considering a matter, the hearing officer shall issue a notice stating that he or she is withdrawing from the matter and setting forth the reasons therefor.

(b) *Motion for Withdrawal.* Any party who has a reasonable, good faith basis to believe that a hearing officer has a personal bias, or is otherwise disqualified from hearing a case, may make a motion to the hearing officer that the hearing officer withdraw. The motion shall be accompanied by an affidavit setting forth in detail the facts alleged to constitute grounds for disqualification. If the hearing officer finds himself or herself not disqualified, he or she shall so rule and shall continue to preside over the proceeding.

Rule 120. Ex parte communications

(a) Except to the extent required for the disposition of *ex parte* matters as authorized by law, the person presiding over an evidentiary hearing may not:

(1) Consult a person or party on a fact in issue, unless on notice and opportunity for all parties to participate; or

(2) Be responsible to or subject to the supervision or direction of an employee or agent engaged in the performance of investigative or prosecuting functions for the Commission.

(b) The Commission's code of behavior regarding *ex parte* communications between persons outside the Commission and decisional employees, 17 CFR 200.110 through 200.114, governs other prohibited communications during a proceeding conducted under the Rules of Practice.

Rule 121. Separation of functions

Any Commission officer, employee or agent engaged in the performance of investigative or prosecutorial functions for the Commission in a proceeding as defined in Rule § 101(a) may not, in that proceeding or one that is factually related, participate or advise in the decision, or in Commission review of the decision pursuant to Section 557 of the Administrative Procedure Act, 5 U.S.C. 557, except as a witness or counsel in the proceeding.

Rule 140. Commission orders and decisions: signature and availability

(a) *Signature Required.* All orders and decisions of the Commission shall be signed by the Secretary or any other person duly authorized by the Commission.

(b) *Availability for Inspection.* Each order and decision shall be available for inspection by the public from the date of entry, unless the order or decision is nonpublic. A nonpublic order or decision shall be available for inspection by any person entitled to inspect it from the date of entry.

(c) *Date of Entry of Orders.* The date of entry of a Commission order shall be the date the order is signed. Such date shall be reflected in the caption of the order, or if there is no caption, in the order itself.

Rule 141. Orders and decisions: service of orders instituting proceedings and other orders and decisions

(a) *Service of an Order Instituting Proceedings.*

(1) *By Whom Made.* The Secretary, or another duly authorized officer of the Commission, shall serve a copy of an order instituting proceedings on each person named in the order as a party. The Secretary may direct an interested division to assist in making service.

(2) *How Made.* (i) *To Individuals.* Notice of a proceeding shall be made to an individual by delivering a copy of the order instituting proceedings to the individual or to an agent authorized by appointment or by law to receive such notice. Delivery means—handing a copy of the order to the individual; or leaving a copy at the individual's office with a clerk or other person in charge thereof; or leaving a copy at the individual's dwelling house or usual place of abode with some person of suitable age and discretion then residing therein; or sending a copy of the order addressed to the individual by U.S. Postal Service certified, registered or Express Mail and obtaining a confirmation of receipt; or giving confirmed telegraphic notice.

(ii) *To Corporations or Entities.* Notice of a proceeding shall be made to a person other than a natural person by delivering a copy of the order instituting proceedings to an officer, managing or general agent, or any other agent authorized by appointment or law to receive such notice, by any method specified in paragraph (a)(2)(i) of this rule, or, in the case of an issuer of a class of securities registered with the Commission, by sending a copy of the order addressed to the most recent address shown on the entity's most recent filing with the Commission by U.S. Postal Service certified, registered, or Express Mail and obtaining a confirmation of attempted delivery.

(iii) *Upon Persons Registered with the Commission.* In addition to any other method of service specified in paragraph (a)(2) of this rule, notice may be made to a person currently registered with the Commission as a broker, dealer, municipal securities dealer, government securities broker, government securities dealer, investment adviser, investment company or transfer agent by sending a copy of the order addressed to the most recent business address shown on the person's registration form by U.S. Postal Service certified, registered or Express

Mail and obtaining a confirmation of attempted delivery.

(iv) *Upon Persons in a Foreign Country.* Notice of a proceeding to a person in a foreign country may be made by any of the following methods:

(A) Any method specified in paragraph (a)(2) of this rule that is not prohibited by the law of the foreign country; or

(B) By any internationally agreed means of service that is reasonably calculated to give notice, such as those authorized by the Hague Convention on the Service Abroad of Judicial and Extrajudicial Documents; or

(C) Any method that is reasonably calculated to give notice:

(*1*) As prescribed by the foreign country's law for service in that country in an action in its courts of general jurisdiction; or

(*2*) As the foreign authority directs in response to a letter rogatory or letter of request; or

(*3*) Unless prohibited by the foreign country's law, by delivering a copy of the order instituting proceedings to the individual personally, or using any form of mail that the Secretary or the interested division addresses and sends to the individual and that requires a signed receipt; or

(D) By any other means not prohibited by international agreement, as the Commission or hearing officer orders.

(v) *In Stop Order Proceedings.* Notwithstanding any other provision of paragraph (a)(2) of this rule, in proceedings pursuant to Sections 8 or 10 of the Securities Act of 1933, 15 U.S.C. 77h or 77j, or Sections 305 or 307 of the Trust Indenture Act of 1939, 15 U.S.C. 77eee or 77ggg, notice of the institution of proceedings shall be made by personal service or confirmed telegraphic notice, or a waiver obtained pursuant to paragraph (a)(4) of this rule.

(vi) *To Persons Registered with Self-Regulatory Organizations.* Notice of a proceeding shall be made to a person registered with a self-regulatory organization by any method specified in paragraph (a)(2)(i) of this rule, or by sending a copy of the order addressed to the most recent address for the person shown in the Central Registration Depository by U.S. Postal Service certified, registered, or Express Mail and obtaining a confirmation of attempted delivery.

(3) *Record of Service.* The Secretary shall maintain a record of service on parties (in hard copy or computerized format), identifying the party given notice, the method of service, the date of service, the address to which service was made, and the person who made service. If a division serves a copy of an order instituting proceedings, the division shall file with the Secretary either an acknowledgement of service by the person served or proof of service consisting of a statement by the person who made service certifying the date and manner of service; the names of the persons served; and their mail or electronic addresses, facsimile numbers, or the addresses of the places of delivery, as appropriate for the manner of service. If service is made in person, the certificate of service shall state, if available, the name of the individual to whom the order was given. If service is made by U.S. Postal Service certified or Express Mail, the Secretary shall maintain the confirmation of receipt or of attempted delivery, and tracking number. If service is made to an agent authorized by appointment to receive service, the certificate of service shall be accompanied by evidence of the appointment.

(4) *Waiver of Service.* In lieu of service as set forth in paragraph (a)(2) of this rule, the party may be provided a copy of the order instituting proceedings by first class mail or other reliable means if a waiver of service is obtained from the party and placed in the record.

(b) *Service of Orders or Decisions Other than an Order Instituting Proceedings.* Written orders or decisions issued by the Commission or by a hearing officer shall be served promptly on each party pursuant to any method of service authorized under paragraph (a) of this rule or 17 CFR 201.150(c)(1)-(3). Such orders or decisions may also be served by facsimile transmission if the party to be served has agreed to accept such service in a writing, signed by the party, and has provided the Commission with information concerning the facsimile machine telephone number and hours of facsimile machine operation. Service of orders or decisions by the Commission, including those entered pursuant to delegated authority, shall be made by the Secretary or, as authorized by the Secretary, by a member of an interested division. Service of orders or decisions issued by a hearing officer shall be made by the Secretary or the hearing officer.

Rule 150. Service of papers by parties

(a) *When Required.* In every proceeding as defined in Rule 101(a), each paper, including each notice of appearance, written motion, brief, or other written communication, shall be served upon each party in the proceeding in accordance with the provisions of this section; provided, however, that absent an order to the contrary, no service shall be required for motions which may be heard *ex parte.*

(b) *Upon a Person Represented by Counsel.* Whenever service is required to be made upon a person represented by counsel who has filed a notice of appearance pursuant to Rule 102, service shall be made pursuant to paragraph (c) of this rule upon counsel, unless service upon the person represented is ordered by the Commission or the hearing officer.

(c) *How Made.* Service shall be made by delivering a copy of the filing. *Delivery* means:

(1) Personal service—handing a copy to the person required to be served; or leaving a copy at the person's office with a clerk or other person in charge thereof, or, if there is no one in charge, leaving it in a conspicuous place therein; or, if the office is closed or the person to be served has no office, leaving it at the person's dwelling house or usual place of abode with some person of suitable age and discretion then residing therein;

(2) Mailing the papers through the U.S. Postal Service by first class, registered, or certified mail or Express Mail delivery addressed to the person;

(3) Sending the papers through a commercial courier service or express delivery service; or

(4) Transmitting the papers by facsimile transmission where the following conditions are met:

(i) The persons so serving each other have provided the Commission and the parties with notice of the facsimile machine telephone number to be used and the hours of facsimile machine operation;

(ii) The transmission is made at such a time that it is received during the Commission's business hours as defined in Rule 104; and

(iii) The sender of the transmission previously has not been served in accordance with Rule 150 with a written notice from the recipient of the transmission declining service by facsimile transmission.

(d) *When Service Is Complete.* Personal service, service by U.S. Postal Service Express Mail or service by a commercial courier or express delivery service is complete upon delivery. Service by mail is complete upon mailing. Service by facsimile is complete upon confirmation of transmission by delivery of a manually signed receipt.

Rule 151. Filing of papers with the Commission: procedure

(a) *When to File.* All papers required to be served by a party upon any person shall be filed contemporaneously with the Commission. Papers required to be filed with the Commission must be received within the time limit, if any, for such filing. Filing with the Commission may be made by facsimile transmission if the party also contemporaneously transmits to the Commission a non-facsimile original with a manual signature. However, any person filing with the Commission by facsimile transmission will be responsible for assuring that the Commission receives a complete and legible filing within the time limit set for such filing.

(b) *Where to File.* Filing of papers with the Commission shall be made by filing them with the Secretary. When a proceeding is assigned to a hearing officer, a person making a filing with the Secretary shall promptly provide to the hearing officer a copy of any such filing, provided, however, that the hearing officer may direct or permit filings to be made with him or her, in which event the hearing officer shall note thereon the filing date and promptly provide the Secretary with either the original or a copy of any such filings.

(c) *To Whom to Direct the Filing.* Unless otherwise provided, where the Commission has assigned a case to a hearing officer, all motions, objections, applications or other filings made during a proceeding prior to the filing of an initial decision therein, or, if no initial decision is to be filed, prior to the time fixed for the filing of briefs with the Commission, shall be directed to and decided by the hearing officer.

(d) *Certificate of Service.* Papers filed with the Commission or a hearing officer shall be accompanied by a certificate stating the name of the person or persons served, the date of service, the method of service and the mailing address or facsimile telephone number to which service was made, if not made in person. If the method of service to any party is different from the method of service to any other party or the method for filing with the Commission, the certificate shall state why a different means of service was used.

Rule 152. Filing of papers: form

(a) *Specifications.* Papers filed in connection with any proceeding as defined in Rule 101(a) shall:

(1) Be on one grade of unglazed white paper measuring 8½ x 11 inches, except that, to the extent that the reduction of larger documents would render them illegible, such documents may be filed on larger paper;

(2) Be typewritten or printed in 12–point or larger typeface or otherwise reproduced by a process that produces permanent and plainly legible copies;

(3) Include at the head of the paper, or on a title page, the name of the Commission, the title of the proceeding, the names of the parties, the subject of the particular paper or pleading, and the file number assigned to the proceeding;

(4) Be paginated with left hand margins at least 1 inch wide, and other margins of at least 1 inch;

(5) Be double-spaced, with single-spaced footnotes and single-spaced indented quotations; and

(6) Be stapled, clipped or otherwise fastened in the upper left corner.

(b) *Signature Required.* All papers must be dated and signed as provided in Rule 153.

(c) *Suitability for Recordkeeping.* Documents which, in the opinion of the Commission, are not suitable for computer scanning or microfilming may be rejected.

(d) *Number of Copies.* An original and three copies of all papers shall be filed, unless filing is made by facsimile in accordance with Rule 151. If filing is made by facsimile, the filer shall also transmit to the Office of the Secretary one non-facsimile original with a manual signature, contemporaneously with the facsimile transmission. The non-facsimile original must be accompanied by a statement of the date on which, and the facsimile number to which, the party made transmission of the facsimile filing.

(e) *Form of Briefs.* All briefs containing more than 10 pages shall include a table of contents, an alphabetized table of cases, a table of statutes, and a table of other authorities cited, with references to the pages of the brief wherein they are cited.

(f) *Scandalous or Impertinent Matter.* Any scandalous or impertinent matter contained in any brief or pleading or in connection with any oral presentation in a proceeding may be stricken on order of the Commission or the hearing officer.

Rule 153. Filing of papers: signature requirement and effect

(a) *General Requirements.* Following the issuance of an order instituting proceedings, every filing of a party represented by counsel shall be signed by at least one counsel of record in his or her name and shall state that counsel's business address and telephone number. A party who acts as his or her own counsel shall sign his or her individual name and state his or her address and telephone number on every filing.

(b) *Effect of Signature.* (1) The signature of a counsel or party shall constitute a certification that:

(i) the person signing the filing has read the filing;

(ii) to the best of his or her knowledge, information, and belief, formed after reasonable inquiry, the filing is well grounded in fact and is warranted by existing law or a good faith argument for the extension, modification, or reversal of existing law; and

(iii) the filing is not made for any improper purpose, such as to harass or to cause unnecessary delay or needless increase in the cost of adjudication.

(2) If a filing is not signed, the hearing officer or the Commission shall strike the filing, unless it is signed promptly after the omission is called to the attention of the person making the filing.

Rule 154. Motions

(a) *Generally.* Unless made during a hearing or conference, a motion shall be in writing, shall state with particularity the grounds therefor, shall set forth the relief or order sought, and shall be accompanied by a written brief of the points and authorities relied upon. All written motions shall be served in accordance with Rule 150, be filed in accordance with Rule 151, meet the requirements of Rule 152, and be signed in accordance with Rule 153. The Commission or the hearing officer may order that an oral motion be submitted in writing. Unless otherwise ordered by the Commission or the hearing officer, if a motion is properly made to the Commission concerning a proceeding to which a hearing officer is assigned, the proceeding before the hearing officer shall continue pending the determination of the motion by the Commission. No oral argument shall be heard on any motion unless the Commission or the hearing officer otherwise directs.

(b) *Opposing and Reply Briefs.* Briefs in opposition to a motion shall be filed within five days after service of the motion. Reply briefs shall be filled within three days after service of the opposition.

(c) *Length Limitation.* No motion (together with the brief in support of the motion), brief in opposition to the motion, or reply brief shall exceed 7,000 words, exclusive of any table of contents or table of authorities. The word limit shall not apply to any addendum that consists solely of copies of applicable cases, pertinent legislative provisions or rules, or relevant exhibits. Requests for leave to file motions and briefs in excess of 7,000 words are disfavored. A motion or brief, together with any accompanying brief, that does not exceed 15 pages in length, exclusive of pages containing the table of contents, table of authorities, and any addendum that consists solely of copies of applicable cases, pertinent legislative provisions, or rules and exhibits, but inclusive of pleadings incorporated by reference, is presumptively considered to contain no more than 7,000 words. Any motion or brief that exceeds these page limits must include a certificate by the attorney, or an unrepresented party, stating that the document complies with the length limitation set forth in this paragraph and stating the number of words in the document. The person preparing the certificate may rely on the word count of a word processing program to prepare the document.

Rule 155. Default; motion to set aside default

(a) A party to a proceeding may be deemed to be in default and the Commission or the hearing officer may determine the proceeding against that party upon consideration of the record, including the order instituting proceedings, the allegations of which may be deemed to be true, if that party fails:

(1) To appear, in person or through a representative, at a hearing or conference of which that party has been notified;

(2) To answer, to respond to a dispositive motion within the time provided, or otherwise to defend the proceeding; or

(3) To cure a deficient filing within the time specified by the commission or the hearing officer pursuant to Rule 180(b).

(b) A motion to set aside a default shall be made within a reasonable time, state the reasons for the failure to appear or defend, and specify the nature of the proposed defense in the proceeding. In order to prevent injustice and on such conditions as may be appropriate, the hearing officer, at any time prior to the filing of the initial decision, or the Commission, at any time, may for good cause shown set aside a default.

Rule 160. Time computation

(a) *Computation.* In computing any period of time prescribed in or allowed by these Rules of Practice or by order of the Commission, the day of the act, event, or default from which the designated period of time begins to run shall not be included. The last day of the period so computed shall be included unless it is a Saturday, Sunday, or Federal legal holiday (as defined in Rule 104), in which event the period runs until the end of the next day that is not a Saturday, Sunday, or Federal legal holiday. Intermediate Saturdays, Sundays, and Federal legal holidays shall be excluded from the computation when the period of time prescribed or allowed is seven days or less, not including any additional time allowed for service by mail in paragraph (b) of this rule. If on the day a filing is to be made, weather or other conditions have caused the Secretary's office or other designated filing location to close, the filing deadline shall be extended to the end of the next day that is neither a Saturday, a Sunday, nor a Federal legal holiday.

(b) *Additional Time for Service by Mail.* If service is made by mail, three days shall be added to the prescribed period for response unless an order of the Commission or the hearing officer specifies a date certain for filing. In the event that an order of the Commission or the hearing officer specifies a date certain for filing, no time shall be added for service by mail.

Rule 161. Extensions of time, postponements and adjournments

(a) *Availability.* Except as otherwise provided by law, the Commission, at any time, or the hearing officer, at any time prior to the filing of his or her initial decision or, if no initial decision is to be filed, at any time prior to the closing of the record, may, for good cause shown, extend or shorten any time limits prescribed by these Rules of Practice for the filing of any papers and may, consistent with paragraphs (b) and (c) of this rule, postpone or adjourn any hearing.

(b) *Considerations in Determining Whether to Extend Time Limits or Grant Postponements, Adjournments and Extensions.* (1) In considering all motions or requests pursuant to paragraph (a) or (b) of this rule, the Commission or the hearing officer should adhere to a policy of strongly disfavoring such requests, except in circumstances where the requesting party makes a strong showing that the denial of the request or motion would substantially prejudice their case. In determining whether to grant any requests, the Commission or hearing officer shall consider, in addition to any other relevant factors:

(i) The length of the proceeding to date;

(ii) The number of postponements, adjournments or extensions already granted;

(iii) The stage of the proceedings at the time of the request;

(iv) The impact of the request on the hearing officer's ability to complete the proceeding in the time specified by the Commission; and

(v) Any other such matters as justice may require.

(2) To the extent that the Commission has chosen a timeline under which the hearing would occur beyond the statutory 60–day deadline, this policy of strongly disfavoring requests for postponement will not apply to a request by a respondent to postpone commencement of a cease and desist proceeding hearing beyond the statutory 60–day period.

(c)(1) *Time Limit.* Postponements, adjournments or extensions of time for filing papers shall not exceed 21 days unless the Commission or the hearing officer states on the record or sets forth in a written order the reasons why a longer period of time is necessary.

(2) *Stay Pending Commission Consideration of Offers of Settlement.* (i) If the Commission staff and one or more respondents in the proceeding file a joint motion notifying the hearing officer that they have agreed in principle to a settlement on all major terms, then the hearing officer shall stay the proceeding as to the settling respondent(s), or in the discretion of the hearing officer as to all respondents, pending completion of Commission consideration of the settlement offer. Any such stay will be contingent upon:

(A) The settling respondent(s) submitting to the Commission staff, within fifteen business days of the stay, a signed offer of settlement in conformance with Rule 240; and

(B) Within twenty business days of receipt of the signed offer, the staff submitting the settlement offer and accompanying recommendation to the Commission for consideration.

(ii) If the parties fail to meet either of these deadlines or if the Commission rejects the offer of settlement, the hearing officer must be promptly notified and, upon notification of the hearing officer, the stay shall lapse and the proceeding will continue. In the circumstance where:

(A) A hearing officer has granted a stay because the parties have "agreed in principle to a settlement;"

(B) The agreement in principle does not materialize into a signed settlement offer within 15 business days of the stay; and

(C) The stay lapses, the hearing officer will not be required to grant another stay related to the settlement process until both parties have notified the hearing officer in writing that a signed settlement offer has been prepared, received by the Commission's staff, and will be submitted to the Commission.

(iii) The granting of any stay pursuant to this paragraph (c) shall stay the timeline pursuant to Rule 360(a).

Rule 180. Sanctions

(a) *Contemptuous Conduct.* (1) *Subject to Exclusion or Suspension.* Contemptuous conduct by any person before the Commission or a hearing officer during any proceeding, including at or in connection with any conference, deposition or hearing, shall be grounds for the Commission or the hearing officer to:

(i) Exclude that person from such deposition, hearing or conference, or any portion thereof; and/or

(ii) Summarily suspend that person from representing others in the proceeding in which such conduct occurred for the duration, or any portion, of the proceeding.

(2) *Review Procedure.* A person excluded from a deposition, hearing or conference, or a counsel summarily suspended from practice for the duration or any portion of a proceeding, may seek review of the exclusion or suspension by filing with the Commission, within three days of the exclusion or suspension order, a motion to vacate the order. The Commission shall consider such motion on an expedited basis as provided in Rule 500.

(3) *Adjournment.* Upon motion by a party represented by counsel subject to an order of exclusion or suspension, an adjournment shall be granted to allow the retention of new counsel. In determining the length of an adjournment, the Commission or hearing officer shall consider, in addition to the factors set forth in Rule 161, the availability of

co-counsel for the party or of other members of a suspended counsel's firm.

(b) *Deficient Filings; Leave to Cure Deficiencies.* The Commission or the hearing officer may reject, in whole or in part, any filing that fails to comply with any requirements of these Rules of Practice or of any order issued in the proceeding in which the filing was made. Any such filings shall not be part of the record. The Commission or the hearing officer may direct a party to cure any deficiencies and to resubmit the filing within a fixed time period.

(c) *Failure to Make Required Filing or to Cure Deficient Filing.* The Commission or the hearing officer may enter a default pursuant to Rule 155, dismiss one or more claims, decide the particular claim(s) at issue against that person, or prohibit the introduction of evidence or exclude testimony concerning that claim if a person fails:

(1) To make a filing required under these Rules of Practice; or

(2) To cure a deficient filing within the time specified by the Commission or the hearing officer pursuant to paragraph (b) of this rule.

Rule 190. Confidential treatment of information in certain filings

(a) *Application.* An application for confidential treatment pursuant to the provisions of Clause 30 of Schedule A of the Securities Act of 1933, 15 U.S.C. 77aa(30), and Rule 406 thereunder, 17 CFR 230.406; Section 24(b)(2) of the Securities Exchange Act of 1934, 15 U.S.C. 78x(b)(2), and Rule 24b–2 thereunder, 17 CFR 240.24b–2; Section 45(a) of the Investment Company Act of 1940, 15 U.S.C. 80a–44(a), and Rule 45a–1 thereunder, 17 CFR 270.45a–1; or Section 210(a) of the Investment Advisers Act of 1940, 15 U.S.C. 80b–10(a), shall be filed with the Secretary. The application shall be accompanied by a sealed copy of the materials as to which confidential treatment is sought.

(b) *Procedure for Supplying Additional Information.* The applicant may be required to furnish in writing additional information with respect to the grounds for objection to public disclosure. Failure to supply the information so requested within 14 days from the date of receipt by the applicant of a notice of the information required shall be deemed a waiver of the objection to public disclosure of that portion of the information to which the additional information relates, unless the Commission or the hearing officer shall otherwise order for good cause shown at or before the expiration of such 14–day period.

(c) *Confidentiality of Materials Pending Final Decision.* Pending the determination of the application for confidential treatment, transcripts, non-final orders including an initial decision, if any, and other materials in connection with the application shall be placed under seal; shall be for the confidential use only of the hearing officer, the Commission, the applicant, and any other parties and counsel; and shall be made available to the public only in accordance with orders of the Commission.

(d) *Public Availability of Orders.* Any final order of the Commission denying or sustaining an application for confidential treatment shall be made public. Any prior findings or opinions relating to an application for confidential treatment under this section shall be made public at such time as the material as to which confidentiality was requested is made public.

Rule 191. Adjudications not required to be determined on the record after notice and opportunity for hearing

(a) *Scope of the Rule.* This rule applies to every case of adjudication, as defined in 5 U.S.C. 551, pursuant to any statute which the Commission administers, where adjudication is not required to be determined on the record after notice and opportunity for hearing and which the Commission has not chosen to determine on the record after notice and opportunity for hearing.

(b) *Procedure.* In every case of adjudication under paragraph (a) of this section, the Commission shall give prompt notice of any adverse action or final disposition to any person who has requested the Commission to make (or not to make) any such adjudication, and furnish to any such person a written statement of reasons therefor. Additional procedures may be specified in rules relating to specific types of such adjudications. Where any such rule provides for the publication of a Commission order, notice of the action or disposition shall be deemed to be given by such publication.

(c) *Contents of the Record.* If the Commission provides notice and opportunity for the submission of written comments by parties to the adjudication or, as the case may be, by other interested persons, written comments received on or before the closing date for comments, unless accorded confidential treatment pursuant to statute or rule of the Commission, become a part of the record of the adjudication. The Commission, in its discretion, may accept and include in the record written comments filed with the Commission after the closing date.

Rule 192. Rulemaking: issuance, amendment and repeal of rules of general application

(a) *By Petition.* Any person desiring the issuance, amendment or repeal of a rule of general application may file a petition therefore with the Secretary. Such petition shall include a statement setting forth the text or the substance of any proposed rule or amendment desired or specifying the rule the repeal of which is desired, and stating the nature of his or her interest and his or her reasons for seeking the issuance, amendment or repeal of the rule. The Secretary shall acknowledge, in writing, receipt of the petition and refer it to the appropriate division or office for consideration and recommendation. Such recommendations shall be transmitted with the petition to the Commission for such action as the Commission deems appropriate. The Secretary shall notify the petitioner of the action taken by the Commission.

(b) *Notice of Proposed Issuance, Amendment or Repeal of Rules.* Except where the Commission finds that notice and public procedure are impracticable, unnecessary, or contrary to the public interest, whenever the Commission proposes to issue, amend, or repeal any rule or regulation of general application other than an interpretive rule; general statement of policy; or rule of agency organization, procedure, or practice; or any matter relating to agency management or personnel or to public property, loans, grants, benefits, or contracts, there shall first be published in the FEDERAL REGISTER a notice of the proposed action. Such notice shall include:

(1) A statement of the time, place, and nature of the rulemaking proceeding, with particular reference to the manner in which interested persons shall be afforded the opportunity to participate in such proceeding;

(2) Reference to the authority under which the rule is proposed; and

(3) The terms or substance of the proposed rule or a description of the subjects and issues involved.

Rule 193. Applications by barred individuals for consent to associate

PRELIMINARY NOTE

This rule governs applications to the Commission by certain persons, barred by Commission order from association with brokers, dealers, municipal securities dealers, government securities brokers, government securities dealers, investment advisers, investment companies or transfer agents, for consent to become so associated. Applications made pursuant to this section must show that the proposed association would be consistent with the public interest. In addition to the information specifically required by the rule, applications should be supplemented, where appropriate, by written statements of individuals (other than the applicant) who are competent to attest to the applicant's character, employment performance, and other relevant information. Intentional misstatements or omissions of fact may constitute criminal violations of 18 U.S.C. 1001 *et seq.* and other provisions of law.

The nature of the supervision that an applicant will receive or exercise as an associated person with a registered entity is an important matter bearing upon the public interest. In meeting the burden of showing that the proposed association is consistent with the public interest, the application and supporting documentation must demonstrate that the proposed supervision, procedures, or terms and conditions of employment are reasonably designed to prevent a recurrence of the conduct that led to imposition of the bar. As an associated person, the applicant will be limited to association in a specified capacity with a particular registered entity and may also be subject to specific terms and conditions.

Normally, the applicant's burden of demonstrating that the proposed association is consistent with the public interest will be difficult to meet where the applicant is to be supervised by, or is to supervise, another barred individual. In addition, where an applicant wishes to become the sole proprietor of a registered entity and thus is seeking Commission consent notwithstanding an absence of supervision, the applicant's burden will be difficult to meet.

In addition to the factors set forth in paragraph (d) of this section, the Commission will consider the nature of the findings that resulted in the bar when making its determination as to whether the proposed association is consistent with the public interest. In this regard, attention is directed to Rule 5(e) of the Commission's Rules on Informal and Other Procedures, 17 CFR 202.5(e). Among other things, Rule 5(e) sets forth the Commission's policy "not to permit a * * * respondent [in an administrative proceeding] to consent to * * * [an] order that imposes a sanction while denying the allegations in the * * * order for proceedings." Consistent with the rationale underlying that policy, and in order to avoid the appearance that an application made pursuant to this section was granted on the basis of such denial, the Commission will not consider any application that attempts to reargue or collaterally attack the findings that resulted in the Commission's bar order.

(a) *Scope of Rule.* Applications for Commission consent to associate, or to change the terms and conditions of association, with a registered broker, dealer, municipal securities dealer, government securities broker, government securities dealer, investment adviser, investment company or transfer agent may be made pursuant to this section where a Commission order bars the individual from association with a registered entity and:

(1) Such barred individual seeks to become associated with an entity that is not a member of a self-regulatory organization; or

(2) The order contains a proviso that application may be made to the Commission after a specified period of time.

(b) *Form of Application.* Each application shall be supported by an affidavit, manually signed by the applicant, that addresses the factors set forth in paragraph (d) of this section. One original and three copies of the application shall be filed pursuant to Rules 151, 152 and 153. Each application shall include as exhibits:

(1) A copy of the Commission order imposing the bar;

(2) An undertaking by the applicant to notify immediately the Commission in writing if any information submitted in support of the application becomes materially false or misleading while the application is pending;

(3) The following forms, as appropriate:

(i) A copy of a completed Form U–4, where the applicant's proposed association is with a broker-dealer or municipal securities dealer;

(ii) A copy of a completed Form MSD–4, where the applicant's proposed association is with a bank municipal securities dealer;

(iii) The information required by Form ADV, 17 CFR 279.1, with respect to the applicant, where the applicant's proposed association is with an investment adviser;

(iv) The information required by Form TA–1, 17 CFR 249b.100, with respect to the applicant, where the applicant's proposed association is with a transfer agent; and

(4) A written statement by the proposed employer that describes:

(i) The terms and conditions of employment and supervision to be exercised over such applicant and, where applicable, by such applicant;

(ii) The qualifications, experience, and disciplinary records of the proposed supervisor(s) of the applicant;

(iii) The compliance and disciplinary history, during the two years preceding the filing of the application, of the office in which the applicant will be employed; and

(iv) The names of any other associated persons in the same office who have previously been barred by the Commission, and whether they are to be supervised by the applicant.

(c) *Required Showing.* The applicant shall make a showing satisfactory to the Commission that the proposed association would be consistent with the public interest.

(d) *Factors to Be Addressed.* The affidavit required by paragraph (b) of this rule shall address each of the following:

(1) The time period since the imposition of the bar;

(2) Any restitution or similar action taken by the applicant to recompense any person injured by the misconduct that resulted in the bar;

(3) The applicant's compliance with the order imposing the bar;

(4) The applicant's employment during the period subsequent to imposition of the bar;

(5) The capacity or position in which the applicant proposes to be associated;

(6) The manner and extent of supervision to be exercised over such applicant and, where applicable, by such applicant;

(7) Any relevant courses, seminars, examinations or other actions completed by the applicant subsequent to imposition of the bar to prepare for his or her return to the securities business; and

(8) Any other information material to the application.

(e) *Notification to Applicant and Written Statement.* In the event an adverse recommendation is proposed by the staff with respect to an application made pursuant to this section, the applicant shall be so advised and provided with a written statement of the reasons for such recommendation. The applicant shall then have 30 days to submit a written statement in response.

(f) *Concurrent Applications.* The Commission will not consider any application submitted pursuant to this section if any other application for consent to associate concerning the same applicant is pending before any self-regulatory organization.

INITIATION OF PROCEEDINGS AND PREHEARING RULES

Rule 200. Initiation of proceedings

(a) *Order Instituting Proceedings: Notice and Opportunity for Hearing.* (1) *Generally.* Whenever an order instituting proceedings is issued by the Commission, appropriate notice thereof shall be given to each party to the proceeding by the Secretary or another duly designated officer of the Commission. Each party shall be given notice of any hearing within a time reasonable in light of the circumstances, in advance of the hearing; provided, however, no prior notice need be given to a respondent if the Commission has authorized the Division of Enforcement to seek a temporary sanction *ex parte*.

(2) *Stop Order Proceedings: Additional Persons Entitled to Notice.* Any notice of a proceeding relating to the issuance of a stop order suspending the effectiveness of a registration statement pursuant to Section 8(d) of the Securities Act of 1933, 15 U.S.C. 77h(d), shall be sent to or served on the issuer; or, in the case of a foreign government or political subdivision thereof, sent to or served on the underwriter; or, in the case of a foreign or territorial person, sent to or served on its duly authorized representative in the United States named in the registration statement, properly directed in the case of telegraphic notice to the address given in such statement. In addition, if such proceeding is commenced within 90 days after the registration statement has become effective, notice of the proceeding shall be given to the agent for service named on the facing sheet of the registration statement and to each other person designated on the facing sheet of the registration statement as a person to whom copies of communications to such agent are to be sent.

(b) *Content of Order.* The order instituting proceedings shall:

(1) State the nature of any hearing;

(2) State the legal authority and jurisdiction under which the hearing is to be held;

(3) Contain a short and plain statement of the matters of fact and law to be considered and determined, unless the order directs an answer pursuant to Rule 220 in which case the order shall set forth the factual and legal basis alleged therefor in such detail as will permit a specific response thereto; and

(4) State the nature of any relief or action sought or taken.

(c) *Time and Place of Hearing.* The time and place for any hearing shall be fixed with due regard for the public interest and the convenience and necessity of the parties, other participants, or their representatives.

(d) *Amendment to Order Instituting Proceedings.* (1) *By the Commission.* Upon motion by a party, the Commission may, at any time, amend an order instituting proceedings to include new matters of fact or law.

(2) *By the Hearing Officer.* Upon motion by a party, the hearing officer may, at any time prior to the filing of an initial decision or, if no initial decision is to be filed, prior to the time fixed for the filing of final briefs with the Commission, amend an order instituting proceedings to include new matters of fact or law that are within the scope of the original order instituting proceedings.

(e) *Publication of Notice of Public Hearings.* Unless otherwise ordered by the Commission, notice of any public hearing shall be given general circulation by release to the public, by publication in the *SEC News Digest* and, where directed, by publication in the FEDERAL REGISTER.

Rule 201. Consolidation and severance of proceedings

(a) *Consolidation.* By order of the Commission or a hearing officer, proceedings involving a common question of law or fact may be consolidated for hearing of any or all the matters at issue in such proceedings. The Commission or the hearing officer may make such orders concerning the conduct of such proceedings as it deems appropriate to avoid unnecessary cost or delay. Consolidation shall not prejudice any rights under these Rules of Practice and shall not affect the right of any party to raise issues that could have been raised if consolidation had not occurred. For purposes of this section, no distinction is made between joinder and consolidation of proceedings.

(b) *Severance.* By order of the Commission, any proceeding may be severed with respect to one or more parties. Any motion to sever must be made solely to the Commission and must include a representation that a settlement offer is pending before the Commission or otherwise show good cause.

Rule 202. Specification of procedures by parties in certain proceedings

(a) *Motion to Specify Procedures.* In any proceeding other than an enforcement or disciplinary proceeding, a proceeding to review a determination by a self-regulatory organization pursuant to Rules 420 and 421, or a proceeding to review a determination of the Board pursuant to Rules 440 and 441, a party may, at any time up to 20 days prior to the start of a hearing, make a motion to specify the procedures necessary or appropriate for the proceeding with particular reference to:

(1) Whether there should be an initial decision by a hearing officer;

(2) Whether any interested division of the Commission may assist in the preparation of the Commission's decision; and

(3) Whether there should be a 30–day waiting period between the issuance of the Commission's order and the date it is to become effective.

(b) *Objections; Effect of Failure to Object.* Any other party may object to the procedures so specified, and such party may specify such additional procedures as it considers necessary or appropriate. In the absence of such objection or such specification of additional procedures, such other party may be deemed to have waived objection to the specified procedures.

(c) *Approval Required.* Any proposal pursuant to paragraph (a) of this rule, even if not objected to by any party, shall be subject to the written approval of the hearing officer.

(d) *Procedure upon Agreement to Waive an Initial Decision.* If an initial decision is waived pursuant to paragraph (a) of this rule, the hearing officer shall notify the Secretary and, unless the Commission directs otherwise within 14 days, no initial decision shall be issued.

Rule 210. Parties, limited participants and amici curiae

(a) *Parties in an Enforcement or Disciplinary Proceeding, a Proceeding to Review a Self-Regulatory Organization Determination, or a Proceeding to Review a Board Determination.* (1) *Generally.* No person shall be granted leave to become a party or a non-party participant on a limited basis in an enforcement or disciplinary proceeding, a proceeding to review a determination by a self-regulatory organization pursuant to Rules 420 and 421, or a proceeding to review a determination by the Board pursuant to Rules 440 and 441, except as authorized by paragraph (c) of this section.

(2) *Disgorgement Proceedings.* In an enforcement proceeding, a person may state his or her views with respect to a proposed plan of disgorgement or file a proof of claim pursuant to Rule 1103.

(b) *Intervention as a Party.* (1) *Generally.* In any proceeding, other than an enforcement proceeding, a disciplinary proceeding, a proceeding to review a self-regulatory determination, or a proceeding to review a Board determination, any person may seek leave to intervene as a party by filing a motion setting forth the person's interest in the proceeding. No person, however, shall be admitted as a party to a proceeding by intervention unless it is determined that leave to participate pursuant to paragraph (c) of this section would be inadequate for the protection of the person's interests. In a proceeding under the Investment Company Act of 1940, any representative of interested security holders, or any other person whose participation in the proceeding may be in the public interest or for the protection of investors, may be admitted as a party upon the filing of a written motion setting forth the person's interest in the proceeding.

(2) *Intervention as of Right.* In proceedings under the Investment Company Act of 1940, any interested State or State agency shall be admitted as a party to any proceeding upon the filing of a written motion requesting leave to be admitted.

(c) *Leave to Participate on a Limited Basis.* In any proceeding, other than an enforcement proceeding, a disciplinary proceeding, a proceeding to review a self-regulatory determination, or a proceeding to review a Board determination, any person may seek leave to participate on a limited basis as a non-party participant as to any matter affecting the person's interests:

(1) *Procedure.* Motions for leave to participate shall be in writing, shall set forth the nature and extent of the movant's interest in the proceeding, and, except where good cause for late filing is shown, shall be filed not later than 20 days prior to the date fixed for the commencement of the hearing. Leave to participate pursuant to this paragraph (c) may include such rights of a party as the hearing officer may deem appropriate. Persons granted leave to participate shall be served in accordance with Rule 150; provided, however, that a party to the proceeding may move that the extent of notice of filings or other papers to be provided to persons granted leave to participate be limited, or may move that the persons granted leave to participate bear the cost of being provided copies of any or all filings or other papers. Persons granted leave to participate shall be bound, except as may be otherwise determined by the hearing officer, by any stipulation between the parties to the proceeding with respect to procedure, including submission of evidence, substitution of exhibits, corrections of the record, the time within which briefs or exceptions may be filed or proposed findings and conclusions may be submitted, the filing of initial decisions, the procedure to be followed in the preparation of decisions and the effective date of the Commission's order in the case. Where the filing of briefs or exceptions or the submission of proposed findings and conclusions are waived by

the parties to the proceedings, a person granted leave to participate pursuant to this paragraph (c) shall not be permitted to file a brief or exceptions or submit proposed findings and conclusions except by leave of the Commission or of the hearing officer.

(2) *Certain Persons Entitled to Leave to Participate.* The hearing officer is directed to grant leave to participate under this paragraph (c) to any person to whom it is proposed to issue any security in exchange for one or more bona fide outstanding securities, claims or property interests, or partly in such exchange and partly for cash, where the Commission is authorized to approve the terms and conditions of such issuance and exchange after a hearing upon the fairness of such terms and conditions.

(3) *Leave to Participate in Certain Commission Proceedings by a Representative of the United States Department of Justice, a United States Attorney's Office, or a Criminal Prosecutorial Authority of any State or any Other Political Subdivision of a State.* The Commission or the hearing officer may grant leave to participate on a limited basis to an authorized representative of the United States Department of Justice, an authorized representative of a United States Attorney, or an authorized representative of any criminal prosecutorial authority of any State or any other political subdivision of a State for the purpose of requesting a stay during the pendency of a criminal investigation or prosecution arising out of the same or similar facts that are at issue in the pending Commission enforcement or disciplinary proceeding. Upon a showing that such a stay is in the public interest or for the protection of investors, the motion for stay shall be favored. A stay granted under this paragraph (c)(3) may be granted for such a period and upon such conditions as the Commission or the hearing officer deems appropriate.

(d) *Amicus Participation.* (1) *Availability.* An amicus brief may be filed only if:

(i) A motion for leave to file the brief has been granted;

(ii) The brief is accompanied by written consent of all parties;

(iii) The brief is filed at the request of the Commission or the hearing officer; or

(iv) The brief is presented by the United States or an officer or agency thereof, or by a State, Territory or Commonwealth.

(2) *Procedure.* An amicus brief may be filed conditionally with the motion for leave. The motion for leave shall identify the interest of the movant and shall state the reasons why a brief of an amicus curiae is desirable. Except as all parties otherwise consent, any amicus curiae shall file its brief within the time allowed the party whose position the amicus will support, unless the Commission or hearing officer; for cause shown, grants leave for a later filing. In the event that a later filing is allowed, the order granting leave to file shall specify when an opposing party may reply to the brief. A motion of an amicus curiae to participate in oral argument will be granted only for extraordinary reasons.

(e) *Permission to State Views.* Any person may make a motion seeking leave to file a memorandum or make an oral statement of his or her views. Any such communication may be included in the record; provided, however, that unless offered and admitted as evidence of the truth of the statements therein made, any assertions of fact submitted pursuant to the provisions of this paragraph (e) will be considered only to the extent that the statements therein made are otherwise supported by the record.

(f) *Modification of Participation Provisions.* The Commission or the hearing officer may, by order, modify the provisions of this section which would otherwise be applicable, and may impose such terms and conditions on the participation of any person in any proceeding as it may deem necessary or appropriate in the public interest.

Rule 220. Answer to allegations

(a) *When Required.* In its order instituting proceedings, the Commission may require any respondent to file an answer to each of the allegations contained therein. Even if not so ordered, any respondent in any proceeding may elect to file an answer. Any other person granted leave by the Commission or the hearing officer to participate on a limited basis in such proceedings pursuant to Rule 210(c) may be required to file an answer.

(b) *When to File.* Except where a different period is provided by rule or by order, a respondent required to file an answer as provided in paragraph (a) of this rule shall do so within 20 days after service upon the respondent of the order instituting proceedings. Persons granted leave to participate on a limited basis in the proceeding pursuant to Rule 210(c) may file an answer within a reasonable time, as determined by the Commission or the hearing officer. If the order instituting proceedings is amended, the Commission or the hearing officer may require that an amended answer be filed and, if such an answer is required, shall specify a date for the filing thereof.

(c) *Contents; effect of failure to deny.* Unless otherwise directed by the hearing officer or the Commission, an answer shall specifically admit, deny, or state that the party does not have, and is unable to obtain, sufficient information to admit or deny each allegation in the order instituting proceedings. When a party intends in good faith to deny only a part of an allegation, the party shall specify so much of it as is true and shall deny only the remainder. A statement of a lack of information shall have the effect of a denial. Any allegation not denied shall be deemed admitted. A respondent must affirmatively state in the answer any avoidance or affirmative defense, including but not limited to res judicata and statute of limitations. In this regard, a respondent must state in the answer whether the respondent relied on the advice of counsel, accountants, auditors, or other professionals in connection with any claim, violation alleged or remedy sought. Failure to do so may be deemed a waiver.

(d) *Motion for More Definite Statement.* A respondent may file with an answer a motion for a more definite statement of specified matters of fact or law to be considered or determined. Such motion shall state the respects in which, and the reasons why, each such matter of fact or law should be required to be made more definite. If the motion is granted, the order granting such motion shall set the periods for filing such a statement and any answer thereto.

(e) *Amendments.* A respondent may amend its answer at any time by written consent of each adverse party or with leave of the Commission or the hearing officer. Leave shall be freely granted when justice so requires.

(f) *Failure to File Answer: Default.* If a respondent fails to file an answer required by this rule within the time provided, such respondent may be deemed in default pursuant to Rule 155(a). A party may make a motion to set aside a default pursuant to Rule 155(b).

Rule 221. Prehearing conference

(a) *Purposes of Conference.* The purposes of a prehearing conference include, but are not limited to:

(1) Expediting the disposition of the proceeding;

(2) Establishing early and continuing control of the proceeding by the hearing officer; and

(3) Improving the quality of the hearing through more thorough preparation.

(b) *Procedure.* On his or her own motion or at the request of a party, the hearing officer may, in his or her discretion, direct counsel or any party to meet for an initial, final or other prehearing conference. Such conferences may be held with or without the hearing officer present as the hearing officer deems appropriate. Where such a conference is held outside the presence of the hearing officer, the hearing officer shall be advised promptly by the parties of any agreements reached. Such conferences also may be held with one or more persons participating by telephone or other remote means.

(c) *Subjects to Be Discussed.* At a prehearing conference consideration may be given and action taken with respect to any and all of the following:

(1) Simplification and clarification of the issues;

(2) Exchange of witness and exhibit lists and copies of exhibits;

(3) Timing of expert witness disclosures and reports, if any;

(4) Stipulations, admissions of fact, and stipulations concerning the contents, authenticity, or admissibility into evidence of documents;

(5) Matters of which official notice may be taken;

(6) The schedule for exchanging prehearing motions or briefs, if any;

(7) The method of service for papers other than Commission orders;

(8) The filing of any motion pursuant to Rule 250;

(9) Settlement of any or all issues;

(10) Determination of hearing dates;

(11) Amendments to the order instituting proceedings or answers thereto;

(12) Production, and timing for completion of the production, of documents as set forth in Rule 230, and prehearing production of documents in response to subpoenas duces tecum as set forth in Rule 232;

(13) Specification of procedures as set forth in Rule 202;

(14) Depositions to be conducted, if any, and date by which depositions shall be completed; and

(15) Such other matters as may aid in the orderly and expeditious disposition of the proceeding.

(d) *Required Prehearing Conference.* Except where the emergency nature of a proceeding would make a prehearing conference clearly inappropriate, at least one prehearing conference should be held.

(e) *Prehearing Orders.* At or following the conclusion of any conference held pursuant to this section, the hearing officer shall enter a ruling or order which recites the agreements reached and any procedural determinations made by the hearing officer.

(f) *Failure to Appear; Default.* Any person who is named in an order instituting proceedings as a person against whom findings may be made or sanctions imposed and who fails to appear, in person or through a representative, at a prehearing conference of which he or she has been duly notified may be deemed in default pursuant to Rule 155(a). A party may make a motion to set aside a default pursuant to Rule 155(b).

Rule 222. Prehearing submissions

(a) *Submissions Generally.* The hearing officer, on his or her own motion, or at the request of a party or other participant, may order any party, including the interested division, to furnish such information as deemed appropriate, including any or all of the following:

(1) An outline or narrative summary of its case or defense;

(2) The legal theories upon which it will rely;

(3) Copies and a list of documents that it intends to introduce at the hearing; and

(4) A list of witnesses who will testify on its behalf, including the witnesses' names, occupations, addresses and a brief summary of their expected testimony.

(b) *Expert Witnesses*—(1) *Information to be supplied; reports.* Each party who intends to call an expert witness shall submit, in addition to the information required by paragraph (a)(4) of this rule, a statement of the expert's qualifications, a listing of other proceedings in which the expert has given expert testimony during the previous four years, and a list of publications authored or co-authored by the expert in the previous ten years. Additionally, if the witness is one retained or specially employed to provide expert testimony in the case or one whose duties as the party's employee regularly involve giving expert testimony, then the party must include in the disclosure a written report—prepared and signed by the witness. The report must contain:

(i) A complete statement of all opinions the witness will express and the basis and reasons for them;

(ii) The facts or data considered by the witness in forming them;

(iii) Any exhibits that will be used to summarize or support them; and

(iv) A statement of the compensation to be paid for the study and testimony in the case.

(2) *Drafts and communications protected.*

(i) Drafts of any report or other disclosure required under this section need not be furnished regardless of the form in which the draft is recorded.

(ii) Communications between a party's attorney and the party's expert witness who is required to provide a report under this section need not be furnished regardless of the form of the communications, except if the communications relate to compensation for the expert's study or testimony, identify facts or data that the party's attorney provided and that the expert considered in forming the opinions to be expressed, or identify assumptions that the party's attorney provided and that the expert relied on in forming the opinions to be expressed.

Rule 230. Enforcement and disciplinary proceedings: availability of documents for inspection and copying

For purposes of this rule, the term documents shall include writings, drawings, graphs, charts, photographs, recordings and other data compilations, including data stored by computer, from which information can be obtained.

(a) *Documents to Be Available for Inspection and Copying.* (1) Unless otherwise provided by this rule, or by order of the Commission or the hearing officer, the Division of Enforcement shall make available for inspection and copying by any party documents obtained by the Division prior to the institution of proceedings, in connection with the investigation leading to the Division's recommendation to institute proceedings. Such documents shall include:

(i) Each subpoena issued;

(ii) Every other written request to persons not employed by the Commission to provide documents or to be interviewed;

(iii) The documents turned over in response to any such subpoenas or other written requests;

(iv) All transcripts and transcript exhibits;

(v) Any other documents obtained from persons not employed by the Commission; and

(vi) Any final examination or inspection reports prepared by the Office of Compliance Inspections and Examinations, the Division of Trading and Markets, or the Division of Investment Management, if the Division of Enforcement intends either to introduce any such report into evidence or to use any such report to refresh the recollection of any witness.

(2) Nothing in this paragraph (a) shall limit the right of the Division to make available any other document, or shall limit the right of a respondent to seek access to or production pursuant to subpoena of any other document, or shall limit the authority of the hearing officer to order the production of any document pursuant to subpoena.

(b) *Documents that may be withheld or redacted.* (1) The Division of Enforcement may withhold a document if:

(i) The document is privileged;

(ii) The document is an internal memorandum, note or writing prepared by a Commission employee, other than an examination or inspection report as specified in paragraph (a)(1)(vi) of this rule, or is otherwise attorney work product and will not be offered in evidence;

(iii) The document would disclose the identity of a confidential source;

(iv) The document reflects only settlement negotiations between the Division of Enforcement and a person or entity who is not a respondent in the proceeding; or

(v) The hearing officer grants leave to withhold a document or category of documents as not relevant to the subject matter of the proceeding or otherwise, for good cause shown.

(2) Unless the hearing officer orders otherwise upon motion, the Division of Enforcement may redact information from a document if:

(i) The information is among the categories set forth in paragraphs (b)(1)(i) through (v) of this section; or

(ii) The information consists of the following with regard to a person other than the respondent to whom the information is being produced:

(A) An individual's social-security number;

(B) An individual's birth date;

(C) The name of an individual known to be a minor; or

(D) A financial account number, taxpayer-identification number, credit card or debit card number, passport number, driver's license number, or state-issued identification number other than the last four digits of the number.

(3) Nothing in this paragraph (b) authorizes the Division of Enforcement in connection with an enforcement or disciplinary proceeding to withhold, contrary to the doctrine of *Brady v. Maryland*, 373 U.S. 83, 87 (1963) documents that contain material exculpatory evidence.

(c) *Withheld Document List.* The hearing officer may require the Division of Enforcement to submit for review a list of documents or categories of documents withheld pursuant to paragraphs (b)(1)(i) through (b)(1)(iv) of this rule or to submit any document withheld, and may determine whether any such document should be made available for inspection and copying. When similar documents are withheld pursuant to paragraphs (b)(1)(i) through (b)(1)(iv) of this rule, those documents may be identified by category instead of by individual document. The hearing officer retains discretion to determine when an identification by category is insufficient.

(d) *Timing of Inspection and Copying.* Unless otherwise ordered by the Commission or the hearing officer, the Division of Enforcement shall commence making documents available to a respondent for inspection and copying pursuant to this section no later than 7 days after the service of the order instituting proceedings. In a proceeding in which a temporary cease-and-desist order is sought pursuant to Rule 510 or a temporary suspension of registration is sought pursuant to Rule 520, documents shall be made available no later than the day after service of the decision as to whether to issue a temporary cease-and-desist order or temporary suspension order.

(e) *Place of Inspection and Copying.* Documents subject to inspection and copying pursuant to this section shall be made available to the respondent for inspection and copying at the Commission office where they are ordinarily maintained, or at such other place as the parties, in writing, may agree. A respondent shall not be given custody of the documents or leave to remove the documents from the Commission's offices pursuant to the requirements of this section other than by written agreement of the Division of Enforcement. Such agreement shall specify the documents subject to the agreement, the date they shall be returned and such other terms or conditions as are appropriate to provide for the safekeeping of the documents.

(f) *Copying Costs and Procedures.* The respondent may obtain a photocopy of any documents made available for inspection. The respondent shall be responsible for the cost of photocopying. Unless otherwise ordered, charges for copies made by the Division of Enforcement at the request of the respondent will be at the rate charged pursuant to the fee schedule at 17 CFR 200.80e for copies. The respondent shall be given access to the documents at the Commission's offices or such other place as the parties may agree during normal business hours for copying of documents at the respondent's expense.

(g) *Issuance of Investigatory Subpoenas After Institution of Proceedings.* The Division of Enforcement shall promptly inform the hearing officer and each party if investigatory subpoenas are issued under the same investigation file number or pursuant to the same order directing private investigation ("formal order") under which the investigation leading to the institution of proceedings was conducted. The hearing officer shall order such steps as necessary and appropriate to assure that the issuance of investigatory subpoenas after the institution of proceedings is not for the purpose of obtaining evidence relevant to the proceedings and that any relevant documents that may be obtained through the use of investigatory subpoenas in a continuing investigation are made available to each respondent for inspection and copying on a timely basis.

(h) *Failure to Make Documents Available—Harmless Error.* In the event that a document required to be made available to a respondent pursuant to this section is not made available by the Division of Enforcement, no rehearing or redecision of a proceeding already heard or decided shall be required, unless the respondent shall establish that the failure to make the document available was not harmless error.

Rule 231. Enforcement and disciplinary proceedings: production of witness statements

(a) *Availability.* Any respondent in an enforcement or disciplinary proceeding may move that the Division of Enforcement produce for inspection and copying any statement of any person called or to be called as a witness by the Division of Enforcement that pertains, or is expected to pertain, to his or her direct testimony and that would be required to be required to be produced pursuant to the Jencks Act, 18 U.S.C. 3500. For purposes of this section, *statement* shall have the meaning set forth in 18 U.S.C. 3500(e). Such production shall be made at a time and place fixed by the hearing officer and shall be made available to any party, provided, however, that the production shall be made under conditions intended to preserve the items to be inspected or copied.

(b) *Failure to Produce—Harmless Error.* In the event that a statement required to be made available for inspection and copying by a respondent is not turned over by the Division of Enforcement, no rehearing or redecision of a proceeding already heard or decided shall be required unless the respondent establishes that the failure to turn over the statement was not harmless error.

Rule 232. Subpoenas

(a) *Availability; Procedure.* In connection with any hearing ordered by the Commission or any deposition permitted under Rule 233, a party may request the issuance of subpoenas requiring the attendance and testimony of witnesses at such depositions or at the designated time and place of hearing, and subpoenas requiring the production of documentary or other tangible evidence returnable at any designated time or place. Unless made on the record at a hearing, requests for issuance of a subpoena shall be made in writing and served on each party pursuant to Rule 150. A person whose request for a subpoena has been denied or modified may not request that any other person issue the subpoena.

(1) *Unavailability of Hearing Officer.* In the event that the hearing officer assigned to a proceeding is unavailable, the party seeking issuance of the subpoena may seek its issuance from the first available of the following persons: The Chief Administrative Law Judge, the law judge most

senior in service as a law judge, the duty officer, any other member of the Commission, or any other person designated by the Commission to issue subpoenas. Requests for issuance of a subpoena made to the Commission, or any member thereof, must be submitted to the Secretary, not to an individual Commissioner.

(2) *Signing May Be Delegated.* A hearing officer may authorize issuance of a subpoena, and may delegate the manual signing of the subpoena to any other person authorized to issue subpoenas.

(b) *Standards for Issuance.* Where it appears to the person asked to issue the subpoena that the subpoena sought may be unreasonable, oppressive, excessive in scope, or unduly burdensome, he or she may, in his or her discretion, as a condition precedent to the issuance of the subpoena, require the person seeking the subpoena to show the general relevance and reasonable scope of the testimony or other evidence sought. If after consideration of all the circumstances, the person requested to issue the subpoena determines that the subpoena or any of its terms is unreasonable, oppressive, excessive in scope, or unduly burdensome, he or she may refuse to issue the subpoena, or issue it only upon such conditions as fairness requires. In making the foregoing determination, the person issuing the subpoena may inquire of the other participants whether they will stipulate to the facts sought to be proved.

(c) *Service.* Service shall be made pursuant to the provisions of Rule 150(b) through (d). The provisions of this paragraph (c) shall apply to the issuance of subpoenas for purposes of investigations, as required by 17 CFR 203.8, as well as depositions and hearings.

(d) *Tender of Fees Required.* When a subpoena ordering the attendance of a person at a hearing or deposition is issued at the instance of anyone other than an officer or agency of the United States, service is valid only if the subpoena is accompanied by a tender to the subpoenaed person of the fees for one day's attendance and mileage specified by paragraph (f) of this section.

(e) *Application to Quash or Modify.* (1) *Procedure.* Any person to whom a subpoena or notice of deposition is directed, or who is an owner, creator or the subject of the documents that are to be produced pursuant to a subpoena, or any party may, prior to the time specified therein for compliance, but in no event more than 15 days after the date of service of such subpoena or notice, request that the subpoena or notice be quashed or modified. Such request shall be made by application filed with the Secretary and served on all parties pursuant to Rule 150. The party on whose behalf the subpoena or notice was issued may, within five days of service of the application, file an opposition to the application. If a hearing officer has been assigned to the proceeding, the application to quash shall be directed to that hearing officer for consideration, even if the subpoena or notice was issued by another person.

(2) *Standards Governing Application to Quash or Modify.* If compliance with the subpoena or notice of deposition would be unreasonable, oppressive, unduly burdensome or would unduly delay the hearing, the hearing officer or the Commission shall quash or modify the subpoena or notice, or may order a response to the subpoena or appearance at a deposition, only upon specified conditions. These conditions may include but are not limited to a requirement that the party on whose behalf the subpoena was issued shall make reasonable compensation to the person to whom the subpoena was addressed for the cost of copying or transporting evidence to the place for return of the subpoena.

(3) *Additional Standards Governing Application to Quash Deposition Notices or Subpoenas Filed Pursuant to Rule 233(a).* The hearing officer or the Commission shall quash or modify a deposition notice or subpoena filed or issued pursuant to Rule 233(a) unless the requesting party demonstrates that the deposition notice or subpoena satisfies the requirements of Rule 233(a), and:

(i) The proposed deponent was a witness of or participant in any event, transaction, occurrence, act, or omission that forms the basis for any claim asserted by the Division of Enforcement, any defense, or anything else required to be included in an answer pursuant to Rule 220(c) by any respondent in the proceeding (this excludes a proposed deponent whose only knowledge of these matters arises from the Division of Enforcement's investigation or the proceeding);

(ii) The proposed deponent is a designated as an "expert witness" under Rule 222(b); provided, however, that the deposition of an expert who is required to submit a written report under Rule 222(b) may only occur after such report is served; or

(iii) The proposed deponent has custody of documents or electronic data relevant to the claims or defenses of any party (this excludes Division of Enforcement or other Commission officers or personnel who have custody of documents or data that was produced by the Division to the respondent).

(f) *Witness Fees and Mileage.* Witnesses summoned before the Commission shall be paid the same fees and mileage that are paid to witnesses in the courts of the United States, and witnesses whose depositions are taken and the persons taking the same shall severally be entitled to the same fees as are paid for like services in the courts of the United States. Witness fees and mileage shall be paid by the party at whose instance the witnesses appear. Except for such witness fees and mileage, each party is responsible for paying any fees and expenses of the expert witnesses whom that party designates under Rule 222(b), for appearance at any deposition or hearing.

Rule 233. Depositions upon oral examination

(a) *Depositions Upon Written Notice.* In any proceeding under the 120-day timeframe designated pursuant to Rule 360(a)(2), depositions upon written notice may be taken as set forth in this paragraph. No other depositions shall be permitted except as provided in paragraph (b) of this section.

(1) If the proceeding involves a single respondent, the respondent may file written notices to depose no more than three persons, and the Division of Enforcement may file written notices to depose no more than three persons.

(2) If the proceeding involves multiple respondents, the respondents collectively may file joint written notices to depose no more than five persons, and the Division of Enforcement may file written notices to depose no more than five persons. The depositions taken under this paragraph (a)(2) shall not exceed a total of five depositions for the Division of Enforcement, and five depositions for all respondents collectively.

(3) *Additional depositions upon motion.* Any side may file a motion with the hearing officer seeking leave to notice up to two additional depositions beyond those permitted pursuant to paragraphs (a)(1) and (2) of this section.

(i) *Procedure.* (A) A motion for additional depositions must be filed no later than 90 days prior to the hearing date. Any party opposing the motion may submit an opposition within five days after service of the motion. No reply shall be permitted. The motion and any oppositions each shall not exceed seven pages in length. These limitations exclusively govern motions under this section; notwithstanding Rule 154(a), any points and authorities shall be included in the motion or opposition, with no separate statement of points and authorities permitted, and none of the requirements in Rule 154(b) or (c) shall apply.

(B) Upon consideration of the motion and any opposing papers, the hearing officer will issue an order either granting or denying the motion. The hearing officer shall consider the motion on an expedited basis.

(C) The proceeding shall not automatically be stayed pending the determination of the motion.

(ii) *Grounds and standards for motion.* A motion under this paragraph (a)(3) shall not be granted unless the additional depositions satisfy Rule 232(e) and the moving side demonstrates a compelling need for the additional depositions by:

(A) Identifying each of the witnesses whom the moving side plans to depose pursuant to paragraph (a)(1) or (2) of this section as well as the additional witnesses whom the side seeks to depose;

(B) Describing the role of each witness and proposed additional witness;

(C) Describing the matters concerning which each witness and proposed additional witness is expected to be questioned, and why the deposition of each witness and proposed additional witness is necessary for the moving side's arguments, claims, or defenses; and

(D) Showing that the additional deposition(s) requested will not be unreasonably cumulative or duplicative.

(iii) If the moving side proposes to take and submit the additional deposition(s) on written questions, as provided in 17 CFR 201.234, the motion shall so state. The motion for additional depositions shall constitute a motion under Rule 234(a), and the moving party is required to submit its questions with its motion under this rule. The procedures for such a deposition shall be governed by Rule 234.

(4) A deponent's attendance may be ordered by subpoena issued pursuant to the procedures in Rule 232; and

(5) The Commission or hearing officer may rule on a motion that a deposition noticed under paragraph (a)(1) or (2) of this section shall not be taken upon a determination under Rule 232(e). The fact that a witness testified during an investigation does not preclude the deposition of that witness.

(b) *Depositions When Witness Is Unavailable.* In addition to depositions permitted under paragraph (a) of this section, the Commission or the hearing officer may grant a party's request to file a written notice of deposition if the requesting party shows that the prospective witness will likely give testimony material to the proceeding; that it is likely the prospective witness, who is then within the United States, will be unable to attend or testify at the hearing because of age, sickness, infirmity, imprisonment, other disability, or absence from the United States, unless it appears that the absence of the witness was procured by the party requesting the deposition; and that the taking of a deposition will serve the interests of justice.

(c) *Service and Contents of Notice.* Notice of any deposition pursuant to this section shall be made in writing and served on each party pursuant to Rule 150. A notice of deposition shall designate by name a deposition officer. The deposition officer may be any person authorized to administer oaths by the laws of the United States or of the place where the deposition is to be held. A notice of deposition also shall state:

(1) The name and address of the witness whose deposition is to be taken;

(2) The time and place of the deposition; provided that a subpoena for a deposition may command a person to attend a deposition only as follows:

(i) Within 100 miles of where the person resides, is employed, or regularly transacts business in person;

(ii) Within the state where the person resides, is employed, or regularly transacts business in person, if the person is a party or a party's officer;

(iii) At such other location that the parties and proposed deponent stipulate; or

(iv) At such other location that the hearing officer or the Commission determines is appropriate; and

(3) The manner of recording and preserving the deposition.

(d) *Producing Documents.* In connection with any deposition pursuant to this section, a party may request the issuance of a subpoena duces tecum under Rule 232. The party conducting the deposition shall serve upon the deponent any subpoena duces tecum so issued. The materials designated for production, as set out in the subpoena, must be listed in the notice of deposition.

(e) *Method of Recording*—(1) *Method stated in the notice.* The party who notices the deposition must state in the notice the method for recording the testimony. Unless the hearing officer or Commission orders otherwise, testimony may be recorded by audio, audiovisual, or stenographic means. The noticing party bears the recording costs. Any party may arrange to transcribe a deposition, at that party's expense. Each party shall bear its own costs for obtaining copies of any transcripts or audio or audiovisual recordings.

(2) *Additional method.* With prior notice to the deponent and other parties, any party may designate another method for recording the testimony in addition to that specified in the original notice. That party bears the expense of the additional record or transcript unless the hearing officer or the Commission orders otherwise.

(f) *By Remote Means.* The parties may stipulate—or the hearing officer or Commission may on motion order—that a deposition be taken by telephone or other remote means. For the purpose of this section, the deposition takes place where the deponent answers the questions.

(g) *Deposition Officer's Duties*—(1) *Before the deposition.* The deposition officer designated pursuant to paragraph (c) of this section must begin the deposition with an on-the-record statement that includes:

(i) The deposition officer's name and business address;

(ii) The date, time, and place of the deposition;

(iii) The deponent's name;

(iv) The deposition officer's administration of the oath or affirmation to the deponent; and

(v) The identity of all persons present.

(2) *Conducting the deposition; avoiding distortion.* If the deposition is recorded non-stenographically, the deposition officer must repeat the items in paragraphs (g)(1)(i) through (iii) of this section at the beginning of each unit of the recording medium. The deponent's and attorneys' appearance or demeanor must not be distorted through recording techniques.

(3) *After the deposition.* At the end of a deposition, the deposition officer must state on the record that the deposition is complete and must set out any stipulations made by the attorneys about custody of the transcript or recording and of the exhibits, or about any other pertinent matters.

(h) *Order and record of the examination*—(1) *Order of examination.* The examination and cross-examination of a deponent shall proceed as they would at the hearing. After putting the deponent under oath or affirmation, the deposition officer must record the testimony by the method designated under paragraph (e) of this section. The testimony must be recorded by the deposition officer personally or by a person acting in the presence and under the direction of the deposition officer. The witness being deposed may have counsel present during the deposition.

(2) *Form of objections stated during the deposition.* An objection at the time of the examination—whether to evidence, to a party's conduct, to the deposition officer's qualifications, to the manner of taking the deposition, or to any other aspect of the deposition—must be noted on the record, but the examination shall still proceed and the testimony shall be taken subject to any objection. An objection must be stated concisely in a nonargumentative and nonsuggestive manner. A person may instruct a deponent not to answer only when necessary to preserve a privilege, to enforce a limitation ordered by the hearing officer or the Commission, or to present a motion to the hearing officer or the Commission for a limitation on the questioning in the deposition.

(i) *Waiver of objections*—(1) *To the notice.* An objection to an error or irregularity in a deposition notice is waived unless promptly served in writing on the party giving the notice.

(2) *To the deposition officer's qualification.* An objection based on disqualification of the deposition officer before whom a deposition is to be taken is waived if not made:

(i) Before the deposition begins; or

(ii) Promptly after the basis for disqualification becomes known or, with reasonable diligence, could have been known.

(3) *To the taking of the deposition*—(i) *Objection to competence, relevance, or materiality.* An objection to a deponent's competence—or to the competence, relevance, or materiality of testimony—is not waived by a failure to make the objection before or during the deposition, unless the ground for it might have been corrected at that time.

(ii) *Objection to an error or irregularity.* An objection to an error or irregularity at an oral examination is waived if:

(A) It relates to the manner of taking the deposition, the form of a question or answer, the oath or affirmation, a party's conduct, or other matters that might have been corrected at that time; and

(B) It is not timely made during the deposition.

(4) *To completing and returning the deposition.* An objection to how the deposition officer transcribed the testimony—or prepared, signed, certified, sealed, endorsed, sent, or otherwise dealt with the deposition—is waived unless a motion to suppress is made promptly after the error or irregularity becomes known or, with reasonable diligence, could have been known

(j) *Duration; Cross-Examination; Motion to Terminate or Limit*—(1) *Duration.* Unless otherwise stipulated or ordered by the hearing officer or the Commission, a deposition is limited to one day of seven hours, including cross-examination as provided in this subsection. In a deposition conducted by or for a respondent, the Division of Enforcement shall be allowed a reasonable amount of time for cross-examination of the deponent. In a deposition conducted by the Division, the respondents collectively shall be allowed a reasonable amount of time for cross examination of the deponent. The hearing officer or the Commission may allow additional time if needed to fairly examine the deponent or if the deponent, another person, or any other circumstance impedes or delays the examination.

(2) *Motion to terminate or limit*—(i) *Grounds.* At any time during a deposition, the deponent or a party may move to terminate or limit it on the ground that it is being conducted in bad faith or in a manner that unreasonably annoys, embarrasses, or oppresses the deponent or party. If the objecting deponent or party so demands, the depo-

sition must be suspended for the time necessary to present the motion to the hearing officer or the Commission.

(ii) *Order*. Upon a motion under paragraph (j)(2)(i) of this section, the hearing officer or the Commission may order that the deposition be terminated or may limit its scope. If terminated, the deposition may be resumed only by order of the hearing officer or the Commission.

(k) *Review by the Witness; Changes*—(1) *Review; statement of changes*. On request by the deponent or a party before the deposition is completed, and unless otherwise ordered by the hearing officer or the Commission, the deponent must be allowed 14 days after being notified by the deposition officer that the transcript or recording is available, unless a longer time is agreed to by the parties or permitted by the hearing officer, in which:

(i) To review the transcript or recording; and

(ii) If there are changes in form or substance, to sign a statement listing the changes and the reasons for making them.

(2) *Changes indicated in the deposition officer's certificate*. The deposition officer must note in the certificate prescribed by paragraph (*l*)(1) of this section whether a review was requested and, if so, must attach any changes the deponent makes during the 14-day period.

(*l*) *Certification and Delivery; Exhibits; Copies of the Transcript or Recording*—(1) *Certification and delivery*. The deposition officer must certify in writing that the witness was duly sworn and that the deposition accurately records the witness's testimony. The certificate must accompany the record of the deposition. Unless the hearing officer orders otherwise, the deposition officer must seal the deposition in an envelope or package bearing the title of the action and marked "Deposition of [witness's name]" and must promptly send it to the attorney or party who arranged for the transcript or recording. The attorney or party must store it under conditions that will protect it against loss, destruction, tampering, or deterioration.

(2) *Documents and Tangible Things*—(i) *Originals and copies*. Documents and tangible things produced for inspection during a deposition must, on a party's request, be marked for identification and attached to the deposition. Any party may inspect and copy them. But if the person who produced them wants to keep the originals, the person may:

(A) Offer copies to be marked, attached to the deposition, and then used as originals—after giving all parties a fair opportunity to verify the copies by comparing them with the originals; or

(B) Give all parties a fair opportunity to inspect and copy the originals after they are marked—in which event the originals may be used as if attached to the deposition.

(ii) *Order regarding the originals*. Any party may move for an order that the originals be attached to the deposition pending final disposition of the case.

(3) *Copies of the transcript or recording*. Unless otherwise stipulated or ordered by the hearing officer or Commission, the deposition officer must retain the stenographic notes of a deposition taken stenographically or a copy of the recording of a deposition taken by another method. When paid reasonable charges, the deposition officer must furnish a copy of the transcript or recording to any party or the deponent, as directed by the party or person paying such charges.

(m) *Presentation of Objections or Disputes*. Any party seeking relief with respect to disputes over the conduct of a deposition may file a motion with the hearing officer to obtain relief as permitted by this part.

Rule 234. Depositions upon written questions

(a) *Availability*. Any deposition permitted under Rule 233 may be taken and submitted on written questions upon motion of any party, for good cause shown, or as stipulated by the parties.

(b) *Procedure*. Written questions shall be filed with the motion. Within 10 days after service of the motion and written questions, any party may file objections to such written questions and any party may file cross-questions. When a deposition is taken pursuant to this section no persons other than the witness, counsel to the witness, the deposition officer, and, if the deposition officer does not act as reporter, a reporter, shall be present at the examination of the witness. No party shall be present or represented unless otherwise permitted by order. The deposition officer shall propound the questions and cross-questions to the witness in the order submitted.

(c) *Additional Requirements*. The order for deposition, filing of the deposition, form of the deposition and use of the deposition in the record shall be governed by paragraphs (c) through (*l*) of Rule 233, except that no cross-examination shall be made.

Rule 235. Introducing prior sworn statements or declarations

(a) At a hearing, any person wishing to introduce a prior, sworn deposition taken pursuant to Rule 233 or 234, investigative testimony, or other sworn statement or a declaration pursuant to 28 U.S.C. 1746, of a witness, not a party, otherwise admissible in the proceeding, may make a motion setting forth the reasons therefor. If only part of a statement or declaration is offered in evidence, the hearing officer may require that all relevant portions of the statement or declaration be introduced. If all of a statement or declaration is offered in evidence, the hearing officer may require that portions not relevant to the proceeding be excluded. A motion to introduce a prior sworn statement or declaration may be granted if:

(1) The witness is dead;

(2) The witness is out of the United States, unless it appears that the absence of the witness was procured by the party offering the prior sworn statement or declaration;

(3) The witness is unable to attend or testify because of age, sickness, infirmity, imprisonment or other disability;

(4) The party offering the prior sworn statement or declaration has been unable to procure the attendance of the witness by subpoena; or

(5) In the discretion of the Commission or the hearing officer, it would be desirable, in the interests of justice, to allow the prior sworn statement or declaration to be used. In making this determination, due regard shall be given to the presumption that witnesses will testify orally in an open hearing. If the parties have stipulated to accept a prior sworn statement or declaration in lieu of live testimony, consideration shall also be given to the convenience of the parties in avoiding unnecessary expense.

(b) *Sworn Statement or Declaration of Party or Agent.* An adverse party may use for any purpose a deposition taken pursuant to Rule 233 or 234, investigative testimony, or other sworn statement or a declaration pursuant to 28 U.S.C. 1746, of a party or anyone who, when giving the sworn statement or declaration, was the party's officer, director, or managing agent.

Rule 240. Settlement

(a) *Availability.* Any person who is notified that a proceeding may or will be instituted against him or her, or any party to a proceeding already instituted, may, at any time, propose in writing an offer of settlement.

(b) *Procedure.* An offer of settlement shall state that it is made pursuant to this section; shall recite or incorporate as a part of the offer the provisions of paragraphs (c)(4) and (5) of this rule; shall be signed by the person making the offer, not by counsel; and shall be submitted to the interested division.

(c) *Consideration of Offers of Settlement.* (1) Offers of settlement shall be considered by the interested division when time, the nature of the proceedings, and the public interest permit.

(2) Where a hearing officer is assigned to a proceeding, the interested division and the party submitting the offer may request that the hearing officer express his or her views regarding the appropriateness of the offer of settlement. A request for the hearing officer to express his or her views on an offer of settlement or otherwise to participate in a settlement conference constitutes a waiver by the persons making the request of any right to claim bias or prejudgment by the hearing officer based on the views expressed.

(3) The interested division shall present the offer of settlement to the Commission with its recommendation, except that, if the division's recommendation is unfavorable, the offer shall not be presented to the Commission unless the person making the offer so requests.

(4) By submitting an offer of settlement, the person making the offer waives, subject to acceptance of the offer:

(i) All hearings pursuant to the statutory provisions under which the proceeding is to be or has been instituted;

(ii) The filing of proposed findings of fact and conclusions of law;

(iii) Proceedings before, and an initial decision by, a hearing officer;

(iv) All post-hearing procedures; and

(v) Judicial review by any court.

(5) By submitting an offer of settlement the person further waives:

(i) Such provisions of the Rules of Practice or other requirements of law as may be construed to prevent any member of the Commission's staff from participating in the preparation of, or advising the Commission as to, any order, opinion, finding of fact, or conclusion of law to be entered pursuant to the offer; and

(ii) Any right to claim bias or prejudgment by the Commission based on the consideration of or discussions concerning settlement of all or any part of the proceeding.

(6) If the Commission rejects the offer of settlement, the person making the offer shall be notified of the Commission's action and the offer of settlement shall be deemed withdrawn. The rejected offer shall not constitute a part of the record in any proceeding against the person making the offer, provided, however, that rejection of an offer of settlement does not affect the continued validity of waivers pursuant to paragraph (c)(5) of this rule with respect to any discussions concerning the rejected offer of settlement.

(7) Final acceptance of any offer of settlement will occur only upon the issuance of findings and an order by the Commission.

Rule 250. Dispositive motions

(a) *Motion for a Ruling on the Pleadings.* No later than 14 days after a respondent's answer has been filed, any party may move for a ruling on the pleadings on one or more claims or defenses, asserting that, even accepting all of the non-movant's factual allegations as true and drawing all reasonable inferences in the non-movant's favor, the movant is entitled to a ruling as a matter of law. The hearing officer shall promptly grant or deny the motion.

(b) *Motion for Summary Disposition in 30- and 75-Day Proceedings.* In any proceeding under the 30- or 75-day timeframe designated pursuant to Rule 360(a)(2), after a respondent's answer has been filed and documents have been made available to that respondent for inspection and copying pursuant to Rule 230, any party may make a motion for summary disposition on one or more claims or defenses, asserting that the undisputed pleaded facts, declarations, affidavits, documentary evidence or facts officially noted pursuant to Rule 323 show that there is no genuine issue with regard to any material fact and that the movant is entitled to summary disposition as a matter of law. The hearing officer shall promptly grant or deny the motion for summary disposition or shall defer decision on the motion. If it appears that a party, for good cause shown, cannot present prior to the hearing facts essential to justify opposition to the motion, the hearing officer shall deny or defer the motion.

(c) *Motion for Summary Disposition in 120-Day Proceedings.* In any proceeding under the 120-day timeframe designated pursuant to Rule 360(a)(2), after a respondent's answer has been filed and documents have been made available to that respondent for inspection and copying pursuant to Rule 230, a party may make a motion for summary disposition on one or more claims or defenses, asserting that the undisputed pleaded facts, declarations, affidavits, deposition transcripts, documentary evidence or facts officially noted pursuant to Rule 323 show that there is no genuine issue with regard to any material fact and that the movant is entitled to summary disposition as a matter of law. A motion for summary disposition shall be made only with leave of the hearing officer. Leave shall be granted only for good cause shown and if consideration of the motion will not delay the scheduled start of the hearing. The hearing officer shall promptly grant or deny the motion for summary disposition or shall defer decision on the motion. If it appears that a party, for good cause shown, cannot present prior to the hearing facts essential to justify opposition to the motion, the hearing officer shall deny or defer the motion.

(d) *Motion for a Ruling as a Matter of Law Following Completion of Case in Chief.* Following the interested division's presentation of its case in chief, any party may make a motion, asserting that the movant is entitled to a ruling as a matter of law on one or more claims or defenses.

(e) *Length Limitation for Dispositive Motions.* Dispositive motions, together with any supporting memorandum of points and authorities (exclusive of any declarations, affidavits, deposition transcripts or other attachments), shall not exceed 9,800 words. Requests for leave to file motions and accompanying documents in excess of 9,800 words are disfavored. A double-spaced motion that does not, together with any accompanying memorandum of points and authorities, exceed 35 pages in length, inclusive of pleadings incorporated by reference (but excluding any declarations, affidavits, deposition transcripts or attachments) in the dispositive motion, is presumptively considered to contain no more than 9,800 words. Any motion that exceeds this page limit must include a certificate by the attorney, or an unrepresented party, stating that the brief complies with the word limit set forth in this paragraph and stating the number of words in the motion. The person preparing the certificate may rely on the word count of a word-processing program to prepare the document.

(f) *Opposition and Reply Length Limitations and Response Time.* A non-moving party may file an opposition to a dispositive motion and the moving party may thereafter file a reply.

(1) *Length limitations.* Any opposition must comply with the length limitations applicable to the movant's motion as set forth in paragraph (e) of this section. Any reply must comply with the length limitations set forth in Rule 154(c).

(2) *Response time.* (i) For motions under paragraphs (a), (b), and (d) of this section, the response times set forth in Rule 154(b) apply to any opposition and reply briefs.

(ii) For motions under paragraph (c) of this section, any opposition must be filed within 21 days after service of such a motion, and any reply must be filed within seven days after service of any opposition.

RULES REGARDING HEARINGS

Rule 300. Hearings

Hearings for the purpose of taking evidence shall be held only upon order of the Commission. All hearings shall be conducted in a fair, impartial, expeditious and orderly manner.

Rule 301. Hearings to be public

All hearings, except hearings on applications for confidential treatment filed pursuant to Rule 190, hearings held to consider a motion for a protective order pursuant to Rule 322, and hearings on *ex parte* application for a temporary cease-and-desist order, shall be public unless otherwise ordered by the Commission on its own motion or the motion of a party. No hearing shall be nonpublic where all respondents request that the hearing be made public.

Rule 302. Record of hearings

(a) *Recordation.* Unless ordered otherwise by the hearing officer or the Commission, all hearings shall be recorded and a written transcript thereof shall be prepared.

(b) *Availability of a Transcript.* Transcripts of public hearings shall be available for purchase at prescribed rates. Transcripts of nonpublic proceedings, and transcripts subject to a protective order pursuant to Rule 322, shall be available for purchase only by parties; provided, however, that any person compelled to submit data or evidence in a hearing may purchase a copy of his or her own testimony.

(c) *Transcript Correction.* Prior to the filing of post-hearing briefs or proposed findings and conclusions, or within such earlier time as directed by the Commission or the hearing officer, a party or witness may make a motion to correct the transcript. Proposed corrections of the transcript may be submitted to the hearing officer by stipulation pursuant to Rule 324, or by motion. Upon notice to all parties to the proceeding, the hearing officer may, by order, specify corrections to the transcript.

Rule 310. Failure to appear at hearings: default

Any person named in an order instituting proceedings as a person against whom findings may be made or sanctions imposed who fails to appear at a hearing of which he or she has been duly notified may be deemed to be in default pursuant to Rule 155(a). A party may make a motion to set aside a default pursuant to Rule 155(b).

Rule 320. Evidence: admissibility

(a) Except as otherwise provided in this section, the Commission or the hearing officer may receive relevant evidence and shall exclude all evidence that is irrelevant, immaterial, unduly repetitious, or unreliable.

(b) Subject to Rule 235, evidence that constitutes hearsay may be admitted if it is relevant, material, and bears satisfactory indicia of reliability so that its use is fair.

Rule 321. Evidence: objections and offers of proof

(a) *Objections.* Objections to the admission or exclusion of evidence must be made on the record and shall be in short form, stating the grounds relied upon. Exceptions to any ruling thereon by the hearing officer need not be noted at the time of the ruling. Such exceptions will be deemed waived on appeal to the Commission, however, unless raised:

(1) Pursuant to interlocutory review in accordance with Rule 400;

(2) In a proposed finding or conclusion filed pursuant to Rule 340; or

(3) In a petition for Commission review of an initial decision filed in accordance with Rule 410.

(b) *Offers of Proof.* Whenever evidence is excluded from the record, the party offering such evidence may make an offer of proof, which shall be included in the record. Excluded material shall be retained pursuant to Rule 350(b).

Rule 322. Evidence: confidential information, protective orders

(a) *Procedure.* In any proceeding as defined in Rule 101(a), a party, any person who is the owner, subject or creator of a document subject to subpoena or which may be introduced as evidence, or any witness who testifies at a hearing may file a motion requesting a protective order to limit from disclosure to other parties or to the public documents or testimony that contain confidential information. The motion should include a general summary or extract of the documents without revealing confidential details. If the movant seeks a protective order against disclosure to other parties as well as the public, copies of the documents shall not be served on other parties. Unless the documents are unavailable, the movant shall file for in camera inspection a sealed copy of the documents as to which the order is sought.

(b) *Basis for Issuance.* Documents and testimony introduced in a public hearing are presumed to be public. A motion for a protective order shall be granted only upon a finding that the harm resulting from disclosure would outweigh the benefits of disclosure.

(c) *Requests for Additional Information Supporting Confidentiality.* A movant under paragraph (a) of this rule may be required to furnish in writing additional information with respect to the grounds for confidentiality. Failure to supply the information so requested within five days from the date of receipt by the movant of a notice of the information required shall be deemed a waiver of the objection to public disclosure of that portion of the documents to which the additional information relates, unless the Commission or the hearing officer shall otherwise order for good cause shown at or before the expiration of such five-day period.

(d) *Confidentiality of Documents Pending Decision.* Pending a determination of a motion under this section, the documents as to which confidential treatment is sought and any other documents that would reveal the confidential information in those documents shall be maintained under seal and shall be disclosed only in accordance with orders of the Commission or the hearing officer. Any order issued in connection with a motion under this section shall be public unless the order would disclose information as to which a protective order has been granted, in which case that portion of the order that would reveal the protected information shall be nonpublic.

Rule 323. Evidence: official notice

Official notice may be taken of any material fact which might be judicially noticed by a district court of the United States, any matter in the public official records of the Commission, or any matter which is peculiarly within the knowledge of the Commission as an expert body. If official notice is requested or taken of a material fact not appearing in the evidence in the record, the parties, upon timely request, shall be afforded an opportunity to establish the contrary.

Rule 324. Evidence: stipulations

The parties may, by stipulation, at any stage of the proceeding agree upon any pertinent facts in the proceeding. A stipulation may be received in evidence and, when received, shall be binding on the parties to the stipulation.

Rule 325. Evidence: presentation under oath or affirmation

A witness at a hearing for the purpose of taking evidence shall testify under oath or affirmation.

Rule 326. Evidence: presentation, rebuttal and cross–examination

In any proceeding in which a hearing is required to be conducted on the record after opportunity for hearing in accord with 5 U.S.C. 556(a), a party is entitled to present its case or defense by oral or documentary evidence, to submit rebuttal evidence, and to conduct such cross-examination as, in the discretion of the Commission or the hearing officer, may be required for a full and true disclosure of the facts. The scope and form of evidence, rebuttal evidence, if any, and cross-examination, if any, in any other proceeding shall be determined by the Commission or the hearing officer in each proceeding.

Rule 340. Proposed findings, conclusions and supporting briefs

(a) *Opportunity to File.* Before an initial decision is issued, each party shall have an opportunity, reasonable in light of all the circumstances, to file in writing proposed findings and conclusions together with, or as a part of, its brief.

(b) *Procedure.* Proposed findings of fact must be supported by citations to specific portions of the record. If successive filings are directed, the proposed findings and conclusions of the party assigned to file first shall be set forth in serially numbered paragraphs, and any counter statement of proposed findings and conclusions must, in addition to any other matter, indicate those paragraphs of the proposals already filed as to which there is no dispute. A reply brief may be filed by the party assigned to file first, or, where simultaneous filings are directed, reply briefs may be filed by each party, within the period prescribed therefor by the hearing officer. No further briefs may be filed except with leave of the hearing officer.

(c) *Time for Filing.* In any proceeding in which an initial decision is to be issued:

(1) At the end of each hearing, the hearing officer shall, by order, after consultation with the parties, prescribe the period within which proposed findings and conclusions and supporting briefs are to be filed. The party or parties directed to file first shall make its or their initial filing within 30 days of the end of the hearing unless the hearing officer, for good cause shown, permits a different period and sets forth in the order the reasons why the different period is necessary.

(2) The total period within which all such proposed findings and conclusions and supporting briefs and any counter statements of proposed findings and conclusions and reply briefs are to be filed shall be no longer than 90 days after the close of the hearing unless the hearing officer, for good cause shown, permits a different period and sets forth in an order the reasons why the different period is necessary.

Rule 350. Record in proceedings before hearing officer; retention of documents; copies

(a) *Contents of the Record.* The record shall consist of:

(1) The order instituting proceedings, each notice of hearing and any amendments;

(2) Each application, motion, submission or other paper, and any amendments, motions, objections, and exceptions to or regarding them;

(3) Each stipulation, transcript of testimony and document or other item admitted into evidence;

(4) Each written communication accepted by the hearing officer pursuant to Rule 210;

(5) With respect to a request to disqualify a hearing officer or to allow the hearing officer's withdrawal under Rule 112, each affidavit or transcript of testimony taken and the decision made in connection with the request;

(6) All motions, briefs and other papers filed on interlocutory appeal;

(7) All proposed findings and conclusions;

(8) Each written order issued by the hearing officer or Commission; and

(9) Any other document or item accepted into the record by the hearing officer.

(b) *Retention of Documents Not Admitted.* Any document offered into evidence but excluded, shall not be considered a part of the record. The Secretary shall retain any such document until the later of the date upon which a Commission order ending the proceeding becomes final, or the conclusion of any judicial review of the Commission's order.

(c) *Substitution of Copies.* A true copy of a document may be substituted for any document in the record or any document retained pursuant to paragraph (b) of this rule.

Rule 351. Transmittal of documents to Secretary; record index; certification

(a) *Transmittal from Hearing Officer to Secretary of Partial Record Index.* The hearing officer may, at any time, transmit to the Secretary motions, exhibits or any other original documents filed with or accepted into evidence by the hearing officer, together with a list of such documents.

(b) *Preparation, Certification of Record Index.* Promptly after the close of the hearing, the hearing officer shall transmit to the Secretary an index of the originals of any motions, exhibits or any other documents filed with or accepted into evidence by the hearing officer that have not been previously transmitted to the Secretary, and the Secretary shall prepare a record index. Prior to issuance of an initial decision, or if no initial decision is to be prepared, within 30 days of the close of the hearing, the Secretary shall transmit the record index to the hearing officer and serve a copy of the record index on each party. Any person may file proposed corrections to the record index with the hearing officer within 15 days of service of the record index. The hearing officer shall, by order, direct whether any corrections to the record index shall be made. The Secretary shall make such corrections, if any, and issue a revised record index. If an initial decision is to be issued, the initial decision shall include a certification that the record consists of the items set forth in the record index or revised record index issued by the Secretary.

(c) *Final Transmittal of Record Items to the Secretary.* After the close of the hearing, the hearing officer shall transmit to the Secretary originals of any motions, exhibits or any other documents filed with, or accepted into evidence by, the hearing officer, or any other portions of the record that have not already been transmitted to the Secretary. Prior to service of the initial decision by the Secretary, or if no initial decision is to be issued, within 60 days of the close of the hearing, the Secretary shall inform the hearing officer if any portions of the record are not in the Secretary's custody.

Rule 360. Initial decision of hearing officer and timing of hearing

(a)(1) *When required.* Unless the Commission directs otherwise, the hearing officer shall prepare an initial decision in any proceeding in which the Commission directs a hearing officer to preside at a hearing, provided, however, that an initial decision may be waived by the parties with the consent of the hearing officer pursuant to Rule 202.

(2) *Time period for filing initial decision and for hearing*—(i) *Initial Decision.* In the order instituting proceedings, the Commission will specify a time period in which the hearing officer's initial decision must be filed with the Secretary. In the Commission's discretion, after consideration of the nature, complexity, and urgency of the subject matter, and with due regard for the public interest and the protection of investors, this time period will be either 30, 75, or 120 days. The time period will run from the occurrence of the following events:

(A) The completion of post-hearing briefing in a proceeding where the hearing has been completed; or

(B) The completion of briefing on a Rule 250 motion in the event the hearing officer has determined that no hearing is necessary; or

(C) The determination by the hearing officer that, pursuant to Rule 155, a party is deemed to be in default and no hearing is necessary.

(ii) *Hearing.* Under the 120-day timeline, the hearing officer shall issue an order scheduling the hearing to begin approximately four months (but no more than ten months) from the date of service of the order instituting the proceeding. Under the 75-day timeline, the hearing officer shall issue an order scheduling the hearing to begin approximately 2-1/2 months (but no more than six months) from the date of service of the order instituting the proceeding. Under the 30-day timeline, the hearing officer shall issue an order scheduling the hearing to begin approximately one month (but no more than four months) from the date of service of the order instituting the proceeding. These deadlines confer no substantive rights on respondents. If a stay is granted pursuant to Rule 161(c)(2)(i) or Rule 210(c)(3), the time period specified in the order instituting proceedings in which the hearing officer's initial decision must be filed with the Secretary, as well as any other time limits established in orders issued by the hearing officer in the proceeding, shall be automatically tolled during the period while the stay is in effect.

(3) *Certification of extension; motion for extension.*

(i) In the event that the hearing officer presiding over the proceeding determines that it will not be possible to file the initial decision within the specified period of time, the hearing officer may certify to the Commission in writing the need to extend the initial decision deadline by up to 30 days for case management purposes. The certification must be issued no later than 30 days prior to the expiration of the time specified for the issuance of an initial decision and be served on the Commission and all parties in the proceeding. If the Commission has not issued an order to the contrary within 14 days after receiving the certification, the extension set forth in the hearing officer's certification shall take effect.

(ii) Either in addition to a certification of extension, or instead of a certification of extension, the Chief Administrative Law Judge may submit a motion to the Commission requesting an extension of the time period for filing the initial decision. First, the hearing officer presiding over the proceeding must consult with the Chief Administrative Law Judge. Following such consultation, the Chief Administrative Law Judge may determine, in his or her discretion, to submit a motion to the Commission requesting an extension of the time period for filing the initial decision. This motion may request an extension of any length but must be filed no later than 15 days prior to the expiration of the time specified in the certification of extension, or if there is no certification of extension, 30 days prior to the expiration of the time specified in the order instituting proceedings. The motion will be served upon all parties in the proceeding, who may file with the Commission statements in support of or in opposition to the motion. If the Commission determines that additional time is necessary or appropriate in the public interest, the Commission shall issue an order extending the time period for filing the initial decision.

(iii) The provisions of this paragraph (a)(3) confer no rights on respondents.

(b) *Content.* An initial decision shall include findings and conclusions, and the reasons or basis therefor, as to all the material issues of fact, law or discretion presented on the record and the appropriate order, sanction, relief, or denial thereof. The initial decision shall also state the time period, not to exceed 21 days after service of the decision, except for good cause shown, within which a petition for review of the initial decision may be filed. The reasons for any extension of time shall be stated in the initial decision. The initial decision shall also include a statement that, as provided in paragraph (d) of this section:

(1) The Commission will enter an order of finality as to each party unless a party or an aggrieved person entitled to review timely files a petition for review of the initial decision or a motion to correct a manifest error of fact in the initial decision with the hearing officer, or the Commission determines on its own initiative to review the initial decision; and

(2) If a party or an aggrieved person entitled to review timely files a petition for review or a motion to correct a manifest error of fact in the initial decision with the hearing officer, or if the Commission takes action to review as to a party or an aggrieved person entitled to review, the initial decision shall not become final as to that party or person.

(c) *Filing, Service and Publication.* The Secretary shall promptly serve the initial decision upon the parties and shall promptly publish notice of the filing thereof on the SEC website; provided, however, that in nonpublic proceedings no notice shall be published unless the Commission otherwise directs.

(d) *Finality.* (1) If a party or an aggrieved person entitled to review timely files a petition for review or a motion to correct a manifest error of fact in the initial decision, or if the Commission on its own initiative orders review of a decision with respect to a party or a person aggrieved who would be entitled to review, the initial decision shall not become final as to that party or person.

(2) If a party or aggrieved person entitled to review fails to file timely a petition for review or a motion to correct a manifest error of fact in the initial decision, and if the Commission does not order review of a decision on its own initiative, the Commission will issue an order that the decision has become final as to that party. The decision becomes final upon issuance of the order. The order of finality shall state the date on which sanctions, if any, take effect. Notice of the order shall be published on the SEC website.

APPEAL TO THE COMMISSION AND COMMISSION REVIEW

Rule 400. Interlocutory review

(a) *Availability.* The Commission may, at any time, on its own motion, direct that any matter be submitted to it for review. Petitions by parties for interlocutory review are disfavored, and the Commission ordinarily will grant a petition to review a hearing officer ruling prior to its consideration of an initial decision only in extraordinary circumstances. The Commission may decline to consider a ruling certified by a hearing officer pursuant to paragraph (c) of this rule or the petition of a party who has been denied certification if it determines that interlocutory review is not warranted or appropriate under the circumstances. This section is the exclusive remedy for review of a hearing officer's ruling prior to Commission consideration of the entire proceeding and is the sole mechanism for appeal of actions delegated pursuant to 17 CFR 200.30–9 and 200.30–10.

(b) *Expedited Consideration.* Interlocutory review of a hearing officer's ruling shall be expedited in every way, consistent with the Commission's other responsibilities.

(c) *Certification Process.* A ruling submitted to the Commission for interlocutory review must be certified in writing by the hearing officer and shall specify the material relevant to the ruling involved. The hearing officer shall not certify a ruling unless:

(1) His or her ruling would compel testimony of Commission members, officers or employees or the production of documentary evidence in their custody; or

(2) Upon application by a party, within five days of the hearing officer's ruling, the hearing officer is of the opinion that:

(i) The ruling involves a controlling question of law as to which there is substantial ground for difference of opinion; and

(ii) An immediate review of the order may materially advance the completion of the proceeding.

(d) *Proceedings Not Stayed.* The filing of an application for review or the grant of review shall not stay proceedings before the hearing officer unless he or she, or the Commission, shall so order. The Commission will not consider the motion for a stay unless the motion shall have first been made to the hearing officer.

Rule 401. Consideration of stays

(a) *Procedure.* A request for a stay shall be made by written motion, filed pursuant to Rule 154, and served on all parties pursuant to Rule 150. The motion shall state the reasons for the relief requested and the facts relied upon, and, if the facts are subject to dispute, the motion shall be supported by affidavits or other sworn statements or copies thereof. Portions of the record relevant to the relief sought, if available to the movant, shall be filed with the motion. The Commission may issue a stay based on such motion or on its own motion.

(b) *Scope of Relief.* The Commission may grant a stay in whole or in part, and may condition relief under this section upon such terms, or upon the implementation of such procedures, as it deems appropriate.

(c) *Stay of a Commission Order.* A motion for a stay of a Commission order may be made by any person aggrieved thereby who would be entitled to review in a federal court of appeals. A motion seeking to stay the effectiveness of a Commission order pending judicial review may be made to the Commission at any time during which the Commission retains jurisdiction over the proceeding.

(d) *Stay of an Action by a Self-Regulatory Organization.* (1) *Availability.* A motion for a stay of an action by a self-regulatory organization for which the Commission is the appropriate regulatory agency, for which action review may be sought pursuant to Rule 420, may be made by any person aggrieved thereby at the time an application for review is filed in accordance with Rule 420 or thereafter.

(2) *Summary Entry.* A stay may be entered summarily, without notice and opportunity for hearing.

(3) *Expedited Consideration.* Where the action complained of has already taken effect and the motion for stay is filed within 10 days of the effectiveness of the action, or where the action complained of, will, by its terms, take effect within five days of the filing of the motion for stay, the consideration of and decision on the motion for a stay shall be expedited in every way, consistent with the Commission's other responsibilities. Where consideration will be expedited, persons opposing the motion for a stay may file a statement in opposition within two days of service of the motion unless the Commission, by written order, shall specify a different period.

(e) *Lifting of Stay of Action by the Public Company Accounting Oversight Board.* (1) *Availability.* Any person aggrieved by a stay of action by the Board entered in accordance with 15 U.S.C. 7215(e) for which review has been sought pursuant to Rule 440 or which the Commission has taken up on its motion pursuant to Rule 441 may make a motion to lift the stay. The Commission may, at any time, on its own motion determine whether to lift the automatic stay.

(2) *Summary Action.* The Commission may lift a stay summarily, without notice and opportunity for hearing.

(3) *Expedited Consideration.* The Commission may expedite consideration of a motion to lift a stay of Board action, consistent with the Commission's other responsibilities. Where consideration is expedited, persons opposing the lifting of the stay may file a statement in opposition within two days of service of the motion requesting lifting of the stay unless the Commission, by written order, shall specify a different period.

Rule 410. Appeal of initial decisions by hearing officers

(a) *Petition for Review; When Available.* In any proceeding in which an initial decision is made by a hearing officer, any party, and any other person who would have been entitled to judicial review of the decision entered therein if the Commission itself had made the decision, may file a petition for review of the decision with the Commission.

(b) *Procedure.* The petition for review of an initial decision shall be filed with the Commission within such time after service of the initial decision as prescribed by the hearing officer pursuant to Rule 360(b) unless a party has filed a motion to correct an initial decision with the hearing officer. If such correction has been sought, a party shall have 21 days from the date of the hearing officer's order resolving the motion to correct to file a petition for review. The petition shall set forth a statement of the issues presented for review under Rule 411(b). In the event a petition for review is filed, any other party to the proceeding may file a cross-petition for review within the original time allowed for seeking review or within ten days from the date that the petition for review was filed, whichever is later.

(c) *Length Limitation.* Except with leave of the Commission, the petition for review shall not exceed three pages in length. Incorporation of pleadings or filings by reference into the petition is not permitted. Motions to file petitions in excess of those limitations are disfavored.

(d) *Financial Disclosure Statement Requirement.* Any person who files a petition for review of an initial decision that asserts that person's inability to pay either disgorgement, interest or a penalty shall file with the opening brief a sworn financial disclosure statement containing the information specified in Rule 630(b).

(e) *Prerequisite to Judicial Review.* Pursuant to Section 704 of the Administrative Procedure Act, 5 U.S.C. 704, a petition to the Commission for review of an initial decision is a prerequisite to the seeking of judicial review of a final order entered pursuant to such decision.

Rule 411. Commission consideration of initial decisions by hearing officers

(a) *Scope of Review.* The Commission may affirm, reverse, modify, set aside or remand for further proceedings, in whole or in part, an initial decision by a hearing officer and may make any findings or conclusions that in its judgment are proper and on the basis of the record.

(b) *Standards for Granting Review Pursuant to a Petition for Review.* (1) Mandatory Review. After a petition for review has been filed, the Commission shall review any initial decision that:

(i) Denies any request for action pursuant to Section 8(a) or Section 8(c) of the Securities Act of 1933, 15 U.S.C. 77h(a), (c), or the first sentence of Section 12(d) of the Exchange Act, 15 U.S.C. 78*l*(d);

(ii) Suspends trading in a security pursuant to Section 12(k) of the Exchange Act, 15 U.S.C. 78*l*(k); or

(iii) Is in a case of adjudication (as defined in 5 U.S.C. 551) not required to be determined on the record after notice and opportunity for hearing (except to the extent there is involved a matter described in 5 U.S.C. 554(a)(1) through (6)).

(2) *Discretionary review.* The Commission may decline to review any other decision. In determining whether to grant review, the Commission shall consider whether the petition for review makes a reasonable showing that:

(i) A prejudicial error was committed in the conduct of the proceeding; or

(ii) The decision embodies:

(A) A finding or conclusion of material fact that is clearly erroneous; or

(B) A conclusion of law that is erroneous; or

(C) An exercise of discretion or decision of law or policy that is important and that the Commission should review.

(c) *Commission Review Other than Pursuant to a Petition for Review.* The Commission may, on its own initiative, order review of any initial decision, or any portion of any initial decision, within 21 days after the end of the period established for filing a petition for review pursuant to Rule 410(b). A party who does not intend to file a petition for review, and who desires the Commission's determination whether to order review on its own initiative to be made in a shorter time, may make a motion for an expedited decision, accompanied by a written statement that the party waives its right to file a petition for review. The vote of one member of the Commission, conveyed to the Secretary, shall be sufficient to bring a matter before the Commission for review.

(d) *Limitations on Matters Reviewed.* Review by the Commission of an initial decision shall be limited to the issues specified in an opening brief that complies with Rule 450(b), or the issues, if any, specified in the briefing schedule order issued pursuant to Rule 450(a). Any exception to an initial decision not supported in an opening brief that complies with Rule 450(b) may, at the discretion of the Commission, be deemed to have been waived by the petitioner. On notice to all parties, however, the Commission may, at any time prior to issuance of its decision, raise and determine any other matters that it deems material, with opportunity for oral or written argument thereon by the parties.

(e) *Summary Affirmance.* (1) At any time within 21 days after the filing of a petition for review pursuant to Rule 410(b), any party may file a motion in accordance with Rule 154 asking that the Commission summarily affirm an initial decision. Any party may file an opposition and reply to such motion in accordance with Rule 154. Pending determination of the motion for summary affirmance, the Commission, in its discretion, may delay issuance of a briefing schedule order pursuant to Rule 450.

(2) Upon consideration of the motion and any opposition or upon its own initiative, the Commission may summarily affirm an initial decision. The Commission may grant summary affirmance if it finds that no issue raised in the initial decision warrants consideration by the Commission of further oral or written argument. The Commission will decline to grant summary affirmance upon a reasonable showing that a prejudicial error was committed in the conduct of the proceeding or that

the decision embodies an exercise of discretion or decision of law or policy that is important and that the Commission should review.

(f) *Failure to Obtain a Majority.* In the event a majority of participating Commissioners do not agree to a disposition on the merits, the initial decision shall be of no effect, and an order will be issued in accordance with this result.

Rule 420. Appeal of determinations by self-regulatory organizations

(a) *Application for Review; When Available.* An application for review by the Commission may be filed by any person who is aggrieved by a determination of a self-regulatory organization with respect to any:

(1) Final disciplinary sanction;

(2) Denial or conditioning of membership or participation;

(3) Prohibition or limitation in respect to access to services offered by that self-regulatory organization or a member thereof; or

(4) Bar from association as to which a notice is required to be filed with the Commission pursuant to Section 19(d)(1) of the Exchange Act, 15 U.S.C. 78s(d)(1).

(b) *Procedure.* As required by section 19(d)(1) of the Securities Exchange Act of 1934, 15 U.S.C. 78s(d)(1), an applicant must file an application for review with the Commission within 30 days after the notice of the determination is filed with the Commission and received by the aggrieved person applying for review. The Commission will not extend this 30-day period, absent a showing of extraordinary circumstances. This section is the exclusive remedy for seeking an extension of the 30-day period.

(c) *Application.* The application shall be filed with the Commission pursuant to Rule 151. The applicant shall serve the application on the self-regulatory organization. The application shall identify the determination complained of and set forth in summary form a brief statement of the alleged errors in the determination and supporting reasons therefor. The application shall state an address where the applicant can be served. The application should not exceed two pages in length. If the applicant will be represented by a representative, the application shall be accompanied by the notice of appearance required by Rule 102(d). Any exception to a determination not supported in an opening brief that complies with Rule 450(b) may, at the discretion of the Commission, be deemed to have been waived by the applicant.

(d) *Determination Not Stayed.* Filing an application for review with the Commission pursuant to paragraph (b) of this section shall not operate as a stay of the complained of determination made by the self-regulatory organization unless the Commission otherwise orders either pursuant to a motion filed in accordance with Rule 401 or on its own motion.

(e) *Certification of the Record; Service of the Index.* Fourteen days after receipt of an application for review or a Commission order for review, the self-regulatory organization shall certify and file with the Commission one copy of the record upon which the action complained of was taken, and shall file with the Commission three copies of an index to such record, and shall serve upon each party one copy of the index.

Rule 421. Commission consideration of determinations by self-regulatory organizations

(a) *Commission Review Other than Pursuant to a Petition for Review.* The Commission may, on its own initiative, order review of any determination by a self-regulatory organization that could be subject to an application for review pursuant to Rule 420(a) within 40 days after notice thereof was filed with the Commission pursuant to Section 19(d)(1) of the Exchange Act, 15 U.S.C. 78s(d)(1).

(b) *Supplemental Briefing.* The Commission may at any time prior to issuance of its decision raise or consider any matter that it deems material, whether or not raised by the parties. Notice to the parties and an opportunity for supplemental briefing with respect to issues not briefed by the parties shall be given where the Commission believes that such briefing would significantly aid the decisional process.

Rule 430. Appeal of actions made pursuant to delegated authority

(a) *Scope of Rule.* Any person aggrieved by an action made by authority delegated in 17 CFR 200.30–1 through 200.30–8 or 17 CFR 200.30–11 through 200.30–18 of this chapter may seek review of the action pursuant to paragraph (b) of this rule.

(b) *Procedure.* (1) *Notice of Intention to Petition for Review.* A party to an action made pursuant to delegated authority, or a person aggrieved by such action, may seek Commission review of the action by filing a written notice of intention to petition for review within five days after actual notice of the action to that party or aggrieved person, or 15 days after publication of the notice of action in the FEDERAL REGISTER, or five days after service of notice of the action on that party or aggrieved person pursuant to Rule 141(b), whichever is the earliest.

(2) *Petition for Review.* Within five days after the filing of a notice of intention to petition for review pursuant to paragraph (b)(1) of this section, the person seeking review shall file a petition for review containing a clear and concise statement of the issues to be reviewed and the reasons why review is appropriate. The petition shall include exceptions to any findings of fact or conclusions of law made, together with supporting reasons for such exceptions based on appropriate citations to such record as may exist. These reasons may be stated in summary form.

(c) *Prerequisite to Judicial Review.* Pursuant to Section 704 of the Administrative Procedure Act, 5 U.S.C. 704, a petition to the Commission for review of an action made by authority delegated in 17 CFR 200.30–1 through 200.30–18 is a prerequisite to the seeking of judicial review of a final order entered pursuant to such an action. Pursuant to 15 U.S.C. 7214(h)(2), any decision by the Commission pursuant to 200.30–11 shall not be reviewable under 15 U.S.C. 78y and shall not be deemed "final agency action" for purposes of 5 U.S.C. 704.

Rule 431. Commission consideration of actions made pursuant to delegated authority

(a) *Scope of Review.* The Commission may affirm, reverse, modify, set aside or remand for further proceedings, in whole or in part, any action made pursuant to authority delegated in 17 CFR 200.30–1 through 200.30–18.

(b) *Standards for Granting Review Pursuant to a Petition for Review.* (1) *Mandatory Review.* After a petition for review has been filed, the Commission shall review any action that it would be required to review pursuant to Rule 411(b)(1) if the action was made as the initial decision of a hearing officer.

(2) *Discretionary Review.* The Commission may decline to review any other action. In determining whether to grant review, the Commission shall consider the factors set forth in Rule 411(b)(2).

(c) *Commission Review Other than Pursuant to a Petition for Review.* The Commission may, on its own initiative, order review of any action made pursuant to delegated authority at any time, provided, however, that where there are one or more parties to the matter, such review shall not be ordered more than ten days after the action. The vote of one member of the Commission, conveyed to the Secretary, shall be sufficient to bring a matter before the Commission for review.

(d) *Required Items in an Order for Review.* In an order granting a petition for review or directing review on the Commission's own initiative, the Commission shall set forth the time within which any party or other person may file a statement in support of or in opposition to the action made by delegated authority and shall state whether a stay shall be granted, if none is in effect, or shall be continued, if in effect pursuant to paragraph (e) of this rule.

(e) *Automatic Stay of Delegated Action.* An action made pursuant to delegated authority shall have immediate effect and be deemed the action of the Commission. Upon filing with the Commission of a notice of intention to petition for review, or upon notice to the Secretary of the vote of a Commissioner that a matter be reviewed, an action made pursuant to delegated authority shall be stayed until the Commission orders otherwise, provided, however, there shall be no automatic stay of an action:

(1) To grant a stay of action by the Commission or a self-regulatory organization as authorized by 17 CFR 200.30–14(g)(5)–(6); or

(2) To commence a subpoena enforcement proceeding as authorized by 17 CFR 200.30–4(a)(10).

(f) *Effectiveness of Stay or of Commission Decision to Modify or Reverse a Delegated Action.* As against any person who shall have acted in reliance upon any action at a delegated level, any stay or any modification or reversal by the Commission of such action shall be effective only from the time such person receives actual notice of such stay, modification or reversal.

Rule 440. Appeal of determinations by the Public Company Accounting Oversight Board

(a) *Application for Review; When Available.* Any person who is aggrieved by a determination of the Board with respect to any final disciplinary sanction, including disapproval of a completed application for registration of a public accounting firm, may file an application for review.

(b) *Procedure.* An aggrieved person may file an application for review with the Commission pursuant to Rule 151 within 30 days after the notice filed by the Board of its determination with the Commission pursuant to Rule 19d–4 is received by the aggrieved person applying for review. The applicant shall serve the application on the Board at the same time. The application shall identify the determination complained of, set forth in summary form a brief statement of alleged errors in the determination and supporting reasons therefor, and state an address where the applicant can be served. The application should not exceed two pages in length. The notice of appearance required by Rule 102(d) shall accompany the application. Any exception to a determination not supported in an opening brief that complies with Rule 450(b) may, at the discretion of the Commission, be deemed to have been waived by the applicant.

(c) *Stay of Determination.* Filing an application for review with the Commission pursuant to paragraph (b) of this rule operates as a stay of the Board's determination unless the Commission otherwise orders either pursuant to a motion filed in accordance with Rule 401(e) or upon its own motion.

(d) *Certification of the Record; Service of the Index.* Within fourteen days after receipt of an application for review, the Board shall certify and file with the Commission one copy of the record upon which it took the complained-of action. The Board shall file with the Commission three copies of an index of such record, and shall serve one copy of the index on each party.

Rule 441. Commission consideration of board determinations

(a) *Commission Review Other than Pursuant to an Application for Review.* The Commission may, on its own initiative, order review of any final disciplinary sanction, including disapproval of a completed application for registration of a public accounting firm, imposed by the Board that could be subject to an application for review pursuant to Rule 440(a) within 40 days after the Board filed notice thereof pursuant to Rule 19d–4 under the Securities Exchange Act of 1934.

(b) *Supplemental Briefing.* The Commission may at any time prior to the issuance of its decision raise or consider any matter that it deems material, whether or not raised by the parties. The Commission will give notice to the parties and an opportunity for supplemental briefing with respect to issues not briefed by the parties where the Commission believes that such briefing could significantly aid the decisional process.

Rule 450. Briefs filed with the Commission

(a) *Briefing Schedule Order.* Other than review ordered pursuant to Rule 431, if review of a determination is mandated by statute, rule, or judicial order or the Commission determines to grant review as a matter of discretion, the Commission shall issue a briefing schedule order directing the party or parties to file opening briefs and specifying particular issues, if any, as to which briefing should be limited or directed. Unless otherwise provided, opening briefs shall be filed within 30 days of the date of the briefing schedule order. Opposition briefs shall be filed within 30 days after the date opening briefs are due. Reply briefs shall be filed within 14 days after the date opposition briefs are due. No briefs in addition to those specified in the briefing schedule order may be filed except with leave of the Commission. The briefing schedule order shall be issued:

(1) At the time the Commission orders review on its own initiative pursuant to Rules 411 or 421, or orders interlocutory review on its own motion pursuant to Rule 400(a); or

(2) Within 21 days, or such longer time as provided by the Commission, after:

(i) The last day permitted for filing a petition for review pursuant to Rule 410(b) or a brief in opposition to a petition for review pursuant to Rule 410(d);

(ii) Receipt by the Commission of an index to the record of a determination of a self-regulatory organization filed pursuant to Rule 420(d);

(iii) Receipt by the Commission of an index to the record of a determination by the Board filed pursuant to Rule 440(d);

(iv) Receipt by the Commission of the mandate of a court of appeals with respect to a judicial remand; or

(v) Certification of a ruling for interlocutory review pursuant to Rule 400(c).

(b) *Contents of Briefs.* Briefs shall be confined to the particular matters at issue. Each exception to the findings or conclusions being reviewed shall be stated succinctly. Exceptions shall be supported by citation to the relevant portions of the record, including references to the specific pages relied upon, and by concise argument including citation of such statutes, decisions and other authorities as may be relevant. If the exception relates to the admission or exclusion of evidence, the substance of the evidence admitted or excluded shall be set forth in the brief, or by citation to the record. Reply briefs shall be confined to matters in opposition briefs of other parties; except as otherwise determined by the Commission in its discretion, any argument raised for the first time in a reply brief shall be deemed to have been waived.

(c) *Length Limitation.* Except with leave of the Commission, opening and opposition briefs shall not exceed 14,000 words and reply briefs shall not exceed 7,000 words, exclusive of pages containing the table of contents, table of authorities, and any addendum that consists solely of copies of applicable cases, pertinent legislative provisions or rules, and exhibits. Incorporation of pleadings or filings by reference into briefs submitted to the Commission is not permitted. Motions to file briefs in excess of these limitations are disfavored.

(d) *Certificate of Compliance.* An opening or opposition brief that does not exceed 30 pages in length, exclusive of pages containing the table of contents, table of authorities, and any addendum that consists solely of copies of applicable cases, pertinent legislative provisions, or rules and exhibits, is presumptively considered to contain no more than 14,000 words. A reply brief that does not exceed 15 pages in length, exclusive of pages containing the table of contents, table of authorities, and any addendum that consists solely of copies of applicable cases, pertinent legislative provisions, or rules and exhibits is presumptively considered to contain no more than 7,000 words. Any brief that exceeds these page limits must include a certificate by the party's representative, or an unrepresented party, stating that the brief complies with the requirements set forth in paragraph (c) of this section and stating the number of words in the brief. The person preparing the certificate may rely on the word count of the word-processing system used to prepare the brief.

Rule 451. Oral argument before the Commission

(a) *Availability.* The Commission, on its own motion or the motion of a party or any other aggrieved person entitled to Commission review, may order oral argument with respect to any matter. Motions for oral argument with respect to whether to affirm all or part of an initial decision by a hearing officer shall be granted unless exceptional circumstances make oral argument impractical or inadvisable. The Commission will consider appeals, motions and other matters properly before it on the basis of the papers filed by the parties without oral argument unless the Commission determines that the presentation of facts and legal arguments in the briefs and record and the decisional process would be significantly aided by oral argument.

(b) *Procedure.* Requests for oral argument shall be made by separate motion accompanying the initial brief on the merits. The Commission shall issue an order as to whether oral argument is to be heard, and if so, the time and place therefor. If oral argument is granted, the time fixed for oral argument shall be changed only by written order of the Commission, for good cause shown. The order shall state at whose request the change is made and the reasons for any such changes. No visual aids may be used at oral argument unless copies have been provided to the Commission and all parties at least five business days before the argument is to be held.

(c) *Time Allowed.* Unless the Commission orders otherwise, not more than one half-hour per side will be allowed for oral argument. The Commission may, in its discretion, determine that several persons have a common interest, and that the interests represented will be considered a single side for purposes of allotting time for oral argument. Time will be divided equally among persons on a single side, provided, however, that by mutual agreement they may reallocate their time among themselves. A request for additional time must be made by motion filed reasonably in advance of the date fixed for argument.

(d) *Participation of Commissioners.* A member of the Commission who was not present at the oral argument may participate in the decision of the proceeding, provided that the member has reviewed the transcript of such argument prior to such participation. The decision shall state whether the required review was made.

Rule 452. Additional evidence

Upon its own motion or the motion of a party, the Commission may allow the submission of additional evidence. A party may file a motion for leave to adduce additional evidence at any time prior to issuance of a decision by the Commission. Such motion shall show with particularity that such additional evidence is material and that there were reasonable grounds for failure to adduce such evidence previously. The Commission may accept or hear additional evidence, may remand the proceeding to a self-regulatory organization, or may remand or refer the proceeding to a hearing officer for the taking of additional evidence as appropriate.

Rule 460. Record before the Commission

The Commission shall determine each matter on the basis of the record.

(a) *Contents of the Record.* (1) In proceedings for final decision before the Commission other than those reviewing a determination by a self-regulatory organization, the record shall consist of:

(i) All items part of the record below in accordance with Rule 350;

(ii) Any petitions for review, cross-petitions or oppositions; and

(iii) All briefs, motions, submissions and other papers filed on appeal or review.

(2) In a proceeding for final decision before the Commission reviewing a determination by a self-regulatory organization, the record shall consist of:

(i) The record certified pursuant to Rule 420(d) by the self-regulatory organization;

(ii) Any application for review; and

(iii) Any submissions, moving papers, and briefs filed on appeal or review.

(3) In a proceeding for final decision before the Commission reviewing a determination of the Board, the record shall consist of:

(i) The record certified pursuant to Rule 440(d) by the Board;

(ii) Any application for review; and

(iii) Any submissions, moving papers, and briefs filed on appeal or review.

(b) *Transmittal of Record to Commission.* Within 14 days after the last date set for filing briefs or such later date as the Commission directs, the Secretary shall transmit the record to the Commission.

(c) *Review of Documents Not Admitted.* Any document offered in evidence but excluded by the hearing officer or the Commission and any document marked for identification but not offered as an exhibit shall not be considered a part of the record before the Commission on appeal but shall be transmitted to the Commission by the Secretary if so requested by the Commission. In the event that the Commission does not request the document, the Secretary shall retain the document not admitted into the record until the later of:

(1) The date upon which the Commission's order becomes final, or

(2) The conclusion of any judicial review of that order.

Rule 470. Reconsideration

(a) *Scope of Rule.* A party or any person aggrieved by a determination in a proceeding may file a motion for reconsideration of a final order issued by the Commission.

(b) *Procedure.* A motion for reconsideration shall be filed within 10 days after service of the order complained of, or within such time as the Commission may prescribe upon motion for extension of time filed by the person seeking reconsideration, if the motion is made within the foregoing 10–day period. The motion for reconsideration shall briefly and specifically state the matters of record alleged to have been erroneously decided, the grounds relied upon, and the relief sought. A motion for reconsideration shall conform to the requirements, including the limitation on the numbers of words, provided in Rule 154. No response to a motion for reconsideration shall be filed unless requested by the Commission. Any response so requested shall comply with Rule 154.

Rule 490. Receipt of petitions for judicial review pursuant to 28 U.S.C. 2112(a)(1)

The Commission officer and office designated pursuant to 28 U.S.C. 2112(a)(1) to receive copies of petitions for review of Commission orders from the persons instituting review in a court of appeals, are the Secretary and the Office of the Secretary at the Commission's Headquarters. Ten copies of each petition shall be submitted. Each copy shall state on its face that it is being submitted to the Commission pursuant to 28 U.S.C. 2112 by the person or persons who filed the petition in the court of appeals.

RULES RELATING TO TEMPORARY ORDERS AND SUSPENSIONS

Rule 500. Expedited consideration of proceedings

Consistent with the Commission's or the hearing officer's other responsibilities, every hearing shall be held and every decision shall be rendered at the earliest possible time in connection with:

(a) An application for a temporary sanction, as defined in Rule 101(a), or a proceeding to determine whether a temporary sanction should be made permanent;

(b) A motion or application to review an order suspending temporarily the effectiveness of an exemption from registration pursuant to Regulations A, B, E or F under the Securities Act, 17 CFR 230.258, 230.336, 230.610 or 230.656; or,

(c) A motion to or petition to review an order suspending temporarily the privilege of appearing before the Commission under Rule 102(e)(3), or a sanction under Rule 180(a)(1).

Rule 510. Temporary cease-and-desist orders: application process

(a) *Procedure.* A request for entry of a temporary cease-and-desist order shall be made by application filed by the Division of Enforcement. The application shall set forth the statutory provision or rule that each respondent is alleged to have violated; the temporary relief sought against each respondent, including whether the respondent would be required to take action to prevent the dissipation or conversion of assets; and whether the relief is sought *ex parte*.

(b) *Accompanying Documents.* The application shall be accompanied by a declaration of facts signed by a person with knowledge of the facts contained therein, a memorandum of points and authorities, a proposed order imposing the temporary relief sought, and, unless relief is sought *ex parte,* a proposed notice of hearing and order to show cause whether the temporary relief should be imposed. If a proceeding for a permanent cease-and-desist order has not already been commenced, a proposed order instituting proceedings to determine whether a permanent cease-and-desist order should be imposed shall also be filed with the application.

(c) *With Whom Filed.* The application shall be filed with the Secretary or, if the Secretary is unavailable, with the duty officer. In no event shall an application be filed with an administrative law judge.

(d) *Record of Proceedings.* Hearings, including *ex parte* presentations made by the Division of Enforcement pursuant to Rule 513, shall be recorded or transcribed pursuant to Rule 302.

Rule 511. Temporary cease-and-desist orders: notice; procedures for hearing

(a) *Notice: How Given.* Notice of an application for a temporary cease-and-desist order shall be made by serving a notice of hearing and order to show cause pursuant to Rule 141(b) or, where timely service of a notice of hearing pursuant to Rule 141(b) is not practicable, by any other means reasonably calculated to give actual notice that a hearing will be held, including telephonic notification of the general subject matter, time, and place of the hearing. If an application is made *ex parte,* pursuant to Rule 513, no notice to a respondent need be given prior to the Commission's consideration of the application.

(b) *Hearing Before the Commission.* Except as provided in paragraph (d) of this rule, hearings on an application for a temporary cease-and-desist order shall be held before the Commission.

(c) *Presiding Officer: Designation.* The Chairman shall preside or designate a Commissioner to preside at the hearing. If the Chairman is absent or unavailable at the time of hearing and no other Commissioner has been designated to preside, the duty officer on the day the hearing begins shall preside or designate another Commissioner to preside.

(d) *Procedure at Hearing.* (1) The presiding officer shall have all those powers of a hearing officer set forth in Rule 111 and shall rule on the admissibility of evidence and other procedural matters, including, but not limited to whether oral testimony will be heard; the time allowed each party for the submission of evidence or argument; and whether post-hearing submission of briefs, proposed findings of fact and conclusions of law will be permitted and if so, the procedures for submission; provided, however, that the person presiding may consult with other Commissioners participating in the hearing on these or any other question of procedure.

(2) Each Commissioner present at the hearing shall be afforded a reasonable opportunity to ask questions of witnesses, if any, or of counsel.

(3) A party or witness may participate by telephone. Alternative means of remote access, including a video link, shall be permitted in the Commission's discretion. Factors the Commission may consider in determining whether to permit alternative means of remote access include, but are not limited to, whether allowing an alternative means of access will delay the hearing, whether the alternative means is reliable, and whether the party proposing its use has made arrangements to pay for its cost.

(4) After a hearing has begun, the Commission may, on its own motion, or the motion of a party, assign a hearing officer to preside at the taking of oral testimony or other evidence and to certify the record of such testimony or other evidence to the Commission within a fixed period of time. No recommended or initial decision shall be made by such a hearing officer.

Rule 512. Temporary cease-and-desist orders: issuance after notice and opportunity for hearing

(a) *Basis for Issuance.* A temporary cease-and-desist order shall be issued only if the Commission determines that the alleged violation or threatened violation specified in an order instituting proceedings whether to enter a permanent cease-and-desist order pursuant to Securities Act Section 8A(a), 15 U.S.C. 77h–1(a), Exchange Act Section 21C(a), 15 U.S.C. 78u–3(a), Investment Company Act Section 9(f)(1), 15 U.S.C. 80a–9(f)(1), or Investment Advisers Act Section 203(k)(1), 15 U.S.C. 80b–3(k)(1), or the continuation thereof, is likely to result in significant dissipation or conversion of assets, significant harm to investors, or substantial harm to the public interest, including, but not limited to, losses to the

Securities Investor Protection Corporation, prior to the completion of proceedings on the permanent cease-and-desist order.

(b) *Content, Scope and Form of Order*. Every temporary cease-and-desist order granted shall:

(1) Describe the basis for its issuance, including the alleged or threatened violations and the harm that is likely to result without the issuance of an order;

(2) Describe in reasonable detail, and not by reference to the order instituting proceedings or any other document, the act or acts the respondent is to take or refrain from taking; and

(3) Be indorsed with the date and hour of issuance.

(c) *Effective Upon Service*. A temporary cease-and-desist order is effective upon service upon the respondent.

(d) *Service: How Made*. Service of a temporary cease-and-desist order shall be made pursuant to Rule 141(a). The person who serves the order shall promptly file a declaration of service identifying the person served, the method of service, the date of service, the address to which service was made and the person who made service; provided, however, failure to file such a declaration shall have no effect on the validity of the service.

(e) *Commission Review*. At any time after the respondent has been served with a temporary cease-and-desist order, the respondent may apply to the Commission to have the order set aside, limited or suspended. The application shall set forth with specificity the facts that support the request.

Rule 513. Temporary cease-and-desist orders: issuance without prior notice and opportunity for hearing

In addition to the requirements for issuance of a temporary cease-and-desist order set forth in Rule 512, the following requirements shall apply if a temporary cease-and-desist order is to be entered without prior notice and opportunity for hearing:

(a) *Basis for Issuance Without Prior Notice and Opportunity for Hearing*. A temporary cease-and-desist order may be issued without notice and opportunity for hearing only if the Commission determines, from specific facts in the record of the proceeding, that notice and hearing prior to entry of an order would be impracticable or contrary to the public interest.

(b) *Content of the Order*. An *ex parte* temporary cease-and-desist order shall state specifically why notice and hearing would have been impracticable or contrary to the public interest.

(c) *Hearing Before the Commission*. If a respondent has been served with a temporary cease-and-desist order entered without a prior Commission hearing, the respondent may apply to the Commission to have the order set aside, limited, or suspended, and if the application is made within 10 days after the date on which the order was served, may request a hearing on such application. The Commission shall hold a hearing and render a decision on the respondent's application at the earliest possible time. The hearing shall begin within two days of the filing of the application unless the applicant consents to a longer period or the Commission, by order, for good cause shown, sets a later date. The Commission shall render a decision on the application within five calendar days of its filing, provided, however, that the Commission, by order, for good cause shown, may extend the time within which a decision may be rendered for a single period of five calendar days, or such longer time as consented to by the applicant. If the Commission does not render its decision within 10 days of the respondent's application or such longer time as consented to by the applicant, the temporary order shall be suspended until a decision is rendered.

(d) *Presiding Officer, Procedure at Hearing*. Procedures with respect to the selection of a presiding officer and the conduct of the hearing shall be in accordance with Rule 511.

Rule 514. Temporary cease-and-desist orders; judicial review; duration

(a) *Availability of Judicial Review*. Judicial review of a temporary cease-and-desist order shall be available as provided in Section 8A(d)(2) of the Securities Act, 15 U.S.C. 77h–1(d)(2), Section 21C(d)(2) of the Exchange Act, 15 U.S.C. 78u–3(d)(2), Section 9(f)(4)(B) of the Investment Company Act, 15 U.S.C. 80a–9(f)(4)(B), or Section 203(k)(4)(B) of the Investment Advisers Act, 15 U.S.C. 80b–3(k)(4)(B).

(b) *Duration*. Unless set aside, limited, or suspended, either by order of the Commission, a court of competent jurisdiction, or a hearing officer acting pursuant to Rule 531, or by operation of Rule 513, a temporary cease-and-desist order shall remain effective and enforceable until the earlier of:

(1) The completion of the proceedings whether a permanent order shall be entered; or

(2) 180 days, or such longer time as consented to by the respondent, after issuance of a briefing

schedule order pursuant to Rule 540(b), if an initial decision whether a permanent order should be entered is appealed.

Rule 520. Suspension of registration of brokers, dealers, or other Exchange Act–registered entities: application

(a) *Procedure.* A request for suspension of a registered broker, dealer, municipal securities dealer, government securities broker, government securities dealer, or transfer agent pending a final determination whether the registration shall be revoked shall be made by application filed by the Division of Enforcement. The application shall set forth the statutory provision or rule that each respondent is alleged to have violated and the temporary suspension sought as to each respondent.

(b) *Accompanying Documents.* The application shall be accompanied by a declaration of facts signed by a person with knowledge of the facts contained therein, a memorandum of points and authorities, a proposed order imposing the temporary suspension of registration sought, and a proposed notice of hearing and order to show cause whether the temporary suspension of registration should be imposed. If a proceeding to determine whether to revoke the registration permanently has not already been commenced, a proposed order instituting proceedings to determine whether a permanent sanction should be imposed shall also be filed with the application.

(c) *With Whom Filed.* The application shall be filed with the Secretary or, if the Secretary is unavailable, with the duty officer. In no event shall an application be filed with an administrative law judge.

(d) *Record of Hearings.* All hearings shall be recorded or transcribed pursuant to Rule 302.

Rule 521. Suspension of registration of brokers, dealers, or other Exchange Act–registered entities: notice and opportunity for hearing on application

(a) *How Given.* Notice of an application to suspend a registration pursuant to Rule 520 shall be made by serving a notice of hearing and order to show cause pursuant to Rule 141(b) or, where timely service of a notice of hearing pursuant to Rule 141(b) is not practicable, by any other means reasonably calculated to give actual notice that a hearing will be held, including telephonic notification of the general subject matter, time, and place of the hearing.

(b) *Hearing: Before Whom Held.* Except as provided in paragraph (d) of this rule, hearings on an application to suspend a registration pursuant to Rule 520 shall be held before the Commission.

(c) *Presiding Officer: Designation.* The Chairman shall preside or designate a Commissioner to preside at the hearing. If the Chairman is absent or unavailable at the time of hearing and no other Commissioner has been designated to preside, the duty officer on the day the hearing begins shall preside or designate another Commissioner to preside.

(d) *Procedure at Hearing.* (1) The presiding officer shall have all those powers of a hearing officer set forth in Rule 111 and shall rule on the admissibility of evidence and other procedural matters, including, but not limited to whether oral testimony will be heard; the time allowed each party for the submission of evidence or argument; and whether post-hearing submission of briefs, proposed findings of fact and conclusions of law will be permitted and if so, the procedures for submission; provided, however, that the person presiding may consult with other Commissioners participating in the hearing on these or any other question of procedure.

(2) Each Commissioner present at the hearing shall be afforded a reasonable opportunity to ask questions of witnesses, if any, or counsel.

(3) A party or witness may participate by telephone. Alternative means of remote access, including a video link, shall be permitted in the Commission's discretion. Factors the Commission may consider in determining whether to permit alternative means of remote access include, but are not limited to, whether allowing an alternative means of access will delay the hearing, whether the alternative means is reliable, and whether the party proposing its use has made arrangements to pay for its cost.

(4) After a hearing has begun, the Commission may, on its own motion or the motion of a party, assign a hearing officer to preside at the taking of oral testimony or other evidence and to certify the record of such testimony or other evidence to the Commission within a fixed period of time. No recommended or initial decision shall be made.

Rule 522. Suspension of registration of brokers, dealers, or other Exchange Act–registered entities: issuance and review of order

(a) *Basis for Issuance.* An order suspending a registration, pending final determination as to whether the registration shall be revoked shall be issued only if the Commission finds that the suspension is necessary or appropriate in the public interest or for the protection of investors.

(b) *Content, Scope and Form of Order.* Each order suspending a registration shall:

(1) Describe the basis for its issuance, including the alleged or threatened violations and the harm that is likely to result without the issuance of an order;

(2) Describe in reasonable detail, and not by reference to the order instituting proceedings or any other document, the act or acts the respondent is to take or refrain from taking; and

(3) Be indorsed with the date and hour of issuance.

(c) *Effective Upon Service.* An order suspending a registration is effective upon service upon the respondent.

(d) *Service: How Made.* Service of an order suspending a registration shall be made pursuant to Rule 141(a). The person who serves the order shall promptly file a declaration of service identifying the person served, the method of service, the date of service, the address to which service was made and the person who made service; provided, however, failure to file such a declaration shall have no effect on the validity of the service.

(e) *Commission Review.* At any time after the respondent has been served with an order suspending a registration, the respondent may apply to the Commission or the hearing officer to have the order set aside, limited, or suspended. The application shall set forth with specificity the facts that support the request.

Rule 523. [Reserved]

Rule 524. Suspension of registrations: duration

Unless set aside, limited or suspended by order of the Commission, a court of competent jurisdiction, or a hearing officer acting pursuant to Rule 531, an order suspending a registration shall remain effective and enforceable until the earlier of:

(a) The completion of the proceedings whether the registration shall be permanently revoked; or

(b) 180 days, or such longer time as consented to by the respondent, after issuance of a briefing schedule order pursuant to Rule 540(b), if an initial decision whether the registration shall be permanently revoked is appealed.

Rule 530. Initial decision on permanent order: timing for submitting proposed findings and preparation of decision

Unless otherwise ordered by the Commission or hearing officer, if a temporary cease-and-desist order or suspension of registration order is in effect, the following time limits shall apply to preparation of an initial decision as to whether such order should be made permanent:

(a) Proposed findings and conclusions and briefs in support thereof shall be filed 30 days after the close of the hearing;

(b) The record in the proceedings shall be served by the Secretary upon the hearing officer three days after the date for the filing of the last brief called for by the hearing officer; and

(c) The initial decision shall be filed with the Secretary at the earliest possible time, but in no event more than 30 days after service of the record, unless the hearing officer, by order, shall extend the time for good cause shown for a period not to exceed 30 days.

Rule 531. Initial decision on permanent order: effect on temporary order

(a) *Specification of Permanent Sanction.* If, at the time an initial decision is issued, a temporary sanction is in effect as to any respondent, the initial decision shall specify:

(1) Which terms or conditions of a temporary cease-and-desist order, if any, shall become permanent; and

(2) Whether a temporary suspension of a respondent's registration, if any, shall be made a permanent revocation of registration.

(b) *Modification of Temporary Order.* If any temporary sanction shall not become permanent under the terms of the initial decision, the hearing officer shall issue a separate order setting aside, limiting or suspending the temporary sanction then in effect in accordance with the terms of the initial decision. The hearing officer shall decline to suspend a term or condition of a temporary cease-and-desist order if it is found that the continued effectiveness of such term or condition is necessary to effectuate any term of the relief ordered in the initial decision, including the payment of disgorgement, interest or penalties. An order modifying temporary sanctions shall be effective 14 days after service. Within one week of service of the order modifying temporary sanctions any party may seek a stay or modification of the order from the Commission pursuant to Rule 401.

Rule 540. Appeal and Commission review of initial decision making a temporary order permanent

(a) *Petition for Review.* Any person who seeks Commission review of an initial decision as to whether a temporary sanction shall be made permanent shall file a petition for review pursuant to Rule 410, provided, however, that the petition must be filed within 10 days after service of the initial decision.

(b) *Review Procedure.* If the Commission determines to grant or order review, it shall issue a briefing schedule order pursuant to Rule 450. Unless otherwise ordered by the Commission, opening briefs shall be filed within 21 days of the order granting or ordering review, and opposition briefs shall be filed within 14 days after opening briefs are filed. Reply briefs shall be filed within seven days after opposition briefs are filed. Oral argument, if granted by the Commission, shall be held within 90 days of the issuance of the briefing schedule order.

Rule 550. Summary suspensions pursuant to Exchange Act Section 12(k)(1)(A)

(a) *Petition for Termination of Suspension.* Any person adversely affected by a suspension pursuant to Section 12(k)(1)(A) of the Exchange Act, 15 U.S.C. 78*l*(k)(1)(A), who desires to show that such suspension is not necessary in the public interest or for the protection of investors may file a sworn petition with the Secretary, requesting that the suspension be terminated. The petition shall set forth the reasons why the petitioner believes that the suspension of trading should not continue and state with particularity the facts upon which the petitioner relies.

(b) *Commission Consideration of a Petition.* The Commission, in its discretion, may schedule a hearing on the matter, request additional written submissions, or decide the matter on the facts presented in the petition and any other relevant facts known to the Commission. If the petitioner fails to cooperate with, obstructs, or refuses to permit the making of an examination by the Commission, such conduct shall be grounds to deny the petition.

RULES REGARDING DISGORGEMENT AND PENALTY PAYMENTS

Rule 600. Interest on sums disgorged

(a) *Interest Required.* Prejudgment interest shall be due on any sum required to be paid pursuant to an order of disgorgement. The disgorgement order shall specify each violation that forms the basis for the disgorgement ordered; the date which, for pur-

Table I to Rule 1001—Civil monetary penalty inflation adjustments for violations from December 10, 1996, through November 2, 2015						
		Date of Violation and Corresponding Penalty				
U.S. Code citation	Civil monetary penalty description	Dec. 10, 1996—Feb. 2, 2001[i]	Feb. 3, 2001—Feb 14, 2005[ii]	Feb. 15, 2005—Mar. 3, 2009[iii]	Mar. 4, 2009—Mar. 5, 2013[i]	Mar. 6, 2013—Nov. 2, 2015[v]
15 U.S.C. 77h-1(g) (Securities Act Sec. 8A(g))	For natural person	N/A	N/A	N/A	$7,500[vi]	$7,500
	For any other person	N/A	N/A	N/A	75,000[vi]	80,000
	For natural person / fraud	N/A	N/A	N/A	75,000[vi]	80,000
	For any other person / fraud	N/A	N/A	N/A	375,000[vi]	400,000
	For natural person / fraud / substantial losses or risk of losses to others or gains to self	N/A	N/A	N/A	150,000[vi]	160,000
	For any other person / fraud / substantial losses or risk of losses to others or gain to self	N/A	N/A	N/A	725,000[vi]	775,000

poses of calculating disgorgement, each such violation was deemed to have occurred; the amount to be disgorged for each such violation; and the total sum to be disgorged. Prejudgment interest shall be due from the first day of the month following each such violation through the last day of the month preceding the month in which payment of disgorgement is made. The order shall state the amount of prejudgment interest owed as of the date of the disgorgement order and that interest shall continue to accrue on all funds owed until they are paid.

(b) *Rate of Interest.* Interest on the sum to be disgorged shall be computed at the underpayment rate of interest established under Section 6621(a)(2) of the Internal Revenue Code, 26 U.S.C. 6621(a)(2), and shall be compounded quarterly. The Commission or the hearing officer may, by order, specify a lower rate of prejudgment interest as to any funds which the respondent has placed in an escrow or otherwise guaranteed for payment of disgorgement upon a final determination of the respondent's liability. Escrow and other guarantee arrangements must be approved by the Commission or the hearing officer prior to entry of the disgorgement order.

Rule 601. Prompt payment of disgorgement, interest and penalties

(a) *Timing of Payments.* Unless otherwise provided, funds due pursuant to an order by the Commission requiring the payment of disgorgement, interest, or penalties shall be paid no later than 21 days after service of the order, and funds due pursuant to an order by a hearing officer shall be paid in accordance with the order of finality issued pursuant to Rule 360(d)(2).

(b) *Stays.* A stay of any order requiring the payment of disgorgement, interest or penalties may be sought at any time pursuant to Rule 401.

(c) *Method of Making Payment.* Payment shall be made by United States postal money order, wire transfer, certified check, bank cashier's check, or bank money order made payable to the Securities and Exchange Commission. The payment shall be mailed or delivered to the office designated by this Commission. Payment shall be accompanied by a letter that identifies the name and number of the case and the name of the respondent making payment. A copy of the letter and the instrument of payment shall be sent to counsel for the Division of Enforcement.

Rules 610–14. [Reserved]

Rule 620. [Reserved]

Rule 630. Inability to pay disgorgement, interest or penalties

(a) *Generally.* In any proceeding in which an order requiring payment of disgorgement, interest or penalties may be entered, a respondent may present evidence of an inability to pay disgorgement, interest or a penalty. The Commission may, in its discretion, or the hearing officer may, in his or her discretion, consider evidence concerning ability to pay in determining whether disgorgement, interest or a penalty is in the public interest.

(b) *Financial Disclosure Statement.* Any respondent who asserts an inability to pay disgorgement, interest or penalties may be required to file a sworn financial disclosure statement and to keep the statement current. The financial statement shall show the respondent's assets; liabilities, income or other funds received and expenses or other payments, from the date of the first violation alleged against that respondent in the order instituting proceedings, or such later date as specified by the Commission or a hearing officer, to the date of the order requiring the disclosure statement to be filed. By order, the Commission or the hearing officer may prescribe the use of the Disclosure of Assets and Financial Information Form (*see* Form D–A at § 209.1 of this chapter) or any other form, may specify other time periods for which disclosure is required, and may require such other information as deemed necessary to evaluate a claim of inability to pay.

(c) *Confidentiality.* Any respondent submitting financial information pursuant to this section or Rule 410(c) may make a motion, pursuant to Rule 322, for the issuance of a protective order against disclosure of the information submitted to the public or to any parties other than the Division of Enforcement. Prior to a ruling on the motion, no party receiving information as to which a motion for a protective order has been made may transfer or convey the information to any other person without the prior permission of the Commission or the hearing officer.

(d) *Service Required.* Notwithstanding any provision of Rule 322, a copy of the financial disclosure statement shall be served on the Division of Enforcement.

(e) *Failure to File Required Financial Information: Sanction.* Any respondent who, after making a claim of inability to pay either disgorgement, interest or a penalty, fails to file a financial disclosure statement when such a filing has been ordered or is required by rule may, in the discretion of the Commission or the hearing officer, be deemed to have waived the claim of inability to pay. No sanction pursuant to Rules 155 or 180 shall be imposed for a failure to file such a statement.

Rule 700. Initiation of proceedings for SRO proposed rule changes

(a) *Rules of Practice Incorporated Herein.* For purposes of these Rules of Practice contained at 17 CFR 201.700–701, the following Rules of Practice are incorporated by reference:

(1) Rule 103, (Construction of Rules);

(2) Rule 104, (Business Hours); and

(3) Rule 160, (Time Computation).

(b) *Institution of Proceedings; Notice and Opportunity to Submit Written Views.*

(1) *Generally.* If the Commission determines to initiate proceedings to determine whether a self-regulatory organization's proposed rule change should be disapproved, it shall provide notice thereof to the self-regulatory organization that filed the proposed rule change, as well as all interested parties and the public, by publication in the Federal Register of the grounds for disapproval under consideration.

(i) *Prior to Notice.* If the Commission determines to institute proceedings prior to initial publication by the Commission of the notice of the self-regulatory organization's proposed rule change in the Federal Register, then the Commission shall publish notice of the proposed rule change simultaneously with a brief summary of the grounds for disapproval under consideration.

(ii) *Subsequent to Notice.* If the Commission determines to institute proceedings subsequent to initial publication by the Commission of the notice of the self-regulatory organization's proposed rule change in the Federal Register, then the Commission shall publish separately in the Federal Register a brief summary of the grounds for disapproval under consideration.

(iii) *Service of an Order Instituting Proceedings.* In addition to publication in the Federal Register of the grounds for disapproval under consideration, the Secretary, or another duly authorized officer of the Commission, shall serve a copy of the grounds for disapproval under consideration to the self-regulatory organization that filed the proposed rule change by serving notice to the person listed as the contact person on the cover page of the Form 19b–4 filing. Notice shall be made by delivering a copy of the order to such contact person either by any method specified in Rule 141(a) or by electronic means including email.

(2) *Notice of the Grounds for Disapproval under Consideration.* The grounds for disapproval under consideration shall include a brief statement of the matters of fact and law on which the Commission instituted the proceedings, including the areas in which the Commission may have questions or may need to solicit additional information on the proposed rule change. The Commission may consider during the course of the proceedings additional matters of fact and law beyond what was set forth in its notice of the grounds for disapproval under consideration.

(3) *Demonstration of Consistency with the Exchange Act.* The burden to demonstrate that a proposed rule change is consistent with the Exchange Act and the rules and regulations issued thereunder that are applicable to the self-regulatory organization is on the self-regulatory organization that proposed the rule change. As reflected in the General Instructions to Form 19b–4, the Form is designed to elicit information necessary for the public to provide meaningful comment on the proposed rule change and for the Commission to determine whether the proposed rule change is consistent with the requirements of the Exchange Act and the rules and regulations thereunder applicable to the self-regulatory organization. The self-regulatory organization must provide all information elicited by the Form, including the exhibits, and must present the information in a clear and comprehensible manner. In particular, the self-regulatory organization must explain why the proposed rule change is consistent with the requirements of the Exchange Act and the rules and regulations thereunder applicable to the self-regulatory organization. A mere assertion

that the proposed rule change is consistent with those requirements, or that another self-regulatory organization has a similar rule in place, is not sufficient. Instead, the description of the proposed rule change, its purpose and operation, its effect, and a legal analysis of its consistency with applicable requirements must all be sufficiently detailed and specific to support an affirmative Commission finding. Any failure of the self-regulatory organization to provide the information elicited by Form 19b–4 may result in the Commission not having a sufficient basis to make an affirmative finding that a proposed rule change is consistent with the Exchange Act and the rules and regulations issued thereunder that are applicable to the self-regulatory organization.

(c) *Conduct of Hearings.*

(1) *Initial Comment Period in Writing.* Unless otherwise specified by the Commission in its notice of grounds for disapproval under consideration, all interested persons will be given an opportunity to submit written data, views, and arguments concerning the proposed rule change under consideration and whether the Commission should approve or disapprove the proposed rule change. The self-regulatory organization that submitted the proposed rule change may file a written statement in support of its proposed rule change demonstrating, in specific detail, how such proposed rule change is consistent with the requirements of the Exchange Act and the rules and regulations thereunder applicable to the self-regulatory organization, including a response to each of the grounds for disapproval under consideration. Such statement may include specific representations or undertakings by the self-regulatory organization. The Commission will specify in the summary of the grounds for disapproval under consideration the length of the initial comment period.

(2) *Oral.* The Commission, in its sole discretion, may determine whether any issues relevant to approval or disapproval would be facilitated by the opportunity for an oral presentation of views.

(3) *Rebuttal.* At the end of the initial comment period, the self-regulatory organization that filed the proposed rule change will be given an opportunity to respond to any comments received. The self-regulatory organization may voluntarily file, or the Commission may request a self-regulatory organization to file, a response to a comment received regarding any aspect of the proposed rule change under consideration to assist the Commission in determining whether the proposed rule change should be disapproved. The Commission will specify in the summary of the grounds for disapproval under consideration the length of the rebuttal period.

(4) *Non-Response.* Any failure by the self-regulatory organization to provide a complete response, within the applicable time period specified, to a comment letter received or to the Commission's grounds for disapproval under consideration may result in the Commission not having a sufficient basis to make an affirmative finding that a proposed rule change is consistent with the Exchange Act and the rules and regulations issued thereunder that are applicable to the self-regulatory organization.

(d) *Record Before the Commission.*

(1) *Filing of Papers with the Commission.* Filing of papers with the Commission shall be made by filing them with the Secretary, including through electronic means. In its notice setting forth the grounds for disapproval under consideration for a proposed rule change, the Commission shall inform interested parties of the methods by which they may submit written comments and arguments for or against Commission approval.

(2) *Public Availability of Materials Received.* During the conduct of the proceedings, the Commission generally will make available publicly all written comments it receives without change. In its notice setting forth the grounds for disapproval under consideration for a proposed rule change, the Commission shall inform interested parties of the methods by which they may view all written communications relating to the proposed rule change between the Commission and any person, other than those that may be withheld from the public in accordance with the provisions of 5 U.S.C. 552.

(3) *Record Before the Commission.* The Commission shall determine each matter on the basis of the record. The record shall consist of the proposed rule change filed on Form 19b–4 by the self-regulatory organization, including all attachments and exhibits thereto, and all written materials received from any interested parties on the proposed rule change, including the self-regulatory

organization that filed the proposed rule change, through the means identified by the Commission as provided in paragraph (1), as well as any written materials that reflect communications between the Commission and any interested parties.

(e) *Amended Notice not Required.* The Commission is not required to amend its notice of grounds for disapproval under consideration in order to consider, during the course of the proceedings, additional matters of fact and law beyond what was set forth in the notice of the grounds for disapproval under consideration.

Rule 701. Issuance of order

At any time following conclusion of the rebuttal period specified in Rule 700(b)(4), the Commission may issue an order approving or disapproving the self-regulatory organization's proposed rule change together with a written statement of the reasons therefor.

INFORMAL PROCEDURES AND SUPPLEMENTARY INFORMATION CONCERNING ADJUDICATORY PROCEEDINGS

Rule 900. Informal procedures and supplementary information concerning adjudicatory proceedings

(a) *Guidelines for the Timely Completion of Proceedings.* (1) Timely resolution of adjudicatory proceedings is one factor in assessing the effectiveness of the adjudicatory program in protecting investors, promoting public confidence in the securities markets and assuring respondents a fair hearing. Establishment of guidelines for the timely completion of key phases of contested administrative proceedings provides a standard for both the Commission and the public to gauge the Commission's adjudicatory program on this criterion. The Commission has directed that:

(i) To the extent possible, a decision by the Commission on review of an interlocutory matter should be completed within 45 days of the date set for filing the final brief on the matter submitted for review.

(ii) To the extent possible, a decision by the Commission on a motion to stay a decision that has already taken effect or that will take effect within five days of the filing of the motion, should be issued within five days of the date set for filing of the opposition to the motion for a stay. If the decision complained of has not taken effect, the Commission's decision should be issued within 45 days of the date set for filing of the opposition to the motion for a stay.

(iii) Ordinarily, a decision by the Commission with respect to an appeal from the initial decision of a hearing officer, a review of a determination by a self-regulatory organization or the Public Company Accounting Oversight Board, or a remand of a prior Commission decision by a court of appeals will be issued within eight months from the completion of briefing on the petition for review, application for review, or remand order. If the Commission determines that the complexity of the issues presented in a petition for review, application for review, or remand order warrants additional time, the decision of the Commission in that matter may be issued within ten months of the completion of briefing.

(iv) If the Commission determines that a decision by the Commission cannot be issued within the period specified in paragraph (a)(1)(iii) of this section, the Commission may extend that period by orders as it deems appropriate in its discretion. The guidelines in this paragraph (a) confer no rights or entitlements on parties or other persons.

(2) The guidelines in this paragraph (a) do not create a requirement that each portion of a proceeding or the entire proceeding be completed within the periods described. Among other reasons, Commission review may require additional time because a matter is unusually complex or because the record is exceptionally long. In addition, fairness is enhanced if the Commission's deliberative process is not constrained by an inflexible schedule. In some proceedings, deliberation may be delayed by the need to consider more urgent matters, to permit the preparation of dissenting opinions, or for other good cause. The guidelines will be used by the Commission as one of several criteria in monitoring and evaluating its adjudicatory program. The guidelines will be examined periodically, and, if necessary, readjusted in light of changes in the pending caseload and the available level of staff resources.

(b) *Reports to the Commission on Pending Cases.* The administrative law judges, the Secretary and the General Counsel have each been delegated authority to issue certain orders or adjudicate certain proceedings. See 17 CFR 200.30–1 through 200.30–18. Proceedings are also assigned to the General Counsel for the preparation of a proposed order or opinion which will then be recommended to the Commission for consideration. In order to improve accountability by and to the Commission for management of the docket, the Commission has directed that confidential status reports with respect to all filed adjudicatory proceedings shall be made periodically to the Commission. These reports will be made through the Secretary, with a minimum frequency established by the Commission. In connection with these periodic reports, if a proceeding pending before the Commission has not been concluded within 30 days of the guidelines established in paragraph (a) of this section, the General Counsel shall specifically apprise the Commission of that fact, and shall describe the procedural posture of the case, project an estimated date for conclusion of the proceeding, and provide such other information as is necessary to enable the Commission to make a determination under paragraph (a)(1)(iv) of this section or to determine whether additional steps are necessary to reach a fair and timely resolution of the matter.

(c) *Publication of Information Concerning the Pending Case Docket.* Ongoing disclosure of information about the adjudication program caseload increases awareness of the importance of the program, facilitates oversight of the program and promotes confidence in the efficiency and fairness of the program by investors, securities industry participants, self-regulatory organizations and other members of the public. The Commission has directed the Secretary to publish in the first and seventh months of each fiscal year summary statistical information about the status of pending adjudicatory proceedings and changes in the Commission's caseload over the prior six months. The report will include the number of cases pending before the administrative law judges and the Commission at the beginning and end of the six-month period. The report will also show increases in the caseload arising from new cases being instituted, appealed or remanded to the Commission and decreases in the caseload arising from the disposition of proceedings by issuance of initial decisions, issuance of final decisions issued on appeal of initial decisions, other dispositions of appeals of initial decisions, final decisions on review of self-regulatory organization determinations, other dispositions on review of self-regulatory organization determinations, and decisions with respect to stays or interlocutory motions. For each category of decision, the report shall also show the median age of the cases at the time of the decision, the number of cases decided within the guidelines for the timely completion of adjudicatory proceedings, and, with respect to appeals from initial decisions, reviews of determinations by self-regulatory organizations or the Public Company Accounting Oversight Board, and remands of prior Commission decisions, the median days from the completion of briefing to the time of the Commission's decision.

SUBPART E-ADJUSTMENT OF CIVIL MONETARY PENALTIES

Rule 1001. Adjustment of civil monetary penalties

(a) For violations from December 10, 1996, through November 2, 2015: As required by the Inflation Adjustment Act of 1990, as amended by the Debt Collection Improvement Act of 1996, the Commission has adjusted the maximum amounts of all civil monetary penalties it administers under the Securities Act of 1933, the Securities Exchange Act of 1934, the Investment Company Act of 1940, the Investment Advisers Act of 1940, and certain penalties under the Sarbanes-Oxley Act of 2002 for inflation in the releases and prior regulations listed in the footnotes to Table I. The penalty amounts provided in Table I apply to violations of these statutes that occurred from December 10, 1996, through November 2, 2015, with each column listing the penalty amounts for violations that occurred in a particular time frame. To determine the penalty amounts for violations that occurred prior to December 10, 1996, please refer to the applicable statutory text. To determine penalty amounts for violations after November 2, 2015, please refer to paragraph (b) of this section.

(b) For violations after November 2, 2015: The Federal Civil Penalties Inflation Adjustment Act, as amended by the Federal Civil Penalties Inflation Adjustment Act Improvements Act of 2015 (28 U.S.C. 2461 note), requires that civil monetary penalties be adjusted on an annual basis for inflation. Pursuant to this requirement, the maximum amounts of all civil monetary penalties under the Securities Act of 1933, the Securities Exchange Act of 1934, the Investment Company Act of 1940, and the Investment Advisers Act of 1940, and certain penalties under the Sarbanes-Oxley Act of 2002 will be adjusted annually for inflation. Notice of these adjusted penalty amounts will be published by the Commission in the Federal Register on or before January 15 of each calendar year and will be available, along with the Commission's prior inflation adjustments, on the Commission's website at https://www.sec.gov/enforce/civil-penalties-inflation-adjustments.htm. The adjusted penalty amounts will apply to all penalties imposed after the effective date of the adjustment (for the first day the adjustment is effective, the prior year's penalty amounts shall apply), for violations that occurred after November 2, 2015. The adjusted penalty amount each year will be the larger of:

(1) The maximum penalty amount for the previous calendar year; or

(2) An amount adjusted for inflation, calculated by multiplying the maximum penalty amount for the previous calendar year by the percentage by which the Consumer Price Index for all Urban Consumers (CPI–U) for the month of October preceding the current calendar year exceeds the CPI–U for the month of October of the calendar year two years prior to the current calendar year, adding that amount to the amount for the previous calendar year, and rounding the total to the nearest dollar.

Table I to Rule 1001—Civil monetary penalty inflation adjustments for violations from December 10, 1996, through November 2, 2015

U.S. Code citation	Civil monetary penalty description	Date of Violation and Corresponding Penalty				
		Dec. 10, 1996—Feb. 2, 2001[i]	Feb. 3, 2001—Feb 14, 2005[ii]	Feb. 15, 2005—Mar. 3, 2009[iii]	Mar. 4, 2009—Mar. 5, 2013[iv]	Mar. 6, 2013—Nov. 2, 2015[v]
15 U.S.C. 77h-1(g) (Securities Act Sec. 8A(g))	For natural person	N/A	N/A	N/A	$7,500[vi]	$7,500
	For any other person	N/A	N/A	N/A	75,000[vi]	80,000
	For natural person / fraud	N/A	N/A	N/A	75,000[vi]	80,000
	For any other person / fraud	N/A	N/A	N/A	375,000[vi]	400,000
	For natural person / fraud / substantial losses or risk of losses to others or gains to self	N/A	N/A	N/A	150,000[vi]	160,000
	For any other person / fraud / substantial losses or risk of losses to others or gain to self	N/A	N/A	N/A	725,000[vi]	775,000

15 U.S.C. 77t(d) (Securities Act Sec. 20(d))	For natural person	$5,500	$6,500	$6,500	7,500	7,500
	For any other person	55,000	60,000	65,000	75,000	80,000
	For natural person / fraud	55,000	60,000	65,000	75,000	80,000
	For any other person / fraud	275,000	300,000	325,000	375,000	400,000
	For natural person / fraud / substantial losses or risk of losses to others	110,000	120,000	130,000	150,000	160,000
	For any other person / fraud / substantial losses or risk of losses to others	550,000	600,000	650,000	725,000	775,000
15 U.S.C. 78u(d)(3) (Exchange Act Sec. 21(d)(3))	For natural person	5,500	6,500	6,500	7,500	7,500
	For any other person	55,000	60,000	65,000	75,000	80,000
	For natural person / fraud	55,000	60,000	65,000	75,000	80,000
	For any other person / fraud	275,000	300,000	325,000	375,000	400,000
	For natural person / fraud / substantial losses or risk of losses to others or gains to self	110,000	120,000	130,000	150,000	160,000
	For any other person / fraud / substantial losses or risk of losses to others or gain to self	550,000	600,000	650,000	725,000	775,000
15 U.S.C. 78u-1(a)(3) (Exchange Act Sec. 21A(a)(3))	Insider Trading – controlling person	1,100,000	1,200,000	1,275,000	1,425,000	1,525,000
15 U.S.C. 78u-2 (Exchange Act Sec. 21B)	For natural person	5,500	6,500	6,500	7,500	7,500
	For any other person	55,000	60,000	65,000	75,000	80,000
	For natural person / fraud	55,000	60,000	65,000	75,000	80,000
	For any other person / fraud	275,000	300,000	325,000	375,000	400,000
	For natural person / fraud / substantial losses or risk of losses to others	110,000	120,000	130,000	150,000	160,000
	For any other person / fraud / substantial losses or risk of losses to others	550,000	600,000	650,000	725,000	775,000
15 U.S.C. 78ff(b) (Exchange Act Sec. 32(b))	Exchange Act / failure to file information documents, reports	110	110	110	110	210

15 U.S.C. 78ff(c)(1)(B) (Exchange Act Sec. 32(c)(1)(B))	Foreign Corrupt Practices – any issuer	11,000	11,000	11,000	16,000	16,000
15 U.S.C. 78ff(c)(2)(B) (Exchange Act Sec. 32(c)(2)(B))	Foreign Corrupt Practices – any agent or stockholder acting on behalf of issuer	11,000	11,000	11,000	16,000	16,000
15 U.S.C. 80a-9(d) (Investment Company Act Sec. 9(d))	For natural person	5,500	6,500	6,500	7,500	7,500
	For any other person	55,000	60,000	65,000	75,000	80,000
	For natural person / fraud	55,000	60,000	65,000	75,000	80,000
	For any other person / fraud	275,000	300,000	325,000	375,000	400,000
	For natural person / fraud / substantial losses or risk of losses to others or gains to self	110,000	120,000	130,000	150,000	160,000
	For any other person / fraud / substantial losses or risk of losses to others or gain to self	550,000	600,000	650,000	725,000	775,000
15 U.S.C. 80a-41(e) (Investment Company Act Sec. 42(e))	For natural person	5,500	6,500	6,500	7,500	7,500
	For any other person	55,000	60,000	65,000	75,000	80,000
	For natural person / fraud	55,000	60,000	65,000	75,000	80,000
	For any other person / fraud	275,000	300,000	325,000	375,000	400,000
	For natural person / fraud / substantial losses or risk of losses to others	110,000	120,000	130,000	150,000	160,000
	For any other person / fraud / substantial losses or risk of losses to others	550,000	600,000	650,000	725,000	775,000

	For natural person	5,500	6,500	6,500	7,500	7,500
	For any other person	55,000	60,000	65,000	75,000	80,000
15 U.S.C. 80b-3(i) (Investment Advisers Act Sec. 203(i))	For natural person / fraud	55,000	60,000	65,000	75,000	80,000
	For any other person / fraud	275,000	300,000	325,000	375,000	400,000
	For natural person / fraud / substantial losses or risk of losses to others or gains to self	110,000	120,000	130,000	150,000	160,000
	For any other person / fraud / substantial losses or risk of losses to others or gain to self	550,000	600,000	650,000	725,000	775,000
15 U.S.C. 80b-9(e) (Investment Advisers Act Sec. 209(e))	For natural person	5,500	6,500	6,500	7,500	7,500
	For any other person	55,000	60,000	65,000	75,000	80,000
	For natural person / fraud	55,000	60,000	65,000	75,000	80,000
	For any other person / fraud	275,000	300,000	325,000	375,000	400,000
	For natural person / fraud / substantial losses or risk of losses to others	110,000	120,000	130,000	150,000	160,000
	For any other person / fraud / substantial losses or risk of losses to others	550,000	600,000	650,000	725,000	775,000
15 U.S.C. 7215(c)(4)(D)(i) (Sarbanes-Oxley Act Sec. 105(c)(4)(D)(i))	For natural person	N/A	100,000[vii]	110,000	120,000	130,000
	For any other person	N/A	2,000,000[vii]	2,100,000	2,375,000	2,525,000
15 U.S.C. 7215(c)(4)(D)(ii) (Sarbanes-Oxley Act Sec. 105(c)(4)(D)(ii))	For natural person	N/A	750,000[vii]	800,000	900,000	950,000
	For any other person	N/A	15,000,000[vii]	15,825,000	17,800,000	18,925,000

[i] Release Nos. 33-7361, 34-37912, IA-1596, IC-22310, dated November 1, 1996 (effective December 9, 1996), previously found at 17 CFR 201.1001 and Table I to Subpart E of Part 201.

[ii] Release Nos. 33-7946, 34-43897, IA-1921, IC-24846, dated January 31, 2001 (effective February 2, 2001), previously found at 17 CFR 201.1002 and Table II to Subpart E of Part 201.

[iii] Release Nos. 33-8530, 34-51136, IA-2348, IC-26748, dated February 9, 2005 (effective February 14, 2005), previously found at 17 CFR 201.1003 and Table III to Subpart E of Part 201.

[iv] Release Nos. 33-9009, 34-59449, IA-2845, IC-28635, dated February 25, 2009 (effective March 3, 2009), previously found at 17 CFR 201.1004 and Table IV to Subpart E of Part 201.

[v] Release Nos. 33-9387, 34-68994, IA-3557, IC-30408, dated February 27, 2013 (effective March 5, 2013), previously found at 17 CFR 201.1005 and Table V to Subpart E of Part 201.

[vi] Effective from July 21, 2010 (enactment of the Dodd-Frank Wall Street Reform and Consumer Protection Act, Pub. L. 111-203), through March 5, 2013.

[vii] Effective from July 30, 2002 (enactment of the Sarbanes-Oxley Act of 2002, Pub. L. 107-204), through February 14, 2005.

F. INFORMAL AND OTHER PROCEDURES

(Cite as 17 CFR § 202.___)

Rule 1. General

(a) The statutes administered by the Commission provide generally (1) for the filing with it of certain statements, such as registration statements, periodic and ownership reports, and proxy solicitation material, and for the filing of certain plans of reorganization, applications and declarations seeking Commission approvals; (2) for Commission determination through formal procedures of matters initiated by private parties or by the Commission; (3) for the investigation and examination of persons and records where necessary to carry out the purposes of the statutes and for enforcement of statutory provisions; and (4) for the adoption of rules and regulations where necessary to effectuate the purposes of the statutes.

(b) In addition to the Commission's rules of practice set forth in 17 CFR 202.201, the Commission has promulgated rules and regulations pursuant to the several statutes it administers (17 CFR 230, 240, 260, 270 and 275). These parts contain substantive provisions and include as well numerous provisions detailing the procedure for meeting specific standards embodied in the statutes. The Commission's rules and regulations under each of the statutes are available in pamphlet form upon request to the Superintendent of Documents, U.S. Government Printing Office, Washington, DC 20402.

(c) The statutes and the published rules, regulations and forms thereunder prescribe the course and method of formal procedures to be followed in Commission proceedings. These are supplemented where feasible by certain informal procedures designed to aid the public and facilitate the execution of the Commission's functions. There follows a brief description of procedures generally followed by the Commission which have not been formalized in rules.

(d) The informal procedures of the Commission are largely concerned with the rendering of advice and assistance by the Commission's staff to members of the public dealing with the Commission. While opinions expressed by members of the staff do not constitute an official expression of the Commission's views, they represent the views of persons who are continuously working with the provisions of the statute involved. And any statement by the director, associate director, assistant director, chief accountant, chief counsel, or chief financial analyst of a division can be relied upon as representing the views of that division. In certain instances an informal statement of the views of the Commission may be obtained. The staff, upon request or on its own motion, will generally present questions to the Commission which involve matters of substantial importance and where the issues are novel or highly complex, although the granting of a request for an informal statement by the Commission is entirely within its discretion.

Rule 2. Pre-filing assistance and interpretative advice

The staff of the Commission renders interpretative and advisory assistance to members of the general public, prospective registrants, applicants and declarants. For example, persons having a question regarding the availability of an exemption may secure informal administrative interpretations of the applicable statute or rule as they relate to the particular facts and circumstances presented. Similarly, persons contemplating filings with the Commission may receive advice of a general nature as to the preparation thereof, including information as to the forms to be used and the scope of the items contained in the forms. Inquiries may be directed to an appropriate officer of the Commission's staff. In addition, informal discussions with members of the staff may be arranged whenever feasible, at the Commission's central office or, except in connection with certain matters under the Investment Company Act of 1940, at one of its regional offices.

Rule 3. Processing of filings

(a) Registration statements, proxy statements, letters of notification, periodic reports, applications for qualification of indentures, and similar documents filed with the Commission under the Securities Act of 1933 and the Trust Indenture Act of 1939, and certain filings under the Securities Exchange Act of 1934 are routed to the Division of Corporation Finance, which passes initially on the adequacy of disclosure and recommends the initial action to be taken. If the filing appears to afford inadequate disclosure, as for example through omission of material information or through violation of accepted accounting principles and practices, the usual practice is to bring the deficiency to the attention of the person who filed the document by letter from the Assistant Director assigned supervision over the particular filing, and to afford a reasonable opportunity to discuss the matter and make the necessary corrections. This informal procedure is not generally employed when the deficiencies appear to stem from careless disregard of the statutes and rules or a deliberate attempt to conceal or mislead or where the Commission deems formal proceedings necessary in the public interest. If an electronic filing is not prepared in accordance with the requirements of the current EDGAR Filer Manual, the filing may be suspended and the filer so notified. Reasonable opportunity will be afforded the filer to make the necessary corrections or resubmit the filing as needed. Where it appears that the filing affords adequate disclosure, acceleration of its effectiveness when appropriate normally will be granted. A similar procedure is followed with respect to filings under the Investment Company Act of 1940 and certain filings relating to investment companies under the Securities Act of 1933, the Securities Exchange Act of 1934, and the Trust Indenture Act of 1939, which are routed to the Division of Investment Management. A similar procedure is also followed in the Commission's Regional Offices with respect to registration statements on Forms SB–1 and SB–2 (17 CFR 239.9 and 239.10) and related filings under the Trust Indenture Act of 1939.

(b)(1) Applications for registration as brokers, dealers, investment advisers, municipal securities dealers and transfer agents are submitted to the Office of Filings and Information Services where they are examined to determine whether all necessary information has been supplied and whether all required financial statements and other documents have been furnished in proper form. Defective applications may be returned with a request for correction or held until corrected before being accepted as a filing. The files of the Commission and other sources of information are considered to determine whether any person connected with the applicant appears to have engaged in activities which would warrant commencement of proceedings on the question of denial of registration. The staff confers with applicants and makes suggestions in appropriate cases for amendments and supplemental information. Where it appears appropriate in the public interest and where a basis therefore exists, denial proceedings may be instituted. Within 45 days of the date of the filing of a broker-dealer, investment adviser or municipal securities dealer application (or within such longer period as to which the applicant consents), the Commission shall by order grant registration or institute proceedings to determine whether registration should be denied. An application for registration as a transfer agent shall become effective within 30 days after receipt of the application (or within such shorter period as the Commission may determine). The Office of Filings and Information Services is also responsible for the processing and substantive examination of statements of beneficial ownership of securities and changes in such ownership filed under the Securities Exchange Act of 1934, and the Investment Company Act of

1940, and for the examination of reports filed pursuant to Rule 144 under the Securities Act of 1933.

(2) Applications for registration as national securities exchanges, or exemption from registration as exchanges by reason of such exchanges' limited volume of transactions filed with the Commission are routed to the Division of Market Regulation, which examines these applications to determine whether all necessary information has been supplied and whether all required financial statements and other documents have been furnished in proper form. Defective applications may be returned with a request for correction or held until corrected before being accepted as a filing. The files of the Commission and other sources of information are considered to determine whether any person connected with the applicant appears to have engaged in activities which would warrant commencement of proceedings on the question of denial of registration. The staff confers with applicants and makes suggestions in appropriate cases for amendments and supplemental information. Where it appears appropriate in the public interest and where a basis therefore exists, denial proceedings may be instituted. Within 90 days of the date of publication of a notice of the filing of an application for registration as a national securities exchange, or exemption from registration by reason of such exchanges' limited volume of transactions (or within such longer period as to which the applicant consents), the Commission shall by order grant registration, or institute proceedings to determine whether registration should be denied as provided in Rule 19(a)(1) under the Securities Exchange Act of 1934.

(3) Notice forms for registration as national securities exchanges pursuant to Section 6(g)(1) of the Securities Exchange Act of 1934 (15 U.S.C. 78f(g)(1)) filed with the Commission are routed to the Division of Market Regulation, which examines these notices to determine whether all necessary information has been supplied and whether all other required documents have been furnished in proper form. Defective notices may be returned with a request for correction or held until corrected before being accepted as a filing.

Rule 3a. Instructions for filing fees

(a) *General Instructions for Remittance of Filing Fees.* Payment of filing fees specified by the following sections shall be made according to the directions listed in this rule: Rule 111 under the Securities Act of 1933, Rule 0–9 under the Securities Exchange Act of 1934, and Rule 0–8 under the Investment Company Act of 1940. All such fees are to be paid through the U.S. Treasury designated lockbox depository and may be paid by wire transfer, certified check, bank cashier's check, United States postal money order, or bank money order pursuant to the specific instructions set forth in paragraph (b) of this rule. Personal checks will not be accepted for payment of fees. To ensure proper posting, all filers must include their Commission-assigned Central Index Key (CIK) number (also known as the Commission-assigned registrant or payor account number) on fee payments. If a third party submits a fee payment, the fee payment must specify the account number to which the fee is to be applied.

(b) *Instructions for Payment of Filing Fees.* Except as provided in paragraph (c) of this rule, these instructions provide direction for remitting fees specified in paragraph (a) of this rule. You may contact the Fee Account Services Branch in the Office of Financial Management at (202) 551–8989 for additional information if you have questions.

(1) *Instructions for Payment of Fees by Wire Transfer (FEDWIRE).* U.S. Bank, N.A. in St. Louis, Missouri is the U.S. Treasury designated lockbox depository and financial agent for Commission filing fee payments. The hours of operation at U.S. Bank are 8:30 a.m. to 6:00 p.m. Eastern time for wire transfers. Any bank or wire transfer service may initiate wire transfers of filing fee payments through the FEDWIRE system to U.S. Bank. A filing entity does not need to establish an account at U.S. Bank in order to remit filing fee payments.

(i) To ensure proper credit and prompt filing acceptance, in all wire transfers of filing fees to the Commission, you must include:

(A) The Commission's account number at U.S. Bank (152307768324); and

(B) The payor's CIK number.

(ii) You may refer to the examples found on the Commission's Web site at http://www.sec.gov for the proper format.

(2) *Instructions for Payment of Fees by Check or Money Order.* To remit a filing fee payment by check (certified or bank cashier's check) or money order (United States postal or bank money order), you must make it payable to the Securities and Exchange Commission, omitting the name or title of any official of the Commission. On the front of the check or money order, you must include the Commission's account number (152307768324) and CIK number of the account to which the fee is

to be applied. U.S. Bank does not accept walk-in deliveries by individuals. You must mail checks or money orders to the following U.S. Bank addresses:

(i) Remittances through the U.S. Postal Service must be sent to the following address: Securities and Exchange Commission, P.O. Box 979081, St. Louis, MO 63197–9000.

(ii) The following address can be used for remittances through other common carriers: U.S. Bank, Government Lockbox 979081, 1005 Convention Plaza, SL–MO–C2–GL, St. Louis, MO 63101.

NOTE TO PARAGRAPH (b). Wire transfers are not instantaneous. The time required to process a wire transfer through the FEDWIRE system, from origination to receipt by U.S. Bank, varies substantially. Specified filings, such as registration statements pursuant to section 6(b) of the Securities Act of 1933 that provide for the registration of securities and mandate the receipt of the appropriate fee payment upon filing, and transactional filings pursuant to the Securities Exchange Act of 1934, such as many proxy statements involving extraordinary business transactions, will not be accepted if sufficient funds have not been received by the Commission at the time of filing. You should obtain from your bank or wire transfer service the reference number of the wire transfer. Having this number can greatly facilitate tracing the funds if any problems occur. If a wire transfer of filing fees does not contain the required information in the proper format, the Commission may not be able to identify the payor and the acceptance of filings may be delayed. To ensure proper credit, you must provide all required information to the sending bank or wire transfer service. Commission data must be inserted in the proper fields. The most critical data are the Commission's account number at U.S. Bank and the Commission-assigned account number identified as the CIK number.

(c) *Special Instructions for Rule 462(b) and Rule 110(d) under the Securities Act of 1933.* Notwithstanding paragraphs (a) and (b) of this rule, for registration statements filed pursuant to Rule 462(b) and Rule 110(d) under the Securities Act of 1933, payment of filing fees for the purposes of this rule may be made by:

(1) The registrant or its agent instructing its bank or a wire transfer service to transmit to the Commission the applicable filing fee by a wire transfer of such amount from the issuer's account or its agent's account to the U.S. Treasury designated lockbox depository as soon as practicable, but no later than the close of the next business day following the filing of the registration statement; and

(2) The registrant submitting with the registration statement at the time of filing a certification that:

(i) The registrant or its agent has so instructed its bank or a wire transfer service;

(ii) The registrant or its agent will not revoke such instructions; and

(iii) The registrant or its agent has sufficient funds in such account to cover the amount of such filing fee.

NOTE TO PARAGRAPH (c). Such instructions may be sent on the date of filing the registration statement after the close of business of such bank or wire transfer service, provided that the registrant undertakes in the certification sent to the Commission with the registration statement that it will confirm receipt of such instructions by the bank or wire transfer service during regular business hours on the following business day.

(d) *Filing Fee Accounts.* A filing fee account is maintained for each filer who submits a filing requiring a fee on the Commission's EDGAR system or who submits funds to the U.S. Treasury designated depository in anticipation of paying a filing fee. Account statements are regularly prepared and provided to account holders. Account holders must maintain a current account address with the Commission to ensure timely access to these statements.

NOTE TO PARAGRAPH (d). The deposit of money into a filing fee account does not constitute payment of a filing fee. Payment of the filing fee occurs at the time the filing is made, commensurate with the drawing down of the balance of the fee account.

(e) *Return of Funds from Inactive Accounts.* Funds held in any filing fee account in which there has not been a deposit, withdrawal or other adjustment for more than 180 calendar days will be returned to the account holder, and account statements will not be sent again until a deposit, withdrawal or other adjustment is made with respect to the account. Filers must maintain a current account address to assure the timely return of funds. It may not be possible to return funds from inactive accounts if the Commission is unable to identify a current account address of an account holder after making reasonable efforts to do so.

NOTE TO PARAGRAPH (e). A company must update its account and other addresses using the EDGAR Web site. This method ensures data integrity and the timeliest update. Simply changing an address in the text of the cover page of a filing made on the EDGAR system will not be sufficient to update the Commission's account address records.

Rule 4. Facilitating administrative hearings

(a) Applications, declarations, and other requests involving formal Commission action after opportunity for hearing are scrutinized by the appropriate division for conformance with applicable statutory standards and Commission rules and generally the filing party is advised of deficiencies. Prior to passing upon applications and declarations the Commission receives the views of all interested persons at public hearings whenever appropriate; hence, any applicant or declarant seeking Commission approval of proposed transactions by a particular time should file his application or declaration in time to allow for the presentation and consideration of such views.

(b) After the staff has had an opportunity to study an application or declaration, interested persons may informally discuss the problems therein raised to the extent that time and the nature of the case permit (e.g., consideration is usually given to whether the proceeding is contested and if so to the nature of the contest). In such event, the staff will, to the extent feasible, advise as to the nature of the issues raised by the filing, the necessity for any amendments to the documents filed, the type of evidence it believes should be presented at the hearing and, in some instances, the nature, form, and contents of documents to be submitted as formal exhibits. The staff will, in addition, generally advise as to Commission policy in past cases which dealt with the same subject matter as the filing under consideration.

(c) During the course of the hearings, the staff is generally available for informal discussions to reconcile bona fide divergent views not only between itself and other persons interested in the proceedings, but among all interested persons; and, when circumstances permit, an attempt is made to narrow, if possible, the issues to be considered at the formal hearing.

(d) In some instances the Commission in the order accompanying its findings and opinion reserves jurisdiction over certain matters relating to the proceeding, such as payment of fees and expenses, accounting entries, terms and conditions relating to securities to be issued, and other matters. In such cases, upon receipt of satisfactory information and data the Commission considers whether further hearing is required before releasing jurisdiction.

Rule 5. Enforcement activities

(a) Where, from complaints received from members of the public, communications from Federal or State agencies, examination of filings made with the Commission, or otherwise, it appears that there may be violation of the acts administered by the Commission or the rules or regulations thereunder, a preliminary investigation is generally made. In such preliminary investigation no process is issued or testimony compelled. The Commission may, in its discretion, make such formal investigations and authorize the use of process as it deems necessary to determine whether any person has violated, is violating, or is about to violate any provision of the federal securities laws or the rules of a self-regulatory organization of which the person is a member or participant. Unless otherwise ordered by the Commission, the investigation or examination is non-public and the reports thereon are for staff and Commission use only.

(b) After investigation or otherwise the Commission may in its discretion take one or more of the following actions: Institution of administrative proceedings looking to the imposition of remedial sanctions, initiation of injunctive proceedings in the courts, and, in the case of a willful violation, reference of the matter to the Department of Justice for criminal prosecution. The Commission may also, on some occasions, refer the matter to, or grant requests for access to its files made by, domestic and foreign governmental authorities or foreign securities authorities, self-regulatory organizations such as stock exchanges or the National Association of Securities Dealers, Inc., and other persons or entities.

(c) Persons who become involved in preliminary or formal investigations may, on their own initiative, submit a written statement to the Commission setting forth their interests and position in regard to the subject matter of the investigation. Upon request, the staff, in its discretion, may advise such persons of the general nature of the investigation, including the indicated violations as they pertain to them, and the amount of time that may be available for preparing and submitting a statement prior to the presentation of a staff recommendation to the Commission for the commencement of an administrative or injunction proceeding. Submissions by interested persons should be forwarded to the appropriate Division Director or Regional Director with a copy to the staff members conducting the investigation and should be clearly referenced to the specific investigation to which they relate. In the event a recommendation for the commencement of an enforcement proceeding is presented by the staff, any submissions by interested persons will be forwarded to the Commission in conjunction with the staff memorandum.

(d) In instances where the staff has concluded its investigation of a particular matter and has determined that it will not recommend the commencement of an enforcement proceeding against a person, the staff, in its discretion, may advise the party that its formal investigation has been terminated.

Such advice if given must in no way be construed as indicating that the party has been exonerated or that no action may ultimately result from the staff's investigation of the particular matter.

(e) The Commission has adopted the policy that in any civil lawsuit brought by it or in any administrative proceeding of an accusatory nature pending before it, it is important to avoid creating, or permitting to be created, an impression that a decree is being entered or a sanction imposed, when the conduct alleged did not, in fact, occur. Accordingly, it hereby announces its policy not to permit a defendant or respondent to consent to a judgment or order that imposes a sanction while denying the allegations in the complaint or order for proceedings. In this regard, the Commission believes that a refusal to admit the allegations is equivalent to a denial, unless the defendant or respondent states that he neither admits nor denies the allegations.

(f) In the course of the Commission's investigations, civil lawsuits, and administrative proceedings, the staff, with appropriate authorization, may discuss with persons involved the disposition of such matters by consent, by settlement, or in some other manner. It is the policy of the Commission, however, that the disposition of any such matter may not, expressly or impliedly, extend to any criminal charges that have been, or may be, brought against any such person or any recommendation with respect thereto. Accordingly, any person involved in an enforcement matter before the Commission who consents, or agrees to consent, to any judgment or order does so solely for the purpose of resolving the claims against him in that investigative, civil, or administrative matter and not for the purpose of resolving any criminal charges that have been, or might be, brought against him. This policy reflects the fact that neither the Commission nor its staff has the authority or responsibility for instituting, conducting, settling, or otherwise disposing of criminal proceedings. That authority and responsibility are vested in the Attorney General and representatives of the Department of Justice.

Rule 6. Adoption, revision, and rescission of rules and regulations of general application

(a) The procedure followed by the Commission in connection with the adoption, revision, and rescission of rules of general application necessarily varies in accordance with the nature of the rule, the extent of public interest therein, and the necessity for speed in its adoption. Rules relating to Commission organization, procedure and management, for example, are generally adopted by the Commission without affording public discussion thereof. On the other hand, in the adoption of substantive rules materially affecting an industry or a segment of the public, such as accounting rules, every feasible effort is made in advance of adoption to receive the views of persons to be affected. In such cases, proposals for the adoption, revision, or rescission of rules are initiated either by the Commission or by members of the public, and to the extent practicable, the practices set forth in paragraph (b) of this rule are observed.

(b) After preliminary consideration by the Commission a draft of the proposed rule is published in the Federal Register and mailed to interested persons (e.g., other interested regulatory bodies, principal registrants or persons to be affected, stock exchanges, professional societies and leading authorities on the subject concerned and other persons requesting such draft) for comments. Unless accorded confidential treatment pursuant to statute or rule of the Commission, written comments filed with the Commission on or before the closing date for comments become a part of the public record upon the proposed rule. The Commission, in its discretion, may accept and include in the public record written comments received by the Commission after the closing date.

(c) Following analysis of comments received, the rule may be adopted in the form published or in a revised form in the light of such comments. In some cases, a revised draft is prepared and published and, where appropriate, an oral hearing may be held before final action upon the proposal. Any interested person may appear at the hearing and/or may submit written comment for consideration in accordance with the Commission's notice of the rulemaking procedure to be followed. The rule in the form in which it is adopted by the Commission is publicly released and is published in the Federal Register.

Rule 7. Submittals

(a) All required statements, reports, applications, etc. must be filed with the principal office of the Commission unless otherwise specified in the Commission's rules, schedules and forms. Reports by exchange members, brokers and dealers required by Rule 17a–5 under the Securities Exchange Act of 1934 must be filed with the appropriate regional office as provided in Rule 255(a) under the Securities Act of 1933, and with the principal office of the Commission and the appropriate regional or district office as provided under Rule 17a–5(a) *et seq.* under the Securities Exchange Act of 1934.

(b) *Electronic Filings.* All documents required to be filed in electronic format with the Commission pursuant to the federal securities laws or the rules and regulations thereunder shall be filed at the principal office in Washington, D.C. via EDGAR by delivery to the Commission of a magnetic tape or diskette, or by direct transmission.

Rule 8. Small entity compliance guides

The following small entity compliance guides are available to the public from the Commission's Publications Room and regional offices:

(a) *Q & A: Small Business and the SEC.*[1]

(b) *The Work of the SEC.*[1]

(c) *Broker-Dealer Registration Package.*

(d) *Investment Adviser Registration Package.*

(e) *Investment Company Registration Package.*

(f) *Examination Information for Broker–Dealers, Transfer Agents, Investment Advisers and Investment Companies.*

1. These items are also available on the Securities and Exchange Commission Web site on the Internet, *http://www.sec.gov.*

Rule 9. Small entity enforcement penalty reduction policy

The Commission's policy with respect to whether to reduce or assess civil money penalties against a small entity is:

(a) The Commission will consider on a case-by-case basis whether to reduce or not assess civil money penalties against a small entity. In determining whether to reduce or not assess penalties against a specific small entity, the following considerations will apply:

(1) Except as provided in paragraph (a)(3) of this rule, penalty reduction will not be available for any small entity if:

(i) The small entity was subject previously to an enforcement action;

(ii) Any of the small entity's violations involved willful or criminal conduct; or

(iii) The small entity did not make a good faith effort to comply with the law.

(2) In considering whether the Commission will reduce or refrain from assessing a civil money penalty, the Commission may consider:

(i) The egregiousness of the violations;

(ii) The isolated or repeated nature of the violations;

(iii) The violator's state of mind when committing the violations;

(iv) The violator's history (if any) of legal or regulatory violations;

(v) The extent to which the violator cooperated during the investigation;

(vi) Whether the violator has engaged in subsequent remedial efforts to mitigate the effects of the violation and to prevent future violations;

(vii) The degree to which a penalty will deter the violator or others from committing future violations; and

(viii) Any other relevant fact.

(3) The Commission also may consider whether to reduce or not assess a civil money penalty against a small entity, including a small entity otherwise excluded from this policy under paragraphs (a)(1)(i)–(iii) of this rule, if the small entity can demonstrate to the Commission's satisfaction that it is financially unable to pay the penalty, immediately or over a reasonable period of time, in whole or in part.

(4) For purposes of this policy, an entity qualifies as "small" if it is a small business or small organization as defined by Commission rules adopted for the purpose of compliance with the Regulatory Flexibility Act.[1] An entity not included in these definitions will be considered "small" for purposes of this policy if it meets the total asset amount that applies to issuers as set forth in Rule 157a under the Securities Act of 1933.[2]

1. Pursuant to the Reg. Flex. Act, 5 U.S.C. Sec. 601(3), the Commission has adopted appropriate definitions of "small business" for purposes of the Reg. Flex. Act. See 17 CFR 270.0–10, 275.0–7, 240.0–10, 230.157, and 260.0–7. The Commission recently proposed amendments to certain of these definitions. Definitions of "Small Business" or "Small Organization" Under the Investment Company Act of 1940, the Investment Advisers Act of 1940, the Securities Exchange Act of 1934, and the Securities Act of 1933, Securities Act Rel. No. 7383, 62 FR 4106 (Jan. 28, 1997). The Commission extended the comment period for the proposed amendments to April 30, 1997, 62 FR 13356 (Mar. 20, 1997). Based on an analysis of the language and legislative history of the Reg. Flex. Act, Congress does not appear to have intended that Act to apply to natural persons (as opposed to individual proprietorships) or to foreign entities. The Commission understands that staff at the Small Business Administration have taken the same position.

2. At present, this threshold is $5 million. Thus, non-regulated entities, such as general partnerships, privately held corporations or professional service organizations, with assets of $5 million or less may qualify for penalty-reduction.

(b) This policy does not create a right or remedy for any person. This policy shall not apply to any remedy that may be sought by the Commission other than civil money penalties, whether or not such other remedy may be characterized as penal or remedial.

Rule 10. Policy statement of the Securities and Exchange Commission concerning subpoenas to members of the news media

Freedom of the press is of vital importance to the mission of the Securities and Exchange Commission. Effective journalism complements the Commission's efforts to ensure that investors receive the full and fair disclosure that the law requires, and that they deserve. Diligent reporting is an essential means of bringing securities law violations to light and ultimately helps to deter illegal conduct. In this Policy Statement the Commission sets forth guidelines for the agency's professional staff to ensure that vigorous enforcement of the federal securities laws is conducted completely consistently with the principles of the First Amendment's guarantee of freedom of the press, and specifically to avoid the issuance of subpoenas to members of the media that might impair the news gathering and reporting functions. These guidelines shall be adhered to by all members of the staff in all cases:

(a) In determining whether to issue a subpoena to a member of the news media, the approach in every case must be to strike the proper balance between the public's interest in the free dissemination of ideas and information and the public's interest in effective enforcement of the federal securities laws.

(b) When the staff investigating a matter determines that a member of the news media may have information relevant to the investigation, the staff should:

(1) Determine whether the information might be obtainable from alternative non-media sources.

(2) Make all reasonable efforts to obtain that information from those alternative sources. Whether all reasonable efforts have been made will depend on the particular circumstances of the investigation, including whether there is an immediate need to preserve assets or protect investors from an ongoing fraud.

(3) Determine whether the information is essential to successful completion of the investigation.

(c) If the information cannot reasonably be obtained from alternative sources and the information is essential to the investigation, then the staff, after seeking approval from the responsible Regional Director, District Administrator, or Associate Director, should contact legal counsel for the member of the news media. Staff should contact a member of the news media directly only if the member is not represented by legal counsel. The purpose of this contact is to explore whether the member may have information essential to the investigation, and to determine the interests of the media with respect to the information. If the nature of the investigation permits, the staff should make clear what its needs are as well as its willingness to respond to particular problems of the media. The staff should consult with the Commission's Office of Public Affairs, as appropriate.

(d) The staff should negotiate with news media members or their counsel, consistently with this Policy Statement, to obtain the essential information through informal channels, avoiding the issuance of a subpoena, if the responsible Regional Director, District Administrator, or Associate Director determines that such negotiations would not substantially impair the integrity of the investigation. Depending on the circumstances of the investigation, informal channels may include voluntary production, informal interviews, or written summaries.

(e) If negotiations are not successful in achieving a resolution that accommodates the Commission's interest in the information and the media's interests without issuing a subpoena, the staff investigating the matter should then consider whether to seek the issuance of a subpoena for the information. The following principles should guide the determination of whether a subpoena to a member of the news media should be issued:

(1) There should be reasonable grounds to believe that the information sought is essential to successful completion of the investigation. The subpoena should not be used to obtain peripheral or nonessential information.

(2) The staff should have exhausted all reasonable alternative means of obtaining the information from non-media sources. Whether all reasonable efforts have been made to obtain the information from alternative sources will depend on the particular circumstances of the investigation, including whether there is an immediate need to preserve assets or protect investors from an ongoing fraud.

(f) If there are reasonable grounds to believe the information sought is essential to the investigation, all reasonable alternative means of obtaining it have been exhausted, and all efforts at negotiation have failed, then the staff investigating the matter shall seek authorization for the subpoena from the Director of the Division of Enforcement. No subpoena shall be issued unless the Director, in consultation with the General Counsel, has authorized its issuance.

(g) In the event the Director of the Division of Enforcement, after consultation with the General Counsel, authorizes the issuance of a subpoena, notice shall immediately be provided to the Chairman of the Commission.

(h) Counsel (or the member of the news media, if not represented by counsel) shall be given reasonable and timely notice of the determination of the Director of the Division of Enforcement to authorize the subpoena and the Director's intention to issue it.

(i) Subpoenas should be negotiated with counsel for the member of the news media to narrowly tailor the request for only essential information. In negotiations with counsel, the staff should attempt to accommodate the interests of the Commission in the information with the interests of the media.

(j) Subpoenas should, wherever possible, be directed at material information regarding a limited subject matter, should cover a reasonably limited period of time, and should avoid requiring production of a large volume of unpublished material. They should give reasonable and timely notice of their demand for documents.

(k) In the absence of special circumstances, subpoenas to members of the news media should be limited to the verification of published information and to surrounding circumstances relating to the accuracy of published information.

(*l*) Because the intent of this policy statement is to protect freedom of the press, news gathering functions, and news media sources, this policy statement does not apply to demands for purely commercial or financial information unrelated to the news gathering function.

(m) Failure to follow this policy may constitute grounds for appropriate disciplinary action. The principles set forth in this statement are not intended to create or recognize any legally enforceable rights in any person.

Rule 12. Policy statement concerning cooperation by individuals in its investigations and related enforcement actions

Cooperation by individuals and entities in the Commission's investigations and related enforcement actions can contribute significantly to the success of the agency's mission. Cooperation can enhance the Commission's ability to detect violations of the federal securities laws, increase the effectiveness and efficiency of the Commission's investigations, and provide important evidence for the Commission's enforcement actions. There is a wide spectrum of tools available to the Commission and its staff for facilitating and rewarding cooperation by individuals, ranging from taking no enforcement action to pursuing reduced charges and sanctions in connection with enforcement actions. As with any cooperation program, there exists some tension between the objectives of holding individuals fully accountable for their misconduct and providing incentives for individuals to cooperate with law enforcement authorities. This policy statement sets forth the analytical framework employed by the Commission and its staff for resolving this tension in a manner that ensures that potential cooperation arrangements maximize the Commission's law enforcement interests. Although the evaluation of cooperation requires a case-by-case analysis of the specific circumstances presented, as described in greater detail below, the Commission's general approach is to determine whether, how much, and in what manner to credit cooperation by individuals by evaluating four considerations: the assistance provided by the cooperating individual in the Commission's investigation or related enforcement actions ("Investigation"); the importance of the underlying matter in which the individual cooperated; the societal interest in ensuring that the cooperating individual is held accountable for his or her misconduct; and the appropriateness of cooperation credit based upon the profile of the cooperating individual. In the end, the goal of the Commission's analysis is to protect the investing public by determining whether the public interest in facilitating and rewarding an individual's cooperation in order to advance the Commission's law enforcement interests justifies the credit awarded to the individual for his or her cooperation.

(a) *Assistance Provided by the Individual.* The Commission assesses the assistance provided by the cooperating individual in the Investigation by considering, among other things:

(1) The value of the individual's cooperation to the Investigation including, but not limited to:

(i) Whether the individual's cooperation resulted in substantial assistance to the Investigation;

(ii) The timeliness of the individual's cooperation, including whether the individual was first to report the misconduct to the Commission or to offer his or her cooperation in the Investigation, and whether the cooperation was provided before he or she had any knowledge of a pending investigation or related action;

(iii) Whether the Investigation was initiated based on information or other cooperation provided by the individual;

(iv) The quality of cooperation provided by the individual, including whether the cooperation was truthful, complete, and reliable; and

(v) The time and resources conserved as a result of the individual's cooperation in the Investigation.

(2) The nature of the individual's cooperation in the Investigation including, but not limited to:

(i) Whether the individual's cooperation was voluntary or required by the terms of an agreement with another law enforcement or regulatory organization;

(ii) The types of assistance the individual provided to the Commission;

(iii) Whether the individual provided non-privileged information, which information was not requested by the staff or otherwise might not have been discovered;

(iv) Whether the individual encouraged or authorized others to assist the staff who might not have otherwise participated in the Investigation; and

(v) Any unique circumstances in which the individual provided the cooperation.

(b) *Importance of the Underlying Matter*. The Commission assesses the importance of the Investigation in which the individual cooperated by considering, among other things:

(1) The character of the Investigation including, but not limited to:

(i) Whether the subject matter of the Investigation is a Commission priority;

(ii) The type of securities violations;

(iii) The age and duration of the misconduct;

(iv) The number of violations; and

(v) The isolated or repetitive nature of the violations.

(2) The dangers to investors or others presented by the underlying violations involved in the Investigation including, but not limited to:

(i) The amount of harm or potential harm caused by the underlying violations;

(ii) The type of harm resulting from or threatened by the underlying violations; and

(iii) The number of individuals or entities harmed.[1]

(c) *Interest in Holding the Individual Accountable*. The Commission assesses the societal interest in holding the cooperating individual fully accountable for his or her misconduct by considering, among other things:

(1) The severity of the individual's misconduct assessed by the nature of the violations and in the context of the individual's knowledge, education, training, experience, and position of responsibility at the time the violations occurred;

(2) The culpability of the individual, including, but not limited to, whether the individual acted with scienter, both generally and in relation to others who participated in the misconduct;

(3) The degree to which the individual tolerated illegal activity including, but not limited to, whether he or she took steps to prevent the violations from occurring or continuing, such as notifying the Commission or other appropriate law enforcement agency of the misconduct or, in the case of a violation involving a business organization, by notifying members of management not involved in the misconduct, the board of directors or the equivalent body not involved in the misconduct, or the auditors of such business organization of the misconduct;

(4) The efforts undertaken by the individual to remediate the harm caused by the violations including, but not limited to, whether he or she paid or agreed to pay disgorgement to injured investors and other victims or assisted these victims and the authorities in the recovery of the fruits and instrumentalities of the violations; and

(5) The sanctions imposed on the individual by other federal or state authorities and industry organizations for the violations involved in the Investigation.

(d) *Profile of the Individual*. The Commission assesses whether, how much, and in what manner it is in the public interest to award credit for cooperation, in part, based upon the cooperating individual's per-

1. Cooperation in Investigations that involve priority matters or serious, ongoing, or widespread violations will be viewed most favorably.

sonal and professional profile by considering, among other things:

(1) The individual's history of lawfulness, including complying with securities laws or regulations;

(2) The degree to which the individual has demonstrated an acceptance of responsibility for his or her past misconduct; and

(3) The degree to which the individual will have an opportunity to commit future violations of the federal securities laws in light of his or her occupation—including, but not limited to, whether he or she serves as: A licensed individual, such as an attorney or accountant; an associated person of a regulated entity, such as a broker or dealer; a fiduciary for other individuals or entities regarding financial matters; an officer or director of public companies; or a member of senior management—together with any existing or proposed safeguards based upon the individual's particular circumstances.

NOTE TO RULE 12. Before the Commission evaluates an individual's cooperation, it analyzes the unique facts and circumstances of the case. The above principles are not listed in order of importance nor are they intended to be all-inclusive or to require a specific determination in any particular case. Furthermore, depending upon the facts and circumstances of each case, some of the principles may not be applicable or may deserve greater weight than others. Finally, neither this statement, nor the principles set forth herein creates or recognizes any legally enforceable rights for any person.

SUBPART A—PUBLIC COMPANY ACCOUNTING OVERSIGHT BOARD (REGULATION P)

Rule 140. Interim Commission review of PCAOB inspection reports

(a) *Definitions.*

(1) *Board* or *PCAOB* means the Public Company Accounting Oversight Board.

(2) *Registered public accounting firm* or *Firm* shall have the meaning set forth in 15 U.S.C. 7201(a)(12).

(3) *Associated person* means a person associated with the registered public accounting firm as defined in 15 U.S.C. 7201(a)(9).

(b) *Reviewable Matters.* A registered public accounting firm may request interim Commission review of an assessment or determination by the PCAOB contained in an inspection report prepared under 15 U.S.C. 7214 and relating to that firm, if the firm:

(1) Has provided the PCAOB with a response, pursuant to the rules of the PCAOB, to the substance of particular items in a draft inspection report and disagrees with the assessments relating to those items contained in any final inspection report prepared by the PCAOB following such response;

(2) Disagrees with an assessment contained in any final inspection report that was not contained in the draft inspection report provided to the firm under 15 U.S.C. 7214(f) or the rules of the PCAOB; or

(3) Disagrees with the determination of the PCAOB that criticisms or defects in the quality control systems of the firm that were identified in an inspection report, but not disclosed to the public, have not been addressed to the satisfaction of the PCAOB within 12 months after the date of that inspection report.

(c) *Procedures for Requesting Interim Commission Review.*

(1) A request for interim Commission review with respect to matters described in paragraph (b) of this section must be submitted to the Commission's Office of the Secretary within 30 calendar days of the following:

(i) The date the firm is provided a copy of the final inspection report described in paragraph (b)(1) or (b)(2) of this section; or

(ii) The date the firm receives notice of the PCAOB's determination described in paragraph (b)(3) of this section.

(2) The PCAOB shall not make publicly available the final inspection report or criticisms or defects in the quality control systems of the firm subject to a determination described in paragraph (b) of this section, as applicable, during the 30–day period during which the firm may request interim Commission review, unless the firm consents in writing to earlier publication of the report.

(3) A request for interim Commission review ("request" or "submission") must be marked "Request for Interim Commission Review With Respect to PCAOB Inspection Report." The request must focus on the specific matters for which relief is requested and succinctly address the issues raised by the PCAOB. The request, to the extent possible, should include, for example:

(i) A copy of the particular inspection report that is the subject of the request;

(ii) The specific assessments or determinations that are the subject of the request;

(iii) The alleged errors or deficiencies in the PCAOB's assessments or determination and the reasons for the firm's position;

(iv) If the matter is being reviewed under paragraph (b)(3) of this section, any actions taken by the registered public accounting firm to address criticisms or defects identified in the inspection report; and

(v) Any supporting documentation relevant to the review.

(4) The firm must provide a copy of its review request to the PCAOB simultaneously with its submission to the Commission.

(5) A timely review request by a firm will operate as a stay of publication of those portions of the final inspection report or criticisms or defects in the quality control systems of the firm subject to a determination described in paragraph (b) of this section, as applicable, that are the subject of the firm's review request, unless the Commission otherwise determines in its own discretion. Upon expiration of the 30-day period during which the firm may request interim Commission review, the PCAOB shall make publicly available the remainder of the final inspection report or criticisms or defects in the quality control systems of the firm that were identified in an inspection report, as applicable, that are not the subject of the firm's review request, unless the Commission otherwise determines that such a result would not be necessary or appropriate.

(6) If the firm fails to make a timely review request, pursuant to Section 104(g)(2) of the Act, the PCAOB shall make publicly available the final inspection report or criticisms or defects in the quality control systems of the firm that were identified in an inspection report, as applicable.

(d) *Procedures for Granting or Denying the Review Request.* Within 30 calendar days of a timely review request, the Commission will notify the firm and the PCAOB as to whether the Commission will exercise its discretion to grant the request for an interim review. If the Commission does not grant the review request, the stay of publication is terminated upon notification to the firm and the PCAOB. If the Commission does grant the review request, the stay of publication shall continue unless the Commission determines otherwise in its own discretion, or unless the firm consents in writing to the PCAOB, with a copy to the Commission, to earlier publication.

(e) *Procedures Where a Review Request has been Granted.*

(1) Where the Commission has notified the firm and the PCAOB that it is granting the request for an interim review, the PCAOB may submit responsive information and documents with the Commission within 15 calendar days of receipt of such notice. The PCAOB must provide a copy of such information and documents simultaneously to the firm.

(2) During the course of the interim review, the Commission may request additional information relating to the PCAOB's assessments or determination under review, and provide a period of up to seven calendar days to respond to such request, from the PCAOB, the firm, and any associated person of the firm. The Commission may grant the firm or the PCAOB a period of up to seven calendar days to respond to any information obtained pursuant to this paragraph. The firm or the PCAOB, as applicable, shall provide simultaneously to the other party all information provided as a result of a request for additional information or responses thereto. The firm with which any associated person from whom information is requested shall provide simultaneously to the PCAOB all information provided as a result of a request for additional information or responses thereto. If the firm (including any associated person) or the PCAOB fails to respond timely to a request from the Commission, such failure may serve as the basis for the Commission to conclude its review and make a determination adverse to the non-responsive party.

(3) The Commission, based on the information submitted by the firm, the PCAOB and any associated persons, shall consider whether the PCAOB's assessments or determination are arbitrary and capricious, or otherwise not consistent with the purposes of the Act.

(4) At the conclusion of its review, the Commission shall inform the firm and the PCAOB in writing that the Commission:

(i) Does not object to all or part of the assessments or determination of the PCAOB and the stay of publication is terminated; or

(ii) Remands to the PCAOB with instructions that the stay of publication is permanent or that the PCAOB take such other actions as the Commission deems necessary or appropriate with respect to publication, including, but not limited to, revising the final inspection report or determinations before publication.

(5) The review pursuant to this section shall be completed and a written notice pursuant to this section shall be sent no more than 75 calendar days after notification to the firm and the PCAOB that the Commission is granting the request for an interim review, unless the Commission extends the period for good cause.

(f) *Treatment of Review.*

(1) Time periods in this section shall be computed as provided in the SEC's Rules of Practice, Rule 160.

(2) Unless otherwise determined by the Commission, the decision to grant or deny a review request and the conclusions of the Commission's review shall be non-public, and the information or documents submitted, created, or obtained by the Commission or its staff in the course of the review shall be deemed non-public. Nothing in this rule shall be construed to impair or limit the ability of any party to request confidential treatment under the Freedom of Information Act, 15 U.S.C. 7215(b)(5), or any other applicable law.

(3) Pursuant to 15 U.S.C. 7214(h)(2), any decision of the Commission as a result of an interim review with respect to a PCAOB inspection report, including whether a request for review is granted or denied, shall not be reviewable under 15 U.S.C. 78y and shall not be deemed to be "final agency action" for purposes of 5 U.S.C. 704.

(4) Any action taken by the Commission relates solely to the publication of the relevant inspection report and does not affect the ability of the Commission or PCAOB to take appropriate action.

(g) *Designation of Address; Representation.*

(1) When a registered public accounting firm first submits a request for interim Commission review, or an associated person first submits information related to a request, the firm or associated person shall submit to the Commission, and keep current, an address at which any notice or other written communication furnished to the firm or associated person may be sent, a contact name and telephone number where the firm or associated person may be reached during business hours and, if represented, the representative's name, business address, and telephone number.

(2) If the firm, PCAOB, or associated person will be represented by a representative, the initial submission of that person shall be accompanied by the notice of appearance required by the SEC Rule of Practice 102(d). The other provisions of Rule 102 with respect to representation before the Commission shall apply.

Rule 170. Initiation of disapproval proceedings for PCAOB proposed rules

Initiation of disapproval proceedings for proposed rules of the Public Company Accounting Oversight Board are subject to the provisions of SEC Rules of Practice 700 and 701 as fully as if it were a *registered securities association*, except that:

(a) *Demonstration of Consistency with the Sarbanes–Oxley Act of 2002.* For purposes of proposed rules of the Public Company Accounting Oversight Board, apply this paragraph in lieu of paragraph (b)(3) of 17 CFR 201.700. The burden to demonstrate that a proposed rule is consistent with the requirements of title I of the Sarbanes–Oxley Act of 2002, and the rules and regulations issued thereunder, or as necessary or appropriate in the public interest or for the protection of investors, is on the Public Company Accounting Oversight Board. In its filing the Public Company Accounting Oversight Board must explain in a clear and comprehensible manner why the proposed rule change is consistent with the requirements of title I of the Sarbanes–Oxley Act of 2002 and the rules and regulations thereunder, or as necessary or appropriate in the public interest or for the protection of investors. A mere assertion that the proposed rule change is consistent with those requirements is not sufficient. Instead, the description of the proposed rule, its purpose and operation, its effect, and a legal analysis of its consistency with applicable requirements must all be sufficiently detailed and specific to support an affirmative Commission finding. Any failure by the Public Company Accounting Oversight Board in its proposed rule filing with the Commission may result in the Commission not having a sufficient basis to make an affirmative finding that a proposed rule change is consistent with the title I of the Sarbanes–Oxley Act of 2002, and the rules and regulations issued thereunder, or as necessary or appropriate in the public interest or for the protection of investors.

(b) For each reference to "the Exchange Act and the rules and regulations thereunder applicable to the self-regulatory organization" apply "title I of the Sarbanes–Oxley Act of 2002, and the rules and regulations issued thereunder applicable to such organization, or as necessary or appropriate in the public interest or for the protection of investors."

Rule 190. Public Company Accounting Oversight Board budget approval process

(a) *Purpose.* These procedures are established in connection with consideration and approval of the budget and the accounting support fee for the Public Company Accounting Oversight Board (PCAOB). Actions attributed to the PCAOB in this section shall be performed as authorized by the Sarbanes–Oxley Act of 2002 and the PCAOB's bylaws.

(b) *Definitions.* For the purposes of this rule, the following definitions shall apply:

(1) *Budget category* means a grouping of similar expenditures within the PCAOB's budget. Budget categories shall include, among others: personnel, training, recruiting and relocation expenses, information technology, consulting and professional fees, travel, administrative expenses, lease costs and related expenses, and capital improvements of facilities.

(2) *Budget justification* means the justification for each annual budget, prepared in concise and specific terms, covering all of the PCAOB's programs and activities, and including, among other things as may be requested by the Commission:

(i) A performance budget for the budget year;

(ii) An analysis of the PCAOB's budget, including a tabular presentation that identifies the budgetary resources required for each program area (with a breakout of resources by budget category); a description of the budgetary resources identified in the budget in the context of the PCAOB's programs and activities; and an explanation of the analysis used to determine the resources needed to accomplish each program and strategic goal that demonstrates that reasonable opportunities for making more efficient and effective use of resources have been explored;

(iii) A description of the relationship between the results or outcomes the PCAOB expects to achieve (as discussed in the PCAOB's strategic plan) and the resources requested in the budget;

(iv) Assumptions underlying the calculation of the working capital reserve as permitted in paragraph (d)(3) of this rule and assumptions underlying PCAOB estimates, including work years, program outputs, base compensation levels and proposed compensation increases, and costs of inputs such as materials or contract costs;

(v) A discussion of any models used to develop PCAOB estimates;

(vi) Detailed funding levels for education, training, and travel of the PCAOB workforce;

(vii) Information sufficient for the Commission to assess current and proposed capital projects and information technology projects; and

(viii) A statement that the PCAOB has considered relative costs and benefits in formulating the programs, projects and activities described in the budget.

(3) *Budget year* means the PCAOB fiscal year that is the subject of the budget prepared and submitted by the PCAOB to the Commission for approval.

(4) *Current year* means the PCAOB fiscal year that precedes the budget year, and is the year in which the PCAOB prepares the budget.

(5) *Performance budget* means a budget that presents what the PCAOB proposes to accomplish in the budget year and what resources these proposals will require, and that serves as the primary basis for the justification of the budget submitted to the Commission for approval. The performance budget includes:

(i) A description of what the PCAOB plans to accomplish, organized by strategic goal;

(ii) Background on what the PCAOB has accomplished, organized by strategic goal;

(iii) Analyses of the strategies the PCAOB uses to influence strategic outcomes, including whether those strategies could be improved and, if so, how they could be improved;

(iv) Analyses of the programs that contribute to each goal and their relative roles and effectiveness;

(v) Performance targets for the budget year and the current year and how the PCAOB expects to achieve those targets, as well as actual performance levels achieved in the year immediately preceding the current year;

(vi) The budgetary resources the PCAOB is requesting to achieve those targets;

(vii) Descriptions of the operations, processes, staff skills, information and other technologies, human resources, capital assets, and other resources to be used in achieving the PCAOB's performance goals; and

(viii) Descriptions of the programs, policies, and management, regulatory, and other initiatives and approaches to be used in achieving the PCAOB's performance goals.

(6) *Preliminary budget* means the draft budget submitted for initial consideration by the Commission, which shall be a complete or substantially complete budget for the budget year, and which is accompanied by a budget justification.

(7) *Program area* means the array of the budgeted amounts and other budget-related data according to the major purpose served, such as registration, inspection, standard-setting, enforcement, and administration.

(8) *Receipts* means collections that result from issuers' payments of accounting support fees; public accounting firms' payment of registration fees and fees associated with annual reports; interest income; and other sources of revenue.

(9) *Strategic plan* means the PCAOB's overarching plan for accomplishing its strategic goals, including forecasts for the current and four following years; estimates of the effect that reasonably foreseeable changes impacting the auditing profession and securities markets could have on program levels; and a discussion of the impact that program levels and changes in methods of program delivery, including advances in technology, could have on program operations and administration.

(10) *Supplemental budget* means a budget or amendment thereto submitted to the Commission for approval subsequent to Commission approval of the budget for the budget year, when:

(i) There is a need for additional funds in a program area;

(ii) Resources are to be applied in a manner not fairly implied in the Commission-approved budget and budget justification, such as when programs are created to perform functions that are not, or to perform functions in a way that is not, fairly implied from the Commission-approved budget and budget justification; or

(iii) Programs described in the Commission-approved budget and budget justification are to be eliminated.

(c) *Timetable.* The timetable for preparation and submission of the annual budget is as follows:

Date	***Event***
On or before March 15	PCAOB provides a narrative of its program issues and outlook for the budget year
On or before April 30	Commission provides economic assumptions and general budgetary guidance to the PCAOB
On or before July 31	PCAOB submits preliminary budget and budget justification for Commission review
August–October	Consultation between Commission and PCAOB; Commission staff conducts review of PCAOB preliminary budget, budget justification and related information
On or before October 31	Commission passback of budget to the PCAOB with proposed revisions
On or before November 30	PCAOB adopts budget and submits it, along with the budget justification, to the Commission
On or before December 23	Commission votes on the PCAOB budget

(d) *Contents of Budget.* (1) To facilitate Commission review and approval, each budget (including each preliminary budget and budget submitted for Commission approval) shall:

(i) Be accompanied by a budget justification.

(ii) Include information for the budget year, the current year, and the year immediately preceding the current year, regarding actual or projected spending by program area, receipts, debt, and employment levels.

(iii) Be consistent with, or explain any deviations from, the economic assumptions and budgetary guidance provided by the Commission.

(iv) Include statements of PCAOB programs, initiatives and strategies for the budget year.

(v) Earmark each amount for a specific budget category within a program area.

(vi) Include planned beginning-of-year and end-of-year headcounts for each program area.

(2) Each budget submitted for Commission approval shall be consistent with the preliminary budget and any revisions proposed by the Commission when the budget was passed from the Commission back to the PCAOB or explain any changes from the preliminary budget and/or such proposed revisions.

(3) In addition to amounts needed to fund disbursements during the budget year, a budget may reflect receipts in amounts needed to fund expected disbursements during a period not to exceed the first five months of the fiscal year immediately following the budget year (the working capital reserve), provided such amounts shall be disbursed only as specified in the following year's budget or in a supplemental budget approved by the Commission.

(4) In approving the budget the Commission may not change the amounts earmarked for programs, program areas, or activities, or any other aspects of the budget; provided, that if the budget is conditionally rather than finally approved, then the Commission may transmit to the Board such proposed changes as are consistent with the preliminary budget and any revisions previously proposed by the Commission when it passed the budget back to the PCAOB. No proposed reduction or increase may be greater than that included in the preliminary budget and any revisions previously proposed by the Commission when it passed the budget back to the PCAOB.

(5) In the event the budget is conditionally approved by the Commission, the PCAOB shall have the opportunity to consider the changes proposed by the Commission and to vote again for final approval of the budget as amended. If this iterative process has not resolved differences between the Commission and the PCAOB by December 23, then the terms of the most recent conditional approval shall become final, and the budget shall be deemed finally approved.

(e) *Limitation on Spending.* (1) The PCAOB shall not spend in a budget year more than the amount specified in the Commission-approved PCAOB budget for that year, regardless of the source of the funds, unless such expenses have been approved by the Commission through a supplemental budget request.

(2) Funds may be disbursed by the PCAOB only in accordance with the Commission approved budget, *provided however*, during the budget year the PCAOB may transfer amounts totaling not more than $1,000,000 into or out of each program area without prior Commission approval. Further, the PCAOB shall not:

(i) Apply its resources in a manner not fairly implied in the Commission-approved budget and budget justification, such as to create programs to perform functions that are not, or to perform functions in a way that is not, fairly implied from the Commission-approved budget and budget justification, or

(ii) Eliminate programs described in the Commission-approved budget and budget justification.

(3) In the event that the Commission has not approved a budget for a PCAOB fiscal year before the beginning of that fiscal year, the PCAOB may spend funds from the reserve and continue to incur obligations as if the PCAOB budget or supplemental budget most recently approved by the Commission were continuing in effect for that fiscal year.

(f) *Supplemental Budget.* (1) The PCAOB may submit to the Commission a request for approval of a supplemental budget subsequent to Commission approval of the budget for the budget year in order to spend any amounts in excess of, or contrary to, the limitations described in paragraphs (e)(1) and (e)(2) of this rule.

(2) To facilitate Commission review and approval, a supplemental budget shall include:

(i) Detailed information regarding the impact of the supplemental budget on each affected program area, including costs by cost category, project or activity;

(ii) A statement regarding how the supplemental budget facilitates the strategic and policy goals of the PCAOB;

(iii) Information indicating why the amount was not included in the budget for the current year, including a description of any subsequent and unforeseen events or circumstances necessitating the supplemental budget request;

(iv) Information indicating why the request should not or cannot be postponed until the next regular annual budget process; and

(v) The proposed source for the funds, including any offsets to be made elsewhere in the PCAOB's programs and activities.

(g) *Maintenance of Records; Reports.* (1) The PCAOB shall maintain, and make available to the Commission or Commission staff upon request, a strategic plan and records in reasonable detail that support each preliminary budget, budget, budget justification, supplemental budget and other report or communication in compliance with this rule, including past and projected receipts, outlays, obligations, and employment levels.

(2) The PCAOB is required to maintain and, within 30 business days after the end of each fiscal quarter, to furnish to the Commission a report of its spending and staffing levels for the quarter just ended, comparing those levels to the levels in the Commission approved budget.

(h) *Publication of Budget.* (1) Following submission of the PCAOB-approved budget to the Commission, such budget and budget justification, subject to any applicable exemption under the Freedom of Information Act, shall be made available to the public. Neither the Commission nor the PCAOB shall publish a preliminary budget, budget, budget justification, or any underlying materials in connection therewith, until such time as the budget is approved by the PCAOB and submitted to the Commission for its approval.

(2) Supplemental budgets shall be made public, following approval by the PCAOB and submission to the Commission, in the same manner as described in paragraph (h)(1) of this rule.

(3) The Commission-approved budget shall be made available to the public at the time of such approval.

(i) *Waivers of Rule Provisions.* The Commission, in its discretion, may waive compliance with any provision of this rule.

G. RULES RELATING TO INVESTIGATIONS

(Cite as 17 CFR § 203.___)

In General

Rule 1. Application of the rules of this part

The rules of this part apply only to investigations conducted by the Commission. They do not apply to adjudicative or rulemaking proceedings.

Rule 2. Information obtained in investigations and examinations

Information or documents obtained by the Commission in the course of any investigation or examination, unless made a matter of public record, shall be deemed non-public, but the Commission approves the practice whereby officials of the Divisions of Enforcement, Corporation Finance, Market Regulation and Investment Management and the Office of International Affairs at the level of Assistant Director or higher, and officials in Regional Offices at the level of Assistant Regional Director or higher, may engage in and may authorize members of the Commission's staff to engage in discussions with persons identified in Rule 24c–1(b) under the Securities Exchange Act of 1934 concerning information obtained in individual investigations or examinations, including formal investigations conducted pursuant to Commission order.

Rule 3. Suspension and disbarment

The provisions of 17 CFR 201.103 (Rule 102(e) of the commissions rules of practice) are hereby made specifically applicable to all investigations.

Formal Investigated Proceedings

Rule 4. Applicability of Rules 4 through 8

(a) Rules 4 through 8 shall be applicable to a witness who is sworn in a proceeding pursuant to a Commission order for investigation or examination, such proceeding being hereinafter referred to as a *formal investigative proceeding.*

(b) Formal investigative proceedings may be held before the Commission, before one or more of its members, or before any officer designated by it for the purpose of taking testimony of witnesses and received other evidence. The term *officer conducting the investigation* shall mean any of the foregoing.

Rule 5. Non-public formal investigative proceedings

Unless otherwise ordered by the Commission, all formal investigative proceedings shall be non-public.

Rule 6. Transcripts

Transcripts, if any, of formal investigative proceedings shall be recorded solely by the official reporter, or by any other person or means designated by the officer conducting the investigation. A person who has submitted documentary evidence or testimony in a formal investigative proceeding shall be entitled, upon written request, to procure a copy of his documentary evidence or a transcript of his testimony on payment of the appropriate fees: *Provided, however,* That in a non-public formal investigative proceeding the Commission may for good cause deny such request. In any event, any witness, upon proper identification, shall have the right to inspect the official transcript of the witness' own testimony.

Rule 7. Rights of witnesses

(a) Any person who is compelled or requested to furnish documentary evidence or testimony at a formal investigative proceeding shall, upon request, be shown the Commission's order of investigation. Copies of formal orders of investigation shall not be furnished, for their retention, to such persons requesting the same except with the express approval of officials in the Regional Offices at the level of Assistant Regional Director or higher, or officials in the Division or Divisions conducting or supervising the investigation at the level of Assistant Director or higher. Such approval shall not be given unless the person granting such approval, in his or her discretion, is satisfied that there exist reasons consistent both with the protection of privacy of persons involved in the investigation and with the unimpeded conduct of the investigation.

(b) Any person compelled to appear, or who appears by request or permission of the Commission, in person at a formal investigative proceeding may be accompanied, represented and advised by counsel, as defined in 17 CFR 201.101(a) (Rule 101(a) of the Commission's rules of practice): *Provided, however,* That all witnesses shall be sequestered, and unless permitted in the discretion of the officer conducting the investigation no witness or the counsel accompanying any such witness shall be permitted to be present during the examination of any other witness called in such proceeding.

(c) The right to be accompanied, represented and advised by counsel shall mean the right of a person testifying to have an attorney present with him during any formal investigative proceeding and to have this attorney (1) advise such person before, during and after the conclusion of such examination, (2) question such person briefly at the conclusion of the examination to clarify any of the answers such person has given, and (3) make summary notes during such examination solely for the use of such person.

(d) Unless otherwise ordered by the Commission, in any public formal investigative proceeding, if the record shall contain implications of wrongdoing by any person, such person shall have the right to appear on the record; and in addition to the rights afforded other witnesses hereby, he shall have a reasonable opportunity of cross-examination and production of rebuttal testimony or documentary evidence. *Reasonable* shall mean permitting persons as full an opportunity to assert their position as may be granted consistent with administrative efficiency and with avoidance of undue delay. The determination of reasonableness in each instance shall be made in the discretion of the officer conducting the investigation.

(e) The officer conducting the investigation may report to the Commission any instances where any witness or counsel has been guilty of dilatory, obstructionist or contumacious conduct during the course of an investigation or any other instance of violation of these rules. The Commission will thereupon take such further action as the circumstances may warrant, including suspension or disbarment of counsel from further appearance or practice before it, in accordance with 17 CFR 201.102(e) (Rule 102(e) of the Commission's rules of practice), or exclusion from further participation in the particular investigation.

Rule 8. Service of subpoenas

Service of subpoenas issued in formal investigative proceedings shall be effected in the manner prescribed by Rule 232(c) of the Commission's Rules of Practice, 17 CFR 201.232(c).

H. STANDARDS OF PROFESSIONAL CONDUCT FOR ATTORNEYS APPEARING AND PRACTICING BEFORE THE COMMISSION IN THE REPRESENTATION OF AN ISSUER

(Cite as 17 CFR § 205.___)

Rule 1. Purpose and scope

This part sets forth minimum standards of professional conduct for attorneys appearing and practicing before the Commission in the representation of an issuer. These standards supplement applicable standards of any jurisdiction where an attorney is admitted or practices and are not intended to limit the ability of any jurisdiction to impose additional obligations on an attorney not inconsistent with the application of this part. Where the standards of a state or other United States jurisdiction where an attorney is admitted or practices conflict with this part, this part shall govern.

Rule 2. Definitions

For purposes of this part, the following definitions apply:

(a) *Appearing and practicing* before the Commission:

(1) Means:

(i) Transacting any business with the Commission, including communications in any form;

(ii) Representing an issuer in a Commission administrative proceeding or in connection with any Commission investigation, inquiry, information request, or subpoena;

(iii) Providing advice in respect of the United States securities laws or the Commission's rules or regulations thereunder regarding any document that the attorney has notice will be filed with or submitted to, or incorporated into any document that will be filed with or submitted to, the Commission, including the provision of such advice in the context of preparing, or participating in the preparation of, any such document; or

(iv) Advising an issuer as to whether information or a statement, opinion, or other writing is required under the United States securities laws or the Commission's rules or regulations thereunder to be filed with or submitted to, or incorporated into any document that will be filed with or submitted to, the Commission; but

(2) Does not include an attorney who:

(i) Conducts the activities in paragraphs (a)(1)(i) through (a)(1)(iv) of this rule other than in the context of providing legal services to an issuer with whom the attorney has an attorney-client relationship; or

(ii) Is a non-appearing foreign attorney.

(b) *Appropriate response* means a response to an attorney regarding reported evidence of a material violation as a result of which the attorney reasonably believes:

(1) That no material violation, as defined in paragraph (i) of this rule, has occurred, is ongoing, or is about to occur;

(2) That the issuer has, as necessary, adopted appropriate remedial measures, including appropriate steps or sanctions to stop any material vio-

lations that are ongoing, to prevent any material violation that has yet to occur, and to remedy or otherwise appropriately address any material violation that has already occurred and to minimize the likelihood of its recurrence; or

(3) That the issuer, with the consent of the issuer's board of directors, a committee thereof to whom a report could be made pursuant to Rule 3(b)(3), or a qualified legal compliance committee, has retained or directed an attorney to review the reported evidence of a material violation and either:

(i) Has substantially implemented any remedial recommendations made by such attorney after a reasonable investigation and evaluation of the reported evidence; or

(ii) Has been advised that such attorney may, consistent with his or her professional obligations, assert a colorable defense on behalf of the issuer (or the issuer's officer, director, employee, or agent, as the case may be) in any investigation or judicial or administrative proceeding relating to the reported evidence of a material violation.

(c) *Attorney* means any person who is admitted, licensed, or otherwise qualified to practice law in any jurisdiction, domestic or foreign, or who holds himself or herself out as admitted, licensed, or otherwise qualified to practice law.

(d) *Breach of fiduciary duty* refers to any breach of fiduciary or similar duty to the issuer recognized under an applicable Federal or State statute or at common law, including but not limited to misfeasance, nonfeasance, abdication of duty, abuse of trust, and approval of unlawful transactions.

(e) *Evidence of a material violation* means credible evidence, based upon which it would be unreasonable, under the circumstances, for a prudent and competent attorney not to conclude that it is reasonably likely that a material violation has occurred, is ongoing, or is about to occur.

(f) *Foreign government issuer* means a foreign issuer as defined in Rule 405 under the Securities Act of 1933 eligible to register securities on Schedule B of the Securities Act of 1933 (15 U.S.C. 77a *et seq.*, Schedule B).

(g) *In the representation of an issuer means providing legal services as an* attorney for an issuer, regardless of whether the attorney is employed or retained by the issuer.

(h) *Issuer* means an issuer (as defined in section 3 of the Securities Exchange Act of 1934 (15 U.S.C. 78c)), the securities of which are registered under section 12 of that Act (15 U.S.C. 78l), or that is required to file reports under section 15(d) of that Act (15 U.S.C. 78o(d)), or that files or has filed a registration statement that has not yet become effective under the Securities Act of 1933 (15 U.S.C. 77a *et seq.*), and that it has not withdrawn, but does not include a foreign government issuer. For purposes of paragraphs (a) and (g) of this rule, the term "issuer" includes any person controlled by an issuer, where an attorney provides legal services to such person on behalf of, or at the behest, or for the benefit of the issuer, regardless of whether the attorney is employed or retained by the issuer.

(i) *Material violation* means a material violation of an applicable United States federal or state securities law, a material breach of fiduciary duty arising under United States federal or state law, or a similar material violation of any United States federal or state law.

(j) *Non-appearing foreign attorney* means an attorney:

(1) Who is admitted to practice law in a jurisdiction outside the United States;

(2) Who does not hold himself or herself out as practicing, and does not give legal advice regarding, United States federal or state securities or other laws (except as provided in paragraph (j)(3)(ii) of this rule); and

(3) Who:

(i) Conducts activities that would constitute appearing and practicing before the Commission only incidentally to, and in the ordinary course of, the practice of law in a jurisdiction outside the United States; or

(ii) Is appearing and practicing before the Commission only in consultation with counsel, other than a non-appearing foreign attorney, admitted or licensed to practice in a state or other United States jurisdiction.

(k) *Qualified legal compliance committee* means a committee of an issuer (which also may be an audit or other committee of the issuer) that:

(1) Consists of at least one member of the issuer's audit committee (or, if the issuer has no audit committee, one member from an equivalent committee of independent directors) and two or more members of the issuer's board of directors who are not employed, directly or indirectly, by the issuer and who are not, in the case of a registered invest-

ment company, "interested persons" as defined in section 2(a)(19) of the Investment Company Act of 1940 (15 U.S.C. 80a–2(a)(19));

(2) Has adopted written procedures for the confidential receipt, retention, and consideration of any report of evidence of a material violation under Rule 3;

(3) Has been duly established by the issuer's board of directors, with the authority and responsibility:

(i) To inform the issuer's chief legal officer and chief executive officer (or the equivalents thereof) of any report of evidence of a material violation (except in the circumstances described in Rule 3(b)(4));

(ii) To determine whether an investigation is necessary regarding any report of evidence of a material violation by the issuer, its officers, directors, employees or agents and, if it determines an investigation is necessary or appropriate, to:

(A) Notify the audit committee or the full board of directors;

(B) Initiate an investigation, which may be conducted either by the chief legal officer (or the equivalent thereof) or by outside attorneys; and

(C) Retain such additional expert personnel as the committee deems necessary; and

(iii) At the conclusion of any such investigation, to:

(A) Recommend, by majority vote, that the issuer implement an appropriate response to evidence of a material violation; and

(B) Inform the chief legal officer and the chief executive officer (or the equivalents thereof) and the board of directors of the results of any such investigation under this rule and the appropriate remedial measures to be adopted; and

(4) Has the authority and responsibility, acting by majority vote, to take all other appropriate action, including the authority to notify the Commission in the event that the issuer fails in any material respect to implement an appropriate response that the qualified legal compliance committee has recommended the issuer to take.

(*l*) *Reasonable* or *reasonably* denotes, with respect to the actions of an attorney, conduct that would not be unreasonable for a prudent and competent attorney.

(m) *Reasonably believes* means that an attorney believes the matter in question and that the circumstances are such that the belief is not unreasonable.

(n) *Report* means to make known to directly, either in person, by telephone, by e-mail, electronically, or in writing.

Rule 3. Issuer as client

(a) *Representing an Issuer*. An attorney appearing and practicing before the Commission in the representation of an issuer owes his or her professional and ethical duties to the issuer as an organization. That the attorney may work with and advise the issuer's officers, directors, or employees in the course of representing the issuer does not make such individuals the attorney's clients.

(b) *Duty to Report Evidence of a Material Violation*. (1) If an attorney, appearing and practicing before the Commission in the representation of an issuer, becomes aware of evidence of a material violation by the issuer or by any officer, director, employee, or agent of the issuer, the attorney shall report such evidence to the issuer's chief legal officer (or the equivalent thereof) or to both the issuer's chief legal officer and its chief executive officer (or the equivalents thereof) forthwith. By communicating such information to the issuer's officers or directors, an attorney does not reveal client confidences or secrets or privileged or otherwise protected information related to the attorney's representation of an issuer.

(2) The chief legal officer (or the equivalent thereof) shall cause such inquiry into the evidence of a material violation as he or she reasonably believes is appropriate to determine whether the material violation described in the report has occurred, is ongoing, or is about to occur. If the chief legal officer (or the equivalent thereof) determines no material violation has occurred, is ongoing, or is about to occur, he or she shall notify the reporting attorney and advise the reporting attorney of the basis for such determination. Unless the chief legal officer (or the equivalent thereof) reasonably believes that no material violation has occurred, is ongoing, or is about to occur, he or she shall take all reasonable steps to cause the issuer to adopt an appropriate response, and shall advise the reporting attorney thereof. In lieu of causing an inquiry under this paragraph (b), a chief legal officer (or the equivalent thereof) may refer a report of evidence of a material violation to a qualified legal compliance committee under paragraph (c)(2) of this rule if the issuer has duly established a quali-

fied legal compliance committee prior to the report of evidence of a material violation.

(3) Unless an attorney who has made a report under paragraph (b)(1) of this rule reasonably believes that the chief legal officer or the chief executive officer of the issuer (or the equivalent thereof) has provided an appropriate response within a reasonable time, the attorney shall report the evidence of a material violation to:

(i) The audit committee of the issuer's board of directors;

(ii) Another committee of the issuer's board of directors consisting solely of directors who are not employed, directly or indirectly, by the issuer and are not, in the case of a registered investment company, "interested persons" as defined in section 2(a)(19) of the Investment Company Act of 1940 (15 U.S.C. 80a–2(a)(19)) (if the issuer's board of directors has no audit committee); or

(iii) The issuer's board of directors (if the issuer's board of directors has no committee consisting solely of directors who are not employed, directly or indirectly, by the issuer and are not, in the case of a registered investment company, "interested persons" as defined in section 2(a)(19) of the Investment Company Act of 1940 (15 U.S.C. 80a–2(a)(19))).

(4) If an attorney reasonably believes that it would be futile to report evidence of a material violation to the issuer's chief legal officer and chief executive officer (or the equivalents thereof) under paragraph (b)(1) of this rule, the attorney may report such evidence as provided under paragraph (b)(3) of this rule.

(5) An attorney retained or directed by an issuer to investigate evidence of a material violation reported under paragraph (b)(1), (b)(3), or (b)(4) of this rule shall be deemed to be appearing and practicing before the Commission. Directing or retaining an attorney to investigate reported evidence of a material violation does not relieve an officer or director of the issuer to whom such evidence has been reported under paragraph (b)(1), (b)(3), or (b)(4) of this rule from a duty to respond to the reporting attorney.

(6) An attorney shall not have any obligation to report evidence of a material violation under this paragraph (b) if:

(i) The attorney was retained or directed by the issuer's chief legal officer (or the equivalent thereof) to investigate such evidence of a material violation and:

(A) The attorney reports the results of such investigation to the chief legal officer (or the equivalent thereof); and

(B) Except where the attorney and the chief legal officer (or the equivalent thereof) each reasonably believes that no material violation has occurred, is ongoing, or is about to occur, the chief legal officer (or the equivalent thereof) reports the results of the investigation to the issuer's board of directors, a committee thereof to whom a report could be made pursuant to paragraph (b)(3) of this rule, or a qualified legal compliance committee; or

(ii) The attorney was retained or directed by the chief legal officer (or the equivalent thereof) to assert, consistent with his or her professional obligations, a colorable defense on behalf of the issuer (or the issuer's officer, director, employee, or agent, as the case may be) in any investigation or judicial or administrative proceeding relating to such evidence of a material violation, and the chief legal officer (or the equivalent thereof) provides reasonable and timely reports on the progress and outcome of such proceeding to the issuer's board of directors, a committee thereof to whom a report could be made pursuant to paragraph (b)(3) of this rule, or a qualified legal compliance committee.

(7) An attorney shall not have any obligation to report evidence of a material violation under this paragraph (b) if such attorney was retained or directed by a qualified legal compliance committee:

(i) To investigate such evidence of a material violation; or

(ii) To assert, consistent with his or her professional obligations, a colorable defense on behalf of the issuer (or the issuer's officer, director, employee, or agent, as the case may be) in any investigation or judicial or administrative proceeding relating to such evidence of a material violation.

(8) An attorney who receives what he or she reasonably believes is an appropriate and timely response to a report he or she has made pursuant to paragraph (b)(1), (b)(3), or (b)(4) of this rule need do nothing more under this rule with respect to his or her report.

(9) An attorney who does not reasonably believe that the issuer has made an appropriate response

within a reasonable time to the report or reports made pursuant to paragraph (b)(1), (b)(3), or (b)(4) of this rule shall explain his or her reasons therefor to the chief legal officer (or the equivalent thereof), the chief executive officer (or the equivalent thereof), and directors to whom the attorney reported the evidence of a material violation pursuant to paragraph (b)(1), (b)(3), or (b)(4) of this rule.

(10) An attorney formerly employed or retained by an issuer who has reported evidence of a material violation under this part and reasonably believes that he or she has been discharged for so doing may notify the issuer's board of directors or any committee thereof that he or she believes that he or she has been discharged for reporting evidence of a material violation under this rule.

(c) *Alternative Reporting Procedures for Attorneys Retained or Employed by an Issuer that has Established a Qualified Legal Compliance Committee.* (1) If an attorney, appearing and practicing before the Commission in the representation of an issuer, becomes aware of evidence of a material violation by the issuer or by any officer, director, employee, or agent of the issuer, the attorney may, as an alternative to the reporting requirements of paragraph (b) of this rule, report such evidence to a qualified legal compliance committee, if the issuer has previously formed such a committee. An attorney who reports evidence of a material violation to such a qualified legal compliance committee has satisfied his or her obligation to report such evidence and is not required to assess the issuer's response to the reported evidence of a material violation.

(2) A chief legal officer (or the equivalent thereof) may refer a report of evidence of a material violation to a previously established qualified legal compliance committee in lieu of causing an inquiry to be conducted under paragraph (b)(2) of this rule. The chief legal officer (or the equivalent thereof) shall inform the reporting attorney that the report has been referred to a qualified legal compliance committee. Thereafter, pursuant to the requirements under Rule 2(k), the qualified legal compliance committee shall be responsible for responding to the evidence of a material violation reported to it under this paragraph (c).

(d) *Issuer Confidences.* (1) Any report under this rule (or the contemporaneous record thereof) or any response thereto (or the contemporaneous record thereof) may be used by an attorney in connection with any investigation, proceeding, or litigation in which the attorney's compliance with this part is in issue.

(2) An attorney appearing and practicing before the Commission in the representation of an issuer may reveal to the Commission, without the issuer's consent, confidential information related to the representation to the extent the attorney reasonably believes necessary:

(i) To prevent the issuer from committing a material violation that is likely to cause substantial injury to the financial interest or property of the issuer or investors;

(ii) To prevent the issuer, in a Commission investigation or administrative proceeding from committing perjury, proscribed in 18 U.S.C. 1621; suborning perjury, proscribed in 18 U.S.C. 1622; or committing any act proscribed in 18 U.S.C. 1001 that is likely to perpetrate a fraud upon the Commission; or

(iii) To rectify the consequences of a material violation by the issuer that caused, or may cause, substantial injury to the financial interest or property of the issuer or investors in the furtherance of which the attorney's services were used.

Rule 4. Responsibilities of supervisory attorneys

(a) An attorney supervising or directing another attorney who is appearing and practicing before the Commission in the representation of an issuer is a supervisory attorney. An issuer's chief legal officer (or the equivalent thereof) is a supervisory attorney under this rule.

(b) A supervisory attorney shall make reasonable efforts to ensure that a subordinate attorney, as defined in Rule 5(a), that he or she supervises or directs conforms to this part. To the extent a subordinate attorney appears and practices before the Commission in the representation of an issuer, that subordinate attorney's supervisory attorneys also appear and practice before the Commission.

(c) A supervisory attorney is responsible for complying with the reporting requirements in Rule 3 when a subordinate attorney has reported to the supervisory attorney evidence of a material violation.

(d) A supervisory attorney who has received a report of evidence of a material violation from a subordinate attorney under Rule 3 may report such evidence to the issuer's qualified legal compliance committee if the issuer has duly formed such a committee.

Rule 5. Responsibility of a subordinate attorneys

(a) An attorney who appears and practices before the Commission in the representation of an issuer on a matter under the supervision or direction of another attorney (other than under the direct supervision or direction of the issuer's chief legal officer (or the equivalent thereof)) is a subordinate attorney.

(b) A subordinate attorney shall comply with this part notwithstanding that the subordinate attorney acted at the direction of or under the supervision of another person.

(c) A subordinate attorney complies with Rule 3 if the subordinate attorney reports to his or her supervising attorney under Rule 3(b) evidence of a material violation of which the subordinate attorney has become aware in appearing and practicing before the Commission.

(d) A subordinate attorney may take the steps permitted or required by Rule 3(b) or (c) if the subordinate attorney reasonably believes that a supervisory attorney to whom he or she has reported evidence of a material violation under Rule 3(b) has failed to comply with Rule 3.

Rule 6. Sanctions and discipline

(a) A violation of this part by any attorney appearing and practicing before the Commission in the representation of an issuer shall subject such attorney to the civil penalties and remedies for a violation of the federal securities laws available to the Commission in an action brought by the Commission thereunder.

(b) An attorney appearing and practicing before the Commission who violates any provision of this part is subject to the disciplinary authority of the Commission, regardless of whether the attorney may also be subject to discipline for the same conduct in a jurisdiction where the attorney is admitted or practices. An administrative disciplinary proceeding initiated by the Commission for violation of this part may result in an attorney being censured, or being temporarily or permanently denied the privilege of appearing or practicing before the Commission.

(c) An attorney who complies in good faith with the provisions of this part shall not be subject to discipline or otherwise liable under inconsistent standards imposed by any state or other United States jurisdiction where the attorney is admitted or practices.

(d) An attorney practicing outside the United States shall not be required to comply with the requirements of this part to the extent that such compliance is prohibited by applicable foreign law.

Rule 7. No private right of action

(a) Nothing in this part is intended to, or does, create a private right of action against any attorney, law firm, or issuer based upon compliance or noncompliance with its provisions.

(b) Authority to enforce compliance with this part is vested exclusively in the Commission.

I. SARBANES–OXLEY ACT OF 2002

15 U.S.C. § 7201 et seq.

(Selected Provisions)

Sec. Act	Tit.	U.S.C.	
1		7201 note	Short Title; Table of Contents
2		7201	Definitions
3		7202	Commission Rules and Enforcement
			TITLE I—PUBLIC COMPANY ACCOUNTING OVERSIGHT BOARD
101		7211	Establishment; Administrative Provisions
102		7212	Registration with the Board
103		7213	Auditing, Quality Control, and Independence Standards and Rules
104		7214	Inspections of Registered Public Accounting Firms
105		7215	Investigations and Disciplinary Proceedings
106		7216	Foreign Public Accounting Firms
107		7217	Commission Oversight of the Board
108		7218	Accounting Standards
109		7219	Funding
110		7220	Definitions
			TITLE II—AUDITOR INDEPENDENCE
201		7231	Services Outside the Scope of Practice of Auditors
202			Preapproval Requirements
203			Audit Partner Rotation
204			Auditor Reports to Audit Committees
205			Conforming Amendments
206			Conflicts of Interest
207		7232	Study of Mandatory Rotation of Registered Public Accounting Firms
208		7233	Commission Authority
209		7234	Considerations by Appropriate State Regulatory Authorities
			TITLE III—CORPORATE RESPONSIBILITY
302		7241	Corporate Responsibility for Financial Reports
303		7242	Improper Influence on Conduct of Audits
304		7243	Forfeiture of Certain Bonuses and Profits
306		7244	Insider Trades During Pension Fund Blackout Periods
307		7245	Rules of Professional Responsibility for Attorneys
308		7246	Fair Funds for Investors
			TITLE IV—ENHANCED FINANCIAL DISCLOSURES
401		7261	Disclosures in Periodic Reports
404		7262	Management Assessment of Internal Controls
405		7263	Exemption
406		7264	Code of Ethics for Senior Financial Officers
407		7265	Disclosure of Audit Committee Financial Expert
408		7266	Enhanced Review of Periodic Disclosures by Issuers
409		78m	Real Time Issuer Disclosures
			TITLE V—ANALYST CONFLICTS OF INTEREST
501	15	78o-6	Treatment of Securities Analysts by Registered Securities Associations and National Securities Exchanges

Sec.			
			TITLE VI—COMMISSION RESOURCES AND AUTHORITY
601	15	78kk	Authorization of Appropriations
602	15	78a *et seq.*	Appearance and Practice Before the Commission
603	15	78u(d)	Federal Court Authority to Impose Penny Stock Bars
604	15	78o	Qualifications of Associated Persons of Brokers and Dealers
			TITLE VII—STUDIES AND REPORTS
701	15	7201 note	GAO Study and Report Regarding Consolidation of Public Accounting Firms
702			Commission Study and Report Regarding Credit Rating Agencies
703			Study and Report on Violators and Violations
704			Study of Enforcement Actions
705			Study of Investment Banks
			TITLE VIII—CORPORATE AND CRIMINAL FRAUD ACCOUNTABILITY
801	18	1501 note	Short Title
802	18	1519	Criminal Penalties for Altering Documents
803	11	523(a)	Debts Nondischargeable if Incurred in Violation of Securities Fraud Laws
804	28	1658 note	Statute of Limitations for Securities Fraud
805	28	994 note	Review of Federal Sentencing Guidelines for Obstruction of Justice and Extensive Criminal Fraud
806	18	1514A	Protection for Employees of Publicly Traded Companies who Provide Evidence of Fraud
807	18	1348	Criminal Penalties for Defrauding Shareholders of Publicly Traded Companies
			TITLE IX—WHITE–COLLAR CRIME PENALTY ENHANCEMENTS
901	18	1341 note	Short Title
902	18	1348	Attempts and Conspiracies to Commit Criminal Fraud Offenses
903	18	1341, 1343	Criminal Penalties for Mail and Wire Fraud
904	29	1131	Criminal Penalties for Violations of the Employee Retirement Income Security Act of 1974
905	18	994(p)	Amendment to Sentencing Guidelines Relating to Certain White–Collar Offenses
906	18	1350	Corporate Responsibility for Financial Reports
			TITLE XI—CORPORATE FRAUD AND ACCOUNTABILITY
1101			Short Title
1102	18	1512	Tampering with a Record or Otherwise Impeding an Official Proceeding
1103	15	78u-3(c)	Temporary Freeze Authority for the Securities and Exchange Commission
1104	28	994(p)	Amendment to the Federal Sentencing Guidelines
1105	15	78u-3, 77h-1	Authority of the Commission to Prohibit Persons from Serving as Officers or Directors
1106	18	78ff(a)	Increased Criminal Penalties under Securities Exchange Act of 1934
1107	18	1513	Retaliation Against Informants

SARBANES–OXLEY ACT OF 2002

Short Title; Table of Contents

Sec. 1. (a) *Short Title.* This Act may be cited as the "Sarbanes–Oxley Act of 2002".

(b) [Table of Contents Omitted]

Definitions

Sec. 2. (a) *In General.* Except as otherwise specifically provided in this Act, in this Act, the following definitions shall apply:

(1) *Appropriate State Regulatory Authority.* The term "appropriate State regulatory authority" means the State agency or other authority responsible for the licensure or other regulation of the practice of accounting in the State or States having jurisdiction over a registered public accounting firm or associated person thereof, with respect to the matter in question.

(2) *Audit.* The term "audit" means an examination of the financial statements of any issuer by an independent public accounting firm in accordance with the rules of the Board or the Commission (or, for the period preceding the adoption of applicable rules of the Board under section 103 of this title, in accordance with then-applicable generally accepted auditing and related standards for such purposes), for the purpose of expressing an opinion on such statements.

(3) *Audit Committee.* The term "audit committee" means—

(A) a committee (or equivalent body) established by and amongst the board of directors of an issuer for the purpose of overseeing the accounting and financial reporting processes of the issuer and audits of the financial statements of the issuer; and

(B) if no such committee exists with respect to an issuer, the entire board of directors of the issuer.

(4) *Audit Report.* The term "audit report" means a document or other record—

(A) prepared following an audit performed for purposes of compliance by an issuer with the requirements of the securities laws; and

(B) in which a public accounting firm either—

(i) sets forth the opinion of that firm regarding a financial statement, report, or other document; or

(ii) asserts that no such opinion can be expressed.

(5) *Board.* The term "Board" means the Public Company Accounting Oversight Board established under section 101 of this title.

(6) *Commission.* The term "Commission" means the Securities and Exchange Commission.

(7) *Issuer.* The term "issuer" means an issuer (as defined in section 3 of the Securities Exchange Act of 1934), the securities of which are registered under section 12 of that Act, or that is required to file reports under section 15(d), or that files or has filed a registration statement that has not yet become effective under the Securities Act of 1933, and that it has not withdrawn.

(8) *Non-Audit Services.* The term "non-audit services" means any professional services provided to an issuer by a registered public accounting firm, other than those provided to an issuer in connection with an audit or a review of the financial statements of an issuer.

(9) *Person Associated with a Public Accounting Firm.*

(A) *In General.* The terms "person associated with a public accounting firm" (or with a "registered public accounting firm") and "associated person of a public accounting firm" (or of a "registered public accounting firm") mean any individual proprietor, partner, shareholder, principal, accountant, or other professional employee of a public accounting firm, or any other independent contractor or entity that, in connection with the preparation or issuance of any audit report—

(i) shares in the profits of, or receives compensation in any other form from, that firm; or

(ii) participates as agent or otherwise on behalf of such accounting firm in any activity of that firm.

(B) *Exemption Authority.* The Board may, by rule, exempt persons engaged only in ministerial tasks from the definition in subparagraph (A), to the extent that the Board determines that any such exemption is consistent with the purposes of this Act, the public interest, or the protection of investors.

(C) *Investigative and Enforcement Authority.* For purposes of sections 7202(c), 7211(c), 7215, and 7217(c) of this title and the rules of the Board and Commission issued thereunder, except to the extent specifically excepted by such rules, the terms defined in subparagraph (A) shall include any person associated, seeking to become associated, or formerly associated with a public accounting firm, except that—

(i) the authority to conduct an investigation of such person under section 7215(b) of this title shall apply only with respect to any act or practice, or omission to act, by the person while such person was associated or seeking to become associated with a registered public accounting firm; and

(ii) the authority to commence a disciplinary proceeding under section 7215(c)(1) of this title, or impose sanctions under section 7215(c)(4) of this title, against such person shall apply only with respect to—

(I) conduct occurring while such person was associated or seeking to become associated with a registered public accounting firm; or

(II) non-cooperation, as described in section 7215(b)(3) of this title, with respect to a demand in a Board investigation for testimony, documents, or other information relating to a period when such person was associated or seeking to become associated with a registered public accounting firm.

(10) *Professional Standards*. The term "professional standards" means—

(A) accounting principles that are—

(i) established by the standard setting body described in section 19(b) of the Securities Act of 1933, as amended by this Act, or prescribed by the Commission under section 19(a) of that Act or section 13(b) of the Securities Exchange Act of 1934; and

(ii) relevant to audit reports for particular issuers, or dealt with in the quality control system of a particular registered public accounting firm; and

(B) auditing standards, standards for attestation engagements, quality control policies and procedures, ethical and competency standards, and independence standards (including rules implementing title II) that the Board or the Commission determines—

(i) relate to the preparation or issuance of audit reports for issuers; and (ii) are established or adopted by the Board under section 103(a), or are promulgated as rules of the Commission.

(11) *Public Accounting Firm*. The term "public accounting firm" means—

(A) a proprietorship, partnership, incorporated association, corporation, limited liability company, limited liability partnership, or other legal entity that is engaged in the practice of public accounting or preparing or issuing audit reports; and

(B) to the extent so designated by the rules of the Board, any associated person of any entity described in subparagraph (A).

(12) *Registered Public Accounting Firm*. The term "registered public accounting firm" means a public accounting firm registered with the Board in accordance with this Act.

(13) *Rules of the Board*. The term "rules of the Board" means the bylaws and rules of the Board (as submitted to, and approved, modified, or amended by the Commission, in accordance with section 107), and those stated policies, practices, and interpretations of the Board that the Commission, by rule, may deem to be rules of the Board, as necessary or appropriate in the public interest or for the protection of investors.

(14) *Security*. The term "security" has the same meaning as in section 3(a) of the Securities Exchange Act of 1934.

(15) *Securities Laws*. The term "securities laws" means the provisions of law referred to in section 3(a)(47) of the Securities Exchange Act of 1934, as amended by this Act, and includes the rules, regulations, and orders issued by the Commission thereunder.

(16) *State*. The term "State" means any State of the United States, the District of Columbia, Puerto Rico, the Virgin Islands, or any other territory or possession of the United States.

(17) *Foreign Auditor Oversight Authority*. The term "foreign auditor oversight authority" means any governmental body or other entity empowered by a foreign government to conduct inspections of public accounting firms or otherwise to administer or enforce laws related to the regulation of public accounting firms.

Commission Rules and Enforcement

Sec. 3. (a) *Regulatory Action*. The Commission shall promulgate such rules and regulations, as may be necessary or appropriate in the public interest or for the protection of investors, and in furtherance of this Act.

(b) *Enforcement.*

(1) *In General.* A violation by any person of this Act, any rule or regulation of the Commission issued under this Act, or any rule of the Board shall be treated for all purposes in the same manner as a violation of the Securities Exchange Act of 1934 or the rules and regulations issued thereunder, consistent with the provisions of this Act, and any such person shall be subject to the same penalties, and to the same extent, as for a violation of that Act or such rules or regulations.

(2) to (4) [Omitted. Subsections amended sections 21, 21C(c)(2), and 12(i) of the Securities Exchange Act of 1934.]

(c) *Effect on Commission Authority.* Nothing in this Act or the rules of the Board shall be construed to impair or limit—

(1) the authority of the Commission to regulate the accounting profession, accounting firms, or persons associated with such firms for purposes of enforcement of the securities laws;

(2) the authority of the Commission to set standards for accounting or auditing practices or auditor independence, derived from other provisions of the securities laws or the rules or regulations thereunder, for purposes of the preparation and issuance of any audit report, or otherwise under applicable law; or

(3) the ability of the Commission to take, on the initiative of the Commission, legal, administrative, or disciplinary action against any registered public accounting firm or any associated person thereof.

TITLE I—PUBLIC COMPANY ACCOUNTING OVERSIGHT BOARD

Establishment; Administrative Provisions

Sec. 101. (a) *Establishment of Board.* There is established the Public Company Accounting Oversight Board, to oversee the audit of companies that are subject to the securities laws, and related matters, in order to protect the interests of investors and further the public interest in the preparation of informative, accurate, and independent audit reports. The Board shall be a body corporate, operate as a nonprofit corporation, and have succession until dissolved by an Act of Congress.

(b) *Status.* The Board shall not be an agency or establishment of the United States Government, and, except as otherwise provided in this Act, shall be subject to, and have all the powers conferred upon a nonprofit corporation by, the District of Columbia Nonprofit Corporation Act. No member or person employed by, or agent for, the Board shall be deemed to be an officer or employee of or agent for the Federal Government by reason of such service.

(c) *Duties of the Board.* The Board shall, subject to action by the Commission under section 107, and once a determination is made by the Commission under subsection (d) of this section—

(1) register public accounting firms that prepare audit reports for issuers, in accordance with section 102;

(2) establish or adopt, or both, by rule, auditing, quality control, ethics, independence, and other standards relating to the preparation of audit reports for issuers, brokers, and dealers, in accordance with section 103;

(3) conduct inspections of registered public accounting firms, in accordance with section 104 and the rules of the Board;

(4) conduct investigations and disciplinary proceedings concerning, and impose appropriate sanctions where justified upon, registered public accounting firms and associated persons of such firms, in accordance with section 105;

(5) perform such other duties or functions as the Board (or the Commission, by rule or order) determines are necessary or appropriate to promote high professional standards among, and improve the quality of audit services offered by, registered public accounting firms and associated persons thereof, or otherwise to carry out this Act, in order to protect investors, or to further the public interest;

(6) enforce compliance with this Act, the rules of the Board, professional standards, and the securities laws relating to the preparation and issuance of audit reports and the obligations and liabilities of accountants with respect thereto, by registered public accounting firms and associated persons thereof; and

(7) set the budget and manage the operations of the Board and the staff of the Board.

(d) *Commission Determination.* The members of the Board shall take such action (including hiring of staff, proposal of rules, and adoption of initial and transitional auditing and other professional standards) as may be necessary or appropriate to enable the Commission to determine, not later than 270 days after the date of enactment of this Act, that the Board is so organized and has the capacity to carry out the requirements of this title, and to enforce compliance with this title by registered public accounting firms and associated persons thereof. The Commission shall be responsible, prior to the appointment of the Board, for the planning for the establishment and administrative transition to the Board's operation.

(e) *Board Membership.*

(1) *Composition.* The Board shall have 5 members, appointed from among prominent individuals of integrity and reputation who have a demonstrated commitment to the interests of investors and the public, and an understanding of the responsibilities for and nature of the financial disclosures required of issuers, brokers, and dealers under the securities laws and the obligations of accountants with respect to the preparation and issuance of audit reports with respect to such disclosures.

(2) *Limitation.* Two members, and only 2 members, of the Board shall be or have been certified public accountants pursuant to the laws of 1 or more States, provided that, if 1 of those 2 members is the chairperson, he or she may not have been a practicing certified public accountant for at least 5 years prior to his or her appointment to the Board.

(3) *Full-Time Independent Service.* Each member of the Board shall serve on a full–time basis, and may not, concurrent with service on the Board, be employed by any other person or engage in any other professional or business activity. No member of the Board may share in any of the profits of, or receive payments from, a public accounting firm (or any other person, as determined by rule of the Commission), other than fixed continuing payments, subject to such conditions as the Commission may impose, under standard arrangements for the retirement of members of public accounting firms.

(4) *Appointment of Board Members.*

(A) *Initial Board.* Not later than 90 days after the date of enactment of this Act, the Commission, after consultation with the Chairman of the Board of Governors of the Federal Reserve System and the Secretary of the Treasury, shall appoint the chairperson and other initial members of the Board, and shall designate a term of service for each.

(B) *Vacancies.* A vacancy on the Board shall not affect the powers of the Board, but shall be filled in the same manner as provided for appointments under this section.

(5) *Term of Service.*

(A) *In General.* The term of service of each Board member shall be 5 years, and until a successor is appointed, except that—

(i) the terms of office of the initial Board members (other than the chairperson) shall expire in annual increments, 1 on each of the first 4 anniversaries of the initial date of appointment; and

(ii) any Board member appointed to fill a vacancy occurring before the expiration of the term for which the predecessor was appointed shall be appointed only for the remainder of that term.

(B) *Term Limitation.* No person may serve as a member of the Board, or as chairperson of the Board, for more than 2 terms, whether or not such terms of service are consecutive.

(6) *Removal from Office.* A member of the Board may be removed by the Commission from office, in accordance with section 107(d)(3), for good cause shown before the expiration of the term of that member.

(f) *Powers of the Board.* In addition to any authority granted to the Board otherwise in this Act, the Board shall have the power, subject to section 107—

(1) to sue and be sued, complain and defend, in its corporate name and through its own counsel, with the approval of the Commission, in any Federal, State, or other court;

(2) to conduct its operations and maintain offices, and to exercise all other rights and powers authorized by this Act, in any State, without regard to any qualification, licensing, or other provision of law in effect in such State (or a political subdivision thereof);

(3) to lease, purchase, accept gifts or donations of or otherwise acquire, improve, use, sell, exchange, or convey, all of or an interest in any property, wherever situated;

(4) to appoint such employees, accountants, attorneys, and other agents as may be necessary or appropriate, and to determine their qualifications,

define their duties, and fix their salaries or other compensation (at a level that is comparable to private sector self–regulatory, accounting, technical, supervisory, or other staff or management positions);

(5) to allocate, assess, and collect accounting support fees established pursuant to section 109, for the Board, and other fees and charges imposed under this title; and

(6) to enter into contracts, execute instruments, incur liabilities, and do any and all other acts and things necessary, appropriate, or incidental to the conduct of its operations and the exercise of its obligations, rights, and powers imposed or granted by this title.

(g) *Rules of the Board.* The rules of the Board shall, subject to the approval of the Commission—

(1) provide for the operation and administration of the Board, the exercise of its authority, and the performance of its responsibilities under this Act;

(2) permit, as the Board determines necessary or appropriate, delegation by the Board of any of its functions to an individual member or employee of the Board, or to a division of the Board, including functions with respect to hearing, determining, ordering, certifying, reporting, or otherwise acting as to any matter, except that—

(A) the Board shall retain a discretionary right to review any action pursuant to any such delegated function, upon its own motion;

(B) a person shall be entitled to a review by the Board with respect to any matter so delegated, and the decision of the Board upon such review shall be deemed to be the action of the Board for all purposes (including appeal or review thereof); and

(C) if the right to exercise a review described in subparagraph (A) is declined, or if no such review is sought within the time stated in the rules of the Board, then the action taken by the holder of such delegation shall for all purposes, including appeal or review thereof, be deemed to be the action of the Board;

(3) establish ethics rules and standards of conduct for Board members and staff, including a bar on practice before the Board (and the Commission, with respect to Board–related matters) of 1 year for former members of the Board, and appropriate periods (not to exceed 1 year) for former staff of the Board; and

(4) provide as otherwise required by this Act.

(h) *Annual Report to the Commission.* The Board shall submit an annual report (including its audited financial statements) to the Commission, and the Commission shall transmit a copy of that report to the Committee on Banking, Housing, and Urban Affairs of the Senate, and the Committee on Financial Services of the House of Representatives, not later than 30 days after the date of receipt of that report by the Commission.

Registration with the Board

Sec. 102. (a) *Mandatory Registration.* It shall be unlawful for any person that is not a registered public accounting firm to prepare or issue, or to participate in the preparation or issuance of, any audit report with respect to any issuer, broker, or dealer, broker, or dealer.

(b) *Applications for Registration.*

(1) *Form of Application.* A public accounting firm shall use such form as the Board may prescribe, by rule, to apply for registration under this section.

(2) *Contents of Applications.* Each public accounting firm shall submit, as part of its application for registration, in such detail as the Board shall specify—

(A) the names of all issuer, brokers, and dealers for which the firm prepared or issued audit reports during the immediately preceding calendar year, and for which the firm expects to prepare or issue audit reports during the current calendar year;

(B) the annual fees received by the firm from each such issuer, broker, or dealer for audit services, other accounting services, and non–audit services, respectively;

(C) such other current financial information for the most recently completed fiscal year of the firm as the Board may reasonably request;

(D) a statement of the quality control policies of the firm for its accounting and auditing practices;

(E) a list of all accountants associated with the firm who participate in or contribute to the preparation of audit reports, stating the license or certification number of each such person, as well as the State license numbers of the firm itself;

(F) information relating to criminal, civil, or administrative actions or disciplinary proceedings pending against the firm or any associated person of the firm in connection with any audit report;

(G) copies of any periodic or annual disclosure filed by an issuer, broker, or dealer with the Commission during the immediately preceding calendar year which discloses accounting disagreements between such issuer, broker, or dealer and the firm in connection with an audit report furnished or prepared by the firm for such issuer, broker, or dealer; and

(H) such other information as the rules of the Board or the Commission shall specify as necessary or appropriate in the public interest or for the protection of investors.

(3) *Consents.* Each application for registration under this subsection shall include—

(A) a consent executed by the public accounting firm to cooperation in and compliance with any request for testimony or the production of documents made by the Board in the furtherance of its authority and responsibilities under this title (and an agreement to secure and enforce similar consents from each of the associated persons of the public accounting firm as a condition of their continued employment by or other association with such firm); and

(B) a statement that such firm understands and agrees that cooperation and compliance, as described in the consent required by subparagraph (A), and the securing and enforcement of such consents from its associated persons, in accordance with the rules of the Board, shall be a condition to the continuing effectiveness of the registration of the firm with the Board.

(c) *Action on Applications.*

(1) *Timing.* The Board shall approve a completed application for registration not later than 45 days after the date of receipt of the application, in accordance with the rules of the Board, unless the Board, prior to such date, issues a written notice of disapproval to, or requests more information from, the prospective registrant.

(2) *Treatment.* A written notice of disapproval of a completed application under paragraph (1) for registration shall be treated as a disciplinary sanction for purposes of sections 105(d) and 107(c).

(d) *Periodic Reports.* Each registered public accounting firm shall submit an annual report to the Board, and may be required to report more frequently, as necessary to update the information contained in its application for registration under this section, and to provide to the Board such additional information as the Board or the Commission may specify, in accordance with subsection (b)(2) of this section.

(e) *Public Availability.* Registration applications and annual reports required by this subsection, or such portions of such applications or reports as may be designated under rules of the Board, shall be made available for public inspection, subject to rules of the Board or the Commission, and to applicable laws relating to the confidentiality of proprietary, personal, or other information contained in such applications or reports, provided that, in all events, the Board shall protect from public disclosure information reasonably identified by the subject accounting firm as proprietary information.

(f) *Registration and Annual Fees.* The Board shall assess and collect a registration fee and an annual fee from each registered public accounting firm, in amounts that are sufficient to recover the costs of processing and reviewing applications and annual reports.

Auditing, Quality Control, and Independence Standards and Rules

Sec. 103. (a) *Auditing, Quality Control, and Ethics Standards.*

(1) *In General.* The Board shall, by rule, establish, including, to the extent it determines appropriate, through adoption of standards proposed by 1 or more professional groups of accountants designated pursuant to paragraph (3)(A) or advisory groups convened pursuant to paragraph (4), and amend or otherwise modify or alter, such auditing and related attestation standards, such quality control standards, such ethics standards, and such independence standards to be used by registered public accounting firms in the preparation and issuance of audit reports, as required by this Act or the rules of the Commission, or as may be necessary or appropriate in the public interest or for the protection of investors.

(2) *Rule Requirements.* In carrying out paragraph (1), the Board—

(A) shall include in the auditing standards that it adopts, requirements that each registered public accounting firm shall—

(i) prepare, and maintain for a period of not less than 7 years, audit work papers, and other information related to any audit report, in sufficient detail to support the conclusions reached in such report;

(ii) provide a concurring or second partner review and approval of such audit report (and other related information), and concurring approval in its issuance, by a qualified person (as prescribed by the Board) associated with the public accounting firm, other than the person in charge of the audit, or by an independent reviewer (as prescribed by the Board); and

(iii) in each audit report for an issuer, describe the scope of the auditor's testing of the internal control structure and procedures of the issuer, required by section 404(b), and present (in such report or in a separate report)—

(I) the findings of the auditor from such testing;

(II) an evaluation of whether such internal control structure and procedures—

(aa) include maintenance of records that in reasonable detail accurately and fairly reflect the transactions and dispositions of the assets of the issuer;

(bb) provide reasonable assurance that transactions are recorded as necessary to permit preparation of financial statements in accordance with generally accepted accounting principles, and that receipts and expenditures of the issuer are being made only in accordance with authorizations of management and directors of the issuer; and

(III) a description, at a minimum, of material weaknesses in such internal controls, and of any material noncompliance found on the basis of such testing.

(B) shall include, in the quality control standards that it adopts with respect to the issuance of audit reports, requirements for every registered public accounting firm relating to—

(i) monitoring of professional ethics and independence from issuers, brokers, and dealers on behalf of which the firm issues audit reports;

(ii) consultation within such firm on accounting and auditing questions;

(iii) supervision of audit work;

(iv) hiring, professional development, and advancement of personnel;

(v) the acceptance and continuation of engagements;

(vi) internal inspection; and

(vii) such other requirements as the Board may prescribe, subject to subsection (a)(1).

(3) *Authority to Adopt Other Standards.*

(A) *In General.* In carrying out this subsection, the Board—

(i) may adopt as its rules, subject to the terms of section 107, any portion of any statement of auditing standards or other professional standards that the Board determines satisfy the requirements of paragraph (1), and that were proposed by 1 or more professional groups of accountants that shall be designated or recognized by the Board, by rule, for such purpose, pursuant to this paragraph or 1 or more advisory groups convened pursuant to paragraph (4); and

(ii) notwithstanding clause (i), shall retain full authority to modify, supplement, revise, or subsequently amend, modify, or repeal, in whole or in part, any portion of any statement described in clause (i).

(B) *Initial and Transitional Standards.* The Board shall adopt standards described in subparagraph (A)(i) as initial or transitional standards, to the extent the Board determines necessary, prior to a determination of the Commission under section 101(d), and such standards shall be separately approved by the Commission at the time of that determination, without regard to the procedures required by section 107 that otherwise would apply to the approval of rules of the Board.

(C) *Transition Period for Emerging Growth Companies.* Any rules of the Board requiring mandatory audit firm rotation or a supplement to the auditor's report in which the auditor would be required to provide additional information about the audit and the financial statements of the issuer (auditor discussion and analysis) shall not apply to an audit of an emerging growth company, as defined in section 3 of the

Securities Exchange Act of 1934. Any additional rules adopted by the Board after the date of enactment of this subparagraph shall not apply to an audit of any emerging growth company, unless the Commission determines that the application of such additional requirements is necessary or appropriate in the public interest, after considering the protection of investors and whether the action will promote efficiency, competition, and capital formation.

(4) *Advisory Groups*. The Board shall convene, or authorize its staff to convene, such expert advisory groups as may be appropriate, which may include practicing accountants and other experts, as well as representatives of other interested groups, subject to such rules as the Board may prescribe to prevent conflicts of interest, to make recommendations concerning the content (including proposed drafts) of auditing, quality control, ethics, independence, or other standards required to be established under this section.

(b) *Independence Standards and Rules*. The Board shall establish such rules as may be necessary or appropriate in the public interest or for the protection of investors, to implement, or as authorized under, title II of this Act.

(c) *Cooperation with Designated Professional Groups of Accountants and Advisory Groups*.

(1) *In General*. The Board shall cooperate on an ongoing basis with professional groups of accountants designated under subsection (a)(3)(A) and advisory groups convened under subsection (a)(4) in the examination of the need for changes in any standards subject to its authority under subsection (a), recommend issues for inclusion on the agendas of such designated professional groups of accountants or advisory groups, and take such other steps as it deems appropriate to increase the effectiveness of the standard setting process.

(2) *Board Responses*. The Board shall respond in a timely fashion to requests from designated professional groups of accountants and advisory groups referred to in paragraph (1) for any changes in standards over which the Board has authority.

(d) *Evaluation of Standard Setting Process*. The Board shall include in the annual report required by section 101(h) the results of its standard setting responsibilities during the period to which the report relates, including a discussion of the work of the Board with any designated professional groups of accountants and advisory groups described in paragraphs (3)(A) and (4) of subsection (a), and its pending issues agenda for future standard setting projects.

Inspections of Registered Public Accounting Firms

Sec. 104. (a)(1) *Inspections Generally*. The Board shall conduct a continuing program of inspections to assess the degree of compliance of each registered public accounting firm and associated persons of that firm with this Act, the rules of the Board, the rules of the Commission, or professional standards, in connection with its performance of audits, issuance of audit reports, and related matters involving issuers.

(2) *Inspections of Audit Reports for Brokers and Dealers*.

(A) The Board may, by rule, conduct and require a program of inspection in accordance with paragraph (1), on a basis to be determined by the Board, of registered public accounting firms that provide one or more audit reports for a broker or dealer. The Board, in establishing such a program, may allow for differentiation among classes of brokers and dealers, as appropriate.

(B) If the Board determines to establish a program of inspection pursuant to subparagraph (A), the Board shall consider in establishing any inspection schedules whether differing schedules would be appropriate with respect to registered public accounting firms that issue audit reports only for one or more brokers or dealers that do not receive, handle, or hold customer securities or cash or are not a member of the Securities Investor Protection Corporation.

(C) Any rules of the Board pursuant to this paragraph shall be subject to prior approval by the Commission pursuant to section 107(b) before the rules become effective, including an opportunity for public notice and comment.

(D) Notwithstanding anything to the contrary in section 102 of this Act, a public accounting firm shall not be required to register with the Board if the public accounting firm is exempt from the inspection program which may be established by the Board under subparagraph (A).

(b) *Inspection Frequency*.

(1) *In General*. Subject to paragraph (2), inspections required by this section shall be conducted—

(A) annually with respect to each registered public accounting firm that regularly provides audit reports for more than 100 issuers; and

(B) not less frequently than once every 3 years with respect to each registered public accounting firm that regularly provides audit reports for 100 or fewer issuers.

(2) *Adjustments to Schedules.* The Board may, by rule, adjust the inspection schedules set under paragraph (1) if the Board finds that different inspection schedules are consistent with the purposes of this Act, the public interest, and the protection of investors. The Board may conduct special inspections at the request of the Commission or upon its own motion.

(c) *Procedures.* The Board shall, in each inspection under this section, and in accordance with its rules for such inspections—

(1) identify any act or practice or omission to act by the registered public accounting firm, or by any associated person thereof, revealed by such inspection that may be in violation of this Act, the rules of the Board, the rules of the Commission, the firm's own quality control policies, or professional standards;

(2) report any such act, practice, or omission, if appropriate, to the Commission and each appropriate State regulatory authority; and

(3) begin a formal investigation or take disciplinary action, if appropriate, with respect to any such violation, in accordance with this Act and the rules of the Board.

(d) *Conduct of Inspections.* In conducting an inspection of a registered public accounting firm under this section, the Board shall—

(1) inspect and review selected audit and review engagements of the firm (which may include audit engagements that are the subject of ongoing litigation or other controversy between the firm and 1 or more third parties), performed at various offices and by various associated persons of the firm, as selected by the Board;

(2) evaluate the sufficiency of the quality control system of the firm, and the manner of the documentation and communication of that system by the firm; and

(3) perform such other testing of the audit, supervisory, and quality control procedures of the firm as are necessary or appropriate in light of the purpose of the inspection and the responsibilities of the Board.

(e) *Record Retention.* The rules of the Board may require the retention by registered public accounting firms for inspection purposes of records whose retention is not otherwise required by section 103 or the rules issued thereunder.

(f) *Procedures for Review.* The rules of the Board shall provide a procedure for the review of and response to a draft inspection report by the registered public accounting firm under inspection. The Board shall take such action with respect to such response as it considers appropriate (including revising the draft report or continuing or supplementing its inspection activities before issuing a final report), but the text of any such response, appropriately redacted to protect information reasonably identified by the accounting firm as confidential, shall be attached to and made part of the inspection report.

(g) *Report.* A written report of the findings of the Board for each inspection under this section, subject to subsection (h), shall be—

(1) transmitted, in appropriate detail, to the Commission and each appropriate State regulatory authority, accompanied by any letter or comments by the Board or the inspector, and any letter of response from the registered public accounting firm; and

(2) made available in appropriate detail to the public (subject to section 105(b)(5)(A), and to the protection of such confidential and proprietary information as the Board may determine to be appropriate, or as may be required by law), except that no portions of the inspection report that deal with criticisms of or potential defects in the quality control systems of the firm under inspection shall be made public if those criticisms or defects are addressed by the firm, to the satisfaction of the Board, not later than 12 months after the date of the inspection report.

(h) *Interim Commission Review.*

(1) *Reviewable Matters.* A registered public accounting firm may seek review by the Commission, pursuant to such rules as the Commission shall promulgate, if the firm—

(A) has provided the Board with a response, pursuant to rules issued by the Board under subsection (f), to the substance of particular items in a draft inspection report, and disagrees with the assessments contained in any final report prepared by the Board following such response; or

(B) disagrees with the determination of the Board that criticisms or defects identified in an inspection report have not been addressed to the satisfaction of the Board within 12 months of the date of the inspection report, for purposes of subsection (g)(2).

(2) *Treatment of Review.* Any decision of the Commission with respect to a review under paragraph (1) shall not be reviewable under section 25 of the Securities Exchange Act of 1934, or deemed to be "final agency action" for purposes of section 704 of title 5, United States Code.

(3) *Timing.* Review under paragraph (1) may be sought during the 30–day period following the date of the event giving rise to the review under subparagraph (A) or (B) of paragraph (1).

Investigations and Disciplinary Proceedings

Sec. 105. (a) *In General.* The Board shall establish, by rule, subject to the requirements of this section, fair procedures for the investigation and disciplining of registered public accounting firms and associated persons of such firms.

(b) *Investigations.*

(1) *Authority.* In accordance with the rules of the Board, the Board may conduct an investigation of any act or practice, or omission to act, by a registered public accounting firm, any associated person of such firm, or both, that may violate any provision of this Act, the rules of the Board, the provisions of the securities laws relating to the preparation and issuance of audit reports and the obligations and liabilities of accountants with respect thereto, including the rules of the Commission issued under this Act, or professional standards, regardless of how the act, practice, or omission is brought to the attention of the Board.

(2) *Testimony and Document Production.* In addition to such other actions as the Board determines to be necessary or appropriate, the rules of the Board may—

(A) require the testimony of the firm or of any person associated with a registered public accounting firm, with respect to any matter that the Board considers relevant or material to an investigation;

(B) require the production of audit work papers and any other document or information in the possession of a registered public accounting firm or any associated person thereof, wherever domiciled, that the Board considers relevant or material to the investigation, and may inspect the books and records of such firm or associated person to verify the accuracy of any documents or information supplied;

(C) request the testimony of, and production of any document in the possession of, any other person, including any client of a registered public accounting firm that the Board considers relevant or material to an investigation under this section, with appropriate notice, subject to the needs of the investigation, as permitted under the rules of the Board; and

(D) provide for procedures to seek issuance by the Commission, in a manner established by the Commission, of a subpoena to require the testimony of, and production of any document in the possession of, any person, including any client of a registered public accounting firm, that the Board considers relevant or material to an investigation under this section.

(3) *Noncooperation with Investigations.*

(A) *In General.* If a registered public accounting firm or any associated person thereof refuses to testify, produce documents, or otherwise cooperate with the Board in connection with an investigation under this section, the Board may—

(i) suspend or bar such person from being associated with a registered public accounting firm, or require the registered public accounting firm to end such association;

(ii) suspend or revoke the registration of the public accounting firm; and

(iii) invoke such other lesser sanctions as the Board considers appropriate, and as specified by rule of the Board.

(B) *Procedure.* Any action taken by the Board under this paragraph shall be subject to the terms of section 107(c).

(4) *Coordination and Referral of Investigations.*

(A) *Coordination.* The Board shall notify the Commission of any pending Board investigation involving a potential violation of the securities laws, and thereafter coordinate its work with the work of the Commission's Division of Enforcement, as necessary to protect an ongoing Commission investigation.

(B) *Referral.* The Board may refer an investigation under this section—

(i) to the Commission;

(ii) to any other Federal functional regulator (as defined in section 509 of the Gramm–Leach–Bliley Act), in the case of an investigation that concerns an audit report for an institution that is subject to the jurisdiction of such regulator; and

(iii) to any other Federal functional regulator (as defined in section 509 of the Gramm–Leach–Bliley Act), in the case of an investigation that concerns an audit report for an institution that is subject to the jurisdiction of such regulator; and

(iv) at the direction of the Commission, to—

(I) the Attorney General of the United States;

(II) the attorney general of 1 or more States; and

(III) the appropriate State regulatory authority.

(5) *Use of Documents.*

(A) *Confidentiality.* Except as provided in subparagraphs (B) and (C), all documents and information prepared or received by or specifically for the Board, and deliberations of the Board and its employees and agents, in connection with an inspection under section 104 or with an investigation under this section, shall be confidential and privileged as an evidentiary matter (and shall not be subject to civil discovery or other legal process) in any proceeding in any Federal or State court or administrative agency, and shall be exempt from disclosure, in the hands of an agency or establishment of the Federal Government, under the Freedom of Information Act, or otherwise, unless and until presented in connection with a public proceeding or released in accordance with subsection (c).

(B) *Availability to Government Agencies.* Without the loss of its status as confidential and privileged in the hands of the Board, all information referred to in subparagraph (A) may—

(i) be made available to the Commission; and

(ii) in the discretion of the Board, when determined by the Board to be necessary to accomplish the purposes of this Act or to protect investors, be made available to—

(I) the Attorney General of the United States;

(II) the appropriate Federal functional regulator (as defined in section 509 of the Gramm–Leach–Bliley Act), other than the Commission and the Director of the Federal Housing Finance Agency, with respect to an audit report for an institution subject to the jurisdiction of such regulator;

(III) State attorneys general in connection with any criminal investigation;

(IV) any appropriate State regulatory authority, each of which shall maintain such information as confidential and privileged; and

(V) a self–regulatory organization, with respect to an audit report for a broker or dealer that is under the jurisdiction of such self–regulatory organization, each of which shall maintain such information as confidential and privileged.

(C) *Availability to Foreign Oversight Authorities.* Without the loss of its status as confidential and privileged in the hands of the Board, all information referred to in subparagraph (A) that relates to a public accounting firm that a foreign government has empowered a foreign auditor oversight authority to inspect or otherwise enforce laws with respect to, may, at the discretion of the Board, be made available to the foreign auditor oversight authority, if—

(i) the Board finds that it is necessary to accomplish the purposes of this Act or to protect investors;

(ii) the foreign auditor oversight authority provides—

(I) such assurances of confidentiality as the Board may request;

(II) a description of the applicable information systems and controls of the foreign auditor oversight authority; and

(III) a description of the laws and regulations of the foreign government of the foreign auditor oversight authority that are relevant to information access; and

(iii) the Board determines that it is appropriate to share such information.

(6) *Immunity*. Any employee of the Board engaged in carrying out an investigation under this Act shall be immune from any civil liability arising out of such investigation in the same manner and to the same extent as an employee of the Federal Government in similar circumstances.

(c) *Disciplinary Procedures*.

(1) *Notification; Recordkeeping*. The rules of the Board shall provide that in any proceeding by the Board to determine whether a registered public accounting firm, or an associated person thereof, should be disciplined, the Board shall—

(A) bring specific charges with respect to the firm or associated person;

(B) notify such firm or associated person of, and provide to the firm or associated person an opportunity to defend against, such charges; and

(C) keep a record of the proceedings.

(2) *Public Hearings*. Hearings under this section shall not be public, unless otherwise ordered by the Board for good cause shown, with the consent of the parties to such hearing.

(3) *Supporting Statement*. A determination by the Board to impose a sanction under this subsection shall be supported by a statement setting forth—

(A) each act or practice in which the registered public accounting firm, or associated person, has engaged (or omitted to engage), or that forms a basis for all or a part of such sanction;

(B) the specific provision of this Act, the securities laws, the rules of the Board, or professional standards which the Board determines has been violated; and (C) the sanction imposed, including a justification for that sanction.

(4) *Sanctions*. If the Board finds, based on all of the facts and circumstances, that a registered public accounting firm or associated person thereof has engaged in any act or practice, or omitted to act, in violation of this Act, the rules of the Board, the provisions of the securities laws relating to the preparation and issuance of audit reports and the obligations and liabilities of accountants with respect thereto, including the rules of the Commission issued under this Act, or professional standards, the Board may impose such disciplinary or remedial sanctions as it determines appropriate, subject to applicable limitations under paragraph (5), including—

(A) temporary suspension or permanent revocation of registration under this title;

(B) temporary or permanent suspension or bar of a person from further association with any registered public accounting firm;

(C) temporary or permanent limitation on the activities, functions, or operations of such firm or person (other than in connection with required additional professional education or training);

(D) a civil money penalty for each such violation, in an amount equal to—

(i) not more than $100,000 for a natural person or $2,000,000 for any other person; and

(ii) in any case to which paragraph (5) applies, not more than $750,000 for a natural person or $15,000,000 for any other person;

(E) censure;

(F) required additional professional education or training; or

(G) any other appropriate sanction provided for in the rules of the Board.

(5) *Intentional or Other Knowing Conduct*. The sanctions and penalties described in subparagraphs (A) through (C) and (D)(ii) of paragraph (4) shall only apply to—

(A) intentional or knowing conduct, including reckless conduct, that results in violation of the applicable statutory, regulatory, or professional standard; or

(B) repeated instances of negligent conduct, each resulting in a violation of the applicable statutory, regulatory, or professional standard.

(6) *Failure to Supervise*.

(A) *In General*. The Board may impose sanctions under this section on a registered accounting firm or upon any person who is, or at the time of the alleged failure reasonably to supervise was, a supervisory person of such firm, if the Board finds that—

(i) the firm has failed reasonably to supervise an associated person, either as required by the rules of the Board relating to auditing or quality control standards, or otherwise, with a view to preventing violations of this Act, the rules of the Board, the provisions of the securities laws relating to the preparation and issuance of audit reports and the obligations and liabilities of accountants with respect thereto, including the rules of the Commission under this Act, or professional standards; and

(ii) such associated person commits a violation of this Act, or any of such rules, laws, or standards.

(B) *Rule of Construction.* No current or former supervisory person of a registered public accounting firm shall be deemed to have failed reasonably to supervise any associated person for purposes of subparagraph (A), if—

(i) there have been established in and for that firm procedures, and a system for applying such procedures, that comply with applicable rules of the Board and that would reasonably be expected to prevent and detect any such violation by such associated person; and

(ii) such person has reasonably discharged the duties and obligations incumbent upon that person by reason of such procedures and system, and had no reasonable cause to believe that such procedures and system were not being complied with.

(7) *Effect of Suspension.*

(A) *Association with a Public Accounting Firm.* It shall be unlawful for any person that is suspended or barred from being associated with a registered public accounting firm under this subsection willfully to become or remain associated with any registered public accounting firm, or for any registered public accounting firm that knew, or, in the exercise of reasonable care should have known, of the suspension or bar, to permit such an association, without the consent of the Board or the Commission.

(B) *Association with an Issuer, Broker, or Dealer.* It shall be unlawful for any person that is suspended or barred from being associated with a registered public accounting firm under this subsection willfully to become or remain associated with any issuer in an accountancy or a financial management capacity, and for any issuer, broker, or dealer that knew, or in the exercise of reasonable care should have known, of such suspension or bar, to permit such an association, without the consent of the Board or the Commission.

(d) *Reporting of Sanctions.*

(1) *Recipients.* If the Board imposes a disciplinary sanction, in accordance with this section, the Board shall report the sanction to—

(A) the Commission;

(B) any appropriate State regulatory authority or any foreign accountancy licensing board with which such firm or person is licensed or certified; and

(C) the public (once any stay on the imposition of such sanction has been lifted).

(2) *Contents.* The information reported under paragraph (1) shall include—

(A) the name of the sanctioned person;

(B) a description of the sanction and the basis for its imposition; and

(C) such other information as the Board deems appropriate.

(e) *Stay of Sanctions.*

(1) *In General.* Application to the Commission for review, or the institution by the Commission of review, of any disciplinary action of the Board shall operate as a stay of any such disciplinary action, unless and until the Commission orders (summarily or after notice and opportunity for hearing on the question of a stay, which hearing may consist solely of the submission of affidavits or presentation of oral arguments) that no such stay shall continue to operate.

(2) *Expedited Procedures.* The Commission shall establish for appropriate cases an expedited procedure for consideration and determination of the question of the duration of a stay pending review of any disciplinary action of the Board under this subsection.

Foreign Public Accounting Firms

Sec. 106. (a) *Applicability to Certain Foreign Firms.*

(1) *In General.* Any foreign public accounting firm that prepares or furnishes an audit report with respect to any issuer, broker, or dealer, shall be subject to this Act and the rules of the Board and the Commission issued under this Act, in the same manner and to the same extent as a public accounting firm that is organized and operates under the laws of the United States or any State, except that registration pursuant to section 102 shall not by itself provide a basis for subjecting such a foreign public accounting firm to the juris-

diction of the Federal or State courts, other than with respect to controversies between such firms and the Board.

(2) *Board Authority*. The Board may, by rule, determine that a foreign public accounting firm (or a class of such firms) that does not issue audit reports nonetheless plays such a substantial role in the preparation and furnishing of such reports for particular issuers, brokers, or dealers, that it is necessary or appropriate, in light of the purposes of this Act and in the public interest or for the protection of investors, that such firm (or class of firms) should be treated as a public accounting firm (or firms) for purposes of registration under, and oversight by the Board in accordance with, this subchapter.

(b) *Production of Documents*.

(1) *Production by Foreign Firms*. If a foreign public accounting firm performs material services upon which a registered public accounting firm relies in the conduct of an audit or interim review, issues an audit report, performs audit work, or conducts interim reviews, the foreign public accounting firm shall—

(A) produce the audit work papers of the foreign public accounting firm and all other documents of the firm related to any such audit work or interim review to the Commission or the Board, upon request of the Commission or the Board; and

(B) be subject to the jurisdiction of the courts of the United States for purposes of enforcement of any request for such documents.

(2) *Other Production*. Any registered public accounting firm that relies, in whole or in part, on the work of a foreign public accounting firm in issuing an audit report, performing audit work, or conducting an interim review, shall—

(A) produce the audit work papers of the foreign public accounting firm and all other documents related to any such work in response to a request for production by the Commission or the Board; and

(B) secure the agreement of any foreign public accounting firm to such production, as a condition of the reliance by the registered public accounting firm on the work of that foreign public accounting firm.

(c) *Exemption Authority*. The Commission, and the Board, subject to the approval of the Commission, may, by rule, regulation, or order, and as the Commission (or Board) determines necessary or appropriate in the public interest or for the protection of investors, either unconditionally or upon specified terms and conditions exempt any foreign public accounting firm, or any class of such firms, from any provision of this Act or the rules of the Board or the Commission issued under this Act.

(d) *Service of Requests or Process*.

(1) *In General*. Any foreign public accounting firm that performs work for a domestic registered public accounting firm shall furnish to the domestic registered public accounting firm a written irrevocable consent and power of attorney that designates the domestic registered public accounting firm as an agent upon whom may be served any request by the Commission or the Board under this section or upon whom may be served any process, pleadings, or other papers in any action brought to enforce this section.

(2) *Specific Audit Work*. Any foreign public accounting firm that performs material services upon which a registered public accounting firm relies in the conduct of an audit or interim review, issues an audit report, performs audit work, or, performs interim reviews, shall designate to the Commission or the Board an agent in the United States upon whom may be served any request by the Commission or the Board under this section or upon whom may be served any process, pleading, or other papers in any action brought to enforce this section.

(e) *Sanctions*. A willful refusal to comply, in whole in or in part, with any request by the Commission or the Board under this section, shall be deemed a violation of this Act.

(f) *Other Means of Satisfying Production Obligations*. Notwithstanding any other provisions of this section, the staff of the Commission or the Board may allow a foreign public accounting firm that is subject to this section to meet production obligations under this section through alternate means, such as through foreign counterparts of the Commission or the Board.

(g) *Definition*. In this section, the term "foreign public accounting firm" means a public accounting firm that is organized and operates under the laws of a foreign government or political subdivision thereof.

Commission Oversight of the Board

Sec. 107. (a) *General Oversight Responsibility.* The Commission shall have oversight and enforcement authority over the Board, as provided in this Act. The provisions of section 17(a)(1) of the Securities Exchange Act of 1934, and of section 17(b)(1) of the Securities Exchange Act of 1934 shall apply to the Board as fully as if the Board were a "registered securities association" for purposes of those sections 17(a)(1) and 17(b)(1).

(b) *Rules of the Board.*

(1) *Definition.* In this section, the term "proposed rule" means any proposed rule of the Board, and any modification of any such rule.

(2) *Prior Approval Required.* No rule of the Board shall become effective without prior approval of the Commission in accordance with this section, other than as provided in section 103(a)(3)(B) with respect to initial or transitional standards.

(3) *Approval Criteria.* The Commission shall approve a proposed rule, if it finds that the rule is consistent with the requirements of this Act and the securities laws, or is necessary or appropriate in the public interest or for the protection of investors.

(4) *Proposed Rule Procedures.* The provisions of paragraphs (1) through (3) of section 19(b) of the Securities Exchange Act of 1934 shall govern the proposed rules of the Board, as fully as if the Board were a "registered securities association" for purposes of that section 19(b), except that, for purposes of this paragraph—

(A) the phrase "consistent with the requirements of this title and the rules and regulations thereunder applicable to such organization" in section 19(b)(2) of that Act shall be deemed to read "consistent with the requirements of title I of the Sarbanes–Oxley Act of 2002, and the rules and regulations issued thereunder applicable to such organization, or as necessary or appropriate in the public interest or for the protection of investors"; and

(B) the phrase "otherwise in furtherance of the purposes of this title" in section 19(b)(3)(C) of that Act shall be deemed to read "otherwise in furtherance of the purposes of title I of the Sarbanes–Oxley Act of 2002".

(5) *Commission Authority to Amend Rules of the Board.* The provisions of section 19(c) of the Securities Exchange Act of 1934 shall govern the abrogation, deletion, or addition to portions of the rules of the Board by the Commission as fully as if the Board were a "registered securities association" for purposes of that section 19(c), except that the phrase "to conform its rules to the requirements of this title and the rules and regulations thereunder applicable to such organization, or otherwise in furtherance of the purposes of this title" in section 19(c) of that Act shall, for purposes of this paragraph, be deemed to read "to assure the fair administration of the Public Company Accounting Oversight Board, conform the rules promulgated by that Board to the requirements of title I of the Sarbanes–Oxley Act of 2002, or otherwise further the purposes of that Act, the securities laws, and the rules and regulations thereunder applicable to that Board".

(c) *Commission Review of Disciplinary Action Taken by the Board.*

(1) *Notice of Sanction.* The Board shall promptly file notice with the Commission of any final sanction on any registered public accounting firm or on any associated person thereof, in such form and containing such information as the Commission, by rule, may prescribe.

(2) *Review of Sanctions.* The provisions of sections 19(d)(2) and 19(e)(1) of the Securities Exchange Act of 1934 shall govern the review by the Commission of final disciplinary sanctions imposed by the Board (including sanctions imposed under section 105(b)(3) for noncooperation in an investigation of the Board), as fully as if the Board were a self-regulatory organization and the Commission were the appropriate regulatory agency for such organization for purposes of those sections 19(d)(2) and 19(e)(1), except that,for purposes of this paragraph—

(A) section 105(e) of this Act (rather than that section 19(d)(2)) shall govern the extent to which application for, or institution by the Commission on its own motion of, review of any disciplinary action of the Board operates as a stay of such action;

(B) references in that section 19(e)(1) to "members" of such an organization shall be deemed to be references to registered public accounting firms;

(C) the phrase "consistent with the purposes of this title" in that section 19(e)(1) shall be deemed to read "consistent with the purposes of this title and title I of the Sarbanes–Oxley Act of 2002";

(D) references to rules of the Municipal Securities Rulemaking Board in that section 19(e)(1) shall not apply; and

(E) the reference to section 19(e)(2) of the Securities Exchange Act of 1934 shall refer instead to section 107(c)(3) of this Act.

(3) *Commission Modification Authority*. The Commission may enhance, modify, cancel, reduce, or require the remission of a sanction imposed by the Board upon a registered public accounting firm or associated person thereof, if the Commission, having due regard for the public interest and the protection of investors, finds, after a proceeding in accordance with this subsection, that the sanction—

(A) is not necessary or appropriate in furtherance of this Act or the securities laws; or

(B) is excessive, oppressive, inadequate, or otherwise not appropriate to the finding or the basis on which the sanction was imposed.

(d) *Censure of the Board; Other Sanctions*.

(1) *Rescission of Board Authority*. The Commission, by rule, consistent with the public interest, the protection of investors, and the other purposes of this Act and the securities laws, may relieve the Board of any responsibility to enforce compliance with any provision of this Act, the securities laws, the rules of the Board, or professional standards.

(2) *Censure of the Board; Limitations*. The Commission may, by order, as it determines necessary or appropriate in the public interest, for the protection of investors, or otherwise in furtherance of the purposes of this Act or the securities laws, censure or impose limitations upon the activities, functions, and operations of the Board, if the Commission finds, on the record, after notice and opportunity for a hearing, that the Board—

(A) has violated or is unable to comply with any provision of this Act, the rules of the Board, or the securities laws; or

(B) without reasonable justification or excuse, has failed to enforce compliance with any such provision or rule, or any professional standard by a registered public accounting firm or an associated person thereof.

(3) *Censure of Board Members; Removal from Office*. The Commission may, as necessary or appropriate in the public interest, for the protection of investors, or otherwise in furtherance of the purposes of this Act or the securities laws, remove from office or censure any person who is, or at the time of the alleged misconduct was, a member of the Board, if the Commission finds, on the record, after notice and opportunity for a hearing, that such member—

(A) has willfully violated any provision of this Act, the rules of the Board, or the securities laws;

(B) has willfully abused the authority of that member; or

(C) without reasonable justification or excuse, has failed to enforce compliance with any such provision or rule, or any professional standard by any registered public accounting firm or any associated person thereof.

Accounting Standards

Sec. 108. (a) [Omitted. Subsection amended section 19 of the Securities Act of 1933.]

(b) *Commission Authority*. The Commission shall promulgate such rules and regulations to carry out section 19(b) of the Securities Act of 1933, as added by this section, as it deems necessary or appropriate in the public interest or for the protection of investors.

(c) *No Effect on Commission Powers*. Nothing in this Act, including this section and the amendment made by this section, shall be construed to impair or limit the authority of the Commission to establish accounting principles or standards for purposes of enforcement of the securities laws.

(d) *Study and Report on Adopting Principles-Based Accounting*.

(1) *Study*. (A) *In General*. The Commission shall conduct a study on the adoption by the United States financial reporting system of a principles-based accounting system.

(B) *Study Topics*. The study required by subparagraph (A) shall include an examination of—

(i) the extent to which principles-based accounting and financial reporting exists in the United States;

(ii) the length of time required for change from a rules-based to a principles-based financial reporting system;

(iii) the feasibility of and proposed methods by which a principles-based system may be implemented; and

(iv) a thorough economic analysis of the implementation of a principles-based system.

(2) *Report.* Not later than 1 year after the date of enactment of this Act, the Commission shall submit a report on the results of the study required by paragraph (1) to the Committee on Banking, Housing, and Urban Affairs of the Senate and the Committee on Financial Services of the House of Representatives.

Funding

Sec. 109. (a) *In General.* The Board, and the standard setting body designated pursuant to section 19(b) of the Securities Act of 1933, as amended by section 108, shall be funded as provided in this section.

(b) *Annual Budgets.* The Board and the standard setting body referred to in subsection (a) of this section shall each establish a budget for each fiscal year, which shall be reviewed and approved according to their respective internal procedures not less than 1 month prior to the commencement of the fiscal year to which the budget pertains (or at the beginning of the Board's first fiscal year, which may be a short fiscal year). The budget of the Board shall be subject to approval by the Commission. The budget for the first fiscal year of the Board shall be prepared and approved promptly following the appointment of the initial five Board members, to permit action by the Board of the organizational tasks contemplated by section 101(d).

(c) *Sources and Uses of Funds.*

(1) *Recoverable Budget Expenses.* The budget of the Board (reduced by any registration or annual fees received under section 102(e) for the year preceding the year for which the budget is being computed), and all of the budget of the standard setting body referred to in subsection (a), for each fiscal year of each of those 2 entities, shall be payable from annual accounting support fees, in accordance with subsections (d) and (e). Accounting support fees and other receipts of the Board and of such standard setting body shall not be considered public monies of the United States.

(2) *Funds Generated from the Collection of Monetary Penalties.* Subject to the availability in advance in an appropriations Act, and notwithstanding subsection (j), all funds collected by the Board as a result of the assessment of monetary penalties shall be used to fund a merit scholarship program for undergraduate and graduate students enrolled in accredited accounting degree programs, which program is to be administered by the Board or by an entity or agent identified by the Board.

(d) *Annual Accounting Support Fee for the Board.*

(1) *Establishment of Fee.* The Board shall establish, with the approval of the Commission, a reasonable annual accounting support fee (or a formula for the computation thereof), as may be necessary or appropriate to establish and maintain the Board. Such fee may also cover costs incurred in the Board's first fiscal year (which may be a short fiscal year), or may be levied separately with respect to such short fiscal year.

(2) *Assessments.* The rules of the Board under paragraph (1) shall provide for the equitable allocation, assessment, and collection by the Board (or an agent appointed by the Board) of the fee established under paragraph (1), among issuers, in accordance with subsection (g), and among brokers and dealers, in accordance with subsection (h), and allowing for differentiation among classes of issuers, brokers and dealers, as appropriate.

(3) *Brokers and Dealers.* The Board shall begin the allocation, assessment, and collection of fees under paragraph (2) with respect to brokers and dealers with the payment of support fees to fund the first full fiscal year beginning after the date of enactment of the Investor Protection and Securities Reform Act of 2010.

(e) *Annual Accounting Support Fee for Standard Setting Body.* The annual accounting support fee for the standard setting body referred to in subsection (a)—

(1) shall be allocated in accordance with subsection (g), and assessed and collected against each issuer, on behalf of the standard setting body, by 1 or more appropriate designated collection agents, as may be necessary or appropriate to pay for the budget and provide for the expenses of that standard setting body, and to provide for an independent, stable source of funding for such body, subject to review by the Commission; and

(2) may differentiate among different classes of issuers.

(f) *Limitation on Fee.* The amount of fees collected under this section for a fiscal year on behalf of the Board or the standards setting body, as the case may be, shall not exceed the recoverable budget expenses of the Board or body, respectively (which may include operating, capital, and accrued items), referred to in subsection (c)(1).

(g) *Allocation of Accounting Support Fees Among Issuers*. Any amount due from issuers (or a particular class of issuers) under this section to fund the budget of the Board or the standard setting body referred to in subsection (a) of this section shall be allocated among and payable by each issuer (or each issuer in a particular class, as applicable) in an amount equal to the total of such amount, multiplied by a fraction—

(1) the numerator of which is the average monthly equity market capitalization of the issuer for the 12-month period immediately preceding the beginning of the fiscal year to which such budget relates; and

(2) the denominator of which is the average monthly equity market capitalization of all such issuers for such 12-month period.

(h) *Allocation of Accounting Support Fees Among Brokers and Dealers*.

(1) *Obligation to Pay*. Each broker or dealer shall pay to the Board the annual accounting support fee allocated to such broker or dealer under this section.

(2) *Allocation*. Any amount due from a broker or dealer (or from a particular class of brokers and dealers) under this section shall be allocated among brokers and dealers and payable by the broker or dealer (or the brokers and dealers in the particular class, as applicable).

(3) *Proportionality*. The amount due from a broker or dealer shall be in proportion to the net capital of the broker or dealer (before or after any adjustments), compared to the total net capital of all brokers and dealers (before or after any adjustments), in accordance with rules issued by the Board.

(i) [Omitted. Subsection amended section 13(b)(2) of the Securities Exchange Act of 1934.]

(j) *Rule of Construction*. Nothing in this section shall be construed to render either the Board, the standard setting body referred to in subsection (a), or both, subject to procedures in Congress to authorize or appropriate public funds, or to prevent such organization from utilizing additional sources of revenue for its activities, such as earnings from publication sales, provided that each additional source of revenue shall not jeopardize, in the judgment of the Commission, the actual and perceived independence of such organization.

(k) *Start-Up Expenses of the Board*. From the unexpended balances of the appropriations to the Commission for fiscal year 2003, the Secretary of the Treasury is authorized to advance to the Board not to exceed the amount necessary to cover the expenses of the Board during its first fiscal year (which may be a short fiscal year).

Definitions

Sec. 110. For the purposes of this title, the following definitions shall apply:

(1) *Audit*. The term "audit" means an examination of the financial statements, reports, documents, procedures, controls, or notices of any issuer, broker, or dealer by an independent public accounting firm in accordance with the rules of the Board or the Commission, for the purpose of expressing an opinion on the financial statements or providing an audit report.

(2) *Audit Report*. The term "audit report" means a document, report, notice, or other record—

(A) prepared following an audit performed for purposes of compliance by an issuer, broker, or dealer with the requirements of the securities laws; and

(B) in which a public accounting firm either—

(i) sets forth the opinion of that firm regarding a financial statement, report, notice, or other document, procedures, or controls; or

(ii) asserts that no such opinion can be expressed.

(3) *Broker*. The term "broker" means a broker (as such term is defined in section 3(a)(4) of the Securities Exchange Act of 1934 that is required to file a balance sheet, income statement, or other financial statement under section 17(e)(1)(A) of such Act, where such balance sheet, income statement, or financial statement is required to be certified by a registered public accounting firm.

(4) *Dealer*. The term "dealer" means a dealer (as such term is defined in section 3(a)(5) of the Securities Exchange Act of 1934 that is required to file a balance sheet, income statement, or other financial statement under section 17(e)(1)(A) of such Act, where such balance sheet, income statement, or financial statement is required to be certified by a registered public accounting firm.

(5) *Professional Standards*. The term "professional standards" means—

(A) accounting principles that are—

(i) established by the standard setting body described in section 19(b) of the Securities Act of 1933, as amended by this Act, or prescribed by the Commission under section 19(a) of that Act or section 13(b) of the Securities Exchange Act of 1934; and

(ii) relevant to audit reports for particular issuers, brokers, or dealers, or dealt with in the quality control system of a particular registered public accounting firm; and

(B) auditing standards, standards for attestation engagements, quality control policies and procedures, ethical and competency standards, and independence standards (including rules implementing title II) that the Board or the Commission determines—

(i) relate to the preparation or issuance of audit reports for issuers, brokers, or dealers; and

(ii) are established or adopted by the Board under section 103(a), or are promulgated as rules of the Commission.

(6) *Self-Regulatory Organization*. The term "self-regulatory organization" has the same meaning as in section 3(a) of the Securities Exchange Act of 1934.

TITLE II—AUDITOR INDEPENDENCE

Services Outside the Scope of Practice of Auditors

Sec. 201. (a) [Omitted. Subsection amended section 10A of the Securities Exchange Act of 1934.]

(b) *Exemption Authority*. The Board may, on a case by case basis, exempt any person, issuer, public accounting firm, or transaction from the prohibition on the provision services under section 10A(g) of the Securities Exchange Act of 1934, to the extent that such exemption is necessary or appropriate in the public interest and is consistent with the protection of investors, and subject to review by the Commission in the same manner as for rules of the Board under section 107.

Sec. 202–206. [Omitted. Subsection amended section 10A of the Securities Exchange Act of 1934.]

Study of Mandatory Rotation of Registered Public Accounting Firms

Sec. 207. (a) *Study and Review Required*. The Comptroller General of the United States shall conduct a study and review of the potential effects of requiring the mandatory rotation of registered public accounting firms.

(b) *Report Required*. Not later than 1 year after the date of enactment of this Act, the Comptroller General shall submit a report to the Committee on Banking, Housing, and Urban Affairs of the Senate and the Committee on Financial Services of the House of Representatives on the results of the study and review required by this section.

(c) *Definition*. For purposes of this section, the term "mandatory rotation" refers to the imposition of a limit on the period of years in which a particular registered public accounting firm may be the auditor of record for a particular issuer.

Commission Authority

Sec. 208. (a) *Commission Regulations*. Not later than 180 days after the date of enactment of this Act, the Commission shall issue final regulations to carry out each of subsections (g) through (*l*) of section 10A of the Securities Exchange Act of 1934, as added by this title.

(b) *Auditor Independence*. It shall be unlawful for any registered public accounting firm (or an associated person thereof, as applicable) to prepare or issue any audit report with respect to any issuer, if the firm or associated person engages in any activity with respect to that issuer prohibited by any of subsections (g) through (*l*) of section 10A of the Securities Exchange Act of 1934, as added by this title, or any rule or regulation of the Commission or of the Board issued thereunder.

Considerations by Appropriate State Regulatory Authorities

Sec. 209. In supervising nonregistered public accounting firms and their associated persons, appropriate State regulatory authorities should make an independent determination of the proper standards applicable, particularly taking into consideration the size and nature of the business of the accounting firms they supervise and the size and nature of the business of the clients of those firms. The standards applied by the Board under this Act should not be presumed to be applicable for purposes of this section for small and medium sized nonregistered public accounting firms.

TITLE III—CORPORATE RESPONSIBILITY

Corporate Responsibility for Financial Reports

Sec. 302. (a) *Regulations Required*. The Commission shall, by rule, require, for each company filing periodic reports under section 13(a) or 15(d) of the

Securities Exchange Act of 1934, that the principal executive officer or officers and the principal financial officer or officers, or persons performing similar functions, certify in each annual or quarterly report filed or submitted under either such section of such Act that—

(1) the signing officer has reviewed the report;

(2) based on the officer's knowledge, the report does not contain any untrue statement of a material fact or omit to state a material fact necessary in order to make the statements made, in light of the circumstances under which such statements were made, not misleading;

(3) based on such officer's knowledge, the financial statements, and other financial information included in the report, fairly present in all material respects the financial condition and results of operations of the issuer as of, and for, the periods presented in the report;

(4) the signing officers—

(A) are responsible for establishing and maintaining internal controls;

(B) have designed such internal controls to ensure that material information relating to the issuer and its consolidated subsidiaries is made known to such officers by others within those entities, particularly during the period in which the periodic reports are being prepared;

(C) have evaluated the effectiveness of the issuer's internal controls as of a date within 90 days prior to the report; and

(D) have presented in the report their conclusions about the effectiveness of their internal controls based on their evaluation as of that date;

(5) the signing officers have disclosed to the issuer's auditors and the audit committee of the board of directors (or persons fulfilling the equivalent function)—

(A) all significant deficiencies in the design or operation of internal controls which could adversely affect the issuer's ability to record, process, summarize, and report financial data and have identified for the issuer's auditors any material weaknesses in internal controls; and

(B) any fraud, whether or not material, that involves management or other employees who have a significant role in the issuer's internal controls; and

(6) the signing officers have indicated in the report whether or not there were significant changes in internal controls or in other factors that could significantly affect internal controls subsequent to the date of their evaluation, including any corrective actions with regard to significant deficiencies and material weaknesses.

(b) *Foreign Reincorporations Have No Effect.* Nothing in this section shall be interpreted or applied in any way to allow any issuer to lessen the legal force of the statement required under this section 302, by an issuer having reincorporated or having engaged in any other transaction that resulted in the transfer of the corporate domicile or offices of the issuer from inside the United States to outside of the United States.

(c) *Deadline.* The rules required by subsection (a) of this section shall be effective not later than 30 days after the date of enactment of this Act.

Improper Influence on Conduct of Audits

Sec. 303. (a) *Rules to Prohibit.* It shall be unlawful, in contravention of such rules or regulations as the Commission shall prescribe as necessary and appropriate in the public interest or for the protection of investors, for any officer or director of an issuer, or any other person acting under the direction thereof, to take any action to fraudulently influence, coerce, manipulate, or mislead any independent public or certified accountant engaged in the performance of an audit of the financial statements of that issuer for the purpose of rendering such financial statements materially misleading.

(b) *Enforcement.* In any civil proceeding, the Commission shall have exclusive authority to enforce this section and any rule or regulation issued under this section.

(c) *No Preemption of Other Law.* The provisions of subsection (a) of this section shall be in addition to, and shall not supersede or preempt, any other provision of law or any rule or regulation issued thereunder.

(d) *Deadline for Rulemaking.* The Commission shall—

(1) propose the rules or regulations required by this section, not later than 90 days after the date of enactment of this Act; and

(2) issue final rules or regulations required by this section, not later than 270 days after the date of enactment of this Act.

Forfeiture of Certain Bonuses and Profits

Sec. 304. (a) *Additional Compensation Prior to Noncompliance with Commission Financial Reporting Requirements.* If an issuer is required to prepare an accounting restatement due to the material noncompliance of the issuer, as a result of misconduct, with any financial reporting requirement under the securities laws, the chief executive officer and chief financial officer of the issuer shall reimburse the issuer for—

(1) any bonus or other incentive-based or equity-based compensation received by that person from the issuer during the 12-month period following the first public issuance or filing with the Commission (whichever first occurs) of the financial document embodying such financial reporting requirement; and

(2) any profits realized from the sale of securities of the issuer during that 12–month period.

(b) *Commission Exemption Authority.* The Commission may exempt any person from the application of subsection (a), as it deems necessary and appropriate.

Insider Trades During Pension Fund Blackout Periods

Sec. 306. (a) *Prohibition of Insider Trading During Pension Fund Blackout Periods.*

(1) *In General.* Except to the extent otherwise provided by rule of the Commission pursuant to paragraph (3), it shall be unlawful for any director or executive officer of an issuer of any equity security (other than an exempted security), directly or indirectly, to purchase, sell, or otherwise acquire or transfer any equity security of the issuer (other than an exempted security) during any blackout period with respect to such equity security if such director or officer acquires such equity security in connection with his or her service or employment as a director or executive officer.

(2) *Remedy.* (A) *In General.* Any profit realized by a director or executive officer referred to in paragraph (1) from any purchase, sale, or other acquisition or transfer in violation of this subsection shall inure to and be recoverable by the issuer, irrespective of any intention on the part of such director or executive officer in entering into the transaction.

(B) *Actions to Recover Profits.* An action to recover profits in accordance with this subsection may be instituted at law or in equity in any court of competent jurisdiction by the issuer, or by the owner of any security of the issuer in the name and in behalf of the issuer if the issuer fails or refuses to bring such action within 60 days after the date of request, or fails diligently to prosecute the action thereafter, except that no such suit shall be brought more than 2 years after the date on which such profit was realized.

(3) *Rulemaking Authorized.* The Commission shall, in consultation with the Secretary of Labor, issue rules to clarify the application of this subsection and to prevent evasion thereof. Such rules shall provide for the application of the requirements of paragraph (1) with respect to entities treated as a single employer with respect to an issuer under section 414(b), (c), (m), or (*o*) of the Internal Revenue Code of 1986 to the extent necessary to clarify the application of such requirements and to prevent evasion thereof. Such rules may also provide for appropriate exceptions from the requirements of this subsection, including exceptions for purchases pursuant to an automatic dividend reinvestment program or purchases or sales made pursuant to an advance election.

(4) *Blackout Period.* For purposes of this subsection, the term "blackout period", with respect to the equity securities of any issuer—

(A) means any period of more than 3 consecutive business days during which the ability of not fewer than 50 percent of the participants or beneficiaries under all individual account plans maintained by the issuer to purchase, sell, or otherwise acquire or transfer an interest in any equity of such issuer held in such an individual account plan is temporarily suspended by the issuer or by a fiduciary of the plan; and

(B) does not include, under regulations which shall be prescribed by the Commission—

(i) a regularly scheduled period in which the participants and beneficiaries may not purchase, sell, or otherwise acquire or transfer an interest in any equity of such issuer, if such period is—

(I) incorporated into the individual account plan; and

(II) timely disclosed to employees before becoming participants under the individual account plan or as a subsequent amendment to the plan; or

(ii) any suspension described in subparagraph (A) that is imposed solely in connection with persons becoming participants or beneficiaries, or ceasing to be participants or beneficiaries, in an individual account plan by reason of a corporate merger, acquisition, divestiture, or similar transaction involving the plan or plan sponsor.

(5) *Individual Account Plan.* For purposes of this subsection, the term "individual account plan" has the meaning provided in section 3(34) of the Employee Retirement Income Security Act of 1974, except that such term shall not include a one-participant retirement plan (within the meaning of section 101(i)(8)(B) of such Act).

(6) *Notice to Directors, Executive Officers, and the Commission.* In any case in which a director or executive officer is subject to the requirements of this subsection in connection with a blackout period (as defined in paragraph (4)) with respect to any equity securities, the issuer of such equity securities shall timely notify such director or officer and the Securities and Exchange Commission of such blackout period.

(b) *Notice Requirements to Participants and Beneficiaries under ERISA.*

(1) [Omitted.]

(2) *Issuance of Initial Guidance and Model Notice.* The Secretary of Labor shall issue initial guidance and a model notice pursuant to section 101(i)(6) of the Employee Retirement Income Security Act of 1974 (as added by this subsection [29 U.S.C. 1021(i)(6)]) not later than January 1, 2003. Not later than 75 days after the date of enactment of this Act, the Secretary shall promulgate interim final rules necessary to carry out the amendments made by this subsection.

(3) *Plan Amendments.* If any amendment made by this subsection requires an amendment to any plan, such plan amendment shall not be required to be made before the first plan year beginning on or after the date of enactment of this Act, if—

(A) during the period after such amendment made by this subsection takes effect and before such first plan year, the plan is operated in good faith compliance with the requirements of such amendment made by this subsection, and

(B) such plan amendment applies retroactively to the period after such amendment made by this subsection takes effect and before such first plan year.

(c) *Effective Date.* The provisions of this section (including the amendments made thereby) shall take effect 180 days after the date of enactment of this Act. Good faith compliance with the requirements of such provisions in advance of the issuance of applicable regulations thereunder shall be treated as compliance with such provisions.

Rules of Professional Responsibility for Attorneys

Sec. 307. Not later than 180 days after the date of enactment of this Act, the Commission shall issue rules, in the public interest and for the protection of investors, setting forth minimum standards of professional conduct for attorneys appearing and practicing before the Commission in any way in the representation of issuers, including a rule—

(1) requiring an attorney to report evidence of a material violation of securities law or breach of fiduciary duty or similar violation by the company or any agent thereof, to the chief legal counsel or the chief executive officer of the company (or the equivalent thereof); and

(2) if the counsel or officer does not appropriately respond to the evidence (adopting, as necessary, appropriate remedial measures or sanctions with respect to the violation), requiring the attorney to report the evidence to the audit committee of the board of directors of the issuer or to another committee of the board of directors comprised solely of directors not employed directly or indirectly by the issuer, or to the board of directors.

Fair Funds for Investors

Sec. 308. (a) *Civil Penalties to be Used for the Relief of Victims.* If, in any judicial or administrative action brought by the Commission under the securities laws, the Commission obtains a civil penalty against any person for a violation of such laws, or such person agrees, in settlement of any such action, to such civil penalty, the amount of such civil penalty shall, on the motion or at the direction of the Commission, be added to and become part of a disgorgement fund or other fund established for the benefit of the victims of such violation.

(b) *Acceptance of Additional Donations.* The Commission is authorized to accept, hold, administer, and utilize gifts, bequests and devises of property, both real and personal, to the United States for a disgorgement fund or other fund described in subsection (a) of this section. Such gifts, bequests, and devises of money and proceeds from sales of other property received as gifts, bequests, or devises shall be deposited in such fund and shall be available for allocation in accordance with subsection (a) of this section.

(c) *Study Required.*

(1) *Subject of Study.* The Commission shall review and analyze—

(A) enforcement actions by the Commission over the five years preceding the date of enactment of this Act that have included proceedings to obtain civil penalties or disgorgements to identify areas where such proceedings may be utilized to efficiently, effectively, and fairly provide restitution for injured investors; and

(B) other methods to more efficiently, effectively, and fairly provide restitution to injured investors, including methods to improve the collection rates for civil penalties and disgorgements.

(2) *Report Required.* The Commission shall report its findings to the Committee on Financial Services of the House of Representatives and the Committee on Banking, Housing, and Urban Affairs of the Senate within 180 days after the date of enactment of this Act, and shall use such findings to revise its rules and regulations as necessary. The report shall include a discussion of regulatory or legislative actions that are recommended or that may be necessary to address concerns identified in the study.

(d) [Omitted.]

TITLE IV—ENHANCED FINANCIAL DISCLOSURES

Disclosures in Periodic Reports

Sec. 401. (a) [Omitted]

(b) *Commission Rules on Pro Forma Figures.* Not later than 180 days after the date of enactment of this Act, the Commission shall issue final rules providing that pro forma financial information included in any periodic or other report filed with the Commission pursuant to the securities laws, or in any public disclosure or press or other release, shall be presented in a manner that—

(1) does not contain an untrue statement of a material fact or omit to state a material fact necessary in order to make the pro forma financial information, in light of the circumstances under which it is presented, not misleading; and

(2) reconciles it with the financial condition and results of operations of the issuer under generally accepted accounting principles.

(c) *Study and Report on Special Purpose Entities.*

(1) *Study Required.* The Commission shall, not later than 1 year after the effective date of adoption of off-balance sheet disclosure rules required by section 13 of the Securities Exchange Act of 1934, as added by this subsection, complete a study of filings by issuers and their disclosures to determine—

(A) the extent of off-balance sheet transactions, including assets, liabilities, leases, losses, and the use of special purpose entities; and

(B) whether generally accepted accounting rules result in financial statements of issuers reflecting the economics of such off-balance sheet transactions to investors in a transparent fashion.

(2) *Report and Recommendations.* Not later than 6 months after the date of completion of the study required by paragraph (1), the Commission shall submit a report to the President, the Committee on Banking, Housing, and Urban Affairs of the Senate, and the Committee on Financial Services of the House of Representatives, setting forth—

(A) the amount or an estimate of the amount of off-balance sheet transactions, including assets, liabilities, leases, and losses of, and the use of special purpose entities by, issuers filing periodic reports pursuant to section 13 or 15 of the Securities Exchange Act of 1934;

(B) the extent to which special purpose entities are used to facilitate off-balance sheet transactions;

(C) whether generally accepted accounting principles or the rules of the Commission result in financial statements of issuers reflecting the economics of such transactions to investors in a transparent fashion;

(D) whether generally accepted accounting principles specifically result in the consolidation of special purpose entities sponsored by an issuer in cases in which the issuer has the majority of the risks and rewards of the special purpose entity; and

(E) any recommendations of the Commission for improving the transparency and quality of reporting off-balance sheet transactions in the financial statements and disclosures required to be filed by an issuer with the Commission.

Management Assessment of Internal Controls

Sec. 404. (a) *Rules Required.* The Commission shall prescribe rules requiring each annual report required by section 13 or 15(d) of the Securities Exchange Act of 1934 to contain an internal control report, which shall—

(1) state the responsibility of management for establishing and maintaining an adequate internal control structure and procedures for financial reporting; and

(2) contain an assessment, as of the end of the most recent fiscal year of the issuer, of the effectiveness of the internal control structure and procedures of the issuer for financial reporting.

(b) *Internal Control Evaluation and Reporting.* With respect to the internal control assessment required by subsection (a), each registered public accounting firm that prepares or issues the audit report for the issuer, other than an issuer that is an emerging growth company (as defined in section 3 of the Securities Exchange Act of 1934), shall attest to, and report on, the assessment made by the management of the issuer. An attestation made under this subsection shall be made in accordance with standards for attestation engagements issued or adopted by the Board. Any such attestation shall not be the subject of a separate engagement.

(c) *Exemption for Smaller Issuers.* Subsection (b) shall not apply with respect to any audit report prepared for an issuer that is neither a "large accelerated filer" nor an "accelerated filer" as those terms are defined in Rule 12b–2 under the Securities Exchange Act of 1934.

Exemption

Sec. 405. Nothing in section 401, 402, or 404, the amendments made by those sections, or the rules of the Commission under those sections shall apply to any investment company registered under section 8 of the Investment Company Act of 1940.

Code of Ethics for Senior Financial Officers

Sec. 406. (a) *Code of Ethics Disclosure.* The Commission shall issue rules to require each issuer, together with periodic reports required pursuant to section 13(a) or 15(d) of the Securities Exchange Act of 1934, to disclose whether or not, and if not, the reason therefor, such issuer has adopted a code of ethics for senior financial officers, applicable to its principal financial officer and comptroller or principal accounting officer, or persons performing similar functions.

(b) *Changes in Codes of Ethics.* The Commission shall revise its regulations concerning matters requiring prompt disclosure on Form 8–K (or any successor thereto) to require the immediate disclosure, by means of the filing of such form, dissemination by the Internet or by other electronic means, by any issuer of any change in or waiver of the code of ethics for senior financial officers.

(c) *Definition.* In this section, the term "code of ethics" means such standards as are reasonably necessary to promote—

(1) honest and ethical conduct, including the ethical handling of actual or apparent conflicts of interest between personal and professional relationships;

(2) full, fair, accurate, timely, and understandable disclosure in the periodic reports required to be filed by the issuer; and

(3) compliance with applicable governmental rules and regulations.

(d) *Deadline for Rulemaking.* The Commission shall—

(1) propose rules to implement this section, not later than 90 days after the date of enactment of this Act; and

(2) issue final rules to implement this section, not later than 180 days after the date of enactment of this Act.

Disclosure of Audit Committee Financial Expert

Sec. 407. (a) *Rules Defining "Financial Expert."* The Commission shall issue rules, as necessary or appropriate in the public interest and consistent with the protection of investors, to require each issuer, together with periodic reports required pursuant to sections 13(a) and 15(d) of the Securities Exchange Act of 1934, to disclose whether or not, and if not, the reasons therefor, the audit committee of that issuer is comprised of at least 1 member who is a financial expert, as such term is defined by the Commission.

(b) *Considerations.* In defining the term "financial expert" for purposes of subsection (a), the Commission shall consider whether a person has, through education and experience as a public accountant or auditor or a principal financial officer, comptroller, or principal accounting officer of an issuer, or from a position involving the performance of similar functions—

(1) an understanding of generally accepted accounting principles and financial statements;

(2) experience in—

(A) the preparation or auditing of financial statements of generally comparable issuers; and

(B) the application of such principles in connection with the accounting for estimates, accruals, and reserves;

(3) experience with internal accounting controls; and

(4) an understanding of audit committee functions.

(c) *Deadline for Rulemaking.* The Commission shall—

(1) propose rules to implement this section, not later than 90 days after the date of enactment of this Act; and

(2) issue final rules to implement this section, not later than 180 days after the date of enactment of this Act.

Enhanced Review of Periodic Disclosures by Issuers

Sec. 408. (a) *Regular and Systematic Review.* The Commission shall review disclosures made by issuers reporting under section 13(a) of the Securities Exchange Act of 1934 (including reports filed on Form 10–K), and which have a class of securities listed on a national securities exchange or traded on an automated quotation facility of a national securities association, on a regular and systematic basis for the protection of investors. Such review shall include a review of an issuer's financial statement.

(b) *Review Criteria.* For purposes of scheduling the reviews required by subsection (a), the Commission shall consider, among other factors—

(1) issuers that have issued material restatements of financial results;

(2) issuers that experience significant volatility in their stock price as compared to other issuers;

(3) issuers with the largest market capitalization;

(4) emerging companies with disparities in price to earning ratios;

(5) issuers whose operations significantly affect any material sector of the economy; and

(6) any other factors that the Commission may consider relevant.

(c) *Minimum Review Period.* In no event shall an issuer required to file reports under section 13(a) or 15(d) of the Securities Exchange Act of 1934 be reviewed under this section less frequently than once every 3 years.

Sec. 409. [Omitted. Section amended section 13 of the Securities Exchange Act of 1934.]

TITLE V—ANALYST CONFLICTS OF INTEREST

Treatment of Securities Analysts by Registered Securities Associations and National Securities Exchanges

Sec. 501. (a) [Omitted. Subsection amended section 15 of The Securities Exchange Act of 1934.]

(b) [Omitted. Subsection amended section 21B(a) of the Securities Exchange Act of 1934.]

(c) *Commission Authority.* The Commission may promulgate and amend its regulations, or direct a registered securities association or national securities exchange to promulgate and amend its rules, to carry out section 15D of the Securities Exchange Act of 1934, as added by this section, as is necessary for the protection of investors and in the public interest.

TITLE VI—COMMISSION RESOURCES AND AUTHORITY

Authorization of Appropriations

Sec. 601. [Omitted. Section amended section 35 of the Securities Exchange Act of 1934.]

Appearance and Practice Before the Commission

Sec. 602. [Omitted. Section amended section 4B of the Securities Exchange Act of 1934.]

Federal Court Authority to Impose Penny Stock Bars

Sec. 603. [Omitted. Section amended section 21(d) the Securities Exchange Act of 1934.]

Qualifications of Associated Persons of Brokers and Dealers

Sec. 604. (a) [Omitted. Subsection amended section 15(b)(4) of the Securities Exchange Act of 1934.]

(b) [Omitted. Subsection amended section 203(e) of the Investment Advisers Act of 1940.]

(c) [Omitted.]

TITLE VII—STUDIES AND REPORTS

GAO Study and Report Regarding Consolidation of Public Accounting Firms

Sec. 701. (a) *Study Required.* The Comptroller General of the United States shall conduct a study

(1) to identify

(A) the factors that have led to the consolidation of public accounting firms since 1989 and the consequent reduction in the number of firms capable of providing audit services to large national and multi-national business organizations that are subject to the securities laws;

(B) the present and future impact of the condition described in subparagraph (A) on capital formation and securities markets, both domestic and international; and

(C) solutions to any problems identified under subparagraph (B), including ways to increase competition and the number of firms capable of providing audit services to large national and multinational business organizations that are subject to the securities laws;

(2) of the problems, if any, faced by business organizations that have resulted from limited competition among public accounting firms, including

(A) higher costs;

(B) lower quality of services;

(C) impairment of auditor independence; or

(D) lack of choice; and

(3) whether and to what extent Federal or State regulations impede competition among public accounting firms.

(b) *Consultation.* In planning and conducting the study under this section, the Comptroller General shall consult with

(1) the Commission;

(2) the regulatory agencies that perform functions similar to the Commission within the other member countries of the Group of Seven Industrialized Nations;

(3) the Department of Justice; and

(4) any other public or private sector organization that the Comptroller General considers appropriate.

(c) *Report Required.* Not later than 1 year after the date of enactment of this Act, the Comptroller General shall submit a report on the results of the study required by this section to the Committee on Banking, Housing, and Urban Affairs of the Senate and the Committee on Financial Services of the House of Representatives.

Commission Study and Report Regarding Credit Rating Agencies

Sec. 702. (a) *Study Required.*

(1) *In General.* The Commission shall conduct a study of the role and function of credit rating agencies in the operation of the securities market.

(2) *Areas of Consideration.* The study required by this subsection shall examine

(A) the role of credit rating agencies in the evaluation of issuers of securities;

(B) the importance of that role to investors and the functioning of the securities markets;

(C) any impediments to the accurate appraisal by credit rating agencies of the financial resources and risks of issuers of securities;

(D) any barriers to entry into the business of acting as a credit rating agency, and any measures needed to remove such barriers;

(E) any measures which may be required to improve the dissemination of information concerning such resources and risks when credit rating agencies announce credit ratings; and

(F) any conflicts of interest in the operation of credit rating agencies and measures to prevent such conflicts or ameliorate the consequences of such conflicts.

(b) *Report Required.* The Commission shall submit a report on the study required by subsection (a) to the President, the Committee on Financial Services of the House of Representatives, and the Committee on Banking, Housing, and Urban Affairs of the Senate not later than 180 days after the date of enactment of this Act.

Study and Report on Violators and Violations

Sec. 703. (a) *Study.* The Commission shall conduct a study to determine, based upon information for the period from January 1, 1998, to December 31, 2001

(1) the number of securities professionals, defined as public accountants, public accounting firms, investment bankers, investment advisers, brokers, dealers, attorneys, and other securities professionals practicing before the Commission

(A) who have been found to have aided and abetted a violation of the Federal securities laws, including rules or regulations promulgated thereunder (collectively referred to in this section as "Federal securities laws"), but who have not been sanctioned, disciplined, or otherwise penalized as a primary violator in any administrative action or civil proceeding, including in any settlement of such an action or proceeding (referred to in this section as "aiders and abettors"); and

(B) who have been found to have been primary violators of the Federal securities laws;

(2) a description of the Federal securities laws violations committed by aiders and abettors and by primary violators, including

(A) the specific provision of the Federal securities laws violated;

(B) the specific sanctions and penalties imposed upon such aiders and abettors and primary violators, including the amount of any monetary penalties assessed upon and collected from such persons;

(C) the occurrence of multiple violations by the same person or persons, either as an aider or abettor or as a primary violator; and

(D) whether, as to each such violator, disciplinary sanctions have been imposed, including any censure, suspension, temporary bar, or permanent bar to practice before the Commission; and

(3) the amount of disgorgement, restitution, or any other fines or payments that the Commission has assessed upon and collected from, aiders and abettors and from primary violators.

(b) *Report.* A report based upon the study conducted pursuant to subsection (a) shall be submitted to the Committee on Banking, Housing, and Urban Affairs of the Senate, and the Committee on Financial Services of the House of Representatives not later than 6 months after the date of enactment of this Act.

Study of Enforcement Actions

Sec. 704. (a) *Study Required.* The Commission shall review and analyze all enforcement actions by the Commission involving violations of reporting requirements imposed under the securities laws, and restatements of financial statements, over the 5–year period preceding the date of enactment of this Act, to identify areas of reporting that are most susceptible to fraud, inappropriate manipulation, or inappropriate earnings management, such as revenue recognition and the accounting treatment of off-balance sheet special purpose entities.

(b) *Report Required.* The Commission shall report its findings to the Committee on Financial Services of the House of Representatives and the Committee on Banking, Housing, and Urban Affairs of the Senate, not later than 180 days after the date of enactment of this Act, and shall use such findings to revise its rules and regulations, as necessary. The report shall include a discussion of regulatory or legislative steps that are recommended or that may be necessary to address concerns identified in the study.

Study of Investment Banks

Sec. 705. (a) *GAO Study.* The Comptroller General of the United States shall conduct a study on whether investment banks and financial advisers assisted public companies in manipulating their earnings and obfuscating their true financial condition. The study should address the rule of investment banks and financial advisers

(1) in the collapse of the Enron Corporation, including with respect to the design and implementation of derivatives transactions, transactions involving special purpose vehicles, and other financial arrangements that may have had the effect of altering the company's reported financial statements in ways that obscured the true financial picture of the company;

(2) in the failure of Global Crossing, including with respect to transactions involving swaps of fiberoptic cable capacity, in the designing transactions that may have had the effect of altering the company's reported financial statements in ways that obscured the true financial picture of the company; and

(3) generally, in creating and marketing transactions which may have been designed solely to enable companies to manipulate revenue streams, obtain loans, or move liabilities off balance sheets without altering the economic and business risks faced by the companies or any other mechanism to obscure a company's financial picture.

(b) *Report.* The Comptroller General shall report to Congress not later than 180 days after the date of enactment of this Act on the results of the study required by this section. The report shall include a discussion of regulatory or legislative steps that are recommended or that may be necessary to address concerns identified in the study.

TITLE VIII—CORPORATE AND CRIMINAL FRAUD ACCOUNTABILITY

Short Title

Sec. 801. *Short Title.* This title may be cited as the "Corporate and Criminal Fraud Accountability Act of 2002"

Criminal Penalties for Altering Documents

Sec. 802. (a) *In General.* Chapter 73 of title 18, United States Code, is amended by adding at the end the following:

§ 1519. Destruction, alteration, or falsification of records in Federal investigations and bankruptcy

Whoever knowingly alters, destroys, mutilates, conceals, covers up, falsifies, or makes a false entry in any record, document, or tangible object with the intent to impede, obstruct, or influence the investigation or proper administration of any matter within the jurisdiction of any department or agency of the United States or any case filed under title 11, or in relation to or contemplation of any such matter or case, shall be fined under this title, imprisoned not more than 20 years, or both.

§ 1520. Destruction of corporate audit records

(a)(1) Any accountant who conducts an audit of an issuer of securities to which section 10A(a) of the Securities Exchange Act of 1934 applies, shall maintain all audit or review workpapers for a period of 5 years from the end of the fiscal period in which the audit or review was concluded.

(2) The Securities and Exchange Commission shall promulgate, within 180 days, after adequate notice and an opportunity for comment, such rules and regulations, as are reasonably necessary, relating to the retention of relevant records such as workpapers, documents that form the basis of an audit or review, memoranda, correspondence, communications, other documents, and records (including electronic records) which are created, sent, or received in connection with an audit or review and contain conclusions, opinions, analyses, or financial data relating to such an audit or review, which is conducted by any accountant who conducts an audit of an issuer of securities to which section 10A(a) of the Securities Exchange Act of 1934 (15 U.S.C. 78j–1(a)) applies. The Commission may, from time to time, amend or supplement the rules and regulations that it is required to promulgate under this section, after adequate notice and an opportunity for comment, in order to ensure that such rules and regulations adequately comport with the purposes of this section.

(b) Whoever knowingly and willfully violates subsection (a)(1), or any rule or regulation promulgated by the Securities and Exchange Commission under subsection (a)(2), shall be fined under this title, imprisoned not more than 10 years, or both.

(c) Nothing in this section shall be deemed to diminish or relieve any person of any other duty or obligation imposed by Federal or State law or regulation to maintain, or refrain from destroying, any document.

(b) [Omitted.]

Debts Nondischargeable if Incurred in Violation of Securities Fraud Laws

Sec. 803. Section 523(a) of title 11, United States Code, is amended

(1) in paragraph (17), by striking "or" after the semicolon;

(2) in paragraph (18), by striking the period at the end and inserting "; or"; and

(3) by adding at the end, the following:

(19) that

(A) is for

(i) the violation of any of the Federal securities laws (as that term is defined in section 3(a)(47) of the Securities Exchange Act of 1934), any of the State securities laws, or any regulation or order issued under such Federal or State securities laws; or

(ii) common law fraud, deceit, or manipulation in connection with the purchase or sale of any security; and

(B) results from

(i) any judgment, order, consent order, or decree entered in any Federal or State judicial or administrative proceeding;

(ii) any settlement agreement entered into by the debtor; or

(iii) any court or administrative order for any damages, fine, penalty, citation, restitutionary payment, disgorgement payment, attorney fee, cost, or other payment owed by the debtor.

Statute of Limitations for Securities Fraud

Sec. 804. (a) *In General.* Section 1658 of title 28, United States Code, is amended—

(1) by inserting "(a)" before "Except"; and

(2) by adding at the end the following:

"(b) Notwithstanding subsection (a), a private right of action that involves a claim of fraud, deceit, manipulation, or contrivance in contravention of a regulatory requirement concerning the securities laws, as defined in section 3(a)(47) of the Securities Exchange Act of 1934, may be brought not later than the earlier of—

"(1) 2 years after the discovery of the facts constituting the violation; or

"(2) 5 years after such violation.".

(b) *Effective Date.* The limitations period provided by section 1658(b) of title 28, United States Code, as added by this section, shall apply to all proceedings addressed by this section that are commenced on or after the date of enactment of this Act.

(c) *No Creation of Actions.* Nothing in this section shall create a new, private right of action.

Review of Federal Sentencing Guidelines for Obstruction of Justice and Extensive Criminal Fraud

Sec. 805. (a) *Enhancement of Fraud and Obstruction of Justice Sentences.* Pursuant to section 994 of title 28, United States Code, and in accordance with this section, the United States Sentencing Commission shall review and amend, as appropriate, the Federal Sentencing Guidelines and related policy statements to ensure that

(1) the base offense level and existing enhancements contained in United States Sentencing Guideline 2J1.2 relating to obstruction of justice are sufficient to deter and punish that activity;

(2) the enhancements and specific offense characteristics relating to obstruction of justice are adequate in cases where

(A) the destruction, alteration, or fabrication of evidence involves

(i) a large amount of evidence, a large number of participants, or is otherwise extensive;

(ii) the selection of evidence that is particularly probative or essential to the investigation; or

(iii) more than minimal planning; or

(B) the offense involved abuse of a special skill or a position of trust;

(3) the guideline offense levels and enhancements for violations of section 1519 or 1520 of title 18, United States Code, as added by this title, are sufficient to deter and punish that activity;

(4) a specific offense characteristic enhancing sentencing is provided under United States Sentencing Guideline 2B1.1 (as in effect on the date of enactment of this Act) for a fraud offense that endangers the solvency or financial security of a substantial number of victims; and

(5) the guidelines that apply to organizations in United States Sentencing Guidelines, chapter 8, are sufficient to deter and punish organizational criminal misconduct.

(b) *Emergency Authority and Deadline for Commission Action.* The United States Sentencing Commission is requested to promulgate the guidelines or amendments provided for under this section as soon as practicable, and in any event not later than 180 days after the date of enactment of this Act, in accordance with the procedures set forth in section 219(a) of the Sentencing Reform Act of 1987, as though the authority under that Act had not expired.

Protection for Employees of Publicly Traded Companies who Provide Evidence of Fraud

Sec. 806. (a) *In General.* Chapter 73 of title 18, United States Code, is amended by inserting after section 1514 the following:

§ 1514A. Civil action to protect against retaliation in fraud cases

(a) *Whistleblowers Protection for Employees of Publicly Traded Companies.* No company with a class of securities registered under section 12 of the Securities Exchange Act of 1934, or that is required to file reports under section 15(d) of the Securities Exchange Act of 1934, or any officer, employee, contractor, subcontractor, or agent of such company, may discharge, demote, suspend, threaten, harass, or in any other manner discriminate against an employee in the terms and conditions of employment because of any lawful act done by the employee

(1) to provide information, cause information to be provided, or otherwise assist in an investigation regarding any conduct which the employee reasonably believes constitutes a violation of section 1341, 1343, 1344, or 1348, any rule or regulation of the Securities and Exchange Commission, or any provision of Federal law relating to

fraud against shareholders, when the information or assistance is provided to or the investigation is conducted by

(A) a Federal regulatory or law enforcement agency;

(B) any Member of Congress or any committee of Congress; or

(C) a person with supervisory authority over the employee (or such other person working for the employer who has the authority to investigate, discover, or terminate misconduct); or

(2) to file, cause to be filed, testify, participate in, or otherwise assist in a proceeding filed or about to be filed (with any knowledge of the employer) relating to an alleged violation of section 1341, 1343, 1344, or 1348, any rule or regulation of the Securities and Exchange Commission, or any provision of Federal law relating to fraud against shareholders.

(b) *Enforcement Action.*

(1) *In General.* A person who alleges discharge or other discrimination by any person in violation of subsection (a) may seek relief under subsection (c), by

(A) filing a complaint with the Secretary of Labor; or

(B) if the Secretary has not issued a final decision within 180 days of the filing of the complaint and there is no showing that such delay is due to the bad faith of the claimant, bringing an action at law or equity for de novo review in the appropriate district court of the United States, which shall have jurisdiction over such an action without regard to the amount in controversy.

(2) *Procedure.*

(A) *In General.* An action under paragraph (1)(A) shall be governed under the rules and procedures set forth in section 42121(b) of title 49, United States Code.

(B) *Exception.* Notification made under section 42121(b)(1) of title 49, United States Code, shall be made to the person named in the complaint and to the employer.

(C) *Burdens of Proof.* An action brought under paragraph (1)(B) shall be governed by the legal burdens of proof set forth in section 42121(b) of title 49, United States Code.

(D) *Statute of Limitations.* An action under paragraph (1) shall be commenced not later than 90 days after the date on which the violation occurs.

(c) *Remedies.*

(1) *In General.* An employee prevailing in any action under subsection (b)(1) shall be entitled to all relief necessary to make the employee whole.

(2) *Compensatory Damages.* Relief for any action under paragraph (1) shall include

(A) reinstatement with the same seniority status that the employee would have had, but for the discrimination;

(B) the amount of back pay, with interest; and

(C) compensation for any special damages sustained as a result of the discrimination, including litigation costs, expert witness fees, and reasonable attorney fees.

(d) *Rights Retained by Employee.* Nothing in this section shall be deemed to diminish the rights, privileges, or remedies of any employee under any Federal or State law, or under any collective bargaining agreement.

(b) [Omitted.]

Criminal Penalties for Defrauding Shareholders of Publicly Traded Companies

Sec. 807. (a) *In General.* Chapter 63 of title 18, United States Code, is amended by adding at the end the following:

§ 1348. Securities fraud

Whoever knowingly executes, or attempts to execute, a scheme or artifice

(1) to defraud any person in connection with any security of an issuer with a class of securities registered under section 12 of the Securities Exchange Act of 1934 or that is required to file reports under section 15(d) of the Securities Exchange Act of 1934; or

(2) to obtain, by means of false or fraudulent pretenses, representations, or promises, any money or property in connection with the purchase or sale of any security of an issuer with a class of securities registered under section 12 of the Securities Exchange Act of 1934 or that is required to file reports under section 15(d) of the Securities Exchange Act of 1934; shall be fined under this title, or imprisoned not more than 25 years, or both.

(b) [Omitted.]

TITLE IX—WHITE–COLLAR CRIME PENALTY ENHANCEMENTS

Short Title

Sec. 901. This title may be cited as the "White–Collar Crime Penalty Enhancement Act of 2002"

Attempts and Conspiracies to Commit Criminal Fraud Offenses

Sec. 902. (a) *In General.* Chapter 63 of title 18, United States Code, is amended by inserting after section 1348 as added by this Act the following:

§ 1349. Attempt and conspiracy

Any person who attempts or conspires to commit any offense under this chapter shall be subject to the same penalties as those prescribed for the offense, the commission of which was the object of the attempt or conspiracy.

(b) [Omitted.]

Criminal Penalties for Mail and Wire Fraud

Sec. 903. (a) *Mail Fraud.* Section 1341 of title 18, United States Code, amended by striking "five" and inserting "20".

(b) *Wire Fraud.* Section 1343 of title 18, United States Code, is amended by striking "five" and inserting "20".

Criminal Penalties for Violations of the Employee Retirement Income Security Act of 1974

Sec. 904. Section 501 of the Employee Retirement Income Security Act of 1974 is amended

(1) by striking "$5,000" and inserting "$100,000";

(2) by striking "one year" and inserting "10 years"; and

(3) by striking "$100,000" and inserting "$500,000".

Amendment to Sentencing Guidelines Relating to Certain White–Collar Offenses

Sec. 905. (a) *Directive to the United States Sentencing Commission.* Pursuant to its authority under section 994(p) of title 18, United States Code, and in accordance with this section, the United States Sentencing Commission shall review and, as appropriate, amend the Federal Sentencing Guidelines and related policy statements to implement the provisions of this Act.

(b) *Requirements.* In carrying out this section, the Sentencing Commission shall

(1) ensure that the sentencing guidelines and policy statements reflect the serious nature of the offenses and the penalties set forth in this Act, the growing incidence of serious fraud offenses which are identified above, and the need to modify the sentencing guidelines and policy statements to deter, prevent, and punish such offenses;

(2) consider the extent to which the guidelines and policy statements adequately address whether the guideline offense levels and enhancements for violations of the sections amended by this Act are sufficient to deter and punish such offenses, and specifically, are adequate in view of the statutory increases in penalties contained in this Act;

(3) assure reasonable consistency with other relevant directives and sentencing guidelines;

(4) account for any additional aggravating or mitigating circumstances that might justify exceptions to the generally applicable sentencing ranges;

(5) make any necessary conforming changes to the sentencing guidelines; and

(6) assure that the guidelines adequately meet the purposes of sentencing, as set forth in section 3553(a)(2) of title 18, United States Code.

(c) *Emergency Authority and Deadline for Commission Action.* The United States Sentencing Commission is requested to promulgate the guidelines or amendments provided for under this section as soon as practicable, and in any event not later than 180 days after the date of enactment of this Act, in accordance with the procedures set forth in section 219(a) of the Sentencing Reform Act of 1987, as though the authority under that Act had not expired.

Corporate Responsibility for Financial Reports

Sec. 906. (a) *In General.* Chapter 63 of title 18, United States Code, is amended by inserting after section 1349, as created by this Act, the following:

§ 1350. Failure of corporate officers to certify financial reports

(a) *Certification of Periodic Financial Reports.* Each periodic report containing financial statements filed by an issuer with the Securities Exchange Commission pursuant to section 13(a) or 15(d) of the Securities Exchange Act of 1934 shall be accompanied by a written statement by the chief executive officer and chief financial officer (or equivalent thereof) of the issuer.

(b) *Content.* The statement required under subsection (a) shall certify that the periodic report containing the financial statements fully complies with the requirements of section 13(a) or 15(d) of the Securities Exchange Act of 1934 and that information contained in the periodic report fairly presents, in all material respects, the financial condition and results of operations of the issuer.

(c) *Criminal Penalties.* Whoever

(1) certifies any statement as set forth in subsections (a) and (b) of this section knowing that the periodic report accompanying the statement does not comport with all the requirements set forth in this section shall be fined not more than $1,000,000 or imprisoned not more than 10 years, or both; or

(2) willfully certifies any statement as set forth in sub-sections (a) and (b) of this section knowing that the periodic report accompanying the statement does not comport with all the requirements set forth in this section shall be fined not more than $5,000,000, or imprisoned not more than 20 years, or both.

(b) [Omitted.]

TITLE XI—CORPORATE FRAUD AND ACCOUNTABILITY

Short Title

Sec. 1101. This title may be cited as the "Corporate Fraud Accountability Act of 2002".

Tampering with a Record or Otherwise Impeding an Official Proceeding

Sec. 1102. Section 1512 of title 18, United States Code, is amended

(1) by redesignating subsections (c) through (i) as subsections (d) through (j), respectively; and

(2) by inserting after subsection (b) the following new subsection:

(c) Whoever corruptly

(1) alters, destroys, mutilates, or conceals a record, document, or other object, or attempts to do so, with the intent to impair the object's integrity or availability for use in an official proceeding; or

(2) otherwise obstructs, influences, or impedes any official proceeding, or attempts to do so, shall be fined under this title or imprisoned not more than 20 years, or both.

Temporary Freeze Authority for the Securities and Exchange Commission

Sec. 1103. [Omitted Section amending section 21C(c) of the Securities Exchange Act of 1934.]

Amendment to the Federal Sentencing Guidelines

Sec. 1104. (a) *Request for Immediate Consideration by the United States Sentencing Commission.* Pursuant to its authority under section 994(p) of title 28, United States Code, and in accordance with this section, the United States Sentencing Commission is requested to

(1) promptly review the sentencing guidelines applicable to securities and accounting fraud and related offenses;

(2) expeditiously consider the promulgation of new sentencing guidelines or amendments to existing sentencing guidelines to provide an enhancement for officers or directors of publicly traded corporations who commit fraud and related offenses; and

(3) submit to Congress an explanation of actions taken by the Sentencing Commission pursuant to paragraph (2) and any additional policy recommendations the Sentencing Commission may have for combating offenses described in paragraph (1).

(b) *Considerations in Review.* In carrying out this section, the Sentencing Commission is requested to

(1) ensure that the sentencing guidelines and policy statements reflect the serious nature of securities, pension, and accounting fraud and the need for aggressive and appropriate law enforcement action to prevent such offenses;

(2) assure reasonable consistency with other relevant directives and with other guidelines;

(3) account for any aggravating or mitigating circumstances that might justify exceptions, including circumstances for which the sentencing guidelines currently provide sentencing enhancements;

(4) ensure that guideline offense levels and enhancements for an obstruction of justice offense are adequate in cases where documents or other physical evidence are actually destroyed or fabricated;

(5) ensure that the guideline offense levels and enhancements under United States Sentencing Guideline 2B1.1 (as in effect on the date of enactment of this Act) are sufficient for a fraud offense when the number of victims adversely involved is significantly greater than 50;

(6) make any necessary conforming changes to the sentencing guidelines; and

(7) assure that the guidelines adequately meet the purposes of sentencing as set forth in section 3553 (a)(2) of title 18, United States Code.

(c) *Emergency Authority and Deadline for Commission.* The United States Sentencing Commission is requested to promulgate the guidelines or amendments provided for under this section as soon as practicable, and in any event not later than the 180 days after the date of enactment of this Act, in accordance with the procedures sent forth in section 21(a) of the Sentencing Reform Act of 1987, as though the authority under that Act had not expired.

Authority of the Commission to Prohibit Persons from Serving as Officers or Directors

Sec. 1105. (a) [Omitted. Subsection amending section 21C of the Securities Exchange Act of 1934.]

(b) [Omitted. Subsection amending section 8A of the Securities Act of 1933.]

Increased Criminal Penalties under Securities Exchange Act of 1934

Sec. 1106. [Omitted. Section amending Section 32(a) of the Securities Exchange Act of 1934]

Retaliation Against Informants

Sec. 1107. (a) *In General.* Section 1513 of title 18, United States Code, is amended by adding at the end the following:

(e) Whoever knowingly, with the intent to retaliate, takes any action harmful to any person, including interference with the lawful employment or livelihood of any person, for providing to a law enforcement officer any truthful information relating to the commission or possible commission of any Federal offense, shall be fined under this title or imprisoned not more than 10 years, or both.

J. DODD–FRANK WALL STREET REFORM AND CONSUMER PROTECTION ACT

Public Law 111–203

(Selected Provisions)

Short Title; Table of Contents

Sec. 1. (a) *Short Title.* This Act may be cited as the "Dodd–Frank Wall Street Reform and Consumer Protection Act".

(b) [Table of Contents Omitted].

Definitions

Sec. 2. As used in this Act, the following definitions shall apply, except as the context otherwise requires or as otherwise specifically provided in this Act:

(1) *Affiliate.* The term "affiliate" has the same meaning as in section 3 of the Federal Deposit Insurance Act.

(2) *Appropriate Federal Banking Agency.* On and after the transfer date, the term "appropriate Federal banking agency" has the same meaning as in section 3(q) of the Federal Deposit Insurance Act, as amended by title III.

(3) *Board of Governors.* The term "Board of Governors" means the Board of Governors of the Federal Reserve System.

(4) *Bureau.* The term "Bureau" means the Bureau of Consumer Financial Protection established under title X.

(5) *Commission.* The term "Commission" means the Securities and Exchange Commission, except in the context of the Commodity Futures Trading Commission.

(6) *Commodity Futures Terms.* The terms "futures commission merchant", "swap", "swap dealer", "swap execution facility", "derivatives clearing organization", "board of trade", "commodity trading advisor", "commodity pool", and "commodity pool operator" have the same meanings as given the terms in section 1a of the Commodity Exchange Act.

(7) *Corporation.* The term "Corporation" means the Federal Deposit Insurance Corporation.

(8) *Council.* The term "Council" means the Financial Stability Oversight Council established under title I.

(9) *Credit Union.* The term "credit union" means a Federal credit union, State credit union, or State-chartered credit union, as those terms are defined in section 101 of the Federal Credit Union Act.

(10) *Federal Banking Agency.* The term

(A) "Federal banking agency" means, individually, the Board of Governors, the Office of the Comptroller of the Currency, and the Corporation; and

(B) "Federal banking agencies" means all of the agencies referred to in subparagraph (A), collectively.

(11) *Functionally Related Subsidiary.* The term "functionally regulated subsidiary" has the same meaning as in section 5(c)(5) of the Bank Holding Company Act of 1956.

(12) *Primary Financial Regulatory Agency.* The term "primary financial regulatory agency" means

(A) the appropriate Federal banking agency, with respect to institutions described in section 3(q) of the Federal Deposit Insurance Act, except to the extent that an institution is or the activities of an institution are otherwise described in subparagraph (B), (C), (D), or (E);

(B) the Securities and Exchange Commission, with respect to—

(i) any broker or dealer that is registered with the Commission under the Securities Exchange Act of 1934, with respect to the activities of the broker or dealer that require the broker or dealer to be registered under that Act;

(ii) any investment company that is registered with the Commission under the Investment Company Act of 1940, with respect to the activities of the investment company that require the investment company to be registered under that Act;

(iii) any investment adviser that is registered with the Commission under the Investment Advisers Act of 1940, with respect to the investment advisory activities of such company and activities that are incidental to such advisory activities;

(iv) any clearing agency registered with the Commission under the Securities Exchange Act of 1934, with respect to the activities of the clearing agency that require the agency to be registered under such Act;

(v) any nationally recognized statistical rating organization registered with the Commission under the Securities Exchange Act of 1934;

(vi) any transfer agent registered with the Commission under the Securities Exchange Act of 1934;

(vii) any exchange registered as a national securities exchange with the Commission under the Securities Exchange Act of 1934;

(viii) any national securities association registered with the Commission under the Securities Exchange Act of 1934;

(ix) any securities information processor registered with the Commission under the Securities Exchange Act of 1934;

(x) the Municipal Securities Rulemaking Board established under the Securities Exchange Act of 1934;

(xi) the Public Company Accounting Oversight Board established under the Sarbanes-Oxley Act of 2002;

(xii) the Securities Investor Protection Corporation established under the Securities Investor Protection Act of 1970; and

(xiii) any security-based swap execution facility, security-based swap data repository, security-based swap dealer or major security-based swap participant registered with the Commission under the Securities Exchange Act of 1934, with respect to the security-based swap activities of the person that require such person to be registered under such Act;

(C) the Commodity Futures Trading Commission, with respect to—

(i) any futures commission merchant registered with the Commodity Futures Trading Commission under the Commodity Exchange Act, with respect to the activities of the futures commission merchant that require the futures commission merchant to be registered under that Act;

(ii) any commodity pool operator registered with the Commodity Futures Trading Commission under the Commodity Exchange Act, with respect to the activities of the commodity pool operator that require the commodity pool operator to be registered under that Act, or a commodity pool, as defined in that Act;

(iii) any commodity trading advisor or introducing broker registered with the Commodity Futures Trading Commission under the Commodity Exchange Act, with respect to the activities of the commodity trading advisor or introducing broker that require the commodity trading adviser or introducing broker to be registered under that Act;

(iv) any derivatives clearing organization registered with the Commodity Futures Trading Commission under the Commodity Exchange Act with respect to the activities of the derivatives clearing organization that require the derivatives clearing organization to be registered under that Act;

(v) any board of trade designated as a contract market by the Commodity Futures Trading Commission under the Commodity Exchange Act;

(vi) any futures association registered with the Commodity Futures Trading Commission under the Commodity Exchange Act;

(vii) any retail foreign exchange dealer registered with the Commodity Futures Trading Commission under the Commodity Exchange Act, with respect to the activities of the retail foreign exchange dealer that require the retail foreign exchange dealer to be registered under that Act;

(viii) any swap execution facility, swap data repository, swap dealer, or major swap participant registered with the Commodity Futures Trading Commission under the Commodity Exchange Act with respect to the swap activities of the person that require such person to be registered under that Act; and

(ix) any registered entity under the Commodity Exchange Act, with respect to the activities of the registered entity that require the registered entity to be registered under that Act;

(D) the State insurance authority of the State in which an insurance company is domiciled, with respect to the insurance activities and activities that are incidental to such insurance activities of an insurance company that is subject to supervision by the State insurance authority under State insurance law; and

(E) the Federal Housing Finance Agency, with respect to Federal Home Loan Banks or the Federal Home Loan Bank System, and with respect to the Federal National Mortgage Association or the Federal Home Loan Mortgage Corporation.

(13) *Prudential Standards.* The term "prudential standards" means enhanced supervision and regulatory standards developed by the Board of Governors under section 165.

(14) *Secretary.* The term "Secretary" means the Secretary of the Treasury.

(15) *Securities Terms.* The—

(A) terms "broker", "dealer", "issuer", "nationally recognized statistical rating organization", "security", and "securities laws" have the same meanings as in section 3 of the Securities Exchange Act of 1934;

(B) term "investment adviser" has the same meaning as in section 202 of the Investment Advisers Act of 1940 and

(C) term "investment company" has the same meaning as in section 3 of the Investment Company Act of 1940.

(16) *State.* The term "State" means any State, commonwealth, territory, or possession of the United States, the District of Columbia, the Commonwealth of Puerto Rico, the Commonwealth of the Northern Mariana Islands, American Samoa, Guam, or the United States Virgin Islands.

(17) *Transfer Date.* The term "transfer date" means the date established under section 311.

(18) *Other Incorporated Definitions*

(A) *Federal Deposit Insurance Act.* The terms "bank", "bank holding company", "control", "deposit", "depository institution", "Federal depository institution", "Federal savings association", "foreign bank", "including", "insured branch", "insured depository institution", "national member bank", "national nonmember bank", "savings association", "State bank", "State depository institution", "State member bank", "State nonmember bank", "State savings association", and "subsidiary" have the same meanings as in section 3 of the Federal Deposit Insurance Act.

(B) *Holding Companies.* The term—

(i) "bank holding company" has the same meaning as in section 2 of the Bank Holding Company Act of 1956;

(ii) "financial holding company" has the same meaning as in section 2(p) of the Bank Holding Company Act of 1956; and

(iii) "savings and loan holding company" has the same meaning as in section 10 of the Home Owners' Loan Act.

TITLE IV—REGULATION OF ADVISERS TO HEDGE FUNDS AND OTHERS

Short Title

Sec. 401. This title may be cited as the "Private Fund Investment Advisers Registration Act of 2010".

Definitions

Sec. 402. [Omitted. Section amended section 202(a) of the Investment Advisers Act of 1940.]

Elimination of Private Adviser Exemption; Limited Exemption for Foreign Private Advisers; Limited Intrastate Exemption

Sec. 403. [Omitted. Section amended section 203(b) of the Investment Advisers Act of 1940.]

Collection of Systemic Risk Data; Reports; Examinations; Disclosures

Sec. 404. [Omitted. Section amended section 204 of the Investment Advisers Act of 1940.]

Disclosure Provision Amendment

Sec. 405. [Omitted. Section amended section 210(c) of the Investment Advisers Act of 1940.]

Clarification of Rulemaking Authority

Sec. 406. [Omitted. Section amended section 211 of the Investment Advisers Act of 1940.]

Exemption of and Reporting by Venture Capital Fund Advisers

Sec. 407. [Omitted. Section amended section 203 of the Investment Advisers Act of 1940.]

Exemption of and Reporting by Certain Private Fund Advisers

Sec. 408. [Omitted. Section amended section 203 of the Investment Advisers Act of 1940.]

Family Offices

Sec. 409. (a) [Omitted. Subsection amended section 202(a)(11) of the Investment Advisers Act of 1940]

(b) *Rulemaking.* The rules, regulations, or orders issued by the Commission pursuant to section 202(a)(11)(G) of the Investment Advisers Act of 1940, as added by this section, regarding the definition of the term "family office" shall provide for an exemption that—

(1) is consistent with the previous exemptive policy of the Commission, as reflected in exemptive orders for family offices in effect on the date of enactment of this Act, and the grandfathering provisions in paragraph (3);

(2) recognizes the range of organizational, management, and employment structures and arrangements employed by family offices; and

(3) does not exclude any person who was not registered or required to be registered under the Investment Advisers Act of 1940 on January 1, 2010 from the definition of the term "family office", solely because such person provides investment advice to, and was engaged before January 1, 2010 in providing investment advice to—

(A) natural persons who, at the time of their applicable investment, are officers, directors, or employees of the family office who—

(i) have invested with the family office before January 1, 2010; and

(ii) are accredited investors, as defined in Regulation D of the Commission (or any successor thereto) under the Securities Act of 1933, or, as the Commission may prescribe by rule, the successors-in-interest thereto;

(B) any company owned exclusively and controlled by members of the family of the family office, or as the Commission may prescribe by rule;

(C) any investment adviser registered under the Investment Adviser Act of 1940 that provides investment advice to the family office and who identifies investment opportunities to the family office, and invests in such transactions on substantially the same terms as the family office invests, but does not invest in other funds advised by the family office, and whose assets as to which the family office directly or indirectly provides investment advice represent, in the aggregate, not more than 5 percent of the value of the total assets as to which the family office provides investment advice.

(c) *Anti Fraud Authority.* A family office that would not be a family office, but for subsection (b)(3), shall be deemed to be an investment adviser for the purposes of paragraphs (1), (2) and (4) of section 206 of the Investment Advisers Act of 1940.

State and Federal Responsibilities; Asset Threshold for Federal Registration of Investment Advisers

Sec. 410. [Omitted. Section amended section 203A(a) of the Investment Advisers Act of 1940.]

Custody of Client Assets

Sec. 411. [Omitted. Section added section 223 to the Investment Advisers Act of 1940.]

Comptroller General Study on Custody Rule Costs

Sec. 412. The Comptroller General of the United States shall—

(1) conduct a study of—

(A) the compliance costs associated with the current Securities and Exchange Commission Rule 204–2 and Rule 206(4)–2 under the Investment Advisers Act of 1940 regarding custody of funds or securities of clients by investment advisers; and

(B) the additional costs if subsection (b)(6) of rule 206(4)–2 relating to operational independence were eliminated; and

(2) submit a report to the Committee on Banking, Housing, and Urban Affairs of the Senate and the Committee on Financial Services of the House of Representatives on the results of such study, not later than 3 years after the date of enactment of this Act.

Adjusting the Accredited Investor Standard

Sec. 413. (a) *In General.* The Commission shall adjust any net worth standard for an accredited investor, as set forth in the rules of the Commission under the Securities Act of 1933, so that the individual net worth of any natural person, or joint net worth with the spouse of that person, at the time of purchase, is more than $1,000,000 (as such amount is adjusted periodically by rule of the Commission), excluding the value of the primary residence of such natural person, except that during the 4-year period that begins on the date of enactment of this Act, any net worth standard shall be $1,000,000, excluding the value of the primary residence of such natural person.

(b) *Review and Adjustment.*

(1) *Initial Review and Adjustment.*

(A) *Initial Review.* The Commission may undertake a review of the definition of the term "accredited investor", as such term applies to natural persons, to determine whether the requirements of the definition, excluding the requirement relating to the net worth standard described in subsection (a), should be adjusted or modified for the protection of investors, in the public interest, and in light of the economy.

(B) *Adjustment of Modification.* Upon completion of a review under subparagraph (A), the Commission may, by notice and comment rulemaking, make such adjustments to the definition of the term "accredited investor", excluding adjusting or modifying the requirement relating to the net worth standard described in subsection (a), as such term applies to natural persons, as the Commission may deem appropriate for the protection of investors, in the public interest, and in light of the economy.

(2) *Subsequent Reviews and Adjustment.*

(A) *Subsequent Reviews.* Not earlier than 4 years after the date of enactment of this Act, and not less frequently than once every 4 years thereafter, the Commission shall undertake a review of the definition, in its entirety, of the term "accredited investor", as defined in Rule 215 under the Securities Act of 1933, or any successor thereto, as such term applies to natural persons, to determine whether the requirements of the definition should be adjusted or modified for the protection of investors, in the public interest, and in light of the economy.

(B) *Adjustment or Modification.* Upon completion of a review under subparagraph (A), the Commission may, by notice and comment rulemaking, make such adjustments to the definition of the term "accredited investor", as defined in Rule 215 under the Securities Act of 1933, or any successor thereto, as such term applies to natural persons, as the Commission may deem appropriate for the protection of investors, in the public interest, and in light of the economy.

Rule of Construction Relating to the Commodities Exchange Act

Sec. 414. [Omitted. Section added section 224 to the Investment Advisers Act of 1940.]

GAO Study and Report of Accredited Investors

Sec. 415. The Comptroller General of the United States shall conduct a study on the appropriate criteria for determining the financial thresholds or other criteria needed to qualify for accredited investor status and eligibility to invest in private funds, and shall submit a report to the Committee on Banking, Housing, and Urban Affairs of the Senate and the Committee on Financial Services of the House of Representatives on the results of such study not later than 3 years after the date of enactment of this Act.

GAO Study on Self-Regulatory Organization for Private Funds

Sec. 416. The Comptroller General of the United States shall—

(1) conduct a study of the feasibility of forming a self-regulatory organization to oversee private funds; and

(2) submit a report to the Committee on Banking, Housing, and Urban Affairs of the Senate and the Committee on Financial Services of the House of Representatives on the results of such study, not later than 1 year after the date of enactment of this Act.

Commission Study and Report on Short Selling

Sec. 417. (a) *Studies.* The Division of Risk, Strategy, and Financial Innovation of the Commission shall conduct—

(1) a study, taking into account current scholarship, on the state of short selling on national securities exchanges and in the over-the-counter markets, with particular attention to the impact of recent rule changes and the incidence of—

(A) the failure to deliver shares sold short; or

(B) delivery of shares on the fourth day following the short Be transaction; and

(2) a study of—

(A) the feasibility, benefits, and costs of requiring reporting publicly, in real time short Be positions of publicly listed securities, or, in the alternative, reporting such short positions in real time only to the Commission and the Financial Industry Regulatory Authority; and

(B) the feasibility, benefits, and costs of conducting a voluntary pilot program in which public companies will agree to have all trades of their shares marked "short", "market maker short", "buy", "buy-to-cover", or "long", and reported in real time through the Consolidated Tape.

(b) *Reports.* The Commission shall submit a report to the Committee on Banking, Housing, and Urban Affairs of the Senate and the Committee on Financial Services of the House of Representatives—

(1) on the results of the study required under subsection (a)(1), including recommendations for market improvements, not later than 2 years after the date of enactment of this Act; and

(2) on the results of the study required under subsection (a)(2), not later than 1 year after the date of enactment of this Act.

Qualified Client Standard

Sec. 418. [Omitted. Section amended section 205(e) of the Investment Advisers Act of 1940.]

Transition Period

Sec. 419. Except as otherwise provided in this title, this title and the amendments made by this title shall become effective 1 year after the date of enactment of this Act, except that any investment adviser may, at the discretion of the investment adviser, register with the Commission under the Investment Advisers Act of 1940 during that 1-year period, subject to the rules of the Commission.

TITLE VII—WALL STREET TRANSPARENCY AND ACCOUNTABILITY

Short Title

Sec. 701. This title may be cited as the "Wall Street Transparency and Accountability Act of 2010".

SUBTITLE A—REGULATION OF OVER-THE-COUNTER SWAPS MARKETS

PART I—REGULATORY AUTHORITY

Definitions

Sec. 711. In this subtitle, the terms "prudential regulator", "swap", "swap dealer", "major swap participant", "swap data repository", "associated person of a swap dealer or major swap participant", "eligible contract participant", "swap execution facility", "security-based swap", "security-based swap dealer", "major security-based swap participant", and "associated person of a security-based swap dealer or major security-based swap participant" have the meanings given the terms in section 1a of the Commodity Exchange Act, including any modification of the meanings under section 721(b) of this Act.

Review of Regulatory Authority

Sec. 712. (a) *Consultation.*

(1) *Commodity Futures Trading Commission.* Before commencing any rulemaking or issuing an order regarding swaps, swap dealers, major swap participants, swap data repositories, derivative clearing organizations with regard to swaps, persons associated with a swap dealer or major swap participant, eligible contract participants, or swap execution facilities pursuant to this subtitle, the Commodity Futures Trading Commission shall consult and coordinate to the extent possible with the Securities and Exchange Commission and the prudential regulators for the purposes of assuring regulatory consistency and comparability, to the extent possible.

(2) *Securities and Exchange Commission.* Before commencing any rulemaking or issuing an order regarding security-based swaps, security-based swap dealers, major security-based swap participants, security-based swap data repositories, clearing agencies with regard to security-based swaps, persons associated with a security-based swap dealer or major security-based swap partic-

ipant, eligible contract participants with regard to security-based swaps, or security-based swap execution facilities pursuant to subtitle B, the Securities and Exchange Commission shall consult and coordinate to the extent possible with the Commodity Futures Trading Commission and the prudential regulators for the purposes of assuring regulatory consistency and comparability, to the extent possible.

(3) *Procedures and Deadline.* Such regulations shall be prescribed in accordance with applicable requirements of title 5, United States Code, and shall be issued in final form not later than 360 days after the date of enactment of this Act.

(4) *Applicability.* The requirements of paragraphs (1) and (2) shall not apply to an order issued—

(A) in connection with or arising from a violation or potential violation of any provision of the Commodity Exchange Act;

(B) in connection with or arising from a violation or potential violation of any provision of the securities laws; or

(C) in any proceeding that is conducted on the record in accordance with sections 556 and 557 of title 5, United States Code.

(5) *Effect.* Nothing in this subsection authorizes any consultation or procedure for consultation that is not consistent with the requirements of subchapter II of chapter 5, and chapter 7, of title 5, United States Code (commonly known as the "Administrative Procedure Act").

(6) *Rules; Orders.* In developing and promulgating rules or orders pursuant to this subsection, each Commission shall consider the views of the prudential regulators.

(7) *Treatment of Similar Products and Entities.*

(A) *In General.* In adopting rules and orders under this subsection, the Commodity Futures Trading Commission and the Securities and Exchange Commission shall treat functionally or economically similar products or entities described in paragraphs (1) and (2) in a similar manner.

(B) *Effect.* Nothing in this subtitle requires the Commodity Futures Trading Commission or the Securities and Exchange Commission to adopt joint rules or orders that treat functionally or economically similar products or entities described in paragraphs (1) and (2) in an identical manner.

(8) *Mixed Swaps.* The Commodity Futures Trading Commission and the Securities and Exchange Commission, after consultation with the Board of Governors, shall jointly prescribe such regulations regarding mixed swaps, as described in section 1a(47)(D) of the Commodity Exchange Act and in section 3(a)(68)(D) of the Securities Exchange Act of 1934, as may be necessary to carry out the purposes of this title.

(b) *Limitation.*

(1) *Commodity Futures Trading Commission.* Nothing in this title, unless specifically provided, confers jurisdiction on the Commodity Futures Trading Commission to issue a rule, regulation, or order providing for oversight or regulation of—

(A) security-based swaps; or

(B) with regard to its activities or functions concerning security-based swaps

(i) security-based swap dealers;

(ii) major security-based swap participants;

(iii) security-based swap data repositories;

(iv) associated persons of a security-based swap dealer or major security-based swap participant;

(v) eligible contract participants with respect to security-based swaps; or

(vi) swap execution facilities with respect to security-based swaps.

(2) *Securities and Exchange Commission.* Nothing in this title, unless specifically provided, confers jurisdiction on the Securities and Exchange Commission or State securities regulators to issue a rule, regulation, or order providing for oversight or regulation of—

(A) swaps; or

(B) with regard to its activities or functions concerning swaps

(i) swap dealers;

(ii) major swap participants;

(iii) swap data repositories;

(iv) persons associated with a swap dealer or major swap participant;

(v) eligible contract participants with respect to swaps; or

(vi) swap execution facilities with respect to swaps.

(3) *Prohibition on Certain Futures Associations and National Securities Associations.*

(A) *Futures Associations.* Notwithstanding any other provision of law (including regulations), unless otherwise authorized by this title, no futures association registered under section 17 of the Commodity Exchange Act may issue a rule, regulation, or order for the oversight or regulation of, or otherwise assert jurisdiction over, for any purpose, any security-based swap, except that this subparagraph shall not limit the authority of a registered futures association to examine for compliance with, and enforce, its rules on capital adequacy.

(B) *National Securities Associations.* Notwithstanding any other provision of law (including regulations), unless otherwise authorized by this title, no national securities association registered under section 15A of the Securities Exchange Act of 1934 may issue a rule, regulation, or order for the oversight or regulation of, or otherwise assert jurisdiction over, for any purpose, any swap, except that this subparagraph shall not limit the authority of a national securities association to examine for compliance with, and enforce, its rules on capital adequacy.

(c) *Objection to Commission Regulation.*

(1) *Filing of Petition for Review.*

(A) *In General.* If either Commission referred to in this section determines that a final rule, regulation, or order of the other Commission conflicts with subsection (a)(7) or (b), then the complaining Commission may obtain review of the final rule, regulation, or order in the United States Court of Appeals for the District of Columbia Circuit by filing in the court, not later than 60 days after the date of publication of the final rule, regulation, or order, a written petition requesting that the rule, regulation, or order be set aside.

(B) *Expedited Proceeding.* A proceeding described in subparagraph (A) shall be expedited by the United States Court of Appeals for the District of Columbia Circuit.

(2) *Transmittal of Petition and Record.*

(A) *In General.* A copy of a petition described in paragraph (1) shall be transmitted not later than 1 business day after the date of filing by the complaining Commission to the Secretary of the responding Commission.

(B) *Duty of Responding Commission.* On receipt of the copy of a petition described in paragraph (1), the responding Commission shall file with the United States Court of Appeals for the District of Columbia Circuit—

(i) a copy of the rule, regulation, or order under review (including any documents referred to therein); and

(ii) any other materials prescribed by the United States Court of Appeals for the District of Columbia Circuit.

(3) *Standard of Review.* The United States Court of Appeals for the District of Columbia Circuit shall—

(A) give deference to the views of neither Commission; and

(B) determine to affirm or set aside a rule, regulation, or order of the responding Commission under this subsection, based on the determination of the court as to whether the rule, regulation, or order is in conflict with subsection (a)(7) or (b), as applicable.

(4) *Judicial Stay.* The filing of a petition by the complaining Commission pursuant to paragraph (1) shall operate as a stay of the rule, regulation, or order until the date on which the determination of the United States Court of Appeals for the District of Columbia Circuit is final (including any appeal of the determination).

(d) *Joint Rulemaking.*

(1) *In General.* Notwithstanding any other provision of this title and subsections (b) and (c), the Commodity Futures Trading Commission and the Securities and Exchange Commission, in consultation with the Board of Governors, shall further define the terms "swap", "security-based swap", "swap dealer", "security-based swap dealer", "major swap participant", "major security-based swap participant", "eligible contract participant", and "security-based swap agreement" in section 1a(47)(A)(v) of the Commodity Exchange Act and section 3(a)(78) of the Securities Exchange Act of 1934.

(2) *Authority of the Commissions.*

(A) *In General.* Notwithstanding any other provision of this title, the Commodity Futures Trading Commission and the Securities and Exchange Commission, in consultation with the Board of Governors, shall jointly adopt such other rules regarding such definitions as the Commodity Futures Trading Commission and the Securities Exchange Commission determine are necessary and appropriate, in the public interest, and for the protection of investors.

(B) *Trade Repository Recordkeeping.* Notwithstanding any other provision of this title, the Commodity Futures Trading Commission and the Securities and Exchange Commission, in consultation with the Board of Governors, shall engage in joint rulemaking to jointly adopt a rule or rules governing the books and records that are required to be kept and maintained regarding security-based swap agreements by persons that are registered as swap data repositories under the Commodity Exchange Act, including uniform rules that specify the data elements that shall be collected and maintained by each repository.

(C) *Books and Records.* Notwithstanding any other provision of this title, the Commodity Futures Trading Commission and the Securities and Exchange Commission, in consultation with the Board of Governors, shall engage in joint rulemaking to jointly adopt a rule or rules governing books and records regarding security-based swap agreements, including daily trading records, for swap dealers, major swap participants, security-based swap dealers, and security-based swap participants.

(D) *Comparable Rules.* Rules and regulations prescribed jointly under this title by the Commodity Futures Trading Commission and the Securities and Exchange Commission shall be comparable to the maximum extent possible, taking into consideration differences in instruments and in the applicable statutory requirements.

(E) *Tracking Uncleared Transactions.* Any rules prescribed under subparagraph (A) shall require the maintenance of records of all activities relating to security-based swap agreement transactions defined under subparagraph (A) that are not cleared.

(F) *Sharing of Information.* The Commodity Futures Trading Commission shall make available to the Securities and Exchange Commission information relating to security-based swap agreement transactions defined in subparagraph (A) that are not cleared.

(3) *Financial Stability Oversight Council.* In the event that the Commodity Futures Trading Commission and the Securities and Exchange Commission fail to jointly prescribe rules pursuant to paragraph (1) or (2) in a timely manner, at the request of either Commission, the Financial Stability Oversight Council shall resolve the dispute—

(A) within a reasonable time after receiving the request;

(B) after consideration of relevant information provided by each Commission; and

(C) by agreeing with 1 of the Commissions regarding the entirety of the matter or by determining a compromise position.

(4) *Joint Interpretation.* Any interpretation of, or guidance by either Commission regarding, a provision of this title, shall be effective only if issued jointly by the Commodity Futures Trading Commission and the Securities and Exchange Commission, after consultation with the Board of Governors, if this title requires the Commodity Futures Trading Commission and the Securities and Exchange Commission to issue joint regulations to implement the provision.

(e) *Global Rulemaking Timeframe.* Unless otherwise provided in this title, or an amendment made by this title, the Commodity Futures Trading Commission or the Securities and Exchange Commission, or both, shall individually, and not jointly, promulgate rules and regulations required of each Commission under this title or an amendment made by this title not later than 360 days after the date of enactment of this Act.

(f) *Rules and Registration Before Final Effective Dates.* Beginning on the date of enactment of this Act and not-withstanding the effective date of any provision of this Act, the Commodity Futures Trading Commission and the Securities and Exchange Commission may, in order to prepare for the effective dates of the provisions of this Act—

(1) promulgate rules, regulations, or orders permitted or required by this Act;

(2) conduct studies and prepare reports and recommendations required by this Act;

(3) register persons under the provisions of this Act; and

(4) exempt persons, agreements, contracts, or transactions from provisions of this Act, under the terms contained in this Act, provided, however, that no action by the Commodity Futures Trading

Commission or the Securities and Exchange Commission described in paragraphs (1) through (4) shall become effective prior to the effective date applicable to such action under the provisions of this Act.

Portfolio Margining Conforming Changes

Sec. 713. (a) [Omitted. Subsection amended section 15(c) of the Securities Exchange Act of 1934.]

(b) [Omitted. Subsection amended section 4d of the Commodity Exchange Act.]

(c) [Omitted. Subsection amended section 20 of the Commodity Exchange Act.]

Abusive Swaps

Sec. 714. The Commodity Futures Trading Commission or the Securities and Exchange Commission, or both, individually may, by rule or order

(1) collect information as may be necessary concerning the markets for any types of—

(A) swap (as defined in section 1a of the Commodity Exchange Act); or—

(B) security-based swap (as defined in section 1a of the Commodity Exchange Act); and

(2) issue a report with respect to any types of swaps or security-based swaps that the Commodity Futures Trading Commission or the Securities and Exchange Commission determines to be detrimental to—

(A) the stability of a financial market; or

(B) participants in a financial market.

Authority to Prohibit Participation in Swap Activities

Sec. 715. Except as provided in section 4 of the Commodity Exchange Act, if the Commodity Futures Trading Commission or the Securities and Exchange Commission determines that the regulation of swaps or security-based swaps markets in a foreign country undermines the stability of the United States financial system, either Commission, in consultation with the Secretary of the Treasury, may prohibit an entity domiciled in the foreign country from participating in the United States in any swap or security-based swap activities.

Prohibition Against Federal Government Bailouts of Swaps Entities

Sec. 716. (a) *Prohibition on Federal Assistance.* Notwithstanding any other provision of law (including regulations), no Federal assistance may be provided to any swaps entity with respect to any swap, security-based swap, or other activity of the swaps entity.

(b) *Definitions.* In this section:

(1) *Federal Assistance.* The term "Federal assistance" means the use of any advances from any Federal Reserve credit facility or discount window that is not part of a program or facility with broad-based eligibility under section 13(3)(A) of the Federal Reserve Act, Federal Deposit Insurance Corporation insurance or guarantees for the purpose of

(A) making any loan to, or purchasing any stock, equity interest, or debt obligation of, any swaps entity;

(B) purchasing the assets of any swaps entity;

(C) guaranteeing any loan or debt issuance of any swaps entity; or

(D) entering into any assistance arrangement (including tax breaks), loss sharing, or profit sharing with any swaps entity.

(2) *Swaps Entity.*

(A) *In General.* The term "swaps entity" means any swap dealer, security-based swap dealer, major swap participant, major security-based swap participant, that is registered under

(i) the Commodity Exchange Act; or

(ii) the Securities Exchange Act of 1934.

(B) *Exclusion.* The term "swaps entity" does not include any major swap participant or major security-based swap participant that is an insured depository institution.

(c) *Affiliates of Insured Depository Institutions.* The prohibition on Federal assistance contained in subsection (a) does not apply to and shall not prevent an insured depository institution from having or establishing an affiliate which is a swaps entity, as long as such insured depository institution is part of a bank holding company, or savings and loan holding company, that is supervised by the Federal Reserve and such swaps entity affiliate complies with sections 23A and 23B of the Federal Reserve Act and such other requirements as the Commodity Futures Trading Commission or the Securities Exchange Commission, as appropriate, and the Board of Governors of the Federal Reserve System, may determine to be necessary and appropriate.

(d) *Only Bona Fide Hedging and Traditional Bank Activities Permitted.* The prohibition in subsection (a) shall apply to any insured depository institution unless the insured depository institution limits its swap or security-based swap activities to:

(1) Hedging and other similar risk mitigating activities directly related to the insured depository institution's activities.

(2) Acting as a swaps entity for swaps or security-based swaps involving rates or reference assets that are permissible for investment by a national bank under the paragraph designated as "Seventh." of section 5136 of the Revised Statutes of the United States, other than as described in paragraph (3).

(3) *Limitation on Credit Default Swaps.* Acting as a swaps entity for credit default swaps, including swaps or security-based swaps referencing the credit risk of asset-backed securities as defined in section 3(a)(77) of the Securities Exchange Act of 1934 (as amended by this Act) shall not be considered a bank permissible activity for purposes of subsection (d)(2) unless such swaps or security-based swaps are cleared by a derivatives clearing organization (as such term is defined in section 1a of the Commodity Exchange Act) or a clearing agency (as such term is defined in section 3 of the Securities Exchange Act) that is registered, or exempt from registration, as a derivatives clearing organization under the Commodity Exchange Act or as a clearing agency under the Securities Exchange Act, respectively.

(e) *Existing Swaps and Security-Based Swaps.* The prohibition in subsection (a) shall only apply to swaps or security-based swaps entered into by an insured depository institution after the end of the transition period described in subsection (f).

(f) *Transition Period.* To the extent an insured depository institution qualifies as a "swaps entity" and would be subject to the Federal assistance prohibition in subsection (a), the appropriate Federal banking agency, after consulting with and considering the views of the Commodity Futures Trading Commission or the Securities Exchange Commission, as appropriate, shall permit the insured depository institution up to 24 months to divest the swaps entity or cease the activities that require registration as a swaps entity. In establishing the appropriate transition period to effect such divestiture or cessation of activities, which may include making the swaps entity an affiliate of the insured depository institution, the appropriate Federal banking agency shall take into account and make written findings regarding the potential impact of such divestiture or cessation of activities on the insured depository institution's (1) mortgage lending, (2) small business lending, (3) job creation, and (4) capital formation versus the potential negative impact on insured depositors and the Deposit Insurance Fund of the Federal Deposit Insurance Corporation. The appropriate Federal banking agency may consider such other factors as may be appropriate. The appropriate Federal banking agency may place such conditions on the insured depository institution's divestiture or ceasing of activities of the swaps entity as it deems necessary and appropriate. The transition period under this subsection may be extended by the appropriate Federal banking agency, after consultation with the Commodity Futures Trading Commission and the Securities and Exchange Commission, for a period of up to 1 additional year.

(g) *Excluded Entities.* For purposes of this section, the term "swaps entity" shall not include any insured depository institution under the Federal Deposit Insurance Act or a covered financial company under title II which is in a conservatorship, receivership, or a bridge bank operated by the Federal Deposit Insurance Corporation.

(h) *Effective Date.* The prohibition in subsection (a) shall be effective 2 years following the date on which this Act is effective.

(i) *Liquidation Required.*

(1) *In General.*

(A) *FDIC Insured Institutions.* All swaps entities that are FDIC insured institutions that are put into receivership or declared insolvent as a result of swap or security-based swap activity of the swaps entities shall be subject to the termination or transfer of that swap or security-based swap activity in accordance with applicable law prescribing the treatment of those contracts. No taxpayer funds shall be used to prevent the receivership of any swap entity resulting from swap or security-based swap activity of the swaps entity.

(B) *Institutions That Pose a Systemic Risk and Are Subject to Heightened Prudential Supervision as Regulated Under Section 113.* All swaps entities that are institutions that pose a systemic risk and are subject to heightened prudential supervision as regulated under section 113, that are put into receivership or declared insolvent as a result of swap or security-based swap activity of the swaps entities shall be subject to the termination or transfer of that swap or security-based swap activity in accordance with applicable law prescribing the treatment of those contracts. No taxpayer funds shall be used to prevent the receivership of any swap entity resulting from swap or security-based swap activity of the swaps entity.

(C) *Non-FDIC Insured, Non-Systemically Significant Institutions Not Subject to Heightened Prudential Supervision as Regulated Under Section 113.* No taxpayer resources shall be used for the orderly liquidation of any swaps entities that are non-FDIC insured, non-systemically significant institutions not subject to heightened prudential supervision as regulated under section 113.

(2) *Recovery of Funds.* All funds expended on the termination or transfer of the swap or security-based swap activity of the swaps entity shall be recovered in accordance with applicable law from the disposition of assets of such swap entity or through assessments, including on the financial sector as provided under applicable law.

(3) *No Losses to Taxpayers.* Taxpayers shall bear no losses from the exercise of any authority under this title.

(j) *Prohibition on Unregulated Combination of Swaps Entities and Banking.* At no time following adoption of the rules in subsection (k) may a bank or bank holding company be permitted to be or become a swap entity unless it conducts its swap or security-based swap activity in compliance with such minimum standards set by its prudential regulator as are reasonably calculated to permit the swaps entity to conduct its swap or security-based swap activities in a safe and sound manner and mitigate systemic risk.

(k) *Rules.* In prescribing rules, the prudential regulator for a swaps entity shall consider the following factors:

(1) The expertise and managerial strength of the swaps entity, including systems for effective oversight.

(2) The financial strength of the swaps entity.

(3) Systems for identifying, measuring and controlling risks arising from the swaps entity's operations.

(4) Systems for identifying, measuring and controlling the swaps entity's participation in existing markets.

(5) Systems for controlling the swaps entity's participation or entry into in new markets and products.

(*l*) *Authority of the Financial Stability Oversight Council.* The Financial Stability Oversight Council may determine that, when other provisions established by this Act are insufficient to effectively mitigate systemic risk and protect taxpayers, that swaps entities may no longer access Federal assistance with respect to any swap, security-based swap, or other activity of the swaps entity. Any such determination by the Financial Stability Oversight Council of a prohibition of federal assistance shall be made on an institution-by-institution basis, and shall require the vote of not fewer than two-thirds of the members of the Financial Stability Oversight Council, which must include the vote by the Chairman of the Council, the Chairman of the Board of Governors of the Federal Reserve System, and the Chairperson of the Federal Deposit Insurance Corporation. Notice and hearing requirements for such determinations shall be consistent with the standards provided in title I.

(m) *Ban on Proprietary Trading in Derivatives.* An insured depository institution shall comply with the prohibition on proprietary trading in derivatives as required by section 619 of the Dodd–Frank Wall Street Reform and Consumer Protection Act.

New Product Approval CFTC–SEC Process

Sec. 717. (a) [Omitted. Subsection amended section 2(a)(1)(C) of the Commodity Exchange Act.]

(b) [Omitted. Subsection added section 3B to the Securities Exchange Act of 1934.]

(c) [Omitted. Subsection amended section 19(b) of the Securities Exchange Act of 1934.]

(d) [Omitted. Subsection amended section 5c(c)(1) of the Commodity Exchange Act.]

Determining Status of Novel Derivative Products

Sec. 718. (a) *Process for Determining the Status of a Novel Derivative Product.*

(1) *Notice.*

(A) *In General.* Any person filing a proposal to list or trade a novel derivative product that may have elements of both securities and contracts of a commodity for future delivery (or options on such contracts or options on commodities) may concurrently provide notice and furnish a copy of such filing with the Securities and Exchange Commission and the Commodity Futures Trading Commission. Any such notice shall state that notice has been made with both Commissions.

(B) *Notification*. If no concurrent notice is made pursuant to subparagraph (A), within 5 business days after determining that a proposal that seeks to list or trade a novel derivative product may have elements of both securities and contracts of Be of a commodity for future delivery (or options on such contracts or options on commodities), the Securities and Exchange Commission or the Commodity Futures Trading Commission, as applicable, shall notify the other Commission and provide a copy of such filing to the other Commission.

(2) *Request for Determination*.

(A) *In General*. No later than 21 days after receipt of a notice under paragraph (1), or upon its own initiative if no such notice is received, the Commodity Futures Trading Commission may request that the Securities and Exchange Commission issue a determination as to whether a product is a security, as defined in section 3(a)(10) of the Securities Exchange Act of 1934.

(B) *Request*. No later than 21 days after receipt of a notice under paragraph (1), or upon its own initiative if no such notice is received, the Securities and Exchange Commission may request that the Commodity Futures Trading Commission issue a determination as to whether a product is a contract of a commodity for future delivery, an option on such a contract, or an option on a commodity subject to the Commodity Futures Trading Commission's exclusive jurisdiction under section 2(a)(1)(A) of the Commodity Exchange Act.

(C) *Requirement Relating to Request*. A request under subparagraph (A) or (B) shall be made by submitting such request, in writing, to the Securities and Exchange Commission or the Commodity Futures Trading Commission, as applicable.

(D) *Effect*. Nothing in this paragraph shall be construed to prevent—

(i) the Commodity Futures Trading Commission from requesting that the Securities and Exchange Commission grant an exemption pursuant to section 36(a)(1) of the Securities Exchange Act of 1934 with respect to a product that is the subject of a filing under paragraph (1); or

(ii) the Securities and Exchange Commission from requesting that the Commodity Futures Trading Commission grant an exemption pursuant to section 4(c)(1) of the Commodity Exchange Act with respect to a product that is the subject of a filing under paragraph (1), *Provided, however*, that nothing in this subparagraph shall be construed to require the Commodity Futures Trading Commission or the Securities and Exchange Commission to issue an exemption requested pursuant to this subparagraph; provided further, That an order granting or denying an exemption described in this subparagraph and issued under paragraph (3)(B) shall not be subject to judicial review pursuant to subsection (b).

(E) *Withdrawal of Request*. A request under subparagraph (A) or (B) may be withdrawn by the Commission making the request at any time prior to a determination being made pursuant to paragraph (3) for any reason by providing written notice to the head of the other Commission.

(3) *Determination*. Notwithstanding any other provision of law, no later than 120 days after the date of receipt of a request—

(A) under subparagraph (A) or (B) of paragraph (2), unless such request has been withdrawn pursuant to paragraph (2)(E), the Securities and Exchange Commission or the Commodity Futures Trading Commission, as applicable, shall, by order, issue the determination requested in subparagraph (A) or (B) of paragraph (2), as applicable, and the reasons therefor; or

(B) under paragraph (2)(D), unless such request has been withdrawn, the Securities and Exchange Commission or the Commodity Futures Trading Commission, as applicable, shall grant an exemption or provide reasons for not granting such exemption, provided that any decision by the Securities and Exchange Commission not to grant such exemption shall not be reviewable under section 25 of the Securities Exchange Act of 1934.

(b) *Judicial Resolution*.

(1) *In General*. The Commodity Futures Trading Commission or the Securities and Exchange Commission may petition the United States Court of Appeals for the District of Columbia Circuit for review of a final order of the other Commission issued pursuant to subsection (a)(3)(A), with re-

spect to a novel derivative product that may have elements of both securities and contracts of Be of a commodity for future delivery (or options on such contracts or options on commodities) that it believes affects its statutory jurisdiction within 60 days after the date of entry of such order, a written petition requesting a review of the order. Any such proceeding shall be expedited by the Court of Appeals.

(2) *Transmittal of Petition and Record.* A copy of a petition described in paragraph (1) shall be transmitted not later than 1 business day after filing by the complaining Commission to the responding Commission. On receipt of the petition, the responding Commission shall file with the court a copy of the order under review and any documents referred to therein, and any other materials prescribed by the court.

(3) *Standard of Review.* The court, in considering a petition filed pursuant to paragraph (1), shall give no deference to, or presumption in favor of, the views of either Commission.

(4) *Judicial Stay.* The filing of a petition by the complaining Commission pursuant to paragraph (1) shall operate as a stay of the order, until the date on which the determination of the court is final (including any appeal of the determination).

Studies

Sec. 719. (a) *Study on Effects of Position Limits on Trading on Exchanges in the United States.*

(1) *Study.* The Commodity Futures Trading Commission, in consultation with each entity that is a designated contract market under the Commodity Exchange Act, shall conduct a study of the effects (if any) of the position limits imposed pursuant to the other provisions of this title on excessive speculation and on the movement of transactions from exchanges in the United States to trading venues outside the United States.

(2) *Report to the Congress.* Within 12 months after the imposition of position limits pursuant to the other provisions of this title, the Commodity Futures Trading Commission, in consultation with each entity that is a designated contract market under the Commodity Exchange Act, shall submit to the Congress a report on the matters described in paragraph (1).

(3) *Required Hearing.* Within 30 legislative days after the submission to the Congress of the report described in paragraph (2), the Committee on Agriculture of the House of Representatives shall hold a hearing examining the findings of the report.

(4) *Biennial Reporting.* In addition to the study required in paragraph (1), the Chairman of the Commodity Futures Trading Commission shall prepare and submit to the Congress biennial reports on the growth or decline of the derivatives markets in the United States and abroad, which shall include assessments of the causes of any such growth or decline, the effectiveness of regulatory regimes in managing systemic risk, a comparison of the costs of compliance at the time of the report for market participants subject to regulation by the United States with the costs of compliance in December 2008 for the market participants, and the quality of the available data. In preparing the report, the Chairman shall solicit the views of, consult with, and address the concerns raised by, market participants, regulators, legislators, and other interested parties.

(b) *Study on Feasibility of Requiring Use of Standardized Algorithmic Descriptions for Financial Derivatives.*

(1) *In General.* The Securities and Exchange Commission and the Commodity Futures Trading Commission shall conduct a joint study of the feasibility of requiring the derivatives industry to adopt standardized computer-readable algorithmic descriptions, which may be used to describe complex and standardized financial derivatives.

(2) *Goals.* The algorithmic descriptions defined in the study shall be designed to facilitate computerized analysis of individual derivative contracts and to calculate net exposures to complex derivatives. The algorithmic descriptions shall be optimized for simultaneous use by—

(A) commercial users and traders of derivatives;

(B) derivative clearing houses, exchanges and electronic trading platforms;

(C) trade repositories and regulator investigations of market activities; and

(D) systemic risk regulators.

The study will also examine the extent to which the algorithmic description, together with standardized and extensible legal definitions, may serve as the binding legal definition of derivative contracts. The study will examine the logistics of possible implementations of standardized algorithmic descriptions for derivatives contracts. The study shall be limited to electronic formats for exchange of derivative contract descriptions and will not contemplate disclosure of proprietary valuation models.

(3) *International Coordination.* In conducting the study, the Securities and Exchange Commission and the Commodity Futures Trading Commission shall coordinate the study with international financial institutions and regulators as appropriate and practical.

(4) *Report.* Within 8 months after the date of the enactment of this Act, the Securities and Exchange Commission and the Commodity Futures Trading Commission shall jointly submit to the Committees on Agriculture and on Financial Services of the House of Representatives and the Committees on Agriculture, Nutrition, and Forestry and on Banking, Housing, and Urban Affairs of the Senate a written report which contains the results of the study required by paragraphs (1) through (3).

(c) *International Swap Regulation.*

(1) *In General.* The Commodity Futures Trading Commission and the Securities and Exchange Commission shall jointly conduct a study

(A) relating to—

(i) swap regulation in the United States, Asia, and Europe; and

(ii) clearing house and clearing agency regulation in the United States, Asia, and Europe; and

(B) that identifies areas of regulation that are similar in the United States, Asia and Europe and other areas of regulation that could be harmonized

(2) *Report.* Not later than 18 months after the date of enactment of this Act, the Commodity Futures Trading Commission and the Securities and Exchange Commission shall submit to the Committee on Agriculture, Nutrition, and Forestry and the Committee on Banking, Housing, and Urban Affairs of the Senate and the Committee on Agriculture and the Committee on Financial Services of the House of Representatives a report that includes a description of the results of the study under subsection (a), including

(A) identification of the major exchanges and their regulator in each geographic area for the trading of swaps and security-based swaps including a listing of the major contracts and their trading volumes and notional values as well as identification of the major swap dealers participating in such markets;

(B) identification of the major clearing houses and clearing agencies and their regulator in each geographic area for the clearing of swaps and security-based swaps, including a listing of the major contracts and the clearing volumes and notional values as well as identification of the major clearing members of such clearing houses and clearing agencies in such markets;

(C) a description of the comparative methods of clearing swaps in the United States, Asia, and Europe; and (D) a description of the various systems used for establishing margin on individual swaps, security-based swaps, and swap portfolios.

(d) *Stable Value Contracts.*

(1) *Determination.*

(A) *Status.* Not later than 15 months after the date of the enactment of this Act, the Securities and Exchange Commission and the Commodity Futures Trading Commission shall, jointly, conduct a study to determine whether stable value contracts fall within the definition of a swap. In making the determination required under this subparagraph, the Commissions jointly shall consult with the Department of Labor, the Department of the Treasury, and the State entities that regulate the issuers of stable value contracts.

(B) *Regulations.* If the Commissions determine that stable value contracts fall within the definition of a swap, the Commissions jointly shall determine if an exemption for stable value contracts from the definition of swap is appropriate and in the public interest. The Commissions shall issue regulations implementing the determinations required under this paragraph. Until the effective date of such regulations, and notwithstanding any other provision of this title, the requirements of this title shall not apply to stable value contracts.

(C) *Legal Certainty.* Stable value contracts in effect prior to the effective date of the regulations described in subparagraph (B) shall not be considered swaps.

(2) *Definition.* For purposes of this subsection, the term "stable value contract" means any contract, agreement, or transaction that provides a crediting interest rate and guaranty or financial assurance of liquidity at contract or book value

prior to maturity offered by a bank, insurance company, or other State or federally regulated financial institution for the benefit of any individual or commingled fund available as an investment in an employee benefit plan (as defined in section 3(3) of the Employee Retirement Income Security Act of 1974, including plans described in section 3(32) of such Act) subject to participant direction, an eligible deferred compensation plan (as defined in section 457(b) of the Internal Revenue Code of 1986) that is maintained by an eligible employer described in section 457(e)(1)(A) of such Code, an arrangement described in section 403(b) of such Code, or a qualified tuition program (as defined in section 529 of such Code).

Memorandum

Sec. 720. (a)(1) The Commodity Futures Trading Commission and the Federal Energy Regulatory Commission shall, not later than 180 days after the date of the enactment of this Act, negotiate a memorandum of understanding to establish procedures for—

(A) applying their respective authorities in a manner so as to ensure effective and efficient regulation in the public interest;

(B) resolving conflicts concerning overlapping jurisdiction between the 2 agencies; and

(C) avoiding, to the extent possible, conflicting or duplicative regulation.

(2) Such memorandum and any subsequent amendments to the memorandum shall be promptly submitted to the appropriate committees of Congress.

(b) The Commodity Futures Trading Commission and the Federal Energy Regulatory Commission shall, not later than 180 days after the date of the enactment of this section, negotiate a memorandum of understanding to share information that may be requested where either Commission is conducting an investigation into potential manipulation, fraud, or market power abuse in markets subject to such Commission's regulation or oversight. Shared information shall remain subject to the same restrictions on disclosure applicable to the Commission initially holding the information.

PART II—REGULATION OF SWAP MARKETS

Definitions

Sec. 721. (a) [Omitted. Subsection amended section 1a of the Commodity Exchange Act.]

(b) *Authority to Define Terms.* The Commodity Futures Trading Commission may adopt a rule to define

(1) the term "commercial risk"; and

(2) any other term included in an amendment to the Commodity Exchange Act made by this subtitle.

(c) *Modification of Definitions.* To include transactions and entities that have been structured to evade this subtitle (or an amendment made by this subtitle), the Commodity Futures Trading Commission shall adopt a rule to further define the terms "swap", "swap dealer", "major swap participant", and "eligible contract participant".

(d) [Omitted. Subsection amended section 4(c)(1) of the Commodity Exchange Act.]

(e) [Omitted. Subsection amended 2(c)(2)(B)(i)(II) of the Commodity Exchange Act.]

(f) *Effective Date.* Notwithstanding any other provision of this Act, the amendments made by subsection (a)(4) shall take effect on June 1, 2010.

Jurisdiction

Sec. 722. (a) [Omitted. Subsection amended section 2(a)(1) of the Commodity Exchange Act.]

(b) [Omitted. Subsection amended section 12 of the Commodity Exchange Act.]

(c) [Omitted. Subsection amended section 2(c)(2)(A) of the Commodity Exchange Act.]

(d) [Omitted. Subsection amended section 2 of the Commodity Exchange Act.]

(e) [Omitted. Subsection amended section 2(a)(1) of the Commodity Exchange Act.]

(f) [Omitted. Subsection amended section 4(c) of the Commodity Exchange Act.]

(g) *Authority of FERC.* Nothing in the Wall Street Transparency and Accountability Act of 2010 or the amendments to the Commodity Exchange Act made by such Act shall limit or affect any statutory enforcement authority of the Federal Energy Regulatory Commission pursuant to section 222 of the Federal Power Act and section 4A of the Natural Gas

Act that existed prior to the date of enactment of the Wall Street Transparency and Accountability Act of 2010.

(h) [Omitted. Subsection added section 1b to the Commodity Exchange Act.]

Clearing

Sec. 723. (a) [Omitted. Subsection amended section 2 of the Commodity Exchange Act.]

(b) [Omitted. Subsection amended section 2(a)(1) of the Commodity Exchange Act.]

(c) *Grandfather Provisions.*

(1) *Legal Certainty for Certain Transactions in Exempt Commodities.* Not later than 60 days after the date of enactment of this Act, a person may submit to the Commodity Futures Trading Commission a petition to remain subject to section 2(h) of the Commodity Exchange Act (as in effect on the day before the date of enactment of this Act).

(2) *Consideration; Authority of Commodity Futures Trading Commission.* The Commodity Futures Trading Commission

(A) shall consider any petition submitted under subparagraph (A) in a prompt manner; and

(B) may allow a person to continue operating subject to section 2(h) of the Commodity Exchange Act (as in effect on the day before the date of enactment of this Act) for not longer than a 1–year period.

(3) *Agricultural Swaps.*

(A) *In General.* Except as provided in subparagraph (B), no person shall offer to enter into, enter into, or confirm the execution of, any swap in an agricultural commodity (as defined by the Commodity Futures Trading Commission).

(B) *Exception.* Notwithstanding subparagraph (A), a person may offer to enter into, enter into, or confirm the execution of, any swap in an agricultural commodity pursuant to section 4(c) of the Commodity Exchange Act or any rule, regulation, or order issued thereunder (including any rule, regulation, or order in effect as of the date of enactment of this Act) by the Commodity Futures Trading Commission to allow swaps under such terms and conditions as the Commission shall prescribe.

(4) *Required Reporting.* If the exception described in section 2(h)(8)(B) of the Commodity Exchange Act applies, the counterparties shall comply with any recordkeeping and transaction reporting requirements that may be prescribed by the Commission with respect to swaps subject to section 2(h)(8)(B) of the Commodity Exchange Act.

Swaps; Segregation and Bankruptcy Treatment

Sec. 724. (a) [Omitted. Subsection amended section 4d of the Commodity Exchange Act.]

(b) [Omitted. Subsection amended section 761 of title 11, of the United States Code (11 U.S.C. 761).]

(c) [Omitted. Subsection amended section 4s of the Commodity Exchange Act.]

Derivatives Clearing Organizations

Sec. 725. (a) [Omitted. Subsection amended section 5b of the Commodity Exchange Act.]

(b) [Omitted. Subsection amended section 5b of the Commodity Exchange Act.]

(c) [Omitted. Subsection amended section 5b(c) of the Commodity Exchange Act.]

(d) *Conflicts of Interest.* The Commodity Futures Trading Commission shall adopt rules mitigating conflicts of interest in connection with the conduct of business by a swap dealer or a major swap participant with a derivatives clearing organization, board of trade, or a swap execution facility that clears or trades swaps in which the swap dealer or major swap participant has a material debt or material equity investment.

(e) [Omitted. Subsection amended section 5b of the Commodity Exchange Act.]

(f) [Omitted. Subsection amended section 8(e) of the Commodity Exchange Act.]

(g) [Omitted. Subsection amended the Legal Certainty for Bank Products Act of 2000 (7 U.S.C. 27 *et seq.*)]

(h) [Omitted. Subsection amended section 5b(f)(1) of the Commodity Exchange Act.]

Rulemaking on Conflict of Interest

Sec. 726. (a) *In General.* In order to mitigate conflicts of interest, not later than 180 days after the date of enactment of the Wall Street Transparency and Accountability Act of 2010, the Commodity Futures Trading Commission shall adopt rules which may include numerical limits on the control of, or the voting rights with respect to, any derivatives clearing organization that clears swaps, or swap execution facility or board of trade designated as a contract market that posts swaps or makes swaps available for trading, by a bank holding company (as defined in section 2 of the Bank Holding Company Act of 1956) with total consolidated assets of $50,000,000,000 or more, a nonbank financial company (as defined in section 102) supervised by the Board, an affiliate of such a bank holding company or nonbank financial company, a swap dealer, major swap participant, or associated person of a swap dealer or major swap participant.

(b) *Purposes.* The Commission shall adopt rules if it determines, after the review described in subsection (a), that such rules are necessary or appropriate to improve the governance of, or to mitigate systemic risk, promote competition, or mitigate conflicts of interest in connection with a swap dealer or major swap participant's conduct of business with, a derivatives clearing organization, contract market, or swap execution facility that clears or posts swaps or makes swaps available for trading and in which such swap dealer or major swap participant has a material debt or equity investment.

(c) *Considerations.* In adopting rules pursuant to this section, the Commodity Futures Trading Commission shall consider any conflicts of interest arising from the amount of equity owned by a single investor, the ability to vote, cause the vote of, or withhold votes entitled to be cast on any matters by the holders of the ownership interest, and the governance arrangements of any derivatives clearing organization that clears swaps, or swap execution facility or board of trade designated as a contract market that posts swaps or makes swaps available for trading.

Public Reporting of Swap Transaction Data

Sec. 727. [Omitted. Section amended section 2(a) of the Commodity Exchange Act.]

Swap Data Repositories

Sec. 728. [Omitted. Section added section 21 to the Commodity Exchange Act.]

Reporting and Recordkeeping

Sec. 729. [Omitted. Section added section 4r to the Commodity Exchange Act.]

Large Swap Trader Reporting

Sec. 730. [Omitted. Section added section 4t to the Commodity Exchange Act.]

Registration and Regulation of Swap Dealers and Major Swap Participants

Sec. 731. [Omitted. Section added section 4s to the Commodity Exchange Act.]

Conflicts of Interest

Sec. 732. [Omitted. Section amended section 4d of the Commodity Exchange Act.]

Swap Execution Facilities

Sec. 733. [Omitted. Section added section 5h to the Commodity Exchange Act.]

Derivatives Transaction Execution Facilities and Exempt Boards of Trade

Sec. 734. (a) *In General.* Sections 5a and 5d of the Commodity Exchange Act are repealed.

(b) [Omitted. Subsection amended section 2 of the Commodity Exchange Act.]

(c) *Ability to Petition Commission.*

(1) *In General.* Prior to the final effective dates in this title, a person may petition the Commodity Futures Trading Commission to remain subject to the provisions of section 5d of the Commodity Exchange Act, as such provisions existed prior to the effective date of this subtitle.

(2) *Consideration of Petition.* The Commodity Futures Trading Commission shall consider any petition submitted under paragraph (1) in a prompt manner and may allow a person to continue operating subject to the provisions of section 5d of the Commodity Exchange Act for up to 1 year after the effective date of this subtitle.

Designated Contract Markets

Sec. 735. (a) [Omitted. Subsection amended section 5 of the Commodity Exchange Act.]

(b) [Omitted. Subsection amended section 5 of the Commodity Exchange Act.]

Margin

Sec. 736. [Omitted. Section amended section 8a(7) of the Commodity Exchange Act.]

Position Limits

Sec. 737. (a) [Omitted. Subsection amended section 4a(a) of the Commodity Exchange Act.]

(b) [Omitted. Subsection amended section 4a(b) of the Commodity Exchange Act.]

(c) [Omitted. Subsection amended section 4a(c) of the Commodity Exchange Act.]

(d) *Effective Date.* This section and the amendments made by this section shall become effective on the date of the enactment of this section.

Foreign Boards of Trade

Sec. 738. (a) [Omitted. Subsection amended section 4(b) of the Commodity Exchange Act.]

(b) [Omitted. Subsection amended section 4 of the Commodity Exchange Act.]

(c) [Omitted. Subsection amended section 22(a) of the Commodity Exchange Act.]

Legal Certainty for Swaps

Sec. 739. [Omitted. Section amended section 22(a) of the Commodity Exchange Act.]

Multilateral Clearing Organizations

Sec. 740. Sections 408 and 409 of the Federal Deposit Insurance Corporation Improvement Act of 1991 (12 U.S.C. 4421, 4422) are repealed.

Enforcement

Sec. 741. (a) [Omitted. Subsection added section 4b–1 to the Commodity Exchange Act.]

(b) [Omitted. Subsection amended sections of the Commodity Exchange Act.]

Retail Commodity Transactions

Sec. 742. [Omitted. Subsection amended section 2(c) of the Commodity Exchange Act.]

(b) [Omitted. Subsection amended section 206(a) of the Gramm–Leach–Bliley Act (Public Law 106–102; 15 U.S.C. 78c note).]

(c) [Omitted. Subsection amended section 2(c) of the Commodity Exchange Act.].

Other Authority

Sec. 743. Unless otherwise provided by the amendments made by this subtitle, the amendments made by this subtitle do not divest any appropriate Federal banking agency, the Commodity Futures Trading Commission, the Securities and Exchange Commission, or other Federal or State agency of any authority derived from any other applicable law.

Restitution Remedies

Sec. 744. [Omitted. Section amended section 6c(d) of the Commodity Exchange Act.]

Enhanced Compliance by Registered Entities

Sec. 745. (a) [Omitted. Subsection amended section 5c(a) of the Commodity Exchange Act.]

(b) [Omitted. Subsection amended section 5c of the Commodity Exchange Act.]

(c) [Omitted. Subsection amended section 5c of the Commodity Exchange Act.]

Insider Trading

Sec. 746. [Omitted. Section amended section 4c(a) of the Commodity Exchange Act.]

Antidisruptive Practices Authority

Sec. 747. [Omitted. Section amended section 4c(a) of the Commodity Exchange Act.]

Commodity Whistleblower Incentives and Protection

Sec. 748. [Omitted. Section added section 23 to the Commodity Exchange Act.]

Conforming Amendments

Sec. 749. (a) [Omitted. Subsection amended section 4d of the Commodity Exchange Act.]

(b) [Omitted. Subsection amended section 4m(3) of the Commodity Exchange Act.]

(c) [Omitted. Subsection amended section 5c of the Commodity Exchange Act.]

(e) [Omitted. Subsection amended section 6(b) of the Commodity Exchange Act.]

(f) [Omitted. Subsection amended section 12(e)(2)(B) of the Commodity Exchange Act.]

Study on Oversight of Carbon Markets

Sec. 750. (a) *Interagency Working Group.* There is established to carry out this section an interagency working group (referred to in this section as the "interagency group") composed of the following members or designees:

(1) The Chairman of the Commodity Futures Trading Commission (referred to in this section as the "Commission"), who shall serve as Chairman of the interagency group.

(2) The Secretary of Agriculture.

(3) The Secretary of the Treasury.

(4) The Chairman of the Securities and Exchange Commission.

(5) The Administrator of the Environmental Protection Agency.

(6) The Chairman of the Federal Energy Regulatory Commission.

(7) The Commissioner of the Federal Trade Commission.

(8) The Administrator of the Energy Information Administration.

(b) *Administrative Support.* The Commission shall provide the interagency group such administrative support services as are necessary to enable the interagency group to carry out the functions of the interagency group under this section.

(c) *Consultation.* In carrying out this section, the inter-agency group shall consult with representatives of exchanges, clearinghouses, self-regulatory bodies, major carbon market participants, consumers, and the general public, as the interagency group determines to be appropriate.

(d) *Study.* The interagency group shall conduct a study on the oversight of existing and prospective carbon markets to ensure an efficient, secure, and transparent carbon market, including oversight of spot markets and derivative markets.

(e) *Report.* Not later than 180 days after the date of enactment of this Act, the interagency group shall submit to Congress a report on the results of the study conducted under subsection (b), including recommendations for the oversight of existing and prospective carbon markets to ensure an efficient, secure, and transparent carbon market, including oversight of spot markets and derivative markets.

Energy and Environmental Markets Advisory Committee

Sec. 751. [Omitted. Section amended section 2(a) of the Commodity Exchange Act.]

International Harmonization

Sec. 752. (a) In order to promote effective and consistent global regulation of swaps and security-based swaps, the Commodity Futures Trading Commission, the Securities and Exchange Commission, and the prudential regulators (as that term is defined in section 1a(39) of the Commodity Exchange Act), as appropriate, shall consult and coordinate with foreign regulatory authorities on the establishment of consistent international standards with respect to the regulation (including fees) of swaps, security-based swaps, swap entities, and security-based swap entities and may agree to such information-sharing arrangements as may be deemed to be necessary or appropriate in the public interest or for the protection of investors, swap counterparties, and security-based swap counterparties.

(b) In order to promote effective and consistent global regulation of contracts of Be of a commodity for future delivery and options on such contracts, the Commodity Futures Trading Commission shall consult and coordinate with foreign regulatory authorities on the establishment of consistent international standards with respect to the regulation of contracts of Be of a commodity for future delivery and options on such contracts, and may agree to such information-sharing arrangements as may be deemed necessary or appropriate in the public interest for the protection of users of contracts of a commodity for future delivery.

Anti-Manipulation Authority

Sec. 753. (a) [Omitted. Subsection amended section 6(c) of the Commodity Exchange Act.]

(b) [Omitted. Subsection amended section 6(d) of the Commodity Exchange Act.]

(c) [Omitted. Subsection amended section 22(a)(1) of the Commodity Exchange Act.]

(d) *Effective Date.*

(1) The amendments made by this section shall take effect on the date on which the final rule promulgated by the Commodity Futures Trading Commission pursuant to this Act takes effect.

(2) Paragraph (1) shall not preclude the Commission from undertaking prior to the effective date any rulemaking necessary to implement the amendments contained in this section.

Effective Date

Sec. 754. Unless otherwise provided in this title, the provisions of this subtitle shall take effect on the later of 360 days after the date of the enactment of this subtitle or, to the extent a provision of this subtitle requires a rulemaking, not less than 60 days after publication of the final rule or regulation implementing such provision of this subtitle.

SUBTITLE B—REGULATION OF SECURITY-BASED SWAP MARKETS

Definitions Under the Securities Exchange Act of 1934

Sec. 761. (a) [Omitted. Section amended section 3(a) of the Securities Exchange Act of 1934.]

(b) *Authority to Further Define Terms.* The Securities and Exchange Commission may, by rule, further define—

(1) the term "commercial risk";

(2) any other term included in an amendment to the Securities Exchange Act of 1934 made by this subtitle; and

(3) the terms "security-based swap", "security-based swap dealer", "major security-based swap participant", and "eligible contract participant", with regard to security-based swaps (as such terms are defined in the amendments made by subsection (a)) for the purpose of including transactions and entities that have been structured to evade this subtitle or the amendments made by this subtitle.

Repeal of Prohibition on Regulation of Security-Based Swap Agreements

Sec. 762. (a) *Repeal.* Sections 206B and 206C of the Gramm-Leach-Bliley Act (Public Law 106–102; 15 U.S.C. 78c note) are repealed.

(b) [Omitted. Section amended section 206A(a) of the Gramm-Leach-Bliley Act (15 U.S.C. 78c note).]

(c) [Omitted. Section amended sections 2A and 17 of the Securities Act of 1933.]

(d) [Omitted. Section amended sections 3 and 9 of the Securities and Exchange Act of 1934.]

Amendments to the Securities Exchange Act of 1934

Sec. 763. (a) [Omitted. Section added section 3B to the Securities Exchange Act of 1934.]

(b) [Omitted. Section amended section 17A of the Securities Exchange Act of 1934.]

(c) [Omitted. Section added section 3D to the Securities Exchange Act of 1934.]

(d) [Omitted. Section amended section 3E to the Securities Exchange Act of 1934.]

(e) [Omitted. Section amended section 6 of the Securities Exchange Act of 1934.]

(f) [Omitted. Section amended section 9(b) of the Securities Exchange Act of 1934.]

(g) [Omitted. Section amended section 9 of the Securities Exchange Act of 1934.]

(h) [Omitted. Section added section 10B to the Securities Exchange Act of 1934.]

(i) [Omitted. Section amended section 13 of the Securities Exchange Act of 1934.]

Registration and Regulation of Security-Based Swap Dealers and Major Security-Based Swap Participants

Sec. 764. (a) [Omitted. Section added section 15F to the Securities Exchange Act of 1934.]

(b) *Savings Clause.* Notwithstanding any other provision of this title, nothing in this subtitle shall be construed as divesting any appropriate Federal banking agency of any authority it may have to establish or enforce, with respect to a person for which such agency is the appropriate Federal banking agency, prudential or other standards pursuant to authority by Federal law other than this title.

Rulemaking on Conflict of Interest

Sec. 765. (a) *In General.* In order to mitigate conflicts of interest, not later than 180 days after the date of enactment of the Wall Street Transparency and Accountability Act of 2010, the Securities and Exchange Commission shall adopt rules which may include numerical limits on the control of, or the voting rights with respect to, any clearing agency that clears security-based swaps, or on the control of any security-based swap execution facility or national securities exchange that posts or makes available for trading security-based swaps, by a bank holding company (as defined in section 2 of the Bank Holding Company Act of 1956) with total consolidated assets of $50,000,000,000 or more, a nonbank financial company (as defined in section 102) supervised by the Board of Governors of the Federal Reserve System, affiliate of such a bank holding company or nonbank financial company, a security-based swap dealer, major security-based swap participant, or person associated with a security-based swap dealer or major security-based swap participant.

(b) *Purposes.* The Securities and Exchange Commission shall adopt rules if the Commission determines, after the review described in subsection (a), that such rules are necessary or appropriate to improve the governance of, or to mitigate systemic risk, promote competition, or mitigate conflicts of interest in connection with a security-based swap dealer or major security-based swap participant's conduct of business with, a clearing agency, national securities exchange, or security-based swap execution facility that clears, posts, or makes available for trading security-based swaps and in which such security-based swap dealer or major security-based swap participant has a material debt or equity investment.

(c) *Considerations.* In adopting rules pursuant to this section, the Securities and Exchange Commission shall consider any conflicts of interest arising from the amount of equity owned by a single investor, the ability to vote, cause the vote of, or withhold votes entitled to be cast on any matters by the holders of the ownership interest, and the governance arrangements of any derivatives clearing organization that clears swaps, or swap execution facility or board of trade designated as a contract market that posts swaps or makes swaps available for trading.

Reporting and Recordkeeping

Sec. 766. (a) [Omitted. Section added section 13A of the Securities Exchange Act of 1934.]

(b) [Omitted. Section amended section 13 of the Securities Exchange Act of 1934.]

(c) [Omitted. Section amended section 13(f)(1) of the Securities Exchange Act of 1934.]

(d) [Omitted. Section amended section 15(b)(4) of the Securities Exchange Act of 1934.]

(e) [Omitted. Section amended section 13 of the Securities Exchange Act of 1934.]

State Gaming and Bucket Shop Laws

Sec. 767. [Omitted. Section amended section 28(a) of the Securities Exchange Act of 1934.]

Amendments to the Securities Act of 1933; Treatment of Security-Based Swaps

Sec. 768. (a) [Omitted. Section amended section 2(a) of the Securities Act of 1933.]

(b) [Omitted. Section amended section 5 of the Securities Act of 1933.]

Definitions Under the Investment Company Act of 1940

Sec. 769. [Omitted. Section amended section 2(a) of the Investment Company Act of 1940.]

Definitions Under the Investment Advisers Act of 1940

Sec. 770. [Omitted. Section amended section 202(a) of the Investment Advisers Act of 1940.]

Other Authority

Sec. 771. Unless otherwise provided by its terms, this subtitle does not divest any appropriate Federal banking agency, the Securities and Exchange Commission, the Commodity Futures Trading Commission, or any other Federal or State agency, of any authority derived from any other provision of applicable law.

Jurisdiction

Sec. 772. (a) [Omitted. Section amended section 36 of the Securities Exchange Act of 1934.]

(b) [Omitted. Section amended section 30 of the Securities Exchange Act of 1934.]

Civil Penalties

Sec. 773. [Omitted. Section amended section 21B of the Securities Exchange Act of 1934.]

Effective Date

Sec. 774. Unless otherwise provided, the provisions of this subtitle shall take effect on the later of 360 days after the date of the enactment of this subtitle or, to the extent a provision of this subtitle requires a rulemaking, not less than 60 days after publication of the final rule or regulation implementing such provision of this subtitle.

TITLE IX—INVESTOR PROTECTIONS AND IMPROVEMENTS TO THE REGULATION OF SECURITIES

Short Title

Sec. 901. This title may be cited as the "Investor Protection and Securities Reform Act of 2010".

SUBTITLE A—INCREASING INVESTOR PROTECTION

Investor Advisory Committee Established

Sec. 911. [Omitted. Section added section 39 to Title I of the Securities Exchange Act of 1934.]

Clarification of Authority of the Commission to Engage in Investor Testing

Sec. 912. [Omitted. Section amended section 19 of the Securities Act of 1933.]

Study and Rulemaking Regarding Obligations of Brokers, Dealers, and Investment Advisers

Sec. 913. (a) *Definition.* For purposes of this section, the term "retail customer" means a natural person, or the legal representative of such natural person, who—

(1) receives personalized investment advice about securities from a broker or dealer or investment adviser; and

(2) uses such advice primarily for personal, family, or household purposes.

(b) *Study*. The Commission shall conduct a study to evaluate—

(1) the effectiveness of existing legal or regulatory standards of care for brokers, dealers, investment advisers, persons associated with brokers or dealers, and persons associated with investment advisers for providing personalized investment advice and recommendations about securities to retail customers imposed by the Commission and a national securities association, and other Federal and State legal or regulatory standards; and

(2) whether there are legal or regulatory gaps, shortcomings, or overlaps in legal or regulatory standards in the protection of retail customers relating to the standards of care for brokers, dealers, investment advisers, persons associated with brokers or dealers, and persons associated with investment advisers for providing personalized investment advice about securities to retail customers that should be addressed by rule or statute.

(c) *Considerations*. In conducting the study required under subsection (b), the Commission shall consider—

(1) the effectiveness of existing legal or regulatory standards of care for brokers, dealers, investment advisers, persons associated with brokers or dealers, and persons associated with investment advisers for providing personalized investment advice and recommendations about securities to retail customers imposed by the Commission and a national securities association, and other Federal and State legal or regulatory standards;

(2) whether there are legal or regulatory gaps, shortcomings, or overlaps in legal or regulatory standards in the protection of retail customers relating to the standards of care for brokers, dealers, investment advisers, persons associated with brokers or dealers, and persons associated with investment advisers for providing personalized investment advice about securities to retail customers that should be addressed by rule or statute;

(3) whether retail customers understand that there are different standards of care applicable to brokers, dealers, investment advisers, persons associated with brokers or dealers, and persons associated with investment advisers in the provision of personalized investment advice about securities to retail customers;

(4) whether the existence of different standards of care applicable to brokers, dealers, investment advisers, persons associated with brokers or dealers, and persons associated with investment advisers is a source of confusion for retail customers regarding the quality of personalized investment advice that retail customers receive;

(5) the regulatory, examination, and enforcement resources devoted to, and activities of, the Commission, the States, and a national securities association to enforce the standards of care for brokers, dealers, investment advisers, persons associated with brokers or dealers, and persons associated with investment advisers when providing personalized investment advice and recommendations about securities to retail customers, including—

(A) the effectiveness of the examinations of brokers, dealers, and investment advisers in determining compliance with regulations;

(B) the frequency of the examinations; and

(C) the length of time of the examinations;

(6) the substantive differences in the regulation of brokers, dealers, and investment advisers, when providing personalized investment advice and recommendations about securities to retail customers;

(7) the specific instances related to the provision of personalized investment advice about securities in which—

(A) the regulation and oversight of investment advisers provide greater protection to retail customers than the regulation and oversight of brokers and dealers; and

(B) the regulation and oversight of brokers and dealers provide greater protection to retail customers than the regulation and oversight of investment advisers;

(8) the existing legal or regulatory standards of State securities regulators and other regulators intended to protect retail customers;

(9) the potential impact on retail customers, including the potential impact on access of retail customers to the range of products and services offered by brokers and dealers, of imposing upon brokers, dealers, and persons associated with brokers or dealers—

(A) the standard of care applied under the Investment Advisers Act of 1940 for providing personalized investment advice about securities to retail customers of investment advisers, as interpreted by the Commission and the courts; and

(B) other requirements of the Investment Advisers Act of 1940;

(10) the potential impact of eliminating the broker and dealer exclusion from the definition of "investment adviser" under section 202(a)(11)(C) of the Investment Advisers Act of 1940, in terms of—

(A) the impact and potential benefits and harm to retail customers that could result from such a change, including any potential impact on access to personalized investment advice and recommendations about securities to retail customers or the availability of such advice and recommendations;

(B) the number of additional entities and individuals that would be required to register under, or become subject to, the Investment Advisers Act of 1940, and the additional requirements to which brokers, dealers, and persons associated with brokers and dealers would become subject, including—

(i) any potential additional associated person licensing, registration, and examination requirements; and

(ii) the additional costs, if any, to the additional entities and individuals; and

(C) the impact on Commission and State resources to—

(i) conduct examinations of registered investment advisers and the representatives of registered investment advisers, including the impact on the examination cycle; and

(ii) enforce the standard of care and other applicable requirements imposed under the Investment Advisers Act of 1940;

(11) the varying level of services provided by brokers, dealers, investment advisers, persons associated with brokers or dealers, and persons associated with investment advisers to retail customers and the varying scope and terms of retail customer relationships of brokers, dealers, investment advisers, persons associated with brokers or dealers, and persons associated with investment advisers with such retail customers;

(12) the potential impact upon retail customers that could result from potential changes in the regulatory requirements or legal standards of care affecting brokers, dealers, investment advisers, persons associated with brokers or dealers, and persons associated with investment advisers relating to their obligations to retail customers regarding the provision of investment advice, including any potential impact on—

(A) protection from fraud;

(B) access to personalized investment advice, and recommendations about securities to retail customers; or

(C) the availability of such advice and recommendations;

(13) the potential additional costs and expenses to—

(A) retail customers regarding and the potential impact on the profitability of their investment decisions; and

(B) brokers, dealers, and investment advisers resulting from potential changes in the regulatory requirements or legal standards affecting brokers, dealers, investment advisers, persons associated with brokers or dealers, and persons associated with investment advisers relating to their obligations, including duty of care, to retail customers; and

(14) any other consideration that the Commission considers necessary and appropriate in determining whether to conduct a rulemaking under subsection (f).

(d) *Report*.

(1) *In General*. Not later than 6 months after the date of enactment of this Act, the Commission shall submit a report on the study required under subsection (b) to—

(A) the Committee on Banking, Housing, and Urban Affairs of the Senate; and

(B) the Committee on Financial Services of the House of Representatives.

(2) *Content Requirements*. The report required under paragraph (1) shall describe the findings, conclusions, and recommendations of the Commission from the study required under subsection (b), including—

(A) a description of the considerations, analysis, and public and industry input that the Commission considered, as required under subsection (b), to make such findings, conclusions, and policy recommendations; and

(B) an analysis of whether any identified legal or regulatory gaps, shortcomings, or overlap in legal or regulatory standards in the protection of retail customers relating to the standards of care for brokers, dealers, investment advisers, persons associated with brokers or dealers, and persons associated with investment advisers for providing personalized investment advice about securities to retail customers.

(e) *Public Comment.* The Commission shall seek and consider public input, comments, and data in order to prepare the report required under subsection (d).

(f) *Rulemaking.* The Commission may commence a rulemaking, as necessary or appropriate in the public interest and for the protection of retail customers (and such other customers as the Commission may by rule provide), to address the legal or regulatory standards of care for brokers, dealers, investment advisers, persons associated with brokers or dealers, and persons associated with investment advisers for providing personalized investment advice about securities to such retail customers. The Commission shall consider the findings conclusions, and recommendations of the study required under subsection (b).

(g) [Omitted. Subsection amended section 15 of the Securities Exchange Act of 1934.]

(h) [Omitted. Subsection amended section 211 of the Investment Advisers Act of 1940.]

Study on Enhancing Investment Adviser Examinations

Sec. 914. (a) *Study Required.*

(1) *In General.* The Commission shall review and analyze the need for enhanced examination and enforcement resources for investment advisers.

(2) *Areas of Consideration.* The study required by this subsection shall examine—

(A) the number and frequency of examinations of investment advisers by the Commission over the 5 years preceding the date of the enactment of this subtitle;

(B) the extent to which having Congress authorize the Commission to designate one or more self–regulatory organizations to augment the Commission's efforts in over–seeing investment advisers would improve the frequency of examinations of investment advisers; and

(C) current and potential approaches to examining the investment advisory activities of dually registered broker–dealers and investment advisers or affiliated broker–dealers and investment advisers.

(b) *Report Required.* The Commission shall report its findings to the Committee on Financial Services of the House of Representatives and the Committee on Banking, Housing, and Urban Affairs of the Senate, not later than 180 days after the date of enactment of this subtitle, and shall use such findings to revise its rules and regulations, as necessary. The report shall include a discussion of regulatory or legislative steps that are recommended or that may be necessary to address concerns identified in the study.

Office of the Investor Advocate

Sec. 915. [Omitted. Section amended section 4 of the Securities Exchange Act of 1934.]

Streamlining of Filing Procedures for Self–Regulatory Organizations

Sec. 916. (a) [Omitted. Subsection amended section 19(b) of the Securities Exchange Act of 1934.]

(b) [Omitted. Subsection amended section 19(b) of the Securities Exchange Act of 1934.]

(c) [Omitted. Subsection amended section 19(b)(3) of the Securities Exchange Act of 1934.]

(d) [Omitted. Subsection amended section 19(b)(4)(D) of the Securities Exchange Act of 1934.]

Study Regarding Financial Literacy Among Investors

Sec. 917. (a) *In General.* The Commission shall conduct a study to identify—

(1) the existing level of financial literacy among retail investors, including subgroups of investors identified by the Commission;

(2) methods to improve the timing, content, and format of disclosures to investors with respect to financial intermediaries, investment products, and investment services;

(3) the most useful and understandable relevant information that retail investors need to make informed financial decisions before engaging a financial intermediary or purchasing an investment product or service that is typically sold to retail investors, including shares of open-end companies, as that term is defined in section 5 of the Investment Company Act of 1940 that are registered under section 8 of that Act;

(4) methods to increase the transparency of expenses and conflicts of interests in transactions involving investment services and products, including shares of open-end companies described in paragraph (3);

(5) the most effective existing private and public efforts to educate investors; and

(6) in consultation with the Financial Literacy and Education Commission, a strategy (including, to the extent practicable, measurable goals and objectives) to increase the financial literacy of investors in order to bring about a positive change in investor behavior.

(b) *Report.* Not later than 2 years after the date of enactment of this Act, the Commission shall submit a report on the study required under subsection (a) to—

(1) the Committee on Banking, Housing, and Urban Affairs of the Senate; and

(2) the Committee on Financial Services of the House of Representatives.

Study Regarding Mutual Fund Advertising

Sec. 918. (a) *In General.* The Comptroller General of the United States shall conduct a study on mutual fund advertising to identify—

(1) existing and proposed regulatory requirements for open-end investment company advertisements;

(2) current marketing practices for the sale of open-end investment company shares, including the use of past performance data, funds that have merged, and incubator funds;

(3) the impact of such advertising on consumers; and

(4) recommendations to improve investor protections in mutual fund advertising and additional information necessary to ensure that investors can make informed financial decisions when purchasing shares.

(b) *Report.* Not later than 18 months after the date of enactment of this Act, the Comptroller General of the United States shall submit a report on the results of the study conducted under subsection (a) to—

(1) the Committee on Banking, Housing, and Urban Affairs of the United States Senate; and

(2) the Committee on Financial Services of the House of Representatives.

Clarification of Commission Authority to Require Investor Disclosures Before Purchase of Investment Products and Services

Sec. 919. [Omitted. Subsection amended section 15 of the Securities Exchange Act of 1934.]

Study on Conflicts of Interest

Sec. 919A. (a) *In General.* The Comptroller General of the United States shall conduct a study—

(1) to identify and examine potential conflicts of interest that exist between the staffs of the investment banking and equity and fixed income securities analyst functions within the same firm; and

(2) to make recommendations to Congress designed to protect investors in light of such conflicts.

(b) *Considerations.* In conducting the study under subsection (a), the Comptroller General shall—

(1) consider—

(A) the potential for investor harm resulting from conflicts, including consideration of the forms of misconduct engaged in by the several securities firms and individuals that entered into the Global Analyst Research Settlements in 2003 (also known as the "Global Settlement");

(B) the nature and benefits of the undertakings to which those firms agreed in enforcement proceedings, including firewalls between research and investment banking, separate reporting lines, dedicated legal and compliance staffs, allocation of budget, physical separation, compensation, employee performance evaluations, coverage decisions, limitations on soliciting investment banking business, disclosures, transparency, and other measures;

(C) whether any such undertakings should be codified and applied permanently to securities firms, or whether the Commission should adopt rules applying any such undertakings to securities firms; and

(D) whether to recommend regulatory or legislative measures designed to mitigate possible adverse consequences to investors arising from the conflicts of interest or to enhance investor protection or confidence in the integrity of the securities markets; and

(2) consult with State attorneys general, State securities officials, the Commission, the Financial Industry Regulatory Authority ("FINRA"), NYSE Regulation, investor advocates, brokers, dealers,

retail investors, institutional investors, and academics.

(c) *Report.* The Comptroller General shall submit a report on the results of the study required by this section to the Committee on Banking, Housing, and Urban Affairs of the Senate and the Committee on Financial Services of the House of Representatives, not later than 18 months after the date of enactment of this Act.

Study on Improved Investor Access to Information on Investment Advisers and Broker-Dealers

Sec. 919B. (a) *Study.*

(1) *In General.* Not later than 6 months after the date of enactment of this Act, the Commission shall complete a study, including recommendations, of ways to improve the access of investors to registration information (including disciplinary actions, regulatory, judicial, and arbitration proceedings, and other information) about registered and previously registered investment advisers, associated persons of investment advisers, brokers and dealers and their associated persons on the existing Central Registration Depository and Investment Adviser Registration Depository systems, as well as identify additional information that should be made publicly available.

(2) *Contents.* The study required by subsection (a) shall include an analysis of the advantages and disadvantages of further centralizing access to the information contained in the 2 systems, including—

(A) identification of those data pertinent to investors; and

(B) the identification of the method and format for displaying and publishing such data to enhance accessibility by and utility to investors.

(b) *Implementation.* Not later than 18 months after the date of completion of the study required by subsection (a), the Commission shall implement any recommendations of the study.

Study on Financial Planners and the Use of Financial Designations

Sec. 919C. (a) *In General.* The Comptroller General of the United States shall conduct a study to evaluate—

(1) the effectiveness of State and Federal regulations to protect investors and other consumers from individuals who hold themselves out as financial planners through the use of misleading titles, designations, or marketing materials;

(2) current State and Federal oversight structure and regulations for financial planners; and

(3) legal or regulatory gaps in the regulation of financial planners and other individuals who provide or offer to provide financial planning services to consumers.

(b) *Considerations.* In conducting the study required under subsection (a), the Comptroller General shall consider—

(1) the role of financial planners in providing advice regarding the management of financial resources, including investment planning, income tax planning, education planning, retirement planning, estate planning, and risk management;

(2) whether current regulations at the State and Federal level provide adequate ethical and professional standards for financial planners;

(3) the possible risk posed to investors and other consumers by individuals who hold themselves out as financial planners or as otherwise providing financial planning services in connection with the sale of financial products, including insurance and securities;

(4) the possible risk posed to investors and other consumers by individuals who otherwise use titles, designations, or marketing materials in a misleading way in connection with the delivery of financial advice;

(6) the ability of investors and other consumers to understand licensing requirements and standards of care that apply to individuals who hold themselves out as financial planners or as otherwise providing financial planning services;

(7) the possible benefits to investors and other consumers of regulation and professional oversight of financial planners; and

(8) any other consideration that the Comptroller General deems necessary or appropriate to effectively execute the study required under subsection (a).

(c) *Recommendations.* In providing recommendations for the appropriate regulation of financial planners and other individuals who provide or offer to provide financial planning services, in order to protect investors and other consumers of financial planning services, the Comptroller General shall consider—

(1) the appropriate structure for regulation of financial planners and individuals providing financial planning services; and

(2) the appropriate scope of the regulations needed to protect investors and other consumers, including but not limited to the need to establish competency standards, practice standards, ethical guidelines, disciplinary authority, and transparency to investors and other consumers.

(d) *Report.*

(1) *In General.* Not later than 180 days after the date of enactment of this Act, the Comptroller General shall submit a report on the study required under subsection (a) to—

(A) the Committee on Banking, Housing, and Urban Affairs of the Senate;

(B) the Special Committee on Aging of the Senate; and

(C) the Committee on Financial Services of the House of Representatives.

(2) *Content Requirements.* The report required under paragraph (1) shall describe the findings and determinations made by the Comptroller General in carrying out the study required under subsection (a), including a description of the considerations, analysis, and government, public, industry, non–profit and consumer input that the Comptroller General considered to make such findings, conclusions, and legislative, regulatory, or other recommendations.

Ombudsman

Sec. 919D. [Omitted. Section amended section 4(g) of the Securities Exchange Act of 1934.]

SUBTITLE B—INCREASING REGULATORY ENFORCEMENT AND REMEDIES

Authority to Restrict Mandatory Pre-Dispute Arbitration

Sec. 921. (a) [Omitted. Subsection amended section 15 of the Securities Exchange Act of 1934.]

(b) [Omitted. Subsection amended section 205 of the Investment Advisers Act of 1940.]

Whistleblower Protection

Sec. 922. (a) [Omitted. Subsection added section 21f to the Securities Exchange Act of 1934.]

(b) [Omitted. Subsection amended section 1514A(a) of title 18, United States Code.]

(c) [Omitted. Subsection amended section 1514A of title 18, United States Code.]

(d) *Study of Whistleblower Protection Program.*

(1) *Study.* The Inspector General of the Commission shall conduct a study of the whistleblower protections established under the amendments made by this section, including—

(A) whether the final rules and regulation issued under the amendments made by this section have made the whistleblower protection program (referred to in this subsection as the program) clearly defined and user-friendly;

(B) whether the program is promoted on the website of the Commission and has been widely publicized;

(C) whether the Commission is prompt in—

(i) responding to—

(I) information provided by whistleblowers; and

(II) applications for awards filed by whistleblowers;

(ii) updating whistleblowers about the status of their applications; and

(iii) otherwise communicating with the interested parties;

(D) whether the minimum and maximum reward levels are adequate to entice whistleblowers to come forward with information and whether the reward levels are so high as to encourage illegitimate whistleblower claims;

(E) whether the appeals process has been unduly burdensome for the Commission;

(F) whether the funding mechanism for the Investor Protection Fund is adequate;

(G) whether, in the interest of protecting investors and identifying and preventing fraud, it would be useful for Congress to consider empowering whistleblowers or other individuals, who have already attempted to pursue the case through the Commission, to have a private right of action to bring suit based on the facts of the same case, on behalf of the Government and themselves, against persons who have committee securities fraud;

(H)(i) whether the exemption under section 552(b)(3) of title 5 (known as the Freedom of Information Act) established in section 21F(h)(2)(A) of the Securities Exchange Act of 1934, as added by this Act, aids whistleblowers in disclosing information to the Commission;

(ii) what impact the exemption described in clause (i) has had on the ability of the public to access information about the regulation and enforcement by the Commission of securities; and

(iii) any recommendations on whether the exemption described in clause (i) should remain in effect; and

(I) such other matters as the Inspector General deems appropriate.

(2) *Report.* Not later than 30 months after the date of enactment of this Act, the Inspector General shall—

(A) submit a report on the findings of the study required under paragraph (1) to the Committee on Banking, Housing, and Urban Affairs of the Senate and the Committee on Financial Services of the House; and

(B) make the report described in subparagraph (A) available to the public through publication of the report on the website of the Commission.

Conforming Amendments for Whistleblower Protection

Sec. 923. (a) *In General.*

(1) [Omitted. Subsection amended section 20(d)(3)(A) of the Securities Act of 1933.]

(2) [Omitted. Subsection amended section 42(e)(3)(A) of the Investment Company Act of 1940.]

(3) [Omitted. Subsection amended section 209(e)(3)(A) of the Investment Company Act of 1940.]

(b) *Securities Exchange Act.*

(1) [Omitted. Subsection amended section 21(d)(3)(C)(i) of the Securities Exchange Act of 1934.]

(2) [Omitted. Subsection amended section 21A of the Securities Exchange Act of 1934.]

Implementation and Transition Provisions for Whistleblower Protection

Sec. 924. (a) *Implementing Rules.* The Commission shall issue final regulations implementing the provisions of section 21F of the Securities Exchange Act of 1934, as added by this subtitle, not later than 270 days after the date of enactment of this Act.

(b) *Original Information.* Information provided to the Commission in writing by a whistleblower shall not lose the status of original information (as defined in section 21F(a)(3) of the Securities Exchange Act of 1934, as added by this subtitle) solely because the whistleblower provided the information prior to the effective date of the regulations, if the information is provided by the whistleblower after the date of enactment of this subtitle.

(c) *Awards.* A whistleblower may receive an award pursuant to section 21F of the Securities Exchange Act of 1934, as added by this subtitle, regardless of whether any violation of a provision of the securities laws, or a rule or regulation thereunder, underlying the judicial or administrative action upon which the award is based, occurred prior to the date of enactment of this subtitle.

(d) *Administration and Enforcement.* The Securities and Exchange Commission shall establish a separate office within the Commission to administer and enforce the provisions of section 21F of the Securities Exchange Act of 1934 (as add by section 922(a)). Such office shall report annually to the Committee on Banking, Housing, and Urban Affairs of the Senate and the Committee on Financial Services of the House of Representatives on its activities, whistleblower complaints, and the response of the Commission to such complaints.

Collateral Bars

Sec. 925. (a) [Omitted. Subsection amended sections 15(b)(6)(A), 15B(c)(4) and 17A(c)(4)(C) of the Securities Exchange Act of 1934.]

(b) [Omitted. Subsection amended section 203(f) of the Investment Advisers Act of 1940.]

Disqualifying Felons and Other Bad Actors From Regulation D Offerings

Sec. 926. Not later than 1 year after the date of enactment of this Act, the Commission shall issue rules for the disqualification of offerings and sales of securities made under Rule 506 under the Securities Act of 1933, that—

(1) are substantially similar to the provisions of Rule 262 under the Securities Act of 1933, or any successor thereto; and

(2) disqualify any offering or sale of securities by a person that—

(A) is subject to a final order of a state securities commission (or an agency or officer of a State performing like functions), a State authority that supervises or examines banks, savings associations, or credit unions, a State insurance commission (or an agency or officer of a

State performing like functions), an appropriate Federal banking agency, or the National Credit Union Administration, that—

(i) bars the person from—

(I) association with an entity regulated by such commission, authority, agency, or officer;

(II) engaging in the business of securities, insurance, or banking; or

(III) engaging in savings association or credit union activities; or

(ii) constitutes a final order based on a violation of any law or regulation that prohibits fraudulent, manipulative, or deceptive conduct within the 10–year period ending on the date of the filing of the offer or sale; or

(B) has been convicted of any felony or misdemeanor in connection with the purchase or Be of any security or involving the making of any false filing with the Commission.

Equal Treatment of Self-Regulatory Organization Rules

Sec. 927. [Omitted. Section amended section 29(a) of the Securities Exchange Act of 1934.]

Clarification that Section 205 of the Investment Advisers Act of 1940 Does Not Apply to State-Registered Advisers

Sec. 928. [Omitted. Section amended section 205(a) of the Investment Advisers Act of 1940.]

Unlawful Margin Lending

Sec. 929. [Omitted. Section amended section 7(c)(1)(A) of the Securities Exchange Act of 1934.]

Protection for Employees of Subsidiaries and Affiliates of Publicly Traded Companies

Sec. 929A. [Omitted. Section amended section 1514A of title 18, United States Code.]

Fair Fund Amendments

Sec. 929B. [Omitted. Section amended section 308 of the Sarbanes–Oxley Act of 2002.]

Increasing the Borrowing Limit on Treasury Loans

Sec. 929C. [Omitted. Section amended section 4(h) of the Securities Investor Protection Act of 1970 (15 U.S.C. 78ddd(h)).]

Lost and Stolen Securities

Sec. 929D. [Omitted. Section amended section 17(f)(1) of the Securities Exchange Act of 1934.]

Nationwide Service of Subpoenas

Sec. 929E. (a) [Omitted. Subsection amended section 22(a) of the Securities Act of 1933.]

(b) [Omitted. Subsection amended section 27 of the Securities Exchange Act of 1934.]

(c) [Omitted. Subsection amended section 44 of the Investment Company Act of 1940.]

(d) [Omitted. Subsection amended section 214 of the Investment Advisers Act of 1940.]

Formerly Associated Persons

Sec. 929F. (a) [Omitted. Subsection amended section 15B(c)(8) of the Securities Exchange Act of 1934.]

(b) [Omitted. Subsection amended section 15C(c) of the Securities Exchange Act of 1934.]

(c) [Omitted. Subsection amended section 21(a)(1) of the Securities Exchange Act of 1934.]

(d) [Omitted. Subsection amended section 21(a)(1) of the Securities Exchange Act of 1934.]

(e) [Omitted. Subsection amended section 19(h)(4) of the Securities Exchange Act of 1934.]

(f) [Omitted. Subsection omitted section 36(a) of the Investment Company Act of 1940.]

(g) *Person Associated With A Public Accounting Firm.*

(1) [Omitted. Subsection amended section 2(a)(9) of the Sarbanes–Oxley Act of 2002.]

(2) [Omitted. Subsection amended section 21(a)(1) of the Securities Exchange Act of 1934.]

(h) [Omitted. Subsection amended section 105(c)(6) of the Sarbanes–Oxley Act of 2002.]

(i) [Omitted. Subsection amended section 107(d)(3) of the Sarbanes–Oxley Act of 2002.]

Streamlined Hiring Authority for Market Specialists

Sec. 929G. (a) [Omitted. Subsection amended section 3114 of title 5, United States Code.]

(b) [Omitted. Subsection amended the table of sections for chapter 31 of title 5, United States Code.]

(c) *Pay Authority.* The Commission may set the rate of pay for experts and consultants appointed under the authority of section 3109 of title 5, United States Code, in the same manner in which it sets the rate of pay for employees of the Commission.

SIPC Reforms

Sec. 929H. [Omitted. Section amended section 9 of he Securities Investor Protection Act of 1970 (15 U.S.C. 78fff–3).]

Protecting Confidentiality of Materials Submitted to the Commission

Sec. 929I. (a) [Omitted. Subsection amended section 24 of the Securities Exchange Act of 1934.]

(b) [Omitted. Subsection amended section 31 of the Investment Company Act of 1940.]

(c) [Omitted. Subsection amended section 210 of the Investment Advisers Act of 1940.]

Expansion of Audit Information to be Produced and Exchanged

Sec. 929J. [Omitted. Section amended section 106 of the Sarbanes–Oxley Act of 2002.]

Sharing Privileged Information With Other Authorities

Sec. 929K. [Omitted. Section amended section 24 of the Securities Exchange Act of 1934.]

Enhanced Application of Antifraud Provisions

Sec. 929L. [Omitted. Section amended sections 9, 10, and 15 of the Securities Exchange Act of 1934.]

Aiding and Abetting Authority Under the Securities Act and the Investment Company Act

Sec. 929M. (a) [Omitted. Subsection amended section 15 of the Securities Act of 1933.]

(b) [Omitted. Subsection amended section 48 of the Investment Company Act of 1940.]

Aiding and Abetting Authority Under the Securities Act and the Investment Company Act

Sec. 929N. [Omitted. Section amended section 209 of the Investment Advisers Act of 1940.]

Aiding and Abetting Standard of Knowledge Satisfied by Recklessness

Sec. 929O. [Omitted. Section amended section 20(e) of the Securities Exchange Act of 1934.]

Strengthening Enforcement by the Commission

Sec. 929P. (a) *Authority to Impose Civil Penalties in Cease and Desist Proceedings.*

(1) [Omitted. Subsection amended section 8A of the Securities Act of 1933.]

(2) [Omitted. Subsection amended section 21B(a) of the Securities Exchange Act of 1934.]

(3) [Omitted. Subsection amended section 9(d)(1) of the Investment Company Act of 1940.]

(4) [Omitted. Subsection amended section 203(i)(1) of the Investment Advisers Act of 1940.]

(b) *Extraterritorial Jurisdiction of the Antifraud Provisions of the Federal Securities Laws.*

(1) [Omitted. Subsection amended section 22 of the Securities Act of 1933.]

(2) [Omitted. Subsection amended section 27 of the Securities Exchange Act of 1934.]

(3) [Omitted. Subsection amended section 214 of the Investment Advisers Act of 1940.]

(c) [Omitted. Subsection amended section 20(a) of the Securities Exchange Act of 1934.]

Revision to Recordkeeping Rule

Sec. 929Q. (a) [Omitted. Subsection amended section 31 of the Investment Company Act of 1940.]

(b) [Omitted. Subsection amended section 204 of the Investment Advisers Act of 1940.]

Beneficial Ownership and Short-Swing Profit Reporting

Sec. 929R. (a) [Omitted. Subsection amended section 13 of the Securities Exchange Act of 1934.]

(b) [Omitted. Subsection amended section 16(a) of the Securities Exchange Act of 1934.]

Fingerprinting

Sec. 929S. [Omitted. Section amended section 17(f)(2) of the Securities Exchange Act of 1934.]

Equal Treatment of Self-Regulatory Organization Rules

Sec. 929T. [Omitted. Section amended section 29(a) of the Securities Exchange Act of 1934.]

Deadline for Completing Examinations, Inspections and Enforcement Actions

Sec. 929U. [Omitted. Section added section 4E to the Securities Exchange Act of 1934.]

Security Investor Protection Act Amendments

Sec. 929V. (a) [Omitted. Subsection amended section 4(d)(1)(C) of the Securities Investor Protection Act of 1970 (15 U.S.C. 78ddd(d)(1)(C)).]

(b) [Omitted. Subsection amended section 14(c) of the Securities Investor Protection Act of 1970 (15 U.S.C. 78jjj(c)).]

(c) [Omitted. Subsection amended section 14 of the Securities Investor Protection Act of 1970 (15 U.S.C. 78jjj).]

Notice to Missing Security Holders

Sec. 929W. [Omitted. Section amended section 17A of the Securities Exchange Act of 1934.]

Short Be Reforms

Sec. 929X. (a) [Omitted. Subsection amended section 13(f) of the Securities Exchange Act of 1934.]

(b) [Omitted. Subsection amended section 9 of the Securities Exchange Act of 1934.]

(c) [Omitted. Subsection amended section 15 of the Securities Exchange Act of 1934.]

Study on Extraterritorial Private Rights of Action

Sec. 929Y. (a) *In General.* The Securities and Exchange Commission of the United States shall solicit public comment and thereafter conduct a study to determine the extent to which private rights of action under the antifraud provisions of the Securities and Exchange Act of 1934 should be extended to cover—

(1) conduct within the United States that constitutes a significant step in the furtherance of the violation, even if the securities transaction occurs outside the United States and involves only foreign investors; and

(2) conduct occurring outside the United States that has a foreseeable substantial effect within the United States.

(b) *Contents.* The study shall consider and analyze, among other things—

(1) the scope of such a private right of action, including whether it should extend to all private actors or whether it should be more limited to extend just to institutional investors or otherwise;

(2) what implications such a private right of action would have on international comity;

(3) the economic costs and benefits of extending a private right of action for transnational securities frauds; and

(4) whether a narrower extraterritorial standard should be adopted.

(c) *Report.* A report of the study shall be submitted and recommendations made to the Committee on Banking, Housing, and Urban Affairs of the Senate and the Committee on Financial Services of the House not later than 18 months after the date of enactment of this Act.

GAO Study on Securities Litigation

Sec. 929Z. (a) *Study.* The Comptroller General of the United States shall conduct a study on the impact of authorizing a private right of action against any person who aids or abets another person in violation of the securities laws. To the extent feasible, this study shall include—

(1) a review of the role of secondary actors in companies issuance of securities;

(2) the courts interpretation of the scope of liability for secondary actors under Federal securities laws after January 14, 2008; and

(3) the types of lawsuits decided under the Private Securities Litigation Act of 1995.

(b) *Report.* Not later than 1 year after the date of enactment of this Act, the Comptroller General shall submit a report to Congress on the findings of the study required under subsection (a).

SUBTITLE C—IMPROVEMENTS TO THE REGULATION OF CREDIT RATING AGENCIES

Findings

Sec. 931. Congress finds the following:

(1) Because of the systemic importance of credit ratings and the reliance placed on credit ratings by individual and institutional investors and financial regulators, the activities and performances of credit rating agencies, including nationally recognized statistical rating organizations, are matters of national public interest, as credit rating agencies are central to capital formation, investor confidence, and the efficient performance of the United States economy.

(2) Credit rating agencies, including nationally recognized statistical rating organizations, play a critical gatekeeper role in the debt market that is functionally similar to that of securities analysts, who evaluate the quality of securities in the equity market, and auditors, who review the financial statements of firms. Such role justifies a similar level of public oversight and accountability.

(3) Because credit rating agencies perform evaluative and analytical services on behalf of clients, much as other financial gatekeepers do, the activities of credit rating agencies are fundamentally commercial in character and should be subject to the same standards of liability and oversight as apply to auditors, securities analysts, and investment bankers.

(4) In certain activities, particularly in advising arrangers of structured financial products on potential ratings of such products, credit rating agencies face conflicts of interest that need to be carefully monitored and that therefore should be addressed explicitly in legislation in order to give clearer authority to the Securities and Exchange Commission.

(5) In the recent financial crisis, the ratings on structured financial products have proven to be inaccurate. This inaccuracy contributed significantly to the mismanagement of risks by financial institutions and investors, which in turn adversely impacted the health of the economy in the United States and around the world. Such inaccuracy necessitates increased accountability on the part of credit rating agencies.

Enhanced Regulation, Accountability, and Transparency of Nationally Recognized Statistical Rating Organizations

Sec. 932. (a) [Omitted. Subsection amended section 15E of the Securities Exchange Act of 1934.]

(b) [Omitted. Subsection amended section 3(a)(62) of the Securities Exchange Act of 1934.]

State of Mind in Private Actions

Sec. 933. (a) [Omitted. Subsection amended section 15E(m) of the Securities Exchange Act of 1934.]

(b) [Omitted. Subsection amended section 21D(b)(2) of the Securities Exchange Act of 1934.]

Referring Tips to Law Enforcement or Regulatory Authorities

Sec. 934. [Omitted. Section amended section 15E of the Securities Exchange Act of 1934.]

Consideration of Information from Sources Other Than the Issuer in Rating Decisions

Sec. 935. [Omitted. Section amended section 15E of the Securities Exchange Act of 1934.]

Qualification Standards for Credit Rating Analysts

Sec. 936. Not later than 1 year after the date of enactment of this Act, the Commission shall issue rules that are reasonably designed to ensure that any person employed by a nationally recognized statistical rating organization to perform credit ratings—

(1) meets standards of training, experience, and competence necessary to produce accurate ratings for the categories of issuers whose securities the person rates; and

(2) is tested for knowledge of the credit rating process.

Timing of Regulations

Sec. 937. Unless otherwise specifically provided in this subtitle, the Commission shall issue final regulations, as required by this subtitle and the amendments made by this subtitle, not later than 1 year after the date of enactment of this Act.

Universal Ratings Symbols

Sec. 938. (a) *Rulemaking*. The Commission shall require, by rule, each nationally recognized statistical rating organization to establish, maintain, and enforce written policies and procedures that—

(1) assess the probability that an issuer of a security or money market instrument will default, fail to make timely payments, or otherwise not make payments to investors in accordance with the terms of the security or money market instrument;

(2) clearly define and disclose the meaning of any symbol used by the nationally recognized statistical rating organization to denote a credit rating; and

(3) apply any symbol described in paragraph (2) in a manner that is consistent for all types of securities and money market instruments for which the symbol is used.

(b) *Rule of Construction*. Nothing in this section shall prohibit a nationally recognized statistical rating organization from using distinct sets of symbols to denote credit ratings for different types of securities or money market instruments.

Removal of Statutory References to Credit Ratings

Sec. 939. (a) [Omitted. Subsection amended The Federal Deposit Insurance Act (12 U.S.C. 1811 et seq.).]

(b) [Omitted. Subsection amended section 1319 of the Federal Housing Enterprises Financial Safety and Soundness Act of 1992 (12 U.S.C. 4519).]

(c) [Omitted. Subsection amended section 6(a)(5)(A)(iv)(I) Investment Company Act of 1940.]

(d) [Omitted. Subsection amended section 5136A of title LXII of the Revised Statutes of the United States (12 U.S.C. 24a).]

(e) [Omitted. Subsection amended section 3(a) Securities Exchange Act of 1934.]

(f) [Omitted. Subsection amended section 3(a)(6) of the amendment in the nature of a substitute to the text of H.R. 4645, as ordered reported from the Committee on Banking, Finance and Urban Affairs on September 22, 1988, as enacted into law by section 555 of Public Law 100–461 (22 U.S.C. 286hh(a)(6)).]

(g) *Effective Date.* The amendments made by this section shall take effect 2 years after the date of enactment of this Act.

(h) *Study and Report.*

(1) *In General.* Commission shall undertake a study on the feasibility and desirability of—

(A) standardizing credit ratings terminology, so that all credit rating agencies issue credit ratings using identical terms;

(B) standardizing the market stress conditions under which ratings are evaluated;

(C) requiring a quantitative correspondence between credit ratings and a range of default probabilities and loss expectations under standardized conditions of economic stress; and

(D) standardizing credit rating terminology across asset classes, so that named ratings correspond to a standard range of default probabilities and expected losses independent of asset class and issuing entity.

(2) *Report.* Not later than 1 year after the date of enactment of this Act, the Commission shall submit to Congress a report containing the findings of the study under paragraph (1) and the recommendations, if any, of the Commission with respect to the study.

Review of Reliance on Ratings

Sec. 939A. (a) *Agency Review.* Not later than 1 year after the date of the enactment of this subtitle, each Federal agency shall, to the extent applicable, review—

(1) any regulation issued by such agency that requires the use of an assessment of the credit-worthiness of a security or money market instrument; and

(2) any references to or requirements in such regulations regarding credit ratings.

(b) *Modifications Required.* Each such agency shall modify any such regulations identified by the review conducted under subsection (a) to remove any reference to or requirement of reliance on credit ratings and to substitute in such regulations such standard of credit-worthiness as each respective agency shall determine as appropriate for such regulations. In making such determination, such agencies shall seek to establish, to the extent feasible, uniform standards of credit-worthiness for use by each such agency, taking into account the entities regulated by each such agency and the purposes for which such entities would rely on such standards of credit-worthiness.

(c) *Report.* Upon conclusion of the review required under subsection (a), each Federal agency shall transmit a report to Congress containing a description of any modification of any regulation such agency made pursuant to subsection (b).

Elimination of Exemption from Fair Disclosure Rule

Sec. 939B. Not later than 90 days after the date of enactment of this subtitle, the Securities Exchange Commission shall revise Regulation FD (17 C.F.R. 243.100) to remove from such regulation the exemption for entities whose primary business is the issuance of credit ratings (17 C.F.R. 243.100(b)(2)(iii)).

Securities and Exchange Commission Study on Strengthening Credit Rating Agency Independence

Sec. 939C. (a) *Study.* The Commission shall conduct a study of—

(1) the independence of nationally recognized statistical rating organizations; and

(2) how the independence of nationally recognized statistical rating organizations affects the ratings issued by the nationally recognized statistical rating organizations.

(b) *Subjects for Evaluation.* In conducting the study under subsection (a), the Commission shall evaluate—

(1) the management of conflicts of interest raised by a nationally recognized statistical rating organization providing other services, including risk management advisory services, ancillary assistance, or consulting services;

(2) the potential impact of rules prohibiting a nationally recognized statistical rating organization that provides a rating to an issuer from providing other services to the issuer; and

(3) any other issue relating to nationally recognized statistical rating organizations, as the Chairman of the Commission determines is appropriate.

(c) *Report.* Not later than 3 years after the date of enactment of this Act, the Chairman of the Commission shall submit to the Committee on Banking, Housing, and Urban Affairs of the Senate and the Committee on Financial Services of the House of Representatives a report on the results of the study conducted under subsection (a), including recommendations, if any, for improving the integrity of ratings issued by nationally recognized statistical rating organizations.

Government Accountability Office Study on Alternative Business Models

Sec. 939D. (a) *Study.* The Comptroller General of the United States shall conduct a study on alternative means for compensating nationally recognized statistical rating organizations in order to create incentives for nationally recognized statistical rating organizations to provide more accurate credit ratings, including any statutory changes that would be required to facilitate the use of an alternative means of compensation.

(b) *Report.* Not later than 18 months after the date of enactment of this Act, the Comptroller General shall submit to the Committee on Banking, Housing, and Urban Affairs of the Senate and the Committee on Financial Services of the House of Representatives a report on the results of the study conducted under subsection (a), including recommendations, if any, for providing incentives to credit rating agencies to improve the credit rating process.

Government Accountability Office Study on the Creation of an Independent Professional Analyst Organization

Sec. 939E. (a) *Study.* The Comptroller General of the United States shall conduct a study on the feasibility and merits of creating an independent professional organization for rating analysts employed by nationally recognized statistical rating organizations that would be responsible for—

(1) establishing independent standards for governing the profession of rating analysts;

(2) establishing a code of ethical conduct; and

(3) overseeing the profession of rating analysts.

(b) *Report.* Not later than 1 year after the date of publication of the rules issued by the Commission pursuant to section 936, the Comptroller General shall submit to the Committee on Banking, Housing, and Urban Affairs of the Senate and the Committee on Financial Services of the House of Representatives a report on the results of the study conducted under subsection (a).

Study and Rulemaking on Assigned Credit Ratings

Sec. 939F. (a) *Definition.* In this section, the term structured finance product means an asset-backed security, as defined in section 3(a)(77) of the Securities Exchange Act of 1934, as added by section 941, and any structured product based on an asset-backed security, as determined by the Commission, by rule.

(b) *Study.* The Commission shall carry out a study of—

(1) the credit rating process for structured finance products and the conflicts of interest associated with the issuer-pay and the subscriber-pay models;

(2) the feasibility of establishing a system in which a public or private utility or a self-regulatory organization assigns nationally recognized statistical rating organizations to determine the credit ratings of structured finance products, including—

(A) an assessment of potential mechanisms for determining fees for the nationally recognized statistical rating organizations;

(B) appropriate methods for paying fees to the nationally recognized statistical rating organizations;

(C) the extent to which the creation of such a system would be viewed as the creation of moral hazard by the Federal Government; and

(D) any constitutional or other issues concerning the establishment of such a system;

(3) the range of metrics that could be used to determine the accuracy of credit ratings; and

(4) alternative means for compensating nationally recognized statistical rating organizations that would create incentives for accurate credit ratings.

(c) *Report and Recommendation.* Not later than 24 months after the date of enactment of this Act, the Commission shall submit to the Committee on Banking, Housing, and Urban Affairs of the Senate and the Committee on Financial Services of the House of Representatives a report that contains—

(1) the findings of the study required under subsection (b); and

(2) any recommendations for regulatory or statutory changes that the Commission determines should be made to implement the findings of the study required under subsection (b).

(d) *Rulemaking.*

(1) *Rulemaking.* After submission of the report under subsection (c), the Commission shall, by rule, as the Commission determines is necessary or appropriate in the public interest or for the protection of investors, establish a system for the assignment of nationally recognized statistical rating organizations to determine the initial credit ratings of structured finance products, in a manner that prevents the issuer, sponsor, or underwriter of the structured finance product from selecting the nationally recognized statistical rating organization that will determine the initial credit ratings and monitor such credit ratings. In issuing any rule under this paragraph, the Commission shall give thorough consideration to the provisions of section 15E(w) of the Securities Exchange Act of 1934, as that provision would have been added by section 939D of H.R. 4173 (111th Congress), as passed by the Senate on May 20, 2010, and shall implement the system described in such section 939D unless the Commission determines that an alternative system would better serve the public interest and the protection of investors.

(2) *Rule of Construction.* Nothing in this subsection may be construed to limit or suspend any other rulemaking authority of the Commission.

Effect of Rule 436(g)

Sec. 939G. Rule 436(g), promulgated by the Securities and Exchange Commission under the Securities Act of 1933, shall have no force or effect.

Sense of Congress

Sec. 939H. It is the sense of Congress that the Securities and Exchange Commission should exercise the rulemaking authority of the Commission under section 15E(h)(2)(B) of the Securities Exchange Act of 1934 to prevent improper conflicts of interest arising from employees of nationally recognized statistical rating organizations providing services to issuers of securities that are unrelated to the issuance of credit ratings, including consulting, advisory, and other services.

SUBTITLE D—IMPROVEMENTS TO THE ASSET-BACKED SECURITIZATION PROCESS

Regulation of Credit Risk Retention

Sec. 941. (a) [Omitted. Subsection amended section 3(a) of the Securities Exchange Act of 1934.]

(b) [Omitted. Subsection added section 15G to the Securities Exchange Act of 1934.]

(c) *Study on Risk Retention.*

(1) *Study.* The Board of Governors of the Federal Reserve System, in coordination and consultation with the Comptroller of the Currency, the Director of the Office of Thrift Supervision, the Chairperson of the Federal Deposit Insurance Corporation, and the Securities and Exchange Commission shall conduct a study of the combined impact on each individual class of asset-backed security established under section 15G(c)(2) of the Securities Exchange Act of 1934, as added by subsection (b), of—

(A) the new credit risk retention requirements contained in the amendment made by subsection (b), including the effect credit risk retention requirements have on increasing the market for Federally subsidized loans; and

(B) the Financial Accounting Statements 166 and 167 issued by the Financial Accounting Standards Board.

(2) *Report.* Not later than 90 days after the date of enactment of this Act, the Board of Governors of the Federal Reserve System shall submit to Congress a report on the study conducted under paragraph (1). Such report shall include statutory

and regulatory recommendations for eliminating any negative impacts on the continued viability of the asset-backed securitization markets and on the availability of credit for new lending identified by the study conducted under paragraph (1).

Disclosures and Reporting for Asset-Backed Securities

Sec. 942. (a) [Omitted. Subsection amended section 15(d) of the Securities Exchange Act of 1934.]

(b) [Omitted. Section amended section 7 of the Securities Act of 1933.]

Representations and Warranties in Asset-Backed Offerings

Sec. 943. Not later than 180 days after the date of enactment of this Act, the Securities and Exchange Commission shall prescribe regulations on the use of representations and warranties in the market for asset-backed securities (as that term is defined in section 3(a)(77) of the Securities Exchange Act of 1934, as added by this subtitle) that—

(1) require each national recognized statistical rating organization to include in any report accompanying a credit rating a description of—

(A) the representations, warranties, and enforcement mechanisms available to investors; and

(B) how they differ from the representations, warranties, and enforcement mechanisms in issuances of similar securities; and

(2) require any securitizer (as that term is defined in section 15G(a) of the Securities Exchange Act of 1934, as added by this subtitle) to disclose fulfilled and unfulfilled repurchase requests across all trusts aggregated by the securitizer, so that investors may identify asset originators with clear underwriting deficiencies.

Exempted Transactions Under the Securities Act of 1933

Sec. 944. (a) [Omitted. Subsection amended section 4 of the Securities Act of 1933.]

(b) [Omitted. Subsection amended section 3(a)(4)(B)(vii)(I) of the Securities Exchange Act of 1934.]

Due Diligence Analysis and Disclosure in Asset-Backed Securities Issues

Sec. 945. [Omitted. Subsection amended section 7 of the Securities Act of 1933.]

Study on the Macroeconomic Effects of Risk Retention Requirements

Sec. 946. (a) *Study Required.* The Chairman of the Financial Services Oversight Council shall carry out a study on the macroeconomic effects of the risk retention requirements under this subtitle, and the amendments made by this subtitle, with emphasis placed on potential beneficial effects with respect to stabilizing the real estate market. Such study shall include—

(1) an analysis of the effects of risk retention on real estate asset price bubbles, including a retrospective estimate of what fraction of real estate losses may have been averted had such requirements been in force in recent years;

(2) an analysis of the feasibility of minimizing real estate price bubbles by proactively adjusting the percentage of risk retention that must be borne by creditors and securitizers of real estate debt, as a function of regional or national market conditions;

(3) a comparable analysis for proactively adjusting mortgage origination requirements;

(4) an assessment of whether such proactive adjustments should be made by an independent regulator, or in a formulaic and transparent manner;

(5) an assessment of whether such adjustments should take place independently or in concert with monetary policy; and

(6) recommendations for implementation and enabling legislation.

(b) *Report.* Not later than the end of the 180-day period beginning on the date of the enactment of this title, the Chairman of the Financial Services Oversight Council shall issue a report to the Congress containing any findings and determinations made in carrying out the study required under subsection (a).

SUBTITLE E—ACCOUNTABILITY AND EXECUTIVE COMPENSATION

Shareholder Vote on Executive Compensation Disclosures

Sec. 951. [Omitted. Section added section 14A to the Securities Exchange Act of 1934.]

Compensation Committee Independence

Sec. 952. (a) [Omitted. Subsection added section 10C to the Securities Exchange Act of 1934.]

(b) *Study and Report.*

(1) *Study.* The Securities and Exchange Commission shall conduct a study and review of the use of compensation consultants and the effects of such use.

(2) *Report.* Not later than 2 years after the date of the enactment of this Act, the Commission shall submit a report to Congress on the results of the study and review required by this subsection.

Executive Compensation Disclosures

Sec. 953. (a) [Omitted. Subsection amended section 14 of the Securities Exchange Act of 1934.]

(b) *Additional Disclosure Requirements.*

(1) *In General.* The Commission shall amend Item 402 of Regulation S–K, to require each issuer, other than an emerging growth company, as that term is defined in section 3(a) of the Securities Exchange Act of 1934, to disclose in any filing of the issuer described in Item 10(a) of Regulation S–K (or any successor thereto)—

(A) the median of the annual total compensation of all employees of the issuer, except the chief executive officer (or any equivalent position) of the issuer;

(B) the annual total compensation of the chief executive officer (or any equivalent position) of the issuer; and

(C) the ratio of the amount described in subparagraph (A) to the amount described in subparagraph (B).

(2) *Total Compensation.* For purposes of this subsection, the total compensation of an employee of an issuer shall be determined in accordance with Item 402(c)(2)(x) of Regulation S–K, as in effect on the day before the date of enactment of this Act.

Recovery of Erroneously Awarded Compensation

Sec. 954. [Omitted. Section added section 10D to the Securities Exchange Act of 1934.]

Disclosure Regarding Employee and Director Hedging

Sec. 955. [Omitted. Section amended section 14 of the Securities Exchange Act of 1934.]

Enhanced Compensation Structure Reporting

Sec. 956. (a) *Enhanced Disclosure and Reporting of Compensation Arrangements.*

(1) *In General.* Not later than 9 months after the date Deadline. of enactment of this title, the appropriate Federal regulators jointly shall prescribe regulations or guidelines to require each covered financial institution to disclose to the appropriate Federal regulator the structures of all incentive-based compensation arrangements offered by such covered financial institutions sufficient to determine whether the compensation structure—

(A) provides an executive officer, employee, director, or principal shareholder of the covered financial institution with excessive compensation, fees, or benefits; or

(B) could lead to material financial loss to the covered financial institution.

(2) *Rules of Construction.* Nothing in this section shall be construed as requiring the reporting of the actual compensation of particular individuals. Nothing in this section shall be construed to require a covered financial institution that does not have an incentive-based payment arrangement to make the disclosures required under this subsection.

(b) *Prohibition on Certain Compensation Arrangements.* Not later than 9 months after the date of enactment of this title, the appropriate Federal regulators shall jointly prescribe regulations or guidelines that prohibit any types of incentive-based payment arrangement, or any feature of any such arrangement, that the regulators determine encourages inappropriate risks by covered financial institutions—

(1) by providing an executive officer, employee, director, or principal shareholder of the covered financial institution with excessive compensation, fees, or benefits; or

(2) that could lead to material financial loss to the covered financial institution.

(c) *Standards.* The appropriate Federal regulators shall—

(1) ensure that any standards for compensation established under subsections (a) or (b) are comparable to the standards established under section of the Federal Deposit Insurance Act for insured depository institutions; and

(2) in establishing such standards under such subsections, take into consideration the compensation standards described in section 39(c) of the Federal Deposit Insurance Act.

(d) *Enforcement.* The provisions of this section and the regulations issued under this section shall be enforced under section 505 of the Gramm–Leach–Bliley Act and, for purposes of such section, a violation of this section or such regulations shall be treated as a violation of subtitle A of title V of such Act.

(e) *Definitions.* As used in this section—

(1) the term "appropriate Federal regulator" means the Board of Governors of the Federal Reserve System, the Office of the Comptroller of the Currency, the Board of Directors of the Federal Deposit Insurance Corporation, the Director of the Office of Thrift Supervision, the National Credit Union Administration Board, the Securities and Exchange Commission, the Federal Housing Finance Agency; and

(2) the term "covered financial institution" means—

(A) a depository institution or depository institution holding company, as such terms are defined in section 3 of the Federal Deposit Insurance Act;

(B) a broker-dealer registered under section 15 of the Securities Exchange Act of 1934;

(C) a credit union, as described in section 19(b)(1)(A)(iv) of the Federal Reserve Act;

(D) an investment advisor, as such term is defined in section 202(a)(11) of the Investment Advisers Act of 1940;

(E) the Federal National Mortgage Association;

(F) the Federal Home Loan Mortgage Corporation; and

(G) any other financial institution that the appropriate Federal regulators, jointly, by rule, determine should be treated as a covered financial institution for purposes of this section.

(f) *Exemption for Certain Financial Institutions.* The requirements of this section shall not apply to covered financial institutions with assets of less than $1,000,000,000.

Voting by Brokers

Sec. 957. [Omitted. Section amended section 6(b) of the Securities Exchange Act of 1934.]

SUBTITLE F—IMPROVEMENTS TO THE MANAGEMENT OF THE SECURITIES AND EXCHANGE COMMISSION

Report and Certification of Internal Supervisory Controls

Sec. 961. (a) *Annual Reports and Certification.* Not later than 90 days after the end of each fiscal year, the Commission shall submit a report to the Committee on Banking, Housing, and Urban Affairs of the Senate and the Committee on Financial Services of the House of Representatives on the conduct by the Commission of examinations of registered entities, enforcement investigations, and review of corporate financial securities filings.

(b) *Contents of Reports.* Each report under subsection (a) shall contain—

(1) an assessment, as of the end of the most recent fiscal year, of the effectiveness of—

(A) the internal supervisory controls of the Commission; and

(B) the procedures of the Commission applicable to the staff of the Commission who perform examinations of registered entities, enforcement investigations, and reviews of corporate financial securities filings;

(2) a certification that the Commission has adequate internal supervisory controls to carry out the duties of the Commission described in paragraph (1)(B); and

(3) a summary by the Comptroller General of the United States of the review carried out under subsection (d).

(c) *Certification.*

(1) *Signature.* The certification under subsection (b)(2) shall be signed by the Director of the Division of Enforcement, the Director of the Division of Corporation Finance, and the Director of the Office of Compliance Inspections and Examinations (or the head of any successor division or office).

(2) *Content of Certification.* Each individual described in paragraph (1) shall certify that the individual—

(A) is directly responsible for establishing and maintaining the internal supervisory controls of the Division or Office of which the individual is the head;

(B) is knowledgeable about the internal supervisory controls of the Division or Office of which the individual is the head;

(C) has evaluated the effectiveness of the internal supervisory controls during the 90–day period ending on the final day of the fiscal year to which the report relates; and

(D) has disclosed to the Commission any significant deficiencies in the design or operation of internal supervisory controls that could adversely affect the ability of the Division or Office to consistently conduct inspections, or investigations, or reviews of filings with professional competence and integrity.

(d) *New Director or Acting Director.* Notwithstanding subsection (a), if the Director of the Division of Enforcement, the Director of the Division of Corporate Finance, or the Director of the Office of Compliance Inspections and Examinations has served as Director of the Division or Office for less than 90 days on the date on which a report is required to be submitted under subsection (a), the Commission may submit the report on the date on which the Director has served as Director for 90 days. If there is no Director of the Division of Enforcement, the Division of Corporate Finance, or the Office of Compliance Inspections and Examinations, on the date on which a report is required to be submitted under subsection (a), the Acting Director of the Division or Office may make the certification required under subsection (c).

(e) *Review by the Comptroller General.*

(1) *Report.* The Comptroller General of the United States shall submit to the Committee on Banking, Housing, and Urban Affairs of the Senate and the Committee on Financial Services of the House of Representatives a report that contains a review of the adequacy and effectiveness of the internal supervisory control structure and procedures described in subsection (b)(1), not less frequently than once every 3 years, at a time to coincide with the publication of the reports of the Commission under this section.

(2) *Authority to Hire Experts.* The Comptroller General of the United States may hire independent consultants with specialized expertise in any area relevant to the duties of the Comptroller General described in this section, in order to assist the Comptroller General in carrying out such duties.

Triennial Report on Personnel Management

Sec. 962. (a) *Triennial Report Required.* Once every 3 years, the Comptroller General of the United States shall submit a report to the Committee on Banking, Housing, and Urban Affairs of the Senate and the Committee on Financial Services of the House of Representatives on the quality of personnel management by the Commission.

(b) *Contents of Report.* Each report under subsection (a) shall include—

(1) an evaluation of—

(A) the effectiveness of supervisors in using the skills, talents, and motivation of the employees of the Commission to achieve the goals of the Commission;

(B) the criteria for promoting employees of the Commission to supervisory positions;

(C) the fairness of the application of the promotion criteria to the decisions of the Commission;

(D) the competence of the professional staff of the Commission;

(E) the efficiency of communication between the units of the Commission regarding the work of the Commission (including communication between divisions and between subunits of a division) and the efforts by the Commission to promote such communication;

(F) the turnover within subunits of the Commission, including the consideration of supervisors whose subordinates have an unusually high rate of turnover;

(G) whether there are excessive numbers of low-level, mid-level, or senior-level managers;

(H) any initiatives of the Commission that increase the competence of the staff of the Commission;

(I) the actions taken by the Commission regarding employees of the Commission who have failed to perform their duties and circumstances under which the Commission has issued to employees a notice of termination; and

(J) such other factors relating to the management of the Commission as the Comptroller General determines are appropriate;

(2) an evaluation of any improvements made with respect to the areas described in paragraph (1) since the date of submission of the previous report; and

(3) recommendations for how the Commission can use the human resources of the Commission more effectively and efficiently to carry out the mission of the Commission.

(c) *Consultation.* In preparing the report under subsection (a), the Comptroller General shall consult with current employees of the Commission, retired employees and other former employees of the Commission, the Inspector General of the Commission, persons that have business before the Commission, any union representing the employees of the Commission, private management consultants, academics, and any other source that the Comptroller General deems appropriate.

(d) *Report by Commission.* Not later than 90 days after the date on which the Comptroller General submits each report under subsection (a), the Commission shall submit to the Committee on Banking, Housing, and Urban Affairs of the Senate and the Committee on Financial Services of the House of Representatives a report describing the actions taken by the Commission in response to the recommendations contained in the report under subsection (a).

(e) *Reimbursements for Cost of Reports.*

(1) *Reimbursements Required.* The Commission shall reimburse the Government Accountability Office for the full cost of making the reports under this section, as billed therefor by the Comptroller General.

(2) *Crediting and Use of Reimbursements.* Such reimbursements shall—

(A) be credited to the appropriation account "salaries and Expenses, Government Accountability Office" current when the payment is received; and

(B) remain available until expended.

(f) *Authority to Hire Experts.* The Comptroller General of the United States may hire independent consultants with specialized expertise in any area relevant to the duties of the Comptroller General described in this section, in order to assist the Comptroller General in carrying out such duties.

Annual Financial Controls Audit

Sec. 963. (a) *Reports of Commission.*

(1) *Annual Reports Required.* Not later than 6 months after the end of each fiscal year, the Commission shall publish and submit to Congress a report that—

(A) describes the responsibility of the management of the Commission for establishing and maintaining an adequate internal control structure and procedures for financial reporting; and

(B) contains an assessment of the effectiveness of the internal control structure and procedures for financial reporting of the Commission during that fiscal year.

(2) *Attestation.* The reports required under paragraph (1) shall be attested to by the Chairman and chief financial officer of the Commission.

(b) *Report By Comptroller General.*

(1) *Report Required.* Not later than 6 months after the end of the first fiscal year after the date of enactment of this Act, the Comptroller General of the United States shall submit a report to Congress that assesses—

(A) the effectiveness of the internal control structure and procedures of the Commission for financial reporting; and

(B) the assessment of the Commission under subsection (a)(1)(B).

(2) *Attestation.* The Comptroller General shall attest to, and report on, the assessment made by the Commission under subsection (a).

(c) *Reimbursements for Cost of Reports.*

(1) *Reimbursements Required.* The Commission shall reimburse the Government Accountability Office for the full cost of making the reports under subsection (b), as billed therefor by the Comptroller General.

(2) *Crediting and Use of Reimbursements.* Such reimbursements shall—

(A) be credited to the appropriation account "salaries and Expenses, Government Accountability Office" current when the payment is received; and

(B) remain available until expended.

Report on Oversight of National Securities Associations

Sec. 964. (a) *Report Required.* Not later than 2 years after the date of enactment of this Act, and every 3 years thereafter, the Comptroller General of the United States shall submit to the Committee on Banking, Housing, and Urban Affairs of the Senate and the Committee on Financial Services of the House of Representatives a report that includes an evaluation of the oversight by the Commission of national securities associations registered under section 15A of the Securities Exchange Act of 1934 (15 U.S.C. 78*o*–3) with respect to—

(1) the governance of such national securities associations, including the identification and management of conflicts of interest by such national securities associations, together with an analysis of the impact of any conflicts of interest on the regulatory enforcement or rulemaking by such national securities associations;

(2) the examinations carried out by the national securities associations, including the expertise of the examiners;

(3) the executive compensation practices of such national securities associations;

(4) the arbitration services provided by the national securities associations;

(5) the review performed by national securities associations of advertising by the members of the national securities associations;

(6) the cooperation with and assistance to State securities administrators by the national securities associations to promote investor protection;

(7) how the funding of national securities associations is used to support the mission of the national securities associations, including—

(A) the methods of funding;

(B) the sufficiency of funds;

(C) how funds are invested by the national securities association pending use; and

(D) the impact of the methods, sufficiency, and investment of funds on regulatory enforcement by the national securities associations;

(8) the policies regarding the employment of former employees of national securities associations by regulated entities;

(9) the ongoing effectiveness of the rules of the national securities associations in achieving the goals of the rules;

(10) the transparency of governance and activities of the national securities associations; and

(11) any other issue that has an impact, as determined by the Comptroller General, on the effectiveness of such national securities associations in performing their mission and in dealing fairly with investors and members;

(b) *Reimbursements for Cost of Reports.*

(1) *Reimbursements Required.* The Commission shall reimburse the Government Accountability Office for the full cost of making the reports under subsection (a), as billed therefor by the Comptroller General.

(2) *Crediting and Use of Reimbursements.* Such reimbursements shall—

(A) be credited to the appropriation account "salaries and Expenses, Government Accountability Office" current when the payment is received; and

(B) remain available until expended.

Compliance Examiners

Sec. 965. [Omitted. Section amended section 4 of the Securities Exchange Act of 1934.]

Suggestion Program for Employees of the Commission

Sec. 966. [Omitted. Subsection added section 4D to the Securities Exchange Act of 1934.]

Commission Organizational Study and Reform

Sec. 967. (a) *Study Required.*

(1) *In General.* Not later than the end of the 90–day period beginning on the date of the enactment of this subtitle, the Securities and Exchange Commission (hereinafter in this section referred to as the "SEC") shall hire an independent consultant of high caliber and with expertise in organizational restructuring and the operations of capital markets to examine the internal operations, structure, funding, and the need for comprehensive reform of the SEC, as well as the SEC's relationship with and the reliance on self-regulatory organizations and other entities relevant to the regulation of securities and the protection of securities investors that are under the SEC's oversight.

(2) *Specific Areas for Study.* The study required under paragraph (1) shall, at a minimum, include the study of—

(A) the possible elimination of unnecessary or redundant units at the SEC;

(B) improving communications between SEC offices and divisions;

(C) the need to put in place a clear chain-of-command structure, particularly for enforcement examinations and compliance inspections;

(D) the effect of high-frequency trading and other technological advances on the market and what the SEC requires to monitor the effect of such trading and advances on the market;

(E) the SEC's hiring authorities, workplace policies, and personal practices, including—

(i) whether there is a need to further streamline hiring authorities for those who are not lawyers, accountants, compliance examiners, or economists;

(ii) whether there is a need for further pay reforms;

(iii) the diversity of skill sets of SEC employees and whether the present skill set diversity efficiently and effectively fosters the SEC's mission of investor protection; and

(iv) the application of civil service laws by the SEC;

(F) whether the SEC's oversight and reliance on self-regulatory organizations promotes efficient and effective governance for the securities markets; and

(G) whether adjusting the SEC's reliance on self-regulatory organizations is necessary to promote more efficient and effective governance for the securities markets.

(b) *Consultant Report.* Not later than the end of the 150–day period after being retained, the independent consultant hired pursuant to subsection (a) (1) shall issue a report to the SEC and the Congress containing—

(1) a detailed description of any findings and conclusions made while carrying out the study required under subsection (a)(1); and

(2) recommendations for legislative, regulatory, or administrative action that the consultant determines appropriate to enable the SEC and other entities on which the consultant reports to perform their statutorily or otherwise mandated missions.

(c) *SEC Report.* Not later than the end of the 6-month period beginning on the date the consultant issues the report under subsection (b), and every 6-months thereafter during the 2-year period following the date on which the consultant issues such report, the SEC shall issue a report to the Committee on Financial Services of the House of Representatives and the Committee on Banking, Housing, and Urban Affairs of the Senate describing the SEC's implementation of the regulatory and administrative recommendations contained in the consultant's report.

Study on SEC Revolving Door

Sec. 968. (a) *Government Accountability Office Study.* The Comptroller General of the United States shall conduct a study that will—

(1) review the number of employees who leave the Securities and Exchange Commission to work for financial institutions regulated by such Commission;

(2) determine how many employees who leave the Securities and Exchange Commission worked on cases that involved financial institutions regulated by such Commission;

(3) review the length of time employees work for the Securities and Exchange Commission before leaving to be employed by financial institutions regulated by such Commission;

(4) review existing internal controls and make recommendations on strengthening such controls to ensure that employees of the Securities and Exchange Commission who are later employed by financial institutions did not assist such institutions in violating any rules or regulations of the Commission during the course of their employment with such Commission;

(5) determine if greater post-employment restrictions are necessary to prevent employees of the Securities and Exchange Commission from being employed by financial institutions after employment with such Commission;

(6) determine if the volume of employees of the Securities and Exchange Commission who are later employed by financial institutions has led to inefficiencies in enforcement;

(7) determine if employees of the Securities and Exchange Commission who are later employed by financial institutions assisted such institutions in circumventing Federal rules and regulations while employed by such Commission;

(8) review any information that may address the volume of employees of the Securities and Exchange Commission who are later employed by financial institutions, and make recommendations to Congress; and

(9) review other additional issues as may be raised during the course of the study conducted under this subsection.

(b) *Report.* Not later than 1 year after the date of the enactment of this subtitle, the Comptroller General of the United States shall submit to the Committee on Financial Services of the House of Representatives and the Committee on Banking, Housing, and Urban Affairs of the Senate a report on the results of the study required by subsection (a).

SUBTITLE G—STRENGTHENING CORPORATE GOVERNANCE

Proxy Access

Sec. 971. (a) [Omitted. Subsection amended section 14(a) of the Securities Exchange Act of 1934.]

(b) *Regulations.* The Commission may issue rules permitting the use by a shareholder of proxy solicitation materials supplied by an issuer of securities for the purpose of nominating individuals to membership on the board of directors of the issuer, under such terms and conditions as the Commission determines are in the interests of shareholders and for the protection of investors.

(c) *Exemptions.* The Commission may, by rule or order, exempt an issuer or class of issuers from the requirement made by this section or an amendment made by this section. In deter-mining whether to make an exemption under this subsection, the Commission shall take into account, among other considerations, whether the requirement in the amendment made by subsection (a) disproportionately burdens small issuers.

Disclosures Regarding Chairman and CEO Structures

Sec. 972. [Omitted. Section added section 14B to the Securities Exchange Act of 1934.]

SUBTITLE H—MUNICIPAL SECURITIES

Regulation of Municipal Securities and Changes to the Board of the MSRB

Sec. 975. (a) [Omitted. Subsection amended section 15B(a) of the Securities Exchange Act of 1934.]

(b) [Omitted. Subsection amended section 15B(b) of the Securities Exchange Act of 1934.]

(c) [Omitted. Subsection amended section 15B(c) of the Securities Exchange Act of 1934.]

(d) [Omitted. Subsection amended section 15B(d)(2) of the Securities Exchange Act of 1934.]

(e) [Omitted. Subsection added section 15B(e) to the Securities Exchange Act of 1934.]

(f) [Omitted. Subsection added section 15A(b)(15) of the Securities Exchange Act of 1934.]

(g) [Omitted. Subsection amended section 15 of the Securities Exchange Act of 1934.]

(h) [Omitted. Subsection amended section 17(a)(1) of the Securities Exchange Act of 1934.]

(i) *Effective Date.* This section, and the amendments made by this section, shall take effect on October 1, 2010.

Government Accountability Office Study of Increased Disclosure to Investors

Sec. 976. (a) *Study.* The Comptroller General of the United States shall conduct a study and review of the disclosure required to be made by issuers of municipal securities.

(b) *Subjects for Evaluation.* In conducting the study under subsection (a), the Comptroller General of the United States shall—

(1) broadly describe—

(A) the size of the municipal securities markets and the issuers and investors; and

(B) the disclosures provided by issuers to investors;

(2) compare the amount, frequency, and quality of disclosures that issuers of municipal securities are required by law to provide for the benefit of municipal securities holders, including the amount of and frequency of disclosures actually provided by issuers of municipal securities, with the amount of and frequency of disclosures that issuers of corporate securities provide for the benefit of corporate securities holders, taking into account the differences between issuers of municipal securities and issuers of corporate securities;

(3) evaluate the costs and benefits to various types of issuers of municipal securities of requiring issuers of municipal bonds to provide additional financial disclosures for the benefit of investors;

(4) evaluate the potential benefit to investors from additional financial disclosures by issuers of municipal bonds; and

(5) make recommendations relating to disclosure requirements for municipal issuers, including the advisability of the repeal or retention of section 15B(d) of the Securities Exchange Act of 1934 (commonly known as the "Tower Amendment").

(c) *Report.* Not later than 24 months after the date of enactment of this Act, the Comptroller General of the United States shall submit a report to Congress on the results of the study conducted under subsection (a), including recommendations for how to improve disclosure by issuers of municipal securities.

Government Accountability Office Study on the Municipal Securities Markets

Sec. 977. (a) *Study.* The Comptroller General of the United States shall conduct a study of the municipal securities markets.

(b) *Report.* Not later than 18 months after the date of enactment of this Act, the Comptroller General of the United States shall submit a report to the Committee on Banking, Housing, and Urban Affairs of the Senate, and the Committee on Financial Services of the House of Representatives, with copies to the Special Committee on Aging of the Senate and the Commission, on the results of the study conducted under subsection (a), including—

(1) an analysis of the mechanisms for trading, quality of trade executions, market transparency, trade reporting, price discovery, settlement clearing, and credit enhancements;

(2) the needs of the markets and investors and the impact of recent innovations;

(3) recommendations for how to improve the transparency, efficiency, fairness, and liquidity of trading in the municipal securities markets, including with reference to items listed in paragraph (1); and

(4) potential uses of derivatives in the municipal securities markets.

(c) *Responses.* Not later than 180 days after receipt of the report required under subsection (b), the Commission shall submit a response to the Committee on Banking, Housing, and Urban Affairs of the Senate, and the Committee on Financial Services of the House of Representatives, with a copy to the Special Committee on Aging of the Senate, stating the actions the Commission has taken in response to the recommendations contained in such report.

Funding for Governmental Accounting Standards Board

Sec. 978. (a) [Omitted. Subsection amended section 19 of the Securities Exchange Act of 1933.]

(b) *Study of Funding for Governmental Accounting Standards Board.*

(1) *Study.* The Comptroller General of the United States shall conduct a study that evaluates—

(A) the role and importance of the Governmental Accounting Standards Board in the municipal securities markets; and

(B) the manner and the level at which the Governmental Accounting Standards Board has been funded.

(2) *Consultation.* In conducting the study required under paragraph (1), the Comptroller General shall consult with the principal organizations representing State governors, legislators, local elected officials, and State and local finance officers.

(3) *Report.* Not later than 180 days after the date of enactment of this Act, the Comptroller General shall submit to the Committee on Banking, Housing, and Urban Affairs of the Senate and the Committee on Financial Services of the House of Representatives a report on the study required under paragraph (1).

Commission Office of Municipal Securities

Sec. 979. (a) *In General.* There shall be in the Commission an Office of Municipal Securities, which shall—

(1) administer the rules of the Commission with respect to the practices of municipal securities brokers and dealers, municipal securities advisors, municipal securities investors, and municipal securities issuers; and

(2) coordinate with the Municipal Securities Rulemaking Board for rulemaking and enforcement actions as required by law.

(b) *Director of the Office.* The head of the Office of Municipal Securities shall be the Director, who shall report to the Chairman.

(c) *Staffing.*

(1) *In General.* The Office of Municipal Securities shall be staffed sufficiently to carry out the requirements of this section.

(2) *Requirement.* The staff of the Office of Municipal Securities shall include individuals with knowledge of and expertise in municipal finance.

SUBTITLE I—PUBLIC COMPANY ACCOUNTING OVERSIGHT BOARD, PORTFOLIO MARGINING, AND OTHER MATTERS

Authority to Share Certain Information with Foreign Authorities

Sec. 981. (a) [Omitted. Subsection amended section 2(a) of the Sarbanes-Oxley Act of 2002.]

(b) [Omitted. Subsection amended section 105(b)(5) of the Sarbanes-Oxley Act of 2002.]

(c) [Omitted. Subsection amended section 105(b)(5)(A) of the Sarbanes–Oxley Act of 2002.]

Oversight of Brokers and Dealers

Sec. 982. (a) [Omitted. Subsection added section 110 to Title I of the Sarbanes–Oxley Act of 2002.]

(b) [Omitted. Subsection amended section 101 of the Sarbanes–Oxley Act of 2002.]

(c) [Omitted. Subsection amended section 105(b)(5)(A) of the Sarbanes–Oxley Act of 2002.]

(d) [Omitted. Subsection amended section 103(a) of the Sarbanes–Oxley Act of 2002.]

(e) [Omitted. Subsection amended section 104(a) of the Sarbanes–Oxley Act of 2002.]

(f) [Omitted. Subsection amended section 105(c)(7)(B) of the Sarbanes–Oxley Act of 2002.]

(g) [Omitted. Subsection amended section 106(a) of the Sarbanes–Oxley Act of 2002.]

(h) [Omitted. Subsection amended section 109 of the Sarbanes–Oxley Act of 2002.]

(i) [Omitted. Subsection amended section 105(b)(4)(B) of the Sarbanes–Oxley Act of 2002.]

(j) [Omitted. Subsection amended section 105(b)(5)(B)(ii) of the Sarbanes–Oxley Act of 2002.]

Portfolio Margining

Sec. 983. (a) [Omitted. Subsection amended section 9(a)(1) of the Securities Investor Protection Act of 1970 (15 U.S.C. 78fff3(a)(1)).]

(b) [Omitted. Subsection amended section 16 of the Securities Investor Protection Act of 1970 (15 U.S.C. 78lll).]

Loan or Borrowing of Securities

Sec. 984. (a) [Omitted. Subsection amended section 10 of the Securities Exchange Act of 1934.]

(b) *Rulemaking Required.* Not later than 2 years after the date of enactment of this Act, the Commission shall promulgate rules that are designed to increase the transparency of information available to brokers, dealers, and investors, with respect to the loan or borrowing of securities.

Technical Corrections to Federal Securities Laws

Sec. 985. (a) *Securities Act of 1933.*

(1) [Omitted. Subsection amended section 3(a)(4) of the Securities Act of 1933.]

(2) [Omitted. Subsection amended section 18 of the Securities Act of 1933.]

(3) [Omitted. Subsection amended section 19(d)(6)(A) of the Securities Act of 1933.]

(4) [Omitted. Subsection amended section 27A(c)(1)(B)(ii) of the Securities Act of 1933.]

(b) *Securities Exchange Act of 1934.*

(1) [Omitted. Subsection amended section 2 of the Securities Exchange Act of 1934.]

(2) [Omitted. Subsection amended section 3 of the Securities Exchange Act of 1934.]

(3) [Omitted. Subsection amended section 10A(i)(1)(B) of the Securities Exchange Act of 1934.]

(4) [Omitted. Subsection amended section 13(b)(1) of the Securities Exchange Act of 1934.]

(5) [Omitted. Subsection amended section 15 of the Securities Exchange Act of 1934.]

(6) [Omitted. Subsection amended section 15C(a)(2) of the Securities Exchange Act of 1934.]

(7) [Omitted. Subsection amended section 17(b)(1)(B)of the Securities Exchange Act of 1934.]

(8) [Omitted. Subsection amended section 21C(c)(2) of the Securities Exchange Act of 1934.]

(c) *Trust Indenture Act of 1939.*

(1) [Omitted. Subsection amended section 304(b) of the Trust Indenture Act of 1939 (15 U.S.C. 77aaa).]

(2) [Omitted. Subsection amended section and 317(a)(1) of the Trust Indenture Act of 1939 (15 U.S.C. 77aaa).]

(d) *Investment Company Act of 1940.*

(1) [Omitted. Subsection amended section 2(a)(19) of the Investment Company Act of 1940.]

(2) [Omitted. Subsection amended section 9(b)(4)(B) of the Investment Company Act of 1940.]

(3) [Omitted. Subsection amended section 12(d)(1)(J) of the Investment Company Act of 1940.]

(4) [Omitted. Subsection amended section 17(f) of the Investment Company Act of 1940.]

(e) *Investment Advisors Act of 1940.*

(1) [Omitted. Subsection amended section 203 of the Investment Advisers Act of 1940.]

(2) [Omitted. Subsection amended section 206(3) of the Investment Advisers Act of 1940.]

(3) [Omitted. Subsection amended section 213(a) the Investment Advisers Act of 1940.]

(4) [Omitted. Subsection amended section 222 of the Investment Advisers Act of 1940.]

Conforming Amendments Relating to Repeal of the Public Utility Holding Company Act of 1935

Sec. 986. (a) *Securities Exchange Act of 1934.*

(1) [Omitted. Subsection amended section 3(a)(47) of the Securities Exchange Act of 1934.]

(2) [Omitted. Subsection amended section 12(k) of the Securities Exchange Act of 1934.]

(3) [Omitted. Subsection amended section 21(h)(2) of the Securities Exchange Act of 1934.]

(b) *Trust Indenture Act of 1939.*

(1) [Omitted. Subsection amended section 303 of the Trust Indenture Act of 1939 (15 U.S.C. 77aaa).]

(2) [Omitted. Subsection amended section 310 of the Trust Indenture Act of 1939 (15 U.S.C. 77aaa).]

(3) [Omitted. Subsection amended section 311of the Trust Indenture Act of 1939 (15 U.S.C. 77aaa).]

(4) [Omitted. Subsection amended sections 323(b) of the Trust Indenture Act of 1939 (15 U.S.C. 77aaa).]

(5) [Omitted. Subsection amended section 326 of the Trust Indenture Act of 1939 (15 U.S.C. 77aaa).]

(c) *Investment Company Act of 1940.*

(1) [Omitted. Subsection amended section 2(a)(44) of the Investment Company Act of 1940.]

(2) [Omitted. Subsection amended section 3(c) of the Investment Company Act of 1940.]

(3) [Omitted. Subsection amended section 38(b) of the Investment Company Act of 1940.]

(4) [Omitted. Subsection amended section 50 of the Investment Company Act of 1940.]

(d) *Investment Advisers Act of 1940.* [Omitted. Subsection amended section 202(a)(21) of the Investment Advisers Act of 1940.]

Amendment to Definition of Material Loss and Nonmaterial Losses to the Deposit Insurance Fund for Purposes of Inspector General Reviews

Sec. 987. (a) [Omitted. Subsection amended section 38(k) of the Federal Deposit Insurance Act (12 U.S.C. 1831o(k)).]

(b) [Omitted. Subsection amended section 38(k) of the Federal Deposit Insurance Act (12 U.S.C. 1831o(k)).]

Amendment to Definition of Material Loss and Nonmaterial Losses to the National Credit Union Share Insurance Fund for Purposes of Inspector General Reviews

Sec. 988. (a) [Omitted. Subsection amended section 216(j) of the Federal Credit Union Act (12 U.S.C. 1790d(j)).]

Government Accountability Office Study on Proprietary Trading

Sec. 989. (a) *Definitions.* In this section—

(1) the term "covered entity" means—

(A) an insured depository institution, an affiliate of an insured depository institution, a bank holding company, a financial holding company, or a subsidiary of a bank holding company or a financial holding company, as those terms are defined in the Bank Holding Company Act of 1956; and

(B) any other entity, as the Comptroller General of the United States may determine; and

(2) the term "proprietary trading" means the act of a covered entity investing as a principal in securities, commodities, derivatives, hedge funds, private equity firms, or such other financial products or entities as the Comptroller General may determine.

(b) *Study.*

(1) *In General.* The Comptroller General of the United States shall conduct a study regarding the risks and conflicts associated with proprietary trading by and within covered entities, including an evaluation of—

(A) whether proprietary trading presents a material systemic risk to the stability of the United States financial system, and if so, the costs and benefits of options for mitigating such systemic risk;

(B) whether proprietary trading presents material risks to the safety and soundness of the covered entities that engage in such activities, and if so, the costs and benefits of options for mitigating such risks;

(C) whether proprietary trading presents material conflicts of interest between covered entities that engage in proprietary trading and the clients of the institutions who use the firm to execute trades or who rely on the firm to manage assets, and if so, the costs and benefits of options for mitigating such conflicts of interest;

(D) whether adequate disclosure regarding the risks and conflicts of proprietary trading is provided to the depositors, trading and asset management clients, and investors of covered entities that engage in proprietary trading, and if not, the costs and benefits of options for the improvement of such disclosure; and

(E) whether the banking, securities, and commodities regulators of institutions that engage in proprietary trading have in place adequate systems and controls to monitor and contain any risks and conflicts of interest related to proprietary trading, and if not, the costs and benefits of options for the improvement of such systems and controls.

(2) *Considerations.* In carrying out the study required under paragraph (1), the Comptroller General shall consider—

(A) current practice relating to proprietary trading;

(B) the advisability of a complete ban on proprietary trading;

(C) limitations on the scope of activities that covered entities may engage in with respect to proprietary trading;

(D) the advisability of additional capital requirements for covered entities that engage in proprietary trading;

(E) enhanced restrictions on transactions between affiliates related to proprietary trading;

(F) enhanced accounting disclosures relating to proprietary trading;

(G) enhanced public disclosure relating to proprietary trading; and

(H) any other options the Comptroller General deems appropriate.

(c) *Report to Congress.* Not later than 15 months after the date of enactment of this Act, the Comptroller General shall submit a report to Congress on the results of the study conducted under subsection (b).

(d) *Access by Comptroller General.* For purposes of conducting the study required under subsection (b), the Comptroller General shall have access, upon request, to any information, data, schedules, books, accounts, financial records, reports, files, electronic communications, or other papers, things, or property belonging to or in use by a covered entity that engages in proprietary trading, and to the officers, directors, employees, independent public accountants, financial advisors, staff, and agents and representatives of a covered entity (as related to the activities of the agent or representative on behalf of the covered entity), at such reasonable times as the Comptroller General may request. The Comptroller General may make and retain copies of books, records, accounts, and other records, as the Comptroller General deems appropriate.

(e) *Confidentiality of Reports.*

(1) *In General.* Except as provided in paragraph (2), the Comptroller General may not disclose information regarding—

(A) any proprietary trading activity of a covered entity, unless such information is disclosed at a level of generality that does not reveal the investment or trading position or strategy of the covered entity for any specific security, commodity, derivative, or other investment or financial product; or

(B) any individual interviewed by the Comptroller General for purposes of the study under subsection (b), unless such information is disclosed at a level of generality that does not reveal—

(i) the name of or identifying details relating to such individual; or

(ii) in the case of an individual who is an employee of a third party that provides professional services to a covered entity believed to be engaged in proprietary trading, the name of or any identifying details relating to such third party.

(2) *Exceptions.* The Comptroller General may disclose the information described in paragraph (1)—

(A) to a department, agency, or official of the Federal Government, for official use, upon request;

(B) to a committee of Congress, upon request; and

(C) to a court, upon an order of such court.

Senior Investor Protections

Sec. 989A. (a) *Definitions.* As used in this section—

(1) the term "eligible entity" means—

(A) a securities commission (or any agency or office performing like functions) of a State that the Office determines has adopted rules on the appropriate use of designations in the offer or Be of securities or the provision of investment advice that meet or exceed the minimum requirements of the NASAA Model Rule on the Use of Senior–Specific Certifications and Professional Designations (or any successor thereto);

(B) the insurance commission (or any agency or office performing like functions) of any State that the Office determines has—

(i) adopted rules on the appropriate use of designations in the Be of insurance products that, to the extent practicable, conform to the minimum requirements of the National Association of Insurance Commissioners Model Regulation on the Use of Senior-Specific Certifications and Professional Designations in the Be of Life Insurance and Annuities (or any successor thereto); and

(ii) adopted rules with respect to fiduciary or suitability requirements in the Be of annuities that meet or exceed the minimum requirements established by the Suitability in Annuity Transactions Model Regulation of the National Association of Insurance Commissioners (or any successor thereto); or

(C) a consumer protection agency of any State, if—

(i) the securities commission (or any agency or office performing like functions) of the State is eligible under subparagraph (A); or

(ii) the insurance commission (or any agency or office performing like functions) of the State is eligible under subparagraph (B);

(2) the term "financial product" means a security, an insurance product (including an insurance product that pays a return, whether fixed or variable), a bank product, and a loan product;

(3) the term "misleading designation"—

(A) means a certification, professional designation, or other purported credential that indicates or implies that a salesperson or adviser has special certification or training in advising or servicing seniors; and

(B) does not include a certification, professional designation, license, or other credential that—

(i) was issued by or obtained from an academic institution having regional accreditation;

(ii) meets the standards for certifications and professional designations outlined by the NASAA Model Rule on the Use of Senior–Specific Certifications and Professional Designations (or any successor thereto) or by the Model Regulations on the Use of Senior–Specific Certifications and Professional Designations in the Be of Life Insurance and Annuities, adopted by the National Association of Insurance Commissioners (or any successor thereto); or

(iii) was issued by or obtained from a State;

(4) the term "misleading or fraudulent marketing" means the use of a misleading designation by a person that sells to or advises a senior in connection with the Be of a financial product;

(5) the term "NASAA" means the North American Securities Administrators Association;

(6) the term "Office" means the Office of Financial Literacy of the Bureau;

(7) the term "senior" means any individual who has attained the age of 62 years or older; and

(8) the term "State" has the same meaning as in section 3 of the Securities Exchange Act of 1934.

(b) *Grants to States for Enhanced Protection of Seniors from Being Misled by False Designations.* The Office shall establish a program under which the Office may make grants to States or eligible entities—

(1) to hire staff to identify, investigate, and prosecute (through civil, administrative, or criminal enforcement actions) cases involving misleading or fraudulent marketing;

(2) to fund technology, equipment, and training for regulators, prosecutors, and law enforcement officers, in order to identify salespersons and advisers who target seniors through the use of misleading designations;

(3) to fund technology, equipment, and training for prosecutors to increase the successful prosecution of salespersons and advisers who target seniors with the use of misleading designations;

(4) to provide educational materials and training to regulators on the appropriateness of the use of designations by salespersons and advisers in connection with the Be and marketing of financial products;

(5) to provide educational materials and training to seniors to increase awareness and understanding of misleading or fraudulent marketing;

(6) to develop comprehensive plans to combat misleading or fraudulent marketing of financial products to seniors; and

(7) to enhance provisions of State law to provide protection for seniors against misleading or fraudulent marketing.

(c) *Applications.* A State or eligible entity desiring a grant under this section shall submit an application to the Office, in such form and in such a manner as the Office may determine, that includes—

(1) a proposal for activities to protect seniors from misleading or fraudulent marketing that are proposed to be funded using a grant under this section, including—

(A) an identification of the scope of the problem of misleading or fraudulent marketing in the State;

(B) a description of how the proposed activities would—

(i) protect seniors from misleading or fraudulent marketing in the Be of financial products, including by proactively identifying victims of misleading and fraudulent marketing who are seniors;

(ii) assist in the investigation and prosecution of those using misleading or fraudulent marketing; and

(iii) discourage and reduce cases of misleading or fraudulent marketing; and

(C) a description of how the proposed activities would be coordinated with other State efforts; and (2) any other information, as the Office determines is appropriate.

(d) *Performance Objectives and Reporting Requirements.* The Office may establish such performance objectives and reporting requirements for States and eligible entities receiving a grant under this section as the Office determines are necessary to carry out and assess the effectiveness of the program under this section.

(e) *Maximum Amount.* The amount of a grant under this section may not exceed—

(1) $500,000 for each of 3 consecutive fiscal years, if the recipient is a State, or an eligible entity of a State, that has adopted rules—

(A) on the appropriate use of designations in the offer or Be of securities or investment advice that meet or exceed the minimum requirements of the NASAA Model Rule on the Use of Senior–Specific Certifications and Professional Designations (or any successor thereto);

(B) on the appropriate use of designations in the sale of insurance products that, to the extent practicable, conform to the minimum requirements of the National Association of Insurance Commissioners Model Regulation on the Use of Senior–Specific Certifications and Professional Designations in the sale of Life Insurance and Annuities (or any successor thereto); and

(C) with respect to fiduciary or suitability requirements in the Be of annuities that meet or exceed the minimum requirements established by the Suitability in Annuity Transactions Model Regulation of the National Association of Insurance Commissioners (or any successor thereto); and

(2) $100,000 for each of 3 consecutive fiscal years, if the recipient is a State, or an eligible entity of a State, that has adopted—

(A) rules on the appropriate use of designations in the offer or Be of securities or investment advice that meet or exceed the minimum requirements of the NASAA Model Rule on the Use of Senior–Specific Certifications and Professional Designations (or any successor thereto); or

(B) rules—

(i) on the appropriate use of designations in the Be of insurance products that, to the extent practicable, conform to the minimum requirements of the National Association of Insurance Commissioners Model Regulation on the Use of Senior–Specific Certifications and Professional Designations in the sale of Life Insurance and Annuities (or any successor thereto); and

(ii) with respect to fiduciary or suitability requirements in the Be of annuities that meet or exceed the minimum requirements established by the Suitability in Annuity Transactions Model Regulation of the National Association of Insurance Commissioners (or any successor thereto).

(f) *Subgrants.* A State or eligible entity that receives a grant under this section may make a subgrant, as the State or eligible entity determines is necessary to carry out the activities funded using a grant under this section.

(g) *Reapplication.* A State or eligible entity that receives a grant under this section may reapply for a grant under this section, notwithstanding the limitations on grant amounts under subsection (e).

(h) *Authorization of Appropriations.* There are authorized to be appropriated to carry out this section, $8,000,000 for each of fiscal years 2011 through 2015.

Designated Federal Entity Inspectors General Independence

Sec. 989B. [Omitted. Section amended section 8G of the Inspector General Act of 1978 (5 U.S.C. App.).]

Strengthening Inspector General Accountability

Sec. 989C. [Omitted. Section amended section 5(a) of the Inspector General Act of 1978 (5 U.S.C. App.).]

Removal of Inspectors General of Designated Federal Entities

Sec. 989D. [Omitted. Section amended section 8G(e) of the Inspector General Act of 1978 (5 U.S.C. App.).]

Additional Oversight of Financial Regulatory System

Sec. 989E. (a) *Council of Inspectors General on Financial Oversight.*

(1) *Establishment and Membership.* There is established a Council of Inspectors General on Financial Oversight (in this section referred to as the "Council of Inspectors General") chaired by the Inspector General of the Department of the Treasury and composed of the inspectors general of the following:

(A) The Board of Governors of the Federal Reserve System.

(B) The Commodity Futures Trading Commission.

(C) The Department of Housing and Urban Development.

(D) The Department of the Treasury.

(E) The Federal Deposit Insurance Corporation.

(F) The Federal Housing Finance Agency.

(G) The National Credit Union Administration.

(H) The Securities and Exchange Commission.

(I) The Troubled Asset Relief Program (until the termination of the authority of the Special Inspector General for such program under section 121(k) of the Emergency Economic Stabilization Act of 2008).

(2) *Duties.*

(A) *Meetings.* The Council of Inspectors General shall meet not less than once each quarter, or more frequently if the chair considers it appropriate, to facilitate the sharing of information among inspectors general and to discuss the ongoing work of each inspector general who is a member of the Council of Inspectors General, with a focus on concerns that may apply to the broader financial sector and ways to improve financial oversight.

(B) *Annual Report.* Each year the Council of Inspectors General shall submit to the Council and to Congress a report including—

(i) for each inspector general who is a member of the Council of Inspectors General, a section within the exclusive editorial control of such inspector general that highlights the concerns and recommendations of such inspector general in such inspector general's ongoing and completed work, with a focus on issues that may apply to the broader financial sector; and

(ii) a summary of the general observations of the Council of Inspectors General based on the views expressed by each inspector general as required by clause (i), with a focus on measures that should be taken to improve financial oversight.

(3) *Working Groups to Evaluate Council.*

(A) *Convening a Working Group.* The Council of Inspectors General may, by majority vote, convene a Council of Inspectors General Working Group to evaluate the effectiveness and internal operations of the Council.

(B) *Personnel and Resources.* The inspectors general who are members of the Council of Inspectors General may detail staff and resources to a Council of Inspectors General Working Group established under this paragraph to enable it to carry out its duties.

(C) *Reports.* A Council of Inspectors General Working Group established under this paragraph shall submit regular reports to the Council and to Congress on its evaluations pursuant to this paragraph.

(b) *Response to Report by Council.* The Council shall respond to the concerns raised in the report of the Council of Inspectors General under subsection (a)(2)(B) for such year.

GAO Study of Person to Person Lending

Sec. 989F. (a) *Study.*

(1) *In General.* The Comptroller General of the United States shall conduct a study of person to person lending to determine the optimal Federal regulatory structure.

(2) *Consultation.* In conducting the study required under paragraph (1), the Comptroller General shall consult with Federal banking agencies, the Commission, consumer groups, outside experts, and the person to person lending industry.

(3) *Content of Study.* The study required under paragraph (1) shall include an examination of—

(A) the regulatory structure as it exists on the date of enactment of this Act, as determined by the Commission, with particular attention to—

(i) the application of the Securities Act of 1933 to person to person lending platforms;

(ii) the posting of consumer loan information on the EDGAR database of the Commission; and

(iii) the treatment of privately held person to person lending platforms as public companies;

(B) the State and other Federal regulators responsible for the oversight and regulation of person to person lending markets;

(C) any Federal, State, or local government or private studies of person to person lending completed or in progress on the date of enactment of this Act;

(D) consumer privacy and data protections, minimum credit standards, anti-money laundering and risk management in the regulatory structure as it exists on the date of enactment of this Act, and whether additional or alternative safeguards are needed; and

(E) the uses of person to person lending.

(b) *Report.*

(1) *In General.* Not later than 1 year after the date of enactment of this Act, the Comptroller General shall submit a report on the study required under subsection (a) to the Committee on Banking, Housing, and Urban Affairs of the Senate and the Committee on Financial Services of the House of Representatives.

(2) *Content of Report.* The report required under paragraph (1) shall include alternative regulatory options, including—

(A) the involvement of other Federal agencies; and

(B) alternative approaches by the Commission and recommendations on whether the alternative approaches are effective.

Exemption for Nonaccelerated Filers

Sec. 989G. (a) [Omitted. Subsection amended section 404 of the Sarbanes–Oxley Act of 2002.]

(b) *Study.* The Securities and Exchange Commission shall conduct a study to determine how the Commission could reduce the burden of complying with section 404(b) of the Sarbanes–Oxley Act of 2002 for companies whose market capitalization is between $75,000,000 and $250,000,000 for the relevant reporting period while maintaining investor protections for such companies. The study shall also consider whether any such methods of reducing the compliance burden or a complete exemption for such companies from compliance with such section would encourage companies to list on exchanges in the United States in their initial public offerings. Not later than 9 months after the date of the enactment of this subtitle, the Commission shall transmit a report of such study to Congress.

Corrective Responses by Heads of Certain Establishments to Deficiencies Identified by Inspectors General

Sec. 989H. The Chairman of the Board of Governors of the Federal Reserve System, the Chairman of the Commodity Futures Trading Commission, the Chairman of the National Credit Union Administration, the Director of the Pension Benefit Guaranty Corporation, and the Chairman of the Securities and Exchange Commission shall each—

(1) take action to address deficiencies identified by a report or investigation of the Inspector General of the establishment concerned; or

(2) certify to both Houses of Congress that no action is necessary or appropriate in connection with a deficiency described in paragraph (1).

GAO Study Regarding Exemption for Smaller Issuers

Sec. 989I. (a) *Study Regarding Exemption for Smaller Issuers.* The Comptroller General of the United States shall carry out a study on the impact of the amendments made by this Act to section 404(b) of the Sarbanes–Oxley Act of 2002, which shall include an analysis of—

(1) whether issuers that are exempt from such section 404(b) have fewer or more restatements of published accounting statements than issuers that are required to comply with such section 404(b);

(2) the cost of capital for issuers that are exempt from such section 404(b) compared to the cost of capital for issuers that are required to comply with such section 404(b);

(3) whether there is any difference in the confidence of investors in the integrity of financial statements of issuers that comply with such section 404(b) and issuers that are exempt from compliance with such section 404(b);

(4) whether issuers that do not receive the attestation for internal controls required under such section 404(b) should be required to disclose the lack of such attestation to investors; and

(5) the costs and benefits to issuers that are exempt from such section 404(b) that voluntarily have obtained the attestation of an independent auditor.

(b) *Report.* Not later than 3 years after the date of enactment of this Act, the Comptroller General shall submit to the Committee on Banking, Housing, and Urban Affairs of the Senate and the Committee on Financial Services of the House of Representatives a report on the results of the study required under subsection (a).

Further Promoting the Adoption of the NAIC Model Regulations That Enhance Protection of Seniors and Other Consumers

Sec. 989J. (a) *In General.* The Commission shall treat as exempt securities described under section 3(a)(8) of the Securities Act of 1933 any insurance or endowment policy or annuity contract or optional annuity contract—

(1) the value of which does not vary according to the performance of a separate account;

(2) that—

(A) satisfies standard nonforfeiture laws or similar requirements of the applicable State at the time of issue; or

(B) in the absence of applicable standard nonforfeiture laws or requirements, satisfies the Model Standard Nonforfeiture Law for Life Insurance or Model Standard Nonforfeiture Law for Individual Deferred Annuities, or any successor model law, as published by the National Association of Insurance Commissioners; and

(3) that is issued—

(A) on and after June 16, 2013, in a State, or issued by an insurance company that is domiciled in a State, that—

(i) adopts rules that govern suitability requirements in the Be of an insurance or endowment policy or annuity contract or optional annuity contract, which shall substantially meet or exceed the minimum requirements established by the Suitability in Annuity Transactions Model Regulation adopted by the National Association of Insurance Commissioners in March 2010; and

(ii) adopts rules that substantially meet or exceed the minimum requirements of any successor modifications to the model regulations described in subparagraph (A) within 5 years of the adoption by the Association of any further successors thereto; or

(B) by an insurance company that adopts and implements practices on a nationwide basis for the Be of any insurance or endowment policy or annuity contract or optional annuity contract that meet or exceed the minimum requirements established by the National Association of Insurance Commissioners Suitability in Annuity Transactions Model Regulation (Model 275), and any successor thereto, and is therefore subject to examination by the State of domicile of the insurance company, or by any other State where the insurance company conducts sales of such products, for the purpose of monitoring compliance under this section.

(b) *Rule of Construction.* Nothing in this section shall be construed to affect whether any insurance or endowment policy or annuity contract or optional annuity contract that is not described in this section is or is not an exempt security under section 3(a)(8) of the Securities Act of 1933.

SUBTITLE J—SECURITIES AND EXCHANGE COMMISSION MATCH FUNDING

Securities and Exchange Commission Match Funding

Sec. 991. (a) *Match Funding Authority.*

(1) [Omitted. Subsection amended section 31 of the Securities Exchange Act of 1934.]

(2) *Effective Date.* The amendments made by this subsection shall take effect on the later of—

(A) October 1, 2011; or

(B) the date of enactment of an Act making a regular appropriation to the Commission for fiscal year 2012.

(b) *Amendments to Registration Fee Provisions.*

(1) [Omitted. Subsection amended section 6(b) of the Securities Act of 1933.]

(2) [Omitted. Subsection amended section 13(e) of the Securities Exchange Act of 1934.]

(3) [Omitted. Subsection amended section 14(g) of the Securities Exchange Act of 1934.]

(4) *Effective Date.* The amendments made by this subsection shall take effect on October 1, 2011, except that for fiscal year 2012, the Commission shall publish the rate established under section 6(b) of the Securities Act of 1933, as amended by this Act, on August 31, 2011.

(c) [Omitted. Subsection amended section 35 of the Securities Exchange Act of 1934.]

(d) *Transmittal of Budget Requests.*

(1) [Omitted. Subsection amended section 31 of the Securities Exchange Act of 1934.]

(2) *Budget of the President.* For the fiscal year 2012, and each fiscal year thereafter, the annual budget for the Administration submitted by the President to Congress shall reflect the amendments made by this section.

(e) *Securities and Exchange Commission Reserve Fund.*

(1) [Omitted. Subsection amended section 4 of the Securities Exchange Act of 1934.]

(2) *Effective Date.* The amendment made by this subsection shall take effect on October 1, 2011.

K. JUMPSTART OUR BUSINESS STARTUPS ACT

Public Law 112–106

Short Title

Sec. 1. This Act may be cited as the "Jumpstart Our Business Startups Act".

Sec. 2. [Table of Contents Omitted].

TITLE I—REOPENING AMERICAN CAPITAL MARKETS TO EMERGING GROWTH COMPANIES

Definitions

Sec. 101. (a) *Securities Act of 1933.* [Omitted. Subsection amended section 2(a) of the Securities Act of 1933.]

(b) *Securities Act of 1934.* [Omitted. Subsection amended section 3(a) of the Securities Exchange Act of 1934.]

(c) *Other Definitions.* As used in this title, the following definitions shall apply:

(1) *Commission.* The term "Commission" means the Securities and Exchange Commission.

(2) *Initial Public Offering Date.* The term "initial public offering date" means the date of the first sale of common equity securities of an issuer pursuant to an effective registration statement under the Securities Act of 1933.

(d) *Effective Date.* Notwithstanding section 2(a)(19) of the Securities Act of 1933 and section 3(a)(80) of the Securities Exchange Act of 1934, an issuer shall not be an emerging growth company for purposes of such Acts if the first sale of common equity securities of such issuer pursuant to an effective registration statement under the Securities Act of 1933 occurred on or before December 8, 2011.

Disclosure Obligations

Sec. 102. (a) *Executive Compensation.*

(1) *Exemption.* [Omitted. Paragraph amended section 14A(e) of the Securities Exchange Act of 1934.]

(2) *Proxies.* [Omitted. Paragraph amended section 14(i) of the Securities Exchange Act of 1934.]

(3) *Compensation Disclosures.* [Omitted. Paragraph amended section 953(b)(1) of the Investor Protection and Securities Reform Act of 2010.]

(b) *Financial Disclosures and Accounting Pronouncements.*

(1) *Securities Act of 1933.* [Omitted. Paragraph amended section 7(a) of the Securities Act of 1933.]

(2) *Securities Exchange Act of 1934.* [Omitted. Paragraph amended section 13(a) of the Securities Exchange Act of 1934.]

(c) *Other Disclosures.* An emerging growth company may comply with Item 301 under Regulation S–K, or any successor thereto, by providing information required by such section with respect to the financial statements of the emerging growth company for each period presented pursuant to section 7(a) of the Securities Act of 1933. An emerging growth company may comply with Item 402 under Regulation S–K, or any successor thereto, by disclosing the same information as any issuer with a market value of outstanding voting and nonvoting common equity held by non-affiliates of less than $75,000,000.

(d) *Simplified Disclosure Requirements.*—With respect to an emerging growth company (as such term is defined under section 2 of the Securities Act of 1933):

(1) *Requirement To Include Notice On Forms S–1 And F–1.*—Not later than 30 days after the date of enactment of this subsection, the Securities and Exchange Commission shall revise its general instructions on Forms S–1 and F–1 to indicate that a registration statement filed (or submitted for confidential review) by an issuer prior to an initial public offering may omit financial information for historical periods otherwise required by regulation S–X (17 CFR 210.1–01 et seq.) as of the time of filing (or confidential submission) of such registration statement, provided that—

(A) the omitted financial information relates to a historical period that the issuer reasonably believes will not be required to be included in the Form S–1 or F–1 at the time of the contemplated offering; and

(B) prior to the issuer distributing a preliminary prospectus to investors, such registration statement is amended to include all financial information required by such regulation S–X at the date of such amendment.

(2) *Reliance By Issuers.*—Effective 30 days after the date of enactment of this subsection, an issuer filing a registration statement (or submitting the statement for confidential review) on Form S–1 or Form F–1 may omit financial information for historical periods otherwise required by regulation S–X (17 CFR 210.1–01 et seq.) as of the time of filing (or confidential submission) of such registration statement, provided that—

(A) the omitted financial information relates to a historical period that the issuer reasonably believes will not be required to be included in the Form S–1 or Form F–1 at the time of the contemplated offering; and

(B) prior to the issuer distributing a preliminary prospectus to investors, such registration statement is amended to include all financial information required by such regulation S–X at the date of such amendment.

Internal Controls Audit

Sec. 103. [Omitted. Section amended Section 404(b) of the Sarbanes–Oxley Act of 2002.]

Auditing Standards

Sec. 104. [Omitted. Section amended Section 103(a)(3) of the Sarbanes–Oxley Act of 2002.]

Availability of Information About Emerging Growth Companies

Sec. 105. (a) *Provision of Research.* [Omitted. Subsection amended section 2(a)(3) of the Securities Act of 1933.]

(b) *Securities Analyst Communications.* [Omitted. Subsection amended section 15D of the Securities Exchange Act of 1934.]

(c) *Expanding Permissible Communications* [Omitted. Subsection amended section 5 of the Securities Act of 1933.]

(d) *Post Offering Communications.* Neither the Commission nor any national securities association registered under section 15A of the Securities Exchange Act of 1934 may adopt or maintain any rule or regulation prohibiting any broker, dealer, or member of a national securities association from publishing or distributing any research report or making a public appearance, with respect to the securities of an emerging growth company, either—

(1) within any prescribed period of time following the initial public offering date of the emerging growth company; or

(2) within any prescribed period of time prior to the expiration date of any agreement between the broker, dealer, or member of a national securities association and the emerging growth company or its shareholders that restricts or prohibits the sale of securities held by the emerging growth company or its shareholders after the initial public offering date.

Other Matters

Sec. 106. (a) *Draft Registration Statements.* [Omitted. Subsection amended section 6 of the Securities Act of 1933.]

(b) *Tick Size.* [Omitted. Subsection amended section 11A(c) of the Securities Exchange Act of 1934.]

Opt–In Right for Emerging Growth Companies

Sec. 107. (a) *In General.* With respect to an exemption provided to emerging growth companies under this title, or an amendment made by this title, an emerging growth company may choose to forgo such exemption and instead comply with the requirements that apply to an issuer that is not an emerging growth company.

(b) *Special Rule.* Notwithstanding subsection (a), with respect to the extension of time to comply with new or revised financial accounting standards provided under section 7(a)(2)(B) of the Securities Act of 1933 and section 13(a) of the Securities Exchange Act of 1934, as added by section 102(b), if an emerging growth company chooses to comply with such standards to the same extent that a non-emerging growth company is required to comply with such standards, the emerging growth company—

(1) must make such choice at the time the company is first required to file a registration statement, periodic report, or other report with the Commission under section 13 of the Securities Exchange Act of 1934 and notify the Securities and Exchange Commission of such choice;

(2) may not select some standards to comply with in such manner and not others, but must comply with all such standards to the same extent that a non-emerging growth company is required to comply with such standards; and

(3) must continue to comply with such standards to the same extent that a non-emerging growth company is required to comply with such standards for as long as the company remains an emerging growth company.

Review of Regulation S–K

Sec. 108. (a) *Review.* The Securities and Exchange Commission shall conduct a review of its Regulation S–K to—

(1) comprehensively analyze the current registration requirements of such regulation; and

(2) determine how such requirements can be updated to modernize and simplify the registration process and reduce the costs and other burdens associated with these requirements for issuers who are emerging growth companies.

(b) *Report.* Not later than 180 days after the date of enactment of this title, the Commission shall transmit to Congress a report of the review conducted under subsection (a). The report shall include the specific recommendations of the Commission on how to streamline the registration process in order to make it more efficient and less burdensome for the Commission and for prospective issuers who are emerging growth companies.

TITLE II—ACCESS TO CAPITAL FOR JOB CREATORS

Modification of Exemption

(a) *Modification of Rules.*

(1) Not later than 90 days after the date of the enactment of this Act, the Securities and Exchange Commission shall revise its rules issued in section 230.506 of title 17, Code of Federal Regulations, to provide that the prohibition against general solicitation or general advertising contained in Rule 502(c) shall not apply to offers and sales of securities made pursuant to Rule 506, provided that all purchasers of the securities are accredited investors. Such rules shall require the issuer to take reasonable steps to verify that purchasers of the securities are accredited investors, using such methods as determined by the Commission. Rule 506 under the Securities Act of 1933, as revised pursuant to this section, shall continue to be treated as a regulation issued under section 4(a)(2) of the Securities Act of 1933.

(2) Not later than 90 days after the date of enactment of this Act, the Securities and Exchange Commission shall revise subsection (d)(1) of Rule 144A under the Securities Act of 1933, to provide that securities sold under such revised exemption may be offered to persons other than qualified institutional buyers, including by means of general solicitation or general advertising, provided that securities are sold only to persons that the seller and any person acting on behalf of the seller reasonably believe is a qualified institutional buyer.

(b) *Consistency in Interpretation.* [Omitted. Subsection amended section 4 of the Securities Act of 1933.]

(c) *Explanation of Exemption.* [Omitted. Subsection amended section 4 of the Securities Act of 1933.]

TITLE III—CROWDFUNDING

Short Title

Sec. 301. This title may be cited as the "Capital Raising Online While Deterring Fraud and Unethical Non-Disclosure Act of 2012" or the "CROWDFUND Act".

Crowdfunding Exemption

Sec. 302. (a) *Securities Act of 1933.* [Omitted. Subsection amended section 4 of the Securities Act of 1933.]

(b) *Requirements to Qualify for Crowdfunding Exemption.* [Omitted. Subsection adds section 4A to the Securities Act of 1933.]

(c) *Rulemaking.* Not later than 270 days after the date of enactment of this Act, the Securities and Exchange Commission (in this title referred to as the "Commission") shall issue such rules as the Commission determines may be necessary or appropriate for the protection of investors to carry out sections 4(a)(6) and section 4A of the Securities Act of 1933, as added by this title. In carrying out this section, the Commission shall consult with any securities commission (or any agency or office performing like functions) of the States, any territory of the United States, and the District of Columbia, which seeks to consult with the Commission, and with any applicable national securities association.

(d) *Disqualification.*

(1) *In General.* Not later than 270 days after the date of enactment of this Act, the Commission shall, by rule, establish disqualification provisions under which—

(A) an issuer shall not be eligible to offer securities pursuant to section 4(a)(6) of the Securities Act of 1933, as added by this title; and

(B) a broker or funding portal shall not be eligible to effect or participate in transactions pursuant to that section 4(a)(6).

(2) *Inclusions.* Disqualification provisions required by this subsection shall—

(A) be substantially similar to the provisions of Rule 262 under the Securities Act of 1933 (or any successor thereto); and

(B) disqualify any offering or sale of securities by a person that—

(i) is subject to a final order of a State securities commission (or an agency or officer of a State performing like functions), a State authority that supervises or examines banks, savings associations, or credit unions, a State insurance commission (or an agency or officer of a State performing like functions), an appropriate Federal banking agency, or the National Credit Union Administration, that—

(I) bars the person from—

(aa) association with an entity regulated by such commission, authority, agency, or officer;

(bb) engaging in the business of securities, insurance, or banking; or

(cc) engaging in savings association or credit union activities; or

(II) constitutes a final order based on a violation of any law or regulation that prohibits fraudulent, manipulative, or deceptive conduct within the 10-year period ending on the date of the filing of the offer or sale; or

(ii) has been convicted of any felony or misdemeanor in connection with the purchase or sale of any security or involving the making of any false filing with the Commission.

Exclusion of Crowdfunding Investors from Shareholder Cap

Sec. 303. (a) *Exemption.* [Omitted. Subsection amends section 12(g) of the Securities Exchange Act of 1934.]

(b) *Rulemaking.* The Commission shall issue a rule to carry out section 12(g)(6) of the Securities Exchange Act of 1934, as added by this section, not later than 270 days after the date of enactment of this Act.

Funding Portal Regulation

Sec. 304. (a) *Exemption.*

(1) *In General.* [Omitted. Paragraph amends section Section 3 of the Securities Exchange Act of 1934.]

(2) *Rulemaking.* The Commission shall issue a rule to carry out section 3(h) of the Securities Exchange Act of 1934, as added by this subsection, not later than 270 days after the date of enactment of this Act.

(b) *Definition.* [Omitted. Subsection amends section 3(a) of the Securities Exchange Act of 1934.]

Relationship with State Law

Sec. 305. (a) *In General.* [Omitted. Subsection amends section 18(b)(4) of the Securities Act of 1933.]

(b) *Clarification of the Preservation of State Enforcement Authority.*

(1) *In General.* The amendments made by subsection (a) relate solely to State registration, documentation, and offering requirements, as described under section 18(a) of Securities Act of 1933, and shall have no impact or limitation on other State authority to take enforcement action with regard to an issuer, funding portal, or any other person or entity using the exemption from registration provided by section 4(a)(6) of that Act.

(2) *Clarification of State Jurisdiction over Unlawful Conduct of Funding Portals and Issuers.* [Omitted. Paragraph amends section 18(c)(1) of the Securities Act of 1933.]

(c) *Notice Filings Permitted.* [Omitted. Subsection amends section 18(c)(2) of the Securities Act of 1933.]

(d) *Funding Portals.*

(1) *State Exemptions and Oversight.* [Omitted. Paragraph amends section 15(i) of the Securities Exchange Act of 1934.]

(2) *State Fraud Authority.* [Omitted. Paragraph amends section 18(c)(1) of the Securities Act of 1933.]

TITLE IV—SMALL COMPANY CAPITAL FORMATION

Authority to Exempt Certain Securities

Sec. 401. (a) *In General.* [Omitted. Subsection amends section 3(b) of the Securities Act of 1933.]

(b) *Treatment as Covered Securities for Purposes of NSMIA.* [Omitted. Subsection amends section 18(b)(4) of the Securities Act of 1933.]

(c) *Conforming Amendment.* [Omitted. Subsection amends section 4(a)(5) of the Securities Act of 1933.]

Study on the Impact of State Blue Sky Laws on Regulation A Offerings

Sec. 402. The Comptroller General shall conduct a study on the impact of State laws regulating securities offerings, or "Blue Sky laws", on offerings made under Regulation A (17 CFR 230.251 et seq.). The Comptroller General shall transmit a report on the findings of the study to the Committee on Financial Services of the House of Representatives, and the Committee on Banking, Housing, and Urban Affairs of the Senate not later than 3 months after the date of enactment of this Act.

TITLE V—PRIVATE COMPANY FLEXIBILITY AND GROWTH

Threshold for Registration

Sec. 501. [Omitted. Subsection amends section 12(g)(1)(A) of the Securities Exchange Act of 1934.]

Employees

Sec. 502. [Omitted. Subsection amends section 12(g)(5) of the Securities Exchange Act of 1934.]

Commission Rulemaking

Sec. 503. The Securities and Exchange Commission shall revise the definition of "held of record" pursuant to section 12(g)(5) of the Securities Exchange Act of 1934 to implement the amendment made by section 502. The Commission shall also adopt safe harbor provisions that issuers can follow when determining whether holders of their securities received the securities pursuant to an employee compensation plan in transactions that were exempt from the registration requirements of section 5 of the Securities Act of 1933.

Commission Study of Enforcement Authority Under Rule 12g5–1

Sec. 504. The Securities and Exchange Commission shall examine its authority to enforce Rule 12g5–1 to determine if new enforcement tools are needed to enforce the anti-evasion provision contained in subsection (b)(3) of the rule, and shall, not later than 120 days after the date of enactment of this Act transmit its recommendations to Congress.

TITLE VI—CAPITAL EXPANSION

Shareholder Threshold for Registration

Sec. 601. (a) [Omitted. Subsection amends section 12 of the Securities Exchange Act of 1934.]

(b) [Omitted. Subsection amends section 15 of the Securities Exchange Act of 1934.]

Rulemaking

Sec. 602. Not later than 1 year after the date of enactment of this Act, the Securities and Exchange Commission shall issue final regulations to implement this title and the amendments made by this title.

TITLE VII—OUTREACH ON CHANGES TO THE LAW

Outreach by the Commission

Sec. 701. The Securities and Exchange Commission shall provide online information and conduct outreach to inform small and medium sized businesses, women owned businesses, veteran owned businesses, and minority owned businesses of the changes made by this Act.

II. RELATED FEDERAL LAWS

COMMODITY EXCHANGE ACT

7 U.S.C. § 1 et seq.

Section Act	7 U.S.C.	
6a	10a	Cooperative Associations and Corporations, Exclusion from Board of Trade
6b	13a	Nonenforcement of Rules of Government or Other Violations
6c	13a–1	Action to Enjoin or Restrain Violations
6d	13a–2	Jurisdiction of States
7	11	Vacation of Request of Designation as Registered Entity
8	12	Public Disclosure
8a	12a	Registration of Commodity Dealers and Associated Persons; Regulation of Contract Markets
8b	12b	Trading Ban Violations
8c	12c	Disciplinary Actions
8d	12d	Commission Action for Non–Compliance with Export Sales Reporting Requirements
9	13	Violations Generally; Punishment; Costs of Prosecution
10	17	Separability of Provisions
11		[Repealed]
12	16	Commission Operations
13	13c	Responsibility of Principal
14	18	Complaints Against Registered Persons
15	19	Consideration of Costs and Benefits and Antitrust Laws
16	20	Market Reports
17	21	Registered Futures Associations
18	22	Research and Information Programs
19	23	Standardized Contracts for Certain Commodities Prohibited
20	24	Regulations Respecting Commodity Broker Debtors
21	24a	Swap Data Repositories
22	25	Private Rights of Action
23	26	Commodity Whistleblower Incentives and Protection

Short Title

Sec. 1. This Act may be cited as the "Commodity Exchange Act."

Definitions

Sec. 1a. As used in this Act:

(1) *Alternative Trading System.* The term "alternative trading system" means an organization, association, or group of persons that—

(A) is registered as a broker or dealer pursuant to section 15(b) of the Securities Exchange Act of 1934 (except paragraph (11) thereof);

(B) performs the functions commonly performed by an exchange (as defined in section 3(a)(1) of the Securities Exchange Act of 1934);

(C) does not—

(i) set rules governing the conduct of subscribers other than the conduct of such subscribers' trading on the alternative trading system; or

(ii) discipline subscribers other than by exclusion from trading; and

(D) is exempt from the definition of the term "exchange" under such section 3(a)(1) by rule or regulation of the Securities and Exchange Commission on terms that require compliance with regulations of its trading functions.

(2) *Appropriate Federal Banking Agency.* The term "appropriate Federal banking agency"

(A) has the meaning given the term in section 3 of the Federal Deposit Insurance Act;

(B) means the Board in the case of a noninsured State bank; and

(C) is the Farm Credit Administration for farm credit system institutions.

(3) *Associated Person of a Security–Based Swap Dealer or Major Security–Based Swap Participant.* The term "associated person of a security-based swap dealer or major security-based swap participant" has the meaning given the term in section 3(a) of the Securities Exchange Act of 1934.

(4) *Associated Person of a Swap Dealer or Major Swap Participant.*

(A) *In General.* The term "associated person of a swap dealer or major swap participant" means a person who is associated with a swap dealer or major swap participant as a partner, officer, employee, or agent (or any person occupying a similar status or performing similar functions), in any capacity that involves—

(i) the solicitation or acceptance of swaps; or

(ii) the supervision of any person or persons so engaged.

(B) *Exclusion*. Other than for purposes of section 4s(b)(6), the term "associated person of a swap dealer or major swap participant" does not include any person associated with a swap dealer or major swap participant the functions of which are solely clerical or ministerial.

(5) *Board*. The term "Board" means the Board of Governors of the Federal Reserve System.

(6) *Board of Trade*. The term "board of trade" means any organized exchange or other trading facility.

(7) *Cleared Swap*. The term "cleared swap" means any swap that is, directly or indirectly, submitted to and cleared by a derivatives clearing organization registered with the Commission.

(8) *Commission*. The term "Commission" means the Commodity Futures Trading Commission established under section 2(a)(2).

(9) *Commodity*. The term "commodity" means wheat, cotton, rice, corn, oats, barley, rye, flaxseed, grain sorghums, mill feeds, butter, eggs, Solanum tuberosum (Irish potatoes), wool, wool tops, fats and oils (including lard, tallow, cottonseed oil, peanut oil, soybean oil, and all other fats and oils), cottonseed meal, cottonseed, peanuts, soybeans, soybean meal, livestock, livestock products, and frozen concentrated orange juice, and all other goods and articles, except onions (as provided by the first section of Public Law 85–839 (7 U.S.C. 13–1)) and motion picture box office receipts (or any index, measure, value, or data related to such receipts), and all services, rights, and interests (except motion picture box office receipts, or any index, measure, value or data related to such receipts) in which contracts for future delivery are presently or in the future dealt in.

(10) *Commodity Pool*.

(A) *In General*. The term "commodity pool" means any investment trust, syndicate, or similar form of enterprise operated for the purpose of trading in commodity interests, including any—

(i) commodity for future delivery, security futures product, or swap;

(ii) agreement, contract, or transaction described in section 2(c)(2)(C)(i) or section 2(c)(2)(D)(i);

(iii) commodity option authorized under section 4c; or

(iv) leverage transaction authorized under section 19.

(B) *Further Definition*. The Commission, by rule or regulation, may include within, or exclude from, the term "commodity pool" any investment trust, syndicate, or similar form of enterprise if the Commission determines that the rule or regulation will effectuate the purposes of this Act.

(11) *Commodity Pool Operator*.

(A) *In General*. The term "commodity pool operator" means any person—

(i) engaged in a business that is of the nature of a commodity pool, investment trust, syndicate, or similar form of enterprise, and who, in connection therewith, solicits, accepts, or receives from others, funds, securities, or property, either directly or through capital contributions, the sale of stock or other forms of securities, or otherwise, for the purpose of trading in commodity interests, including any—

(I) commodity for future delivery, security futures product, or swap;

(II) agreement, contract, or transaction described in section 2(c)(2)(C)(i) or section 2(c)(2)(D)(i);

(III) commodity option authorized under section 4c; or

(IV) leverage transaction authorized under section 19; or

(ii) who is registered with the Commission as a commodity pool operator.

(B) *Further Definition*. The Commission, by rule or regulation, may include within, or exclude from, the term "commodity pool operator" any person engaged in a business that is of the nature of a commodity pool, investment trust, syndicate, or similar form of enterprise if the Commission determines that the rule or regulation will effectuate the purposes of this Act.

(12) *Commodity Trading Advisor*.

(A) *In General*. Except as otherwise provided in this paragraph, the term "commodity trading advisor" means any person who—

(i) for compensation or profit, engages in the business of advising others, either directly or through publications, writings, or electronic media, as to the value of or the advisability of trading in—

(I) any contract of sale of a commodity for future delivery or security futures product, or swap;

(II) any agreement, contract, or transaction described in section 2(c)(2)(C)(i) or section 2(c)(2)(D)(i);

(III) any commodity option authorized under section 4c; or

(IV) any leverage transaction authorized under section 19;

(ii) for compensation or profit, and as part of a regular business, issues or promulgates analyses or reports concerning any of the activities referred to in clause (i);

(iii) is registered with the Commission as a commodity trading advisor; or

(iv) the Commission, by rule or regulation, may include if the Commission determines that the rule or regulation will effectuate the purposes of this Act.

(B) *Exclusions.* Subject to subparagraph (C), the term "commodity trading advisor" does not include—

(i) any bank or trust company or any person acting as an employee thereof;

(ii) any news reporter, news columnist, or news editor of the print or electronic media, or any lawyer, accountant, or teacher;

(iii) any floor broker or futures commission merchant;

(iv) the publisher or producer of any print or electronic data of general and regular dissemination, including its employees;

(v) the fiduciary of any defined benefit plan that is subject to the Employee Retirement Income Security Act of 1974;

(vi) any contract market or derivatives transaction execution facility; and

(vii) such other persons not within the intent of this paragraph as the Commission may specify by rule, regulation, or order.

(C) *Incidental Services.* Subparagraph (B) shall apply only if the furnishing of such services by persons referred to in subparagraph (B) is solely incidental to the conduct of their business or profession.

(D) *Advisors.* The Commission, by rule or regulation, may include within the term "commodity trading advisor", any person advising as to the value of commodities or issuing reports or analyses concerning commodities if the Commission determines that the rule or regulation will effectuate the purposes of this paragraph.

(13) *Contract of Sale.* The term "contract of sale" includes sales, agreements of sale, and agreements to sell.

(14) *Cooperative Association of Producers.* The term "cooperative association of producers" means any cooperative association, corporate, or otherwise, not less than 75 percent in good faith owned or controlled, directly or indirectly, by producers of agricultural products and otherwise complying with the Act of February 18, 1922, including any organization acting for a group of such associations and owned or controlled by such associations, except that business done for or with the United States, or any agency thereof, shall not be considered either member or nonmember business in determining the compliance of any such association with this Act.

(15) *Derivatives Clearing Organization.*

(A) *In General.* The term "derivatives clearing organization" means a clearinghouse, clearing association, clearing corporation, or similar entity, facility, system, or organization that, with respect to an agreement, contract, or transaction—

(i) enables each party to the agreement, contract, or transaction to substitute, through novation or otherwise, the credit of the derivatives clearing organization for the credit of the parties;

(ii) arranges or provides, on a multilateral basis, for the settlement or netting of obligations resulting from such agreements, contracts, or transactions executed by participants in the derivatives clearing organization; or

(iii) otherwise provides clearing services or arrangements that mutualize or transfer among participants in the derivatives clearing organization the credit risk arising from such agreements, contracts, or transactions executed by the participants.

(B) *Exclusions.* The term "derivatives clearing organization" does not include an entity, facility, system, or organization solely because it arranges or provides for—

(i) settlement, netting, or novation of obligations resulting from agreements, contracts, or transactions, on a bilateral basis and without a central counterparty;

(ii) settlement or netting of cash payments through an interbank payment system; or

(iii) settlement, netting, or novation of obligations resulting from a sale of a commodity in a transaction in the spot market for the commodity.

(16) *Electronic Trading Facility*. The term "electronic trading facility" means a trading facility that—

(A) operates by means of an electronic or telecommunications network; and

(B) maintains an automated audit trail of bids, offers, and the matching of orders or the execution of transactions on the facility.

(17) *Eligible Commercial Entity*. The term "eligible commercial entity" means, with respect to an agreement, contract or transaction in a commodity—

(A) an eligible contract participant described in clause (i), (ii), (v), (vii), (viii), or (ix) of paragraph (18)(A) that, in connection with its business—

(i) has a demonstrable ability, directly or through separate contractual arrangements, to make or take delivery of the underlying commodity;

(ii) incurs risks, in addition to price risk, related to the commodity; or

(iii) is a dealer that regularly provides risk management or hedging services to, or engages in market-making activities with, the foregoing entities involving transactions to purchase or sell the commodity or derivative agreements, contracts, or transactions in the commodity;

(B) an eligible contract participant, other than a natural person or an instrumentality, department, or agency of a State or local governmental entity, that—

(i) regularly enters into transactions to purchase or sell the commodity or derivative agreements, contracts, or transactions in the commodity; and

(ii) either—

(I) in the case of a collective investment vehicle whose participants include persons other than—

(aa) qualified eligible persons, as defined in Commission rule 4.7(a);

(bb) accredited investors, as defined in Regulation D of the Securities and Exchange Commission under the Securities Act of 1933, with total assets of $2,000,000; or

(cc) qualified purchasers, as defined in section 2(a)(51)(A) of the Investment Company Act of 1940; in each case as in effect on the date of the enactment of the Commodity Futures Modernization Act of 2000, has, or is one of a group of vehicles under common control or management having in the aggregate, $1,000,000,000 in total assets; or

(II) in the case of other persons, has, or is one of a group of persons under common control or management having in the aggregate, $100,000,000 in total assets; or

(C) such other persons as the Commission shall determine appropriate and shall designate by rule, regulation, or order.

(18) *Eligible Contract Participant*. The term "eligible contract participant" means—

(A) acting for its own account—

(i) a financial institution;

(ii) an insurance company that is regulated by a State, or that is regulated by a foreign government and is subject to comparable regulation as determined by the Commission, including a regulated subsidiary or affiliate of such an insurance company;

(iii) an investment company subject to regulation under the Investment Company Act of 1940 or a foreign person performing a similar role or function subject as such to foreign regulation (regardless of whether each investor in the investment company or the foreign person is itself an eligible contract participant);

(iv) a commodity pool that—

(I) has total assets exceeding $5,000,000; and

(II) is formed and operated by a person subject to regulation under this Act or a foreign person performing a similar role or function subject as such to foreign regulation (regardless of whether each investor in the commodity pool or the foreign person is itself an eligible contract participant) provided, however, that for purposes of section 2(c)(2)(B)(vi) and section 2(c)(2)(C)(vii), the term 'eligible contract participant' shall not include a commodity pool in which any participant is not otherwise an eligible contract participant;

(v) a corporation, partnership, proprietorship, organization, trust, or other entity—

(I) that has total assets exceeding $10,000,000;

(II) the obligations of which under an agreement, contract, or transaction are guaranteed or otherwise supported by a letter of credit or keepwell, support, or other agreement by an entity described in subclause (I), in clause (i), (ii), (iii), (iv), or (vii), or in subparagraph (C); or

(III) that—

(aa) has a net worth exceeding $1,000,000; and

(bb) enters into an agreement, contract, or transaction in connection with the conduct of the entity's business or to manage the risk associated with an asset or liability owned or incurred or reasonably likely to be owned or incurred by the entity in the conduct of the entity's business;

(vi) an employee benefit plan subject to the Employee Retirement Income Security Act of 1974, a governmental employee benefit plan, or a foreign person performing a similar role or function subject as such to foreign regulation—

(I) that has total assets exceeding $5,000,000; or

(II) the investment decisions of which are made by—

(aa) an investment adviser or commodity trading advisor subject to regulation under the Investment Advisers Act of 1940 or this Act;

(bb) a foreign person performing a similar role or function subject as such to foreign regulation;

(cc) a financial institution; or

(dd) an insurance company described in clause (ii), or a regulated subsidiary or affiliate of such an insurance company;

(vii)(I) a governmental entity (including the United States, a State, or a foreign government) or political subdivision of a governmental entity;

(II) a multinational or supranational government entity; or

(III) an instrumentality, agency, or department of an entity described in subclause (I) or (II);

except that such term does not include an entity, instrumentality, agency, or department referred to in subclause (I) or (III) of this clause unless

(aa) the entity, instrumentality, agency, or department is a person described in clause (i), (ii), or (iii) of paragraph 17(A);

(bb) the entity, instrumentality, agency, or department owns and invests on a discretionary basis $50,000,0000 or more in investments; or

(cc) the agreement, contract, or transaction is offered by, and entered into with, an entity that is listed in any of subclauses (I) through (VI) of section 2(c)(2)(B)(ii);

(viii)(I) a broker or dealer subject to regulation under the Securities Exchange Act of 1934 or a foreign person performing a similar role or function subject as such to foreign regulation, except that, if the broker or dealer or foreign person is a natural person or proprietorship, the broker or dealer or foreign person shall not be considered to be an eligible contract participant unless the broker or dealer or foreign person also meets the requirements of clause (v) or (xi);

(II) an associated person of a registered broker or dealer concerning the financial or securities activities of which the registered person makes and keeps records under section 15C(b) or 17(h) of the Securities Exchange Act of 1934;

(III) an investment bank holding company (as defined in section 17(i) of the Securities Exchange Act of 1934);

(ix) a futures commission merchant subject to regulation under this Act or a foreign person performing a similar role or function subject as such to foreign regulation, except that, if the futures commission merchant or foreign person is a natural person or proprietorship, the futures commission merchant or foreign person shall not be considered to be an eligible contract participant unless the futures commission merchant or foreign person also meets the requirements of clause (v) or (xi);

(x) a floor broker or floor trader subject to regulation under this Act in connection with any transaction that takes place on or through the facilities of a registered entity (other than an electronic trading facility with respect to a significant price discovery contract) or an exempt board of trade, or any affiliate thereof, on which such person regularly trades; or

(xi) an individual who has amounts invested on a discretionary basis, the aggregate of which is in excess of—

(I) $10,000,000; or

(II) $5,000,000 and who enters into the agreement, contract, or transaction in order to manage the risk associated with an asset owned or liability incurred, or reasonably likely to be owned or incurred, by the individual;

(B)(i) a person described in clause (i), (ii), (iv), (v), (viii), (ix), or (x) of subparagraph (A) or in subparagraph (C), acting as broker or performing an equivalent agency function on behalf of another person described in subparagraph (A) or (C); or

(ii) an investment adviser subject to regulation under the Investment Advisers Act of 1940, a commodity trading advisor subject to regulation under this Act, a foreign person performing a similar role or function subject as such to foreign regulation, or a person described in clause (i), (ii), (iv), (v), (viii), (ix), or (x) of subparagraph (A) or in subparagraph (C), in any such case acting as investment manager or fiduciary (but excluding a person acting as broker or performing an equivalent agency function) for another person described in subparagraph (A) or (C) and who is authorized by such person to commit such person to the transaction; or

(C) any other person that the Commission determines to be eligible in light of the financial or other qualifications of the person.

(19) *Excluded Commodity*. The term "excluded commodity" means—

(i) an interest rate, exchange rate, currency, security, security index, credit risk or measure, debt or equity instrument, index or measure of inflation, or other macroeconomic index or measure;

(ii) any other rate, differential, index, or measure of economic or commercial risk, return, or value that is—

(I) not based in substantial part on the value of a narrow group of commodities not described in clause (i); or

(II) based solely on one or more commodities that have no cash market;

(iii) any economic or commercial index based on prices, rates, values, or levels that are not within the control of any party to the relevant contract, agreement, or transaction; or

(iv) an occurrence, extent of an occurrence, or contingency (other than a change in the price, rate, value, or level of a commodity not described in clause (i)) that is—

(I) beyond the control of the parties to the relevant contract, agreement, or transaction; and

(II) associated with a financial, commercial, or economic consequence.

(20) *Exempt Commodity*. The term "exempt commodity" means a commodity that is not an excluded commodity or an agricultural commodity.

(21) *Financial Institution*. The term "financial institution" means—

(A) a corporation operating under the fifth undesignated paragraph of section 25 of the Federal Reserve Act, commonly known as "an agreement corporation";

(B) a corporation organized under section 25A of the Federal Reserve Act, commonly known as an "Edge Act corporation";

(C) an institution that is regulated by the Farm Credit Administration;

(D) a Federal credit union or State credit union (as defined in section 101 of the Federal Credit Union Act);

(E) a depository institution (as defined in section 3 of the Federal Deposit Insurance Act);

(F) a foreign bank or a branch or agency of a foreign bank (each as defined in section 1(b) of the International Banking Act of 1978);

(G) any financial holding company (as defined in section 2 of the Bank Holding Company Act of 1956);

(H) a trust company; or

(I) a similarly regulated subsidiary or affiliate of an entity described in any of subparagraphs (A) through (H).

(22) *Floor Broker.*

(A) *In General.* The term "floor broker" means any person—

(i) who, in or surrounding any pit, ring, post, or other place provided by a contract market for the meeting of persons similarly engaged, shall purchase or sell for any other person—

(I) any commodity for future delivery, security futures product, or swap; or

(II) any commodity option authorized under section 4c; or

(ii) who is registered with the Commission as a floor broker.

(B) *Further Definition.* The Commission, by rule or regulation, may include within, or exclude from, the term "floor broker" any person in or surrounding any pit, ring, post, or other place provided by a contract market for the meeting of persons similarly engaged who trades for any other person if the Commission determines that the rule or regulation will effectuate the purposes of this Act.

(23) *Floor Trader.*

(A) *In General.* The term "floor trader" means any person—

(i) who, in or surrounding any pit, ring, post, or other place provided by a contract market for the meeting of persons similarly engaged, purchases, or sells solely for such person's own account—

(I) any commodity for future delivery, security futures product, or swap; or

(II) any commodity option authorized under section 4c; or

(ii) who is registered with the Commission as a floor trader.

(B) *Further Definition.* The Commission, by rule or regulation, may include within, or exclude from, the term "floor trader" any person in or surrounding any pit, ring, post, or other place provided by a contract market for the meeting of persons similarly engaged who trades solely for such person's own account if the Commission determines that the rule or regulation will effectuate the purposes of this Act.

(24) *Foreign Exchange Forward.* The term "foreign exchange forward" means a transaction that solely involves the exchange of 2 different currencies on a specific future date at a fixed rate agreed upon on the inception of the contract covering the exchange.

(25) *Foreign Exchange Swap.* The term "foreign exchange swap" means a transaction that solely involves—

(A) an exchange of 2 different currencies on a specific date at a fixed rate that is agreed upon on the inception of the contract covering the exchange; and

(B) a reverse exchange of the 2 currencies described in subparagraph (A) at a later date and at a fixed rate that is agreed upon on the inception of the contract covering the exchange.

(26) *Foreign Futures Authority.* The term "foreign futures authority" means any foreign government, or any department, agency, governmental body, or regulatory organization empowered by a foreign government to administer or enforce a law, rule, or regulation as it relates to a futures or options matter, or any department or agency of a political subdivision of a foreign government empowered to administer or enforce a law, rule, or regulation as it relates to a futures or options matter.

(27) *Future Delivery.* The term "future delivery" does not include any sale of any cash commodity for deferred shipment or delivery.

(28) *Futures Commission Merchant.*

(A) *In General.* The term "futures commission merchant" means an individual, association, partnership, corporation, or trust—

(i) that—

(I) is—

(aa) engaged in soliciting or in accepting orders for—

(AA) the purchase or sale of a commodity for future delivery;

(BB) a security futures product;

(CC) a swap;

(DD) any agreement, contract, or transaction described in section 2(c)(2)(C)(i) or section 2(c)(2)(D)(I);

(EE) any commodity option authorized under section 4c; or

(FF) any leverage transaction authorized under section 19; or

(bb) acting as a counterparty in any agreement, contract, or transaction described in section 2(c)(2)(C)(i) or section 2(c)(2)(D)(i); and

(II) in or in connection with the activities described in items (aa) or (bb) of subclause (I), accepts any money, securities, or property (or extends credit in lieu thereof) to margin, guarantee, or secure any trades or contracts that result or may result therefrom; or

(ii) that is registered with the Commission as a futures commission merchant.

(B) *Further Definition.* The Commission, by rule or regulation, may include within, or exclude from, the term "futures commission merchant" any person who engages in soliciting or accepting orders for, or acting as a counterparty in, any agreement, contract, or transaction subject to this Act, and who accepts any money, securities, or property (or extends credit in lieu thereof) to margin, guarantee, or secure any trades or contracts that result or may result therefrom, if the Commission determines that the rule or regulation will effectuate the purposes of this Act.

(29) *Hybrid Instrument.* The term "hybrid instrument" means a security having one or more payments indexed to the value, level, or rate of, or providing for the delivery of, one or more commodities.

(30) *Interstate Commerce.* The term "interstate commerce" means commerce—

(A) between any State, territory, or possession, or the District of Columbia, and any place outside thereof; or

(B) between points within the same State, territory, or possession, or the District of Columbia, but through any place outside thereof, or within any territory or possession, or the District of Columbia.

(31) *Introducing Broker.*

(A) *In General.* The term "introducing broker" means any person (except an individual who elects to be and is registered as an associated person of a futures commission merchant)—

(i) who—

(I) is engaged in soliciting or in accepting orders for—

(aa) the purchase or sale of any commodity for future delivery, security futures product, or swap;

(bb) any agreement, contract, or transaction described in section 2(c)(2)(C)(i) or section 2(c)(2)(D)(i);

(cc) any commodity option authorized under section 4c; or

(dd) any leverage transaction authorized under section 19; and

(II) does not accept any money, securities, or property (or extend credit in lieu thereof) to margin, guarantee, or secure any trades or contracts that result or may result therefrom; or

(ii) who is registered with the Commission as an introducing broker.

(B) *Further Definition.* The Commission, by rule or regulation, may include within, or exclude from, the term "introducing broker" any person who engages in soliciting or accepting orders for any agreement, contract, or transaction subject to this Act, and who does not accept any money, securities, or property (or extend credit in lieu thereof) to margin, guarantee, or secure any trades or contracts that result or may result therefrom, if the Commission determines that the rule or regulation will effectuate the purposes of this Act.

(32) *Major Security-Based Swap Participant.* The term "major security-based swap participant" has the meaning given the term in section 3(a) of the Securities Exchange Act of 1934.

(33) *Major Swap Participant.*

(A) *In General.* The term "major swap participant" means any person who is not a swap dealer, and—

(i) maintains a substantial position in swaps for any of the major swap categories as determined by the Commission, excluding—

(I) positions held for hedging or mitigating commercial risk; and

(II) positions maintained by any employee benefit plan (or any contract held by such a plan) as defined in paragraphs (3) and (32) of section 3 of the Employee Retirement Income Security Act of 1974 for the primary purpose of hedging or mitigating any risk directly associated with the operation of the plan;

(ii) whose outstanding swaps create substantial counterparty exposure that could have serious adverse effects on the financial stability of the United States banking system or financial markets; or

(iii)(I) is a financial entity that is highly leveraged relative to the amount of capital it holds and that is not subject to capital requirements established by an appropriate Federal banking agency; and

(II) maintains a substantial position in outstanding swaps in any major swap category as determined by the Commission.

(B) *Definition Of Substantial Position*. For purposes of subparagraph (A), the Commission shall define by rule or regulation the term "substantial position" at the threshold that the Commission determines to be prudent for the effective monitoring, management, and oversight of entities that are systemically important or can significantly impact the financial system of the United States. In setting the definition under this subparagraph, the Commission shall consider the person's relative position in uncleared as opposed to cleared swaps and may take into consideration the value and quality of collateral held against counterparty exposures.

(C) *Scope Of Designation*. For purposes of subparagraph (A), a person may be designated as a major swap participant for 1 or more categories of swaps without being classified as a major swap participant for all classes of swaps.

(D) *Exclusions*. The definition under this paragraph shall not include an entity whose primary business is providing financing, and uses derivatives for the purpose of hedging underlying commercial risks related to interest rate and foreign currency exposures, 90 percent or more of which arise from financing that facilitates the purchase or lease of products, 90 percent or more of which are manufactured by the parent company or another subsidiary of the parent company.

(34) *Member of a Registered Entity; Member of a Derivatives Transaction Execution Facility*. The term "member" means, with respect to a registered entity or derivatives transaction execution facility, an individual, association, partnership, corporation, or trust—

(A) owning or holding membership in, or admitted to membership representation on, the registered entity or derivatives transaction execution facility; or

(B) having trading privileges on the registered entity or derivatives transaction execution facility.

A participant in an alternative trading system that is designated as a contract market pursuant to section 5f is deemed a member of the contract market for purposes of transactions in security futures products through the contract market.

(35) *Narrow-Based Security Index*.

(A) The term "narrow-based security index" means an index—

(i) that has 9 or fewer component securities;

(ii) in which a component security comprises more than 30 percent of the index's weighting;

(iii) in which the five highest weighted component securities in the aggregate comprise more than 60 percent of the index's weighting; or

(iv) in which the lowest weighted component securities comprising, in the aggregate, 25 percent of the index's weighting have an aggregate dollar value of average daily trading volume of less than $50,000,000 (or in the case of an index with 15 or more component securities, $30,000,000), except that if there are two or more securities with equal weighting that could be included in the calculation of the lowest weighted component securities comprising, in the aggregate, 25 percent of the index's weighting, such securities shall be ranked from lowest to highest dollar value of average daily trading volume and shall be included in the calculation based on their ranking starting with the lowest ranked security.

(B) Notwithstanding subparagraph (A), an index is not a narrow-based security index if—

(i)(I) it has at least 9 component securities;

(II) no component security comprises more than 30 percent of the index's weighting; and

(III) each component security is—

(aa) registered pursuant to section 12 of the Securities Exchange Act of 1934;

(bb) one of 750 securities with the largest market capitalization; and

(cc) one of 675 securities with the largest dollar value of average daily trading volume;

(ii) a board of trade was designated as a contract market by the Commodity Futures Trading Commission with respect to a contract of sale for future delivery on the index, before the date of the enactment of the Commodity Futures Modernization Act of 2000;

(iii)(I) a contract of sale for future delivery on the index traded on a designated contract market or registered derivatives transaction execution facility for at least 30 days as a contract of sale for future delivery on an index that was not a narrow-based security index; and

(II) it has been a narrow-based security index for no more than 45 business days over 3 consecutive calendar months;

(iv) a contract of sale for future delivery on the index is traded on or subject to the rules of a foreign board of trade and meets such requirements as are jointly established by rule or regulation by the Commission and the Securities and Exchange Commission;

(v) no more than 18 months have passed since the date of the enactment of the Commodity Futures Modernization Act of 2000 [December 21, 2000] and—

(I) it is traded on or subject to the rules of a foreign board of trade;

(II) the offer and sale in the United States of a contract of sale for future delivery on the index was authorized before the date of the enactment of the Commodity Futures Modernization Act of 2000; and

(III) the conditions of such authorization continue to be met; or

(vi) a contract of sale for future delivery on the index is traded on or subject to the rules of a board of trade and meets such requirements as are jointly established by rule, regulation, or order by the Commission and the Securities and Exchange Commission.

(C) Within 1 year after the date of the enactment of the Commodity Futures Modernization Act of 2000, the Commission and the Securities and Exchange Commission jointly shall adopt rules or regulations that set forth the requirements under subparagraph (B)(iv).

(D) An index that is a narrow-based security index solely because it was a narrow-based security index for more than 45 business days over 3 consecutive calendar months pursuant to clause (iii) of subparagraph (B) shall not be a narrow-based security index for the 3 following calendar months.

(E) For purposes of subparagraphs (A) and (B)—

(i) the dollar value of average daily trading volume and the market capitalization shall be calculated as of the preceding 6 full calendar months; and

(ii) the Commission and the Securities and Exchange Commission shall, by rule or regulation, jointly specify the method to be used to determine market capitalization and dollar value of average daily trading volume.

(36) *Option*. The term "option" means an agreement, contract, or transaction that is of the character of, or is commonly known to the trade as, an "option", "privilege", "indemnity", "bid", "offer", "put", "call", "advance guaranty", or "decline guaranty".

(37) *Organized Exchange*. The term "organized exchange" means a trading facility that—

(A) permits trading—

(i) by or on behalf of a person that is not an eligible contract participant; or

(ii) by persons other than on a principal-to-principal basis; or

(B) has adopted (directly or through another nongovernmental entity) rules that—

(i) govern the conduct of participants, other than rules that govern the submission of orders or execution of transactions on the trading facility; and

(ii) include disciplinary sanctions other than the exclusion of participants from trading.

(38) *Person*. The term "person" imports the plural or singular, and includes individuals, associations, partnerships, corporations, and trusts.

(39) *Prudential Regulator*. The term "prudential regulator" means—

(A) the Board in the case of a swap dealer, major swap participant, security-based swap dealer, or major security-based swap participant that is—

(i) a State-chartered bank that is a member of the Federal Reserve System;

(ii) a State-chartered branch or agency of a foreign bank;

(iii) any foreign bank which does not operate an insured branch;

(iv) any organization operating under section 25A of the Federal Reserve Act or having an agreement with the Board under section 225 of the Federal Reserve Act;

(v) any bank holding company (as defined in section 2 of the Bank Holding Company Act of 1965), any foreign bank (as defined in section 1(b)(7) of the International Banking Act of 1978) that is treated as a bank holding company under section 8(a) of the International Banking Act of 1978, and any subsidiary of such a company or foreign bank (other than a subsidiary that is described in subparagraph (A) or (B) or that is required to be registered with the Commission as a swap dealer or major swap participant under this Act or with the Securities and Exchange Commission as a security-based swap dealer or major security-based swap participant);

(vi) after the transfer date (as defined in section 311 of the Dodd–Frank Wall Street Reform and Consumer Protection Act), any savings and loan holding company (as defined in section 10 of the Home Owners' Loan Act) and any subsidiary of such company (other than a subsidiary that is described in subparagraph (A) or (B) or that is required to be registered as a swap dealer or major swap participant with the Commission under this Act or with the Securities and Exchange Commission as a security-based swap dealer or major security-based swap participant); or

(vii) any organization operating under section 25A of the Federal Reserve Act or having an agreement with the Board under section 25 of the Federal Reserve Act;

(B) the Office of the Comptroller of the Currency in the case of a swap dealer, major swap participant, security-based swap dealer, or major security-based swap participant that is—

(i) a national bank;

(ii) a federally chartered branch or agency of a foreign bank; or

(iii) any Federal savings association;

(C) the Federal Deposit Insurance Corporation in the case of a swap dealer, major swap participant, security-based swap dealer, or major security-based swap participant that is—

(i) a State-chartered bank that is not a member of the Federal Reserve System; or

(ii) any State savings association;

(D) the Farm Credit Administration, in the case of a swap dealer, major swap participant, security-based swap dealer, or major security-based swap participant that is an institution chartered under the Farm Credit Act of 1971; and

(E) the Federal Housing Finance Agency in the case of a swap dealer, major swap participant, security-based swap dealer, or major security-based swap participant that is a regulated entity (as such term is defined in section 1303 of the Federal Housing Enterprises Financial Safety and Soundness Act of 1992).

(40) *Registered Entity*. The term "registered entity" means—

(A) a board of trade designated as a contract market under section 5;

(B) a derivatives clearing organization registered under section 5b;

(C) a board of trade designated as a contract market under section 5f; and

(D) a swap execution facility registered under section 5h;

(E) a swap data repository registered under section 21; and

(F) with respect to a contract that the Commission determines is a significant price discovery contract, any electronic trading facility on which the contract is executed or traded.

(41) *Security*. The term "security" means a security as defined in section 2(a)(1) of the Securities Act of 1933 or section 3(a)(10) of the Securities Exchange Act of 1934.

(42) *Security-Based Swap*. The term "security-based swap" has the meaning given the term in section 3(a) of the Securities Exchange Act of 1934.

(43) *Security-Based Swap Dealer*. The term "security-based swap dealer" has the meaning given the term in section 3(a) of the Securities Exchange Act of 1934.

(44) *Security Future*. The term "security future" means a contract of sale for future delivery of a single security or of a narrow-based security index, including any interest therein or based on the value thereof, except an exempted security under section 3(a)(12) of the Securities Exchange Act of 1934 as in effect on the date of the enactment of the Futures Trading Act of 1982 (other than any municipal security as defined in section 3(a)(29) of the Securities Exchange Act of 1934 as in effect on the date of the

enactment of the Futures Trading Act of 1982). The term "security future" does not include any agreement, contract, or transaction excluded from this Act under section 2(c), 2(d), 2(f), or 2(g) of this Act (as in effect on the date of the enactment of the Commodity Futures Modernization Act of 2000) or title IV of the Commodity Futures Modernization Act of 2000.

(45) *Security Futures Product*. The term "security futures product" means a security future or any put, call, straddle, option, or privilege on any security future.

(46) *Significant Price Discovery Contract*. The term "significant price discovery contract" means an agreement, contract, or transaction subject to section 2(h)(5).

(47) *Swap*.

(A) *In General*. Except as provided in subparagraph (B), the term "swap" means any agreement, contract, or transaction—

(i) that is a put, call, cap, floor, collar, or similar option of any kind that is for the purchase or sale, or based on the value, of 1 or more interest or other rates, currencies, commodities, securities, instruments of indebtedness, indices, quantitative measures, or other financial or economic interests or property of any kind;

(ii) that provides for any purchase, sale, payment, or delivery (other than a dividend on an equity security) that is dependent on the occurrence, nonoccurrence, or the extent of the occurrence of an event or contingency associated with a potential financial, economic, or commercial consequence;

(iii) that provides on an executory basis for the exchange, on a fixed or contingent basis, of 1 or more payments based on the value or level of 1 or more interest or other rates, currencies, commodities, securities, instruments of indebtedness, indices, quantitative measures, or other financial or economic interests or property of any kind, or any interest therein or based on the value thereof, and that transfers, as between the parties to the transaction, in whole or in part, the financial risk associated with a future change in any such value or level without also conveying a current or future direct or indirect ownership interest in an asset (including any enterprise or investment pool) or liability that incorporates the financial risk so transferred, including any agreement, contract, or transaction commonly known as—

(I) an interest rate swap;

(II) a rate floor;

(III) a rate cap;

(IV) a rate collar;

(V) a cross-currency rate swap;

(VI) a basis swap;

(VII) a currency swap;

(VIII) a foreign exchange swap;

(IX) a total return swap;

(X) an equity index swap;

(XI) an equity swap;

(XII) a debt index swap;

(XIII) a debt swap;

(XIV) a credit spread;

(XV) a credit default swap;

(XVI) a credit swap;

(XVII) a weather swap;

(XVIII) an energy swap;

(XIX) a metal swap;

(XX) an agricultural swap;

(XXI) an emissions swap; and

(XXII) a commodity swap;

(iv) that is an agreement, contract, or transaction that is, or in the future becomes, commonly known to the trade as a swap;

(v) including any security-based swap agreement which meets the definition of "swap agreement" as defined in section 206A of the Gramm–Leach–Bliley Act of which a material term is based on the price, yield, value, or volatility of any security or any group or index of securities, or any interest therein; or

(vi) that is any combination or permutation of, or option on, any agreement, contract, or transaction described in any of clauses (i) through (v).

(B) *Exclusions*. The term "swap" does not include—

(i) any contract of sale of a commodity for future delivery (or option on such a contract), leverage contract authorized under section 19, security futures product, or agreement, contract, or transaction described in section 2(c)(2)(C)(i) or section 2(c)(2)(D)(i);

(ii) any sale of a nonfinancial commodity or security for deferred shipment or delivery, so long as the transaction is intended to be physically settled;

(iii) any put, call, straddle, option, or privilege on any security, certificate of deposit, or group or index of securities, including any interest therein or based on the value thereof, that is subject to—

(I) the Securities Act of 1933; and

(II) the Securities Exchange Act of 1934;

(iv) any put, call, straddle, option, or privilege relating to a foreign currency entered into on a national securities exchange registered pursuant to section 6(a) of the Securities Exchange Act of 1934;

(v) any agreement, contract, or transaction providing for the purchase or sale of 1 or more securities on a fixed basis that is subject to—

(I) the Securities Act of 1933; and

(II) the Securities Exchange Act of 1934;

(vi) any agreement, contract, or transaction providing for the purchase or sale of 1 or more securities on a contingent basis that is subject to the Securities Act of 1933 and the Securities Exchange Act of 1934, unless the agreement, contract, or transaction predicates the purchase or sale on the occurrence of a bona fide contingency that might reasonably be expected to affect or be affected by the creditworthiness of a party other than a party to the agreement, contract, or transaction;

(vii) any note, bond, or evidence of indebtedness that is a security, as defined in section 2(a)(1) of the Securities Act of 1933;

(viii) any agreement, contract, or transaction that is—

(I) based on a security; and

(II) entered into directly or through an underwriter (as defined in section 2(a)(11) of the Securities Act of 1933 by the issuer of such security for the purposes of raising capital, unless the agreement, contract, or transaction is entered into to manage a risk associated with capital raising;

(ix) any agreement, contract, or transaction a counterparty of which is a Federal Reserve bank, the Federal Government, or a Federal agency that is expressly backed by the full faith and credit of the United States; and

(x) any security-based swap, other than a security-based swap as described in subparagraph (D).

(C) *Rule of Construction Regarding Master Agreements.*

(i) *In General.* Except as provided in clause (ii), the term "swap" includes a master agreement that provides for an agreement, contract, or transaction that is a swap under subparagraph (A), together with each supplement to any master agreement, without regard to whether the master agreement contains an agreement, contract, or transaction that is not a swap pursuant to subparagraph (A).

(ii) *Exception.* For purposes of clause (i), the master agreement shall be considered to be a swap only with respect to each agreement, contract, or transaction covered by the master agreement that is a swap pursuant to subparagraph (A).

(D) *Mixed Swap.* The term "security-based swap" includes any agreement, contract, or transaction that is as described in section 3(a)(68)(A) of the Securities Exchange Act of 1934 and also is based on the value of 1 or more interest or other rates, currencies, commodities, instruments of indebtedness, indices, quantitative measures, other financial or economic interest or property of any kind (other than a single security or a narrow-based security index), or the occurrence, non-occurrence, or the extent of the occurrence of an event or contingency associated with a potential financial, economic, or commercial consequence (other than an event described in subparagraph (A)(iii)).

(E) *Treatment of Foreign Exchange Swaps and Forwards.*

(i) *In General.* Foreign exchange swaps and foreign exchange forwards shall be considered swaps under this paragraph unless the Secretary makes a written determination under section 1b that either foreign exchange swaps or foreign exchange forwards or both—

(I) should be not be regulated as swaps under this Act; and

(II) are not structured to evade the Dodd–Frank Wall Street Reform and Consumer Protection Act in violation of any rule promulgated by the Commission pursuant to section 721(c) of that Act.

(ii) *Congressional Notice; Effectiveness*. The Secretary shall submit any written determination under clause (i) to the appropriate committees of Congress, including the Committee on Agriculture, Nutrition, and Forestry of the Senate and the Committee on Agriculture of the House of Representatives. Any such written determination by the Secretary shall not be effective until it is submitted to the appropriate committees of Congress.

(iii) *Reporting*. Notwithstanding a written determination by the Secretary under clause (i), all foreign exchange swaps and foreign exchange forwards shall be reported to either a swap data repository, or, if there is no swap data repository that would accept such swaps or forwards, to the Commission pursuant to section 4r within such time period as the Commission may by rule or regulation prescribe.

(iv) *Business Standards*. Notwithstanding a written determination by the Secretary pursuant to clause (i), any party to a foreign exchange swap or forward that is a swap dealer or major swap participant shall conform to the business conduct standards contained in section 4s(h).

(v) *Secretary*. For purposes of this subparagraph, the term "Secretary" means the Secretary of the Treasury.

(F) *Exception for Certain Foreign Exchange Swaps and Forwards*.

(i) *Registered Entities*. Any foreign exchange swap and any foreign exchange forward that is listed and traded on or subject to the rules of a designated contract market or a swap execution facility, or that is cleared by a derivatives clearing organization, shall not be exempt from any provision of this Act or amendments made by the Wall Street Transparency and Accountability Act of 2010 prohibiting fraud or manipulation.

(ii) *Retail Transactions*. Nothing in subparagraph (E) shall affect, or be construed to affect, the applicability of this Act or the jurisdiction of the Commission with respect to agreements, contracts, or transactions in foreign currency pursuant to section 2(c)(2).

(48) *Swap Data Repository*. The term "swap data repository" means any person that collects and maintains information or records with respect to transactions or positions in, or the terms and conditions of, swaps entered into by third parties for the purpose of providing a centralized recordkeeping facility for swaps.

(49) *Swap Dealer*.

(A) *In General*. The term "swap dealer" means any person who—

(i) holds itself out as a dealer in swaps;

(ii) makes a market in swaps;

(iii) regularly enters into swaps with counterparties as an ordinary course of business for its own account; or

(iv) engages in any activity causing the person to be commonly known in the trade as a dealer or market maker in swaps,

provided however, in no event shall an insured depository institution be considered to be a swap dealer to the extent it offers to enter into a swap with a customer in connection with originating a loan with that customer.

(B) *Inclusion*. A person may be designated as a swap dealer for a single type or single class or category of swap or activities and considered not to be a swap dealer for other types, classes, or categories of swaps or activities.

(C) *Exception*. The term "swap dealer" does not include a person that enters into swaps for such person's own account, either individually or in a fiduciary capacity, but not as a part of a regular business.

(D) *De Minimis Exception*. The Commission shall exempt from designation as a swap dealer an entity that engages in a de minimis quantity of swap dealing in connection with transactions with or on behalf of its customers. The Commission shall promulgate regulations to establish factors with respect to the making of this determination to exempt.

(50) *Swap Execution Facility*. The term "swap execution facility" means a trading system or platform in which multiple participants have the ability to execute or trade swaps by accepting bids and offers made by multiple participants in the facility or system, through any means of interstate commerce, including any trading facility, that—

(A) facilitates the execution of swaps between persons; and

(B) is not a designated contract market.

(51) *Trading Facility.*

(A) *In General.* The term "trading facility" means a person or group of persons that constitutes, maintains, or provides a physical or electronic facility or system in which multiple participants have the ability to execute or trade agreements, contracts, or transactions—

(i) by accepting bids or offers made by other participants that are open to multiple participants in the facility or system; or

(ii) through the interaction of multiple bids or multiple offers within a system with a pre-determined non-discretionary automated trade matching and execution algorithm.

(B) *Exclusions.* The term "trading facility" does not include—

(i) a person or group of persons solely because the person or group of persons constitutes, maintains, or provides an electronic facility or system that enables participants to negotiate the terms of and enter into bilateral transactions as a result of communications exchanged by the parties and not from interaction of multiple bids and multiple offers within a predetermined, nondiscretionary automated trade matching and execution algorithm;

(ii) a government securities dealer or government securities broker, to the extent that the dealer or broker executes or trades agreements, contracts, or transactions in government securities, or assists persons in communicating about, negotiating, entering into, executing, or trading an agreement, contract, or transaction in government securities (as the terms "government securities dealer", "government securities broker", and "government securities" are defined in section 3(a) of the Securities Exchange Act of 1934); or

(iii) facilities on which bids and offers, and acceptances of bids and offers effected on the facility, are not binding.

Any person, group of persons, dealer, broker, or facility described in clause (i) or (ii) is excluded from the meaning of the term "trading facility" for the purposes of this Act without any prior specific approval, certification, or other action by the Commission.

(C) *Special Rule.* A person or group of persons that would not otherwise constitute a trading facility shall not be considered to be a trading facility solely as a result of the submission to a derivatives clearing organization of transactions executed on or through the person or group of persons.

Requirements of Secretary of the Treasury Regarding Exemption of Foreign Exchange Swaps and Foreign Exchange Forwards from Definition of the Term "Swap"

Sec. 1b. (a) *Required Considerations.* In determining whether to exempt foreign exchange swaps and foreign exchange forwards from the definition of the term "swap", the Secretary of the Treasury (referred to in this section as the "Secretary") shall consider—

(1) whether the required trading and clearing of foreign exchange swaps and foreign exchange forwards would create systemic risk, lower transparency, or threaten the financial stability of the United States;

(2) whether foreign exchange swaps and foreign exchange forwards are already subject to a regulatory scheme that is materially comparable to that established by this Act for other classes of swaps;

(3) the extent to which bank regulators of participants in the foreign exchange market provide adequate supervision, including capital and margin requirements;

(4) the extent of adequate payment and settlement systems; and

(5) the use of a potential exemption of foreign exchange swaps and foreign exchange forwards to evade otherwise applicable regulatory requirements.

(b) *Determination.* If the Secretary makes a determination to exempt foreign exchange swaps and foreign exchange forwards from the definition of the term "swap", the Secretary shall submit to the appropriate committees of Congress a determination that contains—

(1) an explanation regarding why foreign exchange swaps and foreign exchange forwards are qualitatively different from other classes of swaps in a way that would make the foreign exchange swaps and foreign exchange forwards ill–suited for regulation as swaps; and

(2) an identification of the objective differences of foreign exchange swaps and foreign exchange forwards with respect to standard swaps that warrant an exempted status.

(c) *Effect of Determination.* A determination by the Secretary under subsection (b) shall not exempt any foreign exchange swaps and foreign exchange forwards traded on a designated contract market or swap execution facility from any applicable anti-fraud and anti-manipulation provision under this title.

Jurisdiction of Commission; Liability of Principal for Act of Agent; Commodity Futures Trading Commission; Transaction in Interstate Commerce

Sec. 2. (a) *Jurisdiction of Commission; Commodity Futures Trading Commission.*

(1) *Jurisdiction of Commission.*

(A) *In General.* The Commission shall have exclusive jurisdiction, except to the extent otherwise provided in the Wall Street Transparency and Accountability Act of 2010 (including an amendment made by that Act) and subparagraphs (C), (D), and (I) of this paragraph and subsections (c) and (f), with respect to accounts, agreements (including any transaction which is of the character of, or is commonly known to the trade as, an option, privilege, indemnity, bid, offer, put, call, advance guaranty, or decline guaranty), and transactions involving swaps or contracts of sale of a commodity for future delivery (including significant price discovery contracts), traded or executed on a contract market designated pursuant to section 5 or a swap execution facility pursuant to section 5h of this Act or any other board of trade, exchange, or market, and transactions subject to regulation by the Commission pursuant to section 19 of this Act. Except as hereinabove provided, nothing contained in this section shall (I) supersede or limit the jurisdiction at any time conferred on the Securities and Exchange Commission or other regulatory authorities under the laws of the United States or of any State, or (II) restrict the Securities and Exchange Commission and such other authorities from carrying out their duties and responsibilities in accordance with such laws. Nothing in this section shall supersede or limit the jurisdiction conferred on courts of the United States or any State.

(B) *Liability of Principal for Act of Agent.* The act, omission, or failure of any official, agent, or other person acting for any individual, association, partnership, corporation, or trust within the scope of his employment or office shall be deemed the act, omission, or failure of such individual, association, partnership, corporation, or trust, as well as of such official, agent, or other person.

(C) *Designation of Boards of Trade as Contract Markets; Contracts for Future Delivery; Security Futures Products; Filing with Board of Governors of Federal Reserve System; Judicial Review.* Notwithstanding any other provision of law—

(i)(I) Except as provided in subclause (II), this Act shall not apply to and the Commission shall have no jurisdiction to designate a board of trade as a contract market for any transaction whereby any party to such transaction acquires any put, call, or other option on one or more securities (as defined in section 2(1) of the Securities Act of 1933 or section 3(a)(10) of the Securities Exchange Act of 1934 on the date of enactment of the Futures Trading Act of 1982), including any group or index of such securities, or any interest therein or based on the value thereof.

(II) This Act shall apply to and the Commission shall have jurisdiction with respect to accounts, agreements, and transactions involving, and may permit the listing for trading pursuant to section 5c(c) of, a put, call, or other option on 1 or more securities (as defined in section 2(a)(1) of the Securities Act of 1933 or section 3(a)(10) of the Securities Exchange Act of 1934 on the date of enactment of the Futures Trading Act of 1982), including any group or index of such securities, or any interest therein or based on the value thereof, that is exempted by the Securities and Exchange Commission pursuant to section 36(a)(1) of the Securities Exchange Act of 1934 with the condition that the Commission exercise concurrent jurisdiction over such put, call, or other option; provided, however, that nothing in this paragraph shall be construed to affect the jurisdiction and authority of the Securities and Exchange Commission over such put, call, or other option.

(ii) This Act shall apply to and the Commission shall have exclusive jurisdiction with respect to accounts, agreements (including any transaction which is of the character of, or is commonly known to the trade as, an "option," "privilege," "indemnity," "bid," "offer," "put," "call," "advance guaranty," or "decline guaranty") and transactions involving, and may designate a board of trade as a contract market in, or register a derivatives transaction execution facility that trades or executes, contracts of sale (or options on such contracts) for future delivery of a group or index of securities (or any interest therein or based upon the value thereof): *Provided, however,* That no board of trade shall be designated as a contract market with respect to any such contracts of sale (or options on such contracts) for future delivery, and no derivatives transaction execution facility shall trade or execute such contracts of sale (or options on such contracts) for future delivery, unless the board of trade or the derivatives transaction execution facility, and the applicable contract, meet the following minimum requirements:

(I) Settlement of or delivery on such contract (or option on such contract) shall be effected in cash or by means other than the transfer or receipt of any security, except an exempted security under section 3 of the Securities Act of 1933 or section 3(a)(12) of the Securities Exchange Act of 1934 as in effect on the date of enactment of the Futures Trading Act of 1982 (other than any municipal security, as defined in section 3(a)(29) of the Securities Exchange Act of 1934 on the date of enactment of the Futures Trading Act of 1982);

(II) Trading in such contract (or option on such contract) shall not be readily susceptible to manipulation of the price of such contract (or option on such contract), nor to causing or being used in the manipulation of the price of any underlying security, option on such security or option on a group or index including such securities; and

(III) Such group or index of securities shall not constitute a narrow-based security index.

(iii) If, in its discretion, the Commission determines that a stock index futures contract, notwithstanding its conformance with the requirements in clause (ii) of this subparagraph, can reasonably be used as a surrogate for trading a security (including a security futures product), it may, by order, require such contract and any option thereon be traded and regulated as security futures products as defined in section 3(a)(56) of the Securities Exchange Act of 1934 and section 1a of this Act subject to all rules and regulations applicable to security futures products under this Act and the securities laws as defined in section 3(a)(47) of the Securities Exchange Act of 1934.

(iv) No person shall offer to enter into, enter into, or confirm the execution of any contract of sale (or option on such contract) for future delivery of any security, or interest therein or based on the value thereof, except an exempted security under section 3(a)(12) of the Securities Exchange Act of 1934 as in effect on the date of enactment of the Futures Trading Act of 1982 (other than any municipal security as defined in section 3(a)(29) of the Securities Exchange Act of 1934 on the date of enactment of the Futures Trading Act of 1982), or except as provided in clause (ii) of this subparagraph or subparagraph D, any group or index of such securities or any interest therein or based on the value thereof.

(v)(I) Notwithstanding any other provision of this Act, any contract market in a stock index futures contract (or option thereon) other than a security futures product, or any derivatives transaction execution facility on which such contract or option is traded, shall file with the Board of Governors of the Federal Reserve System any rule establishing or changing the levels of margin (initial and maintenance) for such stock index futures contract (or option thereon) other than security futures products.

(II) The Board may at any time request any contract market or derivatives transaction execution facility to set the margin for any stock index futures contract (or option thereon), other than for any security futures product, at such levels as the Board in its judgment determines are appropriate to preserve the financial integrity of the contract market or derivatives transaction execution facility, or its clearing system, or to prevent systemic risk. If the contract market or derivatives transaction execution facility fails to do so within the time specified by the Board in its request, the Board may direct the contract market or derivatives transaction execution facility to alter or supplement the rules of the contract market or derivatives transaction execution facility as specified in the request.

(III) Subject to such conditions as the Board may determine, the Board may delegate any or all of its authority, relating to margin for any stock index futures contract (or option thereon), other than security futures products, under this clause to the Commission.

(IV) It shall be unlawful for any futures commission merchant to, directly or indirectly, extend or maintain credit to or for, or collect margin from any customer on any security futures product unless such activities comply with the regulations prescribed pursuant to section 7(c)(2)(B) of the Securities Exchange Act of 1934.

(V) Nothing in this clause shall supersede or limit the authority granted to the Commission in section 8a(9) to direct a contract market or registered derivatives transaction execution facility, on finding an emergency to exist, to raise temporary margin levels on any futures contract, or option on the contract covered by this clause, or on any security futures product.

(VI) Any action taken by the Board, or by the Commission acting under the delegation of authority under subclause III, under this clause directing a contract market to alter or supplement a contract market rule shall be subject to review only in the Court of Appeals where the party seeking review resides or has its principal place of business, or in the United States Court of Appeals for the District of Columbia Circuit. The review shall be based on the examination of all information before the Board or the Commission, as the case may be, at the time the determination was made. The court reviewing the action of the Board or the Commission shall not enter a stay or order of mandamus unless the court has determined, after notice and a hearing before a panel of the court, that the agency action complained of was arbitrary, capricious, an abuse of discretion, or otherwise not in accordance with law.

(D) *Jurisdiction and Authority of Securities and Exchange Commission Over Security Futures; Requirements for Security Futures Trading; Periodic or Special Examinations by Commission Representatives.*

(i) Notwithstanding any other provision of this Act, the Securities and Exchange Commission shall have jurisdiction and authority over security futures as defined in section 3(a)(55) of the Securities Exchange Act of 1934, section 2(a)(16) of the Securities Act of 1933, section 2(a)(52) of the Investment Company Act of 1940, and section 202(a)(27) of the Investment Advisers Act of 1940, options on security futures, and persons effecting transactions in security futures and options thereon, and this Act shall apply to and the Commission shall have jurisdiction with respect to accounts, agreements (including any transaction which is of the character of, or is commonly known to the trade as, an "option", "privilege", "indemnity", "bid", "offer", "put", "call", "advance guaranty", or "decline guaranty"), contracts, and transactions involving, and may designate a board of trade as a contract market in, or register a derivatives transaction execution facility that trades or executes, a security futures product as defined in section 1a of this Act: *Provided, however,* That, except as provided in clause (vi) of this subparagraph, no board of trade shall be designated as a contract market with respect to, or registered as a derivatives transaction execution facility for, any such contracts of sale for future delivery unless the board of trade and the applicable contract meet the following criteria:

(I) Except as otherwise provided in a rule, regulation, or order issued pursuant to clause (v) of this subparagraph, any security underlying the security future, including each component security of a narrow-based security index, is registered pursuant to section 12 of the Securities Exchange Act of 1934.

(II) If the security futures product is not cash settled, the board of trade on which the security futures product is traded has arrangements in place with a clearing agency registered pursuant to section 17A of the Securities Exchange Act of 1934 for the payment and delivery of the securities underlying the security futures product.

(III) Except as otherwise provided in a rule, regulation, or order issued pursuant to clause (v) of this subparagraph, the security future is based upon common stock and such other equity securities as the Commission and the Securities and Exchange Commission jointly determine appropriate.

(IV) The security futures product is cleared by a clearing agency that has in place provisions for linked and coordinated clearing with other clearing agencies that clear security futures products, which permits the security futures product to be purchased on a designated contract market, registered derivatives transaction execution facility, national securities exchange registered under section 6(a) of the Securities Exchange Act of 1934, or national securities association registered pursuant to section 15A(a) of the Securities Exchange Act of 1934 and offset on another designated contract market, registered derivatives transaction execution facility, national securities exchange registered under section 6(a) of the Securities Exchange Act of 1934, or national securities association registered pursuant to section 15A(a) of the Securities Exchange Act of 1934.

(V) Only futures commission merchants, introducing brokers, commodity trading advisors, commodity pool operators or associated persons subject to suitability rules comparable to those of a national securities association registered pursuant to section 15A(a) of the Securities Exchange Act of 1934 solicit, accept any order for, or otherwise deal in any transaction in or in connection with the security futures product.

(VI) The security futures product is subject to a prohibition against dual trading in section 4j of this Act and the rules and regulations thereunder or the provisions of section 11(a) of the Securities Exchange Act of 1934 and the rules and regulations thereunder, except to the extent otherwise permitted under the Securities Exchange Act of 1934 and the rules and regulations thereunder.

(VII) Trading in the security futures product is not readily susceptible to manipulation of the price of such security futures product, nor to causing or being used in the manipulation of the price of any underlying security, option on such security, or option on a group or index including such securities;

(VIII) The board of trade on which the security futures product is traded has procedures in place for coordinated surveillance among such board of trade, any market on which any security underlying the security futures product is traded, and other markets on which any related security is traded to detect manipulation and insider trading, except that, if the board of trade is an alternative trading system, a national securities association registered pursuant to section 15A(a) of the Securities Exchange Act of 1934 or national securities exchange registered pursuant to section 6(a) of the Securities Exchange Act of 1934 of which such alternative trading system is a member has in place such procedures.

(IX) The board of trade on which the security futures product is traded has in place audit trails necessary or appropriate to facilitate the coordinated surveillance required in subclause (VIII), except that, if the board of trade is an alternative trading system, a national securities association registered pursuant to section 15A(a) of the Securities Exchange Act of 1934 or national securities exchange registered pursuant to section 6(a) of the Securities Exchange Act of 1934 of which such alternative trading system is a member has rules to require such audit trails.

(X) The board of trade on which the security futures product is traded has in place procedures to coordinate trading halts between such board of trade and markets on which any security underlying the security futures product is traded and other markets on which any related security is traded, except that, if the board of trade is an alternative trading system, a national securities association registered pursuant to section 15A(a) of the Securities Exchange Act of 1934 or national securities exchange registered pursuant to section 6(a) of the Securities Exchange Act of 1934 of which such alternative trading system is a member has rules to require such coordinated trading halts.

(XI) The margin requirements for a security futures product comply with the regulations prescribed pursuant to section 7(c)(2)(B) of the Securities Exchange Act of 1934, except that nothing in this subclause shall be construed to prevent a board of trade from requiring higher margin levels for a security futures product when it deems such action to be necessary or appropriate.

(ii) It shall be unlawful for any person to offer, to enter into, to execute, to confirm the execution of, or to conduct any office or business anywhere in the United States, its territories or possessions, for the purpose of soliciting, or accepting any order for, or otherwise dealing in, any transaction in, or in connection with, a security futures product unless—

(I) the transaction is conducted on or subject to the rules of a board of trade that—

(aa) has been designated by the Commission as a contract market in such security futures product; or

(bb) is a registered derivatives transaction execution facility for the security futures product that has provided a certification with respect to the security futures product pursuant to clause (vii);

(II) the contract is executed or consummated by, through, or with a member of the contract market or registered derivatives transaction execution facility; and

(III) the security futures product is evidenced by a record in writing which shows the date, the parties to such security futures product and their addresses, the property covered, and its price, and each contract market member or registered derivatives transaction execution facility member shall keep the record for a period of 3 years from the date of the transaction, or for a longer period if the Commission so directs, which record shall at all times be open to the inspection of any duly authorized representative of the Commission.

(iii)(I) Except as provided in subclause (II) but notwithstanding any other provision of this Act, no person shall offer to enter into, enter into, or confirm the execution of any option on a security future.

(II) After 3 years after the date of the enactment of the Commodity Futures Modernization Act of 2000, the Commission and the Securities and Exchange Commission may by order jointly determine to permit trading of options on any security future authorized to be traded under the provisions of this Act and the Securities Exchange Act of 1934.

(iv)(I) All relevant records of a futures commission merchant or introducing broker registered pursuant to section 4f(a)(2), floor broker or floor trader exempt from registration pursuant to section 4f(a)(3), associated person exempt from registration pursuant to section 4k(6), or board of trade designated as a contract market in a security futures product pursuant to section 5f shall be subject to such reasonable periodic or special examinations by representatives of the Commission as the Commission deems necessary or appropriate in the public interest, for the protection of investors, or otherwise in furtherance of the purposes of this Act, and the Commission, before conducting any such examination, shall give notice to the Securities and Exchange Commission of the proposed examination and consult with the Securities and Exchange Commission concerning the feasibility and desirability of coordinating the examination with examinations conducted by the Securities and Exchange Commission in order to avoid unnecessary regulatory duplication or undue regulatory burdens for the registrant or board of trade.

(II) The Commission shall notify the Securities and Exchange Commission of any examination conducted of any futures commission merchant or introducing broker registered pursuant to section 4f(a)(2), floor broker or floor trader exempt from registration pursuant to section 4f(a)(3), associated person exempt from registration pursuant to section 4k(6), or board of trade designated as a contract market in a security futures product pursuant to section 5f, and, upon request, furnish to the Securities and Exchange Commission any examination report and data supplied to or prepared by the Commission in connection with the examination.

(III) Before conducting an examination under subclause (I), the Commission shall use the reports of examinations, unless the information sought is unavailable in the reports, of any futures commission merchant or introducing broker registered pursuant to section 4f(a)(2), floor broker or floor trader exempt from registration pursuant to section 4f(a)(3), associated person exempt from registration pursuant to section 4k(6), or board of trade designated as a contract market in a security futures product pursuant to section 5f that is made by the Securities and Exchange Commission, a national securities association registered pursuant to section 15A(a) of the Securities Exchange Act of 1934, or a national securities exchange registered pursuant to section 6(a) of the Securities Exchange Act of 1934.

(IV) Any records required under this subsection for a futures commission merchant or introducing broker registered pursuant to section 4f(a)(2), floor broker or floor trader exempt from registration pursuant to section 4f(a)(3), associated person exempt from registration pursuant to section 4k(6), or board of trade designated as a contract market in a security futures product pursuant to section 5f, shall be limited to records with respect to accounts, agreements, contracts, and transactions involving security futures products.

(v)(I) The Commission and the Securities and Exchange Commission, by rule, regulation, or order, may jointly modify the criteria specified in subclause (I) or (III) of clause (i), including the trading of security futures based on securities other than equity securities, to the extent such modification fosters the development of fair and orderly markets in security futures products, is necessary or appropriate in the public interest, and is consistent with the protection of investors.

(II) The Commission and the Securities and Exchange Commission, by order, may jointly exempt any person from compliance with the criterion specified in clause (i)(IV) to the extent such exemption fosters the development of fair and orderly markets in security futures products, is necessary or appropriate in the public interest, and is consistent with the protection of investors.

(vi)(I) Notwithstanding clauses (i) and (vii), until the compliance date, a board of trade shall not be required to meet the criterion specified in clause (i)(IV).

(II) The Commission and the Securities and Exchange Commission shall jointly publish in the Federal Register a notice of the compliance date no later than 165 days before the compliance date.

(III) For purposes of this clause, the term "compliance date" means the later of—

(aa) 180 days after the end of the first full calendar month period in which the average aggregate comparable share volume for all security futures products based on single equity securities traded on all designated contract markets and registered derivatives transaction execution facilities equals or exceeds 10 percent of the average aggregate comparable share volume of options on single equity securities traded on all national securities exchanges registered pursuant to section 6(a) of the Securities Exchange Act of 1934 and any national securities associations registered pursuant to section 15A(a) of such Act; or

(bb) 2 years after the date on which trading in any security futures product commences under this Act.

(vii) It shall be unlawful for a board of trade to trade or execute a security futures product unless the board of trade has provided the Commission with a certification that the specific security futures product and the board of trade, as applicable, meet the criteria specified in subclauses (I) through (XI) of clause (i), except as otherwise provided in clause (vi).

(E) *Obligation to Address Security Futures Products Traded on Foreign Exchanges.*

(i) To the extent necessary or appropriate in the public interest, to promote fair competition, and consistent with promotion of market efficiency, innovation, and expansion of investment opportunities, the protection of investors, and the maintenance of fair and orderly markets, the Commission and the Securities and Exchange Commission shall jointly issue such rules, regulations, or orders as are necessary and appropriate to permit the offer and sale of a security futures product traded on or subject to the rules of a foreign board of trade to United States persons.

(ii) The rules, regulations, or orders adopted under clause (i) shall take into account, as appropriate, the nature and size of the markets that the securities underlying the security futures product reflects.

(F) *Security Futures Products Traded on Foreign Boards of Trade.*

(i) Nothing in this Act is intended to prohibit a futures commission merchant from carrying security futures products traded on or subject to the rules of a foreign board of trade in the accounts of persons located outside of the United States.

(ii) Nothing in this Act is intended to prohibit any eligible contract participant located in the United States from purchasing or carrying securities futures products traded on or subject to the rules of a foreign board of trade, exchange, or market to the same extent such person may be authorized to purchase or carry other securities traded on a foreign board of trade, exchange, or market so long as any underlying security for such security futures products is traded principally on, by, or through any exchange or market located outside the United States.

(G)(i) Nothing in this paragraph shall limit the jurisdiction conferred on the Securities and Exchange Commission by the Wall Street Transparency and Accountability Act of 2010 with regard to security-based swap agreements as defined pursuant to section 3(a)(78) of the Securities Exchange Act of 1934, and security-based swaps.

(ii) In addition to the authority of the Securities and Exchange Commission described in clause (i), nothing in this subparagraph shall limit or affect any statutory authority of the Commission with respect to an agreement, contract, or transaction described in clause (i).

(H) Notwithstanding any other provision of law, the Wall Street Transparency and Accountability Act of 2010 shall not apply to, and the Commodity Futures Trading Commission shall have no jurisdiction under such Act (or any amendments to the Commodity Exchange Act made by such Act) with respect to, any security other than a security-based swap.

(I)(i) Nothing in this Act shall limit or affect any statutory authority of the Federal Energy Regulatory Commission or a State regulatory authority (as defined in section 3(21) of the Federal Power Act) with respect to an agreement, contract, or transaction that is entered into pursuant to a tariff or rate schedule approved by the Federal Energy Regulatory Commission or a State regulatory authority and is—

(I) not executed, traded, or cleared on a registered entity or trading facility; or

(II) executed, traded, or cleared on a registered entity or trading facility owned or operated by a regional transmission organization or independent system operator.

(ii) In addition to the authority of the Federal Energy Regulatory Commission or a State regulatory authority described in clause (i), nothing in this subparagraph shall limit or affect—

(I) any statutory authority of the Commission with respect to an agreement, contract, or transaction described in clause (i); or

(II) the jurisdiction of the Commission under subparagraph (A) with respect to an agreement, contract, or transaction that is executed, traded, or cleared on a registered entity or trading facility that is not owned or operated by a regional transmission organization or independent system operator (as defined by sections 3(27) and (28) of the Federal Power Act).

(2) *Establishment of Commodity Futures Trading Commission; Composition; Terms of Commissioners.*

(A) There is hereby established, as an independent agency of the United States Government, a Commodity Futures Trading Commission. The Commission shall be composed of five Commissioners who shall be appointed by the President, by and with the advice and consent of the Senate. In nominating persons for appointment, the President shall—

(i) select persons who shall each have demonstrated knowledge in futures trading or its regulation, or the production, merchandising, processing or distribution of one or more of the commodities or other goods and articles, services, rights, and interests covered by this Act; and

(ii) seek to ensure that the demonstrated knowledge of the Commissioners is balanced with respect to such areas.

Not more than three of the members of the Commission shall be members of the same political party. Each Commissioner shall hold office for a term of five years and until his successor is appointed and has qualified, except that he shall not so continue to serve beyond the expiration of the next session of Congress subsequent to the expiration of said fixed term of office, and except (i) any Commissioner appointed to fill a vacancy occurring prior to the expiration of the term for which his predecessor was appointed shall be appointed for the remainder of such term, and (ii) the terms of office of the Commissioners first taking office after the enactment of this paragraph shall expire as designated by the President at the time of nomination, one at the end of one year, one at the end of two years, one at the end of three years, one at the end of four years, and one at the end of five years.

(B) The President shall appoint, by and with the advice and consent of the Senate, a member of the Commission as Chairman, who shall serve as Chairman at the pleasure of the President. An individual may be appointed as Chairman at the same time that person is appointed as a Commissioner. The Chairman shall be the chief administrative officer of the Commission and shall preside at hearings before the Commission. At any time, the President may appoint, by and with the advice and consent of the Senate, a different Chairman, and the Commissioner previously appointed as Chairman may complete that Commissioner's term as a Commissioner.

(3) *Vacancies.* A vacancy in the Commission shall not impair the right of the remaining Commissioners to exercise all the powers of the Commission.

(4) *General Counsel.* The Commission shall have a General Counsel, who shall be appointed by the Commission and serve at the pleasure of the Commission. The General Counsel shall report directly to the Commission and serve as its legal advisor. The Commission shall appoint such other attorneys as may be necessary, in the opinion of the Commission, to assist the General Counsel, represent the Commission in all disciplinary proceedings pending before it, represent the Commission in courts of law whenever appropriate, assist the Department of Justice in handling litigation concerning the Commission in courts of law, and perform such other legal duties and functions as the Commission may direct.

(5) *Executive Director.* The Commission shall have an Executive Director, who shall be appointed by the Commission and serve at the pleasure of the Commission. The Executive Director shall report directly to the Commission and perform such functions and duties as the Commission may prescribe.

(6) *Powers and Functions of Chairman.*

(A) Except as otherwise provided in this paragraph and in paragraphs (4) and (5) of this subsection, the executive and administrative functions of the Commission, including functions of the Commission with respect to the appointment and supervision of personnel employed under the Commission, the distribution of business among such personnel and among administrative units of the Commission, and the use and expenditure of funds, according to budget categories, plans, programs, and priorities established and approved by the Commission, shall be exercised solely by the Chairman.

(B) In carrying out any of his functions under the provisions of this paragraph, the Chairman shall be governed by general policies, plans, priorities, and budgets approved by the Commission and by such regulatory decisions, findings, and determinations as the Commission may by law be authorized to make.

(C) The appointment by the Chairman of the heads of major administrative units under the Commission shall be subject to the approval of the Commission.

(D) Personnel employed regularly and full time in the immediate offices of Commissioners other than the Chairman shall not be affected by the provisions of this paragraph.

(E) There are hereby reserved to the Commission its functions with respect to revising budget estimates and with respect to determining the distribution of appropriated funds according to major programs and purposes.

(F) The Chairman may from time to time make such provisions as he shall deem appropriate authorizing the performance by any officer, employee, or administrative unit under his jurisdiction of any functions of the Chairman under this paragraph.

(7) *Appointment and Compensation.*

(A) *In General.* The Commission may appoint and fix the compensation of such officers, attorneys, economists, examiners, and other employees as may be necessary for carrying out the functions of the Commission under this Act.

(B) *Rates of Pay*. Rates of basic pay for all employees of the Commission may be set and adjusted by the Commission without regard to chapter 51 or subchapter III of chapter 53 of title 5, United States Code.

(C) *Comparability*.

(i) *In General*. The Commission may provide additional compensation and benefits to employees of the Commission if the same type of compensation or benefits are provided by any agency referred to in section 1206(a) of the Financial Institutions Reform, Recovery, and Enforcement Act of 1989 or could be provided by such an agency under applicable provisions of law (including rules and regulations).

(ii) *Consultation*. In setting and adjusting the total amount of compensation and benefits for employees, the Commission shall consult with, and seek to maintain comparability with, the agencies referred to in section 1206(a) of the Financial Institutions Reform, Recovery, and Enforcement Act of 1989.

(8) *Conflict of Interest*. No Commissioner or employee of the Commission shall accept employment or compensation from any person, exchange, or clearinghouse subject to regulation by the Commission under this Act during his term of office, nor shall he participate, directly or indirectly, in any registered entity operations or transactions of a character subject to regulation by the Commission.

(9) *Liaison with Department of Agriculture; Communications with Department of the Treasury, Federal Reserve Board, and Securities and Exchange Commission; Application by a Board of Trade for Designation as a Contract Market for Future Delivery of Securities*.

(A) The Commission shall, in cooperation with the Secretary of Agriculture, maintain a liaison between the Commission and the Department of Agriculture. The Secretary shall take such steps as may be necessary to enable the Commission to obtain information and utilize such services and facilities of the Department of Agriculture as may be necessary in order to maintain effectively such liaison. In addition, the Secretary shall appoint a liaison officer, who shall be an employee of the Office of the Secretary, for the purpose of maintaining a liaison between the Department of Agriculture and the Commission. The Commission shall furnish such liaison officer appropriate office space within the offices of the Commission and shall allow such liaison officer to attend and observe all deliberations and proceedings of the Commission.

(B)(i) The Commission shall maintain communications with the Department of the Treasury, the Board of Governors of the Federal Reserve System, and the Securities and Exchange Commission for the purpose of keeping such agencies fully informed of Commission activities that relate to the responsibilities of those agencies, for the purpose of seeking the views of those agencies on such activities, and for considering the relationships between the volume and nature of investment and trading in contracts of sale of a commodity for future delivery and in securities and financial instruments under the jurisdiction of such agencies.

(ii) When a board of trade applies for designation or registration as a contract market or derivatives transaction execution facility involving transactions for future delivery of any security issued or guaranteed by the United States or any agency thereof, the Commission shall promptly deliver a copy of such application to the Department of the Treasury and the Board of Governors of the Federal Reserve System. The Commission may not designate or register a board of trade as a contract market or derivatives transaction execution facility based on such application until forty-five days after the date the Commission delivers the application to such agencies or until the Commission receives comments from each of such agencies on the application, whichever period is shorter. Any comments received by the Commission from such agencies shall be included as part of the public record of the Commission's designation proceeding. In designating, registering, or refusing, suspending, or revoking the designation or registration of, a board of trade as a contract market or derivatives transaction execution facility involving transactions for future delivery referred to in this clause or in considering any possible action under this Act (including without limitation emergency action under section 8a(9)) with respect to such transactions, the Commission shall take into consideration all comments it receives from the Department of the Treasury and the Board of Governors of the Federal Reserve System and shall consider the effect that any such designation, registration, suspension, revocation, or action may have on the debt financing requirements of the United States Government and the continued efficiency and integrity of the underlying market for government securities.

(iii) The provisions of this subparagraph shall not create any rights, liabilities, or obligations upon which actions may be brought against the Commission.

(10) *Transmittal of Budget Requests and Legislative Recommendations to Congressional Committees.*

(A) Whenever the Commission submits any budget estimate or request to the President or the Office of Management and Budget, it shall concurrently transmit copies of that estimate or request to the House and Senate Appropriations Committees and the House Committee on Agriculture and the Senate Committee on Agriculture, Nutrition, and Forestry.

(B) Whenever the Commission transmits any legislative recommendations, or testimony, or comments on legislation to the President or the Office of Management and Budget, it shall concurrently transmit copies thereof to the House Committee on Agriculture and the Senate Committee on Agriculture, Nutrition, and Forestry. No officer or agency of the United States shall have any authority to require the Commission to submit its legislative recommendations, or testimony, or comments on legislation to any officer or agency of the United States for approval, comments, or review, prior to the submission of such recommendations, testimony, or comments to the Congress. In instances in which the Commission voluntarily seeks to obtain the comments or review of any officer or agency of the United States, the Commission shall include a description of such actions in its legislative recommendations, testimony, or comments on legislation which it transmits to the Congress.

(C) Whenever the Commission issues for official publication any opinion, release, rule, order, interpretation, or other determination on a matter, the Commission shall provide that any dissenting, concurring, or separate opinion by any Commissioner on the matter be published in full along with the Commission opinion, release, rule, order, interpretation, or determination.

(11) *Seal.* The Commission shall have an official seal, which shall be judicially noticed.

(12) *Rules and Regulations.* The Commission is authorized to promulgate such rules and regulations as it deems necessary to govern the operating procedures and conduct of the business of the Commission.

(13) *Public Availability of Swap Transaction Data.*

(A) *Definition of Real-Time Public Reporting.* In this paragraph, the term "real-time public reporting" means to report data relating to a swap transaction, including price and volume, as soon as technologically practicable after the time at which the swap transaction has been executed.

(B) *Purpose.* The purpose of this section is to authorize the Commission to make swap transaction and pricing data available to the public in such form and at such times as the Commission determines appropriate to enhance price discovery.

(C) *General Rule.* The Commission is authorized and required to provide by rule for the public availability of swap transaction and pricing data as follows:

(i) With respect to those swaps that are subject to the mandatory clearing requirement described in subsection (h)(1) (including those swaps that are excepted from the requirement pursuant to subsection (h)(7)), the Commission shall require real-time public reporting for such transactions.

(ii) With respect to those swaps that are not subject to the mandatory clearing requirement described in subsection (h)(1), but are cleared at a registered derivatives clearing organization, the Commission shall require real-time public reporting for such transactions.

(iii) With respect to swaps that are not cleared at a registered derivatives clearing organization and which are reported to a swap data repository or the Commission under subsection (h)(6), the Commission shall require real-time public reporting for such transactions, in a manner that does not disclose the business transactions and market positions of any person.

(iv) With respect to swaps that are determined to be required to be cleared under subsection (h)(2) but are not cleared, the Commission shall require real-time public reporting for such transactions.

(D) *Registered Entities and Public Reporting.* The Commission may require registered entities to publicly disseminate the swap transaction and pricing data required to be reported under this paragraph.

(E) *Rulemaking Required.* With respect to the rule providing for the public availability of transaction and pricing data for swaps described in clauses (i) and (ii) of subparagraph (C), the rule promulgated by the Commission shall contain provisions—

(i) to ensure such information does not identify the participants;

(ii) to specify the criteria for determining what constitutes a large notional swap transaction (block trade) for particular markets and contracts;

(iii) to specify the appropriate time delay for reporting large notional swap transactions (block trades) to the public; and

(iv) that take into account whether the public disclosure will materially reduce market liquidity.

(F) *Timeliness of Reporting.* Parties to a swap (including agents of the parties to a swap) shall be responsible for reporting swap transaction information to the appropriate registered entity in a timely manner as may be prescribed by the Commission.

(G) *Reporting of Swaps to Registered Swap Data Repositories.* Each swap (whether cleared or uncleared) shall be reported to a registered swap data repository.

(14) *Semiannual and Annual Public Reporting of Aggregate Swap Data.*

(A) *In General.* In accordance with subparagraph (B), the Commission shall issue a written report on a semiannual and annual basis to make available to the public information relating to—

(i) the trading and clearing in the major swap categories; and

(ii) the market participants and developments in new products.

(B) *Use; Consultation.* In preparing a report under subparagraph (A), the Commission shall—

(i) use information from swap data repositories and derivatives clearing organizations; and

(ii) consult with the Office of the Comptroller of the Currency, the Bank for International Settlements, and such other regulatory bodies as may be necessary.

(C) *Authority of the Commission.* The Commission may, by rule, regulation, or order, delegate the public reporting responsibilities of the Commission under this paragraph in accordance with such terms and conditions as the Commission determines to be appropriate and in the public interest.

(15) *Energy and Environmental Markets Advisory Committee.*

(A) *Establishment.*

(i) *In General.* An Energy and Environmental Markets Advisory Committee is hereby established.

(ii) *Membership.* The Committee shall have 9 members.

(iii) *Activities.* The Committee's objectives and scope of activities shall be—

(I) to conduct public meetings;

(II) to submit reports and recommendations to the Commission (including dissenting or minority views, if any); and

(III) otherwise to serve as a vehicle for discussion and communication on matters of concern to exchanges, firms, end users, and regulators regarding energy and environmental markets and their regulation by the Commission.

(B) *Requirements.*

(i) *In General.* The Committee shall hold public meetings at such intervals as are necessary to carry out the functions of the Committee, but not less frequently than 2 times per year.

(ii) *Members.* Members shall be appointed to 3-year terms, but may be removed for cause by vote of the Commission.

(C) *Appointment.* The Commission shall appoint members with a wide diversity of opinion and who represent a broad spectrum of interests, including hedgers and consumers.

(D) *Reimbursement.* Members shall be entitled to per diem and travel expense reimbursement by the Commission.

(E) *FACA.* The Committee shall not be subject to the Federal Advisory Committee Act.

(b) *Transaction in Interstate Commerce.* For the purposes of this Act (but not in any wise limiting the foregoing definition of interstate commerce) a transaction in respect to any article shall be considered to be in interstate commerce if such article is part of that current of commerce usual in the commodity trade whereby commodities and commodity products and byproducts thereof are sent from one State with the expectation that they will end their transit, after purchase, in another, including, in addition to cases within the above general description, all cases where purchase or sale is either for shipment to another State, or for manufacture within the State and the shipment outside the State of the products resulting from such manufacture. Articles normally in such current of commerce shall not be considered out of such commerce through resort being had to any means or device intended to remove transactions in respect thereto from the provisions of this Act. For the purpose of this paragraph the word "State" includes Territory, the District of Columbia, possession of the United States, and foreign nation.

(c) *Agreements, Contracts, and Transactions in Foreign Currency, Government Securities, and Certain Other Commodities.*

(1) *In General.* Except as provided in paragraph (2), nothing in this Act (other than, section 5b, or 12(e)(2)(B)) governs or applies to an agreement, contract, or transaction in—

(A) foreign currency;

(B) government securities;

(C) security warrants;

(D) security rights;

(E) resales of installment loan contracts;

(F) repurchase transactions in an excluded commodity; or

(G) mortgages or mortgage purchase commitments.

(2) *Commission Jurisdiction.*

(A) *Agreements, Contracts, and Transactions Traded on an Organized Exchange.* This Act applies to, and the Commission shall have jurisdiction over, an agreement, contract, or transaction described in paragraph (1) that is—

(i) a contract of sale of a commodity for future delivery (or an option on such a contract), or an option on a commodity (other than foreign currency or a security or a group or index of securities), that is executed or traded on an organized exchange;

(ii) a swap; or

(iii) an option on foreign currency executed or traded on an organized exchange that is not a national securities exchange registered pursuant to section 6(a) of the Securities Exchange Act of 1934.

(B) *Agreements, Contracts, and Transactions in Retail Foreign Currency.*

(i) This Act applies to, and the Commission shall have jurisdiction over, an agreement, contract, or transaction in foreign currency that—

(I) is a contract of sale of a commodity for future delivery (or an option on such a contract) or an option (other than an option executed or traded on a national securities exchange registered pursuant to section 6(a) of the Securities Exchange Act of 1934); and

(II) is offered to, or entered into with, a person that is not an eligible contract participant, unless the counterparty, or the person offering to be the counterparty, of the person is—

(aa) a United States financial institution;

(bb) (AA) a broker or dealer registered under section 15(b) (except paragraph (11) thereof) or 15C of the Securities Exchange Act of 1934; or

(BB) an associated person of a broker or dealer registered under section 15(b) (except paragraph (11) thereof) or 15C of the Securities Exchange Act of 1934 concerning the financial or securities activities of which the broker or dealer makes and keeps records under section 15C(b) or 17(h) of the Securities Exchange Act of 1934;

(cc) (AA) a futures commission merchant that is primarily or substantially engaged in the business activities described in section 1a of this Act, is registered under this Act, is not a person described in item (bb) of this subclause, and maintains adjusted net capital equal to or in excess of the dollar amount that applies for purposes of clause (ii) of this subparagraph; or

(BB) an affiliated person of a futures commission merchant that is primarily or substantially engaged in the business activities described in section 1a of this Act, is registered under this Act, and is not a person described in item (bb) of this subclause, if the affiliated person maintains adjusted net capital equal to or in excess of the dollar amount that applies for purposes of clause (ii) of this subparagraph and is not a person described in such item (bb), and the futures commission merchant makes and keeps records under section 4f(c)(2)(B) of this Act concerning the futures and other financial activities of the affiliated person;

(dd)* a financial holding company (as defined in section 2 of the Bank Holding Company Act of 1956); or

(ff)** a retail foreign exchange dealer that maintains adjusted net capital equal to or in excess of the dollar amount that applies for purposes of clause (ii) of this subparagraph and is registered in such capacity with the Commission, subject to such terms and conditions as the Commission shall prescribe, and is a member of a futures association registered under section 17.

(ii) The dollar amount that applies for purposes of this clause is—

(I) $10,000,000, beginning 120 days after the date of the enactment of this clause;

(II) $15,000,000, beginning 240 days after such date of enactment; and

(III) $20,000,000, beginning 360 days after such date of enactment.

(iii) Notwithstanding items (cc) and (gg) of clause (i)(II) of this subparagraph, agreements, contracts, or transactions described in clause (i) of this subparagraph, and accounts or pooled investment vehicles described in clause (vi), shall be subject to subsection (a)(1)(B) of this section and sections 4(b), 4b, 4c(b), 4o, 6(c) and 6(d) (except to the extent that sections 6(c) and 6(d) prohibit manipulation of the market price of any commodity in interstate commerce, or for future delivery on or subject to the rules of any market), 6c, 6d, 8(a), 13(a), and 13(b) if the agreements, contracts, or transactions are offered, or entered into, by a person that is registered as a futures commission merchant or retail foreign exchange dealer, or an affiliated person of a futures commission merchant registered under this Act that is not also a person described in any of item (aa), (bb), (ee), or (ff) of clause (i)(II) of this subparagraph.

(iv)(I) Notwithstanding items (cc) and (gg) of clause (i)(II), a person, unless registered in such capacity as the Commission by rule, regulation, or order shall determine and a member of a futures association registered under section 17, shall not—

(aa) solicit or accept orders from any person that is not an eligible contract participant in connection with agreements, contracts, or transactions described in clause (i) entered into with or to be entered into with a person who is not described in item (aa), (bb), (ee), or (ff) of clause (i)(II);

(bb) exercise discretionary trading authority or obtain written authorization to exercise discretionary trading authority over any account for or on behalf of any person that is not an eligible contract participant in connection with agreements, contracts, or transactions described in clause (i) entered into with or to be entered into with a person who is not described in item (aa), (bb), (ee), or (ff) of clause (i)(II); or

(cc) operate or solicit funds, securities, or property for any pooled investment vehicle that is not an eligible contract participant in connection with agreements, contracts, or transactions described in clause (i) entered into with or to be entered into with a person who is not described in item (aa), (bb), (ee), or (ff) of clause (i)(II).

(II) Subclause (I) of this clause shall not apply to—

* Dodd–Frank redesignated former item (ee) as (dd).

** Dodd–Frank redesignated former item (gg) as (ff).

(aa) any person described in any of item (aa), (bb), (ee), or (ff) of clause (i)(II);

(bb) any such person's associated persons; or

(cc) any person who would be exempt from registration if engaging in the same activities in connection with transactions conducted on or subject to the rules of a contract market or a derivatives transaction execution facility.

(III) Notwithstanding items (cc) and (gg) of clause (i)(II), the Commission may make, promulgate, and enforce such rules and regulations as, in the judgment of the Commission, are reasonably necessary to effectuate any of the provisions of, or to accomplish any of the purposes of, this Act in connection with the activities of persons subject to subclause (I).

(IV) Subclause (III) of this clause shall not apply to—

(aa) any person described in any of item (aa) through (ff) of clause (i)(II);

(bb) any such person's associated persons; or

(cc) any person who would be exempt from registration if engaging in the same activities in connection with transactions conducted on or subject to the rules of a contract market or a derivatives transaction execution facility.

(v) Notwithstanding items (cc) and (gg) of clause (i)(II), the Commission may make, promulgate, and enforce such rules and regulations as, in the judgment of the Commission, are reasonably necessary to effectuate any of the provisions of, or to accomplish any of the purposes of, this Act in connection with agreements, contracts, or transactions described in clause (i) which are offered, or entered into, by a person described in item (cc) or (gg) of clause (i)(II).

(vi) This Act applies to, and the Commission shall have jurisdiction over, an account or pooled investment vehicle that is offered for the purpose of trading, or that trades, any agreement, contract, or transaction in foreign currency described in clause (i).

(C)(i)(I) This subparagraph shall apply to any agreement, contract, or transaction in foreign currency that is—

(aa) offered to, or entered into with, a person that is not an eligible contract participant (except that this subparagraph shall not apply if the counterparty, or the person offering to be the counterparty, of the person that is not an eligible contract participant is a person described in any of item (aa), (bb), (ee), or (ff) of subparagraph (B)(i)(II)); and

(bb) offered, or entered into, on a leveraged or margined basis, or financed by the offeror, the counterparty, or a person acting in concert with the offeror or counterparty on a similar basis.

(II) Subclause (I) of this clause shall not apply to—

(aa) a security that is not a security futures product; or

(bb) a contract of sale that—

(AA) results in actual delivery within 2 days; or

(BB) creates an enforceable obligation to deliver between a seller and buyer that have the ability to deliver and accept delivery, respectively, in connection with their line of business.

(ii)(I) Agreements, contracts, or transactions described in clause (i) of this subparagraph, and accounts or pooled investment vehicles described in clause (vii), shall be subject to subsection (a)(1)(B) of this section and sections 4(b), 4b, 4c(b), 4o, 6(c) and 6(d) (except to the extent that sections 6(c) and 6(d) prohibit manipulation of the market price of any commodity in interstate commerce, or for future delivery on or subject to the rules of any market), 6c, 6d, 8(a), 13(a), and 13(b).

(II) Subclause (I) of this clause shall not apply to—

(aa) any person described in any of item (aa), (bb), (ee), or (ff) of subparagraph (B)(i)(II); or

(bb) any such person's associated persons.

(III) The Commission may make, promulgate, and enforce such rules and regulations as, in the judgment of the Commission, are reasonably necessary to effectuate any of the provisions of or to accomplish any of the purposes of this Act in connection with agreements, contracts, or transactions described in clause (i) of this subparagraph if the agreements, contracts, or transactions are offered, or entered into, by a person that is not described in item (aa) through (ff) of subparagraph (B)(i)(II).

(iii) (I) A person, unless registered in such capacity as the Commission by rule, regulation, or order shall determine and a member of a futures association registered under section 17, shall not—

(aa) solicit or accept orders from any person that is not an eligible contract participant in connection with agreements, contracts, or transactions described in clause (i) of this subparagraph entered into with or to be entered into with a person who is not described in item (aa), (bb), (ee), or (ff) of subparagraph (B)(i)(II);

(bb) exercise discretionary trading authority or obtain written authorization to exercise written trading authority over any account for or on behalf of any person that is not an eligible contract participant in connection with agreements, contracts, or transactions described in clause (i) of this subparagraph entered into with or to be entered into with a person who is not described in item (aa), (bb), (ee), or (ff) of subparagraph (B)(i)(II); or

(cc) operate or solicit funds, securities, or property for any pooled investment vehicle that is not an eligible contract participant in connection with agreements, contracts, or transactions described in clause (i) of this subparagraph entered into with or to be entered into with a person who is not described in item (aa), (bb), (ee), or (ff) of subparagraph (B)(i)(II).

(II) Subclause (I) of this clause shall not apply to—

(aa) any person described in item (aa), (bb), (ee), or (ff) of subparagraph (B)(i)(II);

(bb) any such person's associated persons; or

(cc) any person who would be exempt from registration if engaging in the same activities in connection with transactions conducted on or subject to the rules of a contract market or a derivatives transaction execution facility.

(III) The Commission may make, promulgate, and enforce such rules and regulations as, in the judgment of the Commission, are reasonably necessary to effectuate any of the provisions of, or to accomplish any of the purposes of, this Act in connection with the activities of persons subject to subclause (I).

(IV) Subclause (III) of this clause shall not apply to—

(aa) any person described in item (aa) through (ff) of subparagraph (B)(i)(II);

(bb) any such person's associated persons; or

(cc) any person who would be exempt from registration if engaging in the same activities in connection with transactions conducted on or subject to the rules of a contract market or a derivatives transaction execution facility.

(iv) Sections 4(b) and 4b shall apply to any agreement, contract, or transaction described in clause (i) of this subparagraph as if the agreement, contract, or transaction were a contract of sale of a commodity for future delivery.

(v) This subparagraph shall not be construed to limit any jurisdiction that the Commission may otherwise have under any other provision of this Act over an agreement, contract, or transaction that is a contract of sale of a commodity for future delivery.

(vi) This subparagraph shall not be construed to limit any jurisdiction that the Commission or the Securities and Exchange Commission may otherwise have under any other provision of this Act with respect to security futures products and persons effecting transactions in security futures products.

(vii) This Act applies to, and the Commission shall have jurisdiction over, an account or pooled investment vehicle that is offered for the purpose of trading, or that trades, any agreement, contract, or transaction in foreign currency described in clause (i).

(D) *Retail Commodity Transactions.*

(i) *Applicability.* Except as provided in clause (ii), this subparagraph shall apply to any agreement, contract, or transaction in any commodity that is—

(I) entered into with, or offered to (even if not entered into with), a person that is not an eligible contract participant or eligible commercial entity; and

(II) entered into, or offered (even if not entered into), on a leveraged or margined basis, or financed by the offeror, the counterparty, or a person acting in concert with the offeror or counterparty on a similar basis.

(ii) *Exceptions.* This subparagraph shall not apply to—

(I) an agreement, contract, or transaction described in paragraph (1) or subparagraphs (A), (B), or (C), including any agreement, contract, or transaction specifically excluded from subparagraph (A), (B), or (C);

(II) any security;

(III) a contract of sale that—

(aa) results in actual delivery within 28 days or such other longer period as the Commission may determine by rule or regulation based upon the typical commercial practice in cash or spot markets for the commodity involved; or

(bb) creates an enforceable obligation to deliver between a seller and a buyer that have the ability to deliver and accept delivery, respectively, in connection with the line of business of the seller and buyer; or

(IV) an agreement, contract, or transaction that is listed on a national securities exchange registered under section 6(a) of the Securities Exchange Act of 1934; or

(V) an identified banking product, as defined in section 402(b) of the Legal Certainty for Bank Products Act of 2000.

(iii) *Enforcement.* Sections 4(a), 4(b), and 4b apply to any agreement, contract, or transaction described in clause (i), as if the agreement, contract, or transaction was a contract of sale of a commodity for future delivery.

(iv) *Eligible Commercial Entity.* For purposes of this subparagraph, an agricultural producer, packer, or handler shall be considered to be an eligible commercial entity for any agreement, contract, or transaction for a commodity in connection with the line of business of the agricultural producer, packer, or handler.

(E) *Prohibition.*

(i) *Definition of Federal Regulatory Agency.* In this subparagraph, the term "Federal regulatory agency" means—

(I) the Commission;

(II) the Securities and Exchange Commission;

(III) an appropriate Federal banking agency;

(IV) the National Credit Union Association; and

(V) the Farm Credit Administration.

(ii) *Prohibition.*

(I) *In General.* Except as provided in subclause (II), a person described in subparagraph (B)(i)(II) for which there is a Federal regulatory agency shall not offer to, or enter into with, a person that is not an eligible contract participant, any agreement, contract, or transaction in foreign currency described in subparagraph (B)(i)(I) except pursuant to a rule or regulation of a Federal regulatory agency allowing the agreement, contract, or transaction under such terms and conditions as the Federal regulatory agency shall prescribe.

(II) *Effective Date.* With regard to persons described in subparagraph (B)(i)(II) for which a Federal regulatory agency has issued a proposed rule concerning agreements, contracts, or transactions in foreign currency described in subparagraph (B)(i)(I) prior to the date of enactment of this subclause, subclause (I) shall take effect 90 days after the date of enactment of this subclause.

(iii) *Requirements of Rules and Regulations.*

(I) *In General.* The rules and regulations described in clause (ii) shall prescribe appropriate requirements with respect to—

(aa) disclosure;

(bb) recordkeeping;

(cc) capital and margin;

(dd) reporting;

(ee) business conduct;

(ff) documentation; and

(gg) such other standards or requirements as the Federal regulatory agency shall determine to be necessary.

(II) *Treatment.* The rules or regulations described in clause (ii) shall treat all agreements, contracts, and transactions in foreign currency described in subparagraph (B)(i)(I), and all agreements, contracts, and transactions in foreign currency that are functionally or economically similar to agreements, contracts, or transactions described in subparagraph (B)(i)(I), similarly.

(d) *Swaps.* Nothing in this Act (other than subparagraphs (A), (B), (C), (D), (G), and (H) of subsection (a)(1), subsections (f) and (g), sections 1a, 2(a)(13), 2(c)(2)(A)(ii), 2(e), 2(h), 4(c), 4a, 4b, and 4b–1, subsections (a), (b), and (g) of section 4c, sections 4d, 4e, 4f, 4g, 4h, 4i, 4j, 4k, 4l, 4m, 4n, 4o, 4p, 4r, 4s, 4t, 5, 5b, 5c, 5e, and 5h, subsections (c) and (d) of section 6, sections 6c, 6d, 8, 8a, and 9, subsections (e)(2), (f), and (h) of section 12, subsections (a) and (b) of section 13, sections 17, 20, 21, and 22(a)(4), and any other provision of this Act that is applicable to registered entities or Commission registrants) governs or applies to a swap.

(e) *Limitation on Participation.* It shall be unlawful for any person, other than an eligible contract participant, to enter into a swap unless the swap is entered into on, or subject to the rules of, a board of trade designated as a contract market under section 5.

(f) *Exclusion for Qualifying Hybrid Instruments.*

(1) *In General.* Nothing in this Act (other than section 12(e)(2)(B)) governs or is applicable to a hybrid instrument that is predominantly a security.

(2) *Predominance.* A hybrid instrument shall be considered to be predominantly a security if—

(A) the issuer of the hybrid instrument receives payment in full of the purchase price of the hybrid instrument, substantially contemporaneously with delivery of the hybrid instrument;

(B) the purchaser or holder of the hybrid instrument is not required to make any payment to the issuer in addition to the purchase price paid under subparagraph (A), whether as margin, settlement payment, or otherwise, during the life of the hybrid instrument or at maturity;

(C) the issuer of the hybrid instrument is not subject by the terms of the instrument to mark-to-market margining requirements; and

(D) the hybrid instrument is not marketed as a contract of sale of a commodity for future delivery (or option on such a contract) subject to this Act.

(3) *Mark-to-Market Margining Requirements.* For the purposes of paragraph (2)(C), mark-to-market margining requirements do not include the obligation of an issuer of a secured debt instrument to increase the amount of collateral held in pledge for the benefit of the purchaser of the secured debt instrument to secure the repayment obligations of the issuer under the secured debt instrument.

(g) *Application of Commodity Futures Laws.*

(1) No provision of this Act shall be construed as implying or creating any presumption that—

(A) any agreement, contract, or transaction that is excluded from this Act under section 2(c), 2(d), 2(e), 2(f), or 2(g) of this Act or title IV of the Commodity Futures Modernization Act of 2000, or exempted under section 2(h) or 4(c) of this Act; or

(B) any agreement, contract, or transaction, not otherwise subject to this Act, that is not so excluded or exempted,

is or would otherwise be subject to this Act.

(2) No provision of, or amendment made by, the Commodity Futures Modernization Act of 2000 shall be construed as conferring jurisdiction on the Commission with respect to any such agreement, contract, or transaction, except as expressly provided in section 5a of this Act (to the extent provided in section 5a(g) of this Act), 5b of this Act, or 5d of this Act.

(h) *Clearing Requirement.*

(1) *In General.*

(A) *Standard for Clearing.* It shall be unlawful for any person to engage in a swap unless that person submits such swap for clearing to a derivatives clearing organization that is registered under this Act or a derivatives clearing organization that is exempt from registration under this Act if the swap is required to be cleared.

(B) *Open Access.* The rules of a derivatives clearing organization described in subparagraph (A) shall—

(i) prescribe that all swaps (but not contracts of sale of a commodity for future delivery or options on such contracts) submitted to the derivatives clearing organization with the same terms and conditions are economically equivalent within the derivatives clearing organization and may be offset with each other within the derivatives clearing organization; and

(ii) provide for non-discriminatory clearing of a swap (but not a contract of sale of a commodity for future delivery or option on such contract) executed bilaterally or on or through the rules of an unaffiliated designated contract market or swap execution facility.

(2) *Commission Review.*

(A) *Commission-Initiated Review.*

(i) The Commission on an ongoing basis shall review each swap, or any group, category, type, or class of swaps to make a determination as to whether the swap or group, category, type, or class of swaps should be required to be cleared.

(ii) The Commission shall provide at least a 30–day public comment period regarding any determination made under clause (i).

(B) *Swap Submissions.*

(i) A derivatives clearing organization shall submit to the Commission each swap, or any group, category, type, or class of swaps that it plans to accept for clearing, and provide notice to its members (in a manner to be determined by the Commission) of the submission.

(ii) Any swap or group, category, type, or class of swaps listed for clearing by a derivative clearing organization as of the date of enactment of this subsection shall be considered submitted to the Commission.

(iii) The Commission shall—

(I) make available to the public submissions received under clauses (i) and (ii);

(II) review each submission made under clauses (i) and (ii), and determine whether the swap, or group, category, type, or class of swaps described in the submission is required to be cleared; and

(III) provide at least a 30-day public comment period regarding its determination as to whether the clearing requirement under paragraph (1)(A) shall apply to the submission.

(C) *Deadline.* The Commission shall make its determination under subparagraph (B)(iii) not later than 90 days after receiving a submission made under subparagraphs (B)(i) and (B)(ii), unless the submitting derivatives clearing organization agrees to an extension for the time limitation established under this subparagraph.

(D) *Determination.*

(i) In reviewing a submission made under subparagraph (B), the Commission shall review whether the submission is consistent with section 5b(c)(2).

(ii) In reviewing a swap, group of swaps, or class of swaps pursuant to subparagraph (A) or a submission made under subparagraph (B), the Commission shall take into account the following factors:

(I) The existence of significant outstanding notional exposures, trading liquidity, and adequate pricing data.

(II) The availability of rule framework, capacity, operational expertise and resources, and credit support infrastructure to clear the contract on terms that are consistent with the material terms and trading conventions on which the contract is then traded.

(III) The effect on the mitigation of systemic risk, taking into account the size of the market for such contract and the resources of the derivatives clearing organization available to clear the contract.

(IV) The effect on competition, including appropriate fees and charges applied to clearing.

(V) The existence of reasonable legal certainty in the event of the insolvency of the relevant derivatives clearing organization or 1 or more of its clearing members with regard to the treatment of customer and swap counterparty positions, funds, and property.

(iii) In making a determination under subparagraph (A) or (B)(iii) that the clearing requirement shall apply, the Commission may require such terms and conditions to the requirement as the Commission determines to be appropriate.

(E) *Rules.* Not later than 1 year after the date of the enactment of this subsection, the Commission shall adopt rules for a derivatives clearing organization's submission for review, pursuant to this paragraph, of a swap, or a group, category, type, or class of swaps, that it seeks to accept for clearing. Nothing in this subparagraph limits the Commission from making a determination under subparagraph (B)(iii) for swaps described in subparagraph (B)(ii).

(3) *Stay of Clearing Requirement.*

(A) *In General.* After making a determination pursuant to paragraph (2)(B), the Commission, on application of a counterparty to a swap or on its own initiative, may stay the clearing requirement of paragraph (1) until the Commission completes a review of the terms of the swap (or the group, category, type, or class of swaps) and the clearing arrangement.

(B) *Deadline.* The Commission shall complete a review undertaken pursuant to subparagraph (A) not later than 90 days after issuance of the stay, unless the derivatives clearing organization that clears the swap, or group, category, type, or class of swaps agrees to an extension of the time limitation established under this subparagraph.

(C) *Determination.* Upon completion of the review undertaken pursuant to subparagraph (A), the Commission may—

(i) determine, unconditionally or subject to such terms and conditions as the Commission determines to be appropriate, that the swap, or group, category, type, or class of swaps must be cleared pursuant to this subsection if it finds that such clearing is consistent with paragraph (2)(D); or

(ii) determine that the clearing requirement of paragraph (1) shall not apply to the swap, or group, category, type, or class of swaps.

(D) *Rules.* Not later than 1 year after the date of the enactment of the Wall Street Transparency and Accountability Act of 2010, the Commission shall adopt rules for reviewing, pursuant to this paragraph, a derivatives clearing organization's clearing of a swap, or a group, category, type, or class of swaps, that it has accepted for clearing.

(4) *Prevention of Evasion.*

(A) *In General.* The Commission shall prescribe rules under this subsection (and issue interpretations of rules prescribed under this subsection) as determined by the Commission to be necessary to prevent evasions of the mandatory clearing requirements under this Act.

(B) *Duty of Commission to Investigate and Take Certain Actions.* To the extent the Commission finds that a particular swap, group, category, type, or class of swaps would otherwise be subject to mandatory clearing but no derivatives clearing organization has listed the swap, group, category, type, or class of swaps for clearing, the Commission shall—

(i) investigate the relevant facts and circumstances;

(ii) within 30 days issue a public report containing the results of the investigation; and

(iii) take such actions as the Commission determines to be necessary and in the public interest, which may include requiring the retaining of adequate margin or capital by parties to the swap, group, category, type, or class of swaps.

(C) *Effect on Authority.* Nothing in this paragraph—

(i) authorizes the Commission to adopt rules requiring a derivatives clearing organization to list for clearing a swap, group, category, type, or class of swaps if the clearing of the swap, group, category, type, or class of swaps would threaten the financial integrity of the derivatives clearing organization; and

(ii) affects the authority of the Commission to enforce the open access provisions of paragraph (1)(B) with respect to a swap, group, category, type, or class of swaps that is listed for clearing by a derivatives clearing organization.

(5) *Reporting Transition Rules.* Rules adopted by the Commission under this section shall provide for the reporting of data, as follows:

(A) Swaps entered into before the date of the enactment of this subsection shall be reported to a registered swap data repository or the Commission no later than 180 days after the effective date of this subsection.

(B) Swaps entered into on or after such date of enactment shall be reported to a registered swap data repository or the Commission no later than the later of—

(i) 90 days after such effective date; or

(ii) such other time after entering into the swap as the Commission may prescribe by rule or regulation.

(6) *Clearing Transition Rules.*

(A) Swaps entered into before the date of the enactment of this subsection are exempt from the clearing requirements of this subsection if reported pursuant to paragraph (5)(A).

(B) Swaps entered into before application of the clearing requirement pursuant to this subsection are exempt from the clearing requirements of this subsection if reported pursuant to paragraph (5)(B).

(7) *Exceptions.*

(A) *In General.* The requirements of paragraph (1)(A) shall not apply to a swap if 1 of the counterparties to the swap—

(i) is not a financial entity;

(ii) is using swaps to hedge or mitigate commercial risk; and

(iii) notifies the Commission, in a manner set forth by the Commission, how it generally meets its financial obligations associated with entering into non-cleared swaps.

(B) *Option to Clear.* The application of the clearing exception in subparagraph (A) is solely at the discretion of the counterparty to the swap that meets the conditions of clauses (i) through (iii) of subparagraph (A).

(C) *Financial Entity Definition.*

(i) *In General.* For the purposes of this paragraph, the term "financial entity" means—

(I) a swap dealer;

(II) a security-based swap dealer;

(III) a major swap participant;

(IV) a major security-based swap participant;

(V) a commodity pool;

(VI) a private fund as defined in section 202(a) of the Investment Advisers Act of 1940;

(VII) an employee benefit plan as defined in paragraphs (3) and (32) of section 3 of the Employee Retirement Income Security Act of 1974;

(VIII) a person predominantly engaged in activities that are in the business of banking, or in activities that are financial in nature, as defined in section 4(k) of the Bank Holding Company Act of 1956.

(ii) *Exclusion.* The Commission shall consider whether to exempt small banks, savings associations, farm credit system institutions, and credit unions, including—

(I) depository institutions with total assets of $10,000,000,000 or less;

(II) farm credit system institutions with total assets of $10,000,000,000 or less; or

(III) credit unions with total assets of $10,000,000,000 or less.

(iii) *Limitation.* Such definition shall not include an entity whose primary business is providing financing, and uses derivatives for the purpose of hedging underlying commercial risks related to interest rate and foreign currency exposures, 90 percent or more of which arise from financing that facilitates the purchase or lease of products, 90 percent or more of which are manufactured by the parent company or another subsidiary of the parent company.

(D) *Treatment of Affiliates.*

(i) *In General.* An affiliate of a person that qualifies for an exception under subparagraph (A) (including affiliate entities predominantly engaged in providing financing for the purchase of the merchandise or manufactured goods of the person) may qualify for the exception only if the affiliate—

(I) enters into the swap to hedge or mitigate the commercial risk of the person or other affiliate of the person that is not a financial entity, and the commercial risk that the affiliate is hedging or mitigating has been transferred to the affiliate;

(II) is directly and wholly-owned by another affiliate qualified for the exception under this subparagraph or an entity that is not a financial entity;

(III) is not indirectly majority-owned by a financial entity;

(IV) is not ultimately owned by a parent company that is a financial entity; and

(V) does not provide any services, financial or otherwise, to any affiliate that is a nonbank financial company supervised by the Board of Governors (as defined under section 102 of the Financial Stability Act of 2010).

(ii) *Limitation on Qualifying Affiliates.* The exception in clause (i) shall not apply if the affiliate is—

(I) a swap dealer;

(II) a security-based swap dealer;

(III) a major swap participant;

(IV) a major security-based swap participant;

(V) a commodity pool;

(VI) a bank holding company;

(VII) a private fund, as defined in section 202(a) of the Investment Advisers Act of 1940;

(VIII) an employee benefit plan or government plan, as defined in paragraphs (3) and (32) of section 3 of the Employee Retirement Income Security Act of 1974;

(IX) an insured depository institution;

(X) a farm credit system institution;

(XI) a credit union;

(XII) a nonbank financial company supervised by the Board of Governors (as defined under section 102 of the Financial Stability Act of 2010); or

(XIII) an entity engaged in the business of insurance and subject to capital requirements established by an insurance governmental authority of a State, a territory of the United States, the District of Columbia, a country other than the United States, or a political subdivision of a country other than the United States that is engaged in the supervision of insurance companies under insurance law.

(iii) *Limitation on Affiliates' Affiliates.* Unless the Commission determines, by order, rule, or regulation, that it is in the public interest, the exception in clause (i) shall not apply with respect to an affiliate if the affiliate is itself affiliated with—

(I) a major security-based swap participant;

(II) a security-based swap dealer;

(III) a major swap participant; or

(IV) a swap dealer.

(iv) *Conditions on Transactions.* With respect to an affiliate that qualifies for the exception in clause (i)—

(I) the affiliate may not enter into any swap other than for the purpose of hedging or mitigating commercial risk; and

(II) neither the affiliate nor any person affiliated with the affiliate that is not a financial entity may enter into a swap with or on behalf of any affiliate that is a financial entity or otherwise assume, net, combine, or consolidate the risk of swaps entered into by any such financial entity, except one that is an affiliate that qualifies for the exception under clause (i).

(v) *Transition Rule for Affiliates.* An affiliate, subsidiary, or a wholly owned entity of a person that qualifies for an exception under subparagraph (A) and is predominantly engaged in providing financing for the purchase or lease of merchandise or manufactured goods of the person shall be exempt from the margin requirement described in section 4s(e) of this Act and the clearing requirement described in paragraph (1) with regard to swaps entered into to mitigate the risk of the financing activities for not less than a 2-year period beginning on July 21, 2010.

(vi) *Risk Management Program.* Any swap entered into by an affiliate that qualifies for the exception in clause (i) shall be subject to a centralized risk management program of the affiliate, which is reasonably designed both to monitor and manage the risks associated with the swap and to identify each of the affiliates on whose behalf a swap was entered into.

(E) *Election of Counter Party.*

(i) *Swaps Required to be Cleared.* With respect to any swap that is subject to the mandatory clearing requirement under this subsection and entered into by a swap dealer or a major swap participant with a counterparty that is not a swap dealer, major swap participant, security-based swap dealer, or major security-based swap participant, the counterparty shall have the sole right to select the derivatives clearing organization at which the swap will be cleared.

(ii) *Swaps Not Required to be Cleared.* With respect to any swap that is not subject to the mandatory clearing requirement under this subsection and entered into by a swap dealer or a major swap participant with a counterparty that is not a swap dealer, major swap participant, security-based swap dealer, or major security-based swap participant, the counterparty—

(I) may elect to require clearing of the swap; and

(II) shall have the sole right to select the derivatives clearing organization at which the swap will be cleared.

(F) *Abuse of Exception.* The Commission may prescribe such rules or issue interpretations of the rules as the Commission determines to be necessary to prevent abuse of the exceptions described in this paragraph. The Commission may also request information from those persons claiming the clearing exception as necessary to prevent abuse of the exceptions described in this paragraph.

(8) *Trade Execution.*

(A) *In General.* With respect to transactions involving swaps subject to the clearing requirement of paragraph (1), counterparties shall—

(i) execute the transaction on a board of trade designated as a contract market under section 5; or

(ii) execute the transaction on a swap execution facility registered under 5h or a swap execution facility that is exempt from registration under section 5h(f) of this Act.

(B) *Exception.* The requirements of clauses (i) and (ii) of subparagraph (A) shall not apply if no board of trade or swap execution facility makes the swap available to trade or for swap transactions subject to the clearing exception under paragraph (7).

(i) *Applicability.* The provisions of this Act relating to swaps that were enacted by the Wall Street Transparency and Accountability Act of 2010 (including any rule prescribed or regulation promulgated under that Act), shall not apply to activities outside the United States unless those activities—

(1) have a direct and significant connection with activities in, or effect on, commerce of the United States; or

(2) contravene such rules or regulations as the Commission may prescribe or promulgate as are necessary or appropriate to prevent the evasion of any provision of this Act that was enacted by the Wall Street Transparency and Accountability Act of 2010.

(j) *Committee Approval by Board.* Exemptions from the requirements of subsection (h)(1) to clear a swap and subsection (h)(8) to execute a swap through a board of trade or swap execution facility shall be available to a counterparty that is an issuer of securities that are registered under section 12 of the Securities Exchange Act of 1934 or that is required to file reports pursuant to section 15(d) of the Securities Exchange Act of 1934 only if an appropriate committee of the issuer's board or governing body has reviewed and approved its decision to enter into swaps that are subject to such exemptions.

Findings and Purpose

Sec. 3. (a) *Findings.* The transactions subject to this Act are entered into regularly in interstate and international commerce and are affected with a national public interest by providing a means for managing and assuming price risks, discovering prices, or disseminating pricing information through trading in liquid, fair and financially secure trading facilities.

(b) *Purpose.* It is the purpose of this Act to serve the public interests described in subsection (a) through a system of effective self-regulation of trading facilities, clearing systems, market participants and market professionals under the oversight of the Commission. To foster these public interests, it is further the purpose of this Act to deter and prevent price manipulation or any other disruptions to market integrity; to ensure the financial integrity of all transactions subject to this Act and the avoidance of systemic risk; to protect all market participants from fraudulent or other abusive sales practices and misuses of customer assets; and to promote responsible innovation and fair competition among boards of trade, other markets and market participants.

Regulation of Futures Trading and Foreign Transactions

Sec. 4. (a) *Restriction on Futures Trading.* Unless exempted by the Commission pursuant to subsection (c) or by subsection (e), it shall be unlawful for any person to offer to enter into, to enter into, to execute, to confirm the execution of, or to conduct any office or business anywhere in the United States, its territories or possessions, for the purpose of soliciting or accepting any order for, or otherwise dealing in, any transaction in, or in connection with, a contract for the purchase or sale of a commodity for future delivery (other than a contract which is made on or subject to the rules of a board of trade, exchange, or market located outside the United States, its territories or possessions) unless—

(1) such transaction is conducted on or subject to the rules of a board of trade which has been designated or registered by the Commission as a contract market or derivatives transaction execution facility for such commodity;

(2) such contract is executed or consummated by or through a contract market; and

(3) such contract is evidenced by a record in writing which shows the date, the parties to such contract and their addresses, the property covered and its price, and the terms of delivery: *Provided,* That each contract market or derivatives transaction execution facility member shall keep such record for a period of three years from the date thereof, or for a longer period if the Commission shall so direct, which record shall at all times be open to the inspection of any representative of the Commission or the Department of Justice.

(b) *Regulation of Foreign Transactions by United States Persons.*

(1) *Foreign Boards of Trade.*

(A) *Registration.* The Commission may adopt rules and regulations requiring registration with the Commission for a foreign board of trade that provides the members of the foreign board of trade or other participants located in the United States with direct access to the electronic trading and order matching system of the foreign board of trade, including rules and regulations prescribing procedures and requirements applicable to the registration of such foreign boards of trade. For purposes of this paragraph, "direct access" refers to an explicit grant of authority by a foreign board of trade to an identified member or other participant located in the United States to enter trades directly into the trade matching system of the foreign board of trade. In adopting such rules and regulations, the commission shall consider—

(i) whether any such foreign board of trade is subject to comparable, comprehensive supervision and regulation by the appropriate governmental authorities in the foreign board of trade's home country; and

(ii) any previous commission findings that the foreign board of trade is subject to comparable comprehensive supervision and regulation by the appropriate government authorities in the foreign board of trade's home country.

(B) *Linked Contracts.* The Commission may not permit a foreign board of trade to provide to the members of the foreign board of trade or other participants located in the United States direct access to the electronic trading and order-matching system of the foreign board of trade with respect to an agreement, contract, or transaction that settles against any price (including the daily or final settlement price) of 1 or more contracts listed for trading on a registered entity, unless the Commission determines that—

(i) the foreign board of trade makes public daily trading information regarding the agreement, contract, or transaction that is comparable to the daily trading information published by the registered entity for the 1 or more contracts against which the agreement, contract, or transaction traded on the foreign board of trade settles; and

(ii) the foreign board of trade (or the foreign futures authority that oversees the foreign board of trade)—

(I) adopts position limits (including related hedge exemption provisions) for the agreement, contract, or transaction that are comparable to the position limits (including related hedge exemption provisions) adopted by the registered entity for the 1 or more contracts against which the agreement, contract, or transaction traded on the foreign board of trade settles;

(II) has the authority to require or direct market participants to limit, reduce, or liquidate any position the foreign board of trade (or the foreign futures authority that oversees the foreign board of trade) determines to be necessary to pre-vent or reduce the threat of price manipulation, excessive speculation as described in section 4a, price distortion, or disruption of delivery or the cash settlement process;

(III) agrees to promptly notify the Commission, with regard to the agreement, contract, or transaction that settles against any price (including the daily or final settlement price) of 1 or more contracts listed for trading on a registered entity, of any change regarding—

(aa) the information that the foreign board of trade will make publicly available;

(bb) the position limits that the foreign board of trade or foreign futures authority will adopt and enforce;

(cc) the position reductions required to prevent manipulation, excessive speculation as described in section 4a, price distortion, or disruption of delivery or the cash settlement process; and

(dd) any other area of interest expressed by the Commission to the foreign board of trade or foreign futures authority;

(IV) provides information to the Commission regarding large trader positions in the agreement, contract, or transaction that is comparable to the large trader position information collected by the Commission for the 1 or more contracts against which the agreement, contract, or transaction traded on the foreign board of trade settles; and

(V) provides the Commission such information as is necessary to publish reports on aggregate trader positions for the agreement, contract, or transaction traded on the foreign board of trade that are comparable to such reports on aggregate trader positions for the 1 or more contracts against which the agreement, contract, or transaction traded on the foreign board of trade settles.

(C) *Existing Foreign Boards of Trade.* Subparagraphs (A) and (B) shall not be effective with respect to any foreign board of trade to which, prior to the date of enactment of this paragraph, the Commission granted direct access permission until the date that is 180 days after that date of enactment.

(2) *Persons Located in the United States.*

(A) *In General.* The Commission may adopt rules and regulations proscribing fraud and requiring minimum financial standards, the disclosure of risk, the filing of reports, the keeping of books and records, the safeguarding of customers' funds, and registration with the Commission by any person located in the United States, its territories or possessions, who engages in the offer or sale of any contract of sale of a commodity for future delivery that is made or to be made on or subject to the rules of a board of trade, exchange, or market located outside the United States, its territories or possessions.

(B) *Different Requirements.* Rules and regulations described in subparagraph (A) may impose different requirements for such persons depending upon the particular foreign board of trade, exchange, or market involved.

(C) *Prohibition.* Except as provided in paragraphs (1) and (2), no rule or regulation may be adopted by the Commission under this subsection that that—

(i) requires Commission approval of any contract, rule, regulation, or action of any foreign board of trade, exchange, or market, or clearinghouse for such board of trade, exchange, or market; or

(ii) governs in any way any rule or contract term or action of any foreign board of trade, exchange, or market, or clearinghouse for such board of trade, exchange, or market.

(c) *Public Interest Exemptions.*

(1) In order to promote responsible economic or financial innovation and fair competition, the Commission by rule, regulation, or order, after notice and opportunity for hearing, may (on its own initiative or on application of any person, including any board of trade designated or registered as a contract market or derivatives transaction execution facility for transactions for future delivery

in any commodity under section 5 of this Act) exempt any agreement, contract, or transaction (or class thereof) that is otherwise subject to subsection (a) (including any person or class of persons offering, entering into, rendering advice or rendering other services with respect to, the agreement, contract, or transaction), either unconditionally or on stated terms or conditions or for stated periods and either retroactively or prospectively, or both, from any of the requirements of subsection (a), or from any other provision of this Act (except subparagraphs (C)(ii) and (D) of section 2(a)(1)), except that—

(A) unless the Commission is expressly authorized by any provision described in this subparagraph to grant exemptions, with respect to amendments made by subtitle A of the Wall Street Transparency and Accountability Act of 2010—

(i) with respect to—

(I) paragraphs (2), (3), (4), (5), and (7), paragraph (18)(A)(vii)(III), paragraphs (23), (24), (31), (32), (38), (39), (41), (42), (46), (47), (48), and (49) of section 1a, and sections 2(a)(13), 2(c)(1)(D), 4a(a), 4a(b), 4d(c), 4d(d), 4r, 4s, 5b(a), 5b(b), 5(d), 5(g), 5(h), 5b(c), 5b(i), 8e, and 21; and

(II) section 206(e) of the Gramm–Leach–Bliley Act; and

(ii) in sections 721(c) and 742 of the Dodd–Frank Wall Street Reform and Consumer Protection Act; and

(B) the Commission and the Securities and Exchange Commission may by rule, regulation, or order jointly exclude any agreement, contract, or transaction from section 2(a)(1)(D) if the Commissions determine that the exemption would be consistent with the public interest.

(2) The Commission shall not grant any exemption under paragraph (1) from any of the requirements of subsection (a) unless the Commission determines that—

(A) the requirement should not be applied to the agreement, contract, or transaction for which the exemption is sought and that the exemption would be consistent with the public interest and the purposes of this Act; and

(B) the agreement, contract, or transaction—

(i) will be entered into solely between appropriate persons; and

(ii) will not have a material adverse effect on the ability of the Commission or any contract market or derivatives transaction execution facility to discharge its regulatory or self-regulatory duties under this Act.

(3) For purposes of this subsection, the term "appropriate person" shall be limited to the following persons or classes thereof:

(A) A bank or trust company (acting in an individual or fiduciary capacity).

(B) A savings association.

(C) An insurance company.

(D) An investment company subject to regulation under the Investment Company Act of 1940.

(E) A commodity pool formed or operated by a person subject to regulation under this Act.

(F) A corporation, partnership, proprietorship, organization, trust, or other business entity with a net worth exceeding $1,000,000 or total assets exceeding $5,000,000, or the obligations of which under the agreement, contract or transaction are guaranteed or otherwise supported by a letter of credit or keepwell, support, or other agreement by any such entity or by an entity referred to in subparagraph (A), (B), (C), (H), (I), or (K) of this paragraph.

(G) An employee benefit plan with assets exceeding $1,000,000, or whose investment decisions are made by a bank, trust company, insurance company, investment adviser registered under the Investment Advisers Act of 1940, or a commodity trading advisor subject to regulation under this Act.

(H) Any governmental entity (including the United States, any state, or any foreign government) or political subdivision thereof, or any multinational or supranational entity or any instrumentality, agency, or department of any of the foregoing.

(I) A broker-dealer subject to regulation under the Securities Exchange Act of 1934 acting on its own behalf or on behalf of another appropriate person.

(J) A futures commission merchant, floor broker, or floor trader subject to regulation under this Act acting on its own behalf or on behalf of another appropriate person.

(K) Such other persons that the Commission determines to be appropriate in light of their financial or other qualifications, or the applicability of appropriate regulatory protections.

(4) During the pendency of an application for an order granting an exemption under paragraph (1), the Commission may limit the public availability of any information received from the applicant if the applicant submits a written request to limit disclosure contemporaneous with the application, and the Commission determines that—

(A) the information sought to be restricted constitutes a trade secret; or

(B) public disclosure of the information would result in material competitive harm to the applicant.

(5) The Commission may—

(A) promptly following the enactment of this subsection, or upon application by any person, exercise the exemptive authority granted under paragraph (1) with respect to classes of hybrid instruments that are predominantly securities or depository instruments, to the extent that such instruments may be regarded as subject to the provisions of this Act; or

(B) promptly following the enactment of this subsection, or upon application by any person, exercise the exemptive authority granted under paragraph (1) effective as of October 23, 1974, with respect to classes of swap agreements (as defined in section 101 of title 11, United States Code) that are not part of a fungible class of agreements that are standardized as to their material economic terms, to the extent that such agreements may be regarded as subject to the provisions of this Act.

Any exemption pursuant to this paragraph shall be subject to such terms and conditions as the Commission shall determine to be appropriate pursuant to paragraph (1).

(6) If the Commission determines that the exemption would be consistent with the public interest and the purposes of this Act, the Commission shall, in accordance with paragraphs (1) and (2), exempt from the requirements of this Act an agreement, contract, or transaction that is entered into—

(A) pursuant to a tariff or rate schedule approved or permitted to take effect by the Federal Energy Regulatory Commission;

(B) pursuant to a tariff or rate schedule establishing rates or charges for, or protocols governing, the sale of electric energy approved or permitted to take effect by the regulatory authority of the State or municipality having jurisdiction to regulate rates and charges for the sale of electric energy within the State or municipality; or

(C) between entities described in section 201(f) of the Federal Power Act.

(d) *Effect of Exemption on Investigative Authority of Commission.* The granting of an exemption under this section shall not affect the authority of the Commission under any other provision of this Act to conduct investigations in order to determine compliance with the requirements or conditions of such exemption or to take enforcement action for any violation of any provision of this Act or any rule, regulation or order thereunder caused by the failure to comply with or satisfy such conditions or requirements.

(e) *Liability of Registered Persons Trading on a Foreign Board of Trade.*

(1) *In General.* A person registered with the Commission, or exempt from registration by the Commission, under this Act may not be found to have violated subsection (a) with respect to a transaction in, or in connection with, a contract of sale of a commodity for future delivery if the person

(A) has reason to believe that the transaction and the contract is made on or subject to the rules of a foreign board of trade that is

(i) legally organized under the laws of a foreign country;

(ii) authorized to act as a board of trade by a foreign futures authority; and

(iii) subject to regulation by the foreign futures authority; and

(B) has not been determined by the Commission to be operating in violation of subsection (a).

(2) *Rule of Construction.* Nothing in this subsection shall be construed as implying or creating any presumption that a board of trade, exchange, or market is located outside the United States, or its territories or possessions, for purposes of subsection (a).

Excessive Speculation

Sec. 4a. (a) *Burden on Interstate Commerce; Trading or Position Limits.*

(1) *In General.* Excessive speculation in any commodity under contracts of sale of such commodity for future delivery made on or subject to the rules of contract markets or derivatives transaction execution facilities, or swaps that perform or affect a significant price discovery function with respect to registered entities causing sudden or unreasonable fluctuations or unwarranted changes in the price of such commodity, is an undue and unnecessary burden on interstate commerce in such commodity. For the purpose of diminishing, eliminating, or preventing such burden, the Commission shall, from time to time, after due notice and opportunity for hearing, by rule, regulation, or order, proclaim and fix such limits on the amounts of trading which may be done or positions which may be held by any person, including any group or class of traders under contracts of sale of such commodity for future delivery on or subject to the rules of any contract market or derivatives transaction execution facility, or swaps traded on or subject to the rules of a designated contract market or a swap execution facility, or swaps not traded on or subject to the rules of a designated contract market or a swap execution facility that performs a significant price discovery function with respect to a registered entity as the Commission finds are necessary to diminish, eliminate, or prevent such burden. In determining whether any person has exceeded such limits, the positions held and trading done by any persons directly or indirectly controlled by such person shall be included with the positions held and trading done by such person; and further, such limits upon positions and trading shall apply to positions held by, and trading done by, two or more persons acting pursuant to an expressed or implied agreement or understanding, the same as if the positions were held by, or the trading were done by, a single person. Nothing in this section shall be construed to prohibit the Commission from fixing different trading or position limits for different commodities, markets, futures, or delivery months, or for different number of days remaining until the last day of trading in a contract, or different trading limits for buying and selling operations, or different limits for the purposes of paragraphs (1) and (2) of subsection (b) of this section, or from exempting transactions normally known to the trade as "spreads" or "straddles" or "arbitrage" or from fixing limits applying to such transactions or positions different from limits fixed for other transactions or positions. The word "arbitrage" in domestic markets shall be defined to mean the same as a "spread" or "straddle". The Commission is authorized to define the term "international arbitrage".

(2) *Establishment of Limitations.*

(A) *In General.* In accordance with the standards set forth in paragraph (1) of this subsection and consistent with the good faith exception cited in subsection (b)(2), with respect to physical commodities other than excluded commodities as defined by the Commission, the Commission shall by rule, regulation, or order establish limits on the amount of positions, as appropriate, other than bona fide hedge positions, that may be held by any person with respect to contracts of sale for future delivery or with respect to options on the contracts or commodities traded on or subject to the rules of a designated contract market.

(B) *Timing.*

(i) *Exempt Commodities.* For exempt commodities, the limits required under subparagraph (A) shall be established within 180 days after the date of the enactment of this paragraph.

(ii) *Agricultural Commodities.* For agricultural commodities, the limits required under subparagraph (A) shall be established within 270 days after the date of the enactment of this paragraph.

(C) *Goal.* In establishing the limits required under subparagraph (A), the Commission shall strive to ensure that trading on foreign boards of trade in the same commodity will be subject to comparable limits and that any limits to be imposed by the Commission will not cause price discovery in the commodity to shift to trading on the foreign boards of trade.

(3) *Specific Limitations.* In establishing the limits required in paragraph (2), the Commission, as appropriate, shall set limits—

(A) on the number of positions that may be held by any person for the spot month, each other month, and the aggregate number of positions that may be held by any person for all months; and

(B) to the maximum extent practicable, in its discretion—

(i) to diminish, eliminate, or prevent excessive speculation as described under this section;

(ii) to deter and prevent market manipulation, squeezes, and corners;

(iii) to ensure sufficient market liquidity for bona fide hedgers; and

(iv) to ensure that the price discovery function of the underlying market is not disrupted.

(4) *Significant Price Discovery Function.* In making a determination whether a swap performs or affects a significant price discovery function with respect to regulated markets, the Commission shall consider, as appropriate:

(A) *Price Linkage.* The extent to which the swap uses or otherwise relies on a daily or final settlement price, or other major price parameter, of another contract traded on a regulated market based upon the same underlying commodity, to value a position, transfer or convert a position, financially settle a position, or close out a position.

(B) *Arbitrage.* The extent to which the price for the swap is sufficiently related to the price of another contract traded on a regulated market based upon the same underlying commodity so as to permit market participants to effectively arbitrage between the markets by simultaneously maintaining positions or executing trades in the swaps on a frequent and recurring basis.

(C) *Material Price Reference.* The extent to which, on a frequent and recurring basis, bids, offers, or transactions in a contract traded on a regulated market are directly based on, or are determined by referencing, the price generated by the swap.

(D) *Material Liquidity.* The extent to which the volume of swaps being traded in the commodity is sufficient to have a material effect on another contract traded on a regulated market.

(E) *Other Material Factors.* Such other material factors as the Commission specifies by rule or regulation as relevant to determine whether a swap serves a significant price discovery function with respect to a regulated market.

(5) *Economically Equivalent Contracts.*

(A) Notwithstanding any other provision of this section, the Commission shall establish limits on the amount of positions, including aggregate position limits, as appropriate, other than bona fide hedge positions, that may be held by any person with respect to swaps that are economically equivalent to contracts of sale for future delivery or to options on the contracts or commodities traded on or subject to the rules of a designated contract market subject to paragraph (2).

(B) In establishing limits pursuant to subparagraph (A), the Commission shall—

(i) develop the limits concurrently with limits established under paragraph (2), and the limits shall have similar requirements as under paragraph (3)(B); and

(ii) establish the limits simultaneously with limits established under paragraph (2).

(6) *Aggregate Position Limits.* The Commission shall, by rule or regulation, establish limits (including related hedge exemption provisions) on the aggregate number or amount of positions in contracts based upon the same underlying commodity (as defined by the Commission) that may be held by any person, including any group or class of traders, for each month across—

(A) contracts listed by designated contract markets;

(B) with respect to an agreement contract, or transaction that settles against any price (including the daily or final settlement price) of 1 or more contracts listed for trading on a registered entity, contracts traded on a foreign board of trade that provides members or other participants located in the United States with direct access to its electronic trading and order matching system; and

(C) swap contracts that perform or affect a significant price discovery function with respect to regulated entities.

(7) *Exemptions.* The Commission, by rule, regulation, or order, may exempt, conditionally or unconditionally, any person or class of persons, any swap or class of swaps, any contract of sale of a commodity for future delivery or class of such contracts, any option or class of options, or any transaction or class of transactions from any requirement it may establish under this section with respect to position limits.

(b) *Prohibition on Trading or Positions in Excess of Limits Fixed by Commission.* The Commission shall in such rule, regulation, or order, fix a reasonable time (not to exceed ten days) after the promulgation of the rule, regulation, or order; after which, and until such rule, regulation, or order is suspended, modified, or revoked, it shall be unlawful for any person—

(1) directly or indirectly to buy or sell, or agree to buy or sell, under contracts of sale of such commodity for future delivery on or subject to the rules of the contract market or markets or swap execution facility or facilities with respect to a significant price discovery contract to which the rule, regulation, or order applies, any amount of such commodity during any one business day in excess of any trading limit fixed for one business day by the Commission in such rule, regulation, or order for or with respect to such commodity; or

(2) directly or indirectly to hold or control a net long or a net short position in any commodity for future delivery on or subject to the rules of any contract market or swap execution facility with respect to a significant price discovery contract in excess of any position limit fixed by the Commission for or with respect to such commodity: *Provided*, That such position limit shall not apply to a position acquired in good faith prior to the effective date of such rule, regulation, or order.

(c)(1) *Applicability to Bona Fide Hedging Transactions or Positions.* No rule, regulation, or order issued under subsection (a) of this section shall apply to transactions or positions which are shown to be bona fide hedging transactions or positions, as such terms shall be defined by the Commission by rule, regulation, or order consistent with the purposes of this Act. Such terms may be defined to permit producers, purchasers, sellers, middlemen, and users of a commodity or a product derived therefrom to hedge their legitimate anticipated business needs for that period of time into the future for which an appropriate futures contract is open and available on an exchange. To determine the adequacy of this Act and the powers of the Commission acting thereunder to prevent unwarranted price pressures by large hedgers, the Commission shall monitor and analyze the trading activities of the largest hedgers, as determined by the Commission, operating in the cattle, hog, or pork belly markets and shall report its findings and recommendations to the Senate Committee on Agriculture, Nutrition, and Forestry and the House Committee on Agriculture in its annual reports for at least two years following the date of enactment of the Futures Trading Act of 1982.

(2) For the purposes of implementation of subsection (a)(2) for contracts of sale for future delivery or options on the contracts or commodities, the Commission shall define what constitutes a bona fide hedging transaction or position as a transaction or position that—

(A)(i) represents a substitute for transactions made or to be made or positions taken or to be taken at a later time in a physical marketing channel;

(ii) is economically appropriate to the reduction of risks in the conduct and management of a commercial enterprise; and

(iii) arises from the potential change in the value of—

(I) assets that a person owns, produces, manufactures, processes, or merchandises or anticipates owning, producing, manufacturing, processing, or merchandising;

(II) liabilities that a person owns or anticipates incurring; or

(III) services that a person provides, purchases, or anticipates providing or purchasing; or

(B) reduces risks attendant to a position resulting from a swap that

(i) was executed opposite a counterparty for which the transaction would qualify as a bona fide hedging transaction pursuant to subparagraph (A); or

(ii) meets the requirements of subparagraph (A).

(d) *Persons Subject to Regulation; Applicability to Transactions Made by or on Behalf of United States.* This section shall apply to a person that is registered as a futures commission merchant, an introducing broker, or a floor broker under authority of this Act only to the extent that transactions made by such person are made on behalf of or for the account or benefit of such person. This section shall not apply to transactions made by, or on behalf of, or at the direction of, the United States, or a duly authorized agency thereof.

(e) *Rulemaking Power and Penalties for Violation.* Nothing in this section shall prohibit or impair the adoption by any contract market, derivatives transaction execution facility, or by any other board of trade licensed, designated, or registered by the Commission or by any electronic trading facility of any bylaw, rule, regulation, or resolution fixing limits on the amount of trading which may be done or positions which may be held by any person under contracts of sale of any commodity for future delivery traded on or subject to the rules of such contract market or derivatives transaction execution facility or on an electronic trading facility, or under options on such contracts or commodities traded on or subject to the rules of such contract market, derivatives transaction execution facility, or electronic trading facility or such board of trade: *Provided,* That if the Commission shall have fixed limits under this section for any contract or under section 4c of this Act for any commodity option, then the limits fixed by the bylaws, rules, regulations, and resolutions adopted by such contract market, derivatives transaction execution facility, or electronic trading facility or such board of trade shall not be higher than the limits fixed by the Commission. It shall be a violation of this Act for any person to violate any bylaw, rule, regulation, or resolution of any contract market, derivatives transaction execution facility, or other board of trade licensed, designated, or registered by the Commission or electronic trading facility with respect to a significant price discovery contract fixing limits on the amount of trading which may be done or positions which may be held by any person under contracts of sale of any commodity for future delivery or under options on such contracts or commodities, if such bylaw, rule, regulation, or resolution has been approved by the Commission or certified by a registered entity pursuant to section 5c(c)(1): *Provided,* That the provisions of section 9(a)(5) of this Act shall apply only to those who knowingly violate such limits.

Contracts Designed to Defraud or Mislead

Sec. 4b. (a) *Unlawful Actions.* It shall be unlawful—

(1) for any person, in or in connection with any order to make, or the making of, any contract of sale of any commodity in interstate commerce or for future delivery that is made, or to be made, on or subject to the rules of a designated contract market, for or on behalf of any other person; or

(2) for any person, in or in connection with any order to make, or the making of, any contract of sale of any commodity for future delivery, or swap, that is made, or to be made, for or on behalf of, or with, any other person, other than on or subject to the rules of a designated contract market—

(A) to cheat or defraud or attempt to cheat or defraud the other person;

(B) willfully to make or cause to be made to the other person any false report or statement or willfully to enter or cause to be entered for the other person any false record;

(C) willfully to deceive or attempt to deceive the other person by any means whatsoever in regard to any order or contract or the disposition or execution of any order or contract, or in regard to any act of agency performed, with respect to any order or contract for or, in the case of paragraph (2), with the other person; or

(D)(i) to bucket an order if the order is either represented by the person as an order to be executed, or is required to be executed, on or subject to the rules of a designated contract market; or

(ii) to fill an order by offset against the order or orders of any other person, or willfully and knowingly and without the prior consent of the other person to become the buyer in respect to any selling order of the other person, or become the seller in respect to any buying order of the other person, if the order is either represented by the person as an order to be executed, or is required to be executed, on or subject to the rules of a designated contract market unless the order is executed in accordance with the rules of the designated contract market.

(b) *Clarification.* Subsection (a)(2) of this section shall not obligate any person, in or in connection with a transaction in a contract of sale of a commodity for future delivery, or swap, with another person, to disclose to the other person nonpublic information that may be material to the market price, rate, or level of the commodity or transaction, except as necessary to make any statement made to the other person in or in connection with the transaction not misleading in any material respect.

(c) *Buying and Selling Orders for Commodity.* Nothing in this section or in any other section of this chapter shall be construed to prevent a futures commission merchant or floor broker who shall have in hand, simultaneously, buying and selling orders at the market for different principals for a like quantity of a commodity for future delivery in the same month executing such buying and selling orders at the market price: Provided, That any such execution shall take place on the floor of the exchange where such orders are to be executed at public outcry across the ring and shall be duly reported, recorded, and cleared in the same manner as other orders executed on such exchange: And provided further, That such transactions shall be made in accordance with such rules and regulations as the Commission may promulgate regarding the manner of the execution of such transactions.

(d) *Inapplicability to Transactions on Foreign Exchanges.* Nothing in this section shall apply to any activity that occurs on a board of trade, exchange, or market, or clearinghouse for such board of trade, exchange, or market, located outside the United States, or territories or possessions of the United States, involving any contract of sale of a commodity for future delivery that is made, or to be made, on or subject to the rules of such board of trade, exchange, or market.

(e) It shall be unlawful for any person, directly or indirectly, by the use of any means or instrumentality of interstate commerce, or of the mails, or of any facility of any registered entity, in or in connection with any order to make, or the making of, any contract of sale of any commodity for future delivery (or option on such a contract), or any swap, on a group or index of securities (or any interest therein or based on the value thereof)—

(1) to employ any device, scheme, or artifice to defraud;

(2) to make any untrue statement of a material fact or to omit to state a material fact necessary in order to make the statements made, in the light of the circumstances under which they were made, not misleading; or

(3) to engage in any act, practice, or course of business which operates or would operate as a fraud or deceit upon any person.

Enforcement Authority

Sec. 4b–1. (a) *Commodity Futures Trading Commission.* Except as provided in subsections (b), (c), and (d), the Commission shall have exclusive authority to enforce the provisions of subtitle A of the Wall Street Transparency and Accountability Act of 2010 with respect to any person.

(b) *Prudential Regulators.* The prudential regulators shall have exclusive authority to enforce the provisions of section 4s(e) with respect to swap dealers or major swap participants for which they are the prudential regulator.

(c) *Referrals.*

(1) *Prudential Regulators.* If the prudential regulator for a swap dealer or major swap participant has cause to believe that the swap dealer or major swap participant, or any affiliate or division of the swap dealer or major swap participant, may have engaged in conduct that constitutes a violation of the nonprudential requirements of this Act (including section 4s or rules adopted by the Commission under that section), the prudential regulator may promptly notify the Commission in a written report that includes—

(A) a request that the Commission initiate an enforcement proceeding under this Act; and

(B) an explanation of the facts and circumstances that led to the preparation of the written report.

(2) *Commission.* If the Commission has cause to believe that a swap dealer or major swap participant that has a prudential regulator may have engaged in conduct that constitutes a violation of any prudential requirement of section 4s or rules adopted by the Commission under that section, the Commission may notify the prudential regulator of the conduct in a written report that includes—

(A) a request that the prudential regulator initiate an enforcement proceeding under this Act or any other Federal law (including regulations); and

(B) an explanation of the concerns of the Commission, and a description of the facts and circumstances, that led to the preparation of the written report.

(d) *Backstop Enforcement Authority.*

(1) *Initiation of Enforcement Proceeding by Prudential Regulator.* If the Commission does not initiate an enforcement proceeding before the end of the 90–day period beginning on the date on which the Commission receives a written report under subsection (c)(1), the prudential regulator may initiate an enforcement proceeding.

(2) *Initiation of Enforcement Proceeding by Commission.* If the prudential regulator does not initiate an enforcement proceeding before the end of the 90–day period beginning on the date on which the prudential regulator receives a written report under subsection (c)(2), the Commission may initiate an enforcement proceeding.

Prohibited Transactions

Sec. 4c. (a) *In General.*

(1) *Prohibition.* It shall be unlawful for any person to offer to enter into, enter into, or confirm the execution of a transaction described in paragraph (2) involving the purchase or sale of any commodity for future delivery (or any option on such a transaction or option on a commodity) or swap if the transaction is used or may be used to—

(A) hedge any transaction in interstate commerce in the commodity or the product or byproduct of the commodity;

(B) determine the price basis of any such transaction in interstate commerce in the commodity; or

(C) deliver any such commodity sold, shipped, or received in interstate commerce for the execution of the transaction.

(2) *Transaction.* A transaction referred to in paragraph (1) is a transaction that—

(A)(i) is, of the character of, or is commonly known to the trade as, a "wash sale" or "accommodation trade"; or

(ii) is a fictitious sale; or

(B) is used to cause any price to be reported, registered, or recorded that is not a true and bona fide price.

(3) *Contract of Sale.* It shall be unlawful for any employee or agent of any department or agency of the Federal Government or any Member of Congress or employee of Congress (as such terms are defined under section 2 of the STOCK Act) or any judicial officer or judicial employee (as such terms are defined, respectively, under section 2 of the STOCK Act) who, by virtue of the employment or position of the Member, officer, employee or agent, acquires information that may affect or tend to affect the price of any commodity in interstate commerce, or for future delivery, or any swap, and which information has not been disseminated by the department or agency of the Federal Government holding or creating the information or by Congress or by the judiciary in a manner which makes it generally available to the trading public, or disclosed in a criminal, civil, or administrative hearing, or in a congressional, administrative, or Government Accountability Office report, hearing, audit, or investigation, to use the information in his personal capacity and for personal gain to enter into, or offer to enter into—

(A) a contract of sale of a commodity for future delivery (or option on such a contract);

(B) an option (other than an option executed or traded on a national securities exchange registered pursuant to section 6(a) of the Securities Exchange Act of 1934); or

(C) a swap.

(4) *Nonpublic Information.*

(A) *Imparting of Nonpublic Information.* It shall be unlawful for any employee or agent of any department or agency of the Federal Government or any Member of Congress or employee of Congress or any judicial officer or judicial employee who, by virtue of the employment or position of the Member, officer, employee or agent, acquires information that may affect or tend to affect the price of any commodity in interstate commerce, or for future delivery, or any swap, and which information has not been disseminated by the department or agency of the Federal Government holding or creating the information or by Congress or by the judiciary in a manner which makes it generally available to the trading public, or disclosed in a criminal, civil, or administrative hearing, or in a congressional, administrative, or Government Accountability Office report, hearing, audit, or investigation, to impart the information in his personal capacity and for personal gain with intent to assist another person, directly or indirectly, to use the information to enter into, or offer to enter into—

(i) a contract of sale of a commodity for future delivery (or option on such a contract);

(ii) an option (other than an option executed or traded on a national securities exchange registered pursuant to section 6(a) of the Securities Exchange Act of 1934); or

(iii) a swap.

(B) *Knowing Use.* It shall be unlawful for any person who receives information imparted by any employee or agent of any department or agency of the Federal Government or any Member of Congress or employee of Congress or any judicial officer or judicial employee as described in subparagraph (A) to knowingly use such information to enter into, or offer to enter into—

(i) a contract of sale of a commodity for future delivery (or option on such a contract);

(ii) an option (other than an option executed or traded on a national securities exchange registered pursuant to section 6(a) of the Securities Exchange Act of 1934); or

(iii) a swap.

(C) *Theft of Nonpublic Information.* It shall be unlawful for any person to steal, convert, or misappropriate, by any means whatsoever, information held or created by any department or agency of the Federal Government or by Congress or by the judiciary that may affect or tend to affect the price of any commodity in interstate commerce, or for future delivery, or any swap, where such person knows, or acts in reckless disregard of the fact, that such information has not been disseminated by the department or agency of the Federal Government holding or creating the information or by Congress or by the judiciary in a manner which makes it generally available to the trading public, or disclosed in a criminal, civil, or administrative hearing, or in a congressional, administrative, or Government Accountability Office report, hearing, audit, or investigation, and to use such information, or to impart such information with the intent to assist another person, directly or indirectly, to use such information to enter into, or offer to enter into—

(i) a contract of sale of a commodity for future delivery (or option on such a contract);

(ii) an option (other than an option executed or traded on a national securities exchange registered pursuant to section 6(a) of the Securities Exchange Act of 1934); or

(iii) a swap, provided, however, that nothing in this subparagraph shall preclude a person that has provided information concerning, or generated by, the person, its operations or activities, to any employee or agent of any department or agency of the Federal Government to Congress, any Member of Congress, any employee of Congress, any judicial officer, or any judicial employee, voluntarily or as required by law, from using such information to enter into, or offer to enter into, a contract of sale, option, or swap described in clauses (i), (ii), or (iii).

(5) *Disruptive Practices*. It shall be unlawful for any person to engage in any trading, practice, or conduct on or subject to the rules of a registered entity that—

(A) violates bids or offers;

(B) demonstrates intentional or reckless disregard for the orderly execution of transactions during the closing period; or

(C) is, is of the character of, or is commonly known to the trade as, "spoofing" (bidding or offering with the intent to cancel the bid or offer before execution).

(6) *Rulemaking Authority*. The Commission may make and promulgate such rules and regulations as, in the judgment of the Commission, are reasonably necessary to prohibit the trading practices described in paragraph (5) and any other trading practice that is disruptive of fair and equitable trading.

(7) *Use of Swaps to Defraud*. It shall be unlawful for any person to enter into a swap knowing, or acting in reckless disregard of the fact, that its counterparty will use the swap as part of a device, scheme, or artifice to defraud any third party.

(b) *Regulated Option Trading*. No person shall offer to enter into, enter into, or confirm the execution of, any transaction involving any commodity regulated under this Act which is of the character of, or is commonly known to the trade as, an "option", "privilege", "indemnity", "bid", "offer", "put", "call", "advance guaranty", or "decline guaranty", contrary to any rule, regulation, or order of the Commission prohibiting any such transaction or allowing any such transaction under such terms and conditions as the Commission shall prescribe. Any such order, rule, or regulation may be made only after notice and opportunity for hearing, and the Commission may set different terms and conditions for different markets.

(c) *Regulations for Elimination of Pilot Status of Commodity Option Transactions; Terms and Conditions of Options Trading*. Not later than 90 days after the date of the enactment of the Futures Trading Act of 1986, the Commission shall issue regulations—

(1) to eliminate the pilot status of its program for commodity option transactions involving the trading of options on contract markets, including any numerical restrictions on the number of commodities or option contracts for which a contract market may be designated; and

(2) otherwise to continue to permit the trading of such commodity options under such terms and conditions that the Commission from time to time may prescribe.

(d) *Dealer Options Exempt from Subsections (b) and (c) Prohibitions; Requirements*. Notwithstanding the provisions of subsection (c) of this section—

(1) any person domiciled in the United States who on May 1, 1978, was in the business of granting an option on a physical commodity, other than a commodity specifically set forth in section 2(a) of this Act prior to enactment of the Commodity Futures Trading Commission Act of 1974, and was in the business of buying, selling, producing, or otherwise using that commodity, may contin-

ue to grant or issue options on that commodity in accordance with Commission regulations in effect on August 17, 1978, until thirty days after the effective date of regulations issued by the Commission under clause (2) of this subsection: *Provided,* That if such person files an application for registration under the regulations issued under clause (2) of this subsection within thirty days after the effective date of such regulations, that person may continue to grant or issue options pending a final determination by the Commission on the application; and

(2) the Commission shall issue regulations that permit grantors and futures commission merchants to offer to enter into, enter into, or confirm the execution of, any commodity option transaction on a physical commodity subject to the provisions of subsection (b) of this section, other than a commodity specifically set forth in section 2(a) of this Act prior to enactment of the Commodity Futures Trading Commission Act of 1974, if—

(A) the grantor is a person domiciled in the United States who—

(i) is in the business of buying, selling, producing, or otherwise using the underlying commodity;

(ii) at all times has a net worth of at least $5,000,000 certified annually by an independent public accountant using generally accepted accounting principles;

(iii) notifies the Commission and every futures commission merchant offering the grantor's option if the grantor knows or has reason to believe that the grantor's net worth has fallen below $5,000,000;

(iv) segregates daily, exclusively for the benefit of purchasers, money, exempted securities (within the meaning of section 3(a)(12) of the Securities Exchange Act of 1934), commercial paper, bankers' acceptances, commercial bills, or unencumbered warehouse receipts, equal to an amount by which the value of each transaction exceeds the amount received or to be received by the grantor for such transaction;

(v) provides an identification number for each transaction; and

(vi) provides confirmation of all orders for such transactions executed, including the execution price and a transaction identification number;

(B) the futures commission merchant is a person who—

(i) has evidence that the grantor meets the requirements specified in subclause (A) of this clause;

(ii) treats and deals with all money, securities, or property received from its customers as payment of the purchase price in connection with such transactions, as belonging to such customers until the expiration of the term of the option, or, if the customer exercises the option, until all rights of the customer under the commodity option transaction have been fulfilled;

(iii) records each transaction in its customer's name by the transaction identification number provided by the grantor;

(iv) provides a disclosure statement to its customers, under regulations of the Commission, that discloses, among other things, all costs, including any markups or commissions involved in such transaction; and

(C) the grantor and futures commission merchant comply with any additional uniform and reasonable terms and conditions the Commission may prescribe, including registration with the Commission.

The Commission may permit persons not domiciled in the United States to grant options under this subsection, other than options on a commodity specifically set forth in section 2(a) of this Act prior to enactment of the Commodity Futures Trading Commission Act of 1974, under such additional rules, regulations, and orders as the Commission may adopt to provide protection to purchasers that are substantially the equivalent of those applicable to grantors domiciled in the United States. The Commission may terminate the right of any person to grant, offer, or sell options under this subsection only after a hearing, including a finding that the continuation of such right is contrary to the public interest: *Provided,* That pending the completion of such termination proceedings, the Commission may suspend the right to grant, offer, or sell options of any person whose activities in the Commission's judgment present a substantial risk to the public interest.

(e) *Rules and Regulations.* The Commission may adopt rules and regulations, after public notice and opportunity for a hearing on the record, prohibiting the granting, issuance, or sale of options permitted under subsection (d) of this section if the Commission determines that such options are contrary to the public interest.

(f) *Nonapplicability to Foreign Currency Options.* Nothing in this Act shall be deemed to govern or in any way be applicable to any transaction in an option on foreign currency traded on a national securities exchange.

(g) *Oral Orders.* The Commission shall adopt rules requiring that a contemporaneous written record be made, as practicable, of all orders for execution on the floor or subject to the rules of each contract market or derivatives transaction execution facility placed by a member of the contract market or derivatives transaction execution facility who is present on the floor at the time such order is placed.

Dealing by Unregistered Futures Commission Merchants or Introducing Merchants Prohibited

Sec. 4d. (a) *Futures Commission Merchant Registration Requirements; Duties of Merchants in Handling Customer Receipts.* It shall be unlawful for any person to be a futures commission merchant unless—

(1) such person shall have registered, under this Act, with the Commission as such futures commission merchant and such registration shall not have expired nor been suspended nor revoked; and

(2) such person shall, whether a member or nonmember of a contract market or derivatives transaction execution facility, treat and deal with all money, securities, and property received by such person to margin, guarantee, or secure the trades or contracts of any customer of such person, or accruing to such customer as the result of such trades or contracts, as belonging to such customer. Such money, securities, and property shall be separately accounted for and shall not be commingled with the funds of such commission merchant or be used to margin or guarantee the trades or contracts, or to secure or extend the credit, of any customer or person other than the one for whom the same are held: *Provided, however,* That such money, securities, and property of the customers of such futures commission merchant may, for convenience, be commingled and deposited in the same account or accounts with any bank or trust company or with the clearing house organization of such contract market or derivatives transaction execution facility, and that such share thereof as in the normal course of business shall be necessary to margin, guarantee, secure, transfer, adjust, or settle the contracts or trades of such customers, or resulting market positions, with the clearing-house organization of such contract market or derivatives transaction execution facility or with any member of such contract market or derivatives transaction execution facility, may be withdrawn and applied to such purposes, including the payment of commissions, brokerage, interest, taxes, storage, and other charges, lawfully accruing in connection with such contracts and trades: *Provided, further,* That in accordance with such terms and conditions as the Commission may prescribe by rule, regulation, or order, such money, securities, and property of the customers of such futures commission merchant may be commingled and deposited as provided in this section with any other money, securities, and property received by such futures commission merchant and required by the Commission to be separately accounted for and treated and dealt with as belonging to the customers of such futures commission merchant: *Provided further,* That such money may be invested in obligations of the United States, in general obligations of any State or of any political subdivision thereof, and in obligations fully guaranteed as to principal and interest by the United States, such investments to be made in accordance with such rules and regulations and subject to such conditions as the Commission may prescribe.

(b) *Duties of Clearing Agencies, Depositories, and Others in Handling Customer Receipts.* It shall be unlawful for any person, including but not limited to any clearing agency of a contract market or derivatives transaction execution facility and any depository, that has received any money, securities, or property for deposit in a separate account as provided in paragraph (2) of this section, to hold, dispose of, or use any such money, securities, or property as belonging to the depositing futures commission merchant or any person other than the customers of such futures commission merchant.

(c) *Conflicts of Interest.* The Commission shall require that futures commission merchants and introducing brokers implement conflict-of-interest systems and procedures that—

(1) establish structural and institutional safeguards to ensure that the activities of any person within the firm relating to research or analysis of the price or market for any commodity are separated by appropriate informational partitions within the firm from the review, pressure, or over-

sight of persons whose involvement in trading or clearing activities might potentially bias the judgment or supervision of the persons; and

(2) address such other issues as the Commission determines to be appropriate.

(d) *Designation of Chief Compliance Officer.* Each futures commission merchant shall designate an individual to serve as its Chief Compliance Officer and perform such duties and responsibilities as shall be set forth in regulations to be adopted by the Commission or rules to be adopted by a futures association registered under section 17.

(e) *Rules to Avoid Duplicative Regulation of Dual Registrants.* Consistent with this Act, the Commission, in consultation with the Securities and Exchange Commission, shall issue such rules, regulations, or orders as are necessary to avoid duplicative or conflicting regulations applicable to any futures commission merchant registered with the Commission pursuant to section 4f(a) (except paragraph (2) thereof), that is also registered with the Securities and Exchange Commission pursuant to section 15(b) of the Securities Exchange Act (except paragraph (11) thereof), involving the application of—

(1) section 8, section 15(c)(3), and section 17 of the Securities Exchange Act of 1934 and the rules and regulations thereunder related to the treatment of customer funds, securities, or property, maintenance of books and records, financial reporting or other financial responsibility rules (as defined in section 3(a)(40) of the Securities Exchange Act of 1934), involving security futures products; and

(2) similar provisions of this Act and the rules and regulations thereunder involving security futures products.

(f) *Swaps.*

(1) *Registration Requirement.* It shall be unlawful for any person to accept any money, securities, or property (or to extend any credit in lieu of money, securities, or property) from, for, or on behalf of a swaps customer to margin, guarantee, or secure a swap cleared by or through a derivatives clearing organization (including money, securities, or property accruing to the customer as the result of such a swap), unless the person shall have registered under this Act with the Commission as a futures commission merchant, and the registration shall not have expired nor been suspended nor revoked.

(2) *Cleared Swaps.*

(A) *Segregation Required.* A futures commission merchant shall treat and deal with all money, securities, and property of any swaps customer received to margin, guarantee, or secure a swap cleared by or though a derivatives clearing organization (including money, securities, or property accruing to the swaps customer as the result of such a swap) as belonging to the swaps customer.

(B) *Commingling Prohibited.* Money, securities, and property of a swaps customer described in subparagraph (A) shall be separately accounted for and shall not be commingled with the funds of the futures commission merchant or be used to margin, secure, or guarantee any trades or contracts of any swaps customer or person other than the person for whom the same are held.

(3) *Exceptions.*

(A) *Use of Funds.*

(i) *In General.* Notwithstanding paragraph (2), money, securities, and property of swap customers of a futures commission merchant described in paragraph (2) may, for convenience, be commingled and deposited in the same account or accounts with any bank or trust company or with a derivatives clearing organization.

(ii) *Withdrawal.* Notwithstanding paragraph (2), such share of the money, securities, and property described in clause (i) as in the normal course of business shall be necessary to margin, guarantee, secure, transfer, adjust, or settle a cleared swap with a derivatives clearing organization, or with any member of the derivatives clearing organization, may be withdrawn and applied to such purposes, including the payment of commissions, brokerage, interest, taxes, storage, and other charges, lawfully accruing in connection with the cleared swap.

(B) *Commission Action.* Notwithstanding paragraph (2), in accordance with such terms and conditions as the Commission may prescribe by rule, regulation, or order, any money, securities, or property of the swaps customers of a futures commission merchant described in paragraph (2) may be commingled and deposited in customer accounts with any other money, securities, or property received by the futures commission merchant and required by the Commission to be separately accounted for and treated and dealt with as belonging to the swaps customer of the futures commission merchant.

(4) *Permitted Investments.* Money described in paragraph (2) may be invested in obligations of the United States, in general obligations of any State or of any political subdivision of a State, and in obligations fully guaranteed as to principal and interest by the United States, or in any other investment that the Commission may by rule or regulation prescribe, and such investments shall be made in accordance with such rules and regulations and subject to such conditions as the Commission may prescribe.

(5) *Commodity Contract.* A swap cleared by or through a derivatives clearing organization shall be considered to be a commodity contract as such term is defined in section 761 of title 11, United States Code, with regard to all money, securities, and property of any swaps customer received by a futures commission merchant or a derivatives clearing organization to margin, guarantee, or secure the swap (including money, securities, or property accruing to the customer as the result of the swap).

(6) *Prohibition.* It shall be unlawful for any person, including any derivatives clearing organization and any depository institution, that has received any money, securities, or property for deposit in a separate account or accounts as provided in paragraph (2) to hold, dispose of, or use any such money, securities, or property as belonging to the depositing futures commission merchant or any person other than the swaps customer of the futures commission merchant.

(g) It shall be unlawful for any person to be an introducing broker unless such person shall have registered under this Act with the Commission as an introducing broker and such registration shall not have expired nor been suspended nor revoked.

(h) Notwithstanding subsection (a)(2) or the rules and regulations thereunder, and pursuant to an exemption granted by the Commission under section 4(c) of this Act or pursuant to a rule or regulation, a futures commission merchant that is registered pursuant to section 4f(a)(1) of this Act and also registered as a broker or dealer pursuant to section 15(b)(1) of the Securities Exchange Act of 1934 may, pursuant to a portfolio margining program approved by the Securities and Exchange Commission pursuant to section 19(b) of the Securities Exchange Act of 1934, hold in a portfolio margining account carried as a securities account subject to section 15(c)(3) of the Securities Exchange Act of 1934 and the rules and regulations thereunder, a contract for the purchase or sale of a commodity for future delivery or an option on such a contract, and any money, securities or other property received from a customer to margin, guarantee or secure such a contract, or accruing to a customer as the result of such a contract. The Commission shall consult with the Securities and Exchange Commission to adopt rules to ensure that such transactions and accounts are subject to comparable requirements to the extent practical for similar products.

Dealings by Unregistered Floor Trader or Broker Prohibited

Sec. 4e. It shall be unlawful for any person to act as floor trader in executing purchases and sales, or as floor broker in executing any orders for the purchase or sale, of any commodity for future delivery, or involving any contracts of sale of any commodity for future delivery, on or subject to the rules of any contract market or derivatives transaction execution facility unless such person shall have registered, under this Act, with the Commission as such floor trader or floor broker and such registration shall not have expired nor been suspended nor revoked.

Registration and Financial Requirements; Risk Assessment

Sec. 4f. (a) *Registration of Futures Commission Merchants, Introducing Brokers, and Floor Brokers and Traders.*

(1) Any person desiring to register as a futures commission merchant, introducing broker, floor broker, or floor trader hereunder shall be registered upon application to the Commission. The application shall be made in such form and manner as prescribed by the Commission, giving such information and facts as the Commission may deem necessary concerning the business in which the applicant is or will be engaged, including in the case of an application of a futures commission merchant or an introducing broker, the names and addresses of the managers of all branch offices, and the names of such officers and partners, if a partnership, and of such officers, directors, and stockholders, if a corporation, as the Commission may direct. Such person, when registered hereunder, shall likewise continue to report and furnish to the Commission the above-mentioned information and such other information pertaining to such person's business as the Commission may re-

quire. Each registration shall expire on December 31 of the year for which issued or at such other time, not less than one year from the date of issuance, as the Commission may by rule, regulation, or order prescribe, and shall be renewed upon application therefor unless the registration has been suspended (and the period of such suspension has not expired) or revoked pursuant to the provisions of this Act.

(2) Notwithstanding paragraph (1), and except as provided in paragraph (3), any broker or dealer that is registered with the Securities and Exchange Commission shall be registered as a futures commission merchant or introducing broker, as applicable, if—

(A) the broker or dealer limits its solicitation of orders, acceptance of orders, or execution of orders, or placing of orders on behalf of others involving any contracts of sale of any commodity for future delivery, on or subject to the rules of any contract market or registered derivatives transaction execution facility to security futures products;

(B) the broker or dealer files written notice with the Commission in such form as the Commission, by rule, may prescribe containing such information as the Commission, by rule, may prescribe as necessary or appropriate in the public interest or for the protection of investors;

(C) the registration of the broker or dealer is not suspended pursuant to an order of the Securities and Exchange Commission; and

(D) the broker or dealer is a member of a national securities association registered pursuant to section 15A(a) of the Securities Exchange Act of 1934.

The registration shall be effective contemporaneously with the submission of notice, in written or electronic form, to the Commission.

(3) A floor broker or floor trader shall be exempt from the registration requirements of section 4e and paragraph (1) of this subsection if—

(A) the floor broker or floor trader is a broker or dealer registered with the Securities and Exchange Commission;

(B) the floor broker or floor trader limits its solicitation of orders, acceptance of orders, or execution of orders, or placing of orders on behalf of others involving any contracts of sale of any commodity for future delivery, on or subject to the rules of any contract market to security futures products; and

(C) the registration of the floor broker or floor trader is not suspended pursuant to an order of the Securities and Exchange Commission.

(4)(A) A broker or dealer that is registered as a futures commission merchant or introducing broker pursuant to paragraph (2), or that is a floor broker or floor trader exempt from registration pursuant to paragraph (3), shall be exempt from the following provisions of this Act and the rules thereunder:

(i) Subsections (b), (d), (e), and (g) of section 4c.

(ii) Sections 4d, 4e, and 4h.

(iii) Subsections (b) and (c) of this section.

(iv) Section 4j.

(v) Section 4k(1).

(vi) Section 4p.

(vii) Section 6d.

(viii) Subsections (d) and (g) of section 8.

(ix) Section 16.

(B)(i) Except as provided in clause (ii) of this subparagraph, but notwithstanding any other provision of this Act, the Commission, by rule, regulation, or order, may conditionally or unconditionally exempt any broker or dealer subject to the registration requirement of paragraph (2), or any broker or dealer exempt from registration pursuant to paragraph (3), from any provision of this Act or of any rule or regulation thereunder, to the extent the exemption is necessary or appropriate in the public interest and is consistent with the protection of investors.

(ii) The Commission shall, by rule or regulation, determine the procedures under which an exemptive order under this section shall be granted and may, in its sole discretion, decline to entertain any application for an order of exemption under this section.

(C)(i) A broker or dealer that is registered as a futures commission merchant or introducing broker pursuant to paragraph (2) or an associated person thereof, or that is a floor broker or floor trader exempt from registration pursuant to paragraph (3), shall not be required to become a member of any futures association registered under section 21.

(ii) No futures association registered under section 21 shall limit its members from carrying an account, accepting an order, or transacting business with a broker or dealer that is registered as a futures commission merchant or introducing broker pursuant to paragraph (2) or an associated person thereof, or that is a floor broker or floor trader exempt from registration pursuant to paragraph (3).

(b) *Financial Requirements for Futures Commission Merchants and Introducing Brokers.* Notwithstanding any other provisions of this Act, no person desiring to register as futures commission merchant or as introducing broker shall be so registered unless he meets such minimum financial requirements as the Commission may by regulation prescribe as necessary to insure his meeting his obligation as a registrant, and each person so registered shall at all times continue to meet such prescribed minimum financial requirements: *Provided,* That such minimum financial requirements will be considered met if the applicant for registration or registrant is a member of a contract market or derivatives transaction execution facility and conforms to minimum financial standards and related reporting requirements set by such contract market or derivatives transaction execution facility in its bylaws, rules, regulations, or resolutions and approved by the Commission as adequate to effectuate the purposes of this subsection.

(c) *Risk Assessment for Holding Company Systems.*

(1) As used in this subsection:

(i) The term "affiliated person" means any person directly or indirectly controlling, controlled by, or under common control with a futures commission merchant, as the Commission, by rule or regulation, may determine will effectuate the purposes of this subsection.

(ii) The term "Federal banking agency" shall have the same meaning as the term "appropriate Federal banking agency" in section 3(q) of the Federal Deposit Insurance Act.

(2)(A) Each registered futures commission merchant shall obtain such information and make and keep such records as the Commission, by rule or regulation, prescribes concerning the registered futures commission merchant's policies, procedures, or systems for monitoring and controlling financial and operational risks to it resulting from the activities of any of its affiliated persons, other than a natural person.

(B) The records required under subparagraph (A) shall describe, in the aggregate, each of the futures and other financial activities conducted by, and the customary sources of capital and funding of, those of its affiliated persons whose business activities are reasonably likely to have a material impact on the financial or operational condition of the futures commission merchant, including its adjusted net capital, its liquidity, or its ability to conduct or finance its operations.

(C) The Commission, by rule or regulation, may require summary reports of such information to be filed by the futures commission merchant with the Commission no more frequently than quarterly.

(3)(A) If, as a result of adverse market conditions or based on reports provided to the Commission pursuant to paragraph (2) or other available information, the Commission reasonably concludes that the Commission has concerns regarding the financial or operational condition of any registered futures commission merchant, the Commission may require the futures commission merchant to make reports concerning the futures and other financial activities of any of such person's affiliated persons, other than a natural person, whose business activities are reasonably likely to have a material impact on the financial or operational condition of the futures commission merchant.

(B) The Commission, in requiring reports pursuant to this paragraph, shall specify the information required, the period for which it is required, the time and date on which the information must be furnished, and whether the information is to be furnished directly to the Commission or to a contract market or derivatives transaction execution facility or other self-regulatory organization with primary responsibility for examining the registered futures commission merchant's financial and operational condition.

(4)(A) in developing and implementing reporting requirements pursuant to paragraph (2) with respect to affiliated persons subject to examination by or reporting requirements of a Federal banking agency, the Commission shall consult with and consider the views of each such Federal banking agency. If a Federal banking agency comments in writing on a proposed rule of the Commission under this subsection that has been published for comment, the Commission shall respond in writing to the written comment before adopting the proposed rule. The Commission shall, at the request of the Federal banking agency, publish the comment and response in the Federal Register at the time of publishing the adopted rule.

(B)(i) Except as provided in clause (ii), a registered futures commission merchant shall be considered to have complied with a recordkeeping or reporting requirement adopted pursuant to paragraph (2) concerning an affiliated person that is subject to examination by, or reporting requirements of, a Federal banking agency if the futures commission merchant utilizes for the recordkeeping or reporting requirement copies of reports filed by the affiliated person with the Federal banking agency pursuant to section 5211 of the Revised Statutes, section 9 of the Federal Reserve Act, section 7(a) of the Federal Deposit Insurance Act, section 10(b) of the Home Owners' Loan Act, or section 5 of the Bank Holding Company Act of 1956.

(ii) The Commission may, by rule adopted pursuant to paragraph (2), require any futures commission merchant filing the reports with the Commission to obtain, maintain, or report supplemental information if the Commission makes an explicit finding that the supplemental information is necessary to inform the Commission regarding potential risks to the futures commission merchant. Prior to requiring any such supplemental information, the Commission shall first request the Federal banking agency to expand its reporting requirements to include the information.

(5) Prior to making a request pursuant to paragraph (3) for information with respect to an affiliated person that is subject to examination by or reporting requirements of a Federal banking agency, the Commission shall—

(A) notify the agency of the information required with respect to the affiliated person; and

(B) consult with the agency to determine whether the information required is available from the agency and for other purposes, unless the Commission determines that any delay resulting from the consultation would be inconsistent with ensuring the financial and operational condition of the futures commission merchant or the stability or integrity of the futures markets.

(6) Nothing in this subsection shall be construed to permit the Commission to require any futures commission merchant to obtain, maintain, or furnish any examination report of any Federal banking agency or any supervisory recommendations or analysis contained in the report.

(7) No information provided to or obtained by the Commission from any Federal banking agency pursuant to a request under paragraph (5) regarding any affiliated person that is subject to examination by or reporting requirements of a Federal banking agency may be disclosed to any other person (other than as provided in section 8 or section 8a(6)), without the prior written approval of the Federal banking agency.

(8) The Commission shall notify a Federal banking agency of any concerns of the Commission regarding significant financial or operational risks resulting from the activities of any futures commission merchant to any affiliated person thereof that is subject to examination by or reporting requirements of the Federal banking agency.

(9) The Commission, by rule, regulation, or order, may exempt any person or class of persons under such terms and conditions and for such periods as the Commission shall provide in the rule, regulation, or order, from this subsection and the rules and regulations issued under this subsection. In granting the exemption, the Commission shall consider, among other factors—

(A) whether information of the type required under this subsection is available from a supervisory agency (as defined in section 1101(7) of the Right to Financial Privacy Act of 1978), a State insurance commission or similar State agency, the Securities and Exchange Commission, or a similar foreign regulator;

(B) the primary business of any affiliated person;

(C) the nature and extent of domestic or foreign regulation of the affiliated person's activities;

(D) the nature and extent of the registered futures commission merchant's commodity futures and options activities; and

(E) with respect to the registered futures commission merchant and its affiliated persons, on a consolidated basis, the amount and proportion of assets devoted to, and revenues derived from activities in the United States futures markets.

(10) Information required to be provided pursuant to this subsection shall be subject to section 8. Except as specifically provided in section 8 and

notwithstanding any other provision of law, the Commission shall not be compelled to disclose any information required to be reported under this subsection, or any information supplied to the Commission by any domestic or foreign regulatory agency that relates to the financial or operational condition of any affiliated person of a registered futures commission merchant.

(11) Nothing in paragraphs (1) through (10) shall be construed to supersede or to limit in any way the authority or powers of the Commission pursuant to any other provision of this Act or regulations issued under this Act.

Reporting and Recordkeeping

Sec. 4g. (a) *In General.* Every person registered hereunder as futures commission merchant, introducing broker floor broker, or floor trader shall make such reports as are required by the Commission regarding the transactions and positions of such person, and the transactions and positions of the customer thereof, in commodities for future delivery on any board of trade in the United States or elsewhere, and in any significant price discovery contract traded or executed on an electronic trading facility or any agreement, contract, or transaction that is treated by a derivatives clearing organization, whether registered or not registered, as fungible with a significant price discovery contract; shall keep books and records pertaining to such transactions and positions in such form and manner and for such period as may be required by the Commission; and shall keep such books and records open to inspection by any representative of the Commission or the United States Department of Justice.

(b) *Daily Trading Records: Registered Entities.* Every registered entity shall maintain daily trading records. The daily trading records shall include such information as the Commission shall prescribe by rule.

(c) *Daily Trading Records: Floor Brokers, Introducing Brokers, and Futures Commission Merchants.* Floor brokers, introducing brokers, and futures commission merchants shall maintain daily trading records for each customer in such manner and form as to be identifiable with the trades referred to in subsection (b).

(d) *Daily Trading Records: Form and Reports.* Daily trading records shall be maintained in a form suitable to the Commission for such period as may be required by the Commission. Reports shall be made from the records maintained at such times and at such places and in such form as the Commission may prescribe by rule, order, or regulation in order to protect the public interest and the interest of persons trading in commodity futures.

(e) *Disclosure of Information.* Before the beginning of trading each day, the exchange shall, insofar as is practicable and under terms and conditions specified by the Commission, make public the volume of trading on each type of contract for the previous day and such other information as the Commission deems necessary in the public interest and prescribes by rule, order, or regulation.

(f) *Authority of Commission to Make Separate Determinations Unimpaired.* Nothing contained in this section shall be construed to prohibit the Commission from making separate determinations for different registered entities when such determinations are warranted in the judgment of the Commission.

False Self-Representation as Registered Entity Member Prohibited

Sec. 4h. It shall be unlawful for any person falsely to represent such person to be a member of a registered entity or the representative or agent of such member, or to be a registrant under this Act or the representative or agent of any registrant, in soliciting or handling any order or contract for the purchase or sale of any commodity in interstate commerce or for future delivery, or falsely to represent in connection with the handling of any such order or contract that the same is to be or has been executed on, or by or through a member of, any registered entity.

Reports of Deals Equal to or in Excess of Trading Limits; Books and Records; Cash and Controlled Transactions

Sec. 4i. It shall be unlawful for any person to make any contract for the purchase or sale of any commodity for future delivery on or subject to the rules of any contract market or derivatives transaction execution facility, or any significant price discovery contract traded or executed on an electronic trading facility or any agreement, contract, or transaction that is treated by a derivatives clearing organization, whether registered or not registered, as fungible with a significant price discovery contract—

(1) if such person shall directly or indirectly make such contracts with respect to any commodity or any future of such commodity during any one day in an amount equal to or in excess of such amount as shall be fixed from time to time by the Commission, and

(2) if such person shall directly or indirectly have or obtain a long or short position in any commodity or any future of such commodity equal to or in excess of such amount as shall be fixed from time to time by the Commission,

unless such person files or causes to be filed with the properly designated officer of the Commission such reports regarding any transactions or positions described in clauses (1) and (2) hereof as the Commission may by rule or regulation require and unless, in accordance with rules and regulations of the Commission, such person shall keep books and records of all such transactions and positions and transactions and positions in any such commodity traded on or subject to the rules of any other board of trade or electronic trading facility, and of cash or spot transactions in, and inventories and purchase and sale commitments of such commodity. Such books and records shall show complete details concerning all such transactions, positions, inventories, and commitments, including the names and addresses of all persons having any interest therein, and shall be open at all times to inspection by any representative of the Commission or the Department of Justice. For the purposes of this section, the futures and cash or spot transactions and positions of any person shall include such transactions and positions of any persons directly or indirectly controlled by such person.

Restrictions on Dual Trading in Security Futures Products on Designated Contract Markets and Registered Derivatives Transaction Execution Facilities

Sec. 4j. (a) *Issuance of Regulations.* The Commission shall issue regulations to prohibit the privilege of dual trading in security futures products on each contract market and registered derivatives transaction execution facility. The regulations issued by the Commission under this section—

(1) shall provide that the prohibition of dual trading thereunder shall take effect upon issuance of the regulations; and

(2) shall provide exceptions, as the Commission determines appropriate, to ensure fairness and orderly trading in security futures product markets, including—

(A) exceptions for spread transactions and the correction of trading errors;

(B) allowance for a customer to designate in writing not less than once annually a named floor broker to execute orders for such customer, notwithstanding the regulations to prohibit the privilege of dual trading required under this section; and

(C) other measures reasonably designed to accommodate unique or special characteristics of individual boards of trade or contract markets, to address emergency or unusual market conditions, or otherwise to further the public interest consistent with the promotion of market efficiency, innovation, and expansion of investment opportunities, the protection of investors, and with the purposes of this section.

(b) *"Dual Trading" Defined.* As used in this section, the term "dual trading" means the execution of customer orders by a floor broker during the same trading session in which the floor broker executes any trade in the same contract market or registered derivatives transaction execution facility for—

(1) the account of such floor broker;

(2) an account for which such floor broker has trading discretion; or

(3) an account controlled by a person with whom such floor broker has a relationship through membership in a broker association.

(c) *"Broker Association" Defined.* As used in this section, the term "broker association" shall include two or more contract market members or registered derivatives transaction execution facility members with floor trading privileges of whom at least one is acting as a floor broker, who—

(1) engage in floor brokerage activity on behalf of the same employer,

(2) have an employer and employee relationship which relates to floor brokerage activity,

(3) share profits and losses associated with their brokerage or trading activity, or

(4) regularly share a deck of orders.

Registration of Associates of Futures Commission Merchants, Commodity Pool Operators, and Commodity Trading Advisors

Sec. 4k. (1) It shall be unlawful for any person to be associated with a futures commission merchant as a partner, officer, or employee, or to be associated with an introducing broker as a partner, officer, employee, or agent (or any person occupying a similar status or performing similar functions), in any capacity that involves (i) the solicitation or acceptance of customers' orders (other than in a clerical capacity) or (ii) the supervision of any person or persons so engaged, unless such person is registered with the Commission under this Act as an associated person of such futures commission merchant or of such introducing broker and such registration shall not have expired, been suspended (and the period of suspension has not expired), or been revoked. It shall be unlawful for a futures commission merchant or introducing broker to permit such a person to become or remain associated with the futures commission merchant or introducing broker in any such capacity if such futures commission merchant or introducing broker knew or should have known that such person was not so registered or that such registration had expired, been suspended (and the period of suspension has not expired), or been revoked. Any individual who is registered as a floor broker, futures commission merchant, or introducing broker (and such registration is not suspended or revoked) need not also register under this subsection.

(2) Registration Required. It shall be unlawful for any person to be associated with a commodity pool operator as a partner, officer, employee, consultant, or agent (or any person occupying a similar status or performing similar functions), in any capacity that involves (i) the solicitation of funds, securities, or property for a participation in a commodity pool or (ii) the supervision of any person or persons so engaged, unless such person is registered with the Commission under this Act as an associated person of such commodity pool operator and such registration shall not have expired, been suspended (and the period of suspension has not expired), or been revoked. It shall be unlawful for a commodity pool operator to permit such a person to become or remain associated with the commodity pool operator in any such capacity if the commodity pool operator knew or should have known that such person was not so registered or that such registration had expired, been suspended (and the period of suspension has not expired), or been revoked. Any individual who is registered as a floor broker, futures commission merchant, introducing broker, commodity pool operator, or as an associated person of another category of registrant under this section (and such registration is not suspended or revoked) need not also register under this subsection. The Commission may exempt any person or class of persons from having to register under this subsection by rule, regulation, or order.

(3) Trading Advisor Associated Persons. It shall be unlawful for any person to be associated with a commodity trading advisor as a partner, officer, employee, consultant, or agent (or any person occupying a similar status or performing similar functions), in any capacity which involves (i) the solicitation of a client's or prospective client's discretionary account or (ii) the supervision of any person or persons so engaged, unless such person is registered with the Commission under this Act as an associated person of such commodity trading advisor and such registration shall not have expired, been suspended (and the period of suspension has not expired), or been revoked. It shall be unlawful for a commodity trading advisor to permit such a person to become or remain associated with the commodity trading advisor in any such capacity if the commodity trading advisor knew or should have known that such person was not so registered or that such registration had expired, been suspended (and the period of suspension has not expired), or been revoked. Any individual who is registered as a floor broker, futures commission merchant, introducing broker, commodity trading advisor, or as an associated person of another category of registrant under this section (and such registration is not suspended or revoked) need not also register under this subsection. The Commission may exempt any person or class of persons from having to register under this subsection by rule, regulation, or order.

(4) Registration Procedure. Any person desiring to be registered as an associated person of a futures commission merchant, of an introducing broker, of a commodity pool operator, or of a commodity trading advisor shall make application to the Commission in the form and manner prescribed by the Commission, giving such information and facts as the Commission may deem necessary concerning the applicant. Such person, when registered hereunder, shall likewise continue to report and furnish to the Commission such information as the Commission may require. Such registration shall expire at such time as the Commission may by rule, regulation, or order prescribe.

(5) Duties of Registrant. It shall be unlawful for any registrant to permit a person to become or remain an associated person of such registrant, if the registrant knew or should have known of facts regarding such associated person that are set forth as statutory disqualifications in section 8a(2) of this Act, unless such registrant has notified the Commission of such facts and the Commission has determined that such person should be registered or temporarily licensed.

(6) Duties of Registrant. Any associated person of a broker or dealer that is registered with the Secu-

rities and Exchange Commission, and who limits its solicitation of orders, acceptance of orders, or execution of orders, or placing of orders on behalf of others involving any contracts of sale of any commodity for future delivery or any option on such a contract, on or subject to the rules of any contract market or registered derivatives transaction execution facility to security futures products, shall be exempt from the following provisions of this Act and the rules thereunder:

(A) Subsections (b), (d), (e), and (g) of section 4c.

(B) Sections 4d, 4e, and 4h.

(C) Subsections (b) and (c) of section 4f.

(D) Section 4j.

(E) Paragraph (1) of this section.

(F) Section 4p.

(G) Section 6d.

(H) Subsections (d) and (g) of section 8.

(I) Section 16.

Commodity Trading Advisors and Commodity Pool Operators; Congressional Finding

Sec. 4*l*. It is hereby found that the activities of commodity trading advisors and commodity pool operators are affected with a national public interest in that, among other things—

(1) their advice, counsel, publications, writings, analyses, and reports are furnished and distributed, and their contracts, solicitations, subscriptions, agreements, and other arrangements with clients take place and are negotiated and performed by the use of the mails and other means and instrumentalities of interstate commerce;

(2) their advice, counsel, publications, writings, analyses, and reports customarily relate to and their operations are directed toward and cause the purchase and sale of commodities for future delivery on or subject to the rules of contract markets or derivatives transaction execution facilities; and

(3) the foregoing transactions occur in such volume as to affect substantially transactions on contract markets or derivatives transaction execution facilities.

Use of Mails or Other Means or Instrumentalities of Interstate Commerce by Commodity Trading Advisors and Commodity Pool Operators; Relation to Other Law

Sec. 4m. (1) It shall be unlawful for any commodity trading advisor or commodity pool operator, unless registered under this Act, to make use of the mails or any means or instrumentality of interstate commerce in connection with his business as such commodity trading advisor or commodity pool operator: *Provided,* That the provisions of this section shall not apply to any commodity trading advisor who, during the course of the preceding twelve months, has not furnished commodity trading advice to more than fifteen persons and who does not hold himself out generally to the public as a commodity trading advisor. The provisions of this section shall not apply to any commodity trading advisor who is a (1) dealer, processor, broker, or seller in cash market transactions of any commodity specifically set forth in section 2(a) of this Act prior to the enactment of the Commodity Futures Trading Commission Act of 1974 (or products thereof) or (2) nonprofit, voluntary membership, general farm organization, who provides advice on the sale or purchase of any commodity specifically set forth in section 2(a) of this Act prior to the enactment of the Commodity Futures Trading Commission Act of 1974; if the advice by the person described in clause (1) or (2) of this sentence as a commodity trading advisor is solely incidental to the conduct of that person's business: *Provided,* That such person shall be subject to proceedings under section 14 of this Act.

(2) Nothing in this Act shall relieve any person of any obligation or duty, or affect the availability of any right or remedy available to the Securities and Exchange Commission or any private party arising under the Securities Act of 1933 or the Securities Exchange Act of 1934 governing the issuance, offer, purchase, or sale of securities of a commodity pool, or of persons engaged in transactions with respect to such securities, or reporting by a commodity pool.

(3) *Exception.*

(A) *In General.* Paragraph (1) shall not apply to any commodity trading advisor that is registered with the Securities and Exchange Commission as an investment adviser whose business does not consist primarily of acting as a commodity trading advisor, as defined in section 1a, and that does not act as a commodity trading advisor to any commodity pool that is engaged primarily in trading commodity interests.

(B) *Engaged Primarily.* For purposes of subparagraph (A), a commodity trading advisor or a commodity pool shall be considered to be "engaged primarily" in the business of being a commodity trading advisor or commodity pool if it is or holds itself out to the public as being engaged primarily, or proposes to engage primarily, in the business of advising on commodity interests or investing, reinvesting, owning, holding, or trading in commodity interests, respectively.

(C) *Commodity Interests.* For purposes of this paragraph, commodity interests shall include contracts of sale of a commodity for future delivery, options on such contracts, security futures, swaps, leverage contracts, foreign exchange, spot and forward contracts on physical commodities, and any monies held in an account used for trading commodity interests.

Registration of Commodity Trading Advisors and Commodity Pool Operators; Application; Expiration and Renewal; Recordkeeping and Reports; Disclosure; Statements of Account

Sec. 4n. (1) Any commodity trading advisor or commodity pool operator, or any person who contemplates becoming a commodity trading advisor or commodity pool operator, may register under this Act by filing an application with the Commission. Such application shall contain such information, in such form and detail, as the Commission may, by rules and regulations, prescribe as necessary or appropriate in the public interest, including the following:

(A) the name and form of organization, including capital structure, under which the applicant engages or intends to engage in business; the name of the State under the laws of which he is organized; the location of his principal business office and branch offices, if any; the names and addresses of all partners, officers, directors, and persons performing similar functions or, if the applicant be an individual, of such individual; and the number of employees;

(B) the education, the business affiliations for the past ten years, and the present business affiliations of the applicant and of his partners, officers, directors, and persons performing similar functions and of any controlling person thereof;

(C) the nature of the business of the applicant, including the manner of giving advice and rendering of analyses or reports;

(D) the nature and scope of the authority of the applicant with respect to clients' funds and accounts;

(E) the basis upon which the applicant is or will be compensated; and

(F) such other information as the Commission may require to determine whether the applicant is qualified for registration.

(2) Each registration under this section shall expire on the 30th day of June of each year, or at such other time, not less than one year from the effective date thereof, as the Commission may by rule, regulation, or order prescribe, and shall be renewed upon application therefor subject to the same requirements as in the case of an original application.

(3)(A) Every commodity trading advisor and commodity pool operator registered under this Act shall maintain books and records and file such reports in such form and manner as may be prescribed by the Commission. All such books and records shall be kept for a period of at least three years, or longer if the Commission so directs, and shall be open to inspection by any representative of the Commission or the Department of Justice. Upon the request of the Commission, a registered commodity trading advisor or commodity pool operator shall furnish the name and address of each client, subscriber, or participant, and submit samples or copies of all reports, letters, circulars, memorandums, publications, writings, or other literature or advice distributed to clients, subscribers, or participants, or prospective clients, subscribers, or participants.

(B) Unless otherwise authorized by the Commission by rule or regulation, all commodity trading advisors and commodity pool operators shall make a full and complete disclosure to their subscribers, clients, or participants of all futures market positions taken or held by the individual principals of their organization.

(4) Every commodity pool operator shall regularly furnish statements of account to each participant in his operations. Such statements shall be in such form and manner as may be prescribed by the commission and shall include complete information as to the current status of all trading accounts in which such participant has an interest.

Fraud and Misrepresentation by Commodity Trading Advisors, Commodity Pool Operators, and Associated Persons

Sec. 4*o*. (1) It shall be unlawful for a commodity trading advisor, associated person of a commodity trading advisor, commodity pool operator, or associated person of a commodity pool operator by use of the mails or any means or instrumentality of interstate commerce, directly or indirectly—

(A) to employ any device, scheme, or artifice to defraud any client or participant or prospective client or participant; or

(B) to engage in any transaction, practice, or course of business which operates as a fraud or deceit upon any client or participant or prospective client or participant.

(2) It shall be unlawful for any commodity trading advisor, associated person of a commodity trading advisor, commodity pool operator, or associated person of a commodity pool operator registered under this Act to represent or imply in any manner whatsoever that such person has been sponsored, recommended, or approved, or that such person's abilities or qualifications have in any respect been passed upon, by the United States or any agency or officer thereof. This section shall not be construed to prohibit a statement that a person is registered under this Act as a commodity trading advisor, associated person of a commodity trading advisor, commodity pool operator, or associated person of a commodity pool operator, if such statement is true in fact and if the effect of such registration is not misrepresented.

Standards and Examinations

Sec. 4p. (a) The Commission may specify by rules and regulations appropriate standards with respect to training, experience, and such other qualifications as the Commission finds necessary or desirable to insure the fitness of persons required to be registered with the Commission. In connection therewith, the Commission may prescribe by rules and regulations the adoption of written proficiency examinations to be given to applicants for registration and the establishment of reasonable fees to be charged to such applicants to cover the administration of such examinations. The Commission may further prescribe by rules and regulations that, in lieu of examinations administered by the Commission, futures associations registered under section 17 of this Act, contract markets, or derivatives transaction execution facilities may adopt written proficiency examinations to be given to applicants for registration and charge reasonable fees to such applicants to cover the administration of such examinations. Notwithstanding any other provisions of this section, the Commission may specify by rules and regulations such terms and conditions as it deems appropriate to protect the public interest wherein exception to any written proficiency examination shall be made with respect to individuals who have demonstrated, through training and experience, the degree of proficiency and skill necessary to protect the interests of customers, clients, pool participants, or other members of the public with whom such individuals deal.

(b) The Commission shall issue regulations to require new registrants, within six months after receiving such registration, to attend a training session, and all other registrants to attend periodic training sessions, to ensure that registrants understand their responsibilities to the public under this Act, including responsibilities to observe just and equitable principles of trade, any rule or regulation of the Commission, any rule of any appropriate contract market, derivatives transaction execution facility, registered futures association, or other self-regulatory organization, or any other applicable Federal or state law, rule or regulation.

Special Procedures to Encourage and Facilitate Bona Fide Hedging by Agricultural Producers

Sec. 4q. (a) *Authority*. The Commission shall consider issuing rules or orders which—

(1) prescribe procedures under which each contract market is to provide for orderly delivery, including temporary storage costs, of any agricultural commodity enumerated in section 1a(9) which is the subject of a contract for purchase or sale for future delivery;

(2) increase the ease with which domestic agricultural producers may participate in contract markets, including by addressing cost and margin requirements, so as to better enable the producers to hedge price risk associated with their production;

(3) provide flexibility in the minimum quantities of such agricultural commodities that may be the subject of a contract for purchase or sale for future delivery that is traded on a contract market, to better allow domestic agricultural producers to hedge such price risk; and

(4) encourage contract markets to provide information and otherwise facilitate the participation

of domestic agricultural producers in contract markets.

(b) *Report.* Within 1 year after the date of enactment of this section, the Commission shall submit to the Committee on Agriculture of the House of Representatives and the Committee on Agriculture, Nutrition, and Forestry of the Senate a report on the steps it has taken to implement this section and on the activities of contract markets pursuant to this section.

Reporting and Recordkeeping for Uncleared Swaps

Sec. 4r. (a) *Required Reporting of Swaps not Accepted by any Derivatives Clearing Organization.*

(1) *In General.* Each swap that is not accepted for clearing by any derivatives clearing organization shall be reported to—

(A) a swap data repository described in section 21; or

(B) in the case in which there is no swap data repository that would accept the swap, to the Commission pursuant to this section within such time period as the Commission may by rule or regulation prescribe.

(2) *Transition Rule for Preenactment Swaps.*

(A) *Swaps Entered into Before the Date of Enactment of the Wall Street Transparency and Accountability Act of 2010.* Each swap entered into before the date of enactment of the Wall Street Transparency and Accountability Act of 2010, the terms of which have not expired as of the date of enactment of that Act, shall be reported to a registered swap data repository or the Commission by a date that is not later than—

(i) 30 days after issuance of the interim final rule; or

(ii) such other period as the Commission determines to be appropriate.

(B) *Commission Rulemaking.* The Commission shall promulgate an interim final rule within 90 days of the date of enactment of this section providing for the reporting of each swap entered into before the date of enactment as referenced in subparagraph (A).

(C) *Effective Date.* The reporting provisions described in this section shall be effective upon the enactment of this section.

(3) *Reporting Obligations.*

(A) *Swaps in Which only 1 Counterparty Is a Swap Dealer or Major Swap Participant.* With respect to a swap in which only 1 counterparty is a swap dealer or major swap participant, the swap dealer or major swap participant shall report the swap as required under paragraphs (1) and (2).

(B) *Swaps in Which 1 Counterparty Is a Swap Dealer and the Other a Major Swap Participant.* With respect to a swap in which 1 counterparty is a swap dealer and the other a major swap participant, the swap dealer shall report the swap as required under paragraphs (1) and (2).

(C) *Other Swaps.* With respect to any other swap not described in subparagraph (A) or (B), the counterparties to the swap shall select a counterparty to report the swap as required under paragraphs (1) and (2).

(b) *Duties of Certain Individuals.* Any individual or entity that enters into a swap shall meet each requirement described in subsection (c) if the individual or entity did not

(1) clear the swap in accordance with section 2(h)(1); or

(2) have the data regarding the swap accepted by a swap data repository in accordance with rules (including timeframes) adopted by the Commission under section 21.

(c) *Requirements.* An individual or entity described in subsection (b) shall—

(1) upon written request from the Commission, provide reports regarding the swaps held by the individual or entity to the Commission in such form and in such manner as the Commission may request; and

(2) maintain books and records pertaining to the swaps held by the individual or entity in such form, in such manner, and for such period as the Commission may require, which shall be open to inspection by—

(A) any representative of the Commission;

(B) an appropriate prudential regulator;

(C) the Securities and Exchange Commission;

(D) the Financial Stability Oversight Council; and

(E) the Department of Justice.

(d) *Identical Data.* In prescribing rules under this section, the Commission shall require individuals and entities described in subsection (b) to submit to the Commission a report that contains data that is not less comprehensive than the data required to be collected by swap data repositories under section 21.

Registration and Regulation of Swap Dealers and Major Swap Participants

Sec. 4s. (a) *Registration.*

(1) *Swap Dealers.* It shall be unlawful for any person to act as a swap dealer unless the person is registered as a swap dealer with the Commission.

(2) *Major Swap Participants.* It shall be unlawful for any person to act as a major swap participant unless the person is registered as a major swap participant with the Commission.

(b) *Requirements.*

(1) *In General.* A person shall register as a swap dealer or major swap participant by filing a registration application with the Commission.

(2) *Contents.*

(A) *In General.* The application shall be made inch form and manner as prescribed by the Commission, and shall contain such information, as the Commission considers necessary concerning the business in which the applicant is or will be engaged.

(B) *Continual Reporting.* A person that is registered as a swap dealer or major swap participant shall continue to submit to the Commission reports that contain such information pertaining to the business of the person as the Commission may require.

(3) *Expiration.* Each registration under this section shall expire at such time as the Commission may prescribe by rule or regulation.

(4) *Rules.* Except as provided in subsections (d) and (e), the Commission may prescribe rules applicable to swap dealers and major swap participants, including rules that limit the activities of swap dealers and major swap participants.

(5) *Transition.* Rules under this section shall provide for the registration of swap dealers and major swap participants not later than 1 year after the date of enactment of the Wall Street Transparency and Accountability Act of 2010.

(6) *Statutory Disqualification.* Except to the extent otherwise specifically provided by rule, regulation, or order, it shall be unlawful for a swap dealer or a major swap participant to permit any person associated with a swap dealer or a major swap participant who is subject to a statutory disqualification to effect or be involved in effecting swaps on behalf of the swap dealer or major swap participant, if the swap dealer or major swap participant knew, or in the exercise of reasonable care should have known, of the statutory disqualification.

(c) *Dual Registration.*

(1) *Swap Dealer.* Any person that is required to be registered as a swap dealer under this section shall register with the Commission regardless of whether the person also is a depository institution or is registered with the Securities and Exchange Commission as a security-based swap dealer.

(2) *Major Swap Participant.* Any person that is required to be registered as a major swap participant under this section shall register with the Commission regardless of whether the person also is a depository institution or is registered with the Securities and Exchange Commission as a major security-based swap participant.

(d) *Rulemakings.*

(1) *In General.* The Commission shall adopt rules for persons that are registered as swap dealers or major swap participants under this section.

(2) *Exception for Prudential Requirements.*

(A) *In General.* The Commission may not prescribe rules imposing prudential requirements on swap dealers or major swap participants for which there is a prudential regulator.

(B) *Applicability.* Subparagraph (A) does not limit the authority of the Commission to prescribe rules as directed under this section.

(e) *Capital and Margin Requirements.*

(1) *In General.*

(A) *Swap Dealers and Major Swap Participants that are Banks.* Each registered swap dealer and major swap participant for which there is a prudential regulator shall meet such minimum capital requirements and minimum initial and variation margin requirements as the prudential regulator shall by rule or regulation prescribe under paragraph (2)(A).

(B) *Swap Dealers and Major Swap Participants that are not Banks.* Each registered swap dealer and major swap participant for which there is not a prudential regulator shall meet such minimum capital requirements and minimum initial and variation margin requirements as the Commission shall by rule or regulation prescribe under paragraph (2)(B).

(2) *Rules.*

(A) *Swap Dealers and Major Swap Participants that are Banks.* The prudential regulators, in consultation with the Commission and the Securities and Exchange Commission, shall jointly adopt rules for swap dealers and major swap participants, with respect to their activities as a swap dealer or major swap participant, for which there is a prudential regulator imposing—

(i) capital requirements; and

(ii) both initial and variation margin requirements on all swaps that are not cleared by a registered derivatives clearing organization.

(B) *Swap Dealers and Major Swap Participants that are not Banks.* The Commission shall adopt rules for swap dealers and major swap participants, with respect to their activities as a swap dealer or major swap participant, for which there is not a prudential regulator imposing—

(i) capital requirements; and

(ii) both initial and variation margin requirements on all swaps that are not cleared by a registered derivatives clearing organization.

(C) *Capital.* In setting capital requirements for a person that is designated as a swap dealer or a major swap participant for a single type or single class or category of swap or activities, the prudential regulator and the Commission shall take into account the risks associated with other types of swaps or classes of swaps or categories of swaps engaged in and the other activities conducted by that person that are not otherwise subject to regulation applicable to that person by virtue of the status of the person as a swap dealer or a major swap participant.

(3) *Standards for Capital and Margin.*

(A) *In General.* To offset the greater risk to the swap dealer or major swap participant and the financial system arising from the use of swaps that are not cleared, the requirements imposed under paragraph (2) shall—

(i) help ensure the safety and soundness of the swap dealer or major swap participant; and

(ii) be appropriate for the risk associated with the non–cleared swaps held as a swap dealer or major swap participant.

(B) *Rule of Construction.*

(i) *In General.* Nothing in this section shall limit, or be construed to limit, the authority—

(I) of the Commission to set financial responsibility rules for a futures commission merchant or introducing broker registered pursuant to section 4f(a) (except for section 4f(a)(3)) in accordance with section 4f(b); or

(II) of the Securities and Exchange Commission to set financial responsibility rules for a broker or dealer registered pursuant to section 15(b) of the Securities Exchange Act of 1934 (except for section 15(b)(11) of that Act) in accordance with section 15(c)(3) of the Securities Exchange Act of 1934.

(ii) *Futures Commission Merchants and Other Dealers.* A futures commission merchant, introducing broker, broker, or dealer shall maintain sufficient capital to comply with the stricter of any applicable capital requirements to which such futures commission merchant, introducing broker, broker, or dealer is subject to under this Act or the Securities Exchange Act of 1934.

(C) *Margin Requirements.* In prescribing margin requirements under this subsection, the prudential regulator with respect to swap dealers and major swap participants for which it is the prudential regulator and the Commission with respect to swap dealers and major swap participants for which there is no prudential regulator shall permit the use of noncash collateral, as the regulator or the Commission determines to be consistent with—

(i) preserving the financial integrity of markets trading swaps; and

(ii) preserving the stability of the United States financial system.

(D) *Comparability of Capital and Margin Requirements.*

(i) *In General.* The prudential regulators, the Commission, and the Securities and Exchange Commission shall periodically (but not less frequently than annually) consult on minimum capital requirements and minimum initial and variation margin requirements.

(ii) *Comparability.* The entities described in clause (i) shall, to the maximum extent practicable, establish and maintain comparable minimum capital requirements and minimum initial and variation margin requirements, including the use of non cash collateral, for—

(I) swap dealers; and

(II) major swap participants.

(4) *Applicability with Respect to Counterparties.* The requirements of paragraphs (2)(A)(ii) and (2)(B)(ii), including the initial and variation margin requirements imposed by rules adopted pursuant to paragraphs (2)(A)(ii) and (2)(B)(ii), shall not apply to a swap in which a counterparty qualifies for an exception under section 2(h)(7)(A) of this Act, or an exemption issued under section 6(c)(1) of this Act from the requirements of section 2(h)(1)(A) of this Act for cooperative entities as defined in such exemption, or satisfies the criteria in section 2(h)(7)(D) of this Act.

(f) *Reporting and Recordkeeping.*

(1) *In General.* Each registered swap dealer and major swap participant

(A) shall make such reports as are required by the Commission by rule or regulation regarding the transactions and positions and financial condition of the registered swap dealer or major swap participant;

(B)(i) for which there is a prudential regulator, shall keep books and records of all activities related to the business as a swap dealer or major swap participant in such form and manner and for such period as may be prescribed by the Commission by rule or regulation; and

(ii) for which there is no prudential regulator, shall keep books and records in such form and manner and for such period as may be prescribed by the Commission by rule or regulation;

(C) shall keep books and records described in subparagraph (B) open to inspection and examination by any representative of the Commission; and

(D) shall keep any such books and records relating to swaps defined in section 1a(47)(A)(v) open to inspection and examination by the Securities and Exchange Commission.

(2) *Rules.* The Commission shall adopt rules governing reporting and recordkeeping for swap dealers and major swap participants.

(g) *Daily Trading Records.*

(1) *In General.* Each registered swap dealer and major swap participant shall maintain daily trading records of the swaps of the registered swap dealer and major swap participant and all related records (including related cash or forward transactions) and recorded communications, including electronic mail, instant messages, and recordings of telephone calls, for such period as may be required by the Commission by rule or regulation.

(2) *Information Requirements.* The daily trading records shall include such information as the Commission shall require by rule or regulation.

(3) *Counter Party Records.* Each registered swap dealer and major swap participant shall maintain daily trading records for each counterparty in a manner and form that is identifiable with each swap transaction.

(4) *Audit Trail.* Each registered swap dealer and major swap participant shall maintain a complete audit trail for conducting comprehensive and accurate trade reconstructions.

(5) *Rules.* The Commission shall adopt rules governing daily trading records for swap dealers and major swap participants.

(h) *Business Conduct Standards.*

(1) *In General.* Each registered swap dealer and major swap participant shall conform with such business conduct standards as prescribed in paragraph (3) and as may be prescribed by the Commission by rule or regulation that relate to—

(A) fraud, manipulation, and other abusive practices involving swaps (including swaps that are offered but not entered into);

(B) diligent supervision of the business of the registered swap dealer and major swap participant;

(C) adherence to all applicable position limits; and

(D) such other matters as the Commission determines to be appropriate.

(2) *Responsibilities with Respect to Special Entities.*

(A) *Advising Special Entities.* A swap dealer or major swap participant that acts as an advisor to a special entity regarding a swap shall comply with the requirements of subparagraph (4) with respect to such Special Entity.

(B) *Entering of Swaps with Respect to Special Entities.* A swap dealer that enters into or offers to enter into swap with a Special Entity shall comply with the requirements of subparagraph (5) with respect to such Special Entity.

(C) *Special Entity Defined.* For purposes of this subsection, the term "special entity" means—

(i) a Federal agency;

(ii) a State, State agency, city, county, municipality, or other political subdivision of a State;

(iii) any employee benefit plan, as defined in section 3 of the Employee Retirement Income Security Act of 1974;

(iv) any governmental plan, as defined in section 3 of the Employee Retirement Income Security Act of 1974; or

(v) any endowment, including an endowment that is an organization described in section 501(c)(3) of the Internal Revenue Code of 1986.

(3) *Business Conduct Requirements.* Business conduct requirements adopted by the Commission shall—

(A) establish a duty for a swap dealer or major swap participant to verify that any counterparty meets the eligibility standards for an eligible contract participant;

(B) require disclosure by the swap dealer or major swap participant to any counterparty to the transaction (other than a swap dealer, major swap participant, security-based swap dealer, or major security-based swap participant) of—

(i) information about the material risks and characteristics of the swap;

(ii) any material incentives or conflicts of interest that the swap dealer or major swap participant may have in connection with the swap; and

(iii)(I) for cleared swaps, upon the request of the counterparty, receipt of the daily mark of the transaction from the appropriate derivatives clearing organization; and

(II) for uncleared swaps, receipt of the daily mark of the transaction from the swap dealer or the major swap participant;

(C) establish a duty for a swap dealer or major swap participant to communicate in a fair and balanced manner based on principles of fair dealing and good faith; and

(D) establish such other standards and requirements as the Commission may determine are appropriate in the public interest, for the protection of investors, or otherwise in furtherance of the purposes of this Act.

(4) *Special Requirements for Swap Dealers Acting as Advisors.*

(A) *In General.* It shall be unlawful for a swap dealer or major swap participant—

(i) to employ any device, scheme, or artifice to defraud any Special Entity or prospective customer who is a Special Entity;

(ii) to engage in any transaction, practice, or course of business that operates as a fraud or deceit on any Special Entity or prospective customer who is a Special Entity; or

(iii) to engage in any act, practice, or course of business that is fraudulent, deceptive or manipulative.

(B) *Duty.* Any swap dealer that acts as an advisor to a Special Entity shall have a duty to act in the best interests of the Special Entity.

(C) *Reasonable Efforts.* Any swap dealer that acts as an advisor to a Special Entity shall make reasonable efforts to obtain such information as is necessary to make a reasonable determination that any swap recommended by the swap dealer is in the best interests of the Special Entity, including information relating to—

(i) the financial status of the Special Entity;

(ii) the tax status of the Special Entity;

(iii) the investment or financing objectives of the Special Entity; and

(iv) any other information that the Commission may prescribe by rule or regulation.

(5) *Special Requirements for Swap Dealers as Counter Parties to Special Entities.*

(A) Any swap dealer or major swap participant that offers to enter or enters into a swap with a Special Entity shall—

(i) comply with any duty established by the Commission for a swap dealer or major swap participant, with respect to a counterparty that is an eligible contract participant within the meaning of subclause (I) or (II) of clause (vii) of section 1a(18) of this Act, that requires the swap dealer or major swap participant to have a reasonable basis to believe that the counterparty that is a Special Entity has an independent representative that—

(I) has sufficient knowledge to evaluate the transaction and risks;

(II) is not subject to a statutory disqualification;

(III) is independent of the swap dealer or major swap participant;

(IV) undertakes a duty to act in the best interests of the counterparty it represents;

(V) makes appropriate disclosures;

(VI) will provide written representations to the Special Entity regarding fair pricing and the appropriateness of the transaction; and

(VII) in the case of employee benefit plans subject to the Employee Retirement Income Security act of 1974, is a fiduciary as defined in section 3 of that Act; and

(ii) before the initiation of the transaction, disclose to the Special Entity in writing the capacity in which the swap dealer is acting; and

(B) the Commission may establish such other standards and requirements as the Commission may determine are appropriate in the public interest, for the protection of investors, or otherwise in furtherance of the purposes of this Act.

(6) *Rules.* The Commission shall prescribe rules under this subsection governing business conduct standards for swap dealers and major swap participants.

(7) *Applicability.* This section shall not apply with respect to a transaction that is—

(A) initiated by a Special Entity on an exchange or swap execution facility; and

(B) one in which the swap dealer or major swap participant does not know the identity of the counterparty to the transaction.

(i) *Documentation Standards.*

(1) *In General.* Each registered swap dealer and major swap participant shall conform with such standards as may be prescribed by the Commission by rule or regulation that relate to timely and accurate confirmation, processing, netting, documentation, and valuation of all swaps.

(2) *Rules.* The Commission shall adopt rules governing documentation standards for swap dealers and major swap participants.

(j) *Duties.* Each registered swap dealer and major swap participant at all times shall comply with the following requirements:

(1) *Monitoring of Trading.* The swap dealer or major swap participant shall monitor its trading in swaps to prevent violations of applicable position limits.

(2) *Risk Management Procedures.* The swap dealer or major swap participant shall establish robust and professional risk management systems adequate for managing the day–to–day business of the swap dealer or major swap participant.

(3) *Disclosure of General Information.* The swap dealer or major swap participant shall disclose to the Commission and to the prudential regulator for the swap dealer or major swap participant, as applicable, information concerning—

(A) terms and conditions of its swaps;

(B) swap trading operations, mechanisms, and practices;

(C) financial integrity protections relating to swaps; and

(D) other information relevant to its trading in swaps.

(4) *Ability to Obtain Information.* The swap dealer or major swap participant shall—

(A) establish and enforce internal systems and procedures to obtain any necessary information to perform any of the functions described in this section; and

(B) provide the information to the Commission and to the prudential regulator for the swap dealer or major swap participant, as applicable, on request.

(5) *Conflicts of Interest.* The swap dealer and major swap participant shall implement conflict–of–interest systems and procedures that—

(A) establish structural and institutional safeguards to ensure that the activities of any person within the firm relating to research or analysis of the price or market for any commodity or swap or acting in a role of providing clearing activities or making determinations as to accepting clearing customers are separated by appropriate informational partitions within the firm from the review, pressure or oversight of persons whose involvement in pricing, trading, or clearing activities might potentially bias their judgment or supervision and contravene the core principles of open access and the business conduct standards described in this Act; and

(B) address such other issues as the Commission determines to be appropriate.

(6) *Antitrust Considerations.* Unless necessary or appropriate to achieve the purposes of this Act, a swap dealer or major swap participant shall not—

(A) adopt any process or take any action that results in any unreasonable restraint of trade; or

(B) impose any material anticompetitive burden on trading or clearing.

(7) *Rules.* The Commission shall prescribe rules under this subsection governing duties of swap dealers and major swap participants.

(k) *Designation of Chief Compliance Officer.*

(1) *In General.* Each swap dealer and major swap participant shall designate an individual to serve as a chief compliance officer.

(2) *Duties.* The chief compliance officer shall—

(A) report directly to the board or to the senior officer of the swap dealer or major swap participant;

(B) review the compliance of the swap dealer or major swap participant with respect to the swap dealer and major swap participant requirements described in this section;

(C) in consultation with the board of directors, a body performing a function similar to the board, or the senior officer of the organization, resolve any conflicts of interest that may arise;

(D) be responsible for administering each policy and procedure that is required to be established pursuant to this section;

(E) ensure compliance with this Act (including regulations) relating to swaps, including each rule prescribed by the Commission under this section;

(F) establish procedures for the remediation of non–compliance issues identified by the chief compliance officer through any—

(i) compliance office review;

(ii) look-back;

(iii) internal or external audit finding;

(iv) self-reported error; or

(v) validated complaint; and

(G) establish and follow appropriate procedures for the handling, management response, remediation, retesting, and closing of noncompliance issues.

(3) *Annual Reports.*

(A) *In General.* In accordance with rules prescribed by the Commission, the chief compliance officer shall annually prepare and sign a report that contains a description of—

(i) the compliance of the swap dealer or major swap participant with respect to this Act (including regulations); and

(ii) each policy and procedure of the swap dealer or major swap participant of the chief compliance officer (including the code of ethics and conflict of interest policies).

(B) *Requirements.* A compliance report under subparagraph (A) shall—

(i) accompany each appropriate financial report of the swap dealer or major swap participant that is required to be furnished to the Commission pursuant to this section; and

(ii) include a certification that, under penalty of law, the compliance report is accurate and complete.

(*l*) *Segregation Requirements.*

(1) *Segregation of Assets Held as Collateral in Uncleared Swap Transactions.*

(A) *Notification.* A swap dealer or major swap participant shall be required to notify the counterparty of the swap dealer or major swap participant at the beginning of a swap transaction that the counterparty has the right to require segregation of the funds or other property supplied to margin, guarantee, or secure the obligations of the counterparty.

(B) *Segregation and Maintenance of Funds.* At the request of a counterparty to a swap that provides funds or other property to a swap dealer or major swap participant to margin, guarantee, or secure the obligations of the counterparty, the swap dealer or major swap participant shall—

(i) segregate the funds or other property for the benefit of the counterparty; and

(ii) in accordance with such rules and regulations as the Commission may promulgate, maintain the funds or other property in a segregated account separate from the assets and other interests of the swap dealer or major swap participant.

(2) *Applicability.* The requirements described in paragraph (1) shall—

(A) apply only to a swap between a counterparty and a swap dealer or major swap participant that is not submitted for clearing to a derivatives clearing organization; and

(B)(i) not apply to variation margin payments; or

(ii) not preclude any commercial arrangement regarding—

(I) the investment of segregated funds or other property that may only be invested in such investments as the Commission may permit by rule or regulation; and

(II) the related allocation of gains and losses resulting from any investment of the segregated funds or other property.

(3) *Use of Independent Third–Party Custodians.* The segregated account described in paragraph (1) shall be—

(A) carried by an independent third-party custodian; and

(B) designated as a segregated account for and on behalf of the counterparty.

(4) *Reporting Requirement.* If the counterparty does not choose to require segregation of the funds or other property supplied to margin, guarantee, or secure the obligations of the counterparty, the swap dealer or major swap participant shall report to the counterparty of the swap dealer or major swap participant on a quarterly basis that the back office procedures of the swap dealer or major swap participant relating to margin and collateral requirements are in compliance with the agreement of the counterparties.

Large Swap Trader Reporting

Sec. 4t. (a) *Prohibition.*

(1) *In General.* Except as provided in paragraph (2), it shall be unlawful for any person to enter into any swap that the Commission determines to perform a significant price discovery function with respect to registered entities if—

(A) the person directly or indirectly enters into the swap during any 1 day in an amount equal to or in excess of such amount as shall be established periodically by the Commission; and

(B) the person directly or indirectly has or obtains a position in the swap equal to or in excess of such amount as shall be established periodically by the Commission.

(2) *Exception.* Paragraph (1) shall not apply if—

(A) the person files or causes to be filed with the properly designated officer of the Commission such reports regarding any transactions or positions described in subparagraphs (A) and (B) of paragraph (1) as the Commission may require by rule or regulation; and

(B) in accordance with the rules and regulations of the Commission, the person keeps books and records of all such swaps and any transactions and positions in any related commodity traded on or subject to the rules of any designated contract market or swap execution facility, and of cash or spot transactions in, inventories of, and purchase and sale commitments of, such a commodity.

(b) *Requirements.*

(1) *In General.* Books and records described in subsection (a)(2)(B) shall—

(A) show such complete details concerning all transactions and positions as the Commission may prescribe by rule or regulation;

(B) be open at all times to inspection and examination by any representative of the Commission; and

(C) be open at all times to inspection and examination by the Securities and Exchange Commission, to the extent such books and records relate to transactions in swaps (as that term is defined in section 1a(47)(A)(v)), and consistent with the confidentiality and disclosure requirements of section 8.

(2) *Jurisdiction.* Nothing in paragraph (1) shall affect the exclusive jurisdiction of the Commission to prescribe record–keeping and reporting requirements for large swap traders under this section.

(c) *Applicability.* For purposes of this section, the swaps, futures, and cash or spot transactions and positions of any person shall include the swaps, futures, and cash or spot transactions and positions of any persons directly or indirectly controlled by the person.

(d) *Significant Price Discovery Function.* In making a determination as to whether a swap performs or affects a significant price discovery function with respect to registered entities, the Commission shall consider the factors described in section 4a(a)(3).

Designation of Boards of Trade as Contract Markets

Sec. 5. (a) *Applications.* A board of trade applying to the Commission for designation as a contract market shall submit an application to the Commission that includes any relevant materials and records the Commission may require consistent with this Act.

(b) [Repealed]

(c) *Existing Contract Markets.* A board of trade that is designated as a contract market on the date of the enactment of the Commodity Futures Modernization Act of 2000 shall be considered to be a designated contract market under this section.

(d) *Core Principles for Contract Markets.*

(1) *Designation as Contract Market.*

(A) *In General.* To be designated, and maintain a designation, as a contract market, a board of trade shall comply with—

(i) any core principle described in this subsection; and

(ii) any requirement that the Commission may impose by rule or regulation pursuant to section 8a(5).

(B) *Reasonable Discretion of Contract Market.* Unless otherwise determined by the Commission by rule or regulation, a board of trade described in subparagraph (A) shall have reasonable discretion in establishing the manner in which the board of trade complies with the core principles described in this subsection.

(2) *Compliance with Rules.*

(A) *In General.* The board of trade shall establish, monitor, and enforce compliance with the rules of the contract market, including—

(i) access requirements;

(ii) the terms and conditions of any contracts to be traded on the contract market; and

(iii) rules prohibiting abusive trade practices on the contract market.

(B) *Capacity of Contract Market.* The board of trade shall have the capacity to detect, investigate, and apply appropriate sanctions to any person that violates any rule of the contract market.

(C) *Requirement of Rules.* The rules of the contract market shall provide the board of trade with the ability and authority to obtain any necessary information to perform any function described in this subsection, including the capacity to carry out such international information-sharing agreements as the Commission may require.

(3) *Contracts not Readily Subject to Manipulation.* The board of trade shall list on the contract market only contracts that are not readily susceptible to manipulation.

(4) *Prevention of Market Disruption.* The board of trade shall have the capacity and responsibility to prevent manipulation, price distortion, and disruptions of the delivery or cash-settlement process through market surveillance, compliance, and enforcement practices and procedures, including—

(A) methods for conducting real-time monitoring of trading; and

(B) comprehensive and accurate trade reconstructions.

(5) *Position Limitations or Accountability.*

(A) *In General.* To reduce the potential threat of market manipulation or congestion (especially during trading in the delivery month), the board of trade shall adopt for each contract of the board of trade, as is necessary and appropriate, position limitations or position accountability for speculators.

(B) *Maximum Allowable Position Limitation.* For any contract that is subject to a position limitation established by the Commission pursuant to section 4a(a), the board of trade shall set the position limitation of the board of trade at a level not higher than the position limitation established by the Commission.

(6) *Emergency Authority*. The board of trade, in consultation or cooperation with the Commission, shall adopt rules to provide for the exercise of emergency authority, as is necessary and appropriate, including the authority—

(A) to liquidate or transfer open positions in any contract;

(B) to suspend or curtail trading in any contract; and

(C) to require market participants in any contract to meet special margin requirements.

(7) *Availability of General Information*. The board of trade shall make available to market authorities, market participants, and the public accurate information concerning—

(A) the terms and conditions of the contracts of the contract market; and

(B) (i) the rules, regulations, and mechanisms for executing transactions on or through the facilities of the contract market; and

(ii) the rules and specifications describing the operation of the contract market's—

(I) electronic matching platform; or

(II) trade execution facility.

(8) *Daily Publication of Trading Information*. The board of trade shall make public daily information on settlement prices, volume, open interest, and opening and closing ranges for actively traded contracts on the contract market.

(9) *Execution of Transactions*.

(A) *In General*. The board of trade shall provide a competitive, open, and efficient market and mechanism for executing transactions that protects the price discovery process of trading in the centralized market of the board of trade.

(B) *Rules*. The rules of the board of trade may authorize, for bona fide business purposes—

(i) transfer trades or office trades;

(ii) an exchange of—

(I) futures in connection with a cash commodity transaction;

(II) futures for cash commodities; or

(III) futures for swaps; or

(iii) a futures commission merchant, acting as principal or agent, to enter into or confirm the execution of a contract for the purchase or sale of a commodity for future delivery if the contract is reported, recorded, or cleared in accordance with the rules of the contract market or a derivatives clearing organization.

(10) *Trade Information*. The board of trade shall maintain rules and procedures to provide for the recording and safe storage of all identifying trade information in a manner that enables the contract market to use the information—

(A) to assist in the prevention of customer and market abuses; and

(B) to provide evidence of any violations of the rules of the contract market.

(11) *Financial Integrity of Transactions*. The board of trade shall establish and enforce—

(A) rules and procedures for ensuring the financial integrity of transactions entered into on or through the facilities of the contract market (including the clearance and settlement of the transactions with a derivatives clearing organization); and

(B) rules to ensure—

(i) the financial integrity of any—

(I) futures commission merchant; and

(II) introducing broker; and

(ii) the protection of customer funds.

(12) *Protection of Markets and Market Participants*. The board of trade shall establish and enforce rules—

(A) to protect markets and market participants from abusive practices committed by any party, including abusive practices committed by a party acting as an agent for a participant; and

(B) to promote fair and equitable trading on the contract market.

(13) *Disciplinary Procedures*. The board of trade shall establish and enforce disciplinary procedures that authorize the board of trade to discipline, suspend, or expel members or market participants that violate the rules of the board of trade, or similar methods for performing the same functions, including delegation of the functions to third parties.

(14) *Dispute Resolution*. The board of trade shall establish and enforce rules regarding, and provide

facilities for alternative dispute resolution as appropriate for, market participants and any market intermediaries.

(15) *Governance Fitness Standards.* The board of trade shall establish and enforce appropriate fitness standards for directors, members of any disciplinary committee, members of the contract market, and any other person with direct access to the facility (including any party affiliated with any person described in this paragraph).

(16) *Conflicts of Interest.* The board of trade shall establish and enforce rules—

(A) to minimize conflicts of interest in the decision-making process of the contract market; and

(B) to establish a process for resolving conflicts of interest described in subparagraph (A).

(17) *Composition of Governing Boards of Contract Markets.* The governance arrangements of the board of trade shall be designed to permit consideration of the views of market participants.

(18) *Recordkeeping.* The board of trade shall maintain records of all activities relating to the business of the contract market—

(A) in a form and manner that is acceptable to the Commission; and

(B) for a period of at least 5 years.

(19) *Antitrust Considerations.* Unless necessary or appropriate to achieve the purposes of this Act, the board of trade shall not—

(A) adopt any rule or taking any action that results in any unreasonable restraint of trade; or

(B) impose any material anticompetitive burden on trading on the contract market.

(20) *System Safeguards.* The board of trade shall—

(A) establish and maintain a program of risk analysis and oversight to identify and minimize sources of operational risk, through the development of appropriate controls and procedures, and the development of automated systems, that are reliable, secure, and have adequate scalable capacity;

(B) establish and maintain emergency procedures, backup facilities, and a plan for disaster recovery that allow for the timely recovery and resumption of operations and the fulfillment of the responsibilities and obligations of the board of trade; and

(C) periodically conduct tests to verify that backup resources are sufficient to ensure continued order processing and trade matching, price reporting, market surveillance, and maintenance of a comprehensive and accurate audit trail.

(21) *Financial Resources.*

(A) *In General.* The board of trade shall have adequate financial, operational, and managerial resources to discharge each responsibility of the board of trade.

(B) *Determination of Adequacy.* The financial resources of the board of trade shall be considered to be adequate if the value of the financial resources exceeds the total amount that would enable the contract market to cover the operating costs of the contract market for a 1–year period, as calculated on a rolling basis.

(22) *Diversity of Board of Directors.* The board of trade, if a publicly traded company, shall endeavor to recruit individuals to serve on the board of directors and the other decision-making bodies (as determined by the Commission) of the board of trade from among, and to have the composition of the bodies reflect, a broad and culturally diverse pool of qualified candidates.

(23) *Securities and Exchange Commission.* The board of trade shall keep any such records relating to swaps defined in section 1a(47)(A)(v) open to inspection and examination by the Securities and Exchange Commission.

(e) *Current Agricultural Commodities.*

(1) Subject to paragraph (2) of this subsection, a contract for purchase or sale for future delivery of an agricultural commodity enumerated in section 1a(9) that is available for trade on a contract market, as of the date of the enactment of this subsection, may be traded only on a contract market designated under this section.

(2) In order to promote responsible economic or financial innovation and fair competition, the Commission, on application by any person, after notice and public comment and opportunity for hearing, may prescribe rules and regulations to provide for the offer and sale of contracts for future delivery or options on such contracts to be conducted on a derivatives transaction execution facility.

Sec. 5a. [Repealed]

Derivatives Clearing Organizations

Sec. 5b. (a) *Registration Requirement.**

(1) *In General.* Except as provided in paragraph (2), it shall be unlawful for a derivatives clearing organization, directly or indirectly, to make use of the mails or any means or instrumentality of interstate commerce to perform the functions of a derivatives clearing organization with respect to—

(A) a contract of sale of a commodity for future delivery (or an option on the contract of sale) or option on a commodity, in each case, unless the contract or option is—

(i) excluded from this Act by subsection (a)(1)(C)(i), (c), or (f) of section 2; or

(ii) a security futures product cleared by a clearing agency registered with the Securities and Exchange Commission under the Securities Exchange Act of 1934; or

(B) a swap.

(2) *Exception.* Paragraph (1) shall not apply to a derivatives clearing organization that is registered with the Commission.

(b) *Voluntary Registration.* A person that clears 1 or more agreements, contracts, or transactions that are not required to be cleared under this Act may register with the Commission as a derivatives clearing organization.

(c) *Registration of Derivatives Clearing Organizations.*

(1) *Application.* A person desiring to register as a derivatives clearing organization shall submit to the Commission an application in such form and containing such information as the Commission may require for the purpose of making the determinations required for approval under paragraph (2).

(2) *Core Principles for Derivatives Clearing Organizations.*

(A) *Compliance.*

(i) *In General.* To be registered and to maintain registration as a derivatives clearing organization, a derivatives clearing organization shall comply with each core principle described in this paragraph and any requirement that the Commission may impose by rule or regulation pursuant to section 8a(5).

(ii) *Discretion of Derivatives Clearing Organization.* Subject to any rule or regulation prescribed by the Commission, a derivatives clearing organization shall have reasonable discretion in establishing the manner by which the derivatives clearing organization complies with each core principle described in this paragraph.

(B) *Financial Resources.*

(i) *In General.* Each derivatives clearing organization shall have adequate financial, operational, and managerial resources, as determined by the Commission, to discharge each responsibility of the derivatives clearing organization.

(ii) *Minimum Amount of Financial Resources.* Each derivatives clearing organization shall possess financial resources that, at a minimum, exceed the total amount that would—

(I) enable the organization to meet its financial obligations to its members and participants notwithstanding a default by the member or participant creating the largest financial exposure for that organization in extreme but plausible market conditions; and

(II) enable the derivatives clearing organization to cover the operating costs of the derivatives clearing organization for a period of 1 year (as calculated on a rolling basis).

(C) *Participant and Product Eligibility.*

(i) *In General.* Each derivatives clearing organization shall establish—

(I) appropriate admission and continuing eligibility standards (including sufficient financial resources and operational capacity to meet obligations arising from participation in the derivatives clearing organization) for members of, and participants in, the derivatives clearing organization; and

(II) appropriate standards for determining the eligibility of agreements, contracts,

* Dodd–Frank purported to amend the first sentence of subsection (c) by inserting "or of any swap," before "or has willfully made," however, because of prior amendments, the amendment could not be carried out.

or transactions submitted to the derivatives clearing organization for clearing.

(ii) *Required Procedures.* Each derivatives clearing organization shall establish and implement procedures to verify, on an ongoing basis, the compliance of each participation and membership requirement of the derivatives clearing organization.

(iii) *Requirements.* The participation and membership requirements of each derivatives clearing organization shall—

(I) be objective;

(II) be publicly disclosed; and

(III) permit fair and open access.

(D) *Risk Management.*

(i) *In General.* Each derivatives clearing organization shall ensure that the derivatives clearing organization possesses the ability to manage the risks associated with discharging the responsibilities of the derivatives clearing organization through the use of appropriate tools and procedures.

(ii) *Measurement of Credit Exposure.* Each derivatives clearing organization shall—

(I) not less than once during each business day of the derivatives clearing organization, measure the credit exposures of the derivatives clearing organization to each member and participant of the derivatives clearing organization; and

(II) monitor each exposure described in subclause (I) periodically during the business day of the derivatives clearing organization.

(iii) *Limitation of Exposure to Potential Losses From Defaults.* Each derivatives clearing organization, through margin requirements and other risk control mechanisms, shall limit the exposure of the derivatives clearing organization to potential losses from defaults by members and participants of the derivatives clearing organization to ensure that—

(I) the operations of the derivatives clearing organization would not be disrupted; and

(II) nondefaulting members or participants would not be exposed to losses that nondefaulting members or participants cannot anticipate or control.

(iv) *Margin Requirements.* The margin required from each member and participant of a derivatives clearing organization shall be sufficient to cover potential exposures in normal market conditions.

(v) *Requirements Regarding Models and Parameters.* Each model and parameter used in setting margin requirements under clause (iv) shall be—

(I) risk–based; and

(II) reviewed on a regular basis.

(E) *Settlement Procedures.* Each derivatives clearing organization shall—

(i) complete money settlements on a timely basis (but not less frequently than once each business day);

(ii) employ money settlement arrangements to eliminate or strictly limit the exposure of the derivatives clearing organization to settlement bank risks (including credit and liquidity risks from the use of banks to effect money settlements);

(iii) ensure that money settlements are final when effected;

(iv) maintain an accurate record of the flow of funds associated with each money settlement;

(v) possess the ability to comply with each term and condition of any permitted netting or offset arrangement with any other clearing organization;

(vi) regarding physical settlements, establish rules that clearly state each obligation of the derivatives clearing organization with respect to physical deliveries; and

(vii) ensure that each risk arising from an obligation described in clause (vi) is identified and managed.

(F) *Treatment of Funds.*

(i) *Required Standards and Procedures.* Each derivatives clearing organization shall establish standards and procedures that are designed to protect and ensure the safety of member and participant funds and assets.

(ii) *Holding of Funds and Assets.* Each derivatives clearing organization shall hold member and participant funds and assets in a manner by which to minimize the risk of loss or of delay in the access by the derivatives clearing organization to the assets and funds.

(iii) *Permissible Investments.* Funds and assets invested by a derivatives clearing organization shall be held in instruments with minimal credit, market, and liquidity risks.

(G) *Default Rules and Procedures.*

(i) *In General.* Each derivatives clearing organization shall have rules and procedures designed to allow for the efficient, fair, and safe management of events during which members or participants—

(I) become insolvent; or

(II) otherwise default on the obligations of the members or participants to the derivatives clearing organization.

(ii) *Default Procedures.* Each derivatives clearing organization shall—

(I) clearly state the default procedures of the derivatives clearing organization;

(II) make publicly available the default rules of the derivatives clearing organization; and

(III) ensure that the derivatives clearing organization may take timely action

(aa) to contain losses and liquidity pressures; and

(bb) to continue meeting each obligation of the derivatives clearing organization.

(H) *Rule Enforcement.* Each derivatives clearing organization shall—

(i) maintain adequate arrangements and resources for—

(I) the effective monitoring and enforcement of compliance with the rules of the derivatives clearing organization; and

(II) the resolution of disputes;

(ii) have the authority and ability to discipline, limit, suspend, or terminate the activities of a member or participant due to a violation by the member or participant of any rule of the derivatives clearing organization; and

(iii) report to the Commission regarding rule enforcement activities and sanctions imposed against members and participants as provided in clause (ii).

(I) *System Safeguards.* Each derivatives clearing organization shall—

(i) establish and maintain a program of risk analysis and oversight to identify and minimize sources of operational risk through the development of appropriate controls and procedures, and automated systems, that are reliable, secure, and have adequate scalable capacity;

(ii) establish and maintain emergency procedures, backup facilities, and a plan for disaster recovery that allows for—

(I) the timely recovery and resumption of operations of the derivatives clearing organization; and

(II) the fulfillment of each obligation and responsibility of the derivatives clearing organization; and

(iii) periodically conduct tests to verify that the backup resources of the derivatives clearing organization are sufficient to ensure daily processing, clearing, and settlement.

(J) *Reporting.* Each derivatives clearing organization shall provide to the Commission all information that the Commission determines to be necessary to conduct oversight of the derivatives clearing organization.

(K) *Recordkeeping.* Each derivatives clearing organization shall maintain records of all activities related to the business of the derivatives clearing organization as a derivatives clearing organization—

(i) in a form and manner that is acceptable to the Commission; and

(ii) for a period of not less than 5 years.

(L) *Public Information.*

(i) *In General.* Each derivatives clearing organization shall provide to market participants sufficient information to enable the market participants to identify and evaluate accurately the risks and costs associated with using the services of the derivatives clearing organization.

(ii) *Availability of Information.* Each derivatives clearing organization shall make information concerning the rules and operating and default procedures governing the clearing and settlement systems of the derivatives clearing organization available to market participants.

(iii) *Public Disclosure.* Each derivatives clearing organization shall disclose publicly and to the Commission information concerning—

(I) the terms and conditions of each contract, agreement, and transaction cleared and settled by the derivatives clearing organization;

(II) each clearing and other fee that the derivatives clearing organization charges the members and participants of the derivatives clearing organization;

(III) the margin–setting methodology, and the size and composition, of the financial resource package of the derivatives clearing organization;

(IV) daily settlement prices, volume, and open interest for each contract settled or cleared by the derivatives clearing organization; and

(V) any other matter relevant to participation in the settlement and clearing activities of the derivatives clearing organization.

(M) *Information–Sharing.* Each derivatives clearing organization shall—

(i) enter into, and abide by the terms of, each appropriate and applicable domestic and international information–sharing agreement; and

(ii) use relevant information obtained from each agreement described in clause (i) in carrying out the risk management program of the derivatives clearing organization.

(N) *Antitrust Considerations.* Unless necessary or appropriate to achieve the purposes of this Act, a derivatives clearing organization shall not—

(i) adopt any rule or take any action that results in any unreasonable restraint of trade; or

(ii) impose any material anticompetitive burden.

(O) *Governance Fitness Standards.*

(i) *Governance Arrangements.* Each derivatives clearing organization shall establish governance arrangements that are transparent—

(I) to fulfill public interest requirements; and

(II) to permit the consideration of the views of owners and participants.

(ii) *Fitness Standards.* Each derivatives clearing organization shall establish and enforce appropriate fitness standards for—

(I) directors;

(II) members of any disciplinary committee;

(III) members of the derivatives clearing organization;

(IV) any other individual or entity with direct access to the settlement or clearing activities of the derivatives clearing organization; and

(V) any party affiliated with any individual or entity described in this clause.

(P) *Conflicts of Interest.* Each derivatives clearing organization shall—

(i) establish and enforce rules to minimize conflicts of interest in the decision–making process of the derivatives clearing organization; and

(ii) establish a process for resolving conflicts of interest described in clause (i).

(Q) *Composition of Governing Boards.* Each derivatives clearing organization shall ensure that the composition of the governing board or committee of the derivatives clearing organization includes market participants.

(R) *Legal Risk.* Each derivatives clearing organization shall have a well–founded, transparent, and enforceable legal framework for each aspect of the activities of the derivatives clearing organization.

(3) *Orders Concerning Competition.* A derivatives clearing organization may request the Commission to issue an order concerning whether a rule or practice of the applicant is the least anticompetitive means of achieving the objectives, purposes, and policies of this chapter.

(d) *Existing Derivatives Clearing Organizations.* A derivatives clearing organization shall be deemed to be registered under this section to the extent that the derivatives clearing organization clears agreements, contracts, or transactions for a board of trade that has been designated by the Commission as a contract market for such agreements, contracts, or transactions before December 21, 2000.

(e) *Appointment of Trustee.*

(1) *In General.* If a proceeding under section 5e of this title results in the suspension or revocation of the registration of a derivatives clearing organization, or if a derivatives clearing organization withdraws from registration, the Commission, on notice to the derivatives clearing organization, may apply to the appropriate United States district court where the derivatives clearing organization is located for the appointment of a trustee.

(2) *Assumption of Jurisdiction.* If the Commission applies for appointment of a trustee under paragraph (1)—

(A) the court may take exclusive jurisdiction over the derivatives clearing organization and the records and assets of the derivatives clearing organization, wherever located; and

(B) if the court takes jurisdiction under subparagraph (A), the court shall appoint the Commission, or a person designated by the Commission, as trustee with power to take possession and continue to operate or terminate the operations of the derivatives clearing organization in an orderly manner for the protection of participants, subject to such terms and conditions as the court may prescribe.

(f) *Linking of Regulated Clearing Facilities.*

(1) *In General.* The Commission shall facilitate the linking or coordination of derivatives clearing organizations registered under this chapter with other regulated clearance facilities for the coordinated settlement of cleared transactions. In order to minimize systemic risk, under no circumstances shall a derivatives clearing organization be compelled to accept the counterparty credit risk of another clearing organization.

(2) *Coordination.* In carrying out paragraph (1), the Commission shall coordinate with the Federal banking agencies and the Securities and Exchange Commission.

(g) *Existing Depository Institutions and Clearing Agencies.*

(1) *In General.* A depository institution or clearing agency registered with the Securities and Exchange Commission under the Securities Exchange Act of 1934 that is required to be registered as a derivatives clearing organization under this section is deemed to be registered under this section to the extent that, before the date of enactment of this subsection—

(A) the depository institution cleared swaps as a multi-lateral clearing organization; or

(B) the clearing agency cleared swaps.

(2) *Conversion of Depository Institutions.* A depository institution to which this subsection applies may, by the vote of the shareholders owning not less than 51 percent of the voting interests of the depository institution, be converted into a State corporation, partnership, limited liability company, or similar legal form pursuant to a plan of conversion, if the conversion is not in contravention of applicable State law.

(3) *Sharing of Information.* The Securities and Exchange Commission shall make available to the Commission, upon request, all information determined to be relevant by the Securities and Exchange Commission regarding a clearing agency deemed to be registered with the Commission under paragraph (1).

(h) *Exemptions.* The Commission may exempt, conditionally or unconditionally, a derivatives clearing organization from registration under this section for the clearing of swaps if the Commission determines that the derivatives clearing organization is subject to comparable, comprehensive supervision and regulation by the Securities and Exchange Commission or the appropriate government authorities in the home country of the organization. Such conditions may include, but are not limited to, requiring that the derivatives clearing organization be available for inspection by the Commission and make available all information requested by the Commission.

(i) *Designation of Chief Compliance Officer.*

(1) *In General.* Each derivatives clearing organization shall designate an individual to serve as a chief compliance officer.

(2) *Duties.* The chief compliance officer shall—

(A) report directly to the board or to the senior officer of the derivatives clearing organization;

(B) review the compliance of the derivatives clearing organization with respect to the core principles described in subsection (c)(2);

(C) in consultation with the board of the derivatives clearing organization, a body performing a function similar to the board of the derivatives clearing organization, or the senior officer of the derivatives clearing organization, resolve any conflicts of interest that may arise;

(D) be responsible for administering each policy and procedure that is required to be established pursuant to this section;

(E) ensure compliance with this Act (including regulations) relating to agreements, contracts, or transactions, including each rule prescribed by the Commission under this section;

(F) establish procedures for the remediation of non-compliance issues identified by the compliance officer through any

(i) compliance office review;

(ii) look-back;

(iii) internal or external audit finding;

(iv) self-reported error; or

(v) validated complaint; and

(G) establish and follow appropriate procedures for the handling, management response, remediation, re-testing, and closing of noncompliance issues.

(3) *Annual Reports.*

(A) *In General.* In accordance with rules prescribed by the Commission, the chief compliance officer shall annually prepare and sign a report that contains a description of—

(i) the compliance of the derivatives clearing organization of the compliance officer with respect to this Act (including regulations); and

(ii) each policy and procedure of the derivatives clearing organization of the compliance officer (including the code of ethics and conflict of interest policies of the derivatives clearing organization).

(B) *Requirements.* A compliance report under subparagraph (A) shall—

(i) accompany each appropriate financial report of the derivatives clearing organization that is required to be furnished to the Commission pursuant to this section; and

(ii) include a certification that, under penalty of law, the compliance report is accurate and complete.

(k) *Reporting Requirements.*

(1) *Duty of Derivatives Clearing Organizations.* Each derivatives clearing organization that clears swaps shall provide to the Commission all information that is determined by the Commission to be necessary to perform each responsibility of the Commission under this Act.

(2) *Data Collection and Maintenance Requirements.* The Commission shall adopt data collection and maintenance requirements for swaps cleared by derivatives clearing organizations that are comparable to the corresponding requirements for—

(A) swaps data reported to swap data repositories; and

(B) swaps traded on swap execution facilities.

(3) *Reports on Security–Based Swap Agreements to be Shared with the Securities and Exchange Commission.*

(A) *In General.* A derivatives clearing organization that clears security-based swap agreements (as defined in section 1a(47)(A)(v)) shall, upon request, open to inspection and examination to the Securities and Exchange Commission all books and records relating to such security–based swap agreements, consistent with the confidentiality and disclosure requirements of section 8.

(B) *Jurisdiction.* Nothing in this paragraph shall affect the exclusive jurisdiction of the Commission to prescribe recordkeeping and reporting requirements for a derivatives clearing organization that is registered with the Commission.

(4) *Information Sharing.* Subject to section 8, and upon request, the Commission shall share information collected under paragraph (2) with—

(A) the Board;

(B) the Securities and Exchange Commission;

(C) each appropriate prudential regulator;

(D) the Financial Stability Oversight Council;

(E) the Department of Justice; and

(F) any other person that the Commission determines to be appropriate, including—

(i) foreign financial supervisors (including foreign futures authorities);

(ii) foreign central banks; and

(iii) foreign ministries.

(5) *Confidentiality Agreement*. Before the Commission may share information with any entity described in paragraph (4), the Commission shall receive a written agreement from each entity stating that the entity shall abide by the confidentiality requirements described in section 8 of this Act relating to the information on swap transactions that is provided.

(6) *Public Information*. Each derivatives clearing organization that clears swaps shall provide to the Commission (including any designee of the Commission) information under paragraph (2) in such form and at such frequency as is required by the Commission to comply with the public reporting requirements contained in section 2(a)(13).

Common Provisions Applicable to Registered Entities

Sec. 5c. (a) *Acceptable Business Practices under Core Principles.*

(1) In General. Consistent with the purposes of this Act, the Commission may issue interpretations, or approve interpretations submitted to the Commission, of sections 5(d) and 5b(c)(2), to describe what would constitute an acceptable business practice under such sections.

(2) *Effect of Interpretation*. An interpretation issued under paragraph (1) may provide the exclusive means for complying with each section described in paragraph (1).

(b) *Delegation of Functions under Core Principles.*

(1) *In General*. A contract market, derivatives transaction execution facility, or electronic trading facility with respect to a significant price discovery contract may comply with any applicable core principle through delegation of any relevant function to a registered futures association or a registered entity that is not an electronic trading facility.

(2) *Responsibility*. A contract market, derivatives transaction execution facility, or electronic trading facility that delegates a function under paragraph (1) shall remain responsible for carrying out the function.

(3) *Noncompliance*. If a contract market, derivatives transaction execution facility, or electronic trading facility that delegates a function under paragraph (1) becomes aware that a delegated function is not being performed as required under this Act, the contract market, derivatives transaction execution facility, or electronic trading facility shall promptly take steps to address the noncompliance.

(c) *New Contracts, New Rules, and Rule Amendments.**

(1) *In General*. A registered entity may elect to list for trading or accept for clearing any new contract, or other instrument, or may elect to approve and implement any new rule or rule amendment, by providing to the Commission (and the Secretary of the Treasury, in the case of a contract of sale of a government security for future delivery (or option on such a contract) or a rule or rule amendment specifically related to such a contract) a written certification that the new contract or instrument or clearing of the new contract or instrument, new rule, or rule amendment complies with this Act (including regulations under this Act).

(2) *Rule Review*. The new rule or rule amendment described in paragraph (1) shall become effective, pursuant to the certification of the registered entity and notice of such certification to its members (in a manner to be determined by the Commission), on the date that is 10 business days after the date on which the Commission receives the certification (or such shorter period as determined by the Commission by rule or regulation) unless the Commission notifies the registered entity within such time that it is staying the certification because there exist novel or complex issues that require additional time to analyze, an inadequate explanation by the submitting registered entity, or a potential inconsistency with this Act (including regulations under this Act.

(3) *Stay of Certification for Rules.*

(A) A notification by the Commission pursuant to paragraph (2) shall stay the certification of the new rule or rule amendment for up to an additional 90 days from the date of the notification.

(B) A rule or rule amendment subject to a stay pursuant to subparagraph (A) shall become effective, pursuant to the certification of

* Dodd–Frank made conflicting amendments to 5c(c). See Dodd–Frank Act 717(d), 721(e)(7), 745(b).

the registered entity, at the expiration of the period described in subparagraph (A) unless the Commission—

(i) withdraws the stay prior to that time; or

(ii) notifies the registered entity during such period that it objects to the proposed certification on the grounds that it is inconsistent with this Act (including regulations under this Act).

(C) The Commission shall provide a not less than 30-day public comment period, within the 90-day period in which the stay is in effect as described in subparagraph (A), whenever the Commission reviews a rule or rule amendment pursuant to a notification by the Commission under this paragraph.

(4) *Prior Approval.*

(A) *In General.* A registered entity may request that the Commission grant prior approval to any new contract or other instrument, new rule, or rule amendment.

(B) *Prior Approval Required.* Notwithstanding any other provision of this section, a designated contract market shall submit to the Commission for prior approval each rule amendment that materially changes the terms and conditions, as determined by the Commission, in any contract of sale for future delivery of a commodity specifically enumerated in section 1a(10)* (or any option thereon) traded through its facilities if the rule amendment applies to contracts and delivery months which have already been listed for trading and have open interest.

(C) *Deadline.* If prior approval is requested under subparagraph (A), the Commission shall take final action on the request not later than 90 days after submission of the request, unless the person submitting the request agrees to an extension of the time limitation established under this subparagraph.

(5) *Approval.*

(A) *Rules.* The Commission shall approve a new rule, or rule amendment, of a registered entity unless the Commission finds that the new rule, or rule amendment, is inconsistent with this subtitle (including regulations).

(B) *Contracts and Instruments.* The Commission shall approve a new contract or other instrument unless the Commission finds that the new contract or other instrument would violate this Act (including regulations).

(C) *Special Rule for Review and Approval of Event Contracts and Swaps Contracts.*

(i) *Event Contracts.* In connection with the listing of agreements, contracts, transactions, or swaps in excluded commodities that are based upon the occurrence, extent of an occurrence, or contingency (other than a change in the price, rate, value, or levels of a commodity described in section 1a(2)(i)), by a designated contract market or swap execution facility, the Commission may determine that such agreements, contracts, or transactions are contrary to the public interest if the agreements, contracts, or transactions involve—

(I) activity that is unlawful under any Federal or State law;

(II) terrorism;

(III) assassination;

(IV) war;

(V) gaming; or

(VI) other similar activity determined by the Commission, by rule or regulation, to be contrary to the public interest.

(ii) *Prohibition.* No agreement, contract, or transaction determined by the Commission to be contrary to the public interest under clause (i) may be listed or made available for clearing or trading on or through a registered entity.

(iii) *Swaps Contracts.*

(I) *In General.* In connection with the listing of a swap for clearing by a derivatives clearing organization, the Commission shall determine, upon request or on its own motion, the initial eligibility, or the continuing qualification, of a derivatives clearing organization to clear such a swap under those criteria, conditions, or rules that the Commission, in its discretion, determines.

(II) *Requirements.* Any such criteria, conditions, or rules shall consider—

(aa) the financial integrity of the derivatives clearing organization; and

(bb) any other factors which the Commission determines may be appropriate.

* Probably should be 1a(g). See Dodd–Frank Act 721(e)(7).

(iv) *Deadline.* The Commission shall take final action under clauses (i) and (ii) in not later than 90 days from the commencement of its review unless the party seeking to offer the contract or swap agrees to an extension of this time limitation.

(d) [Deleted]

(e) *Reservation of Emergency Authority.* Nothing in this section shall limit or in any way affect the emergency powers of the Commission provided in section 8a(9).

(f) *Rules to Avoid Duplicative Regulation of Dual Registrants.* Consistent with this Act, each designated contract market and registered derivatives transaction execution facility shall issue such rules as are necessary to avoid duplicative or conflicting rules applicable to any futures commission merchant registered with the Commission pursuant to section 4d(e) of this Act (except paragraph (2) thereof), that is also registered with the Securities and Exchange Commission pursuant to section 15(b) of the Securities Exchange Act of 1934 (except paragraph (11) thereof) with respect to the application of—

(1) rules of such designated contract market or registered derivatives transaction execution facility of the type specified in section 4d(c) of this Act involving security futures products; and

(2) similar rules of national securities associations registered pursuant to section 15A(a) of the Securities Exchange Act of 1934 and national securities exchanges registered pursuant to section 6(g) of such Act involving security futures products.

Sec. 5d. [Repealed].

Suspension or Revocation of Designation as Registered Entity

Sec. 5e. The failure of a registered entity to comply with any provision of this Act, or any regulation or order of the Commission under this Act, shall be cause for the suspension of the registered entity for a period not to exceed 180 days, or revocation of designation as a registered entity, in accordance with the procedures and subject to the judicial review provided in section 6(b).

Designation of Securities Exchanges and Associations as Contract Markets

Sec. 5f. (a) Any board of trade that is registered with the Securities and Exchange Commission as a national securities exchange, is a national securities association registered pursuant to section 15A(a) of the Securities Exchange Act of 1934, or is an alternative trading system shall be a designated contract market in security futures products if—

(1) such national securities exchange, national securities association, or alternative trading system lists or trades no other contracts of sale for future delivery, except for security futures products;

(2) such national securities exchange, national securities association, or alternative trading system files written notice with the Commission in such form as the Commission, by rule, may prescribe containing such information as the Commission, by rule, may prescribe as necessary or appropriate in the public interest or for the protection of customers; and

(3) the registration of such national securities exchange, national securities association, or alternative trading system is not suspended pursuant to an order by the Securities and Exchange Commission.

Such designation shall be effective contemporaneously with the submission of notice, in written or electronic form, to the Commission.

(b)(1) A national securities exchange, national securities association, or alternative trading system that is designated as a contract market pursuant to section 5f shall be exempt from the following provisions of this Act and the rules thereunder:

(A) Subsections (c), (e), and (g) of section 4c.

(B) Section 4j.

(C) Section 5.

(D) Section 5c.

(E) Section 6a.

(F) Section 8(d).

(G) Section 9(f).

(H) Section 16.

(2) An alternative trading system that is a designated contract market under this section shall be required to be a member of a futures association registered under section 17 and shall be exempt from any provision of this Act that would require such alternative trading system to—

(A) set rules governing the conduct of subscribers other than the conduct of such subscribers' trading on such alternative trading system; or

(B) discipline subscribers other than by exclusion from trading.

(3) To the extent that an alternative trading system is exempt from any provision of this Act pursuant to paragraph (2) of this subsection, the futures association registered under section 17 of which the alternative trading system is a member shall set rules governing the conduct of subscribers to the alternative trading system and discipline the subscribers.

(4)(A) Except as provided in subparagraph (B), but notwithstanding any other provision of this Act, the Commission, by rule, regulation, or order, may conditionally or unconditionally exempt any designated contract market in security futures subject to the designation requirement of this section from any provision of this Act or of any rule or regulation thereunder, to the extent such exemption is necessary or appropriate in the public interest and is consistent with the protection of investors.

(B) The Commission shall, by rule or regulation, determine the procedures under which an exemptive order under this section is granted and may, in its sole discretion, decline to entertain any application for an order of exemption under this section.

(C) An alternative trading system shall not be deemed to be an exchange for any purpose as a result of the designation of such alternative trading system as a contract market under this section.

Privacy

Sec. 5g. (a) *Treatment as Financial Institutions.* Notwithstanding section 509(3)(B) of the Gramm–Leach–Bliley Act, any futures commission merchant, commodity trading advisor, commodity pool operator, or introducing broker that is subject to the jurisdiction of the Commission under this Act with respect to any financial activity shall be treated as a financial institution for purposes of title V of such Act with respect to such financial activity.

(b) *Treatment of CFTC as Federal Functional Regulator.* For purposes of title V of such Act, the Commission shall be treated as a Federal functional regulator within the meaning of section 509(2) of such Act and shall prescribe regulations under such title within 6 months after the date of enactment of this section.

Swap Execution Facilities

Sec. 5h. (a) *Registration.*

(1) *In General.* No person may operate a facility for the trading or processing of swaps unless the facility is registered as a swap execution facility or as a designated contract market under this section.

(2) *Dual Registration.* Any person that is registered as a swap execution facility under this section shall register with the Commission regardless of whether the person also is registered with the Securities and Exchange Commission as a swap execution facility.

(b) *Trading and Trade Processing.*

(1) *In General.* Except as specified in paragraph (2), a swap execution facility that is registered under subsection (a) may—

(A) make available for trading any swap; and

(B) facilitate trade processing of any swap.

(2) *Agricultural Swaps.* A swap execution facility may not list for trading or confirm the execution of any swap in an agricultural commodity (as defined by the Commission) except pursuant to a rule or regulation of the Commission allowing the swap under such terms and conditions as the Commission shall prescribe.

(c) *Identification of Facility Used to Trade Swaps by Contract Markets.* A board of trade that operates a contract market shall, to the extent that the board of trade also operates a swap execution facility and uses the same electronic trade execution system for listing and executing trades of swaps on or through the contract market and the swap execution facility, identify whether the electronic trading of such swaps is taking place on or through the contract market or the swap execution facility.

(d) *Rule-Writing.*

(1) The Securities and Exchange Commission and Commodity Futures Trading Commission may promulgate rules defining the universe of swaps that can be executed on a swap execution facility. These rules shall take into account the price and nonprice requirements of the counterparties to a swap and the goal of this section as set forth in subsection (e).

(2) For all swaps that are not required to be executed through a swap execution facility as defined in paragraph (1), such trades may be executed

through any other available means of interstate commerce.

(3) The Securities and Exchange Commission and Commodity Futures Trading Commission shall update these rules as necessary to account for technological and other innovation.

(e) *Rule of Construction.* The goal of this section is to promote the trading of swaps on swap execution facilities and to promote pre-trade price transparency in the swaps market.

(f) *Core Principles for Swap Execution Facilities.*

(1) *Compliance with Core Principles.*

(A) *In General.* To be registered, and maintain registration, as a swap execution facility, the swap execution facility shall comply with

(i) the core principles described in this subsection; and

(ii) any requirement that the Commission may impose by rule or regulation pursuant to section 8a(5).

(B) *Reasonable Discretion of Swap Execution Facility.* Unless otherwise determined by the Commission by rule or regulation, a swap execution facility described in subparagraph (A) shall have reasonable discretion in establishing the manner in which the swap execution facility complies with the core principles described in this subsection.

(2) *Compliance with Rules.* A swap execution facility shall—

(A) establish and enforce compliance with any rule of the swap execution facility, including—

(i) the terms and conditions of the swaps traded or processed on or through the swap execution facility; and

(ii) any limitation on access to the swap execution facility;

(B) establish and enforce trading, trade processing, and participation rules that will deter abuses and have the capacity to detect, investigate, and enforce those rules, including means—

(i) to provide market participants with impartial access to the market; and

(ii) to capture information that may be used in establishing whether rule violations have occurred;

(C) establish rules governing the operation of the facility, including rules specifying trading procedures to be used in entering and executing orders traded or posted on the facility, including block trades; and

(D) provide by its rules that when a swap dealer or major swap participant enters into or facilitates a swap that is subject to the mandatory clearing requirement of section 2(h), the swap dealer or major swap participant shall be responsible for compliance with the mandatory trading requirement under section 2(h)(8).

(3) *Swaps not Readily Susceptible to Manipulation.* The swap execution facility shall permit trading only in swaps that are not readily susceptible to manipulation.

(4) *Monitoring of Trading and Trade Processing.* The swap execution facility shall—

(A) establish and enforce rules or terms and conditions defining, or specifications detailing—

(i) trading procedures to be used in entering and executing orders traded on or through the facilities of the swap execution facility; and

(ii) procedures for trade processing of swaps on or through the facilities of the swap execution facility; and

(B) monitor trading in swaps to prevent manipulation, price distortion, and disruptions of the delivery or cash settlement process through surveillance, compliance, and disciplinary practices and procedures, including methods for conducting real-time monitoring of trading and comprehensive and accurate trade reconstructions.

(5) *Ability to Obtain Information.* The swap execution facility shall—

(A) establish and enforce rules that will allow the facility to obtain any necessary information to perform any of the functions described in this section;

(B) provide the information to the Commission on request; and

(C) have the capacity to carry out such international information-sharing agreements as the Commission may require.

(6) *Position Limits or Accountability.*

(A) *In General.* To reduce the potential threat of market manipulation or congestion, especially during trading in the delivery month, a swap execution facility that is a trading facility shall adopt for each of the contracts of the facility, as is necessary and appropriate, position limitations or position accountability for speculators.

(B) *Position Limits.* For any contract that is subject to a position limitation established by the Commission pursuant to section 4a(a), the swap execution facility shall—

(i) set its position limitation at a level no higher than the Commission limitation; and

(ii) monitor positions established on or through the swap execution facility for compliance with the limit set by the Commission and the limit, if any, set by the swap execution facility.

(7) *Financial Integrity of Transactions.* The swap execution facility shall establish and enforce rules and procedures for ensuring the financial integrity of swaps entered on or through the facilities of the swap execution facility, including the clearance and settlement of the swaps pursuant to section 2(h)(1).

(8) *Emergency Authority.* The swap execution facility shall adopt rules to provide for the exercise of emergency authority, in consultation or cooperation with the Commission, as is necessary and appropriate, including the authority to liquidate or transfer open positions in any swap or to suspend or curtail trading in a swap.

(9) *Timely Publication of Trading Information.*

(A) *In General.* The swap execution facility shall make public timely information on price, trading volume, and other trading data on swaps to the extent prescribed by the Commission.

(B) *Capacity of Swap Execution Facility.* The swap execution facility shall be required to have the capacity to electronically capture and transmit trade information with respect to transactions executed on the facility.

(10) *Recordkeeping and Reporting.*

(A) *In General.* A swap execution facility shall—

(i) maintain records of all activities relating to the business of the facility, including a complete audit trail, in a form and manner acceptable to the Commission for a period of 5 years;

(ii) report to the Commission, in a form and manner acceptable to the Commission, such information as the Commission determines to be necessary or appropriate for the Commission to perform the duties of the Commission under this Act; and

(iii) shall keep any such records relating to swaps defined in section 1a(47)(A)(v) open to inspection and examination by the Securities and Exchange Commission.

(B) *Requirements.* The Commission shall adopt data collection and reporting requirements for swap execution facilities that are comparable to corresponding requirements for derivatives clearing organizations and swap data repositories.

(11) *Antitrust Considerations.* Unless necessary or appropriate to achieve the purposes of this Act, the swap execution facility shall not—

(A) adopt any rules or taking any actions that result in any unreasonable restraint of trade; or

(B) impose any material anticompetitive burden on trading or clearing.

(12) *Conflicts of Interest.* The swap execution facility shall—

(A) establish and enforce rules to minimize conflicts of interest in its decision–making process; and

(B) establish a process for resolving the conflicts of interest.

(13) *Financial Resources.*

(A) *In General.* The swap execution facility shall have adequate financial, operational, and managerial resources to discharge each responsibility of the swap execution facility.

(B) *Determination of Resource Adequacy.* The financial resources of a swap execution facility shall be considered to be adequate if the value of the financial resources exceeds the total amount that would enable the swap execution facility to cover the operating costs of the swap execution facility for a 1–year period, as calculated on a rolling basis.

(14) *System Safeguards.* The swap execution facility shall—

(A) establish and maintain a program of risk analysis and oversight to identify and minimize sources of operational risk, through the development of appropriate controls and procedures, and automated systems, that—

(i) are reliable and secure; and

(ii) have adequate scalable capacity;

(B) establish and maintain emergency procedures, backup facilities, and a plan for disaster recovery that allow for—

(i) the timely recovery and resumption of operations; and

(ii) the fulfillment of the responsibilities and obligations of the swap execution facility; and

(C) periodically conduct tests to verify that the backup resources of the swap execution facility are sufficient to ensure continued—

(i) order processing and trade matching;

(ii) price reporting;

(iii) market surveillance and

(iv) maintenance of a comprehensive and accurate audit trail.

(15) *Designation of Chief Compliance Officer*.

(A) *In General.* Each swap execution facility shall designate an individual to serve as a chief compliance officer.

(B) *Duties.* The chief compliance officer shall—

(i) report directly to the board or to the senior officer of the facility;

(ii) review compliance with the core principles in this subsection;

(iii) in consultation with the board of the facility, a body performing a function similar to that of a board, or the senior officer of the facility, resolve any conflicts of interest that may arise;

(iv) be responsible for establishing and administering the policies and procedures required to be established pursuant to this section;

(v) ensure compliance with this Act and the rules and regulations issued under this Act, including rules prescribed by the Commission pursuant to this section; and

(vi) establish procedures for the remediation of noncompliance issues found during compliance office reviews, look backs, internal or external audit findings, self–reported errors, or through validated complaints.

(C) *Requirements for Procedures.* In establishing procedures under subparagraph (B)(vi), the chief compliance officer shall design the procedures to establish the handling, management response, remediation, retesting, and closing of noncompliance issues.

(D) *Annual Reports.*

(i) *In General.* In accordance with rules prescribed by the Commission, the chief compliance officer shall annually prepare and sign a report that contains a description of—

(I) the compliance of the swap execution facility with this Act; and

(II) the policies and procedures, including the code of ethics and conflict of interest policies, of the swap execution facility.

(ii) *Requirements.* The chief compliance officer shall—

(I) submit each report described in clause (i) with the appropriate financial report of the swap execution facility that is required to be submitted to the Commission pursuant to this section; and

(II) include in the report a certification that, under penalty of law, the report is accurate and complete.

(g) *Exemptions.* The Commission may exempt, conditionally or unconditionally, a swap execution facility from registration under this section if the Commission finds that the facility is subject to comparable, comprehensive supervision and regulation on a consolidated basis by the Securities and Exchange Commission, a prudential regulator, or the appropriate governmental authorities in the home country of the facility.

(h) *Rules.* The Commission shall prescribe rules governing the regulation of alternative swap execution facilities under this section.

Application for Designation—Hearing

Sec. 6. (a) Any person desiring to be designated or registered as a contract market or derivatives transaction execution facility shall make application to the Commission for the designation or registration and accompany the same with a showing that it complies with the conditions set forth in this Act, and with a sufficient assurance that it will continue to comply with [the] the requirements of this Act.

The Commission shall approve or deny an application for designation or registration as a contract market or derivatives transaction execution facility within 180 days of the filing of the application. If the Commission notifies the person that its application is materially incomplete and specifies the deficiencies in the application, the running of the 180-day period shall be stayed from the time of such notification until the application is resubmitted in completed form: *Provided,* That the Commission shall have not less than sixty days to approve or deny the application from the time the application is resubmitted in completed form. If the Commission denies an application, it shall specify the grounds for the denial. In the event of a refusal to designate or register as a contract market or derivatives transaction execution facility any person that has made application therefor, the person shall be afforded an opportunity for a hearing on the record before the commission, with the right to appeal an adverse decision after such hearing to the court of appeals as provided for in other cases in subsection (b) of this section.

(b) The Commission is authorized to suspend for a period not to exceed 6 months or to revoke the designation or registration of any contract market or derivatives transaction execution facility, on a showing that the contract market or derivatives transaction execution facility is not enforcing or has not enforced its rules of government, made a condition of its designation or registration as set forth in sections 5 through 5b or section 5f, or that the contract market or derivatives transaction execution facility or electronic trading facility, or any director, officer, agent, or employee thereof, otherwise is violating or has violated any of the provisions of this Act or any of the rules, regulations, or orders of the Commission thereunder. Such suspension or revocation shall only be made after a notice to the officers of the contract market or derivatives transaction execution facility or electronic trading facility affected and upon a hearing on the record: *Provided,* That such suspension or revocation shall be final and conclusive, unless within fifteen days after such suspension or revocation by the Commission such person appeals to the court of appeals for the circuit in which it has its principal place of business, by filing with the clerk of such court a written petition praying that the order of the Commission be set aside or modified in the manner stated in the petition, together with a bond in such sum as the court may determine, conditioned that such person will pay the costs of the proceedings if the court so directs. The clerk of the court in which such a petition is filed shall immediately cause a copy thereof to be delivered to the Commission and file in the court the record in such proceedings, as provided in section 2112 of title 28, United States Code. The testimony and evidence taken or submitted before the Commission, duly filed as aforesaid as a part of the record, shall be considered by the court of appeals as the evidence in the case. Such a court may affirm or set aside the order of the Commission or may direct it to modify its order. No such order of the Commission shall be modified or set aside by the court of appeals unless it is shown by the person that the order is unsupported by the weight of the evidence or was issued without due notice and a reasonable opportunity having been afforded to such person for a hearing, or infringes the Constitution of the United States, or is beyond the jurisdiction of the Commission.

(c) *Prohibition Regarding Manipulation and False Information.**

(1) *Prohibition Against Manipulation.* It shall be unlawful for any person, directly or indirectly, to use or employ, or attempt to use or employ, in connection with any swap, or a contract of sale of any commodity in interstate commerce, or for future delivery on or subject to the rules of any registered entity, any manipulative or deceptive device or contrivance, in contravention of such rules and regulations as the Commission shall promulgate by not later than 1 year after the date of enactment of the Dodd–Frank Wall Street Reform and Consumer Protection Act, provided no rule or regulation promulgated by the Commission shall require any person to disclose to another person nonpublic information that may be material to the market price, rate, or level of the commodity transaction, except as necessary to make any statement made to the other person in or in connection with the transaction not misleading in any material respect.

(A) *Special Provision for Manipulation by False Reporting.* Unlawful manipulation for purposes of this paragraph shall include, but not be limited to, delivering, or causing to be delivered for transmission through the mails or interstate commerce, by any means of communication whatsoever, a false or misleading or inaccurate report concerning crop or market information or conditions that affect or tend to affect the price of any commodity in interstate commerce, knowing, or acting in reckless disregard of the fact that such report is false, misleading or inaccurate.

* Dodd–Frank purported to amend the first sentence of subsection (c) by inserting "or of any swap," before "or has willfully made," however, because of prior amendments, the amendment could not be carried out.

(B) *Effect on Other Law.* Nothing in this paragraph shall affect, or be construed to affect, the applicability of section 9(a)(2).

(C) *Good Faith Mistakes.* Mistakenly transmitting, in good faith, false or misleading or inaccurate information to a price reporting service would not be sufficient to violate subsection (c)(1)(A).

(2) *Prohibition Regarding False Information.* It shall be unlawful for any person to make any false or misleading statement of a material fact to the Commission, including in any registration application or any report filed with the Commission under this Act, or any other information relating to a swap, or a contract of sale of a commodity, in interstate commerce, or for future delivery on or subject to the rules of any registered entity, or to omit to state in any such statement any material fact that is necessary to make any statement of a material fact made not misleading in any material respect, if the person knew, or reasonably should have known, the statement to be false or misleading.

(3) *Other Manipulation.* In addition to the prohibition in paragraph (1), it shall be unlawful for any person, directly or indirectly, to manipulate or attempt to manipulate the price of any swap, or of any commodity in interstate commerce, or for future delivery on or subject to the rules of any registered entity.

(4) *Enforcement.*

(A) *Authority of Commission.* If the Commission has reason to believe that any person (other than a registered entity) is violating or has violated this subsection, or any other provision of this Act (including any rule, regulation, or order of the Commission promulgated in accordance with this subsection or any other provision of this Act), the Commission may serve upon the person a complaint.

(B) *Contents of Complaint.* A complaint under subparagraph (A) shall—

(i) contain a description of the charges against the person that is the subject of the complaint; and

(ii) have attached or contain a notice of hearing that specifies the date and location of the hearing regarding the complaint.

(C) *Hearing.* A hearing described in subparagraph (B)(ii)—

(i) shall be held not later than 3 days after service of the complaint described in subparagraph (A);

(ii) shall require the person to show cause regarding why—

(I) an order should not be made—

(aa) to prohibit the person from trading on, or subject to the rules of, any registered entity; and

(bb) to direct all registered entities to refuse all privileges to the person until further notice of the Commission; and

(II) the registration of the person, if registered with the Commission in any capacity, should not be suspended or revoked; and

(iii) may be held before—

(I) the Commission; or

(II) an administrative law judge designated by the Commission, under which the administrative law judge shall ensure that all evidence is recorded in written form and submitted to the Commission.

(5) *Subpoena.* For the purpose of securing effective enforcement of the provisions of this Act, for the purpose of any investigation or proceeding under this Act, and for the purpose of any action taken under section 12(f), any member of the Commission or any Administrative Law Judge or other officer designated by the Commission (except as provided in paragraph (7)) may administer oaths and affirmations, subpoena witnesses, compel their attendance, take evidence, and require the production of any books, papers, correspondence, memoranda, or other records that the Commission deems relevant or material to the inquiry.

(6) *Witnesses.* The attendance of witnesses and the production of any such records may be required from any place in the United States, any State, or any foreign country or jurisdiction at any designated place of hearing.

(7) *Service.* A subpoena issued under this section may be served upon any person who is not to be found within the territorial jurisdiction of any court of the United States in such manner as the Federal Rules of Civil Procedure prescribe for service of process in a foreign country, except that a subpoena to be served on a person who is not to be found within the territorial jurisdiction of any

court of the United States may be issued only on the prior approval of the Commission.

(8) *Refusal to Obey.* In case of contumacy by, or refusal to obey a subpoena issued to, any person, the Commission may invoke the aid of any court of the United States within the jurisdiction in which the investigation or proceeding is conducted, or where such person resides or transacts business, in requiring the attendance and testimony of witnesses and the production of books, papers, correspondence, memoranda, and other records. Such court may issue an order requiring such person to appear before the Commission or member or Administrative Law Judge or other officer designated by the Commission, there to produce records, if so ordered, or to give testimony touching the matter under investigation or in question.

(9) *Failure to Obey.* Any failure to obey such order of the court may be punished by the court as a contempt thereof. All process in any such case may be served in the judicial district wherein such person is an inhabitant or transacts business or wherever such person may be found.

(10) *Evidence.* On the receipt of evidence under paragraph (4)(C)(iii), the Commission may—

(A) prohibit the person that is the subject of the hearing from trading on, or subject to the rules of, any registered entity and require all registered entities to refuse the person all privileges on the registered entities for such period as the Commission may require in the order;

(B) if the person is registered with the Commission in any capacity, suspend, for a period not to exceed 180 days, or revoke, the registration of the person;

(C) assess such person—

(i) a civil penalty of not more than an amount equal to the greater of—

(I) $140,000; or

(II) triple the monetary gain to such person for each such violation; or

(ii) in any case of manipulation or attempted manipulation in violation of this subsection or section 9(a)(2), a civil penalty of not more than an amount equal to the greater of—

(I) $1,000,000; or

(II) triple the monetary gain to the person for each such violation; and

(D) require restitution to customers of damages proximately caused by violations of the person.

(11) *Orders.*

(A) *Notice.* The Commission shall provide to a person described in paragraph (10) and the appropriate governing board of the registered entity notice of the order described in paragraph (10) by—

(i) registered mail;

(ii) certified mail; or

(iii) personal delivery.

(B) *Review.*

(i) *In General.* A person described in paragraph (10) may obtain a review of the order or such other equitable relief as determined to be appropriate by a court described in clause (ii).

(ii) *Petition.* To obtain a review or other relief under clause (i), a person may, not later than 15 days after notice is given to the person under clause (i), file a written petition to set aside the order with the United States Court of Appeals—

(I) for the circuit in which the petitioner carries out the business of the petitioner; or

(II) in the case of an order denying registration, the circuit in which the principal place of business of the petitioner is located, as listed on the application for registration of the petitioner.

(C) *Procedure.*

(i) *Duty of Clerk of Appropriate Court.* The clerk of the appropriate court under subparagraph (B)(ii) shall transmit to the Commission a copy of a petition filed under subparagraph (B)(ii).

(ii) *Duty of Commission.* In accordance with section 2112 of title 28, United States Code, the Commission shall file in the appropriate court described in subparagraph (B)(ii) the record theretofore made.

(iii) *Jurisdiction of Appropriate Court.* Upon the filing of a petition under subparagraph (B)(ii), the appropriate court described in subparagraph (B)(ii) may affirm, set aside, or modify the order of the Commission.

(d) *Cease and Desist Orders, Fines.* If any person (other than a registered entity), is violating or has violated subsection (c) or any other provisions of this Act or of the rules, regulations, or orders of the Commission thereunder, the Commission may, upon notice and hearing, and subject to appeal as in other cases provided for in subsection (c), make and enter an order directing that such person shall cease and desist therefrom and, if such person thereafter and after the lapse of the period allowed for appeal of such order or after the affirmance of such order, shall knowingly fail or refuse to obey or comply with such order, such person, upon conviction thereof, shall be fined not more than the higher of $140,000 or triple the monetary gain to such person, or imprisoned for not more than 1 year, or both, except that if such knowing failure or refusal to obey or comply with such order involves any offense within subsection (a) or (b) of section 9, such person, upon conviction thereof, shall be subject to the penalties of said subsection (a) or (b): *Provided*, That any such cease and desist order under this subsection against any respondent in any case of manipulation shall be issued only in conjunction with an order issued against such respondent under subsection (c).*

(e) *Assessment of Money Penalties.*

(1) In determining the amount of the money penalty assessed under subsection (c), the Commission shall consider the appropriateness of such penalty to the gravity of the violation.

(2) Unless the person against whom a money penalty is assessed under subsection (c) shows to the satisfaction of the Commission within fifteen days from the expiration of the period allowed for payment of such penalty that either an appeal as authorized by subsection (c) has been taken or payment of the full amount of the penalty then due has been made, at the end of such fifteen-day period and until such person shows to the satisfaction of the Commission that payment of such amount with interest thereon to date of payment has been made—

(A) such person shall be prohibited automatically from the privileges of all registered entities; and

(B) if such person is registered with the Commission, such registration shall be suspended automatically.

* Dodd–Frank purported to amend the first sentence of subsection (d) by inserting "or of any swap," before "or otherwise is violating"; however, because of prior amendments, the amendment could not be executed.

(3) If a person against whom a money penalty is assessed under subsection (c) takes an appeal and if the Commission prevails or the appeal is dismissed, unless such person shows to the satisfaction of the Commission that payment of the full amount of the penalty then due has been made by the end of thirty days from the date of entry of judgment on the appeal—

(A) such person shall be prohibited automatically from the privileges of all registered entities; and

(B) if such person is registered with the Commission, such registration shall be suspended automatically.

If the person against whom the money penalty is assessed fails to pay such penalty after the lapse of the period allowed for appeal or after the affirmance of such penalty, the Commission may refer the matter to the Attorney General who shall recover such penalty by action in the appropriate United States district court.

(4) Any designated clearing organization that knowingly or recklessly evades or participates in or facilitates an evasion of the requirements of section 2(h) shall be liable for a civil money penalty in twice the amount otherwise available for a violation of section 2(h).

(5) Any swap dealer or major swap participant that knowingly or recklessly evades or participates in or facilitates an evasion of the requirements of section 2(h) shall be liable for a civil money penalty in twice the amount otherwise available for a violation of section 2(h).

(f) *Telemarketing Rules.*

(1) Except as provided in paragraph (2), not later than six months after the effective date of rules promulgated by the Federal Trade Commission under section 3(a) of the Telemarketing and Consumer Fraud and Abuse Prevention Act, the Commission shall promulgate, or require each registered futures association to promulgate, rules substantially similar to such rules to prohibit deceptive and other abusive telemarketing acts or practices by any person registered or exempt from registration under this Act in connection with such person's business as a futures commission merchant, introducing broker, commodity trading advisor, commodity pool operator, leverage transaction merchant, floor broker, or floor trader, or a person associated with any such person.

(2) The Commission is not required to promulgate rules under paragraph (1) if it determines that—

(A) rules adopted by the Commission under this Act provide protection from deceptive and abusive telemarketing by persons described under paragraph (1) substantially similar to that provided by rules promulgated by the Federal Trade Commission under section 3(a) of the Telemarketing and Consumer Fraud and Abuse Prevention Act; or

(B) such a rule promulgated by the Commission is not necessary or appropriate in the public interest, or for the protection of customers in the futures and options markets, or would be inconsistent with the maintenance of fair and orderly markets.

If the Commission determines that an exception described in subparagraph (A) or (B) applies, the Commission shall publish in the Federal Register its determination with the reasons for it.

(g) *Notice of Investigations and Enforcement Actions.* The Commission shall provide the Securities and Exchange Commission with notice of the commencement of any proceeding and a copy of any order entered by the Commission pursuant to subsections (c) and (d) of this section against any futures commission merchant or introducing broker registered pursuant to section 4f(a)(2), any floor broker or floor trader exempt from registration pursuant to section 4f(a)(3), any associated person exempt from registration pursuant to section 4k(6), or any board of trade designated as a contract market pursuant to section 5f.

Cooperative Associations and Corporations, Exclusion from Board of Trade

Sec. 6a. (a) No board of trade which has been designated or registered as a contract market or a derivatives transaction execution facility shall exclude from membership in, and all privileges on, such board of trade, any association or corporation engaged in cash commodity business having adequate financial responsibility which is organized under the cooperative laws of any State, or which has been recognized as a cooperative association of producers by the United States Government or by any agency thereof, if such association or corporation complies and agrees to comply with such terms and conditions as are or may be imposed lawfully upon other members of such board, and as are or may be imposed lawfully upon a cooperative association of producers engaged in cash commodity business, unless such board of trade is authorized by the Commission to exclude such association or corporation from membership and privileges after hearing held upon at least three days' notice subsequent to the filing of complaint by the board of trade: Provided, however, That if any such association or corporation shall fail to meet its obligations with any established clearing house or clearing agency of any contract market, such association or corporation shall be ipso facto debarred from further trading on such contract market, except such trading as may be necessary to close open trades and to discharge existing contracts in accordance with the rules of such contract market applicable in such cases. Such Commission may prescribe that such association or corporation shall have and retain membership and privileges, with or without imposing conditions, or it may permit such board of trade immediately to bar such association or corporation from membership and privileges. Any order of said Commission entered hereunder shall be reviewable by the court of appeals for the circuit in which such association or corporation, or such board of trade, has its principal place of business, on written petition either of such association or corporation, or of such board of trade, under the procedure provided in section 6(b) of this Act, but such order shall not be stayed by the court pending review.

(b) No rule of any board of trade designated or registered as a contract market or a derivatives transaction execution facility shall forbid or be construed to forbid the payment of compensation on a commodity-unit basis, or otherwise, by any federated cooperative association to its regional member-associations for services rendered or to be rendered in connection with any organization work, educational activity, or procurement of patronage, provided no part of any such compensation is returned to patrons (whether members or nonmembers) of such cooperative association, or of its regional or local member-associations, otherwise than as a dividend on capital stock or as a patronage dividend out of the net earnings or surplus of such federated cooperative association.

Nonenforcement of Rules of Government or Other Violations

Sec. 6b. If any registered entity is not enforcing or has not enforced its rules of government made a condition of its designation or registration as set forth in sections 5 through 5c, or if any registered entity, or any director, officer, agent, or employee of any registered entity otherwise is violating or has violated any of the provisions of this Act or any of the rules, regulations, or orders of the Commission thereunder, the Commission may, upon notice and hearing on the record and subject to appeal as in other cases provided for in section 6(b) of this Act, make and enter an order directing that such registered entity, director, officer, agent, or employee shall cease and desist from such violation, and assess a civil penalty of not more than $500,000 for each such violation, or, in any case of manipulation or attempted manipulation in violation of section 6(c), 6(d), or 9(a)(2), a civil penalty of not more than $1,000,000 for each such violation. If such registered entity, director, officer, agent, or employee, after the entry of such a cease and desist order and the lapse of the period allowed for appeal of such order or after the affirmance of such order, shall fail or refuse to obey or comply with such order, such registered entity, director, officer, agent, or employee shall be guilty of a misdemeanor and, upon conviction thereof, shall be fined not more than $500,000 or imprisoned for not less than six months nor more than one year, or both, except that if the failure or refusal to obey or comply with the order involved any offense under section 9(a)(2), the registered entity, director, officer, agent, or employee shall be guilty of a felony and, on conviction, shall be subject to penalties under section 9(a)(2). Each day during which such failure or refusal to obey such cease and desist order continues shall be deemed a separate offense. If the offending registered entity or other person upon whom such penalty is imposed, after the lapse of the period allowed for appeal or after the affirmance of such penalty, shall fail to pay such penalty, the Commission shall refer the matter to the Attorney General who shall recover such penalty by action in the appropriate United States district court. In determining the amount of the money penalty assessed under this section, the Commission shall consider the gravity of the offense, and in the case of a registered entity shall further consider whether the amount of the penalty will materially impair the ability of the registered entity to carry on its operations and duties.

Action to Enjoin or Restrain Violations

Sec. 6c. (a) *Action to Enjoin or Restrain Violations.* Whenever it shall appear to the Commission that any registered entity or other person has engaged, is engaging, or is about to engage in any act or practice constituting a violation of any provision of this chapter or any rule, regulation, or order thereunder, or is restraining trading in any commodity for future delivery or any swap, the Commission may bring an action in the proper district court of the United States or the proper United States court of any territory or other place subject to the jurisdiction of the United States, to enjoin such act or practice, or to enforce compliance with this chapter, or any rule, regulation or order thereunder, and said courts shall have jurisdiction to entertain such actions: Provided, That no restraining order (other than a restraining order which prohibits any person from destroying, altering or disposing of, or refusing to permit authorized representatives of the Commission to inspect, when and as requested, any books and records or other documents or which prohibits any person from withdrawing, transferring, removing, dissipating, or disposing of any funds, assets, or other property, and other than an order appointing a temporary receiver to administer such restraining order and to perform such other duties as the court may consider appropriate) or injunction for violation of the provisions of this chapter shall be issued ex parte by said court.

(b) *Injunction or Restraining Order.* Upon a proper showing, a permanent or temporary injunction or restraining order shall be granted without bond.

(c) *Writs or Other Orders.* Upon application of the Commission, the district courts of the United States and the United States courts of any territory or other place subject to the jurisdiction of the United States shall also have jurisdiction to issue writs of mandamus, or orders affording like relief, commanding any person to comply with the provisions of this chapter or any rule, regulation, or order of the Commission thereunder, including the requirement that such person take such action as is necessary to remove the danger of violation of this chapter or any such rule, regulation, or order: *Provided*, That no such writ of mandamus, or order affording like relief, shall be issued ex parte.

(d) *Civil Penalties*—

(1) *In General.* In any action brought under this section, the Commission may seek and the court shall have jurisdiction to impose, on a proper showing, on any person found in the action to have committed any violation—

(A) a civil penalty in the amount of not more than the greater of $100,000 or triple the monetary gain to the person for each violation; or

(B) in any case of manipulation or attempted manipulation in violation of section 6(c), 6(d), or 9(a)(2), a civil penalty in the amount of not more than the greater of $1,000,000 or triple the monetary gain to the person for each violation.

(2) If a person on whom such a penalty is imposed fails to pay the penalty within the time pre-

scribed in the court's order, the Commission may refer the matter to the Attorney General who shall recover the penalty by action in the appropriate United States district court.

(3) *Equitable Remedies.* In any action brought under this section, the Commission may seek, and the court may impose, on a proper showing, on any person found in the action to have committed any violation, equitable remedies including—

(A) restitution to persons who have sustained losses proximately caused by such violation (in the amount of such losses); and

(B) disgorgement of gains received in connection with such violation.

(e) *Venue and Process.* Any action under this section may be brought in the district wherein the defendant is found or is an inhabitant or transacts business or in the district where the act or practice occurred, is occurring, or is about to occur, and process in such cases may be served in any district in which the defendant is an inhabitant or wherever the defendant may be found.

(f) *Action by Attorney General.* In lieu of bringing actions itself pursuant to this section, the Commission may request the Attorney General to bring the action.

(g) *Notice to Attorney General of Action brought by Commission.* Where the Commission elects to bring the action, it shall inform the Attorney General of such suit and advise him of subsequent developments.

(h) *Notice of Investigations and Enforcement Actions.* The Commission shall provide the Securities and Exchange Commission with notice of the commencement of any proceeding and a copy of any order entered by the Commission against any futures commission merchant or introducing broker registered pursuant to section 4f(a)(2), any floor broker or floor trader exempt from registration pursuant to section 4f(a)(3), any associated person exempt from registration pursuant to section 4k(6), or any board of trade designated as a contract market pursuant to section 5f.

Jurisdiction of States

Sec. 6d. (1) Whenever it shall appear to the attorney general of any State, the administrator of the securities laws of any State, or such other official as a State may designate, that the interests of the residents of that State have been, are being, or may be threatened or adversely affected because any person (other than a contract market, derivatives transaction execution facility, clearinghouse, floor broker, or floor trader) has engaged in, is engaging or is about to engage in, any act or practice constituting a violation of any provision of this Act or any rule, regulation, or order of the Commission thereunder, the State may bring a suit in equity or an action at law on behalf of its residents to enjoin such act or practice, to enforce compliance with this Act, or any rule, regulation, or order of the Commission thereunder, to obtain damages on behalf of their residents, or to obtain such further and other relief as the court may deem appropriate.

(2) The district courts of the United States, the United States courts of any territory, and the District Court of the United States for the District of Columbia, shall have jurisdiction of all suits in equity and actions at law brought under this section to enforce any liability or duty created by this Act or any rule, regulation, or order of the Commission thereunder, or to obtain damages or other relief with respect thereto. Upon proper application, such courts shall also have jurisdiction to issue writs of mandamus, or orders affording like relief, commanding the defendant to comply with the provisions of this Act or any rule, regulation, or order of the Commission thereunder, including the requirement that the defendant take such action as is necessary to remove the danger of violation of this Act or of any such rule, regulation, or order. Upon a proper showing, a permanent or temporary injunction or restraining order shall be granted without bond.

(3) Immediately upon instituting any such suit or action, the State shall serve written notice thereof upon the Commission and provide the Commission with a copy of its complaint, and the Commission shall have the right to (A) intervene in the suit or action and, upon doing so, shall be heard on all matters arising therein, and (B) file petitions for appeal.

(4) Any suit or action brought under this section in a district court of the United States may be brought in the district wherein the defendant is found or is an inhabitant or transacts business or wherein the act or practice occurred, is occurring, or is about to occur, and process in such cases may be served in any district in which the defendant is an inhabitant or wherever the defendant may be found.

(5) For purposes of bringing any suit or action under this section, nothing in this Act shall prevent the attorney general, the administrator of the State

securities laws, or other duly authorized State officials from exercising the powers conferred on them by the laws of such State to conduct investigations or to administer oaths or affirmations or to compel the attendance of witnesses or the production of documentary and other evidence.

(6) For purposes of this section, "State" means any State of the United States, the District of Columbia, the Commonwealth of Puerto Rico, or any territory or possession of the United States.

(7) Nothing contained in this section shall prohibit an authorized State official from proceeding in State court on the basis of an alleged violation of any general civil or criminal antifraud statute of such State.

(8) (A) Nothing in this Act shall prohibit an authorized State official from proceeding in a State court against any person registered under this Act (other than a floor broker, floor trader, or registered futures association) for an alleged violation of any antifraud provision of this Act or any antifraud rule, regulation, or order issued pursuant to the Act.

(B) The State shall give the Commission prior written notice of its intent to proceed before instituting a proceeding in State court as described in this subsection and shall furnish the Commission with a copy of its complaint immediately upon instituting any such proceeding. The Commission shall have the right to (i) intervene in the proceeding and, upon doing so, shall be heard on all matters arising therein, and (ii) file a petition for appeal. The Commission or the defendant may remove such proceeding to the district court of the United States for the proper district by following the procedure for removal otherwise provided by law, except that the petition for removal shall be filed within sixty days after service of the summons and complaint upon the defendant. The Commission shall have the right to appear as amicus curiae in any such proceeding.

Vacation of Request of Designation as Registered Entity

Sec. 7. Any person that has been designated or registered a registered entity in the manner herein provided may have such designation or registration vacated and set aside by giving notice in writing to the Commission requesting that its designation or registration as a registered entity be vacated, which notice shall be served at least ninety days prior to the date named therein as the date when the vacation of designation or registration shall take effect. Upon receipt of such notice the Commission shall forthwith order the vacation of the designation or registration of the registered entity, effective upon the day named in the notice, and shall forthwith send a copy of the notice and its order to all other registered entities. From and after the date upon which the vacation became effective the said person can thereafter be designated or registered again a registered entity by making application to the Commission in the manner herein provided for an original application.

Public Disclosure

Sec. 8. (a)(1) For the efficient execution of the provisions of this Act, and in order to provide information for the use of Congress, the Commission may make such investigations as it deems necessary to ascertain the facts regarding the operations of boards of trade and other persons subject to the provisions of this Act. The Commission may publish from time to time the results of any such investigation and such general statistical information gathered therefrom as it deems of interest to the public: Provided, That except as otherwise specifically authorized in this Act, the Commission may not publish data and information that would separately disclose the business transactions or market positions of any person and trade secrets or names of customers: Provided further, That the Commission may withhold from public disclosure any data or information concerning or obtained in connection with any pending investigation of any person. The Commission shall not be compelled to disclose any information or data obtained from a foreign futures authority if—

(A) the foreign futures authority has in good faith determined and represented to the Commission that disclosure of such information or data by that foreign futures authority would violate the laws applicable to that foreign futures authority; and

(B) the Commission obtains such information pursuant to—

(i) such procedure as the Commission may authorize for use in connection with the administration or enforcement of this Act; or

(ii) a memorandum of understanding with that foreign futures authority;

except that nothing in this subsection shall prevent the Commission from disclosing publicly any information or data obtained by the Commission from a foreign futures authority when such disclosure is made in connection with a congressional proceeding, an administrative or judicial proceeding commenced by the United States or the Commission, in any receivership proceeding involving a receiver appointed in a judicial proceeding commenced by the United States or the Commission, or in any proceeding under title 11 of the United States Code in which the Commission has intervened or in which the Commission has the right to appear and be heard. Nothing in this subsection shall be construed to authorize the Commission to withhold information or data from Congress. For purposes of section 552 of title 5, United States Code, this subsection shall be considered a statute described in subsection (b)(3)(B) of section 552.

(2) In conducting investigations authorized under this subsection or any other provision of this Act, the Commission shall continue, as the Commission determines necessary, to request the assistance of and cooperate with the appropriate Federal agencies in the conduct of such investigations, including undercover operations by such agencies. The Commission and the Department of Justice shall assess the effectiveness of such undercover operations and, within two years of the date of enactment of the Futures Trading Practices Act of 1992, shall recommend to Congress any additional undercover or other authority for the Commission that the Commission or the Department of Justice believes to be necessary.

(3) The Commission shall provide the Securities and Exchange Commission with notice of the commencement of any proceeding and a copy of any order entered by the Commission against any futures commission merchant or introducing broker registered pursuant to section 4f(a)(2), any floor broker or floor trader exempt from registration pursuant to section 4f(a)(3), any associated person exempt from registration pursuant to section 4k(6), or any board of trade designated as a contract market pursuant to section 5f.

(b) The Commission may disclose publicly any data or information that would separately disclose the market positions, business transactions, trade secrets, or names of customers of any person when such disclosure is made in connection with a congressional proceeding, in an administrative or judicial proceeding brought under this Act, in any receivership proceeding involving a receiver appointed in a judicial proceeding brought under this Act, or in any bankruptcy proceeding in which the Commission has intervened or in which the Commission has the right to appear and be heard under title 11 of the United States Code. This subsection shall not apply to the disclosure of data or information obtained by the Commission from a foreign futures authority.

(c) The Commission may make or issue such reports as it deems necessary, or such opinions or orders as may be required under other provisions of law, relative to the conduct of any registered entity or to the transactions of any person found guilty of violating the provisions of this Act or the rules, regulations, or orders of the Commission thereunder in proceedings brought under section 6 of this Act. In any such report or opinion, the Commission may set forth the facts as to any actual transaction or any information referred to in subsection (b) of this section, if such facts or information have previously been disclosed publicly in connection with a congressional proceeding, or in an administrative or judicial proceeding brought under this Act.

(d) The Commission, upon its own initiative or in cooperation with existing governmental agencies, shall investigate the marketing conditions of commodities and commodity products and byproducts, including supply and demand for these commodities, cost to the consumer, and handling and transportation charges. It shall also compile and furnish to producers, consumers, and distributors, by means of regular or special reports, or by such other methods as it deems most effective, information respecting the commodity markets, together with information on supply, demand, prices, and other conditions in this and other countries that affect the markets.

(e) The Commission may disclose and make public, where such information has previously been disclosed publicly in accordance with the provisions of this section, the names and addresses of all traders on the boards of trade on the commodity markets with respect to whom the Commission has information, and any other information in the possession of the Commission relating to the amount of commodities purchased or sold by each such trader. Upon the request of any committee of either House of Congress, acting within the scope of its jurisdiction, the Commission shall furnish to such committee the names and addresses of all traders on such boards of trade with respect to whom the Commission has information, and any other information in the possession of the Commission relating to the amount of any commodity purchased or sold by each such trader. Upon the request of any department or agency of the Government of the United States, acting within the scope of its jurisdiction, the Commission may furnish to such department or agency any information in the possession of the Commission obtained in connection with the administration of this Act. However, any information furnished under this subsection to any Federal department or agency shall not be disclosed by such department or agency except in any action or proceeding under the laws of the United States to which it, the Commission, or the United States is a party. Upon the request of any department or agency of any State or any political subdivision thereof, acting within the scope of its jurisdiction, any foreign futures authority, or any department or agency of any foreign government or any political subdivision thereof, acting within the scope of its jurisdiction, the Commission may furnish to such foreign futures authority, department or agency any information in the possession of the Commission obtained in connection with the administration of this Act. Any information furnished to any department or agency of any State or political subdivision thereof shall not be disclosed by such department or agency except in connection with an adjudicatory action or proceeding brought under this Act or the laws of such State or political subdivision to which such State or political subdivision or any department or agency thereof is a party. The Commission shall not furnish any information to a foreign futures authority or to a department, central bank and ministries, or agency of a foreign government or political subdivision thereof unless the Commission is satisfied that the information will not be disclosed by such foreign futures authority, department, central bank and ministries, or agency except in connection with an adjudicatory action or proceeding brought under the laws of such foreign government or political subdivision to which such foreign government or political subdivision or any department, central bank and ministries, or agency thereof, or foreign futures authority, is a party.

(f) The Commission shall disclose information in its possession pursuant to a subpoena or summons only if—

(1) a copy of the subpoena or summons has been mailed to the last known home or business address of the person who submitted the information that is the subject of the subpoena or summons, if the address is known to the Commission, or, if such mailing would be unduly burdensome, the Commission provides other appropriate notice of the subpoena or summons to such person, and

(2) at least fourteen days have expired from the date of such mailing of the subpoena or summons, or such other notice.

This subsection shall not apply to congressional subpoenas or congressional requests for information.

(g) The Commission shall provide any registration information maintained by the Commission on any registrant upon reasonable request made by any department or agency of any State or any political subdivision thereof. Whenever the Commission determines that such information may be appropriate for use by any department or agency of a State or political subdivision thereof, the Commission shall provide such information without request.

(h) [Omitted]

(i) The Comptroller General of the United States shall conduct reviews and audits of the Commission and make reports thereon. For the purpose of conducting such reviews and audits, the Comptroller General shall be furnished such information regarding the powers, duties, organizations, transactions, operations, and activities of the Commission as the Comptroller General may require and the Comptroller General and the duly authorized representatives of the Comptroller General shall, for the purpose of securing such information, have access to and the right to examine any books, documents, papers, or records of the Commission, except that in reports the Comptroller General shall not include data and information that would separately disclose the business transactions of any person and trade secrets or names of customers, although such data shall be provided upon request by any committee of either House of Congress acting within the scope of its jurisdiction.

Registration of Commodity Dealers and Associated Persons; Regulation of Contract Markets

Sec. 8a. The Commission is authorized—

(1) to register futures commission merchants, associated persons of futures commission merchants, introducing brokers, associated persons of introducing brokers, commodity trading advisors, associated persons of commodity trading advisors, commodity pool operators, associated persons of commodity pool operators, floor brokers, and floor traders upon application in accordance with rules and regulations and in the form and manner to be prescribed by the Commission, which may require the applicant, and such persons associated with

the applicant as the Commission may specify, to be fingerprinted and to submit, or cause to be submitted, such fingerprints to the Attorney General for identification and appropriate processing, and in connection therewith to fix and establish from time to time reasonable fees and charges for registrations and renewals thereof: *Provided,* That notwithstanding any provision of this Act, the Commission may grant a temporary license to any applicant for registration with the Commission pursuant to such rules, regulations, or orders as the Commission may adopt, except that the term of any such temporary license shall not exceed six months from the date of its issuance;

(2) upon notice, but without a hearing and pursuant to such rules, regulations, or orders as the Commission may adopt, to refuse to register, to register conditionally, or to suspend or place restrictions upon the registration of, any person and with such a hearing as may be appropriate to revoke the registration of any person—

(A) if a prior registration of such person in any capacity has been suspended (and the period of such suspension has not expired) or has been revoked;

(B) if registration of such person in any capacity has been refused under the provisions of paragraph (3) of this section within five years preceding the filing of the application for registration or at any time thereafter;

(C) if such person is permanently or temporarily enjoined by order, judgment, or decree of any court of competent jurisdiction (except that registration may not be revoked solely on the basis of such temporary order, judgment, or decree), including an order entered pursuant to an agreement of settlement to which the Commission or any Federal or State agency or other governmental body is a party, from (i) acting as a futures commission merchant, introducing broker, floor broker, floor trader, commodity trading advisor, commodity pool operator, associated person of any registrant under this Act, securities broker, securities dealer, municipal securities broker, municipal securities dealer, transfer agent, clearing agency, securities information processor, investment adviser, investment company, or affiliated person or employee of any of the foregoing or (ii) engaging in or continuing any activity where such activity involves embezzlement, theft, extortion, fraud, fraudulent conversion, misappropriation of funds, securities or property, forgery, counterfeiting, false pretenses, bribery, gambling, or any transaction in or advice concerning contracts of sale of a commodity for future delivery, concerning matters subject to Commission regulation under section 4c or 19, or concerning securities.

(D) if such person has been convicted within ten years preceding the filing of the application for registration or at any time thereafter of any felony that (i) involves any transactions or advice concerning any contract of sale of a commodity for future delivery, or any activity subject to Commission regulation under section 4c or 19 of this Act, or concerning a security, (ii) arises out of the conduct of the business of a futures commission merchant, introducing broker, floor broker, floor trader, commodity trading advisor, commodity pool operator, associated person of any registrant under this Act, securities broker, securities dealer, municipal securities broker, municipal securities dealer, transfer agent, clearing agency, securities information processor, investment adviser, investment company, or an affiliated person or employee of any of the foregoing, (iii) involves embezzlement, theft, extortion, fraud, fraudulent conversion, misappropriation of funds, securities or property, forgery, counterfeiting, false pretenses, bribery, or gambling, or (iv) involves the violation of section 152, 1001, 1341, 1342, 1343, 1503, 1623, 1961, 1962, 1963, or 2314, or chapter 25, 47, 95, or 96 of title 18, United States Code, or section 7201 or 7206 of the Internal Revenue Code of 1986;

(E) if such person, within ten years preceding the filing of the application or at any time thereafter, has been found in a proceeding brought by the Commission or any Federal or State agency or other governmental body, or by agreement of settlement to which the Commission or any Federal or State agency or other governmental body is a party, (i) to have violated any provision of this Act, the Securities Act of 1933, the Securities Exchange Act of 1934, the Public Utility Holding Company Act of 1935, the Trust Indenture Act of 1939, the Investment Advisers Act of 1940, the Investment Company Act of 1940, the Securities Investors Protection Act of 1970, the Foreign Corrupt Practices Act of 1977, chapter 96 of title 18 of the United States Code, or any similar statute of a State or foreign jurisdiction, or any rule, regulation, or order under any such statutes, or the rules of the Municipal Securities Rulemaking Board where such violation involves embezzlement, theft, extortion, fraud, fraudulent conversion, misappropriation of funds, securities or property, forgery, counterfeiting, false pretenses, bribery, or gambling, or (ii) to have willfully aided, abetted, counseled, commanded, induced, or procured such violation by any other person;

(F) if such person is subject to an outstanding order of the Commission denying privileges on any registered entity to such person, denying, suspending, or revoking such person's membership in any registered entity or registered futures association, or barring or suspending such person from being associated with a registrant under this Act or with a member of a registered entity or with a member of a registered futures association;

(G) if, as to any of the matters set forth in this paragraph and paragraph (3), such person willfully made any materially false or misleading statement or omitted to state any material fact in such person's application or any update thereto; or

(H) if refusal, suspension, or revocation of the registration of any principal of such person would be warranted because of a statutory disqualification listed in this paragraph:

Provided, That such person may appeal from a decision to refuse registration, condition registration, suspend, revoke or to place restrictions upon registration made pursuant to the provisions of this paragraph in the manner provided in section 6(c) of this Act; and

Provided further, That for the purposes of paragraphs (2) and (3) of this section, "principal" shall mean, if the person is a partnership, any general partner or, if the person is a corporation, any officer, director, or beneficial owner of at least 10 per centum of the voting shares of the corporation, and any other person that the Commission by rule, regulation, or order determines has the power, directly or indirectly, through agreement or otherwise, to exercise a controlling influence over the activities of such person which are subject to regulation by the Commission;

(3) to refuse to register or to register conditionally any person, if it is found, after opportunity for hearing, that—

(A) such person has been found by the Commission or by any court of competent jurisdiction to have violated, or has consented to findings of a violation of, any provision of this Act, or any rule, regulation, or order thereunder (other than a violation set forth in paragraph (2) of this section), or to have willfully aided, abetted, counseled, commanded, induced, or procured the violation by any other person of any such provision;

(B) such person has been found by any court of competent jurisdiction or by any Federal or State agency or other governmental body, or by agreement of settlement to which any Federal or State agency or other governmental body is a party, (i) to have violated any provision of the Securities Act of 1933, the Securities Exchange Act of 1934, the Public Utility Holding Company Act of 1935, the Trust Indenture Act of 1939, the Investment Advisers Act of 1940, the Investment Company Act of 1940, the Securities Investors Protection Act of 1970, the Foreign Corrupt Practices Act of 1977, or any similar statute of a State or foreign jurisdiction, or any rule, regulation, or order under any such statutes, or the rules of the Municipal Securities Rulemaking Board or (ii) to have willfully aided, abetted, counseled, commanded, induced, or procured such violation by any other person;

(C) such person failed reasonably to supervise another person, who is subject to such person's supervision, with a view to preventing violations of this Act, or of any of the statutes set forth in subparagraph (B) of this paragraph, or of any of the rules, regulations, or orders thereunder, and the person subject to supervision committed such a violation: *Provided,* That no person shall be deemed to have failed reasonably to supervise another person, within the meaning of this subparagraph if (i) there have been established procedures, and a system for applying such procedures, which would reasonably be expected to prevent and detect, insofar as practicable, any such violation by such other person and (ii) such person has reasonably discharged the duties and obligations incumbent upon that person, as supervisor, by reason of such procedures and system, without reasonable cause to believe that such procedures and system were not being complied with;

(D) such person pleaded guilty to or was convicted of a felony other than a felony of the type specified in paragraph (2)(D) of this section, or was convicted of a felony of the type specified in paragraph (2)(D) of this section more than ten years preceding the filing of the application;

(E) such person pleaded guilty to or was convicted of any misdemeanor which (i) involves any transaction or advice concerning any contract of sale of a commodity for future delivery or any activity subject to Commission regulation under section 4c or 19 of this Act or concerning a security, (ii) arises out of the conduct of the business of a futures commission merchant, introducing broker, floor broker, floor trader, commodity trading advisor, commodity pool operator, associated person of any registrant under this Act, securities broker, securities dealer, municipal securities broker, municipal securities dealer, transfer agent, clearing agency, securities information processor, investment adviser, investment company, or an affiliated person or employee of any of the foregoing, (iii) involves embezzlement, theft, extortion, fraud, fraudulent conversion, misappropriation of funds, securities or property, forgery, counterfeiting, false pretenses, bribery, or gambling, (iv) involves the violation of section 152, 1341, 1342, or 1343 or chapter 25, 47, 95, or 96 of title 18, United States Code, or section 7203, 7204, 7205, or 7207 of the Internal Revenue Code of 1986;

(F) such person was debarred by any agency of the United States from contracting with the United States;

(G) such person willfully made any materially false or misleading statement or willfully omitted to state any material fact in such person's application or any update thereto, in any report required to be filed with the Commission by this Act or the regulations thereunder, in any proceeding before the Commission or in any registration disqualification proceeding;

(H) such person has pleaded nolo contendere to criminal charges of felonious conduct, or has been convicted in a State court, in a United States military court, or in a foreign court of conduct which would constitute a felony under Federal law if the offense had been committed under Federal jurisdiction;

(I) in the case of an applicant for registration in any capacity for which there are minimum financial requirements prescribed under this Act or under the rules or regulations of the Commission, such person has not established that such person meets such minimum financial requirements;

(J) such person is subject to an outstanding order denying, suspending, or expelling such person from membership in a registered entity, a registered futures association, any other self-regulatory organization, or any foreign regulatory body that the Commission recognizes as having a comparable regulatory program or barring or suspending such person from being associated with any member or members of such registered entity, association, self-regulatory organization, or foreign regulatory body;

(K) such person has been found by any court of competent jurisdiction or by any Federal or State agency or other governmental body, or by agreement of settlement to which any Federal or State agency or other governmental body is a party, (i) to have violated any statute or any rule, regulation, or order thereunder which involves embezzlement, theft, extortion, fraud, fraudulent conversion, misappropriation of funds, securities or property, forgery, counterfeiting, false pretenses, bribery, or gambling or (ii) to have willfully aided, abetted, counseled, commanded, induced or procured such violation by any other person;

(L) such person has associated with such person* any other person and knows, or in the exercise of reasonable care should know, of facts regarding such other person that are set forth as statutory disqualifications in paragraph (2) of this section, unless such person has notified the Commission of such facts and the Commission has determined that such other person should be registered or temporarily licensed;

(M) there is other good cause; or

(N) any principal, as defined in paragraph (2) of this section, of such person has been or could be refused registration:

Provided, That pending final determination under this paragraph, registration shall not be granted: *Provided further,* That such person may appeal from a decision to refuse registration or to condition registration made pursuant to this paragraph in the manner provided in section 6(c) of this Act;

(4) in accordance with the procedure provided for in section 6(c) of this Act, to suspend, revoke, or place restrictions upon the registration of any

* So in original.

person registered under this Act if cause exists under paragraph (3) of this section which would warrant a refusal of registration of such person, and to suspend or revoke the registration of any futures commission merchant or introducing broker who shall knowingly accept any order for the purchase or sale of any commodity for future delivery on or subject to the rules of any registered entity from any person if such person has been denied trading privileges on any registered entity by order of the Commission under section 6(c) of this Act and the period of denial specified in such order shall not have expired: *Provided,* That such person may appeal from a decision to suspend, revoke, or place restrictions upon registration made pursuant to this paragraph in the manner provided in section 6(c) of this Act;

(5) to make and promulgate such rules and regulations as, in the judgment of the Commission, are reasonably necessary to effectuate any of the provisions or to accomplish any of the purposes of this Act;

(6) to communicate to the proper committee or officer of any registered entity, registered futures association, or self-regulatory organization as defined in section 3(a)(26) of the Securities Exchange Act of 1934, notwithstanding the provisions of section 8 of this Act, the full facts concerning any transaction or market operation, including the names of parties thereto, which in the judgment of the Commission disrupts or tends to disrupt any market or is otherwise harmful or against the best interests of producers, consumers, or investors, or which is necessary or appropriate to effectuate the purposes of this Act: *Provided,* That any information furnished by the Commission under this paragraph shall not be disclosed by such registered entity, registered futures association, or self-regulatory organization except in any self-regulatory action or proceeding;

(7) to alter or supplement the rules of a registered entity insofar as necessary or appropriate by rule or regulation or by order, if after making the appropriate request in writing to a registered entity that such registered entity effect on its own behalf specified changes in its rules and practices, and after appropriate notice and opportunity for hearing, the Commission determines that such registered entity has not made the changes so required, and that such changes are necessary or appropriate for the protection of persons producing, handling, processing, or consuming any commodity traded for future delivery on such registered entity, or the product or byproduct thereof, or for the protection of traders or to insure fair dealing in commodities traded for future delivery on such registered entity. Such rules, regulations, or orders may specify changes with respect to such matters as—

(A) terms or conditions in contracts of sale to be executed on or subject to the rules of such registered entity;

(B) the form or manner of execution of purchases and sales for future delivery;

(C) other trading requirements;

(D) margin requirements, provided that the rules, regulations, or orders shall—

(i) be limited to protecting the financial integrity of the derivatives clearing organization;

(ii) be designed for risk management purposes to protect the financial integrity of transactions; and

(iii) not set specific margin amounts;

(E) safeguards with respect to the financial responsibility of members;

(F) the manner, method, and place of soliciting business, including the content of such solicitations; and

(G) the form and manner of handling, recording, and accounting for customers' orders, transactions, and accounts;

(8) to make and promulgate such rules and regulations with respect to those persons registered under this Act, who are not members of a registered entity, as in the judgment of the Commission are reasonably necessary to protect the public interest and promote just and equitable principles of trade, including but not limited to the manner, method, and place of soliciting business, including the content of such solicitation;

(9) to direct the registered entity, whenever it has reason to believe that an emergency exists, to take such action as in the Commission's judgment is necessary to maintain or restore orderly trading in or liquidation of any futures contract, including, but not limited to, the setting of temporary emergency margin levels on any futures contract, and the fixing of limits that may apply to a market position acquired in good faith prior to the effective date of the Commission's action. The term "emergency" as used herein shall mean,

in addition to threatened or actual market manipulations and corners, any act of the United States or a foreign government affecting a commodity or any other major market disturbance which prevents the market from accurately reflecting the forces of supply and demand for such commodity. Any action taken by the Commission under this paragraph shall be subject to review only in the United States Court of Appeals for the circuit in which the party seeking review resides or has its principal place of business, or in the United States Court of Appeals for the District of Columbia Circuit. Such review shall be based upon an examination of all the information before the Commission at the time the determination was made. The court reviewing the Commission's action shall not enter a stay or order of mandamus unless it has determined, after notice and hearing before a panel of the court, that the agency action complained of was arbitrary, capricious, an abuse of discretion, or otherwise not in accordance with law. Nothing herein shall be deemed to limit the meaning or interpretation given by a registered entity to the terms "market emergency", "emergency", or equivalent language in its own bylaws, rules, regulations, or resolutions;

(10) to authorize any person to perform any portion of the registration functions under this Act, in accordance with rules, notwithstanding any other provision of law, adopted by such person and submitted to the Commission for approval or, if applicable, for review pursuant to section 21(j) of this Act, and subject to the provisions of this Act applicable to registrations granted by the Commission; and

(11)(A) by written notice served on the person and pursuant to such rules, regulations, and orders as the Commission may adopt, to suspend or modify the registration of any person registered under this Act who is charged (in any information, indictment, or complaint authorized by a United States attorney or an appropriate official of any State) with the commission of or participation in a crime involving a violation of this Act, or a violation of any other provision of Federal or State law that would reflect on the honesty or the fitness of the person to act as a fiduciary (including an offense specified in subparagraph (D) or (E) of paragraph (2)) that is punishable by imprisonment for a term exceeding one year, if the Commission determines that continued registration of the person may pose a threat to the public interest or may threaten to impair public confidence in any market regulated by the Commission.

(B) Prior to the suspension or modification of the registration of a person under this paragraph, the person shall be afforded an opportunity for a hearing at which the Commission shall have the burden of showing that the continued registration of the person does, or is likely to, pose a threat to the public interest or threaten to impair public confidence in any market regulated by the Commission.

(C) Any notice of suspension or modification issued under this paragraph shall remain in effect until such information, indictment, or complaint is disposed of or until terminated by the Commission.

(D) On disposition of such information, indictment, or complaint, the Commission may issue and serve on such person an order pursuant to paragraph (2) or (4) to suspend, restrict, or revoke the registration of such person.

(E) A finding of not guilty or other disposition of the charge shall not preclude the Commission from thereafter instituting any other proceedings under this Act.

(F) A person aggrieved by an order issued under this paragraph may obtain review of such order in the same manner and on the same terms and conditions as are provided in section 6(b).

Trading Ban Violations

Sec. 8b. It shall be unlawful for any person, against whom there is outstanding any order of the Commission prohibiting him from trading on or subject to the rules of any registered entity, to make or cause to be made in contravention of such order, any contract for future delivery of any commodity, on or subject to the rules of any registered entity.

Disciplinary Actions

Sec. 8c. (a)(1) Any exchange or the Commission if the exchange fails to act, may suspend, expel, or otherwise discipline any person who is a member of that exchange, or deny any person access to the exchange. Any such action shall be taken solely in accordance with the rules of that exchange.

(2) Any suspension, expulsion, disciplinary, or access denial procedure established by an exchange rule shall provide for written notice to the Commission and to the person who is suspended, expelled, or disciplined, or denied access, within

thirty days, which includes the reasons for the exchange action in the form and manner the Commission prescribes. An exchange shall make public its findings and the reasons for the exchange action in any such proceeding, including the action taken or the penalty imposed, but shall not disclose the evidence therefor, except to the person who is suspended, expelled, or disciplined, or denied access, and to the Commission.

(b) The Commission may, in its discretion and in accordance with such standards and procedures as it deems appropriate, review any decision by an exchange whereby a person is suspended, expelled, otherwise disciplined, or denied access to the exchange. In addition, the Commission may, in its discretion and upon application of any person who is adversely affected by any other exchange action, review such action.

(c) The Commission may affirm, modify, set aside, or remand any exchange decision it reviews pursuant to subsection (b), after a determination on the record whether the action of the exchange was in accordance with the policies of this Act. Subject to judicial review, any order of the Commission entered pursuant to subsection (b) shall govern the exchange in its further treatment of the matter.

(d) The Commission, in its discretion, may order a stay of any action taken pursuant to subsection (a) pending review thereof.

(e)(1) The Commission shall issue regulations requiring each registered entity to establish and make available to the public a schedule of major violations of any rule within the disciplinary jurisdiction of such registered entity.

(2) The regulations issued by the Commission pursuant to this subsection shall prohibit, for a period of time to be determined by the Commission, any individual who is found to have committed any major violation from service on the governing board of any registered entity or registered futures association, or on any disciplinary committee thereof.

Commission Action for Non-Compliance with Export Sales Reporting Requirements

Sec. 8d. The Commission may, in accordance with the procedures provided for in this Act, refuse to register, register conditionally, or suspend, place restrictions upon, or revoke the registration of, any person, and may bar for any period as it deems appropriate any person from using or participating in any manner in any market regulated by the Commission, if such person is subject to a final decision or order of any court of competent jurisdiction or agency of the United States finding such person to have knowingly violated any provision of the export sales reporting requirements of section 812 of the Agricultural Act of 1970, or of any regulation issued thereunder.

Violations Generally; Punishment; Costs of Prosecution

Sec. 9. (a) *Felonies Generally.* It shall be a felony punishable by a fine of not more than $1,000,000 or imprisonment for not more than 10 years, or both, together with the costs of prosecution, for:

(1) Any person registered or required to be registered under this Act, or any employee or agent thereof, to embezzle, steal, purloin, or with criminal intent convert to such person's use or the use of another, any money, securities, or property having a value in excess of $100, which was received by such person or any employee or agent thereof to margin, guarantee, or secure the trades or contracts of any customer or accruing to such customer as a result of such trades or contracts or which otherwise was received from any customer, client, or pool participant in connection with the business of such person. The word "value" as used in this paragraph means face, par, or market value, or cost price, either wholesale or retail, whichever is greater.

(2) Any person to manipulate or attempt to manipulate the price of any commodity in interstate commerce, or for future delivery on or subject to the rules of any registered entity, or of any swap, or to corner or attempt to corner any such commodity or knowingly to deliver or cause to be delivered for transmission through the mails or interstate commerce by telegraph, telephone, wireless, or other means of communication false or misleading or knowingly inaccurate reports concerning crop or market information or conditions that affect or tend to affect the price of any commodity in interstate commerce, or knowingly to violate the provisions of section 4, section 4b, subsections (a) through (e) of subsection 4c, section 4h, section 4o(1), or section 19.

(3) Any person knowingly to make, or cause to be made, any statement in any application, report, or document required to be filed under this Act or any rule or regulation thereunder or any undertaking contained in a registration statement required under this Act, or by any registered entity or registered futures association in connec-

tion with an application for membership, or participation therein or to become associated with a member thereof, which statement was false or misleading with respect to any material fact, or knowingly to omit any material fact required to be stated therein or necessary to make the statements therein not misleading.

(4) Any person willfully to falsify, conceal, or cover up by any trick, scheme, or artifice a material fact, make any false, fictitious, or fraudulent statements or representations, or make or use any false writing or document knowing the same to contain any false, fictitious, or fraudulent statement or entry to a registered entity, board of trade, swap data repository, or futures association designated or registered under this Act acting in furtherance of its official duties under this Act.

(5) Any person willfully to violate any other provision of this Act, or any rule or regulation thereunder, the violation of which is made unlawful or the observance of which is required under the terms of this Act, but no person shall be subject to imprisonment under this paragraph for the violation of any rule or regulation if such person proves that he had no knowledge of such rule or regulation.

(6) Any person to abuse the end user clearing exemption under section 2(h)(4), as determined by the Commission.

(b) *Suspension of Convicted Felons.* Any person convicted of a felony under this section shall be suspended from registration under this Act and shall be denied registration or reregistration for five years or such longer period as the Commission may determine, and barred from using, or participating in any manner in, any market regulated by the Commission for five years or such longer period as the Commission shall determine, on such terms and conditions as the Commission may prescribe, unless the Commission determines that the imposition of such suspension, denial of registration or reregistration, or market bar is not required to protect the public interest. The Commission may upon petition later review such disqualification and market bar and for good cause shown reduce the period thereof.

(c) *Transactions by Commissioners and Commission Employees Prohibited.* It shall be a felony punishable by a fine of not more than $500,000 or imprisonment for not more than five years, or both, together with the costs of prosecution, for any Commissioner of the Commission or any employee or agent thereof, to participate, directly or indirectly, in any transaction in commodity futures or any transaction of the character of or which is commonly known to the trade as an "option", "privilege", "indemnity", "bid", "offer", "put", "call", "advance guaranty", or "decline guaranty", or any transaction for the delivery of any commodity under a standardized contract commonly known to the trade as a margin account, margin contract, leverage account, or leverage contract, or under any contract, account, arrangement, scheme, or device that the Commission determines serves the same function or functions as such a standardized contract, or is marketed or managed in substantially the same manner as such a standardized contract, or for any such person to participate, directly or indirectly, in any investment transaction in an actual commodity if nonpublic information is used in the investment transaction, if the investment transaction is prohibited by rule or regulation of the Commission, or if the investment transaction is effected by means of any instrument regulated by the Commission. The foregoing prohibitions shall not apply to any transaction or class of transactions that the Commission, by rule or regulation, has determined would not be contrary to the public interest or otherwise inconsistent with the purposes of this subsection.

(d) *Use of Information by Commissioners and Commission Employees Prohibited.* It shall be a felony punishable by a fine of not more than $500,000 or imprisonment for not more than five years, or both, together with the costs of prosecution—(1) for any Commissioner of the Commission or any employee or agent thereof who, by virtue of his employment or position, acquires information which may affect or tend to affect the price of any commodity futures or commodity and which information has not been made public to impart such information with intent to assist another person, directly or indirectly, to participate in any transaction in commodity futures, any transaction in an actual commodity, or in any transaction of the character of or which is commonly known to the trade as an "option", "privilege", "indemnity", "bid", "offer", "put", "call", "advance guaranty", or "decline guaranty", or in any transaction for the delivery of any commodity under a standardized contract commonly known to the trade as a margin account, margin contract, leverage account, or leverage contract, or under any contract, account, arrangement, scheme, or device that the Commission determines serves the same function or functions as such a standardized contract, or is marketed or managed in substantially the same manner as such a standardized contract; and (2) for any person to acquire such information from any Commissioner of the Commission or any employee or agent thereof and to use such information in any transaction in commodity futures, any transaction in an actual commodity, or in any transaction of the character of or which is commonly known to the trade as an "option", "privilege", "indemnity", "bid", "offer", "put", "call", "advance guaranty", or "decline guaranty", or in any transaction for the delivery of any commodity under a standardized contract commonly known to the trade as a margin account, margin contract, leverage account, or leverage contract, or under any contract, account, arrangement, scheme, or device that the Commission determines serves the same function or functions as such a standardized contract, or is marketed or managed in substantially the same manner as such a standardized contract.

(e) *Insider Trading Prohibited.* It shall be a felony for any person—

(1) who is an employee, member of the governing board, or member of any committee of a board of trade, registered entity, swap data repository, or registered futures association, in violation of a regulation issued by the Commission, willfully and knowingly to trade for such person's own account, or for or on behalf of any other account, in contracts for future delivery or options thereon, or swaps, on the basis of, or willfully and knowingly to disclose for any purpose inconsistent with the performance of such person's official duties as an employee or member, any material nonpublic information obtained through special access related to the performance of such duties; or

(2) willfully and knowingly to trade for such person's own account, or for or on behalf of any other account, in contracts for future delivery or options thereon on the basis of any material nonpublic information that such person knows was obtained in violation of paragraph (1) from an employee, member of the governing board, or member of any committee of a board of trade, registered entity, or registered futures association.

Such felony shall be punishable by a fine of not more than $500,000, plus the amount of any profits realized from such trading or disclosure made in violation of this subsection, or imprisonment for not more than five years, or both, together with the costs of prosecution.

Separability of Provisions

Sec. 10. If any provision of this Act or the application thereof to any person or circumstances is held invalid, the validity of the remainder of the Act and of the application of such provisions to other persons and circumstances shall not be affected thereby.

Sec. 11. [Repealed]

Commission Operations

Sec. 12. (a) The Commission may cooperate with any Department or agency of the Government, any State, territory, district, or possession, or department, agency, or political subdivision thereof, any foreign futures authority, any department or agency of a foreign government or political subdivision thereof, or any person.

(b)(1) The Commission shall have the authority to employ such investigators, special experts, Administrative Law Judges, clerks, and other employees as it may from time to time find necessary for the proper performance of its duties and as may be from time to time appropriated for by Congress.

(2) The Commission may employ experts and consultants in accordance with section 3109 of title 5 of the United States Code, and compensate such persons at rates not in excess of the maximum daily rate prescribed for GS–18 under section 5332 of title 5 of the United States Code.

(3) The Commission shall also have authority to make and enter into contracts with respect to all matters which in the judgment of the Commission are necessary and appropriate to effectuate the purposes and provisions of this Act, including, but not limited to, the rental of necessary space at the seat of Government and elsewhere.

(4) The Commission may request (in accordance with the procedures set forth in subchapter II of chapter 31 of title 5, United States Code) and the Office of Personnel Management shall authorize pursuant to the request, eight positions in the Senior Executive Service in addition to the number of such positions authorized for the Commission on the date of enactment of this sentence.

(c) All of the expenses of the Commissioners, including all necessary expenses for transportation incurred by them while on official business of the Commission, shall be allowed and paid on the presentation of itemized vouchers therefor approved by the Commission.

(d) There are authorized to be appropriated such sums as are necessary to carry out this Act for each of fiscal years 2008 through 2013.

(e) *Relation to Other Law, Departments, or Agencies.*

(1) Nothing in this Act shall supersede or preempt—

(A) criminal prosecution under any Federal criminal statute;

(B) the application of any Federal or State statute (except as provided in paragraph (2)), including any rule or regulation thereunder, to any transaction in or involving any commodity, product, right, service, or interest—

(i) that is not conducted on or subject to the rules of a registered entity or exempt board of trade;

(ii) (except as otherwise specified by the Commission by rule or regulation) that is not conducted on or subject to the rules of any board of trade, exchange, or market located outside the United States, its territories or possessions; or

(iii) that is not subject to regulation by the Commission under section 4c or 19; or

(C) the application of any Federal or State statute, including any rule or regulation thereunder, to any person required to be registered or designated under this Act who shall fail or refuse to obtain such registration or designation.

(2) This Act shall supersede and preempt the application of any State or local law that prohibits or regulates gaming or the operation of bucket shops (other than antifraud provisions of general applicability) in the case of—

(A) an electronic trading facility excluded under section 2(e) of this Act;

(B) an agreement, contract, or transaction that is excluded from this Act under section 2(c) or 2(f) of this Act or title IV of the Commodity Futures Modernization Act of 2000, or exempted under section 4(c) of this Act (regardless of whether any such agreement, contract, or transaction is otherwise subject to this Act).

(f)(1) On request from a foreign futures authority, the Commission may, in its discretion, provide assistance in accordance with this section if the requesting authority states that the requesting authority is conducting an investigation which it deems necessary to determine whether any person has violated, is violating, or is about to violate any laws, rules or regulations relating to futures or options matters that the requesting authority administers or enforces. The Commission may conduct such investigation as the Commission deems necessary to collect information and evidence pertinent to the request for assistance. Such assistance may be provided without regard to whether the facts stated in the request would also constitute a violation of the laws of the United States.

(2) In deciding whether to provide assistance under this subsection, the Commission shall consider whether—

(A) the requesting authority has agreed to provide reciprocal assistance to the Commission in futures and options matters; and

(B) compliance with the request would prejudice the public interest of the United States.

(3) Notwithstanding any other provision of law, the Commission may accept payment and reimbursement, in cash or in kind, from a foreign futures authority, or made on behalf of such authority, for necessary expenses incurred by the Commission, its members, and employees in carrying out any investigation, or in providing any other assistance to a foreign futures authority, pursuant to this section. Any payment or reimbursement accepted shall be considered a reimbursement to the appropriated funds of the Commission.

(g) Consistent with its responsibilities under section 18, the Commission is directed to facilitate the development and operation of computerized trading as an adjunct to the open outcry auction system. The Commission is further directed to cooperate with the Office of the United States Trade Representative, the Department of the Treasury, the Department of Commerce, and the Department of State in order to remove any trade barriers that may be imposed by a foreign nation on the international use of electronic trading systems.

(h) *Regulation of Swaps as Insurance Under State Law*. A swap—

(1) shall not be considered to be insurance; and

(2) may not be regulated as an insurance contract under the law of any State.

Responsibility of Principal

Sec. 13. (a) Any person who commits, or who willfully aids, abets, counsels, commands, induces, or procures the commission of, a violation of any of the provisions of this Act, or any of the rules, regulations or orders issued pursuant to this Act, or who acts in combination or concert with any other person in any such violation, or who willfully causes an act to be done or omitted which if directly performed or omitted by him or another would be a violation of the provisions of this Act or any of such rules, regulations, or orders may be held responsible for such violation as a principal.

(b) *Controlling Persons.* Any person who, directly or indirectly, controls any person who has violated any provision of this Act or any of the rules, regulations, or orders issued pursuant to this Act may be held liable for such violation in any action brought by the Commission to the same extent as such controlled person. In such action, the Commission has the burden of proving that the controlling person did not act in good faith or knowingly induced, directly or indirectly, the act or acts constituting the violation.

(c) *Minor Violations.* Nothing in this Act shall be construed as requiring the Commission to report minor violations of this Act for prosecution, whenever it appears that the public interest does not require such action.

Complaints Against Registered Persons

Sec. 14. (a) *Petition for Actual Damages.*

(1) Any person complaining of any violation of any provision of this Act or any rule, regulation, or order issued pursuant to this Act by any person who is registered under this Act may, at any time within two years after the cause of action accrues, apply to the Commission for an order awarding—

(A) actual damages proximately caused by such violation. If an award of actual damages is made against a floor broker in connection with the execution of a customer order, and the futures commission merchant which selected the floor broker for the execution of the customer order is held to be responsible under section 2(a)(1) for the floor broker's violation, such futures commission merchant may be required to satisfy such award; and

(B) in the case of any action arising from a willful and intentional violation in the execution of an order on the floor of a registered entity, punitive or exemplary damages equal to no more than two times the amount of such actual damages. If an award of punitive or exemplary damages is made against a floor broker in connection with the execution of a customer order, and the futures commission merchant which selected the floor broker for the execution of the customer order is held to be responsible under section 2(a)(1) for the floor broker's violation, such futures commission merchant may be required to satisfy such award if the floor broker fails to do so, except that such requirement shall apply to the futures commission merchant only if it willfully and intentionally selected the floor broker with the intent to assist or facilitate the floor broker's violation.

(2)(A) An action may be brought under this subsection by any one or more persons described in this subsection for and in behalf of such person or persons and other persons similarly situated, if the Commission permits such actions pursuant to a final rule issued by the Commission.

(B) Not later than two hundred and seventy days after the date of enactment of this paragraph, the Commission shall propose and publish for public comment such rules as are necessary to carry out subparagraph (A). In developing such rules, the Commission shall consider the potential impact of such actions on resources available to the reparations system established under this Act and the relative merits of bringing such actions in Federal court.

(b) *Rules and Regulations; Control Over Right of Appeal.* The Commission may promulgate such rules, regulations, and orders as it deems necessary or appropriate for the efficient and expeditious administration of this section. Notwithstanding any other provision of law, such rules, regulations, and orders may prescribe, or otherwise condition, without limitation, the form, filing, and service of pleadings or orders, the nature and scope of discovery, counterclaims, motion practice (including the grounds for dismissal of any claim or counterclaim), hearings (including the waiver thereof, which may relate to the amount in controversy), rights of appeal, if any, and all other matters governing proceedings before the Commission under this section.

(c) *Bond Requirement When Complainant is Nonresident; Waiver.* In case a complaint is made by a nonresident of the United States, the complainant shall be required, before any formal action is taken on his complaint, to furnish a bond in double the amount of the claim conditioned upon the payment of costs, including a reasonable attorney's fee for the respondent if the respondent shall prevail, and any reparation award that may be issued by the Commission against the complainant on any counterclaim by respondent: *Provided,* That the Commission shall have authority to waive the furnishing of a bond by a complainant who is a resident of a country which permits the filing of a complaint by a resident of the United States without the furnishing of a bond.

(d) *Enforcement of Reparation Award.* (1) If any person against whom an award has been made does not pay the reparation award within the time specified in the Commission's order, the complainant, or any person for whose benefit such order was made, within three years of the date of the order, may file a certified copy of the order of the Commission, in the district court of the United States for the district in which he resides or in which is located the principal place of business of the respondent, for enforcement of such reparation award by appropriate orders. The orders, writs, and processes of such district court may in such case run, be served, and be returnable anywhere in the United States. The petitioner shall not be liable for costs in the district court, nor for costs at any subsequent state of the proceedings, unless they accrue upon his appeal. If the petitioner finally prevails, he shall be allowed a reasonable attorney's fee, to be taxed and collected as a part of the costs of the suit. Subject to the right of appeal under subsection (e) of this section, an order of the Commission awarding reparations shall be final and conclusive.

(2) A reparation award shall be directly enforceable in district court as if it were a judgment pursuant to section 1963 of title 28, United States Code. This paragraph shall operate retroactively from the effective date of its enactment, and shall apply to all reparation awards for which a proceeding described in paragraph (1) is commenced within 3 years of the date of the Commission's order.

(e) *Review.* Any order of the Commission entered hereunder shall be reviewable on petition of any party aggrieved thereby, by the United States Court of Appeals for any circuit in which a hearing was held, or if no hearing was held, any circuit in which the appellee is located under the procedure provided in section 6(c) of this Act. Such appeal shall not be effective unless within 30 days from and after the date of the reparation order the appellant also files with the clerk of the court a bond in double the amount of the reparation awarded against the appellant conditioned upon the payment of the judgment entered by the court, plus interest and costs, including a reasonable attorney's fee for the appellee, if the appellee shall prevail. Such bond shall be in the form of cash, negotiable securities having a market value at least equivalent to the amount of bond prescribed, or the undertaking of a surety company on the approved list of sureties issued by the Treasury Department of the United States. The appellee shall not be liable for costs in said court. If the appellee prevails, he shall be allowed a reasonable attorney's fee to be taxed and collected as a part of his costs.

(f) *Automatic Bar from Trading and Suspension for Noncompliance; Effect of Appeal.* Unless the party against whom a reparation order has been issued shows to the satisfaction of the Commission within fifteen days from the expiration of the period allowed for compliance with such order that either an appeal as herein authorized has been taken or payment of the full amount of the order (or any agreed settlement thereof) has been made, such party shall be prohibited automatically from trading on all registered entities and, if the party is registered with the Commission, such registration shall be suspended automatically at the expiration of such fifteen-day period until such party shows to the satisfaction of the Commission that payment of such amount with interest thereon to date of payment has been made: *Provided,* That if on appeal the appellee prevails or if the appeal is dismissed, the automatic prohibition against trading and suspension of registration shall become effective at the expiration of thirty days from the date of judgment on the appeal, but if the judgment is stayed by a court of competent jurisdiction, the suspension shall become effective ten days after the expiration of such stay, unless prior thereto the judgment of the court has been satisfied.

(g) *Predispute Resolution Agreements for Institutional Customers.* Nothing in this section prohibits a registered futures commission merchant from requiring a customer that is an eligible contract participant, as a condition to the commission merchant's conducting a transaction for the customer, to enter into an agreement waiving the right to file a claim under this section.

Consideration of Costs and Benefits and Antitrust Laws

Sec. 15. (a) *Costs and Benefits.*

(1) *In General.* Before promulgating a regulation under this Act or issuing an order (except as provided in paragraph (3)), the Commission shall consider the costs and benefits of the action of the Commission.

(2) *Considerations.* The costs and benefits of the proposed Commission action shall be evaluated in light of—

(A) considerations of protection of market participants and the public;

(B) considerations of the efficiency, competitiveness, and financial integrity of futures markets;

(C) considerations of price discovery;

(D) considerations of sound risk management practices; and

(E) other public interest considerations.

(3) *Applicability*. This subsection does not apply to the following actions of the Commission:

(A) An order that initiates, is part of, or is the result of an adjudicatory or investigative process of the Commission.

(B) An emergency action.

(C) A finding of fact regarding compliance with a requirement of the Commission.

(b) *Antitrust Laws*. The Commission shall take into consideration the public interest to be protected by the antitrust laws and endeavor to take the least anticompetitive means of achieving the objectives of this Act, as well as the policies and purposes of this Act, in issuing any order or adopting any Commission rule or regulation (including any exemption under section 4(c) or 4c(b)), or in requiring or approving any bylaw, rule, or regulation of a contract market or registered futures association established pursuant to section 17 of this Act.

Market Reports

Sec. 16. (a) The Commission may conduct regular investigations of the markets for goods, articles, services, rights, and interests which are the subject of futures contracts, and furnish reports of the findings of these investigations to the public on a regular basis. These market reports shall, where appropriate, include information on the supply, demand, prices, and other conditions in the United States and other countries with respect to such goods, articles, services, rights, interests, and information respecting the futures markets.

(b) The Commission shall cooperate with the Department of Agriculture and any other Department or Federal agency which makes market investigations to avoid unnecessary duplication of information-gathering activities.

(c) The Department of Agriculture and any other Department or Federal agency which has market information sought by the Commission shall furnish it to the Commission upon the request of any authorized employee of the Commission. The Commission shall abide by any rules of confidentiality applying to such information.

(d) The Commission shall not disclose in such reports data and information which would separately disclose the business transactions or market positions of any person and trade secrets or names of customers except as provided in section 8 of this Act.

(e) This section shall not apply to investigations involving any security underlying a security futures product.

Registered Futures Associations

Sec. 17. (a) Any association of persons may be registered with the Commission as a registered futures association pursuant to subsection (b) of this section, under the terms and conditions hereinafter provided in this section, by filing with the Commission for review and approval a registration statement in such form as the Commission may prescribe, setting forth the information, and accompanied by the documents, below specified:

(1) Data as to its organization, membership, and rules of procedure, and such other information as the Commission may by rules and regulations require as necessary or appropriate in the public interest; and

(2) Copies of its constitution, charter, or articles of incorporation or association, with all amendments thereto, and of its bylaws, and of any rules or instruments corresponding to the foregoing, whatever the name, hereinafter in this section collectively referred to as the "rules of the association".

(b) An applicant association shall not be registered as a futures association unless the Commission finds, under standards established by the Commission, that—

(1) such association is in the public interest and that it will be able to comply with the provisions of this section and the rules and regulations thereunder and to carry out the purposes of this section;

(2) the rules of the association provide that any person registered under this Act, registered entity, or any other person designated pursuant to the rules of the Commission as eligible for membership may become a member of such association, except such as are excluded pursuant to paragraph (3) or (4) of this subsection, or a rule of the association permitted under this paragraph. The rules of the association may restrict membership in such association on such specified basis relat-

ing to the type of business done by its members, or on such other specified and appropriate basis, as appears to the Commission to be necessary or appropriate in the public interest and to carry out the purpose of this section. Rules adopted by the association may provide that the association may, unless the Commission directs otherwise in cases in which the Commission finds it appropriate in the public interest so to direct, deny admission to, or refuse to continue in such association any person if (i) such person, whether prior or subsequent to becoming registered as such, or (ii) any person associated within the meaning of "associated person" as set forth in section 4k of this Act, whether prior or subsequent to becoming so associated, has been and is suspended or expelled from a registered entity or has been and is barred or suspended from being associated with all members of such registered entity, for violation of any rule of such registered entity;

(3) the rules of the association provide that, except with the approval or at the direction of the Commission in cases in which the Commission finds it appropriate in the public interest so to approve or direct, no person shall be admitted to or continued in membership in such association, if such person—

(A) has been and is suspended or expelled from a registered futures association or from a registered entity or has been and is barred or suspended from being associated with all members of such association or from being associated with all members of such registered entity, for violation of any rule of such association or registered entity which prohibits any act or transaction constituting conduct inconsistent with just and equitable principles of trade, or requires any act the omission of which constitutes conduct inconsistent with just and equitable principles of trade;

(B) is subject to an order of the Commission denying, suspending, or revoking his registration pursuant to section 6(c) of this Act, or expelling or suspending him from membership in a registered futures association or a registered entity, or barring or suspending him from being associated with a futures commission merchant;

(C) whether prior or subsequent to becoming a member, by his conduct while associated with a member, was a cause of any suspension, expulsion, or order of the character described in clause (A) or (B) which is in effect with respect to such member, and in entering such a suspension, expulsion, or order, the Commission or any such registered entity or association shall have jurisdiction to determine whether or not any person was a cause thereof; or

(D) has associated with him any person who is known, or in the exercise of reasonable care should be known, to him to be a person who would be ineligible for admission to or continuance in membership under clause (A), (B), or (C) of this paragraph;

(4) the rules of the association provide that, except with the approval or at the direction of the Commission in cases in which the Commission finds it appropriate in the public interest so to approve or direct, no person shall become a member and no natural person shall become a person associated with a member, unless such person is qualified to become a member or a person associated with a member in conformity with specified and appropriate standards with respect to the training, experience, and such other qualifications of such person as the association finds necessary or desirable, and in the case of a member, the financial responsibility of such a member. For the purpose of defining such standards and the application thereof, such rules may—

(A) appropriately classify prospective members (taking into account relevant matters, including type or nature of business done) and persons proposed to be associated with members;

(B) specify that all or any portion of such standard shall be applicable to any such class;

(C) require persons in any such class to pass examinations prescribed in accordance with such rules;

(D) provide that persons in any such class other than prospective members and partners, officers and supervisory employees (which latter term may be defined by such rules and as so defined shall include branch managers of members) of members, may be qualified solely on the basis of compliance with specified standards of training and such other qualifications as the association finds appropriate;

(E) provide that applications to become a member or a person associated with a member shall set forth such facts as the association may prescribe as to the training, experience, and other qualifications (including, in the case of an applicant for membership, financial responsibility) of the applicant and that the association shall adopt procedures for verification of qualifications of the applicant, which may require the applicant to be fingerprinted and to submit, or cause to be submitted, such fingerprints to the Attorney General for identification and appropriate processing. Notwithstanding any other provision of law, such an association may receive from the Attorney General all the results of such identification and processing; and

(F) require any class of persons associated with a member to be registered with the association in accordance with procedures specified by such rules (and any application or document supplemental thereto required by such rules of a person seeking to be registered with such association shall, for the purposes of section 6(c) of the Act, be deemed an application required to be filed under this section);

(5) the rules of the association assure a fair representation of its members in the adoption of any rule of the association or amendment thereto, the selection of its officers and directors, and in all other phases of the administration of its affairs;

(6) the rules of the association provide for the equitable allocation of dues among its members, to defray reasonable expenses of administration;

(7) the rules of the association are designed to prevent fraudulent and manipulative acts and practices, to promote just and equitable principles of trade, in general, to protect the public interest, and to remove impediments to and perfect the mechanism of free and open futures trading;

(8) the rules of the association provide that its members and persons associated with its members shall be appropriately disciplined, by expulsion, suspension, fine, censure, or being suspended or barred from being associated with all members, or any other fitting penalty, for any violation of its rules;

(9) the rules of the association provide a fair and orderly procedure with respect to the disciplining of members and persons associated with members and the denial of membership to any person seeking membership therein or the barring of any person from being associated with a member. In any proceeding to determine whether any member or other person shall be disciplined, such rules shall require that specific charges be brought; that such member or person shall be notified of, and be given an opportunity to defend against, such charges; that a record shall be kept; and that the determination shall include—

(A) a statement setting forth any act or practice in which such member or other person may be found to have engaged, or which such member or other person may be found to have omitted;

(B) a statement setting forth the specific rule or rules of the association of which any such act or practice, or omission to act, is deemed to be in violation;

(C) a statement whether the acts or practices prohibited by such rule or rules, or the omission of any act required thereby, are deemed to constitute conduct inconsistent with just and equitable principles of trade; and

(D) a statement setting forth the penalty imposed;

In any proceeding to determine whether a person shall be denied membership or whether any person shall be barred from being associated with a member, such rules shall provide that the person shall be notified of, and be given an opportunity to be heard upon, the specific grounds for denial or bar which are under consideration; that a record shall be kept; and that the determination shall set forth the specific grounds upon which the denial or bar is based;

(10) the rules of the association provide a fair, equitable, and expeditious procedure through arbitration or otherwise for the settlement of customers' claims and grievances against any member or employee thereof: *Provided,* That

(A) the use of such procedure by a customer shall be voluntary,

(B) the term "customer" as used in this paragraph shall not include another member of the association, and

(C) in the case of a claim arising from a violation in the execution of an order on the floor of a registered entity, such procedure shall provide, to the extent appropriate—

(i) for payment of actual damages proximately caused by such violation. If an award of actual damages is made against a floor broker in connection with the execution of a customer order, and the futures commission merchant which selected the floor broker for the execution of the customer order is held to be responsible under section 2(a)(1) for the floor broker's violation, such futures commission merchant may be required to satisfy such award; and

(ii) where the violation is willful and intentional, for payment to the customer of punitive or exemplary damages, in addition to losses proximately caused by the violation, in an amount equal to no more than two times the amount of such losses. If punitive or exemplary damages are awarded against a floor broker in connection with the execution of a customer order, and the futures commission merchant which selected the floor broker for the execution of such order is held to be responsible under section 2(a)(1) for the floor broker's violation, such futures commission merchant may be required to satisfy the award of punitive or exemplary damages if the floor broker fails to do so, except that such requirement shall apply to the futures commission merchant only if it willfully and intentionally selected the floor broker with the intent to assist or facilitate the floor broker's violation; and

(11) such association provides for meaningful representation on the governing board of such association of a diversity of membership interests and provides that no less than 20 percent of the regular voting members of such board be comprised of qualified nonmembers of or persons who are not regulated by such association.

(12)(A) such association provides on all major disciplinary committees for a diversity of membership sufficient to ensure fairness and to prevent special treatment or preference for any person in the conduct of disciplinary proceedings and the assessment of penalties.

(13) A major disciplinary committee hearing a disciplinary matter shall include—

(A) qualified persons representing segments of the association membership other than that of the subject of the proceeding; and

(B) where appropriate to carry out the purposes of this paragraph, qualified persons who are not members of the association.

(c) *Suspension of Registration.* The Commission may, after notice and opportunity for hearing, suspend the registration of any futures association if it finds that the rules thereof do not conform to the requirements of the Commission, and any such suspension shall remain in effect until the Commission issues an order determining that such rules have been modified to conform with such requirements.

(d) *Nonmembers, Fees and Changes.* In addition to the fees and charges authorized by section 8a(1) of this Act, each person registered under this Act, who is not a member of a futures association registered pursuant to this section, shall pay to the Commission such reasonable fees and charges as may be necessary to defray the costs of additional regulatory duties required to be performed by the Commission because such person is not a member of a registered futures association. The Commission shall establish such additional fees and charges by rules and regulations.

(e) *Nonmembers, Just and Equitable Principles of Trade.* Any person registered under this Act, who is not a member of a futures association registered pursuant to this section, in addition to the other requirements and obligations of this Act and the regulations thereunder shall be subject to such other rules and regulations as the Commission may find necessary to protect the public interest and promote just and equitable principles of trade.

(f) *Grant or Denial of Registration.* Upon filing of an application for registration pursuant to subsection (a), the Commission may by order grant such registration if the requirements of this section are satisfied. If, after appropriate notice and opportunity for hearing, it appears to the Commission that any requirement of this section is not satisfied, the Commission shall by order deny such registration.

(g) *Withdrawal from Registration.* A registered futures association may, upon such reasonable notice as the Commission may deem necessary in the public interest, withdraw from registration by filing with the Commission a written notice of withdrawal in such form as the Commission may by rules and regulations prescribe.

(h) *Commission Review of Association Action.*

(1) If any registered futures association takes any final disciplinary action against a member of the association or a person associated with a member, denies admission to any person seeking membership therein, or bars any person from being associated with a member, the association promptly shall give notice thereof to such member or person and file notice thereof with the Commission. The notice shall be in such form and contain such information as the Commission, by rule or regulation, may prescribe as necessary or appropriate to carry out the purposes of this Act.

(2) Any action with respect to which a registered futures association is required by paragraph (1) to file notice shall be subject to review by the Commission on its motion, or on application by any person aggrieved by the action. Such application shall be filed within 30 days after the date such notice is filed with the Commission and received by the aggrieved person, or within such longer period as the Commission may determine.

(3)(A) Application to the Commission for review, or the institution of review by the Commission on its own motion, shall not operate as a stay of such action unless the Commission otherwise orders, summarily or after notice and opportunity for hearing on the question of a stay (which hearing may consist solely of the submission of affidavits or presentation of oral arguments).

(B) The Commission shall establish procedures for expedited consideration and determination of the question of a stay.

(i) *Proceeding to Review Disciplinary Action.*

(1) In a proceeding to review a final disciplinary action taken by a registered futures association against a member thereof or a person associated with a member, after appropriate notice and opportunity for a hearing (which hearing may consist solely of consideration of the record before the association and opportunity for the presentation of supporting reasons to affirm, modify, or set aside the sanction imposed by the association)—

(A) if the Commission finds that—

(i) the member or person associated with a member has engaged in the acts or practices, or has omitted the acts, that the association has found the member or person to have engaged in or omitted;

(ii) the acts or practices, or omissions to act, are in violation of the rules of the association specified in the determination of the association; and

(iii) such rules are, and were applied in a manner, consistent with the purposes of this Act,

the Commission, by order, shall so declare and, as appropriate, affirm the sanction imposed by the association, modify the sanction in accordance with paragraph (2), or remand the case to the association for further proceedings; or

(B) if the Commission does not make any such finding, the Commission, by order, shall set aside the sanction imposed by the association and, if appropriate, remand the case to the association for further proceedings.

(2) If, after a proceeding under paragraph (1), the Commission finds that any penalty imposed on a member or person associated with a member is excessive or oppressive, having due regard for the public interest, the Commission, by order, shall cancel, reduce, or require the remission of the penalty.

(3) In a proceeding to review the denial of membership in a registered futures association or the barring of any person from being associated with a member, after appropriate notice and opportunity for a hearing (which hearing may consist solely of consideration of the record before the association and opportunity for the presentation of supporting reasons to affirm, modify, or set aside the action of the association)—

(A) if the Commission finds that—

(i) the specific grounds on which the denial or bar is based exist in fact;

(ii) the denial or bar is in accordance with the rules of the association; and

(iii) such rules are, and were applied in a manner, consistent with the purposes of this Act,

the Commission, by order, shall so declare and, as appropriate, affirm or modify the action of the association, or remand the case to the association for further proceedings; or

(B) if the Commission does not make any such finding, the Commission, by order, shall set aside the action of the association and require the association to admit the applicant to membership or permit the person to be associated with a member, or, as appropriate, remand the case to the association for further proceedings.

(4) Any person aggrieved by a final order of the Commission entered under this subsection may file a petition for review with a United States court of appeals in the same manner as provided in section 6(c).

(j) *Changes in Association Rules and Regulations.* Every registered futures association shall file with the Commission in accordance with such rules and regulations as the Commission may prescribe as necessary or appropriate in the public interest, copies of any changes in or additions to the rules of the association, and such other information and documents as the Commission may require to keep current or to supplement the registration statement and documents filed pursuant to subsection (a) of this section. A registered futures association shall submit to the Commission any change in or addition to its rules and may make such rules effective ten days after receipt of such submission by the Commission unless, within the ten-day period, the registered futures association requests review and approval thereof by the Commission or the Commission notifies such registered futures association in writing of its determination to review such rules for approval. The Commission shall approve such rules if such rules are determined by the Commission to be consistent with the requirements of this section and not otherwise in violation of this Act or the regulations issued pursuant to this Act, and the Commission shall disapprove, after appropriate notice and opportunity for hearing, any such rule which the Commission determines at any time to be inconsistent with the requirements of this section or in violation of this Act or the regulations issued pursuant to this Act. If the Commission does not approve or institute disapproval proceedings with respect to any rule within one hundred and eighty days after receipt or within such longer period of time as the registered futures association may agree to, or if the Commission does not conclude a disapproval proceeding with respect to any rule within one year after receipt or within such longer period as the registered futures association may agree to, such rule may be made effective by the registered futures association until such time as the Commission disapproves such rule in accordance with this subsection.

(k) *Abrogation of Association Rules.*

(1) The Commission is authorized by order to abrogate any rule of a registered futures association, if after appropriate notice and opportunity for hearing, it appears to the Commission that such abrogation is necessary or appropriate to assure fair dealing by the members of such association, to assure a fair representation of its members in the administration of its affairs or effectuate the purposes of this section.

(2) The Commission may in writing request any registered futures association to adopt any specified alteration or supplement to its rules with respect to any of the matters hereinafter enumerated. If such association fails to adopt such alteration or supplement within a reasonable time, the Commission is authorized by order to alter or supplement the rules of such association in the manner theretofore requested, or with such modifications of such alteration or supplement as it deems necessary if, after appropriate notice and opportunity for hearing, it appears to the Commission that such alteration or supplement is necessary or appropriate in the public interest or to effectuate the purposes of this section, with respect to—

(A) the basis for, and procedure in connection with, the denial of membership or the barring from being associated with a member or the disciplining of members or persons associated with members, or the qualifications required for members or natural persons associated with members or any class thereof;

(B) the method for adoption of any change in or addition to the rules of the association;

(C) the method of choosing officers and directors.

(*l*) *Suspension or Revocation of Association Registration.* The Commission is authorized, if such action appears to it to be necessary or appropriate in the public interest or to carry out the purposes of this section—

(1) after appropriate notice and opportunity for hearing, by order to suspend for a period not exceeding twelve months or to revoke the registration of a registered futures association, if the Commission finds that such association has violated any provisions of this Act or any rule or regulation thereunder, or has failed to enforce compliance with its own rules, or has engaged in any other activity tending to defeat the purposes of this Act;

(2) after appropriate notice and opportunity for hearing, by order to suspend for a period not exceeding twelve months or to expel from a registered futures association any member thereof, or to suspend for a period not exceeding twelve months or to bar any person from being associated with a member thereof, if the Commission finds that such member or person—

(A) has violated any provision of this Act or any rule or regulation thereunder, or has effected any transaction for any other person who, he had reason to believe, was violating with respect to such transaction any provision of this Act or any rule or regulation thereunder; or

(B) has willfully violated any provision of this Act, as amended, or of any rule, regulation, or order thereunder, or has effected any transaction for any other person who, he had reason to believe, was willfully violating with respect to such transaction any provision of such Act or rule, regulation, or order; and

(3) after appropriate notice and opportunity for hearing, by order to remove from office any officer or director of a registered futures association who, the Commission finds, has willfully failed to enforce the rules of the association, or has willfully abused his authority.

(m) *Compulsory Membership.* Notwithstanding any other provision of law, the Commission may approve rules of futures associations that, directly or indirectly, require persons eligible for membership in such associations to become members of at least one such association, upon a determination by the Commission that such rules are necessary or appropriate to achieve the purposes and objectives of this Act.

(n) *Reports to Congress to Include Association Information.* The Commission shall include in its annual reports to Congress information concerning any futures associations registered pursuant to this section and the effectiveness of such associations in regulating the practices of the members.

(o) *Registration Functions.*

(1) The Commission may require any futures association registered pursuant to this section to perform any portion of the registration functions under this Act with respect to each member of the association other than a registered entity and with respect to each associated person of such member, in accordance with rules, notwithstanding any other provision of law, adopted by such futures association and submitted to the Commission pursuant to section 17(j) of this Act, and subject to the provisions of this Act applicable to registrations granted by the Commission.

(2) In performing any Commission registration function authorized by the Commission under section 8a(10), this section, or any other applicable provisions of this Act, a futures association may issue orders (A) to refuse to register any person, (B) to register conditionally any person, (C) to suspend the registration of any person, (D) to place restrictions on the registration of any person, or (E) to revoke the registration of any person. If such an order is the final decision of the futures association, any person against whom the order has been issued may petition the Commission to review the decision. The Commission may on its own initiative or upon petition decline review or grant review and affirm, set aside, or modify such an order of the futures association; and the findings of the futures association as to the facts, if supported by the weight of the evidence, shall be conclusive. Unless the Commission grants review under this section of an order concerning registration issued by a futures association, the order of the futures association shall be considered to be an order issued by the Commission.

(3) Nothing in this section shall affect the Commission's authority to review the granting of a registration application by a registered futures association that is performing any Commission registration function authorized by the Commission under section 8a(10), this section, or any other applicable provision of this Act.

(4) If a person against whom a futures association has issued a registration order under this subsection petitions the Commission to review that order and the Commission declines to take review, such person may file a petition for review with a United States court of appeals, in accordance with section 6(c) of this Act.

(p) *Member Standards.* Notwithstanding any other provision of this section, each futures association registered under this section on the date of enactment of the Futures Trading Act of 1982, shall adopt and submit for Commission approval not later than ninety days after such date of enactment, and each futures association that applies for registration after such date shall adopt and include with its application for registration, rules of the association that require the association to—

(1) establish training standards and proficiency testing for persons involved in the solicitation of transactions subject to the provisions of this Act, supervisors of such persons, and all persons for which it has registration responsibilities, and a program to audit and enforce compliance with such standards;

(2) establish minimum capital, segregation, and other financial requirements applicable to its members for which such requirements are imposed by the Commission and implement a program to audit and enforce compliance with such requirements, except that such requirements may not be less stringent than those imposed on such firms by this Act or by Commission regulation;

(3) establish minimum standards governing the sales practices of its members and persons associated therewith for transactions subject to the provisions of this Act; and

(4) establish special supervisory guidelines to protect the public interest relating to the solicitation by telephone of new futures or options accounts and make such guidelines applicable to those members determined to require such guidelines in accordance with standards established by the Commission consistent with this Act. Such guidelines may include a requirement that, with respect to a customer with no previous futures or commodity options trading experience, the member may not enter an order for the account of such customer for a period of three days following opening of the account and receipt of a signed acknowledgement by the customer of receipt of a risk disclosure statement.

(q) *Implementation of CFTC Rules.** Each futures association registered under this section shall develop a comprehensive program that fully implements the rules approved by the Commission under this section as soon as practicable but not later than September 30, 1985, in the case of any futures association registered on the date of enactment of the Futures Trading Act of 1982, and not later than two and one-half years after the date of registration in the case of any other futures association registered under this section.

(q) *Major Disciplinary Rule Violations.**

(1) *Schedule.* The Commission shall issue regulations requiring each registered futures association to establish and make available to the public a schedule of major violations of any rule within the disciplinary jurisdiction of such registered futures association.

(2) *Prohibition.* The regulations issued by the Commission pursuant to this subsection shall prohibit, for a period of time to be determined by the Commission, any member of a registered futures association who is found to have committed any major violation from service on the governing board of any registered futures association or registered entity, or on any disciplinary committee thereof.

(r) *Duplicative Regulation of Dual Registrants.* Consistent with this Act, each futures association registered under this section shall issue such rules as are necessary to avoid duplicative or conflicting rules applicable to any futures commission merchant registered with the Commission pursuant to section 4f(a) of this Act (except paragraph (2) thereof), that is also registered with the Securities and Exchange Commission pursuant to section 15(b) of the Securities and Exchange Act of 1934 (except paragraph (11) thereof), with respect to the application of—

(1) rules of such futures association of the type specified in section 4d(e) involving security futures products; and

(2) similar rules of national securities associations registered pursuant to section 15A(a) of the Securities and Exchange Act of 1934 involving security futures products.

* Two subsection (q)'s have been enacted.

Research and Information Programs

Sec. 18. (a) The Commission shall establish and maintain, as part of its ongoing operations, research and information programs to (1) determine the feasibility of trading by computer, and the expanded use of modern information system technology, electronic data processing, and modern communication systems by commodity exchanges, boards of trade, and by the Commission itself for purposes of improving, strengthening, facilitating, or regulating futures trading operations; (2) assist in the development of educational and other informational materials regarding futures trading for dissemination and use among producers, market users, and the general public; and (3) carry out the general purposes of this Act.

(b) The Commission shall include in its annual reports to Congress plans and findings with respect to implementing this section.

Standardized Contracts for Certain Commodities Prohibited

Sec. 19. (a) Except as authorized under subsection (b), no person shall offer to enter into, enter into, or confirm the execution of, any transaction for the delivery of any commodity under a standardized contract commonly known to the trade as a margin account, margin contract, leverage account, or leverage contract, or under any contract, account, arrangement, scheme, or device that the Commission determines serves the same function or functions as such a standardized contract, or is marketed or managed in substantially the same manner as such a standardized contract.

(b)(1) Subject to paragraph (2), no person shall offer to enter into, enter into, or confirm the execution of, any transaction for the delivery of silver bullion, gold bullion, bulk silver coins, bulk gold coins, or platinum under a standardized contract described in subsection (a), contrary to the terms of any rule, regulation, or order that the Commission shall prescribe, which may include terms designed to ensure the financial solvency of the transaction or prevent manipulation or fraud. Such rule, regulation, or order may be made only after notice and opportunity for hearing. The Commission may set different terms and conditions for transactions involving different commodities.

(2) No person may engage in any activity described in paragraph (1) who is not permitted to engage in such activity, by the rules, regulations, and orders of the Commission in effect on the date of the enactment of the Futures Trading Act of 1986, until the Commission permits such person to engage in such activity in accordance with regulations issued in accordance with subsection (c)(2).

(c)(1)(A) Not later than 2 years after the date of the enactment of the Futures Trading Act of 1986, the Commission shall—

(i) with the assistance of a futures association registered under this Act, conduct a survey concerning the persons interested in engaging in the business of offering to enter into, entering into, or confirming the execution of, the transactions described in subsection (b)(1); and

(ii) transmit a report of the results of the survey to the Committee on Agriculture of the House of Representatives and the Committee on Agriculture, Nutrition, and Forestry of the Senate.

(B) Notwithstanding any other provision of law, for purposes of completing such report the Commission may direct, by rule, regulation, or order, a futures association registered under this Act to render such assistance as the Commission shall specify.

(C) Such report shall include the findings and any recommendations of the Commission concerning—

(i) whether such transactions serve an economic purpose;

(ii) the most efficient manner, consistent with the public interest, to permit additional persons to engage in the business of offering to enter into, entering into, and confirming the execution of such transactions; and

(iii) the appropriate regulatory scheme to govern such transactions to ensure the financial solvency of such transactions and to prevent manipulation or fraud.

(2) The report shall also include Commission regulations governing such transactions. The regulations shall provide for permitting additional persons to engage in such transactions. The regulations shall become effective on the expiration of 90 calendar days on which either House of Congress is in session after the date of the transmittal of the report to Congress. The regulations—

(A) may authorize or require, notwithstanding any other provision of law, a futures association registered under this Act to perform such responsibilities in connection with such transactions as the Commission may specify; and

(B) may require that permission for additional persons to engage in such business be given on a gradual basis, so as not to place an undue burden on the resources of the Commission.

(d) This section shall not affect any rights or obligations arising out of any transaction subject to this section, as in effect before the date of the enactment of the Futures Trading Act of 1986, that was entered into, or the execution of which was confirmed, before the date of the enactment of such Act.

Regulations Respecting Commodity Broker Debtors

Sec. 20. (a) Notwithstanding title 11 of the United States Code, the Commission may provide, with respect to a commodity broker that is a debtor under chapter 7 of title 11 of the United States Code, by rule or regulation—

(1) that certain cash, securities, other property, or commodity contracts are to be included in or excluded from customer property or member property;

(2) that certain cash, securities, other property, or commodity contracts are to be specifically identifiable to a particular customer in a specific capacity;

(3) the method by which the business of such commodity broker is to be conducted or liquidated after the date of the filing of the petition under such chapter, including the payment and allocation of margin with respect to commodity contracts not specifically identifiable to a particular customer pending their orderly liquidation;

(4) any persons to which customer property and commodity contracts may be transferred under section 766 of title 11 of the United States Code; and

(5) how the net equity of a customer is to be determined.

(b) As used in this section, the terms "commodity broker", "commodity contract", "customer", "customer property", "member property", "net equity", and "security" have the meanings assigned such terms for the purposes of subchapter IV of chapter 7 of title 11 of the United States Code.

(c) The Commission shall exercise its authority to ensure that securities held in a portfolio margining account carried as a futures account are customer property and the owners of those accounts are customers for the purposes of subchapter IV of chapter 7 of title 11 of the United States Code.

Swap Data Repositories

Sec. 21. (a) *Registration Requirement.*

(1) *Requirement; Authority of Derivatives Clearing Organization.*

(A) *In General.* It shall be unlawful for any person, unless registered with the Commission, directly or indirectly to make use of the mails or any means or instrumentality of interstate commerce to perform the functions of a swap data repository.

(B) *Registration of Derivatives Clearing Organizations.* A derivatives clearing organization may register as a swap data repository.

(2) *Inspection and Examination.* Each registered swap data repository shall be subject to inspection and examination by any representative of the Commission.

(3) *Compliance with Core Principles.*

(A) *In General.* To be registered, and maintain registration, as a swap data repository, the swap data repository shall comply with—

(i) the requirements and core principles described in this section; and

(ii) any requirement that the Commission may impose by rule or regulation pursuant to section 8a(5).

(B) *Reasonable Discretion of Swap Data Repository.* Unless otherwise determined by the Commission by rule or regulation, a swap data repository described in subparagraph (A) shall have reasonable discretion in establishing the manner in which the swap data repository complies with the core principles described in this section.

(b) *Standard Setting.*

(1) *Data Identification.*

(A) *In General.* In accordance with subparagraph (B), the Commission shall prescribe standards that specify the data elements for each swap that shall be collected and maintained by each registered swap data repository.

(B) *Requirement.* In carrying out subparagraph (A), the Commission shall prescribe consistent data element standards applicable to registered entities and reporting counterparties.

(2) *Data Collection and Maintenance.* The Commission shall prescribe data collection and data maintenance standards for swap data repositories.

(3) *Comparability.* The standards prescribed by the Commission under this subsection shall be comparable to the data standards imposed by the Commission on derivatives clearing organizations in connection with their clearing of swaps.

(c) *Duties.* A swap data repository shall—

(1) accept data prescribed by the Commission for each swap under subsection (b);

(2) confirm with both counterparties to the swap the accuracy of the data that was submitted;

(3) maintain the data described in paragraph (1) in such form, in such manner, and for such period as may be required by the Commission;

(4)(A) provide direct electronic access to the Commission (or any designee of the Commission, including another registered entity); and

(B) provide the information described in paragraph (1) in such form and at such frequency as the Commission may require to comply with the public reporting requirements contained in section 2(a)(13);

(5) at the direction of the Commission, establish automated systems for monitoring, screening, and analyzing swap data, including compliance and frequency of end user clearing exemption claims by individual and affiliated entities;

(6) maintain the privacy of any and all swap transaction information that the swap data repository receives from a swap dealer, counterparty, or any other registered entity; and

(7) on a confidential basis pursuant to section 8, upon request, and after notifying the Commission

of the request, make available swap data obtained by the swap data repository, including individual counterparty trade and position data, to—

(A) each appropriate prudential regulator;

(B) the Financial Stability Oversight Council;

(C) the Securities and Exchange Commission;

(D) the Department of Justice; and

(E) any other person that the Commission determines to be appropriate, including—

(i) foreign financial supervisors (including foreign futures authorities);

(ii) foreign central banks;

(iii) foreign ministries; and

(iv) other foreign authorities; and

(8) establish and maintain emergency procedures, backup facilities, and a plan for disaster recovery that allows for the timely recovery and resumption of operations and the fulfillment of the responsibilities and obligations of the organization.

(d) *Confidentiality Agreement.* Before the swap data repository may share information with any entity described in subsection (c)(7), the swap data repository shall receive a written agreement from each entity stating that the entity shall abide by the confidentiality requirements described in section 8 of this Act relating to the information on swap transactions that is provided.

(e) *Designation of Chief Compliance Officer.*

(1) *In General.* Each swap data repository shall designate an individual to serve as a chief compliance officer.

(2) *Duties.* The chief compliance officer shall—

(A) report directly to the board or to the senior officer of the swap data repository;

(B) review the compliance of the swap data repository with respect to the requirements and core principles described in this section;

(C) in consultation with the board of the swap data repository, a body performing a function similar to the board of the swap data repository, or the senior officer of the swap data repository, resolve any conflicts of interest that may arise;

(D) be responsible for administering each policy and procedure that is required to be established pursuant to this section;

(E) ensure compliance with this Act (including regulations) relating to agreements, contracts, or transactions, including each rule prescribed by the Commission under this section;

(F) establish procedures for the remediation of non–compliance issues identified by the chief compliance officer through any—

(i) compliance office review;

(ii) look–back;

(iii) internal or external audit finding;

(iv) self–reported error; or

(v) validated complaint; and

(G) establish and follow appropriate procedures for the handling, management response, remediation, retesting, and closing of noncompliance issues.

(3) *Annual Reports.*

(A) *In General.* In accordance with rules prescribed by the Commission, the chief compliance officer shall annually prepare and sign a report that contains a description of—

(i) the compliance of the swap data repository of the chief compliance officer with respect to this Act (including regulations); and

(ii) each policy and procedure of the swap data repository of the chief compliance officer (including the code of ethics and conflict of interest policies of the swap data repository).

(B) *Requirements.* A compliance report under subparagraph (A) shall—

(i) accompany each appropriate financial report of the swap data repository that is required to be furnished to the Commission pursuant to this section; and

(ii) include a certification that, under penalty of law, the compliance report is accurate and complete.

(f) *Core Principles Applicable to Swap Data Repositories.*

(1) *Antitrust Considerations.* Unless necessary or appropriate to achieve the purposes of this Act, a swap data repository shall not—

(A) adopt any rule or take any action that results in any unreasonable restraint of trade; or

(B) impose any material anticompetitive burden on the trading, clearing, or reporting of transactions.

(2) *Governance Arrangements.* Each swap data repository shall establish governance arrangements that are transparent—

(A) to fulfill public interest requirements; and

(B) to support the objectives of the Federal Government, owners, and participants.

(3) *Conflicts of Interest.* Each swap data repository shall—

(A) establish and enforce rules to minimize conflicts of interest in the decision–making process of the swap data repository; and

(B) establish a process for resolving conflicts of interest described in subparagraph (A).

(4) *Additional Duties Developed by Commission.*

(A) *In General.* The Commission may develop 1 or more additional duties applicable to swap data repositories.

(B) *Consideration of Evolving Standards.* In developing additional duties under subparagraph (A), the Commission may take into consideration any evolving standard of the United States or the international community.

(C) *Additional Duties for Commission Designees.* The Commission shall establish additional duties for any registrant described in section 1a(48) in order to minimize conflicts of interest, protect data, ensure compliance, and guarantee the safety and security of the swap data repository.

(g) *Required Registration for Swap Data Repositories.* Any person that is required to be registered as a swap data repository under this section shall register with the Commission regardless of whether that person is also licensed as a bank or registered with the Securities and Exchange Commission as a swap data repository.

(h) *Rules.* The Commission shall adopt rules governing persons that are registered under this section.

Private Rights of Action

Sec. 22. (a) *Actual Damages; Actionable Transactions Exclusive Remedy.*

(1) Any person (other than a registered entity or registered futures association) who violates this Act or who willfully aids, abets, counsels, induces, or procures the commission of a violation of this Act shall be liable for actual damages resulting from one or more of the transactions referred to in subparagraphs (A) through (D) of this paragraph and caused by such violation to any other person—

(A) who received trading advice from such person for a fee;

(B) who made through such person any contract of sale of any commodity for future delivery (or option on such contract or any commodity) or any swap; or who deposited with or paid to such person money, securities, or property (or incurred debt in lieu thereof) in connection with any order to make such contract or any swap;

(C) who purchased from or sold to such person or placed through such person an order for the purchase or sale of—

(i) an option subject to section 4c of this Act (other than an option purchased or sold on a registered entity or other board of trade);

(ii) a contract subject to section 19 of this Act; or

(iii) an interest or participation in a commodity pool; or

(iv) a swap; or

(D) who purchased or sold a contract referred to in subparagraph (B) hereof or swap if the violation constitutes—

(i) the use or employment of, or an attempt to use or employ, in connection with a swap, or a contract of sale of a commodity, in interstate commerce, or for future delivery on or subject to the rules of any registered entity, any manipulative device or contrivance in contravention of such rules and regulations as the Commission shall promulgate by not later than 1 year after the date of enactment of the Dodd–Frank Wall Street Reform and Consumer Protection Act; or

(ii) a manipulation of the price of any such contract or swap or the price of the commodity underlying such contract or swap.

(2) Except as provided in subsection (b), the rights of action authorized by this subsection and by sections 5(d)(13), 5b(c)(2)(H), and 17(b)(10) of this Act shall be the exclusive remedies under this Act available to any person who sustains loss as a result of any alleged violation of this Act. Nothing in this subsection shall limit or abridge the rights of the parties to agree in advance of a dispute upon any forum for resolving claims under this section, including arbitration.

(3) In any action arising from a violation in the execution of an order on the floor of a registered entity, the person referred to in paragraph (1) shall be liable for—

(A) actual damages proximately caused by such violation. If an award of actual damages is made against a floor broker in connection with the execution of a customer order, and the futures commission merchant which selected the floor broker for the execution of the customer order is held to be responsible under section 2(a)(1) for the floor broker's violation, such futures commission merchant may be required to satisfy such award; and

(B) where the violation is willful and intentional, punitive or exemplary damages equal to no more than two times the amount of such actual damages. If an award of punitive or exemplary damages is made against a floor broker in connection with the execution of a customer order, and the futures commission merchant which selected the floor broker for the execution of the customer order is held to be responsible under section 2(a)(1) for the floor broker's violation, such futures commission merchant may be required to satisfy such award if the floor broker fails to do so, except that such requirement shall apply to the futures commission merchant only if it willfully and intentionally selected the floor broker with the intent to assist or facilitate the floor broker's violation.

(4) *Contract Enforcement Between Eligible Counterparties.*

(A) *In General.* No hybrid instrument sold to any investor shall be void, voidable, or unenforceable, and no party to a hybrid instrument shall be entitled to rescind, or recover any payment made with respect to, the hybrid instrument under this section or any other provision of Federal or State law, based solely on the failure of the hybrid instrument to comply with the terms or conditions of section 2(f) or regulations of the Commission.

(B) *Swaps.* No agreement, contract, or transaction between eligible contract participants or persons reasonably believed to be eligible contract participants shall be void, voidable, or unenforceable, and no party to such agreement, contract, or transaction shall be entitled to rescind, or recover any payment made with respect to, the agreement, contract, or transaction under this section or any other provision of Federal or State law, based solely on the failure of the agreement, contract, or transaction—

(i) to meet the definition of a swap under section 1a; or

(ii) to be cleared in accordance with section 2(h)(1).

(5) *Legal Certainty for Long-Term Swaps Entered into Before the Date of Enactment of the Wall Street Transparency and Accountability Act of 2010.*

(A) *Effect on Swaps.* Unless specifically reserved in the applicable swap, neither the enactment of the Wall Street Transparency and Accountability Act of 2010, nor any requirement under that Act or an amendment made by that Act, shall constitute a termination event, force majeure, illegality, increased costs, regulatory change, or similar event under a swap (including any related credit support arrangement) that would permit a party to terminate, renegotiate, modify, amend, or supplement 1 or more transactions under the swap.

(B) *Position Limits.* Any position limit established under the Wall Street Transparency and Accountability Act of 2010 shall not apply to a position acquired in good faith prior to the effective date of any rule, regulation, or order under the Act that establishes the position limit; provided, however, that such positions shall be attributed to the trader if the trader's position is increased after the effective date of such position limit rule, regulation, or order.

(6) *Contract Enforcement for Foreign Futures Contracts.* A contract of sale of a commodity for future delivery traded or executed on or through the facilities of a board of trade, exchange, or market located outside the United States for purposes of section 4(a) shall not be void, voidable, or unenforceable, and a party to such a contract shall not be entitled to rescind or recover any payment made with respect to the contract, based on the failure of the foreign board of trade to comply with any provision of this Act.

(b) *Liabilities of Organizations and Individuals; Bad Faith Requirement; Exclusive Remedy.*

(1)(A) A registered entity that fails to enforce any bylaw, rule, regulation, or resolution that it is required to enforce by section 5, 5b, 5c, 5h, or 21, (B) a licensed board of trade that fails to enforce any bylaw, rule, regulation, or resolution that it is required to enforce by the Commission, or (C) any registered entity that in enforcing any such bylaw, rule, regulation, or resolution violates this Act or any Commission rule, regulation, or order, shall be liable for actual damages sustained by a person who engaged in any transaction on or subject to the rules of such registered entity to the extent of such person's actual losses that resulted from such transaction and were caused by such failure to enforce or enforcement of such bylaws, rules, regulations, or resolutions.

(2) A registered futures association that fails to enforce any bylaw or rule that is required under section 17 of this Act or in enforcing any such bylaw or rule violates this Act or any Commission rule, regulation, or order shall be liable for actual damages sustained by a person that engaged in any transaction specified in subsection (a) of this section to the extent of such person's actual losses that resulted from such transaction and were caused by such failure to enforce or enforcement of such bylaw or rule.

(3) Any individual who, in the capacity as an officer, director, governor, committee member, or employee of a registered entity or a registered futures association willfully aids, abets, counsels, induces, or procures any failure by any such entity to enforce (or any violation of the Act in enforcing) any bylaw, rule, regulation, or resolution referred to in paragraph (1) or (2) of this subsection, shall be liable for actual damages sustained by a person who engaged in any transaction specified in subsection (a) of this section on, or subject to the rules of, such registered entity or, in the case of an officer, director, governor, committee member, or employee of a registered futures association, any transaction specified in subsection (a) of this section, in either case to the extent of such person's actual losses that resulted from such transaction and were caused by such failure or violation.

(4) A person seeking to enforce liability under this section must establish that the registered entity registered futures association, officer, director, governor, committee member, or employee acted in bad faith in failing to take action or in taking such action as was taken, and that such failure or action caused the loss.

(5) The rights of action authorized by this subsection shall be the exclusive remedy under this Act available to any person who sustains a loss as a result of (A) the alleged failure by a registered entity or registered futures association or by any officer, director, governor, committee member, or employee to enforce any bylaw, rule, regulation, or resolution referred to in paragraph (1) or (2) of this subsection or (B) the taking of action in enforcing any bylaw, rule, regulation, or resolution referred to in this subsection that is alleged to have violated this Act, or any Commission rule, regulation, or order.

(c) *Jurisdiction; Statute of Limitations; Venue; Process.* The United States district courts shall have exclusive jurisdiction of actions brought under this section. Any such action shall be brought not later than two years after the date the cause of action arises. Any action brought under subsection (a) of this section may be brought in any judicial district wherein the defendant is found, resides, or transacts business, or in the judicial district wherein any act or transaction constituting the violation occurs. Process in such action may be served in any judicial district of which the defendant is an inhabitant or wherever the defendant may be found.

(d) [Omitted.]

Commodity Whistleblower Incentives and Protection

Sec. 23. (a) *Definitions.* In this section:

(1) *Covered Judicial or Administrative Action.* The term "covered judicial or administrative action" means any judicial or administrative action brought by the Commission under this Act that results in monetary sanctions exceeding $1,000,000.

(2) *Fund.* The term "Fund" means the Commodity Futures Trading Commission Customer Protection Fund established under subsection (g).

(3) *Monetary Sanctions.* The term "monetary sanctions", when used with respect to any judicial or administrative action means

(A) any monies, including penalties, disgorgement, restitution, and interest ordered to be paid; and

(B) any monies deposited into a disgorgement fund or other fund pursuant to section 308(b) of the Sarbanes–Oxley Act of 2002, as a result of such action or any settlement of such action.

(4) *Original Information.* The term "original information" means information that—

(A) is derived from the independent knowledge or analysis of a whistleblower;

(B) is not known to the Commission from any other source, unless the whistleblower is the original source of the information; and

(C) is not exclusively derived from an allegation made in a judicial or administrative hearing, in a governmental report, hearing, audit, or investigation, or from the news media, unless the whistleblower is a source of the information.

(5) *Related Action*. The term "related action", when used with respect to any judicial or administrative action brought by the Commission under this Act, means any judicial or administrative action brought by an entity described in subclauses (I) through (VI) of subsection (h)(2)(C) that is based upon the original information provided by a whistleblower pursuant to subsection (a) that led to the successful enforcement of the Commission action.

(6) *Successful Resolution*. The term "successful resolution", when used with respect to any judicial or administrative action brought by the Commission under this Act, includes any settlement of such action.

(7) *Whistleblower*. The term "whistleblower" means any individual, or 2 or more individuals acting jointly, who provides information relating to a violation of this Act to the Commission, in a manner established by rule or regulation by the Commission.

(b) *Awards*.

(1) *In General*. In any covered judicial or administrative action, or related action, the Commission, under regulations prescribed by the Commission and subject to subsection (c), shall pay an award or awards to 1 or more whistleblowers who voluntarily provided original information to the Commission that led to the successful enforcement of the covered judicial or administrative action, or related action, in an aggregate amount equal to—

(A) not less than 10 percent, in total, of what has been collected of the monetary sanctions imposed in the action or related actions; and

(B) not more than 30 percent, in total, of what has been collected of the monetary sanctions imposed in the action or related actions.

(2) *Payment of Awards*. Any amount paid under paragraph (1) shall be paid from the Fund.

(c) *Determination of Amount of Award; Denial of Award*.

(1) *Determination of Amount of Award*.

(A) *Discretion*. The determination of the amount of an award made under subsection (b) shall be in the discretion of the Commission.

(B) *Criteria*. In determining the amount of an award made under subsection (b), the Commission—

(i) shall take into consideration—

(I) the significance of the information provided by the whistleblower to the success of the covered judicial or administrative action;

(II) the degree of assistance provided by the whistleblower and any legal representative of the whistleblower in a covered judicial or administrative action;

(III) the programmatic interest of the Commission in deterring violations of the Act (including regulations under the Act) by making awards to whistleblowers who provide information that leads to the successful enforcement of such laws; and

(IV) such additional relevant factors as the Commission may establish by rule or regulation; and

(ii) shall not take into consideration the balance of the Fund.

(2) *Denial of Award*. No award under subsection (b) shall be made—

(A) to any whistleblower who is, or was at the time the whistleblower acquired the original information submitted to the Commission, a member, officer, or employee of—

(i) a appropriate regulatory agency;

(ii) the Department of Justice;

(iii) a registered entity;

(iv) a registered futures association;

(v) a self–regulatory organization as defined in section 3(a) of the Securities Exchange Act of 1934; or

(vi) a law enforcement organization;

(B) to any whistleblower who is convicted of a criminal violation related to the judicial or administrative action for which the whistleblower otherwise could receive an award under this section;

(C) to any whistleblower who submits information to the Commission that is based on the facts underlying the covered action submitted previously by another whistleblower;

(D) to any whistleblower who fails to submit information to the Commission in such form as the Commission may, by rule or regulation, require.

(d) *Representation.*

(1) *Permitted Representation.* Any whistleblower who makes a claim for an award under subsection (b) may be represented by counsel.

(2) *Required Representation.*

(A) *In General.* Any whistleblower who anonymously makes a claim for an award under subsection (b) shall be represented by counsel if the whistleblower submits the information upon which the claim is based.

(B) *Disclosure of Identity.* Prior to the payment of an award, a whistleblower shall disclose the identity of the whistleblower and provide such other information as the Commission may require, directly or through counsel for the whistleblower.

(e) *No Contract Necessary.* No contract with the Commission is necessary for any whistleblower to receive an award under subsection (b), unless otherwise required by the Commission, by rule or regulation.

(f) *Appeals.*

(1) *In General.* Any determination made under this section, including whether, to whom, or in what amount to make awards, shall be in the discretion of the Commission.

(2) *Appeals.* Any determination described in paragraph (1) may be appealed to the appropriate court of appeals of the United States not more than 30 days after the determination is issued by the Commission.

(3) *Review.* The court shall review the determination made by the Commission in accordance with section 7064 of title 5, United States Code.

(g) *Commodity Futures Trading Commission Customer Protection Fund.*

(1) *Establishment.* There is established in the Treasury of the United States a revolving fund to be known as the "Commodity Futures Trading Commission Customer Protection Fund".

(2) *Use of Fund.* The Fund shall be available to the Commission, without further appropriation or fiscal year limitation, for—

(A) the payment of awards to whistleblowers as provided in subsection (a); and

(B) the funding of customer education initiatives designed to help customers protect themselves against fraud or other violations of this Act, or the rules and regulations thereunder.

(3) *Deposits and Credits.* There shall be deposited into or credited to the Fund:

(A) *Monetary Sanctions.* Any monetary sanctions collected by the Commission in any covered judicial or administrative action that is not otherwise distributed to victims of a violation of this Act or the rules and regulations thereunder underlying such action, unless the balance of the Fund at the time the monetary judgment is collected exceeds $100,000,000.

(B) *Additional Amounts.* If the amounts deposited into or credited to the Fund under subparagraph (A) are not sufficient to satisfy an award made under subsection (b), there shall be deposited into or credited to the Fund an amount equal to the unsatisfied portion of the award from any monetary sanction collected by the Commission in any judicial or administrative action brought by the Commission under this Act that is based on information provided by a whistleblower.

(C) *Investment Income.* All income from investments made under paragraph (4).

(4) *Investments.*

(A) *Amounts in Fund may be Invested.* The Commission may request the Secretary of the Treasury to invest the portion of the Fund that is not, in the Commission's judgment, required to meet the current needs of the Fund.

(B) *Eligible Investments.* Investments shall be made by the Secretary of the Treasury in obligations of the United States or obligations that are guaranteed as to principal and interest by the United States, with maturities suitable to the needs of the Fund as determined by the Commission.

(C) *Interest and Proceeds Credited.* The interest on, and the proceeds from the sale or redemption of, any obligations held in the Fund shall be credited to, and form a part of, the Fund.

(5) *Reports to Congress.* Not later than October 30 of each year, the Commission shall transmit to the Committee on Agriculture, Nutrition, and Forestry of the Senate, and the Committee on Agriculture of the House of Representatives a report on—

(A) the Commission's whistleblower award program under this section, including a description of the number of awards granted and the types of cases in which awards were granted during the preceding fiscal year;

(B) customer education initiatives described in paragraph (2)(B) that were funded by the Fund during the preceding fiscal year;

(C) the balance of the Fund at the beginning of the preceding fiscal year;

(D) the amounts deposited into or credited to the Fund during the preceding fiscal year;

(E) the amount of earnings on investments of amounts in the Fund during the preceding fiscal year;

(F) the amount paid from the Fund during the preceding fiscal year to whistleblowers pursuant to subsection (b);

(G) the amount paid from the Fund during the preceding fiscal year for customer education initiatives described in paragraph (2)(B);

(H) the balance of the Fund at the end of the preceding fiscal year; and

(I) a complete set of audited financial statements, including a balance sheet, income statement, and cash flow analysis.

(h) *Protection of Whistleblowers.*

(1) *Prohibition Against Retaliation.*

(A) *In General.* No employer may discharge, demote, suspend, threaten, harass, directly or indirectly, or in any other manner discriminate against, a whistleblower in the terms and conditions of employment because of any lawful act done by the whistleblower—

(i) in providing information to the Commission in accordance with subsection (b); or

(ii) in assisting in any investigation or judicial or administrative action of the Commission based upon or related to such information.

(B) *Enforcement.*

(i) *Cause of Action.* An individual who alleges discharge or other discrimination in violation of subparagraph (A) may bring an action under this subsection in the appropriate district court of the United States for the relief provided in subparagraph (C), unless the individual who is alleging discharge or other discrimination in violation of subparagraph (A) is an employee of the Federal Government, in which case the individual shall only bring an action under section 1221 of title 5, United States Code.

(ii) *Subpoenas.* A subpoena requiring the attendance of a witness at a trial or hearing conducted under this subsection may be served at any place in the United States.

(iii) *Statute of Limitations.* An action under this subsection may not be brought more than 2 years after the date on which the violation reported in subparagraph (A) is committed.

(C) *Relief.* Relief for an individual prevailing in an action brought under subparagraph (B) shall include—

(i) reinstatement with the same seniority status that the individual would have had, but for the discrimination;

(ii) the amount of back pay otherwise owed to the individual, with interest; and

(iii) compensation for any special damages sustained as a result of the discharge or discrimination, including litigation costs, expert witness fees, and reasonable attorney's fees.

(2) *Confidentiality.*

(A) *In General.* Except as provided in subparagraphs (B) and (C), the Commission, and any officer or employee of the Commission, shall not disclose any information, including information provided by a whistleblower to the Commission, which could reasonably be expected to reveal the identity of a whistleblower, except in accordance with the provisions of section 552a of title 5, United States Code, unless and until required to be disclosed to a defendant or respondent in connection with a public proceeding instituted by the Commission or any entity described in subparagraph (C). For purposes of section 552 of title 5, United States Code, this paragraph shall be considered a statute described in subsection (b)(3)(B) of such section 552.

(B) *Effect*. Nothing in this paragraph is intended to limit the ability of the Attorney General to present such evidence to a grand jury or to share such evidence with potential witnesses or defendants in the course of an ongoing criminal investigation.

(C) *Availability to Government Agencies*.

(i) *In General*. Without the loss of its status as confidential in the hands of the Commission, all information referred to in subparagraph (A) may, in the discretion of the Commission, when determined by the Commission to be necessary or appropriate to accomplish the purposes of this Act and protect customers and in accordance with clause (ii), be made available to—

(I) the Department of Justice;

(II) an appropriate department or agency of the Federal Government, acting within the scope of its jurisdiction;

(III) a registered entity, registered futures association, or self-regulatory organization as defined in section 3(a) of the Securities Exchange Act of 1934;

(IV) a State attorney general in connection with any criminal investigation;

(V) an appropriate department or agency of any State, acting within the scope of its jurisdiction; and

(VI) a foreign futures authority.

(ii) *Maintenance of Information*. Each of the entities, agencies, or persons described in clause (i) shall maintain information described in that clause as confidential, in accordance with the requirements in subparagraph (A).

(iii) *Study on Impact of FOIA Exemption on Commodity Futures Trading Commission*.

(I) *Study*. The Inspector General of the Commission shall conduct a study—

(aa) on whether the exemption under section 552(b)(3) of title 5, United States Code (known as the Freedom of Information Act) established in paragraph (2)(A) aids whistleblowers in disclosing information to the Commission;

(bb) on what impact the exemption has had on the public's ability to access information about the Commission's regulation of commodity futures and option markets; and

(cc) to make any recommendations on whether the Commission should continue to use the exemption.

(II) *Report*. Not later than 30 months after the date of enactment of this clause, the Inspector General shall—

(aa) submit a report on the findings of the study required under this clause to the Committee on Banking, Housing, and Urban Affairs of the Senate and the Committee on Financial Services of the House of Representatives; and

(bb) make the report available to the public through publication of a report on the website of the Commission.

(3) *Rights Retained*. Nothing in this section shall be deemed to diminish the rights, privileges, or remedies of any whistleblower under any Federal or State law, or under any collective bargaining agreement.

(*i*) *Rulemaking Authority*. The Commission shall have the authority to issue such rules and regulations as may be necessary or appropriate to implement the provisions of this section consistent with the purposes of this section.

(j) *Implementing Rules*. The Commission shall issue final rules or regulations implementing the provisions of this section not later than 270 days after the date of enactment of the Wall Street Transparency and Accountability Act of 2010.

(k) *Original Information*. Information submitted to the Commission by a whistleblower in accordance with rules or regulations implementing this section shall not lose its status as original information solely because the whistleblower submitted such information prior to the effective date of such rules or regulations, provided such information was submitted after the date of enactment of the Wall Street Transparency and Accountability Act of 2010.

(*l*) *Awards*. A whistleblower may receive an award pursuant to this section regardless of whether any violation of a provision of this Act, or a rule or regulation thereunder, underlying the judicial or administrative action upon which the award is based occurred prior to the date of enactment of the Wall Street Transparency and Accountability Act of 2010.

(m) *Provision of False Information*. A whistleblower who knowingly and willfully makes any false, fictitious, or fraudulent statement or representation, or who makes or uses any false writing or document knowing the same to contain any false, fictitious, or fraudulent statement or entry, shall not be entitled to an award under this section and shall be subject to prosecution under section 1001 of title 18, United States Code.

(n) *Nonenforceability of Certain Provisions Waiving Rights and Remedies or Requiring Arbitration of Disputes.*

(1) *Waiver of Rights and Remedies.* The rights and remedies provided for in this section may not be waived by any agreement, policy form, or condition of employment including by a predispute arbitration agreement.

(2) *Predispute Arbitration Agreements.* No predispute arbitration agreement shall be valid or enforceable, if the agreement requires arbitration of a dispute arising under this section.

FOREIGN CORRUPT PRACTICES ACT OF 1977*

15 U.S.C. § 78dd–1 et seq.

Sec. Act	15 U.S.C.	
101		Short Title
102	78q(b)	Accounting Standards
103	78dd–1	Foreign Corrupt Practices by Issuers
104	78dd–2	Prohibited Foreign Trade Practices by Domestic Concerns
104A	78dd–3	Prohibited Foreign Trade Practices by Persons Other Than Issuers or Domestic Concerns

Short Title

Sec. 101. This title may be cited as the "Foreign Corrupt Practices Act of 1977".

Accounting Standards

Sec. 102. [Amended Section 13(b) of the Securities Exchange Act of 1934.]

Foreign Corrupt Practices by Issuers

Sec. 103. [Added Section 30A to the Securities Exchange Act of 1934.]

Prohibited Foreign Trade Practices by Domestic Concerns

Sec. 104. (a) *Prohibition.* It shall be unlawful for any domestic concern, other than an issuer which is subject to section 30A of the Securities Exchange Act of 1934, or for any officer, director, employee, or agent of such domestic concern or any stockholder thereof acting on behalf of such domestic concern, to make use of the mails or any means or instrumentality of interstate commerce corruptly in furtherance of an offer, payment, promise to pay, or authorization of the payment of any money, or offer, gift, promise to give, or authorization of the giving of anything of value to—

(1) any foreign official for purposes of—

(A)(i) influencing any act or decision of such foreign official in his official capacity, (ii) inducing such foreign official to do or omit to do any act in violation of the lawful duty of such official, or (iii) securing any improper advantage; or

(B) inducing such foreign official to use his influence with a foreign government or instrumentality thereof to affect or influence any act or decision of such government or instrumentality,

in order to assist such domestic concern in obtaining or retaining business for or with, or directing business to, any person;

(2) any foreign political party or official thereof or any candidate for foreign political office for purposes of—

(A)(i) influencing any act or decision of such party, official, or candidate in its or his official capacity, (ii) inducing such party, official, or candidate to do or omit to do an act in violation of the lawful duty of such party, official, or candidate, or (iii) securing any improper advantage; or

(B) inducing such party, official, or candidate to use its or his influence with a foreign government or instrumentality thereof to affect or influence any act or decision of such government or instrumentality,

in order to assist such domestic concern in obtaining or retaining business for or with, or directing business to, any person; or

(3) any person, while knowing that all or a portion of such money or thing of value will be offered, given, or promised, directly or indirectly, to any foreign official, to any foreign political party or official thereof, or to any candidate for foreign political office, for purposes of—

(A)(i) influencing any act or decision of such foreign official, political party, party official, or candidate in his or its official capacity, (ii) inducing such foreign official, political party, party official, or candidate to do or omit to do any act in violation of the lawful duty of such foreign official, political party, party official, or candidate, or (iii) securing any improper advantage; or

* [Eds.] The Foreign Corrupt Practices Act of 1977 was enacted P.L. No. 95–213, 91 Stat. 1494 and was amended in 1988 by P.L. 100–418. The statute also amended Sections 13(b)(1) and 13(d)(1) and added Section 30A of the Securities Exchange Act of 1934.

(B) inducing such foreign official, political party, party official, or candidate to use his or its influence with a foreign government or instrumentality thereof to affect or influence any act or decision of such government or instrumentality,

in order to assist such domestic concern in obtaining or retaining business for or with, or directing business to, any person.

(b) *Exception for Routine Governmental Action.* Subsections (a) and (i) of this section shall not apply to any facilitating or expediting payment to a foreign official, political party, or party official the purpose of which is to expedite or to secure the performance of a routine governmental action by a foreign official, political party, or party official.

(c) *Affirmative Defenses.* It shall be an affirmative defense to actions under subsection (a) or (i) of this section that—

(1) the payment, gift, offer, or promise of anything of value that was made, was lawful under the written laws and regulations of the foreign official's, political party's, party official's, or candidate's country; or

(2) the payment, gift, offer, or promise of anything of value that was made, was a reasonable and bona fide expenditure, such as travel and lodging expenses, incurred by or on behalf of a foreign official, party, party official, or candidate and was directly related to—

(A) the promotion, demonstration, or explanation of products or services; or

(B) the execution or performance of a contract with a foreign government or agency thereof.

(d) *Injunctive Relief.*

(1) When it appears to the Attorney General that any domestic concern to which this section applies, or officer, director, employee, agent, or stockholder thereof, is engaged, or about to engage, in any act or practice constituting a violation of subsection (a) or (i) of this section, the Attorney General may, in his discretion, bring a civil action in an appropriate district court of the United States to enjoin such act or practice, and upon a proper showing, a permanent injunction or a temporary restraining order shall be granted without bond.

(2) For the purpose of any civil investigation which, in the opinion of the Attorney General, is necessary and proper to enforce this section, the Attorney General or his designee are empowered to administer oaths and affirmations, subpoena witnesses, take evidence, and require the production of any books, papers, or other documents which the Attorney General deems relevant or material to such investigation. The attendance of witnesses and the production of documentary evidence may be required from any place in the United States, or any territory, possession, or commonwealth of the United States, at any designated place of hearing.

(3) In case of contumacy by, or refusal to obey a subpoena issued to, any person, the Attorney General may invoke the aid of any court of the United States within the jurisdiction of which such investigation or proceeding is carried on, or where such person resides or carries on business, in requiring the attendance and testimony of witnesses and the production of books, papers, or other documents. Any such court may issue an order requiring such person to appear before the Attorney General or his designee, there to produce records, if so ordered, or to give testimony touching the matter under investigation. Any failure to obey such order of the court may be punished by such court as a contempt thereof.

All process in any such case may be served in the judicial district in which such person resides or may be found. The Attorney General may make such rules relating to civil investigations as may be necessary or appropriate to implement the provisions of this subsection.

(e) *Guidelines by Attorney General.* Not later than 6 months after the date of the enactment of the Foreign Corrupt Practices Act Amendments of 1988, the Attorney General, after consultation with the Securities and Exchange Commission, the Secretary of Commerce, the United States Trade Representative, the Secretary of State, and the Secretary of the Treasury, and after obtaining the views of all interested persons through public notice and comment procedures, shall determine to what extent compliance with this section would be enhanced and the business community would be assisted by further clarification of the preceding provisions of this section and may, based on such determination and to the extent necessary and appropriate, issue—

(1) guidelines describing specific types of conduct, associated with common types of export sales arrangements and business contracts, which for purposes of the Department of Justice's present enforcement policy, the Attorney General de-

termines would be in conformance with the preceding provisions of this section; and

(2) general precautionary procedures which domestic concerns may use on a voluntary basis to conform their conduct to the Department of Justice's present enforcement policy regarding the preceding provisions of this section.

The Attorney General shall issue the guidelines and procedures referred to in the preceding sentence in accordance with the provisions of subchapter II of chapter 5 of title 5, United States Code, and those guidelines and procedures shall be subject to the provisions of chapter 7 of that title.

(f) *Opinions of Attorney General.*

(1) The Attorney General, after consultation with appropriate departments and agencies of the United States and after obtaining the views of all interested persons through public notice and comment procedures, shall establish a procedure to provide responses to specific inquiries by domestic concerns concerning conformance of their conduct with the Department of Justice's present enforcement policy regarding the preceding provisions of this section. The Attorney General shall, within 30 days after receiving such a request, issue an opinion in response to that request. The opinion shall state whether or not certain specified prospective conduct would, for purposes of the Department of Justice's present enforcement policy, violate the preceding provisions of this section. Additional requests for opinions may be filed with the Attorney General regarding other specified prospective conduct that is beyond the scope of conduct specified in previous requests. In any action brought under the applicable provisions of this section, there shall be a rebuttable presumption that conduct, which is specified in a request by a domestic concern and for which the Attorney General has issued an opinion that such conduct is in conformity with the Department of Justice's present enforcement policy, is in compliance with the preceding provisions of this section. Such a presumption may be rebutted by a preponderance of the evidence. In considering the presumption for purposes of this paragraph, a court shall weigh all relevant factors, including but not limited to whether the information submitted to the Attorney General was accurate and complete and whether it was within the scope of the conduct specified in any request received by the Attorney General. The Attorney General shall establish the procedure required by this paragraph in accordance with the provisions of subchapter II of chapter 5 of title 5, United States Code, and that procedure shall be subject to the provisions of chapter 7 of that title.

(2) Any document or other material which is provided to, received by, or prepared in the Department of Justice or any other department or agency of the United States in connection with a request by a domestic concern under the procedure established under paragraph (1), shall be exempt from disclosure under section 552 of title 5, United States Code, and shall not, except with the consent of the domestic concern, by made publicly available, regardless of whether the Attorney General response to such a request or the domestic concern withdraws such request before receiving a response.

(3) Any domestic concern who has made a request to the Attorney General under paragraph (1) may withdraw such request prior to the time the Attorney General issues an opinion in response to such request. Any request so withdrawn shall have no force or effect.

(4) The Attorney General shall, to the maximum extent practicable, provide timely guidance concerning the Department of Justice's present enforcement policy with respect to the preceding provisions of this section to potential exporters and small businesses that are unable to obtain specialized counsel on issues pertaining to such provisions. Such guidance shall be limited to responses to requests under paragraph (1) concerning conformity of specified prospective conduct with the Department of Justice's present enforcement policy regarding the preceding provisions of this section and general explanations of compliance responsibilities and of potential liabilities under the preceding provisions of this section.

(g) *Penalties.*

(1)(A) Any domestic concern that is not a natural person and that violates subsection (a) or (i) of this section shall be fined not more than $2,000,000.

(B) Any domestic concern that is not a natural person and that violates subsection (a) or (i) of this section shall be subject to a civil penalty of not more than $10,000 imposed in an action brought by the Attorney General.

(2)(A) Any natural person that is an officer, director, employee, or agent of a domestic concern, or stockholder acting on behalf of such domestic concern, who willfully violates subsection (a) or (i) of this section shall be fined not more than $100,000 or imprisoned not more than 5 years, or both.

(B) Any natural person that is an officer, director, employee, or agent of a domestic concern, or stockholder acting on behalf of such domestic concern, who violates subsection (a) or (i) of this section shall be subject to a civil penalty of not more than $10,000 imposed in an action brought by the Attorney General.

(3) Whenever a fine is imposed under paragraph (2) upon any officer, director, employee, agent, or stockholder of a domestic concern, such fine may not be paid, directly or indirectly, by such domestic concern.

(h) *Definitions*. For purposes of this section:

(1) The term "domestic concern" means—

(A) any individual who is a citizen, national, or resident of the United States; and

(B) any corporation, partnership, association, joint-stock company, business trust, unincorporated organization, or sole proprietorship which has its principal place of business in the United States, or which is organized under the laws of a State of the United States or a territory, possession, or commonwealth of the United States.

(2)(A) The term "foreign official" means any officer or employee of a foreign government or any department, agency, or instrumentality thereof, or of a public international organization, or any person acting in an official capacity for or on behalf of any such government or department, agency, or instrumentality, or for or on behalf of any such public international organization.

(B) For purposes of subparagraph (A), the term "public international organization" means—

(i) an organization that is designated by Executive order pursuant to section 1 of the International Organizations Immunities Act (22 U.S.C. 288); or

(ii) any other international organization that is designated by the President by Executive order for the purposes of this section, effective as of the date of publication of such order in the Federal Register.

(3)(A) A person's state of mind is "knowing" with respect to conduct, a circumstance, or a result if—

(i) such person is aware that such person is engaging in such conduct, that such circumstance exists, or that such result is substantially certain to occur; or

(ii) such person has a firm belief that such circumstance exists or that such result is substantially certain to occur.

(B) When knowledge of the existence of a particular circumstance is required for an offense, such knowledge is established if a person is aware of a high probability of the existence of such circumstance, unless the person actually believes that such circumstance does not exist.

(4)(A) The term "routine governmental action" means only an action which is ordinarily and commonly performed by a foreign official in—

(i) obtaining permits, licenses, or other official documents to qualify a person to do business in a foreign country;

(ii) processing governmental papers, such as visas and work orders;

(iii) providing police protection, mail pick-up and delivery, or scheduling inspections associated with contract performance or inspections related to transit of goods across country;

(iv) providing phone service, power and water supply, loading and unloading cargo, or protecting perishable products or commodities from deterioration; or

(v) actions of a similar nature.

(B) The term "routine governmental action" does not include any decision by a foreign official whether, or on what terms, to award new business to or to continue business with a particular party, or any action taken by a foreign official involved in the decision-making process to encourage a decision to award new business to or continue business with a particular party.

(5) The term "interstate commerce" means trade, commerce, transportation, or communication among the several States, or between any foreign country and any State or between any State and any place or ship outside thereof, and such term includes the intrastate use of—

(A) a telephone or other interstate means of communication, or

(B) any other interstate instrumentality.

(i) *Alternative Jurisdiction*.

(1) It shall also be unlawful for any United States person to corruptly do any act outside the United States in furtherance of an offer, payment, promise to pay, or authorization of the payment of any money, or offer, gift, promise to give, or authorization of the giving of anything of value to any of the persons or entities set forth in paragraphs (1), (2), and (3) of subsection (a), for the purposes set forth therein, irrespective of whether such United States person makes use of the mails or any means or instrumentality of interstate commerce in furtherance of such offer, gift, payment, promise, or authorization.

(2) As used in this subsection, the term "United States person" means a national of the United States (as defined in section 101 of the Immigration and Nationality Act (8 U.S.C. 1101)) or any corporation, partnership, association, joint-stock company, business trust, unincorporated organization, or sole proprietorship organized under the laws of the United States or any State, territory, possession, or commonwealth of the United States, or any political subdivision thereof.

Prohibited Foreign Trade Practices by Persons Other Than Issuers or Domestic Concerns

Sec. 104A. (a) *Prohibition.* It shall be unlawful for any person other than an issuer that is subject to section 30A of the Securities Exchange Act of 1934 or a domestic concern (as defined in section 104 of this Act), or for any officer, director, employee, or agent of such person or any stockholder thereof acting on behalf of such person, while in the territory of the United States, corruptly to make use of the mails or any means or instrumentality of interstate commerce or to do any other act in furtherance of an offer, payment, promise to pay, or authorization of the payment of any money, or offer, gift, promise to give, or authorization of the giving of anything of value to—

(1) any foreign official for purposes of—

(A)(i) influencing any act or decision of such foreign official in his official capacity, (ii) inducing such foreign official to do or omit to do any act in violation of the lawful duty of such official, or (iii) securing any improper advantage; or

(B) inducing such foreign official to use his influence with a foreign government or instrumentality thereof to affect or influence any act or decision of such government or instrumentality,

in order to assist such person in obtaining or retaining business for or with, or directing business to, any person;

(2) any foreign political party or official thereof or any candidate for foreign political office for purposes of—

(A)(i) influencing any act or decision of such party, official, or candidate in its or his official capacity, (ii) inducing such party, official, or candidate to do or omit to do an act in violation of the lawful duty of such party, official, or candidate, or (iii) securing any improper advantage; or

(B) inducing such party, official, or candidate to use its or his influence with a foreign government or instrumentality thereof to affect or influence any act or decision of such government or instrumentality,

in order to assist such person in obtaining or retaining business for or with, or directing business to, any person; or

(3) any person, while knowing that all or a portion of such money or thing of value will be offered, given, or promised, directly or indirectly, to any foreign official, to any foreign political party or official thereof, or to any candidate for foreign political office, for purposes of—

(A)(i) influencing any act or decision of such foreign official, political party, party official, or candidate in his or its official capacity, (ii) inducing such foreign official, political party, party official, or candidate to do or omit to do any act in violation of the lawful duty of such foreign official, political party, party official, or candidate, or (iii) securing any improper advantage; or

(B) inducing such foreign official, political party, party official, or candidate to use his or its influence with a foreign government or instrumentality thereof to affect or influence any act or decision of such government or instrumentality,

in order to assist such person in obtaining or retaining business for or with, or directing business to, any person.

(b) *Exception for Routine Governmental Action.* Subsection (a) of this section shall not apply to any facilitating or expediting payment to a foreign official, political party, or party official the purpose of which is to expedite or to secure the performance of a routine governmental action by a foreign official, political party, or party official.

(c) *Affirmative Defenses.* It shall be an affirmative defense to actions under subsection (a) of this section that—

(1) the payment, gift, offer, or promise of anything of value that was made, was lawful under the written laws and regulations of the foreign official's, political party's, party official's, or candidate's country; or

(2) the payment, gift, offer, or promise of anything of value that was made, was a reasonable and bona fide expenditure, such as travel and lodging expenses, incurred by or on behalf of a foreign official, party, party official, or candidate and was directly related to—

(A) the promotion, demonstration, or explanation of products or services; or

(B) the execution or performance of a contract with a foreign government or agency thereof.

(d) *Injunctive Relief.*

(1) When it appears to the Attorney General that any person to which this section applies, or officer, director, employee, agent, or stockholder thereof, is engaged, or about to engage, in any act or practice constituting a violation of subsection (a) of this section, the Attorney General may, in his discretion, bring a civil action in an appropriate district court of the United States to enjoin such act or practice, and upon a proper showing, a permanent injunction or a temporary restraining order shall be granted without bond.

(2) For the purpose of any civil investigation which, in the opinion of the Attorney General, is necessary and proper to enforce this section, the Attorney General or his designee are empowered to administer oaths and affirmations, subpoena witnesses, take evidence, and require the production of any books, papers, or other documents which the Attorney General deems relevant or material to such investigation. The attendance of witnesses and the production of documentary evidence may be required from any place in the United States, or any territory, possession, or commonwealth of the United States, at any designated place of hearing.

(3) In case of contumacy by, or refusal to obey a subpoena issued to, any person, the Attorney General may invoke the aid of any court of the United States within the jurisdiction of which such investigation or proceeding is carried on, or where such person resides or carries on business, in requiring the attendance and testimony of witnesses and the production of books, papers, or other documents. Any such court may issue an order requiring such person to appear before the Attorney General or his designee, there to produce records, if so ordered, or to give testimony touching the matter under investigation. Any failure to obey such order of the court may be punished by such court as a contempt thereof.

(4) All process in any such case may be served in the judicial district in which such person resides or may be found. The Attorney General may make such rules relating to civil investigations as may be necessary or appropriate to implement the provisions of this subsection.

(e) *Penalties.*

(1)(A) Any juridical person that violates subsection (a) of this section shall be fined not more than $2,000,000.

(B) Any juridical person that violates subsection (a) of this section shall be subject to a civil penalty of not more than $10,000 imposed in an action brought by the Attorney General.

(2)(A) Any natural person who willfully violates subsection (a) of this section shall be fined not more than $100,000 or imprisoned not more than 5 years, or both.

(B) Any natural person who violates subsection (a) of this section shall be subject to a civil penalty of not more than $10,000 imposed in an action brought by the Attorney General.

(3) Whenever a fine is imposed under paragraph (2) upon any officer, director, employee, agent, or stockholder of a person, such fine may not be paid, directly or indirectly, by such person.

(f) *Definitions.* For purposes of this section:

(1) The term "person", when referring to an offender, means any natural person other than a national of the United States (as defined in section 101 of the Immigration and Nationality Act (8 U.S.C. 1101)) or any corporation, partnership, association, jointstock company, business trust, unincorporated organization, or sole proprietorship organized under the law of a foreign nation or a political subdivision thereof.

(2)(A) The term "foreign official" means any officer or employee of a foreign government or any department, agency, or instrumentality thereof, or of a public international organization, or any person acting in an official capacity for or on behalf of any such government or department, agency, or instrumentality, or for or on behalf of any such public international organization.

(B) For purposes of subparagraph (A), the term "public international organization" means—

(i) an organization that is designated by Executive order pursuant to section 1 of the International Organizations Immunities Act (22 U.S.C. 288); or

(ii) any other international organization that is designated by the President by Executive order for the purposes of this section, effective as of the date of publication of such order in the Federal Register.

(3)(A) A person's state of mind is knowing, with respect to conduct, a circumstance or a result if—

(i) such person is aware that such person is engaging in such conduct, that such circumstance exists, or that such result is substantially certain to occur; or

(ii) such person has a firm belief that such circumstance exists or that such result is substantially certain to occur.

(B) When knowledge of the existence of a particular circumstance is required for an offense, such knowledge is established if a person is aware of a high probability of the existence of such circumstance, unless the person actually believes that such circumstance does not exist.

(4)(A) The term "routine governmental action" means only an action which is ordinarily and commonly performed by a foreign official in—

(i) obtaining permits, licenses, or other official documents to qualify a person to do business in a foreign country;

(ii) processing governmental papers, such as visas and work orders;

(iii) providing police protection, mail pickup and delivery, or scheduling inspections associated with contract performance or inspections related to transit of goods across country;

(iv) providing phone service, power and water supply, loading and unloading cargo, or protecting perishable products or commodities from deterioration; or

(v) actions of a similar nature.

(B) The term "routine governmental action" does not include any decision by a foreign official whether, or on what terms, to award new business to or to continue business with a particular party, or any action taken by a foreign official involved in the decision-making process to encourage a decision to award new business to or continue business with a particular party.

(5) The term "interstate commerce" means trade, commerce, transportation, or communication among the several States, or between any foreign country and any State or between any State and any place or ship outside thereof, and such term includes the intrastate use of—

(A) a telephone or other interstate means of communication, or

(B) any other interstate instrumentality.

MAIL AND WIRE FRAUD STATUTES AND OTHER FEDERAL CRIMINAL PROVISIONS

18 U.S.C. § ___

Frauds and Swindles

§ 1341. Whoever, having devised or intending to devise any scheme or artifice to defraud, or for obtaining money or property by means of false or fraudulent pretenses, representations, or promises, or to sell, dispose of, loan, exchange, alter, give away, distribute, supply, or furnish or procure for unlawful use any counterfeit or spurious coin, obligation, security, or other article, or anything represented to be or intimated or held out to be such counterfeit or spurious article, for the purpose of executing such scheme or artifice or attempting so to do, places in any post office or authorized depository for mail matter, any matter or thing whatever to be sent or delivered by the Postal Service, or deposits or causes to be deposited any matter or thing whatever to be sent or delivered by any private or commercial interstate carrier, or takes or receives therefrom, any such matter or thing, or knowingly causes to be delivered by mail or such carrier according to the direction thereon, or at the place at which it is directed to be delivered by the person to whom it is addressed, any such matter or thing, shall be fined under this title or imprisoned not more than 20 years, or both. If the violation occurs in relation to, or involving any benefit authorized, transported, transmitted, transferred, disbursed, or paid in connection with, a presidentially declared major disaster or emergency (as those terms are defined in section 102 of the Robert T. Stafford Disaster Relief and Emergency Assistance Act (42 U.S.C. 5122)), or affects a financial institution, such person shall be fined not more than $1,000,000 or imprisoned not more than 30 years, or both.

Fictitious Name or Address

§ 1342. Whoever, for the purpose of conducting, promoting, or carrying on by means of the Postal Service, any scheme or device mentioned in section 1341 of this title or any other unlawful business, uses or assumes, or requests to be addressed by, any fictitious, false, or assumed title, name, or address or name other than his own proper name, or takes or receives from any post office or authorized depository of mail matter, any letter, postal card, package, or other mail matter addressed to any such fictitious, false, or assumed title, name, or address, or name other than his own proper name, shall be fined under this title or imprisoned not more than five years, or both.

Fraud by Wire, Radio, or Television

§ 1343. Whoever, having devised or intending to devise any scheme or artifice to defraud, or for obtaining money or property by means of false or fraudulent pretenses, representations, or promises, transmits or causes to be transmitted by means of wire, radio, or television communication in interstate or foreign commerce, any writings, signs, signals, pictures, or sounds for the purpose of executing such scheme or artifice, shall be fined under this title or imprisoned not more than 20 years, or both. If the violation occurs in relation to, or involving any benefit authorized, transported, transmitted, transferred, disbursed, or paid in connection with, a presidentially declared major disaster or emergency (as those terms are defined in section 102 of the Robert T. Stafford Disaster Relief and Emergency Assistance Act (42 U.S.C. 5122)), or affects a financial institution, such person shall be fined not more than $1,000,000 or imprisoned not more than 30 years, or both.

Bank Fraud

§ 1344. Whoever knowingly executes, or attempts to execute, a scheme or artifice—

(1) to defraud a financial institution; or

(2) to obtain any of the moneys, funds, credits, assets, securities, or other property owned by, or under the custody or control of, a financial institution, by means of false or fraudulent pretenses, representations, or promises;

shall be fined not more than $1,000,000 or imprisoned not more than 30 years, or both.

Injunctions Against Fraud

(a)(1) If a person is—

(A) violating or about to violate this chapter or section 287, 371 (insofar as such violation involves a conspiracy to defraud the United States or any agency thereof), or 1001 of this title;

(B) committing or about to commit a banking law violation (as defined in section 3322(d) of this title); or

(C) committing or about to commit a Federal health care offense;

the Attorney General may commence a civil action in any Federal court to enjoin such violation.

(2) If a person is alienating or disposing of property, or intends to alienate or dispose of property, obtained as a result of a banking law violation (as defined in section 3322(d) of this title) or a Federal health care offense or property which is traceable to such violation, the Attorney General may commence a civil action in any Federal court—

(A) to enjoin such alienation or disposition of property; or

(B) for a restraining order to—

(i) prohibit any person from withdrawing, transferring, removing, dissipating, or disposing of any such property or property of equivalent value; and

(ii) appoint a temporary receiver to administer such restraining order.

(3) A permanent or temporary injunction or restraining order shall be granted without bond.

(b) The court shall proceed as soon as practicable to the hearing and determination of such an action, and may, at any time before final determination, enter such a restraining order or prohibition, or take such other action, as is warranted to prevent a continuing and substantial injury to the United States or to any person or class of persons for whose protection the action is brought. A proceeding under this section is governed by the Federal Rules of Civil Procedure, except that, if an indictment has been returned against the respondent, discovery is governed by the Federal Rules of Criminal Procedure.

Definition of "Scheme or Artifice to Defraud"

§ 1346. For the purposes of this chapter, the term "scheme or artifice to defraud" includes a scheme or artifice to deprive another of the intangible right of honest services.

Securities and Commodities Fraud

§ 1348. Whoever knowingly executes, or attempts to execute, a scheme or artifice—

(1) to defraud any person in connection with any commodity for future delivery, or any option on a commodity for future delivery, or class of securities registered under section 12 of the Securities Exchange Act of 1934 (15 U.S.C. 78*l*) or that is required to file reports under section 15(d) of the Securities Exchange Act of 1934 (15 U.S.C. 78*o*(d)); or

(2) to obtain, by means of false or fraudulent pretenses, representations, or promises, any money or property in connection with any commodity for future delivery, or any option on a commodity for future delivery, or the purchase or sale of any security of an issuer with a class of securities registered under section 12 of the Securities Exchange Act of 1934 (15 U.S.C. 78*l*) or that is required to file reports under section 15(d) of the Securities Exchange Act of 1934 (15 U.S.C. 78*o*(d)); shall be fined under this title, or imprisoned not more than 25 years, or both.

Attempt and Conspiracy

§ 1349. Any person who attempts or conspires to commit any offense under this chapter shall be subject to the same penalties as those prescribed for the offense, the commission of which was the object of the attempt or conspiracy.

Failure of Corporate Officers to Certify Financial Reports

§ 1350. (a) *Certification of Periodic Financial Reports.* Each periodic report containing financial statements filed by an issuer with the Securities Exchange Commission pursuant to section 13(a) or 15(d) of the Securities Exchange Act of 1934 (15 U.S.C. 78m(a) or 78*o*(d)) shall be accompanied by a written statement by the chief executive officer and chief financial officer (or equivalent thereof) of the issuer.

(b) *Content.* The statement required under subsection (a) shall certify that the periodic report containing the financial statements fully complies with the requirements of section 13(a) or 15(d) of the Securities Exchange Act of 1934 (15 U.S.C. 78m or 78*o*(d)) and that information contained in the periodic report fairly presents, in all material respects, the financial condition and results of operations of the issuer.

(c) *Criminal Penalties.* Whoever—

(1) certifies any statement as set forth in subsections (a) and (b) of this section knowing that the periodic report accompanying the statement does not comport with all the requirements set forth in this section shall be fined not more than $1,000,000 or imprisoned not more than 10 years, or both; or

(2) willfully certifies any statement as set forth in subsections (a) and (b) of this section knowing that the periodic report accompanying the statement does not comport with all the requirements set forth in this section shall be fined not more than $5,000,000, or imprisoned not more than 20 years, or both.

Destruction, Alteration, or Falsification of Records in Federal Investigations and Bankruptcy

§ 1519. Whoever knowingly alters, destroys, mutilates, conceals, covers up, falsifies, or makes a false entry in any record, document, or tangible object with the intent to impede, obstruct, or influence the investigation or proper administration of any matter within the jurisdiction of any department or agency of the United States or any case filed under title 11, or in relation to or contemplation of any such matter or case, shall be fined under this title, imprisoned not more than 20 years, or both.

Destruction of Corporate Audit Records

§ 1520. (a)(1) Any accountant who conducts an audit of an issuer of securities to which section 10A(a) of the Securities Exchange Act of 1934 (15 U.S.C. 78j–1(a)) applies, shall maintain all audit or review workpapers for a period of 5 years from the end of the fiscal period in which the audit or review was concluded.

(2) The Securities and Exchange Commission shall promulgate, within 180 days, after adequate notice and an opportunity for comment, such rules and regulations, as are reasonably necessary, relating to the retention of relevant records such as workpapers, documents that form the basis of an audit or review, memoranda, correspondence, communications, other documents, and records (including electronic records) which are created, sent, or received in connection with an audit or review and contain conclusions, opinions, analyses, or financial data relating to such an audit or review, which is conducted by any accountant who conducts an audit of an issuer of securities to which section 10A(a) of the Securities Exchange Act of 1934 (15 U.S.C. 78j–1(a)) applies. The Commission may, from time to time, amend or supplement the rules and regulations that it is required to promulgate under this section, after adequate notice and an opportunity for comment, in order to ensure that such rules and regulations adequately comport with the purposes of this section.

(b) Whoever knowingly and willfully violates subsection (a)(1), or any rule or regulation promulgated by the Securities and Exchange Commission under subsection (a)(2), shall be fined under this title, imprisoned not more than 10 years, or both.

(c) Nothing in this section shall be deemed to diminish or relieve any person of any other duty or obligation imposed by Federal or State law or regulation to maintain, or refrain from destroying, any document.

CIVIL ACTION TO PROTECT AGAINST RETALIATION IN FRAUD CASES

18 U.S.C. § 1514A

§ 1514A. (a) *Whistleblower Protection for Employees of Publicly Traded Companies.* No company with a class of securities registered under section 12 of the Securities Exchange Act of 1934, or that is required to file reports under section 15(d) of the Securities Exchange Act of 1934 including any subsidiary or affiliate whose financial information is included in the consolidated financial statements of such company, or nationally recognized statistical rating organization (as defined in section 3(a) of the Securities Exchange Act of 1934) or any officer, employee, contractor, subcontractor, or agent of such company or nationally recognized statistical rating organization, may discharge, demote, suspend, threaten, harass, or in any other manner discriminate against an employee in the terms and conditions of employment because of any lawful act done by the employee—

(1) to provide information, cause information to be provided, or otherwise assist in an investigation regarding any conduct which the employee reasonably believes constitutes a violation of section 1341, 1343, 1344, or 1348, any rule or regulation of the Securities and Exchange Commission, or any provision of Federal law relating to fraud against shareholders, when the information or assistance is provided to or the investigation is conducted by—

(A) a Federal regulatory or law enforcement agency;

(B) any Member of Congress or any committee of Congress; or

(C) a person with supervisory authority over the employee (or such other person working for the employer who has the authority to investigate, discover, or terminate misconduct); or

(2) to file, cause to be filed, testify, participate in, or otherwise assist in a proceeding filed or about to be filed (with any knowledge of the employer) relating to an alleged violation of section 1341, 1343, 1344, or 1348, any rule or regulation of the Securities and Exchange Commission, or any provision of Federal law relating to fraud against shareholders.

(b) *Enforcement Action.*

(1) *In General.* A person who alleges discharge or other discrimination by any person in violation of subsection (a) may seek relief under subsection (c), by—

(A) filing a complaint with the Secretary of Labor; or

(B) if the Secretary has not issued a final decision within 180 days of the filing of the complaint and there is no showing that such delay is due to the bad faith of the claimant, bringing an action at law or equity for de novo review in the appropriate district court of the United States, which shall have jurisdiction over such an action without regard to the amount in controversy.

(2) *Procedure.*

(A) *In General.* An action under paragraph (1)(A) shall be governed under the rules and procedures set forth in section 42121(b) of title 49, United States Code.

(B) *Exception.* Notification made under section 42121(b)(1) of title 49, United States Code, shall be made to the person named in the complaint and to the employer.

(C) *Burdens of Proof.* An action brought under paragraph (1)(B) shall be governed by the legal burdens of proof set forth in section 42121(b) of title 49, United States Code.

(D) *Statute of Limitations.* An action under paragraph (1) shall be commenced not later than 180 days after the date on which the violation occurs, or after the date on which the employee became aware of the violation.

(E) *Jury Trial.* A party to an action brought under paragraph (1)(B) shall be entitled to trial by jury.

(c) *Remedies.*

(1) *In General.* An employee prevailing in any action under subsection (b)(1) shall be entitled to all relief necessary to make the employee whole.

(2) *Compensatory Damages.* Relief for any action under paragraph (1) shall include—

(A) reinstatement with the same seniority status that the employee would have had, but for the discrimination;

(B) the amount of back pay, with interest; and

(C) compensation for any special damages sustained as a result of the discrimination, including litigation costs, expert witness fees, and reasonable attorney fees.

(d) *Rights Retained by Employee.* Nothing in this section shall be deemed to diminish the rights, privileges, or remedies of any employee under any Federal or State law, or under any collective bargaining agreement.

(e) *Nonenforceability of Certain Provisions Waiving Rights and Remedies or Requiring Arbitration of Disputes.*

(1) *Waiver of Rights and Remedies.* The rights and remedies provided for in this section may not be waived by any agreement, policy form, or condition of employment, including by a predispute arbitration agreement.

(2) *Predispute Arbitration Agreements.* No predispute arbitration agreement shall be valid or enforceable, if the agreement requires arbitration of a dispute arising under this section.

III. STATE SECURITIES LAWS

UNIFORM SECURITIES ACT (1956)

With 1958 Amendments

An Act [Relating to securities; prohibiting fraudulent practices in relation thereto; requiring the registration of broker-dealers, agents, investment advisers, and securities; and making uniform the law with reference thereto:]

PART I

FRAUDULENT AND OTHER PROHIBITED PRACTICES

PART II

REGISTRATION OF BROKER–DEALERS, AGENTS, AND INVESTMENT ADVISERS

PART III

REGISTRATION OF SECURITIES

PART IV

GENERAL PROVISIONS

PART I
FRAUDULENT AND OTHER PROHIBITED PRACTICES

§ 101. [Sales and Purchases]

It is unlawful for any person, in connection with the offer, sale, or purchase of any security, directly or indirectly

(1) to employ any device, scheme, or artifice to defraud,

(2) to make any untrue statement of a material fact or to omit to state a material fact necessary in order to make the statements made, in the light of the circumstances under which they are made, not misleading, or

(3) to engage in any act, practice, or course of business which operates or would operate as a fraud or deceit upon any person.

§ 102. [Advisory Activities]

(a) It is unlawful for any person who receives any consideration from another person primarily for advising the other person as to the value of securities or their purchase or sale, whether through the issuance of analyses or reports or otherwise,

(1) to employ any device, scheme, or artifice to defraud the other person, or

(2) to engage in any act, practice, or course of business which operates or would operate as a fraud or deceit upon the other person.

(b) It is unlawful for any investment adviser to enter into, extend, or renew any investment advisory contract unless it provides in writing

(1) that the investment adviser shall not be compensated on the basis of a share of capital gains upon or capital appreciation of the funds or any portion of the funds of the client;

(2) that no assignment of the contract may be made by the investment adviser without the consent of the other party to the contract; and

(3) that the investment adviser, if a partnership, shall notify the other party to the contract of any change in the membership of the partnership within a reasonable time after the change.

Clause (1) does not prohibit an investment advisory contract which provides for compensation based upon the total value of a fund averaged over a definite period, or as of definite dates or taken as of a definite date. "Assignment," as used in clause (2), includes any direct or indirect transfer or hypothecation of an investment advisory contract by the assignor or of a controlling block of the assignor's outstanding voting securities by a security holder of the assignor; but, if the investment adviser is a partnership, no assignment of an investment advisory contract is considered to result from the death or withdrawal of a minority of the members of the investment adviser having only a minority interest in the business of the investment adviser, or from the admission to the investment advisor of one or more members who, after admission, will be only a minority of the members and will have only a minority interest in the business.

(c) It is unlawful for any investment adviser to take or have custody of any securities or funds of any client if

(1) the [Administrator] by rule prohibits custody; or

(2) in the absence of rule, the investment adviser fails to notify the [Administrator] that he has or may have custody.

PART II
REGISTRATION OF BROKER–DEALERS, AGENTS, AND INVESTMENT ADVISERS

§ 201. [Registration Requirements]

(a) It is unlawful for any person to transact business in this state as a broker-dealer or agent unless he is registered under this Act.

(b) It is unlawful for any broker-dealer or issuer to employ an agent unless the agent is registered. The registration of an agent is not effective during any period when he is not associated with a particular broker-dealer registered under this Act or a particular issuer. When an agent begins or terminates a connection with a broker-dealer or issuer, or begins or terminates those activities which make him an agent, the agent as well as the broker-dealer or issuer shall promptly notify the [Administrator].

(c) It is unlawful for any person to transact business in this state as an investment adviser unless (1) he is so registered under this Act, (2) he is registered as a broker-dealer without the imposition of a condition under section 204(b)(5), or (3) his only clients in this state are investment companies as defined in the Investment Company Act of 1940 or insurance companies.

(d) Every registration expires one year from its effective date unless renewed. [The [Administrator] may by rule or order prepare an initial schedule for registration renewals so that subsequent renewals of registrations effective on the effective date of this Act may be staggered by calendar months. For this purpose the [Administrator] may by rule reduce the registration fee proportionately.]

§ 202. [Registration Procedure]

(a) A broker-dealer, agent, or investment adviser may obtain an initial or renewal registration by filing with the [Administrator] an application together with a consent to service of process pursuant to section 414(g). The application shall contain whatever information the [Administrator] by rule requires concerning such matters as (1) the applicant's form and place of organization; (2) the applicant's proposed method of doing business; (3) the qualifications and business history of the applicant; in the case of a broker-dealer or investment adviser, the qualifications and business history of any partner, officer, or director, any person occupying a similar status or performing similar functions, or any person directly or indirectly controlling the broker-dealer or investment adviser; and, in the case of an investment adviser, the qualifications and business history of any employee; (4) any injunction or administrative order or conviction of a misdemeanor involving a security or any aspect of the securities business and any conviction of a felony; and (5) the applicant's financial condition and history. The [Administrator] may by rule or order require an applicant for initial registration to publish an announcement of the application in one or more specified newspapers published in this state. If no denial order is in effect and no proceeding is pending under section 204, registration becomes effective at noon of the thirtieth day after an application is filed. The [Administrator] may by rule or order specify an earlier effective date, and [he] may by order defer the effective date until noon of the thirtieth day after the filing of any amendment. Registration of a broker-dealer automatically constitutes registration of any agent who is a partner, officer, or director, or a person occupying a similar status or performing similar functions.

[(b) Every applicant for initial or renewal registration shall pay a filing fee of $______ in the case of a broker-dealer, $______ in the case of an agent, and $______ in the case of an investment adviser. When application is denied or withdrawn, the [Administrator] shall retain $______ of the fee.]

(c) A registered broker-dealer or investment adviser may file an application for registration of a successor, whether or not the successor is then in existence, for the unexpired portion of the year. There shall be no filing fee.

(d) The [Administrator] may by rule require a minimum capital for registered broker-dealers and investment advisers.

(e) The [Administrator] may by rule require registered broker-dealers, agents, and investment advisers to post surety bonds in amounts up to $10,000, and may determine their conditions. Any appropriate deposit of cash or securities shall be accepted in lieu of any bond so required. No bond may be required of any registrant whose net capital, which may be defined by rule, exceeds $25,000. Every bond shall provide for suit thereon by any person who has a cause of action under section 410 and, if the [Administrator] by rule or order requires, by any person who has a cause of action not arising under this act. Every bond shall provide that no suit may be maintained to enforce any liability on the bond unless brought within two years after the sale or other act upon which it is based.

§ 203. [Post–Registration Provisions]

(a) Every registered broker-dealer and investment adviser shall make and keep such accounts, correspondence, memoranda, papers, books, and other records as the [Administrator] by rule prescribes. All records so required shall be preserved for three years unless the [Administrator] by rule prescribes otherwise for particular types of records.

(b) Every registered broker-dealer and investment adviser shall file such financial reports as the [Administrator] by rule prescribes.

(c) If the information contained in any document filed with the [Administrator] is or becomes inaccurate or incomplete in any material respect, the registrant shall promptly file a correcting amendment unless notification of the correction has been given under section 201(b).

(d) All the records referred to in subsection (a) are subject at any time or from time to time to such reasonable periodic, special, or other examinations by representatives of the [Administrator], within or without this state, as the [Administrator] deems necessary or appropriate in the public interest or for the protection of investors. For the purpose of avoiding unnecessary duplication of examinations, the [Administrator], insofar as [he] deems it practicable in administering this subsection, may cooperate with the securities administrators of other states, the Securities and Exchange Commission, and any national securities exchange or national securities association registered under the Securities Exchange Act of 1934.

§ 204. [Denial, Revocation, Suspension, Cancelation, and Withdrawal of Registration]

(a) The [Administrator] may by order deny, suspend, or revoke any registration if [he] finds (1) that the order is in the public interest and (2) that the applicant or registrant or, in the case of a broker-dealer or investment adviser, any partner, officer, or director, any person occupying a similar status or performing similar functions, or any person directly or indirectly controlling the broker-dealer or investment adviser

(A) has filed an application for registration which as of its effective date, or as of any date after filing in the case of an order denying effectiveness, was incomplete in any material respect or contained any statement which was, in light of the circumstances under which it was made, false or misleading with respect to any material fact;

(B) has willfully violated or willfully failed to comply with any provision of this Act or a predecessor Act or any rule or order under this Act or a predecessor Act;

(C) has been convicted, within the past ten years, of any misdemeanor involving a security or any aspect of the securities business, or any felony;

(D) is permanently or temporarily enjoined by any court of competent jurisdiction from engaging in or continuing any conduct or practice involving any aspect of the securities business;

(E) is the subject of an order of the [Administrator] denying, suspending, or revoking registration as a broker-dealer, agent, or investment adviser;

(F) is the subject of an order entered within the past five years by the securities administrator of any other state or by the Securities and Exchange Commission denying or revoking registration as a broker-dealer, agent, or investment adviser, or the substantial equivalent of those terms as defined in this act, or is the subject of an order of the Securities and Exchange Commission suspending or expelling him from a national securities exchange or national securities association registered under the Securities Exchange Act of 1934,[1] or is the subject of a United States Post Office fraud order; but (i) the [Administrator] may not institute a revocation or suspension proceeding under clause (F) more than one year from the date of the order relied on, and (ii) [he] may not enter an order under clause (F) on the basis of an order under another state act unless that order was based on facts which would currently constitute a ground for an order under this section;

(G) has engaged in dishonest or unethical practices in the securities business;

(H) is insolvent, either in the sense that his liabilities exceed his assets or in the sense that he cannot meet his obligations as they mature; but the [Administrator] may not enter an order against a broker-dealer or investment adviser under this clause without a finding of insolvency as to the broker-dealer or investment adviser; or

(I) is not qualified on the basis of such factors as training, experience, and knowledge of the securities business, except as otherwise provided in subsection (b).

The [Administrator] may by order deny, suspend, or revoke any registration if [he] finds (1) that the order is in the public interest and (2) that the applicant or registrant

(J) has failed reasonably to supervise his agents if he is a broker-dealer or his employees if he is an investment adviser; or

(K) has failed to pay the proper filing fee; but the [Administrator] may enter only a denial order under this clause, and [he] shall vacate any such order when the deficiency has been corrected.

The [Administrator] may not institute a suspension or revocation proceeding on the basis of a fact or transaction known to [him] when registration became effective unless the proceeding is instituted within the next thirty days.

(b) The following provisions govern the application of section 204(a)(2)(I):

(1) The [Administrator] may not enter an order against a broker-dealer on the basis of the lack of qualification of any person other than (A) the broker-dealer himself if he is an individual or (B) an agent of the broker-dealer.

(2) The [Administrator] may not enter an order against an investment adviser on the basis of the lack of qualification of any person other than (A) the investment adviser himself if he is an individual or (B) any other person who represents the investment adviser in doing any of the acts which make him an investment adviser.

(3) The [Administrator] may not enter an order solely on the basis of lack of experience if the applicant or registrant is qualified by training or knowledge or both.

(4) The [Administrator] shall consider that an agent who will work under the supervision of a registered broker-dealer need not have the same qualifications as a broker-dealer.

(5) The [Administrator] shall consider that an investment adviser is not necessarily qualified solely on the basis of experience as a broker-dealer or agent. When [he] finds that an applicant for initial or renewal registration as a broker-dealer is not qualified as an investment adviser, [he] may by order condition the applicant's registration as a broker-dealer upon his not transacting business in this state as an investment adviser.

(6) The [Administrator] may by rule provide for an examination, which may be written or oral or both, to be taken by any class of or all applicants, as well as persons who represent or will represent an investment adviser in doing any of the acts which make him an investment adviser.

(c) The [Administrator] may by order summarily postpone or suspend registration pending final determination of any proceeding under this section. Upon the entry of the order, the [Administrator] shall promptly notify the applicant or registrant, as well as the employer or prospective employer if the applicant or registrant is an agent, that it has been entered and of the reasons therefor and that within fifteen days after the receipt of a written request the matter will be set down for hearing. If no hearing is requested and none is ordered by the [Administrator], the order will remain in effect until it is modified or vacated by the [Administrator]. If a hearing is requested or ordered, the [Administrator], after notice of and opportunity for hearing, may modify or vacate the order or extend it until final determination.

(d) If the [Administrator] finds that any registrant or applicant for registration is no longer in existence or has ceased to do business as a broker-dealer, agent, or investment adviser, or is subject to an adjudication of mental incompetence or to the control of a committee, conservator, or guardian, or cannot be located after reasonable search, the [Administrator] may by order cancel the registration or application.

(e) Withdrawal from registration as a broker-dealer, agent, or investment adviser becomes effective thirty days after receipt of an application to withdraw or within such shorter period of time as the [Administrator] may determine, unless a revocation or suspension proceeding is pending when the application is filed or a proceeding to revoke or suspend or to impose conditions upon the withdrawal is instituted within thirty days after the application is filed. If a proceeding is pending or instituted, withdrawal becomes effective at such time and upon such conditions as the [Administrator] by order determines. If no proceeding is pending or instituted and withdrawal automatically becomes effective, the [Administrator] may nevertheless institute a revocation or suspension proceeding under section 204(a)(2)(B) within one year after withdrawal became effective and enter a revocation or suspension order as of the last date on which registration was effective.

(f) No order may be entered under any part of this section except the first sentence of subsection (c) without (1) appropriate prior notice to the applicant or registrant (as well as the employer or prospective employer if the applicant or registrant is an agent),

(2) opportunity for hearing, and (3) written findings of fact and conclusions of law.

PART III

REGISTRATION OF SECURITIES

§ 301. [Registration Requirement]

It is unlawful for any person to offer or sell any security in this state unless (1) it is registered under this Act or (2) the security or transaction is exempted under section 402.

§ 302. [Registration by Notification]

(a) The following securities may be registered by notification, whether or not they are also eligible for registration by coordination under section 303:

(1) any security whose issuer and any predecessors have been in continuous operation for at least five years if (A) there has been no default during the current fiscal year or within the three preceding fiscal years in the payment of principal, interest, or dividends on any security of the issuer (or any predecessor) with a fixed maturity or a fixed interest or dividend provision, and (B) the issuer and any predecessors during the past three fiscal years have had average net earnings, determined in accordance with generally accepted accounting practices, (i) which are applicable to all securities without a fixed maturity or a fixed interest or dividend provision outstanding at the date the registration statement is filed and equal at least five percent of the amount of such outstanding securities (as measured by the maximum offering price or the market price on a day, selected by the registrant, within thirty days before the date of filing the registration statement, whichever is higher, or book value on a day, selected by the registrant, within ninety days of the date of filing the registration statement to the extent that there is neither a readily determinable market price nor a cash offering price), or (ii) which, if the issuer and any predecessors have not had any security of the type specified in clause (i) outstanding for three full fiscal years, equal at least five percent of the amount (as measured in clause (i)) of all securities which will be outstanding if all the securities being offered or proposed to be offered (whether or not they are proposed to be registered or offered in this state) are issued;

(2) any security (other than a certificate of interest or participation in an oil, gas or mining title or lease or in payments out of production under such a title or lease) registered for nonissuer distribution if (A) any security of the same class has ever been registered under this Act or a predecessor Act, or (B) the security being registered was originally issued pursuant to an exemption under this Act or a predecessor Act.

(b) A registration statement under this section shall contain the following information and be accompanied by the following documents in addition to the information specified in section 305(c) and the consent to service of process required by section 414(g):

(1) a statement demonstrating eligibility for registration by notification;

(2) with respect to the issuer and any significant subsidiary: its name, address, and form of organization; the state (or foreign jurisdiction) and the date of its organization; and the general character and location of its business;

(3) with respect to any person on whose behalf any part of the offering is to be made in a non-issuer distribution: his name and address; the amount of securities of the issuer held by him as of the date of the filing of the registration statement; and a statement of his reasons for making the offering;

(4) a description of the security being registered;

(5) the information and documents specified in clauses (8), (10), and (12) of section 304(b); and

(6) in the case of any registration under section 302(a)(2) which does not also satisfy the conditions of section 302(a)(1), a balance sheet of the issuer as of a date within four months prior to the filing of the registration statement, and a summary of earnings for each of the two fiscal years preceding the date of the balance sheet and for any period between the close of the last fiscal year and the date of the balance sheet, or for the period of the issuer's and any predecessors' existence if less than two years.

(c) If no stop order is in effect and no proceeding is pending under section 306, a registration statement under this section automatically becomes effective at [three o'clock Eastern Standard Time] in the afternoon of the second full business day after the filing of the registration statement or the last amendment, or at such earlier time as the [Administrator] determines.

§ 303. [Registration by Coordination]

(a) Any security for which a registration statement has been filed under the Securities Act of 1933 in connection with the same offering may be registered by coordination.

(b) A registration statement under this section shall contain the following information and be accompanied by the following documents in addition to the information specified in section 305(c) and the consent to service of process required by section 414(g):

(1) three copies of the latest form of prospectus filed under the Securities Act of 1933;

(2) if the [Administrator] by rule or otherwise requires, a copy of the articles of incorporation and by-laws (or their substantial equivalents) currently in effect, a copy of any agreements with or among underwriters, a copy of any indenture or other instrument governing the issuance of the security to be registered, and a specimen or copy of the security;

(3) if the [Administrator] requests, any other information, or copies of any other documents, filed under the Securities Act of 1933; and

(4) an undertaking to forward all future amendments to the federal prospectus, other than an amendment which merely delays the effective date of the registration statement, promptly and in any event not later than the first business day after the day they are forwarded to or filed with the Securities and Exchange Commission, whichever first occurs.

(c) A registration statement under this section automatically becomes effective at the moment the federal registration statement becomes effective if all the following conditions are satisfied: (1) no stop order is in effect and no proceeding is pending under section 306; (2) the registration statement has been on file with the [Administrator] for at least ten days; and (3) a statement of the maximum and minimum proposed offering prices and the maximum underwriting discounts and commissions has been on file for two full business days or such shorter period as the [Administrator] permits by rule or otherwise and the offering is made within those limitations. The registrant shall promptly notify the [Administrator] by telephone or telegram of the date and time when the federal registration statement became effective and the content of the price amendment, if any, and shall promptly file a post-effective amendment containing the information and documents in the price amendment. "Price amendment" means the final federal amendment which includes a statement of the offering price, underwriting and selling discounts or commissions, amount of proceeds, conversion rates, call prices, and other matters dependent upon the offering price. Upon failure to receive the required notification and post-effective amendment with respect to the price amendment, the [Administrator] may enter a stop order, without notice or hearing, retroactively denying effectiveness to the registration statement or suspending its effectiveness until compliance with this subsection, if [he] promptly notifies the registrant by telephone or telegram (and promptly confirms by letter or telegram when [he] notifies by telephone) of the issuance of the order. If the registrant proves compliance with the requirements of this subsection as to notice and post-effective amendment, the stop order is void as of the time of its entry. The [Administrator] may by rule or otherwise waive either or both of the conditions specified in clauses (2) and (3). If the federal registration statement becomes effective before all the conditions in this subsection are satisfied and they are not waived, the registration statement automatically becomes effective as soon as all the conditions are satisfied. If the registrant advises the [Administrator] of the date when the federal registration statement is expected to become effective, the [Administrator] shall promptly advise the registrant by telephone or telegram, at the registrant's expense, whether all the conditions are satisfied and whether [he] then contemplates the institution of a proceeding under section 306; but this advice by the [Administrator] does not preclude the institution of such a proceeding at any time.

§ 304. [Registration by Qualification]

(a) Any security may be registered by qualification.

(b) A registration statement under this section shall contain the following information and be accompanied by the following documents in addition to the information specified in section 305(c) and the consent to service of process required by section 414(g):

(1) with respect to the issuer and any significant subsidiary: its name, address, and form of organization; the state or foreign jurisdiction and date of its organization; the general character and location of its business; a description of its physical

properties and equipment; and a statement of the general competitive conditions in the industry or business in which it is or will be engaged;

(2) with respect to every director and officer of the issuer, or person occupying a similar status or performing similar functions: his name, address, and principal occupation for the past five years; the amount of securities of the issuer held by him as of a specified date within thirty days of the filing of the registration statement; the amount of the securities covered by the registration statement to which he has indicated his intention to subscribe; and a description of any material interest in any material transaction with the issuer or any significant subsidiary effected within the past three years or proposed to be effected;

(3) with respect to persons covered by clause (2): the remuneration paid during the past twelve months and estimated to be paid during the next twelve months, directly or indirectly, by the issuer (together with all predecessors, parents, subsidiaries, and affiliates) to all those persons in the aggregate;

(4) with respect to any person owning of record, or beneficially if known, ten percent or more of the outstanding shares of any class of equity security of the issuer: the information specified in clause (2) other than his occupation;

(5) with respect to every promoter if the issuer was organized within the past three years: the information specified in clause (2), any amount paid to him within that period or intended to be paid to him, and the consideration for any such payment;

(6) with respect to any person on whose behalf any part of the offering is to be made in a non-issuer distribution: his name and address; the amount of securities of the issuer held by him as of the date of the filing of the registration statement; a description of any material interest in any material transaction with the issuer or any significant subsidiary effected within the past three years or proposed to be effected; and a statement of his reasons for making the offering;

(7) the capitalization and long-term debt (on both a current and a pro forma basis) of the issuer and any significant subsidiary, including a description of each security outstanding or being registered or otherwise offered, and a statement of the amount and kind of consideration (whether in the form of cash, physical assets, services, patents, goodwill, or anything else) for which the issuer or any subsidiary has issued any of its securities within the past two years or is obligated to issue any of its securities;

(8) the kind and amount of securities to be offered; the proposed offering price or the method by which it is to be computed; any variation therefrom at which any proportion of the offering is to be made to any person or class of persons other than the underwriters, with a specification of any such person or class; the basis upon which the offering is to be made if otherwise than for cash; the estimated aggregate underwriting and selling discounts or commissions and finders' fees (including separately cash, securities, contracts, or anything else of value to accrue to the underwriters or finders in connection with the offering) or, if the selling discounts or commissions are variable, the basis of determining them and their maximum and minimum amounts; the estimated amounts of other selling expenses, including legal, engineering, and accounting charges; the name and address of every underwriter and every recipient of a finder's fee; a copy of any underwriting or selling-group agreement pursuant to which the distribution is to be made, or the proposed form of any such agreement whose terms have not yet been determined, and a description of the plan of distribution of any securities which are to be offered otherwise than through an underwriter;

(9) the estimated cash proceeds to be received by the issuer from the offering; the purposes for which the proceeds are to be used by the issuer; the amount to be used for each purpose; the order or priority in which the proceeds will be used for the purposes stated; the amounts of any funds to be raised from other sources to achieve the purposes stated; the sources of any such funds; and, if any part of the proceeds is to be used to acquire any property (including goodwill) otherwise than in the ordinary course of business, the names and addresses of the vendors, the purchase price, the names of any persons who have received commissions in connection with the acquisition, and the amounts of any such commissions and any other expense in connection with the acquisition (including the cost of borrowing money to finance the acquisition);

(10) a description of any stock options or other security options outstanding, or to be created in connection with the offering, together with the amount of any such options held or to be held by every person required to be named in clause (2), (4), (5), (6), or (8) and by any person who holds or

will hold ten percent or more in the aggregate of any such options;

(11) the dates of, parties to, and general effect concisely stated of, every management or other material contract made or to be made otherwise than in the ordinary course of business if it is to be performed in whole or in part at or after the filing of the registration statement or was made within the past two years, together with a copy of every such contract; and a description of any pending litigation or proceeding to which the issuer is a party and which materially affects its business or assets (including any such litigation or proceeding known to be contemplated by governmental authorities);

(12) a copy of any prospectus, pamphlet, circular, form letter, advertisement, or other sales literature intended as of the effective date to be used in connection with the offering;

(13) a specimen or copy of the security being registered; a copy of the issuer's articles of incorporation and by-laws, or their substantial equivalents, as currently in effect; and a copy of any indenture or other instrument covering the security to be registered;

(14) a signed or conformed copy of an opinion of counsel as to the legality of the security being registered (with an English translation if it is in a foreign language), which shall state whether the security when sold will be legally issued, fully paid, and non-assessable, and, if a debt security, a binding obligation of the issuer;

(15) the written consent of any accountant, engineer, appraiser, or other person whose profession gives authority to a statement made by him, if any such person is named as having prepared or certified a report or valuation (other than a public and official document or statement) which is used in connection with the registration statement;

(16) a balance sheet of the issuer as of a date within four months prior to the filing of the registration statement; a profit and loss statement and analysis of surplus for each of the three fiscal years preceding the date of the balance sheet and for any period between the close of the last fiscal year and the date of the balance sheet, or for the period of the issuer's and any predecessors' existence if less than three years; and, if any part of the proceeds of the offering is to be applied to the purchase of any business, the same financial statements which would be required if that business were the registrant; and

(17) such additional information as the [Administrator] requires by rule or order.

(c) A registration statement under this section becomes effective when the [Administrator] so orders.

(d) The [Administrator] may by rule or order require as a condition of registration under this section that a prospectus containing any designated part of the information specified in subsection (b) be sent or given to each person to whom an offer is made before or concurrently with (1) the first written offer made to him (otherwise than by means of a public advertisement) by or for the account of the issuer or any other person on whose behalf the offering is being made, or by any underwriter or broker-dealer who is offering part of an unsold allotment or subscription taken by him as a participant in the distribution, (2) the confirmation of any sale made by or for the account of any such person, (3) payment pursuant to any such sale, or (4) delivery of the security pursuant to any such sale, whichever first occurs.

§ 305. [Provisions Applicable to Registration Generally]

(a) A registration statement may be filed by the issuer, any other person on whose behalf the offering is to be made, or a registered broker-dealer.

[(b) Every person filing a registration statement shall pay a filing fee of ______ percent of the maximum aggregate offering price at which the registered securities are to be offered in this state, but the fee shall in no case be less than $______ or more than $______. When a registration statement is withdrawn before the effective date or a pre-effective stop order is entered under section 306, the [Administrator] shall retain $______ of the fee.]

(c) Every registration statement shall specify (1) the amount of securities to be offered in this state; (2) the states in which a registration statement or similar document in connection with the offering has been or is to be filed; and (3) any adverse order, judgment, or decree entered in connection with the offering by the regulatory authorities in each state or by any court or the Securities and Exchange Commission.

(d) Any document filed under this act or a predecessor act [within five years preceding the filing of a registration statement] may be incorporated by reference in the registration statement to the extent that the document is currently accurate.

(e) The [Administrator] may by rule or otherwise permit the omission of any item of information or document from any registration statement.

(f) In the case of a non-issuer distribution, information may not be required under section 304 or 305(j) unless it is known to the person filing the registration statement or to the persons on whose behalf the distribution is to be made, or can be furnished by them without unreasonable effort or expense.

(g) The [Administrator] may by rule or order require as a condition of registration by qualification or coordination (1) that any security issued within the past three years or to be issued to a promoter for a consideration substantially different from the public offering price, or to any person for a consideration other than cash, be deposited in escrow; and (2) that the proceeds from the sale of the registered security in this state be impounded until the issuer receives a specified amount from the sale of the security either in this state or elsewhere.

(h) The [Administrator] may by rule or order require as a condition of registration that any security registered by qualification or coordination be sold only on a specified form of subscription or sale contract, and that a signed or conformed copy of each contract be filed with the [Administrator] or preserved for any period up to three years specified in the rule or order.

(i) Every registration statement is effective for one year from its effective date, or any longer period during which the security is being offered or distributed in a non-exempted transaction by or for the account of the issuer or other person on whose behalf the offering is being made or by any underwriter or broker-dealer who is still offering part of an unsold allotment or subscription taken by him as a participant in the distribution, except during the time a stop order is in effect under section 306. All outstanding securities of the same class as a registered security are considered to be registered for the purpose of any non-issuer transaction (1) so long as the registration statement is effective and (2) between the thirtieth day after the entry of any stop order suspending or revoking the effectiveness of the registration statement under section 306 (if the registration statement did not relate in whole or in part to a non-issuer distribution) and one year from the effective date of the registration statement. A registration statement may not be withdrawn for one year from its effective date if any securities of the same class are outstanding. A registration statement may be withdrawn otherwise only in the discretion of the [Administrator].

(j) So long as a registration statement is effective, the [Administrator] may by rule or order require the person who filed the registration statement to file reports, not more often than quarterly, to keep reasonably current the information contained in the registration statement and to disclose the progress of the offering.

(k) A registration statement relating to a security issued by a face-amount certificate company or a redeemable security issued by an open-end management company or unit investment trust, as those terms are defined in the Investment Company Act of 1940, may be amended after its effective date so as to increase the securities specified as proposed to be offered. Such an amendment becomes effective when the [Administrator] so orders. Every person filing such an amendment shall pay a filing fee, calculated in the manner specified in subsection (b), with respect to the additional securities proposed to be offered.

§ 306. [Denial, Suspension, and Revocation of Registration]

(a) The [Administrator] may issue a stop order denying effectiveness to, or suspending or revoking the effectiveness of, any registration statement if [he] finds (1) that the order is in the public interest and (2) that

(A) the registration statement as of its effective date or as of any earlier date in the case of an order denying effectiveness, or any amendment under section 305(k) as of its effective date, or any report under section 305(j) is incomplete in any material respect or contains any statement which was, in the light of the circumstances under which it was made, false or misleading with respect to any material fact;

(B) any provision of this act or any rule, order, or condition lawfully imposed under this act has been willfully violated, in connection with the offering, by (i) the person filing the registration statement, (ii) the issuer, any partner, officer, or director of the issuer, any person occupying a similar status or performing similar functions, or any person directly or indirectly controlling or controlled by the issuer, but only if the person filing the registration statement is directly or indirectly controlled by or acting for the issuer, or (iii) any underwriter;

(C) the security registered or sought to be registered is the subject of an administrative stop order or similar order or a permanent or temporary injunction of any court of competent jurisdiction entered under any other federal or state act applicable to the offering; but (i) the [Administrator] may not institute a proceeding against an effective registration statement under clause (C) more than one year from the date of the order or injunction relied on, and (ii) [he] may not enter an order under clause (C) on the basis of an order or injunction entered under any other state act unless that order or injunction was based on facts which would currently constitute a ground for a stop order under this section;

(D) the issuer's enterprise or method of business includes or would include activities which are illegal where performed;

(E) the offering has worked or tended to work a fraud upon purchasers or would so operate;

(F) the offering has been or would be made with unreasonable amounts of underwriters' and sellers' discounts, commissions, or other compensation, or promoters' profits or participation, or unreasonable amounts or kinds of options;

(G) when a security is sought to be registered by notification, it is not eligible for such registration;

(H) when a security is sought to be registered by coordination, there has been a failure to comply with the undertaking required by section 303(b)(4); or

(I) the applicant or registrant has failed to pay the proper filing fee; but the [Administrator] may enter only a denial order under this clause and [he] shall vacate any such order when the deficiency has been corrected.

The [Administrator] may not institute a stop-order proceeding against an effective registration statement on the basis of a fact or transaction known to him when the registration statement became effective unless the proceeding is instituted within the next thirty days.

(b) The [Administrator] may by order summarily postpone or suspend the effectiveness of the registration statement pending final determination of any proceeding under this section. Upon the entry of the order, the [Administrator] shall promptly notify each person specified in subsection (c) that it has been entered and of the reasons therefor and that within fifteen days after the receipt of a written request the matter will be set down for hearing. If no hearing is requested and none is ordered by the [Administrator], the order will remain in effect until it is modified or vacated by the [Administrator]. If a hearing is requested or ordered, the [Administrator], after notice of an opportunity for hearing to each person specified in subsection (c), may modify or vacate the order or extend it until final determination.

(c) No stop order may be entered under any part of this section except the first sentence of subsection (b) without (1) appropriate prior notice to the applicant or registrant, the issuer, and the person on whose behalf the securities are to be or have been offered, (2) opportunity for hearing, and (3) written findings of fact and conclusions of law.

(d) The [Administrator] may vacate or modify a stop order if [he] finds that the conditions which prompted entry have changed or that it is otherwise in the public interest to do so.

PART IV

GENERAL PROVISIONS

§ 401. [Definitions]

When used in this Act, unless the context otherwise requires:

(a) "[Administrator]" [substitute any other appropriate term, such as "Commission," "Commissioner," "Secretary," etc.] means the [official or agency designated in section 406(a)].

(b) "Agent" means any individual other than a broker-dealer who represents a broker-dealer or issuer in effecting or attempting to effect purchases or sales of securities. "Agent" does not include an individual who represents an issuer in (1) effecting transactions in a security exempted by clause (1), (2), (3), (10), or (11) of section 402(a), (2) effecting transactions exempted by section 402(b), or (3) effecting transactions with existing employees, partners, or directors of the issuer if no commission or other remuneration is paid or given directly or indirectly for soliciting any person in this state. A partner, officer, or director of a broker-dealer or issuer, or a person occupying a similar status or performing similar functions, is an agent only if he otherwise comes within this definition.

(c) "Broker-dealer" means any person engaged in the business of effecting transactions in securities for the account of others or for his own account. "Broker-dealer" does not include (1) an agent, (2) an issuer, (3) a bank, savings institution, or trust company, or (4) a person who has no place of business in this state if (A) he effects transactions in this state exclusively with or through (i) the issuers of the securities involved in the transactions, (ii) other broker-dealers, or (iii) banks, savings institutions, trust companies, insurance companies, investment companies as defined in the Investment Company Act of 1940,[1] pension or profit-sharing trusts, or other financial institutions or institutional buyers, whether acting for themselves or as trustees, or (B) during any period of twelve consecutive months he does not direct more than fifteen offers to sell or buy into this state in any manner to persons other than those specified in clause (A), whether or not the offeror or any of the offerees is then present in this state.

(d) "Fraud," "deceit," and "defraud" are not limited to common-law deceit.

(e) "Guaranteed" means guaranteed as to payment of principal, interest, or dividends.

(f) "Investment adviser" means any person who, for compensation, engages in the business of advising others, either directly or through publications or writings, as to the value of securities or as to the advisability of investing in, purchasing, or selling securities, or who, for compensation and as a part of a regular business, issues or promulgates analyses or reports concerning securities. "Investment adviser" does not include (1) a bank, savings institution, or trust company; (2) a lawyer, accountant, engineer, or teacher whose performance of these services is solely incidental to the practice of his profession; (3) a broker-dealer whose performance of these services is solely incidental to the conduct of his business as a broker-dealer and who receives no special compensation for them; (4) a publisher of any bona fide newspaper, news magazine, or business or financial publication of general, regular, and paid circulation; (5) a person whose advice, analyses, or reports relate only to securities exempted by section 402(a)(1); (6) a person who has no place of business in this state if (A) his only clients in this state are other investment advisers, broker-dealers, banks, savings institutions, trust companies, insurance companies, investment companies as defined in the Investment Company Act of 1940, pension or profit-sharing trusts, or other financial institutions or institutional buyers, whether acting for themselves or as trustees, or (B) during any period of twelve consecutive months he does not direct business communications into this state in any manner to more than five clients other than those specified in clause (A), whether or not he or any of the persons to whom the communications are directed is then present in this state; or (7) such other persons not within the intent of this paragraph as the [Administrator] may by rule or order designate.

(g) "Issuer" means any person who issues or proposes to issue any security, except that (1) with respect to certificates of deposit, voting-trust certificates, or collateral-trust certificates, or with respect to certificates of interest or shares in an unincorporated investment trust not having a board of directors or persons performing similar functions or of the fixed, restricted management, or unit type, the term "issuer" means the person or persons performing the acts and assuming the duties of depositor or manager pursuant to the provisions of the trust or other agreement or instrument under which the security is issued; and (2) with respect to certificates of interest or participation in oil, gas, or mining titles or leases or in payments out of production under such titles or leases, there is not considered to be any "issuer."

(h) "Non-issuer" means not directly or indirectly for the benefit of the issuer.

(i) "Person" means an individual, a corporation, a partnership, an association, a joint-stock company, a trust where the interests of the beneficiaries are evidenced by a security, an unincorporated organization, a government, or a political subdivision of a government.

(j)(1) "Sale" or "sell" includes every contract of sale of, contract to sell, or disposition of, a security or interest in a security for value.

(2) "Offer" or "offer to sell" includes every attempt or offer to dispose of, or solicitation of an offer to buy, a security or interest in a security for value.

(3) Any security given or delivered with, or as a bonus on account of, any purchase of securities or any other thing is considered to constitute part of the subject of the purchase and to have been offered and sold for value.

(4) A purported gift of assessable stock is considered to involve an offer and sale.

(5) Every sale or offer of a warrant or right to purchase or subscribe to another security of the same or another issuer, as well as every sale or offer of a security which gives the holder a present or future right or privilege to convert into another security of the same or another issuer, is considered to include an offer of the other security.

(6) The terms defined in this subsection do not include (A) any bona fide pledge or loan; (B) any stock dividend, whether the corporation distributing the dividend is the issuer of the stock or not, if nothing of value is given by stockholders for the dividend other than the surrender of a right to a cash or property dividend when each stockholder may elect to take the dividend in cash or property or in stock; (C) any act incident to a class vote by stockholders, pursuant to the certificate of incorporation or the applicable corporation statute, on a merger, consolidation, reclassification of securities, or sale of corporate assets in consideration of the issuance of securities of another corporation; or (D) any act incident to a judicially approved reorganization in which a security is issued in exchange for one or more outstanding securities, claims, or property interests, or partly in such exchange and partly for cash.

(k) "Securities Act of 1933," "Securities Exchange Act of 1934," "Public Utility Holding Company Act of 1935," and "Investment Company Act of 1940" means the federal statutes of those names as amended before or after the effective date of this Act.

(*l*) "Security" means any note; stock; treasury stock; bond; debenture; evidence of indebtedness; certificate of interest or participation in any profit-sharing agreement; collateral-trust certificate; preorganization certificate or subscription; transferable share; investment contract; voting-trust certificate; certificate of deposit for a security; certificate of interest or participation in an oil, gas, or mining title or lease or in payments out of production under such a title or lease; or, in general, any interest or instrument commonly known as a "security," or any certificate of interest or participation in, temporary or interim certificate for, receipt for guarantee of, or warrant or right to subscribe to or purchase any of the foregoing. "Security" does not include any insurance or endowment policy or annuity contract under which an insurance company promises to pay [a fixed sum of] money either in a lump sum or periodically for life or for some other specified period.

(m) "State" means any state, territory, or possession of the United States, the District of Columbia, and Puerto Rico.

§ 402. [Exemptions]

(a) The following securities are exempted from sections 301 and 403:

(1) any security (including a revenue obligation) issued or guaranteed by the United States, any state, any political subdivision of a state, or any agency or corporate or other instrumentality of one or more of the foregoing; or any certificate of deposit for any of the foregoing;

(2) any security issued or guaranteed by Canada, any Canadian province, any political subdivision of any such province, any agency or corporate or other instrumentality of one or more of the foregoing, or any other foreign government with which the United States currently maintains diplomatic relations, if the security is recognized as a valid obligation by the issuer or guarantor;

(3) any security issued by and representing an interest in or a debt of, or guaranteed by, any bank organized under the laws of the United States, or any bank, savings institution, or trust company organized and supervised under the laws of any state;

(4) any security issued by and representing an interest in or a debt of, or guaranteed by, any federal savings and loan association, or any building and loan or similar association organized under the laws of any state and authorized to do business in this state;

(5) any security issued by and representing an interest in or a debt of, or guaranteed by, any insurance company organized under the laws of any state and authorized to do business in this state; [but this exemption does not apply to an annuity contract, investment contract, or similar security under which the promised payments are not fixed in dollars but are substantially dependent upon the investment results of a segregated fund or account invested in securities;]

(6) any security issued or guaranteed by any federal credit union or any credit union, industrial loan association, or similar association organized and supervised under the laws of this state;

(7) any security issued or guaranteed by any railroad, other common carrier, public utility, or holding company which is (A) subject to the jurisdiction of the Interstate Commerce Commission; (B) a registered holding company under the Public Utility Holding Company Act of 1935 or a subsidiary of such a company within the meaning of that act; (C) regulated in respect of its rates and charges by a governmental authority of the United States or any state; or (D) regulated in respect of the issuance or guarantee of the security by a governmental authority of the United States, any state, Canada, or any Canadian province;

(8) any security listed or approved for listing upon notice of issuance on the New York Stock

Exchange, the American Stock Exchange, or the Midwest Stock Exchange [, or listed on the (insert names of appropriate regional stock exchanges)]; any other security of the same issuer which is of senior or substantially equal rank; any security called for by subscription rights or warrants so listed or approved; or any warrant or right to purchase or subscribe to any of the foregoing;

(9) any security issued by any person organized and operated not for private profit but exclusively for religious, educational, benevolent, charitable, fraternal, social, athletic, or reformatory purposes, or as a chamber of commerce or trade or professional association;

(10) any commercial paper which arises out of a current transaction or the proceeds of which have been or are to be used for current transactions, and which evidences an obligation to pay cash within nine months of the date of issuance, exclusive of days of grace, or any renewal of such paper which is likewise limited, or any guarantee of such paper or of any such renewal;

(11) any investment contract issued in connection with an employees' stock purchase, savings, pension, profit-sharing, or similar benefit plan if the [Administrator] is notified in writing thirty days before the inception of the plan or, with respect to plans which are in effect on the effective date of this act, within sixty days thereafter (or within thirty days before they are reopened if they are closed on the effective date of this Act);

[(12) insert any desired exemption for cooperatives.]

(b) The following transactions are exempted from sections 301 and 403:

(1) any isolated non-issuer transaction, whether effected through a broker-dealer or not;

(2) any non-issuer distribution of an outstanding security if (A) a recognized securities manual contains the names of the issuer's officers and directors, a balance sheet of the issuer as of a date within eighteen months, and a profit and loss statement for either the fiscal year preceding that date or the most recent year of operations, or (B) the security has a fixed maturity or a fixed interest or dividend provision and there has been no default during the current fiscal year or within the three preceding years, or during the existence of the issuer and any predecessors if less than three years, in the payment of principal, interest, or dividends on the security;

(3) any non-issuer transaction effected by or through a registered broker-dealer pursuant to an unsolicited order or offer to buy; but the [Administrator] may by rule require that the customer acknowledge upon a specified form that the sale was unsolicited, and that a signed copy of each such form be preserved by the broker-dealer for a specified period;

(4) any transaction between the issuer or other person on whose behalf the offering is made and an underwriter, or among underwriters;

(5) any transaction in a bond or other evidence of indebtedness secured by a real or chattel mortgage or deed of trust, or by an agreement for the sale of real estate or chattels, if the entire mortgage, deed of trust, or agreement, together with all the bonds or other evidences of indebtedness secured thereby, is offered and sold as a unit;

(6) any transaction by an executor, administrator, sheriff, marshal, receiver, trustee in bankruptcy, guardian, or conservator;

(7) any transaction executed by a bona fide pledgee without any purpose of evading this act;

(8) any offer or sale to a bank, savings institution, trust company, insurance company, investment company as defined in the Investment Company Act of 1940, pension or profit-sharing trust, or other financial institution or institutional buyer, or to a broker-dealer, whether the purchaser is acting for itself or in some fiduciary capacity;

(9) any transaction pursuant to an offer directed by the offeror to not more than ten persons (other than those designated in paragraph (8)) in this state during any period of twelve consecutive months, whether or not the offeror or any of the offerees is then present in this state, if (A) the seller reasonably believes that all the buyers in this state (other than those designated in paragraph (8)) are purchasing for investment, and (B) no commission or other remuneration is paid or given directly or indirectly for soliciting any prospective buyer in this state (other than those designated in paragraph (8)); but the [Administrator] may by rule or order, as to any security or transaction or any type of security or transaction, withdraw or further condition this exemption, or increase or decrease the number of offerees permitted, or waive the conditions in Clauses (A) and (B) with or without the substitution of a limitation on remuneration;

(10) any offer or sale of a preorganization certificate or subscription if (A) no commission or other remuneration is paid or given directly or indirectly for soliciting any prospective subscriber, (B) the number of subscribers does not exceed ten, and (C) no payment is made by any subscriber;

(11) any transaction pursuant to an offer to existing security holders of the issuer, including persons who at the time of the transaction are holders of convertible securities, non-transferable warrants, or transferable warrants exercisable within not more than ninety days of their issuance, if (A) no commission or other remuneration (other than a standby commission) is paid or given directly or indirectly for soliciting any security holder in this state, or (B) the issuer first files a notice specifying the terms of the offer and the [Administrator] does not by order disallow the exemption within the next five full business days;

(12) any offer (but not a sale) of a security for which registration statements have been filed under both this Act and the Securities Act of 1933 if no stop order or refusal order is in effect and no public proceeding or examination looking toward such an order is pending under either act.

(c) The [Administrator] may by order deny or revoke any exemption specified in clause (9) or (11) of subsection (a) or in subsection (b) with respect to a specific security or transaction. No such order may be entered without appropriate prior notice to all interested parties, opportunity for hearing, and written findings of fact and conclusions of law, except that the [Administrator] may by order summarily deny or revoke any of the specified exemptions pending final determination of any proceeding under this subsection. Upon the entry of a summary order, the [Administrator] shall promptly notify all interested parties that it has been entered and of the reasons therefor and that within fifteen days of the receipt of a written request the matter will be set down for hearing. If no hearing is requested and none is ordered by the [Administrator], the order will remain in effect until it is modified or vacated by the [Administrator]. If a hearing is requested or ordered, the [Administrator], after notice of and opportunity for hearing to all interested persons, may modify or vacate the order or extend it until final determination. No order under this subsection may operate retroactively. No person may be considered to have violated section 301 or 403 by reason of any offer or sale effected after the entry of an order under this subsection if he sustains the burden of proof that he did not know, and in the exercise of reasonable care could not have known, of the order.

(d) In any proceeding under this act, the burden of proving an exemption or an exception from a definition is upon the person claiming it.

§ 403. [Filing of Sales and Advertising Literature]

The [Administrator] may by rule or order require the filing of any prospectus, pamphlet, circular, form letter, advertisement, or other sales literature or advertising communication addressed or intended for distribution to prospective investors, including clients or prospective clients of an investment adviser unless the security or transaction is exempted by Section 402.

§ 404. [Misleading Filings]

It is unlawful for any person to make or cause to be made, in any document filed with the [Administrator] or in any proceeding under this act, any statement which is, at the time and in the light of the circumstances under which it is made, false or misleading in any material respect.

§ 405. [Unlawful Representations Concerning Registration or Exemption]

(a) Neither (1) the fact that an application for registration under Part II or a registration statement under Part III has been filed nor (2) the fact that a person or security is effectively registered constitutes a finding by the [Administrator] that any document filed under this Act is true, complete, and not misleading. Neither any such fact nor the fact that an exemption or exception is available for a security or a transaction means that the [Administrator] has passed in any way upon the merits or qualifications of, or recommended or given approval to, any person, security, or transaction.

(b) It is unlawful to make, or cause to be made, to any prospective purchaser, customer, or client any representation inconsistent with subsection (a).

§ 406. [Administration of Act]

(a) This Act shall be administered by the [insert name of local administrative agency and any related provisions on method of selection, salary, term of office, budget, selection and remuneration of personnel, annual reports to the legislature or governor, etc., which are appropriate to the particular state].

(b) It is unlawful for the [Administrator] or any of [his] officers or employees to use for personal benefit any information which is filed with or obtained by the [Administrator] and which is not made public.

No provision of this act authorizes the [Administrator] or any of [his] officers or employees to disclose any such information except among themselves or when necessary or appropriate in a proceeding or investigation under this Act. No provision of this act either creates or derogates from any privilege which exists at common law or otherwise when documentary or other evidence is sought under a subpoena directed to the [Administrator] or any of his officers or employees.

[(c) Insert a provision, if desired, covering fees for examinations, filings under section 403, and other miscellaneous filings for which no fees are specified elsewhere in this Act.]

§ 407. [Investigations and Subpoenas]

(a) The [Administrator] in [his] discretion (1) may make such public or private investigations within or outside of this state as [he] deems necessary to determine whether any person has violated or is about to violate any provision of this act or any rule or order hereunder, or to aid in the enforcement of this act or in the prescribing of rules and forms hereunder, (2) may require or permit any person to file a statement in writing, under oath or otherwise as the [Administrator] determines, as to all the facts and circumstances concerning the matter to be investigated, and (3) may publish information concerning any violation of this Act or any rule or order hereunder.

(b) For the purpose of any investigation or proceeding under this Act, the [Administrator] or any officer designated by [him] may administer oaths and affirmations, subpoena witnesses, compel their attendance, take evidence, and require the production of any books, papers, correspondence, memoranda, agreements, or other documents or records which the [Administrator] deems relevant or material to the inquiry.

(c) In case of contumacy by, or refusal to obey a subpoena issued to, any person, the [insert name of appropriate court], upon application by the [Administrator], may issue to the person an order requiring him to appear before the [Administrator], or the officer designated by [him], there to produce documentary evidence if so ordered or to give evidence touching the matter under investigation or in question. Failure to obey the order of the court may be punished by the court as a contempt of court.

(d) No person is excused from attending and testifying or from producing any document or record before the [Administrator], or in obedience to the subpoena of the [Administrator] or any officer designated by [him], or in any proceeding instituted by the [Administrator], on the ground that the testimony or evidence (documentary or otherwise) required of him may tend to incriminate him or subject him to a penalty or forfeiture; but no individual may be prosecuted or subjected to any penalty or forfeiture for or on account of any transaction, matter, or thing concerning which he is compelled, after claiming his privilege against self-incrimination, to testify or produce evidence (documentary or otherwise), except that the individual testifying is not exempt from prosecution and punishment for perjury or contempt committed in testifying.

§ 408. [Injunctions]

Whenever it appears to the [Administrator] that any person has engaged or is about to engage in any Act or practice constituting a violation of any provision of this Act or any rule or order hereunder, [he] may in [his] discretion bring an action in the [insert name of appropriate court] to enjoin the acts or practices and to enforce compliance with this act or any rule or order hereunder. Upon a proper showing a permanent or temporary injunction, restraining order, or writ of mandamus shall be granted and a receiver or conservator may be appointed for the defendant or the defendant's assets. The court may not require the [Administrator] to post a bond.

§ 409. [Criminal Penalties]

(a) Any person who willfully violates any provision of this act except section 404, or who willfully violates any rule or order under this Act, or who willfully violates section 404 knowing the statement made to be false or misleading in any material respect, shall upon conviction be fined not more than $5,000 or imprisoned not more than three years, or both; but no person may be imprisoned for the violation of any rule or order if he proves that he had no knowledge of the rule or order. [No indictment or information may be returned under this act more than five years after the alleged violation.]

(b) The [Administrator] may refer such evidence as is available concerning violations of this Act or of any rule or order hereunder to the [attorney general or the proper district attorney], who may, with or without such a reference, institute the appropriate criminal proceedings under this Act.

(c) Nothing in this act limits the power of the state to punish any person for any conduct which constitutes a crime by statute or at common law.

§ 410. [Civil Liabilities]

(a) Any person who

(1) offers or sells a security in violation of section 201(a), 301, or 405(b), or of any rule or order under section 403 which requires the affirmative approval of sales literature before it is used, or of any condition imposed under section 304(d), 305(g), or 305(h), or

(2) offers or sells a security by means of any untrue statement of a material fact or any omission to state a material fact necessary in order to make the statements made, in the light of the circumstances under which they are made, not misleading (the buyer not knowing of the untruth or omission), and who does not sustain the burden of proof that he did not know, and in the exercise of reasonable care could not have known, of the untruth or omission,

is liable to the person buying the security from him, who may sue either at law or in equity to recover the consideration paid for the security, together with interest at six percent per year from the date of payment, costs, and reasonable attorneys' fees, less the amount of any income received on the security, upon the tender of the security, or for damages if he no longer owns the security.

(b) Every person who directly or indirectly controls a seller liable under subsection (a), every partner, officer, or director of such a seller, every person occupying a similar status or performing similar functions, every employee of such a seller who materially aids in the sale, and every broker-dealer or agent who materially aids in the sale are also liable jointly and severally with and to the same extent as the seller, unless the non-seller who is so liable sustains the burden of proof that he did not know, and in exercise of reasonable care could not have known, of the existence of the facts by reason of which the liability is alleged to exist. There is contribution as in cases of contract among the several persons so liable.

(c) Any tender specified in this section may be made at any time before entry of judgment.

(d) Every cause of action under this statute survives the death of any person who might have been a plaintiff or defendant.

(e) No person may sue under this section more than two years after the contract of sale. No person may sue under this section (1) if the buyer received a written offer, before suit and at a time when he owned the security, to refund the consideration paid together with interest at six percent per year from the date of payment, less the amount of any income received on the security, and he failed to accept the offer within thirty days of its receipt, or (2) if the buyer received such an offer before suit and at a time when he did not own the security, unless he rejected the offer in writing within thirty days of its receipt.

(f) No person who has made or engaged in the performance of any contract in violation of any provision of this act or any rule or order hereunder, or who has acquired any purported right under any such contract with knowledge of the facts by reason of which its making or performance was in violation, may base any suit on the contract.

(g) Any condition, stipulation, or provision binding any person acquiring any security to waive compliance with any provision of this act or any rule or order hereunder is void.

(h) The rights and remedies provided by this act are in addition to any other rights or remedies that may exist at law or in equity, but this act does not create any cause of action not specified in this section or section 202(e).

§ 411. [Judicial Review of Orders]

(a) Any person aggrieved by a final order of the [Administrator] may obtain a review of the order in the [insert name of appropriate court] by filing in court, within sixty days after the entry of the order, a written petition praying that the order be modified or set aside in whole or in part. A copy of the petition shall be forthwith served upon the [Administrator], and thereupon the [Administrator] shall certify and file in court a copy of the filing and evidence upon which the order was entered. When these have been filed, the court has exclusive jurisdiction to affirm, modify, enforce, or set aside the order, in whole or in part. The findings of the [Administrator] as to the facts, if supported by competent, material and substantial evidence, are conclusive. If either party applies to the court for leave to adduce additional material evidence, and shows to the satisfaction of the court that there were reasonable grounds for failure to adduce the evidence in the hearing before the [Administrator], the court may order the additional evidence to be taken before the [Administrator] and to be adduced upon the hearing in such manner and upon such conditions as the court considers proper. The [Administrator] may modify [his] findings and order by reason of the additional evidence and shall file in court the additional evidence together with any modified or new findings or order. [The judgment of the court is final, subject to review by the (insert name of appropriate court).]

(b) The commencement of proceedings under subsection (a) does not, unless specifically ordered by the court, operate as a stay of the [Administrator's] order.

§ 412. [Rules, Forms, Orders, and Hearings]

(a) The [Administrator] may from time to time make, amend, and rescind such rules, forms, and orders as are necessary to carry out the provisions of this Act, including rules and forms governing registration statements, applications, and reports, and defining any terms, whether or not used in this act, insofar as the definitions are not inconsistent with the provisions of this Act. For the purposes of rules and forms the [Administrator] may classify securities, persons, and matters within [his] jurisdiction, and prescribe different requirements for different classes.

(b) No rule, form, or order may be made, amended, or rescinded unless the [Administrator] finds that the action is necessary or appropriate in the public interest or for the protection of investors and consistent with the purposes fairly intended by the policy and provisions of this Act. In prescribing rules and forms the [Administrator] may cooperate with the securities administrators of the other states and the Securities and Exchange Commission with a view to effectuating the policy of this statute to achieve maximum uniformity in the form and content of registration statements, applications, and reports wherever practicable.

(c) The [Administrator] may by rule or order prescribe (1) the form and content of financial statements required under this act, (2) the circumstances under which consolidated financial statements shall be filed, and (3) whether any required financial statements shall be certified by independent or certified public accountants. All financial statements shall be prepared in accordance with generally accepted accounting practices.

(d) All rules and forms of the [Administrator] shall be published.

(e) No provision of this act imposing any liability applies to any act done or omitted in good faith in conformity with any rule, form, or order of the [Administrator], notwithstanding that the rule, form, or order may later be amended or rescinded or be determined by judicial or other authority to be invalid for any reason.

(f) Every hearing in an administrative proceeding shall be public unless the [Administrator] in [his] discretion grants a request joined in by all the respondents that the hearing be conducted privately.

§ 413. [Administrative Files and Opinions]

(a) A document is filed when it is received by the [Administrator].

(b) The [Administrator] shall keep a register of all applications for registration and registration statements which are or have ever been effective under this Act and all denial, suspension, or revocation orders which have been entered under this act. The register shall be open for public inspection.

(c) The information contained in or filed with any registration statement, application, or report may be made available to the public under such rules as the [Administrator] prescribes.

(d) Upon request and at such reasonable charges as [he] prescribes, the [Administrator] shall furnish to any person photostatic or other copies (certified under [his] seal of office if requested) of any entry in the register or any document which is a matter of public record. In any proceeding or prosecution under this act, any copy so certified is prima facie evidence of the contents of the entry or document certified.

(e) The [Administrator] in [his] discretion may honor requests from interested persons for interpretative opinions.

§ 414. [Scope of the Act and Service of Process]

(a) Sections 101, 201(a), 301, 405, and 410 apply to persons who sell or offer to sell when (1) an offer to sell is made in this state, or (2) an offer to buy is made and accepted in this state.

(b) Sections 101, 201(a), and 405 apply to persons who buy or offer to buy when (1) an offer to buy is made in this state, or (2) an offer to sell is made and accepted in this state.

(c) For the purpose of this section, an offer to sell or to buy is made in this state, whether or not either party is then present in this state, when the offer (1) originates from this state or (2) is directed by the offeror to this state and received at the place to which it is directed (or at any post office in this state in the case of a mailed offer).

(d) For the purpose of this section, an offer to buy or to sell is accepted in this state when acceptance (1) is communicated to the offeror in this state and (2) has not previously been communicated to the offeror, orally or in writing, outside this state; and acceptance is communicated to the offeror in this state, whether or not either party is then present in this state, when the offeree directs it to the offeror in this state reasonably believing the offeror to be in this state and it is received at the place to which it is directed (or at any post office in this state in the case of a mailed acceptance).

(e) An offer to sell or to buy is not made in this state when (1) the publisher circulates or there is circulated on his behalf in this state any bona fide newspaper or other publication of general, regular, and paid circulation which is not published in this state, or which is published in this state but has had more than two-thirds of its circulation outside this state during the past twelve months, or (2) a radio or television program originating outside this state is received in this state.

(f) Sections 102 and 201(c), as well as section 405 so far as investment advisers are concerned, apply when any act instrumental in effecting prohibited conduct is done in this state, whether or not either party is then present in this state.

(g) Every applicant for registration under this act and every issuer who proposes to offer a security in this state through any person acting on an agency basis in the common-law sense shall file with the [Administrator], in such form as [he] by rule prescribes, an irrevocable consent appointing the [Administrator] or [his] successor in office to be his attorney to receive service of any lawful process in any non-criminal suit, action, or proceeding against him or his successor executor or administrator which arises under this act or any rule or order hereunder after the consent has been filed, with the same force and validity as if served personally on the person filing the consent. A person who has filed such a consent in connection with a previous registration need not file another. Service may be made by leaving a copy of the process in the office of the [Administrator], but it is not effective unless (1) the plaintiff, who may be the [Administrator] in a suit, action, or proceeding instituted by [him], forthwith sends notice of the service and a copy of the process by registered mail to the defendant or respondent at his last address on file with the [Administrator], and (2) the plaintiff's affidavit of compliance with this subsection is filed in the case on or before the return day of the process, if any, or within such further time as the court allows.

(h) When any person, including any nonresident of this state, engages in conduct prohibited or made actionable by this act or any rule or order hereunder, and he has not filed a consent to service of process under subsection (g) and personal jurisdiction over him cannot otherwise be obtained in this state, that conduct shall be considered equivalent to his appointment of the [Administrator] or [his] successor in office to be his attorney to receive service of any lawful process in any non-criminal suit, action, or proceeding against him or his successor executor or administrator which grows out of that conduct and which is brought under this act or any rule or order hereunder, with the same force and validity as if served on him personally. Service may be made by leaving a copy of the process in the office of the [Administrator], and it is not effective unless (1) the plaintiff, who may be the [Administrator] in a suit, action, or proceeding instituted by [him], forthwith sends notice of the service and a copy of the process by registered mail to the defendant or respondent at his last known address or takes other steps which are reasonably calculated to give actual notice, and (2) the plaintiff's affidavit of compliance with this subsection is filed in the case on or before the return day of the process, if any, or within such further time as the court allows.

(i) When process is served under this section, the court, or the [Administrator] in a proceeding before [him], shall order such continuance as may be necessary to afford the defendant or respondent reasonable opportunity to defend.

§ 415. [Statutory Policy]

This act shall be so construed as to effectuate its general purpose to make uniform the law of those states which enact it and to coordinate the interpretation and administration of this Act with the related federal regulation.

§ 416. [Short Title]

This Act may be cited as the Uniform Securities Act.

§ 417. [Severability of Provisions]

If any provision of this Act or the application thereof to any person or circumstance is held invalid, the invalidity shall not affect other provisions or applications of the Act which can be given effect without the invalid provision or application, and to this end the provisions of this Act are severable.

§ 418. [Repeal and Savings Provisions]

(a) The [identify the existing Act or Acts] is [are] repealed except as saved in this section.

(b) Prior law exclusively governs all suits, actions, prosecutions, or proceedings which are pending or may be initiated on the basis of facts or circumstances occurring before the effective date of this Act, except that no civil suit or action may be maintained to enforce any liability under prior law unless brought within any period of limitation which applied when the cause of action accrued and in any event within two years after the effective date of this Act.

(c) All effective registrations under prior law, all administrative orders relating to such registrations, and all conditions imposed upon such registrations remain in effect so long as they would have remained in effect if this Act had not been passed. They are considered to have been filed, entered, or imposed under this act, but are governed by prior law.

(d) Prior law applies in respect of any offer or sale made within one year after the effective date of this Act pursuant to an offering begun in good faith before its effective date on the basis of an exemption available under prior law.

(e) Judicial review of all administrative orders as to which review proceedings have not been instituted by the effective date of this Act are governed by section 411, except that no review proceeding may be instituted unless the petition is filed within any period of limitation which applied to a review proceeding when the order was entered and in any event within sixty days after the effective date of this Act.

§ 419. [Time of Taking Effect]

This Act shall take effect on [insert date, which should be at least sixty or ninety days after enactment].

UNIFORM SECURITIES ACT (2002)

TABLE OF CONTENTS

[ARTICLE] 1

GENERAL PROVISIONS

[ARTICLE] 2

EXEMPTIONS FROM REGISTRATION OF SECURITIES

[ARTICLE] 3

REGISTRATION OF SECURITIES AND NOTICE FILING OF FEDERAL COVERED SECURITIES

[ARTICLE] 4

BROKER-DEALERS, AGENTS, INVESTMENT ADVISERS, INVESTMENT ADVISER REPRESENTATIVES, AND FEDERAL COVERED INVESTMENT ADVISERS

[ARTICLE] 5

FRAUD AND LIABILITIES

Legislative Note

Each state, the District of Columbia, Guam, and Puerto Rico have enacted an administrative procedure act. The procedural provisions of the Act in some instances are intended to augment the state administrative procedure act. In so doing, this Act differs from other uniform acts promulgated by the National Conference of Commissioners on Uniform State Laws (NCCUSL) in that it contains procedural provisions on topics such as administrative rulemaking and adjudication, service of process, judicial review of administrative adjudications, public records, public hearings, and use immunity. Normally a uniform act promulgated by NCCUSL defers to existing state procedural provisions on such matters. This Act reflects a policy decision that these matters should be addressed in this Act to promote uniformity in securities regulation. When a conflict exists between this Act and a state administrative procedure act, this Act is intended to supersede the state administrative procedure act. When, however, a reference is made in this Act to the state administrative procedure act, this Act is intended to follow the state's existing administrative procedure act.

In general in this Act a rule will apply generally and an order will apply to a specific individual, transaction, or matter, although the term order may also apply generally in those states that permit orders of general applicability.

[ARTICLE] 1

GENERAL PROVISIONS

§ 101. SHORT TITLE. This [Act] may be cited as the Uniform Securities Act (2002).

§ 102. DEFINITIONS. In this [Act], unless the context otherwise requires:

(1) "Administrator" means the [insert title of administrative agency or official].

(2) "Agent" means an individual, other than a broker-dealer, who represents a broker-dealer in

effecting or attempting to effect purchases or sales of securities or represents an issuer in effecting or attempting to effect purchases or sales of the issuer's securities. But a partner, officer, or director of a broker-dealer or issuer, or an individual having a similar status or performing similar functions is an agent only if the individual otherwise comes within the term. The term does not include an individual excluded by rule adopted or order issued under this [Act].

(3) "Bank" means:

(A) a banking institution organized under the laws of the United States;

(B) a member bank of the Federal Reserve System;

(C) any other banking institution, whether incorporated or not, doing business under the laws of a State or of the United States, a substantial portion of the business of which consists of receiving deposits or exercising fiduciary powers similar to those permitted to be exercised by national banks under the authority of the Comptroller of the Currency pursuant to Section 1 of Public Law 87–722 (12 U.S.C. Section 92a), and which is supervised and examined by a state or federal agency having supervision over banks, and which is not operated for the purpose of evading this [Act]; and

(D) a receiver, conservator, or other liquidating agent of any institution or firm included in subparagraph (A), (B), or (C).

(4) "Broker-dealer" means a person engaged in the business of effecting transactions in securities for the account of others or for the person's own account. The term does not include:

(A) an agent;

(B) an issuer;

(C) a bank or savings institution if its activities as a broker-dealer are limited to those specified in subsections 3(a)(4)(B)(i) through (vi), (viii) through (x), and (xi) if limited to unsolicited transactions; 3(a)(5)(B); and 3(a)(5)(C) of the Securities Exchange Act of 1934 (15 U.S.C. Sections 78c(a)(4) and (5)) or a bank that satisfies the conditions described in subsection 3(a)(4)(E) of the Securities Exchange Act of 1934 (15 U.S.C. Section 78c(a)(4));

(D) an international banking institution; or

(E) a person excluded by rule adopted or order issued under this [Act].

(5) "Depository institution" means:

(A) a bank; or

(B) a savings institution, trust company, credit union, or similar institution that is organized or chartered under the laws of a State or of the United States, authorized to receive deposits, and supervised and examined by an official or agency of a State or the United States if its deposits or share accounts are insured to the maximum amount authorized by statute by the Federal Deposit Insurance Corporation, the National Credit Union Share Insurance Fund, or a successor authorized by federal law. The term does not include:

(i) an insurance company or other organization primarily engaged in the business of insurance;

(ii) a Morris Plan bank; or

(iii) an industrial loan company.

(6) "Federal covered investment adviser" means a person registered under the Investment Advisers Act of 1940.

(7) "Federal covered security" means a security that is, or upon completion of a transaction will be, a covered security under Section 18(b) of the Securities Act of 1933 (15 U.S.C. Section 77r(b)) or rules or regulations adopted pursuant to that provision.

(8) "Filing" means the receipt under this [Act] of a record by the administrator or a designee of the administrator.

(9) "Fraud," "deceit," and "defraud" are not limited to common law deceit.

(10) "Guaranteed" means guaranteed as to payment of all principal and all interest.

(11) "Institutional investor" means any of the following, whether acting for itself or for others in a fiduciary capacity:

(A) a depository institution or international banking institution;

(B) an insurance company;

(C) a separate account of an insurance company;

(D) an investment company as defined in the Investment Company Act of 1940;

(E) a broker-dealer registered under the Securities Exchange Act of 1934;

(F) an employee pension, profit-sharing, or benefit plan if the plan has total assets in excess of $10,000,000 or its investment decisions are made by a named fiduciary, as defined in the Employee Retirement Income Security Act of 1974, that is a broker-dealer registered under the Securities Exchange Act of 1934, an investment adviser registered or exempt from registration under the Investment Advisers Act of 1940, an investment adviser registered under this [Act], a depository institution, or an insurance company;

(G) a plan established and maintained by a State, a political subdivision of a State, or an agency or instrumentality of a State or a political subdivision of a State for the benefit of its employees, if the plan has total assets in excess of $10,000,000 or its investment decisions are made by a duly designated public official or by a named fiduciary, as defined in the Employee Retirement Income Security Act of 1974, that is a broker-dealer registered under the Securities Exchange Act of 1934, an investment adviser registered or exempt from registration under the Investment Advisers Act of 1940, an investment adviser registered under this [Act], a depository institution, or an insurance company;

(H) a trust, if it has total assets in excess of $10,000,000, its trustee is a depository institution, and its participants are exclusively plans of the types identified in subparagraph (F) or (G), regardless of the size of their assets, except a trust that includes as participants self-directed individual retirement accounts or similar self-directed plans;

(I) an organization described in Section 501(c)(3) of the Internal Revenue Code (26 U.S.C. Section 501(c)(3)), corporation, Massachusetts trust or similar business trust, limited liability company, or partnership, not formed for the specific purpose of acquiring the securities offered, with total assets in excess of $10,000,000;

(J) a small business investment company licensed by the Small Business Administration under Section 301(c) of the Small Business Investment Act of 1958 (15 U.S.C. Section 681(c)) with total assets in excess of $10,000,000;

(K) a private business development company as defined in Section 202(a)(22) of the Investment Advisers Act of 1940 (15 U.S.C. Section 80b–2(a)(22)) with total assets in excess of $10,000,000;

(L) a federal covered investment adviser acting for its own account;

(M) a "qualified institutional buyer" as defined in Rule 144A(a)(1), other than Rule 144A(a)(1)(i)(H), adopted under the Securities Act of 1933 (17 C.F.R. 230.144A);

(N) a "major U.S. institutional investor" as defined in Rule 15a–6(b)(4)(i) adopted under the Securities Exchange Act of 1934 (17 C.F.R. 240.15a–6);

(O) any other person, other than an individual, of institutional character with total assets in excess of $10,000,000 not organized for the specific purpose of evading this [Act]; or

(P) any other person specified by rule adopted or order issued under this [Act].

(12) "Insurance company" means a company organized as an insurance company whose primary business is writing insurance or reinsuring risks underwritten by insurance companies and which is subject to supervision by the insurance commissioner or a similar official or agency of a State.

(13) "Insured" means insured as to payment of all principal and all interest.

(14) "International banking institution" means an international financial institution of which the United States is a member and whose securities are exempt from registration under the Securities Act of 1933.

(15) "Investment adviser" means a person that, for compensation, engages in the business of advising others, either directly or through publications or writings, as to the value of securities or the advisability of investing in, purchasing, or selling securities or that, for compensation and as a part of a regular business, issues or promulgates analyses or reports concerning securities. The term includes a financial planner or other person that, as an integral component of other financially related services, provides investment advice to others for compensation as part of a business or that holds itself out as providing investment advice to others for compensation. The term does not include:

(A) an investment adviser representative;

(B) a lawyer, accountant, engineer, or teacher whose performance of investment advice is solely incidental to the practice of the person's profession;

(C) a broker-dealer or its agents whose performance of investment advice is solely incidental to the conduct of business as a broker-dealer and that does not receive special compensation for the investment advice;

(D) a publisher of a bona fide newspaper, news magazine, or business or financial publication of general and regular circulation;

(E) a federal covered investment adviser;

(F) a bank or savings institution;

(G) any other person that is excluded by the Investment Advisers Act of 1940 from the definition of investment adviser; or

(H) any other person excluded by rule adopted or order issued under this [Act].

(16) "Investment adviser representative" means an individual employed by or associated with an investment adviser or federal covered investment adviser and who makes any recommendations or otherwise gives investment advice regarding securities, manages accounts or portfolios of clients, determines which recommendation or advice regarding securities should be given, provides investment advice or holds herself or himself out as providing investment advice, receives compensation to solicit, offer, or negotiate for the sale of or for selling investment advice, or supervises employees who perform any of the foregoing. The term does not include an individual who:

(A) performs only clerical or ministerial acts;

(B) is an agent whose performance of investment advice is solely incidental to the individual acting as an agent and who does not receive special compensation for investment advisory services;

(C) is employed by or associated with a federal covered investment adviser, unless the individual has a "place of business" in this State as that term is defined by rule adopted under Section 203A of the Investment Advisers Act of 1940 (15 U.S.C. Section 80b–3a) and is

(i) an "investment adviser representative" as that term is defined by rule adopted under Section 203A of the Investment Advisers Act of 1940 (15 U.S.C. Section 80b–3a); or

(ii) not a "supervised person" as that term is defined in Section 202(a)(25) of the Investment Advisers Act of 1940 (15 U.S.C. Section 80b–2(a)(25)); or

(D) is excluded by rule adopted or order issued under this [Act].

(17) "Issuer" means a person that issues or proposes to issue a security, subject to the following:

(A) The issuer of a voting trust certificate, collateral trust certificate, certificate of deposit for a security, or share in an investment company without a board of directors or individuals performing similar functions is the person performing the acts and assuming the duties of depositor or manager pursuant to the trust or other agreement or instrument under which the security is issued.

(B) The issuer of an equipment trust certificate or similar security serving the same purpose is the person by which the property is or will be used or to which the property or equipment is or will be leased or conditionally sold or that is otherwise contractually responsible for assuring payment of the certificate.

(C) The issuer of a fractional undivided interest in an oil, gas, or other mineral lease or in payments out of production under a lease, right, or royalty is the owner of an interest in the lease or in payments out of production under a lease, right, or royalty, whether whole or fractional, that creates fractional interests for the purpose of sale.

(18) "Nonissuer transaction" or "nonissuer distribution" means a transaction or distribution not directly or indirectly for the benefit of the issuer.

(19) "Offer to purchase" includes an attempt or offer to obtain, or solicitation of an offer to sell, a security or interest in a security for value. The term does not include a tender offer that is subject to Section 14(d) of the Securities Exchange Act of 1934 (15 U.S.C. 78n(d)).

(20) "Person" means an individual; corporation; business trust; estate; trust; partnership; limited liability company; association; joint venture; government; governmental subdivision, agency, or instrumentality; public corporation; or any other legal or commercial entity.

(21) "Place of business" of a broker-dealer, an investment adviser, or a federal covered investment adviser means:

(A) an office at which the broker-dealer, investment adviser, or federal covered investment adviser regularly provides brokerage or investment advice or solicits, meets with, or otherwise communicates with customers or clients; or

(B) any other location that is held out to the general public as a location at which the broker-dealer, investment adviser, or federal covered investment adviser provides brokerage or investment advice or solicits, meets with, or otherwise communicates with customers or clients.

(22) "Predecessor act" means the act repealed by Section 702.

(23) "Price amendment" means the amendment to a registration statement filed under the Securities Act of 1933 or, if an amendment is not filed, the prospectus or prospectus supplement filed under the Securities Act of 1933 that includes a statement of the offering price, underwriting and selling discounts or commissions, amount of proceeds, conversion rates, call prices, and other matters dependent upon the offering price.

(24) "Principal place of business" of a broker-dealer or an investment adviser means the executive office of the broker-dealer or investment adviser from which the officers, partners, or managers of the broker-dealer or investment adviser direct, control, and coordinate the activities of the broker-dealer or investment adviser.

(25) "Record," except in the phrases "of record," "official record," and "public record," means information that is inscribed on a tangible medium or that is stored in an electronic or other medium and is retrievable in perceivable form.

(26) "Sale" includes every contract of sale, contract to sell, or disposition of, a security or interest in a security for value, and "offer to sell" includes every attempt or offer to dispose of, or solicitation of an offer to purchase, a security or interest in a security for value. Both terms include:

(A) a security given or delivered with, or as a bonus on account of, a purchase of securities or any other thing constituting part of the subject of the purchase and having been offered and sold for value;

(B) a gift of assessable stock involving an offer and sale; and

(C) a sale or offer of a warrant or right to purchase or subscribe to another security of the same or another issuer and a sale or offer of a security that gives the holder a present or future right or privilege to convert the security into another security of the same or another issuer, including an offer of the other security.

(27) "Securities and Exchange Commission" means the United States Securities and Exchange Commission.

(28) "Security" means a note; stock; treasury stock; security future; bond; debenture; evidence of indebtedness; certificate of interest or participation in a profit-sharing agreement; collateral trust certificate; preorganization certificate or subscription; transferable share; investment contract; voting trust certificate; certificate of deposit for a security; fractional undivided interest in oil, gas, or other mineral rights; put, call, straddle, option, or privilege on a security, certificate of deposit, or group or index of securities, including an interest therein or based on the value thereof; put, call, straddle, option, or privilege entered into on a national securities exchange relating to foreign currency; or, in general, an interest or instrument commonly known as a "security"; or a certificate of interest or participation in, temporary or interim certificate for, receipt for, guarantee of, or warrant or right to subscribe to or purchase, any of the foregoing. The term:

(A) includes both a certificated and an uncertificated security;

(B) does not include an insurance or endowment policy or annuity contract under which an insurance company promises to pay a fixed [or variable] sum of money either in a lump sum or periodically for life or other specified period;

(C) does not include an interest in a contributory or noncontributory pension or welfare plan subject to the Employee Retirement Income Security Act of 1974;

(D) includes as an "investment contract" an investment in a common enterprise with the expectation of profits to be derived primarily from the efforts of a person other than the investor and a "common enterprise" means an enterprise in which the fortunes of the investor are interwoven with those of either the person offering the investment, a third party, or other investors; and

(E) includes as an "investment contract," among other contracts, an interest in a limited partnership and a limited liability company and an investment in a viatical settlement or similar agreement.

(29) "Self-regulatory organization" means a national securities exchange registered under the Securities Exchange Act of 1934, a national securities association of broker-dealers registered under the Securities Exchange Act of 1934, a clearing agency registered under the Securities Exchange Act of 1934, or the Municipal Securities Rulemaking Board established under the Securities Exchange Act of 1934.

(30) "Sign" means, with present intent to authenticate or adopt a record:

(A) to execute or adopt a tangible symbol; or

(B) to attach or logically associate with the record an electronic symbol, sound, or process.

(31) "State" means a State of the United States, the District of Columbia, Puerto Rico, the United States Virgin Islands, or any territory or insular possession subject to the jurisdiction of the United States.

§ 103. REFERENCES TO FEDERAL STATUTES. "Securities Act of 1933" (15 U.S.C. Section 77a et seq.), "Securities Exchange Act of 1934" (15 U.S.C. Section 78a et seq.), "Public Utility Holding Company Act of 1935"(15 U.S.C. Section 79 et seq.), "Investment Company Act of 1940" (15 U.S.C. Section 80a–1 et seq.), "Investment Advisers Act of 1940" (15 U.S.C. Section 80b–1 et seq.), "Employee Retirement Income Security Act of 1974" (29 U.S.C. Section 1001 et seq.), "National Housing Act" (12 U.S.C. Section 1701 et seq.), "Commodity Exchange Act" (7 U.S.C. Section 1 et seq.), "Internal Revenue Code" (26 U.S.C. Section 1 et seq.), "Securities Investor Protection Act of 1970" (15 U.S.C. Section 78aaa et seq.), "Securities Litigation Uniform Standards Act of 1998" (112 Stat. 3227), "Small Business Investment Act of 1958" (15 U.S.C. Section 661 et seq.), and "Electronic Signatures in Global and National Commerce Act" (15 U.S.C. Section 7001 et seq.) mean those statutes and the rules and regulations adopted under those statutes, as in effect on the date of enactment of this [Act] [, or as later amended].

§ 104. REFERENCES TO FEDERAL AGENCIES. A reference in this [Act] to an agency or department of the United States is also a reference to a successor agency or department.

§ 105. ELECTRONIC RECORDS AND SIGNATURES. This [Act] modifies, limits, and supersedes the federal Electronic Signatures in Global and National Commerce Act, but does not modify, limit, or supersede Section 101(c) of that act (15 U.S.C. Section 7001(c)) or authorize electronic delivery of any of the notices described in Section 103(b) of that act (15 U.S.C. Section 7003(b)). This [Act] authorizes the filing of records and signatures, when specified by provisions of this [Act] or by a rule adopted or order issued under this [Act], in a manner consistent with Section 104(a) of that act (15 U.S.C. Section 7004(a)).

[ARTICLE] 2

EXEMPTIONS FROM REGISTRATION OF SECURITIES

§ 201. EXEMPT SECURITIES. The following securities are exempt from the requirements of Sections 301 through 306 and 504:

(1) a security, including a revenue obligation or a separate security as defined in Rule 131 (17 C.F.R. 230.131) adopted under the Securities Act of 1933, issued, insured, or guaranteed by the United States; by a State; by a political subdivision of a State; by a public authority, agency, or instrumentality of one or more States; by a political subdivision of one or more States; or by a person controlled or supervised by and acting as an instrumentality of the United States under authority granted by the Congress; or a certificate of deposit for any of the foregoing;

(2) a security issued, insured, or guaranteed by a foreign government with which the United States maintains diplomatic relations, or any of its political subdivisions, if the security is recognized as a valid obligation by the issuer, insurer, or guarantor;

(3) a security issued by and representing or that will represent an interest in or a direct obligation of, or be guaranteed by:

(A) an international banking institution;

(B) a banking institution organized under the laws of the United States; a member bank of the Federal Reserve System; or a depository institution a substantial portion of the business of which consists or will consist of receiving deposits or share accounts that are insured to the maximum amount authorized by statute by the Federal Deposit Insurance Corporation, the National Credit Union Share Insurance Fund, or a successor authorized by federal law or exercising fiduciary powers that are similar to those permitted for national banks under the authority of the Comptroller of Currency pursuant to Section 1 of Public Law 87–722 (12 U.S.C. Section 92a); or

(C) any other depository institution, unless by rule or order the administrator proceeds under Section 204;

(4) a security issued by and representing an interest in, or a debt of, or insured or guaranteed by, an insurance company authorized to do business in this State;

(5) a security issued or guaranteed by a railroad, other common carrier, public utility, or public utility holding company that is:

(A) regulated in respect to its rates and charges by the United States or a State;

(B) regulated in respect to the issuance or guarantee of the security by the United States, a State, Canada, or a Canadian province or territory; or

(C) a public utility holding company registered under the Public Utility Holding Company Act of 1935 or a subsidiary of such a registered holding company within the meaning of that act;

(6) a federal covered security specified in Section 18(b)(1) of the Securities Act of 1933 (15 U.S.C. Section 77r(b)(1)) or by rule adopted under that provision or a security listed or approved for listing on another securities market specified by rule under this [Act]; a put or a call option contract; a warrant; a subscription right on or with respect to such securities; or an option or similar derivative security on a security or an index of securities or foreign currencies issued by a clearing agency registered under the Securities Exchange Act of 1934 and listed or designated for trading on a national securities exchange, a facility of a national securities exchange, or a facility of a national securities association registered under the Securities Exchange Act of 1934 or an offer or sale, of the underlying security in connection with the offer, sale, or exercise of an option or other security that was exempt when the option or other security was written or issued; or an option or a derivative security designated by the Securities and Exchange Commission under Section 9(b) of the Securities Exchange Act of 1934 (15 U.S.C. Section 78i(b));

(7) a security issued by a person organized and operated exclusively for religious, educational, benevolent, fraternal, charitable, social, athletic, or reformatory purposes, or as a chamber of commerce, and not for pecuniary profit, no part of the net earnings of which inures to the benefit of a private stockholder or other person, or a security of a company that is excluded from the definition of an investment company under Section 3(c)(10)(B) of the Investment Company Act of 1940 (15 U.S.C. Section 80a–3(c)(10)(B)); except that with respect to the offer or sale of a note, bond, debenture, or other evidence of indebtedness issued by such a person, a rule may be adopted under this [Act] limiting the availability of this exemption by classifying securities, persons, and transactions, imposing different requirements for different classes, specifying with respect to paragraph (B) the scope of the exemption and the grounds for denial or suspension, and requiring an issuer:

(A) to file a notice specifying the material terms of the proposed offer or sale and copies of any proposed sales and advertising literature to be used and provide that the exemption becomes effective if the administrator does not disallow the exemption within the period established by the rule;

(B) to file a request for exemption authorization for which a rule under this [Act] may specify the scope of the exemption, the requirement of an offering statement, the filing of sales and advertising literature, the filing of consent to service of process complying with Section 611, and grounds for denial or suspension of the exemption; or

(C) to register under Section 304;

(8) a member's or owner's interest in, or a retention certificate or like security given in lieu of a cash patronage dividend issued by, a cooperative organized and operated as a nonprofit membership cooperative under the cooperative laws of a State, but not a member's or owner's interest, retention certificate, or like security sold to persons other than bona fide members of the cooperative; and

(9) an equipment trust certificate with respect to equipment leased or conditionally sold to a person, if any security issued by the person would be exempt under this section or would be a federal covered security under Section 18(b)(1) of the Securities Act of 1933 (15 U.S.C. Section 77r(b)(1)).

§ 202. EXEMPT TRANSACTIONS. The following transactions are exempt from the requirements of Sections 301 through 306 and 504:

(1) an isolated nonissuer transaction, whether effected by or through a broker-dealer or not;

(2) a nonissuer transaction by or through a broker-dealer registered, or exempt from registration under this [Act], and a resale transaction by a sponsor of a unit investment trust registered under the Investment Company Act of 1940, in a security of a class that has been outstanding in the hands of the public for at least 90 days, if, at the date of the transaction:

(A) the issuer of the security is engaged in business, the issuer is not in the organizational stage or in bankruptcy or receivership, and the issuer is not a blank check, blind pool, or shell company that has no specific business plan or purpose or has indicated that its primary business plan is to engage in a merger or combination of the business with, or an acquisition of, an unidentified person;

(B) the security is sold at a price reasonably related to its current market price;

(C) the security does not constitute the whole or part of an unsold allotment to, or a subscription or participation by, the broker-dealer as an underwriter of the security or a redistribution; and

(D) a nationally recognized securities manual or its electronic equivalent designated by rule adopted or order issued under this [Act] or a record filed with the Securities and Exchange Commission that is publicly available contains:

(i) a description of the business and operations of the issuer;

(ii) the names of the issuer's executive officers and the names of the issuer's directors, if any;

(iii) an audited balance sheet of the issuer as of a date within 18 months before the date of the transaction or, in the case of a reorganization or merger when the parties to the reorganization or merger each had an audited balance sheet, a pro forma balance sheet for the combined organization; and

(iv) an audited income statement for each of the issuer's two immediately previous fiscal years or for the period of existence of the issuer, whichever is shorter, or, in the case of a reorganization or merger when each party to the reorganization or merger had audited income statements, a pro forma income statement; or

(E) the issuer of the security has a class of equity securities listed on a national securities exchange registered under the Securities Exchange Act of 1934 or designated for trading on the National Association of Securities Dealers Automated Quotation System, unless the issuer of the security is a unit investment trust registered under the Investment Company Act of 1940; or the issuer of the security, including its predecessors, has been engaged in continuous business for at least three years; or the issuer of the security has total assets of at least $2,000,000 based on an audited balance sheet as of a date within 18 months before the date of the transaction or, in the case of a reorganization or merger when the parties to the reorganization or merger each had the audited balance sheet, a pro forma balance sheet for the combined organization;

(3) a nonissuer transaction by or through a broker-dealer registered or exempt from registration under this [Act] in a security of a foreign issuer that is a margin security defined in regulations or rules adopted by the Board of Governors of the Federal Reserve System;

(4) a nonissuer transaction by or through a broker-dealer registered or exempt from registration under this [Act] in an outstanding security if the guarantor of the security files reports with the Securities and Exchange Commission under the reporting requirements of Section 13 or 15(d) of the Securities Exchange Act of 1934 (15 U.S.C. 78m or 78o(d));

(5) a nonissuer transaction by or through a broker-dealer registered or exempt from registration under this [Act] in a security that:

(A) is rated at the time of the transaction by a nationally recognized statistical rating organization in one of its four highest rating categories; or

(B) has a fixed maturity or a fixed interest or dividend, if:

(i) a default has not occurred during the current fiscal year or within the three previous fiscal years or during the existence of the issuer and any predecessor if less than three fiscal years, in the payment of principal, interest, or dividends on the security; and

(ii) the issuer is engaged in business, is not in the organizational stage or in bankruptcy or receivership, and is not and has not been within the previous 12 months a blank check, blind pool, or shell company that has no specific business plan or purpose or has indicated that its primary business plan is to engage in a merger or combination of the business with, or an acquisition of, an unidentified person;

(6) a nonissuer transaction by or through a broker-dealer registered or exempt from registration under this [Act] effecting an unsolicited order or offer to purchase;

(7) a nonissuer transaction executed by a bona fide pledgee without the purpose of evading this [Act];

(8) a nonissuer transaction by a federal covered investment adviser with investments under management in excess of $100,000,000 acting in the exercise of discretionary authority in a signed record for the account of others;

(9) a transaction in a security, whether or not the security or transaction is otherwise exempt, in exchange for one or more bona fide outstanding securities, claims, or property interests, or partly in such exchange and partly for cash, if the terms and conditions of the issuance and exchange or the delivery and exchange and the fairness of the terms and

conditions have been approved by the administrator after a hearing;

(10) a transaction between the issuer or other person on whose behalf the offering is made and an underwriter, or among underwriters;

(11) a transaction in a note, bond, debenture, or other evidence of indebtedness secured by a mortgage or other security agreement if:

(A) the note, bond, debenture, or other evidence of indebtedness is offered and sold with the mortgage or other security agreement as a unit;

(B) a general solicitation or general advertisement of the transaction is not made; and

(C) a commission or other remuneration is not paid or given, directly or indirectly, to a person not registered under this [Act] as a broker-dealer or as an agent;

(12) a transaction by an executor, administrator of an estate, sheriff, marshal, receiver, trustee in bankruptcy, guardian, or conservator;

(13) a sale or offer to sell to:

(A) an institutional investor;

(B) a federal covered investment adviser; or

(C) any other person exempted by rule adopted or order issued under this [Act];

(14) a sale or an offer to sell securities by an issuer, if the transaction is part of a single issue in which:

(A) not more than 25 purchasers are present in this State during any 12 consecutive months, other than those designated in paragraph (13);

(B) a general solicitation or general advertising is not made in connection with the offer to sell or sale of the securities;

(C) a commission or other remuneration is not paid or given, directly or indirectly, to a person other than a broker-dealer registered under this [Act] or an agent registered under this [Act] for soliciting a prospective purchaser in this State; and

(D) the issuer reasonably believes that all the purchasers in this State, other than those designated in paragraph (13), are purchasing for investment;

(15) a transaction under an offer to existing security holders of the issuer, including persons that at the date of the transaction are holders of convertible securities, options, or warrants, if a commission or other remuneration, other than a standby commission, is not paid or given, directly or indirectly, for soliciting a security holder in this State;

(16) an offer to sell, but not a sale, of a security not exempt from registration under the Securities Act of 1933 if:

(A) a registration or offering statement or similar record as required under the Securities Act of 1933 has been filed, but is not effective, or the offer is made in compliance with Rule 165 adopted under the Securities Act of 1933 (17 C.F.R. 230.165); and

(B) a stop order of which the offeror is aware has not been issued against the offeror by the administrator or the Securities and Exchange Commission, and an audit, inspection, or proceeding that is public and that may culminate in a stop order is not known by the offeror to be pending;

(17) an offer to sell, but not a sale, of a security exempt from registration under the Securities Act of 1933 if:

(A) a registration statement has been filed under this [Act], but is not effective;

(B) a solicitation of interest is provided in a record to offerees in compliance with a rule adopted by the administrator under this [Act]; and

(C) a stop order of which the offeror is aware has not been issued by the administrator under this [Act] and an audit, inspection, or proceeding that may culminate in a stop order is not known by the offeror to be pending;

(18) a transaction involving the distribution of the securities of an issuer to the security holders of another person in connection with a merger, consolidation, exchange of securities, sale of assets, or other reorganization to which the issuer, or its parent or subsidiary and the other person, or its parent or subsidiary, are parties;

(19) a rescission offer, sale, or purchase under Section 510;

(20) an offer or sale of a security to a person not a resident of this State and not present in this State if the offer or sale does not constitute a violation of the laws of the State or foreign jurisdiction in which the offeree or purchaser is present and is not part of an unlawful plan or scheme to evade this [Act];

(21) employees' stock purchase, savings, option, profit-sharing, pension, or similar employees' benefit plan, including any securities, plan interests, and guarantees issued under a compensatory benefit plan or compensation contract, contained in a record, established by the issuer, its parents, its majority-owned subsidiaries, or the majority-owned subsidiaries of the issuer's parent for the participation of their employees including offers or sales of such securities to:

(A) directors; general partners; trustees, if the issuer is a business trust; officers; consultants; and advisors;

(B) family members who acquire such securities from those persons through gifts or domestic relations orders;

(C) former employees, directors, general partners, trustees, officers, consultants, and advisors if those individuals were employed by or providing services to the issuer when the securities were offered; and

(D) insurance agents who are exclusive insurance agents of the issuer, or the issuer's subsidiaries or parents, or who derive more than 50 percent of their annual income from those organizations;

(22) a transaction involving:

(A) a stock dividend or equivalent equity distribution, whether the corporation or other business organization distributing the dividend or equivalent equity distribution is the issuer or not, if nothing of value is given by stockholders or other equity holders for the dividend or equivalent equity distribution other than the surrender of a right to a cash or property dividend if each stockholder or other equity holder may elect to take the dividend or equivalent equity distribution in cash, property, or stock;

(B) an act incident to a judicially approved reorganization in which a security is issued in exchange for one or more outstanding securities, claims, or property interests, or partly in such exchange and partly for cash; or

(C) the solicitation of tenders of securities by an offeror in a tender offer in compliance with Rule 162 adopted under the Securities Act of 1933 (17 C.F.R. 230.162); or

(23) a nonissuer transaction in an outstanding security by or through a broker-dealer registered or exempt from registration under this [Act], if the issuer is a reporting issuer in a foreign jurisdiction designated by this paragraph or by rule adopted or order issued under this [Act]; has been subject to continuous reporting requirements in the foreign jurisdiction for not less than 180 days before the transaction; and the security is listed on the foreign jurisdiction's securities exchange that has been designated by this paragraph or by rule adopted or order issued under this [Act], or is a security of the same issuer that is of senior or substantially equal rank to the listed security or is a warrant or right to purchase or subscribe to any of the foregoing. For purposes of this paragraph, Canada, together with its provinces and territories, is a designated foreign jurisdiction and The Toronto Stock Exchange, Inc., is a designated securities exchange. After an administrative hearing in compliance with [the state administrative procedure act], the administrator, by rule adopted or order issued under this [Act], may revoke the designation of a securities exchange under this paragraph, if the administrator finds that revocation is necessary or appropriate in the public interest and for the protection of investors.

§ 203. ADDITIONAL EXEMPTIONS AND WAIVERS. A rule adopted or order issued under this [Act] may exempt a security, transaction, or offer; a rule under this [Act] may exempt a class of securities, transactions, or offers from any or all of the requirements of Sections 301 through 306 and 504; and an order under this [Act] may waive, in whole or in part, any or all of the conditions for an exemption or offer under Sections 201 and 202.

§ 204. DENIAL, SUSPENSION, REVOCATION, CONDITION, OR LIMITATION OF EXEMPTIONS.

(a) [**Enforcement Related Powers.**] Except with respect to a federal covered security or a transaction involving a federal covered security, an order under this [Act] may deny, suspend application of, condition, limit, or revoke an exemption created under Section 201(3)(C), (7) or (8) or 202 or an exemption or waiver created under Section 203 with respect to a specific security, transaction, or offer. An order under this section may be issued only pursuant to the procedures in Section 306(d) or 604 and only prospectively.

(b) [**Knowledge of Order Required.**] A person does not violate Section 301, 303 through 306, 504, or 510 by an offer to sell, offer to purchase, sale, or purchase effected after the entry of an order issued under this section if the person did not know, and in the exercise of reasonable care could not have known, of the order.

[ARTICLE] 3

REGISTRATION OF SECURITIES AND NOTICE FILING OF FEDERAL COVERED SECURITIES

§ 301. SECURITIES REGISTRATION REQUIREMENT. It is unlawful for a person to offer or sell a security in this State unless:

(1) the security is a federal covered security;

(2) the security, transaction, or offer is exempted from registration under Sections 201 through 203; or

(3) the security is registered under this [Act].

§ 302. NOTICE FILING.

(a) [**Required Filing of Records.**] With respect to a federal covered security, as defined in Section 18(b)(2) of the Securities Act of 1933 (15 U.S.C. Section 77r(b)(2)), that is not otherwise exempt under Sections 201 through 203, a rule adopted or order issued under this [Act] may require the filing of any or all of the following records:

(1) before the initial offer of a federal covered security in this State, all records that are part of a federal registration statement filed with the Securities and Exchange Commission under the Securities Act of 1933 and a consent to service of process complying with Section 611 signed by the issuer and the payment of a fee of $[___];

(2) after the initial offer of the federal covered security in this State, all records that are part of an amendment to a federal registration statement filed with the Securities and Exchange Commission under the Securities Act of 1933; and

(3) to the extent necessary or appropriate to compute fees, a report of the value of the federal covered securities sold or offered to persons present in this State, if the sales data are not included in records filed with the Securities and Exchange Commission and payment of a fee of $[___].

(b) [**Notice Filing Effectiveness and Renewal.**] A notice filing under subsection (a) is effective for one year commencing on the later of the notice filing or the effectiveness of the offering filed with the Securities and Exchange Commission. On or before expiration, the issuer may renew a notice filing by filing a copy of those records filed by the issuer with the Securities and Exchange Commission that are required by rule or order under this [Act] to be filed and by paying a renewal fee of $[___]. A previously filed consent to service of process complying with Section 611 may be incorporated by reference in a renewal. A renewed notice filing becomes effective upon the expiration of the filing being renewed.

(c) [**Notice Filings for Federal Covered Securities under Section 18(b)(4)(D).**] With respect to a security that is a federal covered security under Section 18(b)(4)(D) of the Securities Act of 1933(15 U.S.C. Section 77r(b)(4)(D)), a rule under this [Act] may require a notice filing by or on behalf of an issuer to include a copy of Form D, including the Appendix, as promulgated by the Securities and Exchange Commission, and a consent to service of process complying with Section 611 signed by the issuer not later than 15 days after the first sale of the federal covered security in this State and the payment of a fee of $[___]; and the payment of a fee of $[___] for any late filing.

(d) [**Stop Orders.**] Except with respect to a federal security under Section 181(b)(1) of the Securities Act of 1933 (15 U.S.C. Section 77r(b)(1)), if the administrator finds that there is a failure to comply with a notice or fee requirement of this section, the administrator may issue a stop order suspending the offer and sale of a federal covered security in this State. If the deficiency is corrected, the stop order is void as of the time of its issuance and no penalty may be imposed by the administrator.

§ 303. SECURITIES REGISTRATION BY COORDINATION.

(a) [**Registration Permitted.**] A security for which a registration statement has been filed under the Securities Act of 1933 in connection with the same offering may be registered by coordination under this section.

(b) [**Required Records.**] A registration statement and accompanying records under this section must contain or be accompanied by the following records in addition to the information specified in Section 305 and a consent to service of process complying with Section 611:

(1) a copy of the latest form of prospectus filed under the Securities Act of 1933;

(2) a copy of the articles of incorporation and bylaws or their substantial equivalents currently in effect; a copy of any agreement with or among underwriters; a copy of any indenture or other instrument governing the issuance of the security to be registered; and a specimen, copy, or description of the security that is required by rule adopted or order issued under this [Act];

(3) copies of any other information or any other records filed by the issuer under the Securities Act of 1933 requested by the administrator; and

(4) an undertaking to forward each amendment to the federal prospectus, other than an amendment that delays the effective date of the registration statement, promptly after it is filed with the Securities and Exchange Commission.

(c) [**Conditions for Effectiveness of Registration Statement.**] A registration statement under this section becomes effective simultaneously with or subsequent to the federal registration statement when all the following conditions are satisfied:

(1) a stop order under subsection (d) or Section 306 or issued by the Securities and Exchange Commission is not in effect and a proceeding is not pending against the issuer under Section 306; and

(2) the registration statement has been on file for at least 20 days or a shorter period provided by rule adopted or order issued under this [Act].

(d) [**Notice of Federal Registration Statement Effectiveness.**] The registrant shall promptly notify the administrator in a record of the date when the federal registration statement becomes effective and the content of any price amendment and shall promptly file a record containing the price amendment. If the notice is not timely received, the administrator may issue a stop order, without prior notice or hearing, retroactively denying effectiveness to the registration statement or suspending its effectiveness until compliance with this section. The administrator shall promptly notify the registrant of an order by telegram, telephone, or electronic means and promptly confirm this notice by a record. If the registrant subsequently complies with the notice requirements of this section, the stop order is void as of the date of its issuance.

(e) [**Effectiveness of Registration Statement.**] If the federal registration statement becomes effective before each of the conditions in this section is satisfied or is waived by the administrator, the registration statement is automatically effective under this [Act] when all the conditions are satisfied or waived. If the registrant notifies the administrator of the date when the federal registration statement is expected to become effective, the administrator shall promptly notify the registrant by telegram, telephone, or electronic means and promptly confirm this notice by a record, indicating whether all the conditions are satisfied or waived and whether the administrator intends the institution of a proceeding under Section 306. The notice by the administrator does not preclude the institution of such a proceeding.

§ 304. SECURITIES REGISTRATION BY QUALIFICATION.

(a) [**Registration Permitted.**] A security may be registered by qualification under this section.

(b) [**Required Records.**] A registration statement under this section must contain the information or records specified in Section 305, a consent to service of process complying with Section 611, and, if required by rule adopted under this [Act], the following information or records:

(1) with respect to the issuer and any significant subsidiary, its name, address, and form of organization; the State or foreign jurisdiction and date of its organization; the general character and location of its business; a description of its physical properties and equipment; and a statement of the general competitive conditions in the industry or business in which it is or will be engaged;

(2) with respect to each director and officer of the issuer, and other person having a similar status or performing similar functions, the person's name, address, and principal occupation for the previous five years; the amount of securities of the issuer held by the person as of the 30th day before the filing of the registration statement; the amount of the securities covered by the registration statement to which the person has indicated an intention to subscribe; and a description of any material interest of the person in any material transaction with the issuer or a significant subsidiary effected within the previous three years or proposed to be effected;

(3) with respect to persons covered by paragraph (2), the aggregate sum of the remuneration paid to those persons during the previous 12 months and estimated to be paid during the next 12 months, directly or indirectly, by the issuer, and all predecessors, parents, subsidiaries, and affiliates of the issuer;

(4) with respect to a person owning of record or owning beneficially, if known, 10 percent or more of the outstanding shares of any class of equity security of the issuer, the information specified in paragraph (2) other than the person's occupation;

(5) with respect to a promoter, if the issuer was organized within the previous three years, the information or records specified in paragraph (2), any amount paid to the promoter within that peri-

od or intended to be paid to the promoter, and the consideration for the payment;

(6) with respect to a person on whose behalf any part of the offering is to be made in a nonissuer distribution, the person's name and address; the amount of securities of the issuer held by the person as of the date of the filing of the registration statement; a description of any material interest of the person in any material transaction with the issuer or any significant subsidiary effected within the previous three years or proposed to be effected; and a statement of the reasons for making the offering;

(7) the capitalization and long term debt, on both a current and pro forma basis, of the issuer and any significant subsidiary, including a description of each security outstanding or being registered or otherwise offered, and a statement of the amount and kind of consideration, whether in the form of cash, physical assets, services, patents, goodwill, or anything else of value, for which the issuer or any subsidiary has issued its securities within the previous two years or is obligated to issue its securities;

(8) the kind and amount of securities to be offered; the proposed offering price or the method by which it is to be computed; any variation at which a proportion of the offering is to be made to a person or class of persons other than the underwriters, with a specification of the person or class; the basis on which the offering is to be made if otherwise than for cash; the estimated aggregate underwriting and selling discounts or commissions and finders' fees, including separately cash, securities, contracts, or anything else of value to accrue to the underwriters or finders in connection with the offering or, if the selling discounts or commissions are variable, the basis of determining them and their maximum and minimum amounts; the estimated amounts of other selling expenses, including legal, engineering, and accounting charges; the name and address of each underwriter and each recipient of a finder's fee; a copy of any underwriting or selling group agreement under which the distribution is to be made or the proposed form of any such agreement whose terms have not yet been determined; and a description of the plan of distribution of any securities that are to be offered otherwise than through an underwriter;

(9) the estimated monetary proceeds to be received by the issuer from the offering; the purposes for which the proceeds are to be used by the issuer; the estimated amount to be used for each purpose; the order or priority in which the proceeds will be used for the purposes stated; the amounts of any funds to be raised from other sources to achieve the purposes stated; the sources of the funds; and, if a part of the proceeds is to be used to acquire property, including goodwill, otherwise than in the ordinary course of business, the names and addresses of the vendors, the purchase price, the names of any persons that have received commissions in connection with the acquisition, and the amounts of the commissions and other expenses in connection with the acquisition, including the cost of borrowing money to finance the acquisition;

(10) a description of any stock options or other security options outstanding, or to be created in connection with the offering, and the amount of those options held or to be held by each person required to be named in paragraph (2), (4), (5), (6), or (8) and by any person that holds or will hold 10 percent or more in the aggregate of those options;

(11) the dates of, parties to, and general effect concisely stated of each managerial or other material contract made or to be made otherwise than in the ordinary course of business to be performed in whole or in part at or after the filing of the registration statement or that was made within the previous two years, and a copy of the contract;

(12) a description of any pending litigation, action, or proceeding to which the issuer is a party and that materially affects its business or assets, and any litigation, action, or proceeding known to be contemplated by governmental authorities;

(13) a copy of any prospectus, pamphlet, circular, form letter, advertisement, or other sales literature intended as of the effective date to be used in connection with the offering and any solicitation of interest used in compliance with Section 202(17)(B);

(14) a specimen or copy of the security being registered, unless the security is uncertificated; a copy of the issuer's articles of incorporation and bylaws or their substantial equivalents, in effect; and a copy of any indenture or other instrument covering the security to be registered;

(15) a signed or conformed copy of an opinion of counsel concerning the legality of the security being registered, with an English translation if it is in a language other than English, which states whether the security when sold will be validly is-

sued, fully paid, and nonassessable and, if a debt security, a binding obligation of the issuer;

(16) a signed or conformed copy of a consent of any accountant, engineer, appraiser, or other person whose profession gives authority for a statement made by the person, if the person is named as having prepared or certified a report or valuation, other than an official record, that is public, which is used in connection with the registration statement;

(17) a balance sheet of the issuer as of a date within four months before the filing of the registration statement; a statement of income and a statement of cash flows for each of the three fiscal years preceding the date of the balance sheet and for any period between the close of the immediately previous fiscal year and the date of the balance sheet, or for the period of the issuer's and any predecessor's existence if less than three years; and, if any part of the proceeds of the offering is to be applied to the purchase of a business, the financial statements that would be required if that business were the registrant; and

(18) any additional information or records required by rule adopted or order issued under this [Act].

(c) [**Conditions for Effectiveness of Registration Statement.**] A registration statement under this section becomes effective 30 days, or any shorter period provided by rule adopted or order issued under this [Act], after the date the registration statement or the last amendment other than a price amendment is filed, if:

(1) a stop order is not in effect and a proceeding is not pending under Section 306;

(2) the administrator has not issued an order under Section 306 delaying effectiveness; and

(3) the applicant or registrant has not requested that effectiveness be delayed.

(d) [**Delay of Effectiveness of Registration Statement.**] The administrator may delay effectiveness once for not more than 90 days if the administrator determines the registration statement is not complete in all material respects and promptly notifies the applicant or registrant of that determination. The administrator may also delay effectiveness for a further period of not more than 30 days if the administrator determines that the delay is necessary or appropriate.

(e) [**Prospectus Distribution May Be Required.**] A rule adopted or order issued under this [Act] may require as a condition of registration under this section that a prospectus containing a specified part of the information or record specified in subsection (b) be sent or given to each person to which an offer is made, before or concurrently, with the earliest of:

(1) the first offer made in a record to the person otherwise than by means of a public advertisement, by or for the account of the issuer or another person on whose behalf the offering is being made or by an underwriter or broker-dealer that is offering part of an unsold allotment or subscription taken by the person as a participant in the distribution;

(2) the confirmation of a sale made by or for the account of the person;

(3) payment pursuant to such a sale; or

(4) delivery of the security pursuant to such a sale.

§ 305. SECURITIES REGISTRATION FILINGS.

(a) [**Who May File.**] A registration statement may be filed by the issuer, a person on whose behalf the offering is to be made, or a broker-dealer registered under this [Act].

(b) [**Filing Fee.**] A person filing a registration statement shall pay a filing fee of $[____]. If a registration statement is withdrawn before the effective date or a pre-effective stop order is issued under Section 306, the administrator shall retain $[____] of the fee.

(c) [**Status of Offering.**] A registration statement filed under Section 303 or 304 must specify:

(1) the amount of securities to be offered in this State;

(2) the States in which a registration statement or similar record in connection with the offering has been or is to be filed; and

(3) any adverse order, judgment, or decree issued in connection with the offering by a State securities regulator, the Securities and Exchange Commission, or a court.

(d) [**Incorporation by Reference.**] A record filed under this [Act] or the predecessor act within five years preceding the filing of a registration statement may be incorporated by reference in the registration statement to the extent that the record is currently accurate.

(e) [**Nonissuer Distribution.**] In the case of a nonissuer distribution, information or a record may not be required under subsection (i) or Section 304, unless it is known to the person filing the registration statement or to the person on whose behalf the distribution is to be made or unless it can be furnished by those persons without unreasonable effort or expense.

(f) [**Escrow and Impoundment.**] A rule adopted or order issued under this [Act] may require as a condition of registration that a security issued within the previous five years or to be issued to a promoter for a consideration substantially less than the public offering price or to a person for a consideration other than cash be deposited in escrow; and that the proceeds from the sale of the registered security in this State be impounded until the issuer receives a specified amount from the sale of the security either in this State or elsewhere. The conditions of any escrow or impoundment required under this subsection may be established by rule adopted or order issued under this [Act], but the administrator may not reject a depository institution solely because of its location in another State.

(g) [**Form of Subscription.**] A rule adopted or order issued under this [Act] may require as a condition of registration that a security registered under this [Act] be sold only on a specified form of subscription or sale contract and that a signed or conformed copy of each contract be filed under this [Act] or preserved for a period specified by the rule or order, which may not be longer than five years.

(h) [**Effective Period.**] Except while a stop order is in effect under Section 306, a registration statement is effective for one year after its effective date, or for any longer period designated in an order under this [Act] during which the security is being offered or distributed in a nonexempted transaction by or for the account of the issuer or other person on whose behalf the offering is being made or by an underwriter or broker-dealer that is still offering part of an unsold allotment or subscription taken as a participant in the distribution. For the purposes of a nonissuer transaction, all outstanding securities of the same class identified in the registration statement as a security registered under this [Act] are considered to be registered while the registration statement is effective. If any securities of the same class are outstanding, a registration statement may not be withdrawn until one year after its effective date. A registration statement may be withdrawn only with the approval of the administrator.

(i) [**Periodic Reports.**] While a registration statement is effective, a rule adopted or order issued under this [Act] may require the person that filed the registration statement to file reports, not more often than quarterly, to keep the information or other record in the registration statement reasonably current and to disclose the progress of the offering.

(j) [**Posteffective Amendments.**] A registration statement may be amended after its effective date. The posteffective amendment becomes effective when the administrator so orders. If a posteffective amendment is made to increase the number of securities specified to be offered or sold, the person filing the amendment shall pay a registration fee of $[____]. A posteffective amendment relates back to the date of the offering of the additional securities being registered if, within one year after the date of the sale, the amendment is filed and the additional registration fee is paid.

§ 306. DENIAL, SUSPENSION, AND REVOCATION OF SECURITIES REGISTRATION.

(a) [**Stop Orders.**] The administrator may issue a stop order denying effectiveness to, or suspending or revoking the effectiveness of, a registration statement if the administrator finds that the order is in the public interest and that:

(1) the registration statement as of its effective date or before the effective date in the case of an order denying effectiveness, an amendment under Section 305(j) as of its effective date, or a report under Section 305(i), is incomplete in a material respect or contains a statement that, in the light of the circumstances under which it was made, was false or misleading with respect to a material fact;

(2) this [Act] or a rule adopted or order issued under this [Act] or a condition imposed under this [Act] has been willfully violated, in connection with the offering, by the person filing the registration statement; by the issuer, a partner, officer, or director of the issuer or a person having a similar status or performing a similar function; a promoter of the issuer; or a person directly or indirectly controlling or controlled by the issuer; but only if the person filing the registration statement is directly or indirectly controlled by or acting for the issuer; or by an underwriter;

(3) the security registered or sought to be registered is the subject of a permanent or temporary injunction of a court of competent jurisdiction or

an administrative stop order or similar order issued under any federal, foreign, or state law other than this [Act] applicable to the offering, but the administrator may not institute a proceeding against an effective registration statement under this paragraph more than one year after the date of the order or injunction on which it is based, and the administrator may not issue an order under this paragraph on the basis of an order or injunction issued under the securities act of another State unless the order or injunction was based on conduct that would constitute, as of the date of the order, a ground for a stop order under this section;

(4) the issuer's enterprise or method of business includes or would include activities that are unlawful where performed;

(5) with respect to a security sought to be registered under Section 303, there has been a failure to comply with the undertaking required by Section 303(b)(4);

(6) the applicant or registrant has not paid the filing fee, but the administrator shall void the order if the deficiency is corrected; or

(7) the offering:

(A) will work or tend to work a fraud upon purchasers or would so operate; [or]

(B) has been or would be made with unreasonable amounts of underwriters' and sellers' discounts, commissions, or other compensation, or promoters' profits or participations, or unreasonable amounts or kinds of options[; or

(C) is being made on terms that are unfair, unjust, or inequitable].

(b) **[Enforcement of Subsection (a)(7).]** To the extent practicable, the administrator by rule adopted or order issued under this [Act] shall publish standards that provide notice of conduct that violates subsection (a)(7).

(c) **[Institution of Stop Order.]** The administrator may not institute a stop order proceeding against an effective registration statement on the basis of conduct or a transaction known to the administrator when the registration statement became effective unless the proceeding is instituted within 30 days after the registration statement became effective.

(d) **[Summary Process.]** The administrator may summarily revoke, deny, postpone, or suspend the effectiveness of a registration statement pending final determination of an administrative proceeding. Upon the issuance of the order, the administrator shall promptly notify each person specified in subsection (e) that the order has been issued, the reasons for the revocation, denial, postponement, or suspension, and that within 15 days after the receipt of a request in a record from the person the matter will be scheduled for a hearing. If a hearing is not requested and none is ordered by the administrator, within 30 days after the date of service of the order, the order becomes final. If a hearing is requested or ordered, the administrator, after notice of and opportunity for hearing for each person subject to the order, may modify or vacate the order or extend the order until final determination.

(e) **[Procedural Requirements for Stop Order.]** A stop order may not be issued under this section without:

(1) appropriate notice to the applicant or registrant, the issuer, and the person on whose behalf the securities are to be or have been offered;

(2) an opportunity for hearing; and

(3) findings of fact and conclusions of law in a record [in accordance with the state administrative procedure act].

(f) **[Modification or Vacation of Stop Order.]** The administrator may modify or vacate a stop order issued under this section if the administrator finds that the conditions that caused its issuance have changed or that it is necessary or appropriate in the public interest or for the protection of investors.

§ 307. WAIVER AND MODIFICATION. The administrator may waive or modify, in whole or in part, any or all of the requirements of Sections 302, 303, and 304(b) or the requirement of any information or record in a registration statement or in a periodic report filed pursuant to Section 305(i).

[ARTICLE] 4

BROKER-DEALERS, AGENTS, INVESTMENT ADVISERS, INVESTMENT ADVISER REPRESENTATIVES, AND FEDERAL COVERED INVESTMENT ADVISERS

§ 401. BROKER-DEALER REGISTRATION REQUIREMENT AND EXEMPTIONS.

(a) **[Registration Requirement.]** It is unlawful for a person to transact business in this State as a broker-dealer unless the person is registered under this [Act] as a broker-dealer or is exempt from registration as a broker-dealer under subsection (b) or (d).

(b) **[Exemptions from Registration.]** The following persons are exempt from the registration requirement of subsection (a):

(1) a broker-dealer without a place of business in this State if its only transactions effected in this State are with:

(A) the issuer of the securities involved in the transactions;

(B) a broker-dealer registered under this [Act] or not required to be registered as a broker-dealer under this [Act];

(C) an institutional investor;

(D) a nonaffiliated federal covered investment adviser with investments under management in excess of $100,000,000 acting for the account of others pursuant to discretionary authority in a signed record;

(E) a bona fide preexisting customer whose principal place of residence is not in this State and the person is registered as a broker-dealer under the Securities Exchange Act of 1934 or not required to be registered under the Securities Exchange Act of 1934 and is registered under the securities act of the State in which the customer maintains a principal place of residence;

(F) a bona fide preexisting customer whose principal place of residence is in this State but was not present in this State when the customer relationship was established, if:

(i) the broker-dealer is registered under the Securities Exchange Act of 1934 or not required to be registered under the Securities Exchange Act of 1934 and is registered under the securities laws of the State in which the customer relationship was established and where the customer had maintained a principal place of residence; and

(ii) within 45 days after the customer's first transaction in this State, the person files an application for registration as a broker-dealer in this State and a further transaction is not effected more than 75 days after the date on which the application is filed, or, if earlier, the date on which the administrator notifies the person that the administrator has denied the application for registration or has stayed the pendency of the application for good cause;

(G) not more than three customers in this State during the previous 12 months, in addition to those customers specified in subparagraphs (A) through (F) and under subparagraph (H), if the broker-dealer is registered under the Securities Exchange Act of 1934 or not required to be registered under the Securities Exchange Act of 1934 and is registered under the securities act of the State in which the broker-dealer has its principal place of business; and

(H) any other person exempted by rule adopted or order issued under this [Act]; and

(2) a person that deals solely in United States government securities and is supervised as a dealer in government securities by the Board of Governors of the Federal Reserve System, the Comptroller of the Currency, the Federal Deposit Insurance Corporation, or the Office of Thrift Supervision.

(c) **[Limits on Employment or Association.]** It is unlawful for a broker-dealer, or for an issuer engaged in offering, offering to purchase, purchasing, or selling securities in this State, directly or indirectly, to employ or associate with an individual to engage in an activity related to securities transactions in this State if the registration of the individual is suspended or revoked or the individual is barred from employment or association with a broker-dealer, an issuer, an investment adviser, or a federal covered investment adviser by an order of the administrator under this [Act], the Securities and Exchange Commission, or a self-regulatory organization. A broker-dealer or issuer does not violate this subsection if the broker-dealer or issuer did not know and in the exercise of reasonable care could not have known, of the suspension, revocation, or bar. Upon request from a broker-dealer or issuer and for good cause, an order under this [Act] may modify or waive, in whole or in part, the application of the prohibitions of this subsection to the broker-dealer.

(d) **[Foreign Transactions.]** A rule adopted or order issued under this [Act] may permit:

(1) a broker-dealer that is registered in Canada or other foreign jurisdiction and that does not have a place of business in this State to effect transactions in securities with or for, or attempt to effect the purchase or sale of any securities by:

(A) an individual from Canada or other foreign jurisdiction who is temporarily present in this State and with whom the broker-dealer had a bona fide customer relationship before the individual entered the United States;

(B) an individual from Canada or other foreign jurisdiction who is present in this State and whose transactions are in a self-directed tax advantaged retirement plan of which the individual is the holder or contributor in that foreign jurisdiction; or

(C) an individual who is present in this State, with whom the broker-dealer customer relationship arose while the individual was temporarily or permanently resident in Canada or the other foreign jurisdiction; and

(2) an agent who represents a broker-dealer that is exempt under this subsection to effect transactions in securities or attempt to effect the purchase or sale of securities in this State as permitted for a broker-dealer described in paragraph (1).

§ 402. AGENT REGISTRATION REQUIREMENT AND EXEMPTIONS.

(a) [**Registration Requirement.**] It is unlawful for an individual to transact business in this State as an agent unless the individual is registered under this [Act] as an agent or is exempt from registration as an agent under subsection (b).

(b) [**Exemptions from Registration.**] The following individuals are exempt from the registration requirement of subsection (a):

(1) an individual who represents a broker-dealer in effecting transactions in this State limited to those described in Section 15(h)(2) of the Securities Exchange Act of 1934 (15 U.S.C. Section 78(*o*)(2));

(2) an individual who represents a broker-dealer that is exempt under Section 401(b) or (d);

(3) an individual who represents an issuer with respect to an offer or sale of the issuer's own securities or those of the issuer's parent or any of the issuer's subsidiaries, and who is not compensated in connection with the individual's participation by the payment of commissions or other remuneration based, directly or indirectly, on transactions in those securities;

(4) an individual who represents an issuer and who effects transactions in the issuer's securities exempted by Section 202, other than Section 202(11) and (14);

(5) an individual who represents an issuer that effects transactions solely in federal covered securities of the issuer, but an individual who effects transactions in a federal covered security under Section 18(b)(3) or 18(b)(4)(D) of the Securities Act of 1933 (15 U.S.C. Section 77r(b)(3) or 77r(b)(4)(D)) is not exempt if the individual is compensated in connection with the agent's participation by the payment of commissions or other remuneration based, directly or indirectly, on transactions in those securities;

(6) an individual who represents a broker-dealer registered in this State under Section 401(a) or exempt from registration under Section 401(b) in the offer and sale of securities for an account of a nonaffiliated federal covered investment adviser with investments under management in excess of $100,000,000 acting for the account of others pursuant to discretionary authority in a signed record;

(7) an individual who represents an issuer in connection with the purchase of the issuer's own securities;

(8) an individual who represents an issuer and who restricts participation to performing clerical or ministerial acts; or

(9) any other individual exempted by rule adopted or order issued under this [Act].

(c) [**Registration Effective Only While Employed or Associated.**] The registration of an agent is effective only while the agent is employed by or associated with a broker-dealer registered under this [Act] or an issuer that is offering, selling, or purchasing its securities in this State.

(d) [**Limit on Employment or Association.**] It is unlawful for a broker-dealer, or an issuer engaged in offering, selling, or purchasing securities in this State, to employ or associate with an agent who transacts business in this State on behalf of broker-dealers or issuers unless the agent is registered under subsection (a) or exempt from registration under subsection (b).

(e) [**Limit on Affiliations.**] An individual may not act as an agent for more than one broker-dealer or one issuer at a time, unless the broker-dealer or the issuer for which the agent acts are affiliated by direct or indirect common control or are authorized by rule or order under this [Act].

§ 403. INVESTMENT ADVISER REGISTRATION REQUIREMENT AND EXEMPTIONS.

(a) [**Registration Requirement.**] It is unlawful for a person to transact business in this State as an investment adviser unless the person is registered under this [Act] as an investment adviser or is exempt from registration as an investment adviser under subsection (b).

(b) [**Exemptions from Registration.**] The following persons are exempt from the registration requirement of subsection (a):

(1) a person without a place of business in this State that is registered under the securities act of the State in which the person has its principal place of business if its only clients in this State are:

(A) federal covered investment advisers, investment advisers registered under this [Act], or broker-dealers registered under this [Act];

(B) institutional investors;

(C) bona fide preexisting clients whose principal places of residence are not in this State if the investment adviser is registered under the securities act of the State in which the clients maintain principal places of residence; or

(D) any other client exempted by rule adopted or order issued under this [Act];

(2) a person without a place of business in this State if the person has had, during the preceding 12 months, not more than five clients that are resident in this State in addition to those specified under paragraph (1); or

(3) any other person exempted by rule adopted or order issued under this [Act].

(c) [**Limits on Employment or Association.**] It is unlawful for an investment adviser, directly or indirectly, to employ or associate with an individual to engage in an activity related to investment advice in this State if the registration of the individual is suspended or revoked or the individual is barred from employment or association with an investment adviser, federal covered investment adviser, or broker-dealer by an order under this [Act], the Securities and Exchange Commission, or a self-regulatory organization, unless the investment adviser did not know, and in the exercise of reasonable care could not have known, of the suspension, revocation, or bar. Upon request from the investment adviser and for good cause, the administrator, by order, may waive, in whole or in part, the application of the prohibitions of this subsection to the investment adviser.

(d) [**Investment Adviser Representative Registration Required.**] It is unlawful for an investment adviser to employ or associate with an individual required to be registered under this [Act] as an investment adviser representative who transacts business in this State on behalf of the investment adviser unless the individual is registered under Section 404(a) or is exempt from registration under Section 404(b).

§ 404. INVESTMENT ADVISER REPRESENTATIVE REGISTRATION REQUIREMENT AND EXEMPTIONS.

(a) [**Registration Requirement.**] It is unlawful for an individual to transact business in this State as an investment adviser representative unless the individual is registered under this [Act] as an investment adviser representative or is exempt from registration as an investment adviser representative under subsection (b).

(b) [**Exemptions from Registration.**] The following individuals are exempt from the registration requirement of subsection (a):

(1) an individual who is employed by or associated with an investment adviser that is exempt from registration under Section 403(b) or a federal covered investment adviser that is excluded from the notice filing requirements of Section 405; and

(2) any other individual exempted by rule adopted or order issued under this [Act].

(c) [**Registration Effective Only While Employed or Associated.**] The registration of an investment adviser representative is not effective while the investment adviser representative is not employed by or associated with an investment adviser registered under this [Act] or a federal covered investment adviser that has made or is required to make a notice filing under Section 405.

(d) [**Limit on Affiliations.**] An individual may transact business as an investment adviser representative for more than one investment adviser or federal covered investment adviser unless a rule adopted or order issued under this [Act] prohibits or limits an individual from acting as an investment adviser representative for more than one investment adviser or federal covered investment adviser.

(e) [**Limits on Employment or Association.**] It is unlawful for an individual acting as an investment adviser representative, directly or indirectly, to conduct business in this State on behalf of an investment adviser or a federal covered investment adviser if the registration of the individual as an investment adviser representative is suspended or revoked or the individual is barred from employment or association with an investment adviser or a federal covered investment adviser by an order under this [Act], the Securities and Exchange Commission, or a self-regulatory organization. Upon request from a federal covered investment adviser and for good cause, the administrator, by order issued, may waive, in whole or in part, the application of the requirements of this subsection to the federal covered investment adviser.

(f) [**Referral Fees.**] An investment adviser registered under this [Act], a federal covered investment adviser that has filed a notice under Section 405, or a broker-dealer registered under this [Act] is not required to employ or associate with an individual as an investment adviser representative if the only compensation paid to the individual for a referral of investment advisory clients is paid to an investment adviser registered under this [Act], a federal covered investment adviser who has filed a notice under Section 405, or a broker-dealer registered under this [Act] with which the individual is employed or associated as an investment adviser representative.

§ 405. FEDERAL COVERED INVESTMENT ADVISER NOTICE FILING REQUIREMENT.

(a) [**Notice Filing Requirement.**] Except with respect to a federal covered investment adviser described in subsection (b), it is unlawful for a federal covered investment adviser to transact business in this State as a federal covered investment adviser unless the federal covered investment adviser complies with subsection (c).

(b) [**Notice Filing Requirement Not Required.**] The following federal covered investment advisers are not required to comply with subsection (c):

(1) a federal covered investment adviser without a place of business in this State if its only clients in this State are:

(A) federal covered investment advisers, investment advisers registered under this [Act], and broker-dealers registered under this [Act];

(B) institutional investors;

(C) bona fide preexisting clients whose principal places of residence are not in this State; or

(D) other clients specified by rule adopted or order issued under this [Act];

(2) a federal covered investment adviser without a place of business in this State if the person has had, during the preceding 12 months, not more than five clients that are resident in this State in addition to those specified under paragraph (1); and

(3) any other person excluded by rule adopted or order issued under this [Act].

(c) [**Notice Filing Procedure.**] A person acting as a federal covered investment adviser, not excluded under subsection (b), shall file a notice, a consent to service of process complying with Section 611, and such records as have been filed with the Securities and Exchange Commission under the Investment Advisers Act of 1940 required by rule adopted or order issued under this [Act] and pay the fees specified in Section 410(e).

(d) [**Effectiveness of Filing.**] The notice under subsection (c) becomes effective upon its filing.

§ 406. REGISTRATION BY BROKER–DEALER, AGENT, INVESTMENT ADVISER, AND INVESTMENT ADVISER REPRESENTATIVE.

(a) [**Application for Initial Registration.**] A person shall register as a broker-dealer, agent, investment adviser, or investment adviser representative by filing an application and a consent to service of process complying with Section 611, and paying the fee specified in Section 410 and any reasonable fees charged by the designee of the administrator for processing the filing. The application must contain:

(1) the information or record required for the filing of a uniform application; and

(2) upon request by the administrator, any other financial or other information or record that the administrator determines is appropriate.

(b) [**Amendment.**] If the information or record contained in an application filed under subsection (a) is or becomes inaccurate or incomplete in a material respect, the registrant shall promptly file a correcting amendment.

(c) [**Effectiveness of Registration.**] If an order is not in effect and a proceeding is not pending under Section 412, registration becomes effective at noon on the 45th day after a completed application is filed, unless the registration is denied. A rule adopted or order issued under this [Act] may set an earlier effective date or may defer the effective date until noon on the 45th day after the filing of any amendment completing the application.

(d) [**Registration Renewal.**] A registration is effective until midnight on December 31 of the year for which the application for registration is filed. Unless an order is in effect under Section 412, a registration may be automatically renewed each year by filing such records as are required by rule adopted or order issued under this [Act], by paying the fee specified in

Section 410, and by paying costs charged by the designee of the administrator for processing the filings.

(e) [**Additional Conditions or Waivers.**] A rule adopted or order issued under this [Act] may impose such other conditions, not inconsistent with the National Securities Markets Improvement Act of 1996. An order issued under this [Act] may waive, in whole or in part, specific requirements in connection with registration as are in the public interest and for the protection of investors.

§ 407. SUCCESSION AND CHANGE IN REGISTRATION OF BROKER–DEALER OR INVESTMENT ADVISER.

(a) [**Succession.**] A broker-dealer or investment adviser may succeed to the current registration of another broker-dealer or investment adviser or a notice filing of a federal covered investment adviser, and a federal covered investment adviser may succeed to the current registration of an investment adviser or notice filing of another federal covered investment adviser, by filing as a successor an application for registration pursuant to Section 401 or 403 or a notice pursuant to Section 405 for the unexpired portion of the current registration or notice filing.

(b) [**Organizational Change.**] A broker-dealer or investment adviser that changes its form of organization or State of incorporation or organization may continue its registration by filing an amendment to its registration if the change does not involve a material change in its financial condition or management. The amendment becomes effective when filed or on a date designated by the registrant in its filing. The new organization is a successor to the original registrant for the purposes of this [Act]. If there is a material change in financial condition or management, the broker-dealer or investment adviser shall file a new application for registration. A predecessor registered under this [Act] shall stop conducting its securities business other than winding down transactions and shall file for withdrawal of broker-dealer or investment adviser registration within 45 days after filing its amendment to effect succession.

(c) [**Name Change.**] A broker-dealer or investment adviser that changes its name may continue its registration by filing an amendment to its registration. The amendment becomes effective when filed or on a date designated by the registrant.

(d) [**Change of Control.**] A change of control of a broker-dealer or investment adviser may be made in accordance with a rule adopted or order issued under this [Act].

§ 408. TERMINATION OF EMPLOYMENT OR ASSOCIATION OF AGENT AND INVESTMENT ADVISER REPRESENTATIVE AND TRANSFER OF EMPLOYMENT OR ASSOCIATION.

(a) [**Notice of Termination.**] If an agent registered under this [Act] terminates employment by or association with a broker-dealer or issuer, or if an investment adviser representative registered under this [Act] terminates employment by or association with an investment adviser or federal covered investment adviser, or if either registrant terminates activities that require registration as an agent or investment adviser representative, the broker-dealer, issuer, investment adviser, or federal covered investment adviser shall promptly file a notice of termination. If the registrant learns that the broker-dealer, issuer, investment adviser, or federal covered investment adviser has not filed the notice, the registrant may do so.

(b) [**Transfer of Employment or Association.**] If an agent registered under this [Act] terminates employment by or association with a broker-dealer registered under this [Act] and begins employment by or association with another broker-dealer registered under this [Act]; or if an investment adviser representative registered under this [Act] terminates employment by or association with an investment adviser registered under this [Act] or a federal covered investment adviser that has filed a notice under Section 405 and begins employment by or association with another investment adviser registered under this [Act] or a federal covered investment adviser that has filed a notice under Section 405; then upon the filing by or on behalf of the registrant, within 30 days after the termination, of an application for registration that complies with the requirement of Section 406(a) and payment of the filing fee required under Section 410, the registration of the agent or investment adviser representative is:

(1) immediately effective as of the date of the completed filing, if the agent's Central Registration Depository record or successor record or the investment adviser representative's Investment Adviser Registration Depository record or successor record does not contain a new or amended disciplinary disclosure within the previous 12 months; or

(2) temporarily effective as of the date of the completed filing, if the agent's Central Registration Depository record or successor record or the

investment adviser representative's Investment Adviser Registration Depository record or successor record contains a new or amended disciplinary disclosure within the preceding 12 months.

(c) [**Withdrawal of Temporary Registration.**] The administrator may withdraw a temporary registration if there are or were grounds for discipline as specified in Section 412 and the administrator does so within 30 days after the filing of the application. If the administrator does not withdraw the temporary registration within the 30 day period, registration becomes automatically effective on the 31st day after filing.

(d) [**Power to Prevent Registration.**] The administrator may prevent the effectiveness of a transfer of an agent or investment adviser representative under subsection (b)(1) or (2) based on the public interest and the protection of investors.

(e) [**Termination of Registration or Application for Registration.**] If the administrator determines that a registrant or applicant for registration is no longer in existence or has ceased to act as a broker-dealer, agent, investment adviser, or investment adviser representative, or is the subject of an adjudication of incapacity or is subject to the control of a committee, conservator, or guardian, or cannot reasonably be located, a rule adopted or order issued under this [Act] may require the registration be canceled or terminated or the application denied. The administrator may reinstate a canceled or terminated registration, with or without hearing, and may make the registration retroactive.

§ 409. WITHDRAWAL OF REGISTRATION OF BROKER-DEALER, AGENT, INVESTMENT ADVISER, AND INVESTMENT ADVISER REPRESENTATIVE. Withdrawal of registration by a broker-dealer, agent, investment adviser, or investment adviser representative becomes effective 60 days after the filing of the application to withdraw or within any shorter period as provided by rule adopted or order issued under this [Act] unless a revocation or suspension proceeding is pending when the application is filed. If a proceeding is pending, withdrawal becomes effective when and upon such conditions as required by rule adopted or order issued under this [Act]. The administrator may institute a revocation or suspension proceeding under Section 412 within one year after the withdrawal became effective automatically and issue a revocation or suspension order as of the last date on which registration was effective if a proceeding is not pending.

§ 410. FILING FEES.

(a) [**Broker-Dealers.**] A person shall pay a fee of $[____] when initially filing an application for registration as a broker-dealer and a fee of $[____] when filing a renewal of registration as a broker-dealer. If the filing results in a denial or withdrawal, the administrator shall retain $[____] of the fee.

(b) [**Agents.**] The fee for an individual is $[____] when filing an application for registration as an agent, a fee of $[____] when filing a renewal of registration as an agent, and a fee of $[____] when filing for a change of registration as an agent. If the filing results in a denial or withdrawal, the administrator shall retain $[____] of the fee.

(c) [**Investment Advisers.**] A person shall pay a fee of $[____] when filing an application for registration as an investment adviser and a fee of $[____] when filing a renewal of registration as an investment adviser. If the filing results in a denial or withdrawal, the administrator shall retain $[____] of the fee.

(d) [**Investment Adviser Representatives.**] The fee for an individual is $[____] when filing an application for registration as an investment adviser representative, a fee of $[____] when filing a renewal of registration as an investment adviser representative, and a fee of $[____] when filing a change of registration as an investment adviser representative. If the filing results in a denial or withdrawal, the administrator shall retain $[____] of the fee.

(e) [**Federal Covered Investment Advisers.**] A federal covered investment adviser required to file a notice under Section 405 shall pay an initial fee of $[____] and an annual notice fee of $[____].

(f) [**Payment.**] A person required to pay a filing or notice fee under this section may transmit the fee through or to a designee as a rule or order provides under this [Act].

[(g) [**Dual Agent/Investment Adviser Representative.**] An investment adviser representative who is registered as an agent under Section 402 and who represents a person that is both registered as a broker-dealer under Section 401 and registered as an investment adviser under Section 403 or required as a federal covered investment adviser to make a notice filing under Section 405 is not required to pay an initial or annual registration fee for registration as an investment adviser representative.]

§ 411. POST-REGISTRATION REQUIREMENTS.

(a) [**Financial Requirements.**] Subject to Section 15(h) of the Securities Exchange Act of 1934 (15 U.S.C. Section 78o(h)) or Section 222 of the Investment Advisers Act of 1940 (15 U.S.C. Section 80b–22), a rule adopted or order issued under this [Act] may establish minimum financial requirements for broker-dealers registered or required to be registered under this [Act] and investment advisers registered or required to be registered under this [Act].

(b) [**Financial Reports.**] Subject to Section 15(h) of the Securities Exchange Act of 1934 (15 U.S.C. Section 78o(h)) or Section 222(b) of the Investment Advisers Act of 1940 (15 U.S.C. Section 80b–22), a broker-dealer registered or required to be registered under this [Act] and an investment adviser registered or required to be registered under this [Act] shall file such financial reports as are required by a rule adopted or order issued under this [Act]. If the information contained in a record filed under this subsection is or becomes inaccurate or incomplete in a material respect, the registrant shall promptly file a correcting amendment.

(c) [**Recordkeeping.**] Subject to Section 15(h) of the Securities Exchange Act of 1934 (15 U.S.C. Section 78o(h)) or Section 222 of the Investment Advisers Act of 1940 (15 U.S.C. Section 80b–22):

(1) a broker-dealer registered or required to be registered under this [Act] and an investment adviser registered or required to be registered under this [Act] shall make and maintain the accounts, correspondence, memoranda, papers, books, and other records required by rule adopted or order issued under this [Act];

(2) broker-dealer records required to be maintained under paragraph (1) may be maintained in any form of data storage acceptable under Section 17(a) of the Securities Exchange Act of 1934 (15 U.S.C. Section 78q(a)) if they are readily accessible to the administrator; and

(3) investment adviser records required to be maintained under paragraph (1) may be maintained in any form of data storage required by rule adopted or order issued under this [Act].

(d) [**Audits or Inspections.**] The records of a broker-dealer registered or required to be registered under this [Act] and of an investment adviser registered or required to be registered under this [Act] are subject to such reasonable periodic, special, or other audits or inspections by a representative of the administrator, within or without this State, as the administrator considers necessary or appropriate in the public interest and for the protection of investors. An audit or inspection may be made at any time and without prior notice. The administrator may copy, and remove for audit or inspection copies of, all records the administrator reasonably considers necessary or appropriate to conduct the audit or inspection. The administrator may assess a reasonable charge for conducting an audit or inspection under this subsection.

(e) [**Custody and Discretionary Authority Bond or Insurance.**] Subject to Section 15(h) of the Securities Exchange Act of 1934 (15 U.S.C. Section 78o(h)) or Section 222 of the Investment Advisers Act of 1940 (15 U.S.C. Section 80b–22), a rule adopted or order issued under this [Act] may require a broker-dealer or investment adviser that has custody of or discretionary authority over funds or securities of a customer or client to obtain insurance or post a bond or other satisfactory form of security in an amount not to exceed $[____]. The administrator may determine the requirements of the insurance, bond, or other satisfactory form of security. Insurance or a bond or other satisfactory form of security may not be required of a broker-dealer registered under this [Act] whose net capital exceeds, or of an investment adviser registered under this [Act] whose minimum financial requirements exceed, the amounts required by rule or order under this [Act]. The insurance, bond, or other satisfactory form of security must permit an action by a person to enforce any liability on the insurance, bond, or other satisfactory form of security if instituted within the time limitations in Section 509(j)(2).

(f) [**Requirements for Custody.**] Subject to Section 15(h) of the Securities Exchange Act of 1934 (15 U.S.C. Section 78o(h)) or Section 222 of the Investment Advisers Act of 1940 (15 U.S.C. Section 80b–22), an agent may not have custody of funds or securities of a customer except under the supervision of a broker-dealer and an investment adviser representative may not have custody of funds or securities of a client except under the supervision of an investment adviser or a federal covered investment adviser. A rule adopted or order issued under this [Act] may prohibit, limit, or impose conditions on a broker-dealer regarding custody of funds or securities of a customer and on an investment adviser regarding custody of securities or funds of a client.

(g) [**Investment Adviser Brochure Rule.**] With respect to an investment adviser registered or required to be registered under this [Act], a rule adopted or order issued under this [Act] may require that information or other record be furnished or disseminated to clients or prospective clients in this State as necessary or appropriate in the public interest and for the protection of investors and advisory clients.

(h) [**Continuing Education.**] A rule adopted or order issued under this [Act] may require an individual registered under Section 402 or 404 to participate in a continuing education program approved by the Securities and Exchange Commission and administered by a self-regulatory organization or, in the absence of such a program, a rule adopted or order issued under this [Act] may require continuing education for an individual registered under Section 404.

§ 412. DENIAL, REVOCATION, SUSPENSION, WITHDRAWAL, RESTRICTION, CONDITION, OR LIMITATION OF REGISTRATION.

(a) [**Disciplinary Conditions—Applicants.**] If the administrator finds that the order is in the public interest and subsection (d) authorizes the action, an order issued under this [Act] may deny an application, or may condition or limit registration: (1) of an applicant to be a broker-dealer, agent, investment adviser, or investment adviser representative, and (2) if the applicant is a broker-dealer or investment adviser, of any partner, officer, director, person having a similar status or performing similar functions, or person directly or indirectly controlling the broker-dealer or investment adviser.

(b) [**Disciplinary Conditions—Registrants.**] If the administrator finds that the order is in the public interest and subsection (d) authorizes the action an order issued under this [Act] may revoke, suspend, condition, or limit the registration of a registrant and if the registrant is a broker-dealer or investment adviser, any partner, officer, or director, any person having a similar status or performing similar functions, or any person directly or indirectly controlling the broker-dealer or investment adviser. However, the administrator

(1) may not institute a revocation or suspension proceeding under this subsection based on an order issued by another State that is reported to the administrator or designee later than one year after the *date of the order* on which it is based; and

(2) under subsection (d)(5)(A) and (B), may not issue an order on the basis of an order under the state securities act of another State unless the other order was based on conduct for which subsection (d) would authorize the action had the conduct occurred in this State.

(c) [**Disciplinary Penalties—Registrants.**] If the administrator finds that the order is in the public interest and subsection (d)(1) through (6), (8), (9), (10), or (12) and (13) authorizes the action, an order under this [Act] may censure, impose a bar, or impose a civil penalty in an amount not to exceed a maximum of $[____] for a single violation or $[____] for several violations on a registrant and if the registrant is a broker-dealer or investment adviser, any partner, officer, or director, a person having similar functions or any person directly or indirectly controlling the broker-dealer or investment adviser.

(d) [**Grounds for Discipline.**] A person may be disciplined under subsections (a) through (c) if the person:

(1) has filed an application for registration in this State under this [Act] or the predecessor act within the previous 10 years, which, as of the effective date of registration or as of any date after filing in the case of an order denying effectiveness, was incomplete in any material respect or contained a statement that, in light of the circumstances under which it was made, was false or misleading with respect to a material fact;

(2) willfully violated or willfully failed to comply with this [Act] or the predecessor act or a rule adopted or order issued under this [Act] or the predecessor act within the previous 10 years;

(3) has been convicted of a felony or within the previous 10 years has been convicted of a misdemeanor involving a security, a commodity future or option contract, or an aspect of a business involving securities, commodities, investments, franchises, insurance, banking, or finance;

(4) is enjoined or restrained by a court of competent jurisdiction in an action instituted by the administrator under this [Act] or the predecessor act, a State, the Securities and Exchange Commission, or the United States from engaging in or continuing an act, practice, or course of business involving an aspect of a business involving securities, commodities, investments, franchises, insurance, banking, or finance;

(5) is the subject of an order, issued after notice and opportunity for hearing by:

(A) the securities, depository institution, insurance, or other financial services regulator of a State or by the Securities and Exchange Commission or other federal agency denying, revoking, barring, or suspending registration as a broker-dealer, agent, investment adviser, federal covered investment adviser, or investment adviser representative;

(B) the securities regulator of a State or by the Securities and Exchange Commission against a broker-dealer, agent, investment adviser, investment adviser representative, or federal covered investment adviser;

(C) the Securities and Exchange Commission or by a self-regulatory organization suspending or expelling the registrant from membership in the self-regulatory organization;

(D) a court adjudicating a United States Postal Service fraud order;

(E) the insurance regulator of a State denying, suspending, or revoking the registration of an insurance agent; or

(F) a depository institution regulator suspending or barring a person from the depository institution business;

(6) is the subject of an adjudication or determination, after notice and opportunity for hearing, by the Securities and Exchange Commission, the Commodity Futures Trading Commission; the Federal Trade Commission; a federal depository institution regulator, or a depository institution, insurance, or other financial services regulator of a State that the person willfully violated the Securities Act of 1933, the Securities Exchange Act of 1934, the Investment Advisers Act of 1940, the Investment Company Act of 1940, or the Commodity Exchange Act, the securities or commodities law of a State, or a federal or state law under which a business involving investments, franchises, insurance, banking, or finance is regulated;

(7) is insolvent, either because the person's liabilities exceed the person's assets or because the person cannot meet the person's obligations as they mature, but the administrator may not enter an order against an applicant or registrant under this paragraph without a finding of insolvency as to the applicant or registrant;

(8) refuses to allow or otherwise impedes the administrator from conducting an audit or inspection under Section 411(d) or refuses access to a registrant's office to conduct an audit or inspection under Section 411(d);

(9) has failed to reasonably supervise an agent, investment adviser representative, or other individual, if the agent, investment adviser representative, or other individual was subject to the person's supervision and committed a violation of this [Act] or the predecessor act or a rule adopted or order issued under this [Act] or the predecessor act within the previous 10 years;

(10) has not paid the proper filing fee within 30 days after having been notified by the administrator of a deficiency, but the administrator shall vacate an order under this paragraph when the deficiency is corrected;

(11) after notice and opportunity for a hearing, has been found within the previous 10 years:

(A) by a court of competent jurisdiction to have willfully violated the laws of a foreign jurisdiction under which the business of securities, commodities, investment, franchises, insurance, banking, or finance is regulated;

(B) to have been the subject of an order of a securities regulator of a foreign jurisdiction denying, revoking, or suspending the right to engage in the business of securities as a broker-dealer, agent, investment adviser, investment adviser representative, or similar person; or

(C) to have been suspended or expelled from membership by or participation in a securities exchange or securities association operating under the securities laws of a foreign jurisdiction;

(12) is the subject of a cease and desist order issued by the Securities and Exchange Commission or issued under the securities, commodities, investment, franchise, banking, finance, or insurance laws of a State;

(13) has engaged in dishonest or unethical practices in the securities, commodities, investment, franchise, banking, finance, or insurance business within the previous 10 years; or

(14) is not qualified on the basis of factors such as training, experience, and knowledge of the securities business. However, in the case of an application by an agent for a broker-dealer that is a member of a self-regulatory organization or by an individual for registration as an investment adviser representative, a denial order may not be based on this paragraph if the individual has successfully completed all examinations required by subsection (e). The administrator may require an applicant for registration under Section 402 or 404 who has not been registered in a State within the two years preceding the filing of an application in this State to successfully complete an examination.

(e) **[Examinations.]** A rule adopted or order issued under this [Act] may require that an examination, including an examination developed or approved by an organization of securities regulators, be successfully completed by a class of individuals or all individuals. An order issued under this [Act] may waive, in whole or in part, an examination as to an individual and a rule adopted under this [Act] may waive, in whole or in part, an examination as to a class of individuals if the administrator determines that the examination is not necessary or appropriate in the public interest and for the protection of investors.

(f) **[Summary Process.]** The administrator may suspend or deny an application summarily; restrict, condition, limit, or suspend a registration; or censure, bar, or impose a civil penalty on a registrant before final determination of an administrative proceeding. Upon the issuance of an order, the administrator shall promptly notify each person subject to the order that the order has been issued, the reasons for the action, and that within 15 days after the receipt of a request in a record from the person the matter will be scheduled for a hearing. If a hearing is not requested and none is ordered by the administrator within 30 days after the date of service of the order, the order becomes final by operation of law. If a hearing is requested or ordered, the administrator, after notice of and opportunity for hearing to each person subject to the order, may modify or vacate the order or extend the order until final determination.

(g) **[Procedural Requirements.]** An order issued may not be issued under this section, except under subsection (f), without:

(1) appropriate notice to the applicant or registrant;

(2) opportunity for hearing; and

(3) findings of fact and conclusions of law in a record [in accordance with the state administrative procedure act].

(h) **[Control Person Liability.]** A person that controls, directly or indirectly, a person not in compliance with this section may be disciplined by order of the administrator under subsections (a) through (c) to the same extent as the noncomplying person, unless the controlling person did not know, and in the exercise of reasonable care could not have known, of the existence of conduct that is a ground for discipline under this section.

(i) **[Limit on Investigation or Proceeding.]** The administrator may not institute a proceeding under subsection(a), (b), or (c) based solely on material facts actually known by the administrator unless an investigation or the proceeding is instituted within one year after the administrator actually acquires knowledge of the material facts.

[ARTICLE] 5

FRAUD AND LIABILITIES

§ 501. GENERAL FRAUD. It is unlawful for a person, in connection with the offer, sale, or purchase of a security, directly or indirectly:

(1) to employ a device, scheme, or artifice to defraud;

(2) to make an untrue statement of a material fact or to omit to state a material fact necessary in order to make the statement made, in the light of the circumstances under which it is made, not misleading; or

(3) to engage in an act, practice, or course of business that operates or would operate as a fraud or deceit upon another person.

§ 502. PROHIBITED CONDUCT IN PROVIDING INVESTMENT ADVICE.

(a) **[Fraud in Providing Investment Advice.]** It is unlawful for a person that advises others for compensation, either directly or indirectly or through publications or writings, as to the value of securities or the advisability of investing in, purchasing, or selling securities or that, for compensation and as part of a regular business, issues or promulgates analyses or reports relating to securities:

(1) to employ a device, scheme, or artifice to defraud another person; or

(2) to engage in an act, practice, or course of business that operates or would operate as a fraud or deceit upon another person.

(b) **[Rules Defining Fraud.]** A rule adopted under this [Act] may define an act, practice, or course of business of an investment adviser or an investment adviser representative, other than a supervised person of a federal covered investment adviser, as fraudulent, deceptive, or manipulative, and prescribe means reasonably designed to prevent investment advisers and investment adviser representatives, other than supervised persons of a federal covered investment adviser, from engaging in acts, practices, and courses of business defined as fraudulent, deceptive, or manipulative.

(c) **[Rules Specifying Contents of Advisory Contract.]** A rule adopted under this [Act] may specify the contents of an investment advisory contract entered into, extended, or renewed by an investment adviser.

§ 503. EVIDENTIARY BURDEN.

(a) **[Civil.]** In a civil action or administrative proceeding under this [Act], a person claiming an exemption, exception, preemption, or exclusion has the burden to prove the applicability of the claim.

(b) **[Criminal.]** In a criminal proceeding under this [Act], a person claiming an exemption, exception, preemption, or exclusion has the burden of going forward with evidence of the claim.

§ 504. FILING OF SALES AND ADVERTISING LITERATURE.

(a) **[Filing Requirement.]** Except as otherwise provided in subsection (b), a rule adopted or order issued under this [Act] may require the filing of a prospectus, pamphlet, circular, form letter, advertisement, sales literature, or other advertising record relating to a security or investment advice, addressed or intended for distribution to prospective investors, including clients or prospective clients of a person registered or required to be registered as an investment adviser under this [Act].

(b) **[Excluded Communications.]** This section does not apply to sales and advertising literature specified in subsection (a) which relates to a federal covered security, a federal covered investment adviser, or a security or transaction exempted by Section 201, 202, or 203 except as required pursuant to Section 201(7).

§ 505. MISLEADING FILINGS. It is unlawful for a person to make or cause to be made, in a record that is used in an action or proceeding or filed under this [Act], a statement that, at the time and in the light of the circumstances under which it is made, is false or misleading in a material respect, or, in connection with the statement, to omit to state a material fact necessary to make the statement made, in the light of the circumstances under which it was made, not false or misleading.

§ 506. MISREPRESENTATIONS CONCERNING REGISTRATION OR EXEMPTION. The filing of an application for registration, a registration statement, a notice filing under this [Act], the registration of a person, the notice filing by a person, or the registration of a security under this [Act] does not constitute a finding by the administrator that a record filed under this [Act] is true, complete, and not misleading. The filing or registration or the availability of an exemption, exception, preemption, or exclusion for a security or a transaction does not mean that the administrator has passed upon the merits or qualifications of, or recommended or given approval to, a person, security, or transaction. It is unlawful to make, or cause to be made, to a purchaser, customer, client, or prospective customer or client a representation inconsistent with this section.

§ 507. QUALIFIED IMMUNITY. A broker-dealer, agent, investment adviser, federal covered investment adviser, or investment adviser representative is not liable to another broker-dealer, agent, investment adviser, federal covered investment adviser, or investment adviser representative for defamation relating to a statement that is contained in a record required by the administrator, or designee of the administrator, the Securities and Exchange Commission, or a self-regulatory organization, unless the person knew, or should have known at the time that the statement was made, that it was false in a material respect or the person acted in reckless disregard of the statement's truth or falsity.

§ 508. CRIMINAL PENALTIES.

(a) **[Criminal Penalties.]** A person that willfully violates this [Act], or a rule adopted or order issued under this [Act], except Section 504 or the notice filing requirements of Section 302 or 405, or that willfully violates Section 505 knowing the statement made to be false or misleading in a material respect, upon conviction, shall be fined not more than $[____] or imprisoned not more than [____] years, or both. An individual convicted of violating a rule or order under this [Act] may be fined, but may not be imprisoned, if the individual did not have knowledge of the rule or order.

(b) **[Criminal Reference Not Required.]** The [Attorney General or the proper prosecuting attorney] with or without a reference from the administrator, may institute criminal proceedings under this [Act].

(c) **[No Limitation on Other Criminal Enforcement.]** This [Act] does not limit the power of this State to punish a person for conduct that constitutes a crime under other laws of this State.

§ 509. CIVIL LIABILITY.

(a) **[Securities Litigation Uniform Standards Act.]** Enforcement of civil liability under this section is subject to the Securities Litigation Uniform Standards Act of 1998.

(b) [**Liability of Seller to Purchaser.**] A person is liable to the purchaser if the person sells a security in violation of Section 301 or, by means of an untrue statement of a material fact or an omission to state a material fact necessary in order to make the statement made, in light of the circumstances under which it is made, not misleading, the purchaser not knowing the untruth or omission and the seller not sustaining the burden of proof that the seller did not know and, in the exercise of reasonable care, could not have known of the untruth or omission. An action under this subsection is governed by the following:

(1) The purchaser may maintain an action to recover the consideration paid for the security, less the amount of any income received on the security, and interest [at the legal rate of interest] from the date of the purchase, costs, and reasonable attorneys' fees determined by the court, upon the tender of the security, or for actual damages as provided in paragraph (3).

(2) The tender referred to in paragraph (1) may be made any time before entry of judgment. Tender requires only notice in a record of ownership of the security and willingness to exchange the security for the amount specified. A purchaser that no longer owns the security may recover actual damages as provided in paragraph (3).

(3) Actual damages in an action arising under this subsection are the amount that would be recoverable upon a tender less the value of the security when the purchaser disposed of it, and interest [at the legal rate of interest] from the date of the purchase, costs, and reasonable attorneys' fees determined by the court.

(c) [**Liability of Purchaser to Seller.**] A person is liable to the seller if the person buys a security by means of an untrue statement of a material fact or omission to state a material fact necessary in order to make the statement made, in light of the circumstances under which it is made, not misleading, the seller not knowing of the untruth or omission, and the purchaser not sustaining the burden of proof that the purchaser did not know, and in the exercise of reasonable care, could not have known of the untruth or omission. An action under this subsection is governed by the following:

(1) The seller may maintain an action to recover the security, and any income received on the security, costs, and reasonable attorneys' fees determined by the court, upon the tender of the purchase price, or for actual damages as provided in paragraph (3).

(2) The tender referred to in paragraph (1) may be made any time before entry of judgment. Tender requires only notice in a record of the present ability to pay the amount tendered and willingness to take delivery of the security for the amount specified. If the purchaser no longer owns the security, the seller may recover actual damages as provided in paragraph (3).

(3) Actual damages in an action arising under this subsection are the difference between the price at which the security was sold and the value the security would have had at the time of the sale in the absence of the purchaser's conduct causing liability, and interest [at the legal rate of interest] from the date of the sale of the security, costs, and reasonable attorneys' fees determined by the court.

(d) [**Liability of Unregistered Broker–Dealer and Agent.**] A person acting as a broker-dealer or agent that sells or buys a security in violation of Section 401(a), 402(a), or 506 is liable to the customer. The customer, if a purchaser, may maintain an action for recovery of actual damages as specified in subsections (b)(1) through (3), or, if a seller, for a remedy as specified in subsections (c)(1) through (3).

(e) [**Liability of Unregistered Investment Adviser and Investment Adviser Representative.**] A person acting as an investment adviser or investment adviser representative that provides investment advice for compensation in violation of Section 403(a), 404(a), or 506 is liable to the client. The client may maintain an action to recover the consideration paid for the advice, interest [at the legal rate of interest] from the date of payment, costs, and reasonable attorneys' fees determined by the court.

(f) [**Liability for Investment Advice.**] A person that receives directly or indirectly any consideration for providing investment advice to another person and that employs a device, scheme, or artifice to defraud the other person or engages in an act, practice, or course of business that operates or would operate as a fraud or deceit on the other person, is liable to the other person. An action under this subsection is governed by the following:

(1) The person defrauded may maintain an action to recover the consideration paid for the advice and the amount of any actual damages caused by the fraudulent conduct, interest [at the legal rate of interest] from the date of the fraudulent conduct, costs, and reasonable attorneys' fees

determined by the court, less the amount of any income received as a result of the fraudulent conduct.

(2) This subsection does not apply to a broker-dealer or its agents if the investment advice provided is solely incidental to transacting business as a broker-dealer and no special compensation is received for the investment advice.

(g) [**Joint and Several Liability.**] The following persons are liable jointly and severally with and to the same extent as persons liable under subsections (b) through (f):

(1) a person that directly or indirectly controls a person liable under subsections (b) through (f), unless the controlling person sustains the burden of proof that the person did not know, and in the exercise of reasonable care could not have known, of the existence of conduct by reason of which the liability is alleged to exist;

(2) an individual who is a managing partner, executive officer, or director of a person liable under subsections (b) through (f), including an individual having a similar status or performing similar functions, unless the individual sustains the burden of proof that the individual did not know and, in the exercise of reasonable care could not have known, of the existence of conduct by reason of which the liability is alleged to exist;

(3) an individual who is an employee of or associated with a person liable under subsections (b) through (f) and who materially aids the conduct giving rise to the liability, unless the individual sustains the burden of proof that the individual did not know and, in the exercise of reasonable care could not have known, of the existence of conduct by reason of which the liability is alleged to exist; and

(4) a person that is a broker-dealer, agent, investment adviser, or investment adviser representative that materially aids the conduct giving rise to the liability under subsections (b) through (f), unless the person sustains the burden of proof that the person did not know and, in the exercise of reasonable care could not have known, of the existence of conduct by reason of which liability is alleged to exist.

(h) [**Right of Contribution.**] A person liable under this section has a right of contribution as in cases of contract against any other person liable under this section for the same conduct.

(i) [**Survival of Cause of Action.**] A cause of action under this section survives the death of an individual who might have been a plaintiff or defendant.

(j) [**Statute of Limitations.**] A person may not obtain relief:

(1) under subsection (b) for violation of Section 301, or under subsection (d) or (e), unless the action is instituted within one year after the violation occurred; or

(2) under subsection (b), other than for violation of Section 301, or under subsection (c) or (f), unless the action is instituted within the earlier of two years after discovery of the facts constituting the violation or five years after the violation.

(k) [**No Enforcement of Violative Contract.**] A person that has made, or has engaged in the performance of, a contract in violation of this [Act] or a rule adopted or order issued under this [Act], or that has acquired a purported right under the contract with knowledge of conduct by reason of which its making or performance was in violation of this [Act], may not base an action on the contract.

(*l*) [**No Contractual Waiver.**] A condition, stipulation, or provision binding a person purchasing or selling a security or receiving investment advice to waive compliance with this [Act] or a rule adopted or order issued under this [Act] is void.

(m) [**Survival of Other Rights or Remedies.**] The rights and remedies provided by this [Act] are in addition to any other rights or remedies that may exist, but this [Act] does not create a cause of action not specified in this section or Section 411(e).

§ 510. RESCISSION OFFERS. A purchaser, seller, or recipient of investment advice may not maintain an action under Section 509 if:

(1) The purchaser, seller, or recipient of investment advice receives in a record, before the action is instituted:

(A) an offer stating the respect in which liability under Section 509 may have arisen and fairly advising the purchaser, seller, or recipient of investment advice of that person's rights in connection with the offer, and any financial or other information necessary to correct all material misrepresentations or omissions in the information that was required by this [Act] to be furnished to that person at the time of the purchase, sale, or investment advice;

(B) if the basis for relief under this section may have been a violation of Section 509(b), an offer to repurchase the security for cash, payable on delivery of the security, equal to the consideration paid, and interest [at the legal rate of interest] from the date of the purchase, less the amount of any income received on the security, or, if the purchaser no longer owns the security, an offer to pay the purchaser upon acceptance of the offer damages in an amount that would be recoverable upon a tender, less the value of the security when the purchaser disposed of it, and interest [at the legal rate of interest] from the date of the purchase in cash equal to the damages computed in the manner provided in this subsection;

(C) if the basis for relief under this section may have been a violation of Section 509(c), an offer to tender the security, on payment by the seller of an amount equal to the purchase price paid, less income received on the security by the purchaser and interest [at the legal rate of interest] from the date of the sale; or if the purchaser no longer owns the security, an offer to pay the seller upon acceptance of the offer, in cash, damages in the amount of the difference between the price at which the security was purchased and the value the security would have had at the time of the purchase in the absence of the purchaser's conduct that may have caused liability and interest [at the legal rate of interest] from the date of the sale;

(D) if the basis for relief under this section may have been a violation of Section 509(d); and if the customer is a purchaser, an offer to pay as specified in subparagraph (B); or, if the customer is a seller, an offer to tender or to pay as specified in subparagraph (C);

(E) if the basis for relief under this section may have been a violation of Section 509(e), an offer to reimburse in cash the consideration paid for the advice and interest [at the legal rate of interest] from the date of payment; or

(F) if the basis for relief under this section may have been a violation of Section 509(f), an offer to reimburse in cash the consideration paid for the advice, the amount of any actual damages that may have been caused by the conduct, and interest [at the legal rate of interest] from the date of the violation causing the loss;

(2) the offer under paragraph 1 states that it must be accepted by the purchaser, seller, or recipient of investment advice within 30 days after the date of its receipt by the purchaser, seller, or recipient of investment advice or any shorter period, of not less than three days, that the administrator, by order, specifies;

(3) the offeror has the present ability to pay the amount offered or to tender the security under paragraph (1);

(4) the offer under paragraph (1) is delivered to the purchaser, seller, or recipient of investment advice, or sent in a manner that ensures receipt by the purchaser, seller, or recipient of investment advice; and

(5) the purchaser, seller, or recipient of investment advice that accepts the offer under paragraph (1) in a record within the period specified under paragraph (2) is paid in accordance with the terms of the offer.

[ARTICLE] 6
ADMINISTRATION AND JUDICIAL REVIEW

§ 601. ADMINISTRATION.

(a) **[Administration.]** The administrator shall administer this [Act] [insert any related provisions on such matters as method of selection, salary, term of office, selection and remuneration of personnel, and annual reports to the legislature or governor that are appropriate to the particular State].

(b) **[Unlawful Use of Records or Information.]** It is unlawful for the administrator or an officer, employee, or designee of the administrator to use for personal benefit or the benefit of others records or other information obtained by or filed with the administrator that are not public under Section 607(b). This [Act] does not authorize the administrator or an officer, employee, or designee of the administrator to disclose the record or information, except in accordance with Section 602, 607(c), or 608.

(c) **[No Privilege or Exemption Created or Diminished.]** This [Act] does not create or diminish a privilege or exemption that exists at common law, by statute or rule, or otherwise.

(d) **[Investor Education.]** The administrator may develop and implement investor education initiatives to inform the public about investing in securities, with particular emphasis on the prevention and detection of securities fraud. In developing and implementing these initiatives, the administrator may collaborate with public and nonprofit organizations with an interest in investor education. The administrator may accept a grant or donation from a person that is not affiliated with the securities industry or from a nonprofit organization, regardless of whether the organization is affiliated with the securities industry, to develop and implement investor education initiatives. This subsection does not authorize the administrator to require participation or monetary contributions of a registrant in an investor education program.

(e) [**The Securities Investor Education and Training Fund.**] The Securities Investor Education and Training Fund is created to provide funds for the purposes specified in subsection (d). [All monies received by the State by reason of civil penalties pursuant to this [Act] shall be deposited in the Securities Investor Education and Training Fund. The State may insert any other provision concerning appropriations to support this fund as well as procedures for its operations.]

§ 602. INVESTIGATIONS AND SUBPOENAS.

(a) [**Authority to Investigate.**] The administrator may:

(1) conduct public or private investigations within or outside of this State which the administrator considers necessary or appropriate to determine whether a person has violated, is violating, or is about to violate this [Act] or a rule adopted or order issued under this [Act], or to aid in the enforcement of this [Act] or in the adoption of rules and forms under this [Act];

(2) require or permit a person to testify, file a statement, or produce a record, under oath or otherwise as the administrator determines, as to all the facts and circumstances concerning a matter to be investigated or about which an action or proceeding is to be instituted; and

(3) publish a record concerning an action, proceeding, or an investigation under, or a violation of, this [Act] or a rule adopted or order issued under this [Act] if the administrator determines it is necessary or appropriate in the public interest and for the protection of investors.

(b) [**Administrator Powers to Investigate.**] For the purpose of an investigation under this [Act], the administrator or its designated officer may administer oaths and affirmations, subpoena witnesses, seek compulsion of attendance, take evidence, require the filing of statements, and require the production of any records that the administrator considers relevant or material to the investigation.

(c) [**Procedure and Remedies for Noncompliance.**] If a person does not appear or refuses to testify, file a statement, produce records, or otherwise does not obey a subpoena as required by the administrator under this [Act], the administrator [may refer the matter to the Attorney General or the proper attorney, who] may apply to [insert name of the appropriate court] or a court of another State to enforce compliance. The court may:

(1) hold the person in contempt;

(2) order the person to appear before the administrator;

(3) order the person to testify about the matter under investigation or in question;

(4) order the production of records;

(5) grant injunctive relief, including restricting or prohibiting the offer or sale of securities or the providing of investment advice;

(6) impose a civil penalty of not less than $[____] and not greater than $[____] for each violation; and

(7) grant any other necessary or appropriate relief.

(d) [**Application for Relief.**] This section does not preclude a person from applying to [insert name of appropriate court] or a court of another State for relief from a request to appear, testify, file a statement, produce records, or obey a subpoena.

(e) [**Use Immunity Procedure.**] An individual is not excused from attending, testifying, filing a statement, producing a record or other evidence, or obeying a subpoena of the administrator under this [Act] or in an action or proceeding instituted by the administrator under this [Act] on the ground that the required testimony, statement, record, or other evidence, directly or indirectly, may tend to incriminate the individual or subject the individual to a criminal fine, penalty, or forfeiture. If the individual refuses to testify, file a statement, or produce a record or other evidence on the basis of the individual's privilege against self-incrimination, the administrator may apply [to the name of the appropriate court] to compel the testimony, the filing of the statement, the production of the record, or the giving of other evidence. The testimony, record, or other evidence compelled under such an order may not be used, directly or indirectly, against the individual in a criminal case, except in a prosecution for perjury or contempt or otherwise failing to comply with the order.

(f) [**Assistance to Securities Regulator of Another Jurisdiction.**] At the request of the securities regulator of another State or a foreign jurisdiction, the administrator may provide assistance if the requesting regulator states that it is conducting an

investigation to determine whether a person has violated, is violating, or is about to violate a law or rule of the other State or foreign jurisdiction relating to securities matters that the requesting regulator administers or enforces. The administrator may provide the assistance by using the authority to investigate and the powers conferred by this section as the administrator determines is necessary or appropriate. The assistance may be provided without regard to whether the conduct described in the request would also constitute a violation of this [Act] or other law of this State if occurring in this State. In deciding whether to provide the assistance, the administrator may consider whether the requesting regulator is permitted and has agreed to provide assistance reciprocally within its State or foreign jurisdiction to the administrator on securities matters when requested; whether compliance with the request would violate or prejudice the public policy of this State; and the availability of resources and employees of the administrator to carry out the request for assistance.

§ 603. CIVIL ENFORCEMENT.

(a) **[Civil Action Instituted by Administrator.]** If the administrator believes that a person has engaged, is engaging, or is about to engage in an act, practice, or course of business constituting a violation of this [Act] or a rule adopted or order issued under this [Act] or that a person has, is, or is about to engage in an act, practice, or course of business that materially aids a violation of this [Act] or a rule adopted or order issued under this [Act], the administrator may maintain an action in the [insert the name of the court] to enjoin the act, practice, or course of business and to enforce compliance with this [Act] or a rule adopted or order issued under this [Act].

(b) **[Relief Available.]** In an action under this section and on a proper showing, the court may:

(1) issue a permanent or temporary injunction, restraining order, or declaratory judgment;

(2) order other appropriate or ancillary relief, which may include:

(A) an asset freeze, accounting, writ of attachment, writ of general or specific execution, and appointment of a receiver or conservator, that may be the administrator, for the defendant or the defendant's assets;

(B) ordering the administrator to take charge and control of a defendant's property, including investment accounts and accounts in a depository institution, rents, and profits; to collect debts; and to acquire and dispose of property;

(C) imposing a civil penalty up to $[____] for a single violation or up to $[____] for more than one violation; an order of rescission, restitution, or disgorgement directed to a person that has engaged in an act, practice, or course of business constituting a violation of this [Act] or the predecessor act or a rule adopted or order issued under this [Act] or the predecessor act; and

(D) ordering the payment of prejudgment and postjudgment interest; or

(3) order such other relief as the court considers appropriate.

(c) **[No Bond Required.]** The administrator may not be required to post a bond in an action or proceeding under this [Act].

§ 604. ADMINISTRATIVE ENFORCEMENT.

(a) **[Issuance of an Order or Notice.]** If the administrator determines that a person has engaged, is engaging, or is about to engage in an act, practice, or course of business constituting a violation of this [Act] or a rule adopted or order issued under this [Act] or that a person has materially aided, is materially aiding, or is about to materially aid an act, practice, or course of business constituting a violation of this [Act] or a rule adopted or order issued under this [Act], the administrator may:

(1) issue an order directing the person to cease and desist from engaging in the act, practice, or course of business or to take other action necessary or appropriate to comply with this [Act];

(2) issue an order denying, suspending, revoking, or conditioning the exemptions for a broker-dealer under Section 401(b)(1)(D) or (F) or an investment adviser under Section 403(b)(1)(C); or

(3) issue an order under Section 204.

(b) **[Summary Process.]** An order under subsection (a) is effective on the date of issuance. Upon issuance of the order, the administrator shall promptly serve each person subject to the order with a copy of the order and a notice that the order has been entered. The order must include a statement whether the administrator will seek a civil penalty or costs of the investigation, a statement of the reasons for the order, and notice that, within 15 days after receipt of a request in a record from the person, the matter will be scheduled for a hearing. If a person subject to the order does not request a hearing and none is ordered by the administrator within 30 days after the date of service of the order, the order, which may include a civil penalty or costs of the investigation if a civil penalty or costs were sought in the statement accompanying the order, becomes final as to that person by operation of law. If a hearing is requested or ordered, the administrator, after notice of and opportunity for hearing to each person subject to the order, may modify or vacate the order or extend it until final determination.

(c) [**Procedure for Final Order.**] If a hearing is requested or ordered pursuant to subsection (b), a hearing must be held [pursuant to the state administrative procedure act]. A final order may not be issued unless the administrator makes findings of fact and conclusions of law in a record [in accordance with the state administrative procedure act]. The final order may make final, vacate, or modify the order issued under subsection (a).

(d) [**Civil Penalty.**] In a final order under subsection (c), the administrator may impose a civil penalty up to $[____] for a single violation or up to $[____] for more than one violation.

(e) [**Costs.**] In a final order, the administrator may charge the actual cost of an investigation or proceeding for a violation of this [Act] or a rule adopted or order issued under this [Act].

(f) [**Filing of Certified Final Order with Court; Effect of Filing.**] If a petition for judicial review of a final order is not filed in accordance with Section 609, the administrator may file a certified copy of the final order with the clerk of a court of competent jurisdiction. The order so filed has the same effect as a judgment of the court and may be recorded, enforced, or satisfied in the same manner as a judgment of the court.

(g) [**Enforcement by Court; Further Civil Penalty.**] If a person does not comply with an order under this section, the administrator may petition a court of competent jurisdiction to enforce the order. The court may not require the administrator to post a bond in an action or proceeding under this section. If the court finds, after service and opportunity for hearing, that the person was not in compliance with the order, the court may adjudge the person in civil contempt of the order. The court may impose a further civil penalty against the person for contempt in an amount not less than $[____] but not greater than $[____] for each violation and may grant any other relief the court determines is just and proper in the circumstances.

§ 605. RULES, FORMS, ORDERS, INTERPRETATIVE OPINIONS, AND HEARINGS.

(a) [**Issuance and Adoption of Forms, Orders, and Rules.**] The administrator may:

(1) issue forms and orders and, after notice and comment, may adopt and amend rules necessary or appropriate to carry out this [Act] and may repeal rules, including rules and forms governing registration statements, applications, notice filings, reports, and other records;

(2) by rule, define terms, whether or not used in this [Act], but those definitions may not be inconsistent with this [Act]; and

(3) by rule, classify securities, persons, and transactions and adopt different requirements for different classes.

(b) [**Findings and Cooperation.**] Under this [Act], a rule or form may not be adopted or amended, or an order issued or amended, unless the administrator finds that the rule, form, order, or amendment is necessary or appropriate in the public interest or for the protection of investors and is consistent with the purposes intended by this [Act]. In adopting, amending, and repealing rules and forms, Section 608 applies in order to achieve uniformity among the States and coordination with federal laws in the form and content of registration statements, applications, reports, and other records, including the adoption of uniform rules, forms, and procedures.

(c) [**Financial Statements.**] Subject to Section 15(h) of the Securities Exchange Act and Section 222 of the Investment Advisers Act of 1940, the administrator may require that a financial statement filed under this [Act] be prepared in accordance with generally accepted accounting principles in the United States and comply with other requirements specified by rule adopted or order issued under this [Act]. A rule adopted or order issued under this [Act] may establish:

(1) subject to Section 15(h) of the Securities Exchange Act and Section 222 of the Investment Advisors Act of 1940, the form and content of financial statements required under this [Act];

(2) whether unconsolidated financial statements must be filed; and

(3) whether required financial statements must be audited by an independent certified public accountant.

(d) [**Interpretative Opinions.**] The administrator may provide interpretative opinions or issue

determinations that the administrator will not institute a proceeding or an action under this [Act] against a specified person for engaging in a specified act, practice, or course of business if the determination is consistent with this [Act]. A rule adopted or order issued under this [Act] may establish a reasonable charge for interpretative opinions or determinations that the administrator will not institute an action or a proceeding under this [Act].

(e) [**Effect of Compliance.**] A penalty under this [Act] may not be imposed for, and liability does not arise from conduct that is engaged in or omitted in good faith believing it conforms to a rule, form, or order of the administrator under this [Act].

(f) [**Presumption for Public Hearings.**] A hearing in an administrative proceeding under this [Act] must be conducted in public unless the administrator for good cause consistent with this [Act] determines that the hearing will not be so conducted.

§ 606. ADMINISTRATIVE FILES AND OPINIONS.

(a) [**Public Register of Filings.**] The administrator shall maintain, or designate a person to maintain, a register of applications for registration of securities; registration statements; notice filings; applications for registration of broker-dealers, agents, investment advisers, and investment adviser representatives; notice filings by federal covered investment advisers that are or have been effective under this [Act] or the predecessor act; notices of claims of exemption from registration or notice filing requirements contained in a record; orders issued under this [Act] or the predecessor act; and interpretative opinions or no action determinations issued under this [Act].

(b) [**Public Availability.**] The administrator shall make all rules, forms, interpretative opinions, and orders available to the public.

(c) [**Copies of Public Records.**] The administrator shall furnish a copy of a record that is a public record or a certification that the public record does not exist to a person that so requests. A rule adopted under this [Act] may establish a reasonable charge for furnishing the record or certification. A copy of the record certified or a certificate by the administrator of a record's nonexistence is prima facie evidence of a record or its nonexistence.

§ 607. PUBLIC RECORDS; CONFIDENTIALITY.

(a) [**Presumption of Public Records.**] Except as otherwise provided in subsection (b), records obtained by the administrator or filed under this [Act], including a record contained in or filed with a registration statement, application, notice filing, or report, are public records and are available for public examination.

(b) [**Nonpublic Records.**] The following records are not public records and are not available for public examination under subsection (a):

(1) a record obtained by the administrator in connection with an audit or inspection under Section 411(d) or an investigation under Section 602;

(2) a part of a record filed in connection with a registration statement under Sections 301 and 303 through 305 or a record under Section 411(d) that contains trade secrets or confidential information if the person filing the registration statement or report has asserted a claim of confidentiality or privilege that is authorized by law;

(3) a record that is not required to be provided to the administrator or filed under this [Act] and is provided to the administrator only on the condition that the record will not be subject to public examination or disclosure;

(4) a nonpublic record received from a person specified in Section 608(a); [and]

(5) any social security number, residential address, and residential telephone number contained in a record that is filed [and]

(6) a record obtained by the administrator through a designee of the administrator that a rule or order under this [Act] determines has been:

(A) expunged from the administrator's records by the designee; or

(B) determined to be nonpublic or nondisclosable by that designee if the administrator finds the determination to be in the public interest and for the protection of investors.

(c) [**Administrator Discretion to Disclose.**] If disclosure is for the purpose of a civil, administrative, or criminal investigation, action, or proceeding or to a person specified in Section 608(a), the administrator may disclose a record obtained in connection with an audit or inspection under Section 411(d) or a record obtained in connection with an investigation under Section 602.

§ 608. UNIFORMITY AND COOPERATION WITH OTHER AGENCIES.

(a) [**Objective of Uniformity.**] The administrator shall, in its discretion, cooperate, coordinate, consult, and, subject to Section 607, share records and information with the securities regulator of another State, Canada, a Canadian province or territory, a foreign jurisdiction, the Securities and Exchange Commission, the United States Department of Justice, the Commodity Futures Trading Commission, the Federal Trade Commission, the Securities Investor Protection Corporation, a self-regulatory organization, a national or international organization of securities regulators, a federal or state banking and insurance regulator, and a governmental law enforcement agency to effectuate greater uniformity in securities matters among the federal government, self-regulatory organizations, States, and foreign governments.

(b) [**Policies to Consider.**] In cooperating, coordinating, consulting, and sharing records and information under this section and in acting by rule, order, or waiver under this [Act], the administrator shall, in its discretion, take into consideration in carrying out the public interest the following general policies:

(1) maximizing effectiveness of regulation for the protection of investors;

(2) maximizing uniformity in federal and state regulatory standards; and

(3) minimizing burdens on the business of capital formation, without adversely affecting essentials of investor protection.

(c) [**Subjects for Cooperation.**] The cooperation, coordination, consultation, and sharing of records and information authorized by this section includes:

(1) establishing or employing one or more designees as a central depository for registration and notice filings under this [Act] and for records required or allowed to be maintained under this [Act];

(2) developing and maintaining uniform forms;

(3) conducting a joint examination or investigation;

(4) holding a joint administrative hearing;

(5) instituting and prosecuting a joint civil or administrative proceeding;

(6) sharing and exchanging personnel;

(7) coordinating registrations under Sections 301 and 401 through 404 and exemptions under Section 203;

(8) sharing and exchanging records, subject to Section 607;

(9) formulating rules, statements of policy, guidelines, forms, and interpretative opinions and releases;

(10) formulating common systems and procedures;

(11) notifying the public of proposed rules, forms, statements of policy, and guidelines;

(12) attending conferences and other meetings among securities regulators, which may include representatives of governmental and private sector organizations involved in capital formation, deemed necessary or appropriate to promote or achieve uniformity; and

(13) developing and maintaining a uniform exemption from registration for small issuers, and taking other steps to reduce the burden of raising investment capital by small businesses.

§ 609. JUDICIAL REVIEW.

(a) [**Judicial Review of Orders.**] A final order issued by the administrator under this [Act] is subject to judicial review in accordance with [the state administrative procedure act].

[(b) [**Judicial Review of Rules.**] A rule adopted under this [Act] is subject to judicial review in accordance with [the state administrative procedure act].]

§ 610. JURISDICTION.

(a) [**Sales and Offers to Sell.**] Sections 301, 302, 401(a), 402(a), 403(a), 404(a), 501, 506, 509, and 510 do not apply to a person that sells or offers to sell a security unless the offer to sell or the sale is made in this State or the offer to purchase or the purchase is made and accepted in this State.

(b) [**Purchases and Offers to Purchase.**] Sections 401(a), 402(a), 403(a), 404(a), 501, 506, 509, and 510 do not apply to a person that purchases or offers to purchase a security unless the offer to purchase or the purchase is made in this State or the offer to sell or the sale is made and accepted in this State.

(c) [**Offers in this State.**] For the purpose of this section, an offer to sell or to purchase a security is made in this State, whether or not either party is then present in this State, if the offer:

(1) originates from within this State; or

(2) is directed by the offeror to a place in this State and received at the place to which it is directed.

(d) [**Acceptances in this State.**] For the purpose of this section, an offer to purchase or to sell is accepted in this State, whether or not either party is then present in this State, if the acceptance:

(1) is communicated to the offeror in this State and the offeree reasonably believes the offeror to be present in this State and the acceptance is received at the place in this State to which it is directed; and

(2) has not previously been communicated to the offeror, orally or in a record, outside this State.

(e) [**Publications, Radio, Television, or Electronic Communications.**] An offer to sell or to purchase is not made in this State when a publisher circulates or there is circulated on the publisher's behalf in this State a bona fide newspaper or other publication of general, regular, and paid circulation that is not published in this State, or that is published in this State but has had more than two thirds of its circulation outside this State during the previous 12 months or when a radio or television program or other electronic communication originating outside this State is received in this State. A radio or television program, or other electronic communication is considered as having originated in this State if either the broadcast studio or the originating source of transmission is located in this State, unless:

(1) the program or communication is syndicated and distributed from outside this State for redistribution to the general public in this State;

(2) the program or communication is supplied by a radio, television, or other electronic network with the electronic signal originating from outside this State for redistribution to the general public in this State;

(3) the program or communication is an electronic communication that originates outside this State and is captured for redistribution to the general public in this State by a community antenna or cable, radio, cable television, or other electronic system; or

(4) the program or communication consists of an electronic communication that originates in this State, but which is not intended for distribution to the general public in this State.

(f) [**Investment Advice and Misrepresentations.**] Sections 403(a), 404(a), 405(a), 502, 505, and 506 apply to a person if the person engages in an act, practice, or course of business instrumental in effecting prohibited or actionable conduct in this State, whether or not either party is then present in this State.

§ 611. SERVICE OF PROCESS.

(a) [**Signed Consent to Service of Process.**] A consent to service of process complying with Section 611 required by this [Act] must be signed and filed in the form required by a rule or order under this [Act]. A consent appointing the administrator the person's agent for service of process in a noncriminal action or proceeding against the person, or the person's successor or personal representative under this [Act] or a rule adopted or order issued under this [Act] after the consent is filed, has the same force and validity as if the service were made personally on the person filing the consent. A person that has filed a consent complying with this subsection in connection with a previous application for registration or notice filing need not file an additional consent.

(b) [**Conduct Constituting Appointment of Agent for Service.**] If a person, including a nonresident of this State, engages in an act, practice, or course of business prohibited or made actionable by this [Act] or a rule adopted or order issued under this [Act] and the person has not filed a consent to service of process under subsection (a), the act, practice, or course of business constitutes the appointment of the administrator as the person's agent for service of process in a noncriminal action or proceeding against the person or the person's successor or personal representative.

(c) [**Procedure for Service of Process.**] Service under subsection (a) or (b) may be made by providing a copy of the process to the office of the administrator, but it is not effective unless:

(1) the plaintiff, which may be the administrator, promptly sends notice of the service and a copy of the process, return receipt requested, to the defendant or respondent at the address set forth in the consent to service of process or, if a consent to service of process has not been filed, at the last known address, or takes other reasonable steps to give notice; and

(2) the plaintiff files an affidavit of compliance with this subsection in the action or proceeding on or before the return day of the process, if any, or within the time that the court, or the administrator in a proceeding before the administrator, allows.

(d) [**Service in Administrative Proceedings or Civil Actions by Administrator.**] Service pursuant to subsection (c) may be used in a proceeding before the administrator or by the administrator in a civil action in which the administrator is the moving party.

(e) [**Opportunity to Defend.**] If process is served under subsection (c), the court, or the administrator in a proceeding before the administrator, shall order continuances as are necessary or appropriate to afford the defendant or respondent reasonable opportunity to defend.

§ 612. SEVERABILITY CLAUSE. If any provision of this [Act] or its application to any person or circumstances is held invalid, the invalidity does not affect other provisions or applications of this [Act] that can be given effect without the invalid provision or application, and to this end the provisions of this [Act] are severable.

[ARTICLE] 7

TRANSITION

§ 701. EFFECTIVE DATE. This [Act] takes effect on [insert date, which should be at least 60 days after enactment].

§ 702. REPEALS. The following act is repealed: [Insert name of former State securities act].

§ 703. APPLICATION OF ACT TO EXISTING PROCEEDING AND EXISTING RIGHTS AND DUTIES.

(a) [**Applicability of Predecessor Act to Pending Proceedings and Existing Rights.**] The predecessor act exclusively governs all actions or proceedings that are pending on the effective date of this [Act] or may be instituted on the basis of conduct occurring before the effective date of this [Act], but a civil action may not be maintained to enforce any liability under the predecessor act unless instituted within any period of limitation that applied when the cause of action accrued or within five years after the effective date of this [Act], whichever is earlier.

(b) [**Continued Effectiveness under Predecessor Act.**] All effective registrations under the predecessor act, all administrative orders relating to the registrations, rules, statements of policy, interpretative opinions, declaratory rulings, no action determinations, and conditions imposed on the registrations under the predecessor act remain in effect while they would have remained in effect if this [Act] had not been enacted. They are considered to have been filed, issued, or imposed under this [Act], but are exclusively governed by the predecessor act.

(c) [**Applicability of Predecessor Act to Offers or Sales.**] The predecessor act exclusively applies to an offer or sale made within one year after the effective date of this [Act] pursuant to an offering made in good faith before the effective date of this [Act] on the basis of an exemption available under the predecessor act.

NASAA UNIFORM LIMITED OFFERING EXEMPTION

UNIFORM LIMITED OFFERING EXEMPTION

Adopted September 21, 1983

With Amendments Adopted Through April 29, 1989

North American Securities Administrators Association, Inc.

STATUTE

Statute Section. Section ______. The administrator is hereby granted authority to create by rule a limited offering transactional exemption which shall further the objectives of compatibility with federal exemptions and uniformity among the states.

PRELIMINARY NOTES

1. Nothing in this exemption is intended to or should be construed as in any way relieving issuers or persons acting on behalf of issuers from providing disclosure to prospective investors adequate to satisfy the anti-fraud provisions of this state's securities law.

2. In view of the objective of this rule and the purposes and policies underlying this act, the exemption is not available to any issuer with respect to any transaction which, although in technical compliance with this rule, is part of a plan or scheme to evade registration or the conditions or limitations explicitly stated in this rule.

3. Nothing in this rule is intended to relieve registered broker/dealers or agents from the due diligence, suitability, or know your customer standards or any other requirements of law otherwise applicable to such registered persons.

Rule

By authority delegated the administrator in Section ___ of this act to promulgate rules, the following transaction is determined to be exempt from the registration provisions of this act:

1. Any offer or sale of securities offered or sold in compliance with Securities Act of 1933, Regulation D, Rules 505 (and/or 506),[1] including any offer or sale made exempt by application of Rule 508(a), as made effective in Release No. 33–6389 and as amended in Release Nos. 33–6437; 33–6663, 33–6758, and 33–6825, and which satisfies the following further conditions and limitations:

A. No commission, fee or other remuneration shall be paid or given, directly or indirectly, to any person for soliciting any prospective purchaser in this state unless such person is appropriately registered in this state.[2 & 3]

B. No exemption under this rule shall be available for the securities of any issuer if any of the parties described in Securities Act of 1933, Regulation A, Rule 252, section (c), (d), (e) or (f):

1. Has filed a registration statement which is subject of a currently effective registration stop order entered pursuant to any state's

[1] In those states where facts and circumstances permit, it would not be inconsistent with the regulatory objectives of this exemption for a state to elect to accept Rule 506 offerings within the ambit of this exemption. In doing so, however, the state disqualification provisions of this rule should be made applicable.

With inclusion of Rule 506, the major objective of the exemption is not limited to facilitating the capital-raising ability of small business. The removal of the dollar limit makes the exemption available to private placements of all sizes. In large private offerings, the problems associated with determining that all the investors are experienced enough to fully understand the risks of the offering and controlling the manner and scope of the offering so that it does not become a public offering are magnified. Also, and largely because of the removal of the dollar limit, the exemption becomes more attractive to tax shelter investments.

Tax shelter offerings that would be permitted by Rule 506, particularly those with abusively high write-off ratios, involve special facts and circumstances, and enforcement experience shows that they have a greater potential for regulatory concerns and many lack economic substance and fail to contribute to job creation. In recognition of these concerns Rule 506 is not adopted as part of the basic ULOE.

In those states where facts and circumstances permit, it would not be inconsistent with the regulatory objectives of this exemption to further condition the exemption with the following provision:

"In the case of offerings of direct participation programs as defined in Section 34 of Article III of the National Association of Securities Dealers, Inc., Rules of Fair Practice, delivery of a disclosure document containing the information required by Rule 502(b) of Regulation D to individuals covered by Subsections (5), (6) and (7) of Rule 501(a) of Regulation D is required."

[2] In those states where facts and circumstances permit, it would not be inconsistent with the regulatory objectives of this exemption for a state to substitute the following for section 1.A.

a. All persons who offer or sell securities in this state to nonaccredited and/or accredited investors as defined in Securities Act of 1933, Regulation D, Rule 501(a)(5)–(6) shall be appropriately registered in accordance with this state's securities law.

It is a defense to a violation of this subsection if the issuer sustains the burden of proof to establish that he or she did not know and in the exercise of reasonable care could not have known that the person who received a commission, fee or other remuneration was not appropriately registered in this state.

securities law within five years prior to the filing of the notice required under this exemption.

2. Has been convicted within five years prior to the filing of the notice required under this exemption of any felony or misdemeanor in connection with the offer, purchase or sale of any security or any felony involving fraud or deceit, including but not limited to forgery, embezzlement, obtaining money under false pretenses, larceny or conspiracy to defraud.

3. Is currently subject to any state administrative enforcement order or judgment entered by that state's securities administrator within five years prior to the filing of the notice required under this exemption or is subject to any state's administrative enforcement order or judgment in which fraud or deceit, including but not limited to making untrue statements of material facts and omitting to state material facts, was found and the order or judgment was entered within five years prior to the filing of the notice required under this exemption.

4. Is subject to any state's administrative enforcement order or judgment which prohibits, denies or revokes the use of any exemption from registration in connection with the offer, purchase or sale of securities.

5. Is currently subject to any order, judgment, or decree of any court of competent jurisdiction temporarily or preliminarily restraining or enjoining, or is subject to any order, judgment or decree of any court of competent jurisdiction, permanently restraining or enjoining, such party from engaging in or continuing any conduct or practice in connection with the purchase or sale of any security or involving the making of any false filing with the state entered within five years prior to the filing of the notice required under this exemption.

6. The prohibitions of paragraphs 1–3 and 5 above shall not apply if the person subject to the disqualification is duly licensed or registered to conduct securities related business in the state in which the administrative order or judgment was entered against such person or if the broker/dealer employing such party is licensed or registered in this state and the Form B–D filed with this state discloses the order, conviction, judgment or decree relating to such person. No person disqualified under this subsection may act in a capacity other than that for which the person is licensed or registered.

7. Any disqualification caused by this section is automatically waived if the state securities administrator or agency of the state which created the basis for disqualification determines upon a showing of good cause that it is not necessary under the circumstances that the exemption be denied.

It is a defense to a violation of this subsection if issuer sustains the burden of proof to establish that he or she did not know and in the exercise of reasonable care could not have known that a disqualification under this subsection existed.

C. The issuer shall file with the state administrator a notice on Form D (17 CFR 239.500):

1. No later than (10 days prior)[4] to the receipt of consideration or the delivery of a subscription agreement by an investor in this state which results from an offer being made in reliance upon this exemption and at such other times and in the form required under Regulation D, Rule 503 to be filed with the Securities and Exchange Commission.

2. The notice shall contain an undertaking by the issuer to furnish to the state securities administrator, upon written request, the information furnished by the issuer to offerees, except where the state administrator pursuant to regulation requires that the informa-

[3] In those states where facts and circumstances permit, it would not be inconsistent with the regulatory objectives of this exemption for a state to provide for a system or process to simplify and facilitate the registration of broker/dealers and agents which would not otherwise be required to be registered except for this exemption. Such a system or process should as a minimum, grant jurisdiction as well as the ability to effectively limit and control persons offering and selling securities within the state.

It is a defense to a violation of this subsection if the issuer sustains the burden of proof to establish that he or she did not know and in the exercise of reasonable care could not have known that the person who received a commission, fee or other remuneration was not appropriately registered in this state.

[4] In those states where facts and circumstances permit, it would not be inconsistent with the regulatory objectives of this exemption for a state to consider a post sale notice patterned after the notice provisions of Regulation D (Rule 230.503).

tion be filed at the same time with the filing of the notice.[5]

3. Unless otherwise available, included with or in the initial notice shall be a consent to service of process.

4. Every person filing the initial notice provided for in 1 above shall pay a filing fee of ______.

D. In all sales to nonaccredited investors in this state one of the following conditions must be satisfied or the issuer and any person acting on its behalf shall have reasonable grounds to believe and after making reasonable inquiry shall believe that one of the following conditions is satisfied:

1. The investment is suitable for the purchaser upon the basis of the facts, if any, disclosed by the purchaser as to the purchaser's other security holdings, financial situation and needs. For the purpose of this condition only, it may be presumed that if the investment does not exceed 10% of the investor's net worth, it is suitable.

2. The purchaser either alone or with his/her purchaser representative(s) has such knowledge and experience in financial and business matters that he/she is or they are capable of evaluating the merits and risk of the prospective investment.

2. A failure to comply with a term, condition or requirement of Sections 1.A, [C[6]], and D of this rule will not result in loss of the exemption from the requirements of section [301] of this act for any offer or sale to a particular individual or entity if the person relying on the exemption shows:

A. the failure to comply did not pertain to a term, condition or requirement directly intended to protect that particular individual or entity; and

B. the failure to comply was insignificant with respect to the offering as a whole; and

C. a good faith and reasonable attempt was made to comply with all applicable terms, conditions and requirements of Sections 1.A [C], and D.

3. Where an exemption is established only through reliance upon section 2 of this rule, the failure to comply shall nonetheless be actionable by the [administrator] under section [408] of the Act.[7]

4. Transactions which are exempt under this rule may not be combined with offers and sales exempt under any other rule or section of this act, however, nothing in this limitation shall act as an election. Should for any reason the offer and sale fail to comply with all of the conditions for this exemption, the issuer may claim the availability of any other applicable exemption.

5. The administrator may, by rule or order, increase the number of purchasers or waive any other conditions of this exemption.

6. The exemption authorized by this rule shall be known and may be cited as the "Uniform Limited Offering Exemption."

[5] This latter filing requirement is not intended to provide the basis for a fairness type of review of the offering.

[6] In those states which have adopted a post-sale notice patterned after the notice provisions of Regulation D (Rule 230.503) it would not be inconsistent with the regulatory objectives of this exemption to include the notice filing requirements of section 1.C within the substantial compliance provisions of section 2 or to eliminate the filing as a condition and adopt a rule similar to Rule 507.

[7] The cited reference is to the section of the Uniform Securities Act which authorizes the state administrator to bring a civil action to enjoin rule violations. Those states which have authority to bring an administrative enforcement action for rule violations may wish to include a reference to that statutory authority. If the administrator lacks authority to bring enforcement actions based solely on rule violations, he/she may wish to consider a statutory amendment.

ORDER GRANTING TEMPORARY EXEMPTIONS UNDER THE SECURITIES EXCHANGE ACT OF 1934 IN CONNECTION WITH THE PENDING REVISION OF THE DEFINITION OF "SECURITY" TO ENCOMPASS SECURITY–BASED SWAPS*

IT IS HEREBY ORDERED, pursuant to Section 36 of the Exchange Act, that, until the compliance date for final rules that we may adopt further defining the terms "security based swap" and "eligible contract participant," the following exemptions from Exchange Act requirements will apply:

(a) *Temporary Exemption in Connection with Security-Based Swap Activity*:

(1) *Persons Eligible.* The exemption in paragraph (a)(2) of this exemption is available to any person that meets the definition of eligible contract participant as set forth in Section 1a(12) of the Commodity Exchange Act (as in effect on July 20, 2010), other than:

(i) a broker or dealer registered under Section 15(b) of the Exchange Act (other than paragraph (11) thereof); or

(ii) a self-regulatory organization, as defined in Section 3(a)(26) of the Exchange Act; provided, however, that this temporary exemption shall be available to a registered securities association solely with respect to its obligations under Section 19(g)(1)(B) of the Exchange Act to enforce compliance with provisions of its rules (and provisions of the rules of the Municipal Securities Rulemaking Board) that do not apply to positions or activities involving security-based swaps as of July 15, 2011.

(2) *General Scope of Exemption.* Subject to the exclusions in paragraph (a)(3) of this exemption, such person shall be exempt from the provisions of the Exchange Act, and the rules and regulations thereunder, solely in connection with the person's activities involving security-based swaps.

(3) *Exclusions from Exemption.* The exemption in paragraph (a)(2) of this exemption does not extend to the following provisions under the Exchange Act, and the applicable rules or regulations thereunder:

(i) *Antifraud and Anti–Manipulation Provisions.* The antifraud and anti-manipulation provisions of Sections 9(a)(2)(5), 10(b), 15(c)(1), 20(d) and 21A(a)(1) of the Exchange Act, as well as underlying rules prohibiting fraud, manipulation or insider trading (but not prophylactic reporting or recordkeeping requirements), and any provision of the Exchange Act related to the Commission's enforcement authority in connection with violations or potential violations of such provisions.

(ii) *Provisions Added or Amended by the Subtitle B of Title VII of the Dodd–Frank Act.* All Exchange Act provisions related to security-based swaps added or amended by subtitle B of Title VII of the Dodd–Frank Act, including the amended definition of "security" in Section 3(a)(10) of the Exchange Act.

(iii) Provisions applicable to certain securities brokers. The broker registration requirements of Section 15(a)(1) of the Exchange Act, and the other requirements of the Exchange Act and the rules and regulations thereunder that apply to a broker that is not registered with the Commission; provided, however, that this exclusion shall apply only to broker activities by persons that are members of a clearing agency that functions as a central counterparty for security-based swaps and that hold customer funds or securities in connection with security-based swaps. Otherwise, paragraph (a)(2) of this exemption will be available in connection with broker activities involving security-based swaps by persons other than registered broker-dealers or self-regulatory organizations. For these purposes, the term "central counterparty" means a

* On February 5, 2014, the SEC issued an Order Extending Temporary Exemptions under the Securities Exchange Act of 1934 in Connection with the Revision of the Definition of "Security" to Encompass Security–Based Swaps. This order extended the expiration date "until the earlier of such time as the Commission issues an order or rule determining whether any continuing exemptive relief is appropriate for security-based swap activities with respect to any of these Exchange Act provisions" or February 5, 2017. The SEC release number is 34–71485.

clearing agency that interposes itself between the counterparties to security-based swap transactions, acting functionally as the buyer to every seller and the seller to every buyer.

(iv) *Provisions Applicable to Certain Securities Dealers.* The dealer registration requirements of Section 15(a)(1) of the Exchange Act, and the other requirements of the Exchange Act and the rules and regulations thereunder that apply to a dealer that is not registered with the Commission; provided, however, that this exclusion shall not apply, and paragraph (a)(2) of this exemption will be available, in connection with dealing activities involving security-based swaps with counterparties that meet the definition of eligible contract participant as set forth in Section 1a(12) of the Commodity Exchange Act (as in effect on July 20, 2010).

(v) *Additional Provisions.* The following additional provisions under the Exchange Act, or the rules and regulations thereunder:

(A) Paragraphs (42), (43), (44), and (45) of Section 3(a);

(B) Section 5;

(C) Section 6;107

(D) Section 12;

(E) Section 13;

(F) Section 14;

(G) Paragraphs (4) and (6) of Section 15(b);

(H) Section 15(d);

(I) Section 15C;

(J) Section 16; and

(K) Section 17A.

(b) *Temporary Exemption Specific to Security-Based Swap Activities by Registered Brokers and Dealers.*

(1) *In General.* Subject to paragraph (b)(2) of this exemption, a broker or dealer registered under Section 15(b) of the Exchange Act (other than paragraph (11) thereof) shall be exempt from the provisions of the Exchange Act and the rules and regulations thereunder specified in paragraph (a)(2) (subject to the exclusions in paragraph (a)(3) of this exemption) solely with respect to security-based swaps.

(2) *Limited Exemption in Connection with Certain Provisions and Rules.* A registered broker or dealer shall be exempt from the following provisions and rules in connection with security-based swaps solely to the extent that those provisions or rules do not apply to the broker's or dealer's security-based swap positions or activities as of July 15, 2011; provided, however, that the exemption from Rule 15c3–3 under the Exchange Act shall not be available for activities and positions of the registered broker or dealer related to cleared security-based swaps, to the extent that the registered broker or dealer is a member of a clearing agency that functions as a central counterparty for security-based swaps, and holds customer funds or securities in connection with cleared security-based swaps:[1]

(i) Section 7(c);

(ii) Section 15(c)(3);

(iii) Section 17(a);

(iv) Section 17(b);

(v) Regulation T (12 CFR 220.1 *et seq.*);

(vi) Rule 15c3–1;

(vii) Rule 15c3–3;

(viii) Rule 17a–3;

(ix) Rule 17a–4;

(x) Rule 17a–5;

(xi) Rule 17a–8; and

(xii) Rule 17a–13.

IT IS HEREBY FURTHER ORDERED, pursuant to Section 36 of the Exchange Act, that, until the earliest compliance date set forth in any of the final rules regarding registration of security-based swap execution facilities, the following exceptions from Exchange Act requirements will apply:

(a) *Temporary Exemption from Sections 5 and 6 of the Exchange Act.*

(1) Any person other than a clearing agency acting as a central counterparty in security-based swaps shall be exempt from the requirements to register as a national securities exchange under Sections 5 and 6 of the Exchange Act and the rules and regulations thereunder solely in connection with the person's activities involving security-based swaps.

[1] Solely for purposes of this temporary exemption, in addition to the general requirements under the referenced Exchange Act Sections, registered broker-dealers shall only be subject to the enumerated rules under the referenced Exchange Act Sections in connection with security-based swaps.

(2) A broker or dealer shall be exempt from Section 5 of the Exchange Act solely in connection with the broker's or dealer's activities involving security-based swaps that it effects or reports on an exchange that is exempted from registration pursuant to paragraph (a)(1) of this exemption.

(3) Each CDS CCP shall be exempt from the requirements of Sections 5 and 6 of the Exchange Act and the rules and regulations thereunder solely in connection with its calculation of mark-to-market prices for open positions in Cleared CDS, subject to the following conditions:

(i) Each CDS CCP shall report the following information with respect to the calculation of mark-to-market prices for Cleared CDS to the Commission within 30 days of the end of each quarter, and preserve such reports during the life of the enterprise and of any successor enterprise:

(A) The total dollar volume of transactions executed during the quarter, broken down by reference entity, security, or index; and

(B) The total unit volume and/or notional amount executed during the quarter, broken down by reference entity, security, or index;

(ii) The CDS CCP shall establish and maintain adequate safeguards and procedures to protect members' confidential trading information. Such safeguards and procedures shall include:

(A) Limiting access to the confidential trading information of members to those employees of the CDS CCP who are operating the system or responsible for its compliance with this exemption or any other applicable rules; and

(B) Establishing and maintaining standards controlling employees of the CDS CCP trading for their own accounts. The CDS CCP must establish and maintain adequate oversight procedures to ensure that the safeguards and procedures established pursuant to this condition are followed; and

(iii) Each CDS CCP shall directly or indirectly make available to the public on terms that are fair and reasonable and not unreasonably discriminatory:

(A) All end-of-day settlement prices and any other prices with respect to Cleared CDS that it may establish to calculate mark-to-market margin requirements for its clearing members; and

(B) Any other pricing or valuation information with respect to Cleared CDS as is published or distributed by the CDS CCP.

(4) Any member of an CDS CCP shall be exempt from the requirements of Section 5 of the Exchange Act solely to the extent such member uses any facility of the CDS CCP to effect any transaction in Cleared CDS, or to report any such transaction, in connection with the CDS CCP's clearance and risk management process for Cleared CDS.

(b) *Definitions.*

(1) For purposes of this exemption, the term "central counterparty" means a clearing agency that interposes itself between the counterparties to security-based swap transactions, acting functionally as the buyer to every seller and the seller to every buyer.

(2) For purposes of this exemption, the term "CDS CCP" shall mean ICE Trust U.S. LLC, Chicago Mercantile Exchange Inc., and ICE Clear Europe, Limited.

(3) For purposes of this exemption, the term "Cleared CDS" shall mean a credit default swap that is a security-based swap that is submitted (or offered, purchased, or sold on terms providing for submission) to a CDS CCP, that is offered only to, purchased only by, and sold only to persons that meet the definition of eligible contract participant as set forth in Section 1a(12) of the Commodity Exchange Act (as in effect on July 20, 2010) , and in which:

(i) The reference entity, the issuer of the reference security, or the reference security is one of the following:

(A) An entity reporting under the Exchange Act, providing Securities Act rule 144A(d)(4) information, or about which financial information is otherwise publicly available;

(B) A foreign private issuer whose securities are listed outside the United States and that has its principal trading market outside the United States;

(C) A foreign sovereign debt security;

(D) An asset-backed security, as defined in Regulation AB, issued in a registered transaction with publicly available distribution reports; or

(E) An asset-backed security issued or guaranteed by the Federal National Mortgage Association, the Federal Home Loan Mortgage Corporation, or the Government National Mortgage Association; or

(ii) The reference index is an index in which 80% or more of the index's weighting is comprised of the entities or securities described in subparagraph (i).